The National Hockey League

Official Guide & Record Book

2006

THE NATIONAL HOCKEY LEAGUE
Official Guide & Record Book/2006

TERMS & CONDITIONS FOR USING THIS BOOK

ATTENTION: PLEASE READ THIS DOCUMENT CAREFULLY BEFORE USING THIS BOOK (THE "BOOK") AND/OR THE DATA IT CONTAINS (THE "DATA"). INDIVIDUALS OR ENTITIES USING THE BOOK AND/OR THE DATA ("END USERS") AGREE TO BE BOUND BY THE TERMS OF THIS LICENSE. IF YOU DO NOT AGREE TO THE TERMS OF THIS LICENSE, DO NOT USE THE BOOK OR THE DATA AND PROMPTLY RETURN THE UNUSED BOOK AND PROOF OF PAYMENT TO THE FOLLOWING ADDRESS FOR A REFUND:

> Dan Diamond & Associates, Inc.
> 194 Dovercourt Road, Toronto, Ontario, Canada M6J 3C8
> dda.nhl@sympatico.ca.

Dan Diamond & Associates, Inc. (the "Publisher") owns, and retains ownership of, the Data. The Publisher reserves any right not expressly granted to End Users below.

1. License. End-Users are granted a limited, non-exclusive license to do only the following, subject to the restrictions set out in Section 2 below:

    (a) End-Users may use the Book and the Data for personal, non-commercial purposes.

    (b) End-Users may reproduce individual player records, tables and data panels in connection with bona fide private study and research.

    (c) End-Users who are journalists may reproduce individual player records, tables and data panels for use by the broadcast and print media.

2. Restrictions. End-Users may NOT reproduce the Book or the Data, in whole or in part, in any form or by any means, electronic or mechanical, including photocopying, recording, or by any information storage and retrieval system now known or hereafter invented, without written permission from the Publisher. End-Users may NOT sublicense, assign, or distribute (via the World Wide Web or otherwise) copies of the Book or the Data, in whole or in part, to others. END-USERS MAY NOT MODIFY, ADAPT, TRANSLATE, RENT, LEASE, LOAN, RESELL FOR PROFIT, DISTRIBUTE, OR OTHERWISE ASSIGN OR TRANSFER THE BOOK OR THE DATA, OR CREATE DERIVATIVE WORKS BASED UPON THE BOOK OR THE DATA OR ANY PART THEREOF, EXCEPT AS PROVIDED ABOVE.

3. Commercial Users. Commercial users (such as sports reference and sports gaming websites) may obtain a license to use customized Data upon payment of a reasonable fee. Please contact the Publisher at the address provided above.

4. Termination. This License is effective until terminated. This License will terminate immediately without notice from the Publisher if the End User fails to comply with any of its provisions. Upon termination End Users must destroy the Book, the Data and all copies thereof.

5. General. This License will be governed by and construed in accordance with the laws of the province of Ontario and the laws of Canada applicable therein, and shall inure to the benefit of the Publisher and End-Users and their successors, assigns and legal representatives. If any provision of this License is held by a court of competent jurisdiction to be invalid or unenforceable to any extent under applicable law, that provision will be enforced to the maximum extent permissible and the remaining provisions of this License will remain in full force and effect. Any notices or other communications to be sent to the Publisher must be mailed first class, postage prepaid, to the address provided above. This Agreement constitutes the entire agreement between the parties with respect to the subject matter hereof, and all prior proposals, agreements, representations, statements and undertakings are hereby expressly cancelled and superseded. This Agreement may not be changed or amended except by a written instrument executed by a duly authorized officer of the Publisher.

6. Acknowledgment. BY USING THE BOOK OR THE DATA, THE END-USER ACKNOWLEDGES THAT IT HAS READ THIS LICENSE, UNDERSTANDS IT, AND AGREES TO BE BOUND BY ITS TERMS AND CONDITIONS. Should you have any questions concerning this License, contact the Publisher at the address provided above.

Copyright © 2005 by the National Hockey League.

Compiled by the NHL Public Relations Department and the 30 NHL Club Public Relations Directors.

Printed in Canada. All rights reserved under the Pan-American and International Copyright Conventions.

Published in Canada by: Dan Diamond and Associates, Inc., 194 Dovercourt Road, Toronto, Ontario M6J 3C8 Canada
ISBN in Canada 0-920445-98-5

Published in the United States by: Triumph Books, 542 South Dearborn Sreet, Suite 750, Chicago, Illinois 60605   ISBN in USA 1-57243-808-8

Staff

For the NHL: Dave McCarthy, George Puro; Supervising Editor: Greg Inglis; Statistician: Benny Ercolani;
Editorial Staff: John Halligan, David Keon, Dave Baker, Jackie Rinaldi, Kelley Rosset, Julie Young.

Senior Managing Editor: Ralph Dinger	**Associate Managing Editor:** Paul Bontje	**Photo Editor:** Eric Zweig
International Editor: Igor Kuperman	**Production Editors:** John Pasternak, Alex Dubiel	**Publisher:** Dan Diamond

Data Management and Typesetting: Caledon Data Management, Orangeville, Ontario
Film Output and Scanning: Embassy Graphics, Toronto, Ontario
Printing: Sunrise Consulting Inc., Port Perry, Ontario; WebcomLimited, Toronto, Ontario
Production Management: Dan Diamond and Associates, Inc., Toronto, Ontario
Contributors and Photo Credits: see page 671

Distribution

Trade sales and distribution in Canada by:
North 49 Books, 35 Prince Andrew Drive, Toronto, Ontario M3C 2H2   416/449-4000; Fax 416/449-9924
Dan Diamond and Associates, Inc., Toronto   416/531-6535; Fax 416/531-3939   dda.nhl@sympatico.ca   www.nhlofficialguide.com

Trade sales and distribution in the United States by:
Triumph Books, 542 South Dearborn Sreet, Suite 750, Chicago, Illinois 60605   312/939-3330; Fax 312/663-3557

International representatives:
Barkers Worldwide Publications, Unit 6/7 The Elms Centre, Glaziers Lane, Normandy, Guildford, Surrey GU3 2DF England
Tel 011/441/483/811-971; Fax 011/441/483/811-972   sales@bwpu.demon.co.uk   www.bwpu.demon.co.uk

Licensed by the National Hockey League.®

NHL and the NHL Shield are registered trademarks of the National Hockey League.
All NHL logos and marks and team logos and marks depicted herein are the property of the NHL and the respective teams and may not be reproduced without the prior written consent of Enterprises, L.P. © NHL 2004. All Rights Reserved.

The National Hockey League
1251 Avenue of the Americas, 47th Floor, New York, New York 10020-1198
1800 McGill College Ave., Suite 2600, Montreal, Quebec H3A 3J6
50 Bay Street, 11th Floor, Toronto, Ontario M5J 2X8

Table of Contents

141 NHL 2004-05 Player Register
2004-05 Statistics for Players on NHL Rosters in 2003-04

Table of Contents *continued*

Introduction

WELCOME TO *THE NATIONAL HOCKEY LEAGUE OFFICIAL GUIDE & RECORD BOOK* FOR **2005-06.** Like the NHL itself, this 74th edition of the *Guide* includes significant changes and new features. The recent agreement ratified by NHL owners and players ended the lockout that resulted in the cancellation of the 2004-05 season and also had an immediate impact on how teams are built and how the game is played. Much about the NHL has changed for 2005-06 and these changes are reflected in the *Guide & Record Book*.

Players have signed with new clubs in much greater numbers than in a typical off-season. Many rosters are greatly revamped and many clubs appear to have significantly upgraded. The *Guide & Record Book* has stayed current with these changes. The book's final editorial lockdown was delayed until after Labor Day to make sure the *2006 Guide* incorporated the latest free-agent signings, re-signings and trades. A new feature found on page three of each club's four-page section is titled "Key Off-Season Acquisitions and Signings." In addition, on the second page of each club, the 2005-06 Player Personnel panel has been supplemented with a second roster titled "In the System and Recently Drafted" to provide a big-picture view of organizational strengths. Young European players, who may have played with under-18, junior and senior teams for the same club in 2004-05, have only their top-level team listed here. A complete breakdown of any player's 2004-05 season can be found in his data panel in the Prospect, Player or Goaltender Registers. (Clubs begin on page 21; Registers on page 279.)

The NHL's rules and the rink itself have been rethought as well. The League's Competition Committee, which is made up of players, general managers and team owners, obtained approval for a slate of rule changes designed to emphasize entertainment, skill and competition on the ice. A history of the NHL's major rule changes can be found on page 10. A summary of new rules for 2005-06 can be found on page 13 and comparative rink diagrams showing an NHL sheet of ice both in 2005-06 and in 2003-04 are found on page 12.

NHL players again will participate in the Winter Olympics, representing their countries in Turin, Italy, in February of 2006. This will mark the third consecutive Winter Games in which NHL players have participated. In Nagano, Japan, in 1998 and in Salt Lake City, Utah, in 2002 six Olympic medals were won by five different countries. Canada, the Czech Republic, Finland and the United States have won one medal each. Only Russia has been on the podium at both Olympics, finishing with the silver in Nagano and the bronze in Salt Lake City. Men's and women's 2006 Olympic Schedules are found on page 15 along with results, scores and scoring leaders from every Olympic ice hockey tournament since 1920. The Olympic statistics for active NHL players, including their medal wins, are found on page 19.

The new look of the NHL even extended to the 2005 Entry Draft. Because no games were played in 2004-05, the conventional means of determining an order of selection were replaced by a weighted lottery in which every team had a chance to win the first overall selection in the Draft. The terms of this lottery – won by the Pittsburgh Penguins who selected Sidney Crosby – and the resulting order of selection are found on page 225. A further refinement has been made to tables that breakdown draft selections by club, school or major European hockey nation. The order of display has been reversed, so a team's most recent selections are closest to the club's name and all-time drafted player total in the table. The *Guide & Record Book*'s Entry Draft section (page 223) continues to provide full coverage of the most recent Draft, the first two rounds from 2002 to 2004 and the first round plus notable selections for every Entry and Amateur Draft from 1969 to 2001.

Hockey continued to flourish in many locations this past season. Many players who had appeared in the NHL in 2003-04 joined teams in other leagues and on other continents. It became the task of the *NHL Guide & Record Book* editorial team to track these players wherever they played. The resulting compilation of NHLers' 2004-05 statistics has been applied to their individual player and goaltender data panels, but has also been packaged as separate 2004-05 NHL Player and Goaltender Registers. (Players begin on page 141; goaltenders on 155.) World Cup of Hockey, World Championship and World Junior Championship stats have been added to these registers as well.

Also new in the 2006 edition of the *Guide* is the International Ice Hockey Federation's Hall of Fame. It joins the Hockey Hall of Fame in Toronto and the U.S. Hockey Hall of Fame in Eveleth, Minnesota, in a Halls of Fame section that begins on page 244.

The backbone of every edition of the *NHL Guide & Record Book* remains its Prospect, Player and Goaltender Registers which chart more players and span more pages in this edition than ever before. The order of the Registers is as follows: Prospect (page 279), NHL Player (367), Goaltender (605), Retired Player (630) and Retired Goaltender (665). Note that the Goaltender Register combines prospects and NHL goaltenders in the same section.

A key to the abbreviations and symbols used in individual player and goaltender data panels, along with useful information on how to use the Registers, is found on page 278. A list of abbreviations used for league names is found on page 365. Late additions are found on page 366 and each NHL club's minor-pro affiliates are found on page 14. Referees and linesmen are listed on page 8.

These new and expanded features and sections have resulted in a 32-page increase in the *Guide & Record Book*. This 672-page edition is the biggest yet. When the *Guide*'s big-page format was designed in 1984, the book ran 352 pages. Much has been added, of course, and every feature has been enhanced and enhanced again, but the "sell copy" on the back cover of that old edition is particularly appropriate in today's much revamped League. The *Guide & Record Book* remains "Everything Worth Knowing About the NHL."

As always, our thanks to readers, correspondents and members of the media who take the time to comment on the *Guide & Record Book*. Thanks as well to the people working in the communications departments of the NHL's member clubs and to their counterparts in minor pro, junior, college and European hockey. In addition, our efforts to provide statistical detail on players selected at recent Entry Drafts has brought us into contact with coaches, team managers, league conveners, school athletic directors, players' parents and, in some cases, the players themselves, all to nail down early career statistics. People are, as always, overwhelmingly helpful, resulting in enhanced data panels for the Guide's youngest players. (Contributors are listed on 670.)

Best wishes for an enjoyable 2005-06 season.

ACCURACY REMAINS THE *GUIDE & RECORD BOOK*'S TOP PRIORITY.

We appreciate comments and clarification from our readers. Please direct these to:

- Ralph Dinger   Senior Managing Editor, 194 Dovercourt Road, Toronto, Ontario M6J 3C8. e-mail: ralph.dda@sympatico.ca.
- Greg Inglis   47th floor, 1251 Avenue of the Americas, New York, New York 10020-1198 . . . or . . .
- David Keon   50 Bay Street, 11th Floor, Toronto, Ontario, M5J 2X8

Your involvement makes a better book.

NATIONAL HOCKEY LEAGUE

New York, 1251 Avenue of the Americas, 47th Floor, New York, NY 10020-1198, 212/789-2000, Fax: 212/789-2020, PR Fax: 212/789-2080
Montréal, 1800 McGill College Avenue, Suite 2600, Montréal, Québec, H3A 3J6, 514/841-9220, Fax: 514/841-1070
Toronto, 50 Bay Street, 11th Floor, Toronto, Ontario, M5J 2X8, 416/981-2777, Fax: 416/981-2779
NHL Enterprises, L.P. — 1251 Avenue of the Americas, 47th Floor, New York, NY 10020-1198, 212/789-2000, Fax: 212/789-2020
NHL Enterprises Canada, L.P. — 50 Bay Street, 11th Floor, Toronto, Ontario, M5J 2X8, 416/981-2777, Fax: 416/981-2779
NHL Productions/NHL Images — 240 Pegasus Avenue, Northvale, NJ 07647, 201/750-5800, Fax: 201/750-5850

EXECUTIVE

Commissioner ....Gary B. Bettman
Deputy Commissioner ....William Daly
Executive Vice President & Director of Hockey Operations ....Colin Campbell
Executive Vice President & Chief Financial Officer ....Craig Harnett
Director, Administration & Executive Assistant to the Commissioner ....Debbie Jordan

ADMINISTRATION

Director of Administration ....Debbie Jordan
Director, Offices & Facilities ....Andrew Crawford
Manager, Human Resources ....Patrice Distler

BROADCASTING/SCHEDULING

Vice President, Broadcasting & Programming ....Adam Acone
Director, Television Production & Technology ....Onnie Bose
Manager, Business & Special Events ....Phyllis DeCongilio
Vice President, Scheduling, Operations & Research (Montreal) ....Steve Hatze Petros
Director, Research & Scheduling ....Mark Erlichson

NHL PRODUCTIONS

Executive Producer ....Ken Rosen
Vice President ....Patti Fallick
Coordinating Producer ....Darryl Lepik
Director, Operations/Footage ....Peg Walsh
Manager, Video Services ....Chris Cesa

NHL Images
Vice President ....Patti Fallick

COMMUNICATIONS

Group Vice President, Communications ....Bernadette Mansur
Vice President, Media Relations ....Frank Brown
Vice President, Public Relations & Media Services (Toronto) ....Gary Meagher
Chief Statistician (Toronto) ....Benny Ercolani
Director, Communications ....Jamey Horan
Director, Community and Diversity Programming ....Ken Martin
Director, Media Relations ....Amy Sweeney
Director, News Services ....Greg Inglis
Director, Youth Development, NHL Diversity ....Willie O'Ree
Managers, Public Relations (Toronto) ....David Keon, Julie Young

EVENTS AND ENTERTAINMENT

Group Vice President ....Ken Yaffe
Director ....Bill Miller
Senior Manager ....Dean Matsuzaki

FINANCE

Executive Vice President & Chief Financial Officer ....Craig Harnett
Senior Vice President, Finance ....Joseph DeSousa
Vice President, Finance and Office Manager (Montreal) ....Olivia Pietrantonio
Corporate Controller ....Kenneth Cartisano

HOCKEY OPERATIONS

Executive Vice President & Director of Hockey Operations ....Colin Campbell
Senior Vice President, Hockey Operations (Toronto) ....Jim Gregory
Senior Vice President & Director of Officiating (Toronto) ....Stephen Walkom
Vice President, Hockey Operations (Toronto) ....Mike Murphy
Vice President & Managing Director, Central Registry (Toronto) ....Stephen Pellegrini
Director of Systems, Central Registry (Montreal) ....Madeleine Supino
Director of Projects, Central Registry (Toronto) ....Sean MacLeod
Director, Central Scouting (Toronto) ....E.J. McGuire
Director of Alumni Relations (Toronto) ....Patrick Flatley
Managers, Officiating (Toronto) ....Dave Baker, Randy Hall
Consultant (Toronto) ....Frank Bonello
Consultant (Toronto) ....Kris King
Facilities Operation Manager ....Dan Craig
Video Director ....Damian Echevarrieta
Video Coordinator (Toronto) ....Paul Brighty
Video Technologies Consultant ....Jed Dole

INFORMATION TECHNOLOGY

Group Vice President, Information Technology ....Peter DelGiacco
Assistant Director (Montreal) ....Luc Coulombe
Director, Network Services ....Patrick Powers
Manager, Technical Support ....Dan O'Neill
Manager, Statistical Information Systems ....Neil Pierson

LEGAL

Senior Vice President, General Counsel ....David Zimmerman
Vice President, Deputy General Counsel ....Julie Grand
Associate Counsel ....Daniel Ages

PENSION

Vice President and Managing Director, Pension (Montreal) ....Yvon Chamberland
Controller, Pension (Montreal) ....Mary Skiadopoulos
Manager, Pension (Montreal) ....Lise de Jocas

SECURITY

Senior Vice President, Security ....Dennis Cunningham
Senior Director, Security ....Joseph Caporicci
Manager, Security ....Al Young

TELEVISION AND MEDIA VENTURES

Senior Vice President, Television & Media Ventures ....Doug Perlman
Vice President, Television & Business Affairs ....Leslie Gittess
Director, Team Television & Business Affairs ....John Tortora

NHL Interactive CyberEnterprises (NHL ICE)
President, NHL ICE & Senior Vice President, New Business Development ....Keith Ritter
Vice President, Editorial & Production ....Richard Libero
Senior Director, Web Operations ....Grant Nodine

NHL ENTERPRISES

President, NHL Enterprises ....Ed Horne

CONSUMER PRODUCTS MARKETING

Group Vice President, Consumer Products Marketing ....Brian Jennings
Vice President, Consumer Products Marketing ....James Haskins
Senior Director, Retail Sales & Marketing, Canada (Toronto) ....Barry Monaghan
Director, Entertainment Products ....Dave McCarthy
Manager, Center Ice & Sporting Goods ....Richard Villani
Manager, Consumer Products Marketing, Canada (Toronto) ....Angie Andreou

CORPORATE MARKETING

Group Vice President, Corporate Marketing ....Andrew Judelson
Senior Director, Canada (Toronto) ....Laurie Kepron

CREATIVE SERVICES

Associate Director, Creative Services ....Kathy Drew

FAN DEVELOPMENT

Vice President, Fan Development ....Alysse Soll
Manager ....Suzanne Sherman

FINANCE

Vice President, Finance – NHL Enterprises ....Mary McCarthy
Directors, Finance ....Frank Dowling, Scott Weinfeld

INTERNATIONAL

Group Vice President & Managing Director, NHL International ....Ken Yaffe
Director, International Licensing & Special Projects ....Lynn White

NHLE LEGAL AND BUSINESS AFFAIRS

Executive Vice President & General Counsel ....Richard Zahnd
Vice President, Licensing and Trademark Compliance ....Ruth Gruhin
Vice President & Corporate Counsel ....Robert Hawkins
Vice President, Legal & Business Affairs ....Tom Prochnow
Senior Counsel, Legal & Business Affairs ....Matthew Kline
Senior Manager, Intellectual Property ....Alison Nunez

STRATEGIC DEVELOPMENT

Vice President, Club Marketing ....Susan Cohig

BOARD OF GOVERNORS
Chairman of the Board – Harley N. Hotchkiss

Mighty Ducks of Anaheim
Henry Samueli ....Governor
Michael Schulman ....Alternate Governor
Brian Burke ....Alternate Governor
Tim Ryan ....Alternate Governor
Susan Samueli ....Alternate Governor

Atlanta Thrashers
Bruce Levenson ....Governor
Don Waddell ....Alternate Governor
Bernie Mullin..............................Alternate Governor
J. Rutherford Seydel II ....Alternate Governor

Boston Bruins
Jeremy M. Jacobs ....Governor
Jeremy M. Jacobs, Jr. ....Alternate Governor
Louis Jacobs ....Alternate Governor
Charles M. Jacobs ....Alternate Governor
Harry J. Sinden ....Alternate Governor
Mike O'Connell ....Alternate Governor

Buffalo Sabres
B. Thomas Golisano .... Governor
Lawrence Quinn ....Alternate Governor
Daniel J. DiPofi ....Alternate Governor
Darcy Regier ....Alternate Governor

Calgary Flames
Harley N. Hotchkiss......................Governor
N. Murray Edwards ....Alternate Governor
Alvin Libin ....Alternate Governor
Ken King......................................Alternate Governor

Carolina Hurricanes
Peter Karmanos, Jr.......................Governor
Jim Rutherford ....Alternate Governor
Jason Karmanos ....Alternate Governor
Michael Amendola ....Alternate Governor

Chicago Blackhawks
William W. Wirtz ....Governor
Robert J. Pulford ....Alternate Governor
John A. Ziegler, Jr. ....Alternate Governor
Peter R. Wirtz..............................Alternate Governor

Colorado Avalanche
E. Stanley Kroenke........................Governor
Pierre Lacroix..............................Alternate Governor
Paul Andrews..............................Alternate Governor

Columbus Blue Jackets
John H. McConnell........................Governor
John P. McConnell........................Alternate Governor
Doug MacLean..............................Alternate Governor
Mike Priest ....Alternate Governor

Dallas Stars
Thomas O. Hicks..........................Governor
James R. Lites..............................Alternate Governor
Doug Armstrong ....Alternate Governor

Detroit Red Wings
Michael Ilitch ....Governor
Jim Devellano ....Alternate Governor
Christopher Ilitch ....Alternate Governor
Ken Holland ....Alternate Governor

Edmonton Oilers
Cal Nichols ....Governor
Patrick R. LaForge........................Alternate Governor
Kevin Lowe ....Alternate Governor
William K. Butler ....Alternate Governor

Florida Panthers
Alan Cohen..................................Governor
Steven Cohen ....Alternate Governor
Richard Lehman ....Alternate Governor
William A. Torrey..........................Alternate Governor
Jordan Zimmerman ....Alternate Governor
Mike Keenan................................Alternate Governor

Los Angeles Kings
Timothy J. Leiweke........................Governor
Philip F. Anschutz ....Alternate Governor
David Taylor ....Alternate Governor
Shawn Hunter..............................Alternate Governor

Minnesota Wild
Robert O. Naegele, Jr....................Governor
Jac Sperling..................................Alternate Governor
Doug Risebrough ....Alternate Governor

Montréal Canadiens
George N. Gillett, Jr. ....Governor
Pierre Boivin ....Alternate Governor
Fred Steer....................................Alternate Governor
Bob Gainey ....Alternate Governor
Jeff Joyce ....Alternate Governor
Foster Gillett................................Alternate Governor
Dan O'Neill ....Alternate Governor

Nashville Predators
Craig Leipold ....Governor
Steve Violetta..............................Alternate Governor
Ed Lang ....Alternate Governor
David Poile ....Alternate Governor

New Jersey Devils
Lou Lamoriello..............................Governor
Jeff Vanderbeek............................Jeff Vanderbeek
Michael Gilfillan ....Alternate Governor

New York Islanders
Charles B. Wang............................Governor
Sanjay Kumar................................Alternate Governor
Mike Milbury................................Alternate Governor
Michael J. Picker..........................Alternate Governor
Roy E. Reichbach..........................Alternate Governor

New York Rangers
James L. Dolan .... Governor
Glen Sather..................................Alternate Governor
Steve Mills ....Alternate Governor
Hank Ratner ....Alternate Governor

Ottawa Senators
Eugene Melnyk..............................Governor
Roy Mlakar ....Alternate Governor
Sheldon Plener ....Alternate Governor

Philadelphia Flyers
Edward M. Snider..........................Governor
Ronald K. Ryan ....Alternate Governor
Philip I. Weinberg ....Alternate Governor
Bob Clarke ....Alternate Governor
Peter Luukko ....Alternate Governor

Phoenix Coyotes
Steve Ellman................................Governor
Wayne Gretzky..............................Alternate Governor
Doug Moss ....Alternate Governor
Mike Barnett................................Alternate Governor

Pittsburgh Penguins
Kenneth Sawyer ....Governor
Craig Patrick ....Alternate Governor
Ronald Burkle..............................Alternate Governor
Anthony Liberati ....Alternate Governor

St. Louis Blues
William J. Laurie............................Governor
Richard C. Thomas ....Alternate Governor
Brent P. Karasiuk ....Alternate Governor
Mark Sauer ....Alternate Governor
Larry Pleau ....Alternate Governor

San Jose Sharks
Greg Jamison................................Governor
Kevin Compton..............................Alternate Governor
Doug Wilson ....Alternate Governor

Tampa Bay Lightning
Thomas S. Wilson ....Governor
Ronald J. Campbell ....Alternate Governor
Jay H. Feaster ....Alternate Governor

Toronto Maple Leafs
Larry Tanenbaum..........................Governor
Dean Metcalf ....Alternate Governor
Dale Lastman ....Alternate Governor
Richard Peddie ....Alternate Governor
John Ferguson..............................Alternate Governor

Vancouver Canucks
John E. McCaw, Jr.........................Governor
Francesco Aquilini ....Alternate Governor
David M. Nonis ....Alternate Governor

Washington Capitals
Richard M. Patrick ....Governor
Ted Leonsis..................................Alternate Governor
George McPhee ....Alternate Governor

Commissioner and League Presidents

Gary B. Bettman

Gary B. Bettman took office as the NHL's first Commissioner on February 1, 1993. Since the League was formed in 1917, there have been five League Presidents.

NHL President	Years in Office
Frank Calder	1917-1943
Mervyn "Red" Dutton	1943-1946
Clarence Campbell	1946-1977
John A. Ziegler, Jr.	1977-1992
Gil Stein	1992-1993

Hockey Hall of Fame

BCE Place
30 Yonge Street
Toronto, Ontario M5E 1X8
Phone: 416/360-7735
Executive Fax: 416/360-1501
Resource Centre Fax: 416/360-1316
www.hhof.com

William C. Hay – Chairman and Chief Executive Officer
Jeff Denomme – President, C.O.O. and Treasurer
Craig Baines – Vice President, Operations
Ron Ellis – Director, Public Affairs
    and Assistant to the President
Peter Jagla – Vice President, Marketing
Phil Pritchard – Vice President, Resource Centre
    and Curator
Steve Ozimec – Manager, Special Events
    and Hospitality
Craig Campbell – Manager, Resource Centre
    and Archives
Kelly Massé – Manager, Corporate Development
    and Media Relations
Dave Sanford – Photographer

National Hockey League Players' Association

777 Bay Street, Suite 2400
Toronto, Ontario M5G 2C8
Phone: 416/313-2300
Fax: 416/313-2301
www.nhlpa.com

Ted Saskin – Executive Director and General Counsel
Mike Gartner – Director, Business Relations
Kenneth Kim – Director, Marketing
Ian Pulver, Ian Penny, Roland Lee –
        Associate Counsel, Labour
Mike Ouellet – Associate Counsel, Licensing
Steve Larmer – Player Relations
Greg Dick – Senior Manager, Finance and Business
    Administration
Kim Murdoch – Manager, Pensions and Benefits
Devin Smith – Program Manager, Goals & Dreams Fund
Jonathan Weatherdon – Manager, Media Relations

NHL On-Ice Officials

Total NHL Games and 2003-04 Games columns count regular-season games only.

Referees

#	Name	Birthplace	Birthdate	First NHL Game	Total NHL Games	2003-04 Games
9	Blaine Angus	Shawville, Que.	9/25/61	10/17/92	444	54
15	Stephane Auger	Montreal, Que.	12/9/70	4/1/00	240	72
10	Paul Devorski	Guelph, Ont.	8/18/58	10/14/89	895	72
44	Harry Dumas	Mount Laurel, N.J.	7/7/73	12/27/00	28	14
39	Gord Dwyer	Halifax, N.S.	5/18/77			
2	Kerry Fraser	Sarnia, Ont.	5/30/52	4/6/75	1551	72
27	Eric Furlatt	Cap de la Madelaine, Que.	12/2/71	10/8/01	167	72
30	Mike Hasenfratz	Regina, Sask.	7/19/66	10/21/00	249	72
17	Shane Heyer	Summerland, B.C.	2/7/64	*10/1/99	[1]314	72
46	Scott Hoberg	Windsor, Ont.	1/23/71			
8	Dave Jackson	Montreal, Que.	11/28/64	12/23/90	754	72
25	Marc Joannette	Verdun, Que.	11/3/68	10/27/99	289	72
18	Greg Kimmerly	Toronto, Ont.	12/8/64	11/30/96	376	72
12	Don Koharski	Halifax, N.S.	12/2/55	10/14/77	[2]1434	72
48	Tom Kowal	Vernon, B.C.	11/2/67	10/29/99	175	26
40	Steve Kozari	Penticton, B.C.	6/20/73			
37	Bob Langdon	Woodstock, Ont.	3/11/71	11/11/01	57	29
14	Dennis LaRue	Savannah, GA	7/14/59	3/26/91	576	72
28	Chris Lee	Saint John, N.B.	7/7/70	4/2/00	147	72
3	Mike Leggo	North Bay, Ont.	10/7/64	3/3/98	368	72
6	Dan Marouelli	Edmonton, Alta.	7/16/55	11/2/84	1266	72
26	Rob Martell	Winnipeg, Man.	10/21/63	3/14/84	[3]289	72
41	Wes McCauley	Georgetown, Ont.	1/11/72	1/20/03	23	18
7	Bill McCreary	Guelph, Ont.	11/17/55	11/3/84	1305	72
19	Mick McGeough	Regina, Sask.	6/20/57	1/19/89	877	73
34	Brad Meier	Dayton, OH	4/11/67	10/23/99	291	72
36	Dean Morton	Peterborough, Ont.	2/27/68	11/11/00	31	0
13	Dan O'Halloran	Essex, Ont.	3/25/64	10/14/95	447	73
42	Dan O'Rourke	Calgary, Alta.	8/31/72	10/2/99	[4]25	23
20	Tim Peel	Toronto, Ont.	4/27/66	10/21/99	299	73
43	Brian Pochmara	Detroit, MI	11/27/76			
33	Kevin Pollock	Kincardine, Ont.	2/7/70	3/28/00	296	73
5	Chris Rooney	Boston, MA	5/26/74	11/22/00	192	72
38	Francois St. Laurent	Greenfield Park, Que.	6/26/77			
45	Justin St. Pierre	Dolbeau, Que.	2/17/72			
16	Rob Shick	Port Alberni, B.C.	12/4/57	4/6/86	1074	72
49	Jeff Smith	Hamilton, Ont.	9/2/69			
31	Craig Spada	Welland, Ont.	9/7/71	3/28/02	90	71
11	Kelly Sutherland	Victoria, B.C.	4/18/71	12/19/00	232	72
21	Don Van Massenhoven	London, Ont.	7/17/60	11/11/93	692	72
29	Ian Walsh	Philadelphia, PA	5/9/72	10/14/00	134	70
35	Dean Warren	Toronto, Ont.	7/22/63	10/8/99	293	72
23	Brad Watson	Regina, Sask.	10/4/61	2/5/94	396	72

[1] plus 785 games as a linesman. [2] plus 163 games as a linesman. [3] plus 1 game as a linesman. [4] plus 120 games as a linesman.

Linesmen

#	Name	Birthplace	Birthdate	First NHL Game	Total NHL Games	2003-04 Games
75	Derek Amell	Port Colborne, Ont.	9/16/68	10/13/97	433	73
59	Steve Barton	Ottawa, Ont.	12/27/71	11/1/00	210	71
96	David Brisebois	Sudbury, Ont.	4/14/76	10/11/99	165	29
74	Lonnie Cameron	Victoria, B.C.	7/15/64	10/5/96	550	74
67	Pierre Champoux	Ville St-Pierre, Que.	4/18/63	10/8/88	1005	68
76	Michel Cormier	Trois-Rivieres, Que.	5/28/74	10/10/03	71	71
88	Mike Cvik	Calgary, Alta.	7/6/62	10/8/87	1134	71
83	Angelo D'Amico	Etobicoke, Ont.	5/29/74	11/27/00	97	27
60	Pat Dapuzzo	Hoboken, NJ	12/29/58	12/5/84	1368	32
54	Greg Devorski	Guelph, Ont.	8/3/69	10/9/93	714	70
68	Scott Driscoll	Seaforth, Ont.	5/2/68	10/10/92	782	69
66	Darren Gibbs	Edmonton, Alta.	9/30/66	10/1/97	335	0
82	Ryan Galloway	Winnipeg, Man.	7/12/72	10/17/02	98	73
91	Don Henderson	Calgary, Alta.	9/23/68	3/10/95	537	74
71	Brad Kovachik	Woodstock, Ont.	3/7/71	10/10/96	521	72
86	Brad Lazarowich	Vancouver, B.C.	8/4/62	10/9/86	1228	72
78	Brian Mach	Little Falls, MN	4/15/74	10/7/00	274	71
90	Andy McElman	Chicago Heights, IL	8/4/61	10/7/93	718	71
89	Steve Miller	Stratford, Ont.	6/22/72	10/7/00	264	68
97	Jean Morin	Sorel, Que.	8/10/63	10/5/91	827	60
93	Brian Murphy	Dover, NH	12/13/64	10/7/88	[5]928	70
95	Jonny Murray	Beauport, Que.	8/10/74	10/7/00	277	71
70	Derek Nansen	Ottawa, Ont.	12/6/71	10/11/02	136	71
80	Thor Nelson	Westminister, CA	1/6/68	2/16/95	439	63
77	Tim Nowak	Buffalo, NY	9/6/67	10/8/93	728	73
79	Mark Paré	Windsor, Ont.	7/26/57	10/11/79	1814	68
65	Pierre Racicot	Verdun, Que.	2/15/67	10/12/93	747	71
73	Vaughan Rody	Winnipeg, Man.	12/13/68	10/8/00	267	58
52	Dan Schachte	Madison, WI	7/13/58	10/6/82	1538	71
61	Lyle Seitz	Brooks, Alta.	1/22/69	10/6/92	[6]396	73
84	Anthony Sericolo	Troy, NY	7/17/68	10/21/98	370	70
57	Jay Sharrers	Jamaica, West Indies	7/3/67	10/6/90	[7]642	69
92	Mark Shewchuk	Hamilton, Ont.	6/1/75	10/9/03	71	71
56	Mark Wheler	North Battleford, Sask.	9/20/65	10/10/92	814	74

[5] plus 88 games as a referee. [6] plus 10 games as a referee. [7] plus 136 games as a referee.

NHL History

1917 — National Hockey League organized November 26 in Montreal following suspension of operations by the National Hockey Association of Canada Limited (NHA). Montreal Canadiens, Montreal Wanderers, Ottawa Senators and Quebec Bulldogs attended founding meeting. Delegates decided to use NHA rules.

Toronto Arenas were later admitted as fifth team; Quebec decided not to operate during the first season. Quebec players allocated to remaining four teams.

Frank Calder elected president and secretary-treasurer.

First NHL games played December 19, with Toronto only arena with artificial ice. Clubs played 22-game split schedule.

1918 — Emergency meeting held January 3 due to destruction by fire of Montreal Arena which was home ice for both Canadiens and Wanderers.

Wanderers withdrew, reducing the NHL to three teams; Canadiens played remaining home games at 3,250-seat Jubilee rink.

Quebec franchise sold to P.J. Quinn of Toronto on October 18 on the condition that the team operate in Quebec City for 1918-19 season. Quinn did not attend the November League meeting and Quebec did not play in 1918-19.

1919-20 — NHL reactivated Quebec Bulldogs franchise. Former Quebec players returned to the club. New Mount Royal Arena became home of Canadiens. Toronto Arenas changed name to St. Patricks. Clubs played 24-game split schedule.

1920-21 — H.P. Thompson of Hamilton, Ontario made application for the purchase of an NHL franchise. Quebec franchise shifted to Hamilton with other NHL teams providing players to strengthen the club.

1921-22 — Split schedule abandoned. First and second place teams at the end of full schedule to play for championship.

1922-23 — Clubs agreed that players could not be sold or traded to clubs in any other league without first being offered to all other clubs in the NHL. In March, Foster Hewitt broadcasts radio's first hockey game.

1923-24 — Ottawa's new 10,000-seat arena opened. First U.S. franchise granted to Boston for following season.

Dr. Cecil Hart Trophy donated to NHL to be awarded to the player judged most useful to his team.

1924-25 — Canadian Arena Company of Montreal granted a franchise to operate Montreal Maroons. NHL now six team league with two clubs in Montreal. Inaugural game in new Montreal Forum played November 29, 1924 as Canadiens defeated Toronto 7-1. Forum was home rink for the Maroons, but no ice was available in the Canadiens arena November 29, resulting in a shift to the Forum.

Hamilton finished first in the standings, receiving a bye into the finals. But Hamilton players, demanding $200 each for additional games in the playoffs, went on strike. The NHL suspended all players, fining them $200 each. Stanley Cup finalist to be the winner of NHL semi-final between Toronto and Canadiens.

Prince of Wales and Lady Byng trophies donated to NHL.

Clubs played 30-game schedule.

1925-26 — Hamilton club dropped from NHL. Players signed by new New York Americans franchise. Pittsburgh Pirates granted franchise.

Clubs played 36-game schedule.

1926-27 — New York Rangers granted franchise May 15, 1926. Chicago Black Hawks and Detroit Cougars granted franchises September 25, 1926. NHL now ten-team league with an American and a Canadian Division.

Stanley Cup came under the control of NHL. In previous seasons, winners of the now-defunct Western or Pacific Coast leagues would play NHL champion in Cup finals.

Toronto franchise sold to a new company controlled by Hugh Aird and Conn Smythe. Name changed from St. Patricks to Maple Leafs.

Clubs played 44-game schedule.

The Montreal Canadiens donated the Vezina Trophy to be awarded to the team allowing the fewest goals-against in regular season play. The winning team would, in turn, present the trophy to the goaltender playing in the greatest number of games during the season.

1930-31 — Detroit franchise changed name from Cougars to Falcons. Pittsburgh transferred to Philadelphia for one season. Pirates changed name to Philadelphia Quakers. Trading deadline for teams set at February 15 of each year. NHL approved operation of farm teams by Rangers, Americans, Falcons and Bruins. Four-sided electric arena clock first demonstrated.

1931-32 — Philadelphia dropped out. Ottawa withdrew for one season. New Maple Leaf Gardens completed. Clubs played 48-game schedule

1932-33 — Detroit franchise changed name from Falcons to Red Wings. Franchise application received from St. Louis but refused because of additional travel costs. Ottawa team resumed play.

1933-34 — First All-Star Game played as a benefit for injured player Ace Bailey. Leafs defeated All-Stars 7-3 in Toronto.

1934-35 — Ottawa franchise transferred to St. Louis. Team called St. Louis Eagles and consisted largely of Ottawa's players.

1935-36 — Ottawa-St. Louis franchise terminated. Montreal Canadiens finished season with very poor record. To strengthen the club, NHL gave Canadiens first call on the services of all French-Canadian players for three seasons.

1937-38 — Second benefit All-Star game staged November 2 in Montreal in aid of the family of the late Canadiens star Howie Morenz.

Montreal Maroons withdrew from the NHL on June 22, 1938, leaving seven clubs in the League.

1938-39 — Expenses for each club regulated at $5 per man per day for meals and $2.50 per man per day for accommodation.

1939-40 — Benefit All-Star Game played October 29, 1939 in Montreal for the children of the late Albert (Babe) Siebert.

1940-41 — Ross-Tyer puck adopted as the official puck of the NHL. Early in the season it was apparent that this puck was too soft. The Spalding puck was adopted in its place.

On May 16, 1941, Arthur Ross, NHL governor from Boston, donated a perpetual trophy to be awarded annually to the player voted outstanding in the league. Due to wartime restrictions, the trophy was never awarded.

1941-42 — New York Americans changed name to Brooklyn Americans.

1942-43 — Brooklyn Americans withdrew from NHL, leaving six teams: Boston, Chicago, Detroit, Montreal, New York and Toronto. Playoff format saw first-place team play third-place team and second play fourth.

Clubs played 50-game schedule.

Frank Calder, president of the NHL since its inception, died in Montreal. Meryn "Red" Dutton, former manager of the New York Americans, became president. The NHL commissioned the Calder Memorial Trophy to be awarded to the League's outstanding rookie each year.

1945-46 — Philadelphia, Los Angeles and San Francisco applied for NHL franchises.

The Philadelphia Arena Company of the American Hockey League applied for an injunction to prevent the possible operation of an NHL franchise in that city.

1946-47 — Mervyn Dutton retired as president of the NHL prior to the start of the season. He was succeeded by Clarence S. Campbell.

Individual trophy winners and all-star team members to receive $1,000 awards.

Playoff guarantees for players introduced.

Clubs played 60-game schedule.

1947-48 — The first annual All-Star Game for the benefit of the players' pension fund was played when the All-Stars defeated the Stanley Cup Champion Toronto Maple Leafs 4-3 in Toronto on October 13, 1947.

Criteria for awarding Art Ross Trophy changed. Now awarded to top scorer. Elmer Lach was its first winner.

Philadelphia and Los Angeles franchise applications refused.

National Hockey League Pension Society formed.

1949-50 — Clubs played 70-game schedule.

First intra-league draft held April 30, 1950. Clubs allowed to protect 30 players. Remaining players available for $25,000 each.

1951-52 — Referees included in the League's pension plan.

1952-53 — In May of 1952, City of Cleveland applied for NHL franchise. Application denied. In March of 1953, the Cleveland Barons of the AHL challenged the NHL champions for the Stanley Cup. The NHL governors did not accept this challenge.

1953-54 — The James Norris Memorial Trophy presented to the NHL for annual presentation to the League's best defenseman.

Intra-league draft rules amended to allow teams to protect 18 skaters and two goaltenders, claiming price reduced to $15,000.

1954-55 — Each arena to operate an "out-of-town" scoreboard.

1956-57 — Referees and linesmen to wear shirts of black and white vertical stripes. Standardized signals for referees and linesmen introduced.

1960-61 — Canadian National Exhibition, City of Toronto and NHL reach agreement for the construction of a Hockey Hall of Fame on the CNE grounds. Hall opens on August 26, 1961.

1963-64 — Player development league established with clubs operated by NHL franchises located in Minneapolis, St. Paul, Indianapolis, Omaha and, beginning in 1964-65, Tulsa. First universal amateur draft took place. All players of qualifying age (17) unaffected by sponsorship of junior teams available to be drafted.

1964-65 — Conn Smythe Trophy presented to the NHL to be awarded annually to the outstanding player in the Stanley Cup playoffs.

Minimum age of players subject to amateur draft changed to 18.

1965-66 — NHL announced expansion plans for a second six-team division to begin play in 1967-68.

1966-67 — Fourteen applications for NHL franchises received.

Lester Patrick Trophy presented to the NHL to be awarded annually for outstanding service to hockey in the United States.

NHL sponsorship of junior teams ceased, making all players of qualifying age not already on NHL-sponsored lists eligible for the amateur draft.

1967-68 — Six new teams added: California Seals, Los Angeles Kings, Minnesota North Stars, Philadelphia Flyers, Pittsburgh Penguins, St. Louis Blues. New teams to play in West Division. Remaining six teams to play in East Division.

Minimum age of players subject to amateur draft changed to 20.

Clubs played 74-game schedule.

Clarence S. Campbell Trophy awarded to team finishing the regular season in first place in West Division.

California Seals change name to Oakland Seals on December 8, 1967.

1968-69 — Clubs played 76-game schedule.

Amateur draft expanded to cover any amateur player of qualifying age throughout the world.

1970-71 — Two new teams added: Buffalo Sabres and Vancouver Canucks. These teams joined East Division: Chicago switched to West Division. Oakland Seals change name to California Golden Seals prior to season.

Clubs played 78-game schedule.

1971-72 — Playoff format amended. In each division, first to play fourth; second to play third.

1972-73 — Soviet Nationals and Canadian NHL stars play eight-game pre-season series. Canadians win 4-3-1.

Two new teams added. Atlanta Flames join West Division; New York Islanders join East Division.

1974-75 — Two new teams added: Kansas City Scouts and Washington Capitals. Teams realigned into two nine-team conferences, the Prince of Wales made up of the Norris and Adams Divisions, and the Clarence Campbell made up of the Smythe and Patrick Divisions.

Clubs played 80-game schedule.

1976-77 — California franchise transferred to Cleveland. Team named Cleveland Barons. Kansas City franchise transferred to Denver. Team named Colorado Rockies.

1977-78 — Clarence S. Campbell retires as NHL president. Succeeded by John A. Ziegler, Jr.

1978-79 — Cleveland and Minnesota franchises merge, leaving NHL with 17 teams. Merged team placed in Adams Division, playing home games in Minnesota.

Minimum age of players subject to amateur draft changed to 19.

1979-80 — Four new teams added: Edmonton Oilers, Hartford Whalers, Quebec Nordiques and Winnipeg Jets.

Minimum age of players subject to entry draft changed to 18.

1980-81 — Atlanta franchise shifted to Calgary, retaining "Flames" name.

1981-82 — Teams realigned within existing divisions. New groupings based on geographical areas. Unbalanced schedule adopted.

1982-83 — Colorado Rockies franchise shifted to East Rutherford, New Jersey. Team named New Jersey Devils. Franchise moved to Patrick Division from Smythe; Winnipeg moved to Smythe Division from Norris.

NHL History — *continued*

1991-92 — San Jose Sharks added, making the NHL a 22-team league. NHL celebrates 75th Anniversary Season. The 1991-92 regular season suspended due to a players' strike on April 1, 1992. Play resumed April 12, 1992.

1992-93 — Gil Stein named NHL president (October, 1992). Gary Bettman named first NHL Commissioner (February, 1993). Ottawa Senators and Tampa Bay Lightning added, making the NHL a 24-team league. NHL celebrates Stanley Cup Centennial. Clubs played 84-game schedule.

1993-94 — Mighty Ducks of Anaheim and Florida Panthers added, making the NHL a 26-team league. Minnesota franchise shifted to Dallas, team named Dallas Stars. Prince of Wales and Clarence Campbell Conferences renamed Eastern and Western. Adams, Patrick, Norris and Smythe Divisions renamed Northeast, Atlantic, Central and Pacific. Winnipeg moved to Central Division from Pacific; Tampa Bay moved to Atlantic Division from Central; Pittsburgh moved to Northeast Division from Atlantic.

1994-95 — A lockout resulted in the cancellation of 468 games from October 1, 1994 to January 19, 1995. Clubs played a 48-game schedule that began January 20, 1995 and ended May 3, 1995. No inter-conference games were played.

1995-96 — Quebec franchise transferred to Denver. Team named Colorado Avalanche and placed in Pacific Division of Western Conference. Clubs to play 82-game schedule.

1996-97 — Winnipeg franchise transferred to Phoenix. Team named Phoenix Coyotes and placed in Central Division of Western Conference.

1997-98 — Hartford franchise transferred to Raleigh. Team named Carolina Hurricanes and remains in Northeast Division of Eastern Conference.

1998-99 — The addition of the Nashville Predators made the NHL a 27-team league and brought about the creation of two new divisions and a League-wide realignment in preparation for further expansion to 30 teams by 2000-2001. Nashville was added to the Central Division of the Western Conference, while Toronto moved into the Northeast Division of the Eastern Conference. Pittsburgh was shifted from the Northeast to the Atlantic, while Carolina left the Northeast for the newly created Southeast Division of the Eastern Conference. Florida, Tampa Bay and Washington also joined the Southeast. In the Western Conference, Calgary, Colorado, Edmonton and Vancouver make up the new Northwest Division. Dallas and Phoenix moved from the Central to the Pacific Division.

The NHL retired uniform number 99 in honor of all-time scoring leader Wayne Gretzky who retired at the end of the season.

1999-2000 — Atlanta Thrashers added, making the NHL a 28-team league.

2000-01 — Columbus Blue Jackets and Minnesota Wild added, making the NHL a 30-team league.

2003-04 — First outdoor NHL game and largest crowd in League history as 57,167 attend Heritage Classic at Edmonton's Commonwealth Stadium. Montreal defeated Edmonton 4-3, November 22, 2003.

2004-05 — A lockout resulted in the cancellation of the season.

Major Rule Changes

1910-11 — Game changed from two 30-minute periods to three 20-minute periods.

1911-12 — National Hockey Association (forerunner of the NHL) originated six-man hockey, replacing seven-man game.

1917-18 — Goalies permitted to fall to the ice to make saves. Previously a goaltender was penalized for dropping to the ice.

1918-19 — Penalty rules amended. For minor fouls, substitutes not allowed until penalized player had served three minutes. For major fouls, no substitutes for five minutes. For match fouls, no substitutes allowed for the remainder of the game.

With the addition of two lines painted on the ice twenty feet from center, three playing zones were created, producing a forty-foot neutral center ice area in which forward passing was permitted in this neutral zone. Kicking the puck was permitted in this neutral zone.

Tabulation of assists began.

1921-22 — Goaltenders allowed to pass the puck forward up to their own blue line.

Overtime limited to twenty minutes.

Minor penalties changed from three minutes to two minutes.

1923-24 — Match foul defined as actions deliberately injuring or disabling an opponent. For such actions, a player was fined not less than $50 and ruled off the ice for the balance of the game. A player assessed a match penalty may be replaced by a substitute at the end of 20 minutes. Match penalty recipients must meet with the League president who can assess additional punishment.

1925-26 — Delayed penalty rules introduced. Each team must have a minimum of four players on the ice at all times.

Two rules were amended to encourage offense: No more than two defensemen permitted to remain inside a team's own blue line when the puck has left the defensive zone. A faceoff to be called for ragging the puck unless short-handed.

Team captains only players allowed to talk to referees.

Goaltender's leg pads limited to 12-inch width.

Timekeeper's gong to mark end of periods rather than referee's whistle. Teams to dress a maximum of 12 players for each game from a roster of no more than 14 players.

1926-27 — Blue lines repositioned to sixty feet from each goal-line, thereby enlarging the neutral zone and standardizing distance from blue line to goal.

Uniform goal nets adopted throughout NHL with goal posts securely fastened to the ice.

1927-28 — To further encourage offense, forward passes allowed in defending and neutral zones and goaltender's pads reduced in width from 12 to 10 inches.

Game standardized at three twenty-minute periods of stop-time separated by ten-minute intermissions.

Teams to change ends after each period.

Ten minutes of sudden-death overtime to be played if the score is tied after regulation time.

Minor penalty to be assessed to any player other than a goaltender for deliberately picking up the puck while it is in play. Minor penalty to be assessed for deliberately shooting the puck out of play.

The Art Ross goal net adopted as the official net of the NHL.

Maximum length of hockey sticks limited to 53 inches measured from heel of blade to end of handle. No minimum length stipulated.

Home teams given choice of end to defend at start of game.

1928-29 — Forward passing permitted in defensive and neutral zones and into attacking zone if pass receiver is in neutral zone when pass is made. No forward passing allowed inside attacking zone.

Minor penalty to be assessed to any player who delays the game by passing the puck back into his defensive zone.

Ten-minute overtime without sudden-death provision to be played in games tied after regulation time. Games tied after this overtime period declared a draw.

Exclusive of goaltenders, team to dress at least 8 and no more than 12 skaters.

NHL Attendance

Season	Games	Regular Season Attendance	Games	Playoffs Attendance	Total Attendance
1960-61	210	2,317,142	17	242,000	2,559,142
1961-62	210	2,435,424	18	277,000	2,712,424
1962-63	210	2,590,574	16	220,906	2,811,480
1963-64	210	2,732,642	21	309,149	3,041,791
1964-65	210	2,822,635	20	303,859	3,126,494
1965-66	210	2,941,164	16	249,000	3,190,184
1966-67	210	3,084,759	16	248,336	3,333,095
1967-68	444	4,938,043	40	495,089	5,433,132
1968-69	456	5,550,613	33	431,739	5,982,352
1969-70	456	5,992,065	34	461,694	6,453,759
1970-71	546	7,257,677	43	707,633	7,965,310
1971-72	546	7,609,368	36	582,666	8,192,034
1972-73	624	8,575,651	38	624,637	9,200,288
1973-74	624	8,640,978	38	600,442	9,241,420
1974-75	720	9,521,536	51	784,181	10,305,717
1975-76	720	9,103,761	48	726,279	9,830,040
1976-77	720	8,563,890	44	646,279	9,210,169
1977-78	720	8,526,564	45	686,634	9,213,198
1978-79	680	7,758,053	45	694,521	8,452,574
1979-80	840	10,533,623	63	976,699	11,510,322
1980-81	840	10,726,198	68	966,390	11,692,588
1981-82	840	10,710,894	71	1,058,948	11,769,842
1982-83	840	11,020,610	66	1,088,222	12,028,832
1983-84	840	11,359,386	70	1,107,400	12,466,786
1984-85	840	11,633,730	70	1,107,500	12,741,230
1985-86	840	11,621,000	72	1,152,503	12,773,503
1986-87	840	11,855,880	87	1,383,967	13,239,847
1987-88	840	12,117,512	83	1,336,901	13,454,413
1988-89	840	12,417,969	83	1,327,214	13,745,183
1989-90	840	12,579,651	85	1,355,593	13,935,244
1990-91	840	12,343,897	92	1,442,203	13,786,100
1991-92	880	12,769,676	86	1,327,920	14,097,596
1992-93	1,008	14,158,177[1]	83	1,346,034	15,504,211
1993-94	1,092	16,105,604[2]	90	1,440,095	17,545,699
1994-95	624[3]	9,233,884	81	1,329,130	10,563,014
1995-96	1,066	17,041,614	86	1,540,140	18,581,754
1996-97	1,066	17,640,529	82	1,494,878	19,135,407
1997-98	1,066	17,264,678	82	1,507,416	18,772,094
1998-99	1,107	18,001,741	86	1,509,411	19,511,152
1999-2000	1,148	18,800,139	83	1,524,629	20,324,768
2000-01	1,230	20,373,379	86	1,584,011	21,957,390
2001-02	1,230	20,614,613	90	1,691,174	22,305,787
2002-03	1,230	20,408,704	89	1,636,120	22,044,824
2003-04	1,230	20,356,199	89	1,708,691	22,064,890
2004-05	....	....	....	....	....

NHLExpansion: the NHL operated as a six-team league from 1942-43 to 1966-67. Six teams were added in 1967-68:California (later to move to Cleveland), Los Angeles, Minnesota (later to move to Dallas), Philadelphia, Pittsburgh and St. Louis. In 1970-71: Buffalo and Vancouver. In 1972-73: Atlanta (later to move to Calgary) and NYIslanders. In 1974-75: Kansas City (later to move to Colorado and then to New Jersey) and Washington. In 1979-80, Hartford (later to move to Carolina), Edmonton, Quebec (later to move to Colorado) and Winnipeg (later to move to Phoenix). In 1991-92, San Jose. In 1992-93, Ottawa and Tampa Bay. In 1993-94, Anaheim and Florida. In 1998-99, Nashville. In 1999-2000, Atlanta. In 2000-01, Columbus and Minnesota.

[1] Includes 24 neutral site games
[2] Includes 26 neutral site games
[3] Lockout resulted in the cancellation of 468 regular-season games.

Major Rule Changes — *continued*

1929-30 — Forward passing permitted inside all three zones but not permitted across either blue line.

Kicking the puck allowed, but a goal cannot be scored by kicking the puck in.

No more than three players including the goaltender may remain in their defensive zone when the puck has gone up ice. Minor penalties to be assessed for the first two violations of this rule in a game; major penalties thereafter.

Goaltenders forbidden to hold the puck. Pucks caught must be cleared immediately. For infringement of this rule, a faceoff to be taken ten feet in front of the goal with no player except the goaltender standing between the faceoff spot and the goal-line.

Highsticking penalties introduced.

Maximum number of players in uniform increased from 12 to 15.

December 21, 1929 — Forward passing rules instituted at the beginning of the 1929-30 season more than doubled number of goals scored. Partway through the season, these rules were further amended to read, "No attacking player allowed to precede the play when entering the opposing defensive zone." This is similar to modern offside rule.

1930-31 — A player without a complete stick ruled out of play and forbidden from taking part in further action until a new stick is obtained. A player who has broken his stick must obtain a replacement at his bench.

A further refinement of the offside rule stated that the puck must first be propelled into the attacking zone before any player of the attacking side can enter that zone; for infringement of this rule a faceoff to take place at the spot where the infraction took place.

1931-32 — Though there is no record of a team attempting to play with two goaltenders on the ice, a rule was instituted which stated that each team was allowed only one goaltender on the ice at one time.

Attacking players forbidden to impede the movement or obstruct the vision of opposing goaltenders.

Defending players with the exception of the goaltender forbidden from falling on the puck within 10 feet of the net.

1932-33 — Each team to have captain on the ice at all times.

If the goaltender is removed from the ice to serve a penalty, the manager of the club to appoint a substitute.

Match penalty with substitution after five minutes instituted for kicking another player.

1933-34 — Number of players permitted to stand in defensive zone restricted to three including goaltender.

Visible time clocks required in each rink.

Two referees replace one referee and one linesman.

1934-35 — Penalty shot awarded when a player is tripped and thus prevented from having a clear shot on goal, having no player to pass to other than the offending player. Shot taken from inside a 10-foot circle located 38 feet from the goal. The goaltender must not advance more than one foot from his goal-line when the shot is taken.

1937-38 — Rules introduced governing icing the puck.

Penalty shot awarded when a player other than a goaltender falls on the puck within 10 feet of the goal.

1938-39 — Penalty shot modified to allow puck carrier to skate in before shooting.

One referee and one linesman replace two referee system.

Blue line widened to 12 inches.

Maximum number of players in uniform increased from 14 to 15.

1939-40 — A substitute replacing a goaltender removed from ice to serve a penalty may use a goaltender's stick and gloves but no other goaltending equipment.

1940-41 — Flooding ice surface between periods made obligatory.

1941-42 — Penalty shots classified as minor and major. Minor shot to be taken from a line 28 feet from the goal. Major shot, awarded when a player is tripped with only the goaltender to beat, permits the player taking the penalty shot to skate right into the goalkeeper and shoot from point-blank range.

One referee and two linesmen employed to officiate games.

For playoffs, standby minor league goaltenders employed by NHL as emergency substitutes.

1942-43 — Because of wartime restrictions on train scheduling, regular-season overtime was discontinued on November 21, 1942.

Player limit reduced from 15 to 14. Minimum of 12 men in uniform abolished.

1943-44 — Red line at center ice introduced to speed up the game and reduce offside calls. This rule is considered to mark the beginning of the modern era in the NHL.

1945-46 — Goal indicator lights synchronized with official time clock required at all rinks.

1946-47 — System of signals by officials to indicate infractions introduced.

Linesmen from neutral cities employed for all games.

1947-48 — Goal awarded when a player with the puck has an open net to shoot at and a thrown stick prevents the shot on goal. Major penalty to any player who throws his stick in any zone other than defending zone. If a stick is thrown by a player in his defending zone but the thrown stick is not considered to have prevented a goal, a penalty shot is awarded.

All playoff games played until a winner determined, with 20-minute sudden-death overtime periods separated by 10-minute intermissions.

1949-50 — Ice surface painted white.

Clubs allowed to dress 17 players exclusive of goaltenders.

Major penalties incurred by goaltenders served by a member of the goaltender's team instead of resulting in a penalty shot.

1950-51 — Each team required to provide an emergency goaltender in attendance with full equipment at each game for use by either team in the event of illness or injury to a regular goaltender.

1951-52 — Home teams to wear basic white uniforms; visiting teams basic colored uniforms.

Goal crease enlarged from 3 × 7 feet to 4 × 8 feet.

Number of players in uniform reduced to 15 plus goaltenders.

Faceoff circles enlarged from 10-foot to 15-foot radius.

1952-53 — Teams permitted to dress 15 skaters on the road and 16 at home.

1953-54 — Number of players in uniform set at 16 plus goaltenders.

1954-55 — Number of players in uniform set at 18 plus goaltenders up to December 1 and 16 plus goaltenders thereafter. Teams agree to wear colored uniforms at home and white uniforms on the road.

1956-57 — Player serving a minor penalty allowed to return to ice when a goal is scored by opposing team.

1959-60 — Players prevented from leaving their benches to enter into an altercation. Substitutions permitted providing substitutes do not enter into altercation.

1960-61 — Number of players in uniform set at 16 plus goaltenders.

1961-62 — Penalty shots to be taken by the player against whom the foul was committed. In the event of a penalty shot called in a situation where a particular player hasn't been fouled, the penalty shot to be taken by any player on the ice when the foul was committed.

1964-65 — No body contact on faceoffs.

In playoff games, each team to have its substitute goaltender dressed in his regular uniform except for leg pads and body protector. All previous rules governing standby goaltenders terminated.

1965-66 — Teams required to dress two goaltenders for each regular-season game. Maximum stick length increased to 55 inches.

1966-67 — Substitution allowed on coincidental major penalties.

Between-periods intermissions fixed at 15 minutes.

1967-68 — If a penalty incurred by a goaltender is a co-incident major, the penalty to be served by a player of the goaltender's team on the ice at the time the penalty was called. Limit of curvature of hockey stick blade set at 1½ inches.

1969-70 — Limit of curvature of hockey stick blade set at 1 inch.

1970-71 — Home teams to wear basic white uniforms; visiting teams basic colored uniforms.

Limit of curvature of hockey stick blade set at ½ inch.

Minor penalty for deliberately shooting the puck out of the playing area.

1971-72 — Number of players in uniform set at 17 plus 2 goaltenders.

Third man to enter an altercation assessed an automatic game misconduct penalty.

1972-73 — Minimum width of stick blade reduced to 2 inches from 2½ inches.

1974-75 — Bench minor penalty imposed if a penalized player does not proceed directly and immediately to the penalty box.

1976-77 — Rule dealing with fighting amended to provide a major and game misconduct penalty for any player who is clearly the instigator of a fight.

1977-78 — Teams requesting a stick measurement to be assessed a minor penalty in the event that the measured stick does not violate the rules.

1979-80 — Wearing of helmets made mandatory for players entering the NHL.

1980-81 — Maximum stick length increased to 58 inches.

1981-82 — If both of a team's listed goaltenders are incapacitated, the team can dress and play any eligible goaltender who is available.

1982-83 — Number of players in uniform set at 18 plus 2 goaltenders.

1983-84 — Five-minute sudden-death overtime to be played in regular-season games that are tied at the end of regulation time.

1985-86 — Substitutions allowed in the event of co-incidental minor penalties. Maximum stick length increased to 60 inches.

1986-87 — Delayed off-side is no longer in effect once the players of the offending team have cleared the opponents' defensive zone.

1990-91 — The goal lines, blue lines, defensive zone face-off circles and markings all moved one foot out from the end boards, creating 11 feet of room behind the nets and shrinking the neutral zone from 60 to 58 feet.

1991-92 — Video replays employed to assist referees in goal/no goal situations. Size of goal crease increased. Crease changed to semi-circular configuration. Time clock to record tenths of a second in last minute of each period and overtime. Major and game misconduct penalty for checking from behind into boards. Penalties added for crease infringement and unnecessary contact with goaltender. Goal disallowed if puck enters net while a player of the attacking team is standing on the goal crease line, is in the goal crease or places his stick in the goal crease.

1992-93 — No substitutions allowed in the event of coincidental minor penalties called when both teams are at full strength. Minor penalty for attempting to draw a penalty ("diving"). Major and game misconduct penalty for checking from behind into goal frame. Game misconduct penalty for instigating a fight. High sticking redefined to include any use of the stick above waist-height. Previous rule stipulated shoulder-height.

1993-94 — High sticking redefined to allow goals scored with a high stick below the height of the crossbar of the goal frame.

1996-97 — Maximum stick length increased to 63 inches. All players must be clear of the attacking zone prior to the puck being shot into that zone. The opportunity to "tag-up" and return into the zone has been removed.

1998-99 — The league instituted a two-referee system with each team to play 20 regular-season games with two referees and a pair of linesmen. Goal line moved to 13 feet from end boards. Goal crease altered to extend one foot beyond each goal post (eight feet across in total. Sides of crease squared off, extending 4'6". Only the top of the crease remains rounded. Only the top of the crease remains rounded.

1999-2000 — Each team to play 25 home and 25 road games using the two-referee system. Crease rule revised to implement a "no harm, no foul, no video review" standard. Teams to play with four skaters and a goaltender in regular-season overtime. If a goal is scored in regular-season overtime, the winner is awarded two points and the loser one point. In no goal is scored in overtime, both teams are awarded one point.

2000-01 — All games to be played using the two-referee system.

2002-03 — "Hurry-up" faceoff and line-change rules implemented.

2003-04 — Home teams to wear basic colored uniforms; visiting teams basic white uniforms. Maximum length of goaltender's pads set at 38 inches.

2005-06 — The NHL adopted a comprehensive package of rule changes that included the following:

Goal line moved to 11 feet from end boards; blue lines moved to 75 feet from end boards, reducing neutral zone from 54 feet to 50 feet. Center red line eliminated for two-line passes. "Tag-up" off-side rule reinstituted. This rule was previously used from 1986-87 through 1995-96. Goaltender not permitted to play the puck outside a designated trapezoid-shaped area behind the net. A team that ices the puck will not be permitted to make any player substitutions prior to the ensuing faceoff. A player who instigates a fight in the final five minutes of regulation time or at any time of overtime will receive a minor, a major, a misconduct and an automatic one-game suspension. The size of goaltender equipment has been reduced by approximately 11 percent. If a game remains tied after five minutes of overtime, a shootout will be conducted to determine a winner.

See page 13 for more detail on new rules for 2005-06.

NHL RINK DIMENSIONS 2005-06

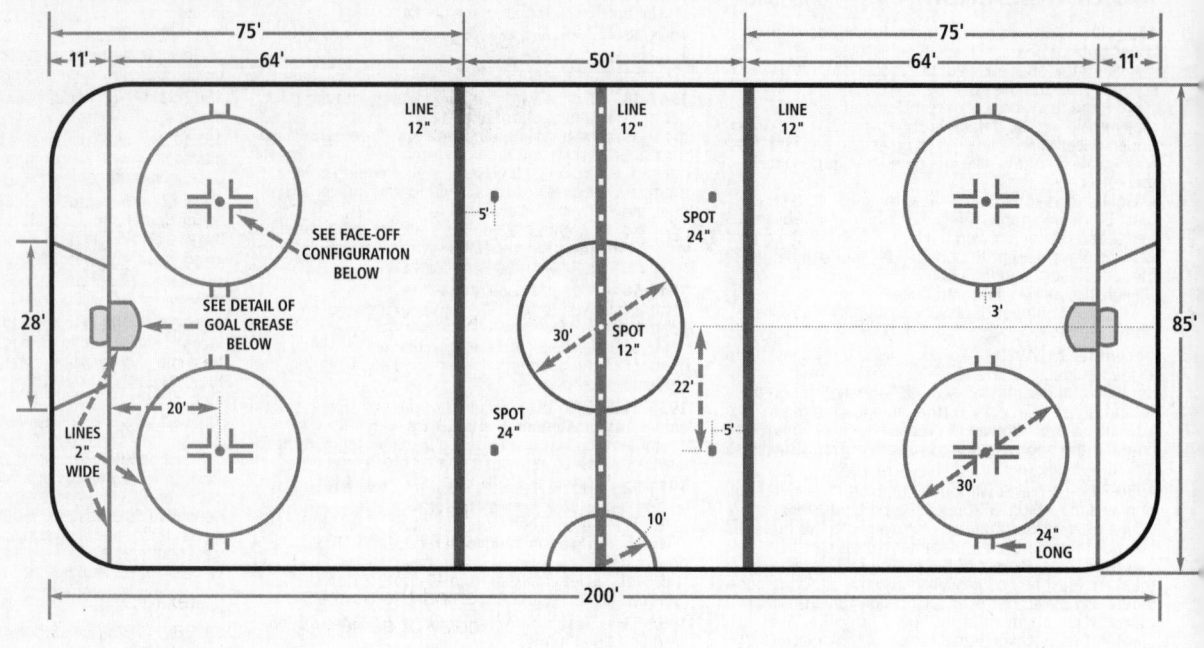

NHL RINK DIMENSIONS 2003-04

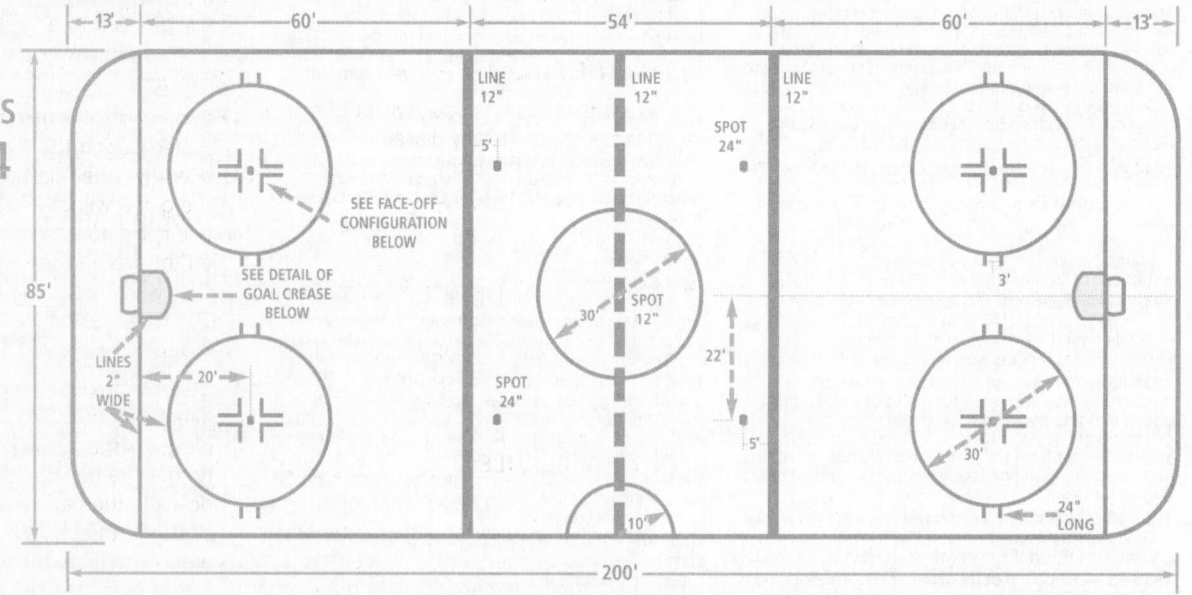

FACEOFF CONFIGURATION

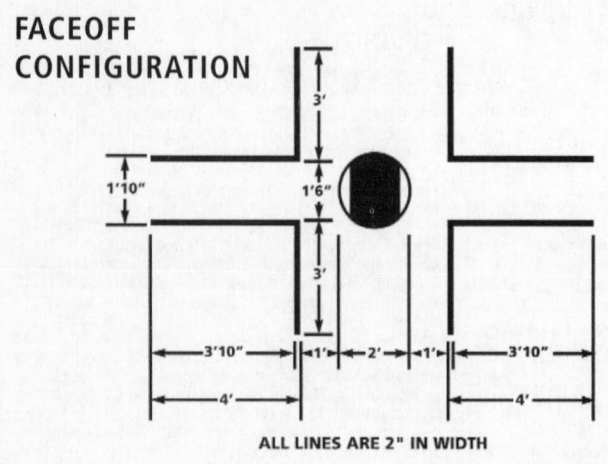

ALL LINES ARE 2" IN WIDTH

CREASE DIMENSIONS

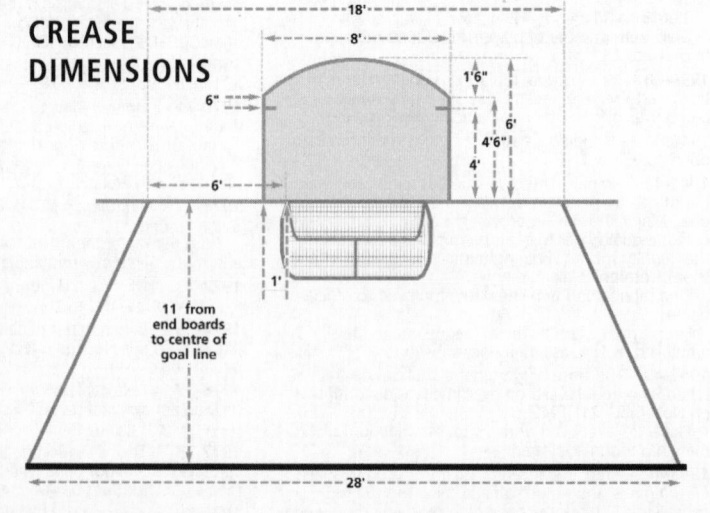

New Rules for 2005-06

DIMENSIONS OF THE RINK

- The neutral-zone edges of the blue lines will be positioned 64 feet from the attacking goal line and 75 feet from the end boards in the attacking zone. There will be an additional four feet in each of the offensive zones between the goal line and blue lines.

- The goal lines will be positioned 11 feet from the end boards, two feet closer to the end boards than previously. The goal line had been at 13 feet since 1998-99.

- The size of the neutral zone will be reduced to 50 feet from 54 feet.

CENTER RED LINE ELIMINATED FOR TWO-LINE PASSES

- Passes from behind the defensive blue line to the attacking blue line will be considered legal. The center red line will be ignored for purposes of a "two-line pass."

OFFSIDE

- During a delayed offside call, the linesman shall nullify the offside violation and allow play to continue if:

  i) All players of the offending Team clear the zone at the same instant (skate contact with the blue line) permitting the attacking players to re-enter the attacking zone, or

  ii) The defending Team passes or carries the puck into the neutral zone.

- The "tag-up" rule was previously used from 1986-87 through 1995-96.

RESTRICTIONS ON GOALIE HANDLING THE PUCK

- A goaltender may not play the puck outside a designated area behind the net. This area is defined by lines that begin on the goal line, six feet from each goal post, and extend diagonally to points 28 feet apart at the end boards. Should a goalie play the puck outside this area behind the goal line, a minor penalty for delay of game will be imposed. The determining factor will be the position of the puck.

ICING THE PUCK

- A team that ices the puck will not be permitted to make any player substitutions prior to the ensuing face-off. The determination of players on-ice will be made when the puck leaves the offending player's stick.

- "Touch" icing will remain the practice, although the Linesman will have discretion to wave off apparent icing infractions on attempted passes if those passes are deemed receivable.

INSTIGATOR RULE

- A player who instigates a fight in the final five minutes of regulation time or at any time of overtime, will receive a minor, a major, a misconduct and an automatic one-game suspension. The length of suspension would double for each additional incident.

- As well, the player's Coach will be fined $10,000 – a fine that would double for each such incident.

GOALTENDER EQUIPMENT

- The dimensions of goaltender equipment will be reduced by approximately 11 percent. In addition to a one-inch reduction (to 11 inches) in the width of legpads, the blocking glove, upper-body protector and pants also will be reduced in size.

SHOOTOUT

- Following a scoreless five-minute overtime, three players from each team participate in the order the coach selects.

- The teams alternate shots. The team with the most goals after each team has taken three shots is declared the winner, unless the outcome is determined earlier in the shootout (example: if Team A is ahead 2-0 after each team has taken two shots).

- If the score remains tied, the shootout will proceed to a "sudden-death" format. No player may shoot twice until everyone who is eligible has shot.

- Regardless of the number of goals scored during the shootout portion of overtime, the final score recorded for the game will give the winning team one more goal than its opponent, based on the score at the end of overtime.

DELAY OF GAME

- When any player, while in his defending zone, shoots the puck directly (non-deflected) out of the playing surface, except where there is no glass, a penalty will be assessed for delaying the game. When the puck is shot into the players' bench, the penalty will not apply. When the puck is shot over the glass behind the players' bench, the penalty will be assessed.

DIVING

- In addition to the minor penalty for diving that may be assessed by the Referee during a game, Hockey Operations will review game videos and assess fines to players who dive or embellish a fall or a reaction, or who feign injury in an attempt to draw penalties. The first such incident will result in a warning letter being sent to the player. The second such incident will result in a $1,000 fine. The third such incident will result in a $2,000 fine. The fourth such incident will result in a one-game suspension.

NHL Clubs' Minor-League Affiliations, 2005-06

NHL CLUB	MINOR-LEAGUE AFFILIATES
Anaheim	Portland Pirates (AHL)
Atlanta	Chicago Wolves (AHL)
	Gwinnett Gladiators (ECHL)
Boston	Providence Bruins (AHL)
Buffalo	Rochester Americans (AHL)
Calgary	Omaha Ak-Sar-Ben Knights (AHL)
	Las Vegas Wranglers (ECHL)
Carolina	Lowell Lock Monsters (AHL)
	Florida Everblades (ECHL)
Chicago	Norfolk Admirals (AHL)
	Greenville Grrrowl (ECHL)
Colorado	Lowell Lock Monsters (AHL)
	San Diego Gulls (ECHL)
Columbus	Syracuse Crunch (AHL)
	Dayton Bombers (ECHL)
Dallas	Iowa Stars (AHL)
	Idaho Steelheads (ECHL)
Detroit	Grand Rapids Griffins (AHL)
	Toledo Storm (ECHL)
Edmonton	Hamilton Bulldogs (AHL)
	Iowa Stars (AHL)
	Greenville Grrrowl (ECHL)
	Odessa Jackalopes (CHL)
Florida	Rochester Americans (AHL)
	Florida Everblades (ECHL)
Los Angeles	Manchester Monarchs (AHL)
	Reading Royals (ECHL)
Minnesota	Houston Aeros (AHL)
	Texas Wildcatters (ECHL)

NHL CLUB	MINOR-LEAGUE AFFILIATES
Montreal	Hamilton Bulldogs (AHL)
	Long Beach Ice Dogs (ECHL)
Nashville	Milwaukee Admirals (AHL)
New Jersey	Albany River Rats (AHL)
NY Islanders	Bridgeport Sound Tigers (AHL)
NY Rangers	Hartford Wolf Pack (AHL)
	Charlotte Checkers (ECHL)
Ottawa	Binghamton Senators (AHL)
	Charlotte Checkers (ECHL)
Philadelphia	Philadelphia Phantoms (AHL)
	Trenton Titans (ECHL)
Phoenix	San Antonio Rampage (AHL)
	Stockton Thunder (ECHL)
	Laredo Bucks (CHL)
Pittsburgh	Wilkes-Barre/Scranton Penguins (AHL)
	Wheeling Nailers (ECHL)
St. Louis	Peoria Rivermen (AHL)
	Alaska Aces (ECHL)
San Jose	Cleveland Barons (AHL)
	Fresno Falcons (ECHL)
	Toledo Storm (ECHL)
Tampa Bay	Springfield Falcons (AHL)
	Johnstown Chiefs (ECHL)
Toronto	Toronto Marlies (AHL)
	Pensacola Ice Pilots (ECHL)
Vancouver	Manitoba Moose (AHL)
	Columbia Inferno (ECHL)
Washington	Hershey Bears (AHL)
	South Carolina Stingrays (ECHL)

NHL Players at the 2006 Olympic Winter Games

As IN 1997-98 AND 2001-02, the NHL's 2005-06 regular season will be interrupted in order to allow the League's players to represent their countries at the Olympic Winter Games in Turin, Italy.

Twelve teams, divided into two groups of six, will play for Olympic gold. Each team will play the five opponents in its group from Feb. 15 to Feb. 21. Canada, Czech Republic, Finland, Germany, Switzerland and Italy will compete in Group A, while Group B will consist of Sweden, Slovakia, USA, Russia, Latvia and Kazakhstan.

The top four teams from each group will advance to the quaterfinals where the two groups crossover: A1 vs B4, A2 vs. B3, B2 vs. A3 and B1 vs. A4. Single-game playoffs will then determine the winner of the quarterfinals (Feb. 22), the semifinals (Feb. 24), the bronze medal game (Feb. 25) and the gold medal game (Feb. 26).

2006 Men's Olympic Hockey Schedule

Start times listed in Eastern Standard Time (EST).
EST is −6 local time in Turin, Italy.
PST is −9 local time in Turin, Italy.

Preliminary Round (round robin)

Feb. 15	Kazakhstan	vs.	Sweden	5:30 am
	Italy	vs.	Canada	7:00 am
	Switzerland	vs.	Finland	9:30 am
	Germany	vs.	Czech Republic	11:00 am
	Russia	vs.	Slovakia	2:00 pm
	Latvia	vs.	USA	3:00 pm
Feb. 16	Finland	vs.	Italy	6:00 am
	Czech Republic	vs.	Switzerland	7:00 am
	Sweden	vs.	Russia	10:00 am
	Slovakia	vs.	Latvia	11:00 am
	Canada	vs.	Germany	2:00 pm
	USA	vs.	Kazakhstan	3:00 pm
Feb. 18	Kazakhstan	vs.	Russia	5:30 am
	Italy	vs.	Germany	7:00 am
	Canada	vs.	Switzerland	9:30 am
	Sweden	vs.	Latvia	11:00 am
	Russia	vs.	USA	2:00 pm
	Czech Republic	vs.	Finland	3:00 pm
Feb. 19	Germany	vs.	Switzerland	6:00 am
	Russia	vs.	Latvia	7:00 am
	Slovakia	vs.	Kazakhstan	10:00 am
	USA	vs.	Sweden	11:00 am
	Czech Republic	vs.	Italy	2:00 pm
	Finland	vs.	Canada	3:00 pm
Feb. 21	Latvia	vs.	Kazakhstan	5:30 am
	Switzerland	vs.	Italy	6:30 am
	Canada	vs.	Czech Republic	9:30 am
	Finland	vs.	Germany	10:30 am
	Sweden	vs.	Slovakia	2:00 pm
	USA	vs.	Russia	2:30 pm

Playoff Round (single elimination)

Feb. 22	Quarterfinals A1 vs. B4		10:30 am
	Quarterfinals A2 vs. B3		11:30 am
	Quarterfinals B2 vs. A3		2:30 pm
	Quarterfinals B1 vs. A4		3:30 pm
Feb. 24	Semifinals		10:30 am
	Semifinals		3:00 pm
Feb. 25	Bronze Medal Game		2:30 pm
Feb. 26	Gold Medal Game		8:00 am

2006 Women's Olympic Hockey Schedule

Start times listed in Eastern Standard Time (EST).
EST is −6 local time in Turin, Italy.
PST is −9 local time in Turin, Italy.

Preliminary Round (round robin)

Feb. 11	Finland	vs.	Germany	7:00 am
	Sweden	vs.	Russia	9:30 am
	United States	vs.	Switzerland	noon
	Canada	vs.	Italy	2:30 pm
Feb. 12	Russia	vs.	Canada	10:30 am
	Germany	vs.	USA	1:00 pm
Feb. 13	Sweden	vs.	Italy	9:00 am
	Finland	vs.	Switzerland	11:30 am
Feb. 14	Italy	vs.	Russia	7:00 am
	Canada	vs.	Sweden	9:30 am
	Switzerland	vs.	Germany	noon
	United States	vs.	Finland	2:30 pm

Playoff Round (single elimination)

Feb. 17	Classification Game A3 vs. B4	7:00 am
	Semifinal A1 vs. B2	11:00 am
	Classification Game B3 vs. A4	12:30 pm
	Semifinal B1 vs. A2	3:00 pm
Feb. 20	7th place game	7:00 am
	Bronze Medal game	10:30 am
	5th place game	11:00 am
	Gold Medal Game	2:30 pm

Cumulative Medal Standings, Women's Olympic Hockey, 1998-2002

		G	S	B	Total	Last Medal
1.	Canada	1	1	0	2	Gold 02
2.	USA	1	1	0	2	Silver 02
3.	Sweden	0	0	1	1	Bronze 02
4.	Finland	0	0	1	1	Bronze 98

Cumulative Medal Standings, Men's Olympic Hockey, 1924-2002

		G	S	B	Total	Last Medal
1.	USSR/Russia*	8	2	2	12	Bronze 02
2.	Canada	6	4	2	12	Gold 02
3.	USA	2	6	1	9	Silver 02
4.	Czechoslovakia/Czech Rep.	1	4	3	8	Gold 98
5.	Sweden	1	2	4	7	Gold 94
6.	Great Britain	1	0	1	2	Gold 36
7.	Finland	0	1	2	3	Bronze 98
8.	W. Germany	0	0	2	2	Bronze 76
9.	Switzerland	0	0	2	2	Bronze 48

* Soviet Union/Russia played as the Unified Team in 1992.

Salt Lake City, Utah, USA • 2002
Men
Preliminary Round
Group A

Team	GP	W	L	T	GF	GA	Pts
Germany	3	3	0	0	10	3	6
Latvia	3	1	1	1	11	12	3
Austria	3	1	2	0	7	9	2
Slovakia	3	0	2	1	8	12	1

Group B

Team	GP	W	L	T	GF	GA	Pts
Belarus	3	2	1	0	5	3	4
Ukraine	3	2	1	0	9	5	4
Switzerland	3	1	1	1	7	9	3
France	3	0	2	1	6	10	1

Final Round
Group C

Team	GP	W	L	T	GF	GA	Pts
Sweden	3	3	0	0	14	4	6
Czech Rep.	3	1	1	1	12	7	3
Canada	3	1	1	1	8	10	3
Germany	3	0	3	0	5	18	0

Group D

Team	GP	W	L	T	GF	GA	Pts
USA	3	2	0	1	16	3	5
Finland	3	2	1	0	11	8	4
Russia	3	1	1	1	9	9	3
Belarus	3	0	3	0	6	22	0

Quarterfinals

Belarus	4	Sweden	3
Russia	2	Czech Republic	1
USA	5	Germany	0
Canada	2	Finland	1

Semifinals

Canada	7	Belarus	1
USA	3	Russia	2

Bronze Medal game

Russia	7	Belarus	2

Gold Medal game

Canada	5	USA	2

2002 Final Rankings, Men

1	Canada
2	USA
3	Russia
4	Belarus
5-8	Czech Republic
5-8	Finland
5-8	Germany
5-8	Sweden
9	Latvia
10	Ukraine
11	Switzerland
12	Austria
13	Slovakia
14	France

2002 Scoring Leaders

Player	Team	GP	G	A	PTS	PIM
Mats Sundin	Sweden	4	5	4	9	10
Brett Hull	USA	6	3	5	8	6
John LeClair	USA	6	6	1	7	2
Joe Sakic	Canada	6	4	3	7	0
Marian Hossa	Slovakia	2	4	2	6	0
J-J Aeschlimann	Switzerland	4	3	3	6	2
Philippe Bozon	France	4	3	3	6	2
Len Soccio	Germany	7	3	3	6	8
Mario Lemieux	Canada	5	2	4	6	2
Steve Yzerman	Canada	6	2	4	6	2
Nicklas Lidstrom	Sweden	4	1	5	6	0
Mike Modano	USA	6	0	6	6	0

2002 Goaltending Leaders
(Minimum 150 Mins)

Player	Team	GP	Min	GA	SO	GAA
Martin Gerber	Switzerland	3	157	4	0	1.52
Martin Brodeur	Canada	5	300	9	0	1.80
Dominik Hasek	Czech Rep.	4	239	8	0	2.01
Mike Richter	USA	4	240	9	1	2.34
N. Khabibulin	Russia	6	359	14	1	2.34
Tommy Salo	Sweden	3	179	7	0	2.35

Nagano, Japan • 1998
Men
Preliminary Round
Group A

Team	GP	W	L	T	GF	GA	Pts
Kazakhstan	3	2	0	1	14	11	5
Slovakia	3	1	1	1	9	9	3
Italy	3	1	2	0	11	11	2
Austria	3	0	1	2	9	12	2

Group B

Team	GP	W	L	T	GF	GA	Pts
Belarus	3	2	0	1	14	4	5
Germany	3	2	1	0	7	9	4
France	3	1	2	0	5	8	2
Japan	3	0	2	1	5	10	1

Final Round
Group A

Team	GP	W	L	T	GF	GA	Pts
Canada	3	3	0	0	12	3	6
Sweden	3	2	1	0	11	7	4
USA	3	1	2	0	8	10	2
Belarus	3	0	3	0	4	15	0

Group B

Team	GP	W	L	T	GF	GA	Pts
Russia	3	3	0	0	15	6	6
Czech Rep.	3	2	1	0	12	4	4
Finland	3	1	2	0	11	9	2
Kazakhstan	3	0	3	0	6	25	0

Quarterfinals

Canada	4	Kazakhstan	1
Czech Republic	4	USA	1
Finland	2	Sweden	1
Russia	4	Belarus	1

Semifinals
Note: SO = Shootout

Czech Republic	2	Canada	1 (SO)
Russia	7	Finland	4

Bronze Medal game

Finland	3	Canada	2

Gold Medal game

Czech Republic	1	Russia	0

1998 Final Rankings, Men

1	Czech Republic
2	Russia
3	Finland
4	Canada
5-8	USA
5-8	Sweden
5-8	Belarus
5-8	Kazakhstan
9	Germany
10	Slovakia
11	France
12	Italy
13	Japan
14	Austria

1998 Scoring Leaders

Player	Team	GP	G	A	PTS	PIM
Teemu Selanne	Finland	5	4	6	10	8
Saku Koivu	Finland	6	2	8	10	4
Pavel Bure	Russia	6	9	0	9	2
Alex. Koreshkov	Kazakhstan	7	3	6	9	2
Phillipe Bozon	France	4	5	2	7	4
K. Shafranov	Kazakhstan	7	4	3	7	6
Dominik Lavoie	Austria	4	5	1	6	8
Jere Lehtinen	Finland	6	4	2	6	2
Alexei Yashin	Russia	6	3	3	6	0
Serge Poudrier	France	6	2	4	6	4
Sergei Fedorov	Russia	6	1	5	6	8

1998 Goaltending Leaders
(Minimum 150 Mins)

Player	Team	GP	Min	GA	SO	GAA
Dominik Hasek	Czech Rep.	6	369	6	2	0.97
Patrick Roy	Canada	6	369	9	1	1.46
M. Shtalenkov	Russia	5	290	8	0	1.65
Tommy Salo	Sweden	4	238	9	0	2.27
Dusty Imoo	Japan	3	189	8	0	2.54
Mike Rosati	Italy	4	215	12	0	3.35

Lillehammer, Norway • 1994
Group A

Team	GP	W	L	T	GF	GA	PTS
Finland	5	5	0	0	25	4	10
Germany	5	3	2	0	11	14	6
Czech Rep.	5	3	2	0	16	11	6
Russia	5	3	2	0	20	14	6
Austria	5	1	4	0	13	28	2
Norway	5	0	5	0	5	19	0

Group B

Team	GP	W	L	T	GF	GA	PTS
Slovakia	5	3	0	2	26	14	8
Canada	5	3	1	1	17	11	7
Sweden	5	3	1	1	23	13	7
USA	5	1	1	3	21	17	5
Italy	5	1	4	0	15	31	2
France	5	0	4	1	11	27	1

Quarterfinals

Canada	3	Czech Rep.	2
Finland	6	USA	1
Sweden	3	Germany	0
Russia	3	Slovakia	2

Semifinals

Canada	5	Finland	3
Sweden	4	Russia	3

Bronze Medal Game

Finland	4	Russia	0

Gold Medal Game *Note: SO = Shootout*

Sweden	3	Canada	2 (SO)

1994 Final Standings
1. Sweden
2. Canada
3. Finland
4. Russia
5. Czech Republic
6. Slovakia
7. Germany
8. USA
9. Italy
10. France
11. Norway
12. Austria

1994 Scoring Leaders

Player	Team	GP	G	A	PTS	PIM
Ziggy Palffy	Slovakia	8	3	7	10	8
Miroslav Satan	Slovakia	8	9	0	9	0
Peter Stastny	Slovakia	8	5	4	9	9
Hakan Loob	Sweden	8	4	5	9	2
Gates Orlando	Italy	7	3	6	9	41
Patrik Juhlin	Sweden	8	7	1	8	16
Jiri Kucera	Czech Rep.	8	6	2	8	4
Marty Dallman	Austria	7	4	4	8	8
Mika Nieminen	Finland	8	3	5	8	0
David Sacco	USA	8	3	5	8	12
Peter Forsberg	Sweden	8	2	6	8	6

Albertville, France • 1992
Group A

Team	GP	W	L	T	GF	GA	PTS
USA	5	4	0	1	18	7	9
Sweden	5	3	0	2	22	11	8
Finland	5	3	0	1	22	11	7
Germany	5	2	3	0	11	12	4
Italy	5	1	4	0	18	24	2
Poland	5	0	5	0	4	30	0

Group B

Team	GP	W	L	T	GF	GA	PTS
Canada	5	4	1	0	28	9	8
Unified Team *5	5	4	1	0	32	10	8
Czech.	5	4	1	0	25	15	8
France	5	2	3	0	14	22	4
Switzerland	5	1	4	0	13	25	2
Norway	5	0	5	0	7	38	0

* Soviet Union/Russia played as Unified Team in 1992.

Medal Round *Note: SO = Shootout*

Canada	4	Germany	3	(SO)
Czechoslovakia	3	Sweden	1	
USA	4	France	1	
Unified Team	6	Finland	1	

Semifinals

Canada	4	Czechoslovakia	2
Unified Team	5	USA	2

Bronze Medal Game

Czechoslovakia	6	USA	1

Gold Medal Game

Unified Team	3	Canada	1

1992 Final Rankings
1. Unified Team
2. Canada
3. Czechoslovakia
4. USA
5. Sweden
6. Germany
7. Finland
8. France
9. Norway
10. Switzerland
11. Poland
12. Italy

1992 Scoring Leaders

Player	Team	GP	G	A	PTS	PIM
Joe Juneau	Canada	8	6	9	15	5
Andrei Khomutov	Unified	8	7	7	14	2
Robert Lang	Czech.	8	5	8	13	8
Teemu Selanne	Finland	8	7	4	11	6
Eric Lindros	Canada	8	5	6	11	5
H. Jarvenpaa	Finland	8	5	6	11	14
V. Bykov	Unified	8	4	7	11	2
Yuri Khmylev	Unified	8	4	6	10	4
Mika Nieminen	Finland	8	4	6	10	6
N. Borschevsky	Unified	8	7	2	9	0

Calgary, Alberta, Canada • 1988
Group A

Team	GP	W	L	T	GF	GA	PTS
Finland	5	3	1	1	22	8	7
Sweden	5	2	0	3	23	10	7
Canada	5	3	1	1	17	12	7
Switzerland	5	3	2	0	19	10	6
Poland	5	0	4	1	3	13	1
France	5	1	4	0	10	41	0

Group B

Team	GP	W	L	T	GF	GA	PTS
Soviet Union	5	5	0	0	32	10	10
W. Germany	5	4	1	0	19	12	8
Czech.	5	3	2	0	23	14	6
USA	5	2	3	0	27	27	4
Austria	5	0	4	1	12	29	1
Norway	5	0	4	1	11	32	1

Final Round

Team	GP	W	L	T	GF	GA	PTS
Soviet Union	5	4	1	0	25	7	8
Finland	5	3	1	1	18	10	7
Sweden	5	2	1	2	15	16	6
Canada	5	2	2	1	17	14	5
W. Germany	5	1	4	0	8	26	2
Czech.	5	1	4	0	12	22	2

1988 Final Rankings
1. Soviet Union
2. Finland
3. Sweden
4. Canada
5. W. Germany
6. Czechoslovakia
7. USA
8. Switzerland
9. Austria
10. Poland
11. France
12. Norway

1988 Scoring Leaders

Player	Team	GP	G	A	PTS	PIM
Vladimir Krutov	Soviet Union	8	6	9	15	0
Igor Larionov	Soviet Union	8	4	9	13	4
V. Fetisov	Soviet Union	8	4	9	13	6
Corey Millen	USA	6	6	5	11	4
Dusan Pasek	Czech.	8	6	5	11	8
Sergei Makarov	Soviet Union	8	3	8	11	10
Erkki Lehtonen	Finland	8	4	6	10	2
Anders Eldebrink	Sweden	8	4	6	10	4
Igor Liba	Czech.	8	4	6	10	10
Gerd Truntschka	W. Germany	8	3	7	10	10
Raimo Helminen	Finland	7	2	8	10	4

Sarajevo, Yugoslavia • 1984
Group A

Team	GP	W	L	T	GF	GA	PTS
Soviet Union	5	5	0	0	42	5	10
Sweden	5	3	1	1	34	15	7
W. Germany	5	3	1	1	27	17	7
Poland	5	1	4	0	16	37	2
Italy	5	1	4	0	15	31	2
Yugoslavia	5	1	4	0	8	37	2

Group B

Team	GP	W	L	T	GF	GA	PTS
Czech.	5	5	0	0	38	7	10
Canada	5	4	1	0	24	10	8
Finland	5	2	2	1	27	19	5
USA	5	1	2	2	16	17	4
Austria	5	1	4	0	13	37	2
Norway	5	0	4	1	15	43	1

Final Round

Team	GP	W	L	T	GF	GA	PTS
Soviet Union	3	3	0	0	16	1	6
Czech.	3	2	1	0	6	2	4
Sweden	3	1	2	0	3	12	2
Canada	3	0	3	0	0	10	0

Consolation Round

Team	GP	W	L	T	GF	GA	PTS
W. Germany	1	1	0	0	7	4	2
USA	1	1	0	0	7	4	2
Finland	1	0	1	0	4	7	0
Poland	1	0	1	0	4	7	0

1984 Final Rankings
1. Soviet Union
2. Czechoslovakia
3. Sweden
4. Canada
5. W. Germany
6. Finland
7. USA
8. Poland

1984 Scoring Leaders

Player	Team	GP	G	A	PTS	PIM
Erich Kuhnhackl	W. Germany	6	8	6	14	12
Peter Gradin	Sweden	7	9	4	13	6
N. Drozdetski	Soviet Union	7	10	2	12	2
V. Fetisov	Soviet Union	7	3	8	11	8
Petri Skriko	Finland	6	6	4	10	8
Vladimir Ruzicka	Czech.	7	4	6	10	4
R. Summanen	Finland	6	4	6	10	4
Darius Rusnak	Czech.	7	4	6	10	6
Jiri Hrdina	Czech.	7	4	6	10	10
Vincent Lukac	Czech.	7	4	5	9	2
Viktor Tjumenev	Soviet Union	6	0	9	9	2

Lake Placid, NY, USA • 1980
Red Division

Team	GP	W	L	T	GF	GA	PTS
Soviet Union	5	5	0	0	51	11	10
Finland	5	3	2	0	26	18	6
Canada	5	3	2	0	28	12	6
Poland	5	2	3	0	15	23	4
Holland	5	1	3	1	16	43	3
Japan	5	0	4	1	7	36	1

Blue Division

Team	GP	W	L	T	GF	GA	PTS
Sweden	5	4	0	1	26	7	9
USA	5	4	0	1	25	10	9
Czech.	5	3	2	0	34	16	6
Romania	5	1	3	1	13	29	3
W. Germany	5	1	4	0	21	30	2
Norway	5	0	4	1	9	36	1

Final Round

Team	GP	W	L	T	GF	GA	PTS
USA	3	2	0	1	10	7	5
Soviet Union	3	2	1	0	16	8	4
Sweden	3	0	1	2	7	14	2
Finland	3	0	2	1	7	11	1

1980 Final Rankings
1. USA
2. Soviet Union
3. Sweden
4. Finland
5. Czechoslovakia
6. Canada
7. Poland
8. Holland
9. Romania
10. W. Germany
11. Norway
12. Japan

1980 Scoring Leaders

Player	Team	GP	G	A	PTS	PIM
Milan Novy	Czech.	6	7	8	15	0
Peter Stastny	Czech.	6	7	7	14	6
Jaroslav Pouzar	Czech.	6	8	5	13	8
Alexander Golikov	Soviet Union	7	6	7	13	6
Jukka Porvari	Finland	7	6	5	11	4
Boris Mikhailov	Soviet Union	7	6	5	11	2
Vladimir Krutov	Soviet Union	7	6	5	11	4
Sergei Makarov	Soviet Union	7	5	6	11	4
Marian Stastny	Czech.	6	5	6	11	4
Mark Johnson	USA	7	5	6	11	6

Innsbruck, Austria • 1976
Group A

Team	GP	W	L	T	GF	GA	PTS
Soviet Union	5	5	0	0	40	11	10
Czech.	5	3	2	0	17	10	6
W. Germany	5	3	0	2	21	24	4
Finland	5	2	3	0	19	18	4
USA	5	2	3	0	15	21	4
Poland	5	0	5	0	9	37	0

Group B

Team	GP	W	L	T	GF	GA	PTS
Romania	5	4	1	0	23	15	8
Austria	5	3	2	0	18	14	6
Japan	5	3	2	0	20	18	6
Yugoslavia	5	3	2	0	22	19	6
Switzerland	5	2	3	0	24	22	4
Bulgaria	5	0	5	0	19	38	0

1976 Final Rankings
1. Soviet Union
2. Czechoslovakia
3. W. Germany
4. Finland
5. USA
6. Poland
7. Romania
8. Austria
9. Japan
10. Yugoslavia
11. Switzerland
12. Bulgaria

1976 Scoring Leaders

Player	Team	GP	G	A	PTS	PIM
Vladimir Shadrin	Soviet Union	5	6	4	10	0
Alexander Maltsev	Soviet Union	5	5	5	10	0
Victor Shalimov	Soviet Union	5	5	5	10	2
Erich Kuhnhackl	W. Germany	5	5	5	10	10
Valeri Kharlamov	Soviet Union	5	3	6	9	6
Ernst Kopf	W. Germany	5	3	5	8	2
Vladimir Petrov	Soviet Union	5	4	3	7	8
A. Yakushev	Soviet Union	5	3	4	7	2
Bob Dobek	USA	5	3	4	7	4
Lorenz Funk	W. Germany	5	2	5	7	4
Victor Zhluktov	Soviet Union	5	1	6	7	2

Sapporo, Japan • 1972
Group A

Team	GP	W	L	T	GF	GA	PTS
Soviet Union	5	4	0	1	33	13	9
USA	5	3	2	0	18	15	6
Czech.	5	3	2	0	26	13	6
Sweden	5	2	2	1	17	13	5
Finland	5	2	3	0	14	24	4
Poland	5	0	5	0	9	39	0

Group B

Team	GP	W	L	T	GF	GA	PTS
W. Germany	4	3	1	0	22	10	6
Norway	4	3	1	0	16	14	6
Japan	4	2	1	1	17	16	5
Switzerland	4	0	2	2	9	16	2
Yugoslavia	4	0	3	1	9	17	1

1972 Final Rankings
1. Soviet Union
2. USA
3. Czechoslovakia
4. Sweden
5. Finland
6. Poland
7. W. Germany
8. Norway
9. Japan
10. Switzerland
11. Yugoslavia

1972 Scoring Leaders

Player	Team	GP	G	A	PTS	PIM
Valeri Kharlamov	Soviet Union	5	9	6	15	2
V. Nedomansky	Czech.	5	6	3	9	0
Vladimir Vikulov	Soviet Union	5	4	5	9	0
Craig Sarner	USA	5	4	5	9	0
Kevin Ahearn	USA	5	4	3	7	0
Alexander Maltsev	Soviet Union	5	2	5	7	0
Anatoli Firsov	Soviet Union	5	2	5	7	0
Yuri Blinov	Soviet Union	5	3	3	6	0
Jiri Kochta	Czech.	5	3	3	6	0
Richard Farda	Czech.	5	1	5	6	0

Grenoble, France • 1968
Group A

Team	GP	W	L	T	GF	GA	PTS
Soviet Union	7	6	1	0	48	10	12
Czech.	7	5	1	1	33	17	11
Canada	7	5	2	0	28	15	10
Sweden	7	4	2	1	23	18	9
Finland	7	3	3	1	17	23	7
USA	7	2	4	1	23	28	5
W. Germany	7	1	6	0	13	39	2
E. Germany	7	0	7	0	13	48	0

Group B

Team	GP	W	L	T	GF	GA	PTS
Yugoslavia	5	5	0	0	33	9	10
Japan	5	4	1	0	27	12	8
Norway	5	3	2	0	15	15	6
Romania	5	2	3	0	22	23	4
Austria	5	1	4	0	12	27	2
France	5	0	5	0	9	32	0

1968 Final Rankings
1. Soviet Union
2. Czechoslovakia
3. Canada
4. Sweden
5. Finland
6. USA
7. W. Germany
8. E. Germany
9. Yugoslavia
10. Japan
11. Norway
12. Romania
13. Austria
14. France

1968 Scoring Leaders

Player	Team	GP	G	A	PTS	PIM
Anatoli Firsov	Soviet Union	7	12	4	16	4
Vladimir Vikulov	Soviet Union	7	2	10	12	2
Vyatch. Starshinov	Soviet Union	7	6	6	12	2
Victor Populanov	Soviet Union	7	6	6	12	10
Josef Golonka	Czech.	7	4	6	10	8
Jan Hrbaty	Czech.	7	2	7	9	2
Fran Huck	Canada	7	4	5	9	10
Marshall Johnston	Canada	7	2	6	8	4
Jack Morrison	USA	7	2	6	8	10
V. Nedomansky	Czech.	7	5	2	7	4

Innsbruck, Austria • 1964
Group A

Team	GP	W	L	T	GF	GA	PTS
Soviet Union	7	7	0	0	54	10	14
Sweden	7	5	2	0	47	16	10
Czech.	7	5	2	0	38	19	10
Canada	7	5	2	0	32	17	10
USA	7	2	5	0	29	33	4
Finland	7	2	5	0	10	31	4
W. Germany	7	2	5	0	13	49	4
Switzerland	7	0	7	0	9	57	0

Group B

Team	GP	W	L	T	GF	GA	PTS
Poland	7	6	1	0	40	13	12
Norway	7	5	2	0	40	19	10
Japan	7	4	2	1	35	31	9
Romania	7	3	3	1	31	28	7
Austria	7	3	3	1	24	28	7
Yugoslavia	7	3	3	1	29	37	7
Italy	7	2	5	0	24	42	4
Hungary	7	0	7	0	14	39	0

1964 Final Rankings
1. Soviet Union
2. Sweden
3. Czechoslovakia
4. Canada
5. USA
6. Finland
7. W. Germany
8. Switzerland
9. Poland
10. Norway
11. Japan
12. Romania
13. Austria
14. Yugoslavia
15. Italy
16. Hungary

1964 Scoring Leaders

Player	Team	GP	G	A	PTS	PIM
Sven Tumba	Sweden	7	8	3	11	0
Ulf Sterner	Sweden	7	6	5	11	0
Victor Yakushev	Soviet Union	7	7	3	10	0
Boris Mayorov	Soviet Union	7	7	3	10	0
Jiri Dolana	Czech.	7	7	3	10	0
Vy. Starshinov	Soviet Union	7	7	3	10	6
Josef Cerny	Czech.	7	5	5	10	2
A. Andersson	Sweden	7	7	2	9	8
K. Loktev	Soviet Union	7	4	5	9	8
Gary Dineen	Canada	7	3	6	9	10

Squaw Valley, CA, USA • 1960
Group A

Team	GP	W	L	T	GF	GA	PTS
Canada	2	2	0	0	24	3	4
Sweden	2	1	1	0	21	5	2
Japan	2	0	2	0	1	38	0

Group B

Team	GP	W	L	T	GF	GA	PTS
Soviet Union	2	2	0	0	16	4	4
W. Germany	2	1	1	0	4	9	2
Finland	2	0	2	0	5	12	0

Group C

Team	GP	W	L	T	GF	GA	PTS
USA	2	2	0	0	19	6	4
Czech.	2	1	1	0	23	6	2
Australia	2	0	2	0	2	30	0

Final Round

Team	GP	W	L	T	GF	GA	PTS
USA	5	5	0	0	29	11	10
Canada	5	4	1	0	31	12	8
Soviet Union	5	2	2	1	24	19	5
Czech.	5	2	3	0	21	23	4
Sweden	5	1	3	1	19	19	3
W. Germany	5	0	5	0	5	45	0

Consolation Round

Team	GP	W	L	T	GF	GA	PTS
Finland	4	3	0	1	50	11	7
Japan	4	2	1	1	32	22	5
Australia	4	0	4	0	8	57	0

1960 Final Rankings
1. USA
2. Canada
3. Soviet Union
4. Czechoslovakia
5. Sweden
6. W. Germany
7. Finland
8. Japan
9. Australia

1960 Scoring Leaders

Player	Team	GP	G	A	PTS	PIM
Fred Etcher	Canada	7	9	12	21	0
Bobby Attersley	Canada	7	6	12	18	4
Bill Cleary	USA	7	7	7	14	2
Bill Christian	USA	7	2	11	13	2
G. Samolenko	Soviet Union	7	8	4	12	0
Lars E. Lundvall	Sweden	7	8	4	12	0
Vaclav Panucek	Czech.	7	7	5	12	0
John Mayasich	USA	7	7	5	12	2
Nisse Nilsson	Sweden	7	7	5	12	4
V. Alexandrov	Soviet Union	7	7	5	12	8
Butch Martin	Canada	7	6	6	12	14
Ronald Petersson	Sweden	7	4	8	12	2

Cortina d'Ampezzo, Italy • 1956
Group A

Team	GP	W	L	T	GF	GA	PTS
Canada	3	3	0	0	30	1	6
W. Germany	3	1	1	1	9	6	3
Italy	3	0	1	2	5	7	2
Austria	3	0	2	1	2	32	1

Group B

Team	GP	W	L	T	GF	GA	PTS
Czech.	2	2	0	0	12	6	4
USA	2	1	1	0	7	4	2
Poland	2	0	2	0	3	12	0

Group C

Team	GP	W	L	T	GF	GA	PTS
Soviet Union	2	2	0	0	15	4	4
Sweden	2	1	1	0	7	10	2
Switzerland	2	0	2	0	8	16	0

Final Round

Team	GP	W	L	T	GF	GA	PTS
Soviet Union	5	5	0	0	25	5	10
USA	5	4	1	0	26	12	8
Canada	5	3	2	0	23	11	6
Sweden	5	1	3	1	10	17	3
Czech.	5	1	4	0	20	30	2
W. Germany	5	0	4	1	6	35	1

Consolation Round

Team	GP	W	L	T	GF	GA	PTS
Italy	3	3	0	0	21	7	6
Poland	3	2	1	0	12	10	4
Switzerland	3	1	2	0	12	8	2
Austria	3	0	3	0	9	19	0

1956 Final Rankings
1. Soviet Union
2. USA
3. Canada
4. Sweden
5. Czechoslovakia
6. W. Germany
7. Italy
8. Poland
9. Switzerland
10. Austria

1956 Scoring Leaders

Player	Team	GP	G	A	PTS	PIM
Jim Logan	Canada	8	7	5	12	2
Paul Knox	Canada	8	7	5	12	2
Vsevolod Bobrov	Soviet Union	7	9	2	11	4
Gerry Theberge	Canada	8	9	2	11	8
Jack McKenzie	Canada	8	7	4	11	4
John Mayasich	USA	7	7	3	10	2
Alexei Guryshev	Soviet Union	7	7	2	9	0
Vlastimil Bubnik	Czech.	7	5	4	9	14
George Scholes	Canada	8	5	3	8	2

Oslo, Norway • 1952

Team	GP	W	L	T	GF	GA	PTS
Canada	8	7	0	1	71	1	15
USA	8	6	1	1	43	21	13
Sweden	8	6	2	0	48	19	12
Czech.	8	6	2	0	47	18	12
Switzerland	8	4	4	0	40	40	8
Poland	8	2	5	1	21	56	5
Finland	8	2	6	0	21	60	4
W. Germany	8	1	6	1	21	53	3
Norway	8	0	8	0	15	46	0

1952 Final Rankings
1. Canada
2. USA
3. Sweden
4. Czechoslovakia
5. Switzerland
6. Poland
7. Finland
8. W. Germany
9. Norway

St. Moritz, Switzerland • 1948

Team	GP	W	L	T	GF	GA	PTS
Canada	7	6	0	1	57	2	13
Czech.	7	6	0	1	76	15	13
Switzerland	7	5	2	0	62	17	10
Sweden	7	4	3	0	53	23	8
Great Britain	7	3	4	0	36	43	6
Poland	7	2	5	0	25	74	4
Austria	7	1	6	0	31	64	2
Italy	7	0	7	0	23	125	0

* USA also competed as an unofficial entry.

1948 Final Rankings
1. Canada
2. Czechoslovakia
3. Switzerland
4. Sweden
5. Great Britain
6. Poland
7. Austria
8. Italy

Garmisch-Partenkirchen, Germany • 1936

Group A

Team	GP	W	L	T	GF	GA	PTS
Canada	3	3	0	0	24	3	6
Austria	3	2	1	0	11	7	4
Poland	3	1	2	0	11	12	2
Latvia	3	0	0	3	3	27	0

Group B

Team	GP	W	L	T	GF	GA	PTS
Germany	3	2	1	0	5	1	4
USA	3	2	1	0	5	2	4
Italy	3	1	2	0	2	5	2
Switzerland	3	1	2	0	1	5	2

Group C

Team	GP	W	L	T	GF	GA	PTS
Czech.	3	3	0	0	10	0	6
Hungary	3	2	1	0	14	5	4
France	3	1	2	0	4	7	2
Belgium	3	0	3	0	4	20	6

Group D

Team	GP	W	L	T	GF	GA	PTS
Great Britain	2	2	0	0	4	0	4
Sweden	2	1	1	0	2	1	2
Japan	2	0	2	0	0	5	0

Group A Semifinal Round

Team	GP	W	L	T	GF	GA	PTS
Great Britain	3	2	0	1	8	3	5
Canada	3	2	1	0	22	4	4
Germany	3	1	1	1	5	8	3
Hungary	3	0	0	3	2	22	0

Group B Semifinal Round

Team	GP	W	L	T	GF	GA	PTS
USA	3	3	0	0	5	1	6
Czech.	3	2	1	0	6	4	4
Sweden	3	1	2	0	3	6	2
Austria	3	0	3	0	1	4	0

Final Round

Team	GP	W	L	T	GF	GA	PTS
Great Britain	3	2	0	1	7	1	5
Canada	3	2	1	0	9	2	4
USA	3	1	1	1	2	1	3
Czech.	3	0	3	0	0	14	0

1936 Final Rankings
1. Great Britain
2. Canada
3. USA
4. Czechoslovakia
5. Germany
5. Sweden
7. Hungary
7. Austria

Lake Placid, NY, USA • 1932

Team	GP	W	L	T	GF	GA	PTS
Canada	6	5	0	1	32	4	11
USA	6	4	1	1	27	5	9
Germany	6	2	4	0	7	26	4
Poland	6	0	6	0	3	34	0

1932 Final Rankings
1. Canada
2. USA
3. Germany
4. Poland

St. Moritz, Switzerland • 1928

Group A

Team	GP	W	L	T	GF	GA	PTS
Great Britain	3	2	1	0	10	6	4
France	3	2	1	0	6	5	4
Belgium	3	2	1	0	9	10	4
Hungary	3	0	3	0	2	6	0

Group B

Team	GP	W	L	T	GF	GA	PTS
Sweden	2	1	0	1	5	2	3
Czech.	2	1	1	0	3	5	2
Poland	2	0	0	1	4	5	1

Group C

Team	GP	W	L	T	GF	GA	PTS
Switzerland	2	1	0	1	5	4	3
Austria	2	0	0	2	4	4	2
Germany	2	0	0	1	0	1	1

Final Round

Team	GP	W	L	T	GF	GA	PTS
Canada	3	3	0	0	38	0	6
Sweden	3	2	1	0	7	12	4
Switzerland	3	1	2	0	4	17	2
Great Britain	3	0	3	0	1	21	0

1928 Final Rankings
1. Canada
2. Sweden
3. Switzerland
4. Great Britain
5. France
5. Czechoslovakia
5. Austria
8. Belgium
8. Poland
8. Germany
11. Hungary

Chamonix, France • 1924

Group A

Team	GP	W	L	T	GF	GA	PTS
Canada	3	3	0	0	85	0	6
Sweden	3	2	1	0	18	25	4
Czech.	3	1	2	0	14	41	2
Switzerland	3	0	3	0	2	53	0

Group B

Team	GP	W	L	T	GF	GA	PTS
USA	3	3	0	0	52	0	6
Great Britain	3	2	1	0	34	16	4
France	3	1	2	0	9	42	2
Belgium	3	0	3	0	8	35	0

Final Round

Team	GP	W	L	T	GF	GA	PTS
Canada	3	3	0	0	47	3	6
USA	3	2	1	0	32	6	4
Great Britain	3	1	2	0	6	33	2
Sweden	3	0	3	0	3	46	0

1924 Final Rankings
1. Canada
2. USA
3. Great Britain
4. Sweden
5. Czechoslovakia
5. France
7. Switzerland
7. Belgium

Antwerp, Belgium • 1920
(unofficial)

Hockey was played at the 1920 Summer Olympics in Antwerp, Belgium. This tournament is not counted in cumulative Winter Olympic Hockey statistics. The IIHF has declared it the first World Championship.

1920 Final Rankings
1. Canada
2. USA
3. Czechoslovakia
4. Sweden
5. Switzerland

Women's Olympic Results and Rankings, 2002 and 1998

Salt Lake City, Utah, USA • 2002
Women

Canada	7	Kazakhstan	0
Sweden	3	Russia	2
USA	10	Germany	0
Finland	4	China	0
Russia	0	Canada	7
Sweden	7	Kazakhstan	0
Finland	3	Germany	1
China	1	USA	12
Kazakhstan	1	Russia	4
USA	5	Finland	0
Germany	5	China	5
Canada	11	Sweden	0

Classification Round

Russia	5	China	0
Germany	4	Kazakhstan	0

Semi-final Games

Canada	7	Finland	3
USA	4	Sweden	0

Seventh-Place Game

China	2	Kazakhstan	1 (OT)

Fifth-Place Game

Russia	5	Germany	0

Bronze Medal Game

Sweden	2	Finland	0

Gold Medal Game

Canada	3	USA	2

2002 Final Rankings, Women
1. Canada
2. USA
3. Sweden
4. Finland
5. Russia
6. Germany
7. China
8. Kazakhstan

Nagano, Japan • 1998
Women

Sweden	0	Finland	6
Canada	13	Japan	0
China	0	USA	5
Finland	11	Japan	1
USA	7	Sweden	1
Canada	2	China	0
Sweden	3	Canada	5
Japan	1	China	6
USA	4	Finland	2
China	3	Sweden	1
USA	10	Japan	0
Finland	2	Canada	4
Japan	0	Sweden	5
Finland	6	China	1
Canada	4	USA	7

Bronze Medal Game

Finland	4	China	1

Gold Medal Game

USA	3	Canada	1

1998 Final Rankings, Women
1. USA
2. Canada
3. Finland
4. China
5. Sweden
6. Japan

Olympic Results, Active NHL Players

Medal	Name	Year	Team	GP	G	A	Pts	PIM	05-06 NHL Club
B	Afinogenov, Maxim	2002	RUS	6	2	2	4	4	BUF
	Albelin, Tommy	1998	SWE	3	0	0	0	4	
	Alfredsson, Daniel	1998	SWE	4	2	3	5	2	OTT
	Alfredsson, Daniel	2002	SWE	4	1	4	5	2	OTT
	Amonte, Tony	1998	USA	4	0	1	1	4	CGY
S	Amonte, Tony	2002	USA	6	2	2	4	0	CGY
	Arvedson, Magnus	2002	SWE	4	0	0	0	0	
S	Aucoin, Adrian	1994	CAN	4	0	0	0	2	CHI
	Axelsson, P.J.	2002	SWE	4	0	0	0	2	BOS
	Berard, Bryan	1998	USA	2	0	0	0	0	CBJ
B	Berg, Aki	1998	FIN	6	0	0	0	6	TOR
	Berg, Aki	2002	FIN	4	1	0	1	2	TOR
	Blake, Rob	1998	CAN	6	1	1	2	2	COL
G	Blake, Rob	2002	CAN	6	1	2	3	2	COL
	Bondra, Peter	1998	SVK	2	1	0	1	25	
	Brandner, Christoph	2002	AUT	4	0	1	1	2	
G	Brewer, Eric	2002	CAN	6	2	0	2	0	ST.L.
	Brind'Amour, Rod	1998	CAN	6	1	2	3	0	CAR
S	Bure, Valeri	1998	RUS	6	1	0	1	0	L.A.
B	Bure, Valeri	2002	RUS	6	1	0	1	2	L.A.
	Cajanek, Petr	2002	CZE	4	0	0	0	0	ST.L.
	Carney, Keith	1998	USA	4	0	0	0	2	ANA
	Chelios, Chris	1984	USA	6	0	4	4	8	DET
	Chelios, Chris	1998	USA	4	2	0	2	2	DET
S	Chelios, Chris	2002	USA	6	1	0	1	4	DET
	Corson, Shayne	1998	CAN	6	1	1	2	4	
	Czerkawski, Mariusz	1992	POL	5	0	1	1	4	
G	Dackell, Andreas	1994	SWE	4	0	0	0	0	
B	Datsyuk, Pavel	2002	RUS	6	1	2	3	0	DET
	Deadmarsh, Adam	1998	USA	4	1	0	1	2	
S	Deadmarsh, Adam	2002	USA	6	1	1	2	2	
	Demitra, Pavol	2002	SVK	2	1	2	3	2	L.A.
	Desjardins, Eric	1998	CAN	6	0	0	0	2	PHI
S	Drury, Chris	2002	USA	6	0	0	0	0	BUF
	Dvorak, Radek	2002	CZE	4	0	0	0	0	EDM
	Ehrhoff, Christian	2002	GER	7	0	0	0	8	S.J.
	Elias, Patrik	2002	CZE	4	1	1	2	0	N.J.
S	Fedorov, Sergei	1998	RUS	6	1	5	6	8	ANA
B	Fedorov, Sergei	2002	RUS	6	2	2	4	4	ANA
	Fedotenko, Ruslan	2002	UKR	1	1	0	1	4	T.B.
	Foote, Adam	1998	CAN	6	0	1	1	4	CBJ
G	Foote, Adam	2002	CAN	6	1	0	1	2	CBJ
G	Forsberg, Peter	1994	SWE	8	2	6	8	6	PHI
	Forsberg, Peter	1998	SWE	4	1	4	5	6	PHI
	Gagne, Simon	2002	CAN	6	1	3	4	0	PHI
S	Gonchar, Sergei	1998	RUS	6	0	2	2	0	PIT
B	Gonchar, Sergei	2002	RUS	6	0	0	0	2	PIT
	Guerin, Bill	1998	USA	4	0	3	3	2	DAL
S	Guerin, Bill	2002	USA	6	4	0	4	4	DAL
	Hagman, Niklas	2002	FIN	4	1	2	3	0	FLA
G	Hamrlik, Roman	1998	CZE	6	1	0	1	2	CGY
	Hamrlik, Roman	2002	CZE	4	0	1	1	2	CGY
	Handzus, Michal	2002	SVK	2	1	0	1	6	PHI
	Hatcher, Derian	1998	USA	4	0	0	0	0	PHI
	Havlat, Martin	2002	CZE	4	3	1	4	27	OTT
	Hecht, Jochen	1998	GER	4	1	0	1	6	BUF
	Hecht, Jochen	2002	GER	4	1	1	2	2	BUF
	Hedican, Bret	1992	USA	8	0	0	0	4	CAR
G	Hejduk, Milan	1998	CZE	4	0	0	0	2	COL
	Hejduk, Milan	2002	CZE	4	1	0	1	0	COL
	Hendrickson, Darby	1994	USA	8	0	0	0	6	
	Hill, Sean	1992	USA	8	2	0	2	6	FLA
	Holmstrom, Tomas	2002	SWE	4	1	0	1	0	DET
	Hossa, Marian	2002	SVK	2	4	2	6	0	ATL
	Hrdina, Jan	2002	CZE	4	0	0	0	0	CBJ
	Hull, Brett	1998	USA	4	2	1	3	0	PHX
S	Hull, Brett	2002	USA	6	3	5	8	6	PHX
G	Iginla, Jarome	2002	CAN	6	3	1	4	0	CGY
G	Jagr, Jaromir	1998	CZE	6	1	4	5	2	NYR
	Jagr, Jaromir	2002	CZE	4	2	3	5	4	NYR
	Johansson, Andreas	1998	SWE	3	0	0	0	2	
S	Johnson, Greg	1994	CAN	8	0	3	3	0	NSH
	Johnson, Craig	1994	USA	8	0	4	4	4	
	Johnsson, Kim	2002	SWE	4	1	1	2	0	PHI
	Jokinen, Olli	2002	FIN	4	2	1	3	0	FLA
G	Jonsson, Kenny	1994	SWE	3	1	0	1	0	NYI
	Jonsson, Kenny	2002	SWE	3	1	0	1	2	NYI
G	Jovanovski, Ed	2002	CAN	6	0	3	3	4	VAN
	Kaberle, Tomas	2002	CZE	4	0	1	1	2	TOR
B	Kapanen, Sami	1994	FIN	8	1	0	1	2	PHI
B	Kapanen, Sami	1998	FIN	6	0	1	1	0	PHI
	Kapanen, Sami	2002	FIN	4	1	2	3	4	PHI
S	Kariya, Paul	1994	CAN	8	3	4	7	2	NSH
G	Kariya, Paul	2002	CAN	6	3	1	4	0	NSH
G	Kasparaitis, Darius	1992	RUS	8	0	2	2	2	NYR
S	Kasparaitis, Darius	1998	RUS	6	0	2	2	6	NYR
B	Kasparaitis, Darius	2002	RUS	6	1	0	1	4	NYR
B	Koivu, Saku	1994	FIN	8	4	3	7	12	MTL
B	Koivu, Saku	1998	FIN	6	2	8	10	4	MTL
	Koltsov, Konstantin	2002	BEL	2	0	0	0	0	PIT
B	Kovalchuk, Ilya	2002	RUS	6	1	2	3	14	ATL
G	Kovalev, Alex	1992	RUS	8	1	2	3	14	MTL
B	Kovalev, Alex	2002	RUS	6	3	1	4	4	MTL
	Kubina, Pavel	2002	CZE	4	0	1	1	0	T.B.
B	Kvasha, Oleg	2002	RUS	5	0	0	0	0	NYI
	Lachance, Scott	1992	USA	8	0	1	1	6	
B	Lang, Robert	1992	CZE	8	5	8	13	8	DET
G	Lang, Robert	1998	CZE	6	0	3	3	0	DET
	Lang, Robert	2002	CZE	4	1	2	3	2	DET
	Langenbrunner, Jamie	1998	USA	3	0	0	0	4	N.J.
	LeClair, John	1998	USA	4	0	1	1	0	PIT
	LeClair, John	2002	USA	6	6	1	7	2	PIT
	Leetch, Brian	1988	USA	6	1	5	6	4	BOS
	Leetch, Brian	1998	USA	4	1	1	2	0	BOS
	Leetch, Brian	2002	USA	6	0	5	5	0	BOS
B	Lehtinen, Jere	1994	FIN	8	3	0	3	0	DAL
B	Lehtinen, Jere	1998	FIN	6	4	2	6	2	DAL
	Lehtinen, Jere	2002	FIN	4	1	2	3	2	DAL
G	Lemieux, Mario	2002	CAN	5	2	4	6	0	PIT
	Lidstrom, Nicklas	1998	SWE	4	1	1	2	2	DET
	Lidstrom, Nicklas	2002	SWE	4	1	5	6	0	DET
B	Linden, Trevor	1998	CAN	6	1	0	1	10	VAN
	Lindgren, Mats	1998	SWE	4	0	0	0	2	
S	Lindros, Eric	1992	CAN	8	5	6	11	5	TOR
	Lindros, Eric	1998	CAN	6	2	3	5	2	TOR
G	Lindros, Eric	2002	CAN	6	1	0	1	8	TOR
	MacInnis, Al	1998	CAN	6	2	0	2	2	
G	MacInnis, Al	2002	CAN	6	0	0	0	8	
	Majesky, Ivan	2002	SVK	4	0	1	1	4	WSH
	Malakhov, Vladimir	1992	RUS	8	0	3	3	4	NYR
B	Malakhov, Vladimir	2002	RUS	6	1	3	4	4	N.J.
	Marchant, Todd	1994	USA	8	1	1	2	6	CBJ
B	Markov, Danny	2002	RUS	5	0	1	1	0	NSH
	McEachern, Shawn	1992	USA	8	1	0	1	10	BOS
	Miller, Kevin	1988	USA	5	1	3	4	4	
S	Miller, Aaron	2002	USA	6	0	0	0	4	L.A.
S	Mironov, Boris	1998	RUS	6	0	2	2	2	
B	Mironov, Boris	2002	RUS	6	1	0	1	2	
	Modano, Mike	1998	USA	4	2	0	2	0	DAL
	Modano, Mike	2002	USA	6	0	6	6	4	DAL
G	Mogilny, Alexander	1988	USSR	6	3	2	5	2	N.J.
S	Morozov, Aleksey	1998	RUS	6	2	2	4	0	PIT
	Naslund, Markus	2002	SWE	4	2	1	3	0	VAN
S	Nedved, Petr	1994	CAN	8	5	1	6	6	PHX
G	Niedermayer, Scott	2002	CAN	6	1	1	2	4	ANA
	Nieminen, Ville	2002	FIN	4	0	1	1	2	NYR
	Nieuwendyk, Joe	1998	CAN	6	2	3	5	2	FLA
G	Nieuwendyk, Joe	2002	CAN	6	1	1	2	0	FLA
B	Niinimaa, Janne	1998	FIN	6	0	3	3	8	NYI
	Niinimaa, Janne	2002	FIN	4	0	3	3	2	NYI
	Nikolishin, Andrei	1994	RUS	8	2	5	7	6	
B	Nikolishin, Andrei	2002	RUS	6	0	1	1	6	
G	Nolan, Owen	2002	CAN	6	0	3	3	2	
	Norstrom, Mattias	1998	SWE	4	1	1	2	L.A.	
	Norstrom, Mattias	2002	SWE	4	0	0	0	0	L.A.
S	Numminen, Teppo	1988	FIN	6	1	4	5	0	BUF
B	Numminen, Teppo	1998	FIN	6	1	1	2	2	BUF
	Numminen, Teppo	2002	FIN	4	0	1	1	0	BUF
	Nylander, Michael	1998	SWE	4	0	0	0	6	NYR
	Nylander, Michael	2002	SWE	4	1	2	3	0	NYR

Olympic Results, Active NHL Players *continued*

Medal	Name	Year	Team	GP	G	A	Pts	PIM	05-06 NHL Club
	Ohlund, Mattias	1998	SWE	4	0	1	1	4	VAN
	Ohlund, Mattias	2002	SWE	4	0	2	2	2	VAN
	Ozolinsh, Sandis	2002	LAT	1	0	4	4	0	ANA
	Palffy, Ziggy	1994	SVK	8	3	7	10	8	PIT
	Palffy, Ziggy	2002	SVK	1	0	0	0	0	PIT
	Patrick, James	1984	CAN	7	0	3	3	4	
G	Peca, Michael	2002	CAN	6	0	2	2	2	EDM
	Pock, Thomas	2002	AUT	4	0	0	0	2	NYR
	Ponikarovsky, Alexei	2002	UKR	4	1	1	2	6	TOR
S	Poti, Tom	2002	USA	6	0	1	1	4	NYR
	Primeau, Keith	1998	CAN	6	2	1	3	4	PHI
G	Pronger, Chris	1998	CAN	6	0	0	0	4	EDM
	Pronger, Chris	2002	CAN	6	0	1	1	2	EDM
S	Rafalski, Brian	2002	USA	6	1	2	3	2	N.J.
	Ragnarsson, Marcus	1998	SWE	3	0	1	1	0	
	Ragnarsson, Marcus	2002	SWE	4	0	2	2	2	
	Recchi, Mark	1998	CAN	5	0	2	2	0	PIT
G	Reichel, Robert	1998	CZE	6	3	0	3	0	
	Reichel, Robert	2002	CZE	4	1	0	1	2	
	Renberg, Mikael	1998	SWE	4	1	2	3	4	
	Renberg, Mikael	2002	SWE	4	1	0	1	4	
	Roenick, Jeremy	1998	USA	4	0	1	1	6	L.A.
S	Roenick, Jeremy	2002	USA	6	1	4	5	2	L.A.
	Rolston, Brian	1994	USA	8	7	0	7	8	MIN
S	Rolston, Brian	2002	USA	6	0	3	3	0	MIN
G	Rucinsky, Martin	1998	CZE	6	3	1	4	4	NYR
	Rucinsky, Martin	2002	CZE	4	0	3	3	2	NYR
	Ruutu, Jarkko	2002	FIN	4	0	0	0	4	VAN
	Sakic, Joe	1998	CAN	4	1	2	3	4	COL
G	Sakic, Joe	2002	CAN	6	4	3	7	0	COL
	Salei, Ruslan	1998	BRS	7	1	0	1	4	ANA
	Salei, Ruslan	2002	BRS	6	2	1	3	4	ANA
	Salo, Sami	2002	FIN	4	0	0	0	0	VAN
B	Samsonov, Sergei	2002	RUS	6	1	2	3	4	BOS
	Satan, Miroslav	1994	SVK	8	9	0	9	0	NYI
	Satan, Miroslav	2002	SVK	2	0	1	1	0	NYI
S	Savage, Brian	1994	CAN	8	2	2	4	6	
	Schneider, Mathieu	1998	USA	4	0	0	0	6	DET
	Seidenberg, Dennis	2002	GER	7	1	1	2	8	PHI
	Selanne, Teemu	1992	FIN	8	7	4	11	6	ANA
B	Selanne, Teemu	1998	FIN	5	4	6	10	8	ANA
	Selanne, Teemu	2002	FIN	4	3	0	3	2	ANA
	Shanahan, Brendan	1998	CAN	6	2	0	2	0	DET
G	Shanahan, Brendan	2002	CAN	6	0	1	1	0	DET
	Skoula, Martin	2002	CZE	4	0	0	0	0	DAL
	Skrastins, Karlis	2002	LAT	1	0	0	0	0	COL
B	Slegr, Jiri	1992	CZE	8	1	1	2	14	BOS
G	Slegr, Jiri	1998	CZE	6	1	0	1	8	BOS
G	Smyth, Ryan	2002	CAN	6	0	1	1	0	EDM
G	Spacek, Jaroslav	1998	CZE	6	0	0	0	4	CHI
	Spacek, Jaroslav	2002	CZE	4	0	0	0	0	CHI
	Stevens, Scott	1998	CAN	6	0	0	0	2	
G	Straka, Martin	1998	CZE	6	1	2	3	0	NYR
	Stumpel, Jozef	2002	SVK	2	2	1	3	0	FLA
	Sturm, Marco	1998	GER	2	0	0	0	0	S.J.
	Sturm, Marco	2002	GER	5	0	1	1	0	S.J.
	Sundin, Mats	1998	SWE	4	3	0	3	4	TOR
	Sundin, Mats	2002	SWE	4	5	4	9	10	TOR
	Sundstrom, Niklas	1998	SWE	4	1	1	2	2	MTL
	Sundstrom, Niklas	2002	SWE	4	1	3	4	0	MTL
	Sykora, Petr	2002	CZE	4	1	0	1	0	ANA
	Tellqvist, Mikael	2002	SWE	3	0	0	0	0	TOR
S	Therien, Chris	1994	CAN	4	0	0	0	4	PHI
B	Timonen, Kimmo	1998	FIN	6	0	1	1	2	NSH
	Timonen, Kimmo	2002	FIN	4	0	1	1	2	NSH
	Tkachuk, Keith	1992	USA	8	1	1	2	12	ST.L.
	Tkachuk, Keith	1998	USA	4	0	2	2	6	ST.L.
S	Tkachuk, Keith	2002	USA	5	2	0	2	2	ST.L.
	Vaananen, Ossi	2002	FIN	2	0	1	1	0	COL
	Vauclair, Julien	2002	SUI	4	1	0	1	2	OTT
	Visnovsky, Lubomir	2002	SVK	3	1	2	3	0	L.A.
	Weight, Doug	1998	USA	4	0	2	2	2	ST.L.
S	Weight, Doug	2002	USA	6	0	3	3	4	ST.L.
	Weinrich, Eric	1988	USA	3	0	0	0	0	ST.L.
S	Woolley, Jason	1992	CAN	8	0	5	5	4	
S	Yashin, Alexei	1998	RUS	6	3	3	6	0	NYI

Medal	Name	Year	Team	GP	G	A	Pts	PIM	05-06 NHL Club
B	Yashin, Alexei	2002	RUS	6	1	1	2	0	NYI
S	York, Mike	2002	USA	6	0	1	1	0	NYI
	Young, Scott	1988	USA	6	2	6	8	4	
	Young, Scott	1992	USA	8	2	1	3	2	
S	Young, Scott	2002	USA	6	4	0	4	2	
	Yzerman, Steve	1998	CAN	6	1	1	2	10	DET
G	Yzerman, Steve	2002	CAN	6	2	4	6	2	DET
	Zamuner, Rob	1998	CAN	6	1	0	1	8	
	Zetterberg, Henrik	2002	SWE	4	0	1	1	0	DET
G	Zhamnov, Alex	1992	RUS	8	0	3	3	8	BOS
S	Zhamnov, Alex	1998	RUS	6	2	1	3	2	BOS
B	Zhamnov, Alex	2002	RUS	6	1	0	1	4	BOS
G	Zhitnik, Alexei	1992	RUS	8	1	0	1	0	NYI
S	Zhitnik, Alexei	1998	RUS	6	0	2	2	2	NYI
G	Zubov, Sergei	1992	RUS	8	0	1	1	0	DAL

Olympic Results, Active NHL Goaltenders

Medal	Name	Year	Team	GPI	W	L	T	Mins	GA	SO	Avg	05-06 NHL Club
	Aebischer, David	2002	SUI	2	1	0	0	81	6	0	4.43	COL
G	Belfour, Ed	2002	CAN	Did not play — backup goaltender								TOR
	Brodeur, Martin	1998	CAN	Did not play — backup goaltender								N.J.
G	Brodeur, Martin	2002	CAN	5	4	0	1	300	9	0	1.80	N.J.
B	Bryzgalov, Ilya	2002	RUS	Did not play — backup goaltender								ANA
S	Burke, Sean	1988	CAN	4	1	2	1	238	12	0	3.02	T.B.
S	Burke, Sean	1992	CAN	7	5	2	0	429	17	0	2.37	T.B.
G	Cechmanek, Roman	1998	CZE	Did not play — backup goaltender								
	Cechmanek, Roman	2002	CZE	Did not play — backup goaltender								
	Divis, Reinhard	2002	AUT	4	1	1	2	238	12	0	3.02	ST.L.
	Dunham, Mike	1992	USA	Did not play — backup goaltender								ATL
	Dunham, Mike	1994	USA	3	0	1	2	180	15	0	5.00	ATL
S	Dunham, Mike	2002	USA	1	1	0	0	60	0	1	0.00	ATL
	Gerber, Martin	2002	SUI	3	1	1	1	158	4	0	1.52	CAR
B	Hasek, Dominik	1988	CZE	5	3	2	0	217	18	1	4.98	OTT
G	Hasek, Dominik	1998	CZE	6	5	1	0	369	6	2	0.97	OTT
	Hasek, Dominik	2002	CZE	4	1	2	1	239	8	0	2.01	OTT
	Hedberg, Johan	1998	SWE	Did not play — backup goaltender								DAL
	Hedberg, Johan	2002	SWE	1	1	0	0	60	1	0	1.00	DAL
G	Hnilicka, Milan	1998	CZE	Did not play — backup goaltender								
	Huet, Cristobal	1998	FRA	2	1	1	0	120	5	0	2.50	MTL
	Huet, Cristobal	2002	FRA	3	0	2	1	179	10	0	3.36	MTL
	Irbe, Arturs	2002	LAT	1	0	1	0	60	4	0	4.00	
	Joseph, Curtis	1998	CAN	Did not play — backup goaltender								PHX
G	Joseph, Curtis	2002	CAN	1	0	1	0	60	5	0	5.00	PHX
G	Khabibulin, Nikolai	1992	RUS	Did not play — backup goaltender								CHI
B	Khabibulin, Nikolai	2002	RUS	6	3	2	1	359	14	1	2.34	CHI
S	Kidd, Trevor	1992	CAN	1	1	0	0	60	0	1	0.00	
	Kolzig, Olie	1998	GER	2	2	0	0	120	2	1	1.00	WSH
S	Legace, Manny	1994	CAN	Did not play — backup goaltender								DET
	Markkanen, Jussi	2002	FIN	Did not play — backup goaltender								EDM
G	Salo, Tommy	1994	SWE	6	5	1	0	370	13	1	2.11	
	Salo, Tommy	1998	SWE	4	2	2	0	238	9	0	2.27	
	Salo, Tommy	2002	SWE	3	2	1	0	179	7	0	2.35	
	Snow, Garth	1994	USA	5	1	3	1	299	17	0	3.41	
	Stana, Rastislav	2002	SVK	1	1	0	0	60	1	0	1.00	WSH
	Tellqvist, Mikael	2002	SWE	Did not play — backup goaltender								TOR

Mighty Ducks of Anaheim

2005-06 Schedule

Oct.	Wed.	5	at Chicago		Mon.	9	Los Angeles
	Sat.	8	at Nashville		Fri.	13	Washington
	Mon.	10	Edmonton		Mon.	16	at Boston*
	Fri.	14	Columbus		Thu.	19	at Ottawa
	Sun.	16	at Minnesota*		Sat.	21	Florida
	Wed.	19	at St. Louis		Mon.	23	at Los Angeles
	Fri.	21	at Detroit		Wed.	25	Edmonton
	Sun.	23	Phoenix*		Thu.	26	at San Jose
	Tue.	25	at Los Angeles		Sat.	28	at Los Angeles*
	Wed.	26	Calgary		Mon.	30	Los Angeles
	Fri.	28	St. Louis	**Feb.**	Wed.	1	San Jose
	Sun.	30	Phoenix*		Sat.	4	at San Jose
Nov.	Tue.	1	Nashville		Mon.	6	at Edmonton
	Thu.	3	at Colorado		Wed.	8	at Calgary
	Fri.	4	San Jose		Fri.	10	at Vancouver
	Sun.	6	Minnesota*		Sun.	12	Chicago*
	Sat.	12	at Phoenix	**Mar.**	Wed.	1	Detroit
	Sun.	13	Dallas*		Fri.	3	Minnesota
	Wed.	16	Dallas		Sun.	5	Columbus*
	Fri.	18	Colorado		Tue.	7	San Jose
	Sun.	20	Vancouver*		Sat.	11	at Phoenix
	Tue.	22	at Phoenix		Sun.	12	Phoenix*
	Wed.	23	at Dallas		Wed.	15	at Detroit
	Fri.	25	Detroit*		Fri.	17	at Chicago
	Sun.	27	Chicago*		Sun.	19	at Columbus*
	Wed.	30	Phoenix		Mon.	20	at Dallas
Dec.	Sat.	3	Atlanta		Wed.	22	Colorado
	Tue.	6	Carolina		Fri.	24	Nashville
	Thu.	8	at Buffalo		Sat.	25	at Phoenix
	Sat.	10	at Montreal		Tue.	28	at Colorado
	Mon.	12	at Toronto		Wed.	29	at Dallas
	Wed.	14	Tampa Bay		Fri.	31	Dallas
	Fri.	16	Los Angeles	**Apr.**	Sun.	2	Vancouver*
	Sun.	18	San Jose*		Tue.	4	Los Angeles
	Tue.	20	at San Jose		Thu.	6	Dallas
	Wed.	21	St. Louis		Sat.	8	at Los Angeles*
	Wed.	28	at Columbus		Mon.	10	at Vancouver
	Sat.	31	at St. Louis*		Tue.	11	at Calgary
Jan.	Sun.	1	at Nashville		Thu.	13	at Edmonton
	Fri.	6	at Dallas		Sat.	15	at San Jose*
	Sat.	7	at Minnesota		Mon.	17	Calgary

* Denotes afternoon game.

Year-by-Year Record

		Home				Road				Overall								
Season	GP	W	L	T	OL	W	L	T	OL	W	L	T	OL	GF	GA	Pts.	Finished	Playoff Result
2004-05	....																	
2003-04	82	19	11	7	4	10	24	3	4	29	35	10	8	184	213	76	4th, Pacific Div.	Out of Playoffs
2002-03	82	22	10	7	2	18	17	2	4	40	27	9	6	203	193	95	2nd, Pacific Div.	Lost Final
2001-02	82	15	19	5	2	14	23	3	1	29	42	8	3	175	198	69	5th, Pacific Div.	Out of Playoffs
2000-01	82	15	20	4	2	10	21	7	3	25	41	11	5	188	245	66	5th, Pacific Div.	Out of Playoffs
1999-2000	82	19	13	7	2	15	20	5	1	34	33	12	3	217	227	83	5th, Pacific Div.	Out of Playoffs
1998-99	82	21	14	6	....	14	20	7	....	35	34	13	....	215	206	83	3rd, Pacific Div.	Lost Conf. Quarter-Final
1997-98	82	12	23	6	....	14	20	7	....	26	43	13	....	205	261	65	6th, Pacific Div.	Out of Playoffs
1996-97	82	23	12	6	....	13	21	7	....	36	33	13	....	245	233	85	2nd, Pacific Div.	Lost Conf. Semi-Final
1995-96	82	22	15	4	....	13	24	4	....	35	39	8	....	234	247	78	4th, Pacific Div.	Out of Playoffs
1994-95	48	11	9	4	....	5	18	1	....	16	27	5	....	125	164	37	6th, Pacific Div.	Out of Playoffs
1993-94	84	14	26	2	....	19	20	3	....	33	46	5	....	229	251	71	4th, Pacific Div.	Out of Playoffs

Rob Niedermayer joined the Mighty Ducks from Calgary late in the 2002-03 season and was a key performer when Anaheim reached the Stanley Cup finals that spring.

Franchise date: June 15, 1993

PACIFIC DIVISION

13th NHL Season

2005-06 Player Personnel

FORWARDS	HT	WT	S	Place of Birth	Date	2004-05 Club
ADAMS, Craig	6-0	200	R	Seria, Brunei	4/26/77	Milano
BRENNAN, Kip	6-4	230	L	Kingston, Ont.	8/27/80	Chicago (AHL)
BRENT, Tim	6-0	188	R	Cambridge, Ont.	3/10/84	Cincinnati (AHL)
FEDOROV, Sergei	6-2	205	L	Pskov, USSR	12/13/69	
FEDORUK, Todd	6-2	235	L	Redwater, Alta.	2/13/79	Philadelphia (AHL)
GETZLAF, Ryan	6-2	210	R	Regina, Sask.	5/10/85	Cgy (WHL)-Cin (AHL)
GILLIES, Trevor	6-3	235	L	Cambridge, Ont.	1/30/79	Hartford
GLENCROSS, Curtis	6-1	195	L	Kindersley, Sask.	12/28/82	Cincinnati (AHL)
HEDSTROM, Jonathan	6-0	200	L	Skelleftea, Sweden	12/27/77	Timra
KONOPKA, Zenon	6-0	206	L	Niagara Falls, Ont.	1/2/81	Cincinnati (AHL)
KUNITZ, Chris	6-0	194	L	Regina, Sask.	9/26/79	Cincinnati (AHL)
LUPUL, Joffrey	6-1	205	R	Edmonton, Alta.	9/23/83	Cincinnati (AHL)
McDONALD, Andy	5-10	186	L	Strathroy, Ont.	8/25/77	Ingolstadt
MOEN, Travis	6-2	210	L	Stewart Valley, Sask.	4/6/82	Norfolk
NIEDERMAYER, Rob	6-2	204	L	Cassiar, B.C.	12/28/74	Ferencvaros
PAHLSSON, Samuel	5-11	212	L	Ornskoldsvik, Sweden	12/17/77	Frolunda
PENNER, Dustin	6-4	245	L	Winkler, Man.	9/28/82	Cincinnati (AHL)
PERREAULT, Joel	6-1	197	R	Montreal, Que.	4/6/83	Cincinnati (AHL)
PERRY, Corey	6-2	202	R	Peterborough, Ont.	5/16/85	London
SELANNE, Teemu	6-0	204	R	Helsinki, Finland	7/3/70	
SYKORA, Petr	6-0	190	L	Plzen, Czhech.	11/19/76	Magnitogorsk

DEFENSEMEN	HT	WT	S	Place of Birth	Date	2004-05 Club
CARNEY, Keith	6-2	216	L	Providence, RI	2/3/70	
MARSHALL, Jason	6-2	200	R	Cranbrook, B.C.	2/22/71	Plzen
NIEDERMAYER, Scott	6-1	200	L	Edmonton, Alta.	8/31/73	
O'BRIEN, Shane	6-2	237	L	Port Hope, Ont.	8/9/83	Cincinnati (AHL)
OZOLINSH, Sandis	6-3	217	L	Riga, Latvia	8/3/72	
ROME, Aaron	6-1	230	L	Nesbitt, Man.	9/27/83	Cincinnati (AHL)
SALEI, Ruslan	6-1	213	L	Minsk, USSR	11/2/74	Kazan
VISHNEVSKI, Vitaly	6-2	203	L	Kharkov, USSR	3/18/80	Voskresensk

GOALTENDERS	HT	WT	C	Place of Birth	Date	2004-05 Club
BRYZGALOV, Ilya	6-3	198	L	Togliatti, USSR	6/22/80	Cincinnati (AHL)
GIGUERE, Jean-Sebastien	6-1	199	L	Montreal, Que.	5/16/77	Hamburg

In the System and Recently Drafted

FORWARDS	HT	WT	S	Place of Birth	Date	2004-05 Club
AUFFREY, Matt	6-2	203	R	Cincinnati, OH	1/3/86	U. of Wisconsin
BAILEY, Jason	6-0	205	R	Ottawa, Ont.	6/4/87	USA U-18
BOLT, Bobby	6-3	219	L	Thunder Bay, Ont.	4/29/87	Kingston
CHAGODAYEV, Alexandr	6-1	185	L	Perm, USSR	1/15/81	
CHISTOV, Stanislav	5-10	193	R	Chelyabinsk, USSR	4/17/83	Cincinnati (AHL)
CHRISTIE, Matt	5-10	185	L	Toronto, Ont.	2/22/85	Miami U.
DAVIS, George	6-1	242	R	North Sydney, N.S.	7/28/83	Kansas City
HYNES, Shane	6-3	224	R	Montreal, Que.	11/7/83	Cornell
JOHANSSON, Tobias	5-11	180	L	Malmo, Sweden	10/22/77	
MARTENSSON, Tony	6-0	189	L	Upplands Vasby, Sweden	6/23/80	Linkoping
MELIN, Bjorn	6-1	178	R	Jonkoping, Sweden	7/4/81	Malmo
MIETTINEN, Tommi	5-10	165	L	Kuopio, Finland	12/3/75	Brynas
MILLER, Andrew	6-2	165	L	Dover, NJ	2/17/84	Michigan State
PARENTEAU, Pierre	5-11	195	R	Hull, Que.	3/24/83	Cincinnati (AHL)
PESONEN, Janne	5-11	180	L	Suomussalmi, Finland	5/11/82	Karpat
PETERS, Geoff	6-1	205	L	Hamilton, Ont.	4/30/78	Rochester
POHANKA, Igor	6-2	210	L	Piestany, Czech.	7/5/83	Cincinnati (AHL)
PRESTBERG, Pelle	5-10	170	L	Jonkoping, Sweden	2/5/75	Farjestad
RYAN, Bobby	6-2	213	R	Cherry Hill, NJ	3/17/87	Owen Sound
RYBIN, Maxim	5-8	182	R	Zhukovsky, USSR	6/15/81	Cherepovets-Spartak
SOUTHERN, Dirk	6-0	177	R	Winnipeg, Man.	8/9/83	Northern Mich.
STEPP, Joel	6-0	215	L	Estevan, Sask.	2/11/83	Cin (AHL)-San Diego
STUSSI, Rene	5-11	183	R	Muri, Switz.	12/13/78	Thurgau
VIHKO, Joonas	5-9	172	R	Helsinki, Finland	4/6/81	HIFK

DEFENSEMEN	HT	WT	S	Place of Birth	Date	2004-05 Club
AHMAOJA, Timo	6-1	180	R	Jyvaskyla, Finland	8/8/78	
ALEN, Juha	6-3	218	L	Tampere, Finland	10/25/81	Ilves
DiPENTA, Joe	6-2	235	L	Barrie, Ont.	2/25/79	Manitoba
HUSKINS, Kent	6-3	215	L	Ottawa, Ont.	5/4/79	Manitoba
KLUBERTANZ, Kyle	6-0	178	R	Madison, WI	9/23/85	U. of Wisconsin
KORSUNOV, Vladimir	6-2	202	L	Moscow, USSR	3/16/83	Spartak
MANTYMAA, Ville	6-3	183	R	Seinajoki, Finland	3/8/85	Tappara
MIKKELSON, Brendan	6-2	180	L	Regina, Sask.	6/22/87	Portland (WHL)
SALCIDO, Brian	6-2	188	L	Los Angeles, CA	4/14/85	Colorado College
SANDSTROM, Jan	6-0	190	L	Pitea, Sweden	1/24/78	Lulea
SAUNDERS, Nathan	6-4	215	R	Charlottetown, P.E.I.	4/25/85	Moncton
SMID, Ladislav	6-3	204	L	Frydlant V Cechach, Czech.	2/1/86	Liberec
SMITH, Jordan	6-2	215	R	Sault Ste. Marie, Ont.	11/4/85	SS Marie-Cin (AHL)
WALLIN, Viktor	6-3	200	L	Jonkoping, Sweden	1/17/80	Nybro

GOALTENDERS	HT	WT	C	Place of Birth	Date	2004-05 Club
ANDERSSON, Andreas	6-0	180	L	Jonkoping, Sweden	4/9/79	Troja
BOUTHILLETTE, Gabriel	6-3	193	L	Sorel, Que.	5/21/85	Acadie-Bathurst
LEVASSEUR, Jean-Philippe	6-0	184	R	Victoriaville, Que.	1/15/87	Rouyn-Noranda

Coach

CARLYLE, RANDY
Coach, Mighty Ducks of Anaheim. Born in Sudbury, Ont., April 19, 1956.

The Mighty Ducks of Anaheim announced Randy Carlyle as head coach on August 1, 2005. Carlyle had spent the 2004-05 season as head coach of the Manitoba Moose, the Vancouver Canucks' primary development affiliate in the American Hockey League. That year, he led Manitoba to a 44-26-3-7 record and an appearance in the Calder Cup semifinals.

In all, Carlyle spent six seasons between 1996 and 2005 as head coach in Manitoba (both in the International and American Hockey Leagues) with his team posting an overall record of 222-159-52-7. He had the additional duties of general manager of the Moose from 1996 to 2000, and served as club president for the 2001-02 season. The Sudbury, Ontario, native helped the Moose to a 47-21-14 record for 108 points in 1998-99, for which he was named the IHL's general manager of the year.

Following the 2001-02 season, Carlyle joined the coaching staff of the Washington Capitals. He served as an assistant coach with Washington for two years (2002 to 2004), before rejoining Manitoba in 2004-05.

Carlyle played 17 seasons in the NHL with Toronto, Pittsburgh and Winnipeg. He appeared in 1,055 games and had 148 goals and 499 assists for 647 points. Known as a fiery, tough-nosed defenseman, he was selected to play in four NHL All-Star Games, winning the Norris Trophy as the league's top defenseman in 1981. At the conclusion of his playing career in 1993, Carlyle remained with the Winnipeg organization's hockey operations staff, eventually becoming an assistant coach for the 1995-96 season.

The chance to play with his brother Rob was a key reason why Scott Niedermayer signed with Anaheim after 12+ seasons in New Jersey.

Coaching Record

Season	Team	Games	Regular Season			Games	Playoffs	
			W	L	T		W	L
1996-97	Manitoba (IHL)	32	16	14	2	....	....	....
1997-98	Manitoba (IHL)	82	39	36	7	3	0	3
1998-99	Manitoba (IHL)	82	47	21	14	5	2	3
99-2000	Manitoba (IHL)	82	37	31	14	2	0	2
2000-01	Manitoba (IHL)	82	39	31	12	13	6	7
2004-05	Manitoba (AHL)	80	44	33	3	14	6	8

Club Records

Team

(Figures in brackets for season records are games played; records for fewest points, wins, ties, losses, goals, goals against are for 70 or more games)

Most Points	95	2002-03 (82)
Most Wins	40	2002-03 (82)
Most Ties	13	1996-97 (82); 1997-98 (82); 1998-99 (82)
Most Losses	46	1993-94 (84)
Most Goals	245	1996-97 (82)
Most Goals Against	261	1997-98 (82)
Fewest Points	65	1997-98 (82)
Fewest Wins	25	2000-01 (82)
Fewest Ties	5	1993-94 (84)
Fewest Losses	27	2002-03 (82)
Fewest Goals	175	2001-02 (82)
Fewest Goals Against	193	2002-03 (82)

Longest Winning Streak

Overall	7	Feb. 20-Mar. 7/99
Home	5	Four times
Away	5	Nov. 26-Dec. 26/99

Longest Undefeated Streak

Overall	12	Feb. 22-Mar. 19/97 (7 wins, 5 ties)
Home	14	Feb. 12-Apr. 9/97 (10 wins, 4 ties)
Away	5	Five times

Longest Losing Streak

Overall	8	Oct. 12-30/96
Home	8	Jan. 10-Feb. 9/01
Away	6	Four times

Longest Winless Streak

Overall	9	Twice
Home	11	Jan. 5-Feb. 14/01 (8 losses, 3 ties)
Away	13	Nov. 1-Dec. 27/03 (11 losses, 2 ties)

Most Shutouts, Season	9	2002-03 (82)
Most PIM, Season	1,843	1997-98 (82)
Most Goals, Game	8	Three times

Individual

Most Seasons	10	Steve Rucchin
Most Games	616	Steve Rucchin
Most Goals, Career	300	Paul Kariya
Most Assists, Career	369	Paul Kariya
Most Points, Career	669	Paul Kariya (300G, 369A)
Most PIM, Career	788	Dave Karpa
Most Shutouts, Career	27	Guy Hebert
Longest Consecutive Games Streak	237	Oleg Tverdovsky (Oct. 2/99-Mar. 24/02)
Most Goals, Season	52	Teemu Selanne (1997-98)
Most Assists, Season	62	Paul Kariya (1998-99)
Most Points, Season	109	Teemu Selanne (1996-97; 51G, 58A)

Most PIM, Season	285	Todd Ewen (1995-96)
Most Points, Defenseman, Season	56	Fredrik Olausson (1998-99; 16G, 40A)
Most Points, Center, Season	67	Steve Rucchin (1996-97; 19G, 48A)
Most Points, Right Wing, Season	109	Teemu Selanne (1996-97; 51G, 58A)
Most Points, Left Wing, Season	108	Paul Kariya (1995-96; 50G, 58A)
Most Points, Rookie, Season	39	Paul Kariya (1994-95; 18G, 21A)
Most Shutouts, Season	8	Jean-Sebastien Giguere (2002-03)
Most Goals, Game	3	Twenty-one times
Most Assists, Game	5	Dmitri Mironov (Dec. 12/97)
Most Points, Game	5	Six times

General Managers' History

Jack Ferreira, 1993-94 to 1997-98; Pierre Gauthier, 1998-99 to 2001-02; Bryan Murray, 2002-03, 2003-04; Al Coates, 2004-05; Brian Burke, 2005-06.

Coaching History

Ron Wilson, 1993-94 to 1996-97; Pierre Page, 1997-98; Craig Hartsburg, 1998-99, 1999-2000; Craig Hartsburg and Guy Charron, 2000-01; Bryan Murray, 2001-02; Mike Babcock, 2002-03 to 2004-05; Randy Carlyle, 2005-06.

Captains' History

Troy Loney, 1993-94; Randy Ladouceur, 1994-95, 1995-96; Paul Kariya, 1996-97; Paul Kariya and Teemu Selanne, 1997-98; Paul Kariya, 1998-99 to 2002-03; Steve Rucchin, 2003-04.

All-time Record vs. Other Clubs

Regular Season

			At Home								On Road								Total					
	GP	W	L	T	OL	GF	GA	PTS	GP	W	L	T	OL	GF	GA	PTS	GP	W	L	T	OL	GF	GA	PTS
Atlanta	4	2	2	0	0	12	9	4	4	3	1	0	0	16	10	6	8	5	3	0	0	28	19	10
Boston	9	2	3	2	2	18	24	8	8	4	4	0	0	24	23	8	17	6	7	2	2	42	47	16
Buffalo	9	2	7	0	0	15	30	4	9	2	4	3	0	20	25	7	18	4	11	3	0	35	55	11
Calgary	26	12	8	6	0	80	69	30	25	9	15	1	0	61	72	19	51	21	23	7	0	141	141	49
Carolina	9	5	3	1	0	29	26	11	9	3	5	1	0	19	23	7	18	8	8	2	0	48	49	18
Chicago	22	12	7	3	0	58	47	27	24	10	12	2	0	58	67	22	46	22	19	5	0	116	114	49
Colorado	21	7	10	3	1	48	53	18	21	6	10	4	1	53	65	17	42	13	20	7	2	101	118	35
Columbus	8	5	2	1	0	24	16	11	8	2	6	0	0	15	23	4	16	7	8	1	0	39	39	15
Dallas	27	11	13	3	0	61	66	25	27	5	19	2	1	52	101	13	54	16	32	5	1	113	167	38
Detroit	22	7	11	4	0	52	65	18	22	2	15	3	2	49	83	9	44	9	26	7	2	101	148	27
Edmonton	26	15	9	2	0	71	64	32	25	8	15	0	2	50	57	18	51	23	24	2	2	121	121	50
Florida	9	3	5	1	0	27	30	7	8	2	3	2	1	17	23	7	17	5	8	3	1	44	53	14
Los Angeles	30	13	6	7	4	100	80	37	30	9	17	4	0	72	89	22	60	22	23	11	4	172	169	59
Minnesota	8	5	2	0	1	19	17	11	8	3	3	2	0	14	13	8	16	8	5	2	1	33	30	19
Montreal	8	3	5	0	0	25	27	6	8	4	2	0	0	19	24	6	16	5	9	2	0	44	51	12
Nashville	12	9	1	0	2	33	20	20	12	5	5	2	0	28	24	12	24	14	6	2	2	61	44	32
New Jersey	10	4	5	1	0	26	26	9	8	1	6	0	1	14	31	3	18	5	11	1	1	40	57	12
NY Islanders	9	2	4	3	0	18	24	7	8	3	4	1	0	23	24	7	17	5	8	4	0	41	48	14
NY Rangers	8	6	1	0	1	32	25	13	9	5	2	1	1	26	23	12	17	11	3	1	2	58	48	25
Ottawa	9	4	3	2	0	21	18	10	8	3	4	1	0	19	24	7	17	7	7	3	0	40	42	17
Philadelphia	9	4	3	2	0	30	28	10	8	2	3	3	0	17	22	7	17	6	6	5	0	47	50	17
Phoenix	27	15	9	3	0	74	67	33	26	13	10	2	1	77	75	29	53	28	19	5	1	151	142	62
Pittsburgh	8	5	3	0	0	29	24	10	9	2	5	2	0	27	29	6	17	7	8	2	0	56	53	16
St. Louis	22	7	13	2	0	54	65	16	22	7	10	3	2	56	67	19	44	14	23	5	2	110	132	35
San Jose	30	11	17	2	0	78	99	24	30	14	13	2	1	80	84	31	60	25	30	4	1	158	183	55
Tampa Bay	8	4	3	1	0	24	20	9	9	5	4	0	0	23	17	10	17	9	7	1	0	47	37	19
Toronto	11	5	5	1	0	34	28	11	15	2	9	4	0	30	50	8	26	7	14	5	0	64	78	19
Vancouver	25	7	10	7	1	59	74	22	26	8	16	2	0	59	91	18	51	15	26	9	1	118	165	40
Washington	9	6	2	1	0	29	22	13	9	5	4	0	0	22	16	10	18	11	6	1	0	51	38	23
Totals	435	193	172	58	12	1180	1163	456	435	145	228	49	13	1040	1275	352	870	338	400	107	25	2220	2438	808

Playoffs

	Series	W	L	GP	W	L	T	GF	GA	Last Mtg.	Rnd.	Result
Dallas	1	1	0	6	4	2	0	14	14	2003	CSF	W 4-2
Detroit	3	1	2	12	4	8	0	24	36	2003	CQF	W 4-0
Minnesota	1	1	0	4	4	0	0	9	1	2003	CF	W 4-0
New Jersey	1	0	1	7	3	4	0	12	19	2003	F	L 3-4
Phoenix	1	1	0	7	4	3	0	17	17	1997	CQF	W 4-3
Totals	7	4	3	36	19	17	0	76	87			

Playoff Results 2005-2000

Year	Round	Opponent	Result	GF	GA
2003	F	New Jersey	L 3-4	12	19
	CF	Minnesota	W 4-0	9	1
	CSF	Dallas	W 4-2	14	14
	CQF	Detroit	W 4-0	10	6

Abbreviations: Round: F - Final; **CF** – conference final; **CSF** – conference quarter-final; **CQF** – conference quarter-final

Carolina totals include Hartford, 1993-94 to 1996-97.
Colorado totals include Quebec, 1993-94 to 1994-95.
Phoenix totals include Winnipeg, 1993-94 to 1995-96.

Key Off-Season Signings/Acquisitions

2004

June 28 • Re-signed C **Andy McDonald**.

　　　30 • Picked up two-year option on D **Keith Carney**.

July 12 • Re-signed D **Vitaly Vishnevski**.

Sept. 15 • Signed 2003 1st-round picks, C/RW **Ryan Getzlaf** (19th overall) and RW **Corey Perry** (28th overall).

2005

June 20 • Named **Brian Burke** executive vice president and general manager.

July 14 • Named **Bob Murray** senior vice president of hockey operations.

　　　29 • Re-signed D **Sandis Ozolinsh**.

　　　29 • Acquired LW **Todd Fedoruk** from Philadelphia for a 2005 2nd-round pick.

　　　31 • Selected RW **Bobby Ryan** (Owen Sound, OHL) with the 2nd overall selection in the 2005 Entry Draft.

Aug. 1 • Named **Randy Carlyle** head coach.

　　　4 • Re-signed C **Rob Niedermayer** and signed D **Scott Niedermayer**.

　　　8 • Signed D **Jason Marshall**.

　　　10 • Named **Dave Farrish** assistant coach.

　　　17 • Named **Newell Brown** assistant coach.

　　　22 • Signed RW **Teemu Selanne**.

　　　24 • Re-signed C **Samuel Pahlsson**.

　　　24 • Signed 2004 1st-round pick (9th overall), D **Ladislav Smid**.

　　　25 • Signed RW **Craig Adams**.

Entry Draft
Selections 2005-1993

2005 Pick		2001 Pick		1997 Pick		1993 Pick	
2	Bobby Ryan	5	Stanislav Chistov	18	Michael Holmqvist	4	Paul Kariya
31	Brendan Mikkelson	35	Mark Popovic	45	Maxim Balmochnykh	30	Nikolai Tsulygin
63	Jason Bailey	69	Joel Stepp	72	Jay Legault	56	Valeri Karpov
127	Bobby Bolt	102	Timo Parssinen	125	Luc Vaillancourt	82	Joel Gagnon
141	Brian Salcido	105	Vladimir Korsunov	178	Tony Mohagen	108	Mikhail Shtalenkov
197	Jean-Philippe Levasseur	118	Brandon Rogers	181	Mat Snesrud	134	Antti Aalto
		137	Joel Perreault	209	Rene Stussi	160	Matt Peterson
2004 Pick		170	Jan Tabacek	235	Tommi Degerman	186	Tom Askey
9	Ladislav Smid	224	Tony Martensson			212	Vitali Kozel
39	Jordan Smith	232	Martin Gerber	**1996 Pick**		238	Anatoli Fedotov
74	Kyle Klubertanz	264	Pierre Parenteau	9	Ruslan Salei	264	David Penney
75	Tim Brent			35	Matt Cullen		
172	Matt Auffrey	**2000 Pick**		117	Brendan Buckley		
203	Gabriel Bouthillette	12	Alexei Smirnov	149	Blaine Russell		
236	Matt Christie	44	Ilya Bryzgalov	172	Timo Ahmaoja		
269	Janne Pesonen	98	Jonas Ronnqvist	198	Kevin Kellett		
		134	Peter Podhradsky	224	Tobias Johwelin		
2003 Pick		153	Bill Cass				
19	Ryan Getzlaf			**1995 Pick**			
28	Corey Perry	**1999 Pick**		4	Chad Kilger		
86	Shane Hynes	44	Jordan Leopold	29	Brian Wesenberg		
90	Juha Alen	83	Niclas Havelid	55	Mike Leclerc		
119	Nathan Saunders	105	Alexandr Chagodayev	107	Igor Nikulin		
186	Andrew Miller	141	Maxim Rybin	133	Peter LeBoutillier		
218	Dirk Southern	173	Jan Sandstrom	159	Mike LaPlante		
250	Shane O'Brien	230	Petr Tenkrat	185	Igor Karpenko		
280	Ville Mantymaa	258	Brian Gornick				
				1994 Pick			
2002 Pick		**1998 Pick**		2	Oleg Tverdovsky		
7	Joffrey Lupul	5	Vitaly Vishnevski	28	Johan Davidsson		
37	Tim Brent	32	Stephen Peat	67	Craig Reichert		
71	Brian Lee	112	Viktor Wallin	80	Byron Briske		
103	Joonas Vihko	150	Trent Hunter	106	Pavel Trnka		
140	George Davis	178	Jesse Fibiger	132	Bates Battaglia		
173	Luke Fritshaw	205	David Bernier	158	Rocky Welsing		
261	Francois Caron	233	Pelle Prestberg	184	Brad Englehart		
267	Chris Petrow	245	Andreas Andersson	236	Tommi Miettinen		
				262	Jeremy Stevenson		

Vice President and General Manager

BURKE, BRIAN
Executive Vice President/General Manager, Mighty Ducks of Anaheim.
Born in Providence, RI, June 30, 1955.

Brian Burke, former president and general manager of the Vancouver Canucks, was named the Mighty Ducks' new executive vice president and general manager. Burke had served as the president and general manager of the Vancouver Canucks from 1998 to 2004. Under his leadership, the team increased its point total four consecutive years from 1999 to 2003. With 104 and 101 points respectively the last two NHL seasons (2002 to 2004), the Canucks joined only Detroit, Ottawa and Philadelphia to record consecutive seasons with at least 100 points. The 2003–04 Canucks finished with a record of 43-24-10-5 for 101 points, winning the Northwest Division. Over his last four seasons with the team, Burke engineered four consecutive seasons of at least 90 points.

Named by The Sporting News as NHL executive of the year in 2001, Burke acquired the majority of the current Canucks roster. Vancouver ranked third in the NHL in goals scored over his last three years with the team (753, behind only Detroit and Ottawa), including a league-leading 254 goals in 2001–02.

One of the most respected and experienced executives in the NHL, Burke originally joined the Canucks in June, 1987 as vice president and director of hockey operations. He left the Canucks in 1992 to become general manager of the Hartford Whalers, before being named NHL senior vice president and director of hockey operations (1993 to 1998). While working at the NHL league office, Burke worked closely with commissioner Gary Bettman on a wide variety of league issues and policies and was the NHL's chief disciplinarian.

Burke was born in New England and raised in Minnesota. He signed with the Philadelphia Flyers in 1977 as a player and was a member of the 1978 Calder Cup champion Maine Mariners. Burke then returned to Harvard Law School, where he graduated in 1981 before practicing law for six years in Boston. During his two stints in Vancouver, Burke was a valued and active member of the community, including his serving on the board of directors for Canuck Place.

Club Directory

Arrowhead Pond of Anaheim

Mighty Ducks of Anaheim
Arrowhead Pond of Anaheim
2695 Katella Ave.
Anaheim, CA 92806
Phone **714/940-2900**
FAX 714/940-2953
Ticket Information 877/WILDWING
www.mightyducks.com
Capacity: 17,174

Executive Management
CEO	Michael Schulman
Executive Vice President/General Manager	Brian Burke
Executive Vice President/COO	Tim Ryan
Senior Vice President, Hockey Operations	Bob Murray
Senior Vice President/CMO	Bob Wagner
V.P. of Amateur Scouting & Player Development	Chuck Fletcher
Vice President of Sales & Marketing	Steve Obert
Assistant GM, Hockey Operations	David McNab
Senior Advisor to the General Manager	Al Coates
Executive Assistant/Travel Coordinator	Maureen Nyeholt
Executive Assistant/Booking & Contracts	JoAnn Armstrong
Executive Assistant/Office Manager	Cheryl Gorman
Executive Assistant	Janet Conley

Coaching Staff
Head Coach	Randy Carlyle
Assistant Coaches	Dave Farrish, Newell Brown

Hockey Club Operations
Director of Professional Scouting	Rick Paterson
Director of Amateur Scouting	Alain Chainey
Scouting Staff	Jeff Crisp, Jan-Åke Danielson, Brent Flahr, Todd Hearty, Konstantin Krylov, Pavel Routa
Head Trainer	Tim Clark
Strength & Conditioning Coach	Sean Skahan
Equipment Manager	Mark O'Neill
Assistant Equipment Manager	John Allaway
Cincinnati Mighty Ducks (AHL) Head Coach	Kevin Dineen
Cincinnati Assistant Coach	Bruce Crowder
Team Physicians	Dr. Ronald Glousman, Dr. Craig Milhouse
Oral Surgeon	Dr. Jeff Pulver
Visiting Team Equipment Attendant	Chris Kincaid

Communications Department
Director of Media & Communications	Alex Gilchrist
Media & Communications Manager	Merit Tully
Media & Communications Coordinator	Ryan Lichtenfels

Finance and Administration
Director of Finance	Mike McGee
Director of Human Resources	Kim Kutcher
Controller	Melody Martin
Human Resources Associate	Pat Navarro
IT Manager	Mike Wing
Accounting Manager/Financial Analyst	Jennifer Boyle
Accounting Assistant	Rob Dumlao
Accounting Clerk	Linda Dubois
IT Associate	Nate Gardner

Ticket Sales and Customer Service
Director of Ticket Sales & Service	Lisa Johnson
Manager of Premium Sales & Services	Ron Campbell
Premium Services Manager	Jana Cannavo
Manager of Group Sales	Ken Bamberg
Manager of Season Sales	Mike Morrow
Group Sales Account Executive	Clint Blevins, Casey Norvall, Tim Savant, Justin Sheppard, Guy Tomcheck

Ticketing
Assistant Ticketing Manager	Jonas Calicdan
Assistant Box Office Manager	Kenda Cavanaugh
Premium Ticket Operations Supervisor	Gina Bulgheroni
Box Office Supervisor	Pat Lally

Community Development
Director of Community Relations & Public Affairs	Wendy Yamagishi
Community Relations Associates	Jesse Tyler, Jennifer Walker

Entertainment
Director of Entertainment/Multi-Media	Rod Murray
Production Manager	Kent French
Editor/Producer	Rich Cooley

Broadcasting
Director of Broadcasting	Aaron Teats
Telecast Director	Mike Levy
Television, KCAL (Ch. 9) & Fox Sports West 2 (Cable)	John Ahlers, Brian Hayward
Radio, Flagship TBA & Mighty Ducks Radio Network	Steve Carroll

Event Operations
Director of Facilities	Kevin Starkey
Director of Event Development	Pete Dropick
Director of Events	Quinn Mackin
Assistant Director of Operations	Brent Mater
Security/Public Safety Manager	Russell Beecher
Event Manager	Jason Davis
Parking Manager	Jeff Grant
Senior Event Manager	Becca Mack

Sales and Marketing
Director of Marketing	Tracie Jones
Director of Sponsorship Sales	Bonner Paddock
Sponsorship Services Manager	Alex Evezich
Marketing Manager	Chris DiPierro
Senior Sales Manager	Greg Rieber
Advertising & Promotions Manager	Allison Wright
Research & Development Coordinator	Richard Jasik
Special Events Coordinator	Jesse Brewer
Website Coordinator	Todd Farrell
Administrative Assistant – Sales & Marketing	Lori Ortiz

Fan Development
Director of Fan Development	Matt Savant
Manager of Fan Development	Joseph Hwang
Fan Development Coordinator	Champ Baginski

Atlanta Thrashers

2005-06 Schedule

Oct.	Wed.	5	at Florida		Wed.	4	at Carolina
	Fri.	7	at Washington		Fri.	6	Pittsburgh
	Sat.	8	Washington		Sat.	7	at Pittsburgh
	Wed.	12	Montreal		Wed.	11	Nashville
	Fri.	14	Toronto		Fri.	13	St. Louis
	Sat.	15	at NY Rangers		Wed.	18	at Dallas
	Thu.	20	Tampa Bay		Thu.	19	at Los Angeles
	Sat.	22	New Jersey		Sat.	21	Tampa Bay
	Tue.	25	at NY Islanders		Tue.	24	Boston
	Thu.	27	at Pittsburgh		Thu.	26	Carolina
	Sat.	29	Tampa Bay		Sat.	28	at Carolina
Nov.	Tue.	1	at Tampa Bay		Tue.	31	Buffalo
	Fri.	4	at Washington	Feb.	Fri.	3	at Florida
	Sat.	5	at Philadelphia		Sat.	4	Florida
	Wed.	9	Pittsburgh		Tue.	7	at Toronto
	Fri.	11	Tampa Bay		Thu.	9	at Ottawa
	Sat.	12	at Carolina		Sat.	11	at Montreal
	Wed.	16	NY Islanders	Mar.	Wed.	1	at Buffalo
	Fri.	18	at Philadelphia		Thu.	2	at Boston
	Sat.	19	at Toronto		Sat.	4	Washington
	Tue.	22	at Montreal		Mon.	6	Florida
	Thu.	24	NY Rangers		Wed.	8	NY Rangers
	Sat.	26	Florida		Fri.	10	Ottawa
	Sun.	27	at Carolina*		Sun.	12	at NY Rangers*
	Tue.	29	Carolina		Thu.	16	NY Islanders
Dec.	Thu.	1	Toronto		Sat.	18	Philadelphia
	Sat.	3	at Anaheim		Mon.	20	Buffalo
	Mon.	5	at Phoenix		Tue.	21	at Boston
	Tue.	6	at San Jose		Thu.	23	New Jersey
	Fri.	9	Columbus		Sat.	25	at NY Islanders
	Sun.	11	Chicago*		Thu.	30	at Tampa Bay
	Tue.	13	Detroit	Apr.	Sat.	1	Carolina
	Thu.	15	at New Jersey		Mon.	3	at Ottawa
	Sat.	17	Florida		Wed.	5	at Florida
	Thu.	22	Washington		Thu.	6	at Tampa Bay
	Fri.	23	at New Jersey		Sat.	8	Carolina
	Mon.	26	Montreal		Tue.	11	at Tampa Bay
	Wed.	28	Philadelphia		Thu.	13	Washington
	Fri.	30	at Buffalo		Sat.	15	Boston
Jan.	Sun.	1	at Washington*		Mon.	17	at Washington
	Mon.	2	Ottawa		Tue.	18	at Florida

* Denotes afternoon game.

Year-by-Year Record

		Home				Road				Overall							
Season	GP	W	L	T	OL	W	L	T	OL	W	L	T	OL	GF	GA	Pts.	Finished	Playoff Result
2004-05	....	....	....	....	....	....	....	....	....									
2003-04	82	18	17	4	2	15	20	4	2	33	37	8	4	214	243	78	2nd, Southeast Div.	Out of Playoffs
2002-03	82	15	19	4	3	16	20	3	2	31	39	7	5	226	284	74	3rd, Southeast Div.	Out of Playoffs
2001-02	82	11	21	9	0	8	26	2	5	19	47	11	5	187	288	54	5th, Southeast Div.	Out of Playoffs
2000-01	82	10	23	6	2	13	22	6	0	23	45	12	2	211	289	60	4th, Southeast Div.	Out of Playoffs
1999-2000	82	9	26	3	3	5	31	4	1	14	57	7	4	170	313	39	5th, Southeast Div.	Out of Playoffs

Vyacheslav Kozlov has finished second and third in team scoring during his first two years with the Thrashers.

Franchise date: June 25, 1997

SOUTHEAST
DIVISION

**7th
NHL
Season**

2005-06 Player Personnel

FORWARDS	HT	WT	S	Place of Birth	Date	2004-05 Club
ABID, Ramzi	6-2	210	L	Montreal, Que.	3/24/80	Wilkes-Barre
AUBIN, Serge	6-1	200	L	Val-d'Or, Que.	2/15/75	Geneve
BABY, Stephen	6-5	230	R	Chicago, IL	1/31/80	Chicago (AHL)
BARNEY, Scott	6-4	210	R	Oshawa, Ont.	3/27/79	
BOULTON, Eric	6-0	225	L	Halifax, N.S.	8/17/76	Columbia
DESBIENS, Guillaume	6-2	205	L	Alma, Que.	4/20/85	Rouyn-Noranda
DOELL, Kevin	5-11	190	L	Saskatoon, Sask.	7/15/79	Chicago (AHL)-Gwinnett
HOLIK, Bobby	6-4	235	R	Jihlava, Czech.	1/1/71	
HOSSA, Marian	6-1	208	L	Stara Lubovna, Czech.	1/12/79	Mora-Trencin
KOVALCHUK, Ilya	6-2	220	R	Tver, USSR	4/15/83	Kazan
KOZLOV, Vyacheslav	5-10	185	L	Voskresensk, USSR	5/3/72	Voskresensk-Kazan
LARSEN, Brad	6-0	200	L	Nakusp, B.C.	6/28/77	Chicago (AHL)
LESSARD, Francis	6-3	225	R	Montreal, Que.	5/30/79	
MacKENZIE, Derek	5-11	180	L	Sudbury, Ont.	6/11/81	Chicago (AHL)
MALONEY, Brian	6-1	205	L	Bassano, Alta.	9/27/78	Chicago (AHL)
MELLANBY, Scott	6-1	210	R	Montreal, Que.	6/11/66	
PETROVICKY, Ronald	6-0	190	L	Zilina, Czechoslovakia	2/15/77	Zilina-Brynas
SANTALA, Tommi	6-2	210	R	Helsinki, Finland	6/27/79	Chicago (AHL)
SAVARD, Marc	5-10	195	L	Ottawa, Ont.	7/17/77	Thurgau-Bern
SCHELL, Brad	6-0	180	L	Scott, Sask.	8/5/84	Gwinnett
SLATER, Jim	6-0	190	L	Petoskey, MI	12/9/82	Michigan State
SMYTH, Adam	6-1	215	R	Wiarton, Ont.	9/8/83	Chicago (AHL)-Gwinnett
STEFAN, Patrik	6-2	210	L	Pribram, Czech.	9/16/80	Ilves
STEWART, Karl	5-10	175	L	Aurora, Ont.	6/30/83	Chicago (AHL)
STUART, Colin	6-1	195	L	Rochester, MN	7/8/82	Chicago (AHL)-Gwinnett
VIGIER, J.P.	6-0	200	R	Notre D. de Lourdes, Man.	9/11/76	Chicago (AHL)

DEFENSEMEN						
COBURN, Braydon	6-5	220	L	Calgary, Alta.	2/27/85	Port (WHL)-Chi (AHL)
de VRIES, Greg	6-3	215	L	Sundridge, Ont.	1/4/73	
DWYER, Jeff	6-1	205	L	Greenwich, CT	11/22/80	Chicago (AHL)-Gwinnett
EXELBY, Garnet	6-1	215	L	Ste. Anne, Man.	8/16/81	
HAVELID, Niclas	6-0	200	L	Stockholm, Sweden	4/12/73	Sodertalje
HNIDY, Shane	6-1	210	R	Neepawa, Man.	11/8/75	Florida (ECHL)
KLOUCEK, Tomas	6-3	225	L	Prague, Czech.	3/7/80	Slavia-Trinec-Liberec
MANSON, Lane	6-8	250	L	Watrous, Sask.	2/14/84	Gwinnett
MODRY, Jaroslav	6-2	225	L	Ceske Budejovice, Czech.	2/27/71	Liberec
POPOVIC, Mark	6-1	207	L	Stoney Creek, Ont.	10/11/82	Cincinnati (AHL)
ROCHE, Travis	6-1	190	R	Grand Cache, Alta.	6/17/78	Chicago (AHL)
SHARROW, Jim	6-2	180	L	Framingham, MA	1/31/85	Halifax
SIPOTZ, Brian	6-7	235	R	South Bend, IN	9/16/81	Chicago (AHL)-Gwinnett
SUTTON, Andy	6-6	245	L	Kingston, Ont.	3/10/75	GCK Zurich-Zurich

GOALTENDERS	HT	WT	C	Place of Birth	Date	2004-05 Club
BERKHOEL, Adam	5-11	190	L	St. Paul, MN	5/16/81	Chicago (AHL)-Gwinnett
DUNHAM, Mike	6-3	200	L	Johnson City, NY	6/1/72	Skelleftea
GARNETT, Michael	6-1	200	L	Saskatoon, Sask.	11/25/82	Chicago (AHL)
HURME, Jani	6-0	190	L	Turku, Finland	1/7/75	
LEHTONEN, Kari	6-3	200	L	Helsinki, Finland	11/16/83	Chicago (AHL)

In the System and Recently Drafted

FORWARDS	HT	WT	S	Place of Birth	Date	2004-05 Club
BOURRET, Alex	5-9	209	L	Drummondville, Que.	10/5/86	Lewiston
BUTSAYEV, Yuri	6-0	195	L	Togliatti, USSR	10/11/78	Togliatti
CAREFOOT, Mitch	6-1	210	R	Dauphin, Man.	1/2/85	Cornell
DOBRYSHKIN, Yuri	6-0	190	R	Penza, USSR	7/19/79	Magnitogorsk
FRETTER, Colton	5-10	190	R	Harrow, Ont.	3/12/82	Michigan State
GRACIK, Juraj	6-3	190	R	Topolcany, Czech.	8/14/86	Tri-City
HAMILTON, Mike	6-1	200	L	Vancouver, B.C.	5/2/83	U. of Maine
ISOSALO, Samu	6-3	205	L	Rauma, Finland	6/10/81	
KAIP, Rylan	6-0	180	R	Wilcox, Sask.	3/19/84	North Dakota
KOZEK, Andrew	5-10	175	L	Revelstoke, B.C.	5/26/86	South Surrey
LAVALLEE, Jordan	6-3	203	L	Corvallis, OR	5/11/86	Quebec
LOGINOV, Denis	6-1	210	L	Kazan, USSR	5/5/85	Kazan
PAINCHAUD, Chad	5-11	175	L	Mississauga, Ont.	5/27/86	Mississauga-Sarnia
POSPISIL, Tomas	6-0	185	R	Sumperk, Czech.	8/25/87	Trinec
SIDDALL, Matt	6-1	205	R	North Vancouver, B.C.	9/26/84	Northern Mich.
STERLING, Brett	5-7	175	L	Los Angeles, CA	4/24/84	Colorado College
STOESZ, Myles	6-1	197	R	Steinbach, Man.	2/13/87	Spokane
TUOMAINEN, Miikka	6-3	210	L	Turku, Finland	5/22/86	TuTo

DEFENSEMEN						
DENNY, Chad	6-2	210	L	Sydney, N.S.	3/27/87	Lewiston
ENSTROM, Tobias	5-9	175	L	Nordingra, Sweden	11/5/84	MODO
LEHMAN, Scott	6-1	200	L	Fort McMurray, Alta.	1/5/86	St. Michael's
LEWIS, Grant	6-3	190	R	Pittsburgh, PA	1/20/85	Dartmouth
NIKULIN, Ilja	6-3	210	L	Moscow, USSR	3/12/82	Dynamo Moscow
NUMMELIN, Petteri	5-10	200	L	Turku, Finland	11/25/72	Lugano
OYSTRICK, Nathan	6-0	195	L	Regina, Sask.	12/17/82	Northern Mich.
VALABIK, Boris	6-7	230	L	Nitra, Czech.	2/14/86	Kitchener
VANNELLI, Michael	6-2	190	R	St. Paul, MN	10/2/83	U. of Minnesota
ZUBAREV, Andrei	6-1	198	L	Ufa, USSR	3/3/87	Ufa

GOALTENDERS	HT	WT	C	Place of Birth	Date	2004-05 Club
PAVELEC, Ondrej	6-2	180	L	Kladno, Czechoslovakia	8/31/87	Kladno-Slany
TURPLE, Dan	6-5	220	L	Oakville, Ont.	1/1/85	Oshawa-Kitchener

Bobby Holik (above) and Marian Hossa are key Atlanta additions for 2005-06.

Vice President and General Manager

WADDELL, DON
Vice President/General Manager, Atlanta Thrashers.
Born in Detroit, MI, August 19, 1958.

As the only general manager in the history of the Atlanta Thrashers, Don Waddell has established a foundation for long-term success in Atlanta by infusing the club with solid veterans to support a talented young line-up.

Despite facing tremendous adversity following the death of Dan Snyder, Waddell's leadership saw the team narrowly miss the playoffs in 2003-04 while setting franchise records for wins (33) and points (78). The team's first step toward achieving this success came during the 2002-03 season when it made a very dramatic second-half turnaround which was keyed by Waddell's decision to hire proven Stanley Cup winner Bob Hartley as coach. Prior to hiring Hartley, Waddell made his own successful NHL coaching debut with a win at Carolina on December 27, 2002. (He served as interim head coach until January 13, 2003.)

Waddell came to the franchise on June 23, 1998 – almost a year to the day after the NHL granted Atlanta a team. He has built the core of the franchise through the NHL Entry Draft and by stockpiling impressive prospects. He made Ilya Kovalchuk the first Russian player selected first overall in the history of the Entry Draft. In the 2002 Entry Draft, Waddell made Kari Lehtonen of Finland the highest-selected European goaltender in NHL draft history.

Waddell has a long-standing relationship with USA Hockey as a player and in management, and served as assistant general manager for the 2004 World Championship and World Cup teams. He was general manager of the 2005 World Championship team. His extensive organizational experience also includes having previously built two professional hockey franchises: the San Diego Gulls and the Orlando Solar Bears of the now-defunct International Hockey League. He's also no stranger to winning through his role as assistant general manager for the Stanley Cup champion Detroit Red Wings during the 1997-98 season.

Waddell's playing experience includes more than nine seasons of professional hockey, mostly in the IHL. He was drafted by the NHL's Los Angeles Kings in 1978 and spent three years with the organization from 1980 to 1983. During a successful amateur career, Waddell helped the U.S. national team win the gold medal at the 1983 B-Pool World Championships. He played Division I hockey at Northern Michigan University from 1976 to 1980, where he majored in business management.

General Managers' History

Don Waddell, 1999-2000 to date.

Captains' History

Kelly Buchberger, 1999-2000; Steve Staios, 2000-01; Ray Ferraro, 2001-02; no captain, 2002-03; Shawn McEachern, 2003-04.

Coaching History

Curt Fraser, 1999-2000 to 2001-02; Curt Fraser, Don Waddell and Bob Hartley, 2002-03; Bob Hartley, 2003-04 to date.

NHL Coaching Record

| Season | Team | Games | Regular Season | | | Playoffs | | |
			W	L	T	Games	W	L
2002-03	Atlanta	10	4	5	1	....	....	....
	NHL Totals	10	4	5	1	....	....	....

Club Records

Team

(Figures in brackets for season records are games played.)

Most Points	78	2003-04 (82)
Most Wins	33	2003-04 (82)
Most Ties	12	2000-01 (82)
Most Losses	57	1999-2000 (82)
Most Goals	226	2002-03 (82)
Most Goals Against	313	1999-2000 (82)
Fewest Points	39	1999-2000 (82)
Fewest Wins	14	1999-2000 (82)
Fewest Ties	7	1999-2000 (82), 2002-03 (82)
Fewest Losses	37	2003-04 (82)
Fewest Goals	170	1999-2000 (82)
Fewest Goals Against	243	2003-04 (82)

Longest Winning Streak

Overall	4	Twice
Home	3	Three times
Away	4	Jan. 13-Feb. 7/03

Longest Undefeated Streak

Overall	5	Oct. 9-18/03 (3 wins, 2 ties)
Home	4	Oct. 9-23/03 (3 wins, 1 tie)
Away	7	Oct. 21-Nov. 13/00 (3 wins, 4 ties)

Longest Losing Streak

Overall	12	Jan. 24-Feb. 20/00
Home	*11	Jan. 24-Mar. 16/00
Away	10	Oct. 6-Nov. 18/01

Longest Winless Streak

Overall	16	Jan. 16-Feb. 20/00 (2 ties, 14 losses)
Home	*17	Jan. 19-Mar. 29/00 (2 ties, 15 losses)
Away	10	Oct. 6-Nov. 18/01 (10 losses)

Most Shutouts, Season	4	2003-04 (82)
Most PIM, Season	1,505	2003-04 (82)
Most Goals, Game	8	Twice

Individual

Most Seasons	5	Four players
Most Games	350	Patrik Stefan
Most Goals, Career	108	Ilya Kovalchuk
Most Assists, Career	104	Patrik Stefan
Most Points, Career	205	Ilya Kovalchuk (108G, 97A)
Most PIM, Career	532	Jeff Odgers
Most Shutouts, Career	5	Milan Hnilicka, Pasi Nurminen

Longest Consecutive Games Streak	136	Ilya Kovalchuk (Nov. 2/02-Feb. 25/04)
Most Goals, Season	41	Dany Heatley (2002-03), Ilya Kovalchuk (2003-04)
Most Assists, Season	49	Vyacheslav Kozlov (2002-03)
Most Points, Season	89	Dany Heatley (2002-03; 41G, 48A)
Most PIM, Season	226	Jeff Odgers (2000-01)

Most Points, Defenseman, Season	31	Yannick Tremblay (1999-2000; 10G, 21A)
Most Points, Center, Season	76	Ray Ferraro (2000-01; 29G, 47A)
Most Points, Right Wing, Season	89	Dany Heatley (2002-03; 41G, 48A)
Most Points, Left Wing, Season	87	Ilya Kovalchuk (2003-04; 41G, 46A)
Most Points, Rookie, Season	67	Dany Heatley (2001-02; 26G, 41A)
Most Shutouts, Season	3	Milan Hnilicka (2001-02), Pasi Nurminen (2003-04)
Most Goals, Game	4	Pascal Rheaume (Jan. 19/02)
Most Assists, Game	4	Andrew Brunette (Dec. 19/00), Ilya Kovalchuk (Jan. 19/02), Marc Savard (Dec. 20/03)
Most Points, Game	5	Four times

* NHL Record.

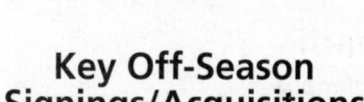

A junior star who twice led the Ontario Hockey League in scoring, Marc Savard collected 52 points (19 goals, 33 assists) in just 45 games with Atlanta in 2003-04.

All-time Record vs. Other Clubs

Regular Season

	At Home							On Road							Total						
	GP	W	L	T	OL	GF	GA	PTS	GP	W	L	T	OL	GF	GA	PTS	GP	W	L	T	OL	GF	GA	PTS
Anaheim	4	1	3	0	0	10	16	2	4	2	2	0	0	9	12	4	8	3	5	0	0	19	28	6
Boston	10	4	6	0	0	28	36	8	10	3	3	2	2	38	36	10	20	7	9	2	2	66	66	18
Buffalo	10	6	2	1	1	31	31	14	10	4	5	0	1	29	43	8	20	10	8	1	1	60	74	22
Calgary	4	3	0	1	0	8	5	7	3	0	3	0	0	6	14	0	7	3	3	1	0	14	19	7
Carolina	13	2	6	3	2	30	38	9	13	2	8	1	2	31	47	7	26	4	14	4	4	61	85	16
Chicago	4	2	2	0	0	14	10	4	2	0	0	0	0	0	6	0	6	2	4	0	0	14	16	4
Colorado	4	1	1	1	1	7	8	4	4	2	2	0	0	10	17	4	8	3	3	1	1	17	25	8
Columbus	3	2	1	0	0	5	6	4	4	2	1	0	1	11	12	5	7	4	2	0	1	16	18	9
Dallas	4	0	3	0	1	9	16	1	4	0	4	0	0	4	9	0	8	0	7	0	1	13	25	1
Detroit	3	0	3	0	0	7	19	0	4	0	2	0	2	8	17	2	7	0	5	0	2	15	36	2
Edmonton	3	1	2	0	0	3	8	2	4	1	2	1	0	11	14	3	7	2	4	1	0	14	22	5
Florida	13	5	3	4	1	40	40	15	13	8	4	1	0	44	31	17	26	13	7	5	1	84	71	32
Los Angeles	4	1	3	0	0	7	16	2	4	1	3	0	0	9	18	2	8	2	6	0	0	16	34	4
Minnesota	2	0	2	0	0	6	10	0	3	0	2	1	0	5	8	1	5	0	4	1	0	11	18	1
Montreal	10	1	7	2	0	12	31	4	10	3	7	0	0	24	34	6	20	4	14	2	0	36	65	10
Nashville	4	2	0	1	1	12	10	6	3	1	2	0	0	6	12	2	7	3	2	1	1	18	22	8
New Jersey	10	1	7	2	0	13	36	4	10	0	3	6	1	20	33	7	20	4	13	3	0	33	69	11
NY Islanders	10	2	6	2	0	27	37	6	10	5	0	0	0	25	36	10	20	7	11	2	0	52	73	16
NY Rangers	10	3	7	0	0	28	34	6	10	6	3	0	0	34	28	13	20	9	10	0	0	62	62	19
Ottawa	10	2	7	1	0	31	45	5	10	3	6	1	0	26	47	7	20	5	13	2	0	57	92	12
Philadelphia	10	2	6	1	1	24	34	6	10	1	7	2	0	28	46	4	20	3	13	3	1	52	80	10
Phoenix	4	1	3	0	0	6	12	2	5	0	4	1	0	7	16	1	9	1	7	1	0	13	28	3
Pittsburgh	10	1	8	0	1	24	39	3	10	2	7	1	0	25	39	5	20	3	15	1	1	49	78	8
St. Louis	4	1	2	1	0	14	16	3	3	0	3	0	0	1	11	0	7	1	5	1	0	15	27	3
San Jose	4	1	2	1	0	7	11	3	4	0	3	0	1	7	16	1	8	1	5	2	0	14	27	4
Tampa Bay	13	8	2	3	0	48	34	19	13	3	8	1	1	29	49	8	26	11	10	4	1	77	83	27
Toronto	9	3	5	0	1	16	31	7	9	3	6	0	0	21	33	7	18	6	10	1	1	37	64	14
Vancouver	3	1	2	0	0	11	12	2	3	1	1	0	1	5	10	3	6	2	3	0	1	16	22	5
Washington	13	6	5	2	0	28	38	14	13	3	1	0	2	29	50	6	26	7	13	5	1	57	88	20
Totals	**205**	**63**	**106**	**26**	**10**	**506**	**673**	**162**	**205**	**57**	**119**	**19**	**10**	**502**	**744**	**143**	**410**	**120**	**225**	**45**	**20**	**1008**	**1417**	**305**

Key Off-Season Signings/Acquisitions

2004

June 26 • Obtained D **Niclas Havelid** from Anaheim for D **Kurtis Foster**.

June 26 • Used the 10th overall pick in the 2004 Entry Draft to select 6'7", 230 lb. D **Boris Valabik** from the OHL Kitchener Rangers.

June 30 • Re-signed LW **Serge Aubin**.

July 1 • Signed D **Jaroslav Modry**.

26 • Signed RW **Scott Mellanby**.

28 • Re-signed C **Patrik Stefan**.

29 • Signed 2003 1st-round pick (8th overall), D **Braydon Coburn**.

Aug. 2 • Re-signed C **Marc Savard**.

4 • Re-signed RW **Ronald Petrovicky**.

5 • Re-signed D **Garnet Exelby**.

2005

July 30 • Obtained D **Shane Hnidy** from Nashville for a 2006 4th-round draft pick.

Aug. 2 • Signed C **Bobby Holik**.

8 • Signed LWs **Eric Boulton** and **Ramzi Abid** and C **Scott Barney**.

11 • Re-signed D **Andy Sutton**, D **Tomas Kloucek**, LW **Brad Larsen** and RW **Francis Lessard**.

16 • Re-signed RW **J.P. Vigier**.

23 • Obtained RW **Marian Hossa** and D **Greg de Vries** from Ottawa for RW **Dany Heatley**.

Sept. 2 • Signed G **Mike Dunham**.

Entry Draft
Selections 2005-1999

2005	
Pick	
16	Alex Bourret
41	Ondrej Pavelec
49	Chad Denny
53	Andrew Kozek
116	Jordan Lavallee
135	Tomas Pospisil
187	Andrei Zubarev
207	Myles Stoesz

2004	
Pick	
10	Boris Valabik
40	Grant Lewis
76	Scott Lehman
106	Chad Painchaud
142	Juraj Gracik
186	Dan Turple
204	Miikka Tuomainen
237	Mitch Carefoot
270	Matt Siddall

2003	
Pick	
8	Braydon Coburn
110	Jim Sharrow
116	Guillaume Desbiens
136	Michael Vannelli
145	Brett Sterling
175	Mike Hamilton
203	Denis Loginov
239	Tobias Enstrom
269	Rylan Kaip

2002	
Pick	
2	Kari Lehtonen
30	Jim Slater
116	Patrick Dwyer
124	Lane Manson
144	Paul Flache
167	Brad Schell
198	Nathan Oystrick
230	Colton Fretter
236	Tyler Boldt
257	Pauli Levokari

2001	
Pick	
1	Ilya Kovalchuk
80	Michael Garnett
100	Brian Sipotz
112	Milan Gajic
135	Colin Stuart
189	Pasi Nurminen
199	Matt Suderman
201	Colin FitzRandolph
262	Mario Cartelli

2000	
Pick	
2	Dany Heatley
31	Ilja Nikulin
42	Libor Ustrnul
107	Carl Mallette
108	Blake Robson
147	Matt McRae
168	Zdenek Smid
178	Jeff Dwyer
180	Darcy Hordichuk
230	Samu Isosalo
242	Evan Nielsen
244	Eric Bowen
288	Mark McRae
290	Simon Gamache

1999	
Pick	
1	Patrik Stefan
30	Luke Sellars
68	Zdenek Blatny
98	David Kaczowka
99	Rob Zepp
128	Derek MacKenzie
159	Yuri Dobryshkin
188	Stephen Baby
217	Garnet Exelby
245	Tommi Santala
246	Raymond DiLauro

Coach

HARTLEY, BOB
Coach, Atlanta Thrashers. Born in Hawkesbury, Ont., September 7, 1960.

Bob Hartley, the second head coach in Thrashers history, has used his experience as a Stanley Cup champion to develop the young talent in the organization. In 2003-04, Hartley helped the team overcome the tragic loss of Dan Snyder and led the club to its best record (33-37-8-4) and a franchise-high 78 points. Hartley joined the Thrashers on January 14, 2003 and became the seventh-fastest coach in NHL history to reach 200 wins with a 4-2 Atlanta victory at New Jersey on February 7, 2003, in his 369th game.

Prior to joining the Thrashers, Hartley guided the Colorado Avalanche to the 2001 Stanley Cup championship. In the 2002 playoffs, he became the first NHL coach to lead his team to the Conference Final in each of his first four seasons with the same club. In 16 seasons as a head coach at the amateur and professional levels, Hartley's teams have qualified for the playoffs 14 times while capturing five league championships. His team's have won at least 40 games eight times and 30 or more contests on 14 occasions. His Avalanche teams won at least 42 games in four consecutive seasons from 1998 to 2002.

Hartley became the second head coach of the Avalanche, and the 11th in franchise history, when he was named to the position on June 30, 1998. He served there until December 18, 2002 and is Colorado's all-time coaching victory leader (193), having guided the Avalanche to four consecutive Northwest Division titles and four straight trips to the Western Conference Final. Hartley guided the 2000-01 Avalanche to its most successful season in franchise history. Colorado established team records for points (118), wins (52) and goals against (192).

Hartley has been a proven winner at every level he has coached. Prior to joining Colorado, Hartley coached four seasons in the American Hockey League from 1994 to 1998, posting a 151-136-33 regular-season record and making four consecutive trips to the playoffs with Cornwall (1994 to 1996) and Hershey (1996 to 1998). He guided Hershey to the 1997 Calder Cup championship. After serving as an assistant coach for Cornwall in 1993-94, Hartley guided the Aces to the Southern Division title in 1994-95, and a trip to the Southern Division Final again in 1995-96. He led Laval to the Quebec Major Junior Hockey League championship and the Memorial Cup in 1993, and compiled an 81-52-7 record in two seasons with Laval from 1991 to 1993.

From 1987 to 1991, Hartley served as head coach for Hawkesbury of the Canadian Junior Hockey League. After enduring an 18-point season his rookie term behind the Hawks' bench, he guided the club to an impressive 117-45-5 mark during the next three seasons, including CJHL championships in 1990 and 1991. His teams dropped just three postseason games in 1990 and 1991, going 24-3 in that span. Overall, his teams in Hawkesbury advanced to the playoffs four consecutive seasons and finished 31-13 in the postseason during that span.

Throughout his coaching career, Hartley has shared a strong sense of dedication with his community. He was honored in his hometown of Hawkesbury, where the local ice arena was renamed Complex Bob Hartley in August 1998 in recognition of his service to the community where he grew up and coached. He has been involved in hockey camps and charitable endeavors throughout his career.

Club Directory

Philips Arena

Atlanta Thrashers
Centennial Tower
101 Marietta St.
Suite 1900
Atlanta, GA 30303
Phone **404/878-3800**
FAX 404/878-3712
www.atlantathrashers.com
Capacity: 18,545

Owners . . . . Bruce Levenson, Rutherford Seydel, Michael Gearon, Jr., Ed Peskowitz, Todd Foreman, Michael Gearon Sr., Beau Turner, Dominique Wilkins

Executive Management – Atlanta Spirit, LLC
President and CEO/Alternate Governor . . . . Bernard J. Mullin
Executive Vice President and General Manager/
    Alternate Governor . . . . Don Waddell
President of Philips Arena . . . . Bob Williams
Executive Vice President and Chief Financial Officer. Bill Duffy
Executive Vice President/Chief Marketing Officer. . . Lou DePaoli
Senior Vice President of Broadcast
    and Corporate Partnerships . . . . Tracy White
Senior Vice President of Communications . . . . Tom Hughes
Senior Vice President of Ticket Sales and Service . . . Jeff Morander
Vice President and Chief Legal Officer. . . . . T. Scott Wilkinson
Vice President of Business Development . . . . David Lee
Vice President of Community Development. . . . . . . LaVerne Henderson
Vice President of Finance. . . . . Phil Ebinger
Vice President of Marketing, Advertising
    and Branding. . . . . Jim Pfeifer
Vice President of Strategic Planning/
    Special Assistant to President. . . . . Ailey Penningroth

Hockey Operations
Vice President and Assistant General Manager . . . . Larry Simmons
Director of Player Personnel. . . . . Jack Ferreira
Director of Amateur Scouting
    and Player Development . . . . Dan Marr
Senior Director of Team Services . . . . Michele Zarzaca
Video Coordinator . . . . Tony Borgford
Assistant to Don Waddell/
    Practice Facility Office Manager . . . . Leisa Ludwin

Coaching Staff
Head Coach . . . . Bob Hartley
Assistant Coaches . . . . Brad McCrimmon, Steve Weeks

Scouting Staff
Head Scout . . . . Marcel Comeau
Full-Time Scouts . . . . Evgeny Bogdanovich, Mark Dobson, Bernd
    Freimuller, Mark Hillier, Peter Mahovlich,
    Bob Owen, John Perpich, Normand Poisson
Part-Time Scouts . . . . Terry Brennan, Pat Carmichael,
    Pentti Katainen

Training Staff
Strength and Conditioning Coach . . . . Ray Bear
Head Athletic Trainer . . . . Craig Brewer
Assistant Athletic Trainer. . . . . Stephen Roberts
Massage Therapist . . . . Inar Treiguts

Equipment Staff
Head Equipment Manager . . . . Bobby Stewart
Assistant Equipment Managers . . . . Joe Guilmet, Jim Guilmet

Medical Staff
Team Physician . . . . Dr. Scott Gillogly
Team Internist. . . . . Dr. William Whaley
Team Dentists . . . . Dr. Gary Saban, Dr. Lawrence Saltzman,
    Dr. Brett Silverman

Public Relations
Senior Director of Public Relations . . . . Rob Koch
Assistant Director of Media Relations . . . . Brian Potter
Manager of Media Relations . . . . John Heid

Coaching Record

		Regular Season				Playoffs		
Season	**Team**	**Games**	**W**	**L**	**T**	**Games**	**W**	**L**
1991-92	Laval (QMJHL)	70	38	27	5	10	4	6
1992-93	Laval (QMJHL)	70	43	25	2	13	12	1
1994-95	Cornwall (AHL)	80	38	33	9	15	8	7
1995-96	Cornwall (AHL)	80	34	39	7	8	3	5
1996-97	Hershey (AHL)	80	43	27	10	23	15	8
1997-98	Hershey (AHL)	80	36	37	7	7	3	4
1998-99	Colorado (NHL)	82	44	28	10	19	11	8
1999-2000	Colorado (NHL)	82	42	29	11	17	11	6
2000-01	Colorado (NHL)	82	52	20	10	23	16	7*
2001-02	Colorado (NHL)	82	45	29	8	21	11	10
2002-03	Colorado (NHL)	31	10	12	9	....	....	....
	Atlanta (NHL)	39	19	15	5	....	....	....
2003-04	Atlanta (NHL)	82	33	41	8	....	....	....
2004-05	Atlanta (NHL)	Season Cancelled						
	NHL Totals	**480**	**245**	**174**	**61**	**80**	**49**	**31**

* Stanley Cup win.

New Bruin Brian Leetch.

Boston Bruins

2005-06 Schedule

Month	Day	Date	Opponent	Month	Day	Date	Opponent
Oct.	Wed.	5	Montreal		Tue.	10	San Jose
	Fri.	7	at Buffalo		Thu.	12	Los Angeles
	Sat.	8	at Pittsburgh		Sat.	14	Dallas*
	Mon.	10	at Tampa Bay		Mon.	16	Anaheim*
	Thu.	13	at Florida		Thu.	19	at Philadelphia
	Sat.	15	at Ottawa		Sat.	21	NY Rangers
	Tue.	18	at Montreal		Mon.	23	at Washington
	Thu.	20	Buffalo		Tue.	24	at Atlanta
	Sat.	22	Pittsburgh		Thu.	26	Washington
	Mon.	24	at Toronto		Sat.	28	NY Islanders
	Wed.	26	at Carolina		Mon.	30	at Ottawa
	Thu.	27	Toronto	**Feb.**	Thu.	2	Montreal
	Sat.	29	New Jersey		Sat.	4	at Montreal*
Nov.	Tue.	1	at NY Islanders		Sun.	5	Carolina*
	Thu.	3	Florida		Wed.	8	at Pittsburgh
	Sat.	5	Pittsburgh		Thu.	9	New Jersey
	Tue.	8	at Philadelphia		Sat.	11	Tampa Bay
	Thu.	10	Ottawa	**Mar.**	Wed.	1	at Carolina
	Sat.	12	at NY Islanders		Thu.	2	Atlanta
	Thu.	17	Toronto		Sat.	4	Buffalo
	Sat.	19	Buffalo		Tue.	7	at Buffalo
	Sun.	20	at NY Rangers		Thu.	9	Montreal
	Wed.	23	at Toronto		Sat.	11	NY Islanders
	Fri.	25	Philadelphia*		Sun.	12	at Buffalo*
	Sat.	26	at Ottawa		Tue.	14	at Toronto
	Tue.	29	at New Jersey		Thu.	16	Ottawa
Dec.	Thu.	1	Ottawa		Sat.	18	Carolina*
	Sat.	3	at Edmonton		Mon.	20	at NY Rangers
	Sun.	4	at Vancouver		Tue.	21	Atlanta
	Wed.	7	at Colorado		Fri.	24	at New Jersey
	Sun.	11	Phoenix*		Sat.	25	Buffalo
	Thu.	15	at Minnesota		Mon.	27	Florida
	Sat.	17	at Calgary		Wed.	29	at Buffalo
	Thu.	22	Toronto	**Apr.**	Sat.	1	at Montreal
	Fri.	23	at Toronto		Tue.	4	at Montreal
	Tue.	27	at Washington		Thu.	6	Toronto
	Wed.	28	at Florida		Sat.	8	NY Rangers*
	Fri.	30	at Tampa Bay		Mon.	10	Washington
Jan.	Mon.	2	Philadelphia*		Tue.	11	at Ottawa
	Thu.	5	Ottawa		Thu.	13	Montreal
	Sat.	7	Tampa Bay		Sat.	15	at Atlanta

* Denotes afternoon game.

Franchise date: November 1, 1924

NORTHEAST DIVISION

82nd NHL Season

Year-by-Year Record

		Home				Road				Overall								
Season	**GP**	**W**	**L**	**T**	**OL**	**W**	**L**	**T**	**OL**	**W**	**L**	**T**	**OL**	**GF**	**GA**	**Pts.**	**Finished**	**Playoff Result**
2004-05	....	....	....	....	....	....	....	....	....	....	....	....	....	....	....	....		
2003-04	82	18	12	9	2	23	7	6	5	41	19	15	7	209	188	104	1st, Northeast Div.	Lost Conf. Quarter-Final
2002-03	82	23	11	5	2	13	20	6	2	36	31	11	4	245	237	87	3rd, Northeast Div.	Lost Conf. Quarter-Final
2001-02	82	23	11	2	5	20	13	4	4	43	24	6	9	236	201	101	1st, Northeast Div.	Lost Conf. Quarter-Final
2000-01	82	21	12	5	3	15	18	3	5	36	30	8	8	227	249	88	4th, Northeast Div.	Out of Playoffs
1999-2000	82	12	17	11	1	12	16	8	5	24	33	19	6	210	248	73	5th, Northeast Div.	Out of Playoffs
1998-99	82	22	10	9	....	17	20	4	....	39	30	13	....	214	181	91	3rd, Northeast Div.	Lost Conf. Semi-Final
1997-98	82	19	16	6	....	20	14	7	....	39	30	13	....	221	194	91	2nd, Northeast Div.	Lost Conf. Quarter-Final
1996-97	82	14	20	7	....	12	27	2	....	26	47	9	....	234	300	61	6th, Northeast Div.	Out of Playoffs
1995-96	82	22	14	5	....	18	17	6	....	40	31	11	....	282	269	91	2nd, Northeast Div.	Lost Conf. Quarter-Final
1994-95	48	15	7	2	....	12	11	1	....	27	18	3	....	150	127	57	3rd, Northeast Div.	Lost Conf. Quarter-Final
1993-94	84	20	14	8	....	22	15	5	....	42	29	13	....	289	252	97	2nd, Northeast Div.	Lost Conf. Semi-Final
1992-93	84	29	10	3	....	22	16	4	....	51	26	7	....	332	268	109	1st, Adams Div.	Lost Div. Semi-Final
1991-92	80	23	11	6	....	13	21	6	....	36	32	12	....	270	275	84	2nd, Adams Div.	Lost Conf. Championship
1990-91	80	26	9	5	....	18	15	7	....	44	24	12	....	299	264	100	1st, Adams Div.	Lost Conf. Championship
1989-90	80	23	13	4	....	23	12	5	....	46	25	9	....	289	232	101	1st, Adams Div.	Lost Final
1988-89	80	17	15	8	....	20	14	6	....	37	29	14	....	289	256	88	2nd, Adams Div.	Lost Div. Final
1987-88	80	24	13	3	....	20	17	3	....	44	30	6	....	300	251	94	2nd, Adams Div.	Lost Final
1986-87	80	25	11	4	....	14	23	3	....	39	34	7	....	301	276	85	3rd, Adams Div.	Lost Div. Semi-Final
1985-86	80	24	9	7	....	13	22	5	....	37	31	12	....	311	288	86	3rd, Adams Div.	Lost Div. Semi-Final
1984-85	80	21	15	4	....	15	19	6	....	36	34	10	....	303	287	82	4th, Adams Div.	Lost Div. Semi-Final
1983-84	80	25	12	3	....	24	13	3	....	49	25	6	....	336	261	104	1st, Adams Div.	Lost Div. Semi-Final
1982-83	80	28	6	6	....	22	14	4	....	50	20	10	....	327	228	110	1st, Adams Div.	Lost Conf. Championship
1981-82	80	24	12	4	....	19	15	6	....	43	27	10	....	323	285	96	2nd, Adams Div.	Lost Div. Final
1980-81	80	26	10	4	....	11	20	9	....	37	30	13	....	316	272	87	2nd, Adams Div.	Lost Prelim. Round
1979-80	80	27	9	4	....	19	12	9	....	46	21	13	....	310	234	105	2nd, Adams Div.	Lost Quarter-Final
1978-79	80	25	10	5	....	18	13	9	....	43	23	14	....	316	270	100	1st, Adams Div.	Lost Semi-Final
1977-78	80	29	6	5	....	22	12	6	....	51	18	11	....	333	218	113	1st, Adams Div.	Lost Final
1976-77	80	27	7	6	....	22	16	2	....	49	23	8	....	312	240	106	1st, Adams Div.	Lost Final
1975-76	80	27	5	8	....	21	10	9	....	48	15	17	....	313	237	113	1st, Adams Div.	Lost Semi-Final
1974-75	80	29	5	6	....	11	21	8	....	40	26	14	....	345	245	94	2nd, Adams Div.	Lost Prelim. Round
1973-74	78	33	4	2	....	19	13	7	....	52	17	9	....	349	221	113	1st, East Div.	Lost Final
1972-73	78	27	10	2	....	24	12	3	....	51	22	5	....	330	235	107	2nd, East Div.	Lost Quarter-Final
1971-72	**78**	**28**	**4**	**7**	....	**26**	**9**	**4**	....	**54**	**13**	**11**	....	**330**	**204**	**119**	**1st, East Div.**	**Won Stanley Cup**
1970-71	78	33	4	2	....	24	10	5	....	57	14	7	....	399	207	121	1st, East Div.	Lost Quarter-Final
1969-70	**76**	**27**	**3**	**8**	....	**13**	**14**	**11**	....	**40**	**17**	**19**	....	**277**	**216**	**99**	**2nd, East Div.**	**Won Stanley Cup**
1968-69	76	29	3	6	....	13	15	10	....	42	18	16	....	303	221	100	2nd, East Div.	Lost Semi-Final
1967-68	74	22	9	6	....	15	18	4	....	37	27	10	....	259	216	84	3rd, East Div.	Lost Quarter-Final
1966-67	70	10	21	4	....	7	22	6	....	17	43	10	....	182	253	44	6th,	Out of Playoffs
1965-66	70	15	17	3	....	6	26	3	....	21	43	6	....	174	275	48	5th,	Out of Playoffs
1964-65	70	12	17	6	....	9	26	0	....	21	43	6	....	166	253	48	6th,	Out of Playoffs
1963-64	70	13	15	7	....	5	25	5	....	18	40	12	....	170	212	48	6th,	Out of Playoffs
1962-63	70	7	18	10	....	7	21	7	....	14	39	17	....	198	281	45	6th,	Out of Playoffs
1961-62	70	9	22	4	....	6	25	4	....	15	47	8	....	177	306	38	6th,	Out of Playoffs
1960-61	70	13	17	5	....	2	25	8	....	15	42	13	....	176	254	43	6th,	Out of Playoffs
1959-60	70	21	11	3	....	7	23	5	....	28	34	8	....	220	241	64	5th,	Out of Playoffs
1958-59	70	21	11	3	....	11	18	6	....	32	29	9	....	205	215	73	2nd,	Lost Semi-Final
1957-58	70	15	14	6	....	12	14	9	....	27	28	15	....	199	194	69	4th,	Lost Final
1956-57	70	20	9	6	....	14	15	6	....	34	24	12	....	195	174	80	3rd,	Lost Final
1955-56	70	14	14	7	....	9	20	6	....	23	34	13	....	147	185	59	5th,	Out of Playoffs
1954-55	70	16	10	9	....	7	16	12	....	23	26	21	....	169	188	67	4th,	Lost Semi-Final
1953-54	70	22	8	5	....	10	20	5	....	32	28	10	....	177	181	74	4th,	Lost Semi-Final
1952-53	70	19	10	6	....	9	19	7	....	28	29	13	....	152	172	69	3rd,	Lost Final
1951-52	70	15	12	8	....	10	17	8	....	25	29	16	....	162	176	66	4th,	Lost Semi-Final
1950-51	70	13	12	10	....	9	18	8	....	22	30	18	....	178	197	62	4th,	Lost Semi-Final
1949-50	70	15	12	8	....	7	20	8	....	22	32	16	....	198	228	60	5th,	Out of Playoffs
1948-49	60	18	10	2	....	11	13	6	....	29	23	8	....	178	163	66	2nd,	Lost Semi-Final
1947-48	60	12	8	10	....	11	16	3	....	23	24	13	....	167	168	59	3rd,	Lost Semi-Final
1946-47	60	18	7	5	....	8	16	6	....	26	23	11	....	190	175	63	3rd,	Lost Semi-Final
1945-46	50	11	5	4	....	13	13	4	....	24	18	8	....	167	156	56	2nd,	Lost Final
1944-45	50	11	12	2	....	5	18	2	....	16	30	4	....	179	219	36	4th,	Lost Semi-Final
1943-44	50	15	8	2	....	4	18	3	....	19	26	5	....	223	268	43	5th,	Out of Playoffs
1942-43	50	17	3	5	....	7	14	4	....	24	17	9	....	195	176	57	2nd,	Lost Final
1941-42	48	17	4	3	....	8	13	3	....	25	17	6	....	160	118	56	3rd,	Lost Semi-Final
1940-41	**48**	**15**	**4**	**5**	....	**12**	**4**	**8**	....	**27**	**8**	**13**	....	**168**	**102**	**67**	**1st,**	**Won Stanley Cup**
1939-40	48	20	3	1	....	11	9	4	....	31	12	5	....	170	98	67	1st,	Lost Semi-Final
1938-39	**48**	**20**	**2**	**2**	....	**16**	**8**	**0**	....	**36**	**10**	**2**	....	**156**	**76**	**74**	**1st,**	**Won Stanley Cup**
1937-38	48	18	3	3	....	12	8	4	....	30	11	7	....	142	89	67	1st, Amn. Div.	Lost Semi-Final
1936-37	48	9	11	4	....	14	7	3	....	23	18	7	....	120	110	53	2nd, Amn. Div.	Lost Quarter-Final
1935-36	48	15	8	1	....	7	12	5	....	22	20	6	....	92	83	50	2nd, Amn. Div.	Lost Quarter-Final
1934-35	48	17	7	0	....	9	9	6	....	26	16	6	....	129	112	58	1st, Amn. Div.	Lost Semi-Final
1933-34	48	11	11	2	....	7	14	3	....	18	25	5	....	111	130	41	4th, Amn. Div.	Out of Playoffs
1932-33	48	19	2	3	....	6	13	5	....	25	15	8	....	124	88	58	1st, Amn. Div.	Lost Semi-Final
1931-32	48	11	10	3	....	4	11	9	....	15	21	12	....	122	117	42	4th, Amn. Div.	Out of Playoffs
1930-31	44	16	1	5	....	12	9	1	....	28	10	6	....	143	90	62	1st, Amn. Div.	Lost Semi-Final
1929-30	44	21	1	0	....	17	4	1	....	38	5	1	....	179	98	77	1st, Amn. Div.	Lost Final
1928-29	**44**	**15**	**6**	**1**	....	**11**	**7**	**4**	....	**26**	**13**	**5**	....	**89**	**52**	**57**	**1st, Amn. Div.**	**Won Stanley Cup**
1927-28	44	13	4	5	....	7	9	6	....	20	13	11	....	77	70	51	1st, Amn. Div.	Lost Semi-Final
1926-27	44	15	7	0	....	6	13	3	....	21	20	3	....	97	89	45	2nd, Amn. Div.	Lost Final
1925-26	36	10	7	1	....	7	8	3	....	17	15	4	....	92	85	38	4th,	Out of Playoffs
1924-25	30	3	12	0	....	3	12	0	....	6	24	0	....	49	119	12	6th,	Out of Playoffs

2005-06 Player Personnel

FORWARDS	HT	WT	S	Place of Birth	Date	2004-05 Club
AXELSSON, P.J.	6-1	184	L	Kungalv, Sweden	2/26/75	Frolunda
BERGERON, Patrice	6-0	186	R	Ancienne-Lorette, Que.	7/24/85	Providence (AHL)
BOYES, Brad	6-1	195	R	Mississauga, Ont.	4/17/82	Providence (AHL)
FITZGERALD, Tom	6-0	190	R	Billerica, MA	8/28/68	
GREEN, Travis	6-2	200	R	Castlegar, B.C.	12/20/70	
GUITE, Ben	6-1	205	R	Montreal, Que.	7/17/78	Providence (AHL)
HEALEY, Eric	6-0	196	L	Hull, MA	1/20/75	Mannheim
HILBERT, Andy	5-11	194	L	Lansing, MI	2/6/81	Providence (AHL)
ISBISTER, Brad	6-4	231	L	Edmonton, Alta.	5/7/77	Innsbruck
LEAHY, Patrick	6-3	200	R	Brighton, MA	6/9/79	Providence (AHL)
MacDONALD, Jason	5-11	210	R	Charlottetown, P.E.I.	4/1/74	St. John's
McEACHERN, Shawn	5-11	200	L	Waltham, MA	2/28/69	Malmo
MURRAY, Glen	6-3	225	R	Halifax, N.S.	11/1/72	
NICKULAS, Eric	5-11	206	R	Hyannis, MA	3/25/75	Norfolk
ORR, Colton	6-3	210	R	Winnipeg, Man.	3/3/82	Providence (AHL)
REICH, Jeremy	6-1	204	L	Craik, Sask.	2/11/79	Syracuse-Houston
ROBINSON, Nathan	5-9	181	L	Scarborough, Ont.	12/31/81	Grand Rapids-Syracuse
SAMSONOV, Sergei	5-8	194	R	Moscow, USSR	10/27/78	Dynamo Moscow
SAMUELSSON, Martin	6-2	200	L	Upplands-Vasby, Sweden	1/25/82	Providence (AHL)
SCATCHARD, Dave	6-3	220	R	Hinton, Alta.	2/20/76	
STROSHEIN, Garret	6-7	245	R	Edmonton, Alta.	4/4/80	Port (AHL)-South Carolina
THOMPSON, Nate	6-0	190	L	Anchorage, AK	10/5/84	Seattle-Providence (AHL)
THORNTON, Joe	6-4	223	L	London, Ont.	7/2/79	Davos
WALTER, Ben	6-1	195	L	Beaconsfield, Que.	5/11/84	U. Mass-Lowell
ZHAMNOV, Alex	6-1	204	L	Moscow, USSR	10/1/70	Chekhov
DEFENSEMEN						
ALBERTS, Andrew	6-4	218	L	Minneapolis, MN	6/30/81	Bos Coll-Prov (AHL)
BOYNTON, Nick	6-2	211	R	Nobleton, Ont.	1/14/79	Nottingham
DALLMAN, Kevin	5-11	205	R	Niagara Falls, Ont.	2/26/81	Providence (AHL)
GILL, Hal	6-7	250	L	Concord, MA	4/6/75	Lukko
GIRARD, Jonathan	5-11	201	R	Rawdon, Que.	5/27/80	
JURCINA, Milan	6-4	233	L	Liptovsky Mikulas, Czech.	6/7/83	Providence (AHL)
LEACH, Jay	6-4	232	L	Syracuse, NY	9/2/79	Providence (AHL)-Trenton
LEETCH, Brian	6-0	185	L	Corpus Christi, TX	3/3/68	
MORAN, Ian	6-0	200	R	Cleveland, OH	8/24/72	Bofors-Nottingham
SIGALET, Jonathan	6-1	185	L	Vancouver, B.C.	2/12/86	Bowling Green
SLEGR, Jiri	6-1	210	L	Jihlava, Czech.	5/30/71	Litvinov
STUART, Mark	6-1	209	L	Rochester, MN	4/27/84	Colorado College
GOALTENDERS	HT	WT	C	Place of Birth	Date	2004-05 Club
BROWN, Mike	6-0	177	L	Syracuse, NY	3/4/85	Saginaw-Owen Sound
RAYCROFT, Andrew	6-0	185	L	Belleville, Ont.	5/4/80	Tappara
SIGALET, Jordan	6-1	180	L	New Westminster, B.C.	2/19/81	Bowling Green
TOIVONEN, Hannu	6-2	191	L	Kalvola, Finland	5/18/84	Providence (AHL)

In the System and Recently Drafted

FORWARDS	HT	WT	S	Place of Birth	Date	2004-05 Club
BITZ, Byron	6-4	200	R	Saskatoon, Sask.	7/21/84	Cornell
BRADFORD, Brock	5-10	170	R	Burnaby, B.C.	1/7/87	Omaha
EVSEEV, Vladislav	6-2	200	L	Moscow, USSR	9/10/84	Dynamo Moscow-Ufa
FROLOV, Pavel	6-1	167	L	Gorky, USSR	6/28/84	
HEDMAN, Anton	6-0	180	L	Stockholm, Sweden	5/15/86	Djurgarden Jr.
HUML, Ivan	6-2	194	L	Kladno, Czech.	9/6/81	Kladno
KALUS, Petr	6-1	189	L	Ostrava, Czech.	6/29/87	Vitkovice
KARSUMS, Martins	5-10	190	R	Riga, Latvia	2/26/86	Moncton
KREJCI, David	5-11	180	R	Sternberk, Czech.	8/24/86	Gatineau
KUBISTA, Jan	6-0	189	L	Kolin, Czech.	4/12/84	Kolin-H. Kralove-Beroun
LEHTONEN, Mikko	6-3	191	R	Espoo, Finland	4/1/87	Blues
LINDSTROM, Andreas	6-5	210	L	Lulea, Sweden	9/1/82	Asploven
RABBIT, Wacey	5-9	169	L	Lethbridge, Alta.	11/16/86	Saskatoon
RODMAN, Marcel	6-1	183	R	Jesenice, Yugoslavia	9/25/81	Jesenice
ROME, Ashton	6-1	202	R	Nesbitt, Man.	12/31/85	Moose Jaw-Red Deer
SOBOTKA, Vladimir	5-10	183	L	Trebic, Czech.	7/2/87	Slavia-Havl. Brod
SODERBERG, Anders	5-6	161	R	Ornskoldsvik, Sweden	10/7/75	Skelleftea
UTKIN, Dmitri	6-0	169	L	Yaroslavl, USSR	6/10/84	Keramin-Brest-Riga 2000
VALCAK, Patrik	6-1	185	L	Ostrava, Czech.	12/16/84	Lincoln-Havirov-Ostrava
VANTUCH, Lukas	6-3	200	L	Jihlava, Czech.	7/20/87	Liberec Jr.
VERSTEEG, Kris	5-10	172	R	Lethbridge, Alta.	5/13/86	Lethbridge
ZINOVJEV, Sergei	5-10	178	L	Novokuznetsk, USSR	3/4/80	Kazan
DEFENSEMEN						
HARIKKALA, Jaakko	6-2	215	L	Kalanti, Finland	3/30/81	Lukko
HUNWICK, Matt	5-11	187	L	Warren, MI	5/21/85	U. of Michigan
JONSSON, Lars	6-1	198	L	Borlange, Sweden	1/2/82	Timra
KULTANEN, Jarno	6-2	198	L	Luumaki, Finland	1/8/73	HIFK
KUTLAK, Zdenek	6-3	221	L	Ceske Budejovice, Czech.	2/13/80	Karlovy Vary
LASHOFF, Matt	6-2	205	L	East Greenbush, NY	9/29/86	Kitchener
MAKELA, Tuukka	6-3	202	L	Helsinki, Finland	5/24/82	HPK
ZHUKOV, Sergei	6-4	187	L	Novosibirsk, USSR	11/23/75	Yaroslavl
GOALTENDERS	HT	WT	C	Place of Birth	Date	2004-05 Club
REGAN, Kevin	6-0	190	L	Boston, MA	7/25/84	New Hampshire

Coach

SULLIVAN, MIKE
Coach, Boston Bruins. Born in Marshfield, MA, February 27, 1968.

The Boston Bruins named Mike Sullivan their head coach on June 23, 2003. He is the 25th head coach in team history and spent the 2003-04 season as the youngest coach in the NHL. In his first season behind the Bruins bench, Sullivan led the team to a first-place finish in the Northeast Division and second in the Eastern Conference with 104 points. The Bruins finished the season with the least amount of regulation losses in the league.

Sullivan began his coaching career with Providence of the AHL when he was hired on July 29, 2002. Under his watch, the Providence Bruins won the North Division with a 44-20-11-5 record and 104 points. The club established a new franchise record with a 19-game home unbeaten streak (16 wins, three ties) from December 6 to February 23. Sullivan's record behind the Providence bench was 41-17-9-4 through March 20, when he was promoted to Boston as an assistant coach under Mike O'Connell. Boston went 3-3-3-0 in the nine remaining regular season games and was eliminated by the eventual Stanley Cup champion New Jersey Devils in five games during the opening round of the playoffs. Sullivan returned to Providence following the NHL playoffs, and was behind the bench for the final three games of Providence's four-game series loss to Manitoba in their AHL playoff series.

Sullivan played four seasons of college hockey at Boston University from 1986-87 through 1989-90 with 61 goals, 77 assists and 104 penalty minutes in 141 career college games. The New York Rangers drafted the center as their fourth pick, 69th overall, in the 1987 NHL Entry Draft, but never signed with the Rangers. He turned professional in 1990, playing the 1990-91 season with San Diego of the International Hockey League before signing with the San Jose Sharks as a free agent in August, 1991 and beginning his 11-year NHL career. He played in San Jose, Calgary, Boston and Phoenix before retiring after the 2001-02 season. His career NHL playing totals were 54 goals and 82 assists for 136 points with 203 penalty minutes in 709 games.

Coaching Record

Season	Team	Games	Regular Season W	L	T	Playoffs Games	W	L
2002-03	Providence (AHL)	71	41	21	9	3	1	2
2003-04	**Boston (NHL)**	**82**	**41**	**26**	**15**	**7**	**3**	**4**
2004-05	Boston (NHL)				Season Cancelled			
	NHL Totals	**82**	**41**	**26**	**15**	**7**	**3**	**4**

Captains' History

No captain, 1924-25 to 1926-27; Lionel Hitchman, 1927-28 to 1930-31; George Owen, 1931-32; Dit Clapper, 1932-33 to 1937-38; Cooney Weiland, 1938-39; Dit Clapper, 1939-40 to 1945-46; Dit Clapper and John Crawford, 1946-47; John Crawford 1947-48 to 1949-50; Milt Schmidt, 1950-51 to 1953-54; Milt Schmidt, Ed Sanford, 1954-55; Fern Flaman, 1955-56 to 1960-61; Don McKenney, 1961-62, 1962-63; Leo Boivin, 1963-64 to 1965-66; John Bucyk, 1966-67; no captain, 1967-68 to 1972-73; John Bucyk, 1973-74 to 1976-77; Wayne Cashman, 1977-78 to 1982-83; Terry O'Reilly, 1983-84, 1984-85; Raymond Bourque, Rick Middleton (co-captains) 1985-86 to 1987-88; Raymond Bourque, 1988-89 to 1999-2000; Jason Allison, 2000-01; no captain, 2001-02; Joe Thornton, 2002-03 to date.

Coaching History

Art Ross, 1924-25 to 1927-28; Cy Denneny, 1928-29; Art Ross, 1929-30 to 1933-34; Frank Patrick, 1934-35, 1935-36; Art Ross, 1936-37 to 1938-39; Cooney Weiland, 1939-40, 1940-41; Art Ross, 1941-42 to 1944-45; Dit Clapper, 1945-46 to 1948-49; Georges Boucher, 1949-50; Lynn Patrick, 1950-51 to 1953-54; Lynn Patrick and Milt Schmidt, 1954-55; Milt Schmidt, 1955-56 to 1960-61; Phil Watson, 1961-62; Phil Watson and Milt Schmidt, 1962-63; Milt Schmidt, 1963-64 to 1965-66; Harry Sinden, 1966-67 to 1969-70; Tom Johnson, 1970-71, 1971-72; Tom Johnson and Bep Guidolin, 1972-73; Bep Guidolin, 1973-74; Don Cherry, 1974-75 to 1978-79; Fred Creighton and Harry Sinden, 1979-80; Gerry Cheevers, 1980-81 to 1983-84; Gerry Cheevers and Harry Sinden, 1984-85; Butch Goring, 1985-86; Butch Goring and Terry O'Reilly, 1986-87; Terry O'Reilly, 1987-88, 1988-89; Mike Milbury, 1989-90, 1990-91; Rick Bowness, 1991-92; Brian Sutter, 1992-93 to 1994-95; Steve Kasper, 1995-96, 1996-97; Pat Burns, 1997-98 to 1999-2000; Pat Burns and Mike Keenan, 2000-01; Robbie Ftorek, 2001-02; Robbie Ftorek and Mike O'Connell, 2002-03; Mike Sullivan, 2003-04 to date.

Club Records

Team

(Figures in brackets for season records are games played; records for fewest points, wins, ties, losses, goals, goals against are for 70 or more games)

Most Points **121** 1970-71 (78)
Most Wins **57** 1970-71 (78)
Most Ties **21** 1954-55 (70)
Most Losses **47** 1961-62 (70), 1996-97 (82)
Most Goals **399** 1970-71 (78)
Most Goals Against **306** 1961-62 (70)
Fewest Points **38** 1961-62 (70)
Fewest Wins **14** 1962-63 (70)
Fewest Ties **5** 1972-73 (78)
Fewest Losses **13** 1971-72 (78)
Fewest Goals **147** 1955-56 (70)
Fewest Goals Against **172** 1952-53 (70)
Longest Winning Streak
Overall .... **14** Dec. 3/29-Jan. 9/30
Home .... ***20** Dec. 3/29-Mar. 18/30
Away .... **8** Feb. 17-Mar. 8/72, Mar. 15-Apr. 14/93
Longest Undefeated Streak
Overall .... **23** Dec. 22/40-Feb. 23/41 (15 wins, 8 ties)
Home .... **27** Nov. 22/70-Mar. 20/71 (26 wins, 1 tie)
Away .... **15** Dec. 22/40-Mar. 16/41 (9 wins, 6 ties)
Longest Losing Streak
Overall .... **11** Dec. 3/24-Jan. 5/25
Home .... ***11** Dec. 8/24-Feb. 17/25
Away .... **14** Dec. 27/64-Feb. 21/65
Longest Winless Streak
Overall .... **20** Jan. 28-Mar. 11/62 (16 losses, 4 ties)
Home .... **11** Dec. 8/24-Feb. 17/25 (11 losses)
Away .... **14** Three times
Most Shutouts, Season **15** 1927-28 (44)
Most PIM, Season **2,443** 1987-88 (80)
Most Goals, Game .... **14** Jan. 21/45 (NYR 3 at Bos. 14)

Individual

Most Seasons .... **21** John Bucyk, Raymond Bourque
Most Games .... **1,518** Raymond Bourque
Most Goals, Career .... **545** John Bucyk
Most Assists, Career .... **1,111** Raymond Bourque
Most Points, Career .... **1,506** Raymond Bourque (395G, 1,111A)
Most PIM, Career .... **2,095** Terry O'Reilly
Most Shutouts, Career .... **74** Tiny Thompson
Longest Consecutive Games Streak .... **418** John Bucyk (Jan. 23/69-Mar. 2/75)
Most Goals, Season .... **76** Phil Esposito (1970-71)
Most Assists, Season .... **102** Bobby Orr (1970-71)
Most Points, Season .... **152** Phil Esposito (1970-71; 76G, 76A)
Most PIM, Season .... **302** Jay Miller (1987-88)
Most Points, Defenseman, Season .... ***139** Bobby Orr (1970-71; 37G, 102A)
Most Points, Center, Season .... **152** Phil Esposito (1970-71; 76G, 76A)
Most Points, Right Wing, Season .... **105** Ken Hodge (1970-71; 43G, 62A), (1973-74; 50G, 55A), Rick Middleton (1983-84; 47G, 58A)
Most Points, Left Wing, Season .... **116** John Bucyk (1970-71; 51G, 65A)
Most Points, Rookie, Season .... **102** Joe Juneau (1992-93; 32G, 70A)
Most Shutouts, Season .... **15** Hal Winkler (1927-28)
Most Goals, Game .... **4** Twenty times
Most Assists, Game .... **6** Ken Hodge (Feb. 9/71), Bobby Orr (Jan. 1/73)
Most Points, Game .... **7** Bobby Orr (Nov. 15/73; 3G, 4A), Phil Esposito (Dec. 19/74; 3G, 4A), Barry Pederson (Apr. 4/82; 3G, 4A), Cam Neely (Oct. 16/88; 3G, 4A)

* NHL Record.

Retired Numbers

2	Eddie Shore	1926-1940
3	Lionel Hitchman	1925-1934
4	Bobby Orr	1966-1976
5	Dit Clapper	1927-1947
7	Phil Esposito	1967-1975
8	Cam Neely	1986-1996
9	John Bucyk	1957-1978
15	Milt Schmidt	1936-1955
24	Terry O'Reilly	1971-1985
77	Raymond Bourque	1979-2000

All-time Record vs. Other Clubs

Regular Season

	At Home								On Road								Total							
	GP	W	L	T	OL	GF	GA	PTS	GP	W	L	T	OL	GF	GA	PTS	GP	W	L	T	OL	GF	GA	PTS
Anaheim	8	4	4	0	0	23	24	8	9	5	2	2	0	24	18	12	17	9	6	2	0	47	42	20
Atlanta	10	5	2	2	1	36	38	13	10	6	3	0	1	30	28	13	20	11	5	2	2	66	66	26
Buffalo	107	61	32	14	0	400	311	136	108	40	52	15	1	322	386	96	215	101	84	29	1	722	697	232
Calgary	47	28	12	6	1	165	130	63	44	22	18	4	0	154	160	48	91	50	30	10	1	319	290	111
Carolina	78	46	25	7	0	274	207	99	76	36	31	9	0	263	252	81	154	82	56	16	0	537	459	180
Chicago	284	161	89	34	0	1023	808	356	286	94	145	45	2	767	926	235	570	255	234	79	2	1790	1734	591
Colorado	62	31	21	9	1	240	192	72	66	36	24	6	0	271	234	78	128	67	45	15	1	511	426	150
Columbus	2	1	1	0	0	8	7	2	3	2	0	0	1	14	3	5	5	3	1	0	1	22	10	7
Dallas	60	41	9	10	0	258	146	92	61	30	17	13	1	220	175	74	121	71	26	23	1	478	321	166
Detroit	287	154	89	43	1	1007	761	352	285	79	153	52	1	720	952	211	572	233	242	95	2	1727	1713	563
Edmonton	30	21	6	3	0	126	80	45	29	15	11	3	0	97	98	33	59	36	17	6	0	223	178	78
Florida	22	8	10	4	0	56	57	20	21	10	8	2	1	58	57	23	43	18	18	6	1	114	114	43
Los Angeles	61	44	11	6	0	287	169	94	61	33	21	7	0	224	210	73	122	77	32	13	0	511	379	167
Minnesota	3	0	3	0	0	4	13	0	2	0	2	0	0	2	7	0	5	0	5	0	0	6	20	0
Montreal	335	155	122	56	2	990	904	368	334	98	189	47	0	790	1120	243	669	253	311	103	2	1780	2024	611
Nashville	5	2	2	1	0	14	9	5	6	4	1	0	1	16	13	9	11	6	3	1	1	30	22	14
New Jersey	56	31	15	8	2	218	171	72	53	27	13	11	2	172	139	67	109	58	28	19	4	390	310	139
NY Islanders	59	32	15	11	1	220	164	76	61	27	24	10	0	199	202	64	120	59	39	21	1	419	366	140
NY Rangers	298	160	95	42	1	1076	834	363	302	116	131	55	0	853	921	287	600	276	226	97	1	1929	1755	650
Ottawa	33	19	9	5	0	123	92	43	31	15	8	3	5	93	78	38	64	34	17	8	5	216	170	81
Philadelphia	76	46	18	11	1	283	211	104	73	31	32	10	0	211	241	72	149	77	50	21	1	494	452	176
Phoenix	30	22	4	4	0	136	92	48	30	14	13	3	0	102	101	31	60	36	17	7	0	238	193	79
Pittsburgh	78	56	16	6	0	343	218	118	80	33	31	15	1	286	273	82	158	89	47	21	1	629	491	200
St. Louis	59	35	14	9	1	247	161	80	59	23	24	9	3	198	188	58	118	58	38	18	4	445	349	138
San Jose	10	7	0	3	0	39	26	17	11	5	4	2	0	38	30	12	21	12	4	5	0	77	56	29
Tampa Bay	23	16	1	6	0	84	49	38	23	10	10	3	0	66	70	23	46	26	11	9	0	150	119	61
Toronto	298	161	89	47	1	967	786	370	299	92	156	51	0	769	1005	235	597	253	245	98	1	1736	1791	605
Vancouver	52	38	7	7	0	217	124	83	51	27	16	8	0	209	166	62	103	65	23	15	0	426	290	145
Washington	56	32	15	9	0	209	151	73	55	26	16	12	1	191	155	65	111	58	31	21	1	400	306	138
Defunct Clubs	164	112	39	13	0	525	306	237	164	79	67	18	0	496	440	176	328	191	106	31	0	1021	746	413
Totals	**2693**	**1529**	**775**	**376**	**13**	**9598**	**7241**	**3447**	**2693**	**1035**	**1222**	**415**	**21**	**7855**	**8648**	**2506**	**5386**	**2564**	**1997**	**791**	**34**	**17453**	**15889**	**5953**

Playoffs

	Series	W	L	GP	W	L	T	GF	GA	Last Mtg.	Rnd.	Result
Buffalo	7	5	2	39	21	18	0	139	130	1999	CSF	L 2-4
Carolina	3	3	0	19	12	7	0	63	48	1999	CQF	W 4-2
Chicago	6	5	1	22	16	5	1	97	63	1978	QF	W 4-0
Colorado	2	1	1	11	6	5	0	37	36	1983	DSF	W 3-1
Dallas	1	0	1	3	0	3	0	13	20	1981	PRE	L 0-3
Detroit	7	4	3	33	19	14	0	96	98	1957	SF	W 4-1
Edmonton	2	0	2	9	1	8	0	20	41	1990	F	L 1-4
Florida	1	0	1	5	1	4	0	16	22	1996	CQF	L 1-4
Los Angeles	2	2	0	13	8	5	0	56	38	1977	QF	W 4-2
Montreal	30	7	23	152	57	95	0	371	469	2004	CQF	L 3-4
New Jersey	4	1	3	23	8	15	0	60	68	2003	CQF	L 1-4
NY Islanders	2	0	2	11	3	8	0	35	49	1983	CF	L 2-4
NY Rangers	9	6	3	42	22	18	2	114	104	1973	QF	L 1-4
Philadelphia	4	2	2	20	11	9	0	60	57	1978	SF	W 4-1
Pittsburgh	4	2	2	19	9	10	0	62	67	1992	CF	L 0-4
St. Louis	2	2	0	8	8	0	0	48	15	1972	SF	W 4-0
Toronto	13	5	8	62	30	31	1	153	150	1974	QF	W 4-0
Washington	2	1	1	10	6	4	0	28	21	1998	CQF	L 2-4
Defunct Clubs	3	1	2	11	4	5	2	20	20			
Totals	**104**	**47**	**57**	**512**	**242**	**264**	**6**	**1488**	**1516**			

Calgary totals include Atlanta Flames, 1972-73 to 1979-80. Carolina totals include Hartford, 1979-80 to 1996-97.
Colorado totals include Quebec, 1979-80 to 1994-95. Dallas totals include Minnesota North Stars, 1967-68 to 1992-93.
New Jersey totals include Kansas City, 1974-75 to 1975-76, and Colorado Rockies, 1976-77 to 1981-82.
Phoenix totals include Winnipeg, 1979-80 to 1995-96.

Playoff Results 2005-2000

Year	Round	Opponent	Result	GF	GA
2004	CQF	Montreal	L 3-4	14	19
2003	CQF	New Jersey	L 1-4	8	13
2002	CQF	Montreal	L 2-4	18	20

Abbreviations: Round: F - Final;
CF - conference final; **CSF** - conference semi-final;
CQF - conference quarter-final;
DSF - division semi-final; **SF** - semi-final;
QF - quarter-final; **PRE** - preliminary round.

Key Off-Season Signings/Acquisitions

2004

July 7 • Re-signed D **Ian Moran**.
28 • Signed RW **Tom Fitzgerald**.

2005

July 31 • Obtained LW **Brad Isbister** from Edmonton for a 2006 4th-round pick.
Aug. 2 • Re-signed RW **Glen Murray**.
2 • Signed RW **Shawn McEachern** and C **Dave Scatchard**.
3 • Signed D **Brian Leetch**.
4 • Signed C **Alexei Zhamnov**.
10 • Re-signed LWs **Sergei Samsonov** and **P.J. Axelsson**.
10 • Re-signed D **Jonathan Girard**.
11 • Re-signed C **Joe Thornton**.
12 • Re-signed D **Jiri Slegr**.
15 • Re-signed C **Brad Boyes**.
17 • Re-signed C **Travis Green**.
30 • Re-signed D **Hall Gill**.

Entry Draft Selections 2005-1991

2005 Pick		2001 Pick		1997 Pick		1993 Pick	
22	Matt Lashoff	19	Shaone Morrisonn	1	Joe Thornton	25	Kevyn Adams
39	Petr Kalus	77	Darren McLachlan	8	Sergei Samsonov	51	Matt Alvey
83	Mikko Lehtonen	111	Matti Kaltiainen	27	Ben Clymer	88	Charles Paquette
100	Jonathan Sigalet	147	Jiri Jakes	54	Mattias Karlin	103	Shawn Bates
106	Vladimir Sobotka	179	Andrew Alberts	63	Lee Goren	129	Andrei Sapozhnikov
154	Wacey Rabbit	209	Jordan Sigalet	81	Karol Bartanus	155	Milt Mastad
172	Lukas Vantuch	241	Milan Jurcina	135	Denis Timofeev	181	Ryan Golden
217	Brock Bradford	282	Marcel Rodman	162	Joel Trottier	207	Hal Gill
				180	Jim Baxter	233	Joel Prpic
2004		**2000**		191	Antti Laaksonen	259	Joakim Persson
Pick		**Pick**		218	Eric Van Acker		
63	David Krejci	7	Lars Jonsson	246	Jay Henderson	**1992**	
64	Martins Karsums	27	Martin Samuelsson			**Pick**	
108	Ashton Rome	37	Andy Hilbert	**1996**		16	Dmitri Kvartalnov
134	Kris Versteeg	59	Ivan Huml	**Pick**		55	Sergei Zholtok
160	Ben Walter	66	Tuukka Makela	8	Johnathan Aitken	112	Scott Bailey
224	Matt Hunwick	73	Sergei Zinovjev	45	Henry Kuster	133	Jiri Dopita
255	Anton Hedman	102	Brett Nowak	53	Eric Naud	136	Grigori Panteleev
		174	Jarno Kultanen	80	Jason Doyle	184	Kurt Seher
2003		204	Chris Berti	100	Trent Whitfield	208	Mattias Timander
Pick		237	Zdenek Kutlak	132	Elias Abrahamsson	232	Chris Crombie
21	Mark Stuart	268	Pavel Kolarik	155	Chris Lane	256	Denis Chervyakov
45	Patrice Bergeron	279	Andreas Lindstrom	182	Thomas Brown	257	Evgeny Pavlov
66	Masi Marjamaki			208	Bob Prier		
107	Byron Bitz	**1999**		234	Anders Soderberg	**1991**	
118	Frank Rediker	**Pick**				**Pick**	
129	Patrik Valcak	21	Nick Boynton	**1995**		18	Glen Murray
153	Mike Brown	56	Matt Zultek	**Pick**		40	Jozef Stumpel
183	Nate Thompson	89	Kyle Wanvig	9	Kyle McLaren	62	Marcel Cousineau
247	Benoit Mondou	118	Jaakko Harikkala	21	Sean Brown	84	Brad Tiley
277	Kevin Regan	147	Seamus Kotyk	47	Paxton Schafer	106	Mariusz Czerkawski
		179	Donald Choukalos	73	Bill McCauley	150	Gary Golczewski
2002		207	Greg Barber	99	Cameron Mann	172	Jay Moser
Pick		236	John Cronin	151	Yevgeny Shaldybin	194	Daniel Hodge
29	Hannu Toivonen	247	Mikko Eloranta	177	P.J. Axelsson	216	Steve Norton
56	Vladislav Evseev	264	Georgy Pujacs	203	Sergei Zhukov	238	Stephen Lombardi
130	Jan Kubista			229	Jonathon Murphy	260	Torsten Kienass
153	Peter Hamerlik	**1998**					
228	Dmitri Utkin	**Pick**		**1994**			
259	Yan Stastny	48	Jonathan Girard	**Pick**			
290	Pavel Frolov	52	Bobby Allen	21	Evgeni Ryabchikov		
		78	Peter Nordstrom	47	Daniel Goneau		
		135	Andrew Raycroft	99	Eric Nickulas		
		165	Ryan Milanovic	125	Darren Wright		
				151	Andre Roy		
				177	Jeremy Schaefer		
				229	John Grahame		
				255	Neil Savary		
				281	Andrei Yakhanov		

Vice President and General Manager

O'CONNELL, MIKE
Vice President/General Manager, Boston Bruins.
Born in Chicago, IL, November 25, 1955.

Mike O'Connell was named the general manager of the Boston Bruins on November 1, 2000, becoming just the sixth man in club history to hold that position. He was involved in all aspects of the on-ice operation of the hockey team over the previous six seasons as the team's assistant general manager and was instrumental in bringing much of the young talent into the organization. In his first four seasons as the club's general manager, Boston has won two Northeast Division titles.

O'Connell's experience as both a player and assistant coach in the National Hockey League, and as a head coach in both the American and International Hockey Leagues, dates back to the 1977-78 season. Raised in Cohasset, MA, he played two years of high school hockey at Archbishop Williams High School in Braintree, MA. He then made what at the time was an unusual move for an American player, jumping to the Ontario Hockey League to play Canadian major junior hockey at the suggestion of Harry Sinden and Tom Johnson. The move proved beneficial as, after two seasons with Kingston of the OHL, he was drafted by Chicago 43rd overall in the 1975 NHL Amateur Draft.

He turned professional with the Blackhawks organization in 1975 and played five-plus seasons with Chicago and their Central Hockey League affiliate in Dallas before coming to Boston on December 18, 1980, in a trade for Al Secord. He enjoyed his best NHL seasons during his six years in a Bruins uniform, recording 50+ point campaigns for three straight years from 1982 to 1985 and representing the team in the 1984 NHL All-Star Game in New Jersey. He was traded to Detroit for Reed Larson on March 10, 1986 and concluded his playing career with the Red Wings at the end of the 1989-90 season.

O'Connell then moved into the coaching ranks, assuming the head coaching position for the IHL's San Diego Gulls in 1990-91. He then returned to the NHL, with Boston as an assistant coach. On June 12, 1992, he was named as the head coach of Boston's American Hockey League affiliate in Providence. Working with many players who also wore a Boston uniform during his tenure, he compiled a 74-71-15 record over a two-year span and won a Northern Division title in 1992-93. He then returned to Boston when he was named the club's assistant general manager on July 5, 1994. He was named as a vice president of the team in 1998. During the 2002-03 season, O'Connell took over behind the bench late in the season.

NHL Coaching Record

		Regular Season				Playoffs		
Season	Team	Games	W	L	T	Games	W	L
2002-03	Boston	9	3	3	3	5	1	4
	NHL Totals	9	3	3	3	5	1	4

Club Directory

TD Banknorth Garden

Boston Bruins
TD Banknorth Garden
100 Legends Way
Boston, MA 02114
Phone **617/624-1900**
FAX 617/523-7184
www.bostonbruins.com
Capacity: 17,565

Executive
Owner & Governor . . . . Jeremy M. Jacobs
Alternate Governors . . . . Charles Jacobs, Jeremy Jacobs Jr., Louis Jacobs, Mike O'Connell, Harry Sinden
President . . . . Harry Sinden
Senior Assistant to the President . . . . Nate Greenberg
Chief Legal Officer . . . . Michael Wall
Chief Financial Officer . . . . Jessica Rahuba
Vice President & General Manager . . . . Mike O'Connell
Assistant General Manager . . . . Jeff Gorton
Executive Vice President . . . . Charles M. Jacobs
Executive Vice President . . . . Richard A. Krezwick
Director of Administration . . . . Dale Hamilton-Powers
Assistant to the President . . . . Joe Curnane
Assistant Director of Administration
  & Travel Coordinator . . . . Carol Gould
Administrative Assistant . . . . Karen Ondo
Executive Secretary . . . . Rita Brandano

Coaching Staff
Head Coach . . . . Mike Sullivan
Assistant Coach . . . . Wayne Cashman
Assistant Coach . . . . Norm Maciver
Goaltending Coach . . . . Bob Essensa
Video Coordinator . . . . Brant Berglund
Team Road Services Coordinator . . . . John Bucyk
Coach, Providence Bruins . . . . Scott Gordon
Assistant Coach, Providence Bruins . . . . Rob Murray

Scouting Staff
Director of Pro Scouting & Player Development . . . . Sean Coady
Director of Amateur Scouting . . . . Scott Bradley
Director of European Scouting . . . . Nikolai Bobrov
Scouting Staff . . . . Gerry Cheevers, Adam Creighton, Daniel Dore, Oto Huscak, Mike McGraw, Tom McVie, Tom Songin, Svenake Svensson

Medical & Training Staff
Strength & Conditioning Coach . . . . John Whitesides
Athletic Trainer . . . . Don DelNegro
Physical Therapist . . . . Scott Waugh
Equipment Manager . . . . Peter Henderson
Assistant Equipment Manager . . . . Chris "Muggsy" Aldrich
Assistant Equipment Manager . . . . Keith Robinson
Head Team Physician/Orthopedist . . . . Dr. Bertram Zarins
Team Psychologist . . . . Dr. Fred Neff

Communications & Marketing Staff
Director of Media Relations . . . . Heidi Holland
Manager of Media Relations . . . . Ryan Nadeau
Director of Marketing & Community Relations . . . . Sue Byrne
Manager of Community Development
  & Special Events . . . . Kerry Collins
Administrative Assistant, Alumni Office . . . . Mal Viola

Ticketing & Finance Staff
Director of Ticket Operations . . . . Matt Brennan
Assistant Director of Ticket Operations . . . . Jim Foley
Ticket Office Receptionist . . . . Jo-Ann Connolly-White
Controller . . . . Rick McGlinchey
Accountant, Payroll & Benefits . . . . Audrey Centeno
Accounts Payable . . . . Linda Bartlett

Television & Radio
Television . . . . New England Sports Network (NESN)
Radio . . . . WBZ (1030 AM) & Bruins Radio Network
Television Broadcasters . . . . Dale Arnold (play-by-play); Andy Brickley (color)
Radio Broadcasters . . . . Dave Goucher (play-by-play); Bob Beers (color)

General Managers' History

Art Ross, 1924-25 to 1953-54; Lynn Patrick, 1954-55 to 1964-65; Hap Emms, 1965-66, 1966-67; Milt Schmidt, 1967-68 to 1971-72; Harry Sinden, 1972-73 to 1999-2000; Harry Sinden and Mike O'Connell, 2000-01; Mike O'Connell, 2001-02 to date.

Buffalo Sabres

2005-06 Schedule

Oct.	Wed.	5	NY Islanders		Sat.	7	New Jersey
	Fri.	7	Boston		Thu.	12	Phoenix
	Sat.	8	at Ottawa		Sat.	14	Los Angeles
	Mon.	10	Pittsburgh		Mon.	16	at Edmonton
	Thu.	13	at Tampa Bay		Thu.	19	at Vancouver
	Sat.	15	at Florida		Sat.	21	at Calgary
	Thu.	20	at Boston		Tue.	24	at NY Rangers
	Sat.	22	NY Rangers		Thu.	26	at Toronto
	Wed.	26	Washington		Tue.	31	at Atlanta
	Fri.	28	at New Jersey	Feb.	Thu.	2	Philadelphia
	Sat.	29	at NY Islanders		Sat.	4	Ottawa
Nov.	Wed.	2	Ottawa		Tue.	7	at Montreal
	Fri.	4	Montreal		Thu.	9	Montreal
	Sat.	5	at Montreal		Sat.	11	Florida
	Wed.	9	Carolina		Sun.	12	at Carolina*
	Fri.	11	Toronto	Mar.	Wed.	1	Atlanta
	Sat.	12	at Ottawa		Fri.	3	Toronto
	Tue.	15	New Jersey		Sat.	4	at Boston
	Thu.	17	Washington		Tue.	7	Boston
	Sat.	19	at Boston		Thu.	9	Tampa Bay
	Tue.	22	NY Rangers		Sat.	11	at Philadelphia*
	Wed.	23	at NY Islanders		Sun.	12	Boston*
	Fri.	25	Montreal		Tue.	14	at Washington
	Sun.	27	at Washington*		Thu.	16	Toronto
	Tue.	29	at Pittsburgh		Sat.	18	at Ottawa
Dec.	Thu.	1	at Montreal		Mon.	20	at Atlanta
	Fri.	2	San Jose		Wed.	22	Carolina
	Sun.	4	at Colorado		Fri.	24	Ottawa
	Thu.	8	Anaheim		Sat.	25	at Boston
	Sun.	11	at Minnesota		Mon.	27	at NY Rangers
	Wed.	14	Dallas		Wed.	29	Boston
	Fri.	16	at Pittsburgh		Thu.	30	at New Jersey
	Sat.	17	Pittsburgh	Apr.	Sat.	1	at Toronto
	Mon.	19	at Philadelphia		Mon.	3	at Toronto
	Thu.	22	at Florida		Wed.	5	Ottawa
	Fri.	23	at Tampa Bay		Fri.	7	Philadelphia
	Mon.	26	NY Islanders		Sat.	8	at Ottawa
	Thu.	29	at Toronto		Wed.	12	Montreal
	Fri.	30	Atlanta		Sat.	15	at Montreal
Jan.	Sun.	1	Florida*		Sun.	16	Toronto*
	Thu.	5	Tampa Bay		Tue.	18	at Carolina

* Denotes afternoon game.

Franchise date: May 22, 1970

NORTHEAST DIVISION

36th NHL Season

Daniel Briere topped the Sabres in scoring during his first full season in Buffalo, collecting 28 goals and establishing career highs with 37 assists and 65 points in 2003-04.

Year-by-Year Record

Season	GP	Home				Road				Overall								Finished	Playoff Result
		W	L	T	OL	W	L	T	OL	W	L	T	OL	GF	GA	Pts.			
2004-05	....																		
2003-04	82	21	13	4	3	16	21	3	1	37	34	7	4	220	221	85	5th, Northeast Div.	Out of Playoffs
2002-03	82	18	16	5	2	9	21	5	6	27	37	10	8	190	219	72	5th, Northeast Div.	Out of Playoffs
2001-02	82	20	16	5	0	15	19	6	1	35	35	11	1	213	200	82	5th, Northeast Div.	Out of Playoffs
2000-01	82	26	12	3	0	20	18	2	1	46	30	5	1	218	184	98	2nd, Northeast Div.	Lost Conf. Semi-Final
1999-2000	82	21	14	5	1	14	18	6	3	35	32	11	4	213	204	85	3rd, Northeast Div.	Lost Conf. Quarter-Final
1998-99	82	23	12	6	....	14	16	11	....	37	28	17	....	207	175	91	4th, Northeast Div.	Lost Final
1997-98	82	20	13	8	....	16	16	9	....	36	29	17	....	211	187	89	3rd, Northeast Div.	Lost Conf. Final
1996-97	82	24	11	6	....	16	19	6	....	40	30	12	....	237	208	92	1st, Northeast Div.	Lost Conf. Semi-Final
1995-96	82	19	17	5	....	14	25	2	....	33	42	7	....	247	262	73	5th, Northeast Div.	Out of Playoffs
1994-95	48	15	8	1	....	7	11	6	....	22	19	7	....	130	119	51	4th, Northeast Div.	Lost Conf. Quarter-Final
1993-94	84	22	17	3	....	21	15	6	....	43	32	9	....	282	218	95	4th, Northeast Div.	Lost Conf. Quarter-Final
1992-93	84	25	15	2	....	13	21	8	....	38	36	10	....	335	297	86	4th, Adams Div.	Lost Div. Final
1991-92	80	22	13	5	....	9	24	7	....	31	37	12	....	289	299	74	3rd, Adams Div.	Lost Div. Semi-Final
1990-91	80	15	13	12	....	16	17	7	....	31	30	19	....	292	278	81	3rd, Adams Div.	Lost Div. Semi-Final
1989-90	80	27	11	2	....	18	16	6	....	45	27	8	....	286	248	98	2nd, Adams Div.	Lost Div. Semi-Final
1988-89	80	25	12	3	....	13	23	4	....	38	35	7	....	291	299	83	3rd, Adams Div.	Lost Div. Semi-Final
1987-88	80	19	14	7	....	18	18	4	....	37	32	11	....	283	305	85	3rd, Adams Div.	Lost Div. Semi-Final
1986-87	80	18	18	4	....	10	26	4	....	28	44	8	....	280	308	64	5th, Adams Div.	Out of Playoffs
1985-86	80	23	16	1	....	14	21	5	....	37	37	6	....	296	291	80	5th, Adams Div.	Out of Playoffs
1984-85	80	23	10	7	....	15	18	7	....	38	28	14	....	290	237	90	3rd, Adams Div.	Lost Div. Semi-Final
1983-84	80	25	9	6	....	23	16	1	....	48	25	7	....	315	257	103	2nd, Adams Div.	Lost Div. Semi-Final
1982-83	80	25	7	8	....	13	22	5	....	38	29	13	....	318	285	89	3rd, Adams Div.	Lost Div. Final
1981-82	80	23	8	9	....	16	18	6	....	39	26	15	....	307	273	93	3rd, Adams Div.	Lost Div. Semi-Final
1980-81	80	21	7	12	....	18	13	9	....	39	20	21	....	327	250	99	1st, Adams Div.	Lost Quarter-Final
1979-80	80	27	5	8	....	20	12	8	....	47	17	16	....	318	201	110	1st, Adams Div.	Lost Semi-Final
1978-79	80	19	13	8	....	17	15	8	....	36	28	16	....	280	263	88	2nd, Adams Div.	Lost Prelim. Round
1977-78	80	25	7	8	....	19	12	9	....	44	19	17	....	288	215	105	2nd, Adams Div.	Lost Quarter-Final
1976-77	80	27	8	5	....	21	16	3	....	48	24	8	....	301	220	104	2nd, Adams Div.	Lost Quarter-Final
1975-76	80	28	7	5	....	18	14	8	....	46	21	13	....	339	240	105	2nd, Adams Div.	Lost Quarter-Final
1974-75	80	28	6	6	....	21	10	9	....	49	16	15	....	354	240	113	1st, Adams Div.	Lost Final
1973-74	78	23	10	6	....	9	24	6	....	32	34	12	....	242	250	76	5th, East Div.	Out of Playoffs
1972-73	78	30	6	3	....	7	21	11	....	37	27	14	....	257	219	88	4th, East Div.	Lost Quarter-Final
1971-72	78	11	19	9	....	5	24	10	....	16	43	19	....	203	289	51	6th, East Div.	Out of Playoffs
1970-71	78	16	13	10	....	8	26	5	....	24	39	15	....	217	291	63	5th, East Div.	Out of Playoffs

2005-06 Player Personnel

FORWARDS	HT	WT	S	Place of Birth	Date	2004-05 Club
AFINOGENOV, Maxim	6-0	190	L	Moscow, USSR	9/4/79	Dynamo Moscow
BARTOVIC, Milan	5-11	197	L	Trencin, Czech.	4/9/81	Rochester
BRIERE, Daniel	5-10	178	R	Gatineau, Que.	10/6/77	Bern
CONNOLLY, Tim	6-1	190	R	Syracuse, NY	5/7/81	Langnau
DRURY, Chris	5-10	200	R	Trumbull, CT	8/20/76	
DUMONT, J.P.	6-1	205	R	Montreal, Que.	4/1/78	Bern
GAUSTAD, Paul	6-4	220	L	Fargo, ND	2/3/82	Rochester
GRIER, Mike	6-1	227	R	Detroit, MI	1/5/75	
HECHT, Jochen	6-1	200	L	Mannheim, W. Germany	6/21/77	Mannheim
KOTALIK, Ales	6-1	227	R	Jindrichuv Hradec, Czech.	12/23/78	Liberec
MacARTHUR, Clarke	6-0	180	L	Lloydminster, Alta.	4/6/85	Medicine Hat-Rochester
MAIR, Adam	6-2	208	R	Hamilton, Ont.	2/15/79	
PAILLE, Dan	6-0	200	L	Welland, Ont.	4/15/84	Rochester
PETERS, Andrew	6-4	240	L	St. Catharines, Ont.	5/5/80	Boden
POMINVILLE, Jason	6-0	186	R	Repentigny, Que.	11/30/82	Rochester
PYATT, Taylor	6-4	227	L	Thunder Bay, Ont.	8/19/81	Hammarby
ROY, Derek	5-9	186	L	Ottawa, Ont.	5/4/83	Rochester
RYAN, Michael	6-1	180	L	Boston, MA	5/16/80	Rochester
TAYLOR, Chris	6-2	192	L	Stratford, Ont.	3/6/72	Rochester
THORBURN, Chris	6-3	220	R	Sault Ste. Marie, Ont.	6/3/83	Rochester
VANEK, Thomas	6-2	210	L	Vienna, Austria	1/19/84	Rochester

DEFENSEMEN	HT	WT	S	Place of Birth	Date	2004-05 Club
CAMPBELL, Brian	6-0	190	L	Strathroy, Ont.	5/23/79	Jokerit
CULLEN, David	6-2	209	R	St. Catharines, Ont.	12/30/76	Rochester
FITZPATRICK, Rory	6-2	208	R	Rochester, NY	1/11/75	Rochester
JILLSON, Jeff	6-3	215	R	North Smithfield, RI	7/24/80	Rochester
KALININ, Dmitri	6-3	206	L	Chelyabinsk, USSR	7/22/80	Magnitogorsk
LYDMAN, Toni	6-1	202	L	Lahti, Finland	9/25/77	HIFK
McKEE, Jay	6-4	200	L	Kingston, Ont.	9/8/77	
NUMMINEN, Teppo	6-2	197	L	Tampere, Finland	7/3/68	
PAETSCH, Nathan	6-0	198	L	Humboldt, Sask.	3/30/83	Rochester
TALLINDER, Henrik	6-3	215	L	Stockholm, Sweden	1/10/79	Linkoping-Bern

GOALTENDERS	HT	WT	C	Place of Birth	Date	2004-05 Club
BIRON, Martin	6-2	170	L	Lac-St-Charles, Que.	8/15/77	
MILLER, Ryan	6-2	170	L	East Lansing, MI	7/17/80	Rochester
NORONEN, Mika	6-2	200	L	Tampere, Finland	6/17/79	HPK

In the System and Recently Drafted

FORWARDS	HT	WT	S	Place of Birth	Date	2004-05 Club
BIZYAYEV, Vasili	6-1	185	L	Moscow, USSR	6/6/82	
DENISOV, Denis	6-0	183	L	Kalinin, USSR	12/31/81	Kazan
DUBEC, Marek	6-0	179	L	Bratislava, Czech.	2/26/82	Olomouc-Vsetin-N Jicin
FABRY, Branislav	6-0	185	L	Bratislava, Czech.	1/15/85	Zilina-Bratislava-Trnava
GERBE, Nathan	5-5	160	L	Oxford, MI	7/24/87	USA U-18
GOGULLA, Philip	6-2	176	L	Dusseldorf, W. Germany	7/31/87	Essen-Koln
HULVA, Jakub	6-0	172	L	Opava, Czech.	5/6/84	Vitkovice-Ostrava-Opava
HUNTER, Dylan	5-11	198	L	Quebec City, Que.	5/21/85	London
KALETA, Patrick	5-11	195	R	Buffalo, NY	6/8/86	Peterborough
KENNEDY, Tim	5-9	170	L	Buffalo, NY	4/30/86	Sioux City
KRYUKOV, Artem	6-3	180	L	Novosibirsk, USSR	3/5/82	Yaroslavl
MANCARI, Mark	6-3	225	R	London, Ont.	7/11/85	Ottawa (OHL)
McMORROW, Sean	6-4	235	R	Vancouver, B.C.	1/19/82	Rochester
NOVOTNY, Jiri	6-2	204	R	Pelhrimov, Czech.	8/12/83	Rochester
SCHEVJEV, Maxim	6-0	178	L	Noginsk, USSR	7/5/84	Elektrostal
STAFFORD, Drew	6-1	202	R	Milwaukee, WI	10/30/85	North Dakota
VONDRKA, Michal	6-0	178	R	Ceske Budejovice, Czech.	5/17/83	Ml. Boleslav- Hr. Kralove-Slavia
ZAGRAPAN, Marek	6-1	195	L	Presov, Czech.	12/6/86	Chicoutimi

DEFENSEMEN	HT	WT	S	Place of Birth	Date	2004-05 Club
ASLUND, Calle	6-2	198	L	Haninge, Sweden	3/29/83	Rio Grande
BURAVCHIKOV, Vyacheslav	6-0	189	L	Moscow, USSR	5/22/87	Krylja Sovetov
BUTLER, Chris	6-1	178	L	St. Louis, MO	10/27/86	Sioux City
CARD, Mike	6-0	201	R	Kitchener, Ont.	2/18/86	Kelowna
CIZEK, Martin	6-1	188	L	Beroun, Czech.	5/17/84	Jihlava-Trebic-Kladno Jr.
EZHOV, Denis	5-11	200	L	Togliatti, USSR	2/28/85	Novokuznetsk
FUNK, Michael	6-4	199	L	Abbotsford, B.C.	8/15/86	Portland (WHL)
GENEROUS, Matt	6-3	185	R	Methuen, MA	5/4/85	N.E. Jr. Falcons
GRAGNANI, Marc-Andre	6-1	180	L	Montreal, Que.	3/11/87	PEI
HEJDA, Jan	6-3	209	L	Prague, Czech.	6/18/78	CSKA
JANIK, Doug	6-2	209	L	Agawam, MA	3/26/80	Rochester
MORROW, Thomas	6-6	198	L	St. Paul, MN	10/21/83	Boston University
ORPIK, Andrew	6-3	200	R	East Amherst, NY	3/12/86	Thayer
SEKERA, Andrej	6-0	191	L	Bojnice, Czech.	6/8/86	Owen Sound
VOROSHNIN, Pavel	6-3	175	L	Chelyabinsk, USSR	3/23/84	Serov

GOALTENDERS	HT	WT	C	Place of Birth	Date	2004-05 Club
DENNIS, Adam	5-11	183	L	Toronto, Ont.	2/8/85	Guelph-London
VALENT, Michal	6-2	176	L	Martin, Czech.	3/5/86	Sparta Jr.-Nymburk

Coaching History

Punch Imlach, 1970-71; Punch Imlach, Floyd Smith and Joe Crozier, 1971-72; Joe Crozier, 1972-73, 1973-74; Floyd Smith, 1974-75 to 1976-77; Marcel Pronovost, 1977-78; Marcel Pronovost and Billy Inglis, 1978-79; Scotty Bowman, 1979-80; Roger Neilson, 1980-81; Jim Roberts and Scotty Bowman, 1981-82; Scotty Bowman 1982-83 to 1984-85; Jim Schoenfeld and Scotty Bowman, 1985-86; Scotty Bowman, Craig Ramsay and Ted Sator, 1986-87; Ted Sator, 1987-88, 1988-89; Rick Dudley, 1989-90, 1990-91; Rick Dudley and John Muckler, 1991-92; John Muckler, 1992-93 to 1994-95; Ted Nolan, 1995-96, 1996-97; Lindy Ruff, 1997-98 to date.

Head Coach

RUFF, LINDY
Head Coach, Buffalo Sabres. Born in Warburg, Alta., February, 17, 1960.

A former captain of the Sabres, Lindy Ruff was appointed as the club's 15th head coach on July 21, 1997. In 1999, he led the Sabres to the Stanley Cup Finals for just the second time in club history. With 253 victories in seven seasons behind the bench, Ruff has surpassed Scotty Bowman (210) as the winningest coach in Sabres history. As a player, Ruff was drafted 32nd overall by the Sabres in the 1979 Entry Draft. He played both defense and left wing in an NHL career that spanned 12 seasons including 608 regular-season games with Buffalo. He became a playing assistant coach with Rochester of the AHL in 1991-92 and San Diego of the IHL in 1992-93. Ruff's San Diego club set a pro hockey record with 62 wins. In 1993-94 he became an NHL assistant coach with the Florida Panthers.

Coaching Record

Season	Team	Games	Regular Season W	L	T	Playoffs Games	W	L
1997-98	Buffalo (NHL)	82	36	29	17	15	10	5
1998-99	Buffalo (NHL)	82	37	28	17	21	14	7
1999-2000	Buffalo (NHL)	82	35	36	11	5	1	4
2000-01	Buffalo (NHL)	82	46	31	5	13	7	6
2001-02	Buffalo (NHL)	82	35	36	11	....	....	....
2002-03	Buffalo (NHL)	82	27	45	10	....	....	....
2003-04	Buffalo (NHL)	82	37	38	7	....	....	....
2004-05	Buffalo (NHL)				Season Cancelled			
	NHL Totals	574	253	243	78	54	32	22

After playing 15 seasons with the Phoenix Coyotes/Winnipeg Jets franchise, Teppo Numminen joins the Sabres after spending the 2003-04 season with Dallas.

Captains' History

Floyd Smith, 1970-71; Gerry Meehan, 1971-72 to 1973-74; Gerry Meehan and Jim Schoenfeld, 1974-75; Jim Schoenfeld, 1975-76, 1976-77; Danny Gare, 1977-78 to 1980-81; Danny Gare and Gilbert Perreault, 1981-82; Gilbert Perreault, 1982-83 to 1985-86; Gilbert Perreault and Lindy Ruff, 1986-87; Lindy Ruff, 1987-88; Lindy Ruff and Mike Foligno, 1988-89; Mike Foligno, 1989-90; Mike Foligno and Mike Ramsey, 1990-91; Mike Ramsey, 1991-92; Mike Ramsey and Pat LaFontaine, 1992-93; Pat LaFontaine and Alexander Mogilny, 1993-94; Pat LaFontaine, 1994-95 to 1996-97; Donald Audette and Michael Peca, 1997-98; Michael Peca, 1998-99, 1999-2000; no captain, 2000-01; Stu Barnes. 2001-02, 2002-03; Miroslav Satan, Chris Drury, James Patrick, J.P. Dumont, Daniel Briere, 2003-04 to date.

Club Records

Team

(Figures in brackets for season records are games played; records for fewest points, wins, ties, losses, goals, goals against are for 70 or more games)

Most Points	113	1974-75 (80)
Most Wins	49	1974-75 (80)
Most Ties	21	1980-81 (80)
Most Losses	44	1986-87 (80)
Most Goals	354	1974-75 (80)
Most Goals Against	308	1986-87 (80)
Fewest Points	51	1971-72 (78)
Fewest Wins	16	1971-72 (78)
Fewest Ties	5	2000-01 (82)
Fewest Losses	16	1974-75 (80)
Fewest Goals	190	2002-03 (82)
Fewest Goals Against	175	1998-99 (82)

Longest Winning Streak
Overall...........10 Jan. 4-23/84
Home.............12 Nov. 12/72-Jan. 7/73,
                    Oct. 13-Dec. 10/89
Away.............*10 Dec. 10/83-Jan. 23/84

Longest Undefeated Streak
Overall...........14 Mar. 6-Apr. 6/80
                    (8 wins, 6 ties)
Home.............21 Oct. 8/72-Jan. 7/73
                    (18 wins, 3 ties)
Away.............10 Dec. 10/83-Jan. 23/84
                    (10 wins)

Longest Losing Streak
Overall............7 Four times
Home..............6 Oct. 10-Nov. 10/93,
                    Mar. 3-Apr. 3/96
Away..............7 Oct. 14-Nov. 7/70,
                    Feb. 6-27/71,
                    Jan. 10-Feb. 3/96

Longest Winless Streak
Overall...........12 Nov. 23-Dec. 20/91
                    (8 losses, 4 ties)
Home.............12 Jan. 27-Mar. 10/91
                    (7 losses, 5 ties)
Away.............23 Oct. 30/71-Feb. 19/72
                    (15 losses, 8 ties)

Most Shutouts, Season....13 1997-98 (82)
Most PIM, Season........*2,713 1991-92 (80)
Most Goals, Game..........14 Jan. 21/75
                    (Wsh. 2 at Buf. 14),
                    Mar. 19/81
                    (Tor. 4 at Buf. 14)

Individual

Most Seasons	17	Gilbert Perreault
Most Games	1,191	Gilbert Perreault
Most Goals, Career	512	Gilbert Perreault
Most Assists, Career	814	Gilbert Perreault
Most Points, Career	1,326	Gilbert Perreault
		(512G, 814A)
Most PIM, Career	3,189	Rob Ray
Most Shutouts, Career	55	Dominik Hasek

Longest Consecutive
Games Streak...........776 Craig Ramsay
                    (Mar. 27/73-Feb. 10/83)
Most Goals, Season..........76 Alexander Mogilny
                    (1992-93)
Most Assists, Season.........95 Pat LaFontaine
                    (1992-93)
Most Points, Season.........148 Pat LaFontaine
                    (1992-93; 53G, 95A)
Most PIM, Season..........354 Rob Ray
                    (1991-92)

Most Points, Defenseman,
Season..................81 Phil Housley
                    (1989-90; 21G, 60A)
Most Points, Center,
Season.................148 Pat LaFontaine
                    (1992-93; 53G, 95A)
Most Points, Right Wing,
Season.................127 Alexander Mogilny
                    (1992-93; 76G, 51A)
Most Points, Left Wing,
Season..................95 Rick Martin
                    (1974-75; 52G, 43A)
Most Points, Rookie,
Season..................74 Rick Martin
                    (1971-72; 44G, 30A)
Most Shutouts, Season.......13 Dominik Hasek (1997-98)
Most Goals, Game...........5 Dave Andreychuk
                    (Feb. 6/86)
Most Assists, Game..........5 Gilbert Perreault
                    (Feb. 1/76, Mar. 9/80,
                    Jan. 4/84),
                    Dale Hawerchuk
                    (Jan. 15/92),
                    Pat LaFontaine
                    (Dec. 31/92, Feb. 10/93)
Most Points, Game............7 Gilbert Perreault
                    (Feb. 1/76; 2G, 5A)

* NHL Record.

Retired Numbers

2	Tim Horton	1972-1974
7	Rick Martin	1971-1981
11	Gilbert Perreault	1970-1987
14	Rene Robert	1971-1979

All-time Record vs. Other Clubs

Regular Season

	At Home								On Road								Total							
	GP	W	L	T	OL	GF	GA	PTS	GP	W	L	T	OL	GF	GA	PTS	GP	W	L	T	OL	GF	GA	PTS
Anaheim	9	4	2	3	0	25	20	11	9	7	2	0	0	30	15	14	18	11	4	3	0	55	35	25
Atlanta	10	6	4	0	0	43	29	12	10	3	5	1	1	31	31	8	20	9	9	1	1	74	60	20
Boston	108	53	39	15	1	386	322	122	107	32	60	14	1	311	400	79	215	85	99	29	2	697	722	201
Calgary	45	27	13	5	0	189	131	59	46	18	17	11	0	146	152	47	91	45	30	16	0	335	283	106
Carolina	77	46	23	7	1	309	226	100	78	35	32	11	0	230	227	81	155	81	55	18	1	539	453	181
Chicago	53	32	14	7	0	199	138	71	51	18	27	6	0	139	164	42	104	50	41	13	0	338	302	113
Colorado	63	36	18	9	0	247	204	81	64	22	31	11	0	197	227	55	127	58	49	20	0	444	431	136
Columbus	4	2	2	0	0	13	9	4	2	0	1	1	0	4	5	1	6	2	3	1	0	17	14	5
Dallas	52	28	13	11	0	188	139	67	54	21	27	6	0	156	173	48	106	49	40	17	0	344	312	115
Detroit	52	33	11	8	0	226	153	74	55	18	31	5	1	159	203	42	107	51	42	13	1	385	356	116
Edmonton	30	10	13	7	0	109	112	27	29	5	21	3	0	74	120	13	59	15	34	10	0	183	232	40
Florida	23	15	5	3	0	64	37	33	21	10	10	1	0	63	59	21	44	25	15	4	0	127	96	54
Los Angeles	53	28	16	9	0	217	157	65	54	23	22	9	0	187	185	55	107	51	38	18	0	404	342	120
Minnesota	3	1	2	0	0	7	8	2	3	2	1	0	0	7	4	4	6	3	3	0	0	14	12	6
Montreal	102	54	29	19	0	317	268	127	103	34	57	12	0	306	392	80	205	88	86	31	0	623	660	207
Nashville	4	0	3	1	0	9	16	1	5	3	2	0	0	9	10	6	9	3	5	1	0	18	26	7
New Jersey	54	31	15	8	0	213	165	70	54	26	18	9	1	177	162	62	108	57	33	17	1	390	327	132
NY Islanders	61	32	19	9	1	197	164	74	61	25	26	9	1	166	172	60	122	57	45	18	2	363	336	134
NY Rangers	68	39	19	10	0	279	212	88	66	23	27	15	1	180	214	62	134	62	46	25	1	459	426	150
Ottawa	31	21	7	3	0	99	48	45	33	16	9	7	1	86	76	40	64	37	16	10	1	185	124	85
Philadelphia	63	32	23	8	0	209	176	72	67	15	39	12	1	162	228	43	130	47	62	20	1	371	404	115
Phoenix	31	20	6	5	0	127	80	45	29	14	13	2	0	92	87	30	60	34	19	7	0	219	167	75
Pittsburgh	71	34	18	17	2	274	190	87	71	17	36	18	0	217	266	52	142	51	54	35	2	491	456	139
St. Louis	52	29	17	6	0	200	164	64	50	14	28	7	1	125	180	36	102	43	45	13	1	325	344	100
San Jose	11	11	0	0	0	52	27	22	10	1	4	4	1	33	36	7	21	12	4	4	1	85	63	29
Tampa Bay	23	13	8	2	0	63	63	28	23	14	6	3	0	70	49	31	46	27	14	5	0	133	112	59
Toronto	69	43	19	6	1	279	184	93	67	27	26	12	2	228	203	68	136	70	45	18	3	507	387	161
Vancouver	52	26	18	8	0	186	152	60	52	16	25	11	0	162	193	43	104	42	43	19	0	348	345	103
Washington	56	35	15	6	0	216	146	76	56	32	15	9	0	196	140	73	112	67	30	15	0	412	286	149
Defunct Clubs	23	13	5	5	0	94	63	31	23	12	8	3	0	97	76	27	46	25	13	8	0	191	139	58
Totals	1353	754	396	197	6	5036	3803	1711	1353	503	626	212	12	4040	4449	1230	2706	1257	1022	409	18	9076	8252	2941

Playoffs

	Series	W	L	GP	W	L	T	GF	GA	Last Mtg.	Rnd.	Result
Boston	7	2	5	39	18	21	0	130	139	1999	CSF	W 4-2
Chicago	2	2	0	9	8	1	0	36	17	1980	QF	W 4-0
Colorado	2	0	2	8	2	6	0	27	35	1985	DSF	L 2-3
Dallas	3	1	2	13	5	8	0	37	39	1999	F	L 2-4
Montreal	7	3	4	35	17	18	0	111	124	1998	CSF	W 4-0
New Jersey	1	0	1	7	3	4	0	14	14	1994	CQF	L 3-4
NY Islanders	3	0	3	16	4	12	0	45	59	1980	SF	L 2-4
NY Rangers	1	1	0	3	2	1	0	11	6	1978	PRE	W 2-1
Ottawa	2	2	0	11	8	3	0	26	19	1999	CQF	W 4-0
Philadelphia	7	2	5	37	14	23	0	96	110	2001	CQF	W 4-2
Pittsburgh	2	0	2	10	4	6	0	26	26	2001	CSF	L 3-4
St. Louis	1	1	0	3	2	1	0	7	8	1976	PRE	W 2-1
Toronto	1	1	0	5	4	1	0	21	16	1999	CF	W 4-1
Vancouver	2	2	0	7	6	1	0	28	14	1981	PRE	W 3-0
Washington	1	0	1	6	2	4	0	11	13	1998	CF	L 2-4
Totals	42	17	25	209	99	110	0	626	639			

Playoff Results 2005-2000

Year	Round	Opponent	Result	GF	GA
2001	CSF	Pittsburgh	L 3-4	17	17
	CQF	Philadelphia	W 4-2	21	13
2000	CQF	Philadelphia	L 1-4	8	14

Abbreviations: Round: F - Final; CF - conference final; **CSF** - conference semi-final; **CQF** - conference quarter-final; **DSF** - division semi-final; **SF** - semi-final; **QF** - quarter-final; **PRE** - preliminary round.

Calgary totals include Atlanta Flames, 1972-73 to 1979-80.
Colorado totals include Quebec, 1979-80 to 1994-95.
New Jersey totals include Kansas City, 1974-75 to 1975-76, and Colorado Rockies, 1976-77 to 1981-82.
Phoenix totals include Winnipeg, 1979-80 to 1995-96.
Carolina totals include Hartford, 1979-80 to 1996-97.
Dallas totals include Minnesota North Stars, 1970-71 to 1992-93.

Key Off-Season Signings/Acquisitions

2004
Sept. 8 • Signed LW **Thomas Vanek**.

2005
Aug. 4 • Signed D **Teppo Numminen**.

4 • Re-signed LW **Taylor Pyatt**.

8 • Re-signed RW **Mike Grier**.

12 • Re-signed G **Martin Biron**, G **Ryan Miller** and D **Brian Campbell**.

15 • Re-signed Cs **Daniel Briere** and **Tim Connolly**, LW **Jochen Hecht**, RWs **Maxim Afinogenov**, **J.P. Dumont** and **Ales Kotalik** and Ds **Jeff Jillson** and **Henrik Tallinder**.

25 • Obtained D **Toni Lydman** from Calgary for a 2006 3rd-round draft pick.

Entry Draft
Selections 2005-1991

2005 Pick		2001 Pick	
13	Marek Zagrapan	22	Jiri Novotny
48	Philip Gogulla	32	Derek Roy
87	Marc-Andre Gragnani	50	Chris Thorburn
96	Chris Butler	55	Jason Pominville
142	Nathan Gerbe	155	Michal Vondrka
182	Adam Dennis	234	Calle Aslund
191	Vyacheslav Buravchikov	247	Marek Dubec
208	Matt Generous	279	Ryan Jorde
227	Andrew Orpik		

2004 Pick		2000 Pick	
13	Drew Stafford	15	Artem Kryukov
43	Michael Funk	48	Gerard Dicaire
71	Andrej Sekera	111	Ghyslain Rousseau
145	Michal Valent	149	Denis Denisov
176	Patrick Kaleta	213	Vasili Bizyayev
207	Mark Mancari	220	Paul Gaustad
241	Mike Card	258	Sean McMorrow
273	Dylan Hunter	277	Ryan Courtney

2003 Pick		1999 Pick	
5	Thomas Vanek	20	Barrett Heisten
65	Branislav Fabry	35	Milan Bartovic
74	Clarke MacArthur	55	Doug Janik
106	Jan Hejda	64	Mike Zigomanis
114	Denis Ezhov	73	Tim Preston
150	Thomas Morrow	117	Karel Mosovsky
172	Pavel Voroshnin	138	Ryan Miller
202	Nathan Paetsch	146	Matt Kinch
235	Jeff Weber	178	Seneque Hyacinthe
266	Louis-Philippe Martin	206	Bret DeCecco
		235	Brad Self
		263	Craig Brunel

2002 Pick		1998 Pick	
11	Keith Ballard	18	Dmitri Kalinin
20	Dan Paille	34	Andrew Peters
76	Michael Tessier	47	Norm Milley
82	John Adams	50	Jaroslav Kristek
108	Jakub Hulva	77	Mike Pandolfo
121	Marty Magers	137	Aaron Goldade
178	Maxim Schevjev	164	Ales Kotalik
208	Radoslav Hecl	191	Brad Moran
241	Dennis Wideman	218	David Moravec
271	Martin Cizek	249	Edo Terglav

1997 Pick		1993 Pick	
21	Mika Noronen	38	Denis Tsygurov
48	Henrik Tallinder	64	Ethan Philpott
69	Maxim Afinogenov	116	Richard Safarik
75	Jeff Martin	142	Kevin Pozzo
101	Luc Theoret	168	Sergei Petrenko
128	Torrey DiRoberto	194	Mike Barrie
156	Brian Campbell	220	Barrie Moore
184	Jeremy Adduono	246	Chris Davis
212	Kamil Piros	272	Scott Nichol
238	Dylan Kemp		

1996 Pick		1992 Pick	
7	Erik Rasmussen	11	David Cooper
27	Cory Sarich	35	Jozef Cierny
33	Darren Van Oene	59	Ondrej Steiner
54	Francois Methot	80	Dean Melanson
87	Kurt Walsh	83	Matthew Barnaby
106	Mike Martone	107	Markus Ketterer
115	Alexei Tezikov	108	Yuri Khmylev
142	Ryan Davis	131	Paul Rushforth
161	Darren Mortier	179	Dean Tiltgen
222	Scott Buhler	203	Todd Simon
		227	Rick Kowalsky
		251	Chris Clancy

1995 Pick		1991 Pick	
14	Jay McKee	13	Philippe Boucher
16	Martin Biron	35	Jason Dawe
42	Mark Dutiaume	57	Jason Young
68	Mathieu Sunderland	72	Peter Ambroziak
94	Matt Davidson	101	Steve Shields
111	Marian Menhart	123	Sean O'Donnell
119	Kevin Popp	124	Brian Holzinger
123	Daniel Bienvenue	145	Chris Snell
172	Brian Scott	162	Jiri Kuntos
198	Mike Zanutto	189	Tony Iob
224	Rob Skrlac	211	Spencer Meany
		233	Mikhail Volkov
		255	Michael Smith

1994 Pick	
17	Wayne Primeau
43	Curtis Brown
69	Rumun Ndur
121	Sergei Klimentiev
147	Cal Benazic
168	Steve Plouffe
173	Shane Hnidy
176	Steve Webb
199	Bob Westerby
225	Craig Millar
251	Mark Polak
277	Shayne Wright

General Managers' History

Punch Imlach, 1970-71 to 1977-78; John Anderson, 1978-79; Scotty Bowman, 1979-80 to 1985-86; Scotty Bowman and Gerry Meehan, 1986-87; Gerry Meehan, 1987-88 to 1992-93; John Muckler, 1993-94 to 1996-97; Darcy Regier, 1997-98 to date.

General Manager

REGIER, DARCY
General Manager, Buffalo Sabres. Born in Swift Current, Sask., Nov. 27, 1957.

Darcy Regier became the sixth general manager of the Buffalo Sabres on June 11, 1997 after a lengthy management apprenticeship in the New York Islanders organization. As a player, Regier played eight pro seasons, including part of the 1977-78 season with the Cleveland Barons and parts of the 1982-83 and 1983-84 campaigns with the New York Islanders.

He began his career as an administrator with the Islanders in 1984-85 and went on to serve in a variety of capacities including director of administration, assistant director of hockey operations, assistant coach and assistant general manager. He also served as an assistant coach with Hartford in 1991-92.

While with the Islanders, Regier benefitted from working with talented managers and coaches including Bill Torrey and Al Arbour. As a minor pro player with Indianapolis of the CHL he became associated with another important influence on his hockey career, current Detroit Red Wing executive Jim Devellano.

Club Directory

HSBC Arena

Buffalo Sabres
HSBC Arena
One Seymour H. Knox III Plaza
Buffalo, NY 14203
Phone **716/855-4100**
Fax 716/855-4110
Tickets, U.S.: 888/GO-SABRES
Canada: 888/669-GOAL
Capacity: 18,690

Executive
Owner . . . . B. Thomas Golisano
Managing Partner . . . . Lawrence Quinn
Chief Operating Officer . . . . Daniel DiPofi

Hockey Department
General Manager . . . . Darcy Regier
Director of Amateur Scouting . . . . Jim Benning
Director of Pro Scouting . . . . Terry Martin
Director of Player Development . . . . Don Luce
Hockey Department Analyst . . . . Mark Jakubowski
Professional Scout . . . . Jon Christiano
Scouting Coordinator . . . . Scott Schranz
Coordinator of Hockey Operations . . . . Mike Bermingham
Hockey Video Analyst . . . . Corey Smith
Travel Coordinator
Scouting Staff . . . . Bo Berglund, Kevin Devine, Iouri Khmylev, Paul Merritt, Darryl Plandowski
Head Coach . . . . Lindy Ruff
Assistant Coaches . . . . Scott Arniel, Brian McCutcheon
Strength & Conditioning Coach . . . . Doug McKenney
Goaltender Coach . . . . Jim Corsi
Administrative Assistant Coach . . . . Jeff Holbrook
Athletic Trainer . . . . Tim Macre
Head Equipment Manager . . . . Rip Simonick
Assistant Equipment Manager . . . . George Babcock
Equipment Assistant . . . . Encil "Porky" Palmer

Medical
Team Doctors . . . . Les Bisson, M.D., Nicholas Aquino, M.D., William Hartrich, M.D.
Oral Surgeon . . . . Steven Jenson, DDS
Team Dentist . . . . Daniel Yustin, DDS, M.S.
Team Doctor Emeritus . . . . John L. Butsch, M.D.

Legal
Director of Legal Affairs/Human Resources . . . . Richard Mugel

Finance & Administration
Director of Finance & Administration . . . . Chuck LaMattina
Accounting Manager . . . . Christine Ivansitz
Payroll & Human Resource Manager . . . . Birgid Haensel
Accounts Payable Clerk . . . . Kim Binkley
Manager of IT Services . . . . Jon Lamont
Executive Assistant . . . . Eleanore MacKenzie
Receptionist . . . . Olive Anticola

Broadcast Production
Director of Technical & Broadcast Operations . . . . . TBA
Staff Producer . . . . Joe Pinter
Staff Director . . . . Eric Grossman
Feature Producer/Editor . . . . Jeff Hill
Producer . . . . Greg Bauch
Broadcast Team . . . . Rick Jeanneret (Play-by-Play), Jim Lorentz (Commentator)

Merchandise
Director of Merchandise . . . . Mike Kaminska
Merchandise Manager – Inventory Control . . . . . . Glenn Barker
Merchandise Manager – Event Sales . . . . Jeff Smith

Marketing
Director of Marketing . . . . Rob Kopacz
Director of Game Presentation . . . . Rich Wall
Database Marketing Manager . . . . Tom Matheny
Promotions Coordinators . . . . Rich Jureller, Jacqueline Tollar
Web Content Coordinator . . . . Brian Wheeler
Game Presentation & Special Events Coordinator . . Jenifer Dunford
Director of Creative Services . . . . Frank Cravotta
Graphic Artist . . . . Vicki Sitek

Public & Community Relations
Director of Public Relations . . . . Michael Gilbert
Manager of Publications & Hockey Information . . . . Kevin Snow
Coordinator of Media Relations . . . . Chris Bandura
Manager of Community Development . . . . Jennifer Neuhard
Youth Hockey Manager . . . . Patrick Fisher
Mascot Coordinator . . . . Ed Grudzinski
Team Photographer . . . . Bill Wippert
Director of Alumni Relations . . . . Larry Playfair
Corporate & Community Relations Liaison . . . . . . Gilbert Perreault

Sales
VP Sales & Business Development . . . . John Livsey
Senior Account Managers . . . . Joe Foy, Amy Fuchs
Rochester Sales Director . . . . Gary Muxworthy

Ticket Sales & Operations
Director of Ticket Operations & Services . . . . John Sinclair
Account Services Manager . . . . Michael Tout
Box Office Manager . . . . Christopher Makowski

HSBC Arena
Director of Arena Operations . . . . Stan Makowski, Jr.
Director of Event Booking . . . . Jennifer Van Rysdam
Arena Marketing Manager . . . . TBA
Director of Lacrosse . . . . Kurt Silcott
Director of Amateur Athletics . . . . Kevin Sylvester
Events Managers . . . . Matt Rabinowitz, Beth Guiliani Gatto
Communications Technician . . . . Mike Queeno
Chief Engineer . . . . Barry Becker

Calgary Flames

2005-06 Schedule

Oct.	Wed.	5	at Minnesota	Sat.	7	at Vancouver
	Fri.	7	at Columbus	Tue.	10	at NY Rangers
	Sun.	9	at Detroit*	Thu.	12	at NY Islanders
	Mon.	10	at Colorado	Sat.	14	at Minnesota
	Thu.	13	Dallas	Thu.	19	Montreal
	Sat.	15	Edmonton	Sat.	21	Buffalo
	Mon.	17	Phoenix	Mon.	23	at Edmonton
	Thu.	20	Edmonton	Tue.	24	at Colorado
	Sat.	22	at Dallas	Thu.	26	at Chicago
	Sun.	23	at Los Angeles	Sun.	29	at Chicago*
	Wed.	26	at Anaheim	Mon.	30	at St. Louis
	Thu.	27	at Phoenix	**Feb.** Wed.	1	Columbus
	Sat.	29	at San Jose	Fri.	3	Vancouver
Nov.	Tue.	1	Minnesota	Mon.	6	at San Jose
	Thu.	3	Columbus	Wed.	8	Anaheim
	Sat.	5	Vancouver	Fri.	10	St. Louis
	Mon.	7	Vancouver	Tue.	28	Vancouver
	Thu.	10	at Phoenix	**Mar.** Thu.	2	St. Louis
	Sat.	12	Colorado	Sat.	4	San Jose
	Mon.	14	Minnesota	Tue.	7	Nashville
	Wed.	16	Detroit	Thu.	9	Dallas
	Fri.	18	Chicago	Sun.	12	at Colorado*
	Mon.	21	at Colorado	Mon.	13	Colorado
	Wed.	23	San Jose	Thu.	16	at Edmonton
	Fri.	25	Edmonton	Sat.	18	at Nashville
	Tue.	29	at Nashville	Sun.	19	at Minnesota
Dec.	Thu.	1	at Detroit	Tue.	21	at Minnesota
	Sat.	3	at Pittsburgh	Thu.	23	at St. Louis
	Tue.	6	at Philadelphia	Fri.	24	at Columbus
	Wed.	7	at New Jersey	Sun.	26	at Dallas*
	Sat.	10	Ottawa	Wed.	29	Los Angeles
	Sat.	17	Boston	Fri.	31	Colorado
	Mon.	19	at Edmonton	**Apr.** Sat.	1	at Edmonton
	Wed.	21	Los Angeles	Mon.	3	Detroit
	Fri.	23	at Vancouver	Wed.	5	Phoenix
	Mon.	26	at Vancouver	Fri.	7	Minnesota
	Tue.	27	Nashville	Sat.	8	at Vancouver
	Thu.	29	Minnesota	Tue.	11	Anaheim
	Sat.	31	Edmonton	Thu.	13	Colorado
Jan.	Mon.	2	Chicago*	Sat.	15	at Los Angeles
	Fri.	6	Toronto	Mon.	17	at Anaheim

Denotes afternoon game.

Franchise date: June 6, 1972
Transferred from Atlanta to Calgary, June 24, 1980.

NORTHWEST DIVISION

34th NHL Season

Miikka Kiprusoff keyed Calgary's run to the Stanley Cup finals during the spring of 2004. His 1.69 goals-against average in 2003-04 was the lowest since the 1939-40 season.

Year-by-Year Record

Season	GP	Home W	L	T	OL	Road W	L	T	OL	Overall W	L	T	OL	GF	GA	Pts.	Finished	Playoff Result
2004-05	....	....				....				....				....	....	....		
2003-04	82	21	14	5	1	21	16	2	2	42	30	7	3	200	176	94	3rd, Northwest Div.	Lost Final
2002-03	82	14	16	10	1	15	20	3	3	29	36	13	4	186	228	75	5th, Northwest Div.	Out of Playoffs
2001-02	82	20	14	5	2	12	21	7	1	32	35	12	3	201	220	79	4th, Northwest Div.	Out of Playoffs
2000-01	82	12	18	9	2	15	18	6	2	27	36	15	4	197	236	73	4th, Northwest Div.	Out of Playoffs
1999-2000	82	20	14	6	1	11	22	4	4	31	36	10	5	211	256	77	4th, Northwest Div.	Out of Playoffs
1998-99	82	15	20	6	....	15	20	6	....	30	40	12	....	211	234	72	3rd, Northwest Div.	Out of Playoffs
1997-98	82	18	17	6	....	8	24	9	....	26	41	15	....	217	252	67	5th, Pacific Div.	Out of Playoffs
1996-97	82	21	18	2	....	11	23	7	....	32	41	9	....	214	239	73	5th, Pacific Div.	Out of Playoffs
1995-96	82	18	18	5	....	16	19	6	....	34	37	11	....	241	240	79	2nd, Pacific Div.	Lost Conf. Quarter-Final
1994-95	48	15	7	2	....	9	10	5	....	24	17	7	....	163	135	55	1st, Pacific Div.	Lost Conf. Quarter-Final
1993-94	84	25	12	5	....	17	17	8	....	42	29	13	....	302	256	97	1st, Pacific Div.	Lost Conf. Quarter-Final
1992-93	84	23	14	5	....	20	16	6	....	43	30	11	....	322	282	97	2nd, Smythe Div.	Lost Div. Semi-Final
1991-92	80	19	14	7	....	12	23	5	....	31	37	12	....	296	305	74	5th, Smythe Div.	Out of Playoffs
1990-91	80	29	8	3	....	17	18	5	....	46	26	8	....	344	263	100	2nd, Smythe Div.	Lost Div. Semi-Final
1989-90	80	28	7	5	....	14	16	10	....	42	23	15	....	348	265	99	1st, Smythe Div.	Lost Div. Semi-Final
1988-89	**80**	**32**	**4**	**4**	....	**22**	**13**	**5**	....	**54**	**17**	**9**	....	**354**	**226**	**117**	**1st, Smythe Div.**	**Won Stanley Cup**
1987-88	80	26	11	3	....	22	12	6	....	48	23	9	....	397	305	105	1st, Smythe Div.	Lost Div. Final
1986-87	80	25	13	2	....	21	18	1	....	46	31	3	....	318	289	95	2nd, Smythe Div.	Lost Div. Semi-Final
1985-86	80	23	11	6	....	17	20	3	....	40	31	9	....	354	315	89	2nd, Smythe Div.	Lost Final
1984-85	80	23	11	6	....	18	16	6	....	41	27	12	....	363	302	94	3rd, Smythe Div.	Lost Div. Semi-Final
1983-84	80	22	11	7	....	12	21	7	....	34	32	14	....	311	314	82	2nd, Smythe Div.	Lost Div. Final
1982-83	80	21	12	7	....	11	22	7	....	32	34	14	....	321	317	78	2nd, Smythe Div.	Lost Div. Final
1981-82	80	20	11	9	....	9	23	8	....	29	34	17	....	334	345	75	3rd, Smythe Div.	Lost Div. Semi-Final
1980-81	80	25	5	10	....	14	22	4	....	39	27	14	....	329	298	92	3rd, Patrick Div.	Lost Semi-Final
1979-80*	80	18	15	7	....	17	17	6	....	35	32	13	....	282	269	83	4th, Patrick Div.	Lost Prelim. Round
1978-79*	80	25	11	4	....	16	20	4	....	41	31	8	....	327	280	90	4th, Patrick Div.	Lost Prelim. Round
1977-78*	80	20	13	7	....	14	14	12	....	34	27	19	....	274	252	87	3rd, Patrick Div.	Lost Prelim. Round
1976-77*	80	22	11	7	....	12	23	5	....	34	34	12	....	264	265	80	3rd, Patrick Div.	Lost Prelim. Round
1975-76*	80	19	14	7	....	16	19	5	....	35	33	12	....	262	237	82	3rd, Patrick Div.	Lost Prelim. Round
1974-75*	80	24	9	7	....	10	22	8	....	34	31	15	....	243	233	83	4th, Patrick Div.	Out of Playoffs
1973-74*	78	17	15	7	....	13	19	7	....	30	34	14	....	214	238	74	4th, West Div.	Lost Quarter-Final
1972-73*	78	16	16	7	....	9	22	8	....	25	38	15	....	191	239	65	7th, West Div.	Out of Playoffs

*Atlanta Flames

2005-06 Player Personnel

FORWARDS	HT	WT	S	Place of Birth	Date	2004-05 Club
AMONTE, Tony	6-0	200	L	Hingham, MA	8/2/70	
BELLEMARE, Thomas	6-3	222	R	Shawinigan, Que.	1/11/84	Texas-Charlotte
COUTURE, Derek	6-2	202	R	Calgary, Alta.	4/24/84	Seattle
CUNNING, Cam	6-2	215	L	Powell River, B.C.	6/4/85	Kamloops-Vancouver (WHL)
DONALLY, Ryan	6-5	227	L	Tecumseh, Ont.	2/4/85	Windsor-Kitchener
DONOVAN, Shean	6-2	200	R	Timmins, Ont.	1/22/75	Geneve
GERMYN, Carsen	5-10	185	R	Campbell River, B.C.	2/22/85	Lowell
IGINLA, Jarome	6-1	208	R	Edmonton, Alta.	7/1/77	
JOHNER, Dustin	5-11	181	R	Estevan, Sask.	3/6/83	Lowell-Las Vegas
JOHNSON, Tyler	6-2	185	R	Edmonton, Alta.	7/11/85	Red Deer
KOBASEW, Chuck	6-1	195	L	Osoyoos, B.C.	4/17/82	Lowell
LANGKOW, Daymond	5-11	192	L	Edmonton, Alta.	9/27/76	
LOMBARDI, Matthew	6-0	195	L	Montreal, Que.	3/18/82	Lowell
LOYNS, Lynn	5-11	205	L	Naicam, Sask.	2/21/81	Lowell
LYNCH, Darren	5-11	181	R	Regina, Sask.	7/7/83	Las Vegas
MacDONALD, Craig	6-1	195	L	Antigonish, N.S.	4/7/77	Lowell
MAKI, Tomi	5-11	172	L	Helsinki, Finland	8/19/83	Jokerit
McCARTY, Darren	6-1	210	R	Burnaby, B.C.	4/1/72	
MOSS, David	6-3	203	L	Dearborn, MI	12/28/81	U. of Michigan
MYHRES, Brantt	6-3	220	R	Edmonton, Alta.	3/18/74	Lowell
NILSON, Marcus	6-2	195	R	Balsta, Sweden	3/1/78	Djurgarden
NYSTROM, Eric	6-1	205	L	Syosset, NY	2/14/83	U. of Michigan
PETERS, Warren	6-0	200	L	Saskatoon, Sask.	7/10/82	Idaho
PRUST, Brandon	5-11	191	L	London, Ont.	3/16/84	London
REINPRECHT, Steve	6-0	195	L	Edmonton, Alta.	5/7/76	Mulhouse
RITCHIE, Byron	5-10	195	L	Burnaby, B.C.	4/24/77	Rogle
SEVERSON, Cam	6-1	215	L	Canora, Sask.	1/15/78	Milwaukee
SIMON, Chris	6-4	235	L	Wawa, Ont.	1/30/72	
TAYLOR, Justin	6-4	200	L	Edmonton, Alta.	1/1/83	Lowell
WIEMER, Jason	6-1	225	L	Kimberley, B.C.	4/14/76	
YELLE, Stephane	6-1	190	L	Ottawa, Ont.	5/9/74	

DEFENSEMEN	HT	WT	S	Place of Birth	Date	2004-05 Club
FERENCE, Andrew	5-10	196	L	Edmonton, Alta.	3/17/79	C. Budejovice
GIORDANO, Mark	6-0	203	L	Toronto, Ont.	5/10/83	Lowell
HAMRLIK, Roman	6-2	210	L	Zlin, Czech.	4/12/74	Zlin
KOMARNISKI, Zenith	6-0	200	L	Edmonton, Alta.	8/13/78	Syracuse
LEOPOLD, Jordan	6-0	193	L	Golden Valley, MN	8/3/80	
MARR, Steve	6-2	218	L	Kamloops, B.C.	6/6/84	Medicine Hat
MONTADOR, Steve	6-0	210	R	Vancouver, B.C.	12/21/79	Mulhouse
PALIN, Brett	6-2	204	L	Nanaimo, B.C.	6/23/84	Kelowna
PARDY, Adam	6-5	211	L	Bonavista, Nfld.	3/29/84	Cape Breton
PHANEUF, Dion	6-3	213	L	Edmonton, Alta.	4/10/85	Red Deer
REGEHR, Richie	6-0	190	R	Rosthern, Sask.	1/17/83	Lowell
REGEHR, Robyn	6-2	226	L	Recife, Brazil	4/19/80	
WARRENER, Rhett	6-2	217	R	Shaunavon, Sask.	1/27/76	

GOALTENDERS	HT	WT	C	Place of Birth	Date	2004-05 Club
KIPRUSOFF, Miikka	6-2	190	L	Turku, Finland	10/26/76	Timra
KRAHN, Brent	6-5	220	L	Winnipeg, Man.	4/2/82	Lowell
McELHINNEY, Curtis	6-3	207	L	London, Ont.	5/23/83	Colorado College
SAUVE, Philippe	6-0	180	L	Buffalo, NY	2/27/80	Mississippi

In the System and Recently Drafted

FORWARDS	HT	WT	S	Place of Birth	Date	2004-05 Club
ARTEMENKOV, Yuri	6-1	174	L	Moscow, USSR	2/3/84	Krylja Sovetov 2-Tver
BOBROV, Viktor	6-1	176	L	Novocheboksarsk, USSR	1/1/84	CSKA 2
BOYD, Dustin	6-0	188	L	Winnipeg, Man.	7/16/86	Moose Jaw
CETKOVSKY, Jiri	6-4	209	L	Prostejov, Czech.	11/4/83	Pardubice-Hr. Kralove
CHUCKO, Kris	6-2	190	R	Burnaby, B.C.	3/13/86	U. of Minnesota
CRACKNELL, Adam	6-2	211	R	Prince Albert, Sask.	7/15/85	Kootenay
DUDA, Radek	6-1	193	L	Skolov, Czech.	1/28/79	Slavia-Plzen
HAMALAINEN, Ville	5-11	178	L	Lappeenranta, Finland	7/6/81	KalPa
HOGG, Kris	5-11	186	L	Salmon Arm, B.C.	6/17/86	Kamloops
NILSON, Patrik	6-0	180	R	Baltsa, Sweden	5/18/81	Las Vegas-Louisiana
PERSSON, Kristofer	6-3	194	L	Umea, Sweden	1/14/84	Skovde
PETER, Emanuel	6-0	198	L	Nieder Uzwil, Switz.	6/9/84	Kloten
RYDER, Dan	5-10	192	R	Bonavista, Nfld.	1/12/87	Peterborough
SCHNEIDER, Matt	6-7	202	R	Vernon, B.C.	7/10/85	Tri-City
SEITSONEN, Aki	6-3	206	R	Riihimaki, Finland	2/5/86	Prince Albert
SHASTIN, Yegor	5-9	172	L	Kiev, USSR	9/10/82	Omsk-St. Petersburg
SUTTER, Brett	5-11	194	L	Viking, Alta.	6/2/87	Kootenay
TARATUKHIN, Andrei	6-0	198	L	Omsk, USSR	2/22/83	Ufa
TRUBACHEV, Yuri	5-9	187	L	Cherepovets, USSR	3/9/83	Cherepovets
VAN DER GULIK, David	5-11	175	L	Abbotsford, B.C.	4/20/83	Boston University
WATT, J.D.	6-1	206	R	Calgary, Alta.	5/25/87	Vancouver (WHL)
WIKNER, Fred	6-1	187	L	Molndal, Sweden	1/1/86	Molndal-Frolunda
ZAINULLIN, Ruslan	6-2	202	L	Kazan, USSR	2/14/82	Spartak

DEFENSEMEN	HT	WT	S	Place of Birth	Date	2004-05 Club
BALDWIN, Gord	6-5	205	L	Winnipeg, Man.	3/1/87	Medicine Hat
FROGREN, Jonas	6-1	190	L	Falun, Sweden	8/28/80	Farjestad
HAJEK, David	5-11	165	L	Chomutov, Czech.	6/13/80	Chomutov
JOHNSSON, Pierre	6-1	183	L	Karlstad, Sweden	2/7/84	Mora
KOKOREV, Dmitri	6-3	198	L	Moscow, USSR	1/9/79	Chekhov
MARTTINEN, Jyri	5-11	190	L	Tikkakoski, Finland	9/1/82	JYP
PELECH, Matt	6-3	227	R	Toronto, Ont.	9/4/87	Sarnia
RAMHOLT, Tim	6-1	194	L	Zurich, Switz.	11/2/84	Zurich
RUMSEY, Myles	6-1	200	R	Winnipeg, Man.	11/5/86	Swift Current
RYABYKIN, Dmitri	6-1	203	R	Chirchik, USSR	3/24/76	Omsk

GOALTENDERS	HT	WT	C	Place of Birth	Date	2004-05 Club
KEETLEY, Matt	6-0	175	R	Medicine Hat, Alta.	4/27/86	Medicine Hat
LALANDE, Kevin	5-11	175	L	Kingston, Ont.	2/19/87	Belleville
MEDVEDEV, Andrei	6-0	211	L	Moscow, USSR	4/1/83	Spartak
SPRATT, James	6-1	194	L	Detroit, MI	11/10/85	Sioux City

Darren McCarty joins Calgary after 11 seasons (and three Stanley Cup championships) with Detroit.

General Managers' History

Cliff Fletcher, 1972-73 to 1990-91; Doug Risebrough, 1991-92 to 1994-95; Doug Risebrough and Al Coates, 1995-96; Al Coates, 1996-97 to 1999-2000; Craig Button, 2000-01 to 2002-03; Darryl Sutter, 2003-04 to date.

Coaching History

Bernie Geoffrion, 1972-73, 1973-74; Bernie Geoffrion and Fred Creighton, 1974-75; Fred Creighton, 1975-76 to 1978-79; Al MacNeil, 1979-80 to 1981-82; Bob Johnson, 1982-83 to 1986-87; Terry Crisp, 1987-88 to 1989-90; Doug Risebrough, 1990-91; Doug Risebrough and Guy Charron, 1991-92; Dave King, 1992-93 to 1994-95; Pierre Page, 1995-96, 1996-97; Brian Sutter, 1997-98 to 1999-2000; Don Hay and Greg Gilbert, 2000-01; Greg Gilbert, 2001-02; Greg Gilbert, Al MacNeil and Darryl Sutter, 2002-03; Darryl Sutter, 2003-04 to date.

Coach and General Manager

SUTTER, DARRYL
Coach/General Manager, Calgary Flames. Born in Viking, Alta., August 19, 1958.

Darryl Sutter was named general manager of the Calgary Flames on April 11, 2003 adding the portfolio to his head coaching position. He had joined the Flames as coach on December 28, 2002. In his first full season with the Flames in 2003-04, Sutter led the team back to the playoffs after a seven-year absence and guided the club on a thrilling run to the seventh game of the Stanley Cup Finals.

Before joining the Flames, Sutter was the San Jose Sharks franchise leader in regular-season games coached (434) and wins (192). Through the 2001-02 season, Sutter became only the second coach in NHL history (Al Arbour, New York Islanders) to improve his team's point total for five consecutive years.

Prior to San Jose, Sutter coached Chicago for three years (1992 to 1995) and spent two seasons (1995 to 1997) with the Blackhawks as a consultant for special assignments. He spent the 1987-88 campaign as a Blackhawks assistant coach to Bob Murdoch and served as an associate coach for Mike Keenan during the 1990-91 and 1991-92 seasons. During his final season as associate coach, the Blackhawks advanced to the Stanley Cup Finals. Sutter spent two seasons coaching the Blackhawks top development affiliate in the IHL, which played in Saginaw (1988-89) and in Indianapolis (1989-90). Under his leadership, the Indianapolis Ice stormed through the regular season with 114 points and won the Turner Cup championship. He was named IHL coach of the year.

As a player, Sutter was selected by Chicago in the ninth round, 179th overall, in the 1978 NHL Entry Draft. During his eight-year career with the Blackhawks from 1979 to 1987, he scored 279 points (161 goals, 118 assists) with 288 penalty minutes in 406 NHL career games. Sutter served as team captain with the Blackhawks for five seasons, beginning in the 1982-83 season through 1986-87 when he was forced to retire prematurely due to a series of injuries.

Darryl is a member of the famous Sutter hockey family, who had six brothers that played in the NHL. They were all inducted into the Alberta Sports Hall of Fame in May 2000 under the Lifetime Achievement category. Along with his brothers, Darryl is very involved in the Sutter Foundation, started by he and his family in Alberta, which raises money for non-profit organizations.

NHL Coaching Record

Season	Team	Games	Regular Season			Playoffs		
			W	L	T	Games	W	L
1992-93	Chicago	84	47	25	12	4	0	4
1993-94	Chicago	84	39	36	9	6	2	4
1994-95	Chicago	48	24	19	5	16	9	7
1997-98	San Jose	82	34	38	10	6	2	4
1998-99	San Jose	82	31	33	18	6	2	4
1999-2000	San Jose	82	35	37	10	12	5	7
2000-01	San Jose	82	40	30	12	6	2	4
2001-02	San Jose	82	44	30	8	12	7	5
2002-03	San Jose	24	8	14	2	....	....	....
	Calgary	46	19	19	8	....	....	....
2003-04	Calgary	82	42	33	7	26	15	11
	NHL Totals	**778**	**363**	**314**	**101**	**94**	**44**	**50**

Club Records

Team

(Figures in brackets for season records are games played; records for fewest points, wins, ties, losses, goals, goals against are for 70 or more games)

Most Points	117	1988-89 (80)
Most Wins	54	1988-89 (80)
Most Ties	19	1977-78 (80)
Most Losses	41	1996-97 (82),
		1997-98 (82),
		1999-2000 (82)
Most Goals	397	1987-88 (80)
Most Goals Against	345	1981-82 (80)
Fewest Points	65	1972-73 (78)
Fewest Wins	25	1972-73 (78)
Fewest Ties	3	1986-87 (80)
Fewest Losses	17	1988-89 (80)
Fewest Goals	186	2002-03 (82)
Fewest Goals Against	176	2003-04 (82)

Longest Winning Streak

Overall	10	Oct. 14-Nov. 3/78
Home	9	Oct. 17-Nov. 15/78,
		Jan. 3-Feb. 5/89,
		Mar. 3-Apr. 1/90,
		Feb. 21-Mar. 14/91
Away	7	Nov. 10-Dec. 4/88

Longest Undefeated Streak

Overall	13	Nov. 10-Dec. 8/88
		(12 wins, 1 tie)
Home	18	Dec. 29/90-Mar. 14/91
		(17 wins, 1 tie)
Away	9	Feb. 20-Mar. 21/88
		(6 wins, 3 ties),
		Nov. 11-Dec. 16/90
		(6 wins, 3 ties)

Longest Losing Streak

Overall	11	Dec. 14/85-Jan. 7/86
Home	6	Dec. 5-31/98
Away	9	Dec. 1/85-Jan. 12/86

Longest Winless Streak

Overall	11	Dec. 14/85-Jan. 7/86
		(11 losses),
		Jan. 5-26/93
		(9 losses, 2 ties)
Home	10	Oct. 21-Dec. 4/00
		(6 losses, 4 ties)
Away	13	Feb. 3-Mar. 29/73
		(10 losses, 3 ties)

Most Shutouts, Season	11	2003-04 (82)
Most PIM, Season	2,643	1991-92 (80)
Most Goals, Game	13	Feb. 10/93
		(S.J. 1 at Cgy. 13)

Individual

Most Seasons	13	Al MacInnis
Most Games	803	Al MacInnis
Most Goals, Career	364	Theoren Fleury
Most Assists, Career	609	Al MacInnis
Most Points, Career	830	Theoren Fleury
		(364G, 466A)
Most PIM, Career	2,405	Tim Hunter
Most Shutouts, Career	20	Dan Bouchard

Longest Consecutive

Games Streak	257	Brad Marsh
		(Oct. 11/78-Nov. 10/81)
Most Goals, Season	66	Lanny McDonald
		(1982-83)
Most Assists, Season	82	Kent Nilsson
		(1980-81)
Most Points, Season	131	Kent Nilsson
		(1980-81; 49G, 82A)
Most PIM, Season	375	Tim Hunter
		(1988-89)

Most Points, Defenseman, Season	103	Al MacInnis
		(1990-91; 28G, 75A)
Most Points, Center, Season	131	Kent Nilsson
		(1980-81; 49G, 82A)
Most Points, Right Wing, Season	110	Joe Mullen
		(1988-89; 51G, 59A)
Most Points, Left Wing, Season	90	Gary Roberts
		(1991-92; 53G, 37A)
Most Points, Rookie, Season	92	Joe Nieuwendyk
		(1987-88; 51G, 41A)
Most Shutouts, Season	5	Dan Bouchard
		(1973-74),
		Phil Myre
		(1974-75),
		Fred Brathwaite
		(1999-2000, 2000-01),
		Roman Turek
		(2001-02)
Most Goals, Game	5	Joe Nieuwendyk
		(Jan. 11/89)
Most Assists, Game	6	Guy Chouinard
		(Feb. 25/81),
		Gary Suter
		(Apr. 4/86)
Most Points, Game	7	Sergei Makarov
		(Feb. 25/90; 2G, 5A)

Records include Atlanta Flames, 1972-73 through 1979-80.

Retired Numbers

9	Lanny McDonald	1981-1989

All-time Record vs. Other Clubs

Regular Season

	At Home								On Road								Total							
	GP	W	L	T	OL	GF	GA	PTS	GP	W	L	T	OL	GF	GA	PTS	GP	W	L	T	OL	GF	GA	PTS
Anaheim	25	15	9	1	0	72	61	31	26	8	10	6	2	69	80	24	51	23	19	7	2	141	141	55
Atlanta	3	3	0	0	0	14	6	6	4	0	3	1	0	5	8	1	7	3	3	1	0	19	14	7
Boston	44	18	22	4	0	160	154	40	47	13	28	6	0	130	165	32	91	31	50	10	0	290	319	72
Buffalo	46	17	18	11	0	152	146	45	45	13	26	5	1	131	189	32	91	30	44	16	1	283	335	77
Carolina	29	21	6	2	0	140	92	44	28	13	10	5	0	103	91	31	57	34	16	7	0	243	183	75
Chicago	63	29	21	13	0	201	188	71	61	22	26	13	0	179	196	57	124	51	47	26	0	380	384	128
Colorado	47	20	17	9	1	160	141	50	47	18	17	11	1	154	165	48	94	38	34	20	2	314	306	98
Columbus	8	5	3	0	0	24	18	10	8	2	6	0	0	16	26	4	16	7	9	0	0	40	44	14
Dallas	62	33	15	14	0	208	155	80	62	21	29	11	1	196	228	54	124	54	44	25	1	404	383	134
Detroit	60	34	20	6	0	228	179	74	59	18	31	10	0	174	215	46	119	52	51	16	0	402	394	120
Edmonton	81	43	29	9	0	324	275	95	81	29	41	10	1	265	306	69	162	72	70	19	1	589	581	164
Florida	8	4	3	1	0	21	20	9	9	4	3	2	0	22	21	10	17	8	6	3	0	43	41	19
Los Angeles	94	55	27	12	0	413	310	122	91	36	45	9	1	316	338	82	185	91	72	21	1	729	648	204
Minnesota	10	5	1	3	1	23	21	14	11	5	4	1	1	20	24	12	21	10	5	4	2	43	45	26
Montreal	49	16	26	7	0	146	164	39	46	12	26	8	0	112	163	32	95	28	52	15	0	258	327	71
Nashville	12	6	2	3	1	35	26	16	13	4	8	1	0	25	39	9	25	10	10	4	1	60	65	25
New Jersey	42	28	6	8	0	184	111	64	45	27	15	3	0	162	128	57	87	55	21	11	0	346	239	121
NY Islanders	49	24	14	11	0	172	145	59	51	17	25	9	0	143	191	43	100	41	39	20	0	315	336	102
NY Rangers	49	27	11	10	1	216	148	65	52	23	22	5	2	184	178	53	101	50	33	15	3	400	326	118
Ottawa	11	6	4	1	0	38	25	13	10	2	5	3	0	24	27	7	21	8	9	4	0	62	52	20
Philadelphia	52	25	18	9	0	208	172	59	51	15	33	3	0	137	199	33	103	40	51	12	0	345	371	92
Phoenix	71	39	22	9	1	295	227	88	70	25	33	11	1	238	264	62	141	64	55	20	2	533	491	150
Pittsburgh	46	27	11	8	0	204	140	62	44	10	24	10	0	133	167	30	90	37	35	18	0	337	307	92
St. Louis	62	29	26	5	2	201	180	65	64	24	31	9	0	195	229	57	126	53	57	14	2	396	409	122
San Jose	32	18	10	4	0	116	87	40	34	17	13	4	0	102	100	38	66	35	23	8	0	218	187	78
Tampa Bay	10	6	4	0	0	32	24	12	10	4	5	1	0	32	31	9	20	10	9	1	0	64	55	21
Toronto	61	34	22	5	0	239	195	73	53	18	28	7	0	189	202	43	114	52	50	12	0	428	397	116
Vancouver	98	57	26	15	0	392	283	129	99	45	35	18	1	327	335	109	197	102	61	33	1	719	618	238
Washington	38	24	7	7	0	157	93	55	41	14	21	6	0	139	153	34	79	38	28	13	0	296	246	89
Defunct Clubs	13	8	4	1	0	51	34	17	13	7	3	3	0	43	33	17	26	15	7	4	0	94	67	34
Totals	**1275**	**676**	**404**	**188**	**7**	**4826**	**3820**	**1547**	**1275**	**466**	**606**	**191**	**12**	**3965**	**4491**	**1135**	**2550**	**1142**	**1010**	**379**	**19**	**8791**	**8311**	**2682**

Playoffs

	Series	W	L	GP	W	L	T	GF	GA	Last Mtg.
Chicago	3	2	1	12	7	5	0	37	33	1996
Dallas	1	0	1	6	2	4	0	18	25	1981
Detroit	2	1	1	8	4	4	0	16	20	2004
Edmonton	5	1	4	30	11	19	0	96	132	1991
Los Angeles	6	2	4	26	13	13	0	102	105	1993
Montreal	2	1	1	11	5	6	0	32	31	1989
NY Rangers	1	0	1	4	1	3	0	8	14	1980
Philadelphia	2	1	1	11	4	7	0	28	43	1981
St. Louis	1	1	0	7	4	3	0	28	22	1986
San Jose	2	1	1	13	7	6	0	51	38	2004
Tampa Bay	1	0	1	7	3	4	0	14	13	2004
Toronto	1	0	1	2	0	2	0	5	9	1979
Vancouver	6	4	2	32	17	15	0	101	96	2004
Winnipeg	3	1	2	13	6	7	0	43	45	1987
Totals	**36**	**15**	**21**	**182**	**84**	**98**	**0**	**579**	**626**	

Playoff Results 2005-2000

Year	Round	Opponent	Result	GF	GA
2004	F	Tampa Bay	L 3-4	14	13
	CF	San Jose	W 4-2	16	12
	CSF	Detroit	W 4-2	11	12
	CQF	Vancouver	W 4-3	19	16

Abbreviations: Round: F - Final;
CF - conference final; **CSF** - conference semi-final;
CQF - conference quarter-final; **DSF** - division
semi-final; **SF** - semi-final; **QF** - quarter-final;
PRE - preliminary round.

Carolina totals include Hartford, 1979-80 to 1996-97.
Colorado totals include Quebec, 1979-80 to 1994-95. Dallas totals include Minnesota North Stars, 1972-73 to 1992-93.
New Jersey totals include Kansas City, 1974-75 to 1975-76, and Colorado Rockies, 1976-77 to 1981-82.
Phoenix totals include Winnipeg, 1979-80 to 1995-96.

Key Off-Season Signings/Acquisitions

2004

Aug. 5 • Signed C **Jason Wiemer**.

26 • Obtained C **Daymond Langkow** from Phoenix for D **Denis Gauthier** and LW **Oleg Saprykin**.

Sept. 15 • Signed D **Dion Phaneuf**.

2005

Aug. 2 • Signed RW **Tony Amonte** and RW **Darren McCarty**.

3 • Re-signed RW **Jarome Iginla**.

4 • Re-signed D **Jordan Leopold**.

9 • Obtained G **Philippe Sauve** from Colorado for a 2006 conditional draft pick.

10 • Re-signed D **Andrew Ference**.

11 • Re-signed C **Steve Reinprecht**.

12 • Re-signed G **Miikka Kiprusoff** and D **Rhett Warrener**.

14 • Signed D **Roman Hamrlik**.

15 • Signed 2002 1st-round pick (10th overall), LW **Eric Nystrom**.

15 • Re-signed RW **Chuck Kobasew** and C **Matthew Lombardi**.

Entry Draft
Selections 2005-1991

2005
Pick
26 Matt Pelech
69 Gord Baldwin
74 Dan Ryder
111 J.D. Watt
128 Kevin Lalande
158 Matt Keetley
179 Brett Sutter
221 Myles Rumsey

2004
Pick
24 Kris Chucko
70 Brandon Prust
98 Dustin Boyd
118 Aki Seitsonen
121 Kris Hogg
173 Adam Pardy
182 Fred Wikner
200 Matt Schneider
213 James Spratt
279 Adam Cracknell

2003
Pick
9 Dion Phaneuf
39 Tim Ramholt
97 Ryan Donally
112 Jamie Tardif
143 Greg Moore
173 Tyler Johnson
206 Thomas Bellemare
240 Cam Cunning
270 Kevin Harvey

2002
Pick
10 Eric Nystrom
39 Brian McConnell
90 Matthew Lombardi
112 Yuri Artemenkov
141 Jiri Cetkovsky
142 Emanuel Peter
146 Viktor Bobrov
159 Kristofer Persson
176 Curtis McElhinney
206 David Van Der Gulik
207 Pierre Johnsson
238 Jyri Marttinen

2001
Pick
14 Chuck Kobasew
41 Andrei Taratukhin
56 Andrei Medvedev
108 Tomi Maki
124 Yegor Shastin
145 James Hakewill
164 Yuri Trubachev
207 Garrett Bembridge
220 David Moss
233 Joe Campbell
251 Ville Hamalainen

2000
Pick
9 Brent Krahn
40 Kurtis Foster
46 Jarret Stoll
116 Levente Szuper
141 Wade Davis
155 Travis Moen
176 Jukka Hentunen
239 David Hajek
270 Micki DuPont

1999
Pick
11 Oleg Saprykin
38 Dan Cavanaugh
77 Craig Anderson
106 Roman Rozakov
135 Matt Doman
153 Jesse Cook
166 Cory Pecker
170 Matt Underhill
190 Blair Stayzer
252 Dmitri Kirilenko

1998
Pick
6 Rico Fata
33 Blair Betts
62 Paul Manning
102 Shaun Sutter
108 Dany Sabourin
120 Brent Gauvreau
192 Radek Duda
206 Jonas Frogren
234 Kevin Mitchell

1997
Pick
6 Daniel Tkaczuk
32 Evan Lindsay
42 John Tripp
51 Dmitri Kokorev
60 Derek Schutz
70 Erik Andersson
92 Chris St. Croix
100 Ryan Ready
113 Martin Moise
140 Ilja Demidov
167 Jeremy Rondeau
223 Dustin Paul

1996
Pick
13 Derek Morris
39 Travis Brigley
40 Steve Begin
73 Dmitri Vlasenkov
89 Toni Lydman
94 Christian Lefebvre
122 Josef Straka
202 Ryan Wade
228 Ronald Petrovicky

1995
Pick
20 Denis Gauthier
46 Pavel Smirnov
72 Rocky Thompson
98 Jan Labraaten
150 Clarke Wilm
176 Ryan Gillis
233 Steve Shirreffs

1994
Pick
19 Chris Dingman
45 Dmitri Ryabykin
77 Chris Clark
91 Ryan Duthie
97 Johan Finnstrom
107 Nils Ekman
123 Frank Appel
149 Patrick Haltia
175 Ladislav Kohn
201 Keith McCambridge
227 Jorgen Jonsson
253 Mike Peluso
279 Pavel Torgaev

1993
Pick
18 Jesper Mattsson
44 Jamie Allison
70 Dan Tompkins
95 Jason Smith
96 Marty Murray
121 Darryl Lafrance
122 John Emmons
148 Andreas Karlsson
200 Derek Sylvester
252 German Titov
278 Burke Murphy

1992
Pick
6 Cory Stillman
30 Chris O'Sullivan
54 Mathias Johansson
78 Robert Svehla
102 Sami Helenius
126 Ravil Yakubov
129 Joel Bouchard
150 Pavel Rajnoha
174 Ryan Mulhern
198 Brandon Carper
222 Jonas Hoglund
246 Andrei Potaichuk

1991
Pick
19 Niklas Sundblad
41 Francois Groleau
52 Sandy McCarthy
63 Brian Caruso
85 Steven Magnusson
107 Jerome Butler
129 Bobby Marshall
140 Matt Hoffman
151 Kelly Harper
173 David St-Pierre
195 David Struch
217 Sergei Zolotov
239 Marko Jantunen
261 Andrei Trefilov

Club Directory

Pengrowth Saddledome

Calgary Flames
Pengrowth Saddledome
P.O. Box 1540 Station M
Calgary, Alberta T2P 3B9
Phone **403/777-4636**
FAX 403/777-2171
www.calgaryflames.com
Capacity: 17,439

Owners: N. Murray Edwards (Chairman), Harley N. Hotchkiss, Alvin G. Libin, Allan P. Markin, Jeff McCaig, Clayton H. Riddell, Byron J. Seaman, Daryl K. Seaman

Executive
President & Chief Executive Officer . . . . Ken King
General Manager & Head Coach . . . . Darryl Sutter
Vice President, Hockey Administration . . . . Michael Holditch
Vice-President, Building Operations . . . . Libby Raines
Vice President, Advertising, Sponsorship
and Marketing . . . . Jim Bagshaw
Vice-President, Sales . . . . Rollie Cyr
Vice-President, Communications . . . . Peter Hanlon
Vice-President, Business Development . . . . Jim Peplinski

Hockey Club Personnel
Head Coach & General Manager . . . . Darryl Sutter
Vice President, Hockey Admin./CFO . . . . Michael Holditch
Director, Hockey Administration . . . . Mike Burke
Assistant Coaches . . . . Jim Playfair, Rich Preston, Rob Cookson
Goaltending Coach . . . . David Marcoux
Team Services Manager . . . . Kelly Chesla
Exec. Asst. to GM and Hockey Ops. . . . . Brenda Koyich
Director of Scouting . . . . Tod Button
Director of Amateur Scouting . . . . Mike Sands
Western Pro Scout . . . . Ron Sutter
Eastern Pro Scout . . . . Tom Webster
Scouts . . . . Tomas Jelinek, Sergei Samoilov, Al Tuer, Craig
Demetrick, Fred Devereaux, Randy Hansch,
Ralph Schmidt, Anders Steen, Rich Thibeau
President, Omaha/Asst. GM Calgary . . . . Doug Soetaert
Head Coach, Omaha . . . . Ryan McGill
Assistant Coach, Omaha . . . . Scott Allen

Medical/Training Staff
Athletic Therapist . . . . Morris Boyer
Assistant Athletic Therapist . . . . Gerry Kurylowich
Strength & Conditioning Coach . . . . Rich Hesketh
Equipment Manager . . . . Gus Thorson
Assistant Equipment Manager . . . . Les Jarvis
Team Physician . . . . Dr. Kelly Brett
Team Physician . . . . Dr. Jim Thorne
Team Dentist . . . . Dr. Bill Blair
Dressing Room Attendant . . . . Jules Carriere
Visiting Dressing Room Attendant . . . . Garland Auvigne

Communications
Vice-President, Communications . . . . Peter Hanlon
Manager, Media Relations . . . . Sean O'Brien
Administrative Assistant, Communications . . . . Bernie Hargrave

Administration
Director of Financial Reporting . . . . Lisa Gutierrez
Controller . . . . Karen Kingham
Exec. Asst. to President/CEO . . . . Judy O'Brien
Exec. Asst. to VP Hockey Admin./CFO . . . . Jill Laws

Marketing/Ticketing
Senior Director, Advertising . . . . Pat Halls
Director, Corporate Sponsorship . . . . Kevin Gross
Corporate, Key Account Manager . . . . Mark Stiles
Advertising/Promotions Manager . . . . Cheryl Sundell
Executive Assistant Marketing . . . . Yvette Mutcheson
Director, Executive Suites . . . . Bob White
Sales Manager . . . . Mike Franco
Customer Service Manager . . . . Marc Leost
Director/Producer, Jumbotron . . . . Carlo Petrini
Entertainment Coordinator . . . . Steve Johnston
Director, Retail/FanAttic. . . . . Kevin Lawton
Publishing . . . . Laurie Wheeler
Mascot . . . . Harvey the Hound

Pengrowth Saddledome
Operations Manager . . . . George Greenwood
Director, Food Services . . . . Art Hernandez
Concessions Manager . . . . Sheila Parisien
Security/Parking Manager . . . . Bob Godun

Miscellaneous Data
Radio Affiliate . . . . The FAN 960 (960 AM)
TV Affiliate . . . . Rogers Sportsnet, CBC-TV, PPV, TSN

Captains' History
Keith McCreary, 1972-73 to 1974-75; Pat Quinn, 1975-76, 1976-77; Tom Lysiak, 1977-78, 1978-79; Jean Pronovost, 1979-80; Brad Marsh, 1980-81; Phil Russell, 1981-82, 1982-83; Lanny McDonald, Doug Risebrough (co-captains), 1983-84; Lanny McDonald, Doug Risebrough, Jim Peplinski (tri-captains), 1984-85 to 1986-87; Lanny McDonald, Jim Peplinski (co-captains), 1987-88; Lanny McDonald, Jim Peplinski, Tim Hunter (tri-captains), 1988-89; Brad McCrimmon, 1989-90; alternating captains, 1990-91; Joe Nieuwendyk, 1991-92 to 1994-95; Theoren Fleury, 1995-96, 1996-97; Todd Simpson, 1997-98, 1998-99; Steve Smith, 1999-2000; Steve Smith and Dave Lowry, 2000-01; Dave Lowry; Bob Boughner and Craig Conroy (co-captains), 2001-02; Bob Boughner and Craig Conroy (co-captains), 2002-03; Jarome Iginla, 2003-04 to date.

Carolina Hurricanes

2005-06 Schedule

Oct.	Wed.	5	at Tampa Bay		Tue.	10	Detroit
	Fri.	7	Pittsburgh		Fri.	13	Nashville
	Sat.	8	at NY Islanders		Sun.	15	St. Louis*
	Wed.	12	Washington		Tue.	17	at Philadelphia
	Sat.	15	at New Jersey		Thu.	19	NY Islanders
	Thu.	20	at Toronto		Sat.	21	at Washington
	Sat.	22	at Washington		Mon.	23	Montreal
	Mon.	24	Ottawa		Wed.	25	at Florida
	Wed.	26	Boston		Thu.	26	at Atlanta
	Fri.	28	Philadelphia		Sat.	28	Atlanta
	Sat.	29	at Pittsburgh		Tue.	31	at Montreal
Nov.	Thu.	3	Toronto	Feb.	Fri.	3	at New Jersey
	Sat.	5	Florida		Sun.	5	at Boston*
	Wed.	9	at Buffalo		Thu.	9	at Tampa Bay
	Fri.	11	at Florida		Fri.	10	Pittsburgh
	Sat.	12	Atlanta		Sun.	12	Buffalo*
	Tue.	15	at Ottawa	Mar.	Wed.	1	Boston
	Thu.	17	NY Rangers		Fri.	3	Florida
	Sat.	19	at NY Rangers*		Sat.	4	at Pittsburgh
	Sun.	20	Tampa Bay		Mon.	6	at NY Rangers
	Tue.	22	Ottawa		Wed.	8	at Philadelphia
	Fri.	25	Toronto		Sat.	11	at Florida
	Sun.	27	Atlanta*		Sun.	12	at Florida*
	Tue.	29	at Atlanta		Tue.	14	NY Rangers
Dec.	Fri.	2	at Dallas		Thu.	16	at Montreal
	Sat.	3	at Phoenix		Sat.	18	at Boston*
	Tue.	6	at Anaheim		Tue.	21	at Toronto
	Thu.	8	at Los Angeles		Wed.	22	at Buffalo
	Sat.	10	at San Jose		Sat.	25	Washington
	Tue.	13	Chicago		Mon.	27	Tampa Bay
	Thu.	15	Columbus		Wed.	29	Washington
	Sat.	17	New Jersey		Fri.	31	Florida
	Tue.	20	Tampa Bay	Apr.	Sat.	1	at Atlanta
	Fri.	23	Florida		Mon.	3	Washington
	Mon.	26	at Tampa Bay		Wed.	5	at Washington
	Wed.	28	at Ottawa		Fri.	7	at Washington
	Thu.	29	Philadelphia		Sat.	8	at Atlanta
	Sat.	31	Montreal		Tue.	11	New Jersey
Jan.	Wed.	4	Atlanta		Fri.	14	Tampa Bay
	Fri.	6	NY Islanders		Sat.	15	at Tampa Bay
	Sat.	7	at NY Islanders		Tue.	18	Buffalo

Denotes afternoon game.

Glen Wesley enters the 2005-06 season just five games behind Kevin Dineen's 708 played for second all-time in Hurricanes history. Ron Francis is the franchise leader at 1,118.

Franchise date: June 22, 1979
Transferred from Hartford to Carolina, June 25, 1997.

SOUTHEAST DIVISION

27th NHL Season

Year-by-Year Record

		Home				Road				Overall							
Season	GP	W	L	T	OL	W	L	T	OL	W	L	T	OL	GF	GA	Pts.	Finished	Playoff Result
2004-05	....	....				....				....				....	....	....		
2003-04	82	13	18	8	2	15	16	6	4	28	34	14	6	172	209	76	3rd, Southeast Div.	Out of Playoffs
2002-03	82	12	17	9	3	10	26	2	3	22	43	11	6	171	240	61	5th, Southeast Div.	Out of Playoffs
2001-02	82	15	13	11	2	20	13	5	3	35	26	16	5	217	217	91	1st, Southeast Div.	Lost Final
2000-01	82	23	15	3	0	15	17	6	3	38	32	9	3	212	225	88	2nd, Southeast Div.	Lost Conf. Quarter-Final
1999-2000	82	20	16	5	0	17	19	5	0	37	35	10	0	217	216	84	3rd, Southeast Div.	Out of Playoffs
1998-99	82	20	12	9	....	14	18	9	....	34	30	18	....	210	202	86	1st, Southeast Div.	Lost Conf. Quarter-Final
1997-98	82	16	18	7	....	17	23	1	....	33	41	8	....	200	219	74	6th, Northeast Div.	Out of Playoffs
1996-97*	82	23	15	3	....	9	24	8	....	32	39	11	....	226	256	75	5th, Northeast Div.	Out of Playoffs
1995-96*	82	22	15	4	....	12	24	5	....	34	39	9	....	237	259	77	4th, Northeast Div.	Out of Playoffs
1994-95*	48	12	10	2	....	7	14	3	....	19	24	5	....	127	141	43	5th, Northeast Div.	Out of Playoffs
1993-94*	84	14	22	6	....	13	26	3	....	27	48	9	....	227	288	63	6th, Northeast Div.	Out of Playoffs
1992-93*	84	12	25	5	....	14	27	1	....	26	52	6	....	284	369	58	5th, Adams Div.	Out of Playoffs
1991-92*	80	13	17	10	....	13	24	3	....	26	41	13	....	247	283	65	4th, Adams Div.	Lost Div. Semi-Final
1990-91*	80	18	16	6	....	13	22	5	....	31	38	11	....	238	276	73	4th, Adams Div.	Lost Div. Semi-Final
1989-90*	80	17	18	5	....	21	15	4	....	38	33	9	....	275	268	85	4th, Adams Div.	Lost Div. Semi-Final
1988-89*	80	21	17	2	....	16	21	3	....	37	38	5	....	299	290	79	4th, Adams Div.	Lost Div. Semi-Final
1987-88*	80	21	14	5	....	14	24	2	....	35	38	7	....	249	267	77	4th, Adams Div.	Lost Div. Semi-Final
1986-87*	80	26	9	5	....	17	21	2	....	43	30	7	....	287	270	93	1st, Adams Div.	Lost Div. Semi-Final
1985-86*	80	21	17	2	....	19	19	2	....	40	36	4	....	332	302	84	4th, Adams Div.	Lost Div. Final
1984-85*	80	17	18	5	....	13	23	4	....	30	41	9	....	268	318	69	5th, Adams Div.	Out of Playoffs
1983-84*	80	19	16	5	....	9	26	5	....	28	42	10	....	288	320	66	5th, Adams Div.	Out of Playoffs
1982-83*	80	13	22	5	....	6	32	2	....	19	54	7	....	261	403	45	5th, Adams Div.	Out of Playoffs
1981-82*	80	13	17	10	....	8	24	8	....	21	41	18	....	264	351	60	5th, Adams Div.	Out of Playoffs
1980-81*	80	14	17	9	....	7	24	9	....	21	41	18	....	292	372	60	4th, Norris Div.	Out of Playoffs
1979-80*	80	22	12	6	....	5	22	13	....	27	34	19	....	303	312	73	4th, Norris Div.	Lost Prelim. Round

* Hartford Whalers

2005-06 Player Personnel

FORWARDS	HT	WT	S	Place of Birth	Date	2004-05 Club
ADAMS, Kevyn	6-1	195	R	Washington, DC	10/8/74	Dusseldorf
AUCOIN, Keith	5-9	185	R	Waltham, MA	11/6/78	Memphis-Providence (AHL)
BOULERICE, Jesse	6-2	215	R	Plattsburgh, NY	8/10/78	
BRENDL, Pavel	6-1	204	R	Opocno, Czech.	3/23/81	Trinec-Olomouc-Jokipojat-Thurgau
BRIND'AMOUR, Rod	6-1	200	L	Ottawa, Ont.	8/9/70	Kloten
COLE, Erik	6-2	200	L	Oswego, NY	11/6/78	Eisbaren Berlin
CULLEN, Matt	6-2	218	L	Virginia, MN	11/2/76	Cortina
DWYER, Gordie	6-3	215	L	Dalhousie, N.B.	1/25/78	Lowell
FORBES, Colin	6-3	215	L	New Westminster, B.C.	2/16/76	Lowell
GOVE, David	5-9	190	L	Centerville, MA	5/4/78	Providence (AHL)
LADD, Andrew	6-2	200	L	Maple Ridge, B.C.	12/12/85	Calgary (WHL)
LaROSE, Chad	5-10	173	R	Fraser, MI	3/27/82	Lowell
STAAL, Eric	6-3	200	L	Thunder Bay, Ont.	10/29/84	Lowell
STILLMAN, Cory	6-0	194	L	Peterborough, Ont.	12/20/73	
VASICEK, Josef	6-4	210	L	Havlickuv Brod, Czech.	9/12/80	Slavia
VRBATA, Radim	6-1	190	R	Mlada Boleslav, Czech.	6/13/81	Liberec
WHITNEY, Ray	5-10	178	R	Fort Saskatchewan, Alta.	5/8/72	
WILLIAMS, Justin	6-1	190	R	Cobourg, Ont.	10/4/81	Lulea
ZIGOMANIS, Mike	6-1	200	R	North York, Ont.	1/17/81	Lowell

DEFENSEMEN	HT	WT	S	Place of Birth	Date	2004-05 Club
COMMODORE, Mike	6-4	230	R	Fort Saskatchewan, Alta.	11/7/79	Lowell
HAJT, Chris	6-3	206	L	Saskatoon, Sask.	7/5/78	Portland (AHL)-Augusta
HEDICAN, Bret	6-2	205	L	St. Paul, MN	8/10/70	
HUTCHINSON, Andrew	6-2	204	R	Evanston, IL	3/24/80	Milwaukee
JOHNSON, Jack	6-1	201	L	Indianapolis, IN	1/13/87	USA U-18
KABERLE, Frantisek	6-1	190	L	Kladno, Czech.	11/8/73	Kladno-MODO
RICHMOND, Danny	6-0	190	L	Chicago, IL	8/1/84	Lowell
ST. JACQUES, Bruno	6-2	210	L	Montreal, Que.	8/22/80	Lowell
TVERDOVSKY, Oleg	6-1	205	L	Donetsk, USSR	5/18/76	Omsk
WALLIN, Niclas	6-3	220	L	Boden, Sweden	2/20/75	Lulea
WARD, Aaron	6-2	225	R	Windsor, Ont.	1/17/73	Ingolstadt
WESLEY, Glen	6-1	205	L	Red Deer, Alta.	10/2/68	

GOALTENDERS	HT	WT	C	Place of Birth	Date	2004-05 Club
GERBER, Martin	6-0	185	L	Burgdorf, Switz.	9/3/74	Langnau-Farjestad
NASTIUK, Kevin	6-2	176	L	Edmonton, Alta.	7/20/85	Medicine Hat
WARD, Cam	6-0	176	L	Sherwood Park, Alta.	2/29/84	Lowell

In the System and Recently Drafted

FORWARDS	HT	WT	S	Place of Birth	Date	2004-05 Club
BARNES, Joe	6-3	212	L	Winnipeg, Man.	6/16/86	Saskatoon
BLANCHARD, Nicolas	6-3	176	L	Granby, Que.	5/31/87	Chicoutimi
ESTRADA, Kevin	5-11	185	L	Surrey, B.C.	5/28/82	Michigan State
FIEDLER, Jonas	6-2	177	R	Jihlava, Czech.	5/29/84	Plymouth-Florida (ECHL)
KAHNBERG, Magnus	6-2	190	L	Kallered, Sweden	2/25/80	Frolunda
NORDGREN, Niklas	5-11	185	R	Ornskoldsvik, Sweden	6/28/79	Timra
OTCENAS, Ondrej	6-2	187	L	Piestany, Czech.	3/6/87	Trencin Jr.
TROJOVSKY, Matej	6-5	220	L	Plzen, Czech.	10/12/84	Swift Current-Pr. Geo.

DEFENSEMEN	HT	WT	S	Place of Birth	Date	2004-05 Club
BORER, Casey	6-2	197	L	Minneapolis, MN	7/28/85	St. Cloud State
CARSON, Brett	6-4	220	R	Regina, Sask.	11/29/85	Calgary (WHL)
HAGEMO, Nathan	5-11	192	R	Minneapolis, MN	10/8/86	U. of Minnesota
KORHONEN, Risto	6-3	202	L	Sotkamo, Finland	11/27/86	Karpat Jr.
KUNES, Timothy	6-1	170	L	Red Bank, N.J.	2/12/87	N.E. Jr. Falcons
LAWSON, Kyle	5-11	192	R	Southfield, MI	1/11/87	USA U-18
STRACHAN, Tyson	6-3	205	R	Melfort, Sask.	10/30/84	Ohio State
VAGNER, Martin	6-1	214	L	Jaromer, Czech.	3/16/84	Acadie-Bathurst
VOJTA, Jakub	6-0	194	R	Usti nad Labem, Czech.	2/8/87	Sparta Jr.
WALSER, Derrick	5-10	196	L	New Glasgow, N.S.	5/12/78	Eisbaren Berlin

GOALTENDERS	HT	WT	C	Place of Birth	Date	2004-05 Club
AKERLUND, Magnus	6-1	183	R	Osby, Sweden	4/25/86	HV 71-Skovde
KOWALSKI, Craig	5-10	190	L	Warren, MI	1/15/81	Florida (ECHL)
MANZATO, Daniel	6-0	178	L	Fribourg, Switz.	1/17/84	Ambri
PETERS, Justin	6-0	209	L	Blyth, Ont.	8/30/86	St. Michael's

Coaching History

Don Blackburn, 1979-80; Don Blackburn and Larry Pleau, 1980-81; Larry Pleau, 1981-82; Larry Kish, Larry Pleau and John Cuniff, 1982- 83; Jack Evans, 1983-84 to 1986-87; Jack Evans and Larry Pleau, 1987-88; Larry Pleau, 1988-89; Rick Ley, 1989-90, 1990-91; Jim Roberts, 1991-92; Paul Holmgren, 1992-93; Paul Holmgren and Pierre Maguire, 1993-94; Paul Holmgren, 1994-95; Paul Holmgren and Paul Maurice, 1995-96; Paul Maurice, 1996-97 to 2002-03; Paul Maurice and Peter Laviolette, 2003-04; Peter Laviolette, 2004-05 to date.

Coach

LAVIOLETTE, PETER
Coach, Carolina Hurricanes. Born in Norwood, MA, December 7, 1964

On December 15, 2003 the Carolina Hurricanes made Peter Laviolette the 11th head coach in team history. Laviolette most recently coached the New York Islanders during the 2001-02 and 2002-03 seasons, and led the Islanders to the playoffs both seasons after the team missed the postseason seven straight times between 1994 and 2001.

Prior to joining the Islanders, Laviolette served as an assistant coach with the Boston Bruins after two years of guiding Boston's AHL affiliate, Providence. In 1998-99, Laviolette led the Providence Bruins to a 56-16-8 regular-season record, and a 15-4 playoff record that culminated with Providence hoisting the Calder Cup and Laviolette being named AHL coach of the year.

Laviolette played 11 seasons of professional hockey, mostly in the AHL and IHL, but did play 12 games with the New York Rangers during the 1988-89 season. He was a member of the 1988 and 1994 U.S. Olympic hockey teams, and captained the 1994 Olympic squad.

In the spring of 2004, Laviolette helped assure the United States a spot in the 2006 Olympic Games in Torino, Italy, when he guided Team USA to a bronze medal at the 2004 World Championship in the Czech Republic. He also served as an assistant to San Jose Sharks head coach Ron Wilson behind the bench for Team USA in the 2004 World Cup of Hockey and was head coach again at the 2005 World Championship.

Coaching Record

			Regular Season			Playoffs		
Season	Team	Games	W	L	T	Games	W	L
1997-98	Wheeling (ECHL)	70	37	24	9	15	8	7
1998-99	Providence (AHL)	80	56	16	8	19	15	4
1999-00	Providence (AHL)	80	33	38	9	14	10	4
2001-02	NY Islanders (NHL)	82	42	32	8	7	3	4
2002-03	NY Islanders (NHL)	82	35	36	11	5	1	4
2003-04	Carolina (NHL)	52	20	26	6	....	....	....
2004-05	Carolina (NHL)				Season Cancelled			
	NHL Totals	216	97	94	25	12	4	8

Carolina marks Cory Stillman's fourth NHL stop, having played previously with Calgary, St. Louis and Tampa Bay. He had a career year with the Lightning in 2003-04.

Captains' History

Rick Ley, 1979-80; Rick Ley and Mike Rogers, 1980-81; Dave Keon, 1981-82; Russ Anderson, 1982-83; Mark Johnson, 1983-84; Mark Johnson and Ron Francis, 1984-85; Ron Francis, 1985-86 to 1990-91; Randy Ladouceur, 1991-92; Pat Verbeek, 1992-93 to 1994-95; Brendan Shanahan, 1995-96; Kevin Dineen, 1996-97, 1997-98; Keith Primeau, 1998-99; Keith Primeau and Ron Francis, 1999-2000; Ron Francis, 2000-01 to 2003-04; Rod Brind'Amour, 2005-06.

Club Records

Team

(Figures in brackets for season records are games played; records for fewest points, wins, ties, losses, goals, goals against are for 70 or more games)

Most Points	93	1986-87 (80)
Most Wins	43	1986-87 (80)
Most Ties	19	1979-80 (80)
Most Losses	54	1982-83 (80)
Most Goals	332	1985-86 (80)
Most Goals Against	403	1982-83 (80)
Fewest Points	45	1982-83 (80)
Fewest Wins	19	1982-83 (80)
Fewest Ties	4	1985-86 (80)
Fewest Losses	26	2001-02 (82)
Fewest Goals	171	2002-03 (82)
Fewest Goals Against	202	1998-99 (82)

Longest Winning Streak
Overall	7	Mar. 16-29/85
Home	5	Mar. 17-29/85
Away	6	Nov. 10-Dec. 7/90

Longest Undefeated Streak
Overall	10	Jan. 20-Feb. 10/82 (6 wins, 4 ties)
Home	9	Dec. 15/00-Jan. 18/01 (8 wins, 1 tie)
Away	8	Nov. 11-Dec. 5/96 (4 wins, 4 ties)

Longest Losing Streak
Overall	9	Feb. 19-Mar. 8/83
Home	6	Feb. 19-Mar. 12/83, Feb. 10-Mar. 3/85
Away	13	Dec. 18/82-Feb. 5/83

Longest Winless Streak
Overall	14	Jan. 4-Feb. 9/92 (8 losses, 6 ties)
Home	13	Jan. 15-Mar. 10/85 (11 losses, 2 ties)
Away	15	Nov. 11/79-Jan. 9/80 (11 losses, 4 ties)

Most Shutouts, Season	8	1998-99 (82)
Most PIM, Season	2,354	1992-93 (84)
Most Goals, Game	11	Feb. 12/84 (Edm. 0 at Hfd. 11), Oct. 19/85 (Mtl. 6 at Hfd. 11), Jan. 17/86 (Que. 6 at Hfd. 11), Mar. 15/86 (Chi. 4 at Hfd. 11)

Individual

Most Seasons	16	Ron Francis
Most Games	1,186	Ron Francis
Most Goals, Career	382	Ron Francis
Most Assists, Career	793	Ron Francis
Most Points, Career	1,175	Ron Francis (382G, 793A)
Most PIM, Career	1,439	Kevin Dineen
Most Shutouts, Career	20	Arturs Irbe
Longest Consecutive Games Streak	419	Dave Tippett (Mar. 3/84-Oct. 7/89)
Most Goals, Season	56	Blaine Stoughton (1979-80)
Most Assists, Season	69	Ron Francis (1989-90)
Most Points, Season	105	Mike Rogers (1979-80; 44G, 61A), (1980-81; 40G, 65A)
Most PIM, Season	358	Torrie Robertson (1985-86)

Most Points, Defenseman, Season	69	Dave Babych (1985-86; 14G, 55A)
Most Points, Center, Season	105	Mike Rogers (1979-80; 44G, 61A), (1980-81; 40G, 65A)
Most Points, Right Wing, Season	100	Blaine Stoughton (1979-80; 56G, 44A)
Most Points, Left Wing, Season	89	Geoff Sanderson (1992-93; 46G, 43A)
Most Points, Rookie, Season	72	Sylvain Turgeon (1983-84; 40G, 32A)
Most Shutouts, Season	6	Arturs Irbe (1998-99, 2000-01), Kevin Weekes (2003-04)
Most Goals, Game	4	Jordy Douglas (Feb. 3/80), Ron Francis (Feb. 12/84)
Most Assists, Game	6	Ron Francis (Mar. 5/87)
Most Points, Game	6	Paul Lawless (Jan. 4/87; 2G, 4A), Ron Francis (Mar. 5/87; 6A), (Oct. 8/89; 3G, 3A)

Records include Hartford Whalers, 1979-80 through 1996-97.

All-time Record vs. Other Clubs

Regular Season

	At Home								On Road								Total							
	GP	W	L	T	OL	GF	GA	PTS	GP	W	L	T	OL	GF	GA	PTS	GP	W	L	T	OL	GF	GA	PTS
Anaheim	9	5	3	1	0	23	19	11	9	3	5	1	0	26	29	7	18	8	8	2	0	49	48	18
Atlanta	13	10	2	1	0	47	31	21	13	8	1	3	1	38	30	20	26	18	3	4	1	85	61	41
Boston	76	31	36	9	0	252	263	71	78	25	46	7	0	207	274	57	154	56	82	16	0	459	537	128
Buffalo	78	32	35	11	0	227	230	75	77	24	45	7	1	226	309	56	155	56	80	18	1	453	539	131
Calgary	28	10	13	5	0	91	103	25	29	6	21	2	0	92	140	14	57	16	34	7	0	183	243	39
Chicago	30	14	12	4	0	97	93	32	29	10	16	3	0	83	117	23	59	24	28	7	0	180	210	55
Colorado	62	23	25	12	1	203	214	61	65	17	39	9	0	191	274	43	127	41	64	21	1	394	488	104
Columbus	4	3	1	0	0	13	11	6	3	2	1	0	0	9	6	4	7	5	2	0	0	22	17	10
Dallas	32	13	15	4	0	101	110	30	29	10	16	2	1	86	115	23	61	23	31	6	1	187	225	53
Detroit	30	17	12	1	0	104	86	35	31	7	16	7	1	86	119	22	61	24	28	8	1	190	205	57
Edmonton	29	11	11	7	0	112	98	29	31	7	19	5	0	92	121	19	60	18	30	12	0	204	219	48
Florida	25	13	9	3	0	73	63	29	26	7	10	8	1	55	74	23	51	20	19	11	1	128	137	52
Los Angeles	31	15	11	5	0	114	115	35	30	10	17	3	0	113	129	23	61	25	28	8	0	227	244	58
Minnesota	2	2	0	0	0	3	0	4	4	1	1	2	0	12	9	4	6	3	1	2	0	15	9	8
Montreal	78	29	36	13	0	224	268	71	75	18	49	7	1	213	309	44	153	47	85	20	1	437	577	115
Nashville	5	2	1	1	1	14	13	6	4	1	3	0	0	7	9	2	9	3	4	1	1	21	22	8
New Jersey	44	18	18	8	0	137	132	44	45	16	24	4	1	140	158	37	89	34	42	12	1	277	290	81
NY Islanders	45	21	18	5	1	152	148	48	44	20	19	4	1	121	132	45	89	41	37	9	2	273	280	93
NY Rangers	43	24	16	3	0	145	137	51	45	14	27	4	0	115	172	32	88	38	43	7	0	260	309	83
Ottawa	27	16	7	4	0	81	65	36	29	13	12	4	0	78	81	30	56	29	19	8	0	159	146	66
Philadelphia	44	13	21	9	1	140	158	36	43	9	27	5	2	107	162	25	87	22	48	14	3	247	320	61
Phoenix	30	14	10	6	0	103	89	34	31	15	14	2	0	112	110	32	61	29	24	8	0	215	199	66
Pittsburgh	48	22	21	5	0	178	177	49	46	17	22	6	1	170	185	41	94	39	43	11	1	348	362	90
St. Louis	31	12	17	2	0	92	97	26	31	9	18	3	1	94	119	22	62	21	35	5	1	186	216	48
San Jose	11	6	5	0	0	34	23	12	11	4	7	0	0	31	50	8	22	10	12	0	0	65	73	20
Tampa Bay	27	15	4	7	1	81	65	38	26	9	14	3	0	67	73	21	53	24	18	10	1	148	138	59
Toronto	37	18	12	6	1	144	119	43	36	18	13	5	0	126	120	41	73	36	25	11	1	270	239	84
Vancouver	29	12	12	5	0	94	100	29	30	10	13	6	1	81	105	27	59	22	25	11	1	175	205	56
Washington	49	15	23	10	1	128	152	41	47	14	29	4	0	118	163	32	96	29	52	14	1	246	315	73
Totals	**997**	**437**	**406**	**147**	**7**	**3207**	**3179**	**1028**	**997**	**324**	**544**	**116**	**13**	**2896**	**3694**	**777**	**1994**	**761**	**950**	**263**	**20**	**6103**	**6873**	**1805**

Playoffs

	Series	W	L	GP	W	L	T	GF	GA	Last Mtg.
Boston	3	0	3	19	7	12	0	48	63	1999
Colorado	2	1	1	9	5	4	0	35	34	1987
Detroit	1	0	1	5	1	4	0	7	14	2002
Montreal	6	1	5	33	12	21	0	91	108	2002
New Jersey	2	1	1	12	6	6	0	17	31	2002
Toronto	1	1	0	6	4	2	0	10	6	2002
Totals	**15**	**4**	**11**	**84**	**35**	**49**	**0**	**208**	**256**	

Playoff Results 2005-2000

Year	Round	Opponent	Result	GF	GA
2002	F	Detroit	L 1-4	7	14
	CF	Toronto	W 4-2	10	6
	CSF	Montreal	W 4-2	21	12
	CQF	New Jersey	W 4-2	9	11
2001	CQF	New Jersey	L 2-4	8	20

Abbreviations: Round: F - Final; **CF** - conference final; **CSF** - conference semi-final; **CQF** - conference quarter-final; **DSF** - division semi-final.

Calgary totals include Atlanta Flames, 1979-80.
Dallas totals include Minnesota North Stars, 1979-80 to 1992-93.
Phoenix totals include Winnipeg, 1979-80 to 1995-96.

Colorado totals include Quebec, 1979-80 to 1994-95.
New Jersey totals include Colorado Rockies, 1979-80 to 1981-82.

Key Off-Season Signings/Acquisitions

2004
May 13 • Signed 2002 1st-round pick (25th overall), G **Cam Ward**.

June 18 • Obtained G **Martin Gerber** from Anaheim for D **Tomas Malec** and a 2004 3rd-round pick.

July 15 • Re-signed D **Niclas Wallin**.
 15 • Signed D **Frantisek Kaberle**.

2005
July 29 • Obtained D **Mike Commodore** from Calgary for a 2005 3rd-round pick.

 31 • Selected D **Jack Johnson** (U.S. National Under-18 Team) with the 3rd overall pick in the 2005 Entry Draft.

Aug. 2 • Signed LW **Cory Stillman**.
 4 • Signed D **Oleg Tverdovsky**.
 7 • Signed LW **Ray Whitney**.
 8 • Signed C **Matt Cullen**.
 9 • Re-signed C **Kevyn Adams**.
 10 • Re-signed RWs **Radim Vrbata** and **Justin Williams**.
 12 • Re-signed LW **Erik Cole** and RW **Jesse Boulerice**.
 15 • Re-signed RW **Pavel Brendl** and D **Bruno St. Jacques**.
 16 • Re-signed D **Glen Wesley**.
 18 • Re-signed F **Josef Vasicek**.

Entry Draft
Selections 2005-1991

2005
Pick
3	Jack Johnson
58	Nathan Hagemo
64	Joe Barnes
94	Jakub Vojta
123	Ondrej Otcenas
145	Timothy Kunes
159	Risto Korhonen
192	Nicolas Blanchard
198	Kyle Lawson

2004
Pick
4	Andrew Ladd
38	Justin Peters
69	Casey Borer
109	Brett Carson
137	Magnus Akerlund
202	Ryan Pottruff
235	Jonas Fiedler
268	Martin Vagner

2003
Pick
2	Eric Staal
31	Danny Richmond
102	Aaron Dawson
126	Kevin Nastiuk
130	Matej Trojovsky
137	Tyson Strachan
198	Shay Stephenson
230	Jamie Hoffmann
262	Ryan Rorabeck

2002
Pick
25	Cam Ward
91	Jesse Lane
160	Daniel Manzato
224	Adam Taylor

2001
Pick
15	Igor Knyazev
46	Mike Zigomanis
91	Kevin Estrada
110	Rob Zepp
181	Daniel Boisclair
211	Sean Curry
244	Carter Trevisani
274	Peter Reynolds

2000
Pick
32	Tomas Kurka
80	Ryan Bayda
97	Niclas Wallin
110	Jared Newman
181	J.D. Forrest
212	Magnus Kahnberg
235	Craig Kowalski
276	Troy Ferguson

1999
Pick
16	David Tanabe
49	Brett Lysak
84	Brad Fast
113	Ryan Murphy
174	Damian Surma
202	Jim Baxter
231	David Evans
237	Antti Jokela
259	Yevgeny Kurilin

1998
Pick
11	Jeff Heerema
70	Kevin Holdridge
71	Erik Cole
91	Josef Vasicek
93	Tommy Westlund
97	Chris Madden
184	Don Smith
208	Jaroslav Svoboda
211	Mark Kosick
239	Brent McDonald

1997
Pick
22	Nikos Tselios
28	Brad DeFauw
80	Francis Lessard
88	Shane Willis
142	Kyle Dafoe
169	Andrew Merrick
195	Niklas Nordgren
199	Randy Fitzgerald
225	Kent McDonell

1996
Pick
34	Trevor Wasyluk
61	Andrei Petrunin
88	Craig MacDonald
104	Steve Wasylko
116	Mark McMahon
143	Aaron Baker
171	Greg Kuznik
197	Kevin Marsh
223	Craig Adams
231	Ashkat Rakhmatullin

1995
Pick
13	Jean-Sebastien Giguere
35	Sergei Fedotov
85	Ian MacNeil
87	Sami Kapanen
113	Hugh Hamilton
165	Byron Ritchie
191	Milan Kostolny
217	Mike Rucinski

1994
Pick
5	Jeff O'Neill
83	Hnat Domenichelli
109	Ryan Risidore
187	Tom Buckley
213	Ashlin Halfnight
230	Matt Ball
239	Brian Regan
265	Steve Nimigon

1993
Pick
2	Chris Pronger
72	Marek Malik
84	Trevor Roenick
115	Nolan Pratt
188	Manny Legace
214	Dmitri Gorenko
240	Wes Swinson
266	Igor Chibirev

1992
Pick
9	Robert Petrovicky
47	Andrei Nikolishin
57	Jan Vopat
79	Kevin Smyth
81	Jason McBain
143	Jarrett Reid
153	Ken Belanger
177	Konstantin Korotkov
201	Greg Zwakman
225	Steven Halko
249	Joacim Esbjors

1991
Pick
9	Patrick Poulin
31	Martin Hamrlik
53	Todd Hall
59	Michael Nylander
75	Jim Storm
119	Mike Harding
141	Brian Mueller
163	Steve Yule
185	Chris Belanger
207	Jason Currie
229	Mike Santonelli
251	Rob Peters

General Managers' History

Jack Kelly, 1979-80, 1980-81; Larry Pleau, 1981-82, 1982-83; Emile Francis, 1983-84 to 1988-89; Eddie Johnston, 1989-90 to 1991-92; Brian Burke, 1992-93; Paul Holmgren, 1993-94; Jim Rutherford, 1994-95 to date.

President and General Manager

RUTHERFORD, JIM
President/General Manager, Carolina Hurricanes.
Born in Beeton, Ont., February 17, 1949.

Jim Rutherford, a former NHL goaltender, is the franchise's seventh general manager and the only general manager of the Carolina Hurricanes. Named to his position on June 28, 1994, Rutherford has always taken an aggressive approach towards improving the fortunes of the franchise through trades and the NHL draft. In 2002, the team reached the Stanley Cup Finals for the first time in history.

A veteran of 13 NHL seasons, Rutherford began his professional goaltending career in 1969 as a first-round selection of the Detroit Red Wings. While playing for Detroit, Pittsburgh, Toronto and Los Angeles, Rutherford collected 14 career shutouts. For five seasons he also served as the Red Wings' player representative. Rutherford also played for Team Canada at the World Championships in Vienna in 1977 and Moscow in 1979.

After his playing days with the Red Wings, Rutherford joined Compuware to serve as the director of hockey operations for Compuware Sports Corporation. Rutherford gained a wealth of experience in youth hockey and junior programs. As a former player, coach, and general manager, his ability to develop players and produce winning programs is widely respected throughout the hockey community.

He started his management career by guiding Compuware Sports Corporation's purchase of the Windsor Spitfires of the Ontario Hockey League in April of 1984. During the next four years, Rutherford acted as general manager of the Spitfires. After the Spitfires advanced to the 1988 Memorial Cup finals, Rutherford led Compuware's efforts to bring the first American-based OHL franchise to Detroit on December 11, 1989. Rutherford was voted the 1987 executive of the year in both the OHL and the Canadian Hockey League and won the OHL executive of the year award again in 1988.

Club Directory

RBC Center

Carolina Hurricanes
1400 Edwards Mill Rd.
Raleigh, NC   27607
Phone **919/467-7825**
FAX 919/462-0123
Tickets 1.866.NHL.CANES
www.carolinahurricanes.com
Capacity: 18,730

Executive Management
CEO/Owner/Governor	Peter Karmanos Jr.
President/General Manager	Jim Rutherford
General Partner	Thomas Thewes
Vice President of Operations/Assistant G.M.	Jason Karmanos
Chief Financial Officer	Mike Amendola
V.P. of Business Operations	Matt West
V.P./General Manager, RBC Center	Davin Olsen

Hockey Operations
Head Coach	Peter Laviolette
Assistant Coaches	Kevin McCarthy, Jeff Daniels
Goaltending Coach/Pro Scout	Greg Stefan
Director of Amateur Scouting	Sheldon Ferguson
Amateur Scouts	Tony MacDonald, Martin Madden, Bert Marshall
Director of Pro Scouting	Marshall Johnston
Pro Scouts	Claude Larose, Ron Smith
Video Coordinator	Chris Huffine
Head Athletic Therapist/ Strength Conditioning Coach	Peter Friesen
Associate Athletic Therapist	Chris Stewart
Equipment Managers	Wally Tatomir, Skip Cunningham, Bob Gorman
Lowell Lock Monsters Head Coach/G.M.	Tom Rowe
Team Services Manager	Brian Tatum
Hockey Event Coordinator	Kelly Kirwin
Motivational Consultant/Community Programs	Doris E. Barksdale

Administration
Receptionists	Mary Lou Ruetz, Janet Davis

Arena Operations
Assistant General Manager, RBC Center	Larry Perkins
Security Manager	Clinton Peterson
Parking Manager	Mike Alexander
Event Services Manager	Jeff Dow
Premium Services Manager	Mary Pat Mooney
Operations Manager	Dan McGowan
Facility Systems Manager	Rick Dunning
Director of Ticket Operations	Bill Nowicki
Box Office Manager	Joe Sousa
Arena Office Manager	Hilman Huskey

Communications
Director of Media Relations	Mike Sundheim
Manager of Media Relations	Kyle Hanlin
Community Relations Manager	Emma Bennett
Community Relations Coordinator	Anne Nelson
Community Relations Assistant	Michael King

Finance/Information Technology
Director of Arena Finance	William Traurig
Accounts Payable	Michael Arrington
Accounts Receivable	Patty Hilliard, Temika Smith-Harris
Payroll/Human Resources Coordinators	Carrie Hubinek, Irene Cantelli

Food and Beverage
Director of Food and Beverage	Michael Bekolay
Concessions Manager	Rick Rhodes
Assistant Concessions Manager/Group Coordinator	Barbara Couch
Chef De Cuisine	Dennis Atkinson, Carols Duclos

Marketing
Director of Marketing/Creative Services	Howard Sadel
Manager of Creative Services	Ben Aycock
Website Producer	David Pond
Graphic Designer	Kara Kelly
Junior Graphic Designer	Nick Kelley
Manager of Promotions and Fan Development	Doug Warf
Youth and Amateur Hockey Coordinator	Paul Strand
Promotions Assistant	John Chase
Mascot Coordinator	George Brown

Gale Force Media
Director, CanesVision and Wolfpack TV	Pete Soto
Producer, CanesVision and Wolfpack TV	Chris Hooks, Don Sill
Graphics Producer, CanesVision and Wolfpack TV	Stephen Rutherford

Merchandise
Retail Operations Manager	James Blitch

Sales
Director of Corporate, Advertising and Broadcast Sales	Mike Hurley
Sponsorship Sales Executives	Meredith Morgan, Paula McGraw, Derrick Pyke, Jessica Tennes
Director of Ticket Sales	Kyle Prairie
Account Executives, Ticket Sales	Peterson J. Avetta, Brian Kapusta, Michael Miller
Corporate and Premium Ticket Sales Executive	Kristin Ryan
Client Relations Executive	D.J. Ketchabaw
Client Relations Representatives	Megan Aukland, Matthew Horton
RBC Center Group Sales Manager	Brian Slais
Group Sales Representative	Dustin Kilpatrick
Ticket Sales Coordinator	Karen Prince

Broadcasters
Television Play-by-Play	John Forslund
Television Analyst	Tripp Tracy
Radio Play-by-Play	Chuck Kaiton
Cable TV Flagship	Fox Sports Net South
Radio Flagship	102.9 FM WWMY

Chicago Blackhawks

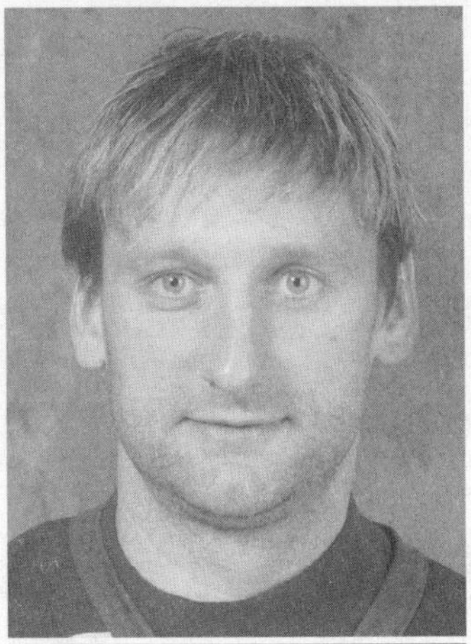

Newcomer Nikolai Khabibulin.

2005-06 Schedule

Month	Day	Date	Opponent
Oct.	Wed.	5	Anaheim
	Fri.	7	San Jose
	Sun.	9	Columbus
	Tue.	11	at St. Louis
	Fri.	14	at Colorado
	Sat.	15	at San Jose
	Tue.	18	at Vancouver
	Sun.	23	Minnesota
	Tue.	25	at Nashville
	Thu.	27	at Detroit
	Sat.	29	Detroit
Nov.	Tue.	1	at Detroit
	Wed.	2	at St. Louis
	Fri.	4	at Dallas
	Sun.	6	Phoenix
	Thu.	10	at St. Louis
	Fri.	11	Los Angeles
	Sun.	13	Edmonton
	Fri.	18	at Calgary
	Sat.	19	at Edmonton
	Tue.	22	at Vancouver
	Sat.	26	at Los Angeles
	Sun.	27	at Anaheim*
	Wed.	30	Los Angeles
Dec.	Fri.	2	at Tampa Bay
	Sat.	3	at Florida
	Wed.	7	NY Rangers
	Sun.	11	at Atlanta*
	Tue.	13	at Carolina
	Thu.	15	at Nashville
	Fri.	16	St. Louis
	Sun.	18	Dallas
	Wed.	21	Nashville
	Fri.	23	Detroit
	Mon.	26	at Columbus
	Wed.	28	St. Louis
	Fri.	30	Columbus
Jan.	Mon.	2	at Calgary*
	Tue.	3	at Edmonton
	Thu.	5	Vancouver
	Sun.	8	Nashville
	Tue.	10	at Washington
	Wed.	11	Philadelphia
	Fri.	13	Pittsburgh
	Sun.	15	New Jersey
	Tue.	17	NY Islanders
	Thu.	19	Colorado
	Fri.	20	at Minnesota
	Sun.	22	Minnesota
	Thu.	26	Calgary
	Sun.	29	Calgary*
Feb.	Thu.	2	at St. Louis
	Sat.	4	at Nashville*
	Tue.	7	at Phoenix
	Wed.	8	at San Jose
	Sat.	11	at Los Angeles*
	Sun.	12	at Anaheim*
Mar.	Wed.	1	Nashville
	Fri.	3	Vancouver
	Sun.	5	Dallas
	Tue.	7	at Columbus
	Thu.	9	Colorado
	Sat.	11	at Detroit
	Sun.	12	Detroit
	Wed.	15	Columbus
	Fri.	17	Anaheim
	Sun.	19	Phoenix*
	Thu.	23	at Phoenix
	Fri.	24	at Dallas
	Sun.	26	San Jose
	Wed.	29	St. Louis
	Fri.	31	at Detroit
Apr.	Sat.	1	at Columbus
	Mon.	3	at Colorado
	Wed.	5	Nashville
	Fri.	7	Edmonton
	Sat.	8	at Nashville
	Tue.	11	at Minnesota
	Thu.	13	Detroit
	Sat.	15	at Columbus
	Sun.	16	Columbus
	Tue.	18	St. Louis

* Denotes afternoon game.

Franchise date: September 25, 1926

WESTERN CONFERENCE
CENTRAL DIVISION

80th NHL Season

Year-by-Year Record

		Home				Road				Overall								
Season	GP	W	L	T	OL	W	L	T	OL	W	L	T	OL	GF	GA	Pts.	Finished	Playoff Result
2004-05	....	....	....	....	....	....	....	....	....	....	....	....	....	....	....	....		
2003-04	82	13	17	6	5	7	26	5	3	20	43	11	8	188	259	59	5th, Central Div.	Out of Playoffs
2002-03	82	17	15	7	2	13	18	6	4	30	33	13	6	207	226	79	3rd, Central Div.	Out of Playoffs
2001-02	82	28	7	5	1	13	20	8	0	41	27	13	1	216	207	96	3rd, Central Div.	Lost Conf. Quarter-Final
2000-01	82	14	21	4	2	15	19	4	3	29	40	8	5	210	246	71	4th, Central Div.	Out of Playoffs
1999-2000	82	16	19	5	1	17	18	5	1	33	37	10	2	242	245	78	3rd, Central Div.	Out of Playoffs
1998-99	82	20	17	4	....	9	24	8	....	29	41	12	....	202	248	70	3rd, Central Div.	Out of Playoffs
1997-98	82	14	19	8	....	16	20	5	....	30	39	13	....	192	199	73	5th, Central Div.	Out of Playoffs
1996-97	82	16	21	4	....	18	14	9	....	34	35	13	....	223	210	81	5th, Central Div.	Lost Conf. Quarter-Final
1995-96	82	22	13	6	....	18	15	8	....	40	28	14	....	273	220	94	2nd, Central Div.	Lost Conf. Semi-Final
1994-95	48	11	10	3	....	13	9	2	....	24	19	5	....	156	115	53	3rd, Central Div.	Lost Conf. Championship
1993-94	84	21	16	5	....	18	20	4	....	39	36	9	....	254	240	87	5th, Central Div.	Lost Conf. Quarter-Final
1992-93	84	25	11	6	....	22	14	6	....	47	25	12	....	279	230	106	1st, Norris Div.	Lost Div. Semi-Final
1991-92	80	23	9	8	....	13	20	7	....	36	29	15	....	257	236	87	2nd, Norris Div.	Lost Final
1990-91	80	28	8	4	....	21	15	4	....	49	23	8	....	284	211	106	1st, Norris Div.	Lost Div. Semi-Final
1989-90	80	25	13	2	....	16	20	4	....	41	33	6	....	316	294	88	1st, Norris Div.	Lost Conf. Championship
1988-89	80	16	14	10	....	11	27	2	....	27	41	12	....	297	335	66	4th, Norris Div.	Lost Conf. Championship
1987-88	80	21	17	2	....	9	24	7	....	30	41	9	....	284	328	69	3rd, Norris Div.	Lost Div. Semi-Final
1986-87	80	18	13	9	....	11	24	5	....	29	37	14	....	290	310	72	3rd, Norris Div.	Lost Div. Semi-Final
1985-86	80	23	12	5	....	16	21	3	....	39	33	8	....	351	349	86	1st, Norris Div.	Lost Div. Semi-Final
1984-85	80	22	16	2	....	16	19	5	....	38	35	7	....	309	299	83	2nd, Norris Div.	Lost Conf. Championship
1983-84	80	25	13	2	....	5	29	6	....	30	42	8	....	277	311	68	4th, Norris Div.	Lost Div. Semi-Final
1982-83	80	29	8	3	....	18	15	7	....	47	23	10	....	338	268	104	1st, Norris Div.	Lost Conf. Championship
1981-82	80	20	13	7	....	10	25	5	....	30	38	12	....	332	363	72	4th, Norris Div.	Lost Conf. Championship
1980-81	80	21	11	8	....	10	22	8	....	31	33	16	....	304	315	78	2nd, Smythe Div.	Lost Prelim. Round
1979-80	80	21	12	7	....	13	15	12	....	34	27	19	....	241	250	87	1st, Smythe Div.	Lost Quarter-Final
1978-79	80	18	12	10	....	11	24	5	....	29	36	15	....	244	277	73	1st, Smythe Div.	Lost Quarter-Final
1977-78	80	20	9	11	....	12	20	8	....	32	29	19	....	230	220	83	1st, Smythe Div.	Lost Quarter-Final
1976-77	80	19	16	5	....	7	27	6	....	26	43	11	....	240	298	63	3rd, Smythe Div.	Lost Prelim. Round
1975-76	80	17	15	8	....	15	15	10	....	32	30	18	....	254	261	82	1st, Smythe Div.	Lost Quarter-Final
1974-75	80	24	12	4	....	13	23	4	....	37	35	8	....	268	241	82	3rd, Smythe Div.	Lost Quarter-Final
1973-74	78	20	6	13	....	21	8	10	....	41	14	23	....	272	164	105	2nd, West Div.	Lost Semi-Final
1972-73	78	26	9	4	....	16	18	5	....	42	27	9	....	284	225	93	1st, West Div.	Lost Final
1971-72	78	28	3	8	....	18	14	7	....	46	17	15	....	256	166	107	1st, West Div.	Lost Semi-Final
1970-71	78	30	6	3	....	19	14	6	....	49	20	9	....	277	184	107	1st, West Div.	Lost Final
1969-70	76	26	7	5	....	19	15	4	....	45	22	9	....	250	170	99	1st, East Div.	Lost Semi-Final
1968-69	76	20	14	4	....	14	19	5	....	34	33	9	....	280	246	77	6th, East Div.	Out of Playoffs
1967-68	74	20	13	4	....	12	13	12	....	32	26	16	....	212	222	80	4th, East Div.	Lost Semi-Final
1966-67	70	24	5	6	....	17	12	6	....	41	17	12	....	264	170	94	1st,	Lost Semi-Final
1965-66	70	21	8	6	....	16	17	2	....	37	25	8	....	240	187	82	2nd,	Lost Semi-Final
1964-65	70	20	13	2	....	14	15	6	....	34	28	8	....	224	176	76	3rd,	Lost Final
1963-64	70	26	4	5	....	10	18	7	....	36	22	12	....	218	169	84	2nd,	Lost Semi-Final
1962-63	70	17	9	9	....	15	12	8	....	32	21	17	....	194	178	81	2nd,	Lost Semi-Final
1961-62	70	20	10	5	....	11	16	8	....	31	26	13	....	217	186	75	3rd,	Lost Final
1960-61	**70**	**20**	**6**	**9**	....	**9**	**18**	**8**	....	**29**	**24**	**17**	....	**198**	**180**	**75**	**3rd,**	**Won Stanley Cup**
1959-60	70	18	11	6	....	10	18	7	....	28	29	13	....	191	180	69	3rd,	Lost Semi-Final
1958-59	70	14	12	9	....	14	17	4	....	28	29	13	....	197	208	69	3rd,	Lost Semi-Final
1957-58	70	15	17	3	....	9	22	4	....	24	39	7	....	163	202	55	5th,	Out of Playoffs
1956-57	70	12	15	8	....	4	24	7	....	16	39	15	....	169	225	47	6th,	Out of Playoffs
1955-56	70	9	19	7	....	10	20	5	....	19	39	12	....	155	216	50	6th,	Out of Playoffs
1954-55	70	6	21	8	....	7	19	9	....	13	40	17	....	161	235	43	6th,	Out of Playoffs
1953-54	70	8	21	6	....	4	30	1	....	12	51	7	....	133	242	31	6th,	Out of Playoffs
1952-53	70	14	11	10	....	13	17	5	....	27	28	15	....	169	175	69	4th,	Lost Semi-Final
1951-52	70	9	19	7	....	8	25	2	....	17	44	9	....	158	241	43	6th,	Out of Playoffs
1950-51	70	8	22	5	....	5	25	5	....	13	47	10	....	171	280	36	6th,	Out of Playoffs
1949-50	70	13	18	4	....	9	20	6	....	22	38	10	....	203	244	54	6th,	Out of Playoffs
1948-49	60	13	12	5	....	8	19	3	....	21	31	8	....	173	211	50	5th,	Out of Playoffs
1947-48	60	10	17	3	....	10	17	3	....	20	34	6	....	195	225	46	6th,	Out of Playoffs
1946-47	60	10	17	3	....	9	20	1	....	19	37	4	....	193	274	42	6th,	Out of Playoffs
1945-46	50	15	5	5	....	8	15	2	....	23	20	7	....	200	178	53	3rd,	Lost Semi-Final
1944-45	50	9	14	2	....	4	16	5	....	13	30	7	....	141	194	33	5th,	Out of Playoffs
1943-44	50	15	6	4	....	7	17	1	....	22	23	5	....	178	187	49	4th,	Lost Final
1942-43	50	14	3	8	....	3	15	7	....	17	18	15	....	179	180	49	5th,	Out of Playoffs
1941-42	48	15	8	1	....	7	15	2	....	22	23	3	....	145	155	47	4th,	Lost Quarter-Final
1940-41	48	11	10	3	....	5	15	4	....	16	25	7	....	112	139	39	5th,	Lost Semi-Final
1939-40	48	15	7	2	....	8	12	4	....	23	19	6	....	112	120	52	4th,	Lost Quarter-Final
1938-39	48	5	13	6	....	7	15	2	....	12	28	8	....	91	132	32	7th,	Out of Playoffs
1937-38	**48**	**10**	**10**	**4**	....	**4**	**15**	**5**	....	**14**	**25**	**9**	....	**97**	**139**	**37**	**3rd, Amn. Div.**	**Won Stanley Cup**
1936-37	48	8	13	3	....	6	14	4	....	14	27	7	....	99	131	35	4th, Amn. Div.	Out of Playoffs
1935-36	48	15	7	2	....	6	12	6	....	21	19	8	....	93	92	50	3rd, Amn. Div.	Lost Quarter-Final
1934-35	48	12	9	3	....	14	8	2	....	26	17	5	....	118	88	57	2nd, Amn. Div.	Lost Quarter-Final
1933-34	**48**	**13**	**4**	**7**	....	**7**	**13**	**4**	....	**20**	**17**	**11**	....	**88**	**83**	**51**	**2nd, Amn. Div.**	**Won Stanley Cup**
1932-33	48	12	7	5	....	4	13	7	....	16	20	12	....	88	101	44	4th, Amn. Div.	Out of Playoffs
1931-32	48	13	5	6	....	5	14	5	....	18	19	11	....	86	101	47	2nd, Amn. Div.	Lost Quarter-Final
1930-31	44	13	8	1	....	11	9	2	....	24	17	3	....	108	78	51	2nd, Amn. Div.	Lost Final
1929-30	44	12	9	1	....	9	9	4	....	21	18	5	....	117	111	47	2nd, Amn. Div.	Lost Quarter-Final
1928-29	44	3	13	6	....	4	16	2	....	7	29	8	....	33	85	22	5th, Amn. Div.	Out of Playoffs
1927-28	44	2	18	2	....	5	16	1	....	7	34	3	....	68	134	17	5th, Amn. Div.	Out of Playoffs
1926-27	44	12	8	2	....	7	14	1	....	19	22	3	....	115	116	41	3rd, Amn. Div.	Lost Quarter-Final

2005-06 Player Personnel

FORWARDS	HT	WT	S	Place of Birth	Date	2004-05 Club
ARNASON, Tyler	5-11	192	L	Oklahoma City, OK	3/16/79	Brynas
BAINES, Ajay	5-10	179	L	Kamloops, B.C.	3/25/78	Norfolk
BARNABY, Matthew	6-0	189	L	Ottawa, Ont.	5/4/73	
BELL, Mark	6-4	205	L	St. Paul's, Ont.	8/5/80	Trondheim
BOLLAND, Dave	6-0	168	R	Toronto, Ont.	6/5/86	London
BOURQUE, Rene	6-2	205	L	Lac La Biche, Alta.	12/10/81	Norfolk
BROWN, Curtis	6-0	196	L	Unity, Sask.	2/12/76	San Diego
CALDER, Kyle	5-11	176	L	Mannville, Alta.	1/5/79	Sodertalje
CULLEN, Mark	5-11	175	L	Moorhead, MN	10/28/78	Houston
DAZE, Eric	6-6	235	L	Montreal, Que.	7/2/75	
DOWD, Jim	6-1	190	R	Brick, NJ	12/25/68	Hamburg
ELLISON, Matt	6-0	192	R	Duncan, B.C.	12/8/83	Norfolk
FRASER, Colin	6-1	182	L	Sicamous, B.C.	1/28/85	Red Deer-Norfolk
HOLMQVIST, Mikael	6-3	205	L	Stockholm, Sweden	6/8/79	Cincinnati (AHL)
KEITH, Matt	6-2	200	R	Edmonton, Alta.	4/11/83	Norfolk
LAING, Quintin	6-2	175	L	Rosetown, Sask.	6/8/79	Norfolk
LAPOINTE, Martin	5-11	215	R	Ville St-Pierre, Que.	9/12/73	
MORGAN, Jason	6-1	200	L	St. John's, Nfld.	10/9/76	Norfolk
RUUTU, Tuomo	6-2	208	L	Vantaa, Finland	2/16/83	
THORNTON, Shawn	6-1	209	R	Oshawa, Ont.	7/23/77	Norfolk
VOROBIEV, Pavel	6-0	194	L	Karaganda, USSR	5/5/82	Norfolk

DEFENSEMEN						
AUCOIN, Adrian	6-2	214	R	Ottawa, Ont.	7/3/73	MODO
BABCHUK, Anton	6-5	202	R	Kiev, USSR	5/6/84	Norfolk
BARINKA, Michal	6-3	217	L	Vyskov, Czech.	6/12/84	Norfolk
BARKER, Cam	6-3	213	L	Winnipeg, Man.	4/4/86	Medicine Hat
BYFUGLIEN, Dustin	6-3	275	R	Minneapolis, MN	3/27/85	Prince George
CULLIMORE, Jassen	6-5	244	L	Simcoe, Ont.	12/4/72	
KEITH, Duncan	6-0	182	L	Winnipeg, Man.	7/16/83	Norfolk
SEABROOK, Brent	6-3	215	R	Richmond, B.C.	4/20/85	Lethbridge-Norfolk
SIMPSON, Todd	6-3	218	L	North Vancouver, B.C.	5/28/73	Herning
SPACEK, Jaroslav	5-11	206	L	Rokycany, Czech.	2/11/74	Plzen-Slavia
VANDERMEER, Jim	6-1	218	L	Caroline, Alta.	2/21/80	Norfolk
WISNIEWSKI, James	6-0	206	R	Canton, MI	2/21/84	Norfolk

GOALTENDERS	HT	WT	C	Place of Birth	Date	2004-05 Club
ANDERSON, Craig	6-2	174	L	Park Ridge, IL	5/21/81	Norfolk
BRODEUR, Mike	6-2	170	L	Calgary, Alta.	3/30/83	Norfolk-Greenville
CRAWFORD, Corey	6-2	183	L	Montreal, Que.	12/31/84	Moncton
KHABIBULIN, Nikolai	6-1	203	L	Sverdlovsk, USSR	1/13/73	Kazan
LEIGHTON, Michael	6-3	186	L	Petrolia, Ont.	5/19/81	Norfolk
MUNRO, Adam	6-2	219	L	St. George, Ont.	11/12/82	Norfolk-Atlantic City

In the System and Recently Drafted

FORWARDS	HT	WT	S	Place of Birth	Date	2004-05 Club
ANDERSSON, Johan	6-1	201	L	Motala, Sweden	5/18/84	Linkoping-Troja
ANTTILA, Marko	6-7	200	R	Lempoala, Finland	3/27/85	Ilves
BERTI, Adam	6-3	193	L	Scarborough, Ont.	7/1/86	Oshawa
BERTRAM, Dan	5-11	175	R	Calgary, Alta.	1/14/87	Boston College
BICKELL, Bryan	6-3	213	L	Bowmanville, Ont.	3/9/86	Ottawa (OHL)
BLUNDEN, Michael	6-3	213	R	Toronto, Ont.	12/15/86	Erie (OHL)
BROPHEY, Evan	6-1	194	L	Kitchener, Ont.	12/3/86	Barrie-Belleville
BROUWER, Troy	6-3	210	R	Vancouver, B.C.	8/17/85	Moose Jaw
BURISH, Adam	6-1	189	R	Madison, WI	1/6/83	U. of Wisconsin
DAVIS, Nathan	6-1	193	L	Cleveland, OH	5/23/86	Miami U.
DOWELL, Jake	6-0	202	L	Eau Claire, WI	3/4/85	U. of Wisconsin
FORD, Matthew	6-1	206	R	West Hills, CA	10/9/84	U. of Wisconsin
GARLOCK, Ryan	6-1	197	L	Iroquois Falls, Ont.	4/24/86	Windsor
HOBSON, Adam	6-0	200	L	Lund, Sweden	1/9/87	Spokane
HROMAS, Karel	6-2	189	L	Beroun, Czech.	1/27/86	Everett
ISTOMIN, Denis	6-0	187	L	Chelyabinsk, USSR	1/12/87	Chelyabinsk
KELL, Trevor	5-11	181	R	Thunder Bay, Ont.	6/23/86	London
KOJEVNIKOV, Alexander	6-3	199	L	Moscow, USSR	4/12/84	Greenville-Dayton
KONTIOLA, Petri	6-0	197	R	Seinajoki, Finland	10/4/84	Tappara
KUCHEJDA, David	5-11	189	L	Havirov, Czech.	6/12/87	C. Budejovice
McCULLOCH, Scott	6-0	198	L	Edmonton, Alta.	3/10/86	Colorado College
NORDQVIST, Jonas	6-3	202	L	Leksand, Sweden	4/26/82	Lulea
PORTER, Chris	6-1	203	L	Toronto, Ont.	5/29/84	North Dakota
SINDEL, Jakub	6-0	172	R	Jihlava, Czech.	1/24/86	Sparta-Trebic-Brandon
SKILLE, Jack	6-1	198	R	Madison, WI	5/19/87	USA U-18
VIUHKOLA, Jari	6-0	165	L	Oulu, Finland	2/27/80	Karpat
WENNERBERG, Mattias	5-11	191	L	Uma, Sweden	8/6/81	MODO-Bjorkloven
YAKUBOV, Mikhail	6-3	202	L	Barnaul, USSR	2/16/82	Norfolk

DEFENSEMEN						
CHARLEBOIS, Joe	6-1	210	R	Potsdam, NY	2/18/86	Sioux City
GRENZY, Michael	6-4	199	L	Niagara Falls, NY	2/6/84	Clarkson
GUSEV, Vladimir	6-2	205	L	Novosibirsk, USSR	11/24/82	Norfolk-Greenville
HJALMARSSON, Niklas	6-3	194	L	Eksjo, Sweden	6/6/87	HV 71
JAASKELAINEN, Teemu	6-1	207	L	Tampere, Finland	6/7/83	Ilves
KANTEE, Kevin	6-2	202	L	Idaho Falls, ID	1/29/84	Jokerit
KUKKONEN, Lasse	6-0	187	L	Oulu, Finland	9/18/81	Karpat
MALMIVAARA, Olli	6-7	220	L	Kajaani, Finland	3/13/82	SaiPa
MAUNU, Mitch	6-1	205	L	Thunder Bay, Ont.	7/30/86	Windsor
TURNER, Brennan	6-3	220	L	Winnipeg, Man.	12/5/86	Notre Dame

GOALTENDERS	HT	WT	C	Place of Birth	Date	2004-05 Club
FALLON, Joseph	6-3	190	L	Bemidji, MN	2/1/85	U. of Vermont

Coach

YAWNEY, TRENT
Coach, Chicago Blackhawks. Born in Hudson Bay, Sask., September 29, 1965.

The Chicago Blackhawks named Trent Yawney the 35th head coach in the team's history on July 7, 2005. Yawney served as the head coach of the Blackhawks' American Hockey League affiliate in Norfolk for five seasons, taking over the coaching reigns of the Admirals on June 23, 2000, for their inaugural season in the AHL.

Under Yawney's guidance, Norfolk won back-to-back South Division titles in 2001–02 and 2002–03. The Admirals made five consecutive playoff appearances and advanced to the conference semifinals twice while seeing over 50 players advance to the Blackhawks during that span. Such players as Tyler Arnason, Mark Bell, Kyle Calder, Craig Anderson, Michael Leighton, Steve McCarthy, Matt Ellison, Matt Keith, Travis Moen, Quintin Laing, Pavel Vorobiev, Mikhail Yakubov, Anton Babchuk and Michal Barinka were developed under Yawney's leadership.

Yawney was honored by The Hockey News as their minor pro coach of the year for the 2003–04 season. The only coach in the AHL to work without an assistant coach, he guided a squad full of rookies which was also depleted by injuries and NHL call-ups to a postseason appearance. The 2004-05 season saw the Admirals establish a new franchise record for wins (43) as well as points (93) during one of the most competitive years in AHL history on the ice.

Yawney was originally drafted by the Blackhawks in the third round, 45th overall, in the 1984 NHL Entry Draft out of Saskatoon in the Western Hockey League. After playing three seasons with the Blades, he joined the Canadian national team in 1985 for three seasons, culminating in the 1988 Winter Olympics in Calgary, Alberta, where he served as captain for Team Canada. Following the Olympics, Yawney joined the Blackhawks making his National Hockey League debut on March 5, 1988. In his 12-year NHL career, Yawney played in 593 regular-season games with the Blackhawks, Calgary Flames and St. Louis Blues recording 27 goals and 102 assists for 129 points with 783 penalty minutes. He also played in 60 career playoff games recording nine goals and 17 assists for 26 points and 81 penalty minutes.

Coaching Record

Season	Team		Regular Season				Playoffs		
		Games	W	L	T	Games	W	L
2000-01	Norfolk (AHL)	80	36	31	13	9	4	5
2001-02	Norfolk (AHL)	80	38	30	12	4	1	3
2002-03	Norfolk (AHL)	80	37	31	12	9	5	4
2003-04	Norfolk (AHL)	80	35	41	4	8	4	4
2004-05	Norfolk (AHL)	80	43	31	6	6	2	4

General Managers' History

Major Frederic McLaughlin, 1926-27 to 1941-42; Bill Tobin, 1942-43 to 1953-54; Tommy Ivan, 1954-55 to 1976-77; Bob Pulford, 1977-78 to 1989-90; Mike Keenan, 1990-91, 1991-92; Mike Keenan and Bob Pulford, 1992-93; Bob Pulford, 1993-94 to 1996-97; Bob Murray, 1997-98, 1998-99; Bob Murray and Bob Pulford, 1999-2000; Mike Smith, 2000-01 to 2002-03; Mike Smith and Bob Pulford, 2003-04; Bob Pulford, 2004-05; Dale Tallon, 2005-06.

Vice President and General Manager

TALLON, DALE
General Manager, Chicago Blackhawks.
Born in Noranda, Que., October 19, 1950.

The Chicago Blackhawks announced on June 21, 2005 that Dale Tallon had been named the eighth general manager in the team's storied history. Tallon, in his second stint with the Blackhawks front office, was named assistant general manager on November 5, 2003. He served four years (1998 to 2002) as the Blackhawks' director of player personnel before he returned to the radio and television booth prior to the 2002-03 season as color analyst for Blackhawk hockey.

Tallon was the Vancouver Canucks' first-round selection and the second player chosen overall (behind Gilbert Perreault, Buffalo) in the 1970 NHL Entry Draft. A defenseman, he immediately jumped into the NHL with the Canucks in the 1970–71 season. Tallon recorded a career-high 17 goals in 69 games with Vancouver during the 1971–72 season and appeared in the 1971 and 1972 NHL All-Star Games.

Tallon was traded to the Blackhawks for Jerry Korab and Gary Smith on May 14,1973. He had his best season as a professional with Chicago in 1975–76 with a career-high 47 assists and 62 points in 80 games. During his five-year Blackhawk career (1973 to 1978), Tallon scored 44 goals and added 112 assists for 156 points with 296 penalty minutes. He was dealt to Pittsburgh on October 9, 1978 and finished his playing career by playing two seasons with the Penguins. During his 10-year NHL career, Tallon scored 98 goals and added 238 assists for 336 points in 642 games. After retiring from the NHL following the 1979–80 season, he served as the Blackhawks color analyst for radio and television broadcasts for 16 seasons.

At the start of the 1998-99 season, Tallon joined the Blackhawk front office as director of player personnel. As he traveled the world scouting hockey, Tallon's knowledge and expertise of the game were honed while aiding in selecting and developing the Blackhawks' young prospects.

Club Records

Team

(Figures in brackets for season records are games played; records for fewest points, wins, ties, losses, goals, goals against are for 70 or more games)

Most Points 107   1970-71 (78),
1971-72 (78)
Most Wins 49   1970-71 (78),
1990-91 (80)
Most Ties 23   1973-74 (78)
Most Losses 51   1953-54 (70),
2003-04 (82)
Most Goals 351   1985-86 (80)
Most Goals Against 363   1981-82 (80)
Fewest Points 31   1953-54 (70)
Fewest Wins 12   1953-54 (70)
Fewest Ties 6   1989-90 (80)
Fewest Losses 14   1973-74 (78)
Fewest Goals *133   1953-54 (70)
Fewest Goals Against 164   1973-74 (78)
Longest Winning Streak
  Overall 8   Dec. 9-26/71,
Jan. 4-21/81
  Home 13   Nov. 11-Dec. 20/70
  Away 7   Dec. 9-29/64
Longest Undefeated Streak
  Overall 15   Jan. 14-Feb. 16/67
(12 wins, 3 ties)
  Home 18   Oct. 11-Dec. 20/70
(16 wins, 2 ties)
  Away 12   Nov. 2-Dec. 16/67
(6 wins, 6 ties)

Longest Losing Streak
  Overall 12   Feb. 25-Mar. 25/51
  Home 9   Feb. 8-Mar. 21/28
  Away 19   Nov. 10-Jan. 29/04
Longest Winless Streak
  Overall 21   Dec. 17/50-Jan. 28/51
(18 losses, 3 ties)
  Home 15   Dec. 16/28-Feb. 28/29
(11 losses, 4 ties)
  Away 22   Dec. 19/50-Mar. 25/51
(20 losses, 2 ties)
Most Shutouts, Season 15   1969-70 (76)
Most PIM, Season 2,663   1991-92 (80)
Most Goals, Game 12   Jan. 30/69
(Chi. 12 at Phi. 0)

Individual

Most Seasons 22   Stan Mikita
Most Games 1,394   Stan Mikita
Most Goals, Career 604   Bobby Hull
Most Assists, Career 926   Stan Mikita
Most Points, Career 1,467   Stan Mikita
(541G, 926A)
Most PIM, Career 1,495   Chris Chelios
Most Shutouts, Career 74   Tony Esposito
Longest Consecutive
  Games Streak 884   Steve Larmer
(Oct. 6/82-Apr. 15/93)
Most Goals, Season 58   Bobby Hull
(1968-69)
Most Assists, Season 87   Denis Savard
(1981-82, 1987-88)
Most Points, Season 131   Denis Savard
(1987-88; 44G, 87A)

Most PIM, Season 408   Mike Peluso
(1991-92)
Most Points, Defenseman,
  Season 85   Doug Wilson
(1981-82; 39G, 46A)
Most Points, Center,
  Season 131   Denis Savard
(1987-88; 44G, 87A)
Most Points, Right Wing,
  Season 101   Steve Larmer
(1990-91; 44G, 57A)
Most Points, Left Wing,
  Season 107   Bobby Hull
(1968-69; 58G, 49A)
Most Points, Rookie,
  Season 90   Steve Larmer
(1982-83; 43G, 47A)
Most Shutouts, Season 15   Tony Esposito
(1969-70)
Most Goals, Game 5   Grant Mulvey
(Feb. 3/82)
Most Assists, Game 6   Pat Stapleton
(Mar. 30/69)
Most Points, Game 7   Max Bentley
(Jan. 28/43; 4G, 3A),
Grant Mulvey
(Feb. 3/82; 5G, 2A)

* NHL Record.

Retired Numbers

1	Glenn Hall	1957-1967
9	Bobby Hull	1957-1972
18	Denis Savard	1980-1990, 1995-1997
21	Stan Mikita	1958-1980
35	Tony Esposito	1969-1984

All-time Record vs. Other Clubs

Regular Season

	At Home								On Road								Total							
	GP	W	L	T	OL	GF	GA	PTS	GP	W	L	T	OL	GF	GA	PTS	GP	W	L	T	OL	GF	GA	PTS
Anaheim	24	12	10	2	0	67	58	26	22	7	12	3	0	47	58	17	46	19	22	5	0	114	116	43
Atlanta	2	2	0	0	0	6	0	4	2	2	0	0	0	10	14	4	4	4	0	0	0	16	14	8
Boston	286	147	94	45	0	926	767	339	284	89	161	34	0	808	1023	212	570	236	255	79	0	1734	1790	551
Buffalo	51	27	17	6	1	164	139	61	53	14	32	7	0	138	199	35	104	41	49	13	1	302	338	96
Calgary	61	26	22	13	0	196	179	65	63	21	28	13	1	188	201	56	124	47	50	26	1	384	380	121
Carolina	29	16	9	3	1	117	83	36	30	12	14	4	0	93	97	28	59	28	23	7	1	210	180	64
Colorado	41	21	14	3	3	144	130	48	39	12	21	6	0	124	158	30	80	33	35	9	3	268	288	78
Columbus	10	7	2	1	0	30	15	15	11	4	5	1	1	34	32	10	21	11	7	2	1	64	47	25
Dallas	110	64	31	15	0	412	289	143	112	44	51	16	1	340	377	105	222	108	82	31	1	752	666	248
Detroit	338	155	130	51	2	1015	951	363	335	99	202	33	1	833	1144	232	673	254	332	84	3	1848	2095	595
Edmonton	44	21	15	7	1	167	152	50	45	18	22	5	0	147	165	41	89	39	37	12	1	314	317	91
Florida	10	5	3	2	0	34	30	12	8	5	2	1	0	30	18	11	18	10	5	3	0	64	48	23
Los Angeles	75	35	31	9	0	261	221	79	74	33	33	8	0	246	245	74	149	68	64	17	0	507	466	153
Minnesota	8	3	4	1	0	17	25	7	8	2	5	0	1	20	28	5	16	5	9	1	1	37	53	12
Montreal	273	93	125	55	0	731	761	241	276	54	173	48	1	653	1067	157	549	147	298	103	1	1384	1828	398
Nashville	17	10	5	1	1	49	39	22	16	6	6	3	1	43	48	16	33	16	11	4	2	92	87	38
New Jersey	46	24	12	10	0	176	127	58	47	16	20	11	0	142	147	43	93	40	32	21	0	318	274	101
NY Islanders	48	26	17	5	0	162	162	57	47	14	18	15	0	141	163	43	95	40	35	20	0	303	325	100
NY Rangers	286	128	115	43	0	870	792	299	285	113	117	55	0	807	841	281	571	241	232	98	0	1677	1633	580
Ottawa	8	4	2	2	0	18	18	10	10	6	4	0	0	30	31	12	18	10	6	2	0	48	49	22
Philadelphia	60	26	15	19	0	205	170	71	62	16	35	11	0	162	204	43	122	42	50	30	0	367	374	114
Phoenix	48	26	12	10	0	184	128	62	50	18	26	5	1	154	164	42	98	44	38	15	1	338	292	104
Pittsburgh	60	39	11	10	0	236	157	88	59	23	29	7	0	190	210	53	119	62	40	17	0	426	367	141
St. Louis	118	65	35	18	0	433	348	148	115	41	56	17	1	356	388	100	233	106	91	35	1	789	736	248
San Jose	25	13	9	2	1	76	77	29	26	10	12	3	1	70	72	24	51	23	21	5	2	146	149	53
Tampa Bay	14	8	4	2	0	45	35	18	14	4	4	2	4	28	26	11	25	12	8	5	0	73	61	29
Toronto	318	156	120	42	0	968	831	354	315	97	164	54	0	821	1071	248	633	253	284	96	0	1789	1902	602
Vancouver	71	47	16	7	1	267	164	102	72	22	34	15	1	210	218	60	143	69	50	22	2	477	382	162
Washington	40	22	12	6	0	151	120	50	41	15	21	5	0	127	145	35	81	37	33	11	0	278	265	85
Defunct Clubs	139	79	40	20	0	408	268	178	140	52	67	21	0	316	346	125	279	131	107	41	0	724	614	303
Totals	**2660**	**1307**	**932**	**410**	**11**	**8535**	**7236**	**3035**	**2660**	**869**	**1376**	**404**	**11**	**7308**	**8900**	**2153**	**5320**	**2176**	**2308**	**814**	**22**	**15843**	**16136**	**5188**

Playoffs

	Series	W	L	GP	W	L	T	GF	GA	Last Mtg.	Rnd.	Result
Boston	6	1	5	22	5	16	1	63	97	1978	QF	L 0-4
Buffalo	2	0	2	9	1	8	0	17	36	1980	QF	L 0-4
Calgary	3	1	2	12	5	7	0	33	37	1996	CQF	W 4-0
Colorado	2	0	2	12	4	8	0	28	49	1997	CQF	L 2-4
Dallas	6	4	2	33	19	14	0	120	118	1991	DSF	L 2-4
Detroit	14	8	6	69	38	31	0	210	190	1995	CF	L 1-4
Edmonton	4	1	3	20	8	12	0	77	102	1992	CF	W 4-0
Los Angeles	1	1	0	5	4	1	0	10	7	1974	QF	W 4-1
Montreal	17	5	12	81	29	50	2	185	261	1976	QF	L 0-4
NY Islanders	2	0	2	6	0	6	0	6	21	1979	QF	L 0-4
NY Rangers	5	4	1	24	14	10	0	66	54	1973	SF	W 4-1
Philadelphia	1	1	0	4	4	0	0	20	8	1971	QF	W 4-0
Pittsburgh	2	1	1	8	4	4	0	24	23	1992	F	L 0-4
St. Louis	10	7	3	50	28	22	0	171	142	2002	CQF	L 1-4
Toronto	9	3	6	38	15	22	1	89	111	1995	CQF	W 4-3
Vancouver	2	1	1	9	5	4	0	24	24	1995	CSF	W 4-0
Defunct Clubs	4	2	2	9								
Totals	**90**	**40**	**50**	**411**	**188**	**218**	**5**	**1159**	**1295**			

Calgary totals include Atlanta Flames, 1972-73 to 1979-80.
Colorado totals include Quebec, 1979-80 to 1994-95.
New Jersey totals include Kansas City, 1974-75 to 1975-76, and Colorado Rockies, 1976-77 to 1981-82.
Phoenix totals include Winnipeg, 1979-80 to 1995-96.
Carolina totals include Hartford, 1979-80 to 1996-97.
Dallas totals include Minnesota North Stars, 1967-68 to 1992-93.

Playoff Results 2005-2000

Year	Round	Opponent	Result	GF	GA
2002	CQF	St. Louis	L 1-4	5	13

Abbreviations: Round: F - Final; **CF** - conference final; **CSF** - conference semi-final; **CQF** - conference quarter-final; **DSF** - division semi-final; **SF** - semi-final; **QF** - quarter-final.

Key Off-Season Signings/Acquisitions

2004

July   2 • Signed C **Curtis Brown** and RW **Matthew Barnaby**.
      15 • Re-signed LWs **Kyle Calder** and **Eric Daze**.
      22 • Signed D **Jassen Cullimore**.

2005

June 21 • Named **Dale Tallon** general manager.

July   7 • Named **Trent Yawney** head coach.
      29 • Signed 2003 1st-round pick (14th overall) D **Brent Seabrook**.

Aug.   2 • Signed D **Adrian Aucoin**.
       4 • Signed RW **Martin Lapointe** and D **Jaroslav Spacek**.
       5 • Signed G **Nikolai Khabibulin** and C **Jim Dowd**.
     10 • Re-signed LW **Mark Bell**.
     11 • Re-signed C **Tyler Arnason**.
     22 • Signed 2004 1st-round pick (3rd overall), D **Cam Barker**.
     23 • Signed D **Todd Simpson**.

Entry Draft
Selections 2005-1991

2005
Pick
7	Jack Skille
43	Michael Blunden
54	Dan Bertram
68	Evan Brophey
108	Niklas Hjalmarsson
113	Nathan Davis
117	Denis Istomin
134	Brennan Turner
167	Joseph Fallon
188	Joe Charlebois
202	David Kuchejda
203	Adam Hobson

2004
Pick
3	Cam Barker
32	Dave Bolland
41	Bryan Bickell
45	Ryan Garlock
54	Jakub Sindel
68	Adam Berti
120	Mitch Maunu
123	Karel Hromas
131	Trevor Kell
140	Jake Dowell
165	Scott McCulloch
196	Petri Kontiola
214	Troy Brouwer
223	Jared Walker
229	Eric Hunter
256	Matthew Ford
260	Marko Anttila

2003
Pick
14	Brent Seabrook
52	Corey Crawford
59	Michal Barinka
151	Lasse Kukkonen
156	Alexei Ivanov
181	Johan Andersson
211	Mike Brodeur
245	Dustin Byfuglien
275	Michael Grenzy
282	Chris Porter

2002
Pick
21	Anton Babchuk
54	Duncan Keith
93	Alexander Kojevnikov
128	Matt Ellison
156	James Wisniewski
188	Kevin Kantee
219	Tyson Kellerman
251	Jason Kostadine
282	Adam Burish

2001
Pick
9	Tuomo Ruutu
29	Adam Munro
59	Matt Keith
73	Craig Anderson
104	Brent MacLellan
115	Vladimir Gusev
119	Alexei Zotkin
142	Tommi Jaminki
174	Alexander Golovin
186	Petr Puncochar
205	Teemu Jaaskelainen
216	Oleg Minakov
268	Jeff Miles

2000
Pick
10	Mikhail Yakubov
11	Pavel Vorobiev
49	Jonas Nordqvist
74	Igor Radulov
106	Scott Balan
117	Olli Malmivaara
151	Alexander Barkunov
177	Michael Ayers
193	Joey Martin
207	Cliff Loya
225	Vladislav Luchkin
240	Adam Berkhoel
262	Peter Flache
271	Reto Von Arx
291	Arne Ramholt

1999
Pick
23	Steve McCarthy
46	Dimitri Levinski
63	Stepan Mokhov
134	Michael Jacobsen
165	Michael Leighton
194	Mattias Wennerberg
195	Yorick Treille
223	Andrew Carver

1998
Pick
8	Mark Bell
94	Matthias Trattnig
156	Kent Huskins
158	Jari Viuhkola
166	Jonathan Pelletier
183	Tyler Arnason
210	Sean Griffin
238	Alexandre Couture
240	Andrei Yershov

1997
Pick
13	Daniel Cleary
16	Ty Jones
39	Jeremy Reich
67	Mike Souza
110	Ben Simon
120	Peter Gardiner
130	Kyle Calder
147	Heath Gordon
174	Jerad Smith
204	Sergei Shikhanov
230	Chris Feil

1996
Pick
31	Remi Royer
42	Jeff Paul
46	Geoff Peters
130	Andy Johnson
184	Mike Vellinga
210	Chris Twerdun
236	Andrei Kozyrev

1995
Pick
19	Dmitri Nabokov
45	Christian Laflamme
71	Kevin McKay
82	Chris Van Dyk
97	Pavel Kriz
146	Marc Magliarditi
149	Marty Wilford
175	Steve Tardif
201	Casey Hankinson
227	Mike Pittman

1994
Pick
14	Ethan Moreau
40	Jean-Yves Leroux
85	Steve McLaren
118	Marc Dupuis
144	Jim Enson
170	Tyler Prosofsky
196	Mike Josephson
222	Lubomir Jandera
248	Lars Weibel
263	Rob Mara

1993
Pick
24	Eric Lecompte
50	Eric Manlow
54	Bogdan Savenko
76	Ryan Huska
90	Eric Daze
102	Patrik Pysz
128	Jonni Vauhkonen
180	Tom White
206	Sergei Petrov
232	Mike Rusk
258	Mike McGhan
284	Tom Noble

1992
Pick
12	Sergei Krivokrasov
36	Jeff Shantz
41	Sergei Klimovich
89	Andy MacIntyre
113	Tim Hogan
137	Gerry Skrypec
161	Mike Prokopec
185	Layne Roland
209	David Hymovitz
233	Richard Raymond

1991
Pick
22	Dean McAmmond
39	Michael Pomichter
44	Jamie Matthews
66	Bobby House
71	Igor Kravchuk
88	Zac Boyer
110	Maco Balkovec
112	Kevin St. Jacques
132	Jacques Auger
154	Scott Kirton
176	Roch Belley
198	Scott MacDonald
220	Alexander Andrievski
242	Mike Larkin
264	Scott Dean

Coaching History
Pete Muldoon, 1926-27; Barney Stanley and Hugh Lehman, 1927-28; Herb Gardiner and Dick Irvin, 1928-29; Tom Shaughnessy and Bill Tobin, 1929-30; Dick Irvin, 1930-31; Bill Tobin, 1931-32; Emil Iverson, Godfrey Matheson and Tommy Gorman, 1932-33; Tommy Gorman, 1933-34; Clem Loughlin, 1934-35 to 1936-37; Bill Stewart, 1937-38; Bill Stewart and Paul Thompson, 1938-39; Paul Thompson, 1939-40 to 1943-44; Paul Thompson and Johnny Gottselig, 1944-45; Johnny Gottselig, 1945-46, 1946-47; Johnny Gottselig and Charlie Conacher, 1947-48; Charlie Conacher, 1948-49, 1949-50; Ebbie Goodfellow, 1950-51, 1951-52; Sid Abel, 1952-53, 1953-54; Frank Eddolls, 1954-55; Dick Irvin, 1955-56; Tommy Ivan, 1956-57; Tommy Ivan and Rudy Pilous, 1957-58; Rudy Pilous, 1958-59 to 1962-63; Billy Reay, 1963-64 to 1975-76; Billy Reay and Bill White, 1976-77; Bob Pulford, 1977-78, 1978-79; Eddie Johnston, 1979-80; Keith Magnuson, 1980-81; Keith Magnuson and Bob Pulford, 1981-82; Orval Tessier, 1982-83, 1983-84; Orval Tessier and Bob Pulford, 1984-85; Bob Pulford, 1985-86, 1986-87; Bob Murdoch, 1987-88; Mike Keenan, 1988-89 to 1991-92; Darryl Sutter, 1992-93 to 1994-95; Craig Hartsburg, 1995-96 to 1997-98; Dirk Graham and Lorne Molleken, 1998-99; Lorne Molleken and Bob Pulford, 1999-2000; Alpo Suhonen, 2000-01; Brian Sutter, 2001-02 to 2003-04; Trent Yawney, 2005-06.

Captains' History
Dick Irvin, 1926-27 to 1928-29; Duke Dukowski, 1929-30; Ty Arbour, 1930-31; Cy Wentworth, 1931-32; Helge Bostrom, 1932-33; Charlie Gardiner, 1933-34; no captain, 1934-35; Johnny Gottselig, 1935-36 to 1939-40; Earl Seibert, 1940-41, 1941-42; Doug Bentley, 1942-43, 1943-44; Clint Smith 1944-45; John Mariucci, 1945-46; Red Hamill, 1946-47; John Mariucci, 1947-48; Gaye Stewart, 1948-49; Doug Bentley, 1949-50; Jack Stewart, 1950-51, 1951-52; Bill Gadsby, 1952-53, 1953-54; Gus Mortson, 1954-55 to 1956-57; no captain, 1957-58; Ed Litzenberger, 1958-59 to 1960-61; Pierre Pilote, 1961-62 to 1967-68, no captain, 1968-69; Pat Stapleton, 1969-70; no captain, 1970-71 to 1974-75; Stan Mikita and Pit Martin, 1975-76; Stan Mikita, Pit Martin and Keith Magnuson, 1976-77; Keith Magnuson, 1977-78, 1978-79; Keith Magnuson and Terry Ruskowski, 1979-80; Terry Ruskowski, 1980-81, 1981-82; Darryl Sutter, 1982-83 to 1984-85; Darryl Sutter and Bob Murray, 1985-86; Darryl Sutter, 1986-87; no captain, 1987-88; Denis Savard and Dirk Graham, 1988-89; Dirk Graham, 1989-90 to 1994-95; Chris Chelios, 1995-96 to 1998-99; Doug Gilmour, 1999-2000; Tony Amonte, 2000-01, 2001-02; Alex Zhamnov, 2002-03, 2003-04.

Club Directory

United Center

Chicago Blackhawks
United Center
1901 W. Madison Street
Chicago, IL 60612
Phone **312/455-7000**
FAX 312/455-7041
www.chicagoblackhawks.com
Capacity: 20,500

President	William W. Wirtz
Senior V.P. and General Manager	Robert J. Pulford
Vice President	Jack Davison
Vice President	Peter R. Wirtz
General Manager	Dale Tallon
Director Player Personnel	Rick Dudley
Special Assistant to G.M.	Stan Bowman
Head Coach	Trent Yawney
Assistant Coach	Denis Savard
Assistant Coach	Bruce Cassidy
Skating Coach	Dan Jansen
Strength & Conditioning Coach	Phil Walker
Goaltending Consultant	Vladislav Tretiak
Goaltending Coach	Stephane Waite
Chief Amateur Scout	Michel Dumas
Amateur Scouts	Ron Anderson, Bruce Franklin, Tim Higgins, Rob Pulford, Chris Valentine
European Scouting Coordinator	Sakari Pietila
European Amateur Scouts	Karl Pavlik, Ruslan Shabanov
Executive Assistant	Cindy Brueck
Video Coordinator	Ike Rhodes

Medical Staff
Head Team Physician, Orthopedics	Michael Terry
Team Physicians, Orthopedics	Sherwin Ho, Bruce Reider
Head Team Physician, Internal Medicine	William Harper
Team Physician, Internal Medicine	Carl Meyer
Team Dentist	Russ Baer
Oral Surgeon	Eric Pulver
Eye Doctor	William Mieler
Head Athletic Trainer	Michael Gapski
Assistant Athletic Trainer	Jeff Thomas
Massage Therapist	Pawel Prylinski
Equipment Manager	Troy Parchman
Assistant Equipment Manager	Scott Boggs
Equipment Manager	Mark DePasquale

Public Relations/Marketing
Exec. Dir. of Communications, Broadcasting and Community Outreach	Jim De Maria
Manager of P.R. & Team Services	Tony Ommen
Director of Community Outreach	Jim Blaney
Manager of Community Outreach	Angela Armbruster
Dir. of In-Kind Giving & Office Mgr.	Barbara Davidson
Communications Manager	Pete Hassen
Website Producer	Adam Kempenaar
Exec. Dir. of Sales & Marketing	Jim Sofranko
Dir. of Corporate Sponsorships	Steve Waight
Account Exec., Corporate Sponsorships	Sara Bailey
Manager, Client Services	Kelly Bodnarchuk
Mgr. of Advertising & Promotions	Evan Hall
Manager, Game Operations	Ben Broder
Executive Assistant	Alison Finley

Finance
Controller	John Kerr
Treasurer	Robert Rinkus
Accounting Manager	Deb Kulir

Ticketing
Exec. Director, Ticket Operations	James K. Bare
Director, Ticket Sales	Doug Ryan
Senior Account Executives	Brad Bober, Ildegardo Esparza, Rich Sommers, Julianna Ilg
Senior Ticket Services Specialist	Kathie Raimondi
Team Photographer	Bill Smith
Assistant Photographer	Joe Oliver
Organist	Frank Pellico
Public Address Announcer	Gene Honda
Website Contributor	Harvey Wittenberg
Radio Station	WSCR (AM 670)
Television Station	Comcast Sports Net Chicago
Broadcasters	Pat Foley, Troy Murray
Radio Studio Host	Jesse Rogers

Colorado Avalanche

After a solid rookie season in 2003-04, John-Michael Liles represented the United States at the World Cup of Hockey and at the World Championship last season.

2005-06 Schedule

Oct.	Wed.	5	at Edmonton		Thu.	5	at Minnesota
	Sat.	8	at Dallas		Sat.	7	Columbus*
	Mon.	10	Calgary		Mon.	9	St. Louis
	Wed.	12	Nashville		Wed.	11	Montreal
	Fri.	14	Chicago		Sat.	14	at Philadelphia*
	Wed.	19	Los Angeles		Tue.	17	Toronto
	Fri.	21	at Edmonton		Thu.	19	at Chicago
	Sat.	22	at Vancouver		Sat.	21	Detroit*
	Tue.	25	Edmonton		Tue.	24	Calgary
	Thu.	27	Vancouver		Thu.	26	Dallas
	Sat.	29	Vancouver		Sat.	28	Vancouver
Nov.	Thu.	3	Anaheim		Tue.	31	Minnesota
	Sat.	5	Dallas	**Feb.**	Thu.	2	at Nashville
	Tue.	8	San Jose		Sat.	4	Detroit*
	Thu.	10	at Vancouver		Tue.	7	Edmonton
	Sat.	12	at Calgary		Thu.	9	at Minnesota
	Mon.	14	Edmonton		Fri.	10	at Columbus
	Wed.	16	at Phoenix		Sun.	12	at Detroit*
	Fri.	18	at Anaheim		Tue.	28	Minnesota
	Sat.	19	at Los Angeles	**Mar.**	Thu.	2	Columbus
	Mon.	21	Calgary		Sat.	4	at Dallas
	Wed.	23	at Detroit		Sun.	5	at Minnesota
	Fri.	25	at Columbus		Tue.	7	at St. Louis
	Sun.	27	Vancouver		Thu.	9	at Chicago
	Tue.	29	at Edmonton		Sun.	12	Calgary*
	Wed.	30	at Vancouver		Mon.	13	at Calgary
Dec.	Sun.	4	Buffalo		Sun.	19	at San Jose*
	Wed.	7	Boston		Mon.	20	at Los Angeles
	Fri.	9	at New Jersey		Wed.	22	at Anaheim
	Sat.	10	at Pittsburgh		Sat.	25	at St. Louis
	Mon.	12	Ottawa		Sun.	26	Edmonton
	Sat.	17	at NY Islanders		Tue.	28	Anaheim
	Sun.	18	at NY Rangers*		Fri.	31	at Calgary
	Tue.	20	at Nashville	**Apr.**	Mon.	3	Chicago
	Thu.	22	Minnesota		Wed.	5	San Jose
	Fri.	23	at Minnesota		Sat.	8	St. Louis*
	Mon.	26	Phoenix		Sun.	9	Minnesota
	Wed.	28	Los Angeles		Tue.	11	Phoenix
	Fri.	30	at San Jose		Thu.	13	at Calgary
	Sat.	31	at Phoenix		Sat.	15	at Vancouver
Jan.	Tue.	3	Nashville		Mon.	17	at Edmonton

* Denotes afternoon game.

Franchise date: June 22, 1979
Transferred from Quebec to Denver, June 21, 1995

NORTHWEST DIVISION

27th NHL Season

Year-by-Year Record

Season	GP	Home W	L	T	OL	Road W	L	T	OL	Overall W	L	T	OL	GF	GA	Pts.	Finished	Playoff Result
2004-05	....																	
2003-04	82	19	14	6	2	21	8	7	5	40	22	13	7	236	198	100	2nd, Northwest Div.	Lost Conf. Semi-Final
2002-03	82	21	9	8	3	21	10	5	5	42	19	13	8	251	194	105	1st, Northwest Div.	Lost Conf. Quarter-Final
2001-02	82	24	12	4	1	21	16	4	0	45	28	8	1	212	169	99	1st, Northwest Div.	Lost Conf. Championship
2000-01	**82**	**28**	**6**	**5**	**2**	**24**	**10**	**5**	**.2**	**52**	**16**	**10**	**4**	**270**	**192**	**118**	**1st, Northwest Div.**	**Won Stanley Cup**
1999-2000	82	25	12	4	0	17	16	7	1	42	28	11	1	233	201	96	1st, Northwest Div.	Lost Conf. Championship
1998-99	82	21	14	6	....	23	14	4	....	44	28	10	....	239	205	98	1st, Northwest Div.	Lost Conf. Championship
1997-98	82	21	10	10	....	18	16	7	....	39	26	17	....	231	205	95	1st, Pacific Div.	Lost Conf. Quarter-Final
1996-97	82	26	10	5	....	23	14	4	....	49	24	9	....	277	205	107	1st, Pacific Div.	Lost Conf. Championship
1995-96	**82**	**24**	**10**	**7**	**....**	**23**	**15**	**3**	**....**	**47**	**25**	**10**	**....**	**326**	**240**	**104**	**1st, Pacific Div.**	**Won Stanley Cup**
1994-95*	48	19	1	4	....	11	12	1	....	30	13	5	....	185	134	65	1st, Northeast Div.	Lost Conf. Quarter-Final
1993-94*	84	19	17	6	....	15	25	2	....	34	42	8	....	277	292	76	5th, Northeast Div.	Out of Playoffs
1992-93*	84	23	17	2	....	24	10	8	....	47	27	10	....	351	300	104	2nd, Adams Div.	Lost Div. Semi-Final
1991-92*	80	18	19	3	....	2	29	9	....	20	48	12	....	255	318	52	5th, Adams Div.	Out of Playoffs
1990-91*	80	9	23	8	....	7	27	6	....	16	50	14	....	236	354	46	5th, Adams Div.	Out of Playoffs
1989-90*	80	8	26	6	....	4	35	1	....	12	61	7	....	240	407	31	5th, Adams Div.	Out of Playoffs
1988-89*	80	16	20	4	....	11	26	3	....	27	46	7	....	269	342	61	5th, Adams Div.	Out of Playoffs
1987-88*	80	15	23	2	....	17	20	3	....	32	43	5	....	271	306	69	5th, Adams Div.	Out of Playoffs
1986-87*	80	20	13	7	....	11	26	3	....	31	39	10	....	267	276	72	4th, Adams Div.	Lost Div. Final
1985-86*	80	23	13	4	....	20	18	2	....	43	31	6	....	330	289	92	1st, Adams Div.	Lost Div. Semi-Final
1984-85*	80	24	13	4	....	17	18	5	....	41	30	9	....	323	275	91	2nd, Adams Div.	Lost Conf. Championship
1983-84*	80	24	11	5	....	18	17	5	....	42	28	10	....	360	278	94	3rd, Adams Div.	Lost Div. Final
1982-83*	80	23	10	7	....	11	24	5	....	34	34	12	....	343	336	80	4th, Adams Div.	Lost Div. Semi-Final
1981-82*	80	24	13	3	....	9	18	13	....	33	31	16	....	356	345	82	4th, Adams Div.	Lost Conf. Championship
1980-81*	80	18	11	11	....	12	21	7	....	30	32	18	....	314	318	78	4th, Adams Div.	Lost Prelim. Round
1979-80*	80	17	16	7	....	8	28	4	....	25	44	11	....	248	313	61	5th, Adams Div.	Out of Playoffs

* Quebec Nordiques

2005-06 Player Personnel

FORWARDS	HT	WT	S	Place of Birth	Date	2004-05 Club
BRUNETTE, Andrew	6-1	210	L	Sudbury, Ont.	8/24/73	
HAHL, Riku	6-1	205	L	Hameenlinna, Finland	11/1/80	HPK
HEALEY, Paul	6-2	198	R	Edmonton, Alta.	3/20/75	San Antonio-Edm (AHL)
HEJDUK, Milan	5-11	185	R	Usti-nad-Labem, Czech.	2/14/76	Pardubice
HINOTE, Dan	6-0	190	R	Leesburg, FL	1/30/77	MODO
KONOWALCHUK, Steve	6-2	207	L	Salt Lake City, UT	11/11/72	
LAAKSONEN, Antti	6-0	180	L	Tammela, Finland	10/3/73	
LAPERRIERE, Ian	6-1	201	R	Montreal, Que.	1/19/74	
MAY, Brad	6-1	217	L	Toronto, Ont.	11/29/71	
McCORMICK, Cody	6-2	200	R	London, Ont.	4/18/83	Hershey
McLEAN, Brett	5-11	194	L	Comox, B.C.	8/14/78	Malmo
RICHARDSON, Brad	5-11	178	L	Belleville, Ont.	2/4/85	Owen Sound
SAKIC, Joe	5-11	195	L	Burnaby, B.C.	7/7/69	
SKLADANY, Frantisek	6-0	185	L	Martin, Czech.	4/22/82	Hershey-Quad City
STEEVES, Ryan	6-0	195	L	Ottawa, Ont.	12/31/82	Hershey
SVAGROVSKY, David	6-3	205	R	Prague, Czech.	12/21/84	Colorado
SVATOS, Marek	5-9	170	L	Kosice, Czech.	6/17/82	Hershey
TANGUAY, Alex	6-0	190	L	Ste-Justine, Que.	11/21/79	Lugano
TURGEON, Pierre	6-1	199	L	Rouyn, Que.	8/28/69	

DEFENSEMEN	HT	WT	S	Place of Birth	Date	2004-05 Club
BLAKE, Rob	6-4	225	R	Simcoe, Ont.	12/10/69	
BOUGHNER, Bob	6-0	203	R	Windsor, Ont.	3/8/71	
BOYCHUK, Johnny	6-2	215	R	Edmonton, Alta.	1/19/84	Hershey
BRISEBOIS, Patrice	6-2	203	R	Montreal, Que.	1/27/71	Kloten
CLARK, Brett	6-1	195	L	Wapella, Sask.	12/23/76	Hershey
FINGER, Jeff	6-2	195	L	Hancock, MI	12/18/79	Hershey
LESCHYSHYN, Curtis	6-1	207	L	Thompson, Man.	9/21/69	
LILES, John-Michael	5-10	185	L	Zionsville, IN	11/25/80	Iserlohn
SAUER, Kurt	6-4	225	L	St. Cloud, MN	1/16/81	
SKRASTINS, Karlis	6-1	212	L	Riga, USSR	7/9/74	Riga 2000
SLOVAK, Tomas	6-1	203	R	Kosice, Czech.	4/5/83	Hershey-Kosice
VAANANEN, Ossi	6-4	215	L	Vantaa, Finland	8/18/80	Jokerit
VIITANEN, Mikko	6-3	220	L	Rajamaki, Finland	2/18/82	Hershey-Reading

GOALTENDERS	HT	WT	C	Place of Birth	Date	2004-05 Club
AEBISCHER, David	6-1	190	L	Fribourg, Switz.	2/7/78	Lugano-Chur
BUDAJ, Peter	6-1	200	L	Bystrica, Czech.	9/18/82	Hershey
KOLESNIK, Vitaly	6-3	198	L	Ust-Kamenogorsk, USSR	8/20/79	Ust-Kamenogorsk
LAWSON, Tom	6-5	200	L	Whitby, Ont.	8/15/79	Hershey
WEIMAN, Tyler	5-11	180	L	Saskatoon, Sask.	6/5/84	Colorado

In the System and Recently Drafted

FORWARDS	HT	WT	S	Place of Birth	Date	2004-05 Club
CORBIN, J.D.	5-10	185	L	Littleton, CO	3/23/85	U. of Denver
DURAND, Chris	6-1	186	R	Saskatoon, Sask.	1/21/87	Seattle
FRITSCHE, Tom	5-11	183	L	Parma, OH	9/30/86	Ohio State
HEMINGWAY, Brett	6-1	185	R	Yorkton, Sask.	9/28/83	New Hampshire
HENSICK, T.J.	5-10	179	R	Lansing, MI	12/10/85	U. of Michigan
JONES, David	6-3	220	R	Guelph, Ont.	8/10/84	Dartmouth
KOVAC, Kristian	6-2	205	R	Kosice, Czech.	1/1/81	Kosice-Trebisov-Presov-Dunaujvaros
McCUTCHEON, Mark	6-0	177	R	Ithaca, NY	5/21/84	Cornell
MERCIER, Justin	5-11	175	L	Erie, PA	6/25/87	USA U-18
ORESKOVICH, Victor	6-2	216	R	Whitby, Ont.	8/15/86	U. of Notre Dame
PARSHIN, Denis	5-9	146	L	Rybinsk, USSR	2/1/86	CSKA
SHEMETOV, Sergei	6-1	185	L	Yaroslavl, USSR	9/3/84	Tyumen
STASTNY, Paul	6-0	201	L	Quebec City, Que.	12/27/85	U. of Denver
STOA, Ryan	6-3	200	L	Bloomington, MN	4/13/87	USA U-18
VIDELL, Linus	6-3	214	L	Skarpnack, Sweden	5/5/85	Sodertalje-Halmstad
WOLSKI, Wojtek	6-3	200	L	Zabrze, Poland	2/24/86	Brampton
YIP, Brandon	6-1	170	R	Vancouver, B.C.	4/25/85	Coquitlam

DEFENSEMEN	HT	WT	S	Place of Birth	Date	2004-05 Club
CUMISKEY, Kyle	5-10	158	L	Abbotsford, B.C.	12/2/86	Kelowna
DEMEN-WILLAUME, Richard	6-3	196	L	Asa, Sweden	1/28/86	Frolunda
KALTEVA, Mikko	6-3	190	L	Hyvinkaa, Finland	5/25/84	Jokerit
LINDSTROM, Sanny	6-2	205	L	Stockholm, Sweden	12/24/79	Timra
LYNCH, Jason	6-3	205	R	North Vancouver, B.C.	5/26/87	Spokane
MACIAS, Raymond	6-1	187	R	Long Beach, CA	9/18/86	Kamloops
McCLELLAN, Stephen	6-1	165	L	Boston, MA	4/22/85	Cushing
PELTIER, Derek	5-11	190	L	Plymounth, MN	3/14/85	U. of Minnesota

GOALTENDERS	HT	WT	C	Place of Birth	Date	2004-05 Club
FRANEK, Petr	5-11	185	L	Most, Czech.	4/6/75	Slavia
KESERICH, Ian	6-3	180	L	Cleveland, OH	1/6/86	Ohio State

Patrice Brisebois joins the Avalanche after 14 seasons in Montreal.

Coach

QUENNEVILLE, JOEL
Coach, Colorado Avalanche. Born in Windsor, Ont., September 15, 1958.

Joel Quenneville returned to the franchise where he began his NHL coaching career in 1994-95 when he was named the fourth head coach in Colorado Avalanche, and the 12th in franchise history on July 7, 2004.

The former Colorado Rockies defenseman was the winningest coach in St. Louis Blues history, compiling a 307-209-77 record while spending 593 regular-season games behind the St. Louis bench, the most of any Blues coach. He reached the personal milestone of 500 career games coached on January 23, 2003 versus Chicago.

Under his guidance, the Blues reached the Western Conference Finals in 2001, the first time the team had done so since 1986, and won the Presidents' Trophy in 1999-2000 with a league-leading and franchise-high 114 points. He served as head coach of the North American All-Stars at the 2001 All-Star Game in Denver, and was named the NHL's coach of the year for 1999-00, capturing the Jack Adams Award.

The former NHL defenseman spent two-and-a-half seasons with the Colorado Avalanche/Quebec Nordiques as an assistant coach prior to being named the Blues' head coach on January 6, 1997. He was instrumental in the Avs' drive for their first Stanley Cup in 1996. He retired as an active player after the 1991-92 season, when he served as a player-coach for the St. John's Maple Leafs (AHL). Quenneville played 13 seasons in the NHL, closing out his career with 54 goals and 136 assists for 190 points adding 705 penalty minutes in 803 games played with Hartford, Washington, New Jersey, Toronto, and the Colorado Rockies. A short time later, he received his first coaching opportunity with the Springfield Indians (AHL) in 1993-94.

Coaching Record

Season	Team	Regular Season				Playoffs		
		Games	W	L	T	Games	W	L
1993-94	Springfield (AHL)	80	29	38	13	6	2	4
1996-97	St. Louis (NHL)	40	18	15	7	6	2	4
1997-98	St. Louis (NHL)	82	45	29	8	10	6	4
1998-99	St. Louis (NHL)	82	37	32	13	13	6	7
1999-2000	St. Louis (NHL)	82	51	20	11	7	3	4
2000-01	St. Louis (NHL)	82	43	27	12	15	9	6
2001-02	St. Louis (NHL)	82	43	31	8	10	5	5
2002-03	St. Louis (NHL)	82	41	30	11	7	3	4
2003-04	St. Louis (NHL)	61	29	25	7	....	....	....
2004-05	Colorado (NHL)			Season Cancelled				
	NHL Totals	593	307	209	68	68	34	34

Coaching History

Jacques Demers, 1979-80; Maurice Filion and Michel Bergeron, 1980-81; Michel Bergeron, 1981-82 to 1986-87; Andre Savard and Ron Lapointe, 1987-88; Ron Lapointe and Jean Perron, 1988-89; Michel Bergeron, 1989-90; Dave Chambers, 1990-91; Dave Chambers and Pierre Page, 1991-92; Pierre Page, 1992-93, 1993-94; Marc Crawford, 1994-95 to 1997-98; Bob Hartley, 1998-99 to 2001-02; Bob Hartley and Tony Granato, 2002-03; Tony Granato, 2003-04; Joel Quenneville, 2004-05 to date.

Captains' History

Marc Tardif, 1979-80, 1980-81; Robbie Ftorek and Andre Dupont, 1981-82; Mario Marois, 1982-83 to 1984-85; Mario Marois and Peter Stastny, 1985-86; Peter Stastny, 1986-87 to 1989-90; Joe Sakic and Steven Finn, 1990-91; Mike Hough, 1991-92; Joe Sakic, 1992-93 to date.

Club Records

Team

(Figures in brackets for season records are games played; records for fewest points, wins, ties, losses, goals, goals against are for 70 or more games)

Most Points	118	2000-01 (82)
Most Wins	52	2000-01 (82)
Most Ties	18	1980-81 (80)
Most Losses	61	1989-90 (80)
Most Goals	360	1983-84 (80)
Most Goals Against	407	1989-90 (80)
Fewest Points	31	1989-90 (80)
Fewest Wins	12	1989-90 (80)
Fewest Ties	5	1987-88 (80)
Fewest Losses	16	2000-01 (82)
Fewest Goals	212	2001-02 (82)
Fewest Goals Against	169	2001-02 (82)

Longest Winning Streak

Overall	12	Jan. 10-Feb. 7/99
Home	10	Nov. 26/83-Jan. 10/84, Mar. 6-Apr. 16/95
Away	7	Jan. 10-Feb. 7/99

Longest Undefeated Streak

Overall	12	Dec. 23/96-Jan. 20/97 (9 wins, 3 ties), Jan. 10-Feb. 7/99 (12 wins)
Home	14	Nov. 19/83-Jan. 21/84 (11 wins, 3 ties)
Away	10	Jan. 10-Mar. 3/99 (8 wins, 2 ties)

Longest Losing Streak

Overall	14	Oct. 21-Nov. 19/90
Home	8	Oct. 21-Nov. 24/90
Away	18	Jan. 18-Apr. 1/90

Longest Winless Streak

Overall	17	Oct. 21-Nov. 25/90 (15 losses, 2 ties)
Home	11	Nov. 14-Dec. 26/89 (7 losses, 4 ties)
Away	33	Oct. 8/91-Feb. 27/92 (25 losses, 8 ties)

Most Shutouts, Season	11	2001-02 (82)
Most PIM, Season	2,104	1989-90 (80)
Most Goals, Game	12	Three times

Individual

Most Seasons	16	Joe Sakic
Most Games	1,155	Joe Sakic
Most Goals, Career	542	Joe Sakic
Most Assists, Career	860	Joe Sakic
Most Points, Career	1,402	Joe Sakic (542G, 860A)
Most PIM, Career	1,562	Dale Hunter
Most Shutouts, Career	37	Patrick Roy

Longest Consecutive

Games Streak	312	Dale Hunter (Oct. 9/80-Mar. 13/84)
Most Goals, Season	57	Michel Goulet (1982-83)
Most Assists, Season	93	Peter Stastny (1981-82)
Most Points, Season	139	Peter Stastny (1981-82; 46G, 93A)
Most PIM, Season	301	Gord Donnelly (1987-88)

Most Points, Defenseman,

Season	82	Steve Duchesne (1992-93; 20G, 62A)

Most Points, Center,

Season	139	Peter Stastny (1981-82; 46G, 93A)

Most Points, Right Wing,

Season	103	Jacques Richard (1980-81; 52G, 51A)

Most Points, Left Wing,

Season	121	Michel Goulet (1983-84; 56G, 65A)

Most Points, Rookie,

Season	109	Peter Stastny (1980-81; 39G, 70A)
Most Shutouts, Season	9	Patrick Roy (2001-02)
Most Goals, Game	5	Mats Sundin (Mar. 5/92), Mike Ricci (Feb. 17/94)
Most Assists, Game	5	Six times
Most Points, Game	8	Peter Stastny (Feb. 22/81; 4G, 4A), Anton Stastny (Feb. 22/81; 3G, 5A)

Records include Quebec Nordiques, 1979-80 through 1994-95.

Retired Numbers

3	J.C. Tremblay*	1972-1979
8	Marc Tardif*	1979-1983
16	Michel Goulet*	1979-1990
77	Raymond Bourque	2000-2001

* Quebec Nordiques

All-time Record vs. Other Clubs

Regular Season

	At Home								On Road								Total							
	GP	W	L	T	OL	GF	GA	PTS	GP	W	L	T	OL	GF	GA	PTS	GP	W	L	T	OL	GF	GA	PTS
Anaheim	21	11	5	4	1	65	53	27	21	11	5	3	2	53	48	27	42	22	10	7	3	118	101	54
Atlanta	4	2	1	0	1	17	10	5	4	2	1	1	0	8	7	5	8	4	2	1	1	25	17	10
Boston	66	24	36	6	0	234	271	54	62	22	31	9	0	192	240	53	128	46	67	15	0	426	511	107
Buffalo	64	31	21	11	1	227	197	74	63	18	35	9	1	204	247	46	127	49	56	20	2	431	444	120
Calgary	47	18	18	11	0	165	154	47	47	18	20	9	0	141	160	45	94	36	38	20	0	306	314	92
Carolina	65	39	17	9	0	274	191	87	62	26	24	12	0	214	203	64	127	65	41	21	0	488	394	151
Chicago	39	21	12	6	0	158	124	48	41	17	21	3	0	130	144	37	80	38	33	9	0	288	268	85
Columbus	8	8	0	0	0	38	10	16	8	6	0	1	1	31	13	14	16	14	0	1	1	69	23	30
Dallas	41	23	11	7	0	150	103	53	41	15	20	5	1	115	131	36	82	38	31	12	1	265	234	89
Detroit	42	20	17	4	1	148	142	45	40	15	23	1	1	120	142	32	82	35	40	5	2	268	284	77
Edmonton	47	24	19	4	0	179	169	52	46	17	24	4	1	137	186	39	93	41	43	8	1	316	355	91
Florida	11	4	4	3	0	30	27	11	11	10	1	0	0	48	30	20	22	14	5	3	0	78	57	31
Los Angeles	42	23	16	3	0	169	140	49	43	13	25	5	0	137	176	31	85	36	41	8	0	306	316	80
Minnesota	11	8	1	2	0	36	22	18	10	6	1	1	2	36	21	15	21	14	2	3	2	72	43	33
Montreal	63	32	26	5	0	216	222	69	64	16	38	10	0	198	261	42	127	48	64	15	0	414	483	111
Nashville	12	6	3	2	1	32	24	15	12	6	2	3	1	45	36	16	24	12	5	5	2	77	60	31
New Jersey	35	18	13	4	0	124	98	40	36	13	19	4	0	121	147	30	71	31	32	8	0	245	245	70
NY Islanders	34	20	11	3	0	123	97	43	32	13	18	1	0	109	129	27	66	33	29	4	0	232	226	70
NY Rangers	35	19	13	3	0	143	130	41	34	11	19	4	0	99	134	26	69	30	32	7	0	242	264	67
Ottawa	15	12	2	1	0	70	41	25	18	7	8	3	0	64	53	17	33	19	10	4	0	134	94	42
Philadelphia	35	12	10	12	1	124	122	37	34	10	21	2	1	91	122	23	69	22	31	14	2	215	244	60
Phoenix	41	21	15	5	0	142	133	47	40	17	15	7	1	142	144	42	81	38	30	12	1	284	277	89
Pittsburgh	32	17	13	2	0	142	122	36	37	17	15	5	0	152	145	39	69	34	28	7	0	294	267	75
St. Louis	41	20	13	7	1	138	111	48	40	14	22	4	0	124	148	32	81	34	35	11	1	262	259	80
San Jose	23	14	4	4	1	82	42	33	24	16	7	1	0	89	65	33	47	30	11	5	1	171	107	66
Tampa Bay	13	8	3	2	0	50	28	18	12	3	8	1	0	32	39	7	25	11	11	3	0	82	67	25
Toronto	29	17	7	5	0	111	87	39	35	15	16	4	0	133	118	34	64	32	23	9	0	244	205	73
Vancouver	47	22	17	8	0	157	133	52	47	23	16	7	1	181	153	54	94	45	33	15	1	338	286	106
Washington	34	15	14	5	0	105	116	35	33	11	18	4	0	105	131	26	67	26	32	9	0	210	247	61
Totals	**997**	**509**	**342**	**138**	**8**	**3649**	**3119**	**1164**	**997**	**388**	**473**	**123**	**13**	**3251**	**3573**	**912**	**1994**	**897**	**815**	**261**	**21**	**6900**	**6692**	**2076**

Playoffs

	Series	W	L	GP	W	L	T	GF	GA	Last Mtg.
Boston	2	1	1	11	5	6	0	36	37	1983
Buffalo	2	2	0	8	6	2	0	35	27	1985
Chicago	2	2	0	12	8	4	0	49	28	1997
Dallas	3	1	2	19	10	9	0	48	47	2004
Detroit	5	3	2	30	17	13	0	79	76	2002
Edmonton	2	1	1	12	7	5	0	35	30	1998
Florida	1	1	0	4	4	0	0	15	4	1996
Hartford	2	1	1	9	5	4	0	34	35	1987
Los Angeles	2	2	0	14	8	6	0	33	23	2002
Minnesota	1	0	1	7	3	4	0	16	20	2003
Montreal	5	2	3	31	14	17	0	85	105	1993
New Jersey	1	1	0	7	4	3	0	19	11	2001
NY Islanders	1	0	1	4	0	4	0	9	18	1982
NY Rangers	1	0	1	6	2	4	0	19	25	1995
Philadelphia	2	0	2	11	4	7	0	29	39	1985
Phoenix	1	1	0	5	4	1	0	17	10	2000
St. Louis	1	1	0	5	4	1	0	17	11	2001
San Jose	3	2	1	19	10	9	0	51	52	2004
Vancouver	1	0	1	4	0	2	0	20	26	2001
Totals	**39**	**23**	**16**	**224**	**122**	**102**	**0**	**667**	**620**	

Calgary totals include Atlanta Flames, 1979-80.
Dallas totals include Minnesota North Stars, 1979-80 to 1992-93.
Phoenix totals include Winnipeg, 1979-80 to 1995-96.

Carolina totals include Hartford, 1979-80 to 1996-97.
New Jersey totals include Colorado Rockies, 1979-80 to 1981-82.

Playoff Results 2005-2000

Year	Round	Opponent	Result	GF	GA
2004	CSF	San Jose	L 2-4	7	14
	CQF	Dallas	W 4-1	19	10
2003	CQF	Minnesota	L 3-4	17	16
2002	CF	Detroit	L 3-4	13	22
	CSF	San Jose	W 4-3	25	21
	CQF	Los Angeles	W 4-3	16	13
2001	F	**New Jersey**	**W 4-3**	**19**	**11**
	CF	St. Louis	W 4-1	17	11
	CSF	Los Angeles	W 4-3	17	10
	CQF	Vancouver	W 4-0	16	9
2000	CF	Dallas	L 3-4	13	14
	CSF	Detroit	W 4-1	13	8
	CQF	Phoenix	W 4-1	17	10

Abbreviations: Round: F - Final; **CF** - conference final; **CSF** - conference semi-final; **CQF** - conference quarter-final; **DSF** - division semi-final.

Key Off-Season Signings/Acquisitions

2004

June 16 • Re-signed LW **Steve Konowalchuk**.

June 30 • Re-signed D **Bob Boughner**.

July 1 • Signed RW **Ian Laperriere**.

2 • Signed LW **Antti Laaksonen**.

7 • Named **Joel Quenneville** head coach and **Tony Granato** assistant coach.

2005

Aug. 3 • Signed C **Pierre Turgeon** and D **Patrice Brisebois**.

4 • Re-signed LW **Alex Tanguay** and D **Kurt Sauer**.

5 • Signed LW **Brad May**.

6 • Signed LW **Andrew Brunette**.

6 • Re-signed RW **Milan Hejduk**.

9 • Re-signed D **Karlis Skrastins**.

12 • Re-signed RWs **Dan Hinote** and **Marek Svatos**.

16 • Re-signed G **David Aebischer**.

17 • Signed D **Curtis Leschyshyn**.

18 • Re-signed D **John-Michael Liles**.

Entry Draft
Selections 2005-1991

2005
Pick
34	Ryan Stoa
44	Paul Stastny
47	Tom Fritsche
52	Chris Durand
88	T.J. Hensick
124	Raymond Macias
166	Jason Lynch
168	Justin Mercier
222	Kyle Cumiskey

2004
Pick
21	Wojtek Wolski
55	Victor Oreskovich
72	Denis Parshin
154	Richard Demen-Williaume
184	Derek Peltier
215	Ian Keserich
239	Brandon Yip
249	J.D. Corbin
281	Stephen McClellan

2003
Pick
63	David Liffiton
131	David Svagrovsky
146	Mark McCutcheon
163	Brad Richardson
204	Linus Videll
225	Brett Hemingway
257	Darryl Yacboski
288	David Jones

2002
Pick
28	Jonas Johansson
61	Johnny Boychuk
94	Eric Lundberg
107	Mikko Kalteva
129	Tom Gilbert
164	Tyler Weiman
195	Taylor Christie
227	Ryan Steeves
258	Sergei Shemetov
289	Sean Collins

2001
Pick
63	Peter Budaj
97	Danny Bois
130	Colt King
143	Frantisek Skladany
144	Cody McCormick
149	Mikko Viitanen
165	Pierre-Luc Emond
184	Scott Horvath
196	Charlie Stephens
227	Marek Svatos

2000
Pick
14	Vaclav Nedorost
47	Jared Aulin
50	Sergei Soin
63	Agris Saviels
88	Kurt Sauer
92	Sergei Klyazmin
119	Brian Fahey
159	John-Michael Liles
189	Chris Bahen
221	Aaron Molnar
252	Darryl Bootland
266	Sean Kotary
285	Blake Ward

1999
Pick
25	Mikhail Kuleshov
45	Martin Grenier
93	Branko Radivojevic
112	Sanny Lindstrom
122	Kristian Kovac
142	Will Magnuson
152	Jordan Krestanovich
158	Anders Lovdahl
183	Riku Hahl
212	Radim Vrbata
240	Jeff Finger

1998
Pick
12	Alex Tanguay
17	Martin Skoula
19	Robyn Regehr
20	Scott Parker
28	Ramzi Abid
38	Philippe Sauve
53	Steve Moore
79	Evgeny Lazarev
141	K.C. Timmons
167	Alexander Riazantsev

1997
Pick
26	Kevin Grimes
53	Graham Belak
55	Rick Berry
78	Ville Nieminen
87	Brad Larsen
133	Aaron Miskovich
161	David Aebischer
217	Doug Schmidt
243	Kyle Kidney
245	Stephen Lafleur

1996
Pick
25	Peter Ratchuk
51	Yuri Babenko
79	Mark Parrish
98	Ben Storey
107	Randy Petruk
134	Luke Curtin
146	Brian Willsie
160	Kai Fischer
167	Dan Hinote
176	Samuel Pahlsson
188	Roman Pylner
214	Matt Scorsune
240	Justin Clark

1995
Pick
25	Marc Denis
51	Nic Beaudoin
77	John Tripp
81	Tomi Kallio
129	Brent Johnson
155	John Cirjak
181	Dan Smith
207	Tomi Hirvonen
228	Chris George

1994
Pick
12	Wade Belak
22	Jeffrey Kealty
35	Josef Marha
61	Sebastien Bety
72	Chris Drury
87	Milan Hejduk
113	Tony Tuzzolino
139	Nicholas Windsor
165	Calvin Elfring
191	Jay Bertsch
217	Tim Thomas
243	Chris Pittman
285	Steven Low

1993
Pick
10	Jocelyn Thibault
14	Adam Deadmarsh
49	Ashley Buckberger
75	Bill Pierce
101	Ryan Tocher
127	Anders Myrvold
137	Nicholas Checco
153	Christian Matte
179	David Ling
205	Petr Franek
231	Vincent Auger
257	Mark Pivetz
283	John Hillman

1992
Pick
4	Todd Warriner
28	Paul Brousseau
29	Tuomas Gronman
52	Manny Fernandez
76	Ian McIntyre
100	Charlie Wasley
124	Paxton Schulte
148	Martin Lepage
172	Mike Jickling
196	Steve Passmore
220	Anson Carter
244	Aaron Ellis

1991
Pick
1	Eric Lindros
24	Rene Corbet
46	Rich Brennan
68	Dave Karpa
90	Patrick Labrecque
103	Bill Lindsay
134	Mikael Johansson
156	Janne Laukkanen
157	Aaron Asp
178	Adam Bartell
188	Brent Brekke
200	Paul Koch
222	Doug Friedman
244	Eric Meloche

General Managers' History
Maurice Filion, 1979-80 to 1987-88; Martin Madden, 1988-89; Martin Madden and Maurice Filion, 1989-90; Pierre Page, 1990-91 to 1993-94; Pierre Lacroix, 1994-95 to date.

President and General Manager

LACROIX, PIERRE
President/General Manager, Colorado Avalanche.
Born in Montreal, Que., August 3, 1948.
Pierre Lacroix was appointed to the general manager's post on May 24, 1994 after 21 years as a respected player agent. In his first season as general manager, his leadership was instrumental in moving the team from 11th to second place in the NHL. Lacroix's second season began with the club's move to Denver. The revamped Avs finished atop the Pacific Division and went on to win the Stanley Cup. He was named NHL executive of the year by *The Hockey News* and became president of the club's hockey operations in August, 1995. The Avalanche have continued to rank among the NHL's top teams, and won the Stanley Cup again in 2001. Colorado won its record-setting ninth consecutive division title in 2002-03.

Club Directory

Pepsi Center

Colorado Avalanche
Pepsi Center
1000 Chopper Circle
Denver, CO 80204
Phone **303/405-1100**
FAX 303/893-0614
Press Box 303/575-1926
www.coloradoavalanche.com
Capacity: 18,007

Owner & Governor	E. Stanley Kroenke
Alternate Governor, President & General Manager	Pierre Lacroix
Head Coach	Joel Quenneville
Assistant Coach	Jacques Cloutier
Assistant Coach	Tony Granato
Special Assistant to the President	Michel Goulet
Assistant to the General Manager	Greg Sherman
Director of Player Personnel	Brad Smith
Director of Player Development/Goaltending Coach	Craig Billington
Senior Director of Hockey Administration	Charlotte Grahame
Video Coordinator	Bryan Vines
Team Services Assistant	Ronnie Jameson
Chief Scout	Jim Hammett
Pro Scout	Garth Joy
Scouts	Glen Cochrane, Paul Fixter, Luc Gauthier, Alan Hepple, Kiril Ladygin, Joni Lehto, Chris O'Sullivan, Don Paarup, Richard Pracey
Strength and Conditioning Coach	Paul Goldberg
Head Athletic Trainer	Matt Sokolowski
Assistant Athletic Trainer	Scott Woodward
Massage Therapist	Gregorio Pradera
Inventory Manager	Wayne Flemming
Head Equipment Manager	Mark Miller
Assistant Equipment Manager	Terry Geer
Assistant Equipment Manager	Cliff Halstead

Communications Department
Senior Vice President, Communications & Team Services	Jean Martineau
Director of Communications	Damen Zier
Director of Media Services/Internet	Brendan McNicholas

Team Information
Home Ice	Pepsi Center
Capacity	18,007
Rink Dimensions	200' × 85'
Team Colors	Burgundy, Silver, Blue and Black
Team Founded	1979 Quebec Nordiques – Relocated to Colorado 1995
Practice Facility	South Suburban Family Sports Center
Minor League Affiliate	Lowell Lock Monsters (AHL)
Television Outlets	Altitude Sports and Entertainment Network
Radio Flagship	KKFN AM-950

Pierre Turgeon enters his first season with the Avalanche just five goals short of 500 for his career.

Columbus Blue Jackets

2005-06 Schedule

Oct.	Wed.	5	at Washington	Sun.	8	at Phoenix	
	Fri.	7	Calgary	Wed.	11	Pittsburgh	
	Sun.	9	at Chicago	Fri.	13	at Tampa Bay	
	Wed.	12	at San Jose	Sat.	14	at Florida	
	Fri.	14	at Anaheim	Mon.	16	NY Rangers	
	Sun.	16	at Los Angeles*	Wed.	18	Detroit	
	Fri.	21	San Jose	Fri.	20	St. Louis	
	Sat.	22	Detroit	Sat.	21	at Nashville	
	Mon.	24	Detroit	Tue.	24	Vancouver	
	Wed.	26	Nashville	Fri.	27	Minnesota	
	Fri.	28	Minnesota	Sat.	28	Nashville	
	Sat.	29	at Minnesota	**Feb.** Wed.	1	at Calgary	
Nov.	Tue.	1	at Edmonton	Thu.	2	at Edmonton	
	Thu.	3	at Calgary	Mon.	6	at Vancouver	
	Fri.	4	at Vancouver	Wed.	8	Los Angeles	
	Wed.	9	St. Louis	Fri.	10	Colorado	
	Fri.	11	Edmonton	Sat.	11	at Nashville	
	Sun.	13	Los Angeles*	**Mar.** Thu.	2	at Colorado	
	Wed.	16	St. Louis	Sat.	4	at Los Angeles*	
	Fri.	18	at Dallas	Sun.	5	at Anaheim*	
	Sun.	20	at Phoenix	Tue.	7	Chicago	
	Wed.	23	Nashville	Thu.	9	Phoenix	
	Fri.	25	Colorado	Sat.	11	Edmonton	
	Sat.	26	at St. Louis	Mon.	13	at St. Louis	
	Wed.	30	at Minnesota	Wed.	15	at Chicago	
Dec.	Thu.	1	at St. Louis	Fri.	17	Vancouver	
	Thu.	8	NY Islanders	Sun.	19	Anaheim*	
	Fri.	9	at Atlanta	Tue.	21	Phoenix	
	Sun.	11	New Jersey*	Fri.	24	Calgary	
	Tue.	13	Philadelphia	Sat.	25	at Detroit	
	Thu.	15	at Carolina	Tue.	28	San Jose	
	Sat.	17	at Nashville	Fri.	31	at St. Louis	
	Tue.	20	at Detroit	**Apr.** Sat.	1	Chicago	
	Wed.	21	Dallas	Mon.	3	at Nashville	
	Fri.	23	Nashville	Fri.	7	at Detroit	
	Mon.	26	Chicago	Sat.	8	Detroit	
	Wed.	28	Anaheim	Tue.	11	at Dallas	
	Fri.	30	at Chicago	Thu.	13	St. Louis	
	Sat.	31	at Detroit	Sat.	15	Chicago	
Jan.	Thu.	5	at San Jose	Sun.	16	at Chicago	
	Sat.	7	at Colorado*	Tue.	18	Dallas	

Denotes afternoon game.

Franchise date: June 25, 1997

CENTRAL DIVISION

6th NHL Season

Year-by-Year Record

Season	GP	Home W	L	T	OL	Road W	L	T	OL	Overall W	L	T	OL	GF	GA	Pts.	Finished	Playoff Result
2004-05	....	....				....				....				....	....	....		
2003-04	82	17	18	4	2	8	27	4	2	25	45	8	4	177	238	62	4th, Central Div.	Out of Playoffs
2002-03	82	20	14	5	2	9	28	3	1	29	42	8	3	213	263	69	5th, Central Div.	Out of Playoffs
2001-02	82	14	18	5	4	8	29	3	1	22	47	8	5	164	255	57	5th, Central Div.	Out of Playoffs
2000-01	82	19	15	4	3	9	24	5	3	28	39	9	6	190	233	71	5th, Central Div.	Out of Playoffs

David Vyborny reached NHL highs in goals (22), assists (31) and points (53) in 2003-04. His assist total led the team, while his goals and points trailed only Rick Nash.

2005-06 Player Personnel

FORWARDS

	HT	WT	S	Place of Birth	Date	2004-05 Club
BALASTIK, Jaroslav	6-0	198	L	Gottwaldov, Czech.	11/28/79	Zlin
BRULE, Gilbert	5-10	175	R	Edmonton, Alta.	1/1/87	Vancouver (WHL)
FRITSCHE, Dan	6-1	198	R	Parma, OH	7/13/85	Sarnia-London
HARTIGAN, Mark	6-1	205	L	Fort St. John, B.C.	10/15/77	Syracuse
HRDINA, Jan	6-0	205	R	Hradec Kralove, Czech.	2/5/76	Kladno
JACKMAN, Tim	6-4	210	R	Minot, ND	11/14/81	Syracuse
LETOWSKI, Trevor	5-10	180	R	Thunder Bay, Ont.	4/5/77	Fribourg
LINDSTROM, Joakim	6-0	187	L	Skelleftea, Sweden	12/5/83	MODO-Syracuse
MALHOTRA, Manny	6-2	215	L	Mississauga, Ont.	5/18/80	Ljubljana-HV 71
MARCHANT, Todd	5-10	180	L	Buffalo, NY	8/12/73	
MOTZKO, Joe	6-0	190	R	Bemidji, MN	3/14/80	Syracuse
MURRAY, Andrew	6-2	210	L	Selkirk, Man.	11/6/81	Bemidji State
NASH, Rick	6-4	206	L	Brampton, Ont.	6/16/84	Davos
PICARD, Alexandre	6-2	190	L	Les Saules, Que.	10/9/85	Lewiston
SANDERSON, Geoff	6-0	190	L	Hay River, N.W.T.	2/1/72	Geneve
SARNO, Peter	5-11	185	L	Toronto, Ont.	7/26/79	Manitoba
SHELLEY, Jody	6-4	225	L	Thompson, Man.	2/7/76	JYP
SIMON, Ben	6-0	195	L	Shaker Heights, OH	6/14/78	Chicago (AHL)
SVITOV, Alexander	6-3	217	L	Omsk, USSR	11/3/82	Syracuse
VYBORNY, David	5-10	189	L	Jihlava, Czech.	6/2/75	Sparta
WRIGHT, Tyler	6-0	190	R	Kamsack, Sask.	4/6/73	Biel
ZHERDEV, Nikolai	6-1	186	R	Kiev, USSR	11/5/84	CSKA

DEFENSEMEN

	HT	WT	S	Place of Birth	Date	2004-05 Club
BEAUCHEMIN, Francois	6-0	214	L	Sorel, Que.	6/4/80	Syracuse
BERARD, Bryan	6-2	220	L	Woonsocket, RI	3/5/77	
FOOTE, Adam	6-2	215	R	Toronto, Ont.	7/10/71	
JOHNSON, Aaron	6-0	197	L	Port Hawkesbury, N.S.	4/30/83	Syracuse
KLESLA, Rostislav	6-3	208	L	Novy Jicin, Czech.	3/21/82	Vsetin-HPK
MacMILLAN, Jeff	6-3	210	L	Durham, Ont.	3/30/79	Hartford
METHOT, Marc	6-3	196	L	Ottawa, Ont.	6/21/85	London
RICHARDSON, Luke	6-4	215	L	Ottawa, Ont.	3/26/69	
SUCHY, Radoslav	6-2	204	L	Kezmarok, Czech.	4/7/76	Poprad
SUGDEN, Brandon	6-4	225	L	Toronto, Ont.	6/23/78	Syracuse
TOLLEFSEN, Ole-Kristian	6-2	200	L	Oslo, Norway	3/29/84	Syracuse-Dayton
WESTCOTT, Duvie	5-11	192	R	Winnipeg, Man.	10/30/77	JYP

GOALTENDERS

	HT	WT	C	Place of Birth	Date	2004-05 Club
DENIS, Marc	6-1	193	L	Montreal, Que.	8/1/77	
LECLAIRE, Pascal	6-2	190	L	Repentigny, Que.	11/7/82	Syracuse
PRUSEK, Martin	6-1	176	L	Ostrava, Czech.	12/11/75	Vitkovice-Znojmo

General Managers' History

Doug MacLean, 2000-01 to date.

President and General Manager

MacLEAN, DOUG
President/General Manager, Columbus Blue Jackets.
Born in Summerside, P.E.I., April 12, 1954.

Doug MacLean was named the first general manager of the Blue Jackets on February 11, 1998. A month later he was named president of the organization and as its top executive, he holds the dual role of overseeing both the business and hockey operations of the franchise as well as the management of Nationwide Arena. MacLean also coached the team for parts of the 2002-03 and 2003-04 seasons.

Under MacLean's guidance, the Blue Jackets have established themselves as one of the most successful business franchises in the NHL. The Blue Jackets have made a significant impact in the Columbus community through its business operations and community service programs.

Prior to joining the Blue Jackets, MacLean served as head coach of the Florida Panthers, where he led his teams into the playoffs in both of his full seasons behind the bench (1995-96, 1996-97). In his first season as an NHL head coach, MacLean led Florida to the Stanley Cup Finals.

MacLean began his NHL coaching career in 1986 as an assistant to Jacques Martin in St. Louis. He spent two seasons with the Blues before joining the Washington Capitals in 1988, assisting Bryan Murray behind the bench. He was named coach of the Capitals' American Hockey League affiliate in Baltimore for the final 35 games of the 1989-90 season.

The following season, MacLean joined Murray on the Detroit Red Wings, serving as an assistant coach for two years. In 1992, MacLean was named assistant general manager of the Red Wings and also served as general manager of the team's AHL affiliate in Adirondack for two years. MacLean followed Murray to the Panthers in 1994, becoming the expansion club's director of player development. He was named head coach on July 24, 1995.

A collegiate hockey player at the University of Prince Edward Island, MacLean graduated with a bachelor's degree in education. He also played for the Montreal Jr. Canadiens and was invited to training camp with the St. Louis Blues in 1974. Following his playing career, MacLean enrolled at the University of Western Ontario, where he received a master's degree in educational psychology. While attending Western, MacLean began his coaching career as an assistant with London of the Ontario Hockey League.

NHL Coaching Record

Season	Team	Regular Season				Playoffs		
		Games	W	L	T	Games	W	L
1995-96	Florida	82	41	31	10	22	12	10
1996-97	Florida	82	35	28	19	5	1	4
1997-98	Florida	23	7	12	4	....	....	....
2002-03	Columbus	42	15	23	4	....	....	....
2003-04	Columbus	37	9	24	4	....	....	....
	NHL Totals	**266**	**107**	**118**	**41**	**27**	**13**	**14**

In the System and Recently Drafted

FORWARDS

	HT	WT	S	Place of Birth	Date	2004-05 Club
BOLL, Jared	6-2	190	R	Crystal Lake, NC	5/13/86	Lincoln
DUPUIS, Philippe	6-0	192	R	Laval, Que.	4/24/85	Rouyn-Noranda
GENOVY, Jeff	6-3	191	L	Kalamazoo, MI	12/4/82	Clarkson
GOERTZEN, Steven	6-1	190	R	Stony Plain, Alta.	5/26/84	Syracuse
GREER, Matt	6-2	190	R	St. Paul, MN	11/21/85	Des Moines
HYVONEN, Hannes	6-2	200	R	Oulu, Finland	8/29/75	Farjestad-Ilves
JARMAN, Kevin	6-0	184	L	Toronto, Ont.	3/12/85	Massachusetts
JOKILA, Janne	5-9	174	L	Turku, Finland	4/22/82	Syracuse-Dayton
KOLARIK, Tyler	5-10	185	R	Philadelphia, PA	1/26/81	Syracuse-Dayton
KONSORADA, Tim	6-0	201	R	Ft. Saskatchewan, Alta.	3/21/84	Brandon
KRACIK, Jaroslav	6-0	178	L	Prague, Czech.	1/18/83	Pisek-Plzen
LUCHINKIN, Sergei	5-11	172	L	Dmitrov, USSR	10/16/76	
MARS, Per	6-3	210	L	Ostersund, Sweden	10/23/82	Tegs
MAULDIN, Greg	5-11	180	R	Boston, MA	6/10/82	Syracuse
McGUIRK, Brian	6-0	191	L	Danvers, MA	7/11/85	Boston University
MOZYAKIN, Sergei	5-10	165	R	Yaroslavl, USSR	3/30/81	CSKA
NEDOROST, Andrej	6-1	198	L	Trencin, Czech.	4/30/80	Magnit.-Nizhnekamsk-Karlovy Vary
PAROULEK, Martin	6-0	193	R	Uherske Hradiste, Czech.	11/4/79	Beroun-Plzen
PETRELL, Lennart	6-3	198	L	Helsinki, Finland	4/13/84	HIFK
PIISPANEN, Arsi	6-3	163	L	Jyvaskyla, Finland	7/23/85	JYP
PINEAULT, Adam	6-1	193	R	Holyoke, MA	5/23/86	Moncton
POHL, Petr	5-11	185	R	Prostejov, Czech.	8/28/86	Gatineau
SANNITZ, Raffaele	6-1	187	L	Mendrisio, Switz.	5/18/83	Syracuse-Dayton
SPANHEL, Martin	6-2	206	L	Zlin, Czech.	7/1/77	Lillehammer IK
STARKOV, Kirill	6-0	194	L	Yekateringurg, USSR	3/31/87	Frolunda Jr.
STREIT, Martin	6-2	202	R	Vyskov, Czech.	2/2/77	Unicov
SUBBOTIN, Dmitri	6-1	183	L	Tomsk, USSR	10/20/77	Omsk
TKACHENKO, Ivan	5-10	183	L	Yaroslavl, USSR	11/9/79	Yaroslavl
VOSTRIKOV, Artem	6-1	175	L	Togliatti, USSR	3/23/83	Krylja Sovetov

DEFENSEMEN

	HT	WT	S	Place of Birth	Date	2004-05 Club
CLITSOME, Grant	6-0	208	L	Gloucester, Ont.	4/14/85	Clarkson
FLOOD, Mark	6-1	189	R	Charlottetown, PEI	9/29/84	Peterborough
GUSKOV, Alexander	6-2	202	L	Nizhny Novgorod, USSR	11/26/76	Kazan-Omsk
HENDRIKX, Trevor	6-2	200	R	Russell, Ont.	3/29/85	Peterborough
KOSMACHEV, Dmitry	6-3	209	R	Nizhny Novgorod, USSR	6/7/85	Nizhny Novgorod
MANNING, Paul	6-4	205	R	Red Deer, Alta.	4/15/79	Hamburg
McQUAID, Adam	6-3	197	R	Charlottetown, P.E.I.	10/12/86	Sudbury
PAGE, Rob	6-1	188	R	Edina, MN	7/9/85	Yale
PETROCHININ, Evgeny	6-2	190	L	Murmansk, USSR	2/7/76	Magnitogorsk
PLEHANOV, Andrei	6-1	187	R	Nizhnekamsk, USSR	7/12/86	Nizhnekamsk-Leninogorsk-Perm 2
RAJAMAKI, Tommi	6-3	206	L	Pori, Finland	2/29/76	
REDLIHS, Jekabs	6-2	185	L	Riga, Latvia	3/29/82	Boston University
REINHART, Derek	6-3	205	R	Rosalind, Alta.	4/20/87	Regina
RUSSELL, Kris	5-10	160	L	Caroline, Alta.	5/2/87	Medicine Hat
VIENNEAU, Justin	6-4	205	L	Saint John, N.B.	2/20/86	Shawinigan
WHARTON, Kyle	6-3	185	L	Ottawa, Ont.	3/3/86	Ottawa (OHL)-SS Marie

GOALTENDERS

	HT	WT	C	Place of Birth	Date	2004-05 Club
LACOSTA, Dan	6-1	186	L	Labrador City, Nfld.	3/28/86	Owen Sound-Barrie
PENNER, Andrew	6-2	205	L	Scarborough, Ont.	12/21/82	Syracuse-Dayton
POPPERLE, Tomas	6-1	187	L	Broumov, Czech.	10/10/84	Beroun-Sparta

One of the league's top defensive defenseman, Adam Foote averaged over 25 minutes of playing time per game in his last six seasons with Colorado.

Club Records

Team

(Figures in brackets for season records are games played.)

Most Points 71 2000-01 (82)
Most Wins 29 2002-03 (82)
Most Ties 9 2000-01 (82)
Most Losses 47 2001-02 (82)
Most Goals 213 2002-03 (82)
Most Goals Against 263 2002-03 (82)
Fewest Points 57 2001-02 (82)
Fewest Wins 22 2001-02 (82)
Fewest Ties 8 2001-02 (82), 2002-03 (82), 2003-04 (82)
Fewest Losses 39 2000-01 (82)
Fewest Goals 164 2001-02 (82)
Fewest Goals Against 233 2000-01 (82)

Longest Winning Streak
Overall .... 4 Nov. 9-Nov. 16/00, Mar. 21-27/04
Home .... 4 Mar. 24-Apr. 8/01, Dec. 31/01-Jan. 16/02
Away .... 3 Jan. 8-11/03

Longest Undefeated Streak
Overall .... 4 Nov. 9-Nov. 16/00 (4 wins), Mar. 21-27/04 (4 wins)
Home .... 6 Jan. 20-Feb. 12/03 (4 wins, 2 ties)
Away .... 4 Jan. 3-11/03 (3 wins, 1 tie)

Longest Losing Streak
Overall .... 8 Nov. 17-Dec. 3/00, Mar. 3-18/04
Home .... 6 Oct. 12-Nov. 9/01
Away .... 11 Mar. 25-Oct. 29/02

Longest Winless Streak
Overall .... 9 Dec. 4-23/03 (8 losses, 1 tie)
Home .... 8 Oct. 4-Nov. 9/01 (6 losses, 2 ties), Dec. 4-31/03 (7 losses, 1 tie)
Away .... 14 Oct. 9-Dec. 23/03 (13 losses, 1 tie)
Most Shutouts, Season 5 2002-03 (82), 2003-04 (82)
Most PIM, Season 1,505 2002-03 (82)
Most Goals, Game .... 7 Three times

Individual

Most Seasons .... 4 Eight players
Most Games .... 315 David Vyborny
Most Goals, Career .... 88 Geoff Sanderson
Most Assists, Career .... 95 Ray Whitney
Most Points, Career .... 168 Geoff Sanderson (88G, 80A)
Most PIM, Career .... 693 Jody Shelley
Most Shutouts, Career ...... 11 Marc Denis
Longest Consecutive
Games Streak .... 161 David Vyborny (Oct. 17/02 to date)
Most Goals, Season .... 41 Rick Nash (2003-04)

Most Assists, Season .... 52 Ray Whitney (2002-03)
Most Points, Season .... 76 Ray Whitney (2002-03; 24G, 52A)
Most PIM, Season .... 249 Jody Shelley (2002-03)
Most Points, Defenseman, Season .... 45 Jaroslav Spacek (2002-03; 9G, 36A)
Most Points, Center, Season .... 68 Andrew Cassels (2002-03; 20G, 48A)
Most Points, Right Wing, Season .... 53 David Vyborny (2003-04; 22G, 31A)
Most Points, Left Wing, Season .... 76 Ray Whitney (2002-03; 24G, 52A)
Most Points, Rookie, Season .... 39 Rick Nash (2002-03; 17G, 22A)
Most Shutouts, Season .... 5 Marc Denis (2002-03, 2003-04)
Most Goals, Game .... 4 Geoff Sanderson (Jan. 11/03)
Most Assists, Game .... 5 Espen Knutsen (Mar. 24/01)
Most Points, Game. .... 5 Espen Knutsen (Mar. 24/01; 5A), Geoff Sanderson (Jan. 11/03; 4G, 1A), Andrew Cassels (Jan. 11/03; 1G, 4A), David Vyborny (Feb. 28/04; 1G, 4A)

Captains' History

Lyle Odelein, 2000-01, 2001-02; Ray Whitney, 2002-03; Luke Richardson, 2003-04 to date.

Goaltender Martin Prusek arrives in Columbus after three seasons with the Senators. He had a 2.12 average in his first full season as an NHL backup in 2003-04.

Key Off-Season Signings/Acquisitions

2004
May 26 • Re-signed LW **Jody Shelley**.
June 25 • Named **Gerard Gallant** head coach and **Dean Blais** associate coach.
June 28 • Claimed LW **Geoff Sanderson** off waivers from Vancouver.
July 6 • Obtained D **Radoslav Suchy** and a 2005 6th-round pick from Phoenix for a 2005 4th-round pick.
Sept. 14 • Re-signed G **Marc Denis** and RW **David Vyborny**.

2005
Aug. 2 • Signed D **Adam Foote**.
3 • Signed D **Bryan Berard**.
4 • Signed G **Martin Prusek**.
8 • Re-signed LW **Rick Nash**.
10 • Signed C **Jan Hrdina**.
15 • Re-signed D **Rostislav Klesla** and G **Pascal Leclaire**.
29 • Signed 2004 1st-round pick (8th overall), RW **Alexandre Picard**.

All-time Record vs. Other Clubs

Regular Season

	At Home								On Road								Total							
	GP	W	L	T	OL	GF	GA	PTS	GP	W	L	T	OL	GF	GA	PTS	GP	W	L	T	OL	GF	GA	PTS
Anaheim	8	6	2	0	0	23	15	12	8	2	4	1	1	16	24	6	16	8	6	1	1	39	39	18
Atlanta	4	2	2	0	0	12	11	4	3	1	2	0	0	6	5	2	7	3	4	0	0	18	16	6
Boston	3	1	2	0	0	3	14	2	2	1	1	0	0	7	8	2	5	2	3	0	0	10	22	4
Buffalo	2	1	0	1	0	5	4	3	4	2	2	0	0	9	13	4	6	3	2	1	0	14	17	7
Calgary	8	6	1	0	1	26	16	13	8	3	5	0	0	18	24	6	16	9	6	0	1	44	40	19
Carolina	3	1	2	0	0	6	9	2	4	1	3	0	0	11	13	2	7	2	5	0	0	17	22	4
Chicago	11	6	4	1	0	32	34	13	10	2	7	1	0	15	30	5	21	8	11	2	0	47	64	18
Colorado	8	1	6	1	0	13	31	3	8	0	8	0	0	10	38	0	16	1	14	1	0	23	69	3
Dallas	8	2	6	0	0	19	26	4	8	0	7	0	1	9	26	1	16	2	13	0	1	28	52	5
Detroit	11	2	4	1	4	21	26	9	10	2	8	0	0	22	39	4	21	4	12	1	4	43	65	13
Edmonton	8	1	4	3	0	20	27	5	8	1	6	0	1	17	31	3	16	2	10	3	1	37	58	8
Florida	2	1	1	0	0	4	4	2	3	1	2	0	0	7	9	2	5	2	3	0	0	11	13	4
Los Angeles	8	5	3	0	0	21	26	10	8	3	4	1	0	16	18	7	16	8	7	1	0	37	44	17
Minnesota	7	5	1	1	0	19	7	11	8	2	5	0	1	16	25	5	15	7	6	1	1	35	32	16
Montreal	1	0	1	0	0	1	3	0	4	2	1	0	1	6	6	5	5	2	2	0	1	7	9	5
Nashville	10	5	4	0	1	23	27	11	11	3	7	1	0	24	29	7	21	8	11	1	1	47	56	18
New Jersey	4	2	2	0	0	13	13	4	2	0	1	1	0	4	5	1	6	2	3	1	0	17	18	5
NY Islanders	4	3	0	1	0	13	7	7	2	2	0	0	0	11	7	4	6	5	0	1	0	24	14	11
NY Rangers	4	3	1	0	0	16	7	6	2	0	1	1	0	5	7	1	6	3	2	1	0	21	14	7
Ottawa	2	0	1	0	1	7	9	1	3	0	2	1	0	6	12	1	5	0	3	1	1	13	21	2
Philadelphia	3	0	1	2	0	6	7	2	2	0	1	0	1	3	7	1	5	0	2	2	1	9	14	3
Phoenix	8	4	3	1	0	19	14	9	8	0	5	3	0	15	24	3	16	4	8	4	0	34	38	12
Pittsburgh	3	1	0	0	2	10	9	4	3	1	2	0	0	9	12	2	6	2	2	0	2	19	21	6
St. Louis	10	4	3	2	1	22	26	11	11	1	8	1	1	23	45	4	21	5	11	3	2	45	71	15
San Jose	8	3	4	0	1	21	20	7	8	1	6	0	1	12	32	3	16	4	10	0	2	33	52	10
Tampa Bay	3	1	1	1	0	5	4	3	3	1	2	0	0	3	5	2	6	2	3	1	0	8	9	5
Toronto	1	1	0	0	0	4	3	2	3	0	2	1	0	4	10	1	4	1	2	1	0	8	13	3
Vancouver	8	2	4	0	2	17	29	6	8	2	5	0	1	23	34	5	16	4	9	0	3	40	63	11
Washington	4	1	2	0	1	11	15	3	2	0	1	1	0	5	8	1	6	1	3	1	1	16	23	4
Totals	164	70	65	18	11	412	443	169	164	34	108	15	7	332	546	90	328	104	173	33	18	744	989	259

Entry Draft
Selections 2005-2000

2005
Pick
6	Gilbert Brule
55	Adam McQuaid
67	Kris Russell
101	Jared Boll
131	Thomas Popperle
177	Derek Reinhart
189	Kirill Starkov
201	Trevor Hendrikx

2004
Pick
8	Alexandre Picard
46	Adam Pineault
59	Kyle Wharton
93	Dan Lacosta
96	Andrei Plehanov
133	Petr Pohl
167	Rob Page
190	Lennart Petrell
198	Justin Vienneau
231	Brian Mcguirk
233	Matt Greer
271	Grant Clitsome

2003
Pick
4	Nikolai Zherdev
46	Dan Fritsche
71	Dmitry Kosmachev
103	Kevin Jarman
104	Philippe Dupuis
138	Arsi Piispanen
168	Marc Methot
200	Alexander Guskov
233	Mathieu Gravel
283	Trevor Hendrikx

2002
Pick
1	Rick Nash
41	Joakim Lindstrom
65	Ole-Kristian Tollefsen
96	Jeff Genovy
98	Ivan Tkachenko
119	Jekabs Redlihs
133	Lasse Pirjeta
168	Tim Konsorada
184	Jaroslav Balastik
199	Greg Mauldin
225	Steven Goertzen
231	Jaroslav Kracik
263	Sergei Mozyakin

2001
Pick
8	Pascal Leclaire
38	Tim Jackman
53	Kiel McLeod
85	Aaron Johnson
87	Per Mars
141	Cole Jarrett
173	Justin Aikins
187	Artem Vostrikov
204	Raffaele Sannitz
236	Ryan Bowness
242	Andrew Murray

2000
Pick
4	Rostislav Klesla
69	Ben Knopp
133	Petteri Nummelin
138	Scott Heffernan
150	Tyler Kolarik
169	Shane Bendera
200	Janne Jokila
231	Peter Zingoni
278	Martin Paroulek
286	Andrej Nedorost
292	Louis Mandeville

Coaching History
Dave King, 2000-01, 2001-02; Dave King and Doug MacLean, 2002-03; Doug MacLean and Gerard Gallant, 2003-04; Gerard Gallant, 2004-05 to date.

Coach

GALLANT, GERARD
Coach, Columbus Blue Jackets.
Born in Summerside, P.E.I., September 2, 1963.

Former NHL All-Star Gerard Gallant joined the Blue Jackets organization July 18, 2000 and served as an assistant coach for three and a half seasons. He took over as the club's interim head coach on January 1, 2004 and was officially named to the position of head coach on June 25.

Originally the Red Wings' sixth pick, 107th overall, in the 1981 Entry Draft, Gallant spent two seasons with Adirondack, Detroit's AHL affiliate. His NHL career began with the Red Wings in 1984 when he notched six goals and 12 assists for 18 points in 32 games as a rookie. Over the next eight years, he averaged 56 points and 72 games played with Detroit, including four consecutive seasons with 70 or more points from 1986 to 1990. Gallant helped Detroit capture three division titles and in 1988-89 he was named a Second Team NHL All-Star after posting a career-high 39 goals, 54 assists and 93 points in 76 games.

Gallant wrapped up his Red Wings career following the 1992-93 season having registered 207 goals, 260 assists, 467 points and 1,600 penalty minutes in 563 games. He signed with the Tampa Bay Lightning as a free agent and played in 51 games during the 1993-94 season. He concluded his NHL career with 211 goals, 269 assists, 480 points and 1,674 penalty minutes in 615 games.

Gallant spent the next five years coaching at the junior hockey and minor pro levels before joining the Blue Jackets organization. He began his coaching career with the Summerside (PEI) Western Capitals, a Canadian Junior A team, midway through the 1995-96 season. In 1996-97, his first full season with the club, he led the squad to the Royal Bank Cup championship, Canada's Junior A national championship tournament, and a 33-11-11 regular season mark. He remained with the club through 1997-98.

Gallant then served as an assistant coach with the Fort Wayne Komets of the International Hockey League in 1998-99 and the following season joined the Louisville Panthers of the American Hockey League as the club's top assistant coach.

Coaching Record

Season	Team	Games	Regular Season W	L	T	Playoffs Games	W	L
2003-04	Columbus (NHL)	45	16	25	4	....	....	....
2004-05	Columbus (NHL)				Season Cancelled			
	NHL Totals	**45**	**16**	**25**	**4**	....	....	....

Club Directory

Nationwide Arena

Columbus Blue Jackets
Nationwide Arena
200 W. Nationwide Blvd.
Columbus, Ohio 43215
Phone **614/246-4625**
FAX 614/246-4007
www.BlueJackets.com
Capacity: 18,136

Ownership
Majority Owner/Governor	John H. McConnell
Alternate Governor	John P. McConnell

Executive Staff
President/General Manager/Alt. Governor	Doug MacLean
Executive Vice-President/Asst. General Manager	Jim Clark
Sr. Vice-President of Business Operations	Larry Hoepfner
Vice-President of Marketing	David Paitson
Vice-President of Corporate Development	Paul D'Aiuto
Vice-President of Ticket Sales	Dan Froehlich
Chief Financial Officer	T.J. LaMendola
General Counsel	Greg Kirstein
Executive Director of Marketing	Marc Gregory
Executive Director of Communications	Todd Sharrock

Hockey Operations
Head Coach	Gerard Gallant
Associate Coach	Dean Blais
Assistant Coach	Gord Murphy
Goaltending Coach, Pro Scout	Rick Wamsley
Director of Player Personnel	Don Boyd
Director of Pro Scouting	Bob Strumm
Director of Player Development	Paul Castron
Manager of Hockey Operations	Chris MacFarland
Manager of Team Services	Jim Rankin
Video Coordinator	Dan Singleton
Administrative Assistant, Hockey Operations	Julie Uhler
Amateur Scouts	Sam McMaster, Wayne Smith, John Williams
Pro Scout	Peter Dineen
European Scout	Kjell Larsson
Regional Scouts	Brian Bates, Scott Fitzgerald, Jukka Holtari, Denis LeBlanc, John McNamara, Artem Telepin Nicholaevich, Bryan Raymond, Andrew Shaw, Milan Tichy
Head Athletic Trainer	Chris Mizer
Strength/Conditioning Coach	Barry Brennan
Massage Therapist	Chris Hannan
Equipment Manager	Tim LeRoy
Assistant Equipment Manager	Jamie Healy
Equipment Assistant	Jason Stypinski

Business Operations
Director of Client Services	Brent Baker
Director of Event Presentation/Production	Kimberly Kershaw
Director of Fan Development	J.D. Kershaw
Director of Community Development	Wendy Bradshaw
Director of Human Resources	Kelley Walton
Director of Retail Operations	Chris Weller
Director of Corporate Sales – Destroyers	Jeff Abbot
Director of Creative Services	Jason Rothwell
Assistant Director of Communications	Jay Levin
Graphic Designer/Manager of Print Production	Will Bennett
Client Services Manager	Heather Popa
Client Services Manager	Cheri Masdea
Account Executive – Corporate Development	Joe Jerele
Manager of Video Production	David Bakalik
Manager of Fan Development	Joel Siegman
Manager of Community Development	Kate Furman
Mascot Coordinator	Jason Zumpano
Video Broadcast Engineer	John Bonitatibus
Human Resources Coordinator	Jennifer Pritz
Payroll Administrator	Christine Parthemore
Retail Operations Warehouse Manager	Ron Smith
Retail Operations Warehouse Associate	Michael LeMaster
Blueline Store Manager	Terry Lowe
Administrative Asst. – Business Development	Gretchen Kyle
Administrative Asst. – Legal, Marketing	Meredith Francis

Finance
Controller	Rich Gross
Staff Accountant	Nora Ludwig
Accounts Payable	Rose Phillips
MIS Manager	Jim Connolly
Office Manager	Rachel Durham
Receptionist	Beth Trexler

Ticket Operations
Senior Director of Tickets Sales/Service	Bill Makris
Director of Ticket Operations/Customer Service	Mark Morris
Mgr. of Ticket Operations/Customer Service	Karen Miller
Manager of Premium Sales/Services	Gabrielle Graf
Inside Sales Manager	Joseph Cote
Account Executive – Group Sales	Clint Fetty
Account Executive – Group Sales	Eric Knauss
Account Executive – Group Sales	Heather Sweeney
Account Executive – Group Sales	Valerie Ott
Account Executive – Season Sales	Cory Rowe
Account Executive – Season Sales	Jim Levin
Season Ticket Service Representative	Katie McMahon
Customer Service Representative	Timothy Hunter
Customer Service Representative	Amanda Horning
Coordinator of Premium Sales/Service	Kristin Anderson

Broadcasting
Director of Broadcasting	Russ Mollohan
Fox Sports Net Play-By-Play Announcer	Jeff Rimer
Fox Sports Net Color Analyst	Brian Engblom
Radio Play-By-Play Announcer	George Matthews
Radio Color Analyst	Bill Davidge

Dallas Stars

Marty Turco has posted a combined goals-against average of 1.91 during his four seasons in the Stars net. He has led the league in goals-against average twice in that time.

2005-06 Schedule

Oct.	Wed.	5	Los Angeles		Mon.	9	at Minnesota
	Sat.	8	Colorado		Thu.	12	Washington
	Tue.	11	Phoenix		Sat.	14	at Boston*
	Thu.	13	at Calgary		Mon.	16	at Montreal
	Fri.	14	at Edmonton		Wed.	18	Atlanta
	Sun.	16	at Vancouver		Fri.	20	Tampa Bay
	Thu.	20	Los Angeles		Mon.	23	Phoenix
	Sat.	22	Calgary		Wed.	25	St. Louis
	Wed.	26	San Jose		Thu.	26	at Colorado
	Fri.	28	Edmonton		Sat.	28	Detroit*
	Sat.	29	at Phoenix		Mon.	30	San Jose
Nov.	Wed.	2	Los Angeles	Feb.	Wed.	1	Nashville
	Fri.	4	Chicago		Sat.	4	at St. Louis*
	Sat.	5	at Colorado		Mon.	6	Nashville
	Mon.	7	Edmonton		Thu.	9	at Phoenix
	Thu.	10	at Nashville		Fri.	10	at San Jose
	Sat.	12	at San Jose		Sun.	12	at Los Angeles*
	Sun.	13	at Anaheim*	Mar.	Thu.	2	at Phoenix
	Wed.	16	at Anaheim		Sat.	4	Colorado
	Fri.	18	Columbus		Sun.	5	at Chicago
	Wed.	23	Anaheim		Tue.	7	at Edmonton
	Fri.	25	Phoenix		Thu.	9	at Calgary
	Sat.	26	at Nashville		Sat.	11	at Vancouver
	Wed.	30	San Jose		Mon.	13	Vancouver
Dec.	Fri.	2	Carolina		Thu.	16	at Los Angeles
	Wed.	7	Florida		Sat.	18	at San Jose*
	Sat.	10	at Toronto		Mon.	20	Anaheim
	Wed.	14	at Buffalo		Wed.	22	Minnesota
	Thu.	15	at Ottawa		Fri.	24	Chicago
	Sun.	18	at Chicago		Sun.	26	Calgary*
	Mon.	19	at Minnesota		Wed.	29	Anaheim
	Wed.	21	at Columbus		Fri.	31	at Anaheim
	Fri.	23	Phoenix	Apr.	Sat.	1	at Los Angeles
	Mon.	26	at St. Louis		Mon.	3	San Jose
	Tue.	27	Detroit		Thu.	6	at Anaheim
	Thu.	29	St. Louis		Sat.	8	at Phoenix
	Sat.	31	Los Angeles		Sun.	9	at San Jose*
Jan.	Mon.	2	at Los Angeles		Tue.	11	Columbus
	Wed.	4	Vancouver		Sat.	15	Minnesota*
	Fri.	6	Anaheim		Mon.	17	at Detroit
	Sun.	8	at Detroit*		Tue.	18	at Columbus

* Denotes afternoon game.

Franchise date: June 5, 1967

Transferred from Minnesota to Dallas, June 9, 1993.

WESTERN CONFERENCE

PACIFIC DIVISION

39th NHL Season

Year-by-Year Record

		Home				Road				Overall							
Season	GP	W	L	T	OL	W	L	T	OL	W	L	T	OL	GF	GA	Pts.	Finished	Playoff Result
2004-05	....	....				....				....				....	....	....		
2003-04	82	26	7	8	0	15	19	5	2	41	26	13	2	194	175	97	2nd, Pacific Div.	Lost Conf. Quarter-Final
2002-03	82	28	5	6	2	18	12	9	2	46	17	15	4	245	169	111	1st, Pacific Div.	Lost Conf. Semi-Final
2001-02	82	18	13	6	4	18	15	7	1	36	28	13	5	215	213	90	4th, Pacific Div.	Out of Playoffs
2000-01	82	26	10	5	0	22	14	3	2	48	24	8	2	241	187	106	1st, Pacific Div.	Lost Conf. Semi-Final
1999-2000	82	21	11	5	4	22	12	5	2	43	23	10	6	211	184	102	1st, Pacific Div.	Lost Final
1998-99	**82**	**29**	**8**	**4**	**....**	**22**	**11**	**8**	**....**	**51**	**19**	**12**		**236**	**168**	**114**	**1st, Pacific Div.**	**Won Stanley Cup**
1997-98	82	26	8	7	....	23	14	4	....	49	22	11	....	242	167	109	1st, Central Div.	Lost Conf. Final
1996-97	82	25	13	3	....	23	13	5	....	48	26	8	....	252	198	104	1st, Central Div.	Lost Conf. Quarter-Final
1995-96	82	14	18	9	....	12	24	5	....	26	42	14	....	227	280	66	6th, Central Div.	Out of Playoffs
1994-95	48	9	10	5	....	8	13	3	....	17	23	8	....	136	135	42	5th, Central Div.	Lost Conf. Quarter-Final
1993-94	84	23	12	7	....	19	17	6	....	42	29	13	....	286	265	97	3rd, Central Div.	Lost Conf. Semi-Final
1992-93*	84	18	17	7	....	18	21	3	....	36	38	10	....	272	293	82	5th, Norris Div.	Out of Playoffs
1991-92*	80	20	16	4	....	12	26	2	....	32	42	6	....	246	278	70	4th, Norris Div.	Lost Div. Semi-Final
1990-91*	80	19	15	6	....	8	24	8	....	27	39	14	....	256	266	68	4th, Norris Div.	Lost Final
1989-90*	80	26	12	2	....	10	28	2	....	36	40	4	....	284	291	76	4th, Norris Div.	Lost Div. Semi-Final
1988-89*	80	17	15	8	....	10	22	8	....	27	37	16	....	258	278	70	3rd, Norris Div.	Lost Div. Semi-Final
1987-88*	80	10	24	6	....	9	24	7	....	19	48	13	....	242	349	51	5th, Norris Div.	Out of Playoffs
1986-87*	80	17	20	3	....	13	20	7	....	30	40	10	....	296	314	70	5th, Norris Div.	Out of Playoffs
1985-86*	80	21	15	4	....	17	18	5	....	38	33	9	....	327	305	85	2nd, Norris Div.	Lost Div. Semi-Final
1984-85*	80	14	19	7	....	11	24	5	....	25	43	12	....	268	321	62	4th, Norris Div.	Lost Div. Final
1983-84*	80	22	14	4	....	17	17	6	....	39	31	10	....	345	344	88	1st, Norris Div.	Lost Conf. Championship
1982-83*	80	23	6	11	....	17	18	5	....	40	24	16	....	321	290	96	2nd, Norris Div.	Lost Div. Final
1981-82*	80	21	7	12	....	16	16	8	....	37	23	20	....	346	288	94	1st, Norris Div.	Lost Div. Semi-Final
1980-81*	80	23	10	7	....	12	18	10	....	35	28	17	....	291	263	87	3rd, Adams Div.	Lost Final
1979-80*	80	25	8	7	....	11	20	9	....	36	28	16	....	311	253	88	3rd, Adams Div.	Lost Semi-Final
1978-79*	80	19	15	6	....	9	25	6	....	28	40	12	....	257	289	68	4th, Adams Div.	Out Of Playoffs
1977-78*	80	12	24	4	....	6	29	5	....	18	53	9	....	218	325	45	5th, Smythe Div.	Out of Playoffs
1976-77*	80	17	14	9	....	6	25	9	....	23	39	18	....	240	310	64	2nd, Smythe Div.	Lost Prelim. Round
1975-76*	80	15	22	3	....	5	31	4	....	20	53	7	....	195	303	47	4th, Smythe Div.	Out of Playoffs
1974-75*	80	17	20	3	....	6	30	4	....	23	50	7	....	221	341	53	4th, Smythe Div.	Out of Playoffs
1973-74	78	18	15	6	....	5	23	11	....	23	38	17	....	235	275	63	7th, West Div.	Out of Playoffs
1972-73	78	26	8	5	....	11	22	6	....	37	30	11	....	254	230	85	3rd, West Div.	Lost Quarter-Final
1971-72	78	22	11	6	....	15	18	6	....	37	29	12	....	212	191	86	2nd, West Div.	Lost Quarter-Final
1970-71	78	16	15	8	....	12	19	8	....	28	34	16	....	191	223	72	4th, West Div.	Lost Semi-Final
1969-70*	76	11	16	11	....	8	19	11	....	19	35	22	....	224	257	60	3rd, West Div.	Lost Quarter-Final
1968-69*	76	11	21	6	....	7	22	9	....	18	43	15	....	189	270	51	6th, West Div.	Out of Playoffs
1967-68*	74	17	12	8	....	10	20	7	....	27	32	15	....	191	226	69	4th, West Div.	Lost Semi-Final

* Minnesota North Stars

2005-06 Player Personnel

FORWARDS	HT	WT	S	Place of Birth	Date	2004-05 Club
ARNOTT, Jason	6-4	220	R	Collingwood, Ont.	10/11/74	
BARNES, Stu	5-11	180	R	Spruce Grove, Alta.	12/25/70	
BURNETT, Garrett	6-3	225	L	Coquitlam, B.C.	9/23/75	Danbury
GUERIN, Bill	6-2	210	R	Worcester, MA	11/9/70	
HAGOS, Yared	6-1	202	L	Stockholm, Sweden	3/27/83	Timra
HOLTET, Marius	6-0	183	R	Hamar, Norway	8/31/84	Houston-Louisiana
JOKINEN, Jussi	5-11	183	L	Kalajoki, Finland	4/1/83	Karpat
KAPANEN, Niko	5-9	180	L	Hameenlinna, Finland	4/29/78	Zug
LEHTINEN, Jere	6-0	200	R	Espoo, Finland	6/24/73	
LESSARD, Junior	6-0	195	R	St-Joseph-de-Beauce, Que.	5/26/80	Houston
MIETTINEN, Antti	5-11	180	R	Hameenlinna, Finland	7/3/80	Hamilton
MODANO, Mike	6-3	205	L	Livonia, MI	6/7/70	
MORROW, Brenden	5-11	210	L	Carlyle, Sask.	1/16/79	Oklahoma City
OLIVER, David	6-0	190	R	Sechelt, B.C.	4/17/71	Guildford
OTT, Steve	6-0	185	L	Summerside, P.E.I.	8/19/82	Hamilton
SIKLENKA, Mike	6-5	224	R	Meadow Lake, Sask.	12/18/79	Klagenfurt
SVOBODA, Jaroslav	6-2	190	L	Cervenka, Czech.	6/1/80	Olomouc-Trinec
TJARNQVIST, Mathias	6-1	183	L	Umea, Sweden	4/15/79	HV 71

DEFENSEMEN						
BELLE, Shawn	6-1	220	L	Edmonton, Alta.	1/3/85	Tri-City
BOUCHER, Philippe	6-3	221	R	Ste-Apollinaire, Que.	3/24/73	
DALEY, Trevor	5-9	197	L	Toronto, Ont.	10/9/83	Hamilton
ERSKINE, John	6-4	215	L	Kingston, Ont.	6/26/80	Houston
KLEMM, Jon	6-2	200	R	Cranbrook, B.C.	1/8/70	
ROBIDAS, Stephane	5-11	188	R	Sherbrooke, Que.	3/3/77	Frankfurt
SKOULA, Martin	6-2	195	L	Litomerice, Czech.	10/28/79	Litvinov
TRAVERSE, Patrick	6-4	207	L	Montreal, Que.	3/14/74	Houston
ZUBOV, Sergei	6-1	200	R	Moscow, USSR	7/22/70	

GOALTENDERS	HT	WT	C	Place of Birth	Date	2004-05 Club
ELLIS, Dan	6-0	185	L	Saskatoon, Sask.	6/19/80	Hamilton
HEDBERG, Johan	6-0	184	L	Leksand, Sweden	5/5/73	Leksand
SMITH, Mike	6-3	189	L	Kingston, Ont.	3/22/82	Houston
TURCO, Marty	5-11	183	L	Sault Ste. Marie, Ont.	8/13/75	Djurgarden

In the System and Recently Drafted

FORWARDS	HT	WT	S	Place of Birth	Date	2004-05 Club
BARARUK, David	6-0	175	L	Moose Jaw, Sask.	5/26/83	Houston-L'siana-Idaho
BERNIKOV, Ruslan	6-3	198	L	Vidnoye, USSR	12/4/77	Togliatti-Cherepovets
CHERNOV, Artem	5-10	176	L	Novokuznetsk, USSR	4/28/82	Spartak-Yunost
CLUNE, Richard	5-11	195	L	Toronto, Ont.	4/25/87	Sarnia
CROMBEEN, Brandon	6-2	200	R	Denver, CO	7/10/85	Barrie
ELOMO, Teemu	5-11	176	L	Turku, Finland	1/13/79	Blues
ERIKSSON, Loui	6-1	183	L	Goteborg, Sweden	7/17/85	Frolunda
GUYER, Gino	5-10	184	L	Grand Rapids, MN	10/14/83	U. of Minnesota
IMMONEN, Jarkko A.	5-11	180	R	Kouvola, Finland	1/18/84	Blues
KARLSSON, Gabriel	6-1	189	L	Borlange, Sweden	1/22/80	Sodertalje
KUKUSHKIN, Sergei	6-2	187	L	Minsk, USSR	7/24/85	N.E. Jr. Falcons-Indiana
LAMMERS, John	5-11	184	L	Bowmanville, Ont.	1/29/86	Lethbridge
LINDGREN, Perttu	6-0	185	L	Tampere, Finland	8/26/87	Ilves
LUNDQVIST, Joel	6-0	185	L	Are, Sweden	3/2/82	Frolunda
McKNIGHT, Matt	6-2	190	R	Red Deer, Alta.	6/14/84	U. Minn-Duluth
MIKKONEN, Tuomas	6-1	183	L	Jyvaskyla, Finland	3/25/83	JYP
NASLUND, Fredrik	6-4	211	R	Bromma, Sweden	2/11/86	Vasteras
NAUROV, Alexander	5-11	191	L	Saratov, USSR	3/4/85	Yaroslavl
NEAL, James	6-2	185	L	Oshawa, Ont.	9/3/87	Plymouth
POLAK, Vojtech	5-11	180	L	Ostrov nad Ohri, Czech.	6/27/85	Jihlava-Kadan-Karl. Vary
SAWADA, Raymond	6-2	195	R	Richmond, B.C.	2/19/85	Cornell
SIDORENKO, Kirill	6-3	187	L	Omsk, USSR	3/30/83	Omsk 2-Samara
TERESCHENKO, Alexei	5-11	176	L	Mozhaisk, USSR	12/16/80	Dynamo Moscow
TOMICA, Marek	6-0	178	L	Prague, Czech.	1/1/81	Slavia
TUOKKO, Marco	6-0	185	L	Raisio, Finland	3/27/79	TPS
VAS, Janos	6-1	183	L	Dunaujvaros, Hungary	1/29/84	Halmstad
VLCEK, Ladislav	5-11	184	L	Kladno, Czech.	9/26/81	Usti n. L.-Olomouc
WANDELL, Tom	6-1	183	L	Sodertalje, Sweden	1/29/87	Sodertalje Jr.
WATHIER, Francis	6-3	198	L	St Isidore, Ont.	12/7/84	Gatineau
WATKINS, Matt	5-10	180	L	Regina, Sask.	11/22/86	Vernon

DEFENSEMEN						
BLAZEK, Michal	6-2	187	L	Vsetin, Czech.	4/2/82	
DONIKA, Mikhail	6-0	185	L	Yaroslavl, USSR	5/15/79	Spartak
FISTRIC, Mark	6-2	232	L	Edmonton, Alta.	6/1/86	Vancouver (WHL)
FRANSSON, Johan	6-1	183	L	Kalix, Sweden	2/18/85	Lulea
GRANATH, Elias	6-1	174	L	Borlange, Sweden	9/6/85	Leksand
GROSSMAN, Nicklas	6-4	187	L	Stockholm, Sweden	1/22/85	Sodertalje
JANCEVSKI, Dan	6-3	212	L	Windsor, Ont.	6/15/81	Hamilton
KHOMITSKY, Vadim	6-1	185	L	Voskresensk, USSR	7/21/82	CSKA
LUDWIG, Trevor	6-1	200	L	Rhinelander, WI	5/24/85	Providence College
NICKERSON, Matt	6-4	230	L	New Haven, CT	1/11/85	Victoriaville
NISKANEN, Matt	6-0	194	L	Virginia, MN	12/6/86	Virginia
SCALZO, Mario	5-9	187	L	St-Hubert, Que.	11/11/84	Victoriaville-Rimouski
VAINIO, Niko	6-1	180	L	Helsinki, Finland	1/24/85	Peterborough
VOMELA, Lukas	6-3	189	L	Ceske Budejovice, Czech.	9/25/85	C. Budej.-Jind. Hradec
WAUGH, Geoff	6-3	210	R	Winnipeg, Man.	8/25/83	Northern Mich.

GOALTENDERS	HT	WT	C	Place of Birth	Date	2004-05 Club
KILPELAINEN, Eero	5-11	152	L	Juva, Finland	5/7/85	Peterborough
McGANN, Pat	5-11	160	R	Evergreen, IL	1/27/87	Team Illinois
STEPHAN, Tobias	6-3	178	L	Zurich, Switz.	1/21/84	Kloten

Coach

TIPPETT, DAVE
Coach, Dallas Stars. Born in Moosomin, Sask., August 25, 1961.

Dallas Stars general manager Doug Armstrong announced the hiring of Dave Tippett as the club's head coach on May 16, 2002. In his first season behind the bench in 2002-03, he led the Stars to the best record in the Western Conference and the second best in the NHL. Tippett had spent the previous three seasons as an assistant coach with the Los Angeles Kings. He served a five-game stint as interim head coach in 2002 while head coach Andy Murray recovered from an auto accident. In all three seasons Tippett was in Los Angeles the Kings qualified for the playoffs. They had reached the postseason just once out of the previous six seasons.

Under Tippett's direction, the Kings power-play led the NHL in 2001-02 with a 20.7 percent success rate. The year before Tippett came aboard the Kings, in 1998-99, the Kings power-play unit ranked 24th in the league. As a highly regarded minor league coach with tremendous work ethic, Tippett posted two 50-win seasons at Houston (International Hockey League) and led the Aeros to the 1999 Turner Cup championship while serving as general manager/head coach. He was also named IHL coach of the year.

Prior to becoming a coach, Tippett played 11 years as a forward in the National Hockey League with the Hartford Whalers, Washington Capitals, Pittsburgh Penguins and Philadelphia Flyers. He ended his playing career in 1995 as a player-assistant coach with the Houston Aeros (IHL). Internationally, he captained the 1984 Canadian Olympic team in Sarajevo, Yugoslavia, and he earned a silver medal as a member of the Canadian Olympic team in Albertville, France, in 1992. He was a member of the 1982 NCAA Division I championship squad at the University of North Dakota with former Stars defenseman Craig Ludwig.

Coaching Record

Season	Team	Games	Regular Season				Playoffs		
			W	L	T	Games	W	L	
1995-96	Houston (IHL)	42	17	18	7	....	....	....	
1996-97	Houston (IHL)	82	44	30	8	13	8	5	
1997-98	Houston (IHL)	82	50	22	10	4	1	3	
1998-99	Houston (IHL)	82	54	15	13	19	11	8	
2002-03	**Dallas (NHL)**	82	46	21	15	12	6	6	
2003-04	**Dallas (NHL)**	82	41	28	13	5	1	4	
2004-05	**Dallas (NHL)**				Season Cancelled				
	NHL Totals	164	87	49	28	17	7	10	

Coaching History

Wren Blair, 1967-68; Wren Blair and John Muckler, 1968-69; Wren Blair and Charlie Burns, 1969-70; Jack Gordon, 1970-71 to 1972-73; Jack Gordon and Parker MacDonald, 1973-74; Jack Gordon and Charlie Burns, 1974-75; Ted Harris, 1975-76, 1976-77; Ted Harris, André Beaulieu and Lou Nanne, 1977-78; Harry Howell and Glen Sonmor, 1978-79; Glen Sonmor, 1979-80 to 1981-82; Glen Sonmor and Murray Oliver, 1982-83; Bill Mahoney, 1983-84, 1984-85; Lorne Henning, 1985-86; Lorne Henning and Glen Sonmor, 1986-87; Herb Brooks, 1987-88; Pierre Page, 1988-89, 1989-90; Bob Gainey, 1990-91 to 1994-95; Bob Gainey and Ken Hitchcock, 1995-96; Ken Hitchcock, 1996-97 to 2000-01; Ken Hitchcock and Rick Wilson, 2001-02; Dave Tippett, 2002-03 to date.

Club Records

Team

(Figures in brackets for season records are games played; records for fewest points, wins, ties, losses, goals, goals against are for 70 or more games)

Most Points	114	1998-99 (82)
Most Wins	51	1998-99 (82)
Most Ties	22	1969-70 (76)
Most Losses	53	1975-76, 1977-78 (80)
Most Goals	346	1981-82 (80)
Most Goals Against	349	1987-88 (80)
Fewest Points	45	1977-78 (80)
Fewest Wins	18	1968-69 (76), 1977-78 (80)
Fewest Ties	4	1989-90 (80)
Fewest Losses	17	2002-03 (82)
Fewest Goals	189	1968-69 (76)
Fewest Goals Against	167	1997-98 (80)

Longest Winning Streak

Overall	7	Mar. 16-28/80, Mar. 16-Apr. 2/97, Nov. 22-Dec. 5/97
Home	11	Nov. 4-Dec. 27/72
Away	7	Three times

Longest Undefeated Streak

Overall	17	Jan. 23-Mar. 20/04 (13 wins, 4 ties)
Home	13	Oct. 28-Dec. 27/72 (12 wins, 1 tie), Nov. 21/79-Jan. 9/80 (10 wins, 3 ties), Jan. 17-Mar. 17/91 (11 wins, 2 ties)
Away	10	Jan. 12-Mar. 4/99 (8 wins, 2 ties)

Longest Losing Streak

Overall	10	Feb. 1-20/76
Home	6	Jan. 17-Feb. 4/70
Away	8	Oct. 19-Nov. 13/75, Jan. 28-Mar. 3/88

Longest Winless Streak

Overall	20	Jan. 15-Feb. 28/70 (15 losses, 5 ties)
Home	12	Jan. 17-Feb. 25/70 (8 losses, 4 ties)
Away	23	Oct. 25/74-Jan. 28/75 (19 losses, 4 ties)

Most Shutouts, Season	11	2000-01 (82), 2002-03 (82)
Most PIM, Season	2,313	1987-88 (80)
Most Goals, Game	15	Nov. 11/81 (Wpg. 2 at Min. 15)

Individual

Most Seasons	16	Neal Broten, Mike Modano
Most Games	1,101	Mike Modano
Most Goals, Career	458	Mike Modano
Most Assists, Career	648	Mike Modano
Most Points, Career	1,106	Mike Modano (458G, 648A)
Most PIM, Career	1,883	Shane Churla
Most Shutouts, Career	27	Ed Belfour
Longest Consecutive Games Streak	442	Danny Grant (Dec. 4/68-Apr. 7/74)
Most Goals, Season	55	Dino Ciccarelli (1981-82), Brian Bellows (1989-90)
Most Assists, Season	76	Neal Broten (1985-86)
Most Points, Season	114	Bobby Smith (1981-82; 43G, 71A)

Most PIM, Season	382	Basil McRae (1987-88)
Most Points, Defenseman, Season	77	Craig Hartsburg (1981-82; 17G, 60A)
Most Points, Center, Season	114	Bobby Smith (1981-82; 43G, 71A)
Most Points, Right Wing, Season	106	Dino Ciccarelli (1981-82; 55G, 51A)
Most Points, Left Wing, Season	99	Brian Bellows (1989-90; 55G, 44A)
Most Points, Rookie, Season	98	Neal Broten (1981-82; 38G, 60A)
Most Shutouts, Season	9	Ed Belfour (1997-98)
Most Goals, Game	5	Tim Young (Jan. 15/79)
Most Assists, Game	5	Murray Oliver (Oct. 24/71), Larry Murphy (Oct. 17/89)
Most Points, Game	7	Bobby Smith (Nov. 11/81; 4G, 3A)

Records include Minnesota North Stars, 1967-68 through 1992-93.

Retired Numbers

7	Neal Broten	1980-1995, 1996-1997
8	Bill Goldsworthy*	1967-1976
19	Bill Masterton*	1967-1968

* Minnesota North Stars

All-time Record vs. Other Clubs

Regular Season

	At Home							On Road							Total						
	GP	W	L	T	OL	GF	GA	PTS	GP	W	L	T	OL	GF	GA	PTS	GP	W	L	T	OL	GF	GA	PTS
Anaheim	27	20	5	2	0	101	52	42	27	13	11	3	0	66	61	29	54	33	16	5	0	167	113	71
Atlanta	4	4	0	0	0	9	4	8	4	4	0	0	0	16	9	8	8	8	0	0	0	25	13	16
Boston	61	18	30	13	0	175	220	49	60	9	41	10	0	146	258	28	121	27	71	23	0	321	478	77
Buffalo	54	27	21	6	0	173	156	60	52	13	28	11	0	139	188	37	106	40	49	17	0	312	344	97
Calgary	62	30	20	11	1	228	196	72	62	15	31	14	2	155	208	46	124	45	51	25	3	383	404	118
Carolina	29	17	10	2	0	115	86	36	32	15	13	4	0	110	101	34	61	32	23	6	0	225	187	70
Chicago	112	52	43	16	1	377	340	121	110	31	64	15	0	289	412	77	222	83	107	31	1	666	752	198
Colorado	41	21	13	5	2	131	115	49	41	11	22	7	1	103	150	30	82	32	35	12	3	234	265	79
Columbus	8	8	0	0	0	26	9	16	8	4	2	0	2	26	19	12	16	14	2	0	0	52	28	28
Detroit	106	51	36	18	1	370	319	121	106	37	53	16	0	336	406	90	212	88	89	34	1	706	725	211
Edmonton	45	24	14	7	0	163	126	55	44	15	20	8	1	145	176	39	89	39	34	15	1	308	302	94
Florida	8	3	2	2	1	25	22	9	10	5	4	1	0	28	21	11	18	8	6	3	1	53	44	20
Los Angeles	84	52	19	13	0	323	218	117	82	28	35	19	0	234	277	75	166	80	54	32	0	557	495	192
Minnesota	8	4	3	1	1	27	18	10	8	4	4	0	0	19	23	8	16	8	6	1	1	46	41	18
Montreal	59	17	30	12	0	153	203	46	58	12	37	9	0	144	250	33	117	29	67	21	0	297	453	79
Nashville	12	10	2	0	0	36	14	20	12	5	6	1	0	23	18	11	24	15	8	1	0	59	42	31
New Jersey	45	26	13	6	0	164	117	58	43	19	21	3	0	132	146	41	88	45	34	9	0	296	263	99
NY Islanders	47	18	20	8	1	139	170	45	48	14	25	8	1	134	176	37	95	32	45	16	2	273	346	82
NY Rangers	61	20	30	11	0	187	221	51	62	15	36	11	0	165	213	41	123	35	66	22	0	352	434	92
Ottawa	11	7	4	0	0	44	28	14	9	5	3	0	1	24	22	11	20	12	7	0	1	68	50	25
Philadelphia	66	27	23	16	0	216	212	70	67	9	42	16	0	150	255	34	133	36	65	32	0	366	467	104
Phoenix	55	27	19	9	0	199	166	63	54	27	23	4	0	182	170	58	109	54	42	13	0	381	336	121
Pittsburgh	64	37	21	6	0	246	213	80	63	19	38	6	0	178	236	44	127	56	59	12	0	424	449	124
St. Louis	115	53	39	22	1	383	334	129	117	32	63	21	1	330	424	86	232	85	102	43	2	713	758	215
San Jose	29	15	10	4	0	81	64	34	30	18	10	1	1	85	68	38	59	33	20	5	1	166	132	72
Tampa Bay	11	7	3	1	0	39	27	15	13	10	1	1	2	37	20	22	24	17	4	3	0	76	47	37
Toronto	97	50	36	11	0	365	306	111	101	35	49	17	0	319	356	87	198	85	85	28	0	684	662	198
Vancouver	71	37	22	12	0	259	211	86	71	30	30	10	1	218	252	71	142	67	52	22	1	477	463	157
Washington	41	21	11	8	1	152	110	51	40	17	15	8	0	129	120	42	81	38	26	16	1	281	230	93
Defunct Clubs	33	19	8	6	0	123	86	44	32	10	16	6	0	84	105	26	65	29	24	12	0	207	191	70
Totals	**1466**	**722**	**506**	**228**	**10**	**5029**	**4363**	**1682**	**1466**	**483**	**743**	**231**	**9**	**4146**	**5151**	**1206**	**2932**	**1205**	**1249**	**459**	**19**	**9175**	**9514**	**2888**

Playoffs

	Series	W	L	GP	W	L	T	GF	GA	Last Mtg.	Rnd.	Result
Anaheim	1	0	1	6	2	4	0	14	14	2003	CSF	L 2-4
Boston	1	1	0	3	3	0	0	20	13	1981	PRE	W 3-0
Buffalo	3	2	1	13	8	5	0	39	37	1999	F	W 4-2
Calgary	1	1	0	6	4	2	0	25	18	1981	SF	W 4-2
Chicago	6	2	4	33	14	19	0	118	120	1991	DSF	W 4-2
Colorado	3	2	1	19	9	10	0	47	48	2004	CQF	L 1-4
Detroit	3	0	3	18	6	12	0	40	55	1998	CF	L 2-4
Edmonton	8	6	2	42	27	15	0	118	104	2003	CQF	W 4-2
Los Angeles	1	1	0	7	4	3	0	26	21	1968	QF	W 4-3
Montreal	2	1	1	13	6	7	0	37	48	1980	QF	W 4-3
New Jersey	1	0	1	6	2	4	0	9	15	2000	F	L 2-4
NY Islanders	1	0	1	5	1	4	0	16	26	1981	F	L 1-4
Philadelphia	2	0	2	11	3	8	0	26	41	1980	SF	L 1-4
Pittsburgh	1	0	1	6	2	4	0	16	28	1991	F	L 1-4
St. Louis	12	6	6	66	34	32	0	197	187	2001	CSF	L 0-4
San Jose	2	2	0	11	8	3	0	31	19	2000	CSF	W 4-1
Toronto	2	2	0	7	4	3	0	35	26	1983	DSF	W 3-1
Vancouver	1	0	1	5	1	4	0	11	18	1994	CSF	L 1-4
Totals	**51**	**26**	**25**	**277**	**140**	**137**	**0**	**825**	**838**			

Calgary totals include Atlanta Flames, 1972-73 to 1979-80.
Colorado totals include Quebec, 1979-80 to 1994-95.
New Jersey totals include Kansas City, 1974-75 to 1975-76, and Colorado Rockies, 1976-77 to 1981-82.
Phoenix totals include Winnipeg, 1979-80 to 1995-96.
Carolina totals include Hartford, 1979-80 to 1996-97.

Playoff Results 2005-2000

Year	Round	Opponent	Result	GF	GA
2004	CQF	Colorado	L 1-4	10	19
2003	CSF	Anaheim	L 2-4	14	14
	CQF	Edmonton	W 4-2	20	11
2001	CSF	St. Louis	L 0-4	6	13
	CQF	Edmonton	W 4-2	16	13
2000	F	New Jersey	L 2-4	9	15
	CF	Colorado	W 4-3	14	13
	CSF	San Jose	W 4-1	15	7
	CQF	Edmonton	W 4-1	14	11

Abbreviations: Round: F - Final;
CF - conference final; **CSF** - conference semi-final;
CQF - conference quarter-final;
DSF - division semi-final; **SF** - semi-final;
QF - quarter-final; **PRE** - preliminary round.

Key Off-Season Signings/Acquisitions

2004

June 25 • Obtained D **Shawn Belle** from St. Louis for G **Jason Bacashihua**.

June 29 • Obtained RW **Jaroslav Svoboda** from Carolina for a 2005 4th-round pick.

Aug. 3 • Re-signed C **Stu Barnes**.

2005

July 31 • Re-signed D **Sergei Zubov**.

Aug. 3 • Re-signed C **Mike Modano**.

3 • Signed D **Martin Skoula**.

5 • Signed G **Johan Hedberg**.

6 • Signed D **Stephane Robidas**.

12 • Re-signed Cs **Niko Kapanen** and **Steve Ott**.

15 • Re-signed C **Jason Arnott**.

19 • Re-signed LW **Brenden Morrow**.

Entry Draft
Selections 2005-1991

2005	**2001**	**1997**	**1993**
Pick	Pick	Pick	Pick
28 Matt Niskanen	26 Jason Bacashihua	25 Brenden Morrow	9 Todd Harvey
33 James Neal	70 Yared Hagos	52 Roman Lyashenko	35 Jamie Langenbrunner
71 Richard Clune	92 Anthony Aquino	77 Steve Gainey	87 Chad Lang
75 Perttu Lindgren	126 Daniel Volrab	105 Marcus Kristoffersson	136 Rick Mrozik
146 Tom Wandell	161 Mike Smith	132 Teemu Elomo	139 Per Svartvadet
160 Matt Watkins	167 Michal Blazek	160 Alexei Timkin	165 Jeremy Stasiuk
223 Pat McGann	192 Jussi Jokinen	189 Jeff McKercher	191 Rob Lurtsema
	255 Marco Rosa	216 Alexei Komarov	243 Jordan Willis
2004	265 Dale Sullivan	242 Brett McLean	249 Bill Lang
Pick	285 Marek Tomica		269 Cory Peterson
28 Mark Fistric		**1996**	
34 Johan Fransson	**2000**	Pick	**1992**
52 Raymond Sawada	Pick	5 Ric Jackman	Pick
56 Nicklas Grossman	25 Steve Ott	70 Jon Sim	34 Jarkko Varvio
86 John Lammers	60 Dan Ellis	90 Mike Hurley	58 Jeff Bes
104 Fredrik Naslund	68 Joel Lundqvist	112 Ryan Christie	88 Jere Lehtinen
183 Trevor Ludwig	91 Alexei Tereschenko	113 Yevgeny Tsybuk	130 Michael Johnson
218 Sergei Kukushkin	123 Vadim Khomitsky	166 Eoin McInerney	154 Kyle Peterson
248 Lukas Vomela	139 Ruslan Bernikov	194 Joel Kwiatkowski	178 Juha Lind
280 Matt McKnight	162 Artem Chernov	220 Nick Bootland	202 Lars Edstrom
	192 Ladislav Vlcek		226 Jeff Romfo
2003	219 Marco Tuokko	**1995**	250 Jeffrey Moen
Pick	224 Antti Miettinen	Pick	
33 Loui Eriksson		11 Jarome Iginla	**1991**
36 Vojtech Polak	**1999**	37 Patrick Cote	Pick
54 Brandon Crombeen	Pick	63 Petr Buzek	8 Richard Matvichuk
99 Matt Nickerson	32 Michael Ryan	69 Sergey Gusev	74 Mike Torchia
134 Alexander Naurov	66 Dan Jancevski	115 Wade Strand	97 Mike Kennedy
144 Eero Kilpelainen	96 Mathias Tjarnqvist	141 Dominic Marleau	118 Mark Lawrence
165 Gino Guyer	126 Jeff Bateman	173 Jeff Dewar	137 Geoff Finch
185 Francis Wathier	156 Gregor Baumgartner	193 Anatoli Koveshnikov	174 Michael Burkett
195 Drew Bagnall	184 Justin Cox	202 Sergei Luchinkin	184 Derek Herlofsky
196 Elias Granath	186 Brett Draney	219 Stephen Lowe	206 Tom Nemeth
259 Niko Vainio	215 Jeff MacMillan		228 Shayne Green
	243 Brian Sullivan	**1994**	250 Jukka Suomalainen
2002	265 Jamie Chamberlain	Pick	
Pick	272 Mikhail Donika	20 Jason Botterill	
26 Martin Vagner		46 Lee Jinman	
32 Janos Vas	**1998**	98 Jamie Wright	
34 Tobias Stephan	Pick	124 Marty Turco	
42 Marius Holtet	39 John Erskine	150 Evgeny Petrochinin	
43 Trevor Daley	57 Tyler Bouck	228 Marty Flichel	
78 Geoff Waugh	86 Gabriel Karlsson	254 Jimmy Roy	
110 Jarkko A. Immonen	153 Pavel Patera	280 Chris Szysky	
147 David Bararuk	173 Niko Kapanen		
180 Kirill Sidorenko	200 Scott Perry		
210 Bryan Hamm			
243 Tuomas Mikkonen			
273 Ned Havern			

Club Directory

American Airlines Center

Dallas Stars
2601 Ave. of the Stars
Frisco, TX 75034
Office Address:
Dr Pepper StarCenter
211 Cowboys Parkway
Irving, TX 75063
Phone **214/387-5500**
FAX 214/387-5610
Ticket Information 214/GO STARS
www.dallasstars.com
Capacity: 18,532

Chairman of the Board & Owner . . . . Thomas O.Hicks
President . . . . James R. Lites
General Manager . . . . Doug Armstrong
Assistant General Managers . . . . Francois Giguere, Les Jackson, Guy Carbonneau
Head Coach . . . . Dave Tippett
Associate Coach . . . . Rick Wilson
Assistant Coaches . . . . Mark Lamb, Andy Moog
Video Coach . . . . Derek MacKinnon
Director, Hockey Administration and Team Services . Lesa Moake
Director, Amateur Scouting . . . . Tim Bernhardt
Director, Professional Scouting . . . . Doug Overton
Scout . . . . Bob Gernander
Professional Scouts . . . . Paul McIntosh, John Weisbrod
Head Athletic Trainer . . . . Dave Surprenant
Head Equipment Manager . . . . Steve Sumner
Strength and Conditioning Coach . . . . J.J. McQueen
Assistant Athletic Trainer . . . . Tommy Alva
Assistant Equipment Manager . . . . Tony Addeo
Equipment Assistant . . . . Chris Davidson-Adams
Administrative Assistant, Hockey Operations . . . . . . Pam Wenzel

Communications
Senior Director, Communications . . . . Rob Scichili
Director, Public Relations . . . . Mark Janko
Manager of Media and Team Services . . . . Jason Rademan

Team Information
Arena . . . . American Airlines Center
2500 Victory Avenue
Dallas, Texas 75219
Capacity 18,532
Colors . . . . Green, Gold, Black
Development Affiliates . . . . Iowa Stars (AHL)
Idaho Steelheads (ECHL)
Television Networks . . . . FSN Southwest, KDFI
Radio Flagship . . . . WBAP 820 AM

Captains' History

Bob Woytowich, 1967-68; Moose Vasko, 1968-69; Claude Larose, 1969-70; Ted Harris, 1970-71 to 1973-74; Bill Goldsworthy, 1974-75, 1975-76; Bill Hogaboam, 1976-77; Nick Beverley, 1977-78; J.P. Parise, 1978-79; Paul Shmyr, 1979-80, 1980-81; Tim Young, 1981-82; Craig Hartsburg, 1982-83; Craig Hartsburg and Brian Bellows, 1983-84; Craig Hartsburg, 1984-85 to 1987-88; Curt Fraser, Bob Rouse and Curt Giles, 1988-89; Curt Giles, 1989-90, 1990-91; Mark Tinordi, 1991-92 to 1993-94; Neal Broten and Derian Hatcher, 1994-95; Derian Hatcher, 1995-96 to 2002-03; Mike Modano, 2003-04 to date.

General Managers' History

Wren Blair, 1967-68 to 1973-74; Jack Gordon, 1974-75 to 1976-77; Lou Nanne, 1977-78 to 1987-88; Jack Ferreira, 1988-89, 1989-90; Bob Clarke 1990-91, 1991-92; Bob Gainey, 1992-93 to 2000-01; Bob Gainey and Doug Armstrong, 2001-02; Doug Armstrong, 2002-03 to date.

General Manager

ARMSTRONG, DOUG
General Manager, Dallas Stars. Born in Sarnia, Ont., September 24, 1964.
Doug Armstrong was in his ninth season as an assistant to Bob Gainey when he was elevated to the position of general manager on January 25, 2002. In his first full season on the job in 2002-03, the Stars had the best record in the Western Conference and the second best in the NHL. Armstrong originally joined the club in 1991. As Gainey's assistant, he worked on contract information and season scheduling and handled the day-to-day operations of the hockey department. In five seasons from 1996 to 2001, he helped Gainey build a team that won five straight division championships, as well as the Presidents' Trophy for the best regular-season record in the NHL twice, and the 1999 Stanley Cup. At the international level, Armstrong served as Team Canada's assistant general manger at the 2002 World Championships in Sweden.

A native of Sarnia, Ontario, Armstrong attended Western Michigan University for two years before transferring to Florida State University in Tallahassee, where he earned his B.S. in Business Administration with a major in marketing.

Durable defenseman Martin Skoula joins the Stars after missing only six games during his first five NHL seasons.

Detroit Red Wings

Steve Yzerman returns in 2005-06.

2005-06 Schedule

Oct.	Wed.	5	St. Louis		Fri.	6	at Nashville
	Thu.	6	at St. Louis		Sun.	8	Dallas*
	Sun.	9	Calgary*		Tue.	10	at Carolina
	Mon.	10	Vancouver		Thu.	12	Philadelphia
	Thu.	13	at Los Angeles		Sat.	14	NY Rangers*
	Sat.	15	at Phoenix		Wed.	18	at Columbus
	Mon.	17	San Jose		Sat.	21	at Colorado*
	Fri.	21	Anaheim		Mon.	23	at Nashville
	Sat.	22	at Columbus		Tue.	24	Nashville
	Mon.	24	at Columbus		Thu.	26	Vancouver
	Thu.	27	Chicago		Sat.	28	at Dallas*
	Sat.	29	at Chicago		Mon.	30	at Minnesota
Nov.	Tue.	1	Chicago	**Feb.**	Wed.	1	St. Louis
	Thu.	3	Edmonton		Sat.	4	at Colorado*
	Sat.	5	Phoenix		Wed.	8	Nashville
	Sun.	6	at St. Louis		Thu.	9	at Nashville
	Wed.	9	Los Angeles		Sun.	12	Colorado*
	Fri.	11	Minnesota		Tue.	28	at San Jose
	Sun.	13	at Vancouver	**Mar.**	Wed.	1	at Anaheim
	Wed.	16	at Calgary		Sat.	4	at Phoenix
	Thu.	17	at Edmonton		Tue.	7	Phoenix
	Sat.	19	St. Louis		Thu.	9	Los Angeles
	Mon.	21	Nashville		Sat.	11	Chicago
	Wed.	23	Colorado		Sun.	12	at Chicago
	Fri.	25	at Anaheim*		Wed.	15	Anaheim
	Sat.	26	at San Jose		Sat.	18	at Edmonton
	Mon.	28	at Los Angeles		Sun.	19	at Vancouver
Dec.	Thu.	1	Calgary		Tue.	21	Nashville
	Sun.	4	NY Islanders*		Thu.	23	San Jose
	Tue.	6	New Jersey		Sat.	25	Columbus
	Fri.	9	at Washington		Mon.	27	at St. Louis
	Mon.	12	Pittsburgh		Fri.	31	Chicago
	Tue.	13	at Atlanta	**Apr.**	Sun.	2	at Minnesota*
	Thu.	15	at Florida		Mon.	3	at Calgary
	Sat.	17	at Tampa Bay		Fri.	7	Columbus
	Tue.	20	Columbus		Sat.	8	at Columbus
	Fri.	23	at Chicago		Tue.	11	Edmonton
	Tue.	27	at Dallas		Thu.	13	at Chicago
	Sat.	31	Columbus		Sat.	15	at St. Louis*
Jan.	Tue.	3	Minnesota		Mon.	17	Dallas
	Thu.	5	St. Louis		Tue.	18	at Nashville

* Denotes afternoon game.

Franchise date: September 25, 1926

80th NHL Season

CENTRAL DIVISION

Year-by-Year Record

		Home				Road				Overall								
Season	GP	W	L	T	OL	W	L	T	OL	W	L	T	OL	GF	GA	Pts.	Finished	Playoff Result
2004-05	....	....	....	....	....	....	....	....	....	....	....	....	....	....	....	....		
2003-04	82	30	7	4	0	18	14	7	2	48	21	11	2	255	189	109	1st, Central Div.	Lost Conf. Semi-Final
2002-03	82	28	6	5	2	20	14	5	2	48	20	10	4	269	203	110	1st, Central Div.	Lost Conf. Quarter-Final
2001-02	**82**	**28**	**7**	**5**	**1**	**23**	**10**	**5**	**3**	**51**	**17**	**10**	**4**	**251**	**187**	**116**	**1st, Central Div.**	**Won Stanley Cup**
2000-01	82	27	9	3	2	22	11	6	2	49	20	9	4	253	202	111	1st, Central Div.	Lost Conf. Quarter-Final
1999-2000	82	28	9	3	1	20	13	7	1	48	22	10	2	278	210	108	2nd, Central Div.	Lost Conf. Semi-Final
1998-99	82	27	12	2	....	16	20	5	....	43	32	7	....	245	202	93	1st, Central Div.	Lost Conf. Semi-Final
1997-98	**82**	**25**	**8**	**8**	....	**19**	**15**	**7**	....	**44**	**23**	**15**	....	**250**	**196**	**103**	**2nd, Central Div.**	**Won Stanley Cup**
1996-97	**82**	**20**	**12**	**9**	....	**18**	**14**	**9**	....	**38**	**26**	**18**	....	**253**	**197**	**94**	**2nd, Central Div.**	**Won Stanley Cup**
1995-96	82	36	3	2	....	26	10	5	....	62	13	7	....	325	181	131	1st, Central Div.	Lost Conf. Championship
1994-95	48	17	4	3	....	16	7	1	....	33	11	4	....	180	117	70	1st, Central Div.	Lost Final
1993-94	84	23	13	6	....	23	17	2	....	46	30	8	....	356	275	100	1st, Central Div.	Lost Conf. Quarter-Final
1992-93	84	25	14	3	....	22	14	6	....	47	28	9	....	369	280	103	2nd, Norris Div.	Lost Div. Semi-Final
1991-92	80	24	12	4	....	19	13	8	....	43	25	12	....	320	256	98	1st, Norris Div.	Lost Div. Final
1990-91	80	26	14	0	....	8	24	8	....	34	38	8	....	273	298	76	3rd, Norris Div.	Lost Div. Semi-Final
1989-90	80	20	14	6	....	8	24	8	....	28	38	14	....	288	323	70	5th, Norris Div.	Out of Playoffs
1988-89	80	20	14	6	....	14	20	6	....	34	34	12	....	313	316	80	1st, Norris Div.	Lost Div. Semi-Final
1987-88	80	24	10	6	....	17	18	5	....	41	28	11	....	322	269	93	1st, Norris Div.	Lost Conf. Championship
1986-87	80	20	14	6	....	14	22	4	....	34	36	10	....	260	274	78	2nd, Norris Div.	Lost Conf. Championship
1985-86	80	10	26	4	....	7	31	2	....	17	57	6	....	266	415	40	5th, Norris Div.	Out of Playoffs
1984-85	80	19	14	7	....	8	27	5	....	27	41	12	....	313	357	66	3rd, Norris Div.	Lost Div. Semi-Final
1983-84	80	18	20	2	....	13	22	5	....	31	42	7	....	298	323	69	3rd, Norris Div.	Lost Div. Semi-Final
1982-83	80	14	19	7	....	7	25	8	....	21	44	15	....	263	344	57	5th, Norris Div.	Out of Playoffs
1981-82	80	15	19	6	....	6	28	6	....	21	47	12	....	270	351	54	6th, Norris Div.	Out of Playoffs
1980-81	80	16	15	9	....	3	28	9	....	19	43	18	....	252	339	56	5th, Norris Div.	Out of Playoffs
1979-80	80	14	21	5	....	12	22	6	....	26	43	11	....	268	306	63	5th, Norris Div.	Out of Playoffs
1978-79	80	15	17	8	....	8	24	8	....	23	41	16	....	252	295	62	5th, Norris Div.	Out of Playoffs
1977-78	80	22	11	7	....	10	23	7	....	32	34	14	....	252	266	78	2nd, Norris Div.	Lost Quarter-Final
1976-77	80	12	22	6	....	4	33	3	....	16	55	9	....	183	309	41	5th, Norris Div.	Out of Playoffs
1975-76	80	17	15	8	....	9	29	2	....	26	44	10	....	226	300	62	4th, Norris Div.	Out of Playoffs
1974-75	80	17	17	6	....	6	28	6	....	23	45	12	....	259	335	58	4th, Norris Div.	Out of Playoffs
1973-74	78	21	12	6	....	8	27	4	....	29	39	10	....	255	319	68	6th, East Div.	Out of Playoffs
1972-73	78	22	12	5	....	15	17	7	....	37	29	12	....	265	243	86	5th, East Div.	Out of Playoffs
1971-72	78	25	11	3	....	8	24	7	....	33	35	10	....	261	262	76	5th, East Div.	Out of Playoffs
1970-71	78	17	15	7	....	5	30	4	....	22	45	11	....	209	308	55	7th, East Div.	Out of Playoffs
1969-70	76	20	11	7	....	20	10	8	....	40	21	15	....	246	199	95	3rd, East Div.	Lost Quarter-Final
1968-69	76	23	8	7	....	10	23	5	....	33	31	12	....	239	221	78	5th, East Div.	Out of Playoffs
1967-68	74	18	15	4	....	9	20	8	....	27	35	12	....	245	257	66	6th, East Div.	Out of Playoffs
1966-67	70	21	11	3	....	6	28	1	....	27	39	4	....	212	241	58	5th,	Out of Playoffs
1965-66	70	20	8	7	....	11	19	5	....	31	27	12	....	221	194	74	4th,	Lost Final
1964-65	70	25	7	3	....	15	16	4	....	40	23	7	....	224	175	87	1st,	Lost Semi-Final
1963-64	70	23	9	3	....	7	20	8	....	30	29	11	....	191	204	71	4th,	Lost Final
1962-63	70	19	10	6	....	13	15	7	....	32	25	13	....	200	194	77	4th,	Lost Final
1961-62	70	17	11	7	....	6	22	7	....	23	33	14	....	184	219	60	5th,	Out of Playoffs
1960-61	70	15	13	7	....	10	16	9	....	25	29	16	....	195	215	66	4th,	Lost Final
1959-60	70	18	14	3	....	8	15	12	....	26	29	15	....	186	197	67	4th,	Lost Semi-Final
1958-59	70	13	17	5	....	12	20	3	....	25	37	8	....	167	218	58	6th,	Out of Playoffs
1957-58	70	16	11	8	....	13	18	4	....	29	29	12	....	176	207	70	3rd,	Lost Semi-Final
1956-57	70	23	7	5	....	15	13	7	....	38	20	12	....	198	157	88	1st,	Lost Semi-Final
1955-56	70	21	6	8	....	9	18	8	....	30	24	16	....	183	148	76	2nd,	Lost Final
1954-55	**70**	**25**	**5**	**5**	....	**17**	**12**	**6**	....	**42**	**17**	**11**	....	**204**	**134**	**95**	**1st,**	**Won Stanley Cup**
1953-54	**70**	**24**	**4**	**7**	....	**13**	**15**	**7**	....	**37**	**19**	**14**	....	**191**	**132**	**88**	**1st,**	**Won Stanley Cup**
1952-53	70	20	5	10	....	16	11	8	....	36	16	18	....	222	133	90	1st,	Lost Semi-Final
1951-52	**70**	**24**	**7**	**4**	....	**20**	**7**	**8**	....	**44**	**14**	**12**	....	**215**	**133**	**100**	**1st,**	**Won Stanley Cup**
1950-51	70	25	3	7	....	19	10	6	....	44	13	13	....	236	139	101	1st,	Lost Semi-Final
1949-50	**70**	**19**	**9**	**7**	....	**18**	**10**	**7**	....	**37**	**19**	**14**	....	**229**	**164**	**88**	**1st,**	**Won Stanley Cup**
1948-49	60	21	6	3	....	13	13	4	....	34	19	7	....	195	145	75	1st,	Lost Final
1947-48	60	16	9	5	....	14	9	7	....	30	18	12	....	187	148	72	2nd,	Lost Final
1946-47	60	14	10	6	....	8	17	5	....	22	27	11	....	190	193	55	4th,	Lost Semi-Final
1945-46	50	16	5	4	....	4	15	6	....	20	20	10	....	146	159	50	4th,	Lost Semi-Final
1944-45	50	19	5	1	....	12	9	4	....	31	14	5	....	218	161	67	2nd,	Lost Final
1943-44	50	18	5	2	....	8	13	4	....	26	18	6	....	214	177	58	2nd,	Lost Semi-Final
1942-43	**50**	**16**	**4**	**5**	....	**9**	**10**	**6**	....	**25**	**14**	**11**	....	**169**	**124**	**61**	**1st,**	**Won Stanley Cup**
1941-42	48	14	7	3	....	5	18	1	....	19	25	4	....	140	147	42	5th,	Lost Final
1940-41	48	14	5	5	....	7	11	6	....	21	16	11	....	112	102	53	3rd,	Lost Final
1939-40	48	11	10	3	....	5	16	3	....	16	26	6	....	91	126	38	5th,	Lost Semi-Final
1938-39	48	14	8	2	....	4	16	4	....	18	24	6	....	107	128	42	5th,	Lost Semi-Final
1937-38	48	8	10	6	....	4	15	5	....	12	25	11	....	99	133	35	4th, Amn. Div.	Out of Playoffs
1936-37	**48**	**14**	**5**	**5**	....	**11**	**9**	**4**	....	**25**	**14**	**9**	....	**128**	**102**	**59**	**1st, Amn. Div.**	**Won Stanley Cup**
1935-36	**48**	**14**	**5**	**5**	....	**10**	**11**	**3**	....	**24**	**16**	**8**	....	**124**	**103**	**56**	**1st, Amn. Div.**	**Won Stanley Cup**
1934-35	48	11	8	5	....	8	14	2	....	19	22	7	....	127	114	45	4th, Amn. Div.	Out of Playoffs
1933-34	48	15	5	4	....	9	9	6	....	24	14	10	....	113	98	58	1st, Amn. Div.	Lost Final
1932-33*	48	17	3	4	....	8	12	4	....	25	15	8	....	111	93	58	2nd, Amn. Div.	Lost Semi-Final
1931-32	48	15	3	6	....	3	17	4	....	18	20	10	....	95	108	46	3rd, Amn. Div.	Lost Quarter-Final
1930-31**	44	10	7	5	....	6	14	2	....	16	21	7	....	102	105	39	4th, Amn. Div.	Out of Playoffs
1929-30	44	9	10	3	....	5	14	3	....	14	24	6	....	117	133	34	4th, Amn. Div.	Out of Playoffs
1928-29	44	11	6	5	....	8	10	4	....	19	16	9	....	72	63	47	3rd, Amn. Div.	Lost Quarter-Final
1927-28	44	9	10	3	....	10	9	3	....	19	19	6	....	88	79	44	4th, Amn. Div.	Out of Playoffs
1926-27***	44	5	16	0	....	7	12	4	....	12	28	4	....	76	105	28	5th, Amn. Div.	Out of Playoffs

* Team name changed to Red Wings. ** Team name changed to Falcons. *** Team named Cougars.

2005-06 Player Personnel

FORWARDS	HT	WT	S	Place of Birth	Date	2004-05 Club
BOOTLAND, Darryl	6-1	194	R	Toronto, Ont.	11/2/81	Grand Rapids
DATSYUK, Pavel	5-11	180	L	Sverdlovsk, USSR	7/20/78	Dynamo Moscow
DRAPER, Kris	5-11	190	L	Toronto, Ont.	5/24/71	
ELLIS, Matt	6-1	190	L	Welland, Ont.	8/31/81	Grand Rapids
FILPPULA, Valtteri	5-11	172	L	Vantaa, Finland	3/20/84	Jokerit
FRANZEN, Johan	6-2	207	L	Landsbro, Sweden	12/23/79	Linkoping
HOLMSTROM, Tomas	6-0	200	L	Pitea, Sweden	1/23/73	Lulea
HUDLER, Jiri	5-9	178	L	Olomouc, Czech.	1/4/84	Vsetin-Grand Rapids
KOPECKY, Tomas	6-3	187	L	Ilava, Czech.	2/5/82	Grand Rapids
LANG, Robert	6-2	216	R	Teplice, Czech.	12/19/70	
MacLEAN, Don	6-2	199	L	Sydney, N.S.	1/14/77	Blues
MALTBY, Kirk	6-0	180	R	Guelph, Ont.	12/22/72	
MANLOW, Eric	6-0	180	L	Belleville, Ont.	4/7/75	Grand Rapids
McDONELL, Kent	6-2	205	R	Williamstown, Ont.	3/1/79	Aylmer-Bergen-Duisburg
MOWERS, Mark	5-11	187	R	Whitesboro, NY	2/16/74	Malmo-Fribourg
SHANAHAN, Brendan	6-3	218	R	Mimico, Ont.	1/23/69	
WILLIAMS, Jason	5-11	185	L	London, Ont.	8/11/80	Assat
YZERMAN, Steve	5-11	185	R	Cranbrook, B.C.	5/9/65	
ZETTERBERG, Henrik	5-11	176	L	Njurunda, Sweden	10/9/80	Timra

DEFENSEMEN						
CHELIOS, Chris	6-1	190	R	Chicago, IL	1/25/62	Motor City
DELMORE, Andy	6-1	200	L	LaSalle, Ont.	12/26/76	Mannheim
FISCHER, Jiri	6-5	225	R	Horovice, Czech.	7/31/80	Liberec-Beroun
HELMER, Bryan	6-1	200	R	Sault Ste. Marie, Ont.	7/15/72	Grand Rapids
KRONWALL, Niklas	5-11	165	L	Stockholm, Sweden	1/12/81	Grand Rapids
LEBDA, Brett	5-11	194	L	Buffalo Grove, IL	1/15/82	Grand Rapids
LIDSTROM, Nicklas	6-2	185	L	Vasteras, Sweden	4/28/70	
LILJA, Andreas	6-3	228	L	Helsingborg, Sweden	7/13/75	Mora-Ambri
MEECH, Derek	5-11	182	L	Winnipeg, Man.	4/21/84	Grand Rapids
QUINCEY, Kyle	6-1	194	L	Kitchener, Ont.	8/12/85	Mississauga
RIVERS, Jamie	6-0	195	L	Ottawa, Ont.	3/16/75	Hershey
SCHNEIDER, Mathieu	5-10	192	L	New York, NY	6/12/69	

GOALTENDERS	HT	WT	C	Place of Birth	Date	2004-05 Club
HOWARD, James	6-0	218	L	Syracuse, NY	3/26/84	U. of Maine
KOOPMANS, Logan	6-2	182	L	Cranbrook, B.C.	5/18/84	Toledo
LEGACE, Manny	5-9	162	L	Toronto, Ont.	2/4/73	Voskresensk
MacDONALD, Joey	6-0	200	L	Pictou, N.S.	2/7/80	Grand Rapids
MacINTYRE, Drew	6-0	173	L	Charlottetown, P.E.I.	6/24/83	Grand Rapids-Toledo
OSGOOD, Chris	5-10	175	L	Peace River, Alta.	11/26/72	

In the System and Recently Drafted

FORWARDS	HT	WT	S	Place of Birth	Date	2004-05 Club
ABDELKADER, Justin	6-1	195	L	Muskegon, MI	2/25/87	Cedar Rapids
AXELSSON, Anton	6-0	183	L	Ytterby, Sweden	1/16/86	Frolunda Jr.
BACKER, Per	6-1	161	L	Grums, Sweden	1/4/82	Farjestad
FORSANDER, Johan	6-1	174	L	Jonkoping, Sweden	4/28/78	Morzine-Avoriaz
GRIGORENKO, Igor	5-10	178	R	Togliatti, USSR	4/9/83	Togliatti-Ufa
HASKINS, Tyler	6-1	177	R	Cleveland, OH	5/26/86	St. Michael's
HELM, Darren	5-11	172	L	Winnipeg, Man.	1/21/87	Medicine Hat
HIMELFARB, Eric	5-9	161	R	Thornhill, Ont.	1/1/83	Grand Rapids
JACKSON, Todd	5-11	170	R	Syracuse, NY	4/10/81	Grand Rapids-Toledo
JAMTIN, Andreas	5-11	185	L	Stockholm, Sweden	5/4/83	HV 71
JOHANSSON, Mikael	5-10	176	L	Arvika, Sweden	6/27/85	Bofors
KOLLAR, Tomas	6-2	211	L	Stockholm, Sweden	4/20/82	Skelleftea-Djurgarden
LOFBERG, Christofer	6-3	189	R	Stockholm, Sweden	10/11/86	Djurgarden
MAXIMENKO, Andrei	5-11	172	R	Moscow, USSR	1/10/81	Saratov-Almetjevsk
McGRATH, Evan	5-11	181	L	Oakville, Ont.	1/14/86	Kitchener
OULAHEN, Ryan	6-1	180	L	Newmarket, Ont.	3/26/85	Brampton
RITOLA, Mattias	6-0	192	L	Borlange, Sweden	3/14/87	Frolunda Jr.-Leksand Jr.
RYNO, Johan	6-4	198	L	Orebro, Sweden	6/5/86	Arboga-Kumla
SEMENOV, Dmitri	5-10	178	L	Moscow, USSR	4/19/82	Novosibirsk
SODERSTROM, Christian	6-1	176	L	Sundsvall, Sweden	10/13/80	Timra
STEEN, Calle	5-11	198	L	Stockholm, Sweden	5/16/80	Farjestad
STOLYAROV, Gennady	6-4	187	L	Moscow, USSR	8/20/86	Chekhov
SUNDIN, Andreas	6-0	185	L	Linkoping, Sweden	3/15/84	Linkoping
SVENSSON, Jimmie	6-1	183	L	Vasteras, Sweden	2/25/82	Troja
TOLSA, Jari	6-0	172	L	Goteborg, Sweden	4/20/81	Frolunda
VALTONEN, Tomek	6-1	198	L	Piotrkow Trybunalski, Pol.	1/8/80	Jokerit

DEFENSEMEN						
BACKSTROM, Nils	6-0	183	R	Stockholm, Sweden	6/29/86	Djurgarden Jr.
BERGGREN, Johan	6-3	176	L	Vastra Amtevik, Sweden	5/18/84	Arboga
BLATAK, Miroslav	5-11	172	L	Gottwaldov, Czech.	5/25/82	Zlin
BLOM, Stefan	6-2	189	L	Stockholm, Sweden	7/30/85	Hammarby Jr.-Arlanda
BYKOV, Dmitri	5-10	169	L	Izhevsk, USSR	5/5/77	Kazan
ERICSSON, Jonathan	6-4	189	L	Karlskrona, Sweden	3/2/84	Sodertalje
KINDL, Jakub	6-3	200	L	Sumperk, Czech.	2/10/87	Kitchener
KOLESOV, Sergei	6-4	187	L	Novopolotsk, USSR	5/22/86	Minsk-Yunost
MAY, Jeff	6-1	186	L	Richmond, B.C.	4/4/87	Prince Albert
MIELONEN, Juho	6-2	180	R	Savonlinna, Finland	3/1/87	Ilves Jr.
PETRASEK, David	6-0	187	R	Jonkoping, Sweden	2/1/76	Malmo
SELUYANOV, Alexander	5-11	172	R	Ufa, USSR	3/24/87	Togliatti
STAMLER, Bretton	6-1	201	R	Calgary, Alta.	3/10/87	Seattle

GOALTENDERS	HT	WT	C	Place of Birth	Date	2004-05 Club
LIV, Stefan	6-0	172	L	Jonkoping, Sweden	12/21/80	HV 71

Coach

BABCOCK, MIKE
Coach, Detroit Red Wings. Born in Manitouwadge, Ont., April 29, 1963.

Mike Babcock became the 26th coach in Detroit Red Wings history on July 14, 2005, bringing a winning track record at all levels of play including college and junior hockey, the American Hockey League, the National Hockey League and the highest level of international competition. He is the only man to coach Team Canada to victories at both the World Junior Championship (1997) and senior World Championship (2004).

Babcock spent two seasons with the Mighty Ducks of Anaheim, leading the team to the Stanley Cup finals in his first season behind the bench in 2002–03. He became the first rookie coach to reach the Finals since Florida's Doug MacLean in 1996. With a four-game sweep over Detroit in the first round of the playoffs, the Ducks became the first team since the 1952 Red Wings (over Toronto) to sweep a defending Stanley Cup champion. Babcock led the team to the best regular season in the club's history with 40 wins and 95 points in 2002–03.

Before joining Anaheim, Babcock spent two seasons as head coach of the Cincinnati Mighty Ducks (2000 to 2002), the primary development affiliate for both Detroit and Anaheim in the American Hockey League. He led the club to a franchise-best 41 wins and 95 points in 2000-01 Babcock moved to Cincinnati after a successful six-year run as the head coach of the Spokane Chiefs of the Western Hockey League (1994 through 2000). He was twice named WHL coach of the year (1996 and 2000) after taking the Chiefs to the league finals in both seasons. He began his WHL coaching career with the Moose Jaw Warriors in 1991–92. In Canadian university play, Babcock won a national championship and was named the coach of the year with the Lethbridge Pronghorns in 1993-94. In 1988, he was named head coach at Red Deer College in Red Deer, Alberta. He spent three seasons at the school, winning the Alberta college championship and coach of the year award in 1989.

Babcock played in the WHL for Saskatoon (1980-81) and Kelowna (1982-83), where he was team captain. In between, he spent a year at the University of Saskatoon. Babcock also played four years at McGill University (1983 to 87), twice being named an All-Star defenseman and team captain. He earned his bachelor's degree in physical education and attended graduate school in sports psychology at McGill.

Coaching History

Art Duncan, 1926-27; Jack Adams, 1927-28 to 1946-47; Tommy Ivan, 1947-48 to 1953-54; Jimmy Skinner, 1954-55 to 1956-57; Jimmy Skinner and Sid Abel, 1957-58; Sid Abel, 1958-59 to 1967-68; Bill Gadsby, 1968-69; Bill Gadsby and Sid Abel, 1969-70; Ned Harkness and Doug Barkley, 1970-71; Doug Barkley and Johnny Wilson, 1971-72; Johnny Wilson, 1972-73; Ted Garvin and Alex Delvecchio, 1973-74; Alex Delvecchio, 1974-75; Doug Barkley and Alex Delvecchio, 1975-76; Alex Delvecchio and Larry Wilson, 1976-77; Bobby Kromm, 1977-78, 1978-79; Bobby Kromm and Ted Lindsay, 1979-80; Ted Lindsay and Wayne Maxner, 1980-81; Wayne Maxner and Billy Dea, 1981-82; Nick Polano, 1982-83 to 1984-85; Harry Neale and Brad Park, 1985-86; Jacques Demers, 1986-87 to 1989-90; Bryan Murray, 1990-91 to 1992-93; Scotty Bowman, 1993-94 to 1997-98; Dave Lewis, Barry Smith (co-coaches) and Scotty Bowman, 1998-99; Scotty Bowman, 1999-2000 to 2001-02; Dave Lewis, 2002-03, 2003-04; Mike Babcock, 2005-06.

Coaching Record

Season	Team		Regular Season				Playoffs		
		Games	W	L	T		Games	W	L
1991-92	Moose Jaw (WHL)	72	33	36	3		4	0	4
1992-93	Moose Jaw (WHL)	72	27	42	3		....	....	....
1993-94	U. of Lethbridge (CIAU)	28	19	7	2		....	....	....
1994-95	Spokane (WHL)	72	32	36	4		11	6	5
1995-96	Spokane (WHL)	72	50	18	4		9	3	6
1996-97	Spokane (WHL)	65	31	30	4		9	4	5
1997-98	Spokane (WHL)	72	45	23	4		18	10	8
1998-99	Spokane (WHL)	72	19	44	9		....	....	....
1999-2000	Spokane (WHL)	72	47	21	4		20	15	5
2000-01	Cincinnati (WHL)	80	41	26	13		4	1	3
2001-02	Cincinnati (WHL)	80	33	33	14		3	1	2
2002-03	Anaheim (NHL)	82	40	33	9		21	15	6
2003-04	Anaheim (NHL)	82	29	43	10		....	....	....
2004-05	Anaheim (NHL)				Season Cancelled				
	NHL Totals	164	69	76	19		21	15	6

Club Records

Team

(Figures in brackets for season records are games played; records for fewest points, wins, ties, losses, goals, goals against are for 70 or more games)

Most Points	131	1995-96 (82)
Most Wins	*62	1995-96 (82)
Most Ties	18	1952-53 (70),
		1980-81 (80),
		1996-97 (82)
Most Losses	57	1985-86 (80)
Most Goals	369	1992-93 (84)
Most Goals Against	415	1985-86 (80)
Fewest Points	40	1985-86 (80)
Fewest Wins	16	1976-77 (80)
Fewest Ties	4	1966-67 (70)
Fewest Losses	13	1950-51 (70),
		1995-96 (82)
Fewest Goals	167	1958-59 (70)
Fewest Goals Against	132	1953-54 (70)

Longest Winning Streak

Overall	9	Mar. 3-21/51,
		Feb. 27-Mar. 20/55,
		Dec. 12-31/95,
		Mar. 3-22/96
Home	14	Jan. 21-Mar. 25/65
Away	7	Mar. 25-Apr. 14/95,
		Feb. 18-Mar. 20/96

Longest Undefeated Streak

Overall	15	Nov. 27-Dec. 28/52
		(8 wins, 7 ties)
Home	19	Dec. 31/00-Apr.7/01
		(17 wins, 2 ties)
Away	15	Oct. 18-Dec. 20/51
		(10 wins, 5 ties)

Longest Losing Streak

Overall	14	Feb. 24-Mar. 25/82
Home	7	Feb. 20-Mar. 25/82
Away	14	Oct. 19-Dec. 21/66

Longest Winless Streak

Overall	19	Feb. 26-Apr. 3/77
		(18 losses, 1 tie)
Home	10	Dec. 11/85-Jan. 18/86
		(9 losses, 1 tie)
Away	26	Dec. 15/76-Apr. 3/77
		(23 losses, 3 ties)

Most Shutouts, Season	13	1953-54 (70)
Most. PIM, Season	2,393	1985-86 (80)
Most Goals, Game	15	Jan. 23/44
		(NYR 0 at Det. 15)

Individual

Most Seasons	25	Gordie Howe
Most Games	1,687	Gordie Howe
Most Goals, Career	786	Gordie Howe
Most Assists, Career	1,023	Gordie Howe
Most Points, Career	1,809	Gordie Howe
		(786G, 1,023A)
Most PIM, Career	2,090	Bob Probert
Most Shutouts, Career	85	Terry Sawchuk

Longest Consecutive

Games Streak	548	Alex Delvecchio
		(Dec. 13/56-Nov. 11/64)
Most Goals, Season	65	Steve Yzerman
		(1988-89)
Most Assists, Season	90	Steve Yzerman
		(1988-89)
Most Points, Season	155	Steve Yzerman
		(1988-89; 65G, 90A)
Most PIM, Season	398	Bob Probert
		(1987-88)

Most Points, Defenseman, Season	77	Paul Coffey
		(1993-94; 14G, 63A)
Most Points, Center, Season	155	Steve Yzerman
		(1988-89; 65G, 90A)
Most Points, Right Wing, Season	103	Gordie Howe
		(1968-69; 44G, 59A)
Most Points, Left Wing, Season	105	John Ogrodnick
		(1984-85; 55G, 50A)
Most Points, Rookie, Season	87	Steve Yzerman
		(1983-84; 39G, 48A)
Most Shutouts, Season	12	Terry Sawchuk
		(1951-52, 1953-54,
		1954-55),
		Glenn Hall
		(1955-56)
Most Goals, Game	6	Syd Howe
		(Feb. 3/44)
Most Assists, Game	*7	Billy Taylor
		(Mar. 16/47)
Most Points, Game	7	Carl Liscombe
		(Nov. 5/42; 3G, 4A),
		Don Grosso
		(Feb. 3/44; 1G, 6A),
		Billy Taylor
		(Mar. 16/47; 7A)

* NHL Record.

Retired Numbers

1	Terry Sawchuk	1949-55, 57-64, 68-69
7	Ted Lindsay	1944-57, 64-65
9	Gordie Howe	1946-1971
10	Alex Delvecchio	1951-1973
12	Sid Abel	1938-43, 45-52

All-time Record vs. Other Clubs

Regular Season

	At Home								On Road								Total							
	GP	W	L	T	OL	GF	GA	PTS	GP	W	L	T	OL	GF	GA	PTS	GP	W	L	T	OL	GF	GA	PTS
Anaheim	22	17	2	3	0	83	49	37	22	11	7	4	0	65	52	26	44	28	9	7	0	148	101	63
Atlanta	4	4	0	0	0	17	8	8	3	3	0	1	0	19	7	6	7	7	0	0	0	36	15	14
Boston	285	154	79	52	0	952	720	360	287	90	153	43	1	1007	224		572	244	232	95	1	1713	1727	584
Buffalo	55	32	18	5	0	203	159	69	52	11	33	8	0	153	226	30	107	43	51	13	0	356	385	99
Calgary	59	31	18	10	0	215	174	72	60	20	34	6	0	179	228	46	119	51	52	16	0	394	402	118
Carolina	31	17	7	7	0	119	86	41	30	12	17	1	0	86	104	25	61	29	24	8	0	205	190	66
Chicago	335	203	98	33	1	1144	833	440	338	132	152	51	3	951	1015	318	673	335	250	84	4	2095	1848	758
Colorado	40	24	15	1	0	142	120	49	42	18	20	4	0	142	148	40	82	42	35	5	0	284	268	89
Columbus	10	8	2	0	0	39	22	16	11	8	2	1	0	26	21	17	21	16	4	1	0	65	43	33
Dallas	106	53	37	16	0	406	336	122	106	37	51	18	0	319	370	92	212	90	88	34	0	725	706	214
Edmonton	44	25	15	3	1	172	146	54	44	14	19	10	1	155	168	39	88	39	34	13	2	327	314	93
Florida	8	4	1	3	0	30	21	11	9	6	1	2	0	27	17	14	17	10	2	5	0	57	38	25
Los Angeles	79	36	30	13	0	300	271	85	80	24	41	14	1	246	321	63	159	60	71	27	1	546	592	148
Minnesota	8	5	2	1	0	32	20	11	8	4	1	2	1	21	18	11	16	9	3	3	1	53	38	22
Montreal	280	130	97	53	0	805	717	313	282	67	172	43	0	636	994	177	562	197	269	96	0	1441	1711	490
Nashville	17	13	1	2	1	69	38	29	16	7	6	2	1	45	40	17	33	20	7	4	2	114	78	46
New Jersey	40	25	13	2	0	164	129	52	40	10	21	9	0	103	138	29	80	35	34	11	0	267	267	81
NY Islanders	45	26	17	2	0	165	135	54	46	19	23	4	0	137	164	42	91	45	40	6	0	302	299	96
NY Rangers	285	164	76	45	0	1004	699	373	284	92	134	58	0	738	868	242	569	256	210	103	0	1742	1567	615
Ottawa	9	6	3	0	0	33	19	12	10	6	3	1	0	29	28	13	19	12	6	1	0	62	47	25
Philadelphia	59	31	18	10	0	210	182	72	58	13	34	11	0	168	230	37	117	44	52	21	0	378	412	109
Phoenix	51	25	18	8	0	200	170	58	49	18	17	14	0	153	149	50	100	43	35	22	0	353	319	108
Pittsburgh	65	40	13	12	0	253	178	92	65	17	44	4	0	195	281	38	130	57	57	16	0	448	459	130
St. Louis	110	52	41	17	0	404	336	121	110	34	54	20	2	308	375	90	220	86	95	37	2	712	711	211
San Jose	25	22	2	1	0	104	45	45	26	14	9	3	0	100	83	31	51	36	11	4	0	204	128	76
Tampa Bay	12	10	1	1	0	47	21	21	14	9	4	1	0	61	43	19	26	19	5	2	0	108	64	40
Toronto	322	168	106	46	2	948	792	384	316	105	164	47	0	846	1045	257	638	273	270	93	2	1794	1837	641
Vancouver	66	41	16	8	1	275	188	91	65	26	29	10	0	210	235	62	131	67	45	18	1	485	423	153
Washington	47	21	15	11	0	161	135	53	46	20	21	5	1	147	168	45	93	41	36	16	0	308	303	98
Defunct Clubs	141	76	40	25	0	430	307	177	141	49	63	29	0	364	375	127	282	125	103	54	0	794	682	304
Totals	**2660**	**1463**	**801**	**390**	**6**	**9146**	**7056**	**3322**	**2660**	**896**	**1329**	**425**	**10**	**7390**	**8918**	**2227**	**5320**	**2359**	**2130**	**815**	**16**	**16536**	**15974**	**5549**

Playoffs

	Series	W	L	GP	W	L	T	GF	GA	Last Mtg.	Rnd.	Result
Anaheim	3	2	1	12	8	4	0	36	24	2003	CQF	L 0-4
Boston	7	3	4	33	14	19	0	98	96	1957	SF	L 1-4
Calgary	2	1	1	8	4	4	0	20	16	2004	CSF	L 2-4
Carolina	1	1	0	5	4	1	0	14	7	2002	F	W 4-1
Chicago	14	6	8	69	31	38	0	190	210	1995	CF	W 4-1
Colorado	5	2	3	30	13	17	0	76	79	2002	CF	W 4-3
Dallas	3	3	0	18	12	6	0	55	40	1998	CF	W 4-2
Edmonton	2	0	2	10	2	8	0	26	39	1988	CF	L 1-4
Los Angeles	2	1	1	10	6	4	0	32	21	2001	CQF	L 2-4
Montreal	12	7	5	62	29	33	0	149	161	1978	QF	L 1-4
Nashville	1	1	0	6	4	2	0	12	9	2004	CQF	W 4-2
New Jersey	1	0	1	4	0	4	0	7	16	1995	F	L 0-4
NY Rangers	5	4	1	23	13	10	0	57	49	1950	F	W 4-3
Philadelphia	1	1	0	4	4	0	0	16	6	1997	F	W 4-0
Phoenix	2	2	0	12	8	4	0	44	28	1998	CQF	W 4-2
St. Louis	7	5	2	40	24	16	0	125	103	2002	CSF	W 4-1
San Jose	2	1	1	7	3	4	0	51	27	1995	CSF	W 4-0
Toronto	23	11	12	117	59	58	0	321	311	1993	DSF	L 3-4
Vancouver	1	1	0	6	4	2	0	22	16	2002	CQF	W 4-2
Washington	1	1	0	4	4	0	0	13	7	1998	F	W 4-0
Defunct Clubs	4	3	1	10	7	2	1	21	13			
Totals	**99**	**56**	**43**	**494**	**257**	**236**	**1**	**1385**	**1278**			

Calgary totals include Atlanta Flames, 1972-73 to 1979-80.
Colorado totals include Quebec, 1979-80 to 1994-95.
New Jersey totals include Kansas City, 1974-75 to 1975-76, and Colorado Rockies, 1976-77 to 1981-82.
Phoenix totals include Winnipeg, 1979-80 to 1995-96.
Carolina totals include Hartford, 1979-80 to 1996-97.
Dallas totals include Minnesota North Stars, 1967-68 to 1992-93.

Playoff Results 2005-2000

Year	Round	Opponent	Result	GF	GA
2004	CSF	Calgary	L 2-4	12	11
	CQF	Nashville	W 4-2	12	9
2003	CQF	Anaheim	L 0-4	6	10
2002	**F**	**Carolina**	**W 4-1**	**14**	**7**
	CF	Colorado	W 4-3	22	13
	CSF	St. Louis	W 4-1	14	11
	CQF	Vancouver	W 4-2	22	16
2001	CQF	Los Angeles	L 2-4	17	15
2000	CSF	Colorado	L 1-4	8	13
	CQF	Los Angeles	W 4-0	15	6

Abbreviations: Round: F - Final; **CF** - conference final; **CSF** - conference semi-final; **CQF** - conference quarter-final; **DSF** - division semi-final; **SF** - semi-final; **QF** - quarter-final.

Entry Draft
Selections 2005-1991

2005
Pick
19	Jakub Kindl
42	Justin Abdelkader
80	Christofer Lofberg
103	Mattias Ritola
132	Darren Helm
137	Johan Ryno
151	Jeff May
175	Juho Mielonen
214	Bretton Stamler

2004
Pick
97	Johan Franzen
128	Evan McGrath
151	Sergei Kolesov
162	Tyler Haskins
192	Anton Axelsson
226	Steven Covington
257	Gennady Stolyarov
290	Nils Backstrom

2003
Pick
64	James Howard
132	Kyle Quincey
164	Ryan Oulahen
170	Andreas Sundin
194	Stefan Blom
226	Tomas Kollar
258	Vladimir Kutny
289	Mikael Johansson

2002
Pick
58	Jiri Hudler
63	Tomas Fleischmann
95	Valtteri Filppula
131	Johan Berggren
166	Logan Koopmans
197	Jimmy Cuddihy
229	Derek Meech
260	Pierre-Olivier Beaulieu
262	Christian Soderstrom
291	Jonathan Ericsson

2001
Pick
62	Igor Grigorenko
121	Drew MacIntyre
129	Miroslav Blatak
157	Andreas Jamtin
195	Nick Pannoni
258	Dmitri Bykov
288	Francois Senez

2000
Pick
29	Niklas Kronwall
38	Tomas Kopecky
102	Stefan Liv
127	Dmitri Semenov
128	Alexander Seluyanov
130	Aaron Van Leusen
187	Per Backer
196	Paul Ballantyne
228	Jimmie Svensson
251	Todd Jackson
260	Yevgeny Bumagin

1999
Pick
120	Jari Tolsa
149	Andrei Maximenko
181	Kent McDonell
210	Henrik Zetterberg
238	Anton Borodkin
266	Ken Davis

1998
Pick
25	Jiri Fischer
55	Ryan Barnes
56	Tomek Valtonen
84	Jake McCracken
111	Brent Hobday
142	Calle Steen
151	Adam DeLeeuw
171	Pavel Datsyuk
198	Jeremy Goetzinger
226	David Petrasek
256	Petja Pietilainen

1997
Pick
49	Yuri Butsayev
76	Petr Sykora
102	Quintin Laing
129	John Wikstrom
157	B.J. Young
186	Mike Laceby
213	Steve Willejto
239	Greg Willers

1996
Pick
26	Jesse Wallin
52	Aren Miller
108	Johan Forsander
135	Michal Podolka
144	Magnus Nilsson
162	Alexandre Jacques
189	Colin Beardsmore
215	Craig Stahl
241	Eugeny Afanasiev

1995
Pick
26	Maxim Kuznetsov
52	Philippe Audet
58	Darryl Laplante
104	Anatoli Ustyugov
125	Chad Wilchynski
126	David Arsenault
156	Tyler Perry
182	Per Eklund
208	Andrei Samokhvalov
234	David Engblom

1994
Pick
23	Yan Golubovsky
49	Mathieu Dandenault
75	Sean Gillam
114	Frederic Deschenes
127	Doug Battaglia
153	Pavel Agarkov
205	Jason Elliot
231	Jeff Mikesch
257	Tomas Holmstrom
283	Toivo Suursoo

1993
Pick
22	Anders Eriksson
48	Jon Coleman
74	Kevin Hilton
97	John Jakopin
100	Benoit Larose
126	Norm Maracle
152	Tim Spitzig
178	Yuri Yeresko
204	Vitezslav Skuta
230	Ryan Shanahan
256	James Kosecki
282	Gordon Hunt

1992
Pick
22	Curtis Bowen
46	Darren McCarty
70	Sylvain Cloutier
118	Mike Sullivan
142	Jason MacDonald
166	Greg Scott
183	Justin Krall
189	C. J. Denomme
214	Jeff Walker
238	Dan McGillis
262	Ryan Bach

1991
Pick
10	Martin Lapointe
32	Jamie Pushor
54	Chris Osgood
76	Mike Knuble
98	Dimitri Motkov
142	Igor Malykhin
186	Jim Bermingham
208	Jason Firth
230	Bart Turner
252	Andrew Miller

Club Directory

Joe Louis Arena

Detroit Red Wings
Joe Louis Arena
600 Civic Center Drive
Detroit, MI 48226
Phone **313/396-7544**
FAX PR: 313/567-0296
Media Hotline: 313/396-7599
www.detroitredwings.com
Capacity: 20,066

Owner/Governor . . . . Mike Ilitch
Owner/Secretary–Treasurer . . . . Marian Ilitch
President & CEO Ilitch Holdings, Inc./Vice-President/
   Alternate Governor Red Wings . . . . Christopher Ilitch
Senior Vice-President/Alternate Governor . . . . Jim Devellano
Vice-President Olympia Entertainment/
   General Counsel Red Wings . . . . Robert E. Carr
General Manager/Alternate Governor . . . . Ken Holland
Assistant General Manager . . . . Jim Nill
Head Coach . . . . Mike Babcock
Assistant Coach . . . . Paul MacLean
Assistant Coach . . . . Todd McLellan
Goaltending Coach . . . . Jim Bedard
Video Coach . . . . Jay Woodcroft
Directory of Hockey Administration . . . . Ryan Martin
Consultant . . . . Scotty Bowman
NHL Scouts . . . . Mark Howe, Dave Lewis, Bob McCammon
Amateur Scouts . . . . Joe McDonnell, Bruce Haralson,
   David Kolb, Mark Leach
Minor League Scout . . . . Glenn Merkosky
Part-Time Scout . . . . Marty Stein
Director of European Scouting . . . . Hakan Andersson
European Scout . . . . Vladimir Havluj
Part-Time European Scout . . . . Evgeni Erfilov
Vice-President of Finance . . . . Paul MacDonald
Executive Assistant . . . . Kathi Wyatt
Accounting Assistant . . . . Bridget Merritt
Athletic Therapist . . . . Piet Van Zant
Assistant Athletic Therapist . . . . Russ Baumann
Equipment Manager . . . . Paul Boyer
Assistant Equipment Manager . . . . Chris Scoppetto
Team Masseur . . . . Sergei Tchekmarev
Senior Director of Communications . . . . John Hahn
Community Relations Manager . . . . Anne Marie Krappmann
Medical Director . . . . Dr. Donald Weaver
Team Physicians . . . . Dr. Anthony Colucci, Dr. Doug Plagens
Team Dentist . . . . Dr. C.J. Regula
Team Photographer . . . . Dave Reginek
Radio Broadcasters, AM 1270
   The Sports Station, WXYT . . . . Ken Kal, Paul Woods
Television Broadcasters, Fox Sports Net – Detroit . . . Ken Daniels, Mickey Redmond

General Manager

HOLLAND, KEN
General Manager, Detroit Red Wings. Born in Vernon, B.C., Nov. 10, 1955.
Ken Holland has served in the Red Wings front office since 1985, and has been the club's general manager since July 18, 1997. He has established himself as one of the most innovative and aggressive GMs in the National Hockey League. Detroit's Stanley Cup victory in 2002 marked the team's second championship under his leadership. Holland began his tenure as the club's general manager after serving as assistant general manager for the previous three seasons. He was elevated to his present position July 18, 1997.

Holland oversees all aspects of hockey operations including all matters relating to player personnel, development, contract negotiations and player movements. He also continues to be Detroit's point person at the NHL Entry Draft, as he has been for the past 13 years.

Holland has deftly handled several different front-office duties for the club over the past 20 years. At the conclusion of his playing days as a goaltender, spending most of his pro career at the American Hockey League level, Holland began his off-ice career in 1985 as a western Canada scout followed by five years as an amateur scouting director before promotions led to his current position as general manager.

A native of Vernon, BC, Holland played in the junior ranks for Medicine Hat (WHL) in 1974-75. He was Toronto's 13th pick (188th overall) in the 1975 draft but never saw action with the Maple Leafs. Holland twice signed with NHL teams as a free agent — in 1980 with Hartford and 1983 with Detroit. He spent most of his pro career with AHL clubs in Binghamton and Springfield, along with Adirondack, but did appear in four NHL games, making his debut with Hartford in 1980-81 and playing three contests for Detroit in 1983-84.

General Managers' History
Art Duncan and Duke Keats, 1926-27; Jack Adams, 1927-28 to 1961-62; Sid Abel, 1962-63 to 1969-70; Sid Abel and Ned Harkness, 1970-71; Ned Harkness, 1971-72 to 1973-74; Alex Delvecchio, 1974-75, 1975-76; Alex Delvecchio and Ted Lindsay, 1976-77; Ted Lindsay, 1977-78 to 1979-80; Jimmy Skinner, 1980-81, 1981-82; Jim Devellano, 1982-83 to 1989-90; Bryan Murray, 1990-91 to 1993-94; Jim Devellano (Senior Vice President), 1994-95 to 1996-97; Ken Holland, 1997-98 to date.

Captains' History
Art Duncan, 1926-27; Reg Noble, 1927-28 to 1929-30; George Hay, 1930-31; Carson Cooper, 1931-32; Larry Aurie, 1932-33; Herbie Lewis, 1933-34; Ebbie Goodfellow, 1934-35; Doug Young, 1935-36 to 1937-38; Ebbie Goodfellow, 1938-39 to 1940-41; Ebbie Goodfellow and Syd Howe, 1941-42; Sid Abel, 1942-43; Mud Bruneteau, Flash Hollett (co-captains), 1943-44; Flash Hollett, 1944-45; Flash Hollett and Sid Abel, 1945-46; Sid Abel, 1946-47 to 1951-52; Ted Lindsay, 1952-53 to 1955-56; Red Kelly, 1956-57, 1957-58; Gordie Howe, 1958-59 to 1961-62; Alex Delvecchio, 1962-63 to 1972-73; Alex Delvecchio, Nick Libett, Red Berenson, Gary Bergman, Ted Harris, Mickey Redmond and Larry Johnston, 1973-74; Marcel Dionne, 1974-75; Danny Grant and Terry Harper, 1975-76; Danny Grant and Dennis Polonich, 1976-77; Dan Maloney and Dennis Hextall, 1977-78; Dennis Hextall, Nick Libett and Paul Woods, 1978-79; Dale McCourt, 1979-80; Errol Thompson and Reed Larson, 1980-81; Reed Larson, 1981-82; Danny Gare, 1982-83 to 1985-86; Steve Yzerman, 1986-87 to date.

Edmonton Oilers

2005-06 Schedule

Oct.	Wed.	5	Colorado
	Sat.	8	Vancouver
	Mon.	10	at Anaheim
	Tue.	11	at Los Angeles
	Fri.	14	Dallas
	Sat.	15	at Calgary
	Tue.	18	Phoenix
	Thu.	20	at Calgary
	Fri.	21	Colorado
	Tue.	25	at Colorado
	Fri.	28	at Dallas
	Sat.	29	at Nashville
Nov.	Tue.	1	Columbus
	Thu.	3	at Detroit
	Fri.	4	at St. Louis
	Mon.	7	at Dallas
	Tue.	8	at Nashville
	Fri.	11	at Columbus
	Sun.	13	at Chicago
	Mon.	14	at Colorado
	Thu.	17	Detroit
	Sat.	19	Chicago
	Mon.	21	San Jose
	Wed.	23	at Minnesota
	Fri.	25	at Calgary
	Tue.	29	Colorado
Dec.	Thu.	1	Vancouver
	Sat.	3	Boston
	Thu.	8	at Philadelphia
	Sat.	10	at NY Islanders
	Tue.	13	at New Jersey
	Thu.	15	Montreal
	Sat.	17	at Vancouver
	Mon.	19	Calgary
	Wed.	21	at Vancouver
	Fri.	23	Los Angeles
	Mon.	26	Minnesota
	Wed.	28	Minnesota
	Fri.	30	Nashville
	Sat.	31	at Calgary
Jan.	Tue.	3	Chicago

	Sat.	7	Toronto*
	Tue.	10	at Pittsburgh
	Thu.	12	at NY Rangers
	Sat.	14	Ottawa
	Mon.	16	Buffalo
	Thu.	19	at San Jose
	Sat.	21	at Phoenix
	Mon.	23	Calgary
	Wed.	25	at Anaheim
	Thu.	26	at Los Angeles
	Sun.	29	at Phoenix
Feb.	Thu.	2	Columbus
	Sat.	4	Vancouver
	Mon.	6	Anaheim
	Tue.	7	at Colorado
	Fri.	10	Minnesota
	Sun.	12	St. Louis*
Mar.	Wed.	1	St. Louis
	Fri.	3	San Jose
	Sun.	5	Nashville*
	Tue.	7	Dallas
	Thu.	9	at San Jose
	Sat.	11	at Columbus
	Sun.	12	at Minnesota
	Tue.	14	at Minnesota
	Thu.	16	Calgary
	Sat.	18	Detroit
	Tue.	21	Vancouver
	Thu.	23	at Vancouver
	Sat.	25	at Vancouver
	Sun.	26	at Colorado
	Tue.	28	Minnesota
	Thu.	30	Los Angeles
Apr.	Sat.	1	Calgary
	Mon.	3	Phoenix
	Thu.	6	at Minnesota
	Fri.	7	at Chicago
	Sun.	9	at St. Louis
	Tue.	11	at Detroit
	Thu.	13	Anaheim
	Mon.	17	Colorado

Denotes afternoon game.

Franchise date: June 22, 1979

NORTHWEST DIVISION

27th
NHL
Season

Year-by-Year Record

Season	GP	Home				Road				Overall						Pts	Finished	Playoff Result
		W	L	T	OL	W	L	T	OL	W	L	T	OL	GF	GA			
2004-05	....																	
2003-04	82	22	12	4	3	14	17	8	2	36	29	12	5	221	208	89	4th, Northwest Div.	Out of Playoffs
2002-03	82	20	12	5	4	16	14	6	5	36	26	11	9	231	230	92	4th, Northwest Div.	Lost Conf. Quarter-Final
2001-02	82	23	14	4	0	15	14	8	4	38	28	12	4	205	182	92	3rd, Northwest Div.	Out of Playoffs
2000-01	82	23	9	7	2	16	19	5	1	39	28	12	3	243	222	93	2nd, Northwest Div.	Lost Conf. Quarter-Final
1999-2000	82	18	11	9	3	14	15	7	5	32	26	16	8	226	212	88	2nd, Northwest Div.	Lost Conf. Quarter-Final
1998-99	82	17	19	5	....	16	18	7	....	33	37	12	....	230	226	78	2nd, Northwest Div.	Lost Conf. Quarter-Final
1997-98	82	20	16	5	....	15	21	5	....	35	37	10	....	215	224	80	3rd, Pacific Div.	Lost Conf. Semi-Final
1996-97	82	21	16	4	....	15	21	5	....	36	37	9	....	252	247	81	3rd, Pacific Div.	Lost Conf. Semi-Final
1995-96	82	15	21	5	....	15	23	3	....	30	44	8	....	240	304	68	5th, Pacific Div.	Out of Playoffs
1994-95	48	11	12	1	....	6	15	3	....	17	27	4	....	136	183	38	5th, Pacific Div.	Out of Playoffs
1993-94	84	17	22	3	....	8	23	11	....	25	45	14	....	261	305	64	6th, Pacific Div.	Out of Playoffs
1992-93	84	16	21	5	....	10	29	3	....	26	50	8	....	242	337	60	5th, Smythe Div.	Out of Playoffs
1991-92	80	22	13	5	....	14	21	5	....	36	34	10	....	295	297	82	3rd, Smythe Div.	Lost Conf. Championship
1990-91	80	22	15	3	....	15	22	3	....	37	37	6	....	272	272	80	3rd, Smythe Div.	Lost Conf. Championship
1989-90	**80**	**23**	**11**	**6**	....	**15**	**17**	**8**	....	**38**	**28**	**14**	....	**315**	**283**	**90**	**2nd, Smythe Div.**	**Won Stanley Cup**
1988-89	80	21	16	3	....	17	18	5	....	38	34	8	....	325	306	84	3rd, Smythe Div.	Lost Div. Semi-Final
1987-88	**80**	**28**	**8**	**4**	....	**16**	**17**	**7**	....	**44**	**25**	**11**	....	**363**	**288**	**99**	**2nd, Smythe Div.**	**Won Stanley Cup**
1986-87	**80**	**29**	**6**	**5**	....	**21**	**18**	**1**	....	**50**	**24**	**6**	....	**372**	**284**	**106**	**1st, Smythe Div.**	**Won Stanley Cup**
1985-86	80	32	6	2	....	24	11	5	....	56	17	7	....	426	310	119	1st, Smythe Div.	Lost Div. Final
1984-85	**80**	**26**	**7**	**7**	....	**23**	**13**	**4**	....	**49**	**20**	**11**	....	**401**	**298**	**109**	**1st, Smythe Div.**	**Won Stanley Cup**
1983-84	**80**	**31**	**5**	**4**	....	**26**	**13**	**1**	....	**57**	**18**	**5**	....	**446**	**314**	**119**	**1st, Smythe Div.**	**Won Stanley Cup**
1982-83	80	25	9	6	....	22	12	6	....	47	21	12	....	424	315	106	1st, Smythe Div.	Lost Final
1981-82	80	31	5	4	....	17	12	11	....	48	17	15	....	417	295	111	1st, Smythe Div.	Lost Div. Semi-Final
1980-81	80	17	13	10	....	12	22	6	....	29	35	16	....	328	327	74	4th, Smythe Div.	Lost Quarter-Final
1979-80	80	17	14	9	....	11	25	4	....	28	39	13	....	301	322	69	4th, Smythe Div.	Lost Prelim. Round

Chris Pronger (left) joined the Oilers in a blockbuster deal with St. Louis on August 2. Michael Peca (right) was acquired from the Islanders the following day.

2005-06 Player Personnel

FORWARDS	HT	WT	S	Place of Birth	Date	2004-05 Club
BAUM, Dan	6-1	189	L	Biggar, Sask.	6/4/83	Edmonton (AHL)
BODIE, Troy	6-4	213	R	Portage La Prairie, Man.	1/25/85	Kelowna
BRODZIAK, Kyle	6-2	198	L	St. Paul, Alta.	5/25/84	Edmonton (AHL)
DiCASMIRRO, Nate	5-11	205	L	Burnsville, MN	9/27/78	Edmonton (AHL)
DVORAK, Radek	6-2	200	R	Tabor, Czech.	3/9/77	C. Budejovice
HARVEY, Todd	6-0	210	R	Hamilton, Ont.	2/17/75	Cambridge
HEMSKY, Ales	6-0	192	R	Pardubice, Czech.	8/13/83	Pardubice
HORCOFF, Shawn	6-1	204	L	Trail, B.C.	9/17/78	Mora
HUNTER, J.J.	6-1	185	L	Shaunavon, Sask.	7/6/80	Edmonton (AHL)
JACQUES, Jean-Francois	6-4	217	L	Terrebonne, Que.	4/29/85	Baie-Comeau-Edm (AHL)
LARAQUE, Georges	6-3	243	R	Montreal, Que.	12/7/76	Solna
MOREAU, Ethan	6-2	220	L	Huntsville, Ont.	9/22/75	Villacher SV
NIINIMAKI, Jesse	6-2	183	L	Tampere, Finland	8/19/83	Ilves-Edmonton (AHL)
PECA, Michael	5-11	190	R	Toronto, Ont.	3/26/74	
PETERSEN, Toby	5-10	197	L	Minneapolis, MN	10/27/78	Edmonton (AHL)
PISANI, Fernando	6-1	205	L	Edmonton, Alta.	12/27/76	Langnau-Asiago
POULIOT, Marc-Antoine	6-1	195	R	Quebec City, Que.	5/22/85	Rimouski
RADUNSKE, Brock	6-4	196	L	Kitchener, Ont.	4/5/83	Edm (AHL)-Greenville
REASONER, Marty	6-1	200	L	Honeoye Falls, NY	2/26/77	Salzburg
RITA, Jani	6-1	206	L	Helsinki, Finland	7/25/81	HPK
SALMELAINEN, Tony	5-9	185	R	Espoo, Finland	8/8/81	Edmonton (AHL)
SCHREMP, Rob	5-11	197	L	Syracuse, NY	7/1/86	London
SMYTH, Ryan	6-1	190	L	Banff, Alta.	2/21/76	
STASTNY, Yan	5-11	175	L	Quebec City, Que.	9/30/82	Nurnberg
STOLL, Jarret	6-1	200	R	Melville, Sask.	6/25/82	Edmonton (AHL)
STORTINI, Zachery	6-3	216	R	Elliot Lake, Ont.	9/11/85	Sudbury
TORRES, Raffi	6-0	216	L	Toronto, Ont.	10/8/81	Edmonton (AHL)
WINCHESTER, Brad	6-5	215	L	Madison, WI	3/1/81	Edmonton (AHL)

DEFENSEMEN						
BERGERON, Marc-Andre	5-10	197	L	St-Louis-de-France, Que.	10/13/80	Brynas
CROSS, Cory	6-5	225	L	Lloydminster, Alta.	1/3/71	
GREENE, Matt	6-3	223	R	Grand Ledge, MI	5/13/83	North Dakota
PLATT, Jason	6-1	210	L	San Francisco, CA	4/29/81	Edmonton (AHL)
PRONGER, Chris	6-6	220	L	Dryden, Ont.	10/10/74	
ROY, Mathieu	6-2	214	R	St-Georges, Que.	8/10/83	Edmonton (AHL)
SEMENOV, Alexei	6-6	235	L	Murmansk, USSR	4/10/81	St. Petersburg
SMITH, Dan	6-3	215	L	Fernie, B.C.	10/19/76	Edmonton (AHL)
SMITH, Jason	6-3	215	R	Calgary, Alta.	11/2/73	
SMITH, Kenny	6-2	209	R	Stoneham, MA	12/31/81	Edm (AHL)-Greenville
STAIOS, Steve	6-1	200	R	Hamilton, Ont.	7/28/73	Lulea
SYVRET, Danny	5-11	203	L	Millgrove, Ont.	6/13/85	London
ULANOV, Igor	6-3	220	L	Krasnokamsk, USSR	10/1/69	

GOALTENDERS	HT	WT	C	Place of Birth	Date	2004-05 Club
CONKLIN, Ty	6-0	184	L	Anchorage, AK	3/30/76	Wolfsburg
DROUIN-DESLAURIERS, Jeff	6-3	175	R	St-Jean-Richelieu, Que.	5/15/84	Edm (AHL)-Greenville
DUBNYK, Devan	6-5	194	L	Regina, Sask.	5/4/86	Kamloops
MARKKANEN, Jussi	6-0	182	L	Imatra, Finland	5/8/75	Togliatti
MORRISON, Mike	6-3	194	R	Medford, MA	7/11/79	Edm (AHL)-Greenville

In the System and Recently Drafted

FORWARDS	HT	WT	S	Place of Birth	Date	2004-05 Club
ALMTORP, Jonas	6-1	190	L	Uppsala, Sweden	11/17/83	Brynas-Almtuna
BRENK, Jake	6-2	187	R	Detroit Lakes, MN	4/16/82	Min. State-Greenville
CARON, Ed	6-2	228	L	Nashua, NH	4/30/82	Greenville
COGLIANO, Andrew	5-9	178	L	Toronto, Ont.	6/14/87	St. Mike's B's
DEE, Robby	6-1	185	L	Minneapolis, MN	4/9/87	Breck
GLASSER, Matthew	5-10	175	L	Saskatoon, Sask.	1/11/87	Fort McMurray
GOULET, Stephane	6-3	185	L	Levis, Que.	1/7/86	Moncton
JOHANSSON, Fredrik	5-11	180	L	Munkedal, Sweden	2/27/84	Vasteras
JOUKOV, Mishail	6-3	187	L	Leningrad, USSR	1/3/85	Kazan-Spartak
McDONALD, Colin	6-2	190	R	New Haven, CT	9/30/84	Providence College
MICKA, Tomas	6-2	180	L	Jihlava, Czech.	6/7/83	Greenville-Tol.-Victoria
MIKHNOV, Alexei	6-5	200	L	Kiev, USSR	8/31/82	Novosibirsk-Yaroslavl
MURATOV, Yevgeny	5-10	178	R	Nizhny Tagil, USSR	1/28/81	Novokuznetsk
MURPHY, Patrick	6-1	195	L	Van Nuys, CA	7/24/83	Northern Mich.
OLSSON, Kalle	6-0	183	L	Munkedal, Sweden	1/31/85	Frolunda-Vaxjo
PAUKOVICH, Geoff	6-4	208	L	Englewood, CO	4/24/86	U. of Denver
PETTERSSON, Fredrik	5-10	183	R	Goteborg, Sweden	6/10/87	Frolunda Jr.
REDDOX, Liam	5-9	179	L	East York, Ont.	1/27/86	Peterborough
ROHLFS, David	6-3	219	R	Ann Arbor, MI	6/4/84	U. of Michigan
SMIRNOV, Oleg	5-11	176	R	Elektrostal, USSR	4/8/80	
SPURGEON, Tyler	5-11	188	L	Edmonton, Alta.	4/10/86	Kelowna
TARVAINEN, Jussi	6-3	215	R	Lahti, Finland	5/31/76	Linkoping
TRUKHNO, Vyacheslav	6-1	196	L	Khimki, USSR	2/22/87	PEI
UMICEVIC, Dragan	6-0	191	R	Kping, Sweden	10/9/84	Sodertalje
VANDE VELDE, Chris	6-1	190	L	Moorhead, MN	3/15/87	Moorhead-Lincoln

DEFENSEMEN						
CHORNEY, Taylor	5-11	182	L	Thunder Bay, Ont.	4/27/87	Shat.-St. Mary's
GILBERT, Tom	6-2	190	R	Minneapolis, MN	1/10/83	U. of Wisconsin
HAAKANA, Kari	6-1	222	L	Outokumpu, Finland	11/8/73	Blues
HRABAL, Josef	6-1	176	L	Prerov, Czech.	3/7/84	Vsetin-Brno-Olomouc
KOLTSOV, Ivan	6-2	182	L	Cherepovets, USSR	3/7/84	Lipetsk-Belgorod
LUOMA, Mikko	6-3	207	L	Jyvaskyla, Finland	6/22/76	Malmo
SVENSK, Mikael	6-2	191	L	Gllstad, Sweden	2/28/83	Halmstad
TESLIUK, Roman	6-1	195	L	Severomorsk, USSR	1/21/86	Kamloops
YOUNG, Bryan	6-1	191	L	Ennismore, Ont.	8/6/86	Peterborough
ZIB, Lukas	6-1	200	R	Ceske Budejovice, Czech.	2/24/77	Perm

GOALTENDERS	HT	WT	C	Place of Birth	Date	2004-05 Club
ANTILA, Kristian	6-3	207	L	Vammala, Finland	1/10/80	Lulea
BJURLING, Bjorn	6-0	205	L	Stockholm, Sweden	8/21/79	Djurgarden
FISHER, Glenn	6-1	165	L	Edmonton, Alta.	4/25/83	U. of Denver

Coaching History

Glen Sather, 1979-80; Bryan Watson and Glen Sather, 1980-81; Glen Sather, 1981-82 to 1988-89; John Muckler, 1989-90, 1990-91; Ted Green, 1991-92, 1992-93; Ted Green and Glen Sather, 1993-94; George Burnett and Ron Low, 1994-95; Ron Low, 1995-96 to 1998-99; Kevin Lowe, 1999-2000; Craig MacTavish, 2000-01 to date.

Coach

MacTAVISH, CRAIG
Coach, Edmonton Oilers. Born in London, Ont., August 15, 1958.

The Edmonton Oilers named Craig MacTavish as their head coach on June 22, 2000. He became the eighth person in the club's NHL history to hold the position. MacTavish joined Kevin Lowe and Glen Sather as head coaches who were former captains of the Oilers.

MacTavish played for 18 seasons in the NHL, including eight-and-three-quarter campaigns with the Oilers. He was instrumental in helping his teams win four Stanley Cup titles; three with Edmonton and one with the New York Rangers. Although he was the last player in the NHL to play without a helmet, MacTavish was known for his aggressive style, combined with above average skills.

MacTavish retired as a player in 1997 and was immediately named an assistant coach with the New York Rangers. He was with the Rangers for two seasons prior to joining the Oilers' coaching staff as an assistant under Kevin Lowe in 1999-2000. He also served as an assistant coach for Team Canada at the 2005 World Championship.

Coaching Record

Season	Team	Games	W	L	T	Games	W	L
			Regular Season				**Playoffs**	
2000-01	Edmonton (NHL)	82	39	31	12	6	2	4
2001-02	Edmonton (NHL)	82	38	32	12	....	....	....
2002-03	Edmonton (NHL)	82	36	35	11	6	2	4
2003-04	Edmonton (NHL)	82	36	34	12	....	....	....
2004-05	Edmonton (NHL)			Season Cancelled				
	NHL Totals	328	149	132	47	12	4	8

General Managers' History

Larry Gordon, 1979-80; Glen Sather, 1980-81 to 1999-2000; Kevin Lowe, 2000-01 to date.

Vice President and General Manager

LOWE, KEVIN
Executive Vice President/General Manager, Edmonton Oilers.
Born in Lachute, Que., April 15, 1959.

The Edmonton Oilers named Kevin Lowe as their general manager on June 9, 2000, filling the position left vacant when Glen Sather resigned on May 19th. Lowe moved into the front office after spending the 1999-2000 season as coach of the Oilers. In his role as Oilers' g.m., Lowe has worked with Wayne Gretzky as assistant executive director of Canada's gold medal-winning team at the 2002 Winter Olympics and at the 2004 World Cup of Hockey.

After a brilliant 19-year playing career with the Edmonton Oilers and New York Rangers, Lowe announced his retirement on July 30, 1998 and joined the Edmonton Oilers coaching staff. He replaced Ron Low as head coach on June 18, 1999.

Lowe was the Oilers' first-ever draft pick when he was selected 1st overall in the 1979 NHL Entry Draft. He went on to play in 1,254 regular-season games and 214 playoff games, winning six Stanley Cup championships; the first five with Edmonton (1984, 1985, 1987, 1988, 1990) followed by a sixth title with the Rangers in 1994. Besides being the first draft choice in Oilers history, Lowe also scored the first goal in team history on October 10, 1979. He holds the Oilers' record for most games played in both the regular season (1,037) and playoffs (172), and became the sixth captain in team history in 1990-91. He was no less a leader off the ice, becoming the only player to win the King Clancy Memorial Trophy and the Budweiser/NHL Man of the Year Award in the same season (1989-90). Both awards are presented for leadership qualities and humanitarian contributions. His work with the Edmonton Christmas Bureau has set the standard for the Oilers' commitment to community involvement.

NHL Coaching Record

Season	Team	Games	W	L	T	Games	W	L
			Regular Season				**Playoffs**	
1999-2000	Edmonton	82	32	34	16	5	1	4
	NHL Totals	82	32	34	16	5	1	4

Club Records

Team

(Figures in brackets for season records are games played; records for fewest points, wins, ties, losses, goals, goals against are for 70 or more games)

Most Points 119   1983-84 (80), 1985-86 (80)
Most Wins 57   1983-84 (80)
Most Ties 16   1980-81 (80), 1999-2000 (82)
Most Losses 50   1992-93 (84)
Most Goals *446   1983-84 (80)
Most Goals Against 337   1992-93 (84)
Fewest Points 60   1992-93 (84)
Fewest Wins 25   1993-94 (84)
Fewest Ties 5   1983-84 (80)
Fewest Losses 17   1981-82 (80), 1985-86 (80)
Fewest Goals 205   2001-02 (82)
Fewest Goals Against 182   2001-02 (82)

Longest Winning Streak
Overall 9   Feb. 20-Mar. 13/01
Home 8   Jan. 19-Feb. 22/85, Feb. 24-Apr. 2/86
Away 8   Dec. 9/86-Jan. 17/87

Longest Undefeated Streak
Overall 15   Oct. 11-Nov. 9/84 (12 wins, 3 ties)
Home 14   Nov. 15/89-Jan. 6/90 (11 wins, 3 ties)
Away 9   Jan. 17-Mar. 2/82 (6 wins, 3 ties), Nov. 23/82-Jan. 18/83 (7 wins, 2 ties)

Longest Losing Streak
Overall 11   Oct. 16-Nov. 7/93
Home 9   Oct. 16-Nov. 24/93
Away 9   Nov. 25-Dec. 30/80

Longest Winless Streak
Overall 14   Oct. 11-Nov. 7/93 (13 losses, 1 tie)
Home 9   Oct. 16-Nov. 24/93 (9 losses)
Away 11   Dec. 18/01-Feb. 8/02 (7 losses, 4 ties)

Most Shutouts, Season 8   1997-98 (82); 2000-01 (82); 2001-02 (82)
Most PIM, Season 2,173   1987-88 (80)
Most Goals, Game 13   Nov. 19/83 (N.J. 4 at Edm. 13), Nov. 8/85 (Van. 0 at Edm. 13)

Individual

Most Seasons 15   Kevin Lowe
Most Games 1,037   Kevin Lowe
Most Goals, Career 583   Wayne Gretzky
Most Assists, Career 1,086   Wayne Gretzky
Most Points, Career 1,669   Wayne Gretzky
Most PIM, Career 1,747   Kelly Buchberger
Most Shutouts, Career 23   Tommy Salo

Longest Consecutive
Games Streak 519   Craig MacTavish (Oct. 11/86-Jan. 2/93)
Most Goals, Season . . . . *92   Wayne Gretzky (1981-82)
Most Assists, Season . . . . . . *163   Wayne Gretzky (1985-86)
Most Points, Season . . . . . . *215   Wayne Gretzky (1985-86; 52G, 163A)
Most PIM, Season 286   Steve Smith (1987-88)

Most Points, Defenseman,
Season 138   Paul Coffey (1985-86; 48G, 90A)

Most Points, Center,
Season . . . . *215   Wayne Gretzky (1985-86; 52G, 163A)

Most Points, Right Wing,
Season 135   Jari Kurri (1984-85; 71G, 64A)

Most Points, Left Wing,
Season 106   Mark Messier (1982-83; 48G, 58A)

Most Points, Rookie,
Season 75   Jari Kurri (1980-81; 32G, 43A)

Most Shutouts, Season 8   Curtis Joseph (1997-98), Tommy Salo (2000-01)

Most Goals, Game 5   Wayne Gretzky (Feb. 18/81, Dec. 30/81, Dec. 15/84, Dec. 6/87), Jari Kurri (Nov. 19/83), Pat Hughes (Feb. 3/84)

Most Assists, Game . . . . *7   Wayne Gretzky (Feb. 15/80, Dec. 11/85, Feb. 14/86)

Most Points, Game 8   Wayne Gretzky (Nov. 19/83; 3G, 5A), (Jan. 4/84; 4G, 4A), Paul Coffey (Mar. 14/86; 2G, 6A)

* NHL Record.

Captains' History

Ron Chipperfield, 1979-80; Blair MacDonald and Lee Fogolin, Jr., 1980-81; Lee Fogolin, Jr., 1981-82, 1982-83; Wayne Gretzky, 1983-84 to 1987-88; Mark Messier, 1988-89 to 1990-91; Kevin Lowe, 1991-92; Craig MacTavish, 1992-93, 1993-94; Shayne Corson, 1994-95; Kelly Buchberger, 1995-96 to 1998-99; Doug Weight, 1999-2000, 2000-01; Jason Smith, 2001-02 to date.

Retired Numbers

3	Al Hamilton	1972-1980
17	Jari Kurri	1980-1990
31	Grant Fuhr	1981-1991
99	Wayne Gretzky	1979-1988

All-time Record vs. Other Clubs

Regular Season

	At Home								On Road								Total							
	GP	W	L	T	OL	GF	GA	PTS	GP	W	L	T	OL	GF	GA	PTS	GP	W	L	T	OL	GF	GA	PTS
Anaheim	25	17	8	0	0	57	50	34	26	9	15	2	0	64	71	20	51	26	23	2	0	121	121	54
Atlanta	4	2	1	0	0	14	11	5	3	2	1	0	0	8	3	4	7	4	2	0	0	22	14	9
Boston	29	11	15	3	0	98	97	25	30	6	20	3	1	80	126	16	59	17	35	6	1	178	223	41
Buffalo	29	21	5	3	0	120	74	45	30	13	10	7	0	112	109	33	59	34	15	10	0	232	183	78
Calgary	81	42	28	10	1	306	265	95	81	29	43	9	0	275	324	67	162	71	71	19	1	581	589	162
Carolina	31	19	7	5	0	121	92	43	29	11	11	7	0	98	112	29	60	30	18	12	0	219	204	72
Chicago	45	22	18	5	0	165	147	49	44	16	21	7	0	152	167	39	89	38	39	12	0	317	314	88
Colorado	46	25	16	4	1	186	137	55	47	19	24	4	0	169	179	42	93	44	40	8	1	355	316	97
Columbus	8	7	1	0	0	31	17	14	8	4	1	3	0	27	20	11	16	11	2	3	0	58	37	25
Dallas	44	21	13	8	2	176	145	52	45	14	23	7	1	126	163	36	89	35	36	15	3	302	308	88
Detroit	44	20	14	10	0	168	155	50	44	16	23	4	0	146	172	37	88	36	37	13	2	314	327	87
Florida	7	4	2	1	0	24	16	9	9	2	5	2	0	24	24	6	16	6	7	3	0	48	40	15
Los Angeles	77	39	23	15	0	347	275	93	77	34	27	15	1	318	298	84	154	73	50	30	1	665	573	177
Minnesota	11	6	1	3	1	24	14	16	10	7	1	1	1	29	22	16	21	13	2	4	2	53	36	32
Montreal	35	18	17	0	0	117	113	36	30	10	16	4	0	95	120	24	65	28	33	4	0	212	218	60
Nashville	12	6	4	0	2	36	34	14	13	6	4	3	0	37	32	15	25	12	8	3	2	73	66	29
New Jersey	31	14	10	6	1	136	114	35	33	16	13	3	1	112	111	36	64	30	23	9	2	248	225	71
NY Islanders	29	16	8	5	0	107	87	37	31	7	15	9	0	110	128	23	60	23	23	14	0	217	215	60
NY Rangers	28	12	13	3	0	101	94	27	30	14	9	6	1	113	112	35	58	26	22	9	1	214	206	62
Ottawa	11	7	2	2	0	39	25	16	10	5	3	2	0	26	19	12	21	12	5	4	0	65	44	28
Philadelphia	28	14	8	6	0	98	83	34	31	9	20	2	0	85	128	20	59	23	28	8	0	183	211	54
Phoenix	72	46	20	6	0	313	234	98	71	37	26	5	3	314	284	82	143	83	46	11	3	627	518	180
Pittsburgh	30	22	7	1	0	148	98	45	30	12	14	3	1	127	117	28	60	34	21	4	1	275	215	73
St. Louis	44	23	17	4	0	161	144	50	44	16	20	7	1	153	157	40	88	39	37	11	1	314	301	90
San Jose	33	19	7	7	0	112	71	45	32	11	14	5	2	100	112	29	65	30	21	12	2	212	183	74
Tampa Bay	10	7	3	0	0	26	21	14	11	6	3	2	0	35	31	14	21	13	6	2	0	61	52	28
Toronto	43	23	13	6	1	178	138	53	37	15	20	2	0	154	154	32	80	38	33	8	1	332	292	85
Vancouver	81	49	22	7	3	356	256	108	82	38	30	12	2	320	295	90	163	87	52	19	5	676	551	198
Washington	29	15	10	4	0	120	91	34	29	9	18	2	0	93	118	20	58	24	28	6	0	213	209	54
Totals	**997**	**547**	**313**	**125**	**12**	**3885**	**3098**	**1231**	**997**	**393**	**450**	**137**	**17**	**3502**	**3693**	**940**	**1994**	**940**	**763**	**262**	**29**	**7387**	**6791**	**2171**

Playoffs

	Series	W	L	GP	W	L	T	GF	GA	Last Mtg.	Rnd.	Result
Boston	2	2	0	9	8	1	0	41	20	1990	F	W 4-1
Calgary	5	4	1	30	19	11	0	132	96	1991	DSF	W 4-3
Chicago	4	3	1	20	12	8	0	102	77	1992	CF	L 0-4
Colorado	2	1	1	12	5	7	0	30	35	1998	CQF	W 4-3
Dallas	8	2	6	42	15	27	0	104	118	2003	CQF	L 2-4
Detroit	2	2	0	10	8	2	0	39	26	1988	CF	W 4-1
Los Angeles	7	5	2	36	24	12	0	154	127	1992	DSF	W 4-2
Montreal	1	1	0	3	3	0	0	15	6	1981	PRE	W 3-0
NY Islanders	3	1	2	15	6	9	0	47	58	1984	F	W 4-1
Philadelphia	3	2	1	15	8	7	0	49	44	1987	F	W 4-3
Vancouver	2	2	0	9	7	2	0	35	20	1992	DF	W 4-2
Winnipeg	6	6	0	26	22	4	0	170	95	1990	DSF	W 4-3
Totals	**45**	**31**	**14**	**227**	**137**	**90**	**0**	**868**	**702**			

Playoff Results 2005-2000

Year	Round	Opponent	Result	GF	GA
2003	CQF	Dallas	L 2-4	11	20
2001	CQF	Dallas	L 2-4	13	16
2000	CQF	Dallas	L 1-4	11	14

Abbreviations: Round: F - Final; **CF** - conference final; **CQF** - conference quarter-final; **DF** - division final; **DSF** - division semi-final; **PRE** - preliminary round.

Calgary totals include Atlanta Flames, 1979-80.
Colorado totals include Quebec, 1979-80 to 1994-95.
New Jersey totals include Colorado Rockies, 1979-80 to 1981-82.

Carolina totals include Hartford, 1979-80 to 1996-97.
Dallas totals include Minnesota North Stars, 1979-80 to 1992-93.
Phoenix totals include Winnipeg, 1979-80 to 1995-96.

Key Off-Season Signings/Acquisitions

2004

Aug. 6 • Re-signed G **Ty Conklin**.
31 • Re-signed D **Alexei Semenov**.
Sept. 10 • Re-signed D **Marc-Andre Bergeron**.
15 • Re-signed D **Jason Smith** and RW **Radek Dvorak**.
15 • Signed RW **Todd Harvey**.

2005

Aug. 2 • Obtained D **Chris Pronger** from St. Louis for Ds **Eric Brewer**, **Doug Lynch** and **Jeff Woywitka**.
3 • Obtained C **Mike Peca** from NY Islanders for C **Mike York** and a conditional draft pick.
5 • Re-signed G **Jussi Markkanen** and D **Igor Ulanov**.
10 • Re-signed Cs **Marty Reasoner** and **Jarret Stoll**.
15 • Re-signed RW **Ales Hemsky**.
16 • Re-signed LW **Raffi Torres**.
19 • Re-signed C **Shawn Horcoff**.
29 • Signed 2005 3rd round pick, 81st overall D **Danny Syvret**.

Entry Draft
Selections 2005-1991

2005
Pick
25	Andrew Cogliano
36	Taylor Chorney
81	Danny Syvret
86	Robby Dee
97	Chris Vande Velde
120	Vyacheslav Trukhno
157	Fredrik Pettersson
220	Matthew Glasser

2004
Pick
14	Devan Dubnyk
25	Rob Schremp
44	Roman Teslyuk
57	Geoff Paukovich
112	Liam Reddox
146	Bryan Young
177	Max Gordichuk
208	Stephane Goulet
242	Tyler Spurgeon
274	Bjorn Bjurling

2003
Pick
22	Marc-Antoine Pouliot
51	Colin McDonald
68	Jean-Francois Jacques
72	Mishail Joukov
94	Zachery Stortini
147	Kalle Olsson
154	David Rohlfs
184	Dragan Umicevic
214	Kyle Brodziak
215	Mathieu Roy
248	Josef Hrabal
278	Troy Bodie

2002
Pick
15	Jesse Niinimaki
31	Jeff Deslauriers
36	Jarret Stoll
44	Matt Greene
79	Brock Radunske
106	Ivan Koltsov
111	Jonas Almtorp
123	invalid pick
148	Glenn Fisher
181	Mikko Luoma
205	J.F. Dufort
211	Patrick Murphy
244	Dwight Helminen
245	Tomas Micka
274	Fredrik Johansson

2001
Pick
13	Ales Hemsky
43	Doug Lynch
52	Ed Caron
84	Kenny Smith
133	Jussi Markkanen
154	Jake Brenk
185	Mikael Svensk
215	Dan Baum
248	Kari Haakana
272	Ales Pisa
278	Shay Stephenson

2000
Pick
17	Alexei Mikhnov
35	Brad Winchester
83	Alexander Liubimov
113	Lou Dickenson
152	Paul Flache
184	Shaun Norrie
211	Joe Cullen
215	Matthew Lombardi
247	Jason Platt
274	Yevgeny Muratov

1999
Pick
13	Jani Rita
36	Alexei Semenov
41	Tony Salmelainen
81	Adam Hauser
91	Mike Comrie
139	Jonathan Fauteux
171	Chris Legg
199	Christian Chartier
256	Tamas Groschl

1998
Pick
13	Michael Henrich
67	Alex Henry
99	Shawn Horcoff
113	Kristian Antila
128	Paul Elliott
144	Oleg Smirnov
159	Trevor Ettinger
186	Mike Morrison
213	Christian Lefebvre
241	Maxim Spiridonov

1997
Pick
14	Michel Riesen
41	Patrick Dovigi
68	Sergei Yerkovich
94	Jonas Elofsson
121	Jason Chimera
141	Peter Sarno
176	Kevin Bolibruck
187	Chad Hinz
205	Chris Kerr
231	Alexander Fomichev

1996
Pick
6	Boyd Devereaux
19	Matthieu Descoteaux
32	Chris Hajt
59	Tom Poti
114	Brian Urick
141	Bryan Randall
168	David Bernier
170	Brandon Lafrance
195	Fernando Pisani
221	John Hultberg

1995
Pick
6	Steve Kelly
31	Georges Laraque
57	Lukas Zib
83	Mike Minard
109	Jan Snopek
161	Martin Cerven
187	Stephen Douglas
213	Jiri Antonin

1994
Pick
4	Jason Bonsignore
6	Ryan Smyth
32	Mike Watt
53	Corey Neilson
60	Brad Symes
79	Adam Copeland
95	Jussi Tarvainen
110	Jon Gaskins
136	Terry Marchant
160	Curtis Sheptak
162	Dmitri Shulga
179	Chris Wickenheiser
185	Rob Guinn
188	Jason Reid
214	Jeremy Jablonski
266	Ladislav Benysek

1993
Pick
7	Jason Arnott
16	Nick Stajduhar
33	David Vyborny
59	Kevin Paden
60	Alexander Kerch
111	Miroslav Satan
163	Alexander Zhurik
189	Martin Bakula
215	Brad Norton
241	Oleg Maltsev
267	Ilja Byakin

1992
Pick
13	Joe Hulbig
37	Martin Reichel
61	Simon Roy
65	Kirk Maltby
96	Ralph Intranuovo
109	Joaquin Gage
157	Steve Gibson
181	Kyuin Shim
190	Colin Schmidt
205	Marko Tuomainen
253	Bryan Rasmussen

1991
Pick
12	Tyler Wright
20	Martin Rucinsky
34	Andrew Verner
56	George Breen
78	Mario Nobili
93	Ryan Haggerty
144	David Oliver
166	Gary Kitching
210	Vegar Barlie
232	Yevgeny Belosheiken
254	Juha Riihijarvi

Rexall Place

Club Directory

Edmonton Oilers
11230 – 110 Street
Edmonton, Alberta T5G 3H7
Phone **780/414-4000**
Press Box 780/409-3780
Ticketing 780/414-4625
Media Lounge 780/409-3778
FAX 780/409-5848
www.edmontonoilers.com
Capacity: 16,389

Owner	Edmonton Investors Group Ltd.
Governor	Cal Nichols
Alternate Governors	Patrick R. LaForge, Kevin Lowe & William Butler
President & Chief Executive Officer	Patrick R. LaForge
Executive Vice-President & General Manager	Kevin Lowe
Vice-President, Hockey Operations	Kevin Prendergast
Assistant General Manager	Scott Howson
Head Coach	Craig MacTavish
Assistant Coaches	Charlie Huddy, Bill Moores, Craig Simpson
Goaltending Coach	Pete Peeters
Video Coach	Brian Ross
Development Coach	Geoff Ward
Dir. of Research, Analysis & Software Dev.	Sean Draper
Scouting Staff	Mike Abbamont, Bob Brown, Bill Dandy, Brad Davis, Lorne Davis, Morey Gare, Kent Hawley, Stu MacGregor, Chris McCarthy, Frank Musil, Kent Nilsson, Dave Semenko, John Stevenson
Executive Assistant to the President	Lisa Stanley
Executive Assistant to the General Manager	Valerie Rendell
Security Advisor	Gary Goulet

Medical and Training Staff
Head Medical Trainer	Ken Lowe
Assistant Medical Trainer	Kim Layton
Head Equipment Manager	Barrie Stafford
Equipment Manager	Lyle Kulchisky
Assistant Equipment Manager	Jeff Lang
Massage Therapist	Stewart Poirier
Team Medical Chief of Staff/Director of Glen Sather Sports Medicine Clinic	Dr. David C. Reid
Team Physicians	Dr. John Clarke, Dr. Dhiron Naidu
Team Dermatologist	Dr. Don Groot
Team Dentists	Dr. Ben Eastwood, Dr. Tony Sneazwell
Fitness Consultants	Dr. Art Quinney, Dr. Gordon Bell
Physical Therapy Consultant	Dr. Dave Magee
Team Optometrist	Dr. Brent Saik
Strength & Conditioning Consultant	Daryl Duke

Communications & Broadcast
Vice President, Communications & Broadcast	Allan Watt
Manager, Communications & Media Relations	J.J. Hebert
Information Coordinator	Steve Knowles
New Media Production Manager	Andreas Schwabe
New Media Production Coordinator	Marc Ciampa
Director of Broadcast	Don Metz
Game Night Director	Glenn Wiun
Game Night Supervisor	Marilyn Riddell

Finance & Administration
V.P. of Finance and Chief Financial Officer	Darryl Boessenkool
Executive Assistant to the CFO & Office Manager	Sherry Smith
Controller	Jason Quilley
Financial Services Coordinator	Corinne McGregor
Payroll Manager	Shawna Quigley
Human Resource Manager	Tandy Kustiak
Accounts Payable Coordinator	Yvonne Weleschuk
Director of Facilities & Events	Craig Tkachuk
IT Manager	Terry Rhoades
Systems Administrator	Rod Pruden

Marketing
Vice Presidnet, Marketing	Stew MacDonald
Director, Marketing	Natalie Minckler
Manager, Corporate Communications	Darren Krill
Manager, E-Marketing & Research	Christine Dmytryshyn
Director, Fan Development & Executive Director, Edmonton Oilers Community Foundation	Gillian Andries
ICE School Coordinator	Sandy VanRiper
Director, Licensing & Special Projects	Nick Wilson
Director, Operations & Events	Craig Tkachuk
Coordinator, Events	Stacey Brockoff
Coordinator, Fan Development	Sandra Psyklywyc
Coordinator, Operations	Chris Delorey
Receptionist	Cheryl Thomas, Sandy Langley

Sales
Vice President, Sales and Sponsorships	Eric Upton

Corporate Sales
Director, Corporate Sales	Brad MacGregor
Corporate Sales Managers	Michael Lake & Daryl Zelinski
Executive Suites Manager	Bob Haromy
Corporate Inventory Specialist	Connie Lloyd
Corporate Sales Coordinators	Bryce Crittenden, Chris Field, Sangelle Rakowski, Angie Zander

Ticket Sales & Service
Director of Ticket Sales and Service	Sean Price
Ticket Sales & Service Department Coordinator	TBA
Sales Account Executives	Melissa Shave, Sheldon Smart, Tyler Waye, Janice Wimberly
Client Service Reps.	Terry Bludd, Tabitha Kobeluck, Blair McGeough, Stephen Slawuta
Inside Sales Representatives	Brad Bistritz, Calvin Brown, Abraham Hajar
Group Sales Specialist	James MacGregro
Ticket Inventory Manager	Jamie Schenknecht
Credit Supervisor	Sangeeta Sundar
Customer Service Representative	Kelly Wylie
Box Office Manager	TBA
Television Outlets	Sportsnet , CBXT TV & TSN
Radio Flagship Station	630 CHED (AM); Rod Phillips (Play-by-play) & Morley Scott (Colour)

Ethan Moreau's career-high 20 goals in 2003-04 were just three back of Ryan Smyth for the Oilers' team lead.

Florida Panthers

2005-06 Schedule

Oct.	Wed.	5	Atlanta
	Fri.	7	Tampa Bay
	Sat.	8	at Tampa Bay
	Mon.	10	at NY Islanders*
	Thu.	13	Boston
	Sat.	15	Buffalo
	Mon.	17	at NY Rangers
	Tue.	18	at New Jersey
	Thu.	20	Washington
	Sat.	22	Ottawa
	Tue.	25	at Pittsburgh
	Thu.	27	at Philadelphia
	Sat.	29	Washington
	Mon.	31	at Toronto
Nov.	Tue.	1	at Montreal
	Thu.	3	at Boston
	Sat.	5	at Carolina
	Wed.	9	NY Rangers
	Fri.	11	Carolina
	Sat.	12	at Philadelphia
	Tue.	15	at Montreal
	Thu.	17	at Ottawa
	Sat.	19	NY Islanders
	Wed.	23	New Jersey
	Fri.	25	Pittsburgh
	Sat.	26	at Atlanta
	Mon.	28	Toronto
Dec.	Sat.	3	Chicago
	Wed.	7	at Dallas
	Thu.	8	at San Jose
	Sat.	10	at Los Angeles*
	Tue.	13	Nashville
	Thu.	15	Detroit
	Sat.	17	at Atlanta
	Sun.	18	at Washington
	Thu.	22	Buffalo
	Fri.	23	at Carolina
	Mon.	26	Philadelphia
	Wed.	28	Boston
	Fri.	30	Montreal
Jan.	Sun.	1	at Buffalo*

	Tue.	3	at New Jersey
	Wed.	4	at NY Islanders
	Sat.	7	at NY Rangers*
	Sun.	8	at Washington*
	Thu.	12	St. Louis
	Sat.	14	Columbus
	Thu.	19	at Phoenix
	Sat.	21	at Anaheim
	Tue.	24	at Tampa Bay
	Wed.	25	Carolina
	Fri.	27	New Jersey
	Mon.	30	Toronto
Feb.	Fri.	3	Atlanta
	Sat.	4	at Atlanta
	Tue.	7	at Washington
	Sat.	11	at Buffalo
	Tue.	28	at Tampa Bay
Mar.	Thu.	2	Montreal
	Fri.	3	at Carolina
	Mon.	6	at Atlanta
	Thu.	9	Ottawa
	Sat.	11	Carolina
	Sun.	12	Carolina*
	Wed.	15	Philadelphia
	Fri.	17	NY Islanders
	Sat.	18	at Washington
	Mon.	20	Tampa Bay
	Wed.	22	Washington
	Fri.	24	NY Rangers
	Mon.	27	at Boston
	Wed.	29	at Pittsburgh
	Fri.	31	at Carolina
Apr.	Sat.	1	Tampa Bay
	Mon.	3	at Tampa Bay
	Wed.	5	Atlanta
	Fri.	7	Pittsburgh
	Sun.	9	Tampa Bay*
	Tue.	11	at Toronto
	Thu.	13	at Ottawa
	Sat.	15	Washington
	Tue.	18	Atlanta

*Denotes afternoon game.

Franchise date: June 14, 1993

EASTERN CONFERENCE

13th NHL Season

SOUTHEAST DIVISION

Year-by-Year Record

Season	GP	Home W	L	T	OL	Road W	L	T	OL	Overall W	L	T	OL	GF	GA	Pts.	Finished	Playoff Result
2004-05	....	....				....				....				....	....	....		
2003-04	82	16	15	7	3	12	20	8	1	28	35	15	4	188	221	75	4th, Southeast Div.	Out of Playoffs
2002-03	82	8	21	7	5	16	15	6	4	24	36	13	9	176	237	70	4th, Southeast Div.	Out of Playoffs
2001-02	82	11	23	3	4	11	21	7	2	22	44	10	6	180	250	60	4th, Southeast Div.	Out of Playoffs
2000-01	82	12	18	7	4	10	20	6	5	22	38	13	9	200	246	66	3rd, Southeast Div.	Out of Playoffs
1999-2000	82	26	9	4	2	17	18	2	4	43	27	6	6	244	209	98	2nd, Southeast Div.	Lost Conf. Quarter-Final
1998-99	82	17	17	7	....	13	17	11	....	30	34	18	....	210	228	78	2nd, Southeast Div.	Out of Playoffs
1997-98	82	11	24	6	....	13	19	9	....	24	43	15	....	203	256	63	6th, Atlantic Div.	Out of Playoffs
1996-97	82	21	12	8	....	14	16	11	....	35	28	19	....	221	201	89	3rd, Atlantic Div.	Lost Conf. Quarter-Final
1995-96	82	25	12	4	....	16	19	6	....	41	31	10	....	254	234	92	3rd, Atlantic Div.	Lost Final
1994-95	48	9	12	3	....	11	10	3	....	20	22	6	....	115	127	46	5th, Atlantic Div.	Out of Playoffs
1993-94	84	15	18	9	....	18	16	8	....	33	34	17	....	233	233	83	5th, Atlantic Div.	Out of Playoffs

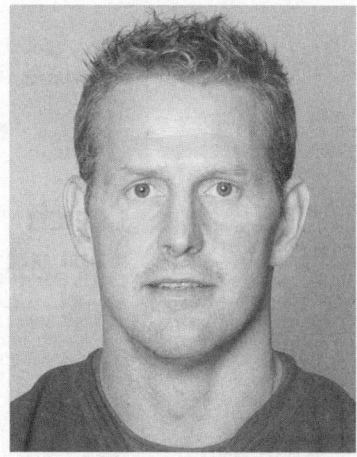

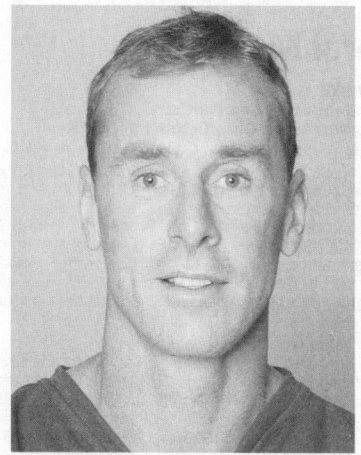

The Panthers acquired 50 seasons and 3,258 games worth of experience over just two days when they signed Gary Roberts (top left), Joe Nieuwendyk (top right) and Martin Gelinas (left) in the summer of 2005.

2005-06 Player Personnel

FORWARDS	HT	WT	S	Place of Birth	Date	2004-05 Club
CAMPBELL, Gregory	6-0	191	L	London, Ont.	12/17/83	San Antonio
GELINAS, Martin	5-11	195	L	Shawinigan, Que.	6/5/70	Morges-Lugano
GRATTON, Chris	6-4	220	L	Brantford, Ont.	7/5/75	
HAGMAN, Niklas	6-0	200	L	Espoo, Finland	12/5/79	Davos
HORTON, Nathan	6-2	201	R	Welland, Ont.	5/29/85	San Antonio
HUSELIUS, Kristian	6-1	190	L	Osterhaninge, Sweden	11/10/78	Rapperswil-Linkoping
JOKINEN, Olli	6-3	205	L	Kuopio, Finland	12/5/78	Kloten-Sodertalje-HIFK
KOLNIK, Juraj	5-10	190	R	Nitra, Czech.	11/13/80	San Antonio
NIEUWENDYK, Joe	6-2	205	L	Oshawa, Ont.	9/10/66	
OLESZ, Rostislav	6-1	207	L	Bilovec, Czech.	10/10/85	Sparta
PAYER, Serge	6-0	192	L	Rockland, Ont.	5/7/79	San Antonio
ROBERTS, Gary	6-2	215	L	North York, Ont.	5/23/66	
STUMPEL, Jozef	6-3	225	R	Nitra, Czech.	7/20/72	Slavia
WEISS, Stephen	5-11	185	L	Toronto, Ont.	4/3/83	San Antonio-Chicago (AHL)
DEFENSEMEN						
BOUWMEESTER, Jay	6-4	210	L	Edmonton, Alta.	9/27/83	San Antonio-Chicago (AHL)
CAIRNS, Eric	6-6	230	L	Oakville, Ont.	6/27/74	London
FOCHT, Dan	6-6	234	L	Regina, Sask.	12/31/77	Hamilton
HILL, Sean	6-0	205	R	Duluth, MN	2/14/70	
KARPOVTSEV, Alexander	6-3	221	R	Moscow, USSR	4/7/70	Novosibirsk-Yaroslavl
KWIATKOWSKI, Joel	6-2	210	L	Kindersley, Sask.	3/22/77	San Antonio-St. John's
MEZEI, Branislav	6-5	236	L	Nitra, Czech.	10/8/80	Trinec-Trencin
VAN RYN, Mike	6-1	202	R	London, Ont.	5/14/79	
GOALTENDERS	**HT**	**WT**	**C**	**Place of Birth**	**Date**	**2004-05 Club**
LUONGO, Roberto	6-3	205	L	Montreal, Que.	4/4/79	
McLENNAN, Jamie	6-0	190	L	Edmonton, Alta.	6/30/71	Guildford
PELLETIER, Jean-Marc	6-3	209	L	Atlanta, GA	3/4/78	Utah-Springfield

General Manager

KEENAN, MIKE
General Manager, Florida Panthers.
Born in Bowmanville, Ont., October 21, 1949.

Mike Keenan became the sixth general manager of the Florida Panthers on May 26, 2004. Previously, he served as interim general manager with Vancouver (1997-98) and as general manager in St. Louis (1994 to 1996) and Chicago (1988 to 1992). During his tenure with these clubs, he traded for players such as Wayne Gretzky (St. Louis), Craig Conroy (St. Louis), Chris Pronger (St. Louis), Todd Bertuzzi (Vancouver), Chris Chelios (Chicago), Michel Goulet (Chicago) and Brent Sutter (Chicago). Serving as both coach and g.m. in Chicago, Keenan posted a mark of 153-126-41 and led the Blackhawks to the Stanley Cup Finals in 1992. His Chicago teams made the playoffs all four years, finishing 33-27 (.550) in the postseason and winning seven of 11 playoff series.

A coaching veteran of 18 seasons, Keenan has spent time behind the bench for seven different NHL clubs including Florida, Boston, Vancouver, St. Louis , NY Rangers, Chicago and Philadelphia. His resume includes three Presidents' Trophies (1985, 1991 and 1994), six division titles (1985, 1986, 1987, 1990, 1991 and 1994), three 50+ win seasons (1984-85, 1985-86 and 1993-94), and five 100+ point seasons (1984-85, 1985-86, 1986-87, 1990-91 and 1993-94). Keenan ranks fifth on the all-time coaching list in both games coached (1,222) and victories (584). Most significantly, he led the Rangers to the 1994 Stanley Cup championship. The Rangers went 52-24-8 under Keenan, going from a non-playoff team to the Presidents' Trophy winner and Stanley Cup champion in a single year. Additionally, Keenan was the general manager/head coach of the championship Team Canada squads that participated in the Canada Cup in 1991 and 1987.

Keenan and Jacques Martin last worked together in Chicago (1988 to 1990), when Keenan served as the team's head coach/general manager and Martin was an assistant coach. Prior to that, the pair worked together when they led the Peterborough Petes to the Memorial Cup Finals in 1980. The duo also played hockey together at St. Lawrence University.

NHL Coaching Record

		Regular Season				Playoffs		
Season	Team	Games	W	L	T	Games	W	L
1984-85	Philadelphia	80	53	20	7	19	12	7
1985-86	Philadelphia	80	53	23	4	5	2	3
1986-87	Philadelphia	80	46	26	8	26	15	11
1987-88	Philadelphia	80	38	33	9	7	3	4
1988-89	Chicago	80	27	41	12	16	9	7
1989-90	Chicago	80	41	33	6	20	10	10
1990-91	Chicago	80	49	23	8	6	2	4
1991-92	Chicago	80	36	29	15	18	12	6
1993-94	NY Rangers	84	52	24	8	23	16	7*
1994-95	St. Louis	48	28	15	5	7	3	4
1995-96	St. Louis	82	32	34	16	13	7	6
1996-97	St. Louis	33	15	17	1	....	....	....
1997-98	Vancouver	63	21	30	12	....	....	....
1998-99	Vancouver	45	15	24	6	....	....	....
2000-01	Boston	74	33	34	7	....	....	....
2001-02	Florida	56	16	32	8	....	....	....
2002-03	Florida	82	24	45	13	....	....	....
2003-04	Florida	15	5	8	2	....	....	....
	NHL Totals	**1222**	**584**	**491**	**147**	**160**	**91**	**69**

* Stanley Cup win.

In the System and Recently Drafted

FORWARDS	HT	WT	S	Place of Birth	Date	2004-05 Club
BEARSON, Zach	6-1	180	R	Houston, TX	6/13/87	Waterloo
BERGLUND, Christian	5-11	190	L	Orebro, Sweden	3/12/80	Farjestad
BOOTH, David	6-0	212	L	Detroit, MI	11/24/84	Michigan State
COLLINS, Dan	6-1	185	R	Syracuse, NY	2/26/87	Plymouth
GLASS, Tanner	6-0	196	L	Regina, Sask.	11/29/83	Dartmouth
GLOBKE, Rob	6-2	200	R	Farmington, MI	10/24/82	San Antonio-Texas
KOIVISTO, Toni	6-0	180	L	Ylitornio, Finland	11/5/82	Lukko
KREPS, Kamil	6-1	190	R	Litomerice, Czech.	11/18/84	San Antonio-Texas
LEGAULT, Olivier	6-5	238	L	Chibougamau, Que.	10/2/86	Lewiston
McARDLE, Kenndal	5-11	190	L	Toronto, Ont.	1/4/87	Moose Jaw
MEYER, Stefan	6-1	194	L	Medicine Hat, Alta.	7/20/85	Medicine Hat
NEDOROST, Vaclav	6-1	190	L	Budejovice, Czech.	3/16/82	Liberec
SHVIDKI, Denis	6-0	195	L	Kharkov, USSR	11/21/80	
SPRUKTS, Janis	6-3	224	L	Riga, Latvia	1/31/82	Riga 2000
STASYUK, Denis	6-1	165	L	Novokuznetsk, USSR	9/2/85	Khabarovsk
STEWART, Anthony	6-1	225	R	LaSalle, Que.	1/5/85	Kingston-San Antonio
TATICEK, Petr	6-3	195	L	Rakovnik, Czech.	9/22/83	San Antonio-Laredo
TRAVIS, Dan	6-3	220	R	Concord, NH	11/26/83	New Hampshire
WICHSER, Adrian	6-0	180	L	Winterthur, Switz.	3/18/80	Lugano
YACHMENEV, Denis	6-1	185	L	Chelyabinsk, USSR	6/4/84	Khabarovsk
DEFENSEMEN						
BAGNALL, Drew	6-3	205	L	Oakbank, Man.	10/26/83	St. Lawrence
BEAVERSON, Luke	6-3	208	L	St. Paul, MN	12/11/84	Alaska-Anchorage
BLANAR, Jan	6-3	185	L	Trencin, Czech.	6/6/83	Hermes
DERLYUK, Roman	6-3	198	L	Leningrad, USSR	10/27/86	Spartak St. Petersburg
DILLON, Spencer	6-4	190	R	Santa Cruz, CA	1/7/85	Green Bay
DUFFY, Matt	6-2	180	R	Portland, ME	3/21/86	N.H. Jr. Monarchs
HAFNER, Peter	6-5	195	R	Summit, NJ	7/26/83	Harvard
JAAKOLA, Topi	6-1	185	L	Oulu, Finland	11/15/83	Karpat
KRAJICEK, Lukas	6-2	185	L	Prostejov, Czech.	3/11/83	San Antonio
LOJEK, Martin	6-5	220	R	Brno, Czech.	8/19/85	Brampton
McNEILL, Grant	6-2	210	L	Vermillion, Alta.	6/8/83	San Antonio-Texas
NASBY, Bret	6-3	188	R	Grimsby, Ont.	3/22/86	Oshawa
NOVAK, Filip	6-1	185	L	Ceske Budejovice, Czech.	5/7/82	San Antonio
PEMBERTON, James	6-4	215	R	Providence, RI	10/2/83	Providence College
SCHAFER, Evan	6-2	221	R	Mankota, Sask.	10/9/85	Prince Albert
SWANSON, Jeremy	6-0	199	L	Nipigon, Ont.	6/21/84	San Antonio-Texas
TOLKUNOV, Dmitri	6-2	200	R	Kiev, USSR	5/5/79	Novosibirsk- Amur Khabarovsk
TUMA, Martin	6-4	209	L	Most, Czech.	9/14/85	SS Marie-San Antonio
UCHEVATOV, Victor	6-4	225	L	Angarsk, USSR	2/10/83	San Antonio
GOALTENDERS	**HT**	**WT**	**C**	**Place of Birth**	**Date**	**2004-05 Club**
FOSTER, Brian	6-1	155	L	Pembroke, NH	2/4/87	N.H. Jr. Monarchs
PLANTE, Tyler	6-2	191	L	Milwaukee, WI	4/16/87	Brandon
SHANTZ, David	6-1	202	L	Burlington, Ont.	5/5/86	Mississauga
VUORIO, Mikael	6-0	165	L	Laitila, Finland	4/1/84	Lukko

Coach

MARTIN, JACQUES
Coach, Florida Panthers. Born in St. Pascal, Ont., October 1, 1952.

Jacques Martin was hired as coach of the Florida Panthers on May 26, 2004, joining the team after eight-and-a-half seasons with the Ottawa Senators. For his career with the Senators, he posted a 341-255-96 regular-season record and stands as the franchise's all-time leader in games coached (692), regular-season wins (341), playoff wins (31) and playoff games coached (69). He is the ninth coach in Panthers history.

Under Martin's guidance, the Senators earned their first Presidents' Trophy and Eastern Conference title, posting a 52-21-8-1 mark in 2002-03. Martin has been nominated for the Jack Adams Award as coach of the year four times. He won the award in 1998-99 and was nominated in 1996-97, 2000-01 and 2002-03. Martin was named as an associate coach for Team Canada's men's hockey team that won gold at the 2002 Olympic Winter Games in Salt Lake City and served in the same capacity with Team Canada at the World Cup of Hockey in 2004.

Martin joined Ottawa after spending the first half of the 1995-96 season with the Stanley Cup champion Colorado Avalanche, where he served as an assistant coach. Martin entered the NHL as head coach of the St. Louis Blues in 1986-87 and 1987-88, leading the Blues to the Norris Division championship in his rookie season. He joined the Blues after guiding the Ontario Hockey League's Guelph Platers to the 1986 Memorial Cup championship and winning OHL coach of the year honors for his efforts.

Coaching Record

		Regular Season				Playoffs		
Season	Team	Games	W	L	T	Games	W	L
1983-84	Peterborough (OHL)	70	43	23	4	....	....	....
1984-85	Peterborough (OHL)	66	42	20	4	....	....	....
1985-86	Guelph (OHL)	66	41	23	2	....	....	....
1986-87	**St. Louis (NHL)**	**80**	**32**	**33**	**15**	**6**	**2**	**4**
1987-88	**St. Louis (NHL)**	**80**	**34**	**38**	**8**	**10**	**5**	**5**
1993-94	Cornwall (AHL)	80	33	36	11	13	8	5
1995-96	**Ottawa (NHL)**	**38**	**10**	**24**	**4**	....	....	....
1996-97	**Ottawa (NHL)**	**82**	**31**	**36**	**15**	**7**	**3**	**4**
1997-98	**Ottawa (NHL)**	**82**	**34**	**33**	**15**	**11**	**5**	**6**
1998-99	**Ottawa (NHL)**	**82**	**44**	**23**	**15**	**4**	**0**	**4**
1999-2000	**Ottawa (NHL)**	**82**	**41**	**30**	**11**	**6**	**2**	**4**
2000-01	**Ottawa (NHL)**	**82**	**48**	**25**	**9**	**4**	**0**	**4**
2001-02	**Ottawa (NHL)**	**80**	**38**	**33**	**9**	**12**	**7**	**5**
2002-03	**Ottawa (NHL)**	**82**	**52**	**22**	**8**	**18**	**11**	**7**
2003-04	**Ottawa (NHL)**	**82**	**43**	**29**	**10**	**7**	**3**	**4**
2004-05	**Florida (NHL)**			Season Cancelled				
	NHL Totals	**852**	**407**	**326**	**119**	**85**	**38**	**47**

Martin stepped aside (with NHL permission) during the final two games of the 2001-02 season in order to allow assistant coach Roger Neilson to reach the 1,000-game plateau, April 11 and 13, 2002.

Club Records

Team

(Figures in brackets for season records are games played; records for fewest points, wins, ties, losses, goals, goals against are for 70 or more games)

Most Points	98	1999-2000 (82)
Most Wins	43	1999-2000 (82)
Most Ties	19	1996-97 (82)
Most Losses	44	2001-02 (82)
Most Goals	254	1995-96 (82)
Most Goals Against	256	1997-98 (82)
Fewest Points	60	2001-02 (82)
Fewest Wins	22	2000-01 (82), 2001-02 (82)
Fewest Ties	6	1999-2000 (82)
Fewest Losses	27	1999-2000 (82)
Fewest Goals	176	2002-03 (82)
Fewest Goals Against	201	1996-97 (82)

Longest Winning Streak
Overall	7	Nov. 2-14/95
Home	5	Nov. 5-14/95
Away	4	Four times

Longest Undefeated Streak
Overall	12	Oct. 5-30/96 (8 wins, 4 ties)
Home	8	Nov. 5-26/95 (7 wins, 1 tie)
Away	7	Twice

Longest Losing Streak
Overall	13	Feb. 7-Mar. 23/98
Home	6	Feb. 25-Mar. 23/98
Away	9	Feb. 9-Mar. 25/02

Longest Winless Streak
Overall	15	Feb. 1-Mar. 23/98 (14 losses, 1 tie)
Home	13	Feb. 5-Mar. 24/03 (11 losses, 2 ties)
Away	16	Jan. 2-Mar. 21/98 (12 losses, 4 ties)

Most Shutouts, Season	7	2002-03 (82)
Most PIM, Season	1,994	2001-02 (82)
Most Goals, Game	10	Nov. 26/97 (Bos. 5 at Fla. 10)

Individual

Most Seasons	9	Paul Laus
Most Games	573	Robert Svehla
Most Goals, Career	157	Scott Mellanby
Most Assists, Career	229	Robert Svehla
Most Points, Career	354	Scott Mellanby (157G, 197A)
Most PIM, Career	1,702	Paul Laus
Most Shutouts, Career	22	Roberto Luongo

Longest Consecutive
Games Streak	300	Robert Svehla (Dec. 23/98-Apr. 14/02)
Most Goals, Season	59	Pavel Bure (2000-01)
Most Assists, Season	53	Viktor Kozlov (1999-2000)
Most Points, Season	94	Pavel Bure (1999-2000; 58G, 36A)
Most PIM, Season	354	Peter Worrell (2001-02)

Most Points, Defenseman, Season	57	Robert Svehla (1995-96; 8G, 49A)
Most Points, Center, Season	70	Viktor Kozlov (1999-2000; 17G, 53A)
Most Points, Right Wing, Season	94	Pavel Bure (1999-2000; 58G, 36A)
Most Points, Left Wing, Season	71	Ray Whitney (1999-2000; 29G, 42A)
Most Points, Rookie, Season	50	Jesse Belanger (1993-94; 17G, 33A)
Most Shutouts, Season	7	Roberto Luongo (2003-04)
Most Goals, Game	4	Mark Parrish (Oct. 30/98); Pavel Bure (Jan. 1/00, Feb. 10/01)
Most Assists, Game	4	Scott Mellanby (Nov. 26/97); Ray Whitney (Oct. 30/00)
Most Points, Game	5	Pavel Bure (Feb. 10/01; 4G, 1A)

Coaching History

Roger Neilson, 1993-94, 1994-95; Doug MacLean, 1995-96, 1996-97; Doug MacLean and Bryan Murray, 1997-98; Terry Murray, 1998-99, 1999-2000; Terry Murray and Duane Sutter, 2000-01; Duane Sutter and Mike Keenan, 2001-02; Mike Keenan, 2002-03; Mike Keenan, Rick Dudley and John Torchetti, 2003-04; Jacques Martin, 2004-05 to date.

Captains' History

Brian Skrudland, 1993-94 to 1996-97; Scott Mellanby, 1997-98 to 2000-01; Pavel Bure, 2001-02; no captain, 2002-03; Olli Jokinen, 2003-04.

General Managers' History

Bob Clarke, 1993-94; Bryan Murray, 1994-95 to 1999-2000; Bryan Murray and Bill Torrey, 2000-01; Bill Torrey and Chuck Fletcher, 2001-02; Rick Dudley, 2002-03, 2003-04; Mike Keenan, 2004-05 to date.

All-time Record vs. Other Clubs

Regular Season

	At Home								On Road								Total							
	GP	W	L	T	OL	GF	GA	PTS	GP	W	L	T	OL	GF	GA	PTS	GP	W	L	T	OL	GF	GA	PTS
Anaheim	8	4	2	2	0	23	17	10	9	5	2	1	1	30	27	12	17	9	4	3	1	53	44	22
Atlanta	13	4	7	1	1	31	44	10	13	4	3	4	2	40	40	14	26	8	10	5	3	71	84	24
Boston	21	9	9	2	1	57	58	21	22	10	8	4	0	57	56	24	43	19	17	6	1	114	114	45
Buffalo	21	10	10	1	0	59	63	21	23	5	14	3	1	37	64	14	44	15	24	4	1	96	127	35
Calgary	9	3	3	2	1	21	22	9	8	3	4	1	0	20	21	7	17	6	7	3	1	41	43	16
Carolina	26	11	5	8	2	74	55	32	25	9	12	3	1	63	73	22	51	20	17	11	3	137	128	54
Chicago	8	2	5	1	0	18	30	5	10	3	5	2	0	30	34	8	18	5	10	3	0	48	64	13
Colorado	11	1	10	0	0	30	48	2	11	4	4	3	0	27	30	11	22	5	14	3	0	57	78	13
Columbus	3	2	0	0	1	9	7	5	2	1	1	0	0	4	4	2	5	3	1	0	1	13	11	7
Dallas	10	4	5	1	0	22	28	9	8	3	3	2	0	22	25	8	18	7	8	3	0	44	53	17
Detroit	9	1	4	2	2	17	27	6	8	1	4	3	0	21	30	5	17	2	8	5	2	38	57	11
Edmonton	9	5	2	2	0	24	24	12	7	2	4	1	0	16	24	5	16	7	6	3	0	40	48	17
Los Angeles	8	4	1	3	0	23	14	11	9	4	5	0	0	29	27	8	17	8	6	3	0	52	41	19
Minnesota	3	1	2	0	0	6	8	2	3	0	2	1	0	1	10	1	6	1	4	1	0	7	18	3
Montreal	22	11	8	3	0	68	61	25	21	10	7	3	1	49	54	24	43	21	15	6	1	117	115	49
Nashville	4	2	0	1	1	11	8	6	5	2	1	2	0	10	8	6	9	4	1	3	1	21	16	12
New Jersey	25	7	13	4	1	53	66	19	24	7	12	3	2	49	72	19	49	14	25	7	3	102	138	38
NY Islanders	25	11	8	6	0	76	74	28	25	11	11	2	1	65	64	25	50	22	19	8	1	141	138	53
NY Rangers	25	10	12	2	1	64	69	23	24	8	12	4	0	59	74	20	49	18	24	6	1	123	143	43
Ottawa	22	9	11	1	1	64	67	20	22	10	8	2	2	60	61	24	44	19	19	3	3	124	128	44
Philadelphia	24	5	17	1	1	57	88	12	25	9	10	6	0	60	65	24	49	14	27	7	1	117	153	36
Phoenix	8	3	5	0	0	23	21	6	10	4	2	3	1	31	25	12	18	7	7	3	1	54	46	18
Pittsburgh	22	13	8	1	0	64	50	27	23	8	10	3	2	68	72	21	45	21	18	4	2	132	122	48
St. Louis	9	2	4	2	1	17	20	7	9	1	7	1	0	12	25	3	18	3	11	3	1	29	45	10
San Jose	9	2	2	5	0	25	27	9	9	2	5	2	0	17	26	6	18	4	7	7	0	42	53	15
Tampa Bay	28	16	6	4	2	81	62	38	28	12	10	6	0	77	60	30	56	28	16	10	2	158	122	68
Toronto	17	5	7	5	0	48	51	15	15	4	9	2	0	34	53	10	32	9	16	7	0	82	104	25
Vancouver	8	3	3	1	1	21	27	8	9	1	3	5	0	19	25	7	17	4	6	6	1	40	52	15
Washington	28	11	12	4	1	70	71	27	28	8	13	5	1	61	86	23	56	19	25	9	3	131	157	50
Totals	**435**	**171**	**181**	**65**	**18**	**1156**	**1207**	**425**	**435**	**151**	**191**	**77**	**16**	**1068**	**1235**	**395**	**870**	**322**	**372**	**142**	**34**	**2224**	**2442**	**820**

Playoffs

	Series	W	L	GP	W	L	T	GF	GA	Last Mtg.	Rnd.	Result
Boston	1	1	0	5	4	1	0	22	16	1996	CQF	W 4-1
Colorado	1	0	1	4	0	4	0	4	15	1996	F	L 0-4
New Jersey	1	0	1	4	0	4	0	6	12	2000	CQF	L 0-4
NY Rangers	1	0	1	5	1	4	0	10	13	1997	CQF	L 1-4
Philadelphia	1	1	0	6	4	2	0	15	11	1996	CSF	W 4-2
Pittsburgh	1	1	0	7	4	3	0	20	15	1996	CF	W 4-3
Totals	**6**	**3**	**3**	**31**	**13**	**18**	**0**	**77**	**82**			

Playoff Results 2005-2000

Year	Round	Opponent	Result	GF	GA
2000	CQF	New Jersey	L 0-4	6	12

Abbreviations: Round: F - Final;
CF - conference final; **CSF** - conference semi-final;
CQF - conference quarter-final.

Colorado totals include Quebec, 1993-94 to 1994-95.
Phoenix totals include Winnipeg, 1993-94 to 1995-96.

Carolina totals include Hartford, 1993-94 to 1996-97.

Entry Draft
Selections 2005-1993

2005
Pick
20	Kenndal McArdle
32	Tyler Plante
90	Dan Collins
93	Olivier Legault
104	Matt Duffy
161	Brian Foster
164	Roman Derlyuk
224	Zach Bearson

2004
Pick
7	Rostislav Olesz
37	David Shantz
53	David Booth
105	Evan Schafer
152	Bret Nasby
267	Spencer Dillon
283	Luke Beaverson

2003
Pick
3	Nathan Horton
25	Anthony Stewart
38	Kamil Kreps
55	Stefan Meyer
105	Martin Lojek
124	James Pemberton
141	Dan Travis
162	Martin Tuma
171	Denis Stasyuk
223	Dany Roussin
234	Petr Kadlec
264	John Hecimovic
265	Tanner Glass

2002
Pick
3	Jay Bouwmeester
9	Petr Taticek
40	Rob Globke
67	Gregory Campbell
134	Topi Jaakola
158	Vince Bellissimo
169	Jeremy Swanson
196	Mikael Vuorio
200	Denis Yachmenev
232	Peter Hafner

2001
Pick
4	Stephen Weiss
24	Lukas Krajicek
34	Greg Watson
64	Tomas Malec
68	Grant McNeill
117	Mike Woodford
136	Billy Thompson
169	Dustin Johner
200	Toni Koivisto
231	Kyle Bruce
263	Jan Blanar
267	Ivan Majesky

2000
Pick
58	Vladimir Sapozhnikov
77	Robert Fried
82	Sean O'Connor
115	Chris Eade
120	Davis Parley
190	Josh Olson
234	Janis Sprukts
253	Mathew Sommerfeld

1999
Pick
12	Denis Shvidki
40	Alex Auld
70	Niklas Hagman
80	Jean-Francois Laniel
103	Morgan McCormick
109	Rod Sarich
169	Brad Woods
198	Travis Eagles
227	Jonathon Charron

1998
Pick
30	Kyle Rossiter
61	Joe DiPenta
63	Lance Ward
89	Ryan Jardine
117	Jaroslav Spacek
148	Chris Ovington
176	B.J. Ketcheson
203	Ian Jacobs
231	Adrian Wichser

1997
Pick
20	Mike Brown
47	Kristian Huselius
56	Vratislav Cech
74	Nick Smith
95	Ivan Novoseltsev
127	Pat Parthenais
155	Keith Delaney
183	Tyler Palmer
211	Doug Schueller
237	Benoit Cote

1996
Pick
20	Marcus Nilson
60	Chris Allen
65	Oleg Kvasha
82	Joey Tetarenko
129	Andrew Long
156	Gaetan Poirier
183	Alexandre Couture
209	Denis Khloptonov
235	Russell Smith

1995
Pick
10	Radek Dvorak
36	Aaron MacDonald
62	Mike O'Grady
80	Dave Duerden
88	Daniel Tjarnqvist
114	Francois Cloutier
166	Peter Worrell
192	Filip Kuba
218	David Lemanowicz

1994
Pick
1	Ed Jovanovski
27	Rhett Warrener
31	Jason Podollan
36	Ryan Johnson
84	David Nemirovsky
105	Dave Geris
157	Matt O'Dette
183	Jason Boudrias
235	Tero Lehtera
261	Per Gustafsson

1993
Pick
5	Rob Niedermayer
41	Kevin Weekes
57	Chris Armstrong
67	Mikael Tjallden
78	Steve Washburn
83	Bill McCauley
109	Todd MacDonald
135	Alain Nasreddine
161	Trevor Doyle
187	Briane Thompson
213	Chad Cabana
239	John Demarco
265	Eric Montreuil

After scoring just 35 goals over his first five NHL seasons, Olli Jokinen scored 36 for Florida in 2002-03, and followed up with 26 in 2003-04.

Club Directory

BankAtlantic Center

Florida Panthers
BankAtlantic Center
One Panther Parkway
Sunrise, FL 33323
Phone **954/835-7000**
FAX 954/835-7700
www.floridapanthers.com
Capacity: 19,250

Executive
General Partner and Chairman of the Board/ Chief Executive Officer/Governor	Alan Cohen
Partner/Pres., Panthers Hockey LLLP & Alt. Gov.	Jordan Zimmerman
Partners	Steve Cohen, David Epstein, Dr. Elliott Hahn, H. Wayne Huizenga, Bernie Kosar, Richard Lehman M.D., Al Maroone, Michael Maroone, Cliff Viner
Alternate Governor	William A. Torrey
Chief Operating Officer	Michael R. Yormark
Sr. VP, Business Relations/Strategic Partnerships	Pedro Goncalves
Sr. VP, Corp Partnerships/Building Operations	Chris Hibbs
Sr. VP, Sales & Marketing	Chad Johnson
G.M., Office Depot Center/V.P., Operations	Brett Stefansson
Executive Assistant	Korrynn Lancaster
Executive Assistant	Cathy Stevenson

Hockey Operations
General Manager	Mike Keenan
Head Coach	Jacques Martin
Assistant Coach	Guy Charron
Goaltending Coach/Pro Scout	Phil Myre
Director, Hockey Operations	Jack Birch
Director, Scouting	Scott Luce
Director, Player Development	Duane Sutter
Director, Hockey Administration	Matt Loughran
Head Equipment Manager	Robert McLean
Strength & Conditioning Coach	Andrew O'Brien
Head Amateur Scout	Darwin Bennett
Pro Scout	Tom Watt
Amateur Scouts	Erin Ginnell, Ron Harris
Part-time Scouts	Dale Degray, Vadim Podrezov, Luke Williams
European Scouts	Niklas Blomgren, Jari Kekalainen
Head Medical Trainer	Jim Pizzutelli
Assistant Equipment Manager	Chris Moody
Video Coach	Pierre Groulx
Coordinator, Team Services	Austin Guhl
Medical Director/Orthopedic Surgeon	Al DeSimone M.D.
Internist	Howard Bush M.D.
Team Dentist	Martin Robins D.D.S.
Orthodontist	George Nicolas, D.M.D.

Communications
VP, Communications	Randy Sieminski
Manager, Communications	Justin Copertino
Manager, Internet Marketing	Lauren Preziosi
Coordinator, Communications	Terri Crolic, Matthew Sacco
Coordinator, Publications & Photography	Tenille Lively

Community Development, Youth Hockey & Broadcasting
VP, Community Development, Youth Hockey & Broadcasting	Randy Moller
Director, Game Presentation and Events	Greg Hanover
Director Community Development/Foundation	Jean Marshall
Coordinator, Community Development	Dave Arias
Coordinator, Special Events & Mascot	Phil Crowhurst
Assistant, Broadcasting & Community Development	Bryan Girsch

Corporate Partnerships
Senior Director, Sponsorship Sales	Jarrett Nasca
Senior Director, Marketing Partnerships	Brette Sadler
Director, New Business Development	Bob Ohrablo
Manager, Corporate Marketing	Susan Ferro
Manager, Marketing Partnerships	Heather Wight
Manager, Marketing Solutions	David Helfman, Chandler Pettit
Manager, New Business Development	Matthew Rickoff
Coordinator, Marketing Partnerships	Micah Goins, Katie Stump

Sales, Service & Marketing
VP, Ticket Sales	RJ Martino
Manager, Marketing	Nadia Abich
Director, Client & Premium Services	Carrie Rubin
Director, Ticket Operations	Sammy Wallace
Manager, Ticket Operations	Orvandis Almonte, Megan Hanney
Coordinator, Box Office	Marcos Jimenez
Manager, Group Sales	Alissa Bavli
Manager, Special Events	Sara Berkowitz
Manager, Inside Sales	Ryan Bringger
Manager, Premium Seating Sales	Ryan McCoy, Jason McDonough
Manager, Sales	Mike Ragan

Finance and Business Support
VP, Finance/CFO	Evelyn Lopez
VP, Human Resources/Payroll	Carol Duncanson
VP, Information Technology	Kelly Moyer
Controller/Senior Director, Accounting	Phillip Reitz
Director, Purchasing	Laura Barrera
Director, Finance	Michael Fallon
Manager, Accounting	Fayon Bryce
Manager, Information Technology	Cindy Moss
Manager, Human Resources	Cheryl Udrich
Coordinator, Human Resources/Payroll	Judith Perez
Coordinator, Workers Comp. and Immigration	Mary Lou Veroline

General Information
Television	Fox Sports Net
Television Announcers	Dave Strader, Denis Potvin, Craig Minervini
Radio Flagship	WQAM (560 AM)
Radio Announcers	Steve Goldstein, Randy Moller
Practice Facility	Incredible ICE

Los Angeles Kings

2005-06 Schedule

Oct.	Wed.	5	at Dallas
	Thu.	6	Phoenix
	Sun.	9	Minnesota*
	Tue.	11	Edmonton
	Thu.	13	Detroit
	Sun.	16	Columbus*
	Wed.	19	at Colorado
	Thu.	20	at Dallas
	Sun.	23	Calgary
	Tue.	25	Anaheim
	Fri.	28	San Jose
	Sat.	29	St. Louis
Nov.	Wed.	2	at Dallas
	Thu.	3	at Phoenix
	Sat.	5	Nashville*
	Wed.	9	at Detroit
	Fri.	11	at Chicago
	Sun.	13	at Columbus*
	Tue.	15	at Nashville
	Thu.	17	Vancouver
	Sat.	19	Colorado
	Tue.	22	at St. Louis
	Thu.	24	at Nashville
	Sat.	26	Chicago
	Mon.	28	Detroit
	Wed.	30	at Chicago
Dec.	Fri.	2	at Ottawa
	Sat.	3	at Montreal
	Tue.	6	at Toronto
	Thu.	8	Carolina
	Sat.	10	Florida*
	Wed.	14	Washington
	Fri.	16	at Anaheim
	Sat.	17	Phoenix
	Mon.	19	at Vancouver
	Wed.	21	at Calgary
	Fri.	23	at Edmonton
	Mon.	26	San Jose
	Wed.	28	at Colorado
	Thu.	29	at Phoenix
	Sat.	31	at Dallas

Jan.	Mon.	2	Dallas
	Thu.	5	Phoenix
	Sat.	7	at San Jose
	Mon.	9	at Anaheim
	Thu.	12	at Boston
	Sat.	14	at Buffalo
	Tue.	17	Tampa Bay
	Thu.	19	Atlanta
	Sat.	21	San Jose*
	Mon.	23	Anaheim
	Tue.	24	at San Jose
	Thu.	26	Edmonton
	Sat.	28	Anaheim*
	Mon.	30	at Anaheim
Feb.	Thu.	2	at Phoenix
	Tue.	7	at Minnesota
	Wed.	8	at Columbus
	Sat.	11	Chicago*
	Sun.	12	Dallas*
Mar.	Thu.	2	Minnesota
	Sat.	4	Columbus*
	Tue.	7	at Minnesota
	Thu.	9	at Detroit
	Sat.	11	at St. Louis
	Mon.	13	at San Jose
	Tue.	14	Phoenix
	Thu.	16	Dallas
	Sat.	18	St. Louis
	Mon.	20	Colorado
	Sat.	25	Nashville
	Mon.	27	at Vancouver
	Wed.	29	at Calgary
	Thu.	30	at Edmonton
Apr.	Sat.	1	Dallas
	Mon.	3	Vancouver
	Tue.	4	at Anaheim
	Thu.	6	San Jose
	Sat.	8	Anaheim*
	Thu.	13	at Phoenix
	Sat.	15	Calgary
	Mon.	17	at San Jose

Denotes afternoon game.

Franchise date: June 5, 1967

WESTERN CONFERENCE

39th NHL Season

PACIFIC DIVISION

Jeremy Roenick (left) brings plenty of personality (and 475 career goals!) to Los Angeles. Pavol Demitra (right) has never scored fewer than 28 goals when he has played at least 70 games. He had 93 points in 2002-03.

Year-by-Year Record

Season	GP	Home W	L	T	OL	Road W	L	T	OL	Overall W	L	T	OL	GF	GA	Pts.	Finished	Playoff Result
2004-05	....	....				....				....				....	....	....		
2003-04	82	15	16	9	1	13	13	7	8	28	29	16	9	205	217	81	3rd, Pacific Div.	Out of Playoffs
2002-03	82	19	19	2	1	14	18	4	5	33	37	6	6	203	221	78	3rd, Pacific Div.	Out of Playoffs
2001-02	82	22	12	6	1	18	15	5	3	40	27	11	4	214	190	95	3rd, Pacific Div.	Lost Conf. Quarter-Final
2000-01	82	20	12	8	1	18	16	5	2	38	28	13	3	252	228	92	3rd, Pacific Div.	Lost Conf. Semi-Final
1999-2000	82	21	13	5	2	18	14	7	2	39	27	12	4	245	228	94	2nd, Pacific Div.	Lost Conf. Quater-Final
1998-99	82	18	20	3	....	14	25	2	....	32	45	5	....	189	222	69	5th, Pacific Div.	Out of Playoffs
1997-98	82	22	16	3	....	16	17	8	....	38	33	11	....	227	225	87	4th, Pacific Div.	Lost Conf. Quater-Final
1996-97	82	18	16	7	....	10	27	4	....	28	43	11	....	214	268	67	6th, Pacific Div.	Out of Playoffs
1995-96	82	16	18	7	....	8	24	9	....	24	40	18	....	256	302	66	6th, Pacific Div.	Out of Playoffs
1994-95	48	7	11	6	....	9	12	3	....	16	23	9	....	142	174	41	4th, Pacific Div.	Out of Playoffs
1993-94	84	18	19	5	....	9	26	7	....	27	45	12	....	294	322	66	5th, Pacific Div.	Out of Playoffs
1992-93	84	22	15	5	....	17	20	5	....	39	35	10	....	338	340	88	3rd, Smythe Div.	Lost Final
1991-92	80	20	11	9	....	15	20	5	....	35	31	14	....	287	296	84	2nd, Smythe Div.	Lost Div. Semi-Final
1990-91	80	26	9	5	....	20	15	5	....	46	24	10	....	340	254	102	1st, Smythe Div.	Lost Div. Final
1989-90	80	21	16	3	....	13	23	4	....	34	39	7	....	338	337	75	4th, Smythe Div.	Lost Div. Final
1988-89	80	25	12	3	....	17	19	4	....	42	31	7	....	376	335	91	2nd, Smythe Div.	Lost Div. Final
1987-88	80	19	18	3	....	11	24	5	....	30	42	8	....	318	359	68	4th, Smythe Div.	Lost Div. Semi-Final
1986-87	80	20	17	3	....	11	24	5	....	31	41	8	....	318	341	70	4th, Smythe Div.	Lost Div. Semi-Final
1985-86	80	9	27	4	....	14	22	4	....	23	49	8	....	284	389	54	5th, Smythe Div.	Out of Playoffs
1984-85	80	20	14	6	....	14	18	8	....	34	32	14	....	339	326	82	4th, Smythe Div.	Lost Div. Semi-Final
1983-84	80	13	19	8	....	10	25	5	....	23	44	13	....	309	376	59	5th, Smythe Div.	Out of Playoffs
1982-83	80	20	13	7	....	7	28	5	....	27	41	12	....	308	365	66	5th, Smythe Div.	Out of Playoffs
1981-82	80	19	15	6	....	5	26	9	....	24	41	15	....	314	369	63	4th, Smythe Div.	Lost Div. Final
1980-81	80	22	11	7	....	21	13	6	....	43	24	13	....	337	290	99	2nd, Norris Div.	Lost Prelim. Round
1979-80	80	18	13	9	....	12	23	5	....	30	36	14	....	290	313	74	2nd, Norris Div.	Lost Prelim. Round
1978-79	80	20	13	7	....	14	21	5	....	34	34	12	....	292	286	80	3rd, Norris Div.	Lost Prelim. Round
1977-78	80	18	16	6	....	13	18	9	....	31	34	15	....	243	245	77	3rd, Norris Div.	Lost Prelim. Round
1976-77	80	20	13	7	....	14	18	8	....	34	31	15	....	271	241	83	2nd, Norris Div.	Lost Quarter-Final
1975-76	80	22	13	5	....	16	20	4	....	38	33	9	....	263	265	85	2nd, Norris Div.	Lost Quarter-Final
1974-75	80	22	7	11	....	20	10	10	....	42	17	21	....	269	185	105	2nd, Norris Div.	Lost Prelim. Round
1973-74	78	22	13	4	....	11	20	8	....	33	33	12	....	233	231	78	3rd, West Div.	Lost Quarter-Final
1972-73	78	21	11	7	....	10	25	4	....	31	36	11	....	232	245	73	6th, West Div.	Out of Playoffs
1971-72	78	14	23	2	....	6	26	7	....	20	49	9	....	206	305	49	7th, West Div.	Out of Playoffs
1970-71	78	17	14	8	....	8	26	5	....	25	40	13	....	239	303	63	5th, West Div.	Out of Playoffs
1969-70	76	12	22	4	....	2	30	6	....	14	52	10	....	168	290	38	6th, West Div.	Out of Playoffs
1968-69	76	19	14	5	....	5	28	5	....	24	42	10	....	185	260	58	4th, West Div.	Lost Semi-Final
1967-68	74	20	13	4	....	11	20	6	....	31	33	10	....	200	224	72	2nd, West Div.	Lost Quarter-Final

2005-06 Player Personnel

FORWARDS	HT	WT	S	Place of Birth	Date	2004-05 Club
ARMSTRONG, Derek	6-0	195	R	Ottawa, Ont.	4/23/73	Geneve-Rapperswil
AVERY, Sean	5-10	185	L	Pickering, Ont.	4/10/80	Pelicans-Motor City
BELANGER, Eric	6-0	185	L	Sherbrooke, Que.	12/16/77	Bolzano
BROWN, Dustin	6-0	195	R	Ithaca, NY	11/4/84	Manchester
BURE, Valeri	5-10	185	R	Moscow, USSR	6/13/74	
CAMMALLERI, Mike	5-9	180	L	Richmond Hill, Ont.	6/8/82	Manchester
CLARKE, Noah	5-9	185	L	LaVerne, CA	6/11/79	Manchester
CONROY, Craig	6-2	197	R	Potsdam, NY	9/4/71	
COWAN, Jeff	6-2	210	L	Scarborough, Ont.	9/27/76	
DEMITRA, Pavol	6-0	206	L	Dubnica, Czech.	11/29/74	Trencin
FLINN, Ryan	6-5	248	L	Halifax, N.S.	4/20/80	Manchester
FROLOV, Alexander	6-3	210	R	Moscow, USSR	6/19/82	CSKA-Dynamo Moscow
GIULIANO, Jeff	5-9	205	L	Nashua, NH	6/20/79	Manchester
HOGEBOOM, Greg	6-0	190	R	Toronto, Ont.	9/26/82	Manchester
KANKO, Petr	5-9	195	L	Pribram, Czech.	2/7/84	Manchester
KLATT, Trent	6-1	210	L	Robbinsdale, MN	1/30/71	
KOPITAR, Anze	6-4	220	L	Jesenice, Yugoslavia	8/24/87	Sodertalje
KOSTOPOULOS, Tom	6-0	200	R	Mississauga, Ont.	1/24/79	Manchester
PARROS, George	6-4	210	R	Washington, PA	12/29/79	Reading-Manchester
PUSHKAREV, Konstantin	6-0	169	L	Ust-Kamenogorsk, USSR	2/12/85	Omsk-Calgary (WHL)
ROBITAILLE, Luc	6-1	215	L	Montreal, Que.	2/17/66	
ROENICK, Jeremy	6-1	196	R	Boston, MA	1/17/70	
RYAN, Matt	5-11	182	L	Sharon, Ont.	11/12/83	Manchester
SMYTH, Brad	6-0	200	R	Ottawa, Ont.	3/13/73	Manchester
TAMBELLINI, Jeff	5-11	186	L	Calgary, Alta.	4/13/84	U. of Michigan
TUKONEN, Lauri	6-2	200	R	Hyvinkaa, Finland	9/1/86	Blues Jr.-Blues

DEFENSEMEN	HT	WT	S	Place of Birth	Date	2004-05 Club
CORVO, Joe	6-1	205	R	Oak Park, IL	6/20/77	Chicago (AHL)
DEMPSEY, Nathan	6-0	190	R	Spruce Grove, Alta.	7/14/74	Eisbaren Berlin
FAST, Brad	6-0	195	L	Fort St. John, B.C.	2/21/80	Lowell-Florida (ECHL)
GLEASON, Tim	6-1	202	L	Southfield, MI	1/29/83	Manchester
GREBESHKOV, Denis	6-1	200	L	Yaroslavl, USSR	10/11/83	Manchester
MILLER, Aaron	6-4	200	R	Buffalo, NY	8/11/71	
MORMINA, Joey	6-6	220	L	Montreal, Que.	6/29/82	Colgate
NORSTROM, Mattias	6-2	210	L	Stockholm, Sweden	1/2/72	Solna
PETIOT, Richard	6-2	190	L	Daysland, Alta.	8/20/82	Colorado College
VISNOVSKY, Lubomir	5-10	188	L	Topolcany, Czech.	8/11/76	Bratislava
WEAVER, Mike	5-9	180	R	Bramalea, Ont.	5/2/78	Manchester
WILFORD, Marty	6-1	212	L	Cobourg, Ont.	4/17/77	Norfolk

GOALTENDERS	HT	WT	C	Place of Birth	Date	2004-05 Club
BRUST, Barry	6-2	210	L	Swan River, Man.	8/8/83	Reading
FUKUFUJI, Yutaka	6-1	160	L	Tokyo, Japan	9/17/82	Bakersfield
GARON, Mathieu	6-2	192	R	Chandler, Que.	1/9/78	Manchester
HAUSER, Adam	6-2	195	L	Bovey, MN	5/27/80	Manchester
LABARBERA, Jason	6-2	205	L	Prince George, B.C.	1/18/80	Hartford
MUNCE, Ryan	6-2	180	L	Mississauga, Ont.	4/16/85	Sarnia

In the System and Recently Drafted

FORWARDS	HT	WT	S	Place of Birth	Date	2004-05 Club
BOYLE, Brian	6-6	222	L	Dorchester, MA	12/18/84	Boston College
CONNE, Flavien	5-9	176	L	Geneva, Switz.	4/1/80	Lugano
CURRY, Mike	6-3	190	R	Fort Benning, GA	9/20/84	U. Minn-Duluth
ERIKSSON, Tim	5-9	161	L	Sodertalje, Sweden	2/5/82	Linkoping
GUERIN, Marty	6-1	190	R	Manchester, NH	5/25/83	Miami U.
HANNUS, Tommi	6-0	180	R	Vantaa, Finland	6/27/80	Pelicans
JOHANSSON, Daniel	5-11	176	L	Ornskoldsvik, Sweden	7/5/81	Vaxjo
JUNTUNEN, Henrik	6-2	185	L	Goteborg, Sweden	4/24/83	Karpat
KARLSSON, Jens	6-3	205	R	Goteborg, Sweden	11/7/82	Rogle-Frolunda
KELLY, Steve	6-2	205	L	Vancouver, B.C.	10/26/76	Mannheim
LEHOUX, Yanick	6-1	200	R	Montreal, Que.	4/8/82	Manchester
LUKACEVIC, Ned	6-0	185	L	Podgorica, Serbia	2/11/86	Spokane
MURRAY, Brady	5-9	165	L	Brandon, Man.	8/17/84	North Dakota
NEILSON, Eric	6-1	201	R	Fredericton, N.B.	8/18/84	Rimouski
PARSE, Scott	6-1	185	R	Kalamazoo, MI	9/5/84	Nebraska-Omaha
PULLIAINEN, Tuukka	5-11	176	L	Turku, Finland	8/25/84	TPS-Jokipojat-TuTo
ROUSSIN, Dany	6-1	190	L	Quebec City, Que.	1/9/85	Rimouski
SEYMOUR, John	6-3	176	L	Scarborough, Ont.	6/16/87	Brampton
SHEFER, Andrei	6-1	194	L	Yekaterinburg, USSR	7/26/81	Cherepovets
SIMONS, Mikael	6-2	200	L	Falun, Sweden	1/15/78	Mora
SULLIVAN, Mike	6-4	190	L	Scarborough, Ont.	9/14/84	Clarkson
TENKANEN, Valtteri	5-11	183	L	Jamsa, Finland	3/27/85	JYP
WERNBLOM, Magnus	6-0	195	L	Kramfors, Sweden	2/3/73	

DEFENSEMEN	HT	WT	S	Place of Birth	Date	2004-05 Club
BAIER, Paul	6-3	212	R	Summit, NJ	2/2/85	Brown U.
FAST, T.J.	6-1	190	L	Calgary, Alta.	9/2/87	Camrose
HERSLEY, Patrik	6-3	205	R	Malmo, Sweden	6/23/86	Malmo
LYUBUSHIN, Mikhail	6-1	183	L	Moscow, USSR	7/24/83	Voskresensk-Chekhov
MANTYLA, Tuukka	5-9	172	L	Tampere, Finland	5/25/81	Lulea
McGINNIS, Ryan	6-1	197	L	Flint, MI	3/3/87	Plymouth
MEYERS, Josh	6-2	180	R	Alexandria, MN	12/7/85	Sioux City
NEMECEK, Jan	6-1	220	L	Pisek, Czech.	2/14/76	Leksand
ZIZKA, Tomas	6-1	198	L	Sternberk, Czech.	10/10/79	Spartak-Slavia

GOALTENDERS	HT	WT	C	Place of Birth	Date	2004-05 Club
GRAHN, Carl	6-0	175	L	Koupolo, Finland	1/8/81	KooKoo
QUICK, Jonathan	6-0	180	L	Milford, CT	1/21/86	Avon Old Farms
TAYLOR, Daniel	5-11	179	L	Plymouth, England	4/28/86	Guelph
ZABA, Matt	6-1	168	L	Yorkton, Sask.	7/14/83	Colorado College

Luc Robitaille has signed on for a 19th NHL season, his 14th in three stints with the Kings.

Vice President and General Manager

TAYLOR, DAVE
Senior Vice President/General Manager, Los Angeles Kings.
Born in Levack, Ont., December 4, 1955.

No player in the history of the Kings ever wore the uniform with more distinction and class than Dave Taylor. For 17 seasons, Taylor gave his all, both on and off the ice, receiving All-Star status for his outstanding play.

Fittingly, after finishing his illustrious career during the 1993-94 season, Taylor remains a key part of the Kings organization, now serving as vice president and general manager for the NHL club. Taylor assumed his current responsibilities on April 22, 1997, becoming the seventh g.m. in team history. He joined the Kings front office four years earlier as an assistant to his predecessor, Sam McMaster.

An All-American hockey player while at Clarkson College, Taylor was relatively unknown when the Kings picked him in the 15th round of the 1975 draft. His grit and work ethic kept him around long enough to hook up with a center named Marcel Dionne, who virtually ignited Taylor's career. As a member of the renowned Triple Crown line with Dionne and left winger Charlie Simmer, Taylor became a prolific scorer and a fearsome checker. Taylor's NHL career stats include a Kings-record 1,111 games, 431 goals, 638 assists and 1,069 points.

A four-time NHL All-Star Game selection, Taylor served as the Kings captain for four seasons (1985-89). After posting career highs in goals (47) and points (112) during the 1980-81 season, Taylor earned a spot on the NHL Second All-Star Team. On April 3, 1995, Taylor's jersey No. 18 was retired, joining Rogie Vachon (No. 30) and Marcel Dionne (No. 16). For all his individual accomplishments in hockey, his crowning glory was reaching the Stanley Cup Finals with the 1992-93 Kings.

Away from the ice, Taylor has worked tirelessly for numerous charities throughout the years. Each year he hosts the Dave Taylor Golf Classic benefiting the Cystic Fibrosis Foundation, which annually raises more than $125,000. In 1991, the NHL honored Taylor's contributions to hockey and the community by awarding him both the Bill Masterton and King Clancy trophies.

General Managers' History

Larry Regan, 1967-68 to 1972-73; Larry Regan and Jake Milford, 1973-74; Jake Milford, 1974-75 to 1976-77; George Maguire, 1977-78 to 1982-83; George Maguire and Rogie Vachon, 1983-84; Rogie Vachon, 1984-85 to 1991-92; Nick Beverley, 1992-93, 1993-94; Sam McMaster, 1994-95 to 1996-97; Dave Taylor, 1997-98 to date.

Captains' History

Bob Wall, 1967-68, 1968-69; Larry Cahan, 1969-70, 1970-71; Bob Pulford, 1971-72, 1972-73; Terry Harper, 1973-74, 1974-75; Mike Murphy, 1975-76 to 1980-81; Dave Lewis, 1981-82, 1982-83; Terry Ruskowski, 1983-84, 1984-85; Dave Taylor, 1985-86 to 1988-89; Wayne Gretzky, 1989-90 to 1991-92; Wayne Gretzky and Luc Robitaille, 1992-93; Wayne Gretzky, 1993-94, 1994-95; Wayne Gretzky and Rob Blake, 1995-96; Rob Blake, 1996-97 to 2000-01; Mattias Norstrom, 2001-02 to date.

Club Records

Team

(Figures in brackets for season records are games played; records for fewest points, wins, ties, losses, goals, goals against are for 70 or more games)

Most Points	**105**	1974-75 (80)
Most Wins	**46**	1990-91 (80)
Most Ties	**21**	1974-75 (80)
Most Losses	**52**	1969-70 (76)
Most Goals	**376**	1988-89 (80)
Most Goals Against	**389**	1985-86 (80)
Fewest Points	**38**	1969-70 (76)
Fewest Wins	**14**	1969-70 (76)
Fewest Ties	**5**	1998-99 (82)
Fewest Losses	**17**	1974-75 (80)
Fewest Goals	**168**	1969-70 (76)
Fewest Goals Against	**185**	1974-75 (80)
Longest Winning Streak		
Overall	**8**	Oct. 21-Nov. 7/72, Feb. 23-Mar. 9/92
Home	**12**	Oct. 10-Dec. 5/92
Away	**8**	Dec. 18/74-Jan. 16/75
Longest Undefeated Streak		
Overall	**11**	Feb. 28-Mar. 24/74 (9 wins, 2 ties)
Home	**13**	Oct. 10-Dec. 8/92 (12 wins, 1 tie)
Away	**11**	Oct. 10-Dec. 11/74 (6 wins, 5 ties)
Longest Losing Streak		
Overall	**11**	Mar. 16-Apr. 4/04
Home	**9**	Feb. 8-Mar. 12/86
Away	**12**	Jan. 11-Feb. 15/70
Longest Winless Streak		
Overall	**17**	Jan. 29-Mar. 5/70 (13 losses, 4 ties)
Home	**9**	Jan. 29-Mar. 5/70 (8 losses, 1 tie), Feb. 8-Mar. 12/86 (9 losses)
Away	**21**	Jan. 11-Apr. 3/70 (17 losses, 4 ties)
Most Shutouts, Season	**10**	2000-01 (82)
Most PIM, Season	**2,247**	1992-93 (84)
Most Goals, Game	**12**	Nov. 29/84 (Van. 1 at L.A. 12)

Individual

Most Seasons	**17**	Dave Taylor
Most Games	**1,111**	Dave Taylor
Most Goals, Career	**550**	Marcel Dionne
Most Assists, Career	**757**	Marcel Dionne
Most Points Career	**1,307**	Marcel Dionne (550G, 757A)
Most PIM, Career	**1,846**	Marty McSorley
Most Shutouts, Career	**32**	Rogie Vachon
Longest Consecutive Games Streak	**324**	Marcel Dionne (Jan. 7/78-Jan. 9/82)
Most Goals, Season	**70**	Bernie Nicholls (1988-89)
Most Assists, Season	**122**	Wayne Gretzky (1990-91)
Most Points, Season	**168**	Wayne Gretzky (1988-89; 54G, 114A)
Most PIM, Season	**399**	Marty McSorley (1992-93)
Most Points, Defenseman, Season	**76**	Larry Murphy (1980-81; 16G, 60A)
Most Points, Center, Season	**168**	Wayne Gretzky (1988-89; 54G, 114A)
Most Points, Right Wing, Season	**112**	Dave Taylor (1980-81; 47G, 65A)
Most Points, Left Wing, Season	***125**	Luc Robitaille (1992-93; 63G, 62A)
Most Points, Rookie, Season	**84**	Luc Robitaille (1986-87; 45G, 39A)
Most Shutouts, Season	**8**	Rogie Vachon (1976-77)
Most Goals, Game	**4**	Sixteen times
Most Assists, Game	**6**	Bernie Nicholls (Dec. 1/88), Tomas Sandstrom (Oct. 9/93)
Most Points, Game	**8**	Bernie Nicholls (Dec. 1/88; 2G, 6A)

* NHL Record.

Coaching History

Red Kelly, 1967-68, 1968-69; Hal Laycoe and Johnny Wilson, 1969-70; Larry Regan, 1970-71; Larry Regan and Fred Glover, 1971-72; Bob Pulford, 1972-73 to 1976-77; Ron Stewart, 1977-78; Bob Berry, 1978-79 to 1980-81; Parker MacDonald and Don Perry, 1981-82; Don Perry, 1982-83; Don Perry, Rogie Vachon and Roger Neilson, 1983-84; Pat Quinn, 1984-85, 1985-86; Pat Quinn and Mike Murphy 1986-87; Mike Murphy, Rogie Vachon and Robbie Ftorek, 1987-88; Robbie Ftorek, 1988-89; Tom Webster, 1989-90 to 1991-92; Barry Melrose, 1992-93, 1993-94; Barry Melrose and Rogie Vachon, 1994-95; Larry Robinson, 1995-96 to 1998-99; Andy Murray, 1999-2000 to date.

Retired Numbers

16	Marcel Dionne	1975-1987
18	Dave Taylor	1977-1994
30	Rogie Vachon	1971-1978
99	Wayne Gretzky	1988-1996

All-time Record vs. Other Clubs

Regular Season

	At Home								On Road								Total							
	GP	W	L	T	OL	GF	GA	PTS	GP	W	L	T	OL	GF	GA	PTS	GP	W	L	T	OL	GF	GA	PTS
Anaheim	30	17	9	4	0	89	72	38	30	10	13	7	0	80	100	27	60	27	22	11	0	169	172	65
Atlanta	4	3	0	0	1	18	9	7	4	3	0	0	1	16	7	7	8	6	0	0	2	34	16	14
Boston	61	21	32	7	1	210	224	50	61	11	44	6	0	169	287	28	122	32	76	13	1	379	511	78
Buffalo	54	22	23	9	0	185	187	53	53	16	28	9	0	157	217	41	107	38	51	18	0	342	404	94
Calgary	91	46	36	9	0	338	316	101	94	27	52	12	3	310	413	69	185	73	88	21	3	648	729	170
Carolina	30	17	10	3	0	129	113	37	31	11	13	5	2	115	114	29	61	28	23	8	2	244	227	66
Chicago	74	33	33	8	0	245	246	74	75	31	34	9	1	221	261	72	149	64	67	17	1	466	507	146
Colorado	43	25	13	5	0	176	137	55	42	16	23	3	0	140	169	35	85	41	36	8	0	316	306	90
Columbus	8	4	3	1	0	18	16	9	8	3	3	0	2	26	21	8	16	7	6	1	2	44	37	17
Dallas	82	35	28	19	0	277	234	89	84	19	50	13	2	218	323	53	166	54	78	32	2	495	557	142
Detroit	80	42	24	14	0	321	246	98	79	30	35	13	1	271	300	74	159	72	59	27	1	592	546	172
Edmonton	77	28	34	15	0	298	318	71	77	23	39	15	0	275	347	61	154	51	73	30	0	573	665	132
Florida	9	5	4	0	0	27	29	10	8	1	4	3	0	14	23	5	17	6	8	3	0	41	52	15
Minnesota	8	2	4	2	0	17	21	6	8	4	1	3	0	21	13	11	16	6	5	5	0	38	34	17
Montreal	65	19	37	9	0	199	256	47	64	8	45	11	0	160	289	27	129	27	82	20	0	359	545	74
Nashville	12	7	4	0	1	36	28	15	12	8	1	3	0	31	16	19	24	15	5	3	1	67	44	34
New Jersey	42	28	8	6	0	201	130	62	43	19	18	5	1	148	142	44	85	47	26	11	1	349	272	106
NY Islanders	45	21	17	7	0	163	143	49	44	15	24	5	0	123	156	35	89	36	41	12	0	286	299	84
NY Rangers	60	23	26	10	1	199	216	57	58	17	35	6	0	172	233	40	118	40	61	16	1	371	449	97
Ottawa	10	8	1	1	0	46	21	17	9	4	4	1	0	28	30	9	19	12	5	2	0	74	51	26
Philadelphia	66	21	37	8	0	193	223	50	63	16	40	7	0	156	244	39	129	37	77	15	0	349	467	89
Phoenix	74	28	31	14	1	294	288	71	76	27	37	11	1	250	301	66	150	55	68	25	2	544	589	137
Pittsburgh	69	44	17	8	0	265	183	96	73	25	38	10	0	233	265	60	142	69	55	18	0	498	448	156
St. Louis	78	35	31	12	0	261	226	82	78	18	49	10	1	195	293	47	156	53	80	22	1	456	519	129
San Jose	37	23	10	4	0	116	88	50	37	12	19	3	3	102	128	30	74	35	29	7	3	218	216	80
Tampa Bay	11	1	8	2	0	24	36	4	10	5	5	0	0	22	23	10	21	6	13	2	0	46	59	14
Toronto	65	34	21	10	0	234	191	78	68	22	34	11	1	223	266	56	133	56	55	21	1	457	457	134
Vancouver	99	51	32	16	0	393	310	118	97	31	49	16	1	300	365	79	196	82	81	32	1	693	675	197
Washington	47	27	13	6	1	187	144	61	46	21	18	7	0	171	185	49	93	48	31	13	1	358	329	110
Defunct Clubs	35	27	6	2	0	141	76	56	34	11	14	9	0	91	109	31	69	38	20	11	0	232	185	87
Totals	**1466**	**697**	**552**	**211**	**6**	**5300**	**4727**	**1611**	**1466**	**464**	**769**	**213**	**20**	**4438**	**5640**	**1161**	**2932**	**1161**	**1321**	**424**	**26**	**9738**	**10367**	**2772**

Playoffs

	Series	W	L	GP	W	L	T	GF	GA	Last Mtg.	Rnd.	Result
Boston	2	0	2	13	5	8	0	38	56	1977	QF	L 2-4
Calgary	6	4	2	26	13	13	0	105	102	1993	DSF	W 4-2
Chicago	1	0	1	5	1	4	0	7	10	1974	QF	L 1-4
Colorado	2	0	2	14	6	8	0	23	33	2002	CQF	L 3-4
Dallas	1	0	1	7	3	4	0	21	26	1968	QF	L 3-4
Detroit	2	1	1	10	4	6	0	21	32	2001	CQF	W 4-2
Edmonton	7	2	5	36	12	24	0	127	154	1992	DSF	L 2-4
Montreal	1	0	1	5	1	4	0	12	15	1993	F	L 1-4
NY Islanders	1	0	1	4	1	3	0	10	21	1980	PRE	L 1-3
NY Rangers	2	0	2	6	1	5	0	14	32	1981	PRE	L 1-3
St. Louis	2	0	2	8	0	8	0	13	32	1998	CQF	L 0-4
Toronto	3	1	2	12	5	7	0	31	41	1993	CF	W 4-3
Vancouver	3	2	1	17	9	8	0	66	60	1993	DF	W 4-2
Defunct Clubs	1	1	0	7	4	3	0	23	25			
Totals	**34**	**11**	**23**	**170**	**65**	**105**	**0**	**511**	**639**			

Playoff Results 2005-2000

Year	Round	Opponent	Result	GF	GA
2002	CQF	Colorado	L 3-4	13	16
2001	CSF	Colorado	L 3-4	10	17
	CQF	Detroit	W 4-2	15	17
2000	CQF	Detroit	L 0-4	6	15

Abbreviations: Round: F - Final; **CF** - conference final; **CSF** - conference semi-final; **CQF** - conference quarter-final; **DF** - division final; **DSF** - division semi-final; **QF** - quarter-final; **PRE** - preliminary round.

Calgary totals include Atlanta Flames, 1972-73 to 1979-80. Carolina totals include Hartford, 1979-80 to 1996-97.
Colorado totals include Quebec, 1979-80 to 1994-95. Dallas totals include Minnesota North Stars, 1967-68 to 1992-93.
New Jersey totals include Kansas City, 1974-75 to 1975-76, and Colorado Rockies, 1976-77 to 1981-82.
Phoenix totals include Winnipeg, 1979-80 to 1995-96.

Key Off-Season Signings/Acquisitions

2004

- May 6 • Re-signed D **Nathan Dempsey**.
- June 26 • Obtained G **Mathieu Garon** and a 2004 3rd-round pick from Montreal for C **Radek Bonk** (Bonk had previously been obtained from Ottawa for a 2004 3rd-round pick).
- July 6 • Signed C **Craig Conroy**.
- 9 • Re-signed D **Lubomir Visnovsky**.
- 16 • Signed RW **Brad Smyth**.
- 31 • Re-signed C **Sean Avery**.

2005

- July 25 • Re-signed LW **Luc Robitaille**.
- Aug. 2 • Signed C **Pavol Demitra**.
- 4 • Obtained C **Jeremy Roenick** and a 2006 3rd-round pick from Philadelphia for future considerations.
- 8 • Re-signed C **Eric Belanger**.
- 10 • Re-signed C **Mike Cammalleri**.
- 12 • Re-signed RW **Alexander Frolov**.
- 12 • Signed RW **Valeri Bure**.
- 15 • Re-signed D **Joe Corvo**.
- 15 • Signed 2003 1st-round pick (27th overall), LW **Jeff Tambellini**.
- 23 • Signed 2004 1st-round pick (11th overall), RW **Lauri Tukonen**.

Entry Draft
Selections 2005-1991

2005
Pick
11	Anze Kopitar
50	Dany Roussin
60	T.J. Fast
72	Jonathan Quick
139	Patrik Hersley
184	Ryan McGinnis
206	Josh Meyers
226	John Seymour

2004
Pick
11	Lauri Tukonen
95	Paul Baier
110	Ned Lukacevic
143	Eric Neilson
174	Scott Parse
205	Mike Curry
220	Maxim Semenov
221	Daniel Taylor
238	Yutaka Fukufuji
264	Valtteri Tenkanen

2003
Pick
13	Dustin Brown
26	Brian Boyle
27	Jeff Tambellini
44	Konstantin Pushkarev
82	Ryan Munce
152	Brady Murray
174	Esa Pirnes
231	Matt Zaba
244	Mike Sullivan
274	Marty Guerin

2002
Pick
18	Denis Grebeshkov
50	Sergei Anshakov
66	Petr Kanko
104	Aaron Rome
115	Mark Rooneem
152	Greg Hogeboom
157	Joel Andresen
185	Ryan Murphy
215	Mikhail Lyubushin
248	Tuukka Pulliainen
279	Connor James

2001
Pick
18	Jens Karlsson
30	Dave Steckel
49	Mike Cammalleri
51	Jaroslav Bednar
83	Henrik Juntunen
116	Richard Petiot
152	Terry Denike
153	Tuukka Mantyla
214	Cristobal Huet
237	Mike Gabinet
277	Sebastien Laplante

2000
Pick
20	Alexander Frolov
54	Andreas Lilja
86	Yanick Lehoux
118	Lubomir Visnovsky
165	Nathan Marsters
201	Yevgeny Fedorov
206	Tim Eriksson
218	Craig Olynick
245	Dan Welch
250	Flavien Conne
282	Carl Grahn

1999
Pick
43	Andrei Shefer
74	Jason Crain
76	Frantisek Kaberle
92	Cory Campbell
104	Brian McGrattan
125	Daniel Johansson
133	Jean-Francois Nogues
193	Kevin Baker
222	George Parros
250	Noah Clarke

1998
Pick
21	Mathieu Biron
46	Justin Papineau
76	Alexei Volkov
103	Kip Brennan
133	Joe Rullier
163	Tomas Zizka
190	Tommi Hannus
217	Jim Henkel
248	Matthew Yeats

1997
Pick
3	Olli Jokinen
15	Matt Zultek
29	Scott Barney
83	Joe Corvo
99	Sean Blanchard
137	Richard Seeley
150	Jeff Katcher
193	Jay Kopischke
220	Konrad Brand

1996
Pick
30	Josh Green
37	Marian Cisar
57	Greg Phillips
84	Mikael Simons
96	Eric Belanger
120	Jesse Black
123	Peter Hogan
190	Stephen Valiquette
193	Kai Nurminen
219	Sebastien Simard

1995
Pick
3	Aki Berg
33	Don MacLean
50	Pavel Rosa
59	Vladimir Tsyplakov
118	Jason Morgan
137	Igor Melyakov
157	Benoit Larose
163	Juha Vuorivirta
215	Brian Stewart

1994
Pick
7	Jamie Storr
33	Matt Johnson
59	Vitali Yachmenev
111	Chris Schmidt
163	Luc Gagne
189	Andrew Dale
215	Jan Nemecek
241	Sergei Shalomai

1993
Pick
42	Shayne Toporowski
68	Jeff Mitchell
94	Bob Wren
105	Frederick Beaubien
117	Jason Saal
120	Tomas Vlasak
146	Jere Karalahti
172	Justin Martin
198	John-Tra Dillabough
224	Martin Strbak
250	Kimmo Timonen
276	Patrick Howald

1992
Pick
39	Justin Hocking
63	Sandy Allan
87	Kevin Brown
111	Jeff Shevalier
135	Rem Murray
207	Magnus Wernblom
231	Ryan Pisiak
255	Jukka Tiilikainen

1991
Pick
42	Guy Leveque
79	Keith Redmond
81	Alexei Zhitnik
108	Pauli Jaks
130	Brett Seguin
152	Kelly Fairchild
196	Craig Brown
218	Mattias Olsson
240	Andre Bouliane
262	Mike Gaul

Club Directory

STAPLES Center

Los Angeles Kings
STAPLES Center
1111 South Figueroa Street
Los Angeles, CA 90015
Phone **213/742-7100**
GM FAX 310/535-4525
www.lakings.com
Capacity: 18,118

Executive
Owner	Philip F. Anschutz
Owner	Edward P. Roski
President/Governor	Timothy J. Leiweke

Hockey Operations
Senior Vice President/General Manager	Dave Taylor
Vice President of Hockey Operations, Assistant General Manager	Kevin Gilmore
Director, Player Personnel	Bill O'Flaherty
Director, Amateur Scouting	Al Murray
Assistant Director of Amateur Scouting	Grant Sonier
Assistant to the General Manager	John Wolf
Hockey Operations Administrator	Lee Callans
Executive Assistant, Hockey Operations	Kely Lyon
Head Coach	Andy Murray
Assistant Coaches	Mark Hardy, Ray Bennett, John Van Boxmeer
Goaltending Consultant	Andy Nowicki
Video Coordinator	Bill Gurney
Director of Pro Scouting	Rob Laird
Pro Scouts	Vaclav Nedomansky, Shawn Dineen
Amateur Scouts	Terry McDonnell, Brent McEwen, John Stanton, Jan Vopat, Ari Vuori, Michel Boucher, Jim Cassidy, Bob Crocker, Mike Donnelly, Tony Gasparini, Viacheslav Golovin, Gary Harker, Barry Martinelli, Peter Nevin, Jerry Sodomlak, Victor Tjumenev

Medical
Athletic Trainer	Peter Demers, ATC
Assistant Athletic Trainer	Rick Burrill, ATC
Rehabilitation Trainer	Robert Zolg, MPT, ATC
Strength and Conditioning Trainer	Mike Kadar, BAPE, MT, CSCS
Team Physician	Dr. Ronald Kvitne (Kerlan-Jobe Orthopaedic Clinic)
Internist	Dr. Michael Mellman
Dentist	Dr. Jeffrey Hoy
Opthamologist	Dr. Howard Lazerson

Equipment Staff
Equipment Manager	Peter Millar
Assistant Equipment Managers	Rick Garcia, Dana Bryson

Communications
Vice President, Communications and Broadcasting	Michael Altieri
Communications Director	Jeff Moeller
Communications Manager	Mike Kalinowski
Assistant, Communications and Broadcasting	Stephanie Krauss

Broadcasters
TV Play-by-Play Announcer	Bob Miller
Radio Play-by-Play Announcer	Nick Nickson
TV Color Commentator	Jim Fox
Radio Color Commentator	Daryl Evans

Miscellaneous
Training Center	Toyota Sports Center
Television	FSN West
Radio Flagship	ESPN Radio 710-KSPN

Coach

MURRAY, ANDY
Coach, Los Angeles Kings. Born in Gladstone, Man., March 3, 1951.

Andy Murray became the 19th head coach in Kings history on June 14, 1999. His coaching experience dates back to 1974 and includes seven seasons as an NHL assistant or associate coach with the Winnipeg Jets (1993 to 1995), Minnesota North Stars (1990 to 1992) and Philadelphia Flyers (1988 to 1990). As an assistant coach in Minnesota, Murray reached the Stanley Cup Finals in 1991.

In addition to his NHL service, Murry brings to the Kings a tremendous amount of internatinal coaching experience. As head coach of the Canadian national team, he guided his team to a 77-29-14 record. He also won the gold medal at the 1997 and 2003 World Championships.

From 1976 to 1978, Murray served his first head coaching position with the Brandon Travelers of the Manitoba Junior Hockey League. He moved on to become head coach for Brandon University from 1978 to 1981, leading the Bobcats to the #1 ranking in Canadian university hockey during his final year. In 1981-82, Murray moved to Switzerland, where for the next seven years he coached several Swiss-A Division teams.

Murray returned to North America as an assistant coach for the Hershey Bears of the American Hockey League in 1987 and helped guide the Bears to the 1988 Calder Cup championship. In 1992, Murray returned to Europe to coach Lugano in Switzerland and then Eisbaren Berlin in Germany a year later. Most recently, Murray served as the head coach for Shattuck-St. Mary's in Faribault, Minnesota, where he led the prep school to a 70-9-2 record and the Midget Triple A USA Hockey national championship in 1998-99.

Coaching Record

Season	Team	Games	Regular Season W	L	T	Playoffs Games	W	L
1999-2000	Los Angeles (NHL)	82	39	31	12	4	0	4
2000-01	Los Angeles (NHL)	82	38	31	13	13	7	6
2001-02	Los Angeles (NHL)	82	40	31	11	7	3	4
2002-03	Los Angeles (NHL)	82	33	43	6	....	....	....
2003-04	Los Angeles (NHL)	82	28	38	16	....	....	....
2004-05	Los Angeles (NHL)			Season Cancelled				
	NHL Totals	**410**	**178**	**174**	**58**	**80**	**49**	**31**

Assistant coach Dave Tippett posted a 2-2-1 record as replacement coach when Murray was sidelined following a car accident, February 26 to March 6, 2002. All games are credited to Murray's coaching record.

Minnesota Wild

2005-06 Schedule

Oct.	Wed.	5	Calgary	Sat.	7	Anaheim
	Sat.	8	at Phoenix	Mon.	9	Dallas
	Sun.	9	at Los Angeles*	Sat.	14	Calgary
	Wed.	12	Vancouver	Mon.	16	Ottawa
	Fri.	14	Vancouver	Wed.	18	Toronto
	Sun.	16	Anaheim*	Fri.	20	Chicago
	Wed.	19	San Jose	Sun.	22	at Chicago
	Sat.	22	at St. Louis	Tue.	24	Phoenix
	Sun.	23	at Chicago	Thu.	26	Nashville
	Tue.	25	Vancouver	Fri.	27	at Columbus
	Fri.	28	at Columbus	Mon.	30	Detroit
	Sat.	29	Columbus	Tue.	31	at Colorado
Nov.	Tue.	1	at Calgary	**Feb.** Thu.	2	at San Jose
	Wed.	2	at Vancouver	Sat.	4	at Phoenix
	Sat.	5	at San Jose	Tue.	7	Los Angeles
	Sun.	6	at Anaheim*	Thu.	9	Colorado
	Tue.	8	Phoenix	Fri.	10	at Edmonton
	Fri.	11	at Detroit	Sun.	12	at Vancouver
	Mon.	14	at Calgary	Tue.	28	at Colorado
	Sat.	19	Nashville	**Mar.** Thu.	2	at Los Angeles
	Wed.	23	Edmonton	Fri.	3	at Anaheim
	Fri.	25	St. Louis*	Sun.	5	Colorado
	Wed.	30	Columbus	Tue.	7	Los Angeles
Dec.	Thu.	1	at Nashville	Fri.	10	at St. Louis
	Sat.	3	at New Jersey*	Sun.	12	Edmonton
	Mon.	5	at NY Rangers	Tue.	14	Edmonton
	Thu.	8	at Pittsburgh	Sun.	19	Calgary
	Sat.	10	at Philadelphia*	Tue.	21	Calgary
	Sun.	11	Buffalo	Wed.	22	at Dallas
	Tue.	13	at NY Islanders	Sat.	25	San Jose
	Thu.	15	Boston	Tue.	28	at Edmonton
	Sat.	17	Montreal	Wed.	29	at Vancouver
	Mon.	19	Dallas	Fri.	31	at Vancouver
	Thu.	22	at Colorado	**Apr.** Sun.	2	Detroit*
	Fri.	23	Colorado	Tue.	4	St. Louis
	Mon.	26	at Edmonton	Thu.	6	Edmonton
	Wed.	28	at Edmonton	Fri.	7	at Calgary
	Thu.	29	at Calgary	Sun.	9	at Colorado
	Sat.	31	Vancouver*	Tue.	11	Chicago
Jan.	Tue.	3	at Detroit	Thu.	13	at Nashville
	Thu.	5	Colorado	Sat.	15	at Dallas*

Denotes afternoon game.

Franchise date: June 25, 1997

WESTERN CONFERENCE

NORTHWEST DIVISION

6th NHL Season

Year-by-Year Record

Season	GP	Home				Road				Overall				GF	GA	Pts.	Finished	Playoff Result
		W	L	T	OL	W	L	T	OL	W	L	T	OL					
2004-05	....	....				....				....				....	....	....		
2003-04	82	19	13	7	2	11	16	13	1	30	29	20	3	188	183	83	5th, Northwest Div.	Out of Playoffs
2002-03	82	25	13	3	0	17	16	7	1	42	29	10	1	198	178	95	3rd, Northwest Div.	Lost Conf. Championship
2001-02	82	14	14	8	5	12	21	4	4	26	35	12	9	195	238	73	5th, Northwest Div.	Out of Playoffs
2000-01	82	14	13	10	4	11	26	3	1	25	39	13	5	168	210	68	5th, Northwest Div.	Out of Playoffs

Though a defensive defenseman, Willie Mitchell's assist totals have improved every season he has played in the NHL. His plus-minus went from -16 in 2001-02 to +13 in 2002-03 and +12 in 2003-04.

2005-06 Player Personnel

FORWARDS	HT	WT	S	Place of Birth	Date	2004-05 Club
BOUCHARD, Pierre-Marc	5-10	165	L	Sherbrooke, Que.	4/27/84	Houston
CHOUINARD, Marc	6-5	218	R	Charlesbourg, Que.	5/6/77	Frisk-Asker
DAIGLE, Alexandre	6-0	195	L	Montreal, Que.	2/7/75	Morges
DUPUIS, Pascal	6-0	196	L	Laval, Que.	4/7/79	Ajoie
FOY, Matt	6-2	219	R	Oakville, Ont.	5/18/83	Houston
GABORIK, Marian	6-1	190	L	Trencin, Czech.	2/14/82	Farjestad-Trencin
KOIVU, Mikko	6-2	205	L	Turku, Finland	3/12/83	Houston
LAW, Kirby	6-1	185	R	McCreary, Man.	3/11/77	Houston
NAZAROV, Andrei	6-5	242	R	Chelyabinsk, USSR	5/22/74	Novokuznetsk-Omsk
O'SULLIVAN, Patrick	5-11	190	L	Winston Salem, NC	2/1/85	Mississauga
ROLSTON, Brian	6-2	210	L	Flint, MI	2/21/73	
TETARENKO, Joey	6-2	215	R	Prince Albert, Sask.	3/3/78	Houston
VEILLEUX, Stephane	6-1	187	L	Beauceville, Que.	11/16/81	Houston
WALLIN, Rickard	6-2	185	L	Stockholm, Sweden	4/19/80	Houston
WALZ, Wes	5-10	180	R	Calgary, Alta.	5/15/70	
WANVIG, Kyle	6-2	219	R	Calgary, Alta.	1/29/81	Houston
WESTRUM, Erik	6-0	204	L	Minneapolis, MN	7/26/79	Utah
WHITE, Todd	5-10	194	L	Kanata, Ont.	5/21/75	Sodertalje

DEFENSEMEN						
BURNS, Brent	6-4	200	R	Ajax, Ont.	3/9/85	Houston
FERGUSON, Scott	6-1	195	L	Camrose, Alta.	1/6/73	
FOSTER, Kurtis	6-5	235	R	Carp, Ont.	11/24/81	Cincinnati (AHL)
HENRY, Alex	6-5	220	L	Elliot Lake, Ont.	10/18/79	Kaufbeuren
KUBA, Filip	6-3	205	L	Ostrava, Czech.	12/29/76	
MITCHELL, Willie	6-3	205	L	Port McNeill, B.C.	4/23/77	
SCHULTZ, Nick	6-1	207	L	Strasbourg, Sask.	8/25/82	Kassel
TJARNQVIST, Daniel	6-2	200	L	Umea, Sweden	10/14/76	Djurgarden
ZYUZIN, Andrei	6-1	215	L	Ufa, USSR	1/21/78	Ufa-Cherepovets

GOALTENDERS	HT	WT	C	Place of Birth	Date	2004-05 Club
FERNANDEZ, Manny	6-0	180	L	Etobicoke, Ont.	8/27/74	Lulea
HARDING, Josh	6-1	180	R	Regina, Sask.	6/18/84	Houston
ROLOSON, Dwayne	6-1	178	L	Simcoe, Ont.	10/12/69	Lukko

In the System and Recently Drafted

FORWARDS	HT	WT	S	Place of Birth	Date	2004-05 Club
BAILEY, Kyle	6-2	182	R	Ponoka, Alta.	10/15/86	Portland (WHL)
BOOGAARD, Derek	6-7	250	R	Saskatoon, Sask.	6/23/82	Houston
BORDELEAU, Patrick	6-5	195	L	Montreal, Que.	3/23/86	Val-d'Or
BROS, Michal	6-1	195	R	Olomouc, Czech.	1/25/76	Sparta
ECKERBLOM, Niklas	6-1	196	L	Vasterhaninge, Sweden	1/4/84	Almtuna
EMMERSON, Riley	6-6	250	L	Burnaby, B.C.	2/7/86	Tri-City
ERICKSON, Mike	6-2	201	R	Eden Prairie, MN	4/12/83	Western Mich.
HANNULA, Mika	5-11	180	L	Huddinge, Sweden	4/2/79	Malmo
IRMEN, Danny	6-0	190	R	Fargo, ND	9/6/84	U. of Minnesota
JONES, Ryan	6-1	200	R	Chatham, Ont.	6/14/84	Miami U.
KASSIAN, Matt	6-4	235	L	Edmonton, Alta.	10/28/86	Van (WHL)-Kamloops
KOLUSZ, Marcin	6-1	180	L	Limanowa, Poland	1/18/85	Nowy Targ
MADSEN, Morten	6-1	185	L	Rodovre, Denmark	1/16/87	Frolunda Jr.
OLVECKY, Peter	6-2	195	L	Trencin, Czech.	10/11/85	Piestany-Trencin
POULIOT, Benoit	6-3	179	L	Alfred, Ont.	9/29/86	Sudbury
ROONEEM, Mark	6-2	185	L	Hinton, Alta.	1/9/83	Houston-L'siana-P'cola
SPRUNGER, Julien	6-4	197	R	Fribourg, Switz.	1/4/86	Fribourg-Ch.-de-Fonds
VOLOSHENKO, Roman	6-1	200	R	Brest, USSR	5/12/86	Krylja Sovetov
WILSON, Kyle	6-0	200	R	Oakville, Ont.	12/15/84	Colgate

DEFENSEMEN						
AIELLO, Anthony	6-1	187	L	Braintree, MA	5/19/86	Thayer
HEID, Chris	6-2	205	L	Langley, B.C.	3/14/83	Houston-L'siana-P'cola
MISHARIN, Grigory	6-0	198	L	Yekaterinburg, USSR	5/11/85	Nizhnekamsk
REITZ, Erik	6-1	210	R	Detroit, MI	7/29/82	Houston
STOKES, Ryan	6-4	220	L	Sarnia, Ont.	6/23/83	Houston-Pensacola
STONER, Clayton	6-3	215	L	Port McNeill, B.C.	2/19/85	Tri-City
THELEN, A.J.	6-3	210	L	Shakopee, Minn.	3/11/86	Michigan State
TYULYAPKIN, Mikhail	6-1	187	L	Gorky, USSR	5/4/84	Novokuznetsk
WOOD, Dustin	6-1	208	L	Scarborough, Ont.	5/21/81	Utah

GOALTENDERS	HT	WT	C	Place of Birth	Date	2004-05 Club
KHUDOBIN, Anton	5-11	176	L	Ust-Kamenogorsk, USSR	5/7/86	Magnitogorsk
KOPRIVA, Miroslav	6-2	176	L	Kladno, Czech.	12/5/83	Kladno-Beroun
WESTBLOM, Kristofer	6-1	155	L	Meadow Lake, Sask.	3/26/87	Kelowna

Coach

LEMAIRE, JACQUES
Coach, Minnesota Wild. Born in LaSalle, Que., September 7, 1945.

The Minnesota Wild announced the signing of Jacques Lemaire as the club's first head coach on June 19, 2000. In 2002-03, he led Minnesota into the playoffs after just three seasons and all the way to the Western Conference Final. He also won the Jack Adams Award as coach of the year. Prior to joining the Wild, Lemaire had spent parts of the previous two seasons as a senior consultant to the general manager for the Montreal Canadiens, the franchise with which he captured eight Stanley Cup championships as a player.

Lemaire spent five seasons behind the New Jersey Devils bench and compiled a 199-122-57 mark. In 1994-95, he coached the Devils to their first Stanley Cup championship. In his first season with the team (1993-94), he was awarded the Jack Adams Award for the first time.

Lemaire began his NHL coaching career with the Montreal Canadiens in 1983-84. He stepped aside as head coach following the 1984-85 campaign and moved to the front office where he held the position of assistant to the managing director. In that role, Lemaire played a part in Montreal's Stanley Cup championships of 1986 and 1993.

Lemaire spent his entire NHL playing career with Montreal from 1967 to 1979 winning the Stanley Cup eight times. He then began his coaching career in Switzerland where he served as player/coach of the Sierre club. He returned to North America in 1981 and was named the first head coach of the Quebec Major Junior Hockey League's expansion Longueuil Chevaliers. In his only season at the helm (1982-83), Lemaire guided the team to the QMJHL finals.

Coaching Record

Season	Team	Games	Regular Season W	L	T	Games	Playoffs W	L
1979-80	Sierre (Switzerland)				UNAVAILABLE			
1980-81	Sierre (Switzerland)				UNAVAILABLE			
1982-83	Longueuil (QMJHL)	70	37	29	4	15	9	6
1983-84	**Montreal (NHL)**	17	7	10	0	15	9	6
1984-85	**Montreal (NHL)**	80	41	27	12	12	6	6
1993-94	**New Jersey (NHL)**	84	47	25	12	20	11	9
1994-95	**New Jersey (NHL)**	48	22	18	8	20	16	4*
1995-96	**New Jersey (NHL)**	82	37	33	12	....	....	....
1996-97	**New Jersey (NHL)**	82	45	23	14	10	5	5
1997-98	**New Jersey (NHL)**	82	48	23	11	6	2	4
2000-01	**Minnesota (NHL)**	82	25	44	13	....	....	....
2001-02	**Minnesota (NHL)**	82	26	44	12	....	....	....
2002-03	**Minnesota (NHL)**	82	42	30	10	18	8	10
2003-04	**Minnesota (NHL)**	82	30	32	20	....	....	....
2004-05	**Minnesota (NHL)**				Season Cancelled			
	NHL Totals	803	370	309	124	101	57	44

* Stanley Cup win.

Joining the Wild from the Ottawa Senators, Todd White has reached the 20-goal plateau during each of his two full NHL seasons.

Club Records

Team

(Figures in brackets for season records are games played.)

Most Points	95	2002-03 (82)
Most Wins	42	2002-03 (82)
Most Ties	20	2003-04 (82)
Most Losses	39	2000-01 (82)
Most Goals	198	2002-03 (82)
Most Goals Against	238	2001-02 (82)
Fewest Points	68	2000-01 (82)
Fewest Wins	25	2000-01 (82)
Fewest Ties	10	2002-03 (82)
Fewest Losses	29	2002-03 (82), 2003-04 (82)
Fewest Goals	168	2000-01 (82)
Fewest Goals Against	178	2002-03 (82)

Longest Winning Streak

Overall	3	Twelve times
Home	5	Feb. 23-Mar. 23/03
Away	2	Eleven times

Longest Undefeated Streak

Overall	9	Dec. 13-30/03 (4 wins, 5 ties)
Home	9	Dec. 13/00-Jan. 10/01 (5 wins, 4 ties)
Away	7	Dec. 6-30/03 (2 wins, 5 ties)

Longest Losing Streak

Overall	5	Mar. 11-19/01, Jan. 28-Feb. 8/02, Mar. 29-Apr. 5/02
Home	4	Oct. 29-Nov. 15/00
Away	5	Three times

Longest Winless Streak

Overall	12	Mar. 11-Apr. 4/01 (9 losses, 3 ties)
Home	8	Feb. 26-Mar. 28/01 (5 losses, 3 ties)
Away	12	Dec. 18/03-Jan. 31/04 (5 losses, 7 ties)

Most Shutouts, Season	7	2003-04 (82)
Most PIM, Season	1,209	2001-02 (82)
Most Goals, Game	8	Mar. 25/04 (Min. 8 at Chi. 2)

Individual

Most Seasons	4	Many players
Most Games	323	Antti Laaksonen
Most Goals, Career	96	Marian Gaborik
Most Assists, Career	112	Marian Gaborik
Most Points, Career	208	Marian Gaborik (96G, 112A)
Most PIM, Career	698	Matt Johnson
Most Shutouts, Career	14	Dwayne Roloson
Longest Consecutive Games Streak	288	Antti Laaksonen (Oct. 6/00-Dec. 29/03)
Most Goals, Season	30	Marian Gaborik (2001-02, 2002-03)
Most Assists, Season	48	Andrew Brunette (2001-02)
Most Points, Season	69	Andrew Brunette (2001-02; 21G, 48A)
Most PIM, Season	201	Matt Johnson (2002-03)

Most Points, Defenseman, Season	34	Lubomir Sekeras (2000-01; 11G, 23A)
Most Points, Center, Season	48	Cliff Ronning (2002-03; 17G, 31A)
Most Points, Right Wing, Season	67	Marian Gaborik (2001-02; 30G, 37A)
Most Points, Left Wing, Season	69	Andrew Brunette (2001-02; 21G, 48A)
Most Points, Rookie, Season	36	Marian Gaborik (2000-01; 18G, 18A)
Most Shutouts, Season	5	Dwayne Roloson (2001-02, 2003-04)
Most Goals, Game	3	Antti Laaksonen (Nov. 26/00), Marian Gaborik (Seven times)
Most Assists, Game	4	Andrew Brunette (Mar. 10/02), Marian Gaborik (Oct. 26/02) Pascal Dupuis (Mar. 25/04)
Most Points, Game	6	Marian Gaborik (Oct. 26/02; 2G, 4A)

General Managers' History

Doug Risebrough, 2000-01 to date.

Coaching History

Jacques Lemaire, 2000-01 to date.

Captains' History

Sean O'Donnell, Scott Pellerin, Wes Walz, Brad Bombardir, Darby Hendrickson, 2000-01; Jim Dowd, Filip Kuba, Brad Brown, Andrew Brunette, 2001-02; Brad Bombardir, Matt Johnson, Sergei Zholtok, 2002-03; Brad Brown, Andrew Brunette, Richard Park, Brad Bombardir, Jim Dowd, 2003-04.

All-time Record vs. Other Clubs

Regular Season

	At Home								On Road								Total							
	GP	W	L	T	OL	GF	GA	PTS	GP	W	L	T	OL	GF	GA	PTS	GP	W	L	T	OL	GF	GA	PTS
Anaheim	8	3	2	2	1	13	14	9	8	3	4	0	1	17	19	7	16	6	6	2	2	30	33	16
Atlanta	3	2	1	0	0	8	5	5	2	2	0	0	0	10	6	4	5	4	1	0	0	18	11	9
Boston	2	2	0	0	0	7	2	4	3	3	0	0	0	13	4	6	5	5	0	0	0	20	6	10
Buffalo	3	1	2	0	0	4	7	2	3	2	1	0	0	8	7	4	6	3	3	0	0	12	14	6
Calgary	11	5	4	1	1	24	20	12	10	2	5	3	0	21	23	7	21	7	9	4	1	45	43	19
Carolina	4	1	1	2	0	9	12	4	2	0	2	0	0	0	3	0	6	1	3	2	0	9	15	4
Chicago	8	6	2	0	0	28	20	12	8	4	3	1	0	25	17	9	16	10	5	1	0	53	37	21
Colorado	10	3	5	1	1	21	36	8	11	1	8	2	0	22	36	4	21	4	13	3	1	43	72	12
Columbus	8	6	2	0	0	25	16	12	7	1	4	1	1	7	19	4	15	7	6	1	1	32	35	16
Dallas	8	4	4	0	0	23	19	8	8	3	4	1	0	18	27	7	16	7	8	1	0	41	46	15
Detroit	8	2	3	2	1	18	21	7	8	2	5	1	0	20	32	5	16	4	8	3	1	38	53	12
Edmonton	10	2	6	1	1	22	29	6	11	2	4	3	2	14	24	9	21	4	10	4	3	36	53	15
Florida	3	2	0	1	0	10	1	5	3	2	1	0	0	8	6	4	6	4	1	1	0	18	7	9
Los Angeles	8	1	4	3	0	13	21	5	8	4	2	2	0	21	17	10	16	5	6	5	0	34	38	15
Montreal	2	1	0	0	1	6	5	3	3	1	1	1	0	8	9	3	5	2	1	1	1	14	14	6
Nashville	8	3	3	2	0	20	18	9	8	1	5	2	0	11	21	4	16	4	7	5	0	31	39	13
New Jersey	3	1	1	1	0	7	8	3	3	0	2	1	0	8	13	1	6	1	3	2	0	15	21	4
NY Islanders	3	2	1	0	0	9	9	4	3	1	2	0	0	6	6	2	6	3	3	0	0	15	15	6
NY Rangers	4	1	2	0	1	11	13	3	3	1	2	0	0	7	10	2	7	2	4	0	1	18	23	5
Ottawa	3	1	0	1	1	10	8	4	2	1	1	0	0	4	2	5	5	2	1	1	1	14	12	6
Philadelphia	2	1	0	1	0	5	3	3	4	1	3	0	0	3	11	2	6	2	3	1	0	8	14	5
Phoenix	8	2	3	2	1	15	17	7	8	2	4	1	1	16	23	6	16	4	7	3	2	31	40	13
Pittsburgh	3	2	0	1	0	9	5	5	3	2	1	0	0	12	6	4	6	4	1	1	0	21	11	9
St. Louis	8	3	1	2	2	19	13	10	8	2	3	3	0	11	15	7	16	5	4	5	2	30	28	17
San Jose	8	4	3	1	0	19	17	9	8	3	4	1	0	14	21	7	16	7	7	2	0	33	38	16
Tampa Bay	3	3	0	0	0	13	8	6	3	1	2	0	0	9	8	3	6	4	1	1	0	22	16	9
Toronto	1	0	1	0	0	0	1	0	3	2	0	0	0	3	11	4	4	0	4	0	0	3	12	0
Vancouver	11	5	4	2	0	27	27	12	10	3	2	3	2	26	28	11	21	8	6	5	2	53	55	23
Washington	3	3	0	0	0	6	1	6	3	1	2	0	0	6	7	2	6	4	2	0	0	12	8	8
Totals	**164**	**72**	**53**	**28**	**11**	**401**	**376**	**183**	**164**	**51**	**79**	**27**	**7**	**348**	**433**	**136**	**328**	**123**	**132**	**55**	**18**	**749**	**809**	**319**

Playoffs

	Series	W	L	GP	W	L	T	GF	GA	Last Mtg.	Rnd.	Result
Anaheim	1	0	1	4	0	4	0	1	9	2003	CF	L 0-4
Colorado	1	1	0	7	4	3	0	16	17	2003	CQF	W 4-3
Vancouver	1	1	0	7	4	3	0	26	17	2003	CSF	W 4-3
Totals	**3**	**2**	**1**	**18**	**8**	**10**	**0**	**43**	**43**			

Playoff Results 2005-2000

Year	Round	Opponent	Result	GF	GA
2003	CF	Anaheim	L 0-4	1	9
	CSF	Vancouver	W 4-3	26	17
	CQF	Colorado	W 4-3	16	17

Abbreviations: Round: CF – conference final; **CSF** – conference semi-final; **CQF** – conference quarter-final.

Key Off-Season Signings/Acquisitions

2004

July 8 • Signed C **Brian Rolston**.

Sept. 14 • Re-signed D **Nick Schultz**.

2005

July 28 • Signed 2003 2nd-round pick (56th overall) C **Patrick O'Sullivan**.

29 • Re-signed RW **Alexandre Daigle**.

30 • Obtained C **Todd White** from Ottawa for a 2005 4th-round pick.

30 • Used to the 4th overall selection in the 2005 Entry Draft to select LW **Benoit Pouliot** (Sudbury, OHL).

Aug. 1 • Signed LW **Andrei Nazarov**.

3 • Re-signed C **Marc Chouinard** and G **Manny Fernandez**.

9 • Re-signed D **Willie Mitchell** and LW **Pierre-Marc Bouchard**.

10 • Re-signed D **Andrei Zyuzin**.

15 • Signed D **Daniel Tjarnqvist**.

19 • Re-signed C **Rickard Wallin**.

Entry Draft
Selections 2005-2000

2005
Pick
4	Benoit Pouliot
57	Matt Kassian
65	Kristofer Westblom
110	Kyle Bailey
122	Morten Madsen
129	Anthony Aiello
199	Riley Emmerson

2004
Pick
12	A.J. Thelen
42	Roman Voloshenko
78	Peter Olvecky
79	Clayton Stoner
111	Ryan Jones
114	Patrick Bordeleau
117	Julien Sprunger
161	Jean-Claude Sawyer
175	Aaron Boogaard
195	Jean-Michel Rizk
206	Anton Khudobin
272	Kyle Wilson

2003
Pick
20	Brent Burns
56	Patrick O'Sullivan
78	Danny Irmen
157	Marcin Kolusz
187	Miroslav Kopriva
207	Grigory Misharin
219	Adam Courchaine
251	Mathieu Melanson
281	Jean-Michel Bolduc

2002
Pick
8	Pierre-Marc Bouchard
38	Josh Harding
72	Mike Erickson
73	Barry Brust
155	Armands Berzins
175	Matt Foy
204	Niklas Eckerblom
237	Christoph Brandner
268	Mikhail Tyulyapkin
269	Mika Hannula

2001
Pick
6	Mikko Koivu
36	Kyle Wanvig
74	Chris Heid
93	Stephane Veilleux
103	Tony Virta
202	Derek Boogaard
239	Jake Riddle

2000
Pick
3	Marian Gaborik
33	Nick Schultz
99	Marc Cavosie
132	Maxim Sushinsky
170	Erik Reitz
199	Brian Passmore
214	Peter Bartos
232	Lubomir Sekeras
255	Eric Johansson

Club Directory

Xcel Energy Center

Minnesota Wild
317 Washington Street
St. Paul, MN 55102
Phone **651/602-6000**
FAX 651/293-9574
Tickets 651/222-9453
www.wild.com
Capacity: 18,064

Founded	2000-01
Home Ice	Xcel Energy Center (18,064)
Practice Facility	Parade Ice Garden
Television	KSTC (Ch. 45) and FSN North (cable)
Radio	WCCO (830 AM)
Colors	Red, Green, Gold, Wheat

Executive Management
Chairman	Bob Naegele, Jr.
Vice Chairman	Jac Sperling
President/General Manager	Doug Risebrough
Executive Vice President, Chief Financial Officer	Pamela Wheelock
Executive Vice President	Matt Majka
Vice President, Sales and Service	Steve Griggs
Vice President/G.M., RiverCentre	Jim Ibister
Vice President/G.M., Xcel Energy Center	Jack Larson
Vice President, Finance and Corporate Controller	Mike Nealy
Vice President, Administration	Mike Reeves
Vice President, Communications and Broadcasting	Bill Robertson

Hockey Operations
Assistant General Manager/Hockey Operations	Tom Lynn
Assistant General Manager/Player Personnel	Tom Thompson
Head Coach	Jacques Lemaire
Assistant Coaches	Mike Ramsey, Mario Tremblay
Goaltending Coach	Bob Mason
Strength and Conditioning Coach	Kirk Olson
Coordinator of Amateur Scouting	Guy Lapointe
Coordinator of Player Development	Barry MacKenzie
Head Athletic Therapist	Don Fuller
Head Equipment Manager	Tony DaCosta
Equipment Manager	Brent Proulx
Director of Hockey Operations	Michael Gibbons
Assistant Athletic Trainer	Mike Vogt
Assistant Equipment Managers	Brent Proulx, Matt Benz
Scouts	Marc Chamard, Paul Charles, Frank Effinger, Branislav Gaborik, Christopher Hamel, Ken Hoodikoff, Jiri Koluch, Doug Mosher, Darryl Porter, Glen Sonmor, Thomas Steen, Matti Vaisanen, Ernie Vargas
Hockey Operations Administrator	Cindy Sweiger
Nutritionist	Carrie Peterson
Executive Assistant, Hockey Operations	Laura Kinzel

Medical
Medical Director	Dr. Sheldon Burns
Orthopedic Surgeon	Dr. Joel Boyd

Communications and Broadcasting
Communications Manager	Aaron Sickman
Media Relations Coordinator	Wayne Carlson
Media Relations Intern	Andy Oberle
Broadcast Coordinator	Maggie Kukar
Radio Production Coordinator	Kevin Falness
Web Content Writer	Glen Andresen
Xcel Energy Center Public Relations Manager	Kathy Ross
Administrative Assistant	Deb Hanson

President and General Manager

RISEBROUGH, DOUG
President/General Manager, Minnesota Wild.
Born in Guelph, Ont., January 29, 1954.

Doug Risebrough was hired as the first executive vice president and general manager of the Minnesota Wild on September 2, 1999. He is responsible for the club's overall hockey operations. His efforts to build a winner through the draft has been exemplified by the success of Marian Gaborik, the club's first-round choice in 2000. The Wild qualified for the playoffs after just three seasons, going all the way to the 2003 Western Conference Final.

After ending his 13-year NHL playing career with the Flames in 1987, Risebrough was named as assistant coach with Calgary and joined Terry Crisp behind the bench. Risebrough was appointed head coach of the Flames on May 18, 1990 and on May 16, 1991, he also assumed the role of general manager. Late in the 1991-92 campaign he directed his energies full-time to general manager, handing the coaching responsibilities over to Guy Charron for the balance of the season. Risebrough served as g.m. in Calgary through the start of the 1995-96 season. He was vice president of hockey operations for the Edmonton Oilers from 1996 to 1999.

Risebrough was Montreal's first selection, seventh overall, in the 1974 Amateur Draft. During his nine years with the Canadiens, he helped his club to four consecutive Stanley Cup championships between 1976 and 1979. He joined the Flames prior to the start of the club's 1982 training camp. During his NHL career, his clubs have won five Stanley Cup titles (1976-1979 as a player and 1989 as an assistant coach with Calgary) and two Presidents' Trophies (1987-88 and 1988-89 as an assistant coach).

NHL Coaching Record

Season	Team	Games	Regular Season W	L	T	Playoffs Games	W	L
1990-91	Calgary	80	46	26	8	7	3	4
1991-92	Calgary	64	25	30	9	....	....	....
	NHL Totals	**144**	**71**	**56**	**17**	**7**	**3**	**4**

Patrick O'Sullivan will have a chance to make the Wild this year after four stellar seasons with the Mississauga IceDogs of the Ontario Hockey League.

Canadiens captain Saku Koivu.

Montreal Canadiens

Year-by-Year Record

Season	GP	Home W	L	T	OL	Road W	L	T	OL	Overall W	L	T	OL	GF	GA	Pts.	Finished	Playoff Result
2004-05																		
2003-04	82	23	13	4	1	18	17	3	3	41	30	7	4	208	192	93	4th, Northeast Div.	Lost Conf. Semi-Final
2002-03	82	16	16	5	4	14	19	3	5	30	35	8	9	206	234	77	4th, Northeast Div.	Out of Playoffs
2001-02	82	21	13	6	1	15	18	6	2	36	31	12	3	207	209	87	4th, Northeast Div.	Lost Conf. Semi-Final
2000-01	82	15	20	4	2	13	20	4	4	28	40	8	6	206	232	70	5th, Northeast Div.	Out of Playoffs
1999-2000	82	18	17	5	1	17	17	4	3	35	34	9	4	196	194	83	4th, Northeast Div.	Out of Playoffs
1998-99	82	21	15	5	....	11	24	6	....	32	39	11	....	184	209	75	5th, Northeast Div.	Out of Playoffs
1997-98	82	15	17	9	....	22	15	4	....	37	32	13	....	235	208	87	4th, Northeast Div.	Lost Conf. Semi-Final
1996-97	82	17	17	7	....	14	19	8	....	31	36	15	....	249	276	77	4th, Northeast Div.	Lost Conf. Quarter-Final
1995-96	82	23	12	6	....	17	20	4	....	40	32	10	....	265	248	90	3rd, Northeast Div.	Lost Conf. Quarter-Final
1994-95	48	15	5	4	....	3	18	3	....	18	23	7	....	125	148	43	6th, Northeast Div.	Out of Playoffs
1993-94	84	26	12	4	....	15	17	10	....	41	29	14	....	283	248	96	3rd, Northeast Div.	Lost Conf. Quarter-Final
1992-93	84	27	13	2	....	21	17	4	....	48	30	6	....	326	280	102	3rd, **Adams Div.**	**Won Stanley Cup**
1991-92	80	27	13	0	....	14	20	6	....	41	28	11	....	267	207	93	1st, Adams Div.	Lost Div. Final
1990-91	80	23	12	5	....	16	18	6	....	39	30	11	....	273	249	89	2nd, Adams Div.	Lost Div. Final
1989-90	80	26	8	6	....	15	20	5	....	41	28	11	....	288	234	93	3rd, Adams Div.	Lost Div. Final
1988-89	80	30	6	4	....	23	12	5	....	53	18	9	....	315	218	115	1st, Adams Div.	Lost Final
1987-88	80	26	8	6	....	19	14	7	....	45	22	13	....	298	238	103	1st, Adams Div.	Lost Div. Final
1986-87	80	27	9	4	....	14	20	6	....	41	29	10	....	277	241	92	2nd, Adams Div.	Lost Conf. Championship
1985-86	80	25	11	4	....	15	22	3	....	40	33	7	....	330	280	87	2nd, **Adams Div.**	**Won Stanley Cup**
1984-85	80	24	10	6	....	17	17	6	....	41	27	12	....	309	262	94	1st, Adams Div.	Lost Div. Final
1983-84	80	19	19	2	....	16	21	3	....	35	40	5	....	286	295	75	4th, Adams Div.	Lost Conf. Championship
1982-83	80	25	6	9	....	17	18	5	....	42	24	14	....	350	286	98	2nd, Adams Div.	Lost Div. Semi-Final
1981-82	80	25	6	9	....	21	11	8	....	46	17	17	....	360	223	109	1st, Adams Div.	Lost Div. Semi-Final
1980-81	80	31	7	2	....	14	15	11	....	45	22	13	....	332	232	103	1st, Norris Div.	Lost Prelim. Round
1979-80	80	30	7	3	....	17	13	10	....	47	20	13	....	328	240	107	1st, Norris Div.	Lost Quarter-Final
1978-79	80	29	6	5	....	23	11	6	....	52	17	11	....	337	204	115	1st, **Norris Div.**	**Won Stanley Cup**
1977-78	80	32	4	4	....	27	6	7	....	59	10	11	....	359	183	129	1st, **Norris Div.**	**Won Stanley Cup**
1976-77	80	33	1	6	....	27	7	6	....	60	8	12	....	387	171	132	1st, **Norris Div.**	**Won Stanley Cup**
1975-76	80	32	3	5	....	26	8	6	....	58	11	11	....	337	174	127	1st, **Norris Div.**	**Won Stanley Cup**
1974-75	80	27	8	5	....	20	6	14	....	47	14	19	....	374	225	113	1st, Norris Div.	Lost Semi-Final
1973-74	78	24	12	3	....	21	12	6	....	45	24	9	....	293	240	99	2nd, East Div.	Lost Quarter-inal
1972-73	78	29	4	6	....	23	6	10	....	52	10	16	....	329	184	120	**1st, East Div.**	**Won Stanley Cup**
1971-72	78	29	3	7	....	17	13	9	....	46	16	16	....	307	205	108	3rd, East Div.	Lost Quarter-Final
1970-71	78	29	7	3	....	13	16	10	....	42	23	13	....	291	216	97	3rd, **East Div.**	**Won Stanley Cup**
1969-70	76	21	9	8	....	17	13	8	....	38	22	16	....	244	201	92	5th, East Div.	Out of Playoffs
1968-69	76	26	7	5	....	20	12	6	....	46	19	11	....	271	202	103	1st, **East Div.**	**Won Stanley Cup**
1967-68	74	26	5	6	....	16	17	4	....	42	22	10	....	236	167	94	1st, **East Div.**	**Won Stanley Cup**
1966-67	70	19	9	7	....	13	16	6	....	32	25	13	....	202	188	77	2nd,	Lost Final
1965-66	70	23	11	1	....	18	10	7	....	41	21	8	....	239	173	90	1st,	**Won Stanley Cup**
1964-65	70	20	8	7	....	16	15	4	....	36	23	11	....	211	185	83	2nd,	**Won Stanley Cup**
1963-64	70	22	7	6	....	14	14	7	....	36	21	13	....	209	167	85	1st,	Lost Semi-Final
1962-63	70	15	10	10	....	13	9	13	....	28	19	23	....	225	183	79	3rd,	Lost Semi-Final
1961-62	70	26	2	7	....	16	12	7	....	42	14	14	....	259	166	98	1st,	Lost Semi-Final
1960-61	70	24	6	5	....	17	13	5	....	41	19	10	....	254	188	92	1st,	Lost Semi-Final
1959-60	70	23	4	8	....	17	14	4	....	40	18	12	....	255	178	92	1st,	**Won Stanley Cup**
1958-59	70	21	8	6	....	18	10	7	....	39	18	13	....	258	158	91	1st,	**Won Stanley Cup**
1957-58	70	23	8	4	....	20	9	6	....	43	17	10	....	250	158	96	1st,	**Won Stanley Cup**
1956-57	70	23	6	6	....	12	17	6	....	35	23	12	....	210	155	82	2nd,	**Won Stanley Cup**
1955-56	70	29	5	1	....	16	10	9	....	45	15	10	....	222	131	100	1st,	**Won Stanley Cup**
1954-55	70	26	5	4	....	15	13	7	....	41	18	11	....	228	157	93	2nd,	Lost Final
1952-53	70	18	12	5	....	10	11	14	....	28	23	19	....	155	148	75	2nd,	**Won Stanley Cup**
1951-52	70	22	8	5	....	12	18	5	....	34	26	10	....	195	164	78	2nd,	Lost Final
1950-51	70	17	10	8	....	8	20	7	....	25	30	15	....	173	184	65	3rd,	Lost Final
1949-50	70	17	8	10	....	12	14	9	....	29	22	19	....	172	150	77	2nd,	Lost Semi-Final
1948-49	60	19	7	4	....	9	15	6	....	28	23	9	....	152	126	65	3rd,	Lost Semi-Final
1947-48	60	13	13	4	....	7	16	7	....	20	29	11	....	147	169	51	5th,	Out of Playoffs
1946-47	60	19	6	5	....	15	10	5	....	34	16	10	....	189	138	78	1st,	Lost Final
1945-46	50	16	6	3	....	12	11	2	....	28	17	5	....	172	134	61	1st,	**Won Stanley Cup**
1944-45	50	21	2	2	....	17	6	2	....	38	8	4	....	228	121	80	1st,	Lost Semi-Final
1943-44	50	22	0	3	....	16	5	4	....	38	5	7	....	234	109	83	1st,	**Won Stanley Cup**
1942-43	50	14	4	7	....	5	15	5	....	19	19	12	....	181	191	50	4th,	Lost Semi-Final
1941-42	48	12	10	2	....	6	17	1	....	18	27	3	....	134	173	39	6th,	Lost Quarter-Final
1940-41	48	11	9	4	....	5	17	2	....	16	26	6	....	121	147	38	6th,	Lost Quarter-Final
1939-40	48	5	14	5	....	5	19	0	....	10	33	5	....	90	167	25	7th,	Out of Playoffs
1938-39	48	8	11	5	....	7	13	4	....	15	24	9	....	115	146	39	6th,	Lost Quarter-Final
1937-38	48	13	4	7	....	5	13	6	....	18	17	13	....	123	128	49	3rd, Cdn. Div.	Lost Quarter-Final
1936-37	48	16	8	0	....	8	10	6	....	24	18	6	....	115	111	54	1st, Cdn. Div.	Lost Semi-Final
1935-36	48	5	11	8	....	6	15	3	....	11	26	11	....	82	123	33	4th, Cdn. Div.	Out of Playoffs
1934-35	48	11	11	2	....	8	12	4	....	19	23	6	....	110	145	44	3rd, Cdn. Div.	Lost Quarter-Final
1933-34	48	16	6	2	....	6	14	4	....	22	20	6	....	99	101	50	2nd, Cdn. Div.	Lost Quarter-Final
1932-33	48	15	5	4	....	3	20	1	....	18	25	5	....	92	115	41	3rd, Cdn. Div.	Lost Quarter-Final
1931-32	48	18	3	3	....	7	13	4	....	25	16	7	....	128	111	57	1st, Cdn. Div.	Lost Semi-Final
1930-31	44	15	3	4	....	11	7	4	....	26	10	8	....	129	89	60	1st, Cdn. Div.	**Won Stanley Cup**
1929-30	44	13	5	4	....	8	9	5	....	21	14	9	....	142	114	51	2nd, **Cdn. Div.**	**Won Stanley Cup**
1928-29	44	12	4	6	....	10	3	9	....	22	7	15	....	71	43	59	1st, Cdn. Div.	Lost Semi-Final
1927-28	44	12	7	3	....	14	4	4	....	26	11	7	....	116	48	59	1st, Cdn. Div.	Lost Semi-Final
1926-27	44	15	5	2	....	13	9	0	....	28	14	2	....	99	67	58	2nd, Cdn. Div.	Lost Semi-Final
1925-26	36	5	12	1	....	6	12	0	....	11	24	1	....	79	108	23	7th,	Out of Playoffs
1924-25	30	10	5	0	....	7	6	2	....	17	11	2	....	93	56	36	3rd,	Lost Final
1923-24	24	10	2	0	....	3	9	0	....	13	11	0	....	59	48	26	2nd,	**Won Stanley Cup**
1922-23	24	10	2	0	....	3	7	2	....	13	9	2	....	73	61	28	2nd,	Lost NHL Final
1921-22	24	8	3	1	....	4	8	0	....	12	11	1	....	88	94	25	3rd,	Out of Playoffs
1920-21	24	9	3	0	....	4	8	0	....	13	11	0	....	112	99	26	3rd and 2nd*	Out of Playoffs
1919-20	24	8	4	0	....	5	7	0	....	13	11	0	....	129	113	26	2nd and 3rd*	Out of Playoffs
1918-19	18	7	2	0	....	3	6	0	....	10	8	0	....	88	78	20	1st and 2nd*	Cup Final but no Decision
1917-18	22	8	3	0	....	5	6	0	....	13	9	0	....	115	84	26	1st and 3rd*	Lost NHL Final

* Season played in two halves with no combined standing at end.
From 1917-18 through 1925-26, NHL champions played against PCHA/WCHL champions for Stanley Cup.

2005-06 Schedule

Oct.					
Wed.	5	at Boston	Sat.	14	San Jose
Thu.	6	at NY Rangers	Mon.	16	Dallas
Sat.	8	at Toronto	Thu.	19	at Calgary
Tue.	11	Ottawa	Sat.	21	at Vancouver
Wed.	12	at Atlanta	Mon.	23	at Carolina
Sat.	15	Toronto	Wed.	25	at Philadelphia
Tue.	18	Boston	Thu.	26	at Ottawa
Sat.	22	NY Islanders	Sat.	28	at Toronto
Tue.	25	Philadelphia	Sat.	31	Carolina
Thu.	27	at Ottawa	**Feb.** Thu.	2	at Boston
Sat.	29	NY Rangers	Sat.	4	Boston*
Mon.	31	at NY Rangers	Sun.	5	Philadelphia*
Nov. Tue.	1	Florida	Tue.	7	Buffalo
Fri.	4	at Buffalo	Thu.	9	at Buffalo
Sat.	5	Buffalo	Sat.	11	Atlanta
Tue.	8	Tampa Bay	Tue.	28	at NY Islanders
Thu.	10	at Pittsburgh	**Mar.** Thu.	2	at Florida
Sat.	12	Toronto	Sat.	4	at Tampa Bay
Tue.	15	Florida	Mon.	6	at Philadelphia
Fri.	18	at New Jersey	Tue.	7	at Toronto
Sat.	19	Washington	Thu.	9	at Boston
Tue.	22	Atlanta	Sat.	11	NY Rangers
Fri.	25	at Buffalo	Mon.	13	Tampa Bay
Sat.	26	at Toronto	Thu.	16	Carolina
Tue.	29	at Ottawa	Sat.	18	Pittsburgh
Dec. Thu.	1	Buffalo	Mon.	20	at Washington
Sat.	3	Los Angeles	Tue.	21	at NY Islanders
Sat.	10	Anaheim	Thu.	23	Toronto
Tue.	13	Phoenix	Sat.	25	Toronto
Thu.	15	at Edmonton	Sun.	26	at Pittsburgh
Sat.	17	at Minnesota	Tue.	28	NY Islanders
Tue.	20	Ottawa	Thu.	30	Washington
Fri.	23	at Washington	**Apr.** Sat.	1	Boston
Mon.	26	at Atlanta	Tue.	4	Boston
Wed.	28	at Tampa Bay	Thu.	6	at Ottawa
Fri.	30	at Florida	Sat.	8	New Jersey
Sat.	31	at Carolina	Mon.	10	Ottawa
Jan. Tue.	3	Pittsburgh	Wed.	12	at Buffalo
Thu.	5	at New Jersey	Thu.	13	at Boston
Sat.	7	Ottawa*	Sat.	15	Buffalo
Wed.	11	at Colorado	Tue.	18	New Jersey

* Denotes afternoon game.

Franchise date: November 22, 1917

EASTERN CONFERENCE

NORTHEAST DIVISION

89th NHL Season

2005-06 Player Personnel

FORWARDS	HT	WT	S	Place of Birth	Date	2004-05 Club
BEGIN, Steve	5-11	195	L	Trois-Rivieres, Que.	6/14/78	Hamilton
BONK, Radek	6-3	220	L	Krnov, Czech.	1/9/76	Trinec-Zlin
BULIS, Jan	6-1	208	L	Pardubice, Czech.	3/18/78	Pardubice
DAGENAIS, Pierre	6-4	217	L	Blainville, Que.	3/4/78	Ajoie
DANDENAULT, Mathieu	6-0	200	R	Sherbrooke, Que.	2/3/76	Asiago
HOSSA, Marcel	6-2	215	L	Ilava, Czech.	10/12/81	Mora
KOIVU, Saku	5-10	181	L	Turku, Finland	11/23/74	TPS
KOVALEV, Alex	6-1	220	L	Togliatti, USSR	2/24/73	Kazan
RIBEIRO, Mike	6-0	177	L	Montreal, Que.	2/10/80	Blues
RYDER, Michael	6-1	196	R	St. John's, Nfld.	3/31/80	Leksand
SUNDSTROM, Niklas	6-0	191	L	Ornskoldsvik, Sweden	6/6/75	Milano
VANDERMEER, Peter	6-0	210	L	Carolina, Alta.	10/14/75	Grand Rapids
ZEDNIK, Richard	6-1	196	L	Bystrica, Czech.	1/6/76	Zvolen

DEFENSEMEN	HT	WT	S	Place of Birth	Date	2004-05 Club
BOUILLON, Francis	5-8	196	L	New York, NY	10/17/75	Leksand
HAINSEY, Ron	6-3	211	L	Bolton, CT	3/24/81	Hamilton
KOMISAREK, Mike	6-4	237	R	Islip Terrace, NY	1/19/82	Hamilton
MARKOV, Andrei	6-0	208	L	Voskresensk, USSR	12/20/78	Dynamo Moscow
RIVET, Craig	6-2	207	R	North Bay, Ont.	9/13/74	TPS
SOURAY, Sheldon	6-4	227	L	Elk Point, Alta.	7/13/76	Farjestad

GOALTENDERS	HT	WT	C	Place of Birth	Date	2004-05 Club
HUET, Cristobal	6-0	194	L	St. Martin D'Heres, France	9/3/75	Mannheim
THEODORE, Jose	5-11	182	R	Laval, Que.	9/13/76	Djurgarden

In the System and Recently Drafted

FORWARDS	HT	WT	S	Place of Birth	Date	2004-05 Club
ANGER, Niklas	6-1	185	L	Gavle, Sweden	7/31/77	Ambri-Sierre
AUBIN, Mathieu	6-2	190	R	Sorel, Que.	9/18/86	Lewiston
BONNEAU, Jimmy	6-3	224	L	Baie-Comeau, Que.	3/22/85	PEI
BUTURLIN, Alexander	5-11	182	L	Moscow, USSR	9/3/81	Togliatti
CHIPCHURA, Kyle	6-3	204	L	Westlock, Alta.	2/19/86	Prince Albert
D'AGOSTINI, Matt	5-11	170	R	Sault Ste. Marie, Ont.	10/23/86	Guelph
ENEQVIST, Johan	6-0	183	L	Nacka, Sweden	1/21/82	Hammarby
FERLAND, Jonathan	6-2	211	R	Quebec City, Que.	2/9/83	Hamilton
GRABOVSKY, Mikhail	5-11	181	L	Potsdam, East Germany	1/31/84	Nizhnekamsk-Yunost
HIGGINS, Christopher	5-11	192	L	Smithtown, NY	6/2/83	Hamilton
IVANANS, Raitis	6-3	220	L	Riga, Latvia	1/1/79	Hamilton
KOSTITSYN, Andrei	6-0	208	R	Novopolosk, USSR	2/3/85	Hamilton
KOSTITSYN, Sergei	5-11	180	L	Novopolotsk, USSR	3/20/87	Gomel
LAMBERT, Michael	6-2	200	L	Trois-Rivieres, Que.	3/10/84	Hamilton-Long Beach
LAPIERRE, Maxim	6-2	201	R	St. Leonard, Que.	3/29/85	PEI
LATENDRESSE, Guillaume	6-1	216	L	Ste-Catherine, Que.	5/24/87	Drummondville
LOCKE, Corey	5-9	175	L	Toronto, Ont.	5/8/84	Hamilton
MIKUS, Juraj	6-1	186	R	Skalica, Slovak.	2/22/87	Skalica
MILROY, Duncan	6-0	197	R	Edmonton, Alta.	2/8/83	Hamilton
PEREZHOGIN, Alexander	6-0	185	L	Ust-Kamenogorsk, USSR	8/10/83	Omsk
PLEKANEC, Tomas	5-10	200	L	Kladno, Czech.	10/31/82	Hamilton
SIDYAKIN, Andrei	5-11	169	L	Ufa, USSR	1/20/79	Ufa
STAAL, Kim	6-0	185	R	Herlev, Denmark	3/10/78	Malmo
STEWART, Greg	6-1	193	L	Kitchener, Ont.	5/21/86	Peterborough
STROM, Peter	6-0	178	R	Snotorp, Sweden	1/14/75	
THINEL, Marc-Andre	6-0	178	L	St-Jerome, Que.	3/24/81	Hamilton
UJCIK, Viktor	5-11	194	L	Jihlava, Czech.	5/24/72	Karpat
URQUHART, Cory	6-3	200	L	Halifax, N.S.	10/1/84	Hamilton-Long Beach
WYMAN, James	6-1	195	R	Edina, MN	2/27/86	Dartmouth

DEFENSEMEN	HT	WT	S	Place of Birth	Date	2004-05 Club
AITKEN, Johnathan	6-4	230	L	Edmonton, Alta.	5/24/78	Manitoba
ARCHER, Andrew	6-4	212	R	Calgary, Alta.	5/15/83	Hamilton
COTE, Jean-Philippe	6-2	213	L	Charlesbourg, Que.	4/22/82	Hamilton
DULAC-LEMELIN, Alex	6-3	190	R	Montreal, Que.	3/17/86	Baie-Comeau
GLEED, Jon	6-2	200	R	Milton, Ont.	1/3/84	Cornell
GUREN, Miloslav	6-2	215	L	Uherske Hradiste, Czech.	9/24/76	Novosibirsk
KORNEEV, Konstantin	5-11	176	L	Moscow, USSR	6/5/84	Kazan
KORPIKARI, Oskari	6-2	210	L	Oulu, Finland	4/5/84	Karpat
KRUCHININ, Andrei	5-11	187	L	Karaganda, USSR	5/18/78	Togliatti
LINHART, Tomas	6-2	209	L	Pardubice, Czech.	2/16/84	Pardubice-Hr. Kralove
MIKKOLA, Ilkka	6-0	189	L	Oulu, Finland	1/18/79	Karpat
O'BYRNE, Ryan	6-5	223	R	Victoria, B.C.	7/19/84	Cornell
PAQUET, Philippe	6-3	200	R	Quebec City, Que.	3/12/87	Salisbury
PAUL, Jeff	6-4	225	R	London, Ont.	3/1/78	Portland (AHL)
STREIT, Mark	5-11	198	L	Englisberg, Switz.	12/11/77	Zurich
VYDARENY, Rene	6-1	198	L	Bratislava, Czech.	5/6/81	Bratislava
YEMELIN, Alexei	6-0	187	L	Kuibyshev, USSR	4/25/86	Togliatti

GOALTENDERS	HT	WT	C	Place of Birth	Date	2004-05 Club
DANIS, Yann	6-0	185	L	Lafontaine, Que.	6/21/81	Hamilton
HALAK, Jaroslav	5-11	171	L	Bratislava, Slovakia	5/13/85	Lewiston
HEINO-LINDBERG, Chris	6-0	163	R	Helsingborg, Sweden	1/29/85	Hammarby
LACASSE, Loic	6-2	175	L	Granby, Que.	4/23/86	Baie-Comeau
MICHAUD, Olivier	5-11	179	L	Beloeil, Que.	9/14/83	Long Beach
PRICE, Carey	6-2	222	L	Vancouver, B.C.	8/16/87	Tri-City
PUURULA, Joni	5-11	180	L	Kokkola, Finland	8/4/82	Ufa-HPK
TARASOV, Vadim	5-11	187	L	Ust-Kamenogorsk, USSR	12/31/76	Novokuznetsk

Coaching History

Jack Laviolette, 1909-10; Adolphe Lecours, 1910-11; Napoleon Dorval, 1911-12, 1912-13; Jimmy Gardner, 1913-14, 1914-15; Newsy Lalonde, 1915-16 to 1920-21; Newsy Lalonde and Léo Dandurand, 1921-22; Léo Dandurand, 1922-23 to 1925-26; Cecil Hart, 1926-27 to 1931-32; Newsy Lalonde, 1932-33, 1933-34; Newsy Lalonde and Léo Dandurand, 1934-35; Sylvio Mantha, 1935-36; Cecil Hart, 1936-37, 1937-38; Cecil Hart and Jules Dugal, 1938-39; Babe Siebert, 1939*; Pit Lepine, 1939-40; Dick Irvin 1940-41 to 1954-55; Toe Blake, 1955-56 to 1967-68; Claude Ruel, 1968-69, 1969-70; Claude Ruel and Al MacNeil 1970-71; Scotty Bowman, 1971-72 to 1978-79; Bernie Geoffrion and Claude Ruel, 1979-80; Claude Ruel, 1980-81; Bob Berry, 1981-82, 1982-83; Bob Berry and Jacques Lemaire, 1983-84; Jacques Lemaire, 1984-85; Jean Perron, 1985-86 to 1987-88; Pat Burns, 1988-89 to 1991-92; Jacques Demers, 1992-93 to 1994-95; Jacques Demers and Mario Tremblay, 1995-96; Mario Tremblay, 1996-97; Alain Vigneault, 1997-98 to 1999-2000; Alain Vigneault and Michel Therrien, 2000-01; Michel Therrien, 2001-02; Michel Therrien and Claude Julien, 2002-03; Claude Julien, 2003-04 to date.

* Named coach in summer but died before 1939-40 season began.

Vice President and General Manager

GAINEY, BOB
Executive Vice President/General Manager, Montreal Canadiens.
Born in Peterborough, Ont., December 13, 1953.

On June 2, 2003, the Montreal Canadiens announced the appointment of Bob Gainey as executive vice president and general manager, effective July 1, 2003. As a player in Montreal, Gainey brought many elements to the Canadiens over his 16-year career.

Described as the world's best all-around player by legendary Soviet national team coach Viktor Tikhonov, Gainey was a tenacious competitor, relentless checker and a respected team leader. His presence helped the Canadiens win the Stanley Cup five times in the decade between 1976 and 1986. He won the Conn Smythe Trophy as playoff MVP in 1979 and was a four-time winner of the Selke Trophy as the NHL's best defensive forward. Gainey was captain of the Canadiens from 1981 until his retirement in 1989. He was elected to the Hockey Hall of Fame in 1992.

Gainey spent a year as a player-coach of the Epinal franchise in France before becoming head coach of the Minnesota North Stars in 1990-91. He was given the g.m.'s job in 1992 and was in the dual role when the Stars relocated to Dallas in 1993. Gainey stepped down as coach on January 8, 1996 to focus solely on the duties of general manager and built a powerhouse club that won five straight division titles from 1996-97 to 2000-01, the Presidents' Trophy in 1998 and 1999, and the Stanley Cup in 1999.

NHL Coaching Record

			Regular Season				Playoffs		
Season	Team	Games	W	L	T		Games	W	L
1990-91	Minnesota	80	27	39	14		23	14	9
1991-92	Minnesota	80	32	42	6		7	3	4
1992-93	Minnesota	84	36	38	10		....	....	....
1993-94	Dallas	84	42	29	13		9	5	4
1994-95	Dallas	48	17	23	8		5	1	4
1995-96	Dallas	39	11	19	9		....	....	....
	NHL Totals	**415**	**165**	**190**	**60**		**44**	**23**	**21**

General Managers' History

Jack Laviolette and Joseph Cattarinich, 1909-1910; George Kennedy, 1910-11 to 1920-21; Leo Dandurand, 1921-22 to 1934-35; Ernest Savard, 1935-36; Cecil Hart, 1936-37 to 1938-39; Jules Dugal, 1939-40; Tom P. Gorman, 1940-41 to 1945-46; Frank J. Selke, 1946-47 to 1963-64; Sam Pollock, 1964-65 to 1977-78; Irving Grundman, 1978-79 to 1982-83; Serge Savard, 1983-84 to 1994-95; Serge Savard and Réjean Houle, 1995-96; Réjean Houle, 1996-97 to 1999-2000; Réjean Houle and Andre Savard, 2000-01; Andre Savard, 2001-02, 2002-03; Bob Gainey, 2003-04 to date.

Captains' History

Jack Laviolette, 1909-10; Newsy Lalonde, 1910-11; Jack Laviolette, 1911-12; Newsy Lalonde, 1912-13; Jimmy Gardner, 1913-14, 1914-15; Howard McNamara, 1915-16; Newsy Lalonde, 1916-17 to 1921-22; Sprague Cleghorn, 1922-23 to 1924-25; Bill Coutu, 1925-26; Sylvio Mantha, 1926-27 to 1931-32; George Hainsworth, 1932-33; Sylvio Mantha, 1933-34 to 1935-36; Babe Siebert, 1936-37 to 1938-39; Walt Buswell, 1939-40; Toe Blake, 1940-41 to 1946-47; Toe Blake and Bill Durnan, 1947-48; Butch Bouchard, 1948-49 to 1955-56; Maurice Richard, 1956-57 to 1959-60; Doug Harvey, 1960-61; Jean Béliveau, 1961-62 to 1970-71; Henri Richard, 1971-72 to 1974-75; Yvan Cournoyer, 1975-76 to 1978-79; Serge Savard, 1979-80, 1980-81; Bob Gainey, 1981-82 to 1988-89; Guy Carbonneau and Chris Chelios (co-captains), 1989-90; Guy Carbonneau, 1990-91 to 1993-94; Kirk Muller and Mike Keane, 1994-95; Mike Keane and Pierre Turgeon, 1995-96; Pierre Turgeon and Vincent Damphousse, 1996-97; Vincent Damphousse, 1997-98, 1998-99; Saku Koivu, 1999-2000 to date.

Club Records

Team

(Figures in brackets for season records are games played; records for fewest points, wins, ties, losses, goals, goals against are for 70 or more games)

Most Points *132 1976-77 (80)
Most Wins 60 1976-77 (80)
Most Ties 23 1962-63 (70)
Most Losses 40 1983-84 (80), 2000-01 (82)
Most Goals 387 1976-77 (80)
Most Goals Against 295 1983-84 (80)
Fewest Points 65 1950-51 (70)
Fewest Wins 25 1950-51 (70)
Fewest Ties 5 1983-84 (80)
Fewest Losses *8 1976-77 (80)
Fewest Goals 155 1952-53 (70)
Fewest Goals Against *131 1955-56 (70)
Longest Winning Streak
Overall .... 12 Jan. 6-Feb. 3/68
Home .... 13 Nov. 2/43-Jan. 8/44, Jan. 30-Mar. 26/77
Away .... 8 Dec. 18/77-Jan. 18/78, Jan. 21-Feb. 21/82
Longest Undefeated Streak
Overall .... 28 Dec. 18/77-Feb. 23/78 (23 wins, 5 ties)
Home .... *34 Nov. 1/76-Apr. 2/77 (28 wins, 6 ties)
Away .... *23 Nov. 27/74-Mar. 12/75 (14 wins, 9 ties)
Longest Losing Streak
Overall .... 12 Feb. 13-Mar. 13/26
Home .... 7 Dec. 16/39-Jan. 18/40, Oct. 28-Nov. 25/00
Away .... 10 Jan. 16-Mar. 13/26
Longest Winless Streak
Overall .... 12 Feb. 13-Mar. 13/26 (12 losses), Nov. 28-Dec. 29/35 (8 losses, 4 ties)
Home .... 15 Dec. 16/39-Mar. 7/40 (12 losses, 3 ties)
Away .... 12 Nov. 26/33-Jan. 28/34 (8 losses, 4 ties), Oct. 20/50-Dec. 13/51 (8 losses, 4 ties)
Most Shutouts, Season *22 1928-29 (44)
Most PIM, Season 1,847 1995-96 (82)
Most Goals, Game .... *16 Mar. 3/20 (Mtl. 16 at Que. 3)

Individual

Most Seasons .... 20 Henri Richard, Jean Béliveau
Most Games .... 1,256 Henri Richard
Most Goals, Career .... 544 Maurice Richard
Most Assists, Career .... 728 Guy Lafleur
Most Points, Career ..... 1,246 Guy Lafleur (518G, 728A)
Most PIM, Career .... 2,248 Chris Nilan
Most Shutouts, Career .... 75 George Hainsworth
Longest Consecutive Games Streak .... 560 Doug Jarvis (Oct. 8/75-Apr. 4/82)
Most Goals, Season .... 60 Steve Shutt (1976-77), Guy Lafleur (1977-78)
Most Assists, Season .... 82 Pete Mahovlich (1974-75)
Most Points, Season .... 136 Guy Lafleur (1976-77; 56G, 80A)
Most PIM, Season .... 358 Chris Nilan (1984-85)
Most Points, Defenseman, Season .... 85 Larry Robinson (1976-77; 19G, 66A)
Most Points, Center, Season .... 117 Pete Mahovlich (1974-75; 35G, 82A)
Most Points, Right Wing, Season .... 136 Guy Lafleur (1976-77; 56G, 80A)
Most Points, Left Wing, Season .... 110 Mats Naslund (1985-86; 43G, 67A)
Most Points, Rookie, Season .... 71 Mats Naslund (1982-83; 26G, 45A), Kjell Dahlin (1985-86; 32G, 39A)
Most Shutouts, Season ...... *22 George Hainsworth (1928-29)
Most Goals, Game .... 6 Newsy Lalonde (Jan. 10/20)
Most Assists, Game .... 6 Elmer Lach (Feb. 6/43)
Most Points, Game .... 8 Maurice Richard (Dec. 28/44; 5G, 3A), Bert Olmstead (Jan. 9/54; 4G, 4A)

* NHL Record.

Retired Numbers

1	Jacques Plante	1952-1963
2	Doug Harvey	1947-1961
4	Jean Béliveau	1950-1971
7	Howie Morenz	1923-1937
9	Maurice Richard	1942-1960
10	Guy Lafleur	1971-1984
16	Henri Richard	1955-1975

All-time Record vs. Other Clubs

Regular Season

	At Home								On Road								Total							
	GP	W	L	T	OL	GF	GA	PTS	GP	W	L	T	OL	GF	GA	PTS	GP	W	L	T	OL	GF	GA	PTS
Anaheim	8	4	2	2	0	24	19	10	8	5	3	0	0	27	25	10	16	9	5	2	0	51	44	20
Atlanta	10	7	3	0	0	34	24	14	10	7	1	2	0	31	12	16	20	14	4	2	0	65	36	30
Boston	334	189	97	47	1	1120	790	426	335	124	152	56	3	904	990	307	669	313	249	103	4	2024	1780	733
Buffalo	103	57	34	12	0	392	306	126	102	29	53	19	1	268	317	78	205	86	87	31	1	660	623	204
Calgary	46	26	12	8	0	163	112	60	49	26	15	7	1	164	146	60	95	52	27	15	1	327	258	120
Carolina	75	50	17	7	1	309	213	108	78	36	27	13	2	268	224	87	153	86	44	20	3	577	437	195
Chicago	276	174	54	48	0	1067	653	396	273	125	93	55	0	761	731	305	549	299	147	103	0	1828	1384	701
Colorado	64	38	15	10	1	261	198	87	63	26	31	5	1	222	216	58	127	64	46	15	2	483	414	145
Columbus	4	1	1	1	1	6	6	4	1	1	0	0	0	3	1	2	5	2	1	1	1	9	7	6
Dallas	58	37	12	9	0	250	144	83	59	30	17	12	0	203	153	72	117	67	29	21	0	453	297	155
Detroit	282	172	67	43	0	994	636	387	280	97	129	53	1	717	805	248	562	269	196	96	1	1711	1441	635
Edmonton	30	16	9	4	1	105	95	37	35	17	16	0	2	113	117	36	65	33	25	4	3	218	212	73
Florida	21	8	9	3	1	54	49	20	22	8	11	3	0	61	68	19	43	16	20	6	1	115	117	39
Los Angeles	64	45	8	11	0	289	160	101	65	37	19	9	0	256	199	83	129	82	27	20	0	545	359	184
Minnesota	3	1	1	1	0	9	8	3	2	1	1	0	0	5	6	2	5	2	2	1	0	14	14	5
Nashville	4	4	0	0	0	15	9	8	4	1	2	1	0	7	14	3	8	5	2	1	0	22	23	11
New Jersey	54	33	15	6	0	182	134	72	54	25	25	4	0	190	160	54	108	58	40	10	0	372	294	126
NY Islanders	60	36	15	9	0	217	168	81	60	24	28	6	2	167	187	56	120	60	43	15	2	384	355	137
NY Rangers	290	190	60	40	0	1125	669	420	290	118	117	54	1	844	835	291	580	308	177	94	1	1969	1504	711
Ottawa	33	17	12	4	0	97	95	38	31	15	14	1	1	87	90	32	64	32	26	5	1	184	185	70
Philadelphia	74	34	25	14	1	254	229	83	73	28	29	16	0	215	223	72	147	62	54	30	1	469	452	155
Phoenix	29	24	3	2	0	142	66	50	29	13	9	7	0	112	94	33	58	37	12	9	0	254	160	83
Pittsburgh	82	62	10	10	0	383	203	134	82	41	28	13	0	290	238	95	164	103	38	23	0	673	441	229
St. Louis	59	41	11	7	0	255	161	89	57	28	14	15	0	195	147	71	116	69	25	22	0	450	308	160
San Jose	11	7	2	2	0	36	20	16	11	4	4	2	1	28	33	11	22	11	6	4	1	64	53	27
Tampa Bay	22	11	10	1	0	59	53	23	23	9	9	5	0	61	55	23	45	20	19	6	0	120	108	46
Toronto	333	198	91	43	1	1162	827	440	333	116	172	45	0	865	1007	277	666	314	263	88	1	2027	1834	717
Vancouver	53	38	10	5	0	244	135	81	55	33	13	8	1	202	146	75	108	71	23	13	1	446	281	156
Washington	60	35	16	8	1	229	127	79	59	24	26	9	0	177	163	57	119	59	42	17	1	406	290	136
Defunct Clubs	231	148	58	25	0	779	469	321	230	98	97	35	0	586	606	231	461	246	155	60	0	1365	1075	552
Totals	**2773**	**1703**	**679**	**382**	**9**	**10256**	**6778**	**3797**	**2773**	**1146**	**1155**	**455**	**17**	**8029**	**8008**	**2764**	**5546**	**2849**	**1834**	**837**	**26**	**18285**	**14786**	**6561**

Playoffs

	Series	W	L	GP	W	L	T	GF	GA	Last Mtg.	Rnd.	Result
Boston	30	23	7	152	95	57	0	469	371	2004	CQF	W 4-3
Buffalo	7	4	3	35	18	17	0	124	111	1998	CSF	L 0-4
Calgary	2	1	1	11	6	5	0	31	32	1989	F	L 2-4
Carolina	6	5	1	33	21	12	0	108	91	2002	CSF	L 2-4
Chicago	17	12	5	81	50	29	2	261	185	1976	QF	W 4-0
Colorado	5	3	2	31	17	14	0	105	85	1993	DSF	W 4-2
Dallas	2	1	1	13	7	6	0	48	37	1980	QF	L 3-4
Detroit	12	5	7	62	33	29	0	161	149	1978	QF	W 4-1
Edmonton	1	0	1	3	0	3	0	6	15	1981	PRE	L 0-3
Los Angeles	1	1	0	5	4	1	0	15	12	1993	F	W 4-1
New Jersey	1	0	1	5	1	4	0	11	22	1997	CQF	L 1-4
NY Islanders	4	3	1	22	14	8	0	64	55	1993	CF	W 4-1
NY Rangers	14	7	7	61	34	25	2	188	158	1996	CQF	L 2-4
Philadelphia	4	3	1	21	14	7	0	72	52	1989	CF	W 4-2
Pittsburgh	1	1	0	6	4	2	0	18	15	1998	CQF	W 4-2
St. Louis	3	3	0	12	12	0	0	42	14	1977	QF	W 4-0
Tampa Bay	1	0	1	4	0	4	0	5	14	2004	CSF	L 0-4
Toronto	15	8	7	71	42	29	0	215	160	1979	QF	W 4-0
Vancouver	1	1	0	5	4	1	0	20	9	1975	QF	W 4-1
Defunct Clubs	11*	6	4	28	15	9	4	70	71			
Totals	**138***	**87**	**50**	**661**	**391**	**262**	**8**	**2033**	**1658**			

* 1919 Final incomplete due to influenza epidemic.

Calgary totals include Atlanta Flames, 1972-73 to 1979-80.
Carolina totals include Hartford, 1979-80 to 1996-97.
Colorado totals include Quebec, 1979-80 to 1994-95.
Dallas totals include Minnesota North Stars, 1967-68 to 1992-93.
New Jersey totals include Kansas City, 1974-75 to 1975-76, and Colorado Rockies, 1976-77 to 1981-82.
Phoenix totals include Winnipeg, 1979-80 to 1995-96.

Playoff Results 2005-2000

Year	Round	Opponent	Result	GF	GA
2004	CSF	Tampa Bay	L 0-4	5	14
	CQF	Boston	W 4-3	19	14
2002	CSF	Carolina	L 2-4	12	21
	CQF	Boston	W 4-2	20	18

Abbreviations: Round: F - Final; **CF** - conference final; **CSF** - conference semi-final; **CQF** - conference quarter-final; **DSF** - division semi-final; **QF** - quarter-final; **PRE** - preliminary round.

Key Off-Season Signings/Acquisitions

2004

June 26 • Obtained C **Radek Bonk** and G **Cristobal Huet** from Los Angeles for G **Mathieu Garon** and a 2004 3rd-round pick.
July 13 • Re-signed C **Steve Begin** and RW **Niklas Sundstrom**.
23 • Re-signed D **Ron Hainsey**.
Aug. 4 • Re-signed RW **Richard Zednik**.
4 • Signed 2003 1st-round pick (10th overall), F **Andrei Kostitsyn**.
Sept. 13 • Re-signed D **Sheldon Souray**.

2005

Aug. 2 • Re-signed D **Francis Bouillon**.
3 • Re-signed RW **Alex Kovalev**.
• Signed D **Mathieu Dandenault**.
8 • Re-signed RW **Pierre Dagenais**.
11 • Re-signed C **Mike Ribeiro** and D **Mike Komisarek**.
12 • Re-signed C **Jan Bulis**.
15 • Re-signed C **Saku Koivu** and LW **Marcel Hossa**.
25 • Re-signed D **Andrei Markov**.
Sept. 2 • Re-signed G **Jose Theodore**.

Entry Draft
Selections 2005-1991

2005
Pick
5	Carey Price
45	Guillaume Latendresse
121	Juraj Mikus
130	Mathieu Aubin
190	Matt D'Agostini
200	Sergei Kostitsyn
229	Philippe Paquet

2004
Pick
18	Kyle Chipchura
84	Alexei Yemelin
100	James Wyman
150	Mikhail Grabovsky
181	Loic Lacasse
212	Jon Gleed
246	Greg Stewart
262	Mark Streit
278	Alex Dulac-Lemelin

2003
Pick
10	Andrei Kostitsyn
40	Cory Urquhart
61	Maxim Lapierre
79	Ryan O'Byrne
113	Corey Locke
123	Danny Stewart
177	Chris Heino-Lindberg
188	Mark Flood
217	Oskari Korpikari
241	Jimmy Bonneau
271	Jaroslav Halak

2002
Pick
14	Christopher Higgins
45	Tomas Linhart
99	Michael Lambert
182	Andre Deveaux
212	Jonathan Ferland
275	Konstantin Korneev

2001
Pick
7	Mike Komisarek
25	Alexander Perezhogin
37	Duncan Milroy
71	Tomas Plekanec
109	Martti Jarventie
171	Eric Himelfarb
203	Andrew Archer
266	Viktor Ujcik

2000
Pick
13	Ron Hainsey
16	Marcel Hossa
78	Jozef Balej
79	Tyler Hanchuck
109	Johan Eneqvist
114	Christian Larrivee
145	Ryan Glenn
172	Scott Selig
182	Petr Chvojka
243	Joni Puurula
275	Jonathan Gauthier

1999
Pick
39	Alexander Buturlin
58	Matt Carkner
97	Chris Dyment
107	Evan Lindsay
136	Dusty Jamieson
145	Marc-Andre Thinel
150	Matt Shasby
167	Sean Dixon
196	Vadim Tarasov
225	Mikko Hyytia
253	Jerome Marois

1998
Pick
16	Eric Chouinard
45	Mike Ribeiro
75	Francois Beauchemin
132	Andrei Bashkirov
152	Gordie Dwyer
162	Andrei Markov
189	Andrei Kruchinin
201	Craig Murray
216	Michael Ryder
247	Darcy Harris

1997
Pick
11	Jason Ward
37	Gregor Baumgartner
65	Ilkka Mikkola
91	Daniel Tetrault
118	Konstantin Sidulov
122	Gennady Razin
145	Jonathan Desroches
172	Ben Guite
197	Petr Kubos
202	Andrei Sidyakin
228	Jarl Espen Ygranes

1996
Pick
18	Matt Higgins
44	Mathieu Garon
71	Arron Asham
92	Kim Staal
99	Etienne Drapeau
127	Daniel Archambault
154	Brett Clark
181	Timo Vertala
207	Mattia Baldi
233	Michel Tremblay

1995
Pick
8	Terry Ryan
60	Miloslav Guren
74	Martin Hohenberger
86	Jonathan Delisle
112	Niklas Anger
138	Boyd Olson
164	Stephane Robidas
190	Greg Hart
216	Eric Houde

1994
Pick
18	Brad Brown
44	Jose Theodore
54	Chris Murray
70	Marko Kiprusoff
74	Martin Belanger
96	Arto Kuki
122	Jimmy Drolet
148	Joel Irving
174	Jessie Rezansoff
200	Peter Strom
226	Tomas Vokoun
252	Chris Aldous
278	Ross Parsons

1993
Pick
21	Saku Koivu
47	Rory Fitzpatrick
73	Sebastien Bordeleau
85	Adam Wiesel
99	Jean-Francois Houle
113	Jeff Lank
125	Dion Darling
151	Darcy Tucker
177	David Ruhly
203	Alan Letang
229	Alexandre Duchesne
255	Brian Larochelle
281	Russell Guzior

1992
Pick
20	David Wilkie
33	Valeri Bure
44	Keli Corpse
68	Craig Rivet
82	Louis Bernard
92	Marc Lamothe
116	Don Chase
140	Martin Sychra
164	Christian Proulx
188	Michael Burman
212	Earl Cronan
236	Trent Cavicchi
260	Hiroyuki Miura

1991
Pick
17	Brent Bilodeau
28	Jim Campbell
43	Craig Darby
61	Yves Sarault
73	Vladimir Vujtek
83	Sylvain Lapointe
100	Brad Layzell
105	Tony Prpic
127	Oleg Petrov
149	Brady Kramer
171	Brian Savage
193	Scott Fraser
215	Greg MacEachern
237	Paul Lepler
259	Dale Hooper

Coach

JULIEN, CLAUDE
Coach, Montreal Canadiens. Born in Blind River, Ont., April 23, 1960.

Claude Julien became head coach of the Montreal Canadiens on January 17, 2003. At the time, he was in his third season as head coach of the Hamilton Bulldogs, the Canadiens' affiliate team in the American Hockey League. In his first full season behind the bench in 2003-04, the Canadiens posted their best record in 10 years and reached the second round of the playoffs.

Julien started his coaching career at the helm of the Ottawa Senators of the Central Junior Hockey League in 1993-94. He later became an assistant coach with the Hull Olympiques of the QMJHL and was promoted to head coach in 1996-97, leading Hull to the Memorial Cup championship that year. Internationally, Julien earned a silver medal as assistant coach and a bronze medal as head coach at the World Junior Championships in 1999 and 2000.

Julien suited up for a total of 14 games as a player in the NHL with the Quebec Nordiques in 1984-85 and 1985-86. He had 40 goals and 206 assists in 409 games as a defenseman in the American Hockey League.

Coaching Record

Season	Team	Games	Regular Season W	L	T	Playoffs Games	W	L
1996-97	Hull (QMJHL)	70	48	19	3	14	12	2
1997-98	Hull (QMJHL)	70	32	37	1	11	6	5
1998-99	Hull (QMJHL)	70	23	38	9	23	15	8
1999-00	Hull (QMJHL)	72	42	24	6	15	9	6
2000-01	Hamilton (AHL)	80	28	46	6	....	....	....
2001-02	Hamilton (AHL)	80	37	33	10	15	10	5
2002-03	Hamilton (AHL)	45	33	9	3	....	....	....
2002-03	**Montreal (NHL)**	**36**	**12**	**21**	**3**	**....**	**....**	**....**
2003-04	**Montreal (NHL)**	**82**	**41**	**34**	**7**	**11**	**4**	**7**
2004-05	**Montreal (NHL)**			Season Cancelled				
	NHL Totals	**118**	**53**	**55**	**10**	**11**	**4**	**7**

Club Directory

Bell Centre

Bell Centre
1260 de La Gauchetière Street W.
Montréal, QC H3B 5E8
Phone: **514/932-2582**
Media Hotline: 514/989-2835
Fax Lines (all area code 514):
Communications 932-8285
Hockey 989-2717
Press Lounge 932-5258
Marketing 925-2145
Community Relations 925-2144
www.canadiens.com
Capacity: 21,273

Executive Management
Chairman and Governor	George N. Gillett Jr.
Vice-Chairman	Jeff Joyce
President, Canadien Hockey Club & Bell Centre & Alternate Governor	Pierre Boivin
Assistant to the President & Alternate Governor	Foster Gillett
Administrative Assistant to the President	Anne Pinsonneault
Executive V.P. Hockey and General Manager & Alternate Governor	Bob Gainey
Chief Financial Officer & Alternate Governor	Fred Steer
Vice-President, Marketing and Sales	Ray Lalonde
Vice-President, Communications and Community Relations	Donald Beauchamp
Vice-President, Operations, Bell Centre	Alain Gauthier
VP & General Manager, Gillett Entertainment Group	Jacques Aubé
President, Effix – Advertising and Sponsorship Sales	François Seigneur
President, Canadiens Alumni	Réjean Houle

Hockey
Assistant General Manager	André Savard
Director of Hockey Operations and Legal Affairs	Julien BriseBois
Director of Player Personnel	Trevor Timmins
Director of Professional Scouting	Pierre Gauthier
Head Coach	Claude Julien
Assistant Coaches	Roland Melanson, Rick Green, Doug Jarvis
Professional Scouts	Richard Green, Gordie Roberts
Scouting Staff	Patrik Allvin, Elmer Benning, William A. Berglund, Vaughn Karpan, Hannu Laine, Dave Mayville, Antonin Routa, Nikolai Vakourov
Team Services & Hockey Administration Manager	Claudine Crépin
Administrative Assistant to the General Manager	Suzanne Charlebois

Medical and Training Staff
Club Physician and Chief Surgeon	Dr. David Mulder
Consultant, Orthopedic Surgeon	Dr. Eric Lenczner
Dentist	Dr. Jean-François Desjardins
Consultant, Ophthalmologist	Dr. John Little
Consultant, Sports Medicine	Dr. Vincent Lacroix
Head Athletic Therapist	Graham Rynbend
Assistant to the Athletic Therapist	Jody van Rees
Strength & Conditioning Coordinator	Scott Livingston
Video Supervisor	Mario Leblanc
Equipment Manager	Pierre Gervais
Assistants to the Equipment Manager	Robert Boulanger, Pierre Ouellette
Visiting team Coordinator	Richard Généreux

Communications
Director of Media Relations	Dominick Saillant
Administrative Assistant to VP Communications	Sylvie Lambert
Communications Coordinator	Michel Lamarche

Community Relations
CEO, Montreal Canadiens Children's Foundation	Robert Sirois
Community Relations Manager	Geneviève Paquette
Coordinator, Montreal Canadiens Children's Foundation	Marie-Christine Boucher
Community Relations Coordinator	Dominique Ladouceur
Coordinator, Canadiens Alumni	Normande Herget

Marketing and Sales
Director, Group Sales and Administration	Pierre Constant
Director, Ticket Sales	Vincent Lucier
Executive Director, Luxury Suites	Richard Primeau
Director, Consumer Products	Matt Zalkowitz
Group Manager, Media and Broadcast	Jon Trzcienski
Manager, Events and Programs	Patrick Boivin
Manager, Game Presentation	Chantal Bunnett
Manager, Guest Services	Sabina D'Ascoli
Manager, Publications & Photos	Carl Lavigne
Manager, Advertising, Broadcast and Promotions	Jonathan Prunier
Manager, Creative Services	Jean Simard
Manager, Group Sales	Stéphane Verret
Team Photographer	Bob Fisher

Ticket Sales and Building Operations
Director of Ticket Office	Cathy D'Ascoli
Assistant Director of Ticket Office	Lucie Masse
Director of Building Operations	Xavier Luydlin
Administrative Assistant to the VP Operations	Maryse Cartwright

Finances
Controller	Dennis McKinley
Assistant Controller	Raymond Lamarche
Director of Information Technology	Pierre-Éric Belzile
Administrative Assistant, Chief Financial Officer	Christine Ouellette

Team Information
Play-by-play – Radio/TV . . Pierre Houde (RDS & SRC), Martin McGuire (CKAC), Rick Moffat (CJAD)
Colormen – Radio/TV . . . . Yvon Pedneault (RDS & SRC), Dany Dubé (CKAC), Murray Wilson (CJAD)
Radio/television flagships . . . . RDS (Cable 33), CKAC (730 AM), CJAD (800 AM)

Nashville Predators

Year-by-Year Record

Season	GP	Home W	L	T	OL	Road W	L	T	OL	Overall W	L	T	OL	GF	GA	Pts.	Finished	Playoff Result
2004-05	....	....				....				....				....	....	....		
2003-04	82	22	10	7	2	16	19	4	2	38	29	11	4	216	217	91	3rd, Central Div.	Lost Conf. Quarter-Final
2002-03	82	18	17	5	1	9	18	8	6	27	35	13	7	183	206	74	4th, Central Div.	Out of Playoffs
2001-02	82	17	16	8	0	11	25	5	0	28	41	13	0	196	230	69	4th, Central Div.	Out of Playoffs
2000-01	82	16	18	7	0	18	18	2	3	34	36	9	3	186	200	80	3rd, Central Div.	Out of Playoffs
1999-2000	82	15	21	3	2	13	19	4	5	28	40	7	7	199	240	70	4th, Central Div.	Out of Playoffs
1998-99	82	15	22	4	....	13	25	3	....	28	47	7	....	190	261	63	4th, Central Div.	Out of Playoffs

2005-06 Schedule

Oct.	Wed.	5	San Jose
	Sat.	8	Anaheim
	Wed.	12	at Colorado
	Thu.	13	at Phoenix
	Sat.	15	at St. Louis
	Thu.	20	St. Louis
	Sat.	22	San Jose
	Tue.	25	Chicago
	Wed.	26	at Columbus
	Sat.	29	Edmonton
Nov.	Tue.	1	at Anaheim
	Wed.	2	at San Jose
	Sat.	5	at Los Angeles*
	Tue.	8	Edmonton
	Thu.	10	Dallas
	Sat.	12	St. Louis
	Tue.	15	Los Angeles
	Sat.	19	at Minnesota
	Mon.	21	at Detroit
	Wed.	23	at Columbus
	Thu.	24	Los Angeles
	Sat.	26	Dallas
	Tue.	29	Calgary
Dec.	Thu.	1	Minnesota
	Sat.	3	Philadelphia
	Wed.	7	at Washington
	Thu.	8	NY Rangers
	Sat.	10	at Tampa Bay
	Tue.	13	at Florida
	Thu.	15	Chicago
	Sat.	17	Columbus
	Tue.	20	Colorado
	Wed.	21	at Chicago
	Fri.	23	at Columbus
	Tue.	27	at Calgary
	Wed.	28	at Vancouver
	Fri.	30	at Edmonton
Jan.	Sun.	1	Anaheim
	Tue.	3	at Colorado
	Wed.	4	at St. Louis
	Fri.	6	Detroit

	Sun.	8	at Chicago
	Tue.	10	NY Islanders
	Wed.	11	at Atlanta
	Fri.	13	at Carolina
	Sun.	15	Pittsburgh
	Thu.	19	New Jersey
	Sat.	21	Columbus
	Mon.	23	Detroit
	Tue.	24	at Detroit
	Thu.	26	at Minnesota
	Sat.	28	at Columbus
Feb.	Wed.	1	at Dallas
	Thu.	2	Colorado
	Sat.	4	Chicago*
	Mon.	6	at Dallas
	Wed.	8	at Detroit
	Thu.	9	Detroit
	Sat.	11	Columbus
Mar.	Wed.	1	at Chicago
	Thu.	2	Vancouver
	Sun.	5	at Edmonton*
	Tue.	7	at Calgary
	Thu.	9	at Vancouver
	Sat.	11	at San Jose*
	Tue.	14	Vancouver
	Thu.	16	Phoenix
	Sat.	18	Calgary
	Mon.	20	St. Louis
	Tue.	21	at Detroit
	Fri.	24	at Anaheim
	Sat.	25	at Los Angeles
	Tue.	28	at Phoenix
Apr.	Sat.	1	St. Louis
	Mon.	3	Columbus
	Wed.	5	at Chicago
	Thu.	6	at St. Louis
	Sat.	8	Chicago
	Tue.	11	at St. Louis
	Thu.	13	Minnesota
	Sat.	15	Phoenix
	Tue.	18	Detroit

* Denotes afternoon game.

Franchise date: June 25, 1997

**8th
NHL
Season**

**CENTRAL
DIVISION**

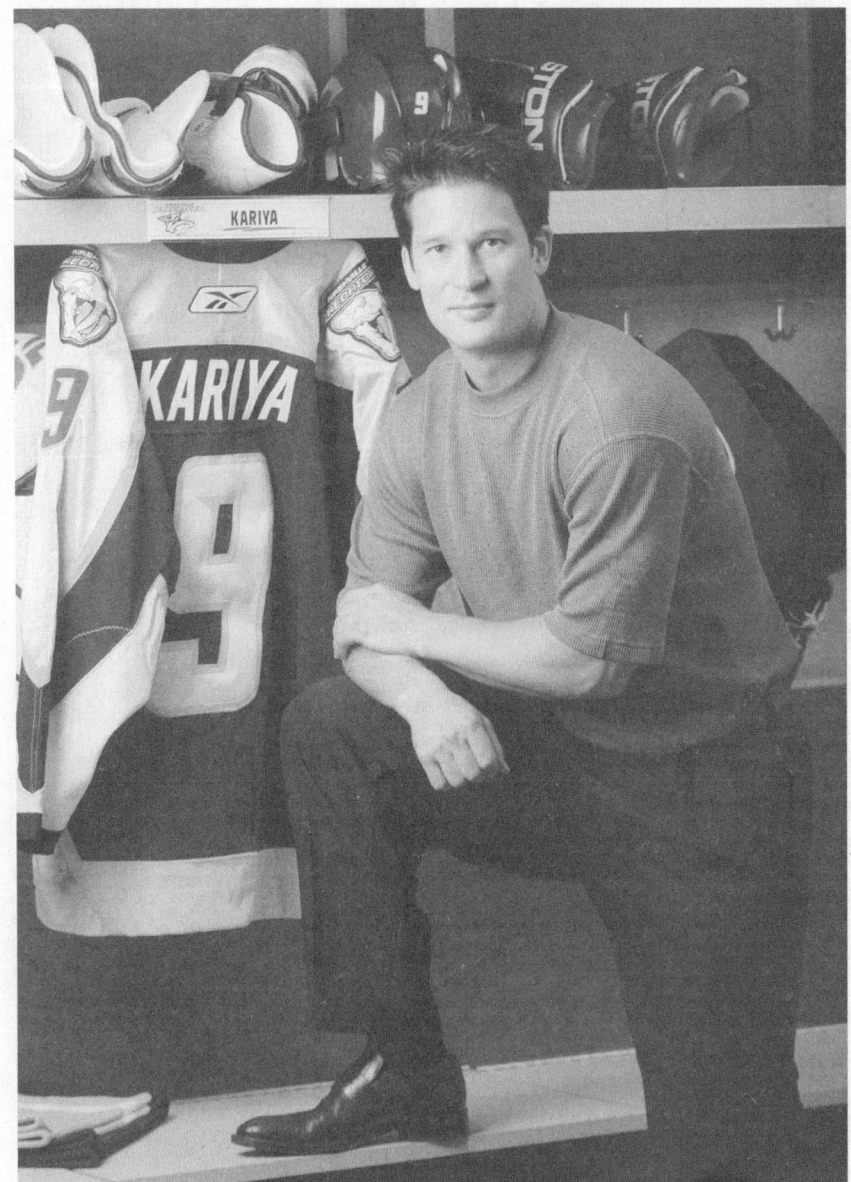

A five-time NHL All-Star, Paul Kariya has collected 705 points (311 goals, 394 assists) over 10 seasons, making him the NHL's highest-scoring active player aged 31 or younger.

2005-06 Player Personnel

FORWARDS	HT	WT	S	Place of Birth	Date	2004-05 Club
BROWN, Paul	6-3	184	R	Edmonton, Alta.	7/21/84	Milwaukee-Trenton
CLASSEN, Greg	6-1	200	L	Aylsham, Sask.	8/24/77	Assat
ERAT, Martin	6-0	195	L	Trebic, Czech.	8/29/81	Zlin
FIDDLER, Vern	5-11	204	L	Edmonton, Alta.	5/9/80	Milwaukee
GAMACHE, Simon	5-10	186	L	Thetford Mines, Que.	1/3/81	Milwaukee
HALL, Adam	6-3	208	R	Kalamazoo, MI	8/14/80	KalPa
HARTNELL, Scott	6-2	210	L	Regina, Sask.	4/18/82	Valerengen
HAYDAR, Darren	5-9	166	L	Toronto, Ont.	10/22/79	Milwaukee
HORDICHUK, Darcy	6-1	215	L	Kamsack, Sask.	8/10/80	
JOHNSON, Greg	5-11	200	L	Thunder Bay, Ont.	3/16/71	
KARIYA, Paul	5-10	176	L	Vancouver, B.C.	10/16/74	
LEGWAND, David	6-2	190	L	Detroit, MI	8/17/80	Basel
NICHOL, Scott	5-8	173	R	Edmonton, Alta.	12/31/74	London
PIVKO, Libor	6-3	214	L	Novy Vicin, Czech.	3/29/80	Milwaukee
ROBITAILLE, Randy	5-11	200	L	Ottawa, Ont.	10/12/75	Zurich
SEGAL, Brandon	6-3	213	R	Richmond, B.C.	7/12/83	Milwaukee-Rockford
SHISHKANOV, Timofei	6-1	209	R	Moscow, USSR	6/10/83	Milwaukee
SMITHSON, Jerred	6-3	194	R	Vernon, B.C.	2/4/79	Milwaukee
STEVENSON, Jeremy	6-1	215	L	San Bernardino, CA	7/28/74	South Carolina
SULLIVAN, Steve	5-9	155	R	Timmins, Ont.	7/6/74	
TOOTOO, Jordin	5-9	194	R	Churchill, Man.	2/2/83	Milwaukee
UPSHALL, Scottie	6-0	197	L	Fort McMurray, Alta.	10/7/83	Milwaukee
WALKER, Scott	5-10	196	R	Cambridge, Ont.	7/19/73	Cambridge-Dundas
YABLONSKI, Jeremy	6-0	240	R	Meadow Lake, Sask.	3/21/80	Milwaukee

DEFENSEMEN						
ALLISON, Jamie	6-1	210	L	Lindsay, Ont.	5/13/75	Cambridge
BROOKBANK, Sheldon	6-2	200	R	Lanigan, Sask.	10/3/80	Cincinnati (AHL)
EATON, Mark	6-2	212	L	Wilmington, DE	5/6/77	Grand Rapids
HAMHUIS, Dan	6-1	200	L	Smithers, B.C.	12/13/82	Milwaukee
KLEIN, Kevin	6-1	195	L	Kitchener, Ont.	12/13/84	Milwaukee-Rockford
MARKOV, Danny	6-1	190	L	Moscow, USSR	7/30/76	Chekhov
SUTER, Ryan	6-1	196	L	Madison, WI	1/21/85	Milwaukee
TIMONEN, Kimmo	5-10	194	L	Kuopio, Finland	3/18/75	Lugano-Brynas-KalPa
WEBER, Shea	6-3	213	R	Sicamous, B.C.	8/14/85	Kelowna
ZANON, Greg	5-11	211	L	Burnaby, B.C.	6/5/80	Milwaukee
ZIDLICKY, Marek	5-11	190	R	Most, Czech.	2/3/77	HIFK

GOALTENDERS	HT	WT	C	Place of Birth	Date	2004-05 Club
FINLEY, Brian	6-3	201	R	Sault Ste. Marie, Ont.	7/13/81	Milwaukee
MASON, Chris	6-0	195	L	Red Deer, Alta.	4/20/76	Valerengen
RINNE, Pekka	6-5	207	L	Kempele, Finland	11/3/82	Karpat
VOKOUN, Tomas	6-0	195	R	Karlovy Vary, Czech.	7/2/76	Znojmo-HIFK

In the System and Recently Drafted

FORWARDS	HT	WT	S	Place of Birth	Date	2004-05 Club
ANDERSSON, Jonas	6-3	204	L	Stockholm, Sweden	2/24/81	Sodertalje-Brynas
ARKHIPOV, Denis	6-3	206	L	Kazan, USSR	5/19/79	Kazan
BALAN, Stanislav	6-2	161	L	Hodonin, Czech.	1/30/86	Hodonin-Zlin Jr.
BETTS, Kaleb	5-10	180	L	Maple Ridge, B.C.	1/10/83	Nebraska-Omaha
CISAR, Marian	6-0	197	R	Bratislava, Czech.	2/25/78	Hannover
DARZINS, Lauris	6-3	190	R	Riga, Latvia	1/28/85	Kelowna
FUGERE, Nick	6-2	238	L	Shawinigan, Que.	9/20/85	Gatineau
GLAZACHEV, Konstantin	6-0	186	R	Arkhangelsk, USSR	2/18/85	Novosibirsk-Yaroslavl
GRASBERG, Gustav	6-0	193	L	Furudal, Sweden	4/6/83	Halmstad
HENTUNEN, Jukka	5-10	194	R	Joroinen, Finland	5/3/74	Fribourg
HORNQVIST, Patric	5-11	178	R	Sollentuna, Sweden	1/1/87	Vasby-Djurgarden Jr.
HUBACEK, Petr	6-2	183	R	Brno, Czech.	9/2/79	Vitkovice
IRGL, Zbynek	5-11	183	R	Vitkovice, Czech.	11/29/80	Vitkovice
MAKI, Ryan	6-2	195	L	Medford, NJ	4/23/85	Harvard
MEIDL, Vaclav	6-4	215	L	Prostejov, Czech.	5/27/86	Plymouth
O'REILLY, Cal	5-11	180	L	Toronto, Ont.	9/30/86	Windsor
PANOV, Konstantin	6-0	195	L	Chelyabinsk, USSR	6/29/80	Chelyabinsk
PLATONOV, Denis	6-3	205	L	Saratov, USSR	11/6/81	Kazan-Nizhnekamsk
RADULOV, Alexander	6-1	180	L	Nizhy Tagil, USSR	7/5/86	Quebec
SANTORELLI, Michael	5-11	180	R	Vancouver, B.C.	12/14/85	Northern Mich.
SETZINGER, Oliver	6-0	197	L	Horn, Austria	7/11/83	HPK
SHAFIGULIN, Grigory	6-2	185	L	Chelyabinsk, USSR	1/13/85	Yaroslavl
SOIN, Sergei	6-0	175	L	Moscow, USSR	3/31/82	CSKA
WIDING, Daniel	6-1	202	R	Gavle, Sweden	4/13/82	Pelicans

DEFENSEMEN						
CHRISTEEN, Mats	6-1	181	L	Sodertalje, Sweden	2/13/82	Solna
FRANSON, Cody	6-4	205	R	Salmon Arm, B.C.	8/8/87	Vancouver (WHL)
HARANT, Tomas	6-3	201	L	Zilina, Czech.	4/28/80	Dynamo Mosc.-K. Vary
HOHENER, Martin	6-1	192	L	Zurich, Switz.	6/23/80	Zurich
KULYASH, Denis	6-2	199	L	Omsk, USSR	5/31/83	CSKA
LAAKSO, Teemu	6-0	187	R	Tuusula, Finland	8/27/87	HIFK
LAVRENTIEV, Anton	6-4	196	R	Kazan, USSR	8/25/83	Novopolotsk
LEHTONEN, Mikko	6-1	194	L	Oulu, Finland	6/12/79	Karpat
MUKHACHEV, Andrei	6-3	196	L	Sverdlovsk, USSR	7/21/80	CSKA
NILSSON, Mattias	6-3	195	L	Ornskoldsvik, Sweden	2/6/82	Hammarby
NISKALA, Janne	5-11	199	L	Rauma, Finland	9/22/81	Lukko
PARENT, Ryan	6-2	183	L	Prince Albert, Sask.	3/17/87	Guelph
SAFRONOV, Kirill	6-2	215	L	Leningrad, USSR	2/26/81	Yaroslavl-Voskresensk
SCHAEFFER, Kevin	6-1	195	R	Huntington, NY	10/16/84	Boston University
SKRBEK, Pavel	6-3	217	L	Kladno, Czech.	8/9/78	Mora
STEHLIK, Richard	6-4	242	L	Skalica, Czech.	6/22/84	Skalica-Trencin
SULZER, Alexander	6-1	207	L	Kaufbeuren, W. Ger.	5/30/84	Dusseldorf-Duisburg
SWITZER, Craig	6-1	195	L	Calgary, Alta.	10/16/84	New Hampshire
TODD, Scott	6-4	221	L	Kingston, Ont.	11/11/86	Oshawa-Windsor

GOALTENDERS	HT	WT	C	Place of Birth	Date	2004-05 Club
HANULJAK, Miroslav	6-4	197	L	Litvinov, Czech.	9/12/84	Havirov-Most
LASSILA, Teemu	6-1	200	L	Helsinki, Finland	3/26/83	TPS
MOIR, Kyle	6-3	193	L	Calgary, Alta.	5/25/86	Swift Current
SIDIKOV, Rustam	6-0	158	L	Moscow, USSR	7/5/85	CSKA 2

Vice President and General Manager

POILE, DAVID
Executive Vice President/General Manager, Nashville Predators.
Born in Toronto, Ont., February 14, 1949.

Since joining the Predators as general manager on July 9, 1997, David Poile has made a commitment to building for the future, surrounding himself with one of the youngest and most talented staffs in the National Hockey League. In 2003-04, Nashville reached the playoffs for the first time in franchise history. Poile has an impressive reputation as an NHL leader and in 2001 he received the Lester Patrick Trophy for his contributions to hockey in the United States. His father, Norman "Bud" Poile, had won the honor in 1989.

Prior to joining Nashville, Poile spent 15 seasons as vice president/general manager of the Washington Capitals. During his tenure in Washington, the Capitals made 14 postseason appearances, winning their only Patrick Division title in 1989 and advancing to the Conference Finals in 1990. During Poile's 15 years in Washington, the Capitals compiled a record of 594-454-132, finished second in the Patrick Division seven times and recorded 90-or-more points seven different seasons.

Poile started his professional hockey career as an administrative assistant for the Atlanta Flames in 1972, shortly after graduating from Northeastern University in Boston. At Northeastern, he was hockey team captain, leading scorer and most valuable player for two years.

In 1977, he was named assistant general manager of the Atlanta Flames (who moved to Calgary in 1980), serving as the manager and coordinator of the Flames farm club.

Poile is a member of the NHL's general managers committee and was instrumental in the NHL's adoption of the instant replay rule in 1991. He was awarded *Inside Hockey*'s man of the year for his leadership on the issue. He was also twice honored as *The Sporting News* NHL executive of the year following the 1982-83 and 1983-84 seasons. Poile served as general manager of the 1998 and 1999 U.S. national team for the World Championships.

Poile was introduced to hockey by watching his father play seven seasons in the NHL. Bud Poile later became general manager for the Vancouver Canucks and the Philadelphia Flyers, both NHL expansion franchises at the time. He was inducted into the Hockey Hall of Fame in 1990.

Tomas Vokoun has emerged as one of the NHL's top goaltenders over his six seasons in Nashville.

Club Records

Team

(Figures in brackets for season records are games played; records for fewest points, wins, ties, losses, goals, goals against are for 70 or more games)

Most Points	91	2003-04 (82)
Most Wins	38	2003-04 (82)
Most Ties	13	2001-02 (82), 2002-03 (82)
Most Losses	47	1998-99 (82)
Most Goals	216	2003-04 (82)
Most Goals Against	261	1998-99 (82)
Fewest Points	63	1998-99 (82)
Fewest Wins	27	2002-03 (82)
Fewest Ties	7	1998-99 (82) 1999-2000 (82)
Fewest Losses	29	2003-04 (82)
Fewest Goals	183	2002-03 (82)
Fewest Goals Against	200	2000-01 (82)

Longest Winning Streak
Overall................ 6 — Nov. 11-Dec. 4/03
Home................. 7 — Feb. 13-Mar. 1/03
Away................. 4 — Nov. 11-Dec. 4/03, Mar. 20-Apr. 4/04

Longest Undefeated Streak
Overall................ 8 — Dec. 18/99-Jan. 1/00 (5 wins, 3 ties)
Home................. 11 — Twice
Away................. 4 — Twice

Longest Losing Streak
Overall................ 7 — Nov. 20-Dec. 2/99
Home................. 6 — Jan. 21-Feb. 15/99, Feb. 26-Mar. 21/02
Away................. 5 — Five times

Longest Winless Streak
Overall................ 15 — Mar. 10-Apr. 6/03 (12 losses (2 in OT), 3 ties)
Home................. 9 — Jan. 21-Mar. 2/99 (8 losses, 1 tie)
Away................. 9 — Three times
Most Shutouts, Season ... 6 — 2000-01 (82)
Most PIM, Season ..... 1,420 — 1998-99 (82)
Most Goals, Game .... 9 — Mar. 4/04 (Nsh. 9 at Pit. 4)

Individual

Most Seasons	6	Many players
Most Games	434	Greg Johnson
Most Goals, Career	91	Scott Walker
Most Assists, Career	145	Cliff Ronning
Most Points, Career	231	Scott Walker (91G, 140A)
Most PIM, Career	429	Scott Walker
Most Shutouts, Career	12	Tomas Vokoun

Longest Consecutive
Games Streak .... 269 — Karlis Skrastins (Feb. 21/00-Apr. 6/03)
Most Goals, Season .... 26 — Cliff Ronning (1999-2000)
Most Assists, Season .... 43 — Cliff Ronning (2000-01)
Most Points, Season .... 67 — Scott Walker (2003-04; 25G, 42A)

Most PIM, Season .... 242 — Patrick Cote (1999-2000)
Most Points, Defenseman, Season .... 53 — Marek Zidlicky (2003-04; 14G, 39A)
Most Points, Center, Season .... 62 — Cliff Ronning (1999-2000; 26G, 36A) (2000-01; 19G, 43A)
Most Points, Right Wing, Season .... 67 — Scott Walker (2003-04; 25G, 42A)
Most Points, Left Wing, Season .... 49 — Martin Erat (2003-04; 16G, 33A)
Most Points, Rookie, Season .... 53 — Marek Zidlicky (2003-04; 14G, 39A)
Most Shutouts, Season .... 4 — Mike Dunham (2000-01)
Most Goals, Game .... 3 — Seven times
Most Assists, Game .... 5 — Mark Zidlicky (Feb. 18/04)
Most Points, Game........... 5 — Mark Zidlicky (Feb. 18/04; 5A), Dan Hamhuis (Mar. 4/04; 1G-4A)

General Managers' History

David Poile, 1998-99 to date.

Coaching History

Barry Trotz, 1998-99 to date.

Captains' History

Tom Fitzgerald, 1998-99 to 2001-02; Greg Johnson, 2002-03 to date.

All-time Record vs. Other Clubs

Regular Season

	At Home								On Road								Total							
	GP	W	L	T	OL	GF	GA	PTS	GP	W	L	T	OL	GF	GA	PTS	GP	W	L	T	OL	GF	GA	PTS
Anaheim	12	5	4	2	1	24	28	13	12	3	8	0	1	20	33	7	24	8	12	2	2	44	61	20
Atlanta	3	2	1	0	0	12	6	4	4	1	2	1	0	10	12	3	7	3	3	1	0	22	18	7
Boston	6	2	4	0	0	13	16	4	5	1	2	1	0	9	14	5	11	4	6	1	0	22	30	9
Buffalo	5	2	2	0	1	10	9	5	4	3	0	1	0	16	9	7	9	5	2	1	1	26	18	12
Calgary	13	8	4	1	0	39	25	17	12	3	4	3	2	26	35	11	25	11	8	4	2	65	60	28
Carolina	4	3	1	0	0	9	7	6	5	2	2	1	0	13	14	5	9	5	3	1	0	22	21	11
Chicago	16	7	6	3	0	48	43	17	17	6	10	1	0	39	49	13	33	13	16	4	0	87	92	30
Colorado	12	3	6	3	0	36	45	9	12	4	5	2	1	24	32	11	24	7	11	5	1	60	77	20
Columbus	11	7	2	1	1	29	24	16	10	5	5	0	0	27	23	10	21	12	7	1	1	56	47	26
Dallas	12	6	5	1	0	28	23	13	12	2	9	0	1	14	36	5	24	8	14	1	1	42	59	18
Detroit	16	7	7	2	0	40	45	16	17	2	11	2	2	38	69	8	33	9	18	4	2	78	114	24
Edmonton	13	4	6	3	0	32	37	11	12	6	5	0	1	34	36	13	25	10	11	3	1	66	73	24
Florida	5	1	2	2	0	8	10	4	4	1	2	1	0	8	11	3	9	2	4	3	0	16	21	7
Los Angeles	12	1	8	3	0	16	31	5	12	5	5	0	2	28	36	12	24	6	13	3	2	44	67	17
Minnesota	8	5	1	2	0	21	11	12	8	2	3	3	0	18	20	7	16	7	4	5	0	39	31	19
Montreal	4	2	1	1	0	14	7	5	4	0	3	0	1	9	15	1	8	2	4	1	1	23	22	6
New Jersey	5	1	4	0	0	9	14	2	5	3	1	0	1	14	15	7	10	4	5	0	1	23	29	9
NY Islanders	5	3	2	0	0	14	16	6	4	2	1	0	1	12	11	5	9	5	3	0	1	26	27	11
NY Rangers	4	2	2	0	0	13	14	4	6	3	2	1	0	15	18	7	10	5	4	1	0	28	32	11
Ottawa	4	2	2	0	0	8	11	4	5	1	4	0	0	7	14	2	9	3	6	0	0	15	25	6
Philadelphia	4	0	2	2	0	4	7	2	5	2	2	1	0	9	17	5	9	2	4	3	0	13	24	7
Phoenix	12	5	5	2	0	32	34	12	12	5	6	0	1	35	33	11	24	10	11	2	1	67	67	23
Pittsburgh	6	4	2	0	0	21	10	8	5	2	1	2	0	17	14	6	11	6	3	2	0	38	24	14
St. Louis	17	5	9	3	0	35	46	13	16	3	10	1	2	23	53	9	33	8	19	4	2	58	99	22
San Jose	12	5	6	1	0	29	34	11	12	5	6	1	0	31	30	11	24	10	12	2	0	60	64	22
Tampa Bay	6	2	4	0	0	12	16	4	4	1	2	0	1	10	11	4	10	3	6	0	1	22	27	8
Toronto	1	1	0	0	0	3	2	2	6	3	2	1	0	18	13	7	7	4	2	1	0	21	15	9
Vancouver	13	5	5	1	2	35	40	13	12	2	9	1	0	28	48	5	25	7	14	2	2	63	88	18
Washington	5	3	1	1	0	16	11	7	4	1	3	0	0	8	10	2	9	4	4	1	0	24	21	9
Totals	246	103	104	34	5	610	622	245	246	80	124	26	16	560	732	202	492	183	228	60	21	1170	1354	447

Playoffs

	Series	W	L	GP	W	L	T	GF	GA	Last Mtg	Rnd.	Result
Detroit	1	0	1	6	2	4	0	9	12	2004	CQF	L 2-4
Totals	1	0	1	6	2	4	0	9	12			

Playoff Results 2005-2000

Year	Round	Opponent	Result	GF	GA
2004	CQF	Detroit	L 2-4	9	12

Abbreviations: Round: CQF - conference quarter-final.

Key Off-Season Signings/Acquisitions

2004

July 19 • Re-signed LW **Jeremy Stevenson**.
Aug. 27 • Re-signed G **Tomas Vokoun**.
Sept. 9 • Signed 2003 1st-round pick (7th overall), D **Ryan Suter**.
  11 • Signed 2003 2nd-round pick (49th overall), D **Shea Weber**.
  15 • Re-signed D **Marek Zidlicky**.

2005

July 27 • Obtained F **Darcy Hordichuk** from Florida for a 2005 4th-round draft pick.
  28 • Re-signed C **Greg Johnson**.
  28 • Exercised options on G **Chris Mason** and C **Vernon Fiddler**.
  31 • Re-signed D **Jamie Allison**.
  31 • Signed 1999 1st-round pick (sixth overall) G **Brian Finley**.
Aug. 2 • Obtained D **Danny Markov** from Philadelphia for a 2006 3rd-round pick.
  4 • Re-signed D **Mark Eaton**.
  5 • Signed LW **Paul Kariya**.
  6 • Signed C **Scott Nichol**.
  10 • Re-signed LW **Scott Hartnell**.
  15 • Re-signed C **David Legwand**.
  16 • Re-signed RW **Steve Sullivan** and D **Dan Hamhuis**.
  19 • Signed C **Randy Robitaille**.
  29 • Re-signed LW **Martin Erat**.

Entry Draft Selections 2005-1998

2005

Pick	
18	Ryan Parent
78	Teemu Laakso
79	Cody Franson
150	Cal O'Reilly
176	Ryan Maki
213	Scott Todd
230	Patric Hornqvist

2004

Pick	
15	Alexander Radulov
81	Vaclav Meidl
107	Nick Fugere
139	Kyle Moir
147	Janne Niskala
178	Michael Santorelli
193	Kevin Schaeffer
209	Stanislav Balan
243	Denis Kulyash
258	Pekka Rinne
275	Craig Switzer

2003

Pick	
7	Ryan Suter
35	Konstantin Glazachev
37	Kevin Klein
49	Shea Weber
76	Richard Stehlik
89	Paul Brown
92	Alexander Sulzer
98	Grigory Shafigulin
117	Teemu Lassila
133	Rustam Sidikov
210	Andrei Mukhachev
213	Miroslav Hanuljak
268	Lauris Darzins

2002

Pick	
6	Scottie Upshall
102	Brandon Segal
138	Patrick Jarrett
172	Mike McKenna
203	Josh Morrow
235	Kaleb Betts
264	Matt Davis
266	Steven Spencer

2001

Pick	
12	Dan Hamhuis
33	Timofei Shishkanov
42	Tomas Slovak
75	Denis Platonov
76	Oliver Setzinger
98	Jordin Tootoo
178	Anton Lavrentiev
240	Gustav Grasberg
271	Mikko Lehtonen

2000

Pick	
6	Scott Hartnell
36	Daniel Widing
72	Mattias Nilsson
89	Libor Pivko
131	Matt Hendricks
137	Mike Stuart
154	Matt Koalska
173	Tomas Harant
197	Zbynek Irgl
203	Jure Penko
236	Mats Christeen
284	Martin Hohener

1999

Pick	
6	Brian Finley
33	Jonas Andersson
52	Adam Hall
54	Andrew Hutchinson
61	Ed Hill
65	Jan Lasak
72	Brett Angel
121	Yevgeny Pavlov
124	Alexandre Krevsun
131	Konstantin Panov
162	Timo Helbling
191	Martin Erat
205	Kyle Kettles
220	Miroslav Durak
248	Darren Haydar

1998

Pick	
2	David Legwand
60	Denis Arkhipov
85	Geoff Koch
88	Kent Sauer
138	Martin Beauchesne
147	Craig Brunel
202	Martin Bartek
230	Karlis Skrastins

Coach

TROTZ, BARRY
Coach, Nashville Predators. Born in Winnipeg, Man., July 15, 1962.

Barry Trotz realized his dream of becoming an NHL head coach on August 6, 1997, after serving four seasons as head coach and director of hockey operations for the American Hockey League's Portland Pirates. He and assistant Paul Gardner spent the 1997-98 season scouting in preparation for the inaugural season of the Predators. In his sixth season behind the bench in 2003-04, Trotz led Nashville into the playoffs for the first time.

Trotz began his coaching career in 1984 as assistant coach with the University of Manitoba for one season, before serving two seasons as the head coach and general manager of the Dauphin Kings Junior Hockey Club from 1985 to 1987. He became head coach of the University of Manitoba during the 1987 season and also served as a scout for the Spokane Chiefs of the Western Hockey League that season. Trotz joined the Washington Capitals organization as their chief western scout during the 1988 season. The Winnipeg, Manitoba native was appointed an assistant coach of the Capitals' American Hockey League affiliate in Baltimore prior to the 1991 season before being named head coach prior to the 1992 season. When the franchise relocated to Portland, he guided the Pirates to two AHL Calder Cup Final appearances in the club's first four seasons. He led the Pirates to a league-best 43-27-10 record, captured the Calder Cup championship and was named the American Hockey League coach of the year following the 1994-95 season.

In 1995, Trotz guided Portland to a new North American professional hockey league record 17-game unbeaten streak (14-0-3) to start the season. He was named head coach for the U.S. team at the American Hockey League All-Star Game in 1996.

Prior to his coaching career, Trotz played junior hockey for the Western Hockey League's Regina Pats from 1979-83. During that time, he recorded 39 goals, 121 assists for 160 points, along with 490 penalty minutes in 204 games.

Coaching Record

		Regular Season				Playoffs		
Season	**Team**	**Games**	**W**	**L**	**T**	**Games**	**W**	**L**
1992-93	Baltimore (AHL)	80	28	40	12	7	3	4
1993-94	Portland (AHL)	80	43	27	10	8	6	2
1994-95	Portland (AHL)	80	46	22	12	7	3	4
1995-96	Portland (AHL)	80	32	38	10	24	14	10
1996-97	Portland (AHL)	80	37	33	10	5	2	3
1998-99	**Nashville (NHL)**	**82**	**28**	**47**	**7**	....	....	....
1999-2000	**Nashville (NHL)**	**82**	**28**	**47**	**7**	....	....	....
2000-01	**Nashville (NHL)**	**82**	**34**	**39**	**9**	....	....	....
2001-02	**Nashville (NHL)**	**82**	**28**	**41**	**13**	....	....	....
2002-03	**Nashville (NHL)**	**82**	**27**	**42**	**13**	....	....	....
2003-04	**Nashville (NHL)**	**82**	**38**	**33**	**11**	**6**	**2**	**4**
2004-05	**Nashville (NHL)**			Season Cancelled				
	NHL Totals	**492**	**183**	**249**	**60**	**6**	**2**	**4**

Club Directory

Gaylord Entertainment Center

Nashville Predators
Gaylord Entertainment Center
501 Broadway
Nashville, TN 37203
Phone **615/770-2300**
FAX 615/770-2309
Ticket Information 615/770-PUCK
www.nashvillepredators.com
Capacity: 17,113

Owner, Chairman and Governor . . . . Craig Leipold
General Partner . . . . Nashville Predators, LLC
Exec. V.P./G.M. & Alt. Gov. . . . . David Poile
Exec. V.P. of Finance & Admin./CFO & Alt. Gov. . . . Ed Lang
Exec. V.P. of Business Affairs & Alt. Gov. . . . . Steve Violetta
Sr. V.P./Communications & Development . . . . Gerry Helper

Hockey Operations
Assistant General Manager . . . . Ray Shero
Head Coach . . . . Barry Trotz
Associate Coach . . . . Brent Peterson
Assistant Coach . . . . Peter Horachek
Goaltending Coach . . . . Mitch Korn
Video Coach . . . . Robert Bouchard
Strength and Conditioning Coach . . . . David Good
Director of Player Personnel/Chief Scout . . . . Paul Fenton
Professional Scouts . . . . Nick Beverley, Dan MacKinnon
North American Amateur Scouts . . . . Gord Donnelly, Jeff Kealty, Rick Knickle, Glen Sanders, David Westby
European Scouts . . . . Lucas Bergman, Janne Kekalainen
Head Athletic Trainer . . . . Dan Redmond
Assistant Athletic Trainer . . . . Eric Claas
Equipment Manager . . . . Pete Rogers
Assistant Equipment Manager . . . . Jeff Camelio
Locker Room Attendant . . . . Craig "Partner" Baugh
Director of Team Services . . . . Gregory Harvey
Hockey Operations Manager . . . . Brandon Walker
Executive Assistant . . . . Jessica Halperin

Team Doctors
Team Physician . . . . Dr. Michael J. Pagnani, MD
Assistant Team Physician . . . . Dr. Blake Garside, MD
Team Dentist . . . . Dr. Cristin Wallace, DDS
Team Ophthalmologist . . . . Dr. Daniel Weikert, MD
Team Plastic Surgeons . . . . Dr. Bryan D. Oslin, MD; Dr. Donald Griffin, MD
Team Neuropsychologist . . . . Dr. Gary S. Solomon, Ph. D.
Team Neurosurgeon . . . . Dr. Carl Hampf, MD
Team Internist . . . . Dr. Richard W. Garman, MD

Communications/Development
Director of Communications . . . . Ken Anderson
Communications Manager . . . . Tim Darling
Internet Development Manager . . . . Doug Brumley
Community Relations Manager . . . . Rebecca Ward
Youth/Amateur Hockey Coordinator . . . . Andee Boiman
Community Relations Coordinator . . . . Erich Wilhelm
Team Photographer . . . . John Russell

Corporate Sales
Vice President of Corporate Partnerships . . . . David Nivison
Account Executives – Corporate Partnerships . . . . . Kristin Fricke, Tom Moulton
Corporate Partnerships Account Manager . . . . Chris Leipold
Corporate Partnerships Account Manager . . . . Kristy Estes-Adoff
Executive Assistant . . . . Gerry Pring

Marketing
Vice President of Marketing . . . . Randy Campbell
Director of Marketing . . . . Bryan Shaffer
Marketing and Special Events Manager . . . . Christel Foley
Entertainment Manager . . . . Adam DeVault
Advertising Manager . . . . Vicki Garrison
Database Marketing Manager . . . . Jason Koettel
Game Operations Coordinator . . . . Brian Campbell
Traffic Coordinator . . . . TBA
Art Director . . . . Jennifer Sheets
Graphic Artist . . . . Chuck Stevens

Premium Seating
Vice President of Premium Seating Service . . . . Susie Masotti
Premium Seating Manager . . . . Britt Kincheloe

Finance/Administration/Human Resources
Senior Director of Finance . . . . Beth Snider
Senior Director of Human Resources . . . . Stephanie Ditenhafer
Payroll Manager . . . . Susan Charnley
Senior Accountant, Predators . . . . Sjar Toney
Accountant, Arena . . . . Melanie Ainsworth
Finance and Human Resources Coordinator . . . . . . Jonathan Norris
Accounts Payable Clerk . . . . Caleb Taylor
Office Coordinator . . . . TBA
Executive Assistant . . . . Elaine Lewis

Tech Ops
Director of Technical Operations . . . . Blake Grant
Information Systems Manager . . . . Albert Woodard
Network Support Technician . . . . Robert Boudreau

Broadcast
Director of Broadcasting . . . . Erik Barnhart
Play-by-Play Announcer . . . . Pete Weber
Color Analyst . . . . Terry Crisp
Manager, Video Production . . . . Mitch Jordan
Videographer/Editor . . . . David White

Ticket Operations
Vice President of Ticket Sales . . . . Scott Wampold
Season Ticket Sales Manager . . . . Nat Harden
Suite and Group Sales Manager . . . . Chris Junghans
Account Executives . . . . Danielle Baker, Michael Ceccarelli, Brad Gillispie, Todd McNamara, Jenny Moss, Jason Mott, Jon Salge, Thomas Tilney, Tiffany Vanek, Tim Wilson
Ticket Operations/Fan Relations Manager . . . . Brad MacLachlan
Ticket Operations Coordinators . . . . Sara Endwright, Mary Jane Rodgers
Fan Relations Representatives . . . . Chris Burton, Courtney Gray
Ticket Sales Coordinator . . . . Kelly Sweeney
Radio Flagship . . . . WGFX 104.5 The Zone, WNSR Sports 56
TV Flagship . . . . FSN South

New Jersey Devils

A fine offensive performer en route to the NHL, John Madden has developed into one of the league's top defensive forwards while averaging 17 goals per year over five NHL seasons.

2005-06 Schedule

Oct.	Wed.	5	Pittsburgh		Sat.	7	at Buffalo
	Fri.	7	at Philadelphia		Mon.	9	Philadelphia
	Sat.	8	NY Rangers		Fri.	13	Vancouver
	Thu.	13	at NY Rangers		Sun.	15	at Chicago
	Sat.	15	Carolina		Tue.	17	at St. Louis
	Tue.	18	Florida		Thu.	19	at Nashville
	Thu.	20	at Pittsburgh		Sat.	21	NY Islanders*
	Sat.	22	at Atlanta		Sun.	22	at NY Rangers
	Wed.	26	Tampa Bay		Tue.	24	at NY Islanders
	Fri.	28	Buffalo		Thu.	26	at Tampa Bay
	Sat.	29	at Boston		Fri.	27	at Florida
Nov.	Tue.	1	Pittsburgh	**Feb.**	Wed.	1	Ottawa
	Thu.	3	NY Rangers		Fri.	3	Carolina
	Sat.	5	at NY Rangers*		Sat.	4	at Toronto
	Tue.	8	NY Islanders		Tue.	7	Tampa Bay
	Fri.	11	at Washington*		Thu.	9	at Boston
	Sat.	12	Washington*		Sat.	11	NY Islanders*
	Tue.	15	at Buffalo	**Mar.**	Wed.	1	Philadelphia
	Fri.	18	Montreal		Thu.	2	at NY Islanders
	Sat.	19	at Ottawa		Sat.	4	NY Rangers
	Wed.	23	at Florida		Tue.	7	at NY Islanders
	Fri.	25	at Tampa Bay		Fri.	10	at Washington
	Tue.	29	Boston		Sat.	11	at Pittsburgh
	Wed.	30	at Philadelphia		Tue.	14	NY Islanders
Dec.	Sat.	3	Minnesota*		Thu.	16	Pittsburgh
	Tue.	6	at Detroit		Sun.	19	Ottawa
	Wed.	7	Calgary		Tue.	21	at Philadelphia
	Fri.	9	Colorado		Thu.	23	at Atlanta
	Sun.	11	at Columbus*		Fri.	24	Boston
	Tue.	13	Edmonton		Sun.	26	Toronto
	Thu.	15	Atlanta		Tue.	28	at Ottawa
	Sat.	17	at Carolina		Thu.	30	Buffalo
	Tue.	20	at NY Rangers	**Apr.**	Sat.	1	at Philadelphia*
	Wed.	21	at NY Islanders		Sun.	2	at Pittsburgh*
	Fri.	23	Atlanta		Wed.	5	Pittsburgh
	Mon.	26	at Toronto		Sat.	8	at Montreal
	Wed.	28	Washington		Sun.	9	NY Rangers
	Thu.	29	at Pittsburgh		Tue.	11	at Carolina
	Sat.	31	Toronto		Thu.	13	Philadelphia
Jan.	Tue.	3	Florida		Sun.	16	Philadelphia*
	Thu.	5	Montreal		Tue.	18	at Montreal

* Denotes afternoon game.

Franchise date: June 11, 1974

Transferred from Denver to New Jersey, June 30, 1982. Previously transferred from Kansas City to Denver.

32nd NHL Season

ATLANTIC DIVISION

Year-by-Year Record

Season	GP	Home W	L	T	OL	Road W	L	T	OL	Overall W	L	T	OL	GF	GA	Pts.	Finished	Playoff Result
2004-05	....	....				....				....				....	....	....		
2003-04	82	22	13	5	1	21	12	7	1	43	25	12	2	213	164	100	2nd, Atlantic Div.	Lost Conf. Quarter-Final
2002-03	**82**	**25**	**11**	**3**	**2**	**21**	**9**	**7**	**4**	**46**	**20**	**10**	**6**	**216**	**166**	**108**	**1st, Atlantic Div.**	**Won Stanley Cup**
2001-02	82	22	13	4	2	19	15	5	2	41	28	9	4	205	187	95	3rd, Atlantic Div.	Lost Conf. Quarter-Final
2000-01	82	24	11	6	0	24	8	6	3	48	19	12	3	295	195	111	1st, Atlantic Div.	Lost Final
1999-2000	**82**	**28**	**9**	**3**	**1**	**17**	**15**	**5**	**4**	**45**	**24**	**8**	**5**	**251**	**203**	**103**	**2nd, Atlantic Div.**	**Won Stanley Cup**
1998-99	82	19	14	8	....	28	10	3	....	47	24	11	....	248	196	105	1st, Atlantic Div.	Lost Conf. Quarter-Final
1997-98	82	29	10	2	....	19	13	9	....	48	23	11	....	225	166	107	1st, Atlantic Div.	Lost Conf. Quarter-Final
1996-97	82	23	9	9	....	22	14	5	....	45	23	14	....	231	182	104	1st, Atlantic Div.	Lost Conf. Semi-Final
1995-96	82	22	17	2	....	15	16	10	....	37	33	12	....	215	202	86	6th, Atlantic Div.	Out of Playoffs
1994-95	**48**	**14**	**4**	**6**	....	**8**	**14**	**2**	....	**22**	**18**	**8**	....	**136**	**121**	**52**	**2nd, Atlantic Div.**	**Won Stanley Cup**
1993-94	84	29	11	2	....	18	14	10	....	47	25	12	....	306	220	106	2nd, Atlantic Div.	Lost Conf. Championship
1992-93	84	24	14	4	....	16	23	3	....	40	37	7	....	308	299	87	4th, Patrick Div.	Lost Div. Semi-Final
1991-92	80	24	12	4	....	14	19	3	....	38	31	11	....	289	259	87	4th, Patrick Div.	Lost Div. Semi-Final
1990-91	80	23	10	7	....	9	23	8	....	32	33	15	....	272	264	79	4th, Patrick Div.	Lost Div. Semi-Final
1989-90	80	22	15	3	....	15	19	6	....	37	34	9	....	295	288	83	2nd, Patrick Div.	Lost Div. Semi-Final
1988-89	80	17	18	5	....	10	23	7	....	27	41	12	....	281	325	66	5th, Patrick Div.	Out of Playoffs
1987-88	80	23	16	1	....	15	20	5	....	38	36	6	....	295	296	82	4th, Patrick Div.	Lost Conf. Championship
1986-87	80	20	17	3	....	9	28	3	....	29	45	6	....	293	368	64	6th, Patrick Div.	Out of Playoffs
1985-86	80	17	21	2	....	11	28	1	....	28	49	3	....	300	374	59	6th, Patrick Div.	Out of Playoffs
1984-85	80	13	21	6	....	9	27	4	....	22	48	10	....	264	346	54	5th, Patrick Div.	Out of Playoffs
1983-84	80	10	28	2	....	7	28	5	....	17	56	7	....	231	350	41	5th, Patrick Div.	Out of Playoffs
1982-83	80	11	20	9	....	6	29	5	....	17	49	14	....	230	338	48	5th, Patrick Div.	Out of Playoffs
1981-82**	80	14	21	5	....	4	28	8	....	18	49	13	....	241	362	49	5th, Smythe Div.	Out of Playoffs
1980-81**	80	15	16	9	....	7	29	4	....	22	45	13	....	258	344	57	5th, Smythe Div.	Out of Playoffs
1979-80**	80	12	20	8	....	7	28	5	....	19	48	13	....	234	308	51	6th, Smythe Div.	Out of Playoffs
1978-79**	80	8	24	8	....	7	29	4	....	15	53	12	....	210	331	42	4th, Smythe Div.	Out of Playoffs
1977-78**	80	17	14	9	....	2	26	12	....	19	40	21	....	257	305	59	2nd, Smythe Div.	Lost Prelim. Round
1976-77**	80	12	20	8	....	8	26	6	....	20	46	14	....	226	307	54	5th, Smythe Div.	Out of Playoffs
1975-76*	80	8	24	8	....	4	32	4	....	12	56	12	....	190	351	36	5th, Smythe Div.	Out of Playoffs
1974-75*	80	12	20	8	....	3	34	3	....	15	54	11	....	184	328	41	5th, Smythe Div.	Out of Playoffs

* Kansas City Scouts. ** Colorado Rockies.

2005-06 Player Personnel

FORWARDS	HT	WT	S	Place of Birth	Date	2004-05 Club
BERGFORS, Nicklas	6-2	190	R	Sodertalje, Sweden	3/7/87	Sodertalje
BRYLIN, Sergei	5-10	190	L	Moscow, USSR	1/13/74	Voskresensk
CLARKSON, Dave	6-1	205	R	Mimico, Ont.	3/31/84	Kitchener
DAVIS, Patrick	6-2	190	R	Sterling, MI	12/28/86	Kitchener
ELIAS, Patrik	6-1	195	L	Trebic, Czech.	4/13/76	Znojmo-Magnitogorsk
FOSTER, Adrian	6-0	205	L	Lethbridge, Alta.	1/15/82	Albany
FRIESEN, Jeff	6-1	205	L	Meadow Lake, Sask.	8/5/76	
GIONTA, Brian	5-7	175	R	Rochester, NY	1/18/79	Albany
GOMEZ, Scott	5-11	200	L	Anchorage, AK	12/23/79	Alaska
JANSSEN, Cam	5-11	205	R	St. Louis, MO	4/15/84	Albany
KHOMUTOV, Ivan	6-3	205	L	Saratov, USSR	3/11/85	Albany
KOZLOV, Viktor	6-5	235	R	Togliatti, USSR	2/14/75	Togliatti
LANGDON, Darren	6-1	205	L	Deer Lake, Nfld.	1/8/71	
LANGENBRUNNER, Jamie	6-1	200	R	Cloquet, MN	7/24/75	Ingolstadt
LEBLOND-LETOURNEAU, Pierre-Luc	6-2	210	L	Levis, Que.	6/4/85	Baie-Comeau
MADDEN, John	5-11	190	L	Barrie, Ont.	5/4/73	HIFK
MARSHALL, Grant	6-1	200	R	Mississauga, Ont.	6/9/73	
MOGILNY, Alexander	6-0	210	L	Khabarovsk, USSR	2/18/69	
MURPHY, Ryan	6-1	210	L	Van Nuys, CA	3/21/79	Albany
NITTEL, Ahren	6-3	225	L	Waterloo, Ont.	12/6/83	Albany
OLIWA, Krzysztof	6-5	245	L	Tychy, Poland	4/12/73	Nowy Targ
PANDOLFO, Jay	6-1	190	L	Winchester, MA	12/27/74	Salzburg
PARISE, Zach	5-11	185	L	Minneapolis, MN	7/28/84	Albany
PIHLMAN, Tuomas	6-3	210	L	Espoo, Finland	11/13/82	Albany
PIKKARAINEN, Ilkka	6-2	200	R	Sonkajarvi, Finland	4/19/81	Albany
RASMUSSEN, Erik	6-1	210	L	Minneapolis, MN	3/28/77	
RHEAUME, Pascal	6-1	220	L	Quebec City, Que.	6/21/73	Albany
RYZNAR, Jason	6-3	205	L	Anchorage, AK	2/19/81	U. of Michigan
SGROI, Mike	6-5	230	L	Toronto, Ont.	8/14/78	Wheeling-Wilkes-Barre
SUGLOBOV, Aleksander	6-0	200	L	Elektrostal, USSR	1/15/82	Albany
SUNDSTROM, Alexander	5-11	190	L	Vancouver, B.C.	3/14/87	Bjorkloven
TALLACKSON, Barry	6-4	210	R	Grafton, ND	4/14/83	U. of Minnesota-Albany
VOROS, Aaron	6-4	190	L	Vancouver, B.C.	7/2/81	Albany
VRANA, Petr	5-10	175	L	Sternberk, Czech.	3/29/85	Halifax

DEFENSEMEN						
ALLEN, Bobby	6-1	205	L	Braintree, MA	11/14/78	Albany
BROOKS, Alex	6-1	205	R	Madison, WI	8/21/76	Albany
BROWN, Sean	6-3	215	L	Oshawa, Ont.	11/5/76	
DeMARCHI, Matt	6-3	190	L	Bemidji, MN	5/4/81	Albany
FRASER, Mark	6-4	195	L	Ottawa, Ont.	9/29/86	Gloucester-Kitchener
HALE, David	6-1	215	L	Colorado Springs, CO	6/18/81	Albany
KESA, Teemu	6-1	190	R	Helsinki, Finland	6/7/81	Albany
MALAKHOV, Vladimir	6-4	230	L	Sverdlovsk, USSR	8/30/68	
MARTIN, Paul	6-1	190	L	Minneapolis, MN	3/5/81	Fribourg
MATVICHUK, Richard	6-2	215	L	Edmonton, Alta.	2/5/73	
McGILLIS, Dan	6-2	230	L	Hawkesbury, Ont.	7/1/72	
MILLER, Bryan	5-10	180	R	Wayne, NJ	2/17/83	Boston University-Albany
RAFALSKI, Brian	5-10	190	L	Dearborn, MI	9/28/73	
REDLIHS, Krisjanis	6-3	190	L	Riga, Latvia	1/15/81	Albany
SCHULTZ, Ray	6-2	215	L	Red Deer, Alta.	11/14/76	Albany
SPENCER, Steven	6-3	220	L	Regina, Sask.	6/16/82	Albany-South Carolina
WHITE, Colin	6-4	215	L	New Glasgow, N.S.	12/12/77	
ZIMMERMAN, Sean	6-2	220	R	Denver, CO	5/24/87	Spokane

GOALTENDERS	HT	WT	C	Place of Birth	Date	2004-05 Club
AHONEN, Ari	6-2	195	L	Jyvaskyla, Finland	2/6/81	Albany
BRODEUR, Martin	6-2	210	L	Montreal, Que.	5/6/72	
CLEMMENSEN, Scott	6-3	205	L	Des Moines, IA	7/23/77	Albany
DISHER, Josh	6-1	170	L	Chatham, Ont.	6/24/85	Erie (OHL)
DOYLE, Frank	6-1	175		Guelph, Ont.	9/8/80	Utah-Idaho

In the System and Recently Drafted

FORWARDS	HT	WT	S	Place of Birth	Date	2004-05 Club
LAINE, Teemu	6-1	200	L	Helsinki, Finland	8/9/82	Tappara
PERKOVICH, Nathan	6-5	195	R	Canton, MI	10/15/85	Chicago
ZAJAC, Travis	6-2	205	R	Winnipeg, Man.	5/13/85	North Dakota

DEFENSEMEN						
ECKFORD, Tyler	6-1	205	L	Vancouver, B.C.	9/8/85	South Surrey
FAYNE, Mark	6-3	195	R	Nashua, NH	5/15/87	Nobles
GLOVER, Dan	6-2	175	L	Delburne, Alta.	5/4/83	Cornell
KADEYKIN, Anton	6-3	205	L	Elektrostal, USSR	5/17/84	
KLIMOV, Valeri	6-2	205	L	Moscow, USSR	7/17/86	Spartak
MIKHAILISHIN, Alexander	6-4	210	L	Neustrelitz, East Germany	2/24/86	Spartak
TARKIR, Zach	6-0	180	R	Fresno, CA	6/28/84	Northern Mich.

GOALTENDERS	HT	WT	C	Place of Birth	Date	2004-05 Club
FRAZEE, Jeff	6-0	184	L	Edina, MN	5/13/87	USA U-18
SMITH, Jason	6-1	170	L	St-Lambert, Que.	7/17/85	Sacred Heart

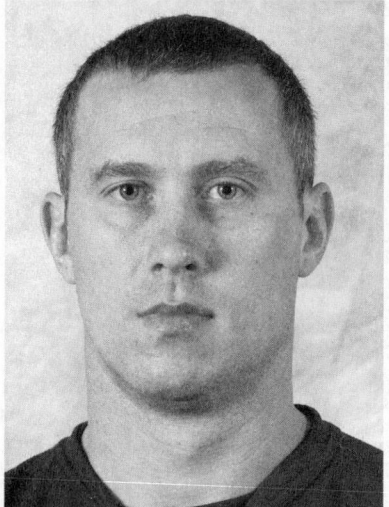

Alexander Mogilny returns to New Jersey, where he scored 43 goals during the 2000-01 season.

Captains' History

Simon Nolet, 1974-75 to 1976-77; Wilf Paiement, 1977-78; Gary Croteau, 1978-79; Mike Christie, Rene Robert and Lanny McDonald, 1979-80; Lanny McDonald, 1980-81; Lanny McDonald and Rob Ramage, 1981-82; Don Lever, 1982-83; Don Lever and Mel Bridgman, 1983-84; Mel Bridgman, 1984-85 to 1986-87; Kirk Muller, 1987-88 to 1990-91; Bruce Driver, 1991-92; Scott Stevens, 1992-93 to 2002-03; Scott Stevens and Scott Neidermayer, 2003-04.

Coaching History

Bep Guidolin, 1974-75; Bep Guidolin, Sid Abel and Eddie Bush, 1975-76; Johnny Wilson, 1976-77; Pat Kelly, 1977-78; Pat Kelly and Aldo Guidolin, 1978-79; Don Cherry, 1979-80; Bill MacMillan, 1980-81; Bert Marshall and Marshall Johnston, 1981-82; Bill MacMillan, 1982-83; Bill MacMillan and Tom McVie, 1983-84; Doug Carpenter, 1984-85 to 1986-87; Doug Carpenter and Jim Schoenfeld, 1987-88; Jim Schoenfeld, 1988-89; Jim Schoenfeld and John Cunniff, 1989-90; John Cunniff and Tom McVie, 1990-91; Tom McVie, 1991-92; Herb Brooks, 1992-93; Jacques Lemaire, 1993-94 to 1997-98; Robbie Ftorek, 1998-99; Robbie Ftorek and Larry Robinson, 1999-2000; Larry Robinson, 2000-01; Larry Robinson and Kevin Constantine, 2001-02; Pat Burns, 2002-03 to 2004-05; Larry Robinson, 2005-06.

Coach

ROBINSON, LARRY
Coach, New Jersey Devils. Born in Winchester, Ont., June 2, 1951.

The New Jersey Devils named Larry Robinson to the position of head coach on July 14, 2005. He is the 13th head coach of the team since the franchise moved to in 1982. Previously, Robinson had spent eight seasons in the Devils organization, including a prior stint as head coach. He was promoted to the position of special assignment coach in August 2002, after re-joining the team as an assistant coach on February 25, 2002. Robinson previously served New Jersey as head coach from March 23, 2000 to January 28, 2002. During the 1999–2000 campaign, Robinson became just the third coach in league history to take over a team in mid-season and go on to win the Stanley Cup.

Robinson re-joined the Devils as an assistant coach on May 26, 1999, after spending the previous four seasons as head coach of the Los Angeles Kings. Robinson was named to that position July 26, 1995, after serving New Jersey as an assistant coach for two seasons, including during the team's first championship in 1994–95. Robinson originally joined the Devils for his first career coaching positions on June 30, 1993, after a one-year absence from hockey.

Robinson played 20 NHL seasons before retiring as a player in 1992. He was elected to the Hockey Hall of Fame in 1995. Among his accomplishments: a six-time Stanley Cup champion with the Montreal Canadiens; a two-time recipient of the Norris Trophy as the NHL's best defenseman (1977, 1980); named to the NHL First All-Star Team three times (1977, 1979, 1980); NHL Second All-Star Team three times (1978, 1981, 1986); and made ten All-Star Game appearances (1974, 1976, 1977, 1978, 1980, 1982, 1986, 1988, 1989, 1992).

Coaching Record

Season	Team	Games	Regular Season W	L	T	Playoffs Games	W	L
1995-96	Los Angeles (NHL)	82	24	40	18	....	....	....
1996-97	Los Angeles (NHL)	82	28	43	11	....	....	....
1997-98	Los Angeles (NHL)	82	38	33	11	4	0	4
1998-99	Los Angeles (NHL)	82	32	45	5	....	....	....
1999-2000	New Jersey (NHL)	8	4	4	0	23	16	7*
2000-01	New Jersey (NHL)	82	48	22	12	25	15	10
2001-02	New Jersey (NHL)	51	21	23	7	....	....	....
	NHL Totals	469	195	210	64	52	31	21

* Stanley Cup win.

Club Records

Team

(Figures in brackets for season records are games played; records for fewest points, wins, ties, losses, goals, goals against are for 70 or more games)

Most Points 111 2000-01 (82)
Most Wins 48 1997-98 (82), 2000-01 (82)
Most Ties 21 1977-78 (80)
Most Losses 56 1975-76 (80), 1983-84 (80)
Most Goals 308 1992-93 (84)
Most Goals Against 374 1985-86 (80)
Fewest Points *36 1975-76 (80)
41 1983-84 (80)
Fewest Wins *12 1975-76 (80)
17 1982-83 (80), 1983-84 (80)
Fewest Ties 3 1985-86 (80)
Fewest Losses 19 2000-01 (82)
Fewest Goals *184 1974-75 (80)
205 2001-02 (82)
Fewest Goals Against 164 2003-04 (82)
Longest Winning Streak
Overall .... 13 Feb. 26-Mar. 23/01
Home .... 8 Oct. 9-Nov. 7/87, Jan. 3-Feb. 4/03
Away .... **10 Feb. 27-Apr. 7/01
Longest Undefeated Streak
Overall .... 13 Four times
Home .... 15 Jan. 8-Mar. 15/97 (9 wins, 6 ties)
Away .... 10 Feb. 27-Apr. 7/01 (10 wins)
Longest Losing Streak
Overall .... *14 Dec. 30/75-Jan. 29/76
10 Oct. 14-Nov. 4/83
Home .... 9 Dec. 22/85-Feb. 6/86
Away .... 12 Oct. 19-Dec. 1/83
Longest Winless Streak
Overall .... *27 Feb. 12-Apr. 4/76 (21 losses, 6 ties)
18 Oct. 20-Nov. 26/82 (14 losses 4 ties)
Home .... *14 Feb. 12-Mar. 30/76 (10 losses, 4 ties), Feb. 4-Mar. 31/79 (12 losses, 2 ties)
9 Dec. 22/85-Feb. 6/86 (9 losses)
Away .... *32 Nov. 12/77-Mar. 15/78 (22 losses, 10 ties)
14 Dec. 26/82-Mar. 5/83 (13 losses, 1 tie)
Most Shutouts, Season 14 2003-04 (82)
Most PIM, Season 2,494 1988-89 (80)
Most Goals, Game .... 9 Nine times

Individual

Most Seasons .... 20 Ken Daneyko
Most Games .... 1,283 Ken Daneyko
Most Goals, Career .... 347 John MacLean
Most Assists, Career .... 364 Scott Niedermayer
Most Points, Career .... 701 John MacLean (347G, 354A)
Most PIM, Career .... 2,519 Ken Daneyko
Most Shutouts, Career .... 75 Martin Brodeur
Longest Consecutive Games Streak .... 388 Ken Daneyko (Nov. 4/89-Mar. 29/94)
Most Goals, Season .... 46 Pat Verbeek (1987-88)
Most Assists, Season .... 60 Scott Stevens (1993-94)
Most Points, Season .... 96 Patrik Elias (2000-01; 40G, 56A)
Most PIM, Season .... 295 Krzysztof Oliwa (1997-98)
Most Points, Defenseman, Season .... 78 Scott Stevens (1993-94; 18G, 60A)
Most Points, Center, Season .... 94 Kirk Muller (1987-88; 37G, 57A)
Most Points, Right Wing, Season .... *87 Wilf Paiement (1977-78; 31G, 56A)
87 John MacLean (1988-89; 42G, 45A)
Most Points, Left Wing, Season .... 96 Patrik Elias (2000-01; 40G, 56A)
Most Points, Rookie, Season .... 70 Scott Gomez (1999-2000; 19G, 51A)
Most Shutouts, Season .... 11 Martin Brodeur (2003-04)
Most Goals, Game .... 4 Five times
Most Assists, Game .... 5 Greg Adams (Oct. 10/85), Kirk Muller (Mar. 25/87), Tom Kurvers (Feb. 13/89), Scott Gomez (Mar. 30/03)
Most Points, Game .... 6 Kirk Muller (Nov. 29/86; 3G, 3A)

* Records include Kansas City Scouts and Colorado Rockies, 1974-75 through 1981-82.
** NHL Record.

All-time Record vs. Other Clubs

Regular Season

	At Home								On Road								Total							
	GP	W	L	T	OL	GF	GA	PTS	GP	W	L	T	OL	GF	GA	PTS	GP	W	L	T	OL	GF	GA	PTS
Anaheim	8	7	1	0	0	31	14	14	10	5	4	1	0	26	26	11	18	12	5	1	0	57	40	25
Atlanta	10	6	3	1	0	33	20	13	10	7	1	2	0	36	13	16	20	13	4	3	0	69	33	29
Boston	53	15	27	11	0	139	172	41	56	17	29	8	2	171	218	44	109	32	56	19	2	310	390	85
Buffalo	54	19	26	9	0	162	177	47	54	15	31	8	0	165	213	38	108	34	57	17	0	327	390	85
Calgary	45	15	27	3	0	128	162	33	42	6	27	8	1	111	184	21	87	21	54	11	1	239	346	54
Carolina	45	25	16	4	0	158	140	54	44	18	17	8	1	132	137	45	89	43	33	12	1	290	277	99
Chicago	47	20	16	11	0	147	142	51	46	12	24	10	0	127	176	34	93	32	40	21	0	274	318	85
Colorado	36	19	13	4	0	147	121	42	35	13	18	4	0	98	124	30	71	32	31	8	0	245	245	72
Columbus	2	1	0	1	0	5	4	3	4	2	2	0	0	13	13	4	6	3	2	1	0	18	17	7
Dallas	43	21	19	3	0	146	132	45	45	13	25	6	1	117	164	33	88	34	44	9	1	263	296	78
Detroit	40	21	10	9	0	138	103	51	40	13	24	2	1	129	164	29	80	34	34	11	1	267	267	80
Edmonton	33	14	16	3	0	111	112	31	31	11	14	6	0	114	136	28	64	25	30	9	0	225	248	59
Florida	24	14	7	3	0	72	49	31	25	14	7	4	0	66	53	32	49	28	14	7	0	138	102	63
Los Angeles	43	19	19	5	0	142	148	43	42	8	27	6	1	130	201	23	85	27	46	11	1	272	349	66
Minnesota	3	2	0	1	0	13	8	5	3	1	1	1	0	8	7	3	6	3	1	2	0	21	15	8
Montreal	54	25	25	4	0	160	190	54	54	15	32	6	1	134	182	37	108	40	57	10	1	294	372	91
Nashville	5	2	3	0	0	15	14	4	5	4	1	0	0	14	9	8	10	6	4	0	0	29	23	12
NY Islanders	84	36	36	11	1	281	289	84	85	19	55	11	0	247	355	49	169	55	91	22	1	528	644	133
NY Rangers	86	45	34	7	0	301	280	97	84	24	39	20	1	255	323	69	170	69	73	27	1	556	603	166
Ottawa	23	13	8	2	0	66	54	28	24	15	5	3	1	60	47	34	47	28	13	5	1	126	101	62
Philadelphia	83	42	33	8	0	283	285	92	85	24	51	10	0	214	322	58	168	66	84	18	0	497	607	150
Phoenix	29	12	11	6	0	95	87	30	31	7	21	3	0	81	114	17	60	19	32	9	0	176	201	47
Pittsburgh	81	39	29	13	0	295	269	91	79	35	39	4	1	269	289	75	160	74	68	17	1	564	558	166
St. Louis	46	22	17	7	0	146	128	51	46	12	26	7	1	143	192	32	92	34	43	14	1	289	320	83
San Jose	12	7	4	1	0	44	24	15	10	6	2	1	1	32	24	14	22	13	6	2	1	76	48	29
Tampa Bay	26	18	5	2	1	93	44	39	25	12	7	5	1	75	59	30	51	30	12	7	2	168	103	69
Toronto	46	17	13	15	1	155	136	50	48	12	31	5	0	138	182	29	94	29	44	20	1	293	318	79
Vancouver	49	20	21	6	2	151	159	48	47	9	27	11	0	130	175	29	96	29	48	17	2	281	334	77
Washington	79	39	32	7	1	240	226	86	79	24	49	6	0	223	308	54	158	63	81	13	1	463	534	140
Defunct Clubs	8	4	2	2	0	25	19	10	8	2	3	3	0	19	27	7	16	6	5	5	0	44	46	17
Totals	**1197**	**559**	**473**	**159**	**6**	**3922**	**3708**	**1283**	**1197**	**375**	**639**	**169**	**14**	**3477**	**4437**	**933**	**2394**	**934**	**1112**	**328**	**20**	**7399**	**8145**	**2216**

Playoffs

	Series	W	L	GP	W	L	T	GF	GA	Last Mtg.	Rnd.	Result
Anaheim	1	1	0	7	4	3	0	19	12	2003	F	W 4-3
Boston	4	3	1	23	15	8	0	68	60	2003	CQF	W 4-1
Buffalo	1	1	0	7	4	3	0	14	14	1994	CQF	W 4-3
Carolina	2	1	1	12	6	6	0	31	17	2002	CQF	L 2-4
Colorado	1	0	1	7	3	4	0	11	19	2001	F	L 3-4
Dallas	1	1	0	6	4	2	0	15	9	2000	F	W 4-2
Detroit	1	1	0	4	4	0	0	16	7	1995	F	W 4-0
Florida	1	1	0	4	4	0	0	12	6	2000	CQF	W 4-0
Montreal	1	1	0	5	4	1	0	22	11	1997	CQF	W 4-1
NY Islanders	1	1	0	6	4	2	0	23	18	1988	DSF	W 4-2
NY Rangers	3	0	3	19	7	12	0	46	56	1997	CSF	L 1-4
Ottawa	2	1	1	13	6	7	0	29	26	2003	CF	W 4-3
Philadelphia	4	2	2	20	9	11	0	50	49	2004	CQF	L 1-4
Pittsburgh	5	2	3	29	15	14	0	86	80	2001	CF	W 4-1
Tampa Bay	1	1	0	5	4	1	0	14	8	2003	CSF	W 4-1
Toronto	2	2	0	13	8	5	0	37	27	2001	CSF	W 4-3
Washington	2	1	1	13	6	7	0	43	44	1990	DSF	L 2-4
Totals	**33**	**20**	**13**	**193**	**107**	**86**	**0**	**536**	**463**			

Playoff Results 2005-2000

Year	Round	Opponent	Result	GF	GA
2004	CQF	Philadelphia	L 1-4	9	14
2003	**F**	**Anaheim**	**W 4-3**	**19**	**12**
	CF	Ottawa	W 4-3	17	13
	CSF	Tampa Bay	W 4-1	14	8
	CQF	Boston	W 4-1	13	8
2002	CQF	Carolina	L 2-4	11	9
2001	F	Colorado	L 3-4	11	19
	CF	Pittsburgh	W 4-1	17	7
	CSF	Toronto	W 4-3	21	18
	CQF	Carolina	W 4-2	20	8
2000	**F**	**Dallas**	**W 4-2**	**15**	**9**
	CF	Philadelphia	W 4-3	18	15
	CSF	Toronto	W 4-2	16	9
	CQF	Florida	W 4-0	12	6

Abbreviations: Round: F – Final; **CF** – conference final; **CSF** – conference semi-final; **CQF** – conference quarter-final; **DSF** – division semi-final.

Calgary totals include Atlanta Flames, 1974-75 to 1979-80.
Colorado totals include Quebec, 1979-80 to 1994-95.
Phoenix totals include Winnipeg, 1979-80 to 1995-96.
Carolina totals include Hartford, 1979-80 to 1996-97.
Dallas totals include Minnesota North Stars, 1974-75 to 1992-93.

Key Off-Season Signings/Acquisitions

2004

Apr. 19 • Signed 2003 1st-round pick (17th overall), C **Zach Parise**.
July 1 • Re-signed C **John Madden** and LW **Jay Pandolfo**.
3 • Signed LW **Darren Langdon**.
8 • Re-signed RW **Grant Marshall**.
12 • Signed D **Richard Matvichuk**.
15 • Signed LW **Krzysztof Oliwa**.
Aug. 13 • Signed Ds **Bobby Allen** and **Ray Schultz**.
19 • Signed C **Sergei Brylin**.
27 • Re-signed C **Erik Rasmussen**.

2005

July 14 • Named **Larry Robinson** head coach.
25 • Exercised option on G **Scott Clemmensen**.
Aug. 4 • Re-signed D **Brian Rafalski**.
4 • Signed Ds **Vladimir Malakhov** and **Dan McGillis**.
11 • Re-signed RW **Jamie Langenbrunner**.
12 • Re-signed LW **Jeff Friesen**, C **Scott Gomez** and RW **Viktor Kozlov**.
13 • Re-signed D **Sean Brown**.
16 • Signed RW **Alexander Mogilny**.
17 • Re-signed RW **Brian Gionta**.
18 • Re-signed D **Colin White**.
19 • Re-signed D **David Hale**.
23 • Re-signed D **Paul Martin**.

Entry Draft
Selections 2005-1991

2005
Pick
23	Nicklas Bergfors
38	Jeff Frazee
84	Mark Fraser
99	Patrick Davis
155	Mark Fayne
170	Sean Zimmerman
218	Alexander Sundstrom

2004
Pick
20	Travis Zajac
155	Alexander Mikhailishin
185	Josh Disher
216	Pierre-Luc Leblond-Letourneau
217	Tyler Eckford
250	Nathan Perkovich
282	Valeri Klimov

2003
Pick
17	Zach Parise
42	Petr Vrana
93	Ivan Khomutov
167	Zach Tarkir
197	Jason Smith
261	Joey Tenute
292	Arseny Bondarev

2002
Pick
51	Anton Kadeykin
53	Barry Tallackson
64	Jason Ryznar
84	Marek Chvatal
85	Ahren Nittel
117	Cam Janssen
154	Krisjanis Redlihs
187	Eric Johansson
218	Ilkka Pikkarainen
250	Dan Glover
281	Bill Kinkel

2001
Pick
28	Adrian Foster
44	Igor Pohanka
48	Tuomas Pihlman
60	Victor Uchevatov
67	Robin Leblanc
72	Brandon Nolan
128	Andrei Posnov
163	Andreas Salomonsson
194	James Massen
229	Aaron Voros
257	Yevgeny Gamalei

2000
Pick
22	David Hale
39	Teemu Laine
56	Aleksander Suglobov
57	Matt DeMarchi
62	Paul Martin
67	Max Birbraer
76	Mike Rupp
125	Phil Cole
135	Mike Danton
164	Matus Kostur
194	Deryk Engelland
198	Ken Magowan
257	Warren McCutcheon

1999
Pick
27	Ari Ahonen
42	Mike Commodore
50	Brett Clouthier
95	Andre Lakos
100	Teemu Kesa
185	Scott Cameron
214	Chris Hartsburg
242	Justin Dziama

1998
Pick
26	Mike Van Ryn
27	Scott Gomez
37	Christian Berglund
82	Brian Gionta
96	Mikko Jokela
105	Pierre Dagenais
119	Anton But
143	Ryan Flinn
172	Jacques Lariviere
199	Erik Jensen
227	Marko Ahosilta
257	Ryan Held

1997
Pick
24	Jean-Francois Damphousse
38	Stanislav Gron
104	Lucas Nehrling
131	Jiri Bicek
159	Sascha Goc
188	Mathieu Benoit
215	Scott Clemmensen
241	Jan Srdinko

1996
Pick
10	Lance Ward
38	Wes Mason
41	Josh DeWolf
47	Pierre Dagenais
49	Colin White
63	Scott Parker
91	Josef Boumedienne
101	Josh MacNevin
118	Glenn Crawford
145	Sean Ritchlin
173	Daryl Andrews
199	Willie Mitchell
205	Jay Bertsch
225	Pasi Petrilainen

1995
Pick
18	Petr Sykora
44	Nathan Perrott
70	Sergei Vyshedkevich
78	David Gosselin
79	Alyn McCauley
96	Henrik Rehnberg
122	Chris Mason
148	Adam Young
174	Richard Rochefort
200	Frederic Henry
226	Colin O'Hara

1994
Pick
25	Vadim Sharifijanov
51	Patrik Elias
71	Sheldon Souray
103	Zdenek Skorepa
129	Christian Gosselin
134	Ryan Smart
155	Luciano Caravaggio
181	Jeff Williams
207	Eric Bertrand
233	Steve Sullivan
259	Scott Swanjord
269	Mike Hanson

1993
Pick
13	Denis Pederson
32	Jay Pandolfo
39	Brendan Morrison
65	Krzysztof Oliwa
110	John Guirestante
143	Steve Brule
169	Nikolai Zavarukhin
195	Thomas Cullen
221	Judd Lambert
247	Jimmy Provencher
273	Mike Legg

1992
Pick
18	Jason Smith
42	Sergei Brylin
66	Cale Hulse
90	Vitali Tomilin
94	Scott McCabe
114	Ryan Black
138	Dan Trebil
162	Geordie Kinnear
186	Stephane Yelle
210	Jeff Toms
234	Heath Weenk
258	Vladislav Yakovenko

1991
Pick
3	Scott Niedermayer
11	Brian Rolston
33	Donevan Hextall
55	Fredrik Lindquist
77	Bradley Willner
121	Curt Regnier
143	David Craievich
165	Paul Wolanski
187	Daniel Reimann
231	Kevin Riehl
253	Jason Hehr

General Managers' History

Sid Abel, 1974-75, 1975-76; Ray Miron, 1976-77 to 1980-81; Bill MacMillan, 1981-82, 1982-83; Bill MacMillan and Max McNab, 1983-84; Max McNab 1984-85 to 1986-87; Lou Lamoriello, 1987-88 to date.

President and General Manager

LAMORIELLO, LOU
CEO/President/General Manager, New Jersey Devils.
Born in Providence, RI, October 21, 1942.

Lou Lamoriello's life-long dedication to the game of hockey was rewarded in 1992 when he was named a recipient of the Lester Patrick Trophy for outstanding service to hockey in the United States. Lamoriello has been president and general manager of the Devils since 1987-88 following more than 20 years with Providence College as a player, coach and administrator. His trades, signings and draft choices helped lead the Devils to their first Stanley Cup championship in 1995 and were followed by victories again in 2000 and 2003. A member of the varsity hockey Friars during his undergraduate days, he became an assistant coach with the college club after graduating in 1963. Lamoriello was later named head coach and in the ensuing 15 years, led his teams to a 248-179-13 record and appearances in 10 post-season tournaments, including the 1983 NCAA Final Four. Lamoriello also served a five-year term as athletic director at Providence and was a co-founder of Hockey East, one of the strongest collegiate hockey conferences in the U.S. He remained as athletic director until he was hired as president of the Devils on April 30, 1987. He assumed the responsibility of general manager on September 10, 1987. He was g.m. of Team USA for the first World Cup of Hockey in 1996 as the U.S. captured the championship. He was also the g.m. for the 1998 U.S. Olympic team.

Club Directory

Continental Airlines Arena

New Jersey Devils
Continental Airlines Arena
50 Route 120 North
P.O. Box 504
East Rutherford, NJ 07073
Phone **201/935-6050**
FAX 201/935-2127
www.newjerseydevils.com
Capacity: 19,040

Chairman/Managing Partner	Jeff Vanderbeek
CEO/President/General Manager	Louis A. Lamoriello
COO/Executive Vice President	Chris Modrzynski
Executive Vice President	Peter S. McMullen
CFO/Vice President	Scott Struble
Vice President, General Counsel	Joseph C. Benedetti
Vice President, Ticket Operations	Terry Farmer
Vice President, Corporate Partnerships	Kenneth F. Ferriter
Vice President, Facilities	Mark Gheduzzi
Vice President, Administration	Gordon Lavalette
Vice President, Information/Publications	Mike Levine
Vice President, Marketing/Community Development	Jason Siegel

Hockey Club Personnel
Head Coach	Larry Robinson
Assistant Coaches	Jacques Laperriere, John MacLean
Goaltending Coach	Jacques Caron
Director, Scouting	David Conte
Assistant Director, Scouting	Claude Carrier
Scouting Staff	Glen Dirk, Milt Fisher, Ferny Flaman, Dan Labraaten, Chris Lamoriello, Vladimir Lokotko, Larry Perris, Marcel Pronovost, Lou Reycroft, Vaclav Slansky, Jr., Geoff Stevens, Ed Thomlinson, Les Widdifield
Pro Scouting Staff	Bob Hoffmeyer, Jan Ludvig, Andre Boudrias, Geordie Kinnear, Gates Orlando
Special Assignments	Pat Burns, Kurt Kleinendorst
Hockey Operations Video Coordinator	Taran Singleton
Scouting Staff Assistant	Callie A. Smith
Medical Trainer	Bill Murray
Strength/Conditioning Coordinator	Michael Vasalani
Equipment Manager	Rich Matthews
Assistant Equipment Managers	Alex Abasto, Scott Sorenson
Massage Therapist	Tommy Plasko
Team Cardiologist	Dr. Joseph Niznik
Team Dentist	Dr. H. Hugh Gardy
Team Optometrist	Dr. Paul Berman
Team Orthopedists	Dr. Barry Fisher, Dr. Len Jaffe
Fitness Consultant	Vladimir Bure
Exercise Physiologist	Dr. Garret Caffrey
Physical Therapist	David Feniger
Video Consultant	Mitch Kaufman
Head Coach, Albany	Robbie Ftorek
Goaltending Coach, Albany	Chris Terreri
Athletic Trainer, Albany	Chris Palmer
Equipment Manager, Albany	Jason McGrath
Assistant Equipment Manager, Albany	Ryan Picard

President's Office
Hockey Ops. Exec. Asst. to CEO/Pres./G.M.	Marie Carnevale
Corporate Exec. Asst. to CEO/Pres./G.M.	Mary K. Morrison
Legal Assistant	Lisa Romero

Operations
Receptionist	Jelsa Belotta
Staff Assistants	Pat Maione, Ken McPeek

Ticket Operations
Director, Ticket Operations	Tom Bates
Ticket Service Managers	Andrea Marchesani, Frank Calandrillo
Director, Group Sales	Neil Desormeaux
Managers, Group Accounts	Don Gleeson, Kevin Quinn, John Tierney

Corporate Partnerships
Director, Corporate Partnerships	Michael DeMartino
Director, Corporate Partner Services	Matt Dugan
Account Manager	Nicole Rivera

Sales
Director, Ticket Sales/Customer Service	David Beck
Assistant Director, Ticket Sales	Vincent Occhipinti
Account Managers	Brooke Alper, Zamen Au, Matt Boiseau, Keith Butler, Kevin Fitzpatrick, Bryan Foxworth, Steven Gero, Kevin Hogan, Craig Ishill, Charlene Romero, Vincent Russo, Aaron Sanders, Glenn Sperber, Jeremy Steiner, Thomas Stocky, Kimberly Torns, Chris Valente
Receptionist, Sales	Jennifer Robinson

Marketing/Community Development
Director, Merchandising	David Perricone
Merchandising Assistant	Adam Manger
Director, Grass Roots Programs	Michael Merolla
Director, Game Entertainment	Anthony Gioia
Manager, Game Entertainment	David Schwinger
Game Entertainment Assistant	Jeff Kemperman
Director, Web Operations/Creative Services	Anthony Bovasso
Staff Assistant	Jennifer Schubert

Communications
Director, Public Relations	Jeff Altstadter
Manager, Communications	Pete Albietz
Staff Assistant	Daniel Beam

Finance
Assistant Contoller	Nicole Florit
Staff Accountants	Mario Deludicibus, Joe Pannia, Kristin Servino
Administrative Assistant	Eileen Philips

Computer Operations
Director, Programming/Computer Operations	Jack Skelley
Programmer/Analyst	Joseph Wyks
Systems Administrator	Mike Tukes

Television/Radio
Television Outlet	FOX Sports Net New York
Broadcasters	Mike Emrick, Play-by-Play, Glenn Resch, Color
Radio Outlet	Sports Radio 66 WFAN
Broadcasters	John Hennessy, Play-by-Play, Randy Velischek, Color

New York Islanders

2005-06 Schedule

Oct.	Wed.	5	at Buffalo
	Sat.	8	Carolina
	Mon.	10	Florida*
	Thu.	13	at Washington
	Sat.	15	at Philadelphia
	Wed.	19	at NY Rangers
	Thu.	20	NY Rangers
	Sat.	22	at Montreal
	Tue.	25	Atlanta
	Thu.	27	at NY Rangers
	Sat.	29	Buffalo
Nov.	Tue.	1	Boston
	Thu.	3	Pittsburgh
	Sat.	5	at Ottawa
	Tue.	8	at New Jersey
	Thu.	10	at Philadelphia
	Sat.	12	Boston
	Mon.	14	at Pittsburgh
	Wed.	16	at Atlanta
	Thu.	17	at Tampa Bay
	Sat.	19	at Florida
	Wed.	23	Buffalo
	Fri.	25	Ottawa*
	Sat.	26	at Philadelphia*
	Tue.	29	Philadelphia
Dec.	Sun.	4	at Detroit*
	Tue.	6	at St. Louis
	Thu.	8	at Columbus
	Sat.	10	Edmonton
	Tue.	13	Minnesota
	Sat.	17	Colorado
	Mon.	19	at Toronto
	Wed.	21	New Jersey
	Fri.	23	Ottawa
	Mon.	26	at Buffalo
	Wed.	28	NY Rangers
	Fri.	30	at Ottawa
Jan.	Mon.	2	Tampa Bay
	Wed.	4	Florida
	Fri.	6	at Carolina
	Sat.	7	Carolina

	Tue.	10	at Nashville
	Thu.	12	Calgary
	Sat.	14	Vancouver
	Tue.	17	at Chicago
	Thu.	19	at Carolina
	Sat.	21	at New Jersey*
	Tue.	24	New Jersey
	Thu.	26	Pittsburgh
	Sat.	28	at Boston
	Tue.	31	Washington
Feb.	Thu.	2	NY Rangers
	Sat.	4	at Pittsburgh
	Mon.	6	Tampa Bay
	Wed.	8	at Philadelphia
	Sat.	11	at New Jersey*
	Tue.	28	Montreal
Mar.	Thu.	2	New Jersey
	Sat.	4	Philadelphia
	Mon.	6	at Washington
	Tue.	7	New Jersey
	Fri.	10	Toronto
	Sat.	11	at Boston
	Tue.	14	at New Jersey
	Thu.	16	at Atlanta
	Fri.	17	at Florida
	Sun.	19	at Tampa Bay*
	Tue.	21	Montreal
	Fri.	24	at Pittsburgh
	Sat.	25	Atlanta
	Tue.	28	at Montreal
	Wed.	29	NY Rangers
	Fri.	31	Pittsburgh
Apr.	Sun.	2	Philadelphia*
	Wed.	5	at Toronto
	Thu.	6	at NY Rangers
	Sat.	8	Washington
	Tue.	11	at NY Rangers
	Thu.	13	Toronto
	Sat.	15	Pittsburgh
	Mon.	17	at Pittsburgh
	Tue.	18	Philadelphia

* Denotes afternoon game.

Franchise date: June 6, 1972

ATLANTIC DIVISION

34th NHL Season

Selected in 2000 as the first goalie to be taken first overall since the NHL Draft became universal in 1969, Rick DiPietro emerged as the Islanders number-one goaltender during the 2003-04 season.

Year-by-Year Record

Season	GP	Home W	L	T	OL	Road W	L	T	OL	Overall W	L	T	OL	GF	GA	Pts.	Finished	Playoff Result
2004-05	....	....								....				....	....	....		
2003-04	82	25	11	4	1	13	18	7	3	38	29	11	4	237	210	91	3rd, Atlantic Div.	Lost Conf. Quarter-Final
2002-03	82	18	18	5	0	17	16	6	2	35	34	11	2	224	231	83	3rd, Atlantic Div.	Lost Conf. Quarter-Final
2001-02	82	21	13	5	2	21	15	3	2	42	28	8	4	239	220	96	2nd, Atlantic Div.	Lost Conf. Quarter-Final
2000-01	82	12	27	1	1	9	24	6	2	21	51	7	3	185	268	52	5th, Atlantic Div.	Out of Playoffs
1999-2000	82	10	25	5	1	14	23	4	0	24	48	9	1	194	275	58	5th, Atlantic Div.	Out of Playoffs
1998-99	82	11	23	7	....	13	25	3	....	24	48	10	....	194	244	58	5th, Atlantic Div.	Out of Playoffs
1997-98	82	17	20	4	....	13	21	7	....	30	41	11	....	212	225	71	4th, Atlantic Div.	Out of Playoffs
1996-97	82	19	18	4	....	10	23	8	....	29	41	12	....	240	250	70	7th, Atlantic Div.	Out of Playoffs
1995-96	82	14	21	6	....	8	29	4	....	22	50	10	....	229	315	54	7th, Atlantic Div.	Out of Playoffs
1994-95	48	10	11	3	....	5	17	2	....	15	28	5	....	126	158	35	7th, Atlantic Div.	Out of Playoffs
1993-94	84	23	15	4	....	13	21	8	....	36	36	12	....	282	264	84	4th, Atlantic Div.	Lost Conf. Quarter-Final
1992-93	84	20	19	3	....	20	18	4	....	40	37	7	....	335	297	87	3rd, Patrick Div.	Lost Conf. Championship
1991-92	80	20	15	5	....	14	20	6	....	34	35	11	....	291	299	79	5th, Patrick Div.	Out of Playoffs
1990-91	80	15	19	6	....	10	26	4	....	25	45	10	....	223	290	60	6th, Patrick Div.	Out of Playoffs
1989-90	80	15	17	8	....	16	21	3	....	31	38	11	....	281	288	73	4th, Patrick Div.	Lost Div. Semi-Final
1988-89	80	19	18	3	....	9	29	2	....	28	47	5	....	265	325	61	6th, Patrick Div.	Out of Playoffs
1987-88	80	24	10	6	....	15	21	4	....	39	31	10	....	308	267	88	1st, Patrick Div.	Lost Div. Semi-Final
1986-87	80	20	15	5	....	15	18	7	....	35	33	12	....	279	281	82	3rd, Patrick Div.	Lost Div. Final
1985-86	80	22	11	7	....	17	18	5	....	39	29	12	....	327	284	90	3rd, Patrick Div.	Lost Div. Semi-Final
1984-85	80	26	11	3	....	14	23	3	....	40	34	6	....	345	312	86	3rd, Patrick Div.	Lost Div. Final
1983-84	80	28	11	1	....	22	15	3	....	50	26	4	....	357	269	104	1st, Patrick Div.	Lost Final
1982-83	**80**	**26**	**11**	**3**	....	**16**	**15**	**9**	....	**42**	**26**	**12**	....	**302**	**226**	**96**	**2nd, Patrick Div.**	**Won Stanley Cup**
1981-82	**80**	**33**	**3**	**4**	....	**21**	**13**	**6**	....	**54**	**16**	**10**	....	**385**	**250**	**118**	**1st, Patrick Div.**	**Won Stanley Cup**
1980-81	**80**	**23**	**6**	**11**	....	**25**	**12**	**3**	....	**48**	**18**	**14**	....	**355**	**260**	**110**	**1st, Patrick Div.**	**Won Stanley Cup**
1979-80	**80**	**26**	**9**	**5**	....	**13**	**19**	**8**	....	**39**	**28**	**13**	....	**281**	**247**	**91**	**2nd, Patrick Div.**	**Won Stanley Cup**
1978-79	80	31	3	6	....	20	12	8	....	51	15	14	....	358	214	116	1st, Patrick Div.	Lost Semi-Final
1977-78	80	29	3	8	....	19	14	7	....	48	17	15	....	334	210	111	1st, Patrick Div.	Lost Quarter-Final
1976-77	80	24	11	5	....	23	10	7	....	47	21	12	....	288	193	106	2nd, Patrick Div.	Lost Semi-Final
1975-76	80	24	8	8	....	18	13	9	....	42	21	17	....	297	190	101	2nd, Patrick Div.	Lost Semi-Final
1974-75	80	22	6	12	....	11	19	10	....	33	25	22	....	264	221	88	3rd, Patrick Div.	Lost Semi-Final
1973-74	78	13	17	9	....	6	24	9	....	19	41	18	....	182	247	56	8th, East Div.	Out of Playoffs
1972-73	78	10	25	4	....	2	35	2	....	12	60	6	....	170	347	30	8th, East Div.	Out of Playoffs

2005-06 Player Personnel

FORWARDS	HT	WT	S	Place of Birth	Date	2004-05 Club
ASHAM, Arron	5-11	209	R	Portage La Prairie, Man.	4/13/78	Visp
BATES, Shawn	6-0	205	R	Melrose, MA	4/3/75	
BERGENHEIM, Sean	5-11	194	L	Helsinki, Finland	2/8/84	Bridgeport
BLAKE, Jason	5-10	180	L	Moorhead, MN	9/2/73	Lugano
COLLEY, Kevin	5-10	175	R	New Haven, CT	1/4/79	Bridgeport
COLLINS, Rob	5-10	174	L	Kitchener, Ont.	3/15/74	Bridgeport
COLLITON, Jeremy	6-2	195	R	Blackie, Alta.	1/13/85	Prince Albert
GODARD, Eric	6-4	227	R	Vernon, B.C.	3/7/80	Bridgeport
HUNTER, Trent	6-3	191	R	Red Deer, Alta.	7/5/80	Nykoping
JARRETT, Cole	6-0	195	L	Sault Ste. Marie, Ont.	1/4/83	Bridgeport
KVASHA, Oleg	6-5	230	R	Moscow, USSR	7/26/78	Cherepovets-CSKA
MAPLETOFT, Justin	6-1	180	L	Lloydminster, Sask.	1/11/81	Bridgeport
MARJAMAKI, Masi	6-2	202	L	Pori, Finland	1/16/85	Moose Jaw
NILSSON, Robert	5-11	176	L	Calgary, Alta.	1/10/85	Almtuna-Hammarby-Djurgarden
NOKELAINEN, Petteri	6-1	187	R	Imatra, Finland	1/16/86	SaiPa
O'MARRA, Ryan	6-1	193	R	Tokyo, Japan	6/9/87	Erie (OHL)
PAPINEAU, Justin	5-10	178	L	Ottawa, Ont.	1/15/80	Bridgeport
PARRISH, Mark	5-11	200	R	Bloomington, MN	2/2/77	
REGIER, Steve	6-4	194	L	Edmonton, Alta.	8/31/84	Bridgeport
SATAN, Miroslav	6-3	190	L	Topolcany, Czech.	10/22/74	Bratislava
SMITH, Wyatt	5-11	200	L	Thief River Falls, MN	2/13/77	Milwaukee
WEINHANDL, Mattias	6-0	183	R	Ljungby, Sweden	6/1/80	MODO
YASHIN, Alexei	6-3	225	R	Sverdlovsk, USSR	11/5/73	Yaroslavl
YORK, Mike	5-10	185	L	Waterford, MI	1/3/78	Iserlohn

DEFENSEMEN						
BOUCHARD, Joel	6-1	209	L	Montreal, Que.	1/23/74	Hartford
CALDWELL, Ryan	6-2	174	L	Deloraine, Man.	6/15/81	Bridgeport
CAMPOLI, Chris	6-0	190	L	North York, Ont.	7/9/84	Bridgeport
GERVAIS, Bruno	6-0	188	R	Longueuil, Que.	10/3/84	Bridgeport
LUKOWICH, Brad	6-1	200	L	Cranbrook, B.C.	8/12/76	Fort Worth (CHL)
MACRI, Vince	6-3	210	R	Bethpage, NY	5/21/81	Bridgeport-Atlantic City
MARTINEK, Radek	6-1	200	R	Havlickuv Brod, Czech.	8/31/76	C. Budejovice
NIINIMAA, Janne	6-1	220	L	Raahe, Finland	5/22/75	Karpat-Malmo
PETTINEN, Tomi	6-3	220	L	Ylojarvi, Finland	6/17/77	Lukko
ROBINSON, Jody	6-2	205	L	New Haven, CT	9/23/78	Bridgeport
ROURKE, Allan	6-1	214	L	Mississauga, Ont.	3/6/80	Lowell
SOPEL, Brent	6-1	205	R	Calgary, Alta.	1/7/77	
ZHITNIK, Alexei	5-11	215	L	Kiev, USSR	10/10/72	Kazan

GOALTENDERS	HT	WT	C	Place of Birth	Date	2004-05 Club
DiPIETRO, Rick	5-11	185	R	Winthrop, MA	9/19/81	
DUBIELEWICZ, Wade	5-10	178	L	Invermere, B.C.	1/30/78	Bridgeport
SNOW, Garth	6-3	200	L	Wrentham, MA	7/28/69	St. Petersburg

In the System and Recently Drafted

FORWARDS	HT	WT	S	Place of Birth	Date	2004-05 Club
ALTAREV, Dmitri	6-3	191	L	Penza, USSR	8/12/80	Penza
AQUINO, Luciano	5-9	198	L	Mississauga, Ont.	1/26/85	Brampton
CHABADA, Martin	6-1	203	R	Prague, Czech.	6/14/77	Sparta
CHERNYKH, Dmitri	6-0	180	L	Voskresensk, USSR	2/27/85	Mechel
COMEAU, Blake	6-1	198	R	Meadow Lake, Sask.	2/18/86	Kelowna
GORBUNOV, Vladimir	6-0	174	L	Moscow, USSR	4/22/82	Ufa-MVD Tver
GUTHRIE, Shea	6-0	187	R	Almonte, Ont.	7/30/87	St. George's
HAMILTON, Jeff	5-10	180	R	Englewood, OH	9/4/77	Hartford
MATEJOVSKY, Radek	6-1	187	R	Praha, Czech.	11/17/77	Plzen
NIELSEN, Frans	5-11	172	L	Herning, Denmark	4/24/84	Malmo
OGORODNIKOV, Sergei	6-0	178	L	Irkutsk, USSR	1/21/86	CSKA
OTTOSSON, Kristofer	5-10	187	L	Stockholm, Sweden	1/9/76	Djurgarden
PITTON, Yevgeny	6-2	196	L	Mississauga, Ont.	5/23/86	Sault Ste. Marie
TUNIK, Yevgeny	6-2	198	L	Kraskovo, USSR	11/17/84	St. Petersburg-Elektrostal-Leninogorsk
UPPER, Dmitri	6-1	185	R	Ust-Kamenogorsk, USSR	7/27/78	CSKA
VOLKOV, Igor	6-0	189	L	Ufa, USSR	1/24/83	Ufa-Dynamo Moscow

DEFENSEMEN						
AXELSSON, Emil	6-3	198	L	Orebro, Sweden	3/19/86	Linkoping Jr.
BRAXENHOLM, Per	6-3	215	L	Karlskrona, Sweden	10/31/83	Morrum
HALVARDSSON, Johan	6-3	198	L	Jonkoping, Sweden	12/26/79	HV 71
HOLUB, Jan	6-3	185	L	Liberec, Czech.	5/3/83	Liberec-Beroun
JONSSON, Kenny	6-3	217	L	Angelholm, Sweden	10/6/74	Rogle
KOHN, Dustin	6-1	182	L	Edmonton, Alta.	2/2/87	Calgary (WHL)
KOROLEV, Evgeny	6-1	214	L	Moscow, USSR	7/24/78	Cherepovets
KUHTINOV, Roman	6-1	207	R	Belgorod, USSR	12/1/75	Magnitogorsk
MASON, Tyrell	6-1	167	L	Grand Prairie, Alta.	3/12/86	Salmon Arm
MRAZEK, Jaroslav	6-3	198	L	Pisek, Czech.	1/14/86	St. Michael's
O'NEILL, Wes	6-4	200	L	Windsor, Ont.	3/3/86	U. of Notre Dame
REHAK, Denis	6-2	196	L	Trencin, Czech.	5/14/85	Technika Brno-Ytong Brno Jr.
STONKUS, Alexei	5-11	175	L	Yaroslavl, USSR	5/6/84	Yaroslavl 2
TUKIO, Arto	5-10	176	L	Tampere, Finland	4/4/81	Frolunda
TUZZOLINO, Nicholas	6-5	225	R	Buffalo, NY	1/19/86	Sarnia

Miroslav Satan joins the Islanders after averaging more than 30 goals per season in seven campaigns with the Buffalo Sabres.

Coach

STIRLING, STEVE
Coach, New York Islanders. Born in Clarkson, Ont., November 19, 1949.

In his first season in 2003-04, Steve Stirling led the Islanders to their third consecutive playoff berth, amassing 91 points. Stirling was named head coach on June 3, 2003, after two successful seasons as skipper of the team's top AHL affiliate in Bridgeport. As the Sound Tigers' first head coach, Stirling led the team to the Calder Cup Finals in the 2001-02 inaugural season, and was named *The Hockey News* Minor Pro Coach of the Year.

Stirling joined the Islanders' organization as a scout in 1997. He served as an assistant coach for the Lowell Lock Monsters, the Islanders' AHL affiliate, from 1998 through 2000 and for the Islanders themselves during the 2000-01 season. He was named the first head coach of the Sound Tigers on July 26, 2001 and led Bridgeport to the AHL's 2001-02 Kilpatrick Trophy regular season championship and Eastern Conference playoff championship before losing to the Chicago Wolves in the 2002 Calder Cup Final.

Stirling first moved into the coaching ranks with the NCAA's Babson College Beavers from 1978 through 1983 and 1985 through 1993. He was the NCAA Division II / III coach of the year in 1980 and again in 1982 and also served as Babson's athletic director from 1986 through 1997. Stirling coached Division I Providence College from 1983 though 1985, leading the Friars to an appearance in the 1985 NCAA National Championship Game.

As a player, Stirling led the Boston University Terriers to appearances in the Beanpot Tournament during each of his three seasons at the school, 1968 to 1971, winning the tournament in 1970 and 1971. As a senior and BU's team captain in 1970-71, he was named Beanpot Most Valuable Player and led the Terriers to the NCAA National Championship. Stirling was inducted into the Beanpot Hall of Fame in February 2003.

Stirling played six seasons, (1971 to 1977), of professional hockey in the AHL and North American Hockey League, as well as in Austria. He spent the bulk of his professional-playing career in the AHL with the Boston Braves (1971 to 1974) and Rochester Americans (1974 to 1977).

Coaching Record

			Regular Season			Playoffs		
Season	Team	Games	W	L	T	Games	W	L
2001-02	Bridgeport (AHL)	80	43	29	8	20	12	8
2002-03	Bridgeport (AHL)	80	40	29	11	9	5	4
2003-04	**NY Islanders (NHL)**	**82**	**38**	**33**	**11**	**5**	**1**	**4**
2004-05	NY Islanders (NHL)			Season Cancelled				
	NHL Totals	**82**	**38**	**33**	**11**	**5**	**1**	**4**

Coaching History

Phil Goyette and Earl Ingarfield, 1972-73; Al Arbour, 1973-74 to 1985-86; Terry Simpson, 1986-87, 1987-88; Terry Simpson and Al Arbour, 1988-89; Al Arbour, 1989-90 to 1993-94; Lorne Henning, 1994-95; Mike Milbury, 1995-96; Mike Milbury and Rick Bowness, 1996-97; Rick Bowness and Mike Milbury, 1997-98; Mike Milbury and Bill Stewart, 1998-99; Butch Goring, 1999-2000; Butch Goring and Lorne Henning, 2000-01; Peter Laviolette, 2001-02, 2002-03; Steve Stirling, 2003-04 to date.

Club Records

Team

(Figures in brackets for season records are games played; records for fewest points, wins, ties, losses, goals, goals against are for 70 or more games)

Most Points 118 1981-82 (80)
Most Wins 54 1981-82 (80)
Most Ties 22 1974-75 (80)
Most Losses 60 1972-73 (78)
Most Goals 385 1981-82 (80)
Most Goals Against 347 1972-73 (78)
Fewest Points 30 1972-73 (78)
Fewest Wins 12 1972-73 (78)
Fewest Ties 4 1983-84 (80)
Fewest Losses 15 1978-79 (80)
Fewest Goals 170 1972-73 (78)
Fewest Goals Against 190 1975-76 (80)
Longest Winning Streak
Overall .... 15 Jan. 21-Feb. 20/82
Home .... 14 Jan. 2-Feb. 25/82
Away .... 8 Feb. 27-Mar. 29/81
Longest Undefeated Streak
Overall .... 15 Three times
Home .... 23 Oct. 17/78-Jan. 27/79 (19 wins, 4 ties), Jan. 2-Apr. 3/82 (21 wins, 2 ties)
Away .... 8 Three times
Longest Losing Streak
Overall .... 12 Dec. 27/72-Jan. 16/73, Nov. 22-Dec. 15/88
Home .... 7 Nov. 13-Dec. 14/99
Away .... 15 Jan. 20-Mar. 31/73
Longest Winless Streak
Overall .... 15 Nov. 22-Dec. 21/72 (12 losses, 3 ties)
Home .... 9 Mar. 2-Apr. 6/99 (7 losses, 2 ties)
Away .... 20 Nov. 3/72-Jan. 13/73 (19 losses, 1 tie)
Most Shutouts, Season 10 1975-76 (80)
Most PIM, Season 1,857 1986-87 (80)
Most Goals, Game .... 11 Dec. 20/83 (Pit. 3 at NYI 11), Mar. 3/84 (NYI 11 at Tor. 6)

Individual

Most Seasons .... 17 Billy Smith
Most Games .... 1,123 Bryan Trottier
Most Goals, Career .... 573 Mike Bossy
Most Assists, Career .... 853 Bryan Trottier
Most Points, Career .... 1,353 Bryan Trottier (500G, 853A)
Most PIM, Career .... 1,879 Mick Vukota
Most Shutouts, Career .... 25 Glenn Resch
Longest Consecutive Games Streak .... 576 Billy Harris (Oct. 7/72-Nov. 30/79)
Most Goals, Season .... 69 Mike Bossy (1978-79)
Most Assists, Season .... 87 Bryan Trottier (1978-79)
Most Points, Season .... 147 Mike Bossy (1981-82; 64G, 83A)
Most PIM, Season .... 356 Brian Curran (1986-87)
Most Points, Defenseman, Season .... 101 Denis Potvin (1978-79; 31G, 70A)
Most Points, Center, Season .... 134 Bryan Trottier (1978-79; 47G, 87A)
Most Points, Right Wing, Season .... 147 Mike Bossy (1981-82; 64G, 83A)
Most Points, Left Wing, Season .... 100 John Tonelli (1984-85; 42G, 58A)
Most Points, Rookie, Season .... 95 Bryan Trottier (1975-76; 32G, 63A)
Most Shutouts, Season .... 7 Glenn Resch (1975-76)
Most Goals, Game .... 5 Bryan Trottier (Dec. 23/78, Feb. 13/82), John Tonelli (Jan. 6/81)
Most Assists, Game .... 6 Mike Bossy (Jan. 6/81)
Most Points, Game .... 8 Bryan Trottier (Dec. 23/78; 5G, 3A)

Captains' History

Ed Westfall, 1972-73 to 1975-76; Ed Westfall and Clark Gillies, 1976-77; Clark Gillies, 1977-78, 1978-79; Denis Potvin, 1979-80 to 1986-87; Brent Sutter, 1987-88 to 1990-91; Brent Sutter and Pat Flatley, 1991-92; Pat Flatley, 1992-93 to 1995-96; no captain, 1996-97; Bryan McCabe and Trevor Linden, 1997-98; Trevor Linden, 1998-99; Kenny Jonsson, 1999-2000, 2000-01; Michael Peca, 2001-02 to 2003-04.

Retired Numbers

5	Denis Potvin	1973-1988
9	Clark Gillies	1974-1986
19	Bryan Trottier	1975-1990
22	Mike Bossy	1977-1987
23	Bob Nystrom	1972-1986
31	Billy Smith	1972-1989

All-time Record vs. Other Clubs

Regular Season

	At Home								On Road								Total							
	GP	W	L	T	OL	GF	GA	PTS	GP	W	L	T	OL	GF	GA	PTS	GP	W	L	T	OL	GF	GA	PTS
Anaheim	8	4	3	1	0	24	23	9	9	4	2	3	0	24	18	11	17	8	5	4	0	48	41	20
Atlanta	10	5	5	0	0	36	25	10	10	6	2	2	0	37	27	14	20	11	7	2	0	73	52	24
Boston	61	24	27	10	0	202	199	58	59	16	31	11	1	164	220	44	120	40	58	21	1	366	419	102
Buffalo	61	27	25	9	0	172	166	63	61	20	31	9	1	164	197	50	122	47	56	18	1	336	363	113
Calgary	51	25	17	9	0	191	143	59	49	14	24	11	0	145	172	39	100	39	41	20	0	336	315	98
Carolina	44	20	20	4	0	132	121	44	45	19	21	5	0	148	152	43	89	39	41	9	0	280	273	87
Chicago	47	18	14	15	0	163	141	51	48	17	26	5	0	162	162	39	95	35	40	20	0	325	303	90
Colorado	32	18	13	1	0	129	109	37	34	11	20	3	0	97	123	25	66	29	33	4	0	226	232	62
Columbus	2	0	2	0	0	7	11	0	4	0	3	1	0	7	13	1	6	0	5	1	0	14	24	1
Dallas	48	26	14	8	0	176	134	60	47	21	18	8	0	170	139	50	95	47	32	16	0	346	273	110
Detroit	46	23	18	4	1	164	137	51	45	17	26	2	0	135	165	36	91	40	44	6	1	299	302	87
Edmonton	31	15	7	9	0	128	110	39	29	8	16	5	0	87	107	21	60	23	23	14	0	215	217	60
Florida	25	12	11	2	0	64	65	26	25	8	11	6	0	74	76	22	50	20	22	8	0	138	141	48
Los Angeles	44	24	15	5	0	156	123	53	45	17	21	7	0	143	163	41	89	41	36	12	0	299	286	94
Minnesota	3	2	1	0	0	6	6	4	3	1	2	0	0	9	9	2	6	3	3	0	0	15	15	6
Montreal	60	30	24	6	0	187	167	66	60	15	36	9	0	168	217	39	120	45	60	15	0	355	384	105
Nashville	4	2	2	0	0	11	12	4	5	2	3	0	0	16	14	4	9	4	5	0	0	27	26	8
New Jersey	85	55	19	11	0	355	247	121	84	37	34	11	2	289	281	87	169	92	53	22	2	644	528	208
NY Rangers	96	54	33	8	1	371	306	117	96	30	55	11	0	284	358	71	192	84	88	19	1	655	664	188
Ottawa	24	5	12	6	1	78	89	17	23	5	13	5	0	62	78	15	47	10	25	11	1	140	167	32
Philadelphia	98	50	33	15	0	356	289	115	95	29	55	11	0	268	340	69	193	79	88	26	0	624	629	184
Phoenix	30	13	9	8	0	113	91	34	30	15	11	4	0	105	96	34	60	28	20	12	0	218	187	68
Pittsburgh	86	46	30	8	2	348	285	102	88	34	39	14	1	310	329	83	174	80	69	22	3	658	614	185
St. Louis	49	25	13	11	0	183	131	61	47	20	17	9	1	153	166	50	96	45	30	20	1	336	297	111
San Jose	11	5	4	2	0	40	35	12	12	6	5	1	0	40	30	13	23	11	9	3	0	80	65	25
Tampa Bay	25	13	11	1	0	78	69	27	26	12	11	2	1	80	67	27	51	25	22	3	1	158	136	54
Toronto	53	30	20	3	0	208	155	63	55	23	27	4	1	184	189	51	108	53	47	7	1	392	344	114
Vancouver	47	26	11	10	0	174	129	62	47	21	23	3	0	153	155	45	94	47	34	13	0	327	284	107
Washington	81	42	37	2	0	298	255	86	81	30	39	11	1	251	267	72	162	72	76	13	1	549	522	158
Defunct Clubs	13	11	0	2	0	75	33	24	13	4	5	4	0	35	41	12	26	15	5	6	0	110	74	36
Totals	**1275**	**650**	**450**	**170**	**5**	**4625**	**3806**	**1475**	**1275**	**462**	**627**	**177**	**9**	**3964**	**4371**	**1110**	**2550**	**1112**	**1077**	**347**	**14**	**8589**	**8177**	**2585**

Playoffs

	Series	W	L	GP	W	L	T	GF	GA	Last Mtg.	Rnd.	Result
Boston	2	2	0	11	8	3	0	49	35	1983	CF	W 4-2
Buffalo	3	3	0	16	12	4	0	59	45	1980	SF	W 4-2
Chicago	2	2	0	6	6	0	0	21	6	1979	QF	W 4-0
Colorado	1	1	0	4	4	0	0	18	9	1982	CF	W 4-0
Dallas	1	1	0	5	4	1	0	26	16	1981	F	W 4-1
Edmonton	3	2	1	15	9	6	0	58	47	1984	F	L 1-4
Los Angeles	1	1	0	4	3	1	0	21	10	1980	PRE	W 3-1
Montreal	4	1	3	22	8	14	0	55	64	1993	CF	L 1-4
New Jersey	1	0	1	6	2	4	0	18	23	1988	DSF	L 2-4
NY Rangers	8	5	3	39	20	19	0	129	132	1994	CQF	L 0-4
Ottawa	1	0	1	5	1	4	0	7	13	2003	CQF	L 1-4
Philadelphia	4	1	3	25	11	14	0	69	83	1987	DF	L 3-4
Pittsburgh	3	3	0	19	11	8	0	67	58	1993	DF	W 4-3
Tampa Bay	1	0	1	5	1	4	0	5	12	2004	CQF	L 1-4
Toronto	3	1	2	17	9	8	0	54	42	2002	CQF	L 3-4
Vancouver	2	2	0	6	6	0	0	26	14	1982	F	W 4-0
Washington	6	5	1	30	18	12	0	99	88	1993	DSF	W 4-2
Totals	**46**	**30**	**16**	**235**	**133**	**102**	**0**	**781**	**697**			

Calgary totals include Atlanta Flames, 1972-73 to 1979-80. Carolina totals include Hartford, 1979-80 to 1996-97.
Colorado totals include Quebec, 1979-80 to 1994-95. Dallas totals include Minnesota North Stars, 1972-73 to 1992-93.
New Jersey totals include Kansas City, 1974-75 to 1975-76, and Colorado Rockies, 1976-77 to 1981-82.
Phoenix totals include Winnipeg, 1979-80 to 1995-96.

Playoff Results 2005-2000

Year	Round	Opponent	Result	GF	GA
2004	CQF	Tampa Bay	L 1-4	5	12
2003	CQF	Ottawa	L 1-4	7	13
2002	CQF	Toronto	L 3-4	21	22

Abbreviations: Round: F – Final;
CF – conference final; **CQF** – conference quarter-final;
DF – division final; **DSF** – division semi-final;
SF – semi-final; **QF** – quarter-final;
PRE – preliminary round.

Key Off-Season Signings/Acquisitions

2004

Aug. 12 • Re-signed D **Janne Niinimaa**.
16 • Re-signed C **Jason Blake**.

2005

Aug. 2 • Signed D **Alexei Zhitnik**.
3 • Obtained C **Mike York** and a conditional draft pick from Edmonton for C **Mike Peca**.
3 • Signed F **Miroslav Satan**.
3 • Obtained D **Brent Sopel** from Vancouver for a 2006 conditional pick.
8 • Named **Brad Shaw** assistant coach.
11 • Signed D **Brad Lukowich**.
12 • Re-signed F **Mattias Weinhandl**.
13 • Re-signed F **Trent Hunter**.
15 • Re-signed Fs **Oleg Kvasha** and **Arron Asham** and D **Radek Martinek**.
19 • Signed D **Joel Bouchard**.
22 • Re-signed F **Shawn Bates**.
23 • Signed 2004 1st-round pick (16th overall), C **Petteri Nokelainen**.
24 • Re-signed C **Justin Papineau**.
30 • Signed 2003 1st-round pick (15th overall), C **Robert Nilsson**.

Entry Draft
Selections 2005-1991

2005
Pick
- 15 Ryan O'Marra
- 46 Dustin Kohn
- 76 Shea Guthrie
- 144 Masi Marjamaki
- 180 Tyrell Mason
- 196 Nicholas Tuzzolino
- 210 Luciano Aquino

2004
Pick
- 16 Petteri Nokelainen
- 47 Blake Comeau
- 82 Sergei Ogorodnikov
- 115 Wes O'Neill
- 148 Steve Regier
- 179 Jaroslav Mrazek
- 210 Emil Axelsson
- 227 Chris Campoli
- 244 Jason Pitton
- 276 Sylvain Michaud

2003
Pick
- 15 Robert Nilsson
- 48 Dmitri Chernykh
- 53 Yevgeny Tunik
- 58 Jeremy Colliton
- 120 Stefan Blaho
- 182 Bruno Gervais
- 212 Denis Rehak
- 238 Cody Blanshan
- 246 Igor Volkov

2002
Pick
- 22 Sean Bergenheim
- 87 Frans Nielsen
- 149 Marcus Paulsson
- 189 Alexei Stonkus
- 220 Brad Topping
- 252 Martin Chabada
- 283 Per Braxenholm

2001
Pick
- 101 Cory Stillman
- 132 Dusan Salficky
- 166 Andy Chiodo
- 197 Jan Holub
- 228 Mike Bray
- 260 Bryan Perez
- 280 Roman Kuhtinov
- 287 Juha-Pekka Ketola

2000
Pick
- 1 Rick DiPietro
- 5 Raffi Torres
- 101 Arto Tukio
- 105 Vladimir Gorbunov
- 136 Dmitri Upper
- 148 Kristofer Ottosson
- 202 Ryan Caldwell
- 264 Dmitri Altarev
- 267 Tomi Pettinen

1999
Pick
- 5 Tim Connolly
- 8 Taylor Pyatt
- 10 Branislav Mezei
- 28 Kristian Kudroc
- 78 Mattias Weinhandl
- 87 Brian Collins
- 101 Juraj Kolnik
- 102 Johan Halvardsson
- 130 Justin Mapletoft
- 140 Adam Johnson
- 163 Bjorn Melin
- 228 Radek Martinek
- 255 Brett Henning
- 268 Tyler Scott

1998
Pick
- 9 Mike Rupp
- 36 Chris Nielsen
- 95 Andy Burnham
- 123 Jiri Dopita
- 155 Kevin Clauson
- 182 Evgeny Korolev
- 209 Frederik Brindamour
- 237 Ben Blais
- 242 Jason Doyle
- 250 Radek Matejovsky

1997
Pick
- 4 Roberto Luongo
- 5 Eric Brewer
- 31 Jeff Zehr
- 59 Jarrett Smith
- 79 Robert Schnabel
- 85 Petr Mika
- 115 Adam Edinger
- 139 Bobby Leavins
- 166 Kris Knoblauch
- 196 Jeremy Symington
- 222 Ryan Clark

1996
Pick
- 3 J.P. Dumont
- 29 Dan LaCouture
- 56 Zdeno Chara
- 83 Tyrone Garner
- 109 Bubba Berenzweig
- 128 Petr Sachl
- 138 Todd Miller
- 165 J.R. Prestifilippo
- 192 Evgeny Korolev
- 218 Mike Muzechka

1995
Pick
- 2 Wade Redden
- 28 Jan Hlavac
- 41 D.J. Smith
- 106 Vladimir Orszagh
- 158 Andrew Taylor
- 210 David MacDonald
- 211 Mike Broda

1994
Pick
- 9 Brett Lindros
- 38 Jason Holland
- 63 Jason Strudwick
- 90 Brad Lukowich
- 112 Mark McArthur
- 116 Albert O'Connell
- 142 Jason Stewart
- 194 Mike Loach
- 203 Peter Hogardh
- 220 Gord Walsh
- 246 Kirk Dewaele
- 272 Dick Tarnstrom

1993
Pick
- 23 Todd Bertuzzi
- 40 Bryan McCabe
- 66 Vladimir Chebaturkin
- 92 Warren Luhning
- 118 Tommy Salo
- 144 Peter LeBoutillier
- 170 Darren Van Impe
- 196 Rod Hinks
- 222 Daniel Johansson
- 248 Stephane Larocque
- 274 Carl Charland

1992
Pick
- 5 Darius Kasparaitis
- 56 Jarrett Deuling
- 104 Thomas Klimt
- 105 Ryan Duthie
- 128 Derek Armstrong
- 152 Vladimir Grachev
- 159 Steve O'Rourke
- 176 Jason Widmer
- 200 Daniel Paradis
- 224 David Wainwright
- 248 Andrei Vasilyev

1991
Pick
- 4 Scott Lachance
- 26 Ziggy Palffy
- 48 Jamie McLennan
- 70 Milan Hnilicka
- 92 Steve Junker
- 114 Rob Valicevic
- 136 Andreas Johansson
- 158 Todd Sparks
- 180 John Johnson
- 202 Robert Canavan
- 224 Marcus Thuresson
- 246 Marty Schriner

General Managers' History

Bill Torrey, 1972-73 to 1991-92; Don Maloney, 1992-93 to 1994-95; Don Maloney and Mike Milbury, 1995-96; Mike Milbury, 1996-97 to date.

General Manager

MILBURY, MIKE
General Manager, New York Islanders. Born in Walpole, MA, June 17, 1952.

Mike Milbury came to the Islanders with 20 years of professional hockey experience with the Boston Bruins — as a player, assistant coach, assistant general manager, general manager and coach on both the NHL and AHL levels. Milbury took over as general manager from Don Maloney on December 12, 1995.

Milbury's recent trades have brought the Islanders established stars like Alexei Yashin, Michael Peca and Adrian Aucoin, while his eye for young talent has yielded new NHL stars such as 2003-04 Calder Trophy nominee Trent Hunter, Mattias Weinhandl and starting goaltender Rick DiPietro. Under Milbury's direction, the Islanders have earned a playoff spot in each of the last three seasons.

Milbury joined the Boston organization after graduating from Colgate University with a degree in urban sociology and enjoyed a 10-year playing career with the team. He retired May 6, 1985 and took over as assistant coach. He returned to the ice late in the 1985-86 season when injuries decimated the Bruins defense.

Milbury's playing career concluded after the 1986-87 season and on July 16, 1987 he took over as coach of the Maine Mariners, Boston's top AHL affiliate. In his first year with the team he guided the Mariners to the AHL's Northern Division title and was named both AHL coach of the year and *The Hockey News* minor league coach of the year.

NHL Coaching Record

Season	Team	Games	Regular Season W	L	T	Playoffs Games	W	L
1989-90	Boston	80	46	25	9	21	13	8
1990-91	Boston	80	44	24	12	19	10	9
1995-96	NY Islanders	82	22	50	10	....	....	....
1996-97	NY Islanders	45	13	23	9	....	....	....
1997-98	NY Islanders	19	8	9	2	....	....	....
	NHL Totals	**306**	**133**	**131**	**42**	**40**	**23**	**17**

Club Directory

Nassau Veterans' Memorial Coliseum

New York Islanders Executive Office
1535 Old Country Rd.
Plainview, NY 11803
Phone **516/501-6700**
FAX 516/501-6850
www.newyorkislanders.com
Arena
Nassau Veterans' Memorial Coliseum
Uniondale, NY 11553
Capacity: 16,234

Owner and Governor . . . . Charles B. Wang
Owner and Alternate Governor . . . . Sanjay Kumar

Operations
Sr. V.P. of Operations/Alternate Governor . . . . Michael J. Picker
General Counsel/Alternate Governor . . . . Roy E. Reichbach
Sr. V.P./Chief Financial Officer . . . . Art McCarthy
Sr. V.P./Public Relations . . . . Paul Lancey
General Manager/Alternate Governor . . . . Mike Milbury
Assistant to Charles B. Wang . . . . Susie Schaefer
Human Resources Manager . . . . Mary Molloy
Executive Assistants . . . . Theresa Doino, Jackie Kraemer
Assistant General Counsel . . . . Jamie Wolf, Ivy Shen
IT Manager . . . . Pawel Tauter
Receptionist . . . . Bonnie Dreher

Finance
Controller . . . . Ralph Sellitti
Assistant Controllers . . . . Ginna Cotton, Jeffrey LaBonte
Payroll Manager . . . . Christine Bowler
Staff Accountant . . . . Laura Ferretti
Accounts Payable . . . . Janet Nelson
Accounting Assistant . . . . Teressa Farino
Ticket Manager . . . . Maria Corvino
Assistant Ticket Manager . . . . Adam Ortiz

Hockey Operations
Head Coach . . . . Steve Stirling
Assistant Coaches . . . . Dan Bylsma, Jack Capuano, Brad Shaw
Goaltending Coach . . . . Sudarshan Maharaj
Manager of Hockey Administration . . . . Joanne Holewa
Assistant Manager of Hockey Operations . . . . Kerry Gwydir
Head Amateur Scout . . . . Tony Feltrin
Director of Pro Scouting . . . . Ken Morrow
Assistant Director of Pro Scouting . . . . Kevin Maxwell
Chief US Regional Scout . . . . Jay Heinbuck
Chief Canada Scout . . . . Doug Gibson
Chief European Amateur Scout . . . . Ryan Jankowski
European Scout . . . . Anders Kallur
Czech and Slovakia Scout . . . . Karel Pavlik
Ontario Scout . . . . Harkie Singh
Russian Scout . . . . Sergei Radchenko
Part-Time Regional Scouts . . . . Brian Hunter, Jim Madigan, David McNamara, Al MacPherson, Mario Saraceno,
Director of Player Development . . . . Dan Marshall
Video Coordinator . . . . Bob Smith

Medical Staff
Director of Medical Services . . . . Dr. Elliot Pellman
Internist . . . . Dr. Damion Martins
Team Orthopedists . . . . Dr. David S. Gazzaniga, Dr. Elliott Hershman, Dr. Kenneth Montgomery
Team Dentists . . . . Dr. Bruce Michnick, Dr. Jan Sherman

Training/Equipment Staff
Head Athletic Trainer . . . . Rich Campbell
Assistant Athletic Trainer . . . . Andy Wetstein
Strength & Conditioning Coach . . . . Garrett Timms
Equipment Manager . . . . Scott Moon
Assistant Equipment Manager . . . . Richard Krouse
Equipment Assistant . . . . Tom Kitz

Sales
Vice President of Sales . . . . Dave Decina
Vice President of Corporate Partnerships . . . . Dean Rivera
Director of Corporate Partnerships . . . . Mary Dolan Grippo
Corporate Partnership Account Managers . . . . James Kilmeade, Kate Larson, Christopher Lombardo, William Presti
Sales Programs Manager . . . . Jessica Rotoli
Customer Service/Telesales Director . . . . Kerry Cornils
Customer Service Manager . . . . Michelle Winter
Corporate Sales Managers . . . . Steve Beisel, Doug Cohen, Jeff Guida
Director of Fan Development . . . . Cliff Gault
Fan Development Coordinator . . . . Nicole D'Addario
Alumni/Community Development Coord. . . . . Bob Nystrom

Game Operations
Director of Games Operations . . . . Matthew Coppola
Avid Editor . . . . Nima Foroush
Merchandise Manager . . . . Danny DiPierri

Communications
Vice President of Communications . . . . Chris Botta
Public Relations Manager . . . . Laurene Gros-Daillon
Media Coordinator . . . . Jim Morlock
Media Assistant . . . . Corey Witt
Office Assistant . . . . Todd Aronovitch

Marketing Services
Vice President of Marketing Services . . . . Dori White
Marketing Services Account Managers . . . . Jessica Sousa Tuttle, Suzanne Keller
Marketing Services Assistant . . . . Mary Cedeno
Creative Services Manager . . . . Thomas Rakoczy
Video Production Manager . . . . Susan Schopp

Team Information
Television Coverage . . . . Fox Sports New York
Television Announcers . . . . Joe Micheletti, Howie Rose
Radio Coverage . . . . Bloomberg Radio, 1130 AM
Radio Broadcasters . . . . Chris King, John Wiedeman

Rangers newcomer Marek Malik

New York Rangers

2005-06 Schedule

Month	Day	Date	Opponent
Oct.	Wed.	5	at Philadelphia
	Thu.	6	Montreal
	Sat.	8	at New Jersey
	Mon.	10	at Washington*
	Thu.	13	New Jersey
	Sat.	15	Atlanta
	Mon.	17	Florida
	Wed.	19	NY Islanders
	Thu.	20	at NY Islanders
	Sat.	22	at Buffalo
	Thu.	27	NY Islanders
	Sat.	29	at Montreal
	Mon.	31	Montreal
Nov.	Thu.	3	at New Jersey
	Sat.	5	New Jersey*
	Mon.	7	Pittsburgh
	Wed.	9	at Florida
	Thu.	10	at Tampa Bay
	Sat.	12	at Pittsburgh
	Tue.	15	at Toronto
	Thu.	17	at Carolina
	Sat.	19	Carolina*
	Sun.	20	Boston
	Tue.	22	at Buffalo
	Thu.	24	at Atlanta
	Sat.	26	Washington
Dec.	Thu.	1	Pittsburgh
	Sat.	3	at Washington
	Mon.	5	Minnesota
	Wed.	7	at Chicago
	Thu.	8	at Nashville
	Sat.	10	at St. Louis
	Tue.	13	Vancouver
	Sun.	18	Colorado*
	Tue.	20	New Jersey
	Thu.	22	Tampa Bay
	Mon.	26	at Ottawa
	Wed.	28	at NY Islanders
	Sat.	31	at Pittsburgh*
Jan.	Tue.	3	Tampa Bay
	Thu.	5	Philadelphia
	Sat.	7	Florida*
	Tue.	10	Calgary
	Thu.	12	Edmonton
	Sat.	14	at Detroit*
	Mon.	16	at Columbus
	Thu.	19	at Pittsburgh
	Sat.	21	at Boston
	Sun.	22	New Jersey
	Tue.	24	Buffalo
	Sat.	28	Pittsburgh
	Mon.	30	Philadelphia
Feb.	Wed.	1	Pittsburgh
	Thu.	2	at NY Islanders
	Sat.	4	at Philadelphia*
	Wed.	8	Ottawa
	Fri.	10	Toronto
	Sat.	11	at Toronto
Mar.	Thu.	2	at Philadelphia
	Sat.	4	at New Jersey
	Mon.	6	Carolina
	Wed.	8	at Atlanta
	Sat.	11	at Montreal
	Sun.	12	Atlanta*
	Tue.	14	at Carolina
	Thu.	16	Washington
	Sat.	18	Toronto
	Mon.	20	Boston
	Wed.	22	Philadelphia
	Fri.	24	at Florida
	Sat.	25	at Tampa Bay
	Mon.	27	Buffalo
	Wed.	29	at NY Islanders
	Thu.	30	at Ottawa
Apr.	Tue.	4	Philadelphia
	Thu.	6	NY Islanders
	Sat.	8	at Boston*
	Sun.	9	at New Jersey
	Tue.	11	NY Islanders
	Thu.	13	at Pittsburgh
	Sat.	15	at Philadelphia*
	Tue.	18	Ottawa

* Denotes afternoon game.

Franchise date: May 15, 1926

EASTERN CONFERENCE

ATLANTIC DIVISION

80th NHL Season

Year-by-Year Record

		Home				Road				Overall								
Season	GP	W	L	T	OL	W	L	T	OL	W	L	T	OL	GF	GA	Pts.	Finished	Playoff Result
2004-05	....	....	....	....	....	....	....	....	....	....	....	....	....	....	....	....		
2003-04	82	13	21	3	4	14	19	4	4	27	40	7	8	206	250	69	4th, Atlantic Div.	Out of Playoffs
2002-03	82	17	18	4	2	15	18	6	2	32	36	10	4	210	231	78	4th, Atlantic Div.	Out of Playoffs
2001-02	82	19	19	2	1	17	19	2	3	36	38	4	4	227	258	80	4th, Atlantic Div.	Out of Playoffs
2000-01	82	17	20	3	1	16	23	2	0	33	43	5	1	250	290	72	4th, Atlantic Div.	Out of Playoffs
1999-2000	82	15	20	5	1	14	18	7	2	29	38	12	3	218	246	73	4th, Atlantic Div.	Out of Playoffs
1998-99	82	17	19	5	....	16	19	6	....	33	38	11	....	217	227	77	4th, Atlantic Div.	Out of Playoffs
1997-98	82	14	18	9	....	11	21	9	....	25	39	18	....	197	231	68	5th, Atlantic Div.	Out of Playoffs
1996-97	82	21	14	6	....	17	20	4	....	38	34	10	....	258	231	86	4th, Atlantic Div.	Lost Conf. Final
1995-96	82	22	10	9	....	19	17	5	....	41	27	14	....	272	237	96	2nd, Atlantic Div.	Lost Conf. Semi-Final
1994-95	48	11	10	3	....	11	13	0	....	22	23	3	....	139	134	47	4th, Atlantic Div.	Lost Conf. Semi-Final
1993-94	**84**	**28**	**8**	**6**	....	**24**	**16**	**2**	....	**52**	**24**	**8**	....	**299**	**231**	**112**	**1st, Atlantic Div.**	**Won Stanley Cup**
1992-93	84	20	17	5	....	14	22	6	....	34	39	11	....	304	308	79	6th, Patrick Div.	Out of Playoffs
1991-92	80	28	8	4	....	22	17	1	....	50	25	5	....	321	246	105	1st, Patrick Div.	Lost Div. Final
1990-91	80	22	11	7	....	14	20	6	....	36	31	13	....	297	265	85	2nd, Patrick Div.	Lost Div. Semi-Final
1989-90	80	20	11	9	....	16	20	4	....	36	31	13	....	279	267	85	1st, Patrick Div.	Lost Div. Final
1988-89	80	21	17	2	....	16	18	6	....	37	35	8	....	310	307	82	3rd, Patrick Div.	Lost Div. Semi-Final
1987-88	80	22	13	5	....	14	21	5	....	36	34	10	....	300	283	82	5th, Patrick Div.	Out of Playoffs
1986-87	80	18	18	4	....	16	20	4	....	34	38	8	....	307	323	76	4th, Patrick Div.	Lost Div. Semi-Final
1985-86	80	20	18	2	....	16	20	4	....	36	38	6	....	280	276	78	4th, Patick Div.	Lost Conf. Championship
1984-85	80	16	18	6	....	10	26	4	....	26	44	10	....	295	345	62	4th, Patrick Div.	Lost Div. Semi-Final
1983-84	80	27	12	1	....	15	17	8	....	42	29	9	....	314	304	93	4th, Patrick Div.	Lost Div. Semi-Final
1982-83	80	24	13	3	....	11	22	7	....	35	35	10	....	306	287	80	4th, Patrick Div.	Lost Div. Final
1981-82	80	19	15	6	....	20	12	8	....	39	27	14	....	316	306	92	2nd, Patrick Div.	Lost Div. Final
1980-81	80	17	13	10	....	13	23	4	....	30	36	14	....	312	317	74	4th, Patrick Div.	Lost Semi-Final
1979-80	80	22	10	8	....	16	22	2	....	38	32	10	....	308	284	86	3rd, Patrick Div.	Lost Quarter-Final
1978-79	80	19	13	8	....	21	16	3	....	40	29	11	....	316	292	91	3rd, Patrick Div.	Lost Final
1977-78	80	18	15	7	....	12	22	6	....	30	37	13	....	279	280	73	4th, Patrick Div.	Lost Prelim. Round
1976-77	80	17	18	5	....	12	19	9	....	29	37	14	....	272	310	72	4th, Patrick Div.	Out of Playoffs
1975-76	80	16	16	8	....	13	26	1	....	29	42	9	....	262	333	67	4th, Patrick Div.	Out of Playoffs
1974-75	80	21	11	8	....	16	18	6	....	37	29	14	....	319	276	88	2nd, Patrick Div.	Lost Prelim. Round
1973-74	78	26	7	6	....	14	17	8	....	40	24	14	....	300	251	94	3rd, East Div.	Lost Semi-Final
1972-73	78	26	8	5	....	21	15	3	....	47	23	8	....	297	208	102	3rd, East Div.	Lost Semi-Final
1971-72	78	26	6	7	....	22	11	6	....	48	17	13	....	317	192	109	2nd, East Div.	Lost Final
1970-71	78	30	2	7	....	19	16	4	....	49	18	11	....	259	177	109	2nd, East Div.	Lost Semi-Final
1969-70	76	22	8	8	....	16	14	8	....	38	22	16	....	246	189	92	4th, East Div.	Lost Quarter-Final
1968-69	76	27	7	4	....	14	19	5	....	41	26	9	....	231	196	91	3rd, East Div.	Lost Quarter-Final
1967-68	74	22	8	7	....	17	15	5	....	39	23	12	....	226	183	90	2nd, East Div.	Lost Quarter-Final
1966-67	70	18	12	5	....	12	16	7	....	30	28	12	....	188	189	72	4th,	Lost Semi-Final
1965-66	70	12	16	7	....	6	25	4	....	18	41	11	....	195	261	47	6th,	Out of Playoffs
1964-65	70	8	19	8	....	12	19	4	....	20	38	12	....	179	246	52	5th,	Out of Playoffs
1963-64	70	14	13	8	....	8	25	2	....	22	38	10	....	186	242	54	5th,	Out of Playoffs
1962-63	70	12	17	6	....	10	19	6	....	22	36	12	....	211	233	56	5th,	Out of Playoffs
1961-62	70	16	11	8	....	10	21	4	....	26	32	12	....	195	207	64	4th,	Lost Semi-Final
1960-61	70	15	15	5	....	7	23	5	....	22	38	10	....	204	248	54	5th,	Out of Playoffs
1959-60	70	10	15	10	....	7	23	5	....	17	38	15	....	187	247	49	6th,	Out of Playoffs
1958-59	70	14	16	5	....	12	16	7	....	26	32	12	....	201	217	64	5th,	Out of Playoffs
1957-58	70	14	15	6	....	18	10	7	....	32	25	13	....	195	188	77	2nd,	Lost Semi-Final
1956-57	70	15	12	8	....	11	18	6	....	26	30	14	....	184	227	66	4th,	Lost Semi-Final
1955-56	70	20	7	8	....	12	21	2	....	32	28	10	....	204	203	74	3rd,	Lost Semi-Final
1954-55	70	10	12	13	....	7	23	5	....	17	35	18	....	150	210	52	5th,	Out of Playoffs
1953-54	70	18	12	5	....	11	19	5	....	29	31	10	....	161	182	68	5th,	Out of Playoffs
1952-53	70	11	14	10	....	6	23	6	....	17	37	16	....	152	211	50	6th,	Out of Playoffs
1951-52	70	16	13	6	....	7	21	7	....	23	34	13	....	192	219	59	5th,	Out of Playoffs
1950-51	70	14	11	10	....	6	18	11	....	20	29	21	....	169	201	61	5th,	Out of Playoffs
1949-50	70	19	12	4	....	9	19	7	....	28	31	11	....	170	189	67	4th,	Lost Final
1948-49	60	13	12	5	....	5	19	6	....	18	31	11	....	133	172	47	6th,	Out of Playoffs
1947-48	60	11	12	7	....	10	14	6	....	21	26	13	....	176	201	55	4th,	Lost Semi-Final
1946-47	60	11	14	5	....	11	18	1	....	22	32	6	....	167	186	50	5th,	Out of Playoffs
1945-46	50	8	12	5	....	5	16	4	....	13	28	9	....	144	191	35	6th,	Out of Playoffs
1944-45	50	7	11	7	....	4	18	3	....	11	29	10	....	154	247	32	6th,	Out of Playoffs
1943-44	50	4	17	4	....	2	22	1	....	6	39	5	....	162	310	17	6th,	Out of Playoffs
1942-43	50	7	13	5	....	4	18	3	....	11	31	8	....	161	253	30	6th,	Out of Playoffs
1941-42	48	15	8	1	....	14	9	1	....	29	17	2	....	177	143	60	1st,	Lost Semi-Final
1940-41	48	13	7	4	....	8	12	4	....	21	19	8	....	143	125	50	4th,	Lost Quarter-Final
1939-40	**48**	**17**	**4**	**3**	....	**10**	**7**	**7**	....	**27**	**11**	**10**	....	**136**	**77**	**64**	**2nd,**	**Won Stanley Cup**
1938-39	48	13	8	3	....	13	8	3	....	26	16	6	....	149	105	58	2nd,	Lost Semi-Final
1937-38	48	15	5	4	....	12	10	2	....	27	15	6	....	149	96	60	2nd, Amn. Div.	Lost Quarter-Final
1936-37	48	9	7	8	....	10	13	1	....	19	20	9	....	117	106	47	3rd, Amn. Div.	Lost Final
1935-36	48	11	6	7	....	8	11	5	....	19	17	12	....	91	96	50	4th, Amn. Div.	Out of Playoffs
1934-35	48	11	8	5	....	11	12	1	....	22	20	6	....	137	139	50	3rd, Amn. Div.	Lost Semi-Final
1933-34	48	11	7	6	....	10	12	2	....	21	19	8	....	120	113	50	3rd, Amn. Div.	Lost Quarter-Final
1932-33	**48**	**12**	**7**	**5**	....	**11**	**10**	**3**	....	**23**	**17**	**8**	....	**135**	**107**	**54**	**3rd, Amn. Div.**	**Won Stanley Cup**
1931-32	48	13	7	4	....	10	10	4	....	23	17	8	....	134	112	54	1st, Amn. Div.	Lost Final
1930-31	44	10	9	3	....	9	7	6	....	19	16	9	....	106	87	47	3rd, Amn. Div.	Lost Semi-Final
1929-30	44	11	5	6	....	6	12	4	....	17	17	10	....	136	143	44	3rd, Amn. Div.	Lost Semi-Final
1928-29	44	12	6	4	....	9	7	6	....	21	13	10	....	72	65	52	2nd, Amn. Div.	Lost Final
1927-28	**44**	**10**	**8**	**4**	....	**9**	**8**	**5**	....	**19**	**16**	**9**	....	**94**	**79**	**47**	**2nd, Amn. Div.**	**Won Stanley Cup**
1926-27	44	13	5	4	....	12	8	2	....	25	13	6	....	95	72	56	1st, Amn. Div.	Lost Quarter-Final

2005-06 Player Personnel

FORWARDS	HT	WT	S	Place of Birth	Date	2004-05 Club
BALEJ, Jozef	6-1	195	R	Myjava, Czech.	2/22/82	Hartford
BETTS, Blair	6-1	211	L	Edmonton, Alta.	2/16/80	Hartford
DAWES, Nigel	5-8	190	L	Winnipeg, Man.	2/9/85	Kootenay
FALARDEAU, Lee	6-4	215	L	Midland, MI	7/22/83	Charlotte-Hartford
GIROUX, Alexandre	6-3	190	L	Quebec City, Que.	6/16/81	Hartford
HELMINEN, Dwight	6-0	190	L	Hancock, MI	6/22/83	Hartford-Charlotte
HOLLWEG, Ryan	5-9	210	L	Downey, CA	4/23/83	Hartford
IMMONEN, Jarkko	6-0	202	R	Rantasalmi, Finland	4/19/82	JYP
JAGR, Jaromir	6-2	224	L	Kladno, Czech.	2/15/72	Kladno-Omsk
JESSIMAN, Hugh	6-5	226	R	New York, NY	3/28/84	Dartmouth
KOZAK, Rick	6-2	215	R	Winnipeg, Man.	8/19/85	Kamloops-Prince Albert
LUNDMARK, Jamie	6-0	200	R	Edmonton, Alta.	1/16/81	Bolzano-Hartford
MOORE, Dominic	6-0	195	L	Thornhill, Ont.	8/3/80	Hartford
MURRAY, Garth	6-1	215	L	Regina, Sask.	9/17/82	Hartford
NIEMINEN, Ville	6-0	200	L	Tampere, Finland	4/6/77	Tappara
NYLANDER, Michael	6-1	195	L	Stockholm, Sweden	10/3/72	Karpat-St. Pete.-Kazan
ORTMEYER, Jed	6-1	191	R	Omaha, NE	9/3/78	Hartford
PRUCHA, Petr	5-10	161	R	Chrudim, Czech.	9/14/82	Pardubice
RUCCHIN, Steve	6-2	211	L	Thunder Bay, Ont.	7/4/71	
RUCINSKY, Martin	6-1	205	L	Most, Czech.	3/11/71	Litvinov
STALS, Juris	6-3	205	L	Riga, Latvia	8/4/82	Charlotte
STRAKA, Martin	5-9	178	L	Plzen, Czech.	9/3/72	Plzen
WARD, Jason	6-3	203	R	Chapleau, Ont.	1/16/79	Hamilton
WELLER, Craig	6-3	195	R	Calgary, Alta.	1/17/81	Hartford
WISEMAN, Chad	6-0	205	L	Burlington, Ont.	3/25/81	Hartford
DEFENSEMEN						
BARANKA, Ivan	6-2	196	L	Ilava, Czech.	5/19/85	Everett-Hartford
GRENIER, Martin	6-5	255	L	Laval, Que.	11/2/80	Charlotte-Hartford
KASPARAITIS, Darius	5-11	215	L	Elektrenai, USSR	10/16/72	Kazan
KONDRATIEV, Maxim	6-1	192	L	Togliatti, USSR	1/20/83	Hartford-Togliatti
LAMPMAN, Bryce	6-1	200	L	Rochester, MN	8/31/82	Hartford
LIFFITON, David	6-2	210	L	Windsor, Ont.	10/18/84	Hartford-Charlotte
MacINTYRE, Steve	6-6	265	L	Brock, Sask.	8/8/80	Hartford-Charlotte
MALIK, Marek	6-5	215	L	Ostrava, Czech.	6/24/75	Vitkovice
PIKKARAINEN, Hannu	5-11	196	L	Helsinki, Finland	10/13/83	HIFK
POECK, Thomas	6-1	208	L	Klagenfurt, Austria	12/2/81	Hartford-Charlotte
POTI, Tom	6-3	210	L	Worcester, MA	3/22/77	
PURINTON, Dale	6-3	228	L	Fort Wayne, IN	10/11/76	Victoria
RAWLYK, Rory	6-3	193	R	Edmonton, Alta.	9/9/83	Hartford-Charlotte
ROZSIVAL, Michal	6-1	212	R	Vlasim, Czech.	9/3/78	Trinec-Pardubice
RULLIER, Joe	6-3	230	R	Montreal, Que.	1/28/80	Manchester
STRUDWICK, Jason	6-3	210	L	Edmonton, Alta.	7/17/75	Ferencvaros
TAYLOR, Jake	6-4	220	R	Rochester, MN	8/1/83	Hartford-Charlotte
TYUTIN, Fedor	6-2	210	L	Izhevsk, USSR	7/19/83	Hartford-St. Petersburg
GOALTENDERS	**HT**	**WT**	**C**	**Place of Birth**	**Date**	**2004-05 Club**
HOLT, Chris	6-2	218	L	Vancouver, B.C.	6/5/85	Nebraska-Omaha
LUNDQVIST, Henrik	6-1	192	L	Are, Sweden	3/2/82	Frolunda
MONTOYA, Al	6-1	190	L	Chicago, IL	2/13/85	U. of Michigan
WEEKES, Kevin	6-0	195	L	Toronto, Ont.	4/4/75	

In the System and Recently Drafted

FORWARDS	HT	WT	S	Place of Birth	Date	2004-05 Club
BAHENSKY, Zdenek	6-2	195	L	Most, Czech.	1/3/86	Saskatoon
BELLER, Greg	6-2	202	L	Vancouver, B.C.	1/22/87	Lake of the Woods-Borderland
BYERS, Dane	6-2	192	L	Nipawin, Sask.	2/21/86	Prince Albert
CALLAHAN, Ryan	5-10	180	R	Rochester, NY	3/21/85	Guelph
CLICHE, Marc-Andre	6-0	177	R	Rouyn-Noranda, Que.	3/23/87	Lewiston
CRABB, Joey	6-1	187	R	Anchorage, AK	4/3/83	Colorado College
DORNIC, Ivan	6-0	183	R	Bratislava, Czech.	4/12/85	Port (WHL)-Trnava-Bratis.
DUBINSKY, Brandon	5-11	203	L	Anchorage, AK	4/29/86	Portland (WHL)
DUPONT, Brodie	6-1	197	L	Russell, Man.	2/17/87	Calgary (WHL)
FOOTE, Jordan	6-3	202	L	Edmonton, Alta.	3/7/85	Michigan Tech
GRAHAM, Bruce	6-6	234	L	Moncton, N.B.	12/2/85	Moncton
HELFENSTEIN, Sven	5-10	176	R	Winterthur, Switz.	7/30/82	GCK Zurich-Zurich
HIRSCHOVITS, Kim	6-1	180	L	Helsinki, Finland	5/9/82	HIFK
JONASEN, Marcus	6-4	215	R	Vasteras, Sweden	1/12/84	Tri-City
KORPIKOSKI, Lauri	6-1	181	L	Turku, Finland	7/28/86	TPS
MAREK, Jan	5-10	178	R	Jindrichuv Hradec, Czech.	12/31/79	Sparta
MOORE, Greg	6-1	215	R	Lisbon, ME	3/26/84	U. of Maine
OLVER, Darin	6-0	182	L	Burnaby, B.C.	3/5/85	Northern Mich.
PETRUZALEK, Jakub	5-9	170	R	Most, Czech.	4/24/85	Ottawa (OHL)
PETTERSTROM, Pontus	6-0	174	L	Nybro, Sweden	4/21/82	Skelleftea
PSURNY, Roman	6-1	170	L	Gottwaldov, Czech.	2/23/86	Medicine Hat
PYATT, Tom	5-11	181	L	Thunder Bay, Ont.	2/14/87	Saginaw
ROCHE, Ken	5-11	202	L	Boston, MA	1/2/84	Boston University
RUSSELL, Ryan	5-9	165	L	Caroline, Alta.	5/2/87	Kootenay
RYAN, Billy	6-1	175	L	Boston, MA	10/23/85	U. of Maine
WALSH, Mike	6-2	220	L	Royal Oak, MI	3/4/83	U. of Notre Dame
DEFENSEMEN						
DUBEN, Premysl	6-3	220	L	Jihlava, Czech.	10/5/81	Jihlava-Trebic-Pisek
FLATT, Dalyn	6-3	217	L	Winnipeg, Man.	10/7/86	Saskatoon
FURRER, Philippe	6-1	187	L	Bern, Switz.	6/16/85	Bern
GUENIN, Nate	6-2	211	R	Sewickley, PA	12/10/82	Ohio State
KALLARSSON, Tomi	6-3	194	L	Lempaala, Finland	3/15/79	
KINCH, Matt	6-0	195	L	Red Deer, Alta.	2/17/80	Salzburg
KOVERKO, Trevor	6-3	218	L	Toronto, Ont.	3/22/87	Owen Sound
LAATIKAINEN, Arto	6-0	187	L	Espoo, Finland	5/24/80	Blues
PAIEMENT, Jonathan	6-1	222	L	Montreal, Que.	3/7/85	Lewiston
POTTER, Corey	6-2	191	R	Lansing, MI	1/5/84	Michigan State
RACHUNEK, Karel	6-2	211	R	Zlin, Czech.	8/27/79	Znojmo-Yaroslavl
REESE, Dylan	6-0	206	R	Pittsburgh, PA	8/29/84	Harvard
RICHTER, Martin	6-1	205	R	Prostejov, Czech.	6/2/77	Sparta
SAUER, Michael	6-2	208	R	St. Cloud, MN	8/7/87	Portland (WHL)
STAAL, Marc	6-3	196	L	Thunder Bay, Ont.	1/13/87	Sudbury
ZHVACHKIN, Leonid	6-3	195	L	Tula, USSR	2/24/83	Krylja Sovetov-Elektrostal-Saratov
GOALTENDERS	**HT**	**WT**	**C**	**Place of Birth**	**Date**	**2004-05 Club**
ASPLUND, Johan	6-1	180	L	Slutskar, Sweden	12/15/80	Nykoping

Coach

RENNEY, TOM
Coach, New York Rangers. Born in Cranbrook, B.C., March 1, 1955.

Tom Renney took over as interim coach of the New York Rangers on February 25, 2004. He was officially named the 33rd head coach in franchise history on July 6. Renney joined the Rangers on July 31, 2000 as director of player personnel and was promoted to vice president, player development on June 21, 2002. In that position, he oversaw all facets of the team's amateur scouting operations, while also assisting with the professional scouting process and player development within the organization. Renney joined the Rangers coaching staff as an assistant coach on July 21, 2003.

From June of 1996 through November, 1997, Renney served as head coach of the Vancouver Canucks. Prior to his return to the National Hockey League in New York, Renney held the position of vice president and head coach of the Canadian national team. Renney rejoined the Canadian Hockey Association in May, 1998. He began his affiliation with the Canadian national team in 1992 and coached Canada's Olympic hockey team to a silver medal at the 1994 Winter Games in Lillehammer, Norway. Later that year, he served as an assistant coach on Team Canada's gold medal-winning team at the World Championships. He won silver again as an assistant coach at the 2005 World Championship. Previously, he won the Memorial Cup with the Kamloops Blazers in 1992.

Coaching Record

		Regular Season				Playoffs, Olympics or World Championships			
Year	Team	Games	W	L	T	Games	W	L	T
1990-91	Kamloops (WHL)	72	50	20	2	12	5	7	0
1991-92	Kamloops (WHL)	72	51	17	4	16	11	5	0
1993-94	Canadian National	63	33	26	4	8	5	2	1*
1994-95	Canadian National	57	37	17	3	8	4	2	2**
1995-96	Canadian National	53	33	12	8	8	4	2	2***
1996-97	**Vancouver (NHL)**	**82**	**35**	**40**	**7**	....	....	....	....
1997-98	**Vancouver (NHL)**	**19**	**4**	**13**	**2**	....	....	....	....
1999-00	Canadian National	56	27	23	6	....	....	....	....
2003-04	**NY Rangers (NHL)**	**20**	**5**	**15**	**0**	....	....	....	....
2004-05	**NY Rangers (NHL)**			Season Cancelled					
	NHL Totals	**121**	**44**	**68**	**9**	....	....	....	....

* Olympics (silver medal)
** World Championships (bronze)
*** World Championships (silver)

Captains' History

Bill Cook, 1926-27 to 1936-37; Art Coulter, 1937-38 to 1941-42; Ott Heller, 1942-43 to 1944-45; Neil Colville 1945-46 to 1948-49; Buddy O'Connor, 1949-50; Frank Eddolls, 1950-51; Frank Eddolls and Allan Stanley, 1951-52; Allan Stanley, 1952-53; Allan Stanley and Don Raleigh, 1953-54; Don Raleigh, 1954-55; Harry Howell, 1955-56, 1956-57; Red Sullivan, 1957-58 to 1960-61; Andy Bathgate, 1961-62, 1962-63; Andy Bathgate and Camille Henry, 1963-64; Camille Henry and Bob Nevin, 1964-65; Bob Nevin 1965-66 to 1970-71; Vic Hadfield, 1971-72 to 1973-74; Brad Park, 1974-75; Brad Park and Phil Esposito, 1975-76; Phil Esposito, 1976-77, 1977-78; Dave Maloney, 1978-79, 1979-80; Dave Maloney, Walt Tkaczuk and Barry Beck, 1980-81; Barry Beck, 1981-82 to 1985-86; Ron Greschner, 1986-87; Ron Greschner and Kelly Kisio, 1987-88; Kelly Kisio, 1988-89 to 1990-91; Mark Messier, 1991-92 to 1996-97; Brian Leetch, 1997-98 to 1999-2000; Mark Messier, 2000-01 to 2003-04.

Coaching History

Lester Patrick, 1926-27 to 1938-39; Frank Boucher, 1939-40 to 1947-48; Frank Boucher and Lynn Patrick, 1948-49; Lynn Patrick, 1949-50; Neil Colville, 1950-51; Neil Colville and Bill Cook, 1951-52; Bill Cook, 1952-53; Frank Boucher and Muzz Patrick, 1953-54; Muzz Patrick, 1954-55; Phil Watson, 1955-56 to 1958-59; Phil Watson and Alf Pike, 1959-60; Alf Pike, 1960-61; Doug Harvey, 1961-62; Muzz Patrick and Red Sullivan, 1962-63; Red Sullivan, 1963-64, 1964-65; Red Sullivan and Emile Francis, 1965-66; Emile Francis, 1966-67, 1967-68; Bernie Geoffrion and Emile Francis, 1968-69; Emile Francis, 1969-70 to 1972-73; Larry Popein and Emile Francis, 1973-74; Emile Francis, 1974-75; Ron Stewart and John Ferguson, 1975-76; John Ferguson, 1976-77; Jean-Guy Talbot, 1977-78; Fred Shero, 1978-79, 1979-80; Fred Shero and Craig Patrick, 1980-81; Herb Brooks, 1981-82 to 1983-84; Herb Brooks and Craig Patrick, 1984-85; Ted Sator, 1985-86; Ted Sator, Tom Webster and Phil Esposito, 1986-87; Michel Bergeron, 1987-88; Michel Bergeron and Phil Esposito, 1988-89; Roger Neilson, 1989-90 to 1991-92; Roger Neilson and Ron Smith, 1992-93; Mike Keenan, 1993-94; Colin Campbell, 1994-95 to 1996-97; Colin Campbell and John Muckler, 1997-98; John Muckler, 1998-99; John Muckler and John Tortorella, 1999-2000; Ron Low, 2000-01, 2001-02; Bryan Trottier and Glen Sather, 2002-03; Glen Sather and Tom Renney, 2003-04; Tom Renney, 2004-05 to date.

Club Records

Team

(Figures in brackets for season records are games played; records for fewest points, wins, ties, losses, goals, goals against are for 70 or more games)

Most Points	112	1993-94 (84)
Most Wins	52	1993-94 (84)
Most Ties	21	1950-51 (70)
Most Losses	44	1984-85 (80)
Most Goals	321	1991-92 (80)
Most Goals Against	345	1984-85 (80)
Fewest Points	47	1965-66 (70)
Fewest Wins	17	1952-53 (70), 1954-55 (70), 1959-60 (70)
Fewest Ties	4	2001-02 (82)
Fewest Losses	17	1971-72 (78)
Fewest Goals	150	1954-55 (70)
Fewest Goals Against	177	1970-71 (78)

Longest Winning Streak

Overall	10	Dec. 19/39-Jan. 13/40, Jan. 19-Feb. 10/73
Home	14	Dec. 19/39-Feb. 25/40
Away	7	Jan. 12-Feb. 12/35, Oct. 28-Nov. 29/78

Longest Undefeated Streak

Overall	19	Nov. 23/39-Jan. 13/40 (14 wins, 5 ties)
Home	26	Mar. 29/70-Jan. 31/71 (19 wins, 7 ties)
Away	11	Nov. 5/39-Jan. 13/40 (6 wins, 5 ties)

Longest Losing Streak

Overall	11	Oct. 30-Nov. 27/43
Home	7	Oct. 20-Nov. 14/76, Mar. 24-Apr. 14/93
Away	10	Oct. 30-Dec. 23/43, Feb. 2-Mar. 15/61

Longest Winless Streak

Overall	21	Jan. 23-Mar. 19/44 (17 losses, 4 ties)
Home	10	Jan. 30-Mar. 19/44 (7 losses, 3 ties)
Away	16	Oct. 9-Dec. 20/52 (12 losses, 4 ties)

Most Shutouts, Season	13	1928-29 (44)
Most PIM, Season	2,018	1989-90 (80)
Most Goals, Game	12	Nov. 21/71 (Cal. 1 at NYR 12)

Individual

Most Seasons	18	Rod Gilbert
Most Games	1,160	Harry Howell
Most Goals, Career	406	Rod Gilbert
Most Assists, Career	741	Brian Leetch
Most Points, Career	1,021	Rod Gilbert (406G, 615A)
Most PIM, Career	1,226	Ron Greschner
Most Shutouts, Career	49	Ed Giacomin

Longest Consecutive

Games Streak	560	Andy Hebenton (Oct. 7/55-Mar. 24/63)
Most Goals, Season	52	Adam Graves (1993-94)
Most Assists, Season	80	Brian Leetch (1991-92)
Most Points, Season	109	Jean Ratelle (1971-72; 46G, 63A)

Most PIM, Season	305	Troy Mallette (1989-90)
Most Points, Defenseman, Season	102	Brian Leetch (1991-92; 22G, 80A)
Most Points, Center, Season	109	Jean Ratelle (1971-72; 46G, 63A)
Most Points, Right Wing, Season	97	Rod Gilbert (1971-72; 43G, 54A), (1974-75; 36G, 61A)
Most Points, Left Wing, Season	106	Vic Hadfield (1971-72; 50G, 56A)
Most Points, Rookie, Season	76	Mark Pavelich (1981-82; 33G, 43A)
Most Shutouts, Season	13	John Ross Roach (1928-29)
Most Goals, Game	5	Don Murdoch (Oct. 12/76), Mark Pavelich (Feb. 23/83)
Most Assists, Game	5	Walt Tkaczuk (Feb. 12/72), Rod Gilbert (Mar. 2/75, Mar. 30/75, Oct. 8/76), Don Maloney (Jan. 3/87), Brian Leetch (Apr. 18/95), Wayne Gretzky (Feb. 15/99)
Most Points, Game	7	Steve Vickers (Feb. 18/76; 3G, 4A)

Retired Numbers

1	Ed Giacomin	1965-1976
7	Rod Gilbert	1960-1978
35	Mike Richter	1989-2003

All-time Record vs. Other Clubs

Regular Season

	At Home							On Road							Total						
	GP	W	L	T	OL	GF	GA	PTS	GP	W	L	T	OL	GF	GA	PTS	GP	W	L	T	OL	GF	GA	PTS
Anaheim	9	3	5	1	0	23	26	7	8	2	6	0	0	25	32	4	17	5	11	1	0	48	58	11
Atlanta	10	3	5	1	1	28	34	8	10	7	3	0	0	34	28	14	20	10	8	1	1	62	62	22
Boston	302	131	116	55	0	921	853	317	298	96	160	42	0	834	1076	234	600	227	276	97	0	1755	1929	551
Buffalo	66	28	23	15	0	214	180	71	68	19	39	10	0	212	279	48	134	47	62	25	0	426	459	119
Calgary	52	24	23	5	0	178	184	53	49	12	27	10	0	148	216	34	101	36	50	15	0	326	400	87
Carolina	45	27	13	4	1	172	115	59	43	16	24	3	0	137	145	35	88	43	37	7	1	309	260	94
Chicago	285	117	113	55	0	841	807	289	286	115	128	43	0	792	870	273	571	232	241	98	0	1633	1677	562
Colorado	34	19	9	4	2	134	99	44	35	13	18	3	1	130	143	30	69	32	27	7	3	264	242	74
Columbus	2	1	0	1	0	7	5	3	4	1	3	0	0	7	16	2	6	2	3	1	0	14	21	5
Dallas	62	36	15	11	0	213	165	83	61	30	19	11	1	221	187	72	123	66	34	22	1	434	352	155
Detroit	284	134	92	58	0	868	738	326	285	76	164	45	0	699	1004	197	569	210	256	103	0	1567	1742	523
Edmonton	30	10	14	6	0	112	113	26	28	13	12	3	0	94	101	29	58	23	26	9	0	206	214	55
Florida	24	12	8	4	0	74	59	28	25	13	9	2	1	69	64	29	49	25	17	6	1	143	123	57
Los Angeles	58	35	17	6	0	233	172	76	60	27	23	10	0	216	199	64	118	62	40	16	0	449	371	140
Minnesota	3	2	1	0	0	10	7	4	4	3	1	0	0	13	11	6	7	5	2	0	0	23	18	10
Montreal	290	118	118	54	0	835	844	290	290	60	190	40	0	669	1125	160	580	178	308	94	0	1504	1969	450
Nashville	6	2	2	1	1	18	15	6	4	2	1	0	1	14	13	5	10	4	3	1	2	32	28	11
New Jersey	84	40	24	20	0	323	255	100	86	34	45	7	0	280	301	75	170	74	69	27	0	603	556	175
NY Islanders	96	55	30	11	0	358	284	121	96	34	54	8	0	306	371	76	192	89	84	19	0	664	655	197
Ottawa	23	11	12	0	0	74	70	22	23	11	8	3	1	65	69	26	46	22	20	3	1	139	139	48
Philadelphia	110	47	39	23	1	353	321	118	109	39	55	14	1	297	355	93	219	86	94	37	2	650	676	211
Phoenix	29	18	9	2	0	128	102	38	31	14	13	4	0	101	107	32	60	32	22	6	0	229	209	70
Pittsburgh	101	51	41	9	0	393	346	111	100	43	40	14	3	365	359	103	201	94	81	23	3	758	705	214
St. Louis	60	44	10	6	0	245	143	94	63	28	25	10	0	202	188	66	123	72	35	16	0	447	331	160
San Jose	10	7	2	1	0	40	29	15	13	9	2	2	0	49	31	20	23	16	4	3	0	89	60	35
Tampa Bay	27	13	11	2	1	87	85	29	25	11	11	3	0	83	86	25	52	24	22	5	1	170	171	54
Toronto	283	120	106	56	1	873	836	297	282	84	158	39	1	741	974	208	565	204	264	95	2	1614	1810	505
Vancouver	54	38	11	5	0	237	139	81	51	33	15	3	0	204	163	69	105	71	26	8	0	441	302	150
Washington	82	38	34	9	1	304	281	86	84	33	41	9	1	273	315	76	166	71	75	18	2	577	596	162
Defunct Clubs	139	87	30	22	0	460	290	196	139	82	34	23	0	441	291	187	278	169	64	45	0	901	581	383
Totals	**2660**	**1271**	**933**	**447**	**9**	**8756**	**7597**	**2998**	**2660**	**960**	**1328**	**361**	**11**	**7721**	**9119**	**2292**	**5320**	**2231**	**2261**	**808**	**20**	**16477**	**16716**	**5290**

Playoffs

	Series	W	L	GP	W	L	T	GF	GA	Last Mtg.	Rnd.	Result
Boston	9	3	6	42	18	22	2	104	114	1973	QF	W 4-1
Buffalo	1	0	1	3	1	2	0	6	11	1978	PRE	L 1-2
Calgary	1	1	0	3	3	1	0	14	8	1980	PRE	W 3-1
Chicago	5	1	4	24	10	14	0	54	66	1973	SF	L 1-4
Colorado	1	1	0	6	4	2	0	25	19	1995	CQF	W 4-2
Detroit	5	1	4	23	10	13	0	49	57	1950	F	L 3-4
Florida	1	1	0	5	4	1	0	13	10	1997	CQF	W 4-1
Los Angeles	2	2	0	6	5	1	0	32	14	1981	PRE	W 3-1
Montreal	14	7	7	61	25	34	2	158	188	1996	CQF	W 4-2
New Jersey	3	3	0	19	12	7	0	56	46	1997	CSF	W 4-1
NY Islanders	8	3	5	39	19	20	0	132	129	1994	CQF	W 4-0
Philadelphia	10	4	6	47	20	27	0	153	157	1997	CF	L 1-4
Pittsburgh	3	0	3	15	3	12	0	45	64	1996	CSF	L 1-4
St. Louis	1	1	0	6	4	2	0	29	22	1981	QF	W 4-2
Toronto	8	5	3	35	19	16	0	86	86	1971	QF	W 4-2
Vancouver	1	1	0	7	4	3	0	21	19	1994	F	W 4-3
Washington	4	2	2	22	11	11	0	71	75	1994	CSF	W 4-1
Defunct Clubs	9	6	3	22	11	7	4	43	29			
Totals	**86**	**42**	**44**	**386**	**183**	**195**	**8**	**1091**	**1114**			

Calgary totals include Atlanta Flames, 1972-73 to 1979-80.
Colorado totals include Quebec, 1979-80 to 1994-95.
New Jersey totals include Kansas City, 1974-75 to 1975-76.
Phoenix totals include Winnipeg, 1979-80 to 1995-96.
Carolina totals include Hartford, 1979-80 to 1996-97.
Dallas totals include Minnesota North Stars, 1967-68 to 1992-93.
and Colorado Rockies, 1976-77 to 1981-82.

Playoff Results 2005-2000

(Last playoff appearance: 1997)

Abbreviations: Round: F – Final;
CF – conference final; **CSF** – conference semi-final;
CQF – conference quarter-final; **SF** – semi-final;
QF – quarter-final; **PRE** – preliminary round.

Key Off-Season Signings/Acquisitions

2004

July 6 • Announced **Tom Renney** would remain as head coach.

22 • Signed D **Jason Strudwick**.

27 • Re-signed D **Dale Purinton**.

Aug. 10 • Signed C **Michael Nylander**.

23 • Named **Mike Pelino** assistant coach.

2005

July 27 • Signed 2004 1st-round pick (sixth overall) G **Al Montoya**.

29 • Signed 2000 7th-round pick G **Henrik Lundqvist**.

29 • Signed 2003 1st-round pick (12th overall) RW **Hugh Jessiman**.

Aug. 2 • Signed D Marek Malik and C **Martin Straka**.

2 • Re-signed G **Kevin Weekes**.

3 • Re-signed LW **Martin Rucinsky**.

4 • Signed LW **Ville Nieminen** and RW **Jason Ward**.

15 • Re-signed D **Tom Poti**.

18 • Re-signed C **Jamie Lundmark**.

23 • Obtained C **Steve Rucchin** from Anaheim for D **Trevor Gillies** and a 2007 conditional draft pick.

Entry Draft
Selections 2005-1991

2005
Pick
12	Marc Staal
40	Michael Sauer
56	Marc-Andre Cliche
66	Brodie Dupont
77	Dalyn Flatt
107	Tom Pyatt
147	Trevor Koverko
178	Greg Beller
211	Ryan Russell

2004
Pick
6	Al Montoya
19	Lauri Korpikoski
36	Darin Olver
48	Dane Byers
51	Bruce Graham
60	Brandon Dubinsky
73	Zdenek Bahensky
80	Billy Ryan
127	Ryan Callahan
135	Roman Psurny
169	Jordan Foote
247	Jonathan Paiement
266	Jakub Petruzalek

2003
Pick
12	Hugh Jessiman
50	Ivan Baranka
75	Ken Roche
122	Corey Potter
149	Nigel Dawes
176	Ivan Dornic
179	Philippe Furrer
180	Chris Holt
209	Dylan Reese
243	Jan Marek

2002
Pick
33	Lee Falardeau
81	Marcus Jonasen
127	Nate Guenin
143	Mike Walsh
177	Jake Taylor
194	Kim Hirschovits
226	Joey Crabb
240	Petr Prucha
270	Rob Flynn

2001
Pick
10	Dan Blackburn
40	Fedor Tyutin
79	Garth Murray
113	Bryce Lampman
139	Shawn Collymore
176	Marek Zidlicky
206	Petr Preucil
226	Pontus Petterstrom
226	Pontus Petterstrom
230	Leonid Zhvachkin
238	Ryan Hollweg
269	Juris Stals

2000
Pick
64	Filip Novak
95	Dominic Moore
112	Premysl Duben
140	Nathan Martz
143	Brandon Snee
175	Sven Helfenstein
205	Henrik Lundqvist
238	Danny Eberly
269	Martin Richter

1999
Pick
4	Pavel Brendl
9	Jamie Lundmark
59	David Inman
79	Johan Asplund
90	Patrick Aufiero
137	Garrett Bembridge
177	Jay Dardis
197	Arto Laatikainen
226	Yevgeny Gusakov
251	Petter Henning
254	Alexei Bulatov

1998
Pick
7	Manny Malhotra
40	Randy Copley
66	Jason Labarbera
114	Boyd Kane
122	Patrick Leahy
131	Tomas Kloucek
180	Stefan Lundqvist
207	Johan Witehall
235	Jan Mertzig

1997
Pick
19	Stefan Cherneski
46	Wes Jarvis
73	Burke Henry
93	Tomi Kallarsson
126	Jason McLean
134	Johan Lindbom
136	Mike York
154	Shawn Degagne
175	Johan Holmqvist
182	Mike Mottau
210	Andrew Proskurnicki
236	Richard Miller

1996
Pick
22	Jeff Brown
48	Daniel Goneau
76	Dmitri Subbotin
131	Colin Pepperall
158	Ola Sandberg
185	Jeff Dessner
211	Ryan McKie
237	Ronnie Sundin

1995
Pick
39	Christian Dube
65	Mike Martin
91	Marc Savard
110	Alexei Vasiliev
117	Dale Purinton
143	Peter Slamiar
169	Jeff Heil
195	Ilya Gorokhov
221	Bob Maudie

1994
Pick
26	Dan Cloutier
52	Rudolf Vercik
78	Adam Smith
100	Alexander Korobolin
104	Sylvain Blouin
130	Martin Ethier
135	Yuri Litvinov
156	David Brosseau
182	Alexei Lazarenko
208	Craig Anderson
209	Vitali Yeremeyev
234	Eric Boulton
260	Radoslav Kropac
267	Jamie Butt
286	Kim Johnsson

1993
Pick
8	Niklas Sundstrom
34	Lee Sorochan
61	Maxim Galanov
86	Sergei Olimpiyev
112	Gary Roach
138	Dave Trofimenkoff
162	Sergei Kondrashkin
164	Todd Marchant
190	Ed Campbell
216	Ken Shepard
242	Andrei Kudinov
261	Pavel Komarov
268	Maxim Smelnitsky

1992
Pick
24	Peter Ferraro
48	Mattias Norstrom
72	Eric Cairns
85	Chris Ferraro
120	Dmitri Starostenko
144	David Dal Grande
168	Matt Oates
192	Mickey Elick
216	Daniel Brierley
240	Vladimir Vorobiev

1991
Pick
15	Alex Kovalev
37	Darcy Werenka
96	Corey Machanic
125	Fredrik Jax
128	Barry Young
147	John Rushin
169	Corey Hirsch
191	Vyachesl Uvayev
213	Jamie Ram
235	Vitali Chinakhov
257	Brian Wiseman

Club Directory

Madison Square Garden

New York Rangers
14th Floor
2 Pennsylvania Plaza
New York, New York 10121
Phone **212/465-6000**
PR FAX 212/465-6494
www.newyorkrangers.com
Capacity: 18,200

Office of the Chairman, Madison Square Garden
President/CEO, Cablevision Systems Corporation;
   Chairman, Madison Square Garden . . . . James L. Dolan
Vice Chairman, Cablevision Systems Corporation;
   Vice Chairman, Madison Square Garden . . . . Hank J. Ratner
President and COO, MSG Sports . . . . Steve Mills
President, G.M., NY Rangers . . . . Glen Sather
President, Basketball Operations, NY Knicks . . . . . . Isiah Thomas

Team Executive Management
President/CEO, Cablevision Systems Corporation;
   Chairman, Madison Square Garden . . . . James L. Dolan
Vice Chairman, Cablevision Systems Corporation;
   Vice Chairman, Madison Square Garden . . . . Hank J. Ratner
President and COO, MSG Sports, Alt. Gov. . . . . Steve Mills
President, G.M. and Alternate Governor . . . . Glen Sather
Senior V.P., Finance and Controller . . . . John Cudmore
Senior V.P., Marketing and Business Operations . . . Michael Golub
Senior V.P., Sports Team Operations . . . . Mark Piazza
Senior V.P., Legal Affairs, MSG . . . . Marc Schoenfeld
Vice President, Marketing . . . . Jeanie Baumgartner
Vice President, Legal and Business Affairs . . . . Rana Dershowitz
Vice President, Public Relations . . . . John Rosasco
Vice President, Publicity – MSG Sports . . . . Dan Schoenberg
Vice President, Sponsorships . . . . Rob Scolaro
Vice President, Team Operations . . . . Darren Blake

Madison Square Garden Executive Management
President, MSG Networks . . . . Michael Bair
Executive Vice President, Finance . . . . Robert Pollichino
Executive Vice President, Ad Sales . . . . TBA
Executive Vice President, Facilities . . . . Tim Hassett
Senior V.P., Sports and Facility Event Sales . . . . . . Joel Fisher
Senior V.P., Communications . . . . Barry Watkins
Senior V.P., Team Sales, Tickets/Suites . . . . Brian Lafemina

Hockey Club Personnel
V.P., Player Personnel and Asst. G.M. . . . . Don Maloney
Head Coach . . . . Tom Renney
V.P., Hockey Administration, R&D . . . . Cameron Hope
Assistant Coaches . . . . Benoit Allaire, Perry Pearn, Mike Pelino
Head Amateur Scout . . . . Gordie Clark
Amateur Scouting Staff . . . . Rich Brown, Ray Clearwater, Andre Beaulieu,
   Jan Gajdosik, Ernie Gare, Vladimir Lutchenko,
   Tim Murray, Christer Rockstom, Shanon Sather
Head Professional Scout . . . . Dave Brown
Professional Scouting Staff . . . . Nick Fotiu, Gilles Leger, Peter Stephan
Medical Trainer . . . . Jim Ramsay
Equipment Manager . . . . Acacio Marques
Assistant Equipment Manager . . . . James Johnson
Massage Therapist . . . . Bruce Lifrieri
Strength and Conditioning Coordinator . . . . Reg Grant
Video Analyst . . . . Jerry Dineen
Mental Skills Coach . . . . Dr. John Phelan
Manager, Madison Square Garden Training Center . . Pat Boller

Medical/Training Staff
Team Physician and Orthopedic Surgeon . . . . Dr. Andrew Feldman
Assistant Team Physician . . . . Dr. Anthony Maddalo
Medical Consultant . . . . Dr. Ronald Weissman
Team Dentists . . . . Dr. Joe Esposito, Dr. Don Salomon,
   Dr. Jeff Shapiro
Sports Psychologist – MSG Sports Teams . . . . Dr. John Phelan

Public Relations Department
Director, Public Relations . . . . Jason Vogel
Manager, Public Relations . . . . TBA
Coordinator, Public Relations . . . . David Martella

Additional Information
Television Network . . . . MSG Network
Radio Network . . . . ESPN Radio 1050

President and General Manager

SATHER, GLEN
President/General Manager, New York Rangers.
Born in High River, Alta., September 2, 1943.

Glen Sather, who spent parts of four seasons with the New York Rangers as a player from 1970 to 1974, became the franchise's 12th president and tenth general manager on June 2, 2000. He also served as coach of the team from January 30, 2003, to February 25, 2004.

Sather joined the Rangers following a 24-year career with the Edmonton Oilers, where he was the architect of five Stanley Cup championships between 1984 and 1990. One of the most respected executives in the National Hockey League, Sather was honored for his tremendous achievements in 1997 by becoming the first member of the Oilers organization to be selected to the Hockey Hall of Fame.

Named coach and vice president of hockey operations for the Oilers when the franchise joined the NHL in June of 1979, Sather became general manager and club president in May of 1980. He coached through the 1988-89 season and also returned for 60 games behind the bench in 1993-94. Sather-coached teams won the Stanley Cup four times in the 1980s. As general manager, Sather was instrumental in the Oilers' fifth Cup triumph in 1990.

He played for six different teams during a 10-year NHL career. He scored 80 goals in 658 games.

NHL Coaching Record

			Regular Season			Playoffs		
Season	Team	Games	W	L	T	Games	W	L
1979-80	Edmonton	80	28	39	13	3	0	3
1980-81	Edmonton	62	25	26	11	9	5	4
1981-82	Edmonton	80	48	17	15	5	2	3
1982-83	Edmonton	80	47	21	12	16	11	5
1983-84	Edmonton	80	57	18	5	19	15	4*
1984-85	Edmonton	80	49	20	11	18	15	3*
1985-86	Edmonton	80	56	17	7	10	6	4
1986-87	Edmonton	80	50	24	6	21	16	5*
1987-88	Edmonton	80	44	25	11	18	16	2*
1988-89	Edmonton	80	38	34	8	7	3	4
1993-94	Edmonton	60	22	27	11	....		
2002-03	NY Rangers	28	11	13	4	....		
2003-04	NY Rangers	62	22	33	7	....		
	NHL Totals	**932**	**497**	**314**	**121**	**126**	**89**	**37**

* Stanley Cup win.

General Managers' History

Lester Patrick, 1926-27 to 1945-46; Frank Boucher, 1946-47 to 1954-55; Muzz Patrick, 1955-56 to 1963-64; Emile Francis, 1964-65 to 1974-75; Emile Francis and John Ferguson, 1975-76; John Ferguson, 1976-77, 1977-78; John Ferguson and Fred Shero, 1978-79; Fred Shero, 1979-80; Fred Shero and Craig Patrick, 1980-81; Craig Patrick, 1981-82 to 1985-86; Phil Esposito, 1986-87 to 1988-89; Neil Smith, 1989-90 to 1999-2000; Glen Sather, 2000-01 to date.

Ottawa Senators

2005-06 Schedule

Oct.	Wed.	5	at Toronto
	Sat.	8	Buffalo
	Mon.	10	Toronto
	Tue.	11	at Montreal
	Sat.	15	Boston
	Fri.	21	at Tampa Bay
	Sat.	22	at Florida
	Mon.	24	at Carolina
	Thu.	27	Montreal
	Sat.	29	at Toronto
	Sun.	30	Philadelphia
Nov.	Wed.	2	at Buffalo
	Thu.	3	Tampa Bay
	Sat.	5	NY Islanders
	Thu.	10	at Boston
	Sat.	12	Buffalo
	Tue.	15	Carolina
	Thu.	17	Florida
	Sat.	19	New Jersey
	Tue.	22	at Carolina
	Fri.	25	at NY Islanders*
	Sat.	26	Boston
	Tue.	29	Montreal
Dec.	Thu.	1	at Boston
	Fri.	2	Los Angeles
	Fri.	9	at Vancouver
	Sat.	10	at Calgary
	Mon.	12	at Colorado
	Thu.	15	Dallas
	Sat.	17	Toronto
	Tue.	20	at Montreal
	Thu.	22	at Philadelphia
	Fri.	23	at NY Islanders
	Mon.	26	NY Rangers
	Wed.	28	Carolina
	Fri.	30	NY Islanders
Jan.	Mon.	2	at Atlanta
	Wed.	4	at Washington
	Thu.	5	at Boston
	Sat.	7	at Montreal*
	Tue.	10	Phoenix

	Thu.	12	San Jose
	Sat.	14	at Edmonton
	Mon.	16	at Minnesota
	Thu.	19	Anaheim
	Sat.	21	Toronto
	Mon.	23	Toronto
	Thu.	26	Montreal
	Mon.	30	Boston
Feb.	Wed.	1	at New Jersey
	Thu.	2	at Pittsburgh
	Sat.	4	at Buffalo
	Mon.	6	Pittsburgh
	Wed.	8	at NY Rangers
	Thu.	9	Atlanta
	Sat.	11	Philadelphia
Mar.	Wed.	1	at Pittsburgh
	Thu.	2	Washington
	Sat.	4	at Toronto
	Mon.	6	at Tampa Bay
	Thu.	9	at Florida
	Fri.	10	at Atlanta
	Sun.	12	at Washington*
	Tue.	14	Tampa Bay
	Thu.	16	at Boston
	Sat.	18	Buffalo
	Sun.	19	at New Jersey
	Tue.	21	Pittsburgh
	Fri.	24	at Buffalo
	Sat.	25	at Philadelphia
	Tue.	28	New Jersey
	Thu.	30	NY Rangers
Apr.	Sat.	1	Washington
	Mon.	3	Atlanta
	Wed.	5	at Buffalo
	Thu.	6	Montreal
	Sat.	8	Buffalo
	Mon.	10	at Montreal
	Tue.	11	Boston
	Thu.	13	Florida
	Sat.	15	at Toronto
	Tue.	18	at NY Rangers

* Denotes afternoon game.

Franchise date: December 16, 1991

EASTERN CONFERENCE

NORTHEAST DIVISION

14th NHL Season

Year-by-Year Record

Season	GP	Home W	L	T	OL	Road W	L	T	OL	Overall W	L	T	OL	GF	GA	Pts.	Finished	Playoff Result
2004-05	....	....	....	....	....	....	....	....	....	....	....	....	....	....	....	....		
2003-04	82	23	8	5	5	20	15	5	1	43	23	10	6	262	189	102	3rd, Northeast Div.	Lost Conf. Quarter-Final
2002-03	82	28	9	3	1	24	12	5	0	52	21	8	1	263	182	113	1st, Northeast Div.	Lost Conf. Championship
2001-02	82	21	13	3	4	18	14	6	3	39	27	9	7	243	208	94	3rd, Northeast Div.	Lost Conf. Semi-Final
2000-01	82	26	7	5	3	22	14	4	1	48	21	9	4	274	205	109	1st, Northeast Div.	Lost Conf. Quarter-Final
1999-2000	82	24	10	5	2	17	18	6	0	41	28	11	2	244	210	95	2nd, Northeast Div.	Lost Conf. Quarter-Final
1998-99	82	22	11	8	....	22	12	7	....	44	23	15	....	239	179	103	1st, Northeast Div.	Lost Conf. Quarter-Final
1997-98	82	18	16	7	....	16	17	8	....	34	33	15	....	193	200	83	5th, Northeast Div.	Lost Conf. Semi-Final
1996-97	82	16	17	8	....	15	19	7	....	31	36	15	....	226	234	77	3rd, Northeast Div.	Lost Conf. Quarter-Final
1995-96	82	8	28	5	....	10	31	0	....	18	59	5	....	191	291	41	6th, Northeast Div.	Out of Playoffs
1994-95	48	5	16	3	....	4	18	2	....	9	34	5	....	117	174	23	7th, Northeast Div.	Out of Playoffs
1993-94	84	8	30	4	....	6	31	5	....	14	61	9	....	201	397	37	7th, Northeast Div.	Out of Playoffs
1992-93	84	9	29	4	....	1	41	0	....	10	70	4	....	202	395	24	6th, Adams Div.	Out of Playoffs

A six-time Vezina Trophy winner in Buffalo and a Stanley Cup champion in Detroit, Dominik Hasek should give the Senators big-game goaltending.

2005-06 Player Personnel

FORWARDS	HT	WT	S	Place of Birth	Date	2004-05 Club
ALFREDSSON, Daniel	5-11	199	R	Goteborg, Sweden	12/11/72	Frolunda
BOCHENSKI, Brandon	6-0	180	R	Blaine, MN	4/4/82	Binghamton
BOIS, Danny	6-1	197	R	Thunder Bay, Ont.	6/1/83	Binghamton
CLOUTHIER, Brett	6-5	225	L	Ottawa, Ont.	6/9/81	Albany-Augusta
EAVES, Patrick	6-0	185	R	Calgary, Alta.	5/1/84	Boston College
FISHER, Mike	6-1	200	R	Peterborough, Ont.	6/5/80	Zug
HAMEL, Denis	6-1	201	L	Lachute, Que.	5/10/77	Binghamton
HAVLAT, Martin	6-1	190	L	Mlada Boleslav, Czech.	4/19/81	Znojmo-Dynamo Moscow-Sparta
HEATLEY, Dany	6-3	215	L	Freiburg, West Germany	1/21/81	Bern-Kazan
HEEREMA, Jeff	6-1	190	R	Thunder Bay, Ont.	1/17/80	Manitoba
KELLY, Chris	6-0	190	L	Toronto, Ont.	11/11/80	Binghamton
MARTINS, Steve	5-9	185	L	Gatineau, Que.	4/13/72	JYP
McGRATTAN, Brian	6-4	225	R	Hamilton, Ont.	9/2/81	Binghamton
NEIL, Chris	6-0	213	R	Markdale, Ont.	6/18/79	Binghamton
SCHAEFER, Peter	5-11	195	L	Yellow Grass, Sask.	7/12/77	Bolzano
SMOLINSKI, Bryan	6-1	208	R	Toledo, OH	12/27/71	Motor City
SPEZZA, Jason	6-2	206	R	Mississauga, Ont.	6/13/83	Binghamton
VARADA, Vaclav	6-0	208	L	Vsetin, Czech.	4/26/76	Vitkovice
VERMETTE, Antoine	6-1	184	L	St-Agapit, Que.	7/20/82	Binghamton
WATSON, Greg	6-0	205	L	Eastend, Sask.	3/2/83	Binghamton

DEFENSEMEN	HT	WT	S	Place of Birth	Date	2004-05 Club
CHARA, Zdeno	6-9	260	L	Trencin, Czech.	3/18/77	Farjestad
KOMADOSKI, Neil	6-2	215	L	Chesterfield, MO	2/10/82	Binghamton
MALEC, Tomas	6-2	193	L	Skalica, Czech.	5/13/82	Cincinnati (AHL)
MESZAROS, Andrej	6-1	200	L	Povazska Bystrica, Czech.	10/13/85	Vancouver (WHL)
PHILLIPS, Chris	6-3	215	L	Calgary, Alta.	3/9/78	Brynas-Brynas
PLATIL, Jan	6-2	195	L	Kladno, Czech.	2/9/83	Binghamton
POTHIER, Brian	6-0	195	R	New Bedford, MA	4/15/77	Binghamton
REDDEN, Wade	6-2	205	L	Lloydminster, Sask.	6/12/77	
SCHUBERT, Christoph	6-2	210	L	Munich, West Germany	2/5/82	Binghamton
VOLCHENKOV, Anton	6-1	227	L	Moscow, USSR	2/25/82	Binghamton
WARD, Lance	6-3	210	L	Lloydminster, Alta.	6/2/78	

GOALTENDERS	HT	WT	C	Place of Birth	Date	2004-05 Club
EMERY, Ray	6-2	198	L	Cayuga, Ont.	9/28/82	Binghamton
GUARD, Kelly	6-1	203	L	Prince Albert, Sask.	6/10/83	Charlotte
HASEK, Dominik	5-11	180	L	Pardubice, Czech.	1/29/65	
THOMPSON, Billy	6-2	200	L	Saskatoon, Sask.	9/24/82	Binghamton

In the System and Recently Drafted

FORWARDS	HT	WT	S	Place of Birth	Date	2004-05 Club
BASS, Cody	6-0	191	R	Owen Sound, Ont.	1/7/87	Mississauga
COOPER, Joe	6-1	199	R	Toronto, Ont.	6/7/85	Miami U.
GREENING, Colin	6-2	191	L	St. John's, Nfld.	3/9/86	Upper Canada
HOOTON, Brock	6-2	208	R	Smithers, B.C.	3/20/83	St. Cloud State
KAIGORODOV, Alexei	6-1	183	L	Chelyabinsk, USSR	7/29/83	Magnitogorsk
KOLEHMAINEN, Janne	6-3	209	L	Lappeenranta, Finland	3/22/86	SaiPa
LOUHIVAARA, Ossi	6-0	179	R	Kotka, Finland	8/21/83	JYP
LUTTINEN, Arttu	5-10	205	L	Helsinki, Finland	9/9/83	HIFK
McILVANE, Matthew	6-0	202	R	Downers Grove, IL	11/2/85	Ohio State
McKENZIE, Jim	6-2	209	R	St. Paul, MN	6/10/84	Michigan State
MIRNOV, Igor	5-11	191	L	Chita, USSR	9/19/84	Dynamo Moscow
NIKULIN, Alexander	6-1	195	L	Moscow, USSR	8/25/85	CSKA
REGIN JENSEN, Peter	6-1	174	L	Herning, Denmark	4/16/86	Herning
WELLER, Shawn	6-1	188	L	Glens Falls, NY	7/8/86	Clarkson
WICK, Roman	6-1	187	L	Kloten, Switz.	12/30/85	Red Deer
WIKNER, John	6-1	179	L	Molndal, Sweden	1/1/86	Molndal-Frolunda Jr.
ZUBOV, Ilja	6-0	176	L	Chelyabinsk, USSR	2/14/87	Chelyabinsk

DEFENSEMEN	HT	WT	S	Place of Birth	Date	2004-05 Club
ANIKEYENKO, Vitali	6-3	200	R	Kiev, USSR	1/2/87	Yaroslavl 2
ATYUSHOV, Vitali	6-1	205	L	Penza, USSR	7/4/79	Magnitogorsk
BJORK, Johan	6-1	176	L	Malmo, Sweden	8/28/84	Malmo-Morrum
COOK, Tim	6-4	190	L	Montclair, NJ	3/13/84	U. of Michigan
GIMAEV, Sergei	6-1	183	L	Moscow, USSR	2/16/84	Cherep.-Novosibirsk
KARLSSON, Mattias	6-2	192	L	Stora, Sweden	4/15/85	Brynas-Almtuna
KUDELKA, Tomas	6-2	176	L	Gottwaldov, Czech.	3/10/87	Zlin
LEE, Brian	6-2	202	R	Fargo, ND	3/26/87	Moorhead-Lincoln
LYAMIN, Kirill	6-2	208	L	Moscow, USSR	1/13/86	CSKA 2
MEGALINSKY, Dmitri	6-2	212	L	Perm, USSR	4/15/85	Yaroslavl
SCHAUER, Stefan	6-1	185	L	Schongau, West Germany	1/12/83	Nurnberg
SEYDOUX, Philippe	6-2	185	L	Bern, Switz.	2/23/85	Kloten

GOALTENDERS	HT	WT	C	Place of Birth	Date	2004-05 Club
ELLIOTT, Brian	6-3	186	L	Newmarket, Ont.	4/9/85	U. of Wisconsin
GLASS, Jeff	6-2	182	L	Calgary, Alta.	11/19/85	Kootenay

Dany Heatley was obtained from Atlanta in a swap for left wing Marian Hossa and defenseman Greg de Vries.

General Manager

MUCKLER, JOHN
General Manager, Ottawa Senators. Born in Midland, Ont., April 3, 1934.

John Muckler was named the sixth general manager in Senators history on June 12, 2002. Prior to his arrival in Ottawa, Muckler served as coach of the New York Rangers from 1997-98 to 1999-2000. Previously, he was general manager of the Buffalo Sabres from 1993 to 1997, and was named NHL executive of the year by *The Sporting News* for the 1996-97 season. Muckler is the first g.m. hired by the Senators to have previous NHL experience as a general manager.

Working for Glen Sather, Muckler enjoyed Edmonton's great 1980s run. He was an assistant coach with the Stanley Cup winners in 1984 and 1985, and designated co-coach during the 1987 and 1988 championship seasons. When Sather gave up the Oilers' coaching reins in 1989, Muckler stepped in and led the team to its fifth Stanley Cup in seven years. In 1991, he left the Oilers for the Buffalo Sabres.

Muckler has been involved in professional hockey since the 1949-50 season. He was a defenseman in the minor leagues for 13 seasons, playing the bulk of his career in the old Eastern Hockey League. His professional coaching career began while he was still a player in 1959 when he took over the New York Rovers of the EHL. He had great success with the team in the 1960s when they were known as the Long Island Ducks. Muckler joined the Minnesota North Stars after NHL expansion in 1967 and spent six seasons in the organization, mostly as a coach and g.m. in the minor leagues. His first NHL coaching job came with the North Stars midway through the 1968-69 season. He later worked in the Rangers and Canucks organizations before joining the Oilers as coach of their Wichita farm club in 1981.

NHL Coaching Record

			Regular Season			Playoffs		
Season	Team	Games	W	L	T	Games	W	L
1968-69	Minnesota	35	6	23	6	....	....	....
1989-90	Edmonton	80	38	28	14	22	16	6*
1990-91	Edmonton	80	37	37	6	18	9	9
1991-92	Buffalo	52	22	22	8	7	3	4
1992-93	Buffalo	84	38	36	10	8	4	4
1993-94	Buffalo	84	43	32	9	7	3	4
1994-95	Buffalo	48	22	19	7	5	1	4
1997-98	NY Rangers	25	8	15	2	....	....	....
1998-99	NY Rangers	82	33	38	11	....	....	....
1999-2000	NY Rangers	78	29	38	11	....	....	....
	NHL Totals	**648**	**276**	**288**	**84**	**67**	**36**	**31**

* Stanley Cup win.

General Managers' History

Mel Bridgman, 1992-93; Randy Sexton, 1993-94, 1994-95; Randy Sexton and Pierre Gauthier, 1995-96; Pierre Gauthier, 1996-97, 1997-98; Rick Dudley, 1998-99; Marshall Johnston, 1999-2000 to 2001-02; John Muckler, 2002-03 to date.

Club Records

Team

(Figures in brackets for season records are games played; records for fewest points, wins, ties, losses, goals, goals against are for 70 or more games)

Most Points	113	2002-03 (82)
Most Wins	52	2002-03 (82)
Most Ties	15	1996-97 (82), 1997-98 (82), 1998-99 (82)
Most Losses	70	1992-93 (84)
Most Goals	274	2000-01 (82)
Most Goals Against	397	1993-94 (84)
Fewest Points	24	1992-93 (84)
Fewest Wins	10	1992-93 (84)
Fewest Ties	4	1992-93 (84)
Fewest Losses	21	2000-01 (82), 2002-03 (82)
Fewest Goals	191	1995-96 (82)
Fewest Goals Against	179	1998-99 (82)

Longest Winning Streak

Overall	7	Oct. 25-Nov. 13/01
Home	8	Nov. 14-Dec. 14/02
Away	6	Mar. 18-Apr. 5/03

Longest Undefeated Streak

Overall	11	Three times
Home	12	Dec. 18/03-Jan. 24/04 (10 wins, 2 ties)
Away	7	Three times

** NHL records do not include neutral site games

Longest Losing Streak

Overall	14	Mar. 2-Apr. 7/93
Home	*11	Oct. 27-Dec. 8/93
Away	*38	Oct. 10/92-Apr. 3/93**

Longest Winless Streak

Overall	21	Oct. 10-Nov. 23/92 (20 losses, 1 tie)
Home	*17	Oct. 28/95-Jan. 27/96 (15 losses, 2 ties)
Away	*38	Oct. 10/92-Apr. 3/93 (38 losses)
Most Shutouts, Season	10	2001-02 (82)
Most PIM, Season	1,716	1992-93 (84)
Most Goals, Game	11	Nov. 13/01 (Ott. 11 at Wsh. 5)

Individual

Most Seasons	10	Radek Bonk
Most Games, Career	689	Radek Bonk
Most Goals, Career	219	Daniel Alfredsson
Most Assists, Career	349	Daniel Alfredsson
Most Points, Career	568	Daniel Alfredsson (219G, 349A)
Most PIM, Career	625	Dennis Vial
Most Shutouts, Career	30	Patrick Lalime
Longest Consecutive Games Streak	292	Alexei Yashin (Dec. 31/95-Apr. 17/99)

Most Goals, Season	45	Marian Hossa (2002-03)
Most Assists, Season	51	Daniel Alfredsson (2002-03)
Most Points, Season	94	Alexei Yashin (1998-99; 44G, 50A)
Most PIM, Season	318	Mike Peluso (1992-93)
Most Points, Defenseman, Season	63	Norm Maciver (1992-93; 17G, 46A)
Most Points, Center, Season	94	Alexei Yashin (1998-99; 44G, 50A)
Most Points, Right Wing, Season	82	Marian Hossa (2003-04; 36G, 46A)
Most Points, Left Wing, Season	72	Shawn McEachern (2000-01; 32G, 40A)
Most Points, Rookie, Season	79	Alexei Yashin (1993-94; 30G, 49A)
Most Shutouts, Season	8	Patrick Lalime (2002-03)
Most Goals, Game	4	Marian Hossa (Jan. 2/03)
Most Assists, Game	5	Marian Hossa (Jan. 4/01)
Most Points, Game	6	Dan Quinn (Oct. 15/95; 3G, 3A), Radek Bonk (Jan. 4/01; 3G, 3A)

* NHL Record.

Coaching History

Rick Bowness, 1992-93 to 1994-95; Rick Bowness, Dave Allison and Jacques Martin, 1995-96; Jacques Martin, 1996-97 to 2000-01; Jacques Martin and Roger Neilson, 2001-02; Jacques Martin, 2002-03, 2003-04; Bryan Murray, 2004-05 to date.

Captains' History

Laurie Boschman, 1992-93; Brad Shaw, Mark Lamb and Gord Dineen, 1993-94; Randy Cunneyworth, 1994-95 to 1997-98; Alexei Yashin, 1998-99; Daniel Alfredsson, 1999-2000 to date.

Retired Numbers

8   Frank Finnigan   1924-1934

All-time Record vs. Other Clubs

Regular Season

	At Home								On Road								Total							
	GP	W	L	T	OL	GF	GA	PTS	GP	W	L	T	OL	GF	GA	PTS	GP	W	L	T	OL	GF	GA	PTS
Anaheim	8	4	3	1	0	24	19	9	9	3	4	2	0	18	21	8	17	7	7	3	0	42	40	17
Atlanta	10	6	1	1	2	47	26	15	10	7	1	1	1	45	31	16	20	13	2	2	3	92	57	31
Boston	31	13	15	3	0	78	93	29	33	9	19	5	0	92	123	23	64	22	34	8	0	170	216	52
Buffalo	33	10	13	7	3	76	86	30	31	7	20	3	1	48	99	18	64	17	33	10	4	124	185	48
Calgary	10	5	1	3	1	27	24	14	11	4	6	1	0	25	38	9	21	9	7	4	1	52	62	23
Carolina	29	12	11	4	2	81	78	30	27	7	16	4	0	65	81	18	56	19	27	8	2	146	159	48
Chicago	10	4	5	0	1	31	30	9	8	2	4	2	0	18	18	6	18	6	9	2	1	49	48	15
Colorado	18	8	7	3	0	53	64	19	15	2	12	1	0	41	70	5	33	10	19	4	0	94	134	24
Columbus	3	2	0	1	0	12	6	5	2	1	0	1	0	9	7	3	5	3	0	2	0	21	13	8
Dallas	9	4	5	0	0	22	24	8	11	4	7	0	0	28	44	8	20	8	12	0	0	50	68	16
Detroit	10	3	5	1	1	28	29	8	9	1	7	0	1	19	33	7	19	4	12	1	2	47	62	15
Edmonton	10	3	5	2	0	19	26	8	11	2	7	2	0	25	39	6	21	5	12	4	0	44	65	14
Florida	22	10	10	2	0	61	60	22	22	12	9	1	0	67	64	25	44	22	19	3	0	128	124	47
Los Angeles	9	4	3	1	1	30	28	10	10	1	8	1	0	21	46	3	19	5	11	2	1	51	74	13
Minnesota	2	1	1	0	0	4	4	2	3	1	1	1	0	8	10	3	5	2	2	1	0	12	14	5
Montreal	31	15	15	1	0	90	87	31	33	12	17	4	0	95	97	28	64	27	32	5	0	185	184	59
Nashville	5	4	1	0	0	15	7	8	4	2	2	0	0	11	8	4	9	6	3	0	0	26	15	12
New Jersey	24	6	14	3	1	47	60	16	23	8	12	2	1	54	66	19	47	14	26	5	2	101	126	35
NY Islanders	23	13	5	5	0	78	62	31	24	13	5	6	0	89	78	32	47	26	10	11	0	167	140	63
NY Rangers	23	9	11	3	0	69	65	21	23	12	11	0	0	70	74	24	46	21	22	3	0	139	139	45
Philadelphia	24	8	10	6	0	65	72	22	23	8	13	2	0	63	73	18	47	16	23	8	0	128	145	40
Phoenix	11	4	6	1	0	29	34	9	10	5	4	1	0	38	34	11	21	9	10	2	0	67	68	20
Pittsburgh	27	8	14	5	0	70	87	21	27	6	16	4	1	64	97	17	54	14	30	9	1	134	184	38
St. Louis	10	4	6	0	0	23	36	8	9	3	4	2	0	25	27	8	19	7	10	2	0	48	63	16
San Jose	9	4	4	1	0	36	26	12	9	4	5	0	0	16	18	8	18	8	9	1	0	52	44	20
Tampa Bay	23	15	8	0	0	88	50	30	23	13	8	2	0	80	70	28	46	28	16	2	0	168	120	58
Toronto	20	12	6	1	1	56	53	26	22	10	10	2	0	60	59	22	42	22	16	3	1	116	112	48
Vancouver	10	5	3	1	1	24	24	12	11	5	5	1	0	26	33	11	21	10	8	2	1	50	57	23
Washington	23	12	9	1	1	84	70	26	24	9	11	4	0	68	76	22	47	21	20	5	1	152	146	48
Totals	477	208	194	60	15	1367	1330	491	477	175	242	55	5	1288	1534	410	954	383	436	115	20	2655	2864	901

Playoffs

	Series	W	L	GP	W	L	T	GF	GA	Last Mtg.	Rnd.	Result
Buffalo	2	0	2	11	3	8	0	19	26	1999	CQF	L 0-4
New Jersey	2	1	1	13	7	6	0	26	29	2003	CF	L 3-4
NY Islanders	1	1	0	5	4	1	0	13	7	2003	CQF	W 4-1
Philadelphia	2	2	0	11	8	3	0	28	12	2003	CSF	W 4-2
Toronto	4	0	4	24	8	16	0	42	57	2004	CQF	L 3-4
Washington	1	0	1	5	1	4	0	7	18	1998	CSF	L 1-4
Totals	12	4	8	69	31	38	0	135	149			

Playoff Results 2005-2000

Year	Round	Opponent	Result	GF	GA
2004	CQF	Toronto	L 3-4	11	14
2003	CF	New Jersey	L 3-4	13	17
	CSF	Philadelphia	W 4-2	17	10
	CQF	NY Islanders	W 4-1	13	7
2002	CSF	Toronto	L 3-4	18	16
	CQF	Philadelphia	W 4-1	11	2
2001	CQF	Toronto	L 0-4	3	10
2000	CQF	Toronto	L 2-4	10	17

Abbreviations: Round: CF – conference final; **CSF** – conference semi-final; **CQF** – conference quarter-final.

Colorado totals include Quebec, 1992-93 to 1994-95.
Dallas totals include Minnesota North Stars, 1992-93.
Carolina totals include Hartford, 1992-93 to 1996-97.
Phoenix totals include Winnipeg, 1992-93 to 1995-96.

Key Off-Season Signings/Acquisitions

2004

June 8 • Named **Bryan Murray** head coach.

July 9 • Named **John Paddock** assistant coach.

Aug. 6 • Re-signed D **Chris Phillips** and F **Peter Schaefer**.

10 • Re-signed D **Zdeno Chara**.

2005

July 27 • Exercised the contract option on G **Dominik Hasek**.

Aug. 2 • Re-signed LW **Denis Hamel**.

10 • Re-signed RW **Martin Havlat** and C **Mike Fisher**.

11 • Re-signed G **Ray Emery**.

12 • Re-signed Cs **Jason Spezza** and **Antoine Vermette**, RW **Chris Neil** and Ds **Anton Volchenkov** and **Christoph Schubert**.

22 • Signed 2003 1st-round pick (29th overall), RW **Patrick Eaves**.

23 • Obtained RW **Dany Heatley** from Ottawa for RW **Marian Hossa** and D **Greg de Vries**.

26 • Signed D **Lance Ward** and RW **Jeff Heerema**.

Entry Draft
Selections 2005-1992

2005
Pick
- 9 Brian Lee
- 70 Vitali Anikeyenko
- 95 Cody Bass
- 98 Ilja Zubov
- 115 Janne Kolehmainen
- 136 Tomas Kudelka
- 186 Dimitri Megalinsky
- 204 Colin Greening

2004
Pick
- 23 Andrej Meszaros
- 58 Kirill Lyamin
- 77 Shawn Weller
- 87 Peter Regin Jensen
- 89 Jeff Glass
- 122 Alexander Nikulin
- 141 Jim McKenzie
- 156 Roman Wick
- 219 Joe Cooper
- 251 Matthew McIlvane
- 284 John Wikner

2003
Pick
- 29 Patrick Eaves
- 67 Igor Mirnov
- 100 Philippe Seydoux
- 135 Mattias Karlsson
- 142 Tim Cook
- 166 Sergei Gimaev
- 228 Will Colbert
- 260 Ossi Louhivaara
- 291 Brian Elliott

2002
Pick
- 16 Jakub Klepis
- 47 Alexei Kaigorodov
- 75 Arttu Luttinen
- 113 Scott Dobben
- 125 Johan Bjork
- 150 Brock Hooton
- 246 Josef Vavra
- 276 Vitali Atyushov

2001
Pick
- 2 Jason Spezza
- 23 Tim Gleason
- 81 Neil Komadoski
- 99 Ray Emery
- 127 Christoph Schubert
- 162 Stefan Schauer
- 193 Brooks Laich
- 218 Jan Platil
- 223 Brandon Bochenski
- 235 Neil Petruic
- 256 Gregg Johnson
- 286 Toni Dahlman

2000
Pick
- 21 Anton Volchenkov
- 45 Mathieu Chouinard
- 55 Antoine Vermette
- 87 Jan Bohac
- 122 Derrick Byfuglien
- 156 Greg Zanon
- 157 Grant Potulny
- 158 Sean Connolly
- 188 Jason Maleyko
- 283 James Demone

1999
Pick
- 26 Martin Havlat
- 48 Simon Lajeunesse
- 62 Teemu Sainomaa
- 94 Chris Kelly
- 154 Andrew Ianiero
- 164 Martin Prusek
- 201 Mikko Ruutu
- 209 Layne Ulmer
- 213 Alexandre Giroux
- 269 Konstantin Gorovikov

1998
Pick
- 15 Mathieu Chouinard
- 44 Mike Fisher
- 58 Chris Bala
- 74 Julien Vauclair
- 101 Petr Schastlivy
- 130 Gavin McLeod
- 161 Chris Neil
- 188 Michel Periard
- 223 Sergei Verenikin
- 246 Rastislav Pavlikovsky

1997
Pick
- 12 Marian Hossa
- 58 Jani Hurme
- 116 Josh Langfeld
- 119 Magnus Arvedson
- 146 Jeff Sullivan
- 173 Robin Bacul
- 203 Nick Gillis
- 229 Karel Rachunek

1996
Pick
- 1 Chris Phillips
- 81 Antti-Jussi Niemi
- 136 Andreas Dackell
- 163 Francois Hardy
- 212 Erich Goldmann
- 216 Ivan Ciernik
- 239 Sami Salo

1995
Pick
- 1 Bryan Berard
- 27 Marc Moro
- 53 Brad Larsen
- 89 Kevin Bolibruck
- 103 Kevin Boyd
- 131 David Hruska
- 183 Kaj Linna
- 184 Ray Schultz
- 231 Erik Kaminski

1994
Pick
- 3 Radek Bonk
- 29 Stan Neckar
- 81 Bryan Masotta
- 131 Mike Gaffney
- 133 Daniel Alfredsson
- 159 Doug Sproule
- 210 Frederic Cassivi
- 211 Danny Dupont
- 237 Stephen MacKinnon
- 274 Antti Tormanen

1993
Pick
- 1 Alexandre Daigle
- 27 Radim Bicanek
- 53 Patrick Charbonneau
- 91 Cosmo Dupaul
- 131 Rick Bodkin
- 157 Sergei Poleschuk
- 183 Jason Disher
- 209 Toby Kvalevog
- 227 Pavol Demitra
- 235 Rick Schuwerk

1992
Pick
- 2 Alexei Yashin
- 25 Chad Penney
- 50 Patrick Traverse
- 73 Radek Hamr
- 98 Daniel Guerard
- 121 Al Sinclair
- 146 Jaroslav Miklenda
- 169 Jay Kenney
- 194 Claude Savoie
- 217 Jake Grimes
- 242 Tomas Jelinek
- 264 Petter Ronnqvist

Coach

MURRAY, BRYAN
Coach, Ottawa Senators. Born in Shawville, Que., December 5, 1942.

Bryan Murray was announced on June 8, 2004, as the fifth head coach in the franchise's new era since returning to the NHL for the 1992-93 season. Murray, who had just completed his 23rd consecutive season in the NHL, resigned as senior vice president and general manager of the Mighty Ducks of Anaheim. He'd been promoted to that post in May 2002, moulding the Ducks into Western Conference champions in 2002-03 before losing in the Stanley Cup to the New Jersey Devils. Murray, named the Ducks' fifth head coach for the 2001-02 season, selected Mike Babcock as his replacement.

Murray joined the NHL coaching fraternity with the Washington Capitals on November 11, 1981, replacing interim head coach Roger Crozier. He remained at the helm of the Capitals for the following eight and half seasons. Beginning with his first full campaign behind the Washington bench (1982-83), the club had winning records and averaged 95 points per season over the next seven years (all playoff teams). Murray won the Jack Adams Award in 1983-84 as the NHL's coach of the year. He enters the 2004-05 season ranked sixth in the NHL in all-time games coached (1,057) and seventh in wins (513). He coached his 1,000th NHL game with Anaheim on November 28, 2001 and earned his 500th victory on January 25, 2002.

A former student of Macdonald College at McGill University, Murray spent four years as the athletic director and coach at the school. He left that post to become head coach of the Regina Pats of the Western Hockey League in 1979-80 where he led the Pats to the WHL championship. Murray took over as coach of the American Hockey League's (AHL) Hershey Bears the next season and was named minor league coach of the year by The Hockey News, after leading Hershey to its best record in 40 years.

Coaching Record

Season	Team	Games	W	L	T	Games	W	L
			Regular Season				**Playoffs**	
1981-82	Washington (NHL)	66	25	28	13	....	....	....
1982-83	Washington (NHL)	80	39	25	16	4	1	3
1983-84	Washington (NHL)	80	48	27	5	8	4	4
1984-85	Washington (NHL)	80	46	25	9	5	2	3
1985-86	Washington (NHL)	80	50	23	7	9	5	4
1986-87	Washington (NHL)	80	38	32	10	7	3	4
1987-88	Washington (NHL)	80	38	33	9	14	7	7
1988-89	Washington (NHL)	80	41	29	10	6	2	4
1989-90	Washington (NHL)	46	18	24	4	....	....	....
1990-91	Detroit (NHL)	80	34	38	8	7	3	4
1991-92	Detroit (NHL)	80	43	25	12	11	4	7
1992-93	Detroit (NHL)	84	47	28	9	7	3	4
1997-98	Florida (NHL)	59	17	31	11	....	....	....
2001-02	Anaheim (NHL)	82	29	45	8	....	....	....
2004-05	Ottawa (NHL)			Season Cancelled				
	NHL Totals	1057	513	413	131	78	34	44

Club Directory

Corel Centre

Ottawa Senators
Corel Centre
1000 Palladium Drive
Ottawa, Ontario
K2V 1A5
Phone **613/599-0250**
FAX 613/599-0358
www.ottawasenators.com
Capacity: 19,153

Executive
Owner, Governor and Chairman . . . . Eugene Melnyk
President, CEO and Alternate Governor. . . . . Roy Mlakar
Chief Operating Officer. . . . . Cyril Leeder
Vice-President and Executive Director, Corel Centre . Tom Conroy
General Manager . . . . John Muckler

Hockey Operations
Assistant General Manager . . . . Peter Chiarelli
Head Coach . . . . Bryan Murray
Director of Player Personnel and Pro Scout . . . . . . Anders Hedberg
Assistant Coaches . . . . John Paddock, Greg Carvel
Conditioning Coach . . . . Randy Lee
Goaltending Coach and Pro Scout. . . . . Ron Low
Video Coach . . . . Tim Pattyson
Director of Player Services . . . . Chad Schella
Assistant to the General Manager . . . . Allison Vaughan
Team Services and Scouting Coordinator. . . . . Alex Lepore
Head Trainer/Therapist . . . . Gerry Townend
Equipment Manager . . . . Scott Allegrino
Assistant Equipment Manager. . . . . Chris Cook
Assistant Athletic Therapist . . . . Andy Playter

Scouts
Director of Amateur Scouting . . . . Frank Jay
Swedish Scout. . . . . Arne Andersen
Scout, Slovak and Czech . . . . Vaclav Burda
Scouts. . . . . George Fargher, Bob Janecyk, Bill McCarthy, Lewis Mongelluzzo, Gord Pell
Pro Scout . . . . Nick Polano
Finnish Scout. . . . . Mikko Ruutu
Scout . . . . Patrick Savard
Russian Scout . . . . Boris Shagas

Communications
Vice-President, Communications . . . . Phil Legault
Director, Communications. . . . . Steve Keogh
Coordinator, Communications . . . . Marlène Joubert

Broadcast Services
Vice-President, Broadcast . . . . Jim Steel

Miscellaneous
Minor League Affiliates . . . . Binghamton Senators (AHL), Charlotte Checkers (ECHL)
Team Colours . . . . Red, black and gold
Radio . . . . Team 1200, CJRC 1150
Television . . . . Rogers Sportsnet, A-Channel and RDS
Team Photographer . . . . Freestyle Photography (André Ringuette)
Anthem Singer . . . . Lyndon Slewidge
Mascot . . . . Spartacat

After a solid season with Ottawa in 2003-04, Jason Spezza led the American Hockey League with 85 assists and 117 points in 2004-05.

Philadelphia Flyers

2005-06 Schedule

Oct.	Wed.	5	NY Rangers
	Fri.	7	New Jersey
	Tue.	11	at Toronto
	Fri.	14	Pittsburgh
	Sat.	15	NY Islanders
	Sat.	22	at Toronto
	Tue.	25	at Montreal
	Thu.	27	Florida
	Fri.	28	at Carolina
	Sun.	30	at Ottawa
Nov.	Thu.	3	Washington
	Sat.	5	Atlanta
	Tue.	8	Boston
	Thu.	10	NY Islanders
	Sat.	12	Florida
	Mon.	14	at Tampa Bay
	Wed.	16	Pittsburgh
	Fri.	18	Atlanta
	Sat.	19	at Pittsburgh
	Tue.	22	Tampa Bay
	Fri.	25	at Boston*
	Sat.	26	NY Islanders
	Tue.	29	at NY Islanders
	Wed.	30	New Jersey
Dec.	Sat.	3	at Nashville
	Tue.	6	Calgary
	Thu.	8	Edmonton
	Sat.	10	Minnesota*
	Tue.	13	at Columbus
	Thu.	15	Vancouver
	Sat.	17	at St. Louis
	Mon.	19	Buffalo
	Thu.	22	Ottawa
	Fri.	23	at Pittsburgh
	Mon.	26	at Florida
	Wed.	28	at Atlanta
	Thu.	29	at Carolina
	Sat.	31	at Washington*
Jan.	Mon.	2	at Boston*
	Thu.	5	at NY Rangers
	Fri.	6	at Washington

	Mon.	9	at New Jersey
	Wed.	11	at Chicago
	Thu.	12	at Detroit
	Sat.	14	Colorado*
	Tue.	17	Carolina
	Thu.	19	Boston
	Sat.	21	at Pittsburgh*
	Mon.	23	Pittsburgh
	Wed.	25	Montreal
	Sat.	28	Tampa Bay*
	Mon.	30	at NY Rangers
Feb.	Thu.	2	at Buffalo
	Sat.	4	NY Rangers*
	Sun.	5	at Montreal*
	Wed.	8	NY Islanders
	Fri.	10	Washington
	Sat.	11	at Ottawa
Mar.	Wed.	1	at New Jersey
	Thu.	2	NY Rangers
	Sat.	4	at NY Islanders
	Mon.	6	Montreal
	Wed.	8	Carolina
	Sat.	11	Buffalo*
	Sun.	12	at Pittsburgh
	Wed.	15	at Florida
	Fri.	17	at Tampa Bay
	Sat.	18	at Atlanta
	Tue.	21	New Jersey
	Wed.	22	at NY Rangers
	Sat.	25	Ottawa
	Tue.	28	Toronto
Apr.	Sat.	1	New Jersey*
	Sun.	2	at NY Islanders*
	Tue.	4	at NY Rangers
	Fri.	7	at Buffalo
	Sat.	8	Toronto
	Tue.	11	Pittsburgh
	Thu.	13	at New Jersey
	Sat.	15	NY Rangers*
	Sun.	16	at New Jersey*
	Tue.	18	at NY Islanders

* Denotes afternoon game.

Franchise date: June 5, 1967

EASTERN CONFERENCE

ATLANTIC DIVISION

39th NHL Season

Year-by-Year Record

Season	GP	Home W	L	T	OL	Road W	L	T	OL	Overall W	L	T	OL	GF	GA	Pts.	Finished	Playoff Result
2004-05	.....																	
2003-04	82	24	11	3	3	16	10	12	3	40	21	15	6	229	186	101	1st, Atlantic Div.	Lost Conf. Final
2002-03	82	21	10	8	2	24	10	5	2	45	20	13	4	211	166	107	2nd, Atlantic Div.	Lost Conf. Semi-Final
2001-02	82	20	13	5	3	22	14	5	0	42	27	10	3	234	192	97	1st, Atlantic Div.	Lost Conf. Quarter-Final
2000-01	82	26	11	4	0	17	14	7	3	43	25	11	3	240	207	100	2nd, Atlantic Div.	Lost Conf. Quarter-Final
1999-2000	82	25	6	7	3	20	16	5	0	45	22	12	3	237	179	105	1st, Atlantic Div.	Lost Conf. Championship
1998-99	82	21	9	11	....	16	17	8	....	37	26	19	....	231	196	93	2nd, Atlantic Div.	Lost Conf. Quarter-Final
1997-98	82	24	11	6	....	18	18	5	....	42	29	11	....	242	193	95	2nd, Atlantic Div.	Lost Conf. Quarter-Final
1996-97	82	23	12	6	....	22	12	7	....	45	24	13	....	274	217	103	2nd, Atlantic Div.	Lost Final
1995-96	82	27	9	5	....	18	15	8	....	45	24	13	....	282	208	103	1st, Atlantic Div.	Lost Conf. Semi-Final
1994-95	48	16	7	1	....	12	9	3	....	28	16	4	....	150	132	60	1st, Atlantic Div.	Lost Conf. Championship
1993-94	84	19	20	3	....	16	19	7	....	35	39	10	....	294	314	80	6th, Atlantic Div.	Out of Playoffs
1992-93	84	23	14	5	....	13	23	6	....	36	37	11	....	319	319	83	5th, Patrick Div.	Out of Playoffs
1991-92	80	22	11	7	....	10	26	4	....	32	37	11	....	252	273	75	6th, Patrick Div.	Out of Playoffs
1990-91	80	18	16	6	....	15	21	4	....	33	37	10	....	252	267	76	5th, Patrick Div.	Out of Playoffs
1989-90	80	17	19	4	....	13	20	7	....	30	39	11	....	290	297	71	6th, Patrick Div.	Out of Playoffs
1988-89	80	22	15	3	....	14	21	5	....	36	36	8	....	307	285	80	4th, Patrick Div.	Lost Conf. Championship
1987-88	80	20	14	6	....	18	19	3	....	38	33	9	....	292	292	85	3rd, Patrick Div.	Lost Div. Semi-Final
1986-87	80	29	9	2	....	17	17	6	....	46	26	8	....	310	245	100	1st, Patrick Div.	Lost Final
1985-86	80	33	6	1	....	20	17	3	....	53	23	4	....	335	241	110	1st, Patrick Div.	Lost Div. Semi-Final
1984-85	80	32	4	4	....	21	16	3	....	53	20	7	....	348	241	113	1st, Patrick Div.	Lost Final
1983-84	80	25	10	5	....	19	16	5	....	44	26	10	....	350	290	98	3rd, Patrick Div.	Lost Div. Semi-Final
1982-83	80	29	8	3	....	20	15	5	....	49	23	8	....	326	240	106	1st, Patrick Div.	Lost Div. Semi-Final
1981-82	80	25	10	5	....	13	21	6	....	38	31	11	....	325	313	87	3rd, Patrick Div.	Lost Div. Semi-Final
1980-81	80	23	9	8	....	18	15	7	....	41	24	15	....	313	249	97	2nd, Patrick Div.	Lost Quarter-Final
1979-80	80	27	5	8	....	21	7	12	....	48	12	20	....	327	254	116	1st, Patrick Div.	Lost Final
1978-79	80	26	10	4	....	14	15	11	....	40	25	15	....	281	248	95	2nd, Patrick Div.	Lost Quarter-Final
1977-78	80	29	6	5	....	16	14	10	....	45	20	15	....	296	200	105	2nd, Patrick Div.	Lost Semi-Final
1976-77	80	33	6	1	....	15	10	15	....	48	16	16	....	323	213	112	1st, Patrick Div.	Lost Semi-Final
1975-76	80	36	2	2	....	15	11	14	....	51	13	16	....	348	209	118	1st, Patrick Div.	Lost Final
1974-75	**80**	**32**	**6**	**2**	....	**19**	**12**	**9**	....	**51**	**18**	**11**	....	**293**	**181**	**113**	**1st, Patrick Div.**	**Won Stanley Cup**
1973-74	**78**	**28**	**6**	**5**	....	**22**	**10**	**7**	....	**50**	**16**	**12**	....	**273**	**164**	**112**	**1st, West Div.**	**Won Stanley Cup**
1972-73	78	27	8	4	....	10	22	7	....	37	30	11	....	296	256	85	2nd, West Div.	Lost Semi-Final
1971-72	78	19	13	7	....	7	25	7	....	26	38	14	....	200	236	66	5th, West Div.	Out of Playoffs
1970-71	78	20	10	9	....	8	23	8	....	28	33	17	....	207	225	73	3rd, West Div.	Lost Quarter-Final
1969-70	76	11	14	13	....	6	21	11	....	17	35	24	....	197	225	58	5th, West Div.	Out of Playoffs
1968-69	76	14	16	8	....	6	19	13	....	20	35	21	....	174	225	61	3rd, West Div.	Lost Quarter-Final
1967-68	74	17	13	7	....	14	19	4	....	31	32	11	....	173	179	73	1st, West Div.	Lost Quarter-Final

Originally drafted by the team back in 1991, Philadelphia fans will finally get the chance to watch Peter Forsberg (left) perform in a Flyers sweater. The deal to acquire Derian Hatcher (right) reunites him with coach Ken Hitchcock.

2005-06 Player Personnel

FORWARDS	HT	WT	S	Place of Birth	Date	2004-05 Club
BRASHEAR, Donald	6-2	235	L	Bedford, IN	1/7/72	Quebec
CARTER, Jeff	6-3	195	R	London, Ont.	1/1/85	Sault Ste. Marie-Phi (AHL)
CHOUINARD, Eric	6-3	215	L	Atlanta, GA	7/8/80	Salzburg
EAGER, Ben	6-3	215	L	Ottawa, Ont.	1/22/84	Philadelphia (AHL)
FORSBERG, Peter	6-0	205	L	Ornskoldsvik, Sweden	7/20/73	MODO
GAGNE, Simon	6-0	190	L	Ste-Foy, Que.	2/29/80	
HANDZUS, Michal	6-5	217	L	Banska Bystrica, Czech.	3/11/77	Zvolen
KAPANEN, Sami	5-10	185	L	Vantaa, Finland	6/14/73	KalPa
KAVANAGH, Pat	6-3	192	R	Ottawa, Ont.	3/14/79	Binghamton
KNUBLE, Mike	6-3	228	R	Toronto, Ont.	7/4/72	Linkoping
MELOCHE, Eric	5-10	197	R	Montreal, Que.	5/1/76	Philadelphia (AHL)
MURPHY, Mark	5-11	200	R	Stoughton, MA	8/6/76	Philadelphia (AHL)
PRIMEAU, Keith	6-5	220	L	Toronto, Ont.	11/24/71	
RADIVOJEVIC, Branko	6-1	209	R	Piestany, Czech.	11/24/80	Vsetin-Lulea
READY, Ryan	6-2	195	L	Peterborough, Ont.	11/7/78	Philadelphia (AHL)
RICHARDS, Mike	5-11	185	L	Kenora, Ont.	2/11/85	Kitch-Phi (AHL)
RUZICKA, Stefan	5-11	189	R	Nitra, Czech.	2/17/85	Owen Sound
SHARP, Patrick	6-0	197	R	Thunder Bay, Ont.	12/27/81	Philadelphia (AHL)
SIM, Jon	5-10	190	L	New Glasgow, N.S.	9/29/77	Utah-Philadelphia (AHL)
STEVENSON, Turner	6-3	220	R	Prince George, B.C.	5/18/72	
UMBERGER, R.J.	6-2	200	L	Pittsburgh, PA	5/3/82	Philadelphia (AHL)
VOCE, Tony	5-8	185	L	Philadelphia, PA	10/30/80	Philadelphia (AHL)

DEFENSEMEN	HT	WT	S	Place of Birth	Date	2004-05 Club
DESJARDINS, Eric	6-1	205	R	Rouyn, Que.	6/14/69	
HATCHER, Derian	6-5	235	L	Sterling Hts., MI	6/4/72	Motor City
HOPE, Joey	6-0	180	R	Anchorage, AK	1/1/82	Philadelphia (AHL)
JOHNSSON, Kim	6-1	205	L	Malmo, Sweden	3/16/76	Ambri
JONES, Randy	6-2	200	L	Quispamsis, N.B.	7/23/81	Philadelphia (AHL)
MEYER, Freddy	5-10	192	L	Sanbornville, NH	1/4/81	Philadelphia (AHL)
PITKANEN, Joni	6-3	200	L	Oulu, Finland	9/19/83	Philadelphia (AHL)
RATHJE, Mike	6-5	235	L	Mannville, Alta.	5/11/74	
SEIDENBERG, Dennis	6-0	200	L	Schwenningen, W. Ger.	7/18/81	Philadelphia (AHL)
SLANEY, John	6-0	189	L	St. John's, Nfld.	2/7/72	Philadelphia (AHL)
THERIEN, Chris	6-5	235	L	Ottawa, Ont.	12/14/71	

GOALTENDERS	HT	WT	C	Place of Birth	Date	2004-05 Club
ESCHE, Robert	6-1	210	L	Whitesboro, NY	1/22/78	
NIITTYMAKI, Antero	6-0	195	L	Turku, Finland	6/18/80	Philadelphia (AHL)
STORR, Jamie	6-2	195	L	Brampton, Ont.	12/28/75	Springfield-Utah

In the System and Recently Drafted

FORWARDS	HT	WT	S	Place of Birth	Date	2004-05 Club
BARANOV, Konstantin	6-2	185	L	Omsk, USSR	1/11/82	Omsk
BEAULIEU, Josh	6-0	180	L	Windsor, Ont.	1/10/87	London
BELLAMY, Rob	6-0	190	R	Providence, RI	5/30/85	U. of Maine
BRUNELLE, Mathieu	5-11	180	L	Warwick, Que.	4/6/83	Trenton-Dayton-Bakersfield
CABANA, Frederik	6-0	182	L	Fleurimont, Que.	5/16/86	Halifax
CLACKSON, Matt	5-11	196	R	Saskatoon, Sask.	4/26/85	Chicago
COTE, Riley	6-1	210	L	Winnipeg, Man.	3/16/82	Philadelphia (AHL)
DOWNIE, Steve	5-10	192	R	Newmarket, Ont.	4/3/87	Windsor
DROZDETSKY, Alexander	6-0	180	L	Moscow, USSR	11/10/81	Kazan-Nizhnekamsk
GRANT, Triston	6-1	223	L	Brandon, Man.	2/2/84	Vancouver (WHL)
GRATTON, Josh	6-2	210	L	Scarborough, Ont.	9/9/82	Phi (AHL)-Trenton
KASPARIK, Pavel	6-2	198	L	Pisek, Czech.	11/11/79	Sparta
KOPECKY, Milan	6-0	180	L	Kolin, Czech.	5/11/81	Slavia
LALIBERTE, David	6-1	194	R	St-Jean-Sur-Richelieu, Que.	3/17/86	PEI
PISELLINI, Gino	6-0	210	R	Melrose Park, IL	8/5/86	Plymouth
PLETKA, Vaclav	5-11	182	L	Mlada Boleslav, Czech.	6/8/79	Trinec
POTULNY, Ryan	6-0	190	L	Grand Forks, ND	9/5/84	U. of Minnesota
ROBINSON, Brent	6-1	195	L	Pointe Claire, Que.	3/18/85	Phi (AHL)-Trenton
ROMY, Kevin	5-11	180	L	La Chaux-de-Fonds, Switz.	1/31/85	Geneve
RUDENKO, Konstantin	5-11	180	R	Ust-Kamenogorsk, USSR	7/23/81	Yaroslavl
SCURKO, Ladislav	6-0	187	L	Spisska Nova Ves, Czech.	4/4/86	Seattle

DEFENSEMEN	HT	WT	S	Place of Birth	Date	2004-05 Club
ANDERSON, R.J.	5-11	180	R	Maple Wood, MN	7/16/86	Centennial
BARTULIS, Oskars	6-2	185	L	Ogre, Latvia	1/21/87	Moncton
FLATTERS, John	6-1	203	L	Calgary, Alta.	6/17/87	Red Deer
GAWRYLETZ, Travis	6-2	190	L	Trail, B.C.	11/2/85	U. Minn-Duluth
KAUPPINEN, Marko	6-0	178	L	Mikkeli, Finland	3/23/79	Mora
PICARD, Alexandre	6-2	214	L	Gatineau, Que.	7/5/85	Halifax-Philadelphia (AHL)
PRINTZ, David	6-5	220	L	Stockholm, Sweden	7/24/80	Phi (AHL)-Trenton
RUGGERI, Rosario	6-1	202	L	Montreal, Que.	6/8/84	Phi (AHL)-Trenton
SKOLNEY, Wade	6-0	197	R	Wynyard, Sask.	6/24/81	Philadelphia (AHL)
TIMONEN, Jussi	6-0	200	L	Kuopio, Finland	6/29/83	SaiPa
WOOD, Stephen	6-3	210	R	Sudbury, MA	8/18/81	Phi (AHL)-Trenton
ZARB, Chris	6-4	176	R	San Diego, CA	1/11/85	Tri-City

GOALTENDERS	HT	WT	C	Place of Birth	Date	2004-05 Club
BEAUCHEMIN, Rejean	6-1	193	L	Winnipeg, Man.	5/3/85	Prince Albert
DUCHESNE, Jeremy	6-0	201	L	Silver Spring, MD	10/17/86	Victoriaville-Halifax
HOSTIKKA, Ville	6-3	209	L	Lappeenranta, Finland	3/21/85	Lukko Jr.
HOULE, Martin	5-10	170	L	Montreal, Que.	2/12/85	Cape Breton
MALEK, Roman	5-11	161	L	Prague, Czech.	9/25/77	Magnitogorsk-Karl. Vary

Coach

HITCHCOCK, KEN
Coach, Philadelphia Flyers. Born in Edmonton, Alta., December 17, 1951.

The Philadelphia Flyers named Ken Hitchcock as their head coach on May 14, 2002. Hitchcock is the 15th head coach in Flyers history. Prior to joining the Flyers, he won a gold medal as an associate coach with Team Canada at the 2002 Winter Olympic Games. (He served the same role with Canada's team at the 2004 World Cup.) Hitchcock served as head coach of the Dallas Stars for parts of seven seasons (1995-96 to 2001-02), compiling a 277-166-60 record in 503 regular season games. Hitchcock served as head coach of Dallas' International Hockey League affiliate, the Kalamazoo Wings/Michigan K-Wings for three seasons, from the 1993-94 season until being named Stars' head coach on January 8, 1996. Prior to joining the Stars' organization, Hitchcock served three seasons as an assistant coach with the Flyers (1990-91 through 1992-93).

Hitchcock joined the Flyers after six seasons as head coach of the Kamloops Blazers of the Western Hockey League from 1984-85 through 1989-90. His .693 winning percentage as head coach at Kamloops is the second highest in the history of the WHL (291-125-15). His international experience also includes serving as an assistant coach for the Team Canada team that captured the gold medal at the 1987 World Junior Championships.

Coaching Record

			Regular Season			Playoffs		
Season	Team	Games	W	L	T	Games	W	L
1984-85	Kamloops (WHL)	71	52	17	2	15	10	5
1985-86	Kamloops (WHL)	72	49	19	4	16	14	2
1986-87	Kamloops (WHL)	72	55	14	3	13	8	5
1987-88	Kamloops (WHL)	72	45	26	1	18	12	6
1988-89	Kamloops (WHL)	72	34	33	5	16	8	8
1989-90	Kamloops (WHL)	72	56	16	0	17	14	3
1993-94	Kalamazoo (IHL)	81	48	26	7	5	1	4
1994-95	Kalamazoo (IHL)	81	43	24	14	16	10	6
1995-96	Michigan (IHL)	40	19	10	11	....	....	....
	Dallas (NHL)	43	15	23	5	....	....	....
1996-97	Dallas (NHL)	82	48	26	8	7	3	4
1997-98	Dallas (NHL)	82	49	22	11	17	10	7
1998-99	Dallas (NHL)	82	51	19	12	23	16	7*
1999-2000	Dallas (NHL)	82	43	29	10	23	14	9
2000-01	Dallas (NHL)	82	48	26	8	10	4	6
2001-02	Dallas (NHL)	50	23	21	6	....	....	....
2002-03	Philadelphia (NHL)	82	45	20	13	13	6	7
2003-04	Philadelphia (NHL)	82	40	27	15	18	11	7
2004-05	Philadelphia (NHL)			Season Cancelled				
NHL Totals		**667**	**362**	**217**	**111**		**64**	**47**

* Stanley Cup win.

Captains' History

Lou Angotti, 1967-68; Ed Van Impe, 1968-69 to 1971-72; Ed Van Impe and Bobby Clarke, 1972-73; Bobby Clarke, 1973-74 to 1978-79; Mel Bridgman, 1979-80, 1980-81; Bill Barber, 1981-82; Bill Barber and Bobby Clarke, 1982-83; Bobby Clarke, 1983-84; Dave Poulin, 1984-85 to 1988-89; Dave Poulin and Ron Sutter, 1989-90; Ron Sutter, 1990-91; Rick Tocchet, 1991-92; no captain, 1992-93; Kevin Dineen, 1993-94; Eric Lindros, 1994-95 to 1998-99; Eric Lindros and Eric Desjardins, 1999-2000; Eric Desjardins, 2000-01; Eric Desjardins and Keith Primeau, 2001-02; Keith Primeau, 2002-03 to date.

Coaching History

Keith Allen, 1967-68, 1968-69; Vic Stasiuk, 1969-70, 1970-71; Fred Shero, 1971-72 to 1977-78; Bob McCammon and Pat Quinn, 1978-79; Pat Quinn, 1979-80, 1980-81; Pat Quinn and Bob McCammon, 1981-82; Bob McCammon, 1982-83, 1983-84; Mike Keenan, 1984-85 to 1987-88; Paul Holmgren, 1988-89 to 1990-91; Paul Holmgren and Bill Dineen, 1991-92; Bill Dineen, 1992-93; Terry Simpson, 1993-94; Terry Murray, 1994-95 to 1996-97; Wayne Cashman and Roger Neilson, 1997-98; Roger Neilson, 1998-99, 1999-2000; Craig Ramsay and Bill Barber, 2000-01; Bill Barber, 2001-02; Ken Hitchcock, 2002-03 to date.

Club Records

Team

(Figures in brackets for season records are games played; records for fewest points, wins, ties, losses, goals, goals against are for 70 or more games)

Most Points **118** 1975-76 (80)
Most Wins **53** 1984-85 (80), 1985-86 (80)
Most Ties ***24** 1969-70 (76)
Most Losses **39** 1989-90 (80), 1993-94 (84)
Most Goals **350** 1983-84 (80)
Most Goals Against **319** 1992-93 (84)
Fewest Points **58** 1969-70 (76)
Fewest Wins **17** 1969-70 (76)
Fewest Ties **4** 1985-86 (80)
Fewest Losses **12** 1979-80 (80)
Fewest Goals **173** 1967-68 (74)
Fewest Goals Against **164** 1973-74 (78)
Longest Winning Streak
Overall .... **13** Oct. 19-Nov. 17/85
Home .... ***20** Jan. 4-Apr. 3/76
Away .... **8** Dec. 22/82-Jan. 16/83
Longest Undefeated Streak
Overall .... ***35** Oct. 14/79-Jan. 6/80 (25 wins, 10 ties)
Home .... **26** Oct. 11/79-Feb. 3/80 (19 wins, 7 ties)
Away .... **16** Oct. 20/79-Jan. 6/80 (11 wins, 5 ties)
Longest Losing Streak
Overall .... **6** Mar. 25-Apr. 4/70, Dec. 5-17/92, Jan. 25-Feb. 5/94
Home .... **5** Jan. 30-Feb. 15/69, Dec. 19/89-Jan. 23/90
Away .... **8** Oct. 25-Nov. 26/72, Mar. 3-29/88
Longest Winless Streak
Overall .... **12** Feb. 24-Mar. 16/99 (8 losses, 4 ties)
Home .... **8** Dec. 19/68-Jan. 18/69 (4 losses, 4 ties), Nov. 17-Dec. 14/91 (4 losses, 4 ties)
Away .... **19** Oct. 23/71-Jan. 27/72 (15 losses, 4 ties)
Most Shutouts, Season **13** 1974-75 (80)
Most PIM, Season **2,621** 1980-81 (80)
Most Goals, Game .... **13** Mar. 22/84 (Pit. 4 at Phi. 13), Oct. 18/84 (Van. 2 at Phi. 13)

Individual

Most Seasons .... **15** Bobby Clarke
Most Games .... **1,144** Bobby Clarke
Most Goals, Career .... **420** Bill Barber
Most Assists, Career .... **852** Bobby Clarke
Most Points, Career .... **1,210** Bobby Clarke (358G, 852A)
Most PIM, Career .... **1,817** Rick Tocchet
Most Shutouts, Career .... **50** Bernie Parent
Longest Consecutive Game Streak .... **484** Rod Brind'Amour (Feb. 24/93-Apr. 18/99)
Most Goals, Season .... **61** Reggie Leach (1975-76)
Most Assists, Season .... **89** Bobby Clarke (1974-75, 1975-76)
Most Points, Season .... **123** Mark Recchi (1992-93; 53G, 70A)
Most PIM, Season .... ***472** Dave Schultz (1974-75)
Most Points, Defenseman, Season .... **82** Mark Howe (1985-86; 24G, 58A)
Most Points, Center, Season .... **119** Bobby Clarke (1975-76; 30G, 89A)
Most Points, Right Wing, Season .... **123** Mark Recchi (1992-93; 53G, 70A)
Most Points, Left Wing, Season .... **112** Bill Barber (1975-76; 50G, 62A)
Most Points, Rookie, Season .... **82** Mikael Renberg (1993-94; 38G, 44A)
Most Shutouts, Season .... **12** Bernie Parent (1973-74, 1974-75)
Most Goals, Game .... **4** Sixteen times
Most Assists, Game .... **6** Eric Lindros (Feb. 26/97)
Most Points, Game .... **8** Tom Bladon (Dec. 11/77; 4G, 4A)

* NHL Record.

Retired Numbers

1	Bernie Parent	1967-1971, 1973-1979
4	Barry Ashbee	1970-1974
7	Bill Barber	1972-1985
16	Bobby Clarke	1969-1984

All-time Record vs. Other Clubs

Regular Season

	At Home								On Road								Total							
	GP	W	L	T	OL	GF	GA	PTS	GP	W	L	T	OL	GF	GA	PTS	GP	W	L	T	OL	GF	GA	PTS
Anaheim	8	3	2	3	0	22	17	9	9	3	3	2	1	28	30	9	17	6	5	5	1	50	47	18
Atlanta	10	7	1	2	0	46	28	16	10	7	2	1	0	34	24	15	20	14	3	3	0	80	52	31
Boston	73	32	30	10	1	241	211	75	76	19	44	11	2	211	283	51	149	51	74	21	3	452	494	126
Buffalo	67	40	15	12	0	228	162	92	63	23	32	8	0	176	209	54	130	63	47	20	0	404	371	146
Calgary	51	33	14	3	1	199	137	70	52	18	25	9	0	172	208	45	103	51	39	12	1	371	345	115
Carolina	43	29	9	5	0	162	107	63	44	22	13	9	0	158	140	53	87	51	22	14	0	320	247	116
Chicago	62	35	16	11	0	204	162	81	60	15	26	19	0	170	205	49	122	50	42	30	0	374	367	130
Colorado	34	22	9	2	1	122	91	47	35	11	11	12	1	122	124	35	69	33	20	14	2	244	215	82
Columbus	2	1	0	1	0	7	3	3	3	1	0	2	0	7	6	4	5	2	0	3	0	14	9	7
Dallas	67	42	9	16	0	255	150	100	66	23	27	16	0	212	216	62	133	65	36	32	0	467	366	162
Detroit	58	34	13	11	0	230	168	79	59	18	31	10	0	182	210	46	117	52	44	21	0	412	378	125
Edmonton	31	20	9	2	0	128	85	42	28	8	14	6	0	83	98	22	59	28	23	8	0	211	183	64
Florida	25	10	8	6	1	65	60	27	24	18	5	1	0	88	57	37	49	28	13	7	1	153	117	64
Los Angeles	63	40	15	7	1	244	156	88	66	37	21	8	0	223	193	82	129	77	36	15	1	467	349	170
Minnesota	4	3	1	0	0	11	3	6	2	0	1	1	0	3	5	1	6	3	2	1	0	14	8	7
Montreal	73	29	27	16	1	223	215	75	74	26	33	14	1	229	254	67	147	55	60	30	2	452	469	142
Nashville	5	2	1	1	1	17	9	6	4	2	0	2	0	7	4	6	9	4	1	3	1	24	13	12
New Jersey	85	51	23	10	1	322	214	113	83	33	42	8	0	285	283	74	168	84	65	18	1	607	497	187
NY Islanders	95	55	27	11	2	340	268	123	98	33	49	15	1	289	356	82	193	88	76	26	3	629	624	205
NY Rangers	109	56	39	14	0	355	297	126	110	40	46	23	1	321	353	104	219	96	85	37	1	676	650	230
Ottawa	23	13	8	2	0	73	63	28	24	10	8	6	0	72	65	26	47	23	16	8	0	145	128	54
Phoenix	31	23	8	0	0	134	83	46	31	16	13	2	0	106	99	34	62	39	21	2	0	240	182	80
Pittsburgh	106	81	17	8	0	446	257	170	106	38	46	22	0	346	373	98	212	119	63	30	0	792	630	268
St. Louis	67	45	12	10	0	264	153	100	68	35	26	7	0	219	194	77	135	80	38	17	0	483	347	177
San Jose	11	6	3	2	0	36	27	14	12	7	3	2	0	31	22	16	23	13	6	4	0	67	49	30
Tampa Bay	25	14	3	7	1	79	46	36	26	16	9	1	0	78	71	33	51	30	12	8	1	157	117	69
Toronto	67	43	16	8	0	254	154	94	67	30	23	14	0	225	210	74	134	73	39	22	0	479	364	168
Vancouver	54	37	16	1	0	234	159	75	51	29	10	12	0	203	144	70	105	66	26	13	0	437	303	145
Washington	83	53	24	6	0	312	219	112	80	34	32	13	1	259	261	82	163	87	56	19	1	571	480	194
Defunct Clubs	34	24	4	6	0	137	67	54	35	13	14	8	0	102	89	34	69	37	18	14	0	239	156	88
Totals	**1466**	**883**	**379**	**193**	**11**	**5390**	**3771**	**1970**	**1466**	**585**	**609**	**264**	**8**	**4641**	**4786**	**1442**	**2932**	**1468**	**988**	**457**	**19**	**10031**	**8557**	**3412**

Playoffs

	Series	W	L	GP	W	L	T	GF	GA	Last Mtg.	Rnd.	Result
Boston	4	2	2	20	9	11	0	57	60	1978	SF	L 1-4
Buffalo	7	5	2	37	23	14	0	110	96	2001	CQF	L 2-4
Calgary	2	1	1	11	7	4	0	43	28	1981	QF	L 3-4
Chicago	1	0	1	4	0	4	0	8	20	1971	QF	L 0-4
Colorado	2	2	0	11	7	4	0	39	29	1985	CF	W 4-2
Dallas	2	2	0	11	8	3	0	41	26	1980	SF	W 4-1
Detroit	1	0	1	4	0	4	0	6	16	1997	F	L 0-4
Edmonton	3	1	2	15	7	8	0	44	49	1987	F	L 3-4
Florida	1	0	1	6	2	4	0	11	15	1996	CSF	L 2-4
Montreal	4	1	3	21	7	14	0	52	72	1989	CF	L 2-4
New Jersey	4	2	2	20	11	9	0	49	50	2004	CQF	W 4-1
NY Islanders	4	3	1	25	14	11	0	83	69	1987	DF	W 4-3
NY Rangers	10	6	4	47	27	20	0	157	153	1997	CF	W 4-1
Ottawa	2	0	2	11	3	8	0	12	28	2003	CSF	L 2-4
Pittsburgh	3	3	0	18	12	6	0	66	51	2000	CSF	W 4-2
St. Louis	2	0	2	11	3	8	0	20	34	1969	QF	L 0-4
Tampa Bay	2	1	1	13	7	6	0	45	34	2004	CF	L 3-4
Toronto	6	5	1	36	22	14	0	119	85	2004	CSF	W 4-2
Vancouver	1	1	0	3	2	1	0	15	9	1979	PRE	W 2-1
Washington	3	1	2	16	7	9	0	55	65	1989	DSF	W 4-2
Totals	**64**	**36**	**28**	**340**	**178**	**162**	**0**	**1032**	**989**			

Calgary totals include Atlanta Flames, 1972-73 to 1979-80. Carolina totals include Hartford, 1979-80 to 1996-97.
Colorado totals include Quebec, 1979-80 to 1994-95. Dallas totals include Minnesota North Stars, 1967-68 to 1992-93.
New Jersey totals include Kansas City, 1974-75 to 1975-76, and Colorado Rockies, 1976-77 to 1981-82.
Phoenix totals include Winnipeg, 1979-80 to 1995-96.

Playoff Results 2005-2000

Year	Round	Opponent	Result	GF	GA
2004	CF	Tampa Bay	L 3-4	19	21
	CSF	Toronto	W 4-2	17	13
	CQF	New Jersey	W 4-1	14	9
2003	CSF	Ottawa	L 2-4	10	17
	CQF	Toronto	W 4-3	24	16
2002	CQF	Ottawa	L 1-4	2	11
2001	CQF	Buffalo	L 2-4	13	21
2000	CF	New Jersey	L 3-4	15	18
	CSF	Pittsburgh	W 4-2	15	14
	CQF	Buffalo	W 4-1	14	8

Abbreviations: Round: F – Final; **CF** – conference final; **CSF** – conference semi-final; **CQF** – conference quarter-final; **DF** – division final; **DSF** – division semi-final; **SF** – semi-final; **QF** – quarter-final; **PRE** – preliminary round.

Key Off-Season Signings/Acquisitions

2004

June 14 • Re-signed C **Keith Primeau**.
June 16 • Signed C **R.J. Umberger**.
July 3 • Signed RWs **Mike Knuble** and **Turner Stevenson**.
Aug. 2 • Re-signed G **Antero Niittymaki**.
6 • Re-signed C **Michal Handzus**.
12 • Re-signed D **Mattias Timander**.
19 • Re-signed LW **Sami Kapanen**.

2005

July 27 • Signed 2003 1st-round draft picks, Cs **Jeff Carter** (11th overall) and **Mike Richards** (24th overall).
Aug. 2 • Signed LW **Jon Sim**.
2 • Signed Ds **Derian Hatcher**, **Mike Rathje** and **Chris Therien**.
3 • Signed C **Peter Forsberg**.
9 • Re-signed LW **Simon Gagne**, RW **Branko Radivojevic**, C **Patrick Sharp** and D **Kim Johnsson**.
10 • Re-signed G **Robert Esche** and D **Dennis Seidenberg**.
22 • Signed G **Jamie Storr**.

Entry Draft
Selections 2005-1991

2005
Pick
29	Steve Downie
91	Oskars Bartulis
119	Jeremy Duchesne
152	Josh Beaulieu
174	John Flatters
215	Matt Clackson

2004
Pick
92	Rob Bellamy
101	R.J. Anderson
124	David Laliberte
144	Chris Zarb
149	Gino Pisellini
170	Ladislav Scurko
171	Frederik Cabana
232	Martin Houle
253	Travis Gawryletz
286	Triston Grant
291	John Carter

2003
Pick
11	Jeff Carter
24	Mike Richards
69	Colin Fraser
81	Stefan Ruzicka
85	Alexandre Picard
87	Ryan Potulny
95	Rick Kozak
108	Kevin Romy
140	David Tremblay
191	Rejean Beauchemin
193	Ville Hostikka

2002
Pick
4	Joni Pitkanen
105	Rosario Ruggeri
126	Konstantin Baranov
161	Dov Grumet-Morris
192	Nikita Korovkin
193	Joey Mormina
201	Mathieu Brunelle

2001
Pick
27	Jeff Woywitka
95	Patrick Sharp
146	Jussi Timonen
150	Bernd Bruckler
158	Roman Malek
172	Dennis Seidenberg
177	Andrei Razin
208	Thierry Douville
225	David Printz

2000
Pick
28	Justin Williams
94	Alexander Drozdetsky
171	Roman Cechmanek
195	Colin Shields
210	John Eichelberger
227	Guillaume Lefebvre
259	Regan Kelly
287	Milan Kopecky

1999
Pick
22	Maxime Ouellet
119	Jeff Feniak
160	Konstantin Rudenko
200	Pavel Kasparik
208	Vaclav Pletka
224	David Nystrom

1998
Pick
22	Simon Gagne
42	Jason Beckett
51	Ian Forbes
109	Jean-Philippe Morin
124	Francis Belanger
139	Garrett Prosofsky
168	Antero Niittymaki
175	Cam Ondrik
195	Tomas Divisek
222	Lubomir Pistek
243	Petr Hubacek
253	Bruno St. Jacques
258	Sergei Skrobot

1997
Pick
30	Jean-Marc Pelletier
50	Pat Kavanagh
62	Kris Mallette
103	Mikhail Chernov
158	Jordon Flodell
164	Todd Fedoruk
214	Marko Kauppinen
240	Par Styf

1996
Pick
15	Dainius Zubrus
64	Chester Gallant
124	Per-Ragna Bergqvist
133	Jesse Boulerice
187	Roman Malov
213	Jeff Milleker

1995
Pick
22	Brian Boucher
48	Shane Kenny
100	Radovan Somik
132	Dmitri Tertyshny
135	Jamie Sokolsky
152	Martin Spanhel
178	Martin Streit
204	Ruslan Shafikov
230	Jeff Lank

1994
Pick
62	Artem Anisimov
88	Adam Magarrell
101	Sebastien Vallee
140	Alex Selivanov
166	Colin Forbes
192	Derek Diener
202	Raymond Giroux
218	Johan Hedberg
244	Andre Payette
270	Jan Lipiansky

1993
Pick
36	Janne Niinimaa
71	Vaclav Prospal
77	Milos Holan
114	Vladimir Krechin
140	Mike Crowley
166	Aaron Israel
192	Paul Healey
218	Tripp Tracy
226	E.J. Bradley
244	Jeff Staples
270	Ken Hemenway

1992
Pick
7	Ryan Sittler
15	Jason Bowen
31	Denis Metlyuk
103	Vladislav Buljin
127	Roman Zolotov
151	Kirk Daubenspeck
175	Claude Jr. Jutras
199	Jonas Hakansson
223	Chris Herperger
247	Patrice Paquin

1991
Pick
6	Peter Forsberg
50	Yanick Dupre
86	Aris Brimanis
94	Yanick Degrace
116	Clayton Norris
122	Dmitry Yushkevich
138	Andrei Lomakin
182	James Bode
204	Josh Bartell
226	Neil Little
248	John Porco

General Managers' History

Bud Poile, 1967-68, 1968-69; Bud Poile and Keith Allen, 1969-70; Keith Allen, 1970-71 to 1982-83; Bob McCammon, 1983-84; Bob Clarke, 1984-85 to 1989-90; Russ Farwell, 1990-91 to 1993-94; Bob Clarke, 1994-95 to date.

General Manager

CLARKE, BOB
General Manager, Philadelphia Flyers.
Born in Flin Flon, Man., August 13, 1949.

Bob Clarke was named general manager of the Philadelphia Flyers on June 15, 1994. Clarke's appointment marked the second time he has served as the Flyers' general manager. The Flin Flon native was the Flyers' vice president and general manager from 1984 to 1990. During his tenure as the team's general manager, the Flyers have won seven divisional titles, three conference championships, reached the Stanley Cup semifinals seven times and the finals three times.

Prior to re-joining the Flyers' family in 1994, Clarke served as vice president and general manager of the Florida Panthers. In 1993-94, their first season in the NHL, the Panthers established NHL records for wins (33) and points (83) by an expansion franchise. Clarke also served as the vice president and general manager of the Minnesota North Stars from 1990 to 1992, guiding the team to the Stanley Cup Finals in 1991.

As a player, the former Philadelphia captain led his club to Stanley Cup championships in 1974 and 1975 and captured numerous individual awards, including the Hart Trophy as the league's most valuable player in 1973, 1975 and 1976. The four-time All-Star also received the Bill Masterton Memorial Trophy (perseverance and dedication) in 1972 and the Frank J. Selke Trophy (top defensive forward) in 1983. He appeared in eight All-Star Games and was elected to the Hockey Hall of Fame in 1987. He was awarded the Lester Patrick Trophy in 1979-80 in recognition of his contribution to hockey in the United States. Clarke appeared in 1,144 regular season games, recording 358 goals and 852 assists for 1,210 points. He added 119 points in 136 playoff games.

Club Directory

Wachovia Center

Philadelphia Flyers
Wachovia Center
3601 South Broad Street
Philadelphia, PA 19148-5290
Phone **215/465-4500**
PR FAX 215/389-9403
www.philadelphiaflyers.com
Capacity: 19,523

Executive Management
Chairman	Ed Snider
President and COO of Comcast-Spectacor	Peter Luukko
President	Ron Ryan
General Manager	Bob Clarke
Executive Vice President	Keith Allen
Governor	Ed Snider
Alternate Governors	Bob Clarke, Peter Luukko, Ron Ryan, Phil Weinberg
Senior Vice President, Sales	Joe Croce
Vice President, Marketing and Communications	Shawn Tilger
Executive Assistants	Lisa D'Aprile, Kate Dreyer, Gina Pelle
Receptionists	Ann Bachich, Debbie Brown

Hockey Club Personnel
Assistant General Manager	Paul Holmgren
Head Coach	Ken Hitchcock
Assistant Coaches	Wayne Fleming, Terry Murray
Goaltending Coach	Reggie Lemelin
Director of Pro Hockey Personnel	Ron Hextall
Scouting Staff	John Chapman, Inge Hammarstrom, Simon Nolet, Dennis Patterson, Chris Pryor, Ilkka Sinisalo, Vaclav Slansky, Evgeny Zimin
Pro Scouts	Al Hill, Dean Lombardi
Assistant to the General Manager	Barry Hanrahan
Video Coordinator	Adam Patterson
Scouting Information Coordinator	Bryan Hardenbergh
Executive Assistant	Dianna Taylor
Receptionist	Sharon Allison

Medical/Training Staff
Team Physicians	Bill DeLong, M.D., Gary Dorshimer, M.D., Jeff Hartzell, M.D., Guy Lanzi, D.M.D.
Athletic Trainer/Strength and Conditioning Coach	Jim McCrossin
Athletic Trainer	Steve Lipinski
Massage Therapist	Brad Smith
Head Equipment Manager	Jim Evers
Equipment Managers	Anthony Oratorio, Harry Bricker, Luke Clarke
Training Center Maintenance	Mike Craytor

Communications Department
Senior Director of Communications	Zack Hill
Director of Media Services and Publications	Joe Klueg
New Media Manager	Kevin Kurz
Communications Assistant	Katie Hammer

Community Relations Department
Director of Community Relations	Maureen McGuckin
Community Relations Coordinator	Donna Katzman
Fan Development Manager	Rob Baer
Publicist	Jill Lipson
Ambassador of Hockey	Bob Kelly
Director of Fan Relations	Joe Kadlec
Fan Relations Assistant	Jerry Callahan

Customer Service Department
Director of Customer Service	Cindy Stutman
Customer Service Account Managers	Kristen Canterbury, Missy Keeler
Customer Service Assistant	Debbie Brown

Game Presentation Department
Manager of Game Presentation	Michael Wurman
Public Address Announcer	Lou Nolan
In-Arena Host/Anthem Singer	Lauren Hart

Marketing Department
Director of Marketing	Linda Mantai
Marketing Coordinator	Scott Bohrer

Ticket Sales Department
Senior Director of Sales	Jim Willits
Sales Coordinator	Jessica Palmer

Ticketing Department
Vice President, Ticket Operations	Cecilia Baker
Ticket Office Administration	Joan Kadlec

Finance Department
Director of Finance	Dave Jablonski
Staff Accountant	Doreen Holmgren
Payroll Accountant	Jim Wineland

Advertising Sales Department
Vice President of Advertising Sales	Brian Monihan
Senior Director of Sales	Adrian Staiti
National Sales Manager	Louis Harmelin
Advertising Sales Managers	Mike Garrity, Bo Koelle
Senior Account Executives	Ray Lyons, Joe Watson
Account Executives	Stephanie Bennett, Bryan Collins, Joe Heyer, Andrew Humphreys, Rich Rodowicz, Meredith Timberlake
Sponsorship Manager	Maura Thomson
Manager of Television Services	Shannan Archer

Premium Seating Department
V.P. of Premium Seating – Sales & Services	Rick Campbell
Manager of Finance and Inventory	Amanda Keen
Director of Premium Seating	Jimmy Dunk
Sales Manager of Premium Seating	Anthony Monaco
Director of Client Services	Tamlyn Shusterman

Comcast-Spectacor Foundation/Flyers Charities
Senior Vice President	Mary Ann Saleski
Executive Director	Fran Tobin
Director	Rita Johanson

Additional Information
TV Rightsholders	Comcast SportsNet, UPN-57 WPSG-TV
Radio Rightsholder	SportsRadio 610 WIP (610 AM)

Phoenix Coyotes

Year-by-Year Record

Season	Home W	L	T	OL	Road W	L	T	OL	Overall W	L	T	OL	GF	GA	Pts.	Finished	Playoff Result
2004-05	....																
2003-04	82	11	19	7	4	11	17	11	2	22	36	18	6	188	245	68	5th, Pacific Div.	Out of Playoffs
2002-03	82	17	16	6	2	14	19	5	3	31	35	11	5	204	230	78	4th, Pacific Div.	Out of Playoffs
2001-02	82	27	8	3	3	13	19	6	3	40	27	9	6	228	210	95	2nd, Pacific Div.	Lost Conf. Quarter-Final
2000-01	82	21	11	7	2	14	16	10	1	35	27	17	3	214	212	90	4th, Pacific Div.	Out of Playoffs
1999-2000	82	22	16	2	1	17	15	6	3	39	31	8	4	232	228	90	3rd, Pacific Div.	Lost Conf. Quarter-Final
1998-99	82	23	13	5	....	16	18	7	....	39	31	12	....	205	197	90	2nd, Pacific Div.	Lost Conf. Quarter-Final
1997-98	82	19	16	6	....	16	19	6	....	35	35	12	....	224	227	82	4th, Central Div.	Lost Conf. Quarter-Final
1996-97	82	15	19	7	....	23	18	0	....	38	37	7	....	240	243	83	3rd, Central Div.	Lost Conf. Quarter-Final
1995-96*	82	22	16	3	....	14	24	3	....	36	40	6	....	275	291	78	5th, Central Div.	Lost Conf. Quarter-Final
1994-95*	48	10	10	4	....	6	15	3	....	16	25	7	....	157	177	39	6th, Central Div.	Out of Playoffs
1993-94*	84	15	23	4	....	9	28	5	....	24	51	9	....	245	344	57	6th, Central Div.	Out of Playoffs
1992-93*	84	23	16	3	....	17	21	4	....	40	37	7	....	322	320	87	4th, Smythe Div.	Lost Div. Semi-Final
1991-92*	80	20	14	6	....	13	18	9	....	33	32	15	....	251	244	81	4th, Smythe Div.	Lost Div. Semi-Final
1990-91*	80	17	18	5	....	9	25	6	....	26	43	11	....	260	288	63	5th, Smythe Div.	Out of Playoffs
1989-90*	80	22	13	5	....	15	19	6	....	37	32	11	....	298	290	85	4th, Smythe Div.	Lost Div. Semi-Final
1988-89*	80	17	18	5	....	9	24	7	....	26	42	12	....	300	355	64	5th, Smythe Div.	Out of Playoffs
1987-88*	80	20	14	6	....	13	22	5	....	33	36	11	....	292	310	77	3rd, Smythe Div.	Lost Div. Semi-Final
1986-87*	80	25	12	3	....	15	20	5	....	40	32	8	....	279	271	88	3rd, Smythe Div.	Lost Div. Final
1985-86*	80	18	19	3	....	8	28	4	....	26	47	7	....	295	372	59	3rd, Smythe Div.	Lost Div. Semi-Final
1984-85*	80	21	13	6	....	22	14	4	....	43	27	10	....	358	332	96	2nd, Smythe Div.	Lost Div. Final
1983-84*	80	17	15	8	....	14	23	3	....	31	38	11	....	340	374	73	4th, Smythe Div.	Lost Div. Semi-Final
1982-83*	80	22	16	2	....	11	23	6	....	33	39	8	....	311	333	74	4th, Smythe Div.	Lost Div. Semi-Final
1981-82*	80	18	13	9	....	15	20	5	....	33	33	14	....	319	332	80	2nd, Norris Div.	Lost Div. Semi-Final
1980-81*	80	7	25	8	....	2	32	6	....	9	57	14	....	246	400	32	6th, Smythe Div.	Out of Playoffs
1979-80*	80	13	19	8	....	7	30	3	....	20	49	11	....	214	314	51	5th, Smythe Div.	Out of Playoffs

* Winnipeg Jets

2005-06 Schedule

Oct.	Wed.	5	at Vancouver
	Thu.	6	at Los Angeles
	Sat.	8	Minnesota
	Tue.	11	at Dallas
	Thu.	13	Nashville
	Sat.	15	Detroit
	Mon.	17	at Calgary
	Tue.	18	at Edmonton
	Thu.	20	at Vancouver
	Sun.	23	at Anaheim*
	Tue.	25	St. Louis
	Thu.	27	Calgary
	Sat.	29	Dallas
	Sun.	30	at Anaheim*
Nov.	Thu.	3	Los Angeles
	Sat.	5	at Detroit
	Sun.	6	at Chicago
	Tue.	8	at Minnesota
	Thu.	10	Calgary
	Sat.	12	Anaheim
	Wed.	16	Colorado
	Sat.	19	at San Jose
	Sun.	20	Columbus
	Tue.	22	Anaheim
	Fri.	25	at Dallas
	Sat.	26	Vancouver
	Wed.	30	at Anaheim
Dec.	Sat.	3	Carolina
	Mon.	5	Atlanta
	Sun.	11	at Boston*
	Tue.	13	at Montreal
	Thu.	15	Tampa Bay
	Sat.	17	at Los Angeles
	Tue.	20	St. Louis
	Thu.	22	San Jose
	Fri.	23	at Dallas
	Mon.	26	at Colorado
	Wed.	28	at San Jose
	Thu.	29	Los Angeles
	Sat.	31	Colorado
Jan.	Thu.	5	at Los Angeles

	Sun.	8	Columbus
	Tue.	10	at Ottawa
	Thu.	12	at Buffalo
	Sat.	14	at Toronto
	Mon.	16	Washington*
	Thu.	19	Florida
	Sat.	21	Edmonton
	Mon.	23	at Dallas
	Tue.	24	at Minnesota
	Thu.	26	at St. Louis
	Sat.	28	San Jose
	Sun.	29	Edmonton
	Tue.	31	Vancouver
Feb.	Thu.	2	Los Angeles
	Sat.	4	Minnesota
	Tue.	7	Chicago
	Thu.	9	Dallas
	Sun.	12	San Jose
Mar.	Thu.	2	Dallas
	Sat.	4	Detroit
	Tue.	7	at Detroit
	Thu.	9	at Columbus
	Sat.	11	Anaheim
	Sun.	12	at Anaheim*
	Tue.	14	at Los Angeles
	Thu.	16	at Nashville
	Sun.	19	at Chicago*
	Tue.	21	at Columbus
	Thu.	23	Chicago
	Sat.	25	Anaheim
	Tue.	28	Nashville
	Thu.	30	at San Jose
Apr.	Sat.	1	at San Jose
	Mon.	3	at Edmonton
	Wed.	5	at Calgary
	Sat.	8	Dallas
	Mon.	10	San Jose
	Tue.	11	at Colorado
	Thu.	13	Los Angeles
	Sat.	15	at Nashville
	Sun.	16	at St. Louis

* Denotes afternoon game.

After establishing career highs with 27 goals, 41 assists and 68 points for Phoenix in 2003-04, Shane Doan earned a spot on Team Canada at the World Cup of Hockey.

Franchise date: June 22, 1979
Transferred from Winnipeg to Phoenix, July 1, 1996

WESTERN
CONFERENCE

27th NHL Season

PACIFIC DIVISION

2005-06 Player Personnel

FORWARDS	HT	WT	S	Place of Birth	Date	2004-05 Club
BATHE, Landon	6-0	218	L	Marlton, NJ	4/9/82	Utah-Idaho
CHIMERA, Jason	6-2	206	L	Edmonton, Alta.	5/2/79	Varese
COMRIE, Mike	5-10	185	L	Edmonton, Alta.	9/11/80	Farjestad
DEVEREAUX, Boyd	6-2	195	L	Seaforth, Ont.	4/16/78	
DOAN, Shane	6-2	216	R	Halkirk, Alta.	10/10/76	
DOULL, Doug	6-2	216	L	Green Bay, N.S.	5/31/74	Utah
GAVEY, Aaron	6-2	189	L	Sudbury, Ont.	2/22/74	Storhamar-Utah
GELECH, Randall	6-3	220	R	Wynard, Sask.	2/2/84	Utah
HULL, Brett	5-11	203	R	Belleville, Ont.	8/9/64	
JOHNSON, Mike	6-2	201	R	Scarborough, Ont.	10/3/74	Farjestad
KEEFE, Sheldon	5-11	185	L	Brampton, Ont.	9/17/80	Utah
KOLANOS, Krysofer	6-3	206	R	Calgary, Alta.	7/27/81	Blues-Krefeld
KOREIS, Jakub	6-3	214	L	Plzen, Czech.	6/26/84	Utah
LECLERC, Mike	6-2	208	L	Winnipeg, Man.	11/10/76	
LUKES, Frantisek	5-9	173	R	Kadan, Czech.	9/25/82	Utah-Idaho
McLACHLAN, Darren	6-1	223	L	Penticton, B.C.	2/16/83	Idaho
McLEOD, Kiel	6-6	230	R	Ft. Saskatchewan, Alta.	12/30/82	Utah
MONYCH, Lance	6-3	203	R	Red Deer, Alta.	7/25/84	Brandon
NAGY, Ladislav	5-11	192	L	Saca, Czech.	6/1/79	Kosice-Mora
NASH, Tyson	5-11	191	L	Edmonton, Alta.	3/11/75	
NEDVED, Petr	6-3	196	L	Liberec, Czech.	12/9/71	Sparta
PODLESAK, Martin	6-6	219	L	Melnik, Czech.	9/26/82	Utah
RICCI, Mike	6-0	200	L	Scarborough, Ont.	10/27/71	
RUPP, Mike	6-5	230	L	Cleveland, OH	1/13/80	Danbury
SAPRYKIN, Oleg	6-0	195	L	Moscow, USSR	2/12/81	CSKA
SJOSTROM, Fredrik	6-1	217	L	Fargelanda, Sweden	5/6/83	Utah
SKALDE, Jarrod	6-0	185	L	Niagara Falls, Ont.	2/26/71	Springfield-Utah
SONNENBERG, Martin	6-0	197	L	Wetaskiwin, Alta.	1/23/78	Utah
TAFFE, Jeff	6-3	201	L	Hastings, MN	2/19/81	Utah

DEFENSEMEN	HT	WT	S	Place of Birth	Date	2004-05 Club
BALLARD, Keith	5-11	208	L	Baudette, MN	11/26/82	Utah
CALLAHAN, Joe	6-3	221	R	Brockton, MA	12/20/82	Utah
FERENCE, Brad	6-3	218	R	Calgary, Alta.	4/2/79	Morzine-Avoriaz
GAUTHIER, Denis	6-3	224	L	Montreal, Que.	10/1/76	
HULSE, Cale	6-3	220	R	Edmonton, Alta.	11/10/73	
JONES, Matt	6-0	215	L	Downers Grove, IL	8/8/83	North Dakota
KNYAZEV, Igor	6-0	208	L	Elektrostal, USSR	1/27/83	Voskresensk
MARA, Paul	6-4	219	L	Ridgewood, NJ	9/7/79	Hannover
McALLISTER, Chris	6-8	250	L	Saskatoon, Sask.	6/16/75	Newcastle
MICHALEK, Zbynek	6-1	199	R	Jindrichuv Hradec, Czech.	12/23/82	Houston
MORRIS, Derek	6-0	220	R	Edmonton, Alta.	8/24/78	
O'DONNELL, Sean	6-3	227	L	Ottawa, Ont.	10/13/71	
SPILLER, Matthew	6-5	233	L	Daysland, Alta.	2/7/83	Utah
TANABE, David	6-1	212	R	White Bear Lake, MN	7/19/80	Rapperswil-Kloten

GOALTENDERS	HT	WT	C	Place of Birth	Date	2004-05 Club
BOUCHER, Brian	6-2	198	L	Woonsocket, RI	1/2/77	HV 71
JOSEPH, Curtis	5-11	190	L	Keswick, Ont.	4/29/67	
LENEVEU, David	6-1	187	L	Fernie, B.C.	5/23/83	Utah
PASSMORE, Steve	5-9	165	L	Thunder Bay, Ont.	1/29/73	Mannheim

In the System and Recently Drafted

FORWARDS	HT	WT	S	Place of Birth	Date	2004-05 Club
BROSNIHAN, Pat	6-4	208	R	Worcester, MA	8/20/86	Worcester
BURKHALTER, Loic	6-0	192	L	La Chaux-de-Fonds, Switz.	2/11/80	Langnau
CORMIER, Kevin	6-3	249	L	Moncton, N.B.	1/27/86	Halifax
ENGASSER, William	6-2	228	L	Edina, MN	9/25/85	Yale
GAGNON, Aaron	5-10	185	R	Quesnel, B.C.	4/24/86	Seattle
HANZAL, Martin	6-5	200	L	Pisek, Czech.	2/20/87	C. Budejovice
KOLARIK, Chad	5-10	170	R	Abington, PA	1/26/86	U. of Michigan
KOUBA, Ladislav	6-2	213	L	Vimperk, Czech.	9/10/83	New Mexico-Idaho
KRYSANOV, Anton	6-3	198	L	Togliatti, USSR	3/25/87	Togliatti
LATENDRESSE, Olivier	5-10	190	L	LaSalle, Que.	2/12/86	Val-d'Or
LEWANDOWSKI, Eduard	6-1	205	L	Krasnoturjinsk, USSR	5/3/80	Koln
LINDSTROM, Liam	6-0	189	L	Edmonton, Alta.	1/12/85	Sundsvall
LISIN, Enver	6-2	190	L	Moscow, USSR	4/22/86	Kazan
PESTUNOV, Dmitri	5-9	196	L	Ust-Kamenogorsk, USSR	1/22/85	Magnitogorsk-Spartak
PORTER, Kevin	5-11	194	L	Detroit, MI	3/12/86	U. of Michigan
TATARINOV, Alexander	5-11	176	L	Sverdlovsk, USSR	4/14/82	Mechel
TOMANEK, Roman	6-1	176	R	Povazka Bystrica, Czech.	1/28/86	Calgary (WHL)
VENALAINEN, Sami	5-11	183	R	Kangasala, Finland	10/14/81	Tappara
WHEELER, Blake	6-5	200	R	Robbinsdale, MN	8/31/86	Green Bay
WINNIK, Daniel	6-2	210	R	Toronto, Ont.	3/6/85	New Hampshire
ZEILER, John	6-0	193	R	Pittsburgh, PA	11/21/82	St. Lawrence

DEFENSEMEN	HT	WT	S	Place of Birth	Date	2004-05 Club
BLINDENBACHER, Severin	5-11	189	R	Bulach, Switz.	3/15/83	Kloten
FORSTER, Beat	6-1	224	L	Herisau, Switz.	2/2/83	Davos-Chur
LUNDSTROM, Per-Anton	6-2	185	L	Umea, Sweden	9/29/77	Wolfsburg
STEPHENSON, Logan	6-2	189	L	Saskatoon, Sask.	2/19/86	Tri-City
SULLIVAN, Sean	6-0	180	L	Boston, MA	3/29/84	Boston University
YANDLE, Keith	6-2	195	L	Boston, MA	9/9/86	Cushing

GOALTENDERS	HT	WT	C	Place of Birth	Date	2004-05 Club
PELLETIER, Pier-Olivier	6-1	175	L	St-Louis, Que.	4/8/87	Drummondville
PIETRASIAK, Jeff	6-1	180	L	Marlboro, MA	4/5/83	New Hampshire

Brett Hull (above) and new coach Wayne Gretzky have combined for 1,635 goals.

Coaching History

Tom McVie and Bill Sutherland, 1979-80; Tom McVie, Bill Sutherland and Mike Smith, 1980-81; Tom Watt, 1981-82, 1982-83; Tom Watt and Barry Long, 1983-84; Barry Long, 1984-85; Barry Long and John Ferguson, 1985-86; Dan Maloney, 1986-87, 1987-88; Dan Maloney and Rick Bowness, 1988-89; Bob Murdoch, 1989-90, 1990-91; John Paddock, 1991-92 to 1993-94; John Paddock and Terry Simpson, 1994-95; Terry Simpson, 1995-96; Don Hay, 1996-97; Jim Schoenfeld, 1997-98, 1998-99; Bob Francis, 1999-2000 to 2002-03; Bob Francis and Rick Bowness, 2003-04; Rick Bowness, 2004-05; Wayne Gretzky, 2005-06.

Coach

GRETZKY, WAYNE
Coach, Phoenix Coyotes. Born in Brantford, Ont., January 26, 1961.

Phoenix Coyotes Chairman and Governor Steve Ellman announced on August 8, 2005 that Wayne Gretzky had agreed to a multiyear contract to serve as head coach of the Phoenix Coyotes. In addition to serving as the Coyotes' head coach, Gretzky also continues as managing partner and alternate governor for the Coyotes, a role that he had performed for the previous four seasons. Gretzky officially joined the franchise on February 15, 2001, when the Ellman and Moyes ownership group completed the purchase of the Coyotes.

Gretzky played 20 seasons in the National Hockey League with Edmonton, Los Angeles, St. Louis and the New York Rangers, dominating the game unlike any player in history. Gretzky helped win four Stanley Cup championships and three Canada Cup tournament titles during his illustrious playing career. He became the NHL's all-time leading goal, assist and point producer for a single season and career (both regular season and playoffs). Gretzky won the Art Ross Trophy as the NHL's leading scorer 10 times, the Hart Trophy as the League's MVP nine times (including eight consecutive seasons) and the Conn Smythe Trophies as playoff MVP twice. He earned the Lady Byng Trophy as the NHL's most gentlemanly player five times and made 18 consecutive All-Star Game appearances, securing three All-Star MVP Awards. Gretzky is an eight-time First All-Star Team member and seven-time Second All-Star Team member. He holds virtually every offensive record in the NHL and his tireless support of the game has contributed significantly to the popularity it enjoys today.

On November 22, 1999 – seven months after his retirement – Gretzky was inducted into the Hockey Hall of Fame in Toronto, becoming the tenth and final player in Hockey Hall of Fame history to have the mandatory three-year waiting period for enshrinement waived by the Hall's board of directors.

Gretzky's incredible success in hockey has continued past his playing career. In a managerial role with Team Canada, Gretzky served as executive director for Team Canada, responsible for assembling Canada's best hockey players at the 2002 Olympic Winter Games in Salt Lake City and again in 2004 at the World Cup of Hockey. Under Gretzky's leadership, Team Canada won the gold medal for the first time in 50 years at the 2002 Olympics. Two years later, Team Canada repeated the feat by winning the 2004 World Cup of Hockey championship. In 2006, once again he will manage Team Canada at the 2006 Winter Olympics in Turin, Italy.

Club Records

Team

(Figures in brackets for season records are games played; records for fewest points, wins, ties, losses, goals, goals against are for 70 or more games)

Most Points	96	1984-85 (80)
Most Wins	43	1984-85 (80)
Most Ties	18	2003-04 (82)
Most Losses	57	1980-81 (80)
Most Goals	358	1984-85 (80)
Most Goals Against	400	1980-81 (80)
Fewest Points	32	1980-81 (80)
Fewest Wins	9	1980-81 (80)
Fewest Ties	6	1995-96 (82)
Fewest Losses	27	1984-85 (80), 2000-01 (82), 2001-02 (82)
Fewest Goals	188	2003-04 (82)
Fewest Goals Against	197	1998-99 (82)

Longest Winning Streak

Overall	9	Mar. 8-27/85
Home	9	Dec. 27/92-Jan. 23/93
Away	8	Feb. 25-Apr. 6/85

Longest Undefeated Streak

Overall	14	Oct. 25-Nov. 28/98 (12 wins, 2 ties)
Home	11	Dec. 23/83-Feb. 5/84 (6 wins, 5 ties), Oct. 15-Dec. 20/98 (10 wins, 1 tie)
Away	9	Feb. 25-Apr. 7/85 (8 wins, 1 tie), Dec. 7/03-Jan. 9/04 (5 wins, 4 ties)

Longest Losing Streak

Overall	10	Nov. 30-Dec. 20/80, Feb. 6-25/94
Home	5	Oct. 29-Nov. 13/93, Mar. 13-23/00
Away	13	Jan. 26-Apr. 14/94

Captains' History

Lars-Erik Sjoberg, 1979-80; Morris Lukowich, 1980-81; Dave Christian, 1981-82; Dave Christian and Lucien DeBlois, 1982-83; Lucien DeBlois, 1983-84; Dale Hawerchuk, 1984-85 to 1988-89; Randy Carlyle, Dale Hawerchuk and Thomas Steen (tri-captains), 1989-90; Randy Carlyle and Thomas Steen (co-captains), 1990-91; Troy Murray, 1991-92; Troy Murray and Dean Kennedy, 1992-93; Dean Kennedy and Keith Tkachuk, 1993-94; Keith Tkachuk, 1994-95; Kris King, 1995-96; Keith Tkachuk, 1996-97 to 2000-01; Teppo Numminen, 2001-02, 2002-03; Shane Doan, 2003-04 to date.

Longest Winless Streak

Overall	*30	Oct. 19-Dec. 20/80 (23 losses, 7 ties)
Home	14	Oct. 19-Dec. 14/80 (9 losses, 5 ties)
Away	18	Oct. 19-Dec. 20/80 (16 losses, 2 ties)

Most Shutouts, Season	9	1998-99 (82)
Most PIM, Season	2,278	1987-88 (80)
Most Goals, Game	12	Feb. 25/85 (Wpg. 12 at NYR 5)

Individual

Most Seasons	15	Teppo Numminen
Most Games	1,098	Teppo Numminen
Most Goals, Career	379	Dale Hawerchuk
Most Assists, Career	553	Thomas Steen
Most Points, Career	929	Dale Hawerchuk (379G, 550A)
Most PIM, Career	1,508	Keith Tkachuk
Most Shutouts, Career	21	Nikolai Khabibulin

Longest Consecutive

Games Streak	475	Dale Hawerchuk (Dec. 19/82-Dec. 10/88)
Most Goals, Season	76	Teemu Selanne (1992-93)
Most Assists, Season	79	Phil Housley (1992-93)
Most Points, Season	132	Teemu Selanne (1992-93; 76G, 56A)
Most PIM, Season	347	Tie Domi (1993-94)

Most Points, Defenseman,

Season	97	Phil Housley (1992-93; 18G, 79A)

Most Points, Center,

Season	130	Dale Hawerchuk (1984-85; 53G, 77A)

Most Points, Right Wing,

Season	132	Teemu Selanne (1992-93; 76G, 56A)

Most Points, Left Wing,

Season	98	Keith Tkachuk (1995-96; 50G, 48A)

Most Points, Rookie,

Season	*132	Teemu Selanne (1992-93; 76G, 56A)

Most Shutouts, Season	8	Nikolai Khabibulin (1998-99)
Most Goals, Game	5	Willy Lindstrom (Mar. 2/82), Alexei Zhamnov (Apr. 1/95)
Most Assists, Game	5	Dale Hawerchuk (Mar. 6/84, Mar. 18/89, Mar. 4/90), Phil Housley (Jan. 18/93), Keith Tkachuk (Feb. 23/01)
Most Points, Game	6	Willy Lindstrom (Mar. 2/82; 5G, 1A), Dale Hawerchuk (Dec. 14/83; 3G, 3A, Mar. 5/88; 2G, 4A, Mar. 18/89; 1G, 5A), Thomas Steen (Oct. 24/84; 2G, 4A), Ed Olczyk (Dec. 21/91; 2G, 4A)

* NHL Record.

Records include Winnipeg Jets, 1979-80 through 1995-96.

Winnipeg Jets Retired Numbers

*9	Bobby Hull	1972-1980
25	Thomas Steen	1981-1995

* Brett Hull will wear this number for Phoenix.

All-time Record vs. Other Clubs

Regular Season

	At Home								On Road								Total							
	GP	W	L	T	OL	GF	GA	PTS	GP	W	L	T	OL	GF	GA	PTS	GP	W	L	T	OL	GF	GA	PTS
Anaheim	26	11	10	2	3	75	77	27	27	9	13	3	2	67	74	23	53	20	23	5	5	142	151	50
Atlanta	5	4	0	1	0	16	7	9	4	3	1	0	0	12	6	6	9	7	1	1	0	28	13	15
Boston	30	13	14	3	0	101	102	29	30	4	22	4	0	92	136	12	60	17	36	7	0	193	238	41
Buffalo	29	13	14	2	0	87	92	28	31	6	20	5	0	80	127	17	60	19	34	7	0	167	219	45
Calgary	70	34	25	11	0	264	238	79	71	23	39	9	0	227	295	55	141	57	64	20	0	491	533	134
Carolina	31	14	14	2	1	110	112	31	30	10	13	6	1	89	103	27	61	24	27	8	2	199	215	58
Chicago	50	27	18	5	0	164	154	59	48	12	26	10	0	128	184	34	98	39	44	15	0	292	338	93
Colorado	40	16	17	7	0	144	142	39	41	15	19	5	2	133	142	37	81	31	36	12	2	277	284	76
Columbus	8	5	0	3	0	24	15	13	8	3	4	1	0	14	19	7	16	8	4	4	0	38	34	20
Dallas	54	23	27	4	0	170	182	50	55	19	27	9	0	166	199	47	109	42	54	13	0	336	381	97
Detroit	49	17	18	14	0	149	153	48	51	18	25	8	0	170	200	44	100	35	43	22	0	319	353	92
Edmonton	71	29	36	5	1	284	314	64	72	20	44	6	2	234	313	48	143	49	80	11	3	518	627	112
Florida	10	3	3	3	1	25	31	10	8	5	3	0	0	21	23	10	18	8	6	3	1	46	54	20
Los Angeles	76	38	26	11	1	301	250	88	74	32	27	14	1	288	294	79	150	70	53	25	2	589	544	167
Minnesota	8	5	2	1	0	23	16	11	8	4	2	2	0	17	15	10	16	9	4	3	0	40	31	21
Montreal	29	9	13	7	0	94	112	25	29	3	24	2	0	66	142	8	58	12	37	9	0	160	254	33
Nashville	12	7	4	0	1	33	35	15	12	5	3	2	2	34	32	14	24	12	7	2	3	67	67	29
New Jersey	31	21	7	1	0	114	81	45	29	11	12	6	0	87	95	28	60	32	19	9	0	201	176	73
NY Islanders	30	11	15	4	0	96	105	26	30	9	13	8	0	91	113	26	60	20	28	12	0	187	218	52
NY Rangers	31	13	13	4	1	107	101	31	29	9	17	2	1	102	128	21	60	22	30	6	2	209	229	52
Ottawa	10	4	5	1	0	34	38	9	11	6	4	1	0	34	29	13	21	10	9	2	0	68	67	22
Philadelphia	31	13	16	2	0	99	106	28	31	8	23	0	0	83	134	16	62	21	39	2	0	182	240	44
Pittsburgh	31	14	13	3	1	116	107	32	30	10	20	0	0	86	120	20	61	24	33	3	1	202	227	52
St. Louis	51	26	18	7	0	166	156	59	50	13	26	11	0	136	182	37	101	39	44	18	0	302	338	96
San Jose	35	18	12	3	2	108	99	41	32	13	15	4	0	99	110	30	67	31	27	7	2	207	209	71
Tampa Bay	11	6	5	0	0	28	26	12	10	5	5	0	0	33	33	10	21	11	10	0	0	61	59	22
Toronto	39	20	13	6	0	161	142	46	43	21	20	2	0	161	157	44	82	41	33	8	0	322	299	90
Vancouver	69	33	26	10	0	256	245	76	72	19	43	10	0	201	272	48	141	52	69	20	0	457	517	124
Washington	30	15	8	7	0	112	105	37	31	8	17	5	1	85	129	22	61	23	25	12	1	197	234	59
Totals	997	462	392	131	12	3461	3343	1067	997	323	527	135	12	3036	3796	793	1994	785	919	266	24	6497	7139	1860

Playoffs

	Series	W	L	GP	W	L	T	GF	GA	Last Mtg.	Rnd.	Result
Anaheim	1	0	1	7	3	4	0	17	17	1997	CQF	L 3-4
Calgary	3	2	1	13	7	6	0	45	43	1987	DSF	W 4-2
Colorado	1	0	1	5	1	4	0	10	17	2000	CQF	L 1-4
Detroit	2	0	2	12	4	8	0	28	44	1998	CQF	L 2-4
Edmonton	6	0	6	26	4	22	0	75	120	1990	DSF	L 3-4
St. Louis	2	0	2	11	4	7	0	29	39	1999	CQF	L 1-4
San Jose	1	0	1	5	1	4	0	7	13	2002	CQF	L 1-4
Vancouver	2	0	2	13	6	7	0	34	50	1993	DSF	L 2-4
Totals	18	2	16	92	29	63	0	245	343			

Calgary totals include Atlanta Flames, 1979-80.
Colorado totals include Quebec, 1979-80 to 1994-95.
New Jersey totals include Colorado Rockies, 1979-80 to 1981-82.
Carolina totals include Hartford, 1979-80 to 1996-97.
Dallas totals include Minnesota North Stars, 1979-80 to 1992-93.

Playoff Results 2005-2000

Year	Round	Opponent	Result	GF	GA
2002	CQF	San Jose	L 1-4	7	13
2000	CQF	Colorado	L 1-4	10	17

Abbreviations: Round: CQF – conference quarter-final; **DSF** – division semi-final.

Key Off-Season Signings/Acquisitions

2004

June 8 • Signed 2002 1st-round pick (11th overall) D **Keith Ballard**.

June 26 • Obtained LW **Jason Chimera** and a 2004 3rd-round pick from Edmonton for 2004 2nd- and 4th-round picks.

June 30 • Re-signed LW **Tyson Nash**.

July 6 • Signed C **Mike Ricci**.

9 • Signed D **Sean O'Donnell**.

Aug. 2 • Re-signed LW **Ladislav Nagy**.

6 • Signed RW **Brett Hull**.

12 • Re-signed C **Mike Comrie**.

17 • Re-signed RW **Mike Johnson**.

26 • Signed C **Petr Nedved**.

26 • Obtained D **Denis Gauthier** and LW **Oleg Saprykhin** for C **Daymond Langkow**.

2005

Aug. 2 • Re-signed G **Brian Boucher**.

5 • Re-signed D **Brad Ference**.

8 • Named **Wayne Gretzky** head coach; named **Rick Tocchet**, **Barry Smith** and **Rick Bowness** associate coaches.

11 • Re-signed D **Derek Morris**.

15 • Re-signed Cs **Krys Kolanos** and **Jeff Taffe**.

17 • Signed G **Curtis Joseph**.

19 • Signed G **Steve Passmore**.

22 • Re-signed D **Paul Mara**.

23 • Obtained LW **Mike Leclerc** from Anaheim for a 2007 conditional draft pick.

Entry Draft Selections 2005-1991

2005
Pick
17 Martin Hanzal
59 Pier-Olivier Pelletier
105 Keith Yandle
148 Anton Krysanov
212 Pat Brosnihan

2004
Pick
5 Blake Wheeler
35 Logan Stephenson
50 Enver Lisin
103 Roman Tomanek
119 Kevin Porter
168 Kevin Cormier
199 Chad Kolarik
240 Aaron Gagnon
261 William Engasser
265 Daniel Winnik

2003
Pick
77 Tyler Redenbach
80 Dmitri Pestunov
115 Liam Lindstrom
178 Ryan Gibbons
208 Randall Gelech
242 Eduard Lewandowski
272 Sean Sullivan
290 Loic Burkhalter

2002
Pick
19 Jakub Koreis
23 Ben Eager
46 David Leneveu
70 Joe Callahan
80 Matt Jones
97 Lance Monych
132 John Zeiler
186 Jeff Pietrasiak
216 Ladislav Kouba
249 Marcus Smith
280 Russell Spence

2001
Pick
11 Fredrik Sjostrom
31 Matthew Spiller
45 Martin Podlesak
78 Beat Forster
148 David Klema
180 Scott Polaski
210 Steve Belanger
243 Frantisek Lukes
273 Severin Blindenbacher

2000
Pick
19 Krystofer Kolanos
53 Alexander Tatarinov
85 Ramzi Abid
160 Nate Kiser
186 Brent Gauvreau
217 Igor Samoilov
249 Sami Venalainen
281 Peter Fabus

1999
Pick
15 Scott Kelman
19 Kirill Safronov
53 Brad Ralph
71 Jason Jaspers
116 Ryan Lauzon
123 Preston Mizzi
168 Erik Lewerstrom
234 Goran Bezina
262 Alexei Litvinenko

1998
Pick
14 Patrick DesRochers
43 Ossi Vaananen
73 Pat O'Leary
100 Ryan Vanbuskirk
115 Jay Leach
116 Josh Blackburn
129 Robert Schnabel
160 Rickard Wallin
187 Erik Westrum
214 Justin Hansen

1997
Pick
43 Juha Gustafsson
96 Scott McCallum
123 Curtis Suter
151 Robert Francz
207 Alexander Andreyev
233 Wyatt Smith

1996
Pick
11 Dan Focht
24 Daniel Briere
62 Per-Anton Lundstrom
119 Richard Lintner
139 Robert Esche
174 Trevor Letowski
200 Nicholas Lent
226 Marc-Etienne Hubert

1995
Pick
7 Shane Doan
32 Marc Chouinard
34 Jason Doig
67 Brad Isbister
84 Justin Kurtz
121 Brian Elder
136 Sylvain Daigle
162 Paul Traynor
188 Jaroslav Obsut
189 Fredrik Loven
214 Rob Deciantis

1994
Pick
30 Deron Quint
56 Dorian Anneck
58 Tavis Hansen
82 Steve Cheredaryk
108 Craig Mills
143 Steve Vezina
146 Chris Kibermanis
186 Ramil Saifullin
212 Henrik Smangs
238 Mike Mader
264 Jason Issel

1993
Pick
15 Mats Lindgren
31 Scott Langkow
43 Alexei Budayev
79 Ruslan Batyrshin
93 Ravil Gusmanov
119 Larry Courville
145 Michal Grosek
171 Martin Woods
197 Adrian Murray
217 Vladimir Potapov
223 Ilja Stashenkov
228 Harijs Vitolinsh
285 Russ Hewson

1992
Pick
17 Sergei Bautin
27 Boris Mironov
60 Jeremy Stevenson
84 Mark Visheau
132 Alexander Alexeyev
155 Artur Oktyabrev
156 Andrei Raisky
204 Nikolai Khabibulin
228 Yevgeny Garanin
229 Teemu Numminen
252 Andrei Karpovstev
254 Ivan Vologzhaninov

1991
Pick
5 Aaron Ward
49 Dmitri Filimonov
91 Juha Ylonen
99 Yan Kaminsky
115 Jeff Sebastian
159 Jeff Ricciardi
181 Sean Gauthier
203 Igor Ulanov
225 Jason Jennings
247 Sergei Sorokin

General Managers' History

John Ferguson, 1979-80 to 1987-88; John Ferguson and Mike Smith, 1988-89; Mike Smith, 1989-90 to 1992-93; Mike Smith and John Paddock, 1993-94; John Paddock, 1994-95, 1995-96; John Paddock and Bobby Smith, 1996-97; Bobby Smith, 1997-98 to 1999-2000; Bobby Smith and Cliff Fletcher, 2000-01; Cliff Fletcher and Michael Barnett, 2001-02; Michael Barnett, 2002-03 to date.

Vice President and General Manager

BARNETT, MICHAEL
Executive Vice President/General Manager, Phoenix Coyotes.
Born in Olds, Alta., October 9, 1948.

Michael Barnett joined the Coyotes as vice president and general manager on August 28, 2001 after serving as president of International Management Group's (IMG) hockey division since 1990. Barnett is the sixth general manager in franchise history and follows in the footsteps of Brian Burke (Vancouver Canucks), Pierre Lacroix (Colorado Avalanche) and Dean Lombardi (San Jose Sharks) as former player agents who have become NHL general managers.

With over 20 years of experience in the game prior to joining the Coyotes, Barnett left IMG as one of hockey's most distinguished and well-respected player agents. Over the years, Barnett earned acclaim for his integrity, vision and success as a negotiator. He developed a reputation within the NHL as one of the most creative and well-informed agents in the industry. He is reunited in Phoenix with his longtime friend Wayne Gretzky, the Coyotes' managing partner. Barnett served as Gretzky's agent for 20 years. He also represented some of the NHL's most high-profile players including Jaromir Jagr, Brett Hull, Paul Coffey, Alexander Mogilny, Owen Nolan, Mats Sundin and Joe Thornton.

Barnett actually began his career in hockey as a player. He played hockey at St. Lawrence University in Canton, New York and later attended the University of Calgary, where he played both intercollegiate hockey and football for three years. In 1973-74, he turned professional with the Chicago Cougars (WHA) playing left wing for their minor league affiliate, the Long Island Cougars (NAHL). The following season (1974-75), while playing for the Roanoke-Valley Rebels (SHL) — the Houston Aeros' (WHA) minor league affiliate — Barnett suffered a career ending eye injury.

In 1980, Barnett opened a Western Canadian sports management agency and began his long-lasting relationship with Gretzky by signing him on as his top client. In 1990, Barnett merged his company with Mark McCormack's IMG and became president of IMG hockey operations.

Club Directory

Glendale Arena

Phoenix Coyotes
5800 W. Glenn Drive, Suite 350
Glendale, AZ 85301
Phone **623/463-8800**
FAX 623/463-8810
Tickets 480/563-PUCK

Glendale Arena
9400 W. Maryland Avenue
Glendale, AZ 85303
Phone 623/772-3200
FAX 623/772-3201
Capacity: 17,799
www.PhoenixCoyotes.com

Chairman and Governor . . . . Steve Ellman
Co-Owner . . . . Jerry Moyes
Managing Partner, Alt. Gov. & Head Coach . . . . . . Wayne Gretzky
President, Chief Operating Officer & Alt. Gov. . . . . . Douglas Moss
Sr. Exec. V.P. of Hockey Operations . . . . Cliff Fletcher
G.M., Exec. V.P. & Alt. Gov. . . . . Michael Barnett
Senior Vice President & Assistant General Manager . Laurence Gilman
General Counsel . . . . Bob Kaufman
Senior Vice President & Chief Marketing Officer . . . Michael Bucek
Senior Vice President, Corporate Sales & Suite Sales Dave Groff
Senior Vice President, Ticket Sales & Services . . . . . . Jim Van Stone
Executive Assistant to the Chairman . . . . Jane Fisher
Executive Assistant to the President . . . . Cheryl Taylor
Executive Assistant to the General Manager . . . . . . Tracey Vaughn

Hockey Operations
Head Coach . . . . Wayne Gretzky
Associate Coaches . . . . Rick Tocchet, Barry Smith, Rick Bowness
Goaltending Coach . . . . Grant Fuhr
Director of Player Personnel . . . . Tom Kurvers
Professional Scouts . . . . Warren Rychel, Rich Sutter
Director of Player Development . . . . Eddie Mio
Amateur Scouts . . . . Gus Badali, Keith Gretzky, Charles Henry, Willy Lindstrom, Steve Lyons, Blair Reid, Greg Royce, Evzen Slansky, Boris Yemeljanov
Director of Hockey Administration . . . . Stuart Judge
Strength & Conditioning Coordinator . . . . Mike Bahn
Athletic Therapist . . . . Chris Broadhurst
Massage Therapist . . . . Jukka Nieminen
Head Equipment Manager . . . . Stan Wilson
Equipment Manager . . . . Tony Silva
Assistant Equipment Manager . . . . Jason Rudee
Video Coordinator . . . . Steve Peters
Power Skating Coach . . . . Mark Chiacio
Manager of Team Services . . . . Lesa Guth
Team Internist . . . . Robert Luberto, D.O.
Team Orthopedic Surgeons . . . . Dr. Doug Freedberg, Dr. Gary Waslewski
Team Dentists . . . . Dr. Lawrence Emmott, Dr. Ron Foeldi
San Antonio (AHL) Head Coach . . . . Pat Conacher
San Antonio (AHL) Assistant Coach . . . . Gord Dineen

Communications
Vice President of Communications . . . . Richard Nairn
Director of Media Relations . . . . Rick Braunstein
Manager of Publications & Media Relations . . . . . . Kevin Crawley

Broadcasting
TV Play-by-Play Announcer . . . . Curt Keilback
TV Color Analyst . . . . Darren Pang
TV/Radio Host . . . . Todd Walsh
Radio Play-by-Play Announcer . . . . Bob Heethuis
Radio Color Analyst . . . . Louie DeBrusk
Manager of Broadcasting . . . . Doug Cannon

Community Relations
Director of Community Relations/
Managing Dir. of Coyotes Charities . . . . Barb Kozuh
Community Relations Coordinator . . . . Susan O'Donnell

Corporate Sales & Service
Corporate Sales Account Executives . . . . Peter Bland, Judd Norris, Joe Perre
Sponsorship Services Representatives . . . . Melissa Lehman, Dana Repp, Laura Vandevier

Finance & Administration
Vice President and Controller . . . . Joe Leibfried
Assistant Controller . . . . Burlenti Shaban
Payroll Administrator . . . . Cheri Sedor

Marketing
Director of Marketing . . . . Dan Brewster
Manager of Advertising & Promotions . . . . Jen Byron
Manager of Game Operations/Special Events . . . . . Mark Iralson
Manager of Integrated Marketing/Promotions . . . . . Stacey Cohen
Manager of New Media . . . . Chad Lynch
Graphic Designer . . . . Scott Jenner
Fan Development Coordinator . . . . Sarah Finecey

Ticket Sales & Service
Vice President, Ticket Sales & Service . . . . Shayne Donohue
Director of Group Sales . . . . Matt Peterson
Director of Inside Sales . . . . Al Guido
Director of Business Development & Service . . . . . . Nick Casarona
Director of Ticket Operations . . . . Douglas Vanderheyden

Security
Director of Security . . . . Jim O'Neal

Suite Sales
Suite Sales Account Executives . . . . Mike Briody, Curtis McKenna
Suite Services Representative . . . . Kate Kost

Phoenix Coyotes & Arena Management Group
Executive Director of Human Resources . . . . Julie Atherton
Legal Counsel . . . . Steve Weinreich

Team Information
Broadcast Television Stations . . . . KTVK-NewsChannel 3, KASW TV-WB6
Cable Television Station . . . . Fox Sports Net
Radio Stations . . . . KDKB 93.3 FM, KDUS 1060 AM

Pittsburgh Penguins

Franchise date: June 5, 1967

EASTERN CONFERENCE

ATLANTIC DIVISION

39th NHL Season

2005-06 Schedule

Oct.	Wed.	5	at New Jersey
	Fri.	7	at Carolina
	Sat.	8	Boston
	Mon.	10	at Buffalo
	Fri.	14	at Philadelphia
	Sat.	15	Tampa Bay
	Thu.	20	New Jersey
	Sat.	22	at Boston
	Tue.	25	Florida
	Thu.	27	Atlanta
	Sat.	29	Carolina
Nov.	Tue.	1	at New Jersey
	Thu.	3	at NY Islanders
	Sat.	5	at Boston
	Mon.	7	at NY Rangers
	Wed.	9	at Atlanta
	Thu.	10	Montreal
	Sat.	12	NY Rangers
	Mon.	14	NY Islanders
	Wed.	16	at Philadelphia
	Sat.	19	Philadelphia
	Tue.	22	Washington
	Fri.	25	at Florida
	Sun.	27	at Tampa Bay*
	Tue.	29	Buffalo
Dec.	Thu.	1	at NY Rangers
	Sat.	3	Calgary
	Thu.	8	Minnesota
	Sat.	10	Colorado
	Mon.	12	at Detroit
	Tue.	13	at St. Louis
	Fri.	16	Buffalo
	Sat.	17	at Buffalo
	Fri.	23	Philadelphia
	Tue.	27	Toronto
	Thu.	29	New Jersey
	Sat.	31	NY Rangers*
Jan.	Mon.	2	at Toronto
	Tue.	3	at Montreal
	Fri.	6	at Atlanta
	Sat.	7	Atlanta

	Tue.	10	Edmonton
	Wed.	11	at Columbus
	Fri.	13	at Chicago
	Sun.	15	at Nashville
	Mon.	16	Vancouver
	Thu.	19	NY Rangers
	Sat.	21	Philadelphia*
	Mon.	23	at Philadelphia
	Wed.	25	Washington
	Thu.	26	at NY Islanders
	Sat.	28	at NY Rangers
Feb.	Wed.	1	at NY Rangers
	Thu.	2	Ottawa
	Sat.	4	NY Islanders
	Mon.	6	at Ottawa
	Wed.	8	Boston
	Fri.	10	at Carolina
	Sat.	11	at Washington
Mar.	Wed.	1	Ottawa
	Sat.	4	Carolina
	Tue.	7	Tampa Bay
	Wed.	8	at Washington
	Sat.	11	New Jersey
	Sun.	12	Philadelphia
	Thu.	16	at New Jersey
	Sat.	18	at Montreal
	Sun.	19	Toronto
	Tue.	21	at Ottawa
	Fri.	24	NY Islanders
	Sun.	26	Montreal
	Wed.	29	Florida
	Fri.	31	at NY Islanders
Apr.	Sun.	2	New Jersey*
	Wed.	5	at New Jersey
	Fri.	7	at Florida
	Sat.	8	at Tampa Bay
	Tue.	11	at Philadelphia
	Thu.	13	NY Rangers
	Sat.	15	at NY Islanders
	Mon.	17	NY Islanders
	Tue.	18	at Toronto

* Denotes afternoon game.

Free agents Ziggy Palffy (left) and Sergei Gonchar (right) are among several new additions in Pittsburgh this season. Palffy has never scored less than 32 goals when playing in at least 63 games.

Year-by-Year Record

| | | Home | | | | Road | | | | Overall | | | | | | | |
Season	GP	W	L	T	OL	W	L	T	OL	W	L	T	OL	GF	GA	Pts.	Finished	Playoff Result
2004-05	....																	
2003-04	82	13	22	6	0	10	25	2	4	23	47	8	4	190	303	58	5th, Atlantic Div.	Out of Playoffs
2002-03	82	15	22	2	2	12	22	4	3	27	44	6	5	189	255	65	5th, Atlantic Div.	Out of Playoffs
2001-02	82	16	20	4	1	12	21	4	4	28	41	8	5	198	249	69	5th, Atlantic Div.	Out of Playoffs
2000-01	82	24	15	2	0	18	13	7	3	42	28	9	3	281	256	96	3rd, Atlantic Div.	Lost Conf. Championship
1999-2000	82	23	11	7	0	14	20	1	6	37	31	8	6	241	236	88	3rd, Atlantic Div.	Lost Conf. Semi-Final
1998-99	82	21	10	10	....	17	20	4	....	38	30	14	....	242	225	90	3rd, Atlantic Div.	Lost Conf. Semi-Final
1997-98	82	21	10	10	....	19	14	8	....	40	24	18	....	228	188	98	1st, Northeast Div.	Lost Conf. Quarter-Final
1996-97	82	25	11	5	....	13	25	3	....	38	36	8	....	285	280	84	2nd, Northeast Div.	Lost Conf. Quarter-Final
1995-96	82	32	9	0	....	17	20	4	....	49	29	4	....	362	284	102	1st, Northeast Div.	Lost Conf. Championship
1994-95	48	18	5	1	....	11	11	2	....	29	16	3	....	181	158	61	2nd, Northeast Div.	Lost Conf. Quarter-Final
1993-94	84	25	9	8	....	19	18	5	....	44	27	13	....	299	285	101	1st, Northeast Div.	Lost Conf. Quarter-Final
1992-93	84	32	6	4	....	24	15	3	....	56	21	7	....	367	268	119	1st, Patrick Div.	Lost Div. Final
1991-92	**80**	**21**	**13**	**6**	....	**18**	**19**	**3**	....	**39**	**32**	**9**	....	**343**	**308**	**87**	**3rd, Patrick Div.**	**Won Stanley Cup**
1990-91	**80**	**25**	**12**	**3**	....	**16**	**21**	**3**	....	**41**	**33**	**6**	....	**342**	**305**	**88**	**1st, Patrick Div.**	**Won Stanley Cup**
1989-90	80	22	15	3	....	10	25	5	....	32	40	8	....	318	359	72	5th, Patrick Div.	Out of Playoffs
1988-89	80	24	13	3	....	16	20	4	....	40	33	7	....	347	349	87	2nd, Patrick Div.	Lost Div. Final
1987-88	80	22	12	6	....	14	23	3	....	36	35	9	....	319	316	81	6th, Patrick Div.	Out of Playoffs
1986-87	80	19	15	6	....	11	23	6	....	30	38	12	....	297	290	72	5th, Patrick Div.	Out of Playoffs
1985-86	80	20	15	5	....	14	23	3	....	34	38	8	....	313	305	76	5th, Patrick Div.	Out of Playoffs
1984-85	80	17	20	3	....	7	31	2	....	24	51	5	....	276	385	53	6th, Patrick Div.	Out of Playoffs
1983-84	80	7	29	4	....	9	29	2	....	16	58	6	....	254	390	38	6th, Patrick Div.	Out of Playoffs
1982-83	80	14	22	4	....	4	31	5	....	18	53	9	....	257	394	45	6th, Patrick Div.	Out of Playoffs
1981-82	80	21	11	8	....	10	25	5	....	31	36	13	....	310	337	75	4th, Patrick Div.	Lost Div. Semi-Final
1980-81	80	21	16	3	....	9	21	10	....	30	37	13	....	302	345	73	3rd, Norris Div.	Lost Prelim. Round
1979-80	80	20	13	7	....	10	24	6	....	30	37	13	....	251	303	73	3rd, Norris Div.	Lost Prelim. Round
1978-79	80	23	12	5	....	13	19	8	....	36	31	13	....	281	279	85	2nd, Norris Div.	Lost Quarter-Final
1977-78	80	16	15	9	....	9	22	9	....	25	37	18	....	254	321	68	4th, Norris Div.	Out of Playoffs
1976-77	80	22	12	6	....	12	21	7	....	34	33	13	....	240	252	81	3rd, Norris Div.	Lost Prelim. Round
1975-76	80	23	11	6	....	12	22	6	....	35	33	12	....	339	303	82	3rd, Norris Div.	Lost Prelim. Round
1974-75	80	25	5	10	....	12	23	5	....	37	28	15	....	326	289	89	3rd, Norris Div.	Lost Quarter-Final
1973-74	78	15	18	6	....	13	23	3	....	28	41	9	....	242	273	65	5th, West Div.	Out of Playoffs
1972-73	78	24	11	4	....	8	26	5	....	32	37	9	....	257	265	73	5th, West Div.	Out of Playoffs
1971-72	78	18	15	6	....	8	23	8	....	26	38	14	....	220	258	66	4th, West Div.	Lost Quarter-Final
1970-71	78	18	12	9	....	3	25	11	....	21	37	20	....	221	240	62	6th, West Div.	Out of Playoffs
1969-70	76	17	13	8	....	9	25	4	....	26	38	12	....	182	238	64	2nd, West Div.	Lost Semi-Final
1968-69	76	12	24	6	....	8	25	5	....	20	45	11	....	189	252	51	5th, West Div.	Out of Playoffs
1967-68	74	15	12	10	....	12	22	3	....	27	34	13	....	195	216	67	5th, West Div.	Out of Playoffs

2005-06 Player Personnel

FORWARDS	HT	WT	S	Place of Birth	Date	2004-05 Club
ARMSTRONG, Colby	6-2	195	R	Lloydminster, Sask.	11/23/82	Wilkes-Barre
BEECH, Kris	6-2	208	L	Salmon Arm, B.C.	2/5/81	Wilkes-Barre
CARCILLO, Daniel	5-11	202	L	King City, Ont.	1/28/85	Sarnia-Mississauga
CHRISTENSEN, Erik	6-1	191	L	Edmonton, Alta.	12/17/83	Wilkes-Barre
CROSBY, Sidney	5-10	175	L	Halifax, N.S.	8/7/87	Rimouski
DIXON, Stephen	5-11	188	L	Halifax, N.S.	9/7/85	Cape Breton
EAVES, Ben	5-8	180	R	Minneapolis, MN	3/27/82	Wilkes-Barre-Wheeling
ENDICOTT, Shane	6-3	214	L	Saskatoon, Sask.	12/21/81	Wilkes-Barre
FATA, Rico	6-0	205	L	Sault Ste. Marie, Ont.	2/12/80	Asiago
FILEWICH, Jonathan	6-2	205	R	Kelowna, B.C.	10/2/84	Lethbridge
HUSSEY, Matt	6-2	215	L	New Haven, CT	5/28/79	Wilkes-Barre
KOLTSOV, Konstantin	6-0	206	L	Minsk, USSR	4/17/81	Minsk-Spartak
KRAFT, Milan	6-4	212	L	Plzen, Czech.	1/17/80	Plzen-Karlovy Vary
LeCLAIR, John	6-3	226	L	St. Albans, VT	7/5/69	
LEFEBVRE, Guillaume	6-1	202	L	Amos, Que.	5/7/81	Wilkes-Barre
LEMIEUX, Mario	6-4	230	R	Montreal, Que.	10/5/65	
MALONE, Ryan	6-4	216	L	Pittsburgh, PA	12/1/79	Blues-Renon-Ambri
MOROZOV, Aleksey	6-1	204	L	Moscow, USSR	2/16/77	Kazan
MURLEY, Matt	6-1	206	L	Troy, NY	12/17/79	Wilkes-Barre
OUELLET, Michel	6-0	201	R	Rimouski, Que.	3/5/82	Wilkes-Barre
PADDOCK, Cam	6-1	191	R	Vancouver, B.C.	3/22/83	Wilkes-Barre-Wheeling
PALFFY, Ziggy	5-10	183	L	Skalica, Czech.	5/5/72	Skalica-Slavia
PIRJETA, Lasse	6-4	225	L	Oulu, Finland	4/4/74	HIFK
RECCHI, Mark	5-10	190	L	Kamloops, B.C.	2/1/68	
ROY, Andre	6-4	221	L	Port Chester, NY	2/8/75	
STONE, Ryan	6-2	200	L	Calgary, Alta.	3/20/85	Brandon
SUROVY, Tomas	6-1	205	L	Banska Bystrica, Czech.	9/24/81	Wilkes-Barre
TALBOT, Maxime	5-11	176	L	Lemoyne, Que.	2/11/84	Wilkes-Barre
VANDENBUSSCHE, Ryan	6-0	200	R	Simcoe, Ont.	2/28/73	Wilkes-Barre

DEFENSEMEN						
BISSONNETTE, Paul	6-3	212	L	Welland, Ont.	3/11/85	Saginaw-Owen Sound
FATA, Drew	6-1	220	L	Sault Ste. Marie, Ont.	7/28/83	Wilkes-Barre-Wheeling
FERNHOLM, Daniel	6-4	218	L	Stockholm, Sweden	12/20/83	Djurgarden-Bolzano
GONCHAR, Sergei	6-2	215	L	Chelyabinsk, USSR	4/13/74	Magnitogorsk
JACKMAN, Ric	6-2	197	R	Toronto, Ont.	6/28/78	Bjorkloven
KOCI, David	6-6	230	L	Prague, Czech.	5/12/81	Wilkes-Barre
LANNON, Ryan	6-2	220	L	Worcester, MA	12/14/82	Harvard
LUPASCHUK, Ross	6-1	210	R	Edmonton, Alta.	1/19/81	Wilkes-Barre
MELICHAR, Josef	6-2	220	L	Ceske Budejovice, Czech.	1/20/79	Sparta
NASREDDINE, Alain	6-1	201	L	Montreal, Que.	7/10/75	Wilkes-Barre
ODELEIN, Lyle	6-0	210	R	Quill Lake, Sask.	7/21/68	
ORPIK, Brooks	6-2	228	L	San Francisco, CA	9/26/80	
ROULEAU, Alexandre	6-1	192	L	Mont-Laurier, Que.	7/29/83	Wheeling-Wilkes-Barre
SCHNEIDER, Andy	6-1	215	L	Grand Forks, ND	7/31/81	North Dakota
SCUDERI, Rob	6-0	214	L	Syosset, NY	12/30/78	Wilkes-Barre
STRBAK, Martin	6-3	210	L	Presov, Czech.	1/15/75	Kosice-CSKA
TARNSTROM, Dick	6-1	205	L	Sundbyberg, Sweden	1/20/75	Sodertalje
WELCH, Noah	6-4	212	L	Brighton, MA	8/26/82	Harvard
WHITNEY, Ryan	6-4	202	L	Boston, MA	2/19/83	Wilkes-Barre

GOALTENDERS	HT	WT	C	Place of Birth	Date	2004-05 Club
CARON, Sebastian	6-1	170	L	Amqui, Que.	6/25/80	Saguenay
CHIODO, Andy	5-11	192	L	Toronto, Ont.	4/25/83	Wheeling-Wilkes-Barre
FLEURY, Marc-Andre	6-1	175	L	Sorel, Que.	11/28/84	Wilkes-Barre
SABOURIN, Dany	6-2	182	L	Val-d'Or, Que.	9/2/80	Wilkes-Barre-Wheeling
THIBAULT, Jocelyn	5-11	169	L	Montreal, Que.	1/12/75	

In the System and Recently Drafted

FORWARDS	HT	WT	S	Place of Birth	Date	2004-05 Club
ANSHAKOV, Sergei	6-3	179	L	Moscow, USSR	1/13/84	CSKA-Ufa
BARTSCHI, Patrik	6-0	199	R	Bulach, Switz.	8/20/84	Kloten
CROWDER, Tim	6-2	180	R	Victoria, B.C.	10/16/86	South Surrey
GERGEN, Michael	5-10	185	L	Hastings, MN	2/17/87	Shat.-St. Mary's
GIFFORD, Brian	6-1	173	L	Fargo, ND	11/12/85	Indiana
GUTIERREZ, Moises	6-3	201	R	San Diego, CA	7/20/86	Kamloops
HAVELKA, Petr	6-2	185	L	Most, Czech.	3/4/79	Plzen-C. Budejovice
IHNACAK, Brian	5-11	178	R	Toronto, Ont.	4/10/85	Brown U.
ISAKOV, Evgeni	6-1	196	L	Krasnoyarsk, USSR	10/13/84	Saratov-Tyumen
JENSEN, Joe	5-11	180	L	Maple Grove, MN	2/6/83	St. Cloud State
JOHNSON, Nick	6-1	183	R	Calgary, Alta.	12/24/85	Dartmouth
KENNEDY, Tyler	5-10	183	R	Sault Ste. Marie, Ont.	7/15/86	Sault Ste. Marie
MALKIN, Evgeni	6-3	186	L	Magnitogorsk, USSR	7/31/86	Magnitogorsk
MORRISON, Jordan	5-11	167	L	Scarborough, Ont.	6/4/86	Peterborough
MOULSON, Matt	6-1	195	L	North York, Ont.	11/1/83	Cornell
SALMONSSON, Johannes	6-2	183	L	Uppsala, Sweden	2/7/86	Almtuna-Djurgarden
SERTICH, Andrew	6-0	175	L	Coleraine, MN	5/6/83	U. of Minnesota
SIVEK, Michal	6-3	214	L	Nachod, Czech.	1/21/81	Sparta
SKVARIDLO, Tomas	6-1	180	L	Zvolen, Czech.	6/19/81	Zvolen
VITALE, Joe	5-11	205	R	St. Louis, MO	8/20/85	Sioux Falls

DEFENSEMEN						
BOLF, Lukas	6-1	190	L	Vrchlabi, Czech.	2/20/85	Barrie
GOLIGOSKI, Alex	5-11	180	R	Grand Rapids, MN	7/30/85	U. of Minnesota
LEINONEN, Tommi	6-2	191	L	Kajaani, Finland	5/14/87	Karpat Jr.
LETANG, Kristopher	5-11	190	R	Montreal, Que.	4/24/87	Val-d'Or
MALENKYKH, Vladimir	6-1	190	L	Togliatti, USSR	10/1/80	Togliatti
NEMEC, Ondrej	6-1	196	R	Trebic, Czech.	4/18/84	Trebic-Vsetin
PAQUET, Jean-Philippe	6-2	202	L	St-George, Que.	1/7/87	Shawinigan
PELUSO, Chris	5-11	180	L	Wadena, MN	8/21/86	Sioux Falls
SERSEN, Michal	6-1	200	L	Celnica, Czech.	12/28/85	Rimouski

GOALTENDERS	HT	WT	C	Place of Birth	Date	2004-05 Club
BROWN, David	6-0	185	L	Stoney Creek, Ont.	2/11/85	U. of Notre Dame
CRAWFORD-WEST, Brandon	6-0	180	R	San Diego, CA	7/1/82	Miami U.
DUBA, Tomas	6-0	176	L	Prague, Czech.	7/2/81	Plzen
GOEPFERT, Robert	5-10	170	L	Ozone Park, NY	5/9/83	St. Cloud State
LEHTO, Mika	5-11	175	L	Vammala, Finland	4/12/79	Tappara

John LeClair joins Mario Lemieux as former 50-goal scorers playing in Pittsburgh.

Coach

OLCZYK, EDDIE
Coach, Pittsburgh Penguins. Born in Chicago, IL, August 16, 1966.

Craig Patrick named former Penguins forward Eddie Olczyk as the successor to Rick Kehoe behind the Pittsburgh bench on June 11, 2003. Olczyk is the 21st head coach in club history and the 18th different person to hold the position. He is also the fifth former Penguins player to guide the team, joining Ken Schinkel, Lou Angotti, Gene Ubriaco and Kehoe. At the time of his hiring, he had no previous coaching experience.

The Chicago native moved to the bench from the broadcast booth, having spent the three previous seasons as a color commentator for Penguins broadcasts on Fox Sports Net. He also covered the Stanley Cup playoffs for ESPN and NHL Radio. Olczyk moved behind the microphone in 2000 after completing a successful 16-year NHL career. Selected by his hometown Blackhawks third overall in the 1984 draft, "Edzo" went on to record 342 goals and 794 points in 1,031 games with Chicago, Toronto, Winnipeg, the New York Rangers, Los Angeles and Pittsburgh. He topped the 30-goal mark five consecutive seasons (1987 to 1992), netted a single-season high 42 goals with the Maple Leafs in 1987-88 and captured the Stanley Cup as a member of the Rangers in 1994.

Olczyk joined the Penguins at the 1997 trade deadline, coming to Pittsburgh from Los Angeles for Glen Murray. He recorded 33 points (15 goals, 18 assists) in 68 regular season games with the Pens and added three goals in 11 postseason contests.

Coaching Record

Season	Team	Games	Regular Season			Playoffs		
			W	L	T	Games	W	L
2003-04	Pittsburgh (NHL)	82	23	51	8	....	....	....
2004-05	Pittsburgh (NHL)				Season Cancelled			
	NHL Totals	82	23	51	8	....	....	....

General Managers' History

Jack Riley, 1967-68 to 1969-70; Red Kelly, 1970-71; Red Kelly and Jack Riley, 1971-72; Jack Riley, 1972-73; Jack Riley and Jack Button, 1973-74; Jack Button, 1974-75; Wren Blair, 1975-76; Wren Blair and Baz Bastien, 1976-77; Baz Bastien, 1977-78 to 1982-83; Eddie Johnston, 1983-84 to 1987-88; Tony Esposito, 1988-89; Tony Esposito and Craig Patrick, 1989-90; Craig Patrick, 1990-91 to date.

Coaching History

Red Sullivan, 1967-68, 1968-69; Red Kelly, 1969-70 to 1971-72; Red Kelly and Ken Schinkel, 1972-73; Ken Schinkel and Marc Boileau, 1973-74; Marc Boileau, 1974-75; Marc Boileau and Ken Schinkel, 1975-76; Ken Schinkel, 1976-77; Johnny Wilson, 1977-78 to 1979-80; Eddie Johnston, 1980-81 to 1982-83; Lou Angotti, 1983-84; Bob Berry, 1984-85 to 1986-87; Pierre Creamer, 1987-88; Gene Ubriaco, 1988-89; Gene Ubriaco and Craig Patrick, 1989-90; Bob Johnson, 1990-91, 1991-92; Scotty Bowman, 1991-92, 1992-93; Eddie Johnston, 1993-94 to 1995-96; Eddie Johnston and Craig Patrick, 1996-97; Kevin Constantine, 1997-98, 1998-99; Kevin Constantine and Herb Brooks, 1999-2000; Ivan Hlinka, 2000-01; Ivan Hlinka and Rick Kehoe, 2001-02; Rick Kehoe, 2002-03; Eddie Olczyk, 2003-04 to date.

Club Records

Team

(Figures in brackets for season records are games played; records for fewest points, wins, ties, losses, goals, goals against are for 70 or more games)

Most Points	119	1992-93 (84)
Most Wins	56	1992-93 (84)
Most Ties	20	1970-71 (78)
Most Losses	58	1983-84 (80)
Most Goals	367	1992-93 (84)
Most Goals Against	394	1982-83 (80)
Fewest Points	38	1983-84 (80)
Fewest Wins	16	1983-84 (80)
Fewest Ties	4	1995-96 (82)
Fewest Losses	21	1992-93 (84)
Fewest Goals	182	1969-70 (76)
Fewest Goals Against	188	1997-98 (82)

Longest Winning Streak

Overall	*17	Mar. 9-Apr. 10/93
Home	11	Jan. 5-Mar. 7/91
Away	7	Mar. 14-Apr. 9/93

Longest Undefeated Streak

Overall	18	Mar. 9-Apr. 14/93 (17 wins, 1 tie)
Home	20	Nov. 30/74-Feb. 22/75 (12 wins, 8 ties)
Away	8	Mar. 14-Apr. 14/93 (7 wins, 1 tie)

Longest Losing Streak

Overall	18	Jan. 13-Feb. 22/04
Home	14	Dec. 31/03-Feb. 22/04
Away	18	Dec. 23/82-Mar. 4/83

Longest Winless Streak

Overall	18	Jan. 2-Feb. 10/83 (17 losses, 1 tie), Jan. 13-Feb. 22/04 (18 losses)
Home	16	Dec. 31/03-Mar. 4/04 (15 losses, 1 tie)
Away	18	Oct. 25/70-Jan. 14/71 (11 losses, 7 ties), Dec. 23/82-Mar. 4/83 (18 losses)

Most Shutouts, Season	9	1998-99 (82)
Most PIM, Season	2,670	1988-89 (80)
Most Goals, Game	12	Mar. 15/75 (Wsh. 1 at Pit. 12), Dec. 26/91 (Tor. 1 at Pit. 12)

Individual

Most Seasons	16	Mario Lemieux
Most Games	889	Mario Lemieux
Most Goals, Career	683	Mario Lemieux
Most Assists, Career	1,018	Mario Lemieux
Most Points, Career	1,701	Mario Lemieux (683G, 1,018A)
Most PIM, Career	1,023	Kevin Stevens
Most Shutouts, Career	22	Tom Barrasso

Longest Consecutive Games Streak ... 320 Ron Schock (Oct. 24/73-Apr. 3/77)

Most Goals, Season	85	Mario Lemieux (1988-89)
Most Assists, Season	114	Mario Lemieux (1988-89)
Most Points, Season	199	Mario Lemieux (1988-89; 85G, 114A)
Most PIM, Season	409	Paul Baxter (1981-82)
Most Points, Defenseman, Season	113	Paul Coffey (1988-89; 30G, 83A)
Most Points, Center, Season	199	Mario Lemieux (1988-89; 85G, 114A)
Most Points, Right Wing, Season	*149	Jaromir Jagr (1995-96; 62G, 87A)
Most Points, Left Wing, Season	123	Kevin Stevens (1991-92; 54G, 69A)
Most Points, Rookie, Season	100	Mario Lemieux (1984-85; 43G, 57A)
Most Shutouts, Season	7	Tom Barrasso (1997-98)
Most Goals, Game	5	Mario Lemieux (Three times)
Most Assists, Game	6	Ron Stackhouse (Mar. 8/75), Greg Malone (Nov. 28/79), Mario Lemieux (Three times)
Most Points, Game	8	Mario Lemieux (Oct. 15/88; 2G, 6A, Dec. 31/88; 5G, 3A)

* NHL Record.

Captains' History

Ab McDonald, 1967-68; no captain, 1968-69 to 1972-73; Ron Schock, 1973-74 to 1976-77; Jean Pronovost, 1977-78; Orest Kindrachuk, 1978-79 to 1980-81; Randy Carlyle, 1981-82 to 1983-84; Mike Bullard, 1984-85, 1985-86; Mike Bullard and Terry Ruskowski, 1986-87; Dan Frawley and Mario Lemieux, 1987-88; Mario Lemieux, 1988-89 to 1993-94; Ron Francis, 1994-95; Mario Lemieux, 1995-96, 1996-97; Ron Francis, 1997-98; Jaromir Jagr, 1998-99 to 2000-01; Mario Lemieux, 2001-02 to date.

Retired Numbers

21	Michel Brière	1969-1970

All-time Record vs. Other Clubs

Regular Season

	At Home								On Road								Total							
	GP	W	L	T	OL	GF	GA	PTS	GP	W	L	T	OL	GF	GA	PTS	GP	W	L	T	OL	GF	GA	PTS
Anaheim	9	5	2	0	0	29	27	12	8	3	4	0	1	24	29	7	17	8	6	2	1	53	56	19
Atlanta	10	8	1	0	1	39	25	17	10	9	1	0	0	39	24	18	20	17	2	0	1	78	49	35
Boston	80	32	33	15	0	273	286	79	78	16	56	6	0	218	343	38	158	48	89	21	0	491	629	117
Buffalo	71	36	17	18	0	266	217	90	71	20	34	17	0	190	274	57	142	56	51	35	0	456	491	147
Calgary	44	24	10	10	0	167	133	58	46	11	27	8	0	140	204	30	90	35	37	18	0	307	337	88
Carolina	46	23	17	6	0	185	170	52	48	21	21	5	1	177	178	48	94	44	38	11	1	362	348	100
Chicago	59	29	23	7	0	210	190	65	60	11	39	10	0	157	236	32	119	40	62	17	0	367	426	97
Colorado	37	15	17	5	0	145	152	35	32	13	16	2	1	122	142	29	69	28	33	7	1	267	294	64
Columbus	3	2	1	0	0	12	9	4	3	2	1	0	0	9	10	4	6	4	2	0	0	21	19	8
Dallas	63	38	19	6	0	236	178	82	64	21	36	6	1	213	246	49	127	59	55	12	1	449	424	131
Detroit	65	44	17	4	0	281	195	92	65	13	39	12	1	178	253	39	130	57	56	16	1	459	448	131
Edmonton	30	15	12	3	0	117	127	33	30	7	22	1	0	98	148	15	60	22	34	4	0	215	275	48
Florida	23	12	8	3	0	72	68	27	22	8	11	1	2	50	64	19	45	20	19	4	2	122	132	46
Los Angeles	73	38	25	10	0	265	233	86	69	17	43	8	1	183	265	43	142	55	68	18	1	448	498	129
Minnesota	3	1	2	0	0	6	12	2	3	0	2	1	0	5	9	1	6	1	4	1	0	11	21	3
Montreal	82	28	40	13	1	238	290	70	82	10	60	10	2	203	383	32	164	38	100	23	3	441	673	102
Nashville	5	1	2	2	0	14	17	4	6	2	4	0	0	10	21	4	11	3	6	2	0	24	38	8
New Jersey	79	40	34	4	1	289	269	85	81	29	38	13	1	269	295	72	160	69	72	17	2	558	564	157
NY Islanders	88	40	34	14	0	329	310	94	86	32	46	8	0	285	348	72	174	72	80	22	0	614	658	166
NY Rangers	100	43	43	14	0	359	365	100	101	41	51	9	0	346	393	91	201	84	94	23	0	705	758	191
Ottawa	27	17	6	4	0	97	64	38	27	14	8	3	2	87	70	33	54	31	14	9	0	184	134	71
Philadelphia	106	46	38	22	0	373	346	114	106	17	78	8	3	257	446	45	212	63	116	30	3	630	792	159
Phoenix	30	20	10	0	0	120	86	40	31	14	14	3	0	107	116	31	61	34	24	3	0	227	202	71
St. Louis	64	32	20	12	0	238	190	76	64	15	41	6	2	171	247	38	128	47	61	18	2	409	437	114
San Jose	9	4	4	1	0	41	32	9	13	6	5	2	0	54	34	14	22	10	9	3	0	95	66	23
Tampa Bay	23	15	5	3	0	90	59	33	23	9	11	2	1	60	75	21	46	24	16	5	1	150	134	54
Toronto	69	36	27	6	0	278	228	78	67	24	31	11	1	213	264	60	136	60	58	17	1	491	492	138
Vancouver	50	33	10	7	0	227	171	73	50	23	22	4	1	187	180	51	100	56	32	11	1	414	351	124
Washington	83	47	29	7	0	322	261	101	86	32	44	9	1	312	358	74	169	79	73	16	1	634	619	175
Defunct Clubs	35	22	6	7	0	148	93	51	34	13	10	11	0	108	101	37	69	35	16	18	0	256	194	88
Totals	**1466**	**746**	**512**	**205**	**3**	**5466**	**4803**	**1700**	**1466**	**453**	**815**	**178**	**20**	**4472**	**5756**	**1104**	**2932**	**1199**	**1327**	**383**	**23**	**9938**	**10559**	**2804**

Playoffs

	Series	W	L	GP	W	L	T	GF	GA	Last Mtg.
Boston	4	2	2	19	10	9	0	67	62	1992
Buffalo	2	2	0	10	6	4	0	26	26	2001
Chicago	2	1	1	8	4	4	0	23	24	1992
Dallas	1	1	0	6	4	2	0	28	16	1991
Florida	1	0	1	7	3	4	0	15	20	1996
Montreal	1	0	1	6	2	4	0	15	18	1998
New Jersey	5	3	2	29	14	15	0	80	86	2001
NY Islanders	3	0	3	19	8	11	0	58	67	1993
NY Rangers	3	3	0	15	12	3	0	64	45	1996
Philadelphia	3	0	3	18	6	12	0	51	66	2000
St. Louis	3	1	2	13	6	7	0	40	45	1981
Toronto	3	0	3	12	4	8	0	27	39	1999
Washington	7	6	1	42	26	16	0	137	121	2001
Defunct Clubs	1	1	0	4	4	0	0	13	6	
Totals	**39**	**20**	**19**	**208**	**109**	**99**	**0**	**644**	**641**	

Playoff Results 2005-2000

Year	Round	Opponent	Result	GF	GA
2001	CF	New Jersey	L 1-4	7	17
	CSF	Buffalo	W 4-3	17	13
	CQF	Washington	W 4-2	14	10
2000	CSF	Philadelphia	L 2-4	14	15
	CQF	Washington	W 4-1	17	8

Abbreviations: Round: F – Final; **CF** – conference final; **CSF** – conference semi-final; **CQF** – conference quarter-final; **DF** – division final; **PRE** – preliminary round.

Calgary totals include Atlanta Flames, 1972-73 to 1979-80.
Colorado totals include Quebec, 1979-80 to 1994-95.
New Jersey totals include Kansas City, 1974-75 to 1975-76, and Colorado Rockies, 1976-77 to 1981-82.
Phoenix totals include Winnipeg, 1979-80 to 1995-96.
Carolina totals include Hartford, 1979-80 to 1996-97.
Dallas totals include Minnesota North Stars, 1967-68 to 1992-93.

Key Off-Season Signings/Acquisitions

2004

June 1 • Signed 2002 1st-round pick (5th overall), D **Ryan Whitney**.

June 26 • Selected C **Evgeni Malkin** with the second overall pick in the 2004 Entry Draft.

July 9 • Signed RW **Mark Recchi**.

12 • Signed RW **Ryan Vandenbussche**.

13 • Re-signed D **Ric Jackman**.

15 • Re-signed Cs **Rico Fata** and **Lasse Pirjeta**.

Sept. 2 • Re-signed LW **Tomas Surovy**.

2005

July 22 • Won the NHL Draft Drawing, earning the right to select first overall in the 2005 Entry Draft.

30 • Selected C **Sidney Crosby** (Rimouski, QMJHL) with the first overall pick in the 2005 Entry Draft.

Aug. 3 • Signed D **Sergei Gonchar**.

4 • Signed RW **Andre Roy**.

8 • Signed RW **Zigmund Palffy**.

10 • Obtained G **Jocelyn Thibault** from Chicago for a 2006 4th-round pick.

10 • Re-signed C **Kris Beech**.

15 • Signed LW **John LeClair** and D **Steve Poapst**.

15 • Re-signed D **Josef Melichar**.

16 • Re-signed RW **Konstantin Koltsov**.

27 • D **Dick Tarnstrom** awarded one-year contract in arbitration.

Sept. 1 • Re-signed LW **Ryan Malone**.

2 • Signed D **Lyle Odelein**.

Entry Draft
Selections 2005-1991

2005
Pick
1 Sidney Crosby
61 Michael Gergen
62 Kristopher Letang
125 Tommi Leinonen
126 Tim Crowder
194 Jean-Philippe Paquet
195 Joe Vitale

2004
Pick
2 Evgeni Malkin
31 Johannes Salmonsson
61 Alex Goligoski
67 Nick Johnson
85 Brian Gifford
99 Tyler Kennedy
130 Michal Sersen
164 Moises Gutierrez
194 Chris Peluso
222 Jordan Morrison
228 David Brown
259 Brian Ihnacak

2003
Pick
1 Marc-Andre Fleury
32 Ryan Stone
70 Jonathan Filewich
73 Daniel Carcillo
121 Paul Bissonnette
161 Evgeni Isakov
169 Lukas Bolf
199 Andy Chiodo
229 Stephen Dixon
232 Joe Jensen
263 Matt Moulson

2002
Pick
5 Ryan Whitney
35 Ondrej Nemec
69 Erik Christensen
101 Daniel Fernholm
136 Andrew Sertich
137 Cam Paddock
171 Robert Goepfert
202 Patrik Bartschi
234 Maxime Talbot
239 Ryan Lannon
265 Dwight Labrosse

2001
Pick
21 Colby Armstrong
54 Noah Welch
86 Drew Fata
96 Alexandre Rouleau
120 Tomas Surovy
131 Ben Eaves
156 Andy Schneider
217 Tomas Duba
250 Brandon Crawford-West

2000
Pick
18 Brooks Orpik
52 Shane Endicott
84 Peter Hamerlik
124 Michel Ouellet
146 David Koci
185 Patrick Foley
216 Jim Abbott
248 Steve Crampton
273 Roman Simicek
280 Nick Boucher

1999
Pick
18 Konstantin Koltsov
51 Matt Murley
57 Jeremy Van Hoof
86 Sebastian Caron
115 Ryan Malone
144 Tomas Skvaridlo
157 Vladimir Malenkykh
176 Doug Meyer
204 Tom Kostopoulos
233 Darcy Robinson
261 Andrew McPherson

1998
Pick
23 Milan Kraft
54 Alexander Zevakhin
80 David Cameron
110 Scott Myers
134 Rob Scuderi
169 Jan Fadrny
196 Joel Scherban
224 Mika Lehto
244 Toby Petersen
254 Matt Hussey

1997
Pick
17 Robert Dome
44 Brian Gaffaney
71 Josef Melichar
97 Alexandre Mathieu
124 Harlan Pratt
152 Petr Havelka
179 Mark Moore
208 Andrew Ference
234 Eric Lind

1996
Pick
23 Craig Hillier
28 Pavel Skrbek
72 Boyd Kane
77 Boris Protsenko
105 Michal Rozsival
150 Peter Bergman
186 Eric Meloche
238 Timo Seikkula

1995
Pick
24 Aleksey Morozov
76 Jean-Sebastien Aubin
102 Oleg Belov
128 Jan Hrdina
154 Alexei Kolkunov
180 Derrick Pyke
206 Sergei Voronov
232 Frank Ivankovic

1994
Pick
24 Chris Wells
50 Richard Park
57 Sven Butenschon
73 Greg Crozier
76 Alexei Krivchenkov
102 Tom O'Connor
128 Clint Johnson
154 Valentin Morozov
161 Serge Aubin
180 Drew Palmer
206 Boris Zelenko
232 Jason Godbout
258 Mikhail Kazakevich
284 Brian Leitza

1993
Pick
26 Stefan Bergkvist
52 Domenic Pittis
62 Dave Roche
104 Jonas Andersson-Junkka
130 Chris Kelleher
156 Patrick Lalime
182 Sean Selmser
208 Larry McMorran
234 Timothy Harberts
260 Leonid Toropchenko
286 Hans Jonsson

1992
Pick
19 Martin Straka
43 Marc Hussey
67 Travis Thiessen
91 Todd Klassen
115 Philippe DeRouville
139 Artem Kopot
163 Jan Alinc
187 Fran Bussey
211 Brian Bonin
235 Brian Callahan

1991
Pick
16 Markus Naslund
38 Rusty Fitzgerald
60 Shane Peacock
82 Joe Tamminen
104 Robert Melanson
126 Brian Clifford
148 Ed Patterson
170 Peter McLaughlin
192 Jeff Lembke
214 Chris Tok
236 Paul Dyck
258 Pasi Huura

Vice President and General Manager

PATRICK, CRAIG
Executive Vice President/General Manager, Pittsburgh Penguins.
Born in Detroit, MI, May 20, 1946.

Known for his calm and patient management style, Craig Patrick has led the Penguins to two Stanley Cup championships, one Presidents' Trophy title and five division championships since taking over as general manager on December 5, 1989. In 2000, he and Mario Lemieux were recipients of the Lester Patrick Trophy for their contributions to hockey in the United States. He was elected to the Hockey Hall of Fame in 2001.

A member of one of hockey's most famous families — including grandfather Lester, father Lynn and uncle Muzz — Patrick played collegiate hockey at the University of Denver and captained the Pioneers to the NCAA championship in 1969. He played eight NHL seasons with four different teams, registering 72 goals and 163 points in 401 games before retiring in 1979. He made the transition to management and coaching when he landed the dual role of assistant coach and assistant g.m. of the 1980 U.S. Olympic team that won the gold medal at Lake Placid.

Patrick joined the New York Rangers organization as director of operations in 1980 and became the youngest general manager in club history one year later. He served in that capacity through the 1985-86 season, leading his team to the playoffs every year.

Prior to joining the Penguins, Patrick spent two years as director of athletics and recreation at the University of Denver.

NHL Coaching Record

Season	Team	Games	Regular Season			Games	Playoffs	
			W	L	T		W	L
1980-81	NY Rangers	60	26	23	11	14	7	7
1984-85	NY Rangers	35	11	22	2	3	0	3
1989-90	Pittsburgh	54	22	26	6	....	....	....
1996-97	Pittsburgh	20	7	10	3	5	1	4
	NHL Totals	**169**	**66**	**81**	**22**	**22**	**8**	**14**

Club Directory

Mellon Arena

Pittsburgh Penguins
Mellon Arena
66 Mario Lemieux Place
Pittsburgh, PA 15219
Phone **412/642-1300**
FAX 412/642-1859
Media Relations FAX 412/642-1322
Capacity: 16,940

Ownership . . . . Mario Lemieux and Ron Burkle and the The Lemieux Group limited partnership

Executive Operations
Chairman/CEO . . . . Mario Lemieux
President . . . . Ken Sawyer
Executive VP/General Manager . . . . Craig Patrick
Vice President, Business & Legal Affairs . . . . Ted Black
Vice President & Controller . . . . Kevin Hart
Vice President, Sales & Marketing . . . . David Soltesz
Vice President, Communications . . . . Tom McMillan
Executive Assistant . . . . Fay McNamara
Receptionist . . . . Kelly Hart
Mailroom Supervisor . . . . Brett Hart

Hockey Operations
Assistant General Manager . . . . Ed Johnston
Head Coach . . . . Eddie Olczyk
Assistant Coaches . . . . Randy Hillier, Joe Mullen
Goaltending Coach . . . . Shane Clifford
Head Scout . . . . Greg Malone
Scouts . . . . Chuck Grillo, Mark Kelley, Gilles Meloche, Neil Shea
Pro Scouts . . . . Rick Kehoe, Glenn Patrick
Head Coach, Wilkes-Barre/Scranton (AHL) . . . . . . Michel Therrien
Assistant Coach, Wilkes-Barre/Scranton (AHL) . . . . Mike Yeo
Strength & Conditioning Coach . . . . John Welday
Equipment Manager . . . . Steve Latin
Assistant Equipment Manager . . . . Paul Flati
Assistant Equipment Manager . . . . Paul DeFazio
Team Physician . . . . Dr. Charles Burke
Head Athletic Trainer . . . . Mark Mortland
Assistant Athletic Trainer . . . . Scott Johnson
Massage Therapist . . . . Dave Sampson
Executive Assistant . . . . Tracey Botsford
Video Coordinator . . . . Paul Fink

Communications
Director of Media Relations . . . . Keith Wehner
Manager of Media Relations . . . . Todd Lepovsky
Manager of Media Relations/Publications . . . . . . Joe Sager
Director of New Media . . . . Jeremy Zimmer
Director of Public/Community Relations . . . . Cindy Himes
Exec. Producer, Penguins Radio Network . . . . Ray Walker
Radio Broadcasters . . . . Paul Steigerwald, Phil Bourque
Director of Amateur Hockey . . . . Mark Shuttleworth
Director of Alumni Relations . . . . Jack Riley

Finance
Accounts Payable . . . . Tawni Love
Senior Accountant . . . . Troy Ussak
Payroll Manager . . . . Andrea Winschel

Ticketing
Senior Director of Ticketing . . . . James Santilli
Director of Ticket Sales and Services . . . . Chad Slencak
Director of Premium & Group Ticket Sales . . . . . . Mike Guiffre
Director of Database Marketing . . . . Jill Shipley
Director of Marketing . . . . Ross Miller
Database Manager . . . . Erin Exley
Sales Account Executives . . . . George Birman, Bonnie Golinski, George Murphy, Chuck Pukansky, David Schleter
Customer Service Representatives . . . . Kathy Davis, Cori Shrader
Inside Sales Representatives . . . . Beth Folcik, Nicole Kyslinger, Danny Smith
Group Sales Account Executive . . . . Mike Zatchey
Box Office Manager . . . . Carol Coulson
Box Office Assistants . . . . Kelly Gabany, Jason Onufer

Corporate Sales
Senior Director of Corporate Sales . . . . Kimberly Bogesdorfer
Directors of Corporate Sales . . . . Carl D'Alicandro, Mark DeAndrea, Brian Magness
Creative Director . . . . Barb Pilarski
Senior Account Service Manager . . . . Lori Weinland
Account Service Manager . . . . Jamie Greenwald
Account Service Coordinator . . . . Ronald Hay
Corporate Sales Liason . . . . Pierre Larouche

Game Night Entertainment
Director of Game Operations & Video Production . . Chirs Devivo
Game Night Producer . . . . Matt Bettinger
Game Night Manager . . . . James Archer
Manager of Arts & Graphics . . . . Dori Minnis
Editors . . . . Steve Finerty, Billy Wareham

General Information
Home Ice . . . . Mellon Arena
Dimensions of Rink . . . . 200 feet by 85 feet
Seating Capacity 16,940
Team Colors . . . . Black, Gold and White
TV Station . . . . Fox Sports Net Pittsburgh
TV Announcers . . . . Mike Lange, Bob Errey
Radio Announcers . . . . Paul Steigerwald, Phil Bourque
Flagship Radio Station . . . . 3WS (94.5FM), Fox Sports Radio 970AM
Minor League Affiliates . . . . Wilkes-Barre/Scranton Penguins (AHL)
Wheeling Nailers (ECHL)

St. Louis Blues

2005-06 Schedule

Oct.	Wed.	5	at Detroit
	Thu.	6	Detroit
	Sat.	8	San Jose
	Tue.	11	Chicago
	Sat.	15	Nashville
	Wed.	19	Anaheim
	Thu.	20	at Nashville
	Sat.	22	Minnesota
	Tue.	25	at Phoenix
	Fri.	28	at Anaheim
	Sat.	29	at Los Angeles
Nov.	Wed.	2	Chicago
	Fri.	4	Edmonton
	Sun.	6	Detroit
	Wed.	9	at Columbus
	Thu.	10	Chicago
	Sat.	12	at Nashville
	Wed.	16	at Columbus
	Sat.	19	at Detroit
	Tue.	22	Los Angeles
	Fri.	25	at Minnesota*
	Sat.	26	Columbus
Dec.	Thu.	1	Columbus
	Tue.	6	NY Islanders
	Thu.	8	at Tampa Bay
	Sat.	10	NY Rangers
	Tue.	13	Pittsburgh
	Fri.	16	at Chicago
	Sat.	17	Philadelphia
	Tue.	20	at Phoenix
	Wed.	21	at Anaheim
	Fri.	23	at San Jose
	Mon.	26	Dallas
	Wed.	28	at Chicago
	Thu.	29	at Dallas
	Sat.	31	Anaheim*
Jan.	Mon.	2	Vancouver
	Wed.	4	Nashville
	Thu.	5	at Detroit
	Mon.	9	at Colorado
	Thu.	12	at Florida
	Fri.	13	at Atlanta
	Sun.	15	at Carolina*
	Tue.	17	New Jersey
	Thu.	19	at Washington
	Fri.	20	at Columbus
	Mon.	23	Vancouver
	Wed.	25	at Dallas
	Thu.	26	Phoenix
	Mon.	30	Calgary
Feb.	Wed.	1	at Detroit
	Thu.	2	Chicago
	Sat.	4	Dallas*
	Wed.	8	at Vancouver
	Fri.	10	at Calgary
	Sun.	12	at Edmonton*
Mar.	Wed.	1	at Edmonton
	Thu.	2	at Calgary
	Sun.	5	at Vancouver
	Tue.	7	Colorado
	Fri.	10	Minnesota
	Sat.	11	Los Angeles
	Mon.	13	Columbus
	Thu.	16	at San Jose
	Sat.	18	at Los Angeles
	Mon.	20	at Nashville
	Tue.	21	San Jose
	Thu.	23	Calgary
	Sat.	25	Colorado
	Mon.	27	Detroit
	Wed.	29	at Chicago
	Fri.	31	Columbus
Apr.	Sat.	1	at Nashville
	Tue.	4	at Minnesota
	Thu.	6	Nashville
	Sat.	8	at Colorado*
	Sun.	9	Edmonton
	Tue.	11	Nashville
	Thu.	13	at Columbus
	Sat.	15	Detroit*
	Sun.	16	Phoenix
	Tue.	18	at Chicago

* Denotes afternoon game.

Franchise date: June 5, 1967

WESTERN NHL CONFERENCE

CENTRAL DIVISION

39th NHL Season

One of the NHL's top playmakers, Doug Weight has had at least 50 assists seven times in 13 full NHL seasons.

Year-by-Year Record

Season	GP	Home W	L	T	OL	Road W	L	T	OL	Overall W	L	T	OL	GF	GA	Pts.	Finished	Playoff Result
2004-05	.....																	
2003-04	82	23	11	7	0	16	19	4	2	39	30	11	2	191	198	91	2nd, Central Div.	Lost Conf. Quarter-Final
2002-03	82	23	11	4	3	18	13	7	3	41	24	11	6	253	222	99	2nd, Central Div.	Lost Conf. Quarter-Final
2001-02	82	27	12	1	1	16	15	7	3	43	27	8	4	227	188	98	2nd, Central Div.	Lost Conf. Semi-Final
2000-01	82	28	5	5	3	15	17	7	2	43	22	12	5	249	195	103	2nd, Central Div.	Lost Conf. Championship
1999-2000	82	24	9	7	1	27	10	4	0	51	19	11	1	248	165	114	1st, Central Div.	Lost Conf. Quarter-Final
1998-99	82	18	17	6	....	19	15	7	....	37	32	13	....	237	209	87	2nd, Central Div.	Lost Conf. Semi-Final
1997-98	82	26	10	5	....	19	19	3	....	45	29	8	....	256	204	98	3rd, Central Div.	Lost Conf. Semi-Final
1996-97	82	17	20	4	....	19	15	7	....	36	35	11	....	236	239	83	4th, Central Div.	Lost Conf. Quarter-Final
1995-96	82	15	17	9	....	17	17	7	....	32	34	16	....	219	248	80	4th, Central Div.	Lost Conf. Semi-Final
1994-95	48	16	6	2	....	12	9	3	....	28	15	5	....	178	135	61	2nd, Central Div.	Lost Conf. Quarter-Final
1993-94	84	23	11	8	....	17	22	3	....	40	33	11	....	270	283	91	4th, Central Div.	Lost Conf. Quarter-Final
1992-93	84	22	13	7	....	15	23	4	....	37	36	11	....	282	278	85	4th, Norris Div.	Lost Div. Final
1991-92	80	25	12	3	....	11	21	8	....	36	33	11	....	279	266	83	3rd, Norris Div.	Lost Div. Semi-Final
1990-91	80	24	9	7	....	23	13	4	....	47	22	11	....	310	250	105	2nd, Norris Div.	Lost Div. Final
1989-90	80	20	15	5	....	17	19	4	....	37	34	9	....	295	279	83	2nd, Norris Div.	Lost Div. Final
1988-89	80	22	11	7	....	11	24	5	....	33	35	12	....	275	285	78	2nd, Norris Div.	Lost Div. Final
1987-88	80	18	17	5	....	16	21	3	....	34	38	8	....	278	294	76	2nd, Norris Div.	Lost Div. Final
1986-87	80	21	12	7	....	11	21	8	....	32	33	15	....	281	293	79	1st, Norris Div.	Lost Div. Semi-Final
1985-86	80	23	11	6	....	14	23	3	....	37	34	9	....	302	291	83	3rd, Norris Div.	Lost Conf. Championship
1984-85	80	21	12	7	....	16	19	5	....	37	31	12	....	299	288	86	1st, Norris Div.	Lost Div. Semi-Final
1983-84	80	23	14	3	....	9	27	4	....	32	41	7	....	293	316	71	2nd, Norris Div.	Lost Div. Final
1982-83	80	16	16	8	....	9	24	7	....	25	40	15	....	285	316	65	4th, Norris Div.	Lost Div. Semi-Final
1981-82	80	22	14	4	....	10	26	4	....	32	40	8	....	315	349	72	3rd, Norris Div.	Lost Div. Final
1980-81	80	29	7	4	....	16	11	13	....	45	18	17	....	352	281	107	1st, Smythe Div.	Lost Quarter-Final
1979-80	80	20	13	7	....	14	21	5	....	34	34	12	....	266	278	80	2nd, Smythe Div.	Lost Prelim. Round
1978-79	80	14	20	6	....	4	30	6	....	18	50	12	....	249	348	48	3rd, Smythe Div.	Out of Playoffs
1977-78	80	12	20	8	....	8	27	5	....	20	47	13	....	195	304	53	4th, Smythe Div.	Out of Playoffs
1976-77	80	22	13	5	....	10	26	4	....	32	39	9	....	239	276	73	1st, Smythe Div.	Lost Quarter-Final
1975-76	80	20	12	8	....	9	25	6	....	29	37	14	....	249	290	72	3rd, Smythe Div.	Lost Prelim. Round
1974-75	80	23	13	4	....	12	18	10	....	35	31	14	....	269	267	84	2nd, Smythe Div.	Lost Prelim. Round
1973-74	78	16	16	7	....	10	24	5	....	26	40	12	....	206	248	64	6th, West Div.	Out of Playoffs
1972-73	78	21	11	7	....	11	23	5	....	32	34	12	....	233	251	76	4th, West Div.	Lost Quarter-Final
1971-72	78	17	17	5	....	11	22	6	....	28	39	11	....	208	247	67	3rd, West Div.	Lost Semi-Final
1970-71	78	23	7	9	....	11	18	10	....	34	25	19	....	223	208	87	2nd, West Div.	Lost Quarter-Final
1969-70	76	24	9	5	....	13	18	7	....	37	27	12	....	224	179	86	1st, West Div.	Lost Final
1968-69	76	21	8	9	....	16	17	5	....	37	25	14	....	204	157	88	1st, West Div.	Lost Final
1967-68	74	18	12	7	....	9	19	9	....	27	31	16	....	177	191	70	3rd, West Div.	Lost Final

2005-06 Player Personnel

FORWARDS	HT	WT	S	Place of Birth	Date	2004-05 Club
BOGUNIECKI, Eric	5-8	192	R	New Haven, CT	5/6/75	Langenthal-Worcester
CAJANEK, Petr	5-11	191	L	Gottwaldov, Czech.	8/18/75	Zlin
DISALVATORE, Jon	6-1	200	R	Bangor, ME	3/30/81	Worcester
DOWNEY, Aaron	6-1	220	R	Shelburne, Ont.	8/27/74	
DRAKE, Dallas	6-1	195	L	Trail, B.C.	2/4/69	
EVANS, Blake	6-1	210	L	Smiley, Sask.	7/2/80	Worcester
GLUMAC, Mike	6-2	205	R	Niagara Falls, Ont.	4/5/80	Worcester
HEMINGWAY, Colin	6-0	194	R	Surrey, B.C.	8/12/80	Worcester-Peoria
HOGGAN, Jeff	6-0	180	L	Hope, B.C.	2/1/78	Worcester
JOHNSON, Ryan	6-1	205	L	Thunder Bay, Ont.	6/14/76	Missouri
LOW, Reed	6-4	227	R	Moose Jaw, Sask.	6/21/76	
MAYERS, Jamal	6-1	212	R	Toronto, Ont.	10/24/74	Hammarby-Missouri
McAMMOND, Dean	5-11	200	L	Grand Cache, Alta.	6/15/73	Albany
McCLEMENT, Jay	6-1	199	L	Kingston, Ont.	3/2/83	Worcester
RYCROFT, Mark	5-11	192	R	Penticton, B.C.	7/12/78	Briancon
SEJNA, Peter	5-9	198	L	Liptovsky Mikulas, Czech.	10/5/79	Worcester
SILLINGER, Mike	5-11	196	R	Regina, Sask.	6/29/71	
TKACHUK, Keith	6-2	231	L	Melrose, MA	3/28/72	
WEIGHT, Doug	5-11	200	L	Warren, MI	1/21/71	Frankfurt
WHITFIELD, Trent	5-11	204	L	Estevan, Sask.	6/17/77	Portland (AHL)

DEFENSEMEN						
BACKMAN, Christian	6-3	208	L	Alingsas, Sweden	4/28/80	Frolunda
BREWER, Eric	6-3	225	L	Vernon, B.C.	4/17/79	
JACKMAN, Barret	6-0	209	L	Trail, B.C.	3/5/81	Missouri
LYNCH, Doug	6-3	214	L	North Vancouver, B.C.	4/4/83	Edmonton (AHL)
MacKENZIE, Aaron	6-0	193	L	Terrace Bay, Ont.	3/7/81	Worcester
ROACH, Andy	5-11	181	R	Mattawan, MI	8/22/73	Lausanne
SALVADOR, Bryce	6-2	215	L	Brandon, Man.	2/11/76	Missouri
STUART, Mike	6-0	200	R	Rochester, MN	8/31/80	Worcester
WALKER, Matt	6-3	227	R	Beaverlodge, Alta.	4/7/80	Worcester
WEINRICH, Eric	6-1	207	L	Roanoke, VA	12/19/66	Villacher SV
WOYWITKA, Jeff	6-2	209	L	Vermilion, Alta.	9/1/83	Edmonton (AHL)

GOALTENDERS	HT	WT	C	Place of Birth	Date	2004-05 Club
BACASHIHUA, Jason	5-11	175	L	Garden City, MI	9/20/82	Worcester
DIVIS, Reinhard	6-0	200	L	Vienna, Austria	7/4/75	Villacher SV
LALIME, Patrick	6-2	191	L	St-Bonaventure, Que.	7/7/74	
SANFORD, Curtis	5-10	187	L	Owen Sound, Ont.	10/5/79	Worcester

In the System and Recently Drafted

FORWARDS	HT	WT	S	Place of Birth	Date	2004-05 Club
AALTONEN, Juhamatti	5-11	163	R	Ii, Finland	6/4/85	Karpat
ALEXANDROV, Viktor	5-11	183	L	Ust-Kamenogorsk, USSR	12/28/85	Novokuznetsk
BACKES, David	6-2	200	R	Blaine, MN	5/1/84	Minnesota State
BIRNER, Michal	6-0	183	L	Litomerice, Czech.	3/2/86	Barrie-Saginaw
BLACK, Greg	6-2	193	R	Surrey, B.C.	5/13/82	
BOUTIN, Jonathan Michel	6-2	187	R	La Pocatiere, Que.	10/21/84	Shawinigan
BROOKS, Brendan	5-10	185	R	St. Catherines, Ont.	11/26/78	Worcester
COLLINS, Brian	6-0	195	R	Shrewsbury, MA	10/13/80	Worcester-Pee Dee-Johnstown
DRAZENOVIC, Nicholas	6-0	172	L	Prince George, B.C.	1/14/87	Prince George
FREDRIKSSON, David	6-2	214	L	Jonkoping, Sweden	10/4/85	HV 71-Morrum
JOHNSON, Jonas	6-2	185	L	Gavle, Sweden	3/23/70	Frolunda
KING, D.J.	6-2	221	L	Meadow Lake, Sask.	1/27/84	Worcester
LEMTYUGOV, Nikolai	6-0	183	L	Miass, USSR	1/15/86	CSKA
MacMURCHY, Ryan	5-11	190	R	Regina, Sask.	4/27/83	U. of Wisconsin
OSHIE, T.J.	5-10	170	L	Mt. Vernon, WA	12/23/86	Warroad-Sioux Falls
RAJAMAKI, Erkki	6-2	205	L	Vantaa, Finland	10/30/78	Worcester
RAMSAY, Ryan	5-11	200	L	Ajax, Ont.	5/18/83	Worcester-Peoria
REAVES, Ryan	6-1	193	R	Winnipeg, Man.	1/20/87	Brandon
RIDDLE, Troy	5-10	175	R	Minneapolis, MN	8/24/81	Worcester-Peoria
SEMIN, Dmitri	5-10	185	L	Moscow, USSR	8/14/83	Spartak
SHKOTOV, Alexei	5-10	175	L	Elektrostal, USSR	6/22/84	Voskresensk-Worcester
SKACHKOV, Yevgeny	6-0	187	R	Penza, USSR	7/14/84	Spartak
SODERBERG, Carl	6-3	198	L	Malmo, Sweden	10/12/85	Morrum-Malmo
STEMPNIAK, Lee	6-0	190	R	Buffalo, NY	2/4/83	Dartmouth
TROLIGA, Tomas	6-4	200	R	Presov, Czech.	4/24/84	Zilina-Presov-Tri-City
VIKINGSTAD, Tore	6-4	204	L	Stavenger, Norway	10/8/75	Dusseldorf
ZAKHAROV, Konstantin	6-1	190	R	Minsk, USSR	5/2/85	

DEFENSEMEN						
BYRNE, Trevor	6-2	208	L	Hingham, MA	5/7/80	Worcester-Peoria
FITZGERALD, Zack	6-1	214	L	Two Harbors, MN	6/16/85	Seattle
GAUTHIER, Mike	6-3	185	R	Vancouver, B.C.	3/26/87	Prince Albert
JACKSON, Scott	6-3	200	L	Salmon Arm, B.C.	2/5/87	Seattle
JONSSON, Robin	6-2	194	R	Upplands Vasby, Swe.	12/10/83	Bofors-Farjestad
NIKITIN, Nikita	6-3	178	L	Omsk, USSR	6/16/86	Omsk
PERVYSHIN, Andrei	5-8	156	L	Arkhangelsk, USSR	2/2/85	Kazan
PLEKHANOV, Dmitri	6-2	185	L	Nizhnekamsk, USSR	3/13/78	
POLAK, Roman	6-1	198	R	Ostrava, Czech.	4/28/86	Kootenay
SCHEFFELMAIER, Brett	6-5	220	R	Coronation, Alta.	3/31/81	Worcester-Peoria
SKOOG, Simon	6-2	218	L	Solvesborg, Sweden	2/17/83	HV 71-Morrum
WELLAR, Patrick	6-3	210	L	Carrot River, Sask.	12/4/83	Worcester-Peoria
WIDEMAN, Dennis	6-0	200	R	Kitchener, Ont.	3/20/83	Worcester

GOALTENDERS	HT	WT	C	Place of Birth	Date	2004-05 Club
BARULIN, Konstantin	6-0	180	L	Karaganda, USSR	9/4/84	Tyumen
BECKFORD-TSEU, Chris	6-2	201	L	Toronto, Ont.	6/22/84	Worcester-Peoria
BISHOP, Ben	6-5	205	L	Denver, CO	11/21/86	Texas
NISSINEN, Tuomas	6-1	176	L	Kuopio, Finland	7/17/83	TuTo-Assat
SCHWARZ, Marek	5-11	176	R	Mlada Boleslav, Czech.	4/1/86	Vancouver (WHL)

Coaching History

Lynn Patrick and Scotty Bowman, 1967-68; Scotty Bowman, 1968-69, 1969-70; Al Arbour and Scotty Bowman, 1970-71; Sid Abel, Bill McCreary and Al Arbour, 1971-72; Al Arbour and Jean-Guy Talbot, 1972-73; Jean-Guy Talbot and Lou Angotti, 1973-74; Lou Angotti, Lynn Patrick and Garry Young, 1974-75; Garry Young, Lynn Patrick and Leo Boivin, 1975-76; Emile Francis, 1976-77; Leo Boivin and Barclay Plager, 1977-78; Barclay Plager, 1978-79; Barclay Plager and Red Berenson, 1979-80; Red Berenson, 1980-81; Red Berenson and Emile Francis, 1981-82; Emile Francis and Barclay Plager, 1982-83; Jacques Demers, 1983-84 to 1985-86; Jacques Martin, 1986-87, 1987-88; Brian Sutter, 1988-89 to 1991-92; Bob Plager and Bob Berry, 1992-93; Bob Berry, 1993-94; Mike Keenan, 1994-95, 1995-96; Mike Keenan, Jim Roberts and Joel Quenneville, 1996-97; Joel Quenneville, 1997-98 to 2002-03; Joel Quenneville and Mike Kitchen, 2003-04; Mike Kitchen, 2004-05 to date.

Coach

KITCHEN, MIKE
Coach, St. Louis Blues. Born in Newmarket, Ont., February 1, 1956.

Mike Kitchen was named head coach of the St. Louis Blues on February 24, 2004. His first game as head coach was on February 26, 2004 at Colorado. Kitchen spent six and a half seasons as the Blues' assistant coach, joining the staff on September 1, 1998. Prior to joining the Blues, he spent nine seasons as an assistant coach for the Toronto Maple Leafs. He joined the Leafs on August 8, 1989 after spending one season as an assistant coach for Newmarket in the American Hockey League.

Kitchen spent eight seasons in the National Hockey League as a defenseman with the Colorado Rockies and the New Jersey Devils. He appeared in 474 games, while recording 12 goals, 62 assists and 370 penalty minutes. Kansas City originally drafted him as the 38th overall choice in the 1976 Entry Draft.

Prior to playing in the NHL, Kitchen spent three seasons with the Toronto Marlboros of the OHA, accumulating 79 points (14 goals, 65 assists) and 429 penalty minutes in 202 games played. He also spent one season with the Rhode Island Reds of the AHL, registering 10 assists and 14 penalty minutes in 14 games played.

Coaching Record

			Regular Season				Playoffs		
Season	Team	Games	W	L	T		Games	W	L
2003-04	St. Louis (NHL)	21	10	7	4		5	1	4
2004-05	St. Louis (NHL)				Season Cancelled				
	NHL Totals	21	10	7	4		5	1	4

Although he's only 26 years old, Eric Brewer has already won Olympic gold, a World Cup title and a pair of World Championships.

Captains' History

Al Arbour, 1967-68 to 1969-70; Red Berenson and Barclay Plager, 1970-71; Barclay Plager, 1971-72 to 1975-76; no captain, 1976-77; Red Berenson, 1977-78; Barry Gibbs, 1978-79; Brian Sutter, 1979-80 to 1987-88; Bernie Federko, 1988-89; Rick Meagher, 1989-90; Scott Stevens, 1990-91; Garth Butcher, 1991-92; Brett Hull, 1992-93 to 1994-95; Brett Hull, Shayne Corson and Wayne Gretzky, 1995-96; no captain, 1996-97; Chris Pronger, 1997-98 to 2001-02; Al MacInnis, 2002-03, 2003-04.

Club Records

Team

(Figures in brackets for season records are games played; records for fewest points, wins, ties, losses, goals, goals against are for 70 or more games)

Most Points	114	1999-2000 (82)
Most Wins	51	1999-2000 (82)
Most Ties	19	1970-71 (78)
Most Losses	50	1978-79 (80)
Most Goals	352	1980-81 (80)
Most Goals Against	349	1981-82 (80)
Fewest Points	48	1978-79 (80)
Fewest Wins	18	1978-79 (80)
Fewest Ties	7	1983-84 (80)
Fewest Losses	18	1980-81 (80)
Fewest Goals	177	1967-68 (74)
Fewest Goals Against	157	1968-69 (76)

Longest Winning Streak

Overall	10	Jan. 3-23/02
Home	9	Jan. 26-Feb. 26/91
Away	*10	Jan. 21-Mar. 2/00

Longest Undefeated Streak

Overall	12	Nov. 10-Dec. 8/68 (5 wins, 7 ties), Nov. 24-Dec. 26/00 (11 wins, 1 tie)
Home	11	Four times
Away	11	Jan. 21-Mar. 4/00 (10 wins, 1 tie)

Longest Losing Streak

Overall	7	Nov. 12-26/67, Feb. 12-25/89
Home	6	Nov. 23-Dec. 19/96
Away	10	Jan. 20-Mar. 8/82

Longest Winless Streak

Overall	12	Jan. 17-Feb. 15/78 (10 losses, 2 ties)
Home	7	Dec. 28/82-Jan. 25/83 (5 losses, 2 ties)
Away	17	Jan. 23-Oct. 9/74 (13 losses, 4 ties)
Most Shutouts, Season	13	1968-69 (76)
Most PIM, Season	2,041	1990-91 (80)
Most Goals, Game	11	Feb. 26/94 (St.L. 11 at Ott. 1)

Individual

Most Seasons	13	Bernie Federko
Most Games	927	Bernie Federko
Most Goals, Career	527	Brett Hull
Most Assists, Career	721	Bernie Federko
Most Points, Career	1,073	Bernie Federko (352G, 721A)
Most PIM, Career	1,786	Brian Sutter
Most Shutouts, Career	16	Glenn Hall

Longest Consecutive

Games Streak	662	Garry Unger (Feb. 7/71-Apr. 8/79)
Most Goals, Season	86	Brett Hull (1990-91)
Most Assists, Season	90	Adam Oates (1990-91)
Most Points, Season	131	Brett Hull (1990-91) (86G, 45A)

Most PIM, Season	306	Bob Gassoff (1975-76)
Most Points, Defenseman, Season	78	Jeff Brown (1992-93; 25G, 53A)
Most Points, Center, Season	115	Adam Oates (1990-91; 25G, 90A)
Most Points, Right Wing, Season	131	Brett Hull (1990-91; 86G, 45A)
Most Points, Left Wing, Season	102	Brendan Shanahan (1993-94; 52G, 50A)
Most Points, Rookie, Season	73	Jorgen Pettersson (1980-81; 37G, 36A)
Most Shutouts, Season	8	Glenn Hall (1968-69)
Most Goals, Game	6	Red Berenson (Nov. 7/68)
Most Assists, Game	5	Brian Sutter (Nov. 22/83), Bernie Federko (Feb. 27/88), Adam Oates (Jan. 26/91), Dallas Drake (Oct. 29/03)
Most Points, Game	7	Red Berenson (Nov. 7/68; 6G, 1A), Garry Unger (Mar. 13/71; 3G, 4A)

* NHL Record.

Retired Numbers

3	Bob Gassoff	1973-1977
8	Barclay Plager	1967-1977
11	Brian Sutter	1976-1988
24	Bernie Federko	1976-1989

All-time Record vs. Other Clubs

Regular Season

	At Home GP	W	L	T	OL	GF	GA	PTS	On Road GP	W	L	T	OL	GF	GA	PTS	Total GP	W	L	T	OL	GF	GA	PTS
Anaheim	22	12	7	3	0	67	56	27	22	13	7	2	0	65	54	28	44	25	14	5	0	132	110	55
Atlanta	3	3	0	0	0	11	6	6	4	2	1	1	0	16	14	5	7	5	1	1	0	27	15	11
Boston	59	27	23	9	0	188	198	63	59	15	35	9	0	161	247	39	118	42	58	18	0	349	445	102
Buffalo	50	29	14	7	0	180	125	65	52	17	29	6	0	164	200	40	102	46	43	13	0	344	325	105
Calgary	64	31	24	9	0	229	195	71	62	28	28	5	1	180	201	62	126	59	52	14	1	409	396	133
Carolina	31	19	9	3	0	119	94	41	31	17	12	2	0	97	92	36	62	36	21	5	0	216	186	77
Chicago	115	57	40	17	1	388	356	132	118	35	63	18	2	348	433	90	233	92	103	35	3	736	789	222
Colorado	40	22	14	4	0	148	124	48	41	14	20	7	0	111	138	35	81	36	34	11	0	259	262	83
Columbus	11	9	1	1	0	45	23	19	10	4	3	2	1	26	22	11	21	13	4	3	1	71	45	30
Dallas	117	64	32	21	0	424	330	149	115	40	53	22	0	334	383	102	232	104	85	43	0	758	713	251
Detroit	110	56	34	20	0	375	308	132	110	41	51	17	1	336	404	100	220	97	85	37	1	711	712	232
Edmonton	44	21	16	7	0	157	153	49	44	17	23	4	0	144	161	38	88	38	39	11	0	301	314	87
Florida	9	7	1	1	0	25	12	15	9	5	2	2	0	20	17	12	18	12	3	3	0	45	29	27
Los Angeles	78	50	18	10	0	293	195	110	78	31	35	12	0	226	261	74	156	81	53	22	0	519	456	184
Minnesota	8	3	2	3	0	15	11	9	8	3	3	2	0	13	19	8	16	6	5	5	0	28	30	17
Montreal	57	14	28	15	0	147	195	43	59	11	41	7	0	161	255	29	116	25	69	22	0	308	450	72
Nashville	16	12	3	1	0	53	23	25	17	9	4	3	1	46	35	22	33	21	7	4	1	99	58	47
New Jersey	46	27	11	7	1	192	143	62	46	17	22	7	0	128	146	41	92	44	33	14	1	320	289	103
NY Islanders	47	18	18	9	2	166	153	47	49	13	25	11	0	131	183	37	96	31	43	20	2	297	336	84
NY Rangers	63	25	28	10	0	188	202	60	60	10	44	6	0	143	245	26	123	35	72	16	0	331	447	86
Ottawa	9	4	3	2	0	27	25	10	10	6	4	0	0	36	23	12	19	10	7	2	0	63	48	22
Philadelphia	68	26	33	7	2	194	219	61	67	12	45	10	0	153	264	34	135	38	78	17	2	347	483	95
Phoenix	50	26	13	11	0	182	136	63	51	18	25	7	1	156	166	44	101	44	38	18	1	338	302	107
Pittsburgh	64	43	15	6	0	247	171	92	64	20	31	12	1	190	238	53	128	63	46	18	1	437	409	145
San Jose	28	18	8	1	1	93	65	38	24	19	4	1	0	85	51	39	52	37	12	2	1	178	116	77
Tampa Bay	11	10	1	0	0	44	24	20	13	5	4	3	1	42	38	14	24	15	5	3	1	86	62	34
Toronto	102	58	29	14	1	348	283	131	99	30	58	11	0	292	369	71	201	88	87	25	1	640	652	202
Vancouver	71	41	21	9	0	265	205	91	72	33	29	9	1	230	214	76	143	74	50	18	1	495	419	167
Washington	41	20	13	8	0	165	127	48	39	15	20	4	0	117	136	34	80	35	33	12	0	282	263	82
Defunct Clubs	32	25	4	3	0	131	55	53	33	11	10	12	0	95	100	34	65	36	14	15	0	226	155	87
Totals	**1466**	**777**	**463**	**218**	**8**	**5106**	**4207**	**1780**	**1466**	**511**	**731**	**214**	**10**	**4246**	**5109**	**1246**	**2932**	**1288**	**1194**	**432**	**18**	**9352**	**9316**	**3026**

Playoffs

	Series	W	L	GP	W	L	T	GF	GA	Last Mtg.	Rnd.	Result
Boston	2	0	2	8	0	8	0	15	48	1972	SF	L 0-4
Buffalo	1	0	1	3	1	2	0	8	7	1976	PRE	L 1-2
Calgary	1	0	1	7	3	4	0	22	28	1986	CF	L 3-4
Chicago	10	3	7	50	22	28	0	142	171	2002	CQF	W 4-1
Colorado	1	0	1	5	1	4	0	11	17	2001	CF	L 1-4
Dallas	12	6	6	66	32	34	0	187	197	2001	CSF	W 4-0
Detroit	7	2	5	40	16	24	0	103	125	2002	CSF	L 1-4
Los Angeles	2	2	0	8	8	0	0	32	13	1998	CQF	W 4-0
Montreal	3	0	3	12	0	12	0	14	42	1977	QF	L 0-4
NY Rangers	1	0	1	6	2	4	0	22	29	1981	QF	L 2-4
Philadelphia	2	2	0	11	8	3	0	34	20	1969	QF	W 4-0
Phoenix	2	2	0	11	7	4	0	39	29	1999	CQF	W 4-3
Pittsburgh	3	2	1	13	7	6	0	45	40	1981	PRE	W 3-2
San Jose	3	1	2	18	8	10	0	47	43	2004	CQF	L 1-4
Toronto	5	3	2	31	17	14	0	88	90	1996	CQF	W 4-2
Vancouver	2	0	2	14	6	8	0	48	44	2003	CQF	L 3-4
Totals	**57**	**23**	**34**	**303**	**138**	**165**	**0**	**857**	**943**			

Calgary totals include Atlanta Flames, 1972-73 to 1979-80.
Colorado totals include Quebec, 1979-80 to 1994-95.
New Jersey totals include Kansas City, 1974-75 to 1975-76, and Colorado Rockies, 1976-77 to 1981-82.
Phoenix totals include Winnipeg, 1979-80 to 1995-96.
Carolina totals include Hartford, 1979-80 to 1996-97.
Dallas totals include Minnesota North Stars, 1967-68 to 1992-93.

Playoff Results 2005-2000

Year	Round	Opponent	Result	GF	GA
2004	CQF	San Jose	L 1-4	9	12
2003	CQF	Vancouver	L 3-4	21	17
2002	CSF	Detroit	L 1-4	11	14
	CQF	Chicago	W 4-1	13	5
2001	CF	Colorado	L 1-4	11	17
	CSF	Dallas	W 4-0	13	6
	CQF	San Jose	W 4-2	16	11
2000	CQF	San Jose	L 3-4	22	20

Abbreviations: Round: CF – conference final; **CSF** – conference semi-final; **CQF** – conference quarter-final; **SF** – semi-final; **QF** – quarter-final; **PRE** – preliminary round.

Key Off-Season Signings/Acquisitions

2004

June 25 • Obtained G **Jason Bacashihua** from Dallas for D **Shawn Belle**.

27 • Obtained G **Patrick Lalime** from Ottawa for a 2005 4th-round pick.

29 • Re-signed G **Reinhard Divis**.

30 • Re-signed RW **Dallas Drake**.

July 1 • Re-signed D **Eric Weinrich**.

12 • Re-signed C **Mike Sillinger**.

Aug. 5 • Re-signed C **Petr Cajanek**.

Sept. 10 • Re-signed D **Christian Backman** and G **Curtis Sanford**.

13 • Re-signed D **Barret Jackman**.

2005

June 22 • Named **Curt Fraser** assistant coach.

July 28 • Excercised option on G **Patrick Lalime**.

Aug. 2 • Obtained Ds **Eric Brewer, Doug Lynch** and **Jeff Woywitka** from Edmonton for D **Chris Pronger**.

9 • Re-signed D **Bryce Salvador** and RW **Eric Boguniecki**.

9 • Signed LW **Dean McAmmond**.

11 • Re-signed RW **Mark Rycroft** and C **Ryan Johnson**.

15 • Re-signed RW **Jamal Mayers**.

Entry Draft
Selections 2005-1991

2005
Pick
24	T.J. Oshie
37	Scott Jackson
85	Ben Bishop
156	Ryan Reaves
169	Mike Gauthier
171	Nicholas Drazenovic
219	Nikolai Lemtyugov

2004
Pick
17	Marek Schwarz
49	Carl Soderberg
83	Viktor Alexandrov
116	Michal Birner
136	Nikita Nikitin
180	Roman Polak
211	David Fredriksson
277	Jonathan Michel Boutin

2003
Pick
30	Shawn Belle
62	David Backes
84	Konstantin Barulin
88	Zack Fitzgerald
101	Konstantin Zakharov
127	Alexandre Bolduc
148	Lee Stempniak
159	Chris Beckford-Tseu
189	Jonathan Lehun
221	Yevgeny Skachkov
253	Andrei Pervyshin
284	Juhamatti Aaltonen

2002
Pick
48	Alexei Shkotov
62	Andrei Mikhnov
89	Tomas Troliga
120	Robin Jonsson
165	Justin Maiser
191	D.J. King
221	Jonas Johnson
253	Tom Koivisto
284	Ryan MacMurchy

2001
Pick
57	Jay McClement
89	Tuomas Nissinen
122	Igor Valeev
159	Dmitri Semin
190	Brett Scheffelmaier
253	Petr Cajanek
270	Grant Jacobsen
283	Simon Skoog

2000
Pick
30	Jeff Taffe
65	Dave Morisset
75	Justin Papineau
96	Antoine Bergeron
129	Troy Riddle
167	Craig Weller
229	Brett Lutes
261	Reinhard Divis
293	Lauri Kinos

1999
Pick
17	Barret Jackman
85	Peter Smrek
114	Chad Starling
143	Trevor Byrne
180	Tore Vikingstad
203	Phil Osaer
221	Colin Hemingway
232	Alexander Khavanov
260	Brian McMeekin
270	James Desmarais

1998
Pick
24	Christian Backman
41	Maxim Linnik
83	Matt Walker
157	Brad Voth
170	Andrei Troschinsky
197	Brad Twordik
225	Yevgeny Pastukh
255	John Pohl

1997
Pick
40	Tyler Rennette
86	Didier Tremblay
98	Jan Horacek
106	Jame Pollock
149	Nicholas Bilotto
177	Ladislav Nagy
206	Bobby Haglund
232	Dmitri Plekhanov
244	Marek Ivan

1996
Pick
14	Marty Reasoner
67	Gordie Dwyer
95	Jonathan Zukiwsky
97	Andrei Petrakov
159	Stephen Wagner
169	Daniel Corso
177	Reed Low
196	Andrej Podkonicky
203	Tony Hutchins
229	Konstantin Shafranov

1995
Pick
49	Jochen Hecht
75	Scott Roche
101	Michal Handzus
127	Jeff Ambrosio
153	Denis Hamel
179	Jean-Luc Grand-Pierre
205	Derek Bekar
209	Libor Zabransky

1994
Pick
68	Stephane Roy
94	Tyler Harlton
120	Edvin Frylen
172	Roman Vopat
198	Steve Noble
224	Marc Stephan
250	Kevin Harper
276	Scott Fankhouser

1993
Pick
37	Maxim Bets
63	Jamie Rivers
89	Jamal Mayers
141	Todd Kelman
167	Mike Buzak
193	Eric Boguniecki
219	Mike Grier
245	Libor Prochazka
271	Alexander Vasilevski
275	Christer Olsson

1992
Pick
38	Igor Korolev
62	Vitali Karamnov
64	Vitali Prokhorov
86	Lee Leslie
134	Bob Lachance
158	Ian Laperriere
160	Lance Burns
180	Igor Boldin
182	Nick Naumenko
206	Todd Harris
230	Yuri Gunko
259	Wade Salzman

1991
Pick
27	Steve Staios
64	Kyle Reeves
65	Nathan LaFayette
87	Grayden Reid
109	Jeff Callinan
131	Bruce Gardiner
153	Terry Hollinger
175	Chris Kenady
197	Jed Fiebelkorn
219	Chris MacKenzie
241	Kevin Rappana
263	Mike Veisor

General Managers' History

Lynn Patrick, 1967-68; Scotty Bowman, 1968-69 to 1970-71; Lynn Patrick, 1971-72; Sid Abel, 1972-73; Charles Catto, 1973-74; Gerry Ehman, 1974-75; Dennis Ball, 1975-76; Emile Francis, 1976-77 to 1982-83; Ron Caron, 1983-84 to 1993-94; Mike Keenan, 1994-95, 1995-96; Mike Keenan and Ron Caron, 1996-97; Larry Pleau, 1997-98 to date.

Vice President and General Manager

PLEAU, LARRY
Senior Vice President/General Manager, St. Louis Blues.
Born in Lynn, MA, June 29, 1947.

Larry Pleau was named general manager on June 9, 1997, becoming the tenth person to hold that position in team history. He has built the Blues into one of the NHL's top teams, winning the President's Trophy in 1999-2000 and reaching the Western Conference Finals in 2000-01. In international hockey, he served as associate general manager of the silver medal-winning 2002 U.S. Olympic team and as general manager of Team USA at the World Championships in 2003 and 2004 (bronze medal) and at the 2004 World Cup.

Pleau joined the Blues after spending eight seasons with the New York Rangers organization, reaching the position of vice president of player development. He joined the Rangers in 1989 as assistant general manager of player development. During Pleau's tenure in New York, the Rangers drafted NHL stars Sergei Zubov, Doug Weight, Alex Kovalev and Niklas Sundstrom. Prior to joining the Rangers, Pleau spent 17 seasons with the Hartford Whalers organization as a player, assistant coach, head coach, general manager and minor league general manager and head coach. He was also instrumental in drafting Ray Ferraro, Ron Francis, Kevin Dineen and Ulf Samuelsson while a member of the Whalers organization.

Pleau played three seasons with the Montreal Canadiens (1969-1972) in the National Hockey League before being the first player signed by the Hartford Whalers of the World Hockey Association. He was a center/left wing for the Whalers from 1972 until his retirement in 1979. He played in 468 regular season games for Hartford, accumulating 157 goals and 215 assists for 372 points. He also played for the 1968 United States Olympic team, the 1969 U.S. national team and went to training camp with Team USA for the 1976 Canada Cup tournament.

NHL Coaching Record

			Regular Season			Playoffs		
Season	Team	Games	W	L	T	Games	W	L
1980-81	Hartford	20	6	12	2	....	....	....
1981-82	Hartford	80	21	41	18	....	....	....
1982-83	Hartford	18	4	13	1	....	....	....
1987-88	Hartford	26	13	13	0	6	2	4
1988-89	Hartford	80	37	38	5	4	0	4
	NHL Totals	**224**	**81**	**117**	**26**	**10**	**2**	**8**

Club Directory

Savvis Center

St. Louis Blues
Savvis Center
1401 Clark Avenue
St. Louis, MO 63103
Phone **314/622-2500**
FAX 314/622-2582
www.stlouisblues.com
Capacity: 19,022

Executive, Paige Sports Entertainment
Owner and Chairman	William J. Laurie
President	Richard C. Thomas
Chief Operating Officer and General Counsel	Brent P. Karasiuk
Director of Admin. & Asst. to the President	Deborah Belsheim
Paralegal and Exec. Asst. to the COO	Linda Munden
Executive Assistant	Meghan O'Connor

Blues Executive Management
President and Chief Executive Officer	Mark Sauer
Sr. V.P. and G.M.	Larry Pleau
Sr. V.P. of Finance & Hockey Admin.	Jerry Jasiek
Sr. V.P. & G.M., Savvis Center	Dennis Petrullo
Vice President of Sales	Bruce Affleck
Vice President of Marketing	Jo Ann Miles
Vice President of Human Resources	Dave Coverstone
Vice President of Building Operations	Fred Corsi
Executive Assistant to the President	Lisa Cwiklowski
Executive Assistant to the G.M.	Donna Lembke
Executive Assistant to the G.M., Savvis Center	Cherri Haynes

Hockey Operations
Asst. G.M./Director of Amateur Scouting	Jarmo Kekalainen
Director of Pro Scouting/Peoria G.M.	Kevin McDonald
Director of Player Evaluation	Ted Hampson
Head Coach	Mike Kitchen
Assistant Coach	Curt Fraser
Goaltending Coach	Keith Allain
Video/Strength and Conditioning Coach	Jamie Kompon
Director of Team Services	Mike Caruso

Training Staff
Athletic Trainer	Ray Barile
Equipment Manager	Bert Godin
Assistant Equipment Manager	Steve Wissman
Equipment Assistant	Ray Halle
Massage Therapist	Jeff Wright

Scouting
Professional Scouts	Wayne Mundey, Bob Berry
Amateur Scouts	Mike Antonovich, Craig Channell, Rick Meagher, Ville Siren
Part-Time Amateur Scouts	Bill Armstrong, Thomas Carlsson, Paul Gallagher, Dan Ginnell, Vladimir Havluj, Jr., Barclay Parneta, Georgi Zhuravlev

Team Doctors
Orthopedic Surgeons	Dr. Jerome Gilden, Dr. Rick Wright, Dr. Matt Matava
Internists	Dr. Aaron Birenbaum, Dr. William Birenbaum
Neurosurgeon	Dr. Ralph Dacey
General Surgery	Dr. Michael Brunt
Plastic Surgery	Dr. Tom Francel
Dentist	Dr. Glenn Edwards
Ophthalmologist	Dr. Gill Grand
Optometrist	Dr. Rex Ghormley
Oral Surgeon	Dr. Ken Kram

Communications
Director of Broadcasting & Communications	Chuck Menke
Communications Coordinator	Scott Bonanni
Communications Coordinator	Rich Jankowski
Marketing/Public Relations Assistant	Donna Ferguson
Team Photographer	Mark Buckner

Marketing
Senior Director of Corporate Sponsorship	Chris Arger
Director of Corporate Sponsorship	Mary Greener
Director of Corporate Sponsorship	Chad Watson
Director of Marketing Programs	Lou Siville
Event Presentation Director	Chris Frome
Client Services Manager	Justine Lundin
Marketing Program Manager	Josh Hardin
Manager of Fan Services	Bob Laurie
KTRS Radio/Community Relations	Bob Plager

Sales
Director of Sales	Jennifer Nevins
Administrative Assistant	Cassandra Martin
Ticket Sales Representatives	Kari Palmer, Randy Walker, Renee Orr, Kim Derringer
Group Sales	Ashley Patey
Customer Service Manager	Jill Hahn
Customer Service Assistant Manager	Paula Barnes Munder
Customer Service Representative	Jill Mahoney
Manager Database/Customer Service Rep.	Jason Penning

Finance
Director of MIS/Accounting	Phil Siddle
Manager of Accounting	Craig Bryant
Payroll Supervisor	Pam Di Rie
Payroll Assistant	Crystal Strasburg
Accountants	Deann Cromer, Chantay Kane, Carrin Stelmach, Emily Hobbs

Team Broadcasters
Radio Station	KTRS 550 AM
Radio Broadcasters	Chris Kerber, Kelly Chase
Television Station	KPLR-TV, WB 11
Regional Sports Network	FSN Midwest
Television Broadcasters	John Kelly, Bernie Federko, Dan McLaughlin

San Jose Sharks

Year-by-Year Record

Season	GP	Home W	L	T	OL	Road W	L	T	OL	Overall W	L	T	OL	GF	GA	Pts.	Finished	Playoff Result
2004-05	....	....	....	....	....	....	....	....	....	....	....	....	....	....	....	....		
2003-04	82	24	8	7	2	19	13	5	4	43	21	12	6	219	183	104	1st, Pacific Div.	Lost Conf. Final
2002-03	82	17	16	5	3	11	21	4	5	28	37	9	8	214	239	73	5th, Pacific Div.	Out of Playoffs
2001-02	82	25	11	3	2	19	16	5	1	44	27	8	3	248	199	99	1st, Pacific Div.	Lost Conf. Semi-Final
2000-01	82	22	14	4	1	18	13	8	2	40	27	12	3	217	192	95	2nd, Pacific Div.	Lost Conf. Quarter-Final
1999-2000	82	21	14	3	3	14	16	7	4	35	30	10	7	225	214	87	4th, Pacific Div.	Lost Conf. Semi-Final
1998-99	82	17	15	9	....	14	18	9	....	31	33	18	....	196	191	80	4th, Pacific Div.	Lost Conf. Quarter-Final
1997-98	82	17	19	5	....	17	19	5	....	34	38	10	....	210	216	78	4th, Pacific Div.	Lost Conf. Quarter-Final
1996-97	82	14	23	4	....	13	24	4	....	27	47	8	....	211	278	62	7th, Pacific Div.	Out of Playoffs
1995-96	82	12	26	3	....	8	29	4	....	20	55	7	....	252	357	47	7th, Pacific Div.	Out of Playoffs
1994-95	48	10	13	1	....	9	12	3	....	19	25	4	....	129	161	42	3rd, Pacific Div.	Lost Conf. Semi-Final
1993-94	84	19	13	10	....	14	22	6	....	33	35	16	....	252	265	82	3rd, Pacific Div.	Lost Conf. Semi-Final
1992-93	84	8	33	1	....	3	38	1	....	11	71	2	....	218	414	24	6th, Smythe Div.	Out of Playoffs
1991-92	80	14	23	3	....	3	35	2	....	17	58	5	....	219	359	39	6th, Smythe Div.	Out of Playoffs

2005-06 Schedule

Oct.	Wed.	5	at Nashville
	Fri.	7	at Chicago
	Sat.	8	at St. Louis
	Wed.	12	Columbus
	Sat.	15	Chicago
	Mon.	17	at Detroit
	Wed.	19	at Minnesota
	Fri.	21	at Columbus
	Sat.	22	at Nashville
	Wed.	26	at Dallas
	Fri.	28	at Los Angeles
	Sat.	29	Calgary
Nov.	Wed.	2	Nashville
	Fri.	4	at Anaheim
	Sat.	5	Minnesota
	Tue.	8	at Colorado
	Sat.	12	Dallas
	Wed.	16	Vancouver
	Sat.	19	Phoenix
	Mon.	21	at Edmonton
	Wed.	23	at Calgary
	Thu.	24	at Vancouver
	Sat.	26	Detroit
	Wed.	30	at Dallas
Dec.	Fri.	2	at Buffalo
	Sat.	3	at Toronto
	Tue.	6	Atlanta
	Thu.	8	Florida
	Sat.	10	Carolina
	Fri.	16	Washington
	Sun.	18	at Anaheim*
	Tue.	20	Anaheim
	Thu.	22	at Phoenix
	Fri.	23	St. Louis
	Mon.	26	at Los Angeles
	Wed.	28	Phoenix
	Fri.	30	Colorado
Jan.	Thu.	5	Columbus
	Sat.	7	Los Angeles
	Tue.	10	at Boston
	Thu.	12	at Ottawa
	Sat.	14	at Montreal
	Mon.	16	Tampa Bay*
	Thu.	19	Edmonton
	Sat.	21	at Los Angeles*
	Tue.	24	Los Angeles
	Thu.	26	Anaheim
	Sat.	28	at Phoenix
	Mon.	30	at Dallas
Feb.	Wed.	1	at Anaheim
	Thu.	2	Minnesota
	Sat.	4	Anaheim
	Mon.	6	Calgary
	Wed.	8	Chicago
	Fri.	10	Dallas
	Sun.	12	at Phoenix
	Tue.	28	Detroit
Mar.	Fri.	3	at Edmonton
	Sat.	4	at Calgary
	Tue.	7	at Anaheim
	Thu.	9	Edmonton
	Sat.	11	Nashville*
	Mon.	13	Los Angeles
	Thu.	16	St. Louis
	Sat.	18	Dallas*
	Sun.	19	Colorado*
	Tue.	21	at St. Louis
	Thu.	23	at Detroit
	Sat.	25	at Minnesota
	Sun.	26	at Chicago
	Tue.	28	at Columbus
	Thu.	30	Phoenix
Apr.	Sat.	1	Phoenix
	Mon.	3	at Dallas
	Wed.	5	at Colorado
	Thu.	6	at Los Angeles
	Sun.	9	Dallas*
	Mon.	10	at Phoenix
	Wed.	12	at Vancouver
	Thu.	13	Vancouver
	Sat.	15	Anaheim*
	Mon.	17	Los Angeles

* Denotes afternoon game.

Franchise date: May 9, 1990

WESTERN NHL CONFERENCE

PACIFIC DIVISION

15th NHL Season

Logging more than 20 minutes of ice time per game through each of his first five seasons, Brad Stuart also contributes offensively from the San Jose blue line.

2005-06 Player Personnel

FORWARDS	HT	WT	S	Place of Birth	Date	2004-05 Club
ARMSTRONG, Riley	5-11	185	R	Saskatoon, Sask.	11/8/84	Cleveland
BERNIER, Steve	6-2	230	R	Quebec City, Que.	3/31/85	Moncton
CAVANAGH, Tom	5-10	178	L	Warwick, RI	3/24/82	Harvard
CHEECHOO, Jonathan	6-1	190	R	Moose Factory, Ont.	7/15/80	HV 71
CLOWE, Ryane	6-2	215	R	St. John's, Nfld.	9/30/82	Cleveland
DIMITRAKOS, Niko	5-10	205	R	Sommerville, MA	5/21/79	Langnau
EKMAN, Nils	6-0	185	L	Stockholm, Sweden	3/11/76	Djurgarden
GOC, Marcel	6-0	195	L	Calw, West Germany	8/24/83	Cleveland
HENNESSY, Joshua	6-0	190	L	Brockton, MA	2/7/85	Quebec
JOSEPH, Shane	5-9	170	R	Brooks, Alta.	7/23/81	Cleveland
KASPAR, Lukas	6-2	198	L	Most, Czech.	9/23/85	Ottawa (OHL)
MARLEAU, Patrick	6-2	220	L	Aneroid, Sask.	9/15/79	
McCAULEY, Alyn	5-11	200	L	Brockville, Ont.	5/29/77	
MICHALEK, Milan	6-2	220	L	Jindrichuv Hradec, Czech.	12/7/84	
MORRIS, Mike	6-1	182	R	Dorchester, MA	7/14/83	Northeastern
OLSON, Glenn	6-4	230	L	Fort McNeil, B.C.	5/1/84	Cleveland-Fresno-Jhnstn
PARKER, Scott	6-5	230	R	Hanford, CA	1/29/78	
PLIHAL, Tomas	6-1	195	L	Frydlant v Cechach, Czech.	3/28/83	Cleveland
PRIMEAU, Wayne	6-4	230	L	Scarborough, Ont.	6/4/76	
PRUDDEN, Josh	5-11	190	L	Andover, MA	1/10/80	Cleveland
RISSMILLER, Pat	6-4	210	L	Belmont, MA	10/26/78	Cleveland
SETOGUCHI, Devin	5-11	186	R	Taber, Alta.	1/1/87	Saskatoon
SMITH, Mark	5-10	215	L	Edmonton, Alta.	10/24/77	Victoria
STEVENSON, Grant	5-11	170	R	Spruce Grove, Alta.	10/15/81	Cleveland-Johnstown
STURM, Marco	6-0	195	L	Dingolfing, W. Ger.	9/8/78	Ingolstadt
THORNTON, Scott	6-3	225	L	London, Ont.	1/9/71	Sodertalje
TREMBLAY, Jonathan	6-3	240	R	Fauquier, Ont.	3/3/84	Cleveland-Johnstown
VALETTE, Craig	6-0	190	L	Shellbrook, Sask.	10/7/82	Cleveland

DEFENSEMEN						
CARKNER, Matt	6-4	235	R	Winchester, Ont.	11/3/80	Cleveland
CARLE, Matthew	6-0	182	L	Anchorage, AK	9/25/84	U. of Denver
CONBOY, Tim	6-1	205	R	Farmington, MN	3/22/82	Cleveland
DAVISON, Rob	6-2	225	L	St. Catharines, Ont.	5/1/80	Cardiff
EHRHOFF, Christian	6-2	195	L	Moers, West Germany	7/6/82	Cleveland
FAHEY, Jim	6-0	205	R	Boston, MA	5/11/79	Cleveland
GORGES, Josh	6-1	190	L	Kelowna, B.C.	8/14/84	
HANNAN, Scott	6-1	220	L	Richmond, B.C.	1/23/79	
McLAREN, Kyle	6-4	225	L	Humboldt, Sask.	6/18/77	
MURRAY, Doug	6-3	245	L	Bromma, Sweden	3/12/80	Cleveland
PREISSING, Tom	6-0	205	R	Rosemount, MN	12/3/78	Krefeld
STAFFORD, Garrett	6-0	190	R	Los Angeles, CA	1/28/80	Cleveland
STUART, Brad	6-2	220	L	Rocky Mountain House, Alta.	11/6/79	
VLASIC, Marc-Edouard	6-1	190	L	Montreal, Que.	3/30/87	Quebec

GOALTENDERS	HT	WT	C	Place of Birth	Date	2004-05 Club
EHELECHNER, Patrick	6-2	169	L	Rosenheim, W. Ger.	9/23/84	Sudbury
NABOKOV, Evgeni	6-0	200	L	Ust-Kamenogorsk, USSR	7/25/75	Magnitogorsk
PATZOLD, Dimitri	6-0	200	L	Ust-Kamenogorsk, USSR	2/3/83	Cleveland
SCHAEFER, Nolan	6-2	200	R	Yellow Grass, Sask.	1/15/80	Cleveland
TOSKALA, Vesa	5-10	190	L	Tampere, Finland	5/20/77	Ilves

In the System and Recently Drafted

FORWARDS	HT	WT	S	Place of Birth	Date	2004-05 Club
FENTON, Paul	5-11	177	L	Springfield, MA	8/26/85	Massachusetts
HOSPELT, Kai	6-1	187	L	Cologne, West Germany	8/23/85	Koln
HULT, Alexander	6-1	200	L	Falun, Sweden	11/19/84	Almtuna-Halden
KOROLYUK, Alexander	5-9	190	L	Moscow, USSR	1/15/76	Chekhov-Voskresensk
LEE, Carter	6-1	190	R	Toms River, NJ	7/2/84	Northeastern
LUCIA, Tony	6-0	165	L	Wayzata, MN	8/23/87	Wayzata-Omaha
MACHO, Michal	6-1	170	R	Martin, Czech.	1/17/82	Bratislava
MITCHELL, Torrey	5-11	175	R	Montreal, Que.	1/30/85	U. of Vermont
PAVELSKI, Joe	5-11	194	L	Plover, WI	7/11/84	U. of Wisconsin
ZALEWSKI, Steven	6-0	185	L	Utica, NY	8/20/86	Clarkson

DEFENSEMEN						
COLBERT, Will	6-3	212	L	Arnprior, Ont.	2/6/85	Ottawa (OHL)
HUTCHINS, Michael	5-11	185	L	Wolfeboro, NH	10/27/82	New Hampshire
JENSEN, Christian	6-3	190	R	Brooklyn, NY	1/6/86	Yale
JOSLIN, Derek	6-1	191	L	Richmond Hill, Ont.	3/17/87	Ottawa (OHL)
MAATTA, Tero	6-1	220	L	Vantaa, Finland	1/2/82	Blues
MacDONALD, David	6-3	200	R	Halifax, N.S.	4/30/85	PEI
O'HANLEY, Brian	6-0	177	L	Quincy, MA	12/18/84	Boston College
SPANG, Dan	6-0	205	L	Winchester, MA	8/18/83	Boston University
VERNACE, Michael	6-2	200	L	Toronto, Ont.	5/26/86	Brampton
WALSH, Tom	6-0	190	L	Arlington, MA	4/22/83	Harvard

GOALTENDERS	HT	WT	C	Place of Birth	Date	2004-05 Club
CHURCHILL, Jason	6-3	184	L	St. John's, Nfld.	11/5/85	Halifax
DAKERS, Taylor	6-1	165	L	Richmond, B.C.	9/14/86	Kootenay
GREISS, Thomas	6-1	192	L	Straubing, West Germany	1/29/86	Koln-Regensburg
MacINTYRE, Derek	6-2	185	L	Elgin, IL	11/1/85	Ferris State
MAHONEY-WILSON, Brian	5-10	150	L	Boston, MA	4/7/86	Walpole
STALOCK, Alex	5-11	170	L	St. Paul, MN	7/28/87	Cedar Rapids

Coaching History

George Kingston, 1991-92, 1992-93; Kevin Constantine, 1993-94, 1994-95; Kevin Constantine and Jim Wiley, 1995-96; Al Sims, 1996-97; Darryl Sutter, 1997-98 to 2001-02; Darryl Sutter and Ron Wilson, 2002-03; Ron Wilson, 2003-04 to date.

Coach

WILSON, RON
Coach, San Jose Sharks. Born in Windsor, Ont., May 28, 1955.

Named head coach of the Sharks on December 4, 2002, Ron Wilson's first full season behind the San Jose bench saw the team rebound from a disappointing 2002-03 campaign in which they finished last in the Pacific Division and 14th in the Western Conference to capture its second Pacific Division title with a franchise-best 104 points. The Sharks finished second overall in the Western Conference and reached the Western Conference Final for the first time.

Prior to spending five seasons with the Washington Capitals, Wilson had served as the first head coach of the expansion Mighty Ducks of Anaheim in 1993 and led the team to its first trip to the Stanley Cup playoffs in 1996-97. In four seasons behind the Anaheim bench, he posted a record of 120-145-31.

Throughout his professional and amateur career, Wilson has enjoyed a long-standing relationship with USA Hockey. In 1996, he led Team USA to the gold medal at the inaugural World Cup of Hockey. He coached the team again at the 2004 tournament. Wilson also coached the U.S. national team at the 1994 and 1996 World Championships, where his teams finished fourth and third respectively. Wilson also served as head coach for Team USA at the 1998 Nagano Winter Olympics.

Born in Windsor, Ontario, but raised in Riverside Rhode Island, Wilson was selected by the Toronto Maple Leafs in the seventh round (132nd overall) of the 1975 NHL Entry Draft. He began his professional career with the Dallas Blackhawks (Central Hockey League) in the spring of 1977 and joined the Maple Leafs for the 1977-78 season. In 177 career games with Toronto and the Minnesota North Stars, Wilson posted 93 points (26 goals, 67 assists). He also played for the U.S. national team in 1975, 1981, 1983 and 1987.

Coaching Record

			Regular Season				Playoffs		
Season	Team	Games	W	L	T		Games	W	L
1993-94	Anaheim (NHL)	84	33	46	5		....	....	....
1994-95	Anaheim (NHL)	48	16	27	5		....	....	....
1995-96	Anaheim (NHL)	82	35	39	8		....	....	....
1996-97	Anaheim (NHL)	82	36	33	13		11	4	7
1997-98	Washington (NHL)	82	40	30	12		21	12	9
1998-99	Washington (NHL)	82	31	45	6		....	....	....
1999-2000	Washington (NHL)	82	44	26	12		5	1	4
2000-01	Washington (NHL)	82	41	31	10		6	2	4
2001-02	Washington (NHL)	82	36	35	11		....	....	....
2002-03	San Jose (NHL)	57	19	31	7		....	....	....
2003-04	San Jose (NHL)	82	43	27	12		17	10	7
2004-05	San Jose (NHL)				Season Cancelled				
NHL Totals		**845**	**374**	**370**	**101**		**60**	**29**	**31**

Drafted at age 17 and an NHL regular at age 18, veteran center Patrick Marleau has recorded 28 goals and 29 assists in each of his last two NHL seasons.

Club Records

Team

(Figures in brackets for season records are games played; records for fewest points, wins, ties, losses, goals, goals against are for 70 or more games)

Most Points	104	2003-04 (82)
Most Wins	44	2001-02 (82)
Most Ties	18	1998-99 (82)
Most Losses	*71	1992-93 (84)
Most Goals	252	1993-94 (84), 1995-96 (82)
Most Goals Against	414	1992-93 (84)
Fewest Points	24	1992-93 (84)
Fewest Wins	11	1992-93 (84)
Fewest Ties	*2	1992-93 (84)
Fewest Losses	33	1998-99 (82)
Fewest Goals	196	1998-99 (82)
Fewest Goals Against	183	2003-04 (82)

Longest Winning Streak

Overall	7	Mar. 24-Apr. 5/94, Jan. 30-Feb. 28/02
Home	5	Jan. 21-Feb. 15/95, Oct. 11-Nov. 3/01
Away	6	Nov. 30-Dec. 19/01

Longest Undefeated Streak

Overall	10	Nov. 27-Dec. 19/01 (9 wins, 1 tie)
Home	7	Oct. 12-Nov. 22/00 (6 wins, 1 tie)
Away	10	Dec. 26/00-Feb. 16/01 (6 wins, 4 ties)

Longest Losing Streak

Overall	*17	Jan. 4-Feb. 12/93
Home	9	Nov. 19-Dec. 19/92
Away	19	Nov. 27/92-Feb. 12/93

Longest Winless Streak

Overall	20	Dec. 29/92-Feb. 12/93 (19 losses, 1 tie)
Home	9	Nov. 19-Dec. 19/92 (9 losses)
Away	19	Nov. 27/92-Feb. 12/93 (19 losses)

Most Shutouts, Season	9	2000-01 (82), 2001-02 (82)
Most PIM, Season	2,134	1992-93 (84)
Most Goals, Game	10	Jan. 13/96 (S.J. 10 at Pit. 8), Mar. 30/02 (CBJ 2 at S.J. 10)

Individual

Most Seasons	11	Mike Rathje
Most Games, Career	671	Mike Rathje
Most Goals, Career	206	Owen Nolan
Most Assists, Career	225	Owen Nolan
Most Points, Career	431	Owen Nolan (206G, 225A)
Most PIM, Career	1,001	Jeff Odgers
Most Shutouts, Career	26	Evgeni Nabokov
Longest Consecutive Games Streak	228	Mike Ricci (Nov. 22/97-Oct. 20/00)
Most Goals, Season	44	Owen Nolan (1999-2000)
Most Assists, Season	52	Kelly Kisio (1992-93)
Most Points, Season	84	Owen Nolan (1999-2000; 44G, 40A)

Most PIM, Season	326	Link Gaetz (1991-92)
Most Points, Defenseman, Season	64	Sandis Ozolinsh (1993-94; 26G, 38A)
Most Points, Center, Season	78	Kelly Kisio (1992-93; 26G, 52A)
Most Points, Right Wing, Season	84	Owen Nolan (1999-2000; 44G, 40A)
Most Points, Left Wing, Season	66	Johan Garpenlov (1992-93; 22G, 44A)
Most Points, Rookie, Season	59	Pat Falloon (1991-92; 25G, 34A)
Most Shutouts, Season	9	Evgeni Nabokov (2003-04)
Most Goals, Game	4	Owen Nolan (Dec. 19/95)
Most Assists, Game	4	Seven times
Most Points, Game	6	Owen Nolan (Oct. 4/99; 3G, 3A)

* NHL Record.

Captains' History

Doug Wilson, 1991-92, 1992-93; Bob Errey, 1993-94; Bob Errey and Jeff Odgers, 1994-95; Jeff Odgers, 1995-96; Todd Gill, 1996-97, 1997-98; Owen Nolan, 1998-99 to 2002-03; Mike Ricci, Vincent Damphousse, Alyn McCauley, Patrick Marleau, 2003-04 to date.

All-time Record vs. Other Clubs

Regular Season

	At Home								On Road								Total							
	GP	W	L	T	OL	GF	GA	PTS	GP	W	L	T	OL	GF	GA	PTS	GP	W	L	T	OL	GF	GA	PTS
Anaheim	30	14	13	2	1	84	80	31	30	17	10	2	1	99	78	37	60	31	23	4	2	183	158	68
Atlanta	4	3	0	1	0	16	7	7	4	2	0	1	1	11	7	6	8	5	0	2	1	27	14	13
Boston	11	4	5	2	0	30	38	10	10	0	7	3	0	26	39	3	21	4	12	5	0	56	77	13
Buffalo	10	5	1	4	0	36	33	14	11	0	11	0	0	27	52	0	21	5	12	4	0	63	85	14
Calgary	34	13	17	4	0	100	102	30	32	10	17	4	1	87	116	25	66	23	34	8	1	187	218	55
Carolina	11	7	4	0	0	50	31	14	11	5	6	0	0	23	34	10	22	12	10	0	0	73	65	24
Chicago	26	13	9	3	1	72	70	30	25	10	11	2	2	77	76	24	51	23	20	5	3	149	146	54
Colorado	24	7	16	1	0	65	89	15	23	5	14	4	0	42	82	14	47	12	30	5	0	107	171	29
Columbus	8	7	0	0	1	32	12	15	8	5	3	0	0	20	21	10	16	12	3	0	1	52	33	25
Dallas	30	11	16	1	2	68	85	25	29	10	15	4	0	64	81	24	59	21	31	5	2	132	166	49
Detroit	26	9	13	3	1	83	100	22	25	2	21	1	1	45	104	6	51	11	34	4	2	128	204	28
Edmonton	32	16	11	5	0	112	100	37	33	7	19	7	0	71	112	21	65	23	30	12	0	183	212	58
Florida	9	5	2	2	0	26	17	12	9	2	5	2	0	27	25	9	18	7	4	7	0	53	42	21
Los Angeles	37	22	12	3	0	128	102	47	37	10	21	4	2	88	116	26	74	32	33	7	2	216	218	73
Minnesota	8	4	3	1	0	21	14	9	8	3	3	1	1	17	19	8	16	7	6	2	1	38	33	17
Montreal	11	5	3	2	1	33	28	13	11	2	7	2	0	20	36	6	22	7	10	4	1	53	64	19
Nashville	12	6	5	1	0	30	31	13	12	6	4	1	1	34	29	14	24	12	9	2	1	64	60	27
New Jersey	10	3	5	1	1	24	32	8	12	4	6	1	1	24	44	10	22	7	11	2	2	48	76	18
NY Islanders	12	5	5	1	1	30	40	12	11	4	5	2	0	35	40	10	23	9	10	3	1	65	80	22
NY Rangers	13	2	9	2	0	31	49	6	10	2	6	1	1	29	40	6	23	4	15	3	1	60	89	12
Ottawa	9	5	4	0	0	18	16	10	9	1	4	4	0	26	36	6	18	6	8	4	0	44	52	16
Philadelphia	12	3	7	2	0	22	31	8	11	3	6	2	0	27	36	8	23	6	13	4	0	49	67	16
Phoenix	32	15	12	4	1	110	99	35	35	14	17	3	1	99	108	32	67	29	29	7	2	209	207	67
Pittsburgh	13	5	6	2	0	34	54	12	9	4	4	1	0	32	41	9	22	9	10	3	0	66	95	21
St. Louis	24	4	18	1	1	51	85	10	28	9	17	1	1	65	93	20	52	13	35	2	2	116	178	30
Tampa Bay	10	3	6	1	0	32	36	7	12	4	6	1	1	31	32	10	22	7	12	2	1	63	68	17
Toronto	15	5	7	3	0	32	40	13	18	4	12	1	0	47	69	10	33	9	19	5	0	79	109	23
Vancouver	34	13	16	5	0	98	106	31	32	10	17	4	1	84	115	25	66	23	33	9	1	182	221	56
Washington	10	6	3	1	0	29	26	13	12	7	5	0	0	36	34	14	22	13	8	1	0	65	60	27
Totals	**517**	**220**	**228**	**58**	**11**	**1497**	**1553**	**509**	**517**	**162**	**276**	**63**	**16**	**1313**	**1715**	**403**	**1034**	**382**	**504**	**121**	**27**	**2810**	**3268**	**912**

Playoffs

	Series	W	L	GP	W	L	T	GF	GA	Last Mtg.	Rnd.	Result
Calgary	2	1	1	13	6	7	0	38	51	2004	CF	L 2-4
Colorado	3	1	2	19	9	10	0	52	51	2004	CSF	W 4-2
Dallas	2	0	2	11	3	8	0	19	31	2000	CSF	L 1-4
Detroit	2	1	1	11	4	7	0	27	51	1995	CSF	L 0-4
Phoenix	1	1	0	5	4	1	0	13	7	2002	CQF	W 4-1
St. Louis	3	2	1	18	10	8	0	43	47	2004	CQF	W 4-1
Toronto	1	0	1	7	3	4	0	21	26	1994	CSF	L 3-4
Totals	**14**	**6**	**8**	**84**	**39**	**45**	**0**	**213**	**264**			

Playoff Results 2005-2000

Year	Round	Opponent	Result	GF	GA
2004	CF	Calgary	L 2-4	12	16
	CSF	Colorado	W 4-2	14	7
	CQF	St. Louis	W 4-1	12	9
2002	CSF	Colorado	L 3-4	21	25
	CQF	Phoenix	W 4-1	13	7
2001	CQF	St. Louis	L 2-4	11	16
2000	CSF	Dallas	L 1-4	7	15
	CQF	St. Louis	W 4-3	20	22

Abbreviations: Round: CF – conference final; **CSF** – conference semi-final; **CQF** – conference quarter-final.

Carolina totals include Hartford, 1991-92 to 1996-97.
Dallas totals include Minnesota North Stars, 1991-92 to 1992-93.

Colorado totals include Quebec, 1991-92 to 1994-95.
Phoenix totals include Winnipeg, 1991-92 to 1995-96.

Key Off-Season Signings/Acquisitions

2004
June 30 • Re-signed C **Mark Smith**.
Aug. 3 • Re-signed G **Vesa Toskala**.
   7 • Re-signed D **Scott Hannan**.
  13 • Re-signed G **Evgeni Nabokov**.

2005
Aug. 9 • Re-signed LW **Nils Ekman**.
  10 • Re-signed C **Wayne Primeau** and D **Tom Preissing**.
  11 • Re-signed D **Kyle McLaren** and RW **Niko Dimitrakos**.
  15 • Re-signed C **Patrick Marleau**, LW **Marco Sturm** and D **Brad Stuart**.

Entry Draft
Selections 2005-1991

2005
Pick
8	Devin Setoguchi
35	Marc-Edouard Vlasic
112	Alex Stalock
140	Taylor Dakers
149	Derek Joslin
162	Paul Fenton
183	Will Colbert
193	Tony Lucia

2004
Pick
22	Lukas Kaspar
94	Thomas Greiss
126	Torrey Mitchell
129	Jason Churchill
153	Steven Zalewski
201	Michael Vernace
225	David MacDonald
234	Derek MacIntyre
288	Brian Mahoney-Wilson
289	Christian Jensen

2003
Pick
6	Milan Michalek
16	Steve Bernier
43	Joshua Hennessy
47	Matthew Carle
139	Patrick Ehelechner
201	Jonathan Tremblay
205	Joe Pavelski
216	Kai Hospelt
236	Alexander Hult
267	Brian O'Hanley
276	Carter Lee

2002
Pick
27	Mike Morris
52	Dan Spang
86	Jonas Fiedler
139	Kris Newbury
163	Tom Walsh
217	Tim Conboy
288	Michael Hutchins

2001
Pick
20	Marcel Goc
106	Christian Ehrhoff
107	Dimitri Patzold
140	Tomas Plihal
175	Ryane Clowe
182	Tom Cavanagh

2000
Pick
41	Tero Maatta
104	Jon Disalvatore
142	Michal Pinc
166	Nolan Schaefer
183	Michal Macho
246	Chad Wiseman
256	Pasi Saarinen

1999
Pick
14	Jeff Jillson
82	Mark Concannon
111	Willie Levesque
155	Niko Dimitrakos
229	Eric Betournay
241	Doug Murray
257	Hannes Hyvonen

1998
Pick
3	Brad Stuart
29	Jonathan Cheechoo
65	Eric Laplante
98	Rob Davison
104	Miroslav Zalesak
127	Brandon Coalter
145	Mikael Samuelsson
185	Robert Mulick
212	Jim Fahey

1997
Pick
2	Patrick Marleau
23	Scott Hannan
82	Adam Colagiacomo
107	Adam Nittel
163	Joe Dusbabek
192	Cam Severson
219	Mark Smith

1996
Pick
2	Andrei Zyuzin
21	Marco Sturm
55	Terry Friesen
102	Matt Bradley
137	Michel Larocque
164	Jake Deadmarsh
191	Cory Cyrenne
217	David Thibeault

1995
Pick
12	Teemu Riihijarvi
38	Peter Roed
64	Marko Makinen
90	Vesa Toskala
116	Miikka Kiprusoff
130	Michal Bros
140	Timo Hakanen
142	Jaroslav Kudrna
167	Brad Mehalko
168	Robert Jindrich
194	Ryan Kraft
220	Mikko Markkanen

1994
Pick
11	Jeff Friesen
37	Angel Nikolov
66	Alexei Yegorov
89	Vaclav Varada
115	Brian Swanson
141	Alexander Korolyuk
167	Sergei Gorbachev
193	Eric Landry
219	Evgeni Nabokov
240	Tomas Pisa
245	Aniket Dhadphale
271	David Beauregard

1993
Pick
6	Viktor Kozlov
28	Shean Donovan
45	Vlastimil Kroupa
58	Ville Peltonen
80	Alexander Osadchy
106	Andrei Buschan
132	Petri Varis
154	Fredrik Oduya
158	Anatoli Filatov
184	Todd Holt
210	Jonas Forsberg
236	Jeff Salajko
262	Jamie Matthews

1992
Pick
3	Mike Rathje
10	Andrei Nazarov
51	Alexander Cherbayev
75	Jan Caloun
99	Marcus Ragnarsson
123	Michal Sykora
147	Eric Bellerose
171	Ryan Smith
195	Chris Burns
219	Alexander Kholomeyev
243	Victor Ignatjev

1991
Pick
2	Pat Falloon
23	Ray Whitney
30	Sandis Ozolinsh
45	Dody Wood
67	Kerry Toporowski
89	Dan Ryder
111	Frank Nilsson
133	Jaroslav Otevrel
155	Dean Grillo
177	Corwin Saurdiff
199	Dale Craigwell
221	Aaron Kriss
243	Mikhail Kravets

General Managers' History

Jack Ferreira, 1991-92; Chuck Grillo (V.P. Director of Player Personnel), 1992-93 to 1995-96; Dean Lombardi, 1996-97 to 2002-03; Doug Wilson, 2003-04 to date.

Vice President and General Manager

WILSON, DOUG
Executive Vice President/General Manager, San Jose Sharks.
Born in Ottawa, Ont., July 5, 1957.

Doug Wilson is the architect of the current San Jose Sharks team that soared to unprecedented heights in 2003-04. After missing the playoffs in 2002-03, the Sharks rebounded to capture the Pacific Division title, setting a franchise record with 104 points, earning the second seed in the Western Conference playoffs and reaching the Western Conference Finals for the first time. The Sharks' record of 43-21-12-8 in 2003-04 was the third-best mark in the NHL and the team's 31-point improvement over the previous season was the largest turnaround in the NHL. The team also finished tied for fourth in the NHL with a franchise-best 183 goals against and was tied for sixth with a 85.3 percent penalty kill.

Doug Wilson officially took over as the Sharks' executive vice president and general manager on May 13, 2003. In his current role, he has overall authority regarding all hockey-related operations. He oversees all player personnel decisions, negotiates player contracts, coordinates the efforts of the team's scouting department, leads the team in its draft-day preparations and administers the club's player evaluation process at all professional, minor and junior levels.

In his previous role as the team's director of pro development (1997 to 2003), the 16-year NHL veteran's primary responsibilities included evaluating talent at all professional and minor league levels and continuous assessment of the Sharks roster and reserve list. In addition, he provided valuable input assisting the club's player development programs and consulting with the hockey department on all major personnel issues, special assignments and contract negotiations.

A first-round choice (sixth overall) of the Blackhawks in 1977 after a stellar junior career with the Ottawa 67s, Wilson played 14 seasons in Chicago and still ranks as the club's highest scoring defenseman in goals (225), assists (554) and points (779). In addition, he led all Blackhawks defensemen in scoring from 10 consecutive seasons (1980-81 through 1990-91) and captured the 1982 Norris Trophy, symbolic of the NHL's top defenseman, when he tallied 39 goals and 85 points – still Blackhawks single-season records for goals and points by a defenseman.

Club Directory

HP Pavilion at San Jose

San Jose Sharks
HP Pavilion at San Jose
525 West Santa Clara Street
San Jose, CA 95113
Phone **408/287-7070**
FAX 408/999-5797
www.sjsharks.com
Capacity: 17,496

San Jose Sports & Entertainment Enterprises Board Members
Kevin Compton, Greg Reyes, Greg Jamison, Tom McEnery, Brent Jones

Investors in SJSEE Include
Blue Line Associates (Kevin Compton, Greg Reyes, Hasso Plattner, Stratton Sclavos, Gary Valenzuela, Harvey Armstrong), William DelBiaggio, George Gund III, Greg Jamison, Floyd Kvamme, Tom McEnery, Gordon Russell, Rudy Staedler

Executive Staff
President & Chief Executive Officer	Greg Jamison
Executive V.P. of Business Operations	Malcolm Bordelon
Executive V.P. & G.M. (HP Pavilion at San Jose)	Jim Goddard
Executive V.P. & General Counsel	Don Gralnek
Executive V.P. & G.M. (Sharks)	Doug Wilson
Executive V.P. & Chief Financial Officer	Charlie Faas
Vice President of Finance	Ken Caveney
Vice President of Sales & Marketing	Kent Russell
Vice President of Building Operations	Rich Sotelo
Vice President and Assistant G.M. (Sharks)	Wayne Thomas
Executive Assistants	Tricia Sullivan, Michelle Simmons, Jeanette Shields

Hockey Operations
Head Coach	Ron Wilson
Assistant Coaches	Tim Hunter, Rob Zettler
Goaltender Coach	Warren Strelow
Special Consultant to the General Manager	John Ferguson
Director of Scouting	Tim Burke
Assistant to the General Manager	Joe Will
Scouts	Gilles Cote, Pat Funk, Jack Gardner, Jim Grillo, Brian Gross, Barry Long, Karel Masopust, Cap Raeder
Player Development Coordinator	Graeme Townshend
Director of Hockey Administration	Rosemary Tebaldi
Video Scouting Coordinator	Bob Friedlander
Team Services Coordinator	Marshall Dickerson
Head Athletic Trainer	Ray Tufts, A.T.,C
Assistant Athletic Trainer and Massage Therapist.	Wes Howard, ATC, CMT
Strength & Conditioning Coach	Mac Read
Equipment Manager	Mike Aldrich
Assistant Equipment Manager	Kurt Harvey
Equipment Assistant & Equipment Transportation	Roy Sneesby
Head Coach, Cleveland Barons (AHL)	Roy Sommer
Assistant Coach, Cleveland Barons (AHL)	David Cunniff
Head Trainer, Cleveland Barons (AHL)	Dave Zenobi
Equipment Manager, Cleveland Barons (AHL)	Rob Kennedy
Asst. Equipment Manager, Cleveland Barons (AHL)	Phil Simon
Team Physician	Arthur J. Ting, M.D.
Team Internist	John Chiu, M.D.
Team Dentist	Robert Bonahoom, D.D.S.
Team Vision Specialist	Vincent S. Zuccaro, O.D., F.A.A.O.
Medical Staff	Warren King, M.D., Mark Sontag, M.D.

SVS&E/Business Operations
Senior Director of Communications	Ken Arnold
Director of Broadcasting	Frank Albin
Director of Ticket Sales	John Castro
Director of Advertising & Promotions	Andrew Ebel
Director of Media Relations	Scott Emmert
Dir. of Fan Development/The Sharks Foundation	Rob Jaynes
Director of Event Presentation	Steve Maroni
Director, Corporate Partnerships	Chris Parker
Director of Suite Sales & Service	Bruce Ross
Director of Communications & Internet Services	Roger Ross
Senior Manager, Corporate Partnerships	Bryan Deierling
Senior Ticket Operations Manager	Scott Fitzsimmons
Senior Service Manager, Corporate Partnerships	Heather Hunter
Manager, Corporate Partnerships	Jennifer Birmingham, Eric Kwait
Account Sales Managers	Patrick Frost, Ted Chuba, Adam King
Account Service Managers	Sharon Holman, Sarah Bauerle, Julie Kennedy
Marketing Manager	Doug Bentz
HP Pavilion Group Sales Manager	Adam King
Creative Services Manager	Michelle Kracht
Suite Service Manager	Kathy Payne-Tovar
Public Relations Manager	Jim Sparaco
Service Manager, Corporate Partnerships	Trisha Holman, Janelle Garcia
Ticket Operations Coordinator	Maria Hernandez
Media Relations Coordinator	Tom Holy
Mascot Operations Coordinator	Tim Patnode
Internet Services Coordinator	Ryan Stenn
Executive Assistant	Mary Grace Miller

Finance
Human Resources Manager	Cathy Chandler
Manager of Information Technology	Joseph Lee
Payroll Administrator	Sue Feachen
Controller	Stephanie Reitz

Building Operations
Director of Ticket Operations	Daniel DeBoer
Director of Booking & Events	Steve Kirsner
Director of Guest Services	Ken Sweezey
Facilities Technical Director	Greg Carrolan
Director of Building Services	Monte Chavez
Chief Engineer	Mark Mullins

Miscellaneous
Television Station	FOX Sports Net
Radio Network Flagship	98.5 K-FOX (KUFX FM)
Television Play-By-Play Broadcaster	Randy Hahn
Television Color Analyst	Drew Remenda
Radio Play-By-Play Broadcaster	Dan Rusanowsky
In Game TV Host	Glen Kuiper
Team Photographers	Don Smith, Rocky Widner
P.A. Announcer	Joe Ike
In Game Host	Danny Miller

Tampa Bay Lightning

2005-06 Schedule

Oct.	Wed.	5	Carolina		Thu.	5	at Buffalo
	Fri.	7	at Florida		Sat.	7	at Boston
	Sat.	8	Florida		Fri.	13	Columbus
	Mon.	10	Boston		Mon.	16	at San Jose*
	Thu.	13	Buffalo		Tue.	17	at Los Angeles
	Sat.	15	at Pittsburgh		Fri.	20	at Dallas
	Sun.	16	at Washington		Sat.	21	at Atlanta
	Thu.	20	at Atlanta		Tue.	24	Florida
	Fri.	21	Ottawa		Thu.	26	New Jersey
	Wed.	26	at New Jersey		Sat.	28	at Philadelphia*
	Fri.	28	Washington		Sun.	29	at Washington*
	Sat.	29	at Atlanta		Tue.	31	Toronto
Nov.	Tue.	1	Atlanta	**Feb.**	Sat.	4	Washington
	Thu.	3	at Ottawa		Mon.	6	at NY Islanders
	Sat.	5	at Toronto		Tue.	7	at New Jersey
	Tue.	8	at Montreal		Thu.	9	Carolina
	Thu.	10	NY Rangers		Sat.	11	at Boston
	Fri.	11	at Atlanta		Tue.	28	Florida
	Mon.	14	Philadelphia	**Mar.**	Sat.	4	Montreal
	Tue.	15	at Washington		Mon.	6	Ottawa
	Thu.	17	NY Islanders		Tue.	7	at Pittsburgh
	Sun.	20	at Carolina		Thu.	9	at Buffalo
	Tue.	22	at Philadelphia		Sat.	11	at Toronto
	Wed.	23	at Washington		Mon.	13	at Montreal
	Fri.	25	New Jersey		Tue.	14	at Ottawa
	Sun.	27	Pittsburgh*		Fri.	17	Philadelphia
	Wed.	30	Toronto		Sun.	19	NY Islanders*
Dec.	Fri.	2	Chicago		Mon.	20	at Florida
	Thu.	8	St. Louis		Thu.	23	Washington
	Sat.	10	Nashville		Sat.	25	NY Rangers
	Wed.	14	at Anaheim		Mon.	27	at Carolina
	Thu.	15	at Phoenix		Thu.	30	Atlanta
	Sat.	17	Detroit	**Apr.**	Sat.	1	at Florida
	Tue.	20	at Carolina		Mon.	3	Florida
	Thu.	22	at NY Rangers		Thu.	6	Atlanta
	Fri.	23	Buffalo		Sat.	8	Pittsburgh
	Mon.	26	Carolina		Sun.	9	at Florida*
	Wed.	28	Montreal		Tue.	11	Atlanta
	Fri.	30	Boston		Fri.	14	at Carolina
Jan.	Mon.	2	at NY Islanders		Sat.	15	Carolina
	Tue.	3	at NY Rangers		Tue.	18	Washington

* Denotes afternoon game.

Year-by-Year Record

Season	GP	Home W	L	T	OL	Road W	L	T	OL	Overall W	L	T	OL	GF	GA	Pts.	Finished	Playoff Result
2004-05	....	..	..	..	..	..	..	..	..	..	..	..	..	....	....	....		
2003-04	**82**	**24**	**10**	**4**	**3**	**22**	**12**	**4**	**3**	**46**	**22**	**8**	**6**	**245**	**192**	**106**	**1st,**	**Southeast Div.**	**Won Stanley Cup**
2002-03	82	22	9	7	3	14	16	9	2	36	25	16	5	219	210	93	1st,	Southeast Div.	Lost Conf. Semi-Final
2001-02	82	16	17	5	3	11	23	6	1	27	40	11	4	178	219	69	3rd,	Southeast Div.	Out of Playoffs
2000-01	82	17	19	3	2	7	28	3	3	24	47	6	5	201	280	59	5th,	Southeast Div.	Out of Playoffs
1999-2000	82	13	20	4	4	6	27	5	3	19	47	9	7	204	310	54	4th,	Southeast Div.	Out of Playoffs
1998-99	82	12	25	4	....	7	29	5	....	19	54	9	....	179	292	47	4th,	Southeast Div.	Out of Playoffs
1997-98	82	11	23	7	....	6	32	3	....	17	55	10	....	151	269	44	7th,	Atlantic Div.	Out of Playoffs
1996-97	82	15	18	8	....	17	22	2	....	32	40	10	....	217	247	74	6th,	Atlantic Div.	Out of Playoffs
1995-96	82	22	14	5	....	16	18	7	....	38	32	12	....	238	248	88	5th,	Atlantic Div.	Lost Conf. Quarter-Final
1994-95	48	10	14	0	....	7	14	3	....	17	28	3	....	120	144	37	6th,	Atlantic Div.	Out of Playoffs
1993-94	84	14	22	6	....	16	21	5	....	30	43	11	....	224	251	71	7th,	Atlantic Div.	Out of Playoffs
1992-93	84	12	27	3	....	11	27	4	....	23	54	7	....	245	332	53	6th,	Norris Div.	Out of Playoffs

Vincent Lecavalier (top left), Martin St. Louis (top right) and Dave Andreychuk (left) were all re-signed to long-term deals by the Stanley Cup champion Lightning. St. Louis also won the Hart and Art Ross trophies in 2003-04.

Franchise date: December 16, 1991

14th NHL Season

SOUTHEAST DIVISION

2005-06 Player Personnel

FORWARDS	HT	WT	S	Place of Birth	Date	2004-05 Club
AFANASENKOV, Dmitry	6-1	195	R	Arkhangelsk, USSR	5/12/80	Togliatti
ANDREYCHUK, Dave	6-4	220	R	Hamilton, Ont.	9/29/63	
ARTYUKHIN, Evgeni	6-5	254	L	Moscow, USSR	4/4/83	Springfield
CAMPBELL, Jim	6-2	205	R	Worcester, MA	4/3/73	Bridgeport-Springfield
CIBAK, Martin	6-1	196	L	Liptovsky Mikulas, Czech.	5/17/80	L. Mikulas-Plzen-Kosice
CRAIG, Ryan	6-2	220	L	Abbotsford, B.C.	1/6/82	Springfield
DiMAIO, Rob	5-10	190	R	Calgary, Alta.	2/19/68	Langnau-Milano
DINGMAN, Chris	6-4	235	L	Edmonton, Alta.	7/6/76	
FEDOTENKO, Ruslan	6-2	195	L	Kiev, Ukraine	1/18/79	
FRITZ, Mitch	6-8	258	L	Osoyoos, B.C.	11/24/80	Springfield
HRDEL, Zbynek	6-4	197	R	Pisek, Czech.	8/19/85	Rimouski
JASPERS, Jason	5-11	207	L	Thunder Bay, Ont.	4/8/81	Utah-Springfield
LECAVALIER, Vincent	6-4	207	L	Ile Bizard, Que.	4/21/80	Kazan
MILLEY, Norm	6-0	211	R	Toronto, Ont.	2/14/80	Rochester
MODIN, Fredrik	6-4	220	L	Sundsvall, Sweden	10/8/74	Timra
PROSPAL, Vaclav	6-2	195	L	Ceske Budejovice, Czech.	2/17/75	C. Budejovice
REID, Darren	6-2	205	R	Lac La Biche, Alta.	5/8/83	Springfield
RICHARDS, Brad	6-1	198	L	Murray Harbour, P.E.I.	5/2/80	Kazan
ST. LOUIS, Martin	5-9	185	L	Laval, Que.	6/18/75	Lausanne
TARNASKY, Nick	6-2	233	L	Rocky Mtn. House, Alta.	11/25/84	Springfield
TAYLOR, Tim	6-1	190	L	Stratford, Ont.	2/6/69	

DEFENSEMEN	HT	WT	S	Place of Birth	Date	2004-05 Club
BOYLE, Dan	5-11	190	R	Ottawa, Ont.	7/12/76	Djurgarden
DICAIRE, Gerard	6-2	190	L	Faro, Yukon	9/14/82	Springfield
EGENER, Mike	6-4	213	L	Lahr, West Germany	9/26/84	Springfield
HELBLING, Timo	6-3	209	R	Basel, Switz.	7/21/81	Kloten
KUBINA, Pavel	6-4	230	R	Celadna, Czech.	4/15/77	Vitkovice
O'BRIEN, Doug	6-1	200	L	St. John's, Nfld.	2/16/84	Springfield-Johnstown
PRATT, Nolan	6-3	203	L	Fort McMurray, Alta.	8/14/75	Duisburg
ROHLOFF, Todd	6-3	213	L	Grand Rapids, IL	1/16/74	Rochester
SARICH, Cory	6-3	204	R	Saskatoon, Sask.	8/16/78	
SYDOR, Darryl	6-1	205	L	Edmonton, Alta.	5/13/72	

GOALTENDERS	HT	WT	C	Place of Birth	Date	2004-05 Club
BURKE, Sean	6-4	211	L	Windsor, Ont.	1/29/67	
EKLUND, Brian	6-5	205	L	Braintree, MA	5/24/80	Springfield
GRAHAME, John	6-2	220	L	Denver, CO	8/31/75	

Coaching History

Terry Crisp, 1992-93 to 1996-97; Terry Crisp, Rick Paterson and Jacques Demers, 1997-98; Jacques Demers, 1998-99; Steve Ludzik, 1999-2000; Steve Ludzik and John Tortorella, 2000-01; John Tortorella, 2001-02 to date.

Coach

TORTORELLA, JOHN
Coach, Tampa Bay Lightning. Born in Boston, MA, June 24, 1958.

John Tortorella took over as head coach in Tampa Bay on January 6, 2001. He led the team to its first Eastern Conference and Stanley Cup championships, as well as its second consecutive Southeast Division championship in 2003-04. He was the winner of the Jack Adams Award as the National Hockey League's top coach after leading the Lightning to franchise records with 46 wins and 106 points before embarking on the successful playoff campaign. His 2003-04 team tallied a franchise-record 245 goals and many of his Lightning players established personal bests in goals, assists and points. He now has 121 wins with the Lightning, ranking him second on the team's all-time wins list.

A 14-year NHL coaching veteran, Tortorella became the fourth head coach in team history when he was named to that position on January 6, 2001. Recognized as one of the top teaching coaches in the game, the Boston native joined the Lightning organization when he was hired on as an associate coach prior to the 2000-01 season.

Tortorella began his playing career at Salem State College before transferring to the University of Maine. He spent three seasons with the Black Bears and was twice named an ECAC All-Star. After playing in Sweden, Tortorella played in the Atlantic Coast Hockey League with Virginia, Hampton Roads, and Erie. He spent two seasons as general manager and head coach of the Virginia Lancers (ACHL) from 1986 to 1988, where he garnered coach of the year honors both years while leading his 1986-87 team to the league championship. He was hired as an assistant coach with the New Haven Nighthawks of the American Hockey League in 1988-89 and became an assistant coach with the Buffalo Sabres the following year. Tortorella remained with the Sabres organization through the 1996-97 season, including two years as coach of their AHL affiliate in Rochester.

Tortorella returned to the NHL in 1997 as an assistant with the Phoenix Coyotes, where he spent two seasons before joining the Rangers for 1999-2000. He served as the Rangers' interim head coach for the final four games of the '99-00 season before joining the Lightning staff.

Coaching Record

Season	Team	Games	Regular Season W	L	T	Playoffs Games	W	L
1995-96	Rochester (AHL)	80	37	38	5	19	15	4
1996-97	Rochester (AHL)	80	40	30	9	10	6	4
1999-2000	NY Rangers (NHL)	4	0	3	1	....	....	....
2000-01	Tampa Bay (NHL)	43	12	30	1	....	....	....
2001-02	Tampa Bay (NHL)	82	27	44	11	....	....	....
2002-03	Tampa Bay (NHL)	82	36	30	16	11	5	6
2003-04	Tampa Bay (NHL)	82	46	28	8	23	16	7
2004-05	Tampa Bay (NHL)		Season Cancelled					
	NHL Totals	293	121	135	37	34	21	13

In the System and Recently Drafted

FORWARDS	HT	WT	S	Place of Birth	Date	2004-05 Club
AKKANEN, Karri	6-6	200	L	Tampere, Finland	1/29/84	Tappara Jr.
ALEXEEV, Nikita	6-5	227	L	Murmansk, USSR	12/27/81	Springfield
BARTANUS, Marek	6-3	194	R	Liptovsky Mikulas, Czech.	2/13/87	Kosice-Trebisov
BEZRUKOV, Dmitri	6-3	187	L	Kazan, USSR	11/9/77	Perm-Nizhny Novgorod
BUT, Anton	6-1	201	L	Kharkov, USSR	7/3/80	Yaroslavl
COLLINS, Dustin	6-3	210	L	Payson, AZ	2/28/85	Northern Mich.
DANILICS, Raimonds	6-3	180	R	Riga, Latvia	7/17/85	Texas-Tri-City-Bismarck
DARBY, Craig	6-4	200	R	Oneida, NY	9/26/72	Springfield
DEVEAUX, Andre	6-3	240	R	Freeport, Bahamas	2/23/84	Springfield
GLUKHOV, Alexei	6-3	176	L	Voskresensk, USSR	4/5/84	Voskresensk-Springfield
HAGGLUND, Johan	6-2	203	L	Ornskoldsvik, Sweden	6/9/82	Hammarby
HENRICH, Adam	6-4	231	L	Thornhill, Ont.	1/19/84	Springfield-Johnstown
JONES, Blair	6-2	193	R	Central Butte, Sask.	9/27/86	Red Deer-Moose Jaw
KAZIONOV, Dmitri	6-3	185	L	Moscow, USSR	5/13/84	Togliatti
KELLER, Justin	5-11	185	L	Nelson, B.C.	3/4/86	Kelowna
KVAPIL, Marek	5-10	187	R	Ilava, Czech.	1/5/85	Slavia Jr.-Saginaw
LASCEK, Stanislav	6-0	195	L	Martin, Czech.	1/17/86	Chicoutimi
LAWRENCE, Chris	6-4	199	R	Toronto, Ont.	2/5/87	Sault Ste. Marie
OLVESTAD, Jimmie	6-1	194	L	Stockholm, Sweden	2/16/80	Djurgarden
PACKARD, Dennis	6-4	234	L	St. Catherines, Ont.	2/9/82	Springfield-Johnstown
PERRIN, Eric	5-9	176	L	Laval, Que.	11/1/75	Hershey
POLUSHIN, Alexander	6-2	212	L	Kirovo-Chepetsk, USSR	5/8/83	CSKA
RACHUNEK, Ivan	5-9	176	L	Zlin, Czech.	7/6/81	Znojmo
SEDOV, Pavel	6-3	200	L	Voskresensk, USSR	1/12/82	Tver-Dmitrov-Ryazan
SMOLENAK, Radek	6-2	180	L	Prague, Czech.	12/3/86	Kingston
SOMERVUORI, Eero	5-10	190	R	Jarvenpaa, Finland	2/7/79	Karpat
SOUCY, J.F.	6-3	205	L	Riviere Du Loup, Que.	3/25/83	Springfield-Johnstown
TOBIN, Mark	6-3	211	L	St. John's, Nfld.	11/26/85	Rimouski
TOFFEY, John	6-3	205	L	Barnstable, MA	11/26/82	Massachusetts
VISHNYAKOV, Albert	6-1	178	R	Almyetevsk, USSR	12/30/83	Dynamo Moscow
WILLIS, Shane	6-1	195	R	Edmonton, Alta.	6/13/77	Springfield

DEFENSEMEN	HT	WT	S	Place of Birth	Date	2004-05 Club
ATHERTON, P.J.	6-2	208	R	Edina, MN	8/16/82	U. of Minnesota
BERGFORS, Henrik	6-4	227	R	Sodertalje, Sweden	5/15/82	Adirondack
ELLIOTT, Brandon	6-4	225	L	Orangeville, Ont.	3/8/84	Miss (OHL)-Sprfld-Vic
FEMENELLA, Art	6-7	255	R	Annandale, NJ	6/6/82	U. of Vermont
GOC, Sascha	6-6	220	R	Calw, West Germany	4/14/79	Mannheim
GRECO, Brady	6-3	195	R	Bryan, OH	3/4/83	Colorado College
HOLMQVIST, Andreas	6-4	195	R	Stockholm, Sweden	7/23/81	Springfield
LUNDIN, Mike	6-1	195	L	Burnsville, MN	9/24/84	U. of Maine
McLAREN, Steve	6-0	227	L	Owen Sound, Ont.	2/3/75	Springfield
MIHALIK, Vladimir	6-7	222	L	Presov, Czech.	1/29/87	Presov
RANGER, Paul	6-2	215	L	Whitby, Ont.	9/12/84	Springfield
ROGERS, Andy	6-5	208	L	Calgary, Alta.	8/25/86	Cgy (WHL)-Pr. George
ROSEHILL, Jay	6-3	210	L	Olds, Alta.	7/16/85	U. Minn-Duluth
SMABY, Matt	6-5	211	L	Minneapolis, MN	10/14/84	North Dakota
WESSBECKER, John	6-1	180	R	Edina, MN	9/15/86	Blake
ZAPLETAL, Jan	6-3	190	R	Brno, Czech.	8/21/86	Regina

GOALTENDERS	HT	WT	C	Place of Birth	Date	2004-05 Club
BEECH, Kevin	6-4	168	L	London, Ont.	9/23/86	Sudbury
BOUTIN, Jonathan	6-2	210	L	Granby, Que.	3/28/81	PEI-Quebec
CEY, Morgan	6-3	177	L	Wilkie, Sask.	10/27/81	U. of Notre Dame
COLEMAN, Gerald	6-4	205	L	Romeoville, IL	4/3/85	London
KOSHECHKIN, Vasily	6-6	210	L	Togliatti, USSR	3/27/83	
NORRENA, Fredrik	6-0	187	L	Pietarsaari, Finland	11/29/73	Linkoping
RAMO, Karri	6-2	192	L	Asikkala, Finland	7/1/86	Pelicans

General Managers' History

Phil Esposito, 1992-93 to 1997-98; Jacques Demers, 1998-99; Rick Dudley, 1999-2000, 2000-01; Rick Dudley and Jay Feaster, 2001-02; Jay Feaster, 2002-03 to date.

Club Records

Team

(Figures in brackets for season records are games played; records for fewest points, wins, ties, losses, goals, goals against are for 70 or more games)

Most Points	106	2003-04 (82)
Most Wins	46	2003-04 (82)
Most Ties	16	2002-03 (82)
Most Losses	55	1997-98 (82)
Most Goals	245	1992-93 (84), 2003-04 (82)
Most Goals Against	332	1992-93 (84)
Fewest Points	44	1997-98 (82)
Fewest Wins	17	1997-98 (82)
Fewest Ties	6	2000-01 (82)
Fewest Losses	22	2003-04 (82)
Fewest Goals	151	1997-98 (82)
Fewest Goals Against	192	2003-04 (82)

Longest Winning Streak
Overall	5	Twice
Home	6	Feb. 15-Mar. 10/96, Nov. 17-Dec. 21/01
Away	4	Jan. 6-13/97

Longest Undefeated Streak
Overall	13	Mar. 7-Apr. 2/03 (7 wins, 6 ties)
Home	9	Feb. 25-Apr. 2/03 (5 wins, 4 ties)
Away	6	Twice

Longest Losing Streak
Overall	13	Jan. 3-Feb. 2/98
Home	10	Jan. 3-Feb. 26/98
Away	11	Oct. 24-Dec. 10/97

Longest Winless Streak
Overall	16	Twice
Home	11	Jan. 2-Feb. 26/98 (10 losses, 1 tie)
Away	17	Dec. 2/99-Feb. 19/00 (14 losses, 3 ties)

Most Shutouts, Season	9	2001-02 (82)
Most PIM, Season	1,823	1997-98 (82)
Most Goals, Game	9	Nov. 8/03 (Pit. 0 at T.B. 9)

Individual

Most Seasons	7	Five players
Most Games, Career	475	Rob Zamuner
Most Goals, Career	146	Vincent Lecavalier
Most Assists, Career	193	Brad Richards
Most Points, Career	327	Vincent Lecavalier (146G, 171A)
Most PIM, Career	782	Chris Gratton
Most Shutouts, Career	14	Nikolai Khabibulin
Longest Consecutive Games Streak	226	Rob Zamuner (Nov. 1/95-Mar. 30/98)
Most Goals, Season	42	Brian Bradley (1992-93)
Most Assists, Season	57	Vaclav Prospal, Brad Richards (2002-03)

Most Points, Season	94	Martin St. Louis (2003-04; 38G, 56A)
Most PIM, Season	258	Enrico Ciccone (1995-96)
Most Points, Defenseman, Season	65	Roman Hamrlik (1995-96; 16G, 49A)
Most Points, Center, Season	86	Brian Bradley (1992-93; 42G, 44A)
Most Points, Right Wing, Season	94	Martin St. Louis (2003-04; 38G, 56A)
Most Points, Left Wing, Season	80	Cory Stillman (2003-04; 25G, 55A)
Most Points, Rookie, Season	62	Brad Richards (2000-01; 21G, 41A)
Most Shutouts, Season	7	Nikolai Khabibulin (2001-02)
Most Goals, Game	4	Chris Kontos (Oct. 7/92)
Most Assists, Game	4	Four times
Most Points, Game	6	Doug Crossman (Nov. 7/92; 3G, 3A)

Captains' History

No captain, 1992-93 to 1994-95; Paul Ysebaert, 1995-96, 1996-97; Paul Ysebaert and Mikael Renberg, 1997-98; Rob Zamuner, 1998-99; Bill Houlder, Chris Gratton and Vincent Lecavalier, 1999-2000; Vincent Lecavalier, 2000-01; no captain, 2001-02; Dave Andreychuk, 2002-03 to date.

All-time Record vs. Other Clubs

Regular Season

	At Home							On Road							Total						
	GP	W	L	T	OL	GF	GA	PTS	GP	W	L	T	OL	GF	GA	PTS	GP	W	L	T	OL	GF	GA	PTS
Anaheim	9	4	5	0	0	17	23	8	8	3	4	1	0	20	24	7	17	7	9	1	0	37	47	15
Atlanta	13	9	2	1	1	49	29	20	13	2	8	3	0	34	48	7	26	11	10	4	1	83	77	27
Boston	23	10	8	3	2	70	66	25	23	1	15	6	1	49	84	9	46	11	23	9	3	119	150	34
Buffalo	23	6	13	3	1	49	70	16	23	8	12	2	1	63	63	19	46	14	25	5	2	112	133	35
Calgary	10	5	4	1	0	31	32	11	10	5	4	0	1	24	32	9	20	9	9	1	1	55	64	20
Carolina	26	14	9	3	0	73	67	31	27	5	14	7	1	65	81	18	53	19	23	10	1	138	148	49
Chicago	11	4	3	3	1	26	28	12	14	4	8	2	0	35	45	10	25	8	11	5	1	61	73	22
Colorado	12	8	3	1	1	39	32	18	13	3	8	2	0	28	50	8	25	11	10	3	1	67	82	26
Columbus	3	2	1	0	0	5	3	4	3	1	1	0	1	4	5	3	6	3	2	1	0	9	8	7
Dallas	13	1	10	2	0	20	37	4	11	3	7	1	0	27	39	7	24	4	17	3	0	47	76	11
Detroit	14	4	8	1	1	43	61	10	12	1	10	1	0	21	47	3	26	5	18	2	1	64	108	13
Edmonton	11	3	5	2	1	31	35	9	10	3	7	0	0	21	26	6	21	6	12	2	1	52	61	15
Florida	28	10	12	6	0	60	77	26	28	8	14	4	2	62	81	22	56	18	26	10	2	122	158	48
Los Angeles	10	5	4	0	1	23	22	11	11	8	1	2	0	36	24	18	21	13	5	2	1	59	46	29
Minnesota	3	1	1	1	0	8	9	3	3	0	3	0	0	8	13	0	6	1	4	1	0	16	22	3
Montreal	23	9	8	5	1	55	61	24	22	10	11	1	0	53	59	21	45	19	19	6	1	108	120	45
Nashville	4	1	1	2	0	11	10	4	6	4	2	0	0	16	12	8	10	5	3	2	0	27	22	12
New Jersey	25	8	12	5	0	59	75	21	26	6	18	2	0	44	93	14	51	14	30	7	0	103	168	35
NY Islanders	26	12	12	2	0	67	80	26	25	11	12	1	1	69	78	24	51	23	24	3	1	136	158	50
NY Rangers	25	11	10	3	1	86	83	26	27	12	12	2	1	85	87	27	52	23	22	5	2	171	170	53
Ottawa	23	8	12	2	1	70	80	19	23	8	15	0	0	50	88	16	46	16	27	2	1	120	168	35
Philadelphia	26	9	15	1	1	71	78	20	25	4	14	7	0	46	79	15	51	13	29	8	1	117	157	35
Phoenix	10	5	5	0	0	33	33	10	11	5	6	0	0	26	28	10	21	10	11	0	0	59	61	20
Pittsburgh	23	12	9	2	0	75	60	26	23	5	14	3	1	59	90	14	46	17	23	5	1	134	150	40
St. Louis	13	5	5	3	0	38	42	13	11	1	9	0	1	24	44	3	24	6	14	3	1	62	86	16
San Jose	12	7	4	1	0	32	31	15	10	6	3	1	0	36	32	13	22	13	7	2	0	68	63	28
Toronto	20	3	15	1	1	42	71	8	21	7	12	1	1	55	76	16	41	10	27	2	2	97	147	24
Vancouver	9	3	5	0	1	31	37	7	9	6	2	1	0	17	40	13	18	3	11	1	2	48	77	10
Washington	29	9	18	2	0	65	93	20	29	7	18	4	0	65	101	18	58	16	36	6	0	130	194	38
Totals	**477**	**188**	**218**	**56**	**15**	**1279**	**1425**	**447**	**477**	**140**	**269**	**56**	**12**	**1142**	**1569**	**348**	**954**	**328**	**487**	**112**	**27**	**2421**	**2994**	**795**

Playoffs

	Series	W	L	GP	W	L	T	GF	GA	Last Mtg.
Calgary	1	1	0	7	4	3	0	13	14	2004
Montreal	1	1	0	4	4	0	0	14	5	2004
New Jersey	1	0	1	5	1	4	0	8	14	2003
NY Islanders	1	1	0	5	4	1	0	12	5	2004
Philadelphia	2	1	1	13	6	7	0	34	45	2004
Washington	1	1	0	6	4	2	0	14	15	2003
Totals	**7**	**5**	**2**	**40**	**23**	**17**	**0**	**95**	**98**	

Playoff Results 2005-2000

Year	Round	Opponent	Result	GF	GA
2004	F	Calgary	W 4-3	13	14
	CF	Philadelphia	W 4-3	21	19
	CSF	Montreal	W 4-0	14	5
	CQF	NY Islanders	W 4-1	12	5
2003	CSF	New Jersey	L 1-4	8	14
	CQF	Washington	W 4-2	14	15

Abbreviations: Round: F – Final;
CF – conference final; **CSF** – conference semi-final;
CQF – conference quarter-final.

Carolina totals include Hartford, 1992-93 to 1996-97.
Dallas totals include Minnesota North Stars, 1992-93.

Colorado totals include Quebec, 1992-93 to 1994-95.
Phoenix totals include Winnipeg, 1992-93 to 1995-96.

Key Off-Season Signings/Acquisitions

2004

July 23 • Re-signed LW **Chris Dingman**.
Aug. 5 • D **Pavel Kubina** awarded two-year contract in arbitration.
8 • Re-signed D **Cory Sarich**.
9 • Re-signed LW **Fredrik Modin**.
16 • Obtained LW **Vaclav Prospal** from Anaheim for a 2005 2nd-round pick.

2005

July 28 • Re-signed Cs **Tim Taylor** and **Martin Cibak**.
30 • Re-signed LW **Ruslan Fedotenko**.
Aug. 5 • Re-signed D **Nolan Pratt**.
9 • Re-signed D **Dan Boyle**.
9 • Signed G **Sean Burke** and RW **Rob DiMaio**.
16 • Re-signed C **Vincent Lecavalier**.
24 • Re-signed RW **Martin St. Louis**.
25 • Re-signed C **Dave Andreychuk**.

Entry Draft
Selections 2005-1992

2005
Pick
30	Vladimir Mihalik
73	Radek Smolenak
89	Chris Lawrence
92	Marek Bartanus
102	Blair Jones
133	Stanislav Lascek
163	Marek Kvapil
165	Kevin Beech
225	John Wessbecker

2004
Pick
30	Andy Rogers
65	Mark Tobin
102	Mike Lundin
158	Brandon Elliott
163	Dustin Collins
188	Jan Zapletal
191	Karri Ramo
245	Justin Keller

2003
Pick
34	Mike Egener
41	Matt Smaby
96	Jonathan Boutin
192	Doug O'Brien
224	Gerald Coleman
227	Jay Rosehill
255	Raimonds Danilics
256	Brady Greco
273	Albert Vishnyakov
286	Zbynek Hrdel
287	Nick Tarnasky

2002
Pick
60	Adam Henrich
100	Dmitri Kazionov
135	Joseph Pearce
162	Gerard Dicaire
170	P.J. Atherton
174	Karri Akkanen
183	Paul Ranger
213	Fredrik Norrena
233	Vasily Koshechkin
255	Ryan Craig
256	Darren Reid
286	Alexei Glukhov
287	John Toffey

2001
Pick
3	Alexander Svitov
47	Alexander Polushin
61	Andreas Holmqvist
94	Evgeni Artukhin
123	Aaron Lobb
138	Paul Lynch
188	Art Femenella
219	Dennis Packard
222	Jeremy Van Hoof
252	J.F. Soucy
259	Dmitri Bezrukov
261	Vitali Smolyaninov
281	Ilja Solarev
289	Henrik Bergfors

2000
Pick
8	Nikita Alexeev
34	Ruslan Zainullin
81	Alexander Kharitonov
126	Johan Hagglund
161	Pavel Sedov
191	Aaron Gionet
222	Marek Priechodsky
226	Brian Eklund
233	Alexander Polukeyev
263	Thomas Ziegler

1999
Pick
47	Sheldon Keefe
67	Evgeny Konstantinov
75	Brett Scheffelmaier
88	Jimmie Olvestad
127	Kaspars Astashenko
148	Michal Lanicek
182	Fedor Fedorov
187	Ivan Rachunek
216	Erkki Rajamaki
244	Mikko Kuparinen

1998
Pick
1	Vincent Lecavalier
64	Brad Richards
72	Dmitry Afanasenkov
92	Eric Beaudoin
121	Curtis Rich
146	Sergei Kuznetsov
174	Brett Allan
194	Oak Hewer
221	Daniel Hulak
229	Chris Lyness
252	Martin Cibak

1997
Pick
7	Paul Mara
33	Kyle Kos
61	Matt Elich
108	Mark Thompson
109	Jan Sulc
112	Karel Betik
153	Andrei Skopintsev
168	Justin Jack
170	Eero Somervuori
185	Samuel St-Pierre
198	Shawn Skolney
224	Paul Comrie

1996
Pick
16	Mario Larocque
69	Curtis Tipler
125	Jason Robinson
152	Nikolai Ignatov
157	Xavier Delisle
179	Pavel Kubina

1995
Pick
5	Daymond Langkow
30	Mike McBain
56	Shane Willis
108	Konstantin Golokhvastov
134	Eduard Pershin
160	Cory Murphy
186	Joe Cardarelli
212	Zac Bierk

1994
Pick
8	Jason Wiemer
34	Colin Cloutier
55	Vadim Epanchintsev
86	Dmitri Klevakin
137	Daniel Juden
138	Bryce Salvador
164	Chris Maillet
190	Alexei Baranov
216	Yuri Smirnov
242	Shawn Gervais
268	Brian White

1993
Pick
3	Chris Gratton
29	Tyler Moss
55	Allan Egeland
81	Marian Kacir
107	Ryan Brown
133	Kiley Hill
159	Matthieu Raby
185	Ryan Nauss
211	Alexandre Laporte
237	Brett Duncan
263	Mark Szoke

1992
Pick
1	Roman Hamrlik
26	Drew Bannister
49	Brent Gretzky
74	Aaron Gavey
97	Brantt Myhres
122	Martin Tanguay
145	Derek Wilkinson
170	Dennis Maxwell
193	Andrew Kemper
218	Marc Tardif
241	Tom MacDonald

Vice President and General Manager

FEASTER, JAY
Executive Vice President/General Manager, Tampa Bay Lightning.
Born in Williamstown, PA, July 30, 1962.

Jay Feaster joined the Lightning on October 20, 1998 and was named general manager on February 10, 2002. He led Tampa Bay to the Stanley Cup in 2003-04 and was named NHL executive of the year by *The Sporting News*. The Lightning enjoyed a storybook season under Feaster's direction in 2003-04, winning a second consecutive Southeast Division title, capturing the top seed in the Eastern Conference and skating off with Lord Stanley's Cup after a hard-fought seven game series against the Calgary Flames. He has been widely praised for bringing continuity and stability to the Lightning franchise.

Feaster, named the fourth general manager in franchise history on February 10, 2002, joined the Lightning on October 20, 1998, from the Hershey Bears of the American Hockey League. He spent three-plus seasons as Tampa Bay's assistant general manager, overseeing all contractual, collective bargaining and NHL legal issues, as well as the organization's scouting department and its minor league affiliates. As general manager, Feaster has developed the Lightning into one of the most competitive and entertaining teams in the NHL. He also served as co-general manager of Team USA for the 2003 World Championships along with Larry Pleau of St. Louis.

To join the Lightning, Feaster resigned his post as president of the Hershey Bears and vice president of Hershey Sports and Entertainment. In that capacity, Feaster oversaw the operations of the Bears, the Hershey Wildcats professional soccer team and HersheyPark Arena/Stadium. In his nine years with the Bears, he led the team to a division title (1993-94) and a Calder Cup Championship (1997), while establishing three consecutive single-season attendance records (1991-92 to 1993-94) and entering into a five-year affiliation agreement with the NHL's Colorado Avalanche.

While in Hershey, Feaster spent time on the advisory boards of the Big 33 Scholarship Foundation, the Four Diamonds Fund at the Pennsylvania State University Milton S. Hershey Medical Center, and the Central PA Chapter of the National Multiple Sclerosis Society. He also taught business law and hotel law as a visiting faculty member at the Lebanon Valley College in Annville, Pennsylvania. Prior to joining the Hershey Company, Feaster practiced law with the firm of McNees, Wallace & Nurick in Harrisburg, Pennsylvania. He is a Summa Cum Laude graduate of Susquehanna University and a Cum Laude graduate of The Georgetown Law Center in Washington, D.C.

Club Directory

St. Pete Times Forum

Tampa Bay Lightning
St. Pete Times Forum
401 Channelside Drive
Tampa, FL 33602
Phone 813/301-6500
FAX 813/301-1480
Ticket Info. 813/301-6600
www.tampabaylightning.com
Capacity: 19,758

Executive Staff
Owner	Palace Sports & Entertainment, Bill Davidson
Pres. of Palace Sports & Entertainment/Governor	Tom Wilson
Pres. of Tampa Bay Lightning/Alt. Governor	Ron Campbell
Executive Vice President, G.M. & Alt. Gov.	Jay H. Feaster
Executive Vice President/Chief Operating Officer	Sean Henry
Executive VP of Corporate Sales & Marketing	Harry Hutt
Vice President of Sponsorship Sales	Rob Keith
Sr. Vice President of Ticket Sales	Dave Bullock
Executive Assistants	Michele Colaianni, Julie Stein
Sr. Vice President Communications	Bill Wickett
Vice President, Legal Affairs/Legal Counsel	Paul Davis
Vice President, Chief Financial Officer	Joe Fada

Hockey Operations
Executive Vice President, G.M. & Alt. Gov.	Jay H. Feaster
Director of Player Personnel	Bill Barber
Assistant General Manager	Claude Loiselle
Assistant to the General Manager	Ryan Belec
Executive Assistant to General Manager	Elizabeth Sylvia
Head Coach	John Tortorella
Associate Coach	Craig Ramsay
Assistant Coach	Jeff Reese
Associate Goaltending Coach	Corey Schwab
Strength & Conditioning Coach	Eric Lawson
Video Coach	Nigel Kirwan
Chief Scout	Jake Goertzen
Scouting Staff	Mikael Andersson, Stephen Baker, Larry Bernard, Dirk Graham, Dave Heitz, Kari Kettunen, Miroslav Prihoda, Darrell Young, Glen Zacharias
Director of Team Services	Phil Thibodeau
Head Medical Trainer	Thomas Mulligan
Assistant Medical Trainer	Jason Serbus
Massage Therapist	Mike Griebel
Equipment Manager	Ray Thill
Assistant Equipment Managers	Dana Heinze, Jim Pickard
Head Coach Springfield Falcons	Dirk Graham
Asst Coach Springfield Falcons	Phil Russell
Head Medical Trainer Springfield Falcons	Adam Rambo
Team Physician	Dr. Ira Guttentag
Director of Alumni	John Tucker

Premium Services
Director of Premium Services	Karrie Yager
Premium Services Ticket Manager	Missy Davis
Premium Services Suite Manager	Lakisha Sharpe
Premium Services Manager	Amanda Graul
Premium Services Suite Coordinators	Leah Heiring, Mandy Morris, Ashley Kemp

Finance
Senior Accountants	Doug Riefler, Dave Weber
Accounts Payable	Donna Clark
Staff Accountants	Jane Sheill

Internal Support Staff
Vice President, Information Services	David Everett
Assistant Information Services Manager	Roberto Camejo, Rosie Chhuor

Box Office
Director of Ticket Operations	Jim Mannino
Assistant Box Office Manager	Alex Bohne

Ticket Sales
Sr. Vice President of Ticket Sales	Dave Bullock
Vice President of Sales	Todd Lambert
Director of Group Sales	Brad Lott
Asst. Dir. of Storm Sales/Sr. Corp. Acct. Mgr.	Ryan West
Outside Sales Manager	Patrick Duffy
Director of Suites Sales	Chris Diiorio
Premium Seating Managers	Paul Wallace, Mike Clough
Sr. Premium Seating Manager	Derek Beeman
Sr. Corporate Account Managers	Mike Warren, Tim Post
Corporate Account Managers	Dan Collins, Alec Nguyen, Robert Mulhearn, Jeremy Dixon, Eric Kistler, Ryan Cook, David Inzerillo, Dean Whaley

Sponsorship Sales & Marketing
Director of Promotions	Mark Gullett
Director of Outside Entertainment	Jason Franke
Director of Corporate Partnerships	Arden Robbins
Director of Marketing Partnerships	Alaina Miller
Director of Event Marketing	Holly Brown
Director of Broadcast Production & Game Ops	Jim Ciotoli
Director of Fan Development	David Cole
Director of Web Services	Martin Quessenberry
Marketing Partnerships Managers	Amanda Hurt, Lauren DeLaney, Mary China
Sr. Corporate Marketing Manager	Scott Shepherd
Corporate Marketing Managers	Amy Baldridge, Craig Smith, Joe Ondrejko, Kraig Obarski
Marketing Manager	Karen Cohn
In-Game Entertainment Coordinator	Hope Reep

Communications
Director of Public Relations	Jay Preble
Media Relations Manager	Brian Breseman
Executive Director of Lightning Foundation	Nancy Crane
Public Relations Coordinator	Brian Dancel
Community Relations Manager	Liz Stowell, Michelle Orf

Broadcast Information
Director of Broadcasting & Programming	Jason Dixon
Television	Sunshine Network
Television Broadcasters	Rick Peckham, Bobby Taylor, Paul Kennedy
Radio	WDAE 620 AM, WHOO 1080 AM (Orlando) WIXC 1060 AM (Melbourne), WDGF 1350 AM (Dade City)
Radio Broadcaster	David Mishkin

New Maple Leaf Jason Allison.

Toronto Maple Leafs

2005-06 Schedule

Month	Day	Date	Opponent	Month	Day	Date	Opponent
Oct.	Wed.	5	Ottawa		Sat.	7	at Edmonton*
	Sat.	8	Montreal		Tue.	10	at Vancouver
	Mon.	10	at Ottawa		Sat.	14	Phoenix
	Tue.	11	Philadelphia		Tue.	17	at Colorado
	Fri.	14	at Atlanta		Wed.	18	at Minnesota
	Sat.	15	at Montreal		Sat.	21	at Ottawa
	Thu.	20	Carolina		Mon.	23	at Ottawa
	Sat.	22	Philadelphia		Thu.	26	Buffalo
	Mon.	24	Boston		Sat.	28	Montreal
	Thu.	27	at Boston		Mon.	30	at Florida
	Sat.	29	Ottawa		Tue.	31	at Tampa Bay
	Mon.	31	Florida	Feb.	Fri.	3	at Washington
Nov.	Thu.	3	at Carolina		Sat.	4	New Jersey
	Sat.	5	Tampa Bay		Tue.	7	Atlanta
	Sun.	6	at Washington*		Fri.	10	at NY Rangers
	Tue.	8	Washington		Sat.	11	NY Rangers
	Fri.	11	at Buffalo		Tue.	28	Washington
	Sat.	12	at Montreal	Mar.	Fri.	3	at Buffalo
	Tue.	15	NY Rangers		Sat.	4	Ottawa
	Thu.	17	at Boston		Tue.	7	Montreal
	Sat.	19	Atlanta		Fri.	10	at NY Islanders
	Wed.	23	Boston		Sat.	11	Tampa Bay
	Fri.	25	at Carolina		Tue.	14	Boston
	Sat.	26	Montreal		Thu.	16	at Buffalo
	Mon.	28	at Florida		Sat.	18	at NY Rangers
	Wed.	30	at Tampa Bay		Sun.	19	at Pittsburgh
Dec.	Thu.	1	at Atlanta		Tue.	21	Carolina
	Sat.	3	San Jose		Thu.	23	at Montreal
	Tue.	6	Los Angeles		Sat.	25	at Montreal
	Sat.	10	Dallas		Sun.	26	at New Jersey
	Mon.	12	Anaheim		Tue.	28	at Philadelphia
	Sat.	17	at Ottawa	Apr.	Sat.	1	Buffalo
	Mon.	19	NY Islanders		Mon.	3	Buffalo
	Thu.	22	at Boston		Wed.	5	NY Islanders
	Fri.	23	Boston		Thu.	6	at Boston
	Mon.	26	New Jersey		Sat.	8	at Philadelphia
	Tue.	27	at Pittsburgh		Tue.	11	Florida
	Thu.	29	Buffalo		Thu.	13	at NY Islanders
	Sat.	31	at New Jersey		Sat.	15	Ottawa
Jan.	Mon.	2	Pittsburgh		Sun.	16	at Buffalo*
	Fri.	6	at Calgary		Tue.	18	Pittsburgh

* Denotes afternoon game.

Franchise date: November 22, 1917

NORTHEAST DIVISION

89th NHL Season

Year-by-Year Record

		Home				Road				Overall								
Season	GP	W	L	T	OL	W	L	T	OL	W	L	T	OL	GF	GA	Pts.	Finished	Playoff Result
2004-05	....	....	....	....	....	....	....	....	....	....	....	....	....	....	....	....		
2003-04	82	22	14	3	2	23	10	7	1	45	24	10	3	242	204	103	2nd, Northeast Div.	Lost Conf. Semi-Final
2002-03	82	24	13	4	0	20	15	3	3	44	28	7	3	236	208	98	2nd, Northeast Div.	Lost Conf. Quarter-Final
2001-02	82	24	11	6	0	19	14	4	4	43	25	10	4	249	207	100	2nd, Northeast Div.	Lost Conf. Championship
2000-01	82	19	11	7	4	18	18	4	1	37	29	11	5	232	207	90	3rd, Northeast Div.	Lost Conf. Semi-Final
1999-2000	82	24	12	5	0	21	15	2	3	45	27	7	3	246	222	100	1st, Northeast Div.	Lost Conf. Semi-Final
1998-99	82	23	13	5	....	22	17	2	....	45	30	7	....	268	231	97	2nd, Northeast Div.	Lost Conf. Championship
1997-98	82	16	20	5	....	14	23	4	....	30	43	9	....	194	237	69	6th, Central Div.	Out of Playoffs
1996-97	82	18	20	3	....	12	24	5	....	30	44	8	....	230	273	68	6th, Central Div.	Out of Playoffs
1995-96	82	19	15	7	....	15	21	5	....	34	36	12	....	247	252	80	3rd, Central Div.	Lost Conf. Quarter-Final
1994-95	48	15	7	2	....	6	12	6	....	21	19	8	....	135	146	50	4th, Central Div.	Lost Conf. Quarter-Final
1993-94	84	23	15	4	....	20	14	8	....	43	29	12	....	280	243	98	2nd, Central Div.	Lost Conf. Championship
1992-93	84	25	11	6	....	19	18	5	....	44	29	11	....	288	241	99	3rd, Norris Div.	Lost Conf. Championship
1991-92	80	21	16	3	....	9	27	4	....	30	43	7	....	234	294	67	5th, Norris Div.	Out of Playoffs
1990-91	80	15	21	4	....	8	25	7	....	23	46	11	....	241	318	57	5th, Norris Div.	Out of Playoffs
1989-90	80	24	14	2	....	14	24	2	....	38	38	4	....	337	358	80	3rd, Norris Div.	Lost Div. Semi-Final
1988-89	80	15	20	5	....	13	26	1	....	28	46	6	....	259	342	62	5th, Norris Div.	Out of Playoffs
1987-88	80	14	20	6	....	7	29	4	....	21	49	10	....	273	345	52	4th, Norris Div.	Lost Div. Semi-Final
1986-87	80	22	14	4	....	10	28	2	....	32	42	6	....	286	319	70	4th, Norris Div.	Lost Div. Final
1985-86	80	16	21	3	....	9	27	4	....	25	48	7	....	311	386	57	4th, Norris Div.	Lost Div. Final
1984-85	80	10	28	2	....	10	24	6	....	20	52	8	....	253	358	48	5th, Norris Div.	Out of Playoffs
1983-84	80	17	16	7	....	9	29	2	....	26	45	9	....	303	387	61	5th, Norris Div.	Out of Playoffs
1982-83	80	20	15	5	....	8	25	7	....	28	40	12	....	293	330	68	3rd, Norris Div.	Lost Div. Semi-Final
1981-82	80	12	20	8	....	8	24	8	....	20	44	16	....	298	380	56	5th, Norris Div.	Out of Playoffs
1980-81	80	14	21	5	....	14	16	10	....	28	37	15	....	322	367	71	5th, Adams Div.	Lost Prelim. Round
1979-80	80	17	19	4	....	18	21	1	....	35	40	5	....	304	327	75	4th, Adams Div.	Lost Prelim. Round
1978-79	80	20	12	8	....	14	21	5	....	34	33	13	....	267	252	81	3rd, Adams Div.	Lost Quarter-Final
1977-78	80	21	13	6	....	20	16	4	....	41	29	10	....	271	237	92	3rd, Adams Div.	Lost Semi-Final
1976-77	80	18	13	9	....	15	19	6	....	33	32	15	....	301	285	81	3rd, Adams Div.	Lost Quarter-Final
1975-76	80	23	12	5	....	11	19	10	....	34	31	15	....	294	276	83	3rd, Adams Div.	Lost Quarter-Final
1974-75	80	19	12	9	....	12	21	7	....	31	33	16	....	280	309	78	3rd, Adams Div.	Lost Quarter-Final
1973-74	78	21	11	7	....	14	16	9	....	35	27	16	....	274	230	86	4th, East Div.	Lost Quarter-Final
1972-73	78	20	12	7	....	7	29	3	....	27	41	10	....	247	279	64	6th, East Div.	Out of Playoffs
1971-72	78	21	11	7	....	12	20	7	....	33	31	14	....	209	208	80	4th, East Div.	Lost Quarter-Final
1970-71	78	24	9	6	....	13	24	2	....	37	33	8	....	248	211	82	4th, East Div.	Lost Quarter-Final
1969-70	76	18	13	7	....	11	21	6	....	29	34	13	....	222	242	71	6th, East Div.	Out of Playoffs
1968-69	76	20	8	10	....	15	18	5	....	35	26	15	....	234	217	85	4th, East Div.	Lost Quarter-Final
1967-68	74	24	9	4	....	9	22	6	....	33	31	10	....	209	176	76	5th, East Div.	Out of Playoffs
1966-67	**70**	**21**	**8**	**6**	**....**	**11**	**19**	**5**	**....**	**32**	**27**	**11**	**....**	**204**	**211**	**75**	**3rd,**	**Won Stanley Cup**
1965-66	70	22	9	4	....	12	16	7	....	34	25	11	....	208	187	79	3rd,	Lost Semi-Final
1964-65	70	17	15	3	....	13	11	11	....	30	26	14	....	204	173	74	4th,	Lost Semi-Final
1963-64	**70**	**22**	**7**	**6**	**....**	**11**	**18**	**6**	**....**	**33**	**25**	**12**	**....**	**192**	**172**	**78**	**3rd,**	**Won Stanley Cup**
1962-63	**70**	**21**	**8**	**6**	**....**	**14**	**15**	**6**	**....**	**35**	**23**	**12**	**....**	**221**	**180**	**82**	**1st,**	**Won Stanley Cup**
1961-62	**70**	**25**	**5**	**5**	**....**	**12**	**17**	**6**	**....**	**37**	**22**	**11**	**....**	**232**	**180**	**85**	**2nd,**	**Won Stanley Cup**
1960-61	70	21	6	8	....	18	13	4	....	39	19	12	....	234	176	90	2nd,	Lost Semi-Final
1959-60	70	20	9	6	....	15	17	3	....	35	26	9	....	199	195	79	2nd,	Lost Final
1958-59	70	17	13	5	....	10	19	6	....	27	32	11	....	189	201	65	4th,	Lost Final
1957-58	70	12	16	7	....	9	22	4	....	21	38	11	....	192	226	53	6th,	Out of Playoffs
1956-57	70	12	16	7	....	9	18	8	....	21	34	15	....	174	192	57	5th,	Out of Playoffs
1955-56	70	19	10	6	....	5	23	7	....	24	33	13	....	153	181	61	4th,	Lost Semi-Final
1954-55	70	14	10	11	....	10	14	11	....	24	24	22	....	147	135	70	3rd,	Lost Semi-Final
1953-54	70	22	6	7	....	10	18	7	....	32	24	14	....	152	131	78	3rd,	Lost Semi-Final
1952-53	70	17	12	6	....	10	18	7	....	27	30	13	....	156	167	67	5th,	Out of Playoffs
1951-52	70	17	10	8	....	12	15	8	....	29	25	16	....	168	157	74	3rd,	Lost Semi-Final
1950-51	**70**	**22**	**8**	**5**	**....**	**19**	**8**	**8**	**....**	**41**	**16**	**13**	**....**	**212**	**138**	**95**	**2nd,**	**Won Stanley Cup**
1949-50	70	18	9	8	....	13	18	4	....	31	27	12	....	176	173	74	3rd,	Lost Semi-Final
1948-49	**60**	**12**	**8**	**10**	**....**	**10**	**17**	**3**	**....**	**22**	**25**	**13**	**....**	**147**	**161**	**57**	**4th,**	**Won Stanley Cup**
1947-48	**60**	**22**	**3**	**5**	**....**	**10**	**12**	**8**	**....**	**32**	**15**	**13**	**....**	**182**	**143**	**77**	**1st,**	**Won Stanley Cup**
1946-47	**60**	**20**	**8**	**2**	**....**	**11**	**11**	**8**	**....**	**31**	**19**	**10**	**....**	**209**	**172**	**72**	**2nd,**	**Won Stanley Cup**
1945-46	50	10	13	2	....	9	11	5	....	19	24	7	....	174	185	45	5th,	Out of Playoffs
1944-45	**50**	**13**	**9**	**3**	**....**	**11**	**13**	**1**	**....**	**24**	**22**	**4**	**....**	**183**	**161**	**52**	**3rd,**	**Won Stanley Cup**
1943-44	50	13	11	1	....	10	12	3	....	23	23	4	....	214	174	50	3rd,	Lost Semi-Final
1942-43	50	17	6	2	....	5	13	7	....	22	19	9	....	198	159	53	3rd,	Lost Semi-Final
1941-42	**48**	**18**	**6**	**0**	**....**	**9**	**12**	**3**	**....**	**27**	**18**	**3**	**....**	**158**	**136**	**57**	**2nd,**	**Won Stanley Cup**
1940-41	48	16	5	3	....	12	9	3	....	28	14	6	....	145	99	62	2nd,	Lost Semi-Final
1939-40	48	15	3	6	....	10	14	0	....	25	17	6	....	134	110	56	3rd,	Lost Final
1938-39	48	13	8	3	....	6	12	6	....	19	20	9	....	114	107	47	3rd,	Lost Final
1937-38	48	13	6	5	....	11	9	4	....	24	15	9	....	151	127	57	1st, Cdn. Div.	Lost Final
1936-37	48	14	9	1	....	8	12	4	....	22	21	5	....	119	115	49	3rd, Cdn. Div.	Lost Quarter-Final
1935-36	48	15	4	5	....	8	15	1	....	23	19	6	....	126	106	52	2nd, Cdn. Div.	Lost Final
1934-35	48	16	6	2	....	14	8	2	....	30	14	4	....	157	111	64	1st, Cdn. Div.	Lost Final
1933-34	48	19	2	3	....	7	11	6	....	26	13	9	....	174	119	61	1st, Cdn. Div.	Lost Semi-Final
1932-33	48	16	4	4	....	8	14	2	....	24	18	6	....	119	111	54	1st, Cdn. Div.	Lost Final
1931-32	**48**	**17**	**4**	**3**	**....**	**6**	**14**	**4**	**....**	**23**	**18**	**7**	**....**	**155**	**127**	**53**	**2nd, Cdn. Div.**	**Won Stanley Cup**
1930-31	44	15	4	3	....	7	9	6	....	22	13	9	....	118	99	53	2nd, Cdn. Div.	Lost Quarter-Final
1929-30	44	10	8	4	....	7	13	2	....	17	21	6	....	116	124	40	4th, Cdn. Div.	Out of Playoffs
1928-29	44	15	5	2	....	6	13	3	....	21	18	5	....	85	69	47	3rd, Cdn. Div.	Lost Semi-Final
1927-28	44	9	8	5	....	9	10	3	....	18	18	8	....	89	88	44	4th, Cdn. Div.	Out of Playoffs
1926-27*	44	10	10	2	....	5	14	3	....	15	24	5	....	79	94	35	5th, Cdn. Div.	Out of Playoffs
1925-26	36	11	5	2	....	1	16	1	....	12	21	3	....	92	114	27	6th,	Out of Playoffs
1924-25	30	10	5	0	....	9	6	0	....	19	11	0	....	90	84	38	2nd,	Lost NHL S-Final
1923-24	24	7	5	0	....	3	9	0	....	10	14	0	....	59	85	20	3rd,	Out of Playoffs
1922-23	24	10	1	1	....	3	9	0	....	13	10	1	....	82	88	27	3rd,	Out of Playoffs
1921-22	**24**	**8**	**4**	**0**	**....**	**5**	**6**	**1**	**....**	**13**	**10**	**1**	**....**	**98**	**97**	**27**	**2nd,**	**Won Stanley Cup**
1920-21	24	9	3	0	....	6	6	0	....	15	9	0	....	105	100	30	2nd and 1st***	Lost NHL Final
1919-20**	24	8	4	0	....	4	8	0	....	12	12	0	....	119	106	24	3rd and 2nd***	Out of Playoffs
1918-19	18	5	4	0	....	0	9	0	....	5	13	0	....	64	92	10	3rd and 3rd***	Out of Playoffs
1917-18	**22**	**10**	**1**	**0**	**....**	**3**	**8**	**0**	**....**	**13**	**9**	**0**	**....**	**108**	**109**	**26**	**2nd and 1st*** **	**Won Stanley Cup**

* Name changed from St. Patricks to Maple Leafs (February, 1927). ** Name changed from Arenas to St. Patricks.
*** Season played in two halves with no combined standing at end.
From 1917-18 through 1925-26, NHL champions played against PCHA/WCHL champions for Stanley Cup.

2005-06 Player Personnel

FORWARDS

	HT	WT	S	Place of Birth	Date	2004-05 Club
ALLISON, Jason	6-3	215	R	North York, Ont.	5/29/75	
ANTROPOV, Nik	6-6	230	L	Ust-Kamenogorsk, USSR	2/18/80	Kazan-Yaroslavl
CZERKAWSKI, Mariusz	6-0	200	L	Radomsko, Poland	4/13/72	Djurgarden
DOMI, Tie	5-10	213	R	Windsor, Ont.	11/1/69	
HOFFMAN, Mike	6-4	240	R	Weymouth, MA	9/20/80	Cleveland
KILGER, Chad	6-4	224	L	Cornwall, Ont.	11/27/76	
KUKUMBERG, Roman	6-1	198	R	Bratislava, Czech.	4/8/80	Nizhnekamsk
LEEB, Brad	5-11	187	R	Red Deer, Alta.	8/27/79	St. John's
LINDROS, Eric	6-4	240	R	London, Ont.	2/28/73	
MITCHELL, John	6-1	182	L	Oakville, Ont.	1/22/85	Plymouth-St. John's
ONDRUS, Ben	6-0	185	R	Sherwood Park, Alta.	6/25/82	St. John's
O'NEILL, Jeff	6-1	195	R	Richmond Hill, Ont.	2/23/76	
PERROTT, Nathan	6-0	225	R	Owen Sound, Ont.	12/8/76	St. John's
POHL, John	6-0	186	R	Rochester, MN	6/29/79	Worcester
PONIKAROVSKY, Alexei	6-4	220	L	Kiev, USSR	4/9/80	Voskresensk
ST. JACQUES, Chris	5-8	181	R	Edmonton, Alta.	1/22/83	St. John's-Pensacola
STAJAN, Matt	6-1	180	L	Mississauga, Ont.	12/19/83	St. John's
STEEN, Alexander	5-11	183	L	Winnipeg, Man.	3/1/84	MODO
SUNDIN, Mats	6-5	231	L	Bromma, Sweden	2/13/71	
TUCKER, Darcy	5-10	178	L	Castor, Alta.	3/15/75	
WELLWOOD, Kyle	5-10	190	R	Windsor, Ont.	5/16/83	St. John's
WILLIAMS, Jeremy	5-11	184	R	Regina, Sask.	1/26/84	St. John's
WILM, Clarke	6-0	202	L	Central Butte, Sask.	10/24/76	St. John's

DEFENSEMEN

	HT	WT	S	Place of Birth	Date	2004-05 Club
BELAK, Wade	6-5	221	R	Saskatoon, Sask.	7/3/76	Coventry
BELL, Brendan	6-1	205	L	Ottawa, Ont.	3/31/83	St. John's
BERG, Aki	6-3	213	L	Turku, Finland	7/28/77	Timra
COLAIACOVO, Carlo	6-1	188	L	Toronto, Ont.	1/27/83	St. John's
D'AMOUR, Dominic	6-3	202	L	LaSalle, Que.	1/28/84	St. John's-Pensacola
HARRISON, Jay	6-4	211	L	Oshawa, Ont.	11/3/82	St. John's
KABERLE, Tomas	6-1	198	L	Rakovnik, Czech.	3/2/78	Kladno
KHAVANOV, Alexander	6-2	205	L	Moscow, USSR	1/30/72	St. Petersburg
KLEE, Ken	6-0	210	R	Indianapolis, IN	4/24/71	
KRONVALL, Staffan	6-3	209	L	Jarfalla, Sweden	9/10/82	Brynas-Djurgarden
MARSH, Tyson	6-1	190	L	Quesnel, B.C	6/20/84	St. John's-Pensacola
McCABE, Bryan	6-2	220	L	St. Catharines, Ont.	6/8/75	HV 71
MORO, Marc	6-1	218	R	Toronto, Ont.	7/17/77	St. John's
PILAR, Karel	6-3	207	R	Prague, Czech.	12/23/77	Sparta
TURON, David	6-3	202	R	Havirov, Czech.	10/4/83	St. J's-P'cola-L'siana
WHITE, Ian	5-10	185	R	Winnipeg, Man.	6/4/84	St. John's
WOZNIEWSKI, Andy	6-4	220	L	Buffalo Grove, IL	5/25/80	St. John's

GOALTENDERS

	HT	WT	C	Place of Birth	Date	2004-05 Club
AUBIN, Jean-Sebastien	5-11	180	L	Montreal, Que.	7/19/77	St. John's
BELFOUR, Ed	5-11	202	L	Carman, Man.	4/21/65	
FORD, Todd	6-4	176	L	Calgary, Alta.	5/1/84	Pensacola
RACINE, Jean-Francois	6-3	194	L	St-Hyacinthe, Que.	4/27/82	St. John's-Memphis
TELLQVIST, Mikael	5-11	194	L	Sundbyberg, Sweden	9/19/79	St. John's

Coach

QUINN, PAT
Coach, Toronto Maple Leafs. Born in Hamilton, Ont., January 29, 1943.

Pat Quinn became the 25th head coach of the Toronto Maple Leafs on June 26, 1998. He added the responsibilities of general manager to his coaching duties on July 14, 1999 and held both jobs until the appointment of John Ferguson on August 29, 2003.

The Maple Leafs have reached the playoffs in each of Quinn's seasons behind the bench and set a club record with 103 points in 2003-04. He is fourth all-time in regular-season NHL games coached (1,236) and wins (616) and is only the fourth coach in franchise history to reach the 200-win mark with the club, joining Punch Imlach, Hap Day and Dick Irvin. Previous to his arrival in Toronto he served as coach and/or general manager with Philadelphia, Los Angeles and Vancouver.

In February 2002, Quinn served as head coach of the Canadian Olympic team and guided Canada to its first hockey gold medal in 50 years of Olympic competition. He also coached Team Canada at the 2004 World Cup.

Quinn received the Jake Milford Award for dedicated service and contribution to hockey in British Columbia in 1994. In 2002, he was inducted into the British Columbia Hockey Hall of Fame and he has also been inducted into the Hamilton Gallery of Distinction. He is active in the community, holding his annual Pat Quinn and Friends golf tournament with the proceeds going to Kids Help Phone, RCMP Drugs and Sport and Hockey Canada.

NHL Coaching Record

			Regular Season				Playoffs		
Season	Team	Games	W	L	T	Games	W	L
1978-79	Philadelphia	30	18	8	4	8	3	5
1979-80	Philadelphia	80	48	12	20	19	13	6
1980-81	Philadelphia	80	41	24	15	12	6	6
1981-82	Philadelphia	72	34	29	9	....	....	....
1984-85	Los Angeles	80	34	32	14	3	0	3
1985-86	Los Angeles	80	23	49	8	....	....	....
1986-87	Los Angeles	42	18	20	4	....	....	....
1990-91	Vancouver	26	9	13	4	6	2	4
1991-92	Vancouver	80	42	26	12	13	6	7
1992-93	Vancouver	84	46	29	9	12	6	6
1993-94	Vancouver	84	41	40	3	24	15	9
1995-96	Vancouver	6	3	3	0	6	2	4
1998-99	Toronto	82	45	30	7	17	9	8
1999-2000	Toronto	82	45	30	7	12	6	6
2000-01	Toronto	82	37	34	11	11	7	4
2001-02	Toronto	82	43	29	10	20	10	10
2002-03	Toronto	82	44	31	7	7	3	4
2003-04	Toronto	82	45	27	10	13	6	7
2004-05	Toronto				Season Cancelled			
NHL Totals		**1236**	**616**	**466**	**154**	**183**	**94**	**89**

Assistant coach Rick Ley posted a 1-1 record as replacement coach when Quinn was sidelined with heart arrythmia, May 21 and 25, 2002. Both games are credited to Quinn's coaching record.

In the System and Recently Drafted

FORWARDS

	HT	WT	S	Place of Birth	Date	2004-05 Club
BERRY, Alex	6-2	195	R	Danvers, MA	3/6/86	Junior Bruins
CEREDA, Luca	6-2	212	L	Lugano, Switz.	9/7/81	Bern
DAHLBERG, Johan	6-2	194	L	Kramfors, Sweden	2/3/87	MODO Jr.
EARL, Robbie	5-10	184	L	Chicago, IL	6/6/85	U. of Wisconsin
KOLOZVARY, Ivan	6-0	179	L	Ilava, Czech.	2/16/83	Trencin-Piest.-Dubnica
MELENOVSKY, Marek	5-10	180	L	Humpolec, Czech.	3/30/77	Trinec
NORTON, Pierce	6-2	195	R	Boston, MA	6/7/85	Thayer
RAU, Chad	5-10	175	R	Eden Prairie, MN	1/18/87	Des Moines
SAGAT, Martin	6-3	191	R	Handlova, Czech.	11/11/84	Kootenay
SHINKAR, Alexander	6-0	176	L	Ufa, USSR	7/3/81	St. Petersburg
SKLENAR, Jaroslav	6-0	172	R	Ivancice, Czech.	11/22/82	
SOCHOR, Jan	6-0	198	R	Usti nad Labem, Czech.	1/17/80	Okla. City-Fresno-Victoria
SOZINOV, Vadim	6-1	185	L	Ust-Kamenogorsk, USSR	6/17/81	
STEBER, Jan	6-3	202	R	Ostrava, Czech.	10/19/85	Halifax
TENKRAT, Petr	5-11	200	R	Kladno, Czech.	5/31/77	Karpat
VOLKOV, Konstantin	6-0	174	L	Kolpino, USSR	2/7/85	Togliatti

DEFENSEMEN

	HT	WT	S	Place of Birth	Date	2004-05 Club
DOHERTY, John	6-4	213	R	Malden, MA	3/25/84	New Hamp.-Des Moines
ORESKOVIC, Phil	6-3	217	R	North York, Ont.	1/26/87	Brampton
SEIKOLA, Markus	6-1	194	R	Laitila, Finland	6/5/82	TPS
SEMENOV, Maxim	6-0	183	L	Kamenogorsk, Kazakhstan	2/9/84	Togliatti
STRALMAN, Anton	6-0	176	R	Tibro, Sweden	8/1/86	Skovde
VELEBNY, Lubos	6-1	189	L	Zvolen, Czech.	2/9/82	Zvolen
VOROBIEV, Dmitri	6-1	211	L	Togliatti, USSR	10/18/85	Togliatti
ZAVORAL, Vaclav	6-0	216	L	Teplice, Czech.	5/22/81	Elmira-Kansas City-Flint

GOALTENDERS

	HT	WT	C	Place of Birth	Date	2004-05 Club
POGGE, Justin	6-3	183	L	Ft. McMurray, Alta.	4/22/86	Pr. George-Cgy (WHL)
RASK, Tuukka	6-2	165	L	Savonlinna, Finland	3/10/87	Ilves

Alexander Khavanov joins the Leafs after four seasons in St. Louis. The Blues selected him with the 232nd pick in the 1999 NHL Entry Draft.

Coaching History

Dick Carroll, 1917-18, 1918-19; Frank Heffernan and Harry Sproule, 1919-20; Frank Carroll, 1920-21; George O'Donohue, 1921-22; George O'Donohue and Charles Querrie, 1922-23; Charles Querrie, 1923-24; Eddie Powers, 1924-25, 1925-26; Charles Querrie, Mike Rodden and Alex Romeril, 1926-27; Conn Smythe, 1927-28 to 1929-30; Conn Smythe and Art Duncan, 1930-31; Art Duncan and Dick Irvin, 1931-32; Dick Irvin, 1932-33 to 1939-40; Hap Day, 1940-41 to 1949-50; Joe Primeau, 1950-51 to 1952-53; King Clancy, 1953-54 to 1955-56; Howie Meeker, 1956-57; Billy Reay, 1957-58; Billy Reay and Punch Imlach, 1958-59; Punch Imlach, 1959-60 to 1968-69; John McLellan, 1969-70 to 1972-73; Red Kelly, 1973-74 to 1976-77; Roger Neilson, 1977-78, 1978-79; Floyd Smith, Dick Duff and Punch Imlach, 1979-80; Punch Imlach, Joe Crozier and Mike Nykoluk, 1980-81; Mike Nykoluk, 1981-82 to 1983-84; Dan Maloney, 1984-85, 1985-86; John Brophy, 1986-87, 1987-88; John Brophy and George Armstrong, 1988-89; Doug Carpenter, 1989-90; Doug Carpenter and Tom Watt, 1990-91; Tom Watt, 1991-92 to 1992-93 to 1994-95; Pat Burns and Nick Beverley, 1995-96; Mike Murphy, 1996-97, 1997-98; Pat Quinn, 1998-99 to date.

Captains' History

Hap Day, 1927-28 to 1936-37; Charlie Conacher, 1937-38; Red Horner, 1938-39, 1939-40; Syl Apps, 1940-41 to 1942-43; Bob Davidson, 1943-44, 1944-45; Syl Apps, 1945-46 to 1947-48; Ted Kennedy, 1948-49 to 1954-55; Sid Smith, 1955-56; Jimmy Thomson, Ted Kennedy, 1956-57; George Armstrong, 1957-58 to 1968-69; Dave Keon, 1969-70 to 1974-75; Darryl Sittler, 1975-76 to 1980-81; Rick Vaive, 1981-82 to 1985-86; no captain, 1986-87 to 1988-89; Rob Ramage, 1989-90, 1990-91; Wendel Clark, 1991-92 to 1993-94; Doug Gilmour, 1994-95 to 1996-97; Mats Sundin, 1997-98 to date.

Club Records

Team

(Figures in brackets for season records are games played; records for fewest points, wins, ties, losses, goals, goals against are for 70 or more games)

Most Points **103** 2003-04 (82)
Most Wins **45** 1998-99 (82), 1999-2000 (82), 2003-04 (82)
Most Ties **22** 1954-55 (70)
Most Losses **52** 1984-85 (80)
Most Goals **337** 1989-90 (80)
Most Goals Against **387** 1983-84 (80)
Fewest Points **48** 1984-85 (80)
Fewest Wins **20** 1981-82 (80), 1984-85 (80)
Fewest Ties **4** 1989-90 (80)
Fewest Losses **16** 1950-51 (70)
Fewest Goals **147** 1954-55 (70)
Fewest Goals Against ***131** 1953-54 (70)

Longest Winning Streak
Overall .... **10** Oct. 7-28/93
Home .... **9** Nov. 11-Dec. 26/53
Away .... **7** Nov. 14-Dec. 15/40, Dec. 4/60-Jan. 5/61

Longest Undefeated Streak
Overall .... **11** Oct. 15-Nov. 8/50 (8 wins, 3 ties), Jan. 6-Feb. 1/94 (7 wins, 4 ties)
Home .... **18** Nov. 28/33-Mar. 10/34 (15 wins, 3 ties), Oct. 31/53-Jan. 23/54 (16 wins, 2 ties)
Away .... **9** Nov. 30/47-Jan. 11/48 (4 wins, 5 ties)

Longest Losing Streak
Overall .... **10** Jan. 15-Feb. 8/67
Home .... **7** Nov. 11-Dec. 5/84
Away .... **11** Feb. 20-Apr. 1/88

Longest Winless Streak
Overall .... **15** Dec. 26/87-Jan. 25/88 (11 losses, 4 ties)
Home .... **11** Dec. 19/87-Jan. 25/88 (7 losses, 4 ties)
Away .... **18** Oct. 6/82-Jan. 5/83 (13 losses, 5 ties)

Most Shutouts, Season **13** 1953-54 (70)
Most PIM, Season **2,419** 1989-90 (80)
Most Goals, Game .... **14** Mar. 16/57 (NYR 1 at Tor. 14)

Individual

Most Seasons .... **21** George Armstrong
Most Games .... **1,187** George Armstrong
Most Goals, Career .... **389** Darryl Sittler
Most Assists, Career .... **620** Borje Salming
Most Points, Career .... **916** Darryl Sittler (389G, 527A)
Most PIM, Career .... **1,777** Tie Domi
Most Shutouts, Career .... **62** Turk Broda
Longest Consecutive Games Streak .... **486** Tim Horton (Feb. 11/61-Feb. 4/68)
Most Goals, Season .... **54** Rick Vaive (1981-82)
Most Assists, Season .... **95** Doug Gilmour (1992-93)
Most Points, Season .... **127** Doug Gilmour (1992-93; 32G, 95A)
Most PIM, Season .... **365** Tie Domi (1997-98)
Most Points, Defenseman, Season .... **79** Ian Turnbull (1976-77; 22G, 57A)
Most Points, Center, Season .... **127** Doug Gilmour (1992-93; 32G, 95A)
Most Points, Right Wing, Season .... **97** Wilf Paiement (1980-81; 40G, 57A)
Most Points, Left Wing, Season .... **99** Dave Andreychuk (1993-94; 53G, 46A)
Most Points, Rookie, Season .... **66** Peter Ihnacak (1982-83; 28G, 38A)
Most Shutouts, Season .... **13** Harry Lumley (1953-54)
Most Goals, Game .... **6** Corb Denneny (Jan. 26/21), Darryl Sittler (Feb. 7/76)
Most Assists, Game .... **6** Babe Pratt (Jan. 8/44), Doug Gilmour (Feb. 13/93)
Most Points, Game .... ***10** Darryl Sittler (Feb. 7/76; 6G, 4A)

* NHL Record.

Retired Numbers

5	Bill Barilko	1946-1951
6	Ace Bailey	1926-1934

Honored Numbers

1	Turk Broda	1936-43, 45-52
	Johnny Bower	1958-1970
7	King Clancy	1930-1937
	Tim Horton	1949-50, 51-70
9	Charlie Conacher	1929-1938
	Ted Kennedy	1942-55, 56-57
10	Syl Apps	1936-43, 45-48
	George Armstrong	1949-50, 51-71
27	Frank Mahovlich	1956-1968
	Darryl Sittler	1970-1982

All-time Record vs. Other Clubs

Regular Season

	At Home								On Road								Total							
	GP	W	L	T	OL	GF	GA	PTS	GP	W	L	T	OL	GF	GA	PTS	GP	W	L	T	OL	GF	GA	PTS
Anaheim	15	9	2	4	0	50	30	22	11	5	5	1	0	28	34	11	26	14	7	5	0	78	64	33
Atlanta	9	5	2	1	1	33	21	12	9	6	3	0	0	31	16	12	18	11	5	1	1	64	37	24
Boston	299	156	92	51	0	1005	769	363	298	90	159	47	2	786	967	229	597	246	251	98	2	1791	1736	592
Buffalo	67	28	27	12	0	203	228	68	69	20	43	6	0	184	279	46	136	48	70	18	0	387	507	114
Calgary	53	28	17	7	1	202	189	64	61	22	32	5	2	195	239	51	114	50	49	12	3	397	428	115
Carolina	36	13	18	5	0	120	126	31	37	13	18	6	0	119	144	32	73	26	36	11	0	239	270	63
Chicago	315	164	97	54	0	1071	821	382	318	120	156	42	0	831	968	282	633	284	253	96	0	1902	1789	664
Colorado	35	16	15	4	0	118	133	36	29	7	17	5	0	87	111	19	64	23	32	9	0	205	244	55
Columbus	3	2	0	1	0	10	4	5	1	0	0	0	1	3	4	1	4	2	0	1	1	13	8	6
Dallas	101	49	35	17	0	356	319	115	97	36	50	11	0	306	365	83	198	85	85	28	0	662	684	198
Detroit	316	164	105	47	0	1045	846	375	322	108	168	46	0	792	968	262	638	272	273	93	0	1837	1814	637
Edmonton	37	20	15	2	0	154	154	42	43	14	22	6	1	138	178	35	80	34	37	8	1	292	332	77
Florida	15	9	4	2	0	53	34	20	17	7	5	5	0	51	48	19	32	16	9	7	0	104	82	39
Los Angeles	68	35	22	11	0	266	223	81	65	21	34	10	0	191	234	52	133	56	56	21	0	457	457	133
Minnesota	3	3	0	0	0	11	3	6	1	1	0	0	0	1	0	2	4	4	0	0	0	12	3	8
Montreal	333	172	116	45	0	1007	865	389	333	92	198	43	0	827	1162	227	666	264	314	88	0	1834	2027	616
Nashville	6	2	3	1	0	13	18	5	1	0	0	0	1	2	3	1	7	2	3	1	1	15	21	6
New Jersey	48	31	12	5	0	182	138	67	46	14	16	15	1	136	155	44	94	45	28	20	1	318	293	111
NY Islanders	55	28	23	4	0	189	184	60	53	20	30	3	0	155	208	43	108	48	53	7	0	344	392	103
NY Rangers	282	159	84	39	0	974	741	357	283	107	118	56	2	836	873	272	565	266	202	95	2	1810	1614	629
Ottawa	22	10	9	2	1	59	60	23	20	7	11	1	1	53	56	16	42	17	20	3	2	112	116	39
Philadelphia	67	23	29	14	1	210	225	61	67	16	42	8	1	154	254	41	134	39	71	22	2	364	479	102
Phoenix	43	20	21	2	0	157	161	42	39	13	20	6	0	142	161	32	82	33	41	8	0	299	322	74
Pittsburgh	67	32	24	11	0	264	213	75	69	27	36	6	0	228	278	60	136	59	60	17	0	492	491	135
St. Louis	99	58	28	11	2	369	292	129	102	30	58	14	0	283	348	74	201	88	86	25	2	652	640	203
San Jose	18	12	4	2	0	69	47	26	15	7	5	3	0	40	32	17	33	19	9	5	0	109	79	43
Tampa Bay	21	13	7	1	0	76	55	27	20	16	3	1	0	71	42	33	41	29	10	2	0	147	97	60
Vancouver	60	28	21	11	0	219	195	67	64	24	29	11	0	216	225	59	124	52	50	22	0	435	420	126
Washington	48	26	16	6	0	211	163	58	50	18	28	4	0	144	182	40	98	44	44	10	0	355	345	98
Defunct Clubs	232	158	53	21	0	860	515	337	233	84	120	29	0	607	745	197	465	242	173	50	0	1467	1260	534
Totals	**2773**	**1473**	**901**	**393**	**6**	**9556**	**7772**	**3345**	**2773**	**945**	**1426**	**390**	**12**	**7637**	**9279**	**2292**	**5546**	**2418**	**2327**	**783**	**18**	**17193**	**17051**	**5637**

Playoffs

	Series	W	L	GP	W	L	T	GF	GA	Last Mtg.	Rnd.	Result
Boston	13	8	5	62	31	30	1	150	153	1974	QF	L 0-4
Buffalo	1	0	1	5	1	4	0	16	21	1999	CF	L 1-4
Calgary	1	1	0	2	2	0	0	9	5	1979	PRE	W 2-0
Carolina	1	0	1	6	2	4	0	6	10	2002	CF	L 2-4
Chicago	9	6	3	38	22	15	1	111	89	1995	CQF	L 3-4
Dallas	2	0	2	7	1	6	0	26	35	1983	DSF	L 1-3
Detroit	23	12	11	117	58	59	0	311	321	1993	DSF	W 4-3
Los Angeles	3	2	1	12	7	5	0	41	31	1993	CF	L 3-4
Montreal	15	7	8	71	29	42	0	160	215	1979	QF	L 0-4
New Jersey	2	0	2	13	5	8	0	27	37	2001	CSF	L 3-4
NY Islanders	3	2	1	17	8	9	0	42	54	2002	CQF	W 4-3
NY Rangers	8	3	5	35	16	19	0	86	86	1971	QF	L 2-4
Ottawa	4	4	0	24	16	8	0	57	42	2004	CQF	W 4-3
Philadelphia	6	1	5	36	14	22	0	85	119	2004	CSF	L 2-4
Pittsburgh	3	3	0	12	8	4	0	39	27	1999	CSF	W 4-2
St. Louis	5	2	3	31	14	17	0	90	88	1996	CQF	L 2-4
San Jose	1	1	0	7	4	3	0	26	21	1994	CSF	W 4-3
Vancouver	1	0	1	5	1	4	0	9	16	1994	CF	L 1-4
Defunct Clubs	8	6	2	24	12	10	2	59	57			
Totals	**109**	**58**	**51**	**524**	**251**	**269**	**4**	**1350**	**1427**			

Calgary totals include Atlanta Flames, 1972-73 to 1979-80. Carolina totals include Hartford, 1979-80 to 1996-97.
Colorado totals include Quebec, 1979-80 to 1994-95. Dallas totals include Minnesota North Stars, 1967-68 to 1992-93.
New Jersey totals include Kansas City, 1974-75 to 1975-76, and Colorado Rockies, 1976-77 to 1981-82.
Phoenix totals include Winnipeg, 1979-80 to 1995-96.

Playoff Results 2005-2000

Year	Round	Opponent	Result	GF	GA
2004	CSF	Philadelphia	L 2-4	13	17
	CQF	Ottawa	W 4-3	14	11
2003	CQF	Philadelphia	L 3-4	16	24
2002	CF	Carolina	L 2-4	6	10
	CSF	Ottawa	W 4-3	16	18
	CQF	NY Islanders	W 4-3	22	21
2001	CSF	New Jersey	L 3-4	18	21
	CQF	Ottawa	W 4-0	10	3
2000	CSF	New Jersey	L 2-4	9	16
	CQF	Ottawa	W 4-2	17	10

Abbreviations: Round: CF – conference final; **CSF** – conference semi-final; **CQF** – conference quarter-final; **DSF** – division semi-final; **QF** – quarter-final; **PRE** – preliminary round.

Key Off-Season Signings/Acquisitions

2004

June 18 • Re-signed D **Ken Klee** and RW **Darcy Tucker**.
June 30 • Re-signed G **Ed Belfour**.
Aug. 5 • Re-signed D **Bryan McCabe**.
6 • Re-signed G **Mikael Tellqvist**.
10 • Re-signed D **Tomas Kaberle**.

2005

July 30 • Obtained RW **Jeff O'Neill** from Carolina for a 2006 conditional pick.
Aug. 5 • Re-signed RW **Tie Domi**.
5 • Signed C **Jason Allison**.
9 • Signed 2002 1st-round pick (24th overall) C **Alexander Steen**.
10 • Signed D **Alexander Khavanov**.
10 • Re-signed Ds **Wade Belak** and **Aki Berg**.
11 • Signed C **Eric Lindros**.
12 • Re-signed C **Nik Antropov** and C **Clarke Wilm**.
18 • Signed G **Jean-Sebastien Aubin**.

Entry Draft
Selections 2005-1991

2005 Pick		2000 Pick		1996 Pick		1992 Pick	
21	Tuukka Rask	24	Brad Boyes	36	Marek Posmyk	8	Brandon Convery
82	Phil Oreskovic	51	Kris Vernarsky	50	Francis Larivee	23	Grant Marshall
153	Alex Berry	70	Mikael Tellqvist	66	Mike Lankshear	77	Nikolai Borschevsky
173	Johan Dahlberg	90	Jean-Francois Racine	68	Konstantin Kalmikov	95	Mark Raiter
216	Anton Stralman	100	Miguel Delisle	86	Jason Sessa	101	Janne Gronvall
228	Chad Rau	179	Vadim Sozinov	103	Vladimir Antipov	106	Chris Deruiter
		209	Markus Seikola	110	Peter Cava	125	Mikael Hakansson
2004 Pick		223	Lubos Velebny	111	Brandon Sugden	149	Patrik Augusta
90	Justin Pogge	254	Alexander Shinkar	140	Dmitri Yakushin	173	Ryan Vandenbussche
113	Roman Kukumberg	265	Jean-Philippe Cote	148	Chris Bogas	197	Wayne Clarke
157	Dmitri Vorobiev			151	Lucio DeMartinis	221	Sergei Simonov
187	Robert Earl	**1999** Pick		178	Reggie Berg	245	Nathan Dempsey
252	Jan Steber	24	Luca Cereda	204	Tomas Kaberle		
285	Pierce Norton	60	Peter Reynolds	230	Jared Hope	**1991** Pick	
		108	Mirko Murovic			47	Yanic Perreault
2003 Pick		110	Jon Zion	**1995** Pick		69	Terry Chitaroni
57	John Doherty	151	Vaclav Zavoral	15	Jeff Ware	102	Alexei Kudashov
91	Martin Sagat	161	Jan Sochor	54	Ryan Pepperall	113	Jeff Perry
125	Konstantin Volkov	211	Vladimir Kulikov	139	Doug Bonner	120	Alexander Kuzminsky
158	John Mitchell	239	Pierre Hedin	145	Yannick Tremblay	135	Martin Prochazka
220	Jeremy Williams	267	Peter Metcalf	171	Marek Melenovsky	160	Dmitri Mironov
237	Shaun Landolt			197	Mark Murphy	164	Robb McIntyre
		1998 Pick		223	Danny Markov	167	Tomas Kucharcik
2002 Pick		10	Nik Antropov			179	Guy Lehoux
24	Alexander Steen	35	Petr Svoboda	**1994** Pick		201	Gary Miller
57	Matt Stajan	69	Jamie Hodson	16	Eric Fichaud	223	Johnathon Kelley
74	Todd Ford	87	Alexei Ponikarovsky	48	Sean Haggerty	245	Chris O'Rourke
88	Dominic D'Amour	126	Morgan Warren	64	Fredrik Modin		
122	David Turon	154	Allan Rourke	126	Mark Deyell		
191	Ian White	181	Jonathan Gagnon	152	Kam White		
222	Scott May	215	Dwight Wolfe	178	Tommi Rajamaki		
254	Jarkko Immonen	228	Michal Travnicek	204	Rob Butler		
285	Staffan Kronvall	236	Sergei Rostov	256	Sergei Berezin		
				282	Doug Nolan		
2001 Pick		**1997** Pick					
17	Carlo Colaiacovo	57	Jeff Farkas	**1993** Pick			
39	Karel Pilar	84	Adam Mair	12	Kenny Jonsson		
65	Brendan Bell	111	Frantisek Mrazek	19	Landon Wilson		
82	Jay Harrison	138	Eric Gooldy	123	Zdenek Nedved		
88	Nicolas Corbeil	165	Hugo Marchand	149	Paul Vincent		
134	Kyle Wellwood	190	Shawn Thornton	175	Jeff Andrews		
168	Maxim Kondratiev	194	Russ Bartlett	201	David Brumby		
183	Jaroslav Sklenar	221	Jonathan Hedstrom	253	Kyle Ferguson		
198	Ivan Kolozvary			279	Mikhail Lapin		
213	Jan Chovan						
246	Tomas Mojzis						
276	Mike Knoepfli						

General Managers' History

Charles Querrie, 1917-18 to 1926-27; Conn Smythe, 1927-28 to 1956-57; Hap Day, 1957-58; Punch Imlach, 1958-59 to 1968-69; Jim Gregory, 1969-70 to 1978-79; Punch Imlach, 1979-80, 1980-81; Punch Imlach and Gerry McNamara, 1981-82; Gerry McNamara, 1982-83 to 1987-88; Gord Stellick, 1988-89; Floyd Smith, 1989-90, 1990-91; Cliff Fletcher, 1991-92 to 1996-97; Ken Dryden, 1997-98, 1998-99; Pat Quinn, 1999-2000 to 2002-03; John Ferguson, 2003-04 to date.

General Manager

FERGUSON, JOHN
General Manager, Toronto Maple Leafs. Born in Montreal, Que., July 7, 1969.

John Ferguson became the 12th person to hold the role of general manager of the Toronto Maple Leafs on August 29, 2003. He is the youngest current general manager in the NHL. In his first year on the job in 2003-04, the Maple Leafs set a club record with 103 points.

Prior to his arrival in Toronto, Ferguson had served as vice-president and director of hockey operations for the St. Louis Blues since February 26, 2001. Prior to that he spent five seasons as assistant general manager with the club. Ferguson was also the president and general manager of the Worcester IceCats, the Blues' top minor league affiliate. He is a former chairman of the American Hockey League's Competition Committee and also served on the league's Legal Affairs Committee.

The son of former Montreal Canadiens great John Ferguson, John Jr. played hockey at Providence College and spent four professional seasons at the American Hockey League level with the Montreal Canadiens and Ottawa Senators organizations from 1989 to 1993. From 1993 to 1996 he was a member of the Ottawa Senators scouting staff as an amateur and professional scout. Before joining the Blues, he served as a player agent.

Club Directory

Air Canada Centre

Toronto Maple Leafs
Air Canada Centre
40 Bay St., Suite 400
Toronto, Ontario M5J 2X2
Phone **416/815-5700**
FAX 416/359-9331
www.mapleleafs.com
Capacity: 18,819

Board of Directors
Lawrence M. Tanenbaum (Chairman of the Board), Robert G. Bertram, James W. Leech, Dean Metcalf, Ivan Fecan, John MacIntyre, Dale H. Lastman, Richard Peddie

Maple Leaf Sports & Entertainment Ltd.
Chairman, NHL Governor	Lawrence M. Tanenbaum
President, CEO and Alternate NHL Governor	Richard Peddie
Alternate NHL Governors	John Ferguson, Dale H. Lastman, Dean Metcalf
Executive V.P., Chief Operating Officer	Tom Anselmi
Executive V.P., CFO and Business Development	Ian Clarke
Executive V.P., G.M., Air Canada Centre	Bob Hunter
Sr. V.P., General Counsel & Corporate Secretary	Robin Brudner
V.P., Communications & Community Development	John Lashway
V.P., People	Mardi Walker
V.P., Programming, Executive Producer, Leafs TV	John Shannon
V.P., Corporate Sales & Service	Dave Hopkinson
V.P., Finance	Kevin Nonomura
V.P., Marketing	Beth Robertson
V.P., Operations	Diego Roccasalva

Maple Leafs Management
V.P. & General Manager	John Ferguson
Head Coach	Pat Quinn
Assistant G.M. & Director of Player Personnel	Mike Penny
Assistant Coaches	Keith Acton, Rick Ley
Player Development Coach	Paul Dennis
Manager, Hockey Admin. & Scouting Coord.	Reid Mitchell
Strength & Conditioning Coach	Matt Nichol
Goaltending Consultant	Steve McKichan
Manager, Team Services	Dave Griffiths
Coordinator, Team Services	Bradley Lynn
Video Analyst	Chris Dennis
Community Representatives	Wendel Clark, Darryl Sittler
Director, Amateur Scouting	Barry Trapp
Professional Scouts	Craig Button, Shawn Simpson
Amateur Scouts	Garth Malarchuk, David Morrison, Mike Palmateer, Mark Yannetti, George Armstrong, Fred Bandel
European Scouts	Thommie Bergman, Jan Kovac, Nikolai Ladygin, Peter Ahola
Travel Coordinator	Mary Speck
Executive Assistant	Ann Clark

Maple Leafs Communications and Community Development
V.P., Communications & Community Development	John Lashway
Director, Media Relations	Pat Park
Coordinator, Media Relations	James Lamont
Manager, Corporate Communications	Rajani Kamath
Director, Community Development	Beverley Deeth
Manager, Community Development, the Leafs Fund	Jennifer Woods
Manager, Youth Hockey Development	Dave De Freitas
Exec. Asst. to John Lashway	Rose Politi

Maple Leafs Medical and Training Staff
Head Athletic Therapist	Kevin Wagner
Assistant Athletic Therapist	Chris Davie
Equipment Manager	Brian Papineau
Assistant Equipment Managers	Bobby Hastings, Scott McKay
Team Doctors	Dr. Noah Forman, Dr. Erin Boynton, Dr. Rob Devenyi
Team Dentist	Dr. Allan Hawryluk

Air Canada Centre
Director, Project Development	Dan Arts
Director, Service and Ticketing	Paul Beirne
Director, Retail Finance	Alldrick Britto
Director, Media Sales	Bob Doherty
Director, Food & Beverage	Michael Doyle
Director, Sales	Jim Edmands
Director, Labour Relations	Les Fisher
Director, Executive Suite Services	Kristy Fletcher
Director, Business Operations, Ricoh Coliseum	Chris Gibbs
Director, Ticket Operations	Donna Henderson
Director, Broadcast Partnerships	Aaron Lafontaine
Director, Restaurant Operations, Executive Chef	Brad Long
Director, Consumer Products	Marc Petitpas
Director, Information Technology	Sasha Puric
Director, Live Production & Technical Services	Jim Roe
Director, Finance	Suzanne Scott
Director, Programming and Event Marketing	Patti-Anne Tarlton
Director, Special Projects	Eric Wong
Legal Counsel	Peter Miller
Manager, Video and Scoreboard Production	Curtis Emerson
Manager, Game Presentation	Mike Ferriman
Manager, Game Operations	Nancy Gilks

Broadcast Information
Radio Play-By-Play	Joe Bowen, Dennis Beyak
Radio Analyst	Jim Ralph
Television Play-By-Play	Joe Bowen (mid-weeks)
Television Analyst	Harry Neale

Leafs TV
V.P., Programming, Executive Producer	John Shannon
Executive Assistant	Karyn Savoia
Coordinating Producer	Frank Hayward
Director of Operations	Duncan Blair
Senior Broadcast Producer	Mark Askin
Director	Jacques Primeau
Senior Producer	Chris Clarke
Producers	Shane O'Neil, Mike Brock
Talent	Brian Duff, Bob Harwood, Paul Hendrick, Rick Vaive

Vancouver Canucks ™

2005-06 Schedule

Oct.	Wed.	5	Phoenix		Sat.	7	Calgary
	Sat.	8	at Edmonton		Tue.	10	Toronto
	Mon.	10	at Detroit		Fri.	13	at New Jersey
	Wed.	12	at Minnesota		Sat.	14	at NY Islanders
	Fri.	14	at Minnesota		Mon.	16	at Pittsburgh
	Sun.	16	Dallas		Thu.	19	Buffalo
	Tue.	18	Chicago		Sat.	21	Montreal
	Thu.	20	Phoenix		Mon.	23	at St. Louis
	Sat.	22	Colorado		Tue.	24	at Columbus
	Tue.	25	at Minnesota		Thu.	26	at Detroit
	Thu.	27	at Colorado		Sat.	28	at Colorado
	Sat.	29	at Colorado		Tue.	31	at Phoenix
Nov.	Wed.	2	Minnesota	Feb. Fri.		3	at Calgary
	Fri.	4	Columbus		Sat.	4	at Edmonton
	Sat.	5	at Calgary		Mon.	6	Columbus
	Mon.	7	at Calgary		Wed.	8	St. Louis
	Thu.	10	Colorado		Fri.	10	Anaheim
	Sun.	13	Detroit		Sun.	12	Minnesota
	Wed.	16	at San Jose		Tue.	28	at Calgary
	Thu.	17	at Los Angeles	Mar. Thu.		2	at Nashville
	Sun.	20	at Anaheim*		Fri.	3	at Chicago
	Tue.	22	Chicago		Sun.	5	St. Louis
	Thu.	24	San Jose		Thu.	9	Nashville
	Sat.	26	at Phoenix		Sat.	11	Dallas
	Sun.	27	at Colorado		Mon.	13	at Dallas
	Wed.	30	Colorado		Tue.	14	at Nashville
Dec.	Thu.	1	at Edmonton		Fri.	17	at Columbus
	Sun.	4	Boston		Sun.	19	Detroit
	Fri.	9	Ottawa		Tue.	21	at Edmonton
	Tue.	13	at NY Rangers		Thu.	23	Edmonton
	Thu.	15	at Philadelphia		Sat.	25	Edmonton
	Sat.	17	Edmonton		Mon.	27	Los Angeles
	Mon.	19	Los Angeles		Wed.	29	Minnesota
	Wed.	21	Edmonton		Fri.	31	Minnesota
	Fri.	23	Calgary	Apr. Sun.		2	at Anaheim*
	Mon.	26	Calgary		Mon.	3	at Los Angeles
	Wed.	28	Nashville		Sat.	8	Calgary
	Sat.	31	at Minnesota*		Mon.	10	Anaheim
Jan.	Mon.	2	at St. Louis		Wed.	12	San Jose
	Wed.	4	at Dallas		Thu.	13	at San Jose
	Thu.	5	at Chicago		Sat.	15	Colorado

Denotes afternoon game.

Franchise date: May 22, 1970

WESTERN CONFERENCE NHL

NORTHWEST DIVISION

36th NHL Season

Trevor Linden has spent 11 full seasons and parts of two others with the Canucks during his 17-year career. He is the club leader in games played (919) and goals scored (292).

Year-by-Year Record

Season	GP	Home W	L	T	OL	Road W	L	T	OL	Overall W	L	T	OL	GF	GA	Pts.	Finished	Playoff Result
2004-05	....																	
2003-04	82	21	13	7	0	22	11	3	5	43	24	10	5	235	194	101	1st, Northwest Div.	Lost Conf. Quarter-Final
2002-03	82	22	13	6	0	23	10	7	1	45	23	13	1	264	208	104	2nd, Northwest Div.	Lost Conf. Semi-Final
2001-02	82	23	11	5	2	19	19	2	1	42	30	7	3	254	211	94	2nd, Northwest Div.	Lost Conf. Quarter-Final
2000-01	82	21	12	5	3	15	16	6	4	36	28	11	7	239	238	90	3rd, Northwest Div.	Lost Conf. Quarter-Final
1999-2000	82	16	14	5	6	14	15	10	2	30	29	15	8	227	237	83	3rd, Northwest Div.	Out of Playoffs
1998-99	82	14	21	6	....	9	26	6	....	23	47	12	....	192	258	58	4th, Northwest Div.	Out of Playoffs
1997-98	82	15	22	4	....	10	21	10	....	25	43	14	....	224	273	64	7th, Pacific Div.	Out of Playoffs
1996-97	82	20	17	4	....	15	23	3	....	35	40	7	....	257	273	77	4th, Pacific Div.	Out of Playoffs
1995-96	82	15	19	7	....	17	16	8	....	32	35	15	....	278	278	79	3rd, Pacific Div.	Lost Conf. Quarter-Final
1994-95	48	10	8	6	....	8	10	6	....	18	18	12	....	153	148	48	2nd, Pacific Div.	Lost Conf. Semi-Final
1993-94	84	20	19	3	....	21	21	0	....	41	40	3	....	279	276	85	2nd, Pacific Div.	Lost Final
1992-93	84	27	11	4	....	19	18	5	....	46	29	9	....	346	278	101	1st, Smythe Div.	Lost Div. Final
1991-92	80	23	10	7	....	19	16	5	....	42	26	12	....	285	250	96	1st, Smythe Div.	Lost Div. Final
1990-91	80	18	17	5	....	10	26	4	....	28	43	9	....	243	315	65	4th, Smythe Div.	Lost Div. Semi-Final
1989-90	80	13	16	11	....	12	25	3	....	25	41	14	....	245	306	64	5th, Smythe Div.	Out of Playoffs
1988-89	80	19	15	6	....	14	24	2	....	33	39	8	....	251	253	74	4th, Smythe Div.	Lost Div. Semi-Final
1987-88	80	15	20	5	....	10	26	4	....	25	46	9	....	272	320	59	5th, Smythe Div.	Out of Playoffs
1986-87	80	17	19	4	....	12	24	4	....	29	43	8	....	282	314	66	5th, Smythe Div.	Out of Playoffs
1985-86	80	17	18	5	....	6	26	8	....	23	44	13	....	282	333	59	4th, Smythe Div.	Lost Div. Semi-Final
1984-85	80	15	21	4	....	10	25	5	....	25	46	9	....	284	401	59	5th, Smythe Div.	Out of Playoffs
1983-84	80	20	16	4	....	12	23	5	....	32	39	9	....	306	328	73	3rd, Smythe Div.	Lost Div. Semi-Final
1982-83	80	20	12	8	....	10	23	7	....	30	35	15	....	303	309	75	3rd, Smythe Div.	Lost Div. Semi-Final
1981-82	80	20	8	12	....	10	25	5	....	30	33	17	....	290	286	77	2nd, Smythe Div.	Lost Final
1980-81	80	17	12	11	....	11	20	9	....	28	32	20	....	289	301	76	3rd, Smythe Div.	Lost Prelim. Round
1979-80	80	14	17	9	....	13	20	7	....	27	37	16	....	256	281	70	3rd, Smythe Div.	Lost Prelim. Round
1978-79	80	15	18	7	....	10	24	6	....	25	42	13	....	217	291	63	2nd, Smythe Div.	Lost Prelim. Round
1977-78	80	13	15	12	....	7	28	5	....	20	43	17	....	239	320	57	3rd, Smythe Div.	Out of Playoffs
1976-77	80	13	21	6	....	12	21	7	....	25	42	13	....	235	294	63	4th, Smythe Div.	Out of Playoffs
1975-76	80	22	11	7	....	11	21	8	....	33	32	15	....	271	272	81	2nd, Smythe Div.	Lost Prelim. Round
1974-75	80	23	12	5	....	15	20	5	....	38	32	10	....	271	254	86	1st, Smythe Div.	Lost Quarter-Final
1973-74	78	14	18	7	....	10	25	4	....	24	43	11	....	224	296	59	7th, East Div.	Out of Playoffs
1972-73	78	17	18	4	....	5	29	5	....	22	47	9	....	233	339	53	7th, East Div.	Out of Playoffs
1971-72	78	14	20	5	....	6	30	3	....	20	50	8	....	203	297	48	7th, East Div.	Out of Playoffs
1970-71	78	17	18	4	....	7	28	4	....	24	46	8	....	229	296	56	6th, East Div.	Out of Playoffs

2005-06 Player Personnel

FORWARDS	HT	WT	S	Place of Birth	Date	2004-05 Club
BERNIER, Marc-Andre	6-4	198	R	Laval, Que.	2/5/85	Halifax
BERTUZZI, Todd	6-3	245	L	Sudbury, Ont.	2/2/75	
BOUCK, Tyler	6-0	196	L	Camrose, Alta.	1/13/80	TPS
BROWN, Mike	6-0	210	R	Northbrook, IL	6/24/85	U. of Michigan
CARTER, Anson	6-1	210	R	Toronto, Ont.	6/6/74	
CHUBAROV, Artem	6-1	189	L	Gorky, USSR	12/12/79	Dynamo Moscow
COOKE, Matt	6-0	205	L	Belleville, Ont.	9/7/78	
FEDOROV, Fedor	6-3	230	L	Appatity, USSR	6/11/81	Spartak-Magnitogorsk
GOREN, Lee	6-3	205	R	Winnipeg, Man.	12/26/77	Manitoba
GREEN, Josh	6-3	215	L	Camrose, Alta.	11/16/77	Manitoba
GUENETTE, Francois-Pierre	6-1	183	R	Laval, Que.	1/18/84	Halifax
KESLER, Ryan	6-2	195	R	Detroit, MI	8/31/84	Manitoba
KING, Jason	6-1	195	L	Corner Brook, Nfld.	9/14/81	Manitoba
LINDEN, Trevor	6-4	215	R	Medicine Hat, Alta.	4/11/70	
MORRISON, Brendan	5-11	190	L	Pitt Meadows, B.C.	8/15/75	Linkoping
PARK, Richard	5-11	190	R	Seoul, South Korea	5/27/76	Malmo-Langnau
RUUTU, Jarkko	6-2	195	L	Vantaa, Finland	8/23/75	HIFK
SCHULTZ, Jesse	6-0	192	R	Strasbourg, Sask.	9/28/82	Manitoba
SEDIN, Daniel	6-1	200	L	Ornskoldsvik, Sweden	9/26/80	MODO
SEDIN, Henrik	6-2	200	L	Ornskoldsvik, Sweden	9/26/80	MODO
SMITH, Nathan	6-2	192	L	Edmonton, Alta.	2/9/82	Manitoba

DEFENSEMEN	HT	WT	S	Place of Birth	Date	2004-05 Club
ALLEN, Bryan	6-4	220	L	Kingston, Ont.	8/21/80	Voskresensk
BAUMGARTNER, Nolan	6-2	205	R	Calgary, Alta.	3/23/76	Manitoba
BIEKSA, Kevin	6-1	195	R	Grimsby, Ont.	6/16/81	Manitoba
BROOKBANK, Wade	6-4	225	L	Lanigan, Sask.	9/29/77	Manitoba
BUTENSCHON, Sven	6-4	215	L	Itzehoe, West Germany	3/22/76	Mannheim
JOVANOVSKI, Ed	6-2	210	L	Windsor, Ont.	6/26/76	
KOLTSOV, Kirill	5-11	183	L	Chelyabinsk, USSR	2/1/83	Manitoba-Omsk
McCARTHY, Steve	6-1	198	L	Trail, B.C.	2/3/81	
McIVER, Nathan	6-2	195	L	Kinkora, P.E.I.	1/6/85	St. Michael's
MOJZIS, Tomas	6-1	192	L	Kolin, Czech.	5/2/82	Manitoba
OHLUND, Mattias	6-2	220	L	Pitea, Sweden	9/9/76	Lulea
RYAN, Prestin	6-0	190	L	Arcola, Sask.	6/29/80	Syracuse
SALO, Sami	6-3	215	R	Turku, Finland	9/2/74	Frolunda
SKINNER, Brett	6-1	195	L	Brandon, Man.	6/28/83	U. of Denver

GOALTENDERS	HT	WT	C	Place of Birth	Date	2004-05 Club
AULD, Alex	6-4	200	L	Cold Lake, Alta.	1/7/81	Manitoba
CLOUTIER, Dan	6-1	185	L	Mont-Laurier, Que.	4/22/76	Klagenfurt
FLAHERTY, Wade	6-0	190	L	Terrace, B.C.	1/11/68	Manitoba
JOHNSON, Brent	6-3	205	L	Farmington, MI	3/12/77	
McVICAR, Rob	6-4	201	L	Hay River, N.W.T.	1/15/82	Manitoba-Columbia

In the System and Recently Drafted

FORWARDS	HT	WT	S	Place of Birth	Date	2004-05 Club
BLIZNAK, Mario	6-0	185	L	Trencin, Czech.	3/6/87	Dubnica
BUTCHER, Matt	6-1	185	L	Bellingham, WA	1/1/87	Chilliwack
DANIELSSON, Nicklas	6-1	169	R	Uppsala, Sweden	12/7/84	Brynas
DUMA, Pavel	6-2	183	L	Karaganda, USSR	6/20/81	
GLADSKIKH, Evgeny	6-0	198	L	Magnitogorsk, USSR	4/24/82	Magnitogorsk
HANSEN, Jannik	6-0	176	R	Herlev, Denmark	3/15/86	Rodovre
KRIKUNOV, Ilya	5-11	169	L	Elektrostal, USSR	2/27/84	Voskresensk
LALIBERTE, John	6-2	190	L	Portland, ME	8/5/83	Boston University
MIKHAILOV, Konstantin	5-11	180	L	Moscow, USSR	2/12/83	Cherep.-Golden Amur-Yunost-Gomel
NOLAN, Brandon	6-1	185	L	Sault Ste. Marie, Ont.	7/18/83	Manitoba
NUSSLI, Thomas	6-4	207	L	Nesskin, Switz.	3/12/82	Basel
RAYMOND, Mason	6-0	165	L	Calgary, Alta.	9/17/85	Camrose
REID, Brandon	5-8	185	R	Kirkland, Que.	3/9/81	Hamburg
SARAUER, Andrew	6-4	194	L	Saskatoon, Sask.	11/17/84	Northern Mich.
TOPOL, Sergei	6-2	183	L	Omsk, USSR	2/15/85	Mechel-Omsk

DEFENSEMEN	HT	WT	S	Place of Birth	Date	2004-05 Club
BOURDON, Luc	6-2	199	L	Shippagan, N.B.	2/16/87	Val-d'Or
BROWNLEE, Chad	6-2	184	R	Kelowna, B.C.	7/12/84	Minnesota State
EDLER, Alexander	6-3	194	L	Stockholm, Sweden	4/21/86	MODO Jr.
FREDHEIM, Kris	6-1	170	R	Campbell River, B.C.	2/23/87	Notre Dame
GROT, Denis	6-0	185	L	Minsk, USSR	6/1/84	Yaroslavl-Novosibirsk-Khabarovsk
JOKELA, Mikko	6-1	210	R	Lappeenranta, Finland	3/4/80	HPK
KANKAANPERA, Markus	6-1	191	L	Skelleftea, Sweden	4/27/80	Jokerit
SCHULZ, David	6-3	201	R	Winkler, Man.	1/3/86	Swift Current

GOALTENDERS	HT	WT	C	Place of Birth	Date	2004-05 Club
ELLIS-PLANTE, Julien	6-0	194	L	Sorel, Que.	1/27/86	Shawinigan
MENSATOR, Lukas	5-8	167	L	Sokolov, Czech.	8/18/84	Karlovy Vary-Pisek-Ml. Boleslav
SCHNEIDER, Cory	6-2	195	L	Salem, MA	3/18/86	Boston College
VINCENT, Alexandre	6-4	193	L	Drummondville, Que.	12/11/86	Chicoutimi

With 278 points from 2001-02 through 2003-04, Markus Naslund is the NHL's top scorer over the last three seasons.

Vice President and General Manager

NONIS, DAVID
Senior Vice President/General Manager, Vancouver Canucks.
Born in Burnaby, B.C., May 25, 1966.

David Nonis was given his first assignment as general manager of an NHL hockey club when he was named to the position by the Vancouver Canucks on May 6, 2004. Nonis had spent the previous six seasons as senior vice president, director of hockey operations and was the Canucks' chief negotiator of player contracts. In his first act as general manager, Nonis appointed Steve Tambellini assistant general manager.

A native of Vancouver, Nonis broke into the NHL with the Canucks in 1990. In his first years he was primarily responsible for corporate contracts, computer scouting and team services. Prior to being named senior vice president in 1998, Nonis served as the National Hockey League's manager of hockey operations for four seasons. In his role with the NHL, Nonis gained a vast knowledge of the collective bargaining agreement and helped finalize sections of the document when the previous edition was drafted during the 1994-95 season. He also worked with the league's arbitration team, which included helping teams prepare for arbitration, researching salaries and interpreting contract language.

Nonis played for the Burnaby Blackhawks of the British Columbia Junior Hockey League from 1982 to 1984. He then played for the University of Maine where he served as captain for two seasons and graduated with a B.A. in 1988. Nonis played one season professionally in Denmark, then returned to Maine in 1989 to serve as graduate assistant under head coach Shawn Walsh. Nonis earned an MBA from the University of Maine in 1990.

Coaching History

Hal Laycoe, 1970-71, 1971-72; Vic Stasiuk, 1972-73; Bill McCreary and Phil Maloney, 1973-74; Phil Maloney, 1974-75, 1975-76; Phil Maloney and Orland Kurtenbach, 1976-77; Orland Kurtenbach, 1977-78; Harry Neale, 1978-79 to 1980-81; Harry Neale and Roger Neilson, 1981-82; Roger Neilson, 1982-83; Roger Neilson and Harry Neale, 1983-84; Bill Laforge and Harry Neale, 1984-85; Tom Watt, 1985-86, 1986-87; Bob McCammon, 1987-88 to 1989-90; Bob McCammon and Pat Quinn, 1990-91; Pat Quinn, 1991-92 to 1993-94; Rick Ley, 1994-95; Rick Ley and Pat Quinn, 1995-96; Tom Renney, 1996-97; Tom Renney and Mike Keenan, 1997-98; Mike Keenan and Marc Crawford, 1998-99; Marc Crawford, 1999-2000 to date.

Club Records

Team

(Figures in brackets for season records are games played; records for fewest points, wins, ties, losses, goals, goals against are for 70 or more games)

Most Points	104	2002-03 (82)
Most Wins	46	1992-93 (84)
Most Ties	20	1980-81 (80)
Most Losses	50	1971-72 (78)
Most Goals	346	1992-93 (84)
Most Goals Against	401	1984-85 (80)
Fewest Points	48	1971-72 (78)
Fewest Wins	20	1971-72 (78),
		1977-78 (80)
Fewest Ties	3	1993-94 (84)
Fewest Losses	24	2002-03 (82)
Fewest Goals	192	1998-99 (82)
Fewest Goals Against	194	2003-04 (82)

Longest Winning Streak

Overall	10	Nov. 9-30/02
Home	9	Nov. 6-Dec. 9/92
Away	8	Dec. 20/03-Jan. 13/04

Longest Undefeated Streak

Overall	14	Jan.26-Feb. 25/03 (10 wins, 4 ties)
Home	18	Nov. 4/92-Jan. 16/93 (16 wins, 2 ties)
Away	9	Feb. 4-Mar. 3/03 (6 wins, 3 ties)

Longest Losing Streak

Overall	10	Oct. 23-Nov. 11/97
Home	6	Dec. 18/70-Jan. 20/71
Away	12	Nov. 28/81-Feb. 6/82

Longest Winless Streak

Overall	13	Nov. 9-Dec. 7/73 (10 losses, 3 ties)
Home	11	Dec. 18/70-Feb. 6/71 (10 losses, 1 tie)
Away	20	Jan. 2-Apr. 2/86 (14 losses, 6 ties)

Most Shutouts, Season	8	1974-75 (80), 2001-02 (82)
Most PIM, Season	2,326	1992-93 (84)
Most Goals, Game	11	Mar. 28/71 (Cal. 5 at Van. 11), Nov. 25/86 (L.A. 5 at Van. 11), Mar. 1/92 (Cgy. 0 at Van. 11)

Individual

Most Seasons	13	Stan Smyl
Most Games	919	Trevor Linden
Most Goals, Career	292	Trevor Linden
Most Assists, Career	411	Stan Smyl
Most Points, Career	680	Trevor Linden (292G, 388A)
Most PIM, Career	2,127	Gino Odjick
Most Shutouts, Career	20	Kirk McLean
Longest Consecutive Games Streak	482	Trevor Linden (Oct. 4/90-Dec. 7/96)
Most Goals, Season	60	Pavel Bure (1992-93, 1993-94)
Most Assists, Season	62	André Boudrias (1974-75)
Most Points, Season	110	Pavel Bure (1992-93; 60G, 50A)
Most PIM, Season	372	Donald Brashear (1997-98)

Most Points, Defenseman, Season	63	Doug Lidster (1986-87; 12G, 51A)
Most Points, Center, Season	91	Patrik Sundstrom (1983-84; 38G, 53A)
Most Points, Right Wing, Season	110	Pavel Bure (1992-93; 60G, 50A)
Most Points, Left Wing, Season	104	Markus Naslund (2002-03; 48G, 56A)
Most Points, Rookie, Season	60	Ivan Hlinka (1981-82; 23G, 37A), Pavel Bure (1991-92; 34G, 26A)
Most Shutouts, Season	7	Dan Cloutier (2001-02)
Most Goals, Game	4	Eleven times
Most Assists, Game	6	Patrik Sundstrom (Feb. 29/84)
Most Points, Game	7	Patrik Sundstrom (Feb. 29/84; 1G, 6A)

Retired Numbers

12	Stan Smyl	1978-1991

General Managers' History

Bud Poile, 1970-71 to 1972-73; Hal Laycoe, 1973-74; Phil Maloney, 1974-75 to 1976-77; Jake Milford, 1977-78 to 1981-82; Harry Neale, 1982-83 to 1984-85; Jack Gordon, 1985-86, 1986-87; Pat Quinn, 1987-88 to 1997-98; Brian Burke, 1998-99 to 2003-04; David Nonis, 2004-05 to date.

Captains' History

Orland Kurtenbach, 1970-71 to 1973-74; no captain, 1974-75; Andre Boudrias, 1975-76; Chris Oddleifson, 1976-77; Don Lever, 1977-78; Don Lever and Kevin McCarthy, 1978-79; Kevin McCarthy, 1979-80 to 1981-82; Stan Smyl, 1982-83 to 1989-90; Dan Quinn, Doug Lidster and Trevor Linden, 1990-91; Trevor Linden, 1991-92 to 1996-97; Mark Messier, 1997-98 to 1999-2000; Markus Naslund, 2000-01 to date.

All-time Record vs. Other Clubs

Regular Season

	At Home								On Road								Total							
	GP	W	L	T	OL	GF	GA	PTS	GP	W	L	T	OL	GF	GA	PTS	GP	W	L	T	OL	GF	GA	PTS
Anaheim	26	16	8	2	0	91	59	34	25	11	7	7	0	74	59	29	51	27	15	9	0	165	118	63
Atlanta	3	1	1	1	0	10	5	3	3	2	1	0	0	12	11	4	6	3	2	1	0	22	16	7
Boston	51	16	26	8	1	166	209	41	52	7	37	7	1	124	217	22	103	23	63	15	2	290	426	63
Buffalo	52	25	16	11	0	193	162	61	52	18	26	8	0	152	186	44	104	43	42	19	0	345	348	105
Calgary	99	36	44	18	1	335	327	91	98	26	57	15	0	283	392	67	197	62	101	33	1	618	719	158
Carolina	30	14	10	6	0	105	81	34	29	12	12	5	0	100	94	29	59	26	22	11	0	205	175	63
Chicago	72	35	22	15	0	218	210	85	71	17	45	7	2	164	267	43	143	52	67	22	2	382	477	128
Colorado	47	17	22	7	1	153	181	42	47	17	21	8	1	133	157	43	94	34	43	15	2	286	338	85
Columbus	8	6	2	0	0	34	23	12	8	4	1	2	1	29	17	11	16	10	3	2	1	63	40	23
Dallas	71	31	29	10	1	252	218	73	71	22	37	12	0	211	259	56	142	53	66	22	1	463	477	129
Detroit	65	29	26	10	0	235	210	68	66	17	40	8	1	188	275	43	131	46	66	18	1	423	485	111
Edmonton	82	32	37	12	1	295	320	77	81	25	47	7	2	256	356	59	163	57	84	19	3	551	676	136
Florida	9	3	1	5	0	25	19	11	8	4	3	1	0	27	21	9	17	7	4	6	0	52	40	20
Los Angeles	97	50	31	16	0	365	300	116	99	32	50	16	1	310	393	81	196	82	81	32	1	675	693	197
Minnesota	10	4	2	3	1	28	26	12	11	4	5	2	0	27	27	10	21	8	7	5	1	55	53	22
Montreal	55	14	33	8	0	146	202	36	53	10	38	5	0	135	244	25	108	24	71	13	0	281	446	61
Nashville	12	9	1	1	0	48	28	19	13	7	5	1	0	40	35	15	25	16	7	2	0	88	63	34
New Jersey	47	27	9	11	0	175	130	65	49	23	20	6	0	159	151	52	96	50	29	17	0	334	281	117
NY Islanders	47	23	21	3	0	155	153	49	47	11	25	10	1	129	174	33	94	34	46	13	1	284	327	82
NY Rangers	51	15	33	3	0	163	204	33	54	11	38	5	0	139	237	27	105	26	71	8	0	302	441	60
Ottawa	11	5	5	1	0	33	26	11	10	4	5	1	0	24	24	9	21	9	10	2	0	57	50	20
Philadelphia	51	10	28	12	1	144	203	33	54	16	36	1	1	159	234	34	105	26	64	13	2	303	437	67
Phoenix	72	43	18	10	1	272	201	97	69	26	32	10	1	245	256	63	141	69	50	20	2	517	457	160
Pittsburgh	50	23	23	4	0	180	187	50	50	10	33	7	0	171	227	27	100	33	56	11	0	351	414	77
St. Louis	72	30	33	9	0	214	230	69	71	21	41	9	0	205	265	51	143	51	74	18	0	419	495	120
San Jose	32	18	10	4	0	115	84	40	34	16	13	5	0	106	98	37	66	34	23	9	0	221	182	77
Tampa Bay	9	7	0	2	0	40	17	16	9	4	3	2	0	37	31	12	18	11	3	4	0	77	48	28
Toronto	64	29	22	11	2	225	216	71	60	21	28	11	0	195	219	53	124	50	50	22	2	420	435	124
Washington	39	18	15	5	1	136	123	42	40	14	21	4	1	120	132	33	79	32	36	9	2	256	255	75
Defunct Clubs	19	14	3	2	0	82	48	30	19	10	8	1	0	71	68	21	38	24	11	3	0	153	116	51
Totals	**1353**	**600**	**532**	**210**	**11**	**4633**	**4402**	**1421**	**1353**	**424**	**735**	**181**	**13**	**4025**	**5126**	**1042**	**2706**	**1024**	**1267**	**391**	**24**	**8658**	**9528**	**2463**

Playoffs

	Series	W	L	GP	W	L	T	GF	GA	Last Mtg.
Buffalo	2	0	2	7	1	6	0	14	28	1981
Calgary	6	2	4	32	15	17	0	96	101	2004
Chicago	2	1	1	9	4	5	0	24	24	1995
Colorado	2	0	2	10	2	8	0	26	40	2001
Dallas	1	1	0	5	4	1	0	18	11	1994
Detroit	1	0	1	6	2	4	0	16	22	2002
Edmonton	2	0	2	9	2	7	0	20	35	1992
Los Angeles	3	1	2	17	8	9	0	60	66	1993
Minnesota	1	0	1	7	3	4	0	17	26	2003
Montreal	1	0	1	5	1	4	0	9	20	1975
NY Islanders	2	0	2	6	0	6	0	14	26	1982
NY Rangers	1	0	1	7	3	4	0	19	21	1994
Philadelphia	1	0	1	3	1	2	0	9	15	1979
St. Louis	2	2	0	14	8	6	0	44	48	2003
Toronto	1	1	0	5	4	1	0	16	9	1994
Winnipeg	2	2	0	13	8	5	0	50	34	1993
Totals	**30**	**10**	**20**	**155**	**66**	**89**	**0**	**452**	**526**	

Calgary totals include Atlanta Flames, 1972-73 to 1979-80.
Colorado totals include Quebec, 1979-80 to 1994-95.
New Jersey totals include Kansas City, 1974-75 to 1975-76, and Colorado Rockies, 1976-77 to 1981-82.
Phoenix totals include Winnipeg, 1979-80 to 1995-96.
Carolina totals include Hartford, 1979-80 to 1996-97.
Dallas totals include Minnesota North Stars, 1970-71 to 1992-93.

Playoff Results 2005-2000

Year	Round	Opponent	Result	GF	GA
2004	CQF	Calgary	L 3-4	16	19
2003	CSF	Minnesota	L 3-4	17	26
	CQF	St. Louis	W 4-3	17	21
2002	CQF	Detroit	L 2-4	16	22
2001	CQF	Colorado	L 0-4	9	16

Abbreviations: Round: F – Final;
CF – conference final; CSF – conference semi-final;
CQF – conference quarter-final; DF – division final;
DSF – division semi-final; QF – quarter-final;
PRE – preliminary round.

Key Off-Season Signings/Acquisitions

2004

May 6 • Named **David Nonis** general manager.

Aug. 19 • Re-signed D **Nolan Baumgartner**.

Sept. 10 • Re-signed G **Alex Auld**.

2005

Aug. 3 • Re-signed LW **Markus Naslund**.

5 • Re-signed C **Brendan Morrison**.

8 • RW **Todd Bertuzzi** reinstated by NHL.

9 • Signed RW **Richard Park**.

10 • Re-signed C **Henrik Sedin** and LW **Daniel Sedin**.

15 • Re-signed C **Jason King** and Ds **Sami Salo** and **Bryan Allen**.

17 • Signed RW **Anson Carter**.

18 • Re-signed G **Dan Cloutier**.

22 • Obtained D **Steve McCarthy** from Chicago for a 2007 3rd-round draft pick.

22 • Signed D **Sven Butenschon**.

23 • Signed LW **Josh Green**.

24 • Re-signed D **Mattias Ohlund**.

Sept. 1 • Re-sign RW **Jarkko Ruutu**.

Entry Draft
Selections 2005-1991

2005
Pick
- 10 Luc Bourdon
- 51 Mason Raymond
- 114 Alexandre Vincent
- 138 Matt Butcher
- 185 Kris Fredheim
- 205 Mario Bliznak

2004
Pick
- 26 Cory Schneider
- 91 Alexander Edler
- 125 Andrew Sarauer
- 159 Mike Brown
- 189 Julien Ellis-Plante
- 254 David Schulz
- 287 Jannik Hansen

2003
Pick
- 23 Ryan Kesler
- 60 Marc-Andre Bernier
- 111 Brandon Nolan
- 128 Ty Morris
- 160 Nicklas Danielsson
- 190 Chad Brownlee
- 222 Francois-Pierre Guenette
- 252 Sergei Topol
- 254 Nathan McIver
- 285 Matthew Hansen

2002
Pick
- 49 Kirill Koltsov
- 55 Denis Grot
- 68 Brett Skinner
- 83 Lukas Mensator
- 114 John Laliberte
- 151 Rob McVicar
- 214 Marc-Andre Roy
- 223 Ilya Krikunov
- 247 Matt Violin
- 277 Thomas Nussli
- 278 Matt Gens

2001
Pick
- 16 R.J. Umberger
- 66 Fedor Fedorov
- 114 Evgeny Gladskikh
- 151 Kevin Bieksa
- 212 Jason King
- 245 Konstantin Mikhailov

2000
Pick
- 23 Nathan Smith
- 71 Thatcher Bell
- 93 Tim Branham
- 144 Pavel Duma
- 208 Brandon Reid
- 241 Nathan Barrett
- 272 Tim Smith

1999
Pick
- 2 Daniel Sedin
- 3 Henrik Sedin
- 69 Rene Vydareny
- 129 Ryan Thorpe
- 172 Josh Reed
- 189 Kevin Swanson
- 218 Markus Kankaanpera
- 271 Darrell Hay

1998
Pick
- 4 Bryan Allen
- 31 Artem Chubarov
- 68 Jarkko Ruutu
- 81 Justin Morrison
- 90 Regan Darby
- 136 David Ytfeldt
- 140 Rick Bertran
- 149 Paul Cabana
- 177 Vincent Malts
- 204 Greg Mischler
- 219 Curtis Valentine
- 232 Jason Metcalfe

1997
Pick
- 10 Brad Ference
- 34 Ryan Bonni
- 36 Harold Druken
- 64 Kyle Freadrich
- 90 Chris Stanley
- 114 David Darguzas
- 117 Matt Cockell
- 144 Matt Cooke
- 148 Larry Shapley
- 171 Rod Leroux
- 201 Denis Martynyuk
- 227 Peter Brady

1996
Pick
- 12 Josh Holden
- 75 Zenith Komarniski
- 93 Jonas Soling
- 121 Tyler Prosofsky
- 147 Nolan McDonald
- 175 Clint Cabana
- 201 Jeff Scissons
- 227 Lubomir Vaic

1995
Pick
- 40 Chris McAllister
- 61 Larry Courville
- 66 Peter Schaefer
- 92 Lloyd Shaw
- 120 Todd Norman
- 144 Brent Sopel
- 170 Stewart Bodtker
- 196 Tyler Willis
- 222 Jason Cugnet

1994
Pick
- 13 Mattias Ohlund
- 39 Robb Gordon
- 42 Dave Scatchard
- 65 Chad Allan
- 92 Mike Dubinsky
- 117 Yanick Dube
- 169 Yuri Kuznetsov
- 195 Rob Trumbley
- 221 Bill Muckalt
- 247 Tyson Nash
- 273 Robert Longpre

1993
Pick
- 20 Mike Wilson
- 46 Rick Girard
- 98 Dieter Kochan
- 124 Scott Walker
- 150 Troy Creurer
- 176 Yevgeni Babariko
- 202 Sean Tallaire
- 254 Bert Robertsson
- 280 Sergei Tkachenko

1992
Pick
- 21 Libor Polasek
- 40 Michael Peca
- 45 Mike Fountain
- 69 Jeff Connolly
- 93 Brent Tully
- 110 Brian Loney
- 117 Adrian Aucoin
- 141 Jason Clark
- 165 Scott Hollis
- 213 Sonny Mignacca
- 237 Mark Wotton
- 261 Aaron Boh

1991
Pick
- 7 Alek Stojanov
- 29 Jassen Cullimore
- 51 Sean Pronger
- 95 Dan Kesa
- 117 John Namestnikov
- 139 Brent Thurston
- 161 Eric Johnson
- 183 David Neilson
- 205 Brad Barton
- 227 Jason Fitzsimmons
- 249 Xavier Majic

Coach

CRAWFORD, MARC
Coach, Vancouver Canucks. Born in Belleville, Ont., February 13, 1961.

Marc Crawford became the Canucks' 15th head coach on January 24, 1999.

Crawford began his NHL coaching career with the Quebec Nordiques in 1994 and won a Stanley Cup in 1996 when the team moved to Denver to become the Colorado Avalanche. As coach of the Canucks, he led the team to 83 points in his first full season behind the bench in 1999-2000, then guided the Canucks back into the playoffs in 2000-01. Under Crawford, the Canucks recorded a franchise high 104 points in 2002-03 and won the Northwest Division title in 2003-04.

Crawford was the head coach for Team Canada at the 1998 Olympics and was an assistant at the 1996 World Cup of Hockey. He began his coaching career as a playing assistant with Fredericton (AHL) for the 1987-88 season. At the end of the year he moved to Milwaukee where he served as an assistant coach for the Canucks' IHL affiliate in 1988-89. He then moved to Cornwall where he served as the Royals' general manager and head coach in 1989-90.

After two seasons with Cornwall, Crawford went on to coach the St. John's Maple Leafs of the AHL before joining the Nordiques in 1994. He received the 1995 Jack Adams Award as the NHL coach of the year, becoming the first rookie coach to win the award since it was inaugurated in 1974.

Crawford played every game of his six-year NHL career with the Vancouver Canucks, recording 19 goals and 31 assists in 176 games.

Coaching Record

Season	Team	Games	Regular Season W	L	T	Playoffs Games	W	L
1989-90	Cornwall (OHL)	66	24	38	4	6	2	4
1990-91	Cornwall (OHL)	66	23	42	1	....	....	....
1991-92	St. John's (AHL)	80	39	29	12	16	11	5
1992-93	St. John's (AHL)	80	41	26	13	9	4	5
1993-94	St. John's (AHL)	80	45	23	12	11	6	5
1994-95	Quebec (NHL)	48	30	13	5	6	2	4
1995-96	Colorado (NHL)	82	47	25	10	22	16	6*
1996-97	Colorado (NHL)	82	49	24	9	17	10	7
1997-98	Colorado (NHL)	82	39	26	17	7	3	4
1998-99	Vancouver (NHL)	37	8	23	6	....	....	....
1999-2000	Vancouver (NHL)	82	30	37	15	....	....	....
2000-01	Vancouver (NHL)	82	36	35	11	4	0	4
2001-02	Vancouver (NHL)	82	42	33	7	6	2	4
2002-03	Vancouver (NHL)	82	45	24	13	14	7	7
2003-04	Vancouver (NHL)	82	43	29	10	7	3	4
2004-05	Vancouver (NHL)				Season Cancelled			
	NHL Totals	741	369	269	103	83	43	40

* Stanley Cup win.

Club Directory

Vancouver Canucks
General Motors Place
800 Griffiths Way
Vancouver, B.C. V6B 6G1
Phone **604/899-4600**
FAX 604/899-4640
www.canucks.com
Capacity: 18,630

General Motors Place

Executive Directory
Chairman, OBSE & Governor, NHL	John E. McCaw Jr.
Deputy Chairman, OBSE & Alt. Gov., NHL	Francesco Aquilini
Deputy Chairman, OBSE & President, CEO	TBD
Senior Vice President, G.M. & Alt. Gov., NHL	David M. Nonis
Chief Operating Officer	TBD
Corporate Counsel	James Conrad
Vice President, Finance	Victor de Bonis
Vice President, People Development	Susanne Haine
Vice President, Broadcast & New Media	Chris Hebb
Vice President & G.M., Arena Operations	Harvey Jones
Vice-President, Customer Sales & Service	Caley Denton
Executive Assistant	Leila Neale

Hockey Operations
Senior Vice-President, G.M. & Alt. Gov.	David M. Nonis
Executive Assistant	Chris Stephens
Vice President & Assistant General Manager	Steve Tambellini
Head Coach	Marc Crawford
Executive Assistant	Lori Meehan
Associate Coaches	Jack McIlhargey, Mike Johnston
Assistant Coach	Barry Smith
Goaltending Coach	Ian Clark
Strength & Conditioning Coach	Roger Takahashi
Director, Player Development	Stan Smyl
General Manager, Manitoba Moose	Craig Heisinger
Head Coach, Manitoba Moose	Alain Vigneault
Assistant Coach, Manitoba Moose	Mike Kelly
Senior Editor, Alumni Liaison	Norm Jewison
Director, Media Relations	TBD
Manager, Media & Player Relations	T.C. Carling
Assistant, Media Relations	Stephanie Maniago
Director, Community Relations	Debbie Butt
Manager, Community Relations	Karen Christiansen
Coordinator, Community Relations	Jessica Danylchuk
Assistant, Community Relations	Tara Clarke

Scouting Staff
Chief Scout	Ron Delorme
Professional Scouts	Lucien DeBlois, Eric Crawford
European Scout	Thomas Gradin
Russian Scout	Sergei Chibisov
Amateur Scouts	Jack McCartan, Barry Dean, Mario Marois, John McMorrow, Gary Lupul, Tim Lenardon, Branislav Pulis, Harold Snepsts
Coordinator, Scouting & Player Information	Jonathan Wall

Medical & Training Staff
Medical Trainer	Mike Burnstein
Assistant Medical Trainers	Jon Sanderson, Marty Dudgeon
Equipment Manager	Pat O'Neill
Assistant Equipment Manager	Jamie Hendricks
Assistant Equipment Trainer	Brian Hamilton
Game Dressing Room Attendants	John Jukitch, Ron Shute
Team Doctors	Dr. Rui Avelar, Dr. Bill Regan, Dr. Mike Wilkinson
Team Dentist	Dr. David Lawson
Team Chiropractor	Dr. Sid Sheard
Team Optometrist	Dr. Alan R. Boyco

Marketing and Creative Services
Director, Marketing	Paul Dal Monte
Marketing Coordinator	Jennifer Murtagh
Graphic Designers	Ken Jones, Kim Sissons

Broadcast
Director, Facilities and In-house Productions	Paul Brettell
Director, Production Services	Mike Hall
Director, Technical Services	Vic Araujo
Multimedia Producer	Jason Steensma
Website Manager	Michael Kinghorn
Broadcast Coordinator	Shannon Baker
Multimedia Editor	Kathy Garland

Business Development
Directors, Business Development	David Altman, Sharon Butler, Tom Mauthe
Director, Sponsorship Services	Darren Moscovitch
Manager, Suite and Sponsorship Services	Deborah Boren
Manager, Business Development	Lui Garcea

Customer Sales and Service
Director, Customer Sales & Service	Jordan Thorsteinson
Manager, Customer Sales & Service	Mary Nagy
Manager, Customer Accounts	Andrew Merai, Josh Bender, Martha Vassos, Aysha Wilkes, David Pan, Chris Wallace

Game Entertainment
Manager, Game Entertainment & Events	Jamie Levchuk
Coordinator, Game Presentation & Events	TBD

Finance and Central Services, Travel, People Development
Controller, Hockey	Patricia Bigonzi
Corporate Controller	Aaron Wilson
Travel Manager	Cathie Moroney
Managers, People Development	Lisa Steiman, Pam Petrie

Authentix, Fan Apparel and Collectibles
Director, Merchandise	TBD
Merchandise Manager	Kristy Pennock
Retail Operations Manager	Jeff Winslade
Retail Operations Coordinator	Danielle Libonati

Washington Capitals

2005-06 Schedule

Oct.	Wed.	5	Columbus
	Fri.	7	Atlanta
	Sat.	8	at Atlanta
	Mon.	10	NY Rangers*
	Wed.	12	at Carolina
	Thu.	13	NY Islanders
	Sun.	16	Tampa Bay
	Thu.	20	at Florida
	Sat.	22	Carolina
	Wed.	26	at Buffalo
	Fri.	28	at Tampa Bay
	Sat.	29	at Florida
Nov.	Thu.	3	at Philadelphia
	Fri.	4	Atlanta
	Sun.	6	Toronto*
	Tue.	8	at Toronto
	Fri.	11	New Jersey*
	Sat.	12	at New Jersey*
	Tue.	15	Tampa Bay
	Thu.	17	at Buffalo
	Sat.	19	at Montreal
	Tue.	22	at Pittsburgh
	Wed.	23	Tampa Bay
	Sat.	26	at NY Rangers
	Sun.	27	Buffalo*
Dec.	Sat.	3	NY Rangers
	Wed.	7	Nashville
	Fri.	9	Detroit
	Wed.	14	at Los Angeles
	Fri.	16	at San Jose
	Sun.	18	Florida
	Thu.	22	at Atlanta
	Fri.	23	Montreal
	Tue.	27	Boston
	Wed.	28	at New Jersey
	Sat.	31	Philadelphia*
Jan.	Sun.	1	Atlanta*
	Wed.	4	Ottawa
	Fri.	6	Philadelphia
	Sun.	8	Florida*
	Tue.	10	Chicago

	Thu.	12	at Dallas
	Fri.	13	at Anaheim
	Mon.	16	at Phoenix*
	Thu.	19	St. Louis
	Sat.	21	Carolina
	Mon.	23	Boston
	Wed.	25	at Pittsburgh
	Thu.	26	at Boston
	Sun.	29	Tampa Bay*
	Tue.	31	at NY Islanders
Feb.	Fri.	3	Toronto
	Sat.	4	at Tampa Bay
	Tue.	7	Florida
	Fri.	10	at Philadelphia
	Sat.	11	Pittsburgh
	Tue.	28	at Toronto
Mar.	Thu.	2	at Ottawa
	Sat.	4	at Atlanta
	Mon.	6	NY Islanders
	Wed.	8	Pittsburgh
	Fri.	10	New Jersey
	Sun.	12	Ottawa*
	Tue.	14	Buffalo
	Thu.	16	at NY Rangers
	Sat.	18	Florida
	Mon.	20	Montreal
	Wed.	22	at Florida
	Thu.	23	at Tampa Bay
	Sat.	25	at Carolina
	Wed.	29	at Carolina
	Thu.	30	at Montreal
Apr.	Sat.	1	at Ottawa
	Mon.	3	at Carolina
	Wed.	5	Carolina
	Fri.	7	Carolina
	Sat.	8	at NY Islanders
	Mon.	10	at Boston
	Thu.	13	at Atlanta
	Sat.	15	at Florida
	Mon.	17	Atlanta
	Tue.	18	at Tampa Bay

* Denotes afternoon game.

Franchise date: June 11, 1974

EASTERN
NHL CONFERENCE

SOUTHEAST DIVISION

32nd NHL Season

Five-year veteran Jeff Halpern is the only Washington-area native ever to play for the Capitals. He grew up a fan of Dale Hunter and Rod Langway.

Year-by-Year Record

Season	GP	Home W	L	T	OL	Road W	L	T	OL	Overall W	L	T	OL	GF	GA	Pts.	Finished	Playoff Result
2004-05	....	....				....				....				....	....	....		
2003-04	82	13	20	6	2	10	26	4	1	23	46	10	3	186	253	59	5th, Southeast Div.	Out of Playoffs
2002-03	82	24	13	2	2	15	16	6	4	39	29	8	6	224	220	92	2nd, Southeast Div.	Lost Conf. Quarter-Final
2001-02	82	21	12	6	2	15	21	5	0	36	33	11	2	228	240	85	2nd, Southeast Div.	Out of Playoffs
2000-01	82	24	9	6	2	17	18	4	2	41	27	10	4	233	211	96	1st, Southeast Div.	Lost Conf. Quarter-Final
1999-2000	82	26	5	8	2	18	19	4	0	44	24	12	2	227	194	102	1st, Southeast Div.	Lost Conf. Quarter-Final
1998-99	82	16	23	2	....	15	22	4	....	31	45	6	....	200	218	68	3rd, Southeast Div.	Out of Playoffs
1997-98	82	23	12	6	....	17	18	6	....	40	30	12	....	219	202	92	3rd, Atlantic Div.	Lost Final
1996-97	82	17	17	5	....	14	23	4	....	33	40	9	....	214	231	75	5th, Atlantic Div.	Out of Playoffs
1995-96	82	21	15	5	....	18	17	6	....	39	32	11	....	234	204	89	4th, Atlantic Div.	Lost Conf. Quarter-Final
1994-95	48	15	6	3	....	7	12	5	....	22	18	8	....	136	120	52	3rd, Atlantic Div.	Lost Conf. Quarter-Final
1993-94	84	17	16	9	....	22	19	1	....	39	35	10	....	277	263	88	3rd, Atlantic Div.	Lost Conf. Semi-Final
1992-93	84	21	15	6	....	22	19	1	....	43	34	7	....	325	286	93	2nd, Patrick Div.	Lost Div. Semi-Final
1991-92	80	25	12	3	....	20	15	5	....	45	27	8	....	330	275	98	2nd, Patrick Div.	Lost Div. Semi-Final
1990-91	80	21	14	5	....	16	22	2	....	37	36	7	....	258	258	81	3rd, Patrick Div.	Lost Div. Final
1989-90	80	19	18	3	....	17	20	3	....	36	38	6	....	284	275	78	3rd, Patrick Div.	Lost Conf. Championship
1988-89	80	25	12	3	....	16	17	7	....	41	29	10	....	305	259	92	1st, Patrick Div.	Lost Div. Semi-Final
1987-88	80	22	14	4	....	16	19	5	....	38	33	9	....	281	249	85	2nd, Patrick Div.	Lost Div. Final
1986-87	80	22	15	3	....	16	17	7	....	38	32	10	....	285	278	86	2nd, Patrick Div.	Lost Div. Semi-Final
1985-86	80	30	8	2	....	20	15	5	....	50	23	7	....	315	272	107	2nd, Patrick Div.	Lost Div. Final
1984-85	80	27	11	2	....	19	14	7	....	46	25	9	....	322	240	101	2nd, Patrick Div.	Lost Div. Semi-Final
1983-84	80	26	11	3	....	22	16	2	....	48	27	5	....	308	226	101	2nd, Patrick Div.	Lost Div. Final
1982-83	80	22	12	6	....	17	13	10	....	39	25	16	....	306	283	94	3rd, Patrick Div.	Lost Div. Semi-Final
1981-82	80	16	16	8	....	10	25	5	....	26	41	13	....	319	338	65	5th, Patrick Div.	Out of Playoffs
1980-81	80	16	17	7	....	10	19	11	....	26	36	18	....	286	317	70	5th, Patrick Div.	Out of Playoffs
1979-80	80	20	14	6	....	7	26	7	....	27	40	13	....	261	293	67	5th, Patrick Div.	Out of Playoffs
1978-79	80	15	19	6	....	9	22	9	....	24	41	15	....	273	338	63	4th, Norris Div.	Out of Playoffs
1977-78	80	10	23	7	....	7	26	7	....	17	49	14	....	195	321	48	5th, Norris Div.	Out of Playoffs
1976-77	80	17	15	8	....	7	27	6	....	24	42	14	....	221	307	62	4th, Norris Div.	Out of Playoffs
1975-76	80	6	26	8	....	5	33	2	....	11	59	10	....	224	394	32	5th, Norris Div.	Out of Playoffs
1974-75	80	7	28	5	....	1	39	0	....	8	67	5	....	181	446	21	5th, Norris Div.	Out of Playoffs

2005-06 Player Personnel

FORWARDS

	HT	WT	S	Place of Birth	Date	2004-05 Club
AULIN, Jared	6-0	192	R	Calgary, Alta.	3/15/82	Portland (AHL)
BRADLEY, Matt	6-3	199	R	Stittsville, Ont.	6/13/78	Dornbirn
CASSELS, Andrew	6-1	185	L	Bramalea, Ont.	7/23/69	
CLARK, Chris	6-0	200	R	South Windsor, CT	3/8/76	Bern-Storhamar
CLYMER, Ben	6-1	199	R	Bloomington, MN	4/11/78	Biel
GORDON, Boyd	6-0	198	R	Unity, Sask.	10/19/83	Portland (AHL)
HALPERN, Jeff	6-0	198	R	Potomac, MD	5/3/76	Ajoie-Kloten
KANE, Boyd	6-2	218	L	Swift Current, Sask.	4/18/78	Philadelphia (AHL)
KLEPIS, Jakub	6-2	200	R	Prague, Czech.	6/5/84	Portland (AHL)
OVECHKIN, Alexander	6-2	212	R	Moscow, USSR	9/17/85	Dynamo Moscow
PEAT, Stephen	6-3	230	R	Princeton, B.C.	3/10/80	Danbury
PETTINGER, Matt	6-1	205	L	Edmonton, Alta.	10/22/80	Ljubljana
ROBITAILLE, Louis	6-1	192	L	Montreal, Que.	3/16/82	Portland (AHL)
SEMIN, Alexander	6-0	181	L	Krasnoyarsk, USSR	3/3/84	Togliatti
SUTHERBY, Brian	6-3	205	L	Edmonton, Alta.	3/1/82	Portland (AHL)
SYKORA, Petr	6-3	206	R	Pardubice, Czech.	12/21/78	Pardubice
WILLSIE, Brian	6-1	195	R	London, Ont.	3/16/78	Ljubljana-Port (AHL)
ZALESAK, Miroslav	6-0	200	L	Skalica, Czech.	1/2/80	Skalica-Litvinov
ZUBRUS, Dainius	6-4	226	L	Elektrenai, USSR	6/16/78	Togliatti

DEFENSEMEN

BIRON, Mathieu	6-6	220	R	Lac-St-Charles, Que.	4/29/80	
BOUMEDIENNE, Josef	6-2	205	L	Stockholm, Sweden	1/12/78	Brynas-Karpat
CUTTA, Jakub	6-3	210	L	Jablonec nad Nisou, Czech.	12/29/81	Portland (AHL)
EMINGER, Steve	6-2	203	R	Woodbridge, Ont.	10/31/83	Portland (AHL)
FORTIN, Jean-Francois	6-2	205	L	Laval, Que.	3/15/79	Portland (AHL)
HEWARD, Jamie	6-2	207	R	Regina, Sask.	3/30/71	Langnau
MAJESKY, Ivan	6-5	230	R	Banska Bystrica, Czech.	9/2/76	Sparta
MORRISONN, Shaone	6-3	205	L	Vancouver, B.C.	12/23/82	Portland (AHL)
MUIR, Bryan	6-4	220	L	Winnipeg, Man.	6/8/73	MODO-Blues
NYCHOLAT, Lawrence	6-0	192	L	Calgary, Alta.	5/7/79	Hartford
WITT, Brendan	6-2	219	L	Humboldt, Sask.	2/20/75	Bracknell
YONKMAN, Nolan	6-6	245	R	Punnichy, Sask.	4/1/81	Portland (AHL)

GOALTENDERS

	HT	WT	C	Place of Birth	Date	2004-05 Club
DAIGNEAULT, Maxime	6-3	202	L	St-Jacques-le-Mineur, Que.	1/23/84	Port (AHL)-S. Carolina
KOLZIG, Olie	6-3	225	L	Johannesburg, South Africa	4/6/70	Eisbaren Berlin
OUELLET, Maxime	6-2	195	L	Beauport, Que.	6/17/81	Portland (AHL)

In the System and Recently Drafted

FORWARDS

	HT	WT	S	Place of Birth	Date	2004-05 Club
BLOMDAHL, Patric	6-1	202	L	Stockholm, Sweden	1/30/84	Linkoping-Nykoping
BOURQUE, Chris	5-7	170	L	Boston, MA	1/29/86	Boston U.-Port (AHL)
DVORAK, Petr	6-0	194	R	Roznov, Czech.	10/11/83	Prostejov-Prerov-Havirov
FEHR, Eric	6-3	186	R	Winkler, Man.	9/7/85	Brandon
FLEISCHMANN, Tomas	6-0	165	L	Koprivnice, Czech.	5/16/84	Portland (AHL)
FUSSEY, Owen	6-0	195	L	Winnipeg, Man.	4/2/83	Portland (AHL)
GORDON, Andrew	5-11	180	R	Halifax, N.S.	12/13/85	St. Cloud State
GUGGISBERG, Peter	5-11	183	R	Davos, Switz.	1/20/85	Davos
HAVEL, Marian	6-0	180	L	Jihlava, Czech.	1/26/84	Jihlava
HUBL, Viktor	6-0	183	L	Chomutov, Czech.	8/13/78	Litvinov
IGNATUSHKIN, Igor	5-11	175	L	Elektrostal, USSR	4/7/84	Elektrostal-Leninogorsk
JOHANSSON, Jonas	6-1	180	R	Jonkoping, Sweden	3/18/84	Port (AHL)-S. Carolina
JOUDREY, Andrew	5-11	191	L	Halifax, N.S.	7/15/84	U. of Wisconsin
LAICH, Brooks	6-2	199	L	Wawota, Sask.	6/23/83	Portland (AHL)
MINK, Graham	6-3	217	R	Stowe, VT	5/21/79	Portland (AHL)
MORIN, Travis	6-2	175	L	Minneapolis, MN	1/9/84	Minnesota State
NEPRYAYEV, Ivan	6-1	180	L	Yaroslavl, USSR	2/4/82	Yaroslavl
NOVAK, Zbynek	6-2	194	L	Kutna Hora, Czech.	7/23/83	
ORLOV, Maxim	6-0	176	L	Moscow, USSR	3/31/81	Saratov
POLCIK, Peter	6-4	190	L	Nitra, Czech.	7/23/83	Trnava-Senica
ROBERTSON, Josh	5-11	186	R	Whitman, MA	8/25/84	Northeastern
SALOMONSSON, Andreas	6-1	200	L	Ornskoldsvik, Sweden	12/19/73	MODO
SALONEN, Pasi	5-11	187	L	Vierumaki, Finland	12/18/85	
STECKEL, Dave	6-5	215	L	Westbend, WI	3/15/82	Manchester
VALDIX, Andreas	5-11	170	L	Malmo, Sweden	12/6/84	Malmo-Halmstad
WERNER, Steve	6-0	197	R	Washington, DC	8/8/84	Massachusetts
YUNKOV , Mikhail	6-0	180	L	Voskresensk, USSR	2/16/86	Krylja Sovetov

DEFENSEMEN

BARTHEL, Clayton	6-2	205	L	Lahr, West Germany	4/2/86	Seattle
BORNHAMMAR, David	6-0	180	L	Lidingo, Sweden	6/15/81	Skovde
DOVGAN, Viktor	6-1	205	L	Moscow, USSR	2/27/87	CSKA 2
FINLEY, Joe	6-7	229	L	Edina, MN	6/29/87	Sioux Falls
GREEN, Mike	6-1	198	R	Calgary, Alta.	10/12/85	Saskatoon
HEDMAN, Oscar	6-0	209	L	Ornskoldsvik, Sweden	4/21/86	MODO
LEPISTO, Sami	6-0	176	L	Espoo, Finland	10/17/84	Jokerit
McNEILL, Patrick	6-0	195	L	Strathroy, Ont.	3/17/87	Saginaw
ODUYA, John	6-0	200	L	Stockholm, Sweden	10/1/81	Djurgarden
PETRE, Henrik	6-1	187	L	Stockholm, Sweden	4/9/79	Mora
POKULOK, Sasha	6-5	220	L	Montreal, Que.	5/25/86	Cornell
RIAZANTSEV, Alexander	6-0	210	R	Moscow, USSR	3/15/80	Yaroslavl
SCHADILOV, Igor	6-2	189	L	Moscow, USSR	6/7/80	Dynamo Moscow
SCHULTZ, Jeff	6-6	212	L	Calgary, Alta.	2/25/86	Calgary (WHL)
TERNAVSKY, Artem	6-3	213	L	Magnitogorsk, USSR	6/2/83	Nizh. Novgo.-Barnaul
THOMAS, Andrew	6-2	196	R	West Bend, WI	11/14/85	U. of Denver
WOTTON, Mark	6-1	195	L	Foxwarren, Man.	11/16/73	St. Petersburg
ZIMAKOV, Sergei	6-1	194	L	Moscow, USSR	1/15/78	Spartak
ZINGER, Dwayne	6-4	216	L	Coronation, Alta.	7/5/76	Portland (AHL)

GOALTENDERS

	HT	WT	C	Place of Birth	Date	2004-05 Club
CASSIVI, Frederic	6-4	215	L	Sorel, Que.	6/12/75	Cincinnati (AHL)
MACHESNEY, Daren	6-0	163	L	Hamilton, Ont.	12/13/86	Brampton
MRAZEK, Justin	6-3	185	L	Regina, Sask.	7/21/85	Union College
MULLER, Robert	5-8	165	L	Rosenheim, W. Ger.	6/25/80	Krefeld
STANA, Rastislav	6-2	184	L	Kosice, Czech.	1/10/80	Sodertalje

Coaching History

Jim Anderson, Red Sullivan and Milt Schmidt, 1974-75; Milt Schmidt and Tom McVie, 1975-76; Tom McVie, 1976-77, 1977-78; Danny Belisle, 1978-79; Danny Belisle and Gary Green, 1979-80; Gary Green, 1980-81; Gary Green, Roger Crozier and Bryan Murray, 1981-82; Bryan Murray, 1982-83 to 1988-89; Bryan Murray and Terry Murray, 1989-90; Terry Murray, 1990-91 to 1992-93; Terry Murray and Jim Schoenfeld, 1993-94; Jim Schoenfeld, 1994-95 to 1996-97; Ron Wilson, 1997-98 to 2001-02; Bruce Cassidy, 2002-03; Bruce Cassidy and Glen Hanlon, 2003-04; Glen Hanlon, 2004-05 to date.

Coach

HANLON, GLEN
Coach, Washington Capitals. Born in Brandon, Man., February 20, 1957.

Glen Hanlon was in his second season as an assistant coach when he was promoted to the position of head coach on December 10, 2003. Previously, Hanlon had served as head coach for Washington's minor-league affiliate, the Portland Pirates, for three seasons.

During his first season at the helm of the Pirates in 1999-2000, Hanlon was named the American Hockey League's coach of the year after guiding Portland to a 46-23-10-1 record and a league-best 48-point turnaround. The Pirates finished with 103 points overall, second best in the AHL's New England Division.

In three seasons leading the Pirates, Hanlon guided the club to two Calder Cup playoff appearances. He finished his tenure posting the second-highest win total (110) in Pirates history.

Before arriving in Portland, Hanlon served eight seasons with the Vancouver Canucks as an assistant coach (1994 to 1999) and goaltending coach (1991 to 1994). He helped lead the Canucks to their first 40-win season in franchise history in 1991-92, and the team advanced to the Stanley Cup Finals in 1994. He also served as an assistant coach with the Canadian national team at the 1998 World Championships in Zurich, Switzerland.

Hanlon appeared in 477 NHL games in 14 seasons as a goaltender between 1977 and 1991, playing with the Vancouver Canucks, St. Louis Blues, New York Rangers and Detroit Red Wings. He posted a career record of 167-202-61, a 3.60 goals-against average and 13 shutouts. He also played 35 career NHL playoff games, compiling an 11-15-0 record, a 3.14 goals-against average and four shutouts.

Coaching Record

Season	Team	Games	Regular Season			Playoffs		
			W	L	T	Games	W	L
1999-00	Portland (AHL)	80	46	24	10	4	1	3
2000-01	Portland (AHL)	80	34	42	4	3	0	3
2001-02	Portland (AHL)	80	30	35	15	....	....	....
2003-04	**Washington (NHL)**	**54**	**15**	**30**	**9**	....	....	....
2004-05	**Washington (NHL)**			Season Cancelled				
	NHL Totals	**54**	**15**	**30**	**9**	....	....	....

Selected first in the 2004 NHL Entry Draft, Alexander Ovechkin is now under contract to the Capitals.

Club Records

Team

(Figures in brackets for season records are games played; records for fewest points, wins, ties, losses, goals, goals against are for 70 or more games)

Most Points	107	1985-86 (80)
Most Wins	50	1985-86 (80)
Most Ties	18	1980-81 (80)
Most Losses	67	1974-75 (80)
Most Goals	330	1991-92 (80)
Most Goals Against	*446	1974-75 (80)
Fewest Points	*21	1974-75 (80)
Fewest Wins	*8	1974-75 (80)
Fewest Ties	5	1974-75 (80), 1983-84 (80)
Fewest Losses	23	1985-86 (80)
Fewest Goals	181	1974-75 (80)
Fewest Goals Against	202	1997-98 (82)

Longest Winning Streak

Overall	10	Jan. 27-Feb. 18/84
Home	10	Jan. 4-Feb. 23/00
Away	6	Feb. 26-Apr. 1/84

Longest Undefeated Streak

Overall	14	Nov. 24-Dec. 23/82 (9 wins, 5 ties), Jan. 17-Feb. 18/84 (13 wins, 1 tie)
Home	13	Nov. 25/92-Jan. 31/93 (9 wins, 4 ties), Dec. 27/99-Feb. 23/00 (11 wins, 2 ties)
Away	10	Nov. 24/82-Jan. 8/83 (6 wins, 4 ties)

Longest Losing Streak

Overall	*17	Feb. 18-Mar. 26/75
Home	*11	Feb. 18-Mar. 30/75
Away	37	Oct. 9/74-Mar. 26/75

Longest Winless Streak

Overall	25	Nov. 29/75-Jan. 21/76 (22 losses, 3 ties)
Home	14	Dec. 3/75-Jan. 21/76 (11 losses, 3 ties)
Away	37	Oct. 9/74-Mar. 26/75 (37 losses)

Most Shutouts, Season	9	1995-96 (82)
Most PIM, Season	2,204	1989-90 (80)
Most Goals, Game	12	Feb. 6/90 (Que. 2 at Wsh. 12), Jan. 11/03 (Fla. 2 at Wsh. 12)

Individual

Most Seasons	15	Calle Johansson
Most Games	983	Calle Johansson
Most Goals, Career	472	Peter Bondra
Most Assists, Career	418	Michal Pivonka
Most Points, Career	825	Peter Bondra (472G, 353A)
Most PIM, Career	2,003	Dale Hunter
Most Shutouts, Career	35	Olaf Kolzig
Longest Consecutive Games Streak	422	Bob Carpenter (Oct. 7/81-Nov. 22/86)
Most Goals, Season	60	Dennis Maruk (1981-82)
Most Assists, Season	76	Dennis Maruk (1981-82)
Most Points, Season	136	Dennis Maruk (1981-82; 60G, 76A)
Most PIM, Season	339	Alan May (1989-90)

Most Points, Defenseman, Season	81	Larry Murphy (1986-87; 23G, 58A)
Most Points, Center, Season	136	Dennis Maruk (1981-82; 60G, 76A)
Most Points, Right Wing, Season	102	Mike Gartner (1984-85; 50G, 52A)
Most Points, Left Wing, Season	87	Ryan Walter (1981-82; 38G, 49A)
Most Points, Rookie, Season	67	Bob Carpenter (1981-82; 32G, 35A), Chris Valentine (1981-82; 30G, 37A)
Most Shutouts, Season	9	Jim Carey (1995-96)
Most Goals, Game	5	Bengt Gustafsson (Jan. 8/84), Peter Bondra (Feb. 5/94)
Most Assists, Game	6	Mike Ridley (Jan. 7/89)
Most Points, Game	7	Dino Ciccarelli (Mar. 18/89; 4G, 3A)

* NHL Record.

Retired Numbers

5	Rod Langway	1982-1993
7	Yvon Labre	1974-1981
32	Dale Hunter	1987-1999

Captains' History

Doug Mohns, 1974-75; Bill Clement and Yvon Labre, 1975-76; Yvon Labre, 1976-77, 1977-78; Guy Charron, 1978-79; Ryan Walter, 1979-80 to 1981-82; Rod Langway, 1982-83 to 1991-92; Rod Langway and Kevin Hatcher, 1992-93; Kevin Hatcher, 1993-94; Dale Hunter, 1994-95 to 1998-99; Adam Oates, 1999-2000, 2000-01; Brendan Witt and Steve Konowalchuk, 2001-02; Steve Konowalchuk, 2002-03, 2003-04.

All-time Record vs. Other Clubs

Regular Season

	At Home								On Road								Total							
	GP	W	L	T	OL	GF	GA	PTS	GP	W	L	T	OL	GF	GA	PTS	GP	W	L	T	OL	GF	GA	PTS
Anaheim	9	4	5	0	0	16	22	8	9	2	6	1	0	22	29	5	18	6	11	1	0	38	51	13
Atlanta	13	9	1	3	0	50	29	21	13	5	6	1	0	38	28	12	26	14	7	5	0	88	57	33
Boston	55	17	26	12	0	155	191	46	56	15	31	9	1	151	209	40	111	32	57	21	1	306	400	86
Buffalo	56	15	31	9	1	140	196	40	56	15	35	6	0	146	216	36	112	30	66	15	1	286	412	76
Calgary	41	21	14	6	0	153	139	48	38	7	24	7	0	93	157	21	79	28	38	13	0	246	296	69
Carolina	47	29	14	4	0	163	118	62	49	24	14	10	1	152	128	59	96	53	28	14	1	315	246	121
Chicago	41	21	15	5	0	145	127	47	40	12	22	6	0	120	151	30	81	33	37	11	0	265	278	77
Colorado	33	18	10	4	1	131	105	41	34	14	15	5	0	116	105	33	67	32	25	9	1	247	210	74
Columbus	2	1	0	1	0	8	5	3	4	3	1	0	0	15	11	6	6	4	1	1	0	23	16	9
Dallas	40	15	17	8	0	120	129	38	41	12	21	8	0	110	152	32	81	27	38	16	0	230	281	70
Detroit	46	21	20	5	0	168	147	47	47	15	20	11	1	135	161	42	93	36	40	16	1	303	308	89
Edmonton	29	18	9	2	0	118	93	38	29	10	15	4	0	91	120	24	58	28	24	6	0	209	213	62
Florida	28	15	7	5	1	86	61	36	28	13	11	4	0	71	70	30	56	28	18	9	1	157	131	66
Los Angeles	46	18	21	7	0	185	171	43	47	14	27	6	0	144	187	34	93	32	48	13	0	329	358	77
Minnesota	3	2	1	0	0	7	6	4	3	0	3	0	0	1	6	0	6	2	4	0	0	8	12	4
Montreal	59	26	24	9	0	163	177	61	60	17	35	8	0	127	229	42	119	43	59	17	0	290	406	103
Nashville	4	3	1	0	0	10	8	6	5	1	3	1	1	11	16	3	9	4	4	1	1	21	24	9
New Jersey	79	49	23	6	1	308	223	105	79	33	36	7	3	226	240	76	158	82	59	13	4	534	463	181
NY Islanders	81	40	30	11	0	267	251	91	81	37	42	2	0	255	298	76	162	77	72	13	0	522	549	167
NY Rangers	84	42	30	9	3	315	273	96	82	35	38	9	0	281	304	79	166	77	68	18	3	596	577	175
Ottawa	24	11	9	4	0	76	68	26	23	10	12	1	0	70	84	21	47	21	21	5	0	146	152	47
Philadelphia	80	33	34	13	0	261	259	79	83	24	53	6	0	219	312	54	163	57	87	19	0	480	571	133
Phoenix	31	18	7	5	1	119	85	42	30	8	15	7	0	105	112	23	61	26	22	12	1	224	197	65
Pittsburgh	86	45	31	9	1	358	312	100	83	29	47	7	0	261	322	65	169	74	78	16	1	619	634	165
St. Louis	39	20	15	4	0	136	117	44	41	13	20	8	0	127	165	34	80	33	35	12	0	263	282	78
San Jose	12	5	7	0	0	34	36	10	10	3	6	1	0	26	29	7	22	8	13	1	0	60	65	17
Tampa Bay	29	18	7	4	0	101	65	40	29	18	9	2	0	93	65	38	58	36	16	6	0	194	130	78
Toronto	50	28	17	4	1	182	144	61	48	16	25	6	1	163	211	39	98	44	42	10	2	345	355	100
Vancouver	40	22	14	4	0	132	120	48	39	16	18	5	0	123	136	37	79	38	32	9	0	255	256	85
Defunct Clubs	10	2	8	0	0	28	42	4	10	4	5	1	0	30	39	9	20	6	13	1	0	58	81	13
Totals	**1197**	**586**	**448**	**153**	**10**	**4135**	**3719**	**1335**	**1197**	**425**	**615**	**150**	**7**	**3522**	**4292**	**1007**	**2394**	**1011**	**1063**	**303**	**17**	**7657**	**8011**	**2342**

Playoffs

	Series	W	L	GP	W	L	T	GF	GA	Last Mtg.
Boston	2	1	1	10	4	6	0	21	28	1998
Buffalo	1	1	0	6	4	2	0	13	11	1998
Detroit	1	0	1	4	0	4	0	7	13	1998
New Jersey	2	1	1	13	7	6	0	44	43	1990
NY Islanders	6	1	5	30	12	18	0	88	99	1993
NY Rangers	4	2	2	22	11	11	0	75	71	1994
Ottawa	1	1	0	5	4	1	0	18	7	1998
Philadelphia	3	2	1	16	9	7	0	65	55	1989
Pittsburgh	7	1	6	42	16	26	0	121	137	2001
Tampa Bay	1	0	1	6	2	4	0	15	14	2003
Totals	**28**	**10**	**18**	**154**	**69**	**85**	**0**	**467**	**478**	

Playoff Results 2005-2000

Year	Round	Opponent	Result	GF	GA
2003	CQF	Tampa Bay	L 2-4	15	14
2001	CQF	Pittsburgh	L 2-4	10	14
2000	CQF	Pittsburgh	L 1-4	8	17

Abbreviations: Round: F – Final; **CF** – conference final; **CSF** – conference semi-final; **CQF** – conference quarter-final; **DSF** – division semi-final.

Calgary totals include Atlanta Flames, 1974-75 to 1979-80.
Colorado totals include Quebec, 1979-80 to 1994-95.
New Jersey totals include Kansas City, 1974-75 to 1975-76, and Colorado Rockies, 1976-77 to 1981-82.
Phoenix totals include Winnipeg, 1979-80, 1995-96.
Carolina totals include Hartford, 1979-80 to 1996-97.
Dallas totals include Minnesota North Stars, 1974-75 to 1992-93.

Key Off-Season Signings/Acquisitions

2004

June 26 • Used the first overall pick in the 2004 Entry Draft to select LW **Alexander Ovechkin**.

2005

July 18 • Named **Dean Evason** assistant coach.

28 • Signed 2003 1st-round pick (18th overall), RW **Eric Fehr**.

Aug. 4 • Obtained RW **Chris Clark** from Calgary for a 2006 conditional pick.

5 • Signed 2004 1st overall pick LW **Alexander Ovechkin**.

8 • Signed RW **Miroslav Zalesak** and LW **Ben Clymer**.

9 • Signed C **Andrew Cassels**.

10 • Signed Ds **Mathieu Biron** and **Ivan Majesky**.

11 • Re-signed D **Jakub Cutta** and C/RW **Jared Aulin**.

12 • Obtained D **Bryan Muir** from Los Angeles for future considerations.

15 • Re-signed LW **Matt Pettinger**.

16 • Re-signed Cs **Jeff Halpern** and **Brian Sutherby**, Ds **Brendan Witt**, **Steve Eminger** and **Shaone Morrisonn** and G **Maxime Ouellet**.

Aug. 17 • Signed 2004 2nd-round pick (33rd overall) C/LW **Chris Bourque**.

18 • Re-signed C/RW **Dainius Zubrus** and D **Jean-Francois Fortin**.

18 • Signed RW **Matt Bradley**.

23 • Signed C **Petr Sykora**.

Entry Draft
Selections 2005-1991

2005 Pick		2001 Pick		1997 Pick		1993 Pick	
14	Sasha Pokulok	58	Nathan Paetsch	9	Nick Boynton	11	Brendan Witt
27	Joe Finley	90	Owen Fussey	35	Jean-Francois Fortin	17	Jason Allison
109	Andrew Thomas	125	Jeff Lucky	89	Curtis Cruickshank	69	Patrick Boileau
118	Patrick McNeill	160	Artem Ternavsky	116	Kevin Caulfield	147	Frank Banham
143	Daren Machesney	191	Zbynek Novak	143	Henrik Petre	173	Daniel Hendrickson
181	Tim Kennedy	221	John Oduya	200	Pierre-Luc Therrien	174	Andrew Brunette
209	Viktor Dovgan	249	Matt Maglione	226	Matt Oikawa	199	Joel Poirier
		254	Peter Polcik			225	Jason Gladney
2004 Pick		275	Robert Muller	**1996** Pick		251	Mark Seliger
1	Alexander Ovechkin	284	Viktor Hubl	4	Alexandre Volchkov	277	Dany Bousquet
27	Jeff Schultz			17	Jaroslav Svejkovsky		
29	Mike Green	**2000** Pick		43	Jan Bulis	**1992** Pick	
33	Chris Bourque	26	Brian Sutherby	58	Sergei Zimakov	14	Sergei Gonchar
62	Mikhail Yunkov	43	Matt Pettinger	74	Dave Weninger	32	Jim Carey
66	Sami Lepisto	61	Jakub Cutta	78	Shawn McNeil	53	Stefan Ustorf
88	Clayton Barthel	121	Ryan Vanbuskirk	85	Justin Davis	71	Martin Gendron
132	Oscar Hedman	163	Ivan Nepryayev	126	Matthew Lahey	119	John Varga
138	Pasi Salonen	289	Bjorn Nord	153	Andrew Van Bruggen	167	Mark Matier
166	Peter Guggisberg			180	Michael Anderson	191	Mike Mathers
197	Andrew Gordon	**1999** Pick		206	Oleg Orekhovsky	215	Brian Stagg
230	Justin Mrazek	7	Kris Beech	232	Chad Cavanagh	239	Gregory Callahan
263	Travis Morin	29	Michal Sivek			263	Billy Jo MacPherson
		31	Charlie Stephens	**1995** Pick			
2003 Pick		34	Ross Lupaschuk	17	Brad Church	**1991** Pick	
18	Eric Fehr	37	Nolan Yonkman	23	Miika Elomo	14	Pat Peake
83	Steve Werner	132	Roman Tvrdon	43	Dwayne Hay	21	Trevor Halverson
109	Andreas Valdix	175	Kyle Clark	93	Sebastien Charpentier	25	Eric Lavigne
155	Josh Robertson	192	David Bornhammar	95	Joel Theriault	36	Jeff Nelson
249	Andrew Joudrey	219	Maxim Orlov	105	Benoit Gratton	58	Steve Konowalchuk
279	Mark Olafson	249	Igor Shadilov	124	Joel Cort	80	Justin Morrison
				147	Frederick Jobin	146	Dave Morissette
2002 Pick		**1998** Pick		199	Vasili Turkovsky	168	Rick Corriveau
12	Steve Eminger	49	Jomar Cruz	225	Scott Swanson	190	Trevor Duhaime
13	Alexander Semin	59	Todd Hornung			209	Rob Leask
17	Boyd Gordon	106	Krys Barch	**1994** Pick		212	Carl Leblanc
59	Maxime Daigneault	107	Chris Corrinet	10	Nolan Baumgartner	234	Rob Puchniak
77	Patrick Wellar	118	Mike Siklenka	15	Alexander Kharlamov	256	Bill Kovacs
92	Derek Krestanovich	125	Erik Wendell	41	Scott Cherrey		
109	Jevon Desautels	179	Nate Forster	93	Matt Herr		
118	Petr Dvorak	193	Rastislav Stana	119	Yanick Jean		
145	Rob Gherson	220	Mike Farrell	145	Dmitri Mekeshkin		
179	Marian Havel	251	Blake Evans	171	Daniel Reja		
209	Joni Lindlof			197	Chris Patrick		
242	Igor Ignatushkin			223	John Tuohy		
272	Patric Blomdahl			249	Richard Zednik		
				275	Sergei Tertyshny		

General Managers' History

Milt Schmidt, 1974-75; Milt Schmidt and Max McNab, 1975-76; Max McNab, 1976-77 to 1980-81; Max McNab and Roger Crozier, 1981-82; David Poile, 1982-83 to 1996-97; George McPhee, 1997-98 to date.

Vice President and General Manager

McPHEE, GEORGE
Vice President/General Manager, Washington Capitals.
Born in Guelph, Ont., July 2, 1958.

On June 9, 1997, George McPhee became the fifth general manager of the Washington Capitals. In his first year on the job, McPhee led the Caps to the Stanley Cup Finals for the first time in franchise history. He has begun rebuilding the Capitals with younger players and used the first overall choice at the 2004 NHL Entry Draft to select Alexander Ovechkin.

Prior to joining the Capitals, McPhee spent five years in the front office of the Vancouver Canucks where he served as vice president of hockey operations and alternate governor. He has earned degrees in both law and business and, while attending law school at Rutgers University, interned at the United States Court of International Trade in 1991.

A back injury forced McPhee to retire as an active player at the conclusion of the 1988-89 season, after a seven year playing career with the New York Rangers and New Jersey Devils. McPhee originally signed as a free agent with the Rangers in July, 1982, after graduating from Bowling Green State University with a business degree. McPhee did not waste any time in college, tallying 40 goals and 48 assists in his freshman season and easily winning CCHA rookie of the year honors. His outstanding collegiate hockey career was capped off when he was named the recipient of the Hobey Baker Award as the top U.S. collegiate player in his senior season. McPhee also earned All-America honors as a senior and finished his career at Bowling Green as the CCHA's all-time leading scorer with 114-153-267. He was the first player in CCHA history to make the Conference's all-academic team three straight seasons.

Club Directory

MCI Center

Washington Capitals
401 Ninth Street, NW, Suite 750
Washington, DC 20004
Phone **202/266-2200**
PR FAX 202/266-2360
www.WashingtonCaps.com
Capacity: 18,277

Ownership (Lincoln Holdings LLC)
Chairman & Majority Owner . . . . Ted Leonsis
President & Owner . . . . Dick Patrick
Owners . . . . Jack Davies, Richard Fairbank, Raul Fernandez, Joshua M. Freeman, Sheila Johnson, Richard Kay, Jeong Kim, Mark D. Lerner, George Stamas
Executive Assistant . . . . Michelle Trostle

Hockey Operations
Vice President & General Manager . . . . George McPhee
Director of Player Personnel. . . . . Brian MacLellan
Director of Legal Affairs/Hockey Admin. . . . . Don Fishman
Head Coach . . . . Glen Hanlon
Assistant Coaches . . . . Jay Leach, Dean Evason
Goaltending Coach. . . . . Dave Prior
Scouting Coordinator . . . . Kris Wagner
Security Representative . . . . James Wiseman
Hockey Operations Assistant . . . . Eric Garvey
Executive Assistant . . . . Katy Headman

Scouting Staff
Director of Amateur Scouting . . . . Ross Mahoney
Pro Scout . . . . Larry Carriere
Amateur Scouts . . . . Steve Bowman, Ed McColgan, Ray Payne, Martin Pouliot, Steve Richmond
European Scouts . . . . Gleb Chistyakov, Vojtech Kucera

Medical Staff
Head Athletic Trainer . . . . Greg Smith
Assistant Athletic Trainer. . . . . Christopher Phillips
Massage Therapist . . . . Curt Millar
Physiologist . . . . Jack Blatherwick
Team Physician . . . . Ben Shaffer, MD
Team Internist . . . . Richard Feldman, MD
Team Ophthalmologist . . . . Michael Herr, MD
Team Dentist. . . . . Howard Salob, DDS

Training Staff
Head Equipment Manager . . . . Doug Shearer
Assistant Equipment Manager. . . . . Craig Leydig
Equipment Assistant . . . . Brian Metzger

Business Operations
Director of Operations. . . . . George Parr
Information Technology Manager . . . . Brian McPartland
Mailroom Coordinator . . . . Keith McCombs
Receptionist . . . . Caitlin Wallace

Communications
Senior Director of Communications . . . . Kurt Kehl
Director of Media Relations . . . . Nate Ewell
Manager of Community Relations . . . . Elizabeth Wodatch
New Media Manager . . . . Sean Parker
Senior Sports Media Producer . . . . Mike Vogel
Communications Coordinator . . . . Carolyn Weaver

Finance
Controller . . . . Keith Burrows
Accounts Payable Manager . . . . Jennifer Simpson
Staff Accountant . . . . Jill Ruehle

Marketing
Director of Game Operations . . . . Mark Tamar
Director of Promotions . . . . Chris Lewis
Coordinator of Amateur Hockey & Alumni Relations . . Justin Guiles
Game Operations Coordinator . . . . James Dowd

Sales
Chief Marketing Officer . . . . Kevin Morgan
Director of Group Sales . . . . Darren Montgomery
Senior Regional Sales Manager, Groups . . . . Tim Bronaugh
Director, Season Ticket Sales . . . . Anthony Aspaas
Regional Sales Managers . . . . Nova Ackerman, Dave Boettinger, Matt MacDonald, Joseph O'Neill, Letitia Petrillo, Harry Schroeder, Audrius Zubrus
Regional Sales Managers, Groups . . . . Jeff Keeney, Matt Winkler

Ticket Operations
Director, Ticket Operations . . . . Gary Brosius
Asst. Director, Ticket Operations . . . . Chris Sheap
Manager, Ticket Operations . . . . Tom Nagle
Coordinator, Ticket Operations . . . . Andre Morales

Guest Services
Director, Guest Services . . . . Greg Monares
Coordinators, Guest Services . . . . Chris Roberts, Julia Pergola

Miscellaneous
Team Photographer . . . . Mitchell Layton

Broadcasting
Television Rights Holder . . . . Comcast SportsNet
Radio Flagship . . . . WTNT AM-570
Television Play-by-Play . . . . Joe Beninati
Television Analyst . . . . Craig Laughlin
Television Reporter . . . . Al Koken
Radio Play-by-Play . . . . Steve Kolbe
Radio Analyst . . . . Ken Sabourin

NHL 2004-05 Player Register

2004-05 Statistics for Players
on NHL Rosters in 2003-04

Team	League	Regular Season					Playoffs				
		GP	G	A	Pts	PIM	GP	G	A	Pts	PIM
ABID, Ramzi LW (ATL.)											
Wilkes-Barre	AHL	78	26	29	55	119	7	0	2	2	18
ADAMS, Craig RW (ANA.)											
Milano	Italy	30	15	14	29	57	15	4	7	11	26
ADAMS, Kevyn C (CAR.)											
Dusseldorf	Germany	9	1	2	3	4	....	....	....	....	....
United States	WC-A	1	0	0	0	0	....	....	....	....	....
AFANASENKOV, Dmitry LW (T.B.)											
Togliatti	Russia	30	2	9	11	12	9	0	0	0	4
AFINOGENOV, Maxim RW (BUF.)											
Russia	W-Cup	4	0	1	1	2	....	....	....	....	....
Dynamo Moscow	Russia	36	13	14	27	91	10	4	4	8	8
Russia	WC-A	9	3	2	5	6	....	....	....	....	....
AITKEN, Johnathan D (MTL.)											
Manitoba	AHL	46	1	6	7	101	1	0	0	0	7
ALFREDSSON, Daniel RW (OTT.)											
Sweden	W-Cup	4	0	6	6	2	....	....	....	....	....
Frolunda	Sweden	15	8	9	17	10	14	12	6	18	8
Sweden	WC-A	9	3	6	9	6	....	....	....	....	....
ALLEN, Bryan D (VAN.)											
Voskresensk	Russia	19	0	3	3	34	....	....	....	....	....
ALLISON, Jamie D (NSH.)											
Cambridge	OHA-Sr.	5	0	3	3	4	....	....	....	....	....
ALLISON, Jason C (TOR.)			DID NOT PLAY								
AMONTE, Tony RW (CGY.)											
United States	W-Cup	5	0	1	1	0	....	....	....	....	....
ANDREYCHUK, Dave LW (T.B.)			DID NOT PLAY								
ANGELSTAD, Mel LW											
Belfast	Britain	30	2	7	9	191	8	0	1	1	42
ANTROPOV, Nik C (TOR.)											
Kazan	Russia	10	2	3	5	6	....	....	....	....	....
Yaroslavl	Russia	26	4	15	19	44	9	3	4	7	18
ARKHIPOV, Denis C (NSH.)											
Kazan	Russia	45	9	8	17	28	4	0	0	0	0
ARMSTRONG, Chris D											
Ingolstadt	Germany	46	5	19	24	36	11	2	6	8	18
ARMSTRONG, Derek C (L.A.)											
Geneve	Swiss	9	6	7	13	18	....	....	....	....	....
Rapperswil	Swiss	3	1	3	4	4	....	....	....	....	....
ARNASON, Tyler C (CHI.)											
Brynas	Sweden	4	0	0	0	0	....	....	....	....	....
ARNOTT, Jason C (DAL.)			DID NOT PLAY								
ASHAM, Arron RW (NYI)											
Visp	Swiss-2	5	2	4	6	6	4	1	1	2	8
AUBIN, Serge LW (ATL.)											
Geneve	Swiss	6	2	1	3	8	3	1	2	3	2
AUCOIN, Adrian D (CHI.)											
MODO	Sweden	14	2	4	6	32	6	1	0	1	16
AUDETTE, Donald RW			DID NOT PLAY								
AVERY, Sean C (L.A.)											
Pelicans	Finland	2	3	0	3	26	....	....	....	....	....
Motor City	UHL	16	15	11	26	149	....	....	....	....	....
AXELSSON, P.J. LW (BOS.)											
Sweden	W-Cup	4	0	0	0	2	....	....	....	....	....
Frolunda	Sweden	45	8	9	17	95	14	1	10	11	18
Sweden	WC-A	7	1	0	1	2	....	....	....	....	....
BABCHUK, Anton D (CHI.)											
Norfolk	AHL	66	8	16	24	88	2	0	0	0	2
BACKMAN, Christian D (ST.L.)											
Frolunda	Sweden	50	4	15	19	40	14	2	7	9	10
Sweden	WC-A	9	1	1	2	6	....	....	....	....	....
BALEJ, Jozef RW (NYR)											
Hartford	AHL	69	20	22	42	46	6	0	0	0	4
BARINKA, Michal D (CHI.)											
Norfolk	AHL	59	1	10	11	77	....	....	....	....	....
BARNABY, Matthew RW (CHI.)			DID NOT PLAY								
BARNES, Ryan LW											
Grand Rapids	AHL	69	7	8	15	167	....	....	....	....	....
Kalamazoo	UHL	11	3	5	8	4	....	....	....	....	....
BARNES, Stu C (DAL.)			DID NOT PLAY								
BARNEY, Scott C (ATL.)			DID NOT PLAY								
BARON, Murray D			DID NOT PLAY								
BARTOVIC, Milan RW (BUF.)											
Rochester	AHL	69	10	18	28	83	9	0	3	3	22
BATES, Shawn C (NYI)			DID NOT PLAY								
BATTAGLIA, Bates LW											
Mississippi	ECHL	25	6	11	17	24	4	0	0	0	10
BAUMGARTNER, Nolan D (VAN.)											
Manitoba	AHL	78	9	30	39	51	14	0	4	4	10
BAYDA, Ryan LW											
Lowell	AHL	80	13	27	40	91	9	3	3	6	4
BEAUDOIN, Eric LW											
San Antonio	AHL	32	6	4	10	21	....	....	....	....	....
Edmonton	AHL	24	3	1	4	9	....	....	....	....	....
BEDNAR, Jaroslav RW											
Omsk	Russia	53	12	16	28	56	10	2	1	3	6
BEECH, Kris C (PIT.)											
Wilkes-Barre	AHL	68	14	48	62	146	11	4	6	10	14
BEGIN, Steve C (MTL.)											
Hamilton	AHL	21	10	3	13	20	4	0	2	2	8
BEKAR, Derek LW											
Dundee	Britain-2	3	2	1	3	4	....	....	....	....	....
Springfield	AHL	51	8	14	22	22	....	....	....	....	....
BELAK, Wade D/RW (TOR.)											
Coventry	Britain	20	3	5	8	109	8	1	1	2	16
BELANGER, Eric C (L.A.)											
Bolzano	Italy	12	13	10	23	20	9	3	7	10	33
BELANGER, Ken LW											
Adirondack	UHL	1	0	0	0	5	....	....	....	....	....
BELL, Mark C (CHI.)											
Trondheim	Norway	25	10	17	27	87	11	6	6	12	44
BERARD, Bryan D (CBJ)			DID NOT PLAY								
BEREHOWSKY, Drake D											
Skelleftea	Sweden-2	18	3	5	8	63	....	....	....	....	....
BERG, Aki D (TOR.)											
Finland	W-Cup	5	0	1	1	2	....	....	....	....	....
Timra	Sweden	47	6	14	20	46	7	0	0	0	6
BERGENHEIM, Sean C (NYI)											
Bridgeport	AHL	61	15	14	29	69	....	....	....	....	....
BERGERON, Marc-Andre D (EDM.)											
Brynas	Sweden	10	3	2	5	72	....	....	....	....	....
Brynas	Sweden-Q	9	1	2	3	8	....	....	....	....	....
BERGERON, Patrice C (BOS.)											
Providence	AHL	68	21	40	61	59	16	5	7	12	4
Canada	WJC-A	6	5	8	13	6	....	....	....	....	....
BERGEVIN, Marc D			DID NOT PLAY								
BERGLUND, Christian LW (FLA.)											
Farjestad	Sweden	48	7	13	20	97	14	2	3	5	56
BERRY, Rick D											
Utah	AHL	45	2	6	8	83	....	....	....	....	....
BERTUZZI, Todd RW (VAN.)			DID NOT PLAY – SUSPENDED								
BETTS, Blair C (NYR)											
Hartford	AHL	16	5	4	9	4	....	....	....	....	....
BEZINA, Goran D											
Geneve	Swiss	34	7	12	19	51	4	0	0	0	8
Switzerland	WC-A	7	1	0	1	8	....	....	....	....	....

Team	League	Regular Season GP	G	A	Pts	PIM	Playoffs GP	G	A	Pts	PIM
BICEK, Jiri RW											
Kosice	Slovakia	54	18	23	41	69	10	6	8	14	4
BIRON, Mathieu D (WSH.)				DID NOT PLAY							
BISHAI, Mike C											
Edmonton	AHL	70	10	24	34	36	....	....	....	....	....
BLAKE, Jason C (NYI)											
United States	W-Cup	4	1	0	1	2	....	....	....	....	....
Lugano	Swiss	7	2	2	4	4	....	....	....	....	....
BLAKE, Rob D (COL.)											
Canada	W-Cup			DID NOT PLAY – INJURED							
BLATNY, Zdenek LW											
Znojmo	CzRep	15	3	4	7	28	....	....	....	....	....
Pelicans	Finland	9	1	1	2	32	....	....	....	....	....
BOGUNIECKI, Eric C (ST.L.)											
Worcester	AHL	30	14	11	25	46	....	....	....	....	....
Langenthal	Swiss-2	10	5	3	8	47	....	....	....	....	....
BOILEAU, Patrick D											
Lausanne	Swiss	29	7	12	19	34	8	4	4	8	20
Lausanne	Swiss-Q	....	....	....	....	....	7	0	1	1	4
BOMBARDIR, Brad D				DID NOT PLAY							
BONDRA, Peter RW											
Slovakia	W-Cup			DID NOT PLAY – INJURED							
Poprad	Slovakia	6	4	2	6	4	....	....	....	....	....
BONK, Radek C (MTL.)											
Trinec	CzRep	27	6	10	16	44	....	....	....	....	....
Zlin	CzRep	6	3	2	5	4	6	0	2	2	8
BONVIE, Dennis RW											
Hershey	AHL	76	4	14	18	357	....	....	....	....	....
BOOTLAND, Darryl RW (DET.)											
Grand Rapids	AHL	78	14	20	34	336	....	....	....	....	....
BOTTERILL, Jason LW											
Rochester	AHL	8	6	2	8	9	....	....	....	....	....
BOUCHARD, Joel D (NYI)											
Hartford	AHL	7	1	2	3	6	6	0	2	2	20
BOUCHARD, Pierre-Marc C (MIN.)											
Houston	AHL	67	12	42	54	46	5	0	1	1	0
BOUCHER, Philippe D (DAL.)				DID NOT PLAY							
BOUCK, Tyler C (VAN.)											
TPS	Finland	40	3	7	10	100	6	1	0	1	12
BOUGHNER, Bob D (COL.)				DID NOT PLAY							
BOUILLON, Francis D (MTL.)											
Leksand	Sweden-2	31	10	21	31	46	....	....	....	....	....
BOULERICE, Jesse RW (CAR.)				DID NOT PLAY							
BOULTON, Eric LW (ATL.)											
Columbia	ECHL	48	23	16	39	124	4	2	3	5	8
BOUMEDIENNE, Josef D (WSH.)											
Karpat	Finland	32	5	10	15	58	12	1	5	6	12
Brynas	Sweden	13	6	0	6	43	....	....	....	....	....
BOUWMEESTER, Jay D (FLA.)											
Canada	W-Cup	4	0	0	0	0	....	....	....	....	....
San Antonio	AHL	64	4	13	17	50	....	....	....	....	....
Chicago	AHL	18	6	3	9	12	18	0	0	0	14
BOYES, Brad C (BOS.)											
Providence	AHL	80	33	42	75	58	16	8	7	15	23
BOYLE, Dan D (T.B.)											
Djurgarden	Sweden	32	9	9	18	47	12	2	3	5	26
Canada	WC-A	9	0	3	3	6	....	....	....	....	....
BOYNTON, Nick D (BOS.)											
Nottingham	Britain	9	1	3	4	4	6	1	2	3	22
BRADLEY, Matt RW (WSH.)											
Dornbirn	Austria-2	6	5	2	7	18	....	....	....	....	....
BRANDNER, Christoph LW											
Houston	AHL	26	5	3	8	15	....	....	....	....	....
BRASHEAR, Donald LW (PHI.)											
Quebec	QNAHL	47	18	32	50	260	8	4	6	10	42
BRENDL, Pavel RW (CAR.)											
Trinec	CzRep	2	0	0	0	0	....	....	....	....	....
Olomouc	CzRep-2	3	0	0	0	12	....	....	....	....	....
Jokipojat	Finland-2	21	9	10	19	48	....	....	....	....	....
Thurgau	Swiss-2			0	3	4	....	....	....	....	....
BRENNAN, Kip LW (ANA.)											
Chicago	AHL	48	7	6	13	267	18	1	1	2	105
BREWER, Eric D (ST.L.)											
Canada	W-Cup	6	1	3	4	4	....	....	....	....	....

Team	League	Regular Season GP	G	A	Pts	PIM	Playoffs GP	G	A	Pts	PIM
BRIERE, Daniel C (BUF.)											
Bern	Swiss	36	16	29	45	26	11	1	6	7	2
BRIGLEY, Travis LW											
Valerengen	Norway	21	8	11	19	43	10	3	4	7	18
BRIMANIS, Aris D											
Worcester	AHL	69	4	13	17	44	....	....	....	....	....
BRIND'AMOUR, Rod C (CAR.)											
Kloten	Swiss	2	2	1	3	0	5	2	4	6	6
BRISEBOIS, Patrice D (COL.)											
Kloten	Swiss	10	3	1	4	2	....	....	....	....	....
BROOKBANK, Wade D (VAN.)											
Manitoba	AHL	68	0	10	10	285	9	0	0	0	10
BROWN, Brad D				DID NOT PLAY							
BROWN, Curtis C/LW (CHI.)											
San Diego	ECHL	47	9	29	38	24	....	....	....	....	....
BROWN, Dustin RW (L.A.)											
Manchester	AHL	79	29	45	74	96	6	5	2	7	10
BROWN, Sean D (N.J.)				DID NOT PLAY							
BRUNETTE, Andrew LW (COL.)				DID NOT PLAY							
BRYLIN, Sergei LW (N.J.)											
Voskresensk	Russia	35	8	19	27	40	....	....	....	....	....
BUCHBERGER, Kelly RW				DID NOT PLAY							
BULIS, Jan C (MTL.)											
Pardubice	CzRep	45	24	25	49	113	16	7	4	11	43
BURE, Valeri RW (L.A.)				DID NOT PLAY							
BURNETT, Garrett LW (DAL.)											
Danbury	UHL	7	0	1	1	48	....	....	....	....	....
BURNS, Brent D (MIN.)											
Houston	AHL	73	11	16	27	57	5	0	0	0	4
BUTENSCHON, Sven D (VAN.)											
Mannheim	Germany	50	1	5	6	54	14	0	1	1	16
BYLSMA, Dan RW				DID NOT PLAY							
CAIRNS, Eric D (FLA.)											
London	Britain	22	2	6	8	85	....	....	....	....	....
CAJANEK, Petr RW (ST.L.)											
Czech Republic	W-Cup	4	1	2	3	0	....	....	....	....	....
Zlin	CzRep	49	10	15	25	91	17	5	4	9	24
Czech Republic	WC-A	9	2	2	4	8	....	....	....	....	....
CALDER, Kyle LW (CHI.)											
Sodertalje	Sweden	12	5	1	6	6	10	5	1	6	2
CAMMALLERI, Mike C (L.A.)											
Manchester	AHL	79	46	63	109	60	6	1	5	6	0
CAMPBELL, Brian D (BUF.)											
Jokerit	Finland	44	12	13	25	12	12	3	4	7	6
CAMPBELL, Gregory LW (FLA.)											
San Antonio	AHL	70	12	16	28	113	....	....	....	....	....
CARNEY, Keith D (ANA.)				DID NOT PLAY							
CARTER, Anson RW (VAN.)				DID NOT PLAY							
CASSELS, Andrew C (WSH.)				DID NOT PLAY							
CHARA, Zdeno D (OTT.)											
Slovakia	W-Cup	4	0	2	2	8	....	....	....	....	....
Farjestad	Sweden	33	10	15	25	132	13	3	5	8	82
Slovakia	WC-A	7	0	2	2	2	....	....	....	....	....
CHARTRAND, Brad C				DID NOT PLAY							
CHEECHOO, Jonathan RW (S.J.)											
HV 71	Sweden	20	5	0	5	10	....	....	....	....	....
CHELIOS, Chris D (DET.)											
United States	W-Cup	5	0	1	1	6	....	....	....	....	....
Motor City	UHL	23	5	19	24	25	....	....	....	....	....
CHIMERA, Jason LW (PHX.)											
Varese	Italy	15	7	3	10	34	5	2	1	3	31
CHISTOV, Stanislav LW (ANA.)											
Cincinnati	AHL	79	15	23	38	141	9	2	1	3	6
CHOUINARD, Eric LW (PHI.)											
Salzburg	Austria	16	5	5	10	42	....	....	....	....	....
CHOUINARD, Marc C (MIN.)											
Frisk-Asker	Norway	9	8	17	26	3	5	2	7	29
CHUBAROV, Artem C (VAN.)											
Russia	W-Cup	4	0	1	1	0	....	....	....	....	....
Dynamo Moscow	Russia	27	4	9	13	10	....	....	....	....	....

Team	League	GP	G	A	Pts	PIM	GP	G	A	Pts	PIM
				Regular Season					Playoffs		
CIBAK, Martin C (T.B.)											
Slovakia	W-Cup	4	1	0	1	0	....	....	....	....	....
L. Mikulas	Slovakia	4	0	0	0	6	....	....	....	....	....
Plzen	CzRep	30	4	11	15	52	....	....	....	....	....
Kosice	Slovakia	6	1	3	4	8	10	2	5	7	36
CIERNIK, Ivan RW											
Wolfsburg	Germany	50	26	22	48	91	7	4	2	6	22
CLARK, Brett D (COL.)											
Hershey	AHL	67	7	37	44	54	....	....	....	....	....
CLARK, Chris RW (WSH.)											
Bern	Swiss	3	0	0	0	6	....	....	....	....	....
Storhamar	Norway	15	10	4	14	86	7	4	4	8	14
CLARKE, Noah LW (L.A.)											
Manchester	AHL	61	21	24	45	24	6	1	0	1	4
CLEARY, Daniel RW											
Mora	Sweden	47	11	26	37	138	....	....	....	....	....
CLYMER, Ben LW (WSH.)											
Biel	Swiss-2	19	11	12	23	30	11	6	11	17	24
COLAIACOVO, Carlo D (TOR.)											
St. John's	AHL	49	4	20	24	59	5	0	1	1	2
COLE, Erik LW (CAR.)											
Eisbaren Berlin	Germany	39	6	21	27	76	8	5	1	6	37
United States	WC-A	7	1	5	6	6	....	....	....	....	....
COMMODORE, Mike D (CAR.)											
Lowell	AHL	73	6	29	35	175	11	1	2	3	18
COMRIE, Mike C (PHX.)											
Farjestad	Sweden	10	1	6	7	10	....	....	....	....	....
CONNOLLY, Tim C (BUF.)											
Langnau	Swiss	16	7	3	10	14	....	....	....	....	....
CONROY, Craig C (L.A.)											
United States	W-Cup	2	0	0	0	0	....	....	....	....	....
COOKE, Matt C (VAN.)				DID NOT PLAY							
CORAZZINI, Carl C											
Providence	AHL	8	0	0	0	0	....	....	....	....	....
Hershey	AHL	52	10	13	23	6	....	....	....	....	....
CORSO, Daniel C											
Kassel	Germany	45	8	30	38	32	7	1	5	6	20
CORSON, Shayne LW				DID NOT PLAY							
CORVO, Joe D (L.A.)											
Chicago	AHL	23	7	7	14	14	18	4	5	9	12
COWAN, Jeff LW (L.A.)				DID NOT PLAY							
CROSS, Cory D (EDM.)				DID NOT PLAY							
CULLEN, Matt C (CAR.)											
Cortina	Italy	36	27	33	60	64	18	8	14	22	32
CULLIMORE, Jassen D (CHI.)				DID NOT PLAY							
CUMMINS, Jim RW				DID NOT PLAY							
CUTTA, Jakub D (WSH.)											
Portland	AHL	63	0	5	5	100	....	....	....	....	....
CZERKAWSKI, Mariusz RW											
Djurgarden	Sweden	46	15	9	24	20	5	1	0	1	2
DACKELL, Andreas RW											
Brynas	Sweden	40	9	13	22	48	....	....	....	....	....
Brynas	Sweden-Q	10	2	6	8	8	....	....	....	....	....
DAGENAIS, Pierre RW (MTL.)											
Ajoie	Swiss-2	7	5	5	10	12	6	7	7	14	6
DAIGLE, Alexandre C (MIN.)											
Morges	Swiss-2	....	....	....	....	....	2	1	1	2	0
DALEY, Trevor D (DAL.)											
Hamilton	AHL	78	7	27	34	109	4	0	1	1	2
DAMPHOUSSE, Vincent C				DID NOT PLAY							
DANDENAULT, Mathieu RW/D (MTL.)											
Asiago	Italy	10	0	2	2	2	9	1	6	7	4
DANTON, Mike C				DID NOT PLAY							
DARBY, Craig C (T.B.)											
Springfield	AHL	70	8	26	34	28	....	....	....	....	....
DARCHE, Mathieu LW											
Hershey	AHL	79	29	25	54	49	....	....	....	....	....
DATSYUK, Pavel C (DET.)											
Russia	W-Cup	4	1	0	1	0	....	....	....	....	....
Dynamo Moscow	Russia	47	15	17	32	16	10	6	3	9	4
Russia	WC-A	9	3	4	7	0	....	....	....	....	....
DAVISON, Rob D (S.J.)											
Cardiff	Britain	24	2	3	5	114	8	0	1	1	12

Team	League	GP	G	A	Pts	PIM	GP	G	A	Pts	PIM
				Regular Season					Playoffs		
DAZE, Eric RW (CHI.)				DID NOT PLAY							
de VRIES, Greg D (ATL.)				DID NOT PLAY							
DEADMARSH, Adam RW				DID NOT PLAY							
DELMORE, Andy D (DET.)											
Mannheim	Germany	50	7	16	23	59	14	1	6	7	12
DEMITRA, Pavol LW (L.A.)											
Slovakia	W-Cup	4	0	2	2	2	....	....	....	....	....
Trencin	Slovakia	54	28	54	82	39	12	4	13	17	14
Slovakia	WC-A	7	2	5	7	2	....	....	....	....	....
DEMPSEY, Nathan D (L.A.)											
Eisbaren Berlin	Germany	10	2	3	5	26	12	0	3	3	14
DESJARDINS, Eric D (PHI.)				DID NOT PLAY							
DEVEREAUX, Boyd C (PHX.)				DID NOT PLAY							
DiMAIO, Rob RW (T.B.)											
Langnau	Swiss	9	2	3	5	8	....	....	....	....	....
Milano	Italy	9	4	8	12	4	15	9	11	20	20
DIMITRAKOS, Niko RW (S.J.)											
Langnau	Swiss	3	0	1	1	2	6	3	3	6	16
DINGMAN, Chris LW (T.B.)				DID NOT PLAY							
DOAN, Shane RW (PHX.)											
Canada	W-Cup	6	1	1	2	2	....	....	....	....	....
Canada	WC-A	9	1	3	4	2	....	....	....	....	....
DOIG, Jason D				DID NOT PLAY							
DOMI, Tie RW (TOR.)				DID NOT PLAY							
DONATO, Ted LW				DID NOT PLAY							
DONOVAN, Shean RW (CGY.)											
Geneve	Swiss	12	5	3	8	30	....	....	....	....	....
DOULL, Doug LW (PHX.)											
Utah	AHL	40	1	1	2	232	....	....	....	....	....
DOWD, Jim C (CHI.)											
Hamburg	Germany	20	4	9	13	12	....	....	....	....	....
DOWNEY, Aaron RW (ST.L.)				DID NOT PLAY							
DRAKE, Dallas RW (ST.L.)				DID NOT PLAY							
DRAPER, Kris C (DET.)											
Canada	W-Cup	5	2	2	4	2	....	....	....	....	....
Canada	WC-A	9	0	2	2	6	....	....	....	....	....
DRUKEN, Harold C											
St. John's	AHL	48	18	20	38	28	....	....	....	....	....
DRURY, Chris C (BUF.)											
United States	W-Cup	5	0	0	0	0	....	....	....	....	....
DUFORT, J.F. LW				DID NOT PLAY							
DUMONT, J.P. RW (BUF.)											
Bern	Swiss	3	2	2	4	6	10	4	1	5	16
DUPUIS, Pascal LW (MIN.)											
Ajoie	Swiss-2	8	5	5	10	26	6	6	8	14	8
DUSABLON, Benoit C				DID NOT PLAY							
DVORAK, Radek RW (EDM.)											
Czech Republic	W-Cup	4	1	0	1	0	....	....	....	....	....
C. Budejovice	CzRep-2	32	23	35	58	18	16	5	13	18	20
Czech Republic	WC-A	9	1	1	2	4	....	....	....	....	....
DWYER, Gordie LW (CAR.)											
Lowell	AHL	56	2	7	9	183	11	1	0	1	54
DYKHUIS, Karl D											
Amsterdam	Nether.	5	1	1	2	36	7	1	3	4	39
EASTWOOD, Mike C				DID NOT PLAY							
EATON, Mark D (NSH.)											
Grand Rapids	AHL	29	3	3	6	21	....	....	....	....	....
EHRHOFF, Christian D (S.J.)											
Germany	W-Cup	4	0	0	0	2	....	....	....	....	....
Cleveland	AHL	79	12	23	35	103	....	....	....	....	....
Germany	WC-A	6	0	1	1	4	....	....	....	....	....
EKMAN, Nils LW (S.J.)											
Djurgarden	Sweden	44	18	27	45	106	12	4	5	9	20
ELIAS, Patrik LW (N.J.)											
Czech Republic	W-Cup	5	2	3	5	10	....	....	....	....	....
Znojmo	CzRep	28	8	20	28	65	....	....	....	....	....
Magnitogorsk	Russia	17	5	9	14	28	....	....	....	....	....
ELLISON, Matt RW (CHI.)											
Norfolk	AHL	71	14	37	51	44	5	0	1	1	2
EMINGER, Steve D (WSH.)											
Portland	AHL	62	3	17	20	40	....	....	....	....	....
ERAT, Martin LW (NSH.)											
Zlin	CzRep	48	20	23	43	129	16	7	5	12	12

Team	League	Regular Season					Playoffs				
		GP	G	A	Pts	PIM	GP	G	A	Pts	PIM
ERIKSSON, Anders D											
HV 71	Sweden	32	1	9	10	54	....	....	....	....	....
ERSKINE, John D (DAL.)											
Houston	AHL	61	3	7	10	238	5	0	1	1	20
EVANS, Brennan D											
Lowell	AHL	51	0	7	7	79	5	0	0	0	2
EXELBY, Garnet D (ATL.)		DID NOT PLAY									
FAHEY, Jim D (S.J.)											
Cleveland	AHL	69	4	22	26	146	....	....	....	....	....
FARRELL, Mike RW		DID NOT PLAY									
FAST, Brad D (L.A.)											
Lowell	AHL	32	1	5	6	23	....	....	....	....	....
Florida	ECHL	14	2	5	7	0	18	1	3	4	6
FATA, Rico RW (PIT.)											
Asiago	Italy	35	18	20	38	36	9	7	5	12	10
FEDOROV, Fedor C (VAN.)											
Spartak	Russia	19	4	7	11	52	....	....	....	....	....
Magnitogorsk	Russia	10	3	0	3	22	5	2	0	2	30
Russia	WC-A	6	0	1	1	2	....	....	....	....	....
FEDOROV, Sergei C (ANA.)		DID NOT PLAY									
FEDORUK, Todd LW (ANA.)											
Philadelphia	AHL	42	4	12	16	142	16	2	2	4	33
FEDOTENKO, Ruslan LW (T.B.)		DID NOT PLAY									
FERENCE, Andrew D (CGY.)											
C. Budejovice	CzRep-2	19	5	6	11	45	12	2	7	9	10
FERENCE, Brad D (PHX.)											
Morzine-Avoriaz	France	17	2	10	12	138	4	1	4	5	10
FERGUSON, Scott D (MIN.)		DID NOT PLAY									
FIDDLER, Vern C (NSH.)											
Milwaukee	AHL	73	20	22	42	70	7	0	0	0	18
FINLEY, Jeff D		DID NOT PLAY									
FISCHER, Jiri D (DET.)											
Czech Republic	W-Cup	4	0	0	0	2	....	....	....	....	....
Liberec	CzRep	27	6	12	18	52	11	1	4	5	22
Beroun	CzRep-2	1	0	1	1	25	....	....	....	....	....
Czech Republic	WC-A	9	0	1	1	4	....	....	....	....	....
FISHER, Mike C (OTT.)											
Zug	Swiss	21	9	18	27	34	9	2	3	5	10
Canada	WC-A	9	0	1	1	4	....	....	....	....	....
FITZGERALD, Tom RW (BOS.)		DID NOT PLAY									
FITZPATRICK, Rory D (BUF.)											
Rochester	AHL	20	1	1	2	18	9	0	1	1	12
FOCHT, Dan D (FLA.)											
Hamilton	AHL	26	2	3	5	84	....	....	....	....	....
FOOTE, Adam D (CBJ)											
Canada	W-Cup	6	0	3	3	0	....	....	....	....	....
FORBES, Colin C (CAR.)											
Lowell	AHL	76	27	37	64	80	11	3	1	4	20
FORSBERG, Peter C (PHI.)											
Sweden	W-Cup	4	1	2	3	0	....	....	....	....	....
MODO	Sweden	33	13	26	39	88	1	0	0	0	2
FORTIN, Jean-Francois D (WSH.)											
Portland	AHL	39	1	8	9	50	....	....	....	....	....
FOSTER, Kurtis D (MIN.)											
Cincinnati	AHL	78	17	25	42	71	9	2	3	5	28
FRANCIS, Ron C		DID NOT PLAY									
FRIESEN, Jeff LW (N.J.)		DID NOT PLAY									
FRITSCHE, Dan C (CBJ)											
Sarnia	OHL	2	1	1	2	0	....	....	....	....	....
London	OHL	28	17	18	35	18	17	9	13	22	12
United States	WJC-A	7	3	4	7	22	....	....	....	....	....
London	M-Cup	4	3	3	6	8	....	....	....	....	....
FROLOV, Alexander LW (L.A.)											
Russia	W-Cup	4	0	2	2	2	....	....	....	....	....
CSKA	Russia	42	20	17	37	10	....	....	....	....	....
Dynamo Moscow	Russia	6	2	1	3	2	6	2	1	3	0
FUSSEY, Owen RW (WSH.)											
Portland	AHL	71	14	12	26	26	....	....	....	....	....
GABORIK, Marian RW (MIN.)											
Slovakia	W-Cup	4	1	0	1	2	....	....	....	....	....
Farjestad	Sweden	12	6	4	10	45	....	....	....	....	....
Trencin	Slovakia	29	25	27	52	46	12	8	9	17	26
Slovakia	WC-A	7	1	3	4	6	....	....	....	....	....

Team	League	Regular Season					Playoffs				
		GP	G	A	Pts	PIM	GP	G	A	Pts	PIM
GAGNE, Simon LW (PHI.)											
Canada	W-Cup	6	1	1	2	0	....	....	....	....	....
Canada	WC-A	9	3	7	10	0	....	....	....	....	....
GAINEY, Steve LW											
Epinal	France	30	10	13	23	97	....	....	....	....	....
GAMACHE, Simon C (NSH.)											
Milwaukee	AHL	80	29	57	86	93	7	6	4	10	18
GAUTHIER, Denis D (PHX.)		DID NOT PLAY									
GELINAS, Martin LW (FLA.)											
Lugano	Swiss	1	0	0	0	0	5	0	1	1	2
Morges	Swiss-2	41	37	21	58	81	4	2	2	4	24
GERNANDER, Ken RW											
Hartford	AHL	66	5	8	13	18	6	1	0	1	0
GILL, Hal D (BOS.)											
United States	W-Cup	DID NOT PLAY – INJURED									
Lukko	Finland	31	2	8	10	110	8	0	0	0	57
United States	WC-A	7	0	0	6		....	....	....	....	....
GIONTA, Brian RW (N.J.)											
Albany	AHL	15	5	7	12	10	....	....	....	....	....
United States	WC-A	7	2	1	3	6	....	....	....	....	....
GIRARD, Jonathan D (BOS.)		DID NOT PLAY – INJURED									
GIROUX, Raymond D											
Houston	AHL	70	13	20	33	54	5	0	0	0	13
GLEASON, Tim D (L.A.)											
Manchester	AHL	67	10	14	24	112	5	0	0	0	4
GOC, Marcel C (S.J.)											
Germany	W-Cup	3	0	1	1	2	....	....	....	....	....
Cleveland	AHL	76	16	34	50	28	....	....	....	....	....
Germany	WC-A	6	2	0	2	0	....	....	....	....	....
GODARD, Eric RW (NYI)											
Bridgeport	AHL	75	7	11	18	295	....	....	....	....	....
GOMEZ, Scott C (N.J.)											
United States	W-Cup	5	1	3	4	0	....	....	....	....	....
Alaska	ECHL	61	13	73	86	69	4	1	3	4	4
GONCHAR, Sergei D (PIT.)											
Russia	W-Cup	4	1	2	3	6	....	....	....	....	....
Magnitogorsk	Russia	40	2	17	19	54	4	1	1	2	6
GORDON, Boyd RW (WSH.)											
Portland	AHL	80	17	22	39	35	....	....	....	....	....
GOREN, Lee RW (VAN.)											
Manitoba	AHL	79	32	30	62	117	14	10	3	13	23
GRAND-PIERRE, Jean-Luc D											
Troja	Sweden-2	21	2	3	5	69	....	....	....	....	....
GRATTON, Benoit C											
Lugano	Swiss	32	6	12	18	81	....	....	....	....	....
GRATTON, Chris C (FLA.)		DID NOT PLAY									
GREBESHKOV, Denis D (L.A.)											
Manchester	AHL	75	5	44	49	87	6	0	4	4	2
GREEN, Josh LW (VAN.)											
Manitoba	AHL	67	21	19	40	72	14	9	5	14	26
GREEN, Mike C											
Nurnberg	Germany	44	11	17	28	38	6	1	3	4	0
GREEN, Travis C (BOS.)		DID NOT PLAY									
GRENIER, Martin D (NYR)											
Hartford	AHL	23	2	5	7	136	5	0	0	0	32
Charlotte	ECHL	4	0	2	2	10	....	....	....	....	....
GRIER, Mike RW (BUF.)		DID NOT PLAY									
GROSEK, Michal LW											
Geneve	Swiss	41	15	21	36	149	....	....	....	....	....
GRUDEN, John D		DID NOT PLAY									
GUERIN, Bill RW (DAL.)											
United States	W-Cup	5	2	2	4	8	....	....	....	....	....
HAGMAN, Niklas LW (FLA.)											
Finland	W-Cup	5	1	0	1	2	....	....	....	....	....
Davos	Swiss	44	17	22	39	20	15	10	7	17	6
Finland	WC-A	7	2	0	2	2	....	....	....	....	....
HAHL, Riku C (COL.)											
Finland	W-Cup	2	1	0	1	0	....	....	....	....	....
HPK	Finland	44	8	13	21	12	10	2	6	8	2
Finland	WC-A	5	0	0	0	2	....	....	....	....	....
HAINSEY, Ron D (MTL.)											
Hamilton	AHL	68	9	14	23	45	4	1	1	2	0
HAJT, Chris D (CAR.)											
Portland	AHL	53	3	6	9	16	....	....	....	....	....
Augusta	ECHL	13	1	4	5	8	....	....	....	....	....

Team	League	Regular Season					Playoffs				
		GP	G	A	Pts	PIM	GP	G	A	Pts	PIM
HALE, David D (N.J.)											
Albany	AHL	30	2	3	5	39	....	....	....	....	....
HALL, Adam RW (NSH.)											
KalPa	Finland-2	36	23	17	40	28	9	2	3	5	4
United States	WC-A	7	1	0	1	2	....	....	....	....	....
HALPERN, Jeff C (WSH.)											
United States	W-Cup	4	0	0	0	7	....	....	....	....	....
Ajoie	Swiss-2	15	5	12	17	52	....	....	....	....	....
Kloten	Swiss	9	7	4	11	6	....	....	....	....	....
United States	WC-A	7	1	0	1	6	....	....	....	....	....
HAMEL, Denis LW (OTT.)											
Binghamton	AHL	80	39	39	78	75	5	1	0	1	4
HAMHUIS, Dan D (NSH.)											
Milwaukee	AHL	76	13	38	51	85	7	0	2	2	10
HAMILTON, Jeff C (NYI)											
Hartford	AHL	60	23	30	53	32	6	4	3	7	0
HAMRLIK, Roman D (CGY.)											
Czech Republic	W-Cup	4	0	2	2	0	....	....	....	....	....
Zlin	CzRep	45	2	14	16	70	17	1	3	4	24
HANDZUS, Michal C (PHI.)											
Slovakia	W-Cup				DID NOT PLAY – INJURED						
Zvolen	Slovakia	33	14	24	38	34	17	5	10	15	6
Slovakia	WC-A	7	3	0	3	2	....	....	....	....	....
HANKINSON, Casey LW											
Cincinnati	AHL	54	4	7	11	92	12	2	4	6	36
Chaux-de-Fonds	Swiss-2	4	2	1	3	6	....	....	....	....	....
HANNAN, Scott D (S.J.)											
Canada	W-Cup	5	0	1	1	4	....	....	....	....	....
Canada	WC-A	9	0	0	0	8	....	....	....	....	....
HARTIGAN, Mark C (CBJ)											
Syracuse	AHL	69	31	28	59	105	....	....	....	....	....
HARTNELL, Scott LW (NSH.)											
Valerengen	Norway	28	17	12	29	103	11	12	7	19	24
HARVEY, Todd RW/C (EDM.)											
Cambridge	OHA-Sr.	16	9	15	24	31	....	....	....	....	....
HATCHER, Derian D (PHI.)											
Motor City	UHL	24	5	12	17	27	....	....	....	....	....
HAVELID, Niclas D (ATL.)											
Sodertalje	Sweden	46	2	2	4	60	10	1	1	2	18
HAVLAT, Martin LW (OTT.)											
Czech Republic	W-Cup	5	3	3	6	2	....	....	....	....	....
Znojmo	CzRep	12	10	4	14	16	....	....	....	....	....
Dynamo Moscow	Russia	10	2	0	2	14	....	....	....	....	....
Sparta	CzRep	9	5	4	9	37	5	0	0	0	20
HEALEY, Paul LW (COL.)											
San Antonio	AHL	62	6	17	23	50	....	....	....	....	....
Edmonton	AHL	17	3	6	9	29	....	....	....	....	....
HEATLEY, Dany RW (OTT.)											
Canada	W-Cup	6	0	2	2	2	....	....	....	....	....
Bern	Swiss	16	14	10	24	58	....	....	....	....	....
Kazan	Russia	11	3	1	4	22	4	2	1	3	4
Canada	WC-A	9	3	4	7	16	....	....	....	....	....
HECHT, Jochen LW (BUF.)											
Germany	W-Cup	4	1	0	1	2	....	....	....	....	....
Mannheim	Germany	48	16	34	50	151	14	10	10	20	14
Germany	WC-A	6	3	1	4	6	....	....	....	....	....
HEDICAN, Bret D (CAR.)					DID NOT PLAY						
HEDIN, Pierre D (TOR.)											
MODO	Sweden	31	3	4	7	28	6	1	0	1	6
HEEREMA, Jeff RW (OTT.)											
Manitoba	AHL	80	14	31	45	67	14	4	6	10	12
HEINS, Shawn D											
Eisbaren Berlin	Germany	49	6	21	27	142	11	3	4	7	24
HEJDUK, Milan RW (COL.)											
Czech Republic	W-Cup	4	3	2	5	2	....	....	....	....	....
Pardubice	CzRep	48	25	26	51	14	16	6	2	8	6
HELMER, Bryan D (DET.)											
Grand Rapids	AHL	80	7	18	25	64	....	....	....	....	....
HEMSKY, Ales RW (EDM.)											
Pardubice	CzRep	47	13	18	31	28	16	4	10	14	26
Czech Republic	WC-A	7	2	0	2	2	....	....	....	....	....
HENDRICKSON, Darby C											
Riga 2000	Latvia	1	1	1	2	0	....	....	....	....	....
Riga 2000	BelOpen	6	2	2	4	26	....	....	....	....	....
HENRY, Alex D (MIN.)											
Kaufbeuren	German-2	26	6	6	12	32	....	....	....	....	....

Team	League	Regular Season					Playoffs				
		GP	G	A	Pts	PIM	GP	G	A	Pts	PIM
HENRY, Burke D											
San Antonio	AHL	24	0	2	2	44	....	....	....	....	....
Milwaukee	AHL	16	0	3	3	28	1	0	0	0	0
HIGGINS, Christopher C (MTL.)											
Hamilton	AHL	76	28	23	51	33	4	3	3	6	4
HILBERT, Andy C/LW (BOS.)											
Providence	AHL	79	37	42	79	83	17	7	14	21	27
HILL, Sean D (FLA.)					DID NOT PLAY						
HINOTE, Dan RW (COL.)											
MODO	Sweden	18	2	1	3	106	5	0	0	0	56
HLAVAC, Jan LW											
Sparta	CzRep	48	10	28	38	34	5	2	0	2	6
Czech Republic	WC-A	6	1	2	3	0	....	....	....	....	....
HNIDY, Shane D (ATL.)											
Florida	ECHL	19	1	4	5	56	17	0	4	4	6
HOLDEN, Josh C											
HPK	Finland	51	21	15	36	94	10	6	1	7	12
HOLIK, Bobby C (ATL.)					DID NOT PLAY						
HOLLAND, Jason D											
Alleghe	Italy	13	3	4	7	6	....	....	....	....	....
Manchester	AHL	53	1	9	10	64	6	1	1	2	0
HOLMQVIST, Mikael C (CHI.)											
Cincinnati	AHL	79	14	32	46	111	11	2	2	4	10
HOLMSTROM, Tomas LW (DET.)											
Sweden	W-Cup	4	3	2	5	8	....	....	....	....	....
Lulea	Sweden	47	14	16	30	50	4	0	0	0	18
HOLZINGER, Brian C					DID NOT PLAY						
HORCOFF, Shawn C (EDM.)											
Mora	Sweden	50	19	27	46	117	....	....	....	....	....
HORDICHUK, Darcy LW (NSH.)					DID NOT PLAY						
HORTON, Nathan C (FLA.)											
San Antonio	AHL	21	5	4	9	21	....	....	....	....	....
HOSSA, Marcel LW (MTL.)											
Mora	Sweden	48	18	6	24	69	....	....	....	....	....
Slovakia	WC-A	2	0	0	0	0	....	....	....	....	....
HOSSA, Marian RW (ATL.)											
Slovakia	W-Cup	4	1	0	1	2	....	....	....	....	....
Mora	Sweden	24	18	14	32	22	....	....	....	....	....
Trencin	Slovakia	25	22	20	42	38	5	4	5	9	14
Slovakia	WC-A	7	4	3	7	6	....	....	....	....	....
HRDINA, Jan C (CBJ)											
Kladno	CzRep	23	4	3	7	38	7	3	3	6	4
HUDLER, Jiri C (DET.)											
Vsetin	CzRep	7	5	2	7	10	....	....	....	....	....
Grand Rapids	AHL	52	12	22	34	10	....	....	....	....	....
HULL, Brett RW (PHX.)											
United States	W-Cup	2	0	0	0	2	....	....	....	....	....
HULL, Jody RW					DID NOT PLAY						
HULSE, Cale D (PHX.)					DID NOT PLAY						
HUML, Ivan LW (BOS.)											
Kladno	CzRep	3	0	0	0	2	1	0	0	0	0
HUNTER, Trent RW (NYI)											
Nykoping	Sweden-2	33	13	12	25	73	4	5	3	8	2
HUSELIUS, Kristian LW (FLA.)											
Linkoping	Sweden	34	14	35	49	10	....	....	....	....	....
Rapperswil	Swiss	....	....	....	....	....	4	1	3	4	2
HUSSEY, Matt C (PIT.)											
Wilkes-Barre	AHL	80	16	14	30	19	10	1	2	3	2
HUTCHINSON, Andrew D (CAR.)											
Milwaukee	AHL	76	10	35	45	79	7	1	3	4	8
IGINLA, Jarome RW (CGY.)											
Canada	W-Cup	6	2	1	3	2	....	....	....	....	....
ISBISTER, Brad LW (BOS.)											
Innsbruck	Austria	11	7	4	11	41	5	3	1	4	6
JACKMAN, Barret D (ST.L.)											
Missouri	UHL	28	3	17	20	61	3	0	0	0	4
JACKMAN, Ric D (PIT.)											
Bjorkloven	Sweden-2	46	13	26	39	209	....	....	....	....	....
JACKMAN, Tim RW (CBJ)											
Syracuse	AHL	73	14	21	35	98	....	....	....	....	....

Team	League	Regular Season					Playoffs				
		GP	G	A	Pts	PIM	GP	G	A	Pts	PIM
JAGR, Jaromir RW (NYR)											
Czech Republic	W-Cup	5	1	1	2	2	....	....	....	....	....
Kladno	CzRep	17	11	17	28	16	....	....	....	....	....
Omsk	Russia	32	16	22	38	63	11	4	10	14	22
Czech Republic	WC-A	8	2	7	9	2	....	....	....	....	....
JANIK, Doug D (BUF.)											
Rochester	AHL	76	2	10	12	196	9	0	2	2	10
JASPERS, Jason C (T.B.)											
Utah	AHL	11	0	3	3	6	....	....	....	....	....
Springfield	AHL	48	12	17	29	45	....	....	....	....	....
JILLSON, Jeff D (BUF.)											
Rochester	AHL	78	12	17	29	46	9	1	1	2	12
JOHANSSON, Andreas C											
Sweden	W-Cup	4	0	0	0	4	....	....	....	....	....
Geneve	Swiss	40	12	26	38	60	4	0	6	6	24
JOHANSSON, Calle D					DID NOT PLAY						
JOHNSON, Aaron D (CBJ)											
Syracuse	AHL	77	6	17	23	140	....	....	....	....	....
JOHNSON, Craig LW											
Hamburg	Germany	42	19	25	44	56	....	....	....	....	....
JOHNSON, Greg C (NSH.)					DID NOT PLAY						
JOHNSON, Matt LW					DID NOT PLAY						
JOHNSON, Mike RW (PHX.)											
Farjestad	Sweden	8	1	2	3	4	6	0	2	2	4
JOHNSON, Ryan C (ST.L.)											
Missouri	UHL	29	7	14	21	12	6	1	0	1	13
JOHNSSON, Kim D (PHI.)											
Sweden	W-Cup	4	1	3	4	0	....	....	....	....	....
Ambri	Swiss	24	4	10	14	61	....	....	....	....	....
JOKINEN, Olli C (FLA.)											
Finland	W-Cup	6	2	1	3	6	....	....	....	....	....
Kloten	Swiss	8	6	1	7	14	....	....	....	....	....
Sodertalje	Sweden	23	13	9	22	52	....	....	....	....	....
HIFK	Finland	14	9	8	17	10	5	2	0	2	24
Finland	WC-A	7	1	4	5	2	....	....	....	....	....
JONES, Randy D (PHI.)											
Philadelphia	AHL	69	5	19	24	32	18	0	5	5	10
JONES, Ty RW					DID NOT PLAY						
JONSSON, Kenny D (NYI)											
Rogle	Sweden-2	11	3	7	10	12	2	0	0	0	2
Sweden	WC-A	6	2	2	4	0	....	....	....	....	....
JOVANOVSKI, Ed D (VAN.)											
Canada	W-Cup	1	0	0	0	0	....	....	....	....	....
Canada	WC-A	9	1	2	3	8	....	....	....	....	....
JUNEAU, Joe C					DID NOT PLAY						
KABERLE, Frantisek D (CAR.)											
Czech Republic	W-Cup					DID NOT PLAY – INJURED					
Kladno	CzRep	22	5	11	16	34	....	....	....	....	....
MODO	Sweden	8	2	2	4	0	6	1	0	1	27
Czech Republic	WC-A	9	1	0	1	4	....	....	....	....	....
KABERLE, Tomas D (TOR.)											
Czech Republic	W-Cup	4	0	1	1	0	....	....	....	....	....
Kladno	CzRep	49	8	31	39	38	7	1	0	1	0
Czech Republic	WC-A	9	1	3	4	4	....	....	....	....	....
KALININ, Dmitri D (BUF.)											
Russia	W-Cup	3	0	0	0	0	....	....	....	....	....
Magnitogorsk	Russia	48	2	8	10	14	5	0	0	0	2
Russia	WC-A	9	0	0	0	0	....	....	....	....	....
KANE, Boyd LW (WSH.)											
Philadelphia	AHL	58	9	15	24	112	21	0	7	7	28
KAPANEN, Niko C (DAL.)											
Finland	W-Cup	6	1	2	3	0	....	....	....	....	....
Zug	Swiss	44	10	33	43	24	9	2	5	7	35
Finland	WC-A	7	1	4	5	8	....	....	....	....	....
KAPANEN, Sami RW (PHI.)											
Finland	W-Cup					DID NOT PLAY – INJURED					
KalPa	Finland-2	10	6	3	9	2	9	5	3	8	4
KARIYA, Paul LW (NSH.)					DID NOT PLAY						
KARPOVTSEV, Alexander D (FLA.)											
Novosibirsk	Russia	5	0	1	1	16	....	....	....	....	....
Yaroslavl	Russia	33	2	5	7	45	9	0	0	0	0
Russia	WC-A	8	0	1	1	2	....	....	....	....	....
KASPARAITIS, Darius D (NYR)											
Russia	W-Cup	4	0	1	1	8	....	....	....	....	....
Kazan	Russia	28	1	3	4	118	3	0	0	0	6

Team	League	Regular Season					Playoffs				
		GP	G	A	Pts	PIM	GP	G	A	Pts	PIM
KAVANAGH, Pat RW (PHI.)											
Binghamton	AHL	80	14	17	31	87	6	0	1	1	10
KEANE, Mike RW					DID NOT PLAY						
KEITH, Matt RW (CHI.)											
Norfolk	AHL	80	18	31	49	74	6	0	1	1	0
KELLY, Chris C/LW (OTT.)											
Binghamton	AHL	77	24	36	60	57	6	1	2	3	11
KELLY, Steve C (L.A.)											
Mannheim	Germany	46	11	22	33	210	12	1	4	5	72
KESLER, Ryan C (VAN.)											
Manitoba	AHL	78	30	27	57	105	14	4	5	9	8
KHAVANOV, Alexander D (TOR.)											
Russia	W-Cup	4	0	1	1	4	....	....	....	....	....
St. Petersburg	Russia	3	0	0	0	27	....	....	....	....	....
KILGER, Chad LW (TOR.)					DID NOT PLAY						
KING, Jason C (VAN.)											
Manitoba	AHL	59	26	27	53	22	....	....	....	....	....
KLATT, Trent RW (L.A.)					DID NOT PLAY						
KLEE, Ken D (TOR.)											
United States	W-Cup	4	0	0	0	0	....	....	....	....	....
KLEMM, Jon D (DAL.)					DID NOT PLAY						
KLESLA, Rostislav D (CBJ)											
Vsetin	CzRep	41	7	17	24	136	....	....	....	....	....
HPK	Finland	9	1	2	3	12	10	0	2	2	12
KLOUCEK, Tomas D (ATL.)											
Slavia	CzRep	29	1	1	2	28	....	....	....	....	....
Trinec	CzRep	11	1	2	3	24	....	....	....	....	....
Liberec	CzRep	8	1	0	1	12	9	0	1	1	35
KNUBLE, Mike RW (PHI.)											
Linkoping	Sweden	49	26	13	39	40	6	0	1	1	2
United States	WC-A	7	4	2	6	8	....	....	....	....	....
KNUTSEN, Espen C											
Djurgarden	Sweden	15	0	8	8	12	....	....	....	....	....
KOBASEW, Chuck C (CGY.)											
Lowell	AHL	79	38	37	75	110	11	6	3	9	27
KOIVU, Saku C (MTL.)											
Finland	W-Cup	6	3	1	4	2	....	....	....	....	....
TPS	Finland	20	8	8	16	28	6	3	2	5	30
KOLANOS, Krystofer C (PHX.)											
Blues	Finland	15	7	9	16	40	....	....	....	....	....
Krefeld	Germany	7	3	2	5	16	....	....	....	....	....
KOLNIK, Juraj RW (FLA.)											
San Antonio	AHL	74	13	16	29	24	....	....	....	....	....
KOLTSOV, Konstantin RW (PIT.)											
Minsk	BelOpen	11	6	2	8	38	....	....	....	....	....
Spartak	Russia	31	6	10	16	48	....	....	....	....	....
Belarus	WC-A	6	3	3	6	2	....	....	....	....	....
KOMARNISKI, Zenith D (CGY.)											
Syracuse	AHL	62	3	11	14	99	....	....	....	....	....
KOMISAREK, Mike D (MTL.)											
Hamilton	AHL	20	1	4	5	49	4	0	1	1	8
KONDRATIEV, Maxim D (NYR)											
Hartford	AHL	13	1	4	5	8	....	....	....	....	....
Togliatti	Russia	32	2	4	6	65	5	0	2	2	0
KONOWALCHUK, Steve LW (COL.)											
United States	W-Cup	5	0	0	0	4	....	....	....	....	....
KOROLEV, Igor C											
Yaroslavl	Russia	60	8	20	28	28	9	1	6	7	2
KOROLYUK, Alexander LW (S.J.)											
Chekhov	Russia-2	42	24	28	52	54	....	....	....	....	....
Voskresensk	Russia	10	4	3	7	14	....	....	....	....	....
KOSTOPOULOS, Tom RW (L.A.)											
Manchester	AHL	64	25	46	71	99	6	0	7	7	10
KOTALIK, Ales RW (BUF.)											
Liberec	CzRep	25	8	8	16	46	12	2	5	7	12
KOVALCHUK, Ilya LW (ATL.)											
Russia	W-Cup	4	1	0	1	4	....	....	....	....	....
Kazan	Russia	53	19	23	42	72	4	0	1	1	0
Russia	WC-A	9	3	3	6	4	....	....	....	....	....
KOVALEV, Alex RW (MTL.)											
Russia	W-Cup	4	2	1	3	4	....	....	....	....	....
Kazan	Russia	35	10	12	22	80	4	0	0	0	8
Russia	WC-A	9	3	4	7	16	....	....	....	....	....

Team	League	Regular Season					Playoffs				
		GP	G	A	Pts	PIM	GP	G	A	Pts	PIM
KOZLOV, Viktor C (N.J.)											
Russia	W-Cup	4	1	0	1	0	....	....	....	....	....
Togliatti	Russia	52	15	22	37	22	10	3	3	6	6
Russia	WC-A	9	1	0	1	0	....	....	....	....	....
KOZLOV, Vyacheslav RW (ATL.)											
Voskresensk	Russia	38	12	18	30	69	....	....	....	....	....
Kazan	Russia	8	2	4	6	0	4	1	0	1	8
KRAFT, Milan C (PIT.)											
Plzen	CzRep	17	2	4	6	6	....	....	....	....	....
Karlovy Vary	CzRep	35	9	10	19	20	....	....	....	....	....
KRAJICEK, Lukas D (FLA.)											
San Antonio	AHL	78	2	22	24	57	....	....	....	....	....
KRESTANOVICH, Jordan LW											
Pensacola	ECHL	69	27	41	68	22	3	1	1	2	0
KROG, Jason C											
Villacher SV	Austria	48	27	33	60	38	3	0	1	1	4
KRONWALL, Niklas D (DET.)											
Grand Rapids	AHL	76	13	40	53	53	....	....	....	....	....
Sweden	WC-A	9	3	3	6	10	....	....	....	....	....
KUBA, Filip D (MIN.)					DID NOT PLAY						
KUBINA, Pavel D (T.B.)											
Czech Republic	W-Cup			DID NOT PLAY – INJURED							
Vitkovice	CzRep	28	6	5	11	46	12	4	6	10	34
Czech Republic	WC-A	9	2	2	4	10	....	....	....	....	....
KUDROC, Kristian D											
Hammarby	Sweden-2	6	0	2	2	65	....	....	....	....	....
KUKKONEN, Lasse D (CHI.)											
Karpat	Finland	55	5	13	18	68	12	0	2	2	6
Finland	WC-A	7	0	0	0	2	....	....	....	....	....
KULESHOV, Mikhail LW											
St. Petersburg	Russia	11	0	0	0	6	....	....	....	....	....
Perm	Russia	23	0	3	3	16	....	....	....	....	....
KUNITZ, Chris LW (ANA.)											
Cincinnati	AHL	54	22	17	39	71	12	1	7	8	20
KURKA, Tomas LW											
Litvinov	CzRep	29	1	5	6	6	....	....	....	....	....
Providence	AHL	40	8	3	11	4	17	4	4	8	13
KUTLAK, Zdenek D (BOS.)											
Karlovy Vary	CzRep	52	5	9	14	26	....	....	....	....	....
KUZNETSOV, Maxim D											
Dynamo Moscow	Russia	10	0	0	0	24	....	....	....	....	....
St. Petersburg	Russia	34	4	6	10	72	....	....	....	....	....
KVASHA, Oleg LW/C (NYI)											
Russia	W-Cup	2	0	1	1	0	....	....	....	....	....
Cherepovets	Russia	22	6	5	11	24	....	....	....	....	....
CSKA	Russia	26	3	6	9	20	....	....	....	....	....
KWIATKOWSKI, Joel D (FLA.)											
San Antonio	AHL	64	13	19	32	76	....	....	....	....	....
St. John's	AHL	17	7	6	13	16	5	0	4	4	23
LAAKSONEN, Antti LW (COL.)											
Finland	W-Cup	1	0	0	0	0	....	....	....	....	....
LACHANCE, Scott D					DID NOT PLAY						
LaCOUTURE, Dan LW											
Providence	AHL	64	12	15	27	52	6	1	1	2	4
LAFLAMME, Christian D											
Kassel	Germany	43	4	12	16	96	7	0	1	1	12
LAICH, Brooks C (WSH.)											
Portland	AHL	68	16	10	26	33	....	....	....	....	....
LAING, Quintin LW (CHI.)											
Norfolk	AHL	66	10	13	23	54	4	0	0	0	0
LAMPMAN, Bryce D (NYR)											
Hartford	AHL	74	7	18	25	74	4	0	0	0	4
LANG, Robert C (DET.)					DID NOT PLAY						
LANGDON, Darren LW (N.J.)					DID NOT PLAY						
LANGENBRUNNER, Jamie RW (N.J.)											
United States	W-Cup	3	0	0	0	4	....	....	....	....	....
Ingolstadt	Germany	11	2	2	4	22	11	1	6	7	6
LANGFELD, Josh RW											
Binghamton	AHL	74	32	25	57	75	6	2	2	4	2
LANGKOW, Daymond C (CGY.)					DID NOT PLAY						
LAPERRIERE, Ian RW (COL.)					DID NOT PLAY						
LAPOINTE, Claude LW/C					DID NOT PLAY						
LAPOINTE, Martin RW (CHI.)					DID NOT PLAY						

Team	League	Regular Season					Playoffs				
		GP	G	A	Pts	PIM	GP	G	A	Pts	PIM
LARAQUE, Georges RW (EDM.)											
Solna	Sweden-3	16	11	5	16	24	....	....	....	....	....
LARIONOV, Igor C					DID NOT PLAY						
LAROSE, Cory C											
Chicago	AHL	80	26	37	63	44	18	6	6	12	29
LARSEN, Brad LW (ATL.)											
Chicago	AHL	75	26	23	49	112	18	4	7	11	22
LAW, Kirby RW (MIN.)											
Houston	AHL	80	25	24	49	134	5	0	1	1	4
LEAHY, Patrick RW (BOS.)											
Providence	AHL	38	1	14	15	18	17	4	6	10	20
LECAVALIER, Vincent C (T.B.)											
Canada	W-Cup	6	2	5	7	8	....	....	....	....	....
Kazan	Russia	30	7	9	16	78	4	1	0	1	6
LeCLAIR, John LW (PIT.)					DID NOT PLAY						
LECLERC, Mike LW (PHX.)					DID NOT PLAY						
LEEB, Brad RW (TOR.)											
St. John's	AHL	48	16	13	29	43	3	2	1	3	0
LEETCH, Brian D (BOS.)											
United States	W-Cup	5	0	1	1	6	....	....	....	....	....
LEGWAND, David C (NSH.)											
Basel	Swiss-2	3	6	2	8	2	19	16	23	39	20
United States	WC-A	7	0	1	1	4	....	....	....	....	....
LEHTINEN, Jere RW (DAL.)											
Finland	W-Cup	6	1	3	4	2	....	....	....	....	....
LEMIEUX, Mario C (PIT.)											
Canada	W-Cup	6	1	4	5	2	....	....	....	....	....
LEOPOLD, Jordan D (CGY.)											
United States	W-Cup			DID NOT PLAY – INJURED							
United States	WC-A	7	0	1	1	0	....	....	....	....	....
LESCHYSHYN, Curtis D (COL.)					DID NOT PLAY						
LESSARD, Francis RW (ATL.)					DID NOT PLAY						
LETOWSKI, Trevor RW (CBJ)											
Fribourg	Swiss	9	4	5	9	6	11	7	9	16	8
LIDSTROM, Nicklas D (DET.)											
Sweden	W-Cup	4	1	0	1	2	....	....	....	....	....
LILES, John-Michael D (COL.)											
United States	W-Cup	2	0	0	0	0	....	....	....	....	....
Iserlohn	Germany	17	5	6	11	24	....	....	....	....	....
United States	WC-A	7	0	0	0	0	....	....	....	....	....
LILJA, Andreas D (DET.)											
Mora	Sweden	44	3	8	11	67	....	....	....	....	....
Ambri	Swiss	....	....	....	....	....	5	0	2	2	6
LINDEN, Trevor RW (VAN.)					DID NOT PLAY						
LINDGREN, Mats C/LW					DID NOT PLAY						
LINDROS, Eric C (TOR.)					DID NOT PLAY						
LINDSAY, Bill RW											
Long Beach	ECHL	32	9	14	23	78	7	2	2	4	12
LING, David RW											
St. John's	AHL	80	28	60	88	152	5	1	1	2	43
LOMBARDI, Matthew C (CGY.)											
Lowell	AHL	9	3	1	4	9	11	0	3	3	16
LOW, Reed RW (ST.L.)					DID NOT PLAY						
LOWRY, Dave LW					DID NOT PLAY						
LOYNS, Lynn LW (CGY.)											
Lowell	AHL	77	7	8	15	42	11	0	0	0	0
LUKOWICH, Brad D (NYI)											
Fort Worth	CHL	16	3	5	8	33	....	....	....	....	....
LUNDMARK, Jamie C (NYR)											
Bolzano	Italy	14	9	9	18	22	....	....	....	....	....
Hartford	AHL	64	14	27	41	146	6	2	4	6	8
LUOMA, Mikko D (EDM.)											
Malmo	Sweden	50	9	9	18	72	....	....	....	....	....
LUPUL, Joffrey C (ANA.)											
Cincinnati	AHL	65	30	26	56	58	12	3	9	12	27
LYDMAN, Toni D (BUF.)											
Finland	W-Cup	6	0	3	3	6	....	....	....	....	....
HIFK	Finland	8	1	2	3	2	5	0	3	3	0
LYNCH, Doug D (ST.L.)											
Edmonton	AHL	74	1	13	14	109	....	....	....	....	....
LYSAK, Brett C											
Iserlohn	Germany	49	9	9	18	151	....	....	....	....	....

Team	League	Regular Season					Playoffs				
		GP	G	A	Pts	PIM	GP	G	A	Pts	PIM
MacDONALD, Craig LW (CGY.)											
Lowell	AHL	71	10	18	28	104	2	0	0	0	0
MacDONALD, Jason RW (BOS.)											
St. John's	AHL	29	4	8	12	152	5	2	0	2	27
MacINNIS, Al D				DID NOT PLAY							
MacKENZIE, Derek C (ATL.)											
Chicago	AHL	78	13	20	33	87	18	5	6	11	33
MacLEAN, Don C (DET.)											
Blues	Finland	51	22	21	43	46	....	....	....	....	....
MacMILLAN, Jeff D (CBJ)											
Hartford	AHL	71	2	5	7	136	6	0	0	0	4
MADDEN, John C (N.J.)											
HIFK	Finland	3	0	0	0	0	....	....	....	....	....
MAIR, Adam C (BUF.)				DID NOT PLAY							
MAJESKY, Ivan D (WSH.)											
Slovakia	W-Cup			DID NOT PLAY – INJURED							
Sparta	CzRep	28	2	6	8	40	5	2	1	3	6
Slovakia	WC-A	1	0	0	0	0	....	....	....	....	....
MALAKHOV, Vladimir D (N.J.)				DID NOT PLAY							
MALEC, Tomas D (OTT.)											
Cincinnati	AHL	66	4	14	18	104	6	0	2	2	10
MALHOTRA, Manny C (CBJ)											
Ljubljana	Slovenia	13	6	7	13	20	....	....	....	....	....
Ljubljana	Interliga	13	7	7	14	16	....	....	....	....	....
HV 71	Sweden	20	5	2	7	16	....	....	....	....	....
MALIK, Marek D (NYR)											
Czech Republic	W-Cup	4	0	0	0	4	....	....	....	....	....
Vitkovice	CzRep	42	1	9	10	50	7	0	0	0	37
MALONE, Ryan LW (PIT.)											
Blues	Finland	9	2	1	3	36	....	....	....	....	....
Renon	Italy	10	6	2	8	20	6	4	4	8	36
Ambri	Swiss	....	....	....	....	....	1	0	0	0	2
MALTBY, Kirk RW (DET.)											
Canada	WC-A	9	1	1	2	8	....	....	....	....	....
MANLOW, Eric C (DET.)											
Grand Rapids	AHL	61	21	20	41	24	....	....	....	....	....
MAPLETOFT, Justin C (NYI)											
Bridgeport	AHL	61	11	24	35	51	....	....	....	....	....
MARA, Paul D (PHX.)											
Hannover	Germany	35	5	13	18	89	....	....	....	....	....
MARCHANT, Todd C (CBJ)				DID NOT PLAY							
MARCHMENT, Bryan D				DID NOT PLAY							
MARKOV, Andrei D (MTL.)											
Russia	W-Cup	2	0	1	1	2	....	....	....	....	....
Dynamo Moscow	Russia	42	7	16	23	76	10	2	0	2	22
Russia	WC-A	9	1	4	5	20	....	....	....	....	....
MARKOV, Danny D (NSH.)											
Russia	W-Cup			DID NOT PLAY – INJURED							
Chekhov	Russia-2	26	5	7	12	16	12	0	3	3	6
MARLEAU, Patrick C (S.J.)											
Canada	WC-A	9	2	2	4	4	....	....	....	....	....
MARSHALL, Grant RW (N.J.)				DID NOT PLAY							
MARSHALL, Jason D (ANA.)											
Plzen	CzRep	11	1	3	4	53	....	....	....	....	....
MARTENSSON, Tony C (ANA.)											
Linkoping	Sweden	50	13	21	34	12	5	0	1	1	0
MARTIN, Paul D (N.J.)											
United States	W-Cup	3	0	1	1	0	....	....	....	....	....
Fribourg	Swiss	11	3	4	7	2	....	....	....	....	....
United States	WC-A	7	0	0	0	2	....	....	....	....	....
MARTINEK, Radek D (NYI)											
C. Budejovice	CzRep-2	30	12	18	30	80	12	2	3	5	6
MARTINS, Steve C (OTT.)											
JYP	Finland	54	13	12	25	66	3	0	0	0	4
MATVICHUK, Richard D (N.J.)				DID NOT PLAY							
MAULDIN, Greg C (CBJ)											
Syracuse	AHL	66	7	20	27	49	....	....	....	....	....
MAY, Brad LW (COL.)				DID NOT PLAY							
MAYERS, Jamal RW (ST.L.)											
Hammarby	Sweden-2	19	9	13	22	36	....	....	....	....	....
Missouri	UHL	13	5	2	7	68	....	....	....	....	....
McALLISTER, Chris D (PHX.)											
Newcastle	Britain-2	14	0	4	4	30	....	....	....	....	....
McAMMOND, Dean LW (ST.L.)											
Albany	AHL	79	19	42	61	72	....	....	....	....	....
McCABE, Bryan D (TOR.)											
HV 71	Sweden	10	1	0	1	30	....	....	....	....	....
McCARTHY, Sandy RW				DID NOT PLAY							
McCARTHY, Steve D (VAN.)				DID NOT PLAY							
McCARTY, Darren RW (CGY.)				DID NOT PLAY							
McCAULEY, Alyn C (S.J.)				DID NOT PLAY							
McCORMICK, Cody C/RW (COL.)											
Hershey	AHL	40	5	6	11	68	....	....	....	....	....
McDONALD, Andy C (ANA.)											
Ingolstadt	Germany	36	13	17	30	26	10	5	2	7	35
McDONELL, Kent RW (DET.)											
Aylmer	OHA-Sr.	5	2	4	6	21	....	....	....	....	....
Bergen	Norway	11	12	3	15	75	....	....	....	....	....
Duisburg	German-2	19	4	9	13	57	10	3	3	6	37
McEACHERN, Shawn RW (BOS.)											
Malmo	Sweden	6	0	1	1	14	....	....	....	....	....
Malmo	Sweden-Q	10	1	1	2	12	....	....	....	....	....
McGILLIS, Dan D (N.J.)				DID NOT PLAY							
McKEE, Jay D (BUF.)				DID NOT PLAY							
McKENNA, Steve LW											
Nottingham	Britain	28	5	6	11	22	....	....	....	....	....
Adelaide	Austral.	19	3	16	19	36	2	0	3	3	2
McKENZIE, Jim LW				DID NOT PLAY							
McLAREN, Kyle D (S.J.)				DID NOT PLAY							
McLAREN, Steve D (T.B.)											
Springfield	AHL	26	1	0	1	78	....	....	....	....	....
McLEAN, Brett C (COL.)											
Malmo	Sweden	38	7	6	13	102	....	....	....	....	....
Malmo	Sweden-Q	9	1	1	2	16	....	....	....	....	....
McNEILL, Grant D (FLA.)											
San Antonio	AHL	40	0	2	2	231	....	....	....	....	....
Texas	ECHL	24	0	3	3	111	....	....	....	....	....
MELICHAR, Josef D (PIT.)											
Sparta	CzRep	13	0	4	4	8	5	0	0	0	6
MELLANBY, Scott RW (ATL.)				DID NOT PLAY							
MELOCHE, Eric RW (PHI.)											
Philadelphia	AHL	63	6	11	17	102	17	3	2	5	18
MESSIER, Eric LW				DID NOT PLAY							
MESSIER, Mark C				DID NOT PLAY							
MEYER, Freddy D (PHI.)											
Philadelphia	AHL	59	6	9	15	71	21	3	9	12	34
MEZEI, Branislav D (FLA.)											
Slovakia	W-Cup	2	0	0	0	0	....	....	....	....	....
Trinec	CzRep	41	1	2	3	68	....	....	....	....	....
Trencin	Slovakia	10	1	1	2	16	12	1	2	3	38
MICHALEK, Milan RW (S.J.)				DID NOT PLAY							
MICHALEK, Zbynek D (PHX.)											
Houston	AHL	76	7	17	24	48	5	1	2	3	4
MIETTINEN, Antti C (DAL.)											
Hamilton	AHL	35	8	20	28	21	4	1	1	2	6
MILLER, Aaron D (L.A.)											
United States	W-Cup	5	0	0	0	4	....	....	....	....	....
United States	WC-A	7	0	2	2	6	....	....	....	....	....
MILLER, Kevin C											
Flint	UHL	7	1	4	5	10	....	....	....	....	....
MILLER, Kip C											
Grand Rapids	AHL	50	13	32	45	17	....	....	....	....	....
MILLEY, Norm RW (T.B.)											
Rochester	AHL	72	12	21	33	46	9	1	2	3	4
MINK, Graham C (WSH.)											
Portland	AHL	63	18	21	39	86	....	....	....	....	....
MIRONOV, Boris D				DID NOT PLAY							
MITCHELL, Willie D (MIN.)				DID NOT PLAY							
MODANO, Mike C (DAL.)											
United States	W-Cup	5	0	6	6	0	....	....	....	....	....
United States	WC-A	7	3	1	4	4	....	....	....	....	....
MODIN, Fredrik LW (T.B.)											
Sweden	W-Cup	4	4	4	8	2	....	....	....	....	....
Timra	Sweden	43	12	24	36	58	7	1	1	2	8
MODRY, Jaroslav D (ATL.)											
Liberec	CzRep	19	3	7	10	24	12	0	4	4	22

		Regular Season					Playoffs				
Team	League	GP	G	A	Pts	PIM	GP	G	A	Pts	PIM
MOEN, Travis LW (ANA.)											
Norfolk	AHL	79	8	12	20	187	6	0	1	1	6
MOGILNY, Alexander RW (N.J.)					DID NOT PLAY						
MONTADOR, Steve D (CGY.)											
Mulhouse	France	15	1	7	8	69	....	....	....	....	....
MOORE, Dominic C (NYR)											
Hartford	AHL	78	19	31	50	78	6	1	1	2	4
MOORE, Steve C					DID NOT PLAY – INJURED						
MORAN, Brad C											
Syracuse	AHL	80	26	46	72	70	....	....	....	....	....
MORAN, Ian D (BOS.)											
Bofors	Sweden-2	7	0	4	4	22	....	....	....	....	....
Nottingham	Britain	9	0	4	4	8	5	0	1	1	2
MOREAU, Ethan LW (EDM.)											
Villacher SV	Austria	16	10	6	16	73	3	4	0	4	0
MORGAN, Gavin C											
Hamilton	AHL	76	10	23	33	147	4	0	0	0	6
MORGAN, Jason C (CHI.)											
Norfolk	AHL	71	9	20	29	116	6	2	2	4	8
MOROZOV, Aleksey RW (PIT.)											
Kazan	Russia	58	20	27	47	30	4	1	1	2	
MORRIS, Derek D (PHX.)					DID NOT PLAY						
MORRISON, Brendan C (VAN.)											
Linkoping	Sweden	45	16	28	44	50	6	0	2	2	10
Canada	WC-A	9	4	0	4	10	....	....	....	....	....
MORRISONN, Shaone D (WSH.)											
Portland	AHL	71	4	14	18	63	....	....	....	....	....
MORROW, Brenden LW (DAL.)											
Canada	W-Cup	1	0	0	0	4	....	....	....	....	....
Oklahoma City	CHL	19	8	14	22	31	....	....	....	....	....
Canada	WC-A	9	0	1	1	6	....	....	....	....	....
MOTZKO, Joe RW (CBJ)											
Syracuse	AHL	79	28	38	66	72	....	....	....	....	....
MOWERS, Mark C (DET.)											
Malmo	Sweden	9	2	0	2	0	....	....	....	....	....
Fribourg	Swiss	3	2	0	2	0	9	9	8	17	12
MUIR, Bryan D (WSH.)											
MODO	Sweden	26	1	5	6	36	....	....	....	....	....
Blues	Finland	11	1	0	1	30	....	....	....	....	....
MURLEY, Matt LW (PIT.)											
Wilkes-Barre	AHL	80	17	24	41	55	11	3	0	3	0
MURRAY, Garth C (NYR)											
Hartford	AHL	55	4	5	9	182	5	1	0	1	8
MURRAY, Glen RW (BOS.)					DID NOT PLAY						
MURRAY, Marty C					DID NOT PLAY						
MURRAY, Rem C/LW					DID NOT PLAY						
MYRVOLD, Anders D											
Valerengen	Norway	40	8	24	32	108	11	2	1	3	24
Norway	WC-B	5	1	5	6	0	....	....	....	....	....
NAGY, Ladislav LW (PHX.)											
Slovakia	W-Cup	4	1	0	1	0	....	....	....	....	....
Kosice	Slovakia	18	9	7	16	40	....	....	....	....	....
Mora	Sweden	19	4	4	8	22	....	....	....	....	....
NASH, Rick LW (CBJ)											
Davos	Swiss	44	26	20	46	83	15	9	2	11	26
Canada	WC-A	9	9	6	15	8	....	....	....	....	....
NASH, Tyson LW (PHX.)					DID NOT PLAY						
NASLUND, Markus LW											
Sweden	W-Cup	4	0	3	3	0	....	....	....	....	....
MODO	Sweden	13	8	9	17	8	6	0	1	1	10
NAZAROV, Andrei LW (MIN.)											
Novokuznetsk	Russia	9	0	0	0	20	....	....	....	....	....
Omsk	Russia	23	0	2	2	153	7	0	0	0	6
NECKAR, Stan D											
C. Budejovice	CzRep-2	16	2	6	8	8	16	0	1	1	18
NEDOROST, Andrej LW (CBJ)											
Magnitogorsk	Russia	12	1	0	1	4	....	....	....	....	....
Nizhnekamsk	Russia	7	0	0	0	4	....	....	....	....	....
Karlovy Vary	CzRep	20	6	5	11	16	....	....	....	....	....
NEDOROST, Vaclav C (FLA.)											
Liberec	CzRep	48	15	18	33	20	6	0	1	1	12
NEDVED, Petr C (PHX.)											
Sparta	CzRep	46	22	13	35	44	5	2	3	5	10

		Regular Season					Playoffs				
Team	League	GP	G	A	Pts	PIM	GP	G	A	Pts	PIM
NEIL, Chris RW (OTT.)											
Binghamton	AHL	22	4	6	10	132	6	1	1	2	26
NICHOL, Scott C (NSH.)											
London	Britain	10	1	7	8	70	....	....	....	....	....
NICKULAS, Eric RW (BOS.)											
Norfolk	AHL	53	11	11	22	32	6	0	3	3	8
NIEDERMAYER, Rob C (ANA.)											
Ferencvaros	Hungary	5	2	1	3	14	....	....	....	....	....
NIEDERMAYER, Scott D (ANA.)											
Canada	W-Cup	6	1	1	2	9	....	....	....	....	....
NIEMINEN, Ville LW (NYR)											
Finland	W-Cup	2	0	0	0	0	....	....	....	....	....
Tappara	Finland	26	14	13	27	32	8	2	4	6	12
NIEUWENDYK, Joe C (FLA.)					DID NOT PLAY						
NIINIMAA, Janne D (NYI)											
Finland	W-Cup	3	0	0	0		....	....	....	....	....
Karpat	Finland	26	3	10	13	30	12	0	5	5	8
Malmo	Sweden	10	0	3	3	34	....	....	....	....	....
NIKOLISHIN, Andrei C											
CSKA	Russia	55	7	20	27	64	....	....	....	....	....
NILSON, Marcus LW (CGY.)											
Sweden	W-Cup	4	1	0	1	4	....	....	....	....	....
Djurgarden	Sweden	48	17	22	39	110	7	1	2	3	10
NOLAN, Owen RW					DID NOT PLAY						
NORSTROM, Mattias D (L.A.)											
Sweden	W-Cup	4	0	0	0		....	....	....	....	....
Solna	Sweden-3	8	1	0	1	4	....	....	....	....	....
Sweden	WC-A	9	0	7	7	2	....	....	....	....	....
NORTON, Brad D					DID NOT PLAY						
NOVOSELTSEV, Ivan RW											
Togliatti	Russia	13	0	2	2	8	....	....	....	....	....
Spartak	Russia	26	5	1	6	47	....	....	....	....	....
NUMMINEN, Teppo D (BUF.)											
Finland	W-Cup	6	0	2	2	0	....	....	....	....	....
NYCHOLAT, Lawrence D (WSH.)											
Hartford	AHL	79	5	38	43	132	6	0	3	3	11
NYLANDER, Michael C (NYR)											
Karpat	Finland	23	5	15	20	22	....	....	....	....	....
St. Petersburg	Russia	8	2	5	7	0	....	....	....	....	....
Kazan	Russia	5	0	1	1	2	....	....	....	....	....
OATES, Adam C					DID NOT PLAY						
ODELEIN, Lyle D (PIT.)					DID NOT PLAY						
O'DONNELL, Sean D (PHX.)					DID NOT PLAY						
OHLUND, Mattias D (VAN.)											
Sweden	W-Cup	4	1	0	1	0	....	....	....	....	....
Lulea	Sweden	2	1	0	1	4	....	....	....	....	....
OLIVER, David RW (DAL.)											
Guildford	Britain-2	16	8	14	22	4	15	3	5	8	31
OLIWA, Krzysztof LW (N.J.)											
Nowy Targ	Poland	....	....	....	....	....	2	0	0	0	12
OLSON, Josh LW											
San Antonio	AHL	53	9	7	16	17	....	....	....	....	....
Hershey	AHL	23	1	2	3	4	....	....	....	....	....
O'NEILL, Jeff RW (TOR.)					DID NOT PLAY						
ORPIK, Brooks D (PIT.)					DID NOT PLAY						
ORR, Colton RW (BOS.)											
Providence	AHL	61	1	6	7	279	17	1	0	1	44
ORSZAGH, Vladimir RW											
Slovakia	W-Cup	4	0	0	0	6	....	....	....	....	....
Zvolen	Slovakia	37	16	14	30	50	17	5	2	7	24
B. Bystrica	Slovak-2	2	2	0	2	4	....	....	....	....	....
Slovakia	WC-A	5	0	1	1	0	....	....	....	....	....
ORTMEYER, Jed C (NYR)											
Hartford	AHL	61	7	20	27	63	6	0	1	1	4
OTT, Steve C (DAL.)											
Hamilton	AHL	67	18	21	39	279	4	0	0	0	20
OZOLINSH, Sandis D (ANA.)					DID NOT PLAY						
PAHLSSON, Samuel C (ANA.)											
Sweden	W-Cup	4	0	0	0	6	....	....	....	....	....
Frolunda	Sweden	48	6	18	24	56	14	4	7	11	24
Sweden	WC-A	9	2	5	7	28	....	....	....	....	....

Team	League	Regular Season					Playoffs				
		GP	G	A	Pts	PIM	GP	G	A	Pts	PIM
PALFFY, Ziggy RW (PIT.)											
Slovakia	W-Cup	DID NOT PLAY – INJURED									
Skalica	Slovakia	8	10	3	13	6	....	....	....	....	....
Slavia	CzRep	41	21	19	40	30	7	5	2	7	2
Slovakia	WC-A	7	5	4	9	10	....	....	....	....	....
PANDOLFO, Jay LW (N.J.)											
Salzburg	Austria	19	5	7	12	0	....	....	....	....	....
PANDOLFO, Mike LW											
Syracuse	AHL	62	8	8	16	18	....	....	....	....	....
PAPINEAU, Justin C (NYI)											
Bridgeport	AHL	59	18	15	33	52	....	....	....	....	....
PARK, Richard RW (VAN.)											
Malmo	Sweden	9	1	3	4	4	....	....	....	....	....
Langnau	Swiss	10	3	0	3	8	6	4	1	5	6
United States	WC-A	5	1	0	1	0	....	....	....	....	....
PARKER, Scott RW (S.J.)											
		DID NOT PLAY									
PARRISH, Mark RW (NYI)											
United States	WC-A	6	5	0	5	6	....	....	....	....	....
PATRICK, James D											
		DID NOT PLAY									
PAYER, Serge C (FLA.)											
San Antonio	AHL	3	1	1	2	4	....	....	....	....	....
PEAT, Stephen RW (WSH.)											
Danbury	UHL	7	0	1	1	45	....	....	....	....	....
PECA, Michael C (EDM.)											
		DID NOT PLAY									
PELLERIN, Scott LW											
		DID NOT PLAY									
PELUSO, Mike RW											
		DID NOT PLAY									
PERREAULT, Yanic C											
		DID NOT PLAY									
PERRIN, Eric C (T.B.)											
Hershey	AHL	80	24	49	73	46	....	....	....	....	....
PERROTT, Nathan RW (TOR.)											
St. John's	AHL	60	16	12	28	276	2	0	0	0	6
PETERS, Andrew LW (BUF.)											
Boden	Sweden-2	22	2	4	6	195	....	....	....	....	....
PETROVICKY, Ronald RW (ATL.)											
Zilina	Slovakia	34	10	9	19	34	....	....	....	....	....
Brynas	Sweden	10	0	5	5	27	....	....	....	....	....
Brynas	Sweden-Q	9	0	2	2	0	....	....	....	....	....
PETTINEN, Tomi D (NYI)											
Lukko	Finland	56	6	14	20	49	9	0	2	2	33
PETTINGER, Matt LW (WSH.)											
Ljubljana	Slovenia	1	0	1	1	0	....	....	....	....	....
Ljubljana	Interliga	7	2	4	6	41	....	....	....	....	....
PHILLIPS, Chris D (OTT.)											
Brynas	Sweden	27	5	3	8	45	....	....	....	....	....
Brynas	Sweden-Q	9	1	2	3	2	....	....	....	....	....
Canada	WC-A	9	0	1	1	8	....	....	....	....	....
PIHLMAN, Tuomas LW (N.J.)											
Albany	AHL	68	9	13	22	48	....	....	....	....	....
PILAR, Karel D (TOR.)											
Sparta	CzRep	52	13	15	28	70	....	....	....	....	....
PIRJETA, Lasse LW (PIT.)											
HIFK	Finland	45	16	20	36	26	5	2	0	2	2
PIRNES, Esa C											
Finland	W-Cup	DID NOT PLAY – INJURED									
Lukko	Finland	47	9	29	38	31	9	1	3	4	2
PIROS, Kamil C											
Voskresensk	Russia	27	2	6	8	8	....	....	....	....	....
PISANI, Fernando RW (EDM.)											
Langnau	Swiss	7	1	3	4	0	....	....	....	....	....
Asiago	Italy	12	1	5	6	6	9	4	6	10	0
PITKANEN, Joni D (PHI.)											
Philadelphia	AHL	76	6	35	41	105	21	3	4	7	16
PITTIS, Domenic C											
Kloten	Swiss	43	17	29	46	110	3	2	2	4	4
PIVKO, Libor LW (NSH.)											
Milwaukee	AHL	56	5	15	20	59	6	0	1	1	2
PLEKANEC, Tomas LW (MTL.)											
Hamilton	AHL	80	29	35	64	68	4	2	4	6	6
POAPST, Steve D											
		DID NOT PLAY									
PODKONICKY, Andrej C											
Liberec	CzRep	24	9	4	13	16	10	3	4	7	4
POECK, Thomas D (NYR)											
Hartford	AHL	50	1	5	6	55	6	0	1	1	8
Charlotte	ECHL	3	0	2	2	2	....	....	....	....	....

Team	League	Regular Season					Playoffs				
		GP	G	A	Pts	PIM	GP	G	A	Pts	PIM
POHL, John C (TOR.)											
Worcester	AHL	13	3	6	9	2	....	....	....	....	....
POLLOCK, Jame D											
Kloten	Swiss	26	4	8	12	34	....	....	....	....	....
Lugano	Swiss	....	....	....	....	....	2	0	1	1	8
POMINVILLE, Jason RW (BUF.)											
Rochester	AHL	78	30	38	68	43	....	....	....	....	....
PONIKAROVSKY, Alexei LW (TOR.)											
Voskresensk	Russia	19	1	5	6	16	....	....	....	....	....
POPOVIC, Mark D (ATL.)											
Cincinnati	AHL	74	1	17	18	47	11	2	3	5	6
POTHIER, Brian D (OTT.)											
Binghamton	AHL	77	12	36	48	64	6	0	1	1	6
POTI, Tom D (NYR)											
		DID NOT PLAY									
PRATT, Nolan D (T.B.)											
Duisburg	German-2	10	2	2	4	14	12	0	3	3	10
PREISSING, Tom D (S.J.)											
Krefeld	Germany	33	1	6	7	32	....	....	....	....	....
PRIMEAU, Keith C (PHI.)											
		DID NOT PLAY									
PRIMEAU, Wayne C (S.J.)											
		DID NOT PLAY									
PRONGER, Chris D (EDM.)											
Canada	W-Cup	DID NOT PLAY – INJURED									
PRONGER, Sean C											
Frankfurt	Germany	51	6	10	16	78	4	0	0	0	6
PROSPAL, Vaclav C (T.B.)											
Czech Republic	W-Cup	4	1	3	4	0	....	....	....	....	....
C. Budejovice	CzRep-2	39	28	60	88	82	16	15	15	30	32
Czech Republic	WC-A	9	2	6	8	4	....	....	....	....	....
PURINTON, Dale D (NYR)											
Victoria	ECHL	25	3	9	12	192	....	....	....	....	....
PUSHOR, Jamie D											
Syracuse	AHL	68	1	9	10	85	....	....	....	....	....
PYATT, Taylor LW (BUF.)											
Hammarby	Sweden-2	24	11	9	20	20	....	....	....	....	....
QUINT, Deron D											
Bolzano	Italy	14	5	11	16	10	9	4	5	9	12
QUINTAL, Stephane D											
Asiago	Italy	10	1	2	3	4	5	2	0	2	4
RACHUNEK, Karel D (NYR)											
Znojmo	CzRep	21	5	6	11	55	....	....	....	....	....
Yaroslavl	Russia	27	6	8	14	69	9	2	0	2	6
RADIVOJEVIC, Branko RW (PHI.)											
Slovakia	W-Cup	4	0	1	1	2	....	....	....	....	....
Vsetin	CzRep	31	7	11	18	114	....	....	....	....	....
Lulea	Sweden	10	6	5	11	8	4	0	0	0	44
RADULOV, Igor LW											
Spartak	Russia	25	2	2	4	22	....	....	....	....	....
Norfolk	AHL	16	0	0	0	16	....	....	....	....	....
RAFALSKI, Brian D (N.J.)											
United States	W-Cup	4	0	3	3	6	....	....	....	....	....
RAGNARSSON, Marcus D											
Sweden	W-Cup	3	0	0	0	0	....	....	....	....	....
Almtuna	Sweden-2	....	....	....	....	....	1	1	0	1	0
RASMUSSEN, Erik LW/C (N.J.)											
		DID NOT PLAY									
RATHJE, Mike D (PHI.)											
		DID NOT PLAY									
RAY, Rob RW											
		DID NOT PLAY									
REASONER, Marty C (EDM.)											
Salzburg	Austria	11	5	4	9	12	....	....	....	....	....
RECCHI, Mark RW (PIT.)											
		DID NOT PLAY									
REDDEN, Wade D (OTT.)											
Canada	W-Cup	2	0	1	1	0	....	....	....	....	....
Canada	WC-A	9	2	3	5	2	....	....	....	....	....
REGEHR, Robyn D (CGY.)											
Canada	W-Cup	6	0	0	0	6	....	....	....	....	....
Canada	WC-A	9	0	0	0	4	....	....	....	....	....
REICH, Jeremy LW (BOS.)											
Syracuse	AHL	50	4	5	9	189	....	....	....	....	....
Houston	AHL	18	3	4	7	34	5	0	1	1	28
REICHEL, Robert C											
Czech Republic	W-Cup	4	0	0	0	2	....	....	....	....	....
Litvinov	CzRep	32	9	19	28	32	....	....	....	....	....
REID, Brandon C (VAN.)											
Hamburg	Germany	45	18	29	47	41	6	0	3	3	4

Team	League	Regular Season					Playoffs				
		GP	G	A	Pts	PIM	GP	G	A	Pts	PIM
REINPRECHT, Steve C (CGY.)											
Mulhouse	France	22	20	27	47	6	10	7	6	13	2
REIRDEN, Todd D											
Houston	AHL	52	3	5	8	56	5	0	0	0	6
RENBERG, Mikael RW											
Lulea	Sweden	22	6	5	11	16	....	....	....	....	....
RHEAUME, Pascal C (N.J.)											
Albany	AHL	78	24	25	49	85					
RIBEIRO, Mike C (MTL.)											
Blues	Finland	17	8	9	17	4					
RICCI, Mike C (PHX.)						DID NOT PLAY					
RICHARDS, Brad C (T.B.)											
Canada	W-Cup	6	1	3	4	0					
Kazan	Russia	6	2	5	7	16					
RICHARDSON, Luke D (CBJ)						DID NOT PLAY					
RISSMILLER, Pat LW (S.J.)											
Cleveland	AHL	69	21	23	44	50					
RITA, Jani LW (EDM.)											
HPK	Finland	56	21	18	39	12	10	7	4	11	4
Finland	WC-A	7	0	2	2	6					
RITCHIE, Byron C (CGY.)											
Rogle	Sweden-2	30	17	16	33	111	2	0	0	0	4
RIVERS, Jamie D (DET.)											
Hershey	AHL	50	7	13	20	46					
RIVET, Craig D (MTL.)											
TPS	Finland	18	3	1	4	28	6	0	0	0	39
ROBERTS, Gary LW (FLA.)						DID NOT PLAY					
ROBIDAS, Stephane D (DAL.)											
Frankfurt	Germany	51	15	32	47	64	6	1	2	3	6
ROBINSON, Nathan C (BOS.)											
Grand Rapids	AHL	50	8	16	24	10					
Syracuse	AHL	19	6	14	20	18					
ROBITAILLE, Luc LW (L.A.)						DID NOT PLAY					
ROBITAILLE, Randy C (NSH.)											
Zurich	Swiss	36	22	45	67	56	15	2	16	18	10
ROCHE, Travis D (ATL.)											
Chicago	AHL	73	12	38	50	59	18	1	6	7	18
ROENICK, Jeremy C (L.A.)											
United States	W-Cup					DID NOT PLAY – INJURED					
ROHLOFF, Todd D (T.B.)											
Rochester	AHL	12	0	1	1	4					
ROLSTON, Brian C/RW (MIN.)											
United States	W-Cup	2	0	0	0	0					
RONNING, Cliff C						DID NOT PLAY					
ROSA, Pavel RW											
Dynamo Moscow	Russia	54	21	23	44	14	8	3	2	5	2
ROSSITER, Kyle D											
Chicago	AHL	33	1	5	6	43					
Wilkes-Barre	AHL	9	0	1	1	5	1	0	0	0	0
ROURKE, Allan D (NYI)											
Lowell	AHL	60	7	9	16	75	11	1	2	3	40
ROY, Andre RW (PIT.)						DID NOT PLAY					
ROY, Derek C (BUF.)											
Rochester	AHL	67	16	45	61	60	9	6	5	11	6
RUCCHIN, Steve C (NYR)						DID NOT PLAY					
RUCINSKY, Martin LW (NYR)											
Czech Republic	W-Cup	4	1	1	2	10					
Litvinov	CzRep	38	15	26	41	87					
Czech Republic	WC-A	9	2	4	6	22					
RUMBLE, Darren D											
Springfield	AHL	10	0	1	1	4					
RUPP, Mike C (PHX.)											
Danbury	UHL	14	5	5	10	30	11	3	4	7	38
RUUTU, Jarkko RW (VAN.)											
Finland	W-Cup	4	0	0	0	6					
HIFK	Finland	50	10	18	28	215	3	0	0	0	41
Finland	WC-A	7	1	0	1	4					
RUUTU, Tuomo C/LW (CHI.)											
Finland	W-Cup	6	1	2	3	4					
RYCROFT, Mark RW (ST.L.)											
Briancon	France	13	8	8	16	18	4	2	1	3	0
RYDER, Michael RW (MTL.)											
Leksand	Sweden-2	42	34	27	61	32	....	....	....	....	....

Team	League	Regular Season					Playoffs				
		GP	G	A	Pts	PIM	GP	G	A	Pts	PIM
SAKIC, Joe C (COL.)											
Canada	W-Cup	6	4	2	6	2	....	....	....	....	....
SALEI, Ruslan D (ANA.)											
Kazan	Russia	35	8	12	20	36	4	0	0	0	2
SALMELAINEN, Tony LW (EDM.)											
Edmonton	AHL	76	22	24	46	26					
SALO, Sami D (VAN.)											
Finland	W-Cup	6	0	1	1	2					
Frolunda	Sweden	41	6	8	14	18	14	1	6	7	2
SALVADOR, Bryce D (ST.L.)											
Missouri	UHL	7	0	0	0	16	3	0	0	0	0
SAMSONOV, Sergei LW (BOS.)											
Russia	W-Cup	4	1	2	3	0					
Dynamo Moscow	Russia	3	1	0	1	0	3	1	2	3	0
SAMUELSSON, Martin RW (BOS.)											
Providence	AHL	64	7	10	17	35	10	1	0	1	6
SAMUELSSON, Mikael RW											
Geneve	Swiss	12	2	4	6	14					
Sodertalje	Sweden	29	7	13	20	45	10	3	3	6	24
Sweden	WC-A	9	1	4	5	4					
SANDERSON, Geoff LW (CBJ)											
Geneve	Swiss	9	4	1	5	29					
SANTALA, Tommi C (ATL.)											
Chicago	AHL	67	8	40	48	83	18	5	6	11	42
SAPRYKIN, Oleg LW (PHX.)											
CSKA	Russia	40	15	8	23	105					
SARICH, Cory D (T.B.)						DID NOT PLAY					
SARNO, Peter C (CBJ)											
Manitoba	AHL	80	16	66	82	53	14	1	8	9	4
SATAN, Miroslav LW (NYI)											
Slovakia	W-Cup	4	0	0	0	4	....	....	....	....	....
Bratislava	Slovakia	18	11	9	20	14	18	15	7	22	16
Slovakia	WC-A	7	2	2	4	8					
SAUER, Kurt D (COL.)						DID NOT PLAY					
SAVAGE, Brian LW						DID NOT PLAY					
SAVARD, Marc C (ATL.)											
Bern	Swiss	5	1	2	3	0					
Thurgau	Swiss-2	13	9	19	28	10					
SCATCHARD, Dave C (BOS.)						DID NOT PLAY					
SCHAEFER, Peter LW (OTT.)											
Bolzano	Italy	15	11	14	25	10	10	1	7	8	12
SCHASTLIVY, Petr LW											
Yaroslavl	Russia	59	15	15	30	28	9	1	3	4	2
SCHNABEL, Robert D											
Sparta	CzRep	47	1	4	5	85	4	0	0	0	12
SCHNEIDER, Mathieu D (DET.)											
United States	W-Cup					DID NOT PLAY – INJURED					
SCHULTZ, Nick D (MIN.)											
Kassel	Germany	46	7	15	22	26	7	0	4	4	6
SCOTT, Richard LW						DID NOT PLAY					
SCOVILLE, Darrel D											
Hershey	AHL	7	0	0	0	11					
Providence	AHL	43	6	7	26						
SCUDERI, Rob D (PIT.)											
Wilkes-Barre	AHL	79	2	18	20	34	11	2	1	3	2
SEDIN, Daniel LW (VAN.)											
MODO	Sweden	49	13	20	33	40	6	0	3	3	6
Sweden	WC-A	9	5	4	9	2					
SEDIN, Henrik C (VAN.)											
MODO	Sweden	44	14	22	36	50	6	1	3	4	6
Sweden	WC-A	9	2	4	6	2					
SEIDENBERG, Dennis D (PHI.)											
Germany	W-Cup	4	0	0	0	0					
Philadelphia	AHL	79	13	28	41	47	18	2	8	10	19
SEJNA, Peter LW (ST.L.)											
Worcester	AHL	64	17	21	38	24					
SEKERAS, Lubomir D											
Nurnberg	Germany	52	4	27	31	48	6	0	1	1	4
SELANNE, Teemu RW (ANA.)											
Finland	W-Cup	6	1	3	4	4					
SEMENOV, Alexei D (EDM.)											
St. Petersburg	Russia	50	0	8	26						

Team	League	Regular Season					Playoffs				
		GP	G	A	Pts	PIM	GP	G	A	Pts	PIM

SEMIN, Alexander LW (WSH.)

Team	League	GP	G	A	Pts	PIM	GP	G	A	Pts	PIM
Togliatti	Russia	50	19	11	30	56	10	1	1	2	0
Russia	WC-A	6	3	0	3	8	....	....	....	....	....

SEVERSON, Cam LW (CGY.)

Milwaukee	AHL	63	6	8	14	255	4	0	0	0	12

SHANAHAN, Brendan LW (DET.)   DID NOT PLAY

SHARP, Patrick C (PHI.)

Philadelphia	AHL	75	23	29	52	80	21	8	13	21	20

SHELLEY, Jody LW (CBJ)

JYP	Finland	11	0	1	1	20	3	0	0	0	25

SHISHKANOV, Timofei LW (NSH.)

Milwaukee	AHL	70	20	15	35	31	6	1	0	1	2

SHVIDKI, Denis RW (FLA.)   DID NOT PLAY

SIKLENKA, Mike RW (DAL.)

Klagenfurt	Austria	39	16	18	34	156	12	6	1	7	44

SILLINGER, Mike C (ST.L.)   DID NOT PLAY

SIM, Jon LW (PHI.)

Utah	AHL	10	2	2	4	12	....	....	....	....	....
Philadelphia	AHL	63	35	26	61	66	21	10	7	17	44

SIMON, Ben LW (CBJ)

Chicago	AHL	53	11	10	21	58	18	1	5	6	44

SIMON, Chris LW (CGY.)   DID NOT PLAY

SIMPSON, Reid LW

Rockford	UHL	15	1	3	4	46	7	0	0	0	18

SIMPSON, Todd D (CHI.)

Herning	Denmark	7	2	3	5	35	16	3	5	8	82

SJOSTROM, Fredrik RW (PHX.)

Utah	AHL	80	14	24	38	57	....	....	....	....	....

SKOULA, Martin D (DAL.)

Czech Republic	W-Cup	2	0	0	0	2	....	....	....	....	....
Litvinov	CzRep	47	4	15	19	101	6	0	0	0	6

SKRASTINS, Karlis D (COL.)

Riga 2000	Latvia	4	0	4	4	0	9	3	10	13	33
Riga 2000	BelOpen	34	8	17	25	30	3	0	0	0	25
Latvia	WC-A	6	2	0	2	2	....	....	....	....	....

SKRLAC, Rob LW

Albany	AHL	52	0	2	2	184	....	....	....	....	....

SLANEY, John D (PHI.)

Philadelphia	AHL	78	14	30	44	39	21	3	7	10	12

SLEGR, Jiri D (BOS.)

Czech Republic	W-Cup	3	1	0	1	2	....	....	....	....	....
Litvinov	CzRep	46	6	23	29	135	6	1	2	3	30
Czech Republic	WC-A	9	0	0	0	6	....	....	....	....	....

SLOAN, Blake RW

Grand Rapids	AHL	78	15	11	26	68	....	....	....	....	....

SMIRNOV, Alexei LW

Cincinnati	AHL	65	9	9	18	53	4	0	0	0	0

SMITH, Jason D (EDM.)   DID NOT PLAY

SMITH, Mark C (S.J.)

Victoria	ECHL	20	6	9	15	41	....	....	....	....	....

SMITH, Nathan C (VAN.)

Manitoba	AHL	72	7	9	16	67	14	2	4	6	20

SMITH, Wyatt C (NYI)

Milwaukee	AHL	69	19	28	47	89	7	1	4	5	10

SMITHSON, Jerred C (NSH.)

Milwaukee	AHL	80	11	11	22	92	5	0	0	0	4

SMOLINSKI, Bryan C (OTT.)

United States	W-Cup	3	1	0	1	0	....	....	....	....	....
Motor City	UHL	21	9	23	32	18	....	....	....	....	....

SMYTH, Ryan LW (EDM.)

Canada	W-Cup	6	3	1	4	2	....	....	....	....	....
Canada	WC-A	9	2	1	3	6	....	....	....	....	....

SOMIK, Radovan RW

Slovakia	W-Cup	1	0	0	0	0	....	....	....	....	....
Martin	Slovak-2	2	1	0	1	0	....	....	....	....	....
Vsetin	CzRep	31	7	16	23	24	....	....	....	....	....
Malmo	Sweden	8	1	0	1	6	....	....	....	....	....
Malmo	Sweden-Q	10	1	3	4	2	....	....	....	....	....

SONNENBERG, Martin LW (PHX.)

Utah	AHL	65	13	13	26	94	....	....	....	....	....

SOPEL, Brent D (NYI)   DID NOT PLAY

SOURAY, Sheldon D (MTL.)

Farjestad	Sweden	39	9	8	17	117	15	1	6	7	77
Canada	WC-A	9	1	1	2	6	....	....	....	....	....

SPACEK, Jaroslav D (CHI.)

Czech Republic	W-Cup	4	0	0	0	0	....	....	....	....	....
Plzen	CzRep	30	3	8	11	26	....	....	....	....	....
Slavia	CzRep	17	4	9	13	29	7	0	2	2	8
Czech Republic	WC-A	9	1	0	1	0	....	....	....	....	....

SPEZZA, Jason C (OTT.)

Binghamton	AHL	80	32	85	117	50	6	1	3	4	6

SPILLER, Matthew D (PHX.)

Utah	AHL	79	4	7	11	160	....	....	....	....	....

ST. JACQUES, Bruno D (CAR.)

Lowell	AHL	68	2	12	14	60	11	1	4	5	4

ST. LOUIS, Martin RW (T.B.)

Canada	W-Cup	6	2	2	4	0	....	....	....	....	....
Lausanne	Swiss	23	9	16	25	16	....	....	....	....	....

STAAL, Eric C (CAR.)

Lowell	AHL	77	26	51	77	88	11	2	8	10	12

STAIOS, Steve D (EDM.)

Lulea	Sweden	7	2	1	3	12	....	....	....	....	....

STAJAN, Matt C (TOR.)

St. John's	AHL	80	23	43	66	43	5	2	2	4	6

STEFAN, Patrik C (ATL.)

Ilves	Finland	37	13	28	41	47	7	1	6	7	4

STEPHENS, Charlie C/RW

Binghamton	AHL	80	7	21	28	64	6	3	0	3	19

STEVENS, Scott D   DID NOT PLAY

STEVENSON, Jeremy LW (NSH.)

South Carolina	ECHL	42	9	20	29	140	3	1	0	1	2

STEVENSON, Turner RW (PHI.)   DID NOT PLAY

STEWART, Karl C (ATL.)

Chicago	AHL	77	16	8	24	226	12	4	2	6	32

STILLMAN, Cory LW (CAR.)   DID NOT PLAY

STOCK, P.J. C   DID NOT PLAY

STOLL, Jarret C (EDM.)

Edmonton	AHL	66	21	17	38	92	....	....	....	....	....

STRAKA, Martin C (NYR)

Czech Republic	W-Cup	5	1	2	3	0	....	....	....	....	....
Plzen	CzRep	45	16	18	34	76	....	....	....	....	....
Czech Republic	WC-A	9	3	1	4	8	....	....	....	....	....

STRBAK, Martin D (PIT.)

Slovakia	W-Cup	4	0	0	0	4	....	....	....	....	....
Kosice	Slovakia	14	1	4	5	14	....	....	....	....	....
CSKA	Russia	36	2	11	13	34	....	....	....	....	....
Slovakia	WC-A	7	2	5	7	10	....	....	....	....	....

STROSHEIN, Garret RW (BOS.)

Portland	AHL	42	0	1	1	109	....	....	....	....	....
South Carolina	ECHL	1	0	0	0	5	....	....	....	....	....

STRUDWICK, Jason D (NYR)

Ferencvaros	Hungary	6	1	2	3	8	....	....	....	....	....

STUART, Brad D (S.J.)   DID NOT PLAY

STUART, Mike D (ST.L.)

Worcester	AHL	70	1	10	11	26	....	....	....	....	....

STUMPEL, Jozef C (FLA.)

Slovakia	W-Cup	4	0	0	0	2	....	....	....	....	....
Slavia	CzRep	52	13	26	39	41	7	4	2	6	10
Slovakia	WC-A	7	0	7	7	6	....	....	....	....	....

STURM, Marco LW (S.J.)

Germany	W-Cup	4	2	0	2	0	....	....	....	....	....
Ingolstadt	Germany	45	22	16	38	56	11	3	4	7	12

STUTZEL, Mike LW

Utah	AHL	52	0	2	2	16	....	....	....	....	....
Idaho	ECHL	14	8	7	15	8	4	1	0	1	6

SUCHY, Radoslav D (CBJ)

Slovakia	W-Cup	3	0	0	0	0	....	....	....	....	....
Poprad	Slovakia	34	5	10	15	24	5	0	0	0	2
Slovakia	WC-A	7	0	0	0	0	....	....	....	....	....

SUGLOBOV, Aleksander RW (N.J.)

Albany	AHL	72	25	21	46	77	....	....	....	....	....

SULLIVAN, Steve RW (NSH.)   DID NOT PLAY

SUNDIN, Mats C (TOR.)

Sweden	W-Cup	4	1	5	6	0	....	....	....	....	....

SUNDSTROM, Niklas RW (MTL.)

Milano	Italy	33	9	27	36	40	15	4	14	18	20

SURMA, Damian C

Florida	ECHL	72	32	28	60	74	19	7	6	13	14

Team	League	Regular Season GP	G	A	Pts	PIM	Playoffs GP	G	A	Pts	PIM
SUROVY, Tomas C (PIT.)											
Wilkes-Barre	AHL	80	17	32	49	43	11	2	6	8	9
SUTHERBY, Brian C (WSH.)											
Portland	AHL	53	10	19	29	115	....	....	....	....	....
SUTTON, Andy D (ATL.)											
GCK Zurich	Swiss-2	18	8	18	26	58	6	2	4	6	16
Zurich	Swiss	8	2	2	4	32	1	0	1	1	2
SVATOS, Marek RW (COL.)											
Hershey	AHL	72	18	28	46	69	....	....	....	....	....
SVITOV, Alexander C (CBJ)											
Syracuse	AHL	69	19	23	42	200	....	....	....	....	....
SVOBODA, Jaroslav LW (DAL.)											
Olomouc	CzRep-2	18	7	6	13	67	....	....	....	....	....
Trinec	CzRep	9	0	2	2	14	....	....	....	....	....
SWANSON, Brian C											
Kassel	Germany	37	14	19	33	16	5	2	2	4	4
SWEENEY, Don D		DID NOT PLAY									
SYDOR, Darryl D (T.B.)		DID NOT PLAY									
SYKORA, Petr RW (ANA.)											
Czech Republic	W-Cup	3	0	1	1	2	....	....	....	....	....
Magnitogorsk	Russia	45	18	13	31	46	5	2	3	5	8
Czech Republic	WC-A	9	2	1	3	4	....	....	....	....	....
TAFFE, Jeff C (PHX.)											
Utah	AHL	27	9	10	19	35	....	....	....	....	....
TALLINDER, Henrik D (BUF.)											
Linkoping	Sweden	44	6	10	16	63	....	....	....	....	....
Bern	Swiss	....	....	....	....	....	10	1	1	2	4
TAMER, Chris D		DID NOT PLAY									
TANABE, David D (PHX.)											
Rapperswil	Swiss	8	4	5	9	4	....	....	....	....	....
Kloten	Swiss	20	3	7	10	18	5	1	4	5	8
TANGUAY, Alex LW (COL.)											
Lugano	Swiss	6	3	3	6	4	....	....	....	....	....
TARNSTROM, Dick D (PIT.)											
Sweden	W-Cup	2	0	0	0	0	....	....	....	....	....
Sodertalje	Sweden	50	7	18	25	46	9	1	0	1	6
TAYLOR, Chris C (BUF.)											
Rochester	AHL	79	21	58	79	50	9	1	8	9	4
TAYLOR, Tim C (T.B.)		DID NOT PLAY									
TETARENKO, Joey RW (MIN.)											
Houston	AHL	15	0	1	1	49	....	....	....	....	....
THERIEN, Chris D (PHI.)		DID NOT PLAY									
THOMAS, Steve LW		DID NOT PLAY									
THORNTON, Joe C (BOS.)											
Canada	W-Cup	6	1	5	6	0	....	....	....	....	....
Davos	Swiss	40	10	44	54	80	14	4	20	24	29
Canada	WC-A	9	6	10	16	4	....	....	....	....	....
THORNTON, Scott LW (S.J.)											
Sodertalje	Sweden	12	2	5	7	10	10	0	3	3	27
THORNTON, Shawn RW (CHI.)											
Norfolk	AHL	71	5	9	14	253	6	0	0	0	8
TIMANDER, Mattias D											
MODO	Sweden	47	3	7	10	60	6	0	1	1	4
TIMONEN, Kimmo D (NSH.)											
Finland	W-Cup	6	1	5	6	2	....	....	....	....	....
Lugano	Swiss	3	0	1	1	0	....	....	....	....	....
Brynas	Sweden	10	5	3	8	8	....	....	....	....	....
KalPa	Finland-2	12	4	13	17	6	8	3	7	10	4
Finland	WC-A	6	2	1	3	6	....	....	....	....	....
TJARNQVIST, Daniel D (MIN.)											
Sweden	W-Cup	3	0	0	0	2	....	....	....	....	....
Djurgarden	Sweden	49	12	12	24	30	12	2	5	7	10
TJARNQVIST, Mathias RW (DAL.)											
HV 71	Sweden	46	8	9	17	18	....	....	....	....	....
TKACHUK, Keith LW (ST.L.)											
United States	W-Cup	5	5	1	6	23	....	....	....	....	....
TOOTOO, Jordin RW (NSH.)											
Milwaukee	AHL	59	10	12	22	266	6	0	0	0	41
TORRES, Raffi LW (EDM.)											
Edmonton	AHL	67	21	25	46	165	....	....	....	....	....
TREMBLAY, Yannick D											
Sherbrooke	QNAHL	36	26	25	51	40	....	....	....	....	....
Mannheim	Germany	14	1	4	5	16	14	2	6	8	6
TRIPP, John RW											
Mannheim	Germany	44	9	16	25	136	14	2	3	5	54
TRNKA, Pavel D											
Plzen	CzRep	47	7	10	17	103	....	....	....	....	....
TUCKER, Darcy RW (TOR.)		DID NOT PLAY									
TURGEON, Pierre C (COL.)		DID NOT PLAY									
TVRDON, Roman C											
Nottingham	Britain	9	2	5	7	6	....	....	....	....	....
TYUTIN, Fedor D (NYR)											
Hartford	AHL	13	2	1	3	10	....	....	....	....	....
St. Petersburg	Russia	35	5	3	8	24	....	....	....	....	....
ULANOV, Igor D (EDM.)		DID NOT PLAY									
ULMER, Layne C											
Hartford	AHL	65	7	30	37	23	6	0	0	0	2
UPSHALL, Scottie RW (NSH.)											
Milwaukee	AHL	62	19	27	46	108	5	2	2	4	8
VAANANEN, Ossi D (COL.)											
Finland	W-Cup	4	1	2	3	0	....	....	....	....	....
Jokerit	Finland	28	2	2	4	30	12	0	0	0	26
Finland	WC-A	7	0	1	1	8	....	....	....	....	....
VALICEVIC, Rob RW											
Flint	UHL	78	36	60	96	38	....	....	....	....	....
VAN ALLEN, Shaun C		DID NOT PLAY									
VAN RYN, Mike D (FLA.)		DID NOT PLAY									
VANDENBUSSCHE, Ryan RW (PIT.)											
Wilkes-Barre	AHL	23	4	7	11	67	11	2	2	4	11
VANDERMEER, Jim D (CHI.)											
Norfolk	AHL	52	3	10	13	164	....	....	....	....	....
VARADA, Vaclav RW (OTT.)											
Vitkovice	CzRep	44	8	19	27	83	11	3	3	6	37
Czech Republic	WC-A	9	1	0	1	2	....	....	....	....	....
VASICEK, Josef C (CAR.)											
Czech Republic	W-Cup	1	0	0	0	0	....	....	....	....	....
Slavia	CzRep	52	20	23	43	42	7	1	6	7	10
Czech Republic	WC-A	8	1	1	2	4	....	....	....	....	....
VAUCLAIR, Julien D											
Lugano	Swiss	42	4	7	11	26	3	0	0	0	2
Switzerland	WC-A	7	0	0	0	10	....	....	....	....	....
VEILLEUX, Stephane LW (MIN.)											
Houston	AHL	59	15	24	39	35	....	....	....	....	....
VERMETTE, Antoine C (OTT.)											
Binghamton	AHL	78	28	45	73	36	6	1	4	5	10
VERNARSKY, Kris C											
Providence	AHL	5	0	1	1	2	....	....	....	....	....
Florida	ECHL	53	16	20	36	47	18	2	7	9	33
VEROT, Darcy LW											
Portland	AHL	36	0	1	1	189	....	....	....	....	....
VIGIER, J.P. RW (ATL.)											
Chicago	AHL	76	29	41	70	56	18	5	6	11	19
VISHNEVSKI, Vitaly D (ANA.)											
Russia	W-Cup	3	0	0	0	0	....	....	....	....	....
Voskresensk	Russia	51	7	17	24	92	....	....	....	....	....
VISNOVSKY, Lubomir D (L.A.)											
Slovakia	W-Cup	4	0	0	0	6	....	....	....	....	....
Bratislava	Slovakia	43	13	25	38	40	14	2	10	12	10
Slovakia	WC-A	7	2	6	8	0	....	....	....	....	....
VOLCHENKOV, Anton D (OTT.)											
Russia	W-Cup	1	0	0	0	0	....	....	....	....	....
Binghamton	AHL	69	10	35	45	62	6	0	3	3	0
VOROBIEV, Pavel RW (CHI.)											
Norfolk	AHL	79	19	25	44	48	6	2	1	3	4
VRBATA, Radim RW (CAR.)											
Liberec	CzRep	45	18	21	39	91	12	3	2	5	0
Czech Republic	WC-A	3	0	1	1	0	....	....	....	....	....
VYBORNY, David RW (CBJ)											
Czech Republic	W-Cup	5	0	0	0	2	....	....	....	....	....
Sparta	CzRep	51	12	34	46	10	5	2	5	7	4
Czech Republic	WC-A	9	1	3	4	8	....	....	....	....	....
WALKER, Matt D (ST.L.)											
Worcester	AHL	20	2	4	6	44	....	....	....	....	....
WALKER, Scott RW (NSH.)											
Cambridge	OHA-Sr.	5	2	6	8	4	....	....	....	....	....
Dundas	OHA-Sr.	3	3	2	5	8	....	....	....	....	....
Canada	WC-A	9	0	0	0	0	....	....	....	....	....
WALLIN, Niclas D (CAR.)											
Lulea	Sweden	39	6	7	13	89	3	0	1	1	6

Team	League	Regular Season					Playoffs				
		GP	G	A	Pts	PIM	GP	G	A	Pts	PIM
WALLIN, Rickard C (MIN.)											
Houston	AHL	79	12	31	43	61	5	1	0	1	29
WALSER, Derrick D (CAR.)											
Eisbaren Berlin	Germany	50	9	14	23	143	12	4	4	8	20
WALZ, Wes C (MIN.)				DID NOT PLAY							
WANVIG, Kyle RW (MIN.)											
Houston	AHL	76	13	17	30	158	5	1	2	3	8
WARD, Aaron D (CAR.)											
Ingolstadt	Germany	8	0	3	3	16	11	1	1	2	16
WARD, Jason RW (NYR)											
Hamilton	AHL	77	20	34	54	66	4	2	1	3	2
WARD, Lance D (OTT.)				DID NOT PLAY							
WARRENER, Rhett D (CGY.)				DID NOT PLAY							
WEAVER, Mike D (L.A.)											
Manchester	AHL	79	1	22	23	61	6	0	1	1	0
WEBB, Steve RW				DID NOT PLAY							
WEIGHT, Doug C (ST.L.)											
United States	W-Cup	5	1	0	1	4	....	....	....	....	....
Frankfurt	Germany	7	6	9	15	26	11	2	10	12	8
United States	WC-A	7	1	5	6	0	....	....	....	....	....
WEINHANDL, Mattias RW (NYI)											
MODO	Sweden	50	26	20	46	18	6	0	0	0	4
Sweden	WC-A	8	0	1	1	0	....	....	....	....	....
WEINRICH, Eric D (ST.L.)											
United States	W-Cup	2	0	0	0	0	....	....	....	....	....
Villacher SV	Austria	10	3	8	11	8	3	0	1	1	6
WEISS, Stephen C (FLA.)											
San Antonio	AHL	62	15	23	38	38	....	....	....	....	....
Chicago	AHL	18	7	9	16	12	18	2	7	9	17
WELLWOOD, Kyle C (TOR.)											
St. John's	AHL	80	38	49	87	20	5	2	2	4	2
WESLEY, Glen D (CAR.)				DID NOT PLAY							
WESTCOTT, Duvie D (CBJ)											
JYP	Finland	46	11	7	18	106	1	2	0	2	25
WESTRUM, Erik C (MIN.)											
Utah	AHL	80	18	15	33	117	....	....	....	....	....
WHITE, Colin D (N.J.)				DID NOT PLAY							
WHITE, Peter C											
Philadelphia	AHL	10	2	6	8	6	....	....	....	....	....
Utah	AHL	70	12	25	37	14	....	....	....	....	....
WHITE, Todd C (MIN.)											
Sodertalje	Sweden	1	0	1	1	4	....	....	....	....	....
WHITFIELD, Trent C (ST.L.)											
Portland	AHL	67	17	38	55	75	....	....	....	....	....
WHITNEY, Ray LW (CAR.)				DID NOT PLAY							
WIEMER, Jason C (CGY.)				DID NOT PLAY							
WILLIAMS, Jason C (DET.)											
Assat	Finland	43	26	17	43	52	2	1	1	2	4
WILLIAMS, Justin RW (CAR.)											
Lulea	Sweden	49	14	18	32	61	4	0	1	1	29
WILLIS, Shane RW (T.B.)											
Springfield	AHL	58	18	16	34	29	....	....	....	....	....
WILLSIE, Brian RW (WSH.)											
Ljubljana	Interliga	12	7	6	13	34	....	....	....	....	....
Ljubljana	Slovenia	2	0	3	3	4	....	....	....	....	....
Portland	AHL	53	23	17	40	47	....	....	....	....	....
WILM, Clarke C (TOR.)											
St. John's	AHL	69	11	16	27	145	5	2	2	4	8
WILSON, Landon RW											
Blues	Finland	37	8	11	19	80	....	....	....	....	....
WISEMAN, Chad LW (NYR)											
Hartford	AHL	60	17	16	33	74	6	1	1	2	6
WITT, Brendan D (WSH.)											
Bracknell	Britain-2	3	1	4	5	0	....	....	....	....	....
WOOLLEY, Jason D											
Flint	UHL	9	4	2	6	4	....	....	....	....	....
WORRELL, Peter LW				DID NOT PLAY							
WRIGHT, Tyler C (CBJ)											
Biel	Swiss-2	7	3	2	5	4	12	8	8	16	44
YABLONSKI, Jeremy LW (NSH.)											
Milwaukee	AHL	32	3	2	5	116	....	....	....	....	....
YAKUBOV, Mikhail C (CHI.)											
Norfolk	AHL	59	12	15	27	43	3	0	0	0	0
YASHIN, Alexei C (NYI)											
Russia	W-Cup	4	1	2	3	4	....	....	....	....	....
Yaroslavl	Russia	10	3	3	6	14	9	3	7	10	10
Russia	WC-A	9	2	1	3	8	....	....	....	....	....
YELLE, Stephane C (CGY.)				DID NOT PLAY							
YONKMAN, Nolan D (WSH.)											
Portland	AHL	32	0	3	3	68	....	....	....	....	....
YORK, Jason D				DID NOT PLAY							
YORK, Mike LW (NYI)											
Iserlohn	Germany	52	16	46	62	77	....	....	....	....	....
United States	WC-A	7	0	1	1	0	....	....	....	....	....
YOUNG, Scott RW											
Memphis	CHL	3	2	1	3	0	....	....	....	....	....
YZERMAN, Steve C (DET.)											
Canada	W-Cup				DID NOT PLAY – INJURED						
ZALESAK, Miroslav RW (WSH.)											
Skalica	Slovakia	18	11	14	25	18	....	....	....	....	....
Litvinov	CzRep	30	6	6	12	26	6	1	1	2	0
ZAMUNER, Rob LW											
Basel	Swiss-2	40	10	24	34	91	12	7	7	14	24
ZEDNIK, Richard RW (MTL.)											
Slovakia	W-Cup	3	0	0	0	0	....	....	....	....	....
Zvolen	Slovakia	36	15	19	34	56	17	9	10	19	12
Slovakia	WC-A	7	1	1	2	10	....	....	....	....	....
ZETTERBERG, Henrik LW (DET.)											
Sweden	W-Cup	4	1	1	2	4	....	....	....	....	....
Timra	Sweden	50	19	31	50	24	7	6	2	8	2
Sweden	WC-A	9	2	4	6	4	....	....	....	....	....
ZHAMNOV, Alex C (BOS.)											
Chekhov	Russia-2	24	5	22	27	20	14	7	7	14	10
ZHERDEV, Nikolai W (CBJ)											
CSKA	Russia	51	19	21	40	62	....	....	....	....	....
ZHITNIK, Alexei D (NYI)											
Kazan	Russia	23	1	8	9	30	4	0	0	0	2
ZIDLICKY, Marek D (NSH.)											
Czech Republic	W-Cup	5	3	1	4	2	....	....	....	....	....
HIFK	Finland	49	11	20	31	91	5	0	3	3	14
Czech Republic	WC-A	9	1	3	4	18	....	....	....	....	....
ZIGOMANIS, Mike C (CAR.)											
Lowell	AHL	76	29	31	60	71	11	4	7	11	8
ZINGER, Dwayne D (WSH.)											
Portland	AHL	58	0	4	4	118	....	....	....	....	....
ZINOVJEV, Sergei C/LW (BOS.)											
Kazan	Russia	54	17	21	38	82	4	1	0	1	12
ZIZKA, Tomas D (L.A.)											
Spartak	Russia	23	0	3	3	32	....	....	....	....	....
Slavia	CzRep	26	2	4	6	26	2	0	0	0	2
ZUBOV, Sergei D (DAL.)				DID NOT PLAY							
ZUBRUS, Dainius RW (WSH.)											
Russia	W-Cup	4	2	1	3	4	....	....	....	....	....
Togliatti	Russia	42	8	11	19	85	10	3	1	4	22
Lithuania	WC-B	4	3	1	4	2	....	....	....	....	....
ZYUZIN, Andrei D (MIN.)											
Ufa	Russia	14	2	1	3	6	....	....	....	....	....
Cherepovets	Russia	10	2	1	3	8	....	....	....	....	....

NHL 2004-05 Goaltender Register

2004-05 Statistics for Goaltenders
on NHL Rosters in 2003-04

Team	League	GP	W	L	T	MIN	GA	SO	Avg.	GP	W	L	Min.	GA	SO	Avg.
AEBISCHER, David (COL.)																
Lugano	Swiss	18	12	2	3	1019	41	0	2.41	4	1	3	240	10	0	2.50
Chur	Swiss-2	....	....	....	....	....	....	....	....	2	....	....	130	4	0	1.84
Switzerland	WC-A	1	0	0	1	60	3	0	3.00							
AHONEN, Ari (N.J.)																
Albany	AHL	38	16	20	1	2195	114	4	3.12							
ANDERSON, Craig (CHI.)																
Norfolk	AHL	15	9	4	1	886	27	2	1.83	6	2	4	356	14	0	2.36
AUBIN, Jean-Sebastien (TOR.)																
St. John's	AHL	23	12	9	0	1336	64	3	2.87	1	0	0	47	1	0	1.27
AULD, Alex (VAN.)																
Manitoba	AHL	50	25	18	4	2764	118	2	2.56	3	0	2	128	7	0	3.29
BACASHIHUA, Jason (ST.L.)																
Worcester	AHL	35	18	13	1	1909	80	2	2.51							
BELFOUR, Ed (TOR.)																
Canada	W-Cup					DID NOT PLAY – INJURED										
BIERK, Zac						DID NOT PLAY										
BIRON, Martin (BUF.)						DID NOT PLAY										
BOUCHER, Brian (PHX.)																
HV 71	Sweden	4	....	....	....	235	13	0	3.32							
BRATHWAITE, Fred																
Kazan	Russia	34	....	....	....	1958	61	9	1.87	2	....	....	128	2	1	0.94
BROCHU, Martin						DID NOT PLAY										
BRODEUR, Martin (N.J.)																
Canada	W-Cup	5	5	0	0	300	5	1	1.00							
Canada	WC-A	7	5	2	0	419	20	0	2.87							
BRYZGALOV, Ilya (ANA.)																
Russia	W-Cup	3	2	1	0	180	7	0	2.34							
Cincinnati	AHL	36	17	13	1	2007	87	4	2.60	7	3	3	314	13	0	2.48
BURKE, Sean (T.B.)						DID NOT PLAY										
CARON, Sebastian (PIT.)																
Saguenay	QNAHL					STATISTICS NOT AVAILABLE										
CASSIVI, Frederic (WSH.)																
Cincinnati	AHL	46	25	18	2	2549	88	10	2.07	8	2	4	444	21	0	2.84
CECHMANEK, Roman																
Czech Republic	W-Cup					DID NOT PLAY – SPARE GOALTENDER										
Vsetin	CzRep	35	....	....	....	1974	88	3	2.67							
CHARPENTIER, Sebastien						DID NOT PLAY										
CHIODO, Andy (PIT.)																
Wheeling	ECHL	22	9	10	2	1259	47	1	2.24							
Wilkes-Barre	AHL	14	5	7	1	788	43	2	3.27	9	5	4	556	23	1	2.48
CHOUINARD, Mathieu																
Cincinnati	AHL	3	1	1	0	153	4	1	1.57							
San Diego	ECHL	27	11	9	3	1453	73	1	3.01							
Peoria	ECHL	1	0	1	0	58	2	0	2.07							
CLEMMENSEN, Scott (N.J.)																
Albany	AHL	46	13	25	5	2645	124	2	2.81							
CLOUTIER, Dan (VAN.)																
Klagenfurt	Austria	13	7	0	5	772	25	1	1.94	10	6	4	590	27	1	2.75
CONKLIN, Ty (EDM.)																
United States	W-Cup					DID NOT PLAY – SPARE GOALTENDER										
Wolfsburg	Germany	11	....	....	....	623	31	0	2.99	7	....	....	414	11	2	1.59
United States	WC-A	3	1	0	2	180	6	0	2.00							
DAFOE, Byron						DID NOT PLAY										
DENIS, Marc (CBJ)						DID NOT PLAY										
DiPIETRO, Rick (NYI)																
United States	W-Cup	1	1	0	0	60	1	0	1.00							
United States	WC-A	4	2	2	0	250	7	1	1.68							
DIVIS, Reinhard (ST.L.)																
Villacher SV	Austria	26	10	10	4	1482	61	2	2.47	3	0	3	169	12	0	4.26
DUBIELEWICZ, Wade (NYI)																
Bridgeport	AHL	43	18	23	1	2539	113	1	2.67							

Team	League	GP	W	L	T	MIN	GA	SO	Avg.	GP	W	L	Min.	GA	SO	Avg.
DUNHAM, Mike (ATL.)																
Skelleftea	Sweden-2	13	....	....	....	726	36	4	2.97							
ELLIS, Dan (DAL.)																
Hamilton	AHL	31	10	19	0	1774	82	1	2.77							
EMERY, Ray (OTT.)																
Binghamton	AHL	51	28	18	5	2993	132	0	2.65	6	2	4	409	14	0	2.05
ESCHE, Robert (PHI.)																
United States	W-Cup	4	1	3	0	237	10	0	2.53							
FERNANDEZ, Manny (MIN.)																
Lulea	Sweden	19	....	....	....	1083	50	2	2.77	3	....	....	159	13	0	4.90
FLAHERTY, Wade (VAN.)																
Manitoba	AHL	36	19	10	3	2010	78	4	2.33	12	8	4	720	29	2	2.42
FLEURY, Marc-Andre (PIT.)																
Wilkes-Barre	AHL	54	26	19	4	3029	127	5	2.52	4	0	2	151	11	0	4.36
GARON, Mathieu (L.A.)																
Manchester	AHL	52	32	14	4	2969	105	8	2.12	6	2	4	285	17	0	3.58
GERBER, Martin (CAR.)																
Langnau	Swiss	20	6	10	4	1220	59	0	2.90							
Farjestad	Sweden	30	20	6	4	1827	58	4	1.90	15	9	6	900	36	1	2.40
Switzerland	WC-A	6	3	3	0	359	10	1	1.67							
GIGUERE, Jean-Sebastien (ANA.)																
Hamburg	Germany	6	....	....	....	301	12	0	2.39	2	....	....	100	7	0	4.20
GRAHAME, John (T.B.)						DID NOT PLAY										
HACKETT, Jeff						DID NOT PLAY										
HASEK, Dominik (OTT.)						DID NOT PLAY										
HEDBERG, Johan (DAL.)																
Leksand	Sweden-2	21	....	....	....	1274	45	1	2.12							
HNILICKA, Milan																
Liberec	CzRep	46	....	....	....	2740	106	5	2.32	12	....	....	702	32	0	2.74
Czech Republic	WC-A	1	1	0	0	60	0	1	0.00							
HOLMQVIST, Johan																
Brynas	Sweden	42	....	....	....	2445	138	1	3.39							
Sweden	WC-A	1	0	1	0	40	3	0	4.50							
HUET, Cristobal (MTL.)																
Mannheim	Germany	36	....	....	....	2001	93	1	2.79	14	....	....	850	40	2	2.82
IRBE, Arturs																
Latvia	WC-A	6	2	3	1	283	7	1	1.48							
JOHNSON, Brent (VAN.)						DID NOT PLAY										
JOSEPH, Curtis (PHX.)						DID NOT PLAY										
KHABIBULIN, Nikolai (CHI.)																
Kazan	Russia	24	....	....	....	1457	40	5	1.65	2	....	....	118	6	0	3.04
KIDD, Trevor																
Orebro	Sweden-3	8	....	....	....	480	19	2	2.37							
KIPRUSOFF, Miikka (CGY.)																
Finland	W-Cup	6	4	1	1	364	9	2	1.48							
Timra	Sweden	46	....	....	....	2719	97	5	2.14	6	....	....	356	13	0	2.19
KOCHAN, Dieter																
Bridgeport	AHL	39	19	19	0	2303	102	2	2.66							
KOLZIG, Olie (WSH.)																
Germany	W-Cup	3	0	3	0	180	10	0	3.34							
Eisbaren Berlin	Germany	8	....	....	....	452	19	2	2.52	3	....	....	178	7	1	2.36
KOTYK, Seamus																
Milwaukee	AHL	23	10	6	1	1138	56	0	2.95	1	0	0	0	0	0	0.00
Rockford	UHL	6	5	1	0	358	6	1	1.00							
KRAHN, Brent (CGY.)																
Lowell	AHL	35	20	11	2	1998	83	6	2.49	1			0	0	0	0.00
LABARBERA, Jason (L.A.)																
Hartford	AHL	53	31	16	2	2937	90	6	1.84	4	1	3	238	9	0	2.27
LALIME, Patrick (ST.L.)						DID NOT PLAY										
LAMOTHE, Marc																
Yaroslavl	Russia	55	....	....	....	3357	90	6	1.61	9	....	....	521	21	0	2.42
LECLAIRE, Pascal (CBJ)																
Syracuse	AHL	14	5	6	3	845	33	2	2.34							

Team	League	GP	W	L	T	MIN	GA	SO	Avg.	GP	W	L	Min.	GA	SO	Avg.
LEGACE, Manny (DET.)																
Voskresensk	Russia	2	..	..	..	89	10	0	6.73	..	..	..	..	..	..	..
LEHTONEN, Kari (ATL.)																
Finland	W-Cup					DID NOT PLAY – SPARE GOALTENDER										
Chicago	AHL	57	38	17	2	3378	128	5	2.27	16	10	6	983	28	2	1.71
LEIGHTON, Michael (CHI.)																
Norfolk	AHL	41	20	16	3	2319	78	7	2.02							
LITTLE, Neil																
Philadelphia	AHL	26	15	7	0	1383	54	3	2.34	2	1	0	25	0	0	0.00
LUONGO, Roberto (FLA.)																
Canada	W-Cup	1	1	0	0	64	3	0	2.82							
Canada	WC-A	2	1	0	1	120	3	1	1.50							
MARKKANEN, Jussi (EDM.)																
Togliatti	Russia	54	..	..	..	3157	63	11	1.20	10	..	..	627	15	1	1.44
MASON, Chris (NSH.)																
Valerengen	Norway	20	..	..	..	1204	36	1	1.79	11	..	..	657	22	1	2.01
McLENNAN, Jamie (FLA.)																
Guildford	Britain-2	3	2	1	0	185	8	0	2.59	7	4	3	385	13	0	2.02
MILLER, Ryan (BUF.)																
Rochester	AHL	63	41	17	4	3741	153	8	2.45	9	5	4	547	24	0	2.63
MORRISON, Mike (EDM.)																
Greenville	ECHL	26	13	10	2	1576	72	1	2.74	1	1	1	150	9	0	3.61
Edmonton	AHL	14	4	5	5	728	21	2	1.73							
MOSS, Tyler																
Edmonton	AHL	50	24	19	4	2870	126	5	2.63							
MUNRO, Adam (CHI.)																
Norfolk	AHL	30	14	10	2	1595	66	4	2.48							
Atlantic City	ECHL	5	2	2	1	272	9	0	1.99							
NABOKOV, Evgeni (S.J.)																
Russia	W-Cup					DID NOT PLAY – INJURED										
Magnitogorsk	Russia	14	..	..	..	808	27	3	2.00	5	..	..	307	13	0	2.53
NIITTYMAKI, Antero (PHI.)																
Philadelphia	AHL	58	33	21	4	3453	119	6	2.07	21	15	5	1269	37	3	1.75
NORONEN, Mika (BUF.)																
HPK	Finland	27	14	8	4	1615	54	1	2.01	9	4	4	482	21	1	2.61
NURMINEN, Pasi																
Pelicans	Finland	16	2	7	6	966	48	0	2.98							
Malmo	Sweden	30	..	..	..	1755	86	3	2.94							
Malmo	Sweden-Q	10	..	..	..	578	20	0	2.08							
Finland	WC-A					DID NOT PLAY – SPARE GOALTENDER										
OSAER, Phil																
San Antonio	AHL	3	1	1	0	121	9	0	4.45							
Texas	ECHL	42	10	27	3	2421	125	1	3.10							
OSGOOD, Chris (DET.)						DID NOT PLAY										
OUELLET, Maxime (WSH.)																
Portland	AHL	40	15	20	3	2305	111	0	2.89							
PASSMORE, Steve (PHX.)																
Mannheim	Germany	21	..	..	..	1110	48	0	2.59							
PELLETIER, Jean-Marc (FLA.)																
Utah	AHL	23	6	12	1	1231	77	0	3.75							
Springfield	AHL	13	2	10	1	715	35	0	2.94							
POTVIN, Felix						DID NOT PLAY										
PRUSEK, Martin (CBJ.)																
Czech Republic	W-Cup					DID NOT PLAY – INJURED										
Vitkovice	CzRep	14	..	..	..	672	28	0	2.50							
Znojmo	CzRep	8	..	..	..	453	18	0	2.38							
RAYCROFT, Andrew (BOS.)																
Tappara	Finland	11	4	5	2	658	32	1	2.92	3	..	0	2	104	11	0	6.36
ROLOSON, Dwayne (MIN.)																
Lukko	Finland	34	20	10	4	2049	70	4	2.05	9	4	5	512	18	2	2.11
SABOURIN, Dany (PIT.)																
Wilkes-Barre	AHL	20	8	8	2	1029	38	1	2.22							
Wheeling	ECHL	27	19	6	1	1579	44	5	1.67							
SALO, Tommy																
Sweden	W-Cup	1	1	0	0	60	2	0	2.00							
MODO	Sweden	36	..	..	..	2165	93	0	2.58	6	..	..	358	19	1	3.18
SANFORD, Curtis (ST.L.)																
Worcester	AHL	50	19	25	2	2743	123	2	2.69							
SAUVE, Philippe (CGY.)																
Mississippi	ECHL	21	13	4	4	1298	56	2	2.59	4	1	3	227	16	0	4.23
SCHAEFER, Nolan (S.J.)																
Cleveland	AHL	43	17	23	1	2418	110	3	2.73							
SCHWAB, Corey						DID NOT PLAY										
SCOTT, Travis																
San Antonio	AHL	59	18	28	4	3211	126	3	2.35							
SHIELDS, Steve						DID NOT PLAY										
SMITH, Mike (DAL.)																
Houston	AHL	45	19	17	3	2408	97	5	2.42	3	1	2	181	4	0	1.33
SNOW, Garth (NYI)																
St. Petersburg	Russia	16	..	..	..	893	41	1	2.75							
STANA, Rastislav (WSH.)																
Slovakia	W-Cup	2	0	1	0	88	6	0	4.08							
Sodertalje	Sweden	45	..	..	..	2562	116	3	2.72	10	..	..	605	22	1	2.18
Slovakia	WC-A	2	1	1	0	92	6	0	3.90							
STORR, Jamie (PHI.)																
Springfield	AHL	30	8	20	2	1697	91	0	3.22							
Utah	AHL	16	6	7	1	885	36	1	2.44							
TELLQVIST, Mikael (TOR.)																
Sweden	W-Cup	3	1	1	1	179	12	0	4.03							
St. John's	AHL	45	24	16	4	2600	115	0	2.65	5	1	4	253	15	0	3.56
THEODORE, Jose (MTL.)																
Canada	W-Cup					DID NOT PLAY – SPARE GOALTENDER										
Djurgarden	Sweden	17	..	..	..	1024	42	0	2.46	12	..	..	728	27	0	2.23
THIBAULT, Jocelyn (PIT.)						DID NOT PLAY										
THOMAS, Tim																
Jokerit	Finland	54	34	13	7	3267	86	15	1.58	12	8	4	721	22	0	1.83
United States	WC-A					DID NOT PLAY – SPARE GOALTENDER										
TOSKALA, Vesa (S.J.)																
Finland	W-Cup					DID NOT PLAY – SPARE GOALTENDER										
Ilves	Finland	3	0	1	2	186	8	0	2.58	6	3	3	358	19	0	3.19
TUGNUTT, Ron						DID NOT PLAY										
TURCO, Marty (DAL.)																
Djurgarden	Sweden	6	..	..	..	356	12	1	2.02							
Canada	WC-A					DID NOT PLAY – SPARE GOALTENDER										
TUREK, Roman																
C. Budejovice	CzRep-2	15	..	..	..	859	23	3	1.61	11	..	..	650	12	6	1.11
UNDERHILL, Matt																
Mississippi	ECHL	24	13	8	3	1450	64	3	2.65							
St. John's	AHL	1	0	0	1	39	0	0	0.00							
Providence	AHL	5	1	2	1	244	12	1	2.95							
Alaska	ECHL	3	3	0	0	180	6	0	2.00	1	1	1	145	8	0	3.31
VALIQUETTE, Stephen																
Hartford	AHL	35	19	11	1	1900	56	7	1.77	2	1	1	118	4	0	2.03
VOKOUN, Tomas (NSH.)																
Czech Republic	W-Cup	5	2	3	0	302	15	0	2.98							
Znojmo	CzRep	27	..	..	..	1599	69	3	2.59							
HIFK	Finland	19	11	4	4	1149	35	2	1.83	4	0	3	205	12	0	3.51
Czech Republic	WC-A	8	7	1	0	499	9	2	1.08							
WEEKES, Kevin (NYR)						DID NOT PLAY										
YEATS, Matthew																
Reading	ECHL	13	8	2	2	780	31	1	2.38							
Idaho	ECHL	4	2	1	1	247	9	0	2.19	2	0	1	66	3	0	2.72

NHL Record Book

Year-By-Year Final Standings & Leading Scorers

*Stanley Cup winner

1917-18

First Half

Team	GP	W	L	T	GF	GA	PTS
Montreal	14	10	4	0	81	47	20
Toronto	14	8	6	0	71	75	16
Ottawa	14	5	9	0	67	79	10
**Mtl. Wanderers	6	1	5	0	17	35	2

**Montreal Arena burned down and Wanderers forced to withdraw from League. Montreal Canadiens and Toronto each counted a win for defaulted games with Wanderers.

Second Half

Team	GP	W	L	T	GF	GA	PTS
*Toronto	8	5	3	0	37	34	10
Ottawa	8	4	4	0	35	35	8
Montreal	8	3	5	0	34	37	6

Leading Scorers

Player	Club	GP	G	A	PTS	PIM
Malone, Joe	Montreal	20	44	4	48	30
Denneny, Cy	Ottawa	20	36	10	46	80
Noble, Reg	Toronto	20	30	10	40	35
Lalonde, Newsy	Montreal	14	23	7	30	51
Denneny, Corb	Toronto	21	20	9	29	14
Cameron, Harry	Toronto	21	17	10	27	28
Pitre, Didier	Montreal	20	17	6	23	29
Gerard, Eddie	Ottawa	20	13	7	20	26
Darragh, Jack	Ottawa	18	14	5	19	26
Nighbor, Frank	Ottawa	10	11	8	19	6
Meeking, Harry	Toronto	21	10	9	19	28

1918-19

First Half

Team	GP	W	L	T	GF	GA	PTS
• Montreal	10	7	3	0	57	50	14
Ottawa	10	5	5	0	39	39	10
Toronto	10	3	7	0	42	49	6

Second Half

Team	GP	W	L	T	GF	GA	PTS
Ottawa	8	7	1	0	32	14	14
Montreal	8	3	5	0	31	28	6
Toronto	8	2	6	0	22	43	4

• NHL Champion. Stanley Cup not awarded due to influenza epidemic.

Leading Scorers

Player	Club	GP	G	A	PTS	PIM
Lalonde, Newsy	Montreal	17	22	10	32	40
Cleghorn, Odie	Montreal	17	22	6	28	22
Nighbor, Frank	Ottawa	18	19	9	28	27
Denneny, Cy	Ottawa	18	18	4	22	58
Pitre, Didier	Montreal	17	14	5	19	12
Skinner, Alf	Toronto	17	12	4	16	26
Cameron, Harry	Tor., Ott.	14	11	3	14	35
Darragh, Jack	Ottawa	14	11	3	14	33
Randall, Ken	Toronto	15	8	6	14	27
Cleghorn, Sprague	Ottawa	18	7	6	13	27

1919-20

First Half

Team	GP	W	L	T	GF	GA	PTS
Ottawa	12	9	3	0	59	23	18
Montreal	12	8	4	0	62	51	16
Toronto	12	5	7	0	52	62	10
Quebec	12	2	10	0	44	81	4

Second Half

Team	GP	W	L	T	GF	GA	PTS
*Ottawa	12	10	2	0	62	41	20
Toronto	12	7	5	0	67	44	14
Montreal	12	5	7	0	67	62	10
Quebec	12	2	10	0	47	96	4

Leading Scorers

Player	Club	GP	G	A	PTS	PIM
Malone, Joe	Quebec	24	39	10	49	12
Lalonde, Newsy	Montreal	23	37	9	46	34
Nighbor, Frank	Ottawa	23	26	15	41	18
Denneny, Corb	Toronto	24	24	12	36	20
Darragh, Jack	Ottawa	23	22	14	36	22
Noble, Reg	Toronto	24	24	9	33	52
Arbour, Amos	Montreal	22	21	5	26	13
Wilson, Cully	Toronto	23	20	6	26	86
Pitre, Didier	Montreal	22	14	12	26	6
Broadbent, Punch	Ottawa	21	19	6	25	40

1920-21

First Half

Team	GP	W	L	T	GF	GA	PTS
*Ottawa	10	8	2	0	49	23	16
Toronto	10	5	5	0	39	47	10
Montreal	10	4	6	0	37	51	8
Hamilton	10	3	7	0	34	38	6

Second Half

Team	GP	W	L	T	GF	GA	PTS
Toronto	14	10	4	0	66	53	20
Montreal	14	9	5	0	75	48	18
Ottawa	14	6	8	0	48	52	12
Hamilton	14	3	11	0	58	94	6

Leading Scorers

Player	Club	GP	G	A	PTS	PIM
Lalonde, Newsy	Montreal	24	33	10	43	36
Dye, Babe	Ham., Tor.	24	35	5	40	32
Denneny, Cy	Ottawa	24	34	5	39	10
Malone, Joe	Hamilton	20	28	9	37	6
Nighbor, Frank	Ottawa	24	19	10	29	10
Noble, Reg	Toronto	24	19	8	27	54
Cameron, Harry	Toronto	24	18	9	27	35
Prodgers, Goldie	Hamilton	24	18	9	27	8
Denneny, Corb	Toronto	20	19	7	26	29
Darragh, Jack	Ottawa	24	11	15	26	20

All-Time Standings of NHL Teams

(ranked by percentage)

Active Clubs

Team	Games	Wins	Losses	Ties	OT Losses	Goals For	Goals Against	Points	Pts %	First Season
Montreal	5546	2849	1834	837	26	18285	14786	6561	.590	1917-18
Philadelphia	2932	1468	988	457	19	10031	8557	3412	.578	1967-68
Boston	5386	2564	1997	791	34	17453	15889	5953	.550	1924-25
Buffalo	2706	1257	1022	409	18	9076	8252	2941	.540	1970-71
Edmonton	1994	940	763	262	29	7387	6791	2171	.538	1979-80
Calgary	2550	1142	1010	379	19	8791	8311	2682	.521	1972-73
Detroit	5320	2359	2130	815	16	16536	15974	5549	.519	1926-27
Colorado	1994	897	815	261	21	6900	6692	2076	.514	1979-80
St. Louis	2932	1288	1194	432	18	9352	9316	3026	.511	1967-68
Toronto	5546	2418	2327	783	18	17193	17051	5637	.506	1917-18
NY Islanders	2550	1112	1077	347	14	8589	8177	2585	.503	1972-73
NY Rangers	5320	2231	2261	808	20	16477	16716	5290	.495	1926-27
Dallas	2932	1205	1249	459	19	9175	9514	2888	.489	1967-68
Chicago	5320	2176	2308	814	22	15843	16136	5188	.486	1926-27
Washington	2394	1011	1063	303	17	7657	8011	2342	.485	1974-75
Pittsburgh	2932	1199	1327	383	23	9938	10559	2804	.474	1967-68
Los Angeles	2932	1161	1321	424	26	9738	10367	2772	.469	1967-68
Minnesota	328	123	132	55	18	749	809	319	.464	2000-01
Ottawa	954	383	436	115	20	2655	2864	901	.462	1992-93
Phoenix	1994	785	919	266	24	6497	7139	1860	.461	1979-80
Florida	870	322	372	142	34	2224	2442	820	.459	1993-94
New Jersey	2394	934	1112	328	20	7399	8145	2216	.457	1974-75
Anaheim	870	338	400	107	25	2220	2438	808	.452	1993-94
Vancouver	2706	1024	1267	391	24	8658	9528	2463	.450	1970-71
Carolina	1994	761	950	263	20	6103	6873	1805	.447	1979-80
San Jose	1034	382	504	121	27	2810	3268	912	.431	1991-92
Nashville	492	183	228	60	21	1170	1354	447	.430	1998-99
Tampa Bay	954	328	487	112	27	2421	2994	795	.408	1992-93
Columbus	328	104	173	33	18	744	989	259	.371	2000-01
Atlanta	410	120	225	45	20	1008	1417	305	.349	1999-2000

Defunct Clubs

Team	Games	Wins	Losses	Ties	Goals For	Goals Against	Points	Pts %	First Season	Last Season
Ottawa Senators	542	258	221	63	1458	1333	579	.534	1917-18	1933-34
Montreal Maroons	622	271	260	91	1474	1405	633	.509	1924-25	1937-38
NY/Brooklyn Americans	784	255	402	127	1643	2182	637	.406	1925-26	1941-42
Hamilton Tigers	126	47	78	1	414	475	95	.377	1920-21	1924-25
Cleveland Barons	160	47	87	26	470	617	120	.375	1976-77	1977-78
Pittsburgh Pirates	212	67	122	23	376	519	157	.370	1925-26	1929-30
Calif./Oakland Seals	698	182	401	115	1826	2580	479	.343	1967-68	1975-76
St. Louis Eagles	48	11	31	6	86	144	28	.292	1934-35	1934-35
Quebec Bulldogs	24	4	20	0	91	177	8	.167	1919-20	1919-20
Montreal Wanderers	6	1	5	0	17	35	2	.167	1917-18	1917-18
Philadelphia Quakers	44	4	36	4	76	184	12	.136	1930-31	1930-31

Calgary totals include Atlanta Flames, 1972-73 to 1979-80.
Carolina totals include Hartford, 1979-80 to 1996-97.
Colorado totals include Quebec, 1979-80 to 1994-95.
Dallas totals include Minnesota North Stars, 1967-68 to 1992-93.
Detroit totals include Cougars, 1926-27 to 1929-30, and Falcons, 1930-31 to 1931-32.
New Jersey totals include Kansas City, 1974-75 to 1975-76, and Colorado Rockies, 1976-77 to 1981-82.
Phoenix totals include Winnipeg, 1979-80 to 1995-96.
Toronto totals include Arenas, 1917-18 to 1918-19, and St. Patricks, 1919-20 to 1925-26.

1921-22

Team	GP	W	L	T	GF	GA	PTS
Ottawa	24	14	8	2	106	84	30
*Toronto	24	13	10	1	98	97	27
Montreal	24	12	11	1	88	94	25
Hamilton	24	7	17	0	88	105	14

Leading Scorers

Player	Club	GP	G	A	PTS	PIM
Broadbent, Punch	Ottawa	24	32	14	46	28
Denneny, Cy	Ottawa	22	27	12	39	20
Dye, Babe	Toronto	24	31	7	38	39
Cameron, Harry	Toronto	24	18	17	35	22
Malone, Joe	Hamilton	24	24	7	31	4
Denneny, Corb	Toronto	24	19	9	28	28
Noble, Reg	Toronto	24	17	11	28	19
Cleghorn, Sprague	Montreal	24	17	9	26	80
Boucher, Georges	Ottawa	23	13	12	25	12
Cleghorn, Odie	Montreal	23	21	3	24	26

1922-23

Team	GP	W	L	T	GF	GA	PTS
*Ottawa	24	14	9	1	77	54	29
Montreal	24	13	9	2	73	61	28
Toronto	24	13	10	1	82	88	27
Hamilton	24	6	18	0	81	110	12

Leading Scorers

Player	Club	GP	G	A	PTS	PIM
Dye, Babe	Toronto	22	26	11	37	19
Denneny, Cy	Ottawa	24	23	11	34	28
Boucher, Billy	Montreal	24	24	7	31	55
Adams, Jack	Toronto	23	19	9	28	42
Roach, Mickey	Hamilton	24	17	10	27	8
Cleghorn, Odie	Montreal	24	19	6	25	14
Boucher, Georges	Ottawa	24	14	9	23	58
Noble, Reg	Toronto	24	12	11	23	47
Wilson, Cully	Hamilton	23	16	5	21	46
Joliat, Aurel	Montreal	24	12	9	21	37

1923-24

Team	GP	W	L	T	GF	GA	PTS
Ottawa	24	16	8	0	74	54	32
*Montreal	24	13	11	0	59	48	26
Toronto	24	10	14	0	59	85	20
Hamilton	24	9	15	0	63	68	18

Leading Scorers

Player	Club	GP	G	A	PTS	PIM
Denneny, Cy	Ottawa	22	22	2	24	10
Boucher, Georges	Ottawa	21	13	10	23	38
Boucher, Billy	Montreal	23	16	6	22	48
Burch, Billy	Hamilton	24	16	6	22	6
Joliat, Aurel	Montreal	24	15	5	20	27
Dye, Babe	Toronto	19	16	3	19	23
Adams, Jack	Toronto	22	14	4	18	51
Noble, Reg	Toronto	23	12	5	17	79
Morenz, Howie	Montreal	24	13	3	16	20
Clancy, King	Ottawa	24	8	8	16	26

1924-25

Team	GP	W	L	T	GF	GA	PTS
Hamilton	30	19	10	1	90	60	39
Toronto	30	19	11	0	90	84	38
• Montreal	30	17	11	2	93	56	36
Ottawa	30	17	12	1	83	66	35
Mtl. Maroons	30	9	19	2	45	65	20
Boston	30	6	24	0	49	119	12

• NHL Champion (Stanley Cup won by Victoria Cougars, WCHL)

Leading Scorers

Player	Club	GP	G	A	PTS	PIM
Dye, Babe	Toronto	29	38	8	46	41
Denneny, Cy	Ottawa	29	27	15	42	16
Joliat, Aurel	Montreal	25	30	11	41	85
Morenz, Howie	Montreal	30	28	11	39	46
Green, Red	Hamilton	30	19	15	34	81
Adams, Jack	Toronto	27	21	10	31	67
Boucher, Billy	Montreal	30	17	13	30	92
Burch, Billy	Hamilton	27	20	7	27	10
Herberts, Jimmy	Boston	30	17	7	24	55
Smith, Hooley	Ottawa	30	10	13	23	81

1925-26

Team	GP	W	L	T	GF	GA	PTS
Ottawa	36	24	8	4	77	42	52
*Mtl. Maroons	36	20	11	5	91	73	45
Pittsburgh	36	19	16	1	82	70	39
Boston	36	17	15	4	92	85	38
NY Americans	36	12	20	4	68	89	28
Toronto	36	12	21	3	92	114	27
Montreal	36	11	24	1	79	108	23

Leading Scorers

Player	Club	GP	G	A	PTS	PIM
Stewart, Nels	Mtl. Maroons	36	34	8	42	119
Denneny, Cy	Ottawa	36	24	12	36	18
Cooper, Carson	Boston	36	28	3	31	10
Herberts, Jimmy	Boston	36	26	5	31	47
Morenz, Howie	Montreal	31	23	3	26	39
Adams, Jack	Toronto	36	21	5	26	52
Joliat, Aurel	Montreal	35	17	9	26	52
Burch, Billy	NY Americans	36	22	3	25	33
Smith, Hooley	Ottawa	28	16	9	25	53
Nighbor, Frank	Ottawa	35	12	13	25	40

1926-27

Canadian Division

Team	GP	W	L	T	GF	GA	PTS
*Ottawa	44	30	10	4	86	69	64
Montreal	44	28	14	2	99	67	58
Mtl. Maroons	44	20	20	4	71	68	44
NY Americans	44	17	25	2	82	91	36
Toronto	44	15	24	5	79	94	35

American Division

Team	GP	W	L	T	GF	GA	PTS
NY Rangers	44	25	13	6	95	72	56
Boston	44	21	20	3	97	89	45
Chicago	44	19	22	3	115	116	41
Pittsburgh	44	15	26	3	79	108	33
Detroit	44	12	28	4	76	105	28

Leading Scorers

Player	Club	GP	G	A	PTS	PIM
Cook, Bill	NY Rangers	44	33	4	37	58
Irvin, Dick	Chicago	43	18	18	36	34
Morenz, Howie	Montreal	44	25	7	32	49
Fredrickson, Frank	Det., Bos.	41	18	13	31	46
Dye, Babe	Chicago	41	25	5	30	14
Bailey, Ace	Toronto	42	15	13	28	82
Boucher, Frank	NY Rangers	44	13	15	28	17
Burch, Billy	NY Americans	43	19	8	27	40
Oliver, Harry	Boston	42	18	6	24	17
Keats, Duke	Bos., Det.	42	16	8	24	52

1927-28

Canadian Division

Team	GP	W	L	T	GF	GA	PTS
Montreal	44	26	11	7	116	48	59
Mtl. Maroons	44	24	14	6	96	77	54
Ottawa	44	20	14	10	78	57	50
Toronto	44	18	18	8	89	88	44
NY Americans	44	11	27	6	63	128	28

American Division

Team	GP	W	L	T	GF	GA	PTS
Boston	44	20	13	11	77	70	51
*NY Rangers	44	19	16	9	94	79	47
Pittsburgh	44	19	17	8	67	76	46
Detroit	44	19	19	6	88	79	44
Chicago	44	7	34	3	68	134	17

Leading Scorers

Player	Club	GP	G	A	PTS	PIM
Morenz, Howie	Montreal	43	33	18	51	66
Joliat, Aurel	Montreal	44	28	11	39	105
Boucher, Frank	NY Rangers	44	23	12	35	15
Hay, George	Detroit	42	22	13	35	20
Stewart, Nels	Mtl. Maroons	41	27	7	34	104
Gagne, Art	Montreal	44	20	10	30	75
Cook, Bun	NY Rangers	44	14	14	28	45
Carson, Bill	Toronto	32	20	6	26	36
Finnigan, Frank	Ottawa	38	20	5	25	34
Cook, Bill	NY Rangers	43	18	6	24	42
Keats, Duke	Det., Chi.	38	14	10	24	60

1928-29

Canadian Division

Team	GP	W	L	T	GF	GA	PTS
Montreal	44	22	7	15	71	43	59
NY Americans	44	19	13	12	53	53	50
Toronto	44	21	18	5	85	69	47
Ottawa	44	14	17	13	54	67	41
Mtl. Maroons	44	15	20	9	67	65	39

American Division

Team	GP	W	L	T	GF	GA	PTS
*Boston	44	26	13	5	89	52	57
NY Rangers	44	21	13	10	72	65	52
Detroit	44	19	16	9	72	63	47
Pittsburgh	44	9	27	8	46	80	26
Chicago	44	7	29	8	33	85	22

Leading Scorers

Player	Club	GP	G	A	PTS	PIM
Bailey, Ace	Toronto	44	22	10	32	78
Stewart, Nels	Mtl. Maroons	44	21	8	29	74
Cooper, Carson	Detroit	43	18	9	27	14
Morenz, Howie	Montreal	42	17	10	27	47
Blair, Andy	Toronto	44	12	15	27	41
Boucher, Frank	NY Rangers	44	10	16	26	8
Oliver, Harry	Boston	43	17	6	23	24
Cook, Bill	NY Rangers	43	15	8	23	41
Ward, Jimmy	Mtl. Maroons	43	14	8	22	46

Seven players tied with 19 points

1929-30

Canadian Division

Team	GP	W	L	T	GF	GA	PTS
Mtl. Maroons	44	23	16	5	141	114	51
*Montreal	44	21	14	9	142	114	51
Ottawa	44	21	15	8	138	118	50
Toronto	44	17	21	6	116	124	40
NY Americans	44	14	25	5	113	161	33

American Division

Team	GP	W	L	T	GF	GA	PTS
Boston	44	38	5	1	179	98	77
Chicago	44	21	18	5	117	111	47
NY Rangers	44	17	17	10	136	143	44
Detroit	44	14	24	6	117	133	34
Pittsburgh	44	5	36	3	102	185	13

Leading Scorers

Player	Club	GP	G	A	PTS	PIM
Weiland, Cooney	Boston	44	43	30	73	27
Boucher, Frank	NY Rangers	42	26	36	62	16
Clapper, Dit	Boston	44	41	20	61	48
Cook, Bill	NY Rangers	44	29	30	59	56
Kilrea, Hec	Ottawa	44	36	22	58	72
Stewart, Nels	Mtl. Maroons	44	39	16	55	81
Morenz, Howie	Montreal	44	40	10	50	72
Himes, Normie	NY Americans	44	28	22	50	15
Lamb, Joe	Ottawa	44	29	20	49	119
Gainor, Dutch	Boston	42	18	31	49	39

1930-31

Canadian Division

Team	GP	W	L	T	GF	GA	PTS
*Montreal	44	26	10	8	129	89	60
Toronto	44	22	13	9	118	99	53
Mtl. Maroons	44	20	18	6	105	106	46
NY Americans	44	18	16	10	76	74	46
Ottawa	44	10	30	4	91	142	24

American Division

Team	GP	W	L	T	GF	GA	PTS
Boston	44	28	10	6	143	90	62
Chicago	44	24	17	3	108	78	51
NY Rangers	44	19	16	9	106	87	47
Detroit	44	16	21	7	102	105	39
Philadelphia	44	4	36	4	76	184	12

Leading Scorers

Player	Club	GP	G	A	PTS	PIM
Morenz, Howie	Montreal	39	28	23	51	49
Goodfellow, Ebbie	Detroit	44	25	23	48	32
Conacher, Charlie	Toronto	37	31	12	43	78
Cook, Bill	NY Rangers	43	30	12	42	39
Bailey, Ace	Toronto	40	23	19	42	46
Primeau, Joe	Toronto	38	9	32	41	18
Stewart, Nels	Mtl. Maroons	42	25	14	39	75
Boucher, Frank	NY Rangers	44	12	27	39	20
Weiland, Cooney	Boston	44	25	13	38	14
Cook, Bun	NY Rangers	44	18	17	35	72
Joliat, Aurel	Montreal	43	13	22	35	73

1931-32

Canadian Division

Team	GP	W	L	T	GF	GA	PTS
Montreal	48	25	16	7	128	111	57
*Toronto	48	23	18	7	155	127	53
Mtl. Maroons	48	19	22	7	142	139	45
NY Americans	48	16	24	8	95	142	40

American Division

Team	GP	W	L	T	GF	GA	PTS
NY Rangers	48	23	17	8	134	112	54
Chicago	48	18	19	11	86	101	47
Detroit	48	18	20	10	95	108	46
Boston	48	15	21	12	122	117	42

Leading Scorers

Player	Club	GP	G	A	PTS	PIM
Jackson, Busher	Toronto	48	28	25	53	63
Primeau, Joe	Toronto	46	13	37	50	25
Morenz, Howie	Montreal	48	24	25	49	46
Conacher, Charlie	Toronto	44	34	14	48	66
Cook, Bill	NY Rangers	48	34	14	48	33
Trottier, Dave	Mtl. Maroons	48	26	18	44	94
Smith, Hooley	Mtl. Maroons	43	11	33	44	49
Siebert, Babe	Mtl. Maroons	48	21	18	39	64
Clapper, Dit	Boston	48	17	22	39	21
Joliat, Aurel	Montreal	48	15	24	39	46

1932-33

Canadian Division

Team	GP	W	L	T	GF	GA	PTS
Toronto	48	24	18	6	119	111	54
Mtl. Maroons	48	22	20	6	135	119	50
Montreal	48	18	25	5	92	115	41
NY Americans	48	15	22	11	91	118	41
Ottawa	48	11	27	10	88	131	32

American Division

Team	GP	W	L	T	GF	GA	PTS
Boston	48	25	15	8	124	88	58
Detroit	48	25	15	8	111	93	58
*NY Rangers	48	23	17	8	135	107	54
Chicago	48	16	20	12	88	101	44

Leading Scorers

Player	Club	GP	G	A	PTS	PIM
Cook, Bill	NY Rangers	48	28	22	50	51
Jackson, Busher	Toronto	48	27	17	44	43
Northcott, Baldy	Mtl. Maroons	48	22	21	43	30
Smith, Hooley	Mtl. Maroons	48	20	21	41	66
Haynes, Paul	Mtl. Maroons	48	16	25	41	18
Joliat, Aurel	Montreal	48	18	21	39	53
Barry, Marty	Boston	48	24	13	37	40
Cook, Bun	NY Rangers	48	22	15	37	35
Stewart, Nels	Boston	47	18	18	36	62
Morenz, Howie	Montreal	46	14	21	35	32
Gagnon, Johnny	Montreal	48	12	23	35	64
Shore, Eddie	Boston	48	8	27	35	102
Boucher, Frank	NY Rangers	46	7	28	35	4

1933-34

Canadian Division

Team	GP	W	L	T	GF	GA	PTS
Toronto	48	26	13	9	174	119	61
Montreal	48	22	20	6	99	101	50
Mtl. Maroons	48	19	18	11	117	122	49
NY Americans	48	15	23	10	104	132	40
Ottawa	48	13	29	6	115	143	32

American Division

Team	GP	W	L	T	GF	GA	PTS
Detroit	48	24	14	10	113	98	58
*Chicago	48	20	17	11	88	83	51
NY Rangers	48	21	19	8	120	113	50
Boston	48	18	25	5	111	130	41

Leading Scorers

Player	Club	GP	G	A	PTS	PIM
Conacher, Charlie	Toronto	42	32	20	52	38
Primeau, Joe	Toronto	45	14	32	46	8
Boucher, Frank	NY Rangers	48	14	30	44	4
Barry, Marty	Boston	48	27	12	39	12
Dillon, Cecil	NY Rangers	48	13	26	39	10
Stewart, Nels	Boston	48	21	17	38	68
Jackson, Busher	Toronto	38	20	18	38	38
Joliat, Aurel	Montreal	48	22	15	37	27
Smith, Reg	Mtl. Maroons	47	18	19	37	58
Thompson, Paul	Chicago	48	20	16	36	17

1934-35

Canadian Division

Team	GP	W	L	T	GF	GA	PTS
Toronto	48	30	14	4	157	111	64
*Mtl. Maroons	48	24	19	5	123	92	53
Montreal	48	19	23	6	110	145	44
NY Americans	48	12	27	9	100	142	33
St. Louis	48	11	31	6	86	144	28

American Division

Team	GP	W	L	T	GF	GA	PTS
Boston	48	26	16	6	129	112	58
Chicago	48	26	17	5	118	88	57
NY Rangers	48	22	20	6	137	139	50
Detroit	48	19	22	7	127	114	45

Leading Scorers

Player	Club	GP	G	A	PTS	PIM
Conacher, Charlie	Toronto	47	36	21	57	24
Howe, Syd	St.L., Det.	50	22	25	47	34
Aurie, Larry	Detroit	48	17	29	46	24
Boucher, Frank	NY Rangers	48	13	32	45	2
Jackson, Busher	Toronto	42	22	22	44	27
Lewis, Herbie	Detroit	47	16	27	43	26
Chapman, Art	NY Americans	47	9	34	43	4
Barry, Marty	Boston	48	20	20	40	33
Schriner, Sweeney	NY Americans	48	18	22	40	6
Stewart, Nels	Boston	47	21	18	39	45
Thompson, Paul	Chicago	48	16	23	39	20

1935-36

Canadian Division

Team	GP	W	L	T	GF	GA	PTS
Mtl. Maroons	48	22	16	10	114	106	54
Toronto	48	23	19	6	126	106	52
NY Americans	48	16	25	7	109	122	39
Montreal	48	11	26	11	82	123	33

American Division

Team	GP	W	L	T	GF	GA	PTS
*Detroit	48	24	16	8	124	103	56
Boston	48	22	20	6	92	83	50
Chicago	48	21	19	8	93	92	50
NY Rangers	48	19	17	12	91	96	50

Leading Scorers

Player	Club	GP	G	A	PTS	PIM
Schriner, Sweeney	NY Americans	48	19	26	45	8
Barry, Marty	Detroit	48	21	19	40	16
Thompson, Paul	Chicago	45	17	23	40	19
Thoms, Bill	Toronto	48	23	15	38	29
Conacher, Charlie	Toronto	44	23	15	38	74
Smith, Hooley	Mtl. Maroons	47	19	19	38	75
Romnes, Doc	Chicago	48	13	25	38	6
Chapman, Art	NY Americans	47	10	28	38	14
Lewis, Herbie	Detroit	45	14	23	37	25
Northcott, Baldy	Mtl. Maroons	48	15	21	36	41

1936-37

Canadian Division

Team	GP	W	L	T	GF	GA	PTS
Montreal	48	24	18	6	115	111	54
Mtl. Maroons	48	22	17	9	126	110	53
Toronto	48	22	21	5	119	115	49
NY Americans	48	15	29	4	122	161	34

American Division

Team	GP	W	L	T	GF	GA	PTS
*Detroit	48	25	14	9	128	102	59
Boston	48	23	18	7	120	110	53
NY Rangers	48	19	20	9	117	106	47
Chicago	48	14	27	7	99	131	35

Leading Scorers

Player	Club	GP	G	A	PTS	PIM
Schriner, Sweeney	NY Americans	48	21	25	46	17
Apps, Syl	Toronto	48	16	29	45	10
Barry, Marty	Detroit	48	17	27	44	6
Aurie, Larry	Detroit	45	23	20	43	20
Jackson, Busher	Toronto	46	21	19	40	12
Gagnon, Johnny	Montreal	48	20	16	36	38
Gracie, Bob	Mtl. Maroons	47	11	25	36	18
Stewart, Nels	Bos., NYA	43	23	12	35	37
Thompson, Paul	Chicago	47	17	18	35	28
Cowley, Bill	Boston	46	13	22	35	4

1937-38

Canadian Division

Team	GP	W	L	T	GF	GA	PTS
Toronto	48	24	15	9	151	127	57
NY Americans	48	19	18	11	110	111	49
Montreal	48	18	17	13	123	128	49
Mtl. Maroons	48	12	30	6	101	149	30

American Division

Team	GP	W	L	T	GF	GA	PTS
Boston	48	30	11	7	142	89	67
NY Rangers	48	27	15	6	149	96	60
*Chicago	48	14	25	9	97	139	37
Detroit	48	12	25	11	99	133	35

Leading Scorers

Player	Club	GP	G	A	PTS	PIM
Drillon, Gordie	Toronto	48	26	26	52	4
Apps, Syl	Toronto	47	21	29	50	9
Thompson, Paul	Chicago	48	22	22	44	14
Mantha, Georges	Montreal	47	23	19	42	12
Dillon, Cecil	NY Rangers	48	21	18	39	6
Cowley, Bill	Boston	48	17	22	39	8
Schriner, Sweeney	NY Americans	49	21	17	38	22
Thoms, Bill	Toronto	48	14	24	38	14
Smith, Clint	NY Rangers	48	14	23	37	0
Stewart, Nels	NY Americans	48	19	17	36	29
Colville, Neil	NY Rangers	45	17	19	36	11

1938-39

Team	GP	W	L	T	GF	GA	PTS
*Boston	48	36	10	2	156	76	74
NY Rangers	48	26	16	6	149	105	58
Toronto	48	19	20	9	114	107	47
NY Americans	48	17	21	10	119	157	44
Detroit	48	18	24	6	107	128	42
Montreal	48	15	24	9	115	146	39
Chicago	48	12	28	8	91	132	32

Leading Scorers

Player	Club	GP	G	A	PTS	PIM
Blake, Toe	Montreal	48	24	23	47	10
Schriner, Sweeney	NY Americans	48	13	31	44	20
Cowley, Bill	Boston	34	8	34	42	2
Smith, Clint	NY Rangers	48	21	20	41	2
Barry, Marty	Detroit	48	13	28	41	4
Apps, Syl	Toronto	44	15	25	40	4
Anderson, Tom	NY Americans	48	13	27	40	14
Gottselig, Johnny	Chicago	48	16	23	39	15
Haynes, Paul	Montreal	47	5	33	38	27
Conacher, Roy	Boston	47	26	11	37	12
Carr, Lorne	NY Americans	46	19	18	37	16
Colville, Neil	NY Rangers	48	18	19	37	12
Watson, Phil	NY Rangers	48	15	22	37	42

1939-40

Team	GP	W	L	T	GF	GA	PTS
Boston	48	31	12	5	170	98	67
*NY Rangers	48	27	11	10	136	77	64
Toronto	48	25	17	6	134	110	56
Chicago	48	23	19	6	112	120	52
Detroit	48	16	26	6	90	126	38
NY Americans	48	15	29	4	106	140	34
Montreal	48	10	33	5	90	168	25

Leading Scorers

Player	Club	GP	G	A	PTS	PIM
Schmidt, Milt	Boston	48	22	30	52	37
Dumart, Woody	Boston	48	22	21	43	16
Bauer, Bobby	Boston	48	17	26	43	2
Drillon, Gordie	Toronto	43	21	19	40	13
Cowley, Bill	Boston	48	13	27	40	24
Hextall, Bryan	NY Rangers	48	24	15	39	52
Colville, Neil	NY Rangers	48	19	19	38	22
Howe, Syd	Detroit	46	14	23	37	17
Blake, Toe	Montreal	48	17	19	36	48
Armstrong, Murray	NY Americans	48	16	20	36	12

1940-41

Team	GP	W	L	T	GF	GA	PTS
*Boston	48	27	8	13	168	102	67
Toronto	48	28	14	6	145	99	62
Detroit	48	21	16	11	112	102	53
NY Rangers	48	21	19	8	143	125	50
Chicago	48	16	25	7	112	139	39
Montreal	48	16	26	6	121	147	38
NY Americans	48	8	29	11	99	186	27

Leading Scorers

Player	Club	GP	G	A	PTS	PIM
Cowley, Bill	Boston	46	17	45	62	16
Hextall, Bryan	NY Rangers	48	26	18	44	16
Drillon, Gordie	Toronto	42	23	21	44	2
Apps, Syl	Toronto	41	20	24	44	6
Patrick, Lynn	NY Rangers	48	20	24	44	12
Howe, Syd	Detroit	48	20	24	44	8
Colville, Neil	NY Rangers	48	14	28	42	28
Wiseman, Eddie	Boston	48	16	24	40	10
Bauer, Bobby	Boston	48	17	22	39	2
Schriner, Sweeney	Toronto	48	24	14	38	6
Conacher, Roy	Boston	40	24	14	38	7
Schmidt, Milt	Boston	44	13	25	38	23

1941-42

Team	GP	W	L	T	GF	GA	PTS
NY Rangers	48	29	17	2	177	143	60
*Toronto	48	27	18	3	158	136	57
Boston	48	25	17	6	160	118	56
Chicago	48	22	23	3	145	155	47
Detroit	48	19	25	4	140	147	42
Montreal	48	18	27	3	134	173	39
Brooklyn	48	16	29	3	133	175	35

Leading Scorers

Player	Club	GP	G	A	PTS	PIM
Hextall, Bryan	NY Rangers	48	24	32	56	30
Patrick, Lynn	NY Rangers	47	32	22	54	18
Grosso, Don	Detroit	48	23	30	53	13
Watson, Phil	NY Rangers	48	15	37	52	48
Abel, Sid	Detroit	48	18	31	49	45
Blake, Toe	Montreal	47	17	28	45	19
Thoms, Bill	Chicago	47	15	30	45	8
Drillon, Gordie	Toronto	48	23	18	41	6
Apps, Syl	Toronto	38	18	23	41	0
Anderson, Tom	Brooklyn	48	12	29	41	54

1942-43

Team	GP	W	L	T	GF	GA	PTS
*Detroit	50	25	14	11	169	124	61
Boston	50	24	17	9	195	176	57
Toronto	50	22	19	9	198	159	53
Montreal	50	19	19	12	181	191	50
Chicago	50	17	18	15	179	180	49
NY Rangers	50	11	31	8	161	253	30

Leading Scorers

Player	Club	GP	G	A	PTS	PIM
Bentley, Doug	Chicago	50	33	40	73	18
Cowley, Bill	Boston	48	27	45	72	10
Bentley, Max	Chicago	47	26	44	70	2
Patrick, Lynn	NY Rangers	50	22	39	61	28
Carr, Lorne	Toronto	50	27	33	60	15
Taylor, Billy	Toronto	50	18	42	60	2
Hextall, Bryan	NY Rangers	50	27	32	59	28
Blake, Toe	Montreal	48	23	36	59	28
Lach, Elmer	Montreal	45	18	40	58	14
O'Connor, Buddy	Montreal	50	15	43	58	2

1943-44

Team	GP	W	L	T	GF	GA	PTS
*Montreal	50	38	5	7	234	109	83
Detroit	50	26	18	6	214	177	58
Toronto	50	23	23	4	214	174	50
Chicago	50	22	23	5	178	187	49
Boston	50	19	26	5	223	268	43
NY Rangers	50	6	39	5	162	310	17

Leading Scorers

Player	Club	GP	G	A	PTS	PIM
Cain, Herb	Boston	48	36	46	82	4
Bentley, Doug	Chicago	50	38	39	77	22
Carr, Lorne	Toronto	50	36	38	74	9
Liscombe, Carl	Detroit	50	36	37	73	17
Lach, Elmer	Montreal	48	24	48	72	23
Smith, Clint	Chicago	50	23	49	72	4
Cowley, Bill	Boston	36	30	41	71	12
Mosienko, Bill	Chicago	50	32	38	70	10
Jackson, Art	Boston	49	28	41	69	8
Bodnar, Gus	Toronto	50	22	40	62	18

1944-45

Team	GP	W	L	T	GF	GA	PTS
Montreal	50	38	8	4	228	121	80
Detroit	50	31	14	5	218	161	67
*Toronto	50	24	22	4	183	161	52
Boston	50	16	30	4	179	219	36
Chicago	50	13	30	7	141	194	33
NY Rangers	50	11	29	10	154	247	32

Leading Scorers

Player	Club	GP	G	A	PTS	PIM
Lach, Elmer	Montreal	50	26	54	80	37
Richard, Maurice	Montreal	50	50	23	73	36
Blake, Toe	Montreal	49	29	38	67	15
Cowley, Bill	Boston	49	25	40	65	2
Kennedy, Ted	Toronto	49	29	25	54	14
Mosienko, Bill	Chicago	50	28	26	54	0
Carveth, Joe	Detroit	50	26	28	54	6
DeMarco, Ab	NY Rangers	50	24	30	54	10
Smith, Clint	Chicago	50	23	31	54	0
Howe, Syd	Detroit	46	17	36	53	6

1945-46

Team	GP	W	L	T	GF	GA	PTS
*Montreal	50	28	17	5	172	134	61
Boston	50	24	18	8	167	156	56
Chicago	50	23	20	7	200	178	53
Detroit	50	20	20	10	146	159	50
Toronto	50	19	24	7	174	185	45
NY Rangers	50	13	28	9	144	191	35

Leading Scorers

Player	Club	GP	G	A	PTS	PIM
Bentley, Max	Chicago	47	31	30	61	6
Stewart, Gaye	Toronto	50	37	15	52	8
Blake, Toe	Montreal	50	29	21	50	2
Smith, Clint	Chicago	50	26	24	50	2
Richard, Maurice	Montreal	50	27	21	48	50
Mosienko, Bill	Chicago	40	18	30	48	12
DeMarco, Ab	NY Rangers	50	20	27	47	20
Lach, Elmer	Montreal	50	13	34	47	34
Kaleta, Alex	Chicago	49	19	27	46	17
Taylor, Billy	Toronto	48	23	18	41	14
Horeck, Pete	Chicago	50	20	21	41	34

1946-47

Team	GP	W	L	T	GF	GA	PTS
Montreal	60	34	16	10	189	138	78
*Toronto	60	31	19	10	209	172	72
Boston	60	26	23	11	190	175	63
Detroit	60	22	27	11	190	193	55
NY Rangers	60	22	32	6	167	186	50
Chicago	60	19	37	4	193	274	42

Leading Scorers

Player	Club	GP	G	A	PTS	PIM
Bentley, Max	Chicago	60	29	43	72	12
Richard, Maurice	Montreal	60	45	26	71	69
Taylor, Billy	Detroit	60	17	46	63	35
Schmidt, Milt	Boston	59	27	35	62	40
Kennedy, Ted	Toronto	60	28	32	60	27
Bentley, Doug	Chicago	52	21	34	55	18
Bauer, Bobby	Boston	58	30	24	54	4
Conacher, Roy	Detroit	60	30	24	54	6
Mosienko, Bill	Chicago	59	25	27	52	2
Dumart, Woody	Boston	60	24	28	52	12

1947-48

Team	GP	W	L	T	GF	GA	PTS
*Toronto	60	32	15	13	182	143	77
Detroit	60	30	18	12	187	148	72
Boston	60	23	24	13	167	168	59
NY Rangers	60	21	26	13	176	201	55
Montreal	60	20	29	11	147	169	51
Chicago	60	20	34	6	195	225	46

Leading Scorers

Player	Club	GP	G	A	PTS	PIM
Lach, Elmer	Montreal	60	30	31	61	72
O'Connor, Buddy	NY Rangers	60	24	36	60	8
Bentley, Doug	Chicago	60	20	37	57	16
Stewart, Gaye	Tor.,-Chi.	61	27	29	56	83
Bentley, Max	Chi., Tor.	59	26	28	54	14
Poile, Bud	Tor.,-Chi.	58	25	29	54	17
Richard, Maurice	Montreal	53	28	25	53	89
Apps, Syl	Toronto	55	26	27	53	12
Lindsay, Ted	Detroit	60	33	19	52	95
Conacher, Roy	Chicago	52	22	27	49	4

1948-49

Team	GP	W	L	T	GF	GA	PTS
Detroit	60	34	19	7	195	145	75
Boston	60	29	23	8	178	163	66
Montreal	60	28	23	9	152	126	65
*Toronto	60	22	25	13	147	161	57
Chicago	60	21	31	8	173	211	50
NY Rangers	60	18	31	11	133	172	47

Leading Scorers

Player	Club	GP	G	A	PTS	PIM
Conacher, Roy	Chicago	60	26	42	68	8
Bentley, Doug	Chicago	58	23	43	66	38
Abel, Sid	Detroit	60	28	26	54	49
Lindsay, Ted	Detroit	50	26	28	54	97
Conacher, Jim	Det., Chi.	59	26	23	49	43
Ronty, Paul	Boston	60	20	29	49	11
Watson, Harry	Toronto	60	26	19	45	0
Reay, Billy	Montreal	60	22	23	45	33
Bodnar, Gus	Chicago	59	19	26	45	14
Peirson, Johnny	Boston	59	22	21	43	45

1949-50

Team	GP	W	L	T	GF	GA	PTS
*Detroit	70	37	19	14	229	164	88
Montreal	70	29	22	19	172	150	77
Toronto	70	31	27	12	176	173	74
NY Rangers	70	28	31	11	170	189	67
Boston	70	22	32	16	198	228	60
Chicago	70	22	38	10	203	244	54

Leading Scorers

Player	Club	GP	G	A	PTS	PIM
Lindsay, Ted	Detroit	69	23	55	78	141
Abel, Sid	Detroit	69	34	35	69	46
Howe, Gordie	Detroit	70	35	33	68	69
Richard, Maurice	Montreal	70	43	22	65	114
Ronty, Paul	Boston	70	23	36	59	8
Conacher, Roy	Chicago	70	25	31	56	16
Bentley, Doug	Chicago	64	20	33	53	28
Peirson, Johnny	Boston	57	27	25	52	49
Prystai, Metro	Chicago	65	29	22	51	31
Guidolin, Bep	Chicago	70	17	34	51	42

1950-51

Team	GP	W	L	T	GF	GA	PTS
Detroit	70	44	13	13	236	139	101
*Toronto	70	41	16	13	212	138	95
Montreal	70	25	30	15	173	184	65
Boston	70	22	30	18	178	197	62
NY Rangers	70	20	29	21	169	201	61
Chicago	70	13	47	10	171	280	36

Leading Scorers

Player	Club	GP	G	A	PTS	PIM
Howe, Gordie	Detroit	70	43	43	86	74
Richard, Maurice	Montreal	65	42	24	66	97
Bentley, Max	Toronto	67	21	41	62	34
Abel, Sid	Detroit	69	23	38	61	30
Schmidt, Milt	Boston	62	22	39	61	33
Kennedy, Ted	Toronto	63	18	43	61	32
Lindsay, Ted	Detroit	67	24	35	59	110
Sloan, Tod	Toronto	70	31	25	56	105
Kelly, Red	Detroit	70	17	37	54	24
Smith, Sid	Toronto	70	30	21	51	10
Gardner, Cal	Toronto	66	23	28	51	42

1951-52

Team	GP	W	L	T	GF	GA	PTS
*Detroit	70	44	14	12	215	133	100
Montreal	70	34	26	10	195	164	78
Toronto	70	29	25	16	168	157	74
Boston	70	25	29	16	162	176	66
NY Rangers	70	23	34	13	192	219	59
Chicago	70	17	44	9	158	241	43

Leading Scorers

Player	Club	GP	G	A	PTS	PIM
Howe, Gordie	Detroit	70	47	39	86	78
Lindsay, Ted	Detroit	70	30	39	69	123
Lach, Elmer	Montreal	70	15	50	65	36
Raleigh, Don	NY Rangers	70	19	42	61	14
Smith, Sid	Toronto	70	27	30	57	6
Geoffrion, Bernie	Montreal	67	30	24	54	66
Mosienko, Bill	Chicago	70	31	22	53	10
Abel, Sid	Detroit	62	17	36	53	32
Kennedy, Ted	Toronto	70	19	33	52	33
Schmidt, Milt	Boston	69	21	29	50	57
Peirson, Johnny	Boston	68	20	30	50	30

1952-53

Team	GP	W	L	T	GF	GA	PTS
Detroit	70	36	16	18	222	133	90
*Montreal	70	28	23	19	155	148	75
Boston	70	28	29	13	152	172	69
Chicago	70	27	28	15	169	175	69
Toronto	70	27	30	13	156	167	67
NY Rangers	70	17	37	16	152	211	50

Leading Scorers

Player	Club	GP	G	A	PTS	PIM
Howe, Gordie	Detroit	70	49	46	95	57
Lindsay, Ted	Detroit	70	32	39	71	111
Richard, Maurice	Montreal	70	28	33	61	112
Hergesheimer, Wally	NY Rangers	70	30	29	59	10
Delvecchio, Alex	Detroit	70	16	43	59	28
Ronty, Paul	NY Rangers	70	16	38	54	20
Prystai, Metro	Detroit	70	16	34	50	12
Kelly, Red	Detroit	70	19	27	46	8
Olmstead, Bert	Montreal	69	17	28	45	83
Mackell, Fleming	Boston	65	27	17	44	63
McFadden, Jim	Chicago	70	23	21	44	29

1953-54

Team	GP	W	L	T	GF	GA	PTS
*Detroit	70	37	19	14	191	132	88
Montreal	70	35	24	11	195	141	81
Toronto	70	32	24	14	152	131	78
Boston	70	32	28	10	177	181	74
NY Rangers	70	29	31	10	161	182	68
Chicago	70	12	51	7	133	242	31

Leading Scorers

Player	Club	GP	G	A	PTS	PIM
Howe, Gordie	Detroit	70	33	48	81	109
Richard, Maurice	Montreal	70	37	30	67	112
Lindsay, Ted	Detroit	70	26	36	62	110
Geoffrion, Bernie	Montreal	54	29	25	54	87
Olmstead, Bert	Montreal	70	15	37	52	85
Kelly, Red	Detroit	62	16	33	49	18
Reibel, Dutch	Detroit	69	15	33	48	18
Sandford, Ed	Boston	70	16	31	47	42
Mackell, Fleming	Boston	67	15	32	47	60
Mosdell, Ken	Montreal	67	22	24	46	64
Ronty, Paul	NY Rangers	70	13	33	46	18

1954-55

Team	GP	W	L	T	GF	GA	PTS
*Detroit	70	42	17	11	204	134	95
Montreal	70	41	18	11	228	157	93
Toronto	70	24	24	22	147	135	70
Boston	70	23	26	21	169	188	67
NY Rangers	70	17	35	18	150	210	52
Chicago	70	13	40	17	161	235	43

Leading Scorers

Player	Club	GP	G	A	PTS	PIM
Geoffrion, Bernie	Montreal	70	38	37	75	57
Richard, Maurice	Montreal	67	38	36	74	125
Béliveau, Jean	Montreal	70	37	36	73	58
Reibel, Dutch	Detroit	70	25	41	66	15
Howe, Gordie	Detroit	64	29	33	62	68
Sullivan, Red	Chicago	69	19	42	61	51
Olmstead, Bert	Montreal	70	10	48	58	103
Smith, Sid	Toronto	70	33	21	54	14
Mosdell, Ken	Montreal	70	22	32	54	82
Lewicki, Danny	NY Rangers	70	29	24	53	8

1955-56

Team	GP	W	L	T	GF	GA	PTS
*Montreal	70	45	15	10	222	131	100
Detroit	70	30	24	16	183	148	76
NY Rangers	70	32	28	10	204	203	74
Toronto	70	24	33	13	153	181	61
Boston	70	23	34	13	147	185	59
Chicago	70	19	39	12	155	216	50

Leading Scorers

Player	Club	GP	G	A	PTS	PIM
Béliveau, Jean	Montreal	70	47	41	88	143
Howe, Gordie	Detroit	70	38	41	79	100
Richard, Maurice	Montreal	70	38	33	71	89
Olmstead, Bert	Montreal	70	14	56	70	94
Sloan, Tod	Toronto	70	37	29	66	100
Bathgate, Andy	NY Rangers	70	19	47	66	59
Geoffrion, Bernie	Montreal	59	29	33	62	66
Reibel, Dutch	Detroit	68	17	39	56	10
Delvecchio, Alex	Detroit	70	25	26	51	24
Creighton, Dave	NY Rangers	70	20	31	51	43
Gadsby, Bill	NY Rangers	70	9	42	51	84

1956-57

Team	GP	W	L	T	GF	GA	PTS
Detroit	70	38	20	12	198	157	88
*Montreal	70	35	23	12	210	155	82
Boston	70	34	24	12	195	174	80
NY Rangers	70	26	30	14	184	227	66
Toronto	70	21	34	15	174	192	57
Chicago	70	16	39	15	169	225	47

Leading Scorers

Player	Club	GP	G	A	PTS	PIM
Howe, Gordie	Detroit	70	44	45	89	72
Lindsay, Ted	Detroit	70	30	55	85	103
Béliveau, Jean	Montreal	69	33	51	84	105
Bathgate, Andy	NY Rangers	70	27	50	77	60
Litzenberger, Ed	Chicago	70	32	32	64	48
Richard, Maurice	Montreal	63	33	29	62	74
McKenney, Don	Boston	69	21	39	60	31
Moore, Dickie	Montreal	70	29	29	58	56
Richard, Henri	Montreal	63	18	36	54	71
Ullman, Norm	Detroit	64	16	36	52	47

1957-58

Team	GP	W	L	T	GF	GA	PTS
*Montreal	70	43	17	10	250	158	96
NY Rangers	70	32	25	13	195	188	77
Detroit	70	29	29	12	176	207	70
Boston	70	27	28	15	199	194	69
Chicago	70	24	39	7	163	202	55
Toronto	70	21	38	11	192	226	53

Leading Scorers

Player	Club	GP	G	A	PTS	PIM
Moore, Dickie	Montreal	70	36	48	84	65
Richard, Henri	Montreal	67	28	52	80	56
Bathgate, Andy	NY Rangers	65	30	48	78	42
Howe, Gordie	Detroit	64	33	44	77	40
Horvath, Bronco	Boston	67	30	36	66	71
Litzenberger, Ed	Chicago	70	32	30	62	63
Mackell, Fleming	Boston	70	20	40	60	72
Béliveau, Jean	Montreal	55	27	32	59	93
Delvecchio, Alex	Detroit	70	21	38	59	22
McKenney, Don	Boston	70	28	30	58	22

1958-59

Team	GP	W	L	T	GF	GA	PTS
*Montreal	70	39	18	13	258	158	91
Boston	70	32	29	9	205	215	73
Chicago	70	28	29	13	197	208	69
Toronto	70	27	32	11	189	201	65
NY Rangers	70	26	32	12	201	217	64
Detroit	70	25	37	8	167	218	58

Leading Scorers

Player	Club	GP	G	A	PTS	PIM
Moore, Dickie	Montreal	70	41	55	96	61
Béliveau, Jean	Montreal	64	45	46	91	67
Bathgate, Andy	NY Rangers	70	40	48	88	48
Howe, Gordie	Detroit	70	32	46	78	57
Litzenberger, Ed	Chicago	70	33	44	77	37
Geoffrion, Bernie	Montreal	59	22	44	66	30
Sullivan, Red	NY Rangers	70	21	42	63	56
Hebenton, Andy	NY Rangers	70	33	29	62	8
McKenney, Don	Boston	70	32	30	62	20
Sloan, Tod	Chicago	59	27	35	62	79

1959-60

Team	GP	W	L	T	GF	GA	PTS
*Montreal	70	40	18	12	255	178	92
Toronto	70	35	26	9	199	195	79
Chicago	70	28	29	13	191	180	69
Detroit	70	26	29	15	186	197	67
Boston	70	28	34	8	220	241	64
NY Rangers	70	17	38	15	187	247	49

Leading Scorers

Player	Club	GP	G	A	PTS	PIM
Hull, Bobby	Chicago	70	39	42	81	68
Horvath, Bronco	Boston	68	39	41	80	60
Béliveau, Jean	Montreal	60	34	40	74	57
Bathgate, Andy	NY Rangers	70	26	48	74	28
Richard, Henri	Montreal	70	30	43	73	66
Howe, Gordie	Detroit	70	28	45	73	46
Geoffrion, Bernie	Montreal	59	30	41	71	36
McKenney, Don	Boston	70	20	49	69	28
Stasiuk, Vic	Boston	69	29	39	68	121
Prentice, Dean	NY Rangers	70	32	34	66	43

1960-61

Team	GP	W	L	T	GF	GA	PTS
Montreal	70	41	19	10	254	188	92
Toronto	70	39	19	12	234	176	90
*Chicago	70	29	24	17	198	180	75
Detroit	70	25	29	16	195	215	66
NY Rangers	70	22	38	10	204	248	54
Boston	70	15	42	13	176	254	43

Leading Scorers

Player	Club	GP	G	A	PTS	PIM
Geoffrion, Bernie	Montreal	64	50	45	95	29
Béliveau, Jean	Montreal	69	32	58	90	57
Mahovlich, Frank	Toronto	70	48	36	84	131
Bathgate, Andy	NY Rangers	70	29	48	77	22
Howe, Gordie	Detroit	64	23	49	72	30
Ullman, Norm	Detroit	70	28	42	70	34
Kelly, Red	Toronto	64	20	50	70	12
Moore, Dickie	Montreal	57	35	34	69	62
Richard, Henri	Montreal	70	24	44	68	91
Delvecchio, Alex	Detroit	70	27	35	62	26

1961-62

Team	GP	W	L	T	GF	GA	PTS
Montreal	70	42	14	14	259	166	98
*Toronto	70	37	22	11	232	180	85
Chicago	70	31	26	13	217	186	75
NY Rangers	70	26	32	12	195	207	64
Detroit	70	23	33	14	184	219	60
Boston	70	15	47	8	177	306	38

Leading Scorers

Player	Club	GP	G	A	PTS	PIM
Hull, Bobby	Chicago	70	50	34	84	35
Bathgate, Andy	NY Rangers	70	28	56	84	44
Howe, Gordie	Detroit	70	33	44	77	54
Mikita, Stan	Chicago	70	25	52	77	97
Mahovlich, Frank	Toronto	70	33	38	71	87
Delvecchio, Alex	Detroit	70	26	43	69	18
Backstrom, Ralph	Montreal	66	27	38	65	29
Ullman, Norm	Detroit	70	26	38	64	54
Hay, Bill	Chicago	60	11	52	63	34
Provost, Claude	Montreal	70	33	29	62	22

1962-63

Team	GP	W	L	T	GF	GA	PTS
*Toronto	70	35	23	12	221	180	82
Chicago	70	32	21	17	194	178	81
Montreal	70	28	19	23	225	183	79
Detroit	70	32	25	13	200	194	77
NY Rangers	70	22	36	12	211	233	56
Boston	70	14	39	17	198	281	45

Leading Scorers

Player	Club	GP	G	A	PTS	PIM
Howe, Gordie	Detroit	70	38	48	86	100
Bathgate, Andy	NY Rangers	70	35	46	81	54
Mikita, Stan	Chicago	65	31	45	76	69
Mahovlich, Frank	Toronto	67	36	37	73	56
Richard, Henri	Montreal	67	23	50	73	57
Béliveau, Jean	Montreal	69	18	49	67	68
Bucyk, John	Boston	69	27	39	66	36
Delvecchio, Alex	Detroit	70	20	44	64	8
Hull, Bobby	Chicago	65	31	31	62	27
Oliver, Murray	Boston	65	22	40	62	38

1963-64

Team	GP	W	L	T	GF	GA	PTS
Montreal	70	36	21	13	209	167	85
Chicago	70	36	22	12	218	169	84
*Toronto	70	33	25	12	192	172	78
Detroit	70	30	29	11	191	204	71
NY Rangers	70	22	38	10	186	242	54
Boston	70	18	40	12	170	212	48

Leading Scorers

Player	Club	GP	G	A	PTS	PIM
Mikita, Stan	Chicago	70	39	50	89	146
Hull, Bobby	Chicago	70	43	44	87	50
Béliveau, Jean	Montreal	68	28	50	78	42
Bathgate, Andy	NYR, Tor.	71	19	58	77	34
Howe, Gordie	Detroit	69	26	47	73	70
Wharram, Kenny	Chicago	70	39	32	71	18
Oliver, Murray	Boston	70	24	44	68	41
Goyette, Phil	NY Rangers	67	24	41	65	15
Gilbert, Rod	NY Rangers	70	24	40	64	62
Keon, Dave	Toronto	70	23	37	60	6

1964-65

Team	GP	W	L	T	GF	GA	PTS
Detroit	70	40	23	7	224	175	87
*Montreal	70	36	23	11	211	185	83
Chicago	70	34	28	8	224	176	76
Toronto	70	30	26	14	204	173	74
NY Rangers	70	20	38	12	179	246	52
Boston	70	21	43	6	166	253	48

Leading Scorers

Player	Club	GP	G	A	PTS	PIM
Mikita, Stan	Chicago	70	28	59	87	154
Ullman, Norm	Detroit	70	42	41	83	70
Howe, Gordie	Detroit	70	29	47	76	104
Hull, Bobby	Chicago	61	39	32	71	32
Delvecchio, Alex	Detroit	68	25	42	67	16
Provost, Claude	Montreal	70	27	37	64	28
Gilbert, Rod	NY Rangers	70	25	36	61	52
Pilote, Pierre	Chicago	68	14	45	59	162
Bucyk, John	Boston	68	26	29	55	24
Backstrom, Ralph	Montreal	70	25	30	55	41
Esposito, Phil	Chicago	70	23	32	55	44

1965-66

Team	GP	W	L	T	GF	GA	PTS
*Montreal	70	41	21	8	239	173	90
Chicago	70	37	25	8	240	187	82
Toronto	70	34	25	11	208	187	79
Detroit	70	31	27	12	221	194	74
Boston	70	21	43	6	174	275	48
NY Rangers	70	18	41	11	195	261	47

Leading Scorers

Player	Club	GP	G	A	PTS	PIM
Hull, Bobby	Chicago	65	54	43	97	70
Mikita, Stan	Chicago	68	30	48	78	58
Rousseau, Bobby	Montreal	70	30	48	78	20
Béliveau, Jean	Montreal	67	29	48	77	50
Howe, Gordie	Detroit	70	29	46	75	83
Ullman, Norm	Detroit	70	31	41	72	35
Delvecchio, Alex	Detroit	70	31	38	69	16
Nevin, Bob	NY Rangers	69	29	33	62	10
Richard, Henri	Montreal	62	22	39	61	47
Oliver, Murray	Boston	70	18	42	60	30

1966-67

Team	GP	W	L	T	GF	GA	PTS
Chicago	70	41	17	12	264	170	94
Montreal	70	32	25	13	202	188	77
*Toronto	70	32	27	11	204	211	75
NY Rangers	70	30	28	12	188	189	72
Detroit	70	27	39	4	212	241	58
Boston	70	17	43	10	182	253	44

Leading Scorers

Player	Club	GP	G	A	PTS	PIM
Mikita, Stan	Chicago	70	35	62	97	12
Hull, Bobby	Chicago	66	52	28	80	52
Ullman, Norm	Detroit	68	26	44	70	26
Wharram, Kenny	Chicago	70	31	34	65	21
Howe, Gordie	Detroit	69	25	40	65	53
Rousseau, Bobby	Montreal	68	19	44	63	58
Esposito, Phil	Chicago	69	21	40	61	40
Goyette, Phil	NY Rangers	70	12	49	61	6
Mohns, Doug	Chicago	61	25	35	60	58
Richard, Henri	Montreal	65	21	34	55	28
Delvecchio, Alex	Detroit	70	17	38	55	10

1967-68

East Division

Team	GP	W	L	T	GF	GA	PTS
*Montreal	74	42	22	10	236	167	94
NY Rangers	74	39	23	12	226	183	90
Boston	74	37	27	10	259	216	84
Chicago	74	32	26	16	212	222	80
Toronto	74	33	31	10	209	176	76
Detroit	74	27	35	12	245	257	66

West Division

Team	GP	W	L	T	GF	GA	PTS
Philadelphia	74	31	32	11	173	179	73
Los Angeles	74	31	33	10	200	224	72
St. Louis	74	27	31	16	177	191	70
Minnesota	74	27	32	15	191	226	69
Pittsburgh	74	27	34	13	195	216	67
Oakland	74	15	42	17	153	219	47

Leading Scorers

Player	Club	GP	G	A	PTS	PIM
Mikita, Stan	Chicago	72	40	47	87	14
Esposito, Phil	Boston	74	35	49	84	21
Howe, Gordie	Detroit	74	39	43	82	53
Ratelle, Jean	NY Rangers	74	32	46	78	18
Gilbert, Rod	NY Rangers	73	29	48	77	12
Hull, Bobby	Chicago	71	44	31	75	39
Ullman, Norm	Det., Tor.	71	35	37	72	28
Delvecchio, Alex	Detroit	74	22	48	70	14
Bucyk, John	Boston	72	30	39	69	8
Wharram, Kenny	Chicago	74	27	42	69	18

1968-69

East Division

Team	GP	W	L	T	GF	GA	PTS
*Montreal	76	46	19	11	271	202	103
Boston	76	42	18	16	303	221	100
NY Rangers	76	41	26	9	231	196	91
Toronto	76	35	26	15	234	217	85
Detroit	76	33	31	12	239	221	78
Chicago	76	34	33	9	280	246	77

West Division

Team	GP	W	L	T	GF	GA	PTS
St. Louis	76	37	25	14	204	157	88
Oakland	76	29	36	11	219	251	69
Philadelphia	76	20	35	21	174	225	61
Los Angeles	76	24	42	10	185	260	58
Pittsburgh	76	20	45	11	189	252	51
Minnesota	76	18	43	15	189	270	51

Leading Scorers

Player	Club	GP	G	A	PTS	PIM
Esposito, Phil	Boston	74	49	77	126	79
Hull, Bobby	Chicago	74	58	49	107	48
Howe, Gordie	Detroit	76	44	59	103	58
Mikita, Stan	Chicago	74	30	67	97	52
Hodge, Ken	Boston	75	45	45	90	75
Cournoyer, Yvan	Montreal	76	43	44	87	31
Delvecchio, Alex	Detroit	72	25	58	83	8
Berenson, Red	St. Louis	76	35	47	82	43
Béliveau, Jean	Montreal	69	33	49	82	55
Mahovlich, Frank	Detroit	76	49	29	78	38
Ratelle, Jean	NY Rangers	75	32	46	78	26

1969-70

East Division

Team	GP	W	L	T	GF	GA	PTS
Chicago	76	45	22	9	250	170	99
*Boston	76	40	17	19	277	216	99
Detroit	76	40	21	15	246	199	95
NY Rangers	76	38	22	16	246	189	92
Montreal	76	38	22	16	244	201	92
Toronto	76	29	34	13	222	242	71

West Division

Team	GP	W	L	T	GF	GA	PTS
St. Louis	76	37	27	12	224	179	86
Pittsburgh	76	26	38	12	182	238	64
Minnesota	76	19	35	22	224	257	60
Oakland	76	22	40	14	169	243	58
Philadelphia	76	17	35	24	197	225	58
Los Angeles	76	14	52	10	168	290	38

Leading Scorers

Player	Club	GP	G	A	PTS	PIM
Orr, Bobby	Boston	76	33	87	120	125
Esposito, Phil	Boston	76	43	56	99	50
Mikita, Stan	Chicago	76	39	47	86	50
Goyette, Phil	St. Louis	72	29	49	78	16
Tkaczuk, Walt	NY Rangers	76	27	50	77	38
Ratelle, Jean	NY Rangers	75	32	42	74	28
Berenson, Red	St. Louis	67	33	39	72	38
Parise, Jean-Paul	Minnesota	74	24	48	72	72
Howe, Gordie	Detroit	76	31	40	71	58
Mahovlich, Frank	Detroit	74	38	32	70	59
Balon, Dave	NY Rangers	76	33	37	70	100
McKenzie, John	Boston	72	29	41	70	114

1970-71

East Division

Team	GP	W	L	T	GF	GA	PTS
Boston	78	57	14	7	399	207	121
NY Rangers	78	49	18	11	259	177	109
*Montreal	78	42	23	13	291	216	97
Toronto	78	37	33	8	248	211	82
Buffalo	78	24	39	15	217	291	63
Vancouver	78	24	46	8	229	296	56
Detroit	78	22	45	11	209	308	55

West Division

Team	GP	W	L	T	GF	GA	PTS
Chicago	78	49	20	9	277	184	107
St. Louis	78	34	25	19	223	208	87
Philadelphia	78	28	33	17	207	225	73
Minnesota	78	28	34	16	191	223	72
Los Angeles	78	25	40	13	239	303	63
Pittsburgh	78	21	37	20	221	240	62
California	78	20	53	5	199	320	45

Leading Scorers

Player	Club	GP	G	A	PTS	PIM
Esposito, Phil	Boston	78	76	76	152	71
Orr, Bobby	Boston	78	37	102	139	91
Bucyk, John	Boston	78	51	65	116	8
Hodge, Ken	Boston	78	43	62	105	113
Hull, Bobby	Chicago	78	44	52	96	32
Ullman, Norm	Toronto	73	34	51	85	24
Cashman, Wayne	Boston	77	21	58	79	100
McKenzie, John	Boston	65	31	46	77	120
Keon, Dave	Toronto	76	38	38	76	4
Béliveau, Jean	Montreal	70	25	51	76	40
Stanfield, Fred	Boston	75	24	52	76	12

1971-72

East Division

Team	GP	W	L	T	GF	GA	PTS
*Boston	78	54	13	11	330	204	119
NY Rangers	78	48	17	13	317	192	109
Montreal	78	46	16	16	307	205	108
Toronto	78	33	31	14	209	208	80
Detroit	78	33	35	10	261	262	76
Buffalo	78	16	43	19	203	289	51
Vancouver	78	20	50	8	203	297	48

West Division

Team	GP	W	L	T	GF	GA	PTS
Chicago	78	46	17	15	256	166	107
Minnesota	78	37	29	12	212	191	86
St. Louis	78	28	39	11	208	247	67
Pittsburgh	78	26	38	14	220	258	66
Philadelphia	78	26	38	14	200	236	66
California	78	21	39	18	216	288	60
Los Angeles	78	20	49	9	206	305	49

Leading Scorers

Player	Club	GP	G	A	PTS	PIM
Esposito, Phil	Boston	76	66	67	133	76
Orr, Bobby	Boston	76	37	80	117	106
Ratelle, Jean	NY Rangers	63	46	63	109	4
Hadfield, Vic	NY Rangers	78	50	56	106	142
Gilbert, Rod	NY Rangers	73	43	54	97	64
Mahovlich, Frank	Montreal	76	43	53	96	36
Hull, Bobby	Chicago	78	50	43	93	24
Cournoyer, Yvan	Montreal	73	47	36	83	15
Bucyk, John	Boston	78	32	51	83	4
Clarke, Bobby	Philadelphia	78	35	46	81	87
Lemaire, Jacques	Montreal	77	32	49	81	26

1972-73

East Division

Team	GP	W	L	T	GF	GA	PTS
*Montreal	78	52	10	16	329	184	120
Boston	78	51	22	5	330	235	107
NY Rangers	78	47	23	8	297	208	102
Buffalo	78	37	27	14	257	219	88
Detroit	78	37	29	12	265	243	86
Toronto	78	27	41	10	247	279	64
Vancouver	78	22	47	9	233	339	53
NY Islanders	78	12	60	6	170	347	30

West Division

Team	GP	W	L	T	GF	GA	PTS
Chicago	78	42	27	9	284	225	93
Philadelphia	78	37	30	11	296	256	85
Minnesota	78	37	30	11	254	230	85
St. Louis	78	32	34	12	233	251	76
Pittsburgh	78	32	37	9	257	265	73
Los Angeles	78	31	36	11	232	245	73
Atlanta	78	25	38	15	191	239	65
California	78	16	46	16	213	323	48

Leading Scorers

Player	Club	GP	G	A	PTS	PIM
Esposito, Phil	Boston	78	55	75	130	87
Clarke, Bobby	Philadelphia	78	37	67	104	80
Orr, Bobby	Boston	63	29	72	101	99
MacLeish, Rick	Philadelphia	78	50	50	100	69
Lemaire, Jacques	Montreal	77	44	51	95	16
Ratelle, Jean	NY Rangers	78	41	53	94	12
Redmond, Mickey	Detroit	76	52	41	93	24
Bucyk, John	Boston	78	40	53	93	12
Mahovlich, Frank	Montreal	78	38	55	93	51
Pappin, Jim	Chicago	76	41	51	92	82

Jean Ratelle led Rangers linemates Rod Gilbert and Vic Hadfield to a 3-4-5 finish behind Boston's Phil Esposito and Bobby Orr in the 1971-72 scoring race.

1973-74
East Division

Team	GP	W	L	T	GF	GA	PTS
Boston	78	52	17	9	349	221	113
Montreal	78	45	24	9	293	240	99
NY Rangers	78	40	24	14	300	251	94
Toronto	78	35	27	16	274	230	86
Buffalo	78	32	34	12	242	250	76
Detroit	78	29	39	10	255	319	68
Vancouver	78	24	43	11	224	296	59
NY Islanders	78	19	41	18	182	247	56

West Division

Team	GP	W	L	T	GF	GA	PTS
*Philadelphia	78	50	16	12	273	164	112
Chicago	78	41	14	23	272	164	105
Los Angeles	78	33	33	12	233	231	78
Atlanta	78	30	34	14	214	238	74
Pittsburgh	78	28	41	9	242	273	65
St. Louis	78	26	40	12	206	248	64
Minnesota	78	23	38	17	235	275	63
California	78	13	55	10	195	342	36

Leading Scorers

Player	Club	GP	G	A	PTS	PIM
Esposito, Phil	Boston	78	68	77	145	58
Orr, Bobby	Boston	74	32	90	122	82
Hodge, Ken	Boston	76	50	55	105	43
Cashman, Wayne	Boston	78	30	59	89	111
Clarke, Bobby	Philadelphia	77	35	52	87	113
Martin, Rick	Buffalo	78	52	34	86	38
Apps Jr., Syl	Pittsburgh	75	24	61	85	37
Sittler, Darryl	Toronto	78	38	46	84	55
MacDonald, Lowell	Pittsburgh	78	43	39	82	14
Park, Brad	NY Rangers	78	25	57	82	148
Hextall, Dennis	Minnesota	78	20	62	82	138

1974-75
PRINCE OF WALES CONFERENCE
Norris Division

Team	GP	W	L	T	GF	GA	PTS
Montreal	80	47	14	19	374	225	113
Los Angeles	80	42	17	21	269	185	105
Pittsburgh	80	37	28	15	326	289	89
Detroit	80	23	45	12	259	335	58
Washington	80	8	67	5	181	446	21

Adams Division

Team	GP	W	L	T	GF	GA	PTS
Buffalo	80	49	16	15	354	240	113
Boston	80	40	26	14	345	245	94
Toronto	80	31	33	16	280	309	78
California	80	19	48	13	212	316	51

CLARENCE CAMPBELL CONFERENCE
Patrick Division

Team	GP	W	L	T	GF	GA	PTS
*Philadelphia	80	51	18	11	293	181	113
NY Rangers	80	37	29	14	319	276	88
NY Islanders	80	33	25	22	264	221	88
Atlanta	80	34	31	15	243	233	83

Smythe Division

Team	GP	W	L	T	GF	GA	PTS
Vancouver	80	38	32	10	271	254	86
St. Louis	80	35	31	14	269	267	84
Chicago	80	37	35	8	268	241	82
Minnesota	80	23	50	7	221	341	53
Kansas City	80	15	54	11	184	328	41

Leading Scorers

Player	Club	GP	G	A	PTS	PIM
Orr, Bobby	Boston	80	46	89	135	101
Esposito, Phil	Boston	79	61	66	127	62
Dionne, Marcel	Detroit	80	47	74	121	14
Lafleur, Guy	Montreal	70	53	66	119	37
Mahovlich, Pete	Montreal	80	35	82	117	64
Clarke, Bobby	Philadelphia	80	27	89	116	125
Robert, Rene	Buffalo	74	40	60	100	75
Gilbert, Rod	NY Rangers	76	36	61	97	22
Perreault, Gilbert	Buffalo	68	39	57	96	36
Martin, Rick	Buffalo	68	52	43	95	72

1975-76
PRINCE OF WALES CONFERENCE
Norris Division

Team	GP	W	L	T	GF	GA	PTS
*Montreal	80	58	11	11	337	174	127
Los Angeles	80	38	33	9	263	265	85
Pittsburgh	80	35	33	12	339	303	82
Detroit	80	26	44	10	226	300	62
Washington	80	11	59	10	224	394	32

Adams Division

Team	GP	W	L	T	GF	GA	PTS
Boston	80	48	15	17	313	237	113
Buffalo	80	46	21	13	339	240	105
Toronto	80	34	31	15	294	276	83
California	80	27	42	11	250	278	65

CLARENCE CAMPBELL CONFERENCE
Patrick Division

Team	GP	W	L	T	GF	GA	PTS
Philadelphia	80	51	13	16	348	209	118
NY Islanders	80	42	21	17	297	190	101
Atlanta	80	35	33	12	262	237	82
NY Rangers	80	29	42	9	262	333	67

Smythe Division

Team	GP	W	L	T	GF	GA	PTS
Chicago	80	32	30	18	254	261	82
Vancouver	80	33	32	15	271	272	81
St. Louis	80	29	37	14	249	290	72
Minnesota	80	20	53	7	195	303	47
Kansas City	80	12	56	12	190	351	36

Leading Scorers

Player	Club	GP	G	A	PTS	PIM
Lafleur, Guy	Montreal	80	56	69	125	36
Clarke, Bobby	Philadelphia	76	30	89	119	136
Perreault, Gilbert	Buffalo	80	44	69	113	36
Barber, Bill	Philadelphia	80	50	62	112	104
Larouche, Pierre	Pittsburgh	76	53	58	111	33
Ratelle, Jean	Bos., NYR	80	36	69	105	18
Mahovlich, Pete	Montreal	80	34	71	105	76
Pronovost, Jean	Pittsburgh	80	52	52	104	24
Sittler, Darryl	Toronto	79	41	59	100	90
Apps Jr., Syl	Pittsburgh	80	32	67	99	24

1976-77
PRINCE OF WALES CONFERENCE
Norris Division

Team	GP	W	L	T	GF	GA	PTS
*Montreal	80	60	8	12	387	171	132
Los Angeles	80	34	31	15	271	241	83
Pittsburgh	80	34	33	13	240	252	81
Washington	80	24	42	14	221	307	62
Detroit	80	16	55	9	183	309	41

Adams Division

Team	GP	W	L	T	GF	GA	PTS
Boston	80	49	23	8	312	240	106
Buffalo	80	48	24	8	301	220	104
Toronto	80	33	32	15	301	285	81
Cleveland	80	25	42	13	240	292	63

CLARENCE CAMPBELL CONFERENCE
Patrick Division

Team	GP	W	L	T	GF	GA	PTS
Philadelphia	80	48	16	16	323	213	112
NY Islanders	80	47	21	12	288	193	106
Atlanta	80	34	34	12	264	265	80
NY Rangers	80	29	37	14	272	310	72

Smythe Division

Team	GP	W	L	T	GF	GA	PTS
St. Louis	80	32	39	9	239	276	73
Minnesota	80	23	39	18	240	310	64
Chicago	80	26	43	11	240	298	63
Vancouver	80	25	42	13	235	294	63
Colorado	80	20	46	14	226	307	54

Leading Scorers

Player	Club	GP	G	A	PTS	PIM
Lafleur, Guy	Montreal	80	56	80	136	20
Dionne, Marcel	Los Angeles	80	53	69	122	12
Shutt, Steve	Montreal	80	60	45	105	28
MacLeish, Rick	Philadelphia	79	49	48	97	42
Perreault, Gilbert	Buffalo	80	39	56	95	30
Young, Tim	Minnesota	80	29	66	95	58
Ratelle, Jean	Boston	78	33	61	94	22
McDonald, Lanny	Toronto	80	46	44	90	77
Sittler, Darryl	Toronto	73	38	52	90	89
Clarke, Bobby	Philadelphia	80	27	63	90	71

1977-78
PRINCE OF WALES CONFERENCE
Norris Division

Team	GP	W	L	T	GF	GA	PTS
*Montreal	80	59	10	11	359	183	129
Detroit	80	32	34	14	252	266	78
Los Angeles	80	31	34	15	243	245	77
Pittsburgh	80	25	37	18	254	321	68
Washington	80	17	49	14	195	321	48

Adams Division

Team	GP	W	L	T	GF	GA	PTS
Boston	80	51	18	11	333	218	113
Buffalo	80	44	19	17	288	215	105
Toronto	80	41	29	10	271	237	92
Cleveland	80	22	45	13	230	325	57

CLARENCE CAMPBELL CONFERENCE
Patrick Division

Team	GP	W	L	T	GF	GA	PTS
NY Islanders	80	48	17	15	334	210	111
Philadelphia	80	45	20	15	296	200	105
Atlanta	80	34	27	19	274	252	87
NY Rangers	80	30	37	13	279	280	73

Smythe Division

Team	GP	W	L	T	GF	GA	PTS
Chicago	80	32	29	19	230	220	83
Colorado	80	19	40	21	257	305	59
Vancouver	80	20	43	17	239	320	57
St. Louis	80	20	47	13	195	304	53
Minnesota	80	18	53	9	218	325	45

Leading Scorers

Player	Club	GP	G	A	PTS	PIM
Lafleur, Guy	Montreal	78	60	72	132	26
Trottier, Bryan	NY Islanders	77	46	77	123	46
Sittler, Darryl	Toronto	80	45	72	117	100
Lemaire, Jacques	Montreal	76	36	61	97	14
Potvin, Denis	NY Islanders	80	30	64	94	81
Bossy, Mike	NY Islanders	73	53	38	91	6
O'Reilly, Terry	Boston	77	29	61	90	211
Perreault, Gilbert	Buffalo	79	41	48	89	20
Clarke, Bobby	Philadelphia	71	21	68	89	83
McDonald, Lanny	Toronto	74	47	40	87	54
Paiement, Wilf	Colorado	80	31	56	87	114

1978-79
PRINCE OF WALES CONFERENCE
Norris Division

Team	GP	W	L	T	GF	GA	PTS
*Montreal	80	52	17	11	337	204	115
Pittsburgh	80	36	31	13	281	279	85
Los Angeles	80	34	34	12	292	286	80
Washington	80	24	41	15	273	338	63
Detroit	80	23	41	16	252	295	62

Adams Division

Team	GP	W	L	T	GF	GA	PTS
Boston	80	43	23	14	316	270	100
Buffalo	80	36	28	16	280	263	88
Toronto	80	34	33	13	267	252	81
Minnesota	80	28	40	12	257	289	68

CLARENCE CAMPBELL CONFERENCE
Patrick Division

Team	GP	W	L	T	GF	GA	PTS
NY Islanders	80	51	15	14	358	214	116
Philadelphia	80	40	25	15	281	248	95
NY Rangers	80	40	29	11	316	292	91
Atlanta	80	41	31	8	327	280	90

Smythe Division

Team	GP	W	L	T	GF	GA	PTS
Chicago	80	29	36	15	244	277	73
Vancouver	80	25	42	13	217	291	63
St. Louis	80	18	50	12	249	348	48
Colorado	80	15	53	12	210	331	42

Leading Scorers

Player	Club	GP	G	A	PTS	PIM
Trottier, Bryan	NY Islanders	76	47	87	134	50
Dionne, Marcel	Los Angeles	80	59	71	130	30
Lafleur, Guy	Montreal	80	52	77	129	28
Bossy, Mike	NY Islanders	80	69	57	126	25
MacMillan, Bob	Atlanta	79	37	71	108	14
Chouinard, Guy	Atlanta	80	50	57	107	14
Potvin, Denis	NY Islanders	73	31	70	101	58
Federko, Bernie	St. Louis	74	31	64	95	14
Taylor, Dave	Los Angeles	78	43	48	91	124
Gillies, Clark	NY Islanders	75	35	56	91	68

1979-80

PRINCE OF WALES CONFERENCE

Norris Division

Team	GP	W	L	T	GF	GA	PTS
Montreal	80	47	20	13	328	240	107
Los Angeles	80	30	36	14	290	313	74
Pittsburgh	80	30	37	13	251	303	73
Hartford	80	27	34	19	303	312	73
Detroit	80	26	43	11	268	306	63

Adams Division

Team	GP	W	L	T	GF	GA	PTS
Buffalo	80	47	17	16	318	201	110
Boston	80	46	21	13	310	234	105
Minnesota	80	36	28	16	311	253	88
Toronto	80	35	40	5	304	327	75
Quebec	80	25	44	11	248	313	61

CLARENCE CAMPBELL CONFERENCE

Patrick Division

Team	GP	W	L	T	GF	GA	PTS
Philadelphia	80	48	12	20	327	254	116
*NY Islanders	80	39	28	13	281	247	91
NY Rangers	80	38	32	10	308	284	86
Atlanta	80	35	32	13	282	269	83
Washington	80	27	40	13	261	293	67

Smythe Division

Team	GP	W	L	T	GF	GA	PTS
Chicago	80	34	27	19	241	250	87
St. Louis	80	34	34	12	266	278	80
Vancouver	80	27	37	16	256	281	70
Edmonton	80	28	39	13	301	322	69
Winnipeg	80	20	49	11	214	314	51
Colorado	80	19	48	13	234	308	51

Leading Scorers

Player	Club	GP	G	A	PTS	PIM
Dionne, Marcel	Los Angeles	80	53	84	137	32
Gretzky, Wayne	Edmonton	79	51	86	137	21
Lafleur, Guy	Montreal	74	50	75	125	12
Perreault, Gilbert	Buffalo	80	40	66	106	57
Rogers, Mike	Hartford	80	44	61	105	10
Trottier, Bryan	NY Islanders	78	42	62	104	68
Simmer, Charlie	Los Angeles	64	56	45	101	65
Stoughton, Blaine	Hartford	80	56	44	100	16
Sittler, Darryl	Toronto	73	40	57	97	62
MacDonald, Blair	Edmonton	80	46	48	94	6
Federko, Bernie	St. Louis	79	38	56	94	24

1980-81

PRINCE OF WALES CONFERENCE

Norris Division

Team	GP	W	L	T	GF	GA	PTS
Montreal	80	45	22	13	332	232	103
Los Angeles	80	43	24	13	337	290	99
Pittsburgh	80	30	37	13	302	345	73
Hartford	80	21	41	18	292	372	60
Detroit	80	19	43	18	252	339	56

Adams Division

Team	GP	W	L	T	GF	GA	PTS
Buffalo	80	39	20	21	327	250	99
Boston	80	37	30	13	316	272	87
Minnesota	80	35	28	17	291	263	87
Quebec	80	30	32	18	314	318	78
Toronto	80	28	37	15	322	367	71

CLARENCE CAMPBELL CONFERENCE

Patrick Division

Team	GP	W	L	T	GF	GA	PTS
*NY Islanders	80	48	18	14	355	260	110
Philadelphia	80	41	24	15	313	249	97
Calgary	80	39	27	14	329	298	92
NY Rangers	80	30	36	14	312	317	74
Washington	80	26	36	18	286	317	70

Smythe Division

Team	GP	W	L	T	GF	GA	PTS
St. Louis	80	45	18	17	352	281	107
Chicago	80	31	33	16	304	315	78
Vancouver	80	28	32	20	289	301	76
Edmonton	80	29	35	16	328	327	74
Colorado	80	22	45	13	258	344	57
Winnipeg	80	9	57	14	246	400	32

Leading Scorers

Player	Club	GP	G	A	PTS	PIM
Gretzky, Wayne	Edmonton	80	55	109	164	28
Dionne, Marcel	Los Angeles	80	58	77	135	70
Nilsson, Kent	Calgary	80	49	82	131	26
Bossy, Mike	NY Islanders	79	68	51	119	32
Taylor, Dave	Los Angeles	72	47	65	112	130
Stastny, Peter	Quebec	77	39	70	109	37
Simmer, Charlie	Los Angeles	65	56	49	105	62
Rogers, Mike	Hartford	80	40	65	105	32
Federko, Bernie	St. Louis	78	31	73	104	47
Richard, Jacques	Quebec	78	52	51	103	39
Middleton, Rick	Boston	80	44	59	103	16
Trottier, Bryan	NY Islanders	73	31	72	103	74

1981-82

CLARENCE CAMPBELL CONFERENCE

Norris Division

Team	GP	W	L	T	GF	GA	PTS
Minnesota	80	37	23	20	346	288	94
Winnipeg	80	33	33	14	319	332	80
St. Louis	80	32	40	8	315	349	72
Chicago	80	30	38	12	332	363	72
Toronto	80	20	44	16	298	380	56
Detroit	80	21	47	12	270	351	54

Smythe Division

Team	GP	W	L	T	GF	GA	PTS
Edmonton	80	48	17	15	417	295	111
Vancouver	80	30	33	17	290	286	77
Calgary	80	29	34	17	334	345	75
Los Angeles	80	24	41	15	314	369	63
Colorado	80	18	49	13	241	362	49

PRINCE OF WALES CONFERENCE

Adams Division

Team	GP	W	L	T	GF	GA	PTS
Montreal	80	46	17	17	360	223	109
Boston	80	43	27	10	323	285	96
Buffalo	80	39	26	15	307	273	93
Quebec	80	33	31	16	356	345	82
Hartford	80	21	41	18	264	351	60

Patrick Division

Team	GP	W	L	T	GF	GA	PTS
*NY Islanders	80	54	16	10	385	250	118
NY Rangers	80	39	27	14	316	306	92
Philadelphia	80	38	31	11	325	313	87
Pittsburgh	80	31	36	13	310	337	75
Washington	80	26	41	13	319	338	65

Leading Scorers

Player	Club	GP	G	A	PTS	PIM
Gretzky, Wayne	Edmonton	80	92	120	212	26
Bossy, Mike	NY Islanders	80	64	83	147	22
Stastny, Peter	Quebec	80	46	93	139	91
Maruk, Dennis	Washington	80	60	76	136	128
Trottier, Bryan	NY Islanders	80	50	79	129	88
Savard, Denis	Chicago	80	32	87	119	82
Dionne, Marcel	Los Angeles	78	50	67	117	50
Smith, Bobby	Minnesota	80	43	71	114	82
Ciccarelli, Dino	Minnesota	76	55	51	106	138
Taylor, Dave	Los Angeles	78	39	67	106	130

1982-83

CLARENCE CAMPBELL CONFERENCE

Norris Division

Team	GP	W	L	T	GF	GA	PTS
Chicago	80	47	23	10	338	268	104
Minnesota	80	40	24	16	321	290	96
Toronto	80	28	40	12	293	330	68
St. Louis	80	25	40	15	285	316	65
Detroit	80	21	44	15	263	344	57

Smythe Division

Team	GP	W	L	T	GF	GA	PTS
Edmonton	80	47	21	12	424	315	106
Calgary	80	32	34	14	321	317	78
Vancouver	80	30	35	15	303	309	75
Winnipeg	80	33	39	8	311	333	74
Los Angeles	80	27	41	12	308	365	66

PRINCE OF WALES CONFERENCE

Adams Division

Team	GP	W	L	T	GF	GA	PTS
Boston	80	50	20	10	327	228	110
Montreal	80	42	24	14	350	286	98
Buffalo	80	38	29	13	318	285	89
Quebec	80	34	34	12	343	336	80
Hartford	80	19	54	7	261	403	45

Patrick Division

Team	GP	W	L	T	GF	GA	PTS
Philadelphia	80	49	23	8	326	240	106
*NY Islanders	80	42	26	12	302	226	96
Washington	80	39	25	16	306	283	94
NY Rangers	80	35	35	10	306	287	80
New Jersey	80	17	49	14	230	338	48
Pittsburgh	80	18	53	9	257	394	45

Leading Scorers

Player	Club	GP	G	A	PTS	PIM
Gretzky, Wayne	Edmonton	80	71	125	196	59
Stastny, Peter	Quebec	75	47	77	124	78
Savard, Denis	Chicago	78	35	86	121	99
Bossy, Mike	NY Islanders	79	60	58	118	20
Dionne, Marcel	Los Angeles	80	56	51	107	22
Pederson, Barry	Boston	77	46	61	107	47
Messier, Mark	Edmonton	77	48	58	106	72
Goulet, Michel	Quebec	80	57	48	105	51
Anderson, Glenn	Edmonton	72	48	56	104	70
Nilsson, Kent	Calgary	80	46	58	104	10
Kurri, Jari	Edmonton	80	45	59	104	22

1983-84

CLARENCE CAMPBELL CONFERENCE

Norris Division

Team	GP	W	L	T	GF	GA	PTS
Minnesota	80	39	31	10	345	344	88
St. Louis	80	32	41	7	293	316	71
Detroit	80	31	42	7	298	323	69
Chicago	80	30	42	8	277	311	68
Toronto	80	26	45	9	303	387	61

Smythe Division

Team	GP	W	L	T	GF	GA	PTS
*Edmonton	80	57	18	5	446	314	119
Calgary	80	34	32	14	311	314	82
Vancouver	80	32	39	9	306	328	73
Winnipeg	80	31	38	11	340	374	73
Los Angeles	80	23	44	13	309	376	59

PRINCE OF WALES CONFERENCE

Adams Division

Team	GP	W	L	T	GF	GA	PTS
Boston	80	49	25	6	336	261	104
Buffalo	80	48	25	7	315	257	103
Quebec	80	42	28	10	360	278	94
Montreal	80	35	40	5	286	295	75
Hartford	80	28	42	10	288	320	66

Patrick Division

Team	GP	W	L	T	GF	GA	PTS
NY Islanders	80	50	26	4	357	269	104
Washington	80	48	27	5	308	226	101
Philadelphia	80	44	26	10	350	290	98
NY Rangers	80	42	29	9	314	304	93
New Jersey	80	17	56	7	231	350	41
Pittsburgh	80	16	58	6	254	390	38

Leading Scorers

Player	Club	GP	G	A	PTS	PIM
Gretzky, Wayne	Edmonton	74	87	118	205	39
Coffey, Paul	Edmonton	80	40	86	126	104
Goulet, Michel	Quebec	75	56	65	121	76
Stastny, Peter	Quebec	80	46	73	119	73
Bossy, Mike	NY Islanders	67	51	67	118	8
Pederson, Barry	Boston	80	39	77	116	64
Kurri, Jari	Edmonton	64	52	61	113	14
Trottier, Bryan	NY Islanders	68	40	71	111	59
Federko, Bernie	St. Louis	79	41	66	107	43
Middleton, Rick	Boston	80	47	58	105	14

1984-85

CLARENCE CAMPBELL CONFERENCE

Norris Division

Team	GP	W	L	T	GF	GA	PTS
St. Louis	80	37	31	12	299	288	86
Chicago	80	38	35	7	309	299	83
Detroit	80	27	41	12	313	357	66
Minnesota	80	25	43	12	268	321	62
Toronto	80	20	52	8	253	358	48

Smythe Division

Team	GP	W	L	T	GF	GA	PTS
*Edmonton	80	49	20	11	401	298	109
Winnipeg	80	43	27	10	358	332	96
Calgary	80	41	27	12	363	302	94
Los Angeles	80	34	32	14	339	326	82
Vancouver	80	25	46	9	284	401	59

PRINCE OF WALES CONFERENCE

Adams Division

Team	GP	W	L	T	GF	GA	PTS
Montreal	80	41	27	12	309	262	94
Quebec	80	41	30	9	323	275	91
Buffalo	80	38	28	14	290	237	90
Boston	80	36	34	10	303	287	82
Hartford	80	30	41	9	268	318	69

Patrick Division

Team	GP	W	L	T	GF	GA	PTS
Philadelphia	80	53	20	7	348	241	113
Washington	80	46	25	9	322	240	101
NY Islanders	80	40	34	6	345	312	86
NY Rangers	80	26	44	10	295	345	62
New Jersey	80	22	48	10	264	346	54
Pittsburgh	80	24	51	5	276	385	53

Leading Scorers

Player	Club	GP	G	A	PTS	PIM
Gretzky, Wayne	Edmonton	80	73	135	208	52
Kurri, Jari	Edmonton	73	71	64	135	30
Hawerchuk, Dale	Winnipeg	80	53	77	130	74
Dionne, Marcel	Los Angeles	80	46	80	126	46
Coffey, Paul	Edmonton	80	37	84	121	97
Bossy, Mike	NY Islanders	76	58	59	117	38
Ogrodnick, John	Detroit	79	55	50	105	30
Savard, Denis	Chicago	79	38	67	105	56
Federko, Bernie	St. Louis	76	30	73	103	27
Gartner, Mike	Washington	80	50	52	102	71

1985-86
CLARENCE CAMPBELL CONFERENCE
Norris Division

Team	GP	W	L	T	GF	GA	PTS
Chicago	80	39	33	8	351	349	86
Minnesota	80	38	33	9	327	305	85
St. Louis	80	37	34	9	302	291	83
Toronto	80	25	48	7	311	386	57
Detroit	80	17	57	6	266	415	40

Smythe Division

Team	GP	W	L	T	GF	GA	PTS
Edmonton	80	56	17	7	426	310	119
Calgary	80	40	31	9	354	315	89
Winnipeg	80	26	47	7	295	372	59
Vancouver	80	23	44	13	282	333	59
Los Angeles	80	23	49	8	284	389	54

PRINCE OF WALES CONFERENCE
Adams Division

Team	GP	W	L	T	GF	GA	PTS
Quebec	80	43	31	6	330	289	92
*Montreal	80	40	33	7	330	280	87
Boston	80	37	31	12	311	288	86
Hartford	80	40	36	4	332	302	84
Buffalo	80	37	37	6	296	291	80

Patrick Division

Team	GP	W	L	T	GF	GA	PTS
Philadelphia	80	53	23	4	335	241	110
Washington	80	50	23	7	315	272	107
NY Islanders	80	39	29	12	327	284	90
NY Rangers	80	36	38	6	280	276	78
Pittsburgh	80	34	38	8	313	305	76
New Jersey	80	28	49	3	300	374	59

Leading Scorers

Player	Club	GP	G	A	PTS	PIM
Gretzky, Wayne	Edmonton	80	52	163	215	52
Lemieux, Mario	Pittsburgh	79	48	93	141	43
Coffey, Paul	Edmonton	79	48	90	138	120
Kurri, Jari	Edmonton	78	68	63	131	22
Bossy, Mike	NY Islanders	80	61	62	123	14
Stastny, Peter	Quebec	76	41	81	122	60
Savard, Denis	Chicago	80	47	69	116	111
Naslund, Mats	Montreal	80	43	67	110	16
Hawerchuk, Dale	Winnipeg	80	46	59	105	44
Broten, Neal	Minnesota	80	29	76	105	47

1986-87
CLARENCE CAMPBELL CONFERENCE
Norris Division

Team	GP	W	L	T	GF	GA	PTS
St. Louis	80	32	33	15	281	293	79
Detroit	80	34	36	10	260	274	78
Chicago	80	29	37	14	290	310	72
Toronto	80	32	42	6	286	319	70
Minnesota	80	30	40	10	296	314	70

Smythe Division

Team	GP	W	L	T	GF	GA	PTS
*Edmonton	80	50	24	6	372	284	106
Calgary	80	46	31	3	318	289	95
Winnipeg	80	40	32	8	279	271	88
Los Angeles	80	31	41	8	318	341	70
Vancouver	80	29	43	8	282	314	66

PRINCE OF WALES CONFERENCE
Adams Division

Team	GP	W	L	T	GF	GA	PTS
Hartford	80	43	30	7	287	270	93
Montreal	80	41	29	10	277	241	92
Boston	80	39	34	7	301	276	85
Quebec	80	31	39	10	267	276	72
Buffalo	80	28	44	8	280	308	64

Patrick Division

Team	GP	W	L	T	GF	GA	PTS
Philadelphia	80	46	26	8	310	245	100
Washington	80	38	32	10	285	278	86
NY Islanders	80	35	33	12	279	281	82
NY Rangers	80	34	38	8	307	323	76
Pittsburgh	80	30	38	12	297	290	72
New Jersey	80	29	45	6	293	368	64

Leading Scorers

Player	Club	GP	G	A	PTS	PIM
Gretzky, Wayne	Edmonton	79	62	121	183	28
Kurri, Jari	Edmonton	79	54	54	108	41
Lemieux, Mario	Pittsburgh	63	54	53	107	57
Messier, Mark	Edmonton	77	37	70	107	73
Gilmour, Doug	St. Louis	80	42	63	105	58
Ciccarelli, Dino	Minnesota	80	52	51	103	92
Hawerchuk, Dale	Winnipeg	80	47	53	100	54
Goulet, Michel	Quebec	75	49	47	96	61
Kerr, Tim	Philadelphia	75	58	37	95	57
Bourque, Raymond	Boston	78	23	72	95	36

1987-88
CLARENCE CAMPBELL CONFERENCE
Norris Division

Team	GP	W	L	T	GF	GA	PTS
Detroit	80	41	28	11	322	269	93
St. Louis	80	34	38	8	278	294	76
Chicago	80	30	41	9	284	328	69
Toronto	80	21	49	10	273	345	52
Minnesota	80	19	48	13	242	349	51

Smythe Division

Team	GP	W	L	T	GF	GA	PTS
Calgary	80	48	23	9	397	305	105
*Edmonton	80	44	25	11	363	288	99
Winnipeg	80	33	36	11	292	310	77
Los Angeles	80	30	42	8	318	359	68
Vancouver	80	25	46	9	272	320	59

PRINCE OF WALES CONFERENCE
Adams Division

Team	GP	W	L	T	GF	GA	PTS
Montreal	80	45	22	13	298	238	103
Boston	80	44	30	6	300	251	94
Buffalo	80	37	32	11	283	305	85
Hartford	80	35	38	7	249	267	77
Quebec	80	32	43	5	271	306	69

Patrick Division

Team	GP	W	L	T	GF	GA	PTS
NY Islanders	80	39	31	10	308	267	88
Washington	80	38	33	9	281	249	85
Philadelphia	80	38	33	9	292	292	85
New Jersey	80	38	36	6	295	296	82
NY Rangers	80	36	34	10	300	283	82
Pittsburgh	80	36	35	9	319	316	81

Leading Scorers

Player	Club	GP	G	A	PTS	PIM
Lemieux, Mario	Pittsburgh	77	70	98	168	92
Gretzky, Wayne	Edmonton	64	40	109	149	24
Savard, Denis	Chicago	80	44	87	131	95
Hawerchuk, Dale	Winnipeg	80	44	77	121	59
Robitaille, Luc	Los Angeles	80	53	58	111	82
Stastny, Peter	Quebec	76	46	65	111	69
Messier, Mark	Edmonton	77	37	74	111	103
Carson, Jimmy	Los Angeles	80	55	52	107	45
Loob, Hakan	Calgary	80	50	56	106	47
Goulet, Michel	Quebec	80	48	58	106	56

1988-89
CLARENCE CAMPBELL CONFERENCE
Norris Division

Team	GP	W	L	T	GF	GA	PTS
Detroit	80	34	34	12	313	316	80
St. Louis	80	33	35	12	275	285	78
Minnesota	80	27	37	16	258	278	70
Chicago	80	27	41	12	297	335	66
Toronto	80	28	46	6	259	342	62

Smythe Division

Team	GP	W	L	T	GF	GA	PTS
*Calgary	80	54	17	9	354	226	117
Los Angeles	80	42	31	7	376	335	91
Edmonton	80	38	34	8	325	306	84
Vancouver	80	33	39	8	251	253	74
Winnipeg	80	26	42	12	300	355	64

PRINCE OF WALES CONFERENCE
Adams Division

Team	GP	W	L	T	GF	GA	PTS
Montreal	80	53	18	9	315	218	115
Boston	80	37	29	14	289	256	88
Buffalo	80	38	35	7	291	299	83
Hartford	80	37	38	5	299	290	79
Quebec	80	27	46	7	269	342	61

Patrick Division

Team	GP	W	L	T	GF	GA	PTS
Washington	80	41	29	10	305	259	92
Pittsburgh	80	40	33	7	347	349	87
NY Rangers	80	37	35	8	310	307	82
Philadelphia	80	36	36	8	307	285	80
New Jersey	80	27	41	12	281	325	66
NY Islanders	80	28	47	5	265	325	61

Leading Scorers

Player	Club	GP	G	A	PTS	PIM
Lemieux, Mario	Pittsburgh	76	85	114	199	100
Gretzky, Wayne	Los Angeles	78	54	114	168	26
Yzerman, Steve	Detroit	80	65	90	155	61
Nicholls, Bernie	Los Angeles	79	70	80	150	96
Brown, Rob	Pittsburgh	68	49	66	115	118
Coffey, Paul	Pittsburgh	75	30	83	113	193
Mullen, Joe	Calgary	79	51	59	110	16
Kurri, Jari	Edmonton	76	44	58	102	69
Carson, Jimmy	Edmonton	80	49	51	100	36
Robitaille, Luc	Los Angeles	78	46	52	98	65

1989-90
CLARENCE CAMPBELL CONFERENCE
Norris Division

Team	GP	W	L	T	GF	GA	PTS
Chicago	80	41	33	6	316	294	88
St. Louis	80	37	34	9	295	279	83
Toronto	80	38	38	4	337	358	80
Minnesota	80	36	40	4	284	291	76
Detroit	80	28	38	14	288	323	70

Smythe Division

Team	GP	W	L	T	GF	GA	PTS
Calgary	80	42	23	15	348	265	99
*Edmonton	80	38	28	14	315	283	90
Winnipeg	80	37	32	11	298	290	85
Los Angeles	80	34	39	7	338	337	75
Vancouver	80	25	41	14	245	306	64

PRINCE OF WALES CONFERENCE
Adams Division

Team	GP	W	L	T	GF	GA	PTS
Boston	80	46	25	9	289	232	101
Buffalo	80	45	27	8	286	248	98
Montreal	80	41	28	11	288	234	93
Hartford	80	38	33	9	275	268	85
Quebec	80	12	61	7	240	407	31

Patrick Division

Team	GP	W	L	T	GF	GA	PTS
NY Rangers	80	36	31	13	279	267	85
New Jersey	80	37	34	9	295	288	83
Washington	80	36	38	6	284	275	78
NY Islanders	80	31	38	11	281	288	73
Pittsburgh	80	32	40	8	318	359	72
Philadelphia	80	30	39	11	290	297	71

Leading Scorers

Player	Club	GP	G	A	PTS	PIM
Gretzky, Wayne	Los Angeles	73	40	102	142	42
Messier, Mark	Edmonton	79	45	84	129	79
Yzerman, Steve	Detroit	79	62	65	127	79
Lemieux, Mario	Pittsburgh	59	45	78	123	78
Hull, Brett	St. Louis	80	72	41	113	24
Nicholls, Bernie	L.A., NYR	79	39	73	112	86
Turgeon, Pierre	Buffalo	80	40	66	106	29
LaFontaine, Pat	NY Islanders	74	54	51	105	38
Coffey, Paul	Pittsburgh	80	29	74	103	95
Sakic, Joe	Quebec	80	39	63	102	27
Oates, Adam	St. Louis	80	23	79	102	30

1990-91
CLARENCE CAMPBELL CONFERENCE
Norris Division

Team	GP	W	L	T	GF	GA	PTS
Chicago	80	49	23	8	284	211	106
St. Louis	80	47	22	11	310	250	105
Detroit	80	34	38	8	273	298	76
Minnesota	80	27	39	14	256	266	68
Toronto	80	23	46	11	241	318	57

Smythe Division

Team	GP	W	L	T	GF	GA	PTS
Los Angeles	80	46	24	10	340	254	102
Calgary	80	46	26	8	344	263	100
Edmonton	80	37	37	6	272	272	80
Vancouver	80	28	43	9	243	315	65
Winnipeg	80	26	43	11	260	288	63

PRINCE OF WALES CONFERENCE
Adams Division

Team	GP	W	L	T	GF	GA	PTS
Boston	80	44	24	12	299	264	100
Montreal	80	39	30	11	273	249	89
Buffalo	80	31	30	19	292	278	81
Hartford	80	31	38	11	238	276	73
Quebec	80	16	50	14	236	354	46

Patrick Division

Team	GP	W	L	T	GF	GA	PTS
*Pittsburgh	80	41	33	6	342	305	88
NY Rangers	80	36	31	13	297	265	85
Washington	80	37	36	7	258	258	81
New Jersey	80	32	33	15	272	264	79
Philadelphia	80	33	37	10	252	267	76
NY Islanders	80	25	45	10	223	290	60

Leading Scorers

Player	Club	GP	G	A	PTS	PIM
Gretzky, Wayne	Los Angeles	78	41	122	163	16
Hull, Brett	St. Louis	78	86	45	131	22
Oates, Adam	St. Louis	61	25	90	115	29
Recchi, Mark	Pittsburgh	78	40	73	113	48
Cullen, John	Pit., Hfd.	78	39	71	110	101
Sakic, Joe	Quebec	80	48	61	109	24
Yzerman, Steve	Detroit	80	51	57	108	34
Fleury, Theoren	Calgary	79	51	53	104	136
MacInnis, Al	Calgary	78	28	75	103	90
Larmer, Steve	Chicago	80	44	57	101	79

1991-92
CLARENCE CAMPBELL CONFERENCE
Norris Division

Team	GP	W	L	T	GF	GA	PTS
Detroit	80	43	25	12	320	256	98
Chicago	80	36	29	15	257	236	87
St. Louis	80	36	33	11	279	266	83
Minnesota	80	32	42	6	246	278	70
Toronto	80	30	43	7	234	294	67

Smythe Division

Team	GP	W	L	T	GF	GA	PTS
Vancouver	80	42	26	12	285	250	96
Los Angeles	80	35	31	14	287	296	84
Edmonton	80	36	34	10	295	297	82
Winnipeg	80	33	32	15	251	244	81
Calgary	80	31	37	12	296	305	74
San Jose	80	17	58	5	219	359	39

PRINCE OF WALES CONFERENCE
Adams Division

Team	GP	W	L	T	GF	GA	PTS
Montreal	80	41	28	11	267	207	93
Boston	80	36	32	12	270	275	84
Buffalo	80	31	37	12	289	299	74
Hartford	80	26	41	13	247	283	65
Quebec	80	20	48	12	255	318	52

Patrick Division

Team	GP	W	L	T	GF	GA	PTS
NY Rangers	80	50	25	5	321	246	105
Washington	80	45	27	8	330	275	98
*Pittsburgh	80	39	32	9	343	308	87
New Jersey	80	38	31	11	289	259	87
NY Islanders	80	34	35	11	291	299	79
Philadelphia	80	32	37	11	252	273	75

Leading Scorers

Player	Club	GP	G	A	PTS	PIM
Lemieux, Mario	Pittsburgh	64	44	87	131	94
Stevens, Kevin	Pittsburgh	80	54	69	123	254
Gretzky, Wayne	Los Angeles	74	31	90	121	34
Hull, Brett	St. Louis	73	70	39	109	48
Robitaille, Luc	Los Angeles	80	44	63	107	95
Messier, Mark	NY Rangers	79	35	72	107	76
Roenick, Jeremy	Chicago	80	53	50	103	98
Yzerman, Steve	Detroit	79	45	58	103	64
Leetch, Brian	NY Rangers	80	22	80	102	26
Oates, Adam	St.L., Bos.	80	20	79	99	22

1992-93
CLARENCE CAMPBELL CONFERENCE
Norris Division

Team	GP	W	L	T	GF	GA	PTS
Chicago	84	47	25	12	279	230	106
Detroit	84	47	28	9	369	280	103
Toronto	84	44	29	11	288	241	99
St. Louis	84	37	36	11	282	278	85
Minnesota	84	36	38	10	272	293	82
Tampa Bay	84	23	54	7	245	332	53

Smythe Division

Team	GP	W	L	T	GF	GA	PTS
Vancouver	84	46	29	9	346	278	101
Calgary	84	43	30	11	322	282	97
Los Angeles	84	39	35	10	338	340	88
Winnipeg	84	40	37	7	322	320	87
Edmonton	84	26	50	8	242	337	60
San Jose	84	11	71	2	218	414	24

PRINCE OF WALES CONFERENCE
Adams Division

Team	GP	W	L	T	GF	GA	PTS
Boston	84	51	26	7	332	268	109
Quebec	84	47	27	10	351	300	104
*Montreal	84	48	30	6	326	280	102
Buffalo	84	38	36	10	335	297	86
Hartford	84	26	52	6	284	369	58
Ottawa	84	10	70	4	202	395	24

Patrick Division

Team	GP	W	L	T	GF	GA	PTS
Pittsburgh	84	56	21	7	367	268	119
Washington	84	43	34	7	325	286	93
NY Islanders	84	40	37	7	335	297	87
New Jersey	84	40	37	7	308	299	87
Philadelphia	84	36	37	11	319	319	83
NY Rangers	84	34	39	11	304	308	79

Leading Scorers

Player	Club	GP	G	A	PTS	PIM
Lemieux, Mario	Pittsburgh	60	69	91	160	38
LaFontaine, Pat	Buffalo	84	53	95	148	63
Oates, Adam	Boston	84	45	97	142	32
Yzerman, Steve	Detroit	84	58	79	137	44
Selanne, Teemu	Winnipeg	84	76	56	132	45
Turgeon, Pierre	NY Islanders	83	58	74	132	26
Mogilny, Alexander	Buffalo	77	76	51	127	40
Gilmour, Doug	Toronto	83	32	95	127	100
Robitaille, Luc	Los Angeles	84	63	62	125	100
Recchi, Mark	Philadelphia	84	53	70	123	95

1993-94
EASTERN CONFERENCE
Northeast Division

Team	GP	W	L	T	GF	GA	PTS
Pittsburgh	84	44	27	13	299	285	101
Boston	84	42	29	13	289	252	97
Montreal	84	41	29	14	283	248	96
Buffalo	84	43	32	9	282	218	95
Quebec	84	34	42	8	277	292	76
Hartford	84	27	48	9	227	288	63
Ottawa	84	14	61	9	201	397	37

Atlantic Division

Team	GP	W	L	T	GF	GA	PTS
*NY Rangers	84	52	24	8	299	231	112
New Jersey	84	47	25	12	306	220	106
Washington	84	39	35	10	277	263	88
NY Islanders	84	36	36	12	282	264	84
Florida	84	33	34	17	233	233	83
Philadelphia	84	35	39	10	294	314	80
Tampa Bay	84	30	43	11	224	251	71

WESTERN CONFERENCE
Central Division

Team	GP	W	L	T	GF	GA	PTS
Detroit	84	46	30	8	356	275	100
Toronto	84	43	29	12	280	243	98
Dallas	84	42	29	13	286	265	97
St. Louis	84	40	33	11	270	283	91
Chicago	84	39	36	9	254	240	87
Winnipeg	84	24	51	9	245	344	57

Pacific Division

Team	GP	W	L	T	GF	GA	PTS
Calgary	84	42	29	13	302	256	97
Vancouver	84	41	40	3	279	276	85
San Jose	84	33	35	16	252	265	82
Anaheim	84	33	46	5	229	251	71
Los Angeles	84	27	45	12	294	322	66
Edmonton	84	25	45	14	261	305	64

Leading Scorers

Player	Club	GP	G	A	PTS	PIM
Gretzky, Wayne	Los Angeles	81	38	92	130	20
Fedorov, Sergei	Detroit	82	56	64	120	34
Oates, Adam	Boston	77	32	80	112	45
Gilmour, Doug	Toronto	83	27	84	111	105
Bure, Pavel	Vancouver	76	60	47	107	86
Roenick, Jeremy	Chicago	84	46	61	107	125
Recchi, Mark	Philadelphia	84	40	67	107	46
Shanahan, Brendan	St. Louis	81	52	50	102	211
Andreychuk, Dave	Toronto	83	53	46	99	98
Jagr, Jaromir	Pittsburgh	80	32	67	99	61

1994-95
EASTERN CONFERENCE
Northeast Division

Team	GP	W	L	T	GF	GA	PTS
Quebec	48	30	13	5	185	134	65
Pittsburgh	48	29	16	3	181	158	61
Boston	48	27	18	3	150	127	57
Buffalo	48	22	19	7	130	119	51
Hartford	48	19	24	5	127	141	43
Montreal	48	18	23	7	125	148	43
Ottawa	48	9	34	5	117	174	23

Atlantic Division

Team	GP	W	L	T	GF	GA	PTS
Philadelphia	48	28	16	4	150	132	60
*New Jersey	48	22	18	8	136	121	52
Washington	48	22	18	8	136	120	52
NY Rangers	48	22	23	3	139	134	47
Florida	48	20	22	6	115	127	46
Tampa Bay	48	17	28	3	120	144	37
NY Islanders	48	15	28	5	126	158	35

WESTERN CONFERENCE
Central Division

Team	GP	W	L	T	GF	GA	PTS
Detroit	48	33	11	4	180	117	70
St. Louis	48	28	15	5	178	135	61
Chicago	48	24	19	5	156	115	53
Toronto	48	21	19	8	135	146	50
Dallas	48	17	23	8	136	135	42
Winnipeg	48	16	25	7	157	177	39

Pacific Division

Team	GP	W	L	T	GF	GA	PTS
Calgary	48	24	17	7	163	135	55
Vancouver	48	18	18	12	153	148	48
San Jose	48	19	25	4	129	161	42
Los Angeles	48	16	23	9	142	174	41
Edmonton	48	17	27	4	136	183	38
Anaheim	48	16	27	5	125	164	37

Leading Scorers

Player	Club	GP	G	A	PTS	PIM
Jagr, Jaromir	Pittsburgh	48	32	38	70	37
Lindros, Eric	Philadelphia	46	29	41	70	60
Zhamnov, Alex	Winnipeg	48	30	35	65	20
Sakic, Joe	Quebec	47	19	43	62	30
Francis, Ron	Pittsburgh	44	11	48	59	18
Fleury, Theoren	Calgary	47	29	29	58	112
Coffey, Paul	Detroit	45	14	44	58	72
Renberg, Mikael	Philadelphia	47	26	31	57	20
LeClair, John	Mtl., Phi.	46	26	28	54	30
Messier, Mark	NY Rangers	46	14	39	53	40
Oates, Adam	Boston	48	12	41	53	8

Colorado's Alex Tanguay ranked among the NHL's leading scorers for the first time in 2003-04.

Tampa Bay's Brad Richards was among three Lightning forwards to crack the top 10 in scoring in 2003-04.

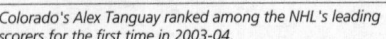

1995-96
EASTERN CONFERENCE
Northeast Division

Team	GP	W	L	T	GF	GA	PTS
Pittsburgh	82	49	29	4	362	284	102
Boston	82	40	31	11	282	269	91
Montreal	82	40	32	10	265	248	90
Hartford	82	34	39	9	237	259	77
Buffalo	82	33	42	7	247	262	73
Ottawa	82	18	59	5	191	291	41

Atlantic Division

Team	GP	W	L	T	GF	GA	PTS
Philadelphia	82	45	24	13	282	208	103
NY Rangers	82	41	27	14	272	237	96
Florida	82	41	31	10	254	234	92
Washington	82	39	32	11	234	204	89
Tampa Bay	82	38	32	12	238	248	88
New Jersey	82	37	33	12	215	202	86
NY Islanders	82	22	50	10	229	315	54

WESTERN CONFERENCE
Central Division

Team	GP	W	L	T	GF	GA	PTS
Detroit	82	62	13	7	325	181	131
Chicago	82	40	28	14	273	220	94
Toronto	82	34	36	12	247	252	80
St. Louis	82	32	34	16	219	248	80
Winnipeg	82	36	40	6	275	291	78
Dallas	82	26	42	14	227	280	66

Pacific Division

Team	GP	W	L	T	GF	GA	PTS
*Colorado	82	47	25	10	326	240	104
Calgary	82	34	37	11	241	240	79
Vancouver	82	32	35	15	278	278	79
Anaheim	82	35	39	8	234	247	78
Edmonton	82	30	44	8	240	304	68
Los Angeles	82	24	40	18	256	302	66
San Jose	82	20	55	7	252	357	47

Leading Scorers

Player	Club	GP	G	A	PTS	PIM
Lemieux, Mario	Pittsburgh	70	69	92	161	54
Jagr, Jaromir	Pittsburgh	82	62	87	149	96
Sakic, Joe	Colorado	82	51	69	120	44
Francis, Ron	Pittsburgh	77	27	92	119	56
Forsberg, Peter	Colorado	82	30	86	116	47
Lindros, Eric	Philadelphia	73	47	68	115	163
Kariya, Paul	Anaheim	82	50	58	108	20
Selanne, Teemu	Wpg., Ana.	79	40	68	108	22
Mogilny, Alexander	Vancouver	79	55	52	107	16
Fedorov, Sergei	Detroit	78	39	68	107	48

1996-97
EASTERN CONFERENCE
Northeast Division

Team	GP	W	L	T	GF	GA	PTS
Buffalo	82	40	30	12	237	208	92
Pittsburgh	82	38	36	8	285	280	84
Ottawa	82	31	36	15	226	234	77
Montreal	82	31	36	15	249	276	77
Hartford	82	32	39	11	226	256	75
Boston	82	26	47	9	234	300	61

Atlantic Division

Team	GP	W	L	T	GF	GA	PTS
New Jersey	82	45	23	14	231	182	104
Philadelphia	82	45	24	13	274	217	103
Florida	82	35	28	19	221	201	89
NY Rangers	82	38	34	10	258	231	86
Washington	82	33	40	9	214	231	75
Tampa Bay	82	32	40	10	217	247	74
NY Islanders	82	29	41	12	240	250	70

WESTERN CONFERENCE
Central Division

Team	GP	W	L	T	GF	GA	PTS
Dallas	82	48	26	8	252	198	104
*Detroit	82	38	26	18	253	197	94
Phoenix	82	38	37	7	240	243	83
St. Louis	82	36	35	11	236	239	83
Chicago	82	34	35	13	223	210	81
Toronto	82	30	44	8	230	273	68

Pacific Division

Team	GP	W	L	T	GF	GA	PTS
Colorado	82	49	24	9	277	205	107
Anaheim	82	36	33	13	245	233	85
Edmonton	82	36	37	9	252	247	81
Vancouver	82	35	40	7	257	273	77
Calgary	82	32	41	9	214	239	73
Los Angeles	82	28	43	11	214	268	67
San Jose	82	27	47	8	211	278	62

Leading Scorers

Player	Club	GP	G	A	PTS	PIM
Lemieux, Mario	Pittsburgh	76	50	72	122	65
Selanne, Teemu	Anaheim	78	51	58	109	34
Kariya, Paul	Anaheim	69	44	55	99	6
LeClair, John	Philadelphia	82	50	47	97	58
Gretzky, Wayne	NY Rangers	82	25	72	97	28
Jagr, Jaromir	Pittsburgh	63	47	48	95	40
Sundin, Mats	Toronto	82	41	53	94	59
Palffy, Ziggy	NY Islanders	80	48	42	90	43
Francis, Ron	Pittsburgh	81	27	63	90	20
Shanahan, Brendan	Hfd., Det.	81	47	41	88	131

1997-98
EASTERN CONFERENCE
Northeast Division

Team	GP	W	L	T	GF	GA	PTS
Pittsburgh	82	40	24	18	228	188	98
Boston	82	39	30	13	221	194	91
Buffalo	82	36	29	17	211	187	89
Montreal	82	37	32	13	235	208	87
Ottawa	82	34	33	15	193	200	83
Carolina	82	33	41	8	200	219	74

Atlantic Division

Team	GP	W	L	T	GF	GA	PTS
New Jersey	82	48	23	11	225	166	107
Philadelphia	82	42	29	11	242	193	95
Washington	82	40	30	12	219	202	92
NY Islanders	82	30	41	11	212	225	71
NY Rangers	82	25	39	18	197	231	68
Florida	82	24	43	15	203	256	63
Tampa Bay	82	17	55	10	151	269	44

WESTERN CONFERENCE
Central Division

Team	GP	W	L	T	GF	GA	PTS
Dallas	82	49	22	11	242	167	109
*Detroit	82	44	23	15	250	196	103
St. Louis	82	45	29	8	256	204	98
Phoenix	82	35	35	12	224	227	82
Chicago	82	30	39	13	192	199	73
Toronto	82	30	43	9	194	237	69

Pacific Division

Team	GP	W	L	T	GF	GA	PTS
Colorado	82	39	26	17	231	205	95
Los Angeles	82	38	33	11	227	225	87
Edmonton	82	35	37	10	215	224	80
San Jose	82	34	38	10	210	216	78
Calgary	82	26	41	15	217	252	67
Anaheim	82	26	43	13	205	261	65
Vancouver	82	25	43	14	224	273	64

Leading Scorers

Player	Club	GP	G	A	PTS	PIM
Jagr, Jaromir	Pittsburgh	77	35	67	102	64
Forsberg, Peter	Colorado	72	25	66	91	94
Bure, Pavel	Vancouver	82	51	39	90	48
Gretzky, Wayne	NY Rangers	82	23	67	90	28
LeClair, John	Philadelphia	82	51	36	87	32
Palffy, Ziggy	NY Islanders	82	45	42	87	34
Francis, Ron	Pittsburgh	81	25	62	87	20
Selanne, Teemu	Anaheim	73	52	34	86	30
Allison, Jason	Boston	81	33	50	83	60
Stumpel, Jozef	Los Angeles	77	21	58	79	53

Robert Lang was among the NHL's leading scorers in 2003-04 while splitting the season between Washington and Detroit.

Cory Stillman had 25 goals and a career-high 55 assists to rank among the scoring leaders with Tampa Bay in 2003-04.

Ottawa's Daniel Alfredsson improved on his offensive totals for the sixth straight season in 2003-04 to rank among the leaders.

1998-99

EASTERN CONFERENCE
Northeast Division

Team	GP	W	L	T	GF	GA	PTS
Ottawa	82	44	23	15	239	179	103
Toronto	82	45	30	7	268	231	97
Boston	82	39	30	13	214	181	91
Buffalo	82	37	28	17	207	175	91
Montreal	82	32	39	11	184	209	75

Atlantic Division

Team	GP	W	L	T	GF	GA	PTS
New Jersey	82	47	24	11	248	196	105
Philadelphia	82	37	26	19	231	196	93
Pittsburgh	82	38	30	14	242	225	90
NY Rangers	82	33	38	11	217	227	77
NY Islanders	82	24	48	10	194	244	58

Southeast Division

Team	GP	W	L	T	GF	GA	PTS
Carolina	82	34	30	18	210	202	86
Florida	82	30	34	18	210	228	78
Washington	82	31	45	6	200	218	68
Tampa Bay	82	19	54	9	179	292	47

WESTERN CONFERENCE
Central Division

Team	GP	W	L	T	GF	GA	PTS
Detroit	82	43	32	7	245	202	93
St Louis	82	37	32	13	237	209	87
Chicago	82	29	41	12	202	248	70
Nashville	82	28	47	7	190	261	63

Pacific Division

Team	GP	W	L	T	GF	GA	PTS
*Dallas	82	51	19	12	236	168	114
Phoenix	82	39	31	12	205	197	90
Anaheim	82	35	34	13	215	206	83
San Jose	82	31	33	18	196	191	80
Los Angeles	82	32	45	5	189	222	69

Northwest Division

Team	GP	W	L	T	GF	GA	PTS
Colorado	82	44	28	10	239	205	98
Edmonton	82	33	37	12	230	226	78
Calgary	82	30	40	12	211	234	72
Vancouver	82	23	47	12	192	258	58

Leading Scorers

Player	Club	GP	G	A	PTS	PIM
Jagr, Jaromir	Pittsburgh	81	44	83	127	66
Selanne, Teemu	Anaheim	75	47	60	107	30
Kariya, Paul	Anaheim	82	39	62	101	40
Forsberg, Peter	Colorado	78	30	67	97	108
Sakic, Joe	Colorado	73	41	55	96	29
Yashin, Alexei	Ottawa	82	44	50	94	54
Lindros, Eric	Philadelphia	71	40	53	93	120
Fleury, Theoren	Cgy., Col.	75	40	53	93	86
LeClair, John	Philadelphia	76	43	47	90	30
Demitra, Pavol	St Louis	82	37	52	89	16

1999-2000

EASTERN CONFERENCE
Northeast Division

Team	GP	W	L	T	OTL	GF	GA	PTS
Toronto	82	45	27	7	3	246	222	100
Ottawa	82	41	28	11	2	244	210	95
Buffalo	82	35	32	11	4	213	204	85
Montreal	82	35	34	9	4	196	194	83
Boston	82	24	33	19	6	210	248	73

Atlantic Division

Team	GP	W	L	T	OTL	GF	GA	PTS
Philadelphia	82	45	22	12	3	237	179	105
*New Jersey	82	45	24	8	5	251	203	103
Pittsburgh	82	37	31	8	6	241	236	88
NY Rangers	82	29	38	12	3	218	246	73
NY Islanders	82	24	48	9	1	194	275	58

Southeast Division

Team	GP	W	L	T	OTL	GF	GA	PTS
Washington	82	44	24	12	2	227	194	102
Florida	82	43	27	6	6	244	209	98
Carolina	82	37	35	10	0	217	216	84
Tampa Bay	82	19	47	9	7	204	310	54
Atlanta	82	14	57	7	4	170	313	39

WESTERN CONFERENCE
Central Division

Team	GP	W	L	T	OTL	GF	GA	PTS
St. Louis	82	51	19	11	1	248	165	114
Detroit	82	48	22	10	2	278	210	108
Chicago	82	33	37	10	2	242	245	78
Nashville	82	28	40	7	7	199	240	70

Pacific Division

Team	GP	W	L	T	OTL	GF	GA	PTS
Dallas	82	43	23	10	6	211	184	102
Los Angeles	82	39	27	12	4	245	228	94
Phoenix	82	39	31	8	4	232	228	90
San Jose	82	35	30	10	7	225	214	87
Anaheim	82	34	33	12	3	217	227	83

Northwest Division

Team	GP	W	L	T	OTL	GF	GA	PTS
Colorado	82	42	28	11	1	233	201	96
Edmonton	82	32	26	16	8	226	212	88
Vancouver	82	30	29	15	8	227	237	83
Calgary	82	31	36	10	5	211	256	77

Leading Scorers

Player	Club	GP	G	A	PTS	PIM
Jagr, Jaromir	Pittsburgh	63	42	54	96	50
Bure, Pavel	Florida	74	58	36	94	16
Recchi, Mark	Philadelphia	82	28	63	91	50
Kariya, Paul	Anaheim	74	42	44	86	24
Selanne, Teemu	Anaheim	79	33	52	85	12
Nolan, Owen	San Jose	78	44	40	84	110
Amonte, Tony	Chicago	82	43	41	84	48
Modano, Mike	Dallas	77	38	43	81	48
Sakic, Joe	Colorado	60	28	53	81	28
Yzerman, Steve	Detroit	78	35	44	79	34

2000-01

EASTERN CONFERENCE
Northeast Division

Team	GP	W	L	T	OTL	GF	GA	PTS
Ottawa	82	48	21	9	4	274	205	109
Buffalo	82	46	30	5	1	218	184	98
Toronto	82	37	29	11	5	232	207	90
Boston	82	36	30	8	8	227	249	88
Montreal	82	28	40	8	6	206	232	70

Atlantic Division

Team	GP	W	L	T	OTL	GF	GA	PTS
New Jersey	82	48	19	12	3	295	195	111
Philadelphia	82	43	25	11	3	240	207	100
Pittsburgh	82	42	28	9	3	281	256	96
NY Rangers	82	33	43	5	1	250	290	72
NY Islanders	82	21	51	7	3	185	268	52

Southeast Division

Team	GP	W	L	T	OTL	GF	GA	PTS
Washington	82	41	27	10	4	233	211	96
Carolina	82	38	32	9	3	212	225	88
Florida	82	22	38	13	9	200	246	66
Atlanta	82	23	45	12	2	211	289	60
Tampa Bay	82	24	47	6	5	201	280	59

WESTERN CONFERENCE
Central Division

Team	GP	W	L	T	OTL	GF	GA	PTS
Detroit	82	49	20	9	4	253	202	111
St. Louis	82	43	22	12	5	249	195	103
Nashville	82	34	36	9	3	186	200	80
Chicago	82	29	40	8	5	210	246	71
Columbus	82	28	39	9	6	190	233	71

Pacific Division

Team	GP	W	L	T	OTL	GF	GA	PTS
Dallas	82	48	24	8	2	241	187	106
San Jose	82	40	27	12	3	217	192	95
Los Angeles	82	38	28	13	3	252	228	92
Phoenix	82	35	27	17	3	214	212	90
Anaheim	82	25	41	11	5	188	245	66

Northwest Division

Team	GP	W	L	T	OTL	GF	GA	PTS
*Colorado	82	52	16	10	4	270	192	118
Edmonton	82	39	28	12	3	243	222	93
Vancouver	82	36	28	11	7	239	238	90
Calgary	82	27	36	15	4	197	236	73
Minnesota	82	25	39	13	5	168	210	68

Leading Scorers

Player	Club	GP	G	A	PTS	PIM
Jagr, Jaromir	Pittsburgh	81	52	69	121	42
Sakic, Joe	Colorado	82	54	64	118	30
Elias, Patrik	New Jersey	82	40	56	96	51
Kovalev, Alex	Pittsburgh	79	44	51	95	96
Allison, Jason	Boston	82	36	59	95	85
Straka, Martin	Pittsburgh	82	27	68	95	38
Bure, Pavel	Florida	82	59	33	92	58
Weight, Doug	Edmonton	82	25	65	90	91
Palffy, Ziggy	Los Angeles	73	38	51	89	20
Forsberg, Peter	Colorado	73	27	62	89	54

New Jersey's Patrick Elias was a top-10 scorer for the second time in his career in 2003-04, having finished third in 2000-01.

Marian Hossa established career highs with 46 assists and 82 points for Ottawa to finish fifth in scoring in 2003-04.

Vancouver's Markus Naslund finished fourth in scoring in 2003-04 after two straight seasons in the #2 spot.

2001-02
EASTERN CONFERENCE
Northeast Division

Team	GP	W	L	T	OTL	GF	GA	PTS
Boston	82	43	24	6	9	236	201	101
Toronto	82	43	25	10	4	249	207	100
Ottawa	82	39	27	9	7	243	208	94
Montreal	82	36	31	12	3	207	209	87
Buffalo	82	35	35	11	1	213	200	82

Atlantic Division

Team	GP	W	L	T	OTL	GF	GA	PTS
Philadelphia	82	42	27	10	3	234	192	97
NY Islanders	82	42	28	8	4	239	220	96
New Jersey	82	41	28	9	4	205	187	95
NY Rangers	82	36	38	4	4	227	258	80
Pittsburgh	82	28	41	8	5	198	249	69

Southeast Division

Team	GP	W	L	T	OTL	GF	GA	PTS
Carolina	82	35	26	16	5	217	217	91
Washington	82	36	33	11	2	228	240	85
Tampa Bay	82	27	40	11	4	178	219	69
Florida	82	22	44	10	6	180	250	60
Atlanta	82	19	47	11	5	187	288	54

WESTERN CONFERENCE
Central Division

Team	GP	W	L	T	OTL	GF	GA	PTS
*Detroit	82	51	17	10	4	251	187	116
St. Louis	82	43	27	8	4	227	188	98
Chicago	82	41	27	13	1	216	207	96
Nashville	82	28	41	13	0	196	230	69
Columbus	82	22	47	8	5	164	255	57

Pacific Division

Team	GP	W	L	T	OTL	GF	GA	PTS
San Jose	82	44	27	8	3	248	199	99
Phoenix	82	40	27	9	6	228	210	95
Los Angeles	82	40	27	11	4	214	190	95
Dallas	82	36	28	13	5	215	213	90
Anaheim	82	29	42	8	3	175	198	69

Northwest Division

Team	GP	W	L	T	OTL	GF	GA	PTS
Colorado	82	45	28	8	1	212	169	99
Vancouver	82	42	30	7	3	254	211	94
Edmonton	82	38	28	12	4	205	182	92
Calgary	82	32	35	12	3	201	220	79
Minnesota	82	26	35	12	9	195	238	73

Leading Scorers

Player	Club	GP	G	A	PTS	PIM
Iginla, Jarome	Calgary	82	52	44	96	77
Naslund, Markus	Vancouver	81	40	50	90	50
Bertuzzi, Todd	Vancouver	72	36	49	85	110
Sundin, Mats	Toronto	82	41	39	80	94
Jagr, Jaromir	Washington	69	31	48	79	30
Sakic, Joe	Colorado	82	26	53	79	18
Demitra, Pavol	St. Louis	82	35	43	78	46
Oates, Adam	Wsh., Phi.	80	14	64	78	28
Modano, Mike	Dallas	78	34	43	77	38
Francis, Ron	Carolina	80	27	50	77	18

2002-03
EASTERN CONFERENCE
Northeast Division

Team	GP	W	L	T	OTL	GF	GA	PTS
Ottawa	82	52	21	8	1	263	182	113
Toronto	82	44	28	7	3	236	208	98
Boston	82	36	31	11	4	245	237	87
Montreal	82	30	35	8	9	206	234	77
Buffalo	82	27	37	10	8	190	219	72

Atlantic Division

Team	GP	W	L	T	OTL	GF	GA	PTS
*New Jersey	82	46	20	10	6	216	166	108
Philadelphia	82	45	20	13	4	211	166	107
NY Islanders	82	35	34	11	2	224	231	83
NY Rangers	82	32	36	10	4	210	231	78
Pittsburgh	82	27	44	6	5	189	255	65

Southeast Division

Team	GP	W	L	T	OTL	GF	GA	PTS
Tampa Bay	82	36	25	16	5	219	210	93
Washington	82	39	29	8	6	224	220	92
Atlanta	82	31	39	7	5	226	284	74
Florida	82	24	36	13	9	176	237	70
Carolina	82	22	43	11	6	171	240	61

WESTERN CONFERENCE
Central Division

Team	GP	W	L	T	OTL	GF	GA	PTS
Detroit	82	48	20	10	4	269	203	110
St. Louis	82	41	24	11	6	253	222	99
Chicago	82	30	33	13	6	207	226	79
Nashville	82	27	35	13	7	183	206	74
Columbus	82	29	42	8	3	213	263	69

Pacific Division

Team	GP	W	L	T	OTL	GF	GA	PTS
Dallas	82	46	17	15	4	245	169	111
Anaheim	82	40	27	9	6	203	193	95
Los Angeles	82	33	37	6	6	203	221	78
Phoenix	82	31	35	11	5	204	230	78
San Jose	82	28	37	9	8	214	239	73

Northwest Division

Team	GP	W	L	T	OTL	GF	GA	PTS
Colorado	82	42	19	13	8	251	194	105
Vancouver	82	45	23	13	1	264	208	104
Minnesota	82	42	29	10	1	198	178	95
Edmonton	82	36	26	11	9	231	230	92
Calgary	82	29	36	13	4	186	228	75

Leading Scorers

Player	Club	GP	G	A	PTS	PIM
Forsberg, Peter	Colorado	75	29	77	106	70
Naslund, Markus	Vancouver	82	48	56	104	52
Thornton, Joe	Boston	77	36	65	101	109
Hejduk, Milan	Colorado	82	50	48	98	52
Bertuzzi, Todd	Vancouver	82	46	51	97	144
Demitra, Pavol	St. Louis	78	36	57	93	32
Murray, Glen	Boston	82	44	48	92	64
Lemieux, Mario	Pittsburgh	67	28	63	91	43
Heatley, Danny	Atlanta	77	41	48	89	58
Palffy, Ziggy	Los Angeles	76	37	48	85	47
Modano, Mike	Dallas	79	28	57	85	30

2003-04
EASTERN CONFERENCE
Northeast Division

Team	GP	W	L	T	OTL	GF	GA	PTS
Boston	82	41	19	15	7	209	188	104
Toronto	82	45	24	10	3	242	204	103
Ottawa	82	43	23	10	6	262	189	102
Montreal	82	41	30	7	4	208	192	93
Buffalo	82	37	34	7	4	220	221	85

Atlantic Division

Team	GP	W	L	T	OTL	GF	GA	PTS
Philadelphia	82	40	21	15	6	229	186	101
New Jersey	82	43	25	12	2	213	164	100
NY Islanders	82	38	29	11	4	237	210	91
NY Rangers	82	27	40	7	8	206	250	69
Pittsburgh	82	23	47	8	4	190	303	58

Southeast Division

Team	GP	W	L	T	OTL	GF	GA	PTS
*Tampa Bay	82	46	22	8	6	245	192	106
Atlanta	82	33	37	8	4	214	243	78
Carolina	82	28	34	14	6	172	209	76
Florida	82	28	35	15	4	188	221	75
Washington	82	23	46	10	3	186	253	59

WESTERN CONFERENCE
Central Division

Team	GP	W	L	T	OTL	GF	GA	PTS
Detroit	82	48	21	11	2	255	189	109
St. Louis	82	39	30	11	2	191	198	91
Nashville	82	38	29	11	4	216	217	91
Columbus	82	25	45	8	4	177	238	62
Chicago	82	20	43	11	8	188	259	59

Pacific Division

Team	GP	W	L	T	OTL	GF	GA	PTS
San Jose	82	43	21	12	6	219	183	104
Dallas	82	41	26	13	2	194	175	97
Los Angeles	82	28	29	16	9	205	217	81
Anaheim	82	29	35	10	8	184	213	76
Phoenix	82	22	36	18	6	188	245	68

Northwest Division

Team	GP	W	L	T	OTL	GF	GA	PTS
Vancouver	82	43	24	10	5	235	194	101
Colorado	82	40	22	13	7	236	198	100
Calgary	82	42	30	7	3	200	176	94
Edmonton	82	36	29	12	5	221	208	89
Minnesota	82	30	29	20	3	188	183	83

Leading Scorers

Player	Club	GP	G	A	PTS	PIM
St. Louis, Martin	Tampa Bay	82	38	56	94	24
Kovalchuk, Ilya	Atlanta	81	41	46	87	63
Sakic, Joe	Colorado	81	33	54	87	42
Naslund, Markus	Vancouver	78	35	49	84	58
Hossa, Marian	Ottawa	81	36	46	82	46
Elias, Patrik	New Jersey	82	38	43	81	44
Alfredsson, Daniel	Ottawa	77	32	48	80	24
Stillman, Cory	Tampa Bay	81	25	55	80	36
Lang, Robert	Wsh., Det.	69	30	49	79	24
Richards, Brad	Tampa Bay	82	26	53	79	12
Tanguay, Alex	Colorado	69	25	54	79	42

2004-05
SEASON CANCELLED

Colorado's Joe Sakic finished third in scoring in 2003-04, his ninth career appearance in the top 10.

Atlanta's Ilya Kovalchuk tied Rick Nash and Jarome Iginla with 41 goals in 2003-04 and finished second with 87 points.

After a breakout season the year before, Tampa Bay's Martin St. Louis won the Art Ross and Hart trophies in 2003-04.

Team Records

Regular Season

FINAL STANDINGS

MOST POINTS, ONE SEASON:
132 – Montreal Canadiens, 1976-77. 60w-8L-12T. 80GP
131 – Detroit Red Wings, 1995-96. 62w-13L-7T. 82GP
129 – Montreal Canadiens, 1977-78. 59w-10L-11T. 80GP

BEST POINTS PERCENTAGE, ONE SEASON:
.875 – Boston Bruins, 1929-30. 38w-5L-1T. 77PTS in 44GP
.830 – Montreal Canadiens, 1943-44. 38w-5L-7T. 83PTS in 50GP
.825 – Montreal Canadiens, 1976-77. 60w-8L-12T. 132PTS in 80GP
.806 – Montreal Canadiens, 1977-78. 59w-10L-11T. 129PTS in 80GP
.800 – Montreal Canadiens, 1944-45. 38w-8L-4T. 80PTS in 50GP

FEWEST POINTS, ONE SEASON:
8 – Quebec Bulldogs, 1919-20. 4w-20L-0T. 24GP
10 – Toronto Arenas, 1918-19. 5w-13L-0T. 18GP
12 – Hamilton Tigers, 1920-21. 6w-18L-0T. 24GP
– Hamilton Tigers, 1922-23. 6w-18L-0T. 24GP
– Boston Bruins, 1924-25. 6w-24L-0T. 30GP
– Philadelphia Quakers, 1930-31. 4w-36L-4T. 44GP

FEWEST POINTS, ONE SEASON (MINIMUM 70-GAME SCHEDULE):
21 – Washington Capitals, 1974-75. 8w-67L-5T. 80GP
24 – Ottawa Senators, 1992-93. 10w-70L-4T. 84GP
– San Jose Sharks, 1992-93. 11w-71L-2T. 84GP
30 – New York Islanders, 1972-73. 12w-60L-6T. 78GP

WORST POINTS PERCENTAGE, ONE SEASON:
.131 – Washington Capitals, 1974-75. 8w-67L-5T. 21PTS in 80GP
.136 – Philadelphia Quakers, 1930-31. 4w-36L-4T. 12PTS in 44GP
.143 – Ottawa Senators, 1992-93. 10w-70L-4T. 24PTS in 84GP
– San Jose Sharks, 1992-93. 11w-71L-2T. 24PTS in 84GP
.148 – Pittsburgh Pirates, 1929-30. 5w-36L-3T. 13PTS in 44GP

TEAM WINS

Most Wins

MOST WINS, ONE SEASON:
62 – Detroit Red Wings, 1995-96. 82GP
60 – Montreal Canadiens, 1976-77. 80GP
59 – Montreal Canadiens, 1977-78. 80GP

MOST HOME WINS, ONE SEASON:
36 – Philadelphia Flyers, 1975-76. 40GP
– **Detroit Red Wings**, 1995-96. 41GP
33 – Boston Bruins, 1970-71. 39GP
– Boston Bruins, 1973-74. 39GP
– Montreal Canadiens, 1976-77. 40GP
– Philadelphia Flyers, 1976-77. 40GP
– New York Islanders, 1981-82. 40GP
– Philadelphia Flyers, 1985-86. 40GP

MOST ROAD WINS, ONE SEASON:
28 – New Jersey Devils, 1998-99. 41GP
27 – Montreal Canadiens, 1976-77. 40GP
– Montreal Canadiens, 1977-78. 40GP
– St. Louis Blues, 1999-2000. 41GP
26 – Boston Bruins, 1971-72. 39GP
– Montreal Canadiens, 1975-76. 40GP
– Edmonton Oilers, 1983-84. 40GP
– Detroit Red Wings, 1995-96. 41GP

Fewest Wins

FEWEST WINS, ONE SEASON:
4 – Quebec Bulldogs, 1919-20. 24GP
– **Philadelphia Quakers**, 1930-31. 44GP
5 – Toronto Arenas, 1918-19. 18GP
Pittsburgh Pirates, 1929-30. 44GP

FEWEST WINS, ONE SEASON (MINIMUM 70-GAME SCHEDULE):
8 – Washington Capitals, 1974-75. 80GP
9 – Winnipeg Jets, 1980-81. 80GP
10 – Ottawa Senators, 1992-93. 84GP

FEWEST HOME WINS, ONE SEASON:
2 – Chicago Blackhawks, 1927-28. 22GP
3 – Boston Bruins, 1924-25. 15GP
– Chicago Blackhawks, 1928-29. 22GP
– Philadelphia Quakers, 1930-31. 22GP

FEWEST HOME WINS, ONE SEASON (MINIMUM 70-GAME SCHEDULE):
6 – Chicago Blackhawks, 1954-55. 35GP
– **Washington Capitals**, 1975-76. 40GP
7 – Boston Bruins, 1962-63. 35GP
– Washington Capitals, 1974-75. 40GP
– Winnipeg Jets, 1980-81. 40GP
– Pittsburgh Penguins, 1983-84. 40GP

FEWEST ROAD WINS, ONE SEASON:
0 – Toronto Arenas, 1918-19. 9GP
– **Quebec Bulldogs**, 1919-20. 12GP
– **Pittsburgh Pirates**, 1929-30. 22GP
1 – Hamilton Tigers, 1921-22. 12GP
– Toronto St. Patricks, 1925-26. 18GP
– Philadelphia Quakers, 1930-31. 22GP
– New York Americans, 1940-41. 24GP
– Washington Capitals, 1974-75. 40GP
* – Ottawa Senators, 1992-93. 41GP

FEWEST ROAD WINS, ONE SEASON (MINIMUM 70-GAME SCHEDULE):
1 – Washington Capitals, 1974-75. 40GP
* – Ottawa Senators, 1992-93. 41GP
2 – Boston Bruins, 1960-61. 35GP
– Los Angeles Kings, 1969-70. 38GP
– New York Islanders, 1972-73. 39GP
– California Golden Seals, 1973-74. 39GP
– Colorado Rockies, 1977-78. 40GP
– Winnipeg Jets, 1980-81. 40GP
– Quebec Nordiques, 1991-92. 40GP

TEAM LOSSES

Fewest Losses

FEWEST LOSSES, ONE SEASON:
5 – Ottawa Senators, 1919-20. 24GP
– **Boston Bruins**, 1929-30. 44GP
– **Montreal Canadiens**, 1943-44. 50GP

FEWEST HOME LOSSES, ONE SEASON:
0 – Ottawa Senators, 1922-23. 12GP
– **Montreal Canadiens**, 1943-44. 25GP
1 – Toronto Arenas, 1917-18. 11GP
– Ottawa Senators, 1918-19. 9GP
– Ottawa Senators, 1919-20. 12GP
– Toronto St. Patricks, 1922-23. 12GP
– Boston Bruins, 1929-30. 22GP
– Boston Bruins, 1930-31. 22GP
– Montreal Canadiens, 1976-77. 40GP
– Quebec Nordiques, 1994-95. 24GP

FEWEST ROAD LOSSES, ONE SEASON:
3 – Montreal Canadiens, 1928-29. 22GP
4 – Ottawa Senators, 1919-20. 12GP
– Montreal Canadiens, 1927-28. 22GP
– Boston Bruins, 1929-30. 20GP
– Boston Bruins, 1940-41. 24GP

FEWEST LOSSES, ONE SEASON (MINIMUM 70-GAME SCHEDULE):
8 – Montreal Canadiens, 1976-77. 80GP
10 – Montreal Canadiens, 1972-73. 78GP
– Montreal Canadiens, 1977-78. 80GP
11 – Montreal Canadiens, 1975-76. 80GP

FEWEST HOME LOSSES, ONE SEASON (MINIMUM 70-GAME SCHEDULE):
1 – Montreal Canadiens, 1976-77. 40GP
2 – Montreal Canadiens, 1961-62. 35GP
– New York Rangers, 1970-71. 39GP
– Philadelphia Flyers, 1975-76. 40GP

FEWEST ROAD LOSSES, ONE SEASON (MINIMUM 70-GAME SCHEDULE):
6 – Montreal Canadiens, 1972-73. 39GP
– **Montreal Canadiens**, 1974-75. 40GP
– **Montreal Canadiens**, 1977-78. 40GP
7 – Detroit Red Wings, 1951-52. 35GP
– Montreal Canadiens, 1976-77. 40GP
– Philadelphia Flyers, 1979-80. 40GP
– Boston Bruins, 2003-04. 41GP

Most Losses

MOST LOSSES, ONE SEASON:
71 – San Jose Sharks, 1992-93. 84GP
70 – Ottawa Senators, 1992-93. 84GP
67 – Washington Capitals, 1974-75. 80GP
61 – Quebec Nordiques, 1989-90. 80GP
– Ottawa Senators, 1993-94. 84GP

MOST HOME LOSSES, ONE SEASON:
*32 – San Jose Sharks, 1992-93. 41GP
29 – Pittsburgh Penguins, 1983-84. 40GP
* – Ottawa Senators, 1993-94. 41GP

MOST ROAD LOSSES, ONE SEASON:
*40 – Ottawa Senators, 1992-93. 41GP
39 – Washington Capitals, 1974-75. 40GP
37 – California Golden Seals, 1973-74. 39GP
* – San Jose Sharks, 1992-93. 41GP

* – Does not include neutral site games

TEAM TIES

Most Ties

MOST TIES, ONE SEASON:
24 – Philadelphia Flyers, 1969-70. 76GP
23 – Montreal Canadiens, 1962-63. 70GP
– Chicago Blackhawks, 1973-74. 78GP

MOST HOME TIES, ONE SEASON:
13 – New York Rangers, 1954-55. 35GP
– **Philadelphia Flyers**, 1969-70. 38GP
– **California Golden Seals**, 1971-72. 39GP
– **California Golden Seals**, 1972-73. 39GP
– **Chicago Blackhawks**, 1973-74. 39GP

MOST ROAD TIES, ONE SEASON:
15 – Philadelphia Flyers, 1976-77. 40GP
14 – Montreal Canadiens, 1952-53. 35GP
– Montreal Canadiens, 1974-75. 40GP
– Philadelphia Flyers, 1975-76. 40GP

Fewest Ties

FEWEST TIES, ONE SEASON (Since 1926-27):
1 – Boston Bruins, 1929-30. 44GP
2 – Montreal Canadiens, 1926-27. 44GP
– New York Americans, 1926-27. 44GP
– Boston Bruins, 1938-39. 48GP
– New York Rangers, 1941-42. 48GP
– San Jose Sharks, 1992-93. 84GP

FEWEST TIES, ONE SEASON (MINIMUM 70-GAME SCHEDULE):
2 – San Jose Sharks, 1992-93. 84GP
3 – New Jersey Devils, 1985-86. 80GP
– Calgary Flames, 1986-87. 80GP
– Vancouver Canucks, 1993-94. 84GP

WINNING STREAKS

LONGEST WINNING STREAK, ONE SEASON:
17 Games – Pittsburgh Penguins, Mar. 9 – Apr. 10, 1993.
15 Games – New York Islanders, Jan. 21 – Feb. 20, 1982.
14 Games – Boston Bruins, Dec. 3, 1929 – Jan. 9, 1930.

LONGEST HOME WINNING STREAK, ONE SEASON:
20 Games – Boston Bruins, Dec. 3, 1929 – Mar. 18, 1930.
– **Philadelphia Flyers**, Jan. 4 – Apr. 3, 1976.

LONGEST ROAD WINNING STREAK, ONE SEASON:
10 Games – Buffalo Sabres, Dec. 10, 1983 – Jan. 23, 1984.
– **St. Louis Blues**, Jan. 21 – Mar. 2, 2000.
– **New Jersey Devils**, Feb. 27 – Apr. 7, 2001.
8 Games – Boston Bruins, Feb. 17 – Mar. 8, 1972.
– Los Angeles Kings, Dec. 18, 1974 – Jan. 16, 1975.
– Montreal Canadiens, Dec. 18, 1977 – Jan. 18, 1978.
– New York Islanders, Feb. 27 – Mar. 29, 1981.
– Montreal Canadiens, Jan. 21 – Feb. 21, 1982.
– Philadelphia Flyers, Dec. 22, 1982 – Jan. 16, 1983.
– Winnipeg Jets, Feb. 25 – Apr. 6, 1985.
– Edmonton Oilers, Dec. 9, 1986 – Jan. 17, 1987.
– Boston Bruins, Mar. 15 – Apr. 14, 1993.
– Detroit Red Wings, Feb. 4 – Mar. 9, 2002.
– Vancouver Canucks, Dec. 20, 2003 – Jan. 13, 2004.

LONGEST WINNING STREAK FROM START OF SEASON:
10 Games – Toronto Maple Leafs, 1993-94.
8 Games – Toronto Maple Leafs, 1934-35.
– Buffalo Sabres, 1975-76.
7 Games – Edmonton Oilers, 1983-84.
– Quebec Nordiques, 1985-86.
– Pittsburgh Penguins, 1986-87.
– Pittsburgh Penguins, 1994-95.

LONGEST HOME WINNING STREAK FROM START OF SEASON:
11 Games – Chicago Blackhawks, 1963-64.
10 Games – Ottawa Senators, 1925-26.
9 Games – Montreal Canadiens, 1953-54.
– Chicago Blackhawks, 1971-72.

LONGEST ROAD WINNING STREAK FROM START OF SEASON:
7 Games – Toronto Maple Leafs, Nov. 14 – Dec. 15, 1940.
– **Philadelphia Flyers**, Oct. 12 – Nov. 16, 1985.

LONGEST WINNING STREAK, INCLUDING PLAYOFFS:
15 Games – Detroit Red Wings, Feb. 27 – Apr. 5, 1955.
(9 regular-season games, 6 playoff games)

LONGEST HOME WINNING STREAK, INCLUDING PLAYOFFS:
24 Games – Philadelphia Flyers, Jan. 4 – Apr. 25, 1976.
(20 regular-season games, 4 playoff games)

LONGEST ROAD WINNING STREAK, INCLUDING PLAYOFFS:
11 Games – New Jersey Devils, Feb. 27 – Apr. 17, 2001.
(10 regular-season games, 1 playoff game)

UNDEFEATED STREAKS

LONGEST UNDEFEATED STREAK, ONE SEASON:
35 Games – Philadelphia Flyers, Oct. 14, 1979 – Jan. 6, 1980. 25w-10T
28 Games – Montreal Canadiens, Dec. 18, 1977 – Feb. 23, 1978. 23w-5T

LONGEST HOME UNDEFEATED STREAK, ONE SEASON:
34 Games – Montreal Canadiens, Nov. 1, 1976 – Apr. 2, 1977. 28w-6T
27 Games – Boston Bruins, Nov. 22, 1970 – Mar. 20, 1971. 26w-1T

LONGEST ROAD UNDEFEATED STREAK, ONE SEASON:
23 Games – Montreal Canadiens, Nov. 27, 1974 – Mar. 12, 1975. 14w-9T
17 Games – Montreal Canadiens, Dec. 18, 1977 – Mar. 1, 1978. 14w-3T

LONGEST UNDEFEATED STREAK FROM START OF SEASON:
15 Games – Edmonton Oilers, 1984-85. 12w-3T
14 Games – Montreal Canadiens, 1943-44. 11w-3T

LONGEST HOME UNDEFEATED STREAK FROM START OF SEASON:
26 Games – Philadelphia Flyers, Oct. 11, 1979 – Feb. 3, 1980. 19w-7T

LONGEST ROAD UNDEFEATED STREAK FROM START OF SEASON:
15 Games – Detroit Red Wings, Oct. 18 – Dec. 20, 1951. 10w-5T

LONGEST UNDEFEATED STREAK, INCLUDING PLAYOFFS:
21 Games – Pittsburgh Penguins, Mar. 9 – Apr. 22, 1993.
17w-1T in regular season and 3w in playoffs.

LONGEST HOME UNDEFEATED STREAK, INCLUDING PLAYOFFS:
38 Games – Montreal Canadiens, Nov. 1, 1976 – Apr. 26, 1977.
28w-6T in regular season and 4w in playoffs.

LONGEST ROAD UNDEFEATED STREAK, INCLUDING PLAYOFFS:
13 Games – Philadelphia Flyers, Feb. 26 – Apr. 21, 1977. 6w-4T in
regular season and 3w in playoffs.
– **Montreal Canadiens**, Feb. 26 – Apr. 20, 1980. 6w-4T in
regular season and 3w in playoffs.
– **New York Islanders**, Mar. 16 – May 1, 1980. 3w-3T in regular
season and 7w in playoffs.

LOSING STREAKS

LONGEST LOSING STREAK, ONE SEASON:
17 Games – Washington Capitals, Feb. 18 – Mar. 26, 1975.
– **San Jose Sharks**, Jan. 4 – Feb. 12, 1993.
15 Games – Philadelphia Quakers, Nov. 29, 1930 – Jan. 8, 1931.

LONGEST HOME LOSING STREAK, ONE SEASON:
14 Games – Pittsburgh Penguins, Dec. 31, 2003 – Feb. 22, 2004.
11 Games – Boston Bruins, Dec. 8, 1924 – Feb. 17, 1925.
– Washington Capitals, Feb. 18 – Mar. 30, 1975.
– Ottawa Senators, Oct. 27 – Dec. 8, 1993.
– Atlanta Thrashers, Jan. 24 – Mar. 16, 2000.

LONGEST ROAD LOSING STREAK, ONE SEASON:
***38 Games – Ottawa Senators**, Oct. 10, 1992 – Apr. 3, 1993.
37 Games – Washington Capitals, Oct. 9, 1974 – Mar. 26, 1975.

LONGEST LOSING STREAK FROM START OF SEASON:
11 Games – New York Rangers, 1943-44.
7 Games – Montreal Canadiens, 1938-39.
– Chicago Blackhawks, 1947-48.
– Washington Capitals, 1983-84.
– Chicago Blackhawks, 1997-98.

LONGEST HOME LOSING STREAK FROM START OF SEASON:
8 Games – Los Angeles Kings, Oct. 13 – Nov. 6, 1971.

LONGEST ROAD LOSING STREAK FROM START OF SEASON:
***38 Games – Ottawa Senators**, Oct. 10, 1992 – Apr. 3, 1993.

WINLESS STREAKS

LONGEST WINLESS STREAK, ONE SEASON:
30 Games – Winnipeg Jets, Oct. 19 – Dec. 20, 1980. 23L-7T
27 Games – Kansas City Scouts, Feb. 12 – Apr. 4, 1976. 21L-6T
25 Games – Washington Capitals, Nov. 29, 1975 – Jan. 21, 1976. 22L-3T

LONGEST HOME WINLESS STREAK, ONE SEASON:
17 Games – Ottawa Senators, Oct. 28, 1995 – Jan. 27, 1996. 15L-2T
– **Atlanta Thrashers**, Jan. 19 – Mar. 29, 2000. 15L-2T
16 Games – Pittsburgh Penguins, Dec. 31, 2003 – Mar. 4, 2004. 15L-1T

LONGEST ROAD WINLESS STREAK, ONE SEASON:
***38 Games – Ottawa Senators**, Oct. 10, 1992 – Apr. 3, 1993. 38L
37 Games – Washington Capitals, Oct. 9, 1974 – Mar. 26, 1975. 37L

LONGEST WINLESS STREAK FROM START OF SEASON:
15 Games – New York Rangers, 1943-44. 14L-1T
11 Games – Pittsburgh Pirates, 1927-28. 8L-3T
– Minnesota North Stars, 1973-74. 5L-6T
– San Jose Sharks, 1995-96. 7L-4T

LONGEST HOME WINLESS STREAK FROM START OF SEASON:
11 Games – Pittsburgh Penguins, Oct. 8 – Nov. 19, 1983. 9L-2T

LONGEST ROAD WINLESS STREAK FROM START OF SEASON:
***38 Games – Ottawa Senators**, Oct. 10, 1992 – Apr. 3, 1993. 38L

NON-SHUTOUT STREAKS

LONGEST NON-SHUTOUT STREAK:
264 Games – Calgary Flames, Nov. 12, 1981 – Jan. 9, 1985.
261 Games – Los Angeles Kings, Mar. 15, 1986 – Oct. 22, 1989.
244 Games – Washington Capitals, Oct. 31, 1989 – Nov. 11, 1993.
236 Games – New York Rangers, Dec. 20, 1989 – Dec. 13, 1992.
230 Games – Quebec Nordiques, Feb. 10, 1980 – Jan. 12, 1983.

LONGEST NON-SHUTOUT STREAK, INCLUDING PLAYOFFS:
264 Games – Los Angeles Kings, Mar. 15, 1986 – Apr. 6, 1989.
(5 playoff games in 1987; 5 in 1988; 2 in 1989).
262 Games – Chicago Blackhawks, Mar. 14, 1970 – Feb. 21, 1973.
(8 playoff games in 1970; 18 in 1971; 8 in 1972).
251 Games – Quebec Nordiques, Feb. 10, 1980 – Jan. 12, 1983.
(5 playoff games in 1981; 16 in 1982).
246 Games – Pittsburgh Penguins, Jan. 7, 1989 – Oct. 26, 1991.
(11 playoff games in 1989; 24 in 1991).

TEAM GOALS

Most Goals

MOST GOALS, ONE SEASON:
446 – Edmonton Oilers, 1983-84. 80GP
426 – Edmonton Oilers, 1985-86. 80GP
424 – Edmonton Oilers, 1982-83. 80GP
417 – Edmonton Oilers, 1981-82. 80GP
401 – Edmonton Oilers, 1984-85. 80GP

MOST GOALS, ONE TEAM, ONE GAME:
16 – Montreal Canadiens, Mar. 3, 1920, at Quebec. Montreal won 16-3.

MOST GOALS, BOTH TEAMS, ONE GAME:
21 – Montreal Canadiens (14), Toronto St. Patricks (7), Jan. 10, 1920, at Montreal.
– **Edmonton Oilers (12), Chicago Blackhawks (9)**, Dec. 11, 1985, at Chicago.
20 – Edmonton Oilers (12), Minnesota North Stars (8), Jan. 4, 1984, at Edmonton.
– Toronto Maple Leafs (11), Edmonton Oilers (9), Jan. 8, 1986, at Toronto.
19 – Montreal Wanderers (10), Toronto Arenas (9), Dec. 19, 1917, at Montreal.
– Montreal Canadiens (16), Quebec Bulldogs (3), Mar. 3, 1920, at Quebec.
– Montreal Canadiens (13), Hamilton Tigers (6), Feb. 26, 1921, at Montreal.
– Boston Bruins (10), New York Rangers (9), Mar. 4, 1944, at Boston.
– Detroit Red Wings (10), Boston Bruins (9), Mar. 16, 1944, at Detroit.
– Vancouver Canucks (10), Minnesota North Stars (9), Oct. 7, 1983, at Vancouver.

MOST GOALS, ONE TEAM, ONE PERIOD:
9 – Buffalo Sabres, Mar. 19, 1981, at Buffalo, second period during 14-4 win over Toronto.
8 – Detroit Red Wings, Jan. 23, 1944, at Detroit, third period during 15-0 win over NY Rangers.
– Boston Bruins, Mar. 16, 1969, at Boston, second period during 11-3 win over Toronto.
– New York Rangers, Nov. 21, 1971, at NY Rangers, third period during 12-1 win over California.
– Philadelphia Flyers, Mar. 31, 1973, at Philadelphia, second period during 10-2 win over NY Islanders.
– Buffalo Sabres, Dec. 21, 1975, at Buffalo, third period during 14-2 win over Washington.
– Minnesota North Stars, Nov. 11, 1981, at Minnesota, second period during 15-2 win over Winnipeg.
– Pittsburgh Penguins, Dec. 17, 1991, at Pittsburgh, second period during 10-2 win over San Jose.
– Washington Capitals, Feb. 3, 1999, at Washington, second period during 10-1 win over Tampa Bay.

MOST GOALS, BOTH TEAMS, ONE PERIOD:
12 – Buffalo Sabres (9), Toronto Maple Leafs (3), Mar. 19, 1981, at Buffalo, second period. Buffalo won 14-4.
– **Edmonton Oilers (6), Chicago Blackhawks (6)**, Dec. 11, 1985, at Chicago, second period. Edmonton won 12-9.
10 – New York Rangers (7), New York Americans (3), Mar. 16, 1939, at NY Americans, third period. NY Rangers won 11-5.
– Toronto Maple Leafs (6), Detroit Red Wings (4), Mar. 17, 1946, at Detroit, third period. Toronto won 11-7.
– Buffalo Sabres (6), Vancouver Canucks (4), Jan. 8, 1976, at Buffalo, third period. Buffalo won 8-5.
– Buffalo Sabres (5), Montreal Canadiens (5), Oct. 26, 1982, at Montreal, first period. Teams tied 7-7.
– Quebec Nordiques (6), Boston Bruins (4), Dec. 7, 1982, at Quebec, second period. Quebec won 10-5.
– Vancouver Canucks (6), Calgary Flames (4), Jan. 16, 1987, at Vancouver, first period. Vancouver won 9-5.
– Detroit Red Wings (7), Winnipeg Jets (3), Nov. 25, 1987, at Detroit, third period. Detroit won 10-8.
– Chicago Blackhawks (5), St. Louis Blues (5), Mar. 15, 1988, at St. Louis, third period. Teams tied 7-7.

MOST CONSECUTIVE GOALS, ONE TEAM, ONE GAME:
15 – Detroit Red Wings, Jan. 23, 1944, at Detroit during 15-0 win over NY Rangers.

Fewest Goals

FEWEST GOALS, ONE SEASON:
33 – Chicago Blackhawks, 1928-29. 44GP
45 – Montreal Maroons, 1924-25. 30GP
46 – Pittsburgh Pirates, 1928-29. 44GP

FEWEST GOALS, ONE SEASON (MINIMUM 70-GAME SCHEDULE):
133 – Chicago Blackhawks, 1953-54. 70GP
147 – Toronto Maple Leafs, 1954-55. 70GP
– Boston Bruins, 1955-56. 70GP
150 – New York Rangers, 1954-55. 70GP

TEAM POWER-PLAY GOALS

MOST POWER-PLAY GOALS, ONE SEASON:
119 – Pittsburgh Penguins, 1988-89. 80GP
113 – Detroit Red Wings, 1992-93. 84GP
111 – New York Rangers, 1987-88. 80GP
110 – Pittsburgh Penguins, 1987-88. 80GP
– Winnipeg Jets, 1987-88, 80GP

TEAM SHORTHAND GOALS

MOST SHORTHAND GOALS, ONE SEASON:
36 – Edmonton Oilers, 1983-84. 80GP
28 – Edmonton Oilers, 1986-87. 80GP
27 – Edmonton Oilers, 1985-86. 80GP
– Edmonton Oilers, 1988-89. 80GP

TEAM GOALS-PER-GAME

HIGHEST GOALS-PER-GAME AVERAGE, ONE SEASON:
5.58 – Edmonton Oilers, 1983-84. 446G in 80GP.
5.38 – Montreal Canadiens, 1919-20. 129G in 24GP.
5.33 – Edmonton Oilers, 1985-86. 426G in 80GP.
5.30 – Edmonton Oilers, 1982-83. 424G in 80GP.
5.23 – Montreal Canadiens, 1917-18. 115G in 22GP.

LOWEST GOALS-PER-GAME AVERAGE, ONE SEASON:
0.75 – Chicago Blackhawks, 1928-29. 33G in 44GP.
1.05 – Pittsburgh Pirates, 1928-29. 46G in 44GP.
1.20 – New York Americans, 1928-29. 53G in 44GP.

TEAM ASSISTS

MOST ASSISTS, ONE SEASON:
737 – Edmonton Oilers, 1985-86. 80GP
736 – Edmonton Oilers, 1983-84. 80GP
706 – Edmonton Oilers, 1981-82. 80GP

FEWEST ASSISTS, ONE SEASON (Since 1926-27):
45 – New York Rangers, 1926-27. 44GP

FEWEST ASSISTS, ONE SEASON (MINIMUM 70-GAME SCHEDULE):
206 – Chicago Blackhawks, 1953-54. 70GP

TEAM TOTAL POINTS

MOST SCORING POINTS, ONE SEASON:
1,182 – Edmonton Oilers, 1983-84. 80GP
1,163 – Edmonton Oilers, 1985-86. 80GP
1,123 – Edmonton Oilers, 1981-82. 80GP

MOST SCORING POINTS, ONE TEAM, ONE GAME:
40 – Buffalo Sabres, Dec. 21, 1975, at Buffalo. Buffalo defeated Washington 14-2, and had 26A.
39 – Minnesota North Stars, Nov. 11, 1981, at Minnesota. Minnesota defeated Winnipeg 15-2, and had 24A.
37 – Detroit Red Wings, Jan. 23, 1944, at Detroit. Detroit defeated NY Rangers 15-0, and had 22A.
– Toronto Maple Leafs, Mar. 16, 1957, at Toronto. Toronto defeated NY Rangers 14-1, and had 23A.
– Buffalo Sabres, Feb. 25, 1978, at Cleveland. Buffalo defeated Cleveland 13-3, and had 24A.
– Calgary Flames, Feb. 10, 1993, at Calgary. Calgary defeated San Jose 13-1, and had 24A.

MOST SCORING POINTS, BOTH TEAMS, ONE GAME:
62 – Edmonton Oilers, Chicago Blackhawks, Dec. 11, 1985, at Chicago. Edmonton won 12-9. Edmonton had 24A, Chicago, 17A.
53 – Quebec Nordiques, Washington Capitals, Feb. 22, 1981, at Washington. Quebec won 11-7. Quebec had 22A, Washington, 13A.
– Edmonton Oilers, Minnesota North Stars, Jan. 4, 1984, at Edmonton. Edmonton won 12-8. Edmonton had 20A, Minnesota, 13A.
– Minnesota North Stars, St. Louis Blues, Jan. 27, 1984, at St. Louis. Minnesota won 10-8. Minnesota had 19A, St. Louis, 16A.
– Toronto Maple Leafs, Edmonton Oilers, Jan. 8, 1986, at Toronto. Toronto won 11-9. Toronto had 17A, Edmonton, 16A.
52 – Montreal Maroons, New York Americans, Feb. 18, 1936, at NY Americans. Teams tied 8-8. NY Americans had 20A, Montreal, 16A. (3A allowed for each goal.)
– Vancouver Canucks, Minnesota North Stars, Oct. 7, 1983, at Vancouver. Vancouver won 10-9. Vancouver had 16A, Minnesota, 17A.

MOST SCORING POINTS, ONE TEAM, ONE PERIOD:
23 – New York Rangers, Nov. 21, 1971, at NY Rangers, third period during 12-1 win over California. NY Rangers had 8G, 15A.
 – **Buffalo Sabres**, Dec. 21, 1975, at Buffalo, third period during 14-2 win over Washington. Buffalo had 8G, 15A.
 – **Buffalo Sabres**, Mar. 19, 1981, at Buffalo, second period during 14-4 win over Toronto. Buffalo had 9G, 14A.
22 – Detroit Red Wings, Jan. 23, 1944, at Detroit, third period during 15-0 win over NY Rangers. Detroit had 8G, 14A.
 – Boston Bruins, Mar. 16, 1969, at Boston, second period during 11-3 win over Toronto. Boston had 8G, 14A.
 – Minnesota North Stars, Nov. 11, 1981, at Minnesota, second period during 15-2 win over Winnipeg. Minnesota had 8G, 14A.
 – Pittsburgh Penguins, Dec. 17, 1991, at Pittsburgh, second period during 10-2 win over San Jose. Pittsburgh had 8G, 14A.
 – Washington Capitals, Feb. 3, 1999, at Washington, second period during 10-1 win over Tampa Bay. Washington had 8G, 14A.

MOST SCORING POINTS, BOTH TEAMS, ONE PERIOD:
35 – Edmonton, Oilers, Chicago Blackhawks, Dec. 11, 1985, at Chicago, second period. Edmonton won 12-9. Edmonton had 6G, 12A; Chicago, 6G, 11A.
31 – Buffalo Sabres, Toronto Maple Leafs, Mar. 19, 1981, at Buffalo, second period. Buffalo won 14-4. Buffalo had 9G, 14A; Toronto, 3G, 5A.
29 – Winnipeg Jets, Detroit Red Wings, Nov. 25, 1987, at Detroit, third period. Detroit won 10-8. Detroit had 7G, 13A; Winnipeg, 3G, 6A.
 – Chicago Blackhawks, St. Louis Blues, Mar. 15, 1988, at St. Louis, third period. Teams tied 7-7. St. Louis had 5G, 10A; Chicago, 5G, 9A.

FASTEST GOALS

FASTEST SIX GOALS, BOTH TEAMS:
3:00 – Quebec Nordiques, Washington Capitals, Feb. 22, 1981, at Washington. Scorers: Peter Stastny, Quebec, 18:51; Pierre Lacroix, Quebec, 19:57 (first period); Anton Stastny, Quebec, 0:34; Jacques Richard, Quebec, 1:07 and 1:37; Rick Green, Washington, 1:51 (second period). Quebec won 11-7.
3:15 – Montreal Canadiens, Toronto Maple Leafs, Jan. 4, 1944, at Montreal, first period. Scorers: Maurice Richard, Montreal, 14:10; Don Webster, Toronto, 15:13; Fern Majeau, Montreal, 15:41; Phil Watson, Montreal, 15:52; Lorne Carr, Toronto, 16:55; Butch Bouchard, Montreal, 17:25. Montreal won 6-3.

FASTEST FIVE GOALS, BOTH TEAMS:
1:24 – Chicago Blackhawks, Toronto Maple Leafs, Oct. 15, 1983, at Toronto, second period. Scorers: Gaston Gingras, Toronto, 16:49; Denis Savard, Chicago, 17:12; Steve Larmer, Chicago, 17:27; Denis Savard, Chicago, 17:42; John Anderson, Toronto, 18:13. Toronto won 10-8.
1:39 – Detroit Red Wings, Toronto Maple Leafs, Nov. 15, 1944, at Toronto, third period. Scorers: Ted Kennedy, Toronto, 10:36 and 10:55; Harold Jackson, Detroit, 11:48; Steve Wojciechowski, Detroit, 12:02; Don Grosso, Detroit, 12:15. Detroit won 8-4.

FASTEST FIVE GOALS, ONE TEAM:
2:07 – Pittsburgh Penguins, Nov. 22, 1972, at Pittsburgh, third period. Scorers: Bryan Hextall, Jr., 12:00; Jean Pronovost, 12:18; Al McDonough, 13:40; Ken Schinkel, 13:49; Ron Schock, 14:07. Pittsburgh defeated St. Louis 10-4.
2:37 – New York Islanders, Jan. 26, 1982, at NY Islanders, first period. Scorers: Duane Sutter, 1:31; John Tonelli, 2:30; Bryan Trottier, 2:46 and 3:31; Duane Sutter, 4:08. NY Islanders defeated Pittsburgh 9-2.
2:55 – Boston Bruins, Dec. 19, 1974, at Boston. Scorers: Bobby Schmautz, 19:13 (first period); Ken Hodge, 0:18; Phil Esposito, 0:43; Don Marcotte, 0:58; John Bucyk, 2:08 (second period). Boston defeated NY Rangers 11-3.

FASTEST FOUR GOALS, BOTH TEAMS:
0:53 – Chicago Blackhawks, Toronto Maple Leafs, Oct. 15, 1983, at Toronto, second period. Scorers: Gaston Gingras, Toronto, 16:49; Denis Savard, Chicago, 17:12; Steve Larmer, Chicago, 17:27; Denis Savard, Chicago, 17:42. Toronto won 10-8.
0:57 – Quebec Nordiques, Detroit Red Wings, Jan. 27, 1990, at Quebec, first period. Scorers: Paul Gillis, Quebec, 18:01; Claude Loiselle, Quebec, 18:12; Joe Sakic, Quebec, 18:27; Jimmy Carson, Detroit, 18:58. Detroit won 8-6.
1:01 – Colorado Rockies, New York Rangers, Jan. 15, 1980, at NY Rangers, first period. Scorers: Doug Sulliman, NY Rangers, 7:52; Eddie Johnstone, NY Rangers, 7:57; Warren Miller, NY Rangers, 8:20; Rob Ramage, Colorado, 8:53. Teams tied 6-6.
 – Chicago Blackhawks, Toronto Maple Leafs, Oct. 15, 1983, at Toronto, second period. Scorers: Denis Savard, Chicago, 17:12; Steve Larmer, Chicago, 17:27; Denis Savard, Chicago, 17:42; John Anderson, Toronto, 18:13. Toronto won 10-8.

FASTEST FOUR GOALS, ONE TEAM:
1:20 – Boston Bruins, Jan. 21, 1945, at Boston, second period. Scorers: Bill Thoms, 6:34; Frank Mario, 7:08 and 7:27; Ken Smith, 7:54. Boston defeated NY Rangers 14-3.

FASTEST THREE GOALS, BOTH TEAMS:
0:15 – Minnesota North Stars, New York Rangers, Feb. 10, 1983, at Minnesota, second period. Scorers: Mark Pavelich, NY Rangers, 19:18; Ron Greschner, NY Rangers, 19:27; Willi Plett, Minnesota, 19:33. Minnesota won 7-5.
0:18 – Montreal Canadiens, New York Rangers, Dec. 12, 1963, at Montreal, first period. Scorers: Dave Balon, Montreal, 0:58; Gilles Tremblay, Montreal, 1:04; Camille Henry, NY Rangers, 1:16. Montreal won 6-4.
 – California Golden Seals, Buffalo Sabres, Feb. 1, 1976, at California, third period. Scorers: Jim Moxey, California, 19:38; Wayne Merrick, California, 19:45; Danny Gare, Buffalo, 19:56. Buffalo won 9-5.

FASTEST THREE GOALS, ONE TEAM:
0:20 – Boston Bruins, Feb. 25, 1971, at Boston, third period. Scorers: John Bucyk, 4:50; Ed Westfall, 5:02; Ted Green, 5:10. Boston defeated Vancouver 8-3.
0:21 – Chicago Blackhawks, Mar. 23, 1952, at NY Rangers, third period. Bill Mosienko scored all three goals, at 6:09, 6:20 and 6:30. Chicago defeated NY Rangers 7-6.
 – Washington Capitals, Nov. 23, 1990, at Washington, first period. Scorers: Michal Pivonka, 16:18; Stephen Leach, 16:29 and 16:39. Washington defeated Pittsburgh 7-3.

FASTEST THREE GOALS FROM START OF PERIOD, BOTH TEAMS:
1:05 – Hartford Whalers, Montreal Canadiens, Mar. 11, 1989, at Montreal, second period. Scorers: Kevin Dineen, Hartford, 0:11; Guy Carbonneau, Montreal, 0:36; Petr Svoboda, Montreal, 1:05. Montreal won 5-3.

FASTEST THREE GOALS FROM START OF PERIOD, ONE TEAM:
0:53 – Calgary Flames, Feb. 10, 1993, at Calgary, third period. Scorers: Gary Suter, 0:17; Chris Lindberg, 0:40; Ron Stern, 0:53. Calgary defeated San Jose 13-1.

FASTEST TWO GOALS, BOTH TEAMS:
0:02 – St. Louis Blues, Boston Bruins, Dec. 19, 1987, at Boston, third period. Scorers: Ken Linseman, Boston, 19:50; Doug Gilmour, St. Louis, 19:52. St. Louis won 7-5.
0:03 – Chicago Blackhawks, Minnesota North Stars, Nov. 5, 1988, at Minnesota, third period. Scorers: Steve Thomas, Chicago, 6:03; Dave Gagner, Minnesota, 6:06. Teams tied 5-5.

FASTEST TWO GOALS, ONE TEAM:
0:03 – Minnesota Wild, Jan. 21, 2004, at Minnesota, third period. Scorers: Jim Dowd, 19:44; Richard Park, 19:47. Minnesota defeated Chicago 4-2.
0:04 – Montreal Maroons, Jan. 3, 1931, at Montreal. Nels Stewart scored both goals, at 8:24 and 8:28. Mtl. Maroons defeated Boston 5-3.
 – Buffalo Sabres, Oct. 17, 1974, at Buffalo, third period. Scorers: Lee Fogolin, Jr., 14:55; Don Luce, 14:59. Buffalo defeated California 6-1.
 – Toronto Maple Leafs, Dec. 29, 1988, at Quebec, third period. Scorers: Ed Olczyk, 5:24; Gary Leeman, 5:28. Toronto defeated Quebec 6-5.
 – Calgary Flames, Oct. 17, 1989, at Quebec, third period. Scorers: Doug Gilmour, 19:45; Paul Ranheim, 19:49. Teams tied 8-8.
 – Winnipeg Jets, Dec. 15, 1995, at Winnipeg, second period. Deron Quint scored both goals, at 7:51 and 7:55. Winnipeg defeated Edmonton 9-4.

FASTEST TWO GOALS FROM START OF GAME, ONE TEAM:
0:24 – Edmonton Oilers, Mar. 28, 1982, at Los Angeles. Scorers: Mark Messier, 0:14; Dave Lumley, 0:24. Edmonton defeated Los Angeles 6-2.
0:27 – Boston Bruins, Feb. 14, 2003, at Florida. Mike Knuble scored both goals, at 0:10 and 0:27. Calgary defeated Hartford 6-1.
0:29 – Pittsburgh Penguins, Dec. 6, 1980, at Pittsburgh. Scorers: George Ferguson, 0:17; Greg Malone, 0:29. Pittsburgh defeated Chicago 6-4.

FASTEST TWO GOALS FROM START OF PERIOD, BOTH TEAMS:
0:14 – New York Rangers, Quebec Nordiques, Nov. 5, 1983, at Quebec, third period. Scorers: Andre Savard, Quebec, 0:08; Pierre Larouche, NY Rangers, 0:14. Teams tied 4-4.
0:26 – Buffalo Sabres, St. Louis Blues, Jan. 3, 1993, at Buffalo, third period. Scorers: Alexander Mogilny, Buffalo, 0:08; Philippe Bozon, St. Louis, 0:26. Buffalo won 6-5.
0:28 – Boston Bruins, Montreal Canadiens, Oct. 11, 1989, at Montreal, third period. Scorers: Jim Wiemer, Boston 0:10; Tom Chorske, Montreal 0:28. Montreal won 4-2.

FASTEST TWO GOALS FROM START OF PERIOD, ONE TEAM:
0:21 – Chicago Blackhawks, Nov. 5, 1983, at Minnesota, second period. Scorers: Ken Yaremchuk, 0:12; Darryl Sutter, 0:21. Minnesota defeated Chicago 10-5.
0:24 – Edmonton Oilers, Mar. 28, 1982, at Los Angeles, first period. Scorers: Mark Messier, 0:14; Dave Lumley, 0:24. Edmonton defeated Los Angeles 6-2.
0:29 – Pittsburgh Penguins, Dec. 6, 1980, at Pittsburgh, first period. Scorers: George Ferguson, 0:17; Greg Malone, 0:29. Pittsburgh defeated Chicago 6-4.

Though he did it all by himself, Bill Mosienko's three goals in 21 seconds ranks second as a team record. Boston's John Bucyk, Ed Westfall and Ted Green scored three times in just 20 seconds on February 25, 1971.

50, 40, 30, 20-GOAL SCORERS

MOST 50-OR-MORE GOAL SCORERS, ONE SEASON:
3 – Edmonton Oilers, 1983-84. 80GP. Wayne Gretzky, 87; Glenn Anderson, 54; Jari Kurri, 52.
– **Edmonton Oilers**, 1985-86. 80GP. Jari Kurri, 68; Glenn Anderson, 54; Wayne Gretzky, 52.
2 – Boston Bruins, 1970-71. 78GP. Phil Esposito, 76; John Bucyk, 51.
– Boston Bruins, 1973-74. 78GP. Phil Esposito, 68; Ken Hodge, 50.
– Philadelphia Flyers, 1975-76. 80GP. Reggie Leach, 61; Bill Barber, 50.
– Pittsburgh Penguins, 1975-76. 80GP. Pierre Larouche, 53; Jean Pronovost, 52.
– Montreal Canadiens, 1976-77. 80GP. Steve Shutt, 60; Guy Lafleur, 56.
– Los Angeles Kings, 1979-80. 80GP. Charlie Simmer, 56; Marcel Dionne, 53.
– Montreal Canadiens, 1979-80. 80GP. Pierre Larouche, 50; Guy Lafleur, 50.
– Los Angeles Kings, 1980-81. 80GP. Marcel Dionne, 58; Charlie Simmer, 56.
– Edmonton Oilers, 1981-82. 80GP. Wayne Gretzky, 92; Mark Messier, 50.
– New York Islanders, 1981-82. 80GP. Mike Bossy, 64; Bryan Trottier, 50.
– Edmonton Oilers, 1984-85. 80GP. Wayne Gretzky, 73; Jari Kurri, 71.
– Washington Capitals, 1984-85. 80GP. Bob Carpenter, 53; Mike Gartner, 50.
– Edmonton Oilers, 1986-87. 80GP. Wayne Gretzky, 62; Jari Kurri, 54.
– Calgary Flames, 1987-88. 80GP. Joe Nieuwendyk, 51; Hakan Loob, 50.
– Los Angeles Kings, 1987-88. 80GP. Jimmy Carson, 55; Luc Robitaille, 53.
– Los Angeles Kings, 1988-89. 80GP. Bernie Nicholls, 70; Wayne Gretzky, 54.
– Calgary Flames, 1988-89. 80GP. Joe Nieuwendyk, 51; Joe Mullen, 51.
– Buffalo Sabres, 1992-93. 84GP. Alexander Mogilny, 76; Pat LaFontaine, 53.
– Pittsburgh Penguins, 1992-93. 84GP. Mario Lemieux, 69; Kevin Stevens, 55.
– St. Louis Blues, 1992-93. 84GP. Brett Hull, 54; Brendan Shanahan, 51.
– St. Louis Blues, 1993-94. 84GP. Brett Hull, 57; Brendan Shanahan, 52.
– Detroit Red Wings, 1993-94. 84GP. Sergei Fedorov, 56; Ray Sheppard, 52.
– Pittsburgh Penguins, 1995-96. 82GP. Mario Lemieux, 69; Jaromir Jagr, 62.

MOST 40-OR-MORE GOAL SCORERS, ONE SEASON:
4 – Edmonton Oilers, 1982-83. 80GP. Wayne Gretzky, 71; Glenn Anderson, 48; Mark Messier, 48; Jari Kurri, 45.
– **Edmonton Oilers**, 1983-84. 80GP. Wayne Gretzky, 87; Glenn Anderson, 54; Jari Kurri, 52; Paul Coffey, 40.
– **Edmonton Oilers**, 1984-85. 80GP. Wayne Gretzky, 73; Jari Kurri, 71; Mike Krushelnyski, 43; Glenn Anderson, 42.
– **Edmonton Oilers**, 1985-86. 80GP. Jari Kurri, 68; Glenn Anderson, 54; Wayne Gretzky, 52; Paul Coffey, 48.
– **Calgary Flames**, 1987-88. 80GP. Joe Nieuwendyk, 51; Hakan Loob, 50; Mike Bullard, 48; Joe Mullen, 40.
3 – Boston Bruins, 1970-71. 78GP. Phil Esposito, 76; John Bucyk, 51; Ken Hodge, 43.
– New York Rangers, 1971-72. 78GP. Vic Hadfield, 50; Jean Ratelle, 46; Rod Gilbert, 43.
– Buffalo Sabres, 1975-76. 80GP. Danny Gare, 50; Rick Martin, 49; Gilbert Perreault, 44.
– Montreal Canadiens, 1979-80. 80GP. Guy Lafleur, 50; Pierre Larouche, 50; Steve Shutt, 47.
– Buffalo Sabres, 1979-80. 80GP. Danny Gare, 56; Rick Martin, 45; Gilbert Perreault, 40.
– Los Angeles Kings, 1980-81. 80GP. Marcel Dionne, 58; Charlie Simmer, 56; Dave Taylor, 47.
– Los Angeles Kings, 1984-85. 80GP. Marcel Dionne, 46; Bernie Nicholls, 46; Dave Taylor, 41.
– New York Islanders, 1984-85. 80GP. Mike Bossy, 58; Brent Sutter, 42; John Tonelli, 42.
– Chicago Blackhawks, 1985-86. 80GP. Denis Savard, 47; Troy Murray, 45; Al Secord, 40.
– Chicago Blackhawks, 1987-88. 80GP. Denis Savard, 44; Rick Vaive, 43; Steve Larmer, 41.
– Edmonton Oilers, 1987-88. 80GP. Craig Simpson, 43; Jari Kurri, 43; Wayne Gretzky, 40.
– Los Angeles Kings, 1988-89. 80GP. Bernie Nicholls, 70; Wayne Gretzky, 54; Luc Robitaille, 46.
– Los Angeles Kings, 1990-91. 80GP. Luc Robitaille, 45; Tomas Sandstrom, 45; Wayne Gretzky, 41.
– Pittsburgh Penguins, 1991-92. 80GP. Kevin Stevens, 54; Mario Lemieux, 44; Joe Mullen, 42.
– Pittsburgh Penguins, 1992-93. 84GP. Mario Lemieux, 69; Kevin Stevens, 55; Rick Tocchet, 48.
– Calgary Flames, 1993-94. 84GP. Gary Roberts, 41; Robert Reichel, 40; Theoren Fleury, 40.
– Pittsburgh Penguins, 1995-96. 82GP. Mario Lemieux, 69; Jaromir Jagr, 62; Petr Nedved, 45.

MOST 30-OR-MORE GOAL SCORERS, ONE SEASON:
6 – Buffalo Sabres, 1974-75. 80GP. Rick Martin, 52; Rene Robert, 40; Gilbert Perreault, 39; Don Luce, 33; Rick Dudley, 31; Danny Gare, 31.
– **New York Islanders**, 1977-78. 80GP. Mike Bossy, 53; Bryan Trottier, 46; Clark Gillies, 35; Denis Potvin, 30; Bob Nystrom, 30; Bob Bourne, 30.
– **Winnipeg Jets**, 1984-85. 80GP. Dale Hawerchuk, 53; Paul MacLean, 41; Laurie Boschman, 32; Brian Mullen, 32; Doug Smail, 31; Thomas Steen, 30.
5 – Chicago Blackhawks, 1968-69. 76GP
– Boston Bruins, 1970-71. 78GP
– Montreal Canadiens, 1971-72. 78GP
– Philadelphia Flyers, 1972-73. 78GP
– Boston Bruins, 1973-74. 78GP
– Montreal Canadiens, 1974-75. 80GP
– Montreal Canadiens, 1975-76. 80GP
– Pittsburgh Penguins, 1975-76. 80GP
– New York Islanders, 1978-79. 80GP
– Detroit Red Wings, 1979-80. 80GP
– Philadelphia Flyers, 1979-80. 80GP
– New York Islanders, 1980-81. 80GP
– St. Louis Blues, 1980-81. 80GP
– Chicago Blackhawks, 1981-82. 80GP
– Edmonton Oilers, 1981-82. 80GP
– Montreal Canadiens, 1981-82. 80GP
– Quebec Nordiques, 1981-82. 80GP
– Washington Capitals, 1981-82. 80GP
– Edmonton Oilers, 1982-83. 80GP
– Edmonton Oilers, 1983-84. 80GP
– Edmonton Oilers, 1984-85. 80GP
– Los Angeles Kings, 1984-85. 80GP
– Edmonton Oilers, 1985-86. 80GP
– Edmonton Oilers, 1986-87. 80GP
– Edmonton Oilers, 1987-88. 80GP
– Edmonton Oilers, 1988-89. 80GP
– Detroit Red Wings, 1991-92. 80GP
– New York Rangers, 1991-92. 80GP
– Pittsburgh Penguins, 1991-92. 80GP
– Detroit Red Wings, 1992-93. 84GP
– Pittsburgh Penguins, 1992-93. 84GP

MOST 20-OR-MORE GOAL SCORERS, ONE SEASON:
11 – Boston Bruins, 1977-78. 80GP. Peter McNab, 41; Terry O'Reilly, 29; Bobby Schmautz, 27; Stan Jonathan, 27; Jean Ratelle, 25; Rick Middleton, 25; Wayne Cashman, 24; Gregg Sheppard, 23; Brad Park, 22; Don Marcotte, 20; Bob Miller, 20.
10 – Boston Bruins, 1970-71. 78GP
– Montreal Canadiens, 1974-75. 80GP
– St. Louis Blues, 1980-81. 80GP

Entering his first season with the Florida Panthers in 2005-06, Gary Roberts was a member of the Calgary Flames in 1993-94. In that season, he scored 41 goals while teammates Robert Reichel and Theoren Fleury each recorded 40.

100-POINT SCORERS

MOST 100 OR-MORE-POINT SCORERS, ONE SEASON:
4 – Boston Bruins, 1970-71. 78GP. Phil Esposito, 76G-76A-152PTS;
   Bobby Orr, 37G-102A-139PTS; John Bucyk, 51G-65A-116PTS;
   Ken Hodge, 43G-62A-105PTS.
 – Edmonton Oilers, 1982-83. 80GP. Wayne Gretzky, 71G-125A-196PTS;
   Mark Messier, 48G-58A-106PTS; Glenn Anderson, 48G-56A-104PTS;
   Jari Kurri, 45G-59A-104PTS.
 – Edmonton Oilers, 1983-84. 80GP. Wayne Gretzky, 87G-118A-205PTS;
   Paul Coffey, 40G-86A-126PTS; Jari Kurri, 52G-61A-113PTS;
   Mark Messier, 37G-64A-101PTS.
 – Edmonton Oilers,1985-86. 80GP. Wayne Gretzky, 52G-163A-215PTS;
   Paul Coffey, 48G-90A-138PTS; Jari Kurri, 68G-63A-131PTS;
   Glenn Anderson, 54G-48A-102PTS.
 – Pittsburgh Penguins,1992-93. 84GP. Mario Lemieux, 69G-91A-160PTS;
   Kevin Stevens, 55G-56A-111PTS; Rick Tocchet, 48G-61A-109PTS;
   Ron Francis, 24G-76A-100PTS.
3 – Boston Bruins, 1973-74. 78GP. Phil Esposito, 68G-77A-145PTS;
   Bobby Orr, 32G-90A-122PTS; Ken Hodge, 50G-55A-105PTS.
 – New York Islanders, 1978-79. 80GP. Bryan Trottier, 47G-87A-134PTS;
   Mike Bossy, 69G-57A-126PTS; Denis Potvin, 31G-70A-101PTS.
 – Los Angeles Kings, 1980-81. 80GP. Marcel Dionne, 58G-77A-135PTS;
   Dave Taylor, 47G-65A-112PTS; Charlie Simmer, 56G-49A-105PTS.
 – Edmonton Oilers, 1984-85. 80GP. Wayne Gretzky, 73G-135A-208PTS;
   Jari Kurri, 71G-64A-135PTS; Paul Coffey, 37G-84A-121PTS.
 – New York Islanders, 1984-85. 80GP. Mike Bossy, 58G-59A-117PTS;
   Brent Sutter, 42G-60A-102PTS; John Tonelli, 42G-58A-100PTS.
 – Edmonton Oilers, 1986-87. 80GP. Wayne Gretzky, 62G-121A-183PTS;
   Jari Kurri, 54G-54A-108PTS; Mark Messier, 37G-70A-107PTS.
 – Pittsburgh Penguins, 1988-89. 80GP. Mario Lemieux, 85G-114A-199PTS;
   Rob Brown, 49G-66A-115PTS; Paul Coffey, 30G-83A-113PTS.
 – Pittsburgh Penguins, 1995-96. 82GP. Mario Lemieux, 69G-92A-161PTS;
   Jaromir Jagr, 62G-87A-149PTS; Ron Francis, 27G-92A-119PTS.

SHOTS ON GOAL

MOST SHOTS, BOTH TEAMS, ONE GAME:
141 – New York Americans, Pittsburgh Pirates, Dec. 26, 1925, at
   NY Americans. NY Americans won 3-1 with 73 shots; Pittsburgh had 68
   shots.

MOST SHOTS, ONE TEAM, ONE GAME:
83 – Boston Bruins, Mar. 4, 1941, at Boston. Boston defeated Chicago 3-2.
73 – New York Americans, Dec. 26, 1925, at NY Americans. NY Americans
   defeated Pittsburgh 3-1.
 – Boston Bruins, Mar. 21, 1991, at Boston. Boston tied Quebec 3-3.
72 – Boston Bruins, Dec. 10, 1970, at Boston. Boston defeated Buffalo 8-2.

MOST SHOTS, ONE TEAM, ONE PERIOD:
33 – Boston Bruins, Mar. 4, 1941, at Boston, second period.
   Boston defeated Chicago 3-2.

TEAM GOALS AGAINST

Fewest Goals Against

FEWEST GOALS AGAINST, ONE SEASON:
42 – Ottawa Senators, 1925-26. 36GP
43 – Montreal Canadiens, 1928-29. 44GP
48 – Montreal Canadiens, 1923-24. 24GP
 – Montreal Canadiens, 1927-28. 44GP

**FEWEST GOALS AGAINST, ONE SEASON
(MINIMUM 70-GAME SCHEDULE):**
131 – Toronto Maple Leafs, 1953-54. 70GP
 – Montreal Canadiens, 1955-56. 70GP
132 – Detroit Red Wings, 1953-54. 70GP
133 – Detroit Red Wings, 1951-52. 70GP
 – Detroit Red Wings, 1952-53. 70GP

LOWEST GOALS-AGAINST-PER-GAME AVERAGE, ONE SEASON:
0.98 – Montreal Canadiens, 1928-29. 43GA in 44GP.
1.09 – Montreal Canadiens, 1927-28. 48GA in 44GP.
1.17 – Ottawa Senators, 1925-26. 42GA in 36GP.

Most Goals Against

MOST GOALS AGAINST, ONE SEASON:
446 – Washington Capitals, 1974-75. 80GP
415 – Detroit Red Wings, 1985-86. 80GP
414 – San Jose Sharks, 1992-93. 84GP
407 – Quebec Nordiques, 1989-90. 80GP
403 – Hartford Whalers, 1982-83. 80GP

HIGHEST GOALS-AGAINST-PER-GAME AVERAGE, ONE SEASON:
7.38 – Quebec Bulldogs, 1919-20. 177GA in 24GP.
6.20 – New York Rangers, 1943-44. 310GA in 50GP.
5.58 – Washington Capitals, 1974-75. 446GA in 80GP.

MOST POWER-PLAY GOALS AGAINST, ONE SEASON:
122 – Chicago Blackhawks, 1988-89. 80GP
120 – Pittsburgh Penguins, 1987-88. 80GP
115 – New Jersey Devils, 1988-89. 80GP
 – Ottawa Senators, 1992-93. 84GP
114 – Los Angeles Kings, 1992-93. 84GP

MOST SHORTHAND GOALS AGAINST, ONE SEASON:
22 – Pittsburgh Penguins, 1984-85. 80GP
 – Minnesota North Stars, 1991-92. 80GP
 – Colorado Avalanche, 1995-96. 82GP
21 – Calgary Flames, 1984-85. 80GP
 – Pittsburgh Penguins, 1989-90. 80GP

SHUTOUTS

MOST SHUTOUTS, ONE SEASON:
22 – Montreal Canadiens, 1928-29. All by George Hainsworth. 44GP
16 – New York Americans, 1928-29. Roy Worters 13; Flat Walsh 3. 44GP
15 – Ottawa Senators, 1925-26. All by Alex Connell. 36GP
 – Ottawa Senators, 1927-28. All by Alex Connell. 44GP
 – Boston Bruins, 1927-28. All by Hal Winkler. 44GP
 – Chicago Blackhawks, 1969-70. All by Tony Esposito. 76GP

MOST CONSECUTIVE SHUTOUTS, ONE SEASON:
6 – Ottawa Senators, Jan. 31 – Feb. 18, 1928. All by Alex Connell.

MOST CONSECUTIVE SHUTOUTS TO START SEASON:
5 – Toronto Maple Leafs, Nov. 13 – 22, 1930. Lorne Chabot 3,
   Benny Grant 2.

MOST GAMES SHUTOUT, ONE SEASON:
20 – Chicago Blackhawks, 1928-29. 44GP

MOST CONSECUTIVE GAMES SHUTOUT:
8 – Chicago Blackhawks, Feb. 7 – 28, 1929.

MOST CONSECUTIVE GAMES SHUTOUT TO START SEASON:
3 – Montreal Maroons, Nov. 11 – 18, 1930.

TEAM PENALTIES

MOST PENALTY MINUTES, ONE SEASON:
2,713 – Buffalo Sabres, 1991-92. 80GP
2,670 – Pittsburgh Penguins, 1988-89. 80GP
2,663 – Chicago Blackhawks, 1991-92. 80GP
2,643 – Calgary Flames, 1991-92. 80GP
2,621 – Philadelphia Flyers, 1980-81. 80GP

MOST PENALTIES, BOTH TEAMS, ONE GAME:
85 – Edmonton Oilers (44), Los Angeles Kings (41), Feb. 28, 1990, at
   Los Angeles. Edmonton received 26 minors, 7 majors, 4 10-minute
   misconducts, 4 game misconducts and 1 match penalty; Los Angeles
   received 26 minors, 9 majors, 3 10-minute misconducts and 3 game
   misconducts.

MOST PENALTY MINUTES, BOTH TEAMS, ONE GAME:
419 – Ottawa Senators (206), Philadelphia Flyers (213), Mar. 5, 2004, at
   Philadelphia. Ottawa received 8 minors, 10 majors, 4 10-minute
   misconducts and 10 game misconducts. Philadelphia received 9 minors,
   11 majors, 4 10-minute misconducts and 10 game misconducts.

MOST PENALTIES, ONE TEAM, ONE GAME:
44 – Edmonton Oilers, Feb. 28, 1990, at Los Angeles. Edmonton received
   26 minors, 7 majors, 6 10-minute misconducts, 4 game misconducts
   and 1 match penalty.
42 – Minnesota North Stars, Feb. 26, 1981, at Boston. Minnesota received
   18 minors, 13 majors, 4 10-minute misconducts and 7 game misconducts.
 – Boston Bruins, Feb. 26, 1981, at Boston vs. Minnesota. Boston received
   20 minors, 13 majors, 3 10-minute misconducts and 6 game misconducts.

MOST PENALTY MINUTES, ONE TEAM, ONE GAME:
213 – Philadelphia Flyers, Mar. 5, 2004, at Philadelphia. Philadelphia received
   9 minors, 11 majors, 4 10-minute misconducts and 10 game misconducts.

MOST PENALTIES, BOTH TEAMS, ONE PERIOD:
67 – Minnesota North Stars (34), Boston Bruins (33), Feb. 26, 1981, at
   Boston, first period. Minnesota received 15 minors, 8 majors, 4 10-minute
misconducts and 7 game misconducts. Boston had 16 minors, 8 majors,
   3 10-minute misconducts and 6 game misconducts.

MOST PENALTY MINUTES, BOTH TEAMS, ONE PERIOD:
409 – Ottawa Senators (200), Philadelphia Flyers (209), Mar. 5, 2004, at
   Philadelphia, third period. Ottawa received 5 minors, 10 majors, 4 10-
   minute misconducts and 10 game misconducts. Philadelphia received 7
   minors, 11 majors, 4 10-minute misconducts and 10 game misconducts.

MOST PENALTIES, ONE TEAM, ONE PERIOD:
34 – Minnesota North Stars, Feb. 26, 1981, at Boston, first period.
   Minnesota received 15 minors, 8 majors, 4 10-minute misconducts and
   7 game misconducts.

MOST PENALTY MINUTES, ONE TEAM, ONE PERIOD:
209 – Philadelphia Flyers, Mar. 5, 2004, at Philadelphia vs. Ottawa, third
   period. Philadelphia received 7 minors, 11 majors, 4 10-minute
   misconducts and 10 game misconducts.
200 – Ottawa Senators, Mar. 5, 2004, at Philadelphia, third period.
   Ottawa received 5 minors, 10 majors, 4 10-minute misconducts and
   10 game misconducts.

NHL Individual Scoring Records - History

Six individual scoring records stand as benchmarks in the history of the game: most goals, single-season and career; most assists, single-season and career; and most points, single-season and career. The evolution of these six records is traced here, beginning with 1917-18, the NHL's first season. New research has resulted in changes to scoring records in the NHL's first nine seasons.

MOST GOALS, ONE SEASON

44 —Joe Malone, Montreal, 1917-18.
   Scored goal #44 against Toronto's Harry Holmes on March 2, 1918 and finished season with 44 goals.
50 —Maurice Richard, Montreal, 1944-45.
   Scored goal #45 against Toronto's Frank McCool on February 25, 1945 and finished the season with 50 goals.
50 —Bernie Geoffrion, Montreal, 1960-61.
   Scored goal #50 against Toronto's Cesare Maniago on March 16, 1961 and finished the season with 50 goals.
50 —Bobby Hull, Chicago, 1961-62.
   Scored goal #50 against NY Rangers' Gump Worsley on March 25, 1962 and finished the season with 50 goals.
54 —Bobby Hull, Chicago, 1965-66.
   Scored goal #51 against NY Rangers' Cesare Maniago on March 12, 1966 and finished the season with 54 goals.
58 —Bobby Hull, Chicago, 1968-69.
   Scored goal #55 against Boston's Gerry Cheevers on March 20, 1969 and finished the season with 58 goals.
76 —Phil Esposito, Boston, 1970-71.
   Scored goal #59 against Los Angeles' Denis DeJordy on March 11, 1971 and finished the season with 76 goals.
92 —Wayne Gretzky, Edmonton, 1981-82.
   Scored goal #77 against Buffalo's Don Edwards on February 24, 1982 and finished the season with 92 goals.

MOST ASSISTS, ONE SEASON

10 —Cy Denneny, Ottawa, 1917-18.
   —Reg Noble, Toronto, 1917-18.
   —Harry Cameron, Toronto, 1917-18.
   —Newsy Lalonde, Montreal, 1918-19.
15 —Frank Nighbor, Ottawa, 1919-20.
   —Jack Darragh, Ottawa, 1920-21.
17 —Harry Cameron, Toronto, 1921-22.
18 —Dick Irvin, Chicago, 1926-27.
   —Howie Morenz, Montreal, 1927-28.
36 —Frank Boucher, NY Rangers, 1929-30.
37 —Joe Primeau, Toronto, 1931-32.
45 —Bill Cowley, Boston, 1940-41.
   —Bill Cowley, Boston, 1942-43.
49 —Clint Smith, Chicago, 1943-44.
54 —Elmer Lach, Montreal, 1944-45.
55 —Ted Lindsay, Detroit, 1949-50.
56 —Bert Olmstead, Montreal, 1955-56.
58 —Jean Beliveau, Montreal, 1960-61.
   —Andy Bathgate, NY Rangers/Toronto, 1963-64.
59 —Stan Mikita, Chicago, 1964-65.
62 —Stan Mikita, Chicago, 1966-67.
77 —Phil Esposito, Boston, 1968-69.
87 —Bobby Orr, Boston, 1969-70.
102 —Bobby Orr, Boston, 1970-71.
109 —Wayne Gretzky, Edmonton, 1980-81.
120 —Wayne Gretzky, Edmonton, 1981-82.
125 —Wayne Gretzky, Edmonton, 1982-83.
135 —Wayne Gretzky, Edmonton, 1984-85.
163 —Wayne Gretzky, Edmonton, 1985-86.

MOST POINTS, ONE SEASON

48 —Joe Malone, Montreal, 1917-18.
49 —Joe Malone, Montreal, 1919-20.
51 —Howie Morenz, Montreal, 1927-28.
73 —Cooney Weiland, Boston, 1929-30.
   —Doug Bentley, Chicago, 1942-43.
82 —Herb Cain, Boston, 1943-44.
86 —Gordie Howe, Detroit, 1950-51.
95 —Gordie Howe, Detroit, 1952-53.
96 —Dickie Moore, Montreal, 1958-59.
97 —Bobby Hull, Chicago, 1965-66.
   —Stan Mikita, Chicago, 1966-67.
126 —Phil Esposito, Boston, 1968-69.
152 —Phil Esposito, Boston, 1970-71.
164 —Wayne Gretzky, Edmonton, 1980-81.
212 —Wayne Gretzky, Edmonton, 1981-82.
215 —Wayne Gretzky, Edmonton, 1985-86.

MOST REGULAR-SEASON GOALS, CAREER

44 —Joe Malone, 1917-18, Montreal.
   Malone led the NHL in goals in the league's first season and finished with 44 goals in 22 games in 1917-18.
54 —Cy Denneny, 1918-19, Ottawa.
   Denneny passed Malone during the 1918-19 season, finishing the year with a two-year total of 54 goals. He held the career goal- scoring mark until 1919-20.
143 —Joe Malone, Montreal, Quebec Bulldogs, Hamilton.
   Malone passed Denneny in 1919-20 and remained the NHL's career goal-scoring leader until 1922-23.
248 —Cy Denneny, Ottawa, Boston.
   Denneny passed Malone with goal #144 in 1922-23 and remained the NHL's career goal-scoring leader until his retirement. He finished with a career total of 248 goals.
271 —Howie Morenz, Montreal, Chicago, NY Rangers.
   Morenz passed Denneny with goal #249 in 1933-34 and finished his career with 271 goals.
324 —Nels Stewart, Montreal Maroons, Boston, NY Americans.
   Stewart passed Morenz with goal #272 in 1936-37 and remained the NHL's career goal-scoring leader until his retirement. He finished his career with 324 goals.
544 —Maurice Richard, Montreal.
   Richard passed Nels Stewart with goal #325 on Nov. 8, 1952 and remained the NHL's career goal-scoring leader until his retirement. He finished his career with 544 goals.
801 —Gordie Howe, Detroit, Hartford.
   Howe passed Richard with goal #545 on Nov. 10, 1963 and remained the NHL's career goal-scoring leader until his retirement. He finished his career with 801 goals.
894 —Wayne Gretzky, Edmonton, Los Angeles, St. Louis, NY Rangers.
   Gretzky passed Gordie Howe with goal #802 on March 23, 1994. He retired as the NHL's current goal-scoring leader with 894.

In brief NHL trials between 1960 and 1966, Cesare Maniago (above) served as a backup to future Hall of Famers Johnny Bower in Toronto, Jacques Plante in Montreal and Ed Giacomin in New York. Maniago played just 55 games in the NHL during that stretch, but allowed Bernie Geoffrion's record-tying 50th goal on March 16, 1961, and Bobby Hull's record-breaking 51st on March 12, 1966. Maniago finally earned steady NHL employment after the Minnesota North Stars selected him in the 1967 Expansion Draft. Hall of Famer Cy Denneny (facing page) surpassed Joe Malone as the NHL's goal-scoring leader in 1922-23. His career totals of 248 goals and 333 points stood as league records until being surpassed by Howie Morenz.

MOST REGULAR-SEASON ASSISTS, CAREER

(minimum 100 assists)

100 —Frank Boucher, Ottawa, NY Rangers.
   In 1930-31, Boucher became the first NHL player to reach the 100-assist milestone.
263 —Frank Boucher, Ottawa, NY Rangers.
   Boucher retired as the NHL's career assist leader in 1938 with 253. He returned to the NHL in 1943-44 and remained the NHL's career assist leader until he was overtaken by Bill Cowley in 1943-44. He finished his career with 263 assists.
353 —Bill Cowley, St. Louis Eagles, Boston.
   Cowley passed Boucher with assist #264 in 1943-44. He retired as the NHL's career assist leader in 1947 with 353.
408 —Elmer Lach, Montreal.
   Lach passed Cowley with assist #354 in 1951-52. He retired as the NHL's career assist leader in 1954 with 408.
1,049 —Gordie Howe, Detroit, Hartford.
   Howe passed Lach with assist #409 in 1957-58. He retired as the NHL's career assist leader in 1980 with 1,049.
1,963 —Wayne Gretzky, Edmonton, Los Angeles, St. Louis, NY Rangers.
   Gretzky passed Howe with assist #1,050 in 1988-89. He retired as the NHL's current career assist leader with 1,963.

MOST REGULAR-SEASON POINTS, CAREER

(minimum 100 points)

100 —Joe Malone, Montreal, Quebec Bulldogs, Hamilton.
   In 1919-20, Malone became the first player in NHL history to record 100 points.
200 —Cy Denneny, Ottawa.
   In 1923-24, Denneny became the first player in NHL history to record 200 points.
300 —Cy Denneny, Ottawa.
   In 1926-27, Denneny became the first player in NHL history to record 300 points.
333 —Cy Denneny, Ottawa, Boston.
   Denneny retired as the NHL's career point-scoring leader in 1929 with 333 points.
472 —Howie Morenz, Montreal, Chicago, NY Rangers.
   Morenz passed Cy Denneny with point #334 in 1931-32. At the time his career ended in 1937, he was the NHL's career point- scoring leader with 472 points.
515 —Nels Stewart, Montreal Maroons, Boston, NY Americans.
   Stewart passed Morenz with point #473 in 1938-39. He retired as the NHL's career point-scoring leader in 1940 with 515 points.
528 —Syd Howe, Ottawa, Philadelphia Quakers, Toronto, St. Louis Eagles, Detroit.
   Howe passed Nels Stewart with point #516 on March 8, 1945. He retired as the NHL's career point-scoring leader in 1946 with 528 points.
548 —Bill Cowley, St. Louis Eagles, Boston.
   Cowley passed Syd Howe with point #529 on Feb. 12, 1947. He retired as the NHL's career point-scoring leader in 1947 with 548 points.
610 —Elmer Lach, Montreal.
   Lach passed Bill Cowley with point #549 on Feb. 23, 1952. He remained the NHL's career point-scoring leader until he was overtaken by Maurice Richard in 1953-54. He finished his career with 623 points.
946 —Maurice Richard, Montreal.
   Richard passed teammate Elmer Lach with point #611 on Dec. 12, 1953. He remained the NHL's career point-scoring leader until he was overtaken by Gordie Howe in 1959-60. He finished his career with 965 points.
1,850 —Gordie Howe, Detroit, Hartford.
   Howe passed Richard with point #947 on Jan. 16, 1960. He retired as the NHL's career point-scoring leader in 1980 with 1,850 points.
2,857 —Wayne Gretzky, Edmonton, Los Angeles, St. Louis, NY Rangers.
   Gretzky passed Howe with point #1,851 on Oct. 15, 1989. He retired as the NHL's current career points leader with 2,857.

Individual Records

Regular Season

SEASONS

MOST SEASONS:
26 – Gordie Howe, Detroit, 1946-47 – 1970-71; Hartford, 1979-80.
25 – Mark Messier, Edmonton, NY Rangers, Vancouver,
1979-80 – 2003-04.
24 – Alex Delvecchio, Detroit, 1950-51 – 1973-74.
– Tim Horton, Toronto, NY Rangers, Pittsburgh, Buffalo,
1949-50, 1951-52 – 1973-74.
23 – John Bucyk, Detroit, Boston, 1955-56 – 1977-78.
– Ron Francis, Hartford, Pittsburgh, Carolina, Toronto, 1981-82 – 2003-04.
– Al MacInnis, Calgary, St. Louis, 1981-82 – 2003-04.

GAMES

MOST GAMES:
1,767 – Gordie Howe, Detroit, 1946-47 – 1970-71; Hartford, 1979-80.
1,756 – Mark Messier, Edmonton, NY Rangers, Vancouver, 1979-80 – 2003-04.
1,731 – Ron Francis, Hartford, Pittsburgh, Carolina, Toronto, 1981-82 – 2003-04.
1,635 – Scott Stevens, Washington, St. Louis, New Jersey, 1982-83 – 2003-04.
1,615 – Larry Murphy, Los Angeles, Washington, Minnesota, Pittsburgh, Toronto, Detroit, 1980-81 – 2000-01.

MOST GAMES, INCLUDING PLAYOFFS:
1,992 – Mark Messier, Edmonton, NY Rangers, Vancouver,
1,756 regular-season games, 236 playoff games.
1,924 – Gordie Howe, Detroit, Hartford, 1,767 regular-season games,
157 playoff games.
1,902 – Ron Francis, Hartford, Pittsburgh, Carolina, Toronto, 1,731 regular-season
games, 171 playoff games.
1,868 – Scott Stevens, Washington, St. Louis, New Jersey, 1,635 regular-season
games, 233 playoff games.
1,830 – Larry Murphy, Los Angeles, Washington, Minnesota, Pittsburgh, Toronto,
Detroit, 1,615 regular-season games, 215 playoff games.

MOST CONSECUTIVE GAMES:
964 – Doug Jarvis, Montreal, Washington, Hartford,
Oct. 8, 1975 – Oct. 10, 1987.
914 – Garry Unger, Toronto, Detroit, St. Louis, Atlanta,
Feb. 24, 1968 – Dec. 21, 1979.
884 – Steve Larmer, Chicago, Oct. 6, 1982 – Apr. 15, 1993.
776 – Craig Ramsay, Buffalo, Mar. 27, 1973 – Feb. 10, 1983.
630 – Andy Hebenton, NY Rangers, Boston, Oct. 7, 1955 – Mar. 22, 1964.

GOALS

MOST GOALS:
894 – Wayne Gretzky, Edmonton, Los Angeles, St. Louis, NY Rangers,
in 20 seasons. 1,487GP
801 – Gordie Howe, Detroit, Hartford, in 26 seasons. 1,767GP
741 – Brett Hull, Calgary, St. Louis, Dallas, Detroit, in 18 seasons. 1,264GP
731 – Marcel Dionne, Detroit, Los Angeles, NY Rangers, in 18 seasons. 1,348GP
717 – Phil Esposito, Chicago, Boston, NY Rangers, in 18 seasons. 1,282GP

MOST GOALS, INCLUDING PLAYOFFS:
1,016 – Wayne Gretzky, Edmonton, Los Angeles, St. Louis, NY Rangers,
894G in 1,487 regular-season games, 122G in 208 playoff games.
869 – Gordie Howe, Detroit, Hartford, 801G in 1,767 regular-season games,
68G in 157 playoff games.
844 – Brett Hull, Calgary, St. Louis, Dallas, Detroit, 741G in 1,264 regular-season
games, 103G in 202 playoff games.
803 – Mark Messier, Edmonton, NY Rangers, Vancouver, 694G in 1,756 regular-
season games, 109G in 236 playoff games.
778 – Phil Esposito, Chicago, Boston, NY Rangers, 717G in 1,282 regular-season
games, 61G in 130 playoff games.

MOST GOALS, ONE SEASON:
92 – Wayne Gretzky, Edmonton, 1981-82. 80GP – 80 game schedule.
87 – Wayne Gretzky, Edmonton, 1983-84. 74GP – 80 game schedule.
86 – Brett Hull, St. Louis, 1990-91. 78GP – 80 game schedule.
85 – Mario Lemieux, Pittsburgh, 1988-89. 76GP – 80 game schedule.
76 – Phil Esposito, Boston, 1970-71. 78GP – 78 game schedule.
– Alexander Mogilny, Buffalo, 1992-93. 77GP – 84 game schedule.
– Teemu Selanne, Winnipeg, 1992-93. 84GP – 84 game schedule.
73 – Wayne Gretzky, Edmonton, 1984-85. 80GP – 80 game schedule.
72 – Brett Hull, St. Louis, 1989-90. 80GP – 80 game schedule.
71 – Wayne Gretzky, Edmonton, 1982-83. 80GP – 80 game schedule.
– Jari Kurri, Edmonton, 1984-85. 73GP – 80 game schedule.
70 – Mario Lemieux, Pittsburgh, 1987-88. 77GP – 80 game schedule.
– Bernie Nicholls, Los Angeles, 1988-89. 79GP – 80 game schedule.
– Brett Hull, St. Louis, 1991-92. 73GP – 80 game schedule.

MOST GOALS, ONE SEASON, INCLUDING PLAYOFFS:
100 – Wayne Gretzky, Edmonton, 1983-84,
87G in 74 regular-season games, 13G in 19 playoff games.
97 – Wayne Gretzky, Edmonton, 1981-82,
92G in 80 regular-season games, 5G in 5 playoff games.
– Mario Lemieux, Pittsburgh, 1988-89,
85G in 76 regular-season games, 12G in 11 playoff games.
– Brett Hull, St. Louis, 1990-91,
86G in 78 regular-season games, 11G in 13 playoff games.
90 – Wayne Gretzky, Edmonton, 1984-85,
73G in 80 regular-season games, 17G in 18 playoff games.
– Jari Kurri, Edmonton, 1984-85,
71G in 80 regular-season games, 19G in 18 playoff games.
85 – Mike Bossy, NY Islanders, 1980-81,
68G in 79 regular-season games, 17G in 18 playoff games.
– Brett Hull, St. Louis, 1989-90,
72G in 80 regular-season games, 13G in 12 playoff games.
83 – Wayne Gretzky, Edmonton, 1982-83,
71G in 73 regular-season games, 12G in 16 playoff games.
– Alexander Mogilny, Buffalo, 1992-93,
76G in 77 regular-season games, 7G in 7 playoff games.

MOST GOALS, 50 GAMES FROM START OF SEASON:
61 – Wayne Gretzky, Edmonton, 1981-82.
Oct. 7, 1981 – Jan. 22, 1982. (80-game schedule)
– Wayne Gretzky, Edmonton, 1983-84.
Oct. 5, 1983 – Jan. 25, 1984. (80-game schedule)
54 – Mario Lemieux, Pittsburgh, 1988-89.
Oct. 7, 1988 – Jan. 31, 1989. (80-game schedule)
53 – Wayne Gretzky, Edmonton, 1984-85.
Oct. 11, 1984 – Jan. 28, 1985. (80-game schedule)
52 – Brett Hull, St. Louis, 1990-91.
Oct. 4, 1990 – Jan. 26, 1991. (80-game schedule)
50 – Maurice Richard, Montreal, 1944-45.
Oct. 28, 1944 – Mar. 18, 1945. (50-game schedule)
– Mike Bossy, NY Islanders, 1980-81.
Oct. 11, 1980 – Jan. 24, 1981. (80-game schedule)
– Brett Hull, St. Louis, 1991-92.
Oct. 5, 1991 – Jan. 28, 1992. (80-game schedule)

MOST GOALS, ONE GAME:
7 – Joe Malone, Quebec, Jan. 31, 1920, at Quebec.
Quebec 10, Toronto 6.
6 – Newsy Lalonde, Montreal, Jan. 10, 1920, at Montreal.
Montreal 14, Toronto 7.
– Joe Malone, Quebec, Mar. 10, 1920, at Quebec.
Quebec 10, Ottawa 4.
– Corb Denneny, Toronto, Jan. 26, 1921, at Toronto.
Toronto 10, Hamilton 3.
– Cy Denneny, Ottawa, Mar. 7, 1921, at Ottawa.
Ottawa 12, Hamilton 5.
– Syd Howe, Detroit, Feb. 3, 1944, at Detroit.
Detroit 12, NY Rangers 2.
– Red Berenson, St. Louis, Nov. 7, 1968, at Philadelphia.
St. Louis 8, Philadelphia 0.
– Darryl Sittler, Toronto, Feb. 7, 1976, at Toronto.
Toronto 11, Boston 4.

Originally drafted by Toronto, Doug Jarvis was traded to Montreal on June 26, 1975, and played his first game on October 8, 1975. He played 964 in a row before retiring on October 10, 1987 to move into coaching with the Hartford Whalers.

Joe Malone of the Quebec Bulldogs (seated in the center of the front row) enjoyed a six-goal game against Ottawa on January 10, 1920 and a record-setting seven-goal game against Toronto three weeks later.

MOST GOALS, ONE ROAD GAME:

6 – Red Berenson, St. Louis, Nov. 7, 1968, at Philadelphia. St. Louis 8, Philadelphia 0.

5 – Joe Malone, Montreal, Dec. 19, 1917, at Ottawa. Montreal 7, Ottawa 4.
  – Red Green, Hamilton, Dec. 5, 1924, at Toronto. Hamilton 10, Toronto 3.
  – Babe Dye, Toronto, Dec. 22, 1924, at Boston. Toronto 10, Boston 1.
  – Punch Broadbent, Mtl. Maroons, Jan. 7, 1925, at Hamilton. Mtl. Maroons 6, Hamilton 2.
  – Don Murdoch, NY Rangers, Oct. 12, 1976, at Minnesota. NY Rangers 10, Minnesota 4.
  – Tim Young, Minnesota, Jan. 15, 1979, at NY Rangers. Minnesota 8, NY Rangers 1.
  – Willy Lindstrom, Winnipeg, Mar. 2, 1982, at Philadelphia. Winnipeg 7, Philadelphia 6.
  – Bengt Gustafsson, Washington, Jan. 8, 1984, at Philadelphia. Washington 7, Philadelphia 1.
  – Wayne Gretzky, Edmonton, Dec. 15, 1984, at St. Louis. Edmonton 8, St. Louis 2.
  – Dave Andreychuk, Buffalo, Feb. 6, 1986, at Boston. Buffalo 8, Boston 6.
  – Mats Sundin, Quebec, Mar. 5, 1992, at Hartford. Quebec 10, Hartford 4.
  – Mario Lemieux, Pittsburgh, Apr. 9, 1993, at NY Rangers. Pittsburgh 10, NY Rangers 4.
  – Mike Ricci, Quebec, Feb. 17, 1994, at San Jose. Quebec 8, San Jose 2.
  – Alex Zhamnov, Winnipeg, Apr. 1, 1995, at Los Angeles. Winnipeg 7, Los Angeles 7.

MOST GOALS, ONE PERIOD:

4 – Busher Jackson, Toronto, Nov. 20, 1934, at St. Louis, third period. Toronto 5, St. Louis 2.
  – Max Bentley, Chicago, Jan. 28, 1943, at Chicago, third period. Chicago 10, NY Rangers 1.
  – Clint Smith, Chicago, Mar. 4, 1945, at Chicago, third period. Chicago 6, Montreal 4.
  – Red Berenson, St. Louis, Nov. 7, 1968, at Philadelphia, second period. St. Louis 8, Philadelphia 0.
  – Wayne Gretzky, Edmonton, Feb. 18, 1981, at Edmonton, third period. Edmonton 9, St. Louis 2.
  – Grant Mulvey, Chicago, Feb. 3, 1982, at Chicago, first period. Chicago 9, St. Louis 5.
  – Bryan Trottier, NY Islanders, Feb. 13, 1982, at NY Islanders, second period. NY Islanders 8, Philadelphia 2.
  – Al Secord, Chicago, Jan. 7, 1987, at Chicago, second period. Chicago 6, Toronto 4.
  – Joe Nieuwendyk, Calgary, Jan. 11, 1989, at Calgary, second period. Calgary 8, Winnipeg 3.
  – Peter Bondra, Washington, Feb. 5, 1994, at Washington, first period. Washington 6, Tampa Bay 3.
  – Mario Lemieux, Pittsburgh, Jan. 26, 1997, at Montreal, third period. Pittsburgh 5, Montreal 2.

ASSISTS

MOST ASSISTS:

1,963 – Wayne Gretzky, Edmonton, Los Angeles, St. Louis, NY Rangers, in 20 seasons. 1,487GP

1,249 – Ron Francis, Hartford, Pittsburgh, Carolina, Toronto, in 23 seasons. 1,731GP
1,193 – Mark Messier, Edmonton, NY Rangers, Vancouver, in 25 seasons. 1,756GP
1,169 – Raymond Bourque, Boston, Colorado, in 22 seasons. 1,612GP
1,135 – Paul Coffey, Edmonton, Pittsburgh, Los Angeles, Detroit, Hartford, Philadelphia, Chicago, Carolina, Boston, in 21 seasons. 1,409GP

MOST ASSISTS, INCLUDING PLAYOFFS:

2,223 – Wayne Gretzky, Edmonton, Los Angeles, St. Louis, NY Rangers, 1,963A in 1,487 regular-season games, 260A in 208 playoff games.
1,379 – Mark Messier, Edmonton, NY Rangers, Vancouver, 1,193A in 1,756 regular-season games, 186A in 236 playoff games.
1,346 – Ron Francis, Hartford, Pittsburgh, Carolina, Toronto, 1,249A in 1,731 regular-season games, 97A in 171 playoff games.
1,308 – Raymond Bourque, Boston, Colorado, 1,169A in 1,612 regular-season games, 139A in 214 playoff games.
1,272 – Paul Coffey, Edmonton, Pittsburgh, Los Angeles, Detroit, Hartford, Philadelphia, Chicago, Carolina, Boston, 1,135A in 1,409 regular-season games, 137A in 194 playoff games.

MOST ASSISTS, ONE SEASON:

163 – Wayne Gretzky, Edmonton, 1985-86. 80GP – 80 game schedule.
135 – Wayne Gretzky, Edmonton, 1984-85. 80GP – 80 game schedule.
125 – Wayne Gretzky, Edmonton, 1982-83. 80GP – 80 game schedule.
122 – Wayne Gretzky, Los Angeles, 1990-91. 78GP – 80 game schedule.
121 – Wayne Gretzky, Edmonton, 1986-87. 79GP – 80 game schedule.
120 – Wayne Gretzky, Edmonton, 1981-82. 80GP – 80 game schedule.
118 – Wayne Gretzky, Edmonton, 1983-84. 74GP – 80 game schedule.
114 – Wayne Gretzky, Los Angeles, 1988-89. 78GP – 80 game schedule.
  – Mario Lemieux, Pittsburgh, 1988-89. 76GP – 80 game schedule.
109 – Wayne Gretzky, Edmonton, 1980-81. 80GP – 80 game schedule.
  – Wayne Gretzky, Edmonton, 1987-88. 64GP – 80 game schedule.
102 – Bobby Orr, Boston, 1970-71. 78GP – 78 game schedule.
  – Wayne Gretzky, Los Angeles, 1989-90. 73GP – 80 game schedule.

MOST ASSISTS, ONE SEASON, INCLUDING PLAYOFFS:

174 – Wayne Gretzky, Edmonton, 1985-86,
163A in 80 regular-season games, 11A in 10 playoff games.
165 – Wayne Gretzky, Edmonton, 1984-85,
135A in 80 regular-season games, 30A in 18 playoff games.
151 – Wayne Gretzky, Edmonton, 1982-83,
125A in 80 regular-season games, 26A in 16 playoff games.
150 – Wayne Gretzky, Edmonton, 1986-87,
121A in 79 regular-season games, 29A in 21 playoff games.
140 – Wayne Gretzky, Edmonton, 1983-84,
118A in 74 regular-season games, 22A in 19 playoff games.
– Wayne Gretzky, Edmonton, 1987-88,
109A in 64 regular-season games, 31A in 19 playoff games.
133 – Wayne Gretzky, Los Angeles, 1990-91,
122A in 78 regular-season games, 11A in 12 playoff games.
131 – Wayne Gretzky, Los Angeles, 1988-89,
114A in 78 regular-season games, 17A in 11 playoff games.
127 – Wayne Gretzky, Edmonton, 1981-82,
120A in 80 regular-season games, 7A in 5 playoff games.
123 – Wayne Gretzky, Edmonton, 1980-81,
109A in 80 regular-season games, 14A in 9 playoff games.
121 – Mario Lemieux, Pittsburgh, 1988-89,
114A in 76 regular-season games, 7A in 11 playoff games.

MOST ASSISTS, ONE GAME:

7 – Billy Taylor, Detroit, Mar. 16, 1947, at Chicago. Detroit 10, Chicago 6.
– **Wayne Gretzky**, Edmonton, Feb. 15, 1980, at Edmonton.
Edmonton 8, Washington 2.
– **Wayne Gretzky**, Edmonton, Dec. 11, 1985, at Chicago.
Edmonton 12, Chicago 9.
– **Wayne Gretzky**, Edmonton, Feb. 14, 1986, at Edmonton.
Edmonton 8, Quebec 2.
6 – Six assists have been recorded in one game on 24 occasions since
Elmer Lach of Montreal first accomplished the feat vs. Boston on
Feb. 6, 1943. The most recent player is Eric Lindros of Philadelphia
on Feb. 26, 1997 at Ottawa.

MOST ASSISTS, ONE ROAD GAME:

7 – Billy Taylor, Detroit, Mar. 16, 1947, at Chicago. Detroit 10, Chicago 6.
– **Wayne Gretzky**, Edmonton, Dec. 11, 1985, at Chicago.
Edmonton 12, Chicago 9.
6 – Bobby Orr, Boston, Jan. 1, 1973, at Vancouver. Boston 8, Vancouver 2.
– Patrik Sundstrom, Vancouver, Feb. 29, 1984, at Pittsburgh.
Vancouver 9, Pittsburgh 5.
– Mario Lemieux, Pittsburgh, Dec. 5, 1992, at San Jose.
Pittsburgh 9, San Jose 4.
– Eric Lindros, Philadelphia, Feb. 26, 1997, at Ottawa.
Philadelphia 8, Ottawa 5.

MOST ASSISTS, ONE PERIOD:

5 – Dale Hawerchuk, Winnipeg, Mar. 6, 1984, at Los Angeles,
second period. Winnipeg 7, Los Angeles 3.
4 – Four assists have been recorded in one period on 63 occasions since
Mickey Roach of Hamilton first accomplished the feat vs. Toronto
on Feb. 23, 1921. The most recent player is Paul Kariya of Anaheim
on Dec. 16, 1998 vs. Nashville.

POINTS

MOST POINTS:

2,857 – Wayne Gretzky, Edmonton, Los Angeles, St. Louis, NY Rangers,
in 20 seasons. 1,487GP (894G-1,963A)
1,887 – Mark Messier, Edmonton, NY Rangers, Vancouver,
in 25 seasons. 1,756GP (694G-1,193A)
1,850 – Gordie Howe, Detroit, Hartford, in 26 seasons. 1,767GP (801G-1,049A)
1,798 – Ron Francis, Hartford, Pittsburgh, Carolina, Toronto,
in 23 seasons. 1,731GP (549G-1,249A)
1,771 – Marcel Dionne, Detroit, Los Angeles, NY Rangers,
in 18 seasons. 1,348GP (731G-1,040A)

MOST POINTS, INCLUDING PLAYOFFS:

3,239 – Wayne Gretzky, Edmonton, Los Angeles, St. Louis, NY Rangers,
2,857PTS in 1,487 regular-season games, 382PTS in 208 playoff games.
2,182 – Mark Messier, Edmonton, NY Rangers, Vancouver,
1,887PTS in 1,756 regular-season games, 295PTS in 236 playoff games.
2,010 – Gordie Howe, Detroit, Hartford,
1,850PTS in 1,767 regular-season games, 160PTS in 157 playoff games.
1,941 – Ron Francis, Hartford, Pittsburgh, Carolina, Toronto,
1,798PTS in 1,731 regular-season games, 143PTS in 171 playoff games
1,902 – Steve Yzerman, Detroit,
1,721PTS in 1,453 regular-season games, 181PTS in 192 playoff games.

MOST POINTS, ONE SEASON:

215 – Wayne Gretzky, Edmonton, 1985-86. 80GP – 80 game schedule.
212 – Wayne Gretzky, Edmonton, 1981-82. 80GP – 80 game schedule.
208 – Wayne Gretzky, Edmonton, 1984-85. 80GP – 80 game schedule.
205 – Wayne Gretzky, Edmonton, 1983-84. 74GP – 80 game schedule.
199 – Mario Lemieux, Pittsburgh, 1988-89. 76GP – 80 game schedule.
196 – Wayne Gretzky, Edmonton, 1982-83. 80GP – 80 game schedule.
183 – Wayne Gretzky, Edmonton, 1986-87. 79GP – 80 game schedule.
168 – Mario Lemieux, Pittsburgh, 1987-88, 77GP – 80 game schedule.
– Wayne Gretzky, Los Angeles, 1988-89. 78GP – 80 game schedule.
164 – Wayne Gretzky, Edmonton, 1980-81. 80GP – 80 game schedule.
163 – Wayne Gretzky, Los Angeles, 1990-91. 78GP – 80 game schedule.
161 – Mario Lemieux, Pittsburgh, 1995-96. 70GP – 82 game schedule.
160 – Mario Lemieux, Pittsburgh, 1992-93. 60GP – 84 game schedule.

MOST POINTS, ONE SEASON, INCLUDING PLAYOFFS:

255 – Wayne Gretzky, Edmonton, 1984-85,
208PTS in 80 regular-season games, 47PTS in 18 playoff games.
240 – Wayne Gretzky, Edmonton, 1983-84,
205PTS in 74 regular-season games, 35PTS in 19 playoff games.
234 – Wayne Gretzky, Edmonton, 1982-83,
196PTS in 80 regular-season games, 38PTS in 16 playoff games.
– Wayne Gretzky, Edmonton, 1985-86,
215PTS in 80 regular-season games, 19PTS in 10 playoff games.
224 – Wayne Gretzky, Edmonton, 1981-82,
212PTS in 80 regular-season games, 12PTS in 5 playoff games.
218 – Mario Lemieux, Pittsburgh, 1988-89,
199PTS in 76 regular-season games, 19PTS in 11 playoff games.
217 – Wayne Gretzky, Edmonton, 1986-87,
183PTS in 79 regular-season games, 34PTS in 21 playoff games.
192 – Wayne Gretzky, Edmonton, 1987-88,
149PTS in 64 regular-season games, 43PTS in 19 playoff games.
190 – Wayne Gretzky, Los Angeles, 1988-89,
168PTS in 78 regular-season games, 22PTS in 11 playoff games.
188 – Mario Lemieux, Pittsburgh, 1995-96,
161PTS in 70 regular-season games, 27PTS in 18 playoff games.
185 – Wayne Gretzky, Edmonton, 1980-81,
164PTS in 80 regular-season games, 21PTS in 9 playoff games.

Many thought Wayne Gretzky would be too small and too slow to succeed in the NHL, but he became the game's most dominant offensive performer. Gretzky enters the NHL coaching fraternity with the Phoenix Coyotes this season.

MOST POINTS, ONE GAME:

10 – Darryl Sittler, Toronto, Feb. 7, 1976, at Toronto, 6G-4A. Toronto 11, Boston 4.

8 – Maurice Richard, Montreal, Dec. 28, 1944, at Montreal, 5G-3A. Montreal 9, Detroit 1.
 – Bert Olmstead, Montreal, Jan. 9, 1954, at Montreal, 4G-4A. Montreal 12, Chicago 1.
 – Tom Bladon, Philadelphia, Dec. 11, 1977, at Philadelphia, 4G-4A. Philadelphia 11, Cleveland 1.
 – Bryan Trottier, NY Islanders, Dec. 23, 1978, at NY Islanders, 5G-3A. NY Islanders 9, NY Rangers 4.
 – Peter Stastny, Quebec, Feb. 22, 1981, at Washington, 4G-4A. Quebec 11, Washington 7.
 – Anton Stastny, Quebec, Feb. 22, 1981, at Washington, 3G-5A. Quebec 11, Washington 7.
 – Wayne Gretzky, Edmonton, Nov. 19, 1983, at Edmonton, 3G-5A. Edmonton 13, New Jersey 4.
 – Wayne Gretzky, Edmonton, Jan. 4, 1984, at Edmonton, 4G-4A. Edmonton 12, Minnesota 8.
 – Paul Coffey, Edmonton, Mar. 14, 1986, at Edmonton, 2G-6A. Edmonton 12, Detroit 3.
 – Mario Lemieux, Pittsburgh, Oct. 15, 1988, at Pittsburgh, 2G-6A. Pittsburgh 9, St. Louis 2.
 – Bernie Nicholls, Los Angeles, Dec. 1, 1988, at Los Angeles, 2G-6A. Los Angeles 9, Toronto 3.
 – Mario Lemieux, Pittsburgh, Dec. 31, 1988, at Pittsburgh, 5G-3A. Pittsburgh 8, New Jersey 6.

MOST POINTS, ONE ROAD GAME:

8 – Peter Stastny, Quebec, Feb. 22, 1981, at Washington. 4G-4A. Quebec 11, Washington 7.
 – Anton Stastny, Quebec, Feb. 22, 1981, at Washington. 3G-5A. Quebec 11, Washington 7.
7 – Red Green, Hamilton, Dec. 5, 1924, at Toronto. 5G-2A. Hamilton 10, Toronto 3.
 – Billy Taylor, Detroit, Mar. 16, 1947, at Chicago. 7A. Detroit 10, Chicago 6.
 – Red Berenson, St. Louis, Nov. 7, 1968, at Philadelphia. 6G-1A. St. Louis 8, Philadelphia 0.
 – Gilbert Perreault, Buffalo, Feb. 1, 1976, at California. 2G-5A. Buffalo 9, California 5.
 – Peter Stastny, Quebec, Apr. 1, 1982, at Boston. 3G-4A. Quebec 8, Boston 5.
 – Wayne Gretzky, Edmonton, Nov. 6, 1983, at Winnipeg. 4G-3A. Edmonton 8, Winnipeg 5.
 – Patrik Sundstrom, Vancouver, Feb. 29, 1984, at Pittsburgh. 1G-6A. Vancouver 9, Pittsburgh 5.
 – Wayne Gretzky, Edmonton, Dec. 11, 1985, at Chicago. 7A. Edmonton 12, Chicago 9.
 – Cam Neely, Boston, Oct. 16, 1988, at Chicago. 3G-4A. Boston 10, Chicago 3.
 – Mario Lemieux, Pittsburgh, Jan. 21, 1989, at Edmonton. 2G-5A. Pittsburgh 7, Edmonton 4.
 – Dino Ciccarelli, Washington, Mar. 18, 1989, at Hartford. 4G-3A. Washington 8, Hartford 2.
 – Mats Sundin, Quebec, Mar. 5, 1992, at Hartford. 5G-2A. Quebec 10, Hartford 4.
 – Mario Lemieux, Pittsburgh, Dec. 5, 1992, at San Jose. 1G-6A. Pittsburgh 9, San Jose 4.
 – Eric Lindros, Philadelphia, Feb. 26, 1997, at Ottawa. 1G-6A. Philadelphia 8, Ottawa 5.

MOST POINTS, ONE PERIOD:

6 – Bryan Trottier, NY Islanders, Dec. 23, 1978, at NY Islanders, second period. 3G-3A. NY Islanders 9, NY Rangers 4.
5 – Bill Cook, NY Rangers, Mar. 12, 1933, at NY Americans third period. 3G-2A. NY Rangers 8, NY Americans 2.
 – Les Cunningham, Chicago, Jan. 28, 1940, at Chicago, third period. 2G-3A. Chicago 8, Montreal 1.
 – Max Bentley, Chicago, Jan. 28, 1943, at Chicago, third period. 4G-1A. Chicago 10, NY Rangers 1.
 – Leo Labine, Boston, Nov. 28, 1954, at Boston, second period. 3G-2A. Boston 6, Detroit 2.
 – Darryl Sittler, Toronto, Feb. 7, 1976, at Toronto, second period. 3G-2A. Toronto 11, Boston 4.
 – Grant Mulvey, Chicago, Feb. 3, 1982, at Chicago, first period. 4G-1A. Chicago 9, St. Louis 5.
 – Dale Hawerchuk, Winnipeg, Mar. 6, 1984, at Los Angeles, second period. 5A. Winnipeg 7, Los Angeles 3.
 – Jari Kurri, Edmonton, Oct. 26, 1984, at Edmonton, second period. 2G-3A. Edmonton 8, Los Angeles 2.
 – Pat Elynuik, Winnipeg, Jan. 20, 1989, at Winnipeg, second period. 2G-3A. Winnipeg 7, Pittsburgh 3.
 – Ray Ferraro, Hartford, Dec. 9, 1989, at Hartford, first period. 3G-2A. Hartford 7, New Jersey 3.
 – Stephane Richer, Montreal, Feb. 14, 1990, at Montreal, first period. 2G-3A. Montreal 10, Vancouver 1.
 – Cliff Ronning, Vancouver, Apr. 15, 1993, at Los Angeles, third period. 3G-2A. Vancouver 8, Los Angeles 6.
 – Peter Forsberg, Colorado, Mar. 3, 1999, at Florida, third period. 2G-3A. Colorado 7, Florida 5.

POWER-PLAY AND SHORTHAND GOALS

MOST POWER-PLAY GOALS, CAREER:

270 – Dave Andreychuk, Buffalo, Toronto, New Jersey, Boston, Colorado, Tampa Bay, in 22 seasons. 1,597GP.
265 – Brett Hull, Calgary, St. Louis, Dallas, Detroit, in 18 seasons. 1,264GP
249 – Phil Esposito, Chicago, Boston, NY Rangers, in 18 seasons. 1,282GP

MOST POWER-PLAY GOALS, ONE SEASON:

34 – Tim Kerr, Philadelphia, 1985-86. 76GP – 80 game schedule.
32 – Dave Andreychuk, Buffalo, Toronto, 1992-93. 83GP – 84 game schedule.
31 – Joe Nieuwendyk, Calgary, 1987-88. 75GP – 80 game schedule.
 – Mario Lemieux, Pittsburgh, 1988-89. 76GP – 80 game schedule.
 – Mario Lemieux, Pittsburgh, 1995-96. 70GP – 82 game schedule.
29 – Michel Goulet, Quebec, 1987-88. 80GP – 80 game schedule.
 – Brett Hull, St. Louis, 1990-91. 78GP – 80 game schedule.
 – Brett Hull, St. Louis, 1992-93. 80GP – 84 game schedule.

MOST SHORTHAND GOALS, ONE SEASON:

13 – Mario Lemieux, Pittsburgh, 1988-89. 76GP – 80 game schedule.
12 – Wayne Gretzky, Edmonton, 1983-84. 74GP – 80 game schedule.
11 – Wayne Gretzky, Edmonton, 1984-85. 80GP – 80 game schedule.
10 – Marcel Dionne, Detroit, 1974-75. 80GP – 80 game schedule.
 – Mario Lemieux, Pittsburgh, 1987-88. 77GP – 80 game schedule.
 – Dirk Graham, Chicago, 1988-89. 80GP – 80 game schedule.

MOST SHORTHAND GOALS, ONE GAME:

3 – Theoren Fleury, Calgary, Mar. 9, 1991, at St. Louis. Calgary 8, St. Louis 4.

OVERTIME SCORING

MOST OVERTIME GOALS, CAREER:

13 – Steve Thomas, Toronto, Chicago, NY Islanders, New Jersey, Anaheim.
 – Sergei Fedorov, Detroit, Anaheim.
 – Mats Sundin, Quebec, Toronto.
12 – Jaromir Jagr, Pittsburgh, Washington.
 – Brett Hull, St. Louis, Dallas, Detroit.
11 – Mario Lemieux, Pittsburgh.
 – Theoren Fleury, Calgary, Colorado, NY Rangers, Chicago.
 – Pierre Turgeon, Buffalo, NY Islanders, Montreal, St. Louis, Dallas.

MOST OVERTIME ASSISTS, CAREER:

18 – Mark Messier, Edmonton, NY Rangers, Vancouver.
17 – Adam Oates, Detroit, St. Louis, Boston, Washington, Philadelphia, Anaheim.
16 – Nicklas Lidstrom, Detroit.
15 – Wayne Gretzky, Edmonton, Los Angeles, St. Louis, NY Rangers.
 – Doug Gilmour, St. Louis, Calgary, Toronto, New Jersey, Chicago, Buffalo, Montreal.

MOST OVERTIME POINTS, CAREER:

26 – Mark Messier, Edmonton, NY Rangers, Vancouver. 8G-18A.
24 – Sergei Fedorov, Detroit, Anaheim. 13G-11A.
23 – Steve Thomas, Toronto, Chicago, NY Islanders, New Jersey, Chicago, Anaheim. 13G-10A.
22 – Mario Lemieux, Pittsburgh. 11G-11A.
 – Adam Oates, Detroit, St. Louis, Boston, Washington, Philadelphia, Anaheim. 5G-17A.
 – Pierre Turgeon, Buffalo, NY Islanders, Montreal, St. Louis, Dallas. 11G-11A.

Sergei Fedorov scored his record-tying 13th career overtime goal with the Mighty Ducks in 2003-04. He also reached the 30-goal plateau for the tenth time in his NHL career during his first season with Anaheim.

SCORING BY A CENTER

MOST GOALS BY A CENTER, CAREER
894 – Wayne Gretzky, Edmonton, Los Angeles, St. Louis, NY Rangers, in 20 seasons. 1,487GP
731 – Marcel Dionne, Detroit, Los Angeles, NY Rangers, in 18 seasons. 1,348GP
717 – Phil Esposito, Chicago, Boston, NY Rangers, in 18 seasons. 1,282GP
694 – Mark Messier, Edmonton, NY Rangers, Vancouver, in 25 seasons. 1,756GP
683 – Mario Lemieux, Pittsburgh, in 16 seasons. 889GP

MOST GOALS BY A CENTER, ONE SEASON:
92 – Wayne Gretzky, Edmonton, 1981-82. 80GP – 80 game schedule.
87 – Wayne Gretzky, Edmonton, 1983-84. 74GP – 80 game schedule.
85 – Mario Lemieux, Pittsburgh, 1988-89. 76GP – 80 game schedule.
76 – Phil Esposito, Boston, 1970-71. 78GP – 78 game schedule.
73 – Wayne Gretzky, Edmonton, 1984-85. 80GP – 80 game schedule.

MOST ASSISTS BY A CENTER, CAREER:
1,963 – Wayne Gretzky, Edmonton, Los Angeles, St. Louis, NY Rangers, in 20 seasons. 1,487GP
1,249 – Ron Francis, Hartford, Pittsburgh, Carolina, Toronto, in 23 seasons. 1,731GP
1,193 – Mark Messier, Edmonton, NY Rangers, Vancouver, in 25 seasons. 1,756GP
1,079 – Adam Oates, Detroit, St. Louis, Boston, Washington, Philadelphia, Anaheim, Edmonton, in 19 seasons. 1,337GP
1,043 – Steve Yzerman, Detroit, in 21 seasons. 1,453GP

MOST ASSISTS BY A CENTER, ONE SEASON:
163 – Wayne Gretzky, Edmonton, 1985-86. 80GP – 80 game schedule.
135 – Wayne Gretzky, Edmonton, 1984-85. 80GP – 80 game schedule.
125 – Wayne Gretzky, Edmonton, 1982-83. 80GP – 80 game schedule.
122 – Wayne Gretzky, Los Angeles, 1990-91. 78GP – 80 game schedule.
121 – Wayne Gretzky, Edmonton, 1986-87. 79GP – 80 game schedule.

MOST POINTS BY A CENTER, CAREER:
2,857 – Wayne Gretzky, Edmonton, Los Angeles, St. Louis, NY Rangers, in 20 seasons. 1,487GP (894G-1,963A)
1,887 – Mark Messier, Edmonton, NY Rangers, Vancouver, in 25 seasons. 1,756GP (694G-1,193A)
1,798 – Ron Francis, Hartford, Pittsburgh, Carolina, Toronto, in 23 seasons. 1,731GP (549G-1,249A)
1,771 – Marcel Dionne, Detroit, Los Angeles, NY Rangers, in 18 seasons. 1,348GP (731G-1,040A)
1,721 – Steve Yzerman, Detroit, in 21 seasons. 1,453GP (678G-1,043A)

MOST POINTS BY A CENTER, ONE SEASON:
215 – Wayne Gretzky, Edmonton, 1985-86. 80GP – 80 game schedule.
212 – Wayne Gretzky, Edmonton, 1981-82. 80GP – 80 game schedule.
208 – Wayne Gretzky, Edmonton, 1984-85. 80GP – 80 game schedule.
205 – Wayne Gretzky, Edmonton, 1983-84. 74GP – 80 game schedule.
199 – Mario Lemieux, Pittsburgh, 1988-89. 76GP – 80 game schedule.

SCORING BY A LEFT WING

MOST GOALS BY A LEFT WING, CAREER:
653 – Luc Robitaille, Los Angeles, Pittsburgh, NY Rangers, Detroit, in 18 seasons. 1,366GP
634 – Dave Andreychuk, Buffalo, Toronto, New Jersey, Boston, Colorado, Tampa Bay, in 22 seasons. 1,597GP
610 – Bobby Hull, Chicago, Winnipeg, Hartford, in 16 seasons. 1,063GP
558 – Brendan Shanahan, New Jersey, St. Louis, Hartford, Detroit, in 17 seasons. 1,268GP
556 – John Bucyk, Detroit, Boston, in 23 seasons. 1,540GP

MOST GOALS BY A LEFT WING, ONE SEASON:
63 – Luc Robitaille, Los Angeles, 1992-93. 84GP – 84 game schedule.
60 – Steve Shutt, Montreal, 1976-77. 80GP – 80 game schedule.
58 – Bobby Hull, Chicago, 1968-69. 74GP – 76 game schedule.
57 – Michel Goulet, Quebec, 1982-83. 80GP – 80 game schedule.
56 – Charlie Simmer, Los Angeles, 1979-80. 64GP – 80 game schedule.
   – Charlie Simmer, Los Angeles, 1980-81. 65GP – 80 game schedule.
   – Michel Goulet, Quebec, 1983-84. 75GP – 80 game schedule.

MOST ASSISTS BY A LEFT WING, CAREER:
813 – John Bucyk, Detroit, Boston, in 23 seasons. 1,540GP
717 – Luc Robitaille, Los Angeles, Pittsburgh, NY Rangers, Detroit, in 18 seasons. 1,366GP
706 – Dave Andreychuk, Buffalo, Toronto, New Jersey, Boston, Colorado, Tampa Bay, in 22 seasons. 1,597GP
604 – Michel Goulet, Quebec, Chicago, in 15 seasons. 1,089GP
593 – Brendan Shanahan, New Jersey, St. Louis, Hartford, Detroit, in 17 seasons. 1,268GP

MOST ASSISTS BY A LEFT WING, ONE SEASON:
70 – Joe Juneau, Boston, 1992-93. 84GP – 84 game schedule.
69 – Kevin Stevens, Pittsburgh, 1991-92. 80GP – 80 game schedule.
67 – Mats Naslund, Montreal, 1985-86. 80GP – 80 game schedule.
65 – John Bucyk, Boston, 1970-71. 78GP – 78 game schedule.
   – Michel Goulet, Quebec, 1983-84. 75GP – 80 game schedule.
64 – Mark Messier, Edmonton, 1983-84. 73GP – 80 game schedule.

MOST POINTS BY A LEFT WING, CAREER:
1,370 – Luc Robitaille, Los Angeles, Pittsburgh, NY Rangers, Detroit, in 18 seasons. 1,366GP (653G-717A)
1,369 – John Bucyk, Detroit, Boston, in 23 seasons. 1,540GP (556G-813A)
1,320 – Dave Andreychuk, Buffalo, Toronto, New Jersey, Boston, Colorado, Tampa Bay, in 22 seasons. 1,597GP (634G-686A)
1,170 – Bobby Hull, Chicago, Winnipeg, Hartford, in 16 seasons. 1,063GP (610G-560A)
1,152 – Michel Goulet, Quebec, Chicago, in 15 seasons. 1,089GP (548G-604A)

MOST POINTS BY A LEFT WING, ONE SEASON:
125 – Luc Robitaille, Los Angeles, 1992-93. 84GP – 84 game schedule.
123 – Kevin Stevens, Pittsburgh, 1991-92. 80GP – 80 game schedule.
121 – Michel Goulet, Quebec, 1983-84. 75GP – 80 game schedule.
116 – John Bucyk, Boston, 1970-71. 78GP – 78 game schedule.
112 – Bill Barber, Philadelphia, 1975-76. 80GP – 80 game schedule.

SCORING BY A RIGHT WING

MOST GOALS BY A RIGHT WING, CAREER:
801 – Gordie Howe, Detroit, Hartford, in 26 seasons. 1,767GP
741 – Brett Hull, Calgary, St. Louis, Dallas, Detroit, in 18 seasons. 1,264GP
708 – Mike Gartner, Washington, Minnesota, NY Rangers, Toronto, Phoenix, in 19 seasons. 1,432GP
608 – Dino Ciccarelli, Minnesota, Washington, Detroit, Tampa Bay, Florida, in 19 seasons. 1,232GP
601 – Jari Kurri, Edmonton, Los Angeles, NY Rangers, Anaheim, Colorado, in 17 seasons. 1,251GP

MOST GOALS BY A RIGHT WING, ONE SEASON:
86 – Brett Hull, St. Louis, 1990-91. 78GP – 80 game schedule.
76 – Alexander Mogilny, Buffalo, 1992-93. 77GP – 84 game schedule.
   – Teemu Selanne, Winnipeg, 1992-93. 84GP – 84 game schedule.
72 – Brett Hull, St. Louis, 1989-90. 80GP – 80 game schedule.
71 – Jari Kurri, Edmonton, 1984-85. 73GP – 80 game schedule.
70 – Brett Hull, St. Louis, 1991-92. 80GP – 80 game schedule.

MOST ASSISTS BY A RIGHT WING, CAREER:
1,049 – Gordie Howe, Detroit, Hartford, in 26 seasons. 1,767GP
797 – Jari Kurri, Edmonton, Los Angeles, NY Rangers, Anaheim, Colorado, in 17 seasons. 1,251GP
793 – Guy Lafleur, Montreal, NY Rangers, Quebec, in 17 seasons. 1,126GP
772 – Jaromir Jagr, Pittsburgh, Washington, NY Rangers, in 14 seasons. 1,027GP
745 – Mark Recchi, Pittsburgh, Philadelphia, Montreal, in 16 seasons. 1,173GP

MOST ASSISTS BY A RIGHT WING, ONE SEASON:
87 – Jaromir Jagr, Pittsburgh, 1995-96. 82GP – 82 game schedule.
83 – Mike Bossy, NY Islanders, 1981-82. 80GP – 80 game schedule.
   – Jaromir Jagr, Pittsburgh, 1998-99. 81GP – 82 game schedule.
80 – Guy Lafleur, Montreal, 1976-77. 80GP – 80 game schedule.
77 – Guy Lafleur, Montreal, 1978-79. 80GP – 80 game schedule.

With 558 goals, Detroit's Brendan Shanahan currently ranks fourth among left wingers in NHL history, sitting between Hall of Famers Bobby Hull (610) and John Bucyk (556).

MOST POINTS BY A RIGHT WING, CAREER:
1,850 – Gordie Howe, Detroit, Hartford, in 26 seasons. 1,767GP (801G-1,049A)
1,398 – Jari Kurri, Edmonton, Los Angeles, NY Rangers, Anaheim, Colorado, in 17 seasons. 1,251GP (601G-797A)
1,390 – Brett Hull, Calgary, St. Louis, Dallas, Detroit, in 18 seasons. 1,264GP (741G-649A)
1,353 – Guy Lafleur, Montreal, NY Rangers, Quebec, in 17 seasons. 1,126GP (560G-793A)
1,335 – Mike Gartner, Washington, Minnesota, NY Rangers, Toronto, Phoenix, in 19 seasons. 1,432GP (708G-627A)

MOST POINTS BY A RIGHT WING, ONE SEASON:
149 – Jaromir Jagr, Pittsburgh, 1995-96. 82GP – 82 game schedule.
147 – Mike Bossy, NY Islanders, 1981-82. 80GP – 80 game schedule.
136 – Guy Lafleur, Montreal, 1976-77. 80GP – 80 game schedule.
135 – Jari Kurri, Edmonton, 1984-85. 73GP – 80 game schedule.
132 – Guy Lafleur, Montreal, 1977-78. 78GP – 80 game schedule.
– Teemu Selanne, Winnipeg, 1992-93. 84GP – 84 game schedule.

SCORING BY A DEFENSEMAN

MOST GOALS BY A DEFENSEMAN, CAREER:
410 – Raymond Bourque, Boston, Colorado, in 22 seasons. 1,612GP
396 – Paul Coffey, Edmonton, Pittsburgh, Los Angeles, Detroit, Hartford, Philadelphia, Chicago, Carolina, Boston, in 21 seasons. 1,409GP
340 – Al MacInnis, Calgary, St. Louis, in 23 seasons. 1,416GP
338 – Phil Housley, Buffalo, Winnipeg, St. Louis, Calgary, New Jersey, Washington, Chicago, Toronto, in 21 seasons. 1,495GP
310 – Denis Potvin, NY Islanders, in 15 seasons. 1,060GP

MOST GOALS BY A DEFENSEMAN, ONE SEASON:
48 – Paul Coffey, Edmonton, 1985-86. 79GP – 80 game schedule.
46 – Bobby Orr, Boston, 1974-75. 80GP – 80 game schedule.
40 – Paul Coffey, Edmonton, 1983-84. 80GP – 80 game schedule.
39 – Doug Wilson, Chicago, 1981-82. 76GP – 80 game schedule.
37 – Bobby Orr, Boston, 1970-71. 78GP – 78 game schedule.
– Bobby Orr, Boston, 1971-72. 76GP – 78 game schedule.
– Paul Coffey, Edmonton, 1984-85. 80GP – 80 game schedule.

MOST GOALS BY A DEFENSEMAN, ONE GAME:
5 – Ian Turnbull, Toronto, Feb. 2, 1977, at Toronto. Toronto 9, Detroit 1.
4 – Harry Cameron, Toronto, Dec. 26, 1917, at Toronto. Toronto 7, Montreal 5.
– Harry Cameron, Montreal, Mar. 3, 1920, at Quebec. Montreal 16, Quebec 3.
– Sprague Cleghorn, Montreal, Jan. 14, 1922, at Montreal. Montreal 10, Hamilton 6.
– John McKinnon, Pittsburgh, Nov. 19, 1929, at Pittsburgh. Pittsburgh 10, Toronto 5.
– Hap Day, Toronto, Nov. 19, 1929, at Pittsburgh. Pittsburgh 10, Toronto 5.
– Tom Bladon, Philadelphia, Dec. 11, 1977, at Philadelphia. Philadelphia 11, Cleveland 1.
– Ian Turnbull, Los Angeles, Dec. 12, 1981, at Los Angeles. Los Angeles 7, Vancouver 5.
– Paul Coffey, Edmonton, Oct. 26, 1984, at Calgary. Edmonton 6, Calgary 5.

MOST ASSISTS BY A DEFENSEMAN, CAREER:
1,169 – Raymond Bourque, Boston, Colorado, in 22 seasons. 1,612GP
1,135 – Paul Coffey, Edmonton, Pittsburgh, Los Angeles, Detroit, Hartford, Philadelphia, Chicago, Carolina, Boston, in 21 seasons. 1,409GP
934 – Al MacInnis, Calgary, St. Louis, in 23 seasons. 1,416GP
929 – Larry Murphy, Los Angeles, Washington, Minnesota, Pittsburgh, Toronto, Detroit, in 21 seasons. 1,615GP
894 – Phil Housley, Buffalo, Winnipeg, St. Louis, Calgary, New Jersey, Washington, Chicago, Toronto, in 21 seasons. 1,495GP

MOST ASSISTS BY A DEFENSEMAN, ONE SEASON:
102 – Bobby Orr, Boston, 1970-71. 78GP – 78 game schedule.
90 – Bobby Orr, Boston, 1973-74. 74GP – 78 game schedule.
– Paul Coffey, Edmonton, 1985-86. 79GP – 80 game schedule.
89 – Bobby Orr, Boston, 1974-75. 80GP – 80 game schedule.
87 – Bobby Orr, Boston, 1969-70. 76GP – 78 game schedule.

MOST ASSISTS BY A DEFENSEMAN, ONE GAME:
6 – Babe Pratt, Toronto, Jan. 8, 1944, at Toronto. Toronto 12, Boston 3.
– **Pat Stapleton**, Chicago, Mar. 30, 1969, at Chicago. Chicago 9, Detroit 5.
– **Bobby Orr**, Boston, Jan. 1, 1973, at Vancouver. Boston 8, Vancouver 2.
– **Ron Stackhouse**, Pittsburgh, Mar. 8, 1975, at Pittsburgh. Pittsburgh 8, Philadelphia 2.
– **Paul Coffey**, Edmonton, Mar. 14, 1986, at Edmonton. Edmonton 12, Detroit 3.
– **Gary Suter**, Calgary, Apr. 4, 1986, at Calgary. Calgary 9, Edmonton 3.

MOST POINTS BY A DEFENSEMAN, CAREER:
1,579 – Raymond Bourque, Boston, Colorado, in 22 seasons. 1,612GP (410G-1,169A)
1,531 – Paul Coffey, Edmonton, Pittsburgh, Los Angeles, Detroit, Hartford, Philadelphia, Chicago, Carolina, Boston, in 21 seasons. 1,409GP (396G-1,135A)
1,274 – Al MacInnis, Calgary, St. Louis, in 23 seasons. 1,416GP (340G-934A)
1,232 – Phil Housley, Buffalo, Winnipeg, St. Louis, Calgary, New Jersey, Washington, Chicago, Toronto, in 21 seasons. 1,495GP (338G-894A)
1,216 – Larry Murphy, Los Angeles, Washington, Minnesota, Pittsburgh, Toronto, Detroit, in 21 seasons. 1,615GP (287G-929A)

MOST POINTS BY A DEFENSEMAN, ONE SEASON:
139 – Bobby Orr, Boston, 1970-71. 78GP – 78 game schedule.
138 – Paul Coffey, Edmonton, 1985-86. 79GP – 80 game schedule.
135 – Bobby Orr, Boston, 1974-75. 80GP – 80 game schedule.
126 – Paul Coffey, Edmonton, 1983-84. 80GP – 80 game schedule.
122 – Bobby Orr, Boston, 1973-74. 74GP – 78 game schedule.

MOST POINTS BY A DEFENSEMAN, ONE GAME:
8 – Tom Bladon, Philadelphia, Dec. 11, 1977, at Philadelphia. 4G-4A. Philadelphia 11, Cleveland 1.
– **Paul Coffey**, Edmonton, Mar. 14, 1986, at Edmonton. 2G-6A. Edmonton 12, Detroit 3.
7 – Bobby Orr, Boston, Nov. 15, 1973, at Boston. 3G-4A. Boston 10, NY Rangers 2.

SCORING BY A GOALTENDER

MOST POINTS BY A GOALTENDER, CAREER:
48 – Tom Barrasso, Buffalo, Pittsburgh, Ottawa, Carolina, Toronto, St. Louis, in 19 seasons. 777GP
46 – Grant Fuhr, Edmonton, Toronto, Buffalo, Los Angeles, St. Louis, Calgary, in 19 seasons. 868GP

MOST POINTS BY A GOALTENDER, ONE SEASON:
14 – Grant Fuhr, Edmonton, 1983-84. 45GP – 80 game schedule.
9 – Curtis Joseph, St. Louis, 1991-92. 60GP – 80 game schedule.
8 – Mike Palmateer, Washington, 1980-81. 49GP – 80 game schedule.
– Grant Fuhr, Edmonton, 1987-88. 75GP – 80 game schedule.
– Ron Hextall, Philadelphia, 1988-89. 64GP – 80 game schedule.
– Tom Barrasso, Pittsburgh, 1992-93. 63GP – 84 game schedule.

MOST POINTS BY A GOALTENDER, ONE GAME:
3 – Jeff Reese, Calgary, Feb. 10, 1993, at Calgary. Calgary 13, San Jose 1.

Doug Wilson, now the general manager of the San Jose Sharks, scored 39 goals for Chicago during his Norris Trophy-winning season of 1981-82. Among defensemen, only Paul Coffey and Bobby Orr have ever had more goals in a single season.

SCORING BY A ROOKIE

MOST GOALS BY A ROOKIE, ONE SEASON:
76 – Teemu Selanne, Winnipeg, 1992-93. 84GP – 84 game schedule.
53 – Mike Bossy, NY Islanders, 1977-78. 73GP – 80 game schedule.
51 – Joe Nieuwendyk, Calgary, 1987-88. 75GP – 80 game schedule.
45 – Dale Hawerchuk, Winnipeg, 1981-82. 80GP – 80 game schedule.
  – Luc Robitaille, Los Angeles, 1986-87. 79GP – 80 game schedule.

MOST GOALS BY A PLAYER IN HIS FIRST NHL SEASON, ONE GAME:
5 – Howie Meeker, Toronto, Jan. 8, 1947, at Toronto. Toronto 10, Chicago 4.
  – **Don Murdoch**, NY Rangers, Oct. 12, 1976, at Minnesota.
  NY Rangers 10, Minnesota 4.

MOST GOALS BY A PLAYER IN HIS FIRST NHL GAME:
3 – Alex Smart, Montreal, Jan. 14, 1943, at Montreal. Montreal 5, Chicago 1.
  – **Real Cloutier**, Quebec, Oct. 10, 1979, at Quebec. Atlanta 5, Quebec 3.

MOST ASSISTS BY A ROOKIE, ONE SEASON:
70 – Peter Stastny, Quebec, 1980-81. 77GP – 80 game schedule.
  – **Joe Juneau**, Boston, 1992-93. 84GP – 84 game schedule.
63 – Bryan Trottier, NY Islanders, 1975-76. 80GP – 80 game schedule.
62 – Sergei Makarov, Calgary, 1989-90. 80GP – 80 game schedule.
60 – Larry Murphy, Los Angeles, 1980-81. 80GP – 80 game schedule.

MOST ASSISTS BY A PLAYER IN HIS FIRST NHL SEASON, ONE GAME:
7 – Wayne Gretzky, Edmonton, Feb. 15, 1980, at Edmonton.
  Edmonton 8, Washington 2.
6 – Gary Suter, Calgary, Apr. 4, 1986, at Calgary. Calgary 9, Edmonton 3.

MOST ASSISTS BY A PLAYER IN HIS FIRST NHL GAME:
4 – Dutch Reibel, Detroit, Oct. 8, 1953, at Detroit. Detroit 4, NY Rangers 1.
  – **Roland Eriksson**, Minnesota, Oct. 6, 1976, at NY Rangers.
  NY Rangers 6, Minnesota 5.
3 – Al Hill, Philadelphia, Feb. 14, 1977, at Philadelphia. Philadelphia 6,
  St. Louis 4.
  – Jarno Kultanen, Boston, Oct. 5, 2000, at Boston. Boston 4, Ottawa 4.
  – Stanislav Chistov, Anaheim, Oct. 10, 2002, at St. Louis. Anaheim 4,
  St. Louis 3.
  – Dominic Moore, NY Rangers, Nov. 1, 2003, at Montreal. NY Rangers 5,
  Montreal 1.

MOST POINTS BY A ROOKIE, ONE SEASON:
132 – Teemu Selanne, Winnipeg, 1992-93. 84GP – 84 game schedule.
109 – Peter Stastny, Quebec, 1980-81. 77GP – 80 game schedule.
103 – Dale Hawerchuk, Winnipeg, 1981-82. 80GP – 80 game schedule.
102 – Joe Juneau, Boston, 1992-93. 84GP – 84 game schedule.
100 – Mario Lemieux, Pittsburgh, 1984-85. 73GP – 80 game schedule.

MOST POINTS BY A PLAYER IN HIS FIRST NHL SEASON, ONE GAME:
8 – Peter Stastny, Quebec, Feb. 22, 1981, at Washington. 4G-4A.
  Quebec 11, Washington 7.
  – **Anton Stastny**, Quebec, Feb. 22, 1981, at Washington. 3G-5A.
  Quebec 11, Washington 7.
7 – Wayne Gretzky, Edmonton, Feb. 15, 1980, at Edmonton. 7A.
  Edmonton 8, Washington 2.
  – Sergei Makarov, Calgary, Feb. 25, 1990, at Calgary. 2G-5A.
  Calgary 10, Edmonton 4.
6 – Wayne Gretzky, Edmonton, Mar. 29, 1980, at Toronto. 2G-4A.
  Edmonton 8, Toronto 5.
  – Gary Suter, Calgary, Apr. 4, 1986, at Calgary. 6A.
  Calgary 9, Edmonton 3.

MOST POINTS BY A PLAYER IN HIS FIRST NHL GAME:
5 – Al Hill, Philadelphia, Feb. 14, 1977, at Philadelphia. 2G-3A.
  Philadelphia 6, St. Louis 4.
4 – Alex Smart, Montreal, Jan. 14, 1943, at Montreal. 3G-1A.
  Montreal 5, Chicago 1.
  – Dutch Reibel, Detroit, Oct. 8, 1953, at Detroit. 4A.
  Detroit 4, NY Rangers 1.
  – Roland Eriksson, Minnesota, Oct. 6, 1976, at NY Rangers. 4A.
  NY Rangers 6, Minnesota 5.
  – Stanislav Chistov, Anaheim, Oct. 10, 2002, at St. Louis. 1G-3A.
  Anaheim 4, St. Louis 3.

SCORING BY A ROOKIE DEFENSEMAN

MOST GOALS BY A ROOKIE DEFENSEMAN, ONE SEASON:
23 – Brian Leetch, NY Rangers, 1988-89. 68GP – 80 game schedule.
22 – Barry Beck, Colorado, 1977-78. 75GP – 80 game schedule.
19 – Reed Larson, Detroit, 1977-78. 75GP – 80 game schedule.
  – Phil Housley, Buffalo, 1982-83. 77GP – 80 game schedule.

MOST ASSISTS BY A ROOKIE DEFENSEMAN, ONE SEASON:
60 – Larry Murphy, Los Angeles, 1980-81. 80GP – 80 game schedule.
55 – Chris Chelios, Montreal, 1984-85. 74GP – 80 game schedule.
50 – Stefan Persson, NY Islanders, 1977-78. 66GP – 80 game schedule.
  – Gary Suter, Calgary, 1985-86. 80GP – 80 game schedule.
49 – Nicklas Lidstrom, Detroit, 1991-92. 80GP – 80 game schedule.

MOST POINTS BY A ROOKIE DEFENSEMAN, ONE SEASON:
76 – Larry Murphy, Los Angeles, 1980-81. 80GP – 80 game schedule.
71 – Brian Leetch, NY Rangers, 1988-89. 68GP – 80 game schedule.
68 – Gary Suter, Calgary, 1985-86. 80GP – 80 game schedule.
66 – Phil Housley, Buffalo, 1982-83. 77GP – 80 game schedule.
65 – Raymond Bourque, Boston, 1979-80. 80GP – 80 game schedule.

Gus Bodnar (on the right beside Bud Poile, shortly after being traded from Toronto to Chicago) scored 15 seconds into his first NHL game on October 30, 1943 for a record that still stands.

PER-GAME SCORING AVERAGES

HIGHEST GOALS-PER-GAME AVERAGE, CAREER
(AMONG PLAYERS WITH 200-OR-MORE GOALS):
.768 – **Mario Lemieux**, Pittsburgh, 1984-85 – 1996-97, 2000-01 – 2003-04, with 683G in 889GP.
.762 – Mike Bossy, NY Islanders, 1977-78 – 1986-87, with 573G in 752GP.
.756 – Cy Denneny, Ottawa, Boston, 1917-18 – 1928-29, with 248G in 328GP.
.742 – Babe Dye, Toronto, Hamilton, Chicago, NY Americans, 1919-20 – 1930-31, with 201G in 271GP.
.623 – Pavel Bure, Vancouver, Florida, NY Rangers, 1991-92 – 2002-03, with 437G in 702GP.

HIGHEST GOALS-PER-GAME AVERAGE, ONE SEASON
(AMONG PLAYERS WITH 20-OR-MORE GOALS):
2.20 – **Joe Malone**, Montreal, 1917-18, with 44G in 20GP.
1.80 – Cy Denneny, Ottawa, 1917-18, with 36G in 20GP.
1.64 – Newsy Lalonde, Montreal, 1917-18, with 23G in 14GP.
1.63 – Joe Malone, Quebec, 1919-20, with 39G in 24GP.
1.61 – Newsy Lalonde, Montreal, 1919-20, with 37G in 23GP.

HIGHEST GOALS-PER-GAME AVERAGE, ONE SEASON
(AMONG PLAYERS WITH 50-OR-MORE GOALS):
1.18 – **Wayne Gretzky**, Edmonton, 1983-84, with 87G in 74GP.
1.15 – Wayne Gretzky, Edmonton, 1981-82, with 92G in 80GP.
– Mario Lemieux, Pittsburgh, 1992-93, with 69G in 60GP.
1.12 – Mario Lemieux, Pittsburgh, 1988-89, with 85G in 76GP.
1.10 – Brett Hull, St. Louis, 1990-91, with 86G in 78GP.
1.02 – Cam Neely, Boston, 1993-94, with 50G in 49GP.
1.00 – Maurice Richard, Montreal, 1944-45, with 50G in 50GP.

HIGHEST ASSISTS-PER-GAME AVERAGE, CAREER
(AMONG PLAYERS WITH 300-OR-MORE ASSISTS):
1.320 – **Wayne Gretzky**, Edmonton, Los Angeles, St. Louis, NY Rangers, 1979-80 – 1998-99, with 1,963A in 1,487GP.
1.145 – Mario Lemieux, Pittsburgh, 1984-85 – 1996-97, 2000-01 – 2003-04, with 1,018A in 889GP.
.982 – Bobby Orr, Boston, Chicago, 1966-67 – 1978-79, with 645A in 657GP.
.905 – Peter Forsberg, Quebec, Colorado, 1994-95 – 2000-01, 2002-03 – 2003-04 with 525A in 580GP.
.808 – Peter Stastny, Quebec, New Jersey, St. Louis, 1980-81 – 1994-95, with 789A in 977GP.

HIGHEST ASSISTS-PER-GAME AVERAGE, ONE SEASON
(AMONG PLAYERS WITH 35-OR-MORE ASSISTS):
2.04 – **Wayne Gretzky, Edmonton**, 1985-86, with 163A in 80GP.
1.70 – Wayne Gretzky, Edmonton, 1987-88, with 109A in 64GP.
1.69 – Wayne Gretzky, Edmonton, 1984-85, with 135A in 80GP.
1.59 – Wayne Gretzky, Edmonton, 1983-84, with 118A in 74GP.
1.56 – Wayne Gretzky, Edmonton, 1982-83, with 125A in 80GP.
– Wayne Gretzky, Los Angeles, 1990-91, with 122A in 78GP.
1.53 – Wayne Gretzky, Edmonton, 1986-87, with 121A in 79GP.
1.52 – Mario Lemieux, Pittsburgh, 1992-93, with 91A in 60GP.
1.50 – Wayne Gretzky, Edmonton, 1981-82, with 120A in 80GP.
– Mario Lemieux, Pittsburgh, 1988-89, with 114A in 76GP.

HIGHEST POINTS-PER-GAME AVERAGE, CAREER:
(AMONG PLAYERS WITH 500-OR-MORE POINTS):
1.921 – **Wayne Gretzky**, Edmonton, Los Angeles, St. Louis, NY Rangers, 1979-80 – 1998-99, with 2,857PTS (894G-1,963A) in 1,487GP.
1.913 – Mario Lemieux, Pittsburgh, 1984-85 – 1996-97, 2000-01 – 2003-04, with 1,701PTS (683G-1,018A) in 889GP.
1.497 – Mike Bossy, NY Islanders, 1977-78 – 1986-87, with 1,126PTS (573G-553A) in 752GP.
1.393 – Bobby Orr, Boston, Chicago, 1966-67 – 1978-79, with 915PTS (270G-645A) in 657GP.
1.314 – Marcel Dionne, Detroit, Los Angeles, NY Rangers, 1971-72 – 1988-89, with 1,771PTS (731G-1,040A) in 1,348GP.

HIGHEST POINTS-PER-GAME AVERAGE, ONE SEASON
(AMONG PLAYERS WITH 50-OR-MORE POINTS):
2.77 – **Wayne Gretzky**, Edmonton, 1983-84, with 205PTS in 74GP.
2.69 – Wayne Gretzky, Edmonton, 1985-86, with 215PTS in 80GP.
2.67 – Mario Lemieux, Pittsburgh, 1992-93, with 160PTS in 60GP.
2.65 – Wayne Gretzky, Edmonton, 1981-82, with 212PTS in 80GP.
2.62 – Mario Lemieux, Pittsburgh, 1988-89, with 199PTS in 76GP.
2.60 – Wayne Gretzky, Edmonton, 1984-85, with 208PTS in 80GP.
2.45 – Wayne Gretzky, Edmonton, 1982-83, with 196PTS in 80GP.
2.33 – Wayne Gretzky, Edmonton, 1987-88, with 149PTS in 64GP.
2.32 – Wayne Gretzky, Edmonton, 1986-87, with 183PTS in 79GP.
2.30 – Mario Lemieux, Pittsburgh, 1995-96, with 161PTS in 70GP.
2.18 – Mario Lemieux, Pittsburgh, 1987-88, with 168PTS in 77GP.
2.15 – Wayne Gretzky, Los Angeles, 1988-89, with 168PTS in 78GP.
2.09 – Wayne Gretzky, Los Angeles, 1990-91, with 163PTS in 78GP.
2.08 – Mario Lemieux, Pittsburgh, 1989-90, with 123PTS in 59GP.

During his time with the Avalanche, Peter Forsberg collected 525 assists in just 580 games. His rate of .905 assists per game trails only Wayne Gretzky, Mario Lemieux and Bobby Orr for players with more than 300 career assists.

SCORING PLATEAUS

MOST 20-OR-MORE GOAL SEASONS:
22 – **Gordie Howe**, Detroit, Hartford, in 26 seasons.
20 – Ron Francis, Hartford, Pittsburgh, Carolina, Toronto, in 23 seasons.
19 – Dave Andreychuk, Buffalo, Toronto, New Jersey, Boston, Colorado, Tampa Bay, in 22 seasons.
17 – Marcel Dionne, Detroit, Los Angeles, NY Rangers, in 18 seasons.
– Mike Gartner, Washington, Minnesota, NY Rangers, Toronto, Phoenix, in 19 seasons.
– Wayne Gretzky, Edmonton, Los Angeles, St. Louis, NY Rangers, in 20 seasons.
– Mark Messier, Edmonton, NY Rangers, Vancouver, in 25 seasons.
– Brett Hull, Calgary, St. Louis, Dallas, Detroit, in 18 seasons.

MOST CONSECUTIVE 20-OR-MORE GOAL SEASONS:
22 – **Gordie Howe**, Detroit, 1949-50 – 1970-71.
17 – Marcel Dionne, Detroit, Los Angeles, NY Rangers, 1971-72 – 1987-88.
– Brett Hull, Calgary, St. Louis, Dallas, Detroit, 1987-88 – 2003-04.
16 – Phil Esposito, Chicago, Boston, NY Rangers, 1964-65 – 1979-80.
– Brendan Shanahan, New Jersey, St. Louis, Hartford, Detroit, 1988-89 – 2003-04.
15 – Mike Gartner, Washington, Minnesota, NY Rangers, Toronto, 1979-80 – 1993-94.

MOST 30-OR-MORE GOAL SEASONS:
17 – Mike Gartner, Washington, Minnesota, NY Rangers, Toronto, Phoenix, in 19 seasons.
14 – Gordie Howe, Detroit, Hartford, in 26 seasons.
– Marcel Dionne, Detroit, Los Angeles, NY Rangers, in 18 seasons.
– Wayne Gretzky, Edmonton, Los Angeles, St. Louis, NY Rangers, in 20 seasons.
13 – Bobby Hull, Chicago, Winnipeg, Hartford, in 16 seasons.
– Phil Esposito, Chicago, Boston, NY Rangers, in 18 seasons.
– Jaromir Jagr, Pittsburgh, Washington, NY Rangers, in 14 seasons.
– Brett Hull, Calgary, St. Louis, Dallas, Detroit, in 18 seasons.

MOST CONSECUTIVE 30-OR-MORE GOAL SEASONS:
15 – Mike Gartner, Washington, Minnesota, NY Rangers, Toronto, 1979-80 – 1993-94.
13 – Bobby Hull, Chicago, 1959-60 – 1971-72.
– Phil Esposito, Boston, NY Rangers, 1967-68 – 1979-80.
– Wayne Gretzky, Edmonton, Los Angeles, 1979-80 – 1991-92.
– Jaromir Jagr, Pittsburgh, Washington, NY Rangers, 1991-92 – 2003-04.

MOST 40-OR-MORE GOAL SEASONS:
12 – Wayne Gretzky, Edmonton, Los Angeles, St. Louis, NY Rangers, in 20 seasons.
10 – Marcel Dionne, Detroit, Los Angeles, NY Rangers, in 18 seasons.
– Mario Lemieux, Pittsburgh, in 15 seasons.
9 – Mike Bossy, NY Islanders, in 10 seasons.
– Mike Gartner, Washington, Minnesota, NY Rangers, Toronto, Phoenix, in 19 seasons.

MOST CONSECUTIVE 40-OR-MORE GOAL SEASONS:
12 – Wayne Gretzky, Edmonton, Los Angeles, 1979-80 – 1990-91.
9 – Mike Bossy, NY Islanders, 1977-78 – 1985-86.
8 – Luc Robitaille, Los Angeles, 1986-87 – 1993-94.
7 – Phil Esposito, Boston, 1968-69 – 1974-75.
– Michel Goulet, Quebec, 1981-82 – 1987-88.
– Jari Kurri, Edmonton, 1982-83 – 1988-89.

MOST 50-OR-MORE GOAL SEASONS:
9 – Mike Bossy, NY Islanders, in 10 seasons.
– **Wayne Gretzky**, Edmonton, Los Angeles, St. Louis, NY Rangers, in 20 seasons.
6 – Guy Lafleur, Montreal, NY Rangers, Quebec, in 17 seasons.
– Marcel Dionne, Detroit, Los Angeles, NY Rangers, in 18 seasons.
– Mario Lemieux, Pittsburgh, in 15 seasons.
5 – Bobby Hull, Chicago, Winnipeg, Hartford, in 16 seasons.
– Phil Esposito, Chicago, Boston, NY Rangers, in 18 seasons.
– Brett Hull, Calgary, St. Louis, Dallas, Detroit, in 17 seasons.
– Steve Yzerman, Detroit, in 20 seasons.
– Pavel Bure, Vancouver, Florida, NY Rangers, in 12 seasons.

MOST CONSECUTIVE 50-OR-MORE GOAL SEASONS:
9 – Mike Bossy, NY Islanders, 1977-78 – 1985-86.
8 – Wayne Gretzky, Edmonton, 1979-80 – 1986-87.
6 – Guy Lafleur, Montreal, 1974-75 – 1979-80.
5 – Phil Esposito, Boston, 1970-71 – 1974-75.
– Marcel Dionne, Los Angeles, 1978-79 – 1982-83.
– Brett Hull, St. Louis, 1989-90 – 1993-94.

MOST 60-OR-MORE GOAL SEASONS:
5 – Mike Bossy, NY Islanders, in 10 seasons.
– **Wayne Gretzky**, Edmonton, Los Angeles, St. Louis, NY Rangers, in 20 seasons.
4 – Phil Esposito, Chicago, Boston, NY Rangers, in 18 seasons.
– Mario Lemieux, Pittsburgh, in 15 seasons.

MOST CONSECUTIVE 60-OR-MORE GOAL SEASONS:
4 – Wayne Gretzky, Edmonton, 1981-82 – 1984-85.
3 – Mike Bossy, NY Islanders, 1980-81 – 1982-83.
– Brett Hull, St. Louis, 1989-90 – 1991-92.
2 – Phil Esposito, Boston, 1970-71 – 1971-72, 1973-74 – 1974-75.
– Jari Kurri, Edmonton, 1984-85 – 1985-86.
– Mario Lemieux, Pittsburgh, 1987-88 – 1988-89.
– Steve Yzerman, Detroit, 1988-89 – 1989-90.
– Pavel Bure, Vancouver, 1992-93 – 1993-94.

MOST 100-OR-MORE POINT SEASONS:
15 – Wayne Gretzky, Edmonton, Los Angeles, St. Louis, NY Rangers, in 20 seasons.
10 – Mario Lemieux, Pittsburgh, in 15 seasons.
8 – Marcel Dionne, Detroit, Los Angeles, NY Rangers, in 18 seasons.
7 – Mike Bossy, NY Islanders, in 10 seasons.
– Peter Stastny, Quebec, New Jersey, St. Louis, in 15 seasons.

MOST CONSECUTIVE 100-OR-MORE POINT SEASONS:
13 – Wayne Gretzky, Edmonton, Los Angeles, 1979-80 – 1991-92.
6 – Bobby Orr, Boston, 1969-70 – 1974-75.
– Guy Lafleur, Montreal, 1974-75 – 1979-80.
– Mike Bossy, NY Islanders, 1980-81 – 1985-86.
– Peter Stastny, Quebec, 1980-81 – 1985-86.
– Mario Lemieux, Pittsburgh, 1984-85 – 1989-90.
– Steve Yzerman, Detroit, 1987-88 – 1992-93.

The longtime captain of the Detroit Red Wings, Steve Yzerman posted six straight 100-point seasons early in his career.

THREE-OR-MORE-GOAL GAMES

MOST THREE-OR-MORE GOAL GAMES, CAREER:
50 – Wayne Gretzky, Edmonton, Los Angeles, St. Louis, NY Rangers, in 20 seasons, 37 three-goal games, 9 four-goal games, 4 five-goal games.
40 – Mario Lemieux, Pittsburgh, in 16 seasons, 27 three-goal games, 10 four-goal games, 3 five-goal games.
39 – Mike Bossy, NY Islanders, in 10 seasons, 30 three-goal games, 9 four-goal games.
33 – Brett Hull, Calgary, St. Louis, Dallas, Detroit, in 18 seasons, 30 three-goal games, 3 four-goal games.
32 – Phil Esposito, Chicago, Boston, NY Rangers, in 18 seasons, 27 three-goal games, 5 four-goal games.

MOST THREE-OR-MORE GOAL GAMES, ONE SEASON:
10 – Wayne Gretzky, Edmonton, 1981-82. 6 three-goal games, 3 four-goal games, 1 five-goal game.
– **Wayne Gretzky**, Edmonton, 1983-84. 6 three-goal games, 4 four-goal games.
9 – Mike Bossy, NY Islanders, 1980-81. 6 three-goal games, 3 four-goal games.
– Mario Lemieux, Pittsburgh, 1988-89. 7 three-goal games, 1 four-goal game, 1 five-goal game.
8 – Brett Hull, St. Louis, 1991-92. 8 three-goal games.
7 – Joe Malone, Montreal, 1917-18. 2 three-goal games, 2 four-goal games, 3 five-goal games.
– Phil Esposito, Boston, 1970-71. 7 three-goal games.
– Rick Martin, Buffalo, 1975-76. 6 three-goal games, 1 four-goal game.
– Alexander Mogilny, Buffalo, 1992-93. 5 three-goal games, 2 four-goal games.

SCORING STREAKS

LONGEST CONSECUTIVE GOAL-SCORING STREAK:
16 Games – Punch Broadbent, Ottawa, 1921-22. 27G
14 Games – Joe Malone, Montreal, 1917-18. 35G
13 Games – Newsy Lalonde, Montreal, 1920-21. 24G
– Charlie Simmer, Los Angeles, 1979-80. 17G
12 Games – Cy Denneny, Ottawa, 1917-18. 23G
– Dave Lumley, Edmonton, 1981-82. 15G
– Mario Lemieux, Pittsburgh, 1992-93. 18G

LONGEST CONSECUTIVE ASSIST-SCORING STREAK:
23 Games – Wayne Gretzky, Los Angeles, 1990-91. 48A
18 Games – Adam Oates, Boston, 1992-93. 28A
17 Games – Wayne Gretzky, Edmonton, 1983-84. 38A
– Paul Coffey, Edmonton, 1985-86. 27A
– Wayne Gretzky, Los Angeles, 1989-90. 35A
16 Games – Jaromir Jagr, Pittsburgh, 2000-01. 24A

LONGEST CONSECUTIVE POINT-SCORING STREAK:
51 Games – Wayne Gretzky, Edmonton, 1983-84. 61G-92A-153PTS
46 Games – Mario Lemieux, Pittsburgh, 1989-90. 39G-64A-103PTS
39 Games – Wayne Gretzky, Edmonton, 1985-86. 33G-75A-108PTS
30 Games – Wayne Gretzky, Edmonton, 1982-83. 24G-52A-76PTS
– Mats Sundin, Quebec, 1992-93. 21G-25A-46PTS

**LONGEST CONSECUTIVE POINT-SCORING STREAK
FROM START OF SEASON:**
51 Games – Wayne Gretzky, Edmonton, 1983-84. 61G-92A-153PTS. Streak ended by Los Angeles and goaltender Markus Mattsson on Jan. 28, 1984.

LONGEST CONSECUTIVE POINT-SCORING STREAK BY A DEFENSEMAN:
28 Games – Paul Coffey, Edmonton, 1985-86. 16G-39A-55PTS
19 Games – Raymond Bourque, Boston, 1987-88. 6G-21A-27PTS
17 Games – Raymond Bourque, Boston, 1984-85. 4G-24A-28PTS
– Brian Leetch, NY Rangers, 1991-92. 5G-24A-29PTS
16 Games – Gary Suter, Calgary, 1987-88. 8G-17A-25PTS
15 Games – Bobby Orr, Boston, 1970-71. 10G-23A-33PTS
– Bobby Orr, Boston, 1973-74. 8G-15A-23PTS
– Steve Duchesne, Quebec, 1992-93. 4G-17A-21PTS
– Chris Chelios, Chicago, 1995-96. 4G-16A-20PTS

FASTEST GOALS AND ASSISTS

FASTEST GOAL FROM START OF A GAME:
0:05 – Doug Smail, Winnipeg, Dec. 20, 1981, at Winnipeg. Winnipeg 5, St. Louis 4.
– **Bryan Trottier**, NY Islanders, Mar. 22, 1984, at Boston. NY Islanders 3, Boston 3.
– **Alexander Mogilny**, Buffalo, Dec. 21, 1991, at Toronto. Buffalo 4, Toronto 1.
0:06 – Henry Boucha, Detroit, Jan. 28, 1973, at Montreal. Detroit 4, Montreal 2.
– Jean Pronovost, Pittsburgh, Mar. 25, 1976, at St. Louis. St. Louis 5, Pittsburgh 2.
0:07 – Charlie Conacher, Toronto, Feb. 6, 1932, at Toronto. Toronto 6, Boston 0.
– Danny Gare, Buffalo, Dec. 17, 1978, at Buffalo. Buffalo 6, Vancouver 3.
– Tiger Williams, Los Angeles, Feb. 14, 1987, at Los Angeles. Los Angeles 5, Harford 2.
0:08 – Ron Martin, NY Americans, Dec. 4, 1932, at NY Americans. NY Americans 4, Montreal 2.
– Chuck Arnason, Colorado, Jan. 28, 1977, at Atlanta. Colorado 3, Atlanta 3.
– Wayne Gretzky, Edmonton, Dec. 14, 1983, at NY Rangers. Edmonton 9, NY Rangers 4.
– Gaetan Duchesne, Washington, Mar. 14, 1987, at St. Louis. Washington 3, St. Louis 3.
– Tim Kerr, Philadelphia, Mar. 7, 1989, at Philadelphia. Philadelphia 4, Edmonton 4.
– Grant Ledyard, Buffalo, Dec. 4, 1991, at Winnipeg. Buffalo 4, Winnipeg 4.
– Brent Sutter, Chicago, Feb. 5, 1995, at Vancouver. Chicago 9, Vancouver 4.
– Paul Kariya, Anaheim, Mar. 9, 1997, at Colorado. Anaheim 2, Colorado 2.
– Tony Hrkac, Dallas, Nov. 7, 1998, at Los Angeles. Dallas 4, Los Angeles 3.
– Sergei Fedorov, Detroit, Nov. 21, 1998, at Vancouver. Detroit 4, Vancouver 2.
– Ronald Petrovicky, Atlanta, Dec. 20, 2003, at Pittsburgh. Atlanta 7, Pittsburgh 4.
– Mike Modano, Dallas, Dec. 27, 2003, at Columbus. Dallas 4, Columbus 3.

FASTEST GOAL FROM START OF A PERIOD:
0:04 – Claude Provost, Montreal, Nov. 9, 1957, at Montreal, second period. Montreal 4, Boston 2.
– **Denis Savard**, Chicago, Jan. 12, 1986, at Chicago, third period. Chicago 4, Hartford 2.

FASTEST GOAL BY A PLAYER IN HIS FIRST NHL GAME:
0:15 – Gus Bodnar, Toronto, Oct. 30, 1943, at Toronto. Toronto 5, NY Rangers 2.
0:18 – Danny Gare, Buffalo, Oct. 10, 1974, at Buffalo. Buffalo 9, Boston 5.
0:20 – Alexander Mogilny, Buffalo, Oct. 5, 1989, at Buffalo. Buffalo 4, Quebec 3.

FASTEST TWO GOALS FROM START OF A GAME:
0:27 – Mike Knuble, Boston, Feb. 14, 2003, at Florida at 0:10 and 0:27. Boston 6, Florida 5.

FASTEST TWO GOALS:
0:04 – Nels Stewart, Mtl. Maroons, Jan. 3, 1931, at Mtl. Maroons at 8:24 and 8:28, third period. Mtl. Maroons 5, Boston 3.
– **Deron Quint**, Winnipeg, Dec. 15, 1995, at Winnipeg at 7:51 and 7:55, second period. Winnipeg 9, Edmonton 4.
0:05 – Pete Mahovlich, Montreal, Feb. 20, 1971, at Montreal at 12:16 and 12:21, third period. Montreal 7, Chicago 1.
0:06 – Jim Pappin, Chicago, Feb. 16, 1972, at Chicago at 2:57 and 3:03, third period. Chicago 3, Philadelphia 3.
– Ralph Backstrom, Los Angeles, Nov. 2, 1972, at Los Angeles at 8:30 and 8:36, third period. Los Angeles 5, Boston 2.
– Lanny McDonald, Calgary, Mar. 22, 1984, at Calgary at 16:23 and 16:29, first period. Detroit 6, Calgary 4.
– Sylvain Turgeon, Hartford, Mar. 28, 1987, at Hartford at 13:59 and 14:05, second period. Hartford 5, Pittsburgh 4.

FASTEST THREE GOALS:
0:21 – Bill Mosienko, Chicago, Mar. 23, 1952, at NY Rangers, against goaltender Lorne Anderson. Mosienko scored at 6:09, 6:20 and 6:30 of third period, all with both teams at full strength. Chicago 7, NY Rangers 6.
0:44 – Jean Béliveau, Montreal, Nov. 5, 1955, at Montreal, against goaltender Terry Sawchuk. Béliveau scored at 0:42, 1:08 and 1:26 of second period, all with Montreal holding a 6-4 man advantage. Montreal 4, Boston 2.

FASTEST THREE ASSISTS:
0:21 – Gus Bodnar, Chicago, Mar. 23, 1952, at NY Rangers, Bodnar assisted on Bill Mosienko's three goals at 6:09, 6:20 and 6:30 of third period. Chicago 7, NY Rangers 6.
0:44 – Bert Olmstead, Montreal, Nov. 5, 1955, at Montreal, Olmstead assisted on Jean Béliveau's three goals at 0:42, 1:08 and 1:26 of second period. Montreal 4, Boston 2.

SHOTS ON GOAL

MOST SHOTS ON GOAL, ONE SEASON:
550 – Phil Esposito, Boston, 1970-71. 78GP – 78 game schedule.
429 – Paul Kariya, Anaheim, 1998-99. 82GP – 82 game schedule.
426 – Phil Esposito, Boston, 1971-72. 76GP – 78 game schedule.
414 – Bobby Hull, Chicago, 1968-69. 74GP – 76 game schedule.

PENALTIES

MOST PENALTY MINUTES, CAREER:
3,966 – Tiger Williams, Toronto, Vancouver, Detroit, Los Angeles, Hartford, in 14 seasons. 962GP
3,565 – Dale Hunter, Quebec, Washington, Colorado, in 19 seasons. 1,407GP
3,406 – Tie Domi, Toronto, NY Rangers, Winnipeg, in 15 seasons. 943GP
3,381 – Marty McSorley, Pittsburgh, Edmonton, Los Angeles, NY Rangers, San Jose, Boston, in 17 seasons. 961GP
3,300 – Bob Probert, Detroit, Chicago, in 17 seasons. 935GP

MOST PENALTY MINUTES, CAREER, INCLUDING PLAYOFFS:
4,421 – Tiger Williams, Toronto, Vancouver, Detroit, Los Angeles, Hartford, 3,966 in 962 regular-season games; 455 in 83 playoff games.
4,294 – Dale Hunter, Quebec, Washington, Colorado, 3,565 in 1,407 regular-season games; 729 in 186 playoff games.
3,755 – Marty McSorley, Pittsburgh, Edmonton, Los Angeles, NY Rangers, San Jose, Boston, 3,381 in 961 regular-season games; 374 in 115 playoff games.
3,644 – Tie Domi, Toronto, NY Rangers, Winnipeg, 3,406 in 943 regular-season games; 238 in 98 playoff games.
3,584 – Chris Nilan, Montreal, NY Rangers, Boston, 3,043 in 688 regular-season games; 541 in 111 playoff games.

MOST PENALTY MINUTES, ONE SEASON:
472 – Dave Schultz, Philadelphia, 1974-75.
409 – Paul Baxter, Pittsburgh, 1981-82.
408 – Mike Peluso, Chicago, 1991-92.
405 – Dave Schultz, Los Angeles, Pittsburgh, 1977-78.

MOST PENALTIES, ONE GAME:
10 – Chris Nilan, Boston, Mar. 31, 1991, at Boston vs. Hartford. 6 minors, 2 majors, 1 10-minute misconduct.
9 – Jim Dorey, Toronto, Oct. 16, 1968, at Toronto vs. Pittsburgh. 4 minors, 2 majors, 2 10-minute misconducts, 1 game misconduct.
– Dave Schultz, Pittsburgh, Apr. 6, 1978, at Detroit. 5 minors, 2 majors, 2 10-minute misconducts.
– Randy Holt, Los Angeles, Mar. 11, 1979, at Philadelphia. 1 minor, 3 majors, 2 10-minute misconducts, 3 game misconducts.
– Russ Anderson, Pittsburgh, Jan. 19, 1980, at Pittsburgh vs. Edmonton. 3 minors, 3 majors, 3 game misconducts.
– Kim Clackson, Quebec, Mar. 8, 1981, at Quebec vs. Chicago. 4 minors, 3 majors, 2 game misconducts.
– Terry O'Reilly, Boston, Dec. 19, 1984, at Hartford. 5 minors, 3 majors, 1 game misconduct.
– Larry Playfair, Los Angeles, Dec. 9, 1986, at NY Islanders. 6 minors, 2 majors, 1 10-minute misconduct.
– Marty McSorley, Los Angeles, Apr. 14, 1992, at Vancouver. 5 minors, 2 majors, 1 10-minute misconduct, 1 game misconduct.
– Reed Low, St. Louis, Dec. 31, 2002, at Detroit. 4 minors, 1 major, 1 10-minute misconduct, 3 game misconducts.

MOST PENALTY MINUTES, ONE GAME:
67 – Randy Holt, Los Angeles, Mar. 11, 1979, at Philadelphia. 1 minor, 3 majors, 2 10-minute misconducts, 3 game misconducts.
57 – Brad Smith, Toronto, Nov. 15, 1986, at Toronto vs. Detroit. 1 minor, 3 majors, 2 10-minute misconducts, 2 game misconducts.
– Reed Low, St. Louis, Feb. 28, 2002, at St. Louis vs. Calgary. 1 minor, 3 majors, 1 10-minute misconduct, 3 game misconducts.

MOST PENALTIES, ONE PERIOD:
   9 – **Randy Holt**, Los Angeles, Mar. 11, 1979, at Philadelphia, first period.
      1 minor, 3 majors, 2 10-minute misconducts, 3 game misconducts.

MOST PENALTY MINUTES, ONE PERIOD:
   67 – **Randy Holt**, Los Angeles, Mar. 11, 1979, at Philadelphia, first period.
      1 minor, 3 majors, 2 10-minute misconducts, 3 game misconducts.

GOALTENDING

MOST GAMES APPEARED IN BY A GOALTENDER, CAREER:
   1,029 – **Patrick Roy**, Montreal, Colorado,1984-85 – 2002-03.
      971 – Terry Sawchuk, Detroit, Boston, Toronto, Los Angeles, NY Rangers,
         1949-50 – 1969-70.
      906 – Glenn Hall, Detroit, Chicago, St. Louis, 1952-53 – 1970-71.
      886 – Tony Esposito, Montreal, Chicago, 1968-69 – 1983-84.
      882 – John Vanbiesbrouck, NY Rangers, Florida, Philadelphia, NY Islanders,
         New Jersey, 1981-82 – 2001-02.

MOST CONSECUTIVE COMPLETE GAMES BY A GOALTENDER:
   502 – **Glenn Hall**, Detroit, Chicago. Played 502 games from beginning of
      1955-56 season through first 12 games of 1962-63 season. In his 503rd
      straight game, Nov. 7, 1962, at Chicago, Hall was removed from the
      game against Boston with a back injury in the first period.

MOST GAMES APPEARED IN BY A GOALTENDER, ONE SEASON:
   79 – **Grant Fuhr**, St. Louis, 1995-96.
   77 – Martin Brodeur, New Jersey, 1995-96.
      – Bill Ranford, Edmonton, Boston, 1995-96.
      – Arturs Irbe, Carolina, 2000-01.
      – Marc Denis, Columbus, 2002-03.

MOST MINUTES PLAYED BY A GOALTENDER, CAREER:
   60,235 – **Patrick Roy**, Montreal, Colorado, 1984-85 – 2002-03.
   57,194 – Terry Sawchuk, Detroit, Boston, Toronto, Los Angeles, NY Rangers,
      1949-50 – 1969-70.

MOST MINUTES PLAYED BY A GOALTENDER, ONE SEASON:
   4,555 – **Martin Brodeur**, New Jersey, 2003-04.
   4,511 – Marc Denis, Columbus, 2002-03.

MOST SHUTOUTS, CAREER:
   103 – **Terry Sawchuk**, Detroit, Boston, Toronto, Los Angeles, NY Rangers,
      in 21 seasons.
   94 – George Hainsworth, Montreal, Toronto, in 11 seasons.
   84 – Glenn Hall, Detroit, Chicago, St. Louis, in 18 seasons.

MOST SHUTOUTS, ONE SEASON:
   22 – **George Hainsworth**, Montreal, 1928-29. 44GP
   15 – Alec Connell, Ottawa, 1925-26. 36GP
      – Alec Connell, Ottawa, 1927-28. 44GP
      – Hal Winkler, Boston, 1927-28. 44GP
      – Tony Esposito, Chicago, 1969-70. 63GP
   14 – George Hainsworth, Montreal, 1926-27. 44GP

LONGEST SHUTOUT SEQUENCE BY A GOALTENDER:
   461:29 – **Alec Connell**, Ottawa, 1927-28, six consecutive shutouts.
      (Forward passing not permitted in attacking zones in 1927-28.)
   343:05 – George Hainsworth, Montreal, 1928-29, four consecutive shutouts.
      (Forward passing not permitted in attacking zones in 1928-29.)
   332:01 – Brian Boucher, Phoenix, 2003-04, five consecutive shutouts.
   324:40 – Roy Worters, NY Americans, 1930-31, four consecutive shutouts.
   309:21 – Bill Durnan, Montreal, 1948-49, four consecutive shutouts.

MOST WINS BY A GOALTENDER, CAREER:
   551 – **Patrick Roy**, Montreal, Colorado, in 19 seasons. 1,029GP
   447 – Terry Sawchuk, Detroit, Boston, Toronto, Los Angeles, NY Rangers,
      in 21 seasons. 971GP
   435 – Jacques Plante, Montreal, NY Rangers, St. Louis, Toronto, Boston,
      in 18 seasons. 837GP
      – Ed Belfour, Chicago, San Jose, Dallas, Toronto,
      in 15 seasons. 856GP
   423 – Tony Esposito, Montreal, Chicago, in 16 seasons. 886GP

MOST WINS BY A GOALTENDER, ONE SEASON:
   47 – **Bernie Parent**, Philadelphia, 1973-74. 73GP
   44 – Bernie Parent, Philadelphia, 1974-75. 68GP
      – Terry Sawchuk, Detroit, 1950-51. 70GP
      – Terry Sawchuk, Detroit, 1951-52. 70GP

LONGEST WINNING STREAK BY A GOALTENDER, ONE SEASON:
   17 – **Gilles Gilbert**, Boston, 1975-76.
   14 – Tiny Thompson, Boston, 1929-30.
      – Ross Brooks, Boston, 1973-74.
      – Don Beaupre, Minnesota, 1985-86.
      – Tom Barrasso, Pittsburgh, 1992-93.

LONGEST UNDEFEATED STREAK BY A GOALTENDER, ONE SEASON:
   32 Games – Gerry Cheevers, Boston, 1971-72. 24w-8T
   31 Games – Pete Peeters, Boston, 1982-83. 26w-5T
   27 Games – Pete Peeters, Philadelphia, 1979-80. 22w-5T

LONGEST UNDEFEATED STREAK BY A GOALTENDER IN HIS FIRST NHL SEASON:
   23 Games –Grant Fuhr, Edmonton, 1981-82. 15w-8T

LONGEST UNDEFEATED STREAK BY A GOALTENDER FROM START OF CAREER:
   16 Games – Patrick Lalime, Pittsburgh, 1996-97. 14w-2T

MOST 40-OR-MORE WIN SEASONS BY A GOALTENDER:
   4 – **Martin Brodeur,** New Jersey, in 12 seasons.
   3 – Terry Sawchuk, Detroit, Boston, Toronto, Los Angeles, NY Rangers,
      in 21 seasons.
      – Jacques Plante, Montreal, NY Rangers, St. Louis, Toronto, Boston,
      in 18 seasons.
   2 – Bernie Parent, Boston, Philadelphia, Toronto, in 13 seasons.
      – Ken Dryden, Montreal, in 8 seasons.
      – Ed Belfour, Chicago, San Jose, Dallas, Toronto, in 15 seasons.

MOST CONSECUTIVE 40-OR-MORE WIN SEASONS BY A GOALTENDER:
   2 – **Terry Sawchuk**, Detroit, 1950-51 – 1951-52.
      – **Bernie Parent**, Philadelphia, 1973-74 – 1974-75.
      – **Ken Dryden**, Montreal, 1975-76 – 1976-77.
      – **Martin Brodeur**, New Jersey, 1999-2000 – 2000-01.

MOST 30-OR-MORE WIN SEASONS BY A GOALTENDER:
   13 – **Patrick Roy**, Montreal, Colorado, in 19 seasons.
   9 – Martin Brodeur, New Jersey, in 12 seasons.
      – Ed Belfour, Chicago, San Jose, Dallas, Toronto, in 15 seasons.
   8 – Tony Esposito, Montreal, Chicago, in 16 seasons.
   7 – Jacques Plante, Montreal, NY Rangers, St. Louis, Toronto, Boston,
      in 18 seasons.
      – Ken Dryden, Montreal, in 8 seasons.

MOST CONSECUTIVE 30-OR-MORE WIN SEASONS BY A GOALTENDER:
   9 – **Martin Brodeur**, New Jersey, 1995-96 – 2003-04.
   8 – Patrick Roy, Montreal, Colorado, 1995-96 – 2002-03.
   7 – Tony Esposito, Chicago, 1969-70 – 1975-76.
   6 – Jacques Plante, Montreal, 1954-55 – 1959-60.
   5 – Terry Sawchuk, Detroit, 1950-51 – 1954-55.
      – Ken Dryden, Montreal, 1974-75 – 1978-79.

MOST LOSSES BY A GOALTENDER, CAREER:
   352 – **Gump Worsley**, NY Rangers, Montreal, Minnesota, in 21 seasons. 861GP
   351 – Gilles Meloche, Chicago, California, Cleveland, Minnesota, Pittsburgh,
      in 18 seasons. 788GP
   346 – John Vanbiesbrouck, NY Rangers, Florida, Philadelphia, NY Islanders,
      New Jersey, in 20 seasons. 882GP
   332 – Terry Sawchuk, Detroit, Boston, Toronto, Los Angeles, NY Rangers,
      in 21 seasons. 971GP

MOST LOSSES BY A GOALTENDER, ONE SEASON:
   48 – **Gary Smith**, California, 1970-71. 71GP
   47 – Al Rollins, Chicago, 1953-54. 66GP
   46 – Peter Sidorkiewicz, Ottawa, 1992-93. 64GP
   44 – Harry Lumley, Chicago, 1951-52. 70GP

Among the NHL records least likely to be eclipsed is Glenn Hall's streak of playing every minute of 502 consecutive games over seven-plus seasons.

Active NHL Players' Three-or-More-Goal Games

Regular Season

Teams named are the ones the players were with at the time of their multiple-scoring games. Players listed alphabetically.

A 20-goal scorer in each of the last three seasons, Marco Sturm recorded a three-goal game on December 23, 1998 against Edmonton.

Player	Team	3-Goals	4-Goals	5-Goals
Alfredsson, Daniel	Ottawa	4	—	—
Allison, Jason	Boston	4	—	—
Amonte, Tony	NYR, Chi.	7	—	—
Andreychuk, Dave	Buf., Tor., Bos.	7	3	1
Antropov, Nik	Toronto	1	—	—
Arnason, Tyler	Chicago	1	—	—
Arnott, Jason	Edm., N.J., Dal.	4	—	—
Audette, Donald	Buf., Atl.	4	—	—
Barnes, Stu	Wpg., Pit.	3	—	—
Battaglia, Bates	Carolina	1	—	—
Belanger, Eric	Los Angeles	1	—	—
Bertuzzi, Todd	Vancouver	3	—	—
Blake, Jason	NY Islanders	1	—	—
Blake, Rob	Los Angeles	1	—	—
Bondra, Peter	Washington	12	5	1
Bonk, Radek	Ottawa	1	—	—
Brind'Amour, Rod	Phi., Car.	2	—	—
Brown, Curtis	Buffalo	1	—	—
Buchberger, Kelly	Edmonton	1	—	—
Bure, Valeri	Calgary	1	—	—
Carter, Anson	Boston	1	—	—
Cassels, Andrew	Vancouver	1	—	—
Cole, Erik	Carolina	2	—	—
Conroy, Craig	St. Louis	1	—	—
Corson, Shayne	Mtl., Edm.	3	—	—
Czerkawski, Mariusz	Edm., NYI	4	—	—
Dackell, Andreas	Ottawa	1	—	—
Daigle, Alexandre	Ott., Phi.	2	—	—
Daze, Eric	Chicago	5	1	—
Deadmarsh, Adam	Col., L.A.	2	—	—
Demitra, Pavol	St. Louis	3	—	—
Devereaux, Boyd	Edmonton	1	—	—
Donovan, Shean	Atlanta	1	—	—
Druken, Harold	Vancouver	1	—	—
Dumont, Jean-Pierre	Chi., Buf.	3	—	—
Dvorak, Radek	NY Rangers	1	1	—
Eastwood, Mike	St. Louis	1	—	—
Elias, Patrik	New Jersey	5	1	—
Fedorov, Sergei	Detroit	4	1	1
Forsberg, Peter	Colorado	6	—	—
Francis, Ron	Hfd., Pit.	10	1	—
Friesen, Jeff	San Jose	2	—	—
Gaborik, Marian	Minnesota	5	—	—
Gagne, Simon	Philadelphia	1	—	—
Gelinas, Martin	Edm., Van.	2	1	—
Gomez, Scott	New Jersey	1	—	—
Gonchar, Sergei	Washington	1	—	—
Gratton, Chris	Tampa Bay	1	—	—
Green, Travis	NY Islanders	1	—	—
Grier, Mike	Edmonton	1	—	—
Grosek, Michal	Buffalo	1	—	—
Guerin, Bill	N.J., Bos.	3	—	—
Handzus, Michal	St. Louis	1	—	—
Harvey, Todd	Dal., S.J.	2	—	—
Havlat, Martin	Ottawa	3	—	—
Heatley, Dany	Atlanta	2	—	—
Hejduk, Milan	Colorado	1	—	—
Hlavac, Jan	NYR, Car.	3	—	—
Holik, Bobby	New Jersey	3	—	—
Holmstrom, Tomas	Detroit	1	—	—
Hossa, Marian	Ottawa	3	1	—
Hull, Brett	Cgy., St.L., Dal., Det.	30	3	—
Iginla, Jarome	Calgary	3	1	—
Jagr, Jaromir	Pittsburgh	10	1	—
Johansson, Andreas	Nashville	1	—	—
Kapanen, Sami	Carolina	3	—	—
Kariya, Paul	Anaheim	8	—	—
Klatt, Trent	Philadelphia	1	—	—
Koivu, Saku	Montreal	1	—	—
Konowalchuk, Steve	Washington	3	—	—
Korolev, Igor	Winnipeg	1	—	—
Kovalchuk, Ilya	Atlanta	3	—	—
Kovalev, Alex	NYR, Pit.	10	—	—
Kozlov, Viktor	Florida	1	—	—
Kozlov, Vyacheslav	Detroit	2	1	—
Laaksonen, Antti	Minnesota	1	—	—
Lang, Robert	Washington	1	—	—
Langkow, Daymond	Phoenix	2	—	—
Laperriere, Ian	Los Angeles	1	—	—
Lapointe, Martin	Det., Bos.	2	—	—
Laraque, Georges	Edmonton	1	—	—
Lecavalier, Vincent	Tampa Bay	3	—	—
LeClair, John	Philadelphia	8	3	—
Lehtinen, Jere	Dallas	2	—	—
Lemieux, Mario	Pittsburgh	27	10	3
Linden, Trevor	Van., Mtl.	5	—	—
Lindros, Eric	Phi., NYR	12	1	—
Lombardi, Matthew	Calgary	1	—	—
MacInnis, Al	Cgy., St.L.	3	—	—
Madden, John	New Jersey	1	1	—
Malakhov, Vladimir	Montreal	1	—	—
Maltby, Kirk	Detroit	1	—	—
Marleau, Patrick	San Jose	1	—	—
McCauley, Alyn	San Jose	1	—	—
McEachern, Shawn	Ott., Atl.	2	—	—
McKenzie, Jim	Phoenix	1	—	—
Mellanby, Scott	St. Louis	—	1	—
Messier, Mark	Edm., NYR	15	4	—
Miller, Kevin	Det., St.L., S.J.	4	—	—
Modano, Mike	Min., Dal.	6	1	—
Modin, Fredrik	Tampa Bay	2	—	—
Mogilny, Alexander	Buf., Van., N.J., Tor.	15	2	—
Morozov, Aleksey	Pittsburgh	2	—	—
Morrison, Brendan	Vancouver	1	—	—
Morrow, Brendan	Dallas	1	—	—
Murray, Glen	L.A., Bos.	5	—	—
Murray, Rem	Edmonton	1	—	—
Nagy, Ladislav	Phoenix	1	—	—
Naslund, Markus	Pit., Van.	8	2	—
Nedved, Petr	Pit., NYR	6	1	—
Nieuwendyk, Joe	Cgy., Dal.	9	3	1
Nolan, Owen	Que., S.J.	9	1	—
Nylander, Michael	Hfd., Chi.	1	1	—
Odelein, Lyle	Montreal	1	—	—
Oliver, David	Edmonton	1	—	—
O'Neill, Jeff	Hfd., Car.	2	—	—
Orszagh, Vladimir	Nashville	1	—	—
Ozolinsh, Sandis	Col., Car.	2	—	—
Palffy, Ziggy	NYI, L.A.	8	—	—
Parrish, Mark	Fla., NYI	3	1	—
Peca, Michael	Buffalo	1	—	—
Perreault, Yanic	L.A., Tor., Mtl.	3	1	—
Petersen, Toby	Pittsburgh	1	—	—
Piros, Kamil	Atlanta	1	—	—
Pisani, Fernando	Edmonton	1	—	—
Primeau, Keith	Philadelphia	1	—	—
Prospal, Vaclav	Anaheim	1	—	—
Pyatt, Taylor	Buffalo	1	—	—
Quint, Deron	Columbus	1	—	—
Recchi, Mark	Pit., Mtl., Phi.	5	—	—
Reichel, Robert	Cgy., NYI	5	—	—
Reinprecht, Steve	Colorado	2	—	—
Rheaume, Pascal	Atlanta	—	1	—
Ricci, Mike	Que., S.J.	1	—	1
Roberts, Gary	Cgy., Car., Tor.	12	1	—
Robitaille, Luc	L.A., Pit.	11	3	—
Roenick, Jeremy	Chi., Phx.	7	2	—
Rolston, Brian	New Jersey	1	—	—
Ronning, Cliff	St.L., Van.	3	—	—
Rucinsky, Martin	Montreal	1	—	—
Sakic, Joe	Que., Col.	13	1	—
Salo, Sami	Ottawa	1	—	—
Samsonov, Sergei	Boston	1	—	—
Sanderson, Geoff	Har., Buf., CBJ	7	1	—
Satan, Miroslav	Buffalo	5	1	—
Savage, Brian	Montreal	6	1	—
Savard, Marc	Calgary	1	1	—
Scatchard, Dave	NY Islanders	2	—	—
Sedin, Daniel	Vancouver	—	1	—
Selanne, Teemu	Wpg., Ana., S.J.	16	2	—
Shanahan, Brendan	N.J., St.L., Hfd., Det.	15	1	—
Smolinski, Bryan	Bos., L.A.	3	—	—
Smyth, Ryan	Edmonton	4	—	—
Souray, Sheldon	Montreal	1	—	—
St. Louis, Martin	Tampa Bay	3	—	—
Stillman, Cory	Cgy., St.L.	3	—	—
Straka, Martin	Pittsburgh	4	—	—
Stumpel, Jozef	Bos., L.A.	2	—	—
Sturm, Marco	San Jose	1	—	—
Sullivan, Steve	Tor., Chi., Nsh.	3	1	—
Sundin, Mats	Que., Tor.	5	—	1
Sydor, Darryl	Dallas	1	—	—
Tanguay, Alex	Colorado	2	—	—
Tenkrat, Petr	Nashville	1	—	—
Thomas, Steve	Chi., NYI	4	2	—
Thornton, Joe	Boston	2	—	—
Thornton, Scott	San Jose	1	—	—
Tkachuk, Keith	Phoenix	7	2	—
Toms, Jeff	NY Rangers	1	—	—
Turgeon, Pierre	Buf., NYI, Mtl., St.L.	15	—	—
Valicevic, Robert	Nashville	1	—	—
Vasicek, Josef	Carolina	1	—	—
Vrbata, Radim	Col., Car.	2	—	—
Vyborny, David	Columbus	1	—	—
Walker, Scott	Nashville	2	—	—
Weight, Doug	Edm., St.L.	2	—	—
Wesley, Glen	Boston	1	—	—
Whitney, Ray	Columbus	1	—	—
Wiemer, Jason	Tampa Bay	1	—	—
Willis, Shane	Carolina	1	—	—
Wright, Tyler	Columbus	3	—	—
Yashin, Alexei	Ott., NYI	8	—	—
Young, Scott	Que., Col.	4	—	—
Yzerman, Steve	Detroit	17	1	—
Zamuner, Rob	Tampa Bay	1	—	—
Zednik, Richard	Washington	1	—	—
Zhamnov, Alex	Wpg., Chi.	5	—	1
Zubrus, Dainus	Montreal	1	—	—

Top 100 All-Time Goal-Scoring Leaders

* active player

Player	Seasons	Games	Goals	Goals per game
1. **Wayne Gretzky**, Edm., L.A., St.L., NYR .	20	1487	**894**	.601
2. **Gordie Howe**, Det., Hfd.	26	1767	**801**	.453
* 3. **Brett Hull**, Cgy., St.L., Dal., Det.	19	1264	**741**	.586
4. **Marcel Dionne**, Det., L.A., NYR	18	1348	**731**	.542
5. **Phil Esposito**, Chi., Bos., NYR	18	1282	**717**	.559
6. **Mike Gartner**, Wsh., Min., NYR, Tor., Phx.	19	1432	**708**	.494
* 7. **Mark Messier**, Edm., NYR, Van.	25	1756	**694**	.395
* 8. **Mario Lemieux**, Pit.	17	889	**683**	.768
* 9. **Steve Yzerman**, Det.	21	1453	**678**	.467
* 10. **Luc Robitaille**, L.A., Pit., NYR, Det.	18	1366	**653**	.478
* 11. **Dave Andreychuk**, Buf., Tor., N.J., Bos., Col., T.B.	22	1597	**634**	.397
12. **Bobby Hull**, Chi., Wpg., Hfd.	16	1063	**610**	.574
13. **Dino Ciccarelli**, Min., Wsh., Det., T.B., Fla.	19	1232	**608**	.494
14. **Jari Kurri**, Edm., L.A., NYR, Ana., Col.	17	1251	**601**	.480
15. **Mike Bossy**, NYI	10	752	**573**	.762
16. **Guy Lafleur**, Mtl., NYR, Que.	17	1126	**560**	.497
* 17. **Brendan Shanahan**, N.J., St.L., Hfd., Det.	17	1268	**558**	.440
18. **John Bucyk**, Det., Bos.	23	1540	**556**	.361
* 19. **Ron Francis**, Hfd., Pit., Car., Tor.	23	1731	**549**	.317
20. **Michel Goulet**, Que., Chi.	15	1089	**548**	.503
21. **Maurice Richard**, Mtl.	18	978	**544**	.556
* 22. **Joe Sakic**, Que., Col.	16	1155	**542**	.469
23. **Stan Mikita**, Chi.	22	1394	**541**	.388
* 24. **Jaromir Jagr**, Pit., Wsh., NYI	14	1027	**537**	.523
* 25. **Joe Nieuwendyk**, Cgy., Dal., N.J., Tor.	18	1177	**533**	.453
26. **Frank Mahovlich**, Tor., Det., Mtl.	18	1181	**533**	.451
27. **Bryan Trottier**, NYI, Pit.	18	1279	**524**	.410
28. **Pat Verbeek**, N.J., Hfd., NYR, Dal., Det.	20	1424	**522**	.367
29. **Dale Hawerchuk**, Wpg., Buf., St.L., Phi.	16	1188	**518**	.436
30. **Gilbert Perreault**, Buf.	17	1191	**512**	.430
31. **Jean Beliveau**, Mtl.	20	1125	**507**	.451
32. **Joe Mullen**, St.L., Cgy., Pit., Bos.	17	1062	**502**	.473
33. **Lanny McDonald**, Tor., Col., Cgy.	16	1111	**500**	.450
34. **Glenn Anderson**, Edm., Tor., NYR, St.L.	16	1129	**498**	.441
* 35. **Pierre Turgeon**, Buf., NYI, Mtl., St.L., Dal.	17	1215	**495**	.407
36. **Jean Ratelle**, NYR, Bos.	21	1281	**491**	.383
37. **Norm Ullman**, Det., Tor.	20	1410	**490**	.348
38. **Brian Bellows**, Min., Mtl., T.B., Ana., Wsh.	17	1188	**485**	.408
39. **Darryl Sittler**, Tor., Phi., Det.	15	1096	**484**	.442
* 40. **Peter Bondra**, Wsh., Ott.	14	984	**477**	.485
* 41. **Jeremy Roenick**, Chi., Phx., Phi.	16	1124	**475**	.423
42. **Bernie Nicholls**, L.A., NYR, Edm., N.J., Chi., S.J.	18	1127	**475**	.421
43. **Denis Savard**, Chi., Mtl., T.B.	17	1196	**473**	.395
44. **Pat LaFontaine**, NYI, Buf., NYR	15	865	**468**	.541
* 45. **Mats Sundin**, Que., Tor.	14	1086	**465**	.428
* 46. **Alexander Mogilny**, Buf., Van., N.J., Tor.	15	956	**461**	.482
* 47. **Mike Modano**, Min., Dal.	16	1101	**458**	.416
* 48. **Mark Recchi**, Pit., Phi., Mtl.	16	1173	**456**	.389
49. **Alex Delvecchio**, Det.	24	1549	**456**	.294
50. **Theoren Fleury**, Cgy., Col., NYR, Chi.	15	1084	**455**	.420
* 51. **Teemu Selanne**, Wpg., Ana., S.J., Col.	12	879	**452**	.514
52. **Doug Gilmour**, St.L., Cgy., Tor., Chi., Buf., Mtl.	20	1474	**450**	.305
53. **Peter Stastny**, Que., N.J., St.L.	15	977	**450**	.461
54. **Rick Middleton**, NYR, Bos.	14	1005	**448**	.446
55. **Rick Vaive**, Van., Tor., Chi., Buf.	13	876	**441**	.503
56. **Steve Larmer**, Chi., NYR.	15	1006	**441**	.438
57. **Rick Tocchet**, Phi., Pit., L.A., Bos., Wsh., Phx.	18	1144	**440**	.385
58. **Pavel Bure**, Van., Fla., NYR	12	702	**437**	.623
59. **Vincent Damphousse**, Tor., Edm., Mtl., S.J.	18	1378	**432**	.313
* 60. **Keith Tkachuk**, Wpg., Phx., St.L.	13	856	**431**	.504
61. **Dave Taylor**, L.A.	17	1111	**431**	.388
* 62. **Sergei Fedorov**, Det., Ana.	14	988	**431**	.436
63. **Yvan Cournoyer**, Mtl.	16	968	**428**	.442
64. **Brian Propp**, Phi., Bos., Min., Hfd.	15	1016	**425**	.418
65. **Steve Shutt**, Mtl., L.A.	13	930	**424**	.456
* 66. **Steve Thomas**, Tor., Chi., NYI, N.J., Ana., Det.	20	1235	**421**	.341
67. **Stephane Richer**, Mtl., N.J., T.B., St.L., Pit.	17	1054	**421**	.399
68. **Bill Barber**, Phi.	14	903	**420**	.465
69. **John MacLean**, N.J., S.J., NYR, Dal.	18	1194	**413**	.346
70. **Garry Unger**, Tor., Det., St.L., Atl., L.A., Edm.	16	1105	**413**	.374
71. **Raymond Bourque**, Bos., Col.	22	1612	**410**	.254
72. **Ray Ferraro**, Hfd., NYI, NYR, L.A., Atl., St.L.	18	1258	**408**	.324
73. **Rod Gilbert**, NYR	18	1065	**406**	.381
74. **John Ogrodnick**, Det., Que., NYR	14	928	**402**	.433

Rick Vaive scored 441 goals in a 13-year career spent with four different teams. He topped the 50-goal plateau for three straight seasons with Toronto in the early 1980s.

Player	Seasons	Games	Goals	Goals per game
* 75. **Gary Roberts**, Cgy., Car., Tor.	18	1029	**397**	.386
76. **Paul Coffey**, Edm., Pit., L.A., Det., Hfd., Phi., Car., Bos.	21	1409	**396**	.281
77. **Dave Keon**, Tor., Hfd.	18	1296	**396**	.306
78. **Cam Neely**, Van., Bos.	13	726	**395**	.544
79. **Pierre Larouche**, Pit., Mtl., Hfd., NYR	14	812	**395**	.486
80. **Tomas Sandstrom**, NYR, L.A., Pit., Det., Ana.	15	983	**394**	.401
81. **Bernie Geoffrion**, Mtl., NYR.	16	883	**393**	.445
* 82. **Tony Amonte**, NYR, Chi., Phx., Phi.	14	1013	**392**	.387
83. **Jean Pronovost**, Pit., Atl., Wsh.	14	998	**391**	.392
84. **Dean Prentice**, NYR, Bos., Det., Pit., Min.	22	1378	**391**	.284
85. **Rick Martin**, Buf., L.A.	11	685	**384**	.561
* 86. **John LeClair**, Mtl., Phi.	14	873	**382**	.438
87. **Reggie Leach**, Bos., Cal., Phi., Det.	13	934	**381**	.408
88. **Ted Lindsay**, Det., Chi.	17	1068	**379**	.355
89. **Claude Lemieux**, Mtl., N.J., Col., Phx., Dal.	20	1197	**379**	.317
90. **Butch Goring**, L.A., NYI, Bos.	16	1107	**375**	.339
91. **Rick Kehoe**, Tor., Pit.	14	906	**371**	.409
92. **Tim Kerr**, Phi., NYR, Hfd.	13	655	**370**	.565
93. **Bernie Federko**, St.L., Det.	14	1000	**369**	.369
94. **Geoff Courtnall**, Bos., Edm., Wsh., St.L., Van.	17	1048	**367**	.350
95. **Jacques Lemaire**, Mtl.	12	853	**366**	.429
96. **Peter McNab**, Buf., Bos., Van., N.J.	14	954	**363**	.381
97. **Brent Sutter**, NYI, Chi.	18	1111	**363**	.327
98. **Ivan Boldirev**, Bos., Cal., Chi., Atl., Van., Det.	15	1052	**361**	.343
99. **Henri Richard**, Mtl.	20	1256	**358**	.285
100. **Bobby Clarke**, Phi.	15	1144	**358**	.313

Top 100 Active Goal-Scoring Leaders

Player	Seasons	Games	Goals	Goals per game
1. **Brett Hull**, Cgy., St.L., Dal., Det.	19	1264	**741**	.586
2. **Mark Messier**, Edm., NYR, Van.	25	1756	**694**	.395
3. **Mario Lemieux**, Pit.	17	889	**683**	.768
4. **Steve Yzerman**, Det.	21	1453	**678**	.467
5. **Luc Robitaille**, L.A., Pit., NYR, Det.	18	1366	**653**	.478
6. **Dave Andreychuk**, Buf., Tor., N.J., Bos., Col., T.B.	22	1597	**634**	.397
7. **Brendan Shanahan**, N.J., St.L., Hfd., Det.	17	1268	**558**	.440
8. **Ron Francis**, Hfd., Pit., Car., Tor.	23	1731	**549**	.317
9. **Joe Sakic**, Que., Col.	16	1155	**542**	.469
10. **Jaromir Jagr**, Pit., Wsh., NYI	14	1027	**537**	.523
11. **Joe Nieuwendyk**, Cgy., Dal., N.J., Tor.	18	1177	**533**	.453
12. **Pierre Turgeon**, Buf., NYI, Mtl., St.L., Dal.	17	1215	**495**	.407
13. **Peter Bondra**, Wsh., Ott.	14	984	**477**	.485
14. **Jeremy Roenick**, Chi., Phx., Phi. . . .	16	1124	**475**	.423
15. **Mats Sundin**, Que., Tor.	14	1086	**465**	.428
16. **Alexander Mogilny**, Buf., Van., N.J., Tor.	15	956	**461**	.482
17. **Mike Modano**, Min., Dal.	16	1101	**458**	.416
18. **Mark Recchi**, Pit., Phi., Mtl.	16	1173	**456**	.389
19. **Teemu Selanne**, Wpg., Ana., S.J., Col. .	12	879	**452**	.514
20. **Keith Tkachuk**, Wpg., Phx., St.L.	13	856	**431**	.504
21. **Sergei Fedorov**, Det., Ana.	14	988	**431**	.436
22. **Steve Thomas**, Tor., Chi., NYI, N.J., Ana., Det.	20	1235	**421**	.341
23. **Gary Roberts**, Cgy., Car., Tor.	18	1029	**397**	.386
24. **Tony Amonte**, NYR, Chi., Phx., Phi. . . .	14	1013	**392**	.387
25. **John LeClair**, Mtl., Phi.	14	873	**382**	.438
26. **Eric Lindros**, Phi., NYR, NYI	11	678	**356**	.525
27. **Rod Brind'Amour**, St.L., Phi., Car.	16	1109	**351**	.317
28. **Owen Nolan**, Que., Col., S.J., Tor. . . .	14	915	**349**	.381
29. **Trevor Linden**, Van., NYI, Mtl., Wsh. . .	16	1161	**349**	.301
30. **Scott Mellanby**, Phi., Edm., Fla., St.L. . .	19	1291	**340**	.263
31. **Al MacInnis**, Cgy., St.L.	23	1416	**340**	.240
32. **Scott Young**, Hfd., Pit., Que., Col., Ana., St.L., Dal.	16	1102	**324**	.294
33. **Ziggy Palffy**, NYI, L.A.	11	642	**318**	.495
34. **Geoff Sanderson**, Hfd., Car., Van., Buf., CBJ	14	928	**316**	.341
35. **Bill Guerin**, N.J., Edm., Bos., Dal.	13	879	**315**	.358
36. **Paul Kariya**, Ana., Col.	10	657	**311**	.473
37. **Cliff Ronning**, St.L., Van., Phx., Nsh., L.A., Min., NYI	18	1137	**306**	.269
38. **Petr Nedved**, Van., St.L., NYR, Pit., Edm.	13	889	**301**	.339
39. **Alex Kovalev**, NYR, Pit., Mtl.	12	849	**292**	.344
40. **Alexei Yashin**, Ott., NYI	10	710	**291**	.410
41. **Markus Naslund**, Pit., Van.	11	790	**290**	.367
42. **Bobby Holik**, Hfd., N.J., NYR	14	1024	**281**	.274
43. **Martin Gelinas**, Edm., Que., Van., Car., Cgy.	16	1052	**269**	.256
44. **Glen Murray**, Bos., Pit., L.A.	13	823	**268**	.326
45. **Keith Primeau**, Det., Car., Phi.	14	900	**265**	.294
46. **Donald Audette**, Buf., L.A., Atl., Dal., Mtl., Fla.	15	735	**260**	.354
47. **Miroslav Satan**, Edm., Buf.	9	704	**259**	.368
48. **Shawn McEachern**, Pit., L.A., Bos., Ott., Atl.	13	883	**254**	.288
49. **Vyacheslav Kozlov**, Det., Buf., Atl. . .	13	800	**252**	.315
50. **Robert Reichel**, Cgy., NYI, Phx., Tor. . . .	11	830	**252**	.304
51. **Jarome Iginla**, Cgy.	9	626	**250**	.399
52. **Alex Zhamnov**, Wpg., Chi., Phi.	12	783	**248**	.317
53. **Jason Arnott**, Edm., N.J., Dal.	11	743	**244**	.328
54. **Brian Leetch**, NYR, NYI, Tor.	17	1144	**242**	.212
55. **Mike Ricci**, Phi., Que., Col., S.J.	14	1014	**233**	.230
56. **Bryan Smolinski**, Bos., Pit., NYI, L.A., Ott.	12	829	**231**	.279
57. **Eric Daze**, Chi.	10	600	**226**	.377
58. **Doug Weight**, NYR, Edm., St.L.	14	912	**224**	.246
59. **Stu Barnes**, Wpg., Fla., Pit., Buf., Dal. . .	13	897	**221**	.246
60. **Daniel Alfredsson**, Ott.	9	629	**219**	.348
61. **Peter Forsberg**, Que., Col.	10	580	**216**	.372
62. **Pavol Demitra**, Ott., St.L.	11	553	**216**	.391
63. **Jeff Friesen**, S.J., Ana., N.J.	10	770	**208**	.270
64. **Martin Rucinsky**, Edm., Que., Col., Mtl., Dal., NYR, St.L., Van.	13	817	**208**	.255
65. **Mariusz Czerkawski**, Bos., Edm., NYI, Mtl.	11	710	**207**	.292
66. **Patrik Elias**, N.J.	9	558	**207**	.371
67. **Ray Whitney**, S.J., Edm., Fla., CBJ, Det.	13	700	**205**	.293
68. **Petr Sykora**, N.J., Ana.	9	608	**202**	.332
69. **Andrew Cassels**, Mtl., Hfd., Cgy., Van., CBJ	15	984	**200**	.203
70. **Todd Bertuzzi**, NYI, Van.	9	628	**198**	.315
71. **Jeff O'Neill**, Hfd., Car.	9	673	**198**	.294
72. **Ryan Smyth**, Edm.	10	642	**198**	.308

Already ranking sixth all-time in Oilers goal scoring with 198, Ryan Smyth has been Edmonton's top marksman five times in nine full seasons.

Player	Seasons	Games	Goals	Goals per game
73. **Milan Hejduk**, Col.	6	470	**197**	.419
74. **Yanic Perreault**, Tor., L.A., Mtl.	11	671	**195**	.291
75. **Martin Straka**, Pit., Ott., NYI, Fla., L.A. .	12	730	**192**	.263
76. **Brian Rolston**, N.J., Col., Bos.	10	736	**190**	.258
77. **Marian Hossa**, Ott.	7	467	**188**	.403
78. **Rob Blake**, L.A., Col.	15	903	**186**	.206
79. **Adam Deadmarsh**, Que., Col., L.A. . . .	9	567	**184**	.325
80. **Cory Stillman**, Cgy., St.L., T.B.	10	645	**184**	.285
81. **Brian Savage**, Mtl., Phx., St.L.	11	608	**183**	.301
82. **Travis Green**, NYI, Ana., Phx., Tor., Bos.	12	857	**182**	.212
83. **Chris Chelios**, Mtl., Chi., Det.	21	1395	**178**	.128
84. **Steve Sullivan**, N.J., Tor., Chi., Nsh. . .	9	597	**175**	.293
85. **Robert Lang**, L.A., Bos., Pit., Wsh., Det.	11	646	**174**	.269
86. **Chris Gratton**, T.B., Phi., Buf., Phx., Col.	11	851	**174**	.204
87. **Valeri Bure**, Mtl., Cgy., Fla., St.L., Dal. .	10	621	**174**	.280
88. **Nicklas Lidstrom**, Det.	13	1016	**173**	.170
89. **Mathieu Schneider**, Mtl., NYI, Tor., NYR, L.A., Det.	16	992	**168**	.169
90. **Mike Keane**, Mtl., Col., NYR, Dal., St.L., Van.	16	1161	**168**	.145
91. **Dallas Drake**, Det., Wpg., Phx., St.L. .	12	822	**166**	.202
92. **Mike Sillinger**, Det., Ana., Van., Phi., T.B., Fla., Ott., CBJ, Phx., St.L.	14	829	**166**	.200
93. **Steve Konowalchuk**, Wsh., Col.	13	769	**165**	.215
94. **Sami Kapanen**, Hfd., Car., Phi.	9	622	**161**	.259
95. **Joe Thornton**, Bos.	7	509	**160**	.314
96. **Anson Carter**, Wsh., Bos., Edm., NYR, NYI, L.A.	8	529	**158**	.299
97. **Sandis Ozolinsh**, S.J., Col., Car., Fla., Ana.	12	779	**158**	.203
98. **Jere Lehtinen**, Dal.	9	568	**157**	.276
99. **Joe Juneau**, Bos., Wsh., Buf., Ott., Phx., Mtl.	13	828	**156**	.188
100. **Patrick Marleau**, S.J.	7	558	**153**	.274

Top 100 All-Time Assist Leaders

* active player

Player	Seasons	Games	Assists	Assists per game
1. **Wayne Gretzky**, Edm., L.A., St.L., NYR .	20	1487	**1963**	1.320
* 2. **Ron Francis**, Hfd., Pit., Car., Tor.	23	1731	**1249**	.722
* 3. **Mark Messier**, Edm., NYR, Van.	25	1756	**1193**	.679
4. **Raymond Bourque**, Bos., Col.	22	1612	**1169**	.725
5. **Paul Coffey**, Edm., Pit., L.A., Det., Hfd., Phi., Chi., Car., Bos.	21	1409	**1135**	.806
6. **Adam Oates**, Det., St.L., Bos., Wsh., Phi., Ana., Edm.	19	1337	**1079**	.807
7. **Gordie Howe**, Det., Hfd.	26	1767	**1049**	.594
* 8. **Steve Yzerman**, Det.	21	1453	**1043**	.718
9. **Marcel Dionne**, Det., L.A., NYR	18	1348	**1040**	.772
* 10. **Mario Lemieux**, Pit.	17	889	**1018**	1.145
11. **Doug Gilmour**, St.L., Cgy., Tor., N.J., Chi., Buf., Mtl.	20	1474	**964**	.654
* 12. **Al MacInnis**, Cgy., St.L.	23	1416	**934**	.660
13. **Larry Murphy**, L.A., Wsh., Min., Pit., Tor., Det.	21	1615	**929**	.575
14. **Stan Mikita**, Chi.	22	1394	**926**	.664
15. **Bryan Trottier**, NYI, Pit.	18	1279	**901**	.704
16. **Phil Housley**, Buf., Wpg., St.L., Cgy., N.J., Wsh., Chi., Tor. . . .	21	1495	**894**	.598
17. **Dale Hawerchuk**, Wpg., Buf., St.L., Phi.	16	1188	**891**	.750
18. **Phil Esposito**, Chi., Bos., NYR	18	1282	**873**	.681
19. **Denis Savard**, Chi., Mtl., T.B.	17	1196	**865**	.723
* 20. **Joe Sakic**, Que., Col.	16	1155	**860**	.745
21. **Bobby Clarke**, Phi.	15	1144	**852**	.745
22. **Alex Delvecchio**, Det.	24	1549	**825**	.533
23. **Gilbert Perreault**, Buf.	17	1191	**814**	.683
24. **John Bucyk**, Det., Bos.	23	1540	**813**	.528
25. **Jari Kurri**, Edm., L.A., NYR, Ana., Col. . .	17	1251	**797**	.637
26. **Guy Lafleur**, Mtl., NYR, Que.	17	1126	**793**	.704
27. **Peter Stastny**, Que., N.J., St.L.	15	977	**789**	.808
* 28. **Pierre Turgeon**, Buf., NYI, Mtl., St.L., Dal.	17	1215	**779**	.641
29. **Jean Ratelle**, NYR, Bos.	21	1281	**776**	.606
30. **Vincent Damphousse**, Tor., Edm., Mtl., S.J.	18	1378	**773**	.561
* 31. **Jaromir Jagr**, Pit., Wsh., NYI	14	1027	**772**	.752
32. **Bernie Federko**, St.L., Det.	14	1000	**761**	.761
* 33. **Brian Leetch**, NYR, NYI, Tor.	17	1144	**754**	.659
34. **Larry Robinson**, Mtl., L.A.	20	1384	**750**	.542
* 35. **Mark Recchi**, Pit., Phi., Mtl.	16	1173	**745**	.635
36. **Denis Potvin**, NYI	15	1060	**742**	.700
37. **Norm Ullman**, Det., Tor.	20	1410	**739**	.524
* 38. **Chris Chelios**, Mtl., Chi., Det.	21	1395	**736**	.528
39. **Bernie Nicholls**, L.A., NYR, Edm., N.J., Chi., S.J.	18	1127	**734**	.651
* 40. **Luc Robitaille**, L.A., Pit., NYR, Det.	18	1366	**717**	.525
41. **Jean Beliveau**, Mtl.	20	1125	**712**	.633
42. **Scott Stevens**, Wsh., St.L., N.J.	22	1635	**712**	.435
43. **Dale Hunter**, Que., Wsh., Col.	19	1407	**697**	.495
44. **Henri Richard**, Mtl.	20	1256	**688**	.548
* 45. **Dave Andreychuk**, Buf., Tor., N.J., Bos., Col., T.B. . . .	22	1597	**686**	.430
46. **Brad Park**, NYR, Bos., Det.	17	1113	**683**	.614
47. **Bobby Smith**, Min., Mtl.	15	1077	**679**	.630
* 48. **Brett Hull**, Cgy., St.L., Dal., Det.	19	1264	**649**	.513
* 49. **Mike Modano**, Min., Dal.	16	1101	**648**	.589
* 50. **Jeremy Roenick**, Chi., Phx., Phi.	16	1124	**645**	.574
51. **Bobby Orr**, Bos., Chi.	12	657	**645**	.982
52. **Gary Suter**, Cgy., Chi., S.J.	17	1145	**641**	.560
53. **Dave Taylor**, L.A.	17	1111	**638**	.574
54. **Darryl Sittler**, Tor., Phi., Det.	15	1096	**637**	.581
55. **Borje Salming**, Tor., Det.	17	1148	**637**	.555
56. **Neal Broten**, Min., Dal., N.J., L.A.	17	1099	**634**	.577
57. **Theoren Fleury**, Cgy., Col., NYR, Chi. . . .	15	1084	**633**	.584
58. **Mike Gartner**, Wsh., Min., NYR, Tor., Phx. . . .	19	1432	**627**	.438
59. **Andy Bathgate**, NYR, Tor., Det., Pit. . . .	17	1069	**624**	.584
* 60. **Mats Sundin**, Que., Tor.	14	1086	**624**	.575
61. **Rod Gilbert**, NYR	18	1065	**615**	.577
62. **Michel Goulet**, Que., Chi.	15	1089	**604**	.555
* 63. **Doug Weight**, NYR, Edm., St.L.	14	912	**604**	.662
64. **Kirk Muller**, N.J., Mtl., NYI, Tor., Fla., Dal. . . .	19	1349	**602**	.446
65. **Glenn Anderson**, Edm., Tor., NYR, St.L.	16	1129	**601**	.532
* 66. **Brendan Shanahan**, N.J., St.L., Hfd., Det.	17	1268	**593**	.468
67. **Dino Ciccarelli**, Min., Wsh., Det., T.B., Fla.	19	1232	**592**	.481
68. **Dave Keon**, Tor., Hfd.	18	1296	**590**	.455
69. **Doug Wilson**, Chi., S.J.	16	1024	**590**	.576
* 70. **Sergei Fedorov**, Det., Ana.	14	988	**588**	.595
71. **Dave Babych**, Wpg., Hfd., Van., Phi., L.A. . . .	19	1195	**581**	.486
72. **Brian Propp**, Phi., Bos., Min., Hfd.	15	1016	**579**	.570

Though not remembered as a playmaker, Dale Hunter (being checked by Jeff Brown) collected an impressive 697 assists in his 19-year career.

Player	Seasons	Games	Assists	Assist per game
73. **Steve Larmer**, Chi., NYR.	15	1006	**571**	.568
74. **Frank Mahovlich**, Tor., Det., Mtl.	18	1181	**570**	.483
75. **Craig Janney**, Bos., St.L., S.J., Wpg., Phx., T.B., NYI	12	760	**563**	.741
* 76. **Cliff Ronning**, St.L., Van., Phx., Nsh., L.A., Min., NYI	18	1137	**563**	.495
77. **Joe Mullen**, St.L., Cgy., Pit., Bos.	17	1062	**561**	.528
78. **Bobby Hull**, Chi., Wpg., Hfd.	16	1063	**560**	.527
* 79. **Rod Brind'Amour**, St.L., Phi., Car.	16	1109	**560**	.505
* 80. **Nicklas Lidstrom**, Det.	13	1016	**553**	.544
81. **Thomas Steen**, Wpg.	14	950	**553**	.582
82. **Mike Bossy**, NYI	10	752	**553**	.735
83. **Tom Lysiak**, Atl., Chi.	13	919	**551**	.600
84. **Ken Linseman**, Phi., Edm., Bos., Tor. . . .	14	860	**551**	.641
* 85. **Alexander Mogilny**, Buf., Van., N.J., Tor. . . .	15	956	**546**	.571
86. **Mark Howe**, Hfd., Phi., Det.	16	929	**545**	.587
87. **Pat LaFontaine**, NYI, Buf., NYR	15	865	**545**	.630
88. **Red Kelly**, Det., Tor.	20	1316	**542**	.412
89. **Pat Verbeek**, N.J., Hfd., NYR, Dal., Det.	20	1424	**541**	.380
90. **Rick Middleton**, NYR, Bos.	14	1005	**540**	.537
91. **Brian Bellows**, Min., Mtl., T.B., Ana., Wsh. . . .	17	1188	**537**	.452
* 92. **Joe Nieuwendyk**, Cgy., Dal., N.J., Tor. . .	18	1177	**529**	.449
* 93. **Peter Forsberg**, Que., Col.	10	580	**525**	.905
94. **Steve Duchesne**, L.A., Phi., Que., St.L., Ott., Det.	16	1113	**525**	.472
95. **Dennis Maruk**, Cal., Cle., Min., Wsh. . . .	14	888	**522**	.588
* 96. **Andrew Cassels**, Mtl., Hfd., Cgy., Van., CBJ. . . .	15	984	**520**	.528
97. **Wayne Cashman**, Bos.	17	1027	**516**	.502
98. **Butch Goring**, L.A., NYI, Bos.	16	1107	**513**	.463
* 99. **Steve Thomas**, Tor., Chi., NYI, N.J., Ana., Det.	20	1235	**512**	.415
100. **Rick Tocchet**, Phi., Pit., L.A., Bos., Wsh., Phx.	18	1144	**512**	.448

Top 100 Active Assist Leaders

Player	Seasons	Games	Assists	Assists per game
1. **Ron Francis**, Hfd., Pit., Car., Tor.	23	1731	**1249**	.722
2. **Mark Messier**, Edm., NYR, Van.	25	1756	**1193**	.679
3. **Steve Yzerman**, Det.	21	1453	**1043**	.718
4. **Mario Lemieux**, Pit.	17	889	**1018**	1.145
5. **Al MacInnis**, Cgy., St.L.	23	1416	**934**	.660
6. **Joe Sakic**, Que., Col.	16	1155	**860**	.745
7. **Pierre Turgeon**, Buf., NYI, Mtl., St.L., Dal.	17	1215	**779**	.641
8. **Jaromir Jagr**, Pit., Wsh., NYI	14	1027	**772**	.752
9. **Brian Leetch**, NYR, NYI, Tor.	17	1144	**754**	.659
10. **Mark Recchi**, Pit., Phi., Mtl.	16	1173	**745**	.635
11. **Chris Chelios**, Mtl., Chi., Det.	21	1395	**736**	.528
12. **Luc Robitaille**, L.A., Pit., NYR, Det.	18	1366	**717**	.525
13. **Dave Andreychuk**, Buf., Tor., N.J., Bos., Col., T.B.	22	1597	**686**	.430
14. **Brett Hull**, Cgy., St.L., Dal., Det.	19	1264	**649**	.513
15. **Mike Modano**, Min., Dal.	16	1101	**648**	.589
16. **Jeremy Roenick**, Chi., Phx., Phi.	16	1124	**645**	.574
17. **Mats Sundin**, Que., Tor.	14	1086	**624**	.575
18. **Doug Weight**, NYR, Edm., St.L.	14	912	**604**	.662
19. **Brendan Shanahan**, N.J., St.L., Hfd., Det.	17	1268	**593**	.468
20. **Sergei Fedorov**, Det., Ana.	14	988	**588**	.595
21. **Cliff Ronning**, St.L., Van., Phx., Nsh., L.A., Min., NYI	18	1137	**563**	.495
22. **Rod Brind'Amour**, St.L., Phi., Car.	16	1109	**560**	.505
23. **Nicklas Lidstrom**, Det.	13	1016	**553**	.544
24. **Alexander Mogilny**, Buf., Van., N.J., Tor.	15	956	**546**	.571
25. **Joe Nieuwendyk**, Cgy., Dal., N.J., Tor.	18	1177	**529**	.449
26. **Peter Forsberg**, Que., Col.	10	580	**525**	.905
27. **Andrew Cassels**, Mtl., Hfd., Cgy., Van., CBJ.	15	984	**520**	.528
28. **Steve Thomas**, Tor., Chi., NYI, N.J., Ana., Det.	20	1235	**512**	.415
29. **Teemu Selanne**, Wpg., Ana., S.J., Col.	12	879	**499**	.568
30. **James Patrick**, NYR, Hfd., Cgy., Buf.	21	1280	**490**	.383
31. **Sergei Zubov**, NYR, Pit., Dal.	12	856	**484**	.565
32. **Trevor Linden**, Van., NYI, Mtl., Wsh.	16	1161	**465**	.401
33. **Eric Lindros**, Phi., NYR, NYI.	11	678	**461**	.680
34. **Alex Zhamnov**, Wpg., Chi., Phi.	12	783	**461**	.589
35. **Teppo Numminen**, Wpg., Phx., Dal.	16	1160	**440**	.379
36. **Tony Amonte**, NYR, Chi., Phx., Phi.	14	1013	**436**	.430
37. **Scott Mellanby**, Phi., Edm., Fla., St.L.	19	1291	**430**	.333
38. **Eric Desjardins**, Mtl., Phi.	16	1098	**419**	.382
39. **Gary Roberts**, Cgy., Car., Tor.	18	1029	**409**	.397
40. **Keith Tkachuk**, Wpg., Phx., St.L.	13	856	**401**	.468
41. **Rob Blake**, L.A., Col.	15	903	**400**	.443
42. **Jozef Stumpel**, Bos., L.A.	13	758	**397**	.524
43. **Paul Kariya**, Ana., Col.	10	657	**394**	.600
44. **Alex Kovalev**, NYR, Pit., Mtl.	12	849	**388**	.457
45. **Owen Nolan**, Que., Col., S.J., Tor.	14	915	**386**	.422
46. **Scott Young**, Hfd., Pit., Que., Col., Ana., St.L., Dal.	16	1102	**384**	.348
47. **Mathieu Schneider**, Mtl., NYI, Tor., NYR, L.A., Det.	16	992	**384**	.387
48. **Glen Wesley**, Bos., Hfd., Car., Tor.	17	1247	**382**	.306
49. **Petr Nedved**, Van., St.L., NYR, Pit., Edm.	13	889	**379**	.426
50. **John LeClair**, Mtl., Phi.	14	873	**379**	.434
51. **Robert Reichel**, Cgy., NYI, Phx., Tor.	11	830	**378**	.455
52. **Alexei Yashin**, Ott., NYI	10	710	**374**	.527
53. **Sandis Ozolinsh**, S.J., Col., Car., Fla., Ana.	12	779	**367**	.471
54. **Scott Niedermayer**, N.J.	13	892	**364**	.408
55. **Peter Bondra**, Wsh., Ott.	14	984	**362**	.368
56. **Bobby Holik**, Hfd., N.J., NYR.	14	1024	**361**	.353
57. **Mike Ricci**, Phi., Que., Col., S.J.	14	1014	**355**	.350
58. **Ziggy Palffy**, NYI, L.A.	11	642	**353**	.550
59. **Daniel Alfredsson**, Ott.	9	629	**349**	.555
60. **Keith Primeau**, Det., Hfd., Car., Phi.	14	900	**347**	.386
61. **Darryl Sydor**, L.A., Dal., CBJ, T.B.	13	943	**342**	.363
62. **Markus Naslund**, Pit., Van.	11	790	**339**	.429
63. **Martin Straka**, Pit., Ott., NYI, Fla., L.A.	12	730	**338**	.463
64. **Ray Whitney**, S.J., Edm., Fla., CBJ, Det.	13	700	**330**	.471
65. **Roman Hamrlik**, T.B., Edm., NYI.	12	873	**324**	.371
66. **Jason Arnott**, Edm., N.J., Dal.	11	743	**324**	.436
67. **Shawn McEachern**, Pit., L.A., Bos., Ott., Atl.	13	883	**317**	.359
68. **Alexei Zhitnik**, L.A., Buf.	12	882	**315**	.357
69. **Bill Guerin**, N.J., Edm., Bos., Dal.	13	879	**308**	.350
70. **Vyacheslav Kozlov**, Det., Buf., Atl.	13	800	**307**	.384
71. **Michael Nylander**, Hfd., Cgy., T.B., Chi., Wsh., Bos.	11	648	**307**	.474
72. **Chris Pronger**, Hfd., St.L.	11	722	**306**	.424
73. **Pavol Demitra**, Ott., St.L.	11	553	**303**	.548

Better known as a sniper with 318 career goals, Ziggy Palffy takes a career total of 353 assists with him from Los Angeles to Pittsburgh.

Player	Games	Assists	Assists per game
74. **Bryan Smolinski**, Bos., Pit., NYI, L.A., Ott.	829	**303**	.366
75. **Eric Weinrich**, N.J., Hfd., Chi., Mtl., Bos., Phi., St.L.	1082	**302**	.279
76. **Mike Keane**, Mtl., Col., NYR, Dal., St.L., Van.	1161	**302**	.260
77. **Martin Rucinsky**, Edm., Que., Col., Mtl., Dal., NYR, St.L., Van.	817	**300**	.367
78. **Chris Gratton**, T.B., Phi., Buf., Phx., Col.	851	**296**	.348
79. **Geoff Sanderson**, Hfd., Car., Van., Buf., CBJ.	928	**296**	.319
80. **Robert Lang**, L.A., Bos., Pit., Wsh., Det.	646	**293**	.454
81. **Stu Barnes**, Wpg., Fla., Pit., Buf., Dal.	897	**292**	.326
82. **Jason Allison**, Wsh., Bos., L.A.	486	**288**	.593
83. **Martin Gelinas**, Edm., Que., Van., Car., Cgy.	1052	**286**	.272
84. **Jeff Friesen**, S.J., Ana., N.J.	770	**285**	.370
85. **Steve Rucchin**, Ana.	616	**279**	.453
86. **Saku Koivu**, Mtl.	497	**278**	.559
87. **Sergei Gonchar**, Wsh., Bos.	669	**277**	.414
88. **Steve Sullivan**, N.J., Tor., Chi., Nsh.	597	**274**	.459
89. **Dallas Drake**, Det., Wpg., Phx., St.L.	822	**267**	.325
90. **Patrice Brisebois**, Mtl.	791	**263**	.332
91. **Joe Thornton**, Bos.	509	**261**	.513
92. **Miroslav Satan**, Edm., Buf.	704	**260**	.369
93. **Todd Bertuzzi**, NYI, Van.	628	**260**	.414
94. **Petr Sykora**, N.J., Ana.	608	**259**	.426
95. **Vladimir Malakhov**, NYI, Mtl., N.J., NYR, Phi.	683	**255**	.373
96. **Glen Murray**, Bos., Pit., L.A.	823	**255**	.310
97. **Jarome Iginla**, Cgy.	626	**253**	.404
98. **Patrik Elias**, N.J.	558	**252**	.452
99. **Cory Stillman**, Cgy., St.L., T.B.	645	**250**	.388
100. **Donald Audette**, Buf., L.A., Atl., Dal., Mtl., Fla.	735	**249**	.339

Top 100 All-Time Point Leaders

* active player

Player	Seasons	Games	Goals	Assists	Points	Points per game
1. **Wayne Gretzky**, Edm., L.A., St.L., NYR	20	1487	894	1963	**2857**	1.921
* 2. **Mark Messier**, Edm., NYR, Van.	25	1756	694	1193	**1887**	1.075
3. **Gordie Howe**, Det., Hfd.	26	1767	801	1049	**1850**	1.047
* 4. **Ron Francis**, Hfd., Pit., Car., Tor.	23	1731	549	1249	**1798**	1.039
5. **Marcel Dionne**, Det., L.A., NYR	18	1348	731	1040	**1771**	1.314
* 6. **Steve Yzerman**, Det.	21	1453	678	1043	**1721**	1.184
* 7. **Mario Lemieux**, Pit.	17	889	683	1018	**1701**	1.913
8. **Phil Esposito**, Chi., Bos., NYR	18	1282	717	873	**1590**	1.240
9. **Raymond Bourque**, Bos., Col.	22	1612	410	1169	**1579**	.980
10. **Paul Coffey**, Edm., Pit., L.A., Det., Hfd., Phi., Chi., Car., Bos.	21	1409	396	1135	**1531**	1.087
11. **Stan Mikita**, Chi.	22	1394	541	926	**1467**	1.052
12. **Bryan Trottier**, NYI, Pit.	18	1279	524	901	**1425**	1.114
13. **Adam Oates**, Det., St.L., Bos., Wsh., Phi., Ana., Edm.	19	1337	341	1079	**1420**	1.062
14. **Doug Gilmour**, St.L., Cgy., Tor., N.J., Chi., Buf., Mtl.	20	1474	450	964	**1414**	.959
15. **Dale Hawerchuk**, Wpg., Buf., St.L., Phi.	16	1188	518	891	**1409**	1.186
* 16. **Joe Sakic**, Que., Col.	16	1155	542	860	**1402**	1.214
17. **Jari Kurri**, Edm., L.A., NYR, Ana., Col.	17	1251	601	797	**1398**	1.118
* 18. **Brett Hull**, Cgy., St.L., Dal., Det.	19	1264	741	649	**1390**	1.100
* 19. **Luc Robitaille**, L.A., Pit., NYR, Det.	18	1366	653	717	**1370**	1.003
20. **John Bucyk**, Det., Bos.	23	1540	556	813	**1369**	.889
21. **Guy Lafleur**, Mtl., NYR, Que.	17	1126	560	793	**1353**	1.202
22. **Denis Savard**, Chi., Mtl., T.B.	17	1196	473	865	**1338**	1.119
23. **Mike Gartner**, Wsh., Min., NYR, Tor., Phx.	19	1432	708	627	**1335**	.932
24. **Gilbert Perreault**, Buf.	17	1191	512	814	**1326**	1.113
* 25. **Dave Andreychuk**, Buf., Tor., N.J., Bos., Col., T.B.	22	1597	634	686	**1320**	.827
* 26. **Jaromir Jagr**, Pit., Wsh., NYI	14	1027	537	772	**1309**	1.275
27. **Alex Delvecchio**, Det.	24	1549	456	825	**1281**	.827
* 28. **Pierre Turgeon**, Buf., NYI, Mtl., St.L., Dal.	17	1215	495	779	**1274**	1.049
* 29. **Al MacInnis**, Cgy., St.L.	23	1416	340	934	**1274**	.900
30. **Jean Ratelle**, NYR, Bos.	21	1281	491	776	**1267**	.989
31. **Peter Stastny**, Que., N.J., St.L.	15	977	450	789	**1239**	1.268
32. **Phil Housley**, Buf., Wpg., St.L., Cgy., N.J., Wsh., Chi., Tor.	21	1495	338	894	**1232**	.824
33. **Norm Ullman**, Det., Tor.	20	1410	490	739	**1229**	.872
34. **Jean Beliveau**, Mtl.	20	1125	507	712	**1219**	1.084
35. **Larry Murphy**, L.A., Wsh., Min., Pit., Tor., Det.	21	1615	287	929	**1216**	.753
36. **Bobby Clarke**, Phi.	15	1144	358	852	**1210**	1.058
37. **Bernie Nicholls**, L.A., NYR, Edm., N.J., Chi., S.J.	18	1127	475	734	**1209**	1.073
38. **Vincent Damphousse**, Tor., Edm., Mtl., S.J.	18	1378	432	773	**1205**	.874
* 39. **Mark Recchi**, Pit., Phi., Mtl.	16	1173	456	745	**1201**	1.024
40. **Dino Ciccarelli**, Min., Wsh., Det., T.B., Fla.	19	1232	608	592	**1200**	.974
41. **Bobby Hull**, Chi., Wpg., Hfd.	16	1063	610	560	**1170**	1.101
42. **Michel Goulet**, Que., Chi.	15	1089	548	604	**1152**	1.058
* 43. **Brendan Shanahan**, N.J., St.L., Hfd., Det.	17	1268	558	593	**1151**	.908
44. **Bernie Federko**, St.L., Det.	14	1000	369	761	**1130**	1.130
45. **Mike Bossy**, NYI	10	752	573	553	**1126**	1.497
46. **Darryl Sittler**, Tor., Phi., Det.	15	1096	484	637	**1121**	1.023
* 47. **Jeremy Roenick**, Chi., Phx., Phi.	16	1124	475	645	**1120**	.996
* 48. **Mike Modano**, Min., Dal.	16	1101	458	648	**1106**	1.005
49. **Frank Mahovlich**, Tor., Det., Mtl.	18	1181	533	570	**1103**	.934
50. **Glenn Anderson**, Edm., Tor., NYR, St.L.	16	1129	498	601	**1099**	.973
* 51. **Mats Sundin**, Que., Tor.	14	1086	465	624	**1089**	1.003
52. **Theoren Fleury**, Cgy., Col., NYR, Chi.	15	1084	455	633	**1088**	1.004
53. **Dave Taylor**, L.A.	17	1111	431	638	**1069**	.962
54. **Pat Verbeek**, N.J., Hfd., NYR, Dal., Det.	20	1424	522	541	**1063**	.746
55. **Joe Mullen**, St.L., Cgy., Pit., Bos.	17	1062	502	561	**1063**	1.001
* 56. **Joe Nieuwendyk**, Cgy., Dal., N.J., Tor.	18	1177	533	529	**1062**	.902
57. **Denis Potvin**, NYI	15	1060	310	742	**1052**	.992
58. **Henri Richard**, Mtl.	20	1256	358	688	**1046**	.833

With 1,309 points, Jaromir Jagr enters the 2005-06 season as the 26th leading scorer in NHL history. He currently ranks ninth among active players.

Player	Seasons	Games	Goals	Assists	Points	Points per game
59. **Bobby Smith**, Min., Mtl.	15	1077	357	679	**1036**	.962
60. **Brian Bellows**, Min., Mtl., T.B., Ana., Wsh.	17	1188	485	537	**1022**	.860
61. **Rod Gilbert**, NYR	18	1065	406	615	**1021**	.959
62. **Dale Hunter**, Que., Wsh., Col.	19	1407	323	697	**1020**	.725
* 63. **Sergei Fedorov**, Det., Ana.	14	988	431	588	**1019**	1.031
64. **Pat LaFontaine**, NYI, Buf., NYR	15	865	468	545	**1013**	1.171
65. **Steve Larmer**, Chi., NYR	15	1006	441	571	**1012**	1.006
* 66. **Alexander Mogilny**, Buf., Van., N.J., Tor.	15	956	461	546	**1007**	1.053
67. **Lanny McDonald**, Tor., Col., Cgy.	16	1111	500	506	**1006**	.905
68. **Brian Propp**, Phi., Bos., Min., Hfd.	15	1016	425	579	**1004**	.988
* 69. **Brian Leetch**, NYR, NYI, Tor.	17	1144	242	754	**996**	.871
70. **Rick Middleton**, NYR, Bos.	14	1005	448	540	**988**	.983
71. **Dave Keon**, Tor., Hfd.	18	1296	396	590	**986**	.761
72. **Andy Bathgate**, NYR, Tor., Det., Pit.	17	1069	349	624	**973**	.910
73. **Maurice Richard**, Mtl.	18	978	544	421	**965**	.987
74. **Kirk Muller**, N.J., Mtl., NYI, Tor., Fla., Dal.	19	1349	357	602	**959**	.711
75. **Larry Robinson**, Mtl., L.A.	20	1384	208	750	**958**	.692
76. **Rick Tocchet**, Phi., Pit., L.A., Bos., Wsh., Phx.	18	1144	440	512	**952**	.832
* 77. **Teemu Selanne**, Wpg., Ana., S.J., Col.	12	879	452	499	**951**	1.082
* 78. **Steve Thomas**, Tor., Chi., NYI, N.J., Ana., Det.	20	1235	421	512	**933**	.755
79. **Neal Broten**, Min., Dal., N.J., L.A.	17	1099	289	634	**923**	.840
80. **Bobby Orr**, Bos., Chi.	12	657	270	645	**915**	1.393
* 81. **Chris Chelios**, Mtl., Chi., Det.	21	1395	178	736	**914**	.655
* 82. **Rod Brind'Amour**, St.L., Phi., Car.	16	1109	351	560	**911**	.821
83. **Scott Stevens**, Wsh., St.L., N.J.	22	1635	196	712	**908**	.555
84. **Ray Ferraro**, Hfd., NYI, NYR, L.A., Atl., St.L.	18	1258	408	490	**898**	.714
85. **Brad Park**, NYR, Bos., Det.	17	1113	213	683	**896**	.805
86. **Butch Goring**, L.A., NYI, Bos.	16	1107	375	513	**888**	.802
87. **Bill Barber**, Phi.	14	903	420	463	**883**	.978
88. **Dennis Maruk**, Cal., Cle., Min., Wsh.	14	888	356	522	**878**	.989
* 89. **Cliff Ronning**, St.L., Van., Phx., Nsh., L.A., Min., NYI	18	1137	306	563	**869**	.764
90. **Ivan Boldirev**, Bos., Cal., Chi., Atl., Van., Det.	15	1052	361	505	**866**	.823
91. **Yvan Cournoyer**, Mtl.	16	968	428	435	**863**	.892
92. **Dean Prentice**, NYR, Bos., Det., Pit., Min.	22	1378	391	469	**860**	.624
93. **Tomas Sandstrom**, NYR, L.A., Pit., Det., Ana.	15	983	394	462	**856**	.871
94. **Ted Lindsay**, Det., Chi.	17	1068	379	472	**851**	.797
95. **Gary Suter**, Cgy., Chi., S.J.	17	1145	203	641	**844**	.737
96. **Tom Lysiak**, Atl., Chi.	13	919	292	551	**843**	.917
97. **John MacLean**, N.J., S.J., NYR, Dal.	18	1194	413	429	**842**	.705
* 98. **Peter Bondra**, Wsh., Ott.	14	984	477	362	**839**	.853
99. **John Tonelli**, NYI, Cgy., L.A., Chi., Que.	14	1028	325	511	**836**	.813
100. **Jacques Lemaire**, Mtl.	12	853	366	469	**835**	.979

Top 100 Active Points Leaders

	Player	Seasons	Games	Goals	Assists	Points	Points per game
1.	**Mark Messier**, Edm., NYR, Van.	25	1756	694	1193	**1887**	1.075
2.	**Ron Francis**, Hfd., Pit., Car., Tor.	23	1731	549	1249	**1798**	1.039
3.	**Steve Yzerman**, Det.	21	1453	678	1043	**1721**	1.184
4.	**Mario Lemieux**, Pit.	17	889	683	1018	**1701**	1.913
5.	**Joe Sakic**, Que., Col.	16	1155	542	860	**1402**	1.214
6.	**Brett Hull**, Cgy., St.L., Dal., Det.	19	1264	741	649	**1390**	1.100
7.	**Luc Robitaille**, L.A., Pit., NYR, Det.	18	1366	653	717	**1370**	1.003
8.	**Dave Andreychuk**, Buf., Tor., N.J., Bos., Col., T.B.	22	1597	634	686	**1320**	.827
9.	**Jaromir Jagr**, Pit., Wsh., NYI	14	1027	537	772	**1309**	1.275
10.	**Al MacInnis**, Cgy., St.L.	23	1416	340	934	**1274**	.900
11.	**Pierre Turgeon**, Buf., NYI, Mtl., St.L., Dal.	17	1215	495	779	**1274**	1.049
12.	**Mark Recchi**, Pit., Phi., Mtl.	16	1173	456	745	**1201**	1.024
13.	**Brendan Shanahan**, N.J., St.L., Hfd., Det.	17	1268	558	593	**1151**	.908
14.	**Jeremy Roenick**, Chi., Phx., Phi.	16	1124	475	645	**1120**	.996
15.	**Mike Modano**, Min., Dal.	16	1101	458	648	**1106**	1.005
16.	**Mats Sundin**, Que., Tor.	14	1086	465	624	**1089**	1.003
17.	**Joe Nieuwendyk**, Cgy., Dal., N.J., Tor.	18	1177	533	529	**1062**	.902
18.	**Sergei Fedorov**, Det., Ana.	14	988	431	588	**1019**	1.031
19.	**Alexander Mogilny**, Buf., Van., N.J., Tor.	15	956	461	546	**1007**	1.053
20.	**Brian Leetch**, NYR, NYI, Tor.	17	1144	242	754	**996**	.871
21.	**Teemu Selanne**, Wpg., Ana., S.J., Col.	12	879	452	499	**951**	1.082
22.	**Steve Thomas**, Tor., Chi., NYI, N.J., Ana., Det.	20	1235	421	512	**933**	.755
23.	**Chris Chelios**, Mtl., Chi., Det.	21	1395	178	736	**914**	.655
24.	**Rod Brind'Amour**, St.L., Phi., Car.	16	1109	351	560	**911**	.821
25.	**Cliff Ronning**, St.L., Van., Phx., Nsh., L.A., Min., NYI	18	1137	306	563	**869**	.764
26.	**Peter Bondra**, Wsh., Ott.	14	984	477	362	**839**	.853
27.	**Keith Tkachuk**, Wpg., Phx., St.L.	13	856	431	401	**832**	.972
28.	**Tony Amonte**, NYR, Chi., Phx., Phi.	14	1013	392	436	**828**	.817
29.	**Doug Weight**, NYR, Edm., St.L.	14	912	224	604	**828**	.908
30.	**Eric Lindros**, Phi., NYR, NYI	11	678	356	461	**817**	1.205
31.	**Trevor Linden**, Van., NYI, Mtl., Wsh.	16	1161	349	465	**814**	.701
32.	**Gary Roberts**, Cgy., Car., Tor.	18	1029	397	409	**806**	.783
33.	**Scott Mellanby**, Phi., Edm., Fla., St.L.	19	1291	340	430	**770**	.596
34.	**John LeClair**, Mtl., Phi.	14	873	382	379	**761**	.872
35.	**Peter Forsberg**, Que., Col.	10	580	216	525	**741**	1.278
36.	**Owen Nolan**, Que., Col., S.J., Tor.	14	915	349	386	**735**	.803
37.	**Nicklas Lidstrom**, Det.	13	1016	173	553	**726**	.715
38.	**Andrew Cassels**, Mtl., Hfd., Cgy., Van., CBJ	15	984	200	520	**720**	.732
39.	**Alex Zhamnov**, Wpg., Chi., Phi.	12	783	248	461	**709**	.905
40.	**Scott Young**, Hfd., Pit., Que., Col., Ana., St.L., Dal.	16	1102	324	384	**708**	.642
41.	**Paul Kariya**, Ana., Col.	10	657	311	394	**705**	1.073
42.	**Petr Nedved**, Van., St.L., NYR, Pit., Edm.	13	889	301	379	**680**	.765
43.	**Alex Kovalev**, NYR, Pit., Mtl.	12	849	292	388	**680**	.801
44.	**Ziggy Palffy**, NYI, L.A.	11	642	318	353	**671**	1.045
45.	**Alexei Yashin**, Ott., NYI	10	710	291	374	**665**	.937
46.	**Bobby Holik**, Hfd., N.J., NYR	14	1024	281	361	**642**	.627
47.	**James Patrick**, NYR, Hfd., Cgy., Buf.	21	1280	149	490	**639**	.499
48.	**Robert Reichel**, Cgy., NYI, Phx., Tor.	11	830	252	378	**630**	.759
49.	**Markus Naslund**, Pit., Van.	11	790	290	339	**629**	.796
50.	**Bill Guerin**, N.J., Edm., Bos., Dal.	13	879	315	308	**623**	.709
51.	**Geoff Sanderson**, Hfd., Car., Van., Buf., CBJ	14	928	316	296	**612**	.659
52.	**Keith Primeau**, Det., Hfd., Car., Phi.	14	900	265	347	**612**	.680
53.	**Sergei Zubov**, NYR, Pit., Dal.	12	856	123	484	**607**	.709
54.	**Mike Ricci**, Phi., Que., Col., S.J.	14	1014	233	355	**588**	.580
55.	**Rob Blake**, L.A., Col.	15	903	186	400	**586**	.649
56.	**Joe Juneau**, Bos., Wsh., Buf., Ott., Phx., Mtl.	13	828	156	416	**572**	.691
57.	**Shawn McEachern**, Pit., L.A., Bos., Ott., Atl.	13	883	254	317	**571**	.647
58.	**Daniel Alfredsson**, Ott.	9	629	219	349	**568**	.903
59.	**Jason Arnott**, Edm., N.J., Dal.	11	743	244	324	**568**	.764
60.	**Vyacheslav Kozlov**, Det., Buf., Atl.	13	800	252	307	**559**	.699
61.	**Martin Gelinas**, Edm., Que., Van., Car., Cgy.	16	1052	269	286	**555**	.528
62.	**Mathieu Schneider**, Mtl., NYI, Tor., NYR, L.A., Det.	16	992	168	384	**552**	.556
63.	**Eric Desjardins**, Mtl., Phi.	16	1098	132	419	**551**	.502
64.	**Teppo Numminen**, Wpg., Phx., Dal.	16	1160	111	440	**551**	.475
65.	**Jozef Stumpel**, Bos., L.A.	13	758	151	397	**548**	.723
66.	**Ray Whitney**, S.J., Edm., Fla., CBJ, Det.	13	700	205	330	**535**	.764
67.	**Bryan Smolinski**, Bos., Pit., NYI, L.A., Ott.	12	829	231	303	**534**	.644
68.	**Martin Straka**, Pit., Ott., NYI, Fla., L.A.	12	730	192	338	**530**	.726
69.	**Sandis Ozolinsh**, S.J., Col., Car., Fla., Ana.	12	779	158	367	**525**	.674
70.	**Glen Murray**, Bos., Pit., L.A.	13	823	268	255	**523**	.635
71.	**Miroslav Satan**, Edm., Buf.	9	704	259	260	**519**	.737
72.	**Pavol Demitra**, Ott., St.L.	11	553	216	303	**519**	.939
73.	**Stu Barnes**, Wpg., Fla., Pit., Buf., Dal.	13	897	221	292	**513**	.572
74.	**Donald Audette**, Buf., L.A., Atl., Dal., Mtl., Fla.	15	735	260	249	**509**	.693
75.	**Martin Rucinsky**, Edm., Que., Col., Mtl., Dal., NYR, St.L., Van.	13	817	208	300	**508**	.622
76.	**Glen Wesley**, Bos., Hfd., Car., Tor.	17	1247	124	382	**506**	.406
77.	**Jarome Iginla**, Cgy.	9	626	250	253	**503**	.804
78.	**Jeff Friesen**, S.J., Ana., N.J.	10	770	208	285	**493**	.640
79.	**Scott Niedermayer**, N.J.	13	892	112	364	**476**	.534
80.	**Mike Keane**, Mtl., Col., NYR, Dal., St.L., Van.	16	1161	168	302	**470**	.405
81.	**Chris Gratton**, T.B., Phi., Buf., Phx., Col.	11	851	174	296	**470**	.552
82.	**Robert Lang**, L.A., Bos., Pit., Wsh., Det.	11	646	174	293	**467**	.723
83.	**Petr Sykora**, N.J., Ana.	9	608	202	259	**461**	.758
84.	**Patrik Elias**, N.J.	9	558	207	252	**459**	.823
85.	**Todd Bertuzzi**, NYI, Van.	9	628	198	260	**458**	.729
86.	**Steve Sullivan**, N.J., Tor., Chi., Nsh.	9	597	175	274	**449**	.752
87.	**Michael Nylander**, Hfd., Cgy., T.B., Chi., Wsh., Bos.	11	648	140	307	**447**	.690
88.	**Roman Hamrlik**, T.B., Edm., NYI	12	873	117	324	**441**	.505
89.	**Cory Stillman**, Cgy., St.L., T.B.	10	645	184	250	**434**	.673
90.	**Dallas Drake**, Det., Wpg., Phx., St.L.	12	822	166	267	**433**	.527
91.	**Steve Rucchin**, Ana.	10	616	153	279	**432**	.701
92.	**Brian Rolston**, N.J., Col., Bos.	10	736	190	242	**432**	.587
93.	**Travis Green**, NYI, Ana., Phx., Tor., Bos.	12	857	182	249	**431**	.503
94.	**Ryan Smyth**, Edm.	10	642	198	232	**430**	.670
95.	**Darryl Sydor**, L.A., Dal., CBJ, T.B.	13	943	85	342	**427**	.453
96.	**Jason Allison**, Wsh., Bos., L.A.	10	486	137	288	**425**	.874
97.	**Sergei Gonchar**, Wsh., Bos.	10	669	148	277	**425**	.635
98.	**Mariusz Czerkawski**, Bos., Edm., NYI, Mtl.	11	710	207	218	**425**	.599
99.	**Joe Thornton**, Bos.	7	509	160	261	**421**	.827
100.	**Jeff O'Neill**, Hfd., Car.	9	673	198	218	**416**	.618

Jeff Friesen enters the 2005-06 season 7 points shy of 500 for his career. He has 208 goals and 285 assists in 770 games.

Top 100 All-Time Games Played Leaders

* active player

Player	Seasons	Games Played
1. **Gordie Howe**, Det., Hfd.	26	1767
* 2. **Mark Messier**, Edm., NYR, Van.	25	1756
* 3. **Ron Francis**, Hfd., Pit., Car., Tor.	23	1731
4. **Scott Stevens**, Wsh., St.L., N.J.	22	1635
5. **Larry Murphy**, L.A., Wsh., Min., Pit., Tor., Det.	21	1615
6. **Raymond Bourque**, Bos., Col.	22	1612
* 7. **Dave Andreychuk**, Buf., Tor., N.J., Bos., Col., T.B.	22	1597
8. **Alex Delvecchio**, Det.	24	1549
9. **John Bucyk**, Det., Bos.	23	1540
10. **Phil Housley**, Buf., Wpg., St.L., Cgy., N.J., Wsh., Chi., Tor.	21	1495
11. **Wayne Gretzky**, Edm., L.A., St.L., NYR	20	1487
12. **Doug Gilmour**, St.L., Cgy., Tor., N.J., Chi., Buf., Mtl.	20	1474
* 13. **Steve Yzerman**, Det.	21	1453
14. **Tim Horton**, Tor., NYR, Pit., Buf.	24	1446
15. **Mike Gartner**, Wsh., Min., NYR, Tor., Phx.	19	1432
16. **Pat Verbeek**, N.J., Hfd., NYR, Dal., Det.	20	1424
* 17. **Al MacInnis**, Cgy., St.L.	23	1416
18. **Harry Howell**, NYR, Oak., Cal., L.A.	21	1411
19. **Norm Ullman**, Det., Tor.	20	1410
20. **Paul Coffey**, Edm., Pit., L.A., Det., Hfd., Phi., Chi., Car., Bos.	21	1409
21. **Dale Hunter**, Que., Wsh., Col.	19	1407
* 22. **Chris Chelios**, Mtl., Chi., Det.	21	1395
23. **Stan Mikita**, Chi.	22	1394
24. **Doug Mohns**, Bos., Chi., Min., Atl., Wsh.	22	1390
25. **Larry Robinson**, Mtl., L.A.	20	1384
26. **Vincent Damphousse**, Tor., Edm., Mtl., S.J.	18	1378
27. **Dean Prentice**, NYR, Bos., Det., Pit., Min.	22	1378
* 28. **Luc Robitaille**, L.A., Pit., NYR, Det.	18	1366
29. **Ron Stewart**, Tor., Bos., St.L., NYR, Van., NYI	21	1353
30. **Kirk Muller**, N.J., Mtl., NYI, Tor., Fla., Dal.	19	1349
31. **Marcel Dionne**, Det., L.A., NYR	18	1348
32. **Adam Oates**, Det., St.L., Bos., Wsh., Phi., Ana., Edm.	19	1337
33. **Guy Carbonneau**, Mtl., St.L., Dal.	19	1318
34. **Red Kelly**, Det., Tor.	20	1316
35. **Dave Keon**, Tor., Hfd.	18	1296
* 36. **Scott Mellanby**, Phi., Edm., Fla., St.L.	19	1291
37. **Ken Daneyko**, N.J.	20	1283
38. **Phil Esposito**, Chi., Bos., NYR	18	1282
39. **Jean Ratelle**, NYR, Bos.	21	1281
* 40. **James Patrick**, NYR, Hfd., Cgy., Buf.	21	1280
41. **Bryan Trottier**, NYI, Pit.	18	1279
* 42. **Brendan Shanahan**, N.J., St.L., Hfd., Det.	17	1268
* 43. **Brett Hull**, Cgy., St.L., Dal., Det.	19	1264
44. **Ray Ferraro**, Hfd., NYI, NYR, L.A., Atl., St.L.	18	1258
45. **Craig Ludwig**, Mtl., NYI, Min., Dal.	17	1256
46. **Henri Richard**, Mtl.	20	1256
47. **Kevin Lowe**, Edm., NYR.	19	1254
48. **Jari Kurri**, Edm., L.A., NYR, Ana., Col.	17	1251
49. **Bill Gadsby**, Chi., NYR, Det.	20	1248
* 50. **Luke Richardson**, Tor., Edm., Phi., CBJ	17	1247
* 51. **Glen Wesley**, Bos., Hfd., Car., Tor.	17	1247
52. **Allan Stanley**, NYR, Chi., Bos., Tor., Phi.	21	1244
* 53. **Steve Thomas**, Tor., Chi., NYI, N.J., Ana., Det.	20	1235
54. **Dino Ciccarelli**, Min., Wsh., Det., T.B., Fla.	19	1232
55. **Brad McCrimmon**, Bos., Phi., Cgy., Det., Hfd., Phx.	18	1222
56. **Ed Westfall**, Bos., NYI	18	1220
57. **Eric Nesterenko**, Tor., Chi.	21	1219
* 58. **Pierre Turgeon**, Buf., NYI, Mtl., St.L., Dal.	17	1215
59. **Marcel Pronovost**, Det., Tor.	21	1206
60. **Claude Lemieux**, Mtl., N.J., Col., Phx., Dal.	20	1197
61. **Denis Savard**, Chi., Mtl., T.B.	17	1196
62. **Dave Babych**, Wpg., Hfd., Van., Phi., L.A.	19	1195
63. **John MacLean**, N.J., S.J., NYR, Dal.	18	1194
64. **Gilbert Perreault**, Buf.	17	1191
* 65. **Marc Bergevin**, Chi., NYI, Hfd., T.B., Det., St.L., Pit., Van.	20	1191
66. **Dale Hawerchuk**, Wpg., Buf., St.L., Phi.	16	1188
67. **Brian Bellows**, Min., Mtl., T.B., Ana., Wsh.	17	1188
68. **Kevin Dineen**, Hfd., Phi., Car., Ott., CBJ	19	1188
69. **George Armstrong**, Tor.	21	1187
* 70. **Kelly Buchberger**, Edm., Atl., L.A., Phx., Pit.	18	1182
71. **Frank Mahovlich**, Tor., Det., Mtl.	18	1181
72. **Bob Carpenter**, Wsh., NYR, L.A., Bos., N.J.	19	1178
* 73. **Joe Nieuwendyk**, Cgy., Dal., N.J., Tor.	18	1177
74. **Don Marshall**, Mtl., NYR, Buf., Tor.	19	1176
* 75. **Mark Recchi**, Pit., Phi., Mtl.	16	1173
76. **Sylvain Cote**, Hfd., Wsh., Tor., Chi., Dal.	19	1171
* 77. **Mike Keane**, Mtl., Col., NYR, Dal., St.L., Van.	16	1161

Only Gordie Howe ranks ahead of Mark Messier when it comes to regular-season games played in the NHL. Messier passed Howe in career points in 2003-04.

Player	Seasons	Games Played
* 78. **Trevor Linden**, Van., NYI, Mtl., Wsh.	16	1161
79. **Bob Gainey**, Mtl.	16	1160
* 80. **Teppo Numminen**, Wpg., Phx., Dal.	16	1160
81. **Kevin Hatcher**, Wsh., Dal., Pit., NYR, Car.	17	1157
82. **Shayne Corson**, Mtl., Edm., St.L., Tor., Dal.	19	1156
* 83. **Joe Sakic**, Que., Col.	16	1155
84. **Adam Graves**, Det., Edm., NYR, S.J.	16	1152
85. **Leo Boivin**, Tor., Bos., Det., Pit., Min.	19	1150
86. **Garry Galley**, L.A., Wsh., Bos., Phi., Buf., NYI	17	1149
87. **Borje Salming**, Tor., Det.	17	1148
88. **Gary Suter**, Cgy., Chi., S.J.	17	1145
89. **Bobby Clarke**, Phi.	15	1144
* 90. **Brian Leetch**, NYR, Tor.	17	1144
91. **Rick Tocchet**, Phi., Pit., L.A., Bos., Wsh., Phx.	18	1144
* 92. **Cliff Ronning**, St.L., Van., Phx., Nsh., L.A., Min., NYI	18	1137
93. **Glenn Anderson**, Edm., Tor., NYR, St.L.	16	1129
94. **Dave Ellett**, Wpg., Tor., N.J., Bos., St.L.	16	1129
95. **Jamie Macoun**, Cgy., Tor., Det.	16	1128
96. **Bob Nevin**, Tor., NYR, Min., L.A.	18	1128
97. **Murray Oliver**, Det., Bos., Tor., Min.	17	1127
98. **Bernie Nicholls**, L.A., NYR, Edm., N.J., Chi., S.J.	18	1127
99. **Guy Lafleur**, Mtl., NYR, Que.	17	1126
100. **Jean Beliveau**, Mtl.	20	1125

Top 100 Active Games Played Leaders

Player	Seasons	Games Played
1. **Mark Messier**, Edm., NYR, Van.	25	1756
2. **Ron Francis**, Hfd., Pit., Car., Tor.	23	1731
3. **Dave Andreychuk**, Buf., Tor., N.J., Bos., Col., T.B.	22	1597
4. **Steve Yzerman**, Det.	21	1453
5. **Al MacInnis**, Cgy., St.L.	23	1416
6. **Chris Chelios**, Mtl., Chi., Det.	21	1395
7. **Luc Robitaille**, L.A., Pit., NYR, Det.	18	1366
8. **Scott Mellanby**, Phi., Edm., Fla., St.L.	19	1291
9. **James Patrick**, NYR, Hfd., Cgy., Buf.	21	1280
10. **Brendan Shanahan**, N.J., St.L., Hfd., Det.	17	1268
11. **Brett Hull**, Cgy., St.L., Dal., Det.	19	1264
12. **Luke Richardson**, Tor., Edm., Phi., CBJ	17	1247
13. **Glen Wesley**, Bos., Hfd., Car., Tor.	17	1247
14. **Steve Thomas**, Tor., Chi., NYI, N.J., Ana., Det.	20	1235
15. **Pierre Turgeon**, Buf., NYI, Mtl., St.L., Dal.	17	1215
16. **Marc Bergevin**, Chi., NYI, Hfd., T.B., Det., St.L., Pit., Van.	20	1191
17. **Kelly Buchberger**, Edm., Atl., L.A., Phx., Pit.	18	1182
18. **Joe Nieuwendyk**, Cgy., Dal., N.J., Tor.	18	1177
19. **Mark Recchi**, Pit., Phi., Mtl.	16	1173
20. **Mike Keane**, Mtl., Col., NYR, Dal., St.L., Van.	16	1161
21. **Trevor Linden**, Van., NYI, Mtl., Wsh.	16	1161
22. **Teppo Numminen**, Wpg., Phx., Dal.	16	1160
23. **Joe Sakic**, Que., Col.	16	1155
24. **Brian Leetch**, NYR, Tor.	17	1144
25. **Cliff Ronning**, St.L., Van., Phx., Nsh., L.A., Min., NYI	18	1137
26. **Jeremy Roenick**, Chi., Phx., Phi.	16	1124
27. **Don Sweeney**, Bos., Dal.	16	1115
28. **Rod Brind'Amour**, St.L., Phi., Car.	16	1109
29. **Scott Young**, Hfd., Pit., Que., Col., Ana., St.L., Dal.	16	1102
30. **Mike Modano**, Min., Dal.	16	1101
31. **Eric Desjardins**, Mtl., Phi.	16	1098
32. **Mats Sundin**, Que., Tor.	14	1086
33. **Eric Weinrich**, N.J., Hfd., Chi., Mtl., Bos., Phi., St.L.	16	1082
34. **Martin Gelinas**, Edm., Que., Van., Car., Cgy.	16	1052
35. **Curtis Leschyshyn**, Que., Col., Wsh., Hfd., Car., Min., Ott.	16	1033
36. **Lyle Odelein**, Mtl., N.J., Phx., CBJ, Chi., Dal., Fla.	15	1029
37. **Gary Roberts**, Cgy., Car., Tor.	18	1029
38. **Jaromir Jagr**, Pit., Wsh., NYR	14	1027
39. **Tom Fitzgerald**, NYI, Fla., Col., Nsh., Chi., Tor.	16	1026
40. **Bobby Holik**, Hfd., N.J., NYR	14	1024
41. **Nicklas Lidstrom**, Det.	13	1016
42. **Mike Ricci**, Phi., Que., Col., S.J.	14	1014
43. **Tony Amonte**, NYR, Chi., Phx., Phi.	14	1013
44. **Mathieu Schneider**, Mtl., NYI, Tor., NYR, L.A., Det.	16	992
45. **Sergei Fedorov**, Det., Ana.	14	988
46. **Murray Baron**, Phi., St.L., Mtl., Phx., Van.	15	988
47. **Peter Bondra**, Wsh., Ott.	14	984
48. **Andrew Cassels**, Mtl., Hfd., Cgy., Van., CBJ	15	984
49. **Alexander Mogilny**, Buf., Van., N.J., Tor.	15	956
50. **Darryl Sydor**, L.A., Dal., CBJ, T.B.	13	943
51. **Tie Domi**, Tor., NYR, Wpg.	15	943
52. **Geoff Sanderson**, Hfd., Car., Van., Buf., CBJ.	14	928
53. **Owen Nolan**, Que., Col., S.J., Tor.	14	915
54. **Doug Weight**, NYR, Edm., St.L.	14	912
55. **Rob Blake**, L.A., Col.	15	903
56. **Keith Primeau**, Det., Hfd., Car., Phi.	14	900
57. **Rob Ray**, Buf., Ott.	15	900
58. **Stu Barnes**, Wpg., Fla., Pit., Buf., Dal.	13	897
59. **Scott Niedermayer**, N.J.	13	892
60. **Petr Nedved**, Van., St.L., NYR, Pit., Edm.	13	889
61. **Bryan Marchment**, Wpg., Chi., Hfd., Edm., T.B., S.J., Col., Tor.	16	889
62. **Mario Lemieux**, Pit.	17	889
63. **Shawn McEachern**, Pit., L.A., Bos., Ott., Atl.	13	883
64. **Alexei Zhitnik**, L.A., Buf.	12	882
65. **Jim McKenzie**, Hfd., Dal., Pit., Wpg., Phx., Ana., Wsh., N.J., Nsh.	15	880
66. **Teemu Selanne**, Wpg., Ana., S.J., Col.	12	879
67. **Bill Guerin**, N.J., Edm., Bos., Dal.	13	879
68. **Claude Lapointe**, Que., Col., Cgy., NYI, Phi.	14	879
69. **Roman Hamrlik**, T.B., Edm., NYI	12	873
70. **John LeClair**, Mtl., Phi.	14	873
71. **Travis Green**, NYI, Ana., Phx., Tor., Bos.	12	857
72. **Sergei Zubov**, NYR, Pit., Dal.	12	856
73. **Keith Tkachuk**, Wpg., Phx., St.L.	13	856
74. **Chris Gratton**, T.B., Phi., Buf., Phx., Col.	11	851
75. **Alex Kovalev**, NYR, Pit., Mtl.	12	849
76. **Derian Hatcher**, Min., Dal., Det.	13	842
77. **Rob DiMaio**, NYI, T.B., Phi., Bos., NYR, Car., Dal.	16	833
78. **Robert Reichel**, Cgy., NYI, Phx., Tor.	11	830

Player	Seasons	Games Played
79. **Bryan Smolinski**, Bos., Pit., NYI, L.A., Ott.	12	829
80. **Mike Sillinger**, Det., Ana., Van., Phi., T.B., Fla., Ott., CBJ, Phx., St.L.	14	829
81. **Glen Murray**, Bos., Pit., L.A.	13	823
82. **Dallas Drake**, Det., Wpg., Phx., St.L.	12	822
83. **Scott Lachance**, NYI, Mtl., Van., CBJ	13	819
84. **Martin Rucinsky**, Edm., Que., Col., Mtl., Dal., NYR, St.L., Van.	13	817
85. **Brad May**, Buf., Van., Phx.	13	804
86. **Vyacheslav Kozlov**, Det., Buf., Atl.	13	800
87. **Adam Foote**, Que., Col.	13	799
88. **Keith Carney**, Buf., Chi., Phx., Ana.	13	798
89. **Bret Hedican**, St.L., Van., Fla., Car.	13	798
90. **Rob Zamuner**, NYR, T.B., Ott., Bos.	13	798
91. **Igor Korolev**, St.L., Wpg., Phx., Tor., Chi.	12	795
92. **Shaun Van Allen**, Edm., Ana., Ott., Dal., Mtl.	13	794
93. **Patrice Brisebois**, Mtl.	14	791
94. **Markus Naslund**, Pit., Van.	11	790
95. **Dmitry Yushkevich**, Phi., Tor., Fla., L.A.	11	786
96. **Alex Zhamnov**, Wpg., Chi., Phi.	12	783
97. **Mike Eastwood**, Tor., Wpg., NYR, St.L., Chi., Pit.	13	783
98. **Trent Klatt**, Min., Dal., Phi., Van., L.A.	13	782
99. **Sandis Ozolinsh**, S.J., Col., Car., Fla., Ana.	12	779
100. **Bill Lindsay**, Que., Fla., Cgy., S.J., Mtl., Atl.	13	777

Before joining the Columbus Blue Jackets for the 2005-06 season, Adam Foote played 799 games on defense for the Colorado Avalanche and Quebec Nordiques.

Goaltending Records

All-Time Shutout Leaders (Minimum 41 Shutouts)

Goaltender	Team	Seasons	Games	Shutouts
Terry Sawchuk	Detroit	14	734	85
(1949-1970)	Boston	2	102	11
	Toronto	3	91	4
	Los Angeles	1	36	2
	NY Rangers	1	8	1
	Total	21	971	**103**
George Hainsworth	Montreal	7½	318	75
(1926-1937)	Toronto	3½	147	19
	Total	11	465	**94**
Glenn Hall	Detroit	4	148	17
(1952-1971)	Chicago	10	618	51
	St. Louis	4	140	16
	Total	18	906	**84**
Jacques Plante	Montreal	11	556	58
(1952-1973)	NY Rangers	2	98	5
	St. Louis	2	69	10
	Toronto	2¾	106	7
	Boston	¼	8	2
	Total	18	837	**82**
Tiny Thompson	Boston	10¼	468	74
(1928-1940)	Detroit	1¾	85	7
	Total	12	553	**81**
Alex Connell	Ottawa	8	293	64
(1924-1937)	Detroit	1	48	6
	NY Americans	1	1	0
	Mtl. Maroons	2	75	11
	Total	12	417	**81**
Tony Esposito	Montreal	1	13	2
(1968-1984)	Chicago	15	873	74
	Total	16	886	**76**
Martin Brodeur	New Jersey	12	740	**75**
(1991-2004)				
Ed Belfour	Chicago	7⅔	415	30
(1988-2004)	San Jose	⅓	13	1
	Dallas	5	307	27
	Toronto	2	121	17
	Total	15	856	**75**
Lorne Chabot	NY Rangers	2	80	21
(1926-1937)	Toronto	5	214	32
	Montreal	1	47	8
	Chicago	1	48	8
	Mtl. Maroons	1	16	2
	NY Americans	1	6	1
	Total	11	411	**72**
Harry Lumley	Detroit	6½	324	26
(1943-1960)	NY Rangers	½	1	0
	Chicago	2	134	5
	Toronto	4	267	34
	Boston	3	78	6
	Total	16	804	**71**
Roy Worters	Pittsburgh Pirates	3	123	22
(1925-1937)	NY Americans	9	360	45
	* Montreal		1	0
	Total	12	484	**67**

Goaltender	Team	Seasons	Games	Shutouts
Patrick Roy	Montreal	11½	551	29
(1984-2003)	Colorado	6½	478	37
	Total	19	1,029	**66**
Turk Broda	Toronto	14	629	**62**
(1936-1952)				
Dominik Hasek	Chicago	2	25	1
(1990-2004)	Buffalo	9	491	55
	Detroit	2	79	7
	Total	13	595	**63**
Clint Benedict	Ottawa	7	158	19
(1917-1930)	Mtl. Maroons	6	204	39
	Total	13	362	**58**
John Ross Roach	Toronto	7	222	13
(1921-1935)	NY Rangers	4	89	30
	Detroit	3	180	15
	Total	14	491	**58**
Bernie Parent	Boston	2	57	1
(1965-1979)	Philadelphia	9½	486	50
	Toronto	1½	65	3
	Total	13	608	**54**
Ed Giacomin	NY Rangers	10¼	539	49
(1965-1978)	Detroit	2¾	71	5
	Total	13	610	**54**
Dave Kerr	Mtl. Maroons	3	101	11
(1930-1941)	NY Americans	1	1	0
	NY Rangers	7	324	40
	Total	11	426	**51**
Rogie Vachon	Montreal	5¼	206	13
(1966-1982)	Los Angeles	6¾	389	32
	Detroit	2	109	4
	Boston	2	91	2
	Total	16	795	**51**
Ken Dryden	Montreal	8	397	**46**
(1970-1979)				
Curtis Joseph	St. Louis	6	280	5
(1989-2004)	Edmonton	3	177	14
	Toronto	4	249	17
	Detroit	2	92	7
	Total	15	498	**43**
Gump Worsley	NY Rangers	10	582	24
(1952-1974)	Montreal	6½	172	16
	Minnesota	4½	107	3
	Total	21	861	**43**
Charlie Gardiner	Chicago	7	316	**42**
(1927-1934)				
Chris Osgood	Detroit	8	389	30
(1993-2004)	NY Islanders	1¾	103	6
	St. Louis	1¼	76	5
	Total	11	568	**41**

*Played 1 game for Montreal in 1929-30.

Ten or More Shutouts, One Season

Number of Shutouts	Goaltender	Team	Season	Length of Schedule
22	George Hainsworth	Montreal	1928-29	44
15	Alex Connell	Ottawa	1925-26	36
	Alex Connell	Ottawa	1927-28	44
	Hal Winkler	Boston	1927-28	44
	Tony Esposito	Chicago	1969-70	76
14	George Hainsworth	Montreal	1926-27	44
13	Clint Benedict	Mtl. Maroons	1926-27	44
	Alex Connell	Ottawa	1926-27	44
	George Hainsworth	Montreal	1927-28	44
	John Ross Roach	NY Rangers	1928-29	44
	Roy Worters	NY Americans	1928-29	44
	Harry Lumley	Toronto	1953-54	70
	Dominik Hasek	Buffalo	1997-98	82
12	Tiny Thompson	Boston	1928-29	44
	Charlie Gardiner	Chicago	1930-31	44
	Terry Sawchuk	Detroit	1951-52	70
	Terry Sawchuk	Detroit	1953-54	70
	Terry Sawchuk	Detroit	1954-55	70
	Glenn Hall	Detroit	1955-56	70
	Bernie Parent	Philadelphia	1973-74	78
	Bernie Parent	Philadelphia	1974-75	80

Number of Shutouts	Goaltender	Team	Season	Length of Schedule
11	Lorne Chabot	NY Rangers	1927-28	44
	Hap Holmes	Detroit	1927-28	44
	Roy Worters	Pittsburgh Pirates	1927-28	44
	Clint Benedict	Mtl. Maroons	1928-29	44
	Joe Miller	Pittsburgh Pirates	1928-29	44
	Lorne Chabot	Toronto	1928-29	44
	Tiny Thompson	Boston	1932-33	48
	Terry Sawchuk	Detroit	1950-51	70
	Dominik Hasek	Buffalo	2000-01	82
	Martin Brodeur	New Jersey	2003-04	82
10	Lorne Chabot	NY Rangers	1926-27	44
	Dolly Dolson	Detroit	1928-29	44
	John Ross Roach	Detroit	1932-33	48
	Charlie Gardiner	Chicago	1933-34	48
	Tiny Thompson	Boston	1935-36	48
	Frank Brimsek	Boston	1938-39	48
	Bill Durnan	Montreal	1948-49	60
	Harry Lumley	Toronto	1952-53	70
	Gerry McNeil	Montreal	1952-53	70
	Tony Esposito	Chicago	1973-74	78
	Ken Dryden	Montreal	1976-77	80
	Martin Brodeur	New Jersey	1996-97	82
	Martin Brodeur	New Jersey	1997-98	82
	Byron Dafoe	Boston	1998-99	82
	Roman Cechmanek	Philadelphia	2000-01	82
	Ed Belfour	Toronto	2003-04	82

All-Time Win Leaders

(Minimum 230 Wins)

Goaltender	Wins	GP	Dec.	Losses	Ties
Patrick Roy	551	1029	997	315	131
Terry Sawchuk	447	971	949	330	172
Jacques Plante	437	837	827	247	145
* Ed Belfour	435	856	827	281	111
Tony Esposito	423	886	880	306	151
Glenn Hall	407	906	896	326	163
* Martin Brodeur	403	740	665	217	105
Grant Fuhr	403	868	812	295	114
* Curtis Joseph	396	798	767	289	90
Mike Vernon	385	781	750	273	92
John Vanbiesbrouck	374	882	839	346	119
Andy Moog	372	713	669	209	88
Tom Barrasso	369	777	732	277	86
Rogie Vachon	355	795	773	291	127
Gump Worsley	335	861	837	352	150
Harry Lumley	330	803	801	329	142
* Chris Osgood	305	568	548	177	66
Billy Smith	305	680	643	233	105
* Sean Burke	304	762	726	321	101
Turk Broda	302	629	627	224	101
Mike Richter	301	666	632	258	73
* Dominik Hasek	296	595	570	192	82
Ron Hextall	296	608	579	214	69
Mike Liut	294	663	639	271	74
Ed Giacomin	289	610	594	208	97
Dan Bouchard	286	655	631	232	113
Tiny Thompson	284	553	553	194	75
Bernie Parent	271	608	590	198	121
Kelly Hrudey	271	677	624	265	88
Gilles Meloche	270	788	752	351	131
Don Beaupre	268	667	620	277	75
* Felix Potvin	266	635	611	260	85
Ken Dryden	258	397	389	57	74
Frank Brimsek	252	514	514	182	80
Johnny Bower	250	552	535	195	90
George Hainsworth	246	465	465	145	74
Pete Peeters	246	489	452	155	51
Kirk McLean	245	612	579	262	72
Bill Ranford	240	647	595	279	76
Reggie Lemelin	236	507	461	162	63
* Olie Kolzig	234	544	517	220	63
Eddie Johnston	234	592	571	257	80
Glenn Resch	231	571	537	224	82
Gerry Cheevers	230	418	406	102	74

* active player

Goals-Against Average Leaders (Minimum 25 games played)

(Exceptions: Minimum 13 games played, 1994-95; minimum 26 games played, 1992-93 to 1993-94; minimum 15 games played, 1917-18 to 1925-26)

Season	Goaltender and Club	GP	Mins.	GA	SO	AVG.
2003-04	Miikka Kiprusoff, San Jose, Calgary	38	2,301	65	4	1.69
2002-03	Marty Turco, Dallas	55	3,203	92	7	1.72
2001-02	Patrick Roy, Colorado	63	3,773	122	9	1.94
2000-01	Marty Turco, Dallas	26	1,266	40	3	1.90
99-2000	Brian Boucher, Philadelphia	35	2,038	65	4	1.91
1998-99	Ron Tugnutt, Ottawa	43	2,508	75	3	1.79
1997-98	Ed Belfour, Dallas	61	3,581	112	9	1.88
1996-97	Martin Brodeur, New Jersey	67	3,838	120	10	1.88
1995-96	Ron Hextall, Philadelphia	53	3,102	112	4	2.17
1994-95	Dominik Hasek, Buffalo	41	2,416	85	5	2.11
1993-94	Dominik Hasek, Buffalo	58	3,358	109	7	1.95
1992-93	Felix Potvin, Toronto	48	2,781	116	2	2.50
1991-92	Patrick Roy, Montreal	67	3,935	155	5	2.36
1990-91	Ed Belfour, Chicago	74	4,127	170	4	2.47
1989-90	Mike Liut, Hartford, Washington	37	2,161	91	4	2.53
1988-89	Patrick Roy, Montreal	48	2,744	113	4	2.47
1987-88	Pete Peeters, Washington	35	1,896	88	2	2.78
1986-87	Brian Hayward, Montreal	37	2,178	102	1	2.81
1985-86	Bob Froese, Philadelphia	51	2,728	116	5	2.55
1984-85	Tom Barrasso, Buffalo	54	3,248	144	5	2.66
1983-84	Pat Riggin, Washington	41	2,299	102	4	2.66
1982-83	Pete Peeters, Boston	62	3,611	142	8	2.36
1981-82	Denis Herron, Montreal	27	1,547	68	3	2.64
1980-81	Richard Sevigny, Montreal	33	1,777	71	2	2.40
1979-80	Bob Sauve, Buffalo	32	1,880	74	4	2.36
1978-79	Ken Dryden, Montreal	47	2,814	108	5	2.30
1977-78	Ken Dryden, Montreal	52	3,071	105	5	2.05
1976-77	Michel Larocque, Montreal	26	1,525	53	4	2.09
1975-76	Ken Dryden, Montreal	62	3,580	121	8	2.03
1974-75	Bernie Parent, Philadelphia	68	4,041	137	12	2.03
1973-74	Bernie Parent, Philadelphia	73	4,314	136	12	1.89
1972-73	Ken Dryden, Montreal	54	3,165	119	6	2.26
1971-72	Tony Esposito, Chicago	48	2,780	82	9	1.77
1970-71	Jacques Plante, Toronto	40	2,329	73	4	1.88
1969-70	Ernie Wakely, St. Louis	30	1,651	58	4	2.11
1968-69	Jacques Plante, St. Louis	37	2,139	70	5	1.96
1967-68	Gump Worsley, Montreal	40	2,213	73	6	1.98
1966-67	Glenn Hall, Chicago	32	1,664	66	2	2.38
1965-66	Johnny Bower, Toronto	35	1,998	75	3	2.25
1964-65	Johnny Bower, Toronto	34	2,040	81	3	2.38
1963-64	Johnny Bower, Toronto	51	3,009	106	5	2.11
1962-63	Don Simmons, Toronto	28	1,680	69	1	2.46
1961-62	Jacques Plante, Montreal	70	4,200	166	4	2.37
1960-61	Charlie Hodge, Montreal	30	1,800	74	4	2.47
1959-60	Jacques Plante, Montreal	69	4,140	175	3	2.54
1958-59	Jacques Plante, Montreal	67	4,000	144	9	2.16
1957-58	Jacques Plante, Montreal	57	3,386	119	9	2.11
1956-57	Jacques Plante, Montreal	61	3,660	122	9	2.00
1955-56	Jacques Plante, Montreal	64	3,840	119	7	1.86
1954-55	Harry Lumley, Toronto	69	4,140	134	8	1.94
1953-54	Harry Lumley, Toronto	69	4,140	128	13	1.86
1952-53	Terry Sawchuk, Detroit	63	3,780	120	9	1.90
1951-52	Terry Sawchuk, Detroit	70	4,200	133	12	1.90
1950-51	Al Rollins, Toronto	40	2,367	70	5	1.77
1949-50	Bill Durnan, Montreal	64	3,840	141	8	2.20
1948-49	Bill Durnan, Montreal	60	3,600	126	10	2.10
1947-48	Turk Broda, Toronto	60	3,600	143	5	2.38
1946-47	Bill Durnan, Montreal	60	3,600	138	4	2.30
1945-46	Bill Durnan, Montreal	40	2,400	104	4	2.60
1944-45	Bill Durnan, Montreal	50	3,000	121	1	2.42
1943-44	Bill Durnan, Montreal	50	3,000	109	2	2.18
1942-43	Johnny Mowers, Detroit	50	3,010	124	6	2.47
1941-42	Frank Brimsek, Boston	47	2,930	115	3	2.35
1940-41	Turk Broda, Toronto	48	2,970	99	5	2.00
1939-40	Dave Kerr, NY Rangers	48	3,000	77	8	1.54
1938-39	Frank Brimsek, Boston	43	2,610	68	10	1.56
1937-38	Tiny Thompson, Boston	48	2,970	89	7	1.80
1936-37	Normie Smith, Detroit	48	2,980	102	6	2.05
1935-36	Tiny Thompson, Boston	48	2,930	82	10	1.68
1934-35	Lorne Chabot, Chicago	48	2,940	88	8	1.80
1933-34	Wilf Cude, Detroit, Montreal	30	1,920	47	5	1.47
1932-33	Tiny Thompson, Boston	48	3,000	88	11	1.76
1931-32	Charlie Gardiner, Chicago	48	2,989	92	4	1.85
1930-31	Roy Worters, NY Americans	44	2,760	74	8	1.61
1929-30	Tiny Thompson, Boston	44	2,680	98	3	2.19
1928-29	George Hainsworth, Montreal	44	2,800	43	22	0.92
1927-28	George Hainsworth, Montreal	44	2,730	48	13	1.05
1926-27	Clint Benedict, Mtl. Maroons	43	2,748	65	13	1.42
1925-26	Alex Connell, Ottawa	36	2,251	42	15	1.12
1924-25	Georges Vezina, Montreal	30	1,860	56	5	1.81
1923-24	Georges Vezina, Montreal	24	1,459	48	3	1.97
1922-23	Clint Benedict, Ottawa	24	1,478	54	4	2.18
1921-22	Clint Benedict, Ottawa	24	1,508	84	2	3.34
1920-21	Clint Benedict, Ottawa	24	1,457	75	2	3.09
1919-20	Clint Benedict, Ottawa	24	1,444	64	5	2.66
1918-19	Clint Benedict, Ottawa	18	1,113	53	2	2.86
1917-18	Georges Vezina, Montreal	21	1,282	84	1	3.93

Active Shutout Leaders

(Minimum 25 Shutouts)

Goaltender	Teams	Seasons	Games	Shutouts
Martin Brodeur	New Jersey	12	740	75
Ed Belfour	Chi., S.J., Dal., Tor.	15	856	75
Dominik Hasek	Chi., Buf., Det.	13	595	63
Curtis Joseph	St.L., Edm., Tor., Det.	15	798	43
Chris Osgood	Det., NYI, St.L.	11	568	41
Jocelyn Thibault	Que., Col., Mtl., Chi.	11	536	36
Nikolai Khabibulin	Wpg., Phx., T.B.	9	476	35
Sean Burke	N.J., Hfd., Car., Van., Phi., Fla., Phx.	16	762	35
Patrick Lalime	Pittsburgh, Ottawa	6	322	33
Olie Kolzig	Washington	13	544	33
Arturs Irbe	S.J., Dal., Van., Car.	13	568	33
Felix Potvin	Tor., NYI, Van., L.A., Bos.	13	635	32
Roman Turek	Dal., St.L., Cal.	8	328	27
Evgeni Nabokov	San Jose	5	258	26
Byron Dafoe	Wsh., L.A., Bos., Atl.	12	415	26
Ron Tugnutt	Que., Edm., Ana., Mtl., Ott., Pit., CBJ, Dal.	16	537	26
Roman Cechmanek	Philadelphia, Los Angeles	4	212	25

All-Time Regular-Season Penalty-Minute Leaders

* active player

	Player	Seasons	Games	Penalty Minutes	Mins. per game
1.	**Tiger Williams**, Tor., Van., Det., L.A., Hfd.	14	962	**3966**	4.12
2.	**Dale Hunter**, Que., Wsh., Col.	19	1407	**3565**	2.53
* 3.	**Tie Domi**, Tor., NYR, Wpg.	15	943	**3406**	3.61
4.	**Marty McSorley**, Pit., Edm., L.A., NYR, S.J., Bos.	17	961	**3381**	3.52
5.	**Bob Probert**, Det., Chi.	16	935	**3300**	3.53
* 6.	**Rob Ray**, Buf., Ott.	15	900	**3207**	3.56
7.	**Craig Berube**, Phi., Tor., Cgy., Wsh., NYI	17	1054	**3149**	2.99
8.	**Tim Hunter**, Cgy., Que., Van., S.J.	16	815	**3146**	3.86
9.	**Chris Nilan**, Mtl., NYR, Bos.	13	688	**3043**	4.42
10.	**Rick Tocchet**, Phi., Pit., L.A., Bos., Wsh., Phx.	18	1144	**2972**	2.60
11.	**Pat Verbeek**, N.J., Hfd., NYR, Dal., Det.	20	1424	**2905**	2.04

All-Time Regular Season NHL Coaching Register

Regular Season, 1917-2005

Coach	Team	Games Coached	Wins	Losses	Ties	Years	Cup Wins	Career
Abel, Sid	Chicago	140	39	79	22	2		
	Detroit	811	340	339	132	12		
	St. Louis	10	3	6	1	1		
	Kansas City	3	0	3	0	1		
	Total	964	382	427	155	16		1952-76
Adams, Jack	Detroit	964	413	390	161	20	3	1927-47
Allen, Keith	Philadelphia	150	51	67	32	2		1967-69
Allison, Dave	Ottawa	25	2	22	1	1		1995-96
Anderson, Jim	Washington	54	4	45	5	1		1974-75
Angotti, Lou	St. Louis	32	6	20	6	2		
	Pittsburgh	80	16	58	6	1		
	Total	112	22	78	12	3		1973-84
Arbour, Al	St. Louis	107	42	40	25	3		
	NY Islanders	1499	739	537	223	19	4	
	Total	1606	781	577	248	22	4	1970-94
Armstrong, George	Toronto	47	17	26	4	1		1988-89
Babcock, Mike	Anaheim	164	69	76	19	3		2002-05
Barber, Bill	Philadelphia	136	73	46	17	2		2000-02
Barkley, Doug	Detroit	77	20	46	11	3		1970-76
Beaulieu, Andre	Minnesota	32	6	23	3	1		1977-78
Belisle, Danny	Washington	96	28	51	17	2		1978-80
Berenson, Red	St. Louis	204	100	72	32	3		1979-82
Bergeron, Michel	Quebec	634	265	283	86	8		
	NY Rangers	158	73	67	18	2		
	Total	792	338	350	104	10		1980-90
Berry, Bob	Los Angeles	240	107	94	39	3		
	Montreal	223	116	71	36	3		
	Pittsburgh	240	88	127	25	3		
	St. Louis	157	73	63	21	2		
	Total	860	384	355	121	11		1978-94
Beverley, Nick	Toronto	17	9	6	2	1		1995-96
Blackburn, Don	Hartford	140	42	63	35	2		1979-81
Blair, Wren	Minnesota	147	48	65	34	3		1967-70
Blake, Toe	Montreal	914	500	255	159	13	8	1955-68
Boileau, Marc	Pittsburgh	151	66	61	24	3		1973-76
Boivin, Leo	St. Louis	97	28	53	16	2		1975-78
Boucher, Frank	NY Rangers	527	181	263	83	11	1	1939-54
Boucher, Georges	Mtl. Maroons	12	6	5	1	1		
	Ottawa	48	13	29	6	1		
	St. Louis	35	9	20	6	1		
	Boston	70	22	32	16	1		
	Total	165	50	86	29	4		1930-50
Bowman, Scotty	St. Louis	238	110	83	45	4		
	Montreal	634	419	110	105	8	5	
	Buffalo	404	210	134	60	7		
	Pittsburgh	164	95	53	16	2	1	
	Detroit	701	410	204	87	9	3	
	Total	2141	1244	584	313	30	9	1967-02
Bowness, Rick	Winnipeg	28	8	17	3	1		
	Boston	80	36	32	12	1		
	Ottawa	235	39	178	18	4		
	NY Islanders	100	38	50	12	2		
	Phoenix	20	2	15	3	2		
	Total	463	123	292	48	10		1988-05
Brooks, Herb	NY Rangers	285	131	113	41	4		
	Minnesota	80	19	48	13	1		
	New Jersey	84	40	37	7	1		
	Pittsburgh	58	29	24	5	1		
	Total	507	219	222	66	7		1981-00
Brophy, John	Toronto	193	64	111	18	3		1986-89
Burnett, George	Edmonton	35	12	20	3	1		1994-95
Burns, Charlie	Minnesota	86	22	50	14	2		1969-75
Burns, Pat	Montreal	320	174	104	42	4		
	Toronto	281	133	107	41	4		
	Boston	254	105	103	46	4		
	New Jersey	164	89	53	22	3	1	
	Total	1019	501	367	151	15	1	1988-05
Bush, Eddie	Kansas City	32	1	23	8	1		1975-76
Campbell, Colin	NY Rangers	269	118	108	43	4		1994-98
Carpenter, Doug	New Jersey	290	100	166	24	4		
	Toronto	91	39	47	5	2		
	Total	381	139	213	29	6		1984-91
Carroll, Dick	Toronto	40	18	22	0	2	1	1917-19
Carroll, Frank	Toronto	24	15	9	0	1		1920-21
Cashman, Wayne	Philadelphia	61	32	20	9	1		1997-98
Cassidy, Bruce	Washington	110	47	54	9	3		2002-05
Chambers, Dave	Quebec	98	19	64	15	2		1990-92
Charron, Guy	Calgary	16	6	7	3	1		
	Anaheim	49	14	28	7	1		
	Total	65	20	35	10	2		1991-01
Cheevers, Gerry	Boston	376	204	126	46	5		1980-85
Cherry, Don	Boston	400	231	105	64	5		
	Colorado	80	19	48	13	1		
	Total	480	250	153	77	6		1974-80

Coach	Team	Games Coached	Wins	Losses	Ties	Years	Cup Wins	Career
Clancy, King	Mtl. Maroons	18	6	11	1	1		
	Toronto	210	80	81	49	3		
	Total	228	86	92	50	4		1937-56
Clapper, Dit	Boston	230	102	88	40	4		1945-49
Cleghorn, Odie	Pittsburgh	168	62	86	20	4		1925-29
Cleghorn, Sprague	Mtl. Maroons	48	19	22	7	1		1931-32
Colville, Neil	NY Rangers	93	26	41	26	2		1950-52
Conacher, Charlie	Chicago	162	56	84	22	3		1947-50
Conacher, Lionel	NY Americans	44	14	25	5	1		1929-30
Constantine, Kevin	San Jose	157	55	78	24	3		
	Pittsburgh	188	86	67	35	3		
	New Jersey	31	20	9	2	1		
	Total	376	161	154	61	7		1993-02
Cook, Bill	NY Rangers	117	34	59	24	2		1951-53
Crawford, Marc	Quebec	48	30	13	5	1		
	Colorado	246	135	75	36	3	1	
	Vancouver	447	204	181	62	7		
	Total	741	369	269	103	11	1	1994-05
Creamer, Pierre	Pittsburgh	80	36	35	9	1		1987-88
Creighton, Fred	Atlanta	348	156	136	56	5		
	Boston	73	40	20	13	1		
	Total	421	196	156	69	6		1974-80
Crisp, Terry	Calgary	240	144	63	33	3	1	
	Tampa Bay	391	142	204	45	6		
	Total	631	286	267	78	9	1	1987-98
Crozier, Joe	Buffalo	192	77	80	35	3		
	Toronto	40	13	22	5	1		
	Total	232	90	102	40	4		1971-81
Crozier, Roger	Washington	1	0	1	0	1		1981-82
Cunniff, John	Hartford	13	3	9	1	1		
	New Jersey	133	59	56	18	2		
	Total	146	62	65	19	3		1982-91
Curry, Alex	Ottawa	36	24	8	4	1		1925-26
Dandurand, Leo	Montreal	163	78	76	9	6	1	1921-35
Day, Hap	Toronto	546	259	206	81	10	5	1940-50
Dea, Billy	Detroit	11	3	8	0	1		1981-82
Delvecchio, Alex	Detroit	245	82	131	32	4		1973-77
Demers, Jacques	Quebec	80	25	44	11	1		
	St. Louis	240	106	106	28	3		
	Detroit	320	137	136	47	4		
	Montreal	221	107	87	27	4	1	
	Tampa Bay	145	34	94	17	2		
	Total	1006	409	467	130	14	1	1979-99
Denneny, Cy	Boston	44	26	13	5	1	1	
	Ottawa	48	11	27	10	1		
	Total	92	37	40	15	2	1	1928-33
Dineen, Bill	Philadelphia	140	60	60	20	2		1991-93
Dudley, Rick	Buffalo	188	85	72	31	3		
	Florida	40	13	18	9	2		
	Total	228	98	90	40	5		1989-05
Duff, Dick	Toronto	2	0	2	0	1		1979-80
Dugal, Jules	Montreal	18	9	6	3	1		1938-39
Duncan, Art	Detroit	33	10	21	2	1		
	Toronto	47	21	16	10	2	1	
	Total	80	31	37	12	3	1	1926-32
Dutton, Red	NY Americans	288	90	151	47	6		
	Brooklyn	48	16	29	3	1		
	Total	336	106	180	50	7		1935-42
Eddolls, Frank	Chicago	70	13	40	17	1		1954-55
Esposito, Phil	NY Rangers	45	24	21	0	2		1986-89
Evans, Jack	California	80	27	42	11	1		
	Cleveland	160	47	87	26	2		
	Hartford	374	163	174	37	5		
	Total	614	237	303	74	8		1975-88
Fashoway, Gordie	Oakland	10	4	5	1	1		1967-68
Ferguson, John	NY Rangers	121	43	59	19	2		
	Winnipeg	14	7	6	1	1		
	Total	135	50	65	20	3		1975-86
Filion, Maurice	Quebec	6	1	3	2	1		1980-81
Francis, Bob	Phoenix	390	165	165	60	5		1999-04
Francis, Emile	NY Rangers	654	342	209	103	10		
	St. Louis	124	46	64	14	3		
	Total	778	388	273	117	13		1965-83
Fraser, Curt	Atlanta	279	64	184	31	4		1999-03
Fredrickson, Frank	Pittsburgh	44	5	36	3	1		1929-30
Ftorek, Robbie	Los Angeles	132	65	56	11	2		
	New Jersey	156	88	49	19	2		
	Boston	155	76	65	14	2		
	Total	443	229	170	44	6		1987-03
Gadsby, Bill	Detroit	78	35	31	12	2		1968-70
Gainey, Bob	Minnesota	244	95	119	30	3		
	Dallas	171	70	71	30	3		
	Total	415	165	190	60	6		1990-96
Gallant, Gerard	Columbus	45	16	25	4	2		2003-05
Gardiner, Herb	Chicago	32	5	23	4	1		1929-30
Gardner, Jimmy	Hamilton	30	19	10	1	1		1924-25
Garvin, Ted	Detroit	11	2	8	1	1		1973-74
Geoffrion, Bernie	NY Rangers	43	22	18	3	1		
	Atlanta	208	77	92	39	3		
	Montreal	30	15	9	6	1		
	Total	281	114	119	48	5		1968-80
Gerard, Eddie	Ottawa	22	9	13	0	1		
	Mtl. Maroons	294	129	122	43	7	1	
	NY Americans	92	34	40	18	2		
	St. Louis	13	2	11	0	1		
	Total	421	174	186	61	11	1	1917-35

Coach	Team	Games Coached	Wins	Losses	Ties	Years	Cup Wins	Career
Gilbert, Greg	Calgary	121	42	62	17	3		2000-03
Gill, David	Ottawa	132	64	41	27	3	1	1926-29
Glover, Fred	Oakland	152	51	76	25	2		
	California	204	45	131	28	4		
	Los Angeles	68	18	42	8	1		
	Total	424	114	249	61	7		1968-74
Goodfellow, Ebbie	Chicago	140	30	91	19	2		1950-52
Gordon, Jackie	Minnesota	289	116	123	50	5		1970-75
Goring, Butch	Boston	93	42	38	13	2		
	NY Islanders	147	41	92	14	2		
	Total	240	83	130	27	4		1985-01
Gorman, Tommy	NY Americans	80	31	33	16	2		
	Chicago	73	28	28	17	2	1	
	Mtl. Maroons	174	74	71	29	4	1	
	Total	327	133	132	62	8	2	1925-38
Gottselig, Johnny	Chicago	187	62	105	20	4		1944-48
Goyette, Phil	NY Islanders	48	6	38	4	1		1972-73
Graham, Dirk	Chicago	59	16	35	8	1		1998-99
Granato, Tony	Colorado	133	72	44	17	2		2002-04
Green, Gary	Washington	157	50	78	29	3		1979-82
Green, Pete	Ottawa	150	94	52	4	6	3	1919-25
Green, Shorty	NY Americans	44	11	27	6	1		1927-28
Green, Ted	Edmonton	188	65	102	21	3		1991-94
Guidolin, Aldo	Colorado	59	12	39	8	1		1978-79
Guidolin, Bep	Boston	104	72	23	9	2		
	Kansas City	125	26	84	15	2		
	Total	229	98	107	24	4		1972-76
Hanlon, Glen	Washington	54	15	30	9	2		2003-05
Harkness, Ned	Detroit	38	12	22	4	1		1970-71
Harris, Ted	Minnesota	179	48	104	27	3		1975-78
Hart, Cecil	Montreal	394	196	125	73	9	2	1926-39
Hartley, Bob	Colorado	359	193	118	48	5	1	
	Atlanta	121	52	56	13	3		
	Total	480	245	174	61	7	1	1998-05
Hartsburg, Craig	Chicago	246	104	102	40	3		
	Anaheim	197	80	88	29	3		
	Total	443	184	190	69	6		1995-01
Harvey, Doug	NY Rangers	70	26	32	12	1		1961-62
Hay, Don	Phoenix	82	38	37	7	1		
	Calgary	68	23	32	13	1		
	Total	150	61	69	20	2		1996-01
Heffernan, Frank	Toronto	12	5	7	0	1		1919-20
Henning, Lorne	Minnesota	158	68	72	18	2		
	NY Islanders	65	19	39	7	2		
	Total	223	87	111	25	4		1985-01
Hitchcock, Ken	Dallas	503	277	166	60	7		
	Philadelphia	164	85	51	28	3		
	Total	667	362	217	88	10	1	1995-05
Hlinka, Ivan	Pittsburgh	86	42	35	9	2		2000-02
Holmgren, Paul	Philadelphia	264	107	126	31	4		
	Hartford	161	54	93	14	4		
	Total	425	161	219	45	8		1988-96
Howell, Harry	Minnesota	11	3	6	2	1		1978-79
Imlach, Punch	Toronto	770	370	275	125	12	4	
	Buffalo	119	32	62	25	2		
	Total	889	402	337	150	14	4	1958-80
Ingarfield, Earl	NY Islanders	30	6	22	2	1		1972-73
Inglis, Bill	Buffalo	56	28	18	10	1		1978-79
Irvin, Dick	Chicago	126	45	62	19	3		
	Toronto	427	216	152	59	9	1	
	Montreal	896	431	313	152	15	3	
	Total	1449	692	527	230	27	4	1928-56
Ivan, Tommy	Detroit	470	262	118	90	7	3	
	Chicago	103	26	56	21	2		
	Total	573	288	174	111	9	3	1947-58
Iverson, Emil	Chicago	21	8	7	6	1		1932-33
Johnson, Bob	Calgary	400	193	155	52	5		
	Pittsburgh	80	41	33	6	1	1	
	Total	480	234	188	58	6	1	1982-91
Johnson, Tom	Boston	208	142	43	23	3	1	1970-73
Johnston, Eddie	Chicago	80	34	27	19	1		
	Pittsburgh	516	232	224	60	7		
	Total	596	266	251	79	8		1979-97
Johnston, Marshall	California	69	13	45	11	2		
	Colorado	56	15	32	9	1		
	Total	125	28	77	20	3		1973-82
Julien, Claude	Montreal	118	53	55	11	2		2002-05
Kasper, Steve	Boston	164	66	78	20	2		1995-97
Keats, Duke	Detroit	11	2	7	2	1		1926-27
Keenan, Mike	Philadelphia	320	190	102	28	4		
	Chicago	320	153	126	41	4		
	NY Rangers	84	52	24	8	1	1	
	St. Louis	163	75	66	22	3		
	Vancouver	108	36	54	18	2		
	Boston	74	33	34	7	1		
	Florida	153	45	85	23	3		
	Total	1222	584	491	147	18	1	1984-04
Kehoe, Rick	Pittsburgh	160	55	91	14	2		2001-03
Kelly, Pat	Colorado	101	22	54	25	2		1977-79
Kelly, Red	Los Angeles	150	55	75	20	2		
	Pittsburgh	274	90	132	52	4		
	Toronto	318	133	123	62	4		
	Total	742	278	330	134	10		1967-77

Coach	Team	Games Coached	Wins	Losses	Ties	Years	Cup Wins	Career
King, Dave	Calgary	216	109	76	31	3		
	Columbus	204	64	119	21	3		
	Total	420	173	195	52	6		1992-03
Kingston, George	San Jose	164	28	129	7	2		1991-93
Kish, Larry	Hartford	49	12	32	5	1		1982-83
Kitchen, Mike	St. Louis	21	10	7	4	2		2003-05
Kromm, Bobby	Detroit	231	79	111	41	3		1977-80
Kurtenbach, Orland	Vancouver	125	36	62	27	2		1976-78
LaForge, Bill	Vancouver	20	4	14	2	1		1984-85
Lalonde, Newsy	Montreal	207	96	97	14	8		
	NY Americans	44	17	25	2	1		
	Ottawa	88	31	45	12	2		
	Total	339	144	167	28	11		1917-35
Lapointe, Ron	Quebec	89	33	50	6	2		1987-89
Laviolette, Peter	NY Islanders	164	77	68	19	2		
	Carolina	52	20	26	6	2		
	Total	216	97	94	25	4		2001-05
Laycoe, Hal	Los Angeles	24	5	18	1	1		
	Vancouver	156	44	96	16	2		
	Total	180	49	114	17	3		1969-72
Lehman, Hugh	Chicago	21	3	17	1	1		1927-28
Lemaire, Jacques	Montreal	97	48	37	12	2		
	New Jersey	378	199	122	57	5	1	
	Minnesota	328	123	150	55	5		
	Total	803	370	309	124	12	1	1983-05
Lepine, Pit	Montreal	48	10	33	5	1		1939-40
LeSueur, Percy	Hamilton	10	3	7	0	1		1923-24
Lewis, Dave*	Detroit	169	100	48	21	4		1998-05

*Shared a record of 4-1-0 with co-coach Barry Smith in 1998-99

Coach	Team	Games Coached	Wins	Losses	Ties	Years	Cup Wins	Career
Ley, Rick	Hartford	160	69	71	20	2		
	Vancouver	124	47	50	27	2		
	Total	284	116	121	47	4		1989-96
Lindsay, Ted	Detroit	29	5	21	3	2		1979-81
Long, Barry	Winnipeg	205	87	93	25	3		1983-86
Loughlin, Clem	Chicago	144	61	63	20	3		1934-37
Lowe, Ron	Edmonton	341	139	162	40	5		
	NY Rangers	164	69	86	9	2		
	Total	505	208	248	49	7		1994-02
Lowe, Kevin	Edmonton	82	32	34	16	1		1999-00
Ludzik, Steve	Tampa Bay	121	31	76	14	2		1999-01
MacDonald, Parker	Minnesota	61	20	30	11	1		
	Los Angeles	42	13	24	5	1		
	Total	103	33	54	16	2		1973-82
MacLean, Doug	Florida	187	83	71	33	3		
	Columbus	79	24	47	8	2		
	Total	266	107	118	41	5		1995-04
MacMillan, Bill	Colorado	80	22	45	13	1		
	New Jersey	100	19	67	14	2		
	Total	180	41	112	27	3		1980-84
MacNeil, Al	Montreal	55	31	15	9	1	1	
	Atlanta	80	35	32	13	1		
	Calgary	171	72	66	33	3		
	Total	306	138	113	55	5		1970-03
MacTavish, Craig	Edmonton	328	149	132	47	5		2000-05
Magnuson, Keith	Chicago	132	49	57	26	2		1980-82
Mahoney, Bill	Minnesota	93	42	39	12	2		1983-85
Maloney, Dan	Toronto	160	45	100	15	2		
	Winnipeg	212	91	93	28	3		
	Total	372	136	193	43	5		1984-89
Maloney, Phil	Vancouver	232	95	105	32	4		1973-77
Mantha, Sylvio	Montreal	48	11	26	11	1		1935-36
Marshall, Bert	Colorado	24	3	17	4	1		1981-82
Martin, Jacques	St. Louis	160	66	71	23	2		
	Ottawa	692	341	255	96	9		
	Florida	....	....	....	....	1		
	Total	852	407	326	119	12		1986-05
Matheson, Godfrey	Chicago	2	0	2	0	1		1932-33
Maurice, Paul	Hartford	152	61	72	19	2		
	Carolina	522	207	235	80	7		
	Total	674	268	307	99	9		1995-04
Maxner, Wayne	Detroit	129	34	68	27	2		1980-82
McCammon, Bob	Philadelphia	218	119	68	31	4		
	Vancouver	294	102	156	36	4		
	Total	512	221	224	67	8		1978-91
McCreary, Bill	St. Louis	24	6	14	4	1		
	Vancouver	41	9	25	7	1		
	California	32	8	20	4	1		
	Total	97	23	59	15	3		1971-75
McGuire, Pierre	Hartford	67	23	37	7	1		1993-94
McLellan, John	Toronto	310	126	139	45	4		1969-73
McVie, Tom	Washington	204	49	122	33	3		
	Winnipeg	105	20	67	18	2		
	New Jersey	153	57	74	22	3		
	Total	462	126	263	73	8		1975-92
Meeker, Howie	Toronto	70	21	34	15	1		1956-57
Melrose, Barry	Los Angeles	209	79	101	29	3		1992-95
Milbury, Mike	Boston	160	90	49	21	2		
	NY Islanders	191	56	111	24	4		
	Total	351	146	160	45	6		1989-99
Molleken, Lorne	Chicago	47	18	21	8	2		1998-00
Muckler, John	Minnesota	35	6	23	6	1		
	Edmonton	160	75	65	20	2	1	
	Buffalo	268	125	109	34	4		
	NY Rangers	185	70	91	24	3		
	Total	648	276	288	84	10	1	1968-00

Coach	Team	Games Coached	Wins	Losses	Ties	Years	Cup Wins	Career
Muldoon, Pete	Chicago	44	19	22	3	1		1926-27
Munro, Dunc	Mtl. Maroons	76	37	29	10	2		1929-31
Murdoch, Bob	Chicago	80	30	41	9	1		
	Winnipeg	160	63	75	22	2		
	Total	240	93	116	31	3		1987-91
Murphy, Mike	Los Angeles	65	20	37	8	2		
	Toronto	164	60	87	17	2		
	Total	229	80	124	25	4		1986-98
Murray, Andy	Los Angeles	410	178	174	58	6		1999-05
Murray, Bryan	Washington	672	343	246	83	9		
	Detroit	244	124	91	29	3		
	Florida	59	17	31	11	1		
	Anaheim	82	29	45	8	1		
	Ottawa	....	....	....	....	1		
	Total	1057	513	413	131	15		1981-05
Murray, Terry	Washington	325	163	134	28	5		
	Philadelphia	212	118	64	30	3		
	Florida	200	79	90	31	3		
	Total	737	360	288	89	11		1989-01
Nanne, Lou	Minnesota	29	7	18	4	1		1977-78
Neale, Harry	Vancouver	407	142	189	76	6		
	Detroit	35	8	23	4	1		
	Total	442	150	212	80	7		1978-86
Neilson, Roger	Toronto	160	75	62	23	2		
	Buffalo	80	39	20	21	1		
	Vancouver	133	51	61	21	3		
	Los Angeles	28	8	17	3	1		
	NY Rangers	280	141	104	35	4		
	Florida	132	53	56	23	2		
	Philadelphia	185	92	60	33	3		
	Ottawa	2	1	1	0	1		
	Total	1000	460	381	159	17		1977-02
Nolan, Ted	Buffalo	164	73	72	19	2		1995-97
Nykoluk, Mike	Toronto	280	89	144	47	4		1980-84
O'Connell, Mike	Boston	9	3	3	3	1		2002-03
O'Donoghue, George	Toronto	29	15	13	1	2	1	1921-23
O'Reilly, Terry	Boston	227	115	86	26	3		1986-89
Olcyck, Ed	Pittsburgh	82	23	51	8	2		2003-05
Oliver, Murray	Minnesota	41	21	12	8	2		1981-83
Olmstead, Bert	Oakland	64	11	37	16	1		1967-68
Paddock, John	Winnipeg	281	106	138	37	4		1991-95
Page, Pierre	Minnesota	160	63	77	20	2		
	Quebec	230	98	103	29	3		
	Calgary	164	66	78	20	2		
	Anaheim	82	26	43	13	1		
	Total	636	253	301	82	8		1988-98
Park, Brad	Detroit	45	9	34	2	1		1985-86
Paterson, Rick	Tampa Bay	8	0	8	0	1		1997-98
Patrick, Craig	NY Rangers	95	37	45	13	2		
	Pittsburgh	74	29	36	9	2		
	Total	169	66	81	22	4		1980-97
Patrick, Frank	Boston	96	48	36	12	2		1934-36
Patrick, Lester	NY Rangers	604	281	216	107	13	2	1926-39
Patrick, Lynn	NY Rangers	107	40	51	16	2		
	Boston	310	117	130	63	5		
	St. Louis	26	8	15	3	3		
	Total	443	165	196	82	10		1948-76
Patrick, Muzz	NY Rangers	136	43	66	27	4		1953-63
Perron, Jean	Montreal	240	126	84	30	3	1	
	Quebec	47	16	26	5	1		
	Total	287	142	110	35	4	1	1985-89
Perry, Don	Los Angeles	168	52	85	31	3		1981-84
Pike, Alf	NY Rangers	123	36	66	21	2		1959-61
Pilous, Rudy	Chicago	387	162	151	74	6	1	1957-63
Plager, Barclay	St. Louis	178	49	96	33	4		1977-83
Plager, Bob	St. Louis	11	4	6	1	1		1992-93
Pleau, Larry	Hartford	224	81	117	26	5		1980-89
Polano, Nick	Detroit	240	79	127	34	3		1982-85
Popein, Larry	NY Rangers	41	18	14	9	1		1973-74
Powers, Eddie	Toronto	66	31	32	3	2		1924-26
Primeau, Joe	Toronto	210	97	71	42	3	1	1950-53
Pronovost, Marcel	Buffalo	104	52	29	23	2		1977-79
Pulford, Bob	Los Angeles	396	178	150	68	5		
	Chicago	433	185	180	68	7		
	Total	829	363	330	136	12		1972-00
Quenneville, Joel	St. Louis	593	307	209	77	8		
	Colorado	....	....	....	....	1		
	Total	593	307	209	77	9		1996-05
Querrie, Charles	Toronto	72	29	38	5	3		1922-27
Quinn, Mike	Quebec	24	4	20	0	1		1919-20
Quinn, Pat	Philadelphia	262	141	73	48	4		
	Los Angeles	202	75	101	26	3		
	Vancouver	280	141	111	28	5		
	Toronto	492	259	181	52	7		
	Total	1236	616	466	154	18		1978-05
Raeder, Cap	San Jose	1	1	0	0	1		2002-03
Ramsay, Craig	Buffalo	21	4	15	2	1		
	Philadelphia	28	12	12	4	1		
	Total	49	16	27	6	2		1986-01
Randall, Ken	Hamilton	14	6	8	0	1		1923-24
Reay, Billy	Toronto	90	26	50	14	2		
	Chicago	1012	516	335	161	14		
	Total	1102	542	385	175	16		1957-77
Regan, Larry	Los Angeles	88	27	47	14	2		1970-72
Renney, Tom	Vancouver	101	39	53	9	2		
	NY Rangers	20	5	15	0	2		
	Total	121	44	68	9	4		1996-05
Risebrough, Doug	Calgary	144	71	56	17	2		1990-92
Roberts, Jim	Buffalo	45	21	16	8	1		
	Hartford	80	26	41	13	1		
	St. Louis	9	3	3	3	1		
	Total	134	50	60	24	3		1981-97
Robinson, Larry	Los Angeles	328	122	161	45	4		
	New Jersey	141	73	49	19	3	1	
	Total	469	195	210	64	7	1	1995-02
Rodden, Mike	Toronto	2	0	2	0	1		1926-27
Romeril, Alex	Toronto	13	7	5	1	1		1926-27
Ross, Art	Mtl. Wanderers	6	1	5	0	1		
	Hamilton	24	6	18	0	1		
	Boston	728	361	277	90	16	1	
	Total	758	368	300	90	18	1	1917-45
Ruel, Claude	Montreal	305	172	82	51	5	2	1968-81
Ruff, Lindy	Buffalo	574	253	243	78	8		1997-05
Sather, Glen	Edmonton	842	464	268	110	11	4	
	NY Rangers	90	33	46	11	2		
	Total	932	497	314	121	13		1979-04
Sator, Ted	NY Rangers	99	41	48	10	2		
	Buffalo	207	96	89	22	3		
	Total	306	137	137	32	5		1985-89
Savard, Andre	Quebec	24	10	13	1	1		1987-88
Schinkel, Ken	Pittsburgh	203	83	92	28	4		1972-77
Schmidt, Milt	Boston	726	245	360	121	11		
	Washington	44	5	34	5	2		
	Total	770	250	394	126	13		1954-76
Schoenfeld, Jim	Buffalo	43	19	19	5	1		
	New Jersey	124	50	59	15	3		
	Washington	249	113	102	34	4		
	Phoenix	164	74	66	24	2		
	Total	580	256	248	78	10		1985-99
Shaughnessy, Tom	Chicago	21	10	8	3	1		1929-30
Shero, Fred	Philadelphia	554	308	151	95	7	2	
	NY Rangers	180	82	74	24	3		
	Total	734	390	225	119	10	2	1971-81
Simpson, Joe	NY Americans	144	42	72	30	3		1932-35
Simpson, Terry	NY Islanders	187	81	82	24	3		
	Philadelphia	84	35	39	10	1		
	Winnipeg	97	43	47	7	2		
	Total	368	159	168	41	6		1986-96
Sims, Al	San Jose	82	27	47	8	1		1996-97
Sinden, Harry	Boston	327	153	116	58	6	1	1966-85
Skinner, Jimmy	Detroit	247	123	78	46	4	1	1954-58
Smeaton, Cooper	Philadelphia	44	4	36	4	1		1930-31
Smith, Alf	Ottawa	18	12	6	0	1		1918-19
Smith, Barry*	Detroit	5	4	1	0	1		1998-99
*Results shared with co-coach Dave Lewis								
Smith, Floyd	Buffalo	241	143	62	36	4		
	Toronto	68	30	33	5	1		
	Total	309	173	95	41	5		1971-80
Smith, Mike	Winnipeg	23	2	17	4	1		1980-81
Smith, Ron	NY Rangers	44	15	22	7	1		1992-93
Smythe, Conn	Toronto	134	57	57	20	4		1927-31
Sonmor, Glen	Minnesota	417	174	161	82	7		1978-87
Sproule, Harry	Toronto	12	7	5	0	1		1919-20
Stanley, Barney	Chicago	23	4	17	2	1		1927-28
Stasiuk, Vic	Philadelphia	154	45	68	41	2		
	California	75	21	38	16	1		
	Vancouver	78	22	47	9	1		
	Total	307	88	153	66	4		1969-73
Stewart, Bill	Chicago	69	22	35	12	2	1	1937-39
Stewart, Bill	NY Islanders	37	11	19	7	1		1998-99
Stewart, Ron	NY Rangers	39	15	20	4	1		
	Los Angeles	80	31	34	15	1		
	Total	119	46	54	19	2		1975-78
Stirling, Steve	NY Islanders	82	38	33	11	2		2003-05
Suhonen, Alpo	Chicago	82	29	45	8	1		2000-01
Sullivan, Red	NY Rangers	196	58	103	35	4		
	Pittsburgh	150	47	79	24	2		
	Washington	18	2	16	0	1		
	Total	364	107	198	59	7		1962-75
Sullivan, Mike	Boston	82	41	26	15	2		2003-05
Sutherland, Bill	Winnipeg	32	7	22	3	2		1979-81
Sutter, Brian	St. Louis	320	153	124	43	4		
	Boston	216	120	73	23	3		
	Calgary	246	87	122	37	3		
	Chicago	246	91	118	37	4		
	Total	1028	451	437	140	14		1988-05
Sutter, Darryl	Chicago	216	110	80	26	3		
	San Jose	434	192	182	60	6		
	Calgary	128	61	52	15	3		
	Total	778	363	314	101	11		1992-05
Sutter, Duane	Florida	72	22	42	8	2		2000-02
Talbot, Jean-Guy	St. Louis	120	52	53	15	2		
	NY Rangers	80	30	37	13	1		
	Total	200	82	90	28	3		1972-78
Tessier, Orval	Chicago	213	99	93	21	3		1982-85
Therrien, Michel	Montreal	190	77	90	23	3		2000-03
Thompson, Paul	Chicago	272	104	127	41	7		1938-45

Coach	Team	Games Coached	Wins	Losses	Ties	Years	Cup Wins	Career
Thompson, Percy	Hamilton	48	13	35	0	2		1920-22
Tippett, Dave	Dallas	164	87	49	28	3		2002-05
Tobin, Bill	Chicago	71	29	29	13	2		1929-32
Torchetti, John	Florida	27	10	13	4	1		2003-04
Tortorella, John	NY Rangers	4	0	3	1	1		
	Tampa Bay	289	121	132	36	5	1	
	Total	293	121	135	37	6	1	1999-05
Tremblay, Mario	Montreal	159	71	63	25	2		1995-97
Trottier, Bryan	NY Rangers	54	21	27	6	1		2002-03
Trotz, Barry	Nashville	492	183	249	60	7		1998-05
Ubriaco, Gene	Pittsburgh	106	50	47	9	2		1988-90
Vachon, Rogie	Los Angeles	10	4	3	3	3		1983-95
Vigneault, Alain	Montreal	266	109	122	35	4		1997-01
Waddell, Don	Atlanta	10	4	5	1	1		2002-03
Watson, Bryan	Edmonton	18	4	9	5	1		1980-81
Watson, Phil	NY Rangers	295	119	124	52	5		
	Boston	84	16	55	13	2		
	Total	379	135	179	65	7		1955-63
Watt, Tom	Winnipeg	181	72	85	24	3		
	Vancouver	160	52	87	21	2		
	Toronto	149	52	80	17	2		
	Total	490	176	252	62	7		1981-92
Webster, Tom	NY Rangers	18	5	9	4	1		
	Los Angeles	240	115	94	31	3		
	Total	258	120	103	35	4		1986-92
Weiland, Cooney	Boston	96	58	20	18	2	1	1939-41
White, Bill	Chicago	46	16	24	6	1		1976-77
Wiley, Jim	San Jose	57	17	37	3	1		1995-96
Wilson, Johnny	Los Angeles	52	9	34	9	1		
	Detroit	145	67	56	22	2		
	Colorado	80	20	46	14	1		
	Pittsburgh	240	91	105	44	3		
	Total	517	187	241	89	7		1969-80
Wilson, Larry	Detroit	36	3	29	4	1		1976-77
Wilson, Rick	Dallas	32	13	12	7	1		2001-02
Wilson, Ron	Anaheim	296	120	145	31	4		
	Washington	410	192	167	51	5		
	San Jose	139	62	58	19	3		
	Total	845	374	370	101	12		1993-05
Young, Garry	California	12	2	7	3	1		

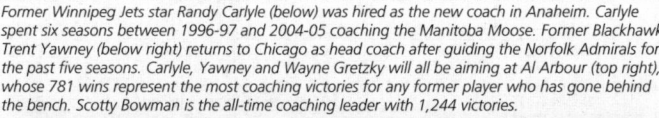

Former Winnipeg Jets star Randy Carlyle (below) was hired as the new coach in Anaheim. Carlyle spent six seasons between 1996-97 and 2004-05 coaching the Manitoba Moose. Former Blackhawk Trent Yawney (below right) returns to Chicago as head coach after guiding the Norfolk Admirals for the past five seasons. Carlyle, Yawney and Wayne Gretzky will all be aiming at Al Arbour (top right), whose 781 wins represent the most coaching victories for any former player who has gone behind the bench. Scotty Bowman is the all-time coaching leader with 1,244 victories.

Year-by-Year Individual Regular-Season Leaders

Season	Goals	G	Assists	A	Points	Pts.	Penalty Minutes	PIM
1917-18	Joe Malone	44	Cy Denneny, Reg Noble, Harry Cameron	10	Joe Malone	48	Joe Hall	100
1918-19	Newsy Lalonde	22	Newsy Lalonde, Eddie Gerard	10	Newsy Lalonde	32	Joe Hall	135
1919-20	Joe Malone	39	Frank Nighbor	15	Joe Malone	49	Cully Wilson	86
1920-21	Babe Dye	35	Jack Darragh	15	Newsy Lalonde	43	Bert Corbeau	86
1921-22	Punch Broadbent	32	Harry Cameron	17	Punch Broadbent	46	Sprague Cleghorn	63
1922-23	Babe Dye	26	Edmond Bouchard	12	Babe Dye	37	Georges Boucher	58
1923-24	Cy Denneny	22	Georges Boucher	10	Cy Denneny	24	Bert Corbeau	55
1924-25	Babe Dye	38	Cy Denneny, Red Green	15	Babe Dye	46	Georges Boucher	95
1925-26	Nels Stewart	34	Frank Nighbor	13	Nels Stewart	42	Bert Corbeau	121
1926-27	Bill Cook	33	Dick Irvin	18	Bill Cook	37	Nels Stewart	133
1927-28	Howie Morenz	33	Howie Morenz	18	Howie Morenz	51	Eddie Shore	165
1928-29	Ace Bailey	22	Frank Boucher	16	Ace Bailey	32	Red Dutton	139
1929-30	Cooney Weiland	43	Frank Boucher	36	Cooney Weiland	73	Joe Lamb	119
1930-31	Charlie Conacher	31	Joe Primeau	32	Howie Morenz	51	Harvey Rockburn	118
1931-32	Charlie Conacher, Bill Cook	34	Joe Primeau	37	Busher Jackson	53	Red Dutton	107
1932-33	Bill Cook	28	Frank Boucher	28	Bill Cook	50	Red Horner	144
1933-34	Charlie Conacher	32	Joe Primeau	32	Charlie Conacher	52	Red Horner	126 *
1934-35	Charlie Conacher	36	Art Chapman	34	Charlie Conacher	57	Red Horner	125
1935-36	Charlie Conacher, Bill Thoms	23	Art Chapman	28	Sweeney Schriner	45	Red Horner	167
1936-37	Larry Aurie, Nels Stewart	23	Syl Apps	29	Sweeney Schriner	46	Red Horner	124
1937-38	Gordie Drillon	26	Syl Apps	29	Gordie Drillon	52	Red Horner	82 *
1938-39	Roy Conacher	26	Bill Cowley	34	Toe Blake	47	Red Dutton	85
1939-40	Bryan Hextall	24	Milt Schmidt	30	Milt Schmidt	52	Red Horner	87
1940-41	Bryan Hextall	26	Bill Cowley	45	Bill Cowley	62	Jimmy Orlando	99
1941-42	Lynn Patrick	32	Phil Watson	37	Bryan Hextall	56	Pat Egan	124
1942-43	Doug Bentley	33	Bill Cowley	45	Doug Bentley	73	Jimmy Orlando	89 *
1943-44	Doug Bentley	38	Clint Smith	49	Herb Cain	82	Mike McMahon	98
1944-45	Maurice Richard	50	Elmer Lach	54	Elmer Lach	80	Pat Egan	86
1945-46	Gaye Stewart	37	Elmer Lach	34	Max Bentley	61	Jack Stewart	73
1946-47	Maurice Richard	45	Billy Taylor	46	Max Bentley	72	Gus Mortson	133
1947-48	Ted Lindsay	33	Doug Bentley	37	Elmer Lach	61	Bill Barilko	147
1948-49	Sid Abel	28	Doug Bentley	43	Roy Conacher	68	Bill Ezinicki	145
1949-50	Maurice Richard	43	Ted Lindsay	55	Ted Lindsay	78	Bill Ezinicki	144
1950-51	Gordie Howe	43	Gordie Howe, Ted Kennedy	43	Gordie Howe	86	Gus Mortson	142
1951-52	Gordie Howe	47	Elmer Lach	50	Gordie Howe	86	Gus Kyle	127
1952-53	Gordie Howe	49	Gordie Howe	46	Gordie Howe	95	Maurice Richard	112
1953-54	Maurice Richard	37	Gordie Howe	48	Gordie Howe	81	Gus Mortson	132
1954-55	Maurice Richard, Bernie Geoffrion	38	Bert Olmstead	48	Bernie Geoffrion	75	Fern Flaman	150
1955-56	Jean Beliveau	47	Bert Olmstead	56	Jean Beliveau	88	Lou Fontinato	202
1956-57	Gordie Howe	44	Ted Lindsay	55	Gordie Howe	89	Gus Mortson	147
1957-58	Dickie Moore	36	Henri Richard	52	Dickie Moore	84	Lou Fontinato	152
1958-59	Jean Beliveau	45	Dickie Moore	55	Dickie Moore	96	Ted Lindsay	184
1959-60	Bobby Hull, Bronco Horvath	39	Don McKenney	49	Bobby Hull	81	Carl Brewer	150
1960-61	Bernie Geoffrion	50	Jean Beliveau	58	Bernie Geoffrion	95	Pierre Pilote	165
1961-62	Bobby Hull	50	Andy Bathgate	56	Bobby Hull, Andy Bathgate	84	Lou Fontinato	167
1962-63	Gordie Howe	38	Henri Richard	50	Gordie Howe	86	Howie Young	273
1963-64	Bobby Hull	43	Andy Bathgate	58	Stan Mikita	89	Vic Hadfield	151
1964-65	Norm Ullman	42	Stan Mikita	59	Stan Mikita	87	Carl Brewer	177
1965-66	Bobby Hull	54	Stan Mikita, Bobby Rousseau, Jean Beliveau	48	Bobby Hull	97	Reggie Fleming	166
1966-67	Bobby Hull	52	Stan Mikita	62	Stan Mikita	97	John Ferguson	177
1967-68	Bobby Hull	44	Phil Esposito	49	Stan Mikita	87	Barclay Plager	153
1968-69	Bobby Hull	58	Phil Esposito	77	Phil Esposito	126	Forbes Kennedy	219
1969-70	Phil Esposito	43	Bobby Orr	87	Bobby Orr	120	Keith Magnuson	213
1970-71	Phil Esposito	76	Bobby Orr	102	Phil Esposito	152	Keith Magnuson	291
1971-72	Phil Esposito	66	Bobby Orr	80	Phil Esposito	133	Bryan Watson	212
1972-73	Phil Esposito	55	Phil Esposito	75	Phil Esposito	130	Dave Schultz	259
1973-74	Phil Esposito	68	Bobby Orr	90	Phil Esposito	145	Dave Schultz	348
1974-75	Phil Esposito	61	Bobby Orr, Bobby Clarke	89	Bobby Orr	135	Dave Schultz	472
1975-76	Reggie Leach	61	Bobby Clarke	89	Guy Lafleur	125	Steve Durbano	370
1976-77	Steve Shutt	60	Guy Lafleur	80	Guy Lafleur	136	Tiger Williams	338
1977-78	Guy Lafleur	60	Bryan Trottier	77	Guy Lafleur	132	Dave Schultz	405
1978-79	Mike Bossy	69	Bryan Trottier	87	Bryan Trottier	134	Tiger Williams	298
1979-80	Charlie Simmer, Danny Gare, Blaine Stoughton	56	Wayne Gretzky	86	Marcel Dionne, Wayne Gretzky	137	Jimmy Mann	287
1980-81	Mike Bossy	68	Wayne Gretzky	109	Wayne Gretzky	164	Tiger Williams	343
1981-82	Wayne Gretzky	92	Wayne Gretzky	120	Wayne Gretzky	212	Paul Baxter	409
1982-83	Wayne Gretzky	71	Wayne Gretzky	125	Wayne Gretzky	196	Randy Holt	275
1983-84	Wayne Gretzky	87	Wayne Gretzky	118	Wayne Gretzky	205	Chris Nilan	338
1984-85	Wayne Gretzky	73	Wayne Gretzky	135	Wayne Gretzky	208	Chris Nilan	358
1985-86	Jari Kurri	68	Wayne Gretzky	163	Wayne Gretzky	215	Joe Kocur	377
1986-87	Wayne Gretzky	62	Wayne Gretzky	121	Wayne Gretzky	183	Tim Hunter	361
1987-88	Mario Lemieux	70	Wayne Gretzky	109	Mario Lemieux	168	Bob Probert	398
1988-89	Mario Lemieux	85	Mario Lemieux, Wayne Gretzky	114	Mario Lemieux	199	Tim Hunter	375
1989-90	Brett Hull	72	Wayne Gretzky	102	Wayne Gretzky	142	Basil McRae	351
1990-91	Brett Hull	86	Wayne Gretzky	122	Wayne Gretzky	163	Rob Ray	350
1991-92	Brett Hull	70	Wayne Gretzky	90	Mario Lemieux	131	Mike Peluso	408
1992-93	Teemu Selanne, Alexander Mogilny	76	Adam Oates	97	Mario Lemieux	160	Marty McSorley	399
1993-94	Pavel Bure	60	Wayne Gretzky	92	Wayne Gretzky	130	Tie Domi	347
1994-95	Peter Bondra	34	Ron Francis	48	Jaromir Jagr, Eric Lindros	70	Enrico Ciccone	225
1995-96	Mario Lemieux	69	Mario Lemieux, Ron Francis	92	Mario Lemieux	161	Matthew Barnaby	335
1996-97	Keith Tkachuk	52	Mario Lemieux, Wayne Gretzky	72	Mario Lemieux	122	Gino Odjick	371
1997-98	Teemu Selanne, Peter Bondra	52	Jaromir Jagr	67	Jaromir Jagr	102	Donald Brashear	372
1998-99	Teemu Selanne	47	Jaromir Jagr	83	Jaromir Jagr	127	Rob Ray	261
99-2000	Pavel Bure	58	Mark Recchi	63	Jaromir Jagr	96	Denny Lambert	219
2000-01	Pavel Bure	59	Jaromir Jagr, Adam Oates	69	Jaromir Jagr	121	Matthew Barnaby	265
2001-02	Jarome Iginla	52	Adam Oates	64	Jarome Iginla	96	Peter Worrell	354
2002-03	Milan Hejduk	50	Peter Forsberg	77	Peter Forsberg	106	Jody Shelley	249
2003-04	Rick Nash, Jarome Iginla, Ilya Kovalchuk	41	Scott Gomez, Martin St. Louis	56	Martin St. Louis	94	Sean Avery	261
2004-05	....		....		....		....	

* Match Misconduct penalty not included in total penalty minutes.
1946-47 was the first season that a Match penalty was automaticaly written into the player's total penalty minutes as 20 minutes.
Beginning in 1947-48 all penalties, Match, Game Misconduct, and Misconduct, are written as 10 minutes.

One Season Scoring Records

Goals-Per-Game Leaders, One Season

(Among players with 20 goals or more in one season)

Player	Team	Season	Games	Goals	Average
Joe Malone	Montreal	1917-18	20	44	2.20
Cy Denneny	Ottawa	1917-18	20	36	1.80
Newsy Lalonde	Montreal	1917-18	14	23	1.64
Joe Malone	Quebec	1919-20	24	39	1.63
Newsy Lalonde	Montreal	1919-20	23	37	1.61
Reg Noble	Toronto	1917-18	20	30	1.50
Babe Dye	Ham., Tor.	1920-21	24	35	1.46
Cy Denneny	Ottawa	1920-21	24	34	1.42
Joe Malone	Hamilton	1920-21	20	28	1.40
Newsy Lalonde	Montreal	1920-21	24	33	1.38
Punch Broadbent	Ottawa	1921-22	24	32	1.33
Babe Dye	Toronto	1924-25	29	38	1.31
Babe Dye	Toronto	1921-22	24	31	1.29
Newsy Lalonde	Montreal	1918-19	17	22	1.29
Odie Cleghorn	Montreal	1918-19	17	22	1.29
Cy Denneny	Ottawa	1921-22	22	27	1.23
Aurel Joliat	Montreal	1924-25	25	30	1.20
Wayne Gretzky	Edmonton	1983-84	74	87	1.18
Babe Dye	Toronto	1922-23	22	26	1.18
Wayne Gretzky	Edmonton	1981-82	80	92	1.15
Mario Lemieux	Pittsburgh	1992-93	60	69	1.15
Frank Nighbor	Ottawa	1919-20	23	26	1.13
Mario Lemieux	Pittsburgh	1988-89	76	85	1.12
Brett Hull	St. Louis	1990-91	78	86	1.10
Cam Neely	Boston	1993-94	49	50	1.02
Maurice Richard	Montreal	1944-45	50	50	1.00
Reg Noble	Toronto	1919-20	24	24	1.00
Corb Denneny	Toronto	1919-20	24	24	1.00
Joe Malone	Hamilton	1921-22	24	24	1.00
Billy Boucher	Montreal	1922-23	24	24	1.00
Cy Denneny	Ottawa	1923-24	22	22	1.00
Alexander Mogilny	Buffalo	1992-93	77	76	0.99
Mario Lemieux	Pittsburgh	1995-96	70	69	0.99
Cooney Weiland	Boston	1929-30	44	43	0.98
Phil Esposito	Boston	1970-71	78	76	0.97
Jari Kurri	Edmonton	1984-85	73	71	0.97

Mario Lemieux is one of only two modern players (along with Wayne Gretzky) to average more than a goal a game in two different seasons. Lemieux had 69 goals in 60 games in 1992-93 and 85 goals in 76 games in 1988-89.

Assists-Per-Game Leaders, One Season

(Among players with 35 assists or more in one season)

Player	Team	Season	Games	Assists	Average
Wayne Gretzky	Edmonton	1985-86	80	163	2.04
Wayne Gretzky	Edmonton	1987-88	64	109	1.70
Wayne Gretzky	Edmonton	1984-85	80	135	1.69
Wayne Gretzky	Edmonton	1983-84	74	118	1.59
Wayne Gretzky	Edmonton	1982-83	80	125	1.56
Wayne Gretzky	Los Angeles	1990-91	78	122	1.56
Wayne Gretzky	Edmonton	1986-87	79	121	1.53
Mario Lemieux	Pittsburgh	1992-93	60	91	1.52
Wayne Gretzky	Edmonton	1981-82	80	120	1.50
Mario Lemieux	Pittsburgh	1988-89	76	114	1.50
Adam Oates	St. Louis	1990-91	61	90	1.48
Wayne Gretzky	Los Angeles	1988-89	78	114	1.46
Wayne Gretzky	Los Angeles	1989-90	73	102	1.40
Wayne Gretzky	Edmonton	1980-81	80	109	1.36
Mario Lemieux	Pittsburgh	1991-92	64	87	1.36
Mario Lemieux	Pittsburgh	1989-90	59	78	1.32
Bobby Orr	Boston	1970-71	78	102	1.31
Mario Lemieux	Pittsburgh	1995-96	70	92	1.31
Mario Lemieux	Pittsburgh	1987-88	77	98	1.27
Bobby Orr	Boston	1973-74	74	90	1.22
Wayne Gretzky	Los Angeles	1991-92	74	90	1.22
Ron Francis	Pittsburgh	1995-96	77	92	1.19
Mario Lemieux	Pittsburgh	1985-86	79	93	1.18
Bobby Clarke	Philadelphia	1975-76	76	89	1.17
Peter Stastny	Quebec	1981-82	80	93	1.16
Adam Oates	Boston	1992-93	84	97	1.15
Doug Gilmour	Toronto	1992-93	83	95	1.14
Wayne Gretzky	Los Angeles	1993-94	81	92	1.14
Paul Coffey	Edmonton	1985-86	79	90	1.14
Bobby Orr	Boston	1969-70	76	87	1.14
Bryan Trottier	NY Islanders	1978-79	76	87	1.14
Bobby Orr	Boston	1972-73	63	72	1.14
Bill Cowley	Boston	1943-44	36	41	1.14
Pat LaFontaine	Buffalo	1992-93	84	95	1.13
Steve Yzerman	Detroit	1988-89	80	90	1.13
Paul Coffey	Pittsburgh	1987-88	46	52	1.13
Bobby Orr	Boston	1974-75	80	89	1.11
Bobby Clarke	Philadelphia	1974-75	80	89	1.11
Paul Coffey	Pittsburgh	1988-89	75	83	1.11
Wayne Gretzky	Los Angeles	1992-93	45	49	1.11
Denis Savard	Chicago	1982-83	78	86	1.10
Denis Savard	Chicago	1981-82	80	87	1.09
Denis Savard	Chicago	1987-88	80	87	1.09
Wayne Gretzky	Edmonton	1979-80	79	86	1.09
Ron Francis	Pittsburgh	1994-95	44	48	1.09
Paul Coffey	Edmonton	1983-84	80	86	1.08
Elmer Lach	Montreal	1944-45	50	54	1.08
Peter Stastny	Quebec	1985-86	76	81	1.07
Jaromir Jagr	Pittsburgh	1995-96	82	87	1.06
Mark Messier	Edmonton	1989-90	79	84	1.06
Peter Forsberg	Colorado	1995-96	82	86	1.05
Paul Coffey	Edmonton	1984-85	80	84	1.05
Marcel Dionne	Los Angeles	1979-80	80	84	1.05
Bobby Orr	Boston	1971-72	76	80	1.05
Mike Bossy	NY Islanders	1981-82	80	83	1.04
Adam Oates	Boston	1993-94	77	80	1.04
Phil Esposito	Boston	1968-69	74	77	1.04
Bryan Trottier	NY Islanders	1983-84	68	71	1.04
Pete Mahovlich	Montreal	1974-75	80	82	1.03
Kent Nilsson	Calgary	1980-81	80	82	1.03
Peter Stastny	Quebec	1982-83	75	77	1.03
Denis Savard	Chicago	1988-89	58	59	1.02
Jaromir Jagr	Pittsburgh	1998-99	81	83	1.02
Doug Gilmour	Toronto	1993-94	83	84	1.01
Bernie Nicholls	Los Angeles	1988-89	79	80	1.01
Guy Lafleur	Montreal	1979-80	74	75	1.01
Guy Lafleur	Montreal	1976-77	80	80	1.00
Marcel Dionne	Los Angeles	1984-85	80	80	1.00
Brian Leetch	NY Rangers	1991-92	80	80	1.00
Bryan Trottier	NY Islanders	1977-78	77	77	1.00
Mike Bossy	NY Islanders	1983-84	67	67	1.00
Jean Ratelle	NY Rangers	1971-72	63	63	1.00
Steve Yzerman	Detroit	1993-94	58	58	1.00
Ron Francis	Hartford	1985-86	53	53	1.00
Guy Chouinard	Calgary	1980-81	52	52	1.00
Elmer Lach	Montreal	1943-44	48	48	1.00

Points-Per-Game Leaders, One Season

(Among players with 50 points or more in one season)

Player	Team	Season	Games	Points	Average	Player	Team	Season	Games	Points	Average
Wayne Gretzky	Edmonton	1983-84	74	205	2.77	Peter Stastny	Quebec	1982-83	75	124	1.65
Wayne Gretzky	Edmonton	1985-86	80	215	2.69	Bobby Orr	Boston	1973-74	74	122	1.65
Mario Lemieux	Pittsburgh	1992-93	60	160	2.67	Kent Nilsson	Calgary	1980-81	80	131	1.64
Wayne Gretzky	Edmonton	1981-82	80	212	2.65	Denis Savard	Chicago	1987-88	80	131	1.64
Mario Lemieux	Pittsburgh	1988-89	76	199	2.62	Wayne Gretzky	Los Angeles	1991-92	74	121	1.64
Wayne Gretzky	Edmonton	1984-85	80	208	2.60	Steve Yzerman	Detroit	1992-93	84	137	1.63
Wayne Gretzky	Edmonton	1982-83	80	196	2.45	Marcel Dionne	Los Angeles	1978-79	80	130	1.63
Wayne Gretzky	Edmonton	1987-88	64	149	2.33	Dale Hawerchuk	Winnipeg	1984-85	80	130	1.63
Wayne Gretzky	Edmonton	1986-87	79	183	2.32	Mark Messier	Edmonton	1989-90	79	129	1.63
Mario Lemieux	Pittsburgh	1995-96	70	161	2.30	Bryan Trottier	NY Islanders	1983-84	68	111	1.63
Mario Lemieux	Pittsburgh	1987-88	77	168	2.18	Pat LaFontaine	Buffalo	1991-92	57	93	1.63
Wayne Gretzky	Los Angeles	1988-89	78	168	2.15	Charlie Simmer	Los Angeles	1980-81	65	105	1.62
Wayne Gretzky	Los Angeles	1990-91	78	163	2.09	Guy Lafleur	Montreal	1978-79	80	129	1.61
Mario Lemieux	Pittsburgh	1989-90	59	123	2.08	Bryan Trottier	NY Islanders	1981-82	80	129	1.61
Wayne Gretzky	Edmonton	1980-81	80	164	2.05	Phil Esposito	Boston	1974-75	79	127	1.61
Mario Lemieux	Pittsburgh	1991-92	64	131	2.05	Steve Yzerman	Detroit	1989-90	79	127	1.61
Bill Cowley	Boston	1943-44	36	71	1.97	Peter Stastny	Quebec	1985-86	76	122	1.61
Phil Esposito	Boston	1970-71	78	152	1.95	Mario Lemieux	Pittsburgh	1996-97	76	122	1.61
Wayne Gretzky	Los Angeles	1989-90	73	142	1.95	Michel Goulet	Quebec	1983-84	75	121	1.61
Steve Yzerman	Detroit	1988-89	80	155	1.94	Wayne Gretzky	Los Angeles	1993-94	81	130	1.60
Bernie Nicholls	Los Angeles	1988-89	79	150	1.90	Bryan Trottier	NY Islanders	1977-78	77	123	1.60
Adam Oates	St. Louis	1990-91	61	115	1.89	Bobby Orr	Boston	1972-73	63	101	1.60
Phil Esposito	Boston	1973-74	78	145	1.86	Guy Chouinard	Calgary	1980-81	52	83	1.60
Jari Kurri	Edmonton	1984-85	73	135	1.85	Elmer Lach	Montreal	1944-45	50	80	1.60
Mike Bossy	NY Islanders	1981-82	80	147	1.84	Pierre Turgeon	NY Islanders	1992-93	83	132	1.59
Jaromir Jagr	Pittsburgh	1995-96	82	149	1.82	Steve Yzerman	Detroit	1987-88	64	102	1.59
Mario Lemieux	Pittsburgh	1985-86	79	141	1.78	Mike Bossy	NY Islanders	1978-79	80	126	1.58
Bobby Orr	Boston	1970-71	78	139	1.78	Paul Coffey	Edmonton	1983-84	80	126	1.58
Jari Kurri	Edmonton	1983-84	64	113	1.77	Marcel Dionne	Los Angeles	1984-85	80	126	1.58
Mario Lemieux	Pittsburgh	2000-01	43	76	1.77	Bobby Orr	Boston	1969-70	76	120	1.58
Pat LaFontaine	Buffalo	1992-93	84	148	1.76	Eric Lindros	Philadelphia	1995-96	73	115	1.58
Bryan Trottier	NY Islanders	1978-79	76	134	1.76	Charlie Simmer	Los Angeles	1979-80	64	101	1.58
Mike Bossy	NY Islanders	1983-84	67	118	1.76	Teemu Selanne	Winnipeg	1992-93	84	132	1.57
Paul Coffey	Edmonton	1985-86	79	138	1.75	Jaromir Jagr	Pittsburgh	1998-99	81	127	1.57
Phil Esposito	Boston	1971-72	76	133	1.75	Bobby Clarke	Philadelphia	1975-76	76	119	1.57
Peter Stastny	Quebec	1981-82	80	139	1.74	Guy Lafleur	Montreal	1975-76	80	125	1.56
Wayne Gretzky	Edmonton	1979-80	79	137	1.73	Dave Taylor	Los Angeles	1980-81	72	112	1.56
Jean Ratelle	NY Rangers	1971-72	63	109	1.73	Denis Savard	Chicago	1982-83	78	121	1.55
Marcel Dionne	Los Angeles	1979-80	80	137	1.71	Ron Francis	Pittsburgh	1995-96	77	119	1.55
Herb Cain	Boston	1943-44	48	82	1.71	Mike Bossy	NY Islanders	1985-86	80	123	1.54
Guy Lafleur	Montreal	1976-77	80	136	1.70	Kevin Stevens	Pittsburgh	1991-92	80	123	1.54
Dennis Maruk	Washington	1981-82	80	136	1.70	Bobby Orr	Boston	1971-72	76	117	1.54
Phil Esposito	Boston	1968-69	74	126	1.70	Mike Bossy	NY Islanders	1984-85	76	117	1.54
Guy Lafleur	Montreal	1974-75	70	119	1.70	Kevin Stevens	Pittsburgh	1992-93	72	111	1.54
Mario Lemieux	Pittsburgh	1986-87	63	107	1.70	Doug Bentley	Chicago	1943-44	50	77	1.54
Adam Oates	Boston	1992-93	84	142	1.69	Doug Gilmour	Toronto	1992-93	83	127	1.53
Bobby Orr	Boston	1974-75	80	135	1.69	Marcel Dionne	Los Angeles	1976-77	80	122	1.53
Marcel Dionne	Los Angeles	1980-81	80	135	1.69	Jaromir Jagr	Pittsburgh	99-2000	63	96	1.52
Guy Lafleur	Montreal	1977-78	78	132	1.69	Eric Lindros	Philadelphia	1996-97	52	79	1.52
Guy Lafleur	Montreal	1979-80	74	125	1.69	Eric Lindros	Philadelphia	1994-95	46	70	1.52
Rob Brown	Pittsburgh	1988-89	68	115	1.69	Marcel Dionne	Detroit	1974-75	80	121	1.51
Jari Kurri	Edmonton	1985-86	78	131	1.68	Mike Bossy	NY Islanders	1980-81	79	119	1.51
Brett Hull	St. Louis	1990-91	78	131	1.68	Paul Coffey	Edmonton	1984-85	80	121	1.51
Phil Esposito	Boston	1972-73	78	130	1.67	Dale Hawerchuk	Winnipeg	1987-88	80	121	1.51
Cooney Weiland	Boston	1929-30	44	73	1.66	Paul Coffey	Pittsburgh	1988-89	75	113	1.51
Alexander Mogilny	Buffalo	1992-93	77	127	1.65	Jaromir Jagr	Pittsburgh	1996-97	63	95	1.51

Bernie Nicholls (surrounded by Luc Robitaille and Steve Duchesne) had one of the most productive seasons in hockey history when he had 70 goals and 80 assists for the Los Angeles Kings in 1988-89.

Columbus's Rick Nash (far right) tied for the NHL lead as a 19-year-old with 41 goals in his second season in 2003-04. Now with Toronto, Eric Lindros (right) had 41 goals as a rookie with Philadelphia in a higher scoring time back in 1992-93.

Rookie Scoring Records

All-Time Top 50 Goal-Scoring Rookies

	Rookie	Team	Position	Season	GP	G	A	PTS
1.	* Teemu Selanne	Winnipeg	Right wing	1992-93	84	**76**	56	132
2.	* Mike Bossy	NY Islanders	Right wing	1977-78	73	**53**	38	91
3.	* Joe Nieuwendyk	Calgary	Center	1987-88	75	**51**	41	92
4.	* Dale Hawerchuk	Winnipeg	Center	1981-82	80	**45**	58	103
	* Luc Robitaille	Los Angeles	Left wing	1986-87	79	**45**	39	84
6.	Rick Martin	Buffalo	Left wing	1971-72	73	**44**	30	74
	Barry Pederson	Boston	Center	1981-82	80	**44**	48	92
8.	* Steve Larmer	Chicago	Right wing	1982-83	80	**43**	47	90
	* Mario Lemieux	Pittsburgh	Center	1984-85	73	**43**	57	100
10.	Eric Lindros	Philadelphia	Center	1992-93	61	**41**	34	75
11.	Darryl Sutter	Chicago	Left wing	1980-81	76	**40**	22	62
	Sylvain Turgeon	Hartford	Left wing	1983-84	76	**40**	32	72
	Warren Young	Pittsburgh	Left wing	1984-85	80	**40**	32	72
14.	* Eric Vail	Atlanta	Left wing	1974-75	72	**39**	21	60
	Anton Stastny	Quebec	Left wing	1980-81	80	**39**	46	85
	* Peter Stastny	Quebec	Center	1980-81	77	**39**	70	109
	Steve Yzerman	Detroit	Center	1983-84	80	**39**	48	87
18.	* Gilbert Perreault	Buffalo	Center	1970-71	78	**38**	34	72
	Neal Broten	Minnesota	Center	1981-82	73	**38**	60	98
	Ray Sheppard	Buffalo	Right wing	1987-88	74	**38**	27	65
	Mikael Renberg	Philadelphia	Left wing	1993-94	83	**38**	44	82
22.	Jorgen Pettersson	St. Louis	Left wing	1980-81	62	**37**	36	73
	Jimmy Carson	Los Angeles	Center	1986-87	80	**37**	42	79
24.	Mike Foligno	Detroit	Right wing	1979-80	80	**36**	35	71
	Mike Bullard	Pittsburgh	Center	1981-82	75	**36**	27	63
	Paul MacLean	Winnipeg	Right wing	1981-82	74	**36**	25	61
	Tony Granato	NY Rangers	Right wing	1988-89	78	**36**	27	63
28.	Marian Stastny	Quebec	Right wing	1981-82	74	**35**	54	89
	Brian Bellows	Minnesota	Right wing	1982-83	78	**35**	30	65
	Tony Amonte	NY Rangers	Right wing	1991-92	79	**35**	34	69
31.	Nels Stewart	Mtl. Maroons	Center	1925-26	36	**34**	8	42
	* Danny Grant	Minnesota	Left wing	1968-69	75	**34**	31	65
	Norm Ferguson	Oakland	Right wing	1968-69	76	**34**	20	54
	Brian Propp	Philadelphia	Left wing	1979-80	80	**34**	41	75
	Wendel Clark	Toronto	Left wing	1985-86	66	**34**	11	45
	* Pavel Bure	Vancouver	Right wing	1991-92	65	**34**	26	60
37.	* Willi Plett	Atlanta	Right wing	1976-77	64	**33**	23	56
	Dale McCourt	Detroit	Center	1977-78	76	**33**	39	72
	Mark Pavelich	NY Rangers	Center	1981-82	79	**33**	43	76
	Ron Flockhart	Philadelphia	Center	1981-82	72	**33**	39	72
	Steve Bozek	Los Angeles	Center	1981-82	71	**33**	23	56
	Jason Arnott	Edmonton	Center	1993-94	78	**33**	35	68
43.	Bill Mosienko	Chicago	Right wing	1943-44	50	**32**	38	70
	Michel Bergeron	Detroit	Right wing	1975-76	72	**32**	27	59
	* Bryan Trottier	NY Islanders	Center	1975-76	80	**32**	63	95
	Don Murdoch	NY Rangers	Right wing	1976-77	59	**32**	24	56
	Jari Kurri	Edmonton	Left wing	1980-81	75	**32**	43	75
	Bobby Carpenter	Washington	Center	1981-82	80	**32**	35	67
	Kjell Dahlin	Montreal	Right wing	1985-86	77	**32**	39	71
	Petr Klima	Detroit	Left wing	1985-86	74	**32**	24	56
	Darren Turcotte	NY Rangers	Right wing	1989-90	76	**32**	34	66
	Joe Juneau	Boston	Center	1992-93	84	**32**	70	102

* Calder Trophy Winner

All-Time Top 50 Point-Scoring Rookies

	Rookie	Team	Position	Season	GP	G	A	PTS
1.	* Teemu Selanne	Winnipeg	Right wing	1992-93	84	76	56	**132**
2.	* Peter Stastny	Quebec	Center	1980-81	77	39	70	**109**
3.	* Dale Hawerchuk	Winnipeg	Center	1981-82	80	45	58	**103**
4.	Joe Juneau	Boston	Center	1992-93	84	32	70	**102**
5.	* Mario Lemieux	Pittsburgh	Center	1984-85	73	43	57	**100**
6.	Neal Broten	Minnesota	Center	1981-82	73	38	60	**98**
7.	* Bryan Trottier	NY Islanders	Center	1975-76	80	32	63	**95**
8.	Barry Pederson	Boston	Center	1981-82	80	44	48	**92**
	* Joe Nieuwendyk	Calgary	Center	1987-88	75	51	41	**92**
10.	* Mike Bossy	NY Islanders	Right wing	1977-78	73	53	38	**91**
11.	* Steve Larmer	Chicago	Right wing	1982-83	80	43	47	**90**
12.	Marian Stastny	Quebec	Right wing	1981-82	74	35	54	**89**
13.	Steve Yzerman	Detroit	Center	1983-84	80	39	48	**87**
14.	* Sergei Makarov	Calgary	Right wing	1989-90	80	24	62	**86**
15.	Anton Stastny	Quebec	Left wing	1980-81	80	39	46	**85**
16.	* Luc Robitaille	Los Angeles	Left wing	1986-87	79	45	39	**84**
17.	Mikael Renberg	Philadelphia	Left wing	1993-94	83	38	44	**82**
18.	Jimmy Carson	Los Angeles	Center	1986-87	80	37	42	**79**
	Sergei Fedorov	Detroit	Center	1990-91	77	31	48	**79**
	Alexei Yashin	Ottawa	Center	1993-94	83	30	49	**79**
21.	Marcel Dionne	Detroit	Center	1971-72	78	28	49	**77**
22.	Larry Murphy	Los Angeles	Defense	1980-81	80	16	60	**76**
	Mark Pavelich	NY Rangers	Center	1981-82	79	33	43	**76**
	Dave Poulin	Philadelphia	Center	1983-84	73	31	45	**76**
25.	Brian Propp	Philadelphia	Left wing	1979-80	80	34	41	**75**
	Jari Kurri	Edmonton	Left wing	1980-81	75	32	43	**75**
	Denis Savard	Chicago	Center	1980-81	76	28	47	**75**
	Mike Modano	Minnesota	Center	1989-90	80	29	46	**75**
	Eric Lindros	Philadelphia	Center	1992-93	61	41	34	**75**
30.	Rick Martin	Buffalo	Left wing	1971-72	73	44	30	**74**
	* Bobby Smith	Minnesota	Center	1978-79	80	30	44	**74**
32.	Jorgen Pettersson	St. Louis	Left wing	1980-81	62	37	36	**73**
33.	* Gilbert Perreault	Buffalo	Center	1970-71	78	38	34	**72**
	Dale McCourt	Detroit	Center	1977-78	76	33	39	**72**
	Ron Flockhart	Philadelphia	Center	1981-82	72	33	39	**72**
	Sylvain Turgeon	Hartford	Left wing	1983-84	76	40	32	**72**
	Warren Young	Pittsburgh	Left wing	1984-85	80	40	32	**72**
	Carey Wilson	Calgary	Center	1984-85	74	24	48	**72**
	Alex Zhamnov	Winnipeg	Center	1992-93	68	25	47	**72**
40.	Mike Foligno	Detroit	Right wing	1979-80	80	36	35	**71**
	Dave Christian	Winnipeg	Center	1980-81	80	28	43	**71**
	Mats Naslund	Montreal	Left wing	1982-83	74	26	45	**71**
	Kjell Dahlin	Montreal	Right wing	1985-86	77	32	39	**71**
	* Brian Leetch	NY Rangers	Defense	1988-89	68	23	48	**71**
45.	Bill Mosienko	Chicago	Right wing	1943-44	50	32	38	**70**
	* Scott Gomez	New Jersey	Center	99-2000	82	19	51	**70**
47.	Roland Eriksson	Minnesota	Center	1976-77	80	25	44	**69**
	Tony Amonte	NY Rangers	Right wing	1991-92	79	35	34	**69**
49.	Jude Drouin	Minnesota	Center	1970-71	75	16	52	**68**
	Pierre Larouche	Pittsburgh	Center	1974-75	79	31	37	**68**
	Ron Francis	Hartford	Center	1981-82	59	25	43	**68**
	* Gary Suter	Calgary	Defense	1985-86	80	18	50	**68**
	Jason Arnott	Edmonton	Center	1993-94	84	33	35	**68**

50-Goal Seasons

Bobby Clarke

Wayne Babych

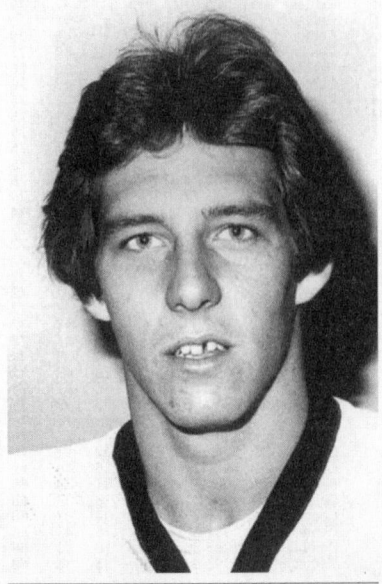

Al Secord

Player	Team	Date of 50th Goal	Score			Goaltender	Player's Game No.	Team Game No.	Total Goals	Total Games	Age When First 50th Scored (Yrs. & Mos.)
Maurice Richard	Mtl.	18-3-45	Mtl. 4	at	Bos. 2	Harvey Bennett	50	50	50	50	23.7
Bernie Geoffrion	Mtl.	16-3-61	Tor. 2	at	Mtl. 5	Cesare Maniago	62	68	50	64	30.1
Bobby Hull	Chi.	25-3-62	Chi. 1	at	NYR 4	Gump Worsley	70	70	50	70	23.2
Bobby Hull	Chi.	2-3-66	Det. 4	at	Chi. 5	Hank Bassen	52	57	54	65	
Bobby Hull	Chi.	18-3-67	Chi. 5	at	Tor. 9	Bruce Gamble	63	66	52	66	
Bobby Hull	Chi.	5-3-69	NYR 4	at	Chi. 4	Ed Giacomin	64	66	58	74	
Phil Esposito	Bos.	20-2-71	at L.A. 5	at	L.A. 5	Denis DeJordy	58	58	76	78	29.0
John Bucyk	Bos.	16-3-71	Bos. 11	at	Det. 4	Roy Edwards	69	69	51	78	35.10
Phil Esposito	Bos.	20-2-72	Bos. 3	at	Chi. 1	Tony Esposito	60	60	66	76	
Bobby Hull	Chi.	2-4-72	Det. 1	at	Chi. 6	Andy Brown	78	78	50	78	
Vic Hadfield	NYR	2-4-72	Mtl. 6	at	NYR 5	Denis DeJordy	78	78	50	78	31.6
Phil Esposito	Bos.	25-3-73	Buf. 1	at	Bos. 6	Roger Crozier	75	75	55	78	
Mickey Redmond	Det.	27-3-73	Det. 8	at	Tor. 1	Ron Low	73	75	52	76	25.3
Rick MacLeish	Phi.	1-4-73	Phi. 4	at	Pit. 5	Cam Newton	78	78	50	78	23.2
Phil Esposito	Bos.	20-2-74	Bos. 5	at	Min. 5	Cesare Maniago	56	56	68	78	
Mickey Redmond	Det.	23-3-74	NYR 3	at	Det. 5	Ed Giacomin	69	71	51	76	
Ken Hodge	Bos.	6-4-74	Bos. 2	at	Mtl. 6	Michel Larocque	75	77	50	76	29.10
Rick Martin	Buf.	7-4-74	St.L. 2	at	Buf. 5	Wayne Stephenson	78	78	52	78	22.9
Phil Esposito	Bos.	8-2-75	Bos. 8	at	Det. 5	Jim Rutherford	54	54	61	79	
Guy Lafleur	Mtl.	29-3-75	K.C. 1	at	Mtl. 4	Denis Herron	66	76	53	70	23.6
Danny Grant	Det.	2-4-75	Wsh. 3	at	Det. 8	John Adams	78	78	50	80	29.2
Rick Martin	Buf.	3-4-75	Bos. 2	at	Buf. 4	Ken Broderick	67	79	52	68	
Reggie Leach	Phi.	14-3-76	Atl. 1	at	Phi. 6	Dan Bouchard	69	69	61	80	25.11
Jean Pronovost	Pit.	24-3-76	Bos. 5	at	Pit. 5	Gilles Gilbert	74	74	52	80	30.3
Guy Lafleur	Mtl.	27-3-76	K.C. 2	at	Mtl. 8	Denis Herron	76	76	56	80	
Bill Barber	Phi.	3-4-76	Buf. 2	at	Phi. 5	Al Smith	79	79	50	80	23.9
Pierre Larouche	Pit.	3-4-76	Wsh. 5	at	Pit. 4	Ron Low	75	79	53	76	20.5
Danny Gare	Buf.	4-4-76	Tor. 2	at	Buf. 5	Gord McRae	79	80	50	79	21.11
Steve Shutt	Mtl.	1-3-77	Mtl. 5	at	NYI 4	Glenn Resch	65	65	60	80	24.8
Guy Lafleur	Mtl.	6-3-77	Mtl. 1	at	Buf. 4	Don Edwards	68	68	56	80	
Marcel Dionne	L.A.	2-4-77	Min. 2	at	L.A. 7	Pete LoPresti	79	79	53	80	25.8
Guy Lafleur	Mtl.	8-3-78	Wsh. 3	at	Mtl. 4	Jim Bedard	63	65	60	78	
Mike Bossy	NYI	1-4-78	Wsh. 2	at	NYI 3	Bernie Wolfe	69	76	53	73	21.2
Mike Bossy	NYI	24-2-79	Det. 1	at	NYI 3	Rogie Vachon	58	58	69	80	
Marcel Dionne	L.A.	11-3-79	L.A. 3	at	Phi. 6	Wayne Stephenson	68	68	59	80	
Guy Lafleur	Mtl.	31-3-79	Pit. 3	at	Mtl. 5	Denis Herron	76	76	52	80	
Guy Chouinard	Atl.	6-4-79	NYR 2	at	Atl. 9	John Davidson	79	79	50	80	22.5
Marcel Dionne	L.A.	12-3-80	L.A. 2	at	Pit. 4	Nick Ricci	70	70	53	80	
Mike Bossy	NYI	16-3-80	NYI 6	at	Chi. 1	Tony Esposito	68	71	51	75	
Charlie Simmer	L.A.	19-3-80	Det. 3	at	L.A. 4	Jim Rutherford	57	73	56	64	26.0
Pierre Larouche	Mtl.	25-3-80	Chi. 4	at	Mtl. 8	Tony Esposito	72	75	50	73	
Danny Gare	Buf.	27-3-80	Det. 1	at	Buf. 10	Jim Rutherford	71	75	56	76	
Blaine Stoughton	Hfd.	28-3-80	Hfd. 4	at	Van. 4	Glen Hanlon	75	75	56	80	27.0
Guy Lafleur	Mtl.	2-4-80	Mtl. 7	at	Det. 2	Rogie Vachon	72	78	50	74	
Wayne Gretzky	Edm.	2-4-80	Min. 1	at	Edm. 1	Gary Edwards	78	79	51	79	19.2
Reggie Leach	Phi.	3-4-80	Wsh. 2	at	Phi. 4	empty net	75	79	50	76	
Mike Bossy	NYI	24-1-81	Que. 3	at	NYI 7	Ron Grahame	50	50	68	79	
Charlie Simmer	L.A.	26-1-81	L.A. 7	at	Que. 5	Michel Dion	51	51	56	65	
Marcel Dionne	L.A.	8-3-81	L.A. 4	at	Wpg. 1	Markus Mattsson	68	68	58	80	
Wayne Babych	St.L.	12-3-81	St.L. 3	at	Mtl. 4	Richard Sevigny	70	68	54	78	22.9
Wayne Gretzky	Edm.	15-3-81	Edm. 3	at	Cgy. 3	Pat Riggin	69	69	55	80	
Rick Kehoe	Pit.	16-3-81	Pit. 7	at	Edm. 6	Eddie Mio	70	70	55	80	29.7
Jacques Richard	Que.	29-3-81	Mtl. 0	at	Que. 4	Richard Sevigny	76	75	52	78	28.6
Dennis Maruk	Wsh.	5-4-81	Det. 2	at	Wsh. 7	Larry Lozinski	80	80	50	80	25.3
Wayne Gretzky	Edm.	30-12-81	Phi. 5	at	Edm. 7	empty net	39	39	92	80	
Dennis Maruk	Wsh.	21-2-82	Wpg. 3	at	Wsh. 6	Doug Soetaert	61	61	60	80	
Mike Bossy	NYI	4-3-82	Tor. 1	at	NYI 10	Michel Larocque	66	66	64	80	
Dino Ciccarelli	Min.	8-3-82	St.L. 1	at	Min. 8	Mike Liut	67	68	55	76	22.1
Rick Vaive	Tor.	24-3-82	St.L. 3	at	Tor. 4	Mike Liut	72	75	54	77	22.10
Blaine Stoughton	Hfd.	28-3-82	Min. 5	at	Hfd. 2	Gilles Meloche	76	76	52	80	
Rick Middleton	Bos.	28-3-82	Bos. 5	at	Buf. 9	Paul Harrison	72	77	51	75	28.11
Marcel Dionne	L.A.	30-3-82	Cgy. 7	at	L.A. 5	Pat Riggin	75	77	50	78	
Mark Messier	Edm.	31-3-82	L.A. 3	at	Edm. 7	Mario Lessard	78	79	50	78	21.3
Bryan Trottier	NYI	3-4-82	Phi. 3	at	NYI 6	Pete Peeters	79	79	50	80	25.9
Lanny McDonald	Cgy.	18-2-83	Cgy. 1	at	Buf. 5	Bob Sauve	60	60	66	80	30.0
Wayne Gretzky	Edm.	19-2-83	Edm. 10	at	Pit. 7	Nick Ricci	60	60	71	80	
Michel Goulet	Que.	5-3-83	Hfd. 3	at	Que. 10	Mike Veisor	67	67	57	80	22.11
Mike Bossy	NYI	12-3-83	Wsh. 2	at	NYI 6	Al Jensen	70	71	60	79	
Marcel Dionne	L.A.	17-3-83	Que. 3	at	L.A. 4	Dan Bouchard	71	71	56	80	
Al Secord	Chi.	20-3-83	Tor. 3	at	Chi. 7	Mike Palmateer	73	73	54	80	25.0
Rick Vaive	Tor.	30-3-83	Tor. 4	at	Det. 2	Gilles Gilbert	76	78	51	78	
Wayne Gretzky	Edm.	7-1-84	Hfd. 3	at	Edm. 5	Greg Millen	42	42	87	74	
Michel Goulet	Que.	8-3-84	Que. 8	at	Pit. 6	Denis Herron	63	69	56	75	
Rick Vaive	Tor.	14-3-84	Min. 3	at	Tor. 3	Gilles Meloche	69	72	52	76	
Mike Bullard	Pit.	14-3-84	Pit. 6	at	L.A. 7	Markus Mattsson	71	72	51	76	23.0
Jari Kurri	Edm.	15-3-84	Edm. 2	at	Mtl. 3	Rick Wamsley	57	73	52	64	23.10
Glenn Anderson	Edm.	21-3-84	Hfd. 3	at	Edm. 5	Greg Millen	76	76	54	80	23.6
Tim Kerr	Phi.	22-3-84	Pit. 4	at	Phi. 13	Denis Herron	74	75	54	79	24.3
Mike Bossy	NYI	31-3-84	NYI 3	at	Wsh. 1	Pat Riggin	67	79	51	67	
Wayne Gretzky	Edm.	26-1-85	Pit. 3	at	Edm. 6	Denis Herron	49	49	73	80	
Jari Kurri	Edm.	3-2-85	Hfd. 3	at	Edm. 6	Greg Millen	50	53	71	73	
Mike Bossy	NYI	5-3-85	Phi. 5	at	NYI 4	Bob Froese	61	65	58	76	
Michel Goulet	Que.	6-3-85	Buf. 3	at	Que. 4	Tom Barrasso	62	73	55	69	
Tim Kerr	Phi.	7-3-85	Wsh. 6	at	Phi. 9	Pat Riggin	63	65	54	74	
John Ogrodnick	Det.	13-3-85	Det. 6	at	Edm. 7	Grant Fuhr	69	69	55	79	25.9
Bob Carpenter	Wsh.	21-3-85	Wsh. 2	at	Mtl. 3	Steve Penney	72	72	53	80	21.9

Player	Team	Date of 50th Goal	Score		Goaltender	Player's Game No.	Team Game No.	Total Goals	Total Games	Age When First 50th Scored (Yrs. & Mos.)
Dale Hawerchuk	Wpg.	29-3-85	Chi. 5	at Wpg. 5	W. Skorodenski	77	77	53	80	21.11
Mike Gartner	Wsh.	7-4-85	Pit. 3	at Wsh. 7	Brian Ford	80	80	50	80	25.5
Jari Kurri	Edm.	4-3-86	Edm. 6	at Van. 2	Richard Brodeur	63	65	68	78	
Mike Bossy	NYI	11-3-86	Cgy. 4	at NYI 8	Reggie Lemelin	67	67	61	80	
Glenn Anderson	Edm.	14-3-86	Det. 3	at Edm. 12	Greg Stefan	63	71	54	72	
Michel Goulet	Que.	17-3-86	Que. 8	at Mtl. 6	Patrick Roy	67	72	53	75	
Wayne Gretzky	Edm.	18-3-86	Wpg. 2	at Edm. 6	Brian Hayward	72	72	52	80	
Tim Kerr	Phi.	20-3-86	Pit. 1	at Phi. 5	Roberto Romano	68	72	58	76	
Wayne Gretzky	Edm.	4-2-87	Edm. 6	at Min. 5	Don Beaupre	55	55	62	79	
Dino Ciccarelli	Min.	7-3-87	Pit. 7	at Min. 3	Gilles Meloche	66	66	52	80	
Mario Lemieux	Pit.	12-3-87	Que. 3	at Pit. 6	Mario Gosselin	53	70	54	63	21.5
Tim Kerr	Phi.	17-3-87	NYR 1	at Phi. 4	J. Vanbiesbrouck	67	71	58	75	
Jari Kurri	Edm.	17-3-87	N.J. 4	at Edm. 7	Craig Billington	69	70	54	79	
Mario Lemieux	Pit.	2-2-88	Wsh. 2	at Pit. 3	Pete Peeters	51	54	70	77	
Steve Yzerman	Det.	1-3-88	Buf. 0	at Det. 4	Tom Barrasso	64	64	50	64	22.10
Joe Nieuwendyk	Cgy.	12-3-88	Buf. 4	at Cgy. 10	Tom Barrasso	66	70	51	75	21.5
Craig Simpson	Edm.	15-3-88	Buf. 4	at Edm. 6	Jacques Cloutier	71	71	56	80	21.1
Jimmy Carson	L.A.	26-3-88	Chi. 5	at L.A. 9	Darren Pang	77	77	55	88	19.8
Luc Robitaille	L.A.	1-4-88	L.A. 6	at Cgy. 3	Mike Vernon	79	79	53	80	21.10
Hakan Loob	Cgy.	3-4-88	Min. 1	at Cgy. 4	Don Beaupre	80	80	50	80	27.9
Stephane Richer	Mtl.	3-4-88	Mtl. 4	at Buf. 4	Tom Barrasso	72	80	50	72	21.10
Mario Lemieux	Pit.	20-1-89	Pit. 3	at Wpg. 7	Pokey Reddick	44	46	85	76	
Bernie Nicholls	L.A.	28-1-89	Edm. 7	at L.A. 6	Grant Fuhr	51	51	70	79	27.7
Steve Yzerman	Det.	5-2-89	Det. 6	at Wpg. 2	Pokey Reddick	55	55	65	80	
Wayne Gretzky	L.A.	4-3-89	Phi. 2	at L.A. 6	Ron Hextall	66	67	54	78	
Joe Nieuwendyk	Cgy.	21-3-89	NYI 1	at Cgy. 4	Mark Fitzpatrick	72	74	51	77	
Joe Mullen	Cgy.	31-3-89	Wpg. 1	at Cgy. 4	Bob Essensa	78	79	51	79	32.1
Brett Hull	St.L.	6-2-90	Tor. 4	at St.L. 6	Jeff Reese	54	54	72	80	25.6
Steve Yzerman	Det.	24-2-90	Det. 3	at NYI 3	Glenn Healy	63	63	62	79	
Cam Neely	Bos.	10-3-90	Bos. 3	at NYI 3	Mark Fitzpatrick	69	71	55	76	24.9
Luc Robitaille	L.A.	31-3-90 -	L.A. 3	at Van. 6	Kirk McLean	79	79	52	80	
Brian Bellows	Min.	22-3-90	Min. 5	at Det. 1	Tim Cheveldae	75	75	55	80	25.6
Pat LaFontaine	NYI	24-3-90	NYI 5	at Edm. 5	Bill Ranford	71	77	54	74	25.1
Stephane Richer	Mtl.	24-3-90	Mtl. 4	at Hfd. 7	Peter Sidorkiewicz	75	77	51	75	
Gary Leeman	Tor.	28-3-90	NYI 6	at Tor. 3	Mark Fitzpatrick	78	78	51	80	26.1
Brett Hull	St.L.	25-1-91	St.L. 9	at Det. 4	David Gagnon	49	49	86	78	
Cam Neely	Bos.	26-3-91	Bos. 7	at Que. 4	empty net	67	78	51	69	
Theoren Fleury	Cgy.	26-3-91	Van. 2	at Cgy. 7	Bob Mason	77	77	51	79	22.9
Steve Yzerman	Det.	30-3-91	NYR 5	at Det. 6	Mike Richter	79	79	51	80	
Brett Hull	St.L.	28-1-92	St.L. 3	at L.A. 3	Kelly Hrudey	50	50	70	73	
Jeremy Roenick	Chi.	7-3-92	Chi. 2	at Bos. 1	Daniel Berthiaume	67	67	53	80	22.2
Kevin Stevens	Pit.	24-3-92	Pit. 3	at Det. 4	Tim Cheveldae	74	74	54	80	26.11
Gary Roberts	Cgy.	31-3-92	Edm. 2	at Cgy. 5	Bill Ranford	73	77	53	76	25.10
Alexander Mogilny	Buf.	3-2-93	Hfd. 2	at Buf. 3	Sean Burke	46	53	76	77	23.11
Teemu Selanne	Wpg.	28-2-93	Min. 6	at Wpg. 7	Darcy Wakaluk	63	63	76	84	22.6
Pavel Bure	Van.	1-3-93	Van. 5	at Buf. 2*	Grant Fuhr	63	63	60	83	21.11
Steve Yzerman	Det.	10-3-93	Det. 6	at Edm. 3	Bill Ranford	70	70	58	84	
Luc Robitaille	L.A.	15-3-93	L.A. 4	at Buf. 2	Grant Fuhr	69	69	63	84	
Brett Hull	St.L.	20-3-93	St.L. 2	at L.A. 3	Robb Stauber	73	73	54	80	
Mario Lemieux	Pit.	21-3-93	Pit. 6	at Edm. 4**	Ron Tugnutt	48	72	69	60	
Kevin Stevens	Pit.	21-3-93	Pit. 6	at Edm. 4**	Ron Tugnutt	62	72	55	72	
Dave Andreychuk	Tor.	23-3-93	Tor. 5	at Wpg. 4	Bob Essensa	72	73	54	83	29.6
Pat LaFontaine	Buf.	28-3-93	Ott. 1	at Buf. 3	Peter Sidorkiewicz	75	75	53	84	
Pierre Turgeon	NYI	2-4-93	NYI 3	at NYR 2	Mike Richter	75	76	58	83	23.8
Mark Recchi	Phi.	3-4-93	T.B. 2	at Phi. 6	J-C Bergeron	77	77	53	84	25.2
Jeremy Roenick	Chi.	15-4-93	Tor. 2	at Chi. 3	Felix Potvin	84	84	50	84	
Brendan Shanahan	St.L.	15-4-93	T.B. 5	at St.L. 6	Pat Jablonski	71	84	51	71	24.3
Cam Neely	Bos.	7-3-94	Wsh. 3	at Bos. 6	Don Beaupre	44	66	50	49	
Sergei Fedorov	Det.	15-3-94	Van. 2	at Det. 5	Kirk McLean	67	69	56	82	24.3
Pavel Bure	Van.	23-3-94	Van. 2	at L.A. 3	empty net	65	73	60	76	
Adam Graves	NYR	23-3-94	NYR 5	at Edm. 3	Bill Ranford	74	74	51	84	25.11
Dave Andreychuk	Tor.	24-3-94	S.J. 2	at Tor. 1	Arturs Irbe	73	74	53	83	
Brett Hull	St.L.	25-3-94	Dal. 3	at St.L. 5	Andy Moog	71	74	52	81	
Ray Sheppard	Det.	29-3-94	Hfd. 2	at Det. 6	Sean Burke	74	76	52	82	27.10
Brendan Shanahan	St.L.	12-4-94	St.L. 5	at Dal. 9	Andy Moog	80	83	52	81	
Mike Modano	Dal.	12-4-94	St.L. 5	at Dal. 9	Curtis Joseph	75	83	50	76	23.11
Mario Lemieux	Pit.	23-2-96	Hfd. 4	at Pit. 5	Sean Burke	50	59	69	70	
Jaromir Jagr	Pit.	23-2-96	Hfd. 4	at Pit. 5	Sean Burke	59	59	62	82	24.0
Alexander Mogilny	Van.	29-2-96	St.L. 2	at Van. 2	Grant Fuhr	60	63	55	79	
Peter Bondra	Wsh.	3-4-96	Wsh. 5	at Buf. 1	Andrei Trefilov	62	77	52	67	28.1
Joe Sakic	Col.	7-4-96	Col. 4	at Dal. 1	empty net	79	79	51	82	26.7
John LeClair	Phi.	10-4-96	Phi. 5	at N.J. 1	Corey Schwab	80	80	51	82	26.7
Keith Tkachuk	Wpg.	12-4-96	L.A. 3	at Wpg. 5	empty net	75	81	50	76	24.0
Paul Kariya	Ana.	14-4-96	Wpg. 2	at Ana. 5	N. Khabibulin	82	82	50	82	21.5
Keith Tkachuk	Phx.	6-4-97	Phx. 1	at Col. 2	Patrick Roy	78	79	52	81	
Teemu Selanne	Ana.	9-4-97	L.A. 1	at Ana. 4	empty net	77	81	51	78	
Mario Lemieux	Pit.	11-4-97	Pit. 2	at Fla. 4	J. Vanbiesbrouck	75	81	50	76	
John LeClair	Phi.	13-4-97	N.J. 4	at Phi. 5	Mike Dunham	82	82	50	82	
Teemu Selanne	Ana.	25-3-98	Ana. 3	at Chi. 2	Jeff Hackett	66	71	52	73	
John LeClair	Phi.	13-4-98	Phi. 1	at Buf. 2	Dominik Hasek	79	79	51	82	
Pavel Bure	Van.	17-4-98	Cgy. 4	at Van. 2	Dwayne Roloson	81	81	51	82	
Peter Bondra	Wsh.	18-4-98	Wsh. 4	at Car. 3	Mike Fountain	75	80	52	76	
Pavel Bure	Fla.	18-3-00	Fla. 4	at NYI 2	empty net	63	71	58	74	
Pavel Bure	Fla.	16-3-01	Pit. 6	at Fla. 3	Johan Hedberg	72	72	59	82	
Joe Sakic	Col.	4-4-01	Ana. 1	at Col. 1	J-S Giguere	80	80	54	82	
Jaromir Jagr	Pit.	4-4-01	T.B. 2	at Pit. 4	Kevin Weekes	80	80	52	81	
Jarome Iginla	Cgy.	7-4-02	Cgy. 2	at Chi. 3	Jocelyn Thibault	79	79	52	82	24.9
Milan Hejduk	Col.	6-4-03	St. L. 2	at Col. 5	Brent Johnson	82	82	50	82	27.1

* neutral site game played at Hamilton; ** neutral site game played at Cleveland

Craig Simpson

Kevin Stevens

Paul Kariya

Marcel Dionne

Guy Chouinard

Rick Middleton

100-Point Seasons

Player	Team	Date of 100th Point	G or A	Score			Player's Game No.	Team Game No.	G - A — PTS	Total Games	Age when first 100th point scored (Yrs. & Mos.)
Phil Esposito	Bos.	2-3-69	(G)	Pit. 0	at	Bos. 4	60	62	49-77 — 126	74	27.1
Bobby Hull	Chi.	20-3-69	(G)	Chi. 5	at	Bos. 5	71	71	58-49 — 107	76	30.2
Gordie Howe	Det.	30-3-69	(G)	Det. 5	at	Chi. 9	76	76	44-59 — 103	76	41.0
Bobby Orr	Bos.	15-3-70	(G)	Det. 5	at	Bos. 5	67	67	33-87 — 120	76	22.11
Phil Esposito	Bos.	6-2-71	(A)	Buf. 3	at	Bos. 4	51	51	76-76 — 152	78	
Bobby Orr	Bos.	20-2-71	(A)	Bos. 4	at	L.A. 5	58	58	37-102 — 139	78	
John Bucyk	Bos.	13-3-71	(G)	Bos. 6	at	Van. 3	68	68	51-65 — 116	78	35.10
Ken Hodge	Bos.	21-3-71	(A)	Buf. 7	at	Bos. 5	72	72	43-62 — 105	78	26.9
Jean Ratelle	NYR	18-2-72	(A)	NYR 2	at	Cal. 2	58	58	46-63 — 109	63	31.4
Phil Esposito	Bos.	19-2-72	(A)	Bos. 6	at	Min. 4	59	59	66-67 — 133	76	
Bobby Orr	Bos.	2-3-72	(A)	Van. 3	at	Bos. 7	64	64	37-80 — 117	76	
Vic Hadfield	NYR	25-3-72	(A)	NYR 3	at	Mtl. 3	74	74	50-56 — 106	78	31.5
Phil Esposito	Bos.	3-3-73	(A)	Bos. 1	at	Mtl. 5	64	64	55-75 — 130	78	
Bobby Clarke	Phi.	29-3-73	(G)	Atl. 2	at	Phi. 4	76	76	37-67 — 104	78	23.7
Bobby Orr	Bos.	31-3-73	(G)	Bos. 3	at	Tor. 7	62	77	29-72 — 101	63	
Rick MacLeish	Phi.	1-4-73	(G)	Phi. 4	at	Pit. 5	78	78	50-50 — 100	78	23.3
Phil Esposito	Bos.	13-2-74	(A)	Bos. 9	at	Cal. 6	53	53	68-77 — 145	78	
Bobby Orr	Bos.	12-3-74	(A)	Buf. 0	at	Bos. 4	62	66	32-90 — 122	74	
Ken Hodge	Bos.	24-3-74	(A)	Mtl. 3	at	Bos. 6	72	72	50-55 — 105	76	
Phil Esposito	Bos.	8-2-75	(A)	Bos. 8	at	Det. 5	54	54	61-66 — 127	79	
Bobby Orr	Bos.	13-2-75	(A)	Bos. 1	at	Buf. 3	57	57	46-89 — 135	80	
Guy Lafleur	Mtl.	7-3-75	(G)	Wsh. 4	at	Mtl. 8	56	66	53-66 — 119	70	24.6
Pete Mahovlich	Mtl.	9-3-75	(G)	Mtl. 5	at	NYR 3	67	67	35-82 — 117	80	29.5
Marcel Dionne	Det.	9-3-75	(A)	Det. 5	at	Phi. 8	67	67	47-74 — 121	80	23.7
Bobby Clarke	Phi.	22-3-75	(A)	Min. 0	at	Phi. 4	72	72	27-89 — 116	80	
Rene Robert	Buf.	5-4-75	(A)	Buf. 4	at	Tor. 2	74	80	40-60 — 100	74	26.4
Guy Lafleur	Mtl.	10-3-76	(G)	Mtl. 5	at	Chi. 1	69	69	56-69 — 125	80	
Bobby Clarke	Phi.	11-3-76	(A)	Buf. 1	at	Phi. 6	64	68	30-89 — 119	76	
Bill Barber	Phi.	18-3-76	(A)	Van. 2	at	Phi. 3	71	71	50-62 — 112	80	23.8
Gilbert Perreault	Buf.	21-3-76	(A)	K.C. 1	at	Buf. 3	73	73	44-69 — 113	80	25.4
Pierre Larouche	Pit.	24-3-76	(A)	Bos. 5	at	Pit. 5	70	74	53-58 — 111	76	20.4
Pete Mahovlich	Mtl.	28-3-76	(A)	Mtl. 2	at	Bos. 2	77	77	34-71 — 105	80	
Jean Ratelle	Bos.	30-3-76	(G)	Buf. 4	at	Bos. 4	77	77	36-69 — 105	80	
Jean Pronovost	Pit.	3-4-76	(A)	Wsh. 5	at	Pit. 4	79	79	52-52 — 104	80	30.4
Darryl Sittler	Tor.	3-4-76	(A)	Bos. 4	at	Tor. 2	78	79	41-59 — 100	79	25.7
Guy Lafleur	Mtl.	26-2-77	(A)	Cle. 3	at	Mtl. 5	63	63	56-80 — 136	80	
Marcel Dionne	L.A.	5-3-77	(G)	Pit. 3	at	L.A. 3	67	67	53-69 — 122	80	
Steve Shutt	Mtl.	27-3-77	(A)	Mtl. 6	at	Det. 0	77	77	60-45 — 105	80	24.9
Bryan Trottier	NYI	25-2-78	(A)	Chi. 1	at	NYI 7	59	60	46-77 — 123	77	21.7
Guy Lafleur	Mtl.	28-2-78	(G)	Det. 3	at	Mtl. 9	69	61	60-72 — 132	78	
Darryl Sittler	Tor.	12-3-78	(A)	Tor. 7	at	Pit. 1	67	67	45-72 — 117	80	
Guy Lafleur	Mtl.	27-2-79	(A)	Mtl. 3	at	NYI 7	61	61	52-77 — 129	80	
Bryan Trottier	NYI	6-3-79	(A)	Buf. 3	at	NYI 2	59	63	47-87 — 134	76	
Marcel Dionne	L.A.	8-3-79	(G)	L.A. 4	at	Buf. 6	66	66	59-71 — 130	80	
Mike Bossy	NYI	11-3-79	(G)	NYI 4	at	Bos. 4	66	66	69-57 — 126	80	22.2
Bob MacMillan	Atl.	15-3-79	(A)	Atl. 4	at	Phi. 5	68	69	37-71 — 108	79	26.6
Guy Chouinard	Atl.	30-3-79	(G)	L.A. 3	at	Atl. 5	75	75	50-57 — 107	80	22.5
Denis Potvin	NYI	8-4-79	(A)	NYI 5	at	NYR 2	73	80	31-70 — 101	73	25.5
Marcel Dionne	L.A.	6-2-80	(A)	L.A. 3	at	Hfd. 7	53	53	53-84 — 137	80	
Guy Lafleur	Mtl.	10-2-80	(A)	Mtl. 3	at	Bos. 2	55	55	50-75 — 125	74	
Wayne Gretzky	Edm.	24-2-80	(A)	Bos. 4	at	Edm. 2	61	62	51-86 — 137	79	19.2
Bryan Trottier	NYI	30-3-80	(A)	NYI 9	at	Que. 6	75	77	42-62 — 104	78	
Gilbert Perreault	Buf.	1-4-80	(A)	Buf. 5	at	Atl. 2	77	77	40-66 — 106	80	
Mike Rogers	Hfd.	4-4-80	(A)	Que. 2	at	Hfd. 9	79	79	44-61 — 105	80	25.5
Charlie Simmer	L.A.	5-4-80	(G)	Van. 5	at	L.A. 3	64	80	56-45 — 101	64	26.0
Blaine Stoughton	Hfd.	6-4-80	(A)	Det. 3	at	Hfd. 5	80	80	56-44 — 100	80	27.0
Wayne Gretzky	Edm.	6-2-81	(G)	Wpg. 4	at	Edm. 10	53	53	55-109 — 164	80	
Marcel Dionne	L.A.	12-2-81	(A)	L.A. 5	at	Chi. 5	58	58	58-77 — 135	80	
Charlie Simmer	L.A.	14-2-81	(A)	Bos. 5	at	L.A. 4	59	59	56-49 — 105	65	
Kent Nilsson	Cgy.	27-2-81	(G)	Hfd. 1	at	Cgy. 5	64	64	49-82 — 131	80	24.6
Mike Bossy	NYI	3-3-81	(G)	Edm. 8	at	NYI 8	65	66	68-51 — 119	79	
Dave Taylor	L.A.	14-3-81	(G)	Min. 4	at	L.A. 10	63	70	47-65 — 112	72	25.3
Mike Rogers	Hfd.	22-3-81	(G)	Tor. 3	at	Hfd. 3	74	74	40-65 — 105	80	
Bernie Federko	St.L.	28-3-81	(A)	Buf. 4	at	St.L. 7	74	76	31-73 — 104	78	24.10
Rick Middleton	Bos.	28-3-81	(A)	Chi. 2	at	Bos. 5	76	76	44-59 — 103	80	27.4
Jacques Richard	Que.	29-3-81	(G)	Mtl. 0	at	Que. 4	75	76	52-51 — 103	78	28.6
Bryan Trottier	NYI	29-3-81	(G)	NYI 5	at	Wsh. 4	69	76	31-72 — 103	73	
Peter Stastny	Que.	29-3-81	(G)	Mtl. 0	at	Que. 4	73	76	39-70 — 109	77	24.6
Wayne Gretzky	Edm.	27-12-81	(G)	L.A. 3	at	Edm. 10	38	38	92-120 — 212	80	
Mike Bossy	NYI	13-2-82	(A)	Phi. 2	at	NYI 8	55	55	64-83 — 147	80	
Peter Stastny	Que.	16-2-82	(A)	Wpg. 3	at	Que. 7	60	60	46-93 — 139	80	
Dennis Maruk	Wsh.	20-2-82	(G)	Wsh. 3	at	Min. 7	60	60	60-76 — 136	80	26.3
Bryan Trottier	NYI	23-2-82	(G)	Chi. 1	at	NYI 5	61	61	50-79 — 129	80	
Denis Savard	Chi.	27-2-82	(A)	Chi. 5	at	L.A. 3	64	64	32-87 — 119	80	21.1
Bobby Smith	Min.	3-3-82	(G)	Det. 4	at	Min. 6	66	66	43-71 — 114	80	24.1
Marcel Dionne	L.A.	6-3-82	(A)	L.A. 6	at	Hfd. 7	64	66	50-67 — 117	78	
Dave Taylor	L.A.	20-3-82	(A)	Pit. 5	at	L.A. 7	71	72	39-67 — 106	78	
Dale Hawerchuk	Wpg.	24-3-82	(G)	L.A. 3	at	Wpg. 5	74	74	45-58 — 103	80	18.11
Dino Ciccarelli	Min.	27-3-82	(G)	Min. 6	at	Bos. 5	72	76	55-52 — 107	76	21.8
Glenn Anderson	Edm.	28-3-82	(G)	Edm. 6	at	L.A. 2	78	78	38-67 — 105	80	21.7
Mike Rogers	NYR	2-4-82	(G)	Pit. 7	at	NYR 5	79	79	38-65 — 103	80	

Player	Team	Date of 100th Point	G or A	Score	Player's Game No.	Team Game No.	G - A PTS	Total Games	Age when first 100th point scored (Yrs. & Mos.)
Wayne Gretzky	Edm.	5-1-83	(A)	Edm. 8 at Wpg. 3	42	42	71-125 — 196	80	
Mike Bossy	NYI	3-3-83	(A)	Tor. 1 at NYI 5	66	67	60-58 — 118	79	
Peter Stastny	Que.	5-3-83	(A)	Hfd. 3 at Que. 10	62	67	47-77 — 124	75	
Denis Savard	Chi.	6-3-83	(G)	Mtl. 4 at Chi. 5	65	67	35-86 — 121	78	
Mark Messier	Edm.	23-3-83	(G)	Edm. 4 at Wpg. 3	73	76	48-58 — 106	77	22.2
Barry Pederson	Bos.	26-3-83	(A)	Hfd. 4 at Bos. 7	73	76	46-61 — 107	77	22.0
Marcel Dionne	L.A.	26-3-83	(A)	Edm. 9 at L.A. 3	75	75	56-51 — 107	80	
Michel Goulet	Que.	27-3-83	(A)	Que. 6 at Buf. 6	77	77	57-48 — 105	80	22.11
Glenn Anderson	Edm.	29-3-83	(A)	Edm. 7 at Van. 4	70	78	48-56 — 104	72	
Jari Kurri	Edm.	29-3-83	(A)	Edm. 7 at Van. 4	78	78	45-59 — 104	80	22.10
Kent Nilsson	Cgy.	29-3-83	(G)	L.A. 3 at Cgy. 5	78	78	46-58 — 104	80	
Wayne Gretzky	Edm.	18-12-83	(G)	Edm. 7 at Wpg. 5	34	34	87-118 — 205	74	
Paul Coffey	Edm.	4-3-84	(A)	Mtl. 1 at Edm. 6	68	68	40-86 — 126	80	22.9
Michel Goulet	Que.	4-3-84	(A)	Que. 1 at Buf. 1	62	67	56-65 — 121	75	
Jari Kurri	Edm.	7-3-84	(G)	Chi. 4 at Edm. 7	53	69	52-61 — 113	64	
Peter Stastny	Que.	8-3-84	(A)	Que. 8 at Pit. 6	69	69	46-73 — 119	80	
Mike Bossy	NYI	8-3-84	(G)	Tor. 5 at NYI 9	56	68	51-67 — 118	67	
Barry Pederson	Bos.	14-3-84	(A)	Bos. 4 at Det. 2	71	71	39-77 — 116	80	
Bryan Trottier	NYI	18-3-84	(A)	NYI 4 at Hfd. 5	62	73	40-71 — 111	68	
Bernie Federko	St.L.	20-3-84	(A)	Wpg. 3 at St.L. 9	75	76	41-66 — 107	79	
Rick Middleton	Bos.	27-3-84	(G)	Bos. 6 at Que. 4	77	77	47-58 — 105	80	
Dale Hawerchuk	Wpg.	27-3-84	(A)	Wpg. 3 at L.A. 3	77	77	37-65 — 102	80	
Mark Messier	Edm.	27-3-84	(G)	Edm. 9 at Cgy. 2	72	79	37-64 — 101	73	
Wayne Gretzky	Edm.	29-12-84	(A)	Det. 3 at Edm. 6	35	35	73-135 — 208	80	
Jari Kurri	Edm.	29-1-85	(G)	Edm. 4 at Cgy. 2	48	51	71-64 — 135	73	
Mike Bossy	NYI	23-2-85	(G)	Bos. 1 at NYI 7	56	60	58-59 — 117	76	
Dale Hawerchuk	Wpg.	25-2-85	(A)	Wpg. 12 at NYR 5	64	64	53-77 — 130	80	
Marcel Dionne	L.A.	5-3-85	(A)	Pit. 0 at L.A. 6	66	66	46-80 — 126	80	
Brent Sutter	NYI	12-3-85	(A)	NYI 6 at St.L. 5	68	68	42-60 — 102	72	22.10
John Ogrodnick	Det.	22-3-85	(A)	NYR 3 at Det. 5	73	73	55-50 — 105	79	25.9
Paul Coffey	Edm.	26-3-85	(G)	Edm. 7 at NYI 5	74	74	37-84 — 121	80	
Denis Savard	Chi.	29-3-85	(A)	Chi. 5 at Wpg. 5	75	76	38-67 — 105	79	
Peter Stastny	Que.	2-4-85	(A)	Bos. 4 at Que. 6	74	77	32-68 — 100	75	
Bernie Federko	St.L.	4-4-85	(A)	NYR 5 at St.L. 4	74	78	30-73 — 103	76	
John Tonelli	NYI	6-4-85	(G)	N.J. 5 at NYI 5	80	80	42-58 — 100	80	28.1
Paul MacLean	Wpg.	6-4-85	(A)	Wpg. 6 at Edm. 5	78	79	41-60 — 101	79	27.1
Bernie Nicholls	L.A.	6-4-85	(A)	Van. 4 at L.A. 4	80	80	46-54 — 100	80	22.9
Mike Gartner	Wsh.	7-4-85	(G)	Pit. 3 at Wsh. 7	80	80	50-52 — 102	80	25.6
Mario Lemieux	Pit.	7-4-85	(G)	Pit. 3 at Wsh. 7	73	80	43-57 — 100	73	19.6
Wayne Gretzky	Edm.	4-1-86	(A)	Hfd. 3 at Edm. 4	39	39	52-163 — 215	80	
Mario Lemieux	Pit.	15-2-86	(G)	Van. 4 at Pit. 9	55	56	48-93 — 141	79	
Paul Coffey	Edm.	19-2-86	(A)	Tor. 5 at Edm. 9	59	60	48-90 — 138	79	
Peter Stastny	Que.	1-3-86	(A)	Buf. 8 at Que. 4	66	68	41-81 — 122	76	
Jari Kurri	Edm.	2-3-86	(G)	Phi. 1 at Edm. 2	62	64	68-63 — 131	78	
Mike Bossy	NYI	8-3-86	(G)	Wsh. 6 at NYI 2	65	65	61-62 — 123	80	
Denis Savard	Chi.	12-3-86	(A)	Buf. 7 at Chi. 6	69	69	47-69 — 116	80	
Mats Naslund	Mtl.	13-3-86	(A)	Mtl. 2 at Bos. 3	70	70	43-67 — 110	80	26.4
Michel Goulet	Que.	24-3-86	(A)	Que. 1 at Min. 0	70	75	53-50 — 103	75	
Glenn Anderson	Edm.	25-3-86	(G)	Edm. 7 at Det. 2	66	74	54-48 — 102	72	
Neal Broten	Min.	26-3-86	(A)	Min. 6 at Tor. 1	76	76	29-76 — 105	80	26.4
Dale Hawerchuk	Wpg.	31-3-86	(A)	Wpg. 5 at L.A. 2	78	78	46-59 — 105	80	
Bernie Federko	St.L.	5-4-86	(G)	Chi. 5 at St.L. 7	79	79	34-68 — 102	80	
Wayne Gretzky	Edm.	11-1-87	(A)	Cgy. 3 at Edm. 5	42	42	62-121 — 183	79	
Jari Kurri	Edm.	14-3-87	(A)	Buf. 3 at Edm. 5	67	68	54-54 — 108	79	
Mario Lemieux	Pit.	18-3-87	(A)	St.L. 4 at Pit. 5	55	72	54-53 — 107	63	
Mark Messier	Edm.	19-3-87	(A)	Edm. 4 at Cgy. 5	71	71	37-70 — 107	77	
Dino Ciccarelli	Min.	30-3-87	(A)	NYR 6 at Min. 5	78	78	52-51 — 103	80	
Doug Gilmour	St.L.	2-4-87	(A)	Buf. 3 at St.L. 5	78	78	42-63 — 105	80	23.10
Dale Hawerchuk	Wpg.	5-4-87	(A)	Wpg. 3 at Cgy. 1	80	80	47-53 — 100	80	
Mario Lemieux	Pit.	20-1-88	(G)	Pit. 8 at Chi. 3	45	48	70-98 — 168	77	
Wayne Gretzky	Edm.	11-2-88	(A)	Edm. 7 at Van. 2	43	56	40-109 — 149	64	
Denis Savard	Chi.	12-2-88	(A)	St.L. 3 at Chi. 4	57	57	44-87 — 131	80	
Dale Hawerchuk	Wpg.	23-2-88	(G)	Wpg. 4 at Pit. 3	61	61	44-77 — 121	80	
Steve Yzerman	Det.	27-2-88	(A)	Det. 4 at Que. 5	63	63	50-52 — 102	64	22.10
Peter Stastny	Que.	8-3-88	(A)	Hfd. 4 at Que. 6	63	67	46-65 — 111	76	
Mark Messier	Edm.	15-3-88	(A)	Buf. 4 at Edm. 6	68	71	37-74 — 111	77	
Jimmy Carson	L.A.	26-3-88	(A)	Chi. 5 at L.A. 9	77	77	55-52 — 107	80	19.8
Hakan Loob	Cgy.	26-3-88	(A)	Van. 1 at Cgy. 6	76	76	50-56 — 106	80	27.9
Mike Bullard	Cgy.	26-3-88	(A)	Van. 1 at Cgy. 6	76	76	48-55 — 103	79	27.1
Michel Goulet	Que.	27-3-88	(A)	Pit. 6 at Que. 3	76	76	48-58 — 106	80	
Luc Robitaille	L.A.	30-3-88	(G)	Cgy. 7 at L.A. 9	78	78	53-58 — 111	80	22.1
Mario Lemieux	Pit.	31-12-88	(A)	N.J. 6 at Pit. 8	36	38	85-114 — 199	76	
Wayne Gretzky	L.A.	21-1-89	(A)	L.A. 4 at Hfd. 5	47	48	54-114 — 168	78	
Bernie Nicholls	L.A.	21-1-89	(A)	L.A. 4 at Hfd. 5	48	48	70-80 — 150	79	
Steve Yzerman	Det.	27-1-89	(G)	Tor. 1 at Det. 8	50	50	65-90 — 155	80	
Rob Brown	Pit.	16-3-89	(A)	Pit. 2 at N.J. 1	60	72	49-66 — 115	68	20.11
Paul Coffey	Pit.	20-3-89	(A)	Pit. 2 at Min. 7	69	74	30-83 — 113	75	
Joe Mullen	Cgy.	23-3-89	(A)	L.A. 2 at Cgy. 4	74	75	51-59 — 110	79	32.1
Jari Kurri	Edm.	29-3-89	(A)	Edm. 5 at Van. 2	75	79	44-58 — 102	76	
Jimmy Carson	Edm.	2-4-89	(A)	Edm. 2 at Cgy. 4	80	80	49-51 — 100	80	
Mario Lemieux	Pit.	28-1-90	(G)	Pit. 2 at Buf. 7	50	50	45-78 — 123	59	
Wayne Gretzky	L.A.	30-1-90	(A)	N.J. 2 at L.A. 5	51	51	40-102 — 142	73	
Steve Yzerman	Det.	19-2-90	(A)	Mtl. 5 at Det. 5	61	61	62-65 — 127	79	
Mark Messier	Edm.	20-2-90	(A)	Van. 2 at Edm. 4	62	62	45-84 — 129	79	
Brett Hull	St.L.	3-3-90	(A)	NYI 4 at St.L. 5	67	67	72-41 — 113	80	25.7
Bernie Nicholls	NYR	12-3-90	(A)	L.A. 6 at NYR 2	70	71	39-73 — 112	79	
Pierre Turgeon	Buf.	25-3-90	(G)	N.J. 4 at Buf. 3	76	76	40-66 — 106	80	20.7
Paul Coffey	Pit.	25-3-90	(A)	Pit. 2 at Hfd. 4	77	77	29-74 — 103	80	
Pat LaFontaine	NYI	27-3-90	(G)	Cgy. 4 at NYI 2	72	78	54-51 — 105	74	25.1
Adam Oates	St.L.	29-3-90	(G)	Pit 4 at St.L. 5	79	79	23-79 — 102	80	27.7

Mike Bossy

Bernie Federko

Glenn Anderson

Dale Hawerchuk

Joe Sakic

Joe Thornton

Player	Team	Date of 100th Point	G or A	Score			Player's Game No.	Team Game No.	G - A PTS	Total Games	Age when first 100th point scored (Yrs. & Mos.)
Joe Sakic	Que.	31-3-90	(G)	Hfd. 3	at	Que. 2	79	79	39-63 — 102	80	20.8
Ron Francis	Hfd.	31-3-90	(G)	Hfd. 3	at	Que. 2	79	79	32-69 — 101	80	27.0
Luc Robitaille	L.A.	1-4-90	(A)	L.A. 4	at	Cgy. 8	80	80	52-49 — 101	80	
Wayne Gretzky	L.A.	30-1-91	(A)	N.J. 4	at	L.A. 2	50	51	41-122 — 163	78	
Brett Hull	St.L.	23-2-91	(G)	Bos. 2	at	St.L. 9	60	62	86-45 — 131	78	
Mark Recchi	Pit.	5-3-91	(G)	Van. 1	at	Pit. 4	66	67	40-73 — 113	78	23.1
Steve Yzerman	Det.	10-3-91	(A)	Det. 4	at	St.L. 1	72	72	51-57 — 108	80	
John Cullen	Hfd.	16-3-91	(G)	N.J. 2	at	Hfd. 6	71	71	39-71 — 110	78	26.7
Adam Oates	St.L.	17-3-91	(A)	St.L. 4	at	Chi. 6	54	73	25-90 — 115	61	
Joe Sakic	Que.	19-3-91	(G)	Edm. 7	at	Que. 6	74	74	48-61 — 109	80	
Steve Larmer	Chi.	24-3-91	(A)	Min. 4	at	Chi. 5	76	76	44-57 — 101	80	29.9
Theoren Fleury	Cgy.	26-3-91	(A)	Van. 2	at	Cgy. 7	77	77	51-53 — 104	79	22.9
Al MacInnis	Cgy.	28-3-91	(A)	Edm. 4	at	Cgy. 4	78	78	28-75 — 103	78	27.8
Brett Hull	St.L.	2-3-92	(G)	St.L. 5	at	Van. 3	66	66	70-39 — 109	73	
Wayne Gretzky	L.A.	3-3-92	(A)	Phi. 1	at	L.A. 4	60	66	31-90 — 121	74	
Kevin Stevens	Pit.	7-3-92	(A)	Pit. 3	at	L.A. 5	66	66	54-69 — 123	80	26.11
Mario Lemieux	Pit.	10-3-92	(A)	Cgy. 2	at	Pit. 5	53	67	44-87 — 131	64	
Luc Robitaille	L.A.	17-3-92	(A)	Wpg. 4	at	L.A. 5	73	73	44-63 — 107	80	
Mark Messier	NYR	22-3-92	(A)	N.J. 2	at	NYR 8	74	75	35-72 — 107	79	
Jeremy Roenick	Chi.	29-3-92	(A)	Tor. 1	at	Chi. 5	77	77	53-50 — 103	80	22.2
Steve Yzerman	Det.	14-4-92	(A)	Det. 7	at	Min. 4	79	80	45-58 — 103	79	
Brian Leetch	NYR	16-4-92	(G)	Pit. 1	at	NYR 7	80	80	22-80 — 102	80	24.1
Mario Lemieux	Pit.	31-12-92	(G)	Tor. 3	at	Pit. 3	38	39	69-91 — 160	60	
Pat LaFontaine	Buf.	10-2-93	(A)	Buf. 6	at	Wpg. 2	55	55	53-95 — 148	84	
Adam Oates	Bos.	14-2-93	(A)	Bos. 3	at	T.B. 3	58	58	45-97 — 142	84	
Steve Yzerman	Det.	24-2-93	(A)	Det. 7	at	Buf. 10	64	64	58-79 — 137	84	
Pierre Turgeon	NYI	28-2-93	(A)	NYI 7	at	Hfd. 6	62	63	58-74 — 132	83	
Doug Gilmour	Tor.	3-3-93	(A)	Min. 1	at	Tor. 3	64	64	32-95 — 127	83	
Alexander Mogilny	Buf.	5-3-93	(A)	Hfd. 4	at	Buf. 2	58	65	76-51 — 127	77	24.1
Mark Recchi	Phi.	7-3-93	(G)	Phi. 3	at	N.J. 7	66	66	53-70 — 123	84	
Teemu Selanne	Wpg.	9-3-93	(G)	Wpg. 4	at	T.B. 2	68	68	76-56 — 132	84	22.7
Luc Robitaille	L.A.	15-3-93	(A)	L.A. 4	at	Buf. 2	69	69	63-62 — 125	84	
Kevin Stevens	Pit.	23-3-93	(A)	S.J. 2	at	Pit. 7	63	73	55-56 — 111	72	
Mats Sundin	Que.	27-3-93	(G)	Phi. 3	at	Que. 8	71	75	47-67 — 114	80	22.1
Pavel Bure	Van.	1-4-93	(G)	Van. 5	at	T.B. 3	77	77	60-50 — 110	83	22.0
Jeremy Roenick	Chi.	4-4-93	(A)	St.L. 4	at	Chi. 5	79	79	50-57 — 107	84	
Craig Janney	St.L.	4-4-93	(G)	St.L. 4	at	Chi. 5	79	79	24-82 — 106	84	25.7
Rick Tocchet	Pit.	7-4-93	(G)	Mtl. 3	at	Pit. 4	77	81	48-61 — 109	80	28.11
Joe Sakic	Que.	8-4-93	(A)	Que. 2	at	Bos. 6	75	81	48-57 — 105	78	
Ron Francis	Pit.	9-4-93	(A)	Pit. 10	at	NYR 4	82	82	24-76 — 100	84	
Brett Hull	St.L.	11-4-93	(G)	Min. 1	at	St.L. 5	78	82	54-47 — 101	80	
Theoren Fleury	Cgy.	11-4-93	(G)	Cgy. 3	at	Van. 6	82	82	34-66 — 100	83	
Joe Juneau	Bos.	14-4-93	(A)	Bos. 4	at	Ott. 2	84	84	32-70 — 102	84	25.3
Wayne Gretzky	L.A.	14-2-94	(A)	Bos. 3	at	L.A. 2	56	56	38-92 — 130	81	
Sergei Fedorov	Det.	1-3-94	(A)	Cgy. 2	at	Det. 5	63	63	56-64 — 120	82	24.2
Doug Gilmour	Tor.	23-3-94	(G)	Tor. 1	at	Fla. 1	74	74	27-84 — 111	83	
Adam Oates	Bos.	26-3-94	(A)	Mtl. 3	at	Bos. 6	68	75	32-80 — 112	77	
Mark Recchi	Phi.	27-3-94	(A)	Ana. 3	at	Phi. 2	76	76	40-67 — 107	84	
Pavel Bure	Van.	28-3-94	(A)	Tor. 2	at	Van. 3	68	76	60-47 — 107	76	
Jeremy Roenick	Chi.	31-3-94	(G)	Chi. 3	at	Wsh. 6	78	78	46-61 — 107	84	
Brendan Shanahan	St.L.	12-4-94	(G)	St.L. 5	at	Dal. 9	80	83	52-50 — 102	81	25.2
Mario Lemieux	Pit.	16-1-96	(G)	Col. 5	at	Pit. 2	38	44	69-92 — 161	70	
Jaromir Jagr	Pit.	6-2-96	(G)	Bos. 5	at	Pit. 6	52	52	62-87 — 149	82	23.11
Ron Francis	Pit.	9-3-96	(A)	N.J. 4	at	Pit. 3	61	66	27-92 — 119	77	
Peter Forsberg	Col.	9-3-96	(A)	Col. 7	at	Van. 5	68	68	30-86 — 116	82	22.7
Joe Sakic	Col.	17-3-96	(A)	Edm. 1	at	Col. 8	70	70	51-69 — 120	82	
Teemu Selanne	Ana.	25-3-96	(A)	Ana. 1	at	Det. 5	70	73	40-68 — 108	79	
Alexander Mogilny	Van.	25-3-96	(A)	L.A. 1	at	Van. 4	72	75	55-52 — 107	79	
Eric Lindros	Phi.	25-3-96	(A)	Hfd. 0	at	Phi. 3	65	73	47-68 — 115	73	23.0
Wayne Gretzky	St.L.	28-3-96	(G)	N.J. 4	at	St.L. 4	76	75	23-79 — 102	80	
Doug Weight	Edm.	30-3-96	(G)	Tor. 4	at	Edm. 3	76	76	25-79 — 104	82	25.3
Sergei Fedorov	Det.	2-4-96	(A)	Det. 3	at	S.J. 6	72	76	39-68 — 107	78	
Paul Kariya	Ana.	7-4-96	(A)	Ana. 5	at	S.J. 3	78	78	50-58 — 108	82	21.5
Mario Lemieux	Pit.	8-3-97	(A)	Phi. 2	at	Pit. 3	61	65	50-72 — 122	76	
Teemu Selanne	Ana.	1-4-97	(A)	Chi. 3	at	Ana. 3	74	78	51-58 — 109	78	
Jaromir Jagr	Pit.	15-4-98	(G)	T.B. 1	at	Pit. 5	76	80	35-67 — 102	77	
Jaromir Jagr	Pit.	13-3-99	(G)	Phi. 0	at	Pit. 4	65	65	44-83 — 127	81	
Teemu Selanne	Ana.	5-4-99	(A)	Ana. 2	at	Det. 3	69	76	47-60 — 107	75	
Paul Kariya	Ana.	17-4-99	(G)	Ana. 3	at	S.J. 3	82	82	39-62 — 101	82	
Jaromir Jagr	Pit.	10-3-01	(G)	Cgy. 3	at	Pit. 6	68	68	52-69 — 121	81	
Joe Sakic	Col.	18-3-01	(G)	Min. 3	at	Col. 4	72	72	54-64 — 118	82	
Markus Naslund	Van.	27-3-03	(A)	Phx. 1	at	Van. 5	78	78	48-56 — 104	82	
Peter Forsberg	Col.	31-3-03	(A)	S.J. 1	at	Col. 3	72	79	29-77 — 106	79	
Joe Thornton	Bos.	4-4-03	(A)	Buf. 5	at	Bos. 8	77	82	36-65 — 101	77	

Five-or-more-Goal Games

Player	Team	Date	Score				Opposing Goaltender
SEVEN GOALS							
Joe Malone	Quebec Bulldogs	Jan. 31/20	Tor. 6	at	Que. 10		Ivan Mitchell
SIX GOALS							
Newsy Lalonde	Montreal	Jan. 10/20	Tor. 7	at	Mtl. 14		Ivan Mitchell
Joe Malone	Quebec Bulldogs	Mar. 10/20	Ott. 4	at	Que. 10		Clint Benedict
Corb Denneny	Toronto St. Pats	Jan. 26/21	Ham. 3	at	Tor. 10		Howard Lockhart
Cy Denneny	Ottawa Senators	Mar. 7/21	Ham. 5	at	Ott. 12		Howard Lockhart
Syd Howe	Detroit	Feb. 3/44	NYR 2	at	Det. 12		Ken McAuley
Red Berenson	St. Louis	Nov. 7/68	St.L. 8	at	Phi. 0		Doug Favell
Darryl Sittler	Toronto	Feb. 7/76	Bos. 4	at	Tor. 11		Dave Reece
FIVE GOALS							
Joe Malone	Montreal	Dec. 19/17	Mtl. 7	at	Ott. 4		Clint Benedict
Harry Hyland	Mtl. Wanderers	Dec. 19/17	Tor. 9	at	Mtl. W. 10		Art Brooks, Sammy Hebert
Joe Malone	Montreal	Jan. 12/18	Ott. 4	at	Mtl. 9		Clint Benedict
Joe Malone	Montreal	Feb. 2/18	Tor. 2	at	Mtl. 11		Hap Holmes
Mickey Roach	Toronto St. Pats	Mar. 6/20	Que. 2	at	Tor. 11		Howard Lockhart
Newsy Lalonde	Montreal	Feb. 16/21	Ham. 5	at	Mtl. 10		Howard Lockhart
Babe Dye	Toronto St. Pats	Dec. 16/22	Mtl. 2	at	Tor. 7		Georges Vezina
Red Green	Hamilton Tigers	Dec. 5/24	Ham. 10	at	Tor. 3		John Ross Roach
Babe Dye	Toronto St. Pats	Dec. 22/24	Tor. 10	at	Bos. 1		Hec Fowler
Punch Broadbent	Mtl. Maroons	Jan. 7/25	Mtl. 6	at	Ham. 2		Jake Forbes
Pit Lepine	Montreal	Dec. 14/29	Ott. 4	at	Mtl. 6		Alex Connell
Howie Morenz	Montreal	Mar. 18/30	NYA 3	at	Mtl. 8		Roy Worters
Charlie Conacher	Toronto	Jan. 19/32	NYA 3	at	Tor. 11		Roy Worters, Al Shields
Ray Getliffe	Montreal	Feb. 6/43	Bos. 3	at	Mtl. 8		Frank Brimsek
Maurice Richard	Montreal	Dec. 28/44	Det. 1	at	Mtl. 9		Harry Lumley
Howie Meeker	Toronto	Jan. 8/47	Chi. 4	at	Tor. 10		Paul Bibeault
Bernie Geoffrion	Montreal	Feb. 19/55	NYR 2	at	Mtl. 10		Gump Worsley
Bobby Rousseau	Montreal	Feb. 1/64	Det. 3	at	Mtl. 9		Roger Crozier
Yvan Cournoyer	Montreal	Feb. 15/75	Chi. 3	at	Mtl. 12		Mike Veisor
Don Murdoch	NY Rangers	Oct. 12/76	NYR 10	at	Min. 4		Gary Smith
Ian Turnbull	Toronto	Feb. 2/77	Det. 1	at	Tor. 9		Ed Giacomin (2), Jim Rutherford (3)
Bryan Trottier	NY Islanders	Dec. 23/78	NYR 4	at	NYI 9		Wayne Thomas (4), John Davidson (1)
Tim Young	Minnesota	Jan. 15/79	Min. 8	at	NYR 1		Doug Soetaert (3), Wayne Thomas (2)
John Tonelli	NY Islanders	Jan. 6/81	Tor. 3	at	NYI 6		Jiri Crha (4), empty net (1)
Wayne Gretzky	Edmonton	Feb. 18/81	St.L. 2	at	Edm. 9		Mike Liut (3), Ed Staniowski (2)
Wayne Gretzky	Edmonton	Dec. 30/81	Phi. 5	at	Edm. 7		Pete Peeters (4), empty net (1)
Grant Mulvey	Chicago	Feb. 3/82	St.L. 5	at	Chi. 9		Mike Liut (4), Gary Edwards (1)
Bryan Trottier	NY Islanders	Feb. 13/82	Phi. 2	at	NYI 8		Pete Peeters
Willy Lindstrom	Winnipeg	Mar. 2/82	Wpg. 7	at	Phi. 6		Pete Peeters
Mark Pavelich	NY Rangers	Feb. 23/83	Hfd. 3	at	NYR 11		Greg Millen
Jari Kurri	Edmonton	Nov. 19/83	N.J. 4	at	Edm. 13		Glenn Resch (3), Ron Low (2)
Bengt Gustafsson	Washington	Jan. 8/84	Wsh. 7	at	Phi. 1		Pelle Lindbergh
Pat Hughes	Edmonton	Feb. 3/84	Cgy. 5	at	Edm. 10		Don Edwards (3), Reggie Lemelin (2)
Wayne Gretzky	Edmonton	Dec. 15/84	Edm. 8	at	St.L. 2		Rick Wamsley (4), Mike Liut(1)
Dave Andreychuk	Buffalo	Feb. 6/86	Buf. 8	at	Bos. 6		Pat Riggin (3), Doug Keans (4)
Wayne Gretzky	Edmonton	Dec. 6/87	Min. 4	at	Edm. 10		Don Beaupre (4), Kari Takko (1)
Mario Lemieux	Pittsburgh	Dec. 31/88	N.J. 6	at	Pit. 8		Bob Sauve (3), Chris Terreri (2)
Joe Nieuwendyk	Calgary	Jan. 11/89	Wpg. 3	at	Cgy. 8		Daniel Berthiaume
Mats Sundin	Quebec	Mar. 5/92	Que. 10	at	Hfd. 4		Peter Sidorkiewicz (3), Kay Whitmore (2)
Mario Lemieux	Pittsburgh	Apr. 9/93	Pit. 10	at	NYR 4		Corey Hirsch (3), Mike Richter (2)
Peter Bondra	Washington	Feb. 5/94	T.B. 3	at	Wsh. 6		Daren Puppa (4), Pat Jablonski (1)
Mike Ricci	Quebec	Feb. 17/94	Que. 8	at	S.J. 2		Arturs Irbe (3), Jimmy Waite (2)
Alex Zhamnov	Winnipeg	Apr. 1/95	Wpg. 7	at	L.A. 7		Kelly Hrudey (3), Grant Fuhr (2)
Mario Lemieux	Pittsburgh	Mar. 26/96	St.L. 4	at	Pit. 8		Grant Fuhr (1), Jon Casey (4)
Sergei Fedorov	Detroit	Dec. 26/96	Wsh. 4	at	Det. 5		Jim Carey

Players' 500th Goals

Regular Season

Player	Team	Date	Game No.	Score				Opposing Goaltender	Total Goals	Total Games
Maurice Richard	Montreal	Oct. 19/57	863	Chi. 1	at	Mtl. 3		Glenn Hall	544	978
Gordie Howe	Detroit	Mar. 14/62	1,045	Det. 2	at	NYR 3		Gump Worsley	801	1,767
Bobby Hull	Chicago	Feb. 21/70	861	NYR. 2	at	Chi. 4		Ed Giacomin	610	1,063
Jean Béliveau	Montreal	Feb. 11/71	1,101	Min. 2	at	Mtl. 6		Gilles Gilbert	507	1,125
Frank Mahovlich	Montreal	Mar. 21/73	1,105	Van. 2	at	Mtl. 3		Dunc Wilson	533	1,181
Phil Esposito	Boston	Dec. 22/74	803	Det. 4	at	Bos. 5		Jim Rutherford	717	1,282
John Bucyk	Boston	Oct. 30/75	1,370	St.L. 2	at	Bos. 3		Yves Bélanger	556	1,540
Stan Mikita	Chicago	Feb. 27/77	1,221	Van. 4	at	Chi. 3		Cesare Maniago	541	1,394
Marcel Dionne	Los Angeles	Dec. 14/82	887	L.A. 2	at	Wsh. 7		Al Jensen	731	1,348
Guy Lafleur	Montreal	Dec. 20/83	918	Mtl. 6	at	N.J. 0		Glenn Resch	560	1,126
Mike Bossy	NY Islanders	Jan. 2/86	647	Bos. 5	at	NYI 7		empty net	573	752
Gilbert Perreault	Buffalo	Mar. 9/86	1,159	N.J. 3	at	Buf. 4		Alain Chevrier	512	1,191
Wayne Gretzky	Edmonton	Nov. 22/86	575	Van. 2	at	Edm. 5		empty net	894	1,487
Lanny McDonald	Calgary	Mar. 21/89	1,107	NYI 1	at	Cgy. 4		Mark Fitzpatrick	500	1,111
Bryan Trottier	NY Islanders	Feb. 13/90	1,104	Cgy. 4	at	NYI 2		Rick Wamsley	524	1,279
Mike Gartner	NY Rangers	Oct. 14/91	936	Wsh. 5	at	NYR 3		Mike Liut	708	1,432
Michel Goulet	Chicago	Feb. 16/92	951	Cgy. 5	at	Chi. 5		Jeff Reese	548	1,089
Jari Kurri	Los Angeles	Oct. 17/92	833	Bos. 6	at	L.A. 8		empty net	601	1,251
Dino Ciccarelli	Detroit	Jan. 8/94	946	Det. 6	at	L.A. 3		Kelly Hrudey	608	1,232
*Mario Lemieux	Pittsburgh	Oct. 26/95	605	Pit. 7	at	NYI 5		Tommy Soderstrom	683	889
*Mark Messier	NY Rangers	Nov. 6/95	1,141	Cgy. 2	at	NYR 4		Rick Tabaracci	694	1,756
*Steve Yzerman	Detroit	Jan. 17/96	906	Col. 2	at	Det. 3		Patrick Roy	678	1,453
Dale Hawerchuk	St. Louis	Jan. 31/96	1,103	St.L. 4	at	Tor. 0		Felix Potvin	518	1,188
*Brett Hull	St. Louis	Dec. 22/96	693	L.A. 4	at	St.L. 7		Stephane Fiset	741	1,264
Joe Mullen	Pittsburgh	Mar. 14/97	1,052	Pit. 3	at	Col. 6		Patrick Roy	502	1,062
*Dave Andreychuk	New Jersey	Mar. 15/97	1,070	Wsh. 2	at	N.J. 3		Bill Ranford	634	1,597
*Luc Robitaille	Los Angeles	Jan. 7/99	928	Buf. 2	at	L.A. 4		Dwayne Roloson	653	1,366
Pat Verbeek	Detroit	Mar. 22/00	1,285	Cgy. 2	at	Det. 2		Fred Brathwaite	522	1,424
*Ron Francis	Carolina	Jan. 2/02	1,533	Bos. 6	at	Car. 3		Byron Dafoe	549	1,731
*Brendan Shanahan	Detroit	Mar. 23/02	1,100	Det. 2	at	Col. 0		Patrick Roy	558	1,268
*Joe Sakic	Colorado	Dec. 11/02	1,044	Col. 1	at	Van. 3		Dan Cloutier	542	1,155
*Joe Nieuwendyk	New Jersey	Jan. 17/03	1,094	N.J. 2	at	Car. 1		Kevin Weekes	533	1,177
*Jaromir Jagr	Washington	Feb. 4/03	928	Wsh. 5	at	T.B. 1		John Grahame	537	1,027

*Active

Bobby Hull became the third player in NHL history to score 50 goals in a season on March 25, 1962. He became the third to score 500 in a career on February 21, 1970.

Players' 1,000th Points

Regular Season

Player	Team	Date	Game No.	G or A	Score				Total Points G	A	PTS	Total Games
Gordie Howe	Detroit	Nov. 27/60	938	(A)	Tor. 0	at	Det. 2		801-1,049	–1,850		1,767
Jean Béliveau	Montreal	Mar. 3/68	911	(G)	Mtl. 2	at	Det. 5		507-712	–1,219		1,125
Alex Delvecchio	Detroit	Feb. 16/69	1,143	(A)	L.A. 3	at	Det. 6		456-825	–1,281		1,549
Bobby Hull	Chicago	Dec. 13/70	909	(A)	Min. 2	at	Chi. 5		610-560	–1,170		1,063
Norm Ullman	Toronto	Oct. 16/71	1,113	(A)	NYR 5	at	Tor. 3		490-739	–1,229		1,410
Stan Mikita	Chicago	Oct. 15/72	924	(A)	St.L. 3	at	Chi. 1		541-926	–1,467		1,394
John Bucyk	Boston	Nov. 9/72	1,144	(A)	Det. 3	at	Bos. 8		556-813	–1,369		1,540
Frank Mahovlich	Montreal	Feb. 17/73	1,090	(A)	Phi. 7	at	Mtl. 6		533-570	–1,103		1,181
Henri Richard	Montreal	Dec. 20/73	1,194	(A)	Mtl. 2	at	Buf. 7		358-688	–1,046		1,256
Phil Esposito	Boston	Feb. 15/74	745	(A)	Bos. 4	at	Van. 2		717-873	–1,590		1,282
Rod Gilbert	NY Rangers	Feb. 19/77	1,027	(G)	NYR 2	at	NYI 5		406-615	–1,021		1,065
Jean Ratelle	Boston	Apr. 3/77	1,007	(G)	Tor. 4	at	Bos. 7		491-776	–1,267		1,281
Marcel Dionne	Los Angeles	Jan. 7/81	740	(G)	L.A. 5	at	Hfd. 3		731-1,040	–1,771		1,348
Guy Lafleur	Montreal	Mar. 4/81	720	(G)	Mtl. 9	at	Wpg. 3		560-793	–1,353		1,126
Bobby Clarke	Philadelphia	Mar. 19/81	922	(G)	Bos. 3	at	Phi. 5		358-852	–1,210		1,144
Gilbert Perreault	Buffalo	Apr. 3/82	871	(A)	Buf. 5	at	Mtl. 4		512-814	–1,326		1,191
Darryl Sittler	Philadelphia	Jan. 20/83	927	(G)	Cgy. 2	at	Phi. 5		484-637	–1,121		1,096
Wayne Gretzky	Edmonton	Dec. 19/84	424	(A)	L.A. 3	at	Edm. 7		894-1,963	–2,875		1,487
Bryan Trottier	NY Islanders	Jan. 29/85	726	(A)	Min. 4	at	NYI 4		524-901	–1,425		1,279
Mike Bossy	NY Islanders	Jan. 24/86	656	(A)	NYI 7	at	Wsh. 5		573-553	–1,126		752
Denis Potvin	NY Islanders	Apr. 4/87	987	(G)	Buf. 6	at	NYI 6		310-742	–1,052		1,060
Bernie Federko	St. Louis	Mar. 19/88	855	(A)	Hfd. 5	at	St.L. 3		369-761	–1,130		1,000
Lanny McDonald	Calgary	Mar. 7/89	1,101	(G)	Wpg. 5	at	Cgy. 9		500-506	–1,006		1,111
Peter Stastny	Quebec	Oct. 19/89	682	(G)	Que. 5	at	Chi. 3		450-789	–1,239		977
Jari Kurri	Edmonton	Jan. 2/90	716	(G)	Edm. 6	at	St.L. 4		601-797	–1,398		1,251
Denis Savard	Chicago	Mar. 11/90	727	(A)	St.L. 6	at	Chi. 4		473-865	–1,338		1,196
Paul Coffey	Pittsburgh	Dec. 22/90	770	(A)	Pit. 4	at	NYI 3		396-1,135	–1,531		1,409
*Mark Messier	Edmonton	Jan. 13/91	822	(A)	Edm. 5	at	Phi. 3		694-1,193	–1,887		1,756
Dave Taylor	Los Angeles	Feb. 5/91	930	(A)	L.A. 3	at	Phi. 2		431-638	–1,069		1,111
Michel Goulet	Chicago	Feb. 23/91	878	(G)	Chi. 3	at	Min. 3		548-604	–1,152		1,089
Dale Hawerchuk	Buffalo	Mar. 8/91	781	(G)	Chi. 5	at	Buf. 3		518-891	–1,409		1,188
Bobby Smith	Minnesota	Nov. 30/91	986	(A)	Min. 4	at	Tor. 3		357-679	–1,036		1,077
Mike Gartner	NY Rangers	Jan. 4/92	971	(A)	NYR 4	at	N.J. 6		708-627	–1,335		1,432
Raymond Bourque	Boston	Feb. 29/92	933	(A)	Wsh. 5	at	Bos. 5		410-1,169	–1,579		1,612
*Mario Lemieux	Pittsburgh	Mar. 24/92	513	(A)	Pit. 3	at	Det. 4		683-1,018	–1,701		889
Glenn Anderson	Toronto	Feb. 22/93	954	(A)	Tor. 8	at	Wsh. 1		498-601	–1,099		1,129
*Steve Yzerman	Detroit	Feb. 24/93	737	(A)	Det. 7	at	Buf. 10		678-1,043	–1,721		1,453
*Ron Francis	Pittsburgh	Oct. 28/93	893	(G)	Que. 7	at	Pit. 3		549-1,249	–1,798		1,731
Bernie Nicholls	New Jersey	Feb. 13/94	858	(A)	N.J. 3	at	T.B. 3		475-734	–1,209		1,127
Dino Ciccarelli	Detroit	Mar. 9/94	957	(G)	Det. 5	at	Cgy. 1		608-592	–1,200		1,232
Brian Propp	Hartford	Mar. 19/94	1,008	(G)	Hfd. 5	at	Phi. 3		425-579	–1,004		1,016
Joe Mullen	Pittsburgh	Feb. 7/95	935	(A)	Fla. 3	at	Pit. 7		502-561	–1,063		1,062
Steve Larmer	NY Rangers	Mar. 8/95	983	(A)	N.J. 4	at	NYR 6		441-571	–1,012		1,006
Doug Gilmour	Toronto	Dec. 23/95	935	(A)	Edm. 1	at	Tor. 6		450-964	–1,414		1,474
Larry Murphy	Toronto	Mar. 27/96	1,228	(G)	Tor. 6	at	Van. 2		287-929	–1,216		1,615
*Dave Andreychuk	New Jersey	Apr. 7/96	998	(G)	NYR 2	at	N.J. 4		634-686	–1,320		1,597
Adam Oates	Washington	Oct. 8/97	830	(G)	Wsh. 6	at	NYI 3		341-1,079	–1,420		1,337
Phil Housley	Washington	Nov. 8/97	1,081	(A)	Edm. 1	at	Wsh. 2		338-894	–1,232		1,495
Dale Hunter	Washington	Jan. 9/98	1,308	(A)	Phi. 1	at	Wsh. 4		323-697	–1,020		1,407
Pat LaFontaine	NY Rangers	Jan. 22/98	847	(G)	Phi. 4	at	NYR 3		468-545	–1,013		865
*Luc Robitaille	Los Angeles	Jan. 29/98	882	(A)	Cgy. 3	at	L.A. 5		653-717	–1,370		1,366
*Al MacInnis	St. Louis	Apr. 7/98	1,056	(G)	St.L. 3	at	Det. 5		340-934	–1,274		1,416
*Brett Hull	Dallas	Nov. 14/98	815	(A)	Dal. 3	at	Bos. 1		741-649	–1,390		1,264
Brian Bellows	Washington	Jan. 2/99	1,147	(A)	Tor. 2	at	Wsh. 5		485-537	–1,022		1,188
*Pierre Turgeon	St. Louis	Oct. 9/99	881	(A)	St.L. 4	at	Edm. 3		495-779	–1,274		1,215
*Joe Sakic	Colorado	Dec. 27/99	810	(A)	St.L. 1	at	Col. 5		542-860	–1,402		1,155
Pat Verbeek	Detroit	Feb. 27/00	1,275	(A)	T.B. 1	at	Det. 3		522-541	–1,063		1,424
*V. Damphousse	San Jose	Oct. 14/00	1,090	(A)	Bos. 2	at	S.J. 5		432-773	–1,205		1,378
*Jaromir Jagr	Pittsburgh	Dec. 30/00	763	(G)	Ott. 3	at	Pit. 5		537-772	–1,309		1,027
*Mark Recchi	Philadelphia	Mar. 13/01	920	(G)	St.L. 2	at	Phi. 5		456-745	–1,201		1,173
Theoren Fleury	NY Rangers	Oct. 29/01	960	(G)	Dal. 2	at	NYR 4		455-633	–1,088		1,084
*B. Shanahan	Detroit	Jan. 12/02	1,073	(G)	Dal. 2	at	Det. 5		558-593	–1,151		1,268
*Jeremy Roenick	Philadelphia	Jan. 30/02	961	(G)	Phi. 1	at	Ott. 3		475-645	–1,120		1,124
*Mike Modano	Dallas	Nov. 15/02	965	(G)	Col. 2	at	Dal. 4		458-648	–1,106		1,101
*Joe Nieuwendyk	New Jersey	Feb. 23/03	1,094	(G)	N.J. 4	at	Pit. 3		533-529	–1,062		1,177
*Mats Sundin	Toronto	Mar. 10/03	994	(G)	Tor. 3	at	Edm. 2		465-624	–1,089		1,086
*Sergei Fedorov	Anaheim	Feb. 14/04	965	(G)	Ana. 2	at	Van. 1		431-588	–1,019		988
*Alexander Mogilny	Toronto	Mar. 15/04	946	(A)	Tor. 6	at	Buf. 5		461-546	–1,007		956

*Active

On March 3, 1968, Jean Beliveau joined Gordie Howe as the only players to that point in NHL history to reach 1,000 career points. On February 11, 1971, he became just the fourth player in history to score 500 goals.

Individual Awards

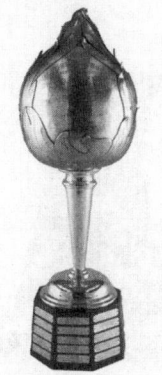

Hart Memorial Trophy

Art Ross Trophy

Calder Memorial Trophy

James Norris Memorial Trophy

HART MEMORIAL TROPHY

An annual award "to the player adjudged to be the most valuable to his team." Winner selected in a poll by the Professional Hockey Writers' Association in the 30 NHL cities at the end of the regular schedule.

History: The Hart Memorial Trophy was presented by the National Hockey League in 1960 after the original Hart Trophy was retired to the Hockey Hall of Fame. The original Hart Trophy was donated to the NHL in 1923 by Dr. David A. Hart, father of Cecil Hart, former manager-coach of the Montreal Canadiens.

Multiple Winners	
Wayne Gretzky	9
Gordie Howe	6
Eddie Shore	4
Mario Lemieux	3
Bobby Clarke	3
Bobby Orr	3
Howie Morenz	3
Nine tied with	2

CALDER MEMORIAL TROPHY

An annual award "to the player selected as the most proficient in his first year of competition in the National Hockey League." Winner selected in a poll by the Professional Hockey Writers' Association at the end of the regular schedule.

History: From 1936-37 until his death in 1943, Frank Calder, NHL President, bought a trophy each year to be given permanently to the outstanding rookie. After Calder's death, the NHL presented the Calder Memorial Trophy in his memory and the trophy is to be kept in perpetuity. To be eligible for the award, a player cannot have played more than 25 games in any single preceding season nor in six or more games in each of any two preceding seasons in any major professional league. Beginning in 1990-91, to be eligible for this award a player must not have attained his twenty-sixth birthday by September 15th of the season in which he is eligible.

Recent Calder Memorial Trophy winners: Barret Jackman, at left with trophy, St. Louis, D, 2002-03 and Andrew Raycroft, above, Boston, G, 2003-04.

ART ROSS TROPHY

An annual award "to the player who leads the league in scoring points at the end of the regular season."

History: Arthur Howie Ross, former manager-coach of the Boston Bruins, presented the trophy to the National Hockey League in 1947. If two players finish the schedule with the same number of points, the trophy is awarded in the following manner: 1. Player with most goals. 2. Player with fewer games played. 3. Player scoring first goal of the season.

Multiple Winners	
Wayne Gretzky	10
Mario Lemieux	6
Gordie Howe	6
Jaromir Jagr	5
Phil Esposito	5
Stan Mikita	4
Guy Lafleur	3
11 tied with	2

JAMES NORRIS MEMORIAL TROPHY

An annual award "to the defense player who demonstrates throughout the season the greatest all-round ability in the position." Winner selected in a poll by the Professional Hockey Writers' Association at the end of the regular schedule.

History: The James Norris Memorial Trophy was presented in 1953 by the four children of the late James Norris in memory of the former owner-president of the Detroit Red Wings.

Multiple Winners	
Bobby Orr	8
Doug Harvey	7
Raymond Bourque	5
Nicklas Lidstrom	3
Chris Chelios	3
Paul Coffey	3
Denis Potvin	3
Pierre Pilote	3
Brian Leetch	2
Rod Langway	2
Larry Robinson	2

Vezina Trophy

Lady Byng Memorial Trophy

Frank J. Selke Trophy

Conn Smythe Trophy

VEZINA TROPHY

An annual award "to the goalkeeper adjudged to be the best at his position" as voted by the general managers of each of the 30 clubs.

History: Leo Dandurand, Louis Letourneau and Joe Cattarinich, former owners of the Montreal Canadiens, presented the trophy to the National Hockey League in 1926-27 in memory of Georges Vezina, outstanding goalkeeper of the Canadiens who collapsed during an NHL game on November 28, 1925, and died of tuberculosis a few months later. Until the 1981-82 season, the goalkeeper(s) of the team allowing the fewest number of goals during the regular season were awarded the Vezina Trophy.

Multiple Winners	
Jacques Plante	7
Dominik Hasek	6
Bill Durnan	6
Ken Dryden	5
Michel Laroque	4
Terry Sawchuk	4
Tiny Thompson	4
Patrick Roy	3
Glenn Hall	3
George Hainsworth	3

LADY BYNG MEMORIAL TROPHY

An annual award "to the player adjudged to have exhibited the best type of sportsmanship and gentlemanly conduct combined with a high standard of playing ability." Winner selected in a poll by the Professional Hockey Writers' Association at the end of the regular schedule.

History: Lady Byng, wife of Canada's Governor-General at the time, presented the Lady Byng Trophy in the 1924-25 season. After Frank Boucher of the New York Rangers won the award seven times in eight seasons, he was given the trophy to keep and Lady Byng donated another trophy in 1936. After Lady Byng's death in 1949, the National Hockey League presented a new trophy, changing the name to Lady Byng Memorial Trophy.

Multiple Winners	
Frank Boucher	7
Wayne Gretzky	5
Red Kelly	4
Ron Francis	3
Bobby Bauer	3
12 tied with	2

FRANK J. SELKE TROPHY

An annual award "to the forward who best excels in the defensive aspects of the game." Winner selected in a poll by the Professional Hockey Writers' Association at the end of the regular schedule.

History: Presented to the National Hockey League in 1977 by the Board of Governors of the NHL in honor of Frank J. Selke, one of the great architects of Montreal and Toronto championship teams.

Multiple Winners	
Bob Gainey	4
Jere Lehtinen	3
Guy Carbonneau	3
Michael Peca	2
Sergei Fedorov	2

WILLIAM M. JENNINGS TROPHY

An annual award "to the goalkeeper(s) having played a minimum of 25 games for the team with the fewest goals scored against it." Winners selected on regular-season play.

History: The Jennings Trophy was presented in 1981-82 by the National Hockey League's Board of Governors to honor the late William M. Jennings, longtime governor and president of the New York Rangers and one of the great builders of hockey in the United States.

Multiple Winners	
Patrick Roy	5
Martin Brodeur	4
Ed Belfour	4
Brian Hayward	3
Dominik Hasek	2
Roman Turek	2

CONN SMYTHE TROPHY

An annual award "to the most valuable player for his team in the playoffs." Winner selected by the Professional Hockey Writers' Association at the conclusion of the final game in the Stanley Cup Finals.

History: Presented by Maple Leaf Gardens Limited in 1964 to honor Conn Smythe, the former coach, manager, president and owner-governor of the Toronto Maple Leafs.

Multiple Winners	
Patrick Roy	3
Mario Lemieux	2
Wayne Gretzky	2
Bernie Parent	2
Bobby Orr	2

William M. Jennings Trophy

Jack Adams Award

Bill Masterton Trophy

Lester Patrick Trophy

Lester B. Pearson Award

JACK ADAMS AWARD

An annual award presented by the National Hockey League Broadcasters' Association to "the NHL coach adjudged to have contributed the most to his team's success." Winner selected by a poll among members of the NHL Broadcasters' Association at the end of the regular season.

History: The award was presented by the NHL Broadcasters' Association in 1974 to commemorate the late Jack Adams, coach and general manager of the Detroit Red Wings, whose lifetime dedication to hockey serves as an inspiration to all who aspire to further the game.

Multiple Winners	
Pat Burns	3
Scotty Bowman	2
Pat Quinn	2
Jacques Demers	2

LESTER PATRICK TROPHY

An annual award "for outstanding service to hockey in the United States." Eligible recipients are players, officials, coaches, executives and referees. Winners are selected by an award committee consisting of the commissioner of the NHL, an NHL governor, a representative of the New York Rangers, a member of the Hockey Hall of Fame builder's section, a member of the Hockey Hall of Fame player's section, a member of the U.S. Hockey Hall of Fame, a member of the NHL Broadcasters' Association and a member of the Professional Hockey Writers' Association. Each except the League Commissioner is rotated annually. The winner receives a miniature of the trophy.

History: Presented by the New York Rangers in 1966 to honor the late Lester Patrick, longtime general manager and coach of the New York Rangers, whose teams finished out of the playoffs only once in his first 16 years with the club.

BILL MASTERTON MEMORIAL TROPHY

An annual award under the trusteeship of the Professional Hockey Writers' Association to "the National Hockey League player who best exemplifies the qualities of perseverance, sportsmanship and dedication to hockey." Winner selected by a poll among the 30 chapters of the PHWA at the end of the regular season. A $2,500 grant from the PHWA is awarded annually to the Bill Masterton Scholarship Fund, based in Bloomington, MN, in the name of the Masterton Trophy winner.

History: The trophy was presented by the NHL Writers' Association in 1968 to commemorate the late Bill Masterton, a player with the Minnesota North Stars, who exhibited to a high degree the qualities of perseverance, sportsmanship and dedication to hockey, and who died January 15, 1968.

LESTER B. PEARSON AWARD

An annual award presented to the NHL's outstanding player as selected by the members of the National Hockey League Players' Association. The winner and the two runners-up receive monetary awards to donate to the grassroots hockey program of their choice, through the NHLPA's Goals & Dreams Fund.

History: The award was first presented in 1970-71 by the NHLPA in honor of the late Lester B. Pearson, former Prime Minister of Canada.

Multiple Winners	
Wayne Gretzky	5
Mario Lemieux	4
Guy Lafleur	3
Jaromir Jagr	2
Dominik Hasek	2
Mark Messier	2
Marcel Dionne	2
Phil Esposito	2

King Clancy Memorial Trophy

Presidents' Trophy

Maurice "Rocket" Richard Trophy

Bud Light Plus-Minus Award

KING CLANCY MEMORIAL TROPHY

An annual award "to the player who best exemplifies leadership qualities on and off the ice and has made a noteworthy humanitarian contribution in his community."

History: The King Clancy Memorial Trophy was presented to the National Hockey League by the Board of Governors in 1988 to honor the late Frank "King" Clancy.

Recent King Clancy Memorial Trophy winners: Brendan Shanahan, at left with trophy, Detroit, 2002-03 and Jarome Iginla, above, Calgary, 2003-04.

PRESIDENTS' TROPHY

An annual award to the club finishing the regular-season with the best overall record.

History: Presented to the National Hockey League in 1985-86 by the NHL Board of Governors to recognize the team compiling the top regular-season record.

Multiple Winners	
Detroit Red Wings	4
Colorado Avalanche	2
Dallas Stars	2
New York Rangers	2
Calgary Flames	2
Edmonton Oilers	2

MAURICE "ROCKET" RICHARD TROPHY

An annual award "presented to the player finishing the regular season as the League's goal-scoring leader."

History: A gift to the NHL from the Montreal Canadiens in 1999, the Maurice "Rocket" Richard Trophy honors one of the game's greatest stars. During his 18-year career with the Canadiens from 1942-43 through 1959-60, Richard was the first player in NHL history to score 50 goals in a season and 500 in his career. He played on eight Stanley Cup champions and led the League in goal scoring five times.

Multiple Winners	
Jarome Iginla	2
Pavel Bure	2

BUD LIGHT PLUS-MINUS AWARD

An annual award "to the player, having played a minimum of 60 games, who leads the League in plus/minus statistics" at the end of the regular season.

History: This award was first presented to the NHL in 1997-98 by Anheuser-Busch Inc. to recognize the League leader in plus-minus statistics. Plus-minus statistics are calculated by giving a player a "plus" when on-ice for an even-strength or short-handed goal scored by his team. He receives a "minus" when on-ice for an even-strength or short-handed goal scored by the opposing team. A plus-minus award has been presented since the 1982-83 season.

Multiple Winners	
Chris Pronger	2

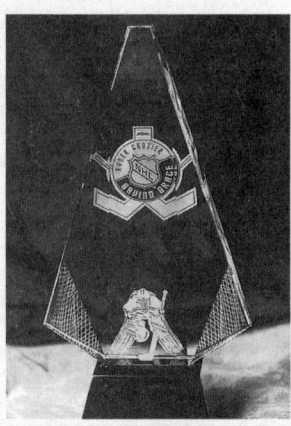

MBNA/Mastercard Roger Crozier
Saving Grace Award

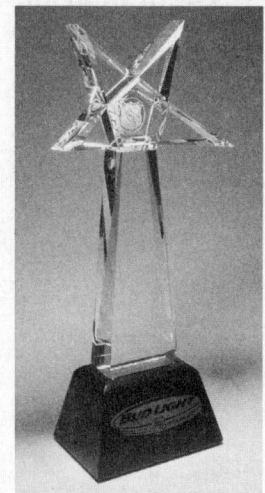

Bud Light NHL All-Star Game
MVP Award

MBNA/MASTERCARD
ROGER CROZIER SAVING GRACE AWARD

An award "presented to the goaltender having played a minimum of 25 games with the NHL's best save percentage during the regular season." The winner receives a monetary award to be donated to the youth hockey or educational program of his choice.

History: This award was first presented to the league in 1999-2000 by MBNA Corporation. It is named for Roger Crozier, one of the NHL's top goaltenders during his career. Crozier joined MBNA America Bank in 1983. He passed away on Jan. 11, 1996. Save percentage is calculated by dividing total saves by total shots faced.

Multiple Winners	
Marty Turco	2

BUD LIGHT NHL ALL-STAR GAME MVP AWARD

1962	Eddie Shack, Tor.	1984	Don Maloney, NYR
1963	Frank Mahovlich, Tor.	1985	Mario Lemieux, Pit.
1964	Jean Beliveau, Mtl.	1986	Grant Fuhr, Edm.
1965	Gordie Howe, Det.	1988	Mario Lemieux, Pit.
1967	Henri Richard, Mtl.	1989	Wayne Gretzky, L.A.
1968	Bruce Gamble, Tor.	1990	Mario Lemieux, Pit.
1969	Frank Mahovlich, Det.	1991	Vincent Damphousse, Tor.
1970	Bobby Hull, Chi.	1992	Brett Hull, St.L.
1971	Bobby Hull, Chi.	1993	Mike Gartner, NYR
1972	Bobby Orr, Bos.	1994	Mike Richter, NYR
1973	Greg Polis, Pit.	1996	Raymond Bourque, Bos.
1974	Garry Unger, St.L.	1997	Mark Recchi, Mtl.
1975	Syl Apps Jr., Pit.	1998	Teemu Selanne, Ana.
1976	Pete Mahovlich, Mtl.	1999	Wayne Gretzky, NYR
1977	Rick Martin, Buf.	2000	Pavel Bure, Fla.
1978	Billy Smith, NYI	2001	Bill Guerin, Bos.
1980	Reggie Leach, Phi.	2002	Eric Daze, Chi.
1981	Mike Liut, St.L.	2003	Dany Heatley, Atl.
1982	Mike Bossy, NYI	2004	Joe Sakic, Col.
1983	Wayne Gretzky, Edm.		

NHL/SHERATON ROAD PERFORMER AWARD

An award "to the players who accumulate the most road points." The player with the most road points at the end of each month is recognized as the monthly winner. At season's end, the player who accrues the most road points during the regular season wins year-end honors. Sheraton will donate one million Starpoints® to the charity of the player's choice. Points can be used for travel expenses including hotel stays, airline tickets and more.

History: This award was introduced for the 2003-04 season by the NHL and Sheraton Hotels & Resorts Worldwide, Inc

NATIONAL HOCKEY LEAGUE INDIVIDUAL AWARD WINNERS

ART ROSS TROPHY

	Winner	Runner-up
2005	....	
2004	Martin St. Louis, T.B.	Ilya Kovalchuk, Atl.
2003	Peter Forsberg, Col.	Markus Naslund, Van.
2002	Jarome Iginla, Cgy.	Markus Naslund, Van.
2001	Jaromir Jagr, Pit.	Joe Sakic, Col.
2000	Jaromir Jagr, Pit.	Pavel Bure, Fla.
1999	Jaromir Jagr, Pit.	Teemu Selanne, Ana.
1998	Jaromir Jagr, Pit.	Peter Forsberg, Col.
1997	Mario Lemieux, Pit.	Teemu Selanne, Ana.
1996	Mario Lemieux, Pit.	Jaromir Jagr, Pit.
1995	Jaromir Jagr, Pit.	Eric Lindros, Phi.
1994	Wayne Gretzky, L.A.	Sergei Fedorov, Det.
1993	Mario Lemieux, Pit.	Pat LaFontaine, Buf.
1992	Mario Lemieux, Pit.	Kevin Stevens, Pit.
1991	Wayne Gretzky, L.A.	Brett Hull, St.L.
1990	Wayne Gretzky, L.A.	Mark Messier, Edm.
1989	Mario Lemieux, Pit.	Wayne Gretzky, L.A.
1988	Mario Lemieux, Pit.	Wayne Gretzky, Edm.
1987	Wayne Gretzky, Edm.	Jari Kurri, Edm.
1986	Wayne Gretzky, Edm.	Mario Lemieux, Pit.
1985	Wayne Gretzky, Edm.	Jari Kurri, Edm.
1984	Wayne Gretzky, Edm.	Paul Coffey, Edm.
1983	Wayne Gretzky, Edm.	Peter Stastny, Que.
1982	Wayne Gretzky, Edm.	Mike Bossy, NYI
1981	Wayne Gretzky, Edm.	Marcel Dionne, L.A.
1980	Marcel Dionne, L.A.	Wayne Gretzky, Edm.
1979	Bryan Trottier, NYI	Marcel Dionne, L.A.
1978	Guy Lafleur, Mtl.	Bryan Trottier, NYI
1977	Guy Lafleur, Mtl.	Marcel Dionne, L.A.
1976	Guy Lafleur, Mtl.	Bobby Clarke, Phi.
1975	Bobby Orr, Bos.	Phil Esposito, Bos.
1974	Phil Esposito, Bos.	Bobby Orr, Bos.
1973	Phil Esposito, Bos.	Bobby Clarke, Phi.
1972	Phil Esposito, Bos.	Bobby Orr, Bos.
1971	Phil Esposito, Bos.	Bobby Orr, Bos.
1970	Bobby Orr, Bos.	Phil Esposito, Bos.
1969	Phil Esposito, Bos.	Bobby Hull, Chi.
1968	Stan Mikita, Chi.	Phil Esposito, Bos.
1967	Stan Mikita, Chi.	Bobby Hull, Chi.
1966	Bobby Hull, Chi.	Stan Mikita, Chi.
1965	Stan Mikita, Chi.	Norm Ullman, Det.
1964	Stan Mikita, Chi.	Bobby Hull, Chi.
1963	Gordie Howe, Det.	Andy Bathgate, NYR
1962	Bobby Hull, Chi.	Andy Bathgate, NYR
1961	Bernie Geoffrion, Mtl.	Jean Beliveau, Mtl.
1960	Bobby Hull, Chi.	Bronco Horvath, Bos.
1959	Dickie Moore, Mtl.	Jean Beliveau, Mtl.
1958	Dickie Moore, Mtl.	Henri Richard, Mtl.
1957	Gordie Howe, Det.	Ted Lindsay, Det.
1956	Jean Beliveau, Mtl.	Gordie Howe, Det.
1955	Bernie Geoffrion, Mtl.	Maurice Richard, Mtl.
1954	Gordie Howe, Det.	Maurice Richard, Mtl.
1953	Gordie Howe, Det.	Ted Lindsay, Det.
1952	Gordie Howe, Det.	Ted Lindsay, Det.
1951	Gordie Howe, Det.	Maurice Richard, Mtl.
1950	Ted Lindsay, Det.	Sid Abel, Det.
1949	Roy Conacher, Chi.	Doug Bentley, Chi.
1948*	Elmer Lach, Mtl.	Buddy O'Connor, NYR
1947	Max Bentley, Chi.	Maurice Richard, Mtl.
1946	Max Bentley, Chi.	Gaye Stewart, Tor.
1945	Elmer Lach, Mtl.	Maurice Richard, Mtl.
1944	Herb Cain, Bos.	Doug Bentley, Chi.
1943	Doug Bentley, Chi.	Bill Cowley, Bos.
1942	Bryan Hextall, NYR	Lynn Patrick, NYR
1941	Bill Cowley, Bos.	Bryan Hextall, NYR
1940	Milt Schmidt, Bos.	Woody Dumart, Bos.
1939	Toe Blake, Mtl.	Sweeney Schriner, NYA
1938	Gordie Drillon, Tor.	Syl Apps, Tor.
1937	Sweeney Schriner, NYA	Syl Apps, Tor.
1936	Sweeney Schriner, NYA	Marty Barry, Det.
1935	Charlie Conacher, Tor.	Syd Howe, St.L., Det.
1934	Charlie Conacher, Tor.	Joe Primeau, Tor
1933	Bill Cook, NYR	Busher Jackson, Tor.
1932	Busher Jackson, Tor.	Joe Primeau, Tor.
1931	Howie Morenz, Mtl.	Ebbie Goodfellow, Det.
1930	Cooney Weiland, Bos.	Frank Boucher, NYR
1929	Ace Bailey, Tor.	Nels Stewart, Mtl.M
1928	Howie Morenz, Mtl.	Aurel Joliat, Mtl.
1927	Bill Cook, NYR	Dick Irvin, Chi.
1926	Nels Stewart, Mtl.M	Cy Denneny, Ott.
1925	Babe Dye, Tor.	Cy Denneny, Ott.
1924	Cy Denneny, Ott.	Billy Boucher, Mtl.
1923	Babe Dye, Tor.	Cy Denneny, Ott.
1922	Punch Broadbent, Ott.	Cy Denneny, Ott.
1921	Newsy Lalonde, Mtl.	Babe Dye, Ham., Tor.
1920	Joe Malone, Que.	Newsy Lalonde, Mtl.
1919	Newsy Lalonde, Mtl.	Odie Cleghorn, Mtl.
1918	Joe Malone, Mtl.	Cy Denneny, Ott.

* Trophy first awarded in 1948.
  Scoring leaders listed from 1918 to 1947.

HART MEMORIAL TROPHY

	Winner	Runner-up
2005	....	
2004	Martin St. Louis, T.B.	Jarome Iginla, Cgy.
2003	Peter Forsberg, Col.	Markus Naslund, Van.
2002	Jose Theodore, Mtl.	Jarome Iginla, Cgy.
2001	Joe Sakic, Col.	Mario Lemieux, Pit.
2000	Chris Pronger, St.L.	Jaromir Jagr, Pit.
1999	Jaromir Jagr, Pit.	Alexei Yashin, Ott.
1998	Dominik Hasek, Buf.	Jaromir Jagr, Pit.
1997	Dominik Hasek, Buf.	Paul Kariya, Ana.
1996	Mario Lemieux, Pit.	Mark Messier, NYR
1995	Eric Lindros, Phi.	Jaromir Jagr, Pit.
1994	Sergei Fedorov, Det.	Dominik Hasek, Buf.
1993	Mario Lemieux, Pit.	Doug Gilmour, Tor.
1992	Mark Messier, NYR	Patrick Roy, Mtl.
1991	Brett Hull, St.L.	Wayne Gretzky, L.A.
1990	Mark Messier, Edm.	Raymond Bourque, Bos.
1989	Wayne Gretzky, L.A.	Mario Lemieux, Pit.
1988	Mario Lemieux, Pit.	Grant Fuhr, Edm.
1987	Wayne Gretzky, Edm.	Raymond Bourque, Bos.
1986	Wayne Gretzky, Edm.	Mario Lemieux, Pit.
1985	Wayne Gretzky, Edm.	Dale Hawerchuk, Wpg.
1984	Wayne Gretzky, Edm.	Rod Langway, Wsh.
1983	Wayne Gretzky, Edm.	Pete Peeters, Bos.
1982	Wayne Gretzky, Edm.	Bryan Trottier, NYI
1981	Wayne Gretzky, Edm.	Mike Liut, St.L.
1980	Wayne Gretzky, Edm.	Marcel Dionne, L.A.
1979	Bryan Trottier, NYI	Guy Lafleur, Mtl.
1978	Guy Lafleur, Mtl.	Bryan Trottier, NYI
1977	Guy Lafleur, Mtl.	Bobby Clarke, Phi.
1976	Bobby Clarke, Phi.	Denis Potvin, NYI
1975	Bobby Clarke, Phi.	Rogie Vachon, L.A.
1974	Phil Esposito, Bos.	Bernie Parent, Phi.
1973	Bobby Clarke, Phi.	Phil Esposito, Bos.
1972	Bobby Orr, Bos.	Ken Dryden, Mtl.
1971	Bobby Orr, Bos.	Phil Esposito, Bos.
1970	Bobby Orr, Bos.	Tony Esposito, Chi.
1969	Phil Esposito, Bos.	Jean Beliveau, Mtl.
1968	Stan Mikita, Chi.	Jean Beliveau, Mtl.
1967	Stan Mikita, Chi.	Ed Giacomin, NYR
1966	Bobby Hull, Chi.	Jean Beliveau, Mtl.
1965	Bobby Hull, Chi.	Norm Ullman, Det.
1964	Jean Beliveau, Mtl.	Bobby Hull, Chi.
1963	Gordie Howe, Det.	Stan Mikita, Chi.
1962	Jacques Plante, Mtl.	Doug Harvey, NYR
1961	Bernie Geoffrion, Mtl.	Johnny Bower, Tor.
1960	Gordie Howe, Det.	Bobby Hull, Chi.
1959	Andy Bathgate, NYR	Gordie Howe, Det.
1958	Gordie Howe, Det.	Andy Bathgate, NYR
1957	Gordie Howe, Det.	Jean Beliveau, Mtl.
1956	Jean Beliveau, Mtl.	Tod Sloan, Tor.
1955	Ted Kennedy, Tor.	Harry Lumley, Tor.
1954	Al Rollins, Chi.	Red Kelly, Det.
1953	Gordie Howe, Det.	Al Rollins, Chi.
1952	Gordie Howe, Det.	Elmer Lach, Mtl.
1951	Milt Schmidt, Bos.	Maurice Richard, Mtl.
1950	Chuck Rayner, NYR	Ted Kennedy, Tor.
1949	Sid Abel, Det.	Bill Durnan, Mtl.
1948	Buddy O'Connor, NYR	Frank Brimsek, Bos.
1947	Maurice Richard, Mtl.	Milt Schmidt, Bos.
1946	Max Bentley, Chi.	Gaye Stewart, Tor.
1945	Elmer Lach, Mtl.	Maurice Richard, Mtl.
1944	Babe Pratt, Tor.	Bill Cowley, Bos.
1943	Bill Cowley, Bos.	Doug Bentley, Chi.
1942	Tom Anderson, Bro.	Syl Apps, Tor.
1941	Bill Cowley, Bos.	Dit Clapper, Bos.
1940	Ebbie Goodfellow, Det.	Syl Apps, Tor.
1939	Toe Blake, Mtl.	Syl Apps, Tor.
1938	Eddie Shore, Bos.	Paul Thompson, Chi.
1937	Babe Siebert, Mtl.	Lionel Conacher, Mtl.M
1936	Eddie Shore, Bos.	Hooley Smith, Mtl.M
1935	Eddie Shore, Bos.	Charlie Conacher, Tor.
1934	Aurel Joliat, Mtl.	Lionel Conacher, Chi.
1933	Eddie Shore, Bos.	Bill Cook, NYR
1932	Howie Morenz, Mtl.	Ching Johnson, NYR
1931	Howie Morenz, Mtl.	Eddie Shore, Bos.
1930	Nels Stewart, Mtl.M.	Lionel Hitchman, Bos.
1929	Roy Worters, NYA	Ace Bailey, Tor.
1928	Howie Morenz, Mtl.	Roy Worters, Pit.
1927	Herb Gardiner, Mtl.	Bill Cook, NYR
1926	Nels Stewart, Mtl.M.	Sprague Cleghorn, Bos.
1925	Billy Burch, Ham.	Howie Morenz, Mtl.
1924	Frank Nighbor, Ott.	Sprague Cleghorn, Mtl.

BUD LIGHT PLUS-MINUS AWARD

2005	....	....
2004	Marek Malik	Vancouver
	Martin St. Louis	Tampa Bay
2003	Peter Forsberg	Colorado
	Milan Hejduk	Colorado
2002	Chris Chelios	Detroit
2001	Patrik Elias	New Jersey
	Joe Sakic	Colorado
2000	Chris Pronger	St. Louis
1999	John LeClair	Philadelphia
1998	Chris Pronger	St. Louis
1997	John LeClair	Philadelphia

WILLIAM M. JENNINGS TROPHY

	Winner	Runner-up
2005	....	
2004	Martin Brodeur, N.J.	Marty Turco, Dal.
2003	Martin Brodeur, N.J.	Marty Turco, Dal.
	Roman Cechmanek, Phi.	Ron Tugnutt, Dal.
	Robert Esche, Phi.	
2002	Patrick Roy, Col.	Tommy Salo, Edm.
2001	Dominik Hasek, Buf.	Ed Belfour, Dal.
		Marty Turco, Dal.
2000	Roman Turek, St.L.	John Vanbiesbrouck, Phi.
		Brian Boucher, Phi.
1999	Ed Belfour, Dal.	Dominik Hasek, Buf.
	Roman Turek, Dal.	
1998	Martin Brodeur, N.J.	Ed Belfour, Dal.
1997	Martin Brodeur, N.J.	Chris Osgood, Det.
	Mike Dunham, N.J.	Mike Vernon, Det.
1996	Chris Osgood, Det.	Martin Brodeur, N.J.
	Mike Vernon, Det.	
1995	Ed Belfour, Chi.	Mike Vernon, Det.
		Chris Osgood, Det.
1994	Dominik Hasek, Buf.	Martin Brodeur, N.J.
	Grant Fuhr, Buf.	Chris Terreri, N.J.
1993	Ed Belfour, Chi.	Felix Potvin, Tor.
		Grant Fuhr, Tor.
1992	Patrick Roy, Mtl.	Ed Belfour, Chi.
1991	Ed Belfour, Chi.	Patrick Roy, Mtl.
1990	Andy Moog, Bos.	Patrick Roy, Mtl.
	Reggie Lemelin, Bos.	Brian Hayward, Mtl.
1989	Patrick Roy, Mtl.	Mike Vernon, Cgy.
	Brian Hayward, Mtl.	Rick Wamsley, Cgy.
1988	Patrick Roy, Mtl.	Clint Malarchuk, Wsh.
	Brian Hayward, Mtl.	Pete Peeters, Wsh.
1987	Patrick Roy, Mtl.	Ron Hextall, Phi.
	Brian Hayward, Mtl.	
1986	Bob Froese, Phi.	Al Jensen, Wsh.
	Darren Jensen, Phi.	Pete Peeters, Wsh.
1985	Tom Barrasso, Buf.	Pat Riggin, Wsh.
	Bob Sauve, Buf.	
1984	Al Jensen, Wsh.	Tom Barrasso, Buf.
	Pat Riggin, Wsh.	Bob Sauve, Buf.
1983	Roland Melanson, NYI	Pete Peeters, Bos.
	Billy Smith, NYI	
1982	Rick Wamsley, Mtl.	Billy Smith, NYI
	Denis Herron, Mtl.	Roland Melanson, NYI

BILL MASTERTON MEMORIAL TROPHY

2005	....	
2004	Bryan Berard	Chicago
2003	Steve Yzerman	Detroit
2002	Saku Koivu	Montreal
2001	Adam Graves	NY Rangers
2000	Ken Daneyko	New Jersey
1999	John Cullen	Tampa Bay
1998	Jamie McLennan	St. Louis
1997	Tony Granato	San Jose
1996	Gary Roberts	Calgary
1995	Pat LaFontaine	Buffalo
1994	Cam Neely	Boston
1993	Mario Lemieux	Pittsburgh
1992	Mark Fitzpatrick	NY Islanders
1991	Dave Taylor	Los Angeles
1990	Gord Kluzak	Boston
1989	Tim Kerr	Philadelphia
1988	Bob Bourne	Los Angeles
1987	Doug Jarvis	Hartford
1986	Charlie Simmer	Boston
1985	Anders Hedberg	NY Rangers
1984	Brad Park	Detroit
1983	Lanny McDonald	Calgary
1982	Glenn Resch	Colorado
1981	Blake Dunlop	St. Louis
1980	Al MacAdam	Minnesota
1979	Serge Savard	Montreal
1978	Butch Goring	Los Angeles
1977	Ed Westfall	NY Islanders
1976	Rod Gilbert	NY Rangers
1975	Don Luce	Buffalo
1974	Henri Richard	Montreal
1973	Lowell MacDonald	Pittsburgh
1972	Bobby Clarke	Philadelphia
1971	Jean Ratelle	NY Rangers
1970	Pit Martin	Chicago
1969	Ted Hampson	Oakland
1968	Claude Provost	Montreal

NHL/SHERATON ROAD PERFORMER AWARD

2005	....	....
2004	Joe Sakic	Colorado

LADY BYNG MEMORIAL TROPHY

	Winner	Runner-up
2005	....	....
2004	Brad Richards, T.B.	Daniel Alfredsson, Ott.
2003	Alexander Mogilny, Tor.	Nicklas Lidstrom, Det.
2002	Ron Francis, Car.	Joe Sakic, Col.
2001	Joe Sakic, Col.	Nicklas Lidstrom, Det.
2000	Pavol Demitra, St.L.	Nicklas Lidstrom, Det.
1999	Wayne Gretzky, NYR.	Nicklas Lidstrom, Det.
1998	Ron Francis, Pit.	Teemu Selanne, Ana.
1997	Paul Kariya, Ana.	Teemu Selanne, Ana.
1996	Paul Kariya, Ana.	Adam Oates, Bos.
1995	Ron Francis, Pit.	Adam Oates, Bos.
1994	Wayne Gretzky, L.A.	Adam Oates, Bos.
1993	Pierre Turgeon, NYI	Adam Oates, Bos.
1992	Wayne Gretzky, L.A.	Joe Sakic, Que.
1991	Wayne Gretzky, L.A.	Brett Hull, St.L.
1990	Brett Hull, St.L.	Wayne Gretzky, L.A.
1989	Joe Mullen, Cgy.	Wayne Gretzky, L.A.
1988	Mats Naslund, Mtl.	Wayne Gretzky, Edm.
1987	Joe Mullen, Cgy.	Wayne Gretzky, Edm.
1986	Mike Bossy, NYI	Jari Kurri, Edm.
1985	Jari Kurri, Edm.	Joe Mullen, St.L.
1984	Mike Bossy, NYI	Rick Middleton, Bos.
1983	Mike Bossy, NYI	Rick Middleton, Bos.
1982	Rick Middleton, Bos.	Mike Bossy, NYI
1981	Rick Kehoe, Pit.	Wayne Gretzky, Edm.
1980	Wayne Gretzky, Edm.	Marcel Dionne, L.A.
1979	Bob MacMillan, Atl.	Marcel Dionne, L.A.
1978	Butch Goring, L.A.	Peter McNab, Bos.
1977	Marcel Dionne, L.A.	Jean Ratelle, Bos.
1976	Jean Ratelle, NYR-Bos.	Jean Pronovost, Pit.
1975	Marcel Dionne, Det.	John Bucyk, Bos.
1974	John Bucyk, Bos.	Lowell MacDonald, Pit.
1973	Gilbert Perreault, Buf.	Jean Ratelle, NYR
1972	Jean Ratelle, NYR	John Bucyk, Bos.
1971	John Bucyk, Bos.	Dave Keon, Tor.
1970	Phil Goyette, St.L.	John Bucyk, Bos.
1969	Alex Delvecchio, Det.	Ted Hampson, Oak.
1968	Stan Mikita, Chi.	John Bucyk, Bos.
1967	Stan Mikita, Chi.	Dave Keon, Tor.
1966	Alex Delvecchio, Det.	Bobby Rousseau, Mtl.
1965	Bobby Hull, Chi.	Alex Delvecchio, Det.
1964	Kenny Wharram, Chi.	Dave Keon, Tor.
1963	Dave Keon, Tor.	Camille Henry, NYR
1962	Dave Keon, Tor.	Claude Provost, Mtl.
1961	Red Kelly, Tor.	Norm Ullman, Det.
1960	Don McKenney, Bos.	Andy Hebenton, NYR
1959	Alex Delvecchio, Det.	Andy Hebenton, NYR
1958	Camille Henry, NYR	Don Marshall, Mtl.
1957	Andy Hebenton, NYR	Dutch Reibel, Det.
1956	Dutch Reibel, Det.	Floyd Curry, Mtl.
1955	Sid Smith, Tor.	Danny Lewicki, NYR
1954	Red Kelly, Det.	Don Raleigh, NYR
1953	Red Kelly, Det.	Wally Hergesheimer, NYR
1952	Sid Smith, Tor.	Red Kelly, Det.
1951	Red Kelly, Det.	Woody Dumart, Bos.
1950	Edgar Laprade, NYR	Red Kelly, Det.
1949	Bill Quackenbush, Det.	Harry Watson, Tor.
1948	Buddy O'Connor, NYR	Syl Apps, Tor.
1947	Bobby Bauer, Bos.	Syl Apps, Tor.
1946	Toe Blake, Mtl.	Clint Smith, Chi.
1945	Bill Mosienko, Chi.	Syd Howe, Det.
1944	Clint Smith, Chi.	Herb Cain, Bos.
1943	Max Bentley, Chi.	Buddy O'Connor, Mtl.
1942	Syl Apps, Tor.	Gordie Drillon, Tor.
1941	Bobby Bauer, Bos.	Gordie Drillon, Tor.
1940	Bobby Bauer, Bos.	Clint Smith, NYR
1939	Clint Smith, NYR	Marty Barry, Det.
1938	Gordie Drillon, Tor.	Clint Smith, NYR
1937	Marty Barry, Det.	Gordie Drillon, Tor.
1936	Doc Romnes, Chi.	Sweeney Schriner, NYA
1935	Frank Boucher, NYR	Russ Blinco, Mtl.M
1934	Frank Boucher, NYR	Joe Primeau, Tor.
1933	Frank Boucher, NYR	Joe Primeau, Tor.
1932	Joe Primeau, Tor.	Frank Boucher, NYR
1931	Frank Boucher, NYR	Normie Himes, NYA
1930	Frank Boucher, NYR	Normie Himes, NYA
1929	Frank Boucher, NYR	Harold Darragh, Pit.
1928	Frank Boucher, NYR	George Hay, Det.
1927	Billy Burch, NYA	Dick Irvin, Chi.
1926	Frank Nighbor, Ott.	Billy Burch, NYA
1925	Frank Nighbor, Ott.	none

KING CLANCY MEMORIAL TROPHY

2005	....	....
2004	Jarome Iginla	Calgary
2003	Brendan Shanahan	Detroit
2002	Ron Francis	Carolina
2001	Shjon Podein	Colorado
2000	Curtis Joseph	Toronto
1999	Rob Ray	Buffalo
1998	Kelly Chase	St. Louis
1997	Trevor Linden	Vancouver
1996	Kris King	Winnipeg
1995	Joe Nieuwendyk	Calgary
1994	Adam Graves	NY Rangers
1993	Dave Poulin	Boston
1992	Raymond Bourque	Boston
1991	Dave Taylor	Los Angeles
1990	Kevin Lowe	Edmonton
1989	Bryan Trottier	NY Islanders
1988	Lanny McDonald	Calgary

VEZINA TROPHY

	Winner	Runner-up
2005	....	
2004	Martin Brodeur, N.J.	Miikka Kiprusoff, Cgy.
2003	Martin Brodeur, N.J.	Marty Turco, Dal.
2002	Jose Theodore, Mtl.	Patrick Roy, Col.
2001	Dominik Hasek, Buf.	Roman Cechmanek, Phi.
2000	Olaf Kolzig, Wsh.	Roman Turek, St.L.
1999	Dominik Hasek, Buf.	Curtis Joseph, Tor.
1998	Dominik Hasek, Buf.	Martin Brodeur, N.J.
1997	Dominik Hasek, Buf.	Martin Brodeur, N.J.
1996	Jim Carey, Wsh.	Chris Osgood, Det.
1995	Dominik Hasek, Buf.	Ed Belfour, Chi.
1994	Dominik Hasek, Buf.	John Vanbiesbrouck, Fla.
1993	Ed Belfour, Chi.	Tom Barrasso, Pit.
1992	Patrick Roy, Mtl.	Kirk McLean, Van.
1991	Ed Belfour, Chi.	Patrick Roy, Mtl.
1990	Patrick Roy, Mtl.	Daren Puppa, Buf.
1989	Patrick Roy, Mtl.	Mike Vernon, Cgy.
1988	Grant Fuhr, Edm.	Tom Barrasso, Buf.
1987	Ron Hextall, Phi.	Mike Liut, Hfd.
1986	John Vanbiesbrouck, NYR	Bob Froese, Phi.
1985	Pelle Lindbergh, Phi.	Tom Barrasso, Buf.
1984	Tom Barrasso, Buf.	Reggie Lemelin, Cgy.
1983	Pete Peeters, Bos.	Roland Melanson, NYI
1982	Billy Smith, NYI	Grant Fuhr, Edm.
1981	Richard Sevigny, Mtl.	Pete Peeters, Phi.
	Denis Herron, Mtl.	Rick St. Croix, Phi.
	Michel Larocque, Mtl.	
1980	Bob Sauve, Buf.	Gerry Cheevers, Bos.
	Don Edwards, Buf.	Gilles Gilbert, Bos.
1979	Ken Dryden, Mtl.	Glenn Resch, NYI
	Michel Larocque, Mtl.	Billy Smith, NYI
1978	Ken Dryden, Mtl.	Bernie Parent, Phi.
	Michel Larocque, Mtl.	Wayne Stephenson, Phi.
1977	Ken Dryden, Mtl.	Glenn Resch, NYI
	Michel Larocque, Mtl.	Billy Smith, NYI
1976	Ken Dryden, Mtl.	Glenn Resch, NYI
		Billy Smith, NYI
1975	Bernie Parent, Phi.	Rogie Vachon, L.A.
		Gary Edwards, L.A.
1974	Bernie Parent, Phi. (tie)	Gilles Gilbert, Bos.
	Tony Esposito, Chi. (tie)	
1973	Ken Dryden, Mtl.	Ed Giacomin, NYR
		Gilles Villemure, NYR
1972	Tony Esposito, Chi.	Cesare Maniago, Min.
	Gary Smith, Chi.	Gump Worsley, Min.
1971	Ed Giacomin, NYR	Tony Esposito, Chi.
	Gilles Villemure, NYR	
1970	Tony Esposito, Chi.	Jacques Plante, St.L.
		Ernie Wakely, St.L.
1969	Jacques Plante, St.L.	Ed Giacomin, NYR
	Glenn Hall, St.L.	
1968	Gump Worsley, Mtl.	Johnny Bower, Tor.
	Rogie Vachon, Mtl.	Bruce Gamble, Tor.
1967	Glenn Hall, Chi.	Charlie Hodge, Mtl.
	Denis Dejordy, Chi.	
1966	Gump Worsley, Mtl.	Glenn Hall, Chi.
	Charlie Hodge, Mtl.	
1965	Terry Sawchuk, Tor.	Roger Crozier, Det.
	Johnny Bower, Tor.	
1964	Charlie Hodge, Mtl.	Glenn Hall, Chi.
1963	Glenn Hall, Chi.	Johnny Bower, Tor.
		Don Simmons, Tor.
1962	Jacques Plante, Mtl.	Johnny Bower, Tor.
1961	Johnny Bower, Tor.	Glenn Hall, Chi.
1960	Jacques Plante, Mtl.	Glenn Hall, Chi.
1959	Jacques Plante, Mtl.	Johnny Bower, Tor.
		Ed Chadwick, Tor.
1958	Jacques Plante, Mtl.	Gump Worsley, NYR
		Marcel Paille, NYR
1957	Jacques Plante, Mtl.	Glenn Hall, Det.
1956	Jacques Plante, Mtl.	Glenn Hall, Det.
1955	Terry Sawchuk, Det.	Harry Lumley, Tor.
1954	Harry Lumley, Tor.	Terry Sawchuk, Det.
1953	Terry Sawchuk, Det.	Gerry McNeil, Mtl.
1952	Terry Sawchuk, Det.	Al Rollins, Tor.
1951	Al Rollins, Tor.	Terry Sawchuk, Det.
1950	Bill Durnan, Mtl.	Harry Lumley, Det.
1949	Bill Durnan, Mtl.	Harry Lumley, Det.
1948	Turk Broda, Tor.	Harry Lumley, Det.
1947	Bill Durnan, Mtl.	Turk Broda, Tor.
1946	Bill Durnan, Mtl.	Frank Brimsek, Bos.
1945	Bill Durnan, Mtl.	Frank McCool, Tor. (tie)
		Harry Lumley, Det. (tie)
1944	Bill Durnan, Mtl.	Paul Bibeault, Tor.
1943	Johnny Mowers, Det.	Turk Broda, Tor.
1942	Frank Brimsek, Bos.	Turk Broda, Tor.
1941	Turk Broda, Tor.	Frank Brimsek, Bos. (tie)
		Johnny Mowers, Det. (tie)
1940	Dave Kerr, NYR	Frank Brimsek, Bos.
1939	Frank Brimsek, Bos.	Dave Kerr, NYR
1938	Tiny Thompson, Bos.	Dave Kerr, NYR
1937	Normie Smith, Det.	Dave Kerr, NYR
1936	Tiny Thompson, Bos.	Mike Karakas, Chi.
1935	Lorne Chabot, Chi.	Alex Connell, Mtl.M
1934	Charlie Gardiner, Chi.	Wilf Cude, Det.
1933	Tiny Thompson, Bos.	John Ross Roach, Det.
1932	Charlie Gardiner, Chi.	Alex Connell, Det.
1931	Roy Worters, NYA	Charlie Gardiner, Chi.
1930	Tiny Thompson, Bos.	Charlie Gardiner, Chi.
1929	George Hainsworth, Mtl.	Tiny Thompson, Bos.
1928	George Hainsworth, Mtl.	Alex Connell, Ott.
1927	George Hainsworth, Mtl.	Clint Benedict, Mtl.M

CALDER MEMORIAL TROPHY

	Winner	Runner-up
2005	....	....
2004	Andrew Raycroft, Bos.	Michael Ryder, Mtl.
2003	Barret Jackman, St.L.	Henrik Zetterberg, Det.
2002	Dany Heatley, Atl.	Ilya Kovalchuk, Atl.
2001	Evgeni Nabokov, S.J.	Brad Richards, T.B.
2000	Scott Gomez, N.J.	Brad Stuart, S.J.
1999	Chris Drury, Col.	Marian Hossa, Ott.
1998	Sergei Samsonov, Bos.	Mattias Ohlund, Van.
1997	Bryan Berard, NYI	Jarome Iginla, Cgy.
1996	Daniel Alfredsson, Ott.	Eric Daze, Chi.
1995	Peter Forsberg, Que.	Jim Carey, Wsh.
1994	Martin Brodeur, N.J.	Jason Arnott, Edm.
1993	Teemu Selanne, Wpg.	Joe Juneau, Bos.
1992	Pavel Bure, Van.	Nicklas Lidstrom, Det
1991	Ed Belfour, Chi.	Sergei Fedorov, Det.
1990	Sergei Makarov, Cgy.	Mike Modano, Min.
1989	Brian Leetch, NYR	Trevor Linden, Van.
1988	Joe Nieuwendyk, Cgy.	Ray Sheppard, Buf.
1987	Luc Robitaille, L.A.	Ron Hextall, Phi.
1986	Gary Suter, Cgy.	Wendel Clark, Tor.
1985	Mario Lemieux, Pit.	Chris Chelios, Mtl.
1984	Tom Barrasso, Buf.	Steve Yzerman, Det.
1983	Steve Larmer, Chi.	Phil Housley, Buf.
1982	Dale Hawerchuk, Wpg.	Barry Pederson, Bos.
1981	Peter Stastny, Que.	Larry Murphy, L.A.
1980	Raymond Bourque, Bos.	Mike Foligno, Det.
1979	Bobby Smith, Min	Ryan Walter, Wsh.
1978	Mike Bossy, NYI	Barry Beck, Col.
1977	Willi Plett, Atl.	Don Murdoch, NYR
1976	Bryan Trottier, NYI	Glenn Resch, NYI
1975	Eric Vail, Atl.	Pierre Larouche, Pit.
1974	Denis Potvin, NYI	Tom Lysiak, Atl.
1973	Steve Vickers, NYR	Bill Barber, Phi.
1972	Ken Dryden, Mtl.	Rick Martin, Buf.
1971	Gilbert Perreault, Buf.	Jude Drouin, Min.
1970	Tony Esposito, Chi.	Bill Fairbairn, NYR
1969	Danny Grant, Min.	Norm Ferguson, Oak.
1968	Derek Sanderson, Bos.	Jacques Lemaire, Mtl.
1967	Bobby Orr, Bos.	Ed Van Impe, Chi.
1966	Brit Selby, Tor.	Bert Marshall, Det.
1965	Roger Crozier, Det.	Ron Ellis, Tor.
1964	Jacques Laperriere, Mtl.	John Ferguson, Mtl.
1963	Kent Douglas, Tor.	Doug Barkley, Det.
1962	Bobby Rousseau, Mtl.	Cliff Pennington, Bos.
1961	Dave Keon, Tor.	Bob Nevin, Tor.
1960	Bill Hay, Chi.	Murray Oliver, Det.
1959	Ralph Backstrom, Mtl.	Carl Brewer, Tor.
1958	Frank Mahovlich, Tor.	Bobby Hull, Chi.
1957	Larry Regan, Bos.	Ed Chadwick, Tor.
1956	Glenn Hall, Det.	Andy Hebenton, NYR
1955	Ed Litzenberger, Chi.	Don McKenney, Bos.
1954	Camille Henry, NYR	Dutch Reibel, Det.
1953	Gump Worsley, NYR	Gord Hannigan, Tor.
1952	Bernie Geoffrion, Mtl.	Hy Buller, NYR
1951	Terry Sawchuk, Det.	Al Rollins, Tor.
1950	Jack Gelineau, Bos.	Phil Maloney, Bos.
1949	Pentti Lund, NYR	Allan Stanley, NYR
1948	Jim McFadden, Det.	Pete Babando, Bos.
1947	Howie Meeker, Tor.	Jim Conacher, Det.
1946	Edgar Laprade, NYR	George Gee, Chi.
1945	Frank McCool, Tor.	Ken Smith, Bos.
1944	Gus Bodnar, Tor.	Bill Durnan, Mtl.
1943	Gaye Stewart, Tor.	Glen Harmon, Mtl.
1942	Grant Warwick, NYR	Buddy O'Connor, Mtl.
1941	John Quilty, Mtl.	Johnny Mowers, Det.
1940	Kilby MacDonald, NYR	Wally Stanowski, Tor.
1939	Frank Brimsek, Bos.	Roy Conacher, Bos.
1938	Cully Dahlstrom, Chi.	Murph Chamberlain, Tor.
1937	Syl Apps, Tor.	Gordie Drillon, Tor.
1936	Mike Karakas, Chi.	Bucko McDonald, Det.
1935	Sweeney Schriner, NYA	Bert Connelly, NYR
1934	Russ Blinco, Mtl.M.	none
1933	Carl Voss, Det.	none

FRANK J. SELKE TROPHY

	Winner	Runner-up
2005	....	....
2004	Kris Draper, Det.	John Madden, N.J.
2003	Jere Lehtinen, Dal.	John Madden, N.J.
2002	Michael Peca, NYI	Craig Conroy, Cgy.
2001	John Madden, N.J.	Joe Sakic, Col.
2000	Steve Yzerman, Det.	Michal Handzus, St.L.
1999	Jere Lehtinen, Dal.	Magnus Arvedson, Ott.
1998	Jere Lehtinen, Dal.	Michael Peca, Buf.
1997	Michael Peca, Buf.	Peter Forsberg, Col.
1996	Sergei Fedorov, Det.	Ron Francis, Pit.
1995	Ron Francis, Pit.	Esa Tikkanen, St.L.
1994	Sergei Fedorov, Det.	Doug Gilmour, Tor.
1993	Doug Gilmour, Tor.	Dave Poulin, Bos.
1992	Guy Carbonneau, Mtl.	Sergei Fedorov, Det.
1991	Dirk Graham, Chi.	Esa Tikkanen, Edm.
1990	Rick Meagher, St.L.	Guy Carbonneau, Mtl.
1989	Guy Carbonneau, Mtl.	Esa Tikkanen, Edm.
1988	Guy Carbonneau, Mtl.	Steve Kasper, Bos.
1987	Dave Poulin, Phi.	Guy Carbonneau, Mtl.
1986	Troy Murray, Chi.	Ron Sutter, Phi.
1985	Craig Ramsay, Buf.	Doug Jarvis, Wsh.
1984	Doug Jarvis, Wsh.	Bryan Trottier, NYI
1983	Bobby Clarke, Phi.	Jari Kurri, Edm.
1982	Steve Kasper, Bos.	Bob Gainey, Mtl.
1981	Bob Gainey, Mtl.	Craig Ramsay, Buf.
1980	Bob Gainey, Mtl.	Craig Ramsay, Buf.
1979	Bob Gainey, Mtl.	Don Marcotte, Bos.
1978	Bob Gainey, Mtl.	Craig Ramsay, Buf.

CONN SMYTHE TROPHY

2005	....	....
2004	Brad Richards	Tampa Bay
2003	Jean-Sebastien Giguere	Anaheim
2002	Nicklas Lidstrom	Detroit
2001	Patrick Roy	Colorado
2000	Scott Stevens	New Jersey
1999	Joe Nieuwendyk	Dallas
1998	Steve Yzerman	Detroit
1997	Mike Vernon	Detroit
1996	Joe Sakic	Colorado
1995	Claude Lemieux	New Jersey
1994	Brian Leetch	NY Rangers
1993	Patrick Roy	Montreal
1992	Mario Lemieux	Pittsburgh
1991	Mario Lemieux	Pittsburgh
1990	Bill Ranford	Edmonton
1989	Al MacInnis	Calgary
1988	Wayne Gretzky	Edmonton
1987	Ron Hextall	Philadelphia
1986	Patrick Roy	Montreal
1985	Wayne Gretzky	Edmonton
1984	Mark Messier	Edmonton
1983	Billy Smith	NY Islanders
1982	Mike Bossy	NY Islanders
1981	Butch Goring	NY Islanders
1980	Bryan Trottier	NY Islanders
1979	Bob Gainey	Montreal
1978	Larry Robinson	Montreal
1977	Guy Lafleur	Montreal
1976	Reggie Leach	Philadelphia
1975	Bernie Parent	Philadelphia
1974	Bernie Parent	Philadelphia
1973	Yvan Cournoyer	Montreal
1972	Bobby Orr	Boston
1971	Ken Dryden	Montreal
1970	Bobby Orr	Boston
1969	Serge Savard	Montreal
1968	Glenn Hall	St. Louis
1967	Dave Keon	Toronto
1966	Roger Crozier	Detroit
1965	Jean Beliveau	Montreal

JAMES NORRIS MEMORIAL TROPHY

	Winner	Runner-up
2005	....	....
2004	Scott Niedermayer, N.J.	Zdeno Chara, Ott.
2003	Nicklas Lidstrom, Det.	Al MacInnis, St.L.
2002	Nicklas Lidstrom, Det.	Chris Chelios, Det.
2001	Nicklas Lidstrom, Det.	Raymond Bourque, Col.
2000	Chris Pronger, St.L.	Nicklas Lidstrom, Det.
1999	Al MacInnis, St.L.	Nicklas Lidstrom, Det.
1998	Rob Blake, L.A.	Nicklas Lidstrom, Det.
1997	Brian Leetch, NYR	V. Konstantinov, Det.
1996	Chris Chelios, Chi.	Raymond Bourque, Bos.
1995	Paul Coffey, Det.	Chris Chelios, Chi.
1994	Raymond Bourque, Bos.	Scott Stevens, N.J.
1993	Chris Chelios, Chi.	Raymond Bourque, Bos.
1992	Brian Leetch, NYR	Raymond Bourque, Bos.
1991	Raymond Bourque, Bos.	Al MacInnis, Cgy.
1990	Raymond Bourque, Bos.	Al MacInnis, Cgy.
1989	Chris Chelios, Mtl	Paul Coffey, Pit.
1988	Raymond Bourque, Bos.	Scott Stevens, Wsh.
1987	Raymond Bourque, Bos.	Mark Howe, Phi.
1986	Paul Coffey, Edm.	Mark Howe, Phi.
1985	Paul Coffey, Edm.	Raymond Bourque, Bos.
1984	Rod Langway, Wsh.	Paul Coffey, Edm.
1983	Rod Langway, Wsh.	Mark Howe, Phi.
1982	Doug Wilson, Chi.	Raymond Bourque, Bos.
1981	Randy Carlyle, Pit.	Denis Potvin, NYI
1980	Larry Robinson, Mtl.	Borje Salming, Tor.
1979	Denis Potvin, NYI	Larry Robinson, Mtl.
1978	Denis Potvin, NYI	Brad Park, Bos.
1977	Larry Robinson, Mtl.	Borje Salming, Tor.
1976	Denis Potvin, NYI	Brad Park, NYR-Bos.
1975	Bobby Orr, Bos.	Denis Potvin, NYI
1974	Bobby Orr, Bos.	Brad Park, NYR
1973	Bobby Orr, Bos.	Guy Lapointe, Mtl.
1972	Bobby Orr, Bos.	Brad Park, NYR
1971	Bobby Orr, Bos.	Brad Park, NYR
1970	Bobby Orr, Bos.	Brad Park, NYR
1969	Bobby Orr, Bos.	Tim Horton, Tor.
1968	Bobby Orr, Bos.	J.C. Tremblay, Mtl
1967	Harry Howell, NYR	Pierre Pilote, Chi.
1966	Jacques Laperriere, Mtl.	Pierre Pilote, Chi.
1965	Pierre Pilote, Chi.	Jacques Laperriere, Mtl.
1964	Pierre Pilote, Chi.	Tim Horton, Tor.
1963	Pierre Pilote, Chi.	Carl Brewer, Tor.
1962	Doug Harvey, NYR	Pierre Pilote, Chi.
1961	Doug Harvey, Mtl.	Marcel Pronovost, Det.
1960	Doug Harvey, Mtl.	Allan Stanley, Tor.
1959	Tom Johnson, Mtl.	Bill Gadsby, NYR
1958	Doug Harvey, Mtl.	Bill Gadsby, NYR
1957	Doug Harvey, Mtl.	Red Kelly, Det.
1956	Doug Harvey, Mtl.	Bill Gadsby, NYR
1955	Doug Harvey, Mtl.	Red Kelly, Det.
1954	Red Kelly, Det.	Doug Harvey, Mtl.

MAURICE "ROCKET" RICHARD TROPHY

2005	....	....
2004	Rick Nash	Columbus
	Jarome Iginla	Calgary
	Ilya Kovalchuk	Atlanta
2003	Milan Hejduk	Colorado
2002	Jarome Iginla	Calgary
2001	Pavel Bure	Florida
2000	Pavel Bure	Florida
1999	Teemu Selanne	Anaheim

LESTER PATRICK TROPHY

2005	....	
2004	Mike Emrick	
	John Davidson	
	Ray Miron	
2003	Raymond Bourque	
	Ron DeGregorio	
	Willie O'Ree	
2002	1960 U.S. Olympic Hockey Team	
	Herb Brooks	
	Larry Pleau	
2001	Scotty Bowman	
	David Poile	
	Gary Bettman	
2000	Mario Lemieux	
	Craig Patrick	
	Lou Vairo	
1999	Harry Sinden	
	1998 U.S. Olympic Women's Hockey Team	
1998	Peter Karmanos	
	Neal Broten	
	John Mayasich	
	Max McNab	
1997	*Seymour H. Knox III	
	Bill Cleary	
	Pat LaFontaine	
1996	George Gund	
	Ken Morrow	
	Milt Schmidt	
1995	Joe Mullen	
	Brian Mullen	
	Bob Fleming	
1994	Wayne Gretzky	
	Robert Ridder	
1993	*Frank Boucher	
	*Mervyn "Red" Dutton	
	Bruce McNall	
	Gil Stein	
1992	Al Arbour	
	Art Berglund	
	Lou Lamoriello	
1991	Rod Gilbert	
	Mike Ilitch	
1990	Len Ceglarski	
1989	Dan Kelly	
	Lou Nanne	
	*Lynn Patrick	
	Bud Poile	
1988	Keith Allen	
	Fred Cusick	
	Bob Johnson	
1987	*Hobey Baker	
	Frank Mathers	
1986	John MacInnes	
	Jack Riley	
1985	Jack Butterfield	
	Arthur M. Wirtz	
1984	John A. Ziegler, Jr.	
	*Arthur Howie Ross	
1983	Bill Torrey	
1982	Emile P. Francis	
1981	Charles M. Schulz	
1980	Bobby Clarke	
	Edward M. Snider	
	Frederick A. Shero	
	1980 U.S. Olympic Hockey Team	
1979	Bobby Orr	
1978	Phil Esposito	
	Tom Fitzgerald	
	William T. Tutt	
	William W. Wirtz	
1977	John P. Bucyk	
	Murray A. Armstrong	
	John Mariucci	
1976	Stanley Mikita	
	George A. Leader	
	Bruce A. Norris	
1975	Donald M. Clark	
	William L. Chadwick	
	Thomas N. Ivan	
1974	Alex Delvecchio	
	Murray Murdoch	
	*Weston W. Adams, Sr.	
	*Charles L. Crovat	
1973	Walter L. Bush, Jr.	
1972	Clarence S. Campbell	
	John A. "Snooks" Kelly	
	Ralph "Cooney" Weiland	
	*James D. Norris	
1971	William M. Jennings	
	*John B. Sollenberger	
	*Terrance G. Sawchuk	
1970	Edward W. Shore	
	*James C. V. Hendy	
1969	Robert M. Hull	
	*Edward J. Jeremiah	
1968	Thomas F. Lockhart	
	*Walter A. Brown	
	*Gen. John R. Kilpatrick	
1967	Gordon Howe	
	*Charles F. Adams	
	*James Norris, Sr.	
1966	J.J. "Jack" Adams	
	* awarded posthumously	

PRESIDENTS' TROPHY

	Winner	Runner-up
2005	....	....
2004	Detroit Red Wings	Tampa Bay Lightning
2003	Ottawa Senators	Dallas Stars
2002	Detroit Red Wings	Boston Bruins
2001	Colorado Avalanche	Detroit Red Wings
2000	St. Louis Blues	Detroit Red Wings
1999	Dallas Stars	New Jersey Devils
1998	Dallas Stars	New Jersey Devils
1997	Colorado Avalanche	Dallas Stars
1996	Detroit Red Wings	Colorado Avalanche
1995	Detroit Red Wings	Quebec Nordiques
1994	New York Rangers	New Jersey Devils
1993	Pittsburgh Penguins	Boston Bruins
1992	New York Rangers	Washington Capitals
1991	Chicago Blackhawks	St. Louis Blues
1990	Boston Bruins	Calgary Flames
1989	Calgary Flames	Montreal Canadiens
1988	Calgary Flames	Montreal Canadiens
1987	Edmonton Oilers	Philadelphia Flyers
1986	Edmonton Oilers	Philadelphia Flyers

LESTER B. PEARSON AWARD

2005	....	....
2004	Martin St. Louis	Tampa Bay
2003	Markus Naslund	Vancouver
2002	Jarome Iginla	Calgary
2001	Joe Sakic	Colorado
2000	Jaromir Jagr	Pittsburgh
1999	Jaromir Jagr	Pittsburgh
1998	Dominik Hasek	Buffalo
1997	Dominik Hasek	Buffalo
1996	Mario Lemieux	Pittsburgh
1995	Eric Lindros	Philadelphia
1994	Sergei Fedorov	Detroit
1993	Mario Lemieux	Pittsburgh
1992	Mark Messier	NY Rangers
1991	Brett Hull	St. Louis
1990	Mark Messier	Edmonton
1989	Steve Yzerman	Detroit
1988	Mario Lemieux	Pittsburgh
1987	Wayne Gretzky	Edmonton
1986	Mario Lemieux	Pittsburgh
1985	Wayne Gretzky	Edmonton
1984	Wayne Gretzky	Edmonton
1983	Wayne Gretzky	Edmonton
1982	Wayne Gretzky	Edmonton
1981	Mike Liut	St. Louis
1980	Marcel Dionne	Los Angeles
1979	Marcel Dionne	Los Angeles
1978	Guy Lafleur	Montreal
1977	Guy Lafleur	Montreal
1976	Guy Lafleur	Montreal
1975	Bobby Orr	Boston
1974	Phil Esposito	Boston
1973	Bobby Clarke	Philadelphia
1972	Jean Ratelle	NY Rangers
1971	Phil Esposito	Boston

JACK ADAMS AWARD

	Winner	Runner-up
2005	....	....
2004	John Tortorella, T.B.	Ron Wilson, S.J.
2003	Jacques Lemaire, Min.	John Tortorella, T.B.
2002	Bob Francis, Phx.	Brian Sutter, Chi.
2001	Bill Barber, Phi.	Scotty Bowman, Det.
2000	Joel Quenneville, St.L.	Alain Vigneault, Mtl.
1999	Jacques Martin, Ott.	Pat Quinn, Tor.
1998	Pat Burns, Bos.	Larry Robinson, L.A.
1997	Ted Nolan, Buf.	Ken Hitchcock, Dal.
1996	Scotty Bowman, Det.	Doug MacLean, Fla.
1995	Marc Crawford, Que.	Scotty Bowman, Det.
1994	Jacques Lemaire, N.J.	Kevin Constantine, S.J.
1993	Pat Burns, Tor.	Brian Sutter, Bos.
1992	Pat Quinn, Van.	Roger Neilson, NYR
1991	Brian Sutter, St.L.	Tom Webster, L.A.
1990	Bob Murdoch, Wpg.	Mike Milbury, Bos.
1989	Pat Burns, Mtl.	Bob McCammon, Van.
1988	Jacques Demers, Det.	Terry Crisp, Cgy.
1987	Jacques Demers, Det.	Jack Evans, Hfd.
1986	Glen Sather, Edm.	Jacques Demers, St.L.
1985	Mike Keenan, Phi.	Barry Long, Wpg.
1984	Bryan Murray, Wsh.	Scotty Bowman, Buf.
1983	Orval Tessier, Chi.	
1982	Tom Watt, Wpg.	
1981	Red Berenson, St.L.	Bob Berry, L.A.
1980	Pat Quinn, Phi.	
1979	Al Arbour, NYI	Fred Shero, NYR
1978	Bobby Kromm, Det.	Don Cherry, Bos.
1977	Scotty Bowman, Mtl.	Tom McVie, Wsh.
1976	Don Cherry, Bos.	
1975	Bob Pulford, L.A.	
1974	Fred Shero, Phi.	

MBNA/MASTERCARD ROGER CROZIER SAVING GRACE AWARD

	Winner	Runner-up
2005	....	....
2004	Dwayne Roloson, Min.	Miikka Kiprusoff, Cgy.
2003	Marty Turco, Dal.	Dwayne Roloson, Min.
2002	Jose Theodore, Mtl.	Patrick Roy, Col.
2001	Marty Turco, Dal.	Mike Dunham, N.J.
2000	Ed Belfour, Dal.	Jose Theodore, Mtl.

NHL Entry Draft

History

Year	Location	Date	Players Drafted
1963	Queen Elizabeth Hotel, Montreal	June 5	21
1964	Queen Elizabeth Hotel, Montreal	June 11	24
1965	Queen Elizabeth Hotel, Montreal	April 27	11
1966	Mount Royal Hotel, Montreal	April 25	24
1967	Queen Elizabeth Hotel, Montreal	June 7	18
1968	Queen Elizabeth Hotel, Montreal	June 13	24
1969	Queen Elizabeth Hotel, Montreal	June 12	84
1970	Queen Elizabeth Hotel, Montreal	June 11	115
1971	Queen Elizabeth Hotel, Montreal	June 10	117
1972	Queen Elizabeth Hotel, Montreal	June 8	152
1973	Mount Royal Hotel, Montreal	May 15	168
1974	NHL Montreal Office	May 28	247
1975	NHL Montreal Office	June 3	217
1976	NHL Montreal Office	June 1	135
1977	NHL Montreal Office	June 14	185
1978	Queen Elizabeth Hotel, Montreal	June 15	234
1979	Queen Elizabeth Hotel, Montreal	August 9	126
1980	Montreal Forum	June 11	210
1981	Montreal Forum	June 10	211
1982	Montreal Forum	June 9	252
1983	Montreal Forum	June 8	242
1984	Montreal Forum	June 9	250
1985	Toronto Convention Centre	June 15	252
1986	Montreal Forum	June 21	252
1987	Joe Louis Arena, Detroit	June 13	252
1988	Montreal Forum	June 11	252
1989	Met Sports Center, Bloomington	June 17	252
1990	B.C. Place, Vancouver	June 16	250
1991	Memorial Auditorium, Buffalo	June 22	264
1992	Montreal Forum	June 20	264
1993	Le Colisee, Quebec	June 26	286
1994	Hartford Civic Center	June 28-29	286
1995	Edmonton Coliseum	July 8	234
1996	Kiel Center, St. Louis	June 22	241
1997	Civic Arena, Pittsburgh	June 21	246
1998	Marine Midland Arena, Buffalo	June 27	258
1999	FleetCenter, Boston	June 26	272
2000	Saddledome, Calgary	June 24-25	293
2001	National Car Rental Center, Florida	June 23-24	289
2002	Air Canada Centre, Toronto	June 22-23	290
2003	Gaylord Entertainment Center, Nashville	June 21-22	292
2004	RBC Center, Raleigh, NC	June 26-27	291
2005	Sheraton Hotel and Towers, Ottawa	July 30	230

First Selections

Year	Player	Pos	Team	Drafted From	Age
1963	Garry Monahan	LW	Montreal	St. Michael's Juveniles	16.7
1964	Claude Gauthier		Detroit	Comite des jeunes (Rosemont)	
1965	Andre Veilleux	RW	NY Rangers	Montreal Ranger Jr. B	
1966	Barry Gibbs	D	Boston	Estevan Bruins	17.7
1967	Rick Pagnutti	D	Los Angeles	Garson Native Sons	20.6
1968	Michel Plasse	G	Montreal	Drummondville Rangers	20.0
1969	Rejean Houle	LW	Montreal	Montreal Jr. Canadiens	19.8
1970	Gilbert Perreault	C	Buffalo	Montreal Jr. Canadiens	19.7
1971	Guy Lafleur	RW	Montreal	Quebec Remparts	19.9
1972	Billy Harris	RW	NY Islanders	Toronto Marlboros	20.4
1973	Denis Potvin	D	NY Islanders	Ottawa 67s	19.7
1974	Greg Joly	D	Washington	Regina Pats	20.0
1975	Mel Bridgman	C	Philadelphia	Victoria Cougars	20.1
1976	Rick Green	D	Washington	London Knights	20.3
1977	Dale McCourt	C	Detroit	St. Catharines Fincups	20.4
1978	Bobby Smith	C	Minnesota	Ottawa 67's	20.4
1979	Rob Ramage	D	Colorado	London Knights	20.5
1980	Doug Wickenheiser	C	Montreal	Regina Pats	19.2
1981	Dale Hawerchuk	C	Winnipeg	Cornwall Royals	18.2
1982	Gord Kluzak	D	Boston	Nanaimo Islanders	18.3
1983	Brian Lawton	C	Minnesota	Mount St. Charles HS	18.11
1984	Mario Lemieux	C	Pittsburgh	Laval Voisins	18.8
1985	Wendel Clark	LW/D	Toronto	Saskatoon Blades	18.7
1986	Joe Murphy	C	Detroit	Michigan State	18.8
1987	Pierre Turgeon	C	Buffalo	Granby Bisons	17.10
1988	Mike Modano	C	Minnesota	Prince Albert Raiders	18.0
1989	Mats Sundin	RW	Quebec	Nacka (Sweden)	18.4
1990	Owen Nolan	RW	Quebec	Cornwall Royals	18.4
1991	Eric Lindros	C	Quebec	Oshawa Generals	18.3
1992	Roman Hamrlik	D	Tampa Bay	ZPS Zlin (Czech.)	18.2
1993	Alexandre Daigle	C	Ottawa	Victoriaville Tigres	18.5
1994	Ed Jovanovski	D	Florida	Windsor Spitfires	18.0
1995	Bryan Berard	D	Ottawa	Detroit Jr. Red Wings	18.4
1996	Chris Phillips	D	Ottawa	Prince Albert Raiders	18.3
1997	Joe Thornton	C	Boston	Sault Ste. Marie	17.11
1998	Vincent Lecavalier	C	Tampa Bay	Rimouski Oceanic	18.2
1999	Patrik Stefan	C	Atlanta	Long Beach Ice Dogs (IHL)	18.9
2000	Rick DiPietro	G	NY Islanders	Boston University	18.9
2001	Ilya Kovalchuk	RW	Atlanta	Spartak (Russia)	18.2
2002	Rick Nash	LW	Columbus	London Knights	18.0
2003	Marc-Andre Fleury	G	Pittsburgh	Cape Breton Screaming Eagles	18.0
2004	Alexander Ovechkin	LW	Washington	Dynamo Moscow (Russia)	18.9
2005	Sidney Crosby	C	Pittsburgh	Rimouski Oceanic	17.11

Draft Summary

Following is a summary of the players drafted from the Ontario Hockey League (OHL), Quebec Major Junior Hockey League (QMJHL), Western Hockey League (WHL), United States colleges, United States high schools, European leagues and other North American leagues since 1969. "Other" may include Canadian and U.S. Jr. A and Jr. B, minor professional leagues (AHL, IHL), midget and other teams playing in leagues not listed above.

Year	Total Picks	OHL Picks	%	QMJHL Picks	%	WHL Picks	%	College Picks	%	Hi School Picks	%	Int'l Picks	%	Other Picks	%
1969	84	36	42.9	11	13.1	20	23.8	7	8.3	-	-	1	1.2	9	10.7
1970	115	51	44.3	13	11.3	22	19.1	16	13.9	-	-	-	-	13	11.3
1971	117	41	35.0	13	11.1	28	23.9	22	18.8	-	-	-	-	13	11.1
1972	152	46	30.3	30	19.7	44	28.9	21	13.8	-	-	-	-	11	7.2
1973	168	56	33.3	24	14.3	49	29.2	25	14.9	-	-	-	-	14	8.3
1974	247	69	27.9	40	16.2	66	26.7	41	16.6	-	-	6	2.4	25	10.1
1975	217	55	25.3	28	12.9	57	26.3	59	27.2	-	-	6	2.8	12	5.5
1976	135	47	34.8	18	13.3	33	24.4	26	19.3	-	-	8	5.9	3	2.2
1977	185	42	22.7	40	21.6	44	23.8	49	26.5	-	-	5	2.7	5	2.7
1978	234	59	25.2	22	9.4	48	20.5	73	31.2	-	-	16	6.8	16	6.8
1979	126	48	38.1	19	15.1	37	29.4	15	11.9	-	-	6	4.8	1	0.8
1980	210	73	34.8	24	11.4	41	19.5	42	20.0	7	3.3	13	6.2	10	4.8
1981	211	59	28.0	28	13.3	37	17.5	21	10.0	17	8.1	32	15.2	17	8.1
1982	252	60	23.8	17	6.7	55	21.8	20	7.9	47	18.7	35	13.9	18	7.1
1983	242	57	23.6	24	9.9	41	16.9	14	5.8	35	14.5	34	14.0	37	15.3
1984	250	55	22.0	16	6.4	37	14.8	22	8.8	44	17.6	40	16.0	36	14.4
1985	252	59	23.4	15	6.0	48	19.0	20	7.9	48	19.0	31	12.3	31	12.3
1986	252	66	26.2	22	8.7	32	12.7	22	8.7	40	15.9	28	11.1	42	16.7
1987	252	32	12.7	17	6.7	36	14.3	40	15.9	69	27.4	38	15.1	20	7.9
1988	252	32	12.7	22	8.7	30	11.9	48	19.0	56	22.2	39	15.5	25	9.9
1989	252	39	15.5	16	6.3	44	17.5	48	19.0	47	18.7	38	15.1	20	7.9
1990	250	39	15.6	14	5.6	33	13.2	38	15.2	57	22.8	53	21.2	16	6.4
1991	264	43	16.3	25	9.5	40	15.2	43	16.3	37	14.0	55	20.8	21	8.0
1992	264	57	21.6	22	8.3	45	17.0	9	3.4	25	9.5	84	31.8	22	8.3
1993	286	60	21.0	23	8.0	44	15.4	17	5.9	33	11.5	78	27.3	31	10.8
1994	286	45	15.7	28	9.8	66	23.1	6	2.1	28	9.8	80	28.0	33	11.5
1995	234	54	23.1	35	15.0	55	23.5	5	2.1	2	0.9	69	29.5	14	6.0
1996	241	51	21.2	31	12.9	54	22.4	6	2.5	5	2.1	58	24.1	16	6.6
1997	246	52	21.1	19	7.7	63	25.6	26	10.6	4	1.6	63	25.6	19	7.7
1998	258	50	19.4	41	15.9	44	17.1	27	10.5	7	2.7	75	29.1	14	5.4
1999	272	52	19.1	20	7.4	40	14.7	36	13.2	9	3.3	94	34.6	21	7.7
2000	293	39	13.3	21	7.2	41	14.0	35	11.9	7	2.4	123	42.0	27	9.2
2001	289	41	14.2	26	9.0	45	15.6	24	8.3	8	2.8	119	41.2	26	9.0
2002	290	35	12.1	23	7.9	43	14.8	41	14.1	6	2.1	110	37.9	32	11.0
2003	292	44	15.1	38	13.0	41	14.0	23	7.9	10	3.4	93	31.8	43	14.7
2004	291	42	14.4	27	9.3	44	15.1	28	9.6	18	6.2	88	30.2	44	15.1
2005	230	43	18.7	23	10.0	43	18.7	13	5.6	18	7.8	50	21.7	40	17.4
Total	**1829**		**21.5**	**875**	**10.3**	**1590**	**18.7**	**1047**	**12.3**	**685**	**8.0**	**1668**	**19.5**	**797**	**9.3**

Total Players Drafted (1969-2005): 8,491

Top prospects at the 2005 NHL Entry Draft pose in Ottawa prior to the event. Left to right, top row: Sidney Crosby (Rimouski, C, 1st by Pittsburgh), Alex Bourret (Lewiston, RW, 16th by Atlanta), Devin Setoguchi (Saskatoon, RW, 8th by San Jose). Middle row: Jack Skille (USA U-18, RW, 7th by Chicago), Ryan Parent (Guelph, D, 18th by Nashville). Bottom row: Luc Bourdon (Val-d'Or, D, 10th by Vancouver), Martin Hanzal (Ceske Budejovice, C, 17th by Phoenix).

Ontario Hockey League Draft Selections by Club

Total	Club	'05	'04	'03	'02	'01	'00	'99	'98	'97	'96	'95	'94	'93	'92	'91	'90	'89	'88	'87	'86	'85	'84	'83	'82	'81	'80	'79	'78	'77	'76	'75	'74	'73	'72	'71	'70	'69
160	Peterborough	2	5	5	1	2	1	4	1	5	4	5	2	4	4	3	4	2	2	5	2	9	3	7	5	3	10	9	6	4	1	8	4	9	5	4	5	5
144	Oshawa	–	3	3	3	1	2	3	4	3	1	10	1	4	4	4	2	4	2	3	6	6	6	5	5	9	2	3	3	1	6	6	7	5	5	3	4	5
137	London	3	6	4	2	2	1	4	8	1	4	1	1	4	3	1	3	3	6	2	3	1	7	3	5	5	2	6	3	4	5	3	6	6	5	1	9	4
136	Kitchener	4	2	1	4	1	1	–	5	3	2	4	2	4	1	3	5	7	1	2	3	6	4	8	5	5	4	4	4	3	1	3	13	4	8	2	6	1
131	Ottawa	2	3	2	–	3	2	6	2	5	2	1	1	4	6	5	5	–	1	2	3	3	2	2	9	4	8	3	5	5	5	6	5	6	4	3	4	2
105	Sudbury	4	0	1	1	2	–	5	5	3	1	2	2	10	2	8	2	1	–	1	3	5	2	–	4	2	7	3	4	4	5	4	6	6	–	–	–	–
104	Sault Ste. Marie	1	3	1	2	1	1	1	4	1	4	3	4	3	7	2	1	3	2	1	7	5	4	6	1	8	3	3	5	1	5	2	5	4	–	–	–	–
93	Kingston	2	–	1	1	2	–	4	1	4	4	3	2	5	3	2	2	–	1	1	4	3	3	1	2	5	8	2	9	4	6	4	4	–	–	–	–	–
74	Windsor	3	2	2	2	2	2	2	1	5	1	4	3	–	3	–	1	2	5	–	7	3	2	2	3	5	3	2	4	1	2	–	–	–	–	–	–	–
66	Guelph	2	2	1	2	4	1	3	5	1	6	5	7	2	2	–	–	4	–	2	8	3	5	1	–	–	–	–	–	–	–	–	–	–	–	–	–	–
62	Saginaw/N. Bay	3	1	2	2	3	2	2	2	1	1	2	7	2	5	2	4	1	3	3	3	3	4	4	–	–	–	–	–	–	–	–	–	–	–	–	–	–
55	Belleville	2	–	–	2	3	1	5	2	5	–	3	3	–	4	1	2	4	–	2	5	4	4	3	–	–	–	–	–	–	–	–	–	–	–	–	–	–
51	Plymouth	3	3	3	3	3	6	2	2	4	3	6	2	7	2	2	–	–	–	–	–	–	–	–	–	–	–	–	–	–	–	–	–	–	–	–	–	–
28	Sarnia	3	–	5	2	1	3	1	3	2	7	1	–	–	–	–	–	–	–	–	–	–	–	–	–	–	–	–	–	–	–	–	–	–	–	–	–	–
25	Owen Sound	2	1	1	1	–	1	–	1	2	3	2	3	4	2	1	1	–	–	–	–	–	–	–	–	–	–	–	–	–	–	–	–	–	–	–	–	–
24	Brampton	4	2	4	3	3	6	2	–	–	–	–	–	–	–	–	–	–	–	–	–	–	–	–	–	–	–	–	–	–	–	–	–	–	–	–	–	–
21	Barrie	–	–	1	1	1	3	6	3	4	2	–	–	–	–	–	–	–	–	–	–	–	–	–	–	–	–	–	–	–	–	–	–	–	–	–	–	–
17	Erie	2	2	–	2	2	3	2	1	3	–	–	–	–	–	–	–	–	–	–	–	–	–	–	–	–	–	–	–	–	–	–	–	–	–	–	–	–
16	St. Michael's	–	4	5	1	5	1	–	–	–	–	–	–	–	–	–	–	–	–	–	–	–	–	–	–	–	–	–	–	–	–	–	–	–	–	–	–	–
8	Mississauga	1	3	2	–	–	2	–	–	–	–	–	–	–	–	–	–	–	–	–	–	–	–	–	–	–	–	–	–	–	–	–	–	–	–	–	–	–
Teams no longer operating																																						
97	Toronto	–	–	–	–	–	–	–	–	–	–	–	–	–	–	–	–	2	2	1	4	3	4	4	6	2	10	4	5	7	4	4	8	6	5	6	7	3
72	Niagara Falls	–	–	–	–	–	–	–	–	–	6	2	3	4	4	4	4	4	–	–	–	–	–	–	6	6	8	5	3	2	–	–	–	–	4	1	2	4
62	Hamilton	–	–	–	–	–	–	–	–	–	–	–	–	–	–	2	–	–	4	4	6	3	–	–	–	–	–	1	8	–	3	7	4	6	4	5	3	2
52	St. Catharines	–	–	–	–	–	–	–	–	–	–	–	–	–	–	–	–	–	–	–	–	–	–	–	–	–	–	–	–	6	4	8	7	4	5	8	5	5
37	Cornwall	–	–	–	–	–	–	–	–	–	–	–	–	–	5	3	3	2	3	3	2	2	3	4	7	–	–	–	–	–	–	–	–	–	–	–	–	–
27	Brantford	–	–	–	–	–	–	–	–	–	–	–	–	–	–	–	–	–	–	–	–	–	2	7	2	5	8	3	–	–	–	–	–	–	–	–	–	–
20	Montreal	–	–	–	–	–	–	–	–	–	–	–	–	–	–	–	–	–	–	–	–	–	–	–	–	–	–	–	–	–	–	–	–	–	1	8	6	5
5	Newmarket	–	–	–	–	–	–	–	–	–	–	–	2	3	–	–	–	–	–	–	–	–	–	–	–	–	–	–	–	–	–	–	–	–	–	–	–	–

Quebec Major Junior Hockey League Draft Selections by Club

Total	Club	'05	'04	'03	'02	'01	'00	'99	'98	'97	'96	'95	'94	'93	'92	'91	'90	'89	'88	'87	'86	'85	'84	'83	'82	'81	'80	'79	'78	'77	'76	'75	'74	'73	'72	'71	'70	'69
73	Shawinigan	1	3	2	2	1	1	1	3	1	4	2	1	1	3	2	–	2	–	1	2	–	2	5	5	2	2	–	–	3	–	3	5	1	6	1	2	3
70	Gatineau/Hull	–	4	4	5	2	–	4	3	–	3	3	1	3	3	3	3	2	2	3	4	–	1	3	–	1	3	–	3	2	2	3	–	–	–	–	–	–
70	Lewiston/Sher.	5	2	1	–	3	–	–	5	1	–	4	2	3	–	–	–	–	–	–	–	–	–	–	2	5	1	4	3	6	5	7	3	4	2	2	–	
52	Drummondville	2	1	1	–	1	1	–	2	2	3	4	1	2	2	4	–	1	4	2	2	2	1	–	–	–	–	–	–	–	–	–	1	2	4	1	4	2
51	Chicoutimi	4	–	1	3	1	1	–	1	2	–	2	3	1	1	–	1	1	2	2	1	3	–	3	1	6	3	1	1	5	–	–	1	–	–	–	–	–
25	Halifax	1	3	6	–	3	2	–	3	3	1	3	–	–	–	–	–	–	–	–	–	–	–	–	–	–	–	–	–	–	–	–	–	–	–	–	–	–
22	Rimouski	2	3	4	–	4	2	2	5	–	–	–	–	–	–	–	–	–	–	–	–	–	–	–	–	–	–	–	–	–	–	–	–	–	–	–	–	–
21	Val-d'Or	2	1	1	1	2	2	3	–	2	4	2	1	–	–	–	–	–	–	–	–	–	–	–	–	–	–	–	–	–	–	–	–	–	–	–	–	–
18	PEI/Mtl. Rocket	2	8	1	3	1	1	2	–	–	–	–	–	–	–	–	–	–	–	–	–	–	–	–	–	–	–	–	–	–	–	–	–	–	–	–	–	–
17	Quebec	2	1	3	1	3	–	3	4	–	–	–	–	–	–	–	–	–	–	–	–	–	–	–	–	–	–	–	–	–	–	–	–	–	–	–	–	–
14	Baie-Comeau	–	3	2	1	3	2	–	3	–	–	–	–	–	–	–	–	–	–	–	–	–	–	–	–	–	–	–	–	–	–	–	–	–	–	–	–	–
14	Moncton	1	2	3	2	–	–	2	2	1	1	–	–	–	–	–	–	–	–	–	–	–	–	–	–	–	–	–	–	–	–	–	–	–	–	–	–	–
12	Cape Breton	–	3	2	2	1	1	–	3	–	–	–	–	–	–	–	–	–	–	–	–	–	–	–	–	–	–	–	–	–	–	–	–	–	–	–	–	–
11	Rouyn-Noranda	1	–	2	–	–	4	1	3	–	–	–	–	–	–	–	–	–	–	–	–	–	–	–	–	–	–	–	–	–	–	–	–	–	–	–	–	–
7	Acadie-Bathurst	–	–	3	2	–	–	2	–	–	–	–	–	–	–	–	–	–	–	–	–	–	–	–	–	–	–	–	–	–	–	–	–	–	–	–	–	–
Teams no longer operating																																						
54	Laval	–	–	–	–	–	–	–	3	1	2	4	5	2	1	4	3	3	1	3	5	–	2	1	2	–	–	1	2	4	1	1	2	–	1	–	–	–
47	Quebec	–	–	–	–	–	–	–	–	–	–	–	–	–	–	–	–	–	–	–	–	3	2	2	1	2	2	3	1	7	3	1	6	6	4	2	1	1
47	Trois Rivieres	–	–	–	–	–	–	–	–	–	–	–	–	–	1	2	1	3	3	1	–	3	–	3	1	2	2	2	3	6	2	3	2	2	2	2	1	–
45	Cornwall	–	–	–	–	–	–	–	–	–	–	–	–	–	–	–	–	–	–	–	–	–	–	–	–	5	5	1	6	1	3	1	8	4	6	2	1	2
32	Montreal	–	–	–	–	–	–	–	–	–	–	–	–	–	–	–	–	–	–	–	–	–	–	–	3	–	3	4	2	3	1	8	4	4	–	–	–	–
30	Granby	–	–	–	–	–	–	–	–	1	3	2	5	1	–	2	–	2	–	4	2	2	3	1	2	–	–	–	–	–	–	–	–	–	–	–	–	–
30	Victoriaville	–	–	–	3	1	3	2	1	2	3	1	1	6	2	–	1	–	4	–	–	–	–	–	–	–	–	–	–	–	–	–	–	–	–	–	–	–
28	Sorel	–	–	–	–	–	–	–	–	–	–	–	–	–	–	–	–	–	–	–	–	–	–	–	–	5	–	–	–	3	1	1	8	1	3	1	3	2
27	Verdun	–	–	–	–	–	–	–	–	–	–	–	–	–	3	–	–	1	3	0	3	–	3	3	–	–	3	3	1	–	–	–	–	–	2	1	1	–
21	Beauport	–	–	–	–	–	–	–	–	3	3	7	3	1	3	1	–	–	–	–	–	–	–	–	–	–	–	–	–	–	–	–	–	–	–	–	–	–
16	St. Jean	–	–	–	–	–	–	–	–	–	–	1	1	2	1	3	–	1	3	0	1	1	–	2	–	–	–	–	–	–	–	–	–	–	–	–	–	–
15	St. Hyacinthe	–	–	–	–	–	–	–	–	–	4	–	4	1	2	1	3	–	–	–	–	–	–	–	–	–	–	–	–	–	–	–	–	–	–	–	–	–
12	Longueuil	–	–	–	–	–	–	–	–	–	–	–	–	–	–	3	2	–	–	1	2	1	2	1	–	–	–	–	–	–	–	–	–	–	–	–	–	–
2	St. Jerome	–	–	–	–	–	–	–	–	–	–	–	–	–	–	–	–	–	–	–	–	–	–	–	–	–	–	–	–	–	–	–	–	–	–	1	–	1

Western Hockey League Draft Selections by Club

Total	Club	'05	'04	'03	'02	'01	'00	'99	'98	'97	'96	'95	'94	'93	'92	'91	'90	'89	'88	'87	'86	'85	'84	'83	'82	'81	'80	'79	'78	'77	'76	'75	'74	'73	'72	'71	'70	'69
104	Regina	1	0	2	1	2	2	4	2	3	4	2	3	–	4	–	1	5	–	2	3	4	4	8	6	5	3	1	4	1	3	5	8	1	5	5	–	–
104	Kamloops	2	5	2	5	2	4	4	1	3	4	5	9	2	3	6	4	5	1	3	4	4	4	4	2	–	–	–	–	4	4	4	4	–	–	–	–	–
103	Portland	3	2	1	2	–	6	1	3	3	1	2	3	4	4	1	1	4	1	3	4	2	5	7	7	6	8	7	8	4	–	–	–	–	–	–	–	–
102	Saskatoon	4	1	–	–	4	1	4	2	2	2	2	4	2	3	2	2	3	4	4	5	1	3	5	5	3	2	2	1	4	3	5	4	8	3	1	–	1
102	Medicine Hat	4	2	3	3	2	–	1	3	2	7	2	6	1	3	3	1	4	1	5	2	6	1	2	1	2	4	–	4	5	3	5	4	6	4	–	–	–
96	Brandon	2	0	3	4	2	–	–	4	5	2	6	5	2	1	1	1	–	3	3	1	2	3	1	2	2	5	10	1	3	–	4	7	2	5	1	3	–
90	Seattle	3	2	5	1	5	4	6	2	8	1	5	5	4	2	3	6	2	4	2	1	3	1	–	6	–	3	2	4	–	–	–	–	–	–	–	–	–
85	Lethbridge	–	2	2	2	1	3	–	1	5	1	3	3	4	3	7	4	3	3	–	1	5	1	2	7	4	1	4	5	3	2	3	–	–	–	–	–	–
80	Prince Albert	2	4	2	1	4	2	3	3	5	3	4	3	5	2	6	4	3	3	1	6	6	2	2	4	–	–	–	–	–	–	–	–	–	–	–	–	–
57	Moose Jaw	3	3	3	3	3	5	1	2	4	4	4	3	2	3	2	1	3	–	3	1	4	–	–	–	–	–	–	–	–	–	–	–	–	–	–	–	–
56	Swift Current	1	2	2	4	1	3	1	2	2	1	4	4	5	1	1	2	2	2	5	–	–	–	–	–	–	–	–	–	–	–	–	6	3	–	1	–	1
56	Spokane	4	1	–	3	3	2	1	1	4	5	4	4	4	7	5	1	2	3	1	–	–	–	–	–	1	–	–	–	–	–	–	–	–	–	–	–	–
51	Tri-City	2	4	1	3	2	2	1	4	1	6	6	2	2	5	3	3	4	–	–	–	–	–	–	–	–	–	–	–	–	–	–	–	–	–	–	–	–
40	Red Deer	1	1	4	4	6	1	1	5	3	4	2	5	3	–	–	–	–	–	–	–	–	–	–	–	–	–	–	–	–	–	–	–	–	–	–	–	–
29	Calgary	2	5	3	2	1	4	6	3	–	3	–	–	–	–	–	–	–	–	–	–	–	–	–	–	–	–	–	–	–	–	–	–	–	–	–	–	–
28	Kelowna	2	4	4	1	1	1	2	2	7	4	–	–	–	–	–	–	–	–	–	–	–	–	–	–	–	–	–	–	–	–	–	–	–	–	–	–	–
21	Prince George	1	2	2	–	4	–	2	4	2	2	2	–	–	–	–	–	–	–	–	–	–	–	–	–	–	–	–	–	–	–	–	–	–	–	–	–	–
14	Kootenay	3	2	1	3	2	1	2	–	–	–	–	–	–	–	–	–	–	–	–	–	–	–	–	–	–	–	–	–	–	–	–	–	–	–	–	–	–
7	Vancouver	3	2	1	1	–	–	–	–	–	–	–	–	–	–	–	–	–	–	–	–	–	–	–	–	–	–	–	–	–	–	–	–	–	–	–	–	–
Teams no longer operating																																						
70	Victoria	–	–	–	–	–	–	–	–	–	–	–	2	2	1	–	2	4	4	2	1	2	4	3	2	6	8	1	3	3	4	7	5	2	2	–	–	–
66	Calgary	–	–	–	–	–	–	–	–	–	–	–	–	–	–	–	–	–	–	–	2	3	3	3	4	5	2	–	3	4	4	4	8	4	7	2	5	3
62	New Westm'r	–	–	–	–	–	–	–	–	–	–	–	–	–	–	–	–	–	1	2	1	1	2	–	–	–	1	5	6	8	5	9	7	8	6	–	–	–
39	Flin Flon	–	–	–	–	–	–	–	–	–	–	–	–	–	–	–	–	–	–	–	–	–	–	–	–	–	–	–	5	1	3	4	7	4	2	5	4	4
38	Edmonton	–	–	–	–	–	–	–	–	4	–	–	–	–	–	–	–	–	–	–	–	–	–	–	–	–	–	2	–	–	2	3	2	6	6	5	4	4
34	Winnipeg	–	–	–	–	–	–	–	–	–	–	–	–	–	–	–	–	–	–	–	–	–	–	1	4	1	–	–	–	4	–	4	4	5	2	4	2	3
13	Billings	–	–	–	–	–	–	–	–	–	–	–	–	–	–	–	–	–	–	–	–	–	–	–	–	2	4	3	4	–	–	–	–	–	–	–	–	–
12	Estevan	–	–	–	–	–	–	–	–	–	–	–	–	–	–	–	–	–	–	–	–	–	–	–	–	–	–	–	–	–	–	–	–	–	–	4	4	4
12	Tacoma	–	–	–	–	–	–	–	–	–	–	2	5	2	3	–	–	–	–	–	–	–	–	–	–	–	–	–	–	–	–	–	–	–	–	–	–	–
11	Kelowna	–	–	–	–	–	–	–	–	–	–	–	–	–	–	–	–	–	–	–	–	5	4	2	–	–	–	–	–	–	–	–	–	–	–	–	–	–
6	Nanaimo	–	–	–	–	–	–	–	–	–	–	–	–	–	–	–	–	–	–	–	–	–	–	1	5	–	–	–	–	–	–	–	–	–	–	–	–	–
2	Vancouver	–	–	–	–	–	–	–	–	–	–	–	–	–	–	–	–	–	–	–	–	–	–	–	–	–	–	–	–	–	–	–	–	–	2	–	–	–

Montreal selected Michael Ryder (top) from Hull in the QMJHL with the 216th pick in the 1998 NHL Entry Draft. Calgary's Jarome Iginla was the Dallas Stars' first choice (11th overall) from Kamloops in the WHL.

U.S. College Hockey Draft Selections by School

Total	School	'05	'04	'03	'02	'01	'00	'99	'98	'97	'96	'95	'94	'93	'92	'91	'90	'89	'88	'87	'86	'85	'84	'83	'82	'81	'80	'79	'78	'77	'76	'75	'74	'73	'72	'71	'70	'69
66	Minnesota	1	0	2	3	–	3	3	1	2	3	2	–	–	1	1	1	2	–	1	1	1	2	–	1	1	1	3	2	5	5	4	4	9	–	–	2	3	1
64	Michigan	1	3	2	3	2	1	2	3	1	3	–	1	1	2	4	5	3	2	1	–	1	1	–	–	4	–	6	1	3	3	2	2	–	–	–	1
50	Boston U.	–	1	–	3	2	1	3	2	1	1	1	–	1	1	2	2	1	3	2	2	1	1	–	1	–	1	5	4	1	1	1	1	–	–	4	–
47	Michigan State	–	2	1	4	–	2	2	1	1	1	–	1	1	1	4	5	4	4	4	1	1	–	2	–	2	–	–	–	1	1	1	1	–	1	1	–
46	Michigan Tech	–	–	1	–	–	–	1	–	1	2	1	–	2	1	1	1	2	2	2	–	1	–	4	1	2	1	4	4	5	2	1	3	–	–
43	Denver	2	1	–	1	–	–	1	–	3	–	–	–	–	–	1	1	4	2	1	–	–	1	–	1	2	2	2	2	1	3	2	4	2	3	1
41	Wisconsin	–	–	–	–	3	2	–	–	–	–	1	–	–	1	–	1	–	1	–	1	1	–	2	3	–	1	–	3	2	4	4	5	4	2	1	–
38	North Dakota	–	1	1	–	1	–	1	–	2	–	–	–	–	1	1	2	–	–	–	1	–	–	1	3	3	3	1	–	1	2	4	1	3	3	2
36	Boston College	1	1	1	3	2	3	–	3	3	2	–	–	–	2	–	2	1	–	–	1	1	2	–	5	–	1	1	–	1	1	–	–	–	1	–
34	Cornell	1	2	2	1	–	2	2	–	1	–	–	–	2	5	2	1	–	2	1	–	1	1	1	–	1	1	–	1	1	1	–	1	1	2	–
34	Harvard	1	–	–	3	2	2	1	2	1	3	–	1	2	–	1	–	–	2	1	1	–	2	–	1	1	–	–	2	2	–	2	–	–	2	–	1	–
34	Providence	–	0	1	1	–	2	–	2	1	–	–	–	–	1	–	1	1	–	2	1	4	5	–	4	3	2	3	–	–	–	–	–
32	Colorado	1	0	2	1	1	2	1	3	–	–	1	–	–	–	2	–	–	1	–	1	–	–	3	–	–	–	2	2	1	3	1	–	–	–	–	1	2
32	Clarkson	–	–	–	–	1	1	3	–	–	–	1	2	3	1	1	1	–	1	1	1	1	1	1	1	2	2	–	2	–	1	2	2	–
31	New Hampshire	–	1	–	1	–	2	1	–	1	–	–	–	–	1	–	–	1	–	2	1	1	2	1	1	4	–	6	3	1	1	–	–
30	Notre Dame	–	2	–	2	1	1	2	–	2	1	–	–	–	–	–	–	1	1	3	–	2	7	–	3	2	–
27	Bowling Green	1	–	–	1	1	–	1	1	1	–	–	1	3	1	2	3	–	–	1	–	1	1	1	1	2	3	1	–
25	RPI	–	–	–	1	2	2	–	1	–	1	3	–	–	2	2	–	1	1	1	2	1	–	1	3	–	1	–
24	Lake Superior	–	–	–	–	–	–	1	–	–	1	3	2	3	–	3	–	1	–	–	3	–	1	1	1	–
23	St. Lawrence	–	–	–	–	–	–	1	–	–	2	1	1	1	1	1	1	–	3	–	4	1	1	–
23	W. Michigan	–	–	1	–	–	1	1	–	–	2	–	4	1	1	1	2	–	2	2	–	2	–	–
22	Northern Mich.	–	2	2	–	1	–	1	–	–	–	1	2	1	4	–	–	1	2	1	–	4	–
21	Ohio State	1	0	1	2	2	–	1	1	–	1	1	1	1	–	2	2	–	–	1	–	1	2	–
21	Maine	–	1	2	–	1	4	1	4	1	1	1	–	2	3	–	1	–	1	1	–
20	Vermont	1	–	–	2	–	1	–	–	1	–	–	–	–	2	1	1	–	1	1	1	1	–	4	–	1	–
20	Miami U.	1	2	–	1	1	–	1	1	–	1	1	2	4	2	1	–
15	Yale	–	2	–	3	–	1	–	–	–	–	2	1	–	–	1	–	2	1	–	1	1	–
13	Brown	–	1	–	–	1	–	–	–	–	1	–	–	–	–	–	1	2	3	1	2	1	–
13	Minn.-Duluth	–	–	–	–	–	–	–	–	1	2	1	2	–	1	1	1	–	–	1	2	–
12	Colgate	–	1	–	1	–	–	–	–	2	2	1	–	–	–	1	2	–	1	–	1	–
10	Northeastern	–	–	–	1	1	–	1	1	–	–	1	1	–	1	1	1	–	1	1	–
10	Princeton	–	–	–	1	–	1	–	–	1	–	–	1	–	1	1	1	1	1	1	–

Colleges with fewer than 10 players drafted: 9 - Dartmouth; 8 - Ferris State, Merrimack; 7 - Mass.-Lowell, St.Cloud State; 6 - Illinois-Chicago, St. Louis; 5 - Pennsylvania, Union College; 4 - Alaska-Anchorage, Mass.-Amherst, Nebraska-Omaha; 3 - Babson College; 2 - Alaska-Fairbanks, Minnesota State (Mankato); 1 - Air Force, American International College, Army, Bemidji State, Greenway, Hamilton, St. Anselem College, St. Thomas, Salem State, San Diego U., Wisconsin-River Falls.

U.S. High and Prep Schools Draft Selections by School (10 or more players drafted)

Total	School	'05	'04	'03	'02	'01	'00	'99	'98	'97	'96	'95	'94	'93	'92	'91	'90	'89	'88	'87	'86	'85	'84	'83	'82	'81	'80
21	Northwood Prep (NY)	–	1	–	–	–	1	–	–	–	–	1	1	–	1	3	1	1	4	2	2	–	2	–	–
20	Cushing Acad. (MA)	1	2	–	–	1	–	1	1	–	2	2	–	1	3	2	3	–	–	1	–	–	–
16	Edina (MN)	–	–	–	–	–	–	–	–	–	1	–	1	2	2	1	–	2	2	4	1	–
16	Belmont Hill (MA)	–	–	–	–	–	–	1	–	2	1	2	3	1	2	1	2	–	1	–
15	Hill-Murray (MN)	–	–	–	–	–	–	–	1	–	–	3	2	–	3	3	–	3	–
14	Catholic Memorial (MA)	–	2	–	–	–	1	–	–	2	1	2	–	2	1	1	–	2	–
13	Deerfield (IL)	–	1	1	–	2	1	–	–	–	–	1	–	2	1	1	–	1	1	–
12	Mount St. Charles (RI)	–	–	–	–	–	–	–	–	–	1	1	2	1	2	–	1	3	1	–
12	Culver Mil. Acad. (IN)	–	–	–	–	–	–	2	2	1	2	2	1	2	–
12	St. Sebastian's (MA)	–	4	1	1	–	–	1	–	1	2	2	–
11	Hotchkiss (CT)	–	1	–	1	–	–	–	2	1	3	–	1	–	1	–
11	Canterbury (CT)	–	1	–	1	–	–	–	–	1	2	–	2	–	3	–	2	–
10	Matignon (MA)	–	–	–	–	–	–	–	–	–	1	–	–	3	–	3	1	1	1
10	Roseau (MN)	–	–	–	–	–	–	–	–	–	1	3	1	–	1	1	1	–	1
10	Choate (CT)	–	–	–	–	1	–	–	–	–	–	1	1	1	–	3	2	1	–

U.S. College and High School Firsts

1967 – First U.S. College Player Drafted
Michigan Tech center Al Karlander was selected 17th overall by the Detroit Red Wings.

1979 – First U.S. College First-Round Selection
Minnesota-born defenseman Mike Ramsey (currently an assistant coach with the Minnesota Wild) was selected 11th overall by the Buffalo Sabres.

1980 – First U.S. High School Player Drafted
Center Jay North of Bloomington-Jefferson H.S. was taken 62nd overall by the Buffalo Sabres in 1980.

1981 – First U.S. High School First- Round Selection
Center Bob Carpenter of St. John's prep school was selected third overall by Washington in 1981.

1983 – First U.S. High School Player Drafted First Overall
Minnesota North Stars selected left winger Brian Lawton from Mount St. Charles H.S. first overall in 1983.

1986 – First U.S. College Player Drafted First Overall
Detroit selected right winger Joe Murphy from Michigan State first overall in 1986.

2005 – Most U.S. College Players Selected in the First Round
The 2005 draft saw eight U.S. college players selected in the first round, the most in Entry Draft history. Seven were selected in the first round in 2003 and 1986, six in 2000, five in 2002, four in 2001 and three in each of the 1986 and 1999 Entry Drafts.

2005 NHL Entry Draft Order of Selection

A weighted lottery system was used to determine the order of selection for all seven rounds of the 2005 NHL Entry Draft. The Pittsburgh Penguins won the Draft Drawing and with it the first overall selection.

The weighted lottery was structured as follows: clubs that neither qualified for the Stanley Cup Playoffs in each of the 2001-02, 2002-03 and 2003-04 seasons, nor were awarded the first overall selection in each of the 2001, 2002, 2003 and 2004 Entry Drafts were assigned a 6.3% chance of receiving the first overall selection. These clubs were the Penguins, Buffalo Sabres, Columbus Blue Jackets and New York Rangers.

Ten clubs met one of the seven criteria listed above and were assigned a 4.2% chance of winning. The remaining 16 clubs met more than one of the criteria and were assigned a 2.1% chance of winning.

Forty-eight balls, numbered one through 48, were placed in a lottery machine. Three ball numbers were randomly assigned to each of the Penguins, Sabres, Blue Jackets and Rangers; two ball numbers were assigned to the 10 clubs with a 4.2% chance; and one ball number was assigned to the 16 clubs with a 2.1% chance. The first ball expelled determined the winner of the first overall draft pick. That ball had been assigned to the Penguins.

After the first overall selection was awarded, another ball was expelled to determine which club, from among the 29 remaining, received the second overall pick. This process was continued until each of the 30 first-round draft positions was assigned.

Picks in Subsequent Rounds
The order of selection for the second round of the Entry Draft was the inverse of the order of selection for the first round (i.e. the club that selected 30th overall in the first round selected first overall in the second round). The order of selection for the third round was the same as the order of selection for the first round. The order of selection alternated each round thereafter.

First-Round Order of Selection

1.	Pittsburgh Penguins	16.	New York Rangers
2.	Mighty Ducks of Anaheim	17.	Phoenix Coyotes
3.	Carolina Hurricanes	18.	Nashville Predators
4.	Minnesota Wild	19.	Detroit Red Wings
5.	Montreal Canadiens	20.	Philadelphia Flyers
6.	Columbus Blue Jackets	21.	Toronto Maple Leafs
7.	Chicago Blackhawks	22.	Boston Bruins
8.	Atlanta Thrashers	23.	New Jersey Devils
9.	Ottawa Senators	24.	St. Louis Blues
10.	Vancouver Canucks	25.	Edmonton Oilers
11.	Los Angeles Kings	26.	Calgary Flames
12.	San Jose Sharks	27.	Colorado Avalanche
13.	Buffalo Sabres	28.	Dallas Stars
14.	Washington Capitals	29.	Florida Panthers
15.	New York Islanders	30.	Tampa Bay Lightning

International

Total	Country	'05	'04	'03	'02	'01	'00	'99	'98	'97	'96	'95	'94	'93	'92	'91	'90	'89	'88	'87	'86	'85	'84	'83	'82	'81	'80	'79	'78	'77	'76	'75	'74	'73	'72	'71	'70	'69
487	USSR/CIS/Russia	11	24	32	33	36	44	29	22	16	17	27	35	31	45	25	14	18	11	2	1	2	1	5	3	–	–	2	–	1	–	–	–	–				
410	Sweden	15	18	19	24	14	24	24	19	14	16	8	17	18	11	11	7	9	14	15	9	16	14	10	14	14	9	5	8	2	5	2	5	–	–	–	–	–
388	CzRep/Slovakia	15	24	20	21	28	28	20	20	17	14	21	18	15	17	9	21	8	5	11	6	8	13	9	13	4	–	1	2	–	–	–	–	–				
289	Finland	8	14	12	26	29	19	17	12	11	7	12	8	9	8	6	9	3	7	6	10	4	10	9	5	12	4	–	2	3	2	3	1	–	–	–	–	1
39	Switzerland	–	4	5	4	5	7	3	2	3	1	–	1	2	–	1	–																					
38	Germany	1	1	4	1	7	1	–	–	1	3	1	1	3	2	1	–	2	1	–	1	2	1	–	2	–	–	2	–									
7	Norway	–	–	–	–	1	–	–	1	–	–	–	–	1	2	–	2	–																				
4	Denmark	–	2	–	–	–	–	–	–	–	–	–	–	–	–	–	1	1																				
2	Japan	–	1	–	–	–	–	–	1																													
2	Poland	–	–	1	–	–	–	–	1																													
1	Scotland	–	–	–	–	–	–	–	–	–	–	–	–																									
1	Hungary	–	–	–	–	1																																

Czech Republic and Slovakia

Total	Club	'05	'04	'03	'02	'01	'00	'99	'98	'97	'96	'95	'94	'93	'92	'91	'90	'89	'88	'87	'86	'85	'84	'83	'82	'81	'80	'79	'78	'77	'76	'75	'74	'73	'72	'71	'70	'69
33	Chemo. Litv.[1]	–	3	2	–	1	–	1	1	2	2	2	4	2	3	1	2	2	–	–	–	2	1	3	–													
29	Dukla Jihlava	–	1	–	–	–	1	–	–	2	2	1	1	1	2	3	1	1	3	–	1	3	4	2	–													
27	Dukla Trencin	1	4	3	–	2	3	2	–	1	–	2	2	–	2	1	1	–	–	–	1	–																
26	Slavia Praha	1	1	2	2	5	3	2	5	4	–	–	1	–	–	–	–	–	1	–	–																	
26	HC Ceske Bud.[2]	2	–	2	–	2	3	1	1	2	1	3	2	1	–	–	–	1	1	2	–																	
25	Sparta Praha	2	4	1	1	2	1	–	1	1	–	1	–	2	1	2	1	2	1	1	2	–	1	–														
22	Slovan Bratis.	–	–	3	1	–	2	2	1	1	1	–	3	–	–	1	–	1	1	1	–	2	–	1	1													
20	ZPS Zlin[3]	1	2	–	–	2	–	2	2	1	–	2	–	1	2	2	–	–	1	1	1	–	1	–														
19	HC Kladno[4]	1	1	1	–	1	1	2	–	–	2	–	2	1	–	2	1	–	–	1	1	–	1	2	–													
17	HC Vitkovice[5]	1	2	–	2	–	1	1	1	–	1	1	1	3	1	–	1	–	–	–	1	–																
13	HC Kosice[6]	1	–	–	–	1	–	1	1	1	1	–	–	1	–	–	2	–	2	1	–																	
13	HC Pardubice[7]	–	–	3	1	–	–	1	2	–	–	–	–	1	–	1	–	2	2	–																		
13	Interconex Plzen[8]	–	–	–	2	1	1	–	1	1	1	–	3	–	1	–	1	1	–	–																		
12	HC Vsetin	–	1	1	3	2	2	–	1	2	–	–	–	–	–	–	–	–	–																			
8	Zetor Brno	–	–	–	–	–	–	–	–	1	–	2	–	3	–	1	–																					
7	HC Olomouc[9]	–	–	–	–	–	–	2	1	–	2	–	1	–	1	–																						
7	AC Nitra	–	–	1	–	1	–	1	–	1	–	1	–	2	–																							
6	ZTK Zvolen	–	–	–	–	2	2	–	1	1	–	1	–																									
6	ZTS Martin	–	1	–	–	1	1	–	2	–	–	–	–	–																								
6	Zelezarny Trinec	1	–	1	1	1	2	–	–	–	–	–																										
4	HC Karlovy Vary	–	–	1	1	1	1	–	–																													
3	HC Liberec	1	1	–	1	–	–																															
3	Havirov	–	–	2	–	1	–																															
3	ZPA Presov	–	–	–	–	1	–	–	1	–																												

Former club names: [1]–CHZ Litvinov, [2]–Motor Ceske Budejovice, [3]–TJ Gottwaldov, [4]–Poldi Kladno, [3]–TJ Gottwaldov, TJ Zlin, [5]–TJ Vitkovice, [6]–VSZ Kosice, [7]–Tesla Pardubice, [8]–Skoda Plzen, [9]–DS Olomouc.

Teams with two players selected: Ingstav Brno, IS Banska Bystrica, Dubnica, Michalovce, Partizan Liptovsky Mikulas, VTJ Pisek, Skalica, Spisska Nova Ves.

Teams with one player selected: Banik Sokolov, KLH Chomutov, Havlickuv Brod, Ostrava, KC SKP Poprad, Povazska Bystrica, Topolcany, HK Trnava, KHM Zvolen.

Finland

Total	Club	'05	'04	'03	'02	'01	'00	'99	'98	'97	'96	'95	'94	'93	'92	'91	'90	'89	'88	'87	'86	'85	'84	'83	'82	'81	'80	'79	'78	'77	'76	'75	'74	'73	'72	'71	'70	'69
34	HIFK Helsinki	1	2	–	5	2	2	4	2	1	–	1	–	2	–	–	1	2	–	1	2	2	1	1	–	1	–	–	1	–	–	–	–	1				
34	Jokerit	–	1	2	6	4	3	1	1	1	–	1	–	3	–	2	–	1	1	–	1	–	1	2	–	–	–											
34	TPS Turku	–	1	1	1	3	3	1	3	3	1	3	2	3	–	–	–	1	1	–	6	1	–															
27	Ilves	3	–	–	2	4	3	1	2	–	–	2	–	1	1	–	2	2	–	2	–	2	1	–														
22	Karpat	2	2	3	3	3	–	1	1	–	–	1	–	1	–	–	2	2	–	1	–	1	–	–														
20	Tappara	–	1	1	2	2	–	2	1	1	–	–	1	–	4	–	–	2	–	–	1	–																
18	Lukko	–	1	1	1	3	1	2	–	–	–	1	–	1	–	1	–	2	–	1	2	–																
15	Blues Espoo	1	1	–	1	2	–	2	–	1	2	–	2	1	1	–	1	–	–																			
14	Assat	–	–	1	–	–	1	1	1	–	1	–	1	–	–	2	2	–	1	–																		
11	JyP Jyvaskyla	–	1	–	2	1	–	3	–	1	–	–	–	1	–	–	–																					
11	HPK	–	–	1	1	3	1	1	1	–	–	1	–	2	–																							
9	KalPa Kuopio	–	1	–	2	1	–	1	–	2	–	1	–																									
8	Reipas Lahti	–	1	–	–	–	1	–	1	–	2	–	1	1	1	–																						
6	SaiPa Lappeen.	1	1	1	–	1	1	–																														
3	Kiekoo-67	–	–	–	–	–	–	–	3																													

Teams with two players selected: KooKoo Kouvola, Sapko Savonlinna, Sport Vaasa, TuTo.

Teams with one player selected: Ahmat Hyvinkaa, Hermes Kokkola, Junkkarit Kalajoki, GrIFK Kauniainen, LeKi, S-Kiekko Seinajoki.

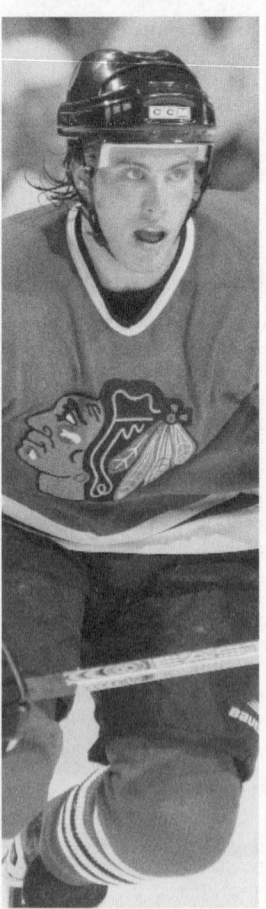

Edmonton selected Shawn Horcoff, above, from Michigan State with the 99th pick in the 1998 Entry Draft. Tuomo Ruutu, at right, was the third member of his family to be selected in the Entry Draft when Chicago picked him ninth in 2001.

NATIONAL HOCKEY LEAGUE
NHL DRAFT 2005 ™

USSR/CIS/Russia

Total	Club	'05	'04	'03	'02	'01	'00	'99	'98	'97	'96	'95	'94	'93	'92	'91	'90	'89	'88	'87	'86	'85	'84	'83	'82	'81	'80	'79	'78	'77	'76	'75	'74	'73	'72	'71	'70	'69
59	CSKA Moscow	1	3	3	–	–	–	3	1	–	3	2	5	3	7	4	3	8	5	1	1	1	–	4	1	–	–	–	1	–	–	–	–	–	–	–	–	–
45	Dynamo Moscow	–	1	1	–	–	2	2	1	1	1	7	1	2	10	7	4	3	2	–	–	–	–	–	–	–	–	–	–	–	–	–	–	–	–	–	–	–
31	Krylja Sovetov	1	2	–	1	1	1	2	1	1	2	3	5	1	3	4	2	1	1	–	–	–	–	–	–	–	–	–	–	–	–	–	–	–	–	–	–	–
23	Lokomotiv Yaro.2	2	–	3	1	1	9	–	4	2	2	1	–	–	–	–	–	–	–	–	–	–	–	–	–	–	–	–	–	–	–	–	–	–	–	–	–	–
22	Spartak Moscow	–	–	–	–	6	–	1	–	–	–	1	6	–	4	1	–	–	–	1	–	1	–	–	1	–	–	–	–	–	–	–	–	–	–	–	–	–
22	Lokomotiv Yaro.[1]	–	–	4	2	–	1	1	3	1	1	5	1	–	–	2	1	–	–	–	–	–	–	–	–	–	–	–	–	–	–	–	–	–	–	–	–	–
16	Chelyabinsk	2	–	–	1	–	–	–	1	1	–	1	1	7	2	–	–	2	–	–	–	–	–	–	–	–	–	–	–	–	–	–	–	–	–	–	–	–
16	Elektrostal	–	–	2	9	1	–	–	–	1	–	–	–	–	3	–	–	–	–	–	–	–	–	–	–	–	–	–	–	–	–	–	–	–	–	–	–	–
16	Dynamo 2	–	–	1	–	–	4	–	3	3	–	–	2	1	2	–	–	–	–	–	–	–	–	–	–	–	–	–	–	–	–	–	–	–	–	–	–	–
16	Lada Togliatti	–	2	–	2	–	2	2	1	3	1	–	–	2	1	–	–	–	–	–	–	–	–	–	–	–	–	–	–	–	–	–	–	–	–	–	–	–
14	Voskresensk	–	–	1	–	1	1	–	2	–	–	–	1	–	2	1	3	1	–	–	–	–	–	1	–	–	–	–	–	–	–	–	–	–	–	–	–	–
12	Severstal Cher.[2]	–	–	2	–	–	1	5	–	–	1	1	–	1	1	–	–	–	–	–	–	–	–	–	–	–	–	–	–	–	–	–	–	–	–	–	–	–
11	SKA St. Pete.[3]	–	–	–	–	2	1	2	–	–	–	–	1	–	1	2	–	–	–	–	–	–	–	–	1	–	–	–	1	–	–	–	–	–	–	–	–	–
11	Sokol Kiev	–	–	–	–	–	–	–	–	–	–	2	–	1	3	2	1	–	1	–	–	–	1	–	–	–	–	–	–	–	–	–	–	–	–	–	–	–
11	HC CSKA	–	–	–	4	–	5	2	–	–	–	–	–	–	–	–	–	–	–	–	–	–	–	–	–	–	–	–	–	–	–	–	–	–	–	–	–	–
10	Pardaugava Riga[4]	–	–	–	–	–	–	–	–	–	–	–	–	1	4	1	–	2	1	–	–	–	–	–	–	–	–	–	–	–	–	1	–	–	–	–	–	–
9	Ust-Kamenogorsk	–	–	1	–	–	–	1	2	–	–	1	2	1	1	–	–	–	–	–	–	–	–	–	–	–	–	–	–	–	–	–	–	–	–	–	–	–
9	Ufa	–	–	1	–	–	1	–	–	1	1	1	2	2	–	–	–	–	–	–	–	–	–	–	–	–	–	–	–	–	–	–	–	–	–	–	–	–
9	Avangard Omsk	–	–	–	1	3	1	–	–	–	1	–	3	–	–	–	–	–	–	–	–	–	–	–	–	–	–	–	–	–	–	–	–	–	–	–	–	–
8	CSKA Moscow 2	1	1	2	–	–	–	–	–	2	2	–	1	–	–	–	–	–	–	–	–	–	–	–	–	–	–	–	–	–	–	–	–	–	–	–	–	–
7	Novokuznetsk	–	1	1	–	1	2	2	–	–	–	–	–	–	–	–	–	–	–	–	–	–	–	–	–	–	–	–	–	–	–	–	–	–	–	–	–	–
6	Nizhnekamsk	–	1	–	–	2	2	–	–	1	–	–	–	–	–	–	–	–	–	–	–	–	–	–	–	–	–	–	–	–	–	–	–	–	–	–	–	–
6	THC Tver	–	3	3	–	1	2	–	–	–	–	–	–	–	–	–	–	–	–	–	–	–	–	–	–	–	–	–	–	–	–	–	–	–	–	–	–	–
5	Perm	–	–	–	1	1	1	–	–	–	–	1	1	–	–	–	–	–	–	–	–	–	–	–	–	–	–	–	–	–	–	–	–	–	–	–	–	–
5	AK Bars Kazan	–	–	1	–	1	1	–	1	–	–	–	1	–	–	–	–	–	–	–	–	–	–	–	–	–	–	–	–	–	–	–	–	–	–	–	–	–
5	Lada Togliatti 2	1	–	–	–	2	2	1	–	–	–	–	–	–	–	–	–	–	–	–	–	–	–	–	–	–	–	–	–	–	–	–	–	–	–	–	–	–
5	Magnitogorsk	–	–	1	1	3	–	–	–	–	–	–	–	–	–	–	–	–	–	–	–	–	–	–	–	–	–	–	–	–	–	–	–	–	–	–	–	–
5	Avangard Omsk 2	–	1	1	–	3	–	–	–	–	–	–	–	–	–	–	–	–	–	–	–	–	–	–	–	–	–	–	–	–	–	–	–	–	–	–	–	–
4	Tivali Minsk[5]	–	–	–	–	–	–	–	–	–	–	–	1	2	–	–	–	–	1	–	–	–	–	–	–	–	–	–	–	–	–	–	–	–	–	–	–	–
4	Nizhny Novgorod[6]	–	–	–	–	–	1	–	–	–	–	–	–	–	2	–	1	–	–	–	–	–	–	–	–	–	–	–	–	–	–	–	–	–	–	–	–	–
4	Krylja Sovetov 2	–	–	–	3	–	–	–	–	–	–	–	–	1	–	–	–	–	–	–	–	–	–	–	–	–	–	–	–	–	–	–	–	–	–	–	–	–
4	CSK VVS Samara	–	–	1	–	1	–	1	–	–	–	1	–	–	–	–	–	–	–	–	–	–	–	–	–	–	–	–	–	–	–	–	–	–	–	–	–	–
4	Dyn-Energ. Yekat.[7]	–	–	1	–	–	–	1	1	–	1	–	–	–	–	–	–	–	–	–	–	–	–	–	–	–	–	–	–	–	–	–	–	–	–	–	–	–
3	Kristall Saratov	–	1	–	–	1	–	–	–	–	–	–	–	1	–	–	–	–	–	–	–	–	–	–	–	–	–	–	–	–	–	–	–	–	–	–	–	–
3	Severstal Cher. 2	–	–	–	1	–	1	1	–	–	–	–	–	–	–	–	–	–	–	–	–	–	–	–	–	–	–	–	–	–	–	–	–	–	–	–	–	–
3	Ak-Bars Kazan 2	–	–	1	–	1	–	1	–	–	–	–	–	–	–	–	–	–	–	–	–	–	–	–	–	–	–	–	–	–	–	–	–	–	–	–	–	–

Former club names: [1]–Torpedo Yaroslavl, [2]–Metallurg Cherepovets, [3]–SKA Leningrad, [4]–Dynamo Riga, HC Riga, [5]–Dynamo Minsk, [6]–Torpedo Gorky, [7]–Avtomobilist Yekaterinburg

Teams with two players selected: Dizelist Penza, Metallurg Novokuznetsk 2, Salavat Yulayev Ufa 2, Spartak Moscow 2, Torpedo Nizhny Novgorod 2, Yunost Minsk.

Teams with one player selected: Amur Khabarovsk, Argus Moscow, HC CSKA Moscow 2, Dynamo Khazov, Dynamo-81 Riga, Gazovik Tyumen, HK Gomel, Izohets St. Petersburg, Kapitan Stupino, Khimik Novopolotsk, Khimik Voskresensk 2, Mechel Chelyabinsk, Metallurg Magnitogorsk 2, Metalurgs Liepaja, Mostovik Kurgan, Neftekhimik Nizhnekamsk, Neftekhimik Nizhnekamsk 2, SKA St. Petersburg 2, Spartak St. Petersburg, Sibir Novosibirsk 2, Stalkers-Juniors, Torpedo Nizhny Novgorod 2, THC Tver, Vityaz Podolsk, Vityaz Podolsk 2.

Sweden

Total	Club	'05	'04	'03	'02	'01	'00	'99	'98	'97	'96	'95	'94	'93	'92	'91	'90	'89	'88	'87	'86	'85	'84	'83	'82	'81	'80	'79	'78	'77	'76	'75	'74	'73	'72	'71	'70	'69
36	Djurgarden	1	2	–	2	1	4	1	–	2	2	3	–	1	1	2	1	1	–	2	1	–	1	2	1	–	2	1	–	–	1	1	1	–	–	–	–	–
36	MoDo	1	1	–	3	–	3	7	–	3	3	–	–	5	2	2	–	–	–	1	–	–	2	–	1	–	–	1	–	–	1	–	–	–	–	–	–	–
32	Farjestad	–	–	–	2	1	–	1	6	3	–	2	–	1	2	1	–	1	–	–	–	2	1	1	1	2	1	–	2	2	–	–	–	–	–	–	–	–
28	Leksand	1	–	2	–	–	5	–	2	–	1	–	2	2	–	2	–	1	2	1	1	2	2	–	1	–	–	1	–	–	–	–	1	–	–	–	–	–
27	Vastra Frolunda	3	4	2	3	3	4	2	1	–	1	1	3	–	1	–	–	1	1	1	–	1	2	–	–	–	–	–	–	–	–	–	–	–	–	–	–	–
24	AIK Solna	–	–	–	1	1	–	3	1	1	–	–	1	–	1	1	1	–	–	–	–	4	–	1	3	2	–	1	1	–	1	–	–	–	–	–	–	–
23	Brynas Gavle	–	–	2	–	2	1	1	2	1	1	–	–	1	–	–	–	–	–	4	–	–	2	1	–	1	1	1	1	–	–	–	1	–	–	–	–	–
21	HV 71	1	2	1	1	–	1	3	4	1	2	–	2	–	–	–	1	–	1	1	–	–	–	–	–	1	–	–	–	–	–	–	–	–	–	–	–	–
19	Sodertalje	3	1	2	–	1	1	–	1	–	–	–	–	1	–	–	–	2	–	–	2	2	2	1	1	1	–	–	1	–	–	–	–	–	–	–	–	–
14	Malmo	1	1	1	4	–	1	1	–	–	2	–	1	1	1	–	–	–	1	–	–	–	–	–	–	–	–	–	–	–	–	–	–	–	–	–	–	–
10	Skelleftea	–	–	–	–	–	–	–	–	1	–	–	–	1	–	–	–	–	1	–	–	–	1	2	1	1	–	–	–	–	1	1	–	–	–	–	–	–
11	Lulea	–	1	–	–	–	2	–	1	1	–	–	–	–	1	–	–	–	1	1	1	–	–	–	–	1	1	–	–	–	–	–	–	–	–	–	–	–
11	Vasteras	–	1	–	1	–	1	–	–	–	–	–	1	1	–	1	1	2	2	–	–	–	–	–	–	–	–	–	–	–	–	–	–	–	–	–	–	–
9	Rogle	–	–	–	–	–	–	1	–	–	–	1	2	2	–	–	–	–	2	1	–	–	–	–	–	–	–	–	–	–	–	–	–	–	–	–	–	–
9	Hammarby	–	–	–	3	–	1	–	–	1	–	–	–	1	1	–	–	–	–	–	–	–	–	–	–	–	1	1	–	–	–	–	–	–	–	–	–	–
8	Timra	–	–	–	1	–	–	1	–	–	–	–	1	–	–	–	–	–	–	–	1	1	–	–	–	2	1	–	–	–	–	–	–	–	–	–	–	–
6	Huddinge	–	–	–	1	1	–	1	–	–	2	–	–	–	–	1	–	–	–	–	–	–	–	–	–	–	–	–	–	–	–	–	–	–	–	–	–	–
6	Mora	–	–	1	–	1	–	–	–	1	1	–	–	–	–	–	–	–	–	–	1	–	–	1	–	–	–	–	–	–	–	–	–	–	–	–	–	–
5	Bjorkloven	1	–	–	–	–	–	–	–	–	–	–	–	–	–	–	–	–	1	–	–	1	–	–	–	1	2	–	–	–	–	–	–	–	–	–	–	–
6	Orebro	–	1	–	–	–	–	–	–	–	–	–	–	–	–	–	–	–	–	1	–	1	–	1	–	–	–	–	1	–	1	–	–	–	–	–	–	–
4	Nacka	–	–	–	–	–	–	–	–	–	–	–	–	–	2	–	–	1	–	–	1	–	–	–	–	–	–	–	–	–	–	–	–	–	–	–	–	–
4	Troja/Ljungby	–	–	1	–	–	–	1	–	–	–	–	–	–	–	–	–	–	1	–	–	1	–	–	–	–	–	–	–	–	–	–	–	–	–	–	–	–
3	Falun	–	–	–	–	–	–	–	–	–	–	–	–	–	–	1	–	–	1	–	–	–	–	–	–	1	–	–	–	–	–	–	–	–	–	–	–	–
3	Team Kiruna	–	–	–	–	–	–	–	–	–	–	–	–	1	–	–	–	–	–	–	–	–	–	–	1	–	–	–	1	–	–	–	–	–	–	–	–	–
3	Boden	–	–	–	–	–	–	–	–	–	–	–	1	–	–	–	–	–	–	–	1	–	–	–	–	–	–	–	–	–	–	–	1	–	–	–	–	–
3	Pitea	–	–	–	–	–	–	–	–	–	–	–	1	–	–	–	1	–	–	–	–	–	–	–	1	–	–	–	–	–	–	–	–	–	–	–	–	–
3	Grums	–	–	–	–	–	1	1	–	–	–	–	1	–	–	–	–	–	–	–	–	–	–	–	–	–	–	–	–	–	–	–	–	–	–	–	–	–
3	Morrum	–	–	–	2	1	–	–	–	–	–	–	–	–	–	–	–	–	–	–	–	–	–	–	–	–	–	–	–	–	–	–	–	–	–	–	–	–
3	Stocksund	–	2	–	–	–	–	–	–	–	–	–	–	–	–	–	–	–	–	–	–	–	–	–	1	–	–	–	–	–	–	–	–	–	–	–	–	–

Teams with two players selected: Hasten, Linkoping, Ostersund.

Teams with one player selected: Almtuna, Arboga, Arvika, Bofors, Danderyd Hockey, Fagersta, Jamtland, Karskoga, Kumla, Stocksund, S/G Hockey 83 Gavle, Skovde, Sunne, Talje, Tingsryd, Tunabro, Uppsala, Vallentuna, Vasby.

2005 Entry Draft Analysis

Country of Origin

Country	Players Drafted
Canada	110
USA	61
Czech Republic	12
Sweden	12
Russia	11
Finland	9
Slovakia	8
Germany	1
Latvia	1
Belarus	1
Denmark	1
Japan	1
Ukraine	1
Slovenia	1

Birth Year

Year	Players Drafted
1987	140
1986	68
1985	21
1984	1

Position

Position	Players Drafted
Defense	87
Center	52
Right Wing	39
Left Wing	29
Goaltender	23

Note: Players drafted in the international category played outside North America in their draft year. European-born players drafted from the OHL, QMJHL, WHL, U.S. colleges or other North American leagues are not counted as International players.

See Country of Origin above

European Draft Firsts

1969 – First European (and Finn) Selected The first European-trained player selected was left winger Tommi Salmelainen taken 66th overall by the St. Louis Blues in 1969.

1974 – First Swede Selected Center Per Alexandersson was selected by the Toronto Maple Leafs 49th overall in 1974. Four other Swedish-born players were selected that year, including defenseman Stefan Persson (214th overall, NY Islanders) who became the first European to play on a Stanley Cup winner. (four times, 1980-83).

1975 – First Russian Selected The Philadelphia Flyers selected center Viktor Khatulev 160th overall in 1975.

1976 – First European Taken in the First Round The California Seals selected Swedish defenseman Bjorn Johansson with their first pick, fifth overall, in the 1976 Amateur Draft.

1976 – First Swiss Player Selected The St. Louis Blues selected center Jacques Soguel 121st overall in 1976.

1978 – First Czechoslovak Selected The Detroit Red Wings selected left winger Ladislav Svozil 194th overall in 1978

1978 – First German Selected The first German players were also drafted in 1978. The Atlanta Flames selected goaltender Bernard Englbrecht 196th overall and St. Louis selected forward Gerd Truntschka 200th overall.

1989 – First European Taken First Overall The Quebec Nordiques selected Swedish center Mats Sundin first overall in 1989.

Notes on 2005 First-Round Selections

1. PITTSBURGH • **SIDNEY CROSBY** • C • With unparalleled vision and great hockey sense, Sidney Crosby is a two-time Canadian Hockey League MVP and the most-anticipated draft pick in over a decade. He is an exceptional skater with a smooth stride and tremendous balance who can shoot the puck hard with a slap shot or with a quick, accurate wrist shot. Crosby is an unselfish player who plays with great poise in all game situations. He won a gold medal with Team Canada at the 2005 World Junior Championship.

2. ANAHEIM • **BOBBY RYAN** • RW • A reliable forward who is well aware of his defensive responsibilities, Bobby Ryan goes to the net fearlessly and is difficult to move from out front. He handles the puck well in traffic and his bent-over skating style makes him solid on his skates. Ryan's very good on-ice vision allows him to move the puck skillfully and his passing abilities are equal on the forehand and backhand. He has very good hockey sense and reads game situations well.

3. CAROLINA • **JACK JOHNSON** • D • A solid two-way defenseman who plays a physical style and a strong positional game, Jack Johnson likes to rush the puck and has very good straightaway speed. He is an outstanding passer with good peripheral vision and has an accurate, low shot from the point. Johnson is a graduate of the U.S. National Team Development Program and won a gold medal with the American team at the 2005 World Under-18 Championship.

4. MINNESOTA • **BENOIT POULIOT** • LW • A very good skater with a long, powerful stride, Benoit Pouliot has good acceleration and speed and is solid on his skates. He has very good offensive instincts and combines skillful puckhandling with good on-ice vision. He has soft hands and a good wrist shot with a quick release. Pouliot can move the puck through a crowd and is effective at setting up teammates. He uses his size and strength effectively to protect the puck.

5. MONTREAL • **CAREY PRICE** • G • A very confident netminder with good lateral movement and strong skating skills, Carey Price uses his size well, staying square and challenging shooters. He has an excellent catching hand and is excellent at controlling rebounds. Price handles the puck well and is good at going behind the net to stop the puck on dump-ins. He uses the "paddle down" technique with good coverage on wrap-arounds and in close situations.

6. COLUMBUS • **GILBERT BRULE** • C • A gifted offensive player, Gilbert Brule is a very good skater with exceptional agility who scores highlight-reel goals with a hard, accurate shot. He does not lose speed while moving laterally and uses his excellent on-ice vision and great hands to create chances for his teammates. Brule is a dynamic, skilled, creative player who finishes checks with authority and does not back down.

7. CHICAGO • **JACK SKILLE** • RW • A power forward who drives aggressively to the net, Jack Skille makes good decisions with the puck and can score in traffic. He is a good skater with straightaway speed and has a quick release on his wrist shot. Skille is a graduate of the U.S. National Team Development Program and won a gold medal with the American team at the 2005 World Under-18 Championship.

8. SAN JOSE• **DEVIN SETOGUCHI** • RW • A strong skater with a quick stride, Devin Setoguchi has a knack for holding on to the puck in traffic. He displays exceptional lateral movement and is outstanding in one-on-one situations. Setoguchi has great awareness of where his teammates are and distributes the puck well. He is a feisty player with a hard, quick, accurate shot and excellent scoring instincts.

9. OTTAWA • **BRIAN LEE** • D • An offensive-minded defenseman with a calm, confident manner, Brian Lee plays his position in the defensive zone very well and has plenty of acceleration when leading a rush. He's an upright skater with short, quick strides who has very good hands and playmaking ability. Lee is a smart player who sees the ice well and has a very good wrist shot from the point. He can get physical.

10. VANCOUVER • **LUC BOURDON** • D • A physical defenseman who finishes his checks with authority, Luc Bourdon uses his strength to clear the front of the net and avoids being tied up. He is an excellent skater with outstanding balance and lateral movement who reaches his top speed easily. Bourdon has an accurate wrist shot and a very good slap shot and can protect the puck well with his body.

11. LOS ANGELES • **ANZE KOPITAR** • C • A good skater with an excellent overall skill level, Anze Kopitar has an excellent understanding of the game. He has smooth hands, a good shot and is tough on face-offs. Kopitar is a hard worker with a good attitude. He represented his native Slovenia at the World Junior Championship, the World Under-18 Championship and the World Championship (where he held his own against NHL players) in 2005.

12. NY RANGERS • **MARC STAAL** • D • Though he is not a punishing checker, Marc Staal is an aggressive defenseman who uses his size well in front of the net and will not back down from confrontations. He finishes his checks well and plays tough along the boards. Staal likes to join the rush and shows patience with the puck. He makes good outlet passes to open teammates and has a good shot. Brother Eric was drafted second overall by the Carolina Hurricanes in 2003.

13. BUFFALO • **MAREK ZAGRAPAN** • C • A very good skater with an effortless, smooth stride, Marek Zagrapan is a nifty playmaker and puckhandler. He sees the ice and reads the play smartly and is poised and patient with the puck. Zagarapan has an accurate wrist shot with a quick release and has added more grit and defensive awareness to his game. He is a key component on the power-play, and is often used on the point to set up teammates for scoring chances.

14. WASHINGTON • **SASHA POKULOK** • D • At 6'5" and 220 pounds, Sasha Pokulok is a towering defenseman who skates well for a big player. He moves the puck quickly and passes it with authority, making safe decisions. Pokulok is a smart player who anticipates the play very well. He competes well for the puck and is aggressive in the corners and in front of the net. Pokulok is a good playmaking defenseman on the power-play with a good, low shot from the point.

15. NY ISLANDERS • **RYAN O'MARRA** • C • Solid on his skates and tough to knock off the puck, Ryan O'Marra sees the ice well and moves the puck effectively through traffic. His soft hands make him a good playmaker and he has a good wrist shot. O'Marra plays a steady two-way game and shows good hustle getting back to his end. He finishes his checks in all areas of the ice and is good on face-offs. He gives a consist effort on every shift, both at home and on the road.

16. ATLANTA • **ALEX BOURRET** • RW • A very good skater who is quick off the mark, Alex Bourret uses his speed, shooting ability and toughness to frustrate the opposition. He carries the puck with poise and confidence and can go end-to-end. He plays the give-and-go very well and is adept at making short passes in tight quarters. His speed makes him hard to contain one-on-one and his tenacious forechecking causes turnovers. He is aggressive and can be abrasive.

17. PHOENIX • **MARTIN HANZAL** • C • A smart player who is agile for his size (6'5" and 200 pounds), Martin Hanzal has very good puckhandling skills and a fair scoring touch around the net. He has excellent hockey sense, sees the ice well and creates scoring chances with quality passes. Hanzal handles himself well in traffic and has a good understanding of his defensive duties. He does not shy away from rough play.

18. NASHVILLE • **RYAN PARENT** • D • An on-ice leader who commands respect from his teammates, Ryan Parent plays in all situations and is especially effective on the penalty kill. He is an outstanding, effortless skater with a long, fluid stride who combines balance, speed and agility both forward and backward. A defensive defenseman, Parent does not lead the rush but contributes to the offense with quick outlet passes.

19. DETROIT • **JAKUB KINDL** • D • A well-rounded, versatile defenseman, Jakub Kindl moves the puck well in open ice but is sometimes prone to giveaways when pressured. He skates very well both with and without the puck and is capable of going end to end on a rush. He has a heavy shot from the point and though he does not initiate a lot of physical play, he does not shy away from that aspect of the game.

20. FLORIDA • **KENNDAL McCARDLE** • LW • A very explosive skater, Kenndal McCardle's quick acceleration enables him to find open holes and create scoring chances. He is extremely strong on his feet and hard to knock off the puck. McCardle handles the puck well in traffic and makes good decisions in those situations. He has a great desire and attitude for the game and works hard through adversity.

21. TORONTO • **TUUKA RASK** • G • A big goalie who covers a lot of the net, Tuuka Rask reads the game very well and plays with confidence. He has a good glove, quick reflexes and plays his angles very well. Rask played mainly in the Finnish junior league in 2004-05, but also saw action with Ilves in the Finnish Elite League. He was the number-one Finnish goalie at both the World Junior Championship and the World Under-18 Championship in 2005.

22. BOSTON • **MATT LASHOFF** • D • An adept passer with good hands, Matt Lashoff makes good decisions on breakout plays and is skillful at finding open teammates in the offensive zone. He's a very strong skater with long, fluid strides and his confidence in his skating allows him to gamble offensively and still recover quickly for his defensive responsibilities. He is capable of going end-to-end with the puck and has a good shot. He can also battle along the boards and out front.

23. NEW JERSEY • **NICKLAS BERGFORS** • W • An excellent skater with fine first-step quickness, Nicklas Bergfors' skill is augmented by a physical element. He is a fine playmaker who also knows how to score. Bergfors is also an effective forechecker who makes things happen with his quick moves. He has an excellent attitude and work ethic. Bergfors represented Sweden at both the World Junior Championship and the World Under-18 Championship in 2005.

24. ST. LOUIS • **T.J. OSHIE** • C • Strong on his skates with good acceleration when needed, T.J. Oshie finds the holes and uses his speed. He has excellent hands and a good shot with a quick release. He's a good stickhandler with quick moves and is inventive moving the puck in tight quarters. Oshie can score in many ways. He beats opponents one-on-one and does not hesitate to be the first one to the puck.

25. EDMONTON • **ANDREW COGLIANO** • C • Excellent vision and hockey sense make Andrew Cogliano adept at getting open in the offensive zone. He is an excellent skater with a smooth, powerful stride who uses a quick burst of speed to catch the opposition flat-footed. He has a very good wrist and snap shot, which he is adept at releasing in full flight. He is not a physical player, but does not shy away from traffic.

26. CALGARY • **MATT PELECH** • D • A good skater with a long, fluid stride, Matt Pelech combines good agility with acceleration and speed. He is solid on his skates and has a good shot, but would rather move the puck with safe outlet passes than lead the rush. He will jump up from the point to support the rush. Pelech is in excellent physical condition and can play a tough, aggressive game. His strong upper body allows him to move players out from in front of the net.

27. WASHINGTON • **JOE FINLEY** • D • Though he stands 6'7" and weighs 229 pounds, Joe Finley has good speed with a long stride and is smooth and light on his skates. He passes the puck well, but is not a great stickhandler. Finley has a very good wrist and slap shot from the point that he keeps low and gets away quickly. He has a physical presence and will punish opponents when finishing the check. He is also effective when pinching down low in the offensive zone.

28. DALLAS • **MATT NISKANEN** • D • A fluid skater who is solid on his feet, Matt Niskanen has very good balance and mobility. An excellent passer and playmaker, he likes to lead the offensive rush and also has a very strong wrist and slap shot. He is a smart player who is never surprised, though his poise and on-ice demeanor can give the mistaken impression that he is not working hard. Niskanen also captained his high school football and baseball teams.

29. PHILADELPHIA • **STEVE DOWNIE** • RW • A creative playmaker who is adept at setting up his teammates for scoring opportunities, Steve Downie also possesses an accurate shot which he gets away quickly, often while on the move. He has very good hockey sense and plays bigger than his size (5'10" and 192 pounds). Downie battles hard in the corners and along the boards and does not show any fear.

30. TAMPA BAY • **VLADIMIR MIHALIK** • D • A giant on the ice at 6'7" and 222 pounds, Vladimir Mihalik moves surprisingly well for his size. He has good puck skills and a very good reach as he uses his long arms to his advantage. He is very competitive and will likely develop more of a physical presence. He has been a regular on the Slovakian team at the World Under-18 Championship the past two years.

Players selected first through tenth in the 2005 NHL Entry Draft. (All rows left to right): Top row: 1. Sidney Crosby, C, Pittsburgh; 2. Bobby Ryan, RW, Anaheim. Second row: 3. Jack Johnson, D, Carolina; 4. Benoit Pouliot, LW, Minnesota. Third row: 5. Carey Price, G, Montreal; 6. Gilbert Brule, C, Columbus. Fourth row: 7. Jack Skille, RW, Chicago; 8. Devin Setoguchi, RW, San Jose. Bottom row: 9. Brian Lee, D, Ottawa; 10. Luc Bourdon, D, Vancouver.

2005 NHL ENTRY DRAFT

Pick	Claimed by	Amateur Club	Position

FIRST ROUND

Pick	Claimed by	Amateur Club	Position
1	Pit.	Sidney Crosby	Rimouski	C
2	Ana.	Bobby Ryan	Owen Sound	RW
3	Car.	Jack Johnson	USA U-18	D
4	Min.	Benoit Pouliot	Sudbury	LW
5	Mtl.	Carey Price	Tri-City	G
6	CBJ	Gilbert Brule	Vancouver	C
7	Chi.	Jack Skille	USA U-18	RW
8	S.J.	Devin Setoguchi	Saskatoon	RW
9	Ott.	Brian Lee	Moorhead	D
10	Van.	Luc Bourdon	Val D'or	D
11	L.A.	Anze Kopitar	Sodertalje Jr.	C
12	NYR	Marc Staal	Sudbury	D
13	Buf.	Marek Zagrapan	Chicoutimi	C
14	Wsh.	Sasha Pokulok	Cornell	D
15	NYI	Ryan O'Marra	Erie	C
16	Atl.	Alex Bourret	Lewiston	RW
17	Phx.	Martin Hanzal	C. Budejovice	C
18	Nsh.	Ryan Parent	Guelph	D
19	Det.	Jakub Kindl	Kitchener	D
20	Fla.	Kenndal McArdle	Moose Jaw	LW
21	Tor.	Tuukka Rask	Ilves Jr.	G
22	Bos.	Matt Lashoff	Kitchener	D
23	N.J.	Nicklas Bergfors	Sodertalje	RW
24	St.L.	T.J. Oshie	Warroad	C
25	Edm.	Andrew Cogliano	St. Mike's B's	C
26	Cgy.	Matt Pelech	Sarnia	D
27	Wsh.	Joe Finley	Sioux Falls	D
28	Dal.	Matt Niskanen	Virginia	D
29	Phi.	Steve Downie	Windsor	RW
30	T.B.	Vladimir Mihalik	Presov	D

SECOND ROUND

Pick	Claimed by	Amateur Club	Position
31	Ana.	Brendan Mikkelson	Portland	D
32	Fla.	Tyler Plante	Brandon	G
33	Dal.	James Neal	Plymouth	LW
34	Col.	Ryan Stoa	USA U-18	C
35	S.J.	Marc-Edouard Vlasic	Quebec	D
36	Edm.	Taylor Chorney	Shat.-St. Mary's	D
37	St.L.	Scott Jackson	Seattle	D
38	N.J.	Jeff Frazee	USA U-18	G
39	Bos.	Petr Kalus	Vitkovice Jr.	LW
40	NYR	Michael Sauer	Portland	D
41	Atl.	Ondrej Pavelec	Kladno Jr.	G
42	Det.	Justin Abdelkader	Cedar Rapids	LW
43	Chi.	Michael Blunden	Erie	RW
44	Col.	Paul Stastny	U. of Denver	C
45	Mtl.	Guillaume Latendresse	Drummondville	RW
46	NYI	Dustin Kohn	Calgary	D
47	Col.	Tom Fritsche	Ohio State	LW
48	Buf.	Philip Gogulla	Koln	RW
49	Atl.	Chad Denny	Lewiston	D
50	L.A.	Dany Roussin	Rimouski	LW
51	Van.	Mason Raymond	Camrose	LW
52	Col.	Chris Durand	Seattle	C
53	Atl.	Andrew Kozek	South Surrey	W
54	Chi.	Dan Bertram	Boston College	RW
55	CBJ	Adam McQuaid	Sudbury	D
56	NYR	Marc-Andre Cliche	Lewiston	RW
57	Min.	Matt Kassian	Kamloops	LW
58	Car.	Nathan Hagemo	U. of Minnesota	D
59	Phx.	Pier-Olivier Pelletier	Drummondville	G
60	L.A.	T.J. Fast	Camrose	D
61	Pit.	Michael Gergen	Shat.-St. Mary's	W

THIRD ROUND

Pick	Claimed by	Amateur Club	Position
62	Pit.	Kristopher Letang	Val D'or	D
63	Ana.	Jason Bailey	USA U-18	RW
64	Car.	Joe Barnes	Saskatoon	C
65	Min.	Kristofer Westblom	Kelowna	G
66	NYR	Brodie Dupont	Calgary	C
67	CBJ	Kris Russell	Medicine Hat	D
68	Chi.	Evan Brophey	Belleville	C/LW
69	Cgy.	Gord Baldwin	Medicine Hat	D
70	Ott.	Vitali Anikeyenko	Yaroslavl 2	D
71	Dal.	Richard Clune	Sarnia	LW
72	L.A.	Jonathan Quick	Avon Old Farms	G
73	T.B.	Radek Smolenak	Kingston	LW
74	Cgy.	Dan Ryder	Peterborough	C
75	Dal.	Perttu Lindgren	Ilves Jr.	C
76	NYI	Shea Guthrie	St. George's	W
77	NYR	Dalyn Flatt	Saskatoon	D
78	Nsh.	Teemu Laakso	HIFK	D
79	Nsh.	Cody Franson	Vancouver	D
80	Det.	Christofer Lofberg	Djurgarden Jr.	C
81	Edm.	Danny Syvret	London	D
82	Tor.	Phil Oreskovic	Brampton	D
83	Bos.	Mikko Lehtonen	Blues Jr.	RW
84	N.J.	Mark Fraser	Kitchener	D
85	St.L.	Ben Bishop	Texas	G
86	Edm.	Robby Dee	Breck	C/W
87	Buf.	Marc-Andre Gragnani	P.E.I.	D
88	Col.	T.J. Hensick	U. of Michigan	C
89	T.B.	Chris Lawrence	Sault Ste. Marie	C
90	Fla.	Dan Collins	Plymouth	RW
91	Phi.	Oskars Bartulis	Moncton	D

FOURTH ROUND

Pick	Claimed by	Amateur Club	Position
92	T.B.	Marek Bartanus	Kosice	RW
93	Fla.	Olivier Legault	Lewiston	LW
94	Car.	Jakub Vojta	Sparta Jr.	D
95	Ott.	Cody Bass	Mississauga	C
96	Buf.	Chris Butler	Sioux City	D
97	Edm.	Chris Vande Velde	Moorhead	C
98	Ott.	Ilja Zubov	Chelyabinsk	C
99	N.J.	Patrick Davis	Kitchener	LW
100	Bos.	Jonathan Sigalet	Bowling Green	D
101	CBJ	Jared Boll	Lincoln	RW
102	T.B.	Blair Jones	Moose Jaw	C
103	Det.	Mattias Ritola	Leksand Jr.	RW
104	Fla.	Matt Duffy	N.H. Jr. Monarchs	D
105	Phx.	Keith Yandle	Cushing	D
106	Bos.	Vladimir Sobotka	Slavia	C
107	NYR	Tom Pyatt	Saginaw	C
108	Chi.	Niklas Hjalmarsson	HV 71 Jr.	D
109	Wsh.	Andrew Thomas	U. of Denver	D
110	Min.	Kyle Bailey	Portland	C
111	Cgy.	J.D. Watt+E59	Vancouver	RW
112	S.J.	Alex Stalock	Cedar Rapids	G
113	Chi.	Nathan Davis	Miami University	C/LW
114	Van.	Alexandre Vincent	Chicoutimi	G
115	Ott.	Janne Kolehmainen	SaiPa	LW
116	Atl.	Jordan Lavallee	Quebec	LW
117	Chi.	Denis Istomin	Chelyabinsk	RW
118	Phx.	Patrick McNeill	Saginaw	D
119	Phi.	Jeremy Duchesne	Halifax	G
120	Edm.	Vyacheslav Trukhno	Prince Edward	LW
121	Mtl.	Juraj Mikus	Skalica	RW
122	Min.	Morten Madsen	Frolunda Jr.	RW
123	Car.	Ondrej Otcenas	Trencin Jr.	C
124	Col.	Raymond Macias	Kamloops	D
125	Pit.	Tommi Leinonen	Karpat Jr.	D

FIFTH ROUND

Pick	Claimed by	Amateur Club	Position
126	Pit.	Tim Crowder	South Surrey	RW
127	Ana.	Bobby Bolt	Kingston	LW
128	Cgy.	Kevin Lalande	Belleville	G
129	Min.	Anthony Aiello	Thayer	D
130	Mtl.	Mathieu Aubin	Lewiston	C
131	CBJ	Tomas Popperle	Sparta	G
132	Det.	Darren Helm	Medicine Hat	C/LW
133	T.B.	Stanislav Lascek	Chicoutimi	RW
134	Chi.	Brennan Turner	Notre Dame	D
135	Atl.	Tomas Pospisil	Trinec Jr.	D
136	Ott.	Tomas Kudelka	Zlin Jr.	D
137	Det.	Johan Ryno	Kumla Jr.	W
138	Van.	Matt Butcher	Chilliwack	C
139	L.A.	Patrik Hersley	Malmo Jr.	D
140	S.J.	Taylor Dakers	Kootenay	G
141	Ana.	Brian Salcido	Colorado College	D
142	Buf.	Nathan Gerbe	USA U-18	C
143	Wsh.	Daren Machesney	Brampton	G
144	NYI	Masi Marjamaki	Moose Jaw	RW
145	Car.	Timothy Kunes	N.E. Jr. Falcons	D
146	Dal.	Tom Wandell	Sodertalje Jr.	C
147	NYR	Trevor Koverko	Owen Sound	D
148	Phx.	Anton Krysanov	Togliatti 2	C
149	S.J.	Derek Joslin	Ottawa	D
150	Nsh.	Cal O'Reilly	Windsor	C
151	Det.	Jeff May	Prince Albert	D
152	Phi.	Josh Beaulieu	London	C
153	Tor.	Alex Berry	Junior Bruins	RW
154	Bos.	Wacey Rabbit	Saskatoon	C
155	N.J.	Mark Fayne	Nobles	D
156	St.L.	Ryan Reaves	Brandon	RW
157	Edm.	Fredrik Pettersson	Frolunda Jr.	LW
158	Cgy.	Matt Keetley	Medicine Hat	G
159	Car.	Risto Korhonen	Karpat Jr.	D
160	Dal.	Matt Watkins	Vernon	RW
161	Fla.	Brian Foster	N.H. Jr. Monarchs	G
162	S.J.	Paul Fenton	U. Mass-Amherst	Forward

SIXTH ROUND

Pick	Claimed by	Amateur Club	Position
163	T.B.	Marek Kvapil	Saginaw	RW
164	Fla.	Roman Derlyuk	Spartak St. Petersburg	D
165	T.B.	Kevin Beech	Sudbury	G
166	Col.	Jason Lynch	Spokane	D
167	Chi.	Joseph Fallon	U. of Vermont	G
168	Col.	Justin Mercier	USA U-18	C/W
169	St.L.	Mike Gauthier	Prince Albert	D
170	N.J.	Sean Zimmerman	Spokane	D
171	St.L.	Nicholas Drazenovic	Prince George	C
172	Bos.	Lukas Vantuch	Liberec Jr.	RW
173	Tor.	Johan Dahlberg	MODO Jr.	LW
174	Phi.	John Flatters	Red Deer	D
175	Det.	Juho Mielonen	Ilves Jr.	D
176	Nsh.	Ryan Maki	Harvard	RW
177	CBJ	Derek Reinhart	Regina	D
178	NYR	Greg Beller	Lake of the Woods	W
179	Cgy.	Brett Sutter	Kootenay	C/LW
180	NYI	Tyrell Mason	Salmon Arm	D
181	Wsh.	Tim Kennedy	Sioux City	LW
182	Buf.	Adam Dennis	London	G
183	S.J.	William Colbert	Ottawa	D
184	L.A.	Ryan McGinnis	Plymouth	D
185	Van.	Kris Fredheim	Notre Dame	D

Pick	Claimed by	Amateur Club	Position
186 Ott.	Dimitri Megalinsky	Yaroslavl	D
187 Atl.	Andrei Zubarev	Ufa 2	D
188 Chi.	Joe Charlebois	Sioux City	D
189 CBJ	Kirill Starkov	Frolunda Jr.	C
190 Mtl.	Matt D'Agostini	Guelph.	RW
191 Buf.	Vyacheslav Buravchikov	Krylja Sovetov	D
192 Car.	Nicolas Blanchard	Chicoutimi	C
193 S.J.	Tony Lucia	Wayzata	LW
194 Pit.	Jean-Philippe Paquet	Shawinigan	D

SEVENTH ROUND

Pick	Claimed by	Amateur Club	Position
195 Pit.	Joe Vitale	Sioux Falls	C
196 NYI	Nicholas Tuzzolino	Sarnia	D
197 Ana.	Jean-Philippe Levasseur	Rouyn Noranda	G
198 Car.	Kyle Lawson	USA U-18	D
199 Min.	Riley Emmerson	Tri-City	D
200 Mtl.	Sergei Kostitsyn	Gomel	LW
201 CBJ	Trevor Hendrikx	Peterborough	D
202 Chi.	David Kuchejda	C. Budejovice Jr.	RW
203 Chi.	Adam Hobson	Spokane	C
204 Ott.	Colin Greening	Upper Canada College	C/LW
205 Van.	Mario Bliznak	Dubnica	C
206 L.A.	Josh Meyers	Sioux City	D
207 Atl.	Myles Stoesz	Spokane	D
208 Buf.	Matt Generous	N.E. Jr. Falcons.	D
209 Wsh.	Viktor Dovgan	CSKA Moscow 2	D
210 NYI	Luciano Aquino	Brampton	C/LW
211 NYR	Ryan Russell	Kootenay	C
212 Phx.	Pat Brosnihan	Worcester	RW
213 Nsh.	Scott Todd	Windsor	D
214 Det.	Bretton Stamler	Seattle	D
215 Phi.	Matthew Clackson	Chicago	LW
216 Tor.	Anton Stralman	Skovde	D
217 Bos.	Brock Bradford	Omaha	C
218 N.J.	Alexander Sundstrom	Bjorkloven.	C/W
219 St.L.	Nikolai Lemtyugov	CSKA.	W
220 Edm.	Matthew Glasser	Fort McMurray	LW
221 Cgy.	Myles Rumsey	Swift Current.	D
222 Col.	Kyle Cumiskey	Kelowna	D
223 Dal.	Pat McGann	Team Illinois.	G
224 Fla.	Zach Bearson	Waterloo	RW
225 T.B.	John Wessbecker	Blake	D
226 L.A.	John Seymour	Brampton	LW
227 Buf.	Andrew Orpik	Thayer	C
228 Tor.	Chad Rau	Des Moines	C
229 Mtl.	Philippe Paquet	Salisbury	D
230 Nsh.	Patric Hornqvist	Vasby.	W

First Two Rounds
2004–2002

2004
FIRST ROUND

Pick	Claimed by	Amateur Club	Position
1 Wsh.	Alexander Ovechkin	Dynamo	LW
2 Pit.	Evgeni Malkin	Magnitogorsk	C
3 Chi.	Cam Barker	Medicine Hat.	D
4 Car.	Andrew Ladd	Calgary	LW
5 Phx.	Blake Wheeler	Breck	RW
6 NYR	Al Montoya	U. of Michigan	G
7 Fla.	Rostislav Olesz	Vitkovice	C
8 CBJ	Alexandre Picard	Lewiston	LW
9 Ana.	Ladislav Smid	Liberec	D
10 Atl.	Boris Valabik	Kitchener	D
11 L.A.	Lauri Tukonen	Blues Espoo	RW
12 Min.	A.J. Thelen	Michigan State	D
13 Buf.	Drew Stafford	U. of North Dakota	RW
14 Edm.	Devan Dubnyk	Kamloops	G
15 Nsh.	Alexander Radulov	Tver	LW
16 NYI	Petteri Nokelainen	SaiPa	C
17 St.L.	Marek Schwarz	Sparta Praha	G
18 Mtl.	Kyle Chipchura	Prince Albert	C
19 NYR	Lauri Korpikoski	TPS Turku Jr.	LW
20 N.J.	Travis Zajac	Salmon Arm	C
21 Col.	Wojtek Wolski	Brampton	LW
22 S.J.	Lukas Kaspar	Litvinov	RW
23 Ott.	Andrej Meszaros	Trencin	D
24 Cgy.	Kris Chucko	Salmon Arm	RW
25 Edm.	Rob Schremp	London	C
26 Van.	Cory Schneider	Phillips-Andover	G
27 Wsh.	Jeff Schultz	Calgary	D
28 Dal.	Mark Fistric	Vancouver	D
29 Wsh.	Mike Green	Saskatoon	D
30 T.B.	Andy Rogers	Calgary	D

SECOND ROUND

Pick	Claimed by	Amateur Club	Position
31 Pit.	Johannes Salmonsson	Djurgarden	LW
32 Chi.	Dave Bolland	London	C/RW
33 Wsh.	Christopher Bourque	Cushing Academy	C
34 Dal.	Johan Fransson	Lulea	D
35 Phx.	Logan Stephenson	Tri-City	D
36 NYR	Darin Olver	Northern Michigan.	C
37 Fla.	David Shantz	Mississauga	G
38 Car.	Justin Peters	St. Michael's	G
39 Ana.	Jordan Smith	Sault Ste. Marie	D
40 Atl.	Grant Lewis	Dartmouth	D
41 Chi.	Bryan Bickell	Ottawa	LW
42 Min.	Roman Voloshenko	Krylja Sovetov	LW
43 Buf.	Michael Funk	Portland	D
44 Edm.	Roman Teslyuk	Kamloops	D
45 Chi.	Ryan Garlock	Windsor	C
46 CBJ	Adam Pineault	Boston College	RW
47 NYI	Blake Comeau	Kelowna	RW
48 NYR	Dane Byers	Prince Albert	LW
49 St.L.	Carl Soderberg	Malmo	C
50 Phx.	Enver Lisin	Saratov	RW
51 NYR	Bruce Graham	Moncton	C
52 Dal.	Raymond Sawada	Nanaimo	RW
53 Fla.	David Booth	Michigan State	LW
54 Chi.	Jakub Sindel	Sparta Praha	C
55 Col.	Victor Oreskovich	Green Bay	RW
56 Dal.	Nikolas Grossmann	Sodertalje Jr.	D
57 Edm.	Geoff Paukovich	U.S. Nat'l U-18	LW
58 Ott.	Kirill Lyamin	CSKA Moscow.	D
59 CBJ	Kyle Wharton	Ottawa	D
60 NYR	Brandon Dubinsky	Portland	C
61 Pit.	Alex Goligoski	Sioux Falls	D
62 Wsh.	Michail Yunkov	Krylja	C
63 Bos.	David Krejci	Kladno Jr.	C
64 Bos.	Martins Karsums	Moncton	RW
65 T.B.	Mark Tobin	Rimouski	LW

Carolina selected Eric Staal second overall behind Marc-Andre Fleury in the 2003 NHL Entry Draft. The New York Rangers selected his brother Marc with the 12th pick in 2005.

2003
FIRST ROUND

Pick	Claimed by	Amateur Club	Position
1 Pit.	Marc-Andre Fleury	Cape Breton	G
2 Car.	Eric Staal	Peterborough	C
3 Fla.	Nathan Horton	Oshawa	C
4 CBJ	Nikolai Zherdev	CSKA Moscow.	W
5 Buf.	Thomas Vanek	U. of Minnesota	LW
6 S.J.	Milan Michalek	Budejovice	RW
7 Nsh.	Ryan Suter	U.S. National U-18	D
8 Atl.	Braydon Coburn	Portland.	D
9 Cgy.	Dion Phaneuf	Red Deer	D
10 Mtl.	Andrei Kostitsyn	CSKA Moscow 2	RW
11 Phi.	Jeff Carter	Sault Ste. Marie	C
12 NYR	Hugh Jessiman	Dartmouth	RW
13 L.A.	Dustin Brown	Guelph	RW
14 Chi.	Brent Seabrook	Lethbridge	D
15 NYI	Robert Nilsson	Leksand	RW
16 S.J.	Steve Bernier	Moncton	RW
17 N.J.	Zach Parise	North Dakota	C
18 Wsh.	Eric Fehr	Brandon	RW
19 Ana.	Ryan Getzlaf	Calgary	C
20 Min.	Brent Burns	Brampton	RW
21 Bos.	Mark Stuart	Colorado College	D
22 Edm.	Marc-Antoine Pouliot	Rimouski	C
23 Van.	Ryan Kesler	Ohio State	C
24 Phi.	Mike Richards	Kitchener	C
25 Fla.	Anthony Stewart	Kingston	C
26 L.A.	Brian Boyle	St. Sebastian's H.S.	C
27 L.A.	Jeff Tambellini	U. of Michigan	LW
28 Ana.	Corey Perry	London	RW
29 Ott.	Patrick Eaves	Boston College	RW
30 St.L.	Shawn Belle	Tri-City	D

SECOND ROUND

Pick	Claimed by	Amateur Club	Position
31 Car.	Danny Richmond	U. of Michigan	D
32 Pit.	Ryan Stone	Brandon.	C
33 Dal.	Loui Eriksson	Vastra Frolunda Jr.	LW
34 T.B.	Mike Egener	Calgary	D
35 Nsh.	Konstantin Glazachev	Yaroslavl	LW
36 Dal.	Vojtech Polak	Karlovy Vary	RW
37 Nsh.	Kevin Klein	St. Michael's.	D
38 Fla.	Kamil Kreps	Brampton.	C
39 Cgy.	Tim Ramholt	Zurich	D
40 Mtl.	Cory Urquhart	Montreal	C
41 T.B.	Matt Smaby	Shattuck St. Mary's H.S.	D
42 N.J.	Petr Vrana	Halifax.	LW
43 S.J.	Joshua Hennessy	Quebec	C
44 L.A.	Konstantin Pushkarev	Ust-Kamenogorsk	RW
45 Bos.	Patrice Bergeron-Cleary	Acadie-Bathurst	C
46 CBJ	Dan Fritsche	Sarnia	C
47 S.J.	Matthew Carle	River City	D
48 NYI	Dmitri Chernykh	Khimik Voskresensk	RW
49 Nsh.	Shea Weber	Kelowna	D
50 NYR	Ivan Baranka	Dubnica Jr.	D
51 Edm.	Colin McDonald	New England.	RW
52 Chi.	Corey Crawford	Moncton	G
53 NYI	Yevgeni Tunik	Elektrostal	C
54 Dal.	Brandon Crombeen	Barrie	RW
55 Fla.	Stefan Meyer	Medicine Hat	LW
56 Min.	Patrick O'Sullivan	Mississauga	C
57 Tor.	John Doherty	Phillips-Andover	D
58 NYI	Jeremy Colliton	Prince Albert	C
59 Chi.	Michal Barinka	Budejovice	D
60 Van.	Marc-Andre Bernier	Halifax	RW
61 Mtl.	Maxim Lapierre.	Montreal	C
62 St.L.	David Backes	Lincoln.	C
63 Col.	David Liffiton	Plymouth	D
64 Det.	James Howard	U. of Maine	G
65 Buf.	Branislav Fabry	Bratislava Jr.	LW
66 Bos.	Masi Marjamaki	Red Deer	LW
67 Ott.	Igor Mirnov	Dynamo.	LW
68 Edm.	Jean-Francois Jacques	Baie-Comeau	LW

2002
FIRST ROUND

Pick	Claimed by	Amateur Club	Position
1 CBJ	Rick Nash	London	LW
2 Atl.	Kari Lehtonen	Jokerit	G
3 Fla.	Jay Bouwmeester	Medicine Hat	D
4 Phi.	Joni Pitkanen	Karpat	D
5 Pit.	Ryan Whitney	Boston U.	D
6 Nsh.	Scottie Upshall	Kamloops	RW
7 Ana.	Joffrey Lupul	Medicine Hat	C
8 Min.	Pierre-Marc Bouchard	Chicoutimi	C
9 Fla.	Petr Taticek	Sault Ste. Marie	C
10 Cgy.	Eric Nystrom	U. of Michigan	LW
11 Buf.	Keith Ballard	U. of Minnesota	D
12 Wsh.	Steve Eminger	Kitchener	D
13 Wsh.	Alexander Semin	Chelyabinsk	LW
14 Mtl.	Christopher Higgins	Yale	C
15 Edm.	Jesse Niinimaki	Ilves Tampere	C
16 Ott.	Jakub Klepis	Portland.	C
17 Wsh.	Boyd Gordon	Red Deer	RW
18 L.A.	Denis Grebeshkov	Yaroslavl	D
19 Phx.	Jakub Koreis	Plzen	C
20 Buf.	Dan Paille	Guelph	LW
21 Chi.	Anton Babchuk	Elektrostal	D
22 NYI	Sean Bergenheim	Jokerit	LW
23 Phx.	Ben Eager	Oshawa	LW
24 Tor.	Alexander Steen	Vastra Frolunda	C
25 Car.	Cam Ward	Red Deer	G
26 Dal.	Martin Vagner	Hull	D
27 S.J.	Mike Morris	St. Sebastian's H.S.	RW
28 Col.	Jonas Johansson	HV 71 Jonkoping Jr.	RW
29 Bos.	Hannu Toivonen	HPK Jr.	G
30 Atl.	Jim Slater	Michigan State	C

SECOND ROUND

Pick	Claimed by	Amateur Club	Position
31 Edm.	Jeff Deslauriers	Chicoutimi	G
32 Dal.	Janos Vas	Malmo Jr.	LW
33 NYR	Lee Falardeau	Michigan State	C
34 Dal.	Tobias Stephan	Chur	G
35 Pit.	Ondrej Nemec	Vsetin	D
36 Edm.	Jarret Stoll	Kootenay	C
37 Ana.	Tim Brent	St. Michael's.	C
38 Min.	Josh Harding	Regina.	G
39 Cgy.	Brian McConnell	Boston U.	C
40 Fla.	Rob Globke	Notre Dame	C
41 CBJ	Joakim Lindstrom	MoDo Ornskoldsvik	C
42 Dal.	Marius Holtet	Farjestad Jr.	C
43 Dal.	Trevor Daley	Sault Ste. Marie	D
44 Edm.	Matt Greene	Green Bay	D
45 Mtl.	Tomas Linhart	Pardubice Jr.	D
46 Phx.	David Leneveu	Cornell	G
47 Ott.	Alexei Kaigorodov	Magnitogorsk	C
48 St.L.	Alexei Shkotov	Elektrostal Jr.	RW
49 Van.	Kirill Koltsov	Omsk.	D
50 L.A.	Sergei Anshakov	CSKA Moscow	LW
51 N.J.	Anton Kadeikin	Elektrostal	D
52 S.J.	Dan Spang	Winchester H.S.	D
53 N.J.	Barry Tallackson	U. of Minnesota.	C
54 Chi.	Duncan Keith	Michigan State.	D
55 Van.	Denis Grot	Elektrostal	D
56 Bos.	Vladislav Yevseyev	CSKA Moscow	LW
57 Tor.	Matt Stajan	Belleville	C
58 Det.	Jiri Hudler	Vsetin	C
59 Wsh.	Maxime Daigneault	Val-d'Or.	G
60 T.B.	Adam Henrich	Brampton	LW
61 Col.	Johnny Boychuk	Calgary	D
62 St.L.	Andrei Mikhnov	Sudbury	C
63 Det.	Tomas Fleischmann	Vitkovice Jr.	LW

First Round and Other Notable Selections 2001–1969

2001

FIRST ROUND

Pick	Claimed by	Player	Amateur Club	Position
1	Atl.	Ilya Kovalchuk	Krylja Sovetov	LW
2	Ott.	Jason Spezza	Windsor	C
3	T.B.	Alexander Svitov	Avangard Omsk	C
4	Fla.	Stephen Weiss	Plymouth	C
5	Ana.	Stanislav Chistov	Avangard Omsk	LW
6	Min.	Mikko Koivu	TPS Turku	C
7	Mtl.	Mike Komisarek	U. of Michigan	D
8	CBJ	Pascal Leclaire	Halifax	G
9	Chi.	Tuomo Ruutu	Jokerit	C/LW
10	NYR	Dan Blackburn	Kootenay	G
11	Phx.	Fredrik Sjostrom	Vastra Frolunda	RW
12	Nsh.	Dan Hamhuis	Prince George	D
13	Edm.	Ales Hemsky	Hull	RW
14	Cgy.	Chuck Kobasew	Boston College	C
15	Car.	Igor Knyazev	Spartak	D
16	Van.	R.J. Umberger	Ohio State	C
17	Tor.	Carlo Colaiacovo	Erie	D
18	L.A.	Jens Karlsson	Vastra Frolunda	RW
19	Bos.	Shaone Morrisonn	Kamloops	D
20	S.J.	Marcel Goc	Schwenningen	C
21	Pit.	Colby Armstrong	Red Deer	RW
22	Buf.	Jiri Novotny	Budejovice	C
23	Ott.	Tim Gleason	Windsor	D
24	Fla.	Lukas Krajicek	Peterborough	D
25	Mtl.	Alexander Perezhogin	Avangard Omsk	C
26	Dal.	Jason Bacashihua	Chicago (NAHL)	G
27	Phi.	Jeff Woywitka	Red Deer	D
28	N.J.	Adrian Foster	Saskatoon	C
29	Chi.	Adam Munro	Erie	G
30	L.A.	Dave Steckel	Ohio State	C

OTHER NOTABLE SELECTIONS

Pick	Claimed by	Player	Amateur Club	Position
39	Tor.	Karel Pilar	Litvinov	D
49	L.A.	Mike Cammalleri	U. of Michigan	C
66	Van.	Fedor Fedorov	Sudbury	LW
98	Nsh.	Jordin Tootoo	Brandon	RW
106	S.J.	Christoph Ehrhoff	Krefeld	D
132	NYI	Dusan Salficky	Plzen	G
172	Phi.	Denis Seidenberg	Mannheim	D
176	Nsh.	Marek Zidlicky	HIFK	D
189	Atl.	Pasi Nurminen	Jokerit	G
214	L.A.	Cristobel Huet	Lugano	G
232	Ana.	Martin Gerber	Langnau	G
253	St.L.	Petr Cajanek	Zlin	RW

2000

FIRST ROUND

Pick	Claimed by	Player	Amateur Club	Position
1	NYI	Rick DiPietro	Boston U.	G
2	Atl.	Dany Heatley	U. of Wisconsin	RW
3	Min.	Marian Gaborik	Dukla Trencin	RW
4	CBJ	Rostislav Klesla	Brampton	D
5	NYI	Raffi Torres	Brampton	LW
6	Nsh.	Scott Hartnell	Prince Albert	LW
7	Bos.	Lars Jönsson	Leksand	D
8	T.B.	Nikita Alexeev	Erie	RW
9	Cgy.	Brent Krahn	Calgary	G
10	Chi.	Mikhail Yakubov	Lada Togliatti	C
11	Chi.	Pavel Vorobiev	Yaroslavl	RW
12	Ana.	Alexei Smirnov	Tver	LW
13	Mtl.	Ron Hainsey	U. of Mass-Lowell	D
14	Col.	Vaclav Nedorost	Budejovice	C
15	Buf.	Artem Kryukov	Yaroslavl	C
16	Mtl.	Marcel Hossa	Portland	LW
17	Edm.	Alexei Mikhnov	Yaroslavl	LW
18	Pit.	Brooks Orpik	Boston College	D
19	Phx.	Krys Kolanos	Boston College	C
20	L.A.	Alexander Frolov	Yaroslavl 2	LW
21	Ott.	Anton Volchenkov	HC Moscow	D
22	N.J.	David Hale	Sioux City	D
23	Van.	Nathan Smith	Swift Current	C
24	Tor.	Brad Boyes	Erie	C
25	Dal.	Steve Ott	Windsor	C
26	Wsh.	Brian Sutherby	Moose Jaw	C
27	Bos.	Martin Samuelsson	MoDo Ornskoldsvik	RW
28	Phi.	Justin Williams	Plymouth	RW
29	Det.	Niklas Kronwall	Djurgarden	D
30	St.L.	Jeff Taffe	U. of Minnesota	C

OTHER NOTABLE SELECTIONS

Pick	Claimed by	Player	Amateur Club	Position
33	Min.	Nick Schultz	Prince Albert	D
43	Wsh.	Matt Pettinger	Calgary	LW
44	Ana.	Ilya Bryzgalov	Lada Togliatti	G
46	Cgy.	Jarrett Stoll	Kootenay	C
54	L.A.	Andreas Lilja	Malmo	D
76	N.J.	Michael Rupp	Erie	LW
97	Car.	Niclas Wallin	Brynas	D
118	L.A.	Lubomir Visnovsky	Bratislava	D

Pick	Claimed by	Player	Amateur Club	Position
155	Cgy.	Travis Moen	Kelowna	LW
159	Col.	John-Michael Liles	Michigan State	D
171	Phi.	Roman Cechmanek	Vsetin	G
232	Min.	Lubomir Sekeras	Trinec	D

1999

FIRST ROUND

Pick	Claimed by	Player	Amateur Club	Position
1	Atl.	Patrik Stefan	Long Beach	C
2	Van.	Daniel Sedin	MoDo Ornskoldsvik	LW
3	Van.	Henrik Sedin	MoDo Ornskoldsvik	C
4	NYR	Pavel Brendl	Calgary	RW
5	NYI	Tim Connolly	Erie	C
6	Nsh.	Brian Finley	Barrie	G
7	Wsh.	Kris Beech	Calgary	C
8	NYI	Taylor Pyatt	Sudbury	LW
9	NYR	Jamie Lundmark	Moose Jaw	C
10	NYI	Branislav Mezei	Belleville	D
11	Cgy.	Oleg Saprykin	Seattle	LW
12	Fla.	Denis Shvidki	Barrie	RW
13	Edm.	Jani Rita	Jokerit	LW
14	S.J.	Jeff Jillson	U. of Michigan	D
15	Phx.	Scott Kelman	Seattle	C
16	Car.	David Tanabe	U. of Wisconsin	D
17	St.L.	Barret Jackman	Regina	D
18	Pit.	Konstantin Koltsov	Cherepovets	RW
19	Phx.	Kirill Safronov	St. Petersburg	D
20	Buf.	Barrett Heisten	U. of Maine	LW
21	Bos.	Nick Boynton	Ottawa	D
22	Phi.	Maxime Ouellet	Quebec	G
23	Chi.	Steve McCarthy	Kootenay	D
24	Tor.	Luca Cereda	Ambri	C
25	Col.	Mikhail Kuleshov	Cherepovets	LW
26	Ott.	Martin Havlat	Trinec	LW
27	N.J.	Ari Ahonen	JyP HT Jr.	G
28	NYI	Kristian Kudroc	Michalovce	D

OTHER NOTABLE SELECTIONS

Pick	Claimed by	Player	Amateur Club	Position
42	N.J.	Mike Commodore	North Dakota	D
70	Fla.	Niklas Hagman	HIFK Helsinki	LW
76	L.A.	Frantisek Kaberle	MoDo Ornskoldsvik	D
83	Ana.	Niclas Havelid	Malmo	D
91	Edm.	Mike Comrie	U. of Michigan	C
115	Pit.	Ryan Malone	Omaha	LW
191	Nsh.	Martin Erat	ZPS Zlin Jr.	LW
210	Det.	Henrik Zetterberg	Timra	LW
212	Col.	Radim Vrbata	Hull	RW
230	Ana.	Petr Tenkrat	Kladno	RW
232	St.L.	Alexander Khavanov	Dynamo	D
247	Bos.	Mikko Eloranta	TPS Turku	LW

1998

FIRST ROUND

Pick	Claimed by	Player	Amateur Club	Position
1	T.B.	Vincent Lecavalier	Rimouski	C
2	Nsh.	David Legwand	Plymouth	C
3	S.J.	Brad Stuart	Regina	D
4	Van.	Bryan Allen	Oshawa	D
5	Ana.	Vitaly Vishnevski	Yaroslavl 2	D
6	Cgy.	Rico Fata	London	RW
7	NYR	Manny Malhotra	Guelph	C
8	Chi.	Mark Bell	Ottawa	C
9	NYI	Mike Rupp	Erie	RW
10	Tor.	Nik Antropov	Ust-Kamenogorsk	C
11	Car.	Jeff Heerema	Sarnia	RW
12	Col.	Alex Tanguay	Halifax	LW
13	Edm.	Michael Henrich	Barrie	RW
14	Phx.	Patrick DesRochers	Sarnia	G
15	Ott.	Mathieu Chouinard	Shawinigan	G
16	Mtl.	Eric Chouinard	Quebec	LW
17	Col.	Martin Skoula	Barrie	D
18	Buf.	Dmitri Kalinin	Chelyabinsk	D
19	Col.	Robyn Regehr	Kamloops	D
20	Col.	Scott Parker	Kelowna	RW
21	L.A.	Mathieu Biron	Shawinigan	D
22	Phi.	Simon Gagne	Quebec	LW
23	Pit.	Milan Kraft	Keramika Plzen Jr.	C
24	St.L.	Christian Backman	Vastra Frolunda Jr.	D
25	Det.	Jiri Fischer	Hull	D
26	N.J.	Mike Van Ryn	U. of Michigan	D
27	N.J.	Scott Gomez	Tri-City	C

OTHER NOTABLE SELECTIONS

Pick	Claimed by	Player	Amateur Club	Position
29	S.J.	Jonathan Cheechoo	Belleville	RW
43	Phx.	Ossi Vaananen	Jokerit Jr.	D
44	Ott.	Mike Fisher	Sudbury	C
48	Bos.	Jonathan Girard	Laval	D
60	Nsh.	Denis Arkhipov	Ak Bars Kazan	C
64	T.B.	Brad Richards	Rimouski	C
91	Car.	Josef Vasicek	Slavia Praha Jr.	C
99	Edm.	Shawn Horcoff	Michigan State	C
117	Fla.	Jaroslav Spacek	Farjestad Karlstad	D
135	Bos.	Andrew Raycroft	Sudbury	G
150	Ana.	Trent Hunter	Prince George	RW
171	Det.	Pavel Datsyuk	Yekateringburg	C
216	Mtl.	Michael Rider	Hull	RW
230	Nsh.	Karlis Skrastins	TPS Turku	D

1997

FIRST ROUND

Pick	Claimed by	Player	Amateur Club	Position
1	Bos.	Joe Thornton	Sault Ste. Marie	C
2	S.J.	Patrick Marleau	Seattle	C
3	L.A.	Olli Jokinen	HIFK Helsinki	C
4	NYI	Roberto Luongo	Val-d'Or	G
5	NYI	Eric Brewer	Prince George	D
6	Cgy.	Daniel Tkaczuk	Barrie	C
7	T.B.	Paul Mara	Sudbury	D
8	Bos.	Sergei Samsonov	Detroit	LW
9	Wsh.	Nick Boynton	Ottawa	D
10	Van.	Brad Ference	Spokane	D
11	Mtl.	Jason Ward	Erie	RW
12	Ott.	Marian Hossa	Dukla Trencin	RW
13	Chi.	Daniel Cleary	Belleville	RW
14	Edm.	Michel Riesen	Biel-Bienne	RW
15	L.A.	Matt Zultek	Ottawa	LW
16	Chi.	Ty Jones	Spokane	RW
17	Pit.	Robert Dome	Las Vegas (IHL)	RW
18	Ana.	Mikael Holmqvist	Djurgarden	C
19	NYR	Stefan Cherneski	Brandon	RW
20	Fla.	Mike Brown	Red Deer	LW
21	Buf.	Mika Noronen	Tappara Tampere	G
22	Car.	Nikos Tselios	Belleville	D
23	S.J.	Scott Hannan	Kelowna	D
24	N.J.	J-F Damphousse	Moncton	G
25	Dal.	Brenden Morrow	Portland	LW
26	Col.	Kevin Grimes	Kingston	D

OTHER NOTABLE SELECTIONS

Pick	Claimed by	Player	Amateur Club	Position
27	Bos.	Ben Clymer	Minnesota-Duluth	LW
70	Cgy.	Erik Andersson	U. of Denver	C
95	Fla.	Ivan Novoseltsev	Krylja Sovetov	RW
119	Ott.	Magnus Arvedson	Farjestad Karlstad	LW
130	Chi.	Kyle Calder	Regina	LW
136	NYR	Mike York	Michigan State	LW
144	Van.	Matt Cooke	Windsor	C
177	St.L.	Ladislav Nagy	Dragon Presov	LW
191	Bos.	Antti Laaksonen	U. of Denver	LW
242	Chi.	Brett McLean	Kelowna	C

1996

FIRST ROUND

Pick	Claimed by	Player	Amateur Club	Position
1	Ott.	Chris Phillips	Prince Albert	D
2	S.J.	Andrei Zyuzin	Salavat Yulayev Ufa	D
3	NYI	J.P. Dumont	Val-d'Or	RW
4	Wsh.	Alexandre Volchkov	Barrie	C
5	Dal.	Ric Jackman	Sault Ste. Marie	D
6	Edm.	Boyd Devereaux	Kitchener	C
7	Buf.	Erik Rasmussen	U. of Minnesota	LW/C
8	Bos.	Johnathan Aitken	Medicine Hat	D
9	Ana.	Ruslan Salei	Las Vegas (IHL)	D
10	N.J.	Lance Ward	Red Deer	D
11	Phx.	Dan Focht	Tri-City	D
12	Van.	Josh Holden	Regina	C
13	Cgy.	Derek Morris	Regina	D
14	St.L.	Marty Reasoner	Boston College	C
15	Phi.	Dainius Zubrus	Pembroke Jr. A	RW
16	T.B.	Mario Larocque	Hull	D
17	Wsh.	Jaroslav Svejkovsky	Tri-City	RW
18	Mtl.	Matt Higgins	Moose Jaw	C
19	Edm.	Matthieu Descoteaux	Shawinigan	D
20	Fla.	Marcus Nilson	Djurgarden	LW
21	S.J.	Marco Sturm	Landshut	LW
22	NYR	Jeff Brown	Sarnia	D
23	Pit.	Craig Hillier	Ottawa	G
24	Phx.	Daniel Briere	Drummondville	C
25	Col.	Peter Ratchuk	Shattuck St. Mary's H.S.	D
26	Det.	Jesse Wallin	Red Deer	D

OTHER NOTABLE SELECTIONS

Pick	Claimed by	Player	Amateur Club	Position
35	Ana.	Matt Cullen	St. Cloud State	C
49	N.J.	Colin White	Hull	D
56	NYI	Zdeno Chara	Dukla Trencin	D
59	Edm.	Tom Poti	Cushing Academy	D
65	Fla.	Oleg Kvasha	CSKA Moscow	LW/C
79	Col.	Mark Parrish	St. Cloud State	RW
136	Ott.	Andreas Dackell	Brynas Gavle	RW
139	Phx.	Robert Esche	Detroit	G
174	Phx.	Trevor Letowski	Sarnia	RW
179	T.B.	Pavel Kubina	Vitkovice	D
204	Tor.	Tomas Kaberle	Kladno	D

1995

FIRST ROUND

Pick	Claimed by		Amateur Club	Position
1	Ott.	Bryan Berard	Detroit	D
2	NYI	Wade Redden	Brandon	D
3	L.A.	Aki Berg	Kiekko-67 Turku	D
4	Ana.	Chad Kilger	Kingston	C
5	T.B.	Daymond Langkow	Tri-City	C
6	Edm.	Steve Kelly	Prince Albert	C
7	Wpg.	Shane Doan	Kamloops	RW
8	Mtl.	Terry Ryan	Tri-City	LW
9	Bos.	Kyle McLaren	Tacoma	D
10	Fla.	Radek Dvorak	HC Ceske Budejovice	RW
11	Dal.	Jarome Iginla	Kamloops	RW
12	S.J.	Teemu Riihijarvi	Kiekko-Espoo	LW
13	Hfd.	Jean-Sebastien Giguere	Halifax	G
14	Buf.	Jay McKee	Niagara Falls	D
15	Tor.	Jeff Ware	Oshawa	D
16	Buf.	Martin Biron	Beauport	G
17	Wsh.	Brad Church	Prince Albert	LW
18	N.J.	Petr Sykora	Detroit	RW
19	Chi.	Dmitri Nabokov	Krylja Sovetov	C/LW
20	Cgy.	Denis Gauthier	Drummondville	D
21	Bos.	Sean Brown	Belleville	D
22	Phi.	Brian Boucher	Tri-City	G
23	Wsh.	Miika Elomo	Kiekko-67 Turku	LW
24	Pit.	Aleksey Morozov	Krylja Sovetov	RW
25	Col.	Marc Denis	Chicoutimi	G
26	Det.	Maxim Kuznetsov	Dynamo	D

OTHER NOTABLE SELECTIONS

Pick	Claimed by		Amateur Club	Position
31	Edm.	Georges Laraque	St-Jean	RW
45	Chi.	Christian Laflamme	Beauport	D
59	L.A.	Vladimir Tsyplakov	Fort Wayne IHL	LW
67	Wpg.	Brad Isbister	Portland	LW
79	N.J.	Alyn McCauley	Ottawa	C
87	Hfd.	Sami Kapanen	HIFK Helsinki	RW
91	NYR	Marc Savard	Oshawa	C
101	St.L.	Michal Handzus	IS Banska Bystrica	C
116	S.J.	Miikka Kiprusoff	TPS Turku Jr.	G
128	Pit.	Jan Hrdina	Seattle	C
145	Tor.	Yannick Tremblay	Beauport	D
166	Fla.	Peter Worrell	Hull	LW
177	Bos.	P.J. Axelsson	Vastra Frolunda	LW
223	Tor.	Danny Markov	Spartak	D

Milan Hedjuk was drafted when the Colorado franchise was still based in Quebec. The Nordiques took him with their sixth choice (87th overall) in the 1994 Entry Draft.

1994

FIRST ROUND

Pick	Claimed by		Amateur Club	Position
1	Fla.	Ed Jovanovski	Windsor	D
2	Ana.	Oleg Tverdovsky	Krylja Sovetov	D
3	Ott.	Radek Bonk	Las Vegas (IHL)	C
4	Edm.	Jason Bonsignore	Niagara Falls	C
5	Hfd.	Jeff O'Neill	Guelph	RW
6	Edm.	Ryan Smyth	Moose Jaw	LW
7	L.A.	Jamie Storr	Owen Sound	G
8	T.B.	Jason Wiemer	Portland	C
9	NYI	Brett Lindros	Kingston	RW
10	Wsh.	Nolan Baumgartner	Kamloops	D
11	S.J.	Jeff Friesen	Regina	LW
12	Que.	Wade Belak	Saskatoon	D/RW
13	Van.	Mattias Ohlund	Pitea	D
14	Chi.	Ethan Moreau	Niagara Falls	LW
15	Wsh.	Alexander Kharlamov	CSKA Moscow	C
16	Tor.	Eric Fichaud	Chictoutimi	G
17	Buf.	Wayne Primeau	Owen Sound	C
18	Mtl.	Brad Brown	North Bay	D
19	Cgy.	Chris Dingman	Brandon	LW
20	Dal.	Jason Botterill	U. of Michigan	LW
21	Bos.	Evgeni Ryabchikov	Molot Perm	G
22	Que.	Jeffrey Kealty	Catholic Memorial H.S.	D
23	Det.	Yan Golubovsky	Dynamo 2	D
24	Pit.	Chris Wells	Seattle	C
25	N.J.	Vadim Sharifijanov	Salavat Yulayev Ufa	LW
26	NYR	Dan Cloutier	Sault Ste. Marie	G

OTHER NOTABLE SELECTIONS

Pick	Claimed by		Amateur Club	Position
27	Fla.	Rhett Warrener	Saskatoon	D
43	Buf.	Curtis Brown	Moose Jaw	C/LW
49	Det.	Mathieu Dandenault	Sherbrooke	RW/D
51	N.J.	Patrik Elias	Kladno	C
64	Tor.	Fredrik Modin	Timra	LW
87	Que.	Milan Hejduk	Pardubice	RW
124	Dal.	Marty Turco	Cambridge Jr. A	G
132	Ana.	Bates Battaglia	Caledon Jr. A	LW
133	Ott.	Daniel Alfredsson	Vastra Frolunda	RW
210	N.J.	Steve Sullivan	Sault Ste. Marie	RW
219	S.J.	Evegeni Nabokov	Ust-Kamengorsk	G
272	NYI	Dick Tarnstrom	AIK Solna	D

1993

FIRST ROUND

Pick	Claimed by		Amateur Club	Position
1	Ott.	Alexandre Daigle	Victoriaville	C
2	Hfd.	Chris Pronger	Peterborough	D
3	T.B.	Chris Gratton	Kingston	C
4	Ana.	Paul Kariya	U. of Maine	LW
5	Fla.	Rob Niedermayer	Medicine Hat	C
5	Det.	Benoit Larose	Laval	D
6	S.J.	Viktor Kozlov	Dynamo	C
7	Edm.	Jason Arnott	Oshawa	C
8	NYR	Niklas Sundstrom	MoDo Ornskoldsvik	RW
9	Dal.	Todd Harvey	Detroit	RW/C
10	Que.	Jocelyn Thibault	Sherbrooke	G
11	Wsh.	Brendan Witt	Seattle	D
12	Tor.	Kenny Jonsson	Rogle Angelholm	D
13	N.J.	Denis Pederson	Prince Albert	C/RW
14	Que.	Adam Deadmarsh	Portland	RW
15	Wpg.	Mats Lindgren	Skelleftea	C/LW
16	Edm.	Nick Stajduhar	London	D
17	Wsh.	Jason Allison	London	C
18	Cgy.	Jesper Mattsson	Malmo	C
19	Tor.	Landon Wilson	Dubuque Jr. A	RW
20	Van.	Mike Wilson	Sudbury	D
21	Mtl.	Saku Koivu	TPS Turku	C
22	Det.	Anders Eriksson	MoDo Ornskoldsvik	D
23	NYI	Todd Bertuzzi	Guelph	RW
24	Chi.	Eric Lecompte	Hull	LW
25	Bos.	Kevyn Adams	Miami of Ohio	C
26	Pit.	Stefan Bergkvist	Leksand	D

OTHER NOTABLE SELECTIONS

Pick	Claimed by		Amateur Club	Position
28	S.J.	Shean Donovan	Ottawa	RW
71	Phi.	Vaclav Prospal	Motor Ceske Budejovice	C
72	Hfd.	Marek Malik	Vitkovice	D
90	Chi.	Eric Daze	Beauport	RW
111	Edm.	Miroslav Satan	Dukla Trencin	LW
118	NYI	Tommy Salo	Vasteras	G
124	Van.	Scott Walker	Owen Sound	RW
151	Mtl.	Darcy Tucker	Kamloops	RW
164	NYR	Todd Marchant	Clarkson	C
207	Bos.	Hal Gill	Nashoba H.S.	D
219	St.L.	Mike Grier	St. Sebastian's H.S.	RW
227	Ott.	Pavol Demitra	Dukla Trencin	LW
252	Cgy.	German Titov	TPS Turku	LW

1992

FIRST ROUND

Pick	Claimed by		Amateur Club	Position
1	T.B.	Roman Hamrlik	ZPS Zlin	D
2	Ott.	Alexei Yashin	Dynamo	C
3	S.J.	Mike Rathje	Medicine Hat	D
4	Que.	Todd Warriner	Windsor	LW
5	NYI	Darius Kasparaitis	Dynamo	D
6	Cgy.	Cory Stillman	Windsor	LW
7	Phi.	Ryan Sittler	Nichols H.S.	LW
8	Tor.	Brandon Convery	Sudbury	C
9	Hfd.	Robert Petrovicky	Dukla Trencin	C
10	S.J.	Andrei Nazarov	Dynamo	LW
11	Buf.	David Cooper	Medicine Hat	D
12	Chi.	Sergei Krivokrasov	CSKA Moscow	RW
13	Edm.	Joe Hulbig	St. Sebastian's H.S.	LW
14	Wsh.	Sergei Gonchar	Chelyabinsk	D
15	Phi.	Jason Bowen	Tri-City	D
16	Bos.	Dmitri Kvartalnov	San Diego (IHL)	LW
17	Wpg.	Sergei Bautin	Dynamo	D
18	N.J.	Jason Smith	Regina	D
19	Pit.	Martin Straka	HC Skoda Plzen	C
20	Mtl.	David Wilkie	Kamloops	D
21	Van.	Libor Polasek	Vitkovice	C
22	Det.	Curtis Bowen	Ottawa	LW
23	Tor.	Grant Marshall	Ottawa	RW
24	NYR	Peter Ferraro	Waterloo Jr. A	LW

OTHER NOTABLE SELECTIONS

Pick	Claimed by		Amateur Club	Position
27	Wpg.	Boris Mironov	CSKA Moscow	D
33	Mtl.	Valeri Bure	Spokane	RW
36	Chi.	Jeff Shantz	Regina	C
38	St.L.	Igor Korolev	Dynamo	C
40	Van.	Michael Peca	Ottawa	C
42	N.J.	Sergei Brylin	CSKA Moscow	C
46	Det.	Darren McCarty	Bellevile	RW
48	NYR	Mattias Norstrom	AIK Solna	D
65	Edm.	Kirk Maltby	Owen Sound	RW
78	Cgy.	Robert Svehla	Dukla Trencin	D
83	Buf.	Matthew Barnaby	Beauport	RW
158	St.L.	Ian Laperriere	Drummondville	C/RW
186	N.J.	Stephane Yelle	Oshawa	C
204	Wpg.	Nikolai Khabibulin	CSKA Moscow	G

1991

FIRST ROUND

Pick	Claimed by		Amateur Club	Position
1	Que.	Eric Lindros	Oshawa	C
2	S.J.	Pat Falloon	Spokane	RW
3	N.J.	Scott Niedermayer	Kamloops	D
4	NYI	Scott Lachance	Boston U.	D
5	Wpg.	Aaron Ward	U. of Michigan	D
6	Phi.	Peter Forsberg	MoDo Ornskoldsvik	C
7	Van.	Alek Stojanov	Hamilton	RW
8	Min.	Richard Matvichuk	Saskatoon	D
9	Hfd.	Patrick Poulin	St-Hyacinthe	C
10	Det.	Martin Lapointe	Laval	RW
11	N.J.	Brian Rolston	Detroit Compuware Jr. A	C/RW
12	Edm.	Tyler Wright	Swift Current	C
13	Buf.	Philippe Boucher	Granby	D
14	Wsh.	Pat Peake	Detroit	C
15	NYR	Alex Kovalev	Dynamo	RW
16	Pit.	Markus Naslund	MoDo Ornskoldsvik	LW
17	Mtl.	Brent Bilodeau	Seattle	D
18	Bos.	Glen Murray	Sudbury	RW
19	Cgy.	Niklas Sundblad	AIK Solna	RW
20	Edm.	Martin Rucinsky	CHZ Litvinov	LW
21	Wsh.	Trevor Halverson	North Bay	LW
22	Chi.	Dean McAmmond	Prince Albert	LW

OTHER NOTABLE SELECTIONS

Pick	Claimed by		Amateur Club	Position
23	S.J.	Ray Whitney	Spokane	LW
26	NYI	Ziggy Palffy	AC Nitra	RW
30	S.J.	Sandis Ozolinsh	Dynamo Riga	D
40	Bos.	Jozef Stumpel	AC Nitra	C
52	Cgy.	Sandy McCarthy	Laval	RW
58	Wsh.	Steve Konowalchuk	Portland	LW
59	Hfd.	Michael Nylander	Huddinge	C
71	Chi.	Igor Kravchuk	CSKA Moscow	D
81	L.A.	Alexei Zhitnik	Sokol Kiev	D
103	Que.	Bill Lindsay	Tri-City	RW
106	Bos.	Mariusz Czerkawski	GKS Tychy	RW
122	Phi.	Dmitry Yushkevich	Yaroslavl	D
203	Wpg.	Igor Ulanov	Khimik Voskresensk	D

1990

FIRST ROUND

Pick	Claimed by		Amateur Club	Position
1	Que.	Owen Nolan	Cornwall	RW
2	Van.	Petr Nedved	Seattle	C
3	Det.	Keith Primeau	Niagara Falls	C
4	Phi.	Mike Ricci	Peterborough	C
5	Pit.	Jaromir Jagr	Kladno	RW
6	NYI	Scott Scissons	Saskatoon	C
7	L.A.	Darryl Sydor	Kamloops	D
8	Min.	Derian Hatcher	North Bay	D
9	Wsh.	John Slaney	Cornwall	D
10	Tor.	Drake Berehowsky	Kingston	D
11	Cgy.	Trevor Kidd	Brandon	G
12	Mtl.	Turner Stevenson	Seattle	RW
13	NYR	Michael Stewart	Michigan State	D
14	Buf.	Brad May	Niagara Falls	LW
15	Hfd.	Mark Greig	Lethbridge	RW
16	Chi.	Karl Dykhuis	Hull	D
17	Edm.	Scott Allison	Prince Albert	C
18	Van.	Shawn Antoski	North Bay	LW
19	Wpg.	Keith Tkachuk	Malden Catholic H.S.	LW
20	N.J.	Martin Brodeur	St-Hyacinthe	G
21	Bos.	Bryan Smolinski	Michigan State	C

OTHER NOTABLE SELECTIONS

Pick	Claimed by		Amateur Club	Position
23	Van.	Jiri Slegr	CHZ Litvinov	D
31	Tor.	Felix Potvin	Chicoutimi	G
34	NYR	Doug Weight	Lake Superior State	C
36	Hfd.	Geoff Sanderson	Swift Current	LW
45	Det.	Vyacheslav Kozlov	Khimik Voskresensk	RW
85	NYR	Sergei Zubov	CSKA Moscow	D
86	Van.	Gino Odjick	Laval	RW
97	Buf.	Richard Smehlik	Vitkovice	D
133	L.A.	Robert Lang	CHZ Litvinov	C
156	Wsh.	Peter Bondra	Kosice	RW
177	Wsh.	Ken Klee	Bowling Green	D
244	NYR	Sergei Nemchinov	Krylja Sovetov	LW

Pick	Claimed by	Amateur Club	Position

In 1989, Mats Sundin became the first European player to be taken first overall in the NHL Entry Draft when he was selected by the Quebec Nordiques.

1989
FIRST ROUND

Pick	Claimed by	Amateur Club	Position
1	Que.	Mats Sundin	Nacka	C
2	NYI	Dave Chyzowski	Kamloops	LW
3	Tor.	Scott Thornton	Belleville	LW
4	Wpg.	Stu Barnes	Tri-City	C
5	N.J.	Bill Guerin	Springfield Jr. B	RW
6	Chi.	Adam Bennett	Sudbury	D
7	Min.	Doug Zmolek	John Marshall H.S.	D
8	Van.	Jason Herter	North Dakota	D
9	St.L.	Jason Marshall	Vernon Jr. A	D
10	Hfd.	Bobby Holik	Dukla Jihlava	C
11	Det.	Mike Sillinger	Regina	C
12	Tor.	Rob Pearson	Belleville	RW
13	Mtl.	Lindsay Vallis	Seattle	D
14	Buf.	Kevin Haller	Regina	D
15	Edm.	Jason Soules	Niagara Falls	D
16	Pit.	Jamie Heward	Regina	D
17	Bos.	Shayne Stevenson	Kitchener	RW
18	N.J.	Jason Miller	Medicine Hat	LW
19	Wsh.	Olie Kolzig	Tri-City	G
20	NYR	Steven Rice	Kitchener	RW
21	Tor.	Steve Bancroft	Belleville	D

OTHER NOTABLE SELECTIONS

Pick	Claimed by	Amateur Club	Position
22	Que.	Adam Foote	Sault Ste. Marie	D
23	NYI	Travis Green	Spokane	C
53	Det.	Nicklas Lidstrom	Vasteras	D
62	Wpg.	Kris Draper	Canadian National	C
73	Hfd.	Jim McKenzie	Victoria	LW
74	Det.	Sergei Fedorov	CSKA Moscow	C
82	Wsh.	Trent Klatt	Osseo H.S.	RW
113	Van.	Pavel Bure	CSKA Moscow	RW
116	Det.	Dallas Drake	Northern Michigan	RW
183	Buf.	Donald Audette	Laval	RW
196	Min.	Arturs Irbe	Dynamo Riga	G
221	Det.	Vladimir Konstantinov	CSKA Moscow	D

1988
FIRST ROUND

Pick	Claimed by	Amateur Club	Position
1	Min.	Mike Modano	Prince Albert	C
2	Van.	Trevor Linden	Medicine Hat	RW
3	Que.	Curtis Leschyshyn	Saskatoon	D
4	Pit.	Darrin Shannon	Windsor	LW
5	Que.	Daniel Dore	Drummondville	RW
6	Tor.	Scott Pearson	Kingston	LW
7	L.A.	Martin Gelinas	Hull	LW
8	Chi.	Jeremy Roenick	Thayer Academy	C
9	St.L.	Rod Brind'Amour	Notre Dame Jr. A	C
10	Wpg.	Teemu Selanne	Jokerit	RW
11	Hfd.	Chris Govedaris	Toronto	LW
12	N.J.	Corey Foster	Peterborough	D
13	Buf.	Joel Savage	Victoria	RW
14	Phi.	Claude Boivin	Drummondville	LW
15	Wsh.	Reggie Savage	Victoriaville	C
16	NYI	Kevin Cheveldayoff	Brandon	D
17	Det.	Kory Kocur	Saskatoon	RW
18	Bos.	Rob Cimetta	Toronto	W
19	Edm.	Francois Leroux	St-Jean	D
20	Mtl.	Eric Charron	Trois-Rivieres	D
21	Cgy.	Jason Muzzatti	Michigan State	G

OTHER NOTABLE SELECTIONS

Pick	Claimed by	Amateur Club	Position
27	Tor.	Tie Domi	Peterborough	RW
60	Bos.	Steve Heinze	Lawrence Academy	RW
67	Pit.	Mark Recchi	Kamloops	RW
68	NYR	Tony Amonte	Thayer Academy	RW
89	Buf.	Alexander Mogilny	CSKA Moscow	RW
97	Buf.	Rob Ray	Cornwall	RW
120	Wsh.	Dmitri Khristich	Sokol Kiev	LW/C
163	NYI	Marty McInnis	Milton Academy	RW
198	St.L.	Bret Hedican	North St. Paul H.S.	D
234	Que.	Claude Lapointe	Laval	LW/C

1987
FIRST ROUND

Pick	Claimed by	Amateur Club	Position
1	Buf.	Pierre Turgeon	Granby	C
2	N.J.	Brendan Shanahan	London	LW
3	Bos.	Glen Wesley	Portland	D
4	L.A.	Wayne McBean	Medicine Hat	D
5	Pit.	Chris Joseph	Seattle	D
6	Min.	Dave Archibald	Portland	C/LW
7	Tor.	Luke Richardson	Peterborough	D
8	Chi.	Jimmy Waite	Chicoutimi	G
9	Que.	Bryan Fogarty	Kingston	D
10	NYR	Jay More	New Westminster	D
11	Det.	Yves Racine	Longueuil	D
12	St.L.	Keith Osborne	North Bay	RW
13	NYI	Dean Chynoweth	Medicine Hat	D
14	Bos.	Stephane Quintal	Granby	D
15	Que.	Joe Sakic	Swift Current	C
16	Wpg.	Bryan Marchment	Belleville	D
17	Mtl.	Andrew Cassels	Ottawa	C
18	Hfd.	Jody Hull	Peterborough	RW
19	Cgy.	Bryan Deasley	U. of Michigan	LW
20	Phi.	Darren Rumble	Kitchener	D
21	Edm.	Peter Soberlak	Swift Current	LW

OTHER NOTABLE SELECTIONS

Pick	Claimed by	Amateur Club	Position
25	Cgy.	Stephane Matteau	Hull	LW
33	Mtl.	John LeClair	Bellows Academy	LW
38	Mtl.	Eric Desjardins	Granby	D
44	Mtl.	Mathieu Schneider	Cornwall	D
71	Tor.	Joe Sacco	Medford H.S.	RW
108	Van.	Garry Valk	Sherwood Park Jr. A	RW
110	Phi.	Shawn McEachern	Matignon H.S.	RW
159	St.L.	Guy Hebert	Hamilton College	G
166	Cgy.	Theoren Fleury	Moose Jaw	RW

1986
FIRST ROUND

Pick	Claimed by	Amateur Club	Position
1	Det.	Joe Murphy	Michigan State	RW
2	L.A.	Jimmy Carson	Verdun	C
3	N.J.	Neil Brady	Medicine Hat	C
4	Pit.	Zarley Zalapski	Canadian National	D
5	Buf.	Shawn Anderson	Canadian National	D
6	Tor.	Vincent Damphousse	Laval	C
7	Van.	Dan Woodley	Portland	RW
8	Wpg.	Pat Elynuik	Prince Albert	RW
9	NYR	Brian Leetch	Avon Old Farms H.S.	D
10	St.L.	Jocelyn Lemieux	Laval	RW
11	Hfd.	Scott Young	Boston U.	RW
12	Min.	Warren Babe	Lethbridge	LW
13	Bos.	Craig Janney	Boston College	C
14	Chi.	Everett Sanipass	Verdun	LW
15	Mtl.	Mark Pederson	Medicine Hat	LW
16	Cgy.	George Pelawa	Bemidji H.S.	RW
17	NYI	Tom Fitzgerald	Austin Prep	RW
18	Que.	Ken McRae	Sudbury	C
19	Wsh.	Jeff Greenlaw	Canadian National	LW
20	Phi.	Kerry Huffman	Guelph	D
21	Edm.	Kim Issel	Prince Albert	RW

OTHER NOTABLE SELECTIONS

Pick	Claimed by	Amateur Club	Position
22	Det.	Adam Graves	Windsor	LW
27	Mtl.	Benoit Brunet	Hull	LW
29	Wpg.	Teppo Numminen	Tappara Tampere	D
47	Buf.	Bob Corkum	U. of Maine	C
57	Mtl.	Jyrki Lumme	Ilves Tampere	D
67	Pit.	Rob Brown	Kamloops	RW
72	NYR	Mark Janssens	Regina	C
85	Det.	Johan Garpenlov	Nacka	LW
114	NYR	Darren Turcotte	North Bay	C
141	Mtl.	Lyle Odelein	Moose Jaw	D
143	NYI	Rich Pilon	Prince Albert AAA	D
167	Phi.	Murray Baron	Vernon Jr. A	D

1985
FIRST ROUND

Pick	Claimed by	Amateur Club	Position
1	Tor.	Wendel Clark	Saskatoon	LW/D
2	Pit.	Craig Simpson	Michigan State	LW
3	N.J.	Craig Wolanin	Kitchener	D
4	Van.	Jim Sandlak	London	RW
5	Hfd.	Dana Murzyn	Calgary	D
6	NYI	Brad Dalgarno	Hamilton	RW
7	NYR	Ulf Dahlen	Ostersund	LW
8	Det.	Brent Fedyk	Regina	LW
9	L.A.	Craig Duncanson	Sudbury	LW
10	L.A.	Dan Gratton	Oshawa	C
11	Chi.	Dave Manson	Prince Albert	D
12	Mtl.	Jose Charbonneau	Drummondville	RW
13	NYI	Derek King	Sault Ste. Marie	LW
14	Buf.	Calle Johansson	Vastra Frolunda	D
15	Que.	David Latta	Kitchener	LW
16	Mtl.	Tom Chorske	Minneapolis SW H.S.	LW
17	Cgy.	Chris Biotti	Belmont Hill H.S.	D
18	Wpg.	Ryan Stewart	Kamloops	C
19	Wsh.	Yvon Corriveau	Toronto	LW
20	Edm.	Scott Metcalfe	Kingston	LW
21	Phi.	Glen Seabrooke	Peterborough	C

OTHER NOTABLE SELECTIONS

Pick	Claimed by	Amateur Club	Position
24	N.J.	Sean Burke	Toronto	G
27	Cgy.	Joe Nieuwendyk	Cornell	C
28	NYR	Mike Richter	Northwood Prep	G
32	N.J.	Eric Weinrich	North Yarmouth Academy	D
35	Buf.	Benoit Hogue	St-Jean	C
44	St.L.	Nelson Emerson	Stratford Jr.A	RW
52	Bos.	Bill Ranford	New Westminster	G
81	Wpg.	Fredrik Olausson	Farjestad Karlstad	D
113	Det.	Randy McKay	Michigan Tech	RW
119	Buf.	Joe Reekie	Cornwall	D
188	Edm.	Kelly Buchberger	Moose Jaw	RW
214	Van.	Igor Larionov	CSKA Moscow	C

1984
FIRST ROUND

Pick	Claimed by	Amateur Club	Position
1	Pit.	Mario Lemieux	Laval	C
2	N.J.	Kirk Muller	Guelph	LW
3	Chi.	Eddie Olczyk	Team USA	C
4	Tor.	Al Iafrate	Belleville	D
5	Mtl.	Petr Svoboda	CHZ Litvinov	D
6	L.A.	Craig Redmond	U. of Denver	D
7	Det.	Shawn Burr	Kitchener	LW/C
8	Mtl.	Shayne Corson	Brantford	LW
9	Pit.	Doug Bodger	Kamloops	D
10	Van.	J.J. Daigneault	Longueuil	D
11	Hfd.	Sylvain Cote	Quebec	D
12	Cgy.	Gary Roberts	Ottawa	LW
13	Min.	David Quinn	Kent H.S.	D
14	NYR	Terry Carkner	Peterborough	D
15	Que.	Trevor Stienburg	Guelph	RW
16	Pit.	Roger Belanger	Kingston	C
17	Wsh.	Kevin Hatcher	North Bay	D
18	Buf.	Mikael Andersson	Vastra Frolunda	LW
19	Bos.	Dave Pasin	Prince Albert	RW
20	NYI	Duncan MacPherson	Saskatoon	D
21	Edm.	Selmar Odelein	Regina	D

OTHER NOTABLE SELECTIONS

Pick	Claimed by	Amateur Club	Position
25	Tor.	Todd Gill	Windsor	D
27	Phi.	Scott Mellanby	Henry Carr Jr. B	RW
29	Mtl.	Stephane Richer	Granby	RW
38	Cgy.	Paul Ranheim	Edina H.S.	LW
51	Mtl.	Patrick Roy	Granby	G
59	Wsh.	Michal Pivonka	Kladno	C
60	Buf.	Ray Sheppard	Cornwall	RW
117	Cgy.	Brett Hull	Penticton Jr. A	RW
119	NYR	Kjell Samuelsson	Leksand	D
134	St.L.	Cliff Ronning	New Westminster	C
166	Bos.	Don Sweeney	St. Paul's H.S.	D
171	L.A.	Luc Robitaille	Hull	LW
180	Cgy.	Gary Suter	U. of Wisconsin	D

1983
FIRST ROUND

Pick	Claimed by	Amateur Club	Position
1	Min.	Brian Lawton	Mount St. Charles H.S.	LW
2	Hfd.	Sylvain Turgeon	Hull	LW
3	NYI	Pat LaFontaine	Verdun	C
4	Det.	Steve Yzerman	Peterborough	C
5	Buf.	Tom Barrasso	Acton-Boxborough	G
6	N.J.	John MacLean	Oshawa	RW
7	Tor.	Russ Courtnall	Victoria	RW
8	Wpg.	Andrew McBain	North Bay	RW
9	Van.	Cam Neely	Portland	RW
10	Buf.	Normand Lacombe	New Hampshire	RW
11	Buf.	Adam Creighton	Ottawa	C
12	NYR	Dave Gagner	Brantford	C
13	Cgy.	Dan Quinn	Belleville	C
14	Wpg.	Bobby Dollas	Laval	D
15	Pit.	Bob Errey	Peterborough	LW
16	NYI	Gerald Diduck	Lethbridge	D

Pick	Claimed by		Amateur Club	Position
17	Mtl.	Alfie Turcotte	Portland	C
18	Chi.	Bruce Cassidy	Ottawa	D
19	Edm.	Jeff Beukeboom	Sault Ste. Marie	D
20	Hfd.	David Jensen	Lawrence Academy	C
21	Bos.	Nevin Markwart	Regina	LW

OTHER NOTABLE SELECTIONS

Pick	Claimed by		Amateur Club	Position
26	Mtl.	Claude Lemieux	Trois-Rivieres	RW
46	Det.	Bob Probert	Brantford	LW
60	Chi.	Marc Bergevin	Chicoutimi	D
82	Edm.	Esa Tikkanen	HIFK Helsinki	LW
88	Det.	Petr Klima	Dukla Jihlava	W
91	Det.	Joe Kocur	Saskatoon	RW
103	L.A.	Garry Galley	Bowling Green	D
114	Van.	Dave Lowry	London	LW
125	Phi.	Rick Tocchet	Sault Ste. Marie	RW
150	N.J.	Viacheslav Fetisov	CSKA Moscow	D
207	Chi.	Dominik Hasek	Pardubice	G
223	Buf.	Uwe Krupp	Koln	D
241	Cgy.	Sergei Makarov	CSKA Moscow	RW

1982

FIRST ROUND

Pick	Claimed by		Amateur Club	Position
1	Bos.	Gord Kluzak	Billings	D
2	Min.	Brian Bellows	Kitchener	LW
3	Tor.	Gary Nylund	Portland	D
4	Phi.	Ron Sutter	Lethbridge	C
5	Wsh.	Scott Stevens	Kitchener	D
6	Buf.	Phil Housley	South St. Paul H.S.	D
7	Chi.	Ken Yaremchuk	Portland	C
8	N.J.	Rocky Trottier	Nanaimo	RW
9	Buf.	Paul Cyr	Victoria	LW
10	Pit.	Rich Sutter	Lethbridge	RW
11	Van.	Michel Petit	Sherbrooke	D
12	Wpg.	Jim Kyte	Cornwall	D
13	Que.	David Shaw	Kitchener	D
14	Hfd.	Paul Lawless	Windsor	LW
15	NYR	Chris Kontos	Toronto	LW/C
16	Buf.	Dave Andreychuk	Oshawa	LW
17	Det.	Murray Craven	Medicine Hat	LW
18	N.J.	Ken Daneyko	Seattle	D
19	Mtl.	Alain Heroux	Chicoutimi	LW
20	Edm.	Jim Playfair	Portland	D
21	NYI	Pat Flatley	U. of Wisconsin	RW

OTHER NOTABLE SELECTIONS

Pick	Claimed by		Amateur Club	Position
36	NYR	Tomas Sandstrom	Farjestad Karlstad	RW
43	N.J.	Pat Verbeek	Sudbury	RW
45	Tor.	Ken Wregget	Lethbridge	G
56	Hfd.	Kevin Dineen	U. of Denver	RW
60	Bos.	Dave Reid	Peterborough	LW
67	Hfd.	Ulf Samuelsson	Leksand	D
75	Wpg.	Dave Ellett	Ottawa Jr. A	D
80	Min.	Bob Rouse	Nanaimo	D
88	Hfd.	Ray Ferraro	Penticton Jr. A	C
119	Phi.	Ron Hextall	Brandon	G
120	NYR	Tony Granato	Northwood Prep	RW
134	St.L.	Doug Gilmour	Cornwall	C
140	Phi.	Dave Brown	Saskatoon	RW
181	Que.	Mike Hough	Kitchener	LW
183	NYR	Kelly Miller	Michigan State	LW

1981

FIRST ROUND

Pick	Claimed by		Amateur Club	Position
1	Wpg.	Dale Hawerchuk	Cornwall	C
2	L.A.	Doug Smith	Ottawa	C
3	Wsh.	Bob Carpenter	St. John's Prep	C
4	Hfd.	Ron Francis	Sault Ste. Marie	C
5	Col.	Joe Cirella	Oshawa	D
6	Tor.	Jim Benning	Portland	D
7	Mtl.	Mark Hunter	Brantford	RW
8	Edm.	Grant Fuhr	Victoria	G
9	NYR	James Patrick	Prince Albert	D
10	Van.	Garth Butcher	Regina	D
11	Que.	Randy Moller	Lethbridge	D
12	Chi.	Tony Tanti	Oshawa	RW
13	Min.	Ron Meighan	Niagara Falls	D
14	Bos.	Normand Leveille	Chicoutimi	LW
15	Cgy.	Al MacInnis	Kitchener	D
16	Phi.	Steve Smith	Sault Ste. Marie	D
17	Buf.	Jiri Dudacek	Kladno	RW
18	Mtl.	Gilbert Delorme	Chicoutimi	D
19	Mtl.	Jan Ingman	Farjestad Karlstad	LW
20	St.L.	Marty Ruff	Lethbridge	D
21	NYI	Paul Boutilier	Sherbrooke	D

OTHER NOTABLE SELECTIONS

Pick	Claimed by		Amateur Club	Position
40	Mtl.	Chris Chelios	Moose Jaw	D
56	Cgy.	Mike Vernon	Calgary	G
72	NYR	John Vanbiesbrouck	Sault Ste. Marie	G
108	Col.	Bruce Driver	U. of Wisconsin	D
111	Edm.	Steve Smith	London	D
116	Que.	Mike Eagles	Kitchener	C/LW
145	Mtl.	Tom Kurvers	Minnesota-Duluth	D
152	Wsh.	Gaetan Duchesne	Quebec	LW

1980

FIRST ROUND

Pick	Claimed by		Amateur Club	Position
1	Mtl.	Doug Wickenheiser	Regina	C
2	Wpg.	Dave Babych	Portland	D
3	Chi.	Denis Savard	Montreal	C
4	L.A.	Larry Murphy	Peterborough	D
5	Wsh.	Darren Veitch	Regina	D
6	Edm.	Paul Coffey	Kitchener	D
7	Van.	Rick Lanz	Oshawa	D
8	Hfd.	Fred Arthur	Cornwall	D
9	Pit.	Mike Bullard	Brantford	C
10	L.A.	Jim Fox	Ottawa	RW
11	Det.	Mike Blaisdell	Regina	RW
12	St.L.	Rik Wilson	Kingston	D
13	Cgy.	Denis Cyr	Montreal	RW
14	NYR	Jim Malone	Toronto	C
15	Chi.	Jerome Dupont	Toronto	D
16	Min.	Brad Palmer	Victoria	LW
17	NYI	Brent Sutter	Red Deer Jr. A	C
18	Bos.	Barry Pederson	Victoria	C
19	Col.	Paul Gagne	Windsor	LW
20	Buf.	Steve Patrick	Brandon	RW
21	Phi.	Mike Stothers	Kingston	D

OTHER NOTABLE SELECTIONS

Pick	Claimed by		Amateur Club	Position
37	Min.	Don Beaupre	Sudbury	G
38	NYI	Kelly Hrudey	Medicine Hat	G
39	Cgy.	Steve Konroyd	Oshawa	D
46	Det.	Mark Osborne	Niagara Falls	LW
61	Mtl.	Craig Ludwig	North Dakota	D
69	Edm.	Jari Kurri	Jokerit	RW
73	L.A.	Bernie Nicholls	Kingston	C
80	NYI	Greg Gilbert	Toronto	LW
81	Bos.	Steve Kasper	Verdun	C
106	Col.	Aaron Broten	Minnesota-Duluth	LW/C
120	Chi.	Steve Larmer	Niagara Falls	RW
124	Mtl.	Mike McPhee	RPI	LW
128	Wpg.	Brian Mullen	U.S. Jr. National	RW
132	Edm.	Andy Moog	Billings	G
133	Van.	Doug Lidster	Colorado College	D
167	Buf.	Randy Cunneyworth	Ottawa	LW

1979

FIRST ROUND

Pick	Claimed by		Amateur Club	Position
1	Col.	Rob Ramage	London	D
2	St.L.	Perry Turnbull	Portland	C
3	Det.	Mike Foligno	Sudbury	RW
4	Wsh.	Mike Gartner	Niagara Falls	RW
5	Van.	Rick Vaive	Sherbrooke	RW
6	Min.	Craig Hartsburg	Sault Ste. Marie	D
7	Chi.	Keith Brown	Portland	D
8	Bos.	Raymond Bourque	Verdun	D
9	Tor.	Laurie Boschman	Brandon	C
10	Min.	Tom McCarthy	Oshawa	LW
11	Buf.	Mike Ramsey	U. of Minnesota	D
12	Atl.	Paul Reinhart	Kitchener	D
13	NYR	Doug Sulliman	Kitchener	RW
14	Phi.	Brian Propp	Brandon	LW
15	Bos.	Brad McCrimmon	Brandon	D
16	L.A.	Jay Wells	Kingston	D
17	NYI	Duane Sutter	Lethbridge	RW
18	Hfd.	Ray Allison	Brandon	RW
19	Wpg.	Jimmy Mann	Sherbrooke	RW
20	Que.	Michel Goulet	Quebec	LW
21	Edm.	Kevin Lowe	Quebec	D

OTHER NOTABLE SELECTIONS

Pick	Claimed by		Amateur Club	Position
26	Van.	Brent Ashton	Saskatoon	LW
30	L.A.	Mark Hardy	Montreal	D
32	Buf.	Lindy Ruff	Lethbridge	D/LW
37	Mtl.	Mats Naslund	Brynas Gavle	LW
40	Wpg.	Dave Christian	North Dakota	RW
41	Que.	Dale Hunter	Sudbury	C
42	Min.	Neal Broten	Minnesota-Duluth	C
44	Mtl.	Guy Carbonneau	Chicoutimi	C
48	Edm.	Mark Messier	St. Albert Jr. A	C
54	Atl.	Tim Hunter	Seattle	RW
66	Det.	John Ogrodnick	New Westminster	LW
69	Edm.	Glenn Anderson	U. of Denver	RW
75	Atl.	Jim Peplinski	Toronto	RW
83	Que.	Anton Stastny	Slovan Bratislava	LW
89	Van.	Dirk Graham	Regina	RW/LW
103	Wpg.	Thomas Steen	Leksand	C
120	Bos.	Mike Krushelnyski	Montreal	LW/C

1978

FIRST ROUND

Pick	Claimed by		Amateur Club	Position
1	Min.	Bobby Smith	Ottawa	C
2	Wsh.	Ryan Walter	Seattle	C/LW
3	St.L.	Wayne Babych	Portland	RW
4	Van.	Bill Derlago	Brandon	C
5	Col.	Mike Gillis	Kingston	LW
6	Phi.	Behn Wilson	Kingston	D
7	Phi.	Ken Linseman	Kingston	C
8	Mtl.	Danny Geoffrion	Cornwall	RW
9	Det.	Willie Huber	Hamilton	D
10	Chi.	Tim Higgins	Ottawa	RW
11	Atl.	Brad Marsh	London	D
12	Det.	Brent Peterson	Portland	C
13	Buf.	Larry Playfair	Portland	D
14	Phi.	Danny Lucas	Sault Ste. Marie	RW
15	NYI	Steve Tambellini	Lethbridge	C
16	Bos.	Al Secord	Hamilton	LW
17	Mtl.	Dave Hunter	Sudbury	LW
18	Wsh.	Tim Coulis	Hamilton	LW

OTHER NOTABLE SELECTIONS

Pick	Claimed by		Amateur Club	Position
19	Min.	Steve Payne	Ottawa	LW
21	Tor.	Joel Quenneville	Windsor	D
26	NYR	Don Maloney	Kitchener	LW
32	Buf.	Tony McKegney	Kingston	LW
40	Van.	Stan Smyl	New Westminster	RW
54	Min.	Curt Giles	Minnesota-Duluth	D
55	Wsh.	Bengt-Ake Gustafsson	Farjestad Karlstad	RW
93	NYR	Tom Laidlaw	Northern Michigan	D
103	Mtl.	Keith Acton	Peterborough	C
109	St.L.	Paul MacLean	Hull	RW
153	Bos.	Craig MacTavish	University of Lowell	C
173	St.L.	Risto Siltanen	Ilves Tampere	D
179	Chi.	Darryl Sutter	Lethbridge	LW
231	Mtl.	Chris Nilan	Northeastern	RW

1977

FIRST ROUND

Pick	Claimed by		Amateur Club	Position
1	Det.	Dale McCourt	St. Catharines	C
2	Col.	Barry Beck	New Westminster	D
3	Wsh.	Robert Picard	Montreal	D
4	Van.	Jere Gillis	Sherbrooke	LW
5	Cle.	Mike Crombeen	Kingston	RW
6	Chi.	Doug Wilson	Ottawa	D
7	Min.	Brad Maxwell	New Westminster	D
8	NYR	Lucien DeBlois	Sorel	C
9	St.L.	Scott Campbell	London	D
10	Mtl.	Mark Napier	Toronto	RW
11	Tor.	John Anderson	Toronto	RW
12	Tor.	Trevor Johansen	Toronto	D
13	NYR	Ron Duguay	Sudbury	C/RW
14	Buf.	Ric Seiling	St. Catharines	RW/C
15	NYI	Mike Bossy	Laval	RW
16	Bos.	Dwight Foster	Kitchener	RW
17	Phi.	Kevin McCarthy	Winnipeg	D
18	Mtl.	Norm Dupont	Montreal	LW

OTHER NOTABLE SELECTIONS

Pick	Claimed by		Amateur Club	Position
25	Min.	Dave Semenko	Brandon	LW
33	NYI	John Tonelli	Toronto	LW
36	Mtl.	Rod Langway	New Hampshire	D
43	Mtl.	Alain Cote	Chicoutimi	LW
54	Mtl.	Gordie Roberts	Victoria	D
62	NYR	Mario Marois	Quebec	D
66	Pit.	Mark Johnson	U. of Wisconsin	C
102	Pit.	Greg Millen	Peterborough	G
118	Atl.	Bobby Gould	New Hampshire	RW
135	Phi.	Pete Peeters	Medicine Hat	G
162	Mtl.	Craig Laughlin	Clarkson	RW

1976

FIRST ROUND

Pick	Claimed by		Amateur Club	Position
1	Wsh.	Rick Green	London	D
2	Pit.	Blair Chapman	Saskatoon	RW
3	Min.	Glen Sharpley	Hull	C
4	Det.	Fred Williams	Saskatoon	C
5	Cal.	Bjorn Johansson	Orebro	D
6	NYR	Don Murdoch	Medicine Hat	RW
7	St.L.	Bernie Federko	Saskatoon	C
8	Atl.	Dave Shand	Peterborough	D
9	Chi.	Real Cloutier	Quebec	RW
10	Atl.	Harold Phillipoff	New Westminster	LW
11	K.C.	Paul Gardner	Oshawa	C
12	Mtl.	Peter Lee	Ottawa	RW
13	Mtl.	Rod Schutt	Sudbury	LW
14	NYI	Alex McKendry	Sudbury	W
15	Wsh.	Greg Carroll	Medicine Hat	C
16	Bos.	Clayton Pachal	New Westminster	C/LW
17	Phi.	Mark Suzor	Kingston	D
18	Mtl.	Bruce Baker	Ottawa	RW

Pick	Claimed by	Amateur Club	Position

OTHER NOTABLE SELECTIONS

20	St.L.	Brian Sutter	Lethbridge	LW
22	Det.	Reed Larson	Minnesota-Duluth	D
30	Tor.	Randy Carlyle	Sudbury	D
42	NYR	Mike McEwen	Toronto	D
45	Chi.	Thomas Gradin	MoDo Ornskoldsvik	C
47	Pit.	Morris Lukowich	Medicine Hat	LW
56	St.L.	Mike Liut	Bowling Green	G
64	Atl.	Kent Nilsson	Djurgarden	C
68	NYI	Ken Morrow	Bowling Green	D
133	Mtl.	Ron Wilson	St. Catharines	C

1975

FIRST ROUND

1	Phi.	Mel Bridgman	Victoria	C
2	K.C.	Barry Dean	Medicine Hat	LW
3	Cal.	Ralph Klassen	Saskatoon	C
4	Min.	Bryan Maxwell	Medicine Hat	D
5	Det.	Rick Lapointe	Victoria	D
6	Tor.	Don Ashby	Calgary	C
7	Chi.	Greg Vaydik	Medicine Hat	C
8	Atl.	Richard Mulhern	Sherbrooke	D
9	Mtl.	Robin Sadler	Edmonton	D
10	Van.	Rick Blight	Brandon	RW
11	NYI	Pat Price	Saskatoon	D
12	NYR	Wayne Dillon	Toronto	C
13	Pit.	Gord Laxton	New Westminster	G
14	Bos.	Doug Halward	Peterborough	D
15	Mtl.	Pierre Mondou	Montreal	C
16	L.A.	Tim Young	Ottawa	C

OTHER NOTABLE SELECTIONS

17	Buf.	Bob Sauve	Laval	G
21	Cal.	Dennis Maruk	London	C
24	Tor.	Doug Jarvis	Peterborough	C
43	Chi.	Mike O'Connell	Kingston	D
57	Cal.	Greg Smith	Colorado College	D
80	Atl.	Willi Plett	St. Catharines	RW
108	Phi.	Paul Holmgren	U. of Minnesota	RW
210	L.A.	Dave Taylor	Clarkson	RW

1974

FIRST ROUND

1	Wsh.	Greg Joly	Regina	D
2	K.C.	Wilf Paiement	St. Catharines	RW
3	Cal.	Rick Hampton	St. Catharines	LW/D
4	NYI	Clark Gillies	Regina	LW
5	Mtl.	Cam Connor	Flin Flon	RW
6	Min.	Doug Hicks	Flin Flon	D
7	Mtl.	Doug Risebrough	Kitchener	C
8	Pit.	Pierre Larouche	Sorel	C
9	Det.	Bill Lochead	Oshawa	LW
10	Mtl.	Rick Chartraw	Kitchener	D/RW
11	Buf.	Lee Fogolin Jr.	Oshawa	D
12	Mtl.	Mario Tremblay	Montreal	RW
13	Tor.	Jack Valiquette	Sault Ste. Marie	C
14	NYR	Dave Maloney	Kitchener	D
15	Mtl.	Gord McTavish	Sudbury	C
16	Chi.	Grant Mulvey	Calgary	RW
17	Cal.	Ron Chipperfield	Brandon	C
18	Bos.	Don Larway	Swift Current	RW

OTHER NOTABLE SELECTIONS

22	NYI	Bryan Trottier	Swift Current	C
25	Bos.	Mark Howe	Toronto	D
29	Buf.	Danny Gare	Calgary	RW
31	Tor.	Tiger Williams	Swift Current	LW
32	NYR	Ron Greschner	New Westminster	D
38	K.C.	Bob Bourne	Saskatoon	C
39	Cal.	Charlie Simmer	Sault Ste. Marie	LW
52	Chi.	Bob Murray	Cornwall	D
59	Van.	Harold Snepsts	Edmonton	D
70	Chi.	Terry Ruskowski	Swift Current	C
125	Phi.	Reggie Lemelin	Sherbrooke	G
199	Mtl.	Dave Lumley	New Hampshire	RW
214	NYI	Stefan Persson	Brynas Gavle	D

1973

FIRST ROUND

1	NYI	Denis Potvin	Ottawa	D
2	Atl.	Tom Lysiak	Medicine Hat	C
3	Van.	Dennis Ververgaert	London	RW
4	Tor.	Lanny McDonald	Medicine Hat	RW
5	St.L.	John Davidson	Calgary	G
6	Bos.	Andre Savard	Quebec	C
7	Pit.	Blaine Stoughton	Flin Flon	RW
8	Mtl.	Bob Gainey	Peterborough	LW
9	Van.	Bob Dailey	Toronto	D
10	Tor.	Bob Neely	Peterborough	LW
11	Det.	Terry Richardson	New Westminster	G
12	Buf.	Morris Titanic	Sudbury	LW
13	Chi.	Darcy Rota	Edmonton	LW
14	NYR	Rick Middleton	Oshawa	RW
15	Tor.	Ian Turnbull	Ottawa	D
16	Atl.	Vic Mercredi	New Westminster	C

OTHER NOTABLE SELECTIONS

21	Atl.	Eric Vail	Sudbury	LW
27	Pit.	Colin Campbell	Peterborough	D
30	NYR	Pat Hickey	Hamilton	LW
33	NYI	Dave Lewis	Saskatoon	D
49	NYI	Andre St. Laurent	Montreal	C
85	Atl.	Ken Houston	Chatham Jr. B	RW
130	Cal.	Larry Patey	Braintree H.S.	C
134	Pit.	Gord Lane	New Westminster	D
162	Atl.	Greg Fox	U. of Michigan	D

1972

FIRST ROUND

1	NYI	Billy Harris	Toronto	RW
2	Atl.	Jacques Richard	Quebec	LW
3	Van.	Don Lever	Niagara Falls	LW
4	Mtl.	Steve Shutt	Toronto	LW
5	Buf.	Jim Schoenfeld	Niagara Falls	D
6	Mtl.	Michel Larocque	Ottawa	G
7	Phi.	Bill Barber	Kitchener	LW
8	Mtl.	Dave Gardner	Toronto	C
9	St.L.	Wayne Merrick	Ottawa	C
10	NYR	Al Blanchard	Kitchener	LW
11	Tor.	George Ferguson	Toronto	C
12	Min.	Jerry Byers	Kitchener	LW
13	Chi.	Phil Russell	Edmonton	D
14	Mtl.	John Van Boxmeer	Guelph	D
15	NYR	Bob MacMillan	St. Catharines	RW
16	Bos.	Mike Bloom	St. Catharines	LW

OTHER NOTABLE SELECTIONS

17	NYI	Lorne Henning	New Westminster	C
23	Phi.	Tom Bladon	Edmonton	D
33	NYI	Bob Nystrom	Calgary	RW
39	Phi.	Jimmy Watson	Calgary	D
55	Phi.	Al MacAdam	University of PEI	RW
85	Buf.	Peter McNab	U. of Denver	C
97	NYI	Richard Brodeur	Cornwall	G
139	Tor.	Pat Boutette	Minnesota-Duluth	C/RW
144	NYI	Garry Howatt	Flin Flon	LW

1971

FIRST ROUND

1	Mtl.	Guy Lafleur	Quebec	RW
2	Det.	Marcel Dionne	St. Catharines	C
3	Van.	Jocelyn Guevremont	Montreal	D
4	St.L.	Gene Carr	Flin Flon	C
5	Buf.	Rick Martin	Montreal	LW
6	Bos.	Ron Jones	Edmonton	D
7	Mtl.	Chuck Arnason	Flin Flon	RW
8	Phi.	Larry Wright	Regina	C
9	Phi.	Pierre Plante	Drummondville	RW
10	NYR	Steve Vickers	Toronto	LW
11	Mtl.	Murray Wilson	Ottawa	LW
12	Chi.	Dan Spring	Edmonton	C
13	NYR	Steve Durbano	Toronto	D
14	Bos.	Terry O'Reilly	Oshawa	RW

OTHER NOTABLE SELECTIONS

17	Van.	Bobby Lalonde	Montreal	C
19	Buf.	Craig Ramsay	Peterborough	LW
20	Mtl.	Larry Robinson	Kitchener	D
22	Tor.	Rick Kehoe	Hamilton	RW
33	Buf.	Bill Hajt	Saskatoon	D
48	L.A.	Neil Komadoski	Winnipeg	D
55	NYR	Jerry Butler	Hamilton	RW

1970

FIRST ROUND

1	Buf.	Gilbert Perreault	Montreal	C
2	Van.	Dale Tallon	Toronto	D
3	Bos.	Reggie Leach	Flin Flon	RW
4	Bos.	Rick MacLeish	Peterborough	C
5	Mtl.	Ray Martyniuk	Flin Flon	G
6	Mtl.	Chuck Lefley	Canadian National	LW
7	Pit.	Greg Polis	Estevan	LW
8	Tor.	Darryl Sittler	London	C
9	Bos.	Ron Plumb	Peterborough	D
10	Cal.	Chris Oddleifson	Winnipeg	C
11	NYR	Norm Gratton	Montreal	LW
12	Det.	Serge Lajeunesse	Montreal	D/RW
13	Bos.	Bob Stewart	Oshawa	D
14	Chi.	Dan Maloney	London	LW

OTHER NOTABLE SELECTIONS

18	Phi.	Bill Clement	Ottawa	C
22	Tor.	Errol Thompson	Charlottetown Sr.	LW
25	NYR	Mike Murphy	Toronto	RW
27	Bos.	Dan Bouchard	London	G
32	Phi.	Bob Kelly	Oshawa	LW
40	Det.	Yvon Lambert	Drummondville	LW
59	L.A.	Billy Smith	Cornwall	G
70	Chi.	Gilles Meloche	Verdun	G
88	Oak.	Terry Murray	Ottawa	D
103	Tor.	Ron Low	Dauphin Jr. A	G

1969

FIRST ROUND

1	Mtl.	Rejean Houle	Montreal	W
2	Mtl.	Marc Tardif	Montreal	LW
3	Bos.	Don Tannahill	Niagara Falls	LW
4	Bos.	Frank Spring	Edmonton	RW
5	Min.	Dick Redmond	St. Catharines	D
6	Phi.	Bob Currier	Cornwall	C
7	Oak.	Tony Featherstone	Peterborough	RW
8	NYR	Andre Dupont	Montreal	D
9	Tor.	Ernie Moser	Estevan	RW
10	Det.	Jim Rutherford	Hamilton	G
11	Bos.	Ivan Boldirev	Oshawa	C
12	NYR	Pierre Jarry	Ottawa	LW

OTHER NOTABLE SELECTIONS

17	Phi.	Bobby Clarke	Flin Flon	C
18	Oak.	Ron Stackhouse	Peterborough	D
25	Min.	Gilles Gilbert	London	G
26	Pit.	Michel Briere	Shawinigan	C
51	L.A.	Butch Goring	Dauphin Jr. A	C
52	Phi.	Dave Schultz	Sorel	LW
55	Tor.	Brian Spencer	Swift Current	LW
64	Phi.	Don Saleski	Regina	RW

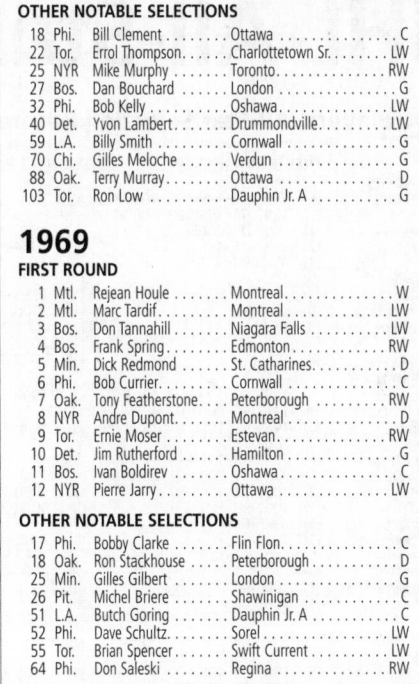

Dale Tallon was chosen second overall by the expansion Vancouver Canucks in 1970 after a spin of the wheel gave Buffalo – the NHL's other expansion club – the first pick. The Sabres selected Gilbert Perreault.

NHL All-Stars

Active Players' All-Star Selection Records

	First Team Selections	Second Team Selections	Total
GOALTENDERS			
Dominik Hasek	(6) 1993-94; 1994-95; 1996-97; 1997-98; 1998-99; 2000-01.	(0)	6
Martin Brodeur	(2) 2002-03; 2003-04.	(2) 1996-97; 1997-98.	4
Ed Belfour	(2) 1990-91; 1992-93.	(1) 1994-95	3
Olie Kolzig	(1) 99-2000.	(0)	1
Chris Osgood	(0)	(1) 1995-96.	1
Byron Dafoe	(0)	(1) 1998-99.	1
Roman Cechmanek	(0)	(1) 2000-01.	1
Jose Theodore	(0)	(1) 2001-02.	1
Marty Turco	(0)	(1) 2002-03.	1
Roberto Luongo	(0)	(1) 2003-04.	1
DEFENSEMEN			
Chris Chelios	(5) 1988-89; 1992-93; 1994-95; 1995-96; 2001-02.	(2) 1990-91; 1996-97.	7
Al MacInnis	(4) 1989-90; 1990-91; 1998-99; 2002-03.	(3) 1986-87; 1988-89; 1993-94.	7
Nicklas Lidstrom	(6) 1997-98; 1998-99; 99-2000; 2000-01; 2001-02; 2002-03.	(0)	6
Brian Leetch	(2) 1991-92; 1996-97.	(3) 1990-91; 1993-94; 1995-96.	5
Rob Blake	(1) 1997-98.	(3) 99-2000; 2000-01; 2001-02.	4
Chris Pronger	(1) 99-2000.	(2) 1997-98; 2003-04.	3
Scott Niedermayer	(1) 2003-04.	(1) 2002-03.	2
Eric Desjardins	(0)	(2) 1998-99; 99-2000.	2
Sergei Gonchar	(0)	(2) 2001-02; 2002-03.	2
Sandis Ozolinsh	(1) 1996-97.	(0)	1
Zdeno Chara	(1) 2003-04.	(0)	1
Derian Hatcher	(0)	(1) 2002-03.	1
Bryan McCabe	(0)	(1) 2003-04.	1
CENTERS			
Mario Lemieux	(5) 1987-88; 1988-89; 1992-93; 1995-96; 1996-97.	(4) 1985-86; 1986-87; 1991-92; 2000-01.	9
Peter Forsberg	(3) 1997-98; 1998-99; 2002-03.	(0)	3
Joe Sakic	(3) 2000-01; 2001-02; 2003-04.	(0)	3
Mark Messier	(2) 1989-90; 1991-92.	(0)	2
Eric Lindros	(1) 1994-95.	(1) 1995-96.	2
Mats Sundin	(0)	(2) 2001-02; 2003-04.	2
Sergei Fedorov	(1) 1993-94.	(0)	1
Steve Yzerman	(1) 99-2000.	(0)	1
Alex Zhamnov	(0)	(1) 1994-95.	1
Alexei Yashin	(0)	(1) 1998-99.	1
Mike Modano	(0)	(1) 99-2000.	1
Joe Thornton	(0)	(1) 2002-03.	1
RIGHT WINGERS			
Jaromir Jagr	(6) 1994-95; 1995-96; 1997-98; 1998-99; 99-2000; 2000-01.	(1) 1996-97.	7
Teemu Selanne	(2) 1992-93; 1996-97.	(2) 1997-98; 1998-99.	4
Brett Hull	(3) 1989-90; 1990-91; 1991-92.	(0)	3
Jarome Iginla	(1) 2001-02.	(1) 2003-04.	2
Alexander Mogilny	(0)	(2) 1992-93; 1995-96.	2
Todd Bertuzzi	(1) 2002-03.	(0)	1
Martin St. Louis	(1) 2003-04.	(0)	1
Mark Recchi	(0)	(1) 1991-92.	1
Bill Guerin	(0)	(1) 2001-02.	1
Milan Hejduk	(0)	(1) 2002-03.	1
LEFT WINGERS			
Luc Robitaille	(5) 1987-88; 1988-89; 1989-90; 1990-91; 1992-93.	(3) 1986-87; 1991-92; 2000-01.	8
Paul Kariya	(3) 1995-96; 1996-97; 1998-99.	(2) 99-2000; 2002-03.	5
John LeClair	(2) 1994-95; 1997-98.	(3) 1995-96; 1996-97; 1998-99.	5
Mark Messier	(2) 1981-82; 1982-83.	(1) 1983-84.	3
Markus Naslund	(3) 2001-02; 2002-03; 2003-04.	(0)	3
Brendan Shanahan	(2) 1993-94; 99-2000.	(1) 2001-02.	3
Keith Tkachuk	(0)	(2) 1994-95; 1997-98.	2
Patrik Elias	(1) 2000-01.	(0)	1
Ilya Kovalchuk	(0)	(1) 2003-04.	1

Leading NHL All-Stars 1930-31 to 2003-04

Player	Pos	Team	NHL Seasons	First Team Selections	Second Team Selections	Total Selections
Howe, Gordie	RW	Detroit	26	12	9	21
Bourque, Raymond	D	Bos., Col.	22	13	6	19
Gretzky, Wayne	C	Edm., L.A., NYR	20	8	7	15
Richard, Maurice	RW	Montreal	18	8	6	14
Hull, Bobby	LW	Chicago	16	10	2	12
Harvey, Doug	D	Mtl., NYR	19	10	1	11
Hall, Glenn	G	Det., Chi., St.L.	18	7	4	11
Beliveau, Jean	C	Montreal	20	6	4	10
Seibert, Earl	D	NYR, Chi.	15	4	6	10
Orr, Bobby	D	Boston	12	8	1	9
Lindsay, Ted	LW	Detroit	17	8	1	9
* Lemieux, Mario	C	Pittsburgh	16	5	4	9
Mahovlich, Frank	LW	Tor., Det., Mtl.	18	3	6	9
Shore, Eddie	D	Boston	14	7	1	8
Esposito, Phil	C	Boston	18	6	2	8
Kelly, Red	D	Detroit	20	6	2	8
Mikita, Stan	C	Chicago	22	6	2	8
Bossy, Mike	RW	NY Islanders	10	5	3	8
Pilote, Pierre	D	Chicago	14	5	3	8
* Robitaille, Luc	LW	Los Angeles	18	5	3	8
Coffey, Paul	D	Edm., Pit., Det.	21	4	4	8
Brimsek, Frank	G	Boston	10	2	6	8
* Jagr, Jaromir	RW	Pittsburgh	14	6	1	7
Potvin, Denis	D	NY Islanders	15	5	2	7
Park, Brad	D	NYR, Bos.	17	5	2	7
* Chelios, Chris	D	Mtl., Chi.	21	5	2	7
* MacInnis, Al	D	Cgy., St.L.	23	4	3	7
Plante, Jacques	G	Mtl., Tor.	18	3	4	7
Gadsby, Bill	D	Chi., NYR, Det.	20	3	4	7
Sawchuk, Terry	G	Detroit	21	3	4	7
Durnan, Bill	G	Montreal	7	6	0	6
* Hasek, Dominik	G	Buffalo	12	6	0	6
* Lidstrom, Niklas	D	Detroit	13	6	0	6
Lafleur, Guy	RW	Montreal	17	6	0	6
Dryden, Ken	G	Montreal	8	5	1	6
Roy, Patrick	G	Montreal	19	4	2	6
Clapper, Dit	RW/D	Boston	20	3	3	6
Robinson, Larry	D	Montreal	20	3	3	6
Horton, Tim	D	Toronto	24	3	3	6
Salming, Borje	D	Toronto	17	1	5	6
Cowley, Bill	C	Boston	13	4	1	5
Jackson, Busher	LW	Toronto	15	4	1	5
* Messier, Mark	LW/C	Edm., NYR	25	4	1	5
* Kariya, Paul	LW	Anaheim	10	3	2	5
Conacher, Charlie	RW	Toronto	12	3	2	5
Stewart, Jack	D	Detroit	12	3	2	5
Blake, Toe	LW	Montreal	14	3	2	5
Lach, Elmer	C	Montreal	14	3	2	5
Quackenbush, Bill	D	Det., Bos.	14	3	2	5
Goulet, Michel	LW	Quebec	15	3	2	5
Esposito, Tony	G	Chicago	16	3	2	5
Reardon, Ken	D	Montreal	7	2	3	5
Apps, Syl	C	Toronto	10	2	3	5
* LeClair, John	LW	Mtl., Phi.	14	2	3	5
Giacomin, Ed	G	NY Rangers	13	2	3	5
* Leetch, Brian	D	NY Rangers	16	2	3	5
Kurri, Jari	RW	Edmonton	17	2	3	5
Stevens, Scott	D	Wsh., N.J.	21	2	3	5

Position Leaders in All-Star Selections

Position	Player	First Team	Second Team	Total	Position	Player	First Team	Second Team	Total
GOAL	Glenn Hall	7	4	11	LEFT WING	Bobby Hull	10	2	12
	Frank Brimsek	2	6	8		Ted Lindsay	8	1	9
	Jacques Plante	3	4	7		Frank Mahovlich	3	6	9
	Terry Sawchuk	3	4	7		* Luc Robitaille	5	3	8
	Bill Durnan	6	0	6					
	* Dominik Hasek	6	0	6	RIGHT WING	Gordie Howe	12	9	21
	Ken Dryden	5	1	6		Maurice Richard	8	6	14
	Patrick Roy	4	2	6		Mike Bossy	5	3	8
						* Jaromir Jagr	6	1	7
DEFENSE	Raymond Bourque	13	6	19		Guy Lafleur	6	0	6
	Doug Harvey	10	1	11					
	Earl Seibert	4	6	10	CENTER	Wayne Gretzky	8	7	15
	Bobby Orr	8	1	9		Jean Beliveau	6	4	10
	Eddie Shore	7	1	8		* Mario Lemieux	5	4	9
	Red Kelly	6	2	8		Phil Esposito	6	2	8
	Pierre Pilote	5	3	8		Stan Mikita	6	2	8
	Paul Coffey	4	4	8					

* active player

All-Star Teams

1930-2005

Voting for the NHL All-Star Team is conducted among the representatives of the Professional Hockey Writers' Association at the end of the season.

Following is a list of the First and Second All-Star Teams since their inception in 1930-31.

2004-05

No All-Star Team selected

2003-04

First Team		Second Team
Martin Brodeur, N.J.	G	Roberto Luongo, Fla.
Scott Niedermayer, N.J.	D	Chris Pronger, St.L.
Zdeno Chara, Ott.	D	Bryan McCabe, Tor.
Joe Sakic, Col.	C	Mats Sundin, Tor.
Martin St. Louis, T.B.	RW	Jarome Iginla, Cgy.
Markus Naslund, Van.	LW	Ilya Kovalchuk, Atl.

2002-03

First Team		Second Team
Martin Brodeur, N.J.	G	Marty Turco, Dal.
Al MacInnis, St.L.	D	Sergei Gonchar, Wsh.
Nicklas Lidstrom, Det.	D	Derian Hatcher, Dal.
Peter Forsberg, Col.	C	Joe Thornton, Bos.
Todd Bertuzzi, Van.	RW	Milan Hejduk, Col.
Markus Naslund, Van.	LW	Paul Kariya, Ana.

2001-02

First Team		Second Team
Patrick Roy, Col.	G	Jose Theodore, Mtl.
Nicklas Lidstrom, Det.	D	Rob Blake, L.A. Col.
Chris Chelios, Det.	D	Sergei Gonchar, Wsh.
Joe Sakic, Col.	C	Mats Sundin, Tor.
Jarome Iginla, Cgy.	RW	Bill Guerin, Bos.
Markus Naslund, Van.	LW	Brendan Shanahan, Det.

2000-01

First Team		Second Team
Dominik Hasek, Buf.	G	Roman Cechmanek, Phi.
Nicklas Lidstrom, Det.	D	Rob Blake, L.A. Col.
Raymond Bourque, Col.	D	Scott Stevens, N.J.
Joe Sakic, Col.	C	Mario Lemieux, Pit.
Jaromir Jagr, Pit.	RW	Pavel Bure, Fla.
Patrik Elias, N.J.	LW	Luc Robitaille, L.A.

1999-2000

First Team		Second Team
Olaf Kolzig, Wsh.	G	Roman Turek, St.L.
Chris Pronger, St.L.	D	Rob Blake, L.A.
Nicklas Lidstrom, Det.	D	Eric Desjardins, Phi.
Steve Yzerman, Det.	C	Mike Modano, Dal.
Jaromir Jagr, Pit.	RW	Pavel Bure, Fla.
Brendan Shanahan, Det.	LW	Paul Kariya, Ana.

1998-99

First Team		Second Team
Dominik Hasek, Buf.	G	Byron Dafoe, Bos.
Al MacInnis, St.L.	D	Raymond Bourque, Bos.
Nicklas Lidstrom, Det.	D	Eric Desjardins, Phi.
Peter Forsberg, Col.	C	Alexei Yashin, Ott.
Jaromir Jagr, Pit.	RW	Teemu Selanne, Ana.
Paul Kariya, Ana.	LW	John LeClair, Phi.

1997-98

First Team		Second Team
Dominik Hasek, Buf.	G	Martin Brodeur, N.J.
Nicklas Lidstrom, Det.	D	Chris Pronger, St.L.
Rob Blake, L.A.	D	Scott Niedermayer, N.J.
Peter Forsberg, Col.	C	Wayne Gretzky, NYR
Jaromir Jagr, Pit.	RW	Teemu Selanne, Ana.
John LeClair, Phi.	LW	Keith Tkachuk, Phx.

1996-97

First Team		Second Team
Dominik Hasek, Buf.	G	Martin Brodeur, N.J.
Brian Leetch, NYR	D	Chris Chelios, Chi.
Sandis Ozolinsh, Col.	D	Scott Stevens, N.J.
Mario Lemieux, Pit.	C	Wayne Gretzky, NYR
Teemu Selanne, Ana.	RW	Jaromir Jagr, Pit.
Paul Kariya, Ana.	LW	John LeClair, Phi.

1995-96

First Team		Second Team
Jim Carey, Wsh.	G	Chris Osgood, Det.
Chris Chelios, Chi.	D	V. Konstantinov, Det.
Raymond Bourque, Bos.	D	Brian Leetch, NYR
Mario Lemieux, Pit.	C	Eric Lindros, Phi.
Jaromir Jagr, Pit.	RW	Alexander Mogilny, Van.
Paul Kariya, Ana.	LW	John LeClair, Phi.

1994-95

First Team		Second Team
Dominik Hasek, Buf.	G	Ed Belfour, Chi.
Paul Coffey, Det.	D	Raymond Bourque, Bos.
Chris Chelios, Chi.	D	Larry Murphy, Pit.
Eric Lindros, Phi.	C	Alexei Zhamnov, Wpg.
Jaromir Jagr, Pit.	RW	Theoren Fleury, Cgy.
John LeClair, Mtl., Phi.	LW	Keith Tkachuk, Wpg.

1993-94

First Team		Second Team
Dominik Hasek, Buf.	G	John Vanbiesbrouck, Fla.
Raymond Bourque, Bos.	D	Al MacInnis, Cgy.
Scott Stevens, N.J.	D	Brian Leetch, NYR
Sergei Fedorov, Det.	C	Wayne Gretzky, L.A.
Pavel Bure, Van.	RW	Cam Neely, Bos.
Brendan Shanahan, St.L.	LW	Adam Graves, NYR

1992-93

First Team		Second Team
Ed Belfour, Chi.	G	Tom Barrasso, Pit.
Chris Chelios, Chi.	D	Larry Murphy, Pit.
Raymond Bourque, Bos.	D	Al Iafrate, Wsh.
Mario Lemieux, Pit.	C	Pat LaFontaine, Buf.
Teemu Selanne, Wpg.	RW	Alexander Mogilny, Buf.
Luc Robitaille, L.A.	LW	Kevin Stevens, Pit.

1991-92

First Team		Second Team
Patrick Roy, Mtl.	G	Kirk McLean, Van.
Brian Leetch, NYR	D	Phil Housley, Wpg.
Raymond Bourque, Bos.	D	Scott Stevens, N.J.
Mark Messier, NYR	C	Mario Lemieux, Pit.
Brett Hull, St.L.	RW	Mark Recchi, Pit., Phi.
Kevin Stevens, Pit.	LW	Luc Robitaille, L.A.

1990-91

First Team		Second Team
Ed Belfour, Chi.	G	Patrick Roy, Mtl.
Raymond Bourque, Bos.	D	Chris Chelios, Chi.
Al MacInnis, Cgy.	D	Brian Leetch, NYR
Wayne Gretzky, L.A.	C	Adam Oates, St.L.
Brett Hull, St.L.	RW	Cam Neely, Bos.
Luc Robitaille, L.A.	LW	Kevin Stevens, Pit.

1989-90

First Team		Second Team
Patrick Roy, Mtl.	G	Daren Puppa, Buf.
Raymond Bourque, Bos.	D	Paul Coffey, Pit.
Al MacInnis, Cgy.	D	Doug Wilson, Chi.
Mark Messier, Edm.	C	Wayne Gretzky, L.A.
Brett Hull, St.L.	RW	Cam Neely, Bos.
Luc Robitaille, L.A.	LW	Brian Bellows, Min.

1988-89

First Team		Second Team
Patrick Roy, Mtl.	G	Mike Vernon, Cgy.
Chris Chelios, Mtl.	D	Al MacInnis, Cgy.
Paul Coffey, Pit.	D	Raymond Bourque, Bos.
Mario Lemieux, Pit.	C	Wayne Gretzky, L.A.
Joe Mullen, Cgy.	RW	Jari Kurri, Edm.
Luc Robitaille, L.A.	LW	Gerard Gallant, Det.

1987-88

First Team		Second Team
Grant Fuhr, Edm.	G	Patrick Roy, Mtl.
Raymond Bourque, Bos.	D	Gary Suter, Cgy.
Scott Stevens, Wsh.	D	Brad McCrimmon, Cgy.
Mario Lemieux, Pit.	C	Wayne Gretzky, Edm.
Hakan Loob, Cgy.	RW	Cam Neely, Bos.
Luc Robitaille, L.A.	LW	Michel Goulet, Que.

1986-87

First Team		Second Team
Ron Hextall, Phi.	G	Mike Liut, Hfd.
Raymond Bourque, Bos.	D	Larry Murphy, Wsh.
Mark Howe, Phi.	D	Al MacInnis, Cgy.
Wayne Gretzky, Edm.	C	Mario Lemieux, Pit.
Jari Kurri, Edm.	RW	Tim Kerr, Phi.
Michel Goulet, Que.	LW	Luc Robitaille, L.A.

1985-86

First Team		Second Team
John Vanbiesbrouck, NYR	G	Bob Froese, Phi.
Paul Coffey, Edm.	D	Larry Robinson, Mtl.
Mark Howe, Phi.	D	Raymond Bourque, Bos.
Wayne Gretzky, Edm.	C	Mario Lemieux, Pit.
Mike Bossy, NYI	RW	Jari Kurri, Edm.
Michel Goulet, Que.	LW	Mats Naslund, Mtl.

1984-85

First Team		Second Team
Pelle Lindbergh, Phi.	G	Tom Barrasso, Buf.
Paul Coffey, Edm.	D	Rod Langway, Wsh.
Raymond Bourque, Bos.	D	Doug Wilson, Chi.
Wayne Gretzky, Edm.	C	Dale Hawerchuk, Wpg.
Jari Kurri, Edm.	RW	Mike Bossy, NYI
John Ogrodnick, Det.	LW	John Tonelli, NYI

1983-84

First Team		Second Team
Tom Barrasso, Buf.	G	Pat Riggin, Wsh.
Rod Langway, Wsh.	D	Paul Coffey, Edm.
Raymond Bourque, Bos.	D	Denis Potvin, NYI
Wayne Gretzky, Edm.	C	Bryan Trottier, NYI
Mike Bossy, NYI	RW	Jari Kurri, Edm.
Michel Goulet, Que.	LW	Mark Messier, Edm.

1982-83

First Team		Second Team
Pete Peeters, Bos.	G	Roland Melanson, NYI
Mark Howe, Phi.	D	Raymond Bourque, Bos.
Rod Langway, Wsh.	D	Paul Coffey, Edm.
Wayne Gretzky, Edm.	C	Denis Savard, Chi.
Mike Bossy, NYI	RW	Lanny McDonald, Cgy.
Mark Messier, Edm.	LW	Michel Goulet, Que.

1981-82

First Team		Second Team
Billy Smith, NYI	G	Grant Fuhr, Edm.
Doug Wilson, Chi.	D	Paul Coffey, Edm.
Raymond Bourque, Bos.	D	Brian Engblom, Mtl.
Wayne Gretzky, Edm.	C	Bryan Trottier, NYI
Mike Bossy, NYI	RW	Rick Middleton, Bos.
Mark Messier, Edm.	LW	John Tonelli, NYI

First Team			Second Team

1980-81

First Team	Pos	Second Team
Mike Liut, St.L.	G	Mario Lessard, L.A.
Denis Potvin, NYI	D	Larry Robinson, Mtl.
Randy Carlyle, Pit.	D	Raymond Bourque, Bos.
Wayne Gretzky, Edm.	C	Marcel Dionne, L.A.
Mike Bossy, NYI	RW	Dave Taylor, L.A.
Charlie Simmer, L.A.	LW	Bill Barber, Phi.

1979-80

First Team	Pos	Second Team
Tony Esposito, Chi.	G	Don Edwards, Buf.
Larry Robinson, Mtl.	D	Borje Salming, Tor.
Raymond Bourque, Bos.	D	Jim Schoenfeld, Buf.
Marcel Dionne, L.A.	C	Wayne Gretzky, Edm.
Guy Lafleur, Mtl.	RW	Danny Gare, Buf.
Charlie Simmer, L.A.	LW	Steve Shutt, Mtl.

1978-79

First Team	Pos	Second Team
Ken Dryden, Mtl.	G	Glenn Resch, NYI
Denis Potvin, NYI	D	Borje Salming, Tor.
Larry Robinson, Mtl.	D	Serge Savard, Mtl.
Bryan Trottier, NYI	C	Marcel Dionne, L.A.
Guy Lafleur, Mtl.	RW	Mike Bossy, NYI
Clark Gillies, NYI	LW	Bill Barber, Phi.

1977-78

First Team	Pos	Second Team
Ken Dryden, Mtl.	G	Don Edwards, Buf.
Denis Potvin, NYI	D	Larry Robinson, Mtl.
Brad Park, Bos.	D	Borje Salming, Tor.
Bryan Trottier, NYI	C	Darryl Sittler, Tor.
Guy Lafleur, Mtl.	RW	Mike Bossy, NYI
Clark Gillies, NYI	LW	Steve Shutt, Mtl.

1976-77

First Team	Pos	Second Team
Ken Dryden, Mtl.	G	Rogie Vachon, L.A.
Larry Robinson, Mtl.	D	Denis Potvin, NYI
Borje Salming, Tor.	D	Guy Lapointe, Mtl.
Marcel Dionne, L.A.	C	Gilbert Perreault, Buf.
Guy Lafleur, Mtl.	RW	Lanny McDonald, Tor.
Steve Shutt, Mtl.	LW	Rick Martin, Buf.

1975-76

First Team	Pos	Second Team
Ken Dryden, Mtl.	G	Glenn Resch, NYI
Denis Potvin, NYI	D	Brad Park, Bos.
Brad Park, Bos.	D	Guy Lapointe, Mtl.
Bobby Clarke, Phi.	C	Gilbert Perreault, Buf.
Guy Lafleur, Mtl.	RW	Reggie Leach, Phi.
Bill Barber, Phi.	LW	Rick Martin, Buf.

1974-75

First Team	Pos	Second Team
Bernie Parent, Phi.	G	Rogie Vachon, L.A.
Bobby Orr, Bos.	D	Guy Lapointe, Mtl.
Denis Potvin, NYI	D	Borje Salming, Tor.
Bobby Clarke, Phi.	C	Phil Esposito, Bos.
Guy Lafleur, Mtl.	RW	René Robert, Buf.
Rick Martin, Buf.	LW	Steve Vickers, NYR

1973-74

First Team	Pos	Second Team
Bernie Parent, Phi.	G	Tony Esposito, Chi.
Bobby Orr, Bos.	D	Bill White, Chi.
Brad Park, NYR	D	Barry Ashbee, Phi.
Phil Esposito, Bos.	C	Bobby Clarke, Phi.
Ken Hodge, Bos.	RW	Mickey Redmond, Det.
Rick Martin, Buf.	LW	Wayne Cashman, Bos.

1972-73

First Team	Pos	Second Team
Ken Dryden, Mtl.	G	Tony Esposito, Chi.
Bobby Orr, Bos.	D	Brad Park, NYR
Guy Lapointe, Mtl.	D	Bill White, Chi.
Phil Esposito, Bos.	C	Bobby Clarke, Phi.
Mickey Redmond, Det.	RW	Yvan Cournoyer, Mtl.
Frank Mahovlich, Mtl.	LW	Dennis Hull, Chi.

1971-72

First Team	Pos	Second Team
Tony Esposito, Chi.	G	Ken Dryden, Mtl.
Bobby Orr, Bos.	D	Bill White, Chi.
Brad Park, NYR	D	Pat Stapleton, Chi.
Phil Esposito, Bos.	C	Jean Ratelle, NYR
Rod Gilbert, NYR	RW	Yvan Cournoyer, Mtl.
Bobby Hull, Chi.	LW	Vic Hadfield, NYR

1970-71

First Team	Pos	Second Team
Ed Giacomin, NYR	G	Jacques Plante, Tor.
Bobby Orr, Bos.	D	Brad Park, NYR
J.C. Tremblay, Mtl.	D	Pat Stapleton, Chi.
Phil Esposito, Bos.	C	Dave Keon, Tor.
Ken Hodge, Bos.	RW	Yvan Cournoyer, Mtl.
John Bucyk, Bos.	LW	Bobby Hull, Chi.

1969-70

First Team	Pos	Second Team
Tony Esposito, Chi.	G	Ed Giacomin, NYR
Bobby Orr, Bos.	D	Carl Brewer, Det.
Brad Park, NYR	D	Jacques Laperriere, Mtl.
Phil Esposito, Bos.	C	Stan Mikita, Chi.
Gordie Howe, Det.	RW	John McKenzie, Bos.
Bobby Hull, Chi.	LW	Frank Mahovlich, Det.

1968-69

First Team	Pos	Second Team
Glenn Hall, St.L.	G	Ed Giacomin, NYR
Bobby Orr, Bos.	D	Ted Green, Bos.
Tim Horton, Tor.	D	Ted Harris, Mtl.
Phil Esposito, Bos.	C	Jean Béliveau, Mtl.
Gordie Howe, Det.	RW	Yvan Cournoyer, Mtl.
Bobby Hull, Chi.	LW	Frank Mahovlich, Det.

1967-68

First Team	Pos	Second Team
Gump Worsley, Mtl.	G	Ed Giacomin, NYR
Bobby Orr, Bos.	D	J.C. Tremblay, Mtl.
Tim Horton, Tor.	D	Jim Neilson, NYR
Stan Mikita, Chi.	C	Phil Esposito, Bos.
Gordie Howe, Det.	RW	Rod Gilbert, NYR
Bobby Hull, Chi.	LW	John Bucyk, Bos.

1966-67

First Team	Pos	Second Team
Ed Giacomin, NYR	G	Glenn Hall, Chi.
Pierre Pilote, Chi.	D	Tim Horton, Tor.
Harry Howell, NYR	D	Bobby Orr, Bos.
Stan Mikita, Chi.	C	Norm Ullman, Det.
Kenny Wharram, Chi.	RW	Gordie Howe, Det.
Bobby Hull, Chi.	LW	Don Marshall, NYR

1965-66

First Team	Pos	Second Team
Glenn Hall, Chi.	G	Gump Worsley, Mtl.
Jacques Laperriere, Mtl.	D	Allan Stanley, Tor.
Pierre Pilote, Chi.	D	Pat Stapleton, Chi.
Stan Mikita, Chi.	C	Jean Béliveau, Mtl.
Gordie Howe, Det.	RW	Bobby Rousseau, Mtl.
Bobby Hull, Chi.	LW	Frank Mahovlich, Tor.

1964-65

First Team	Pos	Second Team
Roger Crozier, Det.	G	Charlie Hodge, Mtl.
Pierre Pilote, Chi.	D	Bill Gadsby, Det.
Jacques Laperriere, Mtl.	D	Carl Brewer, Tor.
Norm Ullman, Det.	C	Stan Mikita, Chi.
Claude Provost, Mtl.	RW	Gordie Howe, Det.
Bobby Hull, Chi.	LW	Frank Mahovlich, Tor.

1963-64

First Team	Pos	Second Team
Glenn Hall, Chi.	G	Charlie Hodge, Mtl.
Pierre Pilote, Chi.	D	Moose Vasko, Chi.
Tim Horton, Tor.	D	Jacques Laperriere, Mtl.
Stan Mikita, Chi.	C	Jean Béliveau, Mtl.
Kenny Wharram, Chi.	RW	Gordie Howe, Det.
Bobby Hull, Chi.	LW	Frank Mahovlich, Tor.

1962-63

First Team	Pos	Second Team
Glenn Hall, Chi.	G	Terry Sawchuk, Det.
Pierre Pilote, Chi.	D	Tim Horton, Tor.
Carl Brewer, Tor.	D	Moose Vasko, Chi.
Stan Mikita, Chi.	C	Henri Richard, Mtl.
Gordie Howe, Det.	RW	Andy Bathgate, NYR
Frank Mahovlich, Tor.	LW	Bobby Hull, Chi.

1961-62

First Team	Pos	Second Team
Jacques Plante, Mtl.	G	Glenn Hall, Chi.
Doug Harvey, NYR	D	Carl Brewer, Tor.
Jean-Guy Talbot, Mtl.	D	Pierre Pilote, Chi.
Stan Mikita, Chi.	C	Dave Keon, Tor.
Andy Bathgate, NYR	RW	Gordie Howe, Det.
Bobby Hull, Chi.	LW	Frank Mahovlich, Tor.

1960-61

First Team	Pos	Second Team
Johnny Bower, Tor.	G	Glenn Hall, Chi.
Doug Harvey, Mtl.	D	Allan Stanley, Tor.
Marcel Pronovost, Det.	D	Pierre Pilote, Chi.
Jean Béliveau, Mtl.	C	Henri Richard, Mtl.
Bernie Geoffrion, Mtl.	RW	Gordie Howe, Det.
Frank Mahovlich, Tor.	LW	Dickie Moore, Mtl.

1959-60

First Team	Pos	Second Team
Glenn Hall, Chi.	G	Jacques Plante, Mtl.
Doug Harvey, Mtl.	D	Allan Stanley, Tor.
Marcel Pronovost, Det.	D	Pierre Pilote, Chi.
Jean Béliveau, Mtl.	C	Bronco Horvath, Bos.
Gordie Howe, Det.	RW	Bernie Geoffrion, Mtl.
Bobby Hull, Chi.	LW	Dean Prentice, NYR

1958-59

First Team	Pos	Second Team
Jacques Plante, Mtl.	G	Terry Sawchuk, Det.
Tom Johnson, Mtl.	D	Marcel Pronovost, Det.
Bill Gadsby, NYR	D	Doug Harvey, Mtl.
Jean Béliveau, Mtl.	C	Henri Richard, Mtl.
Andy Bathgate, NYR	RW	Gordie Howe, Det.
Dickie Moore, Mtl.	LW	Alex Delvecchio, Det.

1957-58

First Team	Pos	Second Team
Glenn Hall, Chi.	G	Jacques Plante, Mtl.
Doug Harvey, Mtl.	D	Fern Flaman, Bos.
Bill Gadsby, NYR	D	Marcel Pronovost, Det.
Henri Richard, Mtl.	C	Jean Béliveau, Mtl.
Gordie Howe, Det.	RW	Andy Bathgate, NYR
Dickie Moore, Mtl.	LW	Camille Henry, NYR

1956-57

First Team	Pos	Second Team
Glenn Hall, Det.	G	Jacques Plante, Mtl.
Doug Harvey, Mtl.	D	Fern Flaman, Bos.
Red Kelly, Det.	D	Bill Gadsby, NYR
Jean Béliveau, Mtl.	C	Ed Litzenberger, Chi.
Gordie Howe, Det.	RW	Maurice Richard, Mtl.
Ted Lindsay, Det.	LW	Real Chevrefils, Bos.

1955-56

First Team	Pos	Second Team
Jacques Plante, Mtl.	G	Glenn Hall, Det.
Doug Harvey, Mtl.	D	Red Kelly, Det.
Bill Gadsby, NYR	D	Tom Johnson, Mtl.
Jean Béliveau, Mtl.	C	Tod Sloan, Tor.
Maurice Richard, Mtl.	RW	Gordie Howe, Det.
Ted Lindsay, Det.	LW	Bert Olmstead, Mtl.

1954-55

First Team	Pos	Second Team
Harry Lumley, Tor.	G	Terry Sawchuk, Det.
Doug Harvey, Mtl.	D	Bob Goldham, Det.
Red Kelly, Det.	D	Fern Flaman, Bos.
Jean Béliveau, Mtl.	C	Ken Mosdell, Mtl.
Maurice Richard, Mtl.	RW	Bernie Geoffrion, Mtl.
Sid Smith, Tor.	LW	Danny Lewicki, NYR

First Team		Second Team
1953-54		
Harry Lumley, Tor.	G	Terry Sawchuk, Det.
Red Kelly, Det.	D	Bill Gadsby, Chi.
Doug Harvey, Mtl.	D	Tim Horton, Tor.
Ken Mosdell, Mtl.	C	Ted Kennedy, Tor.
Gordie Howe, Det.	RW	Maurice Richard, Mtl.
Ted Lindsay, Det.	LW	Ed Sandford, Bos.
1952-53		
Terry Sawchuk, Det.	G	Gerry McNeil, Mtl.
Red Kelly, Det.	D	Bill Quackenbush, Bos.
Doug Harvey, Mtl.	D	Bill Gadsby, Chi.
Fleming MacKell, Bos.	C	Alex Delvecchio, Det.
Gordie Howe, Det.	RW	Maurice Richard, Mtl.
Ted Lindsay, Det.	LW	Bert Olmstead, Mtl.
1951-52		
Terry Sawchuk, Det.	G	Jim Henry, Bos.
Red Kelly, Det.	D	Hy Buller, NYR
Doug Harvey, Mtl.	D	Jimmy Thomson, Tor.
Elmer Lach, Mtl.	C	Milt Schmidt, Bos.
Gordie Howe, Det.	RW	Maurice Richard, Mtl.
Ted Lindsay, Det.	LW	Sid Smith, Tor.
1950-51		
Terry Sawchuk, Det.	G	Chuck Rayner, NYR
Red Kelly, Det.	D	Jimmy Thomson, Tor.
Bill Quackenbush, Bos.	D	Leo Reise Jr., Det.
Milt Schmidt, Bos.	C	Sid Abel, Det.
		Ted Kennedy (tied), Tor.
Gordie Howe, Det.	RW	Maurice Richard, Mtl.
Ted Lindsay, Det.	LW	Sid Smith, Tor.
1949-50		
Bill Durnan, Mtl.	G	Chuck Rayner, NYR
Gus Mortson, Tor.	D	Leo Reise Jr., Det.
Ken Reardon, Mtl.	D	Red Kelly, Det.
Sid Abel, Det.	C	Ted Kennedy, Tor.
Maurice Richard, Mtl.	RW	Gordie Howe, Det.
Ted Lindsay, Det.	LW	Tony Leswick, NYR
1948-49		
Bill Durnan, Mtl.	G	Chuck Rayner, NYR
Bill Quackenbush, Det.	D	Glen Harmon, Mtl.
Jack Stewart, Det.	D	Ken Reardon, Mtl.
Sid Abel, Det.	C	Doug Bentley, Chi.
Maurice Richard, Mtl.	RW	Gordie Howe, Det.
Roy Conacher, Chi.	LW	Ted Lindsay, Det.
1947-48		
Turk Broda, Tor.	G	Frank Brimsek, Bos.
Bill Quackenbush, Det.	D	Ken Reardon, Mtl.
Jack Stewart, Det.	D	Neil Colville, NYR
Elmer Lach, Mtl.	C	Buddy O'Connor, NYR
Maurice Richard, Mtl.	RW	Bud Poile, Chi.
Ted Lindsay, Det.	LW	Gaye Stewart, Chi.
1946-47		
Bill Durnan, Mtl.	G	Frank Brimsek, Bos.
Ken Reardon, Mtl.	D	Jack Stewart, Det.
Butch Bouchard, Mtl.	D	Bill Quackenbush, Det.
Milt Schmidt, Bos.	C	Max Bentley, Chi.
Maurice Richard, Mtl.	RW	Bobby Bauer, Bos.
Doug Bentley, Chi.	LW	Woody Dumart, Bos.
1945-46		
Bill Durnan, Mtl.	G	Frank Brimsek, Bos.
Jack Crawford, Bos.	D	Ken Reardon, Mtl.
Butch Bouchard, Mtl.	D	Jack Stewart, Det.
Max Bentley, Chi.	C	Elmer Lach, Mtl.
Maurice Richard, Mtl.	RW	Bill Mosienko, Chi.
Gaye Stewart, Tor.	LW	Toe Blake, Mtl.
Dick Irvin, Mtl.	Coach	Johnny Gottselig, Chi.
1944-45		
Bill Durnan, Mtl.	G	Mike Karakas, Chi.
Butch Bouchard, Mtl.	D	Glen Harmon, Mtl.
Flash Hollett, Det.	D	Babe Pratt, Tor.
Elmer Lach, Mtl.	C	Bill Cowley, Bos.
Maurice Richard, Mtl.	RW	Bill Mosienko, Chi.
Toe Blake, Mtl.	LW	Syd Howe, Det.
Dick Irvin, Mtl.	Coach	Jack Adams, Det.

First Team		Second Team
1943-44		
Bill Durnan, Mtl.	G	Paul Bibeault, Tor.
Earl Seibert, Chi.	D	Butch Bouchard, Mtl.
Babe Pratt, Tor.	D	Dit Clapper, Bos.
Bill Cowley, Bos.	C	Elmer Lach, Mtl.
Lorne Carr, Tor.	RW	Maurice Richard, Mtl.
Doug Bentley, Chi.	LW	Herb Cain, Bos.
Dick Irvin, Mtl.	Coach	Hap Day, Tor.
1942-43		
Johnny Mowers, Det.	G	Frank Brimsek, Bos.
Earl Seibert, Chi.	D	Jack Crawford, Bos.
Jack Stewart, Det.	D	Flash Hollett, Bos.
Bill Cowley, Bos.	C	Syl Apps, Tor.
Lorne Carr, Tor.	RW	Bryan Hextall, NYR
Doug Bentley, Chi.	LW	Lynn Patrick, NYR
Jack Adams, Det.	Coach	Art Ross, Bos.
1941-42		
Frank Brimsek, Bos.	G	Turk Broda, Tor.
Earl Seibert, Chi.	D	Pat Egan, Bro.
Tom Anderson, Bro.	D	Bucko McDonald, Tor.
Syl Apps, Tor.	C	Phil Watson, NYR
Bryan Hextall, NYR	RW	Gordie Drillon, Tor.
Lynn Patrick, NYR	LW	Sid Abel, Det.
Frank Boucher, NYR	Coach	Paul Thompson, Chi.
1940-41		
Turk Broda, Tor.	G	Frank Brimsek, Bos.
Dit Clapper, Bos.	D	Earl Seibert, Chi.
Wally Stanowski, Tor.	D	Ott Heller, NYR
Bill Cowley, Bos.	C	Syl Apps, Tor.
Bryan Hextall, NYR	RW	Bobby Bauer, Bos.
Sweeney Schriner, Tor.	LW	Woody Dumart, Bos.
Cooney Weiland, Bos.	Coach	Dick Irvin, Mtl.
1939-40		
Dave Kerr, NYR	G	Frank Brimsek, Bos.
Dit Clapper, Bos.	D	Art Coulter, NYR
Ebbie Goodfellow, Det.	D	Earl Seibert, Chi.
Milt Schmidt, Bos.	C	Neil Colville, NYR
Bryan Hextall, NYR	RW	Bobby Bauer, Bos.
Toe Blake, Mtl.	LW	Woody Dumart, Bos.
Paul Thompson, Chi.	Coach	Frank Boucher, NYR
1938-39		
Frank Brimsek, Bos.	G	Earl Robertson, NYA
Eddie Shore, Bos.	D	Earl Seibert, Chi.
Dit Clapper, Bos.	D	Art Coulter, NYR
Syl Apps, Tor.	C	Neil Colville, NYR
Gordie Drillon, Tor.	RW	Bobby Bauer, Bos.
Toe Blake, Mtl.	LW	Johnny Gottselig, Chi.
Art Ross, Bos.	Coach	Red Dutton, NYA
1937-38		
Tiny Thompson, Bos.	G	Dave Kerr, NYR
Eddie Shore, Bos.	D	Art Coulter, NYR
Babe Siebert, Mtl.	D	Earl Seibert, Chi.
Bill Cowley, Bos.	C	Syl Apps, Tor.
Cecil Dillon, NYR	RW	
Gordie Drillon, Tor.	(tied)	
Paul Thompson, Chi.	LW	Toe Blake, Mtl.
Lester Patrick, NYR	Coach	Art Ross, Bos.
1936-37		
Normie Smith, Det.	G	Wilf Cude, Mtl.
Babe Siebert, Mtl.	D	Earl Seibert, Chi.
Ebbie Goodfellow, Det.	D	Lionel Conacher, Mtl. M.
Marty Barry, Det.	C	Art Chapman, NYA
Larry Aurie, Det.	RW	Cecil Dillon, NYR
Busher Jackson, Tor.	LW	Sweeney Schriner, NYA
Jack Adams, Det.	Coach	Cecil Hart, Mtl.
1935-36		
Tiny Thompson, Bos.	G	Wilf Cude, Mtl.
Eddie Shore, Bos.	D	Earl Seibert, Chi.
Babe Siebert, Bos.	D	Ebbie Goodfellow, Det.
Hooley Smith, Mtl. M.	C	Bill Thoms, Tor.
Charlie Conacher, Tor.	RW	Cecil Dillon, NYR
Sweeney Schriner, NYA	LW	Paul Thompson, Chi.
Lester Patrick, NYR	Coach	Tommy Gorman, Mtl. M.

First Team		Second Team
1934-35		
Lorne Chabot, Chi.	G	Tiny Thompson, Bos.
Eddie Shore, Bos.	D	Cy Wentworth, Mtl. M.
Earl Seibert, NYR	D	Art Coulter, Chi.
Frank Boucher, NYR	C	Cooney Weiland, Det.
Charlie Conacher, Tor.	RW	Dit Clapper, Bos.
Busher Jackson, Tor.	LW	Aurel Joliat, Mtl.
Lester Patrick, NYR	Coach	Dick Irvin, Tor.
1933-34		
Charlie Gardiner, Chi.	G	Roy Worters, NYA
King Clancy, Tor.	D	Eddie Shore, Bos.
Lionel Conacher, Chi.	D	Ching Johnson, NYR
Frank Boucher, NYR	C	Joe Primeau, Tor.
Charlie Conacher, Tor.	RW	Bill Cook, NYR
Busher Jackson, Tor.	LW	Aurel Joliat, Mtl.
Lester Patrick, NYR	Coach	Dick Irvin, Tor.
1932-33		
John Ross Roach, Det.	G	Charlie Gardiner, Chi.
Eddie Shore, Bos.	D	King Clancy, Tor.
Ching Johnson, NYR	D	Lionel Conacher, Mtl. M.
Frank Boucher, NYR	C	Howie Morenz, Mtl.
Bill Cook, NYR	RW	Charlie Conacher, Tor.
Baldy Northcott, Mtl M.	LW	Busher Jackson, Tor.
Lester Patrick, NYR	Coach	Dick Irvin, Tor.
1931-32		
Charlie Gardiner, Chi.	G	Roy Worters, NYA
Eddie Shore, Bos.	D	Sylvio Mantha, Mtl.
Ching Johnson, NYR	D	King Clancy, Tor.
Howie Morenz, Mtl.	C	Hooley Smith, Mtl. M.
Bill Cook, NYR	RW	Charlie Conacher, Tor.
Busher Jackson, Tor.	LW	Aurel Joliat, Mtl.
Lester Patrick, NYR	Coach	Dick Irvin, Tor.
1930-31		
Charlie Gardiner, Chi.	G	Tiny Thompson, Bos.
Eddie Shore, Bos.	D	Sylvio Mantha, Mtl.
King Clancy, Tor.	D	Ching Johnson, NYR
Howie Morenz, Mtl.	C	Frank Boucher, NYR
Bill Cook, NYR	RW	Dit Clapper, Bos.
Aurel Joliat, Mtl.	LW	Bun Cook, NYR
Lester Patrick, NYR	Coach	Dick Irvin, Chi.

All-Star Game Results

Year	Venue	Score	Coaches	Attendance
2004	Minnesota	East 6, West 4	Pat Quinn, Dave Lewis	19,434
2003	Florida	West 6, East 5	Marc Crawford, Jacques Martin	19,250
2002	Los Angeles	World 8, North America 5	Scotty Bowman, Pat Quinn	18,118
2001	Colorado	North America 14, World 12	Joel Quenneville, Jacques Martin	18,646
2000	Toronto	World 9, North America 4	Scotty Bowman, Pat Quinn	19,300
1999	Tampa Bay	North America 8, World 6	Lindy Ruff, Ken Hitchcock	19,758
1998	Vancouver	North America 8, World 7	Jacques Lemaire, Ken Hitchcock	18,422
1997	San Jose	East 11, West 7	Doug MacLean, Ken Hitchcock	17,422
1996	Boston	East 5, West 4	Doug MacLean, Scotty Bowman	17,565
1994	NY Rangers	East 9, West 8	Jacques Demers, Barry Melrose	18,200
1993	Montreal	Wales 16, Campbell 6	Scotty Bowman, Mike Keenan	17,137
1992	Philadelphia	Campbell 10, Wales 6	Bob Gainey, Scotty Bowman	17,380
1991	Chicago	Campbell 11, Wales 5	John Muckler, Mike Milbury	18,472
1990	Pittsburgh	Wales 12, Campbell 7	Pat Burns, Terry Crisp	16,236
1989	Edmonton	Campbell 9, Wales 5	Glen Sather, Terry O'Reilly	17,503
1988	St. Louis	Wales 6, Campbell 5 OT	Mike Keenan, Glen Sather	17,878
1986	Hartford	Wales 4, Campbell 3 OT	Mike Keenan, Glen Sather	15,100
1985	Calgary	Wales 6, Campbell 4	Al Arbour, Glen Sather	16,825
1984	New Jersey	Wales 7, Campbell 6	Al Arbour, Glen Sather	18,939
1983	NY Islanders	Campbell 9, Wales 3	Roger Neilson, Al Arbour	15,230
1982	Washington	Wales 4, Campbell 2	Al Arbour, Glen Sonmor	18,130
1981	Los Angeles	Campbell 4, Wales 1	Pat Quinn, Scotty Bowman	15,761
1980	Detroit	Wales 6, Campbell 3	Scotty Bowman, Al Arbour	21,002
1978	Buffalo	Wales 3, Campbell 2 OT	Scotty Bowman, Fred Shero	16,433
1977	Vancouver	Wales 4, Campbell 3	Scotty Bowman, Fred Shero	15,607
1976	Philadelphia	Wales 7, Campbell 5	Floyd Smith, Fred Shero	16,436
1975	Montreal	Wales 7, Campbell 1	Bep Guidolin, Fred Shero	16,080
1974	Chicago	West 6, East 4	Billy Reay, Scotty Bowman	16,426
1973	NY Rangers	East 5, West 4	Tom Johnson, Billy Reay	16,986
1972	Minnesota	East 3, West 2	Al MacNeil, Billy Reay	15,423
1971	Boston	West 2, East 1	Scotty Bowman, Harry Sinden	14,790
1970	St. Louis	East 4, West 1	Claude Ruel, Scotty Bowman	16,587
1969	Montreal	East 3, West 3	Toe Blake, Scotty Bowman	16,260
1968	Toronto	Toronto 4, All-Stars 3	Punch Imlach, Toe Blake	15,753
1967	Montreal	Montreal 3, All-Stars 0	Toe Blake, Sid Abel	14,284
1965	Montreal	All-Stars 5, Montreal 2	Billy Reay, Toe Blake	13,529
1964	Toronto	All-Stars 3, Toronto 2	Sid Abel, Punch Imlach	14,232
1963	Toronto	All-Stars 3, Toronto 3	Sid Abel, Punch Imlach	14,034
1962	Toronto	Toronto 4, All-Stars 1	Punch Imlach, Rudy Pilous	14,236
1961	Chicago	All-Stars 3, Chicago 1	Sid Abel, Rudy Pilous	14,534
1960	Montreal	All-Stars 2, Montreal 1	Punch Imlach, Toe Blake	13,949
1959	Montreal	Montreal 6, All-Stars 1	Toe Blake, Punch Imlach	13,818
1958	Montreal	Montreal 6, All-Stars 3	Toe Blake, Milt Schmidt	13,989
1957	Montreal	All-Stars 5, Montreal 3	Milt Schmidt, Toe Blake	13,003
1956	Montreal	All-Stars 1, Montreal 1	Jim Skinner, Toe Blake	13,095
1955	Detroit	Detroit 3, All-Stars 1	Jim Skinner, Dick Irvin	10,111
1954	Detroit	All-Stars 2, Detroit 2	King Clancy, Jim Skinner	10,689
1953	Montreal	All-Stars 3, Montreal 1	Lynn Patrick, Dick Irvin	14,153
1952	Detroit	1st Team 1, 2nd Team 1	Tommy Ivan, Dick Irvin	10,680
1951	Toronto	1st Team 2, 2nd Team 2	Joe Primeau, Dick Irvin	11,469
1950	Detroit	Detroit 7, All-Stars 1	Tommy Ivan, Lynn Patrick	9,166
1949	Toronto	All-Stars 3, Toronto 1	Tommy Ivan, Hap Day	13,541
1948	Chicago	All-Stars 3, Toronto 1	Tommy Ivan, Hap Day	12,794
1947	Toronto	All-Stars 4, Toronto 3	Dick Irvin, Hap Day	14,169

There was no All-Star contest during the calendar year of 1966 because the game was moved from the start of season to mid-season. In 1979, the Challenge Cup series between the Soviet Union and Team NHL replaced the All-Star Game. In 1987, Rendez-Vous '87, two games between the Soviet Union and Team NHL replaced the All-Star Game. Rendez-Vous '87 scores: game one, NHL All-Stars 4, Soviet Union 3; game two, Soviet Union 5, NHL All-Stars 3. No All-Star Games were played in 1995 and 2005.

Eddie Shore was a First-Team All-Star seven times in nine seasons between 1930-31 and 1938-39. He also played in All-Star benefit games in 1934, 1937 and 1939 which were forerunners to the annual NHL All-Star Game.

NHL ALL-ROOKIE TEAM

Voting for the NHL All-Rookie Team is conducted among the representatives of the Professional Hockey Writers' Association at the end of the season. The rookie all-star team was first selected for the 1982-83 season.

2004-05
Goal	
Defense	
Defense	No All-Rookie Team selected
Forward	
Forward	
Forward	

2003-04
Goal	Andrew Raycroft, Boston
Defense	John-Michael Liles, Colorado
Defense	Joni Pitkanen, Philadelphia
Forward	Trent Hunter, NY Islanders
Forward	Ryan Malone, Pittsburgh
Forward	Michael Ryder, Montreal

2002-03
Goal	Sebastian Caron, Pittsburgh
Defense	Jay Bouwmeester, Florida
Defense	Barret Jackman, St. Louis
Forward	Tyler Arnason, Chicago
Forward	Rick Nash, Columbus
Forward	Henrik Zetterberg, Detroit

2001-02
Goal	Dan Blackburn, NY Rangers
Defense	Nick Boynton, Boston
Defense	Rostislav Klesla, Columbus
Forward	Dany Heatley, Atlanta
Forward	Ilya Kovalchuk, Atlanta
Forward	Kristian Huselius, Florida

2000-01
Goal	Evgeni Nabokov, San Jose
Defense	Lubomir Visnovsky, Los Angeles
Defense	Colin White, New Jersey
Forward	Martin Havlat, Ottawa
Forward	Brad Richards, Tampa Bay
Forward	Shane Willis, Carolina

1999-2000
Goal	Brian Boucher, Philadelphia
Defense	Brian Rafalski, New Jersey
Defense	Brad Stuart, San Jose
Forward	Simon Gagne, Philadelphia
Forward	Scott Gomez, New Jersey
Forward	Michael York, NY Rangers

1998-99
Goal	Jamie Storr, Los Angeles
Defense	Tom Poti, Edmonton
Defense	Sami Salo, Ottawa
Forward	Chris Drury, Colorado
Forward	Milan Hejduk, Colorado
Forward	Marian Hossa, Ottawa

1997-98
Goal	Jamie Storr, Los Angeles
Defense	Mattias Ohlund, Vancouver
Defense	Derek Morris, Calgary
Forward	Sergei Samsonov, Boston
Forward	Patrick Elias, New Jersey
Forward	Mike Johnson, Toronto

1996-97
Goal	Patrick Lalime, Pittsburgh
Defense	Bryan Berard, NY Islanders
Defense	Janne Niinimaa, Philadelphia
Forward	Jarome Iginla, Calgary
Forward	Jim Campbell, St. Louis
Forward	Sergei Berezin, Toronto

1995-96
Goal	Corey Hirsch, Vancouver
Defense	Ed Jovanovski, Florida
Defense	Kyle McLaren, Boston
Forward	Daniel Alfredsson, Ottawa
Forward	Eric Daze, Chicago
Forward	Petr Sykora, New Jersey

1994-95
Goal	Jim Carey, Washington
Defense	Chris Therien, Philadelphia
Defense	Kenny Jonsson, Toronto
Forward	Peter Forsberg, Quebec
Forward	Jeff Friesen, San Jose
Forward	Paul Kariya, Anaheim

1993-94
Goal	Martin Brodeur, New Jersey
Defense	Chris Pronger, Hartford
Defense	Boris Mironov, Wpg./Edm.
Forward	Jason Arnott, Edmonton
Forward	Mikael Renberg, Philadelphia
Forward	Oleg Petrov, Montreal

1992-93
Goal	Felix Potvin, Toronto
Defense	Vladimir Malakhov, NY Islanders
Defense	Scott Niedermayer, New Jersey
Forward	Eric Lindros, Philadelphia
Forward	Teemu Selanne, Winnipeg
Forward	Joe Juneau, Boston

1991-92
Goal	Dominik Hasek, Chicago
Defense	Nicklas Lidstrom, Detroit
Defense	Vladimir Konstantinov, Detroit
Forward	Kevin Todd, New Jersey
Forward	Tony Amonte, NY Rangers
Forward	Gilbert Dionne, Montreal

1990-91
Goal	Ed Belfour, Chicago
Defense	Eric Weinrich, New Jersey
Defense	Rob Blake, Los Angeles
Forward	Sergei Fedorov, Detroit
Forward	Ken Hodge, Boston
Forward	Jaromir Jagr, Pittsburgh

1989-90
Goal	Bob Essensa, Winnipeg
Defense	Brad Shaw, Hartford
Defense	Geoff Smith, Edmonton
Forward	Mike Modano, Minnesota
Forward	Sergei Makarov, Calgary
Forward	Rod Brind'Amour, St. Louis

1988-89
Goal	Peter Sidorkiewicz, Hartford
Defense	Brian Leetch, NY Rangers
Defense	Zarley Zalapski, Pittsburgh
Forward	Trevor Linden, Vancouver
Forward	Tony Granato, NY Rangers
Forward	David Volek, NY Islanders

1987-88
Goal	Darren Pang, Chicago
Defense	Glen Wesley, Boston
Defense	Calle Johansson, Buffalo
Forward	Joe Nieuwendyk, Calgary
Forward	Ray Sheppard, Buffalo
Forward	Iain Duncan, Winnipeg

1986-87
Goal	Ron Hextall, Philadelphia
Defense	Steve Duchesne, Los Angeles
Defense	Brian Benning, St. Louis
Forward	Jimmy Carson, Los Angeles
Forward	Jim Sandlak, Vancouver
Forward	Luc Robitaille, Los Angeles

1985-86
Goal	Patrick Roy, Montreal
Defense	Gary Suter, Calgary
Defense	Dana Murzyn, Hartford
Forward	Mike Ridley, NY Rangers
Forward	Kjell Dahlin, Montreal
Forward	Wendel Clark, Toronto

1984-85
Goal	Steve Penney, Montreal
Defense	Chris Chelios, Montreal
Defense	Bruce Bell, Quebec
Forward	Mario Lemieux, Pittsburgh
Forward	Tomas Sandstrom, NY Rangers
Forward	Warren Young, Pittsburgh

1983-84
Goal	Tom Barrasso, Buffalo
Defense	Thomas Eriksson, Philadelphia
Defense	Jamie Macoun, Calgary
Forward	Steve Yzerman, Detroit
Forward	Hakan Loob, Calgary
Forward	Sylvain Turgeon, Hartford

1982-83
Goal	Pelle Lindbergh, Philadelphia
Defense	Scott Stevens, Washington
Defense	Phil Housley, Buffalo
Forward	Dan Daoust, Mtl./Tor.
Forward	Steve Larmer, Chicago
Forward	Mats Naslund, Montreal

All-Star Game Records
1947 through 2004

TEAM RECORDS

MOST GOALS, BOTH TEAMS, ONE GAME:
26 — North America 14, World 12, 2001 at Colorado
22 — Wales 16, Campbell 6, 1993 at Montreal
19 — Wales 12, Campbell 7, 1990 at Pittsburgh
18 — East 11, West 7, 1997 at San Jose
17 — East 9, West 8, 1994 at NY Rangers
16 — Campbell 11, Wales 5, 1991 at Chicago
— Campbell 10, Wales 6, 1992 at Philadelphia
15 — North America 8, World 7, 1998 at Vancouver

FEWEST GOALS, BOTH TEAMS, ONE GAME:
2 — First Team All-Stars 1, Second Team All-Stars 1, 1952 at Detroit
— NHL All-Stars 1, Montreal Canadiens 1, 1956 at Montreal
3 — NHL All-Stars 2, Montreal Canadiens 1, 1960 at Montreal
— Montreal Canadiens 3, NHL All-Stars 0, 1967 at Montreal
— West 2, East 1, 1971 at Boston

MOST GOALS, ONE TEAM, ONE GAME:
16 — Wales 16, Campbell 6, 1993 at Montreal
14 — North America 14, World 12, 2001 at Colorado
12 — Wales 12, Campbell 7, 1990 at Pittsburgh
— World 12, North America 14, 2001 at Colorado
11 — Campbell 11, Wales 5, 1991 at Chicago
— East 11, West 7, 1997 at San Jose

FEWEST GOALS, ONE TEAM, ONE GAME:
0 — NHL All-Stars 0, Montreal Canadiens 3, 1967 at Montreal
1 — 17 times (1981, 1975, 1971, 1970, 1962, 1961, 1960, 1959, both teams 1956, 1955, 1953, both teams 1952, 1950, 1949, 1948)

MOST SHOTS, BOTH TEAMS, ONE GAME (SINCE 1955):
102 — 1994 at NY Rangers — East 9 (56 shots),
West 8 (46 shots)
98 — 2001 at Colorado — North America 14 (53 shots),
World 12 (45 shots)
90 — 1993 at Montreal — Wales 16 (49 shots),
Campbell 6 (41 shots)
89 — 2002 at Los Angeles — World 8 (39 shots),
North America 5 (50 shots)

FEWEST SHOTS, BOTH TEAMS, ONE GAME (SINCE 1955):
52 — 1978 at Buffalo — Campbell 2 (12 shots)
Wales 3 (40 shots)
53 — 1960 at Montreal — NHL All-Stars 2 (27 shots)
Montreal Canadiens 1 (26 shots)
55 — 1956 at Montreal — NHL All-Stars 1 (28 shots)
Montreal Canadiens 1 (27 shots)
— 1971 at Boston — West 2 (28 shots)
East 1 (27 shots)

MOST SHOTS, ONE TEAM, ONE GAME (SINCE 1955):
56 — 1994 at NY Rangers — East (9-8 vs. West)
53 — 2001 at Colorado — North America (14-12 vs. World)
50 — 2002 at Los Angeles — North America (5-8 vs. World)
49 — 1993 at Montreal — Wales (16-6 vs. Campbell)
— 1999 at Tampa Bay — North America (8-6 vs. World)

FEWEST SHOTS, ONE TEAM, ONE GAME (SINCE 1955):
12 — 1978 at Buffalo — Campbell (2-3 vs. Wales)
17 — 1970 at St. Louis — West (1-4 vs. East)
23 — 1961 at Chicago — Chicago Black Hawks (1-3 vs. NHL All-Stars)
24 — 1976 at Philadelphia — Campbell (5-7 vs. Wales)

MOST POWER-PLAY GOALS, BOTH TEAMS, ONE GAME (SINCE 1950):
3 — 1953 at Montreal — NHL All-Stars 3 (2 power-play goals),
Montreal Canadiens 1 (1 power-play goal)
— 1954 at Detroit — NHL All-Stars 2 (1 power-play goal)
Detroit Red Wings 2 (2 power-play goals)
— 1958 at Montreal — NHL All-Stars 3 (1 power-play goal)
Montreal Canadiens 6 (2 power-play goals)

FEWEST POWER-PLAY GOALS, BOTH TEAMS, ONE GAME (SINCE 1950):
0 — 22 times (1952, 1959, 1960, 1967, 1968, 1969, 1972, 1973, 1976, 1980, 1981, 1984, 1985, 1992, 1994, 1996, 1999, 2000, 2001, 2002, 2003, 2004)

FASTEST TWO GOALS, BOTH TEAMS, FROM START OF GAME:
0:37 — 1970 at St. Louis — Jacques Laperriere of East scored at 0:20 and Dean Prentice of West scored at 0:37. Final score: East 4, West 1.
2:15 — 1998 at Vancouver — Teemu Selanee scored at 0:53 and Jaromir Jagr scored at 2:15 for World. Final score: North America 8, World 7.
3:37 — 1993 at Montreal — Mike Gartner scored at 3:15 and at 3:37 for Wales. Final score: Wales 16, Campbell 6.

FASTEST TWO GOALS, BOTH TEAMS:
0:08 — 1997 at San Jose — Owen Nolan scored at 18:54 and 19:02 of second period for West. Final Score: East 11, West 7.
0:10 — 1976 at Philadelphia — Dennis Ververgaert scored at 4:33 and at 4:43 of third period for Campbell. Final score: Wales 7, Campbell 5.
0:13 — 1998 at Vancouver — Teemu Selanne scored at 4:00 of first period for World and John LeClair scored at 4:13 for North America. Final score: North America 8, World 7.

FASTEST THREE GOALS, BOTH TEAMS:
1:08 — 1993 at Montreal — all by Wales — Mike Gartner scored at 3:15 and at 3:37 of first period; Peter Bondra scored at 4:23. Final score: Wales 16, Campbell 6.
1:14 — 1994 at NY Rangers — Bob Kudelski scored at 9:46 of first period for East; Sergei Fedorov scored at 10:20 for West; Eric Lindros scored at 11:00 for East. Final score: East 9, West 8.
1:23 — 1999 at Tampa Bay — Mats Sundin scored at 2:57 of third period for World; Darryl Sydor scored at 4:02 for North America; Sergei Zubov scored at 4:20 for World. Final score: North America 8, World 6.

FASTEST FOUR GOALS, BOTH TEAMS:
2:24 — 1997 at San Jose — Brendan Shanahan scored at 16:38 of second period for West; Dale Hawerchuk scored at 17:28 for East; Owen Nolan scored at 18:54 and 19:02 for West. Final score: East 11, West 7.
2:57 — 2002 at Los Angeles — Sergei Fedorov scored at 16:59 of third period for World; Markus Naslund scored at 18:17 for World; Alex Zhamnov scored at 19:12 for World; Sami Kapanen scored at 19:56 for World. Final score: World 8, North America 5.
3:04 — 1997 at San Jose — Mark Recchi scored at 15:32 of first period for East; Dale Hawerchuk scored at 16:19 for East; Pavel Bure scored at 17:36 for West; Paul Kariya scored at 18:36 for West. Final score: East 11, West 7.

FASTEST TWO GOALS, ONE TEAM, FROM START OF GAME:
2:15 — 1998 at Vancouver — World — Teemu Selanee scored at 0:53 and Jaromir Jagr scored at 2:15. Final score: North America 8, World 7.
3:37 — 1993 at Montreal — Wales — Mike Gartner scored at 3:15 and at 3:37. Final score: Wales 16, Campbell 6.
4:19 — 1980 at Detroit — Wales — Larry Robinson scored at 3:58 and Steve Payne scored at 4:19. Final score: Wales 6, Campbell 3.

FASTEST TWO GOALS, ONE TEAM:
0:08 — 1997 at San Jose — West — Owen Nolan scored at 18:54 and at 19:02 of second period. Final score: East 11, West 7.
0:10 — 1976 at Philadelphia — Campbell — Dennis Ververgaert scored at 4:33 and at 4:43 of third period. Final score: Wales 7, Campbell 5.
0:14 — 1989 at Edmonton — Campbell — Steve Yzerman and Gary Leeman scored at 17:21 and 17:35 of second period. Final score: Campbell 9, Wales 5.

FASTEST THREE GOALS, ONE TEAM:
1:08 — 1993 at Montreal — Wales — Mike Gartner scored at 3:15 and 3:37 of first period; Peter Bondra scored at 4:23. Final score: Wales 16, Campbell 6.
1:32 — 1980 at Detroit — Wales — Ron Stackhouse scored at 11:40 of third period; Craig Hartsburg scored at 12:40; Reed Larson scored at 13:12. Final score: Wales 6, Campbell 3.
1:39 — 2002 at Los Angeles — Markus Naslund scored at 18:17 of third period; Alex Zhamnov scored at 19:12; Sami Kapanen scored at 19:56. Final score: World 8, North America 5.

FASTEST FOUR GOALS, ONE TEAM:
2:57 — 2002 at Los Angeles — World — Sergei Fedorov scored at 16:59 of third period; Markus Naslund scored at 18:17; Alex Zhamnov scored at 19:12; Sami Kapanen scored at 19:56. Final score: World 8, North America 5.
4:19 — 1992 at Philadelphia — Campbell — Brian Bellows scored at 7:40 of second period; Jeremy Roenick scored at 8:13; Theoren Fleury scored at 11:06; Brett Hull scored at 11:59. Final score: Campbell 10, Wales 6.
4:26 — 1980 at Detroit — Wales — Ron Stackhouse scored at 11:40 of third period; Craig Hartsburg scored at 12:40; Reed Larson scored at 13:12; Real Cloutier scored at 16:06. Final score: Wales 6, Campbell 3.

MOST GOALS, BOTH TEAMS, ONE PERIOD:
10 — 1997 at San Jose — Second period — East (6), West (4).
Final score: East 11, West 7.
— 2001 at Colorado — Second period — North America (6), World (4).
Final score: North America 14, World 12.
— 2001 at Colorado — Third period — North America (5), World (5).
Final score: North America 14, World 12.
9 — 1990 at Pittsburgh — First period — Wales (7), Campbell (2).
Final score: Wales 12, Campbell 7.

MOST GOALS, ONE TEAM, ONE PERIOD:
7 — 1990 at Pittsburgh — First period — Wales. Final score: Wales 12, Campbell 7.
6 — 1983 at NY Islanders — Third period — Campbell.
Final score: Campbell 9, Wales 3.
 — 1992 at Philadelphia — Second period — Campbell.
Final score: Campbell 10, Wales 6.
 — 1993 at Montreal — First period — Wales.
Final score: Wales 16, Campbell 6.
 — 1993 at Montreal — Second period — Wales.
Final score: Wales 16, Campbell 6.
 — 1997 at San Jose — Second period — East.
Final score: East 11, West 7.
 — 2001 at Colorado — Second period — North America.
Final score: North America 14, World 12.

MOST SHOTS, BOTH TEAMS, ONE PERIOD:
39 — 1994 at NY Rangers — Second period — West (21), East (18).
Final score: East 9, West 8.
 — 2001 at Colorado — Third period — World (23), North America (16).
Final score: North America 14, World 12.
36 — 1990 at Pittsburgh — Third period — Campbell (22), Wales (14).
Final score: Wales 12, Campbell 7.
 — 1994 at NY Rangers — First period — East (19), West (17).
Final score: East 9, West 8.
 — 2002 at Los Angeles — Third period — North America (20), World (16).
Final score: World 8, North America 5.

MOST SHOTS, ONE TEAM, ONE PERIOD:
23 — 2001 at Colorado — Third period — World.
Final score: North America 14, World 12.
22 — 1990 at Pittsburgh — Third period — Campbell.
Final score: Wales 12, Campbell 7.
 — 1991 at Chicago — Third period — Wales.
Final score: Campbell 11, Wales 5.
 — 1993 at Montreal — First period — Wales.
Final score: Wales 16, Campbell 6.

FEWEST SHOTS, BOTH TEAMS, ONE PERIOD:
9 — 1971 at Boston — Third period — East (2), West (7).
Final score: West 2, East 1.
 — 1980 at Detroit — Second period — Campbell (4), Wales (5).
Final score: Wales 6, Campbell 3.
13 — 1982 at Washington — Third period — Campbell (6), Wales (7).
Final score: Wales 4, Campbell 2.
14 — 1978 at Buffalo — First period — Campbell (7), Wales (7).
Final score: Wales 3, Campbell 2.
 — 1986 at Hartford — First period — Campbell (6), Wales (8).
Final score: Wales 4, Campbell 3.

FEWEST SHOTS, ONE TEAM, ONE PERIOD:
2 — 1971 at Boston — Third period — East.
Final score: West 2, East 1.
 — 1978 at Buffalo — Second period — Campbell.
Final score: Wales 3, Campbell 2.
3 — 1978 at Buffalo — Third period — Campbell.
Final score: Wales 3, Campbell 2.
4 — 1955 at Detroit — First period — NHL All-Stars.
Final score: Detroit Red Wings 3, NHL All-Stars 1.
 — 1980 at Detroit — Second period — Campbell.
Final score: Wales 6, Campbell 3.

INDIVIDUAL RECORDS

Games

MOST GAMES PLAYED:
23 — **Gordie Howe** from 1948 through 1980
19 — Raymond Bourque from 1981 through 2001
18 — Wayne Gretzky from 1980 through 1999
15 — Frank Mahovlich from 1959 through 1974
 — Mark Messier from 1982 through 2004

Goals

MOST GOALS (CAREER):
13 — **Wayne Gretzky** in 18GP
 — **Mario Lemieux** in 10GP
10 — Gordie Howe in 23GP
 8 — Frank Mahovlich in 15GP
 — Luc Robitaille in 8GP
 — Teemu Selanne in 9GP

MOST GOALS, ONE GAME:
 4 — **Wayne Gretzky,** Campbell, 1983
 — **Mario Lemieux,** Wales, 1990
 — **Vince Damphousse,** Campbell, 1991
 — **Mike Gartner,** Wales, 1993
 — **Dany Heatley,** East, 2003
 3 — Ted Lindsay, Detroit, 1950
 — Mario Lemieux, Wales, 1988
 — Pierre Turgeon, Wales, 1993
 — Mark Recchi, East, 1997
 — Owen Nolan, West, 1997
 — Teemu Selanne, World, 1998
 — Pavel Bure, World, 2000
 — Bill Guerin, North America, 2001
 — Joe Sakic, West, 2004

MOST GOALS, ONE PERIOD:
 4 — **Wayne Gretzky,** Campbell, Third period, 1983
 3 — Mario Lemieux, Wales, First period, 1990
 — Vince Damphousse, Campbell, Third period, 1991
 — Mike Gartner, Wales, First period, 1993

Assists

MOST ASSISTS (CAREER):
14 — **Mark Messier** in 15GP
13 — Raymond Bourque in 19GP
12 — Adam Oates in 5GP
 — Mats Sundin in 8GP
 — Joe Sakic in 11GP
 — Wayne Gretzky in 18GP

MOST ASSISTS, ONE GAME:
 5 — **Mats Naslund,** Wales, 1988
 4 — Raymond Bourque, Wales, 1985
 — Adam Oates, Campbell, 1991
 — Adam Oates, Wales, 1993
 — Mark Recchi, Wales, 1993
 — Pierre Turgeon, East, 1994
 — Fredrik Modin, World, 2001

MOST ASSISTS, ONE PERIOD:
 4 — **Adam Oates,** Wales, First period, 1993
 3 — Mark Messier, Campbell, Third period, 1983

Joe Sakic looks on as Theo Fleury and Paul Kariya celebrate after Kariya set up Fleury just 49 seconds into the 2001 All-Star Game. The 26 goals scored that year are the most ever in an All-Star Game.

Points

MOST POINTS, CAREER:
25 — Wayne Gretzky (13G-12A in 18GP)
23 — Mario Lemieux (13G-10A in 10GP)
20 — Mark Messier (6G-14A in 15GP)
19 — Gordie Howe (10G-9A in 23GP)
18 — Joe Sakic (6G-12A in 11GP)

MOST POINTS, ONE GAME:
 6 — Mario Lemieux, Wales, 1988 (3G-3A)
 5 — Mats Naslund, Wales, 1988 (5A)
  — Adam Oates, Campbell, 1991 (1G-4A)
  — Mike Gartner, Wales, 1993 (4G-1A)
  — Mark Recchi, Wales, 1993 (1G-4A)
  — Pierre Turgeon, Wales, 1993 (3G-2A)
  — Bill Guerin, North America, 2001 (3G-2A)
  — Dany Heatley, East, 2003 (4G-1A)

MOST POINTS, ONE PERIOD:
 4 — Wayne Gretzky, Campbell, Third period, 1983 (4G)
  — **Mike Gartner,** Wales, First period, 1993 (3G-1A)
  — **Adam Oates,** Wales, First period, 1993 (4A)
 3 — Gordie Howe, NHL All-Stars, Second period, 1965 (1G-2A)
  — Pete Mahovlich, Wales, First period, 1976 (1G-2A)
  — Mark Messier, Campbell, Third period, 1983 (3A)
  — Mario Lemieux, Wales, Second period, 1988 (1G-2A)
  — Mario Lemieux, Wales, First period, 1990 (3G)
  — Vince Damphousse, Campbell, Third period, 1991 (3G)
  — Mark Recchi, Wales, Second period, 1993 (1G-2A)
  — Tony Amonte, North America, Second period, 2001 (2G-1A)
  — Daniel Alfredsson, East, Second period, 2004 (2G-1A)

Power-Play Goals

MOST POWER-PLAY GOALS, CAREER:
 6 — Gordie Howe in 23GP
 3 — Bobby Hull in 12GP
  — Maurice Richard in 13GP

Fastest Goals

FASTEST GOAL FROM START OF GAME:
0:19 — Ted Lindsay, Detroit, 1950
0:20 — Jacques Laperriere, East, 1970
0:21 — Mario Lemieux, Wales, 1990
0:35 — Vincent Damphousse, North America, 2002
0:36 — Chico Maki, West, 1971

FASTEST GOAL FROM START OF A PERIOD:
0:17 — Raymond Bourque, North America, 1999 (second period)
0:19 — Ted Lindsay, Detroit, 1950 (first period)
  — Rick Tocchet, Wales, 1993 (second period)
0:20 — Jacques Laperriere, East, 1970 (first period)
0:21 — Mario Lemieux, Wales, 1990 (first period)
0:26 — Wayne Gretzky, Campbell, 1982 (second period)

FASTEST TWO GOALS (ONE PLAYER) FROM START OF GAME:
3:37 — Mike Gartner, Wales, 1993, at 3:15 and 3:37.
4:00 — Teemu Selanne, World, 1998, at 0:53 and 4:00
5:25 — Wally Hergesheimer,. NHL All-Stars, 1953, at 4:06 and 5:25.

FASTEST TWO GOALS (ONE PLAYER) FROM START OF A PERIOD:
3:37 — Mike Gartner, Wales, 1993, at 3:15 and 3:37 of first period.
4:00 — Teemu Selanne, World, 1998, at 0:53 and 4:00 of first period.
4:43 — Dennis Ververgaert, Campbell, 1976, at 4:33 and 4:43 of third period.

FASTEST TWO GOALS (ONE PLAYER):
0:08 — Owen Nolan, West, 1997. Scored at 18:54 and 19:02 of second period.
0:10 — Dennis Ververgaert, Campbell, 1976. Scored at 4:33 and 4:43 of third period.
0:22 — Mike Gartner, Wales, 1993. Scored at 3:15 and 3:37 of first period.

Penalties

MOST PENALTY MINUTES:
25 — Gordie Howe in 23GP
21 — Gus Mortson in 9GP
16 — Harry Howell in 7GP

Goaltenders

MOST GAMES PLAYED:
13 — Glenn Hall from 1955 through 1969
11 — Terry Sawchuk from 1950 through 1968
  — Patrick Roy from 1988 through 2003
 8 — Jacques Plante from 1956 through 1970
  — Martin Brodeur from 1996 through 2004

MOST MINUTES PLAYED:
540 — Glenn Hall in 13GP
467 — Terry Sawchuk in 11GP
370 — Jacques Plante in 8GP
230 — Patrick Roy in 11GP
209 — Turk Broda in 4GP

MOST GOALS AGAINST:
29 — Patrick Roy in 11GP
22 — Glenn Hall in 13GP
21 — Mike Vernon in 5GP
19 — Terry Sawchuk in 11GP
18 — Jacques Plante in 8GP
  — Andy Moog in 4GP

BEST GOALS-AGAINST-AVERAGE AMONG THOSE WITH AT LEAST TWO GAMES PLAYED:
0.68 — Gilles Villemure in 3GP
1.49 — Gerry McNeil in 3GP
1.50 — Johnny Bower in 4GP
1.51 — Frank Brimsek in 3GP
1.64 — Gump Worsley in 4GP

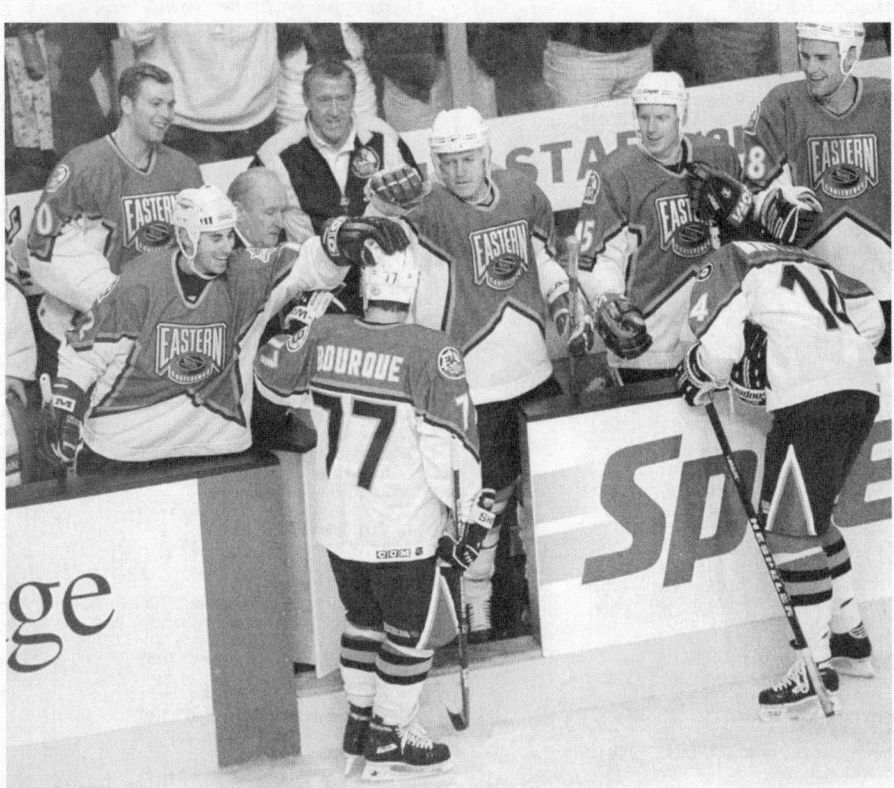

Raymond Bourque is seen here accepting congratulations for a goal scored in the 1996 All-Star Game. At the 1999 Game, his goal 17 seconds into the second period set a new All-Star record.

Hockey Hall of Fame

(Year of induction is listed after each Honoured Members name)

Location: BCE Place, at the corner of Front and Yonge Streets in the heart of downtown Toronto. Easy access from all major highways running into Toronto. Close to TTC and Union Station.

Telephone: administration (416) 360-7735; information (416) 360-7765.

Public Hours of Operation: Open every day except Christmas Day, New Year's Day and Induction Day (November 8, 2004). Please call our information number (above) or visit our website (below) for times.

The Hockey Hall of Fame can be booked for private functions after hours.

Website address: www.hhof.com

History: The Hockey Hall of Fame was established in 1943. Members were first honoured in 1945. On August 26, 1961, the Hockey Hall of Fame opened its doors to the public in a building located on the grounds of the Canadian National Exhibition in Toronto. The Hockey Hall of Fame relocated to its new site at BCE Place and welcomed the hockey world on June 18, 1993.

Honour Roll: There are 339 Honoured Members in the Hockey Hall of Fame. 232 have been inducted as players, 93 as builders and 14 as Referees/Linesmen. In addition, there are 74 media honourees.

Founding/Premiere Sponsors: IBM Canada, Imperial Oil, International Ice Hockey Federation, Kodak Canada, MCI Canada, Molson Canada, National Hockey League, National Hockey League Players' Association, Panasonic Canada, Pepsi-Cola Canada, Sun Media (Toronto)/The Toronto Sun, The Sports Network (TSN/RDS).

Cam Neely enters the Hockey Hall of Fame this year with Soviet legend Valeri Kharlamov and builder Murray Costello. Neely reached the 50-goal plateau three times in his career, including scoring 50 goals in just 49 games in 1993-94.

PLAYERS

* Abel, Sidney Gerald 1969
* Adams, John James "Jack" 1959
* Apps, Charles Joseph Sylvanus "Syl" 1961
  Armstrong, George Edward 1975
* Bailey, Irvine Wallace "Ace" 1975
* Bain, Donald H. "Dan" 1945
* Baker, Hobart "Hobey" 1945
  Barber, William Charles "Bill" 1990
* Barry, Martin J. "Marty" 1965
  Bathgate, Andrew James "Andy" 1978
* Bauer, Robert Theodore "Bobby" 1996
  Béliveau, Jean Arthur 1972
* Benedict, Clinton S. 1965
* Bentley, Douglas Wagner 1964
* Bentley, Maxwell H. L. 1966
* Blake, Hector "Toe" 1966
  Boivin, Leo Joseph 1986
* Boon, Richard R. "Dickie" 1952
  Bossy, Michael 1991
  Bouchard, Emile Joseph "Butch" 1966
* Boucher, Frank 1958
* Boucher, Georges "Buck" 1960
  Bourque, Raymond 2004
  Bower, John William 1976
* Bowie, Russell 1945
* Brimsek, Francis Charles 1966
* Broadbent, Harry L. "Punch" 1962
* Broda, Walter Edward "Turk" 1967
  Bucyk, John Paul 1981
* Burch, Billy 1974
* Cameron, Harold Hugh "Harry" 1962
  Cheevers, Gerald Michael "Gerry" 1985
* Clancy, Francis Michael "King" 1958
* Clapper, Aubrey "Dit" 1947
  Clarke, Robert "Bobby" 1987
* Cleghorn, Sprague 1958
  Coffey, Paul 2004
* Colville, Neil MacNeil 1967
* Conacher, Charles W. 1961
* Conacher, Lionel Pretoria 1994
* Conacher, Roy Gordon 1998
* Connell, Alex 1958
* Cook, Fred "Bun" 1995
* Cook, William Osser 1952
* Coulter, Arthur Edmund 1974
  Cournoyer, Yvan Serge 1982
* Cowley, William Mailes 1968
* Crawford, Samuel Russell "Rusty" 1962
* Darragh, John Proctor "Jack" 1962
* Davidson, Allan M. "Scotty" 1950
* Day, Clarence Henry "Hap" 1961
  Delvecchio, Alex 1977
* Denneny, Cyril "Cy" 1959
  Dionne, Marcel 1992
* Drillon, Gordon Arthur 1975

* Drinkwater, Charles Graham 1950
  Dryden, Kenneth Wayne 1983
* Dumart, Woodrow "Woody" 1992
* Dunderdale, Thomas 1974
* Durnan, William Ronald 1964
* Dutton, Mervyn A. "Red" 1958
* Dye, Cecil Henry "Babe" 1970
  Esposito, Anthony James "Tony" 1988
  Esposito, Philip Anthony 1984
* Farrell, Arthur F. 1965
  Federko, Bernie 2002
  Fetisov, Viacheslav 2001
* Flaman, Ferdinand Charles "Fern" 1990
* Foyston, Frank 1958
* Fredrickson, Frank 1958
  Fuhr, Grant 2003
  Gadsby, William Alexander 1970
  Gainey, Bob 1992
* Gardiner, Charles Robert "Chuck" 1945
* Gardiner, Herbert Martin "Herb" 1958
* Gardner, James Henry "Jimmy" 1962
  Gartner, Michael Alfred 2001
  Geoffrion, Jos. A. Bernard "Boom Boom" 1972
* Gerard, Eddie 1945
  Giacomin, Edward "Eddie" 1987
  Gilbert, Rodrigue Gabriel "Rod" 1982
  Gillies, Clark 2002
* Gilmour, Hamilton Livingstone "Billy" 1962
* Goheen, Frank Xavier "Moose" 1952
* Goodfellow, Ebenezer R. "Ebbie" 1963
  Goulet, Michel 1998
* Grant, Michael "Mike" 1950
* Green, Wilfred "Shorty" 1962
  Gretzky, Wayne Douglas 1999
* Griffis, Silas Seth "Si" 1950
* Hainsworth, George 1961
  Hall, Glenn Henry 1975
* Hall, Joseph Henry 1961
* Harvey, Douglas Norman 1973
  Hawerchuk, Dale Martin 2001
* Hay, George 1958
* Hern, William Milton "Riley" 1962
* Hextall, Bryan Aldwyn 1969
* Holmes, Harry "Hap" 1972
* Hooper, Charles Thomas "Tom" 1962
* Horner, George Reginald "Red" 1965
* Horton, Miles Gilbert "Tim" 1977
  Howe, Gordon 1972
* Howe, Sydney Harris 1965
  Howell, Henry Vernon "Harry" 1979
  Hull, Robert Marvin 1983
* Hutton, John Bower "Bouse" 1962
* Hyland, Harry M. 1962
* Irvin, James Dickenson "Dick" 1958
* Jackson, Harvey "Busher" 1971

* Johnson, Ernest "Moose" 1952
* Johnson, Ivan "Ching" 1958
  Johnson, Thomas Christian 1970
* Joliat, Aurel 1947
* Keats, Gordon "Duke" 1958
  Kelly, Leonard Patrick "Red" 1969
  Kennedy, Theodore Samuel "Teeder" 1966
  Keon, David Michael 1986
* Kharlamov, Valeri 2005
  Kurri, Jari 2001
  Lach, Elmer James 1966
  Lafleur, Guy Damien 1988
  LaFontaine, Pat 2003
* Lalonde, Edouard Charles "Newsy" 1950
  Langway, Rod Corry 2002
  Laperriere, Jacques 1987
  Lapointe, Guy 1993
  Laprade, Edgar 1993
* Laviolette, Jean Baptiste "Jack" 1962
* Lehman, Hugh 1958
  Lemaire, Jacques Gerard 1984
  Lemieux, Mario 1997
* LeSueur, Percy 1961
* Lewis, Herbert A. 1989
  Lindsay, Robert Blake Theodore "Ted" 1966
* Lumley, Harry 1980
* MacKay, Duncan "Mickey" 1952
  Mahovlich, Frank William 1981
* Malone, Joseph "Joe" 1950
* Mantha, Sylvio 1960
* Marshall, John "Jack" 1965
* Maxwell, Fred G. "Steamer" 1962
  McDonald, Lanny 1992
* McGee, Frank 1945
* McGimsie, William George "Billy" 1962
* McNamara, George 1958
  Mikita, Stanley 1983
  Moore, Richard Winston "Dickie" 1974
* Moran, Patrick Joseph "Paddy" 1958
* Morenz, Howie 1945
* Mosienko, William "Billy" 1965
  Mullen, Joseph P. 2000
  Murphy, Larry 2004
  Neely, Cam 2005
* Nighbor, Frank 1947
* Noble, Edward Reginald "Reg" 1962
* O'Connor, Herbert William "Buddy" 1988
* Oliver, Harry 1967
  Olmstead, Murray Bert "Bert" 1985
  Orr, Robert Gordon 1979
  Parent, Bernard Marcel 1984
  Park, Douglas Bradford "Brad" 1988
* Patrick, Joseph Lynn 1980
* Patrick, Lester 1947
  Perreault, Gilbert 1990

* Phillips, Tommy 1945
Pilote, Joseph Albert Pierre Paul 1975
* Pitre, Didier "Pit" 1962
* Plante, Joseph Jacques Omer 1978
Potvin, Denis 1991
* Pratt, Walter "Babe" 1966
* Primeau, A. Joseph 1963
Pronovost, Joseph René Marcel 1978
Pulford, Bob 1991
* Pulford, Harvey 1945
* Quackenbush, Hubert George "Bill" 1976
* Rankin, Frank 1961
Ratelle, Joseph Gilbert Yvan Jean "Jean" 1985
* Rayner, Claude Earl "Chuck" 1973
Reardon, Kenneth Joseph 1966
Richard, Joseph Henri 1979
* Richard, Joseph Henri Maurice "Rocket" 1961
* Richardson, George Taylor 1950
* Roberts, Gordon 1971
Robinson, Larry 1995
* Ross, Arthur Howie 1945
* Russel, Blair 1965
* Russell, Ernest 1965
* Ruttan, J.D. "Jack" 1962
Salming, Borje Anders 1996
Savard, Denis Joseph 2000
Savard, Serge 1986
* Sawchuk, Terrance Gordon "Terry" 1971
* Scanlan, Fred 1965
Schmidt, Milton Conrad "Milt" 1961
* Schriner, David "Sweeney" 1962
* Seibert, Earl Walter 1963
* Seibert, Oliver Levi 1961
* Shore, Edward W. "Eddie" 1947
Shutt, Stephen 1993
* Siebert, Albert C. "Babe" 1964
* Simpson, Harold Edward "Bullet Joe" 1962
Sittler, Darryl Glen 1989
* Smith, Alfred E. 1962
Smith, Clint 1991
* Smith, Reginald "Hooley" 1972
* Smith, Thomas James 1973
Smith, William John "Billy" 1993
Stanley, Allan Herbert 1981
* Stanley, Russell "Barney" 1962
Stastny, Peter 1998
* Stewart, John Sherratt "Black Jack" 1964
* Stewart, Nelson "Nels" 1962
* Stuart, Bruce 1961
* Stuart, Hod 1945
* Taylor, Frederick "Cyclone" (O.B.E.) 1947
* Thompson, Cecil R. "Tiny" 1959
Tretiak, Vladislav 1989
* Trihey, Col. Harry J. 1950
Trottier, Bryan 1997
Ullman, Norman V. Alexander "Norm" 1982
* Vezina, Georges 1945
* Walker, John Phillip "Jack" 1960
* Walsh, Martin "Marty" 1962
* Watson, Harry E. 1962
Watson, Harry 1994
* Weiland, Ralph "Cooney" 1971
* Westwick, Harry 1962
* Whitcroft, Fred 1962
* Wilson, Gordon Allan "Phat" 1962
Worsley, Lorne John "Gump" 1980
* Worters, Roy 1969

BUILDERS

* Adams, Charles 1960
* Adams, Weston W. 1972
* Ahearn, Thomas Franklin "Frank" 1962
* Ahearne, John Francis "Bunny" 1977
* Allan, Sir Montagu (C.V.O.) 1945
Allen, Keith 1992
Arbour, Alger Joseph "Al" 1996
* Ballard, Harold Edwin 1977
* Bauer, Father David 1989
* Bickell, John Paris 1978
Bowman, Scotty 1991
* Brown, George V. 1961
* Brown, Walter A. 1962
* Buckland, Frank 1975
Bush, Walter Sr. 2000
Butterfield, Jack Arlington 1980
* Calder, Frank 1947
* Campbell, Angus D. 1964
* Campbell, Clarence Sutherland 1966
* Cattarinich, Joseph 1977

Costello, Murray 2005
* Dandurand, Joseph Viateur "Leo" 1963
* Dilio, Francis Paul 1964
* Dudley, George S. 1958
* Dunn, James A. 1968
Fletcher, Cliff 2004
Francis, Emile 1982
* Gibson, Dr. John L. "Jack" 1976
* Gorman, Thomas Patrick "Tommy" 1963
* Griffiths, Frank A. 1993
* Hanley, William 1986
* Hay, Charles 1974
* Hendy, James C. 1968
* Hewitt, Foster 1965
* Hewitt, William Abraham 1947
* Hume, Fred J. 1962
Illitch, Mike 2003
* Imlach, George "Punch" 1984
* Ivan, Thomas N. 1974
* Jennings, William M. 1975
* Johnson, Bob 1992
* Juckes, Gordon W. 1979
* Kilpatrick, Gen. John Reed 1960
Kilrea, Brian Blair 2003
* Knox, Seymour H. III 1993
* Leader, George Alfred 1969
* LeBel, Robert 1970
* Lockhart, Thomas F. 1965
* Loicq, Paul 1961
* Mariucci, John 1985
* Mathers, Frank 1992
* McLaughlin, Major Frederic 1963
* Milford, John "Jake" 1984
* Molson, Hon. Hartland de Montarville 1973
Morrison, Ian "Scotty" 1999
* Murray, Monsignor Athol 1998
* Neilson, Roger 2002
* Nelson, Francis 1947
* Norris, Bruce A. 1969
* Norris, Sr., James 1958
* Norris, James Dougan 1962
* Northey, William M. 1947
* O'Brien, John Ambrose 1962
O'Neill, Brian 1994
* Page, Fred 1993
Patrick, Craig 2001
* Patrick, Frank 1958
* Pickard, Allan W. 1958
* Pilous, Rudy 1985
* Poile, Norman "Bud" 1990
Pollock, Samuel Patterson Smyth 1978
* Raymond, Sen. Donat 1958
* Robertson, John Ross 1947
* Robinson, Claude C. 1947
* Ross, Philip D. 1976
* Sabetzki, Dr. Gunther 1995
Sather, Glen 1997
* Selke, Frank J. 1960
Sinden, Harry James 1983
* Smith, Frank D. 1962
* Smythe, Conn 1958
Snider, Edward M. 1988
* Stanley of Preston, Lord (G.C.B.) 1945
* Sutherland, Cap. James T. 1947
* Tarasov, Anatoli V. 1974
Torrey, Bill 1995
* Turner, Lloyd 1958
* Tutt, William Thayer 1978
* Voss, Carl Potter 1974
* Waghorne, Fred 1961
* Wirtz, Arthur Michael 1971
Wirtz, William W. "Bill" 1976
Ziegler, John A. Jr. 1987

REFEREES/LINESMEN

Armstrong, Neil 1991
Ashley, John George 1981
Chadwick, William L. 1964
* D'Amico, John 1993
* Elliott, Chaucer 1961
* Hayes, George William 1988
* Hewitson, Robert W. 1963
* Ion, Fred J. "Mickey" 1961
Pavelich, Matt 1987
* Rodden, Michael J. "Mike" 1962
* Smeaton, J. Cooper 1961
Storey, Roy Alvin "Red" 1967
Udvari, Frank Joseph 1973
Van Hellemond, Andy 1999

Elmer Ferguson Memorial Award Winners

In recognition of distinguished members of the newspaper profession whose words have brought honor to journalism and to hockey. Selected by the Professional Hockey Writers' Association.

* Barton, Charlie, Buffalo-Courier Express 1985
* Beauchamp, Jacques, Montreal Matin/Journal de Montréal 1984
* Brennan, Bill, Detroit News 1987
* Burchard, Jim, New York World Telegram 1984
* Burnett, Red, Toronto Star 1984
* Carroll, Dink, Montreal Gazette 1984
* Coleman, Jim, Southam Newspapers 1984
Conway, Russ, Eagle-Tribune 1999
* Damata, Ted, Chicago Tribune 1984
Delano, Hugh, New York Post 1991
Desjardins, Marcel, Montréal La Presse 1984
Duhatschek, Eric, Calgary Herald/Globe and Mail 2001
* Dulmage, Jack, Windsor Star 1984
Dunnell, Milt, Toronto Star 1984
Dupont, Kevin Paul, Boston Globe 2002
Elliott, Helene, Los Angeles Times 2005
Farber, Michael, Montreal Gazette/Sports Illustrated 2003
* Ferguson, Elmer, Montreal Herald/Star 1984
* Fitzgerald, Tom, Boston Globe 1984
Frayne, Trent, Toronto Telegram/Globe and Mail/Sun 1984
Gatecliff, Jack, St. Catherines Standard 1995
Gross, George, Toronto Telegram/Sun 1985
Johnston, Dick, Buffalo News 1986
Kelley, Jim, Buffalo News 2004
* Laney, Al, New York Herald-Tribune 1984
* Larochelle, Claude, Le Soleil 1989
L'Esperance, Zotique, Journal de Montréal/le Petit Journal 1985
* MacLeod, Rex, Toronto Globe and Mail/Star 1987
Matheson, Jim, Edmonton Journal 2000
* Mayer, Charles, Journal de Montréal/la Patrie 1985
* McKenzie, Ken, The Hockey News 1997
Monahan, Leo, Boston Daily Record/Record-American/Herald American 1986
Moriarty, Tim, UPI/Newsday 1986
Nichols, Joe, New York Times 1984
* O'Brien, Andy, Weekend Magazine 1985
Orr, Frank, Toronto Star 1989
Olan, Ben, New York Associated Press 1987
* O'Meara, Basil, Montreal Star 1984
Pedneault, Yvon, La Presse/Journal de Montréal 1998
* Proudfoot, Jim, Toronto Star 1988
Raymond, Bertrand, Journal de Montréal 1990
Rosa, Fran, Boston Globe 1987
Strachan, Al, Globe and Mail/Toronto Sun 1993
* Vipond, Jim, Toronto Globe and Mail 1984
Walter, Lewis, Detroit Times 1984
* Young, Scott, Toronto Globe and Mail/Telegram 1988

Foster Hewitt Memorial Award Winners

In recognition of members of the radio and television industry who made outstanding contributions to their profession and the game during their career in hockey broadcasting. Selected by the NHL Broadcasters' Association.

Cole, Bob, Hockey Night in Canada 1996
Cusick, Fred, Boston 1984
* Darling, Ted, Buffalo 1994
* Gallivan, Danny, Montreal 1984
Garneau, Richard, Montreal 1999
* Hart, Gene, Philadelphia 1997
* Hewitt, Foster, Toronto 1984
Irvin, Dick, Montreal 1988
Kaiton, Chuck, Hartford/Carolina 2004
* Kelly, Dan, St. Louis 1989
Lange, Mike, Pittsburgh 2001
* Lecavelier, René, Montreal 1984
Lynch, Budd, Detroit 1985
Martyn, Bruce, Detroit 1991
McDonald, Jiggs, Los Angeles, Atlanta, NY Islanders 1990
McFarlane, Brian, Hockey Night in Canada 1995
* McKnight, Wes, Toronto 1986
Meeker, Howie, Hockey Night in Canada 1998
Messina, Sal, New York 2005
Miller, Bob, Los Angeles 2000
Pettit, Lloyd, Chicago 1986
Phillips, Rod, Edmonton 2003
Robson, Jim, Vancouver 1992
Shaver, Al, Minnesota 1993
* Smith, Doug, Montreal 1985
Tremblay, Gilles, La Soirée du Hockey 2002
Wilson, Bob, Boston 1987

* Deceased

6th Annual Hockey Hall of Fame Game
Saturday, November 5, 2005
Tampa Bay Lightning vs. Toronto Maple Leafs
at Air Canada Centre in Toronto.

United States Hockey Hall of Fame

The United States Hockey Hall of Fame was opened on June 21, 1973 as the national shrine of American Hockey. It is dedicated to honoring the sport of ice hockey in the United States by preserving those precious memories and legends of the game. It is located in Eveleth, Minnesota, 60 miles north of Duluth on Highway 53. The facility is open Monday to Saturday, 9 a.m. to 5 p.m. and Sundays from 10 a.m. to 3 p.m. Admission is $8.00 for adults, $7.00 for seniors and youths (13-17) and $6.00 for children (6-12). Children under 6 are free. Call for any further information: 1-800-443-7825 or 218-744-5167. Web site address: www.ushockeyhall.com

There are now 123 enshrined members consisting of 75 players, 24 coaches, 20 administrators, one player/administrator, one referee and two teams. New members are inducted annually in the fall and must have made a significant contribution towards hockey in the United States during the course of their career. A special Wayne Gretzky Award pays tribute to international individuals who have made major contributions to hockey in the USA. Support for the Hall of Fame comes from sponsorships, admissions, gift store sales, special events and grants from the hockey community and government agencies.

PLAYERS

* Abel, Clarence "Taffy" 1973
* Baker, Hobart "Hobey" 1973
* Bartholome, Earl 1977
* Bessone, Peter 1978
  Blake, Robert 1985
  Boucha, Henry 1995
* Brimsek, Frank 1973
  Broten, Neal 2000
  Cavanagh, Joe 1994
* Chaisson, Ray 1974
* Chase, John P. 1973
  Christian, Dave 2001
  Christian, Roger 1989
  Christian, William "Bill" 1984
  Cleary, Robert 1981
  Cleary, William 1976
* Conroy, Anthony 1975
  Coppo, Paul, 2004
  Curran, Mike 1998
* Dahlstrom, Carl "Cully" 1973
* Desjardins, Victor 1974
* Desmond, Richard 1988
* Dill, Robert 1979
  Dougherty, Richard "Dick"
* Everett, Doug 1974
  Fusco, Mark 2002
  Fusco, Scott 2002
  Ftorek, Robbie 1991
* Garrison, John B. 1973
  Garrity, Jack 1986
* Goheen, Frank "Moose" 1973
  Grant, Wally 1994
* Harding, Austin "Austie" 1975
  Housley, Phil 2004
  Howe, Mark 2003
* Iglehart, Stewart 1975
  Johnson, Mark 2004
  Johnson, Paul 2001
* Johnson, Virgil 1974
* Karakas, Mike 1973
  Kirrane, Jack 1987
  Lafontaine, Pat 2003
* Lane, Myles J. 1973
  Langevin, David R. 1993
  Langway, Rod 1999
  Larson, Reed 1996
* Linder, Joseph 1975
* LoPresti, Sam L. 1973
* Mariucci, John 1973
  Matchefts, John 1991
* Mather, Bruce 1998
  Mayasich, John 1976
  McCartan, Jack 1983
* Moe, William 1974
  Morrow, Ken 1995
* Moseley, Fred 1975
  Mullen, Joe 1998
* Murray, Sr., Hugh "Muzz" 1987
* Nelson, Hubert "Hub" 1978
* Nyrop, William D. 1997
* Olson , Eddie 1977
* Owen, Jr., George 1973
* Palmer, Winthrop 1973
  Paradise, Robert 1989
* Purpur, Clifford "Fido" 1974
  Ramsey, Mike 2001
*Riley, Joe 2002
  Riley, William 1977
  Roberts, Gordie 1999
* Romnes, Elwin "Doc" 1973
* Rondeau, Richard 1985
  Sheehy, Timothy K. 1997
* Williams, Thomas 1981
* Winters, Frank "Coddy" 1973
* Yackel, Ken 1986

COACHES

* Almquist, Oscar 1983
  Bessone, Amo 1992
  Brooks, Herbert 1990
  Ceglarski, Len 1992
* Cuniff, John
* Fullerton, James 1992
  Gambucci, Sergio 1996
* Gordon, Malcolm K. 1973
  Harkness, Nevin D. "Ned" 1994
  Heyliger, Victor 1974
* Holt, Jr. Charles E. 1997
  Ikola, Willard 1990
* Jeremiah, Edward J. 1973
* Johnson, Bob 1991
* Kelley, John "Snooks" 1974
  Kelley, John H. "Jack" 1993
  Patrick, Craig 1996
* Pleban, Jon "Connie" 1990
  Riley, Jack 1979
* Ross, Larry 1988
* Thompson, Clifford, R. 1973
* Stewart, William 1982
* Winsor, Alfred "Ralph" 1973
  Woog, Doug 2002

ADMINISTRATORS

* Brown, George V. 1973
* Brown, Walter A. 1973
  Bush, Walter 1980
* Clark, Donald 1978
  Claypool, James 1995
* Gibson, J.C. "Doc" 1973
  Ilitch, Mike 2004
* Jennings, William M. 1981
* Kahler, Nick 1980
* Lockhart, Thomas F. 1973
* Marvin, Cal 1982
  Palazzari, Doug 2000
  Pleau, Larry 2000
* Ridder, Robert 1976
* Schulz, Charles M. 1993
  Trumble, Harold 1985
* Tutt, William Thayer 1973
* Watson, Sid 1999
  Wirtz, William W. "Bill" 1984
* Wright, Lyle Z.1973

PLAYER/ADMINISTRATOR

Nanne, Lou 1998

REFEREE

Chadwick, William 1974

TEAMS

1960 Olympic Team, 2000
1980 Olympic Team, 2003

WAYNE GRETZKY INTERNATIONAL AWARD

Wayne Gretzky 1999
The Howe family 2000
Scotty Morrison 2001
Scotty Bowman 2002
Bobby Hull 2003
* Herb Brooks 2004

*Deceased

Frank Brimsek became a charter member of the United States Hockey Hall of Fame in 1973. A star with the Boston Bruins from 1938 to 1949, Brimsek hailed from Eveleth, Minnesota.

International Ice Hockey Federation Hall of Fame

The IIHF Hall of Fame was founded in 1997.

Candidates for election as Honoured Members in the player category shall be chosen on the basis of their playing ability, sportsmanship, character and their contribution to their team or teams and to the game of ice hockey in general.

Candidates for election as Honoured Members in the builder category shall be chosen on the basis of their coaching, managerial or executive ability, where applicable, their sportsmanship and character, and their contribution to their organization or organizations and to the game of ice hockey in general.

Candidates for election as Honoured Members in the referee or linesman category shall be chosen on the basis of their officiating ability, sportsmanship, character and their contribution to the game of ice hockey in general.

Inductees' names are followed by their country and year of induction.

Pictured here in front of 1980 Team USA backup Steve Janaszak during a "pre-Miracle" exhibition game in Madison Square Garden, longtime Soviet captain Boris Mikhailov participated at the Olympics in 1972, 1976 and 1980, the Canada-Russia series in 1972 and 11 World Championships from 1969 to1980.

PLAYERS

Balderis, Helmut, LAT, 1998
Ball, Rudi, GER, 2004
Bergqvist, Sven, SWE, 1999
Bjorn, Lars, SWE, 1998
Bobrov, Vsevolod, RUS, 1997
Bourbonnais, Roger, CAN, 1999
Bubnik, Vlastimil, CzRep, 1997
Cattini, Ferdinand, SUI, 1998
Cattini, Hans, SUI, 1998
Christian, Bill, USA, 1998
Cleary, Bill, USA, 1997
Craig, Jim, USA, 1999
Crosby, Gerry, USA, 1997
Curran, Mike, USA, 1999
Davydov, Vitaly, RUS, 2004
Drobny, Jaroslav, CzRep, 1997
Dzurilla, Vladimir, SVK, 1998
Erhardt, Carl, G.B., 1998
Fetisov, Vyacheslav, RUS, 2005
Firsov, Anatoli, RUS, 1998
Golonka, Josef, SVK, 1998
Gretzky, Wayne, CAN, 2000
Gustafsson, Bengt-Ake, SWE, 2003
Gut, Karel, CzRep, 1998
Hedberg, Anders, SWE, 1997
Hlinka, Ivan, CzRep, 2002
Holecek, Jiri, CzRep, 1998
Holik, Jiri, CzRep, 1999
Holmqvist, Leif, SWE, 1999
Huck, Fran, CAN, 1999
Jaenecke, Gustav, GER, 1998
Johnson, Mark, USA, 1999
Johnston, Marshall, CAN, 1998
Jonsson, Tomas, SWE, 2000
Jutila, Timo, FIN, 2003
Keinonen, Matti, FIN, 2002
Kharlamov, Valeri, RUS, 1998
Kiessling, Udo, GER, 2000
Kuhnhackl, Erich, GER, 1997
Kurri, Jari, FIN, 2000
Kuzkin, Viktor, RUS, 2005
Lacarriere, Jacques, FRA, 1998
Loob, Hakan, SWE, 1998
Lundquist, Vic, CAN, 1997
Machac, Oldrich, CzRep, 1999
MacKenzie, Barry, CAN, 1999

Makarov, Sergei, RUS, 2001
Malecek, Josef, CzRep, 2003
Maltsev, Alexander, RUS, 1999
Marjamaki, Pekka, FIN, 1998
Martin, Seth, CAN, 1997
Martinec, Vladimir, CzRep, 2001
Mayasich, John, USA, 1997
Mayorov, Boris, RUS, 1999
McCartan, Jack, USA, 1998
McLeod, Jackie, CAN, 1999
Mikhailov, Boris, RUS, 2000
Nanne, Lou, USA, 2004
Naslund, Mats, SWE, 2005
Nedomansky, Vaclav, CzRep, 1997
Nilsson, Nisse, SWE, 2002
O'Malley, Terry, CAN, 1998
Oksanen, Lasse, FIN, 1999
Pana, Eduard, ROM, 1998
Patton, Peter, G.B., 2002
Pettersson, Ronald, SWE, 2004
Pospisil, Frantisek, CzRep, 1999
Puschnig, Josef, AUT, 1999
Ragulin, Alexander, RUS, 1997
Rampf, Hans, GER, 2001
Salming, Borje, SWE, 1998
Schloder, Alois, GER, 2005
Sinden, Harry, CAN, 1997
Sologubov, Nikolai, RUS, 2004
Stastny, Peter, SVK, 2000
Sterner, Ulf, SWE, 2001
Stoltz, Roland, SWE, 1999
Tikal, Frantisek, CzRep, 2004
Torriani, Bibi, SUI, 1997
Tretiak, Vladislav, RUS, 1997
Tumba, Sven, SWE, 1997
Valtonen, Jorma, FIN, 1999
Vasiliev, Valeri, RUS, 1998
Watson, Harry, CAN, 1998
Yakushev, Alexander, RUS, 2003
Ylonen, Urpo, FIN, 1997
Zabrodsky, Vladimir, CzRep, 1997
Ziesche, Joachim, GER, 1999

BUILDERS

Ahearne, Bunny, G.B., 1997
Aljancic Sr., Ernest, SLO, 2002
Bauer, Father David, CAN, 1997
Berglund, Curt, SWE, 2003
Brooks, Herb, USA, 1999
Brown, Walter, USA, 1997
Buckna, Mike, CAN, 2004
Calcaterra, Enrico, ITA, 1999
Chernyshev, Arkady, RUS, 1999
Eklow, Rudolf, SWE, 1999
Grunander, Arne, SWE, 1997
Henschel, Heinz, GER, 2003
Hewitt, William, CAN, 1998
Holmes, Derek, CAN, 1999
Horsky, Ladislav, SVK, 2004
Hviid, Jorgen, DEN, 2005
Johannessen, Tore, NOR, 1999
Juckes, Gordon, CAN, 1997
Kawabuchi, Tsutomu, JPN, 2004
King, Dave, CAN, 2001
Kostka, Vladimir, CzRep, 1997
LeBel, Bob, CAN, 1997
Lindblad, Harry, FIN, 1999
Loicq, Paul, BEL, 1997
Luhti, Cesar W., SUI, 1998
Magnus, Louis, FRA, 1997
Pasztor, Gyorgy, HUN, 2001
Renwick, Gordon, CAN, 2002
Ridder, Bob, USA, 1998

Riley, Jack, USA, 1998
Sabetzki, Dr. Gunther, GER, 1997
Starovoitov, Andrei, RUS, 1997
Starsi, Jan, SVK, 1999
Stromberg, Arne, SWE, 1998
Stubb, Goran, FIN, 2000
Subrt, Miroslav, CzRep, 2004
Tarasov, Anatoli, RUS, 1997
Tikhonov, Viktor, RUS, 1998
Trumble, Hal, USA, 1999
Tsutsumi, Yoshiaki, JPN, 1999
Tutt, Thayer, USA, 2002
Unsinn, Xaver, GER, 1998
Wasservogel, Walter, AUT, 1997
Yurzinov, Vladimir, RUS, 2002

REFEREES

Adamec, Quido, CzRep, 2005
Dahlberg, Ove, SWE, 2004
Karandin, Yuri, RUS, 2004
Kompalla, Josef, GER, 2003
Wiitala, Unto, FIN, 2003

Stanley Cup Record Book

History: The Stanley Cup, the oldest trophy competed for by professional athletes in North America, was donated by Frederick Arthur, Lord Stanley of Preston and son of the Earl of Derby, in 1893. Lord Stanley purchased the trophy for 10 guineas ($50 at that time) for presentation to the amateur hockey champions of Canada. Since 1910, when the National Hockey Association took possession of the Stanley Cup, the trophy has been the symbol of professional hockey supremacy. It has been competed for only by NHL teams since 1926-27 and has been under the exclusive control of the NHL since 1947.

Stanley Cup Standings

1918-2005
(ranked by Cup wins)

Teams	Cup Wins	Yrs.	Series	Wins	Losses	Games	Wins	Losses	Ties	Goals For	Goals Against	Winning %
Montreal	23 [1]	74	137 [2]	86	50	661	391	262	8	2033	1658	.598
Toronto	13	64	109	58	51	524	251	269	4	1350	1427	.483
Detroit	10	53	99	56	43	494	257	236	1	1385	1278	.521
Boston	5	62	104	47	57	512	242	264	6	1488	1516	.479
Edmonton	5	19	45	31	14	227	137	90	0	868	702	.604
NY Rangers	4	48	86	42	44	386	183	195	8	1091	1114	.484
NY Islanders	4	20	46	30	16	235	133	102	0	781	697	.566
Chicago	3	53	90	40	50	411	188	218	5	1176	1311	.464
New Jersey [3]	3	16	33	20	13	193	107	86	0	536	463	.554
Philadelphia	2	30	64	36	28	340	178	162	0	1032	989	.524
Pittsburgh	2	21	39	20	19	208	109	99	0	644	641	.524
Colorado [4]	2	18	39	23	16	224	122	102	0	667	620	.545
Dallas [5]	1	26	51	26	25	277	140	137	0	825	838	.505
Calgary [6]	1	22	36	15	21	182	84	98	0	579	626	.462
Tampa Bay	1	3	7	5	2	40	23	17	0	95	98	.575
St. Louis	0	34	57	23	34	303	138	165	0	857	943	.455
Buffalo	0	25	42	17	25	209	99	110	0	626	639	.474
Los Angeles	0	23	34	11	23	170	65	105	0	511	649	.382
Vancouver	0	20	30	10	20	155	66	89	0	452	526	.426
Washington	0	18	28	10	18	154	69	85	0	467	478	.448
Phoenix [7]	0	16	18	2	16	92	29	63	0	245	343	.315
Carolina [8]	0	11	15	4	11	84	35	49	0	208	256	.417
San Jose	0	8	14	6	8	84	39	45	0	213	264	.464
Ottawa [9]	0	8	12	4	8	69	31	38	0	135	149	.449
Florida	0	3	6	3	3	31	13	18	0	77	82	.419
Anaheim	0	3	7	4	3	36	19	17	0	76	87	.528
Minnesota	0	1	3	2	1	18	8	10	0	43	43	.444

[1] Montreal also won the Stanley Cup in 1916.
[2] 1919 final incomplete due to influenza epidemic.
[3] Includes totals of Colorado Rockies 1976-82.
[4] Includes totals of Quebec 1979-95.
[5] Includes totals of Minnesota North Stars 1967-93.
[6] Includes totals of Atlanta Flames 1972-80.
[7] Includes totals of Winnipeg 1979-96.
[8] Includes totals of Hartford 1979-97.
[9] Modern Ottawa franchise only 1992 to date.

Stanley Cup Winners Prior to Formation of NHL in 1917

Season	Champions	Manager	Coach
1916-17	Seattle Metropolitans	Pete Muldoon	Pete Muldoon
1915-16	Montreal Canadiens	George Kennedy	George Kennedy
1914-15	Vancouver Millionaires	Frank Patrick	Frank Patrick
1913-14	Toronto Blueshirts	Jack Marshall	Scotty Davidson*
1912-13**	Quebec Bulldogs	M.J. Quinn	Joe Malone*
1911-12	Quebec Bulldogs	M.J. Quinn	C. Nolan
1910-11	Ottawa Senators		Bruce Stuart*
1909-10	Montreal Wanderers (Mar. 1910)	Dickie Boon	Pud Glass*
1909-10	Ottawa Senators (Jan. 1910)		Bruce Stuart*
1908-09	Ottawa Senators		Bruce Stuart*
1907-08	Montreal Wanderers	Dickie Boon	Cecil Blachford
1906-07	Montreal Wanderers (Mar. 1907)	Dickie Boon	Cecil Blachford
1906-07	Kenora Thistles (Jan./Mar. 1907)	F.A. Hudson	Tom Phillips*
1905-06	Montreal Wanderers (Mar. 1906)	Cecil Blachford*	
1905-06	Ottawa Silver Seven (Feb. 1906)		Alf Smith
1904-05	Ottawa Silver Seven		Alf Smith
1903-04	Ottawa Silver Seven		Alf Smith
1902-03	Ottawa Silver Seven (Mar. 1903)		Alf Smith
1902-03	Montreal A.A.A. (Feb. 1903)		C. McKerrow
1901-02	Montreal A.A.A. (Mar. 1902)		C. McKerrow
1901-02	Winnipeg Victorias (Jan. 1902)		
1900-01	Winnipeg Victorias		Dan Bain*
1899-1900	Montreal Shamrocks		Harry Trihey*
1898-99	Montreal Shamrocks (Mar. 1899)		Harry Trihey*
1898-99	Montreal Victorias (Feb. 1899)		Mike Grant*
1897-98	Montreal Victorias		Frank Richardson
1896-97	Montreal Victorias		Mike Grant*
1895-96	Montreal Victorias (Dec. 1896)		Mike Grant*
1895-96	Winnipeg Victorias (Feb. 1896)		Jack Armitage
1894-95	Montreal Victorias		Mike Grant*
1893-94	Montreal A.A.A.		
1892-93	Montreal A.A.A.		

* In the early years the teams were frequently run by the Captain. *Indicates Captain

Stanley Cup Winners

Year	W-L-T in Finals	Winner	Coach	Finalist	Coach
2005	....	....		....	....
2004	4-3	Tampa Bay	John Tortorella	Calgary	Darryl Sutter
2003	4-3	New Jersey	Pat Burns	Anaheim	Mike Babcock
2002	4-1	Detroit	Scotty Bowman	Carolina	Paul Maurice
2001	4-3	Colorado	Bob Hartley	New Jersey	Larry Robinson
2000	4-2	New Jersey	Larry Robinson	Dallas	Ken Hitchcock
1999	4-2	Dallas	Ken Hitchcock	Buffalo	Lindy Ruff
1998	4-0	Detroit	Scotty Bowman	Washington	Ron Wilson
1997	4-0	Detroit	Scotty Bowman	Philadelphia	Terry Murray
1996	4-0	Colorado	Marc Crawford	Florida	Doug MacLean
1995	4-0	New Jersey	Jacques Lemaire	Detroit	Scotty Bowman
1994	4-3	NY Rangers	Mike Keenan	Vancouver	Pat Quinn
1993	4-1	Montreal	Jacques Demers	Los Angeles	Barry Melrose
1992	4-0	Pittsburgh	Scotty Bowman	Chicago	Mike Keenan
1991	4-2	Pittsburgh	Bob Johnson	Minnesota	Bob Gainey
1990	4-1	Edmonton	John Muckler	Boston	Mike Milbury
1989	4-2	Calgary	Terry Crisp	Montreal	Pat Burns
1988	4-0	Edmonton	Glen Sather	Boston	Terry O'Reilly
1987	4-3	Edmonton	Glen Sather	Philadelphia	Mike Keenan
1986	4-1	Montreal	Jean Perron	Calgary	Bob Johnson
1985	4-1	Edmonton	Glen Sather	Philadelphia	Mike Keenan
1984	4-1	Edmonton	Glen Sather	NY Islanders	Al Arbour
1983	4-0	NY Islanders	Al Arbour	Edmonton	Glen Sather
1982	4-0	NY Islanders	Al Arbour	Vancouver	Roger Neilson
1981	4-1	NY Islanders	Al Arbour	Minnesota	Glen Sonmor
1980	4-2	NY Islanders	Al Arbour	Philadelphia	Pat Quinn
1979	4-1	Montreal	Scotty Bowman	NY Rangers	Fred Shero
1978	4-2	Montreal	Scotty Bowman	Boston	Don Cherry
1977	4-0	Montreal	Scotty Bowman	Boston	Don Cherry
1976	4-0	Montreal	Scotty Bowman	Philadelphia	Fred Shero
1975	4-2	Philadelphia	Fred Shero	Buffalo	Floyd Smith
1974	4-2	Philadelphia	Fred Shero	Boston	Bep Guidolin
1973	4-2	Montreal	Scotty Bowman	Chicago	Billy Reay
1972	4-2	Boston	Tom Johnson	NY Rangers	Emile Francis
1971	4-3	Montreal	Al MacNeil	Chicago	Billy Reay
1970	4-0	Boston	Harry Sinden	St. Louis	Scotty Bowman
1969	4-0	Montreal	Claude Ruel	St. Louis	Scotty Bowman
1968	4-0	Montreal	Toe Blake	St. Louis	Scotty Bowman
1967	4-2	Toronto	Punch Imlach	Montreal	Toe Blake
1966	4-2	Montreal	Toe Blake	Detroit	Sid Abel
1965	4-3	Montreal	Toe Blake	Chicago	Billy Reay
1964	4-3	Toronto	Punch Imlach	Detroit	Sid Abel
1963	4-1	Toronto	Punch Imlach	Detroit	Sid Abel
1962	4-2	Toronto	Punch Imlach	Chicago	Rudy Pilous
1961	4-2	Chicago	Rudy Pilous	Detroit	Sid Abel
1960	4-0	Montreal	Toe Blake	Toronto	Punch Imlach
1959	4-1	Montreal	Toe Blake	Toronto	Punch Imlach
1958	4-2	Montreal	Toe Blake	Boston	Milt Schmidt
1957	4-1	Montreal	Toe Blake	Boston	Milt Schmidt
1956	4-1	Montreal	Toe Blake	Detroit	Jimmy Skinner
1955	4-3	Detroit	Jimmy Skinner	Montreal	Dick Irvin
1954	4-3	Detroit	Tommy Ivan	Montreal	Dick Irvin
1953	4-1	Montreal	Dick Irvin	Boston	Lynn Patrick
1952	4-0	Detroit	Tommy Ivan	Montreal	Dick Irvin
1951	4-1	Toronto	Joe Primeau	Montreal	Dick Irvin
1950	4-3	Detroit	Tommy Ivan	NY Rangers	Lynn Patrick
1949	4-0	Toronto	Hap Day	Detroit	Tommy Ivan
1948	4-0	Toronto	Hap Day	Detroit	Tommy Ivan
1947	4-2	Toronto	Hap Day	Montreal	Dick Irvin
1946	4-1	Montreal	Dick Irvin	Boston	Dit Clapper
1945	4-3	Toronto	Hap Day	Detroit	Jack Adams
1944	4-0	Montreal	Dick Irvin	Chicago	Paul Thompson
1943	4-0	Detroit	Jack Adams	Boston	Art Ross
1942	4-3	Toronto	Hap Day	Detroit	Jack Adams
1941	4-0	Boston	Cooney Weiland	Detroit	Ebbie Goodfellow
1940	4-2	NY Rangers	Frank Boucher	Toronto	Dick Irvin
1939	4-1	Boston	Art Ross	Toronto	Dick Irvin
1938	3-1	Chicago	Bill Stewart	Toronto	Dick Irvin
1937	3-2	Detroit	Jack Adams	NY Rangers	Lester Patrick
1936	3-1	Detroit	Jack Adams	Toronto	Dick Irvin
1935	3-0	Mtl. Maroons	Tommy Gorman	Toronto	Dick Irvin
1934	3-1	Chicago	Tommy Gorman	Detroit	Herbie Lewis
1933	3-1	NY Rangers	Lester Patrick	Toronto	Dick Irvin
1932	3-0	Toronto	Dick Irvin	NY Rangers	Lester Patrick
1931	3-2	Montreal	Cecil Hart	Chicago	Dick Irvin
1930	2-0	Montreal	Cecil Hart	Boston	Art Ross
1929	2-0	Boston	Cy Denneny	NY Rangers	Lester Patrick
1928	3-2	NY Rangers	Lester Patrick	Mtl. Maroons	Eddie Gerard
1927	2-0-2	Ottawa	Dave Gill	Boston	Art Ross
		The National Hockey League assumed control of Stanley Cup competition after 1926			
1926	3-1	Mtl. Maroons	Eddie Gerard	Victoria	Lester Patrick
1925	3-1	Victoria	Lester Patrick	Montreal	Leo Dandurand
1924	2-0	Montreal	Leo Dandurand	Cgy. Tigers	Eddie Oatman
	2-0			Van. Maroons	Art Duncan/Frank Patrick
1923	2-0	Ottawa	Pete Green	Edm. Eskimos	Ken McKenzie
	3-1			Van. Maroons	Lloyd Cook/Frank Patrick
1922	3-2	Tor. St. Pats	George O'Donoghue	Van. Millionaires	Lloyd Cook/Frank Patrick
1921	3-2	Ottawa	Pete Green	Van. Millionaires	Lloyd Cook/Frank Patrick
1920	3-2	Ottawa	Pete Green	Seattle	Pete Muldoon
1919	2-2-1	No decision - series between Montreal and Seattle cancelled due to influenza epidemic			
1918	3-2	Tor. Arenas	Dick Carroll	Van. Millionaires	Frank Patrick

Championship Trophies

PRINCE OF WALES TROPHY

Beginning with the 1993-94 season, the club which advances to the Stanley Cup Finals as the winner of the Eastern Conference Championship is presented with the Prince of Wales Trophy.

History: His Royal Highness, the Prince of Wales, donated the trophy to the National Hockey League in 1924. From 1927-28 through 1937-38, the award was presented to the team finishing first in the American Division of the NHL. (The team finishing first in the Canadian Division received the O'Brien Trophy during these years.) From 1938-39, when the NHL reverted to one section, to 1966-67, it was presented to the team winning the NHL regular-season championship. With expansion in 1967-68, it again became a divisional trophy, awarded to the regular-season champions of the East Division through to the end of the 1973-74 season. Beginning in 1974-75, it was awarded to the regular-season winner of the conference bearing the name of the trophy. From 1981-82 to 1992-93 the trophy was presented to the playoff champion in the Wales Conference. Since 1993-94, the trophy has been presented to the playoff champion in the Eastern Conference.

Prince of Wales Trophy

Stanley Cup

PRINCE OF WALES TROPHY WINNERS

2004-05	....	1963-64	Montreal Canadiens
2003-04	Tampa Bay Lightning	1962-63	Toronto Maple Leafs
2002-03	New Jersey Devils	1961-62	Montreal Canadiens
2001-02	Carolina Hurricanes	1960-61	Montreal Canadiens
2000-01	New Jersey Devils	1959-60	Montreal Canadiens
99-2000	New Jersey Devils	1958-59	Montreal Canadiens
1998-99	Buffalo Sabres	1957-58	Montreal Canadiens
1997-98	Washington Capitals	1956-57	Detroit Red Wings
1996-97	Philadelphia Flyers	1955-56	Montreal Canadiens
1995-96	Florida Panthers	1954-55	Detroit Red Wings
1994-95	New Jersey Devils	1953-54	Detroit Red Wings
1993-94	New York Rangers	1952-53	Detroit Red Wings
1992-93	Montreal Canadiens	1951-52	Detroit Red Wings
1991-92	Pittsburgh Penguins	1950-51	Detroit Red Wings
1990-91	Pittsburgh Penguins	1949-50	Detroit Red Wings
1989-90	Boston Bruins	1948-49	Detroit Red Wings
1988-89	Montreal Canadiens	1947-48	Toronto Maple Leafs
1987-88	Boston Bruins	1946-47	Montreal Canadiens
1986-87	Philadelphia Flyers	1945-46	Montreal Canadiens
1985-86	Montreal Canadiens	1944-45	Montreal Canadiens
1984-85	Philadelphia Flyers	1943-44	Montreal Canadiens
1983-84	New York Islanders	1942-43	Detroit Red Wings
1982-83	New York Islanders	1941-42	New York Rangers
1981-82	New York Islanders	1940-41	Boston Bruins
1980-81	Montreal Canadiens	1939-40	Boston Bruins
1979-80	Buffalo Sabres	1938-39	Boston Bruins
1978-79	Montreal Canadiens	1937-38	Boston Bruins
1977-78	Montreal Canadiens	1936-37	Detroit Red Wings
1976-77	Montreal Canadiens	1935-36	Detroit Red Wings
1975-76	Montreal Canadiens	1934-35	Boston Bruins
1974-75	Buffalo Sabres	1933-34	Detroit Red Wings
1973-74	Boston Bruins	1932-33	Boston Bruins
1972-73	Montreal Canadiens	1931-32	New York Rangers
1971-72	Boston Bruins	1930-31	Boston Bruins
1970-71	Boston Bruins	1929-30	Boston Bruins
1969-70	Chicago Blackhawks	1928-29	Boston Bruins
1968-69	Montreal Canadiens	1927-28	Boston Bruins
1967-68	Montreal Canadiens	1926-27	Ottawa Senators
1966-67	Chicago Blackhawks	1925-26	Montreal Maroons
1965-66	Montreal Canadiens	1924-25	Montreal Canadiens
1964-65	Detroit Red Wings	1923-24	Montreal Canadiens

CLARENCE S. CAMPBELL BOWL

Beginning with the 1993-94 season, the club which advances to the Stanley Cup Finals as the winner of the Western Conference Championship is presented with the Clarence S. Campbell Bowl.

History: Presented by the member clubs in 1968 for perpetual competition by the National Hockey League in recognition of the services of Clarence S. Campbell, President of the NHL from 1946 to 1977. From 1967-68 through 1973-74, the trophy was awarded to the regular-season champions of the West Division. Beginning in 1974-75, it was awarded to the regular-season winner of the conference bearing the name of the trophy. From 1981-82 to 1992-93 the trophy was presented to the playoff champion in the Campbell Conference. Since 1993-94, the trophy has been presented to the playoff champion in the Western Conference. The trophy itself is a hallmark piece made of sterling silver and was crafted by a British silversmith in 1878.

Clarence S. Campbell Bowl

CLARENCE S. CAMPBELL BOWL WINNERS

2004-05	....	1985-86	Calgary Flames
2003-04	Calgary Flames	1984-85	Edmonton Oilers
2002-03	Anaheim Mighty Ducks	1983-84	Edmonton Oilers
2001-02	Detroit Red Wings	1982-83	Edmonton Oilers
2000-01	Colorado Avalanche	1981-82	Vancouver Canucks
99-2000	Dallas Stars	1980-81	New York Islanders
1998-99	Dallas Stars	1979-80	Philadelphia Flyers
1997-98	Detroit Red Wings	1978-79	New York Islanders
1996-97	Detroit Red Wings	1977-78	New York Islanders
1995-96	Colorado Avalanche	1976-77	Philadelphia Flyers
1994-95	Detroit Red Wings	1975-76	Philadelphia Flyers
1993-94	Vancouver Canucks	1974-75	Philadelphia Flyers
1992-93	Los Angeles Kings	1973-74	Philadelphia Flyers
1991-92	Chicago Blackhawks	1972-73	Chicago Blackhawks
1990-91	Minnesota North Stars	1971-72	Chicago Blackhawks
1989-90	Edmonton Oilers	1970-71	Chicago Blackhawks
1988-89	Calgary Flames	1969-70	St. Louis Blues
1987-88	Edmonton Oilers	1968-69	St. Louis Blues
1986-87	Edmonton Oilers	1967-68	Philadelphia Flyers

Stanley Cup Winners

Rosters and Final Series Scores

2004-05 — No Cup Winner — Regular season and playoffs cancelled due to labor dispute.

2003-04 — Tampa Bay Lightning — Dave Andreychuk (Captain), Dimitry Afanasenkov, Dan Boyle, Martin Cibak, Ben Clymer, Jassen Cullimore, Chris Dingman, Ruslan Fedotenko, John Grahame, Nikolai Khabibulin, Pavel Kubina, Vincent Lecavalier, Brad Lukowich, Fredrik Modin, Stan Neckar, Eric Perrin, Nolan Pratt, Brad Richards, Andre Roy, Darren Rumble, Martin St. Louis, Cory Sarich, Cory Stillman, Darryl Sydor, Tim Taylor, Bill Davidson (Owner), Tom Wilson (Governor), Ron Campbell (President), Jay Feaster (General Manager), Bill Barber (Director of Player Personnel), John Tortorella (Head Coach), Craig Ramsay (Associate Coach), Jeff Reese (Assistant Coach), Eric Lawson (Strength and Conditioning Coach), Nigel Kirwan (Video Coach), Jake Goertzen (Head Scout), Rick Paterson (Chief Professional Scout), Dirk Graham (Pro Scout), Ryan Belec (Assistant to the GM), Kathy Paterson (Hockey Operations Executive Assistant), Phil Thibodeau (Director of Team Services), Thomas Mulligan (Trainer), Adam Rambo (Assistant Trainer), Mike Griebel (Massage Therapist), Ray Thill (Equipment Manager), Dana Heinze, Jim Pickard (Assistant Equipment Managers).

Scores: May 25, at Tampa Bay - Calgary 4, Tampa Bay 1; May 27, at Tampa Bay - Tampa Bay 4, Calgary 1; May 29, at Calgary - Calgary 3, Tampa Bay 0; May 31, at Calgary - Tampa Bay 1, Calgary 0; June 3, at Tampa Bay - Calgary 3, Tampa Bay 2; June 5, at Calgary - Tampa Bay 3, Calgary 2; June 7, at Tampa Bay - Tampa Bay 2, Calgary 1.

2002-03 — New Jersey Devils — Scott Stevens (Captain), Tommy Albelin, Martin Brodeur, Sergei Brylin, Ken Daneyko, Patrik Elias, Jeff Friesen, Brian Gionta, Scott Gomez, Jamie Langenbrunner, John Madden, Grant Marshall, Jim McKenzie, Scott Niedermayer, Joe Nieuwendyk, Jay Pandolfo, Brian Rafalski, Pascal Rheaume, Michael Rupp, Corey Schwab, Richard Smehlik, Turner Stevenson, Oleg Tverdovsky, Colin White, Raymond G. Chambers (Owner), Lewis Katz (Owner), Peter Simon (Chairman), Lou Lamoriello (CEO/President/General Manager), Pat Burns (Head Coach), Bob Carpenter (Assistant Coach), John MacLean (Assistant Coach), Jacques Caron (Goaltending Coach), Larry Robinson (Special Assignment Coach), David Conte (Director, Scouting), Claude Carrier (Assistant Director, Scouting), Chris Lamoriello (Scout/Albany GM), Milt Fisher (Scout), Dan Labraaten (Scout), Marcel Pronovost (Scout), Bob Hoffmeyer (Pro Scout), Jan Ludvig (Pro Scout), Dr. Barry Fisher (Orthopedist), Chris Modrzynski (Exec. VP), Terry Farmer (VP), Vladimir Bure (Fitness Consultant), Taran Singleton (Hockey Operations), Bill Murray (Medical Trainer), Michael Vasalani (Strength/Conditioning Coordinator), Rich Matthews (Equipment Manager), Juergen Merz (Massage Therapist), Alex Abasto (Assistant Equipment Manager).

Scores: May 27, at New Jersey - New Jersey 3, Anaheim 0; May 29, at New Jersey - New Jersey 3, Anaheim 0; May 31, at Anaheim - Anaheim 3, New Jersey 2; June 2, at Anaheim - Anaheim 1, New Jersey 0; June 5, at New Jersey - New Jersey 6, Anaheim 3; June 7, at Anaheim - Anaheim 5, New Jersey 2; June 9, at New Jersey - New Jersey 3, Anaheim 0.

2001-02 — Detroit Red Wings — Steve Yzerman (Captain), Chris Chelios, Mathieu Dandenault, Pavel Datsyuk, Boyd Devereaux, Kris Draper, Steve Duchesne, Sergei Fedorov, Jiri Fischer, Dominik Hasek, Tomas Holmstrom, Brett Hull, Igor Larionov, Manny Legace, Nicklas Lidstrom, Kirk Maltby, Darren McCarty, Fredrik Olausson, Luc Robitaille, Brendan Shanahan, Jiri Slegr, Jason Williams, Michael Ilitch (Owner/Governor) Marian Ilitch (Owner/Secretary Treasurer), Ronald Ilitch, Michael Ilitch Jr., Lisa Ilitch Murray, Atanas Ilitch, Carole Ilitch, Jim Devallano (Senior Vice President), Christopher Ilitch (Vice President), Denise Ilitch (Alternate Governor), Ken Holland (General Manager), Jim Nill (Assistant General Manager), Scotty Bowman (Head Coach), Dave Lewis (Associate Coach), Barry Smith (Associate Coach), Jim Bedard (Goaltending Consultant), Joe Kocur (Video Coordinator), John Wharton (Athletic Trainer), Paul Boyer (Equipment Manager), Piet Van Zant (Assistant Athletic Trainer), Paul MacDonald (Senior Director of Finance), Nancy Beard (Executive Assistant), Dan Belisle (Pro Scout), Mark Howe (Pro Scout), Bob McCammon (Pro Scout), Hakan Andersson (Director of European Scouting), Mark Leach (Scout), Bruce Haralson (Scout), Joe McDonnell (Scout), Glenn Merkosky (Scout).

Scores: June 4, at Detroit - Carolina 3, Detroit 2; June 6, at Detroit - Detroit 3, Carolina 1; June 8, at Carolina - Detroit 3, Carolina 2; June 10, at Carolina - Detroit 3, Carolina 0; June 13, at Detroit - Detroit 3, Carolina 1.

2000-01 — Colorado Avalanche — Joe Sakic (Captain), David Aebischer, Rob Blake, Raymond Bourque, Greg de Vries, Chris Dingman, Chris Drury, Adam Foote, Peter Forsberg, Milan Hejduk, Dan Hinote, Jon Klemm, Eric Messier, Bryan Muir, Ville Nieminen, Scott Parker, Shjon Podein, Nolan Pratt, Dave Reid, Steve Reinprecht, Patrick Roy, Martin Skoula, Alex Tanguay, Stephane Yelle, E. Stanley Kroenke (Owner/Governor), Pierre Lacroix (President and General Manager), Bob Hartley (Head Coach), Jacques Cloutier (Assistant Coach), Bryan Trottier (Assistant Coach), Paul Fixter (Video Coach), Francois Giguere (Vice President of Hockey Operations), Brian MacDonald (Assistant General Manager), Michel Goulet (Vice President of Player Personnel), Jean Martineau (Vice President of Communications/Team Services), Pat Karns (Head Athletic Trainer), Matthew Sokolowski (Assistant Athletic Trainer), Wayne Flemming (Equipment Manager), Mark Miller (Equipment Manager), Dave Randolph (Assistant Equipment Manager), Paul Goldberg (Strength and Conditioning Coach), Gregorio Pradera (Massage Therapist), Brad Smith (Pro Scout), Jim Hammett (Chief Scout), Garth Joy, Steve Lyons, Joni Lehto, Orval Tessier (Scouts), Charlotte Grahame (Director of Hockey Operations).

Scores: May 26, at Colorado - Colorado 5, New Jersey 0; May 29, at Colorado - New Jersey 2, Colorado 1; May 31, at New Jersey - Colorado 3, New Jersey 1; June 2, at New Jersey - New Jersey 3, Colorado 2; June 4, at Colorado - New Jersey 4, Colorado 1; June 7, at New Jersey - Colorado 4, New Jersey 0; June 9, at Colorado - Colorado 3, New Jersey 1.

1999-2000 — New Jersey Devils — Scott Stevens (Captain), Jason Arnott, Brad Bombardir, Martin Brodeur, Steve Brule, Sergei Brylin, Ken Daneyko, Patrik Elias, Scott Gomez, Bobby Holik, Steve Kelly, Claude Lemieux, John Madden, Vladimir Malakhov, Randy McKay, Alexander Mogilny, Sergei Nemchinov, Scott Niedermayer, Krzysztof Oliwa, Jay Pandolfo, Brian Rafalski, Ken Sutton, Petr Sykora, Chris Terreri, Colin White, Dr. John J. McMullen (Owner/Chairman), Peter S. McMullen (Owner), Lou Lamoriello (President/General Manager), Larry Robinson (Head Coach), Viacheslav Fetisov (Assistant Coach), Bob Carpenter (Assistant Coach), Jacques Caron (Goaltending Coach), John Cunniff (AHL Coach), David Conte (Director of Scouting), Milt Fisher (Scout), Claude Carrier (Assistant Director of Scouting), Dan Labraaten (Scout), Marcel Pronovost (Scout), Bob Hoffmeyer (Pro Scout), Dr. Barry Fisher (Orthopedist), Dennis Gendron (AHL Assistant Coach), Robbie Ftorek (Coach), Vladimir Bure (Consultant), Taran Singleton (Hockey Operations), Marie Carnevale (Hockey Operations), Callie Smith (Hockey Operations), Bill Murray (Medical Trainer), Michael Vasalani (Strength/Conditioning Coordinator), Dana McGuane (Equipment Manager), Juergen Merz (Massage Therapist), Harry Bricker (Assistant Equipment Manager), Lou Centanni (Assistant Equipment Manager).

Scores: May 30, at New Jersey - New Jersey 7, Dallas 3; June 1, at New Jersey - Dallas 2, New Jersey 1; June 3, at Dallas - New Jersey 2, Dallas 1; June 5, at Dallas - New Jersey 3, Dallas 1; June 8, at New Jersey - Dallas 1 - New Jersey 0; at Dallas, New Jersey 2 - Dallas 1.

1998-99 — Dallas Stars — Derian Hatcher (Captain), Ed Belfour, Guy Carbonneau, Shawn Chambers, Benoit Hogue, Tony Hrkac, Brett Hull, Mike Keane, Jamie Langenbrunner, Jere Lehtinen, Craig Ludwig, Grant Marshall, Richard Matvichuk, Mike Modano, Joe Nieuwendyk, Derek Plante, Dave Reid, Jon Sim, Brian Skrudland, Blake Sloan, Darryl Sydor, Roman Turek, Pat Verbeek, Sergei Zubov, Thomas Hicks (Chairman of the Board and Owner), Jim Lites (President), Bob Gainey (Vice President, Hockey Operations and General Manager), Doug Armstrong (Assistant General Manager), Craig Button (Director of Player Personnel), Ken Hitchcock (Head Coach), Doug Jarvis (Assistant Coach), Rick Wilson (Assistant Coach), Rick McLaughlin (Vice President and Chief Financial Officer), Jeff Cogen (Vice President, Marketing and Promotion), Bill Strong (Vice President, Marketing and Broadcasting), Tim Bernhardt (Director of Amateur Scouting), Doug Overton (Director of Pro Scouting), Bob Gernander (Chief Scout), Stu MacGregor (Western Scout), Dave Suprenant (Medical Trainer), Dave Smith (Equipment Manager), Rich Matthews (Equipment Manager), J.J. McQueen (Strength and Conditioning Coach), Rick St. Croix (Goaltending Consultant), Dan Stuchal (Director of Team Services), Larry Kelly (Director of Public Relations).

Scores: June 8, at Dallas - Buffalo 3, Dallas 2; June 10, at Dallas - Dallas 4, Buffalo 2; June 12, at Buffalo - Dallas 2, Buffalo 1; June 15, at Buffalo - Buffalo 2, Dallas 1; June 17, at Dallas - Dallas 2, Buffalo 0; June 19, at Buffalo - Dallas 2, Buffalo 1.

1997-98 — Detroit Red Wings — Steve Yzerman (Captain), Doug Brown, Mathieu Dandenault, Kris Draper, Anders Eriksson, Sergei Fedorov, Viacheslav Fetisov, Brent Gilchrist, Kevin Hodson, Tomas Holmstrom, Mike Knuble, Joe Kocur, Vladimir Konstantinov, Vyacheslav Kozlov, Martin Lapointe, Igor Larionov, Nicklas Lidstrom, Jamie Macoun, Kirk Maltby, Darren McCarty, Dmitri Mironov, Larry Murphy, Chris Osgood, Bob Rouse, Brendan Shanahan, Aaron Ward, Mike Ilitch, (Owner/Chairman), Marian Ilitch (Owner), Atanas Ilitch (Vice President), Christopher Ilitch (Vice President), Denise Ilitch, Ronald Ilitch, Michael Ilitch Jr., Lisa Ilitch Murray, Carole Ilitch Trepeck, Jim Devellano (Senior Vice President), Scotty Bowman (Head Coach), Ken Holland (General Manager), Don Waddell (Assistant General Manager), Barry Smith (Associate Coach), Dave Lewis (Associate Coach), Jim Bedard (Goaltending Consultant), Jim Nill (Director of Player Development), Dan Belisle (Pro Scout), Mark Howe (Pro Scout), Hakan Andersson (Director of European Scouting), Mark Leach (USA Scout), Moe McDonnell (Eastern Scout), Bruce Haralson (Western Scout), John Wharton (Athletic Trainer), Paul Boyer (Equipment Manager) Tim Abbott (Assistant Equipment Manager), Bob Huddleston (Masseur), Sergei Mnatsakanov (Masseur), Wally Crossman (Dressing Room Assistant).

Scores: June 9, at Detroit — Detroit 2, Washington 1; June 11, at Detroit — Detroit 5, Washington 4; June 13, at Washington — Detroit 2, Washington 1; June 16, at Washington — Detroit 4, Washington 1.

1996-97 — Detroit Red Wings — Steve Yzerman (Captain), Doug Brown, Mathieu Dandenault, Kris Draper, Sergei Fedorov, Viacheslav Fetisov, Kevin Hodson, Tomas Holmstrom, Joe Kocur, Vladimir Konstantinov, Vyacheslav Kozlov, Martin Lapointe, Igor Larionov, Nicklas Lidstrom, Kirk Maltby, Darren McCarty, Larry Murphy, Chris Osgood, Jamie Pushor, Bob Rouse, Tomas Sandstrom, Brendan Shanahan, Tim Taylor, Mike Vernon, Aaron Ward, Mike Ilitch (Owner/Chairman), Marian Ilitch (Owner), Atanas Ilitch (Vice President), Christopher Ilitch (Vice President), Denise Ilitch Lites, Ronald Ilitch, Michael Ilitch, Jr., Lisa Ilitch Murray, Carole Ilitch Trepeck, Jim Devellano (Senior Vice President), Scotty Bowman (Head Coach/Director of Player Personnel), Ken Holland (Assistant General Manager), Barry Smith (Associate Coach), Dave Lewis (Associate Coach), Mike Krushelnyski (Assistant Coach). Jim Nill (Director of Player Development), Dan Belisle (Pro Scout), Mark Howe (Pro Scout), Hakan Andersson (Director of European Scouting), John Wharton (Athletic Trainer), Paul Boyer (Equipment Manager) Tim Abbott (Assistant Equipment Manager), Sergei Mnatsakanov (Masseur).

Scores: May 31, at Philadelphia — Detroit 4, Philadelphia 2; June 3, at Philadelphia — Detroit 4, Philadelphia 2; June 5, at Detroit — Detroit 6, Philadelphia 1; June 7, at Detroit — Detroit 2, Philadelphia 1.

1995-96 — Colorado Avalanche — Joe Sakic (Captain), Rene Corbet, Adam Deadmarsh, Stephane Fiset, Adam Foote, Peter Forsberg, Alexei Gusarov, Dave Hannan, Valeri Kamensky, Mike Keane, Jon Klemm, Uwe Krupp, Sylvain Lefebvre, Claude Lemieux, Curtis Leschyshyn, Troy Murray, Sandis Ozolinsh, Mike Ricci, Patrick Roy, Warren Rychel, Chris Simon, Craig Wolanin, Stephane Yelle, Scott Young, Charlie Lyons (Chairman, CEO), Pierre Lacroix (Exec. V.P., G.M.), Marc Crawford (Head Coach), Joel Quenneville (Assistant Coach), Jacques Cloutier (Assistant Coach), Francois Giguere (Assistant General Manager), Michel Goulet (Director of Player Personnel), Dave Draper (Chief Scout), Jean Martineau (Director of Public Relations), Pat Karns (Trainer), Matthew Sokolowski (Assistant Trainer), Rob McLean (Equipment Manager), Mike Kramer (Assistant Equipment Manager), Brock Gibbins (Assistant Equipment Manager), Skip Allen (Strength and Conditioning Coach), Paul Fixter (Video Coordinator), Leo Vyssokov (Massage Therapist).

Scores: June 4, at Colorado — Colorado 3, Florida 1; June 6, at Colorado — Colorado 8, Florida 1; June 8, at Florida — Colorado 3, Florida 2; June 10, at Florida — Colorado 1, Florida 0.

1994-95 — New Jersey Devils — Scott Stevens (Captain), Tommy Albelin, Martin Brodeur, Neal Broten, Sergei Brylin, Bob Carpenter, Shawn Chambers, Tom Chorske, Danton Cole, Ken Daneyko, Kevin Dean, Jim Dowd, Bruce Driver (Alternate Captain), Bill Guerin, Bobby Holik, Claude Lemieux, John MacLean (Alternate Captain), Chris McAlpine, Randy McKay, Scott Niedermayer, Mike Peluso, Stephane Richer, Brian Rolston, Chris Terreri, Valeri Zelepukin, Dr. John J. McMullen (Owner/Chairman), Peter S. McMullen (Owner), Lou Lamoriello (President/General Manager), Jacques Lemaire (Head Coach), Jacques Caron (Goaltender Coach), Dennis Gendron (Assistant Coach), Larry Robinson (Assistant Coach), Robbie Ftorek (AHL Coach), Alex Abasto (Assistant Equipment Manager), Bob Huddleston (Massage Therapist), David Nichols (Equipment Manager), Ted Schuch (Medical Trainer), Mike Vasalani (Strength Coach), David Conte (Director of Scouting) Claude Carrier (Scout), Milt Fisher (Scout), Dan Labraaten (Scout), Marcel Pronovost (Scout).

Scores: June 17, at Detroit — New Jersey 2, Detroit 1; June 20, at Detroit — New Jersey 4, Detroit 2; June 22, at New Jersey — New Jersey 5, Detroit 2; June 24, at New Jersey — New Jersey 5, Detroit 2.

1993-94 — New York Rangers — Mark Messier (Captain), Brian Leetch, Kevin Lowe, Adam Graves, Steve Larmer, Glenn Anderson, Jeff Beukeboom, Greg Gilbert, Mike Hartman, Glenn Healy, Mike Hudson, Alexander Karpovtsev, Joe Kocur, Alexei Kovalev, Nick Kypreos, Doug Lidster, Stephane Matteau, Craig MacTavish, Sergei Nemchinov, Brian Noonan, Ed Olczyk, Mike Richter, Esa Tikkanen, Jay Wells, Sergei Zubov, Neil Smith (President, General Manager and Governor), Robert Gutkowski, Stanley Jaffe, Kenneth Munoz (Governors), Larry Pleau (Assistant General Manager), Mike Keenan (Head Coach), Colin Campbell (Associate Coach), Dick Todd (Assistant Coach), Matthew Loughren (Manager, Team Operations), Barry Watkins (Director, Communications), Christer Rockstrom, Tony Feltrin, Martin Madden, Herb Hammond, Darwin Bennett (Scouts), Dave Smith, Joe Murphy, Mike Folga, Bruce Lifrieri (Trainers).

Scores: May 31, at New York — Vancouver 3, NY Rangers 2; June 2, at New York — NY Rangers 3, Vancouver 1; June 4, at Vancouver — NY Rangers 5, Vancouver 1; June 7, at Vancouver — NY Rangers 4, Vancouver 2; June 9, at New York — Vancouver 6, at NY Rangers 3; June 11, at Vancouver — Vancouver 4, NY Rangers 1; June 14, at New York — NY Rangers 3, Vancouver 2.

1992-93 — Montreal Canadiens — Guy Carbonneau (Captain), Patrick Roy, Mike Keane, Eric Desjardins, Stephan Lebeau, Mathieu Schneider, J-J Daigneault, Denis Savard, Lyle Odelein, Todd Ewen, Kirk Muller, John LeClair, Gilbert Dionne, Benoit Brunet, Patrice Brisebois, Paul Di Pietro, Andre Racicot, Donald Dufresne, Mario Roberge, Sean Hill, Ed Ronan, Kevin Haller, Vincent Damphousse, Brian Bellows, Gary Leeman, Rob Ramage, Ronald Corey (President), Serge Savard (Managing Director & Vice-President Hockey), Jacques Demers (Head Coach), Jacques Laperriere (Assistant Coach), Charles Thiffault (Assistant Coach), Francois Allaire (Goaltending Instructor), Jean Béliveau (Senior Vice-President, Corporate Affairs), Fred Steer (Vice-President, Finance & Adminstration), Aldo Giampaolo (Vice-President, Operations), Bernard Brisset (Vice-President, Marketing & Communications), André Boudrias (Assistant to the Managing Director & Director of Scouting), Jacques Lemaire (Assistant to the Managing Director), Gaeten Lefebvre (Athletic Trainer), John Shipman (Assistant to the Athletic Trainer), Eddy Palchak (Equipment Manager), Pierre Gervais (Assistant to the Equipment Manager), Robert Boulanger (Assistant to the Equipment Manager), Pierre Ouellete (Assistant to the Equipment Manager).

Scores: June 1, at Montreal — Los Angeles 4, Montreal 1; June 2, at Montreal — Montreal 3, Los Angeles 2; June 5, at Los Angeles — Montreal 4, Los Angeles 3; June 7, at Los Angeles — Montreal 3, Los Angeles 2; June 9, at Montreal — Montreal 4, Los Angeles 1.

1991-92 — Pittsburgh Penguins — Mario Lemieux (Captain), Ron Francis, Bryan Trottier, Kevin Stevens, Bob Errey, Phil Bourque, Troy Loney, Rick Tocchet, Joe Mullen, Jaromir Jagr, Jiri Hrdina, Shawn McEachern, Ulf Samuelsson, Kjell Samuelsson, Larry Murphy, Gordie Roberts, Jim Paek, Paul Stanton, Tom Barrasso, Ken Wregget, Jay Caufield, Jamie Leach, Wendell Young, Grant Jennings, Peter Taglianetti, Jock Callander, Dave Michayluk, Mike Needham, Jeff Chychrun, Ken Priestlay, Jeff Daniels, Howard Baldwin (Owner and President), Morris Belzberg (Owner), Thomas Ruta (Owner), Donn Patton (Executive Vice President and Chief Financial Officer), Paul Martha (Executive Vice President and General Counsel), Craig Patrick (Executive Vice President and General Manager), Bob Johnson (Coach), Scotty Bowman (Director of Player Development and Coach), Barry Smith, Rick Kehoe, Pierre McGuire, Gilles Meloche, Rick Paterson (Assistant Coaches), Steve Latin (Equipment Manager), Skip Thayer (Trainer), John Welday (Strength and Conditioning Coach), Greg Malone, Les Binkley, Charlie Hodge, John Gill, Ralph Cox (Scouts).
Scores: May 26, at Pittsburgh — Pittsburgh 5, Chicago 4; May 28, at Pittsburgh — Pittsburgh 3, Chicago 1; May 30, at Chicago — Pittsburgh 1, Chicago 0; June 1, at Chicago — Pittsburgh 6, Chicago 5.

1990-91 — Pittsburgh Penguins — Mario Lemieux (Captain), Paul Coffey, Randy Hillier, Bob Errey, Tom Barrasso, Phil Bourque, Jay Caufield, Ron Francis, Randy Gilhen, Jiri Hrdina, Jaromir Jagr, Grant Jennings, Troy Loney, Joe Mullen, Larry Murphy, Jim Paek, Frank Pietrangelo, Barry Pederson, Mark Recchi, Gordie Roberts, Ulf Samuelsson, Paul Stanton, Kevin Stevens, Peter Taglianetti, Bryan Trottier, Scott Young, Wendell Young, Edward J. DeBartolo, Sr. (Owner), Marie D. DeBartolo York (President), Paul Martha (Vice-President & General Counsel), Craig Patrick (General Manager), Scotty Bowman (Director of Player Development & Recruitment), Bob Johnson (Coach), Rick Kehoe (Assistant Coach), Gilles Meloche (Goaltending Coach & Scout), Rick Paterson (Assistant Coach), Barry Smith (Assistant Coach), Steve Latin (Equipment Manager), Skip Thayer (Trainer), John Welday (Strength & Conditioning Coach), Greg Malone (Scout).
Scores: May 15, at Pittsburgh — Minnesota 5, Pittsburgh 4; May 17, at Pittsburgh — Pittsburgh 4, Minnesota 1; May 19, at Minnesota — Minnesota 3, Pittsburgh 1; May 21, at Minnesota — Pittsburgh 5, Minnesota 3; May 23, at Pittsburgh — Pittsburgh 6, Minnesota 4; May 25, at Minnesota — Pittsburgh 8, Minnesota 0.

1989-90 — Edmonton Oilers — Kevin Lowe, Steve Smith, Jeff Beukeboom, Mark Lamb, Joe Murphy, Glenn Anderson, Mark Messier (Captain), Adam Graves, Craig MacTavish, Kelly Buchberger, Jari Kurri, Craig Simpson, Martin Gelinas, Randy Gregg, Charlie Huddy, Geoff Smith, Reijo Ruotsalainen, Craig Muni, Bill Ranford, Dave Brown, Pokey Reddick, Petr Klima, Esa Tikkanen, Grant Fuhr, Peter Pocklington (Owner), Glen Sather (President/General Manager), John Muckler (Coach), Ted Green (Co-Coach), Ron Low (Ass't Coach), Bruce MacGregor (Ass't General Manager), Barry Fraser (Director of Player Personnel), John Blackwell (Director of Operations, AHL), Ace Bailey, Ed Chadwick, Lorne Davis, Harry Howell, Matti Vaisanen and Albert Reeves (Scouts), Bill Tuele (Director of Public Relations), Werner Baum (Controller), Dr. Gordon Cameron (Medical Chief of Staff), Dr. David Reid (Team Physician), Barrie Stafford (Athletic Trainer), Ken Lowe (Athletic Therapist), Stuart Poirier (Massage Therapist), Lyle Kulchisky (Ass't Trainer).
Scores: May 15, at Boston — Edmonton 3, Boston 2; May 18, at Boston — Edmonton 7, Boston 2; May 20, at Edmonton — Boston 2, Edmonton 1; May 22, at Edmonton — Edmonton 5, Boston 1; May 24, at Boston — Edmonton 4, Boston 1.

1988-89 — Calgary Flames — Mike Vernon, Rick Wamsley, Al MacInnis, Brad McCrimmon, Dana Murzyn, Ric Nattress, Joe Mullen, Lanny McDonald (Co-captain), Gary Roberts, Colin Patterson, Hakan Loob, Theoren Fleury, Jiri Hrdina, Tim Hunter (Ass't. captain), Gary Suter, Mark Hunter, Jim Peplinski (Co-captain), Joe Nieuwendyk, Brian MacLellan, Joel Otto, Jamie Macoun, Doug Gilmour, Rob Ramage. Norman Green, Harley Hotchkiss, Norman Kwong, Sonia Scurfield, B.J. Seaman, D.K. Seaman (Owners), Cliff Fletcher (President and General Manager), Al MacNeil (Ass't General Manager), Al Coates (Ass't to the President), Terry Crisp (Head Coach), Doug Risebrough, Tom Watt (Ass't Coaches), Glenn Hall (Goaltending Consultant), Jim Murray (Trainer), Bob Stewart (Equipment Manager), Al Murray (Ass't Trainer).
Scores: May 14, at Calgary — Calgary 3, Montreal 2; May 17, at Calgary — Montreal 4, Calgary 2; May 19, at Montreal — Montreal 4, Calgary 3; May 21, at Montreal — Calgary 4, Montreal 2; May 23, at Calgary — Calgary 3, Montreal 2; May 25, at Montreal — Calgary 4, Montreal 2.

1987-88 — Edmonton Oilers — Keith Acton, Glenn Anderson, Jeff Beukeboom, Geoff Courtnall, Grant Fuhr, Randy Gregg, Wayne Gretzky (Captain), Dave Hannan, Charlie Huddy, Mike Krushelnyski, Jari Kurri, Normand Lacombe, Kevin Lowe, Craig MacTavish, Kevin McClelland, Marty McSorley, Mark Messier, Craig Muni, Bill Ranford, Craig Simpson, Steve Smith, Esa Tikkanen, Peter Pocklington (Owner), Glen Sather (General Manager/Coach), John Muckler (Co-Coach), Ted Green (Ass't Coach), Bruce MacGregor (Ass't General Manager), Barry Fraser (Director of Player Personnel), Bill Tuele (Director of Public Relations), Dr. Gordon Cameron (Team Physician), Peter Millar (Athletic Therapist), Barrie Stafford (Trainer), Juergen Mers (Massage Therapist), Lyle Kulchisky (Ass't Trainer).
Scores: May 18, at Edmonton — Edmonton 2, Boston 1; May 20, at Edmonton — Edmonton 4, Boston 2; May 22, at Boston — Edmonton 6, Boston 3; May 24, at Boston — Boston 3, Edmonton 3 (suspended due to power failure); May 26, at Edmonton — Edmonton 6, Boston 3.

1986-87 — Edmonton Oilers — Glenn Anderson, Jeff Beukeboom, Kelly Buchberger, Paul Coffey, Grant Fuhr, Randy Gregg, Wayne Gretzky (Captain), Charlie Huddy, Dave Hunter, Mike Krushelnyski, Jari Kurri, Moe Lemay, Kevin Lowe, Craig MacTavish, Kevin McClelland, Marty McSorley, Mark Messier, Andy Moog, Craig Muni, Kent Nilsson, Jaroslav Pouzar, Reijo Ruotsalainen, Steve Smith, Esa Tikkanen, Peter Pocklington (Owner), Glen Sather (General Manager/Coach), John Muckler (Co-Coach), Ted Green (Ass't Coach), Ron Low (Ass't Coach), Bruce MacGregor (Ass't. General Manager), Barry Fraser (Director of Player Personnel), Peter Millar (Athletic Therapist), Barrie Stafford (Trainer), Lyle Kulchisky (Ass't Trainer).
Scores: May 17, at Edmonton — Edmonton 4, Philadelphia 2; May 20, at Edmonton — Edmonton 3, Philadelphia 2; May 22, at Philadelphia — Philadelphia 5, Edmonton 3; May 24, at Philadelphia — Edmonton 4, Philadelphia 1; May 26, at Edmonton — Philadelphia 4, Edmonton 3; May 28, at Philadelphia — Philadelphia 3, Edmonton 2; May 31, at Edmonton — Edmonton 3, Philadelphia 1.

1985-86 — Montreal Canadiens — Bob Gainey (Captain), Doug Soetaert, Patrick Roy, Rick Green, David Maley, Ryan Walter, Serge Boisvert, Mario Tremblay, Bobby Smith, Craig Ludwig, Tom Kurvers, Kjell Dahlin, Larry Robinson, Guy Carbonneau, Chris Chelios, Petr Svoboda, Mats Naslund, Lucien DeBlois, Steve Rooney, Gaston Gingras, Mike Lalor, Chris Nilan, John Kordic, Claude Lemieux, Mike McPhee, Brian Skrudland, Stephane Richer, Ronald Corey (President), Serge Savard (General Manager), Jean Perron (Coach), Jacques Laperrière (Ass't. Coach), Jean Béliveau (Vice President), Francois-Xavier Seigneur (Vice President), Fred Steer (Vice President), Jacques Lemaire (Ass't General Manager), André Boudrias (Ass't. General Manager), Claude Ruel (Scouting), Yves Belanger (Athletic Therapist), Gaetan Lefebvre (Ass't. Athletic Therapist), Eddy Palchak (Trainer), Sylvain Toupin (Ass't. Trainer).
Scores: May 16, at Calgary — Calgary 5, Montreal 2; May 18, at Calgary — Montreal 3, Calgary 2; May 20, at Montreal — Montreal 5, Calgary 3; May 22, at Montreal — Montreal 1, Calgary 0; May 24, at Calgary — Montreal 4, Calgary 3.

1984-85 — Edmonton Oilers — Glenn Anderson, Billy Carroll, Paul Coffey, Lee Fogolin, Grant Fuhr, Randy Gregg, Wayne Gretzky (Captain), Charlie Huddy, Pat Hughes, Dave Hunter, Don Jackson, Mike Krushelnyski, Jari Kurri, Willy Lindstrom, Kevin Lowe, Dave Lumley, Kevin McClelland, Larry Melnyk, Mark Messier, Andy Moog, Mark Napier, Jaroslav Pouzar, Dave Semenko, Esa Tikkanen, Peter Pocklington (Owner), Glen Sather (General Manager/Coach), John Muckler (Ass't. Coach), Ted Green (Ass't. Coach), Bruce MacGregor (Ass't. General Manager), Barry Fraser (Director of Player Personnel/Chief Scout), Peter Millar (Athletic Therapist), Barrie Stafford, Lyle Kulchisky (Trainers).
Scores: May 21, at Philadelphia — Philadelphia 4, Edmonton 1; May 23, at Philadelphia — Edmonton 3, Philadelphia 1; May 25, at Edmonton — Edmonton 4, Philadelphia 3; May 28, at Edmonton — Edmonton 5, Philadelphia 3; May 30, at Edmonton — Edmonton 8, Philadelphia 3.

1983-84 — Edmonton Oilers — Glenn Anderson, Paul Coffey, Pat Conacher, Lee Fogolin, Grant Fuhr, Randy Gregg, Wayne Gretzky (Captain), Charlie Huddy, Pat Hughes, Dave Hunter, Don Jackson, Jari Kurri, Willy Lindstrom, Ken Linseman, Kevin Lowe, Dave Lumley, Kevin McClelland, Mark Messier, Andy Moog, Jaroslav Pouzar, Dave Semenko, Peter Pocklington (Owner), Glen Sather (General Manager/Coach), John Muckler (Ass't. Coach), Ted Green (Ass't. Coach), Bruce MacGregor (Ass't. General Manager), Barry Fraser (Director of Player Personnel/Chief Scout), Peter Millar (Athletic Therapist), Barrie Stafford (Trainer).
Scores: May 10, at New York — Edmonton 1, NY Islanders 0; May 12, at New York — NY Islanders 6, Edmonton 1; May 15, at Edmonton — Edmonton 7, NY Islanders 2; May 17, at Edmonton — Edmonton 7, NY Islanders 2; May 19, at Edmonton — Edmonton 5, NY Islanders 2.

1982-83 — New York Islanders — Mike Bossy, Bob Bourne, Paul Boutilier, Billy Carroll, Greg Gilbert, Clark Gillies, Butch Goring, Mats Hallin, Tomas Jonsson, Anders Kallur, Gord Lane, Dave Langevin, Mike McEwen, Rollie Melanson, Wayne Merrick, Ken Morrow, Bob Nystrom, Stefan Persson, Denis Potvin (Captain), Billy Smith, Brent Sutter, Duane Sutter, John Tonelli, Bryan Trottier, Al Arbour (Coach), Lorne Henning (Ass't Coach), Bill Torrey (General Manager), Ron Waske, Jim Pickard (Trainers).
Scores: May 10, at Edmonton — NY Islanders 2, Edmonton 0; May 12, at Edmonton — NY Islanders 6, Edmonton 3; May 14, at New York — NY Islanders 5, Edmonton 1; May 17, at New York — NY Islanders 4, Edmonton 2

1981-82 — New York Islanders — Mike Bossy, Bob Bourne, Billy Carroll, Butch Goring, Greg Gilbert, Clark Gillies, Tomas Jonsson, Anders Kallur, Gord Lane, Dave Langevin, Hector Marini, Mike McEwen, Rollie Melanson, Wayne Merrick, Ken Morrow, Bob Nystrom, Stefan Persson, Denis Potvin (Captain), Billy Smith, Brent Sutter, Duane Sutter, John Tonelli, Bryan Trottier, Al Arbour (Coach), Lorne Henning (Ass't Coach), Bill Torrey (General Manager), Jim Devellano (ass't. general manager/dir. of scouting), Ron Waske, Jim Pickard (Trainers).
Scores: May 8, at New York — NY Islanders 6, Vancouver 5; May 11, at New York — NY Islanders 6, Vancouver 4; May 13, at Vancouver — NY Islanders 3, Vancouver 0; May 16, at Vancouver — NY Islanders 3, Vancouver 1

1980-81 — New York Islanders — Denis Potvin (Captain), Mike McEwen, Ken Morrow, Gord Lane, Bob Lorimer, Stefan Persson, Dave Langevin, Mike Bossy, Bryan Trottier, Butch Goring, Wayne Merrick, Clark Gillies, John Tonelli, Bob Nystrom, Billy Carroll, Bob Bourne, Hector Marini, Anders Kallur, Duane Sutter, Garry Howatt, Lorne Henning, Billy Smith, Rollie Melanson, Al Arbour (Coach), Bill Torrey (General Manager), Jim Devellano (Chief Scout), Ron Waske, Jim Pickard (Trainers).
Scores: May 12, at New York — NY Islanders 6, Minnesota 3; May 14, at New York — NY Islanders 6, Minnesota 3; May 17, at Minnesota — NY Islanders 7, Minnesota 5; May 19, at Minnesota— Minnesota 4, NY Islanders 2; May 21, at New York — NY Islanders 5, Minnesota 1.

1979-80 — New York Islanders — Gord Lane, Jean Potvin, Bob Lorimer, Denis Potvin (Captain), Stefan Persson, Ken Morrow, Dave Langevin, Duane Sutter, Garry Howatt, Clark Gillies, Lorne Henning, Wayne Merrick, Bob Bourne, Steve Tambellini, Bryan Trottier, Mike Bossy, Bob Nystrom, John Tonelli, Anders Kallur, Butch Goring, Alex McKendry, Glenn Resch, Billy Smith, Al Arbour (Coach), Bill Torrey (General Manager), Jim Devellano (Chief Scout), Ron Waske, Jim Pickard (Trainers).
Scores: May 13, at Philadelphia — NY Islanders 4, Philadelphia 3; May 15, at Philadelphia — Philadelphia 8, NY Islanders 3; May 17, at New York — NY Islanders 6, Philadelphia 2; May 19, at New York — NY Islanders 5, Philadelphia 2; May 22 at Philadelphia — Philadelphia 6, NY Islanders 3; May 24, at New York — NY Islanders 5, Philadelphia 4.

1978-79 — Montreal Canadiens — Ken Dryden, Larry Robinson, Serge Savard, Guy Lapointe, Brian Engblom, Gilles Lupien, Rick Chartraw, Guy Lafleur, Steve Shutt, Jacques Lemaire, Yvan Cournoyer (Captain), Réjean Houle, Pierre Mondou, Bob Gainey, Doug Jarvis, Yvon Lambert, Doug Risebrough, Pierre Larouche, Mario Tremblay, Cam Connor, Pat Hughes, Rod Langway, Mark Napier, Michel Larocque, Richard Sévigny, Scotty Bowman (Coach), Irving Grundman (Managing Director), Eddy Palchak, Pierre Meilleur (Trainers).
Scores: May 13, at Montreal — NY Rangers 4, Montreal 1; May 15, at Montreal — Montreal 6, NY Rangers 2; May 17, at New York — Montreal 4, NY Rangers 1; May 19, at New York — Montreal 4, NY Rangers 3; May 21 at Montreal — Montreal 4, NY Rangers 1.

1977-78 — Montreal Canadiens — Ken Dryden, Larry Robinson, Serge Savard, Guy Lapointe, Bill Nyrop, Pierre Bouchard, Brian Engblom, Gilles Lupien, Rick Chartraw, Guy Lafleur, Steve Shutt, Jacques Lemaire, Yvan Cournoyer (Captain), Réjean Houle, Pierre Mondou, Bob Gainey, Doug Jarvis, Yvon Lambert, Doug Risebrough, Pierre Larouche, Mario Tremblay, Michel Larocque, Murray Wilson, Scotty Bowman (Coach), Sam Pollock (General Manager), Eddy Palchak, Pierre Meilleur (Trainers).
Scores: May 13, at Montreal — Montreal 4, Boston 1; May 16, at Montreal — Montreal 3, Boston 2; May 18, at Boston — Boston 4, Montreal 0; May 21, at Boston — Boston 4, Montreal 3; May 23, at Montreal — Montreal 4, Boston 1; May 25, at Boston — Montreal 4, Boston 1.

1976-77 — Montreal Canadiens — Ken Dryden, Guy Lapointe, Larry Robinson, Serge Savard, Jimmy Roberts, Rick Chartraw, Bill Nyrop, Pierre Bouchard, Brian Engblom, Yvan Cournoyer (Captain), Guy Lafleur, Jacques Lemaire, Steve Shutt, Pete Mahovlich, Murray Wilson, Doug Jarvis, Yvon Lambert, Bob Gainey, Doug Risebrough, Mario Tremblay, Rejean Houle, Pierre Mondou, Mike Polich, Michel Larocque, Scotty Bowman (Coach), Sam Pollock (General Manager), Eddy Palchak, Pierre Meilleur (Trainers).
Scores: May 7, at Montreal — Montreal 7, Boston 3; May 10, at Montreal — Montreal 3, Boston 0; May 12, at Boston — Montreal 4, Boston 2; May 14, at Boston — Montreal 2, Boston 1.

1975-76 — Montreal Canadiens — Ken Dryden, Serge Savard, Guy Lapointe, Larry Robinson, Bill Nyrop, Pierre Bouchard, Jimmy Roberts, Guy Lafleur, Steve Shutt, Pete Mahovlich, Yvan Cournoyer (Captain), Jacques Lemaire, Yvon Lambert, Bob Gainey, Doug Jarvis, Doug Risebrough, Murray Wilson, Mario Tremblay, Rick Chartraw, Michel Larocque, Scotty Bowman (Coach), Sam Pollock (General Manager), Eddy Palchak, Pierre Meilleur (Trainers).
Scores: May 9, at Montreal — Montreal 4, Philadelphia 3; May 11, at Montreal — Montreal 2, Philadelphia 1; May 13, at Philadelphia — Montreal 3, Philadelphia 2; May 16, at Philadelphia — Montreal 5, Philadelphia 3.

1974-75 — Philadelphia Flyers — Bernie Parent, Wayne Stephenson, Ed Van Impe, Tom Bladon, André Dupont, Joe Watson, Jimmy Watson, Ted Harris, Larry Goodenough, Rick MacLeish, Bobby Clarke (Captain), Bill Barber, Reggie Leach, Gary Dornhoefer, Ross Lonsberry, Bob Kelly, Terry Crisp, Don Saleski, Dave Schultz, Orest Kindrachuk, Bill Clement, Fred Shero (Coach), Keith Allen (general manager), Frank Lewis, Jim McKenzie (Trainers).
Scores: May 15, at Philadelphia — Philadelphia 4, Buffalo 1; May 18, at Philadelphia — Philadelphia 2, Buffalo 1; May 20, at Buffalo — Buffalo 5, Philadelphia 4; May 22, at Buffalo — Buffalo 4, Philadelphia 2; May 25, at Philadelphia — Philadelphia 5, Buffalo 1; May 27, at Buffalo — Philadelphia 2, Buffalo 0.

1973-74 — Philadelphia Flyers — Bernie Parent, Ed Van Impe, Tom Bladon, André Dupont, Joe Watson, Jimmy Watson, Barry Ashbee, Bill Barber, Dave Schultz, Don Saleski, Gary Dornhoefer, Terry Crisp, Bobby Clarke (Captain), Simon Nolet, Ross Lonsberry, Rick MacLeish, Bill Flett, Orest Kindrachuk, Bill Clement, Bob Kelly, Bruce Cowick, Al MacAdam, Bobby Taylor, Fred Shero (Coach), Keith Allen (General Manager), Frank Lewis, Jim McKenzie (Trainers).
Scores: May 7, at Boston — Boston 3, Philadelphia 2; May 9, at Boston — Philadelphia 3, Boston 2; May 12, at Philadelphia — Philadelphia 4, Boston 1; May 14, at Philadelphia — Philadelphia 4, Boston 2; May 16, at Boston — Boston 5, Philadelphia 1; May 19, at Philadelphia — Philadelphia 1, Boston 0.

1972-73 — Montreal Canadiens — Ken Dryden, Guy Lapointe, Serge Savard, Larry Robinson, Jacques Laperrière, Bob Murdoch, Pierre Bouchard, Jimmy Roberts, Yvan Cournoyer, Frank Mahovlich, Jacques Lemaire, Pete Mahovlich, Marc Tardif, Henri Richard (Captain), Réjean Houle, Guy Lafleur, Chuck Lefley, Claude Larose, Murray Wilson, Steve Shutt, Michel Plasse, Scotty Bowman (Coach), Sam Pollock (General Manager), Eddy Palchak, Bob Williams (Trainers).
Scores: April 29, at Montreal — Montreal 8, Chicago 3; May 1, at Montreal — Montreal 4, Chicago 1; May 3, at Chicago — Chicago 7, Montreal 4; May 6, at Chicago — Montreal 4, Chicago 0; May 8, at Montreal — Chicago 8, Montreal 7; May 10, at Chicago — Montreal 6, Chicago 4.

1971-72 — Boston Bruins — Gerry Cheevers, Eddie Johnston, Bobby Orr, Ted Green, Carol Vadnais, Dallas Smith, Don Awrey, Phil Esposito, Ken Hodge, John Bucyk, Mike Walton, Wayne Cashman, Garnet Bailey, Derek Sanderson, Fred Stanfield, Ed Westfall, John McKenzie, Don Marcotte, Garry Peters, Chris Hayes, Tom Johnson (Coach), Milt Schmidt (General Manager), Dan Canney, John Forristall (Trainers).
Scores: April 30, at Boston — Boston 6, NY Rangers 5; May 2, at Boston — Boston 2, NY Rangers 1; May 4, at New York — NY Rangers 5, Boston 2; May 7, at New York — Boston 3, NY Rangers 2; May 9, at Boston — NY Rangers 3, Boston 2; May 11, at New York — Boston 3, NY Rangers 0.

1970-71 — Montreal Canadiens — Ken Dryden, Rogie Vachon, Jacques Laperrière, J.C. Tremblay, Guy Lapointe, Terry Harper, Pierre Bouchard, Jean Béliveau (Captain), Marc Tardif, Yvan Cournoyer, Réjean Houle, Claude Larose, Henri Richard, Phil Roberto, Pete Mahovlich, Leon Rochefort, John Ferguson, Bobby Sheehan, Jacques Lemaire, Frank Mahovlich, Bob Murdoch, Chuck Lefley, Al MacNeil (Coach), Sam Pollock (General Manager), Yvon Belanger, Eddy Palchak (Trainers).
Scores: May 4, at Chicago — Chicago 2, Montreal 1; May 6, at Chicago — Chicago 5, Montreal 3; May 9, at Montreal — Montreal 4, Chicago 2; May 11, at Montreal — Montreal 5, Chicago 2; May 13, at Chicago — Chicago 2, Montreal 0; May 16, at Montreal — Montreal 4, Chicago 3; May 18, at Chicago — Montreal 3, Chicago 2.

1969-70 — Boston Bruins — Gerry Cheevers, Eddie Johnston, Bobby Orr, Rick Smith, Dallas Smith, Bill Speer, Gary Doak, Don Awrey, Phil Esposito, Ken Hodge, John Bucyk, Wayne Carleton, Wayne Cashman, Derek Sanderson, Fred Stanfield, Ed Westfall, John McKenzie, Jim Lorentz, Don Marcotte, Bill Lesuk, Danny Schock, Harry Sinden (Coach), Milt Schmidt (General Manager), Dan Canney, John Forristall (Trainers).
Scores: May 3, at St. Louis — Boston 6, St. Louis 1; May 5, at St. Louis — Boston 6, St. Louis 2; May 7, at Boston — Boston 4, St. Louis 1; May 10, at Boston — Boston 4, St. Louis 3.

1968-69 — Montreal Canadiens — Gump Worsley, Rogie Vachon, Jacques Laperrière, J.C. Tremblay, Ted Harris, Serge Savard, Terry Harper, Larry Hillman, Jean Béliveau (Captain), Ralph Backstrom, Dick Duff, Yvan Cournoyer, Claude Provost, Bobby Rousseau, Jacques Lemaire, Lucien Grenier, Tony Esposito, Claude Ruel (Coach), Sam Pollock (General Manager), Larry Aubut, Eddy Palchak (Trainers).
Scores: April 27, at Montreal — Montreal 3, St. Louis 1; April 29, at Montreal — Montreal 3, St. Louis 1; May 1 at St. Louis — Montreal 4, St. Louis 0; May 4, at St. Louis — Montreal 2, St. Louis 1.

1967-68 — Montreal Canadiens — Gump Worsley, Rogie Vachon, Jacques Laperrière, J.C. Tremblay, Ted Harris, Serge Savard, Carol Vadnais, Jean Béliveau (Captain), Gilles Tremblay, Ralph Backstrom, Dick Duff, Claude Larose, Yvan Cournoyer, Claude Provost, Bobby Rousseau, Henri Richard, John Ferguson, Danny Grant, Jacques Lemaire, Mickey Redmond, Toe Blake (Coach), Sam Pollock (General Manager), Larry Aubut, Eddy Palchak (Trainers).
Scores: May 5, at St. Louis — Montreal 3, St. Louis 2; May 7, at St. Louis — Montreal 1, St. Louis 0; May 9, at Montreal — Montreal 4, St. Louis 3; May 11, at Montreal — Montreal 3, St. Louis 2.

1966-67 — Toronto Maple Leafs — Johnny Bower, Terry Sawchuk, Larry Hillman, Marcel Pronovost, Tim Horton, Bob Baun, Aut Erickson, Allan Stanley, Red Kelly, Ron Ellis, George Armstrong (Captain), Pete Stemkowski, Dave Keon, Mike Walton, Jim Pappin, Bob Pulford, Brian Conacher, Eddie Shack, Frank Mahovlich, Milan Marcetta, Larry Jeffrey, Bruce Gamble, Punch Imlach (Manager-Coach), Bob Haggart (Trainer).
Scores: April 20, at Montreal — Toronto 2, Montreal 6; April 22, at Montreal — Toronto 3, Montreal 0; April 25, at Toronto — Toronto 3, Montreal 2; April 27, at Toronto — Toronto 2, Montreal 6; April 29, at Montreal — Toronto 4, Montreal 1; May 2, at Toronto — Toronto 3, Montreal 1.

1965-66 — Montreal Canadiens — Gump Worsley, Charlie Hodge, J.C. Tremblay, Ted Harris, Jean-Guy Talbot, Terry Harper, Jacques Laperrière, Noel Price, Jean Béliveau (Captain), Ralph Backstrom, Dick Duff, Gilles Tremblay, Yvan Cournoyer, Claude Provost, Bobby Rousseau, Henri Richard, Dave Balon, John Ferguson, Leon Rochefort, Jimmy Roberts, Toe Blake (Coach), Sam Pollock (general manager), Larry Aubut, Andy Galley (Trainers).
Scores: April 24, at Montreal — Detroit 3, Montreal 2; April 26, at Montreal — Detroit 5, Montreal 2; April 28, at Detroit — Montreal 4, Detroit 2; May 1, at Detroit — Montreal 2, Detroit 1; May 3, at Montreal — Montreal 5, Detroit 1; May 5, at Detroit — Montreal 3, Detroit 2.

1964-65 — Montreal Canadiens — Gump Worsley, Charlie Hodge, J.C. Tremblay, Ted Harris, Jean-Guy Talbot, Terry Harper, Jacques Laperrière, Jean Gauthier, Noel Picard, Jean Béliveau (Captain), Ralph Backstrom, Dick Duff, Claude Larose, Yvan Cournoyer, Claude Provost, Bobby Rousseau, Henri Richard, Dave Balon, John Ferguson, Red Berenson, Jimmy Roberts, Toe Blake (Coach), Sam Pollock (general manager), Larry Aubut, Andy Galley (Trainers).
Scores: April 17, at Montreal — Montreal 3, Chicago 2; April 20, at Montreal — Montreal 2, Chicago 0; April 22, at Chicago — Montreal 1, Chicago 3; April 25, at Chicago — Montreal 1, Chicago 5; April 7, at Montreal — Montreal 6, Chicago 0; April 29, at Chicago — Montreal 1, Chicago 2; May 1, at Montreal — Montreal 4, Chicago 0.

1963-64 — Toronto Maple Leafs — Johnny Bower, Don Simmons, Carl Brewer, Tim Horton, Bob Baun, Allan Stanley, Larry Hillman, Al Arbour, Red Kelly, Gerry Ehman, Andy Bathgate, George Armstrong (Captain), Ron Stewart, Dave Keon, Billy Harris, Don McKenney, Jim Pappin, Bob Pulford, Eddie Shack, Frank Mahovlich, Ed Litzenberger, Punch Imlach (Manager-Coach), Bob Haggert (Trainer).
Scores April 11, at Toronto — Toronto 3, Detroit 2; April 14, at Toronto — Toronto 3, Detroit 4; April 16, at Detroit — Toronto 3, Detroit 4; April 18, at Detroit — Toronto 4, Detroit 2; April 21, at Toronto — Toronto 1, Detroit 2; April 23, at Detroit — Toronto 4, Detroit 3; April 25, at Toronto — Toronto 4, Detroit 0.

1962-63 — Toronto Maple Leafs — Johnny Bower, Don Simmons, Carl Brewer, Tim Horton, Kent Douglas, Allan Stanley, Bob Baun, Larry Hillman, Red Kelly, Dick Duff, George Armstrong (Captain), Bob Nevin, Ron Stewart, Dave Keon, Billy Harris, Bob Pulford, Eddie Shack, Ed Litzenberger, Frank Mahovlich, John MacMillan, Punch Imlach (Manager-Coach), Bob Haggert (Trainer).
Scores: April 9, at Toronto — Toronto 4, Detroit 2; April 11, at Toronto — Toronto 4, Detroit 2; April 14, at Detroit — Toronto 2, Detroit 3; April 16, at Detroit — Toronto 4, Detroit 2; April 18, at Toronto — Toronto 3, Detroit 1.

1961-62 — Toronto Maple Leafs — Johnny Bower, Don Simmons, Carl Brewer, Tim Horton, Bob Baun, Allan Stanley, Al Arbour, Larry Hillman, Red Kelly, Dick Duff, George Armstrong (Captain), Frank Mahovlich, Bob Nevin, Ron Stewart, Billy Harris, Bert Olmstead, Bob Pulford, Eddie Shack, Dave Keon, Ed Litzenberger, John MacMillan, Punch Imlach (Manager-Coach), Bob Haggert (Trainer).
Scores: April 10, at Toronto — Toronto 4, Chicago 1; April 12, at Toronto — Toronto 3, Chicago 2; April 15, at Chicago — Toronto 0, Chicago 3; April 17, at Chicago — Toronto 1, Chicago 4; April 19, at Toronto —Toronto 8, Chicago 4; April 22, at Chicago — Toronto 2, Chicago 1.

1960-61 — Chicago Black Hawks — Glenn Hall, Al Arbour, Pierre Pilote, Moose Vasko, Jack Evans, Dollard St. Laurent, Reggie Fleming, Tod Sloan, Ron Murphy, Ed Litzenberger (Captain), Bill Hay, Wayne Hillman, Bobby Hull, Ab McDonald, Eric Nesterenko, Kenny Wharram, Earl Balfour, Stan Mikita, Murray Balfour, Chico Maki, Wayne Hicks, Tommy Ivan (Manager), Rudy Pilous (Coach), Nick Garen (Trainer).
Scores: April 6, at Chicago — Chicago 3, Detroit 2; April 8, at Detroit — Detroit 3, Chicago 1; April 10, at Chicago — Chicago 3, Detroit 1; April 12, at Detroit — Detroit 2, Chicago 1; April 14, at Chicago — Chicago 6, Detroit 3; April 16, at Detroit — Chicago 5, Detroit 1.

1959-60 — Montreal Canadiens — Jacques Plante, Charlie Hodge, Doug Harvey, Tom Johnson, Bob Turner, Jean-Guy Talbot, Albert Langlois, Ralph Backstrom, Jean Béliveau, Marcel Bonin, Bernie Geoffrion, Phil Goyette, Bill Hicke, Don Marshall, Ab McDonald, Dickie Moore, André Pronovost, Claude Provost, Henri Richard, Maurice Richard (Captain), Frank Selke (Manager), Toe Blake (Coach), Hector Dubois, Larry Aubut (Trainers).
Scores: April 7, at Montreal — Montreal 4, Toronto 2; April 9, at Montreal — Montreal 2, Toronto 1; April 12, at Toronto — Montreal 5, Toronto 2; April 14, at Toronto — Montreal 4, Toronto 0.

1958-59 — Montreal Canadiens — Jacques Plante, Charlie Hodge, Doug Harvey, Tom Johnson, Bob Turner, Jean-Guy Talbot, Albert Langlois, Bernie Geoffrion, Ralph Backstrom, Bill Hicke, Maurice Richard (Captain), Dickie Moore, Claude Provost, Ab McDonald, Henri Richard, Marcel Bonin, Phil Goyette, Don Marshall, André Pronovost, Jean Béliveau, Frank Selke (Manager), Toe Blake (Coach), Hector Dubois, Larry Aubut (Trainers).
Scores: April 9, at Montreal — Montreal 5, Toronto 3; April 11, at Montreal — Montreal 3, Toronto 1; April 14, at Toronto — Montreal 3, Toronto 2; April 16, at Toronto — Montreal 5, Toronto 3.

1957-58 — Montreal Canadiens — Jacques Plante, Gerry McNeil, Doug Harvey, Tom Johnson, Bob Turner, Dollard St-Laurent, Jean-Guy Talbot, Albert Langlois, Jean Béliveau, Bernie Geoffrion, Maurice Richard (Captain), Dickie Moore, Claude Provost, Floyd Curry, Bert Olmstead, Henri Richard, Marcel Bonin, Phil Goyette, Don Marshall, André Pronovost, Connie Broden, Ab McDonald, Frank Selke (Manager), Toe Blake (Coach), Hector Dubois, Larry Aubut (Trainers).
Scores: April 8, at Montreal —Montreal 2, Boston 1; April 10, at Montreal — Boston 5, Montreal 2; April 13, at Boston — Montreal 3, Boston 0; April 15, at Boston — Boston 3, Montreal 1; April 17, at Montreal — Montreal 3, Boston 2; April 20, at Boston — Montreal 5, Boston 3.

1956-57 — Montreal Canadiens — Jacques Plante, Gerry McNeil, Doug Harvey, Tom Johnson, Bob Turner, Dollard St-Laurent, Jean-Guy Talbot, Jean Béliveau, Bernie Geoffrion, Floyd Curry, Dickie Moore, Maurice Richard (Captain), Claude Provost, Bert Olmstead, Henri Richard, Phil Goyette, Don Marshall, André Pronovost, Connie Broden, Frank Selke (Manager), Toe Blake (Coach), Hector Dubois, Larry Aubut (Trainers).
Scores: April 6, at Montreal — Montreal 5, Boston 1; April 9, at Montreal — Montreal 1, Boston 0; April 11, at Boston — Montreal 4, Boston 2; April 14, at Boston — Boston 2, Montreal 0; April 16, at Montreal — Montreal 5, Boston 1.

1955-56 — Montreal Canadiens — Jacques Plante, Doug Harvey, Butch Bouchard (Captain), Bob Turner, Tom Johnson, Jean-Guy Talbot, Dollard St-Laurent, Jean Béliveau, Bernie Geoffrion, Bert Olmstead, Floyd Curry, Jackie Leclair, Maurice Richard, Dickie Moore, Henri Richard, Ken Mosdell, Don Marshall, Claude Provost, Frank Selke (Manager), Toe Blake (Coach), Hector Dubois (Trainer).
Scores: March 31, at Montreal — Montreal 6, Detroit 4; April 3, at Montreal — Montreal 5, Detroit 1; April 5, at Detroit — Detroit 3, Montreal 1; April 8, at Detroit — Montreal 3, Detroit 0; April 10, at Montreal — Montreal 3, Detroit 1.

1954-55 — Detroit Red Wings — Terry Sawchuk, Red Kelly, Bob Goldham, Marcel Pronovost, Benny Woit, Jim Hay, Larry Hillman, Ted Lindsay (Captain), Tony Leswick, Gordie Howe, Alex Delvecchio, Marty Pavelich, Glen Skov, Earl Reibel, Johnny Wilson, Bill Dineen, Vic Stasiuk, Marcel Bonin, Jack Adams (Manager), Jimmy Skinner (Coach), Carl Mattson (Trainer).
Scores: April 3, at Detroit — Detroit 4, Montreal 2; April 5, at Detroit — Detroit 7, Montreal 1, April 7, at Montreal — Montreal 4, Detroit 2; April 9, at Montreal — Montreal 5, Detroit 3; April 10, at Detroit — Detroit 5, Montreal 1; April 12, at Montreal — Montreal 6, Detroit 3; April 14, at Detroit — Detroit 3, Montreal 1.

1953-54 — Detroit Red Wings — Terry Sawchuk, Red Kelly, Bob Goldham, Benny Woit, Marcel Pronovost, Al Arbour, Keith Allen, Ted Lindsay (Captain), Tony Leswick, Gordie Howe, Marty Pavelich, Alex Delvecchio, Gilles Dube, Metro Prystai, Glen Skov, Johnny Wilson, Bill Dineen, Jimmy Peters, Earl Reibel, Vic Stasiuk, Jack Adams (Manager), Tommy Ivan (Coach), Carl Mattson (Trainer).
Scores: April 4, at Detroit — Detroit 3, Montreal 1; April 6, at Detroit — Montreal 3, Detroit 1; April 8, at Montreal — Detroit 5, Montreal 2; April 10, at Montreal — Detroit 2, Montreal 0; April 11, at Detroit — Montreal 1, Detroit 0; April 13, at Montreal — Montreal 4, Detroit 1; April 16, at Detroit — Detroit 2, Montreal 1.

1952-53 — Montreal Canadiens — Gerry McNeil, Jacques Plante, Doug Harvey, Butch Bouchard (Captain), Tom Johnson, Dollard St. Laurent, Bud MacPherson, Maurice Richard, Elmer Lach, Paul Meger, Bert Olmstead, Bernie Geoffrion, Floyd Curry, Paul Masnick, Billy Reay, Dickie Moore, Ken Mosdell, Dick Gamble, John McCormack, Lorne Davis, Calum MacKay, Eddie Mazur, Frank Selke (Manager), Dick Irvin (Coach), Hector Dubois (Trainer).
Scores: April 9, at Montreal — Montreal 4, Boston 2; April 11, at Montreal — Boston 4, Montreal 1; April 12, at Boston — Montreal 3, Boston 0; April 14, at Boston — Montreal 7, Boston 3; April 16, at Montreal — Montreal 1, Boston 0.

1951-52 — Detroit Red Wings — Terry Sawchuk, Bob Goldham, Benny Woit, Red Kelly, Leo Reise Jr., Marcel Pronovost, Ted Lindsay, Tony Leswick, Gordie Howe, Metro Prystai, Marty Pavelich, Sid Abel (Captain), Glen Skov, Alex Delvecchio, John Wilson, Vic Stasiuk, Larry Zeidel, Jack Adams (Manager) Tommy Ivan (Coach), Carl Mattson (Trainer).
Scores: April 10, at Montreal — Detroit 3, Montreal 1; April 12, at Montreal — Detroit 2, Montreal 1; April 13, at Detroit — Detroit 3, Montreal 0; April 15, at Detroit — Detroit 3, Montreal 0.

1950-51 — Toronto Maple Leafs — Turk Broda, Al Rollins, Jimmy Thomson, Gus Mortson, Bill Barilko, Bill Juzda, Fern Flaman, Hugh Bolton, Ted Kennedy (Captain), Sid Smith, Tod Sloan, Cal Gardner, Howie Meeker, Harry Watson, Max Bentley, Joe Klukay, Danny Lewicki, Ray Timgren, Fleming Mackell, John McCormack, Bob Hassard, Conn Smythe (Manager), Joe Primeau (Coach), Tim Daly (Trainer).
Scores: April 11, at Toronto — Toronto 3, Montreal 2; April 14, at Toronto — Montreal 3, Toronto 2; April 17, at Montreal — Toronto 2, Montreal 1; April 19, at Montreal — Toronto 3, Montreal 2; April 21, at Toronto — Toronto 3, Montreal 2.

1949-50 — Detroit Red Wings — Harry Lumley, Jack Stewart, Leo Reise Jr., Clare Martin, Doug McKay, Al Dewsbury, Lee Fogolin, Marcel Pronovost, Red Kelly, Gord Haidy, Ted Lindsay, Sid Abel (Captain), Gordie Howe, George Gee, Jimmy Peters, Marty Pavelich, Jim McFadden, Pete Babando, Max McNab, Gerry Couture, Joe Carveth, Steve Black, Johnny Wilson, Larry Wilson, Jack Adams (Manager), Tommy Ivan (Coach), Carl Mattson (Trainer).
Scores: April 11, at Detroit — Detroit 4, NY Rangers 1; April 13, at Toronto* — NY Rangers 3, Detroit 1; April 15, at Toronto — Detroit 4, NY Rangers 0; April 18, at Detroit — NY Rangers 4, Detroit 3; April 20, at Detroit — NY Rangers 2, Detroit 1; April 22, at Detroit — Detroit 5, NY Rangers 4; April 23, at Detroit — Detroit 4, NY Rangers 3.

* Ice was unavailable in Madison Square Garden and Rangers elected to play second and third games on Toronto ice.

Johnny Bower watches while Tim Horton ties up Henri Richard. Between them, the Toronto Maple Leafs and Montreal Canadiens won the Stanley Cup nine times in 10 years from 1959-60 to 1968-69.

1948-49 — Toronto Maple Leafs — Turk Broda, Jimmy Thomson, Gus Mortson, Bill Barilko, Garth Boesch, Bill Juzda, Ted Kennedy (Captain), Howie Meeker, Vic Lynn, Harry Watson, Bill Ezinicki, Cal Gardner, Max Bentley, Joe Klukay, Sid Smith, Don Metz, Ray Timgren, Fleming Mackell, Harry Taylor, Bob Dawes, Tod Sloan, Conn Smythe (Manager), Hap Day (Coach), Tim Daly (Trainer).
Scores: April 8, at Detroit — Toronto 3, Detroit 2; April 10, at Detroit — Toronto 3, Detroit 1; April 13, at Toronto — Toronto 3, Detroit 1; April 16, at Toronto — Toronto 3, Detroit 1.

1947-48 — Toronto Maple Leafs — Turk Broda, Jimmy Thomson, Wally Stanowski, Garth Boesch, Bill Barilko, Gus Mortson, Phil Samis, Syl Apps (Captain), Bill Ezinicki, Harry Watson, Ted Kennedy, Howie Meeker, Vic Lynn, Nick Metz, Max Bentley, Joe Klukay, Les Costello, Don Metz, Sid Smith, Conn Smythe (Manager), Hap Day (Coach), Tim Daly (Trainer).
Scores: April 7, at Toronto — Toronto 5, Detroit 3; April 10, at Toronto — Toronto 4, Detroit 2; April 11, at Detroit — Toronto 2, Detroit 0; April 14, at Detroit — Toronto 7, Detroit 2.

1946-47 — Toronto Maple Leafs — Turk Broda, Garth Boesch, Gus Mortson, Jimmy Thomson, Wally Stanowski, Bill Barilko, Harry Watson, Bud Poile, Ted Kennedy, Syl Apps (Captain), Don Metz, Nick Metz, Bill Ezinicki, Vic Lynn, Howie Meeker, Gaye Stewart, Joe Klukay, Gus Bodnar, Bob Goldham, Conn Smythe (Manager), Hap Day (Coach), Tim Daly (Trainer).
Scores: April 8, at Montreal — Montreal 6, Toronto 0; April 10, at Montreal — Toronto 4, Montreal 0; April 12, at Toronto — Toronto 4, Montreal 2; April 15, at Toronto — Toronto 2, Montreal 1; April 17, at Montreal — Montreal 3, Toronto 1; April 19, at Toronto — Toronto 2, Montreal 1.

1945-46 — Montreal Canadiens — Elmer Lach, Toe Blake (Captain), Maurice Richard, Bob Fillion, Dutch Hiller, Murph Chamberlain, Ken Mosdell, Buddy O'Connor, Glen Harmon, Jimmy Peters, Butch Bouchard, Billy Reay, Ken Reardon, Leo Lamoureux, Frank Eddolls, Gerry Plamondon, Bill Durnan, Tommy Gorman (Manager), Dick Irvin (Coach), Ernie Cook (Trainer).
Scores: March 30, at Montreal — Montreal 4, Boston 3; April 2, at Montreal — Montreal 3, Boston 2; April 4, at Boston — Montreal 4, Boston 2; April 7, at Boston — Boston 3, Montreal 2; April 9, at Montreal — Montreal 6, Boston 3.

1944-45 — Toronto Maple Leafs — Don Metz, Frank McCool, Wally Stanowski, Reg Hamilton, Moe Morris, John McCreedy, Tom O'Neill, Ted Kennedy, Babe Pratt, Gus Bodnar, Art Jackson, Jack McLean, Mel Hill, Nick Metz, Bob Davidson (Captain), Sweeney Schriner, Lorne Carr, Conn Smythe (Manager), Frank Selke (Business Manager), Hap Day (Coach), Tim Daly (Trainer).
Scores: April 6, at Detroit — Toronto 1, Detroit 0; April 8, at Detroit — Toronto 2, Detroit 0; April 12, at Toronto — Toronto 1, Detroit 0; April 14, at Toronto — Detroit 5, Toronto 3; April 19, at Detroit — Detroit 2, Toronto 0; April 21, at Toronto — Detroit 1, Toronto 0; April 22, at Detroit — Toronto 2, Detroit 1.

1943-44 — Montreal Canadiens — Toe Blake (Captain), Maurice Richard, Elmer Lach, Ray Getliffe, Murph Chamberlain, Phil Watson, Butch Bouchard, Glen Harmon, Buddy O'Connor, Gerry Heffernan, Mike McMahon, Leo Lamoureux, Fern Majeau, Bob Fillion, Bill Durnan, Tommy Gorman (Manager), Dick Irvin (Coach), Ernie Cook (Trainer).
Scores: April 4, at Montreal — Montreal 5, Chicago 1; April 6, at Chicago — Montreal 3, Chicago 1; April 9, at Chicago — Montreal 3, Chicago 2; April 13, at Montreal — Montreal 5, Chicago 4.

1942-43 — Detroit Red Wings — Jack Stewart, Jimmy Orlando, Sid Abel (Captain), Alex Motter, Harry Watson, Joe Carveth, Mud Bruneteau, Eddie Wares, Johnny Mowers, Cully Simon, Don Grosso, Carl Liscombe, Connie Brown, Syd Howe, Les Douglas, Harold Jackson, Joe Fisher, Jack Adams (Manager), Ebbie Goodfellow (Playing Coach), Honey Walker (Trainer).
Scores: April 1, at Detroit — Detroit 6, Boston 2; April 4, at Detroit — Detroit 4, Boston 3; April 7, at Boston — Detroit 4, Boston 0; April 8, at Boston — Detroit 2, Boston 0.

1941-42 — Toronto Maple Leafs — Wally Stanowski, Syl Apps (Captain), Bob Goldham, Gordie Drillon, Hank Goldup, Ernie Dickens, Sweeney Schriner, Bucko McDonald, Bob Davidson, Nick Metz, Bingo Kampman, Don Metz, Gaye Stewart, Turk Broda, John McCreedy, Lorne Carr, Pete Langelle, Billy Taylor, Conn Smythe (Manager), Hap Day (Coach), Frank Selke (Business Manager), Tim Daly (Trainer).
Scores: April 4, at Toronto — Detroit 3, Toronto 2; April 7, at Toronto — Detroit 4, Toronto 2; April 9, at Detroit — Detroit 5, Toronto 2; April 12, at Detroit — Toronto 4, Detroit 3; April 14, at Toronto — Toronto 9, Detroit 3; April 16, at Detroit — Toronto 3, Detroit 0; April 18, at Toronto — Toronto 3, Detroit 1.

1940-41 — Boston Bruins — Bill Cowley, Des Smith, Dit Clapper (Captain), Frank Brimsek, Flash Hollett, Jack Crawford, Bobby Bauer, Pat McReavy, Herb Cain, Mel Hill, Milt Schmidt, Woody Dumart, Roy Conacher, Terry Reardon, Art Jackson, Eddie Wiseman, Art Ross (Manager), Cooney Weiland (Coach), Win Green (Trainer).
Scores: April 6, at Boston — Detroit 2, Boston 3; April 8, at Boston — Detroit 1, Boston 2; April 10, at Detroit — Boston 4, Detroit 2; April 12, at Detroit — Boston 3, Detroit 1.

1939-40 — New York Rangers — Dave Kerr, Art Coulter (Captain), Ott Heller, Alex Shibicky, Mac Colville, Neil Colville, Phil Watson, Lynn Patrick, Clint Smith, Muzz Patrick, Babe Pratt, Bryan Hextall, Kilby MacDonald, Dutch Hiller, Alf Pike, Stan Smith, Lester Patrick (Manager), Frank Boucher (Coach), Harry Westerby (Trainer).
Scores: April 2, at New York — NY Rangers 2, Toronto 1; April 3, at New York — NY Rangers 6, Toronto 2; April 6, at Toronto — NY Rangers 1, Toronto 2; April 9, at Toronto — NY Rangers 0, Toronto 3; April 11, at Toronto — NY Rangers 2, Toronto 1; April 13, at Toronto — NY Rangers 3, Toronto 2.

1938-39 — Boston Bruins — Bobby Bauer, Mel Hill, Flash Hollett, Roy Conacher, Gord Pettinger, Charlie Sands, Milt Schmidt, Woody Dumart, Jack Crawford, Ray Getliffe, Frank Brimsek, Eddie Shore, Dit Clapper, Bill Cowley, Jack Portland, Red Hamill, Cooney Weiland (Captain), Art Ross (Manager-Coach), Win Green (Trainer).
Scores: April 6, at Boston — Toronto 1, Boston 2; April 9, at Boston — Toronto 3, Boston 2; April 11, at Toronto — Toronto 1, Boston 3; April 13, at Toronto — Toronto 0, Boston 2; April 16, at Boston — Toronto 1, Boston 3.

1937-38 — Chicago Black Hawks — Art Wiebe, Carl Voss, Harold Jackson, Mike Karakas, Mush March, Jack Shill, Earl Seibert, Cully Dahlstrom, Alex Levinsky, Johnny Gottselig (Captain), Lou Trudel, Pete Palangio, Bill MacKenzie, Doc Romnes, Paul Thompson, Roger Jenkins, Alfie Moore, Bert Connelly, Virgil Johnson, Paul Goodman, Bill Stewart (Manager-Coach), Eddie Froelich (Trainer).
Scores: April 5, at Toronto — Chicago 3, Toronto 1; April 7, at Toronto — Chicago 1, Toronto 5; April 10, at Chicago — Chicago 2, Toronto 1; April 12, at Chicago — Chicago 4, Toronto 1.

1936-37 — Detroit Red Wings — Normie Smith, Pete Kelly, Larry Aurie, Herbie Lewis, Hec Kilrea, Mud Bruneteau, Syd Howe, Wally Kilrea, Jimmy Franks, Bucko McDonald, Gord Pettinger, Ebbie Goodfellow, John Gallagher, Ralph Bowman, John Sorrell, Marty Barry, Earl Robertson, John Sherf, Howie Mackie, Rolly Roulston, Doug Young (Captain), Jack Adams (Manager-Coach), Honey Walker (Trainer).
Scores: April 6, at New York — Detroit 1, NY Rangers 5; April 8, at Detroit — Detroit 4, NY Rangers 2; April 11, at Detroit — Detroit 0, NY Rangers 1; April 13, at Detroit — Detroit 1, NY Rangers 0; April 15, at Detroit — Detroit 3, NY Rangers 0.

1935-36 — Detroit Red Wings — John Sorrell, Syd Howe, Marty Barry, Herbie Lewis, Mud Bruneteau, Wally Kilrea, Hec Kilrea, Gord Pettinger, Bucko McDonald, Ralph Bowman, Pete Kelly, Doug Young (Captain), Ebbie Goodfellow, Normie Smith, Larry Aurie, Jack Adams (Manager-Coach), Honey Walker (Trainer).
Scores: April 5, at Detroit — Detroit 3, Toronto 1; April 7, at Detroit — Detroit 9, Toronto 4; April 9, at Toronto — Detroit 3, Toronto 4; April 11, at Toronto — Detroit 3, Toronto 2.

1934-35 — Montreal Maroons — Lionel Conacher, Cy Wentworth, Alex Connell, Toe Blake, Stewart Evans, Earl Robinson, Bill Miller, Dave Trottier, Jimmy Ward, Baldy Northcott, Hooley Smith, Russ Blinco, Al Shields, Sammy McManus, Gus Marker, Bob Gracie, Herb Cain, Tommy Gorman (Manager-Coach), Bill O'Brien (Trainer).
Scores: April 4, at Toronto — Mtl. Maroons 3, Toronto 2; April 6, at Toronto — Mtl. Maroons 3, Toronto 1; April 9, at Montreal — Mtl. Maroons 4, Toronto 1.

1933-34 — Chicago Black Hawks — Clarence Abel, Rosie Couture, Lou Trudel, Lionel Conacher, Paul Thompson, Leroy Goldsworthy, Art Coulter, Roger Jenkins, Don McFadyen, Tom Cook, Doc Romnes, Johnny Gottselig, Mush March, Johnny Sheppard, Charlie Gardiner (Captain), Bill Kendall, Tommy Gorman (Manager-Coach), Eddie Froelich (Trainer).
Scores: April 3, at Detroit — Chicago 2, Detroit 1; April 5, at Detroit — Chicago 4, Detroit 1; April 8, at Chicago — Detroit 5, Chicago 2; April 10, at Chicago — Chicago 1, Detroit 0.

1932-33 — New York Rangers — Ching Johnson, Butch Keeling, Frank Boucher, Art Somers, Babe Siebert, Bun Cook, Andy Aitkenhead, Ott Heller, Oscar Asmundson, Gord Pettinger, Doug Brennan, Cecil Dillon, Bill Cook (Captain), Murray Murdoch, Earl Seibert, Lester Patrick (Manager-Coach), Harry Westerby (Trainer).
Scores: April 4, at New York — NY Rangers 5, Toronto 1; April 8, at Toronto — NY Rangers 3, Toronto 1; April 11, at Toronto — Toronto 3, NY Rangers 2; April 13, at Toronto — NY Rangers 1, Toronto 0.

1931-32 — Toronto Maple Leafs — Charlie Conacher, Busher Jackson, King Clancy, Andy Blair, Red Horner, Lorne Chabot, Alex Levinsky, Joe Primeau, Harold Darragh, Baldy Cotton, Frank Finnigan, Hap Day (Captain), Ace Bailey, Bob Gracie, Fred Robertson, Earl Miller, Conn Smythe (Manager), Dick Irvin (Coach), Tim Daly (Trainer).
Scores: April 5, at New York — Toronto 6, NY Rangers 4; April 7, at Boston* — Toronto 6, NY Rangers 2; April 9, at Toronto — Toronto 6, NY Rangers 4.

* Ice was unavailable in Madison Square Garden and Rangers elected to play the second game on neutral ice.

1930-31 — Montreal Canadiens — George Hainsworth, Wildor Larochelle, Marty Burke, Sylvio Mantha (Captain), Howie Morenz, Johnny Gagnon, Aurel Joliat, Armand Mondou, Pit Lepine, Albert Leduc, Georges Mantha, Art Lesieur, Nick Wasnie, Bert McCaffrey, Gus Rivers, Jean Pusie, Léo Dandurand (Manager), Cecil Hart (Coach), Ed Dufour (Trainer).
Scores: April 3, at Chicago — Montreal 2, Chicago 1; April 5, at Chicago — Chicago 2, Montreal 1; April 9, at Montreal — Chicago 3, Montreal 2; April 11, at Montreal — Montreal 4, Chicago 2; April 14, at Montreal — Montreal 2, Chicago 0.

1929-30 — Montreal Canadiens — George Hainsworth, Marty Burke, Sylvio Mantha (Captain), Howie Morenz, Bert McCaffrey, Aurel Joliat, Albert Leduc, Pit Lepine, Wildor Larochelle, Nick Wasnie, Gerry Carson, Armand Mondou, Georges Mantha, Gus Rivers, Léo Dandurand (Manager), Cecil Hart (Coach), Ed Dufour (Trainer).
Scores: April 1, at Boston — Montreal 3, Boston 0; April 3, at Montreal — Montreal 4, Boston 3.

1928-29 — Boston Bruins — Tiny Thompson, Eddie Shore, Lionel Hitchman (Captain), Percy Galbraith, Mickey Mackay, Red Green, Dutch Gainor, Harry Oliver, Eddie Rodden, Dit Clapper, Cooney Weiland, Lloyd Klein, Cy Denneny (Playing Coach), Bill Carson, George Owen, Myles Lane, Art Ross (Manager), Win Green (Trainer).
Scores: March 28, at Boston — Boston 2, NY Rangers 0; March 29, at New York — Boston 2, NY Rangers 1.

1927-28 — New York Rangers — Lorne Chabot, Clarence Abel, Leo Bourgeault, Ching Johnson, Bill Cook (Captain), Bun Cook, Frank Boucher, Bill Boyd, Murray Murdoch, Paul Thompson, Alex Gray, Joe Miller, Patsy Callighen, Lester Patrick (Manager-Coach), Harry Westerby (Trainer).
Scores: April 5, at Montreal — Mtl. Maroons 2, NY Rangers 0; April 7, at Montreal — NY Rangers 2, Mtl. Maroons 1; April 10, at Montreal — Mtl. Maroons 2, NY Rangers 0; April 12, at Montreal — NY Rangers 1, Mtl. Maroons 0; April 14, at Montreal — NY Rangers 2, Mtl. Maroons 1.

1926-27 — Ottawa Senators — Alex Connell, King Clancy, Georges Boucher, Ed Gorman, Frank Finnigan, Alex Smith, Hec Kilrea, Hooley Smith, Cy Denneny, Frank Nighbor, Jack Adams, Milt Halliday, Dave Gill (Manager-Coach).
Scores: April 7, at Boston — Ottawa 0, Boston 0; April 9, at Boston — Ottawa 3, Boston 1; April 11, at Ottawa — Boston 1, Ottawa 1; April 13, at Ottawa — Ottawa 3, Boston 1.

1925-26 — Montreal Maroons — Clint Benedict, Reg Noble, Frank Carson, Dunc Munro, Nels Stewart, Punch Broadbent, Babe Siebert, Chuck Dinsmore, Merlyn Phillips, Hobie Kitchen, Sam Rothschild, Albert Holway, George Horne, Bernie Brophy, Eddie Gerard (Manager-Coach), Bill O'Brien (Trainer).
Scores: March 30, at Montreal — Mtl. Maroons 3, Victoria 0; April 1, at Montreal — Mtl. Maroons 3, Victoria 0; April 3, at Montreal — Victoria 3, Mtl. Maroons 2; April 6, at Montreal — Mtl. Maroons 2, Victoria 0.

The series in the spring of 1926 ended the annual playoffs between the champions of the East and the champions of the West. Since 1926-27 the annual playoffs in the National Hockey League have decided the Stanley Cup champions.

1924-25 — Victoria Cougars — Hap Holmes, Clem Loughlin, Gord Fraser, Frank Fredrickson, Jack Walker, Gizzy Hart, Harold Halderson, Frank Foyston, Wally Elmer, Harry Meeking, Jocko Anderson, Lester Patrick (Manager-Coach).
Scores: March 21, at Victoria — Victoria 5, Montreal 2; March 23, at Vancouver — Victoria 3, Montreal 1; March 27, at Victoria — Montreal 4, Victoria 2; March 30, at Victoria — Victoria 6, Montreal 1.

The Stanley Cup champion Seattle Metropolitans of 1917 were: Bobby Rowe, Cully Wilson, Jack Walker, Bernie Morris, Frank Foyston, Jim Riley, Roy Rickey, Ed Carpenter and Hap Holmes.
All but Riley and Carpenter were back in 1919 (although Morris didn't play) for the 1919 Stanley Cup series that was canceled by the worldwide flu epidemic.

1923-24 — Montreal Canadiens — Georges Vezina, Sprague Cleghorn (Captain), Billy Coutu, Howie Morenz, Aurel Joliat, Billy Boucher, Odie Cleghorn, Sylvio Mantha, Bobby Boucher, Billy Bell, Billy Cameron, Joe Malone, Charles Fortier, Leo Dandurand (Manager-Coach).
Scores: March 18, at Montreal — Montreal 3, Van. Maroons 2; March 20, at Montreal — Montreal 2, Van. Maroons 1. March 22, at Montreal — Montreal 6, Cgy. Tigers 1; March 25, at Ottawa* — Montreal 3, Cgy. Tigers 0.
* Game transferred to Ottawa to benefit from artificial ice surface.

1922-23 — Ottawa Senators — Georges Boucher, Lionel Hitchman, Frank Nighbor, King Clancy, Harry Helman, Clint Benedict, Jack Darragh, Eddie Gerard, Cy Denneny, Punch Broadbent, Tommy Gorman (Manager), Pete Green (Coach), F. Dolan (Trainer).
Scores: March 16, at Vancouver — Ottawa 1, Van. Maroons 0; March 19, at Vancouver — Van. Maroons 4, Ottawa 1; March 23, at Vancouver — Ottawa 3, Van. Maroons 2; March 26, at Vancouver — Ottawa 5, Van. Maroons 1; March 29, at Vancouver — Ottawa 2, Edm. Eskimos 1; March 31, at Vancouver — Ottawa 1, Edm. Eskimos 0.

1921-22 — Toronto St. Pats — Ted Stackhouse, Corb Denneny, Rod Smylie, Lloyd Andrews, John Ross Roach, Harry Cameron, Billy Stuart, Babe Dye, Ken Randall, Reg Noble, Eddie Gerard (borrowed for one game from Ottawa), Stan Jackson, Ivan Mitchell, Charlie Querrie (Manager), George O'Donoghue (Coach).
Scores: March 17, at Toronto — Van. Millionaires 4, Toronto 3; March 20, at Toronto — Toronto 2, Van. Millionaires 1; March 23, at Toronto — Van. Millionaires 3, Toronto 0; March 25, at Toronto — Toronto 6, Van. Millionaires 0; March 28, at Toronto — Toronto 5, Van. Millionaires 1.

1920-21 — Ottawa Senators — Jack MacKell, Jack Darragh, Morley Bruce, Georges Boucher, Eddie Gerard, Clint Benedict, Sprague Cleghorn, Frank Nighbor, Punch Broadbent, Cy Denneny, Leth Graham, Tommy Gorman (Manager),Pete Green (Coach), F. Dolan (Trainer).
Scores: March 21, at Vancouver — Van. Millionaires 2, Ottawa 1; March 24, at Vancouver — Ottawa 4, Van. Millionaires 3; March 28, at Vancouver — Ottawa 3, Van. Millionaires 2; March 31, at Vancouver — Van. Millionaires 3, Ottawa 2; April 4, at Vancouver — Ottawa 2, Van. Millionaires 1.

1919-20 — Ottawa Senators — Jack MacKell, Jack Darragh, Morley Bruce, Horrace Merrill, Georges Boucher, Eddie Gerard, Clint Benedict, Sprague Cleghorn, Frank Nighbor, Punch Broadbent, Cy Denneny, Tommy Gorman (Manager), Pete Green (Coach).
Scores: March 22, at Ottawa — Ottawa 3, Seattle 2; March 24, at Ottawa — Ottawa 3, Seattle 0; March 27, at Ottawa — Seattle 3, Ottawa 1; March 30, at Toronto* — Seattle 5, Ottawa 2; April 1, at Toronto* — Ottawa 6, Seattle 1.
* Games transferred to Toronto to benefit from artificial ice surface.

1918-19 — No decision, Series halted by Spanish influenza epidemic, illness of several players and death of Joe Hall of Montreal Canadiens from flu. Five games had been played when the series was halted, each team having won two and tied one. The results are shown:
Scores: March 19, at Seattle — Seattle 7, Montreal 0; March 22, at Seattle — Montreal 4, Seattle 2; March 24, at Seattle — Seattle 7, Montreal 2; March 26, at Seattle — Montreal 0, Seattle 0; March 30, at Seattle — Montreal 4, Seattle 3.

1917-18 — Toronto Arenas — Rusty Crawford, Harry Meeking, Ken Randall, Corb Denneny, Harry Cameron, Jack Adams, Alf Skinner, Harry Mummery, Hap Holmes, Reg Noble, Sammy Hebert, Jack Coughlin, Charlie Querrie (Manager), Dick Carroll (Coach), Frank Carroll (Trainer).
Scores: March 20, at Toronto — Toronto 5, Van. Millionaires 3; March 23, at Toronto — Toronto 6, Van. Millionaires 3; March 26, at Toronto — Van. Millionaires 8, Toronto 1; March 28, at Toronto — Van. Millionaires 8, Toronto 1; March 30, at Toronto — Toronto 2, Van. Millionaires 1.

1916-17 — Seattle Metropolitans — Hap Holmes, Ed Carpenter, Cully Wilson, Jack Walker, Bernie Morris, Frank Foyston, Roy Rickey, Jim Riley, Bobby Rowe (Captain), Peter Muldoon (Manager).
Scores: March 17, at Seattle — Montreal 8, Seattle 4; March 20, at Seattle — Seattle 6, Montreal 1; March 23, at Seattle — Seattle 4, Montreal 1; March 25, at Seattle — Seattle 9, Montreal 1.

1915-16 — Montreal Canadiens — Georges Vezina, Bert Corbeau, Jack Laviolette, Newsy Lalonde, Louis Berlinquette, Goldie Prodgers, Howard McNamara (Captain), Didier Pitre, Skene Ronan, Amos Arbour, Skinner Poulin, Jack Fournier, George Kennedy (Manager).
Scores: March 20, at Montreal — Portland 2, Montreal 0; March 22, at Montreal — Montreal 2, Portland 1; March 25, at Montreal — Montreal 6, Portland 3; March 28, at Montreal — Portland 6, Montreal 5; March 30, at Montreal — Montreal 2, Portland 1.

1914-15 — Vancouver Millionaires — Ken Mallen, Frank Nighbor, Cyclone Taylor, Hugh Lehman, Lloyd Cook, Mickey Mackay, Barney Stanley, Jim Seaborn, Si Griffis (Captain), Johnny Matz, Frank Patrick (Playing Manager).
Scores: March 22, at Vancouver — Van. Millionaires 6, Ottawa 2; March 24, at Vancouver — Van. Millionaires 8, Ottawa 3; March 26, at Vancouver — Van. Millionaires 12, Ottawa 3.

1913-14 — Toronto Blueshirts — Con Corbeau, Roy McGiffen, Jack Walker, George McNamara, Cully Wilson, Frank Foyston, Harry Cameron, Hap Holmes, Scotty Davidson (Captain), Harriston, Jack Marshall (Playing Manager), Frank and Dick Carroll (Trainers).
Scores: March 14, at Toronto — Toronto 5, Victoria 2; March 17, at Toronto — Toronto 6, Victoria 5; March 19, at Toronto — Toronto 2, Victoria 1.

1912-13 — Quebec Bulldogs — Joe Malone, Joe Hall, Paddy Moran, Harry Mummery, Tommy Smith, Jack Marks, Rusty Crawford, Billy Creighton, Jeff Malone, Rocket Power, M.J. Quinn (Manager), D. Beland (Trainer).
Scores: March 8, at Quebec — Que. Bulldogs 14, Sydney 3; March 10, at Quebec — Que. Bulldogs 6, Sydney 2.

Victoria challenged Quebec but the Bulldogs refused to put the Stanley Cup in competition so the two teams played an exhibition series with Victoria winning two games to one by scores of 7-5, 3-6, 6-1. It was the first meeting between the Eastern champions and the Western champions. The following year, and until the Western Hockey League disbanded after the 1926 playoffs, the Cup went to the winner of the series between East and West.

1911-12 — Quebec Bulldogs — Goldie Prodgers, Joe Hall, Walter Rooney, Paddy Moran, Jack Marks, Jack McDonald, Eddie Oatman, George Leonard, Joe Malone (Captain), C. Nolan (Coach), M.J. Quinn (Manager), D. Beland (Trainer).
Scores: March 11, at Quebec — Que. Bulldogs 9, Moncton 3; March 13, at Quebec — Que. Bulldogs 8, Moncton 0.

Prior to 1912, teams could challenge the Stanley Cup champions for the title, thus there was more than one Championship Series played in most of the seasons between 1894 and 1911.

1910-11 — Ottawa Senators — Hamby Shore, Percy LeSueur, Jack Darragh, Bruce Stuart, Marty Walsh, Bruce Ridpath, Fred Lake, Dubbie Kerr, Alex Currie, Horace Gaul.
Scores: March 13, at Ottawa — Ottawa 7, Galt 4; March 16, at Ottawa — Ottawa 13, Port Arthur 4.

1909-10 (March) **— Montreal Wanderers** — Cecil Blachford, Moose Johnson, Ernie Russell, Riley Hern, Harry Hyland, Jack Marshall, Pud Glass (Captain), Jimmy Gardner, Dickie Boon (Manager).
Scores: March 12, at Montreal — Mtl. Wanderers 7, Berlin (Kitchener) 3.

1909-10 (January) **— Ottawa Senators** — Dubbie Kerr, Fred Lake, Percy LeSueur, Ken Mallen, Bruce Ridpath, Gord Roberts, Hamby Shore, Bruce Stuart, Marty Walsh.
Scores: January 5, at Ottawa — Ottawa 12, Galt 3; January 7, at Ottawa — Ottawa 3, Galt 1; January 18, at Ottawa — Ottawa 8, Edmonton 4; January 20, at Ottawa — Ottawa 13, Edmonton 7.

1908-09 — Ottawa Senators — Fred Lake, Percy LeSueur, Cyclone Taylor, Billy Gilmour, Dubbie Kerr, Edgar Dey, Marty Walsh, Bruce Stuart (Captain).
Scores: Ottawa, as champions of the Eastern Canada Hockey Association took over the Stanley Cup in 1909 and, although a challenge was accepted by the Cup trustees from Winnipeg Shamrocks, games could not be arranged because of the lateness of the season. No other challenges were made in 1909. The following season — 1909-10 — however, the Senators accepted two challenges as defending Cup Champions. The first was against Galt in a two-game, total-goals series, and the second against Edmonton, also a two-game, total-goals series. Results: January 5, at Ottawa —Ottawa 12, Galt 3; January 7, at Ottawa — Ottawa 3, Galt 1. January 18, at Ottawa — Ottawa 8, Edm. Eskimos 4; January 20, at Ottawa — Ottawa 13, Edm. Eskimos 7.

1907-08 — Montreal Wanderers — Riley Hern, Art Ross, Walter Smaill, Pud Glass, Bruce Stuart, Ernie Russell, Moose Johnson, Cecil Blachford (Captain), Tom Hooper, Larry Gilmour, Ernie Liffiton, Dickie Boon (Manager).
Scores: Wanderers accepted four challenges for the Cup: January 9, at Montreal — Mtl. Wanderers 9, Ott. Victorias 3; January 13, at Montreal — Mtl. Wanderers 13, Ott. Victorias 1; March 10, at Montreal — Mtl. Wanderers 11, Wpg. Maple Leafs 5; March 12, at Montreal — Mtl. Wanderers 9, Wpg. Maple Leafs 3; March 14, at Montreal — Mtl. Wanderers 6, Toronto (OPHL) 4. At start of following season, 1908-09, Wanderers were challenged by Edmonton. Results: December 28, at Montreal — Mtl. Wanderers 7, Edm. Eskimos 3; December 30, at Montreal — Edm. Eskimos 7, Mtl. Wanderers 6. Total goals: Mtl. Wanderers 13, Edm. Eskimos 10.

1906-07 — (March 25) **— Montreal Wanderers** — Billy Strachan, Riley Hern, Lester Patrick, Hod Stuart, Pud Glass, Ernie Russell, Cecil Blachford (Captain), Moose Johnson, Rod Kennedy, Jack Marshall, Dickie Boon (Manager).

1906-07 — (March 18) **— Kenora Thistles** — Eddie Giroux, Si Griffis, Tom Hooper, Fred Whitcroft, Alf Smith, Harry Westwick, Roxy Beaudro, Tom Phillips (Captain), Russell Phillips.
Scores: March 16, at Winnipeg — Kenora 8, Brandon 6; March 18, at Winnipeg — Kenora 4, Brandon 1; March 23, at Winnipeg — Mtl. Wanderers 7, Kenora 2; March 25, at Winnipeg — Kenora 6, Mtl. Wanderers 5. Total goals: Mtl. Wanderers 12, Kenora 8.

1906-07 — (January) **— Kenora Thistles** — Eddie Giroux, Art Ross, Si Griffis, Tom Hooper, Billy McGimsie, Roxy Beaudro, Tommy Phillips (Captain), Joe Hall, Russell Phillips.
Scores: January 17, at Montreal — Kenora 4, Mtl. Wanderers 2; Jan. 21, at Montreal — Kenora 8, Mtl. Wanderers 6.

1905-06 — (March) **— Montreal Wanderers** — Henri Menard, Billy Strachan, Rod Kennedy, Lester Patrick, Pud Glass, Ernie Russell, Moose Johnson, Cecil Blachford (Captain), Josh Arnold, Dickie Boon (Manager).
Scores: March 14, at Montreal — Mtl. Wanderers 9, Ottawa 1; March 17, at Ottawa — Ottawa 9, Mtl. Wanderers 3. Total goals: Mtl. Wanderers 12, Ottawa 10. Wanderers accepted a challenge from New Glasgow, N.S., prior to the start of the 1906-07 season. Results: December 27, at Montreal — Mtl. Wanderers 10, New Glasgow 3; December 29, at Montreal — Mtl. Wanderers 7, New Glasgow 2.

1905-06 — (February) **— Ottawa Silver Seven** — Harvey Pulford (Captain), Arthur Moore, Harry Westwick, Frank McGee, Alf Smith (Playing Coach), Billy Gilmour, Billy Hague, Percy LeSueur, Harry Smith, Tommy Smith, Dion, Ebbs.
Scores: February 27, at Ottawa — Ottawa 16, Queen's University 7; February 28, at Ottawa — Ottawa 12, Queen's University 7; March 6, at Ottawa — Ottawa 6, Smiths Falls 5; March 8, at Ottawa — Ottawa 8, Smiths Falls 2.

1904-05 — Ottawa Silver Seven — Dave Finnie, Harvey Pulford (Captain), Arthur Moore, Harry Westwick, Frank McGee, Alf Smith (Playing Coach), Billy Gilmour, Frank White, Horace Gaul, Hamby Shore, Bones Allen.
Scores: January 13, at Ottawa — Ottawa 9, Dawson City 2; January 16, at Ottawa — Ottawa 23, Dawson City 2; March 7, at Ottawa — Rat Portage 9, Ottawa 3; March 9, at Ottawa — Ottawa 4, Rat Portage 2; March 11, at Ottawa — Ottawa 5, Rat Portage 4.

1903-04 — Ottawa Silver Seven — Suddy Gilmour, Arthur Moore, Frank McGee, Bouse Hutton, Billy Gilmour, Jim McGee, Harry Westwick, Harvey Pulford (Captain), Scott, Alf Smith (Playing Coach).
Scores: December 30, at Ottawa — Ottawa 9, Wpg. Rowing Club 1; January 1, at Ottawa — Wpg. Rowing Club 6, Ottawa 2; January 4, at Ottawa — Ottawa 2, Wpg. Rowing Club 0. February 23, at Ottawa — Ottawa 6, Tor. Marlboros 3; February 25, at Ottawa — Ottawa 11, Tor. Marlboros 2; March 2, at Montreal — Ottawa 5, Mtl. Wanderers 5. Following the tie game, a new two-game series was ordered to be played in Ottawa but the Wanderers refused unless the tie game was replayed in Montreal. When no settlement could be reached, the series was abandoned and Ottawa retained the Cup and accepted a two-game challenge from Brandon. Results: (both games at Ottawa), March 9, Ottawa 6, Brandon 3; March 11, Ottawa 9, Brandon 3.

1902-03 — (March) **— Ottawa Silver Seven** — Suddy Gilmour, Percy Sims, Bouse Hutton, Dave Gilmour, Billy Gilmour, Harry Westwick, Frank McGee, F.H. Wood, A.A. Fraser, Charles Spittal, Harvey Pulford (Captain), Arthur Moore, Alf Smith (coach.)
Scores: March 7, at Montreal — Ottawa 1, Mtl. Victorias 1; March 10, at Ottawa — Ottawa 8, Mtl. Victorias 0. Total goals: Ottawa 9, Mtl. Victorias 1; March 12, at Ottawa — Ottawa 6, Rat Portage 2; March 14, at Ottawa — Ottawa 4, Rat Portage 2.

1902-03 — (February) **— Montreal AAA** — Tom Hodge, Dickie Boon, Billy Nicholson, Tommy Phillips, Art Hooper, Billy Bellingham, Charles Liffiton, Jack Marshall, Jimmy Gardner, Cecil Blachford, George Smith.
Scores: January 29, at Montreal — Mtl. AAA 8, Wpg. Victorias 1; January 31, at Montreal — Wpg. Victorias 2, Mtl. AAA 2; February 2, at Montreal — Wpg. Victorias 4, Mtl. AAA 2; February 4, at Montreal — Mtl. AAA 5, Wpg. Victorias 1.

1901-02 — (March) **— Montreal AAA** — Tom Hodge, Dickie Boon, Billy Nicholson, Archie Hooper, Billy Bellingham, Charles Liffiton, Jack Marshall, Roland Elliott, Jimmy Gardner.
Scores: March 13, at Winnipeg — Wpg. Victorias 1, Mtl. AAA 0; March 15, at Winnipeg — Mtl. AAA 5, Wpg. Victorias 0; March 17, at Winnipeg — Mtl. AAA 2, Wpg. Victorias 1.

1901-02 — (January) **— Winnipeg Victorias** — Burke Wood, Tony Gingras, Charles Johnstone, Rod Flett, Magnus Flett, Dan Bain (Captain), Fred Scanlon, F. Cadham, G. Brown.
Scores: January 21, at Winnipeg — Wpg. Victorias 5, Tor Wellingtons 3; January 23, at Winnipeg — Wpg. Victorias 5, Tor. Wellingtons 3.

1900-01 — Winnipeg Victorias — Burke Wood, Jack Marshall, Tony Gingras, Charles Johnstone, Rod Flett, Magnus Flett, Dan Bain (Captain), Art Brown.
Scores: January 29, at Montreal — Wpg. Victorias 4, Mtl. Shamrocks 3; January 31, at Montreal — Wpg. Victorias 2, Mtl. Shamrocks 1.

1899-1900 — Montreal Shamrocks — Joe McKenna, Frank Tansey, Frank Wall, Art Farrell, Fred Scanlon, Harry Trihey (Captain), Jack Brannen.
Scores: February 12, at Montreal — Mtl. Shamrocks 4, Wpg. Victorias 3; February 14, at Montreal — Wpg. Victorias 3, Mtl. Shamrocks 2; February 16, at Montreal — Mtl. Shamrocks 5, Wpg. Victorias 4; March 5, at Montreal — Mtl. Shamrocks 10, Halifax 2; March 7, at Montreal — Mtl. Shamrocks 11, Halifax 0.

1898-99 — (March) **— Montreal Shamrocks** — Joe McKenna, Frank Tansey, Frank Wall, Harry Trihey (Captain), Art Farrell, Fred Scanlon, Jack Brannen, John Dobby, Charles Hoerner.
Scores: March 14, at Montreal — Mtl. Shamrocks 6, Queen's University 2.

1898-99 — (February) **— Montreal Victorias** — Gordon Lewis, Mike Grant, Graham Drinkwater, Cam Davidson, Bob McDougall, Ernie McLea, Frank Richardson, Jack Ewing, Russell Bowie, Douglas Acer, Fred McRobie.
Scores: February 15, at Montreal — Mtl. Victorias 2, Wpg. Victorias 1; February 18, at Montreal — Mtl. Victorias 3, Wpg. Victorias 2.

1897-98 — Montreal Victorias — Gordon Lewis, Hartland McDougall, Mike Grant, Graham Drinkwater, Cam Davidson, Bob McDougall, Ernie McLea, Frank Richardson (Captain), Jack Ewing. The Victorias as champions of the Amateur Hockey Association, retained the Cup and were not called upon to defend it.

1896-97 — Montreal Victorias — Gordon Lewis, Harold Henderson, Mike Grant (Captain), Cam Davidson, Graham Drinkwater, Bob McDougall, Ernie McLea, Shirley Davidson, Hartland McDougall, Jack Ewing, Percy Molson, David Gillilan, McLellan.
Scores: December 27, at Montreal — Mtl. Victorias 15, Ott. Capitals 2.

1895-96 — (December) **— Montreal Victorias** — Harold Henderson, Mike Grant (Captain), Bob McDougall, Graham Drinkwater, Shirley Davidson, Ernie McLea, W. Wallace, Robert Jones, Cam Davidson, David Gillilan, Stanley Willett.
Scores: December 30, at Winnipeg — Mtl. Victorias 6, Wpg. Victorias 5.

1895-96 — (February) **— Winnipeg Victorias** — Whitey Merritt, Rod Flett, Fred Higginbotham, Jack Armitage (Captain), Tote Campbell, Dan Bain, Bobby Benson, Attie Howard.
Scores: February 14, at Montreal — Wpg. Victorias 2, Mtl. Victorias 0.

1894-95 — Montreal Victorias — Robert Jones, Harold Henderson, Mike Grant (Captain), Shirley Davidson, Bob McDougall, Norman Rankin, Graham Drinkwater, Roland Elliot, William Pullan, Hartland McDougall, Art Fenwick, A. McDougall. Montreal Victorias, as champions of the Amateur Hockey Association, were prepared to defend the Stanley Cup. However, the Stanley Cup trustees had already accepted a challenge match between the 1894 champion Montreal AAA and Queen's University. It was declared that if Montreal AAA defeated Queen's University, Montreal Victorias would be declared Stanley Cup champions. If Queen's University won, the Cup would go to the university club. In a game played March 9, 1895, Montreal AAA defeated Queen's University 5-1. As a result, Montreal Victorias were awarded the Stanley Cup.

1893-94 — Montreal AAA — Herb Collins, Allan Cameron, George James, Billy Barlow, Clare Mussen, Archie Hodgson, Haviland Routh, Alex Irving, James Stewart, E. O'Brien, A.C. (Toad) Wand, A.B. Kingan.
Scores: March 17, at Mtl. Victorias — Mtl. AAA 3, Mtl. Victorias 2; March 22, at Montreal — Mtl. AAA 3, Ott. Capitals 1.

1892-93 — Montreal AAA — Tom Paton, James Stewart, Allan Cameron, Haviland Routh, Archie Hodgson, Billy Barlow, A.B. Kingan, G.S. Lowe.
In accordance with the terms governing the presentation of the Stanley Cup, it was awarded for the first time to the Montreal AAA as champions of the Amateur Hockey Association in 1893. Once Montreal AAA had been declared holders of the Stanley Cup, any Canadian hockey team could challenge for the trophy.

All-Time NHL Playoff Formats

1917-18 — The regular-season was split into two halves. The winners of both halves faced each other in a two-game, total-goals series for the NHL championship and the right to meet the PCHA champion in the best-of-five Stanley Cup Finals.

1918-19 — Same as 1917-18, except that the Stanley Cup Finals was extended to a best-of-seven series.

1919-20 — Same as 1917-1918, except that Ottawa won both halves of the split regular-season schedule to earn an automatic berth into the best-of-five Stanley Cup Finals against the PCHA champions.

1921-22 — The top two teams at the conclusion of the regular-season faced each other in a two-game, total-goals series for the NHL championship. The NHL champion then moved on to play the winner of the PCHA-WCHL playoff series in the best-of-five Stanley Cup Finals.

1922-23 — The top two teams at the conclusion of the regular-season faced each other in a two-game, total-goals series for the NHL championship. The NHL champion then moved on to play the PCHA champion in the best-of-three Stanley Cup Semi-Finals, and the winner of the Semi-Finals played the WCHL champion, which had been given a bye, in the best-of-three Stanley Cup Finals.

1923-24 — The top two teams at the conclusion of the regular-season faced each other in a two-game, total-goals series for the NHL championship. The NHL champion then moved on to play the loser of the PCHA-WCHL playoff (the winner of the PCHA-WCHL playoff earned a bye into the Stanley Cup Finals) in the best-of-three Stanley Cup Semi-Finals. The winner of this series met the PCHA-WCHL playoff winner in the best-of-three Stanley Cup Finals.

1924-25 — The first place team (Hamilton) at the conclusion of the regular-season was supposed to play the winner of a two-game, total-goals series between the second (Toronto) and third (Montreal) place clubs. However, Hamilton refused to abide by this new format, demanding greater compensation than offered by the League. Thus, Toronto and Montreal played their two-game, total-goals series, and the winner (Montreal) earned the NHL title and then played the WCHL champion (Victoria) in the best-of-five Stanley Cup Finals.

1925-26 — The format which was intended for 1924-25 went into effect. The winner of the two-game, total-goals series between the second and third place teams squared off against the first place team in the two-game, total-goals NHL championship series. The NHL champion then moved on to play the WHL champion in the best-of-five Stanley Cup Finals.

After the 1925-26 season, the NHL was the only major professional hockey league still in existence and consequently took over sole control of the Stanley Cup competition.

1926-27 — The 10-team league was divided into two divisions — Canadian and American — of five teams apiece. In each division, the winner of the two-game, total-goals series between the second and third place teams faced the first place team in a two-game, total-goals series for the division title. The two division title winners then met in the best-of-five Stanley Cup Finals.

1928-29 — Both first place teams in the two divisions played each other in a best-of-five series. Both second place teams in the two divisions played each other in a two-game, total-goals series as did the two third place teams. The winners of these latter two series then played each other in a best-of-three series for the right to meet the winner of the series between the two first place clubs. This Stanley Cup Final was a best-of-three.

> Series A: First in Canadian Division vs. first in American (best-of-five)
> Series B: Second in Canadian Division vs. second in American (two-game, total-goals)
> Series C: Third in Canadian Division vs. third in American (two-game, total-goals)
> Series D: Winner of Series B vs. winner of Series C (best-of-three)
> Series E: Winner of Series A vs. winner of Series D (best-of-three) for Stanley Cup

1931-32 — Same as 1928-29, except that Series D was changed to a two-game, total-goals format and Series E was changed to best-of-five.

1936-37 — Same as 1931-32, except that Series B, C, and D were each best-of-three.

1938-39 — With the NHL reduced to seven teams, the two-division system was replaced by one seven-team league. Based on final regular-season standings, the following playoff format was adopted:

> Series A: First vs. Second (best-of-seven)
> Series B: Third vs. Fourth (best-of-three)
> Series C: Fifth vs. Sixth (best-of-three)
> Series D: Winner of Series B vs. winner of Series C (best-of-three)
> Series E: Winner of Series A vs. winner of Series D (best-of-seven)

1942-43 — With the NHL reduced to six teams (the "original six"), only the top four finishers qualified for playoff action. The best-of-seven Semi-Finals pitted Team #1 vs. Team #3 and Team #2 vs. Team #4. The winners of each Semi-Final series met in the best-of-seven Stanley Cup Finals.

1967-68 — When it doubled in size from 6 to 12 teams, the NHL once again was divided into two divisions — East and West — of six teams apiece. The top four clubs in each division qualified for the playoffs (all series were best-of-seven):

> Series A: Team #1 (East) vs. Team #3 (East)
> Series B: Team #2 (East) vs. Team #4 (East)
> Series C: Team #1 (West) vs. Team #3 (West)
> Series D: Team #2 (West) vs. Team #4 (West)
> Series E: Winner of Series A vs. winner of Series B
> Series F: Winner of Series C vs. winner of Series D
> Series G: Winner of Series E vs. Winner of Series F

1970-71 — Same as 1967-68 except that Series E matched the winners of Series A and D, and Series F matched the winners of Series B and C.

1971-72 — Same as 1970-71, except that Series A and C matched Team #1 vs. Team #4, and Series B and D matched Team #2 vs. Team #3.

1974-75 — With the League now expanded to 18 teams in four divisions, a completely new playoff format was introduced. First, the #2 and #3 teams in each of the four divisions were pooled together in the Preliminary round. These eight (#2 and #3) clubs were ranked #1 to #8 based on regular-season record:

> Series A: Team #1 vs. Team #8 (best-of-three)
> Series B: Team #2 vs. Team #7 (best-of-three)
> Series C: Team #3 vs. Team #6 (best-of-three)
> Series D: Team #4 vs. Team #5 (best-of-three)
The winners of this Preliminary round then pooled together with the four division winners, which had received byes into this Quarter-Final round. These eight teams were again ranked #1 to #8 based on regular-season record:
> Series E: Team #1 vs. Team #8 (best-of-seven)
> Series F: Team #2 vs. Team #7 (best-of-seven)
> Series G: Team #3 vs. Team #6 (best-of-seven)
> Series H: Team #4 vs. Team #5 (best-of-seven)
The four Quarter-Finals winners, which moved on to the Semi-Finals, were then ranked #1 to #4 based on regular season record:
> Series I: Team #1 vs. Team #4 (best-of-seven)
> Series J: Team #2 vs. Team #3 (best-of-seven)
> Series K: Winner of Series I vs. winner of Series J (best-of-seven)

1977-78 — Same as 1974-75, except that the Preliminary round consisted of the #2 teams in the four divisions and the next four teams based on regular-season record (not their standings within their divisions).

1979-80 — With the addition of four WHA franchises, the League expanded its playoff structure to include 16 of its 21 teams. The four first place teams in the four divisions automatically earned playoff berths. Among the 17 other clubs, the top 12, according to regular-season record, also earned berths. All 16 teams were then pooled together and ranked #1 to #16 based on regular-season record:

> Series A: Team #1 vs. Team #16 (best-of-five)
> Series B: Team #2 vs. Team #15 (best-of-five)
> Series C: Team #3 vs. Team #14 (best-of-five)
> Series D: Team #4 vs. Team #13 (best-of-five)
> Series E: Team #5 vs. Team #12 (best-of-five)
> Series F: Team #6 vs. Team #11 (best-of-five)
> Series G: Team #7 vs. Team #10 (best-of-five)
> Series H: Team #8 vs. Team # 9 (best-of-five)

The eight Preliminary round winners, ranked #1 to #8 based on regular-season record, moved on to the Quarter-Finals:
Series I: Team #1 vs. Team #8 (best-of-seven)
Series J: Team #2 vs. Team #7 (best-of-seven)
Series K: Team #3 vs. Team #6 (best-of-seven)
Series L: Team #4 vs. Team #5 (best-of-seven)
The four Quarter-Finals winners, ranked #1 to #4 based on regular-season record, moved on to the semi-finals:
Series M: Team #1 vs. Team #4 (best-of-seven)
Series N: Team #2 vs. Team #3 (best-of-seven)
Series O: Winner of Series M vs. winner of Series N (best-of-seven)

1981-82 — The first four teams in each division earned playoff berths. In each division, the first-place team opposed the fourth-place team and the second-place team opposed the third-place team in a best-of-five Division Semi-Final series (DSF). In each division, the two winners of the DSF met in a best-of-seven Division Final series (DF). The two DF winners in each conference met in a best-of-seven Conference Final series (CF). In the Prince of Wales Conference, the Adams Division winner opposed the Patrick Division winner; in the Clarence Campbell Conference, the Smythe Division winner opposed the Norris Division winner. The two CF winners met in a best-of-seven Stanley Cup Final (F) series.

1986-87 — Division Semi-Final series changed from best-of-five to best-of-seven.

1993-94 — The NHL's playoff draw is conference-based rather than division-based. At the conclusion of the regular season, the top eight teams in each of the Eastern and Western Conferences qualify for the playoffs. The teams that finish in first place in each of the League's divisions are seeded first and second in each conference's playoff draw and are assured of home ice advantage in the first two playoff rounds. The remaining teams are seeded based on their regular-season point totals. In each conference, the team seeded #1 plays #8; #2 vs. #7; #3 vs. #6; and #4 vs. #5. All series are best-of-seven with home ice rotating on a 2-2-1-1-1 basis, with the exception of matchups between Central and Pacific Division teams. These matchups will be played on a 2-3-2 basis to reduce travel. In a 2-3-2 series, the team with the most points will have its choice to start the series at home or on the road. The Eastern Conference champion will face the Western Conference champion in the Stanley Cup Final.

1994-95 — Same as 1993-94, except that in first, second or third-round playoff series involving Central and Pacific Division teams, the team with the better record has the choice of using either a 2-3-2 or a 2-2-1-1-1 format. When a 2-3-2 format is selected, the higher-ranked team also has the choice of playing games 1, 2, 6 and 7 at home or playing games 3, 4 and 5 at home. The format for the Stanley Cup Final remains 2-2-1-1-1.

1998-99 — The NHL's clubs are re-aligned into two conferences each consisting of three divisions. The number of teams qualifying for the Stanley Cup Playoffs remains unchanged at 16.

First-round playoff berths will be awarded to the first-place team in each division as well as to the next five best teams based on regular-season point totals in each conference. The three division winners in each conference will be seeded first through third, in order of points, for the playoffs and the next five best teams, in order of points, will be seeded fourth through eighth. In each conference, the team seeded #1 will play #8; #2 vs. #7; #3 vs. #6; and #4 vs. #5 in the quarterfinal round. Home-ice in the Conference Quarter-Finals is granted to those teams seeded first through fourth in each conference.

In the Conference Semi-Finals and Conference Finals, teams will be re-seeded according to the same criteria as the Conference Quarter-Finals. Higher seeded teams will have home-ice advantage.

Home-ice advantage for the Stanley Cup Finals will be determined by points.

All series remain best-of-seven.

Stanley Cup champions in 1970 (pictured here) and again in 1972, the Boston Bruins made the NHL playoffs for a record 29 consecutive seasons from 1968 to 1996.

Team Records

1918-2004

GAMES PLAYED

MOST GAMES PLAYED BY ALL TEAMS, ONE PLAYOFF YEAR:
92 — 1991. There were 51 DSF, 24 DF, 11 CF and 6 F games.
90 — 1994. There were 48 CQF, 23 CSF, 12 CF and 7 F games.
— 2002. There were 47 CQF, 25 CSF, 13 CF and 5 F games.

MOST GAMES PLAYED, ONE TEAM, ONE PLAYOFF YEAR:
26 — Philadelphia Flyers, 1987. Won DSF 4-2 vs. NY Rangers, DF 4-3 vs. NY Islanders, CF 4-2 vs. Montreal, and lost F 4-3 vs. Edmonton.
— **Calgary Flames,** 2004. Won DSF 4-3 vs. Vancouver, DF 4-2 vs. Detroit, CF 4-2 vs. San Jose, and lost F 4-3 vs. Tampa Bay.
25 — New Jersey Devils, 2001. Won CQF 4-2 vs. Carolina, CSF 4-3 vs. Toronto, CF 4-1 vs. Pittsburgh, and lost F 4-3 vs. Colorado.

PLAYOFF APPEARANCES

MOST STANLEY CUP CHAMPIONSHIPS:
23 — Montreal Canadiens (1924-30-31-44-46-53-56-57-58-59-60-65-66-68-69-71-73-76-77-78-79-86-93)
13 — Toronto Maple Leafs (1918-22-32-42-45-47-48-49-51-62-63-64-67)
10 — Detroit Red Wings (1936-37-43-50-52-54-55-97-98-02)

MOST CONSECUTIVE STANLEY CUP CHAMPIONSHIPS:
5 — Montreal Canadiens (1956-57-58-59-60)
4 — Montreal Canadiens (1976-77-78-79)
— NY Islanders (1980-81-82-83)

MOST FINAL SERIES APPEARANCES:
32 — Montreal Canadiens in 86-year history.
22 — Detroit Red Wings in 77-year history.
21 — Toronto Maple Leafs in 86-year history.

MOST CONSECUTIVE FINAL SERIES APPEARANCES:
10 — Montreal Canadiens, (1951-60, inclusive)
5 — Montreal Canadiens, (1965-69, inclusive)
— NY Islanders, (1980-84, inclusive)

MOST YEARS IN PLAYOFFS:
74 — Montreal Canadiens in 87-year history.
64 — Toronto Maple Leafs in 87-year history.
62 — Boston Bruins in 80-year history.

MOST CONSECUTIVE PLAYOFF APPEARANCES:
29 — Boston Bruins (1968-96, inclusive)
28 — Chicago Blackhawks (1970-97, inclusive)
25 — St. Louis Blues (1980-2004, inclusive)
24 — Montreal Canadiens (1971-94, inclusive)
21 — Montreal Canadiens (1949-69, inclusive)

TEAM WINS

MOST HOME WINS, ONE TEAM, ONE PLAYOFF YEAR:
12 — New Jersey Devils, 2003 in 13 home games.
11 — Edmonton Oilers, 1988 in 11 home games.
10 — Edmonton Oilers, 1985 in 10 home games.
— Montreal Canadiens, 1986 in 11 home games.
— Montreal Canadiens, 1993 in 11 home games.

MOST ROAD WINS, ONE TEAM, ONE PLAYOFF YEAR:
10 — New Jersey Devils, 1995. Won three at Boston in CQF; two at Pittsburgh in CSF; three at Philadelphia in CF; and two at Detroit in F.
— **New Jersey Devils,** 2000. Won two at Florida in CQF; two at Toronto in CSF; three at Philadelphia in CF; and three at Dallas in F.
— **Calgary Flames,** 2004. Won three at Vancouver in DSF; two at Detroit in DF; three at San Jose in CF; and two at Tampa Bay in F.
8 — NY Islanders, 1980. Won two at Los Angeles in PR; three at Boston in QF; two at Buffalo in SF; and one at Philadelphia in F.
— Philadelphia Flyers, 1987. Won two at NY Rangers in DSF; two at NY Islanders in DF; three at Montreal in CF; and one at Edmonton in F.
— Edmonton Oilers, 1990. Won three at Winnipeg in DSF; two at Los Angeles in DF; two at Chicago in CF and three at Boston in F.
— Pittsburgh Penguins, 1992. Won two at Washington in DSF; two at NY Rangers in DF; two at Boston in CF; and two at Chicago in F.
— Vancouver Canucks, 1994. Won three at Calgary in CQF; two at Dallas in CSF; one at Toronto in CF; and two at NY Rangers in F.
— Colorado Avalanche, 1996. Won two at Vancouver in CQF; two at Chicago in CSF; two at Detroit in CF; and two at Florida in F.
— Detroit Red Wings, 1998. Won two at Phoenix in CQF; three at St. Louis in CSF; one at Dallas in CF; and two at Washington in F.
— Colorado Avalanche, 1999. Won three at San Jose in CQF; three at Detroit in CSF; and two at Dallas in CF.
— New Jersey Devils, 2001. Won two at Carolina in CQF; two at Toronto in CSF; two at Pittsburgh in CF; and two at Colorado in F.
— Detroit Red Wings, 2002. Won three at Vancouver in CQF; one at St. Louis in CSF; two at Colorado in CF; and two at Carolina in F.

MOST ROAD WINS, ALL TEAMS, ONE PLAYOFF YEAR:
46 — 1987. Of 87 games played, road teams won 46 (22 DSF, 14 DF, 8 CF and 2 in F).

MOST OVERTIME WINS, ONE TEAM, ONE PLAYOFF YEAR:
10 — Montreal Canadiens, 1993. Won two vs. Quebec in DSF; three vs. Buffalo in DF; two vs. NY Islanders in CF; and three vs. Los Angeles in F.
7 — Carolina Hurricanes, 2002. Won two vs. New Jersey in CQF; one vs. Montreal in CSF; three vs. Toronto in CF; and one vs. Detroit in F.
— Anaheim Mighty Ducks, 2003. Won two vs. Detroit in CQF; two vs. Dallas in CSF; one vs. Minnesota in CF; and two vs. New Jersey in F.

MOST OVERTIME WINS AT HOME, ONE TEAM, ONE PLAYOFF YEAR:
4 — St. Louis Blues, 1968. Won one vs. Philadelphia in QF; three vs. Minnesota in SF.
— **Montreal Canadiens, 1993.** Won one vs. Quebec in DSF; one vs. Buffalo in DF, one vs. NY Islanders in CF; one vs. Los Angeles in F.

MOST OVERTIME WINS ON THE ROAD, ONE TEAM, ONE PLAYOFF YEAR:
6 — Montreal Canadiens, 1993. Won one vs. Quebec in DSF; two vs. Buffalo in DF; one vs. NY Islanders in CF; two vs. Los Angeles in F.

TEAM LOSSES

MOST LOSSES, ONE TEAM, ONE PLAYOFF YEAR:
11 — **Philadelphia Flyers, 1987.** Lost two vs. NY Rangers in DSF; three vs. NY Islanders in DF; two vs. Montreal in CF; four vs. Edmonton in F.
— **Calgary Flames, 2004.** Lost three vs. Vancouver in CQF; two vs. Detroit in CSF; two vs. San Jose in CF; four vs. Tampa Bay in F

MOST HOME LOSSES, ONE TEAM, ONE PLAYOFF YEAR:
7 — **Calgary Flames, 2004.** Lost two vs. Vancouver in DSF; one vs. Detroit in DF; two vs. San Jose in CF; two vs. Tampa Bay in F.
6 — Philadelphia Flyers, 1987. Lost one vs. NY Rangers in DSF; two vs. NY Islanders in DF; two vs. Montreal in CF; one vs. Edmonton in F.
— Washington Capitals, 1998. Lost two vs. Boston in CQF; two vs. Buffalo in CF; two vs. Detroit in F.
— Colorado Avalanche, 1999. Lost two vs. San Jose in CQF; two vs. Detroit in CSF; two vs. Dallas in CF.
— New Jersey Devils, 2001. Lost one vs. Carolina in CQF; two vs. Toronto in CSF; one vs. Pittsburgh in CF; two vs. Colorado in F.
— Minnesota Wild, 2003. Lost two vs. Colorado in CQF; two vs. Vancouver in CSF; two vs. Anaheim in CF.

MOST ROAD LOSSES, ONE TEAM, ONE PLAYOFF YEAR:
7 — **New Jersey Devils, 2003.** Lost one at Boston in CQF; one at Tampa Bay in CSF; two at Ottawa in CF; three at Anaheim in F.

MOST OVERTIME LOSSES, ONE TEAM, ONE PLAYOFF YEAR:
4 — **Montreal Canadiens, 1951.** Lost four vs. Toronto in F.
— **St. Louis Blues, 1968.** Lost one vs. Philadelphia in QF; one vs. Minnesota in SF; two vs. Montreal in F.
— **New York Rangers, 1979.** Lost one vs. Philadelphia in QF; two vs. NY Islanders in SF; one vs. Montreal in F.
— **Los Angeles Kings, 1991.** Lost one vs. Vancouver in DSF; three vs. Edmonton in DF.
— **Los Angeles Kings, 1993.** Lost one vs. Toronto in CF; three vs. Montreal in F.
— **New Jersey Devils, 1994.** Lost one vs. Buffalo in CQF; one vs. Boston in CSF; two vs. NY Rangers in CF.
— **Chicago Blackhawks, 1995.** Lost one vs. Toronto in CQF; three vs. Detroit in CF.
— **Philadelphia Flyers, 1996.** Lost two vs. Tampa Bay in CQF; two vs. Florida in CSF.
— **Dallas Stars, 1999.** Lost two vs. St. Louis in CSF; one vs. Colorado in CF; one vs. Buffalo in F.
— **Detroit Red Wings, 2002.** Lost one vs. Vancouver in CQF; two vs. Colorado in CF; one vs. Carolina in F.
— **New Jersey Devils, 2003.** Lost two vs. Ottawa in CF; two vs. Anaheim in F.

MOST OVERTIME LOSSES AT HOME, ONE TEAM, ONE PLAYOFF YEAR:
4 — **Detroit Red Wings, 2002.** Lost one vs. Vancouver in CQF; two vs. Colorado in CF; one vs. Carolina in F.

MOST OVERTIME LOSSES ON THE ROAD, ONE TEAM, ONE PLAYOFF YEAR:
3 — **Los Angeles Kings, 1991.** Lost one at Vancouver in DSF; two at Edmonton in DF.
— **Chicago Blackhawks, 1995.** Lost one at Toronto in CQF; two at Detroit in CF.
— **St. Louis Blues, 1996.** Lost two at Toronto in CQF; one at Detroit in CSF.
— **Dallas Stars, 1999.** Lost two at St. Louis in CSF; one at Colorado in CF.
— **New Jersey Devils, 2003.** Lost one at Ottawa in CF; two at Anaheim in F.

PLAYOFF WINNING STREAKS

LONGEST PLAYOFF WINNING STREAK:
14 — **Pittsburgh Penguins.** Streak started on May 9, 1992 as Pittsburgh won the first of three straight games in DF vs. NY Rangers. Continued with four wins vs. Boston in 1992 CF and four wins vs. Boston in 1992 CF and four wins vs. Chicago in 1992 F. Pittsburgh then won the first three games of 1993 DSF vs. New Jersey. New Jersey ended the streak April 25, 1993, at New Jersey with a 4-1 win vs. Pittsburgh in the fourth game of 1993 DSF.
12 — Edmonton Oilers. Streak started on May 15, 1984 as Edmonton won the first of three straight games in F vs. NY Islanders. Continued with three wins vs. Los Angeles in 1985 DSF and four wins vs. Winnipeg in 1985 DF. Edmonton then won the first two games of 1985 CF vs. Chicago. Chicago ended the streak May 9, 1985, at Chicago with a 5-2 win vs. Edmonton in the third game of 1985 CF.

MOST CONSECUTIVE WINS, ONE TEAM, ONE PLAYOFF YEAR:
11 — **Chicago Blackhawks** in 1992. Chicago won last three games of DSF vs. St. Louis to win series 4-2, defeated Detroit 4-0 in DF and Edmonton 4-0 in CF.
— **Pittsburgh Penguins** in 1992. Pittsburgh won last three games of DF vs. NY Rangers to win series 4-2, defeated Boston 4-0 in CF and Chicago 4-0 in F.
— **Montreal Canadiens** in 1993. Montreal won last four games of DSF vs. Quebec to win series 4-2, defeated Buffalo 4-0 in DF and won first three games of CF vs. NY Islanders.

PLAYOFF LOSING STREAKS

LONGEST PLAYOFF LOSING STREAK:
16 — **Chicago Black Hawks.** Streak started April 20, 1975 at Chicago with a 6-2 loss in fourth game of QF vs. Buffalo won by Buffalo 4-1. Continued with four consecutive losses vs. Montreal in 1976 QF and two straight losses vs. NY Islanders in 1977 best-of-three PRE. Chicago then lost four games vs. Boston in 1978 QF and four games vs. NY Islanders in 1979 QF. Chicago ended the streak April 8, 1980, at Chicago with a 3-2 win vs. St. Louis in the opening game of 1980 PRE.
— Los Angeles Kings. Streak started June 3, 1993 at Montreal with a 3-2 loss in second game of F vs. Montreal, won by Montreal 4-1. Los Angeles failed to qualify for the playoffs for the next four years. Then Los Angeles lost four games vs. St. Louis in 1998 CQF; missed the 1999 playoffs and lost four games vs. Detroit in 2002 CQF. Los Angeles then lost the first two games of 2001 CQF vs. Detroit. Los Angeles ended the streak April 15, 2001, at Los Angeles with a 2-1 win.

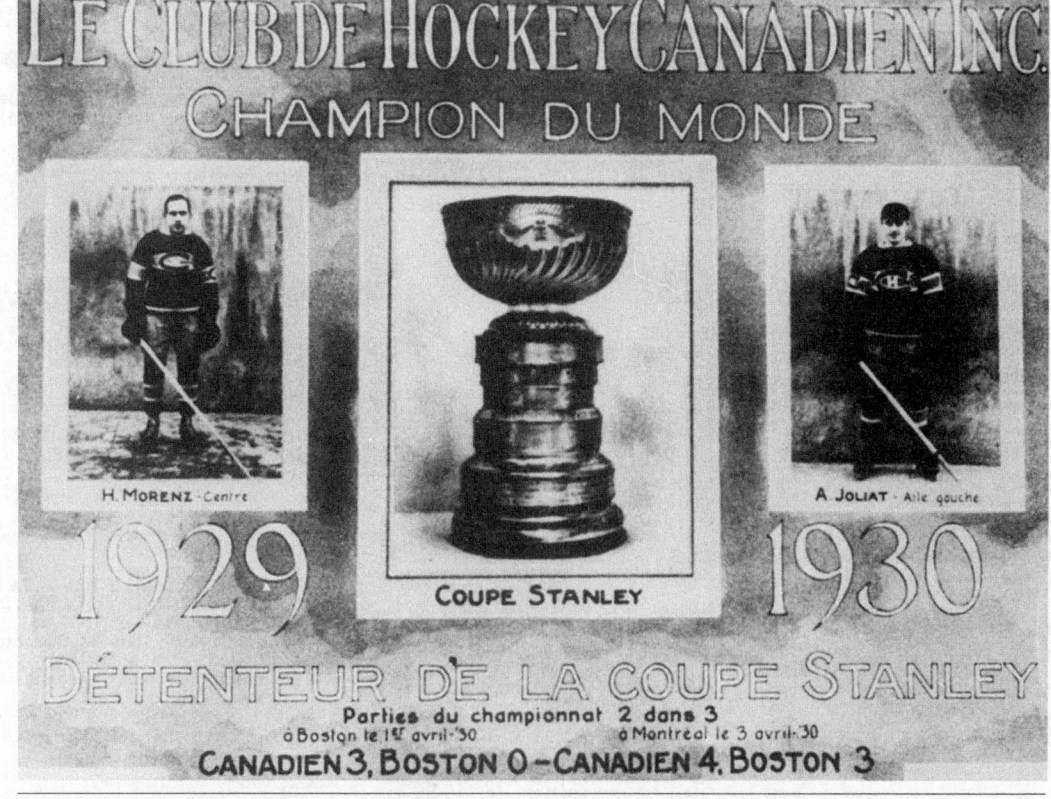

Led by Howie Morenz and Aurel Joliat, the Montreal Canadiens of 1929-30 won the first of back-to-back Stanley Cup titles, the second and third of Montreal's NHL-record 23 championships.

MOST GOALS IN A SERIES, ONE TEAM

MOST GOALS, ONE TEAM, ONE PLAYOFF SERIES:
44 — Edmonton Oilers in 1985 CF. Edmonton won best-of-seven series 4-2, outscoring Chicago 44-25.
35 — Edmonton Oilers in 1983 DF. Edmonton won best-of-seven series 4-1, outscoring Calgary 35-13.
— Calgary Flames in 1995 CQF. Calgary lost best-of-seven series 4-3, outscoring San Jose 35-26.

MOST GOALS, ONE TEAM, TWO-GAME SERIES:
11 — Buffalo Sabres in 1977 PRE. Buffalo won best-of-three series 2-0, outscoring Minnesota 11-3.
— **Toronto Maple Leafs** in 1978 PRE. Toronto won best-of-three series 2-0, outscoring Los Angeles 11-3.

MOST GOALS, ONE TEAM, THREE-GAME SERIES:
23 — Chicago Blackhawks in 1985 DSF. Chicago won best-of-five series 3-0, outscoring Detroit 23-8.
20 — Minnesota North Stars in 1981 PRE. Minnesota won best-of-five series 3-0, outscoring Boston 20-13.
— NY Islanders in 1981 PRE. NY Islanders won best-of-five series 3-0, outscoring Toronto 20-4.

MOST GOALS, ONE TEAM, FOUR-GAME SERIES:
28 — Boston Bruins in 1972 SF. Boston won best-of-seven series 4-0, outscoring St. Louis 28-8.

MOST GOALS, ONE TEAM, FIVE-GAME SERIES:
35 — Edmonton Oilers in 1983 DF. Edmonton won best-of-seven series 4-1, outscoring Calgary 35-13.
32 — Edmonton Oilers in 1987 DSF. Edmonton won best-of-seven series 4-1, outscoring Los Angeles 32-20.
30 — Calgary Flames in 1988 DSF. Calgary won best-of-seven series 4-1, outscoring Los Angeles 30-18.

MOST GOALS, ONE TEAM, SIX-GAME SERIES:
44 — Edmonton Oilers in 1985 CF. Edmonton won best-of-seven series 4-2, outscoring Chicago 44-25.
33 — Montreal Canadiens in 1973 F. Montreal won best-of-seven series 4-2, outscoring Chicago 33-23.
— Chicago Blackhawks in 1985 DF. Chicago won best-of-seven series 4-2, outscoring Minnesota 33-29.
— Los Angeles Kings in 1993 DSF. Los Angeles won best-of-seven series 4-2, outscoring Calgary 33-28.

MOST GOALS, ONE TEAM, SEVEN-GAME SERIES:
35 — Calgary Flames in 1995 CQF. Calgary lost best-of-seven series 4-3, outscoring San Jose 35-26.
33 — Philadelphia Flyers in 1976 QF. Philadelphia won best-of-seven series 4-3, outscoring Toronto 33-23.
— Boston Bruins in 1983 DF. Boston won best-of-seven series 4-3, outscoring Buffalo 33-23.
— Edmonton Oilers in 1984 DF. Edmonton won best-of-seven series 4-3, outscoring Calgary 33-27.

FEWEST GOALS IN A SERIES, ONE TEAM

FEWEST GOALS, ONE TEAM, TWO-GAME SERIES:
0 — Toronto St. Patricks in 1921 NHL F. Toronto lost two-game, total-goals series 7-0 vs. Ottawa.
— **New York Americans** in 1929 SF. NY Americans lost two-game, total-goals series 1-0 vs. NY Rangers.
— **New York Rangers** in 1931 SF. NY Rangers lost two-game, total-goals series 3-0 vs. Chicago.
— **Chicago Black Hawks** in 1935 SF. Chicago lost two-game, total-goals series 1-0 vs. Mtl. Maroons.
— **Montreal Maroons** in 1937 SF. Mtl. Maroons lost best-of-three series 2-0, outscored by NY Rangers 5-0.
— **New York Americans** in 1939 QF. NY Americans lost best-of-three series 2-0, outscored by Toronto 5-0.

FEWEST GOALS, ONE TEAM, THREE-GAME SERIES:
1 — Montreal Maroons in 1936 SF. Mtl. Maroons lost best-of-five series 3-0, outscored by Detroit 6-1.

FEWEST GOALS, ONE TEAM, FOUR-GAME SERIES:
1 — Minnesota Wild in 2003 CF. Minnesota lost best-of-seven series 4-0, outscored by Anaheim 9-1.

FEWEST GOALS, ONE TEAM, FIVE-GAME SERIES:
2 — Philadelphia Flyers in 2002 CQF. Ottawa won best-of-seven series 4-1, while outscoring Philadelphia 11-2.

FEWEST GOALS, ONE TEAM, SIX-GAME SERIES:
5 — Boston Bruins in 1951 SF. Toronto won best-of-seven series 4-1 with 1 tie, outscoring Boston 17-5.

FEWEST GOALS, ONE TEAM, SEVEN-GAME SERIES:
9 — Toronto Maple Leafs, in 1945 F. Toronto won best-of-seven series 4-3; teams tied in scoring 9-9.
— **Detroit Red Wings,** in 1945 F. Toronto won best-of-seven series 4-3; teams tied in scoring 9-9.

The 1984-85 Chicago Blackhawks were involved in the two highest-scoring playoff series in NHL history. Darryl Sutter had 12 goals in 15 playoff games in the spring of 1985.

MOST GOALS IN A SERIES, BOTH TEAMS

MOST GOALS, BOTH TEAMS, ONE PLAYOFF SERIES:
69 — Edmonton Oilers (44), Chicago Black Hawks (25) in 1985 CF. Edmonton won best-of-seven series 4-2.
62 — Chicago Black Hawks (33), Minnesota North Stars (29) in 1985 DF. Chicago won best-of-seven series 4-2.
61 — Los Angeles Kings (33), Calgary Flames (28) in 1993 DSF. Los Angeles won best-of-seven series 4-2.
— Calgary Flames (35), San Jose Sharks (26) in 1995 CQF. San Jose won best-of-seven series 4-3.

MOST GOALS, BOTH TEAMS, TWO-GAME SERIES:
17 — Toronto St. Patricks (10), Montreal Canadiens (7) in 1918 NHL F. Toronto won two-game total-goals series.
15 — Boston Bruins (10), Chicago Black Hawks (5) in 1927 QF. Boston won two-game total-goals series.
— Pittsburgh Penguins (9), St. Louis Blues (6) in 1975 PRE. Pittsburgh won best-of-three series 2-0.

MOST GOALS, BOTH TEAMS, THREE-GAME SERIES:
33 — Minnesota North Stars (20), Boston Bruins (13) in 1981 PRE. Minnesota won best-of-five series 3-0.
31 — Chicago Black Hawks (23), Detroit Red Wings (8) in 1985 DSF. Chicago won best-of-five series 3-0.
28 — Toronto Maple Leafs (18), New York Rangers (10) in 1932 F. Toronto won best-of-five series 3-0.

MOST GOALS, BOTH TEAMS, FOUR-GAME SERIES:
36 — Boston Bruins (28), St. Louis Blues (8) in 1972 SF. Boston won best-of-seven series 4-0.
— **Minnesota North Stars (18), Toronto Maple Leafs (18)** in 1983 DSF. Minnesota won best-of-five series 3-1.
— **Edmonton Oilers (25), Chicago Black Hawks (11)** in 1983 CF. Edmonton won best-of-seven series 4-0.
35 — New York Rangers (23), Los Angeles Kings (12) in 1981 PRE. NY Rangers won best-of-five series 3-1.

MOST GOALS, BOTH TEAMS, FIVE-GAME SERIES:
52 — Edmonton Oilers (32), Los Angeles Kings (20) in 1987 DSF. Edmonton won best-of-seven series 4-1.
50 — Los Angeles Kings (27), Edmonton Oilers (23) in 1982 DSF. Los Angeles won best-of-five series 3-2.
48 — Edmonton Oilers (35), Calgary Flames (13) in 1983 DF. Edmonton won best-of-seven series 4-1.
— Calgary Flames (30), Los Angeles Kings (18) in 1988 DSF. Calgary won best-of-seven series 4-1.

MOST GOALS, BOTH TEAMS, SIX-GAME SERIES:
69 — Edmonton Oilers (44), Chicago Black Hawks (25) in 1985 CF. Edmonton won best-of-seven series 4-2.
62 — Chicago Black Hawks (33), Minnesota North Stars (29) in 1985 DF. Chicago won best-of-seven series 4-2.
61 — Los Angeles Kings (33), Calgary Flames (28) in 1993 DSF. Los Angeles won best-of-seven series 4-2.

MOST GOALS, BOTH TEAMS, SEVEN-GAME SERIES:
61 — Calgary Flames (35), San Jose Sharks (26) in 1995 CQF. San Jose won series 4-3.
60 — Edmonton Oilers (33), Calgary Flames (27) in 1984 DF. Edmonton won best-of-seven series 4-3.

FEWEST GOALS IN A SERIES, BOTH TEAMS

FEWEST GOALS, BOTH TEAMS, TWO-GAME SERIES:
1 — New York Rangers (1), New York Americans (0) in 1929 SF. NY Rangers won two-game total-goals series.
— Montreal Maroons (1), Chicago Black Hawks (0) in 1935 SF. Mtl. Maroons won two-game total-goals series.

FEWEST GOALS, BOTH TEAMS, THREE-GAME SERIES:
7 — Boston Bruins (5), Montreal Canadiens (2) in 1929 SF. Boston won best-of-five series 3-0.
— Detroit Red Wings (6), Montreal Maroons (1) in 1936 SF. Detroit won best-of-five series 3-0.

FEWEST GOALS, BOTH TEAMS, FOUR-GAME SERIES:
9 — Toronto Maple Leafs (7), Boston Bruins (2) in 1935 SF. Toronto won best-of-five series 3-1.

FEWEST GOALS, BOTH TEAMS, FIVE-GAME SERIES:
11 — Montreal Maroons (6), New York Rangers (5) in 1928 F. NY Rangers won best-of-five series 3-2.

FEWEST GOALS, BOTH TEAMS, SIX-GAME SERIES:
16 — Carolina Hurricanes (10), Toronto Maple Leafs (6) in 2002 CF. Carolina won best-of-seven series 4-2.

FEWEST GOALS, BOTH TEAMS, SEVEN-GAME SERIES:
18 — Toronto Maple Leafs (9), Detroit Red Wings (9) in 1945 F. Toronto won best-of-seven series 4-3.

MOST GOALS IN A GAME OR PERIOD

MOST GOALS, ONE TEAM, ONE GAME:
13 — Edmonton Oilers April 9, 1987, vs. Los Angeles at Edmonton. Edmonton won 13-3.
12 — Los Angeles Kings, April 10, 1990, vs. Calgary at Los Angeles. Los Angeles won 12-4.
11 — Montreal Canadiens, March 30, 1944, vs. Toronto at Montreal. Montreal won 11-0.
— Edmonton Oilers, May 4, 1985, vs. Chicago at Edmonton. Edmonton won 11-2.

MOST GOALS, ONE TEAM, ONE PERIOD:
7 — Montreal Canadiens (6), March 30, 1944, vs. Toronto at Montreal, third period. Montreal won 11-0.

MOST GOALS, BOTH TEAMS, ONE GAME:
18 — Los Angeles Kings (10), Edmonton Oilers (8), April 7, 1982, at Edmonton. Los Angeles won best-of-five DSF 3-2.
17 — Pittsburgh Penguins (10), Philadelphia Flyers (7), April 25, 1989, at Pittsburgh. Pittsburgh won best-of-seven DF 4-3.
16 — Edmonton Oilers (13), Los Angeles Kings (3), April 9, 1987, at Edmonton. Edmonton won best-of-seven DSF 4-1.
— Los Angeles Kings (12), Calgary Flames (4), April 10, 1990, at Los Angeles. Los Angeles won best-of-seven DF 4-2.

MOST GOALS, BOTH TEAMS, ONE PERIOD:
9 — New York Rangers (6), Philadelphia Flyers (3), April 24, 1979, third period, at Philadelphia. NY Rangers won 8-3.
— **Los Angeles Kings (5), Calgary Flames (4),** April 10, 1990, second period, at Los Angeles. Los Angeles won 12-4.
8 — Chicago Black Hawks (5), Montreal Canadiens (3), May 8, 1973, second period, at Montreal. Chicago won 8-7.
— Chicago Black Hawks (5), Edmonton Oilers (3), May 12, 1985, first period, at Chicago. Chicago won 8-6.
— Edmonton Oilers (6), Winnipeg Jets (2), April 6, 1988, third period, at Edmonton. Edmonton won 7-4.
— Hartford Whalers (5), Montreal Canadiens (3), April 10, 1988, third period, at Montreal. Hartford won 7-5.
— Vancouver Canucks (5), New York Rangers (3), June 9, 1994, third period, at NY Rangers. Vancouver won 6-3.

TEAM POWER-PLAY GOALS

MOST POWER-PLAY GOALS BY ALL TEAMS, ONE PLAYOFF YEAR:
199 — 1988 in 83 games.

MOST POWER-PLAY GOALS, ONE TEAM, ONE PLAYOFF YEAR:
35 — Minnesota North Stars, 1991 in 23 games.
32 — Edmonton Oilers, 1988 in 18 games.
31 — New York Islanders, 1981 in 18 games.

MOST POWER-PLAY GOALS, ONE TEAM, ONE SERIES:
15 — New York Islanders in 1980 F vs. Philadelphia. NY Islanders won series 4-2.
— **Minnesota North Stars** in 1991 DSF vs. Chicago. Minnesota won series 4-2.
13 — New York Islanders in 1981 QF vs. Edmonton. NY Islanders won series 4-2.
— Calgary Flames in 1986 CF vs. St. Louis. Calgary won series 4-3.
12 — Toronto Maple Leafs in 1976 QF vs. Philadelphia. Philadelphia won series 4-3.

MOST POWER-PLAY GOALS, BOTH TEAMS, ONE SERIES:
21 — New York Islanders (15), Philadelphia Flyers (6) in 1980 best-of-seven F won by NY Islanders 4-2.
— **New York Islanders (13), Edmonton Oilers (8)** in 1981 best-of-seven QF won by NY Islanders 4-2.
— **Philadelphia Flyers (11), Pittsburgh Penguins (10)** in 1989 best-of-seven DF won by Philadelphia 4-3.
— **Minnesota North Stars (15), Chicago Black Hawks (6)** in 1991 best-of-seven DSF won by Minnesota 4-2.
20 — Toronto Maple Leafs (12), Philadelphia Flyers (8) in 1976 best-of-seven QF won by Philadelphia 4-3.

MOST POWER-PLAY GOALS, ONE TEAM, ONE GAME:
6 — Boston Bruins, April 2, 1969, at Boston vs. Toronto. Boston won 10-0.

MOST POWER-PLAY GOALS, BOTH TEAMS, ONE GAME:
8 — Minnesota North Stars (4), St. Louis Blues (4), April 24, 1991, at Minnesota. Minnesota won 8-4.
7 — Minnesota North Stars (4), Edmonton Oilers (3), April 28, 1984, at Minnesota. Edmonton won 8-5.
— Philadelphia Flyers (4), NY Rangers (3), April 13, 1985, at NY Rangers. Philadelphia won 6-5.
— Chicago Black Hawks (5), Edmonton Oilers (2), April 28, 1984, at Minnesota. Edmonton won 8-5.
— Edmonton Oilers (5), Los Angeles Kings (2), April 9, 1987, at Edmonton. Edmonton won 13-3.
— Vancouver Canucks (4), Calgary Flames (3), April 9, 1989, at Vancouver. Vancouver won 5-3.

MOST POWER-PLAY GOALS, ONE TEAM, ONE PERIOD:
4 — Toronto Maple Leafs, March 26, 1936, second period vs. Boston at Toronto. Toronto won 8-3.
— **Minnesota North Stars,** April 28, 1984, second period vs. Edmonton at Minnesota. Edmonton won 8-5.
— **Boston Bruins,** April 11, 1991, third period vs. Hartford at Boston. Boston won 6-1.
— **Minnesota North Stars,** April 24, 1991, second period vs. St. Louis at Minnesota. Minnesota won 8-4.
— **St. Louis Blues,** April 27, 1998, third period at Los Angeles. St. Louis won 4-3.

MOST POWER-PLAY GOALS, BOTH TEAMS, ONE PERIOD:
5 — Minnesota North Stars (4), Edmonton Oilers (1), April 28, 1984, at Minnesota. Edmonton won 8-5.
— **Vancouver Canucks (3), Calgary Flames (2),** April 9, 1989, at Vancouver. Vancouver won 5-3.
— **Minnesota North Stars (4), St. Louis Blues (1),** April 24, 1991, at Minnesota. Minnesota won 8-4.

TEAM SHORTHAND GOALS

MOST SHORTHAND GOALS BY ALL TEAMS, ONE PLAYOFF YEAR:
33 — 1988, in 83 games.

MOST SHORTHAND GOALS, ONE TEAM, ONE PLAYOFF YEAR:
10 — Edmonton Oilers, 1983, in 16 games.
9 — New York Islanders, 1981, in 19 games.
8 — Philadelphia Flyers, 1989, in 19 games.

MOST SHORTHAND GOALS, ONE TEAM, ONE SERIES:
6 — **Calgary Flames** in 1995 vs. San Jose in best-of-seven CQF won by San Jose 4-3.
 — **Vancouver Canucks** in 1995 vs. St. Louis in best-of-seven CQF won by Vancouver 4-3.
5 — NY Rangers in 1979 vs. Philadelphia in best-of-seven QF won by NY Rangers 4-1.
 — Edmonton Oilers in 1983 vs. Calgary in best-of-seven DF won by Edmonton 4-1.

MOST SHORTHAND GOALS, BOTH TEAMS, ONE SERIES:
7 — **Boston Bruins (4), NY Rangers (3),** in 1958 SF won by Boston 4-2.
 — **Edmonton Oilers (5), Calgary Flames (2),** in 1983 DF won by Edmonton 4-1.
 — **Vancouver Canucks (6), St. Louis Blues (1),** in 1995 CQF won by Vancouver 4-3.

MOST SHORTHAND GOALS, ONE TEAM, ONE GAME:
3 — **Boston Bruins,** April 11, 1981, at Minnesota North Stars. Minnesota won 6-3.
 — **New York Islanders,** April 17, 1983, at NY Rangers. NY Rangers won 7-6.
 — **Toronto Maple Leafs,** May 8, 1994, at San Jose Sharks. Toronto won 8-3.

MOST SHORTHAND GOALS, BOTH TEAMS, ONE GAME:
4 — **Boston Bruins (3), Minnesota North Stars (1),** April 11, 1981, at Minnesota. Minnesota won 6-3.
 — **New York Islanders (3), New York Rangers (1),** April 17, 1983, at NY Rangers. NY Rangers won 7-6.
 — **Toronto Maple Leafs (3), San Jose Sharks (1),** May 8, 1994, at San Jose. Toronto won 8-3.
3 — Toronto Maple Leafs (2), Detroit Red Wings (1), April 5, 1947, at Toronto. Toronto won 6-1.
 — New York Rangers (2), Boston Bruins (1), April 1, 1958, at Boston. NY Rangers won 5-2.
 — Minnesota North Stars (2), Philadelphia Flyers (1), May 4, 1980, at Minnesota. Philadelphia won 5-3.
 — Winnipeg Jets (2), Edmonton Oilers (1), April 9, 1988, at Winnipeg. Winnipeg won 6-4.
 — New York Islanders (2), New Jersey Devils (1), April 14, 1988, at New Jersey. New Jersey won 6-5.
 — Montreal Canadiens (2), New Jersey Devils (1), April 17, 1997, at New Jersey. New Jersey won 5-2.
 — Dallas Stars (2), San Jose Sharks (1), May 5, 2000, at San Jose. Dallas won 5-4.

MOST SHORTHAND GOALS, ONE TEAM, ONE PERIOD:
2 — **Toronto Maple Leafs,** April 5, 1947, first period vs. Detroit at Toronto. Toronto won 6-1.
 — **Toronto Maple Leafs,** April 13, 1965, first period vs. Montreal at Toronto. Montreal won 4-3.
 — **Boston Bruins,** April 20, 1969, first period vs. Montreal at Boston. Boston won 3-2.
 — **Boston Bruins,** April 8, 1970, second period vs. NY Rangers at Boston. Boston won 8-2.
 — **Boston Bruins,** April 30, 1972, first period vs. NY Rangers at Boston. Boston won 6-5.
 — **Chicago Black Hawks,** May 3, 1973, first period vs. Montreal at Chicago. Chicago won 7-4.
 — **Montreal Canadiens,** April 23, 1978, first period at Detroit. Montreal won 8-0.
 — **New York Islanders,** April 8, 1980, second period vs. Los Angeles at NY Islanders. NY Islanders won 8-1.
 — **Los Angeles Kings,** April 9, 1980, first period at NY Islanders. Los Angeles won 6-3.
 — **Boston Bruins,** April 13, 1980, second period at Pittsburgh. Boston won 8-3.
 — **Minnesota North Stars,** May 4, 1980, second period vs. Philadelphia at Minnesota. Philadelphia won 5-3.
 — **Boston Bruins,** April 11, 1981, third period at Minnesota North Stars. Minnesota won 6-3.
 — **New York Islanders,** May 12, 1981, first period vs. Minnesota North Stars at NY Islanders. NY Islanders won 6-3.
 — **Montreal Canadiens,** April 7, 1982, third period vs. Quebec at Montreal. Montreal won 5-1.
 — **Edmonton Oilers,** April 24, 1983, third period vs. Chicago at Edmonton. Edmonton won 8-4.
 — **Winnipeg Jets,** April 14, 1985, second period at Calgary. Winnipeg won 5-3.
 — **Boston Bruins,** April 6, 1988, first period vs. Buffalo at Boston. Boston won 7-3.
 — **New York Islanders,** April 14, 1988, third period at New Jersey. New Jersey won 6-5.
 — **Detroit Red Wings,** April 29, 1993, second period at Toronto. Detroit won 7-3.
 — **Toronto Maple Leafs,** May 8, 1994, third period at San Jose. Toronto won 8-3.
 — **Calgary Flames,** May 11, 1995, first period at San Jose. Calgary won 9-2.
 — **Vancouver Canucks,** May 15, 1995, second period at St. Louis. Vancouver won 6-5.
 — **Montreal Canadiens,** April 17, 1997, second period at New Jersey. New Jersey won 5-2.
 — **Philadelphia Flyers,** April 26, 1997, first period vs. Pittsburgh at Philadelphia. Philadelphia won 6-3.
 — **Phoenix Coyotes,** April 24, 1998, second period at Detroit. Phoenix won 7-4.
 — **Buffalo Sabres,** April 27, 1998, second period vs. Philadelphia at Buffalo. Buffalo won 6-1.
 — **San Jose Sharks,** April 30, 1999, third period at Colorado. San Jose won 7-3.
 — **Detroit Red Wings,** April 27, 2002, second period at Vancouver. Detroit won 6-4.

MOST SHORTHAND GOALS, BOTH TEAMS, ONE PERIOD:
3 — **Toronto Maple Leafs (2), Detroit Red Wings (1),** April 5, 1947, first period at Toronto. Toronto won 6-1.
 — **Toronto Maple Leafs (2), San Jose Sharks (1),** May 8, 1994, third period at San Jose. Toronto won 8-3.

FASTEST GOALS

FASTEST FIVE GOALS, BOTH TEAMS:
3:06 — **Minnesota North Stars, Chicago Black Hawks,** April 21, 1985, at Chicago. Keith Brown scored for Chicago at 1:12 of the second period; Ken Yaremchuk, Chicago, 1:27; Dino Ciccarelli, Minnesota, 2:48; Tony McKegney, Minnesota, 4:07; and Curt Fraser, Chicago, 4:18. Chicago won 6-2 and won best-of-seven DF 4-2.
3:20 — Minnesota North Stars, Philadelphia Flyers, April 29, 1980, at Philadelphia. Paul Shmyr scored for Minnesota at 13:20 of the first period; Steve Christoff, Minnesota, 13:59; Ken Linseman, Philadelphia, 14:54; Tom Gorence, Philadelphia, 15:36; and Ken Linseman, Philadelphia, 16:40. Minnesota won 6-5. Philadelphia won best-of-seven SF 4-1.
4:00 — Los Angeles Kings, Detroit Red Wings, April 15, 2000, at Detroit. Brendan Shanahan scored for Detroit at 0:55 of the first period; Martin Lapointe, Detroit, 1:33; Luc Robitaille, Los Angeles, 2:04; Kris Draper, Detroit, 3:32; and Ziggy Palffy, Los Angeles, 4:55. Detroit won 8-5 and best-of-seven CQF 4-0.

FASTEST FIVE GOALS, ONE TEAM:
3:36 — **Montreal Canadiens,** March 30, 1944, at Montreal vs. Toronto. Toe Blake scored at 7:58 and 8:37 the first period; Maurice Richard, 9:17; Ray Getliffe, 10:33; and Buddy O'Connor, 11:34. Canadiens won 11-0 and best-of-seven SF 4-1.

FASTEST FOUR GOALS, BOTH TEAMS:
1:33 — **Toronto Maple Leafs, Philadelphia Flyers,** April 20, 1976, at Philadelphia. Don Saleski scored for Philadelphia at 10:04 of the second period; Bob Neely, Toronto, 10:42; Gary Dornhoefer, Philadelphia, 11:24; and Don Saleski, Philadelphia, 11:37. Philadelphia won 7-1 and best-of-seven SF 4-3.
1:34 — **Calgary Flames, Montreal Canadiens,** May 20, 1986, at Montreal. Joel Otto scored for Calgary at 17:59 of the first period; Bobby Smith, Montreal, 18:25; Mats Naslund, Montreal, 19:17; and Bob Gainey, Montreal, 19:33. Montreal won 5-3 and best-of-seven F 4-1.
1:38 — **Boston Bruins, Philadelphia Flyers,** April 26, 1977, at Philadelphia. Gregg Sheppard scored for Boston at 14:01 of the second period; Mike Milbury, 15:01; Gary Dornhoefer, Philadelphia, 15:16; and Jean Ratelle, Boston, 15:39. Boston won 5-4 and best-of-seven SF 4-0.

FASTEST FOUR GOALS, ONE TEAM:
2:35 — **Montreal Canadiens,** March 30, 1944, at Montreal. Toe Blake scored at 7:58 and 8:37 of the third period; Maurice Richard, 9:17; and Ray Getliffe, 10:33. Montreal won 11-0 and best-of-seven SF 4-1.

FASTEST THREE GOALS, BOTH TEAMS:
0:21 — **Chicago Black Hawks, Edmonton Oilers,** May 7, 1985, at Edmonton. Behn Wilson scored for Chicago at 19:22 of the third period; Jari Kurri, Edmonton, 19:36; and Glenn Anderson, Edmonton, 19:43. Edmonton won 7-3 and best-of-seven CF 4-2.
0:27 — Phoenix Coyotes, Detroit Red Wings, April 24, 1998, at Detroit. Jeremy Roenick scored for Phoenix at 13:24 of the second period; Mathieu Dandenault, Detroit, 13:32; and Keith Tkachuk, Phoenix, 13:51. Phoenix won 7-4. Detroit won best-of-seven CQF 4-2.
0:30 — Pittsburgh Penguins, Chicago Black Hawks, June 1, 1992, at Chicago. Dirk Graham scored for Chicago at 6:21 of the first period; Kevin Stevens, Pittsburgh, 6:33; and Dirk Graham, Chicago, 6:51. Pittsburgh won 6-5 and best-of-seven F 4-0.

FASTEST THREE GOALS, ONE TEAM:
0:23 — **Toronto Maple Leafs,** April 12, 1979, at Toronto vs. Atlanta Flames. Darryl Sittler scored at 4:04 and 4:16 of the first period; and Ron Ellis, 4:27. Toronto won 7-4 and best-of-three PRE 2-0.
0:38 — New York Rangers, April 12, 1986, at NY Rangers vs. Philadelphia. Jim Weimer scored at 12:29 of the third period; Bob Brooke, 12:43; and Ron Greschner, 13:07. NY Rangers won 5-2 and best-of-five DSF 3-2.
 — Colorado Avalanche, April 18, 2001, at Vancouver. Peter Forsberg scored at 9:11 of the third period; Joe Sakic, 9:28; and Eric Messier, 9:49. Colorado won 5-1 and best-of-seven CQF 4-0.

FASTEST TWO GOALS, BOTH TEAMS:
0:05 — **Pittsburgh Penguins, Buffalo Sabres,** April 14, 1979, at Buffalo. Gilbert Perreault scored for Buffalo at 12:59 of the first period; and Jim Hamilton, Pittsburgh, 13:04. Pittsburgh won 4-3 and best-of-three PRE 2-1.
0:08 — St. Louis Blues, Minnesota North Stars, April 9, 1989, at Minnesota. Bernie Federko scored for St. Louis at 2:28 of the third period; and Perry Berezan, Minnesota, 2:36. Minnesota won 5-4. St. Louis won best-of-seven DSF 4-1.
 — Phoenix Coyotes, Detroit Red Wings, April 24, 1998, at Detroit. Jeremy Roenick scored for Phoenix at 13:24 of the second period; and Mathieu Dandenault, Detroit, 13:32. Phoenix won 7-4. Detroit won best-of-seven CQF 4-2.

FASTEST TWO GOALS, ONE TEAM:
0:05 — **Detroit Red Wings,** April 11, 1965, at Detroit vs. Chicago. Norm Ullman scored at 17:35 and 17:40 of the second period. Detroit won 4-2. Chicago won best-of-seven SF 4-3.

Tomas Vokoun recorded the first playoff victory in Nashville Predators history with a 3-1 win over Detroit on April 11, 2004. Two days later, he recorded the team's first playoff shutout.

OVERTIME

SHORTEST OVERTIME:
0:09 — Montreal Canadiens, Calgary Flames, May 18, 1986, at Calgary. Montreal won 3-2 on Brian Skrudland's goal at 0:09 of the first overtime period. Montreal won best-of-seven F 4-1.
0:11 — New York Islanders, New York Rangers, April 11, 1975, at NY Rangers. NY Islanders won 4-3 on J.P. Parise's goal at 0:11 of the first overtime period. NY Islanders won best-of-three PRE 2-1.

LONGEST OVERTIME:
116:30 — Detroit Red Wings, Montreal Maroons, March 24, 1936, at Montreal. Mtl. Maroons won 1-0 on Mud Bruneteau's goal at 16:30 of the sixth overtime period. Detroit won best-of-five SF 3-0.

MOST OVERTIME GAMES, ONE PLAYOFF YEAR:
28 — 1993. Of 85 games played, 28 went into overtime.
26 — 2001. Of 86 games played, 26 went into overtime.
22 — 2003. Of 89 games played, 22 went into overtime.
21 — 1999. Of 86 games played, 21 went into overtime.

FEWEST OVERTIME GAMES, ONE PLAYOFF YEAR:
0 — 1963. None of the 16 games went into overtime, the only year since 1926 that no overtime was required in any playoff series.

MOST OVERTIME GAMES, ONE SERIES:
5 — Toronto Maple Leafs, Montreal Canadiens in 1951. Toronto won best-of-seven F 4-1.
4 — Toronto Maple Leafs, Boston Bruins in 1933. Toronto won best-of-five SF 3-2.
— Boston Bruins, NY Rangers in 1939. Boston won best-of-seven SF 4-3.
— St. Louis Blues, Minnesota North Stars in 1968. St. Louis won best-of-seven SF 4-3.
— Dallas Stars, St. Louis Blues in 1999. Dallas won best-of-seven CSF 4-2.
— Dallas Stars, Edmonton Oilers in 2001. Dallas won best-of-seven CQF 4-2.

THREE-OR-MORE GOAL GAMES

MOST THREE-OR-MORE GOAL GAMES BY ALL TEAMS, ONE PLAYOFF YEAR:
12 — 1983 in 66 games.
— **1988** in 83 games.
11 — 1985 in 70 games.
— 1992 in 86 games.

MOST THREE-OR-MORE GOAL GAMES, ONE TEAM, ONE PLAYOFF YEAR:
6 — Edmonton Oilers in 16 games, 1983.
— **Edmonton Oilers** in 18 games, 1985.

SHUTOUTS

MOST SHUTOUTS, ONE PLAYOFF YEAR, ALL TEAMS:
25 — 2002. Of 90 games played, Detroit had 6; Ottawa had 4; Carolina, Colorado, St. Louis and Toronto had 3 each; while Los Angeles, New Jersey and Philadelphia had 1 each.
23 — 2004. Of 89 games played, Tampa Bay, Calgary had 5 each; Toronto, San Jose had 3 each; while Boston, Colorado, Detroit, Montreal, Nashville, NY Islanders and Philadelphia had 1 each.
19 — 2001. Of 86 games played, Colorado, New Jersey had 4 each, Toronto had 3, Pittsburgh and Los Angeles had 2 each, while Buffalo, Washington, Detroit and San Jose had 1 each.

FEWEST SHUTOUTS, ONE PLAYOFF YEAR, ALL TEAMS:
0 — 1959. 18 games played.

MOST SHUTOUTS, BOTH TEAMS, ONE SERIES:
5 — Toronto Maple Leafs (3), Detroit Red Wings (2), in 1945. Toronto won best-of-seven series F 4-3.
— **Toronto Maple Leafs (3), Detroit Red Wings (2),** in 1950. Toronto won best-of-seven SF 4-3.

TEAM PENALTIES

FEWEST PENALTIES, BOTH TEAMS, BEST-OF-SEVEN SERIES:
19 — Detroit Red Wings, Toronto Maple Leafs in 1945 F. Detroit received 10 minors, Toronto received 9 minors. Detroit won best-of-seven series 4-3.

FEWEST PENALTIES, ONE TEAM, BEST-OF-SEVEN SERIES:
9 — Toronto Maple Leafs in 1945 F vs. Detroit. Toronto received 9 minors. Detroit won best-of-seven series 4-3.

MOST PENALTIES, BOTH TEAMS, ONE SERIES:
218 — New Jersey Devils, Washington Capitals in 1988 DF. New Jersey received 97 minors, 11 majors, 9 misconducts and 1 match penalty. Washington received 80 minors, 11 majors, 8 misconducts and 1 match penalty. New Jersey won best-of-seven series 4-3.

MOST PENALTY MINUTES, BOTH TEAMS, ONE SERIES:
654 — New Jersey Devils (349), Washington Capitals (305) in 1988 DF. New Jersey won best-of-seven series 4-3.

MOST PENALTIES, ONE TEAM, ONE SERIES:
118 — New Jersey Devils in 1988 DF vs. Washington. New Jersey received 97 minors, 11 majors, 9 misconducts and 1 match penalty. New Jersey won best-of-seven series 4-3.

MOST PENALTY MINUTES, ONE TEAM, ONE SERIES:
349 — New Jersey Devils in 1988 DF vs. Washington. New Jersey won best-of-seven series 4-3.

MOST PENALTIES, BOTH TEAMS, ONE GAME:
66 — Detroit Red Wings (33), St. Louis Blues (33), April 12, 1991, at St. Louis. St. Louis won 6-1.
63 — Minnesota North Stars (34), Chicago Black Hawks (29), April 6, 1990, at Chicago. Chicago won 5-3.
62 — New Jersey Devils (32), Washington Capitals (30), April 22, 1988, at New Jersey. New Jersey won 10-4.

MOST PENALTY MINUTES, BOTH TEAMS, ONE GAME:
298 — Detroit Red Wings (152), St. Louis Blues (146), April 12, 1991, at St. Louis. Detroit received 33 penalties; St. Louis received 33 penalties. St. Louis won 6-1.
267 — New York Rangers (142), Los Angeles Kings (125), April 9, 1981, at Los Angeles. NY Rangers received 31 penalties; Los Angeles received 28 penalties. Los Angeles won 5-4.

MOST PENALTIES, ONE TEAM, ONE GAME:
34 — Minnesota North Stars, April 6, 1990, at Chicago. Chicago won 5-3.
33 — Detroit Red Wings, April 12, 1991, at St. Louis. St. Louis won 6-1.
— St. Louis Blues, April 12, 1991, at St. Louis vs. Detroit. St. Louis won 6-1.

MOST PENALTY MINUTES, ONE TEAM, ONE GAME:
152 — Detroit Red Wings, April 12, 1991, at St. Louis. St. Louis won 6-1.
146 — St. Louis Blues, April 12, 1991, at St. Louis vs. Detroit. St. Louis won 6-1.
142 — New York Rangers, April 9, 1981, at Los Angeles. Los Angeles won 5-4.

MOST PENALTIES, BOTH TEAMS, ONE PERIOD:
43 — New York Rangers (24), Los Angeles Kings (19), April 9, 1981, first period at Los Angeles. Los Angeles won 5-4.

MOST PENALTY MINUTES, BOTH TEAMS, ONE PERIOD:
248 — New York Islanders (124), Boston Bruins (124), April 17, 1980, first period at Boston. NY Islanders won 5-4.

MOST PENALTIES, ONE TEAM, ONE PERIOD:
24 — New York Rangers, April 9, 1981, first period at Los Angeles. Los Angeles won 5-4.

MOST PENALTY MINUTES, ONE TEAM, ONE PERIOD:
125 — New York Rangers, April 9, 1981, first period at Los Angeles. Los Angeles won 5-4.

Individual Records

GAMES PLAYED

MOST YEARS IN PLAYOFFS:
  21 — Raymond Bourque, Boston, Colorado (1980-96 inclusive;
     98-2001 inclusive)
  20 — Gordie Howe, Detroit, Hartford
     — Larry Robinson, Montreal, Los Angeles
     — Larry Murphy, Los Angeles, Washington, Minnesota, Pittsburgh, Toronto,
       Detroit
     — Scott Stevens, Washington, St. Louis, New Jersey
     — Chris Chelios, Montreal, Chicago, Detroit

MOST CONSECUTIVE YEARS IN PLAYOFFS:
  20 — Larry Robinson, Montreal, Los Angeles (1973-92, inclusive).
  19 — Brett Hull, Calgary, St. Louis, Dallas, Detroit (1986-2004, inclusive).
  18 — Larry Murphy, Los Angeles, Washington, Minnesota, Pittsburgh, Toronto,
     Detroit (1984-2001, inclusive).
  17 — Brad Park, NY Rangers, Boston, Detroit (1969-85, inclusive).
     — Raymond Bourque, Boston (1980-96, inclusive).

MOST PLAYOFF GAMES:
  240 — Patrick Roy, Montreal, Colorado
  236 — Mark Messier, Edmonton, NY Rangers
  233 — Claude Lemieux, Montreal, New Jersey, Colorado, Phoenix
  231 — Guy Carbonneau, Montreal, St. Louis, Dallas
  227 — Larry Robinson, Montreal, Los Angeles

GOALS

MOST GOALS IN PLAYOFFS (CAREER):
  122 — Wayne Gretzky, Edmonton, Los Angeles, St. Louis, NY Rangers
  109 — Mark Messier, Edmonton, NY Rangers
  106 — Jari Kurri, Edmonton, Los Angeles, NY Rangers, Anaheim
  100 — Brett Hull, Calgary, St. Louis, Dallas, Detroit
  93 — Glenn Anderson, Edmonton, Toronto, NY Rangers, St. Louis

MOST GOALS, ONE PLAYOFF YEAR:
  19 — Reggie Leach, Philadelphia, 1976. 16 games.
     — Jari Kurri, Edmonton, 1985. 18 games.
  18 — Joe Sakic, Colorado, 1996. 22 games.
  17 — Newsy Lalonde, Montreal, 1919. 10 games.
     — Mike Bossy, NY Islanders, 1981. 18 games.
     — Steve Payne, Minnesota, 1981. 19 games.
     — Mike Bossy, NY Islanders, 1982. 19 games.
     — Mike Bossy, NY Islanders, 1983. 19 games.
     — Wayne Gretzky, Edmonton, 1985. 18 games.
     — Kevin Stevens, Pittsburgh, 1991. 24 games.

MOST GOALS IN ONE SERIES (OTHER THAN FINAL):
  12 — Jari Kurri, Edmonton, in 1985 CF, 6 games vs. Chicago.
  11 — Newsy Lalonde, Montreal, in 1919 NHL F, 5 games vs. Ottawa.
  10 — Tim Kerr, Philadelphia, in 1989 DF, 7 games vs. Pittsburgh.
  9 — Reggie Leach, Philadelphia, in 1976 SF, 5 games vs. Boston.
     — Bill Barber, Philadelphia, in 1980 SF, 5 games vs. Minnesota.
     — Mike Bossy, NY Islanders, in 1983 CF, 6 games vs. Boston.
     — Mario Lemieux, Pittsburgh, in 1989 DF, 7 games vs. Philadelphia.

MOST GOALS IN FINAL SERIES (NHL PLAYERS ONLY):
  9 — Babe Dye, Toronto, in 1922, 5 games vs. Van. Millionaires.
  8 — Alf Skinner, Toronto, in 1918, 5 games vs. Van. Millionaires.
  7 — Jean Beliveau, Montreal, in 1956, 5 games vs. Detroit.
     — Mike Bossy, NY Islanders, in 1982, 4 games vs. Vancouver.
     — Wayne Gretzky, Edmonton, in 1985, 5 games vs. Philadelphia.

MOST GOALS, ONE GAME:
  5 — Newsy Lalonde, Montreal, March 1, 1919, at Montreal. Final score:
     Montreal 6, Ottawa 3.
     — Maurice Richard, Montreal, March 23, 1944, at Montreal. Final score:
     Montreal 5, Toronto 1.
     — Darryl Sittler, Toronto, April 22, 1976, at Toronto. Final score:
     Toronto 8, Philadelphia 5.
     — Reggie Leach, Philadelphia, May 6, 1976, at Philadelphia. Final score:
     Philadelphia 6, Boston 3.
     — Mario Lemieux, Pittsburgh, April 25, 1989, at Pittsburgh. Final score:
     Pittsburgh 10, Philadelphia 7.

MOST GOALS, ONE PERIOD:
  4 — Tim Kerr, Philadelphia, April 13, 1985, at NY Rangers, second period. Final
     score: Philadelphia 6, NY Rangers 5.
     — Mario Lemieux, Pittsburgh, April 25, 1989, at Pittsburgh vs. Philadelphia,
     first period. Final score: Pittsburgh 10, Philadelphia 7.

ASSISTS

MOST ASSISTS IN PLAYOFFS (CAREER):
  260 — Wayne Gretzky, Edmonton, Los Angeles, St. Louis, NY Rangers
  186 — Mark Messier, Edmonton, NY Rangers
  139 — Raymond Bourque, Boston, Colorado
  137 — Paul Coffey, Edmonton, Pittsburgh, Los Angeles, Detroit, Philadelphia,
     Carolina
  128 — Doug Gilmour, St. Louis, Calgary, Toronto, New Jersey, Buffalo, Montreal

MOST ASSISTS, ONE PLAYOFF YEAR:
  31 — Wayne Gretzky, Edmonton, 1988. 19 games.
  30 — Wayne Gretzky, Edmonton, 1985. 18 games.
  29 — Wayne Gretzky, Edmonton, 1987. 21 games.
  28 — Mario Lemieux, Pittsburgh, 1991. 23 games.
  26 — Wayne Gretzky, Edmonton, 1983. 16 games.

MOST ASSISTS IN ONE SERIES (OTHER THAN FINAL):
  14 — Rick Middleton, Boston, in 1983 DF, 7 games vs. Buffalo.
     — Wayne Gretzky, Edmonton, in 1985 CF, 6 games vs. Chicago.
  13 — Wayne Gretzky, Edmonton, in 1987 DSF, 5 games vs. Los Angeles.
     — Doug Gilmour, Toronto, in 1994 CSF, 7 games vs. San Jose.
  11 — Al MacInnis, Calgary, in 1984 DF, 7 games vs. Edmonton.
     — Mark Messier, Edmonton, in 1989 DSF, 7 games vs. Los Angeles.
     — Mike Ridley, Washington, in 1992 DSF, 7 games vs. Pittsburgh.
     — Ron Francis, Pittsburgh, in 1995 CQF, 7 games vs. Washington.
  10 — Fleming Mackell, Boston, in 1958 SF, 6 games vs. NY Rangers.
     — Stan Mikita, Chicago, in 1962 SF, 6 games vs. Montreal.
     — Bob Bourne, NY Islanders, in 1983 DF, 6 games vs. NY Rangers.
     — Wayne Gretzky, Edmonton, in 1988 DSF, 5 games vs. Winnipeg.
     — Mario Lemieux, Pittsburgh, in 1992 DSF, 6 games vs. Washington.

MOST ASSISTS IN FINAL SERIES:
  10 — Wayne Gretzky, Edmonton, in 1988, 4 games plus suspended game vs.
     Boston.
  9 — Jacques Lemaire, Montreal, in 1973, 6 games vs. Chicago.
     — Wayne Gretzky, Edmonton, in 1987, 7 games vs. Philadelphia.
     — Larry Murphy, Pittsburgh, in 1991, 6 games vs. Minnesota.

MOST ASSISTS, ONE GAME:
  6 — Mikko Leinonen, NY Rangers, April 8, 1982, at NY Rangers. Final score:
     NY Rangers 7, Philadelphia 3.
     — Wayne Gretzky, Edmonton, April 9, 1987, at Edmonton. Final score:
     Edmonton 13, Los Angeles 3.
  5 — Toe Blake, Montreal, March 23, 1944, at Montreal. Final score: Montreal 5,
     Toronto 1.
     — Maurice Richard, Montreal, March 27, 1956, at Montreal. Final score:
     Montreal 7, NY Rangers 0.
     — Bert Olmstead, Montreal, March 30, 1957, at Montreal. Final score:
     Montreal 8, NY Rangers 3.
     — Don McKenney, Boston, April 5, 1958, at Boston. Final score: Boston 8,
     NY Rangers 2.
     — Stan Mikita, Chicago, April 4, 1973, at Chicago. Final score: Chicago 7,
     St. Louis 1.
     — Wayne Gretzky, Edmonton, April 8, 1981, at Montreal. Final score:
     Edmonton 6, Montreal 3.
     — Paul Coffey, Edmonton, May 14, 1985, at Edmonton. Final score:
     Edmonton 10, Chicago 5.
     — Doug Gilmour, St. Louis, April 15, 1986, at Minnesota. Final score: St. Louis 6,
     Minnesota 3.
     — Risto Siltanen, Quebec, April 14, 1987, at Hartford. Final score: Quebec 7,
     Hartford 5.
     — Patrik Sundstrom, New Jersey, April 22, 1988, at New Jersey. Final score:
     New Jersey 10, Washington 4.
     — Geoff Courtnall, St. Louis, April 23, 1998, at St. Louis. Final score:
     St. Louis 8, Los Angeles 3.

MOST ASSISTS, ONE PERIOD:
  3 — Three assists by one player in one period of a playoff game has been recorded
     on 74 occasions. Chris Chelios of the Detroit Red Wings is the most recent to
     equal this mark with 3 assists in the second period at Vancouver, April 27,
     2002. Final score: Detroit 6, Vancouver 4.
     — Wayne Gretzky has had 3 assists in one period 5 times; Raymond Bourque, 3
     times; Toe Blake, Jean Beliveau, Doug Harvey and Bobby Orr, twice each. Joe
     Primeau of Toronto was the first player to be credited with 3 assists in one
     period of a playoff game; third period at Boston vs. NY Rangers, April 7,
     1932. Final score: Toronto 6, NY Rangers 2.

POINTS

MOST POINTS IN PLAYOFFS (CAREER):
  382 — Wayne Gretzky, Edmonton, Los Angeles, St. Louis, NY Rangers,
     122G, 260A
  295 — Mark Messier, Edmonton, NY Rangers, 109G, 186A
  233 — Jari Kurri, Edmonton, Los Angeles, NY Rangers, Anaheim, 106G, 127A
  214 — Glenn Anderson, Edmonton, Toronto, NY Rangers, St. Louis, 93G, 121A
  196 — Paul Coffey, Edmonton, Pittsburgh, Los Angeles, Detroit, Philadelphia,
     Carolina, 59G, 137A

MOST POINTS, ONE PLAYOFF YEAR:
  47 — Wayne Gretzky, Edmonton, in 1985. 17 goals, 30 assists in 18 games.
  44 — Mario Lemieux, Pittsburgh, in 1991. 16 goals, 28 assists in 23 games.
  43 — Wayne Gretzky, Edmonton, in 1988. 12 goals, 31 assists in 19 games.
  40 — Wayne Gretzky, Los Angeles, in 1993. 15 goals, 25 assists in 24 games.
  38 — Wayne Gretzky, Edmonton, in 1983. 12 goals, 26 assists in 16 games.

MOST POINTS IN ONE SERIES (OTHER THAN FINAL):

19 — Rick Middleton, Boston, in 1983 DF, 7 games vs. Buffalo. 5 goals, 14 assists.

18 — Wayne Gretzky, Edmonton, in 1985 CF, 6 games vs. Chicago. 4 goals, 14 assists.

17 — Mario Lemieux, Pittsburgh, in 1992 DSF, 6 games vs. Washington. 7 goals, 10 assists.

16 — Barry Pederson, Boston, in 1983 DF, 7 games vs. Buffalo. 7 goals, 9 assists.
   — Doug Gilmour, Toronto, in 1994 CSF, 7 games vs. San Jose. 3 goals, 13 assists.

15 — Jari Kurri, Edmonton, in 1985 CF, 6 games vs. Chicago. 12 goals, 3 assists.
   — Wayne Gretzky, Edmonton, in 1987 DSF, 5 games vs. Los Angeles. 2 goals, 13 assists.
   — Tim Kerr, Philadelphia, in 1989 DF, 7 games vs. Pittsburgh. 10 goals, 5 assists.
   — Mario Lemieux, Pittsburgh, in 1991 CF, 6 games vs. Boston. 6 goals, 9 assists.

MOST POINTS IN FINAL SERIES:

13 — Wayne Gretzky, Edmonton, in 1988, 4 games plus suspended game vs. Boston. 3 goals, 10 assists.

12 — Gordie Howe, Detroit, in 1955, 7 games vs. Montreal. 5 goals, 7 assists.
   — Yvan Cournoyer, Montreal, in 1973, 6 games vs. Chicago. 6 goals, 6 assists.
   — Jacques Lemaire, Montreal, in 1973, 6 games vs. Chicago. 3 goals, 9 assists.
   — Mario Lemieux, Pittsburgh, in 1991, 5 games vs. Minnesota. 5 goals, 7 assists.

MOST POINTS, ONE GAME:

8 — Patrik Sundstrom, New Jersey, April 22, 1988, at New Jersey in 10-4 win over Washington. Sundstrom had 3 goals, 5 assists.
   — **Mario Lemieux, Pittsburgh,** April 25, 1989, at Pittsburgh in 10-7 win over Philadelphia. Lemieux had 5 goals, 3 assists.

7 — Wayne Gretzky, Edmonton, April 17, 1983, at Calgary in 10-2 win. Gretzky had 4 goals, 3 assists.
   — Wayne Gretzky, Edmonton, April 25,1985, at Winnipeg in 8-3 win. Gretzky had 3 goals, 4 assists.
   — Wayne Gretzky, Edmonton, April 9, 1987, at Edmonton in 13-3 win over Los Angeles. Gretzky had 1 goal, 6 assists.

6 — Dickie Moore, Montreal, March 25, 1954, at Montreal in 8-1 win over Boston. Moore had 2 goals, 4 assists.
   — Phil Esposito, Boston, April 2, 1969, at Boston in 10-0 win over Toronto. Esposito had 4 goals, 2 assists.
   — Darryl Sittler, Toronto, April 22, 1976, at Toronto in 8-5 win over Philadelphia. Sittler had 5 goals, 1 assist.
   — Guy Lafleur, Montreal, April 11, 1977, at Montreal in 7-2 win over St. Louis. Lafleur had 3 goals, 3 assists.
   — Mikko Leinonen, NY Rangers, April 8, 1982, at NY Rangers in 7-3 win over Philadelphia. Leinonen had 6 assists.
   — Paul Coffey, Edmonton, May 14, 1985, at Edmonton in 10-5 win over Chicago. Coffey had 1 goal, 5 assists.
   — John Anderson, Hartford, April 12, 1986, at Hartford in 9-4 win over Quebec. Anderson had 2 goals, 4 assists.
   — Mario Lemieux, Pittsburgh, April 23, 1992, at Pittsburgh in 6-4 win over Washington. Lemieux had 3 goals, 3 assists.
   — Geoff Courtnall, St. Louis, April 23, 1998, at St. Louis in 8-3 win over Los Angeles. Courtnall had 1 goal, 5 assists.

MOST POINTS, ONE PERIOD:

4 — Maurice Richard, Montreal, March 29, 1945, at Montreal, third period, in 10-3 win vs. Toronto. 3 goals, 1 assist.
   — **Dickie Moore,** Montreal, March 25, 1954, at Montreal, first period, in 8-1 win vs. Boston. 2 goals, 2 assists.
   — **Barry Pederson,** Boston, April 8, 1982, at Boston, second period, in 7-3 win vs. Buffalo. 3 goals, 1 assist.
   — **Peter McNab,** Boston, April 11, 1982, at Buffalo, second period, in 5-2 win vs. Buffalo. 1 goal, 3 assists.
   — **Tim Kerr,** Philadelphia, April 13, 1985, at NY Rangers, second period, in 6-5 win vs. NY Rangers. 4 goals.
   — **Ken Linseman,** Boston, April 14, 1985, at Boston, second period, in 7-6 win vs. Montreal. 2 goals, 2 assists.
   — **Wayne Gretzky,** Edmonton, April 12, 1987, at Los Angeles, third period, in 6-3 win vs. Los Angeles. 1 goal, 3 assists.
   — **Glenn Anderson,** Edmonton, April 6, 1988, at Edmonton, third period, in 7-4 win vs. Winnipeg. 3 goals, 1 assist.
   — **Mario Lemieux,** Pittsburgh, April 25, 1989, at Pittsburgh, first period, in 10-7 win vs. Philadelphia. 4 goals.
   — **Dave Gagner,** Minnesota North Stars, April 8, 1991, at Minnesota, first period, in 6-5 loss vs. Chicago. 2 goals, 2 assists.
   — **Mario Lemieux,** Pittsburgh, April 23, 1992, at Pittsburgh, second period, in 6-4 win vs. Washington. 2 goals, 2 assists.
   — **Alexander Mogilny,** New Jersey, April 28, 2001, at New Jersey, second period, in 6-5 win vs. Toronto. 1 goal, 3 assists.

POWER-PLAY GOALS

MOST POWER-PLAY GOALS IN PLAYOFFS (CAREER):

38 — Brett Hull, St. Louis, Dallas, Detroit
35 — Mike Bossy, NY Islanders
34 — Dino Ciccarelli, Minnesota, Washington, Detroit
   — Wayne Gretzky, Edmonton, Los Angeles, St. Louis, NY Rangers
29 — Mario Lemieux, Pittsburgh

MOST POWER-PLAY GOALS, ONE PLAYOFF YEAR:

9 — Mike Bossy, NY Islanders, 1981. 18 games vs. Toronto, Edmonton, NY Rangers and Minnesota.
   — **Cam Neely, Boston,** 1991. 19 games vs. Hartford, Montreal and Pittsburgh.
8 — Tim Kerr, Philadelphia, 1989. 19 games.
   — John Druce, Washington, 1990. 15 games.
   — Brian Propp, Minnesota, 1991. 23 games.
   — Mario Lemieux, Pittsburgh, 1992. 15 games.

MOST POWER-PLAY GOALS, ONE PLAYOFF SERIES:

6 — Chris Kontos, Los Angeles, 1989 DSF vs. Edmonton, won by Los Angeles 4-3.

5 — Andy Bathgate, Detroit, 1966 SF vs. Chicago, won by Detroit 4-2.
   — Denis Potvin, NY Islanders, 1981 QF vs. Edmonton, won by NY Islanders 4-2.
   — Ken Houston, Calgary, 1981 QF vs. Philadelphia, won by Calgary 4-3.
   — Rick Vaive, Chicago, 1988 DSF vs. St. Louis, won by St. Louis 4-1.
   — Tim Kerr, Philadelphia, 1989 DF vs. Pittsburgh, won by Philadelphia 4-3.
   — Mario Lemieux, Pittsburgh, 1989 DF vs. Philadelphia, won by Philadelphia 4-3.
   — John Druce, Washington, 1990 DF vs. NY Rangers, won by Washington 4-1.
   — Pat LaFontaine, Buffalo, 1992 DSF vs. Boston, won by Boston 4-3.
   — Adam Graves, NY Rangers, 1996 CQF vs Montreal, won by NY Rangers 4-2.

MOST POWER-PLAY GOALS, ONE GAME:

3 — Syd Howe, Detroit, March 23, 1939, at Detroit vs. Montreal. Detroit won 7-3.
   — **Sid Smith, Toronto,** April 10, 1949, at Detroit. Toronto won 3-1.
   — **Phil Esposito, Boston,** April 2, 1969, at Boston vs. Toronto. Boston won 10-0.
   — **John Bucyk, Boston,** April 21, 1974, at Boston vs. Chicago. Boston won 8-6.
   — **Denis Potvin, NY Islanders,** April 17, 1981, at NY Islanders vs. Edmonton. NY Islanders won 6-3.
   — **Tim Kerr, Philadelphia,** April 13, 1985, at NY Rangers. Philadelphia won 6-5.
   — **Jari Kurri, Edmonton,** April 9, 1987, at Edmonton vs. Los Angeles. Edmonton won 13-3.
   — **Mark Johnson, New Jersey,** April 22, 1988, at New Jersey vs. Washington. New Jersey won 10-4.
   — **Dino Ciccarelli, Detroit,** April 29, 1993, at Toronto. Detroit won 7-3.
   — **Dino Ciccarelli, Detroit,** May 11, 1995, at Dallas. Detroit won 5-1.
   — **Valeri Kamensky, Colorado,** April 24, 1997, at Colorado vs. Chicago. Colorado won 7-0.

MOST POWER-PLAY GOALS, ONE PERIOD:

3 — Tim Kerr, Philadelphia, April 13, 1985, at NY Rangers, second period in 6-5 win.

2 — Two power-play goals have been scored by one player in one period on 55 occasions. Charlie Conacher of Toronto was the first to score two power-play goals in one period, setting the mark with two power-play goals in the second period at Toronto vs. Boston, March 26, 1936. Final score: Toronto 8, Boston 3. Brad Richards of the Tampa Bay Lightning is the most recent to equal this mark with two power-play goals in the second period at Calgary, June 5, 2004. Final score: Tampa Bay 3, Calgary 2.

SHORTHAND GOALS

MOST SHORTHAND GOALS IN PLAYOFFS (CAREER):

14 — Mark Messier, Edmonton, NY Rangers
11 — Wayne Gretzky, Edmonton, Los Angeles, St. Louis
10 — Jari Kurri, Edmonton, Los Angeles, NY Rangers
8 — Ed Westfall, Boston, NY Islanders
   — Hakan Loob, Calgary

MOST SHORTHAND GOALS, ONE PLAYOFF YEAR:

3 — Derek Sanderson, Boston, 1969. 1 vs. Toronto in QF, won by Boston 4-0; 2 vs. Montreal in SF, won by Montreal, 4-2.
   — **Bill Barber, Philadelphia,** 1980. All vs. Minnesota in SF, won by Philadelphia 4-1.
   — **Lorne Henning, NY Islanders,** 1980. 1 vs. Boston in QF, won by NY Islanders 4-1; 1 vs. Buffalo in SF, won by NY Islanders 4-2, 1 vs. Philadelphia in F, won by NY Islanders 4-2.
   — **Wayne Gretzky, Edmonton,** 1983. 2 vs. Winnipeg in DSF, won by Edmonton 3-0; 1 vs. Calgary in DF, won by Edmonton 4-1.
   — **Wayne Presley, Chicago,** 1989. All vs. Detroit in DSF, won by Chicago 4-2.
   — **Todd Marchant, Edmonton,** 1997. 1 vs. Dallas in CQF, won by Edmonton 4-3; 2 vs. Colorado in CSF, won by Colorado 4-1.

Boston's Ken Linseman is one of only 12 NHL players to collect four points in a single playoff period. Linseman did it versus Montreal on April 14, 1985.

MOST SHORTHAND GOALS, ONE PLAYOFF SERIES:
3 — **Bill Barber, Philadelphia,** 1980 SF vs. Minnesota, won by Philadelphia 4-1.
   — **Wayne Presley, Chicago,** 1989 DSF vs. Detroit, won by Chicago 4-2.
2 — Mac Colville, NY Rangers, 1940 SF vs. Boston, won by NY Rangers 4-2.
   — Jerry Toppazzini, Boston, 1958 SF vs. NY Rangers, won by Boston 4-2.
   — Dave Keon, Toronto, 1963 F vs. Detroit, won by Toronto 4-1.
   — Bob Pulford, Toronto, 1964 F vs. Detroit, won by Toronto 4-3.
   — Serge Savard, Montreal, 1968 F vs. St. Louis, won by Montreal 4-0.
   — Derek Sanderson, Boston, 1969 SF vs. Montreal, won by Montreal 4-2.
   — Bryan Trottier, NY Islanders, 1980 PR vs. Los Angeles, won by NY Islanders 3-1.
   — Bobby Lalonde, Boston, 1981 PR vs. Minnesota, won by Minnesota 3-0.
   — Butch Goring, NY Islanders, 1981 SF vs. NY Rangers, won by NY Islanders 4-0.
   — Wayne Gretzky, Edmonton, 1983 DSF vs. Winnipeg, won by Edmonton 3-0.
   — Mark Messier, Edmonton, 1983 DF vs. Calgary, won by Edmonton 4-1.
   — Jari Kurri, Edmonton, 1983 CF vs. Chicago, won by Edmonton 4-0.
   — Wayne Gretzky, Edmonton, 1985 DF vs. Winnipeg, won by Edmonton 4-0.
   — Kevin Lowe, Edmonton, 1987 F vs. Philadelphia, won by Edmonton 4-3.
   — Bob Gould, Washington, 1988 DSF vs. Philadelphia, won by Washington 4-3.
   — Dave Poulin, Philadelphia, 1989 DF vs. Pittsburgh, won by Philadelphia 4-3.
   — Russ Courtnall, Montreal, 1991 DF vs. Boston, won by Boston 4-3.
   — Sergei Fedorov, Detroit, 1992 DSF vs. Minnesota, won by Detroit 4-3.
   — Mark Messier, NY Rangers, 1992 DSF vs. New Jersey, won by NY Rangers 4-3.
   — Tom Fitzgerald, NY Islanders, 1993 DF vs. Pittsburgh, won by NY Islanders 4-3.
   — Mark Osborne, Toronto, 1994 CSF vs. San Jose, won by Toronto 4-3.
   — Tony Amonte, Chicago, 1997 CQF vs. Colorado, won by Colorado 4-2.
   — Brian Rolston, New Jersey, 1997 CQF vs. Montreal, won by New Jersey 4-1.
   — Rod Brind'Amour, Philadelphia, 1997 CQF vs. Pittsburgh, won by Philadelphia 4-1.
   — Todd Marchant, Edmonton, 1997 CSF vs. Colorado, won by Colorado 4-1.
   — Jeremy Roenick, Phoenix, 1998 CQF vs. Detroit, won by Detroit 4-2.
   — Vincent Damphousse, San Jose, 1999 CQF vs. Colorado, won by Colorado 4-2.
   — Dixon Ward, Buffalo, 1999 CF vs. Toronto, won by Buffalo 4-1.
   — Curtis Brown, Buffalo, 2001 CSF vs. Pittsburgh, won by Pittsburgh 4-3.

MOST SHORTHAND GOALS, ONE GAME:
2 — **Dave Keon, Toronto,** April 18, 1963, at Toronto, in 3-1 win vs. Detroit.
   — **Bryan Trottier, NY Islanders,** April 8, 1980, at NY Islanders, in 8-1 win vs. Los Angeles.
   — **Bobby Lalonde, Boston,** April 11, 1981, at Minnesota, in 6-3 loss vs. Minnesota.
   — **Wayne Gretzky, Edmonton,** April 6, 1983, at Edmonton, in 6-3 win vs. Winnipeg.
   — **Jari Kurri, Edmonton,** April 24, 1983, at Edmonton, in 8-3 win vs. Chicago.
   — **Mark Messier, NY Rangers,** April 21, 1992, at NY Rangers, in 7-3 loss vs. New Jersey.
   — **Tom Fitzgerald, NY Islanders,** May 8, 1993, at NY Islanders, in 6-5 win vs. Pittsburgh.
   — **Rod Brind'Amour, Philadelphia,** April 26, 1997, at Philadelphia, in 6-3 win vs. Pittsburgh.
   — **Jeremy Roenick, Phoenix,** April 24, 1998, at Detroit, in 7-4 win vs. Detroit.
   — **Vincent Damphousse, San Jose,** April 30, 1999, at Colorado, in 7-3 win by San Jose.

MOST SHORTHAND GOALS, ONE PERIOD:
2 — **Bryan Trottier, NY Islanders,** April 8, 1980, second period, at NY Islanders, in 8-1 win vs. Los Angeles.
   — **Bobby Lalonde, Boston,** April 11, 1981, third period, at Minnesota, in 6-3 loss vs. Minnesota.
   — **Jari Kurri, Edmonton,** April 24, 1983, third period, at Edmonton, in 8-4 win vs. Chicago.
   — **Rod Brind'Amour, Philadelphia,** April 26, 1997, first period, at Philadelphia, in 6-3 win vs. Pittsburgh.
   — **Jeremy Roenick, Phoenix,** April 24, 1998, second period, at Detroit, in 7-4 win by Phoenix.
   — **Vincent Damphousse, San Jose,** April 30, 1999, third period, at Colorado, in 7-3 win vs. Colorado.

GAME-WINNING GOALS

MOST GAME-WINNING GOALS IN PLAYOFFS, CAREER:
24 — **Wayne Gretzky, Edmonton, Los Angeles, St. Louis, NY Rangers**
   — **Brett Hull, St. Louis, Dallas, Detroit**
19 — Claude Lemieux, Montreal, New Jersey, Colorado
18 — Maurice Richard, Montreal
17 — Mike Bossy, NY Islanders
   — Glenn Anderson, Edmonton, Toronto, NY Rangers, St. Louis
   — Joe Sakic, Colorado

MOST GAME-WINNING GOALS, ONE PLAYOFF YEAR:
7 — **Brad Richards, Tampa Bay,** 2004. 23 games.
6 — Joe Sakic, Colorado, 1996. 22 games.
   — Joe Nieuwendyk, Dallas, 1999. 23 games.
5 — Mike Bossy, NY Islanders, 1983. 19 games.
   — Jari Kurri, Edmonton, 1987. 21 games.
   — Bobby Smith, Minnesota, 1991. 23 games.
   — Mario Lemieux, Pittsburgh, 1992. 15 games.

MOST GAME-WINNING GOALS, ONE PLAYOFF SERIES:
4 — **Mike Bossy, NY Islanders,** 1983 CF vs. Boston, won by NY Islanders 4-2.

OVERTIME GOALS

MOST OVERTIME GOALS IN PLAYOFFS, CAREER:
6 — **Maurice Richard, Montreal** (1 in 1946; 3 in 1951; 1 in 1957; 1 in 1958)
   — **Joe Sakic, Colorado** (2 in 1996; 1 in 1998; 1 in 2001; 2 in 2004)
5 — Glenn Anderson, Edmonton, Toronto, St. Louis
4 — Bob Nystrom, NY Islanders
   — Dale Hunter, Quebec, Washington
   — Wayne Gretzky, Edmonton, Los Angeles
   — Stephane Richer, Montreal, New Jersey
   — Joe Murphy, Edmonton, Chicago
   — Esa Tikkanen, Edmonton, NY Rangers
   — Jaromir Jagr, Pittsburgh
   — Kirk Muller, Montreal, Dallas
   — Jeremy Roenick, Chicago, Philadelphia

MOST OVERTIME GOALS, ONE PLAYOFF YEAR:
3 — **Mel Hill, Boston,** 1939. All vs. NY Rangers in best-of-seven SF, won by Boston 4-3.
   — **Maurice Richard, Montreal,** 1951. 2 vs. Detroit in best-of-seven SF, won by Montreal 4-2; 1 vs. Toronto best-of-seven F, won by Toronto 4-1.

MOST OVERTIME GOALS, ONE PLAYOFF SERIES:
3 — **Mel Hill, Boston,** 1939, SF vs. NY Rangers, won by Boston 4-3. Hill scored at 59:25 of overtime March 21 for a 2-1 win; at 8:24 of overtime, March 23 for a 3-2 win; and at 48:00 of overtime, April 2 for a 2-1 win.

San Jose's Vincent Damphousse is the most recent of 10 NHL players to score two shorthanded goals in one game, accomplishing the feat on April 30, 1999.

SCORING BY A DEFENSEMAN

MOST GOALS BY A DEFENSEMAN, ONE PLAYOFF YEAR:
12 — Paul Coffey, Edmonton, 1985. 18 games.
11 — Brian Leetch, NY Rangers, 1994. 23 games.
 9 — Bobby Orr, Boston, 1970. 14 games.
  — Brad Park, Boston, 1978. 15 games.
 8 — Denis Potvin, NY Islanders, 1981. 18 games.
  — Raymond Bourque, Boston, 1983. 17 games.
  — Denis Potvin, NY Islanders, 1983. 20 games.
  — Paul Coffey, Edmonton, 1984. 19 games.

MOST GOALS BY A DEFENSEMAN, ONE GAME:
3 — Bobby Orr, Boston, April 11, 1971, at Montreal. Final score: Boston 5, Montreal 2.
  — **Dick Redmond, Chicago,** April 4, 1973, at Chicago. Final score: Chicago 7, St. Louis 1.
  — **Denis Potvin, NY Islanders,** April 17, 1981, at NY Islanders. Final score: NY Islanders 6, Edmonton 3.
  — **Paul Reinhart, Calgary,** April 14, 1983, at Edmonton. Final score: Edmonton 6, Calgary 3.
  — **Doug Halward, Vancouver,** April 7, 1984, at Vancouver. Final score: Vancouver 7, Calgary 0.
  — **Paul Reinhart, Calgary,** April 8, 1984, at Vancouver. Final score: Calgary 5, Vancouver 1.
  — **Al Iafrate, Washington,** April 26, 1993, at Washington. Final score: Washington 6, NY Islanders 4.
  — **Eric Desjardins, Montreal,** June 3, 1993, at Montreal. Final score: Montreal 3, Los Angeles 2.
  — **Gary Suter, Chicago,** April 24, 1994, at Chicago. Final score: Chicago 4, Toronto 3.
  — **Brian Leetch, NY Rangers,** May 22, 1995, at Philadelphia. Final score: Philadelphia 4, NY Rangers 3.
  — **Andy Delmore, Philadelphia,** May 7, 2000, at Philadelphia. Final score: Philadelphia 6, Pittsburgh 3.

MOST ASSISTS BY A DEFENSEMAN, ONE PLAYOFF YEAR:
25 — Paul Coffey, Edmonton, 1985. 18 games.
24 — Al MacInnis, Calgary, 1989. 22 games.
23 — Brian Leetch, NY Rangers, 1994. 23 games.
19 — Bobby Orr, Boston, 1972. 15 games.
18 — Raymond Bourque, Boston, 1988. 23 games.
  — Raymond Bourque, Boston, 1991. 19 games.
  — Larry Murphy, Pittsburgh, 1991. 23 games.

MOST ASSISTS BY A DEFENSEMAN, ONE GAME:
5 — Paul Coffey, Edmonton, May 14, 1985 at Edmonton vs. Chicago. Edmonton won 10-5.
  — **Risto Siltanen, Quebec,** April 14, 1987 at Hartford. Quebec won 7-5.

MOST POINTS BY A DEFENSEMAN, ONE PLAYOFF YEAR:
37 — Paul Coffey, Edmonton, 1985. 12 goals, 25 assists in 18 games.
34 — Brian Leetch, NY Rangers, 1994. 11 goals, 23 assists in 23 games.
31 — Al MacInnis, Calgary, 1989. 7 goals, 24 assists in 22 games.
25 — Denis Potvin, NY Islanders, 1981. 8 goals, 17 assists in 18 games.
  — Raymond Bourque, Boston, 1991. 7 goals, 18 assists in 19 games.

MOST POINTS BY A DEFENSEMAN, ONE GAME:
6 — Paul Coffey, Edmonton, May 14, 1985 at Edmonton vs. Chicago. 1 goal, 5 assists. Edmonton won 10-5.
 5 — Eddie Bush, Detroit, April 9, 1942, at Detroit vs. Toronto. 1 goal, 4 assists. Detroit won 5-2.
  — Bob Dailey, Philadelphia, May 1, 1980, at Philadelphia vs. Minnesota. 1 goal, 4 assists. Philadelphia won 7-0.
  — Denis Potvin, NY Islanders, April 17, 1981, at NY Islanders vs. Edmonton. 3 goals, 2 assists. NY Islanders won 6-3.
  — Risto Siltanen, Quebec, April 14, 1987, at Hartford. 5 assists. Quebec won 7-5.

SCORING BY A ROOKIE

MOST GOALS BY A ROOKIE, ONE PLAYOFF YEAR:
14 — Dino Ciccarelli, Minnesota, 1981. 19 games.
11 — Jeremy Roenick, Chicago, 1990. 20 games.
10 — Claude Lemieux, Montreal, 1986. 20 games.
 9 — Pat Flatley, NY Islanders, 1984. 21 games.
 8 — Steve Christoff, Minnesota, 1980. 14 games.
  — Brad Palmer, Minnesota, 1981. 19 games.
  — Mike Krushelnyski, Boston, 1983. 17 games.
  — Bob Joyce, Boston, 1988. 23 games.

MOST POINTS BY A ROOKIE, ONE PLAYOFF YEAR:
21 — Dino Ciccarelli, Minnesota, 1981. 14 goals, 7 assists in 19 games.
20 — Don Maloney, NY Rangers, 1979. 7 goals, 13 assists in 18 games.

THREE-OR-MORE-GOAL GAMES

MOST THREE-OR-MORE-GOAL GAMES IN PLAYOFFS, CAREER:
10 — Wayne Gretzky, Edmonton, Los Angeles, NY Rangers. Eight three-goal games; two four-goal games.
 7 — Maurice Richard, Montreal. Four three-goal games; two four-goal games; one five-goal game.
  — Jari Kurri, Edmonton. Six three-goal games; one four-goal game.
 6 — Dino Ciccarelli, Minnesota, Washington, Detroit. Five three-goal games; one four-goal game.
 5 — Mike Bossy, NY Islanders. Four three-goal games; one four-goal game.

MOST THREE-OR-MORE-GOAL GAMES, ONE PLAYOFF YEAR:
4 — Jari Kurri, Edmonton, 1985. 1 four-goal game, 3 three-goal games.
 3 — Mark Messier, Edmonton, 1983. 3 three-goal games.
  — Mike Bossy, NY Islanders, 1983. 1 four-goal game, 2 three-goal games
 2 — Newsy Lalonde, Montreal, 1919. 1 five-goal game, 1 four-goal game.
  — Maurice Richard, Montreal, 1944. 1 five-goal game; 1 three-goal game.
  — Doug Bentley, Chicago, 1944. 2 three-goal games.
  — Norm Ullman, Detroit, 1964. 2 three-goal games.
  — Phil Esposito, Boston, 1970. 2 three-goal games.
  — Pit Martin, Chicago, 1973. 2 three-goal games.
  — Rick MacLeish, Philadelphia, 1975. 2 three-goal games.
  — Lanny McDonald, Toronto, 1977. 1 four-goal game; 1 three-goal game.
  — Wayne Gretzky, Edmonton, 1981. 2 three-goal games.
  — Wayne Gretzky, Edmonton, 1983. 2 four-goal games.
  — Wayne Gretzky, Edmonton, 1985. 2 three-goal games.
  — Petr Klima, Detroit, 1988. 2 three-goal games.
  — Cam Neely, Boston, 1991. 2 three-goal games.
  — Wayne Gretzky, NY Rangers, 1997. 2 three-goal games.
  — Daniel Alfredsson, Ottawa, 1998. 2 three-goal games.
  — Patrick Marleau, San Jose, 2004. 2 three-goal games.

MOST THREE-OR-MORE-GOAL GAMES, ONE PLAYOFF SERIES:
3 — Jari Kurri, Edmonton, 1985 CF vs. Chicago, won by Edmonton 4-2. Kurri scored 3 goals May 7 at Edmonton in 7-3 win, 3 goals May 14 at Edmonton in 10-5 win and 4 goals May 16 at Chicago in 8-2 win.
 2 — Doug Bentley, Chicago, 1944 SF vs. Detroit, won by Chicago 4-1. Bentley scored 3 goals Mar. 28 at Chicago in 7-1 win and 3 goals Mar. 30 at Detroit in 5-2 win.
  — Norm Ullman, Detroit, 1964 SF vs. Chicago, won by Detroit 4-3. Ullman scored 3 goals Mar. 29 at Chicago in 5-4 win and 3 goals April 7 at Detroit in 7-2 win.
  — Mark Messier, Edmonton, 1983 DF vs. Calgary, won by Edmonton 4-1. Messier scored 4 goals April 14 at Edmonton in 6-3 win and 3 goals April 17 at Calgary in 10-2 win.
  — Mike Bossy, NY Islanders, 1983 CF vs. Boston, won by NY Islanders 4-2. Bossy scored 3 goals May 3 at NY Islanders in 8-3 win and 4 goals May 7 at New York in 8-4 win.

SCORING STREAKS

LONGEST CONSECUTIVE GOAL-SCORING STREAK, ONE PLAYOFF YEAR:
10 Games — Reggie Leach, Philadelphia, 1976. Streak started April 17 at Toronto and ended May 9 at Montreal. He scored one goal in each of eight games; two in one game; and five in another; a total of 15 goals.

LONGEST CONSECUTIVE POINT-SCORING STREAK, ONE PLAYOFF YEAR:
18 games — Bryan Trottier, NY Islanders, 1981. 11 goals, 18 assists, 29 points.
17 games — Wayne Gretzky, Edmonton, 1988. 12 goals, 29 assists, 41 points.
  — Al MacInnis, Calgary, 1989. 7 goals, 19 assists, 26 points.

LONGEST CONSECUTIVE POINT-SCORING STREAK, MORE THAN ONE PLAYOFF YEAR:
27 games — Bryan Trottier, NY Islanders, 1980, 1981 and 1982. 7 games in 1980 (3 goals, 5 assists, 8 points), 18 games in 1981 (11 goals, 18 assists, 29 points), and two games in 1982 (2 goals, 3 assists, 5 points). Total points, 42.
19 games — Wayne Gretzky, Edmonton, Los Angeles, 1988 and 1989. 17 games in 1988 (12 goals, 29 assists, 41 points with Edmonton), 2 games in 1989 (1 goal, 2 assists, 3 points with Los Angeles). Total points, 44.
  — Al MacInnis, Calgary, 1989 and 1990. 17 games in 1989 (7 goals, 19 assists, 26 points), and two games in 1990 (2 goals, 1 assist, 3 points). Total points, 29.

FASTEST GOALS

FASTEST GOAL FROM START OF GAME:
0:06 — Don Kozak, Los Angeles, April 17, 1977, at Los Angeles vs. Boston and goaltender Gerry Cheevers. Los Angeles won 7-4.
0:07 — Bob Gainey, Montreal, May 5, 1977, at NY Islanders vs. goaltender Chico Resch. Montreal won 2-1.
  — Terry Murray, Philadelphia, April 12, 1981, at Quebec vs. goaltender Dan Bouchard. Quebec won 4-3 in overtime.

FASTEST GOAL FROM START OF PERIOD (OTHER THAN FIRST):
0:06 — Pelle Eklund, Philadelphia, April 25, 1989, at Pittsburgh vs. goaltender Tom Barrasso, second period. Pittsburgh won 10-7.
0:09 — Bill Collins, Minnesota, April 9, 1968, at Minnesota vs. Los Angeles and goaltender Wayne Rutledge, third period. Minnesota won 7-5.
  — Dave Balon, Minnesota, April 25, 1968, at St. Louis vs. goaltender Glenn Hall, third period. Minnesota won 5-1.
  — Murray Oliver, Minnesota, April 8, 1971, at St. Louis vs. goaltender Ernie Wakely, third period. St. Louis won 4-2.
  — Clark Gillies, NY Islanders, April 15, 1977, at Buffalo vs. goaltender Don Edwards, third period. NY Islanders won 4-3.
  — Eric Vail, Atlanta, April 11, 1978, at Atlanta vs. Detroit and goaltender Ron Low, third period. Detroit won 5-3.
  — Stan Smyl, Vancouver, April 10, 1979, at Philadelphia vs. goaltender Wayne Stephenson, third period. Vancouver won 3-2.
  — Wayne Gretzky, Edmonton, April 6, 1983, at Edmonton vs. Winnipeg and goaltender Brian Hayward, second period. Edmonton won 6-3.
  — Mark Messier, Edmonton, April 16, 1984, at Calgary vs. goaltender Don Edwards, third period. Edmonton won 5-3.
  — Brian Skrudland, Montreal, May 18, 1986, at Calgary vs. goaltender Mike Vernon, first overtime period. Montreal won 3-2.

FASTEST TWO GOALS:
0:05 — Norm Ullman, Detroit, April 11, 1965, at Detroit vs. Chicago and goaltender Glenn Hall. Ullman scored at 17:35 and 17:40 of second period. Detroit won 4-2.

FASTEST TWO GOALS FROM START OF A GAME:
    1:08 — **Dick Duff, Toronto,** April 9, 1963, at Toronto vs. Detroit and goaltender Terry Sawchuk. Duff scored at 0:49 and 1:08. Toronto won 4-2.

FASTEST TWO GOALS FROM START OF A PERIOD:
    0:35 — **Pat LaFontaine, NY Islanders,** May 19, 1984, at Edmonton vs. goaltender Andy Moog. LaFontaine scored at 0:13 and 0:35 of third period. Edmonton won 5-2.

PENALTIES

MOST PENALTY MINUTES IN PLAYOFFS, CAREER:
    729 — **Dale Hunter, Quebec, Washington, Colorado**
    541 — Chris Nilan, Montreal, NY Rangers, Boston
    529 — Claude Lemieux, Montreal, New Jersey, Colorado, Phoenix
    471 — Rick Tocchet, Philadelphia, Pittsburgh, Boston, Phoenix
    466 — Willi Plett, Atlanta, Calgary, Minnesota, Boston

MOST PENALTIES, ONE GAME:
    8 — **Forbes Kennedy, Toronto,** April 2, 1969, at Boston. Kennedy was assessed 4 minors, 2 majors, 1 10-minute misconduct, 1 game misconduct. Boston won 10-0.
    — **Kim Clackson, Pittsburgh,** April 14, 1980, at Boston. Clackson was assessed 5 minors, 2 majors, 1 10-minute misconduct. Boston won 6-2.

MOST PENALTY MINUTES, ONE GAME:
    42 — **Dave Schultz, Philadelphia,** April 22, 1976, at Toronto. Schultz was assessed 1 minor, 2 majors, 1 10-minute misconduct and 2 game-misconducts. Toronto won 8-5.

MOST PENALTIES, ONE PERIOD AND MOST PENALTY MINUTES, ONE PERIOD:
6 Penalties; 39 Minutes — **Ed Hospodar, NY Rangers,** April 9, 1981, at Los Angeles, first period. Hospodar was assessed 2 minors, 1 major, 1 10-minute misconduct, 2 game misconducts. Los Angeles won 5-4.

GOALTENDING

MOST PLAYOFF GAMES APPEARED IN BY A GOALTENDER, CAREER:
    247 — **Patrick Roy, Montreal, Colorado**
    161 — Ed Belfour, Chicago, Dallas, Toronto
    150 — Grant Fuhr, Edmonton, Buffalo, St. Louis
    144 — Martin Brodeur, New Jersey
    138 — Mike Vernon, Calgary, Detroit, San Jose, Florida

MOST MINUTES PLAYED BY A GOALTENDER, CAREER:
    15,209 — **Patrick Roy, Montreal, Colorado**
    9,945 — Ed Belfour, Chicago, Dallas, Toronto
    9,000 — Martin Brodeur, New Jersey
    8,834 — Grant Fuhr, Edmonton, Buffalo, St. Louis
    8,214 — Mike Vernon, Calgary, Detroit, San Jose, Florida

MOST MINUTES PLAYED BY A GOALTENDER, ONE PLAYOFF YEAR:
    1,655 — **Miikka Kiprusoff, Calgary,** 2004. 26 games.
    1,544 — Kirk McLean, Vancouver, 1994. 24 games.
        — Ed Belfour, Dallas, 1999. 23 games.
    1,540 — Ron Hextall, Philadelphia, 1987. 26 games.
    1,505 — Martin Brodeur, New Jersey, 2001. 25 games.

MOST SHUTOUTS IN PLAYOFFS (CAREER):
    23 — **Patrick Roy, Montreal, Colorado**
    20 — Martin Brodeur, New Jersey
    16 — Curtis Joseph, St. Louis, Edmonton, Toronto
    14 — Clint Benedict, Ottawa, Mtl. Maroons
        — Jacques Plante, Montreal, St. Louis
        — Ed Belfour, Chicago, Dallas, Toronto

MOST SHUTOUTS, ONE PLAYOFF YEAR:
    7 — **Martin Brodeur, New Jersey,** 2003. 24 games.
    6 — Dominik Hasek, Detroit, 2002. 23 games.
    5 — Jean-Sebastien Giguere, Anaheim, 2003. 21 games.
        — Nikolai Khabibulin, Tampa Bay, 2004. 23 games.
        — Miikka Kiprusoff, Calgary, 2004. 26 games.

MOST SHUTOUTS, ONE PLAYOFF SERIES:
    3 — **Clint Benedict, Mtl. Maroons,** 1926 F vs. Victoria. 4 games.
        — **Dave Kerr, NY Rangers,** 1940 SF vs. Boston. 6 games.
        — **Frank McCool, Toronto,** 1945 F vs. Detroit. 7 games.
        — **Turk Broda, Toronto,** 1950 SF vs. Detroit. 7 games.
        — **Felix Potvin, Toronto,** 1994 CQF vs. Chicago. 6 games.
        — **Martin Brodeur, New Jersey,** 1995 CQF vs. Boston. 7 games.
        — **Brent Johnson, St. Louis,** 2002 CQF vs. Chicago. 5 games.
        — **Patrick Lalime, Ottawa,** 2002 CQF vs. Philadelphia. 5 games.
        — **Jean-Sebastien Giguere, Anaheim,** 2003 CF vs. Minnesota. 4 games.
        — **Martin Brodeur, New Jersey,** 2003 F vs. Anaheim. 7 games.
        — **Ed Belfour, Toronto,** 2004 CQF vs. Ottawa. 7 games.
        — **Nikolai Khabibulin, Tampa Bay,** 2004 CQF vs. NY Islanders. 5 games.

MOST WINS BY A GOALTENDER, (CAREER):
    151 — **Patrick Roy, Montreal, Colorado**
    92 — Grant Fuhr, Edmonton, Buffalo, St. Louis
    88 — Billy Smith, NY Islanders
        — Ed Belfour, Chicago, Dallas, Toronto
    84 — Martin Brodeur, New Jersey

MOST WINS BY A GOALTENDER, ONE PLAYOFF YEAR:
    16 — Sixteen wins by a goaltender in one playoff year has been recorded on 16 occasions. Nikolai Khabibulin of the Tampa Bay Lightning is the most recent to equal this mark, posting a record of 16 wins and 7 losses in 23 games in 2004. It was first accomplished by Grant Fuhr in 1988.

MOST CONSECUTIVE WINS BY A GOALTENDER, MORE THAN ONE PLAYOFF YEAR:
    14 — **Tom Barrasso, Pittsburgh,** 1992, 1993; 3 wins vs. NY Rangers in 1992 DF, won by Pittsburgh 4-2; 4 wins vs. Boston in 1992 CF, won Pittsburgh 4-0; 4 wins vs. Chicago in 1992 F, won by Pittsburgh 4-0; 3 wins vs. New Jersey in 1993 DSF, won by Pittsburgh 4-1.

MOST CONSECUTIVE WINS BY A GOALTENDER, ONE PLAYOFF YEAR:
    11 — **Ed Belfour, Chicago,** 1992. 3 wins vs. St. Louis in DSF, won by Chicago 4-2; 4 wins vs. Detroit in DF, won by Chicago 4-0; and 4 wins vs. Edmonton in CF, won by Chicago 4-0.
        — **Tom Barrasso, Pittsburgh,** 1992. 3 wins vs. NY Rangers in DF, won by Pittsburgh 4-2; 4 wins vs. Boston in CF, won by Pittsburgh 4-0; and 4 wins vs. Chicago in F, won by Pittsburgh 4-0.
        — **Patrick Roy, Montreal,** 1993. 4 wins vs. Quebec in DSF, won by Montreal 4-2; 4 wins vs. Buffalo in DF, won by Montreal 4-0; and 3 wins vs. NY Islanders in CF, won by Montreal 4-1.

LONGEST SHUTOUT SEQUENCE:
270:08 — **George Hainsworth,** Montreal, 1930. Hainsworth's shutout streak began after Murray Murdoch scored a goal for the NY Rangers at 15:34 of the first period in the first game of a SF series on March 28, 1930. Hainsworth did not allow another goal in the final 113:18 of that game, won by Montreal 2-1 at 8:52 of the 4th overtime period. Hainsworth then shutout the NY Rangers in the next and final game of the series on March 30, 1930, won by Montreal 2-0. The streak continued with a 3-0 win over Boston in the opening game of the F series on April 1, 1930. His streak ended on April 3, 1930 when Boston's Eddie Shore scored at 16:50 of the second period in the second game of the F series.

MOST CONSECUTIVE SHUTOUTS:
    3 — **Clint Benedict, Mtl. Maroons,** 1926. Benedict shut out Ottawa 1-0, Mar. 27; he then shut out Victoria twice, 3-0, Mar. 30; 3-0, Apr. 1. Mtl. Maroons won NHL F vs. Ottawa 2 goals to 1 and won the best-of-five F vs. Victoria 3-1.
        — **John Ross Roach, NY Rangers,** 1929. Roach shut out NY Americans twice, 0-0, Mar. 19; 1-0, Mar. 21; he then shut out Toronto 1-0, Mar. 24. NY Rangers won QF vs. NY Americans 1 goal to 0 and won the best-of-three SF vs. Toronto 2-0.
        — **Frank McCool, Toronto,** 1945. McCool shut out Detroit 1-0, April 6; 2-0, April 8; 1-0, April 12. Toronto won the best-of-seven F 4-3.
        — **Brent Johnson, St. Louis,** 2002. Johnson shut out Chicago three times; 2-0, April 20; 4-0, April 21; 1-0, April 23. St. Louis won the best-of-seven CQF 4-1.
        — **Patrick Lalime, Ottawa,** 2002. Lalime shut out Philadelphia three times; 3-0, April 20; 3-0, April 22; 3-0, April 24. Ottawa won the best-of-seven CQF 4-1.
        — **Jean-Sebastien Giguere, Anaheim,** 2003. Giguere shut out Minnesota 1-0, May 10; 2-0, May 12; 4-0, May 14. Anaheim won the best-of-seven CF 4-0.

Early Playoff Records

1893-1918
Team Records

MOST GOALS, BOTH TEAMS, ONE GAME:
    25 — **Ottawa Silver Seven, Dawson City** at Ottawa, Jan. 16, 1905. Ottawa 23, Dawson City 2. Ottawa won best-of-three series 2-0.

MOST GOALS, ONE TEAM, ONE GAME:
    23 — **Ottawa Silver Seven** at Ottawa, Jan. 16, 1905. Ottawa defeated Dawson City 23-2.

MOST GOALS, BOTH TEAMS, BEST-OF-THREE SERIES:
    42 — **Ottawa Silver Seven, Queen's University** at Ottawa, 1906. Ottawa defeated Queen's 16-7, Feb. 27, and 12-7, Feb. 28.

MOST GOALS, ONE TEAM, BEST-OF-THREE SERIES:
    32 — **Ottawa Silver Seven** in 1905 at Ottawa. Defeated Dawson City 9-2, Jan. 13, and 23-2, Jan. 16.

MOST GOALS, BOTH TEAMS, BEST-OF-FIVE SERIES:
    39 — **Toronto Arenas, Vancouver Millionaires** at Toronto, 1918. Toronto won 5-3, Mar. 20; 6-3, Mar. 26; 2-1, Mar. 30. Vancouver won 6-4, Mar. 23, and 8-1, Mar. 28. Toronto scored 18 goals; Vancouver 21.

MOST GOALS, ONE TEAM, BEST-OF-FIVE SERIES:
    26 — **Vancouver Millionaires** in 1915 at Vancouver. Defeated Ottawa Senators 6-2, Mar. 22; 8-3, Mar. 24; and 12-3, Mar. 26.

Individual Records

MOST GOALS IN PLAYOFFS:
    63 — **Frank McGee, Ottawa Silver Seven,** in 22 playoff games. Seven goals in four games, 1903; 21 goals in eight games, 1904; 18 goals in four games, 1905; 17 goals in six games, 1906.

MOST GOALS, ONE PLAYOFF SERIES:
    15 — **Frank McGee, Ottawa Silver Seven,** in two games in 1905 at Ottawa. Scored one goal, Jan. 13, in 9-2 victory over Dawson City and 14 goals, Jan. 16, in 23-2 victory.

MOST GOALS, ONE PLAYOFF GAME:
    14 — **Frank McGee, Ottawa Silver Seven,** at Ottawa, Jan. 16, 1905, in 23-2 victory over Dawson City.

FASTEST THREE GOALS:
    40 Seconds — **Marty Walsh, Ottawa Senators,** at Ottawa, March 16, 1911, at 3:00, 3:10, and 3:40 of third period. Ottawa defeated Port Arthur 13-4.

All-Time Playoff Goal Leaders since 1918

(40 or more goals)

Player	Teams	Yrs.	GP	G
Wayne Gretzky	Edm., L.A., St.L., NYR	16	208	122
* Mark Messier	Edm., NYR, Van.	17	236	109
Jari Kurri	Edm., L.A., NYR, Ana., Col.	15	200	106
* Brett Hull	Cgy., St.L., Dal., Det.	19	202	103
Glenn Anderson	Edm., Tor., NYR, St.L.	15	225	93
Mike Bossy	NYI	10	129	85
Maurice Richard	Mtl.	15	133	82
Claude Lemieux	Mtl., N.J., Col., Phx., Dal.	17	233	80
Jean Beliveau	Mtl.	17	162	79
* Joe Sakic	Que., Col.	11	153	78
* Mario Lemieux	Pit.	8	107	76
Dino Ciccarelli	Min., Wsh., Det., T.B., Fla.	14	141	73
Esa Tikkanen	Edm., NYR, St.L., N.J., Van., Fla., Wsh.	13	186	72
Bryan Trottier	NYI, Pit.	17	221	71
* Steve Yzerman	Det.	19	192	70
Gordie Howe	Det., Hfd.	20	157	68
* Jaromir Jagr	Pit., Wsh., NYI	12	146	67
* Joe Nieuwendyk	Cgy., Dal., N.J., Tor.	16	158	66
Denis Savard	Chi., Mtl., T.B.	16	169	66
Yvan Cournoyer	Mtl.	12	147	64
Brian Propp	Phi., Bos., Min., Hfd.	13	160	64
Bobby Smith	Min., Mtl.	13	184	64
Bobby Hull	Chi., Wpg., Hfd.	14	119	62
Phil Esposito	Chi., Bos., NYR	15	130	61
Jacques Lemaire	Mtl.	11	145	61
Joe Mullen	St.L., Cgy., Pit., Bos.	15	143	60
Doug Gilmour	St.L., Cgy., Tor., N.J., Chi., Buf., Mtl.	17	182	60
Stan Mikita	Chi.	18	155	59
Paul Coffey	Edm., Pit., L.A., Det., Hfd., Phi., Chi., Car., Bos.	16	194	59
Guy Lafleur	Mtl., NYR, Que.	14	128	58
Bernie Geoffrion	Mtl., NYR	16	132	58
* Luc Robitaille	L.A., Pit., NYR, Det.	15	159	58
Cam Neely	Van., Bos.	9	93	57
* Peter Forsberg	Que., Col.	10	133	57
Steve Larmer	Chi., NYR	13	140	56
Denis Potvin	NYI	14	185	56
Rick MacLeish	Phi., Hfd., Pit., Det.	11	114	54
* Steve Thomas	Tor., Chi., NYI, N.J., Ana., Det.	16	174	54
Bill Barber	Phi.	11	129	53
Stephane Richer	Mtl., N.J., T.B., St.L., Pit.	13	134	53
Rick Tocchet	Phi., Pit., L.A., Bos., Wsh., Phx.	13	145	52
* Brendan Shanahan	N.J., St.L., Hfd., Det.	15	151	52
* Jeremy Roenick	Chi., Phx., Phi.	15	136	51
Frank Mahovlich	Tor., Det., Mtl.	14	137	51
Brian Bellows	Min., Mtl., T.B., Ana., Wsh.	13	143	51
* Mike Modano	Min., Dal.	12	144	51
Steve Shutt	Mtl., L.A.	12	99	50
* Sergei Fedorov	Det., Ana.	13	162	50
Henri Richard	Mtl.	18	180	49
Reggie Leach	Bos., Cal., Phi., Det.	8	94	47
Ted Lindsay	Det., Chi.	16	133	47
Clark Gillies	NYI, Buf.	13	164	47
Kevin Stevens	Pit., Bos., L.A., NYR, Phi.	7	103	46
Dickie Moore	Mtl., Tor., St.L.	14	135	46
* Ron Francis	Hfd., Pit., Car., Tor.	17	171	46
Rick Middleton	NYR, Bos.	12	114	45
Lanny McDonald	Tor., Col., Cgy.	13	117	44
* Scott Young	Hfd., Pit., Que., Col., Ana., St.L., Dal.	14	141	44
Ken Linseman	Phi., Edm., Bos., Tor.	11	113	43
Mike Gartner	Wsh., Min., NYR, Tor., Phx.	15	122	43
* Dave Andreychuk	Buf., Tor., N.J., Bos., Col., T.B.	18	162	43
* Vyacheslav Kozlov	Det., Buf., Atl.	9	114	42
Bernie Nicholls	L.A., NYR, Edm., N.J., Chi., S.J.	13	118	42
Bobby Clarke	Phi.	13	136	42
* John LeClair	Mtl., Phi.	14	154	42
Adam Oates	Det., St.L., Bos., Wsh., Phi., Ana., Edm.	15	163	42
Dale Hunter	Que., Wsh., Col.	18	186	42
John Bucyk	Det., Bos.	14	124	41
Vincent Damphousse	Tor., Edm., Mtl., S.J.	14	140	41
Raymond Bourque	Bos., Col.	21	214	41
Tim Kerr	Phi., NYR, Hfd.	10	81	40
Peter McNab	Buf., Bos., Van., N.J.	10	107	40
* Mark Recchi	Pit., Phi., Mtl.	10	110	40
Bob Bourne	NYI, L.A.	13	139	40
John Tonelli	NYI, Cgy., L.A., Chi., Que.	13	172	40

* Active

All-Time Playoff Assist Leaders since 1918

(60 or more assists)

Player	Teams	Yrs.	GP	A
Wayne Gretzky	Edm., L.A., St.L., NYR	16	208	260
* Mark Messier	Edm., NYR, Van.	17	236	186
Raymond Bourque	Bos., Col.	21	214	139
Paul Coffey	Edm., Pit., L.A., Det., Hfd., Phi., Chi., Car., Bos.	16	194	137
Doug Gilmour	St.L., Cgy., Tor., N.J., Chi., Buf., Mtl.	17	182	128
Jari Kurri	Edm., L.A., NYR, Ana., Col.	15	200	127
* Al MacInnis	Cgy., St.L.	19	177	121
Glenn Anderson	Edm., Tor., NYR, St.L.	15	225	121
Larry Robinson	Mtl., L.A.	20	227	116
Larry Murphy	L.A., Wsh., Min., Pit., Tor., Det.	20	215	115
Adam Oates	Det., St.L., Bos., Wsh., Phi., Ana., Edm.	15	163	114
* Sergei Fedorov	Det., Ana.	13	162	113
Bryan Trottier	NYI, Pit.	17	221	113
* Steve Yzerman	Det.	19	192	111
Denis Savard	Chi., Mtl., T.B.	16	169	109
Denis Potvin	NYI	14	185	108
* Chris Chelios	Mtl., Chi., Det.	20	222	107
* Peter Forsberg	Que., Col.	10	133	97
Jean Beliveau	Mtl.	17	162	97
* Ron Francis	Hfd., Pit., Car., Tor.	17	171	97
* Mario Lemieux	Pit.	8	107	96
Bobby Smith	Min., Mtl.	13	184	96
Gordie Howe	Det., Hfd.	20	157	92
Scott Stevens	Wsh., St.L., N.J.	20	233	92
* Joe Sakic	Que., Col.	11	153	91
Stan Mikita	Chi.	18	155	91
Brad Park	NYR, Bos., Det.	17	161	90
* Jaromir Jagr	Pit., Wsh., NYI	12	146	87
* Brett Hull	Cgy., St.L., Dal., Det.	19	202	87
Craig Janney	Bos., St.L., S.J., Wpg., Phx., T.B., NYI	11	120	86
Brian Propp	Phi., Bos., Min., Hfd.	13	160	84
* Nicklas Lidstrom	Det.	13	168	82
Henri Richard	Mtl.	18	180	80
* Sergei Zubov	NYR, Pit., Dal.	10	142	79
Jacques Lemaire	Mtl.	11	145	78
Claude Lemieux	Mtl., N.J., Col., Phx., Dal.	17	233	78
Ken Linseman	Phi., Edm., Bos., Tor.	11	113	77
Bobby Clarke	Phi.	13	136	77
Guy Lafleur	Mtl., NYR, Que.	14	128	76
Phil Esposito	Chi., Bos., NYR	15	130	76
* Mike Modano	Min., Dal.	12	144	76
Dale Hunter	Que., Wsh., Col.	18	186	76
Mike Bossy	NYI	10	129	75
Steve Larmer	Chi., NYR	13	140	75
John Tonelli	NYI, Cgy., L.A., Chi., Que.	13	172	75
Peter Stastny	Que., N.J., St.L.	12	93	72
Bernie Nicholls	L.A., NYR, Edm., N.J., Chi., S.J.	13	118	72
Brian Bellows	Min., Mtl., T.B., Ana., Wsh.	13	143	71
Gilbert Perreault	Buf.	11	90	70
Geoff Courtnall	Bos., Edm., Wsh., St.L., Van.	15	156	70
* Brian Leetch	NYR, NYI, Tor.	8	95	69
Dale Hawerchuk	Wpg., Buf., St.L., Phi.	15	97	69
Alex Delvecchio	Det.	14	121	69
* Luc Robitaille	L.A., Pit., NYR, Det.	15	159	69
Bobby Hull	Chi., Wpg., Hfd.	14	119	67
* Sandis Ozolinsh	S.J., Col., Car., Fla., Ana.	9	134	67
Frank Mahovlich	Tor., Det., Mtl.	14	137	67
Igor Larionov	Van., S.J., Det., Fla., N.J.	13	150	67
Bobby Orr	Bos., Chi.	8	74	66
Bernie Federko	St.L., Det.	11	91	66
Jean Ratelle	NYR, Bos.	15	123	66
Charlie Huddy	Edm., L.A., Buf., St.L.	14	183	66
* Jeremy Roenick	Chi., Phx., Phi.	15	136	65
* Brendan Shanahan	N.J., St.L., Hfd., Det.	15	151	65
Dickie Moore	Mtl., Tor., St.L.	14	135	64
Doug Harvey	Mtl., NYR, Det., St.L.	15	137	64
Neal Broten	Min., Dal., N.J., L.A.	13	135	63
Vincent Damphousse	Tor., Edm., Mtl., S.J.	14	140	63
Yvan Cournoyer	Mtl.	12	147	63
John Bucyk	Det., Bos.	14	124	62
Doug Wilson	Chi., S.J.	12	95	61
Steve Duchesne	L.A., Phi., Que., St.L., Ott., Det.	14	121	61
Kevin Stevens	Pit., Bos., L.A., NYR, Phi.	7	103	60
* Pierre Turgeon	Buf., NYI, Mtl., St.L., Dal.	14	104	60
* Trevor Linden	Van., NYI, Mtl., Wsh.	11	112	60
Bernie Geoffrion	Mtl., NYR	16	132	60
Rick Tocchet	Phi., Pit., L.A., Bos., Wsh., Phx.	13	145	60
Esa Tikkanen	Edm., NYR, St.L., N.J., Van., Fla., Wsh.	13	186	60

All-Time Playoff Point Leaders since 1918

(105 or more points)

Player	Teams	Yrs.	GP	G	A	Pts.
Wayne Gretzky	Edm., L.A., St.L., NYR	16	208	122	260	382
* Mark Messier	Edm., NYR, Van.	17	236	109	186	295
Jari Kurri	Edm., L.A., NYR, Ana., Col.	15	200	106	127	233
Glenn Anderson	Edm., Tor., NYR, St.L.	15	225	93	121	214
Paul Coffey	Edm., Pit., L.A., Det., Hfd., Phi., Chi., Car., Bos.	16	194	59	137	196
* Brett Hull	Cgy., St.L., Dal., Det.	19	202	103	87	190
Doug Gilmour	St.L., Cgy., Tor., N.J., Chi., Buf., Mtl.	17	182	60	128	188
Bryan Trottier	NYI, Pit.	17	221	71	113	184
* Steve Yzerman	Det.	19	192	70	111	181
Raymond Bourque	Bos., Col.	21	214	41	139	180
Jean Beliveau	Mtl.	17	162	79	97	176
Denis Savard	Chi., Mtl., T.B.	16	169	66	109	175
* Mario Lemieux	Pit.	8	107	76	96	172
* Joe Sakic	Que., Col.	11	153	78	91	169
Denis Potvin	NYI	14	185	56	108	164
* Sergei Fedorov	Det., Ana.	13	162	50	113	163
Mike Bossy	NYI	10	129	85	75	160
Gordie Howe	Det., Hfd.	20	157	68	92	160
* Al MacInnis	Cgy., St.L.	19	177	39	121	160
Bobby Smith	Min., Mtl.	13	184	64	96	160
Claude Lemieux	Mtl., N.J., Col., Phx., Dal.	17	233	80	78	158
Adam Oates	Det., St.L., Bos., Wsh., Phi., Ana., Edm.	15	163	42	114	156
* Peter Forsberg	Que., Col.	10	133	57	97	154
* Jaromir Jagr	Pit., Wsh., NYI	12	146	67	87	154
Larry Murphy	L.A., Wsh., Min., Pit., Tor., Det.	20	215	37	115	152
Stan Mikita	Chi.	18	155	59	91	150
Brian Propp	Phi., Bos., Min., Hfd.	13	160	64	84	148
Larry Robinson	Mtl., L.A.	20	227	28	116	144
* Ron Francis	Hfd., Pit., Car., Tor.	17	171	46	97	143
Jacques Lemaire	Mtl.	11	145	61	78	139
Phil Esposito	Chi., Bos., NYR	15	130	61	76	137
* Chris Chelios	Mtl., Chi., Det.	20	222	30	107	137
Guy Lafleur	Mtl., NYR, Que.	14	128	58	76	134
Esa Tikkanen	Edm., NYR, St.L., N.J., Van., Fla., Wsh.	13	186	72	60	132
Steve Larmer	Chi., NYR	13	140	56	75	131
Bobby Hull	Chi., Wpg., Hfd.	14	119	62	67	129
Henri Richard	Mtl.	18	180	49	80	129
* Mike Modano	Min., Dal.	12	144	51	76	127
Yvan Cournoyer	Mtl.	12	147	64	63	127
* Luc Robitaille	L.A., Pit., NYR, Det.	15	159	58	69	127
Maurice Richard	Mtl.	15	133	82	44	126
Brad Park	NYR, Bos., Det.	17	161	35	90	125
Brian Bellows	Min., Mtl., T.B., Ana., Wsh.	13	143	51	71	122
Ken Linseman	Phi., Edm., Bos., Tor.	11	113	43	77	120
Bobby Clarke	Phi.	13	136	42	77	119
Bernie Geoffrion	Mtl., NYR	16	132	58	60	118
Frank Mahovlich	Tor., Det., Mtl.	14	137	51	67	118
Dino Ciccarelli	Min., Wsh., Det., T.B., Fla.	14	141	73	45	118
Dale Hunter	Que., Wsh., Col.	18	186	42	76	118
Scott Stevens	Wsh., St.L., N.J.	20	233	26	92	118
* Brendan Shanahan	N.J., St.L., Hfd., Det.	15	151	52	65	117
* Jeremy Roenick	Chi., Phx., Phi.	15	136	51	65	116
* Joe Nieuwendyk	Cgy., Dal., N.J., Tor.	16	158	66	50	116
* Nicklas Lidstrom	Det.	13	168	34	82	116
John Tonelli	NYI, Cgy., L.A., Chi., Que.	13	172	40	75	115
Bernie Nicholls	L.A., NYR, Edm., N.J., Chi., S.J.	13	118	42	72	114
Rick Tocchet	Phi., Pit., L.A., Bos., Wsh., Phx.	13	145	52	60	112
Craig Janney	Bos., St.L., S.J., Wpg., Phx., T.B., NYI	11	120	24	86	110
Dickie Moore	Mtl., Tor., St.L.	14	135	46	64	110
Geoff Courtnall	Bos., Edm., Wsh., St.L., Van.	15	156	39	70	109
Bill Barber	Phi.	11	129	53	55	108
Rick MacLeish	Phi., Hfd., Pit., Det.	11	114	54	53	107
* Steve Thomas	Tor., Chi., NYI, N.J., Ana., Det.	16	174	54	53	107
Kevin Stevens	Pit., Bos., L.A., NYR, Phi.	7	103	46	60	106
Joe Mullen	St.L., Cgy., Pit., Bos.	15	143	60	46	106
Peter Stastny	Que., N.J., St.L.	12	93	33	72	105

Three-or-more-Goal Games, Playoffs 1918 – 2005

Player	Team	Date	City	Total Goals	Opposing Goaltender	Score	
Wayne Gretzky (10)	Edm.	Apr. 11/81	Edm.	3	Richard Sevigny	Edm. 6	Mtl. 2
		Apr. 19/81	Edm.	3	Billy Smith	Edm. 5	NYI 2
		Apr. 6/83	Edm.	4	Brian Hayward	Edm. 6	Wpg. 3
		Apr. 17/83	Cgy.	4	Reggie Lemelin	Edm. 10	Cgy. 2
		Apr. 25/85	Wpg.	3	Brian Hayward (2)		
					Marc Behrend (1)	Edm. 8	Wpg. 3
		May 25/85	Edm.	3	Pelle Lindbergh	Edm. 4	Phi. 3
		Apr. 24/86	Cgy.	3	Mike Vernon	Edm. 7	Cgy. 4
	L.A.	May 29/93	Tor.	3	Felix Potvin	L.A. 5	Tor. 4
	NYR	Apr. 23/97	NYR	3	John Vanbiesbrouck	NYR 3	Fla. 2
		May 18/97	Phi.	3	Garth Snow	NYR 5	Phi. 4
Maurice Richard (7)	Mtl.	Mar. 23/44	Mtl.	5	Paul Bibeault	Mtl. 5	Tor. 1
		Apr. 6/44	Chi.	3	Mike Karakas	Mtl. 3	Chi. 1
		Mar. 29/45	Mtl.	4	Frank McCool	Mtl. 10	Tor. 3
		Apr. 14/53	Bos.	3	Gord Henry	Mtl. 7	Bos. 3
		Mar. 20/56	Mtl.	3	Gump Worsley	Mtl. 7	NYR 1
		Apr. 6/57	Mtl.	4	Don Simmons	Mtl. 5	Bos. 1
		Apr. 1/58	Det.	3	Terry Sawchuk	Mtl. 4	Det. 3
Jari Kurri (7)	Edm.	Apr. 4/84	Edm.	3	Doug Soetaert (1)		
					Mike Veisor (2)	Edm. 9	Wpg. 2
		Apr. 25/85	Wpg.	3	Brian Hayward (2)		
					Marc Behrend (1)	Edm. 8	Wpg. 3
		May 7/85	Edm.	3	Murray Bannerman	Edm. 7	Chi. 3
		May 14/85	Edm.	3	Murray Bannerman	Edm. 10	Chi. 5
		May 16/85	Chi.	4	Murray Bannerman	Edm. 8	Chi. 2
		Apr. 9/87	Edm.	4	Rollie Melanson (2)		
					Darren Eliot (2)	Edm. 13	L.A. 3
		May 18/90	Bos.	3	Andy Moog (2)		
					Reggie Lemelin (1)	Edm. 7	Bos. 2
Dino Ciccarelli (6)	Min.	May 5/81	Min.	3	Pat Riggin	Min. 7	Cgy. 4
		Apr. 10/82	Min.	3	Murray Bannerman	Min. 7	Chi. 1
	Wsh.	Apr. 5/90	N.J.	3	Sean Burke	Wsh. 5	N.J. 4
		Apr. 25/92	Pit.	4	Tom Barrasso (1)		
					Ken Wregget (3)	Wsh. 7	Pit. 2
	Det.	Apr. 29/93	Tor.	3	Felix Potvin (2)		
					Daren Puppa (1)	Det. 7	Tor. 3
		May 11/95	Dal.	3	Andy Moog (2)		
					Darcy Wakaluk (1)	Det. 5	Dal. 1
Mike Bossy (5)	NYI	Apr. 16/79	NYI	3	Tony Esposito	NYI 6	Chi. 2
		May 8/82	NYI	3	Richard Brodeur	NYI 6	Van. 5
		Apr. 10/83	Wsh.	3	Al Jensen	NYI 6	Wsh. 3
		May 3/83	NYI	3	Pete Peeters	NYI 8	Bos. 3
		May 7/83	NYI	4	Pete Peeters	NYI 8	Bos. 4
Phil Esposito (4)	Bos.	Apr. 2/69	Bos.	4	Bruce Gamble	Bos. 10	Tor. 0
		Apr. 8/70	Bos.	3	Ed Giacomin	Bos. 8	NYR 2
		Apr. 19/70	Chi.	3	Tony Esposito	Bos. 6	Chi. 3
		Apr. 8/75	Bos.	3	Tony Esposito (2)		
					Michel Dumas (1)	Bos. 8	Chi. 2
Mark Messier (4)	Edm.	Apr. 14/83	Edm.	4	Reggie Lemelin	Edm. 6	Cgy. 3
		Apr. 17/83	Cgy.	3	Reggie Lemelin (1)	Edm. 10	Cgy. 2
					Don Edwards (2)		
		Apr. 26/83	Edm.	3	Murray Bannerman	Edm. 8	Chi. 2
	NYR	May 25/94	N.J.	3	Martin Brodeur (2)	NYR 4	N.J. 2
					ENG (1)		
Steve Yzerman (4)	Det.	Apr. 6/89	Det.	3	Alain Chevrier	Chi. 5	Det. 4
		Apr. 4/91	St.L.	3	Vincent Riendeau (2)	Det. 6	St.L. 3
					Pat Jablonski (1)		
		May 8/96	St.L.	3	Jon Casey	St.L. 5	Det. 4
		Apr. 21/99	Det.	3	Guy Hebert (2)	Det. 5	Ana. 3
					Pat Jablonski (1)		
Bernie Geoffrion (3)	Mtl.	Mar. 27/52	Mtl.	3	Jim Henry	Mtl. 4	Bos. 0
		Apr. 7/55	Mtl.	3	Terry Sawchuk	Mtl. 4	Det. 2
		Mar. 30/57	Mtl.	3	Gump Worsley	Mtl. 8	NYR 3
Norm Ullman (3)	Det.	Mar. 29/64	Chi.	3	Glenn Hall	Det. 5	Chi. 4
		Apr. 7/64	Det.	3	Glenn Hall (2)		
					Denis DeJordy (1)	Det. 7	Chi. 2
		Apr. 11/65	Det.	3	Glenn Hall	Det. 4	Chi. 2
John Bucyk (3)	Bos.	May 3/70	St.L.	3	Jacques Plante (1)		
					Ernie Wakely (2)	Bos. 6	St.L. 1
		Apr. 20/72	Bos.	3	Jacques Caron (1)		
					Ernie Wakely (2)	Bos. 10	St.L. 2
		Apr. 21/74	Bos.	3	Tony Esposito	Bos. 8	Chi. 6
Rick MacLeish (3)	Phi.	Apr. 11/74	Phi.	3	Phil Myre	Phi. 5	Atl. 1
		Apr. 13/75	Phi.	3	Gord McRae	Phi. 6	Tor. 3
		May 13/75	Phi.	3	Glenn Resch	Phi. 4	NYI 1
Denis Savard (3)	Chi.	Apr. 19/82	Chi.	3	Mike Liut	Chi. 7	StL. 4
		Apr. 10/86	Chi.	4	Ken Wregget	Tor. 6	Chi. 4
		Apr. 9/88	St.L.	3	Greg Millen	Chi. 6	St.L. 3
Tim Kerr (3)	Phi.	Apr. 13/85	NYR	4	Glen Hanlon	Phi. 6	NYR 5
		Apr. 20/87	Phi.	3	Kelly Hrudey	Phi. 4	NYI 2
		Apr. 19/89	Pit.	3	Tom Barrasso	Phi. 4	Pit. 2
Cam Neely (3)	Bos.	Apr. 9/87	Mtl.	3	Patrick Roy	Mtl. 4	Bos. 3
		Apr. 5/91	Bos.	3	Peter Sidorkiewicz	Bos. 4	Hfd. 3
		Apr. 25/91	Bos.	3	Patrick Roy	Bos. 4	Mtl. 1
Petr Klima (3)	Det.	Apr. 7/88	Tor.	3	Alan Bester (2)		
					Ken Wregett (1)	Det. 6	Tor. 2
		Apr. 21/88	St.L.	3	Greg Millen	Det. 6	St.L. 0
	Edm.	May 4/91	Edm.	3	Jon Casey	Edm. 7	Min. 2
Esa Tikkanen (3)	Edm.	May 22/88	Edm.	3	Reggie Lemelin	Edm. 6	Bos. 3
		Apr. 16/91	Cgy.	3	Mike Vernon	Edm. 5	Cgy. 4
		Apr. 26/92	L.A.	3	Kelly Hrudey (2)	Edm. 5	L.A. 2
					Tom Askey (1)		
Mike Gartner (3)	NYR	Apr. 13/90	NYR	3	Mark Fitzpatrick (2)		
					Glenn Healy (1)	NYR 6	NYI 5
		Apr. 27/92	NYR	3	Chris Terreri	NYR 8	N.J. 5
	Tor.	Apr. 25/96	Tor.	3	Jon Casey	Tor. 5	St.L. 4
Mario Lemieux (3)	Pit.	Apr. 25/89	Pit.	5	Ron Hextall	Pit. 10	Phi. 7
		Apr. 23/92	Pit.	3	Don Beaupre	Pit. 6	Wsh. 4
		May 11/96	Pit.	3	Mike Richter	Pit. 7	NYR 3
Newsy Lalonde (2)	Mtl.	Mar. 1/19	Mtl.	5	Clint Benedict	Mtl. 6	Ott. 3
		Mar. 22/19	Sea.	4	Hap Holmes	Mtl. 4	Sea. 2

Player	Team	Date	City	Total Goals	Opposing Goaltender	Score	
Howie Morenz (2)	Mtl.	Mar. 22/24	Mtl.	3	Charles Reid	Mtl. 6	Cgy.T. 1
		Mar. 27/25	Mtl.	3	Hap Holmes	Mtl. 4	Vic. 2
Doug Bentley (2)	Chi.	Mar. 28/44	Chi.	3	Connie Dion	Chi. 7	Det. 1
		Mar. 30/44	Det.	3	Connie Dion	Chi. 5	Det. 2
Toe Blake (2)	Mtl.	Mar. 22/38	Mtl.	3	Mike Karakas	Mtl. 6	Chi. 4
		Mar. 26/46	Chi.	3	Mike Karakas	Mtl. 7	Chi. 2
Ted Kennedy (2)	Tor.	Apr. 14/45	Tor.	3	Harry Lumley	Det. 5	Tor. 3
		Mar. 27/48	Tor.	4	Frank Brimsek	Tor. 5	Bos. 3
F. St. Marseille (2)	St.L.	Apr. 28/70	St.L.	3	Al Smith	St.L. 5	Pit. 0
		Apr. 6/72	Min.	3	Cesare Maniago	Min. 6	St.L. 5
Bobby Hull (2)	Chi.	Apr. 7/63	Det.	3	Terry Sawchuk	Det. 7	Chi. 4
		Apr. 9/72	Pit.	3	Jim Rutherford	Chi. 6	Pit. 5
Pit Martin (2)	Chi.	Apr. 4/73	Chi.	3	Wayne Stephenson	Chi. 7	St.L. 1
		May 10/73	Chi.	3	Ken Dryden	Mtl. 6	Chi. 4
Yvan Cournoyer (2)	Mtl.	Apr. 5/73	Mtl.	3	Dave Dryden	Mtl. 7	Buf. 3
		Apr. 11/74	Mtl.	3	Ed Giacomin	Mtl. 4	NYR 1
Guy Lafleur (2)	Mtl.	May 1/75	Mtl.	3	Roger Crozier (1)		
					Gerry Desjardins (2)	Mtl. 7	Buf. 0
		Apr. 11/77	Mtl.	3	Ed Staniowski	Mtl. 7	St.L. 2
Lanny McDonald (2)	Tor.	Apr. 9/77	Pit.	3	Denis Herron	Tor. 5	Pit. 2
		Apr. 17/77	Tor.	4	Wayne Stephenson	Phi. 6	Tor. 5
Bill Barber (2)	Phi.	May 4/80	Min.	4	Gilles Meloche	Phi. 5	Min. 3
		Apr. 9/81	Phi.	3	Dan Bouchard	Phi. 8	Que. 5
Bryan Trottier (2)	NYI	Apr. 8/80	NYI	3	Doug Keans	NYI 8	L.A. 1
		Apr. 8/81	NYI	3	Michel Larocque	NYI 5	Tor. 1
Butch Goring (2)	L.A.	Apr. 9/77	L.A.	3	Phil Myre	L.A. 4	Atl. 2
	NYI	May 17/81	Min.	3	Gilles Meloche	NYI 7	Min. 5
Paul Reinhart (2)	Cgy.	Apr. 14/83	Edm.	3	Andy Moog	Edm. 6	Cgy. 3
		Apr. 8/84	Van	3	Richard Brodeur	Cgy. 5	Van. 1
Brian Propp (2)	Phi.	Apr. 22/81	Phi.	3	Pat Riggin	Phi. 9	Cgy. 4
		Apr. 21/85	Phi.	3	Billy Smith	Phi. 5	NYI 2
Peter Stastny (2)	Que.	Apr. 5/83	Bos.	3	Pete Peeters	Bos. 4	Que. 3
		Apr. 11/87	Que.	3	Mike Liut (2)		
					Steve Weeks (1)	Que. 5	Hfd. 1
Michel Goulet (2)	Que.	Apr. 23/85	Que.	3	Steve Penney	Que. 7	Mtl. 6
		Apr. 12/87	Que.	3	Mike Liut	Que. 4	Hfd. 1
Glenn Anderson (2)	Edm.	Apr. 26/83	Edm.	4	Murray Bannerman	Edm. 8	Chi. 2
		Apr. 6/88	Wpg.	3	Daniel Berthiaume	Edm. 7	Wpg. 4
Peter Zezel (2)	Phi.	Apr. 13/86	NYR	3	John Vanbiesbrouck	Phi. 7	NYR 1
	St.L.	Apr. 11/89	St.L.	3	Jon Casey (2)		
					Kari Takko (1)	St.L. 6	Min. 1
Geoff Courtnall (2)	Van.	Apr. 4/91	L.A.	3	Kelly Hrudey	Van. 6	L.A. 5
		Apr. 30/92	Van.	3	Rick Tabaracci	Van. 5	Win. 0
Joe Sakic (2)	Que.	May 6/95	Que.	3	Mike Richter	Que. 5	NYR 4
	Col.	Apr. 25/96	Col.	3	Corey Hirsch	Col. 5	Van. 4
Daniel Alfredsson (2)	Ott.	Apr. 28/98	Ott.	3	Martin Brodeur	Ott. 4	N.J. 3
		May 11/98	Ott.	3	Olaf Kolzig	Ott. 4	Wsh. 3
Patrick Marleau (2)	S.J.	Apr. 10/04	S.J.	3	Chris Osgood	S.J. 3	St.L. 1
		Apr. 22/04	S.J.	3	David Aebischer	S.J. 5	Col. 2
Harry Meeking	Tor.	Mar. 11/18	Tor.	3	Georges Vezina	Tor. 7	Mtl. 3
Alf Skinner	Tor.	Mar. 23/18	Tor.	3	Hugh Lehman	Van.M. 6	Tor. 4
Joe Malone	Mtl.	Feb. 23/19	Mtl.	3	Clint Benedict	Mtl. 8	Ott. 4
Odie Cleghorn	Mtl.	Feb. 27/19	Ott.	3	Clint Benedict	Mtl. 5	Ott. 3
Jack Darragh	Ott.	Apr. 1/20	Tor.	3	Hap Holmes	Ott. 6	Sea. 1
George Boucher	Ott.	Mar. 10/21	Ott.	3	Jake Forbes	Ott. 5	Tor. 0
Babe Dye	Tor.	Mar. 28/22	Tor.	4	Hugh Lehman	Tor. 5	Van.M. 1
Percy Galbraith	Bos.	Mar. 31/27	Bos.	3	Hugh Lehman	Bos. 4	Chi. 4
Busher Jackson	Tor.	Apr. 5/32	NYR	3	John Ross Roach	Tor. 6	NYR 4
Frank Boucher	NYR	Apr. 9/32	Tor.	3	Lorne Chabot	Tor. 6	NYR 4
Charlie Conacher	Tor.	Mar. 26/36	Tor.	3	Tiny Thompson	Tor. 8	Bos. 3
Syd Howe	Det.	Mar. 23/39	Det.	3	Claude Bourque	Det. 7	Mtl. 3
Bryan Hextall	NYR	Apr. 3/40	NYR	3	Turk Broda	NYR 6	Tor. 2
Joe Benoit	Mtl.	Mar. 22/41	Mtl.	3	Sam LoPresti	Mtl. 4	Chi. 3
Syl Apps	Tor.	Mar. 25/41	Tor.	3	Frank Brimsek	Tor. 7	Bos. 2
Jack McGill	Bos.	Mar. 29/42	Bos.	3	Johnny Mowers	Det. 6	Bos. 4
Don Metz	Tor.	Apr. 14/42	Tor.	3	Johnny Mowers	Tor. 9	Det. 3
Mud Bruneteau	Det.	Apr. 1/43	Det.	3	Frank Brimsek	Det. 6	Bos. 2
Don Grosso	Det.	Apr. 7/43	Bos.	3	Frank Brimsek	Det. 4	Bos. 0
Carl Liscombe	Det.	Apr. 3/45	Bos.	4	Paul Bibeault	Det. 5	Bos. 3
Billy Reay	Mtl.	Apr. 1/47	Bos.	4	Frank Brimsek	Mtl. 5	Bos. 1
Gerry Plamondon	Mtl.	Mar. 24/49	Det.	3	Harry Lumley	Mtl. 4	Det. 3
Sid Smith	Tor.	Apr. 10/49	Det.	3	Harry Lumley	Tor. 3	Det. 1
Pentti Lund	NYR	Apr. 2/50	NYR	3	Bill Durnan	NYR 4	Mtl. 1
Ted Lindsay	Det.	Apr. 5/55	Det.	4	Charlie Hodge (1)		
					Jacques Plante (3)	Det. 7	Mtl. 1
Gordie Howe	Det.	Apr. 10/55	Det.	3	Jacques Plante	Det. 5	Mtl. 1
Phil Goyette	Mtl.	Mar. 25/58	Mtl.	3	Terry Sawchuk	Mtl. 8	Det. 1
Jerry Toppazzini	Bos.	Apr. 5/58	Bos.	3	Gump Worsley	Bos. 8	NYR 2
Bob Pulford	Tor.	Apr. 19/62	Tor.	3	Glenn Hall	Tor. 8	Chi. 4
Dave Keon	Tor.	Apr. 9/64	Mtl.	3	Charlie Hodge (2)	Tor. 3	Mtl. 1
					ENG (1)		
Henri Richard	Mtl.	Apr. 20/67	Mtl.	3	Terry Sawchuk (2)		
					Johnny Bower (1)	Mtl. 6	Tor. 2
Rosaire Paiement	Phi.	Apr. 13/68	Phi.	3	Glenn Hall (1)		
					Seth Martin (2)	Phi. 6	St.L. 1
Jean Beliveau	Mtl.	Apr. 20/68	Mtl.	3	Denis DeJordy	Mtl. 4	Chi. 1
Red Berenson	St.L.	Apr. 15/69	St.L.	3	Gerry Desjardins	St.L. 4	L.A. 0
Ken Schinkel	Pit.	Apr. 11/70	Oak.	3	Gary Smith	Pit. 5	Oak. 2
Jim Pappin	Chi.	Apr. 11/71	Phi.	3	Bruce Gamble	Chi. 6	Phi. 2
Bobby Orr	Bos.	Apr. 11/71	Mtl.	3	Ken Dryden	Bos. 5	Mtl. 2
Jacques Lemaire	Mtl.	Apr. 20/71	Mtl.	3	Gump Worsley	Mtl. 7	Min. 2
Vic Hadfield	NYR	Apr. 22/71	NYR	3	Tony Esposito	NYR 4	Chi. 1
Fred Stanfield	Bos.	Apr. 18/72	Bos.	3	Jacques Caron	Bos. 6	St.L. 1
Ken Hodge	Bos.	Apr. 30/72	Bos.	3	Ed Giacomin	Bos. 6	NYR 5
Dick Redmond	Chi.	Apr. 4/73	Chi.	3	Wayne Stephenson	Chi. 7	St.L. 1
Steve Vickers	NYR	Apr. 10/73	Bos.	3	Ross Brooks (2)		
					Eddie Johnston (1)	NYR 6	Bos. 3
Tom Williams	L.A.	Apr. 14/74	L.A.	3	Mike Veisor	L.A. 5	Chi. 1
Marcel Dionne	L.A.	Apr. 15/76	L.A.	3	Gilles Gilbert	L.A. 6	Bos. 4
Don Saleski	Phi.	Apr. 20/76	Phi.	3	Wayne Thomas	Phi. 7	Tor. 1
Darryl Sittler	Tor.	Apr. 22/76	Tor.	5	Bernie Parent	Tor. 8	Phi. 5

Player	Team	Date	City	Total Goals	Opposing Goaltender	Score	
Reggie Leach	Phi.	May 6/76	Phi.	5	Gilles Gilbert	Phi. 6	Bos. 3
Jim Lorentz	Buf.	Apr. 7/77	Min.	3	Pete LoPresti (2)		
					Gary Smith (1)	Buf. 7	Min. 1
Bobby Schmautz	Bos.	Apr. 11/77	Bos.	3	Rogie Vachon	Bos. 8	L.A. 3
Billy Harris	NYI	Apr. 23/77	Mtl.	3	Ken Dryden	Mtl. 4	NYI 3
George Ferguson	Tor.	Apr. 11/78	Tor.	3	Rogie Vachon	Tor. 7	L.A. 3
Jean Ratelle	Bos.	May 3/79	Bos.	3	Ken Dryden	Bos. 4	Mtl. 3
Stan Jonathan	Bos.	May 8/79	Bos.	3	Ken Dryden	Bos. 5	Mtl. 2
Ron Duguay	NYR	Apr. 20/80	NYR	3	Pete Peeters	NYR 4	Phi. 2
Steve Shutt	Mtl.	Apr. 22/80	Mtl.	3	Gilles Meloche	Mtl. 6	Min. 2
Gilbert Perreault	Buf.	May 6/80	NYI	3	Billy Smith (2)		
					ENG (1)	Buf. 7	NYI 4
Paul Holmgren	Phi.	May 15/80	Phi.	3	Billy Smith	Phi. 8	NYI 3
Steve Payne	Min.	Apr. 8/81	Bos.	3	Rogie Vachon	Min. 5	Bos. 4
Denis Potvin	NYI	Apr. 17/81	NYI	3	Andy Moog	NYI 6	Edm. 3
Barry Pederson	Bos.	Apr. 8/82	Bos.	3	Don Edwards	Bos. 7	Buf. 3
Duane Sutter	NYI	Apr. 15/83	NYI	3	Glen Hanlon	NYI 5	NYR 0
Doug Halward	Van.	Apr. 7/84	Van.	3	Reggie Lemelin (2)		
					Don Edwards (1)	Van. 7	Cgy. 0
Jorgen Pettersson	St.L.	Apr. 8/84	Det.	3	Eddie Mio	St.L. 3	Det. 2
Clark Gillies	NYI	May 12/84	NYI	3	Grant Fuhr	NYI 6	Edm. 1
Ken Linseman	Bos.	Apr. 14/85	Bos.	3	Steve Penney	Bos. 7	Mtl. 6
Dave Andreychuk	Buf.	Apr. 14/85	Buf.	3	Dan Bouchard	Buf. 7	Que. 4
Greg Paslawski	St.L.	Apr. 15/86	Min.	3	Don Beaupre	St.L. 6	Min. 3
Doug Risebrough	Cgy.	May 4/86	Cgy.	3	Rick Wamsley	Cgy. 8	St.L. 2
Mike McPhee	Mtl.	Apr. 11/87	Bos.	3	Doug Keans	Mtl. 5	Bos. 4
John Ogrodnick	Que.	Apr. 14/87	Hfd.	3	Mike Liut	Que. 7	Hfd. 5
Pelle Eklund	Phi.	May 10/87	Mtl.	3	Patrick Roy (1)		
					Brian Hayward (2)	Phi. 6	Mtl. 3
John Tucker	Buf.	Apr. 9/88	Bos.	4	Andy Moog	Buf. 6	Bos. 2
Tony Hrkac	St.L.	Apr. 10/88	St.L.	4	Darren Pang	St.L. 6	Chi. 5
Hakan Loob	Cgy.	Apr. 10/88	Cgy.	3	Glenn Healy	Cgy. 7	L.A. 3
Ed Olczyk	Tor.	Apr. 12/88	Tor.	3	Greg Stefan (2)		
					Glen Hanlon (1)	Tor. 6	Det. 5
Aaron Broten	N.J.	Apr. 20/88	N.J.	3	Pete Peeters	N.J. 5	Wsh. 2
Mark Johnson	N.J.	Apr. 22/88	Wsh.	4	Pete Peeters	N.J. 10	Wsh. 4
Patrik Sundstrom	N.J.	Apr. 22/88	Wsh.	3	Pete Peeters (2)		
					Clint Malarchuk (1)	N.J. 10	Wsh. 4
Bob Brooke	Min.	Apr. 5/89	St.L.	3	Greg Millen	St.L. 4	Min. 3
Chris Kontos	L.A.	Apr. 6/89	L.A.	3	Grant Fuhr	L.A. 5	Edm. 2
Wayne Presley	Chi.	Apr. 13/89	Chi.	3	Greg Stefan (1)		
					Glen Hanlon (2)	Chi. 7	Det. 1
Tony Granato	L.A.	Apr. 10/90	L.A.	3	Mike Vernon (1)		
					Rick Wamsley (2)	L.A. 12	Cgy. 4
Tomas Sandstrom	L.A.	Apr. 10/90	L.A.	3	Mike Vernon (1)		
					Rick Wamsley (2)	L.A. 12	Cgy. 4
Dave Taylor	L.A.	Apr. 10/90	L.A.	3	Mike Vernon (1)		
					Rick Wamsley (2)	L.A. 12	Cgy. 4
Bernie Nicholls	NYR	Apr. 19/90	NYR	3	Mike Liut	NYR 7	Wsh. 3
John Druce	Wsh.	Apr. 21/90	NYR	3	John Vanbiesbrouck	Wsh. 6	NYR 3
Adam Oates	St.L.	Apr. 12/91	St.L.	3	Tim Chevaldae	St.L. 6	Det. 1
Luc Robitaille	L.A.	Apr. 26/91	L.A.	3	Grant Fuhr	L.A. 5	Edm. 2
Ray Sheppard	Det.	Apr. 24/92	Min.	3	Jon Casey	Min. 5	Det. 2
Pavel Bure	Van.	Apr. 28/92	Wpg.	3	Rick Tabaracci	Van. 8	Wpg. 3
Joe Murphy	Edm.	May 6/92	Edm.	3	Kirk McLean	Edm. 5	Van. 2
Ron Francis	Pit.	May 9/92	Pit.	3	Mike Richter (2)		
					John V'brouck (1)	Pit. 5	NYR. 4
Kevin Stevens	Pit.	May 21/92	Bos.	4	Andy Moog	Pit. 5	Bos. 2
Dirk Graham	Chi.	Jun. 1/92	Chi.	3	Tom Barrasso	Pit. 6	Chi. 5
Brian Noonan	Chi.	Apr. 18/93	Chi.	3	Curtis Joseph	St.L. 4	Chi. 3
Dale Hunter	Wsh.	Apr. 20/93	Wsh.	3	Glenn Healy	NYI 5	Wsh. 4
Teemu Selanne	Wpg.	Apr. 23/93	Wpg.	3	Kirk McLean	Wpg. 5	Van. 4
Ray Ferraro	NYI	Apr. 26/93	Wsh.	4	Don Beaupre	Wsh. 6	NYI 4
Al Iafrate	Wsh.	Apr. 26/93	Wsh.	3	Glenn Healy (2)		
					Mark Fitzpatrick (1)	Wsh. 6	NYI 4
Paul Di Pietro	Mtl.	Apr. 28/93	Mtl.	3	Ron Hextall	Mtl. 6	Que. 2
Wendel Clark	Tor.	May 27/93	L.A.	3	Kelly Hrudey	L.A. 5	Tor. 4
Eric Desjardins	Mtl.	Jun. 3/93	Mtl.	3	Kelly Hrudey	Mtl. 3	L.A. 2
Tony Amonte	Chi.	Apr. 23/94	Chi.	4	Felix Potvin	Chi. 5	Tor. 4
Gary Suter	Chi.	Apr. 24/94	Chi.	3	Felix Potvin	Chi. 4	Tor. 3
Ulf Dahlen	S.J.	May 6/94	S.J.	3	Felix Potvin	S.J. 5	Tor. 2
Mike Sullivan	Cgy.	May 11/95	S.J.	3	Arturs Irbe (2)		
					Wade Flaherty (1)	Cgy. 9	S.J. 2
Theoren Fleury	Cgy.	May 13/95	S.J.	4	Arturs Irbe (3)		
					ENG (1)	Cgy. 6	S.J. 4
Brendan Shanahan	St.L.	May 13/95	Van.	3	Kirk McLean	St.L. 5	Van. 2
John LeClair	Phi.	May 21/95	Phi.	3	Mike Richter	Phi. 5	NYR 4
Brian Leetch	NYR	May 22/95	Phi.	3	Ron Hextall	Phi. 4	NYR 3
Trevor Linden	Van.	Apr. 25/96	Col.	3	Patrick Roy	Col. 5	Van. 4
Jaromir Jagr	Pit.	May 11/96	Pit.	3	Mike Richter	Pit. 7	NYR 3
Peter Forsberg	Col.	Jun. 6/96	Col.	3	John Vanbiesbrouck	Col. 8	Fla. 1
Valeri Zelepukin	N.J.	Apr. 22/97	Mtl.	3	Jocelyn Thibault	N.J. 6	Mtl. 4
Valeri Kamensky	Col.	Apr. 24/97	Col.	3	Jeff Hackett (2)		
					Chris Terreri (1)	Col. 7	Chi. 0
Eric Lindros	Phi.	May 20/97	NYR	3	Mike Richter	Phi. 6	NYR 3
Matthew Barnaby	Buf.	May 10/98	Buf.	3	Andy Moog (2)	Buf. 6	Mtl. 3
					ENG (1)		
Martin Straka	Pit.	Apr. 25/99	Pit.	3	Martin Brodeur	Pit. 4	N.J. 2
Martin Lapointe	Det.	Apr. 15/00	Det.	3	Stephane Fiset (2)	Det. 8	L.A. 5
					Jamie Storr (1)		
Doug Weight	Edm.	Apr. 16/00	Edm.	3	Ed Belfour	Edm. 5	Dal. 2
Bill Guerin	Edm.	Apr. 18/00	Edm.	3	Ed Belfour	Dal. 4	Edm. 3
Scott Young	St.L.	Apr. 23/00	S.J.	3	Steve Shields	St.L. 6	S.J. 2
Andy Delmore	Phi.	May 7/00	Phi.	3	Ron Tugnutt (2)	Phi. 6	Pit. 3
					Peter Skudra (1)		
Brett Hull	Det.	Apr. 27/02	Van.	3	Peter Skudra	Det. 6	Van. 4
Keith Tkachuk	St.L.	May 7/02	St.L.	3	Dominik Hasek	St.L. 6	Det. 1
Darren McCarty	Det.	May 18/02	Det.	3	Patrick Roy	Det. 5	Col. 3
Alexander Mogilny	Tor.	Apr. 9/03	Phi.	3	Roman Cechmanek (2)	Tor. 5	Phi. 3
					ENG (1)		
Mike Sillinger	St.L.	Apr. 12/04	St.L.	3	Evgeni Nabokov (2)	St.L. 4	S.J. 1
					ENG (1)		
Keith Primeau	Phi.	May 2/04	Phi.	3	Ed Belfour (2)	Phi. 7	Tor. 2
					Trevor Kidd (1)		

Leading Playoff Scorers, 1918–2005

Season	Player and Club	Games Played	Goals	Assists	Points
2004-05	....	....	....	....	....
2003-04	Brad Richards, Tampa Bay	23	12	14	26
2002-03	Jamie Langenbrunner, New Jersey	24	11	7	18
	Scott Niedermayer, New Jersey	24	2	16	18
2001-02	Peter Forsberg, Colorado	20	9	18	27
2000-01	Joe Sakic, Colorado	21	13	13	26
99-2000	Brett Hull, Dallas	23	11	13	24
1998-99	Peter Forsberg, Colorado	19	8	16	24
1997-98	Steve Yzerman, Detroit	22	6	18	24
1996-97	Eric Lindros, Philadelphia	19	12	14	26
1995-96	Joe Sakic, Colorado	22	18	16	34
1994-95	Sergei Fedorov, Detroit	17	7	17	24
1993-94	Brian Leetch, NY Rangers	23	11	23	34
1992-93	Wayne Gretzky, Los Angeles	24	15	25	40
1991-92	Mario Lemieux, Pittsburgh	15	16	18	34
1990-91	Mario Lemieux, Pittsburgh	23	16	28	44
1989-90	Craig Simpson, Edmonton	22	16	15	31
	Mark Messier, Edmonton	22	9	22	31
1988-89	Al MacInnis, Calgary	22	7	24	31
1987-88	Wayne Gretzky, Edmonton	19	12	31	43
1986-87	Wayne Gretzky, Edmonton	21	5	29	34
1985-86	Doug Gilmour, St. Louis	19	9	12	21
	Bernie Federko, St. Louis	19	7	14	21
1984-85	Wayne Gretzky, Edmonton	18	17	30	47
1983-84	Wayne Gretzky, Edmonton	19	13	22	35
1982-83	Wayne Gretzky, Edmonton	16	12	26	38
1981-82	Bryan Trottier, NY Islanders	19	6	23	29
1980-81	Mike Bossy, NY Islanders	18	17	18	35
1979-80	Bryan Trottier, NY Islanders	21	12	17	29
1978-79	Jacques Lemaire, Montreal	16	11	12	23
	Guy Lafleur, Montreal	16	10	13	23
1977-78	Guy Lafleur, Montreal	15	10	11	21
	Larry Robinson, Montreal	15	4	17	21
1976-77	Guy Lafleur, Montreal	14	9	17	26
1975-76	Reggie Leach, Philadelphia	16	19	5	24
1974-75	Rick MacLeish, Philadelphia	17	11	9	20
1973-74	Rick MacLeish, Philadelphia	17	13	9	22
1972-73	Yvan Cournoyer, Montreal	17	15	10	25
1971-72	Phil Esposito, Boston	15	9	15	24
	Bobby Orr, Boston	15	5	19	24
1970-71	Frank Mahovlich, Montreal	20	14	13	27
1969-70	Phil Esposito, Boston	14	13	14	27
1968-69	Phil Esposito, Boston	10	8	10	18
1967-68	Bill Goldsworthy, Minnesota	14	8	7	15
1966-67	Jim Pappin, Toronto	12	7	8	15
1965-66	Norm Ullman, Detroit	12	6	9	15
1964-65	Bobby Hull, Chicago	14	10	7	17
1963-64	Gordie Howe, Detroit	14	9	10	19
1962-63	Gordie Howe, Detroit	11	7	9	16
	Norm Ullman, Detroit	11	4	12	16
1961-62	Stan Mikita, Chicago	12	6	15	21
1960-61	Gordie Howe, Detroit	11	4	11	15
	Pierre Pilote, Chicago	12	3	12	15
1959-60	Henri Richard, Montreal	8	3	9	12
	Bernie Geoffrion, Montreal	8	2	10	12
1958-59	Dickie Moore, Montreal	11	5	12	17
1957-58	Fleming Mackell, Boston	12	5	14	19
1956-57	Bernie Geoffrion, Montreal	11	11	7	18
1955-56	Jean Béliveau, Montreal	10	12	7	19
1954-55	Gordie Howe, Detroit	11	9	11	20
1953-54	Dickie Moore, Montreal	11	5	8	13
1952-53	Ed Sandford, Boston	11	8	3	11
1951-52	Ted Lindsay, Detroit	8	5	2	7
	Floyd Curry, Montreal	11	4	3	7
	Metro Prystai, Detroit	8	2	5	7
	Gordie Howe, Detroit	8	2	5	7
1950-51	Maurice Richard, Montreal	11	9	4	13
	Max Bentley, Toronto	11	2	11	13
1949-50	Pentti Lund, NY Rangers	12	6	5	11
1948-49	Gordie Howe, Detroit	11	8	3	11
1947-48	Ted Kennedy, Toronto	9	8	6	14
1946-47	Maurice Richard, Montreal	10	6	5	11
1945-46	Elmer Lach, Montreal	9	5	12	17
1944-45	Joe Carveth, Detroit	14	5	6	11
1943-44	Toe Blake, Montreal	9	7	11	18
1942-43	Carl Liscombe, Detroit	10	6	8	14
1941-42	Don Grosso, Detroit	12	8	6	14
	Syl Apps, Toronto	13	5	9	14
1940-41	Milt Schmidt, Boston	11	5	6	11
1939-40	Phil Watson, NY Rangers	12	3	6	9
	Neil Colville, NY Rangers	12	2	7	9
1938-39	Bill Cowley, Boston	12	3	11	14
1937-38	Johnny Gottselig, Chicago	10	5	3	8
	Gordie Drillon, Toronto	7	7	1	8
1936-37	Marty Barry, Detroit	10	4	7	11
1935-36	Frank Boll, Toronto	9	7	3	10
1934-35	Baldy Northcott, Mtl. Maroons	7	4	1	5
	Busher Jackson, Toronto	7	3	2	5
	Cy Wentworth, Mtl. Maroons	7	3	2	5
	Charlie Conacher, Toronto	7	1	4	5
1933-34	Larry Aurie, Detroit	9	3	7	10
1932-33	Cecil Dillon, NY Rangers	8	8	2	10
1931-32	Frank Boucher, NY Rangers	7	3	6	9
1930-31	Cooney Weiland, Boston	5	6	3	9
1929-30	Marty Barry, Boston	6	3	3	6
	Cooney Weiland, Boston	6	1	5	6
1928-29	Andy Blair, Toronto	4	3	0	3
	Butch Keeling, NY Rangers	6	3	0	3
	Ace Bailey, Toronto	4	1	2	3
1927-28	Frank Boucher, NY Rangers	9	7	3	10
1926-27	Harry Oliver, Boston	8	4	2	6
	Percy Galbraith, Boston	8	3	3	6
1925-26	Nels Stewart, Mtl. Maroons	8	6	3	9
1924-25	Howie Morenz, Montreal	6	7	1	8
1923-24	Howie Morenz, Montreal	6	7	3	10
1922-23	Punch Broadbent, Ottawa	8	6	1	7
1921-22	Babe Dye, Toronto	7	11	1	12
1920-21	Cy Denneny, Ottawa	7	4	2	6
1919-20	Frank Nighbor, Ottawa	5	6	1	7
	Jack Darragh, Ottawa	5	5	2	7
1918-19	Newsy Lalonde, Montreal	10	17	2	19
1917-18	Alf Skinner, Toronto	7	8	3	11

Overtime Games since 1918

Abbreviations: Teams/Cities: — **Ana.** - Anaheim; **Atl.** - Atlanta; **Bos.** - Boston; **Buf.** - Buffalo; **Cgy.** - Calgary; **Cgy. T.** - Calgary Tigers (Western Canada Hockey League); **Chi.** - Chicago; **Col.** - Colorado; **Dal.** - Dallas; **Det.** - Detroit; **Edm.** - Edmonton; **Edm. E.** - Edmonton Eskimos (WCHL); **Fla.** - Florida; **Hfd.** - Hartford; **L.A.** - Los Angeles; **Min.** - Minnesota; **Mtl.** - Montreal; **Mtl. M.** - Montreal Maroons; **N.J.** - New Jersey; **NYA** - NY Americans; **NYI** - New York Islanders; **NYR** - New York Rangers; **Oak.** - Oakland; **Ott.** - Ottawa; **Phi.** - Philadelphia; **Phx.** - Phoenix; **Pit.** - Pittsburgh; **Que.** - Quebec; **St.L.** - St. Louis; **Sea.** - Seattle Metropolitans (Pacific Coast Hockey Association); **S.J.** - San Jose; **T.B.** - Tampa Bay; **Tor.** - Toronto; **Van.** - Vancouver; **Van. M.** - Vancouver Millionaires (PCHA); **Vic.** - Victoria Cougars (WCHL); **Wpg.** - Winnipeg; **Wsh.** - Washington.

SERIES — **CF** - conference final; **CQF** - conference quarter-final; **CSF** - conference semi-final; **DF** - division final; **DSF** - division semi-final; **F** - final; **PRE** - preliminary round; **QF** - quarter-final; **SF** - semi-final.

Date	City	Series	Score		Scorer	Overtime	Series Winner
Mar. 26/19	Sea.	F	Mtl. 0	Sea. 0	no scorer	20:00	....
Mar. 30/19	Sea.	F	Mtl. 4	Sea. 3	Odie Cleghorn	15:57	....
Mar. 20/22	Tor.	F	Tor. 2	Van. M. 1	Babe Dye	4:50	Tor.
Mar. 29/23	Van.	F	Ott. 2	Edm. E. 1	Cy Denneny	2:08	Ott.
Mar. 31/27	Mtl.	QF	Mtl. 1	Mtl. M. 0	Howie Morenz	12:05	Mtl.
Apr. 7/27	Bos.	F	Ott. 0	Bos. 0	no scorer	20:00	Ott.
Apr. 11/27	Ott.	F	Bos. 1	Ott. 1	no scorer	20:00	Ott.
Apr. 3/28	Mtl.	QF	Mtl. M. 1	Mtl. 0	Russell Oatman	8:20	Mtl. M.
Apr. 7/28	Mtl.	F	NYR 2	Mtl. M. 1	Frank Boucher	7:05	NYR
Mar. 21/29	NYR	QF	NYR 1	NYA 0	Butch Keeling	29:50	NYR
Mar. 26/29	Tor.	SF	NYR 2	Tor. 1	Frank Boucher	2:03	NYR
Mar. 20/30	Mtl.	SF	Bos. 2	Mtl. M. 1	Harry Oliver	45:35	Bos.
Mar. 25/30	Bos.	SF	Mtl. M. 1	Bos. 0	Archie Wilcox	26:27	Bos.
Mar. 26/30	Mtl.	QF	Chi. 2	Mtl. 2	Howie Morenz (Mtl.)	51:43	Mtl.
Mar. 28/30	Mtl.	SF	Mtl. 2	NYR 1	Gus Rivers	68:52	Mtl.
Mar. 24/31	Bos.	SF	Bos. 5	Mtl. 4	Cooney Weiland	18:56	Mtl.
Mar. 26/31	Chi.	QF	Chi. 2	Tor. 1	Stew Adams	19:20	Chi.
Mar. 28/31	Mtl.	SF	Mtl. 4	Bos. 3	Georges Mantha	5:10	Mtl.
Apr. 1/31	Mtl.	SF	Mtl. 3	Bos. 2	Wildor Larochelle	19:00	Mtl.
Apr. 5/31	Chi.	F	Chi. 2	Mtl. 1	Johnny Gottselig	24:50	Mtl.
Apr. 9/31	Mtl.	F	Chi. 3	Mtl. 2	Cy Wentworth	53:50	Mtl.
Mar. 26/32	Mtl.	SF	NYR 4	Mtl. 3	Fred Cook	59:32	NYR
Apr. 2/32	Tor.	SF	Tor. 3	Mtl. M. 2	Bob Gracie	17:59	Tor.
Mar. 25/33	Bos.	SF	Bos. 2	Tor. 1	Marty Barry	14:14	Tor.
Mar. 28/33	Bos.	SF	Tor. 1	Bos. 0	Busher Jackson	15:03	Tor.
Mar. 30/33	Tor.	SF	Bos. 2	Tor. 1	Eddie Shore	4:23	Tor.
Apr. 3/33	Tor.	SF	Tor. 1	Bos. 0	Ken Doraty	104:46	Tor.
Apr. 13/33	Tor.	F	NYR 1	Tor. 0	Bill Cook	7:33	NYR
Mar. 22/34	Tor.	SF	Det. 2	Tor. 1	Herbie Lewis	1:33	Det.
Mar. 25/34	Chi.	QF	Chi. 1	Mtl. 1	Mush March (Chi)	11:05	Chi.
Apr. 3/34	Det.	F	Chi. 2	Det. 1	Paul Thompson	21:10	Chi.
Apr. 10/34	Chi.	F	Chi. 1	Det. 0	Mush March	30:05	Chi.
Mar. 23/35	Bos.	SF	Bos. 1	Tor. 0	Dit Clapper	33:26	Tor.
Mar. 26/35	Chi.	QF	Mtl. M. 1	Chi. 0	Baldy Northcott	4:02	Mtl. M.
Mar. 30/35	Tor.	SF	Tor. 2	Bos. 1	Pep Kelly	1:36	Tor.
Apr. 4/35	Tor.	F	Mtl. M. 3	Tor. 2	Dave Trottier	5:28	Mtl. M.
Mar. 24/36	Mtl.	SF	Det. 1	Mtl. M. 0	Mud Bruneteau	116:30	Det.
Apr. 9/36	Tor.	F	Tor. 4	Det. 3	Buzz Boll	0:31	Det.
Mar. 25/37	NYR	QF	NYR 2	Tor. 1	Babe Pratt	13:05	NYR
Apr. 1/37	Mtl.	SF	Det. 2	Mtl. 1	Hec Kilrea	51:49	Det.
Mar. 22/38	NYR	QF	NYA 2	NYR 1	John Sorrell	21:25	NYA
Mar. 24/38	Tor.	SF	Tor. 1	Bos. 0	George Parsons	21:31	Tor.
Mar. 26/38	Mtl.	QF	Chi. 3	Mtl. 2	Paul Thompson	11:49	Chi.
Mar. 27/38	NYR	QF	NYA 3	NYR 2	Lorne Carr	60:40	NYA
Mar. 29/38	Bos.	SF	Tor. 3	Bos. 2	Gordie Drillon	10:04	Tor.
Mar. 31/38	Chi.	SF	Chi. 1	NYA 0	Cully Dahlstrom	33:01	Chi.
Mar. 21/39	NYR	SF	Bos. 2	NYR 1	Mel Hill	59:25	Bos.
Mar. 23/39	Bos.	SF	Bos. 3	NYR 2	Mel Hill	8:24	Bos.
Mar. 26/39	Det.	QF	Det. 1	Mtl. 0	Marty Barry	7:47	Det.
Mar. 30/39	Bos.	SF	NYR 2	Bos. 1	Clint Smith	17:19	Bos.
Apr. 1/39	Tor.	SF	Tor. 5	Det. 4	Gordie Drillon	5:42	Tor.
Apr. 2/39	Bos.	SF	Bos. 2	NYR 1	Mel Hill	48:00	Bos.
Apr. 9/39	Bos.	F	Tor. 3	Bos. 2	Doc Romnes	10:38	Bos.
Mar. 19/40	Det.	QF	Det. 2	NYA 1	Syd Howe	0:25	Det.
Mar. 19/40	Tor.	QF	Tor. 3	Chi. 2	Syl Apps	6:35	Tor.
Apr. 2/40	NYR	F	NYR 2	Tor. 1	Alf Pike	15:30	NYR
Apr. 11/40	Tor.	F	NYR 2	Tor. 1	Muzz Patrick	31:43	NYR
Apr. 13/40	Tor.	F	NYR 3	Tor. 2	Bryan Hextall	2:07	NYR
Mar. 20/41	Det.	QF	Det. 2	NYR 1	Gus Giesebrecht	12:01	Det.
Mar. 22/41	Mtl.	QF	Mtl. 4	Chi. 3	Charlie Sands	34:04	Chi.
Mar. 29/41	Bos.	SF	Tor. 2	Bos. 1	Pete Langelle	17:31	Bos.
Mar. 30/41	Chi.	SF	Det. 2	Chi. 1	Gus Giesebrecht	9:15	Det.
Mar. 22/42	Chi.	QF	Bos. 2	Chi. 1	Des Smith	6:51	Bos.
Mar. 21/43	Bos.	SF	Bos. 5	Mtl. 4	Don Gallinger	12:30	Bos.
Mar. 23/43	Det.	SF	Tor. 3	Det. 2	Jack McLean	70:18	Det.
Mar. 25/43	Mtl.	SF	Bos. 3	Mtl. 2	Busher Jackson	3:20	Bos.
Mar. 30/43	Tor.	SF	Det. 3	Tor. 2	Adam Brown	9:21	Det.
Mar. 30/43	Bos.	SF	Bos. 5	Mtl. 4	Ab DeMarco	3:41	Bos.
Apr. 13/44	Mtl.	F	Mtl. 5	Chi. 4	Toe Blake	9:12	Mtl.
Mar. 27/45	Tor.	SF	Tor. 4	Mtl. 3	Gus Bodnar	12:36	Tor.
Mar. 29/45	Det.	SF	Det. 3	Bos. 2	Mud Bruneteau	17:12	Det.
Apr. 21/45	Tor.	F	Det. 1	Tor. 0	Ed Bruneteau	14:16	Tor.
Mar. 28/46	Bos.	SF	Bos. 4	Det. 3	Don Gallinger	9:51	Bos.
Mar. 30/46	Mtl.	F	Mtl. 4	Bos. 3	Maurice Richard	9:08	Mtl.
Apr. 2/46	Mtl.	F	Mtl. 3	Bos. 2	Jimmy Peters	16:55	Mtl.
Apr. 7/46	Bos.	F	Bos. 3	Mtl. 2	Terry Reardon	15:13	Mtl.
Mar. 26/47	Tor.	SF	Tor. 3	Det. 2	Howie Meeker	3:05	Tor.
Mar. 27/47	Mtl.	SF	Mtl. 2	Bos. 1	Ken Mosdell	5:38	Mtl.
Apr. 3/47	Mtl.	SF	Mtl. 4	Bos. 3	John Quilty	36:40	Mtl.
Apr. 15/47	Tor.	F	Tor. 2	Mtl. 1	Syl Apps	16:36	Tor.
Mar. 24/48	Tor.	SF	Tor. 5	Bos. 4	Nick Metz	17:03	Tor.
Mar. 22/49	Det.	SF	Det. 2	Mtl. 1	Max McNab	44:52	Det.
Mar. 24/49	Det.	SF	Mtl. 4	Det. 3	Gerry Plamondon	2:59	Det.
Mar. 26/49	Tor.	SF	Bos. 5	Tor. 4	Woody Dumart	16:14	Tor.
Apr. 8/49	Det.	F	Tor. 3	Det. 2	Joe Klukay	17:31	Tor.
Apr. 4/50	Tor.	SF	Det. 2	Tor. 1	Leo Reise Jr.	20:38	Det.
Apr. 4/50	Mtl.	SF	Mtl. 3	NYR 2	Elmer Lach	15:19	NYR
Apr. 9/50	Det.	SF	Det. 1	Tor. 0	Leo Reise Jr.	8:39	Det.
Apr. 18/50	Det.	F	NYR 4	Det. 3	Don Raleigh	8:34	Det.
Apr. 20/50	Det.	F	NYR 2	Det. 1	Don Raleigh	1:38	Det.
Apr. 23/50	Det.	F	Det. 4	NYR 3	Pete Babando	28:31	Det.
Mar. 27/51	Det.	SF	Mtl. 3	Det. 2	Maurice Richard	61:09	Mtl.
Mar. 29/51	Det.	SF	Mtl. 1	Det. 0	Maurice Richard	42:20	Mtl.
Mar. 31/51	Tor.	SF	Bos. 1	Tor. 1	no scorer	20:00	Tor.
Apr. 11/51	Tor.	F	Tor. 3	Mtl. 2	Sid Smith	5:51	Tor.
Apr. 14/51	Tor.	F	Mtl. 3	Tor. 2	Maurice Richard	2:55	Tor.
Apr. 17/51	Mtl.	F	Tor. 2	Mtl. 1	Ted Kennedy	4:47	Tor.
Apr. 19/51	Mtl.	F	Tor. 3	Mtl. 2	Harry Watson	5:15	Tor.
Apr. 21/51	Tor.	F	Tor. 3	Mtl. 2	Bill Barilko	2:53	Tor.
Apr. 6/52	Bos.	SF	Mtl. 3	Bos. 2	Paul Masnick	27:49	Mtl.
Mar. 29/53	Bos.	SF	Bos. 2	Det. 1	Jack McIntyre	12:29	Bos.
Mar. 29/53	Chi.	SF	Chi. 2	Mtl. 1	Al Dewsbury	5:18	Mtl.
Apr. 16/53	Mtl.	F	Mtl. 1	Bos. 0	Elmer Lach	1:22	Mtl.
Apr. 1/54	Det.	SF	Det. 4	Tor. 3	Ted Lindsay	21:01	Det.
Apr. 11/54	Det.	F	Mtl. 1	Det. 0	Ken Mosdell	5:45	Det.
Apr. 16/54	Det.	F	Det. 2	Mtl. 1	Tony Leswick	4:29	Det.
Mar. 29/55	Bos.	SF	Mtl. 4	Bos. 3	Don Marshall	3:05	Mtl.
Mar. 24/56	Tor.	SF	Det. 5	Tor. 4	Ted Lindsay	4:22	Det.
Mar. 28/57	NYR	SF	NYR 4	Mtl. 3	Andy Hebenton	13:38	Mtl.
Apr. 4/57	Mtl.	SF	Mtl. 4	NYR 3	Maurice Richard	1:11	Mtl.
Mar. 27/58	NYR	SF	Bos. 4	NYR 3	Jerry Toppazzini	4:46	Bos.
Mar. 30/58	Det.	SF	Mtl. 2	Det. 1	André Pronovost	11:52	Mtl.
Apr. 17/58	Mtl.	F	Mtl. 3	Bos. 2	Maurice Richard	5:45	Mtl.
Mar. 28/59	Tor.	SF	Tor. 3	Bos. 2	Gerry Ehman	5:02	Tor.
Mar. 31/59	Tor.	SF	Tor. 3	Bos. 2	Frank Mahovlich	11:21	Tor.
Apr. 14/59	Tor.	F	Tor. 3	Mtl. 2	Dick Duff	10:06	Mtl.
Mar. 26/60	Mtl.	SF	Mtl. 4	Chi. 3	Doug Harvey	8:38	Mtl.
Mar. 27/60	Det.	SF	Tor. 5	Det. 4	Frank Mahovlich	43:00	Tor.
Mar. 29/60	Det.	SF	Det. 2	Tor. 1	Gerry Melnyk	1:54	Tor.
Mar. 22/61	Tor.	SF	Tor. 3	Det. 2	George Armstrong	24:51	Det.
Mar. 26/61	Chi.	SF	Chi. 2	Mtl. 1	Murray Balfour	52:12	Chi.
Apr. 5/62	Tor.	SF	Tor. 3	NYR 2	Red Kelly	24:23	Tor.
Apr. 2/64	Det.	SF	Chi. 3	Det. 2	Murray Balfour	8:21	Det.
Apr. 14/64	Tor.	F	Det. 4	Tor. 3	Larry Jeffrey	7:52	Tor.
Apr. 23/64	Det.	F	Tor. 4	Det. 3	Bob Baun	1:43	Tor.
Apr. 6/65	Tor.	SF	Tor. 3	Mtl. 2	Dave Keon	4:17	Mtl.
Apr. 13/65	Tor.	SF	Mtl. 4	Tor. 3	Claude Provost	16:33	Mtl.
May 5/66	Det.	F	Mtl. 3	Det. 2	Henri Richard	2:20	Mtl.
Apr. 13/67	NYR	SF	Mtl. 2	NYR 1	John Ferguson	6:28	Mtl.
Apr. 25/67	Tor.	F	Tor. 3	Mtl. 2	Bob Pulford	28:26	Tor.
Apr. 10/68	St.L.	QF	St.L. 3	Phi. 2	Larry Keenan	24:10	St.L.
Apr. 16/68	St.L.	QF	Phi. 2	St.L. 1	Don Blackburn	31:18	St.L.
Apr. 16/68	Min.	QF	Min. 4	L.A. 3	Milan Marcetta	9:11	Min.
Apr. 22/68	Min.	SF	Min. 3	St.L. 2	Parker MacDonald	3:41	St.L.
Apr. 27/68	St.L.	SF	St.L. 4	Min. 3	Gary Sabourin	1:32	St.L.
Apr. 28/68	Mtl.	SF	Mtl. 4	Chi. 3	Jacques Lemaire	2:14	Mtl.
Apr. 29/68	St.L.	SF	St.L. 3	Min. 2	Bill McCreary	17:27	St.L.
May 3/68	St.L.	SF	St.L. 2	Min. 1	Ron Schock	22:50	St.L.
May 5/68	St.L.	F	Mtl. 3	St.L. 2	Jacques Lemaire	1:41	Mtl.
May 9/68	Mtl.	F	Mtl. 4	St.L. 3	Bobby Rousseau	1:13	Mtl.
Apr. 2/69	Oak.	QF	L.A. 5	Oak. 4	Ted Irvine	0:19	L.A.
Apr. 10/69	Mtl.	SF	Mtl. 3	Bos. 2	Ralph Backstrom	0:42	Mtl.
Apr. 13/69	Mtl.	SF	Mtl. 4	Bos. 3	Mickey Redmond	4:55	Mtl.
Apr. 24/69	Bos.	SF	Mtl. 2	Bos. 1	Jean Béliveau	31:28	Mtl.
Apr. 12/70	Oak.	QF	Pit. 3	Oak. 2	Michel Briere	8:28	Pit.
May 10/70	Bos.	F	Bos. 4	St.L. 3	Bobby Orr	0:40	Bos.
Apr. 15/71	Tor.	QF	NYR 2	Tor. 1	Bob Nevin	9:07	NYR
Apr. 18/71	Chi.	SF	NYR 2	Chi. 1	Pete Stemkowski	1:37	Chi.
Apr. 27/71	Chi.	SF	Chi. 3	NYR 2	Bobby Hull	6:35	Chi.
Apr. 29/71	NYR	SF	NYR 3	Chi. 2	Pete Stemkowski	41:29	Chi.
May 4/71	Chi.	F	Chi. 2	Mtl. 1	Jim Pappin	21:11	Mtl.
Apr. 6/72	Bos.	QF	Tor. 4	Bos. 3	Jim Harrison	2:58	Bos.
Apr. 6/72	Min.	QF	Min. 6	St.L. 5	Bill Goldsworthy	1:36	St.L.
Apr. 9/72	Pit.	QF	Chi. 6	Pit. 5	Pit Martin	0:12	Chi.
Apr. 16/72	Min.	QF	St.L. 2	Min. 1	Kevin O'Shea	10:07	St.L.
Apr. 1/73	Mtl.	QF	Buf. 3	Mtl. 2	René Robert	9:18	Mtl.
Apr. 10/73	Phi.	QF	Phi. 3	Min. 2	Gary Dornhoefer	8:35	Phi.
Apr. 14/73	Mtl.	SF	Phi. 5	Mtl. 4	Rick MacLeish	2:56	Mtl.
Apr. 17/73	Mtl.	SF	Mtl. 4	Phi. 3	Larry Robinson	6:45	Mtl.
Apr. 14/74	Tor.	QF	Bos. 4	Tor. 3	Ken Hodge	1:27	Bos.
Apr. 14/74	Atl.	QF	Phi. 4	Atl. 3	Dave Schultz	5:40	Phi.
Apr. 16/74	Mtl.	QF	NYR 3	Mtl. 2	Ron Harris	4:07	NYR
Apr. 23/74	Chi.	SF	Chi. 4	Bos. 3	Jim Pappin	3:48	Bos.
Apr. 28/74	NYR	SF	NYR 2	Phi. 1	Rod Gilbert	4:20	Phi.
May 9/74	Bos.	F	Phi. 3	Bos. 2	Bobby Clarke	12:01	Phi.
Apr. 8/75	L.A.	PRE	L.A. 3	Tor. 2	Mike Murphy	8:53	Tor.
Apr. 10/75	Tor.	PRE	Tor. 3	L.A. 2	Blaine Stoughton	10:19	Tor.
Apr. 10/75	Chi.	PRE	Chi. 4	Bos. 3	Ivan Boldirev	7:33	Chi.
Apr. 11/75	NYR	PRE	NYI 4	NYR 3	Jean-Paul Parise	0:11	NYI
Apr. 17/75	Chi.	QF	Chi. 5	Buf. 4	Stan Mikita	2:31	Buf.
Apr. 19/75	Tor.	QF	Phi. 4	Tor. 3	André Dupont	1:45	Phi.
Apr. 22/75	Mtl.	QF	Mtl. 5	Van. 4	Guy Lafleur	17:06	Mtl.
Apr. 27/75	Buf.	SF	Buf. 6	Mtl. 5	Danny Gare	4:42	Buf.
May 1/75	Phi.	SF	Phi. 5	NYI 4	Bobby Clarke	2:56	Phi.
May 6/75	Buf.	SF	Buf. 5	Mtl. 4	René Robert	5:56	Buf.
May 7/75	NYI	SF	NYI 4	Phi. 3	Jude Drouin	1:53	Phi.
May 20/75	Buf.	F	Buf. 5	Phi. 4	René Robert	18:29	Phi.
Apr. 8/76	Buf.	PRE	Buf. 3	St.L. 2	Danny Gare	11:43	Buf.
Apr. 9/76	Buf.	PRE	Buf. 2	St.L. 1	Don Luce	14:27	Buf.
Apr. 13/76	Bos.	QF	L.A. 3	Bos. 2	Butch Goring	0:27	Bos.
Apr. 13/76	Buf.	QF	Buf. 3	NYI 2	Danny Gare	14:04	NYI
Apr. 22/76	L.A.	QF	L.A. 4	Bos. 3	Butch Goring	18:28	Bos.
Apr. 29/76	Phi.	SF	Phi. 2	Bos. 1	Reggie Leach	13:38	Phi.
Apr. 15/77	Tor.	QF	Phi. 4	Tor. 3	Rick MacLeish	2:55	Phi.
Apr. 17/77	Tor.	QF	Phi. 6	Tor. 5	Reggie Leach	19:10	Phi.
Apr. 24/77	Phi.	SF	Bos. 4	Phi. 3	Rick Middleton	2:57	Bos.
Apr. 26/77	Phi.	SF	Bos. 5	Phi. 4	Terry O'Reilly	30:07	Bos.
May 3/77	Mtl.	SF	NYI 4	Mtl. 3	Billy Harris	3:58	Mtl.

Date	City	Series	Score		Scorer	Overtime	Series Winner
May 14/77	Bos.	F	Mtl. 2	Bos. 1	Jacques Lemaire	4:32	Mtl.
Apr. 11/78	Phi.	PRE	Phi. 3	Col. 2	Mel Bridgman	0:23	Phi.
Apr. 13/78	NYR	PRE	NYR 4	Buf. 3	Don Murdoch	1:37	Buf.
Apr. 19/78	Bos.	QF	Bos. 4	Chi. 3	Terry O'Reilly	1:50	Bos.
Apr. 19/78	NYI	QF	NYI 3	Tor. 2	Mike Bossy	2:50	Tor.
Apr. 21/78	Chi.	QF	Bos. 4	Chi. 3	Peter McNab	10:17	Bos.
Apr. 25/78	NYI	QF	NYI 2	Tor. 1	Bob Nystrom	8:02	Tor.
Apr. 29/78	NYI	QF	Tor. 2	NYI 1	Lanny McDonald	4:13	Tor.
May 2/78	Bos.	SF	Bos. 3	Phi. 2	Rick Middleton	1:43	Bos.
May 16/78	Mtl.	F	Mtl. 3	Bos. 2	Guy Lafleur	13:09	Mtl.
May 21/78	Bos.	F	Bos. 4	Mtl. 3	Bobby Schmautz	6:22	Mtl.
Apr. 12/79	L.A.	PRE	NYR 2	L.A. 1	Phil Esposito	6:11	NYR
Apr. 14/79	Buf.	PRE	Pit. 4	Buf. 3	George Ferguson	0:47	Pit.
Apr. 16/79	Phi.	QF	Phi. 3	NYR 2	Ken Linseman	0:44	NYR
Apr. 18/79	NYI	QF	NYI 1	Chi. 0	Mike Bossy	2:31	NYI
Apr. 21/79	Tor.	QF	Mtl. 4	Tor. 3	Cam Connor	25:25	Mtl.
Apr. 22/79	Tor.	QF	Mtl. 5	Tor. 4	Larry Robinson	4:14	Mtl.
Apr. 28/79	NYI	SF	NYI 4	NYR 3	Denis Potvin	8:02	NYR
May 3/79	NYR	SF	NYI 3	NYR 2	Bob Nystrom	3:40	NYR
May 3/79	Bos.	SF	Bos. 4	Mtl. 3	Jean Ratelle	3:46	Mtl.
May 10/79	Mtl.	SF	Mtl. 5	Bos. 4	Yvon Lambert	9:33	Mtl.
May 19/79	NYR	F	Mtl. 4	NYR 3	Serge Savard	7:25	Mtl.
Apr. 8/80	NYR	PRE	NYR 2	Atl. 1	Steve Vickers	0:33	NYR
Apr. 8/80	Phi.	PRE	Phi. 4	Edm. 3	Bobby Clarke	8:06	Phi.
Apr. 8/80	Chi.	PRE	Chi. 3	St.L. 2	Doug Lecuyer	12:34	Chi.
Apr. 11/80	Hfd.	PRE	Mtl. 4	Hfd. 3	Yvon Lambert	0:29	Mtl.
Apr. 11/80	Tor.	PRE	Min. 4	Tor. 3	Al MacAdam	0:32	Min.
Apr. 11/80	L.A.	PRE	NYI 4	L.A. 3	Ken Morrow	6:55	NYI
Apr. 11/80	Edm.	PRE	Phi. 3	Edm. 2	Ken Linseman	23:56	Phi.
Apr. 16/80	Bos.	QF	NYI 2	Bos. 1	Clark Gillies	1:02	NYI
Apr. 17/80	Bos.	QF	NYI 5	Bos. 4	Bob Bourne	1:24	NYI
Apr. 21/80	NYI	QF	Bos. 4	NYI 3	Terry O'Reilly	17:13	NYI
May 1/80	Buf.	SF	NYI 2	Buf. 1	Bob Nystrom	21:20	NYI
May 13/80	Phi.	F	NYI 4	Phi. 3	Denis Potvin	4:07	NYI
May 24/80	NYI	F	NYI 5	Phi. 4	Bob Nystrom	7:11	NYI
Apr. 8/81	Buf.	PRE	Buf. 3	Van. 2	Alan Haworth	5:00	Buf.
Apr. 8/81	Bos.	PRE	Min. 5	Bos. 4	Steve Payne	3:34	Min.
Apr. 11/81	Chi.	PRE	Cgy. 5	Chi. 4	Willi Plett	35:17	Cgy.
Apr. 12/81	Que.	PRE	Que. 4	Phi. 3	Dale Hunter	0:37	Phi.
Apr. 14/81	St.L.	PRE	St.L. 4	Pit. 3	Mike Crombeen	25:16	St.L.
Apr. 16/81	Buf.	QF	Min. 4	Buf. 3	Steve Payne	0:22	Min.
Apr. 20/81	Min.	QF	Buf. 5	Min. 4	Craig Ramsay	16:32	Min.
Apr. 20/81	Edm.	QF	NYI 5	Edm. 4	Ken Morrow	5:41	NYI
Apr. 7/82	Min.	DSF	Chi. 3	Min. 2	Greg Fox	3:34	Chi.
Apr. 8/82	Edm.	DSF	Edm. 3	L.A. 2	Wayne Gretzky	6:20	L.A.
Apr. 8/82	Van.	DSF	Van. 2	Cgy. 1	Tiger Williams	14:20	Van.
Apr. 10/82	Pit.	DSF	Pit. 2	NYI 1	Rick Kehoe	4:14	NYI
Apr. 10/82	L.A.	DSF	L.A. 6	Edm. 5	Daryl Evans	2:35	L.A.
Apr. 13/82	Mtl.	DSF	Que. 3	Mtl. 2	Dale Hunter	0:22	Que.
Apr. 13/82	NYI	DSF	NYI 4	Pit. 3	John Tonelli	6:19	NYI
Apr. 16/82	Van.	DF	L.A. 3	Van. 2	Steve Bozek	4:33	Van.
Apr. 18/82	Que.	DF	Que. 3	Bos. 2	Wilf Paiement	11:44	Que.
Apr. 18/82	NYR	DF	NYI 4	NYR 3	Bryan Trottier	3:00	NYI
Apr. 18/82	L.A.	DF	Van. 4	L.A. 3	Colin Campbell	1:23	Van.
Apr. 21/82	St.L.	DF	St.L. 3	Chi. 2	Bernie Federko	3:28	Chi.
Apr. 23/82	Que.	DF	Bos. 6	Que. 5	Peter McNab	10:54	Que.
Apr. 27/82	Chi.	CF	Van. 2	Chi. 1	Jim Nill	28:58	Van.
May 1/82	Que.	CF	NYI 5	Que. 4	Wayne Merrick	16:52	NYI
May 8/82	NYI	F	NYI 6	Van. 5	Mike Bossy	19:58	NYI
Apr. 5/83	Bos.	DSF	Bos. 4	Que. 3	Barry Pederson	1:46	Bos.
Apr. 6/83	Cgy.	DSF	Cgy. 4	Van. 3	Eddy Beers	12:27	Cgy.
Apr. 7/83	Min.	DSF	Min. 5	Tor. 4	Bobby Smith	5:03	Min.
Apr. 10/83	Tor.	DSF	Min. 5	Tor. 4	Dino Ciccarelli	8:05	Min.
Apr. 10/83	Van.	DSF	Cgy. 4	Van. 3	Greg Meredith	1:06	Cgy.
Apr. 18/83	Min.	DF	Chi. 4	Min. 3	Rich Preston	10:34	Chi.
Apr. 24/83	Bos.	DF	Bos. 3	Buf. 2	Brad Park	1:52	Bos.
Apr. 5/84	Edm.	DSF	Edm. 5	Wpg. 4	Randy Gregg	0:21	Edm.
Apr. 7/84	Det.	DSF	St.L. 4	Det. 3	Mark Reeds	37:07	St.L.
Apr. 8/84	Det.	DSF	St.L. 3	Det. 2	Jorgen Pettersson	2:42	St.L.
Apr. 10/84	NYI	DSF	NYI 3	NYR 2	Ken Morrow	8:56	NYI
Apr. 13/84	Min.	DF	St.L. 4	Min. 3	Doug Gilmour	16:16	Min.
Apr. 13/84	Edm.	DF	Cgy. 6	Edm. 5	Carey Wilson	3:42	Edm.
Apr. 13/84	NYI	DF	NYI 5	Wsh. 4	Anders Kallur	7:35	NYI
Apr. 16/84	Mtl.	DF	Que. 4	Mtl. 3	Bo Berglund	3:00	Mtl.
Apr. 20/84	Cgy.	DF	Cgy. 5	Edm. 4	Lanny McDonald	1:04	Edm.
Apr. 22/84	Min.	DF	Min. 4	St.L. 3	Steve Payne	6:00	Min.
Apr. 10/85	Phi.	DSF	Phi. 5	NYR 4	Mark Howe	8:01	Phi.
Apr. 10/85	Wsh.	DSF	Wsh. 4	NYI 3	Alan Haworth	2:28	NYI
Apr. 10/85	Edm.	DSF	Edm. 3	L.A. 2	Lee Fogolin	3:01	Edm.
Apr. 10/85	Wpg.	DSF	Wpg. 5	Cgy. 4	Brian Mullen	7:56	Wpg.
Apr. 11/85	Wsh.	DSF	Wsh. 2	NYI 1	Mike Gartner	21:23	NYI
Apr. 13/85	L.A.	DSF	Edm. 4	L.A. 3	Glenn Anderson	0:46	Edm.
Apr. 18/85	Mtl.	DF	Que. 2	Mtl. 1	Mark Kumpel	12:23	Que.
Apr. 23/85	Que.	DF	Que. 7	Mtl. 6	Dale Hunter	18:36	Que.
Apr. 25/85	Min.	DF	Chi. 7	Min. 6	Darryl Sutter	21:57	Chi.
Apr. 28/85	Chi.	DF	Min. 5	Chi. 4	Dennis Maruk	1:14	Chi.
Apr. 30/85	Min.	DF	Chi. 6	Min. 5	Darryl Sutter	15:41	Chi.
May 2/85	Mtl.	DF	Que. 3	Mtl. 2	Peter Stastny	2:22	Que.
May 5/85	Que.	CF	Que. 2	Phi. 1	Peter Stastny	6:20	Phi.
Apr. 9/86	Que.	DSF	Hfd. 3	Que. 2	Sylvain Turgeon	2:36	Hfd.
Apr. 12/86	Wpg.	DSF	Cgy. 4	Wpg. 3	Lanny McDonald	8:25	Cgy.
Apr. 17/86	Wsh.	DF	NYR 4	Wsh. 3	Brian MacLellan	1:16	NYR
Apr. 20/86	Edm.	DF	Edm. 6	Cgy. 5	Glenn Anderson	1:04	Cgy.
Apr. 23/86	Hfd.	DF	Hfd. 2	Mtl. 1	Kevin Dineen	1:07	Mtl.
Apr. 23/86	NYR	DF	NYR 6	Wsh. 5	Bob Brooke	2:40	NYR
Apr. 26/86	St L.	DF	St L. 4	Tor. 3	Mark Reeds	7:11	St L.
Apr. 29/86	Mtl.	DF	Mtl. 2	Hfd. 1	Claude Lemieux	5:55	Mtl.
May 5/86	NYR	CF	Mtl. 4	NYR 3	Claude Lemieux	9:41	Mtl.
May 12/86	St L.	CF	St L. 6	Cgy. 5	Doug Wickenheiser	7:30	Cgy.
May 18/86	Cgy.	F	Mtl. 3	Cgy. 2	Brian Skrudland	0:09	Mtl.
Apr. 8/87	Hfd.	DSF	Hfd. 3	Que. 2	Paul MacDermid	2:20	Que.
Apr. 9/87	Mtl.	DSF	Mtl. 4	Bos. 3	Mats Naslund	2:38	Mtl.
Apr. 9/87	St.L.	DSF	Tor. 3	St.L. 2	Rick Lanz	10:17	Tor.
Apr. 11/87	Wpg.	DSF	Cgy. 3	Wpg. 2	Mike Bullard	3:53	Wpg.
Apr. 11/87	Chi.	DSF	Det. 4	Chi. 3	Shawn Burr	4:51	Det.
Apr. 16/87	Que.	DSF	Que. 5	Hfd. 4	Peter Stastny	6:05	Que.
Apr. 18/87	Wsh.	DSF	NYI 3	Wsh. 2	Pat LaFontaine	68:47	NYI
Apr. 21/87	Edm.	DF	Edm. 3	Wpg. 2	Glenn Anderson	0:36	Edm.
Apr. 26/87	Que.	DF	Mtl. 3	Que. 2	Mats Naslund	5:30	Mtl.
Apr. 27/87	Tor.	DF	Tor. 3	Det. 2	Mike Allison	9:31	Det.
May 4/87	Phi.	CF	Phi. 4	Mtl. 3	Ilkka Sinislao	9:11	Phi.
May 20/87	Edm.	F	Edm. 3	Phi. 2	Jari Kurri	6:50	Edm.
Apr. 6/88	NYI	DSF	NYI 4	N.J. 3	Pat LaFontaine	6:11	N.J.
Apr. 10/88	Phi.	DSF	Phi. 5	Wsh. 4	Murray Craven	1:18	Wsh.
Apr. 10/88	N.J.	DSF	NYI 5	N.J. 4	Brent Sutter	15:07	N.J.
Apr. 10/88	Buf.	DSF	Buf. 6	Bos. 5	John Tucker	5:32	Bos.
Apr. 12/88	Det.	DSF	Tor. 6	Det. 5	Ed Olczyk	0:34	Det.
Apr. 16/88	Wsh.	DSF	Wsh. 5	Phi. 4	Dale Hunter	5:57	Wsh.
Apr. 21/88	Cgy.	DF	Edm. 5	Cgy. 4	Wayne Gretzky	7:54	Edm.
May 4/88	Bos.	CF	N.J. 3	Bos. 2	Doug Brown	17:46	Bos.
May 9/88	Det.	CF	Edm. 4	Det. 3	Jari Kurri	11:02	Edm.
Apr. 5/89	St.L.	DSF	St.L. 4	Min. 3	Brett Hull	11:55	St.L.
Apr. 5/89	Cgy.	DSF	Van. 4	Cgy. 3	Paul Reinhart	2:47	Cgy.
Apr. 6/89	St.L.	DSF	St.L. 4	Min. 3	Rick Meagher	5:30	St.L.
Apr. 6/89	Det.	DSF	Chi. 5	Det. 4	Duane Sutter	14:36	Chi.
Apr. 8/89	Hfd.	DSF	Mtl. 5	Hfd. 4	Stephane Richer	5:01	Mtl.
Apr. 8/89	Phi.	DSF	Wsh. 4	Phi. 3	Kelly Miller	0:51	Phi.
Apr. 9/89	Hfd.	DSF	Mtl. 4	Hfd. 3	Russ Courtnall	15:12	Mtl.
Apr. 15/89	Cgy.	DSF	Cgy. 4	Van. 3	Joel Otto	19:21	Cgy.
Apr. 18/89	Cgy.	DF	Cgy. 4	L.A. 3	Doug Gilmour	7:47	Cgy.
Apr. 19/89	Mtl.	DF	Mtl. 3	Bos. 2	Bobby Smith	12:24	Mtl.
Apr. 20/89	St.L.	DF	St.L. 5	Chi. 4	Tony Hrkac	33:49	Chi.
Apr. 21/89	Phi.	DF	Pit. 4	Phi. 3	Phil Bourque	12:08	Phi.
May 8/89	Chi.	CF	Cgy. 2	Chi. 1	Al MacInnis	15:05	Cgy.
May 9/89	Mtl.	CF	Phi. 2	Mtl. 1	Dave Poulin	5:02	Mtl.
May 19/89	Mtl.	F	Mtl. 4	Cgy. 3	Ryan Walter	38:08	Cgy.
Apr. 5/90	N.J.	DSF	Wsh. 5	N.J. 4	Dino Ciccarelli	5:34	Wsh.
Apr. 6/90	Edm.	DSF	Edm. 3	Wpg. 2	Mark Lamb	4:21	Edm.
Apr. 8/90	Tor.	DSF	St.L. 6	Tor. 5	Sergio Momesso	6:04	St.L.
Apr. 8/90	L.A.	DSF	L.A. 2	Cgy. 1	Tony Granato	8:37	L.A.
Apr. 9/90	Mtl.	DSF	Mtl. 2	Buf. 1	Brian Skrudland	12:35	Mtl.
Apr. 9/90	NYI	DSF	NYI 4	NYR 3	Brent Sutter	20:59	NYR
Apr. 10/90	Wpg.	DSF	Wpg. 4	Edm. 3	Dave Ellett	21:08	Edm.
Apr. 14/90	L.A.	DSF	L.A. 4	Cgy. 3	Mike Krushelnyski	23:14	L.A.
Apr. 15/90	Hfd.	DSF	Hfd. 3	Bos. 2	Kevin Dineen	12:30	Bos.
Apr. 21/90	Bos.	DF	Bos. 5	Mtl. 4	Garry Galley	3:42	Bos.
Apr. 24/90	L.A.	DF	Edm. 6	L.A. 5	Joe Murphy	4:42	Edm.
Apr. 25/90	Wsh.	DF	Wsh. 4	NYR 3	Rod Langway	0:34	Wsh.
Apr. 27/90	NYR	DF	Wsh. 2	NYR 1	John Druce	6:48	Wsh.
May 15/90	Bos.	F	Edm. 3	Bos. 2	Petr Klima	55:13	Edm.
Apr. 4/91	Chi.	DSF	Min. 4	Chi. 3	Brian Propp	4:14	Min.
Apr. 5/91	Pit.	DSF	Pit. 5	N.J. 4	Jaromir Jagr	8:52	Pit.
Apr. 6/91	L.A.	DSF	L.A. 3	Van. 2	Wayne Gretzky	11:08	L.A.
Apr. 8/91	Van.	DSF	Van. 2	L.A. 1	Cliff Ronning	3:12	L.A.
Apr. 11/91	NYR	DSF	Wsh. 5	NYR 4	Dino Ciccarelli	6:44	Wsh.
Apr. 11/91	Mtl.	DSF	Mtl. 4	Buf. 3	Russ Courtnall	5:56	Mtl.
Apr. 14/91	Edm.	DSF	Cgy. 2	Edm. 1	Theoren Fleury	4:40	Edm.
Apr. 16/91	Cgy.	DSF	Edm. 5	Cgy. 4	Esa Tikkanen	6:58	Edm.
Apr. 18/91	L.A.	DF	L.A. 4	Edm. 3	Luc Robitaille	2:13	Edm.
Apr. 19/91	Bos.	DF	Mtl. 4	Bos. 3	Stephane Richer	0:27	Bos.
Apr. 19/91	Pit.	DF	Pit. 7	Wsh. 6	Kevin Stevens	8:10	Pit.
Apr. 20/91	L.A.	DF	Edm. 4	L.A. 3	Petr Klima	24:48	Edm.
Apr. 22/91	Edm.	DF	Edm. 4	L.A. 3	Esa Tikkanen	20:48	Edm.
Apr. 27/91	Mtl.	DF	Mtl. 3	Bos. 2	Shayne Corson	17:47	Bos.
Apr. 28/91	Edm.	DF	Edm. 4	L.A. 3	Craig MacTavish	16:57	Edm.
May 3/91	Bos.	CF	Bos. 5	Pit. 4	Vladimir Ruzicka	8:14	Pit.
Apr. 21/92	Bos.	DSF	Bos. 3	Buf. 2	Adam Oates	11:14	Bos.
Apr. 22/92	Min.	DSF	Det. 5	Min. 4	Yves Racine	1:15	Det.
Apr. 22/92	St.L.	DSF	St.L. 5	Chi. 4	Brett Hull	23:33	Chi.
Apr. 25/92	Buf.	DSF	Bos. 5	Buf. 4	Ted Donato	2:08	Bos.
Apr. 28/92	Min.	DSF	Det. 1	Min. 0	Sergei Fedorov	16:13	Det.
Apr. 29/92	Hfd.	DSF	Hfd. 2	Mtl. 1	Yvon Corriveau	0:24	Mtl.
May 1/92	Mtl.	DSF	Mtl. 3	Hfd. 2	Russ Courtnall	25:26	Mtl.
May 3/92	Van.	DF	Edm. 4	Van. 3	Joe Murphy	8:36	Edm.
May 5/92	Mtl.	DF	Bos. 3	Mtl. 2	Peter Douris	3:12	Bos.
May 7/92	Pit.	DF	NYR 6	Pit. 5	Kris King	1:29	Pit.
May 9/92	Pit.	DF	Pit. 5	NYR 4	Ron Francis	2:47	Pit.
May 17/92	Pit.	CF	Pit. 4	Bos. 3	Jaromir Jagr	9:44	Pit.
May 20/92	Edm.	CF	Chi. 4	Edm. 3	Jeremy Roenick	2:45	Chi.
Apr. 18/93	Bos.	DSF	Buf. 5	Bos. 4	Bob Sweeney	11:03	Buf.
Apr. 18/93	Que.	DSF	Que. 3	Mtl. 2	Scott Young	16:49	Mtl.
Apr. 20/93	Wsh.	DSF	NYI 5	Wsh. 4	Brian Mullen	34:50	NYI
Apr. 22/93	Mtl.	DSF	Mtl. 2	Que. 1	Vincent Damphousse	10:30	Mtl.
Apr. 22/93	Buf.	DSF	Buf. 4	Bos. 3	Yuri Khmylev	1:05	Buf.
Apr. 22/93	NYI	DSF	NYI 4	Wsh. 3	Ray Ferraro	4:46	NYI
Apr. 24/93	Buf.	DSF	Buf. 6	Bos. 5	Brad May	4:48	Buf.
Apr. 24/93	NYI	DSF	NYI 4	Wsh. 3	Ray Ferraro	25:40	NYI
Apr. 25/93	St.L.	DSF	St.L. 4	Chi. 3	Craig Janney	10:43	St.L.
Apr. 26/93	Que.	DSF	Mtl. 5	Que. 4	Kirk Muller	8:17	Mtl.
Apr. 27/93	Det.	DSF	Tor. 5	Det. 4	Mike Foligno	2:05	Tor.
Apr. 27/93	Van.	DSF	Wpg. 4	Van. 3	Teemu Selanne	6:18	Van.
Apr. 29/93	Wpg.	DSF	Van. 4	Wpg. 3	Greg Adams	4:30	Van.
May 1/93	Det.	DSF	Tor. 4	Det. 3	Nikolai Borschevsky	2:35	Tor.
May 3/93	Tor.	DF	Tor. 2	St.L. 1	Doug Gilmour	23:16	Tor.
May 4/93	Mtl.	DF	Mtl. 4	Buf. 3	Guy Carbonneau	2:50	Mtl.
May 5/93	Tor.	DF	St.L. 2	Tor. 1	Jeff Brown	23:03	Tor.
May 6/93	Buf.	DF	Mtl. 4	Buf. 3	Gilbert Dionne	8:28	Mtl.
May 8/93	Buf.	DF	Mtl. 4	Buf. 3	Kirk Muller	11:37	Mtl.
May 11/93	Van.	DF	L.A. 4	Van. 3	Gary Shuchuk	26:31	L.A.
May 14/93	Pit.	DF	NYI 4	Pit. 3	Dave Volek	5:16	NYI
May 18/93	Mtl.	CF	Mtl. 4	NYI 3	Stephan Lebeau	26:21	Mtl.
May 20/93	NYI	CF	Mtl. 2	NYI 1	Guy Carbonneau	12:34	Mtl.
May 25/93	Tor.	CF	Tor. 3	L.A. 2	Glenn Anderson	19:20	L.A.
May 27/93	L.A.	CF	L.A. 5	Tor. 4	Wayne Gretzky	1:41	L.A.
Jun. 3/93	Mtl.	F	Mtl. 3	L.A. 2	Eric Desjardins	0:51	Mtl.
Jun. 5/93	L.A.	F	Mtl. 4	L.A. 3	John LeClair	0:34	Mtl.

Date	City	Series	Score		Scorer	Overtime	Series Winner
Jun. 7/93	L.A.	F	Mtl. 3	L.A. 2	John LeClair	14:37	Mtl.
Apr. 20/94	Tor.	CQF	Tor. 1	Chi. 0	Todd Gill	2:15	Tor.
Apr. 22/94	St.L.	CQF	Dal. 5	St.L. 4	Paul Cavallini	8:34	Dal.
Apr. 24/94	Chi.	CQF	Chi. 4	Tor. 3	Jeremy Roenick	1:23	Tor.
Apr. 25/94	Bos.	CQF	Mtl. 2	Bos. 1	Kirk Muller	17:18	Bos.
Apr. 26/94	Cgy.	CQF	Van. 2	Cgy. 1	Geoff Courtnall	7:15	Van.
Apr. 27/94	Buf.	CQF	Buf. 1	N.J. 0	Dave Hannan	65:43	N.J.
Apr. 28/94	Van.	CQF	Van. 3	Cgy. 2	Trevor Linden	16:43	Van.
Apr. 30/94	Cgy.	CQF	Van. 4	Cgy. 3	Pavel Bure	22:20	Van.
May 3/94	N.J.	CSF	Bos. 6	N.J. 5	Don Sweeney	9:08	N.J.
May 7/94	Bos.	CSF	N.J. 5	Bos. 4	Stephane Richer	14:19	N.J.
May 8/94	Van.	CSF	Van. 2	Dal. 1	Sergio Momesso	11:01	Van.
May 12/94	Tor.	CSF	Tor. 3	S.J. 2	Mike Gartner	8:53	Tor.
May 15/94	NYR	CF	N.J. 4	NYR 3	Stephane Richer	35:23	NYR
May 16/94	Tor.	CF	Tor. 3	Van. 2	Peter Zezel	16:55	Van.
May 19/94	N.J.	CF	NYR 3	N.J. 2	Stephane Matteau	26:13	NYR
May 24/94	Van.	CF	Van. 4	Tor. 3	Greg Adams	20:14	Van.
May 27/94	NYR	CF	NYR 2	N.J. 1	Stephane Matteau	24:24	NYR
May 31/94	NYR	F	Van. 3	NYR 2	Greg Adams	19:26	NYR
May 7/95	Phi.	CQF	Phi. 4	Buf. 3	Karl Dykhuis	10:06	Phi.
May 9/95	Cgy.	CQF	S.J. 5	Cgy. 4	Ulf Dahlen	12:21	S.J.
May 12/95	NYR	CQF	NYR 3	Que. 2	Steve Larmer	8:09	NYR
May 12/95	N.J.	CQF	N.J. 1	Bos. 0	Randy McKay	8:51	N.J.
May 14/95	Pit.	CQF	Pit. 6	Wsh. 5	Luc Robitaille	4:30	Pit.
May 15/95	St.L.	CQF	Van. 6	St.L. 5	Cliff Ronning	1:48	Van.
May 17/95	Tor.	CQF	Tor. 5	Chi. 4	Randy Wood	10:00	Chi.
May 19/95	Cgy.	CQF	S.J. 5	Cgy. 4	Ray Whitney	21:54	S.J.
May 21/95	Phi.	CSF	Phi. 5	NYR 4	Eric Desjardins	7:03	Phi.
May 21/95	Chi.	CSF	Chi. 2	Van. 1	Joe Murphy	9:04	Chi.
May 22/95	Phi.	CSF	Phi. 4	NYR 3	Kevin Haller	0:25	Phi.
May 25/95	Van.	CSF	Chi. 3	Van. 2	Chris Chelios	6:22	Chi.
May 26/95	N.J.	CSF	N.J. 2	Pit. 1	Neal Broten	18:36	N.J.
May 27/95	Van.	CSF	Chi. 4	Van. 3	Chris Chelios	5:35	Chi.
Jun. 1/95	Det.	CF	Det. 2	Chi. 1	Nicklas Lidstrom	1:01	Det.
Jun. 6/95	Chi.	CF	Det. 4	Chi. 3	Vladimir Konstantinov	29:25	Det.
Jun. 7/95	N.J.	CF	Phi. 3	N.J. 2	Eric Lindros	4:19	N.J.
Jun. 11/95	Det.	CF	Det. 2	Chi. 1	Vyacheslav Kozlov	22:25	Det.
Apr. 16/96	NYR	CQF	Mtl. 3	NYR 2	Vincent Damphousse	5:04	NYR
Apr. 18/96	Tor.	CQF	Tor. 5	St.L. 4	Mats Sundin	4:02	St.L.
Apr. 18/96	Phi.	CQF	T.B. 2	Phi. 1	Brian Bellows	9:05	Phi.
Apr. 21/96	St.L.	CQF	St.L. 3	Tor. 2	Glenn Anderson	1:24	St.L.
Apr. 21/96	T.B.	CQF	T.B. 5	Phi. 4	Alexander Selivanov	2:04	Phi.
Apr. 23/96	Cgy.	CQF	Chi. 2	Cgy. 1	Joe Murphy	50:02	Chi.
Apr. 24/96	Wsh.	CQF	Pit. 3	Wsh. 2	Petr Nedved	79:15	Pit.
Apr. 25/96	Col.	CQF	Col. 5	Van. 4	Joe Sakic	0:51	Col.
Apr. 25/96	Tor.	CQF	Tor. 5	St.L. 4	Mike Gartner	7:31	St.L.
May 2/96	Col.	CSF	Chi. 3	Col. 2	Jeremy Roenick	6:29	Col.
May 6/96	Chi.	CSF	Chi. 4	Col. 3	Sergei Krivokrasov	0:46	Col.
May 8/96	St.L.	CSF	St.L. 5	Det. 4	Igor Kravchuk	3:23	Det.
May 8/96	Chi.	CSF	Col. 3	Chi. 2	Joe Sakic	44:33	Col.
May 9/96	Fla.	CSF	Fla. 4	Phi. 3	Dave Lowry	4:06	Fla.
May 12/96	Phi.	CSF	Fla. 2	Phi. 1	Mike Hough	28:05	Fla.
May 13/96	Chi.	CSF	Col. 4	Chi. 3	Sandis Ozolinsh	25:18	Col.
May 16/96	Det.	CSF	Det. 1	St.L. 0	Steve Yzerman	21:15	Det.
May 19/96	Det.	CF	Col. 3	Det. 2	Mike Keane	17:31	Col.
Jun. 10/96	Fla.	F	Col. 1	Fla. 0	Uwe Krupp	44:31	Col.
Apr. 20/97	Chi.	CQF	Chi. 4	Col. 3	Sergei Krivokrasov	31:03	Col.
Apr. 20/97	Edm.	CQF	Edm. 4	Dal. 3	Kelly Buchberger	9:15	Edm.
Apr. 22/97	NYR	CQF	NYR 4	Fla. 3	Esa Tikkanen	16:29	NYR
Apr. 23/97	Ott.	CQF	Ott. 1	Buf. 0	Daniel Alfredsson	2:34	Buf.
Apr. 24/97	Mtl.	CQF	Mtl. 4	N.J. 3	Patrice Brisebois	47:37	N.J.
Apr. 25/97	Fla.	CQF	NYR 3	Fla. 2	Esa Tikkanen	12:02	NYR
Apr. 25/97	Dal.	CQF	Edm. 1	Dal. 0	Ryan Smyth	20:22	Edm.
Apr. 27/97	Phx.	CQF	Ana. 3	Phx. 2	Paul Kariya	7:29	Ana.
Apr. 29/97	Buf.	CQF	Buf. 3	Ott. 2	Derek Plante	5:24	Buf.
Apr. 29/97	Dal.	CQF	Edm. 4	Dal. 3	Todd Marchant	12:26	Edm.
May 2/97	Det.	CSF	Det. 2	Ana. 1	Martin Lapointe	0:59	Det.
May 4/97	Det.	CSF	Det. 3	Ana. 2	Vyacheslav Kozlov	41:31	Det.
May 8/97	Ana.	CSF	Det. 3	Ana. 2	Brendan Shanahan	37:03	Det.
May 9/97	Phi.	CSF	Buf. 5	Phi. 4	Ed Ronan	6:24	Phi.
May 9/97	Edm.	CSF	Col. 3	Edm. 2	Claude Lemieux	8:35	Col.
May 11/97	N.J.	CSF	NYR 2	N.J. 1	Adam Graves	14:08	NYR
Apr. 22/98	N.J.	CQF	Ott. 2	N.J. 1	Bruce Gardiner	5:58	Ott.
Apr. 23/98	Pit.	CQF	Mtl. 3	Pit. 2	Benoit Brunet	18:43	Mtl.
Apr. 24/98	Wsh.	CQF	Bos. 4	Wsh. 3	Darren Van Impe	20:54	Wsh.
Apr. 26/98	Ott.	CQF	Ott. 2	N.J. 1	Alexei Yashin	2:47	Ott.
Apr. 26/98	Bos.	CQF	Wsh. 3	Bos. 2	Joe Juneau	26:31	Wsh.
Apr. 26/98	Edm.	CQF	Col. 5	Edm. 4	Joe Sakic	15:25	Edm.
Apr. 28/98	S.J.	CQF	S.J. 1	Dal. 0	Andrei Zyuzin	6:31	Dal.
May 1/98	Phi.	CQF	Buf. 3	Phi. 2	Michal Grosek	5:40	Buf.
May 2/98	S.J.	CQF	Dal. 3	S.J. 2	Mike Keane	3:43	Dal.
May 3/98	Bos.	CQF	Wsh. 3	Bos. 2	Brian Bellows	15:24	Wsh.
May 3/98	Buf.	CSF	Buf. 3	Mtl. 2	Geoff Sanderson	2:37	Buf.
May 11/98	Edm.	CSF	Dal. 1	Edm. 0	Benoit Hogue	13:07	Dal.
May 12/98	Mtl.	CSF	Buf. 5	Mtl. 4	Michael Peca	21:24	Buf.
May 12/98	St.L.	CSF	Det. 3	St.L. 2	Brendan Shanahan	31:12	Det.
May 25/98	Wsh.	CF	Wsh. 3	Buf. 2	Todd Krygier	3:01	Wsh.
May 28/98	Buf.	CF	Wsh. 4	Buf. 3	Peter Bondra	9:37	Wsh.
Jun. 3/98	Dal.	CF	Dal. 3	Det. 2	Jamie Langenbrunner	0:46	Det.
Jun. 4/98	Buf.	CF	Wsh. 3	Buf. 2	Joe Juneau	6:24	Wsh.
Jun. 11/98	Det.	F	Det. 5	Wsh. 4	Kris Draper	15:24	Det.
Apr. 23/99	Ott.	CQF	Buf. 3	Ott. 2	Miroslav Satan	30:35	Buf.
Apr. 24/99	Car.	CQF	Car. 3	Bos. 2	Ray Sheppard	17:05	Bos.
Apr. 24/99	Phx.	CQF	Phx. 4	St.L. 3	Shane Doan	8:58	St.L.
Apr. 26/99	S.J.	CQF	Col. 2	S.J. 1	Milan Hejduk	7:53	Col.
Apr. 27/99	Edm.	CQF	Dal. 3	Edm. 2	Joe Nieuwendyk	57:34	Dal.
Apr. 30/99	Tor.	CQF	Tor. 2	Phi. 1	Yanic Perreault	11:51	Tor.
Apr. 30/99	Car.	CQF	Bos. 4	Car. 3	Anson Carter	34:45	Bos.
Apr. 30/99	Phx..	CQF	St.L. 2	Phx. 1	Scott Young	5:43	St.L.
May 2/99	Pit.	CQF	Pit. 3	N.J. 2	Jaromir Jagr	8:59	Pit.
May 3/99	S.J.	CQF	Col. 3	S.J. 2	Milan Hejduk	13:12	Col.
May 4/99	Phx.	CQF	St.L. 1	Phx. 0	Pierre Turgeon	17:59	St.L.
May 7/99	Col.	CSF	Det. 3	Col. 2	Kirk Maltby	4:18	Col.
May 8/99	Dal.	CSF	Dal. 5	St.L. 4	Joe Nieuwendyk	8:22	Dal.
May 10/99	St.L.	CSF	St.L. 3	Dal. 2	Pavol Demitra	2:43	Dal.
May 12/99	St.L.	CSF	St.L. 3	Dal. 2	Pierre Turgeon	5:52	Dal.
May 13/99	Pit.	CSF	Tor. 3	Pit. 2	Sergei Berezin	2:18	Tor.
May 17/99	Pit.	CSF	Tor. 4	Pit. 3	Garry Valk	1:57	Tor.
May 17/99	St.L.	CSF	Dal. 2	St.L. 1	Mike Modano	2:21	Dal.
May 28/99	Col.	CF	Col. 3	Dal. 2	Chris Drury	19:29	Dal.
Jun. 8/99	Dal.	F	Buf. 3	Dal. 2	Jason Woolley	15:30	Dal.
Jun. 19/99	Buf.	F	Dal. 2	Buf. 1	Brett Hull	54:51	Dal.
Apr. 15/00	Pit.	CQF	Pit. 2	Wsh. 1	Jaromir Jagr	5:49	Pit.
Apr. 18/00	Buf.	CQF	Buf. 3	Phi. 2	Stu Barnes	4:42	Phi.
Apr. 22/00	Tor.	CQF	Tor. 2	Ott. 1	Steve Thomas	14:47	Tor.
May 2/00	Pit.	CSF	Phi. 4	Pit. 3	Andy Delmore	11:01	Phi.
May 3/00	Det.	CSF	Col. 3	Det. 2	Chris Drury	10:21	Col.
May 4/00	Pit.	CSF	Phi. 2	Pit. 1	Keith Primeau	92:01	Phi.
May 23/00	Dal.	CF	Dal. 3	Col. 2	Joe Nieuwendyk	12:10	Dal.
Jun. 8/00	N.J.	F	Dal. 1	N.J. 0	Mike Modano	46:21	N.J.
Jun. 10/00	Dal.	F	N.J. 2	Dal. 1	Jason Arnott	28:20	N.J.
Apr. 11/01	Dal.	CQF	Dal. 2	Edm. 1	Jamie Langenbrunner	2:08	Dal.
Apr. 13/01	Ott.	CQF	Tor. 1	Ott. 0	Mats Sundin	10:49	Tor.
Apr. 14/01	Phi.	CQF	Buf. 4	Phi. 3	Jay McKee	18:02	Buf.
Apr. 15/01	Edm.	CQF	Dal. 3	Edm. 2	Benoit Hogue	19:48	Dal.
Apr. 16/01	Tor.	CQF	Tor. 3	Ott. 2	Cory Cross	2:16	Tor.
Apr. 16/01	Van.	CQF	Col. 4	Van. 3	Peter Forsberg	2:50	Col.
Apr. 17/01	Buf.	CQF	Buf. 4	Phi. 3	Curtis Brown	6:13	Buf.
Apr. 17/01	Edm.	CQF	Edm. 2	Dal. 1	Mike Comrie	17:19	Dal.
Apr. 18/01	Car.	CQF	Car. 3	N.J. 2	Rod Brind'Amour	:46	N.J.
Apr. 18/01	Pit.	CQF	Wsh. 4	Pit. 3	Jeff Halpern	4:01	Pit.
Apr. 18/01	L.A.	CQF	L.A. 4	Det. 3	Eric Belanger	2:36	L.A.
Apr. 19/01	Dal.	CQF	Dal. 4	Edm. 3	Kirk Muller	8:01	Dal.
Apr. 19/01	St.L.	CQF	St.L. 3	S.J. 2	Bryce Salvador	9:54	St.L.
Apr. 23/01	Pit.	CQF	Pit. 4	Wsh. 3	Martin Straka	13:04	Pit.
Apr. 23/01	L.A.	CQF	L.A. 3	Det. 2	Adam Deadmarsh	4:48	L.A.
Apr. 26/01	Col.	CSF	L.A. 4	Col. 3	Jaroslav Modry	14:23	Col.
Apr. 28/01	N.J.	CSF	N.J. 6	Tor. 5	Randy McKay	5:31	N.J.
May 1/01	Tor.	CSF	N.J. 3	Tor. 2	Brian Rafalski	7:00	N.J.
May 1/01	St.L.	CSF	St.L. 3	Dal. 2	Cory Stillman	29:26	St.L.
May 5/01	Buf.	CSF	Buf. 3	Pit. 2	Stu Barnes	8:34	Pit.
May 6/01	L.A.	CSF	L.A. 1	Col. 0	Glen Murray	22:41	Col.
May 8/01	Pit.	CSF	Pit. 3	Buf. 2	Martin Straka	11:29	Pit.
May 10/01	Buf.	CSF	Pit. 3	Buf. 2	Darius Kasparaitis	13:01	Pit.
May 16/01	St.L.	CF	St.L. 4	Col. 3	Scott Young	30:27	Col.
May 18/01	St.L.	CF	Col. 4	St.L. 3	Stephane Yelle	4:23	Col.
May 21/01	Col.	CF	Col. 2	St.L. 1	Joe Sakic	:24	Col.
Apr. 17/02	Phi.	CQF	Phi. 1	Ott. 0	Ruslan Fedotenko	7:47	Ott.
Apr. 17/02	Det.	CQF	Van. 4	Det. 3	Henrik Sedin	13:59	Det.
Apr. 19/02	Car.	CQF	Car. 2	N.J. 1	Bates Battaglia	15:26	Car.
Apr. 24/02	Car.	CQF	Car. 3	N.J. 2	Josef Vasicek	8:16	Car.
Apr. 25/02	Col.	CQF	L.A. 1	Col. 0	Craig Johnson	2:19	Col.
Apr. 26/02	Phi.	CQF	Ott. 2	Phi. 1	Martin Havlat	7:33	Ott.
May 4/02	Tor.	CSF	Tor. 3	Ott. 2	Gary Roberts	44:30	Tor.
May 7/02	Mtl.	CSF	Mtl. 2	Car. 1	Donald Audette	2:26	Car.
May 9/02	Mtl.	CSF	Car. 4	Mtl. 3	Niclas Wallin	3:14	Car.
May 13/02	S.J.	CSF	Col. 2	S.J. 1	Peter Forsberg	2:47	Col.
May 19/02	Car.	CF	Car. 2	Tor. 1	Niclas Wallin	13:42	Car.
May 20/02	Det.	CF	Col. 4	Det. 3	Chris Drury	2:17	Det.
May 21/02	Tor.	CF	Car. 2	Tor. 1	Jeff O'Neill	6:01	Car.
May 22/02	Col.	CF	Det. 2	Col. 1	Fredrik Olausson	12:44	Det.
May 27/02	Det.	CF	Col. 2	Det. 1	Peter Forsberg	6:24	Det.
May 28/02	Tor.	CF	Car. 2	Tor. 1	Martin Gelinas	8:05	Car.
Jun. 4/02	Det.	F	Car. 3	Det. 2	Ron Francis	:58	Det.
Jun. 8/02	Car.	F	Det. 3	Car. 2	Igor Larionov	54:47	Det.
Apr. 10/03	Det.	CQF	Ana. 2	Det. 1	Paul Kariya	43:18	Ana.
Apr. 14/03	NYI	CQF	Ott. 3	NYI 2	Todd White	22:25	Ott.
Apr. 14/03	Tor.	CQF	Tor. 4	Phi. 3	Tomas Kaberle	27:20	Phi.
Apr. 15/03	Wsh.	CQF	T.B. 4	Wsh. 3	Vincent Lecavalier	2:29	T.B.
Apr. 16/03	Tor.	CQF	Phi. 3	Tor. 2	Mark Recchi	53:54	Phi.
Apr. 16/03	Ana.	CQF	Ana. 3	Det. 2	Steve Rucchin	6:53	Ana.
Apr. 20/03	Wsh.	CQF	T.B. 2	Wsh. 1	Martin St. Louis	44:03	T.B.
Apr. 21/03	Tor.	CQF	Tor. 2	Phi. 1	Travis Green	30:51	Phi.
Apr. 21/03	Min.	CQF	Min. 3	Col. 2	Richard Park	4:22	Min.
Apr. 22/03	Col.	CQF	Min. 3	Col. 2	Andrew Brunette	3:25	Min.
Apr. 24/03	Dal.	CSF	Ana. 4	Dal. 3	Petr Sykora	80:48	Ana.
Apr. 25/03	Van.	CSF	Van. 4	Min. 3	Trent Klatt	3:42	Min.
Apr. 26/03	N.J.	CSF	N.J. 3	T.B. 2	Jamie Langenbrunner	2:09	N.J.
Apr. 26/03	Dal.	CSF	Ana. 3	Dal. 2	Mike Leclerc	1:44	Ana.
Apr. 29/03	Phi.	CSF	Ott. 3	Phi. 2	Wade Redden	6:43	Ott.
May 2/03	Min.	CSF	Van. 3	Min. 2	Brent Sopel	15:52	Min.
May 2/03	N.J.	CSF	N.J. 2	T.B. 1	Grant Marshall	51:12	N.J.
May 10/03	Min.	CF	Ana. 1	Min. 0	Petr Sykora	28:06	Ana.
May 10/03	Ott.	CF	Ott. 3	N.J. 2	Shaun Van Allen	3:08	N.J.
May 21/03	N.J.	CF	Ott. 2	N.J. 1	Chris Phillips	15:51	N.J.
May 31/03	Ana.	F	Ana. 3	N.J. 2	Ruslan Salei	6:59	N.J.
Jun. 2/03	Ana.	F	Ana. 1	N.J. 0	Steve Thomas	0:39	N.J.
Apr. 8/04	S.J.	CQF	S.J. 1	St.L. 0	Niko Dimitrakos	9:16	S.J.
Apr. 9/04	Bos.	CQF	Bos. 2	Mtl. 1	PatriceBergeron	1:26	Mtl.
Apr. 12/04	Dal.	CQF	Dal. 4	Col. 3	Steve Ott	2:11	Col.
Apr. 13/04	Mtl.	CQF	Bos. 4	Mtl. 3	Glen Murray	29:27	Mtl.
Apr. 14/04	Dal.	CQF	Col. 3	Dal. 2	Marek Svatos	25:21	Col.
Apr. 16/04	T.B.	CQF	T.B. 3	NYI 2	Martin St. Louis	4:07	T.B.
Apr. 17/04	Cgy.	CQF	Van. 5	Cgy 4	Brendan Morrison	42:28	Cgy.
Apr. 18/04	Ott.	CQF	Ott. 2	Tor. 1	Mike Fisher	21:47	Tor.
Apr. 19/04	Van.	CQF	Cgy. 3	Van. 2	Martin Gelinas	1:25	Cgy.
Apr. 22/04	Det.	CSF	Cgy. 2	Det. 1	Marcus Nilson	2:39	Cgy.
Apr. 27/04	Mtl.	CSF	T.B. 4	Mtl 3	Brad Richards	1:05	T.B.
Apr. 28/04	Col	CSF	Col. 1	S.J. 0	Joe Sakic	5:15	S.J.
May 1/04	S.J.	CSF	Col. 2	S.J. 1	Joe Sakic	1:54	S.J.
May 3/04	Cgy	CSF	Cgy. 1	Det. 0	Martin Gelinas	19:13	Cgy.
May 4/04	Phi.	CSF	Phi. 3	Tor. 2	Jeremy Roenick	7:39	Phi.
May 9/04	S.J.	CF	Cgy. 4	S.J. 3	Steve Montador	18:43	Cgy.
May 20/04	Phi.	CF	Phi. 5	T.B. 4	Simon Gagne	18:18	T.B.
Jun. 3/04	T.B.	F	Cgy. 3	T.B. 2	Oleg Saprykin	14:40	T.B.
Jun. 5/04	Cgy.	F	T.B. 3	Cgy. 2	Martin St. Louis	20:33	T.B.

NHL Playoff Coaching Records

Coach	Team	Games Coached	Wins	Losses	Ties	Playoff Years	Cup Wins	Career
Abel, Sid	Chicago	7	3	4	0	1		
	Detroit	69	29	40	0	8		
	Total	76	32	44	0	9		1952-76
Adams, Jack	Detroit	105	52	52	1	15	3	1927-47
Allen, Keith	Philadelphia	11	3	8	0	2		1967-69
Arbour, Al	St. Louis	11	4	7	0	1		
	NY Islanders	198	119	79	0	15	4	
	Total	209	123	86	0	16	4	1970-94
Babcock, Mike	Anaheim	21	15	6	0	1		2002-05
Barber, Bill	Philadelphia	11	3	8	0	2		2000-02
Berenson, Red	St. Louis	14	5	9	0	2		1979-82
Bergeron, Michel	Quebec	68	31	37	0	7		1980-90
Berry, Bob	Los Angeles	10	2	8	0	3		
	Montreal	8	2	6	0	2		
	St. Louis	15	7	8	0	2		
	Total	33	11	22	0	7		1978-94
Beverley, Nick	Toronto	6	2	4	0	1		1995-96
Blackburn, Don	Hartford	3	0	3	0	1		1979-81
Blair, Wren	Minnesota	14	7	7	0	1		1967-70
Blake, Toe	Montreal	119	82	37	0	13	8	1955-68
Boileau, Marc	Pittsburgh	9	5	4	0	1		1973-76
Boivin, Leo	St. Louis	3	1	2	0	1		1975-78
Boucher, Frank	NY Rangers	27	13	14	0	4	1	1939-50
Boucher, Georges	Mtl. Maroons	2	0	2	0	1		1930-50
Bowman, Scotty	St. Louis	52	26	26	0	4		
	Montreal	98	70	28	0	8	5	
	Buffalo	36	18	18	0	5		
	Pittsburgh	33	23	10	0	2	1	
	Detroit	134	86	48	0	9	3	
	Total	353	223	130	0	28	9	1967-02
Bowness, Rick	Boston	15	8	7	0	1		1988-05
Brooks, Herb	NY Rangers	24	12	12	0	3		
	New Jersey	5	1	4	0	1		
	Pittsburgh	11	6	5	0	1		
	Total	40	19	21	0	5		1981-00
Brophy, John	Toronto	19	9	10	0	2		1986-89
Burns, Charlie	Minnesota	6	2	4	0	1		1969-75
Burns, Pat	Montreal	56	30	26	0	4		
	Toronto	46	23	23	0	3		
	Boston	18	8	10	0	3		
	New Jersey	29	17	12	0	2	1	
	Total	149	78	71	0	11	1	1988-05
Campbell, Colin	NY Rangers	36	18	18	0	3		1994-98
Carpenter, Doug	Toronto	5	1	4	0	1		1984-91
Carroll, Dick	Toronto	7	4	3	0	1	1	1917-19
Cassidy, Bruce	Washington	6	2	4	0	1		2002-04
Cheevers, Gerry	Boston	34	15	19	0	4		1980-85
Cherry, Don	Boston	55	31	24	0	5		1974-80
Clancy, King	Toronto	14	2	12	0	3		1937-56
Clapper, Dit	Boston	25	8	17	0	4		1945-49
Cleghorn, Odie	Pittsburgh	4	1	2	1	2		1925-29
Cleghorn, Sprague	Mtl. Maroons	4	1	1	2	1		1931-32
Constantine, Kevin	San Jose	25	11	14	0	2		
	Pittsburgh	19	8	11	0	2		
	New Jersey	6	2	4	0	1		
	Total	50	21	29	0	5		1993-02
Crawford, Marc	Quebec	6	2	4	0	1		
	Colorado	46	29	17	0	3	1	
	Vancouver	31	12	19	0	4		
	Total	83	43	40	0	8	1	1994-05
Creighton, Fred	Atlanta	9	2	7	0	4		1974-80
Crisp, Terry	Calgary	37	22	15	0	3	1	
	Tampa Bay	6	2	4	0	1		
	Total	43	24	19	0	4	1	1987-98
Crozier, Joe	Buffalo	6	2	4	0	1		1971-81
Cunniff, John	New Jersey	6	2	4	0	1		1982-91
Curry, Alex	Ottawa	2	0	1	1	1		1925-26
Dandurand, Leo	Montreal	16	10	6	0	4	1	1921-35
Day, Hap	Toronto	80	49	31	0	9	5	1940-50
Demers, Jacques	St. Louis	33	16	17	0	3		
	Detroit	38	20	18	0	3		
	Montreal	27	19	8	0	2	1	
	Total	98	55	43	0	8	1	1979-99
Denneny, Cy	Boston	5	5	0	0	1	1	1928-33
Dudley, Rick	Buffalo	12	4	8	0	2		1989-04
Dugal, Jules	Montreal	3	1	2	0	1		1938-39
Duncan, Art	Toronto	2	0	1	1	1		1926-32
Dutton, Red	NY Americans	16	6	10	0	4		1935-42
Esposito, Phil	NY Rangers	10	2	8	0	2		1986-89
Evans, Jack	Hartford	16	8	8	0	2		1975-88
Ferguson, John	Winnipeg	3	0	3	0	1		1975-86
Francis, Bob	Phoenix	10	2	8	0	2		1999-04
Francis, Emile	NY Rangers	75	34	41	0	9		
	St. Louis	14	5	9	0	2		
	Total	89	39	50	0	11		1965-83
Ftorek, Robbie	Los Angeles	16	5	11	0	2		
	New Jersey	7	3	4	0	1		
	Boston	6	2	4	0	1		
	Total	29	10	19	0	4		1987-02
Gainey, Bob	Minnesota	30	17	13	0	2		
	Dallas	14	6	8	0	2		
	Total	44	23	21	0	4		1990-96
Geoffrion, Bernie	Atlanta	4	0	4	0	1		1968-80
Gerard, Eddie	Mtl. Maroons	25	11	9	5	5	1	1917-35
Gill, David	Ottawa	8	3	2	3	2	1	1926-29
Glover, Fred	Oakland	11	3	8	0	1		1968-74
Gordon, Jackie	Minnesota	25	11	14	0	3		1970-75
Goring, Butch	Boston	3	0	3	0	1		1985-01
Gorman, Tommy	NY Americans	2	0	1	1	1		
	Chicago	8	6	1	1	1	1	
	Mtl. Maroons	15	7	6	2	3	1	
	Total	25	13	8	4	5	2	1925-38
Gottselig, Johnny	Chicago	4	0	4	0	1		1944-48
Granato, Tony	Colorado	18	9	9	0	2		2002-04
Green, Pete	Ottawa	26	14	9	3	6	3	1919-25
Green, Ted	Edmonton	16	8	8	0	1		1991-94
Guidolin, Bep	Boston	21	11	10	0	2		1972-76
Harris, Ted	Minnesota	2	0	2	0	1		1975-78
Hart, Cecil	Montreal	37	16	17	4	8	2	1926-39
Hartley, Bob	Colorado	80	49	31	0	4	1	1998-05
Hartsburg, Craig	Chicago	16	8	8	0	2		
	Anaheim	4	0	4	0	1		
	Total	20	8	12	0	3		1995-01
Harvey, Doug	NY Rangers	6	2	4	0	1		1961-62
Hay, Don	Phoenix	7	3	4	0	1		1996-01
Henning, Lorne	Minnesota	5	2	3	0	1		1985-01
Hitchcock, Ken	Dallas	80	47	33	0	5	1	
	Philadelphia	31	17	14	0	2		
	Total	111	64	47	0	7	1	1995-05
Hlinka, Ivan	Pittsburgh	18	9	9	0	1		2000-02
Holmgren, Paul	Philadelphia	19	10	9	0	1		1988-96
Imlach, Punch	Toronto	92	44	48	0	11	4	1958-80
Inglis, Bill	Buffalo	3	1	2	0	1		1978-79
Irvin, Dick	Chicago	9	5	3	1	1		
	Toronto	66	33	32	1	9	1	
	Montreal	115	62	53	2	14	3	
	Total	190	100	88	2	24	4	1928-56
Ivan, Tommy	Detroit	67	36	31	0	6	3	1947-58
Johnson, Bob	Calgary	52	25	27	0	5		
	Pittsburgh	24	16	8	0	1	1	
	Total	76	41	35	0	6	1	1982-91
Johnson, Tom	Boston	22	15	7	0	2	1	1970-73
Johnston, Eddie	Chicago	7	3	4	0	1		
	Pittsburgh	46	22	24	0	5		
	Total	53	25	28	0	6		1979-97
Julien, Claude	Montreal	11	4	7	0	1		2002-05
Kasper, Steve	Boston	5	1	4	0	1		1995-97
Keenan, Mike	Philadelphia	57	32	25	0	4		
	Chicago	60	33	27	0	4		
	NY Rangers	23	16	7	0	1	1	
	St. Louis	20	10	10	0	2		
	Total	160	91	69	0	11	1	1984-04
Kelly, Pat	Colorado	2	0	2	0	1		1977-79
Kelly, Red	Los Angeles	18	7	11	0	2		
	Pittsburgh	14	6	8	0	2		
	Toronto	30	11	19	0	4		
	Total	62	24	38	0	8		1967-77
King, Dave	Calgary	20	8	12	0	3		1992-02
Kitchen, Mike	St. Louis	5	1	4	0	1		2003-05
Kromm, Bobby	Detroit	7	3	4	0	1		1977-80
Lalonde, Newsy	Montreal	16	7	6	3	4		
	Ottawa	2	0	1	1	1		
	Total	18	7	7	4	5		1917-35
Laviolette, Peter	NY Islanders	12	4	8	0	2		2001-05
Lemaire, Jacques	Montreal	27	15	12	0	2		
	New Jersey	56	34	22	0	4	1	
	Minnesota	18	8	10	0	1		
	Total	101	57	44	0	7	1	1983-05
Lewis, Dave	Detroit	16	6	10	0	2		1998-05
Ley, Rick	Hartford	13	5	8	0	2		
	Vancouver	11	4	7	0	1		
	Total	24	9	15	0	3		1989-96
Long, Barry	Winnipeg	11	3	8	0	2		1983-86
Loughlin, Clem	Chicago	4	1	2	1	2		1934-37
Low, Ron	Edmonton	28	10	18	0	3		1994-02
Lowe, Kevin	Edmonton	5	1	4	0	1		1999-00
MacLean, Doug	Florida	27	13	14	0	2		1995-04
MacNeil, Al	Montreal	20	12	8	0	1	1	
	Atlanta	4	1	3	0	1		
	Calgary	19	9	10	0	2		
	Total	43	22	21	0	4	1	1970-82
MacTavish, Craig	Edmonton	12	4	8	0	2		2000-05
Magnuson, Keith	Chicago	3	0	3	0	1		1980-82
Mahoney, Bill	Minnesota	16	7	9	0	1		1983-85
Maloney, Dan	Toronto	10	6	4	0	2		
	Winnipeg	15	5	10	0	2		
	Total	25	11	14	0	3		1984-89
Maloney, Phil	Vancouver	7	1	6	0	2		1973-77

Coach	Team	Games Coached	Wins	Losses	Ties	Playoff Years	Cup Wins	Career
Martin, Jacques	St. Louis	16	7	9	0	2		
	Ottawa	69	31	38	0	8		
	Total	85	38	47	0	10		1986-05
Maurice, Paul	Carolina	35	17	18	0	3		1995-04
McCammon, Bob	Philadelphia	10	1	9	0	3		
	Vancouver	7	3	4	0	1		
	Total	17	4	13	0	4		1978-91
McLellan, John	Toronto	11	3	8	0	2		1969-73
McVie, Tom	New Jersey	14	6	8	0	2		1975-92
Melrose, Barry	Los Angeles	24	13	11	0	1		1992-95
Milbury, Mike	Boston	40	23	17	0	2		1989-98
Muckler, John	Edmonton	40	25	15	0	2	1	
	Buffalo	27	11	16	0	4		
	Total	67	36	31	0	6	1	1968-00
Muldoon, Pete	Chicago	2	0	1	1	1		1926-27
Munro, Dunc	Mtl. Maroons	4	1	3	0	1		1929-31
Murdoch, Bob	Chicago	5	1	4	0	1		
	Winnipeg	7	3	4	0	1		
	Total	12	4	8	0	2		1987-91
Murphy, Mike	Los Angeles	5	1	4	0	1		1986-98
Murray, Andy	Los Angeles	24	10	14	0	3		1999-05
Murray, Bryan	Washington	53	24	29	0	7		
	Detroit	25	10	15	0	3		
	Total	78	34	44	0	10		1981-05
Murray, Terry	Washington	39	18	21	0	4		
	Philadelphia	46	28	18	0	3		
	Florida	4	0	4	0	1		
	Total	89	46	43	0	8		1989-01
Neale, Harry	Vancouver	14	3	11	0	4		1978-86
Neilson, Roger	Toronto	19	8	11	0	2		
	Buffalo	8	4	4	0	1		
	Vancouver	21	12	9	0	2		
	NY Rangers	29	13	16	0	3		
	Philadelphia	29	14	15	0	3		
	Total	106	51	55	0	11		1977-02
Nolan, Ted	Buffalo	12	5	7	0	1		1995-97
Nykoluk, Mike	Toronto	7	1	6	0	2		1980-84
O'Connell, Mike	Boston	5	1	4	0	1		2002-03
O'Donoghue, George	Toronto	7	4	2	1	1	1	1921-23
O'Reilly, Terry	Boston	37	17	19	1	3		1986-89
Oliver, Murray	Minnesota	13	5	8	0	2		1981-83
Paddock, John	Winnipeg	13	5	8	0	2		1991-95
Page, Pierre	Minnesota	12	4	8	0	2		
	Quebec	6	2	4	0	1		
	Calgary	4	0	4	0	1		
	Total	22	6	16	0	4		1988-98
Patrick, Craig	NY Rangers	17	7	10	0	2		
	Pittsburgh	5	1	4	0	1		
	Total	22	8	14	0	3		1980-97
Patrick, Frank	Boston	6	2	4	0	2		1934-36
Patrick, Lester	NY Rangers	65	32	26	7	12	2	1926-39
Patrick, Lynn	NY Rangers	12	7	5	0	1		
	Boston	28	9	18	1	4		
	Total	40	16	23	1	5		1948-76
Perron, Jean	Montreal	48	30	18	0	3	1	1985-89
Perry, Don	Los Angeles	10	4	6	0	1		1981-84
Pilous, Rudy	Chicago	41	19	22	0	5	1	1957-63
Plager, Barclay	St. Louis	4	1	3	0	1		1977-83
Pleau, Larry	Hartford	10	2	8	0	2		1980-89
Polano, Nick	Detroit	7	1	6	0	2		1982-85
Powers, Eddie	Toronto	2	0	2	0	1		1924-26
Primeau, Joe	Toronto	15	8	6	1	2	1	1950-53
Pronovost, Marcel	Buffalo	8	3	5	0	1		1977-79
Pulford, Bob	Los Angeles	26	10	16	0	4		
	Chicago	45	17	28	0	6		
	Total	71	27	44	0	10		1972-00
Quenneville, Joel	St. Louis	68	34	34	0	7		1996-05
Quinn, Pat	Philadelphia	39	22	17	0	3		
	Los Angeles	3	0	3	0	1		
	Vancouver	61	31	30	0	5		
	Toronto	80	41	39	0	6		
	Total	183	94	89	0	15		1978-05

Coach	Team	Games Coached	Wins	Losses	Ties	Playoff Years	Cup Wins	Career
Reay, Billy	Chicago	116	56	60	0	12		1957-77
Risebrough, Doug	Calgary	7	3	4	0	1		1990-92
Roberts, Jim	Hartford	7	3	4	0	1		1981-97
Robinson, Larry	Los Angeles	4	0	4	0	1		
	New Jersey	48	31	17	0	2	1	
	Total	52	31	21	0	3	1	1995-02
Ross, Art	Boston	65	27	33	5	11	1	1917-45
Ruel, Claude	Montreal	27	18	9	0	3	1	1968-81
Ruff, Lindy	Buffalo	54	32	22	0	4		1997-05
Sather, Glen	Edmonton	127	89	37	1	10	4	1979-04
Sator, Ted	NY Rangers	16	8	8	0	1		
	Buffalo	11	3	8	0	2		
	Total	27	11	16	0	3		1985-89
Schinkel, Ken	Pittsburgh	6	2	4	0	2		1972-77
Schmidt, Milt	Boston	34	15	19	0	4		1954-76
Schoenfeld, Jim	New Jersey	20	11	9	0	1		
	Washington	24	10	14	0	3		
	Phoenix	13	5	8	0	2		
	Total	57	26	31	0	6		1985-99
Shero, Fred	Philadelphia	83	48	35	0	6	2	
	NY Rangers	27	15	12	0	2		
	Total	110	63	47	0	8	2	1971-81
Simpson, Terry	NY Islanders	20	9	11	0	2		
	Winnipeg	6	2	4	0	1		
	Total	26	11	15	0	3		1986-96
Sinden, Harry	Boston	43	24	19	0	5	1	1966-85
Skinner, Jimmy	Detroit	26	14	12	0	3	1	1954-58
Smith, Alf	Ottawa	5	1	4	0	1		1918-19
Smith, Floyd	Buffalo	32	16	16	0	3		1971-80
Smythe, Conn	Toronto	4	2	2	0	1		1927-31
Sonmor, Glen	Minnesota	43	25	18	0	3		1978-87
Stasiuk, Vic	Philadelphia	4	0	4	0	1		1969-73
Stewart, Bill	Chicago	10	7	3	0	1	1	1937-39
Stewart, Ron	Los Angeles	2	0	2	0	1		1975-78
Stirling, Steve	NY Islanders	5	1	4	0	1		2003-05
Sullivan, Mike	Boston	7	3	4	0	1		2003-05
Sutter, Brian	St. Louis	41	20	21	0	4		
	Boston	22	7	15	0	3		
	Chicago	5	1	4	0	1		
	Total	68	28	40	0	8		1988-05
Sutter, Darryl	Chicago	26	11	15	0	3		
	San Jose	42	18	24	0	5		
	Calgary	26	15	11	0	1		
	Total	94	44	50	0	9		1992-05
Talbot, Jean-Guy	St. Louis	5	1	4	0	1		
	NY Rangers	3	1	2	0	1		
	Total	8	2	6	0	2		1972-78
Tessier, Orval	Chicago	18	9	9	0	2		1982-85
Therrien, Michel	Montreal	12	6	6	0	1		2000-02
Thompson, Paul	Chicago	19	7	12	0	4		1938-45
Tippett, Dave	Dallas	17	7	10	0	2		2002-05
Tobin, Bill	Chicago	4	1	2	1	2		1929-32
Tortorella, John	Tampa Bay	34	21	13	0	2	1	1999-05
Tremblay, Mario	Montreal	11	3	8	0	2		1995-97
Trotz, Barry	Nashville	6	2	4	0	1		1998-05
Ubriaco, Gene	Pittsburgh	11	7	4	0	1		1988-90
Vigneault, Alain	Montreal	10	4	6	0	1		1997-01
Watson, Phil	NY Rangers	16	4	12	0	3		1955-63
Watt, Tom	Winnipeg	7	1	6	0	2		
	Vancouver	3	0	3	0	1		
	Total	10	1	9	0	3		1981-92
Webster, Tom	Los Angeles	28	12	16	0	3		1986-92
Weiland, Cooney	Boston	17	10	7	0	2	1	1939-41
White, Bill	Chicago	2	0	2	0	1		1976-77
Wilson, Johnny	Pittsburgh	12	4	8	0	2		1969-80
Wilson, Ron	Anaheim	11	4	7	0	1		
	Washington	32	15	17	0	3		
	San Jose	17	10	7	0	1		
	Total	60	29	31	0	5		1993-05
Young, Garry	St. Louis	2	0	2	0	1		1972-76

Claude Julien (far left) guided the Montreal Canadiens to their record 74th playoff appearance in 2004. Barry Trotz (left) guided Nashville to its first.

Penalty Shots in Stanley Cup Playoff Games

Date	Player	Goaltender	Scored	Final Score	Series
Mar. 25/37	Lionel Conacher, Mtl. Maroons	Tiny Thompson, Boston	No	Mtl. M. 0 at Bos. 4	QF
Apr. 15/37	Alex Shibicky, NY Rangers	Earl Robertson, Detroit	No	NYR 0 at Det. 3	F
Mar. 24/38	Mush March, Chicago	Wilf Cude, Montreal	No	Mtl. 0 at Chi. 4	QF
Apr. 10/38	Art Wiebe, Chicago	Turk Broda, Toronto	No	Tor. 1 at Chi. 2	F
Mar. 24/42	Charlie Sands, Montreal	Johnny Mowers, Detroit	No	Det. 0 at Mtl. 5	QF
Apr. 13/44	Virgil Johnson, Chicago	Bill Durnan, Montreal	No	Chi. 4 at Mtl. 5*	F
Apr. 9/68	Wayne Connelly, Minnesota	Terry Sawchuk, Los Angeles	Yes	L.A. 5 at Min. 7	QF
Apr. 27/68	Jim Roberts, St. Louis	Cesare Maniago, Minnesota	No	St.L. 4 at Min. 3	SF
May 16/71	Frank Mahovlich, Montreal	Tony Esposito, Chicago	No	Chi. 3 at Mtl. 4	F
May 7/75	Bill Barber, Philadelphia	Glenn Resch, NY Islanders	No	Phi. 3 at NYI 4*	SF
Apr. 20/79	Mike Walton, Chicago	Glenn Resch, NY Islanders	No	NYI 4 at Chi. 0	QF
Apr. 9/81	Peter McNab, Boston	Don Beaupre, Minnesota	No	Min. 5 at Bos. 4*	PR
Apr. 17/81	Anders Hedberg, NY Rangers	Mike Liut, St. Louis	Yes	NYR 6 at St.L. 4	QF
Apr. 9/83	Denis Potvin, NY Islanders	Pat Riggin, Washington	No	NYI 6 at Wsh. 2	DSF
Apr. 28/84	Wayne Gretzky, Edmonton	Don Beaupre, Minnesota	Yes	Edm. 8 at Min. 5	CF
May 1/84	Mats Naslund, Montreal	Billy Smith, NY Islanders	No	Mtl. 1 at NYI 3	CF
Apr. 14/85	Bob Carpenter, Washington	Billy Smith, NY Islanders	No	Wsh. 4 at NYI. 6	DF
May 28/85	Ron Sutter, Philadelphia	Grant Fuhr, Edmonton	No	Phi. 3 at Edm. 5	F
May 30/85	Dave Poulin, Philadelphia	Grant Fuhr, Edmonton	No	Phi. 3 at Edm. 8	F
Apr. 9/88	John Tucker, Buffalo	Andy Moog, Boston	Yes	Bos. 2 at Buf. 6	DSF
Apr. 9/88	Petr Klima, Detroit	Allan Bester, Toronto	Yes	Det. 6 at Tor. 3	DSF
Apr. 8/89	Neal Broten, Minnesota	Greg Millen, St. Louis	Yes	St.L. 5 at Min. 3	DSF
Apr. 4/90	Al MacInnis, Calgary	Kelly Hrudey, Los Angeles	Yes	L.A. 5 at Cgy. 3	DSF
Apr. 5/90	Randy Wood, NY Islanders	Mike Richter, NY Rangers	No	NYI 1 at NYR 2	DSF
May 3/90	Kelly Miller, Washington	Andy Moog, Boston	No	Wsh. 3 at Bos. 5	CF
May 18/90	Petr Klima, Edmonton	Reggie Lemelin, Boston	No	Edm. 7 at Bos. 2	F
Apr. 6/91	Basil McRae, Minnesota	Ed Belfour, Chicago	Yes	Min. 2 at Chi. 5	DSF
Apr. 10/91	Steve Duchesne, Los Angeles	Kirk McLean, Vancouver	Yes	L.A. 6 at Van. 1	DSF
May 11/92	Jaromir Jagr, Pittsburgh	John Vanbiesbrouck, NYR	Yes	Pit. 3 at NYR 2	DF
May 13/92	Shawn McEachern, Pittsburgh	John Vanbiesbrouck, NYR	No	NYR 1 at Pit. 5	DF
June 7/94	Pavel Bure, Vancouver	Mike Richter, NYR	No	NYR 4 at Van. 2	F
May 9/95	Patrick Poulin, Chicago	Felix Potvin, Toronto	No	Tor. 3 at Chi. 0	CQF
May 10/95	Michal Pivonka, Washington	Tom Barrasso, Pittsburgh	No	Pit. 2 at Wsh. 6	CQF
Apr. 24/96	Joe Juneau, Washington	Ken Wregget, Pittsburgh	No	Pit. 3 at Wsh. 2**	CQF
May 11/97	Eric Lindros, Philadelphia	Steve Shields, Buffalo	Yes	Phi. 6 at Buf. 3	CSF
Apr. 23/98	Alexei Morozov, Pittsburgh	Andy Moog, Montreal	No	Mtl. 3 at Pit. 2**	CQF
Apr. 22/99	Mats Sundin, Toronto	John Vanbiesbrouck, Phi.	No	Phi. 3 at Tor. 0	CQF
May 29/99	Mats Sundin, Toronto	Dominik Hasek, Buffalo	Yes	Tor. 2 at Buf. 5	CF
Apr. 16/00	Eric Desjardins, Philadelphia	Dominik Hasek, Buffalo	No	Phi. 2 at Buf. 0	CQF
Apr. 11/01	Mark Recchi, Philadelphia	Dominik Hasek, Buffalo	No	Buf. 2 at Phi. 1	CSF
May 2/01	Martin Straka, Pittsburgh	Dominik Hasek, Buffalo	No	Buf. 5 at Pit. 2	CSF
May 12/01	Joe Sakic, Colorado	Roman Turek, St. Louis	Yes	St.L. 1 at Col. 4	CF
Apr. 21/02	Todd Bertuzzi, Vancouver	Dominik Hasek, Detroit	No	Det. 3 at Van. 1	CQF
Apr. 24/02	Shawn Bates, NY Islanders	Curtis Joseph, Toronto	Yes	Tor. 3 at NYI 4	CQF
Apr. 26/02	Mike Johnson, Phoenix	Evgeni Nabokov, San Jose	Yes	Phx. 1 at S.J. 4	CQF
Apr. 15/03	Dainius Zubrus, Washington	Nikolai Khabibulin, Tampa Bay	No	T.B. 4 at Wsh. 3	CQF
Apr. 21/03	Robert Reichel, Toronto	Roman Cechmanek, Philadelphia	No	Phi. 1 at Tor. 2	CQF
Apr. 7/04	Steve Sullivan, Nashville	Manny Legace, Detroit	No	Nsh. 1 at Det. 3	CQF

Detroit's Manny Legace is the most recent goalie to have stopped a penalty shot in the playoffs, turning back Nashville's Steve Sullivan on April 7, 2004.

Overtime Record of Current Teams

(Listed by number of OT games played)

Team	Overall				Home				Road			
	GP	W	L	T	GP	W	L	T Last OT Game	GP	W	L	T Last OT Game
Montreal	125	70	53	2	59	37	21	1 Apr. 27/04	66	33	32	1 Apr. 9/04
Toronto	106	54	51	1	68	36	31	1 May 4/04	38	18	20	0 Apr. 18/04
Boston	100	40	57	3	46	21	24	1 Apr. 9/04	54	19	33	2 Apr. 13/04
Detroit	76	33	43	0	45	16	29	0 Apr. 22/04	31	17	14	0 May 3/04
NY Rangers	63	30	33	0	27	12	15	0 Apr. 22/97	36	18	18	0 May 11/97
Chicago	62	30	30	2	30	16	13	1 Apr. 20/97	32	14	17	1 May 2/96
Philadelphia	58	28	30	0	26	13	13	0 May 20/04	32	15	17	0 May 4/04
Dallas[1]	54	24	30	0	27	11	16	0 Apr. 14/04	27	13	14	0 May 1/01
St. Louis	50	27	23	0	26	20	6	0 May 18/01	24	7	14	0 Apr. 8/04
Colorado[2]	49	28	21	0	19	9	10	0 Apr. 22/03	30	19	11	0 Apr. 14/04
Buffalo	46	25	21	0	26	16	10	0 May 10/01	20	9	11	0 May 8/01
NY Islanders	40	29	11	0	18	14	4	0 Apr. 14/03	22	15	7	0 Apr. 16/04
Edmonton	38	21	17	0	21	11	10	0 Apr. 17/01	17	10	7	0 Apr. 19/01
Calgary[3]	37	16	21	0	17	5	12	0 Jun. 5/04	20	11	9	0 Jun. 3/04
Los Angeles	35	17	18	0	19	11	8	0 May 6/01	16	6	10	0 Apr. 25/02
Vancouver	35	17	18	0	15	6	9	0 Apr. 19/04	20	11	9	0 Apr. 17/04
New Jersey[4]	33	10	23	0	14	5	9	0 May 21/03	19	5	14	0 Jun. 2/03
Washington	31	14	17	0	12	5	7	0 Apr. 20/03	19	9	10	0 Apr. 23/01
Pittsburgh	28	15	13	0	18	10	8	0 May 8/01	10	5	5	0 May 10/01
Carolina[5]	23	14	9	0	14	9	5	0 Jun. 8/02	9	5	4	0 Jun. 4/02
Ottawa	16	9	7	0	6	4	2	0 Apr. 18/04	10	5	5	0 May 21/03
San Jose	13	4	9	0	8	2	6	0 May 9/04	5	2	3	0 Apr. 28/04
Phoenix[6]	12	5	7	0	8	3	5	0 May 4/99	4	2	2	0 Apr. 27/93
Anaheim	11	8	3	0	4	3	1	0 Jun. 2/03	7	5	2	0 May 10/03
Tampa Bay	11	7	4	0	3	2	1	0 Jun. 3/04	8	5	3	0 Jun. 5/04
Florida	5	2	3	0	3	1	2	0 Apr. 25/97	2	1	1	0 Apr. 22/97
Minnesota	5	2	3	0	3	1	2	0 May 10/03	2	1	1	0 Apr. 25/03

[1] Totals include those of Minnesota North Stars 1967-93.
[2] Totals include those of Quebec 1979-95.
[3] Totals include those of Atlanta Flames 1972-80.
[4] Totals include those of Kansas City and Colorado Rockies 1974-82.
[5] Totals include those of Hartford 1979-97.
[6] Totals include those of Winnipeg 1979-96.

Mike Johnson is the most recent player to have scored on a penalty shot in the playoffs, beating San Jose's Evgeni Nabokov for Phoenix's lone goal on April 26, 2002.

Ten Longest Overtime Games

Date	City	Series	Score				Scorer	Overtime	Series Winner
Mar. 24/36	Mtl.	SF	Det. 1		Mtl. M. 0		Mud Bruneteau	116:30	Det.
Apr. 3/33	Tor.	SF	Tor. 1		Bos. 0		Ken Doraty	104:46	Tor.
May 4/00	Pit.	CSF	Phi. 2		Pit. 1		Keith Primeau	92:01	Phi.
Apr. 24/03	Dal.	CSF	Ana. 4		Dal. 3		Petr Sykora	80:48	Ana.
Apr. 24/96	Wsh.	CQF	Pit. 3		Wsh. 2		Petr Nedved	79:15	Pit.
Mar. 23/43	Det.	SF	Tor. 3		Det. 2		Jack McLean	70:18	Det.
Mar. 28/30	Mtl.	SF	Mtl. 2		NYR 1		Gus Rivers	68:52	Mtl.
Apr. 18/87	Wsh.	DSF	NYI 3		Wsh. 2		Pat LaFontaine	68:47	NYI
Apr. 27/94	Buf.	CQF	Buf. 1		N.J. 0		Dave Hannan	65:43	N.J.
Mar. 27/51	Det.	SF	Mtl. 3		Det. 2		Maurice Richard	61:09	Mtl.

Key to Prospect, NHL Player and Goaltender Registers

Demographics: Position, shooting side (catching hand for goaltenders), height, weight, place and date of birth as well as draft information, if any, is located on this line.

Major Junior, NCAA, minor pro, senior European and NHL clubs form a permanent part of each player's data panel. If a player sees action with more than one club in any of the above categories, a separate line is included for each one.

Olympic Team statistics are also listed.

Player's NHL organization as of September 6, 2005. This includes players under contract, unsigned draft choices and other players on reserve lists. Free agents as of this date show a blank here.

The complete career data panels of players with NHL experience who announced their retirement before the start of the 2005-06 season are included in the 2005-06 Player Register. These newly-retired players also show a blank here.

Each NHL club's minor-pro affiliates are listed on page 14.

							Regular Season										Playoffs					
Season	Club	League	GP	G	A	Pts	PIM	PP	SH	GW	S	%	+/-	TF	F%	Min	GP	G	A	Pts	PIM	PP	SH	W	Min

DRURY, Chris   (DROO-ree, KRIHS)   **BUF.**

Center. Shoots right. 5'10", 200 lbs.   Born, Trumbull, CT, August 20, 1976. Quebec's 5th choice, 72nd overall, in 1994 Entry Draft.

Season	Club	League	GP	G	A	Pts	PIM	PP	SH	GW	S	%	+/-	TF	F%	Min	GP	G	A	Pts	PIM	PP	SH	W	Min
1991-92	Fairfield Prep	High-CT	25	22	27	49		....	....	....	....	....	....	....	....	....		....	....	....	....	....			
1992-93	Fairfield Prep	High-CT	24	25	32	57	15	....	....	....	....	....	....	....	....	....		....	....	....	....	....			
1993-94	Fairfield Prep	High-CT	24	37	18	55		....	....	....	....	....	....	....	....	....		....	....	....	....	....			
1994-95	Boston University	H-East	39	12	15	27	38	....	....	....	....	....	....	....	....	....		....	....	....	....	....			
1995-96	Boston University	H-East	37	35	33	*68	46	....	....	....	....	....	....	....	....	....		....	....	....	....	....			
1996-97	Boston University	H-East	41	*38	24	62	64	....	....	....	....	....	....	....	....	....		....	....	....	....	....			
1997-98	Boston University	H-East	38	28		57	88	....	....	....	....	....	....	....	....	....		....	....	....	....	....			
1998-99	Colorado	NHL	79	20	24	44	62	6	0	3	138	14.5	9	418	46.9	13:15	19	6	2	8	1	0	0	4	11:28
99-2000	Colorado	NHL	82	20	47	67	42	7	0	2	213	9.4	8	1321	53.1	18:33	17	4	10	14	1	1	0	2	18:30
2000-01 ♦	Colorado	NHL	71	24	41	65	47	11	0	5	204	11.8	6	552	55.1	18:03	23	11	5	16	2	2	0	2	19:06
2001-02	Colorado	NHL	82	21	25	46	38	5	0	6	236	8.9	1	1139	53.2	17:57	21	5	7	12	10	1	0	3	17:01
	United States	Olympics	6	0	0	0	0																	
2002-03	Calgary	NHL	80	23	30	53	33	5	1	5	224	10.3	-9	942	53.8	18:33									
2003-04	Buffalo	NHL	76	18	35	53	68	5	1	2	152	11.8	8	1491	54.9	18:04									
2004-05			DID NOT PLAY																					
	NHL Totals		470	126	202	328	290	39	2	23	1167	10.8		5863	53.4	17:24	80	26	24	50	22	4	0	11	16:37

Hockey East Second All-Star Team (1996, 1997) • NCAA East Second All-American Team (1996) • Hockey East Player of the Year (1997, 1998) • NCAA East First All-American Team (1997, 1998) • NCAA Championship All-Tournament Team (1997) • Hockey East First All-Star Team (1998) • Hobey Baker Memorial Award (Top U.S. Collegiate Player) (1998) • NHL All-Rookie Team (1999) • Calder Memorial Trophy (1999)

Diamond (♦) indicates member of Stanley Cup-winning team.

Asterisk (*) indicates league leader in this statistical category.

Indicates that player did not participate in a professional, junior or college league for an entire season.

All-Star Team selections and awards are listed below player's year-by-year data.

NHL All-Star Game appearances are listed above trade notes.

Pronunciation of Player Names

United Press International phonetic style.

AY	long A as in mate
A	short A as in cat
AI	nasal A as on air
AH	short A as in father
AW	broad A as in talk
EE	long E as in meat
EH	short E as in get
UH	hollow E as in the
AY	French long E with acute accent as in Pathe
IH	middle E as in pretty
EW	EW dipthong as in few
IGH	long I as in time
EE	French long I as in machine
IH	short I as in pity
OH	long O as in note
AH	short O as in hot
AW	broad O as in fought
OI	OI dipthong as in noise
OO	long double OO as in fool
U	short double O as in foot
OW	OW dipthong as in how
EW	long U as in mule
OO	long U as in rule
U	middle U as in put
UH	short U as in shut or hurt
K	hard C as in cat
S	soft C as in cease
SH	soft CH as in machine
CH	hard CH or TCH as in catch
Z	hard S as in bells
S	soft S as in sun
G	hard G as in gang
J	soft G as in general
ZH	soft J as in French version of Joliet
KH	gutteral CH as in Scottish version of Loch

Trade and free agent signing dates are based on when the player's contract is filed with NHL Central Registry. This date often differs from the date when the club announces that it has made a trade or come to terms with a free agent.

All trades, free agent signings and other transactions involving NHL clubs are listed in chronological order. First draft selection for players who re-enter the NHL Entry Draft is noted here. Other special notes are also listed here. These are highlighted with a bullet (•).

THIS **74**TH EDITION OF THE *NHL Official Guide & Record Book* is the seventh to include additional statistical categories for forwards and defensemen in the National Hockey League. These categories are, from left to right in the sample panel above, power-play goals (PP), shorthand goals (SH), game-winning goals (GW), shots on goal (S), percentage of shots that score (%), plus-minus rating (+/–), total faceoffs taken (TF), faceoff winning percentage (F%), and average time-on-ice per game played (Min).

To integrate this data, the Player Register has been is split into two sections. The Prospect Register presents data on players who have yet to play in the NHL. The NHL Player Register, containing more information and a photo of each player, lists all active players who have appeared in an NHL regular-season or playoff game at any time.

Goaltenders, whether prospects or active NHLers, are included in one register.

Registers (with their starting page) are presented in the following order: Prospects (279), NHL Players (367), Goaltenders (605), Retired Players (630) and Retired Goaltenders (665).

League abbreviations, page 365

Late additions to the Registers, page 366.

Some information is unavailable at press time. Readers are encouraged to contribute. See page 5 for contact names and addresses.

2005-06 Prospect Register

Note: The 2005-06 Prospect Register lists forwards and defensemen only. Goaltenders are listed separately. The Prospect Register lists every player drafted in the 2005 Entry Draft, players on NHL Reserve Lists and other players who have not yet played in the NHL. Trades and roster changes are current as of September 6, 2005.

Abbreviations: A – assists; **G** – goals; **GP** – games played;
PIM – penalties in minutes; **Pts** – points; ***** – league-leading total.

NHL Player Register begins on page 367.
Goaltender Register begins on page 605.
League Abbreviations are listed on page 365.

AALTONEN, Juhamatti   (AL-toh-nehn, YOO-haw-MAH-tee)   **ST.L.**

Right wing. Shoots right. 5'11", 163 lbs.   Born, Ii, Finland, June 4, 1985.
(St. Louis' 12th choice, 284th overall, in 2003 Entry Draft).

			Regular Season					Playoffs				
Season	Club	League	GP	G	A	Pts	PIM	GP	G	A	Pts	PIM
2001-02	Karpat Oulu U18	Fin-U18	23	9	11	20	28	2	0	0	0	0
2002-03	Karpat Oulu Jr.	Finland-Jr.	33	9	16	25	8	1	0	0	0	7
	Karpat Oulu U18	Fin-U18	2	5	1	6	6	....	....	....	....	....
	Karpat Oulu	Finland	1	0	0	0	0	....	....	....	....	....
2003-04	Karpat Oulu Jr.	Finland-Jr.	32	30	15	45	32	3	1	0	1	2
	Karpat Oulu	Finland	8	0	0	0	2	....	....	....	....	....
2004-05	Karpat Oulu	Finland	6	0	0	0	0	....	....	....	....	....
	Karpat Oulu Jr.	Finland-Jr.	34	27	23	50	38	5	0	2	2	22

ABDELKADER, Justin   (abdehl-KAY-durh, JUHS-tihn)   **DET.**

Left wing. Shoots left. 6'1", 195 lbs.   Born, Muskegon, MI, February 25, 1987.
(Detroit's 2nd choice, 42nd overall, in 2005 Entry Draft).

			Regular Season					Playoffs				
Season	Club	League	GP	G	A	Pts	PIM	GP	G	A	Pts	PIM
2003-04	Muskegon M.S.	High-MI	28	37	43	80	....	....	....	....	....	....
2004-05	Cedar Rapids	USHL	60	27	25	52	86	11	0	4	4	8

Signed Letter of Intent to attend **Michigan State** (CCHA) in fall of 2005.

AIELLO, Anthony   (igh-EHL-oh, AN-thu-nee)   **MIN.**

Defense. Shoots left. 6'1", 187 lbs.   Born, Braintree, MA, May 19, 1986.
(Minnesota's 6th choice, 129th overall, in 2005 Entry Draft).

			Regular Season					Playoffs				
Season	Club	League	GP	G	A	Pts	PIM	GP	G	A	Pts	PIM
2003-04	Thayer Academy	High-MA	33	11	26	37	....	....	....	....	....	....
2004-05	Thayer Academy	High-MA	30	7	27	34	42	....	....	....	....	....

Signed Letter of Intent to attend **Boston College** (H-East) in fall of 2005.

AKKANEN, Karri   (ah-KAHN-uhn, KAH-ree)   **T.B.**

Center. Shoots right. 6'6", 200 lbs.   Born, Tampere, Finland, January 29, 1984.
(Tampa Bay's 6th choice, 174th overall, in 2002 Entry Draft).

			Regular Season					Playoffs				
Season	Club	League	GP	G	A	Pts	PIM	GP	G	A	Pts	PIM
2000-01	Ilves Tampere U18	Fin-U18	32	5	10	15	20	....	....	....	....	....
2001-02	Ilves Tampere U18	Fin-U18	15	6	6	12	30	4	0	1	1	4
	Ilves Tampere Jr.	Finland-Jr.	5	0	1	1	4	....	....	....	....	....
2002-03	Ilves Tampere	Finland	21	0	1	1	0	....	....	....	....	....
	Ilves Tampere U18	Fin-U18	11	1	6	7	65	....	....	....	....	....
	Ilves Tampere Jr.	Finland-Jr.	13	6	14	20	16	....	....	....	....	....
2003-04	Ilves Tampere Jr.	Finland-Jr.	4	0	1	1	22	....	....	....	....	....
	Tappara Jr.	Finland-Jr.	31	4	8	12	58	14	4	3	7	16
2004-05	Tappara Jr.	Finland-Jr.	29	6	6	12	42	4	0	0	0	16

ALBERTS, Andrew   (AL-buhrts, AN-droo)   **BOS.**

Defense. Shoots left. 6'4", 218 lbs.   Born, Minneapolis, MN, June 30, 1981.
(Boston's 5th choice, 179th overall, in 2001 Entry Draft).

			Regular Season					Playoffs				
Season	Club	League	GP	G	A	Pts	PIM	GP	G	A	Pts	PIM
1998-99	Benide	High-MN	26	10	25	35	....	....	....	....	....	....
99-2000	Waterloo	USHL	49	2	2	4	55	4	0	0	0	12
2000-01	Waterloo	USHL	54	4	10	14	128	....	....	....	....	....
2001-02	Boston College	H-East	38	2	10	12	52	....	....	....	....	....
2002-03	Boston College	H-East	39	6	16	22	60	....	....	....	....	....
2003-04	Boston College	H-East	42	4	12	16	64	....	....	....	....	....
2004-05	Boston College	H-East	30	4	12	16	67	....	....	....	....	....
	Providence Bruins	AHL	8	0	0	0	16	16	1	4	5	40

Hockey East Second All-Star Team (2004) • NCAA East First All-American Team (2004, 2005) • Hockey East First All-Star Team (2005)

ALEN, Juha   (AL-ehn, YOO-haw)   **ANA.**

Defense. Shoots left. 6'3", 218 lbs.   Born, Tampere, Finland, October 25, 1981.
(Anaheim's 4th choice, 90th overall, in 2003 Entry Draft).

			Regular Season					Playoffs				
Season	Club	League	GP	G	A	Pts	PIM	GP	G	A	Pts	PIM
1998-99	KooVee Jr.	Finland-Jr.	36	6	7	13	42	....	....	....	....	....
99-2000	KooVee Jr.	Finland-Jr.	22	2	4	6	28	....	....	....	....	....
2000-01	Ilves Tampere Jr.	Finland-Jr.	42	2	12	14	62	....	....	....	....	....
2001-02	Soo Indians	NAHL	54	10	10	20	46	2	0	1	1	0
2002-03	Northern Mich.	CCHA	40	4	19	23	64	....	....	....	....	....
2003-04	Cincinnati	AHL	59	2	3	5	64	9	0	0	0	14
2004-05	Ilves Tampere	Finland	7	0	0	0	16	2	0	0	0	0

• Missed majority of 2004-05 season recovering from off-season foot injury.

ALEXANDROV, Viktor   (al-ehx-AN-drawv, VIHK-tohr)   **ST.L.**

Left wing. Shoots left. 5'11", 183 lbs.   Born, Ust-Kamenogorsk, USSR, December 28, 1985.
(St. Louis' 3rd choice, 83rd overall, in 2004 Entry Draft).

			Regular Season					Playoffs				
Season	Club	League	GP	G	A	Pts	PIM	GP	G	A	Pts	PIM
2001-02	Ust-Kamenogorsk	Russia-2	45	12	17	29	48	2	0	1	1	2
2002-03	Yaroslavl	Russia	2	0	0	0	2	....	....	....	....	....
	Energiya Kemerovo	Russia-2	15	2	4	6	12	....	....	....	....	....
	Novokuznetsk	Russia	11	0	0	0	4	....	....	....	....	....
2003-04	Novokuznetsk	Russia	57	5	4	9	26	4	1	1	2	4
2004-05	Novokuznetsk	Russia	50	8	10	18	16	4	1	1	2	0

ALMTORP, Jonas   (AHLM-tohrp, YOH-nuhs)   **EDM.**

Center. Shoots left. 6'1", 190 lbs.   Born, Uppsala, Sweden, November 17, 1983.
(Edmonton's 7th choice, 111th overall, in 2002 Entry Draft).

			Regular Season					Playoffs				
Season	Club	League	GP	G	A	Pts	PIM	GP	G	A	Pts	PIM
99-2000	MoDo U18	Swe-U18	22	*19	12	31	*55	....	....	....	....	....
	Malmo Jr.	Swe-Jr.	7	1	0	1	0	....	....	....	....	....
2000-01	MoDo U18	Swe-U18	12	11	1	12	30	....	....	....	....	....
	Malmo Jr.	Swe-Jr.	27	19	7	26	38	7	6	1	7	10
2001-02	MODO	Sweden	3	0	0	0	0	....	....	....	....	....
	Malmo Jr.	Swe-Jr.	37	26	18	44	102	2	1	1	2	4
2002-03	MODO	Sweden	28	1	1	2	22	....	....	....	....	....
	Ornskoldsviks SK	Sweden-2	12	5	4	9	49	....	....	....	....	....
	Malmo Jr.	Swe-Jr.	5	2	2	4	12	....	....	....	....	....
2003-04	Sundsvall	Sweden-2	32	9	9	18	65	3	0	0	0	0
	MODO	Sweden	20	0	0	0	4	....	....	....	....	....
	Malmo Jr.	Swe-Jr.	3	0	0	0	14	....	....	....	....	....
2004-05	Brynas IF Gavle	Sweden	3	0	0	0	0	....	....	....	....	....
	Almtuna	Sweden-2	44	16	20	36	56	3	0	3	3	2

ALTAREV, Dmitri   (al-ta-REHV, dih-MEE-tree)   **NYI**

Left wing. Shoots left. 6'3", 191 lbs.   Born, Penza, USSR, August 12, 1980.
(NY Islanders' 8th choice, 264th overall, in 2000 Entry Draft).

			Regular Season					Playoffs				
Season	Club	League	GP	G	A	Pts	PIM	GP	G	A	Pts	PIM
1997-98	Dizelist Penza 2	Russia-3	57	15	8	23	83	....	....	....	....	....
1998-99	Dizelist Penza 2	Russia-4	35	4	3	7	30	....	....	....	....	....
	Dizelist Penza	Russia-2	6	2	0	2	8	....	....	....	....	....
99-2000	Dizelist Penza 2	Russia-3	44	10	8	18	25	....	....	....	....	....
2000-01	Nizhny Novgorod	Russia	36	1	2	3	26	....	....	....	....	....
2001-02	Nizh. Novgorod 2	Russia-3	10	5	6	11	12	....	....	....	....	....
	Nizhny Novgorod	Russia	32	2	3	5	42	....	....	....	....	....
2002-03	Dizel Penza	Russia-3	47	22	26	48	106	....	....	....	....	....
2003-04	Dizel Penza	Russia-2	56	19	20	39	86	4	1	0	1	8
2004-05	Dizel Penza	Russia-2	52	13	11	24	72	4	1	0	1	8

ANDERSON, R.J.   (AN-duhr-suhn, AHR-JAY)   **PHI.**

Defense. Shoots right. 5'11", 180 lbs.   Born, Maple Wood, MN, July 16, 1986.
(Philadelphia's 2nd choice, 101st overall, in 2004 Entry Draft).

			Regular Season					Playoffs				
Season	Club	League	GP	G	A	Pts	PIM	GP	G	A	Pts	PIM
2002-03	Centennial	High-MN	24	6	35	41	10	....	....	....	....	....
2003-04	Centennial	High-MN	30	29	56	85	34	....	....	....	....	....
	Team Northeast	UMEHL	24	9	16	25	....	....	....	....	....	....
2004-05	Centennial	High-MN	28	23	36	59	....	....	....	....	....	....

Signed Letter of Intent to attend **Minnesota** (WCHA), November 18, 2004.

ANDERSSON, Johan (AN-duhr-suhn, YOH-hahn) **CHI.**

Center. Shoots left. 6'1", 201 lbs. Born, Motala, Sweden, May 18, 1984.
(Chicago's 6th choice, 181st overall, in 2003 Entry Draft).

			Regular Season					Playoffs				
Season	Club	League	GP	G	A	Pts	PIM	GP	G	A	Pts	PIM
2000-01	IF Troja-Ljungby	Sweden-2	3	0	0	0	0	....	....	....	....	....
2001-02	IF Troja-Ljungby	Sweden-2	42	2	0	2	10	5	2	0	2	2
2002-03	IF Troja-Ljungby	Sweden-2	20	8	4	12	16	....	....	....	....	....
2003-04	IF Troja-Ljungby	Sweden-2	43	13	11	24	94	....	....	....	....	....
2004-05	Linkopings HC Jr.	Swe-Jr.	2	0	2	2	4	....	....	....	....	....
	IF Troja-Ljungby	Sweden-2	21	6	5	11	37	....	....	....	....	....
	Linkopings HC	Sweden	29	1	2	3	14	4	0	0	0	2

ANGER, Niklas (AN-guhr, NIHK-lahs) **MTL.**

Right wing. Shoots left. 6'1", 185 lbs. Born, Gavle, Sweden, July 31, 1977.
(Montreal's 5th choice, 112th overall, in 1995 Entry Draft).

			Regular Season					Playoffs				
Season	Club	League	GP	G	A	Pts	PIM	GP	G	A	Pts	PIM
1993-94	Djurgarden Jr.	Swe-Jr.	2	0	0	0	0	....	....	....	....	....
1994-95	Djurgarden Jr.	Swe-Jr.	30	14	12	26	26	....	....	....	....	....
	Djurgarden	Sweden	1	0	0	0	0	....	....	....	....	....
1995-96	Djurgarden Jr.	Swe-Jr.	24	13	16	29	26	....	....	....	....	....
	Djurgarden	Sweden	10	0	0	0	2	....	....	....	....	....
1996-97	Djurgarden Jr.	Swe-Jr.	2	1	2	3	0	....	....	....	....	....
	Arlanda HC Marsta	Sweden-2	16	5	9	14	6	....	....	....	....	....
	Linkopings HC	Sweden-2	10	2	2	4	10	14	3	7	10	2
	Djurgarden	Sweden	4	0	0	0	0	....	....	....	....	....
1997-98	Djurgarden	Sweden	45	2	5	7	37	12	0	1	1	2
1998-99	AIK Solna Jr.	Swe-Jr.	1	0	0	0	0	....	....	....	....	....
	AIK Solna	Sweden	47	6	6	12	16	....	....	....	....	....
99-2000	AIK Solna	Sweden	50	11	13	24	14	....	....	....	....	....
2000-01	AIK Solna	Sweden	50	5	10	15	22	5	0	1	1	2
2001-02	AIK Solna	Sweden	50	12	20	32	16	....	....	....	....	....
2002-03	Brynas IF Gavle	Sweden	48	20	12	32	28	....	....	....	....	....
2003-04	Brynas IF Gavle	Sweden	50	11	15	26	26	....	....	....	....	....
2004-05	HC Ambri-Piotta	Swiss	1	1	1	2	0	....	....	....	....	....
	Sierre	Swiss-2	44	25	60	85	28	14	7	13	20	8

ANIKEYENKO, Vitali (ah-nih-KEH-ehn-koh, vih-TAL-ee) **OTT.**

Defense. Shoots right. 6'3", 200 lbs. Born, Kiev, USSR, January 2, 1987.
(Ottawa's 2nd choice, 70th overall, in 2005 Entry Draft).

			Regular Season					Playoffs				
Season	Club	League	GP	G	A	Pts	PIM	GP	G	A	Pts	PIM
2003-04	Yaroslavl 2	Russia-3	40	2	9	11	68	....	....	....	....	....
2004-05	Yaroslavl 2	Russia-3	58	3	11	14	62	....	....	....	....	....

ANSHAKOV, Sergei (an-sha-KAHV, SAIR-gay) **PIT.**

Left wing. Shoots left. 6'3", 179 lbs. Born, Moscow, USSR, January 13, 1984.
(Los Angeles' 2nd choice, 50th overall, in 2002 Entry Draft).

			Regular Season					Playoffs				
Season	Club	League	GP	G	A	Pts	PIM	GP	G	A	Pts	PIM
2000-01	Dyno. Moscow 18	Exhib.	6	7	1	8	2	....	....	....	....	....
2001-02	HK CSKA 2	Russia-3	3	3	1	4	0	....	....	....	....	....
	HK CSKA Moscow	Russia-2	46	20	12	22	10	....	....	....	....	....
2002-03	CSKA Moscow	Russia	25	1	2	3	4	....	....	....	....	....
2003-04	CSKA Moscow	Russia	33	3	2	5	12	....	....	....	....	....
2004-05	CSKA Moscow	Russia	11	0	0	0	2	....	....	....	....	....
	Ufa	Russia	23	9	3	12	4	....	....	....	....	....

Traded to **Pittsburgh** by **Los Angeles** with Martin Strbak for Martin Straka, November 30, 2003. Loaned to **Ufa** (Russia) by **CSKA** (Russia), December 20, 2004.

ANTTILA, Marko (AN-tih-la, MAHR-koh) **CHI.**

Right wing. Shoots right. 6'7", 200 lbs. Born, Lempoala, Finland, March 27, 1985.
(Chicago's 17th choice, 260th overall, in 2004 Entry Draft).

			Regular Season					Playoffs				
Season	Club	League	GP	G	A	Pts	PIM	GP	G	A	Pts	PIM
2003-04	LeKi Lempaala	Finland-Jr.	12	11	11	22	26	....	....	....	....	....
	LeKi Lempaala	Finland-4	22	19	19	38	30	....	....	....	....	....
2004-05	Ilves Tampere Jr.	Finland-Jr.	27	14	6	20	44	9	5	7	12	14
	Ilves Tampere	Finland	28	2	1	3	10	3	0	0	0	0

AQUINO, Luciano (a-KEE-noh, LEW-CHI-a-noh) **NYI**

Center/Left wing. Shoots left. 5'9", 198 lbs. Born, Mississauga, Ont., January 26, 1985.
(NY Islanders' 7th choice, 210th overall, in 2005 Entry Draft).

			Regular Season					Playoffs				
Season	Club	League	GP	G	A	Pts	PIM	GP	G	A	Pts	PIM
2003-04	U. of Maine	H-East	20	4	5	9	8	....	....	....	....	....
2004-05	Brampton	OHL	65	25	46	71	80	....	....	....	....	....

ARCHER, Andrew (AHR-chuhr, AN-droo) **MTL.**

Defense. Shoots right. 6'4", 212 lbs. Born, Calgary, Alta., May 15, 1983.
(Montreal's 7th choice, 203rd overall, in 2001 Entry Draft).

			Regular Season					Playoffs				
Season	Club	League	GP	G	A	Pts	PIM	GP	G	A	Pts	PIM
1998-99	Richmond Hill	OMHA	STATISTICS NOT AVAILABLE									
99-2000	Oshawa Generals	OHL	47	0	1	1	24	3	0	1	1	2
2000-01	Oshawa Generals	OHL	2	0	0	0	4	....	....	....	....	....
	Guelph Storm	OHL	50	0	2	2	59	4	0	0	0	4
2001-02	Guelph Storm	OHL	58	3	10	13	76	9	0	2	2	16
2002-03	Guelph Storm	OHL	65	2	16	18	138	11	2	2	4	18
2003-04	Hamilton Bulldogs	AHL	30	0	1	1	23	3	0	0	0	0
	Columbus	ECHL	6	0	1	1	19	....	....	....	....	....
2004-05	Hamilton Bulldogs	AHL	68	1	10	11	112	3	0	0	0	2

• Missed majority of 2003-04 season recovering from hernia injury suffered in training camp, September 15, 2003.

ARMSTRONG, Colby (AHRM-stawng, KOHL-bee) **PIT.**

Right wing. Shoots right. 6'2", 195 lbs. Born, Lloydminster, Sask., November 23, 1982.
(Pittsburgh's 1st choice, 21st overall, in 2001 Entry Draft).

			Regular Season					Playoffs				
Season	Club	League	GP	G	A	Pts	PIM	GP	G	A	Pts	PIM
1998-99	Sask. Contacts	SMHL	33	21	19	40	103	....	....	....	....	....
	Red Deer Rebels	WHL	1	0	1	1	0	....	....	....	....	....
99-2000	Red Deer Rebels	WHL	68	13	25	38	122	2	0	1	1	11
2000-01	Red Deer Rebels	WHL	72	36	42	78	156	21	6	6	12	29
2001-02	Red Deer Rebels	WHL	64	27	41	68	115	23	6	10	16	32
2002-03	Wilkes-Barre	AHL	73	7	11	18	76	3	0	0	0	4
2003-04	Wilkes-Barre	AHL	67	10	17	27	71	24	3	1	4	45
2004-05	Wilkes-Barre	AHL	80	18	37	55	89	10	4	2	6	14

ARMSTRONG, Riley (AHRM-strawng, RIGH-lee) **S.J.**

Right wing. Shoots right. 5'11", 185 lbs. Born, Saskatoon, Sask., November 8, 1984.

			Regular Season					Playoffs				
Season	Club	League	GP	G	A	Pts	PIM	GP	G	A	Pts	PIM
2001-02	Yorkton Terriers	SMHL	42	43	34	77	....	....	....	....	....	....
2002-03	Kootenay Ice	WHL	65	6	10	16	69	10	0	1	1	14
2003-04	Everett Silvertips	WHL	69	18	26	44	119	21	5	4	9	46
2004-05	Cleveland Barons	AHL	70	8	11	19	117	....	....	....	....	....

Signed as a free agent by **San Jose**, September 15, 2004.

ARTEMENKOV, Yuri (ahr-TUH-mehn-kahv, YOO-ree) **CGY.**

Right wing. Shoots left. 6'1", 174 lbs. Born, Moscow, USSR, February 3, 1984.
(Calgary's 4th choice, 112th overall, in 2002 Entry Draft).

			Regular Season					Playoffs				
Season	Club	League	GP	G	A	Pts	PIM	GP	G	A	Pts	PIM
99-2000	Russia	Nat-Tm	5	1	1	2	0	....	....	....	....	....
2000-01	Krylja Sovetov 2	Russia-3	2	0	0	0	4	....	....	....	....	....
2001-02	Krylja Sovetov 2	Russia-3	32	24	15	42	10	....	....	....	....	....
2002-03	Krylja Sovetov	Russia	3	0	0	0	0	....	....	....	....	....
	Krylja Sovetov 2	Russia-3	7	2	2	4	12	....	....	....	....	....
	Kirovo-Chepetsk	Russia-2	1	0	0	0	0	....	....	....	....	....
2003-04	Krylja Sovetov	Russia-2	27	3	1	4	6	....	....	....	....	....
2004-05	Krylja Sovetov 2	Russia-3	36	15	8	23	18	....	....	....	....	....
	HK Tver	Russia-3	STATISTICS NOT AVAILABLE									

ARTYUKHIN, Evgeni (ahr-TYEW-khin, yehv-GEH-nee) **T.B.**

Right wing. Shoots left. 6'5", 254 lbs. Born, Moscow, USSR, April 4, 1983.
(Tampa Bay's 4th choice, 94th overall, in 2001 Entry Draft).

			Regular Season					Playoffs				
Season	Club	League	GP	G	A	Pts	PIM	GP	G	A	Pts	PIM
99-2000	Vityaz Podolsk 2	Russia-3	26	9	8	17	46	....	....	....	....	....
	Vityaz Podolsk	Russia-2	3	0	0	0	2	....	....	....	....	....
2000-01	Vityaz Podolsk	Russia	24	0	1	1	14	....	....	....	....	....
2001-02	Vityaz Podolsk 2	Russia-3	4	3	1	4	6	....	....	....	....	....
	Vityaz Podolsk	Russia-2	49	15	7	22	94	12	0	1	1	18
2002-03	Moncton Wildcats	QMJHL	53	13	27	40	204	6	1	2	3	29
2003-04	Hershey Bears	AHL	36	3	3	6	111	....	....	....	....	....
	Pensacola	ECHL	6	1	0	1	14	....	....	....	....	....
2004-05	Springfield Falcons	AHL	62	9	19	28	142	....	....	....	....	....

ASLUND, Calle (AZ-luhnd, KAL-ee) **BUF.**

Defense. Shoots left. 6'2", 198 lbs. Born, Haninge, Sweden, March 29, 1983.
(Buffalo's 6th choice, 234th overall, in 2001 Entry Draft).

			Regular Season					Playoffs				
Season	Club	League	GP	G	A	Pts	PIM	GP	G	A	Pts	PIM
99-2000	Huddinge IK U18	Swe-U18	17	1	5	6	48	....	....	....	....	....
2000-01	Huddinge IK U18	Swe-U18	8	1	3	4	30	....	....	....	....	....
	Huddinge IK Jr.	Swe-Jr.	7	0	1	1	14	....	....	....	....	....
2001-02	Huddinge IK Jr.	Swe-Jr.	27	1	6	7	66	....	....	....	....	....
	Huddinge IK	Sweden-2	26	0	0	0	47	....	....	....	....	....
2002-03	Huddinge IK Jr.	Swe-Jr.	5	0	2	2	16	3	0	0	0	25
	Huddinge IK	Sweden-2	37	3	3	6	66	2	0	0	0	6
2003-04	Huddinge IK	Sweden-2	46	1	1	2	123	....	....	....	....	....
	Huddinge IK Jr.	Swe-Jr.	1	0	1	1	2	....	....	....	....	....
2004-05	Rio Grande	CHL	59	1	5	6	89	....	....	....	....	....

Signed as a free agent by **Rio Grande** (CHL), October 27, 2004.

ATHERTON, P.J. (A-thur-tuhn, PEE-JAY) **T.B.**

Defense. Shoots right. 6'2", 208 lbs. Born, Edina, MN, August 16, 1982.
(Tampa Bay's 5th choice, 170th overall, in 2002 Entry Draft).

			Regular Season					Playoffs				
Season	Club	League	GP	G	A	Pts	PIM	GP	G	A	Pts	PIM
99-2000	Edina Hornets	High-MN	38	7	15	22	....	....	....	....	....	....
	Cedar Rapids	USHL	5	0	1	1	4	....	....	....	....	....
2000-01	Cedar Rapids	USHL	43	4	9	13	99	4	2	0	2	10
2001-02	Cedar Rapids	USHL	51	7	22	29	101	8	0	0	0	14
2002-03	U. of Minnesota	WCHA	20	2	2	4	20	....	....	....	....	....
2003-04	U. of Minnesota	WCHA	28	0	2	2	36	....	....	....	....	....
2004-05	U. of Minnesota	WCHA	17	2	2	4	22	....	....	....	....	....

ATYUSHOV, Vitali (a-tew-SHAWF, vih-TAL-ee) **OTT.**

Defense. Shoots left. 6'1", 205 lbs. Born, Penza, USSR, July 4, 1979.
(Ottawa's 8th choice, 276th overall, in 2002 Entry Draft).

			Regular Season					Playoffs				
Season	Club	League	GP	G	A	Pts	PIM	GP	G	A	Pts	PIM
1997-98	Krylja Sovetov	Russia	4	0	0	0	2	....	....	....	....	....
1998-99	Dizelist Penza 2	Russia-4	2	1	1	2	2	....	....	....	....	....
	Dizelist Penza	Russia-2	22	0	0	0	22	....	....	....	....	....
	Krylja Sovetov	Russia	17	1	0	1	20	....	....	....	....	....
	Krylja Sovetov	Russia-Q	21	0	5	5	50	....	....	....	....	....
99-2000	Perm	Russia	38	4	0	4	50	3	0	0	0	12
2000-01	Perm	Russia	44	3	9	12	32	....	....	....	....	....
2001-02	Perm	Russia	51	4	8	12	66	....	....	....	....	....
2002-03	Ak Bars Kazan	Russia	33	0	9	9	12	2	0	0	0	0
2003-04	Magnitogorsk	Russia	56	5	9	14	26	14	2	3	5	6
2004-05	Magnitogorsk	Russia	58	6	18	24	42	5	2	0	2	0

AUBIN, Mathieu (oh-BEHN, MAT-yew) **MTL.**

Center. Shoots right. 6'2", 190 lbs. Born, Sorel, Que., September 18, 1986.
(Montreal's 4th choice, 130th overall, in 2005 Entry Draft).

			Regular Season					Playoffs				
Season	Club	League	GP	G	A	Pts	PIM	GP	G	A	Pts	PIM
2001-02	Antoine-Girouard	QAAA	19	5	10	15	10	....	....	....	....	....
2002-03	Antoine-Girouard	QAAA	42	19	35	54	28	....	....	....	....	....
	Sherbrooke	QMJHL	1	0	0	0	0	....	....	....	....	....
2003-04	Lewiston	QMJHL	68	19	23	42	34	7	1	1	2	2
2004-05	Lewiston	QMJHL	49	19	26	45	24	8	3	6	9	6

AUCOIN, Keith (oh-KOIN, KEETH) CAR.

Center. Shoots right. 5'9", 185 lbs. Born, Waltham, MA, November 6, 1978.

			Regular Season					Playoffs				
Season	Club	League	GP	G	A	Pts	PIM	GP	G	A	Pts	PIM
1997-98	Norwich University	ECAC-3	26	19	14	33	....	....	....	....	....	....
1998-99	Norwich University	ECAC-3	31	33	39	72	....	....	....	....	....	....
99-2000	Norwich University	ECAC-3	31	36	41	77	14	....	....	....	....	....
2000-01	Norwich University	ECAC-3	28	26	30	56	26	....	....	....	....	....
2001-02	Lowell	AHL	30	6	10	16	8	....	....	....	....	....
	Florida Everblades	ECHL	1	0	2	2	0	....	....	....	....	....
	BC Icemen	UHL	44	23	35	58	42	10	3	5	8	4
2002-03	Providence Bruins	AHL	78	25	49	74	71	4	0	1	1	6
2003-04	Cincinnati	AHL	80	18	30	48	64	9	0	3	3	4
2004-05	Memphis	CHL	5	4	5	9	10	....	....	....	....	....
	Providence Bruins	AHL	72	21	45	66	49	17	4	*14	18	18

ECAC-3 First All-Star Team (2000, 2001) • ECAC-3 Player of the Year (2000, 2001)

Signed as a free agent by **Lowell** (AHL), June 19, 2001. Signed as a free agent by **Providence** (AHL), August 2, 2002. Signed as a free agent by **Anaheim**, August 29, 2003. Signed to a PTO (tryout) contract by **Providence** (AHL), November 4, 2004, Signed as a free agent by **Providence** (AHL), December 9, 2004. Signed as a free agent by **Carolina**, August 4, 2005.

AUFFREY, Matt (AWF-ree, MAT) ANA.

Right wing. Shoots right. 6'2", 203 lbs. Born, Cincinnati, OH, January 3, 1986.
(Anaheim's 5th choice, 172nd overall, in 2004 Entry Draft).

			Regular Season					Playoffs				
Season	Club	League	GP	G	A	Pts	PIM	GP	G	A	Pts	PIM
2001-02	Syracuse	OPJHL	....	33	39	72	....	....	....	....	....	....
2002-03	USA U-17	USDP	63	11	18	29	68	....	....	....	....	....
2003-04	USA U-18	USDP	54	14	16	30	....	....	....	....	....	....
2004-05	U. of Wisconsin	WCHA	25	3	5	8	18	....	....	....	....	....

AXELSSON, Anton (AHX-ehl-suhn, AN-tawn) DET.

Left wing. Shoots left. 6', 183 lbs. Born, Ytterby, Sweden, January 16, 1986.
(Detroit's 5th choice, 192nd overall, in 2004 Entry Draft).

			Regular Season					Playoffs				
Season	Club	League	GP	G	A	Pts	PIM	GP	G	A	Pts	PIM
2003-04	V.Frolunda Jr.	Swe-Jr.	28	7	10	17	14	10	2	3	5	2
2004-05	Frolunda Jr.	Swe-Jr.	33	12	30	42	14	6	2	5	7	0

AXELSSON, Emil (AHX-ehl-suhn, eh-MIHL) NYI

Defense. Shoots left. 6'3", 198 lbs. Born, Orebro, Sweden, March 19, 1986.
(NY Islanders' 7th choice, 210th overall, in 2004 Entry Draft).

			Regular Season					Playoffs				
Season	Club	League	GP	G	A	Pts	PIM	GP	G	A	Pts	PIM
2002-03	HC Orebro 90 Jr.	Swe-Jr.	27	7	9	16	2	....	....	....	....	....
2003-04	HC Orebro 90	Sweden-2	49	4	0	4	116	....	....	....	....	....
2004-05	Linkopings HC Jr.	Swe-Jr.	21	0	1	1	32	....	....	....	....	....

BABY, Stephen (BAY-bee, STEE-vehn) ATL.

Right wing. Shoots right. 6'5", 230 lbs. Born, Chicago, IL, January 31, 1980.
(Atlanta's 8th choice, 188th overall, in 1999 Entry Draft).

			Regular Season					Playoffs				
Season	Club	League	GP	G	A	Pts	PIM	GP	G	A	Pts	PIM
1997-98	Green Bay	USHL	56	17	17	34	85	4	1	3	4	8
1998-99	Green Bay	USHL	55	23	24	47	83	6	1	1	2	4
99-2000	Cornell Big Red	ECAC	31	4	10	14	52	....	....	....	....	....
2000-01	Cornell Big Red	ECAC	32	8	20	28	47	....	....	....	....	....
2001-02	Cornell Big Red	ECAC	35	9	23	32	42	....	....	....	....	....
2002-03	Cornell Big Red	ECAC	36	8	*33	41	60	....	....	....	....	....
2003-04	Chicago Wolves	AHL	68	14	12	26	72	10	1	4	5	6
2004-05	Chicago Wolves	AHL	64	6	3	9	115	6	0	0	0	12

ECAC Second All-Star Team (2002, 2003) • NCAA East Second All-American Team (2003)

BACKER, Per (BAK-uhr, PAIR) DET.

Right wing. Shoots left. 6'1", 161 lbs. Born, Grums, Sweden, January 4, 1982.
(Detroit's 7th choice, 187th overall, in 2000 Entry Draft).

			Regular Season					Playoffs				
Season	Club	League	GP	G	A	Pts	PIM	GP	G	A	Pts	PIM
1998-99	Grums IK	Sweden-2	17	1	1	2	4	....	....	....	....	....
99-2000	Grums IK	Sweden-2	46	12	10	22	24	....	....	....	....	....
2000-01	Bofors	Sweden-2	27	9	10	19	10	....	....	....	....	....
2001-02	Farjestad	Sweden	47	4	8	12	12	10	5	1	6	10
2002-03	Farjestad	Sweden	49	11	16	27	46	12	1	1	2	12
2003-04	Farjestad	Sweden	49	7	6	13	24	17	0	0	0	8
2004-05	Farjestad	Sweden	49	3	3	6	18	15	1	1	2	2

BACKES, David (BA-kuhs, DAY-vihd) ST.L.

Center. Shoots right. 6'2", 200 lbs. Born, Blaine, MN, May 1, 1984.
(St. Louis' 2nd choice, 62nd overall, in 2003 Entry Draft).

			Regular Season					Playoffs				
Season	Club	League	GP	G	A	Pts	PIM	GP	G	A	Pts	PIM
99-2000	Spring Lake Park	High-MN	24	17	20	37	....	....	....	....	....	....
2000-01	Spring Lake Park	High-MN	24	29	46	75	....	....	....	....	....	....
2001-02	Chicago Steel	USHL	25	31	36	67	....	2	1	1	2	....
	Lincoln Stars	USHL	30	11	10	21	54	3	0	0	0	2
2002-03	Lincoln Stars	USHL	57	28	41	69	126	7	4	1	5	17
2003-04	Minnesota State	WCHA	39	16	21	37	66	....	....	....	....	....
2004-05	Minnesota State	WCHA	38	17	23	40	55	....	....	....	....	....

USHL First All-Star Team (2003) • WCHA All-Rookie Team (2004)

BACKSTROM, Nils (BAK-struhm, NIHLS) DET.

Defense. Shoots right. 6', 183 lbs. Born, Stockholm, Sweden, June 29, 1986.
(Detroit's 8th choice, 290th overall, in 2004 Entry Draft).

			Regular Season					Playoffs				
Season	Club	League	GP	G	A	Pts	PIM	GP	G	A	Pts	PIM
2003-04	Stocksund Jr.	Swe-Jr.	12	1	6	7	26	....	....	....	....	....
2004-05	Djurgarden Jr.	Swe-Jr.	31	0	5	5	75	....	....	....	....	....

BAGNALL, Drew (BAG-nuhl, DROO) FLA.

Defense. Shoots left. 6'3", 205 lbs. Born, Oakbank, Man., October 26, 1983.
(Dallas' 9th choice, 195th overall, in 2003 Entry Draft).

			Regular Season					Playoffs				
Season	Club	League	GP	G	A	Pts	PIM	GP	G	A	Pts	PIM
2000-01	Battlefords	SJHL	58	7	20	27	205	....	....	....	....	....
2001-02	Battlefords	SJHL	60	16	23	39	247	....	....	....	....	....
2002-03	Battlefords	SJHL	55	17	46	63	248	4	0	1	1	4
2003-04	St. Lawrence	ECAC	40	5	13	18	61	....	....	....	....	....
2004-05	St. Lawrence	ECAC	37	7	12	19	68	....	....	....	....	....

Traded to **Florida** by **Dallas** with Dallas' 2nd round compensatory choice (later traded to Phoenix - Phoenix selected Enver Lisin) in 2004 Entry Draft for Valeri Bure, March 8, 2004.

BAHENSKY, Zdenek (ba-HEHN-skee, z'DEHN-ehk) NYR

Right wing. Shoots left. 6'2", 195 lbs. Born, Most, Czech., January 3, 1986.
(NY Rangers' 7th choice, 73rd overall, in 2004 Entry Draft).

			Regular Season					Playoffs				
Season	Club	League	GP	G	A	Pts	PIM	GP	G	A	Pts	PIM
2001-02	Litvinov U17	CzR-U17	46	16	17	33	102	2	0	0	0	0
2002-03	Litvinov U17	CzR-U17	3	2	3	5	4	....	....	....	....	....
	Litvinov Jr.	CzRep-Jr.	31	4	2	6	8	....	....	....	....	....
2003-04	Litvinov Jr.	CzRep-Jr.	52	14	15	29	204	2	1	1	2	14
2004-05	Saskatoon Blades	WHL	66	14	17	31	101	4	0	0	0	2

BAIER, Paul (BAI-uhr, PAWL) L.A.

Defense. Shoots right. 6'3", 212 lbs. Born, Summit, NJ, February 2, 1985.
(Los Angeles' 2nd choice, 95th overall, in 2004 Entry Draft).

			Regular Season					Playoffs				
Season	Club	League	GP	G	A	Pts	PIM	GP	G	A	Pts	PIM
2002-03	Deerfield Academy	High-MA	25	2	15	17	24	....	....	....	....	....
2003-04	Deerfield Academy	High-MA	23	6	4	10	22	....	....	....	....	....
2004-05	Brown U.	ECAC	32	2	8	10	24	....	....	....	....	....

BAILEY, Jason (BAY-lee, JAY-sohn) ANA.

Right wing. Shoots right. 6', 205 lbs. Born, Ottawa, Ont., June 4, 1987.
(Anaheim's 3rd choice, 63rd overall, in 2005 Entry Draft).

			Regular Season					Playoffs				
Season	Club	League	GP	G	A	Pts	PIM	GP	G	A	Pts	PIM
2003-04	Nepean Raiders	CJHL	45	14	14	28	119	18	2	7	9	35
2004-05	USA U-18	USDP	39	5	6	11	141	....	....	....	....	....
	USA U-17&U-18	NAHL	13	2	4	6	50	....	....	....	....	....

Signed Letter of Intent to attend **Michigan** (CCHA), November 22, 2004.

BAILEY, Kyle (BAY-lee, KIGHL) MIN.

Center. Shoots right. 6'2", 182 lbs. Born, Ponoka, Alta., October 15, 1986.
(Minnesota's 4th choice, 110th overall, in 2005 Entry Draft).

			Regular Season					Playoffs				
Season	Club	League	GP	G	A	Pts	PIM	GP	G	A	Pts	PIM
2002-03	Leduc Oil Kings	AMHL	35	23	19	42	56	....	....	....	....	....
	Portland	WHL	4	1	1	2	0	6	0	0	0	0
2003-04	Portland	WHL	70	9	15	24	85	5	0	1	1	0
2004-05	Portland	WHL	67	11	22	33	116	7	0	2	2	11

BAINES, Ajay (BAYNZ, AY-JAY) CHI.

Center. Shoots left. 5'10", 179 lbs. Born, Kamloops, B.C., March 25, 1978.

			Regular Season					Playoffs				
Season	Club	League	GP	G	A	Pts	PIM	GP	G	A	Pts	PIM
1994-95	Kamloops	BCAHA	52	45	79	124	139	....	....	....	....	....
1995-96	Kamloops Blazers	WHL	68	14	29	43	43	....	....	....	....	....
1996-97	Kamloops Blazers	WHL	70	32	43	75	106	5	4	1	5	6
1997-98	Kamloops Blazers	WHL	72	34	25	59	88	....	....	....	....	....
1998-99	Kamloops Blazers	WHL	72	33	32	65	145	15	7	6	13	20
99-2000	Greenville Grrrowl	ECHL	67	24	31	55	102	15	2	5	7	13
2000-01	Norfolk Admirals	AHL	73	18	18	36	92	9	0	1	1	2
2001-02	Norfolk Admirals	AHL	80	16	28	44	70	4	0	1	1	0
2002-03	Norfolk Admirals	AHL	74	8	14	22	108	9	2	1	3	18
2003-04	Norfolk Admirals	AHL	80	15	27	42	81	8	1	3	4	13
2004-05	Norfolk Admirals	AHL	70	7	16	23	60	6	3	2	5	16

Signed as a free agent by **Chicago**, August 1, 2001.

BALAN, Stanislav (BAY-luhn, STAN-ihs-lahv) NSH.

Center. Shoots left. 6'2", 161 lbs. Born, Hodonin, Czech., January 30, 1986.
(Nashville's 8th choice, 209th overall, in 2004 Entry Draft).

			Regular Season					Playoffs				
Season	Club	League	GP	G	A	Pts	PIM	GP	G	A	Pts	PIM
2001-02	HC Zlin Jr.	CzRep-Jr.	48	21	23	44	60	4	1	1	2	0
2002-03	HC Zlin Jr.	CzRep-Jr.	35	24	21	45	59	3	2	0	2	16
2003-04	HC Zlin Jr.	CzRep-Jr.	53	23	33	56	122	5	2	0	2	31
	HC Hame Zlin	CzRep	4	1	0	1	2	....	....	....	....	....
2004-05	SHK Hodonin	CzRep-3	5	3	2	5	20	....	....	....	....	....
	HC Zlin Jr.	CzRep-Jr.	37	10	13	23	131	2	0	0	0	2

BALASTIK, Jaroslav (ba-LASH-tihk, YAHR-roh-slav) CBJ

Right wing. Shoots left. 6', 198 lbs. Born, Gottwaldov, Czech., November 28, 1979.
(Columbus' 9th choice, 184th overall, in 2002 Entry Draft).

			Regular Season					Playoffs				
Season	Club	League	GP	G	A	Pts	PIM	GP	G	A	Pts	PIM
1996-97	AC ZPS Zlin Jr.	CzRep-Jr.	45	27	24	51	....	....	....	....	....	....
1997-98	HC ZPS Zlin Jr.	CzRep-Jr.	36	21	35	56	....	7	2	3	5	....
	HC ZPS Barum Zlin	CzRep	6	0	2	2	....	....	....	....	....	....
1998-99	HC ZPS Zlin Jr.	CzRep-Jr.	....	....	....	....	....	2	0	0	0	....
	HC ZPS Barum Zlin	CzRep	41	4	8	12	12	9	1	0	1	27
99-2000	HC Zlin Jr.	CzRep-Jr.	4	5	5	10	2	....	....	....	....	....
	Zlin	CzRep	48	7	10	17	0	4	0	1	1	2
2000-01	Zlin	CzRep	52	8	17	25	32	6	1	1	2	6
2001-02	Zlin	CzRep	50	25	19	44	32	11	3	5	8	14
2002-03	HC Hame Zlin	CzRep	31	14	8	22	26	....	....	....	....	....
	HPK Hameenlinna	Finland	13	5	7	12	2	13	4	3	7	6
2003-04	HC Hame Zlin	CzRep	51	*29	18	47	54	17	*9	9	*18	32
2004-05	HC Hame Zlin	CzRep	52	*30	16	46	74	17	4	9	13	*52

BALDWIN, Gord (BAHLD-wihn, GOHRD) **CGY.**

Defense. Shoots left. 6'5", 205 lbs. Born, Winnipeg, Man., March 1, 1987.
(Calgary's 2nd choice, 69th overall, in 2005 Entry Draft).

			Regular Season					Playoffs				
Season	Club	League	GP	G	A	Pts	PIM	GP	G	A	Pts	PIM
2003-04	Wpg. Thrashers	MMHL	39	5	16	21	66	....	....	....	....	....
2004-05	Medicine Hat	WHL	66	3	8	11	73	....	....	....	....	....

BALLANTYNE, Paul (BAL-uhn-tughn, PAWL)

Defense. Shoots right. 6'3", 200 lbs. Born, Waterloo, Ont., July 16, 1982.
(Detroit's 8th choice, 196th overall, in 2000 Entry Draft).

			Regular Season					Playoffs				
Season	Club	League	GP	G	A	Pts	PIM	GP	G	A	Pts	PIM
1997-98	Waterloo Lions	OMHA	30	4	16	20	55	....	....	....	....	....
	Waterloo Siskins	OHA-B	1	0	0	0	0	....	....	....	....	....
1998-99	Sault Ste. Marie	OHL	53	0	6	6	33	5	1	0	1	4
99-2000	Sault Ste. Marie	OHL	58	4	15	19	60	17	2	3	5	17
2000-01	Sault Ste. Marie	OHL	63	12	28	40	60	....	....	....	....	....
2001-02	Sault Ste. Marie	OHL	68	4	24	28	40	6	1	1	2	8
2002-03	Grand Rapids	AHL	7	0	0	0	8	....	....	....	....	....
	Toledo Storm	ECHL	56	10	16	26	41	7	0	1	1	2
2003-04	Toledo Storm	ECHL	54	13	23	36	20	....	....	....	....	....
	Grand Rapids	AHL	9	1	1	2	6	....	....	....	....	....
	Louisiana	ECHL	3	1	0	1	0	7	1	0	1	0
2004-05	Grand Rapids	AHL	23	0	1	1	10	....	....	....	....	....
	Toledo Storm	ECHL	31	5	10	15	21	4	0	0	0	7

BALLARD, Keith (BAL-uhrd, KEETH) **PHX.**

Defense. Shoots left. 5'11", 208 lbs. Born, Baudette, MN, November 26, 1982.
(Buffalo's 1st choice, 11th overall, in 2002 Entry Draft).

			Regular Season					Playoffs				
Season	Club	League	GP	G	A	Pts	PIM	GP	G	A	Pts	PIM
99-2000	USA U-18	USDP	58	12	21	33	....	....	....	....	....	....
2000-01	Omaha Lancers	USHL	56	22	29	51	168	10	1	6	7	8
2001-02	U. of Minnesota	WCHA	41	10	13	23	42	....	....	....	....	....
2002-03	U. of Minnesota	WCHA	41	12	29	41	78	....	....	....	....	....
2003-04	U. of Minnesota	WCHA	37	11	25	36	83	....	....	....	....	....
2004-05	Utah Grizzlies	AHL	60	2	18	20	88	....	....	....	....	....

USHL First All-Star Team (2001) • WCHA All-Rookie Team (2002) • WCHA First All-Star Team (2003, 2004) • NCAA West First All-American Team (2004)

Traded to **Colorado** by **Buffalo** for Steve Reinprecht, July 3, 2003. Traded to **Phoenix** by **Colorado** with Derek Morris for Ossi Vaananen, Chris Gratton and Phoenix's 2nd round choice (Paul Stastny) in 2005 Entry Draft, March 8, 2004.

BARANKA, Ivan (ba-RAN-kuh, IGH-vuhn) **NYR**

Defense. Shoots left. 6'2", 196 lbs. Born, Ilava, Czech., May 19, 1985.
(NY Rangers' 2nd choice, 50th overall, in 2003 Entry Draft).

			Regular Season					Playoffs				
Season	Club	League	GP	G	A	Pts	PIM	GP	G	A	Pts	PIM
2002-03	Dubnica Jr.	Slovak-Jr.	27	1	7	8	44	....	....	....	....	....
	Dubnica	Slovak-2	2	0	0	0	0	....	....	....	....	....
2003-04	Everett Silvertips	WHL	58	3	12	15	69	20	3	5	8	26
2004-05	Everett Silvertips	WHL	64	7	16	23	64	11	3	1	4	6
	Hartford Wolf Pack	AHL	....	....	....	....	....	1	0	0	0	0

BARANOV, Konstantin (buh-RA-nawf, kawn-stuhn-TEEN) **PHI.**

Right wing. Shoots left. 6'2", 185 lbs. Born, Omsk, USSR, January 11, 1982.
(Philadelphia's 3rd choice, 126th overall, in 2002 Entry Draft).

			Regular Season					Playoffs				
Season	Club	League	GP	G	A	Pts	PIM	GP	G	A	Pts	PIM
1998-99	Omsk 2	Russia-4	23	18	8	26	40	....	....	....	....	....
	Avangard Omsk	Russia	1	0	0	0	0	2	0	0	0	0
99-2000	Omsk 2	Russia-3	33	15	8	23	46	....	....	....	....	....
	Avangard Omsk	Russia	1	0	0	0	2	....	....	....	....	....
2000-01	Kristall Saratov	Russia-2	26	6	9	15	26	....	....	....	....	....
	Ufa	Russia	8	1	0	1	4	....	....	....	....	....
2001-02	Avangard Omsk	Russia	5	0	0	0	6	....	....	....	....	....
	Mechel	Russia	6	1	2	3	2	....	....	....	....	....
	Lada Togliatti	Russia	20	2	4	6	18	3	0	2	2	0
2002-03	Avangard Omsk	Russia	6	0	1	1	2	....	....	....	....	....
	Ufa	Russia	11	2	2	4	0	....	....	....	....	....
	CSKA Moscow	Russia	14	4	1	5	10	....	....	....	....	....
	Omsk 2	Russia-3	3	4	6	10	2	....	....	....	....	....
2003-04	Avangard Omsk	Russia	51	6	10	16	50	11	2	2	4	6
2004-05	Omsk 2	Russia-3	7	5	7	12	20	....	....	....	....	....
	Avangard Omsk	Russia	21	3	2	5	16	....	....	....	....	....

BARARUK, David (BAIR-a-ruhk, DAY-vihd) **DAL.**

Center. Shoots left. 6', 175 lbs. Born, Moose Jaw, Sask., May 26, 1983.
(Dallas' 8th choice, 147th overall, in 2002 Entry Draft).

			Regular Season					Playoffs				
Season	Club	League	GP	G	A	Pts	PIM	GP	G	A	Pts	PIM
99-2000	Moose Jaw	WHL	21	0	2	2	0	2	0	0	0	0
2000-01	Moose Jaw	WHL	53	6	9	15	9	3	0	0	0	0
2001-02	Moose Jaw	WHL	72	33	29	62	31	12	3	2	5	0
2002-03	Moose Jaw	WHL	66	29	64	93	44	13	5	9	14	4
2003-04	Utah Grizzlies	AHL	52	5	7	12	4	....	....	....	....	....
	Idaho Steelheads	ECHL	16	7	8	15	4	15	5	9	14	2
2004-05	Houston Aeros	AHL	15	2	2	4	0	....	....	....	....	....
	Louisiana	ECHL	42	14	22	36	10	....	....	....	....	....
	Idaho Steelheads	ECHL	....	....	....	....	....	4	1	2	3	0

WHL East Second All-Star Team (2003)

BARKER, Cam (BAR-kuhr, KAM) **CHI.**

Defense. Shoots left. 6'3", 213 lbs. Born, Winnipeg, Man., April 4, 1986.
(Chicago's 1st choice, 3rd overall, in 2004 Entry Draft).

			Regular Season					Playoffs				
Season	Club	League	GP	G	A	Pts	PIM	GP	G	A	Pts	PIM
2001-02	Cornwall Colts	CJHL	72	6	23	29	132	....	....	....	....	....
	Medicine Hat	WHL	3	0	1	1	0	....	....	....	....	....
2002-03	Medicine Hat	WHL	64	10	37	47	79	11	3	4	7	17
2003-04	Medicine Hat	WHL	69	21	44	65	105	20	3	9	12	18
2004-05	Medicine Hat	WHL	52	15	33	48	99	12	3	3	6	16

BARNES, Joe (BAHRNZ, JOH) **CAR.**

Center. Shoots left. 6'3", 212 lbs. Born, Winnipeg, Man., June 16, 1986.
(Carolina's 3rd choice, 64th overall, in 2005 Entry Draft).

			Regular Season					Playoffs				
Season	Club	League	GP	G	A	Pts	PIM	GP	G	A	Pts	PIM
2001-02	Winnipeg Sharks	MMHL	STATISTICS NOT AVAILABLE									
	Saskatoon Blades	WHL	1	0	0	0	0	....	....	....	....	....
2002-03	Saskatoon Blades	WHL	54	9	7	16	48	....	....	....	....	....
2003-04	Saskatoon Blades	WHL	58	5	17	22	90	....	....	....	....	....
2004-05	Saskatoon Blades	WHL	72	30	32	62	73	4	0	1	1	0

BARRETT, Nathan (BAIR-uht, NAY-thun)

Center. Shoots left. 6', 189 lbs. Born, Vancouver, B.C., August 3, 1981.
(Vancouver's 6th choice, 241st overall, in 2000 Entry Draft).

			Regular Season					Playoffs				
Season	Club	League	GP	G	A	Pts	PIM	GP	G	A	Pts	PIM
1996-97	Langley Lions	BCAHA	90	107	109	216	96	....	....	....	....	....
1997-98	Tri-City Americans	WHL	47	1	1	2	23	....	....	....	....	....
1998-99	Tri-City Americans	WHL	33	9	9	18	19	....	....	....	....	....
	Lethbridge	WHL	22	12	9	21	19	4	1	0	1	0
99-2000	Lethbridge	WHL	72	44	38	82	38	....	....	....	....	....
2000-01	Lethbridge	WHL	70	46	53	99	66	5	1	1	2	6
2001-02	Lethbridge	WHL	72	45	*62	*107	100	4	0	1	1	6
2002-03	St. John's	AHL	69	9	22	31	35	....	....	....	....	....
2003-04	St. John's	AHL	49	17	21	38	41	....	....	....	....	....
2004-05	St. John's	AHL	61	17	22	39	34	3	0	1	1	0

WHL East Second All-Star Team (2001) • WHL East First All-Star Team (2002)

Signed as a free agent by **Toronto**, July 31, 2002.

BARTANUS, Marek (bahr-TA-nuhs, MAHR-ehk) **T.B.**

Right wing. Shoots right. 6'3", 194 lbs. Born, Liptovsky Mikulas, Czech., February 13, 1987.
(Tampa Bay's 4th choice, 92nd overall, in 2005 Entry Draft).

			Regular Season					Playoffs				
Season	Club	League	GP	G	A	Pts	PIM	GP	G	A	Pts	PIM
2003-04	HC Kosice U18	Svk-U18	4	3	2	5	2	....	....	....	....	....
	HC Kosice Jr.	Slovak-Jr.	41	23	11	34	40	3	1	2	3	8
2004-05	HC Kosice	Slovakia	24	2	1	3	2	....	....	....	....	....
	VTJ Trebisov	Slovak-2	1	0	0	0	0	....	....	....	....	....
	HC Kosice Jr.	Slovak-Jr.	34	14	14	28	99	8	1	1	2	16

BARTHEL, Clayton (bahr-TEHL, KLAY-tuhn) **WSH.**

Defense. Shoots left. 6'2", 205 lbs. Born, Lahr, West Germany, April 2, 1986.
(Washington's 7th choice, 88th overall, in 2004 Entry Draft).

			Regular Season					Playoffs				
Season	Club	League	GP	G	A	Pts	PIM	GP	G	A	Pts	PIM
2001-02	Kelowna AA	BCAHA	40	13	15	28	....	....	....	....	....	....
2002-03	Seattle	WHL	62	1	8	9	48	15	1	1	2	10
2003-04	Seattle	WHL	72	3	14	17	125	....	....	....	....	....
2004-05	Seattle	WHL	68	5	13	18	93	12	1	2	3	16

BARTSCHI, Patrik (BAIRT-chee, PAT-rihk) **PIT.**

Center/Right wing. Shoots right. 6', 199 lbs. Born, Bulach, Switz., August 20, 1984.
(Pittsburgh's 8th choice, 202nd overall, in 2002 Entry Draft).

			Regular Season					Playoffs				
Season	Club	League	GP	G	A	Pts	PIM	GP	G	A	Pts	PIM
99-2000	Kloten Flyers Jr.	Swiss-Jr.	26	12	14	26	14	....	....	....	....	....
2000-01	Kloten Flyers Jr.	Swiss-Jr.	36	38	30	68	14	6	11	3	14	6
	Kloten Flyers	Swiss	2	0	0	0	0	....	....	....	....	....
	HC Thurgau	Swiss-2	1	1	0	1	0	....	....	....	....	....
2001-02	Kloten Flyers Jr.	Swiss-Jr.	9	10	7	17	4	2	3	2	5	2
	Kloten Flyers	Swiss	24	4	4	8	8	11	2	2	4	2
2002-03	Kloten Flyers	Swiss	44	21	16	37	39	5	1	3	4	4
2003-04	Kloten Flyers	Swiss	40	12	24	36	6	....	....	....	....	....
2004-05	Kloten Flyers	Swiss	28	7	8	15	12	5	2	0	2	6

BARTULIS, Oskars (bahr-TEW-lihs, AWHS-kahrs) **PHI.**

Defense. Shoots left. 6'2", 185 lbs. Born, Ogre, Latvia, January 21, 1987.
(Philadelphia's 2nd choice, 91st overall, in 2005 Entry Draft).

			Regular Season					Playoffs				
Season	Club	League	GP	G	A	Pts	PIM	GP	G	A	Pts	PIM
2001-02	Prizma '83 Riga	EEHL-B	3	1	0	1	2	....	....	....	....	....
	Prizma '83 Riga	Latvia	6	0	1	1	2	....	....	....	....	....
2002-03	Prizma '83 Riga	EEHL-B	12	5	5	10	12	....	....	....	....	....
	Vilki Riga	Latvia	....	0	1	1	12	....	....	....	....	....
2003-04	CSKA Moscow 2	Russia-3	65	3	9	12	....	....	....	....	....	....
2004-05	Moncton Wildcats	QMJHL	62	5	19	24	55	12	1	1	2	16

QMJHL All-Rookie Team (2005) • Canadian Major Junior All-Rookie Team (2005)

BASS, Cody (BAS, KOH-dee) **OTT.**

Center. Shoots right. 6', 191 lbs. Born, Owen Sound, Ont., January 7, 1987.
(Ottawa's 3rd choice, 95th overall, in 2005 Entry Draft).

			Regular Season					Playoffs				
Season	Club	League	GP	G	A	Pts	PIM	GP	G	A	Pts	PIM
2003-04	Mississauga	OHL	61	3	7	10	30	24	2	3	5	21
2004-05	Mississauga	OHL	66	11	17	28	103	5	1	1	2	8

BATHE, Landon (BAYTH, LAN-duhn) **PHX.**

Left wing. Shoots left. 6', 218 lbs. Born, Marlton, NJ, April 9, 1982.

			Regular Season					Playoffs				
Season	Club	League	GP	G	A	Pts	PIM	GP	G	A	Pts	PIM
99-2000	Des Moines	USHL	40	2	2	4	117	3	0	1	1	6
2000-01	Danville Wings	NAHL	44	2	7	9	155	....	....	....	....	....
2001-02	Tulsa Crude	USHL	32	4	2	6	180	....	....	....	....	....
2002-03	Milwaukee	AHL	3	0	0	0	6	5	0	0	0	21
	Macon Trax	ACHL	54	12	15	27	207	3	0	0	0	4
2003-04	Milwaukee	AHL	6	0	0	0	22	....	....	....	....	....
	Toledo Storm	ECHL	56	4	6	10	182	....	....	....	....	....
2004-05	Utah Grizzlies	AHL	1	0	0	0	2	....	....	....	....	....
	Idaho Steelheads	ECHL	30	2	4	6	63	....	....	....	....	....

Signed as a free agent by **Phoenix**, September 15, 2004.

BAUM, Dan (BAWM, DAN) **EDM.**

Center. Shoots left. 6'1", 189 lbs. Born, Biggar, Sask., June 4, 1983.
(Edmonton's 8th choice, 215th overall, in 2001 Entry Draft).

			Regular Season					Playoffs				
Season	Club	League	GP	G	A	Pts	PIM	GP	G	A	Pts	PIM
99-2000	Prince George	WHL	55	6	10	16	82	12	1	0	1	19
2000-01	Prince George	WHL	59	9	14	23	169	6	1	2	3	27
2001-02	Prince George	WHL	72	32	35	67	197	6	5	3	8	25
2002-03	Prince George	WHL	72	32	41	73	218	5	2	0	2	9
2003-04	Toronto	AHL	37	4	6	10	154	3	0	1	1	0
	Columbus	ECHL	3	0	0	0	7	....	....	....	....	....
2004-05	Edmonton	AHL	48	3	4	7	206	....	....	....	....	....

BEARSON, Zach (BEER-suhn, ZAK) **FLA.**

Right wing. Shoots right. 6'1", 180 lbs. Born, Houston, TX, June 13, 1987.
(Florida's 8th choice, 224th overall, in 2005 Entry Draft).

			Regular Season					Playoffs				
Season	Club	League	GP	G	A	Pts	PIM	GP	G	A	Pts	PIM
2002-03	Team Illinois	MWEHL	....	21	29	50	....	....	....	....	....	....
2003-04	Waterloo	USHL	53	7	11	18	65	9	4	1	5	12
2004-05	Waterloo	USHL	51	18	18	36	56	5	0	1	1	2

Signed Letter of Intent to attend **Wisconsin** (WCHA), August 29, 2004.

BEAULIEU, Josh (BOI-loh, JAWSH) **PHI.**

Center. Shoots left. 6', 180 lbs. Born, Windsor, Ont., January 10, 1987.
(Philadelphia's 4th choice, 152nd overall, in 2005 Entry Draft).

			Regular Season					Playoffs				
Season	Club	League	GP	G	A	Pts	PIM	GP	G	A	Pts	PIM
2003-04	London Knights	OHL	41	3	6	9	32	9	0	0	0	5
2004-05	London Knights	OHL	65	9	13	22	159	13	2	3	5	13

BEAVERSON, Luke (BEE-vuhr-suhn, LEWK) **FLA.**

Defense. Shoots left. 6'3", 208 lbs. Born, St. Paul, MN, December 11, 1984.
(Florida's 7th choice, 283rd overall, in 2004 Entry Draft).

			Regular Season					Playoffs				
Season	Club	League	GP	G	A	Pts	PIM	GP	G	A	Pts	PIM
2003-04	Green Bay	USHL	57	1	6	7	141	....	....	....	....	....
2004-05	Alaska-Anchorage	WCHA	37	0	2	2	48	....	....	....	....	....

BECKETT, Jason (BEH-keht, JAY-suhn)

Defense. Shoots right. 6'3", 218 lbs. Born, Lethbridge, Alta., July 23, 1980.
(Philadelphia's 2nd choice, 42nd overall, in 1998 Entry Draft).

			Regular Season					Playoffs				
Season	Club	League	GP	G	A	Pts	PIM	GP	G	A	Pts	PIM
1997-98	Seattle	WHL	71	1	11	12	241	5	0	0	0	16
1998-99	Seattle	WHL	70	4	26	30	195	11	0	1	1	40
99-2000	Seattle	WHL	70	3	15	18	183	7	1	1	2	12
2000-01	Trenton Titans	ECHL	17	2	2	4	24	15	0	1	1	26
	Philadelphia	AHL	56	2	10	12	107	....	....	....	....	....
2001-02	Philadelphia	AHL	9	0	0	0	11	....	....	....	....	....
	Milwaukee	AHL	28	2	4	6	56	....	....	....	....	....
	Trenton Titans	ECHL	14	1	1	2	49	3	0	0	0	4
2002-03	Milwaukee	AHL	64	2	10	12	130	6	0	1	1	12
2003-04	Houston Aeros	AHL	72	4	7	11	168	2	0	0	0	7
2004-05	Syracuse Crunch	AHL	5	0	0	0	6	....	....	....	....	....
	Pensacola	ECHL	64	10	17	27	140	4	0	0	0	10

Traded to **Nashville** by **Philadelphia** with Petr Hubacek for Yves Sarault, January 11, 2002. Signed as a free agent by **Minnesota**, August 6, 2003. Loaned to **Syracuse** (AHL) by **Houston** (AHL) for the loan of Jeremy Reich, March 10, 2005.

BELAK, Graham (BEE-lak, GRAY-ham)

Left wing. Shoots left. 6'5", 230 lbs. Born, Saskatoon, Sask., August 1, 1979.
(Colorado's 2nd choice, 53rd overall, in 1997 Entry Draft).

			Regular Season					Playoffs				
Season	Club	League	GP	G	A	Pts	PIM	GP	G	A	Pts	PIM
1993-94	North Battleford	SMBHL	50	3	14	17	110	5	0	3	3	30
1994-95	North Battleford	SMBHL	48	10	20	30	152	....	....	....	....	....
1995-96	North Battleford	SJHL	55	3	14	17	110	....	....	....	....	....
1996-97	Edmonton Ice	WHL	61	3	5	8	251	....	....	....	....	....
1997-98	Edmonton Ice	WHL	47	5	5	10	168	....	....	....	....	....
	Hershey Bears	AHL	1	0	0	0	15	....	....	....	....	....
1998-99	Kootenay Ice	WHL	45	3	1	4	201	7	0	0	0	38
99-2000	Kootenay Ice	WHL	49	4	9	13	197	21	2	3	5	*61
2000-01	U. of Alberta	CWUAA	1	0	0	0	0	....	....	....	....	....
2001-02	Bridgeport	AHL	7	0	0	0	5	....	....	....	....	....
	Trenton Titans	ECHL	60	6	6	12	305	....	....	....	....	....
2002-03	Bridgeport	AHL	30	0	1	1	60	2	0	0	0	0
	Trenton Titans	ECHL	2	0	0	0	15	....	....	....	....	....
	Cincinnati	ECHL	40	1	0	1	157	....	....	....	....	....
2003-04	Bridgeport	AHL	72	1	2	3	220	7	0	1	1	29
2004-05	Bridgeport	AHL	45	2	1	3	149	....	....	....	....	....

BELL, Brendan (BEHL, BREHN-duhn) **TOR.**

Defense. Shoots left. 6'1", 205 lbs. Born, Ottawa, Ont., March 31, 1983.
(Toronto's 3rd choice, 65th overall, in 2001 Entry Draft).

			Regular Season					Playoffs				
Season	Club	League	GP	G	A	Pts	PIM	GP	G	A	Pts	PIM
1998-99	Ott. Jr. Senators	CJHL	54	7	20	27	46	....	....	....	....	....
99-2000	Ottawa 67's	OHL	48	1	32	33	34	5	0	1	1	4
2000-01	Ottawa 67's	OHL	68	7	32	39	59	20	1	11	12	22
2001-02	Ottawa 67's	OHL	67	10	36	46	56	13	2	5	7	25
2002-03	Ottawa 67's	OHL	55	14	39	53	46	23	8	19	27	25
2003-04	St. John's	AHL	74	7	18	25	72	....	....	....	....	....
2004-05	St. John's	AHL	75	6	25	31	57	5	0	1	1	2

OHL First All-Star Team (2003) • Canadian Major Junior First All-Star Team (2003) • Canadian Major Junior Defenseman of the Year (2003)

BELLAMY, Rob (BEHL-ah-mee, RAWB) **PHI.**

Right wing. Shoots right. 6', 190 lbs. Born, Providence, RI, May 30, 1985.
(Philadelphia's 1st choice, 92nd overall, in 2004 Entry Draft).

			Regular Season					Playoffs				
Season	Club	League	GP	G	A	Pts	PIM	GP	G	A	Pts	PIM
2002-03	Berkshire Bears	High-MA	32	21	21	42	128	....	....	....	....	....
2003-04	N.E. Jr. Coyotes	EJHL	36	19	21	40	95	....	....	....	....	....
2004-05	U. of Maine	H-East	28	3	4	7	34	....	....	....	....	....

BELLE, Shawn (BEHL, SHAWN) **DAL.**

Defense. Shoots left. 6'1", 220 lbs. Born, Edmonton, Alta., January 3, 1985.
(St. Louis' 1st choice, 30th overall, in 2003 Entry Draft).

			Regular Season					Playoffs				
Season	Club	League	GP	G	A	Pts	PIM	GP	G	A	Pts	PIM
99-2000	K of C Squires	AMBHL	34	7	20	27	36	....	....	....	....	....
2000-01	K of C Squires	AMBHL	39	18	30	48	69	....	....	....	....	....
	Regina Pats	WHL	4	0	3	3	0	....	....	....	....	....
	Tri-City Americans	WHL	2	0	1	1	0	....	....	....	....	....
2001-02	Tri-City Americans	WHL	64	1	17	18	51	5	2	1	3	2
2002-03	Tri-City Americans	WHL	66	7	14	21	79	....	....	....	....	....
2003-04	Tri-City Americans	WHL	55	9	20	29	68	11	3	5	8	15
2004-05	Tri-City Americans	WHL	62	13	32	45	76	5	1	1	2	6

Rights traded to **Dallas** by **St. Louis** for Jason Bacashihua, June 25, 2004.

BELLEMARE, Thomas (BEHL-mahr, TAW-muhs) **CGY.**

Right wing. Shoots right. 6'3", 222 lbs. Born, Shawinigan, Que., January 11, 1984.
(Calgary's 7th choice, 206th overall, in 2003 Entry Draft).

			Regular Season					Playoffs				
Season	Club	League	GP	G	A	Pts	PIM	GP	G	A	Pts	PIM
2002-03	Drummondville	QMJHL	67	5	3	8	474	....	....	....	....	....
2003-04	Drummondville	QMJHL	60	2	5	7	181	7	0	0	0	2
2004-05	Texas Wildcatters	ECHL	29	0	1	1	82	....	....	....	....	....
	Charlotte	ECHL	36	4	2	6	117	15	0	2	2	20

BELLER, Greg (BEHL-uhr, GREHG) **NYR**

Wing. Shoots left. 6'2", 202 lbs. Born, Vancouver, B.C., January 22, 1987.
(NY Rangers' 8th choice, 178th overall, in 2005 Entry Draft).

			Regular Season					Playoffs				
Season	Club	League	GP	G	A	Pts	PIM	GP	G	A	Pts	PIM
2004-05	Lake of the Woods	High-MN	21	23	25	48	38	....	....	....	....	....
	Borderland	SIJHL	6	2	5	7	0	2	0	1	1	2

BELLISSIMO, Vince (behl-IHS-ih-moh, VIHNTS)

Center. Shoots right. 6', 199 lbs. Born, Toronto, Ont., December 14, 1982.
(Florida's 6th choice, 158th overall, in 2002 Entry Draft).

			Regular Season					Playoffs				
Season	Club	League	GP	G	A	Pts	PIM	GP	G	A	Pts	PIM
99-2000	St. Mike's B's	OPJHL	47	30	29	59	31	....	....	....	....	....
2000-01	St. Mike's B's	OPJHL	47	32	64	96	28	6	6	8	14	....
2001-02	Topeka	USHL	61	37	39	76	33	....	....	....	....	....
2002-03	Western Mich.	CCHA	37	19	17	36	18	....	....	....	....	....
2003-04	Western Mich.	CCHA	38	13	27	40	42	....	....	....	....	....
2004-05	Western Mich.	CCHA	35	17	20	37	81	....	....	....	....	....
	San Antonio	AHL	12	3	3	6	2	....	....	....	....	....

USHL First All-Star Team (2002) • USHL Top Forward (2002) • CCHA All-Rookie Team (2003)

BERGFORS, Henrik (BAIRG-fohrz, HEHN-rihk) **T.B.**

Defense. Shoots right. 6'4", 227 lbs. Born, Sodertalje, Sweden, May 15, 1982.
(Tampa Bay's 14th choice, 289th overall, in 2001 Entry Draft).

			Regular Season					Playoffs				
Season	Club	League	GP	G	A	Pts	PIM	GP	G	A	Pts	PIM
99-2000	AIK Solna Jr.	Swe-Jr.	12	0	1	1	6	....	....	....	....	....
2000-01	Sodertalje SK Jr.	Swe-Jr.	14	1	0	1	16	....	....	....	....	....
2001-02	Sodertalje SK Jr.	Swe-Jr.	40	4	4	8	62	2	1	0	1	2
2002-03	Sodertalje SK	Sweden	8	0	0	0	0	....	....	....	....	....
	HC Orebro 90	Sweden-2	18	0	0	0	60	....	....	....	....	....
	Sodertalje SK Jr.	Swe-Jr.	7	0	2	2	29	....	....	....	....	....
2003-04	Wichita Thunder	CHL	DID NOT PLAY – INJURED									
2004-05	Adirondack	UHL	62	0	4	4	44	3	0	0	0	0

• Missed entire 2003-04 season recovering from shoulder injury suffered in pre-season game vs. Tulsa (CHL), September 10, 2003.

BERGFORS, Nicklas (BUHRG-fohrs, NIHK-las) **N.J.**

Right wing. Shoots right. 6'2", 190 lbs. Born, Sodertalje, Sweden, March 7, 1987.
(New Jersey's 1st choice, 23rd overall, in 2005 Entry Draft).

			Regular Season					Playoffs				
Season	Club	League	GP	G	A	Pts	PIM	GP	G	A	Pts	PIM
2002-03	Sodertalje SK U18	Swe-U18	4	4	4	8	0	....	....	....	....	....
	Sodertalje SK Jr.	Swe-Jr.	13	1	5	6	4	....	....	....	....	....
2003-04	Sodertalje SK U18	Swe-U18	5	14	4	18	4	2	0	1	1	6
	Sodertalje SK Jr.	Swe-Jr.	31	13	17	30	22	2	1	1	2	0
2004-05	Sodertalje SK Jr.	Swe-Jr.	21	18	16	34	25	3	0	3	3	4
	Sodertalje SK	Sweden	25	1	0	1	2	2	0	0	0	0

BERGGREN, Johan (BUHR-gruhn, YOH-han) **DET.**

Defense. Shoots left. 6'3", 176 lbs. Born, Vastra Amtevik, Sweden, May 18, 1984.
(Detroit's 4th choice, 131st overall, in 2002 Entry Draft).

			Regular Season					Playoffs				
Season	Club	League	GP	G	A	Pts	PIM	GP	G	A	Pts	PIM
2001-02	HC Sunne	Sweden-3	25	1	7	8	22	....	....	....	....	....
2002-03	Sunne IK Jr.	Swe-Jr.	12	4	0	4	20	....	....	....	....	....
	HC Sunne	Sweden-3	36	1	10	11	40	....	....	....	....	....
2003-04	Sodertalje SK	Sweden	43	0	1	1	20	....	....	....	....	....
	Sodertalje SK Jr.	Swe-Jr.	25	1	7	8	28	2	0	0	0	0
2004-05	IFK Arboga IK	Sweden-2	53	4	8	12	44	....	....	....	....	....

BERNIER, Marc-Andre (BAIRN-yay, MAHRK-AWN-dray) **VAN.**

Right wing. Shoots right. 6'4", 198 lbs. Born, Laval, Que., February 5, 1985.
(Vancouver's 2nd choice, 60th overall, in 2003 Entry Draft).

			Regular Season					Playoffs				
Season	Club	League	GP	G	A	Pts	PIM	GP	G	A	Pts	PIM
99-2000	Laval-Laurentides	QAAA	15	2	3	5	10	9	1	0	1	2
2000-01	Laval-Laurentides	QAAA	26	6	12	18	16	8	3	2	5	6
2001-02	Halifax	QMJHL	49	0	6	6	20	2	0	0	0	0
2002-03	Halifax	QMJHL	67	29	29	58	43	21	9	8	17	8
2003-04	Cape Breton	QMJHL	58	27	23	50	27	5	1	3	4	2
2004-05	Halifax	QMJHL	65	27	23	50	51	12	4	5	9	8

BERNIER, Steve (BAIRN-yay, STEEV) **S.J.**

Right wing. Shoots right. 6'2", 230 lbs. Born, Quebec City, Que., March 31, 1985.
(San Jose's 2nd choice, 16th overall, in 2003 Entry Draft).

			Regular Season					Playoffs				
Season	Club	League	GP	G	A	Pts	PIM	GP	G	A	Pts	PIM
1998-99	Quebec AA Aces	QAHA	28	33	23	56	24	....	....	....	....	....
99-2000	Quebec AA Aces	QAHA	26	12	23	35	42	....	....	....	....	....
2000-01	Ste-Foy	QAAA	39	17	35	52	48	16	9	17	26	8
2001-02	Moncton Wildcats	QMJHL	66	31	28	59	51	....	....	....	....	....
2002-03	Moncton Wildcats	QMJHL	71	49	52	101	90	2	1	0	1	2
2003-04	Moncton Wildcats	QMJHL	66	36	46	82	80	20	7	10	17	17
2004-05	Moncton Wildcats	QMJHL	68	35	36	71	114	12	6	13	19	22

QMJHL All-Rookie Team (2002) • QMJHL Second All-Star Team (2003, 2004)

BERNIKOV, Ruslan (BAIR-nih-kahf, roos-LAHN) **DAL.**

Right wing. Shoots left. 6'3", 198 lbs. Born, Vidnoye, USSR, December 4, 1977.
(Dallas' 6th choice, 139th overall, in 2000 Entry Draft).

			Regular Season					Playoffs				
Season	Club	League	GP	G	A	Pts	PIM	GP	G	A	Pts	PIM
1996-97	Dyn'o Moscow 2	Russia-3	32	11	4	15	20	....	....	....	....	....
	Dynamo Moscow	Russia	2	0	0	0	0	....	....	....	....	....
1997-98	Yekaterinburg 2	Russia-3	2	1	1	2	0	....	....	....	....	....
	Yekaterinburg	Russia	43	7	7	14	55	....	....	....	....	....
1998-99	Dynamo Moscow	Russia	6	0	1	1	2	....	....	....	....	....
	Krylja Sovetov	Russia	20	3	1	4	24	....	....	....	....	....
	CSKA Moscow	Russia	1	0	0	0	0	....	....	....	....	....
	Cherepovets	Russia	5	0	0	0	0	1	0	0	0	0
99-2000	Dynamo Moscow	Russia	6	2	1	3	2	....	....	....	....	....
	Amur Khabarovsk	Russia	14	3	6	9	10	5	3	1	4	2
2000-01	Amur Khabarovsk	Russia	33	1	4	5	40	....	....	....	....	....
2001-02	Amur Khabarovsk	Russia	38	7	10	17	20	....	....	....	....	....
2002-03	Krylja Sovetov	Russia	50	15	10	25	40	....	....	....	....	....
2003-04	Lada Togliatti	Russia	49	8	10	18	51	6	0	0	0	4
2004-05	Lada Togliatti	Russia	16	3	1	4	14	....	....	....	....	....
	Cherepovets	Russia	33	9	6	15	8	....	....	....	....	....

BERRY, Alex (BAIR-ee, Al-ehx) **TOR.**

Right wing. Shoots right. 6'2", 195 lbs. Born, Danvers, MA, March 6, 1986.
(Toronto's 3rd choice, 153rd overall, in 2005 Entry Draft).

			Regular Season					Playoffs				
Season	Club	League	GP	G	A	Pts	PIM	GP	G	A	Pts	PIM
2003-04	Cushing	High-MA	31	19	16	35	50	....	....	....	....	....
2004-05	Junior Bruins	EJHL	53	17	25	42	170	....	....	....	....	....

Signed Letter of Intent to attend **Massachusetts** (H-East) in fall of 2005.

BERTI, Adam (BUHR-tee, A-duhm) **CHI.**

Left wing. Shoots left. 6'3", 193 lbs. Born, Scarborough, Ont., July 1, 1986.
(Chicago's 6th choice, 68th overall, in 2004 Entry Draft).

			Regular Season					Playoffs				
Season	Club	League	GP	G	A	Pts	PIM	GP	G	A	Pts	PIM
2001-02	Oshawa Electric	OMHA	STATISTICS NOT AVAILABLE									
2002-03	Oshawa Generals	OHL	15	3	3	6	12	....	....	....	....	....
2003-04	Oshawa Generals	OHL	66	17	29	46	44	7	0	2	2	4
2004-05	Oshawa Generals	OHL	66	23	28	51	53	....	....	....	....	....

BERTRAM, Dan (BUHR-truhm, DAN) **CHI.**

Right wing. Shoots right. 5'11", 175 lbs. Born, Calgary, Alta., January 14, 1987.
(Chicago's 3rd choice, 54th overall, in 2005 Entry Draft).

			Regular Season					Playoffs				
Season	Club	League	GP	G	A	Pts	PIM	GP	G	A	Pts	PIM
2003-04	Camrose Kodiaks	AJHL	44	22	33	55	....	....	....	....	....	....
2004-05	Boston College	H-East	39	9	8	17	58	....	....	....	....	....

AJHL Rookie of the Year (2004)

BETTS, Kaleb (BEHTZ, KAHL-uhb) **NSH.**

Center. Shoots left. 5'10", 180 lbs. Born, Maple Ridge, B.C., January 10, 1983.
(Nashville's 6th choice, 235th overall, in 2002 Entry Draft).

			Regular Season					Playoffs				
Season	Club	League	GP	G	A	Pts	PIM	GP	G	A	Pts	PIM
2000-01	Chilliwack Chiefs	BCHL	58	17	20	37	79	....	....	....	....	....
2001-02	Chilliwack Chiefs	BCHL	54	35	37	72	92	....	....	....	....	....
2002-03	Nebraska-Omaha	CCHA	DID NOT PLAY – ACADEMICALLY INELIGIBLE									
2003-04	Nebraska-Omaha	CCHA	35	9	13	22	48	....	....	....	....	....
2004-05	Nebraska-Omaha	CCHA	32	5	11	16	88	....	....	....	....	....

BEZRUKOV, Dmitri (behz-ROO-kahv, dih-MEE-tree) **T.B.**

Left wing. Shoots left. 6'3", 187 lbs. Born, Kazan, USSR, November 9, 1977.
(Tampa Bay's 11th choice, 259th overall, in 2001 Entry Draft).

			Regular Season					Playoffs				
Season	Club	League	GP	G	A	Pts	PIM	GP	G	A	Pts	PIM
1997-98	Nizhnekamsk 2	Russia-3	8	0	1	1	6	....	....	....	....	....
	Nizhnekamsk	Russia	14	5	3	8	4	....	....	....	....	....
1998-99	Nizhnekamsk 2	Russia-4	1	3	0	3	0	....	....	....	....	....
	Nizhnekamsk	Russia	39	4	6	10	18	3	1	0	1	2
99-2000	Nizhnekamsk 2	Russia-3	4	0	0	0	6	....	....	....	....	....
	Leninogorsk	Russia-2	8	2	1	3	8	....	....	....	....	....
	Nizhnekamsk	Russia	28	5	6	11	45	3	0	1	1	2
2000-01	Nizhnekamsk	Russia	35	7	10	17	54	4	0	2	2	2
2001-02	Nizhnekamsk	Russia	38	5	6	11	45	....	....	....	....	....
2002-03	Spartak Moscow	Russia	51	10	12	22	24	....	....	....	....	....
2003-04	Nizhnekamsk	Russia	17	1	3	4	10	....	....	....	....	....
	Cherepovets 2	Russia-3	12	7	10	17	20	....	....	....	....	....
	Cherepovets	Russia	8	0	0	0	0	....	....	....	....	....
2004-05	Perm	Russia	27	1	3	4	18	....	....	....	....	....
	Nizhny Novgorod	Russia-2	18	7	5	12	16	6	0	1	1	4

BICKELL, Bryan (bih-KEHL, BRIGH-uhn) **CHI.**

Left wing. Shoots left. 6'3", 213 lbs. Born, Bowmanville, Ont., March 9, 1986.
(Chicago's 3rd choice, 41st overall, in 2004 Entry Draft).

			Regular Season					Playoffs				
Season	Club	League	GP	G	A	Pts	PIM	GP	G	A	Pts	PIM
2000-01	Tor. Red Wings	GTHL	68	24	26	50	20	5	3	1	4	4
2001-02	Tor. Red Wings	GTHL	65	31	41	72	76	2	2	2	4	0
2002-03	Ottawa 67's	OHL	50	7	10	17	4	20	5	3	8	12
2003-04	Ottawa 67's	OHL	59	20	16	36	76	7	3	0	3	11
2004-05	Ottawa 67's	OHL	66	22	32	54	95	21	5	12	17	32

BIEKSA, Kevin (BEEKS-ah, KEH-vihn) **VAN.**

Defense. Shoots right. 6'1", 195 lbs. Born, Grimsby, Ont., June 16, 1981.
(Vancouver's 4th choice, 151st overall, in 2001 Entry Draft).

			Regular Season					Playoffs				
Season	Club	League	GP	G	A	Pts	PIM	GP	G	A	Pts	PIM
1997-98	Burlington	OPJHL	27	0	3	3	10	....	....	....	....	....
1998-99	Burlington	OPJHL	49	8	29	37	83	....	....	....	....	....
99-2000	Burlington	OPJHL	49	6	27	33	139	....	....	....	....	....
2000-01	Bowling Green	CCHA	35	4	9	13	90	....	....	....	....	....
2001-02	Bowling Green	CCHA	40	5	10	15	68	....	....	....	....	....
2002-03	Bowling Green	CCHA	34	8	17	25	92	....	....	....	....	....
2003-04	Bowling Green	CCHA	38	7	15	22	66	....	....	....	....	....
	Manitoba Moose	AHL	4	0	2	2	2	....	....	....	....	....
2004-05	Manitoba Moose	AHL	80	12	27	39	192	14	1	1	2	52

AHL All-Rookie Team (2005)

BIRNER, Michal (BUHR-nuhr, MEE-khahl) **ST.L.**

Left wing. Shoots left. 6', 183 lbs. Born, Litomerice, Czech., March 2, 1986.
(St. Louis' 4th choice, 116th overall, in 2004 Entry Draft).

			Regular Season					Playoffs				
Season	Club	League	GP	G	A	Pts	PIM	GP	G	A	Pts	PIM
2000-01	Slavia U17	CzR-U17	48	16	24	40	20	7	0	1	1	6
2001-02	Slavia U17	CzR-U17	46	24	34	58	28	21	1	0	1	0
2002-03	Slavia U17	CzR-U17	5	5	6	11	14	5	4	3	7	20
	HC Slavia Praha Jr.	CzRep-Jr.	31	4	8	12	10	3	1	0	1	2
2003-04	HC Slavia Praha Jr.	CzRep-Jr.	55	25	35	60	112	2	0	1	1	4
	HC Slavia Praha	CzRep	1	0	0	0	0	....	....	....	....	....
2004-05	Barrie Colts	OHL	28	4	10	14	12	....	....	....	....	....
	Saginaw Spirit	OHL	31	7	21	28	29	....	....	....	....	....

BISSONNETTE, Paul (bih-sawn-EHT, PAWL) **PIT.**

Defense. Shoots left. 6'3", 212 lbs. Born, Welland, Ont., March 11, 1985.
(Pittsburgh's 5th choice, 121st overall, in 2003 Entry Draft).

			Regular Season					Playoffs				
Season	Club	League	GP	G	A	Pts	PIM	GP	G	A	Pts	PIM
2000-01	Welland	OMHA	STATISTICS NOT AVAILABLE									
2001-02	North Bay	OHL	57	3	3	6	21	5	0	0	0	2
2002-03	Saginaw Spirit	OHL	67	7	16	23	57	....	....	....	....	....
2003-04	Saginaw Spirit	OHL	67	5	14	19	96	....	....	....	....	....
2004-05	Saginaw Spirit	OHL	28	1	6	7	46	....	....	....	....	....
	Owen Sound	OHL	35	2	11	13	46	8	1	3	4	2

BITZ, Byron (BIHTZ, BIGH-ruhn) **BOS.**

Right wing. Shoots right. 6'4", 200 lbs. Born, Saskatoon, Sask., July 21, 1984.
(Boston's 4th choice, 107th overall, in 2003 Entry Draft).

			Regular Season					Playoffs				
Season	Club	League	GP	G	A	Pts	PIM	GP	G	A	Pts	PIM
2000-01	Saskatoon	SMBHL	40	17	35	52	....	....	....	....	....	....
2001-02	Saskatoon	SMHL	41	25	48	73	69	11	12	10	22	9
2002-03	Nanaimo Clippers	BCHL	58	27	46	73	59	....	....	....	....	....
2003-04	Cornell Big Red	ECAC	31	5	16	21	36	....	....	....	....	....
2004-05	Cornell Big Red	ECAC	29	5	10	15	20	....	....	....	....	....

BJORK, Johan (b'YAWRK, YOH-han) **OTT.**

Defense. Shoots left. 6'1", 176 lbs. Born, Malmo, Sweden, August 28, 1984.
(Ottawa's 5th choice, 125th overall, in 2002 Entry Draft).

			Regular Season					Playoffs				
Season	Club	League	GP	G	A	Pts	PIM	GP	G	A	Pts	PIM
99-2000	Malmo U18	Swe-U18	8	0	1	1	8	....	....	....	....	....
2000-01	Malmo Jr.	Swe-Jr.	22	0	2	2	12	....	....	....	....	....
	Malmo U18	Swe-U18	3	0	0	0	8	....	....	....	....	....
2001-02	Malmo Jr.	Swe-Jr.	36	1	4	5	72	3	0	0	0	2
2002-03	Malmo	Sweden	21	0	0	0	6	....	....	....	....	....
	Malmo Jr.	Swe-Jr.	22	7	12	19	36	6	0	2	2	6
	IK Pantern Malmo	Sweden-3	STATISTICS NOT AVAILABLE									
2003-04	Malmo U18	Swe-U18	16	4	5	9	6	3	0	0	0	0
	Malmo	Sweden	27	1	0	1	6	....	....	....	....	....
2004-05	Malmo Jr.	Swe-Jr.	4	0	0	0	41	....	....	....	....	....
	Malmo	Sweden	31	0	0	0	6	....	....	....	....	....
	Morrums GoIS IK	Sweden-2	30	0	3	3	14	....	....	....	....	....

BLACK, Greg (BLAK, GREHG) **ST.L.**

Center. Shoots right. 6'2", 193 lbs. Born, Surrey, B.C., May 13, 1982.

			Regular Season					Playoffs				
Season	Club	League	GP	G	A	Pts	PIM	GP	G	A	Pts	PIM
1998-99	South Surrey	BCHL	STATISTICS NOT AVAILABLE									
	Seattle	WHL	2	0	0	0	0	....	....	....	....	....
99-2000	Seattle	WHL	63	8	7	15	114	7	0	1	1	14
2000-01	Seattle	WHL	59	9	11	20	178	....	....	....	....	....
2001-02	Seattle	WHL	63	27	18	45	205	11	5	2	7	37
2002-03	Seattle	WHL	71	36	27	63	203	8	5	5	10	14
2003-04	Worcester IceCats	AHL	39	4	5	9	129	10	0	0	0	10
	Peoria Rivermen	ECHL	15	5	2	7	69	....	....	....	....	....
2004-05			DID NOT PLAY – INJURED									

Signed as a free agent by **St. Louis**, March 20, 2003. • Missed entire 2004-05 season recovering from an elbow injury suffered in a pre-season game, October 2, 2004.

BLANAR, Jan (BLAH-nuhr, YAHN) **FLA.**

Defense. Shoots left. 6'3", 185 lbs. Born, Trencin, Czech., June 6, 1983.
(Florida's 11th choice, 263rd overall, in 2001 Entry Draft).

			Regular Season					Playoffs				
Season	Club	League	GP	G	A	Pts	PIM	GP	G	A	Pts	PIM
1997-98	Dukla Trencin Jr.	Slovak-Jr.	22	0	2	2	2	....	....	....	....	....
1998-99	Dukla Trencin Jr.	Slovak-Jr.	45	2	8	10	20	....	....	....	....	....
99-2000	Dukla Trencin Jr.	Slovak-Jr.	47	8	7	15	18	....	....	....	....	....
2000-01	Dukla Trencin Jr.	Slovak-Jr.	35	3	6	9	16	....	....	....	....	....
2001-02	Dukla Trencin Jr.	Slovak-Jr.	42	3	12	15	....	....	....	....	....	....
	Dukla Trencin	Slovakia	11	0	0	0	2	....	....	....	....	....
2002-03	Dukla Trencin Jr.	Slovak-Jr.	42	3	11	14	40	3	0	1	1	10
	Dukla Trencin	Slovakia	2	0	0	0	0	2	0	0	0	0
2003-04	L. Mikulas	Slovakia	13	0	0	0	0	....	....	....	....	....
	Dubnica	Slovak-2	16	1	4	5	31	9	0	2	2	4
2004-05	Hermes Kokkola	Finland-2	38	2	7	9	54	3	0	0	0	4

BLANCHARD, Nicolas (BLAN-shard, NIHK-o-las) **CAR.**

Center. Shoots left. 6'3", 176 lbs. Born, Granby, Que., May 31, 1987.
(Carolina's 8th choice, 192nd overall, in 2005 Entry Draft).

			Regular Season					Playoffs				
Season	Club	League	GP	G	A	Pts	PIM	GP	G	A	Pts	PIM
2003-04	Antoine-Girouard	QAAA	42	24	28	52	28	13	9	6	15	4
2004-05	Chicoutimi	QMJHL	69	13	26	39	31	17	2	2	4	10

BLATAK, Miroslav (BLAT-ak, MEER-oh-slav) **DET.**

Defense. Shoots left. 5'11", 172 lbs. Born, Gottwaldov, Czech., May 25, 1982.
(Detroit's 3rd choice, 129th overall, in 2001 Entry Draft).

			Regular Season					Playoffs				
Season	Club	League	GP	G	A	Pts	PIM	GP	G	A	Pts	PIM
99-2000	HC Vsetin U17	CzR-U17	30	0	0	0	12	....	....	....	....	....
	HC Vsetin Jr.	CzRep-Jr.	12	0	2	2	10	....	....	....	....	....
2000-01	HC Vsetin U17	CzR-U17	33	7	8	15	56	....	....	....	....	....
	HC Vsetin Jr.	CzRep-Jr.	12	2	4	6	54	7	0	6	6	6
	Zlin	CzRep	8	0	2	2	0	6	0	0	0	0
2001-02	Jihlava Jr.	CzRep-Jr.	3	0	0	0	0	....	....	....	....	....
	HC Zlin Jr.	CzRep-Jr.	3	0	0	0	8	....	....	....	....	....
	HC Dukla Jihlava	CzRep-2	1	0	0	0	0	2	0	0	0	0
	Zlin	CzRep	39	4	7	11	18	11	1	2	3	8
2002-03	HC Hame Zlin	CzRep	49	4	12	16	34	....	....	....	....	....
2003-04	HC Hame Zlin	CzRep	50	5	10	15	34	17	3	3	6	10
2004-05	HC Hame Zlin	CzRep	52	4	8	12	30	17	2	4	6	18

BLINDENBACHER, Severin (blihn-duhn-BAH-khur, SEH-vuhr-ihn) **PHX.**

Defense. Shoots right. 5'11", 189 lbs. Born, Bulach, Switz., March 15, 1983.
(Phoenix's 9th choice, 273rd overall, in 2001 Entry Draft).

			Regular Season					Playoffs				
Season	Club	League	GP	G	A	Pts	PIM	GP	G	A	Pts	PIM
1998-99	EHC Kloten Jr.	Swiss-Jr.	5	0	2	2	4	....	....	....	....	....
99-2000	Kloten Flyers Jr.	Swiss-Jr.	30	8	10	18	18	4	1	1	2	8
2000-01	Kloten Flyers	Swiss	27	0	2	2	17	9	0	0	0	10
2001-02	Kloten Flyers	Swiss	38	1	3	4	22	10	0	2	2	10
	Kloten Flyers Jr.	Swiss-Jr.	....	....	....	....	....	1	0	1	1	2
2002-03	Kloten Flyers	Swiss	43	4	19	23	52	5	1	0	1	4
2003-04	Kloten Flyers	Swiss	34	4	10	14	58	....	....	....	....	....
2004-05	Kloten Flyers	Swiss	41	10	15	25	66	5	1	3	4	10

BLIZNAK, Mario (BLIZH-nak, MAHR-ee-oh) **VAN.**

Center. Shoots left. 6', 185 lbs. Born, Trencin, Czech., March 6, 1987.
(Vancouver's 6th choice, 205th overall, in 2005 Entry Draft).

			Regular Season					Playoffs				
Season	Club	League	GP	G	A	Pts	PIM	GP	G	A	Pts	PIM
2003-04	Dubnica U18	Svk-U18	46	25	26	51	62	....	....	....	....	....
	Dubnica Jr.	Slovak-Jr.	2	1	0	1	2	....	....	....	....	....
2004-05	Dubnica U18	Svk-U18	14	5	8	13	45	....	....	....	....	....
	Dubnica Jr.	Slovak-Jr.	36	22	17	39	38	....	....	....	....	....
	Dubnica	Slovakia	19	0	0	0	14	....	....	....	....	....

BLOM, Stefan (BLAWM, STEH-fan) **DET.**

Defense. Shoots left. 6'2", 189 lbs. Born, Stockholm, Sweden, July 30, 1985.
(Detroit's 5th choice, 194th overall, in 2003 Entry Draft).

			Regular Season					Playoffs				
Season	Club	League	GP	G	A	Pts	PIM	GP	G	A	Pts	PIM
2002-03	Hammarby U18	Swe-U18	18	3	0	0	4	....	....	....	....	....
	Hammarby Jr.	Swe-Jr.	27	4	2	6	12	2	0	0	0	0
2003-04	Djurgarden Jr.	Swe-Jr.	33	2	5	7	16	....	....	....	....	....
2004-05	Hammarby Jr.	Swe-Jr.	18	0	2	2	16	....	....	....	....	....
	Arlanda	Sweden-3	10	0	2	2	8	....	....	....	....	....

BLOMDAHL, Patric (BLAWM-dahl, PAT-rihk) **WSH.**

Right wing. Shoots left. 6'1", 202 lbs. Born, Stockholm, Sweden, January 30, 1984.
(Washington's 13th choice, 272nd overall, in 2002 Entry Draft).

			Regular Season					Playoffs				
Season	Club	League	GP	G	A	Pts	PIM	GP	G	A	Pts	PIM
2000-01	AIK Solna U18	Swe-U18	9	5	1	6	35	....	....	....	....	....
2001-02	AIK Solna U18	Swe-U18	3	0	0	0	2	....	....	....	....	....
	AIK Solna Jr.	Swe-Jr.	20	7	6	13	18	....	....	....	....	....
2002-03	AIK Solna Jr.	Swe-Jr.	19	6	5	11	107	....	....	....	....	....
	AIK Solna	Sweden-2	12	1	0	1	10	....	....	....	....	....
2003-04	AIK Solna Jr.	Swe-Jr.	8	4	1	5	43	....	....	....	....	....
	AIK Solna	Sweden-2	48	9	5	14	46	5	0	0	0	0
2004-05	Linkopings HC	Sweden	4	0	0	0	4	....	....	....	....	....
	Nykoping	Sweden-2	47	7	5	12	64	4	0	0	0	0

BLUNDEN, Michael (BLUHN-dehn, MIGHK-uhl) **CHI.**

Right wing. Shoots right. 6'3", 213 lbs. Born, Toronto, Ont., December 15, 1986.
(Chicago's 2nd choice, 43rd overall, in 2005 Entry Draft).

			Regular Season					Playoffs				
Season	Club	League	GP	G	A	Pts	PIM	GP	G	A	Pts	PIM
2002-03	Erie Otters	OHL	63	10	7	17	55	....	....	....	....	....
2003-04	Erie Otters	OHL	52	22	17	39	53	3	0	0	0	0
2004-05	Erie Otters	OHL	61	22	19	41	75	2	0	0	0	2

BOBROV, Viktor (bawb-RAWV, VIHK-tohr) **CGY.**

Center. Shoots left. 6'1", 176 lbs. Born, Novocheboksarsk, USSR, January 1, 1984.
(Calgary's 7th choice, 146th overall, in 2002 Entry Draft).

			Regular Season					Playoffs				
Season	Club	League	GP	G	A	Pts	PIM	GP	G	A	Pts	PIM
99-2000	Nizh. Novgorod 2	Russia-3	6	6	1	7	0	....	....	....	....	....
2000-01	CSKA Moscow 2	Russia-3	31	30	17	47	32	4	4	3	7	4
2001-02	HK CSKA 2	Russia-3	36	11	16	27	20	....	....	....	....	....
2002-03	Elektrostal	Russia-2	48	7	7	14	16	....	....	....	....	....
2003-04	Kristall Elektrostal	Russia-2	60	6	10	16	38	....	....	....	....	....
2004-05	CSKA Moscow 2	Russia-3	STATISTICS NOT AVAILABLE									

BOCHENSKI, Brandon (boh-CHEHN-skee, BRAN-duhn) **OTT.**

Right wing. Shoots right. 6', 180 lbs. Born, Blaine, MN, April 4, 1982.
(Ottawa's 9th choice, 223rd overall, in 2001 Entry Draft).

			Regular Season					Playoffs				
Season	Club	League	GP	G	A	Pts	PIM	GP	G	A	Pts	PIM
99-2000	Blaine Bengals	High-MN	28	32	30	62	....	....	....	....	....	....
2000-01	Lincoln Stars	USHL	55	*47	33	80	22	11	5	7	12	4
2001-02	North Dakota	WCHA	36	17	15	32	34	....	....	....	....	....
2002-03	North Dakota	WCHA	43	35	27	62	42	....	....	....	....	....
2003-04	North Dakota	WCHA	41	27	33	60	40	....	....	....	....	....
2004-05	Binghamton	AHL	75	34	36	70	16	6	1	0	1	2

USHL First All-Star Team (2001) • USHL Rookie of the Year (2001) • WCHA All-Rookie Team (2002) • WCHA Rookie of the Year (2002) • WCHA Second All-Star Team (2003) • WCHA First All-Star Team (2004) • NCAA West First All-American Team (2004) • AHL All-Rookie Team (2005)

BODIE, Troy (BOH-dee, TROI) **EDM.**

Right wing. Shoots right. 6'4", 213 lbs. Born, Portage La Prairie, Man., January 25, 1985.
(Edmonton's 12th choice, 278th overall, in 2003 Entry Draft).

			Regular Season					Playoffs				
Season	Club	League	GP	G	A	Pts	PIM	GP	G	A	Pts	PIM
2001-02	Central Plains	MMMHL	40	22	21	43	10	....	....	....	....	....
2002-03	Kelowna Rockets	WHL	35	4	4	8	36	11	1	1	2	2
2003-04	Kelowna Rockets	WHL	71	8	12	20	112	17	7	3	10	6
2004-05	Kelowna Rockets	WHL	72	24	24	48	96	24	4	13	17	26

BOIS, Danny (BOIZ, DA-nee) **OTT.**

Right wing. Shoots right. 6'1", 197 lbs. Born, Thunder Bay, Ont., June 1, 1983.
(Colorado's 2nd choice, 97th overall, in 2001 Entry Draft).

			Regular Season					Playoffs				
Season	Club	League	GP	G	A	Pts	PIM	GP	G	A	Pts	PIM
1998-99	Thunder Bay Kings	TBMHL	15	7	12	19	28	....	....	....	....	....
99-2000	Wellington Dukes	OPJHL	37	15	20	35	115	....	....	....	....	....
2000-01	London Knights	OHL	66	21	16	37	218	5	2	1	3	19
2001-02	London Knights	OHL	62	16	14	30	256	12	2	2	4	47
2002-03	London Knights	OHL	56	19	13	32	207	13	4	6	10	38
2003-04	London Knights	OHL	52	14	25	39	242	7	4	4	8	29
2004-05	Binghamton	AHL	72	2	4	6	287	6	0	1	1	2

Signed as a free agent by **Ottawa**, April 30, 2004.

BOLF, Lukas (BAWLF, LOO-kahsh) **PIT.**

Defense. Shoots left. 6'1", 190 lbs. Born, Vrchlabi, Czech., February 20, 1985.
(Pittsburgh's 7th choice, 169th overall, in 2003 Entry Draft).

			Regular Season					Playoffs				
Season	Club	League	GP	G	A	Pts	PIM	GP	G	A	Pts	PIM
99-2000	Karlovy Vary Jr.	CzRep-Jr.	43	2	7	9	57	....	....	....	....	....
2000-01	Sparta U17	CzR-U17	42	4	13	17	54	....	....	....	....	....
2001-02	HPK U18	Fin-U18	6	1	5	6	12	1	0	0	0	0
	HPK Jr.	Finland-Jr.	25	0	4	4	18	5	0	0	0	2
	Sparta Jr.	CzRep-Jr.	21	2	3	5	35	....	....	....	....	....
2002-03	Sparta Jr.	CzRep-Jr.	28	3	7	10	....	....	....	....	....	....
2003-04	Barrie Colts	OHL	56	2	18	20	42	12	0	2	2	26
2004-05	Barrie Colts	OHL	56	6	25	31	59	6	0	2	2	8

BOLL, Jared (BAWL, JAIR-ehd) **CBJ**

Right wing. Shoots right. 6'2", 190 lbs. Born, Crystal Lake, NC, May 13, 1986.
(Columbus' 4th choice, 101st overall, in 2005 Entry Draft).

			Regular Season					Playoffs				
Season	Club	League	GP	G	A	Pts	PIM	GP	G	A	Pts	PIM
2003-04	Lincoln Stars	USHL	57	6	8	14	*176	....	....	....	....	....
2004-05	Lincoln Stars	USHL	59	23	24	47	*294	4	1	3	4	25

BOLLAND, Dave (BOHL-uhnd, DAYV) **CHI.**

Center. Shoots right. 6', 168 lbs. Born, Toronto, Ont., June 5, 1986.
(Chicago's 2nd choice, 32nd overall, in 2004 Entry Draft).

			Regular Season					Playoffs				
Season	Club	League	GP	G	A	Pts	PIM	GP	G	A	Pts	PIM
2000-01	Tor. Red Wings	GTHL	95	79	67	146	....	....	....	....	....	....
2001-02	Tor. Red Wings	GTHL	36	35	35	70	40	....	....	....	....	....
2002-03	London Knights	OHL	64	7	10	17	21	14	2	1	3	2
2003-04	London Knights	OHL	65	37	30	67	58	15	3	10	13	18
2004-05	London Knights	OHL	66	34	51	85	97	18	11	14	25	30

BOLT, Bobby (BOHLT, BAW-bee) **ANA.**

Left wing. Shoots left. 6'3", 219 lbs. Born, Thunder Bay, Ont., April 29, 1987.
(Anaheim's 4th choice, 127th overall, in 2005 Entry Draft).

			Regular Season					Playoffs				
Season	Club	League	GP	G	A	Pts	PIM	GP	G	A	Pts	PIM
2003-04	Strathroy Rockets	OHA-B	39	5	14	19	41	....	....	....	....	....
	London Knights	OHL	8	1	0	1	2	....	....	....	....	....
2004-05	Kingston	OHL	67	11	14	25	92	....	....	....	....	....

BONNEAU, Jimmy (BAW-noh, JIHM-mee) **MTL.**

Left wing. Shoots left. 6'3", 224 lbs. Born, Baie-Comeau, Que., March 22, 1985.
(Montreal's 10th choice, 241st overall, in 2003 Entry Draft).

			Regular Season					Playoffs				
Season	Club	League	GP	G	A	Pts	PIM	GP	G	A	Pts	PIM
2000-01	Jonquiere Elites	QAAA	1	0	0	0	0	....	....	....	....	....
2001-02	Jonquiere Elites	QAAA	40	5	10	15	55	3	1	1	2	2
2002-03	Montreal Rocket	QMJHL	65	1	5	6	261	7	0	0	0	12
2003-04	PEI Rocket	QMJHL	70	7	12	19	263	11	1	0	1	12
2004-05	PEI Rocket	QMJHL	70	11	11	22	234	....	....	....	....	....

BOOGAARD, Derek (BOO-gard, DAIR-ihk) **MIN.**

Left wing. Shoots right. 6'7", 250 lbs. Born, Saskatoon, Sask., June 23, 1982.
(Minnesota's 6th choice, 202nd overall, in 2001 Entry Draft).

			Regular Season					Playoffs				
Season	Club	League	GP	G	A	Pts	PIM	GP	G	A	Pts	PIM
1998-99	Regina Caps	SJHL	35	2	3	5	166	....	....	....	....	....
99-2000	Regina Pats	WHL	5	0	0	0	17	....	....	....	....	....
	Prince George	WHL	33	0	0	0	149	....	....	....	....	....
2000-01	Prince George	WHL	61	1	8	9	245	6	1	0	1	31
2001-02	Prince George	WHL	2	0	0	0	16	....	....	....	....	....
	Medicine Hat	WHL	46	1	8	9	178	....	....	....	....	....
2002-03	Medicine Hat	WHL	27	1	2	3	65	....	....	....	....	....
	Louisiana	ECHL	33	1	2	3	240	2	0	0	0	0
2003-04	Houston Aeros	AHL	53	0	4	4	207	2	0	1	1	16
2004-05	Houston Aeros	AHL	56	1	4	5	259	5	0	0	0	38

BOOTH, David   (BOOTH, DAY-vihd)   **FLA.**

Left wing. Shoots left. 6', 212 lbs.   Born, Detroit, MI, November 24, 1984.
(Florida's 3rd choice, 53rd overall, in 2004 Entry Draft).

| | | | Regular Season | | | | | Playoffs | | | | |
Season	Club	League	GP	G	A	Pts	PIM	GP	G	A	Pts	PIM
2000-01	Det. Compuware	NAHL	42	17	13	30	44	2	1	0	1	2
2001-02	USA U-18	USDP	58	17	12	29	41	....	....	....	....	....
2002-03	Michigan State	CCHA	39	17	19	36	53	....	....	....	....	....
2003-04	Michigan State	CCHA	30	8	10	18	30	....	....	....	....	....
2004-05	Michigan State	CCHA	29	7	9	16	30	....	....	....	....	....

CCHA All-Rookie Team (2003)

BORDELEAU, Patrick   (BOHR-duh-loh, PAT-rihk)   **MIN.**

Left wing. Shoots left. 6'5", 195 lbs.   Born, Montreal, Que., March 23, 1986.
(Minnesota's 6th choice, 114th overall, in 2004 Entry Draft).

| | | | Regular Season | | | | | Playoffs | | | | |
Season	Club	League	GP	G	A	Pts	PIM	GP	G	A	Pts	PIM
2002-03	Gatineau Intrepide	QAAA	39	8	13	21	50	....	....	....	....	....
2003-04	Val-d'Or Foreurs	QMJHL	68	7	11	18	97	7	1	1	2	8
2004-05	Val-d'Or Foreurs	QMJHL	63	14	24	38	51	....	....	....	....	....

BORER, Casey   (BOHR-uhr, KAY-see)   **CAR.**

Defense. Shoots left. 6'2", 197 lbs.   Born, Minneapolis, MN, July 28, 1985.
(Carolina's 3rd choice, 69th overall, in 2004 Entry Draft).

| | | | Regular Season | | | | | Playoffs | | | | |
Season	Club	League	GP	G	A	Pts	PIM	GP	G	A	Pts	PIM
2002-03	USA U-18	USDP	56	3	4	7	46	....	....	....	....	....
2003-04	St. Cloud State	WCHA	31	0	8	8	18	....	....	....	....	....
2004-05	St. Cloud State	WCHA	35	0	11	11	40	....	....	....	....	....

BORNHAMMAR, David   (BOHRN-ham-uhr, DAY-vihd)   **WSH.**

Defense. Shoots left. 6', 180 lbs.   Born, Lidingo, Sweden, June 15, 1981.
(Washington's 8th choice, 192nd overall, in 1999 Entry Draft).

| | | | Regular Season | | | | | Playoffs | | | | |
Season	Club	League	GP	G	A	Pts	PIM	GP	G	A	Pts	PIM
1997-98	AIK Solna Jr.	Swe-Jr.	13	0	1	1	10	....	....	....	....	....
1998-99	AIK Solna Jr.	Swe-Jr.	33	5	5	10	30	....	....	....	....	....
99-2000	Kelowna Rockets	WHL	62	3	24	27	36	2	0	0	0	0
2000-01	AIK Solna Jr.	Swe-Jr.	10	0	3	3	37	....	....	....	....	....
	AIK Solna	Sweden	37	4	2	6	57	4	0	1	1	0
2001-02	AIK Solna	Sweden	48	1	6	7	34	....	....	....	....	....
	AIK Solna	Sweden-Q	8	0	1	1	4	....	....	....	....	....
2002-03	AIK Solna	Sweden-2	50	8	9	17	32	4	1	0	1	8
2003-04	Blue Devils Weiden	German-2	25	5	8	13	18	....	....	....	....	....
2004-05	Skovde IK	Sweden-2	26	3	8	11	20	....	....	....	....	....

• Name when drafted was David Johansson.

BOURDON, Luc   (BOOR-duhn, LEWK)   **VAN.**

Defense. Shoots left. 6'2", 199 lbs.   Born, Shippagan, N.B., February 16, 1987.
(Vancouver's 1st choice, 10th overall, in 2005 Entry Draft).

| | | | Regular Season | | | | | Playoffs | | | | |
Season	Club	League	GP	G	A	Pts	PIM	GP	G	A	Pts	PIM
2003-04	Val-d'Or Foreurs	QMJHL	64	2	6	8	58	7	1	0	1	4
2004-05	Val-d'Or Foreurs	QMJHL	70	13	19	32	117	....	....	....	....	....

BOURQUE, Chris   (BOHRK, KRIHS)   **WSH.**

Center. Shoots left. 5'7", 170 lbs.   Born, Boston, MA, January 29, 1986.
(Washington's 4th choice, 33rd overall, in 2004 Entry Draft).

| | | | Regular Season | | | | | Playoffs | | | | |
Season	Club	League	GP	G	A	Pts	PIM	GP	G	A	Pts	PIM
2002-03	Cushing	High-MA	28	31	26	57	49	....	....	....	....	....
2003-04	Cushing	High-MA	31	37	53	90	96	....	....	....	....	....
2004-05	Boston University	H-East	35	10	13	23	50	....	....	....	....	....
	Portland Pirates	AHL	6	1	1	2	2	....	....	....	....	....

Hockey East All-Rookie Team (2005)

BOURQUE, Rene   (BOHRK, reh-NAY)   **CHI.**

Left wing. Shoots left. 6'2", 205 lbs.   Born, Lac La Biche, Alta., December 10, 1981.

| | | | Regular Season | | | | | Playoffs | | | | |
Season	Club	League	GP	G	A	Pts	PIM	GP	G	A	Pts	PIM
2000-01	U. of Wisconsin	WCHA	32	10	5	15	18	....	....	....	....	....
2001-02	U. of Wisconsin	WCHA	38	12	7	19	26	....	....	....	....	....
2002-03	U. of Wisconsin	WCHA	40	19	8	27	54	....	....	....	....	....
2003-04	U. of Wisconsin	WCHA	42	16	20	36	74	....	....	....	....	....
2004-05	Norfolk Admirals	AHL	78	33	27	60	105	6	1	0	1	8

AHL All-Rookie Team (2005) • Dudley "Red" Garrett Memorial Trophy (Top Rookie - AHL) (2005)
Signed as a free agent by **Chicago**, July 29, 2004.

BOURRET, Alex   (boo-RAY, AL-ehx)   **ATL.**

Right wing. Shoots left. 5'9", 209 lbs.   Born, Drummondville, Que., October 5, 1986.
(Atlanta's 1st choice, 16th overall, in 2005 Entry Draft).

| | | | Regular Season | | | | | Playoffs | | | | |
Season	Club	League	GP	G	A	Pts	PIM	GP	G	A	Pts	PIM
2001-02	Magog	QAAA	40	26	34	60	105	....	....	....	....	....
2002-03	Sherbrooke	QMJHL	61	13	15	28	73	12	1	1	2	10
2003-04	Lewiston	QMJHL	65	22	41	63	94	7	4	5	9	20
2004-05	Lewiston	QMJHL	65	31	55	86	172	8	6	8	14	25

QMJHL Second All-Star Team (2005)

BOUTIN, Jonathan Michel   (boo-TEHN, JAWN-ah-thuhn-mee-SHEHL)   **ST.L.**

Right wing. Shoots right. 6'2", 187 lbs.   Born, La Pocatiere, Que., October 21, 1984.
(St. Louis' 8th choice, 277th overall, in 2004 Entry Draft).

| | | | Regular Season | | | | | Playoffs | | | | |
Season	Club	League	GP	G	A	Pts	PIM	GP	G	A	Pts	PIM
2002-03	Shawinigan	QMJHL	62	8	13	21	72	9	2	0	2	10
2003-04	Shawinigan	QMJHL	70	31	29	60	76	11	2	2	4	19
2004-05	Shawinigan	QMJHL	70	23	30	53	65	4	0	1	1	14

BOYCHUK, Johnny   (BOI-chuhk, JAW-nee)   **COL.**

Defense. Shoots right. 6'2", 215 lbs.   Born, Edmonton, Alta., January 19, 1984.
(Colorado's 2nd choice, 61st overall, in 2002 Entry Draft).

| | | | Regular Season | | | | | Playoffs | | | | |
Season	Club	League	GP	G	A	Pts	PIM	GP	G	A	Pts	PIM
1998-99	Edm. Cycle	AMBHL	36	8	20	28	59	....	....	....	....	....
99-2000	Edm. Cycle	AMHL	35	6	17	23	59	....	....	....	....	....
2000-01	Calgary Hitmen	WHL	66	4	8	12	61	12	1	1	2	17
2001-02	Calgary Hitmen	WHL	70	8	32	40	85	7	1	1	2	6
2002-03	Calgary Hitmen	WHL	40	8	18	26	58	....	....	....	....	....
	Moose Jaw	WHL	27	5	17	22	32	13	2	6	8	29
2003-04	Moose Jaw	WHL	62	13	20	33	71	10	1	9	10	9
2004-05	Hershey Bears	AHL	80	3	12	15	69	....	....	....	....	....

BOYD, Dustin   (BOID, DUHS-tihn)   **CGY.**

Center. Shoots left. 6', 188 lbs.   Born, Winnipeg, Man., July 16, 1986.
(Calgary's 3rd choice, 98th overall, in 2004 Entry Draft).

| | | | Regular Season | | | | | Playoffs | | | | |
Season	Club	League	GP	G	A	Pts	PIM	GP	G	A	Pts	PIM
2001-02	Winnipeg Warriors	MMMHL	40	50	57	107	16	....	....	....	....	....
2002-03	Moose Jaw	WHL	63	11	17	28	15	13	0	3	3	2
2003-04	Moose Jaw	WHL	72	18	22	40	40	10	2	2	4	8
2004-05	Moose Jaw	WHL	66	26	35	61	57	5	1	2	3	2

BOYLE, Brian   (BOIL, BRIGH-uhn)   **L.A.**

Center. Shoots left. 6'6", 222 lbs.   Born, Dorchester, MA, December 18, 1984.
(Los Angeles' 2nd choice, 26th overall, in 2003 Entry Draft).

| | | | Regular Season | | | | | Playoffs | | | | |
Season	Club	League	GP	G	A	Pts	PIM	GP	G	A	Pts	PIM
2000-01	St. Sebastian's	High-MA	25	20	19	39	....	....	....	....	....	....
2001-02	St. Sebastian's	High-MA	28	21	26	47	22	....	....	....	....	....
2002-03	St. Sebastian's	High-MA	31	32	31	62	46	....	....	....	....	....
2003-04	Boston College	H-East	35	5	3	8	36	....	....	....	....	....
2004-05	Boston College	H-East	40	19	8	27	64	....	....	....	....	....

BRADFORD, Brock   (BRAD-fohrd, BRAHK)   **BOS.**

Center. Shoots right. 5'10", 170 lbs.   Born, Burnaby, B.C., January 7, 1987.
(Boston's 8th choice, 217th overall, in 2005 Entry Draft).

| | | | Regular Season | | | | | Playoffs | | | | |
Season	Club	League	GP	G	A	Pts	PIM	GP	G	A	Pts	PIM
2002-03	Richmond	PIJHL	18	12	12	24	....	....	....	....	....	....
	Coquitlam Express	BCHL	36	11	23	34	14	....	....	....	....	....
2003-04	Coquitlam Express	BCHL	57	36	49	85	....	....	....	....	....	....
2004-05	Omaha Lancers	USHL	60	24	33	57	16	5	0	1	1	0

Signed Letter of Intent to attend **Boston College** (H-East), November 3, 2004.

BRAXENHOLM, Per   (BRAX-ehn-hohlm, PAIR)   **NYI**

Defense. Shoots left. 6'3", 215 lbs.   Born, Karlskrona, Sweden, October 31, 1983.
(NY Islanders' 7th choice, 283rd overall, in 2002 Entry Draft).

| | | | Regular Season | | | | | Playoffs | | | | |
Season	Club	League	GP	G	A	Pts	PIM	GP	G	A	Pts	PIM
2001-02	Morrums GoIS IK	Sweden-2	25	0	2	2	2	....	....	....	....	....
	Kallinge/Ronneby	Sweden-4	1	0	1	1	4	....	....	....	....	....
2002-03	Morrums GoIS IK	Sweden-2	37	1	1	2	8	....	....	....	....	....
2003-04	Morrums GoIS IK	Sweden-2	27	1	0	1	18	....	....	....	....	....
2004-05	Morrums GoIS IK	Sweden-2	50	4	4	8	38	....	....	....	....	....

BRENK, Jake   (BREHNK, JAYK)   **EDM.**

Center. Shoots right. 6'2", 187 lbs.   Born, Detroit Lakes, MN, April 16, 1982.
(Edmonton's 6th choice, 154th overall, in 2001 Entry Draft).

| | | | Regular Season | | | | | Playoffs | | | | |
Season	Club	League	GP	G	A	Pts	PIM	GP	G	A	Pts	PIM
99-2000	Breck Mustangs	High-MN	28	18	23	41	....	....	....	....	....	....
2000-01	Breck Mustangs	High-MN	22	28	30	58	22	....	....	....	....	....
2001-02	Minnesota State	WCHA	21	3	3	6	6	....	....	....	....	....
2002-03	Minnesota State	WCHA	36	3	9	12	38	....	....	....	....	....
2003-04	Minnesota State	WCHA	30	4	7	11	36	....	....	....	....	....
2004-05	Minnesota State	WCHA	33	6	13	19	18	....	....	....	....	....
	Greenville Grrrowl	ECHL	11	2	1	3	0	2	0	0	0	0

BRENT, Tim   (BREHNT, TIHM)   **ANA.**

Center. Shoots right. 6', 188 lbs.   Born, Cambridge, Ont., March 10, 1984.
(Anaheim's 3rd choice, 75th overall, in 2004 Entry Draft).

| | | | Regular Season | | | | | Playoffs | | | | |
Season	Club	League	GP	G	A	Pts	PIM	GP	G	A	Pts	PIM
99-2000	Cambridge	OHA-B	40	19	16	35	42	....	....	....	....	....
2000-01	St. Michael's	OHL	64	9	19	28	31	18	2	8	10	6
2001-02	St. Michael's	OHL	61	19	40	59	52	14	7	12	19	20
2002-03	St. Michael's	OHL	60	24	42	66	74	19	7	17	24	14
2003-04	St. Michael's	OHL	53	26	41	67	105	18	4	13	17	24
2004-05	Cincinnati	AHL	46	5	13	18	42	12	0	1	1	6

• Re-entered NHL Entry Draft. Originally Anaheim's 2nd choice, 37th overall, in 2002 Entry Draft.

BRODZIAK, Kyle   (brohd-ZEE-ak, KIGHL)   **EDM.**

Center. Shoots right. 6'2", 198 lbs.   Born, St. Paul, Alta., May 25, 1984.
(Edmonton's 9th choice, 214th overall, in 2003 Entry Draft).

| | | | Regular Season | | | | | Playoffs | | | | |
Season	Club	League	GP	G	A	Pts	PIM	GP	G	A	Pts	PIM
99-2000	Ft. Saskatchewan	AMBHL	36	23	33	56	57	....	....	....	....	....
	Moose Jaw	WHL	2	0	0	0	0	....	....	....	....	....
2000-01	Moose Jaw	WHL	57	2	8	10	49	3	0	0	0	0
2001-02	Moose Jaw	WHL	72	8	12	20	56	12	0	3	3	11
2002-03	Moose Jaw	WHL	72	32	30	62	84	13	5	3	8	16
2003-04	Moose Jaw	WHL	70	39	54	93	58	10	5	4	9	10
2004-05	Edmonton	AHL	56	6	26	32	49	....	....	....	....	....

WHL East First All-Star Team (2004)

BROOKBANK, Sheldon (BRUK-bank, SHEHL-dohn) **NSH.**

Defense. Shoots right. 6'2", 200 lbs. Born, Lanigan, Sask., October 3, 1980.

			Regular Season					Playoffs				
Season	**Club**	**League**	**GP**	**G**	**A**	**Pts**	**PIM**	**GP**	**G**	**A**	**Pts**	**PIM**
2000-01	Humboldt Broncos	SJHL	59	14	35	49	281	....	....	....	....	....
2001-02	Grand Rapids	AHL	6	0	1	1	24	....	....	....	....	....
	Mississippi	ECHL	62	8	21	29	137	10	1	4	5	27
2002-03	Grand Rapids	AHL	69	2	11	13	136	15	1	3	4	28
2003-04	Cincinnati	AHL	74	2	9	11	216	9	0	2	2	20
2004-05	Cincinnati	AHL	60	1	11	12	181	11	0	0	0	40

Signed as a free agent by **Anaheim**, July 21, 2003. Signed as a free agent by **Nashville**, August 4, 2005.

BROOKS, Alex (BROOKS, AL-ehx) **N.J.**

Defense. Shoots right. 6'1", 205 lbs. Born, Madison, WI, August 21, 1976.

			Regular Season					Playoffs				
Season	**Club**	**League**	**GP**	**G**	**A**	**Pts**	**PIM**	**GP**	**G**	**A**	**Pts**	**PIM**
1993-94	Madison Capitols	USHL	13	3	11	14	....	....	....	....	....	....
1994-95	Madison West	High-WI	24	13	28	41	....	....	....	....	....	....
1995-96	Green Bay	USHL	46	3	22	25	....	....	....	....	....	....
1996-97	U. of Wisconsin	WCHA	DID NOT PLAY – INJURED									
1997-98	U. of Wisconsin	WCHA	40	1	4	5	72	....	....	....	....	....
1998-99	U. of Wisconsin	WCHA	37	0	3	3	73	....	....	....	....	....
99-2000	U. of Wisconsin	WCHA	41	4	10	14	78	....	....	....	....	....
2000-01	U. of Wisconsin	WCHA	41	3	16	19	76	....	....	....	....	....
2001-02	Jokerit Helsinki	Finland	53	1	3	4	109	12	0	0	0	11
2002-03	Albany River Rats	AHL	66	0	7	7	56	....	....	....	....	....
2003-04	Albany River Rats	AHL	77	2	6	8	100	....	....	....	....	....
2004-05	Albany River Rats	AHL	63	0	6	6	83	....	....	....	....	....

• Missed entire 1996-97 season recovering from back injury suffered during off-season training, August, 1996. Signed as a free agent by **New Jersey**, July 12, 2002.

BROPHEY, Evan (BROH-fee, EH-vehn) **CHI.**

Center/Left wing. Shoots left. 6'1", 194 lbs. Born, Kitchener, Ont., December 3, 1986.
(Chicago's 4th choice, 68th overall, in 2005 Entry Draft).

			Regular Season					Playoffs				
Season	**Club**	**League**	**GP**	**G**	**A**	**Pts**	**PIM**	**GP**	**G**	**A**	**Pts**	**PIM**
2002-03	Barrie Colts	OHL	61	12	14	26	36	6	0	0	0	2
2003-04	Barrie Colts	OHL	67	14	11	25	63	12	4	3	7	4
2004-05	Barrie Colts	OHL	10	3	7	10	13	....	....	....	....	....
	Belleville Bulls	OHL	53	25	36	61	42	5	2	1	3	2

BROS, Michal (BROHSH, MEE-khahl) **MIN.**

Center. Shoots right. 6'1", 195 lbs. Born, Olomouc, Czech., January 25, 1976.
(San Jose's 6th choice, 130th overall, in 1995 Entry Draft).

			Regular Season					Playoffs				
Season	**Club**	**League**	**GP**	**G**	**A**	**Pts**	**PIM**	**GP**	**G**	**A**	**Pts**	**PIM**
1994-95	HC Olomouc Jr.	CzRep-Jr.	34	29	32	61	....	....	....	....	....	....
1995-96	HC Olomouc	CzRep	35	8	11	19	....	4	2	0	2	....
1996-97	HC Olomouc	CzRep	50	13	14	27	28	....	....	....	....	....
1997-98	HC Petra Vsetin	CzRep	47	14	18	32	28	10	3	1	4	2
	HC Petra Vsetin	EuroHL	9	3	0	3	2	....	....	....	....	....
1998-99	HC Slovnaft Vsetin	CzRep	42	10	18	28	18	12	1	3	4	....
99-2000	HC Sparta Praha	CzRep	49	6	30	36	49	9	1	3	4	4
2000-01	HC Sparta Praha	CzRep	27	3	13	16	22	13	4	6	10	8
2001-02	HC Sparta Praha	CzRep	48	19	29	48	71	13	7	*11	*18	8
2002-03	HC Sparta Praha	CzRep	40	13	17	30	90	10	2	4	6	8
2003-04	HC Sparta Praha	CzRep	46	15	25	40	60	13	1	3	4	6
2004-05	HC Sparta Praha	CzRep	44	7	14	21	63	3	1	0	1	0

Claimed by **Minnesota** from **San Jose** in Expansion Draft, June 23, 2000.

BROSNIHAN, Pat (BRAWS-nih-han, PAT) **PHX.**

Right wing. Shoots right. 6'4", 208 lbs. Born, Worcester, MA, August 20, 1986.
(Phoenix's 5th choice, 212th overall, in 2005 Entry Draft).

			Regular Season					Playoffs				
Season	**Club**	**League**	**GP**	**G**	**A**	**Pts**	**PIM**	**GP**	**G**	**A**	**Pts**	**PIM**
2003-04	Worcester	High-MA	25	28	26	54	30	....	....	....	....	....
2004-05	Worcester	High-MA	26	20	44	64	48	....	....	....	....	....

Signed Letter of Intent to attend **Yale** (ECAC) in fall of 2005.

BROUWER, Troy (BROW-uhr, TROI) **CHI.**

Right wing. Shoots right. 6'3", 210 lbs. Born, Vancouver, B.C., August 17, 1985.
(Chicago's 13th choice, 214th overall, in 2004 Entry Draft).

			Regular Season					Playoffs				
Season	**Club**	**League**	**GP**	**G**	**A**	**Pts**	**PIM**	**GP**	**G**	**A**	**Pts**	**PIM**
2001-02	Moose Jaw	WHL	13	0	0	0	7	....	....	....	....	....
2002-03	Moose Jaw	WHL	59	9	12	21	54	13	1	2	3	14
2003-04	Moose Jaw	WHL	72	23	26	49	111	10	3	0	3	12
2004-05	Moose Jaw	WHL	71	22	25	47	132	5	1	2	3	8

BROWN, Marc (BROWN, MAHRK)

Left wing. Shoots left. 6'1", 196 lbs. Born, White Rock, B.C., March 10, 1979.

			Regular Season					Playoffs				
Season	**Club**	**League**	**GP**	**G**	**A**	**Pts**	**PIM**	**GP**	**G**	**A**	**Pts**	**PIM**
1995-96	Abbotsford Pilots	PIJHL	35	20	15	35	15	....	....	....	....	....
1996-97	Spokane Chiefs	WHL	52	4	8	12	37	2	0	0	0	0
1997-98	Spokane Chiefs	WHL	41	10	15	25	35	....	....	....	....	....
	Prince Albert	WHL	23	6	8	14	21	....	....	....	....	....
1998-99	Prince Albert	WHL	72	35	45	80	47	14	12	6	18	6
99-2000	Worcester IceCats	AHL	72	13	11	24	24	17	3	1	4	0
2000-01	Worcester IceCats	AHL	34	9	10	19	27	10	0	1	1	6
2001-02	Worcester IceCats	AHL	74	30	25	55	42	3	2	2	4	0
2002-03	Worcester IceCats	AHL	58	13	15	28	24	....	....	....	....	....
2003-04	Worcester IceCats	AHL	65	14	20	34	34	7	0	1	1	0
2004-05	Augsburg	Germany	28	2	9	11	61	5	0	1	1	0

Signed as a free agent by **St. Louis**, September 24, 1999. • Missed majority of 2000-01 season recovering from abdominal injury suffered in training camp, September 27, 2000. Signed as a free agent by **Augsburg** (Germany), August, 2004.

BROWN, Mike (BROWN, MIGHK) **VAN.**

Right wing. Shoots right. 6', 210 lbs. Born, Northbrook, IL, June 24, 1985.
(Vancouver's 4th choice, 159th overall, in 2004 Entry Draft).

			Regular Season					Playoffs				
Season	**Club**	**League**	**GP**	**G**	**A**	**Pts**	**PIM**	**GP**	**G**	**A**	**Pts**	**PIM**
2000-01	Chicago Chill	USAHA	66	27	23	50	....	....	....	....	....	....
2001-02	USA U-17	USDP	63	11	15	26	69	....	....	....	....	....
2002-03	USA U-18	USDP	43	5	6	11	45	....	....	....	....	....
2003-04	U. of Michigan	CCHA	42	8	5	13	51	....	....	....	....	....
2004-05	U. of Michigan	CCHA	35	3	5	8	95	....	....	....	....	....

BROWN, Paul (BROWN, PAWL) **NSH.**

Right wing. Shoots right. 6'3", 184 lbs. Born, Edmonton, Alta., July 21, 1984.
(Nashville's 6th choice, 89th overall, in 2003 Entry Draft).

			Regular Season					Playoffs				
Season	**Club**	**League**	**GP**	**G**	**A**	**Pts**	**PIM**	**GP**	**G**	**A**	**Pts**	**PIM**
99-2000	Prince George	BCAHA	65	84	120	204	260	....	....	....	....	....
	Regina Pats	WHL	3	0	0	0	0	....	....	....	....	....
2000-01	Regina Pats	WHL	33	3	1	4	83	....	....	....	....	....
	Kamloops Blazers	WHL	30	6	11	17	118	2	0	0	0	4
2001-02	Kamloops Blazers	WHL	37	7	12	19	130	1	0	0	0	0
2002-03	Kamloops Blazers	WHL	67	21	36	57	231	6	3	0	3	20
2003-04	Kamloops Blazers	WHL	59	11	20	31	222	5	0	1	1	13
2004-05	Milwaukee	AHL	20	3	2	5	90	7	2	0	2	25
	Trenton Titans	ECHL	20	2	4	6	63	12	5	6	11	32

• Missed majority of 2001-02 season recovering from off-season ankle injury, August 20, 2001.

BROWNLEE, Chad (BROWN-lee, CHAD) **VAN.**

Defense. Shoots right. 6'2", 184 lbs. Born, Kelowna, B.C., July 12, 1984.
(Vancouver's 6th choice, 190th overall, in 2003 Entry Draft).

			Regular Season					Playoffs				
Season	**Club**	**League**	**GP**	**G**	**A**	**Pts**	**PIM**	**GP**	**G**	**A**	**Pts**	**PIM**
2001-02	Vernon Vipers	BCHL	55	6	12	18	62	....	....	....	....	....
2002-03	Vernon Vipers	BCHL	58	8	16	24	63	18	2	7	9	14
2003-04	Minnesota State	WCHA	35	2	1	3	44	....	....	....	....	....
2004-05	Minnesota State	WCHA	36	1	1	2	60	....	....	....	....	....

BRULE, Gilbert (broo-LAY, zhihl-BAIR) **CBJ**

Center. Shoots right. 5'10", 175 lbs. Born, Edmonton, Alta., January 1, 1987.
(Columbus' 1st choice, 6th overall, in 2005 Entry Draft).

			Regular Season					Playoffs				
Season	**Club**	**League**	**GP**	**G**	**A**	**Pts**	**PIM**	**GP**	**G**	**A**	**Pts**	**PIM**
2002-03	Quesnel	BCHL	48	32	25	57	71	....	....	....	....	....
	Vancouver Giants	WHL	1	0	0	0	0	4	1	0	1	0
2003-04	Vancouver Giants	WHL	67	25	35	60	100	11	4	5	9	10
2004-05	Vancouver Giants	WHL	70	39	48	87	169	6	1	3	4	8

WHL West First All-Star Team (2005) • Canadian Major Junior Scholastic Player of the Year (2005)

BRUNELLE, Mathieu (broo-nehl, MA-tyew) **PHI.**

Left wing. Shoots left. 5'11", 180 lbs. Born, Warwick, Que., April 6, 1983.
(Philadelphia's 7th choice, 201st overall, in 2002 Entry Draft).

			Regular Season					Playoffs				
Season	**Club**	**League**	**GP**	**G**	**A**	**Pts**	**PIM**	**GP**	**G**	**A**	**Pts**	**PIM**
99-2000	Magog	QAAA	42	26	31	57	64	19	8	7	15	20
2000-01	Victoriaville Tigres	QMJHL	65	7	11	18	39	13	1	1	2	0
2001-02	Victoriaville Tigres	QMJHL	72	43	64	107	105	14	7	6	13	35
2002-03	Victoriaville Tigres	QMJHL	39	21	29	50	75	....	....	....	....	....
	Hull Olympiques	QMJHL	31	17	19	36	42	20	*22	16	38	20
2003-04	Philadelphia	AHL	7	0	1	1	2	....	....	....	....	....
	Trenton Titans	ECHL	64	26	30	56	100	....	....	....	....	....
2004-05	Trenton Titans	ECHL	37	12	9	21	51	....	....	....	....	....
	Dayton Bombers	ECHL	13	2	6	8	32	....	....	....	....	....
	Bakersfield	ECHL	18	13	4	17	12	5	1	1	2	6

Traded to **Dayton** (ECHL) by **Trenton** (ECHL) for Mike Schutte, February 3, 2005.

BUCKLEY, Brendan (BUHK-lee, BREHN-duhn)

Defense. Shoots right. 6', 205 lbs. Born, Boston, MA, February 26, 1977.
(Anaheim's 3rd choice, 117th overall, in 1996 Entry Draft).

			Regular Season					Playoffs				
Season	**Club**	**League**	**GP**	**G**	**A**	**Pts**	**PIM**	**GP**	**G**	**A**	**Pts**	**PIM**
1994-95	Boston Jr. Bruins	Exhib.	48	22	43	65	164	....	....	....	....	....
1995-96	Boston College	H-East	34	0	4	4	72	....	....	....	....	....
1996-97	Boston College	H-East	38	2	6	8	90	....	....	....	....	....
1997-98	Boston College	H-East	41	1	12	13	69	....	....	....	....	....
1998-99	Boston College	H-East	43	1	13	14	75	....	....	....	....	....
99-2000	Cincinnati	AHL	4	0	0	0	6	....	....	....	....	....
	Quad City	UHL	61	1	10	11	73	9	1	0	1	10
2000-01	Wilkes-Barre	AHL	63	2	8	10	62	21	0	2	2	33
2001-02	Wilkes-Barre	AHL	80	1	19	20	116	....	....	....	....	....
2002-03	Wilkes-Barre	AHL	80	2	6	8	99	6	0	0	0	2
2003-04	Wilkes-Barre	AHL	45	2	4	6	61	....	....	....	....	....
	Syracuse Crunch	AHL	30	0	4	4	40	7	0	0	0	14
2004-05	Worcester IceCats	AHL	63	3	13	16	128	....	....	....	....	....

Signed as a free agent by **Pittsburgh**, September 28, 2000. Traded to **Columbus** by **Pittsburgh** for Pauli Levokari, February 10, 2004. Signed as a free agent by **Worcester** (AHL), October 25, 2004.

BURAVCHIKOV, Vyacheslav (burh-AV-chih-kawf, VYACH-ih-slav) **BUF.**

Defense. Shoots left. 6', 189 lbs. Born, Moscow, USSR, May 22, 1987.
(Buffalo's 7th choice, 191st overall, in 2005 Entry Draft).

			Regular Season					Playoffs				
Season	**Club**	**League**	**GP**	**G**	**A**	**Pts**	**PIM**	**GP**	**G**	**A**	**Pts**	**PIM**
2003-04	Krylja Sovetov 2	Russia-3	STATISTICS NOT AVAILABLE									
2004-05	Krylja Sovetov 2	Russia-3	15	5	6	11	22	....	....	....	....	....
	Krylja Sovetov	Russia-2	26	4	1	5	14	3	0	0	0	2

BURISH, Adam (BUHR-ish, A-duhm) **CHI.**

Right wing. Shoots right. 6'1", 189 lbs. Born, Madison, WI, January 6, 1983.
(Chicago's 9th choice, 282nd overall, in 2002 Entry Draft).

			Regular Season					Playoffs				
Season	**Club**	**League**	**GP**	**G**	**A**	**Pts**	**PIM**	**GP**	**G**	**A**	**Pts**	**PIM**
2000-01	Edgewood	High-WI	22	25	30	55	22	....	....	....	....	....
2001-02	Green Bay	USHL	61	24	33	57	122	1	0	0	0	0
2002-03	U. of Wisconsin	WCHA	19	0	6	6	32	....	....	....	....	....
2003-04	U. of Wisconsin	WCHA	43	6	13	19	63	....	....	....	....	....
2004-05	U. of Wisconsin	WCHA	41	13	7	20	41	....	....	....	....	....

BURKHALTER, Loic (buhrk-HAHL-tuhr, LOIK) PHX.

Center. Shoots left. 6', 192 lbs. Born, La Chaux-de-Fonds, Switz., February 11, 1980.
(Phoenix's 8th choice, 290th overall, in 2003 Entry Draft).

			Regular Season					Playoffs				
Season	Club	League	GP	G	A	Pts	PIM	GP	G	A	Pts	PIM
1996-97	Chaux-de-Fonds	Swiss	24	1	0	1	0	....	....	....	....	....
1997-98	Chaux-de-Fonds Jr.	Swiss-Jr.	4	4	2	6	16	....	....	....	....	....
	Chaux-de-Fonds	Swiss	36	3	4	7	8	12	1	0	1	2
1998-99	Chaux-de-Fonds	Swiss-2	38	19	29	48	28	12	4	8	12	10
99-2000	Rapperswil	Swiss	44	7	5	12	16	11	2	9	11	0
2000-01	Rapperswil	Swiss	31	7	5	12	20	4	1	1	2	0
2001-02	HC Ambri-Piotta	Swiss	44	9	12	21	28	6	2	2	4	6
2002-03	HC Ambri-Piotta	Swiss	44	12	22	34	42	4	1	0	1	2
2003-04	HC Ambri-Piotta	Swiss	47	21	26	47	40	7	1	2	3	4
2004-05	Langnau	Swiss	44	9	14	23	32	6	1	3	4	10

BUT, Anton (BOOT, AN-tawn) T.B.

Left wing. Shoots left. 6'1", 201 lbs. Born, Kharkov, USSR, July 3, 1980.
(New Jersey's 7th choice, 119th overall, in 1998 Entry Draft).

			Regular Season					Playoffs				
Season	Club	League	GP	G	A	Pts	PIM	GP	G	A	Pts	PIM
1995-96	Yaroslavl 2	CIS-2	60	30	12	42	10	....	....	....	....	....
1996-97	Yaroslavl 2	Russia-3	70	30	20	50	20	....	....	....	....	....
1997-98	Yaroslavl 2	Russia-2	48	12	5	17	28	....	....	....	....	....
1998-99	Yaroslavl 2	Russia-3	22	12	8	20	59	....	....	....	....	....
	Torpedo Yaroslavl	Russia	5	0	0	0	0	....	....	....	....	....
99-2000	Yaroslavl 2	Russia-3	1	0	0	0	2	....	....	....	....	....
	Torpedo Yaroslavl	Russia	26	2	5	7	16	8	2	1	3	0
2000-01	Yaroslavl	Russia	42	14	6	20	14	11	1	3	4	8
2001-02	Yaroslavl	Russia	48	14	11	25	14	6	0	1	1	2
2002-03	Yaroslavl	Russia	44	16	13	29	16	9	1	2	3	6
2003-04	Yaroslavl	Russia	51	11	10	21	24	3	0	0	0	0
2004-05	Yaroslavl	Russia	60	12	22	34	58	8	3	3	6	0

Rights traded to **Tampa Bay** by **New Jersey** with Josef Boumedienne and Sascha Goc for Andrei Zyuzin, November 9, 2001.

BUTCHER, Matt (BUH-chuhr, MAT) VAN.

Center. Shoots left. 6'1", 185 lbs. Born, Bellingham, WA, January 1, 1987.
(Vancouver's 4th choice, 138th overall, in 2005 Entry Draft).

			Regular Season					Playoffs				
Season	Club	League	GP	G	A	Pts	PIM	GP	G	A	Pts	PIM
2003-04	Chilliwack Chiefs	BCHL	48	7	18	25	73	11	3	1	4	14
2004-05	Chilliwack Chiefs	BCHL	59	27	28	55	94	....	....	....	....	....

Signed Letter of Intent to attend **Northern Michigan** (CCHA) in fall of 2005.

BUTLER, Chris (BUHT-luhr, KRIHS) BUF.

Defense. Shoots left. 6'1", 178 lbs. Born, St. Louis, MO, October 27, 1986.
(Buffalo's 4th choice, 96th overall, in 2005 Entry Draft).

			Regular Season					Playoffs				
Season	Club	League	GP	G	A	Pts	PIM	GP	G	A	Pts	PIM
2003-04	Sioux City	USHL	55	3	6	9	37	7	0	1	1	6
2004-05	Sioux City	USHL	60	6	22	28	90	13	1	6	7	10

USHL First All-Star Team (2005)

Signed Letter of Intent to attend **Denver** (ECAC) in fall of 2005.

BUTURLIN, Alexander (boo-tuhr-LIHN, AL-ehx-an-DEHR) MTL.

Right wing. Shoots left. 5'11", 182 lbs. Born, Moscow, USSR, September 3, 1981.
(Montreal's 1st choice, 39th overall, in 1999 Entry Draft).

			Regular Season					Playoffs				
Season	Club	League	GP	G	A	Pts	PIM	GP	G	A	Pts	PIM
1997-98	CSKA Moscow 2	Russia-3	50	12	15	27	46	....	....	....	....	....
	CSKA Moscow	Russia	2	0	0	0	0	....	....	....	....	....
1998-99	CSKA Moscow	Russia	16	1	0	1	6	3	1	0	1	2
99-2000	Sarnia Sting	OHL	57	20	27	47	46	7	4	2	6	12
2000-01	Sarnia Sting	OHL	57	28	37	65	27	4	3	1	4	0
2001-02	Ufa	Russia	32	3	3	6	42	....	....	....	....	....
2002-03	Lada Togliatti	Russia	49	6	14	20	71	10	3	0	3	4
2003-04	Lada Togliatti	Russia	53	7	13	20	78	6	0	1	1	4
2004-05	Lada Togliatti	Russia	56	9	11	20	46	10	3	6	9	8

BYERS, Dane (BIGH-uhrs, DAYN) NYR

Left wing. Shoots left. 6'2", 192 lbs. Born, Nipawin, Sask., February 21, 1986.
(NY Rangers' 4th choice, 48th overall, in 2004 Entry Draft).

			Regular Season					Playoffs				
Season	Club	League	GP	G	A	Pts	PIM	GP	G	A	Pts	PIM
2002-03	Prince Albert	WHL	49	8	6	14	46	....	....	....	....	....
2003-04	Prince Albert	WHL	51	9	8	17	134	6	1	2	3	17
2004-05	Prince Albert	WHL	65	11	9	20	181	17	4	6	10	18

BYFUGLIEN, Dustin (bigh-FEWG-lehn, DUHS-tihn) CHI.

Defense. Shoots right. 6'3", 275 lbs. Born, Minneapolis, MN, March 27, 1985.
(Chicago's 8th choice, 245th overall, in 2003 Entry Draft).

			Regular Season					Playoffs				
Season	Club	League	GP	G	A	Pts	PIM	GP	G	A	Pts	PIM
2001-02	Chicago Mission	MAHL	52	32	30	62	40	....	....	....	....	....
	Brandon	WHL	3	0	0	0	0	....	....	....	....	....
2002-03	Brandon	WHL	8	1	1	2	4	....	....	....	....	....
	Prince George	WHL	48	9	28	37	74	5	1	3	4	12
2003-04	Prince George	WHL	66	16	29	45	137	....	....	....	....	....
2004-05	Prince George	WHL	64	22	36	58	184	....	....	....	....	....

BYRNE, Trevor (BUHR-ne, TREH-vuhr) ST.L.

Defense. Shoots left. 6'2", 208 lbs. Born, Hingham, MA, May 7, 1980.
(St. Louis' 4th choice, 143rd overall, in 1999 Entry Draft).

			Regular Season					Playoffs				
Season	Club	League	GP	G	A	Pts	PIM	GP	G	A	Pts	PIM
1997-98	Deerfield Academy	High-MA	25	5	14	19	16	....	....	....	....	....
1998-99	Deerfield Academy	High-MA	25	9	19	28	22	....	....	....	....	....
99-2000	Dartmouth	ECAC	30	3	9	12	40	....	....	....	....	....
2000-01	Dartmouth	ECAC	34	5	21	26	52	....	....	....	....	....
2001-02	Dartmouth	ECAC	32	5	16	21	38	....	....	....	....	....
2002-03	Dartmouth	ECAC	34	8	16	24	28	....	....	....	....	....
2003-04	Worcester IceCats	AHL	63	7	13	20	22	9	2	2	4	2
	Peoria Rivermen	ECHL	6	0	0	0	0	....	....	....	....	....
2004-05	Worcester IceCats	AHL	40	1	6	7	18	....	....	....	....	....
	Peoria Rivermen	ECHL	33	6	12	18	28	....	....	....	....	....

ECAC Second All-Star Team (2001, 2002, 2003)

CABANA, Frederik (kah-BAH-nuh, FREHD-uhr-ihk) PHI.

Center/Left wing. Shoots left. 6', 182 lbs. Born, Fleurimont, Que., May 16, 1986.
(Philadelphia's 7th choice, 171st overall, in 2004 Entry Draft).

			Regular Season					Playoffs				
Season	Club	League	GP	G	A	Pts	PIM	GP	G	A	Pts	PIM
2001-02	Magog	QAAA	37	20	16	36	124	7	1	4	5	12
2002-03	Halifax	QMJHL	62	4	10	14	65	24	7	1	8	50
2003-04	Halifax	QMJHL	70	17	21	38	78	....	....	....	....	....
2004-05	Halifax	QMJHL	59	10	24	34	47	11	6	6	12	11

CALDWELL, Ryan (KAWLD-wehl, RIGH-uhn) NYI

Defense. Shoots left. 6'2", 174 lbs. Born, Deloraine, Man., June 15, 1981.
(NY Islanders' 7th choice, 202nd overall, in 2000 Entry Draft).

			Regular Season					Playoffs				
Season	Club	League	GP	G	A	Pts	PIM	GP	G	A	Pts	PIM
1998-99	Shat.-St. Mary's	High-MN	29	24	55	79	22	....	....	....	....	....
99-2000	Thunder Bay Flyers	USHL	46	3	20	23	152	....	....	....	....	....
2000-01	U. of Denver	WCHA	36	3	20	23	76	....	....	....	....	....
2001-02	U. of Denver	WCHA	40	3	16	19	76	....	....	....	....	....
2002-03	U. of Denver	WCHA	38	5	14	19	58	....	....	....	....	....
2003-04	U. of Denver	WCHA	42	15	12	27	96	....	....	....	....	....
2004-05	Bridgeport	AHL	73	2	19	21	65	....	....	....	....	....

WCHA All-Rookie Team (2001) • WCHA Second All-Star Team (2004) • NCAA West First All-American Team (2004) • NCAA Championship All-Tournament Team (2004)

CALLAHAN, Joe (kal-AH-han, JOH) PHX.

Defense. Shoots right. 6'3", 221 lbs. Born, Brockton, MA, December 20, 1982.
(Phoenix's 4th choice, 70th overall, in 2002 Entry Draft).

			Regular Season					Playoffs				
Season	Club	League	GP	G	A	Pts	PIM	GP	G	A	Pts	PIM
2001-02	Yale	ECAC	31	3	8	11	20	....	....	....	....	....
2002-03	Yale	ECAC	32	2	11	13	38	....	....	....	....	....
2003-04	Yale	ECAC	31	6	14	20	38	....	....	....	....	....
	Springfield Falcons	AHL	13	0	4	4	12	....	....	....	....	....
2004-05	Utah Grizzlies	AHL	75	4	7	11	66	....	....	....	....	....

CALLAHAN, Ryan (kal-AH-han, RIGH-uhn) NYR

Right wing. Shoots right. 5'10", 180 lbs. Born, Rochester, NY, March 21, 1985.
(NY Rangers' 9th choice, 127th overall, in 2004 Entry Draft).

			Regular Season					Playoffs				
Season	Club	League	GP	G	A	Pts	PIM	GP	G	A	Pts	PIM
2002-03	Guelph Storm	OHL	59	14	17	31	47	11	0	3	3	2
2003-04	Guelph Storm	OHL	68	36	32	68	86	22	*13	8	21	20
2004-05	Guelph Storm	OHL	60	28	26	54	108	4	1	1	2	6

CAMPBELL, Ed (KAM-behl, EHD)

Defense. Shoots left. 6'2", 204 lbs. Born, Worcester, MA, November 26, 1974.
(NY Rangers' 9th choice, 190th overall, in 1993 Entry Draft).

			Regular Season					Playoffs				
Season	Club	League	GP	G	A	Pts	PIM	GP	G	A	Pts	PIM
1992-93	Omaha Lancers	USHL	42	9	19	28	160	....	....	....	....	....
1993-94	U. Mass-Lowell	H-East	40	8	16	24	114	....	....	....	....	....
1994-95	U. Mass-Lowell	H-East	34	6	24	30	105	....	....	....	....	....
1995-96	U. Mass-Lowell	H-East	39	6	33	39	*107	....	....	....	....	....
1996-97	Binghamton	AHL	74	5	17	22	108	4	0	0	0	2
1997-98	Hartford Wolf Pack	AHL	9	0	1	1	9	14	0	2	2	33
	Fort Wayne	IHL	50	10	5	15	147	....	....	....	....	....
1998-99	Hartford Wolf Pack	AHL	18	0	3	3	24	7	0	3	3	14
	Fort Wayne	IHL	46	1	16	17	137	....	....	....	....	....
99-2000	Orlando	IHL	81	2	7	9	217	3	0	0	0	6
2000-01	Worcester IceCats	AHL	78	5	27	32	207	10	1	0	1	10
2001-02	Worcester IceCats	AHL	70	3	15	18	172	3	0	0	0	5
2002-03	Grand Rapids	AHL	80	0	12	12	140	15	0	1	1	22
2003-04	Providence Bruins	AHL	67	1	8	9	92	2	0	0	0	2
2004-05	Hershey Bears	AHL	1	0	0	0	0	....	....	....	....	....
	Milwaukee	AHL	12	0	1	1	10	....	....	....	....	....
	Bridgeport	AHL	44	1	2	3	45	....	....	....	....	....

Signed as a free agent by **St. Louis**, July 1, 2001. Signed as a free agent by **Detroit**, August 5, 2002. Signed as a free agent by **Boston**, July 31, 2003. Signed as a free agent by **Hershey** (AHL), September 28, 2004. Signed to a PTO (tryout) contract by **Milwaukee** (AHL), October 30, 2004. Signed as a free agent by **Bridgeport** (AHL), January 15, 2005.

CAMPOLI, Chris (kam-POH-lee, KRIHS) NYI

Defense. Shoots left. 6', 190 lbs. Born, North York, Ont., July 9, 1984.
(NY Islanders' 8th choice, 227th overall, in 2004 Entry Draft).

			Regular Season					Playoffs				
Season	Club	League	GP	G	A	Pts	PIM	GP	G	A	Pts	PIM
2001-02	Erie Otters	OHL	68	2	24	26	117	20	0	5	5	18
2002-03	Erie Otters	OHL	60	8	40	48	82	....	....	....	....	....
2003-04	Erie Otters	OHL	67	20	46	66	66	8	0	6	6	16
2004-05	Bridgeport	AHL	79	15	34	49	78	....	....	....	....	....

OHL Humanitarian Player of the Year (2004) • Canadian Major Junior Humanitarian Player of the Year (2004) • AHL All-Rookie Team (2005)

CARCILLO, Daniel (KAR-sihl-oh, DAN-yuhl) PIT.

Left wing. Shoots left. 5'11", 202 lbs. Born, King City, Ont., January 28, 1985.
(Pittsburgh's 4th choice, 73rd overall, in 2003 Entry Draft).

			Regular Season					Playoffs				
Season	Club	League	GP	G	A	Pts	PIM	GP	G	A	Pts	PIM
2001-02	Milton Merchants	OHA-B	47	15	16	31	162	....	....	....	....	....
2002-03	Sarnia Sting	OHL	68	29	37	66	157	6	0	4	4	14
2003-04	Sarnia Sting	OHL	61	30	29	59	148	4	1	2	3	12
2004-05	Sarnia Sting	OHL	12	2	7	9	40	....	....	....	....	....
	Mississauga	OHL	20	8	10	18	75	5	3	1	4	18

CARD, Mike (KARD, MIGHK) BUF.

Defense. Shoots right. 6', 201 lbs. Born, Kitchener, Ont., February 18, 1986.
(Buffalo's 7th choice, 241st overall, in 2004 Entry Draft).

			Regular Season					Playoffs				
Season	Club	League	GP	G	A	Pts	PIM	GP	G	A	Pts	PIM
2002-03	Kelowna Rockets	WHL	61	7	22	29	41	19	2	6	8	12
2003-04	Kelowna Rockets	WHL	72	6	12	18	47	17	2	4	6	20
2004-05	Kelowna Rockets	WHL	72	10	35	45	85	24	2	5	7	38

CAREFOOT, Mitch (KAIR-fut, MIHTCH) **ATL.**

Center. Shoots right. 6'1", 210 lbs. Born, Dauphin, Man., January 2, 1985.
(Atlanta's 8th choice, 237th overall, in 2004 Entry Draft).

			Regular Season					Playoffs				
Season	Club	League	GP	G	A	Pts	PIM	GP	G	A	Pts	PIM
2002-03	Salmon Arm	BCHL	56	19	36	55	51	11	4	3	7	26
2003-04	Cornell Big Red	ECAC	31	6	1	7	14	....	....	....	....	....
2004-05	Cornell Big Red	ECAC	31	4	7	11	8	....	....	....	....	....

CARKNER, Matt (KARK-nehr, MAT) **S.J.**

Defense. Shoots right. 6'4", 235 lbs. Born, Winchester, Ont., November 3, 1980.
(Montreal's 2nd choice, 58th overall, in 1999 Entry Draft).

			Regular Season					Playoffs				
Season	Club	League	GP	G	A	Pts	PIM	GP	G	A	Pts	PIM
1996-97	Winchester Hawks	OHA-B	29	1	18	19	....	....	....	....	....	....
1997-98	Peterborough	OHL	57	0	6	6	121	4	0	0	0	2
1998-99	Peterborough	OHL	60	2	16	18	173	5	0	0	0	20
99-2000	Peterborough	OHL	62	3	13	16	177	5	0	1	1	6
2000-01	Peterborough	OHL	53	8	8	16	128	7	0	3	3	25
2001-02	Cleveland Barons	AHL	74	0	3	3	335	....	....	....	....	....
2002-03	Cleveland Barons	AHL	39	1	4	5	104	....	....	....	....	....
2003-04	Cleveland Barons	AHL	60	2	11	13	115	9	0	3	3	39
2004-05	Cleveland Barons	AHL	73	0	10	10	192	....	....	....	....	....

Signed as a free agent by **San Jose**, June 6, 2001. • Missed majority of 2002-03 season recovering from knee injury suffered in game vs. Utah (AHL), January 4, 2003.

CARLE, Matthew (KARL, MA-thew) **S.J.**

Defense. Shoots left. 6', 182 lbs. Born, Anchorage, AK, September 25, 1984.
(San Jose's 4th choice, 47th overall, in 2003 Entry Draft).

			Regular Season					Playoffs				
Season	Club	League	GP	G	A	Pts	PIM	GP	G	A	Pts	PIM
99-2000	Alaska All-Stars	AASHA	42	14	28	42	....	....	....	....	....	....
2000-01	USA U-17	USDP	68	1	5	6	31	....	....	....	....	....
2001-02	USA U-18	USDP	64	4	15	19	51	....	....	....	....	....
2002-03	River City Lancers	USHL	59	12	30	42	98	11	2	2	4	20
2003-04	U. of Denver	WCHA	30	5	20	25	33	....	....	....	....	....
2004-05	U. of Denver	WCHA	43	13	31	44	68	....	....	....	....	....

USHL First All-Star Team (2003) • USHL Defenseman of the Year (2003) • WCHA All-Rookie Team (2004) • WCHA First All-Star Team (2005) • NCAA West First All-American Team (2005) • NCAA Championship All-Tournament Team (2005)

CARON, Ed (kahr-OHN, EHD) **EDM.**

Center. Shoots left. 6'2", 228 lbs. Born, Nashua, NH, April 30, 1982.
(Edmonton's 3rd choice, 52nd overall, in 2001 Entry Draft).

			Regular Season					Playoffs				
Season	Club	League	GP	G	A	Pts	PIM	GP	G	A	Pts	PIM
1998-99	Exeter	High-NH	31	39	30	69	28	....	....	....	....	....
99-2000	Exeter	High-NH	26	22	26	48	24	....	....	....	....	....
2000-01	Exeter	High-NH	17	30	20	50	42	....	....	....	....	....
2001-02	New Hampshire	H-East	34	6	7	13	51	....	....	....	....	....
2002-03	Yale	ECAC	DID NOT PLAY – TRANSFERRED COLLEGES									
2003-04	New Hampshire	H-East	35	5	1	6	61	....	....	....	....	....
2004-05	Greenville Grrrowl	ECHL	54	10	9	19	23	4	0	0	0	4

• Left **New Hampshire** (H-East) and signed Letter of Intent to attend **Yale** (ECAC), April 26, 2002. • Left **Yale** (ECAC) and returned to **New Hampshire** (H-East), January 16, 2003.

CARSON, Brett (KAR-suhn, BREHT) **CAR.**

Defense. Shoots right. 6'4", 220 lbs. Born, Regina, Sask., November 29, 1985.
(Carolina's 4th choice, 109th overall, in 2004 Entry Draft).

			Regular Season					Playoffs				
Season	Club	League	GP	G	A	Pts	PIM	GP	G	A	Pts	PIM
99-2000	Pipestone Valley	SSMHL	8	0	0	0	0	....	....	....	....	....
2000-01	Pipestone Valley	SSMHL	31	5	17	22	20	....	....	....	....	....
2001-02	Yorkton Terriers	SMHL	41	16	37	53	32	....	....	....	....	....
	Moose Jaw	WHL	6	0	0	0	0	12	2	0	2	0
2002-03	Moose Jaw	WHL	28	1	4	5	28	....	....	....	....	....
	Calgary Hitmen	WHL	30	3	6	9	4	5	2	1	3	0
2003-04	Calgary Hitmen	WHL	71	5	27	32	49	7	0	0	0	6
2004-05	Calgary Hitmen	WHL	61	8	16	24	61	8	2	2	4	8

CARTER, Jeff (KAR-tuhr, JEHF) **PHI.**

Center. Shoots right. 6'3", 195 lbs. Born, London, Ont., January 1, 1985.
(Philadelphia's 1st choice, 11th overall, in 2003 Entry Draft).

			Regular Season					Playoffs				
Season	Club	League	GP	G	A	Pts	PIM	GP	G	A	Pts	PIM
2000-01	Strathroy Rockets	OHA-B	49	27	20	47	10	....	....	....	....	....
2001-02	Sault Ste. Marie	OHL	63	18	17	35	12	4	0	0	0	2
2002-03	Sault Ste. Marie	OHL	61	35	36	71	55	4	0	2	2	2
2003-04	Sault Ste. Marie	OHL	57	36	30	66	26	....	....	....	....	....
	Philadelphia	AHL	....	....	....	....	....	12	4	1	5	0
2004-05	Sault Ste. Marie	OHL	55	34	40	74	40	7	5	5	10	6
	Philadelphia	AHL	3	0	1	1	4	21	12	11	23	12

OHL Second All-Star Team (2004) • OHL First All-Star Team (2005) • Canadian Major Junior Sportsman of the Year (2005) • Canadian Major Junior First All-Star Team (2005)

CAVANAGH, Tom (KAV-a-naw, TAWM) **S.J.**

Left wing. Shoots left. 5'10", 178 lbs. Born, Warwick, RI, March 24, 1982.
(San Jose's 6th choice, 182nd overall, in 2001 Entry Draft).

			Regular Season					Playoffs				
Season	Club	League	GP	G	A	Pts	PIM	GP	G	A	Pts	PIM
1997-98	Toll Gate Titans	High-RI	15	5	17	22	6	4	2	8	10	4
1998-99	Toll Gate Titans	High-RI	15	9	20	29	26	5	5	4	9	6
99-2000	Toll Gate Titans	High-RI	18	25	29	*54	28	5	0	12	12	9
2000-01	Exeter	High-NH	31	*42	40	82	34	....	....	....	....	....
2001-02	Harvard Crimson	ECAC	34	8	17	25	4	....	....	....	....	....
2002-03	Harvard Crimson	ECAC	34	14	13	27	31	....	....	....	....	....
2003-04	Harvard Crimson	ECAC	36	16	20	36	26	....	....	....	....	....
2004-05	Harvard Crimson	ECAC	34	10	19	29	22	....	....	....	....	....

ECAC Second All-Star Team 2005)

CAVANAUGH, Dan (KAV-a-naw, DAN)

Center. Shoots right. 6'1", 190 lbs. Born, Springfield, MA, March 3, 1980.
(Calgary's 2nd choice, 38th overall, in 1999 Entry Draft).

			Regular Season					Playoffs				
Season	Club	League	GP	G	A	Pts	PIM	GP	G	A	Pts	PIM
1995-96	N.E. Jr. Whalers	EJHL	43	8	7	15	....	....	....	....	....	....
1996-97	N.E. Jr. Coyotes	EJHL	56	23	46	69	....	....	....	....	....	....
1997-98	N.E. Jr. Coyotes	EJHL	38	31	*47	*78	58	13	8	12	30	....
1998-99	Boston University	H-East	36	6	8	14	60	....	....	....	....	....
99-2000	Boston University	H-East	40	9	25	34	62	....	....	....	....	....
2000-01	Boston University	H-East	35	7	21	28	43	....	....	....	....	....
2001-02	Houston Aeros	AHL	70	3	16	19	41	5	0	0	0	0
2002-03	Houston Aeros	AHL	77	13	13	26	126	23	2	2	4	20
2003-04	Houston Aeros	AHL	73	16	23	39	94	2	0	1	1	2
2004-05	Houston Aeros	AHL	66	8	14	22	128	5	0	0	0	13

Rights traded to **Minnesota** by **Calgary** with Calgary's 8th round choice (Jake Riddle) in 2001 Entry Draft for Mike Vernon, June 23, 2000.

CAVOSIE, Marc (kuh-VOI-see, MAHRK)

Center. Shoots left. 6', 173 lbs. Born, Albany, NY, August 6, 1981.
(Minnesota's 3rd choice, 99th overall, in 2000 Entry Draft).

			Regular Season					Playoffs				
Season	Club	League	GP	G	A	Pts	PIM	GP	G	A	Pts	PIM
1995-96	Albany	High-NY	22	8	27	31	....	....	....	....	....	....
1996-97	Albany	High-NY	28	26	45	71	....	....	....	....	....	....
1997-98	Albany	High-NY	28	38	33	71	....	....	....	....	....	....
1998-99	Albany	High-NY	28	23	20	43	32	....	....	....	....	....
99-2000	RPI Engineers	ECAC	29	11	17	28	10	....	....	....	....	....
2000-01	RPI Engineers	ECAC	28	13	16	29	47	....	....	....	....	....
2001-02	RPI Engineers	ECAC	36	23	*27	*50	44	....	....	....	....	....
2002-03	Houston Aeros	AHL	54	5	14	19	24	19	3	5	8	12
2003-04	Houston Aeros	AHL	75	10	21	31	37	2	1	0	1	0
2004-05	Houston Aeros	AHL	60	3	17	20	10	4	0	0	0	2

ECAC First All-Star Team (2002) • ECAC Player of the Year (2002)

CEREDA, Luca (suh-REH-duh, LOO-ka) **TOR.**

Center. Shoots left. 6'2", 212 lbs. Born, Lugano, Switz., September 7, 1981.
(Toronto's 1st choice, 24th overall, in 1999 Entry Draft).

			Regular Season					Playoffs				
Season	Club	League	GP	G	A	Pts	PIM	GP	G	A	Pts	PIM
1996-97	HC Ambri-Piotta	Swiss	35	13	8	21	....	....	....	....	....	....
1997-98	HC Ambri-Piotta	Swiss	28	17	27	44	24	....	....	....	....	....
1998-99	Ambri Jr.	Swiss-Jr.	3	4	3	7	20	....	....	....	....	....
	HC Ambri-Piotta	Swiss	38	6	10	16	8	15	0	6	6	4
99-2000	HC Ambri-Piotta	Swiss	44	1	5	6	14	9	0	1	1	2
2000-01	Ottawa 67's	OHL	DID NOT PLAY									
2001-02	St. John's	AHL	71	5	8	13	23	11	2	1	3	10
2002-03	St. John's	AHL	68	7	18	25	26	....	....	....	....	....
2003-04	St. John's	AHL	22	0	2	2	8	....	....	....	....	....
	SC Bern	Swiss	9	1	3	4	22	15	4	0	4	4
2004-05	SC Bern	Swiss	37	1	1	2	6	11	0	1	1	2

• Missed entire 2000-01 season recovering from heart surgery, October 19, 2000. • Loaned to **Bern** (Swiss) by **Toronto**, January 21, 2004.

CETKOVSKY, Jiri (tseht-KAWF-skee, YIH-ree) **CGY.**

Center. Shoots left. 6'4", 209 lbs. Born, Prostejov, Czech., November 4, 1983.
(Calgary's 5th choice, 141st overall, in 2002 Entry Draft).

			Regular Season					Playoffs				
Season	Club	League	GP	G	A	Pts	PIM	GP	G	A	Pts	PIM
99-2000	HC Prostejov Jr.	CzRep-Jr.	5	3	2	5	0	....	....	....	....	....
	MBL Olomouc U17	CzR-U17	25	7	3	10	18	....	....	....	....	....
2000-01	HC Prostejov Jr.	CzRep-Jr.	28	7	7	14	75	....	....	....	....	....
2001-02	HC Zlin Jr.	CzRep-Jr.	30	9	6	15	44	....	....	....	....	....
2002-03	Calgary Hitmen	WHL	57	5	2	7	126	5	0	0	0	15
2003-04	HK Prostejov Jr.	CzRep-Jr.	23	7	7	14	86	6	2	2	4	28
	Prostejov	CzRep-2	13	4	0	4	14	....	....	....	....	....
2004-05	Pardubice	CzRep	1	0	0	0	0	....	....	....	....	....
	Hr. Kralove	CzRep-2	49	4	8	12	58	2	0	0	0	0

CHABADA, Martin (KHA-ba-da, MAHR-tehn) **NYI**

Left wing. Shoots right. 6'1", 203 lbs. Born, Prague, Czech., June 14, 1977.
(NY Islanders' 6th choice, 252nd overall, in 2002 Entry Draft).

			Regular Season					Playoffs				
Season	Club	League	GP	G	A	Pts	PIM	GP	G	A	Pts	PIM
1996-97	HC Sparta Praha	EuroHL	1	0	0	0	0	4	0	0	0	2
	HC Sparta Praha	CzRep	16	1	2	3	4	4	0	1	1	2
1997-98	HC Sparta Praha	EuroHL	4	0	1	1	4	....	....	....	....	....
	HC Sparta Praha	CzRep	40	7	12	19	57	11	1	0	1	4
1998-99	HC Sparta Praha	EuroHL	6	1	1	2	10	2	2	1	3	6
	HC Sparta Praha	CzRep	39	3	9	12	14	1	0	0	0	0
99-2000	HC Sparta Praha	CzRep	35	7	12	19	12	9	2	2	4	4
2000-01	HC Sparta Praha	CzRep	43	9	10	19	36	12	0	0	0	8
2001-02	HC Sparta Praha	CzRep	51	19	21	40	113	13	4	7	11	4
2002-03	Bridgeport	AHL	66	17	13	30	50	9	3	4	7	4
2003-04	Bridgeport	AHL	10	2	3	5	0	....	....	....	....	....
	HC Sparta Praha	CzRep	31	8	18	26	65	13	7	3	10	22
2004-05	HC Sparta Praha	CzRep	50	19	15	34	84	5	0	2	2	16

Signed as a free agent by **Sparta** (CzRep), November 6, 2003.

CHARLEBOIS, Joe (SHAHR-luh-bwah, JOH) **CHI.**

Defense. Shoots right. 6'1", 210 lbs. Born, Potsdam, NY, February 18, 1986.
(Chicago's 10th choice, 188th overall, in 2005 Entry Draft).

			Regular Season					Playoffs				
Season	Club	League	GP	G	A	Pts	PIM	GP	G	A	Pts	PIM
2002-03	Cornwall Colts	CJHL	59	2	18	20	....	....	....	....	....	....
2003-04	USA U-18	USDP	54	1	3	4	20	....	....	....	....	....
2004-05	Sioux City	USHL	59	1	24	25	146	7	1	1	2	6

Signed Letter of Intent to attend **New Hampshire** (H-East) in fall of 2005.

CHERNOV, Artem (chair-NAHF, AR-tehm) DAL.

Center. Shoots left. 5'10", 176 lbs. Born, Novokuznetsk, USSR, April 28, 1982.
(Dallas' 7th choice, 162nd overall, in 2000 Entry Draft).

			Regular Season					Playoffs				
Season	Club	League	GP	G	A	Pts	PIM	GP	G	A	Pts	PIM
1997-98	Novokuznetsk 2	Russia-3	4	0	0	0	0	....	....	....	....	....
1998-99	Novokuznetsk 2	Russia-4	32	9	7	16	14	....	....	....	....	....
99-2000	Magnitogorsk	Russia	10	2	3	5	0	5	0	0	0	0
2000-01	Magnitogorsk	Russia	44	15	17	32	30	....	....	....	....	....
2001-02	Avangard Omsk	Russia	43	6	5	11	4	....	....	....	....	....
2002-03	Avangard Omsk	Russia	48	9	10	19	6	12	1	1	2	4
2003-04	Omsk 2	Russia-3	STATISTICS NOT AVAILABLE									
2004-05	Spartak Moscow	Russia	6	0	0	0	2	....	....	....	....	....
	Yunost-Minsk	BelOpen	20	8	9	17	16	12	3	5	8	4

CHERNYKH, Dmitri (TCHAIR-nihk, dih-MEE-tree) NYI

Right wing. Shoots left. 6', 180 lbs. Born, Voskresensk, USSR, February 27, 1985.
(NY Islanders' 2nd choice, 48th overall, in 2003 Entry Draft).

			Regular Season					Playoffs				
Season	Club	League	GP	G	A	Pts	PIM	GP	G	A	Pts	PIM
2001-02	Voskresensk 2	Russia-3	28	9	6	15	32	....	....	....	....	....
	Voskresensk	Russia-2	7	0	0	0	2	....	....	....	....	....
2002-03	Voskresensk	Russia-2	29	5	4	9	29	....	....	....	....	....
	Voskresensk 2	Russia-3	1	0	0	0	18	....	....	....	....	....
2003-04	CSKA Moscow	Russia	27	2	2	4	0	....	....	....	....	....
2004-05	Mechel	Russia-2	22	1	5	6	6	4	1	0	1	0

CHIPCHURA, Kyle (chip-CHUHR-a, KIGHL) MTL.

Center. Shoots left. 6'3", 204 lbs. Born, Westlock, Alta., February 19, 1986.
(Montreal's 1st choice, 18th overall, in 2004 Entry Draft).

			Regular Season					Playoffs				
Season	Club	League	GP	G	A	Pts	PIM	GP	G	A	Pts	PIM
2000-01	Spruce Grove	AMBHL	36	26	34	60	48	....	....	....	....	....
2001-02	Ft. Saskatchewan	AMHL	33	15	36	51	78	17	16	20	36	....
2002-03	Prince Albert	WHL	63	9	21	30	89	....	....	....	....	....
2003-04	Prince Albert	WHL	64	15	33	48	118	6	2	4	6	12
2004-05	Prince Albert	WHL	28	14	18	32	32	14	4	7	11	25

CHORNEY, Taylor (CHOHR-nee, TAY-luhr) EDM.

Defense. Shoots left. 5'11", 182 lbs. Born, Thunder Bay, Ont., April 27, 1987.
(Edmonton's 2nd choice, 36th overall, in 2005 Entry Draft).

			Regular Season					Playoffs				
Season	Club	League	GP	G	A	Pts	PIM	GP	G	A	Pts	PIM
2003-04	Shat.-St. Mary's	High-MN	74	12	44	56	58	....	....	....	....	....
2004-05	Shat.-St. Mary's	High-MN	50	4	30	34	52	....	....	....	....	....

Signed Letter of Intent to attend **North Dakota** (WCHA), November 19, 2004.

CHRISTEEN, Mats (KRIHS-teen, MATS) NSH.

Defense. Shoots left. 6'1", 181 lbs. Born, Sodertalje, Sweden, February 13, 1982.
(Nashville's 11th choice, 236th overall, in 2000 Entry Draft).

			Regular Season					Playoffs				
Season	Club	League	GP	G	A	Pts	PIM	GP	G	A	Pts	PIM
99-2000	Sodertalje SK U18	Swe-U18	5	0	1	1	8	....	....	....	....	....
	Sodertalje SK Jr.	Swe-Jr.	30	1	0	1	30	4	1	0	1	6
2000-01	Sodertalje SK Jr.	Swe-Jr.	19	2	8	10	16	....	....	....	....	....
	Sodertalje SK	Sweden-2	15	0	3	3	4	....	....	....	....	....
2001-02	Sodertalje SK Jr.	Swe-Jr.	19	3	7	10	47	2	0	0	0	4
	Tierps HK	Sweden-2	15	3	1	4	14	....	....	....	....	....
	Sodertalje SK	Sweden	6	0	0	0	0	....	....	....	....	....
2002-03	Sodertalje SK Jr.	Swe-Jr.	13	3	3	6	62	....	....	....	....	....
	Sodertalje SK	Sweden	10	0	0	0	0	....	....	....	....	....
	HC Orebro 90	Sweden-2	9	2	0	2	10	....	....	....	....	....
2003-04			OUT OF HOCKEY – RETIRED									
2004-05	AIK Solna	Sweden-3	39	6	5	11	120	....	....	....	....	....

• Missed entire 2003-04 season pursuing a modelling career.

CHRISTENSEN, Erik (KRIHS-tehn-suhn, AIR-ihk) PIT.

Center. Shoots left. 6'1", 191 lbs. Born, Edmonton, Alta., December 17, 1983.
(Pittsburgh's 3rd choice, 69th overall, in 2002 Entry Draft).

			Regular Season					Playoffs				
Season	Club	League	GP	G	A	Pts	PIM	GP	G	A	Pts	PIM
1998-99	Leduc Oil Kings	AMBHL	36	34	42	76	70	....	....	....	....	....
99-2000	Kamloops Blazers	WHL	66	9	5	14	41	4	0	0	0	2
2000-01	Kamloops Blazers	WHL	72	21	23	44	36	4	1	1	2	0
2001-02	Kamloops Blazers	WHL	70	22	36	58	68	4	0	0	0	4
2002-03	Kamloops Blazers	WHL	67	*54	54	*108	60	6	1	7	8	14
2003-04	Kamloops Blazers	WHL	29	10	14	24	40	....	....	....	....	....
	Brandon	WHL	34	17	21	38	20	11	8	4	12	8
2004-05	Wilkes-Barre	AHL	77	14	13	27	33	11	1	6	7	4

WHL West First All-Star Team (2003)

CHRISTIE, Matt (KRIHS-tee, MAT) ANA.

Center. Shoots left. 5'10", 185 lbs. Born, Toronto, Ont., February 22, 1985.
(Anaheim's 7th choice, 236th overall, in 2004 Entry Draft).

			Regular Season					Playoffs				
Season	Club	League	GP	G	A	Pts	PIM	GP	G	A	Pts	PIM
2002-03	Aurora Tigers	OPJHL	40	21	30	51	22	15	6	7	13	10
2003-04	Miami U.	CCHA	41	21	14	35	22	....	....	....	....	....
2004-05	Miami U.	CCHA	33	15	21	36	14	....	....	....	....	....

CHUCKO, Kris (CHUH-koh, KRIHS) CGY.

Left wing. Shoots right. 6'2", 190 lbs. Born, Burnaby, B.C., March 13, 1986.
(Calgary's 1st choice, 24th overall, in 2004 Entry Draft).

			Regular Season					Playoffs				
Season	Club	League	GP	G	A	Pts	PIM	GP	G	A	Pts	PIM
2002-03	Salmon Arm	BCHL	59	14	19	33	80	11	5	3	8	12
2003-04	Salmon Arm	BCHL	53	32	55	87	161	14	10	9	19	36
2004-05	U. of Minnesota	WCHA	44	10	11	21	61	....	....	....	....	....

CIZEK, Martin (CHEE-zhehk, MAHR-tehn) BUF.

Defense. Shoots left. 6'1", 188 lbs. Born, Beroun, Czech., May 17, 1984.
(Buffalo's 10th choice, 271st overall, in 2002 Entry Draft).

			Regular Season					Playoffs				
Season	Club	League	GP	G	A	Pts	PIM	GP	G	A	Pts	PIM
99-2000	HC Slavia Praha Jr.	CzRep-Jr.	46	1	11	12	24	....	....	....	....	....
2000-01	HC Slavia Praha Jr.	CzRep-Jr.	53	14	10	24	26	....	....	....	....	....
2001-02	HC Slavia Praha Jr.	CzRep-Jr.	42	2	6	8	30	....	....	....	....	....
2002-03	Plymouth Whalers	OHL	58	2	7	9	40	18	1	1	2	6
2003-04	HC Kladno Jr.	CzRep-Jr.	50	9	23	32	34	7	0	3	3	2
	Beroun	CzRep-2	8	0	0	0	2	1	0	0	0	0
2004-05	HC Dukla Jihlava	CzRep	1	0	0	0	0	....	....	....	....	....
	Jihlava Jr.	CzRep-Jr.	8	4	3	7	6	....	....	....	....	....
	Trebic	CzRep-2	10	0	1	1	6	....	....	....	....	....
	HC Kladno Jr.	CzRep-Jr.	13	5	3	8	4	10	1	4	5	8

CLACKSON, Matt (KLAK-suhn, MA-thyew) PHI.

Left wing. Shoots right. 5'11", 196 lbs. Born, Saskatoon, Sask., April 26, 1985.
(Philadelphia's 6th choice, 215th overall, in 2005 Entry Draft).

			Regular Season					Playoffs				
Season	Club	League	GP	G	A	Pts	PIM	GP	G	A	Pts	PIM
2003-04	Chicago Steel	USHL	42	5	4	9	108	5	0	1	1	8
2004-05	Chicago Steel	USHL	56	10	15	25	270	....	....	....	....	....

Signed Letter of Intent to attend **Western Michigan** (CCHA) in fall of 2005.

CLARKSON, Dave (KLAHRK-suhn, DAYV) N.J.

Center. Shoots right. 6'1", 205 lbs. Born, Mimico, Ont., March 31, 1984.

			Regular Season					Playoffs				
Season	Club	League	GP	G	A	Pts	PIM	GP	G	A	Pts	PIM
2001-02	Belleville Bulls	OHL	22	2	7	9	34	8	1	1	2	6
2002-03	Belleville Bulls	OHL	3	0	0	0	11	....	....	....	....	....
	Kitchener Rangers	OHL	54	17	11	28	122	21	4	3	7	23
2003-04	Kitchener Rangers	OHL	55	22	17	39	173	....	....	....	....	....
2004-05	Kitchener Rangers	OHL	51	33	21	54	145	15	6	2	8	40

Signed as a free agent by **New Jersey**, August 12, 2005.

CLICHE, Marc-Andre (Kligh-SHAY, MAHRK-AWN-dray) NYR

Right wing. Shoots right. 6', 177 lbs. Born, Rouyn-Noranda, Que., March 23, 1987.
(NY Rangers' 3rd choice, 56th overall, in 2005 Entry Draft).

			Regular Season					Playoffs				
Season	Club	League	GP	G	A	Pts	PIM	GP	G	A	Pts	PIM
2003-04	Lewiston	QMJHL	52	8	10	18	17	7	1	2	3	0
2004-05	Lewiston	QMJHL	19	4	4	8	8	....	....	....	....	....

CLITSOME, Grant (KLIHT-suhm, GRANT) CBJ

Defense. Shoots left. 6', 208 lbs. Born, Gloucester, Ont., April 14, 1985.
(Columbus' 12th choice, 271st overall, in 2004 Entry Draft).

			Regular Season					Playoffs				
Season	Club	League	GP	G	A	Pts	PIM	GP	G	A	Pts	PIM
2003-04	Nepean Raiders	CJHL	55	13	26	39	67	17	1	10	11	6
2004-05	Clarkson Knights	ECAC	39	2	11	13	36	....	....	....	....	....

CLOUTHIER, Brett (KLOO-tyay, BREHT) OTT.

Left wing. Shoots left. 6'5", 225 lbs. Born, Ottawa, Ont., June 9, 1981.
(New Jersey's 3rd choice, 50th overall, in 1999 Entry Draft).

			Regular Season					Playoffs				
Season	Club	League	GP	G	A	Pts	PIM	GP	G	A	Pts	PIM
1997-98	Kanata Valley	CJHL	50	12	10	22	135	....	....	....	....	....
1998-99	Kingston	OHL	64	8	14	22	227	5	1	1	2	4
99-2000	Kingston	OHL	65	13	26	39	*266	5	2	0	2	17
2000-01	Kingston	OHL	68	28	29	57	165	4	1	0	1	10
2001-02	Albany River Rats	AHL	62	4	0	4	109	....	....	....	....	....
2002-03	Albany River Rats	AHL	74	6	7	13	220	....	....	....	....	....
2003-04	Albany River Rats	AHL	39	1	0	1	122	....	....	....	....	....
	Cincinnati	ECHL	12	3	3	6	14	....	....	....	....	....
2004-05	Albany River Rats	AHL	46	0	4	4	168	....	....	....	....	....
	Augusta Lynx	ECHL	11	1	1	2	14	....	....	....	....	....

Signed as a free agent by **Ottawa**, August 19, 2005.

CLOWE, Ryane (KLOH, RIGH-uhn) S.J.

Right wing. Shoots right. 6'2", 215 lbs. Born, St. John's, Nfld., September 30, 1982.
(San Jose's 5th choice, 175th overall, in 2001 Entry Draft).

			Regular Season					Playoffs				
Season	Club	League	GP	G	A	Pts	PIM	GP	G	A	Pts	PIM
2000-01	Rimouski Oceanic	QMJHL	32	15	10	25	43	11	8	1	9	12
2001-02	Rimouski Oceanic	QMJHL	53	28	45	73	120	7	1	6	7	2
2002-03	Rimouski Oceanic	QMJHL	17	8	19	27	44	....	....	....	....	....
	Montreal Rocket	QMJHL	43	18	30	48	60	7	3	7	10	6
2003-04	Cleveland Barons	AHL	72	11	29	40	97	8	3	1	4	9
2004-05	Cleveland Barons	AHL	74	27	35	62	101	....	....	....	....	....

CLUNE, Richard (KLOON, RIH-chuhrd) DAL.

Left wing. Shoots left. 5'11", 195 lbs. Born, Toronto, Ont., April 25, 1987.
(Dallas' 3rd choice, 71st overall, in 2005 Entry Draft).

			Regular Season					Playoffs				
Season	Club	League	GP	G	A	Pts	PIM	GP	G	A	Pts	PIM
2003-04	Sarnia Sting	OHL	58	3	13	16	72	5	0	1	1	0
2004-05	Sarnia Sting	OHL	68	21	13	34	103	....	....	....	....	....

COBURN, Braydon (KOH-buhrn, BRAY-duhn) ATL.

Defense. Shoots left. 6'5", 220 lbs. Born, Calgary, Alta., February 27, 1985.
(Atlanta's 1st choice, 8th overall, in 2003 Entry Draft).

			Regular Season					Playoffs				
Season	Club	League	GP	G	A	Pts	PIM	GP	G	A	Pts	PIM
2000-01	Notre Dame	SMHL	32	3	19	22	70	....	....	....	....	....
	Portland	WHL	2	0	1	1	0	14	0	4	4	2
2001-02	Portland	WHL	68	4	33	37	100	7	1	1	2	9
2002-03	Portland	WHL	53	3	16	19	147	7	0	1	1	8
2003-04	Portland	WHL	55	10	20	30	92	5	0	1	1	10
2004-05	Portland	WHL	60	12	32	44	144	7	1	5	6	6
	Chicago Wolves	AHL	3	0	1	1	5	18	0	1	1	36

WHL Rookie of the Year (2002) • WHL West First All-Star Team (2004, 2005)

COGLIANO, Andrew (kawg-LEE-a-noh, AN-droo) EDM.

Center. Shoots left. 5'9", 178 lbs. Born, Toronto, Ont., June 14, 1987.
(Edmonton's 1st choice, 25th overall, in 2005 Entry Draft).

			Regular Season					Playoffs				
Season	Club	League	GP	G	A	Pts	PIM	GP	G	A	Pts	PIM
2002-03	Vaughan	GTHL	58	39	54	93	122	....	....	....	....	....
2003-04	St. Mike's B's	OPJHL	36	26	47	73	14	24	11	20	31	12
2004-05	St. Mike's B's	OPJHL	49	36	*66	*102	33	25	*22	*24	*46	20

Signed Letter of Intent to attend **Michigan** (CCHA), November 22, 2004.

COLBERT, Will (KOHL-buhrt, WIHL) S.J.

Defense. Shoots left. 6'3", 212 lbs. Born, Arnprior, Ont., February 6, 1985.
(San Jose's 7th choice, 183rd overall, in 2005 Entry Draft).

			Regular Season					Playoffs				
Season	Club	League	GP	G	A	Pts	PIM	GP	G	A	Pts	PIM
2001-02	Pembroke	CJHL	52	2	6	8	20	....	....	....	....	....
2002-03	Ottawa 67's	OHL	56	1	6	7	23	23	1	5	6	7
2003-04	Ottawa 67's	OHL	55	3	18	21	28	7	0	4	4	0
2004-05	Ottawa 67's	OHL	68	6	26	32	65	21	3	8	11	8

• Re-entered NHL Entry Draft. Originally Ottawa's 7th choice, 228th overall, in 2003 Entry Draft.

COLE, Phil (KOHL, FIHL)

Defense. Shoots left. 6'4", 205 lbs. Born, Winnipeg, Man., September 6, 1982.
(New Jersey's 8th choice, 125th overall, in 2000 Entry Draft).

			Regular Season					Playoffs				
Season	Club	League	GP	G	A	Pts	PIM	GP	G	A	Pts	PIM
1997-98	Winnipeg Sharks	MMMHL	45	0	18	18	68	5	0	4	4	2
1998-99	Lethbridge	WHL	45	2	1	3	64	4	0	0	0	0
99-2000	Lethbridge	WHL	51	1	6	7	112	....	....	....	....	....
2000-01	Lethbridge	WHL	63	6	15	21	129	1	0	0	0	2
2001-02	Lethbridge	WHL	33	3	13	16	87	....	....	....	....	....
	Vancouver Giants	WHL	6	0	1	1	18	....	....	....	....	....
	Medicine Hat	WHL	15	1	5	6	49	....	....	....	....	....
2002-03	Albany River Rats	AHL	4	0	0	0	6	....	....	....	....	....
	Columbus	ECHL	51	4	5	9	135	....	....	....	....	....
2003-04	Albany River Rats	AHL	39	1	3	4	80	....	....	....	....	....
	Cincinnati	ECHL	12	1	0	1	33	....	....	....	....	....
2004-05	Albany River Rats	AHL	18	0	0	0	16	....	....	....	....	....
	Augusta Lynx	ECHL	42	1	4	5	80	....	....	....	....	....

COLLEY, Kevin (KAW-lee, KEH-vihn) NYI

Center. Shoots right. 5'10", 175 lbs. Born, New Haven, CT, January 4, 1979.

			Regular Season					Playoffs				
Season	Club	League	GP	G	A	Pts	PIM	GP	G	A	Pts	PIM
1996-97	Oshawa Generals	OHL	64	19	17	36	46	16	2	4	6	25
1997-98	Oshawa Generals	OHL	57	27	41	68	107	7	1	5	6	14
1998-99	Oshawa Generals	OHL	63	39	62	101	68	14	7	13	20	32
99-2000	Hartford Wolf Pack	AHL	5	0	0	0	2	....	....	....	....	....
	Charlotte	ECHL	5	2	1	3	10	....	....	....	....	....
	Dayton Bombers	ECHL	24	8	6	14	111	2	1	0	1	4
2000-01	Pensacola	ECHL	23	6	11	17	44	....	....	....	....	....
	New Orleans Brass	ECHL	23	11	8	19	27	8	1	1	2	12
2001-02	Providence Bruins	AHL	4	0	1	1	27	....	....	....	....	....
	Atlantic City	ECHL	41	23	30	53	90	....	....	....	....	....
	Rochester	AHL	25	3	4	7	70	2	0	1	1	0
2002-03	Syracuse Crunch	AHL	16	2	3	5	6	....	....	....	....	....
	Atlantic City	ECHL	50	33	38	71	190	17	*13	7	20	27
	Worcester IceCats	AHL	6	1	1	2	27	....	....	....	....	....
2003-04	Bridgeport	AHL	78	12	19	31	122	3	1	0	1	12
2004-05	Bridgeport	AHL	59	11	13	24	212	....	....	....	....	....

Signed as a free agent by **NY Islanders**, June 10, 2004.

COLLINS, Dan (KAW-lihns, DAN) FLA.

Right wing. Shoots right. 6'1", 185 lbs. Born, Syracuse, NY, February 26, 1987.
(Florida's 3rd choice, 90th overall, in 2005 Entry Draft).

			Regular Season					Playoffs				
Season	Club	League	GP	G	A	Pts	PIM	GP	G	A	Pts	PIM
2002-03	Syracuse	OPJHL	35	14	12	26	58	....	....	....	....	....
2003-04	Plymouth Whalers	OHL	59	9	13	22	30	9	0	1	1	0
2004-05	Plymouth Whalers	OHL	68	25	21	46	60	4	0	0	0	6

COLLINS, Dustin (KAWL-ihns, DUHS-tihn) T.B.

Center/Left wing. Shoots left. 6'3", 210 lbs. Born, Payson, AZ, February 28, 1985.
(Tampa Bay's 5th choice, 163rd overall, in 2004 Entry Draft).

			Regular Season					Playoffs				
Season	Club	League	GP	G	A	Pts	PIM	GP	G	A	Pts	PIM
2001-02	USA U-17	USDP	63	6	10	16	38	....	....	....	....	....
2002-03	USA U-18	USDP	53	6	11	17	31	....	....	....	....	....
2003-04	Northern Mich.	CCHA	37	1	5	6	30	....	....	....	....	....
2004-05	Northern Mich.	CCHA	25	2	1	3	28	....	....	....	....	....

COLLINS, Rob (KAW-lihns, RAWB) NYI

Center. Shoots right. 5'10", 174 lbs. Born, Kitchener, Ont., March 15, 1974.

			Regular Season					Playoffs				
Season	Club	League	GP	G	A	Pts	PIM	GP	G	A	Pts	PIM
1998-99	Ferris State	CCHA	36	3	9	12	14	....	....	....	....	....
99-2000	Ferris State	CCHA	38	11	20	31	39	....	....	....	....	....
2000-01	Ferris State	CCHA	35	15	17	32	23	....	....	....	....	....
2001-02	Ferris State	CCHA	36	15	33	48	30	....	....	....	....	....
	Grand Rapids	AHL	5	0	2	2	0	....	....	....	....	....
2002-03	Grand Rapids	AHL	73	11	20	31	16	15	3	8	11	10
2003-04	Bridgeport	AHL	75	9	23	32	42	7	3	5	8	10
2004-05	Bridgeport	AHL	78	23	39	62	67	....	....	....	....	....

CCHA First All-Star Team (2002) • NCAA West Second All-American Team (2002)

Signed as a free agent by **NY Islanders**, July, 2003.

COLLINS, Sean (KAW-lihns, SHAWN)

Left wing. Shoots left. 5'9", 180 lbs. Born, Boston, MA, February 9, 1983.
(Colorado's 10th choice, 289th overall, in 2002 Entry Draft).

			Regular Season					Playoffs				
Season	Club	League	GP	G	A	Pts	PIM	GP	G	A	Pts	PIM
1997-98	Reading	High-MA	22	32	26	58	....	....	....	....	....	....
1998-99	Reading	High-MA	25	32	35	67	....	....	....	....	....	....
99-2000	Reading	High-MA	22	37	42	79	....	....	....	....	....	....
2000-01	Reading	High-MA	24	28	36	64	....	....	....	....	....	....
2001-02	New Hampshire	H-East	40	20	25	45	4	....	....	....	....	....
2002-03	New Hampshire	H-East	41	22	8	30	12	....	....	....	....	....
2003-04	New Hampshire	H-East	41	16	26	42	28	....	....	....	....	....
2004-05	New Hampshire	H-East	42	19	*37	*56	26	....	....	....	....	....

Hockey East Rookie of the Year (2002) • Hockey East Second All-Star Team (2005) • NCAA East First All-American Team (2005)

COLLITON, Jeremy (KAW-lih-tuhn, JAIR-eh-mee) NYI

Center. Shoots right. 6'2", 195 lbs. Born, Blackie, Alta., January 13, 1985.
(NY Islanders' 4th choice, 58th overall, in 2003 Entry Draft).

			Regular Season					Playoffs				
Season	Club	League	GP	G	A	Pts	PIM	GP	G	A	Pts	PIM
99-2000	Airdrie Express	AMHL	33	16	25	41	28	....	....	....	....	....
2000-01	Crowsnest Pass	AJHL	63	18	30	48	98	....	....	....	....	....
2001-02	Prince Albert	WHL	68	11	21	32	53	....	....	....	....	....
2002-03	Prince Albert	WHL	58	20	28	48	76	....	....	....	....	....
2003-04	Prince Albert	WHL	62	24	26	50	73	6	5	5	10	8
2004-05	Prince Albert	WHL	41	16	30	46	25	17	3	4	7	21

COMEAU, Blake (KOH-moh, BLAYK) NYI

Right wing. Shoots right. 6'1", 198 lbs. Born, Meadow Lake, Sask., February 18, 1986.
(NY Islanders' 2nd choice, 47th overall, in 2004 Entry Draft).

			Regular Season					Playoffs				
Season	Club	League	GP	G	A	Pts	PIM	GP	G	A	Pts	PIM
2001-02	Sask. Contacts	SMHL	42	27	33	60	72	....	....	....	....	....
	Kelowna Rockets	WHL	3	0	0	0	4	....	....	....	....	....
2002-03	Kelowna Rockets	WHL	54	5	18	23	77	19	2	1	3	20
2003-04	Kelowna Rockets	WHL	71	10	23	33	123	17	4	2	6	23
2004-05	Kelowna Rockets	WHL	65	24	23	47	108	24	6	12	18	34

CONBOY, Tim (KAWN-boy, TIHM) S.J.

Defense. Shoots right. 6'1", 205 lbs. Born, Farmington, MN, March 22, 1982.
(San Jose's 6th choice, 217th overall, in 2002 Entry Draft).

			Regular Season					Playoffs				
Season	Club	League	GP	G	A	Pts	PIM	GP	G	A	Pts	PIM
99-2000	Brainerd	High-MN	22	20	26	46	....	....	....	....	....	....
2000-01	Rochester	USHL	51	5	9	14	256	....	....	....	....	....
2001-02	Rochester	USHL	14	1	6	7	65	....	....	....	....	....
	Topeka	USHL	29	4	15	19	128	....	....	....	....	....
2002-03	St. Cloud State	WCHA	31	3	12	15	48	....	....	....	....	....
2003-04	St. Cloud State	WCHA	32	5	5	10	68	....	....	....	....	....
	Cleveland Barons	AHL	....	....	....	....	....	3	0	3	3	4
2004-05	Cleveland Barons	AHL	61	4	11	15	134	....	....	....	....	....

CONNE, Flavien (KAW-neh, FLA-vee-ehn) L.A.

Center. Shoots left. 5'9", 176 lbs. Born, Geneva, Switz., April 1, 1980.
(Los Angeles' 10th choice, 250th overall, in 2000 Entry Draft).

			Regular Season					Playoffs				
Season	Club	League	GP	G	A	Pts	PIM	GP	G	A	Pts	PIM
1995-96	Geneve Jr.	Swiss-Jr.	22	39	27	56	32	....	....	....	....	....
1996-97	Geneve	Swiss-2	30	9	8	17	8	5	1	1	2	4
1997-98	Geneve Jr.	Swiss-Jr.	37	15	12	27	57	3	0	2	2	2
	Geneve	Swiss-2	9	11	6	17	12	....	....	....	....	....
	HC Ambri-Piotta	Swiss	1	0	0	0	0	....	....	....	....	....
1998-99	Fribourg Jr.	Swiss-Jr.	1	1	1	2	2	....	....	....	....	....
	Fribourg	Swiss	37	14	14	28	59	4	4	1	5	6
	Fribourg	EuroHL	3	0	0	0	0	....	....	....	....	....
99-2000	Fribourg	Swiss	44	19	22	41	38	4	0	1	1	0
2000-01	HC Lugano	Swiss	42	9	14	23	8	15	2	6	8	37
2001-02	HC Lugano	Swiss	44	12	13	25	20	5	1	1	2	0
	Switzerland	Olympics	1	0	0	0	0	....	....	....	....	....
2002-03	HC Lugano	Swiss	42	15	23	38	32	16	4	4	8	10
2003-04	HC Lugano	Swiss	32	11	13	24	18	16	8	4	12	12
2004-05	HC Lugano	Swiss	21	2	6	8	18	5	1	1	2	4

COOK, Tim (KUK, TIHM) OTT.

Defense. Shoots right. 6'4", 190 lbs. Born, Montclair, NJ, March 13, 1984.
(Ottawa's 5th choice, 142nd overall, in 2003 Entry Draft).

			Regular Season					Playoffs				
Season	Club	League	GP	G	A	Pts	PIM	GP	G	A	Pts	PIM
2000-01	Hotchkiss	High-CT	22	2	10	12	22	....	....	....	....	....
2001-02	Omaha Lancers	USHL	42	2	4	6	39	5	0	1	1	2
2002-03	River City Lancers	USHL	59	3	12	15	62	10	0	2	2	18
2003-04	U. of Michigan	CCHA	24	0	2	2	28	....	....	....	....	....
2004-05	U. of Michigan	CCHA	36	0	0	0	54	....	....	....	....	....

COOPER, Joe (KOO-puhr, JOH) OTT.

Right wing. Shoots right. 6'1", 199 lbs. Born, Toronto, Ont., June 7, 1985.
(Ottawa's 9th choice, 219th overall, in 2004 Entry Draft).

			Regular Season					Playoffs				
Season	Club	League	GP	G	A	Pts	PIM	GP	G	A	Pts	PIM
2002-03	St. Mike's B's	OPJHL	44	15	30	45	121	....	....	....	....	....
2003-04	Miami U.	CCHA	34	1	0	1	66	....	....	....	....	....
2004-05	Miami U.	CCHA	36	1	7	8	43	....	....	....	....	....

CORBIN, J.D. (KOHR-bihn, JAY-DEE) COL.

Left wing. Shoots left. 5'10", 185 lbs. Born, Littleton, CO, March 23, 1985.
(Colorado's 8th choice, 249th overall, in 2004 Entry Draft).

			Regular Season					Playoffs				
Season	Club	League	GP	G	A	Pts	PIM	GP	G	A	Pts	PIM
2001-02	USA U-17	USDP	43	6	13	19	46	....	....	....	....	....
2002-03	USA U-18	USDP	51	8	13	21	....	....	....	....	....	....
2003-04	U. of Denver	WCHA	39	3	6	9	18	....	....	....	....	....
2004-05	U. of Denver	WCHA	41	1	18	19	22	....	....	....	....	....

CORMIER, Kevin (KOHR-mee-ay, KEH-vihn) **PHX.**

Left wing. Shoots left. 6'3", 249 lbs. Born, Moncton, N.B., January 27, 1986.
(Phoenix's 6th choice, 168th overall, in 2004 Entry Draft).

			Regular Season					Playoffs				
Season	**Club**	**League**	**GP**	**G**	**A**	**Pts**	**PIM**	**GP**	**G**	**A**	**Pts**	**PIM**
2003-04	Moncton	MJrHL	42	3	2	5	235	4	0	0	0	52
	Halifax	QMJHL	1	0	0	0	5	....	....	....	....	....
2004-05	Halifax	QMJHL	60	2	5	7	235	9	0	0	0	8

COTE, Jean-Philippe (KOH-tay, zhawn-fihl-EEP) **MTL.**

Defense. Shoots left. 6'2", 213 lbs. Born, Charlesbourg, Que., April 22, 1982.
(Toronto's 10th choice, 265th overall, in 2000 Entry Draft).

			Regular Season					Playoffs				
Season	**Club**	**League**	**GP**	**G**	**A**	**Pts**	**PIM**	**GP**	**G**	**A**	**Pts**	**PIM**
1998-99	Ste-Foy	QAAA	38	10	24	34	34	17	1	8	9	17
	Quebec Remparts	QMJHL	8	0	0	0	2	....	....	....	....	....
99-2000	Quebec Remparts	QMJHL	34	0	10	10	15	....	....	....	....	....
	Cape Breton	QMJHL	28	0	4	4	21	4	0	1	1	4
2000-01	Cape Breton	QMJHL	71	6	29	35	90	12	0	0	0	18
2001-02	Cape Breton	QMJHL	61	4	20	24	72	16	1	6	7	38
2002-03	Cape Breton	QMJHL	16	1	3	4	12	....	....	....	....	....
	Acadie-Bathurst	QMJHL	48	8	18	26	87	11	2	3	5	20
2003-04	Hamilton Bulldogs	AHL	75	2	7	9	79	10	0	4	4	24
2004-05	Hamilton Bulldogs	AHL	51	1	8	9	58	4	0	1	1	0

Signed as a free agent by **Montreal**, August 19, 2004.

COTE, Riley (COH-tay, RIGH-lee) **PHI.**

Left wing. Shoots left. 6'1", 210 lbs. Born, Winnipeg, Man., March 16, 1982.

			Regular Season					Playoffs				
Season	**Club**	**League**	**GP**	**G**	**A**	**Pts**	**PIM**	**GP**	**G**	**A**	**Pts**	**PIM**
1998-99	Prince Albert	WHL	37	3	2	5	63	9	0	0	0	9
99-2000	Prince Albert	WHL	67	6	7	13	71	3	1	0	1	2
2000-01	Prince Albert	WHL	64	17	35	52	114	....	....	....	....	....
2001-02	Prince Albert	WHL	67	28	23	51	134	....	....	....	....	....
2002-03	St. John's	AHL	6	0	0	0	5	....	....	....	....	....
	Memphis	CHL	51	8	6	14	241	14	1	0	1	54
2003-04	Syracuse Crunch	AHL	9	0	0	0	19	....	....	....	....	....
	Dayton Bombers	ECHL	57	6	11	17	258	....	....	....	....	....
2004-05	Philadelphia	AHL	61	4	7	11	280	13	0	0	0	6

Signed as a free agent by **Philadelphia**, August 23, 2005.

COUTURE, Derek (coh-TYOOR, DAI-ihk) **CGY.**

Right wing. Shoots right. 6'2", 202 lbs. Born, Calgary, Alta., April 24, 1984.

			Regular Season					Playoffs				
Season	**Club**	**League**	**GP**	**G**	**A**	**Pts**	**PIM**	**GP**	**G**	**A**	**Pts**	**PIM**
2001-02	Saskatoon Blades	WHL	61	6	10	16	159	7	0	0	0	10
2002-03	Saskatoon Blades	WHL	70	17	20	37	160	6	1	2	3	13
2003-04	Saskatoon Blades	WHL	45	3	9	12	99	....	....	....	....	....
2004-05	Seattle	WHL	71	20	18	38	154	12	3	6	9	18

Signed as a free agent by **Calgary**, August 5, 2005.

CRABB, Joey (KRAB, JOH-ee) **NYR**

Right wing. Shoots right. 6'1", 187 lbs. Born, Anchorage, AK, April 3, 1983.
(NY Rangers' 7th choice, 226th overall, in 2002 Entry Draft).

			Regular Season					Playoffs				
Season	**Club**	**League**	**GP**	**G**	**A**	**Pts**	**PIM**	**GP**	**G**	**A**	**Pts**	**PIM**
99-2000	USA U-17	USDP	55	13	10	23	69	....	....	....	....	....
2000-01	USA U-18	USDP	60	12	13	25	40	....	....	....	....	....
2001-02	Green Bay	USHL	61	15	27	42	94	7	4	8	12	21
2002-03	Colorado College	WCHA	35	4	4	8	40	....	....	....	....	....
2003-04	Colorado College	WCHA	39	15	12	27	20	....	....	....	....	....
2004-05	Colorado College	WCHA	43	16	16	32	44	....	....	....	....	....

CRACKNELL, Adam (krak-NEHL, A-duhm) **CGY.**

Right wing. Shoots right. 6'2", 211 lbs. Born, Prince Albert, Sask., July 15, 1985.
(Calgary's 10th choice, 279th overall, in 2004 Entry Draft).

			Regular Season					Playoffs				
Season	**Club**	**League**	**GP**	**G**	**A**	**Pts**	**PIM**	**GP**	**G**	**A**	**Pts**	**PIM**
2002-03	Kootenay Ice	WHL	67	7	4	11	37	11	0	0	0	2
2003-04	Kootenay Ice	WHL	72	26	35	61	63	4	1	1	2	2
2004-05	Kootenay Ice	WHL	72	19	29	48	65	16	8	8	16	6

CRAIG, Ryan (KRAIG, RIGH-uhn) **T.B.**

Center. Shoots left. 6'2", 220 lbs. Born, Abbotsford, B.C., January 6, 1982.
(Tampa Bay's 10th choice, 255th overall, in 2002 Entry Draft).

			Regular Season					Playoffs				
Season	**Club**	**League**	**GP**	**G**	**A**	**Pts**	**PIM**	**GP**	**G**	**A**	**Pts**	**PIM**
1997-98	Abbotsford	BCAHA	80	118	120	238	110	....	....	....	....	....
	Brandon	WHL	1	0	0	0	0	....	....	....	....	....
1998-99	Brandon	WHL	54	11	12	23	46	5	0	0	0	4
99-2000	Brandon	WHL	65	17	19	36	40	....	....	....	....	....
2000-01	Brandon	WHL	70	38	33	71	49	6	3	0	3	7
2001-02	Brandon	WHL	52	29	35	64	52	19	11	10	21	13
2002-03	Brandon	WHL	60	42	32	74	69	17	5	8	13	29
2003-04	Hershey Bears	AHL	61	4	8	12	24	....	....	....	....	....
	Pensacola	ECHL	5	3	5	8	0	2	0	1	1	0
2004-05	Springfield Falcons	AHL	80	27	14	41	50	....	....	....	....	....

WHL East First All-Star Team (2003) • Canadian Major Junior Humanitarian Player of the Year (2003)

CROMBEEN, Brandon (KRAWM-been, BRAN-duhn) **DAL.**

Right wing. Shoots right. 6'2", 200 lbs. Born, Denver, CO, July 10, 1985.
(Dallas' 3rd choice, 54th overall, in 2003 Entry Draft).

			Regular Season					Playoffs				
Season	**Club**	**League**	**GP**	**G**	**A**	**Pts**	**PIM**	**GP**	**G**	**A**	**Pts**	**PIM**
2000-01	Newmarket	OPJHL	35	14	14	28	63	....	....	....	....	....
2001-02	Barrie Colts	OHL	60	12	13	25	118	20	1	1	2	31
2002-03	Barrie Colts	OHL	63	22	24	46	133	6	1	0	1	8
2003-04	Barrie Colts	OHL	62	21	29	50	154	12	5	7	12	35
2004-05	Barrie Colts	OHL	63	31	18	49	111	6	2	4	6	35

CROSBY, Sidney (KRAWZ-bee, SIHD-nee) **PIT.**

Center. Shoots left. 5'10", 175 lbs. Born, Halifax, N.S., August 7, 1987.
(Pittsburgh's 1st choice, 1st overall, in 2005 Entry Draft).

			Regular Season					Playoffs				
Season	**Club**	**League**	**GP**	**G**	**A**	**Pts**	**PIM**	**GP**	**G**	**A**	**Pts**	**PIM**
2002-03	Shat.-St. Mary's	High-MN	57	72	90	162	....	....	....	....	....	....
2003-04	Rimouski Oceanic	QMJHL	59	54	*81	*135	74	9	7	9	16	10
2004-05	Rimouski Oceanic	QMJHL	62	*66	*102	*168	84	13	*14	*17	*31	16

QMJHL All-Rookie Team (2004) • QMJHL First All-Star Team (2004, 2005) • QMJHL Player of the Year (2004, 2005) • Canadian Major Junior First All-Star Team (2004, 2005) • Canadian Major Junior Rookie of the Year (2004) • Canadian Major Junior Player of the Year (2004, 2005) • Memorial Cup All-Star Team (2005) • Ed Chynoweth Trophy (Memorial Cup Tournament Leading Scorer) (2005)

CROWDER, Tim (KROW-duhr, TIHM) **PIT.**

Right wing. Shoots right. 6'2", 180 lbs. Born, Victoria, B.C., October 16, 1986.
(Pittsburgh's 5th choice, 126th overall, in 2005 Entry Draft).

			Regular Season					Playoffs				
Season	**Club**	**League**	**GP**	**G**	**A**	**Pts**	**PIM**	**GP**	**G**	**A**	**Pts**	**PIM**
2002-03	Powell River Kings	BCHL	52	6	6	12	....	....	....	....	....	....
2003-04	Powell River Kings	BCHL	57	21	34	55	44	7	3	3	6	8
2004-05	South Surrey	BCHL	56	23	27	50	30	....	....	....	....	....

Signed Letter of Intent to attend **Michigan State** (CCHA) in fall of 2005.

CULLEN, Joe (KUH-lehn, JOH)

Center. Shoots left. 6'1", 210 lbs. Born, Virginia, MN, February 14, 1981.
(Edmonton's 7th choice, 211th overall, in 2000 Entry Draft).

			Regular Season					Playoffs				
Season	**Club**	**League**	**GP**	**G**	**A**	**Pts**	**PIM**	**GP**	**G**	**A**	**Pts**	**PIM**
1997-98	Moorhead Spuds	High-MN	23	18	18	36	....	....	....	....	....	....
1998-99	USA U-18	USDP	52	11	15	26	33	....	....	....	....	....
99-2000	Colorado College	WCHA	29	4	6	10	30	....	....	....	....	....
2000-01	Colorado College	WCHA	34	8	12	20	38	....	....	....	....	....
2001-02	Colorado College	WCHA	43	9	12	21	42	....	....	....	....	....
2002-03	Colorado College	WCHA	42	20	15	35	56	....	....	....	....	....
2003-04	Toronto	AHL	69	14	16	30	30	3	0	0	0	2
2004-05	Edmonton	AHL	30	3	9	12	16	....	....	....	....	....
	San Antonio	AHL	38	3	3	6	20	....	....	....	....	....

Loaned to **San Antonio** (AHL) by **Edmonton** (AHL), January 3, 2005.

CULLEN, Mark (KUH-lehn, MAHRK) **CHI.**

Center. Shoots left. 5'11", 175 lbs. Born, Moorhead, MN, October 28, 1978.

			Regular Season					Playoffs				
Season	**Club**	**League**	**GP**	**G**	**A**	**Pts**	**PIM**	**GP**	**G**	**A**	**Pts**	**PIM**
1996-97	Fargo High	High-ND	30	20	45	65	....	....	....	....	....	....
1997-98	Fargo-Moorhead	USHL	30	17	37	54	16	4	3	0	3	25
1998-99	Colorado College	WCHA	42	8	25	33	22	....	....	....	....	....
99-2000	Colorado College	WCHA	37	11	20	31	22	....	....	....	....	....
2000-01	Colorado College	WCHA	31	20	33	53	26	....	....	....	....	....
2001-02	Colorado College	WCHA	43	14	36	50	14	....	....	....	....	....
2002-03	Houston Aeros	AHL	72	22	25	47	20	15	3	7	10	4
2003-04	Houston Aeros	AHL	53	10	28	38	28	2	0	0	0	0
2004-05	Houston Aeros	AHL	64	10	24	34	26	5	1	1	2	0

USHL All-Rookie Team (1998) • USHL Rookie of the Year (1998) • WCHA First All-Star Team (2001, 2002) • NCAA West Second All-American Team (2001)

Signed as a free agent by **Minnesota**, April 8, 2002.

CUMISKEY, Kyle (kuh-MIHS-kee, KIGHL) **COL.**

Defense. Shoots left. 5'10", 158 lbs. Born, Abbotsford, B.C., December 2, 1986.
(Colorado's 9th choice, 222nd overall, in 2005 Entry Draft).

			Regular Season					Playoffs				
Season	**Club**	**League**	**GP**	**G**	**A**	**Pts**	**PIM**	**GP**	**G**	**A**	**Pts**	**PIM**
2002-03	Penticton Panthers	BCHL	59	10	11	21	36	....	....	....	....	....
2003-04	Kelowna Rockets	WHL	54	2	7	9	20	17	0	0	0	0
2004-05	Kelowna Rockets	WHL	72	4	36	40	47	24	0	13	13	12

CUNNING, Cam (KUH-nihng, KAM) **CGY.**

Left wing. Shoots left. 6'2", 215 lbs. Born, Powell River, B.C., June 4, 1985.
(Calgary's 8th choice, 240th overall, in 2003 Entry Draft).

			Regular Season					Playoffs				
Season	**Club**	**League**	**GP**	**G**	**A**	**Pts**	**PIM**	**GP**	**G**	**A**	**Pts**	**PIM**
2002-03	Kamloops Blazers	WHL	71	7	12	19	54	6	1	0	1	2
2003-04	Kamloops Blazers	WHL	65	14	13	27	62	5	1	1	2	10
2004-05	Kamloops Blazers	WHL	39	14	8	22	63	....	....	....	....	....
	Vancouver Giants	WHL	30	3	7	10	19	6	1	3	4	14

CURRY, Mike (KUH-ree) **L.A.**

Right wing. Shoots right. 6'3", 190 lbs. Born, Fort Benning, GA, September 20, 1984.
(Los Angeles' 6th choice, 205th overall, in 2004 Entry Draft).

			Regular Season					Playoffs				
Season	**Club**	**League**	**GP**	**G**	**A**	**Pts**	**PIM**	**GP**	**G**	**A**	**Pts**	**PIM**
2002-03	Sioux City	USHL	52	6	13	19	58	4	1	2	3	2
2003-04	Sioux City	USHL	60	20	20	40	119	7	2	5	7	16
2004-05	U. Minn-Duluth	WCHA	22	3	6	9	35	....	....	....	....	....

CURRY, Sean (KUH-ree, SHAWN)

Defense. Shoots right. 6'4", 230 lbs. Born, Burnsville, MN, April 29, 1982.
(Carolina's 6th choice, 211th overall, in 2001 Entry Draft).

			Regular Season					Playoffs				
Season	**Club**	**League**	**GP**	**G**	**A**	**Pts**	**PIM**	**GP**	**G**	**A**	**Pts**	**PIM**
99-2000	Burnsville	High-MN	23	8	18	26	....	....	....	....	....	....
2000-01	Tri-City Americans	WHL	72	5	12	17	113	....	....	....	....	....
2001-02	Tri-City Americans	WHL	36	6	6	12	84	....	....	....	....	....
	Medicine Hat	WHL	24	4	13	17	43	....	....	....	....	....
2002-03	Lowell	AHL	35	0	2	2	62	....	....	....	....	....
	Florida Everblades	ECHL	32	1	6	7	77	1	0	0	0	0
2003-04	Lowell	AHL	74	1	8	9	66	....	....	....	....	....
2004-05	Lowell	AHL	61	2	7	9	103	7	0	1	1	4

D'AGOSTINI, Matt (DAG-uh-stee-noh, MAT) **MTL.**

Right wing. Shoots right. 5'11", 170 lbs. Born, Sault Ste. Marie, Ont., October 23, 1986.
(Montreal's 5th choice, 190th overall, in 2005 Entry Draft).

			Regular Season					Playoffs				
Season	**Club**	**League**	**GP**	**G**	**A**	**Pts**	**PIM**	**GP**	**G**	**A**	**Pts**	**PIM**
2003-04	Soo North Stars	GNML	36	36	23	59	41	....	....	....	....	....
2004-05	Guelph Storm	OHL	59	24	22	46	29	4	0	2	2	8

DAHLBERG, Johan (DAHL-buhrg, YO-han) **TOR.**

Left wing. Shoots left. 6'2", 194 lbs. Born, Kramfors, Sweden , February 3, 1987.
(Toronto's 4th choice, 173rd overall, in 2005 Entry Draft).

			Regular Season					Playoffs				
Season	**Club**	**League**	**GP**	**G**	**A**	**Pts**	**PIM**	**GP**	**G**	**A**	**Pts**	**PIM**
2002-03	Kramfors	Sweden-3	19	2	0	2	19	....	....	....	....	....
2003-04	MODO U18	Swe-U18	14	3	2	5	64	3	0	0	0	14
	MODO Jr.	Swe-Jr.	1	0	0	0	0	....	....	....	....	....
2004-05	MODO Jr.	Swe-Jr.	33	10	5	15	78	4	0	0	0	4

DALLMAN, Kevin (DAL-mahn, KEH-vihn) **BOS.**

Defense. Shoots right. 5'11", 195 lbs. Born, Niagara Falls, Ont., February 26, 1981.

			Regular Season					Playoffs				
Season	**Club**	**League**	**GP**	**G**	**A**	**Pts**	**PIM**	**GP**	**G**	**A**	**Pts**	**PIM**
1996-97	Niagara Falls	OHA-B	3	0	1	1	2	....	....	....	....	....
1997-98	Niagara Falls	OHA-B	47	13	25	38	42	....	....	....	....	....
1998-99	Guelph Storm	OHL	68	8	30	38	52	11	1	4	5	2
99-2000	Guelph Storm	OHL	67	13	46	59	38	6	0	2	2	11
2000-01	Guelph Storm	OHL	66	25	52	77	88	1	0	0	0	0
2001-02	Guelph Storm	OHL	67	23	63	86	68	9	8	8	16	22
2002-03	Providence Bruins	AHL	72	2	19	21	53	....	....	....	....	....
2003-04	Providence Bruins	AHL	65	6	23	29	44	2	0	0	0	0
2004-05	Providence Bruins	AHL	71	8	26	34	48	17	4	6	10	20

Memorial Cup Tournament All-Star Team (2002)

Signed as a free agent by **Boston**, July 18, 2002.

D'AMOUR, Dominic (dah-MOHR, DOHM-ihn-ihk) **TOR.**

Defense. Shoots left. 6'3", 202 lbs. Born, LaSalle, Que., January 28, 1984.
(Toronto's 4th choice, 88th overall, in 2002 Entry Draft).

			Regular Season					Playoffs				
Season	**Club**	**League**	**GP**	**G**	**A**	**Pts**	**PIM**	**GP**	**G**	**A**	**Pts**	**PIM**
99-2000	Charles-Lemoyne	QAAA	35	3	8	11	47	16	1	1	2	14
2000-01	Charles-Lemoyne	QAAA	11	1	4	5	36	....	....	....	....	....
	Rouyn-Noranda	QMJHL	18	0	0	0	10	....	....	....	....	....
2001-02	Hull Olympiques	QMJHL	68	5	5	10	225	12	0	3	3	32
2002-03	Hull Olympiques	QMJHL	65	5	25	30	211	17	2	3	5	51
2003-04	Gatineau	QMJHL	61	15	38	53	211	15	3	6	9	*41
2004-05	St. John's	AHL	26	1	1	2	60	1	0	0	0	0
	Pensacola	ECHL	22	4	8	12	33	4	0	0	0	2

DANIELSSON, Nicklas (DAN-yehl-suhn, NIHK-las) **VAN.**

Right wing. Shoots right. 6'1", 169 lbs. Born, Uppsala, Sweden, December 7, 1984.
(Vancouver's 5th choice, 160th overall, in 2003 Entry Draft).

			Regular Season					Playoffs				
Season	**Club**	**League**	**GP**	**G**	**A**	**Pts**	**PIM**	**GP**	**G**	**A**	**Pts**	**PIM**
2001-02	Calgary Bruins	CBHL	9	6	8	14	12	....	....	....	....	....
	Brynas IF Gavle Jr.	Swe-Jr.	42	15	14	29	74	....	....	....	....	....
	Cardiff Devils	Britain-2	13	3	5	8	2	....	....	....	....	....
2002-03	Brynas IF Gavle Jr.	Swe-Jr.	21	21	12	33	24	2	1	0	1	2
	Brynas IF Gavle	Sweden	26	0	4	4	10	....	....	....	....	....
	Brynas IF Gavle	Sweden-Q	6	0	0	0	4	....	....	....	....	....
2003-04	Brynas IF Gavle	Sweden	47	6	0	6	22	....	....	....	....	....
	Brynas IF Gavle Jr.	Swe-Jr.	10	8	8	16	12	5	3	1	4	48
	Almtuna	Sweden-2	4	1	1	2	6	....	....	....	....	....
2004-05	Brynas IF Gavle	Sweden	30	0	1	1	2	....	....	....	....	....

DANILICS, Raimonds (da-NIH-likhs, RAY-mawndz) **T.B.**

Forward. Shoots right. 6'3", 180 lbs. Born, Riga, Latvia, July 17, 1985.
(Tampa Bay's 7th choice, 255th overall, in 2003 Entry Draft).

			Regular Season					Playoffs				
Season	**Club**	**League**	**GP**	**G**	**A**	**Pts**	**PIM**	**GP**	**G**	**A**	**Pts**	**PIM**
2000-01	Daugavpils Jr.	Latvia-Jr.	20	6	8	14	....	....	....	....	....	....
	Prizma Riga	Latvia	2	0	0	0	0	....	....	....	....	....
2001-02	Daugavpils Jr.	Latvia-Jr.	16	4	5	9	10	....	....	....	....	....
2002-03	Daugavpils Jr.	Latvia-Jr.	14	4	5	9	18	....	....	....	....	....
	Daugavpils	EEHL-B	18	7	15	22	29	....	....	....	....	....
2003-04	Lukko Rauma Jr.	Finland-Jr.	27	0	0	0	12	....	....	....	....	....
2004-05	Tri-City Storm	USHL	7	2	0	2	6	....	....	....	....	....
	Texas Tornado	NAHL	13	0	5	5	9	....	....	....	....	....
	Bismarck Bobcats	NAHL	25	3	9	12	0	2	0	1	1	0

DARZINS, Lauris (DAHR-zihnzh, LOW-rihs) **NSH.**

Forward. Shoots right. 6'3", 190 lbs. Born, Riga, Latvia, January 28, 1985.
(Nashville's 13th choice, 268th overall, in 2003 Entry Draft).

			Regular Season					Playoffs				
Season	**Club**	**League**	**GP**	**G**	**A**	**Pts**	**PIM**	**GP**	**G**	**A**	**Pts**	**PIM**
2001-02	Lukko Rauma U18	Fin-U18	7	4	1	5	4	....	....	....	....	....
	Lukko Rauma Jr.	Finland-Jr.	5	1	0	1	0	....	....	....	....	....
2002-03	Lukko Rauma U18	Fin-U18	13	10	10	20	6	....	....	....	....	....
	Lukko Rauma Jr.	Finland-Jr.	13	6	4	10	6	....	....	....	....	....
2003-04	Lukko Rauma Jr.	Finland-Jr.	35	17	8	25	14	....	....	....	....	....
2004-05	Kelowna Rockets	WHL	53	19	15	34	38	24	7	7	14	10

DAVIS, George (DAY-vihs, JOHRJ) **ANA.**

Right wing. Shoots right. 6'1", 242 lbs. Born, North Sydney, N.S., July 28, 1983.
(Anaheim's 5th choice, 140th overall, in 2002 Entry Draft).

			Regular Season					Playoffs				
Season	**Club**	**League**	**GP**	**G**	**A**	**Pts**	**PIM**	**GP**	**G**	**A**	**Pts**	**PIM**
2000-01	Cape Breton	QMJHL	44	0	1	1	196	5	0	0	0	14
2001-02	Cape Breton	QMJHL	46	4	1	5	274	16	1	2	3	18
2002-03	Cape Breton	QMJHL	43	5	8	13	182	....	....	....	....	....
	Halifax	QMJHL	25	0	2	2	89	25	1	3	4	32
2003-04	Halifax	QMJHL	46	2	10	12	155	....	....	....	....	....
	Cincinnati	AHL	7	0	0	0	9	....	....	....	....	....
2004-05	Kansas City	UHL	60	4	4	8	207	....	....	....	....	....

DAVIS, Nathan (DAY-vihs, NAY-thuhn) **CHI.**

Center/Left wing. Shoots left. 6'1", 193 lbs. Born, Cleveland, OH, May 23, 1986.
(Chicago's 6th choice, 113th overall, in 2005 Entry Draft).

			Regular Season					Playoffs				
Season	**Club**	**League**	**GP**	**G**	**A**	**Pts**	**PIM**	**GP**	**G**	**A**	**Pts**	**PIM**
2002-03	USA U-17	USDP	27	5	2	7	6	....	....	....	....	....
2003-04	USA U-18	USDP	57	10	14	24	33	....	....	....	....	....
2004-05	Miami U.	CCHA	38	14	11	25	30	....	....	....	....	....

DAVIS, Patrick (DAY-vihs, PAT-rihk) **N.J.**

Left wing. Shoots right. 6'2", 190 lbs. Born, Sterling, MI, December 28, 1986.
(New Jersey's 4th choice, 99th overall, in 2005 Entry Draft).

			Regular Season					Playoffs				
Season	**Club**	**League**	**GP**	**G**	**A**	**Pts**	**PIM**	**GP**	**G**	**A**	**Pts**	**PIM**
2002-03	Detroit Belle Tire	MWEHL	STATISTICS NOT AVAILABLE									
	Sioux City	USHL	16	3	2	5	8	1	0	0	0	2
2003-04	Kitchener Rangers	OHL	27	8	10	18	21	....	....	....	....	....
2004-05	Kitchener Rangers	OHL	59	20	30	50	41	14	3	4	7	20

DAWES, Nigel (DAWZ, NIGH-juhl) **NYR**

Left wing. Shoots left. 5'8", 190 lbs. Born, Winnipeg, Man., February 9, 1985.
(NY Rangers' 5th choice, 149th overall, in 2003 Entry Draft).

			Regular Season					Playoffs				
Season	**Club**	**League**	**GP**	**G**	**A**	**Pts**	**PIM**	**GP**	**G**	**A**	**Pts**	**PIM**
2000-01	Winnipeg Warriors	MMMHL	36	55	41	96	74	....	....	....	....	....
2001-02	Kootenay Ice	WHL	54	15	19	34	14	22	9	6	15	8
2002-03	Kootenay Ice	WHL	72	47	45	92	54	11	4	8	12	6
2003-04	Kootenay Ice	WHL	56	47	23	70	31	4	1	2	3	10
	Hartford Wolf Pack	AHL	4	0	0	0	0	....	....	....	....	....
2004-05	Kootenay Ice	WHL	63	50	26	76	30	12	5	10	15	5

WHL West Second All-Star Team (2003) • WHL West First All-Star Team (2004, 2005)

DEE, Robby (DEE, RAWB-ee) **EDM.**

Center/Wing. Shoots left. 6'1", 185 lbs. Born, Minneapolis, MN, April 9, 1987.
(Edmonton's 4th choice, 86th overall, in 2005 Entry Draft).

			Regular Season					Playoffs				
Season	**Club**	**League**	**GP**	**G**	**A**	**Pts**	**PIM**	**GP**	**G**	**A**	**Pts**	**PIM**
2004-05	Breck Mustangs	High-MN	28	49	38	87	14	....	....	....	....	....

DeMARCHI, Matt (dih-MAHR-shee, MAT) **N.J.**

Defense. Shoots left. 6'3", 190 lbs. Born, Bemidji, MN, May 4, 1981.
(New Jersey's 4th choice, 57th overall, in 2000 Entry Draft).

			Regular Season					Playoffs				
Season	**Club**	**League**	**GP**	**G**	**A**	**Pts**	**PIM**	**GP**	**G**	**A**	**Pts**	**PIM**
1997-98	North Iowa	USHL	34	1	2	3	66	10	0	1	1	19
1998-99	North Iowa	USHL	53	4	14	18	131	....	....	....	....	....
99-2000	U. of Minnesota	WCHA	39	1	6	7	82	....	....	....	....	....
2000-01	U. of Minnesota	WCHA	39	4	9	13	*149	....	....	....	....	....
2001-02	U. of Minnesota	WCHA	36	3	8	11	112	....	....	....	....	....
2002-03	U. of Minnesota	WCHA	44	8	9	17	130	....	....	....	....	....
2003-04	Albany River Rats	AHL	52	4	10	14	78	....	....	....	....	....
2004-05	Albany River Rats	AHL	61	1	6	7	85	....	....	....	....	....

NCAA Championship All-Tournament Team (2003)

DEMEN-WILLAUME, Richard (deh-MEHN-WIHL-awm, RIH-kahrd) **COL.**

Defense. Shoots left. 6'3", 196 lbs. Born, Asa, Sweden, January 28, 1986.
(Colorado's 4th choice, 154th overall, in 2004 Entry Draft).

			Regular Season					Playoffs				
Season	**Club**	**League**	**GP**	**G**	**A**	**Pts**	**PIM**	**GP**	**G**	**A**	**Pts**	**PIM**
2001-02	V.Frolunda U18	Swe-U18	13	2	2	4	14	3	1	0	1	2
	V.Frolunda Jr.	Swe-Jr.	1	0	0	0	0	....	....	....	....	....
2002-03	V.Frolunda Jr.	Swe-Jr.	22	0	6	6	14	5	0	1	1	6
	V.Frolunda U18	Swe-U18	1	0	0	0	2	7	1	2	3	4
2003-04	V.Frolunda Jr.	Swe-Jr.	35	6	7	13	22	....	....	....	....	....
2004-05	Frolunda	Sweden	9	0	0	0	0	1	0	0	0	0
	Frolunda Jr.	Swe-Jr.	32	3	12	15	63	6	1	1	2	22

DENISOV, Denis (den-NEES-ahf, deh-NEES) **BUF.**

Left wing. Shoots left. 6', 183 lbs. Born, Kalinin, USSR, December 31, 1981.
(Buffalo's 4th choice, 149th overall, in 2000 Entry Draft).

			Regular Season					Playoffs				
Season	**Club**	**League**	**GP**	**G**	**A**	**Pts**	**PIM**	**GP**	**G**	**A**	**Pts**	**PIM**
1997-98	HK CSKA Moscow	Russia	7	0	0	0	4	....	....	....	....	....
1998-99	HK CSKA Moscow	Russia-2	42	1	6	7	16	....	....	....	....	....
99-2000	HK Moscow	Russia-2	39	1	8	9	16	....	....	....	....	....
2000-01	HK Moscow	Russia-2	41	0	3	3	6	....	....	....	....	....
2001-02	Krylja Sovetov	Russia	47	3	4	7	37	....	....	....	....	....
	Krylja Sovetov 2	Russia-3	3	0	1	1	18	....	....	....	....	....
2002-03	Ufa	Russia	50	2	8	10	12	3	0	1	1	0
2003-04	Ak Bars Kazan	Russia	51	4	11	15	34	7	0	0	0	4
2004-05	Ak Bars Kazan	Russia	57	4	7	11	30	4	0	0	0	2

DENNY, Chad (DEHN-ee, CHAD) **ATL.**

Defense. Shoots left. 6'2", 210 lbs. Born, Sydney, N.S., March 27, 1987.
(Atlanta's 3rd choice, 49th overall, in 2005 Entry Draft).

			Regular Season					Playoffs				
Season	**Club**	**League**	**GP**	**G**	**A**	**Pts**	**PIM**	**GP**	**G**	**A**	**Pts**	**PIM**
2003-04	Lewiston	QMJHL	41	3	6	9	19	7	0	0	0	11
2004-05	Lewiston	QMJHL	53	8	18	26	98	8	2	2	4	14

DERLYUK, Roman (duhr-LYUHK, ROH-muhn) **FLA.**

Defense. Shoots left. 6'3", 198 lbs. Born, Leningrad, USSR, October 27, 1986.
(Florida's 7th choice, 164th overall, in 2005 Entry Draft).

			Regular Season					Playoffs				
Season	**Club**	**League**	**GP**	**G**	**A**	**Pts**	**PIM**	**GP**	**G**	**A**	**Pts**	**PIM**
2003-04	Lok. St. Pet.	Russia-3	STATISTICS NOT AVAILABLE									
2004-05	Spartak St. Pet.	Russia-2	51	0	3	3	74	....	....	....	....	....

DESBIENS, Guillaume (deh-BYEHN, gwee-AHM) **ATL.**

Right wing. Shoots left. 6'2", 205 lbs. Born, Alma, Que., April 20, 1985.
(Atlanta's 3rd choice, 116th overall, in 2003 Entry Draft).

			Regular Season					Playoffs				
Season	**Club**	**League**	**GP**	**G**	**A**	**Pts**	**PIM**	**GP**	**G**	**A**	**Pts**	**PIM**
2001-02	Rouyn-Noranda	QMJHL	65	14	10	24	115	4	1	1	2	9
2002-03	Rouyn-Noranda	QMJHL	64	15	18	33	233	4	0	0	0	4
2003-04	Rouyn-Noranda	QMJHL	58	20	21	41	199	11	2	2	4	24
2004-05	Rouyn-Noranda	QMJHL	56	27	16	43	206	10	1	4	5	25

DEVEAUX, Andre (de-VOH, AWN-dray) T.B.

Center. Shoots right. 6'3", 240 lbs. Born, Freeport, Bahamas, February 23, 1984.
(Montreal's 4th choice, 182nd overall, in 2002 Entry Draft).

			Regular Season					Playoffs				
Season	**Club**	**League**	**GP**	**G**	**A**	**Pts**	**PIM**	**GP**	**G**	**A**	**Pts**	**PIM**
99-2000	Fort Erie	OHA-B	STATISTICS NOT AVAILABLE									
2000-01	Belleville Bulls	OHL	58	3	6	9	65	10	3	6	9	6
2001-02	Belleville Bulls	OHL	64	8	13	21	89	11	1	2	3	30
2002-03	Belleville Bulls	OHL	34	6	12	18	93	....	....	....	....	....
	Owen Sound	OHL	29	9	10	19	33	4	2	2	4	6
2003-04	Owen Sound	OHL	64	16	30	46	151	7	3	3	6	21
2004-05	Springfield Falcons	AHL	73	4	8	12	210	....	....	....	....	....

Signed as a free agent by **Tampa Bay**, September 15, 2004.

DICAIRE, Gerard (dih-KAIR, zhehr-AHR) T.B.

Defense. Shoots left. 6'2", 190 lbs. Born, Faro, Yukon, September 14, 1982.
(Tampa Bay's 4th choice, 162nd overall, in 2002 Entry Draft).

			Regular Season					Playoffs				
Season	**Club**	**League**	**GP**	**G**	**A**	**Pts**	**PIM**	**GP**	**G**	**A**	**Pts**	**PIM**
1997-98	Tumble Ridge	NWJHL	35	15	28	43	63	....	....	....	....	....
1998-99	Prince George	BCHL	51	6	22	28	28	....	....	....	....	....
99-2000	Seattle	WHL	68	11	25	36	38	7	0	1	1	6
2000-01	Seattle	WHL	69	15	36	51	33	9	0	2	2	2
2001-02	Seattle	WHL	41	4	25	29	25	....	....	....	....	....
	Kootenay Ice	WHL	25	2	21	23	9	22	1	14	15	24
2002-03	Kootenay Ice	WHL	72	15	44	59	79	11	2	6	8	12
2003-04	Utah Grizzlies	AHL	53	2	7	9	36	....	....	....	....	....
2004-05	Springfield Falcons	AHL	47	3	4	7	20	....	....	....	....	....

• Re-entered NHL Entry Draft. Originally Buffalo's 2nd choice, 48th overall, in 2000 Entry Draft.
WHL West Second All-Star Team (2001, 2003)

DiCASMIRRO, Nate (dee-CAZ-MIHR-oh, NAYT) EDM.

Left wing. Shoots left. 5'11", 205 lbs. Born, Burnsville, MN, September 27, 1978.

			Regular Season					Playoffs				
Season	**Club**	**League**	**GP**	**G**	**A**	**Pts**	**PIM**	**GP**	**G**	**A**	**Pts**	**PIM**
1996-97	North Iowa	USHL	51	18	22	40	86	12	0	6	6	22
1997-98	North Iowa	USHL	52	29	45	74	118	11	5	5	10	34
1998-99	St. Cloud State	WCHA	34	6	8	14	46	....	....	....	....	....
99-2000	St. Cloud State	WCHA	40	19	24	43	26	....	....	....	....	....
2000-01	St. Cloud State	WCHA	32	9	20	29	26	....	....	....	....	....
2001-02	St. Cloud State	WCHA	41	17	33	50	58	....	....	....	....	....
	Hamilton Bulldogs	AHL	1	0	0	0	0	10	0	5	5	6
2002-03	Hamilton Bulldogs	AHL	49	5	12	17	22	16	2	1	3	8
2003-04	Toronto	AHL	71	17	18	35	37	2	0	1	1	0
2004-05	Edmonton	AHL	77	7	18	25	48	....	....	....	....	....

USHL First All-Star Team (1998) • USHL MVP (1998) • WCHA Second All-Star Team (2002)
Signed as a free agent by **Edmonton**, May 28, 2002.

DILLON, Spencer (DIH-luhn, SPEHN-suhr) FLA.

Defense. Shoots right. 6'4", 190 lbs. Born, Santa Cruz, CA, January 7, 1985.
(Florida's 6th choice, 267th overall, in 2004 Entry Draft).

			Regular Season					Playoffs				
Season	**Club**	**League**	**GP**	**G**	**A**	**Pts**	**PIM**	**GP**	**G**	**A**	**Pts**	**PIM**
2003-04	Salmon Arm	BCHL	42	0	7	7	160	14	0	2	2	22
2004-05	Green Bay	USHL	54	1	2	3	91	....	....	....	....	....

DISALVATORE, Jon (dih-sal-vuh-TOH-ray, JAWN) ST.L.

Right wing. Shoots right. 6'1", 200 lbs. Born, Bangor, ME, March 30, 1981.
(San Jose's 2nd choice, 104th overall, in 2000 Entry Draft).

			Regular Season					Playoffs				
Season	**Club**	**League**	**GP**	**G**	**A**	**Pts**	**PIM**	**GP**	**G**	**A**	**Pts**	**PIM**
1997-98	N.E. Jr. Coyotes	EJHL	38	24	41	65	....	....	....	....	....	....
1998-99	N.E. Jr. Coyotes	EJHL	48	44	76	*120	38	....	....	....	....	....
99-2000	Providence College	H-East	38	15	12	27	12	....	....	....	....	....
2000-01	Providence College	H-East	36	9	16	25	29	....	....	....	....	....
2001-02	Providence College	H-East	38	16	26	42	6	....	....	....	....	....
2002-03	Providence College	H-East	36	19	29	48	12	....	....	....	....	....
2003-04	Cleveland Barons	AHL	74	22	24	46	30	8	1	1	2	2
2004-05	Worcester IceCats	AHL	79	22	23	45	42	....	....	....	....	....

Signed as a free agent by **St. Louis**, June 30, 2004.

DIXON, Stephen (DIHX-uhn, STEE-vehn) PIT.

Center. Shoots left. 5'11", 188 lbs. Born, Halifax, N.S., September 7, 1985.
(Pittsburgh's 9th choice, 229th overall, in 2003 Entry Draft).

			Regular Season					Playoffs				
Season	**Club**	**League**	**GP**	**G**	**A**	**Pts**	**PIM**	**GP**	**G**	**A**	**Pts**	**PIM**
2001-02	Cape Breton	QMJHL	64	16	15	31	12	16	3	5	8	12
2002-03	Cape Breton	QMJHL	72	28	42	70	54	4	0	0	0	6
2003-04	Cape Breton	QMJHL	55	22	50	72	33	5	1	0	1	0
2004-05	Cape Breton	QMJHL	45	17	34	51	40	....	....	....	....	....

DOBRYSHKIN, Yuri (doh-BRIHSH-kihn, yew-REE) ATL.

Left wing. Shoots right. 6', 190 lbs. Born, Penza, USSR, July 19, 1979.
(Atlanta's 7th choice, 159th overall, in 1999 Entry Draft).

			Regular Season					Playoffs				
Season	**Club**	**League**	**GP**	**G**	**A**	**Pts**	**PIM**	**GP**	**G**	**A**	**Pts**	**PIM**
1996-97	Krylja Sovetov 2	Russia-3	35	13	5	18	42	....	....	....	....	....
	Krylja Sovetov	Russia	2	0	0	0	0	2	0	0	0	0
1997-98	Krylja Sovetov 2	Russia-3	26	12	5	17	68	....	....	....	....	....
	Krylja Sovetov	Russia	22	4	0	4	12	....	....	....	....	....
1998-99	Krylja Sovetov	Russia	50	11	5	16	86	....	....	....	....	....
99-2000	Ak Bars Kazan	Russia	27	6	9	15	24	17	2	0	2	10
2000-01	Ak Bars Kazan	Russia	40	10	5	15	32	4	2	0	2	2
2001-02	Ak Bars Kazan	Russia	38	9	8	17	22	11	0	2	2	6
2002-03	Cherepovets	Russia	49	19	7	26	82	12	5	2	7	12
2003-04	Cherepovets	Russia	53	11	7	18	75	....	....	....	....	....
2004-05	Magnitogorsk	Russia	54	14	6	20	42	2	0	0	0	0

DOELL, Kevin (DOH-ehl, KEH-vihn) ATL.

Center. Shoots left. 5'11", 190 lbs. Born, Saskatoon, Sask., July 15, 1979.

			Regular Season					Playoffs				
Season	**Club**	**League**	**GP**	**G**	**A**	**Pts**	**PIM**	**GP**	**G**	**A**	**Pts**	**PIM**
99-2000	U. of Denver	WCHA	40	8	15	23	18	....	....	....	....	....
2000-01	U. of Denver	WCHA	36	9	10	19	26	....	....	....	....	....
2001-02	U. of Denver	WCHA	41	20	23	43	28	....	....	....	....	....
2002-03	U. of Denver	WCHA	41	25	26	51	34	....	....	....	....	....
2003-04	Chicago Wolves	AHL	8	1	1	2	6	1	0	0	0	0
	Gwinnett	ECHL	63	33	41	74	88	13	1	6	7	12
2004-05	Chicago Wolves	AHL	45	4	8	12	69	....	....	....	....	....
	Gwinnett	ECHL	11	6	9	15	14	8	2	1	3	14

ECHL All-Rookie Team (2004) • ECHL Rookie of the Year (2004)
Signed as a free agent by **Atlanta**, June 30, 2004.

DOHERTY, John (DOH-her-tee, JAWN) TOR.

Defense. Shoots right. 6'4", 213 lbs. Born, Malden, MA, March 25, 1984.
(Toronto's 1st choice, 57th overall, in 2003 Entry Draft).

			Regular Season					Playoffs				
Season	**Club**	**League**	**GP**	**G**	**A**	**Pts**	**PIM**	**GP**	**G**	**A**	**Pts**	**PIM**
2001-02	Andover	High-MA	24	5	18	23	....	....	....	....	....	....
2002-03	Andover	High-MA	24	12	12	24	40	....	....	....	....	....
	N.H. Jr. Monarchs	EJHL	11	1	4	5	36	....	....	....	....	....
2003-04	New Hampshire	H-East	16	1	2	3	6	....	....	....	....	....
2004-05	New Hampshire	H-East	4	0	0	0	2	....	....	....	....	....
	Des Moines	USHL	39	9	7	16	96	....	....	....	....	....

DONALLY, Ryan (DAWN-ah-lee, RIGH-uhn) CGY.

Left wing. Shoots left. 6'5", 227 lbs. Born, Tecumseh, Ont., February 4, 1985.
(Calgary's 3rd choice, 97th overall, in 2003 Entry Draft).

			Regular Season					Playoffs				
Season	**Club**	**League**	**GP**	**G**	**A**	**Pts**	**PIM**	**GP**	**G**	**A**	**Pts**	**PIM**
2001-02	Windsor Spitfires	OHL	53	6	7	13	77	16	0	2	2	6
2002-03	Windsor Spitfires	OHL	65	11	15	26	108	7	0	1	1	8
2003-04	Windsor Spitfires	OHL	44	8	14	22	93	....	....	....	....	....
2004-05	Windsor Spitfires	OHL	29	2	3	5	87	....	....	....	....	....
	Kitchener Rangers	OHL	21	1	2	3	45	13	0	0	0	12

DONIKA, Mikhail (DAW-nih-ka, mih-kigh-EHL) DAL.

Defense. Shoots left. 6', 185 lbs. Born, Yaroslavl, USSR, May 15, 1979.
(Dallas' 11th choice, 272nd overall, in 1999 Entry Draft).

			Regular Season					Playoffs				
Season	**Club**	**League**	**GP**	**G**	**A**	**Pts**	**PIM**	**GP**	**G**	**A**	**Pts**	**PIM**
1996-97	Yaroslavl 2	Russia-3	15	3	5	8	6	....	....	....	....	....
	Torpedo Yaroslavl	Russia	22	1	0	1	6	2	0	0	0	0
1997-98	Yaroslavl 2	Russia-2	19	1	2	3	32	....	....	....	....	....
	Torpedo Yaroslavl	Russia	30	0	2	2	14	....	....	....	....	....
1998-99	Yaroslavl 2	Russia-3	6	2	1	3	4	....	....	....	....	....
	Torpedo Yaroslavl	Russia	37	0	1	1	10	....	....	....	....	....
99-2000	Torpedo Yaroslavl	Russia	35	0	1	1	22	10	0	0	0	4
2000-01	Dynamo Moscow	Russia	43	1	3	4	12	....	....	....	....	....
2001-02	Amur Khabarovsk	Russia	51	1	3	4	66	....	....	....	....	....
2002-03	Spartak Moscow	Russia	51	4	7	11	16	....	....	....	....	....
2003-04	Spartak Moscow	Russia-2	55	4	14	18	14	12	2	1	3	2
2004-05	Spartak Moscow	Russia	49	0	2	2	34	....	....	....	....	....

DORNIC, Ivan (DOHR-nihch, ee-VAHN) NYR

Center. Shoots right. 6', 183 lbs. Born, Bratislava, Czech., April 12, 1985.
(NY Rangers' 6th choice, 176th overall, in 2003 Entry Draft).

			Regular Season					Playoffs				
Season	**Club**	**League**	**GP**	**G**	**A**	**Pts**	**PIM**	**GP**	**G**	**A**	**Pts**	**PIM**
2001-02	Bratislava Jr.	Slovak-Jr.	17	7	7	14	33	....	....	....	....	....
2002-03	Bratislava Jr.	Slovak-Jr.	33	13	13	26	45	....	....	....	....	....
	Bratislava	Slovakia	8	1	0	1	0	....	....	....	....	....
2003-04	Portland	WHL	54	6	8	14	28	5	0	0	0	4
2004-05	Portland	WHL	8	0	1	1	5	....	....	....	....	....
	HK Trnava	Slovak-2	6	3	2	5	2	3	0	0	0	4
	Bratislava Jr.	Slovak-Jr.	10	7	5	12	26	1	0	1	1	2
	Bratislava	Slovakia	24	2	2	4	2	16	2	0	2	2

DOVGAN, Viktor (DAWV-guhn, VIHK-tohr) WSH.

Defense. Shoots left. 6'1", 205 lbs. Born, Moscow, USSR, February 27, 1987.
(Washington's choice, 209th overall, in 2005 Entry Draft).

			Regular Season					Playoffs				
Season	**Club**	**League**	**GP**	**G**	**A**	**Pts**	**PIM**	**GP**	**G**	**A**	**Pts**	**PIM**
2003-04	CSKA Moscow 2	Russia-3	STATISTICS NOT AVAILABLE									
2004-05	CSKA Moscow 2	Russia-3	STATISTICS NOT AVAILABLE									

DOWELL, Jake (DOW-uhl, JAYK) CHI.

Center. Shoots left. 6', 202 lbs. Born, Eau Claire, WI, March 4, 1985.
(Chicago's 10th choice, 140th overall, in 2004 Entry Draft).

			Regular Season					Playoffs				
Season	**Club**	**League**	**GP**	**G**	**A**	**Pts**	**PIM**	**GP**	**G**	**A**	**Pts**	**PIM**
2000-01	Eau Claire Mem.	High-WI	24	25	30	55	....	....	....	....	....	....
2001-02	USA U-17	USDP	55	10	13	23	65	....	....	....	....	....
2002-03	USA U-18	USDP	63	10	19	29	67	....	....	....	....	....
2003-04	U. of Wisconsin	WCHA	37	6	13	19	48	....	....	....	....	....
2004-05	U. of Wisconsin	WCHA	38	12	14	26	74	....	....	....	....	....

DOWNIE, Steve (DOW-nee, STEEV) PHI.

Right wing. Shoots right. 5'10", 192 lbs. Born, Newmarket, Ont., April 3, 1987.
(Philadelphia's 1st choice, 29th overall, in 2005 Entry Draft).

			Regular Season					Playoffs				
Season	**Club**	**League**	**GP**	**G**	**A**	**Pts**	**PIM**	**GP**	**G**	**A**	**Pts**	**PIM**
2002-03	Aurora Tigers	OPJHL	34	12	13	25	55	....	....	....	....	....
2003-04	Windsor Spitfires	OHL	49	7	9	16	90	4	0	1	1	27
2004-05	Windsor Spitfires	OHL	61	21	52	73	179	11	4	5	9	49

DRAZENOVIC, Nicholas (DRAY-zehn-oh-vihk, NIHK-oh-las) ST.L.

Center. Shoots left. 6', 172 lbs. Born, Prince George, B.C., January 14, 1987.
(St. Louis' 6th choice, 171st overall, in 2005 Entry Draft).

			Regular Season					Playoffs				
Season	**Club**	**League**	**GP**	**G**	**A**	**Pts**	**PIM**	**GP**	**G**	**A**	**Pts**	**PIM**
2003-04	Prince George	WHL	65	7	30	37	38	....	....	....	....	....
2004-05	Prince George	WHL	72	18	38	56	24	....	....	....	....	....

DROZDETSKY, Alexander (drawz-DEHT-skee, al-ehx-AN-duhr) PHI.

Right wing. Shoots left. 6', 180 lbs. Born, Moscow, USSR, November 10, 1981.
(Philadelphia's 2nd choice, 94th overall, in 2000 Entry Draft).

			Regular Season					Playoffs				
Season	Club	League	GP	G	A	Pts	PIM	GP	G	A	Pts	PIM
1997-98	St. Petersburg 2	Russia-3	19	0	1	1	0	....	....	....	....	....
1998-99	St. Petersburg 2	Russia-4	24	5	3	8	12	....	....	....	....	....
99-2000	St. Petersburg 2	Russia-3	4	4	1	5	2	....	....	....	....	....
	SKA St. Petersburg	Russia	32	2	0	2	10	4	0	0	0	0
2000-01	SKA St. Petersburg	Russia	42	6	7	13	74	....	....	....	....	....
2001-02	CSKA Moscow	Russia	49	11	6	17	26	....	....	....	....	....
2002-03	CSKA Moscow	Russia	46	14	13	27	30	....	....	....	....	....
2003-04	Ak Bars Kazan	Russia	57	16	15	31	62	1	0	0	0	2
2004-05	Ak Bars Kazan	Russia	32	3	4	7	28	....	....	....	....	....
	Ak Bars Kazan 2	Russia-3	....	10	8	18	....	....	....	....	....	....
	Nizhnekamsk	Russia	7	5	1	6	4	....	....	....	....	....

DUBEC, Marek (DOO-behts, MAIR-ehk) BUF.

Left wing. Shoots left. 6', 179 lbs. Born, Bratislava, Czech., February 26, 1982.
(Buffalo's 7th choice, 247th overall, in 2001 Entry Draft).

			Regular Season					Playoffs				
Season	Club	League	GP	G	A	Pts	PIM	GP	G	A	Pts	PIM
1996-97	Bratislava Jr.	Slovak-Jr.	47	19	8	27	20	....	....	....	....	....
1997-98	Bratislava Jr.	Slovak-Jr.	40	17	18	35	59	....	....	....	....	....
1998-99	Bratislava Jr.	Slovak-Jr.	47	23	20	43	38	....	....	....	....	....
99-2000	Bratislava Jr.	Slovak-Jr.	36	16	10	26	61	....	....	....	....	....
2000-01	HC Vsetin Jr.	CzRep-Jr.	45	27	15	42	52	8	7	2	9	20
2001-02	HC Vsetin Jr.	CzRep-Jr.	18	12	9	21	32	....	....	....	....	....
	HC Vsetin	CzRep	5	1	0	1	0	4	2	0	2	4
2002-03	HC Vsetin	CzRep	22	2	4	6	24	4	0	0	0	2
	HC Vsetin Jr.	CzRep-Jr.	8	6	6	12	24	5	1	0	1	12
	Trebic	CzRep-2	16	3	2	5	24	....	....	....	....	....
2003-04	HC Hame Zlin	CzRep	5	0	1	1	2	....	....	....	....	....
	HC Vsetin	CzRep	41	7	6	13	73	....	....	....	....	....
	HC Slezan Opava	CzRep-2	3	0	1	1	2	....	....	....	....	....
	HC Sareza Ostrava	CzRep-3	....	....	....	....	....	1	0	0	0	4
2004-05	HC Olomouc	CzRep-2	4	2	1	3	2	....	....	....	....	....
	HC Vsetin	CzRep	40	4	0	4	26	....	....	....	....	....
	TJ Novy Jicin	CzRep-3	3	2	1	3	2	1	0	0	0	2

DUBEN, Premysl (DUH-behn, PREHM-uh-suhl) NYR

Defense. Shoots left. 6'3", 220 lbs. Born, Jihlava, Czech., October 5, 1981.
(NY Rangers' 3rd choice, 112th overall, in 2000 Entry Draft).

			Regular Season					Playoffs				
Season	Club	League	GP	G	A	Pts	PIM	GP	G	A	Pts	PIM
1997-98	Jihlava Jr.	CzRep-Jr.	25	1	6	7	34	....	....	....	....	....
1998-99	Jihlava Jr.	CzRep-Jr.	41	1	5	6	18	....	....	....	....	....
99-2000	Jihlava Jr.	CzRep-Jr.	27	4	2	6	36	....	....	....	....	....
	HC Dukla Jihlava	CzRep-2	19	0	1	1	10	14	0	1	1	4
2000-01	HC Dukla Jihlava	CzRep-2	5	0	0	0	10	....	....	....	....	....
	Baie-Comeau	QMJHL	32	0	8	8	36	9	1	0	1	12
2001-02	Jihlava Jr.	CzRep-Jr.	13	0	5	5	20	....	....	....	....	....
	HC Dukla Jihlava	CzRep-2	33	0	1	1	36	6	0	0	0	2
2002-03	HC Dukla Jihlava	CzRep-2	24	0	1	1	20	12	0	0	0	10
2003-04	Havl. Brod	CzRep-3	12	0	1	1	12	....	....	....	....	....
	HC Dukla Jihlava	CzRep-2	20	0	0	0	47	14	0	0	0	16
2004-05	HC Dukla Jihlava	CzRep	2	0	0	0	0	....	....	....	....	....
	Trebic	CzRep-2	18	1	1	2	16	....	....	....	....	....
	IHC Pisek	CzRep-2	8	0	1	1	50	....	....	....	....	....

DUBINSKY, Brandon (DOO-bihn-skee, BRAN-duhn) NYR

Center. Shoots left. 5'11", 203 lbs. Born, Anchorage, AK, April 29, 1986.
(NY Rangers' 6th choice, 60th overall, in 2004 Entry Draft).

			Regular Season					Playoffs				
Season	Club	League	GP	G	A	Pts	PIM	GP	G	A	Pts	PIM
2001-02	Alaska All-Stars	AASHA	37	14	24	38	....	....	....	....	....	....
2002-03	Portland	WHL	44	8	18	26	35	7	2	2	4	10
2003-04	Portland	WHL	71	30	48	78	137	5	0	2	2	6
2004-05	Portland	WHL	68	23	36	59	160	7	4	5	9	8

WHL West Second All-Star Team (2004)

DUDA, Radek (DOO-duh, RA-dehk) CGY.

Right wing. Shoots left. 6'1", 193 lbs. Born, Skolov, Czech., January 28, 1979.
(Calgary's 7th choice, 192nd overall, in 1998 Entry Draft).

			Regular Season					Playoffs				
Season	Club	League	GP	G	A	Pts	PIM	GP	G	A	Pts	PIM
1994-95	Sokolov Jr.	CzRep-Jr.	36	67	37	104	....	....	....	....	....	....
1995-96	Sparta Jr.	CzRep-Jr.	39	15	10	25	....	....	....	....	....	....
1996-97	Sparta Jr.	CzRep-Jr.	21	9	14	23	....	....	....	....	....	....
	Sokolov Jr.	CzRep-Jr.	1	0	0	0	....	....	....	....	....	....
	HC Sparta Praha	CzRep	....	....	....	....	....	1	0	0	0	0
1997-98	HC Sparta Praha	CzRep	39	3	3	6	41	10	0	2	2	6
1998-99	Regina Pats	WHL	65	24	31	55	139	....	....	....	....	....
99-2000	Lethbridge	WHL	69	42	64	106	193	....	....	....	....	....
2000-01	HC Keramika Plzen	CzRep	24	5	6	11	49	....	....	....	....	....
	HC Sparta Praha	CzRep	18	2	1	3	66	....	....	....	....	....
2001-02	HC Keramika Plzen	CzRep	49	17	18	35	156	6	1	5	6	18
2002-03	HC Keramika Plzen	CzRep	13	5	8	13	47	....	....	....	....	....
	HC Slavia Praha	CzRep	31	12	15	27	105	17	7	3	10	40
2003-04	Ak Bars Kazan	Russia	41	6	9	15	58	3	1	1	2	2
2004-05	HC Slavia Praha	CzRep	32	6	4	10	52	....	....	....	....	....
	Plzen	CzRep	16	3	6	9	55	....	....	....	....	....

DUFFY, Matt (DUHF-ee, MAT) FLA.

Defense. Shoots right. 6'2", 180 lbs. Born, Portland, ME, March 21, 1986.
(Florida's 5th choice, 104th overall, in 2005 Entry Draft).

			Regular Season					Playoffs				
Season	Club	League	GP	G	A	Pts	PIM	GP	G	A	Pts	PIM
2003-04	N.H. Jr. Monarchs	EJHL	33	9	13	22	....	....	....	....	....	....
2004-05	N.H. Jr. Monarchs	EJHL	54	19	26	45	147	....	....	....	....	....

Signed Letter of Intent to attend **Maine** (H-East), November 17, 2004.

DULAC-LEMELIN, Alex (doo-LAK-leh-MUH-lehn, AL-ehx) MTL.

Defense. Shoots right. 6'3", 190 lbs. Born, Montreal, Que., March 17, 1986.
(Montreal's 9th choice, 278th overall, in 2004 Entry Draft).

			Regular Season					Playoffs				
Season	Club	League	GP	G	A	Pts	PIM	GP	G	A	Pts	PIM
2003-04	Baie-Comeau	QMJHL	67	2	11	13	35	3	0	0	0	0
2004-05	Baie-Comeau	QMJHL	63	8	19	27	54	6	0	2	2	15

DUPONT, Brodie (DOO-pohnt, BROH-dee) NYR

Center. Shoots left. 6'1", 197 lbs. Born, Russell, Man., February 17, 1987.
(NY Rangers' 4th choice, 66th overall, in 2005 Entry Draft).

			Regular Season					Playoffs				
Season	Club	League	GP	G	A	Pts	PIM	GP	G	A	Pts	PIM
2003-04	Swan Valley	MJHL	51	25	16	41	88	12	5	1	6	36
	Calgary Hitmen	WHL	2	0	1	1	0	....	....	....	....	....
2004-05	Calgary Hitmen	WHL	70	14	11	25	111	12	2	8	10	21

DUPUIS, Philippe (doo-PWEE, fihl-EEP) CBJ

Center. Shoots right. 6', 192 lbs. Born, Laval, Que., April 24, 1985.
(Columbus' 5th choice, 104th overall, in 2003 Entry Draft).

			Regular Season					Playoffs				
Season	Club	League	GP	G	A	Pts	PIM	GP	G	A	Pts	PIM
2000-01	Laval-Laurentides	QAAA	46	16	27	43	74	8	1	5	6	30
2001-02	Hull Olympiques	QMJHL	67	7	14	21	59	12	6	5	11	14
2002-03	Hull Olympiques	QMJHL	68	22	34	56	89	20	2	4	6	22
2003-04	Gatineau	QMJHL	60	18	37	55	77	15	6	10	16	14
2004-05	Rouyn-Noranda	QMJHL	62	34	50	84	60	10	5	3	8	8

DURAND, Chris (DUHR-and, KRIHS) COL.

Center. Shoots right. 6'1", 186 lbs. Born, Saskatoon, Sask., January 21, 1987.
(Colorado's 4th choice, 52nd overall, in 2005 Entry Draft).

			Regular Season					Playoffs				
Season	Club	League	GP	G	A	Pts	PIM	GP	G	A	Pts	PIM
2002-03	Sask. Contacts	SMHL	39	9	18	27	38	....	....	....	....	....
2003-04	Seattle	WHL	60	17	26	43	71	....	....	....	....	....
2004-05	Seattle	WHL	66	19	34	53	76	12	0	1	1	14

DVORAK, Petr (duv-VOHR-ak, PEE-tuhr) WSH.

Center. Shoots right. 6', 194 lbs. Born, Roznov, Czech., October 11, 1983.
(Washington's 8th choice, 118th overall, in 2002 Entry Draft).

			Regular Season					Playoffs				
Season	Club	League	GP	G	A	Pts	PIM	GP	G	A	Pts	PIM
99-2000	HC Havirov Jr.	CzRep-Jr.	47	28	28	56	79	....	....	....	....	....
2000-01	HC Havirov Jr.	CzRep-Jr.	36	12	15	27	18	....	....	....	....	....
	HC Femax Havirov	CzRep	1	0	0	0	0	....	....	....	....	....
2001-02	HC Havirov Jr.	CzRep-Jr.	40	24	25	49	90	....	....	....	....	....
	Sumperk	CzRep-2	1	0	1	1	0	....	....	....	....	....
	HC Femax Havirov	CzRep	7	0	0	0	0	....	....	....	....	....
2002-03	Regina Pats	WHL	64	16	23	39	30	5	2	1	3	2
2003-04	HC Havirov Jr.	CzRep-Jr.	15	6	6	12	47	....	....	....	....	....
	HC Havirov	CzRep-2	26	5	4	9	22	....	....	....	....	....
2004-05	Prostejov	CzRep-3	3	0	0	0	4	....	....	....	....	....
	HC Minor Prerov	CzRep-3	3	1	1	2	2	....	....	....	....	....
	HC Havirov	CzRep-2	27	5	3	8	8	....	....	....	....	....

DWYER, Jeff (DWIGH-uhr, JEHF) ATL.

Defense. Shoots left. 6'1", 205 lbs. Born, Greenwich, CT, November 22, 1980.
(Atlanta's 8th choice, 178th overall, in 2000 Entry Draft).

			Regular Season					Playoffs				
Season	Club	League	GP	G	A	Pts	PIM	GP	G	A	Pts	PIM
1996-97	Choate-Rosemary	High-CT	28	5	11	16	....	....	....	....	....	....
1997-98	Choate-Rosemary	High-CT	28	9	14	23	....	....	....	....	....	....
1998-99	Choate-Rosemary	High-CT	27	8	22	30	....	....	....	....	....	....
99-2000	Choate-Rosemary	High-CT	25	11	30	41	25	....	....	....	....	....
2000-01	Yale	ECAC	31	3	18	21	16	....	....	....	....	....
2001-02	Yale	ECAC	31	6	9	15	16	....	....	....	....	....
2002-03	Yale	ECAC	32	1	17	18	26	....	....	....	....	....
2003-04	Yale	ECAC	30	4	11	15	38	....	....	....	....	....
	Chicago Wolves	AHL	11	0	0	0	4	....	....	....	....	....
2004-05	Chicago Wolves	AHL	9	0	2	2	6	....	....	....	....	....
	Gwinnett	ECHL	2	0	0	0	5	....	....	....	....	....

• Missed majority of 2004-05 season recovering from groin injury suffered in game vs. Milwaukee (AHL), November 5, 2004.

DYMENT, Chris (DIGH-mehnt, KRIHS)

Defense. Shoots right. 6'3", 207 lbs. Born, Reading, MA, October 24, 1979.
(Montreal's 3rd choice, 97th overall, in 1999 Entry Draft).

			Regular Season					Playoffs				
Season	Club	League	GP	G	A	Pts	PIM	GP	G	A	Pts	PIM
1997-98	Reading	High-MA	22	22	22	44	15	....	....	....	....	....
1998-99	Boston University	H-East	25	1	5	6	16	....	....	....	....	....
99-2000	Boston University	H-East	42	11	20	31	42	....	....	....	....	....
2000-01	Boston University	H-East	37	1	10	11	38	....	....	....	....	....
2001-02	Boston University	H-East	38	7	18	25	24	....	....	....	....	....
2002-03	Houston Aeros	AHL	40	2	3	5	64	17	0	1	1	8
2003-04	Houston Aeros	AHL	13	1	0	1	12	....	....	....	....	....
	Springfield Falcons	AHL	23	0	1	1	16	....	....	....	....	....
2004-05	Providence Bruins	AHL	48	3	4	7	112	5	0	0	0	0

Hockey East First All-Star Team (2000) • NCAA East Second All-American Team (2000) • Hockey East Second All-Star Team (2002)

Traded to **Minnesota** by **Montreal** for Minnesota's 5th round choice (later traded to Calgary – Calgary selected Jiri Cetkovsky) in 2002 Entry Draft, May 25, 2002. Traded to **Phoenix** by **Minnesota** for Michael Schutte, December 9, 2003. Signed as a free agent by **Boston**, September 8, 2004.

EAGER, Ben (EE-guhr, BEHN) PHI.

Left wing. Shoots left. 6'3", 215 lbs. Born, Ottawa, Ont., January 22, 1984.
(Phoenix's 2nd choice, 23rd overall, in 2002 Entry Draft).

			Regular Season					Playoffs				
Season	Club	League	GP	G	A	Pts	PIM	GP	G	A	Pts	PIM
99-2000	Ott. Jr. Senators	CJHL	50	8	11	19	119	....	....	....	....	....
2000-01	Oshawa Generals	OHL	61	4	6	10	120	....	....	....	....	....
2001-02	Oshawa Generals	OHL	63	14	23	37	255	5	0	1	1	13
2002-03	Oshawa Generals	OHL	58	16	24	40	216	8	0	4	4	8
2003-04	Oshawa Generals	OHL	61	25	27	52	204	7	2	3	5	31
	Philadelphia	AHL	5	0	0	0	0	3	0	1	1	8
2004-05	Philadelphia	AHL	66	7	10	17	232	16	1	1	2	71

Traded to **Philadelphia** by **Phoenix** with Sean Burke and Branko Radivojevic for Mike Comrie, February 9, 2004.

EARL, Robbie (UHRL, RAW-bee) TOR.

Left wing. Shoots left. 5'10", 184 lbs. Born, Chicago, IL, June 6, 1985.
(Toronto's 4th choice, 187th overall, in 2004 Entry Draft).

			Regular Season					Playoffs				
Season	Club	League	GP	G	A	Pts	PIM	GP	G	A	Pts	PIM
2000-01	L.A. Jr. Kings	Cal-Am	29	48	22	70	....	....	....	....	....	....
2001-02	USA U-17	USDP	58	22	16	38	39	....	....	....	....	....
2002-03	USA U-18	USDP	53	20	13	33	76	....	....	....	....	....
2003-04	U. of Wisconsin	WCHA	42	14	13	27	46	....	....	....	....	....
2004-05	U. of Wisconsin	WCHA	41	20	24	44	62	....	....	....	....	....

WCHA All-Rookie Team (2004) • WCHA Second All-Star Team (2005)

EAVES, Ben (EEVZ, BEHN) PIT.

Center. Shoots right. 5'8", 180 lbs. Born, Minneapolis, MN, March 27, 1982.
(Pittsburgh's 6th choice, 131st overall, in 2001 Entry Draft).

			Regular Season					Playoffs				
Season	Club	League	GP	G	A	Pts	PIM	GP	G	A	Pts	PIM
1998-99	Minnesota Selects	USAHA	71	68	88	156	12	....	....	....	....	....
99-2000	Shat.-St. Mary's	High-MN	57	47	71	118	16	....	....	....	....	....
2000-01	Boston College	H-East	40	13	26	39	12	....	....	....	....	....
2001-02	Boston College	H-East	23	13	26	39	12	....	....	....	....	....
2002-03	Boston College	H-East	36	18	*39	*57	18	....	....	....	....	....
2003-04	Boston College	H-East	26	9	25	34	4	....	....	....	....	....
2004-05	Wilkes-Barre	AHL	43	4	6	10	12	7	0	0	0	0
	Wheeling Nailers	ECHL	2	1	0	1	0	....	....	....	....	....

Hockey East Second All-Star Team (2002) • Hockey East First All-Star Team (2003) • Hockey East Player of the Year (2003) (co-winner - Michael Ayers) • NCAA East First All-American Team (2003)

EAVES, Patrick (EEVZ, PAT-rihk) OTT.

Right wing. Shoots right. 6', 185 lbs. Born, Calgary, Alta., May 1, 1984.
(Ottawa's 1st choice, 29th overall, in 2003 Entry Draft).

			Regular Season					Playoffs				
Season	Club	League	GP	G	A	Pts	PIM	GP	G	A	Pts	PIM
99-2000	Shat.-St. Mary's	High-MN	50	23	24	47	....	....	....	....	....	....
2000-01	USA U-17	USDP	47	19	19	38	78	....	....	....	....	....
	United States	Nat-Tm	12	8	8	16	18	....	....	....	....	....
2001-02	USA U-18	USDP	49	25	28	53	142	....	....	....	....	....
	United States	Nat-Tm	11	6	12	18	47	....	....	....	....	....
2002-03	Boston College	H-East	14	10	8	18	61	....	....	....	....	....
2003-04	Boston College	H-East	34	18	23	41	66	....	....	....	....	....
2004-05	Boston College	H-East	36	19	29	48	36	....	....	....	....	....

Hockey East Second All-Star Team (2004) • NCAA East Second All-American Team (2004) • Hockey East First All-Star Team (2005) • NCAA East First All-American Team (2005)

• Missed majority of 2002-03 season recovering from neck injury suffered in game vs. Maine (H-East), December 7, 2002.

ECKERBLOM, Niklas (EK-kuhr-blawm, NIHK-las) MIN.

Center. Shoots left. 6'1", 196 lbs. Born, Vasterhaninge, Sweden, January 4, 1984.
(Minnesota's 7th choice, 204th overall, in 2002 Entry Draft).

			Regular Season					Playoffs				
Season	Club	League	GP	G	A	Pts	PIM	GP	G	A	Pts	PIM
99-2000	Djurgarden U18	Swe-U18	13	5	3	8	37	....	....	....	....	....
2000-01					DID NOT PLAY							
2001-02	Djurgarden U18	Swe-U18	5	9	2	11	8	....	....	....	....	....
	Djurgarden Jr.	Swe-Jr.	1	0	0	0	0	....	....	....	....	....
2002-03	Djurgarden Jr.	Swe-Jr.	6	0	2	2	4	....	....	....	....	....
	Djurgarden	Sweden	10	0	1	1	0	5	0	0	0	0
	Trangsunds IF	Sweden-3	19	0	3	3	12	....	....	....	....	....
2003-04	Djurgarden Jr.	Swe-Jr.	19	14	7	21	66	....	....	....	....	....
	Djurgarden	Sweden	38	0	0	0	8	3	0	0	0	0
	Hammarby	Sweden-2	1	0	0	0	0	....	....	....	....	....
2004-05	Almtuna	Sweden-2	45	9	4	13	82	3	0	0	0	2

ECKFORD, Tyler (EHK-fuhrd, TIGH-luhr) N.J.

Defense. Shoots left. 6'1", 205 lbs. Born, Vancouver, B.C., September 8, 1985.
(New Jersey's 5th choice, 217th overall, in 2004 Entry Draft).

			Regular Season					Playoffs				
Season	Club	League	GP	G	A	Pts	PIM	GP	G	A	Pts	PIM
2003-04	South Surrey	BCHL	58	7	30	37	101	13	2	8	10	34
2004-05	South Surrey	BCHL	60	22	43	65	93	25	4	15	19	46

EDLER, Alexander (EHD-luhr, al-EHX-AN-duhr) VAN.

Defense. Shoots left. 6'3", 194 lbs. Born, Stockholm, Sweden, April 21, 1986.
(Vancouver's 2nd choice, 91st overall, in 2004 Entry Draft).

			Regular Season					Playoffs				
Season	Club	League	GP	G	A	Pts	PIM	GP	G	A	Pts	PIM
2001-02	Jamtland	Exhib.	8	0	1	1	2	....	....	....	....	....
2002-03	Jamtland	Exhib.	8	2	1	3	0	....	....	....	....	....
2003-04	Jamtland Jr.	Swe-Jr.	6	0	3	3	6	....	....	....	....	....
	Jamtland	Sweden-3	24	3	6	9	20	....	....	....	....	....
2004-05	MODO Jr.	Swe-Jr.	33	8	15	23	40	5	1	0	1	6

EGENER, Mike (EHG-eh-nuhr, MIGHK) T.B.

Defense. Shoots left. 6'4", 213 lbs. Born, Lahr, West Germany, September 26, 1984.
(Tampa Bay's 1st choice, 34th overall, in 2003 Entry Draft).

			Regular Season					Playoffs				
Season	Club	League	GP	G	A	Pts	PIM	GP	G	A	Pts	PIM
99-2000	Calgary Bruins	CMHA	27	4	9	13	88	....	....	....	....	....
2000-01	Calgary Hitmen	WHL	52	1	0	1	91	6	0	0	0	5
2001-02	Calgary Hitmen	WHL	68	2	7	9	175	6	0	0	0	23
2002-03	Calgary Hitmen	WHL	40	2	8	10	210	3	1	0	1	8
2003-04	Calgary Hitmen	WHL	64	1	16	17	228	7	1	1	2	47
2004-05	Springfield Falcons	AHL	45	3	2	5	183	....	....	....	....	....

ELLIOTT, Brandon (EHL-lee-awt, BRAN-duhn) T.B.

Defense. Shoots left. 6'4", 225 lbs. Born, Orangeville, Ont., March 8, 1984.
(Tampa Bay's 4th choice, 158th overall, in 2004 Entry Draft).

			Regular Season					Playoffs				
Season	Club	League	GP	G	A	Pts	PIM	GP	G	A	Pts	PIM
2001-02	Orangeville	OHA-B		STATISTICS NOT AVAILABLE								
	Mississauga	OHL	7	0	0	0	14	....	....	....	....	....
2002-03	Collingwood Blues	OPJHL		STATISTICS NOT AVAILABLE								
2003-04	Collingwood Blues	OPJHL	25	6	15	21	138	....	....	....	....	....
	Mississauga	OHL	30	0	4	4	89	13	0	0	0	32
2004-05	Mississauga	OHL	22	1	4	5	74	....	....	....	....	....
	Springfield Falcons	AHL	2	0	0	0	7	....	....	....	....	....
	Victoria	ECHL	13	0	2	2	41	....	....	....	....	....

ELLIS, Matt (EH-lihs, MAT) DET.

Left wing. Shoots left. 6'1", 190 lbs. Born, Welland, Ont., August 31, 1981.

			Regular Season					Playoffs				
Season	Club	League	GP	G	A	Pts	PIM	GP	G	A	Pts	PIM
1998-99	St. Michael's	OHL	47	10	8	18	6	....	....	....	....	....
99-2000	St. Michael's	OHL	59	15	20	35	20	....	....	....	....	....
2000-01	St. Michael's	OHL	68	21	24	45	19	18	4	8	12	6
2001-02	St. Michael's	OHL	66	38	51	89	20	15	8	6	14	6
2002-03	Toledo Storm	ECHL	71	27	32	59	34	7	3	5	8	0
2003-04	Grand Rapids	AHL	64	5	10	15	23	4	0	0	0	2
2004-05	Grand Rapids	AHL	79	18	23	41	59	....	....	....	....	....

Signed as a free agent by **Detroit**, May 10, 2002.

ELOMO, Teemu (eh-LOH-moh, TEE-moo) DAL.

Left wing. Shoots left. 5'11", 176 lbs. Born, Turku, Finland, January 13, 1979.
(Dallas' 5th choice, 132nd overall, in 1997 Entry Draft).

			Regular Season					Playoffs				
Season	Club	League	GP	G	A	Pts	PIM	GP	G	A	Pts	PIM
1994-95	TPS Turku U18	Fin-U18	8	5	2	7	12	2	1	0	1	0
1995-96	TPS Turku U18	Fin-U18	17	9	8	17	28	....	....	....	....	....
	TPS Turku Jr.	Finland-Jr.	2	0	0	0	0	....	....	....	....	....
	Kiekko-67 Turku	Finland-2	11	1	0	1	14	6	2	0	2	8
1996-97	TPS Turku Jr.	Finland-Jr.	9	6	2	8	16	....	....	....	....	....
	Kiekko-67 Turku	Finland-2	15	4	3	7	24	....	....	....	....	....
	TPS Turku	Finland	6	0	1	1	0	3	0	0	0	2
1997-98	TPS Turku	Finland	26	3	3	6	14	3	1	0	1	2
	TPS Turku	EuroHL	3	0	0	0	2	....	....	....	....	....
1998-99	TPS Turku	Finland	34	4	8	12	16	5	0	0	0	2
99-2000	TPS Turku	Finland	52	9	7	16	28	11	3	2	5	0
2000-01	TPS Turku	Finland	56	2	10	12	44	10	1	3	4	0
2001-02	Blues Espoo	Finland	49	12	14	26	66	3	0	0	0	14
2002-03	Blues Espoo	Finland	54	13	29	42	60	7	1	1	2	4
2003-04	Blues Espoo	Finland	55	11	12	23	34	9	5	1	6	14
2004-05	Blues Espoo	Finland	55	8	19	27	48	....	....	....	....	....

EMMERSON, Riley (EHM-uhr-sohn, RIGH-lee) MIN.

Right wing. Shoots left. 6'6", 250 lbs. Born, Burnaby, B.C., February 7, 1986.
(Minnesota's 7th choice, 199th overall, in 2005 Entry Draft).

			Regular Season					Playoffs				
Season	Club	League	GP	G	A	Pts	PIM	GP	G	A	Pts	PIM
2003-04	Chilliwack Chiefs	BCHL	52	0	6	6	137	6	0	0	0	0
2004-05	Tri-City Americans	WHL	35	0	0	0	61	....	....	....	....	....

ENEQVIST, Johan (EHN-uh-kvist, YOH-han) MTL.

Left wing. Shoots left. 6', 183 lbs. Born, Nacka, Sweden, January 21, 1982.
(Montreal's 5th choice, 109th overall, in 2000 Entry Draft).

			Regular Season					Playoffs				
Season	Club	League	GP	G	A	Pts	PIM	GP	G	A	Pts	PIM
99-2000	Leksands IF U18	Swe-U18	5	1	1	2	28	....	....	....	....	....
	Leksands IF Jr.	Swe-Jr.	36	10	13	23	36	2	0	0	0	0
2000-01	Leksands IF Jr.	Swe-Jr.	21	19	15	34	2	2	1	1	2	4
	Leksands IF	Sweden	2	0	0	0	0	....	....	....	....	....
2001-02	Leksands IF Jr.	Swe-Jr.	7	3	6	9	18	....	....	....	....	....
	Leksands IF	Sweden-2	45	3	7	10	24	....	....	....	....	....
2002-03	Leksands IF	Sweden	42	2	6	8	77	5	0	0	0	6
2003-04	Hammarby	Sweden-2	53	11	20	31	38	....	....	....	....	....
2004-05	Hammarby Jr.	Swe-Jr.	2	0	1	1	24	....	....	....	....	....
	Hammarby	Sweden-2	41	8	18	26	28	....	....	....	....	....

ENGASSER, William (EHN-gahs-uhr, WIHL-yuhm) PHX.

Left wing. Shoots left. 6'2", 228 lbs. Born, Edina, MN, September 25, 1985.
(Phoenix's 9th choice, 261st overall, in 2004 Entry Draft).

			Regular Season					Playoffs				
Season	Club	League	GP	G	A	Pts	PIM	GP	G	A	Pts	PIM
2000-01	Blake Bears	High-MN	5	1	2	3	....	....	....	....	....	....
2001-02	Blake Bears	High-MN	26	7	24	31	....	....	....	....	....	....
2002-03	Blake Bears	High-MN	28	17	26	43	52	....	....	....	....	....
2003-04	Blake Bears	High-MN	28	22	30	52	20	....	....	....	....	....
	Team Southwest	UMEHL	24	9	5	14	....	....	....	....	....	....
2004-05	Yale	ECAC	21	2	0	2	10	....	....	....	....	....

ENSTROM, Tobias (EHN-stuhm, toh-BEE-uhs) ATL.

Defense. Shoots left. 5'9", 175 lbs. Born, Nordingra, Sweden, November 5, 1984.
(Atlanta's 8th choice, 239th overall, in 2003 Entry Draft).

			Regular Season					Playoffs				
Season	Club	League	GP	G	A	Pts	PIM	GP	G	A	Pts	PIM
99-2000	MoDo U18	Swe-U18	3	0	0	0	0	....	....	....	....	....
2000-01	MoDo U18	Swe-U18	16	7	6	13	18	....	....	....	....	....
	Malmo Jr.	Swe-Jr.	1	0	0	0	0	....	....	....	....	....
2001-02	Malmo Jr.	Swe-Jr.	21	1	7	8	10	2	1	1	2	2
2002-03	Malmo Jr.	Swe-Jr.	7	4	6	10	31	....	....	....	....	....
	MODO	Sweden	42	1	5	6	16	6	0	1	1	4
2003-04	MODO	Sweden	33	1	4	5	6	6	1	1	2	2
2004-05	MODO	Sweden	49	4	10	14	24	2	0	0	0	0

ERICKSON, Mike (AIR-ihk-suhn, MIGHK) MIN.

Right wing. Shoots right. 6'2", 201 lbs. Born, Eden Prairie, MN, April 12, 1983.
(Minnesota's 3rd choice, 72nd overall, in 2002 Entry Draft).

			Regular Season					Playoffs				
Season	Club	League	GP	G	A	Pts	PIM	GP	G	A	Pts	PIM
1998-99	Eden Prairie Eagles	High-MN	23	24	18	42	....	....	....	....	....	....
99-2000	Eden Prairie Eagles	High-MN	25	38	25	63	....	....	....	....	....	....
2000-01	Eden Prairie Eagles	High-MN	22	24	26	50	....	....	....	....	....	....
	Des Moines	USHL	4	0	0	0	0	3	0	0	0	0
2001-02	U. of Minnesota	WCHA	9	1	2	3	2	....	....	....	....	....
2002-03	U. of Minnesota	WCHA	16	0	2	2	4	....	....	....	....	....
	Des Moines	USHL	28	12	18	30	10	4	1	3	4	0
2003-04	Des Moines	USHL	58	*37	24	61	23	3	1	2	3	0
2004-05	Western Mich.	CCHA	34	13	11	24	18	....	....	....	....	....

• Missed majority of 2001-02 season recovering from foot injury suffered in game vs. U. of Minnesota-Duluth (WCHA), November 17, 2001. • Granted leave of absence by U. of Minnesota (WCHA), January 14, 2003. • Signed as a free agent by **Des Moines** (USHL), January 14, 2003.

ERIKSSON, Loui (AIR-ihk-suhn, LOO-ee) **DAL.**

Left wing. Shoots left. 6'1", 183 lbs. Born, Goteborg, Sweden, July 17, 1985.
(Dallas' 1st choice, 33rd overall, in 2003 Entry Draft).

			Regular Season					Playoffs				
Season	**Club**	**League**	**GP**	**G**	**A**	**Pts**	**PIM**	**GP**	**G**	**A**	**Pts**	**PIM**
2000-01	V.Frolunda U18	Swe-U18	9	5	3	8	4	....	....	....	....	....
	V.Frolunda Jr.	Swe-Jr.	1	0	0	0	0	....	....	....	....	....
2001-02	V.Frolunda U18	Swe-U18	1	1	0	1	0	....	....	....	....	....
	V.Frolunda Jr.	Swe-Jr.	35	7	15	22	2	8	2	3	5	2
2002-03	V.Frolunda Jr.	Swe-Jr.	30	16	15	31	10	8	4	6	10	4
2003-04	V.Frolunda	Sweden	46	8	5	13	4	10	1	5	6	0
2004-05	Frolunda	Sweden	39	5	9	14	4	12	0	0	0	0

ERIKSSON, Tim (AIR-ihk-suhn, TIHM) **L.A.**

Center. Shoots left. 5'9", 161 lbs. Born, Sodertalje, Sweden, February 5, 1982.
(Los Angeles' 7th choice, 206th overall, in 2000 Entry Draft).

			Regular Season					Playoffs				
Season	**Club**	**League**	**GP**	**G**	**A**	**Pts**	**PIM**	**GP**	**G**	**A**	**Pts**	**PIM**
1997-98	Sodertalje SK Jr.	Swe-Jr.	11	7	12	19	10	....	....	....	....	....
1998-99	V.Frolunda Jr.	Swe-Jr.	29	7	8	15	6	....	....	....	....	....
99-2000	V.Frolunda Jr.	Swe-Jr.	36	16	25	41	82	....	....	....	....	....
2000-01	Hammarby Jr.	Swe-Jr.	1	2	1	3	0	....	....	....	....	....
	Hammarby	Sweden-2	38	10	21	31	18	14	1	5	6	2
2001-02	Hammarby	Sweden-2	44	10	30	40	34	2	0	1	1	0
2002-03	Linkopings HC	Sweden	49	2	8	10	8	....	....	....	....	....
	Linkopings HC	Sweden-Q	10	1	4	5	16	....	....	....	....	....
2003-04	Linkopings HC	Sweden	50	10	16	26	39	5	0	0	0	4
2004-05	Linkopings HC	Sweden	47	3	8	11	14	6	0	0	0	0

ESTRADA, Kevin (eh-STRA-duh, KEH-vihn) **CAR.**

Right wing. Shoots left. 5'11", 185 lbs. Born, Surrey, B.C., May 28, 1982.
(Carolina's 3rd choice, 91st overall, in 2001 Entry Draft).

			Regular Season					Playoffs				
Season	**Club**	**League**	**GP**	**G**	**A**	**Pts**	**PIM**	**GP**	**G**	**A**	**Pts**	**PIM**
1997-98	Chilliwack Chiefs	BCHL	35	1	5	6	17	....	....	....	....	....
1998-99	Chilliwack Chiefs	BCHL	58	13	29	42	58	....	....	....	....	....
99-2000	Chilliwack Chiefs	BCHL	45	9	20	29	29	30	6	27	33	14
2000-01	Chilliwack Chiefs	BCHL	59	34	*84	*118	65	....	....	....	....	....
2001-02	Michigan State	CCHA	40	4	7	11	24	....	....	....	....	....
2002-03	Michigan State	CCHA	35	7	4	11	16	....	....	....	....	....
2003-04	Michigan State	CCHA	34	6	10	16	43	....	....	....	....	....
2004-05	Michigan State	CCHA	26	3	1	4	16	....	....	....	....	....

EVANS, Blake (EH-vans, BLAYK) **ST.L.**

Center. Shoots left. 6'1", 210 lbs. Born, Smiley, Sask., July 2, 1980.
(Washington's 10th choice, 251st overall, in 1998 Entry Draft).

			Regular Season					Playoffs				
Season	**Club**	**League**	**GP**	**G**	**A**	**Pts**	**PIM**	**GP**	**G**	**A**	**Pts**	**PIM**
1995-96	Sask. Contacts	SMHL	41	15	23	38	84	....	....	....	....	....
1996-97	Spokane Chiefs	WHL	53	4	7	11	19	7	0	0	0	0
1997-98	Spokane Chiefs	WHL	16	6	5	11	29	....	....	....	....	....
	Tri-City Americans	WHL	57	13	29	42	102	....	....	....	....	....
1998-99	Tri-City Americans	WHL	72	18	29	47	131	12	0	4	4	16
99-2000	Tri-City Americans	WHL	72	27	43	70	110	4	1	0	1	6
2000-01	Tri-City Americans	WHL	40	28	31	59	70	....	....	....	....	....
	Regina Pats	WHL	27	24	19	43	50	6	6	2	8	8
2001-02	Peoria Rivermen	ECHL	43	17	20	37	26	....	....	....	....	....
	Worcester IceCats	AHL	28	4	5	9	18	3	0	0	0	2
2002-03	Worcester IceCats	AHL	78	13	21	34	79	3	0	0	0	0
2003-04	Worcester IceCats	AHL	80	21	23	44	91	10	2	3	5	10
2004-05	Worcester IceCats	AHL	67	14	24	38	60	....	....	....	....	....

WHL East Second All-Star Team (2001)

Signed as a free agent by **St. Louis**, April 11, 2001.

EVSEEV, Vladislav (yehv-SAY-ehv, VLA-dih-slav) **BOS.**

Left wing. Shoots left. 6'2", 200 lbs. Born, Moscow, USSR, September 10, 1984.
(Boston's 2nd choice, 56th overall, in 2002 Entry Draft).

			Regular Season					Playoffs				
Season	**Club**	**League**	**GP**	**G**	**A**	**Pts**	**PIM**	**GP**	**G**	**A**	**Pts**	**PIM**
99-2000	Dyn'o Moscow 2	Russia-3	5	2	3	5	6	....	....	....	....	....
2000-01	Dyn'o Moscow 2	Russia-3	6	5	2	7	2	....	....	....	....	....
2001-02	CSKA Moscow 2	Russia-3	8	2	1	3	2	....	....	....	....	....
	HK CSKA Moscow	Russia-2	15	2	5	7	10	....	....	....	....	....
2002-03	Dynamo Moscow	Russia	22	1	1	2	2	1	0	0	0	0
2003-04	Vityaz Podolsk	Russia-2	8	1	2	3	2	7	0	0	0	2
2004-05	Dynamo Moscow	Russia	12	1	1	2	2	....	....	....	....	....
	Ufa	Russia	5	0	0	0	2	....	....	....	....	....

EZHOV, Denis (YEHZH-awf, DEH-nihs) **BUF.**

Defense. Shoots left. 5'11", 200 lbs. Born, Togliatti, USSR, February 28, 1985.
(Buffalo's 5th choice, 114th overall, in 2003 Entry Draft).

			Regular Season					Playoffs				
Season	**Club**	**League**	**GP**	**G**	**A**	**Pts**	**PIM**	**GP**	**G**	**A**	**Pts**	**PIM**
99-2000	Lada Togliatti 2	Russia-3	4	0	0	0	4	....	....	....	....	....
2000-01	Lada Togliatti 2	Russia-3	STATISTICS NOT AVAILABLE									
2001-02	Lada Togliatti 2	Russia-3	4	2	4	6	6	....	....	....	....	....
	Lada Togliatti	Russia	15	0	0	0	6	....	....	....	....	....
2002-03	Lada Togliatti 2	Russia-3	15	2	7	9	4	....	....	....	....	....
	CSK VVS Samara	Russia-2	9	0	1	1	8	....	....	....	....	....
2003-04	Novokuznetsk	Russia	19	0	1	1	2	3	0	0	0	0
	CSKA Moscow 2	Russia-3	4	1	2	3	2	....	....	....	....	....
2004-05	Novokuznetsk	Russia	28	0	0	0	16	4	0	0	0	2

FABRY, Branislav (FA-bree, BRAN-ih-slav) **BUF.**

Left wing. Shoots left. 6', 185 lbs. Born, Bratislava, Czech., January 15, 1985.
(Buffalo's 2nd choice, 65th overall, in 2003 Entry Draft).

			Regular Season					Playoffs				
Season	**Club**	**League**	**GP**	**G**	**A**	**Pts**	**PIM**	**GP**	**G**	**A**	**Pts**	**PIM**
2000-01	Bratislava Jr.	Slovak-Jr.	47	22	25	47	....	....	....	....	....	....
2001-02	Bratislava Jr.	Slovak-Jr.	48	29	37	66	....	....	....	....	....	....
2002-03	Bratislava Jr.	Slovak-Jr.	32	12	15	27	84	....	....	....	....	....
	Bratislava	Slovakia	8	0	0	0	0	....	....	....	....	....
2003-04	Bratislava Jr.	Slovak-Jr.	4	5	2	7	14	....	....	....	....	....
	Bratislava	Slovakia	44	1	6	7	2	5	0	0	0	0
2004-05	MsHK SKP Zilina	Slovakia	12	0	1	1	2	....	....	....	....	....
	Bratislava	Slovakia	10	0	0	0	0	....	....	....	....	....
	HK Trnava	Slovak-2	11	3	4	7	2	....	....	....	....	....
	Bratislava Jr.	Slovak-Jr.	21	9	12	21	44	3	1	0	1	0

FALARDEAU, Lee (FAL-ahr-doh, LEE) **NYR**

Center. Shoots left. 6'4", 215 lbs. Born, Midland, MI, July 22, 1983.
(NY Rangers' 1st choice, 33rd overall, in 2002 Entry Draft).

			Regular Season					Playoffs				
Season	**Club**	**League**	**GP**	**G**	**A**	**Pts**	**PIM**	**GP**	**G**	**A**	**Pts**	**PIM**
99-2000	USA U-17	USDP	61	9	14	23	....	....	....	....	....	....
2000-01	USA U-18	USDP	61	10	21	31	26	....	....	....	....	....
2001-02	Michigan State	CCHA	34	4	10	14	24	....	....	....	....	....
2002-03	Michigan State	CCHA	39	9	6	15	39	....	....	....	....	....
2003-04	Michigan State	CCHA	35	5	5	10	28	....	....	....	....	....
2004-05	Charlotte	ECHL	55	18	17	35	52	14	7	1	8	14
	Hartford Wolf Pack	AHL	3	0	0	0	0	....	....	....	....	....

FAST, T.J. (FAST, TEE-JAY) **L.A.**

Defense. Shoots left. 6'1", 190 lbs. Born, Calgary, Alta., September 2, 1987.
(Los Angeles' 3rd choice, 60th overall, in 2005 Entry Draft).

			Regular Season					Playoffs				
Season	**Club**	**League**	**GP**	**G**	**A**	**Pts**	**PIM**	**GP**	**G**	**A**	**Pts**	**PIM**
2003-04	Cgy. North Stars	AMHL	31	7	7	14	42	....	....	....	....	....
2004-05	Camrose Kodiaks	AJHL	58	8	28	36	40	....	....	....	....	....

AJHL All-Rookie Team (2005)

Signed Letter of Intent to attend **Denver** (ECAC) in fall of 2005.

FATA, Drew (FA-tuh, DROO) **PIT.**

Defense. Shoots left. 6'1", 220 lbs. Born, Sault Ste. Marie, Ont., July 28, 1983.
(Pittsburgh's 3rd choice, 86th overall, in 2001 Entry Draft).

			Regular Season					Playoffs				
Season	**Club**	**League**	**GP**	**G**	**A**	**Pts**	**PIM**	**GP**	**G**	**A**	**Pts**	**PIM**
1998-99	S.S. Marie AA	NOHA	46	4	16	20	55	....	....	....	....	....
99-2000	St. Mike's B's	OPJHL	49	9	18	27	144	....	....	....	....	....
2000-01	St. Michael's	OHL	58	5	15	20	134	18	1	3	4	26
2001-02	St. Michael's	OHL	67	7	21	28	175	15	1	9	10	38
2002-03	St. Michael's	OHL	35	6	13	19	66	....	....	....	....	....
	Kingston	OHL	34	2	17	19	64	....	....	....	....	....
2003-04	Wilkes-Barre	AHL	23	1	2	3	26	....	....	....	....	....
	Wheeling Nailers	ECHL	28	6	10	16	61	4	0	0	0	8
2004-05	Wilkes-Barre	AHL	32	1	1	2	88	5	0	1	1	37
	Wheeling Nailers	ECHL	22	0	1	1	55	....	....	....	....	....

FAYNE, Mark (FAYN, MAHRK) **N.J.**

Defense. Shoots right. 6'3", 195 lbs. Born, Nashua, NH, May 15, 1987.
(New Jersey's 5th choice, 155th overall, in 2005 Entry Draft).

			Regular Season					Playoffs				
Season	**Club**	**League**	**GP**	**G**	**A**	**Pts**	**PIM**	**GP**	**G**	**A**	**Pts**	**PIM**
2003-04	Nobles	High-MA	20	3	5	8	14	....	....	....	....	....
2004-05	Nobles	High-MA	24	1	17	18	16	....	....	....	....	....

FEHR, Eric (FAIR, AIR-ihk) **WSH.**

Right wing. Shoots right. 6'3", 186 lbs. Born, Winkler, Man., September 7, 1985.
(Washington's 1st choice, 18th overall, in 2003 Entry Draft).

			Regular Season					Playoffs				
Season	**Club**	**League**	**GP**	**G**	**A**	**Pts**	**PIM**	**GP**	**G**	**A**	**Pts**	**PIM**
2000-01	Pembina Valley	MMMHL	36	45	13	58	30	....	....	....	....	....
	Brandon	WHL	4	0	0	0	0	....	....	....	....	....
2001-02	Brandon	WHL	63	11	16	27	29	12	1	1	2	0
2002-03	Brandon	WHL	70	26	29	55	76	17	4	8	12	26
2003-04	Brandon	WHL	71	50	34	84	129	7	5	0	5	16
2004-05	Brandon	WHL	71	*59	52	*111	91	24	16	16	*32	47

WHL East First All-Star Team (2005) • WHL Player of the Year (2005)

FEMENELLA, Art (feh-meh-NEHL-uh, AHRT) **T.B.**

Defense. Shoots right. 6'7", 255 lbs. Born, Annandale, NJ, June 6, 1982.
(Tampa Bay's 7th choice, 188th overall, in 2001 Entry Draft).

			Regular Season					Playoffs				
Season	**Club**	**League**	**GP**	**G**	**A**	**Pts**	**PIM**	**GP**	**G**	**A**	**Pts**	**PIM**
1998-99	USA U-17	USDP	51	0	2	2	135	....	....	....	....	....
99-2000	USA U-18	USDP	54	0	8	8	156	....	....	....	....	....
	Sioux City	USHL	3	0	0	0	7	....	....	....	....	....
2000-01	Sioux City	USHL	52	1	1	2	*252	3	0	0	0	2
2001-02	Sioux City	USHL	56	1	10	11	215	12	0	1	1	32
2002-03	Sioux City	USHL	48	1	6	7	197	....	....	....	....	....
2003-04	U. of Vermont	ECAC	27	1	0	1	67	....	....	....	....	....
2004-05	U. of Vermont	ECAC	21	0	0	0	32	....	....	....	....	....

FENTON, Paul (FEHN-tuhn, PAWL) **S.J.**

Forward. Shoots left. 5'11", 177 lbs. Born, Springfield, MA, August 26, 1985.
(San Jose's 6th choice, 162nd overall, in 2005 Entry Draft).

			Regular Season					Playoffs				
Season	**Club**	**League**	**GP**	**G**	**A**	**Pts**	**PIM**	**GP**	**G**	**A**	**Pts**	**PIM**
2002-03	N.E. Jr. Coyotes	EJHL	35	8	17	25	....	....	....	....	....	....
2003-04	N.E. Jr. Coyotes	EJHL	37	16	17	33	61	....	....	....	....	....
2004-05	Massachusetts	H-East	36	12	12	24	24	....	....	....	....	....

Hockey East All-Rookie Team (2005)

FERLAND, Jonathan (fair-LAWN, JAWN-ah-thun) **MTL.**

Right wing. Shoots right. 6'2", 211 lbs. Born, Quebec City, Que., February 9, 1983.
(Montreal's 5th choice, 212th overall, in 2002 Entry Draft).

			Regular Season					Playoffs				
Season	**Club**	**League**	**GP**	**G**	**A**	**Pts**	**PIM**	**GP**	**G**	**A**	**Pts**	**PIM**
1998-99	Laval-Laurentides	QAAA	42	18	17	35	50	....	....	....	....	....
99-2000	Moncton Wildcats	QMJHL	52	3	6	9	21	11	0	1	1	0
2000-01	Acadie-Bathurst	QMJHL	70	17	11	28	135	13	0	4	4	47
2001-02	Acadie-Bathurst	QMJHL	55	28	46	74	104	10	2	10	12	8
2002-03	Acadie-Bathurst	QMJHL	68	45	44	89	94	11	4	5	9	16
2003-04	Hamilton Bulldogs	AHL	70	5	10	15	43	10	0	0	0	6
2004-05	Hamilton Bulldogs	AHL	62	6	8	14	24	4	0	0	0	4

FERNHOLM, Daniel (FUHRN-hohlm, DAN-yehl) **PIT.**

Defense. Shoots left. 6'4", 218 lbs. Born, Stockholm, Sweden, December 20, 1983.
(Pittsburgh's 4th choice, 101st overall, in 2002 Entry Draft).

			Regular Season					Playoffs				
Season	Club	League	GP	G	A	Pts	PIM	GP	G	A	Pts	PIM
99-2000	Mora IK Jr.	Swe-Jr.	33	3	3	6	8	1	0	0	0	0
2000-01	Mora IK Jr.	Swe-Jr.	3	0	1	1	2	....	....	....	....	....
	Mora IK	Sweden-2	2	0	0	0	0	....	....	....	....	....
2001-02	Djurgarden Jr.	Swe-Jr.	8	6	13	19	12	3	0	0	0	0
2002-03	Huddinge IK	Sweden-2	39	6	10	16	20	2	1	0	1	0
	Huddinge IK Jr.	Swe-Jr.	1	0	0	0	2	....	....	....	....	....
2003-04	Hammarby	Sweden-2	15	1	3	4	6	....	....	....	....	....
	Djurgarden	Sweden	37	4	7	11	28	4	0	0	0	4
2004-05	Djurgarden Jr.	Swe-Jr.	2	0	0	0	4	....	....	....	....	....
	HC Forst Bolzano	Italy	7	0	2	2	2	....	....	....	....	....
	Djurgarden	Sweden	31	3	2	5	22	11	0	0	0	14

FIEDLER, Jonas (FIHD-luhr, YOH-nahsh) **CAR.**

Right wing. Shoots right. 6'2", 177 lbs. Born, Jihlava, Czech., May 29, 1984.
(Carolina's 7th choice, 235th overall, in 2004 Entry Draft).

			Regular Season					Playoffs				
Season	Club	League	GP	G	A	Pts	PIM	GP	G	A	Pts	PIM
99-2000	Jihlava Jr.	CzRep-Jr.	48	11	11	22	48	....	....	....	....	....
2000-01	Jihlava Jr.	CzRep-Jr.	44	29	33	62	167	....	....	....	....	....
2001-02	Plymouth Whalers	OHL	68	8	12	20	27	6	0	1	1	4
2002-03	Plymouth Whalers	OHL	63	7	21	28	59	18	5	9	14	10
2003-04	Plymouth Whalers	OHL	63	18	28	46	83	9	1	6	7	16
2004-05	Plymouth Whalers	OHL	61	19	18	37	71	4	1	0	1	2
	Florida Everblades	ECHL	2	0	0	0	0	....	....	....	....	....

• Re-entered NHL Entry Draft. Originally San Jose's 3rd choice, 86th overall, in 2002 Entry Draft.

FILEWICH, Jonathan (FIGHL-uh-which, JAWN-ah-thun) **PIT.**

Right wing. Shoots right. 6'2", 205 lbs. Born, Kelowna, B.C., October 2, 1984.
(Pittsburgh's 3rd choice, 70th overall, in 2003 Entry Draft).

			Regular Season					Playoffs				
Season	Club	League	GP	G	A	Pts	PIM	GP	G	A	Pts	PIM
1998-99	Sherwood Park	AMBHL	36	29	43	72	90	....	....	....	....	....
99-2000	Sherwood Park	AMHL	33	28	20	48	59	....	....	....	....	....
	Prince George	WHL	3	0	0	0	0	....	....	....	....	....
2000-01	Prince George	WHL	61	9	16	25	32	....	....	....	....	....
2001-02	Prince George	WHL	66	13	19	32	23	7	2	0	2	2
2002-03	Prince George	WHL	51	27	27	54	45	5	1	1	2	2
2003-04	Prince George	WHL	72	30	25	55	52	....	....	....	....	....
2004-05	Lethbridge	WHL	68	42	38	80	26	5	1	1	2	2

FILIPOWICZ, Jayme (fihl-ih-POW-its, JAY-mee)

Defense. Shoots left. 6'2", 215 lbs. Born, Arlington Heights, IL, June 15, 1976.

			Regular Season					Playoffs				
Season	Club	League	GP	G	A	Pts	PIM	GP	G	A	Pts	PIM
1993-94	Rochester	USHL	47	7	16	23	52	....	....	....	....	....
1994-95	Dubuque	USHL	35	4	10	14	....	....	....	....	....	....
1995-96	Dubuque	USHL	45	7	16	23	52	....	....	....	....	....
1996-97	New Hampshire	H-East	35	3	16	19	43	....	....	....	....	....
1997-98	New Hampshire	H-East	38	3	28	31	47	....	....	....	....	....
1998-99	New Hampshire	H-East	41	8	30	38	56	....	....	....	....	....
99-2000	Milwaukee	IHL	76	9	23	32	118	3	0	1	1	0
2000-01	Milwaukee	IHL	68	0	13	13	101	2	0	0	0	2
2001-02	Quebec Citadelles	AHL	63	0	7	7	107	1	0	0	0	2
2002-03	Saint John Flames	AHL	63	2	13	15	106	....	....	....	....	....
	Richmond	ECHL	20	1	8	9	36	....	....	....	....	....
2003-04	Hartford Wolf Pack	AHL	63	2	6	8	116	7	0	1	1	2
2004-05	Providence Bruins	AHL	78	2	7	9	124	16	2	1	3	20

Hockey East First All-Star Team (1999) • NCAA East Second All-American Team (1999) • NCAA Championship All-Tournament Team (1999)

Signed as a free agent by **Nashville**, June 17, 1999. Signed to a PTO (tryout) contract by **Providence** (AHL), September 28, 2004. Signed as a free agent by **Providence** (AHL), October 27, 2004.

FILPPULA, Valtteri (FIHL-poo-luh, VAL-tuhr-ee) **DET.**

Center. Shoots left. 5'11", 172 lbs. Born, Vantaa, Finland, March 20, 1984.
(Detroit's 3rd choice, 95th overall, in 2002 Entry Draft).

			Regular Season					Playoffs				
Season	Club	League	GP	G	A	Pts	PIM	GP	G	A	Pts	PIM
2000-01	Jokerit U18	Fin-U18	31	18	29	47	4	....	....	....	....	....
	Jokerit Helsinki Jr.	Finland-Jr.	1	0	1	1	0	....	....	....	....	....
2001-02	Jokerit U18	Fin-U18	1	0	1	1	0	....	....	....	....	....
	Jokerit Helsinki Jr.	Finland-Jr.	40	8	15	23	14	9	4	9	13	2
2002-03	Jokerit Helsinki Jr.	Finland-Jr.	35	16	37	53	39	11	4	10	14	4
2003-04	Jokerit Helsinki	Finland	49	5	13	18	6	....	....	....	....	....
2004-05	Jokerit Helsinki	Finland	55	10	20	30	20	12	5	6	11	2

FINGER, Jeff (FIHN-guhr, JEHF) **COL.**

Defense. Shoots left. 6'2", 195 lbs. Born, Hancock, MI, December 18, 1979.
(Colorado's 11th choice, 240th overall, in 1999 Entry Draft).

			Regular Season					Playoffs				
Season	Club	League	GP	G	A	Pts	PIM	GP	G	A	Pts	PIM
1997-98	Green Bay	USHL	51	5	9	14	208	4	0	0	0	18
1998-99	Green Bay	USHL	54	11	28	39	199	6	0	3	3	14
99-2000	Green Bay	USHL	55	13	35	48	15	14	3	11	14	40
2000-01	St. Cloud State	WCHA	41	4	5	9	84	....	....	....	....	....
2001-02	St. Cloud State	WCHA	42	6	20	26	105	....	....	....	....	....
2002-03	St. Cloud State	WCHA	24	5	8	13	46	....	....	....	....	....
2003-04	Hershey Bears	AHL	63	2	9	11	88	....	....	....	....	....
	Reading Royals	ECHL	10	2	5	7	24	....	....	....	....	....
2004-05	Hershey Bears	AHL	75	4	12	16	125	....	....	....	....	....

FINLEY, Joe (FIHN-lee, JOH) **WSH.**

Defense. Shoots left. 6'7", 229 lbs. Born, Edina, MN, June 29, 1987.
(Washington's 2nd choice, 27th overall, in 2005 Entry Draft).

			Regular Season					Playoffs				
Season	Club	League	GP	G	A	Pts	PIM	GP	G	A	Pts	PIM
2004-05	Sioux Falls	USHL	55	3	10	13	181	....	....	....	....	....

Signed Letter of Intent to attend **North Dakota** (WCHA) in fall of 2005.

FISTRIC, Mark (FIHST-rihc, MAHRK) **DAL.**

Defense. Shoots left. 6'2", 232 lbs. Born, Edmonton, Alta., June 1, 1986.
(Dallas' 1st choice, 28th overall, in 2004 Entry Draft).

			Regular Season					Playoffs				
Season	Club	League	GP	G	A	Pts	PIM	GP	G	A	Pts	PIM
2000-01	Edmonton MLAC	AMBHL	34	13	13	26	144	....	....	....	....	....
2001-02	Edmonton MLAC	AMHL	30	8	10	18	85	....	....	....	....	....
	Vancouver Giants	WHL	4	0	2	2	0	....	....	....	....	....
2002-03	Vancouver Giants	WHL	63	2	7	9	81	4	0	0	0	8
2003-04	Vancouver Giants	WHL	72	1	11	12	192	11	0	2	2	10
2004-05	Vancouver Giants	WHL	15	1	5	6	32	6	1	1	2	16

FITZGERALD, Zack (fihtz-JAIR-uhld, ZAK) **ST.L.**

Defense. Shoots left. 6'1", 214 lbs. Born, Two Harbors, MN, June 16, 1985.
(St. Louis' 4th choice, 88th overall, in 2003 Entry Draft).

			Regular Season					Playoffs				
Season	Club	League	GP	G	A	Pts	PIM	GP	G	A	Pts	PIM
2000-01	Duluth East	High-MN	26	1	7	8	44	....	....	....	....	....
2001-02	Seattle	WHL	61	3	7	10	214	10	0	2	2	19
2002-03	Seattle	WHL	64	8	14	22	232	15	0	4	4	33
2003-04	Seattle	WHL	58	4	15	19	163	....	....	....	....	....
2004-05	Seattle	WHL	65	7	18	25	*244	9	0	3	3	24

FLACHE, Paul (FLAK, PAWL)

Defense. Shoots right. 6'5", 220 lbs. Born, Toronto, Ont., March 4, 1982.
(Atlanta's 5th choice, 144th overall, in 2002 Entry Draft).

			Regular Season					Playoffs				
Season	Club	League	GP	G	A	Pts	PIM	GP	G	A	Pts	PIM
1998-99	Cobourg Cougars	OPJHL	41	1	6	7	50	....	....	....	....	....
99-2000	Brampton	OHL	54	1	0	1	59	6	0	0	0	8
2000-01	Brampton	OHL	68	8	16	24	100	9	1	1	2	18
2001-02	Brampton	OHL	68	9	35	44	148	....	....	....	....	....
2002-03	Greenville Grrrowl	ECHL	46	1	9	10	64	4	0	4	4	6
2003-04	Chicago Wolves	AHL	9	2	2	4	12	....	....	....	....	....
	Gwinnett	ECHL	62	3	15	18	114	10	2	2	4	4
2004-05	Chicago Wolves	AHL	61	3	12	15	172	....	....	....	....	....
	Gwinnett	ECHL	3	1	2	3	4	....	....	....	....	....

• Re-entered NHL Entry Draft. Originally Edmonton's 5th choice, 152nd overall, in 2000 Entry Draft.

FLATT, Dalyn (FLAT, DA-lihn) **NYR**

Defense. Shoots left. 6'3", 217 lbs. Born, Winnipeg, Man., October 7, 1986.
(NY Rangers' 5th choice, 77th overall, in 2005 Entry Draft).

			Regular Season					Playoffs				
Season	Club	League	GP	G	A	Pts	PIM	GP	G	A	Pts	PIM
2001-02	Interlake Lightning	MMHL	51	2	16	18	148	....	....	....	....	....
	Saskatoon Blades	WHL	2	0	0	0	0	....	....	....	....	....
2002-03	Swan Valley	MJHL	51	1	12	13	286	....	....	....	....	....
2003-04	Saskatoon Blades	WHL	41	0	2	2	91	....	....	....	....	....
2004-05	Saskatoon Blades	WHL	72	1	18	19	237	4	0	0	0	12

FLATTERS, John (FLAT-uhrs, JAWN) **PHI.**

Defense. Shoots left. 6'1", 203 lbs. Born, Calgary, Alta., June 17, 1987.
(Philadelphia's 5th choice, 174th overall, in 2005 Entry Draft).

			Regular Season					Playoffs				
Season	Club	League	GP	G	A	Pts	PIM	GP	G	A	Pts	PIM
2003-04	Notre Dame	SMHL	43	1	11	12	116	....	....	....	....	....
2004-05	Red Deer Rebels	WHL	53	0	2	2	117	7	0	0	0	2

FLEISCHMANN, Tomas (FLIGHSH-muhn, TAW-mash) **WSH.**

Left wing. Shoots left. 6', 165 lbs. Born, Koprivnice, Czech., May 16, 1984.
(Detroit's 2nd choice, 63rd overall, in 2002 Entry Draft).

			Regular Season					Playoffs				
Season	Club	League	GP	G	A	Pts	PIM	GP	G	A	Pts	PIM
99-2000	HC Vitkovice Jr.	CzRep-Jr.	46	9	13	22	6	....	....	....	....	....
2000-01	HC Vitkovice U17	CzR-U17	30	28	34	62	8	....	....	....	....	....
	HC Vitkovice Jr.	CzRep-Jr.	21	4	9	13	8	....	....	....	....	....
2001-02	HC Vitkovice Jr.	CzRep-Jr.	46	26	35	51	16	....	....	....	....	....
	TJ Novy Jicin	CzRep-3	8	3	2	5	8	7	3	4	7	35
2002-03	Moose Jaw	WHL	65	21	50	71	36	12	4	11	15	6
2003-04	Moose Jaw	WHL	60	33	42	75	32	10	3	4	7	10
2004-05	Portland Pirates	AHL	53	7	12	19	14	....	....	....	....	....

WHL East Second All-Star Team (2004)

Traded to **Washington** by **Detroit** with Detroit's 1st round choice (Mike Green) in 2004 Entry Draft and Detroit's 4th round choice in 2006 Entry Draft for Robert Lang, February 27, 2004.

FLOOD, Mark (FLUD, MAHRK) **CBJ**

Defense. Shoots right. 6'1", 189 lbs. Born, Charlottetown, PEI, September 29, 1984.
(Montreal's 8th choice, 188th overall, in 2003 Entry Draft).

			Regular Season					Playoffs				
Season	Club	League	GP	G	A	Pts	PIM	GP	G	A	Pts	PIM
2000-01	Charlotwn AAA	PEIHA	STATISTICS NOT AVAILABLE									
	Charlotwn Abbies	MJrHL	11	0	2	2	2	....	....	....	....	....
2001-02	Peterborough	OHL	57	1	4	5	21	6	0	0	0	2
2002-03	Peterborough	OHL	68	5	24	29	18	7	1	2	3	0
2003-04	Peterborough	OHL	68	15	29	44	30	....	....	....	....	....
2004-05	Peterborough	OHL	60	4	38	42	14	14	2	7	9	0

Signed as a free agent by **Columbus**, August 22, 2005.

FOOTE, Jordan (FUT, JOHN-dan) **NYR**

Left wing. Shoots left. 6'3", 202 lbs. Born, Edmonton, Alta., March 7, 1985.
(NY Rangers' 11th choice, 169th overall, in 2004 Entry Draft).

			Regular Season					Playoffs				
Season	Club	League	GP	G	A	Pts	PIM	GP	G	A	Pts	PIM
2003-04	Nanaimo Clippers	BCHL	58	23	26	49	73	....	....	....	....	....
2004-05	Michigan Tech	WCHA	13	1	1	2	6	....	....	....	....	....

FORD, Matthew (FOHRD, MA-thew) **CHI.**

Right wing. Shoots right. 6'1", 206 lbs. Born, West Hills, CA, October 9, 1984.
(Chicago's 16th choice, 256th overall, in 2004 Entry Draft).

			Regular Season					Playoffs				
Season	Club	League	GP	G	A	Pts	PIM	GP	G	A	Pts	PIM
2003-04	Sioux Falls	USHL	60	*37	31	68	60	....	....	....	....	....
2004-05	U. of Wisconsin	WCHA	21	5	5	10	18	....	....	....	....	....

FORSANDER, Johan (fohr-SAHN-duhr, YOH-hahn) DET.

Left wing. Shoots left. 6'1", 174 lbs. Born, Jonkoping, Sweden, April 28, 1978.
(Detroit's 3rd choice, 108th overall, in 1996 Entry Draft).

			Regular Season					Playoffs				
Season	Club	League	GP	G	A	Pts	PIM	GP	G	A	Pts	PIM
1994-95	HV 71 Jr.	Swe-Jr.	25	2	2	4	6	....	....	....	....	....
1995-96	HV 71 Jr.	Swe-Jr.	27	15	8	23	12	....	....	....	....	....
	HV 71 Jonkoping	Sweden	6	0	0	0	0	3	0	0	0	2
1996-97	HV 71 Jr.	Swe-Jr.	6	7	3	10	6	....	....	....	....	....
	HV 71 Jonkoping	Sweden	44	3	2	5	6	5	0	0	0	0
1997-98	HV 71 Jr.	Swe-Jr.	5	1	1	2	6	....	....	....	....	....
	HV 71 Jonkoping	Sweden	46	3	2	5	12	5	0	0	0	0
1998-99	HV 71 Jonkoping	Sweden	48	5	4	9	6	....	....	....	....	....
99-2000	HV 71 Jonkoping	Sweden	48	9	9	18	6	6	0	0	0	4
2000-01	HV 71 Jonkoping	Sweden	DID NOT PLAY – INJURED									
2001-02	Djurgarden	Sweden	48	5	6	11	16	5	0	0	0	4
2002-03	Djurgarden	Sweden	41	1	2	3	49	10	2	2	4	4
2003-04	AIK Solna	Sweden-2	48	11	21	32	48	5	0	4	4	10
2004-05	Morzine-Avoriaz	France	27	19	26	45	28	4	3	2	5	18

• Missed entire 2000-01 season recovering from foot injury suffered in training camp, September 2, 2000.

FORSTER, Beat (FOHRS-tuhr, BEE-at) PHX.

Defense. Shoots left. 6'1", 224 lbs. Born, Herisau, Switz., February 2, 1983.
(Phoenix's 4th choice, 78th overall, in 2001 Entry Draft).

			Regular Season					Playoffs				
Season	Club	League	GP	G	A	Pts	PIM	GP	G	A	Pts	PIM
99-2000	HC Davos Jr.	Swiss-Jr.	34	4	15	19	40	6	1	0	1	6
2000-01	HC Davos Jr.	Swiss-Jr.	27	6	7	13	44	....	....	....	....	....
	SC Herisau	Swiss-2	3	0	0	0	16	....	....	....	....	....
	HC Davos	Swiss	7	0	0	0	6	3	0	0	0	2
2001-02	HC Davos Jr.	Swiss-Jr.	4	2	2	4	12	....	....	....	....	....
	HC Davos	Swiss	33	1	3	4	51	16	0	1	1	2
2002-03	HC Davos	Swiss	30	1	4	5	24	17	0	1	1	16
2003-04	HC Davos	Swiss	44	3	8	11	34	6	0	0	0	36
2004-05	HC Davos	Swiss	29	3	4	7	28	15	1	0	1	10
	EHC Chur	Swiss-2	....	....	....	....	....	1	0	1	1	2

FOSTER, Adrian (FAW-stuhr, AY-dree-uhn) N.J.

Center. Shoots left. 6', 205 lbs. Born, Lethbridge, Alta., January 15, 1982.
(New Jersey's 1st choice, 28th overall, in 2001 Entry Draft).

			Regular Season					Playoffs				
Season	Club	League	GP	G	A	Pts	PIM	GP	G	A	Pts	PIM
1997-98	Calgary Buffaloes	AMHL	36	26	54	80	50	9	3	14	17	18
1998-99	Calgary Canucks	AJHL	18	15	17	32	18	....	....	....	....	....
99-2000	Saskatoon Blades	WHL	7	1	2	3	6	....	....	....	....	....
2000-01	Saskatoon Blades	WHL	5	0	5	5	4	....	....	....	....	....
2001-02	Saskatoon Blades	WHL	13	9	3	12	18	....	....	....	....	....
	Brandon	WHL	14	5	10	15	23	15	4	11	15	14
2002-03	Albany River Rats	AHL	9	3	0	3	4	....	....	....	....	....
2003-04	Albany River Rats	AHL	44	8	13	21	25	....	....	....	....	....
2004-05	Albany River Rats	AHL	51	6	11	17	27	....	....	....	....	....

• Missed majority of 1998-99 season recovering from ankle injury. • Missed majority of 1999-2000, 2000-01, 2001-02 and 2002-03 seasons recovering from abdominal injury, October, 1999.

FOY, Matt (FOI, MAT) MIN.

Right wing. Shoots right. 6'2", 219 lbs. Born, Oakville, Ont., May 18, 1983.
(Minnesota's 6th choice, 175th overall, in 2002 Entry Draft).

			Regular Season					Playoffs				
Season	Club	League	GP	G	A	Pts	PIM	GP	G	A	Pts	PIM
2000-01	Wexford Raiders	OPJHL	47	43	49	92	30	....	....	....	....	....
2001-02	Merrimack College	H-East	31	7	17	24	48	....	....	....	....	....
2002-03	Ottawa 67's	OHL	68	61	71	132	112	21	11	20	31	47
2003-04	Houston Aeros	AHL	51	11	13	24	74	1	0	0	0	0
2004-05	Houston Aeros	AHL	69	12	13	25	78	5	1	2	3	6

OHL First All-Star Team (2003)

• Officially announced intention to withdraw from **Merrimack** (H-East) for academic reasons, May 30, 2002.

FRANSON, Cody (FRAN-suhn, KOH-dee) NSH.

Defense. Shoots right. 6'4", 205 lbs. Born, Salmon Arm, B.C., August 8, 1987.
(Nashville's 3rd choice, 79th overall, in 2005 Entry Draft).

			Regular Season					Playoffs				
Season	Club	League	GP	G	A	Pts	PIM	GP	G	A	Pts	PIM
2002-03	Sicamous	BCAHA	65	44	82	126	42	....	....	....	....	....
	Vancouver Giants	WHL	3	0	0	0	0	....	....	....	....	....
2003-04	Beaver Valley	KIJHL	48	10	22	32	70	....	....	....	....	....
	Trail Smoke Eaters	BCHL	2	0	1	1	0	....	....	....	....	....
	Vancouver Giants	WHL	2	0	0	0	0	....	....	....	....	....
2004-05	Vancouver Giants	WHL	64	2	11	13	44	4	0	1	1	0

FRANSSON, Johan (FRAN-suhn, YOH-hahn) DAL.

Defense. Shoots left. 6'1", 183 lbs. Born, Kalix, Sweden, February 18, 1985.
(Dallas' 2nd choice, 34th overall, in 2004 Entry Draft).

			Regular Season					Playoffs				
Season	Club	League	GP	G	A	Pts	PIM	GP	G	A	Pts	PIM
2000-01	Kalix HF	Sweden-3	19	0	6	6	8	....	....	....	....	....
2001-02	Lulea HF U18	Swe-U18	5	2	0	2	0	....	....	....	....	....
	Lulea HF Jr.	Swe-Jr.	29	4	4	8	28	5	0	1	1	8
2002-03	Lulea HF Jr.	Swe-Jr.	24	2	4	6	67	....	....	....	....	....
	Lulea HF U18	Swe-U18	2	0	0	0	2	....	....	....	....	....
	Lulea HF	Sweden	3	0	0	0	0	....	....	....	....	....
2003-04	Lulea HF Jr.	Swe-Jr.	5	0	2	2	10	....	....	....	....	....
	Lulea HF	Sweden	44	3	3	6	28	2	0	0	0	4
2004-05	Lulea HF Jr.	Swe-Jr.	1	1	1	2	0	7	1	2	3	4
	Lulea HF	Sweden	43	1	6	7	30	3	0	0	0	0

FRANZEN, Johan (FRAN-zehn, YOH-hahn) DET.

Left wing. Shoots left. 6'2", 207 lbs. Born, Landsbro, Sweden, December 23, 1979.
(Detroit's 1st choice, 97th overall, in 2004 Entry Draft).

			Regular Season					Playoffs				
Season	Club	League	GP	G	A	Pts	PIM	GP	G	A	Pts	PIM
2001-02	Linkopings HC	Sweden	36	2	6	8	64	....	....	....	....	....
2002-03	Linkopings HC	Sweden	37	2	4	6	14	....	....	....	....	....
2003-04	Linkopings HC	Sweden	49	12	18	30	26	5	0	1	1	8
2004-05	Linkopings HC	Sweden	43	7	7	14	45	6	2	0	2	16

FRASER, Colin (FRAY-zuhr, KAW-lihn) CHI.

Center. Shoots left. 6'1", 182 lbs. Born, Sicamous, B.C., January 28, 1985.
(Philadelphia's 3rd choice, 69th overall, in 2003 Entry Draft).

			Regular Season					Playoffs				
Season	Club	League	GP	G	A	Pts	PIM	GP	G	A	Pts	PIM
2000-01	Port Coquitlam	PIJHL	38	16	24	40	90	8	2	2	4	21
2001-02	Red Deer Rebels	WHL	67	11	31	42	126	23	2	1	3	39
2002-03	Red Deer Rebels	WHL	69	15	37	52	192	22	7	6	13	40
2003-04	Red Deer Rebels	WHL	70	24	29	53	174	19	5	9	14	24
2004-05	Red Deer Rebels	WHL	63	24	43	67	148	7	2	5	7	8
	Norfolk Admirals	AHL	3	0	0	0	20	6	1	0	1	2

Canadian Major Junior Humanitarian Player of the Year (2005)

Traded to **Chicago** by **Philadelphia** with Jim Vandermeer and Los Angeles' 2nd round choice (previously acquired, Chicago selected Bryan Bickell) in 2004 Entry Draft for Alex Zhamnov and Washington's 4th round choice (previously acquired, Philadelphia selected R.J. Anderson) in 2004 Entry Draft, February 19, 2004.

FRASER, Mark (FRAY-zuhr, MAHRK) N.J.

Defense. Shoots left. 6'4", 195 lbs. Born, Ottawa, Ont., September 29, 1986.
(New Jersey's 3rd choice, 84th overall, in 2005 Entry Draft).

			Regular Season					Playoffs				
Season	Club	League	GP	G	A	Pts	PIM	GP	G	A	Pts	PIM
2004-05	Gloucester	CJHL	STATISTICS NOT AVAILABLE									
	Kitchener Rangers	OHL	58	0	8	8	96	15	0	3	3	26

FREDHEIM, Kris (FREHD-highm, KRIHS) VAN.

Defense. Shoots right. 6'1", 170 lbs. Born, Campbell River, B.C., February 23, 1987.
(Vancouver's 5th choice, 185th overall, in 2005 Entry Draft).

			Regular Season					Playoffs				
Season	Club	League	GP	G	A	Pts	PIM	GP	G	A	Pts	PIM
2003-04	Notre Dame	SMHL	41	9	21	30	38	....	....	....	....	....
2004-05	Notre Dame	SJHL	50	2	15	17	28	....	....	....	....	....

FREDRIKSSON, David (FREHD-rihk-suhn, DAY-vihd) ST.L.

Wing. Shoots left. 6'2", 214 lbs. Born, Jonkoping, Sweden, October 4, 1985.
(St. Louis' 7th choice, 211th overall, in 2004 Entry Draft).

			Regular Season					Playoffs				
Season	Club	League	GP	G	A	Pts	PIM	GP	G	A	Pts	PIM
2001-02	HV 71 Jr.	Swe-Jr.	14	6	2	8	20	....	....	....	....	....
2002-03	HV 71 Jr.	Swe-Jr.	27	9	10	19	24	8	10	0	10	10
	HV 71 Jonkoping	Sweden	1	0	0	0	0	....	....	....	....	....
2003-04	HV 71 Jr.	Swe-Jr.	18	9	3	12	42	2	1	0	1	2
	HV 71 Jonkoping	Sweden	9	0	0	0	2	6	0	0	0	0
2004-05	HV 71 Jr.	Swe-Jr.	19	8	5	13	48	....	....	....	....	....
	Morrums GoIS IK	Sweden-2	2	1	0	1	2	....	....	....	....	....
	HV 71 Jonkoping	Sweden	18	0	0	0	0	....	....	....	....	....

FRETTER, Colton (FREH-tuhr, KOHL-tuhn) ATL.

Center. Shoots right. 5'10", 190 lbs. Born, Harrow, Ont., March 12, 1982.
(Atlanta's 8th choice, 230th overall, in 2002 Entry Draft).

			Regular Season					Playoffs				
Season	Club	League	GP	G	A	Pts	PIM	GP	G	A	Pts	PIM
99-2000	Chatham Maroons	OHA-B	40	12	22	34	34	....	....	....	....	....
2000-01	Chatham Maroons	OHA-B	54	33	39	72	....	15	7	6	13	....
2001-02	Chatham Maroons	OHA-B	52	51	53	104	62	15	5	3	8	2
2002-03	Michigan State	CCHA	35	7	15	22	36	....	....	....	....	....
2003-04	Michigan State	CCHA	39	6	11	17	22	....	....	....	....	....
2004-05	Michigan State	CCHA	40	20	24	44	28	....	....	....	....	....

FRITSCHE, Tom (FRIHCH, TAWM) COL.

Left wing. Shoots left. 5'11", 183 lbs. Born, Parma, OH, September 30, 1986.
(Colorado's 3rd choice, 47th overall, in 2005 Entry Draft).

			Regular Season					Playoffs				
Season	Club	League	GP	G	A	Pts	PIM	GP	G	A	Pts	PIM
2002-03	USA U-17	USDP	63	21	20	41	59	....	....	....	....	....
2003-04	USA U-18	USDP	57	24	27	51	46	....	....	....	....	....
2004-05	Ohio State	CCHA	42	11	*34	45	38	....	....	....	....	....

CCHA All-Rookie Team (2005) • CCHA Second All-Star Team (2005)

FRITZ, Mitch (JOO-lee-A-noh, JEHF) T.B.

Left wing. Shoots left. 6'8", 258 lbs. Born, Osoyoos, B.C., November 24, 1980.

			Regular Season					Playoffs				
Season	Club	League	GP	G	A	Pts	PIM	GP	G	A	Pts	PIM
1998-99	Kelowna Rockets	WHL	52	9	0	9	156	2	0	0	0	0
99-2000	Kelowna Rockets	WHL	58	4	2	6	204	5	0	0	0	0
2000-01	Lowell	AHL	5	0	0	0	20	....	....	....	....	....
	Tallahassee	ECHL	42	5	3	8	79	....	....	....	....	....
2001-02	Hamilton Bulldogs	AHL	13	0	0	0	37	....	....	....	....	....
	Columbus	ECHL	45	3	7	10	284	....	....	....	....	....
	Saint John Flames	AHL	11	0	0	0	34	....	....	....	....	....
2002-03	Milwaukee	AHL	13	1	2	3	33	....	....	....	....	....
	Columbus	ECHL	33	2	4	6	144	....	....	....	....	....
2003-04	Worcester IceCats	AHL	4	0	0	0	10	4	0	0	0	4
	Columbus	ECHL	64	3	9	12	149	....	....	....	....	....
2004-05	Springfield Falcons	AHL	45	3	1	4	179	....	....	....	....	....

Signed as a free agent by **Tampa Bay**, August 5, 2005.

FROGREN, Jonas (FREW-grehn, YOH-nuhs) CGY.

Defense. Shoots left. 6'1", 190 lbs. Born, Falun, Sweden, August 28, 1980.
(Calgary's 8th choice, 206th overall, in 1998 Entry Draft).

			Regular Season					Playoffs				
Season	Club	League	GP	G	A	Pts	PIM	GP	G	A	Pts	PIM
1996-97	Farjestad Jr.	Swe-Jr.	20	2	7	9	4	....	....	....	....	....
1997-98	Farjestad Jr.	Swe-Jr.	28	5	6	11	12	2	1	0	1	0
1998-99	Farjestad Jr.	Swe-Jr.	28	10	8	18	16	6	0	2	2	10
	Farjestad	Sweden	22	0	0	0	2	....	....	....	....	....
	Farjestad	EuroHL	5	0	0	0	0	2	0	0	0	0
99-2000	Bofors	Sweden-2	43	2	7	9	40	....	....	....	....	....
2000-01	Farjestad	Sweden	49	3	0	3	10	16	0	0	0	4
	Farjestad Jr.	Swe-Jr.	1	0	0	0	0	....	....	....	....	....
2001-02	Farjestad	Sweden	50	3	6	9	18	10	0	0	0	4
2002-03	Farjestad	Sweden	50	1	7	8	48	14	0	0	0	16
2003-04	Farjestad	Sweden	47	5	5	10	38	17	2	0	2	6
2004-05	Farjestad	Sweden	34	1	0	1	26	15	0	2	2	2

FUGERE, Nick (FOO-jhair, NIHK) **NSH.**

Left wing. Shoots left. 6'2", 238 lbs. Born, Shawinigan, Que., September 20, 1985.
(Nashville's 3rd choice, 107th overall, in 2004 Entry Draft).

			Regular Season					Playoffs				
Season	Club	League	GP	G	A	Pts	PIM	GP	G	A	Pts	PIM
2001-02	Hull Olympiques	QMJHL	65	7	2	9	180	12	2	1	3	70
2002-03	Hull Olympiques	QMJHL	60	15	9	24	247	19	3	3	6	28
2003-04	Gatineau	QMJHL	54	10	13	23	121	15	3	4	7	11
2004-05	Gatineau	QMJHL	63	10	13	23	173	10	2	4	6	16

FUNK, Michael (FUHNK, MIGH-kuhl) **BUF.**

Defense. Shoots left. 6'4", 199 lbs. Born, Abbotsford, B.C., August 15, 1986.
(Buffalo's 2nd choice, 43rd overall, in 2004 Entry Draft).

			Regular Season					Playoffs				
Season	Club	League	GP	G	A	Pts	PIM	GP	G	A	Pts	PIM
2001-02	Abbotsford Hawks	BCAHA	72	9	24	33	84	....	....	....	....	....
2002-03	Portland	WHL	68	1	15	16	54	7	0	1	1	15
2003-04	Portland	WHL	71	3	25	28	86	5	0	1	1	6
2004-05	Portland	WHL	71	8	22	30	84	7	1	1	2	4

FURRER, Philippe (FUHR-ruhr, fihl-EEP) **NYR**

Defense. Shoots left. 6'1", 187 lbs. Born, Bern, Switz., June 16, 1985.
(NY Rangers' 7th choice, 179th overall, in 2003 Entry Draft).

			Regular Season					Playoffs				
Season	Club	League	GP	G	A	Pts	PIM	GP	G	A	Pts	PIM
2000-01	SC Bern Jr.	Swiss-Jr.	....	....	....	....	....	3	0	0	0	0
2001-02	SC Bern Jr.	Swiss-Jr.	29	5	11	16	31	1	0	0	0	0
	SC Bern	Swiss	10	0	0	0	0	....	....	....	....	....
2002-03	SC Bern Jr.	Swiss-Jr.	11	1	11	12	12	....	....	....	....	....
	SC Bern	Swiss	27	0	1	1	6	13	0	0	0	2
2003-04	SC Bern	Swiss	DID NOT PLAY – INJURED									
2004-05	SC Bern	Swiss	37	3	3	6	14	11	1	1	2	4

• Missed entire 2003-04 season recovering from hip injury suffered during 2002-03 season.

GAGNON, Aaron (GAN-YAWN, AIR-ruhn) **PHX.**

Center. Shoots right. 5'10", 185 lbs. Born, Quesnel, B.C., April 24, 1986.
(Phoenix's 8th choice, 240th overall, in 2004 Entry Draft).

			Regular Season					Playoffs				
Season	Club	League	GP	G	A	Pts	PIM	GP	G	A	Pts	PIM
2001-02	North Okanoghan	BCAHA	41	59	59	118	60	....	....	....	....	....
	Seattle	WHL	2	0	0	0	0	....	....	....	....	....
2002-03	Seattle	WHL	60	5	13	18	14	15	3	2	5	4
2003-04	Seattle	WHL	63	21	15	36	29	....	....	....	....	....
2004-05	Seattle	WHL	72	31	34	65	29	12	4	5	9	16

WHL West First All-Star Team (2005)

GARLOCK, Ryan (GAHR-lawk, RIGH-uhn) **CHI.**

Center. Shoots left. 6'1", 197 lbs. Born, Iroquois Falls, Ont., April 24, 1986.
(Chicago's 4th choice, 45th overall, in 2004 Entry Draft).

			Regular Season					Playoffs				
Season	Club	League	GP	G	A	Pts	PIM	GP	G	A	Pts	PIM
2001-02	Timmins Rangers	NOBHL	34	*34	31	*65	62	....	....	....	....	....
2002-03	Guelph Storm	OHL	51	3	12	15	26	11	1	1	2	0
2003-04	Guelph Storm	OHL	36	16	18	34	32	....	....	....	....	....
	Windsor Spitfires	OHL	16	3	10	13	12	4	1	0	1	6
2004-05	Windsor Spitfires	OHL	68	33	35	68	62	1	0	0	0	2

GAUTHIER, Mike (GOH-tyay, MIGHK) **ST.L.**

Defense. Shoots right. 6'3", 185 lbs. Born, Vancouver, B.C., March 26, 1987.
(St. Louis' 5th choice, 169th overall, in 2005 Entry Draft).

			Regular Season					Playoffs				
Season	Club	League	GP	G	A	Pts	PIM	GP	G	A	Pts	PIM
2002-03	Delta Ice Hawks	PIJHL	36	6	15	21	288	....	....	....	....	....
	Prince Albert	WHL	3	0	0	0	2	....	....	....	....	....
2003-04	Prince Albert	WHL	52	1	0	1	130	5	0	0	0	2
2004-05	Prince Albert	WHL	40	2	1	3	93	13	0	0	0	18

GAWRYLETZ, Travis (GAW-reh-lehtz, TRA-vihs) **PHI.**

Defense. Shoots right. 6'2", 190 lbs. Born, Trail, B.C., November 2, 1985.
(Philadelphia's 9th choice, 253rd overall, in 2004 Entry Draft).

			Regular Season					Playoffs				
Season	Club	League	GP	G	A	Pts	PIM	GP	G	A	Pts	PIM
2002-03	Trail Smoke Eaters	BCHL	56	4	28	32	42	14	6	6	12	10
2003-04	Trail Smoke Eaters	BCHL	51	9	21	30	51	10	1	3	4	6
2004-05	U. Minn-Duluth	WCHA	35	4	1	5	26	....	....	....	....	....

BCHL All-Rookie Team (2003) • BCHL Interior Division First All-Star Team (2004)

GELECH, Randall (GEH-lehkh, RAN-duhl) **PHX.**

Center. Shoots right. 6'3", 220 lbs. Born, Wynard, Sask., February 2, 1984.
(Phoenix's 5th choice, 208th overall, in 2003 Entry Draft).

			Regular Season					Playoffs				
Season	Club	League	GP	G	A	Pts	PIM	GP	G	A	Pts	PIM
2000-01	Kelowna Rockets	WHL	51	1	9	10	19	6	0	0	0	4
2001-02	Kelowna Rockets	WHL	48	6	2	8	33	15	2	1	3	15
2002-03	Kelowna Rockets	WHL	67	25	20	45	93	19	8	4	12	17
2003-04	Kelowna Rockets	WHL	71	30	19	49	117	17	10	4	14	22
2004-05	Utah Grizzlies	AHL	76	15	12	27	72	....	....	....	....	....

Memorial Cup Tournament All-Star Team (2004)

GENEROUS, Matt (GEHN-uhr-uhs, MAT) **BUF.**

Defense. Shoots right. 6'3", 185 lbs. Born, Methuen, MA, May 4, 1985.
(Buffalo's 8th choice, 208th overall, in 2005 Entry Draft).

			Regular Season					Playoffs				
Season	Club	League	GP	G	A	Pts	PIM	GP	G	A	Pts	PIM
2003-04	N.E. Jr. Falcons	EJHL	43	6	9	15	134	....	....	....	....	....
2004-05	N.E. Jr. Falcons	EJHL	49	8	16	24	105	....	....	....	....	....

Signed Letter of Intent to attend **St. Lawrence** (ECAC) in fall of 2005.

GENOVY, Jeff (jeh-NOH-vee, JEHF) **CBJ**

Left wing. Shoots left. 6'3", 191 lbs. Born, Kalamazoo, MI, December 4, 1982.
(Columbus' 4th choice, 96th overall, in 2002 Entry Draft).

			Regular Season					Playoffs				
Season	Club	League	GP	G	A	Pts	PIM	GP	G	A	Pts	PIM
1998-99	Soo Hawks	GLHL	43	10	10	20	39	....	....	....	....	....
99-2000	West. Michigan	MMHL	STATISTICS NOT AVAILABLE									
	Det. Compuware	NAHL	9	0	3	3	2	2	0	0	0	0
2000-01	Soo Indians	NAHL	54	12	14	26	26	8	0	1	1	4
2001-02	Des Moines	USHL	52	23	23	46	86	3	1	4	5	2
2002-03	Clarkson Knights	ECAC	34	5	8	13	45	....	....	....	....	....
2003-04	Clarkson Knights	ECAC	36	2	7	9	42	....	....	....	....	....
2004-05	Clarkson Knights	ECAC	25	3	4	7	39	....	....	....	....	....

GERBE, Nathan (GUHR-bee, NAY-thuhn) **BUF.**

Center. Shoots left. 5'5", 160 lbs. Born, Oxford, MI, July 24, 1987.
(Buffalo's 5th choice, 142nd overall, in 2005 Entry Draft).

			Regular Season					Playoffs				
Season	Club	League	GP	G	A	Pts	PIM	GP	G	A	Pts	PIM
2002-03	River City Lancers	USHL	25	3	3	6	49	7	1	1	2	2
2003-04	USA U-17	USDP	58	25	19	44	153	....	....	....	....	....
2004-05	USA U-17&U-18	NAHL	12	7	5	12	25	....	....	....	....	....
	USA U-18	USDP	38	13	16	29	73	....	....	....	....	....

Signed Letter of Intent to attend **Boston College** (H-East) in fall of 2005.

GERGEN, Michael (GUHR-gehn, MIGHK-uhl) **PIT.**

Wing. Shoots left. 5'10", 185 lbs. Born, Hastings, MN, February 17, 1987.
(Pittsburgh's 2nd choice, 61st overall, in 2005 Entry Draft).

			Regular Season					Playoffs				
Season	Club	League	GP	G	A	Pts	PIM	GP	G	A	Pts	PIM
2003-04	Shat.-St. Mary's	High-MN	71	29	26	55	52	....	....	....	....	....
2004-05	Shat.-St. Mary's	High-MN	69	64	53	117	110	....	....	....	....	....

Signed Letter of Intent to attend **Minnesota-Duluth** (WCHA) in fall of 2005.

GERMYN, Carsen (JUHR-mihn, KAHR-sehn) **CGY.**

Right wing. Shoots right. 5'10", 185 lbs. Born, Campbell River, B.C., February 22, 1985.

			Regular Season					Playoffs				
Season	Club	League	GP	G	A	Pts	PIM	GP	G	A	Pts	PIM
1998-99	Kelowna Rockets	WHL	59	6	10	16	61	5	0	0	0	2
99-2000	Kelowna Rockets	WHL	71	16	29	45	111	5	3	3	6	4
2000-01	Kelowna Rockets	WHL	71	35	52	87	102	6	2	6	8	10
2001-02	Kelowna Rockets	WHL	23	10	18	28	43	....	....	....	....	....
	Red Deer Rebels	WHL	37	23	25	48	83	23	4	12	16	24
2002-03	Red Deer Rebels	WHL	63	26	33	59	108	23	4	9	13	25
2003-04	Norfolk Admirals	AHL	77	11	16	27	104	6	1	0	1	2
2004-05	Lowell	AHL	60	9	11	20	115	10	0	0	0	25

Signed as a free agent by **Calgary**, July 6, 2004.

GERVAIS, Bruno (ZHUR-vay, BROO-noh) **NYI**

Defense. Shoots right. 6', 188 lbs. Born, Longueuil, Que., October 3, 1984.
(NY Islanders' 6th choice, 182nd overall, in 2003 Entry Draft).

			Regular Season					Playoffs				
Season	Club	League	GP	G	A	Pts	PIM	GP	G	A	Pts	PIM
99-2000	Antoine-Girouard	QAAA	6	0	0	0	0	4	0	0	0	0
2000-01	Antoine-Girouard	QAAA	40	8	27	35	46	7	4	2	6	8
2001-02	Acadie-Bathurst	QMJHL	65	4	12	16	42	16	3	1	4	8
2002-03	Acadie-Bathurst	QMJHL	72	22	28	50	73	11	3	5	8	14
2003-04	Acadie-Bathurst	QMJHL	23	4	6	10	28	....	....	....	....	....
2004-05	Bridgeport	AHL	76	8	22	30	58	....	....	....	....	....

QMJHL Second All-Star Team (2003)

Missed majority of 2003-04 season recovering from knee injury suffered during Team Canada Jr. training camp, December 12, 2003.

GETZLAF, Ryan (GEHTZ-laf, RIGH-uhn) **ANA.**

Center. Shoots right. 6'2", 210 lbs. Born, Regina, Sask., May 10, 1985.
(Anaheim's 1st choice, 19th overall, in 2003 Entry Draft).

			Regular Season					Playoffs				
Season	Club	League	GP	G	A	Pts	PIM	GP	G	A	Pts	PIM
2000-01	Regina Rangers	SBHL	41	33	41	74	189	....	....	....	....	....
	Reg. Pat Cdns.	SMHL	8	4	3	7	8	....	....	....	....	....
2001-02	Calgary Hitmen	WHL	63	9	9	18	34	7	2	1	3	4
2002-03	Calgary Hitmen	WHL	70	29	39	68	121	5	1	1	2	6
2003-04	Calgary Hitmen	WHL	49	28	47	75	97	7	5	1	6	12
2004-05	Calgary Hitmen	WHL	51	29	25	54	102	12	4	13	17	18
	Cincinnati	AHL	....	....	....	....	....	10	1	4	5	4

WHL East First All-Star Team (2004) • WHL East Second All-Star Team (2005)

GIFFORD, Brian (GIH-fuhrd, BRIGH-uhn) **PIT.**

Center. Shoots left. 6'1", 173 lbs. Born, Fargo, ND, November 12, 1985.
(Pittsburgh's 5th choice, 85th overall, in 2004 Entry Draft).

			Regular Season					Playoffs				
Season	Club	League	GP	G	A	Pts	PIM	GP	G	A	Pts	PIM
2002-03	Moorhead Spuds	High-MN	30	18	20	38	32	....	....	....	....	....
2003-04	Moorhead Spuds	High-MN	26	19	37	56	26	....	....	....	....	....
2004-05	Indiana Ice	USHL	55	13	10	23	80	3	1	0	1	0

GILBERT, Tom (GIHL-buhrt, TAWM) **EDM.**

Defense. Shoots right. 6'2", 190 lbs. Born, Minneapolis, MN, January 10, 1983.
(Colorado's 5th choice, 129th overall, in 2002 Entry Draft).

			Regular Season					Playoffs				
Season	Club	League	GP	G	A	Pts	PIM	GP	G	A	Pts	PIM
99-2000	Bloomington-Jeff.	High-MN	18	7	18	25	....	....	....	....	....	....
2000-01	Bloomington-Jeff.	High-MN	23	20	18	38	....	....	....	....	....	....
	Chicago Steel	USHL	1	0	0	0	0	....	....	....	....	....
2001-02	Chicago Steel	USHL	57	13	15	28	62	4	0	0	0	4
2002-03	U. of Wisconsin	WCHA	39	7	13	20	36	....	....	....	....	....
2003-04	U. of Wisconsin	WCHA	39	6	15	21	36	....	....	....	....	....
2004-05	U. of Wisconsin	WCHA	41	8	9	17	48	....	....	....	....	....

Traded to **Edmonton** by **Colorado** for Tommy Salo and Edmonton's 6th round choice (Justin Mercier) in 2005 Entry Draft, March 8, 2004.

GILL, Aaron (GIHL, AIR-ruhn)

Center. Shoots right. 6', 180 lbs. Born, Rochester, MN, March 5, 1980.

			Regular Season					Playoffs				
Season	Club	League	GP	G	A	Pts	PIM	GP	G	A	Pts	PIM
1997-98	Rochester	USHL	56	11	12	23	6	....	....	....	....	....
1998-99	Rochester	USHL	56	10	20	30	35	....	....	....	....	....
99-2000	Rochester	USHL	55	27	23	50	43	....	....	....	....	....
2000-01	U. of Notre Dame	CCHA	38	11	15	26	37	....	....	....	....	....
2001-02	U. of Notre Dame	CCHA	38	8	14	22	20	....	....	....	....	....
2002-03	U. of Notre Dame	CCHA	38	13	12	25	14	....	....	....	....	....
2003-04	U. of Notre Dame	CCHA	39	17	21	38	16	....	....	....	....	....
	Cleveland Barons	AHL	6	1	0	1	2	3	0	0	0	0
2004-05	Cleveland Barons	AHL	75	4	5	9	16	....	....	....	....	....

CCHA Second All-Star Team (2004)

Signed to a PTO (tryout) contract by **Cleveland** (AHL), April 2, 2004. Signed as a free agent by **San Jose**, April 23, 2004.

GILLIES, Trevor (GIHL-ees, TREH-vuhr) **ANA.**

Left wing. Shoots left. 6'3", 235 lbs. Born, Cambridge, Ont., January 30, 1979.

			Regular Season					Playoffs				
Season	Club	League	GP	G	A	Pts	PIM	GP	G	A	Pts	PIM
1996-97	North Bay	OHL	26	0	3	3	72	....	....	....	....	....
1997-98	North Bay	OHL	2	0	0	0	4	....	....	....	....	....
	Sarnia Sting	OHL	17	0	1	1	33	....	....	....	....	....
	Oshawa Generals	OHL	45	1	2	3	184	7	0	1	1	12
1998-99	Oshawa Generals	OHL	66	6	9	15	270	11	0	2	2	28
99-2000	Lowell	AHL	8	0	0	0	38	....	....	....	....	....
	Mississippi	ECHL	53	0	6	6	202	....	....	....	....	....
2000-01	Greensboro	ECHL	63	1	6	7	303	....	....	....	....	....
	Worcester IceCats	AHL	....	....	....	....	....	6	0	0	0	24
2001-02	Providence Bruins	AHL	5	0	0	0	21	....	....	....	....	....
	Augusta Lynx	ECHL	46	0	1	1	*269	....	....	....	....	....
	Richmond	ECHL	18	0	1	1	*51	....	....	....	....	....
2002-03	Lowell	AHL	25	0	1	1	132	....	....	....	....	....
	Richmond	ECHL	6	0	0	0	20	....	....	....	....	....
	Peoria Rivermen	ECHL	24	0	1	1	180	....	....	....	....	....
2003-04	Springfield Falcons	AHL	61	2	1	3	277	....	....	....	....	....
2004-05	Hartford Wolf Pack	AHL	49	0	2	2	277	....	....	....	....	....

Signed as a free agent by **NY Rangers**, July 20, 2004. Traded to **Anaheim** by **NY Rangers** with a conditional choice in 2007 Entry Draft for Steve Rucchin, August 23, 2005.

GIMAEV, Sergei (gih-MIGH-ehv, SAIR-gay) **OTT.**

Defense. Shoots left. 6'1", 183 lbs. Born, Moscow, USSR, February 16, 1984.
(Ottawa's 6th choice, 166th overall, in 2003 Entry Draft).

			Regular Season					Playoffs				
Season	Club	League	GP	G	A	Pts	PIM	GP	G	A	Pts	PIM
2001-02	CSKA Moscow 2	Russia-3	36	0	10	10	50	....	....	....	....	....
2002-03	Cherepovets	Russia	11	0	0	0	4	....	....	....	....	....
2003-04	Cherepovets	Russia	50	1	3	4	32	....	....	....	....	....
2004-05	Cherepovets	Russia	5	0	1	1	2	....	....	....	....	....
	Sibir Novosibirsk	Russia	31	1	6	7	34	....	....	....	....	....

GIORDANO, Mark (jee-ohr-DAN-oh, MAHRK) **CGY.**

Defense. Shoots left. 6', 203 lbs. Born, Toronto, Ont., May 10, 1983.

			Regular Season					Playoffs				
Season	Club	League	GP	G	A	Pts	PIM	GP	G	A	Pts	PIM
2002-03	Owen Sound	OHL	68	18	30	48	109	4	1	3	4	2
2003-04	Owen Sound	OHL	65	14	35	49	72	7	1	3	4	5
2004-05	Lowell	AHL	66	6	10	16	85	11	0	1	1	41

Signed as a free agent by **Calgary**, July 6, 2004.

GIROUX, Alexandre (ZHIH-roo, al-ehx-AN-dreh) **NYR**

Center/Left wing. Shoots left. 6'3", 190 lbs. Born, Quebec City, Que., June 16, 1981.
(Ottawa's 9th choice, 213th overall, in 1999 Entry Draft).

			Regular Season					Playoffs				
Season	Club	League	GP	G	A	Pts	PIM	GP	G	A	Pts	PIM
1997-98	Ste-Foy	QAAA	42	28	30	58	96	....	....	....	....	....
1998-99	Hull Olympiques	QMJHL	67	15	22	37	124	22	2	2	4	8
99-2000	Hull Olympiques	QMJHL	72	52	47	99	117	15	12	6	18	30
2000-01	Hull Olympiques	QMJHL	38	31	32	63	62	....	....	....	....	....
	Rouyn-Noranda	QMJHL	25	13	14	27	56	9	2	6	8	22
2001-02	Grand Rapids	AHL	70	11	16	27	74	....	....	....	....	....
2002-03	Binghamton	AHL	67	19	16	35	101	10	1	0	1	10
2003-04	Binghamton	AHL	59	19	23	42	79	....	....	....	....	....
	Hartford Wolf Pack	AHL	16	6	3	9	13	16	3	4	7	28
2004-05	Hartford Wolf Pack	AHL	78	32	22	54	128	6	3	3	6	23

Traded to **NY Rangers** by **Ottawa** with Karel Rachunek for Greg De Vries, March 9, 2004.

GIULIANO, Jeff **L.A.**

Left wing. Shoots left. 5'9", 205 lbs. Born, Nashua, NH, June 20, 1979.

			Regular Season					Playoffs				
Season	Club	League	GP	G	A	Pts	PIM	GP	G	A	Pts	PIM
1998-99	Boston College	H-East	43	5	15	20	10	....	....	....	....	....
99-2000	Boston College	H-East	42	10	13	23	16	....	....	....	....	....
2000-01	Boston College	H-East	43	14	22	36	28	....	....	....	....	....
2001-02	Boston College	H-East	38	11	24	35	14	....	....	....	....	....
2002-03	Manchester	AHL	47	4	11	15	8	3	1	0	1	0
	Reading Royals	ECHL	38	7	23	30	6	....	....	....	....	....
2003-04	Manchester	AHL	80	6	14	20	16	1	0	0	0	0
2004-05	Manchester	AHL	69	8	16	24	21	2	0	0	0	0

Signed as a free agent by **Los Angeles**, August 12, 2005.

GLADSKIKH, Evgeny (glad-SKEEKH, ehv-GEH-nee) **VAN.**

Right wing. Shoots left. 6', 198 lbs. Born, Magnitogorsk, USSR, April 24, 1982.
(Vancouver's 3rd choice, 114th overall, in 2001 Entry Draft).

			Regular Season					Playoffs				
Season	Club	League	GP	G	A	Pts	PIM	GP	G	A	Pts	PIM
1998-99	Magnitogorsk 2	Russia-4	16	3	3	6	6	....	....	....	....	....
99-2000	Magnitogorsk 2	Russia-3	39	17	2	19	24	....	....	....	....	....
	Magnitogorsk	Russia	1	0	0	0	0	....	....	....	....	....
2000-01	Magnitogorsk 2	Russia-3	11	10	7	17	6	....	....	....	....	....
	Magnitogorsk	Russia	31	3	5	8	10	12	0	2	2	2
2001-02	Magnitogorsk	Russia	32	5	6	11	6	4	0	0	0	4
2002-03	Magnitogorsk	Russia	42	4	7	11	18	3	0	0	0	2
2003-04	Magnitogorsk	Russia	47	13	13	26	22	14	3	1	4	10
2004-05	Magnitogorsk 2	Russia-3	2	0	2	2	0	....	....	....	....	....
	Magnitogorsk	Russia	42	11	12	23	24	4	1	0	1	4

GLASS, Tanner (GLAS, TA-nuhr) **FLA.**

Forward. Shoots left. 6', 196 lbs. Born, Regina, Sask., November 29, 1983.
(Florida's 13th choice, 265th overall, in 2003 Entry Draft).

			Regular Season					Playoffs				
Season	Club	League	GP	G	A	Pts	PIM	GP	G	A	Pts	PIM
2000-01	Yorkton Mallers	SMHL	39	31	29	60	120	4	3	1	4	10
2001-02	Penticton Panthers	BCHL	57	11	28	39	171	....	....	....	....	....
2002-03	Penticton Panthers	BCHL	32	15	25	40	108	....	....	....	....	....
	Nanaimo Clippers	BCHL	18	8	14	22	46	....	....	....	....	....
2003-04	Dartmouth	ECAC	26	4	7	11	18	....	....	....	....	....
2004-05	Dartmouth	ECAC	33	7	8	15	32	....	....	....	....	....

GLASSER, Matthew (GLAS-uhr, MA-thyew) **EDM.**

Left wing. Shoots left. 5'10", 175 lbs. Born, Saskatoon, Sask., January 11, 1987.
(Edmonton's 8th choice, 220th overall, in 2005 Entry Draft).

			Regular Season					Playoffs				
Season	Club	League	GP	G	A	Pts	PIM	GP	G	A	Pts	PIM
2003-04	Fort McMurray	AJHL	55	13	12	25	24	....	....	....	....	....
2004-05	Fort McMurray	AJHL	62	25	24	49	14	....	....	....	....	....

Signed Letter of Intent to attend **Denver** (ECAC) in fall of 2005.

GLAZACHEV, Konstantin (GLAH-zuh-chehv, kawn-stuhn-TIHN) **NSH.**

Left wing. Shoots right. 6', 186 lbs. Born, Arkhangelsk, USSR, February 18, 1985.
(Nashville's 2nd choice, 35th overall, in 2003 Entry Draft).

			Regular Season					Playoffs				
Season	Club	League	GP	G	A	Pts	PIM	GP	G	A	Pts	PIM
2001-02	Yaroslavl 2	Russia-3	7	5	6	11	6	....	....	....	....	....
2002-03	Yaroslavl 2	Russia-3	STATISTICS NOT AVAILABLE									
	Yaroslavl	Russia	13	3	4	7	4	4	0	0	0	0
2003-04	Yaroslavl	Russia	35	4	3	7	4	2	0	0	0	0
	Yaroslavl 2	Russia-3	9	6	5	11	8	....	....	....	....	....
2004-05	Sibir Novosibirsk	Russia	24	4	9	13	6	....	....	....	....	....
	Yaroslavl	Russia	9	0	3	3	2	....	....	....	....	....
	Yaroslavl 2	Russia-3	20	17	9	26	14	....	....	....	....	....

GLEED, Jon (GLEED, JAWN) **MTL.**

Defense. Shoots right. 6'2", 200 lbs. Born, Milton, Ont., January 3, 1984.
(Montreal's 6th choice, 212th overall, in 2004 Entry Draft).

			Regular Season					Playoffs				
Season	Club	League	GP	G	A	Pts	PIM	GP	G	A	Pts	PIM
2001-02	Brampton Capitals	OPJHL	45	3	15	18	39	....	....	....	....	....
2002-03	Cornell Big Red	ECAC	12	0	1	1	10	....	....	....	....	....
2003-04	Cornell Big Red	ECAC	28	3	3	6	18	....	....	....	....	....
2004-05	Cornell Big Red	ECAC	30	1	5	6	43	....	....	....	....	....

GLENCROSS, Curtis (GLEHN-kraws, KUHR-tis) **ANA.**

Center. Shoots left. 6'1", 195 lbs. Born, Kindersley, Sask., December 28, 1982.

			Regular Season					Playoffs				
Season	Club	League	GP	G	A	Pts	PIM	GP	G	A	Pts	PIM
2001-02	Brooks Bandits	AJHL	....	42	26	68	....	....	....	....	....	....
2002-03	Alaska-Anchorage	WCHA	35	11	12	23	79	....	....	....	....	....
2003-04	Alaska-Anchorage	WCHA	37	21	13	34	79	....	....	....	....	....
	Cincinnati	AHL	7	2	1	3	6	9	1	6	7	10
2004-05	Cincinnati	AHL	51	6	3	9	63	12	2	0	2	10

Signed as a free agent by **Anaheim**, March 25, 2004.

GLOBKE, Rob (GLAWB-kee, RAWB) **FLA.**

Center. Shoots right. 6'2", 200 lbs. Born, Farmington, MI, October 24, 1982.
(Florida's 3rd choice, 40th overall, in 2002 Entry Draft).

			Regular Season					Playoffs				
Season	Club	League	GP	G	A	Pts	PIM	GP	G	A	Pts	PIM
1998-99	Det. Compuware	NAHL	55	8	14	22	111	7	1	2	3	2
99-2000	USA U-18	USDP	54	15	21	36	68	....	....	....	....	....
2000-01	U. of Notre Dame	CCHA	33	17	9	26	74	....	....	....	....	....
2001-02	U. of Notre Dame	CCHA	33	11	11	22	79	....	....	....	....	....
2002-03	U. of Notre Dame	CCHA	40	21	15	36	44	....	....	....	....	....
2003-04	U. of Notre Dame	CCHA	39	19	21	40	42	....	....	....	....	....
2004-05	San Antonio	AHL	63	6	6	12	21	....	....	....	....	....
	Texas Wildcatters	ECHL	10	8	4	12	13	....	....	....	....	....

CCHA Second All-Star Team (2004)

GLOVER, Dan (GLUH-vuhr, DAN) **N.J.**

Defense. Shoots left. 6'2", 175 lbs. Born, Delburne, Alta., May 4, 1983.
(New Jersey's 10th choice, 250th overall, in 2002 Entry Draft).

			Regular Season					Playoffs				
Season	Club	League	GP	G	A	Pts	PIM	GP	G	A	Pts	PIM
2000-01	Red Deer Chiefs	AMHL	35	1	5	6	40	....	....	....	....	....
2001-02	Camrose Kodiaks	AJHL	55	1	10	11	110	....	....	....	....	....
2002-03	Camrose Kodiaks	AJHL	61	5	14	19	118	27	0	6	6	32
2003-04	Cornell Big Red	ECAC	23	1	2	3	20	....	....	....	....	....
2004-05	Cornell Big Red	ECAC	15	0	1	1	6	....	....	....	....	....

GLUMAC, Mike (GLOO-kmak, MIGHK) **ST.L.**

Right wing. Shoots right. 6'2", 205 lbs. Born, Niagara Falls, Ont., April 5, 1980.

			Regular Season					Playoffs				
Season	Club	League	GP	G	A	Pts	PIM	GP	G	A	Pts	PIM
1997-98	Newmarket	OPJHL	36	16	16	32	57	....	....	....	....	....
1998-99	Miami U.	CCHA	35	2	0	2	44	....	....	....	....	....
99-2000	Miami U.	CCHA	36	8	5	13	52	....	....	....	....	....
2000-01	Miami U.	CCHA	37	9	10	19	46	....	....	....	....	....
2001-02	Miami U.	CCHA	36	15	8	23	28	....	....	....	....	....
2002-03	Pee Dee Pride	ECHL	69	37	32	69	49	....	....	....	....	....
	Cleveland Barons	AHL	2	0	0	0	0	....	....	....	....	....
2003-04	Worcester IceCats	AHL	80	28	24	52	74	10	3	3	6	11
2004-05	Worcester IceCats	AHL	45	12	17	29	27	....	....	....	....	....

ECHL All-Rookie Team (2003)

Signed as a free agent by **Pee Dee** (ECHL), August 28, 2002. Signed as a free agent by **Worcester** (AHL), October 6, 2003. Signed as a free agent by **St. Louis**, June 29, 2004.

GOERTZEN, Steven (GUHRT-sehn, STEEV-ehn) CBJ

Right wing. Shoots right. 6'1", 190 lbs. Born, Stony Plain, Alta., May 26, 1984.
(Columbus' 11th choice, 225th overall, in 2002 Entry Draft).

			Regular Season					Playoffs				
Season	**Club**	**League**	**GP**	**G**	**A**	**Pts**	**PIM**	**GP**	**G**	**A**	**Pts**	**PIM**
99-2000	Spruce Grove	AMBHL	36	16	17	33	30	....	....	....	....	....
2000-01	St. Albert Raiders	AMHL	34	11	19	30	70	....	....	....	....	....
	St. Albert Saints	AJHL	1	0	0	0	0	....	....	....	....	....
2001-02	Seattle	WHL	66	6	9	15	45	11	2	0	2	4
2002-03	Seattle	WHL	71	12	19	31	95	14	4	3	7	9
2003-04	Seattle	WHL	69	15	18	33	115	....	....	....	....	....
	Syracuse Crunch	AHL	8	0	3	3	4	1	0	0	0	0
2004-05	Syracuse Crunch	AHL	57	2	7	9	100	....	....	....	....	....

GOGULLA, Philip (GOH-goo-lah, FIL-uhp) BUF.

Right wing. Shoots left. 6'2", 176 lbs. Born, Dusseldorf, West Germany, July 31, 1987.
(Buffalo's 2nd choice, 48th overall, in 2005 Entry Draft).

			Regular Season					Playoffs				
Season	**Club**	**League**	**GP**	**G**	**A**	**Pts**	**PIM**	**GP**	**G**	**A**	**Pts**	**PIM**
2002-03	Krefelder EV Jr.	Ger-Jr.	32	11	23	34	42	2	0	0	0	2
2003-04	Krefelder EV Jr.	Ger-Jr.	35	35	44	79	22	2	0	2	2	27
2004-05	Essen	German-2	3	0	0	0	0	....	....	....	....	....
	Koln Jr.	Ger-Jr.	7	4	5	9	18	....	....	....	....	....
	Kolner Haie	Germany	47	1	1	2	14	7	0	0	0	2

GOLIGOSKI, Alex (goh-lih-GAW-skee, AL-ehx) PIT.

Defense. Shoots right. 5'11", 180 lbs. Born, Grand Rapids, MN, July 30, 1985.
(Pittsburgh's 3rd choice, 61st overall, in 2004 Entry Draft).

			Regular Season					Playoffs				
Season	**Club**	**League**	**GP**	**G**	**A**	**Pts**	**PIM**	**GP**	**G**	**A**	**Pts**	**PIM**
2002-03	Grand Rapids	High-MN	28	14	20	34	22	....	....	....	....	....
2003-04	Grand Rapids	High-MN	26	25	31	56	16	....	....	....	....	....
	Sioux Falls	USHL	10	0	2	2	6	....	....	....	....	....
2004-05	U. of Minnesota	WCHA	33	5	15	20	44	....	....	....	....	....

WCHA All-Rookie Team (2005)

GORBUNOV, Vladimir (gohr-buh-NAHF, vla-DIH-meer) NYI

Right wing. Shoots left. 6', 174 lbs. Born, Moscow, USSR, April 22, 1982.
(NY Islanders' 4th choice, 105th overall, in 2000 Entry Draft).

			Regular Season					Playoffs				
Season	**Club**	**League**	**GP**	**G**	**A**	**Pts**	**PIM**	**GP**	**G**	**A**	**Pts**	**PIM**
99-2000	HK Moscow	Russia-2	22	11	7	18	32	....	....	....	....	....
2000-01	HK Moscow	Russia-2	43	10	14	24	63	....	....	....	....	....
2001-02	HK CSKA Moscow	Russia-2	46	16	18	34	22	....	....	....	....	....
	CSKA Moscow 2	Russia-3	3	1	1	2	0	....	....	....	....	....
2002-03	CSKA Moscow	Russia	35	5	5	10	46	....	....	....	....	....
	CSKA Moscow 2	Russia-3	STATISTICS NOT AVAILABLE									
2003-04	CSKA Moscow	Russia	34	4	7	11	56	....	....	....	....	....
2004-05	Ufa	Russia	1	0	0	0	0	....	....	....	....	....
	HK MVD Tver	Russia-2	36	4	15	19	48	11	2	1	3	8

GORDON, Andrew (GOHR-duhn, AN-droo) WSH.

Right wing. Shoots right. 5'11", 180 lbs. Born, Halifax, N.S., December 13, 1985.
(Washington's 11th choice, 197th overall, in 2004 Entry Draft).

			Regular Season					Playoffs				
Season	**Club**	**League**	**GP**	**G**	**A**	**Pts**	**PIM**	**GP**	**G**	**A**	**Pts**	**PIM**
2002-03	Notre Dame	SJHL	58	20	27	47	12	....	....	....	....	....
2003-04	Notre Dame	SJHL	55	20	44	64	12	....	....	....	....	....
2004-05	St. Cloud State	WCHA	38	9	8	17	6	....	....	....	....	....

GORGES, Josh (GOHR-juhz, JAWSH) S.J.

Defense. Shoots left. 6'1", 190 lbs. Born, Kelowna, B.C., August 14, 1984.

			Regular Season					Playoffs				
Season	**Club**	**League**	**GP**	**G**	**A**	**Pts**	**PIM**	**GP**	**G**	**A**	**Pts**	**PIM**
2000-01	Kelowna Rockets	WHL	57	4	6	10	24	6	1	1	2	4
2001-02	Kelowna Rockets	WHL	72	7	34	41	74	15	1	7	8	8
2002-03	Kelowna Rockets	WHL	54	11	48	59	76	19	3	17	20	16
2003-04	Kelowna Rockets	WHL	62	11	31	42	38	17	2	13	15	6
2004-05	Cleveland Barons	AHL	74	4	8	12	37	....	....	....	....	....

WHL West Second All-Star Team (2003) • WHL West First All-Star Team (2004) • George Parsons Trophy (Memorial Cup Tournament Most Sportsmanlike Player) (2004)

Signed as a free agent by **San Jose**, September 20, 2002.

GOULET, Stephane (goo-LAY, STEH-fan) EDM.

Right wing. Shoots left. 6'3", 185 lbs. Born, Levis, Que., January 7, 1986.
(Edmonton's 8th choice, 208th overall, in 2004 Entry Draft).

			Regular Season					Playoffs				
Season	**Club**	**League**	**GP**	**G**	**A**	**Pts**	**PIM**	**GP**	**G**	**A**	**Pts**	**PIM**
2002-03	Levis	QAAA	42	39	29	68	70	....	....	....	....	....
2003-04	Quebec Remparts	QMJHL	54	6	8	14	14	5	0	0	0	2
2004-05	Moncton Wildcats	QMJHL	69	22	25	47	37	12	3	7	10	12

GOVE, David (GOHV, DAYV) CAR.

Center. Shoots left. 5'9", 190 lbs. Born, Centerville, MA, May 4, 1978.

			Regular Season					Playoffs				
Season	**Club**	**League**	**GP**	**G**	**A**	**Pts**	**PIM**	**GP**	**G**	**A**	**Pts**	**PIM**
1997-98	Western Mich.	CCHA	36	8	7	15	8	....	....	....	....	....
1998-99	Western Mich.	CCHA	33	9	14	23	12	....	....	....	....	....
99-2000	Western Mich.	CCHA	36	18	28	46	22	....	....	....	....	....
2000-01	Western Mich.	CCHA	39	22	37	59	16	....	....	....	....	....
	Orlando	IHL	9	1	1	2	2	1	0	0	0	0
2001-02	Grand Rapids	AHL	17	2	4	6	8	....	....	....	....	....
	Johnstown Chiefs	ECHL	54	17	32	49	32	8	1	3	4	4
2002-03	San Antonio	AHL	72	15	20	35	30	3	0	1	1	0
	Laredo Bucks	CHL	8	4	12	16	15	....	....	....	....	....
2003-04	Utah Grizzlies	AHL	75	14	22	36	28	....	....	....	....	....
2004-05	Providence Bruins	AHL	70	13	18	31	30	17	3	3	6	14

Signed as a free agent by **Carolina**, August 4, 2005.

GRABOVSKY, Mikhail (gra-BAWV-skee, mih-kigh-EHL) MTL.

Center. Shoots left. 5'11", 181 lbs. Born, Potsdam, East Germany, January 31, 1984.
(Montreal's 4th choice, 150th overall, in 2004 Entry Draft).

			Regular Season					Playoffs				
Season	**Club**	**League**	**GP**	**G**	**A**	**Pts**	**PIM**	**GP**	**G**	**A**	**Pts**	**PIM**
2001-02	HC Minsk	Belarus	26	10	7	17	16	....	....	....	....	....
2002-03	HC Minsk	Belarus	STATISTICS NOT AVAILABLE									
2003-04	Nizhnekamsk	Russia	45	6	11	17	26	5	0	0	0	4
2004-05	Nizhnekamsk	Russia	60	16	20	36	32	3	2	0	2	2
	Yunost-Minsk	BelOpen	....	....	....	....	....	5	2	4	6	6

GRACIK, Juraj (GRAH0chihk, YUH-righ) ATL.

Right wing. Shoots right. 6'3", 190 lbs. Born, Topolcany, Czech., August 14, 1986.
(Atlanta's 5th choice, 142nd overall, in 2004 Entry Draft).

			Regular Season					Playoffs				
Season	**Club**	**League**	**GP**	**G**	**A**	**Pts**	**PIM**	**GP**	**G**	**A**	**Pts**	**PIM**
2002-03	Topolcany Jr.	Slovak-Jr.	24	10	7	17	28	....	....	....	....	....
2003-04	Topolcany Jr.	Slovak-Jr.	28	22	12	34	78	....	....	....	....	....
	Topolcany	Slovak-2	28	16	8	24	8	4	1	0	1	0
2004-05	Tri-City Americans	WHL	33	4	2	6	18	....	....	....	....	....

GRAGNANI, Marc-Andre (GRUH-na-nee, MAHRK-AWN-dray) BUF.

Defense. Shoots left. 6'1", 180 lbs. Born, Montreal, Que., March 11, 1987.
(Buffalo's 3rd choice, 87th overall, in 2005 Entry Draft).

			Regular Season					Playoffs				
Season	**Club**	**League**	**GP**	**G**	**A**	**Pts**	**PIM**	**GP**	**G**	**A**	**Pts**	**PIM**
2002-03	West Island Lions	QAAA	34	3	15	18	22	....	....	....	....	....
2003-04	PEI Rocket	QMJHL	61	2	13	15	42	11	0	0	0	4
2004-05	PEI Rocket	QMJHL	68	10	29	39	48	....	....	....	....	....

GRAHAM, Bruce (GRAY-uhm, BROOS) NYR

Center. Shoots left. 6'6", 234 lbs. Born, Moncton, N.B., December 2, 1985.
(NY Rangers' 5th choice, 51st overall, in 2004 Entry Draft).

			Regular Season					Playoffs				
Season	**Club**	**League**	**GP**	**G**	**A**	**Pts**	**PIM**	**GP**	**G**	**A**	**Pts**	**PIM**
2001-02	Moncton Flyers	NBMHL	STATISTICS NOT AVAILABLE									
	Moncton Wildcats	QMJHL	3	0	0	0	0	....	....	....	....	....
2002-03	Moncton Wildcats	QMJHL	66	15	13	28	80	6	0	2	2	0
2003-04	Moncton Wildcats	QMJHL	68	24	33	57	89	18	0	14	14	4
2004-05	Moncton Wildcats	QMJHL	47	23	19	42	56	12	4	5	9	19

GRANATH, Elias (GRA-nuth, EHL-ee-ahs) DAL.

Defense. Shoots left. 6'1", 174 lbs. Born, Borlange, Sweden, September 6, 1985.
(Dallas' 10th choice, 196th overall, in 2003 Entry Draft).

			Regular Season					Playoffs				
Season	**Club**	**League**	**GP**	**G**	**A**	**Pts**	**PIM**	**GP**	**G**	**A**	**Pts**	**PIM**
2001-02	Leksands IF U18	Swe-U18	11	0	1	1	8	4	0	0	0	2
	Leksands IF Jr.	Swe-Jr.	6	0	0	0	0	1	0	0	0	0
2002-03	Leksands IF Jr.	Swe-Jr.	29	0	4	4	49	....	....	....	....	....
	Leksands IF U18	Swe-U18	6	0	2	2	0	2	0	1	1	8
2003-04	Leksands IF Jr.	Swe-Jr.	25	4	4	8	34	....	....	....	....	....
	Leksands IF	Sweden-Q	10	0	0	0	4	....	....	....	....	....
2004-05	Leksands IF	Sweden-2	35	3	3	6	24	....	....	....	....	....
	Leksands IF Jr.	Swe-Jr.	5	0	2	2	8	5	1	0	1	2

GRANT, Triston (GRANT, TRIHS-tuhn) PHI.

Left wing. Shoots left. 6'1", 223 lbs. Born, Brandon, Man., February 2, 1984.
(Philadelphia's 10th choice, 286th overall, in 2004 Entry Draft).

			Regular Season					Playoffs				
Season	**Club**	**League**	**GP**	**G**	**A**	**Pts**	**PIM**	**GP**	**G**	**A**	**Pts**	**PIM**
2000-01	Neepawa Natives	MJHL	STATISTICS NOT AVAILABLE									
	Lethbridge	WHL	23	2	0	2	75	5	0	0	0	11
2001-02	Lethbridge	WHL	36	8	1	9	110	....	....	....	....	....
	Vancouver Giants	WHL	21	2	4	6	53	....	....	....	....	....
2002-03	Vancouver Giants	WHL	72	10	10	20	200	4	0	0	0	10
2003-04	Vancouver Giants	WHL	69	10	8	18	267	11	1	1	2	33
2004-05	Vancouver Giants	WHL	70	20	12	32	193	6	1	0	1	8

GRASBERG, Gustav (GRAHS-buhrg, GOO-stahv) NSH.

Center. Shoots left. 6', 193 lbs. Born, Furudal, Sweden, April 6, 1983.
(Nashville's 8th choice, 240th overall, in 2001 Entry Draft).

			Regular Season					Playoffs				
Season	**Club**	**League**	**GP**	**G**	**A**	**Pts**	**PIM**	**GP**	**G**	**A**	**Pts**	**PIM**
99-2000	Mora IK U18	Swe-U18	1	0	0	0	6	....	....	....	....	....
	Mora IK Jr.	Swe-Jr.	37	10	15	25	44	....	....	....	....	....
2000-01	Mora IK Jr.	Swe-Jr.	15	6	4	10	40	2	1	2	3	4
	Mora IK	Sweden-2	12	1	0	1	4	....	....	....	....	....
	Mora IK U18	Swe-U18	7	3	4	7	12	7	1	2	3	10
2001-02	Mora IK Jr.	Swe-Jr.	1	0	0	0	8	....	....	....	....	....
	Mora IK	Sweden-2	46	13	7	20	72	3	0	0	0	2
2002-03	Hammarby	Sweden-2	28	5	7	12	62	....	....	....	....	....
	Hammarby Jr.	Swe-Jr.	8	4	4	8	14	....	....	....	....	....
2003-04	Bofors	Sweden-2	46	2	6	8	66	5	0	0	0	0
2004-05	Halmstad	Sweden-2	42	6	6	12	22	2	1	0	1	0

GRATTON, Josh (grah-TOHN, JAWSH) PHI.

Left wing. Shoots left. 6'2", 210 lbs. Born, Scarborough, Ont., September 9, 1982.

			Regular Season					Playoffs				
Season	**Club**	**League**	**GP**	**G**	**A**	**Pts**	**PIM**	**GP**	**G**	**A**	**Pts**	**PIM**
2000-01	Sudbury Wolves	OHL	44	5	13	18	110	9	1	1	2	25
2001-02	Sudbury Wolves	OHL	14	5	4	9	47	....	....	....	....	....
	Kingston	OHL	46	14	14	28	140	1	1	0	1	7
2002-03	Windsor Spitfires	OHL	62	26	30	56	192	6	2	1	3	8
2003-04	Cincinnati	AHL	21	2	2	4	69	8	0	0	0	35
	San Diego Gulls	ECHL	30	4	6	10	239	....	....	....	....	....
2004-05	Philadelphia	AHL	57	9	5	14	246	21	3	3	6	78
	Trenton Titans	ECHL	1	0	0	0	0	....	....	....	....	....

Signed as a free agent by **Philadelphia**, July 27, 2004.

GRECO, Brady (GREH-koh, BRAY-dee) T.B.

Defense. Shoots right. 6'3", 195 lbs. Born, Bryan, OH, March 4, 1983.
(Tampa Bay's 8th choice, 256th overall, in 2003 Entry Draft).

			Regular Season					Playoffs				
Season	Club	League	GP	G	A	Pts	PIM	GP	G	A	Pts	PIM
1997/00	Edgewood	High-WI	66	29	33	62	....	....	....	....	....	....
2000-01	Billings Bulls	AWHL	STATISTICS NOT AVAILABLE									
2001-02	Michigan Tech	WCHA	24	1	9	10	28	....	....	....	....	....
2002-03	Chicago Steel	USHL	57	9	20	29	225	....	....	....	....	....
2003-04	Colorado College	WCHA	28	7	5	12	22	....	....	....	....	....
2004-05	Colorado College	WCHA	26	4	2	6	36	....	....	....	....	....

• Statistics for **Edgewood** (High-WI) are career totals for 1997-2000 seasons.

GREEN, Mike (GREEN, MIGHK) WSH.

Defense. Shoots right. 6'1", 198 lbs. Born, Calgary, Alta., October 12, 1985.
(Washington's 3rd choice, 29th overall, in 2004 Entry Draft).

			Regular Season					Playoffs				
Season	Club	League	GP	G	A	Pts	PIM	GP	G	A	Pts	PIM
2000-01	Cgy. North Stars	AMHL	36	4	23	27	34	....	....	....	....	....
	Saskatoon Blades	WHL	7	0	2	2	0	....	....	....	....	....
2001-02	Saskatoon Blades	WHL	62	3	20	23	57	7	0	1	1	2
2002-03	Saskatoon Blades	WHL	72	6	36	42	70	6	0	2	2	6
2003-04	Saskatoon Blades	WHL	59	14	25	39	92	....	....	....	....	....
2004-05	Saskatoon Blades	WHL	67	14	52	66	105	4	0	0	0	6

WHL East First All-Star Team (2005)

GREENE, Matt (GREEN, MAT) EDM.

Defense. Shoots right. 6'3", 223 lbs. Born, Grand Ledge, MI, May 13, 1983.
(Edmonton's 4th choice, 44th overall, in 2002 Entry Draft).

			Regular Season					Playoffs				
Season	Club	League	GP	G	A	Pts	PIM	GP	G	A	Pts	PIM
2000-01	USA U-18	USDP	54	0	10	10	59	....	....	....	....	....
2001-02	Green Bay	USHL	55	4	20	24	150	7	0	1	1	31
2002-03	North Dakota	WCHA	39	0	4	4	*135	....	....	....	....	....
2003-04	North Dakota	WCHA	40	1	16	17	86	....	....	....	....	....
2004-05	North Dakota	WCHA	43	2	8	10	*126	....	....	....	....	....

USHL Second All-Star Team (2002)

GREENING, Colin (GREEN-ihng, CAW-lihn) OTT.

Center/Left wing. Shoots left. 6'2", 191 lbs. Born, St. John's, Nfld., March 9, 1986.
(Ottawa's 8th choice, 204th overall, in 2005 Entry Draft).

			Regular Season					Playoffs				
Season	Club	League	GP	G	A	Pts	PIM	GP	G	A	Pts	PIM
2003-04	Upper Canada	High-ON	STATISTICS NOT AVAILABLE									
2004-05	Upper Canada	High-ON	35	24	22	46	24	....	....	....	....	....

GREER, Matt (GREER, MAT) CBJ

Wing. Shoots right. 6'2", 190 lbs. Born, St. Paul, MN, November 21, 1985.
(Columbus' 11th choice, 233rd overall, in 2004 Entry Draft).

			Regular Season					Playoffs				
Season	Club	League	GP	G	A	Pts	PIM	GP	G	A	Pts	PIM
2003-04	White Bear	High-MN	27	25	19	44	....	....	....	....	....	....
2004-05	Des Moines	USHL	60	14	18	32	16	....	....	....	....	....

Signed Letter of Intent to attend **Minnesota-Duluth** (WCHA) in fall of 2005.

GRENZY, Michael (GREHN-zee, MIGH-kuhl) CHI.

Defense. Shoots left. 6'4", 199 lbs. Born, Niagara Falls, NY, February 6, 1984.
(Chicago's 9th choice, 275th overall, in 2003 Entry Draft).

			Regular Season					Playoffs				
Season	Club	League	GP	G	A	Pts	PIM	GP	G	A	Pts	PIM
99-2000	Toronto Marlboros	MTHL	56	7	34	41	....	....	....	....	....	....
2000-01	USA U-17	USDP	69	0	1	1	23	....	....	....	....	....
2001-02	USA U-17	USDP	33	0	5	5	36	....	....	....	....	....
	USA U-18	USDP	18	0	1	1	2	....	....	....	....	....
2002-03	Chicago Steel	USHL	51	3	13	16	48	....	....	....	....	....
2003-04	Clarkson Knights	ECAC	22	2	3	5	36	....	....	....	....	....
2004-05	Clarkson Knights	ECAC	37	4	7	11	26	....	....	....	....	....

GRIGORENKO, Igor (grih-goh-REHN-koh, EE-gohr) DET.

Right wing. Shoots right. 5'10", 178 lbs. Born, Togliatti, USSR, April 9, 1983.
(Detroit's 1st choice, 62nd overall, in 2001 Entry Draft).

			Regular Season					Playoffs				
Season	Club	League	GP	G	A	Pts	PIM	GP	G	A	Pts	PIM
1998-99	Lada Togliatti 2	Russia-4	19	3	3	6	2	....	....	....	....	....
99-2000	Lada Togliatti 2	Russia-3	38	17	18	35	36	....	....	....	....	....
2000-01	Lada Togliatti 2	Russia-3	6	5	4	9	....	....	....	....	....	....
	CSK VVS Samara	Russia-2	39	10	10	20	....	....	....	....	....	....
	Lada Togliatti	Russia	....	....	....	....	....	5	1	0	1	4
2001-02	Lada Togliatti	Russia	41	8	9	17	58	4	1	0	1	2
2002-03	Lada Togliatti	Russia	47	19	11	30	82	10	1	*6	7	10
2003-04	Lada Togliatti 2	Russia-3	6	2	2	4	0	2	0	1	1	0
	Lada Togliatti	Russia	....	....	....	....	....	3	0	0	0	0
2004-05	Lada Togliatti	Russia	11	0	1	1	6	....	....	....	....	....
	Ufa	Russia	30	11	7	18	22	....	....	....	....	....

• Missed majority of 2003-04 season recovering from injuries suffered in automobile accident, May 16, 2003.

GROSSMAN, Nicklas (GROHS-man, NIH-kluhs) DAL.

Defense. Shoots left. 6'4", 187 lbs. Born, Stockholm, Sweden, January 22, 1985.
(Dallas' 4th choice, 56th overall, in 2004 Entry Draft).

			Regular Season					Playoffs				
Season	Club	League	GP	G	A	Pts	PIM	GP	G	A	Pts	PIM
2002-03	Sodertalje SK Jr.	Swe-Jr.	34	1	1	2	32	....	....	....	....	....
2003-04	Sodertalje SK Jr.	Swe-Jr.	33	1	2	3	32	2	0	0	0	0
	Sodertalje SK	Sweden	1	0	0	0	0	....	....	....	....	....
2004-05	Sodertalje SK Jr.	Swe-Jr.	12	3	6	9	8	1	0	0	0	0
	Sodertalje SK	Sweden	31	0	2	2	14	9	0	0	0	0

GROT, Denis (GROHT, DEH-nihs) VAN.

Defense. Shoots left. 6', 185 lbs. Born, Minsk, USSR, June 1, 1984.
(Vancouver's 2nd choice, 55th overall, in 2002 Entry Draft).

			Regular Season					Playoffs				
Season	Club	League	GP	G	A	Pts	PIM	GP	G	A	Pts	PIM
2000-01	Yaroslavl 2	Russia-3	34	5	1	6	10	....	....	....	....	....
	Russia	Nat-Tm	5	0	2	2	8	....	....	....	....	....
2001-02	Yaroslavl 2	Russia-3	14	1	0	1	10	....	....	....	....	....
	Elektrostal 2	Russia-3	3	0	1	1	2	....	....	....	....	....
	Elektrostal	Russia-2	33	1	1	2	42	....	....	....	....	....
2002-03	HK Lipetsk	Russia-2	27	4	4	8	28	....	....	....	....	....
2003-04	Yaroslavl	Russia	31	0	2	2	4	3	0	0	0	2
2004-05	Yaroslavl 2	Russia-3	20	2	3	5	22	....	....	....	....	....
	Yaroslavl	Russia	1	0	0	0	2	....	....	....	....	....
	Sibir Novosibirsk	Russia	23	0	4	4	32	....	....	....	....	....
	Amur Khabarovsk	Russia-2	9	1	5	6	2	12	0	0	0	31

GROULX, Danny (GROO, DA-nee)

Defense. Shoots left. 6', 205 lbs. Born, LaSalle, Que., June 23, 1981.

			Regular Season					Playoffs				
Season	Club	League	GP	G	A	Pts	PIM	GP	G	A	Pts	PIM
1996-97	Charles-Lemoyne	QAAA	40	2	26	28	....	15	3	15	18	....
1997-98	Val-d'Or Foreurs	QMJHL	63	4	16	20	61	19	1	4	5	18
1998-99	Val-d'Or Foreurs	QMJHL	36	3	26	29	55	....	....	....	....	....
	Acadie-Bathurst	QMJHL	36	2	15	17	51	18	0	2	2	6
99-2000	Victoriaville Tigres	QMJHL	66	12	55	67	131	6	0	4	4	14
2000-01	Victoriaville Tigres	QMJHL	72	16	71	87	164	13	2	19	21	46
2001-02	Victoriaville Tigres	QMJHL	68	29	83	112	165	22	9	*30	39	68
2002-03	Grand Rapids	AHL	71	3	7	10	52	7	0	1	1	7
2003-04	Grand Rapids	AHL	79	8	13	21	93	3	0	0	0	0
2004-05	Grand Rapids	AHL	53	1	11	12	90	....	....	....	....	....
	Manitoba Moose	AHL	16	2	6	8	16	13	1	3	4	14

QMJHL First All-Star Team (2001, 2002) • Canadian Major Junior First All-Star Team (2002) • Memorial Cup Tournament All-Star Team (2002) • Stafford Smythe Memorial Trophy (Memorial Cup Tournament MVP) (2002)

Signed as a free agent by **Detroit**, August 12, 2002. Loaned to **Manitoba** (AHL) by **Detroit** (Grand Rapids-AHL) for cash, March 15, 2005. Signed as a free agent by **Kassel** (Russia), August 25, 2005.

GUENETTE, Francois-Pierre (gwih-NEHT, frahn-SWUH-PEE-air) VAN.

Center. Shoots right. 6'1", 183 lbs. Born, Laval, Que., January 18, 1984.
(Vancouver's 7th choice, 222nd overall, in 2003 Entry Draft).

			Regular Season					Playoffs				
Season	Club	League	GP	G	A	Pts	PIM	GP	G	A	Pts	PIM
99-2000	Laval-Laurentides	QAAA	33	15	18	33	14	9	3	6	9	2
2000-01	Laval-Laurentides	QAAA	41	17	27	44	47	8	3	8	11	4
2001-02	Halifax	QMJHL	35	2	11	13	14	11	3	4	7	0
2002-03	Halifax	QMJHL	72	38	49	87	24	24	10	17	27	12
2003-04	Cape Breton	QMJHL	69	34	51	85	26	5	0	2	2	2
2004-05	Halifax	QMJHL	70	21	38	59	46	13	4	11	15	4

GUENIN, Nate (GEH-nihn, NAYT) NYR

Defense. Shoots right. 6'2", 211 lbs. Born, Sewickley, PA, December 10, 1982.
(NY Rangers' 3rd choice, 127th overall, in 2002 Entry Draft).

			Regular Season					Playoffs				
Season	Club	League	GP	G	A	Pts	PIM	GP	G	A	Pts	PIM
99-2000	Pittsburgh Hornets	AAHA	40	3	10	13	122	....	....	....	....	....
2000-01	Green Bay	USHL	54	2	11	13	70	4	1	1	2	6
2001-02	Green Bay	USHL	56	4	11	15	150	7	3	3	6	10
2002-03	Ohio State	CCHA	42	2	9	11	85	....	....	....	....	....
2003-04	Ohio State	CCHA	29	2	15	17	92	....	....	....	....	....
2004-05	Ohio State	CCHA	41	2	12	14	136	....	....	....	....	....

USHL All-Rookie Team (2001) • CCHA Second All-Star Team (2005)

GUERIN, Marty (GAIR-ihn, MAHR-tee) L.A.

Right wing. Shoots right. 6'1", 190 lbs. Born, Manchester, NH, May 25, 1983.
(Los Angeles' 10th choice, 274th overall, in 2003 Entry Draft).

			Regular Season					Playoffs				
Season	Club	League	GP	G	A	Pts	PIM	GP	G	A	Pts	PIM
2000-01	Omaha Lancers	USHL	42	3	5	8	24	7	0	0	0	0
2001-02	Omaha Lancers	USHL	31	12	11	33	16	....	....	....	....	....
	Des Moines	USHL	7	2	1	3	2	....	....	....	....	....
2002-03	Des Moines	USHL	60	27	33	60	30	4	1	3	4	6
2003-04	Miami U.	CCHA	41	14	19	33	18	....	....	....	....	....
2004-05	Miami U.	CCHA	34	15	18	33	42	....	....	....	....	....

GUGGISBERG, Peter (GUH-gihs-buhrg, PEE-tuhr) WSH.

Right wing. Shoots right. 5'11", 183 lbs. Born, Davos, Switz., January 20, 1985.
(Washington's 10th choice, 166th overall, in 2004 Entry Draft).

			Regular Season					Playoffs				
Season	Club	League	GP	G	A	Pts	PIM	GP	G	A	Pts	PIM
2000-01	Langnau Jr.	Swiss-Jr.	12	3	3	6	0	2	1	0	1	2
2001-02	Langnau Jr.	Swiss-Jr.	15	12	4	16	2	4	2	3	5	4
	Langnau	Swiss	....	....	....	....	....	6	0	1	1	0
2002-03	Langnau Jr.	Swiss-Jr.	10	7	10	17	0	5	2	1	3	32
	Langnau	Swiss	34	6	7	13	0	....	....	....	....	....
2003-04	HC Davos	Swiss	39	11	9	20	2	6	0	0	0	4
2004-05	HC Davos	Swiss	36	12	7	19	8	15	3	5	8	4

GUITE, Ben (GEE-tay, BEHN) BOS.

Right wing. Shoots right. 6'1", 205 lbs. Born, Montreal, Que., July 17, 1978.
(Montreal's 8th choice, 172nd overall, in 1997 Entry Draft).

			Regular Season					Playoffs				
Season	Club	League	GP	G	A	Pts	PIM	GP	G	A	Pts	PIM
1994-95	Lac St-Louis Lions	QAAA	40	9	12	21	....	4	0	0	0	0
1995-96	Capital District	Exhib.	STATISTICS NOT AVAILABLE									
1996-97	U. of Maine	H-East	34	7	7	14	21	....	....	....	....	....
1997-98	U. of Maine	H-East	32	6	12	18	20	....	....	....	....	....
1998-99	U. of Maine	H-East	40	12	16	28	30	....	....	....	....	....
99-2000	U. of Maine	H-East	40	22	14	36	36	....	....	....	....	....
2000-01	Tallahassee	ECHL	68	11	18	29	34	....	....	....	....	....
2001-02	Bridgeport	AHL	68	12	18	30	39	....	....	....	....	....
	Cincinnati	AHL	10	2	5	7	4	3	0	0	0	2
2002-03	Cincinnati	AHL	80	13	16	29	44	....	....	....	....	....
2003-04	Bridgeport	AHL	79	6	18	24	73	7	0	0	0	6
2004-05	Providence Bruins	AHL	77	9	15	24	69	17	3	4	7	34

Signed as a free agent by **NY Islanders**, August, 2001. Traded to **Anaheim** by **NY Islanders** with the rights to Bjorn Mellin for Dave Roche, March 19, 2002. Signed as a free agent by **NY Rangers**, September 16, 2003. Signed as a free agent by **Bridgeport** (AHL), October 10, 2003. Signed to a PTO (tryout) contract by **Providence** (AHL), September 28, 2004. Signed as a free agent by **Boston**, August 15, 2005.

GUSEV, Vladimir (GOO-sehv, vla-DIH-meer) CHI.

Defense. Shoots left. 6'2", 205 lbs. Born, Novosibirsk, USSR, November 24, 1982.
(Chicago's 6th choice, 115th overall, in 2001 Entry Draft).

			Regular Season					Playoffs				
Season	Club	League	GP	G	A	Pts	PIM	GP	G	A	Pts	PIM
99-2000	Novokuznetsk 2	Russia-3	21	1	0	1	52	....	....	....	....	....
	Magnitogorsk	Russia	....	....	....	....	....	3	0	0	0	0
2000-01	Amur Khabarovsk	Russia	1	0	0	0	0	....	....	....	....	....
	Sibir Novosibirsk 2	Russia-3	3	0	0	0	8	....	....	....	....	....
	Sibir Novosibirsk	Russia-2	1	0	0	0	0	....	....	....	....	....
	Omsk 2	Russia-3	4	1	0	1	4	....	....	....	....	....
2001-02	Sibir Novosibirsk	Russia-2	42	1	3	4	82	....	....	....	....	....
2002-03	Sibir Novosibirsk 2	Russia-3	28	6	12	18	42	....	....	....	....	....
2003-04	Norfolk Admirals	AHL	10	0	1	1	10	....	....	....	....	....
	Florence Pride	ECHL	55	5	9	14	59	....	....	....	....	....
2004-05	Norfolk Admirals	AHL	2	0	0	0	6	....	....	....	....	....
	Greenville Grrrowl	ECHL	70	8	11	19	113	4	0	0	0	6

GUSKOV, Alexander (goos-KAWF, ahl-ehx-AN-duhr) CBJ

Defense. Shoots left. 6'2", 202 lbs. Born, Nizhny Novgorod, USSR, November 26, 1976.
(Columbus' 8th choice, 200th overall, in 2003 Entry Draft).

			Regular Season					Playoffs				
Season	Club	League	GP	G	A	Pts	PIM	GP	G	A	Pts	PIM
1996-97	Motor Zavolzhje	Russia-2	32	3	3	6	20	....	....	....	....	....
1997-98	Motor Zavolzhje	Russia-2	24	2	4	6	26	....	....	....	....	....
	Lada Togliatti	Russia	10	0	1	1	8	....	....	....	....	....
1998-99	Chelyabinsk	Russia	11	2	0	2	4	....	....	....	....	....
	Lada Togliatti	Russia	30	1	3	4	10	5	0	0	0	4
99-2000	Nizhnekamsk	Russia	36	4	17	21	40	4	0	0	0	4
2000-01	Nizhnekamsk	Russia	43	4	9	13	24	4	0	0	0	0
2001-02	Yaroslavl	Russia	51	9	9	18	28	9	1	2	3	2
2002-03	Yaroslavl	Russia	48	10	17	27	32	10	1	1	2	6
2003-04	Yaroslavl	Russia	51	9	12	21	18	3	0	0	0	0
2004-05	Ak Bars Kazan	Russia	18	3	4	7	52	....	....	....	....	....
	Avangard Omsk	Russia	35	4	9	13	47	9	1	1	2	4

Signed as a free agent by **Kazan** (Russia), September, 2004. Signed as a free agent by **Omsk** (Russia), December, 2004.

GUTHRIE, Shea (GUHTH-ree, SHAY) NYI

Wing. Shoots right. 6', 187 lbs. Born, Almonte, Ont., July 30, 1987.
(NY Islanders' 3rd choice, 76th overall, in 2005 Entry Draft).

			Regular Season					Playoffs				
Season	Club	League	GP	G	A	Pts	PIM	GP	G	A	Pts	PIM
2004-05	St. George's	High-RI	25	31	26	57	20	....	....	....	....	....

Signed Letter of Intent to attend **Clarkson** (ECAC) in fall of 2005.

GUTIERREZ, Moises (gih-TAIR-ehz, MOI-zihs) PIT.

Right wing. Shoots right. 6'3", 201 lbs. Born, San Diego, CA, July 20, 1986.
(Pittsburgh's 8th choice, 164th overall, in 2004 Entry Draft).

			Regular Season					Playoffs				
Season	Club	League	GP	G	A	Pts	PIM	GP	G	A	Pts	PIM
2002-03	Kamloops Blazers	WHL	60	2	8	10	50	6	1	2	3	0
2003-04	Kamloops Blazers	WHL	71	7	12	19	107	5	1	0	1	6
2004-05	Kamloops Blazers	WHL	68	9	20	29	125	2	0	1	1	4

GUYER, Gino (GIGH-uhr, JEE-noh) DAL.

Center. Shoots left. 5'10", 184 lbs. Born, Grand Rapids, MN, October 14, 1983.
(Dallas' 7th choice, 165th overall, in 2003 Entry Draft).

			Regular Season					Playoffs				
Season	Club	League	GP	G	A	Pts	PIM	GP	G	A	Pts	PIM
2000-01	Lincoln Stars	USHL	5	2	2	4	2	10	3	5	8	0
2001-02	Greenway Raiders	High-MN	26	35	50	85	18	....	....	....	....	....
	Lincoln Stars	USHL	15	7	10	17	0	4	0	1	1	0
2002-03	U. of Minnesota	WCHA	41	13	16	29	10	....	....	....	....	....
2003-04	U. of Minnesota	WCHA	44	11	21	32	14	....	....	....	....	....
2004-05	U. of Minnesota	WCHA	44	12	20	32	10	....	....	....	....	....

HAFNER, Peter (HAF-nuhr, PEE-tuhr) FLA.

Defense. Shoots right. 6'5", 195 lbs. Born, Summit, NJ, July 26, 1983.
(Florida's 10th choice, 232nd overall, in 2002 Entry Draft).

			Regular Season					Playoffs				
Season	Club	League	GP	G	A	Pts	PIM	GP	G	A	Pts	PIM
2000-01	Taft Eagles	High-CT	24	1	9	10	12	....	....	....	....	....
2001-02	Taft Eagles	High-CT	26	2	19	21	20	....	....	....	....	....
2002-03	Harvard Crimson	ECAC	25	0	2	2	14	....	....	....	....	....
2003-04	Harvard Crimson	ECAC	35	1	6	7	16	....	....	....	....	....
2004-05	Harvard Crimson	ECAC	34	2	3	5	30	....	....	....	....	....

HAGEMO, Nathan (HAG-eh-moh, NAY-thuhn) CAR.

Defense. Shoots right. 5'11", 192 lbs. Born, Minneapolis, MN, October 8, 1986.
(Carolina's 2nd choice, 58th overall, in 2005 Entry Draft).

			Regular Season					Playoffs				
Season	Club	League	GP	G	A	Pts	PIM	GP	G	A	Pts	PIM
2002-03	USA U-17 & U-18	USDP	70	5	12	17	95	....	....	....	....	....
2003-04	USA U-18	USDP	51	8	19	27	59	....	....	....	....	....
2004-05	U. of Minnesota	WCHA	25	2	7	9	22	....	....	....	....	....

HAGGLUND, Johan (HAG-luhnd, YOH-hahn) T.B.

Center. Shoots left. 6'2", 203 lbs. Born, Ornskoldsvik, Sweden, June 9, 1982.
(Tampa Bay's 4th choice, 126th overall, in 2000 Entry Draft).

			Regular Season					Playoffs				
Season	Club	League	GP	G	A	Pts	PIM	GP	G	A	Pts	PIM
1998-99	Malmo Jr.	Swe-Jr.	28	16	22	38	52	....	....	....	....	....
99-2000	MoDo U18	Swe-U18	7	1	2	3	8	....	....	....	....	....
	Malmo Jr.	Swe-Jr.	35	7	10	17	75	2	1	0	1	0
2000-01	Malmo Jr.	Swe-Jr.	21	9	9	18	66	....	....	....	....	....
2001-02	HC Orebro 90	Sweden-2	36	6	4	10	50	....	....	....	....	....
2002-03	HC Orebro 90	Sweden-2	19	8	6	14	26	....	....	....	....	....
	Hammarby	Sweden-2	7	1	1	2	6	....	....	....	....	....
2003-04	Hammarby	Sweden-2	43	6	7	13	32	....	....	....	....	....
2004-05	Hammarby Jr.	Swe-Jr.	2	1	3	4	4	....	....	....	....	....
	Hammarby	Sweden-2	43	7	7	14	50	....	....	....	....	....

HAGOS, Yared (HA-gohs, YAIR-ehd) DAL.

Center. Shoots left. 6'1", 202 lbs. Born, Stockholm, Sweden, March 27, 1983.
(Dallas' 2nd choice, 70th overall, in 2001 Entry Draft).

			Regular Season					Playoffs				
Season	Club	League	GP	G	A	Pts	PIM	GP	G	A	Pts	PIM
1998-99	AIK Solna Jr.	Swe-Jr.	32	8	12	20	22	....	....	....	....	....
99-2000	AIK Solna U18	Swe-U18	13	4	6	10	6	....	....	....	....	....
	AIK Solna Jr.	Swe-Jr.	17	6	4	10	10	....	....	....	....	....
2000-01	AIK Solna Jr.	Swe-Jr.	24	8	13	21	46	2	2	1	3	2
	AIK Solna	Sweden	....	....	....	....	....	5	0	0	0	0
2001-02	AIK Solna Jr.	Swe-Jr.	1	0	3	3	2	1	0	2	2	0
	AIK Solna	Sweden	45	4	6	10	36	....	....	....	....	....
	AIK Solna	Sweden-Q	9	0	0	0	12	....	....	....	....	....
2002-03	AIK Solna	Sweden-2	49	10	22	32	67	4	0	1	1	2
	AIK Solna Jr.	Swe-Jr.	1	0	1	1	0	....	....	....	....	....
2003-04	Timra IK	Sweden	48	9	11	20	75	10	3	1	4	6
2004-05	Timra IK	Sweden	49	6	15	21	38	7	1	0	1	2

HAJEK, David (HIGH-ehk, DAV-vihd) CGY.

Defense. Shoots left. 5'11", 165 lbs. Born, Chomutov, Czech., June 13, 1980.
(Calgary's 8th choice, 239th overall, in 2000 Entry Draft).

			Regular Season					Playoffs				
Season	Club	League	GP	G	A	Pts	PIM	GP	G	A	Pts	PIM
1996-97	VTZ Chomutov Jr.	CzRep-Jr.	36	8	14	22	30	4	0	0	0	2
1997-98	VTZ Chomutov Jr.	CzRep-Jr.	36	3	9	12	18	....	....	....	....	....
1998-99	Melville	SJHL	25	10	19	29	....	....	....	....	....	....
	Spokane Chiefs	WHL	27	0	3	3	10	....	....	....	....	....
99-2000	KLH Chomutov Jr.	CzRep-Jr.	7	1	5	6	14	....	....	....	....	....
	KLH Chomutov	CzRep-2	28	1	5	6	14	12	1	3	4	10
2000-01	Kladno	CzRep	40	1	1	2	66	....	....	....	....	....
2001-02	Kladno	CzRep	48	0	7	7	16	5	0	1	1	4
2002-03	Kladno	CzRep-2	4	0	0	0	0	....	....	....	....	....
	Hr. Kralove	CzRep-2	4	0	1	1	4	....	....	....	....	....
	Hradec Kralove	Czech-Q	6	0	1	1	2	....	....	....	....	....
2003-04	Karlovy Vary	CzRep	33	2	5	7	6	....	....	....	....	....
	KLH Chomutov	CzRep-2	13	1	3	4	12	....	....	....	....	....
2004-05	KLH Chomutov	CzRep-2	45	11	18	29	68	10	0	4	4	8

HALVARDSSON, Johan (HAL-vahrds-sohn, YOH-hahn) NYI

Defense. Shoots left. 6'3", 198 lbs. Born, Jonkoping, Sweden, December 26, 1979.
(NY Islanders' 8th choice, 102nd overall, in 1999 Entry Draft).

			Regular Season					Playoffs				
Season	Club	League	GP	G	A	Pts	PIM	GP	G	A	Pts	PIM
1997-98	HV 71 Jr.	Swe-Jr.	28	5	5	10	65	....	....	....	....	....
1998-99	HV 71 Jonkoping	Sweden	17	1	2	3	33	....	....	....	....	....
99-2000	HV 71 Jonkoping	Sweden	46	0	3	3	75	5	0	0	0	8
2000-01	HV 71 Jonkoping	Sweden	33	0	0	0	24	....	....	....	....	....
2001-02	HV 71 Jonkoping	Sweden	3	0	0	0	0	....	....	....	....	....
2002-03	HV 71 Jonkoping	Sweden	39	0	1	1	14	7	0	0	0	0
2003-04	HV 71 Jonkoping	Sweden	11	0	4	4	39	17	1	3	4	41
	IK Oskarshamn	Sweden-2	32	3	4	7	94	....	....	....	....	....
2004-05	HV 71 Jonkoping	Sweden	36	2	3	5	46	....	....	....	....	....

• Missed majority of 2001-02 season recovering from knee injury suffered in game vs. Sodertalje (Sweden), September 23, 2001.

HAMALAINEN, Ville (ha-muh-LAY-nuhn, VIHL-ee) CGY.

Left wing. Shoots left. 5'11", 178 lbs. Born, Lappeenranta, Finland, July 6, 1981.
(Calgary's 11th choice, 251st overall, in 2001 Entry Draft).

			Regular Season					Playoffs				
Season	Club	League	GP	G	A	Pts	PIM	GP	G	A	Pts	PIM
1997-98	SaiPa Jr.	Finland-Jr.	31	8	27	35	24	....	....	....	....	....
1998-99	SaiPa Jr.	Finland-Jr.	12	6	26	32	26	14	10	12	22	22
	SaiPa	Finland	12	1	0	1	8	....	....	....	....	....
99-2000	SaiPa	Finland	47	6	4	10	20	....	....	....	....	....
	KooKoo Kouvola	Finland-2	3	0	1	1	2	....	....	....	....	....
	SaiPa Jr.	Finland-Jr.	1	2	2	4	2	2	1	1	2	2
2000-01	SaiPa	Finland	42	0	4	4	10	....	....	....	....	....
	SaiPa Jr.	Finland-Jr.	1	1	1	2	0	....	....	....	....	....
2001-02	SaiPa	Finland	51	4	9	13	24	....	....	....	....	....
	SaiPa Jr.	Finland-Jr.	5	4	4	8	2	9	5	6	11	18
2002-03	FPS Forssa	Finland-2	13	4	8	12	6	....	....	....	....	....
	Tappara Tampere	Finland	35	1	2	3	6	6	0	0	0	2
2003-04	KalPa Kuopio	Finland-2	45	21	25	46	36	11	0	7	7	6
2004-05	KalPa Kuopio	Finland-2	44	13	27	40	40	9	2	7	9	2

HAMILTON, Mike (HAM-ihl-tuhn, MIGHK) **ATL.**

Forward. Shoots left. 6'1", 200 lbs. Born, Vancouver, B.C., May 2, 1983.
(Atlanta's 6th choice, 175th overall, in 2003 Entry Draft).

			Regular Season					Playoffs				
Season	**Club**	**League**	**GP**	**G**	**A**	**Pts**	**PIM**	**GP**	**G**	**A**	**Pts**	**PIM**
99-2000	Peninsula Panthers	VIJHL	44	33	42	75	94	....	....	....	....	....
2000-01	Peninsula Panthers	VIJHL	19	15	20	35	106	....	....	....	....	....
	Victoria Salsa	BCHL	31	2	5	7	18	....	....	....	....	....
2001-02	Victoria Salsa	BCHL	13	5	2	7	14	....	....	....	....	....
	Merritt	BCHL	45	23	36	59	64	....	....	....	....	....
2002-03	Merritt	BCHL	56	42	51	95	133	....	....	....	....	....
2003-04	U. of Maine	H-East	29	7	6	13	40	....	....	....	....	....
2004-05	U. of Maine	H-East	38	3	15	18	49	....	....	....	....	....

HANNULA, Mika (HAH-noo-lah, MEE-kah) **MIN.**

Right wing. Shoots left. 5'11", 180 lbs. Born, Huddinge, Sweden, April 2, 1979.
(Minnesota's 10th choice, 269th overall, in 2002 Entry Draft).

			Regular Season					Playoffs				
Season	**Club**	**League**	**GP**	**G**	**A**	**Pts**	**PIM**	**GP**	**G**	**A**	**Pts**	**PIM**
1996-97	AIK Solna Jr.	Swe-Jr.	26	4	4	8	58	....	....	....	....	....
1997-98	Djurgarden Jr.	Swe-Jr.	14	10	6	16	22	2	1	1	2	0
	Lukko Rauma Jr.	Finland-Jr.	6	2	0	2	36	....	....	....	....	....
1998-99	Lidingo HC	Sweden-2	32	10	0	10	47	....	....	....	....	....
99-2000	Hammarby	Sweden-2	43	10	10	20	53	2	0	0	0	2
2000-01	Malmo Jr.	Swe-Jr.	1	1	1	2	0	....	....	....	....	....
	Malmo	Sweden	45	2	9	11	26	8	3	2	5	14
2001-02	Malmo	Sweden	41	10	7	17	14	5	2	1	3	0
2002-03	Malmo	Sweden	49	15	15	30	72	....	....	....	....	....
2003-04	Houston Aeros	AHL	67	9	18	27	59	....	....	....	....	....
2004-05	Malmo	Sweden	47	14	9	23	71	....	....	....	....	....

Signed as a free agent by **Malmo** (Sweden), May 12, 2004.

HANNUS, Tommi (HA-nuhs, TAW-mee) **L.A.**

Left wing. Shoots right. 6', 180 lbs. Born, Vantaa, Finland, June 27, 1980.
(Los Angeles' 7th choice, 190th overall, in 1998 Entry Draft).

			Regular Season					Playoffs				
Season	**Club**	**League**	**GP**	**G**	**A**	**Pts**	**PIM**	**GP**	**G**	**A**	**Pts**	**PIM**
1995-96	TPS Turku U18	Fin-U18	1	1	0	1	2	....	....	....	....	....
1996-97	TPS Turku Jr.	Finland-Jr.	27	7	7	14	6	....	....	....	....	....
	TPS Turku U18	Fin-U18	18	7	7	14	6	6	4	2	6	10
1997-98	TPS Turku Jr.	Finland-Jr.	19	6	3	9	4	....	....	....	....	....
	TPS Turku U18	Fin-U18	9	5	4	9	8	....	....	....	....	....
1998-99	TPS Turku Jr.	Finland-Jr.	8	5	4	9	22	....	....	....	....	....
	TuTo Turku	Finland-2	18	6	4	10	16	8	0	2	2	8
99-2000	TPS Turku Jr.	Finland-Jr.	3	4	3	7	6	....	....	....	....	....
	TuTo Turku	Finland-2	27	11	6	17	20	....	....	....	....	....
	Assat Pori	Finland	13	1	0	1	4	....	....	....	....	....
2000-01	TuTo Turku	Finland-2	29	9	8	17	16	11	*7	7	14	*24
2001-02	TPS Turku	Finland	47	4	2	6	6	3	1	0	1	0
2002-03	Jokerit Helsinki	Finland	31	1	0	1	25	....	....	....	....	....
	Kiekko-Vantaa	Finland-2	14	7	7	14	4	12	3	5	8	8
2003-04	Pelicans Lahti	Finland	55	15	4	19	20	....	....	....	....	....
2004-05	Pelicans Lahti	Finland	53	17	5	22	32	....	....	....	....	....

HANSEN, Jannik (HAHN-suhn, YAH-nih) **VAN.**

Wing. Shoots right. 6', 176 lbs. Born, Herlev, Denmark, March 15, 1986.
(Vancouver's 7th choice, 287th overall, in 2004 Entry Draft).

			Regular Season					Playoffs				
Season	**Club**	**League**	**GP**	**G**	**A**	**Pts**	**PIM**	**GP**	**G**	**A**	**Pts**	**PIM**
2002-03	Rodovre	Denmark	15	0	0	0	0	....	....	....	....	....
	Malmo U18	Swe-U18	12	8	7	15	2	3	2	0	2	0
2003-04	Rodovre	Denmark	35	12	7	19	48	....	....	....	....	....
2004-05	Rodovre	Denmark	32	17	17	34	40	5	3	1	4	24

HANZAL, Martin (HAHN-zuhl, MAHR-tihn) **PHX.**

Center. Shoots left. 6'5", 200 lbs. Born, Pisek, Czech., February 20, 1987.
(Phoenix's 1st choice, 17th overall, in 2005 Entry Draft).

			Regular Season					Playoffs				
Season	**Club**	**League**	**GP**	**G**	**A**	**Pts**	**PIM**	**GP**	**G**	**A**	**Pts**	**PIM**
2002-03	C. Budejovice U17	CzR-U17	47	24	30	54	28	7	1	3	4	25
2003-04	C. Budejovice U17	CzR-U17	2	0	2	2	2	2	1	0	1	4
	C. Budejovice Jr.	CzRep-Jr.	53	15	7	22	32	....	....	....	....	....
2004-05	C. Budejovice Jr.	CzRep-Jr.	37	22	22	44	80	2	1	2	3	2
	C. Budejovice	CzRep-2	15	1	2	3	2	6	0	0	0	6

HARANT, Tomas (HAH-rant, TAW-mahsh) **NSH.**

Defense. Shoots left. 6'3", 201 lbs. Born, Zilina, Czech., April 28, 1980.
(Nashville's 8th choice, 173rd overall, in 2000 Entry Draft).

			Regular Season					Playoffs				
Season	**Club**	**League**	**GP**	**G**	**A**	**Pts**	**PIM**	**GP**	**G**	**A**	**Pts**	**PIM**
1995-96	HKP Zilina Jr.	Slovak-Jr.	46	3	9	12	142	....	....	....	....	....
1996-97	HKP Zilina Jr.	Slovak-Jr.	44	1	4	5	18	....	....	....	....	....
1997-98	HK SKP Zilina Jr.	Slovak-Jr.	41	5	7	12	72	....	....	....	....	....
	HK SKP Zilina	Slovak-2	5	0	0	0	0	....	....	....	....	....
1998-99	HK SKP Zilina Jr.	Slovak-Jr.	33	1	6	7	108	....	....	....	....	....
99-2000	HK SKP PChZ Zilina	Slovak-2	26	0	3	3	34	....	....	....	....	....
2000-01	HC Trinec Jr.	CzRep-Jr.	5	1	2	3	8	1	0	0	0	4
	HC Ocelari Trinec	CzRep	15	1	2	3	14	....	....	....	....	....
2001-02	MsHK SKP Zilina	Slovakia	51	2	3	5	46	4	0	0	0	4
2002-03	Havirov	CzRep	19	0	1	1	40	....	....	....	....	....
	MsHK SKP Zilina	Slovakia	28	2	3	5	86	4	1	0	1	24
2003-04	Dynamo Moscow	Russia	31	1	0	1	18	3	0	0	0	0
2004-05	Dynamo Moscow	Russia	1	0	0	0	2	....	....	....	....	....
	Karlovy Vary	CzRep	37	1	5	6	57	....	....	....	....	....

HARIKKALA, Jaakko (HAHR-ee-kuh-lah, YAH-koh) **BOS.**

Defense. Shoots left. 6'2", 215 lbs. Born, Kalanti, Finland, March 30, 1981.
(Boston's 4th choice, 118th overall, in 1999 Entry Draft).

			Regular Season					Playoffs				
Season	**Club**	**League**	**GP**	**G**	**A**	**Pts**	**PIM**	**GP**	**G**	**A**	**Pts**	**PIM**
1997-98	Jaa-Kotkat	Finland-2	5	0	2	2	8	....	....	....	....	....
	Jaa-Kotkat	Finland-2	45	2	6	8	65	....	....	....	....	....
1998-99	Lukko Rauma Jr.	Finland-Jr.	11	1	3	4	22	....	....	....	....	....
	Lukko Rauma	Finland	35	0	0	0	10	....	....	....	....	....
99-2000	Lukko Rauma	Finland	24	0	0	0	2	....	....	....	....	....
	Lukko Rauma Jr.	Finland-Jr.	19	1	8	9	40	7	1	1	2	31
2000-01	Lukko Rauma Jr.	Finland-Jr.	2	2	0	2	2	....	....	....	....	....
	Jaa-Kotkat	Finland-2	10	0	2	2	16	....	....	....	....	....
	Lukko Rauma	Finland	10	0	0	0	0	....	....	....	....	....
2001-02	Lukko Rauma	Finland	47	4	8	12	40	....	....	....	....	....
	Lukko Rauma Jr.	Finland-Jr.	3	0	1	1	0	....	....	....	....	....
2002-03	Lukko Rauma	Finland	54	7	6	13	48	....	....	....	....	....
2003-04	Lukko Rauma	Finland	55	4	4	8	26	4	0	0	0	0
2004-05	Lukko Rauma	Finland	36	1	0	1	18	3	0	0	0	0

HARRISON, Jay (HAIR-ih-suhn, JAY) **TOR.**

Defense. Shoots left. 6'4", 211 lbs. Born, Oshawa, Ont., November 3, 1982.
(Toronto's 4th choice, 82nd overall, in 2001 Entry Draft).

			Regular Season					Playoffs				
Season	**Club**	**League**	**GP**	**G**	**A**	**Pts**	**PIM**	**GP**	**G**	**A**	**Pts**	**PIM**
1997-98	Oshawa	OHA-B	42	1	11	12	143	....	....	....	....	....
1998-99	Brampton	OHL	63	1	14	15	108	....	....	....	....	....
99-2000	Brampton	OHL	68	2	18	20	139	6	0	2	2	15
2000-01	Brampton	OHL	53	4	15	19	112	9	1	1	2	17
2001-02	Brampton	OHL	61	12	31	43	116	....	....	....	....	....
	St. John's	AHL	7	0	1	1	2	10	0	0	0	4
	Memphis	CHL	....	....	....	....	....	1	0	0	0	2
2002-03	St. John's	AHL	72	2	8	10	72	....	....	....	....	....
2003-04	St. John's	AHL	70	4	5	9	141	....	....	....	....	....
2004-05	St. John's	AHL	60	0	4	4	108	4	0	1	1	14

OHL All-Rookie Team (1999)

HARTSBURG, Chris (HAHRTZ-buhrg, KRIHS)

Right wing. Shoots right. 6', 200 lbs. Born, Edina, MN, May 30, 1980.
(New Jersey's 7th choice, 214th overall, in 1999 Entry Draft).

			Regular Season					Playoffs				
Season	**Club**	**League**	**GP**	**G**	**A**	**Pts**	**PIM**	**GP**	**G**	**A**	**Pts**	**PIM**
1995-96	Cambridge	OHA-B	46	12	15	27	10	....	....	....	....	....
1996-97	Cambridge	OHA-B	47	14	19	33	29	....	....	....	....	....
1997-98	Omaha Lancers	USHL	54	16	19	35	58	12	2	2	4	20
1998-99	Colorado College	WCHA	34	6	4	10	60	....	....	....	....	....
99-2000	Colorado College	WCHA	33	3	2	5	50	....	....	....	....	....
2000-01	Colorado College	WCHA	41	8	7	15	38	....	....	....	....	....
2001-02	Colorado College	WCHA	40	14	8	22	50	....	....	....	....	....
2002-03	Albany River Rats	AHL	40	7	3	10	22	....	....	....	....	....
2003-04	Albany River Rats	AHL	51	4	5	9	26	....	....	....	....	....
2004-05	Colorado Eagles	CHL	46	13	16	29	60	16	3	9	12	26

CHL Playoff MVP (2005)

Signed as a free agent by **Colorado** (CHL), September 28, 2004.

HASKINS, Tyler (HA-skihns, TIGH-luhr) **DET.**

Center. Shoots right. 6'1", 177 lbs. Born, Cleveland, OH, May 26, 1986.
(Detroit's 4th choice, 162nd overall, in 2004 Entry Draft).

			Regular Season					Playoffs				
Season	**Club**	**League**	**GP**	**G**	**A**	**Pts**	**PIM**	**GP**	**G**	**A**	**Pts**	**PIM**
2001-02	Sioux City	USHL	46	3	8	11	20	12	1	0	1	15
2002-03	Guelph Storm	OHL	54	7	14	21	14	11	3	2	5	10
2003-04	Guelph Storm	OHL	9	1	3	4	2	....	....	....	....	....
	St. Michael's	OHL	54	17	24	41	30	18	5	4	9	10
2004-05	St. Michael's	OHL	62	12	20	32	64	10	6	4	10	20

HAVEL, Marian (HAH-vuhl, MAIR-ee-uhn) **WSH.**

Center/Left wing. Shoots left. 6', 180 lbs. Born, Jihlava, Czech., January 26, 1984.
(Washington's 10th choice, 179th overall, in 2002 Entry Draft).

			Regular Season					Playoffs				
Season	**Club**	**League**	**GP**	**G**	**A**	**Pts**	**PIM**	**GP**	**G**	**A**	**Pts**	**PIM**
99-2000	Jihlava Jr.	CzRep-Jr.	50	35	22	57	70	....	....	....	....	....
	Sioux City	USHL	4	0	1	1	0	....	....	....	....	....
2000-01	Jihlava U17	CzR-U17	7	11	18	29	36	....	....	....	....	....
	Jihlava Jr.	CzRep-Jr.	14	9	10	19	64	....	....	....	....	....
	HC Dukla Jihlava	CzRep-2	26	2	2	4	14	....	....	....	....	....
2001-02	Vancouver Giants	WHL	67	17	16	33	83	....	....	....	....	....
2002-03	Vancouver Giants	WHL	5	1	2	3	12	....	....	....	....	....
	Swift Current	WHL	56	8	19	27	46	4	0	0	0	2
2003-04	Plzen	CzRep	2	0	0	0	2	....	....	....	....	....
	HC Dukla Jihlava	CzRep-2	31	3	3	6	8	15	2	1	3	8
2004-05	Jihlava Jr.	CzRep-Jr.	39	27	32	59	182	....	....	....	....	....
	HC Dukla Jihlava	CzRep	30	0	2	2	8	....	....	....	....	....

HAVELKA, Petr (huh-VEHL-kah, PEE-tuhr) **PIT.**

Left wing. Shoots left. 6'2", 185 lbs. Born, Most, Czech., March 4, 1979.
(Pittsburgh's 6th choice, 152nd overall, in 1997 Entry Draft).

			Regular Season					Playoffs				
Season	**Club**	**League**	**GP**	**G**	**A**	**Pts**	**PIM**	**GP**	**G**	**A**	**Pts**	**PIM**
1995-96	Sparta Jr.	CzRep-Jr.	40	15	10	25	....	....	....	....	....	....
1996-97	Sparta Jr.	CzRep-Jr.	22	14	13	27	....	....	....	....	....	....
	HC Sparta Praha	CzRep	....	....	....	....	....	1	0	0	0	0
1997-98	Sparta Jr.	CzRep-Jr.	DID NOT PLAY – INJURED									
1998-99	Sparta Jr.	CzRep-Jr.	5	7	3	10	....	4	1	1	2	....
	HC Velvana Kladno	CzRep	5	0	0	0	0	....	....	....	....	....
99-2000	Sparta Jr.	CzRep-Jr.	2	1	0	1	0	....	....	....	....	....
	Beroun	CzRep-2	5	2	4	6	29	....	....	....	....	....
	HC Velvana Kladno	CzRep	6	1	2	3	2	....	....	....	....	....
	HC Sparta Praha	CzRep	10	0	1	1	0	3	0	0	0	0
2000-01	Beroun	CzRep-2	3	0	0	0	0	....	....	....	....	....
	HC Sparta Praha	CzRep	....	....	....	....	....	7	1	0	1	2
2001-02	Sparta Jr.	CzRep-Jr.	2	1	0	1	0	....	....	....	....	....
	Usti n. L.	CzRep-3	2	0	0	0	2	....	....	....	....	....
	HC Sparta Praha	CzRep	35	3	4	7	12	6	0	0	0	2
2002-03	HC Sparta Praha	CzRep	47	10	6	16	38	8	1	3	4	0
2003-04	HC Sparta Praha	CzRep	6	1	1	2	2	....	....	....	....	....
	BK Mlada Boleslav	CzRep-2	3	1	2	3	2	....	....	....	....	....
2004-05	Plzen	CzRep	8	1	1	2	10	....	....	....	....	....
	C. Budejovice	CzRep-2	33	3	4	7	18	16	1	0	1	4

HEALEY, Eric (HEE-lee, AIR-ihk) BOS.

Left wing. Shoots left. 6', 196 lbs. Born, Hull, MA, January 20, 1975.

			Regular Season					Playoffs				
Season	Club	League	GP	G	A	Pts	PIM	GP	G	A	Pts	PIM
1993-94	New England	NEJHL	37	61	76	137	....	....	....	....	....	....
1994-95	RPI Engineers	ECAC	37	13	11	24	35	....	....	....	....	....
1995-96	RPI Engineers	ECAC	35	18	22	40	57	....	....	....	....	....
1996-97	RPI Engineers	ECAC	36	30	26	56	63	....	....	....	....	....
1997-98	RPI Engineers	ECAC	35	21	27	48	42	....	....	....	....	....
1998-99	Saint John Flames	AHL	64	14	24	38	77	....	....	....	....	....
	Orlando	IHL	13	5	4	9	13	8	1	0	1	12
99-2000	Springfield Falcons	AHL	32	14	15	29	51	1	0	0	0	2
2000-01	Springfield Falcons	AHL	66	16	17	33	53	....	....	....	....	....
2001-02	Manchester	AHL	65	24	34	58	45	5	2	2	4	8
	Jackson Bandits	ECHL	2	1	1	2	0	....	....	....	....	....
2002-03	Manchester	AHL	75	*42	31	73	47	3	1	0	1	2
2003-04	Chicago Wolves	AHL	71	31	20	51	52	10	3	6	9	10
2004-05	Adler Mannheim	Germany	50	16	13	29	54	13	2	4	6	12

ECAC Second All-Star Team (1997) • NCAA East Second All-American Team (1997, 1998) • ECAC First All-Star Team (1998) • Fred T. Hunt Memorial Award (Sportsmanship – AHL) (2003) (co-winner - Chris Ferraro)

Signed as a free agent by **Calgary**, September 22, 1998. Signed as a free agent by **Phoenix**, July 26, 1999. Signed to a PTO (try-out) contract by **Manchester** (AHL), September 30, 2001. Signed as a free agent by **Atlanta**, August 12, 2003. Signed as a free agent by **Mannheim** (Germany), July 9, 2004. Signed as a free agent by **Boston**, August 15, 2005.

HEDLUND, Andy (HEHD-luhnd, AN-dee)

Defense. Shoots left. 6'3", 215 lbs. Born, Osseo, MN, May 16, 1978.

			Regular Season					Playoffs				
Season	Club	League	GP	G	A	Pts	PIM	GP	G	A	Pts	PIM
1997-98	Fargo-Moorhead	USHL	56	4	12	16	135	4	0	4	4	0
1998-99	Minnesota State	WCHA	34	1	2	3	34	....	....	....	....	....
99-2000	Minnesota State	WCHA	36	4	2	6	58	....	....	....	....	....
2000-01	Minnesota State	WCHA	38	6	6	12	64	....	....	....	....	....
2001-02	Minnesota State	WCHA	37	5	10	15	48	....	....	....	....	....
	Trenton Titans	ECHL	2	0	0	0	0	6	0	0	0	6
2002-03	Trenton Titans	ECHL	13	1	2	3	14	....	....	....	....	....
	Binghamton	AHL	59	1	7	8	48	10	0	0	0	0
2003-04	Binghamton	AHL	80	4	19	23	108	2	0	0	0	2
2004-05	Binghamton	AHL	75	2	13	15	103	6	0	2	2	25

Signed as a free agent by **Trenton** (ECHL), March 28, 2002. Signed as a free agent by **Binghamton** (AHL), November 3, 2002. Signed as a free agent by **Ottawa**, December 18, 2003.

HEDMAN, Anton (HEHD-man, AN-tawn) BOS.

Forward. Shoots left. 6', 180 lbs. Born, Stockholm, Sweden, May 15, 1986.
(Boston's 7th choice, 255th overall, in 2004 Entry Draft).

			Regular Season					Playoffs				
Season	Club	League	GP	G	A	Pts	PIM	GP	G	A	Pts	PIM
2003-04	Stocksund Jr.	Swe-Jr.	14	5	5	10	14	....	....	....	....	....
2004-05	Djurgarden Jr.	Swe-Jr.	32	14	9	23	119	....	....	....	....	....

HEDMAN, Oscar (HEHD-man, AWS-kuhr) WSH.

Defense. Shoots left. 6', 209 lbs. Born, Ornskoldsvik, Sweden, April 21, 1986.
(Washington's 8th choice, 132nd overall, in 2004 Entry Draft).

			Regular Season					Playoffs				
Season	Club	League	GP	G	A	Pts	PIM	GP	G	A	Pts	PIM
2002-03	MODO U18	Swe-U18	14	4	5	9	8	6	2	1	3	32
	Malmo Jr.	Swe-Jr.	5	0	1	1	2	....	....	....	....	....
2003-04	Malmo Jr.	Swe-Jr.	25	7	11	18	28	8	3	3	6	6
	MODO U18	Swe-U18	3	3	1	4	2	2	0	3	3	0
	MODO	Sweden	24	1	2	3	6	6	0	0	0	0
2004-05	MODO Jr.	Swe-Jr.	7	2	2	4	12	5	0	1	1	4
	MODO	Sweden	43	1	3	4	18	4	0	0	0	0

HEID, Chris (HIGHD, KRIHS) MIN.

Defense. Shoots left. 6'2", 205 lbs. Born, Langley, B.C., March 14, 1983.
(Minnesota's 3rd choice, 74th overall, in 2001 Entry Draft).

			Regular Season					Playoffs				
Season	Club	League	GP	G	A	Pts	PIM	GP	G	A	Pts	PIM
1998-99	Kamloops	BCAHA	58	26	34	60	65	....	....	....	....	....
	Spokane Chiefs	WHL	1	0	0	0	0	....	....	....	....	....
99-2000	Spokane Chiefs	WHL	44	1	7	8	25	6	0	0	0	4
2000-01	Spokane Chiefs	WHL	51	2	15	17	76	12	0	4	4	12
2001-02	Spokane Chiefs	WHL	69	7	28	35	56	11	1	4	5	8
2002-03	Spokane Chiefs	WHL	60	9	36	45	66	11	2	11	13	10
2003-04	Houston Aeros	AHL	58	3	10	13	35	....	....	....	....	....
2004-05	Houston Aeros	AHL	19	0	5	5	20	....	....	....	....	....
	Louisiana	ECHL	17	2	6	8	14	....	....	....	....	....
	Pensacola	ECHL	....	....	....	....	....	4	0	1	1	2

HEJDA, Jan (HAY-dah, YAHN) BUF.

Defense. Shoots left. 6'3", 209 lbs. Born, Prague, Czech., June 18, 1978.
(Buffalo's 4th choice, 106th overall, in 2003 Entry Draft).

			Regular Season					Playoffs				
Season	Club	League	GP	G	A	Pts	PIM	GP	G	A	Pts	PIM
1997-98	HC Slavia Praha	CzRep	44	2	5	7	51	5	0	0	0	6
1998-99	HC Slavia Praha	CzRep	34	1	2	3	38	....	....	....	....	....
99-2000	HC Slavia Praha	CzRep	26	1	2	3	14	....	....	....	....	....
	HC Femax Havirov	CzRep	7	0	2	2	6	....	....	....	....	....
	HC Stadion Liberec	CzRep-2	1	0	0	0	4	....	....	....	....	....
2000-01	HC Slavia Praha	CzRep	38	2	6	8	70	11	3	0	3	12
	SK Kadan	CzRep-2	8	1	0	1	6	....	....	....	....	....
2001-02	HC Slavia Praha	CzRep	42	9	8	17	52	9	1	1	2	14
2002-03	HC Slavia Praha	CzRep	52	6	11	17	44	17	5	8	13	12
2003-04	CSKA Moscow	Russia	60	1	5	6	26	....	....	....	....	....
2004-05	CSKA Moscow	Russia	60	2	11	13	59	....	....	....	....	....

HELBLING, Timo (HEHL-blihng, TEE-moh) T.B.

Defense. Shoots right. 6'3", 209 lbs. Born, Basel, Switz., July 21, 1981.
(Nashville's 11th choice, 162nd overall, in 1999 Entry Draft).

			Regular Season					Playoffs				
Season	Club	League	GP	G	A	Pts	PIM	GP	G	A	Pts	PIM
1997-98	HC Davos Jr.	Swiss-Jr.	34	6	6	12	38	....	....	....	....	....
1998-99	HC Davos Jr.	Swiss-Jr.	28	5	10	15	116	2	1	3	4	35
	HC Davos	Swiss	44	0	0	0	8	4	0	0	0	0
99-2000	HC Davos	Swiss	44	0	0	0	49	5	0	0	0	0
2000-01	Windsor Spitfires	OHL	54	7	14	21	90	7	0	2	2	11
	Milwaukee	IHL	....	....	....	....	....	1	0	0	0	0
2001-02	Milwaukee	AHL	67	2	6	8	59	....	....	....	....	....
2002-03	Milwaukee	AHL	23	0	1	1	37	....	....	....	....	....
	Toledo Storm	ECHL	35	3	8	11	75	7	0	1	1	2
2003-04	Milwaukee	AHL	37	0	2	2	46	....	....	....	....	....
	Utah Grizzlies	AHL	23	3	2	5	47	....	....	....	....	....
2004-05	Kloten Flyers	Swiss	44	2	9	11	120	5	1	3	4	8

Traded to **Tampa Bay** by **Nashville** for Tampa Bay's 8th round choice (Pekka Rinne) in 2004 Entry Draft, February 25, 2004. Signed as a free agent by **Kloten** (Swiss), June 17, 2004.

HELFENSTEIN, Sven (hehl-fehn-SHTIGHN, SVEHN) NYR

Left wing. Shoots right. 5'10", 176 lbs. Born, Winterthur, Switz., July 30, 1982.
(NY Rangers' 6th choice, 175th overall, in 2000 Entry Draft).

			Regular Season					Playoffs				
Season	Club	League	GP	G	A	Pts	PIM	GP	G	A	Pts	PIM
1997-98	EHC Kloten Jr.	Swiss-Jr.	31	6	8	14	14	....	....	....	....	....
1998-99	EHC Kloten Jr.	Swiss-Jr.	33	25	18	43	14	7	5	3	8	2
	EHC Kloten	Swiss	2	0	0	0	0	....	....	....	....	....
99-2000	EHC Kloten	Swiss	40	6	3	9	28	6	0	1	1	0
2000-01	Kloten Flyers Jr.	Swiss-Jr.	2	3	3	6	0	....	....	....	....	....
	Kloten Flyers	Swiss	8	1	1	2	0	....	....	....	....	....
	Chaux-de-Fonds	Swiss	23	2	8	10	6	12	1	3	4	6
	HC Thurgau	Swiss-2	4	2	1	3	8	....	....	....	....	....
2001-02	SC Bern	Swiss	35	2	10	12	39	6	0	0	0	4
	SC Bern Jr.	Swiss-Jr.	....	....	....	....	....	4	4	2	6	2
2002-03	SC Bern	Swiss	32	2	3	5	14	11	0	0	0	4
	EHC Biel-Bienne	Swiss-2	11	3	4	7	12	....	....	....	....	....
2003-04	ZSC Lions Zurich	Swiss	38	5	8	13	6	13	2	1	3	6
	GCK Lions Zurich	Swiss-2	9	4	7	11	2	....	....	....	....	....
2004-05	GCK Lions Zurich	Swiss-2	1	2	3	5	0	....	....	....	....	....
	ZSC Lions Zurich	Swiss	38	8	8	16	18	15	2	2	4	2

HELM, Darren (HEHLM, DAIR-ehn) DET.

Center/Left wing. Shoots left. 5'11", 172 lbs. Born, Winnipeg, Man., January 21, 1987.
(Detroit's 5th choice, 132nd overall, in 2005 Entry Draft).

			Regular Season					Playoffs				
Season	Club	League	GP	G	A	Pts	PIM	GP	G	A	Pts	PIM
2003-04	Selkirk Fishermen	MJBHL	34	39	32	71	34	....	....	....	....	....
2004-05	Medicine Hat	WHL	72	10	14	24	27	13	2	6	8	10

HELMINEN, Dwight (HEHL-mih-nehn, DWIGHT) NYR

Center. Shoots left. 6', 190 lbs. Born, Hancock, MI, June 22, 1983.
(Edmonton's 12th choice, 244th overall, in 2002 Entry Draft).

			Regular Season					Playoffs				
Season	Club	League	GP	G	A	Pts	PIM	GP	G	A	Pts	PIM
1998-99	Det. Compuware	MNHL	32	9	7	16	....	....	....	....	....	....
99-2000	USA U-17	USDP	30	7	10	17	8	....	....	....	....	....
	USA U-18	USDP	51	6	10	16	6	....	....	....	....	....
2000-01	USA U-18	USDP	67	21	44	65	30	....	....	....	....	....
2001-02	U. of Michigan	CCHA	39	10	8	18	10	....	....	....	....	....
2002-03	U. of Michigan	CCHA	39	17	16	33	34	....	....	....	....	....
2003-04	U. of Michigan	CCHA	41	17	11	28	4	....	....	....	....	....
2004-05	Charlotte	ECHL	28	5	16	21	10	15	7	3	10	2
	Hartford Wolf Pack	AHL	41	2	7	9	10	....	....	....	....	....

Traded to **NY Rangers** by **Edmonton** with Stephen Valiquette and Edmonton's 2nd round compensatory choice (Dane Byers) in 2004 Entry Draft and future considerations for Petr Nedved and Jussi Markkanen, March 3, 2004.

HEMINGWAY, Brett (HEH-mihng-way, BREHT) COL.

Right wing. Shoots right. 6'1", 185 lbs. Born, Yorkton, Sask., September 28, 1983.
(Colorado's 6th choice, 225th overall, in 2003 Entry Draft).

			Regular Season					Playoffs				
Season	Club	League	GP	G	A	Pts	PIM	GP	G	A	Pts	PIM
2000-01	Port Coquitlam	PIJHL	36	22	19	41	24	....	....	....	....	....
2001-02	Coquitlam Express	BCHL	60	45	39	84	31	....	....	....	....	....
2002-03	Coquitlam Express	BCHL	60	42	50	92	50	7	7	5	12	4
2003-04	New Hampshire	H-East	34	7	12	19	8	....	....	....	....	....
2004-05	New Hampshire	H-East	42	22	21	43	14	....	....	....	....	....

Hockey East All-Rookie Team (2004)

HEMINGWAY, Colin (HEH-mihng-way, CAW-lihn) ST.L.

Right wing. Shoots right. 6', 194 lbs. Born, Surrey, B.C., August 12, 1980.
(St. Louis' 7th choice, 221st overall, in 1999 Entry Draft).

			Regular Season					Playoffs				
Season	Club	League	GP	G	A	Pts	PIM	GP	G	A	Pts	PIM
1996-97	Port Coquitlam	PIJHL	34	23	24	47	52	....	....	....	....	....
1997-98	South Surrey	BCHL	58	12	16	28	46	....	....	....	....	....
1998-99	South Surrey	BCHL	59	40	64	104	52	....	....	....	....	....
99-2000	New Hampshire	H-East	22	3	5	8	6	....	....	....	....	....
2000-01	New Hampshire	H-East	37	9	18	27	16	....	....	....	....	....
2001-02	New Hampshire	H-East	40	*33	33	66	30	....	....	....	....	....
2002-03	New Hampshire	H-East	40	22	25	47	51	....	....	....	....	....
2003-04	Worcester IceCats	AHL	13	2	0	2	11	....	....	....	....	....
	Peoria Rivermen	ECHL	36	20	24	44	34	2	0	0	0	0
2004-05	Worcester IceCats	AHL	24	5	2	7	6	....	....	....	....	....
	Peoria Rivermen	ECHL	20	8	10	18	6	....	....	....	....	....

Hockey East First All-Star Team (2002) • Hockey East Second All-Star Team (2003) • NCAA East Second All-American Team (2003)

HENDRIKX, Trevor (HEHN-drihx, TREH-vuhr) **CBJ**

Defense. Shoots right. 6'2", 200 lbs. Born, Russell, Ont., March 29, 1985.
(Columbus' 8th choice, 201st overall, in 2005 Entry Draft).

			Regular Season					Playoffs				
Season	Club	League	GP	G	A	Pts	PIM	GP	G	A	Pts	PIM
2000-01	Gloucester	OPJHL	26	2	3	5	25	....	....	....	....	....
2001-02	Peterborough	OHL	46	1	3	4	37	5	0	0	0	4
2002-03	Peterborough	OHL	56	1	8	9	128	7	0	0	0	4
2003-04	Peterborough	OHL	63	8	24	32	208	....	....	....	....	....
2004-05	Peterborough	OHL	68	15	33	48	100	14	5	7	12	14

• Re-entered NHL Entry Draft. Originally Columbus' 10th choice, 283rd overall, in 2003 Entry Draft.

HENNESSY, Joshua (HEHN-eh-see, JAW-shoo-wuh) **S.J.**

Center. Shoots left. 6', 190 lbs. Born, Brockton, MA, February 7, 1985.
(San Jose's 3rd choice, 43rd overall, in 2003 Entry Draft).

			Regular Season					Playoffs				
Season	Club	League	GP	G	A	Pts	PIM	GP	G	A	Pts	PIM
2000-01	Milton Academy	High-MA	28	20	30	50	20	....	....	....	....	....
2001-02	Quebec Remparts	QMJHL	70	20	20	40	24	9	3	9	12	8
2002-03	Quebec Remparts	QMJHL	72	33	51	84	44	11	6	9	15	10
2003-04	Quebec Remparts	QMJHL	59	40	42	82	55	....	....	....	....	....
2004-05	Quebec Remparts	QMJHL	68	35	50	85	39	12	2	9	11	6

HENRICH, Adam (HEHN-rihch, A-duhm) **T.B.**

Left wing. Shoots left. 6'4", 231 lbs. Born, Thornhill, Ont., January 19, 1984.
(Tampa Bay's 1st choice, 60th overall, in 2002 Entry Draft).

			Regular Season					Playoffs				
Season	Club	League	GP	G	A	Pts	PIM	GP	G	A	Pts	PIM
99-2000	Don Mills Flyers	GTHL	54	30	52	82	86	....	....	....	....	....
2000-01	Brampton	OHL	48	5	4	9	27	9	0	0	0	6
2001-02	Brampton	OHL	66	33	30	63	92	....	....	....	....	....
2002-03	Brampton	OHL	63	31	33	64	84	11	4	1	5	25
2003-04	Brampton	OHL	65	29	29	58	146	12	5	1	6	24
2004-05	Springfield Falcons	AHL	63	10	16	26	97	....	....	....	....	....
	Johnstown Chiefs	ECHL	6	2	1	3	15	....	....	....	....	....

HENSICK, T.J. (HEHN-sihk, TEE-JAY) **COL.**

Center. Shoots right. 5'10", 179 lbs. Born, Lansing, MI, December 10, 1985.
(Colorado's 5th choice, 88th overall, in 2005 Entry Draft).

			Regular Season					Playoffs				
Season	Club	League	GP	G	A	Pts	PIM	GP	G	A	Pts	PIM
2001-02	USA U-17	USDP	63	25	30	55	8	....	....	....	....	....
2002-03	USA U-18	USDP	58	30	31	61	11	....	....	....	....	....
2003-04	U. of Michigan	CCHA	43	12	*34	46	38	....	....	....	....	....
2004-05	U. of Michigan	CCHA	39	23	32	55	24	....	....	....	....	....

CCHA All-Rookie Team (2004) • CCHA First All-Star Team (2004, 2005) • CCHA Rookie of the Year (2004) • NCAA West First All-American Team (2005)

HERSLEY, Patrik (HUHRS-lee, PAT-rihk) **L.A.**

Defense. Shoots right. 6'3", 205 lbs. Born, Malmo, Sweden, June 23, 1986.
(Los Angeles' 5th choice, 139th overall, in 2005 Entry Draft).

			Regular Season					Playoffs				
Season	Club	League	GP	G	A	Pts	PIM	GP	G	A	Pts	PIM
2002-03	Malmo U18	Swe-U18	9	3	4	7	53	4	1	2	3	4
	Malmo Jr.	Swe-Jr.	16	0	2	2	4	1	0	0	0	0
2003-04	Malmo U18	Swe-U18	2	2	0	2	4	....	....	....	....	....
	Malmo Jr.	Swe-Jr.	17	1	4	5	16	....	....	....	....	....
2004-05	Malmo Jr.	Swe-Jr.	31	8	14	22	104	....	....	....	....	....
	Malmo	Sweden	8	0	1	1	0	....	....	....	....	....
	Malmo	Sweden-Q	6	0	0	0	2	....	....	....	....	....

HIRSCHOVITS, Kim (HUHR-shoh-vihts, KIHM) **NYR**

Center. Shoots left. 6'1", 180 lbs. Born, Helsinki, Finland, May 9, 1982.
(NY Rangers' 6th choice, 194th overall, in 2002 Entry Draft).

			Regular Season					Playoffs				
Season	Club	League	GP	G	A	Pts	PIM	GP	G	A	Pts	PIM
1998-99	HIFK Helsinki U18	Fin-U18	34	21	11	32	54	....	....	....	....	....
99-2000	HIFK Helsinki Jr.	Finland-Jr.	40	10	11	21	45	3	0	1	1	0
2000-01	HIFK Helsinki Jr.	Finland-Jr.	35	24	20	44	41	9	6	6	12	4
	HIFK Helsinki	Finland	2	0	0	0	0	....	....	....	....	....
2001-02	Chicago Steel	USHL	6	2	2	4	6	....	....	....	....	....
	HIFK Helsinki	Finland	45	6	10	16	24	....	....	....	....	....
	HIFK Helsinki Jr.	Finland-Jr.	5	4	7	11	8	4	3	6	9	0
	KJT Jarvenpaa	Finland-2	3	1	2	3	6	....	....	....	....	....
2002-03	HIFK Helsinki	Finland	55	4	11	15	26	4	0	0	0	0
	KJT Jarvenpaa	Finland-2	3	1	2	3	6	....	....	....	....	....
2003-04	HIFK Helsinki	Finland	56	7	12	19	56	13	1	3	4	8
2004-05	HIFK Helsinki	Finland	55	8	13	21	61	5	0	1	1	16

HJALMARSSON, Niklas (HJAHL-mahr-suhn, NIHK-las) **CHI.**

Defense. Shoots left. 6'3", 194 lbs. Born, Eksjo, Sweden , June 6, 1987.
(Chicago's 5th choice, 108th overall, in 2005 Entry Draft).

			Regular Season					Playoffs				
Season	Club	League	GP	G	A	Pts	PIM	GP	G	A	Pts	PIM
2003-04	HV 71 Jr.	Swe-Jr.	15	1	3	4	14	2	0	0	0	8
2004-05	HV 71 U18	Swe-U18	3	0	2	2	4	....	....	....	....	....
	HV 71 Jr.	Swe-Jr.	31	4	11	15	87	....	....	....	....	....
	HV 71 Jonkoping	Sweden	14	0	0	0	0	....	....	....	....	....

HOBSON, Adam (HAWB-sohn, A-duhm) **CHI.**

Center. Shoots left. 6', 200 lbs. Born, Lund, Sweden, January 9, 1987.
(Chicago's 12th choice, 203rd overall, in 2005 Entry Draft).

			Regular Season					Playoffs				
Season	Club	League	GP	G	A	Pts	PIM	GP	G	A	Pts	PIM
2002-03	Abbotsford Pilots	PIJHL	38	20	28	48	....	....	....	....	....	....
	Spokane Chiefs	WHL	1	0	0	0	2	....	....	....	....	....
2003-04	Spokane Chiefs	WHL	63	4	5	9	35	4	0	0	0	0
2004-05	Spokane Chiefs	WHL	72	10	27	37	47	....	....	....	....	....

HOFFMAN, Mike **TOR.**

Right wing. Shoots right. 6'4", 240 lbs. Born, Weymouth, MA, September 20, 1980.

			Regular Season					Playoffs				
Season	Club	League	GP	G	A	Pts	PIM	GP	G	A	Pts	PIM
2002-03	Connecticut	MAAC	28	2	8	10	24	....	....	....	....	....
2003-04	Connecticut	MAAC	3	0	0	0	2	....	....	....	....	....
	Worcester IceCats	AHL	15	0	0	0	20	....	....	....	....	....
	Peoria Rivermen	ECHL	25	2	7	9	16	8	0	1	1	6
2004-05	Cleveland Barons	AHL	58	1	7	8	170	....	....	....	....	....

Signed as a free agent by **Cleveland** (AHL), September 22, 2004. Signed as a free agent by **Toronto**, August 12, 2005.

HOGEBOOM, Greg (HOH-guh-BOOM, GREHG) **L.A.**

Right wing. Shoots right. 6', 190 lbs. Born, Toronto, Ont., September 26, 1982.
(Los Angeles' 6th choice, 152nd overall, in 2002 Entry Draft).

			Regular Season					Playoffs				
Season	Club	League	GP	G	A	Pts	PIM	GP	G	A	Pts	PIM
99-2000	Wexford Raiders	OPJHL	48	32	47	79	44	....	....	....	....	....
2000-01	Miami U.	CCHA	38	8	5	13	20	....	....	....	....	....
2001-02	Miami U.	CCHA	36	14	9	23	22	....	....	....	....	....
2002-03	Miami U.	CCHA	41	24	18	42	16	....	....	....	....	....
2003-04	Miami U.	CCHA	41	19	23	42	16	....	....	....	....	....
	Manchester	AHL	3	0	1	1	0	....	....	....	....	....
2004-05	Manchester	AHL	14	1	0	1	10	....	....	....	....	....

CCHA Second All-Star Team (2004)

HOGG, Kris (HAWG, KRIHS) **CGY.**

Left wing. Shoots left. 5'11", 186 lbs. Born, Salmon Arm, B.C., June 17, 1986.
(Calgary's 5th choice, 121st overall, in 2004 Entry Draft).

			Regular Season					Playoffs				
Season	Club	League	GP	G	A	Pts	PIM	GP	G	A	Pts	PIM
2002-03	Kamloops Blazers	WHL	58	5	2	7	12	5	1	0	1	0
2003-04	Kamloops Blazers	WHL	72	24	14	38	79	5	0	1	1	6
2004-05	Kamloops Blazers	WHL	68	18	22	40	131	6	0	3	3	10

HOGGAN, Jeff (HOH-guhn, JEHF) **ST.L.**

Right wing. Shoots left. 6', 180 lbs. Born, Hope, B.C., February 1, 1978.

			Regular Season					Playoffs				
Season	Club	League	GP	G	A	Pts	PIM	GP	G	A	Pts	PIM
1998-99	Powell River Kings	BCHL	STATISTICS NOT AVAILABLE									
99-2000	Nebraska-Omaha	CCHA	34	16	9	25	82	....	....	....	....	....
2000-01	Nebraska-Omaha	CCHA	42	12	17	29	78	....	....	....	....	....
2001-02	Nebraska-Omaha	CCHA	41	24	21	45	92	....	....	....	....	....
	Houston Aeros	AHL	....	....	....	....	....	4	0	0	0	2
2002-03	Houston Aeros	AHL	65	6	5	11	45	14	1	2	3	23
2003-04	Houston Aeros	AHL	77	21	15	36	88	2	0	1	1	4
2004-05	Worcester IceCats	AHL	47	16	9	25	55	....	....	....	....	....

CCHA First All-Star Team (2002) • NCAA West Second All-American Team (2002)

Signed to a try-out contract by **Houston** (AHL), April 4, 2002. Signed as a free agent by **Minnesota**, August 20, 2002. Signed as a free agent by **Worcester** (AHL), September, 2004. Signed as a free agent by **St. Louis**, August 2, 2005.

HOHENER, Martin (HOH-ehn-uhr, MAHR-tihn) **NSH.**

Defense. Shoots left. 6'1", 192 lbs. Born, Zurich, Switz., June 23, 1980.
(Nashville's 12th choice, 284th overall, in 2000 Entry Draft).

			Regular Season					Playoffs				
Season	Club	League	GP	G	A	Pts	PIM	GP	G	A	Pts	PIM
1996-97	EHC Kloten Jr.	Swiss-Jr.	37	4	7	11	....	....	....	....	....	....
1997-98	EHC Kloten Jr.	Swiss-Jr.	25	2	9	11	31	....	....	....	....	....
	EHC Bulach	Swiss-2	4	0	0	0	0	....	....	....	....	....
1998-99	EHC Kloten Jr.	Swiss-Jr.	21	5	8	13	22	2	1	0	1	2
	EHC Kloten	Swiss	20	0	1	1	2	9	0	1	1	0
99-2000	EHC Kloten	Swiss	44	4	2	6	20	5	0	1	1	2
2000-01	Kloten Flyers	Swiss	35	4	5	9	32	9	0	1	1	6
2001-02	Kloten Flyers	Swiss	44	4	12	16	12	9	0	1	1	2
	Switzerland	Olympics	4	0	0	0	0	....	....	....	....	....
2002-03	Kloten Flyers	Swiss	30	0	2	2	8	3	0	0	0	4
2003-04	Geneve	Swiss	39	7	12	19	16	12	0	3	3	8
2004-05	ZSC Lions Zurich	Swiss	27	1	1	2	30	15	0	0	0	12

HOLLWEG, Ryan (HOHL-wehg, RIGH-uhn) **NYR**

Center. Shoots left. 5'9", 210 lbs. Born, Downey, CA, April 23, 1983.
(NY Rangers' 10th choice, 238th overall, in 2001 Entry Draft).

			Regular Season					Playoffs				
Season	Club	League	GP	G	A	Pts	PIM	GP	G	A	Pts	PIM
1998-99	Langley Hornets	BCHL	58	14	40	54	187	....	....	....	....	....
	Grandview	PIJHL	41	23	27	50	135	....	....	....	....	....
99-2000	Medicine Hat	WHL	54	19	27	46	107	....	....	....	....	....
2000-01	Medicine Hat	WHL	65	19	39	58	125	....	....	....	....	....
2001-02	Medicine Hat	WHL	58	30	40	70	121	....	....	....	....	....
	Hartford Wolf Pack	AHL	8	1	1	2	2	9	0	2	2	19
2002-03	Medicine Hat	WHL	4	1	1	2	8	....	....	....	....	....
2003-04	Medicine Hat	WHL	52	25	32	57	117	20	6	9	15	22
2004-05	Hartford Wolf Pack	AHL	73	8	6	14	239	6	1	0	1	9

Missed majority of 2002-03 season recovering from head injury suffered in game vs. Vancouver (WHL), October 8, 2002.

HOLMQVIST, Andreas (HOHLM-kvihst, ahn-DRAY-uhs) **T.B.**

Defense. Shoots right. 6'4", 195 lbs. Born, Stockholm, Sweden, July 23, 1981.
(Tampa Bay's 3rd choice, 61st overall, in 2001 Entry Draft).

			Regular Season					Playoffs				
Season	Club	League	GP	G	A	Pts	PIM	GP	G	A	Pts	PIM
99-2000	Hammarby Jr.	Swe-Jr.	33	8	12	20	16	6	1	2	3	4
2000-01	Hammarby Jr.	Swe-Jr.	47	6	15	21	40	....	....	....	....	....
2001-02	Hammarby	Sweden-2	42	11	13	24	97	....	....	....	....	....
2002-03	Linkopings HC	Sweden	43	4	9	13	28	....	....	....	....	....
	Linkopings HC	Sweden-Q	10	0	0	0	4	....	....	....	....	....
2003-04	Hamilton Bulldogs	AHL	4	0	0	0	0	....	....	....	....	....
	Pensacola	ECHL	63	4	33	37	16	5	0	4	4	0
2004-05	Springfield Falcons	AHL	42	3	9	12	22	....	....	....	....	....

HOLTET, Marius (HOHL-teht, MAIR-ee-uhs) DAL.

Center. Shoots right. 6', 183 lbs. Born, Hamar, Norway, August 31, 1984.
(Dallas' 4th choice, 42nd overall, in 2002 Entry Draft).

			Regular Season					Playoffs				
Season	Club	League	GP	G	A	Pts	PIM	GP	G	A	Pts	PIM
2000-01	Farjestad U18	Swe-U18	5	3	1	4	16	....	....	....	....	....
	Farjestad Jr.	Swe-Jr.	18	2	2	4	18	....	....	....	....	....
2001-02	Farjestad Jr.	Swe-Jr.	37	12	7	19	70	....	....	....	....	....
2002-03	Skare BK Karlstad	Sweden-3	STATISTICS NOT AVAILABLE									
	Bofors	Sweden-2	14	1	1	2	8	2	0	0	0	2
2003-04	Bofors	Sweden-2	43	11	3	14	90	5	2	0	2	4
2004-05	Houston Aeros	AHL	54	7	5	12	48	1	0	0	0	0
	Louisiana	ECHL	4	0	0	0	0	....	....	....	....	....

HOLUB, Jan (HOH-luhb, YAN) NYI

Defense. Shoots left. 6'3", 185 lbs. Born, Liberec, Czech., May 3, 1983.
(NY Islanders' 4th choice, 197th overall, in 2001 Entry Draft).

			Regular Season					Playoffs				
Season	Club	League	GP	G	A	Pts	PIM	GP	G	A	Pts	PIM
99-2000	Liberec Jr.	CzRep-Jr.	2	0	0	0	0	....	....	....	....	....
	HC Liberec 18	CzRep-Jr.	33	2	5	7	65	....	....	....	....	....
2000-01	HC Liberec Jr.	CzRep-Jr.	43	0	6	6	42	....	....	....	....	....
2001-02	HC Liberec Jr.	CzRep-Jr.	11	2	0	2	24	....	....	....	....	....
	Jablonec nad Nisou	CzRep-3	3	0	0	0	2	....	....	....	....	....
	HC Tygri Liberec	CzRep-3	30	1	3	4	22	12	0	0	0	2
2002-03	Liberec	CzRep	21	2	2	4	4	....	....	....	....	....
	HC Liberec Jr.	CzRep-Jr.	13	0	6	6	63	8	0	1	1	8
2003-04	Liberec	CzRep	30	1	0	1	22	....	....	....	....	....
	HC Liberec Jr.	CzRep-Jr.	1	0	1	1	0	....	....	....	....	....
	Beroun	CzRep-2	17	2	3	5	26	....	....	....	....	....
2004-05	Liberec	CzRep	30	1	3	4	18	....	....	....	....	....
	Beroun	CzRep-2	20	0	2	2	16	....	....	....	....	....

HOOTON, Brock (HOO-tuhn, BRAWK) OTT.

Right wing. Shoots right. 6'2", 208 lbs. Born, Smithers, B.C., March 20, 1983.
(Ottawa's 6th choice, 150th overall, in 2002 Entry Draft).

			Regular Season					Playoffs				
Season	Club	League	GP	G	A	Pts	PIM	GP	G	A	Pts	PIM
1998-99	Smithers Selects	BCAHA	40	30	55	85	30	....	....	....	....	....
99-2000	Campbell River	VIJHL	40	8	17	25	8	....	....	....	....	....
2000-01	Quesnel	BCHL	60	11	26	37	....	....	....	....	....	....
2001-02	Quesnel	BCHL	60	34	50	84	33	....	....	....	....	....
2002-03	St. Cloud State	WCHA	26	1	6	7	14	....	....	....	....	....
2003-04	St. Cloud State	WCHA	35	5	10	15	4	....	....	....	....	....
2004-05	St. Cloud State	WCHA	38	5	7	12	10	....	....	....	....	....

HOPE, Joey (HOHP, JOH-ee) PHI.

Defense. Shoots right. 6', 180 lbs. Born, Anchorage, AK, January 1, 1982.

			Regular Season					Playoffs				
Season	Club	League	GP	G	A	Pts	PIM	GP	G	A	Pts	PIM
1998-99	USA U-17	USDP	43	4	7	11	125	....	....	....	....	....
99-2000	USA U-18	USDP	47	5	13	18	66	....	....	....	....	....
2000-01	Prince George	WHL	13	1	3	4	6	....	....	....	....	....
	Portland	WHL	56	6	24	30	103	13	1	7	8	10
2001-02	Portland	WHL	64	9	27	36	124	3	0	2	2	8
2002-03	Portland	WHL	54	12	27	39	142	....	....	....	....	....
2003-04	Philadelphia	AHL	48	0	4	4	32	9	0	1	1	6
	Trenton Titans	ECHL	4	0	2	2	0	....	....	....	....	....
2004-05	Philadelphia	AHL	16	2	2	4	12	....	....	....	....	....

Signed as a free agent by **Philadelphia**, July 14, 2003.

HORNQVIST, Patric (HOHRN-kwihst, PAT-rihk) NSH.

Right wing. Shoots right. 5'11", 178 lbs. Born, Sollentuna, Sweden, January 1, 1987.
(Nashville's 7th choice, 230th overall, in 2005 Entry Draft).

			Regular Season					Playoffs				
Season	Club	League	GP	G	A	Pts	PIM	GP	G	A	Pts	PIM
2003-04	Vasby Jr.	Swe-Jr.	10	7	10	17	30	....	....	....	....	....
	Vasby	Sweden-3	32	8	5	13	26	....	....	....	....	....
2004-05	Vasby	Sweden-3	28	12	12	24	36	....	....	....	....	....
	Djurgarden Jr.	Swe-Jr.	5	3	0	3	2	....	....	....	....	....

HOSPELT, Kai (HAWS-pehlt, KIGH) S.J.

Forward. Shoots left. 6'1", 187 lbs. Born, Cologne, West Germany, August 23, 1985.
(San Jose's 8th choice, 216th overall, in 2003 Entry Draft).

			Regular Season					Playoffs				
Season	Club	League	GP	G	A	Pts	PIM	GP	G	A	Pts	PIM
2000-01	Kolner EC Jr.	Ger-Jr.	35	25	18	43	16	....	....	....	....	....
2001-02	Koln Jr.	Ger-Jr.	40	51	55	106	10	5	6	2	8	4
2002-03	Koln Jr.	Ger-Jr.	29	39	42	81	20	3	2	5	7	2
	Kolner Haie	Germany	21	0	2	2	0	6	0	1	1	0
2003-04	Kolner Haie	Germany	47	2	2	4	18	6	0	0	0	2
2004-05	Kolner Haie	Germany	23	1	1	2	6	....	....	....	....	....

HRABAL, Josef (huh-RA-buhl, YOH-sehf) EDM.

Defense. Shoots left. 6'1", 176 lbs. Born, Prerov, Czech., August 17, 1985.
(Edmonton's 11th choice, 248th overall, in 2003 Entry Draft).

			Regular Season					Playoffs				
Season	Club	League	GP	G	A	Pts	PIM	GP	G	A	Pts	PIM
2001-02	HC Vsetin U17	CzR-U17	38	4	2	6	18	....	....	....	....	....
2002-03	HC Vsetin Jr.	CzRep-Jr.	30	6	7	13	12	9	2	4	6	10
	HC Vsetin	CzRep	6	0	0	0	4	....	....	....	....	....
2003-04	HC Vsetin	CzRep	13	0	0	0	2	....	....	....	....	....
	HC Vsetin Jr.	CzRep-Jr.	46	12	8	20	54	7	1	0	1	2
2004-05	HC Vsetin	CzRep	23	0	2	2	8	....	....	....	....	....
	HC Kometa Brno	CzRep-2	1	0	0	0	0	....	....	....	....	....
	HC Olomouc	CzRep-2	7	0	0	0	6	....	....	....	....	....
	HC Vsetin Jr.	CzRep-Jr.	19	6	8	14	42	8	3	4	7	16

HRDEL, Zbynek (HUHR-duhl, ZBIGH-nek) T.B.

Center. Shoots right. 6'4", 197 lbs. Born, Pisek, Czech., August 19, 1985.
(Tampa Bay's 10th choice, 286th overall, in 2003 Entry Draft).

			Regular Season					Playoffs				
Season	Club	League	GP	G	A	Pts	PIM	GP	G	A	Pts	PIM
2000-01	Sparta U17	CzR-U17	46	11	11	22	22	....	....	....	....	....
2001-02	Sparta U17	CzR-U17	31	24	19	43	42	6	4	3	7	2
2002-03	Rimouski Oceanic	QMJHL	65	10	14	24	131	....	....	....	....	....
2003-04	Rimouski Oceanic	QMJHL	54	15	31	46	41	9	4	6	10	4
2004-05	Rimouski Oceanic	QMJHL	56	23	35	58	47	13	8	7	15	10

HROMAS, Karel (huh-ROM-mahs, KAH-rehl) CHI.

Left wing. Shoots left. 6'2", 189 lbs. Born, Beroun, Czech., January 27, 1986.
(Chicago's 8th choice, 123rd overall, in 2004 Entry Draft).

			Regular Season					Playoffs				
Season	Club	League	GP	G	A	Pts	PIM	GP	G	A	Pts	PIM
2000-01	Sparta U17	CzR-U17	34	4	18	22	6	....	....	....	....	....
2001-02	Sparta U17	CzR-U17	39	19	15	34	55	6	3	2	5	6
2002-03	Sparta U17	CzR-U17	1	3	1	4	0	....	....	....	....	....
	Sparta Jr.	CzRep-Jr.	32	6	7	13	14	3	0	1	1	4
2003-04	Sparta Jr.	CzRep-Jr.	21	10	10	20	16	....	....	....	....	....
	HC Sparta Praha	CzRep	13	0	0	0	0	2	0	0	0	0
2004-05	Everett Silvertips	WHL	65	18	11	29	22	11	2	2	4	4

HUBL, Viktor (HEW-buhl, VIHK-tohr) WSH.

Left wing. Shoots left. 6', 183 lbs. Born, Chomutov, Czech., August 13, 1978.
(Washington's 10th choice, 284th overall, in 2001 Entry Draft).

			Regular Season					Playoffs				
Season	Club	League	GP	G	A	Pts	PIM	GP	G	A	Pts	PIM
1997-98	VTZ Chomutov	CzRep-2	50	18	17	35	....	....	....	....	....	....
1998-99	KLH Chomutov	CzRep-2	5	2	1	3	....	....	....	....	....	....
	Litvinov	CzRep	27	2	6	8	10	....	....	....	....	....
99-2000	KLH Chomutov	CzRep-2	8	2	4	6	4	....	....	....	....	....
	Litvinov	CzRep	36	6	9	15	16	....	....	....	....	....
2000-01	HC Slavia Praha	CzRep	50	16	24	40	24	11	0	2	2	6
2001-02	HC Slavia Praha	CzRep	48	11	14	25	34	8	0	1	1	6
2002-03	Litvinov	CzRep	39	8	13	21	30	....	....	....	....	....
2003-04	Litvinov	CzRep	52	9	17	26	24	....	....	....	....	....
2004-05	Litvinov	CzRep	52	16	15	31	14	6	1	1	2	6

HULT, Alexander (HUHLT, al-EHX-AN-duhr) S.J.

Center. Shoots left. 6'1", 200 lbs. Born, Falun, Sweden, November 19, 1984.
(San Jose's 9th choice, 236th overall, in 2003 Entry Draft).

			Regular Season					Playoffs				
Season	Club	League	GP	G	A	Pts	PIM	GP	G	A	Pts	PIM
2000-01	HV 71 U18	Swe-U18	13	4	12	16	24	....	....	....	....	....
2001-02	HV 71 U18	Swe-U18	1	0	0	0	2	....	....	....	....	....
	HV 71 Jr.	Swe-Jr.	35	11	7	18	87	....	....	....	....	....
	HV 71 Jonkoping	Sweden	....	....	....	....	....	1	0	0	0	0
2002-03	HV 71 Jr.	Swe-Jr.	24	11	14	25	24	....	....	....	....	....
	HV 71 Jonkoping	Sweden	1	0	0	0	2	....	....	....	....	....
	Tranas AIF	Sweden-2	5	1	0	1	0	....	....	....	....	....
2003-04	IK Oskarshamn	Sweden-2	29	2	7	9	22	....	....	....	....	....
	HV 71 Jonkoping	Sweden	3	0	0	0	2	....	....	....	....	....
	Djurgarden Jr.	Swe-Jr.	11	6	10	16	16	....	....	....	....	....
	Djurgarden	Sweden	8	0	0	0	0	3	0	0	0	0
2004-05	Almtuna	Sweden-2	30	3	3	6	16	....	....	....	....	....
	IK Comet Halden	Norway	18	2	7	9	56	....	....	....	....	....
	IK Comet Halden	Norway-Q	5	2	3	5	2	....	....	....	....	....

HULVA, Jakub (HUHL-vuh, YA-kuhb) BUF.

Right wing. Shoots left. 6', 172 lbs. Born, Opava, Czech., May 6, 1984.
(Buffalo's 5th choice, 108th overall, in 2002 Entry Draft).

			Regular Season					Playoffs				
Season	Club	League	GP	G	A	Pts	PIM	GP	G	A	Pts	PIM
99-2000	HC Vitkovice Jr.	CzRep-Jr.	49	20	34	54	38	....	....	....	....	....
2000-01	HC Vitkovice U17	CzR-U17	30	28	40	68	22	....	....	....	....	....
	HC Vitkovice Jr.	CzRep-Jr.	20	5	6	11	6	....	....	....	....	....
	HC Vitkovice	CzRep	1	0	0	0	0	....	....	....	....	....
2001-02	HC Vitkovice Jr.	CzRep-Jr.	45	25	24	49	36	....	....	....	....	....
	HC Slezan Opava	CzRep-2	4	0	0	0	2	....	....	....	....	....
	HC Vitkovice	CzRep	1	0	0	0	0	2	0	0	0	0
2002-03	HC Vitkovice Jr.	CzRep-Jr.	28	13	16	29	28	1	0	3	3	2
	HC Slezan Opava	CzRep-2	6	0	0	0	0	....	....	....	....	....
	HC Vitkovice	CzRep	5	0	1	1	0	3	0	0	0	0
2003-04	HC Vitkovice Jr.	CzRep-Jr.	13	11	7	18	28	....	....	....	....	....
	HC Slezan Opava	CzRep-2	19	8	3	11	8	....	....	....	....	....
	HC Vitkovice	CzRep	20	0	1	1	2	4	1	0	1	0
2004-05	HC Vitkovice Jr.	CzRep-Jr.	1	1	2	3	2	....	....	....	....	....
	HC Sareza Ostrava	CzRep-2	8	1	0	1	0	....	....	....	....	....
	HC Slezan Opava	CzRep-2	12	4	7	11	8	....	....	....	....	....
	HC Vitkovice Steel	CzRep	42	5	3	8	0	2	0	1	1	0

HUNTER, Dylan (HUHN-tuhr, DIH-luhn) BUF.

Left wing. Shoots left. 5'11", 198 lbs. Born, Quebec City, Que., May 21, 1985.
(Buffalo's 8th choice, 273rd overall, in 2004 Entry Draft).

			Regular Season					Playoffs				
Season	Club	League	GP	G	A	Pts	PIM	GP	G	A	Pts	PIM
2001-02	London Knights	OHL	54	6	21	27	38	6	1	1	2	10
2002-03	London Knights	OHL	68	11	31	42	41	14	3	3	6	8
2003-04	London Knights	OHL	64	26	53	79	47	15	4	10	14	10
2004-05	London Knights	OHL	67	31	73	104	64	18	10	11	21	16

OHL First All-Star Team (2005)

HUNTER, J.J. (HUHN-tuhr, JAY-JAY) EDM.

Right wing. Shoots left. 6'1", 185 lbs. Born, Shaunavon, Sask., July 6, 1980.

			Regular Season					Playoffs				
Season	Club	League	GP	G	A	Pts	PIM	GP	G	A	Pts	PIM
1998-99	Kelowna Rockets	WHL	66	18	32	50	61	6	1	2	3	2
99-2000	Kelowna Rockets	WHL	66	22	26	48	61	5	1	0	1	2
2000-01	Kelowna Rockets	WHL	12	1	5	6	4	....	....	....	....	....
	Prince Albert	WHL	58	28	17	45	40	....	....	....	....	....
2001-02	Hamilton Bulldogs	AHL	1	0	0	0	0	1	0	0	0	0
	Columbus	ECHL	60	23	22	45	59	....	....	....	....	....
2002-03	Hamilton Bulldogs	AHL	2	0	0	0	2	....	....	....	....	....
	Columbus	ECHL	70	17	36	53	82	....	....	....	....	....
2003-04	Columbus	ECHL	4	2	1	3	2	....	....	....	....	....
	Toronto	AHL	56	12	16	28	53	3	1	1	2	2
2004-05	Edmonton	AHL	64	13	11	24	51	....	....	....	....	....

Signed as a free agent by **Edmonton**, August 19, 2002.

HUNWICK, Matt (HUHN-wihk, MAT) BOS.

Defense. Shoots left. 5'11", 187 lbs. Born, Warren, MI, May 21, 1985.
(Boston's 6th choice, 224th overall, in 2004 Entry Draft).

			Regular Season					Playoffs				
Season	Club	League	GP	G	A	Pts	PIM	GP	G	A	Pts	PIM
2001-02	USA U-17	USDP	43	5	5	10	36	....	....	....	....	....
2002-03	USA U-18	USDP	48	8	18	26	63	....	....	....	....	....
2003-04	U. of Michigan	CCHA	41	1	14	15	62	....	....	....	....	....
2004-05	U. of Michigan	CCHA	40	6	19	25	60	....	....	....	....	....

CCHA All-Rookie Team (2004) • CCHA Second All-Star Team (2005)

HUSKINS, Kent (HUHS-kihns, KEHNT) ANA.

Defense. Shoots left. 6'3", 215 lbs. Born, Ottawa, Ont., May 4, 1979.
(Chicago's 3rd choice, 156th overall, in 1998 Entry Draft).

			Regular Season					Playoffs				
Season	Club	League	GP	G	A	Pts	PIM	GP	G	A	Pts	PIM
1995-96	Kanata Valley	CJHL	49	6	21	27	18	....	....	....	....	....
1996-97	Kanata Valley	CJHL	53	11	36	47	89	....	....	....	....	....
1997-98	Clarkson Knights	ECAC	35	2	8	10	46	....	....	....	....	....
1998-99	Clarkson Knights	ECAC	37	5	11	16	28	....	....	....	....	....
99-2000	Clarkson Knights	ECAC	28	2	16	18	30	....	....	....	....	....
2000-01	Clarkson Knights	ECAC	35	6	28	34	22	....	....	....	....	....
2001-02	Norfolk Admirals	AHL	65	4	11	15	44	4	0	1	1	0
2002-03	Norfolk Admirals	AHL	80	5	22	27	48	9	2	2	4	4
2003-04	San Antonio	AHL	79	5	14	19	42	....	....	....	....	....
2004-05	Manitoba Moose	AHL	65	5	11	16	41	14	0	2	2	12

ECAC First All-Star Team (2000, 2001) • NCAA East First All-American Team (2001)

Signed as a free agent by **Florida**, August 14, 2003. Signed as a free agent by **Manitoba** (AHL), September 16, 2004. Signed as a free agent by **Anaheim**, August 30, 2005.

HUTCHINS, Michael (HUHCH-ihns, MIGH-kuhl) S.J.

Defense. Shoots left. 5'11", 185 lbs. Born, Wolfeboro, NH, October 27, 1982.
(San Jose's 7th choice, 288th overall, in 2002 Entry Draft).

			Regular Season					Playoffs				
Season	Club	League	GP	G	A	Pts	PIM	GP	G	A	Pts	PIM
99-2000	St. Paul's School	High-NH	30	5	12	17	....	....	....	....	....	....
2000-01	St. Paul's School	High-NH	27	8	27	35	36	....	....	....	....	....
2001-02	Des Moines	USHL	60	7	30	37	133	3	0	1	1	2
2002-03	New Hampshire	H-East	DID NOT PLAY – FRESHMAN									
2003-04	New Hampshire	H-East	22	1	0	1	34	....	....	....	....	....
2004-05	New Hampshire	H-East	19	0	5	5	10	....	....	....	....	....

HYNES, Shane (HIGHNZ, SHAYN) ANA.

Right wing. Shoots right. 6'3", 224 lbs. Born, Montreal, Que., November 7, 1983.
(Anaheim's 3rd choice, 86th overall, in 2003 Entry Draft).

			Regular Season					Playoffs				
Season	Club	League	GP	G	A	Pts	PIM	GP	G	A	Pts	PIM
99-2000	Cgy. AAA Flames	AMHL	30	8	12	20	20	....	....	....	....	....
2000-01	Cgy. AAA Flames	AMHL	28	18	21	38	76	....	....	....	....	....
2001-02	Nanaimo Clippers	BCHL	50	38	36	74	183	....	....	....	....	....
2002-03	Cornell Big Red	ECAC	32	11	9	20	36	....	....	....	....	....
2003-04	Cornell Big Red	ECAC	30	9	9	18	54	....	....	....	....	....
2004-05	Cornell Big Red	ECAC	33	7	21	28	40	....	....	....	....	....

IGNATUSHKIN, Igor (ihg-nah-TOOSH-kihn, EE-gohr) WSH.

Center. Shoots left. 5'11", 175 lbs. Born, Elektrostal, USSR, April 7, 1984.
(Washington's 12th choice, 242nd overall, in 2002 Entry Draft).

			Regular Season					Playoffs				
Season	Club	League	GP	G	A	Pts	PIM	GP	G	A	Pts	PIM
99-2000	Elektrostal 2	Russia-3	5	0	0	0	0	....	....	....	....	....
2000-01	Team Center 84	Exhib.	5	1	1	2	0	....	....	....	....	....
	Elektrostal 2	Russia-3	STATISTICS NOT AVAILABLE									
2001-02	Elektrostal 2	Russia-3	6	2	3	5	6	....	....	....	....	....
	Elektrostal	Russia-2	46	1	4	5	20	....	....	....	....	....
2002-03	Elektrostal	Russia-2	36	9	10	19	8	....	....	....	....	....
2003-04	Kristall Elektrostal	Russia-2	49	6	2	8	22	....	....	....	....	....
2004-05	Kristall Elektrostal	Russia-2	45	9	3	12	28	....	....	....	....	....
	Leninogorsk	Russia-2	6	1	1	2	6	4	1	0	1	4

IHNACAK, Brian (ih-NAH-chehk, BRIGH-uhn) PIT.

Center. Shoots right. 5'11", 178 lbs. Born, Toronto, Ont., April 10, 1985.
(Pittsburgh's 12th choice, 259th overall, in 2004 Entry Draft).

			Regular Season					Playoffs				
Season	Club	League	GP	G	A	Pts	PIM	GP	G	A	Pts	PIM
2001-02	St. Mike's B's	OPJHL	48	6	13	19	22	....	....	....	....	....
2002-03	St. Mike's B's	OPJHL	46	40	46	86	66	10	8	7	15	8
2003-04	Brown U.	ECAC	31	10	20	30	20	....	....	....	....	....
2004-05	Brown U.	ECAC	30	12	11	23	30	....	....	....	....	....

ECAC All-Rookie Team (2004) • ECAC Rookie of the Year (2004) (co-winner - David McKee)

IMMONEN, Jarkko (IH-moh-nihn, YAHR-koh) NYR

Center. Shoots right. 6', 202 lbs. Born, Rantasalmi, Finland, April 19, 1982.
(Toronto's 8th choice, 254th overall, in 2002 Entry Draft).

			Regular Season					Playoffs				
Season	Club	League	GP	G	A	Pts	PIM	GP	G	A	Pts	PIM
1997-98	SaPKo Jr.	Finland-Jr.	14	8	12	20	0	....	....	....	....	....
1998-99	SaPKo Savonlinna	Finland-2	36	2	2	4	6	....	....	....	....	....
99-2000	SaPKo Savonlinna	Finland-2	42	18	16	34	34	....	....	....	....	....
2000-01	TuTo Turku	Finland-2	41	20	20	40	22	11	5	7	12	10
	TuTo Turku Jr.	Finland-Jr.	1	0	1	1	2	1	0	0	0	6
2001-02	Assat Pori	Finland	44	0	2	2	6	....	....	....	....	....
	Assat Pori Jr.	Finland-Jr.	3	1	1	2	4	8	5	1	6	10
2002-03	JYP Jyvaskyla	Finland	56	10	23	33	34	7	1	1	2	8
2003-04	JYP Jyvaskyla	Finland	52	23	26	49	28	2	0	0	0	0
2004-05	JYP Jyvaskyla	Finland	54	19	28	47	24	3	0	2	2	2

Traded to **NY Rangers** by **Toronto** with Maxim Kondratiev, Toronto's 1st round choice (later traded to Calgary - Calgary selected Kris Chucko) in 2004 Entry Draft and Toronto's 2nd round choice (Michael Sauer) in 2005 Entry Draft for Brian Leetch and Edmonton's 4th round choice (previously acquired, Toronto selected Roman Kukumberg) in 2004 Entry Draft, March 3, 2004.

IRGL, Zbynek (UHR-guhl, ZBIH-nehk) NSH.

Center. Shoots right. 5'11", 183 lbs. Born, Vitkovice, Czech., November 29, 1980.
(Nashville's 9th choice, 197th overall, in 2000 Entry Draft).

			Regular Season					Playoffs				
Season	Club	League	GP	G	A	Pts	PIM	GP	G	A	Pts	PIM
1996-97	HC Vitkovice Jr.	CzRep-Jr.	43	44	22	66	....	....	....	....	....	....
1997-98	HC Vitkovice Jr.	CzRep-Jr.	37	17	10	27	....	....	....	....	....	....
1998-99	HC Vitkovice Jr.	CzRep-Jr.	18	9	8	17	....	....	....	....	....	....
	HC Vitkovice	CzRep	33	2	2	4	6	4	0	0	0	....
99-2000	HC Dukla Jihlava	CzRep-2	1	0	0	0	0	....	....	....	....	....
	HC Vitkovice	CzRep	47	7	5	12	10	....	....	....	....	....
2000-01	HC Vitkovice	CzRep	37	0	1	1	8	4	0	0	0	0
	HC Slezan Opava	CzRep-2	9	3	2	5	2	....	....	....	....	....
	HC Vitkovice Jr.	CzRep-Jr.	4	6	3	9	2	....	....	....	....	....
2001-02	HC Vitkovice	CzRep	39	2	8	10	8	13	4	0	4	6
2002-03	HC Vitkovice	CzRep	51	6	7	13	14	5	0	1	1	0
2003-04	HC Vitkovice	CzRep	51	19	16	35	18	4	1	0	1	6
2004-05	HC Vitkovice Steel	CzRep	50	21	10	31	51	11	1	1	2	33

IRMEN, Danny (UHR-mehn, DA-nee) MIN.

Center. Shoots right. 6', 190 lbs. Born, Fargo, ND, September 6, 1984.
(Minnesota's 3rd choice, 78th overall, in 2003 Entry Draft).

			Regular Season					Playoffs				
Season	Club	League	GP	G	A	Pts	PIM	GP	G	A	Pts	PIM
2001-02	Lincoln Stars	USHL	61	17	36	53	....	....	....	....	....	....
2002-03	Lincoln Stars	USHL	45	21	34	55	78	10	8	6	14	17
2003-04	U. of Minnesota	WCHA	44	14	8	22	40	....	....	....	....	....
2004-05	U. of Minnesota	WCHA	44	24	19	43	66	....	....	....	....	....

USHL Second All-Star Team (2003) • USHL Playoff MVP (2003)

ISAKOV, Evgeni (ih-SA-kawf, ehv-GEH-nee) PIT.

Right wing. Shoots left. 6'1", 196 lbs. Born, Krasnoyarsk, USSR, October 13, 1984.
(Pittsburgh's 6th choice, 161st overall, in 2003 Entry Draft).

			Regular Season					Playoffs				
Season	Club	League	GP	G	A	Pts	PIM	GP	G	A	Pts	PIM
99-2000	Rubin Tyumen 2	Russia-3	7	0	2	2	16	....	....	....	....	....
2000-01	Rubin Tyumen 2	Russia-3	....	....	....	....	....	....	....	....	....	....
	Gazovik Tyumen	Russia-3	11	1	1	2	12	....	....	....	....	....
2001-02	Gazovik Tyumen	Russia-2	19	2	2	4	2	....	....	....	....	....
	Elektrostal	Russia-2	29	3	2	5	24	....	....	....	....	....
	Elektrostal 2	Russia-3	11	3	3	6	43	....	....	....	....	....
2002-03	Cherepovets	Russia	36	0	3	3	12	1	0	0	0	0
2003-04	Cherepovets	Russia	38	3	2	5	18	....	....	....	....	....
	Cherepovets 2	Russia-3	14	4	8	12	48	....	....	....	....	....
2004-05	Kristall Saratov	Russia-2	1	0	0	0	0	....	....	....	....	....
	Tyumen 2	Russia-3	2	1	3	4	14	....	....	....	....	....
	Gazovik Tyumen	Russia-2	4	0	2	2	2	3	0	0	0	2

ISOSALO, Samu (ee-soh-SA-low, SA-moo) ATL.

Right wing. Shoots left. 6'3", 205 lbs. Born, Rauma, Finland, June 10, 1981.
(Atlanta's 10th choice, 230th overall, in 2000 Entry Draft).

			Regular Season					Playoffs				
Season	Club	League	GP	G	A	Pts	PIM	GP	G	A	Pts	PIM
1996-97	Lukko Rauma U18	Fin-U18	21	5	6	11	45	....	....	....	....	....
	Lukko Rauma Jr.	Finland-Jr.	1	0	0	0	0	....	....	....	....	....
1997-98	Lukko Rauma Jr.	Finland-Jr.	34	21	19	40	48	....	....	....	....	....
1998-99	North Bay	OHL	59	13	12	25	19	4	0	0	0	4
99-2000	North Bay	OHL	48	17	25	42	26	3	0	0	0	0
2000-01	Lukko Rauma Jr.	Finland-Jr.	14	11	9	20	42	3	1	2	3	0
	Jaa-Kotkat	Finland-2	3	2	1	3	2	....	....	....	....	....
	Lukko Rauma	Finland	31	1	1	2	33	1	0	0	0	0
2001-02	Lukko Rauma Jr.	Finland-Jr.	2	0	3	3	2	....	....	....	....	....
	Lukko Rauma	Finland	4	0	0	0	2	....	....	....	....	....
2002-03	Lukko Rauma	Finland	52	5	5	10	6	....	....	....	....	....
2003-04			DID NOT PLAY – INJURED									
2004-05			DID NOT PLAY – INJURED									

Did not play in 2003-04 and 2004-05 seasons due to knee injury.

ISTOMIN, Denis (ihst-OH-mihn, DEH-nihs) CHI.

Right wing. Shoots left. 6', 187 lbs. Born, Chelyabinsk, USSR, January 12, 1987.
(Chicago's 7th choice, 117th overall, in 2005 Entry Draft).

			Regular Season					Playoffs				
Season	Club	League	GP	G	A	Pts	PIM	GP	G	A	Pts	PIM
2003-04	Magnitogorsk 2	Russia-3	3	2	1	3	2	....	....	....	....	....
2004-05	Chelyabinsk 2	Russia-3	1	0	0	0	0	....	....	....	....	....
	Chelyabinsk	Russia-2	42	11	5	16	24	8	1	1	2	4

IVANANS, Raitis (ih-VAH-nehns, RIGH-this) MTL.

Left wing. Shoots left. 6'3", 220 lbs. Born, Riga, Latvia, January 1, 1979.

			Regular Season					Playoffs				
Season	Club	League	GP	G	A	Pts	PIM	GP	G	A	Pts	PIM
1997-98	Flint Generals	UHL	18	0	1	1	20	....	....	....	....	....
1998-99	Macon Whoopee	CHL	16	1	1	2	20	....	....	....	....	....
	Tulsa Oilers	CHL	32	2	7	9	39	....	....	....	....	....
99-2000	Pensacola	ECHL	59	3	7	10	146	2	0	0	0	0
2000-01	Hershey Bears	AHL	2	0	0	0	0	....	....	....	....	....
	New Haven	UHL	66	4	10	14	270	8	1	0	1	4
2001-02	Toledo Storm	ECHL	16	2	2	4	59	....	....	....	....	....
	Baton Rouge	ECHL	40	4	5	9	180	....	....	....	....	....
2002-03	Milwaukee	AHL	17	0	0	0	38	1	0	0	0	15
	Rockford IceHogs	UHL	50	4	2	6	208	....	....	....	....	....
2003-04	Milwaukee	AHL	54	1	7	8	166	7	0	1	1	17
	Rockford IceHogs	UHL	1	0	0	0	0	....	....	....	....	....
2004-05	Hamilton Bulldogs	AHL	75	2	5	7	259	2	0	1	1	0

Signed as a free agent by **Montreal**, July 16, 2004

JAAKOLA, Topi (YAH-koh-luh, TOH-pee) FLA.

Defense. Shoots left. 6'1", 185 lbs. Born, Oulu, Finland, November 15, 1983.
(Florida's 5th choice, 134th overall, in 2002 Entry Draft).

			Regular Season					Playoffs				
Season	Club	League	GP	G	A	Pts	PIM	GP	G	A	Pts	PIM
99-2000	Karpat Oulu Jr.	Finland-Jr.	36	5	12	17	71	5	1	1	2	4
2000-01	Karpat Oulu Jr.	Finland-Jr.	35	4	10	14	47	6	0	2	2	6
	Karpat Oulu	Finland	4	0	0	0	2	....	....	....	....	....
2001-02	Karpat Oulu Jr.	Finland-Jr.	3	0	0	0	2	2	1	0	1	4
	Karpat Oulu	Finland	44	0	4	4	18	4	0	0	0	4
2002-03	Karpat Oulu	Finland	52	2	2	4	18	15	0	0	0	8
2003-04	Karpat Oulu	Finland	52	0	4	4	12	14	0	1	1	6
2004-05	Karpat Oulu	Finland	33	1	3	4	6	....	....	....	....	....

JAASKELAINEN, Teemu (yas-keh-LIGH-nuhn, TEE-moo) CHI.

Defense. Shoots left. 6'1", 207 lbs. Born, Tampere, Finland, June 7, 1983.
(Chicago's 11th choice, 205th overall, in 2001 Entry Draft).

			Regular Season					Playoffs				
Season	Club	League	GP	G	A	Pts	PIM	GP	G	A	Pts	PIM
99-2000	Ilves Tampere U18	Fin-U18	36	5	1	6	20	....	....	....	....	....
2000-01	Ilves Tampere U18	Fin-U18	5	1	1	2	16	....	....	....	....	....
	Ilves Tampere Jr.	Finland-Jr.	41	4	1	5	30	....	....	....	....	....
2001-02	Ilves Tampere Jr.	Finland-Jr.	13	1	6	7	8	....	....	....	....	....
	Ilves Tampere	Finland	38	0	0	0	24	3	0	0	0	0
2002-03	Ilves Tampere	Finland	48	1	4	5	16	....	....	....	....	....
	Ilves Tampere Jr.	Finland-Jr.	7	3	4	7	4	....	....	....	....	....
2003-04	Ilves Tampere	Finland	44	6	3	9	14	7	0	0	0	0
	Ilves Tampere Jr.	Finland-Jr.	1	0	0	0	2	....	....	....	....	....
2004-05	Ilves Tampere	Finland	51	4	7	11	26	7	0	0	0	4

JACINA, Greg (ja-SEE-nah, GREHG)

Left wing. Shoots right. 6', 203 lbs. Born, Guelph, Ont., May 22, 1982.

			Regular Season					Playoffs				
Season	Club	League	GP	G	A	Pts	PIM	GP	G	A	Pts	PIM
99-2000	Owen Sound	OHL	66	12	29	41	62	....	....	....	....	....
2000-01	Owen Sound	OHL	57	25	26	51	101	4	0	1	1	15
2001-02	Owen Sound	OHL	33	15	20	35	64	....	....	....	....	....
	Mississauga	OHL	28	14	26	40	43	....	....	....	....	....
2002-03	Mississauga	OHL	56	19	47	66	114	5	6	5	11	17
2003-04	San Antonio	AHL	13	0	4	4	22	....	....	....	....	....
	Augusta Lynx	ECHL	58	15	23	38	170	....	....	....	....	....
2004-05	San Antonio	AHL	78	11	20	31	150	....	....	....	....	....

Signed as a free agent by **Florida**, August 12, 2003.

JACKSON, Scott (JAK-suhn, SKAWT) ST.L.

Defense. Shoots left. 6'3", 200 lbs. Born, Salmon Arm, B.C., February 5, 1987.
(St. Louis' 2nd choice, 37th overall, in 2005 Entry Draft).

			Regular Season					Playoffs				
Season	Club	League	GP	G	A	Pts	PIM	GP	G	A	Pts	PIM
2002-03	Sicamous Eagles	KIJHL	45	2	20	22	20	....	....	....	....	....
	Seattle	WHL	2	0	0	0	2	....	....	....	....	....
2003-04	Seattle	WHL	66	4	9	13	17	....	....	....	....	....
2004-05	Seattle	WHL	72	6	16	22	46	12	1	2	3	4

JACKSON, Todd (JAK-suhn, TAWD) DET.

Right wing. Shoots right. 5'11", 170 lbs. Born, Syracuse, NY, April 10, 1981.
(Detroit's 10th choice, 251st overall, in 2000 Entry Draft).

			Regular Season					Playoffs				
Season	Club	League	GP	G	A	Pts	PIM	GP	G	A	Pts	PIM
1998-99	USA U-17	USDP	53	11	9	20	56	....	....	....	....	....
99-2000	USA U-17	USDP	29	8	10	18	25	....	....	....	....	....
	USA U-18	USDP	23	8	6	14	12	....	....	....	....	....
2000-01	U. of Maine	H-East	39	4	8	12	8	....	....	....	....	....
2001-02	U. of Maine	H-East	39	7	21	28	10	....	....	....	....	....
2002-03	U. of Maine	H-East	39	13	13	26	22	....	....	....	....	....
2003-04	U. of Maine	H-East	44	21	12	33	34	....	....	....	....	....
2004-05	Grand Rapids	AHL	30	0	2	2	10	....	....	....	....	....
	Toledo Storm	ECHL	35	12	13	25	24	4	0	0	0	2

Hockey East Second All-Star Team (2004) • NCAA East Second All-American Team (2004)

JACQUES, Jean-Francois (ZHAWK, ZHAWN-fran-SWUH) EDM.

Left wing. Shoots left. 6'4", 217 lbs. Born, Terrebonne, Que., April 29, 1985.
(Edmonton's 3rd choice, 68th overall, in 2003 Entry Draft).

			Regular Season					Playoffs				
Season	Club	League	GP	G	A	Pts	PIM	GP	G	A	Pts	PIM
2000-01	Cap-d-Madeleine	QAAA	39	22	13	35	28	10	5	8	13	14
2001-02	Baie-Comeau	QMJHL	66	10	14	24	136	5	1	0	1	2
2002-03	Baie-Comeau	QMJHL	67	12	21	33	123	12	4	2	6	13
2003-04	Baie-Comeau	QMJHL	59	20	24	44	70	4	1	0	1	4
2004-05	Baie-Comeau	QMJHL	69	36	42	78	56	6	3	5	8	6
	Edmonton	AHL	6	0	0	0	5	....	....	....	....	....

JAMES, Connor (JAYMZ, KAW-nuhr)

Right wing. Shoots right. 5'10", 168 lbs. Born, Calgary, Alta., August 25, 1982.
(Los Angeles' 11th choice, 279th overall, in 2002 Entry Draft).

			Regular Season					Playoffs				
Season	Club	League	GP	G	A	Pts	PIM	GP	G	A	Pts	PIM
1998-99	Calgary Buffaloes	AMHL	36	33	53	86	20	....	....	....	....	....
99-2000	Calgary Royals	AJHL	64	36	57	93	41	....	....	....	....	....
2000-01	U. of Denver	WCHA	38	8	19	27	14	....	....	....	....	....
2001-02	U. of Denver	WCHA	41	16	26	42	18	....	....	....	....	....
2002-03	U. of Denver	WCHA	41	20	23	43	12	....	....	....	....	....
2003-04	U. of Denver	WCHA	40	13	25	38	16	....	....	....	....	....
2004-05	Manchester	AHL	14	2	1	3	10	3	0	0	0	0
	Bakersfield	ECHL	51	21	25	46	34	5	3	1	4	0

NCAA Championship All-Tournament Team (2004)

JAMTIN, Andreas (yahm-TEEN, ahn-DRAY-uhs) DET.

Right wing. Shoots left. 5'11", 185 lbs. Born, Stockholm, Sweden, May 4, 1983.
(Detroit's 4th choice, 157th overall, in 2001 Entry Draft).

			Regular Season					Playoffs				
Season	Club	League	GP	G	A	Pts	PIM	GP	G	A	Pts	PIM
1998-99	AIK Solna Jr.	Swe-Jr.	44	33	29	62	105	....	....	....	....	....
99-2000	Farjestad Jr.	Swe-Jr.	28	6	6	12	36	....	....	....	....	....
2000-01	Farjestad U18	Swe-U18	1	1	0	1	2	....	....	....	....	....
	Farjestad Jr.	Swe-Jr.	13	5	8	13	83	....	....	....	....	....
	Farjestad	Sweden	1	0	0	0	0	....	....	....	....	....
2001-02	AIK Solna	Sweden	42	2	3	5	55	....	....	....	....	....
	AIK Solna Jr.	Swe-Jr.	12	12	15	27	61	1	2	2	4	2
	AIK Solna	Sweden-Q	10	1	2	3	4	....	....	....	....	....
2002-03	AIK Solna	Sweden-2	28	14	15	29	62	....	....	....	....	....
2003-04	HV 71 Jonkoping	Sweden	39	5	13	18	105	16	3	3	6	*68
2004-05	HV 71 Jonkoping	Sweden	42	6	12	18	155	....	....	....	....	....

JANCEVSKI, Dan (jan-SEHV-skee, DAN) DAL.

Defense. Shoots left. 6'3", 212 lbs. Born, Windsor, Ont., June 15, 1981.
(Dallas' 2nd choice, 66th overall, in 1999 Entry Draft).

			Regular Season					Playoffs				
Season	Club	League	GP	G	A	Pts	PIM	GP	G	A	Pts	PIM
1995-96	Riverside Selects	OMHA	59	9	22	31	67	....	....	....	....	....
1996-97	Windsor Lions	OMHA	47	6	20	26	99	....	....	....	....	....
1997-98	Tecumseh	OHA-B	49	3	11	14	145	....	....	....	....	....
1998-99	London Knights	OHL	68	2	12	14	115	25	1	7	8	24
99-2000	London Knights	OHL	59	8	15	23	138	....	....	....	....	....
2000-01	London Knights	OHL	39	4	23	27	95	....	....	....	....	....
	Sudbury Wolves	OHL	31	3	14	17	42	12	0	9	9	17
2001-02	Utah Grizzlies	AHL	77	0	13	13	147	5	0	0	0	4
2002-03	Utah Grizzlies	AHL	76	1	10	11	172	2	0	1	1	12
2003-04	Utah Grizzlies	AHL	80	5	17	22	171	....	....	....	....	....
2004-05	Hamilton Bulldogs	AHL	80	6	20	26	163	4	0	0	0	2

JANSSEN, Cam (JAN-suhn, KAM) N.J.

Right wing. Shoots right. 5'11", 205 lbs. Born, St. Louis, MO, April 15, 1984.
(New Jersey's 6th choice, 117th overall, in 2002 Entry Draft).

			Regular Season					Playoffs				
Season	Club	League	GP	G	A	Pts	PIM	GP	G	A	Pts	PIM
2000-01	St. Louis Jr. Blues	CSJHL	45	1	2	3	244	....	....	....	....	....
2001-02	Windsor Spitfires	OHL	64	5	17	22	*268	10	0	0	0	13
2002-03	Windsor Spitfires	OHL	50	1	12	13	211	7	0	1	1	22
2003-04	Windsor Spitfires	OHL	35	4	9	13	144	....	....	....	....	....
	Guelph Storm	OHL	29	7	4	11	125	22	3	3	6	49
2004-05	Albany River Rats	AHL	70	1	3	4	337	....	....	....	....	....

JARMAN, Kevin (JAR-muhn, KEH-vihn) CBJ

Left wing. Shoots left. 6', 184 lbs. Born, Toronto, Ont., March 12, 1985.
(Columbus' 4th choice, 103rd overall, in 2003 Entry Draft).

			Regular Season					Playoffs				
Season	Club	League	GP	G	A	Pts	PIM	GP	G	A	Pts	PIM
2001-02	Stouffville Spirit	OPJHL	44	20	13	33	53	....	....	....	....	....
2002-03	Stouffville Spirit	OPJHL	46	41	39	80	49	11	5	3	8	6
2003-04	Massachusetts	H-East	34	4	6	10	28	....	....	....	....	....
2004-05	Massachusetts	H-East	37	7	14	21	52	....	....	....	....	....

JARRETT, Cole (JAIR-reht, KOHL) NYI

Wing. Shoots left. 6', 195 lbs. Born, Sault Ste. Marie, Ont., January 4, 1983.
(Columbus' 6th choice, 141st overall, in 2001 Entry Draft).

			Regular Season					Playoffs				
Season	Club	League	GP	G	A	Pts	PIM	GP	G	A	Pts	PIM
1998-99	Waterloo Siskins	OHA-B	44	6	10	16	43	4	2	2	4	5
99-2000	Plymouth Whalers	OHL	57	3	7	10	47	23	3	7	10	19
2000-01	Plymouth Whalers	OHL	60	12	36	48	98	19	6	12	18	29
2001-02	Plymouth Whalers	OHL	51	14	24	38	92	6	1	1	2	18
2002-03	Plymouth Whalers	OHL	58	14	41	55	138	14	5	6	11	29
2003-04	Bridgeport	AHL	59	2	14	16	38	....	....	....	....	....
2004-05	Bridgeport	AHL	61	7	13	20	65	....	....	....	....	....

Signed as a free agent by **NY Islanders**, September 9, 2003.

JENSEN, Christian (JEHN-suhn, KRIHS-tyehn) S.J.

Defense. Shoots right. 6'3", 190 lbs. Born, Brooklyn, NY, January 6, 1986.
(San Jose's 10th choice, 289th overall, in 2004 Entry Draft).

			Regular Season					Playoffs				
Season	Club	League	GP	G	A	Pts	PIM	GP	G	A	Pts	PIM
2003-04	New Jersey Jrs.	AJHL	48	6	23	29	62	....	....	....	....	....
2004-05	Yale	ECAC	29	11	9	20	25	....	....	....	....	....

JENSEN, Joe (JEHN-suhn, JOH) PIT.

Center. Shoots left. 5'11", 180 lbs. Born, Maple Grove, MN, February 6, 1983.
(Pittsburgh's 10th choice, 232nd overall, in 2003 Entry Draft).

			Regular Season					Playoffs				
Season	Club	League	GP	G	A	Pts	PIM	GP	G	A	Pts	PIM
2000-01	Sioux City	USHL	56	14	20	34	59	8	2	4	6	12
2001-02	Sioux City	USHL	57	20	26	46	135	3	0	0	0	6
2002-03	St. Cloud State	WCHA	37	9	9	18	14	....	....	....	....	....
2003-04	St. Cloud State	WCHA	38	10	14	24	42	....	....	....	....	....
2004-05	St. Cloud State	WCHA	40	12	14	26	36	....	....	....	....	....

JESSIMAN, Hugh (JEHS-ih-muhn, HEW) NYR

Right wing. Shoots right. 6'5", 226 lbs. Born, New York, NY, March 28, 1984.
(NY Rangers' 1st choice, 12th overall, in 2003 Entry Draft).

			Regular Season					Playoffs				
Season	Club	League	GP	G	A	Pts	PIM	GP	G	A	Pts	PIM
2001-02	Brunswick Bruins	High-CT	18	25	27	52	40	....	....	....	....	....
2002-03	Dartmouth	ECAC	34	23	24	47	48	....	....	....	....	....
2003-04	Dartmouth	ECAC	34	16	17	33	71	....	....	....	....	....
2004-05	Dartmouth	ECAC	12	1	1	2	18	....	....	....	....	....

ECAC All-Rookie Team (2003) • ECAC Rookie of the Year (2003) • ECAC Second All-Star Team (2004)

JOHANSSON, Daniel (yoh-HAN-suhn, DAN-yehl) L.A.

Center. Shoots left. 5'11", 176 lbs. Born, Ornskoldsvik, Sweden, July 5, 1981.
(Los Angeles' 6th choice, 125th overall, in 1999 Entry Draft).

			Regular Season					Playoffs				
Season	Club	League	GP	G	A	Pts	PIM	GP	G	A	Pts	PIM
1997-98	Malmo Jr.	Swe-Jr.	6	0	0	0	0	....	....	....	....	....
1998-99	Malmo Jr.	Swe-Jr.	43	10	19	29	....	....	....	....	....	....
99-2000	Malmo Jr.	Swe-Jr.	35	11	21	32	34	....	....	....	....	....
	MoDo	EuroHL	2	0	0	0	0	....	....	....	....	....
2000-01	Bodens IK	Sweden-2	36	4	3	7	10	4	0	0	0	0
2001-02	Bodens IK	Sweden-2	37	2	3	5	10	....	....	....	....	....
	Vaxjo Lakers HC	Sweden-3	8	2	5	7	6	....	....	....	....	....
2002-03	Vaxjo Lakers HC	Sweden-3	44	6	18	24		....	....	....	....	....
2003-04	Vaxjo Lakers HC	Sweden-2	46	6	8	14	6	5	0	0	0	0
2004-05	Vaxjo Lakers HC	Sweden-2	42	5	9	14	30	2	0	1	1	0

JOHANSSON, Eric (joh-HAHN-suhn, AIR-ihk)

Center. Shoots left. 6', 195 lbs. Born, Edmonton, Alta., January 7, 1982.
(New Jersey's 8th choice, 187th overall, in 2002 Entry Draft).

			Regular Season					Playoffs				
Season	Club	League	GP	G	A	Pts	PIM	GP	G	A	Pts	PIM
1997-98	Edmonton CAC	AMHA	22	13	10	23	19	....	....	....	....	....
	St. Albert Saints	AJHL	17	2	5	7	17	....	....	....	....	....
1998-99	Tri-City Americans	WHL	48	8	14	22	20	6	1	1	2	2
99-2000	Tri-City Americans	WHL	72	24	36	60	38	4	0	0	0	2
2000-01	Tri-City Americans	WHL	72	36	44	80	72	....	....	....	....	....
2001-02	Tri-City Americans	WHL	69	44	59	103	73	5	1	2	3	5
2002-03	Albany River Rats	AHL	66	7	9	16	24	....	....	....	....	....
2003-04	Albany River Rats	AHL	63	7	19	26	32	....	....	....	....	....
2004-05	Albany River Rats	AHL	22	2	9	11	6	....	....	....	....	....
	Augusta Lynx	ECHL	42	15	21	36	36	....	....	....	....	....

• Re-entered NHL Entry Draft. Originally Minnesota's 9th choice, 255th overall, in 2000 Entry Draft.

WHL West Second All-Star Team (2002)

JOHANSSON, Fredrik (yoh-HAHN-suhn, FREHD-rihk) EDM.

Center. Shoots left. 5'11", 180 lbs. Born, Munkedal, Sweden, February 27, 1984.
(Edmonton's 14th choice, 274th overall, in 2002 Entry Draft).

			Regular Season					Playoffs				
Season	Club	League	GP	G	A	Pts	PIM	GP	G	A	Pts	PIM
2000-01	V.Frolunda Jr.	Swe-Jr.	22	3	4	7	8	3	0	1	1	4
	V.Frolunda U18	Swe-U18	6	5	1	6	4	....	....	....	....	....
2001-02	V.Frolunda Jr.	Swe-Jr.	42	13	23	36	39	....	....	....	....	....
	V.Frolunda U18	Swe-U18	1	0	1	1	0	....	....	....	....	....
2002-03	V.Frolunda Jr.	Swe-Jr.	30	13	34	47	24	3	0	2	2	2
	V.Frolunda	Sweden	9	0	0	0	2	5	0	0	0	0
2003-04	V.Frolunda Jr.	Swe-Jr.	7	1	2	3	4	4	2	4	6	0
	Halmstad	Sweden-2	1	0	0	0	0	....	....	....	....	....
	V.Frolunda	Sweden	48	1	3	4	6	10	0	0	0	0
2004-05	Vasteras	Sweden-2	46	15	15	30	32	5	0	3	3	8

JOHANSSON, Jonas (yoh-HAHN-suhn, YOH-nuhs) WSH.

Right wing. Shoots right. 6'1", 180 lbs. Born, Jonkoping, Sweden, March 18, 1984.
(Colorado's 1st choice, 28th overall, in 2002 Entry Draft).

			Regular Season					Playoffs				
Season	Club	League	GP	G	A	Pts	PIM	GP	G	A	Pts	PIM
99-2000	HV 71 Jr.	Swe-Jr.	9	6	3	9	2	2	0	0	0	4
2000-01	HV 71 Jr.	Swe-Jr.	27	13	8	21	14	2	1	0	1	0
2001-02	HV 71 Jr.	Swe-Jr.	26	15	19	34	20	....	....	....	....	....
	HV 71 Jonkoping	Sweden	5	0	0	0	0	2	0	0	0	0
2002-03	Kamloops Blazers	WHL	26	10	25	35	8	6	1	2	3	4
2003-04	Kamloops Blazers	WHL	72	18	19	37	70	5	2	2	4	4
2004-05	Portland Pirates	AHL	50	3	6	9	8	....	....	....	....	....
	South Carolina	ECHL	5	4	2	6	10	....	....	....	....	....

Traded to **Washington** by **Colorado** with Bates Battaglia for Steve Konowalchuk and Washington's 3rd round choice (later traded to Carolina – Carolina selected Casey Borer) in 2004 Entry Draft, October 22, 2003.

JOHANSSON, Mikael (yoh-HAHN-suhn), MIGH-kuhl) DET.

Center. Shoots left. 5'10", 176 lbs. Born, Arvika, Sweden, June 27, 1985.
(Detroit's 8th choice, 289th overall, in 2003 Entry Draft).

			Regular Season					Playoffs				
Season	Club	League	GP	G	A	Pts	PIM	GP	G	A	Pts	PIM
2001-02	Truro Bearcats	MJrHL	31	1	13	14	34	6	0	0	0	6
2002-03	Arvika HC	Sweden-3	30	13	28	41	89	....	....	....	....	....
2003-04	Skare BK Karlstad	Sweden-3	10	1	5	6	6	....	....	....	....	....
2004-05	Bofors	Sweden-2	45	5	7	12	22	5	0	0	0	0

JOHNER, Dustin (JAW-nuhr, DUHS-tihn) CGY.

Center. Shoots right. 5'11", 181 lbs. Born, Estevan, Sask., March 6, 1983.
(Florida's 8th choice, 169th overall, in 2001 Entry Draft).

			Regular Season					Playoffs				
Season	Club	League	GP	G	A	Pts	PIM	GP	G	A	Pts	PIM
1998-99	Red Deer Rebels	AMBHL	36	35	29	64	42	....	....	....	....	....
99-2000	Red Deer Chiefs	AMHL	36	24	31	55	80	....	....	....	....	....
	Seattle	WHL	6	0	1	1	0	....	....	....	....	....
2000-01	Seattle	WHL	72	25	31	56	45	9	1	5	6	6
2001-02	Seattle	WHL	71	33	48	81	71	8	4	3	7	8
2002-03	Seattle	WHL	71	36	41	77	97	15	7	6	13	14
2003-04	Seattle	WHL	71	26	31	57	54	....	....	....	....	....
	South Carolina	ECHL	4	2	4	6	0	7	4	3	7	4
2004-05	Lowell	AHL	23	4	8	12	12	11	1	0	1	4
	Las Vegas	ECHL	51	22	26	48	42	....	....	....	....	....

Signed as a free agent by **Calgary**, July 6, 2004.

JOHNSON, Jack (JAWN-suhn, JAK) CAR.

Defense. Shoots left. 6'1", 201 lbs. Born, Indianapolis, IN, January 13, 1987.
(Carolina's 1st choice, 3rd overall, in 2005 Entry Draft).

			Regular Season					Playoffs				
Season	Club	League	GP	G	A	Pts	PIM	GP	G	A	Pts	PIM
2002-03	Shat.-St. Mary's	High-MN	48	15	27	42	....	....	....	....	....	....
2003-04	USA U-17	USDP	60	15	21	36	171	....	....	....	....	....
2004-05	USA U-17&U-18	NAHL	12	7	10	17	57	....	....	....	....	....
	USA U-18	USDP	38	12	19	31	143	....	....	....	....	....

Signed Letter of Intent to attend **Michigan** (CCHA), November 22, 2004.

JOHNSON, Jonas (YAWN-suhn, YEW-nuhs) ST.L.

Center. Shoots left. 6'2", 185 lbs. Born, Gavle, Sweden, March 23, 1970.
(St. Louis' 7th choice, 221st overall, in 2002 Entry Draft).

			Regular Season					Playoffs				
Season	Club	League	GP	G	A	Pts	PIM	GP	G	A	Pts	PIM
1987-88	S/G Gavle	Sweden-2	13	4	3	7	0	....	....	....	....	....
1988-89	S/G Gavle	Sweden-2	27	5	3	8	10	....	....	....	....	....
1989-90	S/G Gavle	Sweden-2	24	13	6	19	8	2	1	1	2	0
1990-91	IF Bjorkloven Umea	Sweden-2	36	10	15	25	32	2	0	0	0	0
1991-92	Brynas IF Gavle	Sweden	36	6	9	15	8	5	3	0	3	0
1992-93	Brynas IF Gavle	Sweden	39	8	16	24	24	10	6	4	10	6
1993-94	Brynas IF Gavle	Sweden	39	11	16	27	14	7	2	1	3	8
1994-95	Brynas IF Gavle	Sweden	39	9	15	24	26	14	4	6	10	14
1995-96	Brynas IF Gavle	Sweden	22	11	6	17	12	....	....	....	....	....
	Brynas IF Gavle	Sweden-Q	18	6	25	31	4	10	1	9	10	8
1996-97	EV Landshut	Germany	48	7	19	26	6	7	2	0	2	4
1997-98	EV Landshut	Germany	48	8	6	14	26	6	0	1	1	8
1998-99	V.Frolunda	Sweden	46	13	21	34	44	4	1	1	2	6
99-2000	V.Frolunda	Sweden	50	17	18	35	73	5	0	2	2	6
2000-01	V.Frolunda	Sweden	50	15	29	44	75	5	4	3	7	12
2001-02	V.Frolunda	Sweden	50	14	31	45	24	10	3	3	6	4
2002-03	V.Frolunda	Sweden	49	12	23	35	24	16	3	3	6	27
2003-04	V.Frolunda	Sweden	49	14	14	28	68	10	3	5	8	2
2004-05	Frolunda	Sweden	48	18	9	27	34	14	2	*10	12	8

JOHNSON, Nick (JAWN-suhn, NIHK) PIT.

Right wing. Shoots right. 6'1", 183 lbs. Born, Calgary, Alta., December 24, 1985.
(Pittsburgh's 4th choice, 67th overall, in 2004 Entry Draft).

			Regular Season					Playoffs				
Season	Club	League	GP	G	A	Pts	PIM	GP	G	A	Pts	PIM
2002-03	St. Albert Saints	AJHL	60	21	30	51	10	....	....	....	....	....
2003-04	St. Albert Saints	AJHL	51	35	36	71	33	4	0	2	2	0
2004-05	Dartmouth	ECAC	35	18	17	35	16	....	....	....	....	....

ECAC All-Rookie Team 2005)

JOHNSON, Tyler (JAWN-suhn, TIGH-luhr) CGY.

Center. Shoots right. 6'2", 185 lbs. Born, Edmonton, Alta., July 11, 1985.
(Calgary's 6th choice, 173rd overall, in 2003 Entry Draft).

			Regular Season					Playoffs				
Season	Club	League	GP	G	A	Pts	PIM	GP	G	A	Pts	PIM
2000-01	Leduc Oil Kings	AMHL	1	0	0	0	0	....	....	....	....	....
	Leduc Oil Barons	AMBHL	36	21	31	52	57	4	3	4	7	6
2001-02	Leduc Oil Kings	AMHL	18	4	18	22	26	....	....	....	....	....
	Moose Jaw	WHL	24	2	1	3	11	10	0	0	0	2
2002-03	Moose Jaw	WHL	49	8	6	14	39	13	2	1	3	9
2003-04	Moose Jaw	WHL	22	2	2	4	12	....	....	....	....	....
	Red Deer Rebels	WHL	35	7	9	16	19	19	5	5	10	18
2004-05	Red Deer Rebels	WHL	55	10	19	29	51	7	1	4	5	8

JOKILA, Janne (YOHK-ih-luh, YAH-nee) CBJ

Left wing. Shoots left. 5'9", 174 lbs. Born, Turku, Finland, April 22, 1982.
(Columbus' 7th choice, 200th overall, in 2000 Entry Draft).

			Regular Season					Playoffs				
Season	Club	League	GP	G	A	Pts	PIM	GP	G	A	Pts	PIM
1997-98	TPS Turku U18	Fin-U18	30	11	10	21	28	6	3	1	4	2
1998-99	TPS Turku Jr.	Finland-Jr.	36	17	15	32	77	....	....	....	....	....
99-2000	TPS Turku Jr.	Finland-Jr.	35	10	7	17	32	13	3	3	6	4
2000-01	TPS Turku Jr.	Finland-Jr.	22	15	15	30	30	2	0	1	1	4
	TPS Turku	Finland	2	0	0	0	0	....	....	....	....	....
	SaiPa	Finland	8	1	1	2	0	....	....	....	....	....
2001-02	TPS Turku	Finland	14	1	1	2	4	....	....	....	....	....
	SaiPa	Finland	12	0	0	0	2	....	....	....	....	....
	Lukko Rauma	Finland	14	0	1	1	18	....	....	....	....	....
2002-03	River City Lancers	USHL	45	15	17	32	57	7	1	5	6	4
2003-04	Syracuse Crunch	AHL	7	0	0	0	0	....	....	....	....	....
	Dayton Bombers	ECHL	69	17	23	40	69	....	....	....	....	....
2004-05	Syracuse Crunch	AHL	2	0	0	0	0	....	....	....	....	....
	Dayton Bombers	ECHL	70	24	22	46	78	....	....	....	....	....

JOKINEN, Jussi (YOH-kih-nihn, YOO-see) DAL.

Center. Shoots left. 5'11", 183 lbs. Born, Kalajoki, Finland, April 1, 1983.
(Dallas' 7th choice, 192nd overall, in 2001 Entry Draft).

			Regular Season					Playoffs				
Season	Club	League	GP	G	A	Pts	PIM	GP	G	A	Pts	PIM
99-2000	Karpat Oulu Jr.	Finland-Jr.	28	4	6	10	14	....	....	....	....	....
	Karpat Oulu U18	Fin-U18	15	6	25	31	14	6	2	3	5	0
2000-01	Karpat Oulu U18	Fin-U18	1	2	1	3	0	....	....	....	....	....
	Karpat Oulu Jr.	Finland-Jr.	41	18	31	49	69	6	2	2	4	0
2001-02	Karpat Oulu	Finland	54	10	6	16	34	4	1	0	1	0
	Karpat Oulu Jr.	Finland-Jr.	2	4	1	5	2	1	1	1	2	0
2002-03	Karpat Oulu	Finland	51	14	23	37	10	15	2	1	3	33
2003-04	Karpat Oulu	Finland	55	15	23	38	20	15	3	4	7	6
2004-05	Karpat Oulu	Finland	56	23	24	47	24	12	3	4	7	2

JONASEN, Marcus (YOH-nuh-suhn, MAHR-kuhs) NYR

Left wing. Shoots right. 6'4", 215 lbs. Born, Vasteras, Sweden, January 12, 1984.
(NY Rangers' 2nd choice, 81st overall, in 2002 Entry Draft).

			Regular Season					Playoffs				
Season	Club	League	GP	G	A	Pts	PIM	GP	G	A	Pts	PIM
2001-02	Calgary Bruins	CBHL	3	2	1	3	0	....	....	....	....	....
	Vasteras Jr.	Swe-Jr.	3	0	0	0	4	....	....	....	....	....
	Cardiff Devils	Britain-2	13	3	5	8	6	....	....	....	....	....
	Vasteras	Sweden-3	16	2	1	3	6	....	....	....	....	....
2002-03	Hammarby Jr.	Swe-Jr.	27	16	9	25	28	2	1	0	1	2
2003-04	Tri-City Americans	WHL	43	12	14	26	28	11	4	4	8	8
2004-05	Tri-City Americans	WHL	70	21	20	41	59	5	1	2	3	2

JONES, Blair (JOHNZ, BLAYR) T.B.

Center. Shoots right. 6'2", 193 lbs. Born, Central Butte, Sask., September 27, 1986.
(Tampa Bay's 5th choice, 102nd overall, in 2005 Entry Draft).

			Regular Season					Playoffs				
Season	Club	League	GP	G	A	Pts	PIM	GP	G	A	Pts	PIM
2002-03	Bethune	SBHL	STATISTICS NOT AVAILABLE									
	Red Deer Rebels	WHL	37	3	4	7	17	10	1	0	1	0
2003-04	Red Deer Rebels	WHL	72	9	22	31	55	19	1	5	6	24
2004-05	Red Deer Rebels	WHL	39	7	18	25	48	....	....	....	....	....
	Moose Jaw	WHL	29	7	18	25	30	5	2	5	7	8

JONES, David (JOHNZ, DAY-vihd) COL.

Right wing. Shoots right. 6'3", 220 lbs. Born, Guelph, Ont., August 10, 1984.
(Colorado's 8th choice, 288th overall, in 2003 Entry Draft).

			Regular Season					Playoffs				
Season	Club	League	GP	G	A	Pts	PIM	GP	G	A	Pts	PIM
2000-01	PoCo Bucs	PIJHL	40	18	11	29	33	....	....	....	....	....
2001-02	Coquitlam Express	BCHL	59	19	32	51	62	....	....	....	....	....
2002-03	Coquitlam Express	BCHL	35	9	19	28	55	7	2	6	8	8
2003-04	Coquitlam Express	BCHL	53	33	60	93	78	7	3	6	9	4
2004-05	Dartmouth	ECAC	34	9	5	14	26	....	....	....	....	....

JONES, Matt (JOHNZ, MAT) PHX.

Defense. Shoots left. 6', 215 lbs. Born, Downers Grove, IL, August 8, 1983.
(Phoenix's 5th choice, 80th overall, in 2002 Entry Draft).

			Regular Season					Playoffs				
Season	Club	League	GP	G	A	Pts	PIM	GP	G	A	Pts	PIM
99-2000	Green Bay	USHL	54	1	4	5	59	13	0	0	0	2
2000-01	Green Bay	USHL	52	3	10	13	58	4	0	0	0	2
2001-02	North Dakota	WCHA	37	2	5	7	20	....	....	....	....	....
2002-03	North Dakota	WCHA	39	1	6	7	26	....	....	....	....	....
2003-04	North Dakota	WCHA	41	7	14	21	40	....	....	....	....	....
2004-05	North Dakota	WCHA	45	6	11	17	66	....	....	....	....	....

WCHA Second All-Star Team (2004)

JONES, Ryan (JOHNZ, RIGH-uhn) MIN.

Right wing. Shoots right. 6'1", 200 lbs. Born, Chatham, Ont., June 14, 1984.
(Minnesota's 5th choice, 111th overall, in 2004 Entry Draft).

			Regular Season					Playoffs				
Season	Club	League	GP	G	A	Pts	PIM	GP	G	A	Pts	PIM
2002-03	Chatham Maroons	OHA-B	38	12	11	23	42	....	....	....	....	....
2003-04	Chatham Maroons	OHA-B	46	39	30	69	64	17	17	9	26	25
2004-05	Miami U.	CCHA	38	8	7	15	79	....	....	....	....	....

JONSSON, Lars (YAWN-suhn, LARZ) BOS.

Defense. Shoots left. 6'1", 198 lbs. Born, Borlange, Sweden, January 2, 1982.
(Boston's 1st choice, 7th overall, in 2000 Entry Draft).

			Regular Season					Playoffs				
Season	Club	League	GP	G	A	Pts	PIM	GP	G	A	Pts	PIM
1998-99	Leksands IF Jr.	Swe-Jr.	40	4	8	12	42	....	....	....	....	....
99-2000	Leksands IF Jr.	Swe-Jr.	34	16	22	38	50	2	0	0	0	0
	Leksands IF	Sweden	5	0	0	0	4	....	....	....	....	....
2000-01	Leksands IF Jr.	Swe-Jr.	7	1	3	4	6	....	....	....	....	....
	Leksands IF	Sweden	31	2	1	3	12	....	....	....	....	....
2001-02	Leksands IF Jr.	Swe-Jr.	3	2	1	3	4	1	0	0	0	0
	Leksands IF	Sweden-2	28	1	7	8	59	....	....	....	....	....
2002-03	Leksands IF	Sweden	21	0	0	0	12	5	0	0	0	2
	IF Bjorkloven Umea	Sweden-2	9	3	4	7	10	....	....	....	....	....
	IFK Arboga IK	Sweden-2	4	0	0	0	4	....	....	....	....	....
2003-04	Leksands IF	Sweden	50	3	9	12	30	....	....	....	....	....
	Leksands IF	Sweden-Q	4	1	0	1	2	....	....	....	....	....
2004-05	Timra IK	Sweden	50	5	6	11	32	7	0	0	0	2

JONSSON, Robin (YAWN-suhn, RAW-bihn) ST.L.

Defense. Shoots right. 6'2", 194 lbs. Born, Upplands Vasby, Sweden, December 10, 1983.
(St. Louis' 4th choice, 120th overall, in 2002 Entry Draft).

			Regular Season					Playoffs				
Season	Club	League	GP	G	A	Pts	PIM	GP	G	A	Pts	PIM
99-2000	Farjestad U18	Swe-U18	8	0	0	0	24	....	....	....	....	....
	Farjestad Jr.	Swe-Jr.	18	2	2	4	12	....	....	....	....	....
2000-01	Farjestad Jr.	Swe-Jr.	24	3	8	11	34	....	....	....	....	....
	Farjestad	Sweden	....	....	....	....	....	1	0	0	0	0
2001-02	Bofors	Sweden-2	55	3	4	7	36	....	....	....	....	....
	Farjestad	Sweden	1	0	0	0	0	....	....	....	....	....
2002-03	Bofors	Sweden-2	7	0	2	2	6	....	....	....	....	....
2003-04	Farjestad	Sweden	28	0	0	0	10	....	....	....	....	....
	Bofors	Sweden-2	18	3	3	6	18	5	0	1	1	6
2004-05	Bofors	Sweden-2	11	1	1	2	24	....	....	....	....	....
	Farjestad	Sweden	47	0	2	2	12	15	0	0	0	2

• Missed majority of 2002-03 season recovering from cancer surgery, October 30, 2002.

JOSEPH, Shane (JOH-sehf, SHAYN) S.J.

Center. Shoots right. 5'9", 170 lbs. Born, Brooks, Alta., July 23, 1981.

			Regular Season					Playoffs				
Season	Club	League	GP	G	A	Pts	PIM	GP	G	A	Pts	PIM
1997-98	Medicine Hat	AMHL	35	23	34	57	20	....	....	....	....	....
1998-99	Bow Valley Eagles	AJHL	60	36	34	70	14	....	....	....	....	....
99-2000	Minnesota State	WCHA	5	0	0	0	0	....	....	....	....	....
2000-01	Minnesota State	WCHA	16	0	5	5	2	....	....	....	....	....
2001-02	Minnesota State	WCHA	38	20	11	31	0	....	....	....	....	....
2002-03	Minnesota State	WCHA	41	29	36	65	6	....	....	....	....	....
2003-04	Minnesota State	WCHA	39	19	24	43	2	....	....	....	....	....
	Cleveland Barons	AHL	12	4	5	9	0	9	5	4	9	0
2004-05	Cleveland Barons	AHL	67	10	22	32	8	....	....	....	....	....

WCHA First All-Star Team (2003) • NCAA West Second All-American Team (2003)

• Missed majority of 1999-2000 season recovering from knee injury suffered in game vs. St. Cloud State (WCHA), November 11, 1999. Signed to a PTO (tryout) contract by **Cleveland** (AHL), March 17, 2004. Signed as a free agent by **San Jose**, June 27, 2004.

JOSLIN, Derek (JAWS-lihn, DEH-rihk) S.J.

Defense. Shoots left. 6'1", 191 lbs. Born, Richmond Hill, Ont., March 17, 1987.
(San Jose's 5th choice, 149th overall, in 2005 Entry Draft).

			Regular Season					Playoffs				
Season	Club	League	GP	G	A	Pts	PIM	GP	G	A	Pts	PIM
2002-03	Vaughan	GTHL	60	9	18	27	72	....	....	....	....	....
2003-04	Aurora Tigers	OPJHL	36	4	12	16	....	....	....	....	....	....
	Ottawa 67's	OHL	7	0	0	0	4	....	....	....	....	....
2004-05	Ottawa 67's	OHL	68	6	24	30	44	21	0	3	3	24

JOUDREY, Andrew (JOO-dree, AN-droo) WSH.

Center. Shoots left. 5'11", 191 lbs. Born, Halifax, N.S., July 15, 1984.
(Washington's 5th choice, 249th overall, in 2003 Entry Draft).

			Regular Season					Playoffs				
Season	Club	League	GP	G	A	Pts	PIM	GP	G	A	Pts	PIM
2000-01	Dartmouth	NSMHL	82	51	70	121	....	....	....	....	....	....
2001-02	Notre Dame	SJHL	57	24	38	62	14	....	....	....	....	....
2002-03	Notre Dame	SJHL	53	27	51	78	16	....	....	....	....	....
2003-04	U. of Wisconsin	WCHA	42	7	15	22	2	....	....	....	....	....
2004-05	U. of Wisconsin	WCHA	41	7	17	24	18	....	....	....	....	....

JOUKOV, Mishail (ZHOO-kawv, mee-shigh-EHL) EDM.

Left wing. Shoots left. 6'3", 187 lbs. Born, Leningrad, USSR, January 3, 1985.
(Edmonton's 4th choice, 72nd overall, in 2003 Entry Draft).

			Regular Season					Playoffs				
Season	Club	League	GP	G	A	Pts	PIM	GP	G	A	Pts	PIM
2000-01	Mora IK Jr.	Swe-Jr.	28	9	14	23	6	9	2	4	6	0
2001-02	IFK Arboga IK	Sweden-2	37	4	9	13	12	3	1	0	1	2
2002-03	IFK Arboga IK	Sweden-2	41	9	14	23	30	3	3	1	4	0
2003-04	Vasteras	Sweden-2	44	5	12	17	16	....	....	....	....	....
	HV 71 Jonkoping	Sweden	3	0	0	0	0	....	....	....	....	....
2004-05	Ak Bars Kazan 2	Russia-3	....	8	11	19	....	....	....	....	....	....
	Spartak Moscow	Russia	13	1	2	3	2	....	....	....	....	....
	Ak Bars Kazan	Russia	2	0	0	0	0	....	....	....	....	....

JUNTUNEN, Henrik (YUN-tuh-nehn, HEHN-rihk) L.A.

Right wing. Shoots right. 6'2", 185 lbs. Born, Goteborg, Sweden, April 24, 1983.
(Los Angeles' 5th choice, 83rd overall, in 2001 Entry Draft).

			Regular Season					Playoffs				
Season	Club	League	GP	G	A	Pts	PIM	GP	G	A	Pts	PIM
99-2000	Karpat Oulu Jr.	Finland-Jr.	34	16	7	23	18	5	0	0	0	2
2000-01	Karpat Oulu Jr.	Finland-Jr.	17	4	4	8	12	....	....	....	....	....
	Karpat Oulu	Finland	....	....	....	....	....	2	0	0	0	0
2001-02	Karpat Oulu Jr.	Finland-Jr.	34	19	11	30	42	3	1	1	2	0
	Karpat Oulu	Finland	13	0	0	0	2	....	....	....	....	....
2002-03	Karpat Oulu	Finland	50	5	4	9	30	15	2	0	2	4
	Karpat Oulu Jr.	Finland-Jr.	2	0	0	0	0	....	....	....	....	....
2003-04	Karpat Oulu	Finland	50	4	8	12	30	13	0	1	1	25
2004-05	Karpat Oulu	Finland	52	6	4	10	20	10	0	0	0	2

JURCINA, Milan (YEWR-chee-nah, MEE-lan) BOS.

Defense. Shoots right. 6'4", 233 lbs. Born, Liptovsky Mikulas, Czech., June 7, 1983.
(Boston's 7th choice, 241st overall, in 2001 Entry Draft).

			Regular Season					Playoffs				
Season	Club	League	GP	G	A	Pts	PIM	GP	G	A	Pts	PIM
99-2000	L. Mikulas Jr.	Slovak-Jr.	STATISTICS NOT AVAILABLE									
2000-01	Halifax	QMJHL	68	0	5	5	56	6	0	2	2	12
2001-02	Halifax	QMJHL	61	4	16	20	58	13	5	3	8	10
2002-03	Halifax	QMJHL	51	15	13	28	102	25	6	6	12	40
2003-04	Providence Bruins	AHL	73	5	12	17	52	2	0	1	1	2
2004-05	Providence Bruins	AHL	79	6	17	23	92	17	1	3	4	30

KADEYKIN, Anton (ka-DAY-kihn, AN-tawn) N.J.

Defense. Shoots left. 6'3", 205 lbs. Born, Elektrostal, USSR, May 17, 1984.
(New Jersey's 1st choice, 51st overall, in 2002 Entry Draft).

			Regular Season					Playoffs				
Season	Club	League	GP	G	A	Pts	PIM	GP	G	A	Pts	PIM
99-2000	Elektrostal 2	Russia-3	5	0	0	0	0	....	....	....	....	....
2000-01	Elektrostal 2	Russia-3	3	0	1	1	2	....	....	....	....	....
	Russia	Exhib.	5	0	1	1	6	....	....	....	....	....
2001-02	Elektrostal 2	Russia-3	21	2	2	4	46	....	....	....	....	....
	Elektrostal	Russia-2	20	0	0	0	16	....	....	....	....	....
2002-03	Sarnia Sting	OHL	55	2	8	10	34	6	0	1	1	0
2003-04	Sarnia Sting	OHL	39	0	2	2	38	3	0	0	0	0
2004-05			DID NOT PLAY – INJURED									

Missed entire 2004-05 season recovering from shoulder injury.

KAHNBERG, Magnus (KAHN-buhrg, MAG-nuhs) CAR.

Left wing. Shoots left. 6'2", 190 lbs. Born, Kallered, Sweden, February 25, 1980.
(Carolina's 6th choice, 212th overall, in 2000 Entry Draft).

			Regular Season					Playoffs				
Season	Club	League	GP	G	A	Pts	PIM	GP	G	A	Pts	PIM
1997-98	V.Frolunda U18	Swe-U18	11	15	6	21	6	8	5	8	13	6
	V.Frolunda Jr.	Swe-Jr.	28	6	7	13	8	2	0	0	0	0
1998-99	V.Frolunda Jr.	Swe-Jr.	34	23	18	41	4	4	1	1	2	0
99-2000	V.Frolunda Jr.	Swe-Jr.	35	45	21	66	30	6	7	4	11	4
	V.Frolunda	Sweden	4	0	0	0	0	....	....	....	....	....
2000-01	V.Frolunda U18	Swe-U18	1	8	1	9	0	....	....	....	....	....
	V.Frolunda Jr.	Swe-Jr.	2	*2	1	3	2	....	....	....	....	....
	V.Frolunda	Sweden	50	8	6	14	6	5	0	0	0	2
2001-02	V.Frolunda	Sweden	50	14	11	25	24	10	5	0	5	2
2002-03	V.Frolunda	Sweden	50	14	20	34	22	15	2	6	8	12
2003-04	V.Frolunda	Sweden	50	*33	16	*49	20	10	5	2	7	10
2004-05	Frolunda	Sweden	46	15	8	23	22	13	5	1	6	4

KAIGORODOV, Alexei (kay-goh-ROH-dahv, al-EHX-ay) OTT.

Center. Shoots left. 6'1", 183 lbs. Born, Chelyabinsk, USSR, July 29, 1983.
(Ottawa's 2nd choice, 47th overall, in 2002 Entry Draft).

			Regular Season					Playoffs				
Season	Club	League	GP	G	A	Pts	PIM	GP	G	A	Pts	PIM
1998-99	Magnitogorsk 2	Russia-4	10	6	4	10	2	....	....	....	....	....
99-2000	Magnitogorsk 2	Russia-3	19	2	3	5	8	....	....	....	....	....
2000-01	Magnitogorsk 2	Russia-3	45	12	30	42	26	....	....	....	....	....
2001-02	Magnitogorsk	Russia	46	4	12	16	20	9	0	3	3	2
2002-03	Magnitogorsk	Russia	46	8	14	22	20	3	0	1	1	0
2003-04	Magnitogorsk	Russia	49	4	12	16	24	14	2	2	4	4
2004-05	Magnitogorsk	Russia	57	15	34	49	40	5	0	3	3	2

KAIP, Rylan (KAYP, RIH-luhn) ATL.

Center. Shoots right. 6', 180 lbs. Born, Wilcox, Sask., March 19, 1984.
(Atlanta's 9th choice, 269th overall, in 2003 Entry Draft).

			Regular Season					Playoffs				
Season	Club	League	GP	G	A	Pts	PIM	GP	G	A	Pts	PIM
2000-01	Notre Dame	SJHL	5	0	0	0	0	1	0	0	0	0
2001-02	Notre Dame	SJHL	61	14	18	32	77	....	....	....	....	....
2002-03	Notre Dame	SJHL	57	20	36	56	164	6	1	6	7	21
2003-04	Notre Dame	SJHL	54	30	36	66	133	4	1	1	2	6
2004-05	North Dakota	WCHA	22	0	4	4	20	....	....	....	....	....

KALETA, Patrick (ka-LEH-tuh, PAT-rihk) BUF.

Right wing. Shoots right. 5'11", 195 lbs. Born, Buffalo, NY, June 8, 1986.
(Buffalo's 5th choice, 176th overall, in 2004 Entry Draft).

			Regular Season					Playoffs				
Season	Club	League	GP	G	A	Pts	PIM	GP	G	A	Pts	PIM
2002-03	Peterborough	OHL	67	7	9	16	67	7	0	0	0	6
2003-04	Peterborough	OHL	67	14	14	28	124	....	....	....	....	....
2004-05	Peterborough	OHL	62	24	28	52	146	14	3	3	6	30

KALTEVA, Mikko (KAL-tuh-vah, MEE-koh) COL.

Defense. Shoots left. 6'3", 190 lbs. Born, Hyvinkaa, Finland, May 25, 1984.
(Colorado's 4th choice, 107th overall, in 2002 Entry Draft).

			Regular Season					Playoffs				
Season	Club	League	GP	G	A	Pts	PIM	GP	G	A	Pts	PIM
2000-01	Jokerit U18	Fin-U18	11	1	4	5	6	6	3	1	4	2
	Jokerit Helsinki Jr.	Finland-Jr.	34	0	3	3	12	....	....	....	....	....
2001-02	Jokerit Helsinki Jr.	Finland-Jr.	29	5	3	8	10	1	0	0	0	0
	Jokerit U18	Fin-U18	....	....	....	....	....	8	2	2	4	0
2002-03	Jokerit U18	Fin-U18	34	7	8	15	30	10	2	4	6	4
2003-04	Jokerit Helsinki Jr.	Finland-Jr.	39	14	10	24	42	3	0	0	0	0
	Jokerit Helsinki	Finland	2	0	0	0	0	8	0	0	0	2
2004-05	Jokerit Helsinki Jr.	Finland-Jr.	24	2	9	11	40	....	....	....	....	....
	Jokerit Helsinki	Finland	2	0	0	0	0	2	0	0	0	0

KALUS, Petr (KA-luhs, PEE-tuhr) BOS.

Left wing. Shoots left. 6'1", 189 lbs. Born, Ostrava, Czech., June 29, 1987.
(Boston's 2nd choice, 39th overall, in 2005 Entry Draft).

			Regular Season					Playoffs				
Season	Club	League	GP	G	A	Pts	PIM	GP	G	A	Pts	PIM
2002-03	HC Ostrava U17	CzR-U17	18	3	19	22	14	....	....	....	....	....
	HC Vitkovice U17	CzR-U17	10	3	1	4	37	....	....	....	....	....
	HC Vitkovice Jr.	CzRep-Jr.	11	0	0	0	4	....	....	....	....	....
2003-04	HC Vitkovice U17	CzR-U17	9	7	5	12	60	7	3	5	8	2
	HC Vitkovice Jr.	CzRep-Jr.	41	8	8	16	67	....	....	....	....	....
2004-05	HC Vitkovice Jr.	CzRep-Jr.	39	20	11	31	161	2	2	0	2	25
	HC Vitkovice Steel	CzRep	1	0	0	0	0	....	....	....	....	....

KANKAANPERA, Markus (kan-kahn-PEHR-a, MAHR-kus) VAN.

Defense. Shoots left. 6'1", 191 lbs. Born, Skelleftea, Sweden, April 27, 1980.
(Vancouver's 7th choice, 218th overall, in 1999 Entry Draft).

			Regular Season					Playoffs				
Season	Club	League	GP	G	A	Pts	PIM	GP	G	A	Pts	PIM
1995-96	JyP HT U18	Fin-U18	9	1	1	2	4	....	....	....	....	....
1996-97	JyP HT Jyvaskyla Jr.	Finland-Jr.	33	3	5	8	83	....	....	....	....	....
1997-98	JyP Jyvaskyla U18	Fin-U18	13	4	10	14	18	5	3	2	5	6
	JyP Jyvaskyla Jr.	Finland-Jr.	32	0	0	0	2	....	....	....	....	....
1998-99	JyP Jyvaskyla Jr.	Finland-Jr.	1	0	0	0	4	....	....	....	....	....
	JYP Jyvaskyla	Finland	50	0	2	2	85	3	0	0	0	0
99-2000	JyP Jyvaskyla Jr.	Finland-Jr.	3	1	1	2	2	3	0	1	1	6
	JYP Jyvaskyla	Finland	47	0	5	5	87	....	....	....	....	....
2000-01	JYP Jyvaskyla	Finland	53	5	4	9	60	....	....	....	....	....
2001-02	HPK Hameenlinna	Finland	51	4	3	7	80	8	0	0	0	10
2002-03	Jokerit Helsinki	Finland	52	1	4	5	94	10	1	2	3	6
2003-04	Jokerit Helsinki	Finland	55	6	6	12	101	8	1	1	2	8
2004-05	Jokerit Helsinki	Finland	51	0	3	3	71	7	0	3	3	6

KANKO, Petr (KAN-koh, PEE-tuhr) L.A.

Right wing. Shoots left. 5'9", 195 lbs. Born, Pribram, Czech., February 7, 1984.
(Los Angeles' 3rd choice, 66th overall, in 2002 Entry Draft).

			Regular Season					Playoffs				
Season	Club	League	GP	G	A	Pts	PIM	GP	G	A	Pts	PIM
2000-01	Sparta Jr.	CzRep-Jr.	43	27	10	37	80	....	....	....	....	....
	HC Sparta Praha	CzRep	6	1	0	1	0	....	....	....	....	....
2001-02	Kitchener Rangers	OHL	61	28	32	60	54	4	0	2	2	0
2002-03	Kitchener Rangers	OHL	60	33	34	67	123	20	11	16	27	17
2003-04	Kitchener Rangers	OHL	55	26	42	68	97	5	2	2	4	10
	Manchester	AHL	6	1	3	4	0	6	1	3	4	2
2004-05	Manchester	AHL	60	4	14	18	118	6	0	0	0	18

KANTEE, Kevin (KAN-tee, KEH-vihn) CHI.

Defense. Shoots left. 6'2", 202 lbs. Born, Idaho Falls, ID, January 29, 1984.
(Chicago's 6th choice, 188th overall, in 2002 Entry Draft).

			Regular Season					Playoffs				
Season	Club	League	GP	G	A	Pts	PIM	GP	G	A	Pts	PIM
99-2000	Jokerit Helsinki Jr.	Finland-Jr.	13	0	2	2	6	....	....	....	....	....
2000-01	Jokerit Helsinki Jr.	Finland-Jr.	34	10	8	18	16	6	0	2	2	4
2001-02	Jokerit Helsinki Jr.	Finland-Jr.	34	2	7	9	16	1	0	0	0	0
	Jokerit U18	Fin-U18	1	2	0	2	12	5	2	1	3	....
2002-03	Jokerit Helsinki Jr.	Finland-Jr.	34	5	17	22	34	11	3	4	7	16
2003-04	Jokerit Helsinki Jr.	Finland-Jr.	26	1	17	18	38	3	0	0	0	0
	Jokerit Helsinki	Finland	19	0	1	1	4	6	0	1	1	2
2004-05	Jokerit Helsinki Jr.	Finland-Jr.	11	3	11	14	4	....	....	....	....	....
	Jokerit Helsinki	Finland	46	0	3	3	14	12	0	0	0	0

KARLSSON, Gabriel (KARLS-suhn, ga-BREE-ehl) DAL.

Center. Shoots left. 6'1", 189 lbs. Born, Borlange, Sweden, January 22, 1980.
(Dallas' 3rd choice, 86th overall, in 1998 Entry Draft).

			Regular Season					Playoffs				
Season	Club	League	GP	G	A	Pts	PIM	GP	G	A	Pts	PIM
1996-97	HV 71 Jr.	Swe-Jr.	25	7	9	16	....	....	....	....	....	....
1997-98	HV 71 Jr.	Swe-Jr.	27	11	15	26	32	....	....	....	....	....
	HV 71 Jonkoping	Sweden	1	0	0	0	0	....	....	....	....	....
1998-99	HV 71 Jr.	Swe-Jr.	12	4	9	13	4	....	....	....	....	....
	HV 71 Jonkoping	Sweden	33	2	1	3	2	....	....	....	....	....
99-2000	HV 71 Jonkoping	Sweden	50	5	3	8	12	6	0	0	0	2
2000-01	Assat Pori	Finland	17	2	2	4	6	....	....	....	....	....
	Leksands IF	Sweden	35	9	8	17	10	....	....	....	....	....
2001-02	Sodertalje SK	Sweden	47	8	7	15	18	....	....	....	....	....
2002-03	Sodertalje SK	Sweden	39	4	3	7	12	....	....	....	....	....
	Sodertalje SK Jr.	Swe-Jr.	1	0	1	1	0	....	....	....	....	....
2003-04	Sodertalje SK	Sweden	50	7	10	17	65	....	....	....	....	....
2004-05	Sodertalje SK Jr.	Swe-Jr.	1	0	0	0	0	....	....	....	....	....
	Sodertalje SK	Sweden	44	3	6	9	14	9	0	0	0	0

KARLSSON, Jens (KARLS-suhn, YEHNZ) L.A.

Right wing. Shoots right. 6'3", 205 lbs. Born, Goteborg, Sweden, November 7, 1982.
(Los Angeles' 1st choice, 18th overall, in 2001 Entry Draft).

			Regular Season					Playoffs				
Season	Club	League	GP	G	A	Pts	PIM	GP	G	A	Pts	PIM
1997-98	V.Frolunda Jr.	Swe-Jr.	17	2	3	5	4	....	....	....	....	....
1998-99	V.Frolunda U18	Swe-U18	32	27	17	44	110	4	2	2	4	0
99-2000	V.Frolunda U18	Swe-U18	3	6	3	9	6	....	....	....	....	....
	V.Frolunda Jr.	Swe-Jr.	32	24	13	37	82	6	3	0	3	42
2000-01	V.Frolunda Jr.	Swe-Jr.	25	20	15	35	154	1	0	1	1	2
	IF Molndal Hockey	Sweden-2	5	1	1	2	35	....	....	....	....	....
	V.Frolunda	Sweden	19	2	0	2	4	5	1	3	4	50
2001-02	V.Frolunda	Sweden	46	6	9	15	44	10	1	0	1	18
	V.Frolunda Jr.	Swe-Jr.	....	....	....	....	....	2	0	1	1	12
2002-03	V.Frolunda	Sweden	45	5	6	11	101	11	3	2	5	41
2003-04	V.Frolunda	Sweden	50	3	13	16	62	10	4	0	4	6
2004-05	Rogle	Sweden-2	10	2	7	9	20	....	....	....	....	....
	Frolunda	Sweden	39	1	3	4	57	6	0	0	0	2

KARLSSON, Mattias (KARL-suhn, MA-tee-uhs) OTT.

Defense. Shoots left. 6'2", 192 lbs. Born, Stora, Sweden, April 15, 1985.
(Ottawa's 4th choice, 135th overall, in 2003 Entry Draft).

			Regular Season					Playoffs				
Season	Club	League	GP	G	A	Pts	PIM	GP	G	A	Pts	PIM
2001-02	Brynas U18	Swe-U18	5	2	1	3	6	....	....	....	....	....
	Brynas IF Gavle Jr.	Swe-Jr.	13	0	1	1	12	....	....	....	....	....
2002-03	Brynas IF Gavle Jr.	Swe-Jr.	27	11	6	17	93	2	0	0	0	4
	Brynas IF Gavle	Sweden	3	0	0	0	0	....	....	....	....	....
	Brynas IF Gavle	Sweden-Q	3	0	0	0	0	....	....	....	....	....
2003-04	Brynas IF Gavle Jr.	Swe-Jr.	20	5	8	13	67	5	0	4	4	10
	Brynas IF Gavle	Sweden	39	0	0	0	6	....	....	....	....	....
2004-05	Brynas IF Gavle Jr.	Swe-Jr.	13	3	5	8	40	....	....	....	....	....
	Almtuna	Sweden-2	22	0	2	2	18	....	....	....	....	....
	Brynas IF Gavle	Sweden	9	0	0	0	2	....	....	....	....	....
	Brynas IF Gavle	Sweden-Q	1	0	0	0	0	....	....	....	....	....

KARSUMS, Martins (KAHR-suhmz, MAHR-tihnsh) BOS.

Right wing. Shoots right. 5'10", 190 lbs. Born, Riga, Latvia, February 26, 1986.
(Boston's 2nd choice, 64th overall, in 2004 Entry Draft).

			Regular Season					Playoffs				
Season	Club	League	GP	G	A	Pts	PIM	GP	G	A	Pts	PIM
2000-01	Prizma '83 Riga Jr.	Latvia-Jr.	2	0	0	0	0	....	....	....	....	....
	Lido Nafta Jr.	Latvia-Jr.	18	8	6	14	....	....	....	....	....	....
2001-02	Prizma '83 Riga	EEHL-B	16	7	8	15	4	....	....	....	....	....
	Prizma '83 Riga	Latvia	6	4	1	5	4	....	....	....	....	....
2002-03	HK Riga 2000	EEHL	2	0	0	0	0	....	....	....	....	....
	Vilki Riga	Latvia	STATISTICS NOT AVAILABLE									
2003-04	Moncton Wildcats	QMJHL	60	30	23	53	76	20	8	9	17	14
2004-05	Moncton Wildcats	QMJHL	30	14	12	26	31	2	0	0	0	0

QMJHL All-Rookie Team (2004)

KASPAR, Lukas (kas-PAHR, LOO-kahsh) S.J.

Right wing. Shoots left. 6'2", 198 lbs. Born, Most, Czech., September 23, 1985.
(San Jose's 1st choice, 22nd overall, in 2004 Entry Draft).

			Regular Season					Playoffs				
Season	Club	League	GP	G	A	Pts	PIM	GP	G	A	Pts	PIM
2000-01	Litvinov U17	CzR-U17	48	27	19	46	64	6	2	3	5	0
2001-02	Litvinov U17	CzR-U17	48	35	41	76	143	2	1	1	2	0
2002-03	Litvinov	CzRep	9	1	1	2	2	....	....	....	....	....
	Litvinov Jr.	CzRep-Jr.	26	14	14	28	40	....	....	....	....	....
2003-04	Litvinov Jr.	CzRep-Jr.	23	21	14	35	56	1	0	0	0	0
	Litvinov	CzRep	37	4	2	6	10	....	....	....	....	....
	Usti n. L.	CzRep-2	1	1	0	1	0	....	....	....	....	....
	SK HC Banik Most	CzRep-3	....	....	....	....	....	1	0	0	0	2
2004-05	Ottawa 67's	OHL	59	21	30	51	45	21	6	14	20	8

KASPARIK, Pavel (kas-PAHR-ihk, PAH-vehl) PHI.

Center. Shoots left. 6'2", 198 lbs. Born, Pisek, Czech., November 11, 1979.
(Philadelphia's 4th choice, 200th overall, in 1999 Entry Draft).

			Regular Season					Playoffs				
Season	Club	League	GP	G	A	Pts	PIM	GP	G	A	Pts	PIM
1996-97	VTJ Jitex Pisek Jr.	CzRep-Jr.	36	12	5	17	....	....	....	....	....	....
1997-98	VTJ Jitex Pisek Jr.	CzRep-Jr.	39	21	19	40	....	....	....	....	....	....
	VTJ Jitex Pisek	CzRep-2	15	3	3	6	....	....	....	....	....	....
1998-99	IHC Pisek Jr.	CzRep-Jr.	7	2	3	5	....	....	....	....	....	....
	IHC Pisek	CzRep-2	51	20	23	43	....	....	....	....	....	....
99-2000	IHC Pisek	CzRep-2	24	6	9	15	....	....	....	....	....	....
	HC Femax Havirov	CzRep	1	0	0	0	0	....	....	....	....	....
	HC Sparta Praha	CzRep	22	1	1	2	0	....	....	....	....	....
2000-01	Karlovy Vary	CzRep	29	1	2	3	20	....	....	....	....	....
	HC Sparta Praha	CzRep	19	5	1	6	18	13	2	0	2	12
2001-02	HC Sparta Praha	CzRep	50	14	11	25	10	13	2	0	2	4
2002-03	HC Sparta Praha	CzRep	21	0	4	4	4	....	....	....	....	....
	Liberec	CzRep	30	8	9	17	26	....	....	....	....	....
2003-04	Liberec	CzRep	52	12	16	28	89	....	....	....	....	....
2004-05	HC Sparta Praha	CzRep	46	4	8	12	41	5	0	0	0	0

KASSIAN, Matt (KAS-ee-uhn, MAT) MIN.

Left wing. Shoots left. 6'4", 235 lbs. Born, Edmonton, Alta., October 28, 1986.
(Minnesota's 2nd choice, 57th overall, in 2005 Entry Draft).

			Regular Season					Playoffs				
Season	Club	League	GP	G	A	Pts	PIM	GP	G	A	Pts	PIM
2002-03	Sherwood Park	AJHL	33	5	7	12	38	....	....	....	....	....
2003-04	Vancouver Giants	WHL	37	1	0	1	42	3	0	0	0	4
2004-05	Vancouver Giants	WHL	41	0	3	3	89	....	....	....	....	....
	Kamloops Blazers	WHL	28	3	0	3	83	6	1	2	3	14

KAUPPINEN, Marko (KOW-pih-nehn, MAHR-koh) **PHI.**

Defense. Shoots left. 6', 178 lbs. Born, Mikkeli, Finland, March 23, 1979.
(Philadelphia's 7th choice, 214th overall, in 1997 Entry Draft).

			Regular Season					Playoffs				
Season	**Club**	**League**	**GP**	**G**	**A**	**Pts**	**PIM**	**GP**	**G**	**A**	**Pts**	**PIM**
1995-96	Jukurit Mikkeli	Finland-3	19	1	5	6	10	3	0	0	0	0
1996-97	JyP HT Jyvaskyla Jr.	Finland-Jr.	29	2	3	5	14	7	0	0	0	29
	JyP HT U18	Fin-U18	12	1	6	7	16	....	....	....	....	....
1997-98	JyP Jyvaskyla Jr.	Finland-Jr.	16	2	4	6	16	....	....	....	....	....
	Diskos Jyvaskyla	Finland-2	2	2	1	3	0	....	....	....	....	....
	JYP Jyvaskyla	Finland	33	2	6	8	26	....	....	....	....	....
1998-99	JyP Jyvaskyla Jr.	Finland-Jr.	3	2	1	3	6	....	....	....	....	....
	JYP Jyvaskyla	Finland	49	5	7	12	56	3	0	0	0	6
99-2000	Jokerit Helsinki Jr.	Finland-Jr.	5	0	3	3	8	1	1	0	1	4
	Jokerit Helsinki	Finland	47	4	9	13	16	10	1	3	4	2
2000-01	AIK Solna	Sweden	4	0	0	0	4	....	....	....	....	....
	Jokerit Helsinki	Finland	48	5	7	12	41	5	0	0	0	8
	Kiekko-Vantaa	Finland-2	1	0	0	0	9	....	....	....	....	....
2001-02	TPS Turku	Finland	55	4	9	13	55	5	1	0	1	2
2002-03	TPS Turku	Finland	53	3	10	13	52	7	0	0	0	27
2003-04	TPS Turku	Finland	42	1	3	4	18	13	0	1	1	14
2004-05	Mora IK	Sweden	50	6	11	17	32	....	....	....	....	....

KAZIONOV, Dmitri (ka-zee-OH-nahv, dih-MEE-tree) **T.B.**

Center. Shoots left. 6'3", 185 lbs. Born, Moscow, USSR, May 13, 1984.
(Tampa Bay's 2nd choice, 100th overall, in 2002 Entry Draft).

			Regular Season					Playoffs				
Season	**Club**	**League**	**GP**	**G**	**A**	**Pts**	**PIM**	**GP**	**G**	**A**	**Pts**	**PIM**
99-2000	Dyn'o Moscow 2	Russia-3	2	1	0	1	0	....	....	....	....	....
2000-01	THK Tver	Russia-2	33	1	1	2	6	....	....	....	....	....
2001-02	HK CSKA Moscow	Russia-2	2	0	1	1	0	....	....	....	....	....
	HK CSKA 2	Russia-3	10	1	0	1	4	....	....	....	....	....
	Lada Togliatti	Russia	3	0	0	0	0	....	....	....	....	....
	Lada Togliatti 2	Russia-3	16	10	9	19	0	....	....	....	....	....
2002-03	Lada Togliatti	Russia	5	0	1	1	4	....	....	....	....	....
	Lada Togliatti 2	Russia-3	34	14	13	27	26	....	....	....	....	....
2003-04	Lada Togliatti 2	Russia-3	5	3	2	5	0	4	0	0	0	0
	Lada Togliatti	Russia	47	5	5	10	34	5	0	0	0	4
2004-05	Lada Togliatti	Russia	46	3	7	10	32	2	0	0	0	0

KEITH, Duncan (KEETH, DUHN-kuhn) **CHI.**

Defense. Shoots left. 6', 182 lbs. Born, Winnipeg, Man., July 16, 1983.
(Chicago's 2nd choice, 54th overall, in 2002 Entry Draft).

			Regular Season					Playoffs				
Season	**Club**	**League**	**GP**	**G**	**A**	**Pts**	**PIM**	**GP**	**G**	**A**	**Pts**	**PIM**
1998-99	Penticton	BCAHA	44	51	57	108	45	....	....	....	....	....
99-2000	Penticton Panthers	BCHL	59	9	27	36	37	....	....	....	....	....
2000-01	Penticton Panthers	BCHL	60	18	64	82	61	9	4	6	10	18
2001-02	Michigan State	CCHA	41	3	12	15	18	....	....	....	....	....
2002-03	Michigan State	CCHA	15	3	6	9	8	....	....	....	....	....
	Kelowna Rockets	WHL	37	11	35	46	60	19	3	11	14	12
2003-04	Norfolk Admirals	AHL	75	7	18	25	44	8	1	1	2	6
2004-05	Norfolk Admirals	AHL	79	9	17	26	78	6	0	0	0	14

• Left **Michigan State** (CCHA) and signed as a free agent by **Kelowna** (WHL), December 27, 2002.

KELL, Trevor (KEHL, TREH-vuhr) **CHI.**

Right wing. Shoots right. 5'11", 181 lbs. Born, Thunder Bay, Ont., June 23, 1986.
(Chicago's 9th choice, 131st overall, in 2004 Entry Draft).

			Regular Season					Playoffs				
Season	**Club**	**League**	**GP**	**G**	**A**	**Pts**	**PIM**	**GP**	**G**	**A**	**Pts**	**PIM**
2002-03	Wellington Dukes	OPJHL	42	13	17	30	24	....	....	....	....	....
2003-04	London Knights	OHL	62	9	14	23	48	15	7	8	15	14
2004-05	London Knights	OHL	63	16	17	33	57	12	1	4	5	14

KELLER, Justin (KEHL-uhr, JUHS-tihn) **T.B.**

Left wing. Shoots left. 5'11", 185 lbs. Born, Nelson, B.C., March 4, 1986.
(Tampa Bay's 8th choice, 245th overall, in 2004 Entry Draft).

			Regular Season					Playoffs				
Season	**Club**	**League**	**GP**	**G**	**A**	**Pts**	**PIM**	**GP**	**G**	**A**	**Pts**	**PIM**
2001-02	Spokane Chiefs	WHL	25	7	6	13	10	....	....	....	....	....
	Saskatoon Blades	WHL	36	7	6	13	6	2	0	0	0	2
2002-03	Saskatoon Blades	WHL	2	0	0	0	0	....	....	....	....	....
	Regina Pats	WHL	16	3	3	6	6	....	....	....	....	....
2003-04	Kelowna Rockets	WHL	72	25	21	46	44	17	4	5	9	18
2004-05	Kelowna Rockets	WHL	72	31	22	53	103	23	12	10	22	44

KELLY, Regan (KEHL-lee, REE-guhn)

Defense. Shoots left. 6'2", 200 lbs. Born, Watrous, Sask., March 9, 1981.
(Philadelphia's 7th choice, 259th overall, in 2000 Entry Draft).

			Regular Season					Playoffs				
Season	**Club**	**League**	**GP**	**G**	**A**	**Pts**	**PIM**	**GP**	**G**	**A**	**Pts**	**PIM**
1997-98	Tisdale Trojans	SMHL	41	2	13	15	24	....	....	....	....	....
1998-99	Nipawin Hawks	SJHL	52	4	14	18	30	....	....	....	....	....
99-2000	Nipawin Hawks	SJHL	46	8	21	29	20	....	....	....	....	....
2000-01	Providence College	H-East	36	4	21	25	58	....	....	....	....	....
2001-02	Providence College	H-East	38	6	10	16	48	....	....	....	....	....
2002-03	St. John's	AHL	71	3	15	18	36	....	....	....	....	....
2003-04	St. John's	AHL	55	2	9	11	42	....	....	....	....	....
2004-05	St. John's	AHL	52	0	10	10	76	2	0	0	0	0

Hockey East All-Rookie Team (2001) • Hockey East All-Tournament Team (2001)

Rights traded to **Toronto** by **Philadelphia** for Chris McAllister, September 26, 2000.

KENNEDY, Tim (KEH-nuh-dee, TIHM) **BUF.**

Left wing. Shoots left. 5'9", 170 lbs. Born, Buffalo, NY, April 30, 1986.
(Washington's 6th choice, 181st overall, in 2005 Entry Draft).

			Regular Season					Playoffs				
Season	**Club**	**League**	**GP**	**G**	**A**	**Pts**	**PIM**	**GP**	**G**	**A**	**Pts**	**PIM**
2003-04	Sioux City	USHL	56	9	10	19	42	7	2	2	4	6
2004-05	Sioux City	USHL	54	30	31	61	112	13	*6	*11	*17	18

USHL Second All-Star Team (2005)

Traded to **Buffalo** by **Washington** for Buffalo's 6th round choice in 2006 Entry Draft, July 30, 2005. Signed Letter of Intent to attend **Michigan State** (CCHA) in fall of 2005.

KENNEDY, Tyler (KEH-nuh-dee, TIGH-luhr) **PIT.**

Center. Shoots right. 5'10", 183 lbs. Born, Sault Ste. Marie, Ont., July 15, 1986.
(Pittsburgh's 6th choice, 99th overall, in 2004 Entry Draft).

			Regular Season					Playoffs				
Season	**Club**	**League**	**GP**	**G**	**A**	**Pts**	**PIM**	**GP**	**G**	**A**	**Pts**	**PIM**
2002-03	Sault Ste. Marie	OHL	61	5	10	15	28	4	0	0	0	0
2003-04	Sault Ste. Marie	OHL	63	16	26	42	28	....	....	....	....	....
2004-05	Sault Ste. Marie	OHL	61	21	36	57	37	4	1	3	4	4

KESA, Teemu (KEH-sah, TEE-moo) **N.J.**

Defense. Shoots right. 6'1", 190 lbs. Born, Helsinki, Finland, June 7, 1981.
(New Jersey's 5th choice, 100th overall, in 1999 Entry Draft).

			Regular Season					Playoffs				
Season	**Club**	**League**	**GP**	**G**	**A**	**Pts**	**PIM**	**GP**	**G**	**A**	**Pts**	**PIM**
1996-97	Tappara Jr.	Finland-Jr.	32	1	5	6	58	4	1	0	4	29
1997-98	Ilves Tampere U18	Fin-U18	33	8	1	9	78	....	....	....	....	....
1998-99	Ilves Tampere U18	Fin-U18	24	4	5	9	146	10	0	0	0	12
	Ilves Tampere Jr.	Finland-Jr.	6	0	1	1	10	....	....	....	....	....
99-2000	Ilves Tampere Jr.	Finland-Jr.	31	1	7	8	92	....	....	....	....	....
	Ilves Tampere	Finland	5	0	0	0	8	....	....	....	....	....
2000-01	Ilves Tampere Jr.	Finland-Jr.	4	1	0	1	4	....	....	....	....	....
	Sport Vaasa	Finland-2	1	0	1	1	0	....	....	....	....	....
2001-02	Lukko Rauma	Finland	34	2	0	2	32	....	....	....	....	....
	Lukko Rauma Jr.	Finland-Jr.	3	0	4	4	4	....	....	....	....	....
2002-03	Lukko Rauma	Finland	37	1	0	1	22	....	....	....	....	....
2003-04	Lukko Rauma	Finland	49	2	2	4	62	....	....	....	....	....
2004-05	Albany River Rats	AHL	60	3	7	10	61	....	....	....	....	....

KHOMITSKY, Vadim (khoh-MIHT-skee, va-DEEM) **DAL.**

Defense. Shoots left. 6'1", 185 lbs. Born, Voskresensk, USSR, July 21, 1982.
(Dallas' 5th choice, 123rd overall, in 2000 Entry Draft).

			Regular Season					Playoffs				
Season	**Club**	**League**	**GP**	**G**	**A**	**Pts**	**PIM**	**GP**	**G**	**A**	**Pts**	**PIM**
1998-99	Voskresensk	Russia	9	0	0	0	10	....	....	....	....	....
99-2000	Voskresensk	Russia-2	17	0	0	0	31	....	....	....	....	....
	HK Moscow	Russia-2	11	0	1	1	10	....	....	....	....	....
2000-01	HK Moscow	Russia-2	44	2	7	9	89	....	....	....	....	....
2001-02	HK CSKA Moscow	Russia-2	68	2	18	20	63	....	....	....	....	....
2002-03	CSKA Moscow	Russia	51	3	2	5	58	....	....	....	....	....
2003-04	CSKA Moscow	Russia	54	3	3	6	46	....	....	....	....	....
2004-05	CSKA Moscow	Russia	60	1	5	6	105	....	....	....	....	....

KHOMUTOV, Ivan (khoh-moo-TAWF, ee-VAHN) **N.J.**

Right wing. Shoots left. 6'3", 205 lbs. Born, Saratov, USSR, March 11, 1985.
(New Jersey's 3rd choice, 93rd overall, in 2003 Entry Draft).

			Regular Season					Playoffs				
Season	**Club**	**League**	**GP**	**G**	**A**	**Pts**	**PIM**	**GP**	**G**	**A**	**Pts**	**PIM**
2001-02	HK CSKA 2	Russia-3	30	11	8	19	14	....	....	....	....	....
2002-03	Elektrostal	Russia-2	20	1	1	2	8	....	....	....	....	....
2003-04	London Knights	OHL	40	9	12	21	25	15	3	1	4	7
2004-05	Albany River Rats	AHL	66	6	11	17	30	....	....	....	....	....

KINCH, Matt (KIHNCH, MATT) **NYR**

Defense. Shoots left. 6', 195 lbs. Born, Red Deer, Alta., February 17, 1980.
(Buffalo's 8th choice, 146th overall, in 1999 Entry Draft).

			Regular Season					Playoffs				
Season	**Club**	**League**	**GP**	**G**	**A**	**Pts**	**PIM**	**GP**	**G**	**A**	**Pts**	**PIM**
1995-96	Red Deer	AMHL	35	6	17	23	31	....	....	....	....	....
	Calgary Hitmen	WHL	1	0	1	1	2	....	....	....	....	....
1996-97	Calgary Hitmen	WHL	64	10	22	32	31	....	....	....	....	....
1997-98	Calgary Hitmen	WHL	55	7	24	31	13	18	3	2	5	4
1998-99	Calgary Hitmen	WHL	68	14	69	83	16	21	8	15	23	59
99-2000	Calgary Hitmen	WHL	62	14	61	75	24	13	2	12	14	8
2000-01	Calgary Hitmen	WHL	70	18	66	84	52	12	3	6	9	6
2001-02	Hartford Wolf Pack	AHL	40	1	7	8	4	....	....	....	....	....
	Charlotte	ECHL	26	3	12	15	13	5	3	2	5	0
2002-03	Hartford Wolf Pack	AHL	66	7	22	29	28	2	0	0	0	0
2003-04	Hartford Wolf Pack	AHL	67	1	19	20	38	1	0	0	0	0
2004-05	Salzburg	Austria	37	1	12	13	18	....	....	....	....	....

WHL East First All-Star Team (1999, 2001) • Memorial Cup Tournament All-Star Team (1999) • Canadian Major Junior Sportsman of the Year (1999) • WHL East Second All-Star Team (2000) • Canadian Major Junior First All-Star Team (2001)

Signed as a free agent by **NY Rangers**, June 26, 2001. Signed as a free agent by **Salzburg** (Austria), September, 2004.

KINDL, Jakub (KEEHN-duhl, YA-kuhb) **DET.**

Defense. Shoots left. 6'3", 200 lbs. Born, Sumperk, Czech., February 10, 1987.
(Detroit's 1st choice, 19th overall, in 2005 Entry Draft).

			Regular Season					Playoffs				
Season	**Club**	**League**	**GP**	**G**	**A**	**Pts**	**PIM**	**GP**	**G**	**A**	**Pts**	**PIM**
2002-03	HC Pardubice U17	CzR-U17	3	0	3	3	10	....	....	....	....	....
	HC Pardubice Jr.	CzRep-Jr.	27	0	3	3	46	....	....	....	....	....
	Pardubice	CzRep	1	0	0	0	0	....	....	....	....	....
2003-04	HC Pardubice U17	CzR-U17	2	0	1	1	6	....	....	....	....	....
	HC Pardubice Jr.	CzRep-Jr.	48	4	14	18	108	....	....	....	....	....
	Hr. Kralove	CzRep-2	1	0	0	0	0	1	0	0	0	0
2004-05	Kitchener Rangers	OHL	62	3	11	14	92	12	0	0	0	22

KING, D.J. (KIHNG, DEE-JAY) **ST.L.**

Center. Shoots left. 6'2", 221 lbs. Born, Meadow Lake, Sask., January 27, 1984.
(St. Louis' 6th choice, 191st overall, in 2002 Entry Draft).

			Regular Season					Playoffs				
Season	**Club**	**League**	**GP**	**G**	**A**	**Pts**	**PIM**	**GP**	**G**	**A**	**Pts**	**PIM**
2000-01	Beardy's	SMHL	52	30	28	58	120	....	....	....	....	....
2001-02	Lethbridge	WHL	65	10	14	24	104	....	....	....	....	....
2002-03	Lethbridge	WHL	55	15	17	32	139	....	....	....	....	....
2003-04	Lethbridge	WHL	35	8	15	23	102	....	....	....	....	....
	Kelowna Rockets	WHL	28	5	2	7	80	17	1	6	7	16
2004-05	Worcester IceCats	AHL	74	6	8	14	178	....	....	....	....	....

KLEIN, Kevin (KLIGHN, KEH-vihn) **NSH.**

Defense. Shoots right. 6'1", 195 lbs. Born, Kitchener, Ont., December 13, 1984.
(Nashville's 3rd choice, 37th overall, in 2003 Entry Draft).

			Regular Season					Playoffs				
Season	Club	League	GP	G	A	Pts	PIM	GP	G	A	Pts	PIM
99-2000	Kitchener Midgets	OMHA	54	12	29	41	40	....	....	....	....	....
2000-01	St. Michael's	OHL	58	3	16	19	21	18	0	5	5	17
2001-02	St. Michael's	OHL	68	5	22	27	35	15	2	7	9	12
2002-03	St. Michael's	OHL	67	11	33	44	88	17	1	9	10	8
2003-04	St. Michael's	OHL	5	0	1	1	2	....	....	....	....	....
	Guelph Storm	OHL	46	6	23	29	40	22	10	11	21	12
2004-05	Milwaukee	AHL	65	4	12	16	22	7	0	0	0	11
	Rockford IceHogs	UHL	3	2	1	3	0	....	....	....	....	....

KLEPIS, Jakub (KLEH-pihsh, YA-kuhb) **WSH.**

Center. Shoots right. 6', 200 lbs. Born, Prague, Czech., June 5, 1984.
(Ottawa's 1st choice, 16th overall, in 2002 Entry Draft).

			Regular Season					Playoffs				
Season	Club	League	GP	G	A	Pts	PIM	GP	G	A	Pts	PIM
99-2000	HC Slavia Praha Jr.	CzRep-Jr.	48	14	26	40	30	....	....	....	....	....
2000-01	HC Slavia Praha Jr.	CzRep-Jr.	52	21	25	46	82	....	....	....	....	....
2001-02	Portland	WHL	70	14	50	64	111	7	0	3	3	22
2002-03	HC Slavia Praha	CzRep	38	2	6	8	22	4	0	0	0	6
	HC Slavia Praha Jr.	CzRep-Jr.	11	4	5	9	59	3	0	3	3	4
2003-04	HC Slavia Praha	CzRep	44	4	9	13	43	17	5	3	8	10
2004-05	Portland Pirates	AHL	78	13	14	27	76	....	....	....	....	....

Traded to **Buffalo** by **Ottawa** for Vaclav Varada and Buffalo's 5th round choice (Tim Cook) in 2003 Entry Draft, February 25, 2003. Traded to **Washington** by **Buffalo** for Mike Grier, March 9, 2004.

KLIMOV, Valeri (KLEE-mawf, VAL-uhr-ee) **N.J.**

Defense. Shoots left. 6'3", 200 lbs. Born, Moscow, USSR, July 17, 1986.
(New Jersey's 7th choice, 282nd overall, in 2004 Entry Draft).

			Regular Season					Playoffs				
Season	Club	League	GP	G	A	Pts	PIM	GP	G	A	Pts	PIM
2001-02	Spartak Moscow 2	Russia-3	24	1	1	2	6	....	....	....	....	....
2002-03	Spartak Moscow 2	Russia-3	5	2	1	3	8	....	....	....	....	....
2003-04	Spartak Moscow 2	Russia-3	4	1	0	1	0	....	....	....	....	....
2004-05	Spartak Moscow	Russia	6	0	0	0	2	....	....	....	....	....

KLUBERTANZ, Kyle (KLOO-buhr-tanz, KIGHL) **ANA.**

Defense. Shoots right. 6', 178 lbs. Born, Madison, WI, September 23, 1985.
(Anaheim's 3rd choice, 74th overall, in 2004 Entry Draft).

			Regular Season					Playoffs				
Season	Club	League	GP	G	A	Pts	PIM	GP	G	A	Pts	PIM
2002-03	Green Bay	USHL	60	8	26	34	74	....	....	....	....	....
2003-04	Green Bay	USHL	57	6	21	27	124	....	....	....	....	....
2004-05	U. of Wisconsin	WCHA	41	3	15	18	64	....	....	....	....	....

WCHA All-Rookie Team (2005)

KNYAZEV, Igor (kuh-NYA-zhev, EE-gohr) **PHX.**

Defense. Shoots left. 6', 208 lbs. Born, Elektrostal, USSR, January 27, 1983.
(Carolina's 1st choice, 15th overall, in 2001 Entry Draft).

			Regular Season					Playoffs				
Season	Club	League	GP	G	A	Pts	PIM	GP	G	A	Pts	PIM
99-2000	Spartak Moscow 2	Russia-3	13	2	4	6	74	....	....	....	....	....
	Spartak Moscow	Russia-2	26	1	1	2	6	....	....	....	....	....
2000-01	Spartak Moscow	Russia-2	53	6	5	11	101	....	....	....	....	....
2001-02	Spartak Moscow	Russia	3	0	0	0	8	....	....	....	....	....
	Spartak Moscow 2	Russia-3	2	0	1	1	0	....	....	....	....	....
	Ak Bars Kazan	Russia	14	0	1	1	4	3	0	0	0	0
2002-03	Lowell	AHL	68	2	5	7	68	....	....	....	....	....
2003-04	Springfield Falcons	AHL	72	1	6	7	61	....	....	....	....	....
2004-05	Voskresensk	Russia	29	0	2	2	57	....	....	....	....	....

Traded to **Phoenix** by **Carolina** with David Tanabe for Danny Markov and future considerations (Edmonton's 3rd round choice (previously acquired, later traded to NY Rangers - NY Rangers selected Billy Ryan) in 2004 Entry Draft, June 26, 2004), June 21, 2003. Signed as a free agent by **Voskresensk** (Russia), September, 2004.

KOALSKA, Matt (KOHL-skuh, MAT)

Center. Shoots left. 6'1", 196 lbs. Born, St. Paul, MN, May 16, 1980.
(Nashville's 7th choice, 154th overall, in 2000 Entry Draft).

			Regular Season					Playoffs				
Season	Club	League	GP	G	A	Pts	PIM	GP	G	A	Pts	PIM
1998-99	Hill-Murray	High-MN	26	20	50	70	18	....	....	....	....	....
99-2000	Twin Cities	USHL	57	24	34	58	19	13	5	5	10	4
2000-01	U. of Minnesota	WCHA	42	10	24	34	36	....	....	....	....	....
2001-02	U. of Minnesota	WCHA	44	10	23	33	34	....	....	....	....	....
2002-03	U. of Minnesota	WCHA	41	9	31	40	26	....	....	....	....	....
2003-04	U. of Minnesota	WCHA	44	13	26	39	44	....	....	....	....	....
2004-05	Bridgeport	AHL	60	7	8	15	22	....	....	....	....	....

Signed as a free agent by **NY Islanders**, August 11, 2004.

KOCI, David (KOH-chee, DAY-vihd) **PIT.**

Defense. Shoots left. 6'6", 230 lbs. Born, Prague, Czech., May 12, 1981.
(Pittsburgh's 5th choice, 146th overall, in 2000 Entry Draft).

			Regular Season					Playoffs				
Season	Club	League	GP	G	A	Pts	PIM	GP	G	A	Pts	PIM
1997-98	Sparta Jr.	CzRep-Jr.	41	2	9	11	105	....	....	....	....	....
1998-99	Hvezda Praha Jr.	CzRep-Jr.	22	1	3	4	36	....	....	....	....	....
	Sparta Jr.	CzRep-Jr.	7	0	0	0	4	....	....	....	....	....
99-2000	Sparta Jr.	CzRep-Jr.	47	0	6	6	124	....	....	....	....	....
2000-01	Prince George	WHL	70	2	7	9	155	6	0	0	0	20
2001-02	Wilkes-Barre	AHL	26	1	3	4	98	....	....	....	....	....
	Wheeling Nailers	ECHL	33	2	4	6	105	....	....	....	....	....
2002-03	Wilkes-Barre	AHL	9	0	0	0	4	....	....	....	....	....
	Wheeling Nailers	ECHL	48	0	1	1	103	....	....	....	....	....
2003-04	Wilkes-Barre	AHL	78	1	7	8	298	10	0	0	0	24
2004-05	Wilkes-Barre	AHL	68	1	8	9	311	....	....	....	....	....

KOHN, Dustin (KOHN, DUHS-tihn) **NYI**

Defense. Shoots left. 6'1", 182 lbs. Born, Edmonton, Alta., February 2, 1987.
(NY Islanders' 2nd choice, 46th overall, in 2005 Entry Draft).

			Regular Season					Playoffs				
Season	Club	League	GP	G	A	Pts	PIM	GP	G	A	Pts	PIM
2003-04	Calgary Hitmen	WHL	52	3	6	9	13	7	0	1	1	2
2004-05	Calgary Hitmen	WHL	71	8	35	43	61	12	0	4	4	6

KOIVISTO, Toni (KOI-vihs-toh, TOH-nee) **FLA.**

Left wing. Shoots left. 6', 180 lbs. Born, Ylitornio, Finland, November 5, 1982.
(Florida's 9th choice, 200th overall, in 2001 Entry Draft).

			Regular Season					Playoffs				
Season	Club	League	GP	G	A	Pts	PIM	GP	G	A	Pts	PIM
1997-98	Lukko Rauma U18	Fin-U18	10	10	4	14	0	....	....	....	....	....
1998-99	Lukko Rauma U18	Fin-U18	8	6	5	11	2	....	....	....	....	....
	Lukko Rauma Jr.	Finland-Jr.	24	5	2	7	8	....	....	....	....	....
99-2000	Lukko Rauma Jr.	Finland-Jr.	32	21	12	33	8	8	2	1	3	0
	Lukko Rauma	Finland	11	1	0	1	2	....	....	....	....	....
2000-01	Lukko Rauma	Finland	47	5	1	6	6	2	0	0	0	0
	Lukko Rauma Jr.	Finland-Jr.	16	9	15	24	6	1	0	0	0	0
	Jaa-Kotkat	Finland-2	2	0	0	0	0	....	....	....	....	....
2001-02	Lukko Rauma Jr.	Finland-Jr.	6	7	3	10	2	....	....	....	....	....
	Lukko Rauma	Finland	52	4	10	14	8	....	....	....	....	....
2002-03	Lukko Rauma	Finland	56	7	6	13	16	....	....	....	....	....
2003-04	Lukko Rauma	Finland	54	4	8	12	57	4	0	0	0	0
2004-05	Lukko Rauma	Finland	56	17	10	27	16	9	1	2	3	2

KOIVU, Mikko (KOI-voo, MEE-koh) **MIN.**

Center. Shoots left. 6'2", 205 lbs. Born, Turku, Finland, March 12, 1983.
(Minnesota's 1st choice, 6th overall, in 2001 Entry Draft).

			Regular Season					Playoffs				
Season	Club	League	GP	G	A	Pts	PIM	GP	G	A	Pts	PIM
99-2000	TPS Turku Jr.	Finland-Jr.	41	8	17	25	40	13	1	4	5	8
2000-01	TPS Turku Jr.	Finland-Jr.	26	9	36	45	26	4	2	2	4	8
	TPS Turku	Finland	21	0	1	1	2	....	....	....	....	....
2001-02	TPS Turku	Finland	48	4	3	7	34	8	0	3	3	4
	TPS Turku Jr.	Finland-Jr.	2	0	1	1	12	....	....	....	....	....
2002-03	TPS Turku	Finland	37	7	13	20	20	7	2	2	4	6
2003-04	TPS Turku	Finland	45	6	24	30	36	13	1	7	8	8
2004-05	Houston Aeros	AHL	67	20	28	48	47	5	1	0	1	2

KOJEVNIKOV, Alexander (kuh-ZHEHV-nih-kahv, al-ehx-AN-duhr) **CHI.**

Left wing. Shoots left. 6'3", 199 lbs. Born, Moscow, USSR, April 12, 1984.
(Chicago's 3rd choice, 93rd overall, in 2002 Entry Draft).

			Regular Season					Playoffs				
Season	Club	League	GP	G	A	Pts	PIM	GP	G	A	Pts	PIM
2001-02	Krylja Sovetov 2	Russia-3	32	12	15	27	59	....	....	....	....	....
2002-03	Krylja Sovetov	Russia	5	0	0	0	4	....	....	....	....	....
	Krylja Sovetov 2	Russia-3	3	1	2	3	28	....	....	....	....	....
2003-04	Val-d'Or Foreurs	QMJHL	19	10	4	14	22	....	....	....	....	....
	Quebec Remparts	QMJHL	16	3	4	7	16	4	0	2	2	4
2004-05	Greenville Grrrowl	ECHL	56	11	7	18	46	....	....	....	....	....
	Dayton Bombers	ECHL	2	0	1	1	2	....	....	....	....	....

KOKOREV, Dmitri (KOH-koh-rehf, DEH-mee-tree) **CGY.**

Defense. Shoots left. 6'3", 198 lbs. Born, Moscow, USSR, January 9, 1979.
(Calgary's 4th choice, 51st overall, in 1997 Entry Draft).

			Regular Season					Playoffs				
Season	Club	League	GP	G	A	Pts	PIM	GP	G	A	Pts	PIM
1996-97	Dyn'o Moscow 2	Russia-3	27	2	4	6	24	....	....	....	....	....
	Dynamo Moscow	Russia	1	0	0	0	0	....	....	....	....	....
1997-98	Dynamo Moscow	Russia	24	1	2	3	20	....	....	....	....	....
1998-99	Dynamo Moscow	Russia	26	0	1	1	20	8	1	0	1	0
	Dyn'o Moscow 2	Russia-3	14	0	2	2	20	....	....	....	....	....
99-2000	THK Tver	Russia-2	20	6	3	9	32	....	....	....	....	....
	Dynamo Moscow	Russia	22	0	1	1	14	1	0	0	0	0
2000-01	Dynamo Moscow	Russia	5	0	1	1	4	....	....	....	....	....
2001-02	CSKA Moscow 2	Russia-3	11	2	2	4	22	....	....	....	....	....
	CSKA Moscow	Russia	32	1	3	4	32	....	....	....	....	....
2002-03	Sibir Novosibirsk	Russia	26	0	1	1	59	....	....	....	....	....
2003-04	Spartak Moscow	Russia-2	15	0	0	0	10	....	....	....	....	....
	Kristall Elektrostal	Russia-2	10	0	1	1	16	....	....	....	....	....
2004-05	Vityaz Chekhov	Russia-2	48	4	11	15	64	15	1	3	4	22

KOLARIK, Chad (koh-LAHR-ihk, CHAD) **PHX.**

Center. Shoots right. 5'10", 170 lbs. Born, Abington, PA, January 26, 1986.
(Phoenix's 7th choice, 199th overall, in 2004 Entry Draft).

			Regular Season					Playoffs				
Season	Club	League	GP	G	A	Pts	PIM	GP	G	A	Pts	PIM
2002-03	USA U-17	USDP	65	30	32	62	47	....	....	....	....	....
2003-04	USA U-18	USDP	55	21	24	45	20	....	....	....	....	....
2004-05	U. of Michigan	CCHA	42	18	17	35	53	....	....	....	....	....

KOLARIK, Tyler (koh-LAHR-ihk, TIGH-luhr) **CBJ**

Center. Shoots right. 5'10", 185 lbs. Born, Philadelphia, PA, January 26, 1981.
(Columbus' 5th choice, 150th overall, in 2000 Entry Draft).

			Regular Season					Playoffs				
Season	Club	League	GP	G	A	Pts	PIM	GP	G	A	Pts	PIM
99-2000	Deerfield Academy	High-MA	26	31	22	53	8	....	....	....	....	....
	NY/Mid-Atlantic	MBHL	3	4	3	7	0	....	....	....	....	....
2000-01	Harvard Crimson	ECAC	32	13	15	28	36	....	....	....	....	....
2001-02	Harvard Crimson	ECAC	32	9	21	30	32	....	....	....	....	....
2002-03	Harvard Crimson	ECAC	30	15	13	28	20	....	....	....	....	....
2003-04	Harvard Crimson	ECAC	36	12	18	30	24	....	....	....	....	....
2004-05	Syracuse Crunch	AHL	2	0	0	0	0	....	....	....	....	....
	Dayton Bombers	ECHL	49	16	16	32	67	....	....	....	....	....

KOLEHMAINEN, Janne (koh-leh-MAYN-ehn, YA-nee) **OTT.**

Left wing. Shoots left. 6'3", 209 lbs. Born, Lappeenranta, Finland, March 22, 1986.
(Ottawa's 5th choice, 115th overall, in 2005 Entry Draft).

			Regular Season					Playoffs				
Season	Club	League	GP	G	A	Pts	PIM	GP	G	A	Pts	PIM
2002-03	SaiPa U18	Fin-U18	23	11	8	19	77	....	....	....	....	....
	SaiPa Jr.	Finland-Jr.	1	0	0	0	0	....	....	....	....	....
2003-04	SaiPa U18	Fin-U18	6	3	1	4	18	....	....	....	....	....
	SaiPa Jr.	Finland-Jr.	30	4	7	11	26	4	3	0	3	4
	SaiPa	Finland	6	0	0	0	2	....	....	....	....	....
2004-05	SaiPa Jr.	Finland-Jr.	13	2	4	6	24	2	1	1	2	0
	SaiPa	Finland	29	1	1	2	8	....	....	....	....	....

KOLESOV, Sergei (KOH-leh-sawf, SAIR-gay) DET.

Defense. Shoots left. 6'4", 187 lbs. Born, Novopolotsk, USSR, May 22, 1986.
(Detroit's 3rd choice, 151st overall, in 2004 Entry Draft).

			Regular Season					Playoffs				
Season	Club	League	GP	G	A	Pts	PIM	GP	G	A	Pts	PIM
2003-04	Dynamo Minsk	Belarus	STATISTICS NOT AVAILABLE									
2004-05	Dynamo Minsk	BelOpen	37	2	6	8	24	....	....	....	....	....
	Yunost-Minsk	BelOpen	1	0	0	0	2	9	0	0	0	4

KOLLAR, Tomas (koh-LAHR, TAW-mash) DET.

Left wing. Shoots left. 6'2", 211 lbs. Born, Stockholm, Sweden, April 20, 1982.
(Detroit's 6th choice, 226th overall, in 2003 Entry Draft).

			Regular Season					Playoffs				
Season	Club	League	GP	G	A	Pts	PIM	GP	G	A	Pts	PIM
99-2000	Hammarby Jr.	Swe-Jr.	42	10	15	25	52	....	....	....	....	....
2000-01	Hammarby Jr.	Swe-Jr.	8	2	4	6	12	....	....	....	....	....
	Hammarby	Sweden-2	23	3	2	5	10	....	....	....	....	....
2001-02	Hammarby	Sweden-2	46	9	9	18	24	2	3	0	3	2
	Hammarby Jr.	Swe-Jr.	3	0	3	3	6	2	1	0	1	0
2002-03	Hammarby	Sweden-2	27	10	8	18	45	....	....	....	....	....
2003-04	Djurgarden	Sweden	50	6	8	14	22	4	0	0	0	0
2004-05	Skelleftea AIK HK	Sweden-2	17	9	5	14	16	....	....	....	....	....
	Djurgarden	Sweden	32	1	6	7	46	12	0	1	1	30

KOLOZVARY, Ivan (KOH-lohzh-vah-ree, EE-vahn) TOR.

Center. Shoots left. 6', 179 lbs. Born, Ilava, Czech., February 16, 1983.
(Toronto's 9th choice, 198th overall, in 2001 Entry Draft).

			Regular Season					Playoffs				
Season	Club	League	GP	G	A	Pts	PIM	GP	G	A	Pts	PIM
1998-99	Dukla Trencin Jr.	Slovak-Jr.	46	13	24	37	12	....	....	....	....	....
99-2000	Dukla Trencin Jr.	Slovak-Jr.	51	10	27	37	14	....	....	....	....	....
2000-01	Dukla Trencin Jr.	Slovak-Jr.	39	13	10	23	14	....	....	....	....	....
	Dukla Trencin	Slovakia	14	0	0	0	2	7	0	2	2	2
2001-02	Dukla Trencin	Slovakia	31	1	5	6	2	5	1	1	2	0
2002-03	Dukla Trencin	Slovakia	48	6	11	17	28	12	2	2	4	4
2003-04	Dukla Trencin	Slovakia	48	5	11	16	14	4	0	0	0	2
2004-05	Dukla Trencin	Slovakia	16	1	4	5	2	....	....	....	....	....
	SHK 37 Piestany	Slovak-2	5	3	3	6	10	....	....	....	....	....
	Dubnica	Slovakia	18	4	8	12	8	....	....	....	....	....
	Dubnica	Slovak-Q	....	....	....	....	....	6	3	1	4	4

KOLTSOV, Ivan (kohlt-SAHV, ee-VAHN) EDM.

Defense. Shoots left. 6'2", 182 lbs. Born, Cherepovets, USSR, March 7, 1984.
(Edmonton's 6th choice, 106th overall, in 2002 Entry Draft).

			Regular Season					Playoffs				
Season	Club	League	GP	G	A	Pts	PIM	GP	G	A	Pts	PIM
2001-02	Cherepovets 2	Russia-3	27	2	2	4	24	....	....	....	....	....
2002-03	Leninogorsk	Russia-2	1	0	1	1	2	....	....	....	....	....
	Cherepovets 2	Russia-3	34	4	7	11	26	....	....	....	....	....
2003-04	Cherepovets 2	Russia-3	14	2	2	4	20	....	....	....	....	....
2004-05	HK Lipetsk	Russia-2	10	2	0	2	2	....	....	....	....	....
	HK Belgorod	Russia-2	30	1	2	3	32	....	....	....	....	....

KOLTSOV, Kirill (kohlt-SAHV, kih-RIHL) VAN.

Defense. Shoots left. 5'11", 183 lbs. Born, Chelyabinsk, USSR, February 1, 1983.
(Vancouver's 1st choice, 49th overall, in 2002 Entry Draft).

			Regular Season					Playoffs				
Season	Club	League	GP	G	A	Pts	PIM	GP	G	A	Pts	PIM
1998-99	Streetsville Derbys	OPJHL	20	5	7	12	4	....	....	....	....	....
99-2000	Omsk 2	Russia-3	27	0	7	7	30	....	....	....	....	....
	Avangard Omsk	Russia	2	0	0	0	0	....	....	....	....	....
2000-01	Avangard Omsk	Russia	39	0	1	1	20	16	1	3	4	12
2001-02	Avangard Omsk	Russia	41	1	5	6	34	11	1	0	1	8
2002-03	Avangard Omsk	Russia	45	4	8	12	54	12	1	3	4	8
2003-04	Manitoba Moose	AHL	74	7	25	32	62	....	....	....	....	....
2004-05	Manitoba Moose	AHL	28	3	14	17	42	....	....	....	....	....
	Avangard Omsk	Russia	22	2	2	4	46	10	0	1	1	18

KOLUSZ, Marcin (KOH-loosh, MART-sihn) MIN.

Right wing. Shoots left. 6'1", 180 lbs. Born, Limanowa, Poland, January 18, 1985.
(Minnesota's 4th choice, 157th overall, in 2003 Entry Draft).

			Regular Season					Playoffs				
Season	Club	League	GP	G	A	Pts	PIM	GP	G	A	Pts	PIM
2000-01	Nowy Targ	Poland	5	0	0	0	2	....	....	....	....	....
2001-02	Nowy Targ Jr.	Poland-Jr.	11	13	5	18	22	....	....	....	....	....
2002-03	Nowy Targ	Poland	30	2	4	6	10	2	0	0	0	0
2003-04	Vancouver Giants	WHL	64	6	12	18	19	6	1	0	1	0
2004-05	Nowy Targ	Poland	28	5	8	13	12	7	0	5	5	16

KOMADOSKI, Neil (koh-mah-DAW-skee, NEEL) OTT.

Defense. Shoots left. 6'2", 215 lbs. Born, Chesterfield, MO, February 10, 1982.
(Ottawa's 3rd choice, 81st overall, in 2001 Entry Draft).

			Regular Season					Playoffs				
Season	Club	League	GP	G	A	Pts	PIM	GP	G	A	Pts	PIM
1997-98	Aurora Tigers	OPJHL	1	0	0	0	0	....	....	....	....	....
1998-99	USA U-17	USDP	1	1	0	1	0	....	....	....	....	....
	USA U-18	USDP	50	8	7	15	202	....	....	....	....	....
99-2000	USA U-18	USDP	49	3	11	14	222	....	....	....	....	....
2000-01	U. of Notre Dame	CCHA	30	2	5	7	106	....	....	....	....	....
2001-02	U. of Notre Dame	CCHA	37	2	9	11	100	....	....	....	....	....
2002-03	U. of Notre Dame	CCHA	40	1	23	24	46	....	....	....	....	....
2003-04	U. of Notre Dame	CCHA	39	5	15	20	48	....	....	....	....	....
	Binghamton	AHL	3	0	0	0	2	1	0	0	0	0
2004-05	Binghamton	AHL	36	2	1	3	68	....	....	....	....	....

KONOPKA, Zenon (kuh-NOHP-kah, ZEH-nohn) ANA.

Center. Shoots left. 6', 206 lbs. Born, Niagara Falls, Ont., January 2, 1981.

			Regular Season					Playoffs				
Season	Club	League	GP	G	A	Pts	PIM	GP	G	A	Pts	PIM
1998-99	Ottawa 67's	OHL	56	7	8	15	62	7	0	0	0	2
99-2000	Ottawa 67's	OHL	59	8	11	19	107	11	1	2	3	8
2000-01	Ottawa 67's	OHL	66	20	45	65	120	20	7	13	20	47
2001-02	Ottawa 67's	OHL	61	18	68	86	100	13	8	6	14	49
2002-03	Wilkes-Barre	AHL	4	0	1	1	9	....	....	....	....	....
	Wheeling Nailers	ECHL	68	22	48	70	231	....	....	....	....	....
2003-04	Utah Grizzlies	AHL	43	7	4	11	198	....	....	....	....	....
	Idaho Steelheads	ECHL	23	6	22	28	82	17	9	8	17	30
2004-05	Cincinnati	AHL	75	17	29	46	212	12	3	3	6	26

ECHL All-Rookie Team (2003)

Signed as a free agent by **Utah** (AHL), September 10, 2003. Signed as a free agent by **Anaheim**, September 1, 2004.

KONSORADA, Tim (kawn-sohr-A-duh, TIHM) CBJ

Right wing. Shoots right. 6', 201 lbs. Born, Ft. Saskatchewan, Alta., March 21, 1984.
(Columbus' 8th choice, 168th overall, in 2002 Entry Draft).

			Regular Season					Playoffs				
Season	Club	League	GP	G	A	Pts	PIM	GP	G	A	Pts	PIM
1998-99	Ft. Saskatchewan	ABHL	36	26	45	71	8	....	....	....	....	....
99-2000	Ft. Saskatchewan	AMHL	34	11	23	34	6	....	....	....	....	....
	Brandon	WHL	5	1	2	3	0	....	....	....	....	....
2000-01	Brandon	WHL	67	9	14	23	33	5	2	3	5	11
2001-02	Brandon	WHL	71	17	28	45	36	19	2	11	13	8
2002-03	Brandon	WHL	72	22	48	70	74	17	4	10	14	19
2003-04	Brandon	WHL	25	3	18	21	23	11	2	5	7	8
2004-05	Brandon	WHL	71	29	58	87	43	19	4	11	15	14

KONTIOLA, Petri (KAWN-tee-oh-la, PEH-tree) CHI.

Forward. Shoots right. 6', 197 lbs. Born, Seinajoki, Finland, October 4, 1984.
(Chicago's 12th choice, 196th overall, in 2004 Entry Draft).

			Regular Season					Playoffs				
Season	Club	League	GP	G	A	Pts	PIM	GP	G	A	Pts	PIM
2002-03	Tappara Jr.	Finland-Jr.	36	7	10	17	12	8	3	3	6	0
2003-04	Tappara Jr.	Finland-Jr.	12	3	12	15	8	10	4	4	8	10
	Tappara Tampere	Finland	39	4	9	13	29	3	1	1	2	0
2004-05	Tappara Jr.	Finland-Jr.	1	1	0	1	0	....	....	....	....	....
	Tappara Tampere	Finland	54	8	17	25	24	8	2	2	4	2

KOPECKY, Milan (koh-PEHTS-kee, MEE-lan) PHI.

Left wing. Shoots left. 6', 180 lbs. Born, Kolin, Czech., May 11, 1981.
(Philadelphia's 8th choice, 287th overall, in 2000 Entry Draft).

			Regular Season					Playoffs				
Season	Club	League	GP	G	A	Pts	PIM	GP	G	A	Pts	PIM
1998-99	Sparta Jr.	CzRep-Jr.	49	14	21	35	....	....	....	....	....	....
99-2000	HC Slavia Praha Jr.	CzRep-Jr.	36	17	7	24	24	7	5	3	8	0
	HC Slavia Praha	CzRep	2	0	0	0	0	....	....	....	....	....
2000-01	HC Slavia Praha Jr.	CzRep-Jr.	38	19	17	36	36	....	....	....	....	....
	SC Kolin	CzRep-3	8	2	4	6	2	....	....	....	....	....
2001-02	HC Slavia Praha Jr.	CzRep-Jr.	3	2	0	2	4	....	....	....	....	....
	Beroun	CzRep-2	36	10	9	19	16	....	....	....	....	....
	HC Slavia Praha	CzRep	....	....	....	....	....	1	0	0	0	0
2002-03	HC Slavia Praha	CzRep	33	4	6	10	20	17	2	1	3	8
	Beroun	CzRep-2	7	2	4	6	6	....	....	....	....	....
2003-04	HC Slavia Praha	CzRep	49	5	6	11	20	19	3	0	3	12
2004-05	HC Slavia Praha	CzRep	52	6	4	10	24	7	0	0	0	4

KOPECKY, Tomas (koh-PEHTS-kee, TAW-mahsh) DET.

Center. Shoots left. 6'3", 187 lbs. Born, Ilava, Czech., February 5, 1982.
(Detroit's 2nd choice, 38th overall, in 2000 Entry Draft).

			Regular Season					Playoffs				
Season	Club	League	GP	G	A	Pts	PIM	GP	G	A	Pts	PIM
1997-98	Dukla Trencin Jr.	Slovak-Jr.	41	19	22	41	....	....	....	....	....	....
1998-99	Dukla Trencin Jr.	Slovak-Jr.	44	13	16	29	18	....	....	....	....	....
99-2000	Dukla Trencin Jr.	Slovak-Jr.	14	8	9	17	36	....	....	....	....	....
	Dukla Trencin	Slovakia	52	3	4	7	24	5	0	0	0	0
2000-01	Lethbridge	WHL	49	22	28	50	52	5	1	1	2	6
	Cincinnati	AHL	1	0	0	0	0	....	....	....	....	....
2001-02	Lethbridge	WHL	60	34	42	76	94	4	2	1	3	15
	Cincinnati	AHL	2	1	1	2	6	2	0	0	0	0
2002-03	Grand Rapids	AHL	70	17	21	38	32	14	0	0	0	6
2003-04	Grand Rapids	AHL	48	6	6	12	28	1	0	0	0	2
2004-05	Grand Rapids	AHL	48	8	8	16	35	....	....	....	....	....

KOPITAR, Anze (KOH-pee-tahr, AN-zheh) L.A.

Center. Shoots left. 6'4", 220 lbs. Born, Jesenice, Yugoslavia, August 24, 1987.
(Los Angeles' 1st choice, 11th overall, in 2005 Entry Draft).

			Regular Season					Playoffs				
Season	Club	League	GP	G	A	Pts	PIM	GP	G	A	Pts	PIM
2002-03	Jesenice U18	Sloven-U18	14	38	38	76	10	....	....	....	....	....
	Jesenice Jr.	Sloven-Jr.	20	15	12	27	8	....	....	....	....	....
	Kranjska Gora	Slovenia	11	4	4	8	4	....	....	....	....	....
2003-04	Jesenice Jr.	Sloven-Jr.	25	32	28	60	16	....	....	....	....	....
	Kranjska Gora	Slovenia	21	14	11	25	10	4	1	1	2	0
2004-05	Sodertalje SK U18	Swe-U18	1	1	2	3	0	1	0	0	0	2
	Sodertalje SK Jr.	Swe-Jr.	30	28	21	49	26	2	1	1	2	0
	Sodertalje SK	Sweden	5	0	0	0	0	10	0	0	0	0

KOREIS, Jakub (KOHR-ays, YA-kuhb) PHX.

Center. Shoots left. 6'3", 214 lbs. Born, Plzen, Czech, June 26, 1984.
(Phoenix's 1st choice, 19th overall, in 2002 Entry Draft).

			Regular Season					Playoffs				
Season	Club	League	GP	G	A	Pts	PIM	GP	G	A	Pts	PIM
99-2000	HC Plzen U17	CzR-U17	41	21	22	43	44	....	....	....	....	....
	HC Plzen Jr.	CzRep-Jr.	3	2	1	3	2	....	....	....	....	....
2000-01	HC Plzen U17	CzR-U17	9	7	10	17	28	....	....	....	....	....
	HC Plzen Jr.	CzRep-Jr.	43	14	15	29	83	....	....	....	....	....
2001-02	HC Plzen Jr.	CzRep-Jr.	23	14	14	28	38	....	....	....	....	....
	HC Keramika Plzen	CzRep	20	3	0	3	10	....	....	....	....	....
2002-03	HC Keramika Plzen	CzRep	23	1	6	7	8	....	....	....	....	....
	HC Plzen Jr.	CzRep-Jr.	10	3	5	8	28	....	....	....	....	....
2003-04	Guelph Storm	OHL	48	11	28	39	85	22	8	10	18	24
2004-05	Utah Grizzlies	AHL	79	5	6	11	96	....	....	....	....	....

KORHONEN, Risto (KOHR-hoh-nehn, REE-stoh) **CAR.**

Defense. Shoots left. 6'3", 202 lbs. Born, Sotkamo, Finland, November 27, 1986.
(Carolina's 7th choice, 159th overall, in 2005 Entry Draft).

			Regular Season					Playoffs				
Season	**Club**	**League**	**GP**	**G**	**A**	**Pts**	**PIM**	**GP**	**G**	**A**	**Pts**	**PIM**
2002-03	Karpat Oulu U18	Fin-U18	10	1	6	7	10	1	0	0	0	2
	Karpat Oulu Jr.	Finland-Jr.	24	1	2	3	22	2	0	0	0	0
2003-04	Karpat Oulu U18	Fin-U18	6	0	2	2	18	....	....	....	....	....
	Karpat Oulu Jr.	Finland-Jr.	36	1	3	4	30	5	0	0	0	6
2004-05	Karpat Oulu Jr.	Finland-Jr.	36	5	12	17	73	....	....	....	....	....

KORNEEV, Konstantin (kor-NEE-ehv, kawn-stuhn-TIHN) **MTL.**

Defense. Shoots left. 5'11", 176 lbs. Born, Moscow, USSR, June 5, 1984.
(Montreal's 6th choice, 275th overall, in 2002 Entry Draft).

			Regular Season					Playoffs				
Season	**Club**	**League**	**GP**	**G**	**A**	**Pts**	**PIM**	**GP**	**G**	**A**	**Pts**	**PIM**
99-2000	Krylja Sovetov 2	Russia-3	1	0	0	0	0	....	....	....	....	....
2000-01	Russia Jr.	Exhib.	12	0	4	4	10	....	....	....	....	....
2001-02	Krylja Sovetov 2	Russia-3	26	9	19	28	44	....	....	....	....	....
	Krylja Sovetov	Russia	4	0	2	2	0	2	0	0	0	2
2002-03	Krylja Sovetov	Russia	49	2	8	10	28	....	....	....	....	....
2003-04	Ak Bars Kazan	Russia	55	1	4	5	8	8	0	1	1	2
2004-05	Ak Bars Kazan 2	Russia-3	....	6	16	22	....	....	....	....	....	....
	Ak Bars Kazan	Russia	35	0	4	4	10	1	0	0	0	0

KORPIKARI, Oskari (kohr-pih-KAH-ree, AWS-kahr-ee) **MTL.**

Defense. Shoots left. 6'2", 210 lbs. Born, Oulu, Finland, April 5, 1984.
(Montreal's 9th choice, 217th overall, in 2003 Entry Draft).

			Regular Season					Playoffs				
Season	**Club**	**League**	**GP**	**G**	**A**	**Pts**	**PIM**	**GP**	**G**	**A**	**Pts**	**PIM**
2001-02	Karpat Oulu U18	Fin-U18	22	7	3	10	16	2	0	0	0	0
	Karpat Oulu Jr.	Finland-Jr.	5	0	0	0	0	....	....	....	....	....
2002-03	Karpat Oulu Jr.	Finland-Jr.	23	3	7	10	8	2	0	0	0	0
	Karpat Oulu	Finland	23	0	1	1	4	15	0	0	0	6
2003-04	Karpat Oulu	Finland	35	0	1	1	14	7	0	0	0	2
	Karpat Oulu Jr.	Finland-Jr.	7	3	1	4	8	....	....	....	....	....
2004-05	Karpat Oulu	Finland	21	0	0	0	10	....	....	....	....	....
	Karpat Oulu Jr.	Finland-Jr.	13	6	6	12	10	5	1	4	5	36

KORPIKOSKI, Lauri (kohr-pih-KAWS-kee, LOW-ree) **NYR**

Left wing. Shoots left. 6'1", 181 lbs. Born, Turku, Finland, July 28, 1986.
(NY Rangers' 2nd choice, 19th overall, in 2004 Entry Draft).

			Regular Season					Playoffs				
Season	**Club**	**League**	**GP**	**G**	**A**	**Pts**	**PIM**	**GP**	**G**	**A**	**Pts**	**PIM**
2002-03	TPS Turku Jr.	Finland-Jr.	21	7	4	11	10	....	....	....	....	....
2003-04	TPS Turku Jr.	Finland-Jr.	36	12	8	20	20	8	5	5	10	20
2004-05	TPS Turku Jr.	Finland-Jr.	3	3	0	3	0	....	....	....	....	....
	TPS Turku	Finland	41	0	6	6	12	6	1	0	1	0

KORSUNOV, Vladimir (KOHR-suhn-ahv, vla-DIH-meer) **ANA.**

Defense. Shoots left. 6'2", 202 lbs. Born, Moscow, USSR, March 16, 1983.
(Anaheim's 5th choice, 105th overall, in 2001 Entry Draft).

			Regular Season					Playoffs				
Season	**Club**	**League**	**GP**	**G**	**A**	**Pts**	**PIM**	**GP**	**G**	**A**	**Pts**	**PIM**
99-2000	Spartak Moscow 2	Russia-3	22	1	11	12	60	....	....	....	....	....
2000-01	Spartak Moscow 2	Russia-3	2	1	0	1	8	....	....	....	....	....
2001-02	Spartak Moscow	Russia	40	0	3	3	28	....	....	....	....	....
2002-03	Spartak Moscow	Russia	42	1	4	5	50	....	....	....	....	....
2003-04	Spartak Moscow	Russia-2	56	1	8	9	66	5	1	0	1	6
2004-05	Spartak Moscow	Russia	43	4	7	11	54	....	....	....	....	....

KOSMACHEV, Dmitry (kaws-ma-CHEHV, dih-MEE-tree) **CBJ**

Defense. Shoots right. 6'3", 209 lbs. Born, Nizhny Novgorod, USSR, June 7, 1985.
(Columbus' 3rd choice, 71st overall, in 2003 Entry Draft).

			Regular Season					Playoffs				
Season	**Club**	**League**	**GP**	**G**	**A**	**Pts**	**PIM**	**GP**	**G**	**A**	**Pts**	**PIM**
2001-02	HK CSKA 2	Russia-3	6	1	0	1	2	....	....	....	....	....
	HK CSKA Moscow	Russia-2	49	0	1	1	12	....	....	....	....	....
2002-03	CSKA Moscow	Russia	27	0	0	0	2	....	....	....	....	....
2003-04	CSKA Moscow	Russia	34	0	2	2	12	....	....	....	....	....
2004-05	Nizhny Novgorod	Russia-2	34	3	4	7	22	15	0	1	1	0

KOSTITSYN, Andrei (kaws-TIHT-sihn, AWN-dray) **MTL.**

Wing. Shoots right. 6', 208 lbs. Born, Novopolosk, USSR, February 3, 1985.
(Montreal's 1st choice, 10th overall, in 2003 Entry Draft).

			Regular Season					Playoffs				
Season	**Club**	**League**	**GP**	**G**	**A**	**Pts**	**PIM**	**GP**	**G**	**A**	**Pts**	**PIM**
2000-01	Novopolotsk	Belarus	1	2	1	3	2	....	....	....	....	....
	Novopolotsk	EEHL	5	1	0	1	0	....	....	....	....	....
	Yunost Minsk	Belarus	3	1	4	5	8	....	....	....	....	....
	HC Vitebsk	Belarus	17	17	6	23	42	....	....	....	....	....
2001-02	Novopolotsk	Belarus	17	9	6	15	28	....	....	....	....	....
	Novopolotsk	EEHL	29	9	8	17	16	....	....	....	....	....
	Yunost Minsk	Belarus	6	2	0	2	8	....	....	....	....	....
2002-03	CSKA Moscow	Russia	6	0	0	0	2	....	....	....	....	....
	Voskresensk	Russia-2	2	1	1	2	0	....	....	....	....	....
	Yunost Minsk	Belarus	4	6	4	10	43	....	....	....	....	....
	CSKA Moscow 2	Russia-3	3	2	2	4	25	....	....	....	....	....
2003-04	CSKA Moscow 2	Russia-3	STATISTICS NOT AVAILABLE									
	CSKA Moscow	Russia	12	0	1	1	2	....	....	....	....	....
	Yunost Minsk	Belarus	STATISTICS NOT AVAILABLE									
2004-05	Hamilton Bulldogs	AHL	66	12	11	23	24	3	0	0	0	0

KOSTITSYN, Sergei (kaws-TIHT-sihn, SAIR-gay) **MTL.**

Left wing. Shoots left. 5'11", 180 lbs. Born, Novopolotsk, USSR, March 20, 1987.
(Montreal's 6th choice, 200th overall, in 2005 Entry Draft).

			Regular Season					Playoffs				
Season	**Club**	**League**	**GP**	**G**	**A**	**Pts**	**PIM**	**GP**	**G**	**A**	**Pts**	**PIM**
2003-04	HK Gomel	EEHL	6	0	1	1	0	....	....	....	....	....
	HK Gomel 2	EEHL-B	6	7	2	9	14	....	....	....	....	....
	Yunior Minsk	EEHL-B	STATISTICS NOT AVAILABLE									
	Yunior Minsk	Belarus	3	0	0	0	0	....	....	....	....	....
	HK Gomel	Belarus	22	5	4	9	4	11	1	2	3	8
2004-05	HK Gomel	BelOpen	40	4	10	14	24	4	2	0	2	12

KOUBA, Ladislav (KOH-bah, LA-dih-slahv) **PHX.**

Left wing. Shoots left. 6'2", 213 lbs. Born, Vimperk, Czech., September 10, 1983.
(Phoenix's 9th choice, 216th overall, in 2002 Entry Draft).

			Regular Season					Playoffs				
Season	**Club**	**League**	**GP**	**G**	**A**	**Pts**	**PIM**	**GP**	**G**	**A**	**Pts**	**PIM**
99-2000	HC Plzen Jr.	CzRep-Jr.	34	28	20	48	....	....	....	....	....	....
2000-01	Red Deer Rebels	WHL	62	5	7	12	29	3	0	0	0	2
2001-02	Red Deer Rebels	WHL	62	16	14	30	33	23	5	3	8	6
2002-03	Red Deer Rebels	WHL	68	12	28	40	48	23	5	6	11	4
2003-04	Adirondack	UHL	26	7	4	11	6	....	....	....	....	....
	Springfield Falcons	AHL	3	0	0	0	2	....	....	....	....	....
	Red Deer Rebels	WHL	25	2	10	12	23	19	4	2	6	8
2004-05	Idaho Steelheads	ECHL	10	0	0	0	2	....	....	....	....	....
	New Mexico	CHL	30	6	11	17	24	....	....	....	....	....

KOVAC, Kristian (KOH-vach, KRIHST-yan) **COL.**

Right wing. Shoots right. 6'2", 205 lbs. Born, Kosice, Czech., January 1, 1981.
(Colorado's 5th choice, 122nd overall, in 1999 Entry Draft).

			Regular Season					Playoffs				
Season	**Club**	**League**	**GP**	**G**	**A**	**Pts**	**PIM**	**GP**	**G**	**A**	**Pts**	**PIM**
1997-98	HC Kosice Jr.	Slovak-Jr.	47	22	11	33	103	....	....	....	....	....
1998-99	HC VSZ Kosice Jr.	Slovak-Jr.	39	30	20	50	73	2	1	0	1	2
	HC VSZ Kosice	Slovakia	6	0	0	0	2	....	....	....	....	....
99-2000	Victoriaville Tigres	QMJHL	65	11	18	29	50	5	0	0	0	4
2000-01	Victoriaville Tigres	QMJHL	51	10	20	30	38	13	2	3	5	4
2001-02	HC Kosice	Slovakia	26	5	9	14	10	11	0	0	0	4
2002-03	HC Kosice	Slovakia	48	6	8	14	54	7	1	0	1	2
2003-04	HC Kosice	Slovakia	38	11	12	23	12	....	....	....	....	....
2004-05	HC Kosice	Slovakia	12	0	1	1	6	....	....	....	....	....
	VTJ Trebisov	Slovak-2	1	0	0	0	0	....	....	....	....	....
	PHK Presov	Slovak-2	9	6	4	10	2	....	....	....	....	....
	Dunaujvaros	Hungary	6	2	1	3	0	....	....	....	....	....

KOVERKO, Trevor (KOH-vehr-koh, TREH-vuhr) **NYR**

Defense. Shoots left. 6'3", 218 lbs. Born, Toronto, Ont., March 22, 1987.
(NY Rangers' 7th choice, 147th overall, in 2005 Entry Draft).

			Regular Season					Playoffs				
Season	**Club**	**League**	**GP**	**G**	**A**	**Pts**	**PIM**	**GP**	**G**	**A**	**Pts**	**PIM**
2003-04	North York	OPJHL	42	2	7	9	82	....	....	....	....	....
2004-05	Owen Sound	OHL	66	1	12	13	83	8	0	2	2	2

KOZAK, Rick (KOH-zak, RIHK) **NYR**

Right wing. Shoots right. 6'2", 215 lbs. Born, Winnipeg, Man., August 19, 1985.
(Philadelphia's 7th choice, 95th overall, in 2003 Entry Draft).

			Regular Season					Playoffs				
Season	**Club**	**League**	**GP**	**G**	**A**	**Pts**	**PIM**	**GP**	**G**	**A**	**Pts**	**PIM**
2000-01	Norman	MMMHL	31	17	27	44	166	....	....	....	....	....
2001-02	Swan Valley	MJHL	35	14	21	35	103	4	0	0	0	4
	Prince George	WHL	4	0	0	0	11	....	....	....	....	....
2002-03	Swan Valley	MJHL	25	17	20	37	99	....	....	....	....	....
	Brandon	WHL	38	9	6	15	87	16	6	5	11	51
2003-04	Brandon	WHL	25	5	3	8	83	....	....	....	....	....
	Kamloops Blazers	WHL	29	9	6	15	77	5	1	0	1	12
	Hartford Wolf Pack	AHL	2	0	1	1	0	....	....	....	....	....
2004-05	Kamloops Blazers	WHL	12	3	0	3	33	....	....	....	....	....
	Prince Albert	WHL	39	11	13	24	152	17	6	3	9	58

Traded to **NY Rangers** by **Philadelphia** with Philadelphia's 2nd round choice (later traded to Atlanta - Atlanta selected Ondrej Pavelec) in 2005 Entry Draft for Vladimir Malakhov, March 8, 2004.

KOZEK, Andrew (KOH-zehk, AN-droo) **ATL.**

Wing. Shoots left. 5'10", 175 lbs. Born, Revelstoke, B.C., May 26, 1986.
(Atlanta's 4th choice, 53rd overall, in 2005 Entry Draft).

			Regular Season					Playoffs				
Season	**Club**	**League**	**GP**	**G**	**A**	**Pts**	**PIM**	**GP**	**G**	**A**	**Pts**	**PIM**
2003-04	South Surrey	BCHL	58	19	22	41	67	....	....	....	....	....
2004-05	South Surrey	BCHL	60	48	49	97	81	....	....	....	....	....

Signed Letter of Intent to attend **North Dakota** (WCHA), November 19, 2004.

KRACIK, Jaroslav (KRAH-chihk, YAHR-roh-slav) **CBJ**

Right wing. Shoots left. 6', 178 lbs. Born, Prague, Czech., January 18, 1983.
(Columbus' 12th choice, 231st overall, in 2002 Entry Draft).

			Regular Season					Playoffs				
Season	**Club**	**League**	**GP**	**G**	**A**	**Pts**	**PIM**	**GP**	**G**	**A**	**Pts**	**PIM**
99-2000	HC Plzen U17	CzR-U17	45	31	36	67	28	....	....	....	....	....
	HC Plzen Jr.	CzRep-Jr.	6	1	0	1	2	....	....	....	....	....
2000-01	HC Plzen Jr.	CzRep-Jr.	47	20	28	48	16	....	....	....	....	....
2001-02	HC Plzen Jr.	CzRep-Jr.	39	14	35	49	46	....	....	....	....	....
	HC Klatovy	CzRep-3	6	5	3	8	0	....	....	....	....	....
	HC Keramika Plzen	CzRep	4	0	1	1	0	2	0	0	0	0
2002-03	HC Plzen Jr.	CzRep-Jr.	33	11	17	28	40	1	0	1	1	0
	HC Keramika Plzen	CzRep	4	0	0	0	0	....	....	....	....	....
	Usti n. L.	CzRep-2	9	1	1	2	4	4	0	0	0	0
2003-04	HC Plzen Jr.	CzRep-Jr.	46	32	47	79	107	....	....	....	....	....
	Plzen	CzRep	19	2	2	4	18	12	0	6	6	2
2004-05	IHC Pisek	CzRep-2	3	0	0	0	0	....	....	....	....	....
	Plzen	CzRep	41	5	11	16	2	....	....	....	....	....

KREJCI, David (KRIGH-chee, DAY-vihd) **BOS.**

Center. Shoots right. 5'11", 180 lbs. Born, Sternberk, Czech., August 24, 1986.
(Boston's 1st choice, 63rd overall, in 2004 Entry Draft).

			Regular Season					Playoffs				
Season	**Club**	**League**	**GP**	**G**	**A**	**Pts**	**PIM**	**GP**	**G**	**A**	**Pts**	**PIM**
2000-01	HC Olomouc U17	CzR-U17	26	2	6	8	4	3	1	1	2	0
2001-02	HC Trinec U17	CzR-U17	48	32	27	59	30	6	2	4	6	2
2002-03	HC Trinec U17	CzR-U17	22	12	24	36	42	....	....	....	....	....
	HC Trinec Jr.	CzRep-Jr.	12	4	5	9	2	12	5	5	10	8
2003-04	HC Kladno Jr.	CzRep-Jr.	50	23	37	60	37	7	3	6	9	4
2004-05	Gatineau	QMJHL	62	22	41	63	31	10	2	7	9	10

KREPS, Kamil (KREHPS, KA-mihl) FLA.

Center. Shoots right. 6'1", 190 lbs. Born, Litomerice, Czech., November 18, 1984.
(Florida's 3rd choice, 38th overall, in 2003 Entry Draft).

			Regular Season					Playoffs				
Season	Club	League	GP	G	A	Pts	PIM	GP	G	A	Pts	PIM
99-2000	Litvinov Jr.	CzRep-Jr.	48	18	16	34	10	....	....	....	....	....
2000-01	Litvinov Jr.	CzRep-Jr.	47	16	23	39	6	6	2	6	8	10
2001-02	Brampton	OHL	68	19	24	43	14	....	....	....	....	....
2002-03	Brampton	OHL	53	19	42	61	12	11	3	5	8	4
2003-04	Brampton	OHL	57	19	27	46	19	12	7	8	15	2
2004-05	San Antonio	AHL	58	5	6	11	11	....	....	....	....	....
	Texas Wildcatters	ECHL	12	5	6	11	6	....	....	....	....	....

KRIKUNOV, Ilya (krih-koo-NAWF, IHL-yah) VAN.

Left wing. Shoots left. 5'11", 169 lbs. Born, Elektrostal, USSR, February 27, 1984.
(Vancouver's 8th choice, 223rd overall, in 2002 Entry Draft).

			Regular Season					Playoffs				
Season	Club	League	GP	G	A	Pts	PIM	GP	G	A	Pts	PIM
2000-01	Elektrostal 2	Russia-3	4	0	0	0	2	....	....	....	....	....
2001-02	Elektrostal 2	Russia-3	5	3	6	9	4	....	....	....	....	....
	Elektrostal	Russia-2	48	12	10	22	28	....	....	....	....	....
2002-03	Elektrostal	Russia-2	48	19	9	28	34	....	....	....	....	....
2003-04	Voskresensk	Russia	50	10	9	19	14	....	....	....	....	....
2004-05	Voskresensk	Russia	58	9	14	23	20	....	....	....	....	....

KRONVALL, Staffan (KRAWN-wahl, STAH-fuhn) TOR.

Defense. Shoots left. 6'3", 209 lbs. Born, Jarfalla, Sweden, September 10, 1982.
(Toronto's 9th choice, 285th overall, in 2002 Entry Draft).

			Regular Season					Playoffs				
Season	Club	League	GP	G	A	Pts	PIM	GP	G	A	Pts	PIM
99-2000	Huddinge IK Jr.	Swe-Jr.	34	2	0	2	38	....	....	....	....	....
	Huddinge IK U18	Swe-U18	7	0	3	3	0	....	....	....	....	....
2000-01	Huddinge IK Jr.	Swe-Jr.	23	6	1	7	16	....	....	....	....	....
	Huddinge IK	Sweden-3	1	0	0	0	0	....	....	....	....	....
2001-02	Huddinge IK	Sweden-2	42	4	7	11	30	....	....	....	....	....
	Huddinge IK Jr.	Swe-Jr.	1	0	0	0	0	4	2	1	3	27
2002-03	Djurgarden	Sweden	50	5	13	18	46	12	3	2	5	18
2003-04	Djurgarden	Sweden	44	1	5	6	54	4	0	1	1	2
2004-05	Brynas IF Gavle	Sweden	3	0	1	1	4	....	....	....	....	....
	Djurgarden Jr.	Swe-Jr.	5	2	4	6	0	....	....	....	....	....
	Djurgarden	Sweden	35	1	4	5	43	12	2	0	2	10

KRUCHININ, Andrei (kroo-CHIHN-ihn, AWN-dray) MTL.

Defense. Shoots left. 5'11", 187 lbs. Born, Karaganda, USSR, May 18, 1978.
(Montreal's 7th choice, 189th overall, in 1998 Entry Draft).

			Regular Season					Playoffs				
Season	Club	League	GP	G	A	Pts	PIM	GP	G	A	Pts	PIM
1996-97	Lada Togliatti	Russia	19	0	1	1	8	11	0	0	0	0
1997-98	Lada Togliatti	Russia	43	0	4	4	73	....	....	....	....	....
1998-99	Lada Togliatti	Russia	41	1	4	5	56	6	0	1	1	2
99-2000	CSK VVS Samara	Russia	6	1	0	1	0	....	....	....	....	....
	Lada Togliatti	Russia	25	1	2	3	24	6	1	0	1	4
2000-01	Perm	Russia	14	1	3	4	10	....	....	....	....	....
	Lada Togliatti	Russia	14	0	2	2	12	3	0	0	0	0
2001-02	Avangard Omsk	Russia	21	0	0	0	6	....	....	....	....	....
	Nizhnekamsk	Russia	17	1	3	4	8	....	....	....	....	....
2002-03	Nizhnekamsk	Russia	30	1	6	7	16	....	....	....	....	....
2003-04	Nizhnekamsk	Russia	49	2	6	8	53	5	1	1	2	4
2004-05	Lada Togliatti	Russia	32	3	4	7	24	7	0	1	1	2

KRYSANOV, Anton (KREE-sa-nahf, AN-tawn) PHX.

Center. Shoots left. 6'3", 198 lbs. Born, Togliatti, USSR, March 25, 1987.
(Phoenix's 4th choice, 148th overall, in 2005 Entry Draft).

			Regular Season					Playoffs				
Season	Club	League	GP	G	A	Pts	PIM	GP	G	A	Pts	PIM
2002-03	Lada Togliatti 2	Russia-3	9	1	3	4	2	....	....	....	....	....
2003-04	Lada Togliatti 2	Russia-3	18	2	3	5	2	....	....	....	....	....
2004-05	Lada Togliatti 2	Russia-3	34	13	13	26	32	....	....	....	....	....
	Lada Togliatti	Russia	15	1	0	1	2	....	....	....	....	....

KRYUKOV, Artem (KREE-oo-kahf, AHR-tehm) BUF.

Center. Shoots left. 6'3", 180 lbs. Born, Novosibirsk, USSR, March 5, 1982.
(Buffalo's 1st choice, 15th overall, in 2000 Entry Draft).

			Regular Season					Playoffs				
Season	Club	League	GP	G	A	Pts	PIM	GP	G	A	Pts	PIM
1997-98	Torpedo Yaroslavl	Russia	7	0	0	0	2	....	....	....	....	....
1998-99	Yaroslavl 2	Russia-3	20	2	2	4	6	....	....	....	....	....
99-2000	Yaroslavl 2	Russia-3	14	1	1	2	12	....	....	....	....	....
	Torpedo Yaroslavl	Russia	3	0	0	0	4	....	....	....	....	....
2000-01	Yaroslavl 2	Russia-3	6	0	0	0	2	11	0	0	0	8
	SKA St. Petersburg	Russia	14	0	2	2	14	....	....	....	....	....
2001-02	Yaroslavl	Russia	15	1	3	4	10	6	1	0	1	8
2002-03	Sibir Novosibirsk	Russia	9	0	0	0	27	....	....	....	....	....
2003-04	Yaroslavl 2	Russia-3	30	5	4	9	26	....	....	....	....	....
	Yaroslavl	Russia	4	0	2	2	0	....	....	....	....	....
2004-05	Yaroslavl	Russia	60	8	9	17	44	7	1	0	1	4

KUBISTA, Jan (KOO-bihsh-tuh, YAHN) BOS.

Right wing. Shoots left. 6', 189 lbs. Born, Kolin, Czech., April 12, 1984.
(Boston's 3rd choice, 130th overall, in 2002 Entry Draft).

			Regular Season					Playoffs				
Season	Club	League	GP	G	A	Pts	PIM	GP	G	A	Pts	PIM
99-2000	HC Pardubice U17	CzR-U17	44	16	18	34	10	....	....	....	....	....
	SC Kolin Jr.	CzRep-Jr.	5	4	2	6	0	....	....	....	....	....
2000-01	HC Pardubice U17	CzR-U17	53	33	24	57	61	8	6	7	13	16
	HC Pardubice Jr.	CzRep-Jr.	1	0	1	1	0	....	....	....	....	....
2001-02	HC Pardubice Jr.	CzRep-Jr.	48	12	12	24	36	....	....	....	....	....
2002-03	HC Pardubice Jr.	CzRep-Jr.	32	16	11	27	40	....	....	....	....	....
	Pardubice	CzRep	9	1	1	2	0	....	....	....	....	....
	Hr. Kralove	CzRep-2	2	0	0	0	0	....	....	....	....	....
2003-04	Pardubice	CzRep	3	0	0	0	0	....	....	....	....	....
	Hr. Kralove	CzRep-2	5	0	0	0	0	....	....	....	....	....
	HC Pardubice Jr.	CzRep-Jr.	39	22	23	45	80	....	....	....	....	....
2004-05	Kolin	CzRep-3	2	0	0	0	0	....	....	....	....	....
	Hr. Kralove	CzRep-2	22	1	5	6	0	....	....	....	....	....
	Beroun	CzRep-2	8	0	1	1	0	1	0	0	0	0

KUCHEJDA, David (koo-HAY-dah, DAH-vihd) CHI.

Right wing. Shoots left. 5'11", 189 lbs. Born, Havirov, Czech., June 12, 1987.
(Chicago's 11th choice, 202nd overall, in 2005 Entry Draft).

			Regular Season					Playoffs				
Season	Club	League	GP	G	A	Pts	PIM	GP	G	A	Pts	PIM
2002-03	C. Budejovice U17	CzR-U17	45	23	29	52	34	6	3	4	7	6
2003-04	C. Budejovice U17	CzR-U17	3	2	1	3	31	2	1	0	1	16
	C. Budejovice Jr.	CzRep-Jr.	47	7	12	19	40	....	....	....	....	....
2004-05	C. Budejovice	CzRep-2	1	0	0	0	0	....	....	....	....	....
	C. Budejovice Jr.	CzRep-Jr.	42	12	28	40	142	2	1	1	2	2

KUDELKA, Tomas (koo-DEHL-kah, TAW-mash) OTT.

Defense. Shoots left. 6'2", 176 lbs. Born, Gottwaldov, Czech., March 10, 1987.
(Ottawa's 6th choice, 136th overall, in 2005 Entry Draft).

			Regular Season					Playoffs				
Season	Club	League	GP	G	A	Pts	PIM	GP	G	A	Pts	PIM
2002-03	HC Zlin U17	CzR-U17	45	1	16	17	28	3	1	0	1	12
2003-04	HC Zlin U17	CzR-U17	1	0	0	0	2	3	0	0	0	0
	HC Zlin Jr.	CzRep-Jr.	51	1	12	13	95	7	0	0	0	0
	HC Hame Zlin	CzRep	3	0	0	0	0	....	....	....	....	....
2004-05	HC Zlin Jr.	CzRep-Jr.	38	9	8	17	38	....	....	....	....	....
	HC Hame Zlin	CzRep	4	0	0	0	6	....	....	....	....	....

KUHTINOV, Roman (kukh-TEEN-nawv, ROH-muhn) NYI

Defense. Shoots right. 6'1", 207 lbs. Born, Belgorod, USSR, December 1, 1975.
(NY Islanders' 7th choice, 280th overall, in 2001 Entry Draft).

			Regular Season					Playoffs				
Season	Club	League	GP	G	A	Pts	PIM	GP	G	A	Pts	PIM
1997-98	Raichikhinsk	Russia-3	36	18	8	26	46	....	....	....	....	....
1998-99	Novokuznetsk	Russia	42	2	9	11	26	6	0	0	0	2
99-2000	Novokuznetsk	Russia	37	2	6	8	28	14	1	1	2	8
2000-01	Novokuznetsk	Russia	44	7	10	17	36	....	....	....	....	....
2001-02	Ufa	Russia	51	11	10	21	74	....	....	....	....	....
2002-03	Ufa	Russia	50	4	7	11	72	3	2	0	2	4
2003-04	Cherepovets	Russia	54	2	6	8	46	....	....	....	....	....
2004-05	Magnitogorsk	Russia	53	3	8	11	24	5	0	0	0	2

KUIPER, Nick (KIGH-puhr, NIHK)

Defense. Shoots right. 6'3", 215 lbs. Born, Beaconsfield, Que., February 12, 1982.

			Regular Season					Playoffs				
Season	Club	League	GP	G	A	Pts	PIM	GP	G	A	Pts	PIM
1998-99	Lac St-Louis Lions	QAAA	42	3	23	26	36	5	0	3	3	4
99-2000	Hawkesbury	CJHL	46	7	22	29	40	....	....	....	....	....
2000-01	Hawkesbury	CJHL	32	7	10	17	22	....	....	....	....	....
	Massachusetts	H-East	13	0	1	1	2	....	....	....	....	....
2001-02	Massachusetts	H-East	32	2	9	11	10	....	....	....	....	....
2002-03	Massachusetts	H-East	36	3	3	6	34	....	....	....	....	....
2003-04	Massachusetts	H-East	37	5	5	10	72	....	....	....	....	....
2004-05	Norfolk Admirals	AHL	73	3	5	8	109	5	0	0	0	2

Signed as a free agent by **Chicago**, March 31, 2004.

KUKUMBERG, Roman (KOO-kuhm-buhrg, ROH-muhn) TOR.

Center. Shoots right. 6'1", 198 lbs. Born, Bratislava, Czech., April 8, 1980.
(Toronto's 2nd choice, 113th overall, in 2004 Entry Draft).

			Regular Season					Playoffs				
Season	Club	League	GP	G	A	Pts	PIM	GP	G	A	Pts	PIM
2001-02	Dukla Trencin	Slovakia	46	12	9	21	20	4	0	0	0	2
2002-03	Dukla Trencin	Slovakia	53	18	18	36	60	12	6	5	11	12
2003-04	Dukla Trencin	Slovakia	51	16	20	36	93	11	4	8	12	14
2004-05	Nizhnekamsk	Russia	55	10	11	21	40	3	0	0	0	4

KUKUSHKIN, Sergei (koo-KOOSH-kihn, SAIR-gay) DAL.

Center. Shoots left. 6'2", 187 lbs. Born, Minsk, USSR, July 24, 1985.
(Dallas' 8th choice, 218th overall, in 2004 Entry Draft).

			Regular Season					Playoffs				
Season	Club	League	GP	G	A	Pts	PIM	GP	G	A	Pts	PIM
2003-04	Yunost Minsk	Belarus	STATISTICS NOT AVAILABLE									
2004-05	N.E. Jr. Falcons	EJHL	21	9	13	22	30	....	....	....	....	....
	Indiana Ice	USHL	19	1	2	3	50	....	....	....	....	....

KULYASH, Denis (kuh-L'YASH, DEH-nihs) NSH.

Defense. Shoots left. 6'2", 199 lbs. Born, Omsk, USSR, May 31, 1983.
(Nashville's 9th choice, 243rd overall, in 2004 Entry Draft).

			Regular Season					Playoffs				
Season	Club	League	GP	G	A	Pts	PIM	GP	G	A	Pts	PIM
2003-04	CSK VVS Samara 2	Russia-3	STATISTICS NOT AVAILABLE									
	CSKA Moscow	Russia	10	1	0	1	8	....	....	....	....	....
2004-05	CSKA Moscow	Russia	59	8	10	18	58	....	....	....	....	....

KUNES, Timothy (KOONZ, TIHM-oh-thee) CAR.

Defense. Shoots left. 6'1", 170 lbs. Born, Red Bank, NJ, February 12, 1987.
(Carolina's 6th choice, 145th overall, in 2005 Entry Draft).

			Regular Season					Playoffs				
Season	Club	League	GP	G	A	Pts	PIM	GP	G	A	Pts	PIM
2003-04	N.E. Jr. Falcons	EJHL	45	4	19	23	20	....	....	....	....	....
2004-05	N.E. Jr. Falcons	EJHL	50	12	28	40	51	....	....	....	....	....

Signed Letter of Intent to attend **Boston College** (H-East) in fall of 2005.

KVAPIL, Marek (kuh-VAH-puhl, MAHR-ehk) T.B.

Right wing. Shoots right. 5'10", 187 lbs. Born, Ilava, Czech., January 5, 1985.
(Tampa Bay's 7th choice, 163rd overall, in 2005 Entry Draft).

			Regular Season					Playoffs				
Season	Club	League	GP	G	A	Pts	PIM	GP	G	A	Pts	PIM
2002-03	HC Slavia Praha Jr.	CzRep-Jr.	33	9	4	13	4	2	0	0	0	0
2003-04	HC Slavia Praha Jr.	CzRep-Jr.	42	19	17	36	43	2	1	0	1	0
	HC Slavia Praha	CzRep	11	0	0	0	0	....	....	....	....	....
	HC Kometa Brno	CzRep-2	4	0	2	2	4	....	....	....	....	....
2004-05	HC Slavia Praha Jr.	CzRep-Jr.	8	6	4	10	8	....	....	....	....	....
	Saginaw Spirit	OHL	53	25	37	62	14	....	....	....	....	....

LAAKSO, Teemu (LAK-soh, TEE-moo) **NSH.**

Defense. Shoots right. 6', 187 lbs. Born, Tuusula, Finland, August 27, 1987.
(Nashville's 2nd choice, 78th overall, in 2005 Entry Draft).

			Regular Season					Playoffs				
Season	**Club**	**League**	**GP**	**G**	**A**	**Pts**	**PIM**	**GP**	**G**	**A**	**Pts**	**PIM**
2002-03	KJT Jarvenpaa U18	Fin-U18	18	2	5	7	24	....	....	....	....	....
2003-04	HIFK Helsinki Jr.	Finland-Jr.	41	3	6	9	20	3	0	1	1	0
2004-05	HIFK Helsinki Jr.	Finland-Jr.	20	5	4	9	18	....	....	....	....	....
	HIFK Helsinki	Finland	15	0	2	2	2	....	....	....	....	....
	HIFK Helsinki U18	Fin-U18	....	....	....	....	....	1	0	0	0	0

LAATIKAINEN, Arto (lah-tee-KIGH-nuhn, AHR-toh) **NYR**

Defense. Shoots left. 6', 187 lbs. Born, Espoo, Finland, May 24, 1980.
(NY Rangers' 8th choice, 197th overall, in 1999 Entry Draft).

			Regular Season					Playoffs				
Season	**Club**	**League**	**GP**	**G**	**A**	**Pts**	**PIM**	**GP**	**G**	**A**	**Pts**	**PIM**
1996-97	Kiekko-Espoo Jr.	Finland-Jr.	34	2	9	11	34	....	....	....	....	....
	Kiekko-Espoo U18	Fin-U18	11	2	5	7	2	....	....	....	....	....
1997-98	Kiekko-Espoo U18	Fin-U18	7	2	1	3	6	....	....	....	....	....
	Kiekko-Espoo Jr.	Finland-Jr.	35	7	9	16	24	5	2	0	2	2
1998-99	Blues Espoo Jr.	Finland-Jr.	3	0	1	1	4	1	1	1	2	0
	Blues Espoo	Finland	48	0	6	6	14	4	0	2	2	2
99-2000	Blues Espoo Jr.	Finland-Jr.	1	0	0	0	2	....	....	....	....	....
	Blues Espoo	Finland	51	6	5	11	12	4	1	0	1	4
2000-01	Blues Espoo	Finland	54	5	9	14	38	....	....	....	....	....
	KJT Jarvenpaa	Finland-2	1	1	1	2	0	....	....	....	....	....
2001-02	Blues Espoo	Finland	56	5	6	11	32	3	0	0	0	0
2002-03	Blues Espoo	Finland	51	1	8	9	24	7	0	3	3	4
2003-04	Blues Espoo	Finland	55	4	20	24	30	....	....	....	....	....
2004-05	Blues Espoo	Finland	56	7	8	15	32	....	....	....	....	....

LADD, Andrew (LAD, AN-droo) **CAR.**

Left wing. Shoots left. 6'2", 200 lbs. Born, Maple Ridge, B.C., December 12, 1985.
(Carolina's 1st choice, 4th overall, in 2004 Entry Draft).

			Regular Season					Playoffs				
Season	**Club**	**League**	**GP**	**G**	**A**	**Pts**	**PIM**	**GP**	**G**	**A**	**Pts**	**PIM**
2000-01	Okanagan Chiefs	BCAHA	6	4	8	12	10	....	....	....	....	....
2001-02	Port Coquitlam	BCAHA	50	50	41	91	49	....	....	....	....	....
	Vancouver Giants	WHL	1	0	0	0	0	....	....	....	....	....
2002-03	Coquitlam Express	BCHL	58	15	40	55	61	....	....	....	....	....
2003-04	Calgary Hitmen	WHL	71	30	45	75	119	7	1	6	7	10
2004-05	Calgary Hitmen	WHL	65	19	26	45	167	12	7	4	11	18

LAINE, Teemu (LIGH-neh, TEE-moo) **N.J.**

Right wing. Shoots left. 6'1", 200 lbs. Born, Helsinki, Finland, August 9, 1982.
(New Jersey's 2nd choice, 39th overall, in 2000 Entry Draft).

			Regular Season					Playoffs				
Season	**Club**	**League**	**GP**	**G**	**A**	**Pts**	**PIM**	**GP**	**G**	**A**	**Pts**	**PIM**
1997-98	Jokerit U18	Fin-U18	20	20	24	44	54	5	1	3	4	4
1998-99	Jokerit Helsinki Jr.	Finland-Jr.	29	20	17	37	83	6	0	2	2	6
99-2000	Jokerit Helsinki Jr.	Finland-Jr.	23	5	9	14	42	....	....	....	....	....
	Jokerit Helsinki	Finland	14	1	1	2	8	....	....	....	....	....
2000-01	Jokerit Helsinki Jr.	Finland-Jr.	4	1	2	3	18	1	0	0	0	0
	Kiekko-Vantaa	Finland-2	18	2	4	6	30	....	....	....	....	....
	Jokerit Helsinki	Finland	25	3	2	5	10	5	1	0	1	2
2001-02	Jokerit Helsinki Jr.	Finland-Jr.	8	9	5	14	50	1	0	0	0	2
	Kiekko-Vantaa	Finland-2	9	6	4	10	4	....	....	....	....	....
	Jokerit Helsinki	Finland	38	0	1	1	45	7	0	0	0	2
2002-03	Jokerit Helsinki	Finland	53	7	5	12	52	9	1	1	2	2
2003-04	Jokerit Helsinki	Finland	56	5	8	13	50	8	1	1	2	2
2004-05	Tappara Tampere	Finland	53	7	10	17	60	5	0	1	1	14

LAKOS, Andre (LA-kaws, AWN-dray)

Defense. Shoots right. 6'6", 230 lbs. Born, Vienna, Austria, July 29, 1979.
(New Jersey's 4th choice, 95th overall, in 1999 Entry Draft).

			Regular Season					Playoffs				
Season	**Club**	**League**	**GP**	**G**	**A**	**Pts**	**PIM**	**GP**	**G**	**A**	**Pts**	**PIM**
1995-96	Montreal-Bourassa	QAAA	40	2	13	15	68	....	....	....	....	....
1996-97	Shelburne Wolves	MTJHL	36	5	12	17	47	....	....	....	....	....
1997-98	St. Michael's	OHL	49	2	10	12	54	....	....	....	....	....
1998-99	Barrie Colts	OHL	62	4	23	27	40	12	3	3	6	8
99-2000	Albany River Rats	AHL	65	1	7	8	41	5	0	2	2	4
2000-01	Albany River Rats	AHL	51	1	20	21	29	....	....	....	....	....
2001-02	Albany River Rats	AHL	36	0	3	3	24	....	....	....	....	....
	Utah Grizzlies	AHL	26	0	1	1	28	1	0	0	0	0
	Austria	Olympics	4	0	0	0	6	....	....	....	....	....
2002-03	Augusta Lynx	ECHL	5	0	2	2	8	....	....	....	....	....
2003-04	Vienna Capitals	Austria	48	6	19	25	75	....	....	....	....	....
2004-05	Syracuse Crunch	AHL	51	1	12	13	51	....	....	....	....	....

Traded to **Dallas** by **New Jersey** with future considerations for Valeri Kamensky, January 16, 2002. Signed as a free agent by **Columbus**, July 7, 2004. Signed as a free agent by **Salzburg** (Austria), May 5, 2005.

LALIBERTE, David (lal-IH-buhr-tee, DAY-vihd) **PHI.**

Right wing. Shoots right. 6'1", 194 lbs. Born, St-Jean-Sur-Richelieu, Que., March 17, 1986.
(Philadelphia's 3rd choice, 124th overall, in 2004 Entry Draft).

			Regular Season					Playoffs				
Season	**Club**	**League**	**GP**	**G**	**A**	**Pts**	**PIM**	**GP**	**G**	**A**	**Pts**	**PIM**
2001-02	Antoine-Girouard	QAAA	41	21	21	42	14	15	8	9	17	6
2002-03	Montreal Rocket	QMJHL	66	15	14	29	10	6	3	0	3	2
2003-04	PEI Rocket	QMJHL	70	21	22	43	51	11	1	3	4	6
2004-05	PEI Rocket	QMJHL	41	23	13	36	36	....	....	....	....	....

LALIBERTE, John (lal-IH-buhr-tee, JAWN) **VAN.**

Right wing. Shoots left. 6'2", 190 lbs. Born, Portland, ME, August 5, 1983.
(Vancouver's 5th choice, 114th overall, in 2002 Entry Draft).

			Regular Season					Playoffs				
Season	**Club**	**League**	**GP**	**G**	**A**	**Pts**	**PIM**	**GP**	**G**	**A**	**Pts**	**PIM**
99-2000	Thornton	High-ME	STATISTICS NOT AVAILABLE									
	Exeter Snow Devils	EJHL	32	37	40	77	60	....	....	....	....	....
2000-01	Exeter Snow Devils	EJHL	53	33	42	75	42	....	....	....	....	....
2001-02	N.H. Jr. Monarchs	EJHL	35	39	44	*83	60	....	8	12	20	....
2002-03	Boston University	H-East	26	5	6	11	12	....	....	....	....	....
2003-04	Boston University	H-East	35	5	11	16	20	....	....	....	....	....
2004-05	Boston University	H-East	40	12	18	30	45	....	....	....	....	....

LAMBERT, Michael (lam-BAIR, MIGH-kuhl) **MTL.**

Left wing. Shoots left. 6'2", 200 lbs. Born, Trois-Rivieres, Que., March 10, 1984.
(Montreal's 3rd choice, 99th overall, in 2002 Entry Draft).

			Regular Season					Playoffs				
Season	**Club**	**League**	**GP**	**G**	**A**	**Pts**	**PIM**	**GP**	**G**	**A**	**Pts**	**PIM**
1998-99	Cap-d-Madeleine	QAAA	3	0	0	0	0	....	....	....	....	....
99-2000	Cap-d-Madeleine	QAAA	42	20	16	36	38	1	0	2	2	0
2000-01	Acadie-Bathurst	QMJHL	23	2	5	7	15	....	....	....	....	....
	Montreal Rocket	QMJHL	33	6	12	18	14	....	....	....	....	....
2001-02	Montreal Rocket	QMJHL	71	29	24	53	111	7	1	6	7	15
2002-03	Montreal Rocket	QMJHL	71	28	32	60	53	7	2	2	4	10
2003-04	PEI Rocket	QMJHL	67	42	42	84	53	11	6	7	13	6
2004-05	Hamilton Bulldogs	AHL	40	3	4	7	18	....	....	....	....	....
	Long Beach	ECHL	18	5	4	9	26	7	5	1	6	14

LAMMERS, John (LA-muhrs, JAWN) **DAL.**

Left wing. Shoots left. 5'11", 184 lbs. Born, Bowmanville, Ont., January 29, 1986.
(Dallas' 5th choice, 86th overall, in 2004 Entry Draft).

			Regular Season					Playoffs				
Season	**Club**	**League**	**GP**	**G**	**A**	**Pts**	**PIM**	**GP**	**G**	**A**	**Pts**	**PIM**
2001-02	Langley Bantams	BCAHA	64	51	69	120	30	....	....	....	....	....
	Lethbridge	WHL	5	0	0	0	0	....	....	....	....	....
2002-03	Lethbridge	WHL	53	17	15	32	11	....	....	....	....	....
2003-04	Lethbridge	WHL	62	21	24	45	31	....	....	....	....	....
2004-05	Lethbridge	WHL	66	17	30	47	43	5	0	0	0	2

LANNON, Ryan (LA-nuhn, RIGH-uhn) **PIT.**

Defense. Shoots left. 6'2", 220 lbs. Born, Worcester, MA, December 14, 1982.
(Pittsburgh's 10th choice, 239th overall, in 2002 Entry Draft).

			Regular Season					Playoffs				
Season	**Club**	**League**	**GP**	**G**	**A**	**Pts**	**PIM**	**GP**	**G**	**A**	**Pts**	**PIM**
1998-99	USA U-17	USDP	56	3	4	7	36	....	....	....	....	....
99-2000	Cushing	High-MA	STATISTICS NOT AVAILABLE									
2000-01	Cushing	High-MA	STATISTICS NOT AVAILABLE									
2001-02	Harvard Crimson	ECAC	34	0	2	2	38	....	....	....	....	....
2002-03	Harvard Crimson	ECAC	34	3	11	14	39	....	....	....	....	....
2003-04	Harvard Crimson	ECAC	35	0	9	9	36	....	....	....	....	....
2004-05	Harvard Crimson	ECAC	33	1	12	13	34	....	....	....	....	....

LAPIERRE, Maxim (la-PEE-air, MAX-ihm) **MTL.**

Center. Shoots right. 6'2", 201 lbs. Born, St. Leonard, Que., March 29, 1985.
(Montreal's 3rd choice, 61st overall, in 2003 Entry Draft).

			Regular Season					Playoffs				
Season	**Club**	**League**	**GP**	**G**	**A**	**Pts**	**PIM**	**GP**	**G**	**A**	**Pts**	**PIM**
2001-02	Cap-d-Madeleine	QAAA	42	14	27	41	44	10	3	5	8	16
	Montreal Rocket	QMJHL	9	2	0	2	2	....	....	....	....	....
2002-03	Montreal Rocket	QMJHL	72	22	21	43	55	7	1	3	4	6
2003-04	PEI Rocket	QMJHL	67	25	36	61	138	11	7	2	9	14
2004-05	PEI Rocket	QMJHL	69	25	27	52	139	....	....	....	....	....

LaROSE, Chad (lah-ROHZ, CHAD) **CAR.**

Right wing. Shoots right. 5'10", 173 lbs. Born, Fraser, MI, March 27, 1982.

			Regular Season					Playoffs				
Season	**Club**	**League**	**GP**	**G**	**A**	**Pts**	**PIM**	**GP**	**G**	**A**	**Pts**	**PIM**
99-2000	Sioux Falls	USHL	54	29	26	55	28	3	0	1	1	0
2000-01	Sioux Falls	USHL	24	11	22	33	50	....	....	....	....	....
	Plymouth Whalers	OHL	32	18	7	25	24	19	10	10	20	22
2001-02	Plymouth Whalers	OHL	53	32	27	59	40	6	3	4	7	16
2002-03	Plymouth Whalers	OHL	67	61	56	117	52	15	9	8	17	25
2003-04	Lowell	AHL	36	7	9	16	29	....	....	....	....	....
	Florida Everblades	ECHL	41	16	19	35	16	14	3	4	7	20
2004-05	Lowell	AHL	66	20	22	42	32	11	3	5	8	10

OHL Second All-Star Team (2003)

Signed as a free agent by **Carolina**, August 6, 2003.

LASCEK, Stanislav (LASH-chehk, STAHN-ihs-lahv) **T.B.**

Right wing. Shoots left. 6', 195 lbs. Born, Martin, Czech., January 17, 1986.
(Tampa Bay's 6th choice, 133rd overall, in 2005 Entry Draft).

			Regular Season					Playoffs				
Season	**Club**	**League**	**GP**	**G**	**A**	**Pts**	**PIM**	**GP**	**G**	**A**	**Pts**	**PIM**
2002-03	HKm Zvolen	Slovakia	1	0	0	0	2	....	....	....	....	....
	HKm Zvolen B	Slovak-2	19	2	4	6	29	....	....	....	....	....
2003-04	Chicoutimi	QMJHL	59	17	40	57	49	18	5	13	18	30
2004-05	Chicoutimi	QMJHL	53	18	72	90	42	17	4	18	22	26

LASHOFF, Matt (LASH-awf, MAT) **BOS.**

Defense. Shoots left. 6'2", 205 lbs. Born, East Greenbush, NY, September 29, 1986.
(Boston's 1st choice, 22nd overall, in 2005 Entry Draft).

			Regular Season					Playoffs				
Season	**Club**	**League**	**GP**	**G**	**A**	**Pts**	**PIM**	**GP**	**G**	**A**	**Pts**	**PIM**
2002-03	USA U-17	USDP	62	3	8	11	67	....	....	....	....	....
2003-04	Kitchener Rangers	OHL	62	5	19	24	94	5	0	1	1	0
2004-05	Kitchener Rangers	OHL	44	4	18	22	44	13	0	3	3	18

LATENDRESSE, Guillaume (lah-TEHN-drehs, gee-OHM) **MTL.**

Right wing. Shoots left. 6'1", 216 lbs. Born, Ste-Catherine, Que., May 24, 1987.
(Montreal's 2nd choice, 45th overall, in 2005 Entry Draft).

			Regular Season					Playoffs				
Season	**Club**	**League**	**GP**	**G**	**A**	**Pts**	**PIM**	**GP**	**G**	**A**	**Pts**	**PIM**
2003-04	Drummondville	QMJHL	53	24	25	49	66	....	....	....	....	....
2004-05	Drummondville	QMJHL	65	29	49	78	76	6	6	4	10	7

QMJHL All-Rookie Team (2004)

LATENDRESSE, Olivier (la-TEHN-drehs, oh-LIHV-ee-ay) **PHX.**

Center. Shoots left. 5'10", 190 lbs. Born, LaSalle, Que., February 12, 1986.

			Regular Season					Playoffs				
Season	**Club**	**League**	**GP**	**G**	**A**	**Pts**	**PIM**	**GP**	**G**	**A**	**Pts**	**PIM**
2002-03	Val-d'Or Foreurs	QMJHL	55	11	14	25	22	8	0	2	2	0
2003-04	Val-d'Or Foreurs	QMJHL	53	19	46	65	44	7	1	5	6	14
2004-05	Val-d'Or Foreurs	QMJHL	68	27	47	74	34	....	....	....	....	....

Signed as a free agent by **Phoenix**, September 15, 2004.

LAVALLEE, Jordan (LAV-alee, JOHR-dahn) ATL.

Left wing. Shoots left. 6'3", 203 lbs. Born, Corvallis, OR, May 11, 1986.
(Atlanta's 5th choice, 116th overall, in 2005 Entry Draft).

			Regular Season					Playoffs				
Season	Club	League	GP	G	A	Pts	PIM	GP	G	A	Pts	PIM
2002-03	Quebec Remparts	QMJHL	55	3	6	9	54	11	0	1	1	0
2003-04	Quebec Remparts	QMJHL	69	11	16	27	111	5	2	0	2	6
2004-05	Quebec Remparts	QMJHL	64	40	26	66	108	13	5	2	7	26

LAVRENTIEV, Anton (lahv-REHN-tee-yehv, AN-tawn) NSH.

Defense. Shoots right. 6'4", 196 lbs. Born, Kazan, USSR, August 25, 1983.
(Nashville's 7th choice, 178th overall, in 2001 Entry Draft).

			Regular Season					Playoffs				
Season	Club	League	GP	G	A	Pts	PIM	GP	G	A	Pts	PIM
2000-01	Ak Bars Kazan 2	Russia-3	STATISTICS NOT AVAILABLE									
2001-02	Sudbury Wolves	OHL	10	0	0	0	17	....	....	....	....	....
	Ak Bars Kazan 2	Russia-3	STATISTICS NOT AVAILABLE									
2002-03	Yuzhny Ural Orsk	Russia-2	13	0	1	1	14	....	....	....	....	....
2003-04	HK Rybinsk	Russia-2	31	2	1	3	49	....	....	....	....	....
2004-05	Novopolotsk	BelOpen	23	2	3	5	26	1	0	0	0	2

LAWRENCE, Chris (LOH-rehnts, KRIHS) T.B.

Center. Shoots right. 6'4", 199 lbs. Born, Toronto, Ont., February 5, 1987.
(Tampa Bay's 3rd choice, 89th overall, in 2005 Entry Draft).

			Regular Season					Playoffs				
Season	Club	League	GP	G	A	Pts	PIM	GP	G	A	Pts	PIM
2003-04	Sault Ste. Marie	OHL	62	7	6	13	34	....	....	....	....	....
2004-05	Sault Ste. Marie	OHL	68	11	40	51	57	7	3	3	6	4

LAWSON, Kyle (LAW-suhn, KIGHL) CAR.

Defense. Shoots right. 5'11", 192 lbs. Born, Southfield, MI, January 11, 1987.
(Carolina's 9th choice, 198th overall, in 2005 Entry Draft).

			Regular Season					Playoffs				
Season	Club	League	GP	G	A	Pts	PIM	GP	G	A	Pts	PIM
2003-04	Det. Honeybaked	MWEHL	61	17	41	58	68	....	....	....	....	....
	Texarkana Bandits	NAHL	....	....	....	....	....	3	0	1	1	0
2004-05	USA U-17&U-18	NAHL	8	1	3	4	0	....	....	....	....	....
	USA U-18	USDP	31	3	15	18	6	....	....	....	....	....

Signed Letter of Intent to attend **Notre Dame** (CCHA) in fall of 2005.

LAWSON, Lucas (LAW-suhn, LOO-kuhs)

Center. Shoots left. 6'1", 195 lbs. Born, Braeside, Ont., August 10, 1979.

			Regular Season					Playoffs				
Season	Club	League	GP	G	A	Pts	PIM	GP	G	A	Pts	PIM
1998-99	Kanata Valley	CJHL	50	40	45	85	124	3	2	10	12	0
99-2000	U. of Maine	H-East	23	2	3	5	12	....	....	....	....	....
2000-01	U. of Maine	H-East	39	9	11	20	16	....	....	....	....	....
2001-02	U. of Maine	H-East	44	18	13	31	37	....	....	....	....	....
2002-03	U. of Maine	H-East	39	21	16	37	18	....	....	....	....	....
	Hartford Wolf Pack	AHL	....	....	....	....	....	2	0	0	0	0
2003-04	Charlotte	ECHL	26	11	13	24	10	....	....	....	....	....
	Hartford Wolf Pack	AHL	32	3	4	7	27	5	0	0	0	0
2004-05	Hartford Wolf Pack	AHL	51	4	11	15	32	3	0	0	0	0

Hockey East Second All-Star Team (2003)

Signed as a free agent by **NY Rangers**, April 4, 2003. Signed as a free agent by **JYP** (Finland), August 31, 2005.

LEACH, Jay (LEECH, JAY) BOS.

Defense. Shoots left. 6'4", 232 lbs. Born, Syracuse, NY, September 2, 1979.
(Phoenix's 5th choice, 115th overall, in 1998 Entry Draft).

			Regular Season					Playoffs				
Season	Club	League	GP	G	A	Pts	PIM	GP	G	A	Pts	PIM
1994-95	John Marshall	High-MN	10	0	0	0	14	....	....	....	....	....
1995-96	John Marshall	High-MN	11	1	2	3	8	4	0	0	0	0
	Capital District	Exhib.	53	3	8	11	33	....	....	....	....	....
1996-97	Capital District	Exhib.	57	8	50	58	140	....	....	....	....	....
1997-98	Providence College	H-East	32	0	8	8	29	....	....	....	....	....
1998-99	Providence College	H-East	33	1	8	9	42	....	....	....	....	....
99-2000	Providence College	H-East	37	1	9	10	101	....	....	....	....	....
2000-01	Providence College	H-East	40	4	21	25	104	....	....	....	....	....
2001-02	Mississippi	ECHL	70	3	13	16	116	10	1	1	2	8
2002-03	Springfield Falcons	AHL	9	0	0	0	0	....	....	....	....	....
	Augusta Lynx	ECHL	65	8	11	19	162	....	....	....	....	....
2003-04	Providence Bruins	AHL	3	0	0	0	4	....	....	....	....	....
	Long Beach	ECHL	3	0	1	1	4	....	....	....	....	....
	Bridgeport	AHL	23	0	1	1	33	7	0	1	1	10
	Trenton Titans	ECHL	31	2	11	13	45	....	....	....	....	....
2004-05	Providence Bruins	AHL	62	4	5	9	92	17	0	0	0	28
	Trenton Titans	ECHL	11	0	2	2	17	....	....	....	....	....

Hockey East All-Academic Team (2000)

Signed as a free agent by **Boston**, September 26, 2003.

LEBDA, Brett (LEHB-dah, BREHT) DET.

Defense. Shoots left. 5'11", 194 lbs. Born, Buffalo Grove, IL, January 15, 1982.

			Regular Season					Playoffs				
Season	Club	League	GP	G	A	Pts	PIM	GP	G	A	Pts	PIM
2000-01	U. of Notre Dame	CCHA	39	7	19	26	109	....	....	....	....	....
2001-02	U. of Notre Dame	CCHA	34	6	8	14	54	....	....	....	....	....
2002-03	U. of Notre Dame	CCHA	40	7	14	21	48	....	....	....	....	....
2003-04	U. of Notre Dame	CCHA	39	6	18	24	42	....	....	....	....	....
	Grand Rapids	AHL	6	0	1	1	0	4	0	0	0	2
2004-05	Grand Rapids	AHL	80	2	10	12	34	....	....	....	....	....

CCHA All-Rookie Team (2001) • CCHA Second All-Star Team (2004)

Signed as a free agent by **Detroit**, April 1, 2004.

LEBLOND-LETOURNEAU, Pierre-Luc (leh-TOOR-noh-leh-BLAWN) N.J.

Left wing. Shoots left. 6'2", 210 lbs. Born, Levis, Que., June 4, 1985.
(New Jersey's 4th choice, 216th overall, in 2004 Entry Draft).

			Regular Season					Playoffs				
Season	Club	League	GP	G	A	Pts	PIM	GP	G	A	Pts	PIM
2003-04	Baie-Comeau	QMJHL	62	2	3	5	198	4	0	0	0	6
2004-05	Baie-Comeau	QMJHL	67	1	6	7	229	6	0	1	1	10

LEE, Brian (LEE, BRIGH-uhn) OTT.

Defense. Shoots right. 6'2", 202 lbs. Born, Fargo, ND, March 26, 1987.
(Ottawa's 1st choice, 9th overall, in 2005 Entry Draft).

			Regular Season					Playoffs				
Season	Club	League	GP	G	A	Pts	PIM	GP	G	A	Pts	PIM
2003-04	Moorhead Spuds	High-MN	29	10	38	48	....	....	....	....	....	....
2004-05	Moorhead Spuds	High-MN	25	12	26	38	....	....	....	....	....	....
	Lincoln Stars	USHL	12	0	3	3	4	4	2	3	5	2

Signed Letter of Intent to attend **North Dakota** (WCHA), November 19, 2004.

LEE, Carter (LEE, KAHR-tuhr) S.J.

Forward. Shoots right. 6'1", 190 lbs. Born, Toms River, NJ, July 2, 1984.
(San Jose's 11th choice, 276th overall, in 2003 Entry Draft).

			Regular Season					Playoffs				
Season	Club	League	GP	G	A	Pts	PIM	GP	G	A	Pts	PIM
2001-02	Christian Bros.	High-NJ	34	10	9	19	45	....	....	....	....	....
2002-03	Canterbury	High-CT	35	38	22	60	40	....	....	....	....	....
2003-04	Canterbury	High-CT	30	19	26	45	40	....	....	....	....	....
2004-05	Northeastern	H-East	11	2	1	3	4	....	....	....	....	....

LEGAULT, Olivier (luh-GOH, OH-lihv-ee-ay) FLA.

Left wing. Shoots left. 6'5", 238 lbs. Born, Chibougamau, Que., October 2, 1986.
(Florida's 4th choice, 93rd overall, in 2005 Entry Draft).

			Regular Season					Playoffs				
Season	Club	League	GP	G	A	Pts	PIM	GP	G	A	Pts	PIM
2002-03	Sherbrooke	QMJHL	27	0	0	0	85	5	0	0	0	0
2003-04	Lewiston	QMJHL	54	0	2	2	115	7	0	0	0	9
2004-05	Lewiston	QMJHL	55	1	3	4	131	7	0	0	0	8

LEHMAN, Scott (LAY-man, SKAWT) ATL.

Defense. Shoots left. 6'1", 200 lbs. Born, Fort McMurray, Alta., January 5, 1986.
(Atlanta's 3rd choice, 76th overall, in 2004 Entry Draft).

			Regular Season					Playoffs				
Season	Club	League	GP	G	A	Pts	PIM	GP	G	A	Pts	PIM
2002-03	St. Michael's	OHL	53	3	10	13	50	19	1	3	4	34
2003-04	St. Michael's	OHL	66	5	27	32	189	18	2	2	4	38
2004-05	St. Michael's	OHL	57	2	19	21	189	10	2	2	4	31

LEHOUX, Yanick (luh-HOO, YAH-nihk) L.A.

Center. Shoots right. 6'1", 200 lbs. Born, Montreal, Que., April 8, 1982.
(Los Angeles' 3rd choice, 86th overall, in 2000 Entry Draft).

			Regular Season					Playoffs				
Season	Club	League	GP	G	A	Pts	PIM	GP	G	A	Pts	PIM
1997-98	Cap-d-Madeleine	QAAA	42	29	50	79	26	....	....	....	....	....
1998-99	Baie-Comeau	QMJHL	63	10	20	30	31	....	....	....	....	....
99-2000	Baie-Comeau	QMJHL	67	31	61	92	14	6	1	2	3	2
2000-01	Baie-Comeau	QMJHL	70	67	68	135	62	11	8	16	24	0
2001-02	Baie-Comeau	QMJHL	66	56	69	125	63	5	5	4	9	0
	Manchester	AHL	....	....	....	....	....	1	0	0	0	0
2002-03	Manchester	AHL	78	16	21	37	26	1	0	0	0	0
2003-04	Manchester	AHL	66	14	28	42	22	5	2	3	5	16
2004-05	Manchester	AHL	38	23	31	54	16	....	....	....	....	....

QMJHL Second All-Star Team (2002)

LEHTONEN, Mikko (LEHT-oh-nehn, MEE-koh) NSH.

Defense. Shoots left. 6'1", 194 lbs. Born, Oulu, Finland, June 12, 1979.
(Nashville's 9th choice, 271st overall, in 2001 Entry Draft).

			Regular Season					Playoffs				
Season	Club	League	GP	G	A	Pts	PIM	GP	G	A	Pts	PIM
1995-96	Karpat Oulu U18	Fin-U18	15	4	5	9	30	....	....	....	....	....
1996-97	Karpat Oulu Jr.	Finland-Jr.	35	6	19	25	82	....	....	....	....	....
1997-98	Karpat Oulu Jr.	Finland-Jr.	20	3	4	7	40	....	....	....	....	....
	Karpat Oulu U18	Fin-U18	11	5	7	12	31	....	....	....	....	....
1998-99	Karpat Oulu Jr.	Finland-Jr.	22	7	8	15	51	....	....	....	....	....
	Karpat Oulu	Finland-2	2	0	0	0	0	....	....	....	....	....
	Karpat Oulu U18	Fin-U18	13	6	14	20	14	....	....	....	....	....
99-2000	Karpat Oulu	Finland-2	45	5	10	15	26	6	0	0	0	4
2000-01	Karpat Oulu	Finland	54	6	9	15	58	9	0	3	3	4
2001-02	Karpat Oulu	Finland	55	8	11	19	32	4	1	1	2	4
2002-03	Karpat Oulu	Finland	55	5	12	17	50	15	3	1	4	22
2003-04	Karpat Oulu	Finland	53	5	13	18	62	12	2	4	6	8
2004-05	Karpat Oulu	Finland	53	11	17	28	28	12	3	3	6	12

LEHTONEN, Mikko (LEH-tih-nehn, MEE-koh) BOS.

Right wing. Shoots right. 6'3", 191 lbs. Born, Espoo, Finland, April 1, 1987.
(Boston's 3rd choice, 83rd overall, in 2005 Entry Draft).

			Regular Season					Playoffs				
Season	Club	League	GP	G	A	Pts	PIM	GP	G	A	Pts	PIM
2002-03	Blues Espoo U18	Fin-U18	11	1	3	4	2	1	0	0	0	0
2003-04	Blues Espoo U18	Fin-U18	20	8	7	15	22	....	....	....	....	....
	Blues Espoo Jr.	Finland-Jr.	19	3	0	3	0	5	0	0	0	0
2004-05	Blues Espoo U18	Fin-U18	2	0	2	2	0	....	....	....	....	....
	Blues Espoo Jr.	Finland-Jr.	37	6	9	15	38	6	3	1	4	0
	Blues Espoo	Finland	1	0	0	0	0	....	....	....	....	....

LEINONEN, Tommi (LEIH-noh-nehn, TAW-mee) PIT.

Defense. Shoots left. 6'2", 191 lbs. Born, Kajaani, Finland, May 14, 1987.
(Pittsburgh's 4th choice, 125th overall, in 2005 Entry Draft).

			Regular Season					Playoffs				
Season	Club	League	GP	G	A	Pts	PIM	GP	G	A	Pts	PIM
2003-04	Karpat Oulu U18	Fin-U18	28	9	3	12	30	2	0	0	0	0
2004-05	Karpat Oulu U18	Fin-U18	1	0	0	0	0	....	....	....	....	....
	Karpat Oulu Jr.	Finland-Jr.	36	9	11	20	16	1	0	0	0	0

LEMTYUGOV, Nikolai (LEHM-tyuh-gawf, NIH-koh-ligh) ST.L.

Right wing. Shoots left. 6', 183 lbs. Born, Miass, USSR, January 15, 1986.
(St. Louis' 7th choice, 219th overall, in 2005 Entry Draft).

			Regular Season					Playoffs				
Season	Club	League	GP	G	A	Pts	PIM	GP	G	A	Pts	PIM
2003-04	CSKA Moscow 2	Russia-3	STATISTICS NOT AVAILABLE									
2004-05	CSKA Moscow 2	Russia-3	STATISTICS NOT AVAILABLE									
	CSKA Moscow	Russia	11	1	1	2	16	....	....	....	....	....

LEPISTO, Sami (LEH-pihs-toh, SA-mee) **WSH.**

Defense. Shoots left. 6', 176 lbs. Born, Espoo, Finland, October 17, 1984.
(Washington's 6th choice, 66th overall, in 2004 Entry Draft).

			Regular Season					Playoffs				
Season	Club	League	GP	G	A	Pts	PIM	GP	G	A	Pts	PIM
2001-02	Jokerit Helsinki Jr.	Finland-Jr.	14	0	5	5	21	....	....	....	....	....
	Jokerit U18	Fin-U18	20	8	14	22	36	8	4	8	12	12
2002-03	Jokerit Helsinki Jr.	Finland-Jr.	36	5	14	19	34	11	1	5	6	8
2003-04	Jokerit Helsinki	Finland	53	3	4	7	20	8	0	1	1	4
2004-05	Jokerit Helsinki	Finland	55	7	18	25	44	12	1	7	8	12

LESSARD, Junior (leh-SAHRD, JOO-nyuhr) **DAL.**

Right wing/Center. Shoots right. 6', 195 lbs. Born, St-Joseph-de-Beauce, Que., May 26, 1980.

			Regular Season					Playoffs				
Season	Club	League	GP	G	A	Pts	PIM	GP	G	A	Pts	PIM
99-2000	Portage Terriers	MJHL	60	60	48	108	61	....	....	....	....	....
2000-01	U. Minn-Duluth	WCHA	36	4	8	12	12	....	....	....	....	....
2001-02	U. Minn-Duluth	WCHA	39	17	13	30	50	....	....	....	....	....
2002-03	U. Minn-Duluth	WCHA	40	21	16	37	20	....	....	....	....	....
2003-04	U. Minn-Duluth	WCHA	45	*32	31	*63	34	....	....	....	....	....
2004-05	Houston Aeros	AHL	71	11	11	22	25	5	1	0	1	0

WCHA First All-Star Team (2004) • WCHA Player of the Year (2004) • NCAA West First All-American Team (2004) • NCAA Championship All-Tournament Team (2004) • Hobey Baker Memorial Award (Top U.S. Collegiate Player) (2004)

Signed as a free agent by **Dallas**, April 15, 2004.

LETANG, Kristopher (leh-TANG, KRIHS-tuh-fuhr) **PIT.**

Defense. Shoots right. 5'11", 190 lbs. Born, Montreal, Que., April 24, 1987.
(Pittsburgh's 3rd choice, 62nd overall, in 2005 Entry Draft).

			Regular Season					Playoffs				
Season	Club	League	GP	G	A	Pts	PIM	GP	G	A	Pts	PIM
2002-03	Antoine-Girouard	QAAA	42	2	10	12	34	....	....	....	....	....
2003-04	Antoine-Girouard	QAAA	39	12	41	53	94	13	7	9	16	38
2004-05	Val-d'Or Foreurs	QMJHL	70	13	19	32	79	....	....	....	....	....

QMJHL All-Rookie Team (2005) • Canadian Major Junior All-Rookie Team (2005)

LEWANDOWSKI, Eduard (luh-wan-DOW-skee, EHD-wahrd) **PHX.**

Left wing. Shoots left. 6'1", 205 lbs. Born, Krasnoturjinsk, USSR, May 3, 1980.
(Phoenix's 6th choice, 242nd overall, in 2003 Entry Draft).

			Regular Season					Playoffs				
Season	Club	League	GP	G	A	Pts	PIM	GP	G	A	Pts	PIM
1997-98	Wilhelmshaven	German-2	48	19	12	31	46	....	....	....	....	....
1998-99	Wilhelmshaven	German-3	49	35	21	56	96	....	....	....	....	....
99-2000	Wilhelmshaven	German-2	48	15	26	41	104	....	....	....	....	....
2000-01	Wilhelmshaven	German-2	47	22	30	52	97	....	....	....	....	....
2001-02	Eisbaren Berlin	Germany	59	7	15	22	57	4	0	0	0	2
2002-03	Kolner Haie	Germany	46	6	14	20	46	13	3	3	6	43
2003-04	Kolner Haie	Germany	52	16	17	33	85	5	1	2	3	16
2004-05	Kolner Haie	Germany	49	19	20	39	49	6	1	1	2	33

LEWIS, Grant (LOO-ihs, GRANT) **ATL.**

Defense. Shoots right. 6'3", 190 lbs. Born, Pittsburgh, PA, January 20, 1985.
(Atlanta's 2nd choice, 40th overall, in 2004 Entry Draft).

			Regular Season					Playoffs				
Season	Club	League	GP	G	A	Pts	PIM	GP	G	A	Pts	PIM
2002-03	Pittsburgh Forge	NAHL	50	2	7	9	59	....	....	....	....	....
2003-04	Dartmouth	ECAC	34	3	22	25	57	....	....	....	....	....
2004-05	Dartmouth	ECAC	33	5	17	22	32	....	....	....	....	....

ECAC All-Rookie Team (2004) • ECAC First All-Star Team (2004)

LIFFITON, David (LIH-fih-tuhn, DAY-vihd) **NYR**

Defense. Shoots left. 6'2", 210 lbs. Born, Windsor, Ont., October 18, 1984.
(Colorado's 1st choice, 63rd overall, in 2003 Entry Draft).

			Regular Season					Playoffs				
Season	Club	League	GP	G	A	Pts	PIM	GP	G	A	Pts	PIM
2000-01	Aylmer Aces	OHA-B	51	1	9	10	51	....	....	....	....	....
2001-02	Plymouth Whalers	OHL	62	3	9	12	65	6	0	0	0	0
2002-03	Plymouth Whalers	OHL	64	5	11	16	139	18	1	3	4	29
2003-04	Plymouth Whalers	OHL	44	2	9	11	85	9	0	0	0	12
2004-05	Hartford Wolf Pack	AHL	33	0	1	1	74	....	....	....	....	....
	Charlotte	ECHL	16	0	2	2	18	15	1	4	5	27

Traded to **NY Rangers** by **Colorado** with Chris McAllister and Florida's 2nd round choice (previously acquired, later traded back to Florida – Florida selected David Shantz) in 2004 Entry Draft for Matthew Barnaby and NY Rangers' 3rd round choice (Denis Parshin) in 2004 Entry Draft, March 8, 2004.

LINDGREN, Perttu (LIHND-gruhn, PUHR-too) **DAL.**

Center. Shoots left. 6', 185 lbs. Born, Tampere, Finland, August 26, 1987.
(Dallas' 4th choice, 75th overall, in 2005 Entry Draft).

			Regular Season					Playoffs				
Season	Club	League	GP	G	A	Pts	PIM	GP	G	A	Pts	PIM
2003-04	Ilves Tampere U18	Fin-U18	24	11	17	28	26	....	....	....	....	....
	Ilves Tampere Jr.	Finland-Jr.	2	0	0	0	0	....	....	....	....	....
2004-05	Ilves Tampere Jr.	Finland-Jr.	38	12	29	41	2	10	7	10	17	4
	Ilves Tampere	Finland	2	0	0	0	0	....	....	....	....	....

LINDSTROM, Andreas (LIHND-struhm, an-DRAY-uhs) **BOS.**

Right wing. Shoots left. 6'5", 210 lbs. Born, Lulea, Sweden, September 1, 1982.
(Boston's 12th choice, 279th overall, in 2000 Entry Draft).

			Regular Season					Playoffs				
Season	Club	League	GP	G	A	Pts	PIM	GP	G	A	Pts	PIM
99-2000	Lulea HF Jr.	Swe-Jr.	9	2	2	4	14	....	....	....	....	....
2000-01	Lulea HF Jr.	Swe-Jr.	21	8	6	14	18	....	....	....	....	....
	Lulea HF	Sweden	3	0	0	0	0	8	1	0	1	0
2001-02	Lulea HF	Sweden	....	....	....	....	....	1	0	0	0	4
	Lulea HF Jr.	Swe-Jr.	17	5	4	9	40	2	1	0	1	6
2002-03	Bodens IK	Sweden-2	35	0	2	2	24	....	....	....	....	....
2003-04	Asploven	Sweden-3	33	13	9	22	82	....	....	....	....	....
2004-05	Asploven	Sweden-3	21	7	7	14	55	....	....	....	....	....

LINDSTROM, Joakim (LIHND-struhm, YOH-ah-kihm) **CBJ**

Center. Shoots left. 6', 187 lbs. Born, Skelleftea, Sweden, December 5, 1983.
(Columbus' 2nd choice, 41st overall, in 2002 Entry Draft).

			Regular Season					Playoffs				
Season	Club	League	GP	G	A	Pts	PIM	GP	G	A	Pts	PIM
99-2000	MoDo U18	Swe-U18	17	6	*14	20	32	....	....	....	....	....
	Malmo Jr.	Swe-Jr.	10	4	4	8	2	....	....	....	....	....
2000-01	Malmo Jr.	Swe-Jr.	12	7	14	21	46	4	2	3	5	24
	MoDo	Sweden	10	2	3	5	2	7	0	1	1	0
2001-02	Malmo Jr.	Swe-Jr.	10	9	6	15	67	....	....	....	....	....
	IF Troja-Ljungby	Sweden-2	3	0	0	0	12	....	....	....	....	....
	MODO	Sweden	42	4	3	7	20	14	3	5	8	8
2002-03	MODO	Sweden	29	4	2	6	14	6	1	1	2	2
	Malmo Jr.	Swe-Jr.	2	5	1	6	8	....	....	....	....	....
	Ornskoldsviks SK	Sweden-2	2	1	1	2	4	....	....	....	....	....
2003-04	MODO	Sweden	15	0	2	2	0	....	....	....	....	....
	Sundsvall	Sweden-2	2	0	5	5	0	....	....	....	....	....
2004-05	MODO Jr.	Swe-Jr.	2	4	1	5	0	....	....	....	....	....
	MODO	Sweden	37	2	3	5	24	....	....	....	....	....
	Syracuse Crunch	AHL	13	4	4	8	0	....	....	....	....	....

LINDSTROM, Liam (LIHND-struhm, LEE-uhm) **PHX.**

Center. Shoots left. 6', 189 lbs. Born, Edmonton, Alta., January 12, 1985.
(Phoenix's 3rd choice, 115th overall, in 2003 Entry Draft).

			Regular Season					Playoffs				
Season	Club	League	GP	G	A	Pts	PIM	GP	G	A	Pts	PIM
2000-01	Mora IK U18	Swe-U18	14	3	4	7	14	....	....	....	....	....
	Mora IK Jr.	Swe-Jr.	1	0	0	0	2	1	0	0	0	0
2001-02	Mora IK U18	Swe-U18	2	2	0	2	0	1	1	0	1	4
	Mora IK Jr.	Swe-Jr.	25	5	8	13	12	....	....	....	....	....
2002-03	Mora IK U18	Swe-U18	4	3	1	4	8	....	....	....	....	....
	Mora IK Jr.	Swe-Jr.	20	3	7	10	57	....	....	....	....	....
	Mora IK	Sweden-2	13	0	0	0	0	....	....	....	....	....
2003-04	Sundsvall	Sweden-2	26	0	0	0	4	2	0	0	0	0
2004-05	Sundsvall	Sweden-2	51	5	4	9	30	....	....	....	....	....

LINDSTROM, Sanny (LIHND-struhm, SAN-nee) **COL.**

Defense. Shoots left. 6'2", 205 lbs. Born, Stockholm, Sweden, December 24, 1979.
(Colorado's 4th choice, 112th overall, in 1999 Entry Draft).

			Regular Season					Playoffs				
Season	Club	League	GP	G	A	Pts	PIM	GP	G	A	Pts	PIM
1997-98	Huddinge IK	Sweden-2	32	6	6	12	46	....	....	....	....	....
1998-99	Huddinge IK	Sweden-2	37	4	4	8	65	....	....	....	....	....
99-2000	Hershey Bears	AHL	42	1	2	3	57	....	....	....	....	....
	Baton Rouge	ECHL	11	1	2	3	16	....	....	....	....	....
2000-01	Hershey Bears	AHL	24	0	0	0	61	....	....	....	....	....
	Quad City	UHL	5	1	1	2	10	....	....	....	....	....
2001-02	Quad City	UHL	38	4	23	27	71	12	0	3	3	20
	Hershey Bears	AHL	2	0	0	0	0	....	....	....	....	....
2002-03	Timra IK	Sweden	39	1	1	2	81	9	0	1	1	0
2003-04	Timra IK	Sweden	48	1	3	4	91	10	2	0	2	24
2004-05	Timra IK	Sweden	50	5	6	11	109	7	0	1	1	10

• Missed majority of 2000-01 season recovering from knee injury suffered in practice, March 5, 2000.

LINHART, Tomas (LIHN-hart, TAW-mash) **MTL.**

Defense. Shoots left. 6'2", 209 lbs. Born, Pardubice, Czech., February 16, 1984.
(Montreal's 2nd choice, 45th overall, in 2002 Entry Draft).

			Regular Season					Playoffs				
Season	Club	League	GP	G	A	Pts	PIM	GP	G	A	Pts	PIM
99-2000	HC Pardubice U17	CzR-U17	45	2	8	10	83	....	....	....	....	....
2000-01	HC Pardubice U17	CzR-U17	23	5	7	12	82	....	....	....	....	....
	HC Pardubice Jr.	CzRep-Jr.	29	1	6	7	12	4	0	0	0	0
2001-02	HC Pardubice Jr.	CzRep-Jr.	38	2	4	6	28	....	....	....	....	....
	Sumperk	CzRep-2	1	0	0	0	2	....	....	....	....	....
2002-03	Mississauga	OHL	27	0	2	2	12	....	....	....	....	....
	London Knights	OHL	28	0	2	2	18	1	0	0	0	0
2003-04	HC Pardubice Jr.	CzRep-Jr.	24	3	6	9	67	....	....	....	....	....
	Hr. Kralove	CzRep-2	24	1	1	2	12	3	0	0	0	0
	Pardubice	CzRep	6	0	0	0	0	5	0	0	0	2
2004-05	HC Pardubice Jr.	CzRep-Jr.	2	0	1	1	8	....	....	....	....	....
	Hr. Kralove	CzRep-2	16	0	3	3	20	5	0	1	1	35
	Pardubice	CzRep	29	1	1	2	14	16	0	0	0	2

LISIN, Enver (LIH-sihn, EHN-vuhr) **PHX.**

Right wing. Shoots left. 6'2", 190 lbs. Born, Moscow, USSR, April 22, 1986.
(Phoenix's 3rd choice, 50th overall, in 2004 Entry Draft).

			Regular Season					Playoffs				
Season	Club	League	GP	G	A	Pts	PIM	GP	G	A	Pts	PIM
2001-02	Dyn'o Moscow 2	Russia-3	6	3	0	3	14	....	....	....	....	....
2002-03	Dyn'o Moscow 2	Russia-3	STATISTICS NOT AVAILABLE									
2003-04	Dyn'o Moscow 2	Russia-3	STATISTICS NOT AVAILABLE									
	Kristall Saratov	Russia-2	35	10	6	16	30	4	1	0	1	0
2004-05	Ak Bars Kazan 2	Russia-3	....	4	3	7						
	Ak Bars Kazan	Russia	53	8	4	12	4	3	0	0	0	0

LOCKE, Corey (LAWK, KOHR-ee) **MTL.**

Center. Shoots left. 5'9", 175 lbs. Born, Toronto, Ont., May 8, 1984.
(Montreal's 5th choice, 113th overall, in 2003 Entry Draft).

			Regular Season					Playoffs				
Season	Club	League	GP	G	A	Pts	PIM	GP	G	A	Pts	PIM
2000-01	Newmarket	OPJHL	49	34	51	85	16	16	10	12	22	14
2001-02	Ottawa 67's	OHL	55	18	25	43	18	13	6	7	13	10
2002-03	Ottawa 67's	OHL	66	*63	*88	*151	83	23	*19	19	*38	30
2003-04	Ottawa 67's	OHL	65	*51	67	*118	82	7	7	3	10	10
2004-05	Hamilton Bulldogs	AHL	78	16	27	43	20	4	0	0	0	2

OHL First All-Star Team (2003, 2004) • OHL Player of the Year (2003, 2004) • Canadian Major Junior First All-Star Team (2003, 2004) • Canadian Major Junior Player of the Year (2003)

LOFBERG, Christofer (LAWF-buhrg, KRIHS-tah-fuhr) **DET.**

Center. Shoots right. 6'3", 189 lbs. Born, Stockholm, Sweden, October 11, 1986.
(Detroit's 3rd choice, 80th overall, in 2005 Entry Draft).

			Regular Season					Playoffs				
Season	Club	League	GP	G	A	Pts	PIM	GP	G	A	Pts	PIM
2002-03	AIK Solna U18	Swe-U18	13	8	4	12	18	....	....	....	....	....
	AIK Solna Jr.	Swe-Jr.	3	1	0	1	0	4	0	0	0	0
2003-04	Huddinge IK U18	Swe-U18	2	1	0	1	0	....	....	....	....	....
	Huddinge IK Jr.	Swe-Jr.	36	3	12	15	20	....	....	....	....	....
2004-05	Djurgarden Jr.	Swe-Jr.	30	21	13	34	49	....	....	....	....	....
	Djurgarden	Sweden	1	0	0	0	0	....	....	....	....	....

LOGINOV, Denis (LOG-gih-nawv, DEH-nihs ATL.

Center. Shoots left. 6'1", 210 lbs. Born, Kazan, USSR, May 5, 1985.
(Atlanta's 7th choice, 203rd overall, in 2003 Entry Draft).

			Regular Season					Playoffs				
Season	Club	League	GP	G	A	Pts	PIM	GP	G	A	Pts	PIM
99-2000	Ak Bars Kazan 2	Russia-3	4	0	0	0	0	....	....	....	....	....
2000-01	Ak Bars Kazan 2	Russia-3	STATISTICS NOT AVAILABLE									
2001-02	Ak Bars Kazan 2	Russia-3	38	6	10	16	40	....	....	....	....	....
	Team Volga	Exhib.	3	0	3	3	27	....	....	....	....	....
2002-03	Ak Bars Kazan 2	Russia-3	52	17	24	41	98	....	....	....	....	....
	Perm	Russia	1	0	0	0	0	....	....	....	....	....
2003-04	Ak Bars Kazan	Russia	16	2	1	3	0	7	1	0	1	6
2004-05	Ak Bars Kazan	Russia	2	0	0	0	0	....	....	....	....	....

LOJEK, Martin (LOI-yehk, MAHR-tehn) FLA.

Defense. Shoots right. 6'5", 220 lbs. Born, Brno, Czech., August 19, 1985.
(Florida's 5th choice, 105th overall, in 2003 Entry Draft).

			Regular Season					Playoffs				
Season	Club	League	GP	G	A	Pts	PIM	GP	G	A	Pts	PIM
2000-01	HC Pardubice Jr.	CzRep-Jr.	48	2	2	4	42	7	0	0	0	6
2001-02	HC Pardubice Jr.	CzRep-Jr.	40	2	4	6	24	7	1	0	1	2
2002-03	Brampton	OHL	65	1	13	14	47	11	0	1	1	6
2003-04	Brampton	OHL	68	3	17	20	37	12	0	4	4	2
2004-05	Brampton	OHL	58	1	12	13	58	6	0	0	0	6

LOUHIVAARA, Ossi (loo-hih-VAH-rah, AW-see) OTT.

Forward. Shoots right. 6', 179 lbs. Born, Kotka, Finland, August 21, 1983.
(Ottawa's 8th choice, 260th overall, in 2003 Entry Draft).

			Regular Season					Playoffs				
Season	Club	League	GP	G	A	Pts	PIM	GP	G	A	Pts	PIM
2001-02	Titaanit Kotka Jr.	Finland-Jr.	34	13	14	27	10	3	1	1	2	0
	Banik CHZ Sokolov	CzRep-3	32	10	12	22	10	....	....	....	....	....
	HC Banik Most	CzRep-3	....	....	....	....	....	2	1	2	3	2
2002-03	KooKoo Kouvola	Finland-2	44	20	15	35	20	9	1	3	4	4
2003-04	KooKoo Kouvola	Finland-2	41	13	17	30	4	9	1	1	2	2
2004-05	JYP Jyvaskyla	Finland	56	4	9	13	12	3	0	0	0	0

LUCIA, Tony (Loo-CHEE-ah, TOH-nee) S.J.

Left wing. Shoots left. 6', 165 lbs. Born, Wayzata, MN, August 23, 1987.
(San Jose's 8th choice, 193rd overall, in 2005 Entry Draft).

			Regular Season					Playoffs				
Season	Club	League	GP	G	A	Pts	PIM	GP	G	A	Pts	PIM
2003-04	Wayzata	High-MN	31	13	22	35	....	....	....	....	....	....
2004-05	Wayzata	High-MN	24	27	36	63	32	....	....	....	....	....
	Omaha Lancers	USHL	11	1	0	1	0	....	....	....	....	....

LUDWIG, Trevor (LUHD-wihg, TREH-vuhr) DAL.

Defense. Shoots left. 6'1", 200 lbs. Born, Rhinelander, WI, May 24, 1985.
(Dallas' 7th choice, 183rd overall, in 2004 Entry Draft).

			Regular Season					Playoffs				
Season	Club	League	GP	G	A	Pts	PIM	GP	G	A	Pts	PIM
2002-03	Texas Tornado	NAHL	55	4	5	9	39	....	....	....	....	....
2003-04	Texas Tornado	NAHL	54	5	25	30	50	....	....	....	....	....
2004-05	Providence College	H-East	33	1	6	7	36	....	....	....	....	....

NAHL All-Rookie Team (2003) • NAHL First All-Star Team (2004)

LUKACEVIC, Ned (loo-kuh-SAY-vihk, NEHD) L.A.

Left wing. Shoots left. 6', 185 lbs. Born, Podgorica, Serbia, February 11, 1986.
(Los Angeles' 3rd choice, 110th overall, in 2004 Entry Draft).

			Regular Season					Playoffs				
Season	Club	League	GP	G	A	Pts	PIM	GP	G	A	Pts	PIM
2000-01	Port Coquitlam	BCAHA	60	42	48	90	....	....	....	....	....	....
2001-02	Port Coquitlam	BCAHA	70	40	55	95	60	....	....	....	....	....
	Spokane Chiefs	WHL	1	1	0	1	0	....	....	....	....	....
2002-03	Spokane Chiefs	WHL	31	0	4	4	29	4	0	1	1	0
2003-04	Spokane Chiefs	WHL	72	19	14	33	65	4	1	1	2	2
2004-05	Spokane Chiefs	WHL	71	18	28	46	52	....	....	....	....	....

LUKES, Frantisek (LOO-kehsh, FRAHN-tih-sehk) PHX.

Left wing. Shoots right. 5'9", 173 lbs. Born, Kadan, Czech., September 25, 1982.
(Phoenix's 8th choice, 243rd overall, in 2001 Entry Draft).

			Regular Season					Playoffs				
Season	Club	League	GP	G	A	Pts	PIM	GP	G	A	Pts	PIM
99-2000	Litvinov Jr.	CzRep-Jr.	36	15	13	28	....	....	....	....	....	....
2000-01	St. Michael's	OHL	61	23	33	56	37	18	4	9	13	12
2001-02	St. Michael's	OHL	63	27	37	64	50	15	7	11	18	16
2002-03	St. Michael's	OHL	62	27	46	73	55	19	8	15	23	28
2003-04	Springfield Falcons	AHL	63	8	20	28	30	....	....	....	....	....
2004-05	Utah Grizzlies	AHL	12	0	2	2	20	....	....	....	....	....
	Idaho Steelheads	ECHL	59	18	22	40	30	3	0	1	1	10

LUNDBOHM, Bryan (LUHND-bawm, BRIGH-uhn)

Right wing. Shoots left. 5'10", 184 lbs. Born, Roseau, MN, August 24, 1977.

			Regular Season					Playoffs				
Season	Club	League	GP	G	A	Pts	PIM	GP	G	A	Pts	PIM
1996-97	Lincoln Stars	USHL	52	12	33	45	33	14	8	4	12	20
1997-98	Lincoln Stars	USHL	55	26	38	64	10	9	2	7	9	0
1998-99	North Dakota	WCHA	32	2	9	11	4	....	....	....	....	....
99-2000	North Dakota	WCHA	44	22	22	44	14	....	....	....	....	....
2000-01	North Dakota	WCHA	46	*32	37	69	38	....	....	....	....	....
2001-02	Milwaukee	AHL	79	11	23	34	63	....	....	....	....	....
2002-03	Milwaukee	AHL	80	9	17	26	63	6	1	5	6	0
2003-04	HC Sierre	Swiss-2	10	6	8	14	8	....	....	....	....	....
	Milwaukee	AHL	28	6	8	14	8	....	....	....	....	....
2004-05	Fort Worth	CHL	26	10	20	30	28	....	....	....	....	....
	Grand Rapids	AHL	3	0	0	0	0	....	....	....	....	....
	Milwaukee	AHL	47	7	12	19	36	4	0	0	0	0

USHL First All-Star Team (1998) • WCHA First All-Star Team (2001) • NCAA West Second All-American Team (2001) • NCAA Championship All-Tournament Team (2001)

Signed as a free agent by **Nashville**, May 1, 2001. Signed as a free agent by **Sierre** (Swiss-2), September 5, 2003. Signed as a free agent by **Milwaukee** (AHL), November 25, 2003. • Missed majority of 2003-04 season recovering from groin injury suffered in game vs. Philadelphia (AHL), January 31, 2004. Signed as a free agent by **Fort Worth** (CHL), October 19, 2004. Signed as a free agent by **Grand Rapids** (AHL), November 17, 2004. Signed as a free agent by **Milwaukee** (AHL), December 28, 2004.

LUNDIN, Mike (LUHN-dihn, MIGHK) T.B.

Defense. Shoots left. 6'1", 195 lbs. Born, Burnsville, MN, September 24, 1984.
(Tampa Bay's 3rd choice, 102nd overall, in 2004 Entry Draft).

			Regular Season					Playoffs				
Season	Club	League	GP	G	A	Pts	PIM	GP	G	A	Pts	PIM
2002-03	Apple Valley	High-MN	27	8	20	27	....	....	....	....	....	....
2003-04	U. of Maine	H-East	44	3	16	19	34	....	....	....	....	....
2004-05	U. of Maine	H-East	40	1	13	14	2	....	....	....	....	....

LUNDQVIST, Joel (LOOND-kvihst, JOHL) DAL.

Center. Shoots left. 6', 185 lbs. Born, Are, Sweden, March 2, 1982.
(Dallas' 3rd choice, 68th overall, in 2000 Entry Draft).

			Regular Season					Playoffs				
Season	Club	League	GP	G	A	Pts	PIM	GP	G	A	Pts	PIM
1997-98	Rogle Jr.	Swe-Jr.	59	36	40	76	....	....	....	....	....	....
1998-99	V.Frolunda U18	Swe-U18	32	26	38	64	37	4	3	1	4	2
99-2000	V.Frolunda U18	Swe-U18	4	2	4	6	4	....	....	....	....	....
	V.Frolunda Jr.	Swe-Jr.	25	7	12	19	2	6	2	3	5	2
2000-01	V.Frolunda Jr.	Swe-Jr.	18	14	27	41	12	....	....	....	....	....
	IF Molndal Hockey	Sweden-2	26	18	13	31	22	....	....	....	....	....
	V.Frolunda	Sweden	9	0	0	0	0	....	....	....	....	....
2001-02	V.Frolunda	Sweden	46	12	14	26	28	10	1	3	4	8
	V.Frolunda Jr.	Swe-Jr.	....	....	....	....	....	1	0	0	0	0
2002-03	V.Frolunda	Sweden	50	17	20	37	113	16	6	3	9	12
2003-04	V.Frolunda	Sweden	49	9	14	23	48	10	2	2	4	8
2004-05	Frolunda	Sweden	50	7	12	19	38	13	2	5	7	57

LUTTINEN, Arttu (LOO-tuh-nehn, AHR-too) OTT.

Left wing. Shoots left. 5'10", 205 lbs. Born, Helsinki, Finland, September 9, 1983.
(Ottawa's 3rd choice, 75th overall, in 2002 Entry Draft).

			Regular Season					Playoffs				
Season	Club	League	GP	G	A	Pts	PIM	GP	G	A	Pts	PIM
99-2000	HIFK Helsinki Jr.	Finland-Jr.	17	5	9	14	10	2	0	0	0	2
2000-01	Ilves Tampere U18	Fin-U18	20	14	20	34	141	....	....	....	....	....
	HIFK Helsinki Jr.	Finland-Jr.	8	4	2	6	4	8	0	1	1	2
2001-02	HIFK Helsinki Jr.	Finland-Jr.	24	16	17	23	60	1	0	0	0	0
2002-03	HIFK Helsinki	Finland	41	4	4	8	10	1	0	0	0	0
	HIFK Helsinki Jr.	Finland-Jr.	10	8	9	17	52	8	4	6	10	20
2003-04	HIFK Helsinki	Finland	50	1	7	8	12	12	0	0	0	0
2004-05	HIFK Helsinki	Finland	56	12	13	25	67	5	1	0	1	0

LYAMIN, Kirill (L'YAH-mihn, kih-RIHL) OTT.

Defense. Shoots left. 6'2", 208 lbs. Born, Moscow, USSR, January 13, 1986.
(Ottawa's 2nd choice, 58th overall, in 2004 Entry Draft).

			Regular Season					Playoffs				
Season	Club	League	GP	G	A	Pts	PIM	GP	G	A	Pts	PIM
2001-02	Moscow 18	Exhib.	5	0	3	3	4	....	....	....	....	....
2002-03	CSKA Moscow 2	Russia-3	5	0	0	0	10	....	....	....	....	....
	Moscow 18	Exhib.	5	0	0	0	6	....	....	....	....	....
2003-04	CSKA Moscow	Russia	28	0	3	3	12	....	....	....	....	....
	CSKA Moscow 2	Russia-3	STATISTICS NOT AVAILABLE									
2004-05	CSKA Moscow 2	Russia-3	STATISTICS NOT AVAILABLE									

LYNCH, Darren (LIHNCH, DAIR-uhn) CGY.

Right wing. Shoots right. 5'11", 181 lbs. Born, Regina, Sask., July 7, 1983.

			Regular Season					Playoffs				
Season	Club	League	GP	G	A	Pts	PIM	GP	G	A	Pts	PIM
1998-99	Reg. Pat Cdns.	SMHL	44	33	30	63	20	....	....	....	....	....
	Lethbridge	WHL	1	0	0	0	2	....	....	....	....	....
99-2000	Lethbridge	WHL	50	3	5	8	19	....	....	....	....	....
2000-01	Lethbridge	WHL	27	4	4	8	9	5	0	1	1	14
2001-02	Vancouver Giants	WHL	72	30	31	61	51	....	....	....	....	....
2002-03	Vancouver Giants	WHL	70	29	53	82	44	4	0	0	0	6
2003-04	Vancouver Giants	WHL	71	22	37	59	51	11	5	4	9	6
2004-05	Las Vegas	ECHL	54	15	14	29	26	....	....	....	....	....

Signed as a free agent by **Calgary**, September 27, 2002.

LYNCH, Jason (LIHNCH, JAY-sohn) COL.

Defense. Shoots right. 6'3", 205 lbs. Born, North Vancouver, B.C., May 26, 1987.
(Colorado's 7th choice, 166th overall, in 2005 Entry Draft).

			Regular Season					Playoffs				
Season	Club	League	GP	G	A	Pts	PIM	GP	G	A	Pts	PIM
2002-03	Coquitlam	BCAHA	48	2	47	49	65	....	....	....	....	....
	Spokane Chiefs	WHL	1	0	0	0	0	....	....	....	....	....
2003-04	Spokane Chiefs	WHL	38	0	0	0	52	2	0	0	0	0
2004-05	Spokane Chiefs	WHL	67	1	4	5	78	....	....	....	....	....

LYUBUSHIN, Mikhail (l'yoo-BOOSH-ihn, mih-kigh-EHL) L.A.

Defense. Shoots left. 6'1", 183 lbs. Born, Moscow, USSR, July 24, 1983.
(Los Angeles' 9th choice, 215th overall, in 2002 Entry Draft).

			Regular Season					Playoffs				
Season	Club	League	GP	G	A	Pts	PIM	GP	G	A	Pts	PIM
99-2000	Vityaz Podolsk 2	Russia-3	24	2	2	4	69	....	....	....	....	....
2000-01	Krylja Sovetov	Russia-2	2	0	1	1	0	1	0	0	0	0
2001-02	Krylja Sovetov 2	Russia-3	20	3	6	9	24	....	....	....	....	....
	THK Tver	Russia-2	22	1	0	1	18	....	....	....	....	....
	Krylja Sovetov	Russia	13	0	1	1	14	3	0	0	0	0
2002-03	Krylja Sovetov	Russia	49	0	6	6	26	....	....	....	....	....
2003-04	Dynamo Moscow	Russia	38	1	2	3	18	2	0	0	0	2
2004-05	Voskresensk	Russia	21	1	2	3	16	....	....	....	....	....
	Vityaz Chekhov	Russia-2	8	0	2	2	6	14	1	0	1	8

MAATTA, Tero (MAH-tuh, TEH-roh) **S.J.**

Defense. Shoots left. 6'1", 220 lbs. Born, Vantaa, Finland, January 2, 1982.
(San Jose's 1st choice, 41st overall, in 2000 Entry Draft).

			Regular Season					Playoffs				
Season	**Club**	**League**	**GP**	**G**	**A**	**Pts**	**PIM**	**GP**	**G**	**A**	**Pts**	**PIM**
1997-98	Jokerit U18	Fin-U18	28	4	7	11	10	2	0	0	0	2
1998-99	Jokerit Helsinki Jr.	Finland-Jr.	38	4	8	12	75	8	1	3	4	6
99-2000	Jokerit U18	Fin-U18	13	4	10	14	24	1	0	0	0	25
	Jokerit Helsinki Jr.	Finland-Jr.	31	4	4	8	53	....	....	....	....	....
2000-01	Blues Espoo Jr.	Finland-Jr.	6	0	1	1	6	....	....	....	....	....
	KJT Jarvenpaa	Finland-2	6	0	3	3	31	....	....	....	....	....
	Blues Espoo	Finland	44	4	4	8	24	....	....	....	....	....
2001-02	Blues Espoo Jr.	Finland-Jr.	8	2	6	8	2	....	....	....	....	....
	Blues Espoo	Finland	51	4	6	10	65	3	0	0	0	0
2002-03	Assat Pori	Finland	7	0	0	0	29	....	....	....	....	....
	Blues Espoo	Finland	43	0	3	3	56	7	0	1	1	4
2003-04	Blues Espoo	Finland	56	1	14	15	41	9	0	1	1	8
2004-05	Blues Espoo	Finland	56	2	11	13	40	....	....	....	....	....

MacARTHUR, Clarke (muh-KAR-thuhr, KLAHRK) **BUF.**

Left wing. Shoots left. 6', 180 lbs. Born, Lloydminster, Alta., April 6, 1985.
(Buffalo's 3rd choice, 74th overall, in 2003 Entry Draft).

			Regular Season					Playoffs				
Season	**Club**	**League**	**GP**	**G**	**A**	**Pts**	**PIM**	**GP**	**G**	**A**	**Pts**	**PIM**
99-2000	Lloydminster	CABHL	24	19	45	64	51	5	9	6	15	4
2000-01	Strathcona	AMBHL	38	36	63	99	44	8	6	2	8	10
2001-02	Drayton Valley	AJHL	61	22	40	62	33	16	5	8	13	34
2002-03	Medicine Hat	WHL	70	23	52	75	104	11	3	6	9	8
2003-04	Medicine Hat	WHL	62	35	40	75	93	20	8	10	18	16
2004-05	Medicine Hat	WHL	58	30	44	74	100	13	3	8	11	18
	Rochester	AHL	....	....	....	....	....	3	0	1	1	0

Memorial Cup Tournament All-Star Team (2004) • WHL East First All-Star Team (2005)

MacDONALD, David (MAK-DAWN-uhld, DAY-vihd) **S.J.**

Defense. Shoots right. 6'3", 200 lbs. Born, Halifax, N.S., April 30, 1985.
(San Jose's 7th choice, 225th overall, in 2004 Entry Draft).

			Regular Season					Playoffs				
Season	**Club**	**League**	**GP**	**G**	**A**	**Pts**	**PIM**	**GP**	**G**	**A**	**Pts**	**PIM**
2003-04	N.E. Jr. Coyotes	EJHL	37	1	5	6	81	....	....	....	....	....
2004-05	PEI Rocket	QMJHL	66	0	5	5	78	....	....	....	....	....

MACHO, Michal (MA-khoh, MEE-khahl) **S.J.**

Center. Shoots right. 6'1", 170 lbs. Born, Martin, Czech., January 17, 1982.
(San Jose's 5th choice, 183rd overall, in 2000 Entry Draft).

			Regular Season					Playoffs				
Season	**Club**	**League**	**GP**	**G**	**A**	**Pts**	**PIM**	**GP**	**G**	**A**	**Pts**	**PIM**
1995-96	Martin U18	Svk-U18	12	0	6	6	2	....	....	....	....	....
1996-97	Martin U18	Svk-U18	52	43	44	87	50	....	....	....	....	....
1997-98	Martin U18	Svk-U18	46	41	54	95	58	....	....	....	....	....
	Martin Jr.	Slovak-Jr.	9	3	4	7	0	....	....	....	....	....
1998-99	King's-Edgehill	High-NS	50	45	55	100	....	....	....	....	....	....
	Martin Jr.	Slovak-Jr.	2	2	3	5	0	....	....	....	....	....
99-2000	Martin Jr.	Slovak-Jr.	30	38	44	82	....	....	....	....	....	....
	Martin	Slovak-2	8	1	5	6	4	....	....	....	....	....
2000-01	MHC Martin	Slovakia	37	5	10	15	12	3	1	1	2	2
2001-02	MHC Martin	Slovakia	40	12	8	20	20	....	....	....	....	....
2002-03	Bratislava	Slovakia	51	5	4	9	26	12	1	0	1	0
2003-04	Bratislava	Slovakia	33	7	7	14	14	12	5	3	8	26
2004-05	Bratislava	Slovakia	44	8	20	28	14	12	0	0	0	2

MACIAS, Raymond (mah-CHEE-ahs, RAY-muhnd) **COL.**

Defense. Shoots right. 6'1", 187 lbs. Born, Long Beach, CA, September 18, 1986.
(Colorado's 6th choice, 124th overall, in 2005 Entry Draft).

			Regular Season					Playoffs				
Season	**Club**	**League**	**GP**	**G**	**A**	**Pts**	**PIM**	**GP**	**G**	**A**	**Pts**	**PIM**
2002-03	L.A. Jr. Kings	Cal-Am	49	37	26	63	100	....	....	....	....	....
	Kamloops Blazers	WHL	4	0	0	0	0	2	0	0	0	0
2003-04	Kamloops Blazers	WHL	69	12	17	29	14	5	2	0	2	0
2004-05	Kamloops Blazers	WHL	69	12	35	47	18	2	0	0	0	0

MacINTYRE, Steve (MAK-ihn-tighr, STEEV) **NYR**

Defense. Shoots left. 6'6", 265 lbs. Born, Brock, Sask., August 8, 1980.

			Regular Season					Playoffs				
Season	**Club**	**League**	**GP**	**G**	**A**	**Pts**	**PIM**	**GP**	**G**	**A**	**Pts**	**PIM**
2002-03	St. Jean Mission	QSPHL	10	1	1	2	68	....	....	....	....	....
	Muskegon Fury	UHL	54	2	1	3	279	5	0	0	0	24
2003-04	Hartford Wolf Pack	AHL	3	0	0	0	0	....	....	....	....	....
	Charlotte	ECHL	61	1	4	5	217	....	....	....	....	....
	Jacksonville	WHA2	6	0	2	2	18	5	0	1	1	17
2004-05	Hartford Wolf Pack	AHL	27	1	1	2	207	....	....	....	....	....
	Charlotte	ECHL	46	1	4	5	214	11	0	4	4	17

Signed as a free agent by **NY Rangers**, August 15, 2005.

MacKENZIE, Aaron (muh-KEHN-zee, AIR-ruhn) **ST.L.**

Defense. Shoots left. 6', 193 lbs. Born, Terrace Bay, Ont., March 7, 1981.

			Regular Season					Playoffs				
Season	**Club**	**League**	**GP**	**G**	**A**	**Pts**	**PIM**	**GP**	**G**	**A**	**Pts**	**PIM**
1998-99	Thunder Bay Flyers	USHL	49	8	12	20	123	3	0	1	1	0
99-2000	U. of Denver	WCHA	40	1	9	10	56	....	....	....	....	....
2000-01	U. of Denver	WCHA	37	2	6	8	45	....	....	....	....	....
2001-02	U. of Denver	WCHA	39	5	18	23	30	....	....	....	....	....
2002-03	U. of Denver	WCHA	41	11	21	32	33	....	....	....	....	....
2003-04	Worcester IceCats	AHL	66	5	9	14	108	10	0	2	2	10
2004-05	Worcester IceCats	AHL	75	2	13	15	106	....	....	....	....	....

WCHA First All-Star Team (2003)

Signed as a free agent by **Worcester** (AHL), October 6, 2003. Signed as a free agent by **St. Louis**, June 29, 2004.

MacMURCHY, Ryan (mak-MUHR-chee, RIGH-uhn) **ST.L.**

Right wing. Shoots right. 5'11", 190 lbs. Born, Regina, Sask., April 27, 1983.
(St. Louis' 9th choice, 284th overall, in 2002 Entry Draft).

			Regular Season					Playoffs				
Season	**Club**	**League**	**GP**	**G**	**A**	**Pts**	**PIM**	**GP**	**G**	**A**	**Pts**	**PIM**
1998-99	Regina Capitals	SMHL	40	18	15	33	....	....	....	....	....	....
99-2000	Regina Capitals	SMHL	38	23	44	67	....	....	....	....	....	....
2000-01	Vernon Vipers	BCHL	30	4	6	10	....	....	....	....	....	....
2001-02	Notre Dame	AJHL	61	32	52	84	63	11	2	5	7	13
2002-03	U. of Wisconsin	WCHA	39	10	14	24	69	....	....	....	....	....
2003-04	U. of Wisconsin	WCHA	43	15	13	28	95	....	....	....	....	....
2004-05	U. of Wisconsin	WCHA	40	11	22	33	88	....	....	....	....	....

MACRI, Vince (MA-kree, VIHNS) **NYI**

Defense. Shoots right. 6'3", 210 lbs. Born, Bethpage, NY, May 21, 1981.

			Regular Season					Playoffs				
Season	**Club**	**League**	**GP**	**G**	**A**	**Pts**	**PIM**	**GP**	**G**	**A**	**Pts**	**PIM**
99-2000	Exeter	High-NH	....	10	21	31	....	....	....	....	....	....
2000-01	Brown U.	ECAC	16	1	1	2	16	....	....	....	....	....
2001-02	Brown U.	ECAC	25	1	5	6	40	....	....	....	....	....
2002-03	Brown U.	ECAC	34	4	6	10	49	....	....	....	....	....
2003-04	Brown U.	ECAC	31	6	9	52	....	....	....	....	....	....
	Bridgeport	AHL	3	0	1	1	5	....	....	....	....	....
2004-05	Bridgeport	AHL	27	1	0	1	4	....	....	....	....	....
	Atlantic City	ECHL	49	5	9	14	99	1	0	0	0	0

Signed as a free agent by **NY Islanders**, March, 2004.

MADSEN, Morten (MAD-sehn, MOHR-tuhn) **MIN.**

Right wing. Shoots left. 6'1", 185 lbs. Born, Rodovre, Denmark, January 16, 1987.
(Minnesota's 5th choice, 122nd overall, in 2005 Entry Draft).

			Regular Season					Playoffs				
Season	**Club**	**League**	**GP**	**G**	**A**	**Pts**	**PIM**	**GP**	**G**	**A**	**Pts**	**PIM**
2003-04	V.Frolunda U18	Swe-U18	11	13	8	21	0	7	3	1	4	4
	V.Frolunda Jr.	Swe-Jr.	16	3	2	5	0	1	0	0	0	0
2004-05	Frolunda U18	Swe-U18	2	1	2	3	0	6	7	7	14	6
	Frolunda Jr.	Swe-Jr.	32	7	14	21	14	6	3	2	5	0

MAKELA, Tuukka (MA-kuh-luh TUH-kuh) **BOS.**

Defense. Shoots left. 6'3", 202 lbs. Born, Helsinki, Finland, May 24, 1982.
(Boston's 5th choice, 66th overall, in 2000 Entry Draft).

			Regular Season					Playoffs				
Season	**Club**	**League**	**GP**	**G**	**A**	**Pts**	**PIM**	**GP**	**G**	**A**	**Pts**	**PIM**
1997-98	HIFK Helsinki Jr.	Finland-Jr.	5	0	0	0	4	....	....	....	....	....
1998-99	HIFK Helsinki Jr.	Finland-Jr.	32	1	1	2	20	3	0	1	1	0
99-2000	HIFK Helsinki Jr.	Finland-Jr.	36	2	5	7	22	2	0	0	0	0
2000-01	Montreal Rocket	QMJHL	9	2	1	3	14	....	....	....	....	....
2001-02	HPK Jr.	Finland-Jr.	12	3	0	3	26	7	2	2	4	18
	HPK Hameenlinna	Finland	49	2	3	5	44	8	0	0	0	10
2002-03	HPK Hameenlinna	Finland	52	1	5	6	86	13	0	0	0	14
2003-04	HPK Hameenlinna	Finland	54	3	1	4	44	8	0	1	1	6
2004-05	HPK Hameenlinna	Finland	39	2	2	4	34	8	0	0	0	31

• Missed majority of 2000-01 season recovering from head injury suffered in game vs. Rouyn-Noranda (QMJHL), September 20, 2000.

MAKI, Ryan (MA-kee, RIGH-uhn) **NSH.**

Right wing. Shoots right. 6'2", 195 lbs. Born, Medford, NJ, April 23, 1985.
(Nashville's 5th choice, 176th overall, in 2005 Entry Draft).

			Regular Season					Playoffs				
Season	**Club**	**League**	**GP**	**G**	**A**	**Pts**	**PIM**	**GP**	**G**	**A**	**Pts**	**PIM**
2001-02	USA U-17	USDP	48	7	22	29	30	....	....	....	....	....
2002-03	USA U-18	USDP	52	6	6	12	26	....	....	....	....	....
2003-04	Harvard Crimson	ECAC	34	4	4	8	18	....	....	....	....	....
2004-05	Harvard Crimson	ECAC	30	10	9	19	20	....	....	....	....	....

MAKI, Tomi (MA-kee, TAW-mee) **CGY.**

Right wing. Shoots left. 5'11", 172 lbs. Born, Helsinki, Finland, August 19, 1983.
(Calgary's 4th choice, 108th overall, in 2001 Entry Draft).

			Regular Season					Playoffs				
Season	**Club**	**League**	**GP**	**G**	**A**	**Pts**	**PIM**	**GP**	**G**	**A**	**Pts**	**PIM**
99-2000	Jokerit Helsinki Jr.	Finland-Jr.	33	6	1	7	12	3	0	0	0	0
2000-01	Jokerit U18	Fin-U18	10	4	9	13	4	6	4	3	7	0
	Jokerit Helsinki Jr.	Finland-Jr.	39	7	8	15	10	2	0	0	0	2
2001-02	Jokerit Helsinki Jr.	Finland-Jr.	29	12	13	25	12	1	0	0	0	2
	Kiekko-Vantaa	Finland-2	5	0	0	0	0	....	....	....	....	....
	Jokerit Helsinki	Finland	8	0	1	1	2	....	....	....	....	....
2002-03	Jokerit Helsinki Jr.	Finland-Jr.	14	4	4	8	12	11	3	3	6	4
	Jokerit Helsinki	Finland	18	2	2	4	4	1	0	0	0	0
	Kiekko-Vantaa	Finland-2	5	0	0	0	0	....	....	....	....	....
2003-04	Jokerit Helsinki	Finland	50	5	5	10	14	8	0	0	0	0
2004-05	Jokerit Helsinki	Finland	51	1	4	5	14	12	1	1	2	2

MALENKYKH, Vladimir (MAH-lihn-keh, vla-DIH-meer) **PIT.**

Defense. Shoots left. 6'1", 190 lbs. Born, Togliatti, USSR, October 1, 1980.
(Pittsburgh's 7th choice, 157th overall, in 1999 Entry Draft).

			Regular Season					Playoffs				
Season	**Club**	**League**	**GP**	**G**	**A**	**Pts**	**PIM**	**GP**	**G**	**A**	**Pts**	**PIM**
1997-98	Lada Togliatti 2	Russia-3	39	6	4	10	112	....	....	....	....	....
1998-99	Lada Togliatti 2	Russia-4	38	6	3	9	68	....	....	....	....	....
	Lada Togliatti	Russia	9	0	0	0	2	....	....	....	....	....
99-2000	Lada Togliatti 2	Russia-3	34	7	9	16	98	....	....	....	....	....
	CSK VVS Samara	Russia	7	0	1	1	14	....	....	....	....	....
	Lada Togliatti	Russia	1	0	0	0	0	....	....	....	....	....
	CSK VVS Samara 2	Russia-3	1	0	1	1	2	....	....	....	....	....
2000-01	Lada Togliatti	Russia	25	1	1	2	14	5	0	0	0	26
2001-02	Lada Togliatti	Russia	47	5	4	9	88	4	0	0	0	2
2002-03	Lada Togliatti	Russia	30	3	1	4	36	10	0	0	0	6
2003-04	Lada Togliatti	Russia	44	2	4	6	42	3	0	0	0	0
2004-05	Lada Togliatti	Russia	37	1	4	5	20	....	....	....	....	....

MALKIN, Evgeni (MAHL-kihn, ehv-GEH-nee) **PIT.**

Center. Shoots left. 6'3", 186 lbs. Born, Magnitogorsk, USSR, July 31, 1986.
(Pittsburgh's 1st choice, 2nd overall, in 2004 Entry Draft).

			Regular Season					Playoffs				
Season	**Club**	**League**	**GP**	**G**	**A**	**Pts**	**PIM**	**GP**	**G**	**A**	**Pts**	**PIM**
2003-04	Magnitogorsk 2	Russia-3	2	1	0	1	8	....	....	....	....	....
	Magnitogorsk	Russia	34	3	9	12	12	....	....	....	....	....
2004-05	Magnitogorsk 2	Russia-3	2	1	1	2	2	....	....	....	....	....
	Magnitogorsk	Russia	52	12	20	32	24	5	0	4	4	0

MALMIVAARA, Olli (mal-MIH-vah-ruh, OH-lee) CHI.

Defense. Shoots left. 6'7", 220 lbs. Born, Kajaani, Finland, March 13, 1982.
(Chicago's 6th choice, 117th overall, in 2000 Entry Draft).

			Regular Season					Playoffs				
Season	Club	League	GP	G	A	Pts	PIM	GP	G	A	Pts	PIM
1998-99	Jokerit U18	Fin-U18	35	1	8	9	10	7	0	0	0	2
99-2000	Jokerit U18	Fin-U18	8	3	4	7	8	1	0	0	0	2
	Jokerit Helsinki Jr.	Finland-Jr.	27	3	3	6	12	12	0	2	2	2
2000-01	Jokerit Helsinki Jr.	Finland-Jr.	33	10	13	23	24	2	0	0	0	0
	Kiekko-Vantaa	Finland-2	4	1	0	1	2	....	....	....	....	....
	Jokerit Helsinki	Finland	5	0	0	0	2	....	....	....	....	....
2001-02	Jokerit Helsinki Jr.	Finland-Jr.	2	0	1	1	0	....	....	....	....	....
	Jokerit Helsinki	Finland	53	0	6	6	16	11	0	0	0	2
2002-03	Jokerit Helsinki	Finland	42	1	0	1	22	5	0	0	0	0
	Kiekko-Vantaa	Finland-2	2	1	1	2	2	....	....	....	....	....
2003-04	Jokerit Helsinki	Finland	25	1	0	1	2	....	....	....	....	....
	SaiPa	Finland	11	1	0	1	6	....	....	....	....	....
2004-05	SaiPa	Finland	56	9	1	10	89	....	....	....	....	....

MALONEY, Brian (muh-LOH-nee, BRIGH-uhn) ATL.

Left wing. Shoots left. 6'1", 205 lbs. Born, Bassano, Alta., September 27, 1978.

			Regular Season					Playoffs				
Season	Club	League	GP	G	A	Pts	PIM	GP	G	A	Pts	PIM
1997-98	Olds Grizzlys	AJHL	31	21	13	34	....	....	....	....	....	....
	Chilliwack Chiefs	BCHL	27	4	12	16	36	....	....	....	....	....
1998-99	Chilliwack Chiefs	BCHL	60	40	75	115	121	....	....	....	....	....
99-2000	Michigan State	CCHA	42	12	19	31	87	....	....	....	....	....
2000-01	Michigan State	CCHA	41	15	22	37	86	....	....	....	....	....
2001-02	Michigan State	CCHA	37	17	16	33	71	....	....	....	....	....
2002-03	Michigan State	CCHA	39	19	16	35	48	....	....	....	....	....
	Chicago Wolves	AHL	4	0	1	1	11	....	....	....	....	....
2003-04	Chicago Wolves	AHL	69	9	11	20	56	10	1	1	2	17
2004-05	Chicago Wolves	AHL	77	7	10	17	164	18	2	1	3	38

Signed as a free agent by **Atlanta**, April 2, 2003.

MANCARI, Mark (man-KAH-ree, MAHRK) BUF.

Right wing. Shoots right. 6'3", 225 lbs. Born, London, Ont., July 11, 1985.
(Buffalo's 6th choice, 207th overall, in 2004 Entry Draft).

			Regular Season					Playoffs				
Season	Club	League	GP	G	A	Pts	PIM	GP	G	A	Pts	PIM
2001-02	Ottawa 67's	OHL	34	3	3	6	10	2	0	1	1	0
2002-03	Ottawa 67's	OHL	61	8	11	19	20	11	2	1	3	2
2003-04	Ottawa 67's	OHL	67	29	36	65	56	7	5	3	8	11
2004-05	Ottawa 67's	OHL	64	36	32	68	86	21	*14	10	24	24

MANSON, Lane (MAN-suhn, LAYN) ATL.

Defense. Shoots left. 6'8", 250 lbs. Born, Watrous, Sask., February 14, 1984.
(Atlanta's 4th choice, 124th overall, in 2002 Entry Draft).

			Regular Season					Playoffs				
Season	Club	League	GP	G	A	Pts	PIM	GP	G	A	Pts	PIM
99-2000	North Battleford	SMBHL	41	7	12	19	110	....	....	....	....	....
2000-01	North Battleford	MMMHL	40	14	12	26	180	....	....	....	....	....
2001-02	Moose Jaw	WHL	67	4	3	7	88	12	0	1	1	6
2002-03	Moose Jaw	WHL	66	0	5	5	192	13	0	0	0	12
2003-04	Moose Jaw	WHL	72	3	9	12	253	10	0	2	2	18
2004-05	Gwinnett	ECHL	71	5	12	17	127	8	0	3	3	20

MANTYLA, Tuukka (man-TYEW-la, TOO-OO-kuh) L.A.

Defense. Shoots left. 5'9", 172 lbs. Born, Tampere, Finland, May 25, 1981.
(Los Angeles' 8th choice, 153rd overall, in 2001 Entry Draft).

			Regular Season					Playoffs				
Season	Club	League	GP	G	A	Pts	PIM	GP	G	A	Pts	PIM
1997-98	Tappara U18	Fin-U18	31	2	23	25	49	....	....	....	....	....
	Tappara Jr.	Finland-Jr.	2	0	0	0	0	6	0	0	0	4
1998-99	Tappara U18	Fin-U18	10	4	4	8	42	....	....	....	....	....
	Tappara Jr.	Finland-Jr.	34	5	13	18	42	....	....	....	....	....
99-2000	Tappara Jr.	Finland-Jr.	7	2	5	7	22	5	2	5	7	4
	Tappara Tampere	Finland	43	2	8	10	16	4	0	0	0	0
2000-01	Tappara Tampere	Finland	53	6	14	20	32	10	2	2	4	10
2001-02	Tappara Tampere	Finland	56	5	10	15	70	10	2	4	6	8
2002-03	Tappara Tampere	Finland	54	3	19	22	58	15	0	2	2	6
2003-04	Lulea HF	Sweden	43	6	10	16	67	5	0	0	0	2
2004-05	Lulea HF	Sweden	48	8	14	22	44	4	1	0	1	4

MANTYMAA, Ville (man-T'YUH-mah, VIHL-ee) ANA.

Defense. Shoots right. 6'3", 183 lbs. Born, Seinajoki, Finland, March 8, 1985.
(Anaheim's 9th choice, 280th overall, in 2003 Entry Draft).

			Regular Season					Playoffs				
Season	Club	League	GP	G	A	Pts	PIM	GP	G	A	Pts	PIM
2001-02	Tappara U18	Fin-U18	1	0	0	0	2	....	....	....	....	....
	Tappara Jr.	Finland-Jr.	32	4	2	6	24	....	....	....	....	....
2002-03	Tappara Jr.	Finland-Jr.	33	3	12	15	26	8	2	0	2	4
	Tappara Tampere	Finland	8	0	0	0	0	1	0	0	0	0
2003-04	Pelicans Lahti	Finland	2	0	0	0	0	....	....	....	....	....
	Tappara Tampere	Finland	19	0	2	2	8	....	....	....	....	....
	Tappara Jr.	Finland-Jr.	21	1	7	8	14	14	0	3	3	8
2004-05	Tappara Jr.	Finland-Jr.	13	0	6	6	14	4	0	1	1	2
	Tappara Tampere	Finland	32	1	1	2	18	8	0	1	1	0

MAREK, Jan (MAIR-ehk, YAHN) NYR

Center. Shoots right. 5'10", 178 lbs. Born, Jindrichuv Hradec, Czech., December 31, 1979.
(NY Rangers' 10th choice, 243rd overall, in 2003 Entry Draft).

			Regular Season					Playoffs				
Season	Club	League	GP	G	A	Pts	PIM	GP	G	A	Pts	PIM
1998-99	Trinec	CzRep	32	2	2	4	2	6	0	0	0	0
99-2000	HC Trinec Jr.	CzRep-Jr.	6	5	5	10	10	1	0	0	0	0
	HC Slezan Opava	CzRep-2	3	0	1	1	4	....	....	....	....	....
	Jind. Hradec	CzRep-2	4	0	3	3	10	....	....	....	....	....
	HC Ocelari Trinec	CzRep	32	1	5	6	4	2	0	0	0	0
2000-01	HC Ocelari Trinec	CzRep	38	7	4	11	2	....	....	....	....	....
2001-02	HC Ocelari Trinec	CzRep	52	13	27	40	44	6	1	3	4	6
2002-03	HC Ocelari Trinec	CzRep	51	*32	30	62	42	12	6	4	10	22
2003-04	HC Sparta Praha	CzRep	50	21	30	51	62	11	4	9	13	26
2004-05	HC Sparta Praha	CzRep	38	7	21	28	26	5	2	2	4	2

MARJAMAKI, Masi (mahr-juh-MA-kee, MAH-see) NYI

Right wing. Shoots left. 6'2", 202 lbs. Born, Pori, Finland, January 16, 1985.
(NY Islanders' 4th choice, 144th overall, in 2005 Entry Draft).

			Regular Season					Playoffs				
Season	Club	League	GP	G	A	Pts	PIM	GP	G	A	Pts	PIM
2001-02	Assat Pori U18	Fin-U18	24	6	16	22	93	1	0	1	1	2
	Assat Pori Jr.	Finland-Jr.	1	0	0	0	0	5	3	2	5	2
2002-03	Red Deer Rebels	WHL	65	15	20	35	56	23	1	2	3	20
2003-04	Red Deer Rebels	WHL	28	6	8	14	46	....	....	....	....	....
	Moose Jaw	WHL	35	15	10	25	57	10	1	3	4	15
2004-05	Moose Jaw	WHL	51	14	32	46	49	5	1	2	3	5

• Re-entered NHL Entry Draft. Originally Boston's 3rd choice, 66th overall, in 2003 Entry Draft.

MARR, Steve (MAHR, STEEV) CGY.

Defense. Shoots left. 6'2", 218 lbs. Born, Kamloops, B.C., June 6, 1984.

			Regular Season					Playoffs				
Season	Club	League	GP	G	A	Pts	PIM	GP	G	A	Pts	PIM
2001-02	Medicine Hat	WHL	63	0	0	0	50	....	....	....	....	....
2002-03	Medicine Hat	WHL	54	3	11	14	95	11	0	1	1	22
2003-04	Medicine Hat	WHL	71	2	9	11	80	20	1	2	3	*50
2004-05	Medicine Hat	WHL	54	11	8	19	105	13	2	3	5	22

Signed as a free agent by **Calgary**, August 5, 2005.

MARS, Per (MAHRZ, PAIR) CBJ

Center. Shoots left. 6'3", 210 lbs. Born, Ostersund, Sweden, October 23, 1982.
(Columbus' 5th choice, 87th overall, in 2001 Entry Draft).

			Regular Season					Playoffs				
Season	Club	League	GP	G	A	Pts	PIM	GP	G	A	Pts	PIM
2000-01	Brynas IF Gavle Jr.	Swe-Jr.	23	7	7	14	62	....	....	....	....	....
	Brynas IF Gavle	Sweden	6	0	0	0	0	2	0	0	0	0
2001-02	Brynas IF Gavle	Sweden	12	0	0	0	14	....	....	....	....	....
	Tierps HK	Sweden-2	29	1	4	5	22	11	1	0	1	35
2002-03	Brynas IF Gavle	Sweden	7	0	0	0	2	....	....	....	....	....
	Lincoln Stars	USHL	42	9	9	18	60	9	1	2	3	14
2003-04	IF Bjorkloven Umea	Sweden-2	46	4	1	5	67	....	....	....	....	....
2004-05	Tegs SK Umea	Sweden-2	42	7	6	13	67	....	....	....	....	....

MARSH, Tyson (MAHRSH, TIGH-suhn) TOR.

Defense. Shoots left. 6'1", 190 lbs. Born, Quesnel, B.C, June 20, 1984.

			Regular Season					Playoffs				
Season	Club	League	GP	G	A	Pts	PIM	GP	G	A	Pts	PIM
2000-01	Quesnel	BCHL	52	4	2	6	25	....	....	....	....	....
2001-02	Vancouver Giants	WHL	69	2	14	16	85	....	....	....	....	....
2002-03	Vancouver Giants	WHL	68	3	15	18	143	3	0	1	1	4
2003-04	Vancouver Giants	WHL	67	3	18	21	102	11	0	3	3	4
2004-05	St. John's	AHL	21	0	1	1	30	....	....	....	....	....
	Pensacola	ECHL	23	1	2	3	29	4	0	0	0	2

Signed as a free agent by **Toronto**, September 18, 2002.

MARTTINEN, Jyri (MAHR-tih-nehn, YUHR-ee) CGY.

Defense. Shoots left. 5'11", 190 lbs. Born, Tikkakoski, Finland, September 1, 1982.
(Calgary's 12th choice, 238th overall, in 2002 Entry Draft).

			Regular Season					Playoffs				
Season	Club	League	GP	G	A	Pts	PIM	GP	G	A	Pts	PIM
1998-99	JyP Jyvaskyla U18	Fin-U18	22	1	3	4	12	5	0	0	0	0
99-2000	JyP Jyvaskyla U18	Fin-U18	14	7	4	11	22	....	....	....	....	....
	JyP Jyvaskyla Jr.	Finland-Jr.	3	0	0	0	2	....	....	....	....	....
2000-01	JyP Jyvaskyla Jr.	Finland-Jr.	40	2	8	10	73	6	1	1	2	6
	JYP Jyvaskyla	Finland	8	1	0	1	6	....	....	....	....	....
2001-02	JYP Jyvaskyla	Finland	50	1	4	5	67	....	....	....	....	....
	JyP Jyvaskyla Jr.	Finland-Jr.	5	0	2	2	2	1	0	0	0	0
2002-03	JYP Jyvaskyla	Finland	29	3	2	5	32	....	....	....	....	....
2003-04	JYP Jyvaskyla	Finland	54	6	13	19	115	2	0	0	0	2
2004-05	JYP Jyvaskyla	Finland	46	3	1	4	60	3	0	2	2	0

MASON, Tyrell (MAY-sohn, TIGH-rehl) NYI

Defense. Shoots left. 6'1", 167 lbs. Born, Grand Prairie, Alta., March 12, 1986.
(NY Islanders' 5th choice, 180th overall, in 2005 Entry Draft).

			Regular Season					Playoffs				
Season	Club	League	GP	G	A	Pts	PIM	GP	G	A	Pts	PIM
2003-04	Salmon Arm	BCHL	59	7	29	36	36	....	....	....	....	....
2004-05	Salmon Arm	BCHL	51	6	36	42	78	....	....	....	....	....

Signed Letter of Intent to attend **Clarkson** (ECAC) in fall of 2005.

MATEJOVSKY, Radek (ma-teh-YAHV-skee, ra-DEHK) NYI

Right wing. Shoots right. 6'1", 187 lbs. Born, Praha, Czech., November 17, 1977.
(NY Islanders' 9th choice, 250th overall, in 1998 Entry Draft).

			Regular Season					Playoffs				
Season	Club	League	GP	G	A	Pts	PIM	GP	G	A	Pts	PIM
1992-93	C. Budejovice Jr.	Czech-Jr.	25	38	24	62	....	....	....	....	....	....
1993-94	Slavia Praha Jr.	CzRep-Jr.	45	30	26	56	....	....	....	....	....	....
1994-95	HC Slavia Praha Jr.	CzRep-Jr.	28	7	8	15	12	....	....	....	....	....
1995-96	HC Slavia Praha Jr.	CzRep-Jr.	47	37	21	58	24	....	....	....	....	....
1996-97	HC Slavia Praha Jr.	CzRep-Jr.	4	1	1	2	....	....	....	....	....	....
	H+S Beroun	CzRep-2	12	3	1	4	18	....	....	....	....	....
	HC Slavia Praha	CzRep	41	3	4	7	10	3	0	0	0	0
1997-98	HC Slavia Praha	CzRep	52	9	4	13	24	3	0	0	0	0
1998-99	HC Dukla Jihlava	CzRep	52	12	10	22	57	....	....	....	....	....
	HC Dukla Jihlava	CzRep-Q	7	3	3	6	41	....	....	....	....	....
99-2000	HC Slavia Praha	CzRep	25	4	3	7	22	....	....	....	....	....
	Pardubice	CzRep	25	2	4	6	18	3	0	0	0	0
2000-01	HC Slavia Praha	CzRep	39	6	8	14	63	11	1	2	3	18
2001-02	HC Slavia Praha	CzRep	35	3	1	4	42	9	0	0	0	6
2002-03	HC Keramika Plzen	CzRep	42	7	11	18	126	....	....	....	....	....
2003-04	Plzen	CzRep	52	9	8	17	121	12	2	4	6	49
2004-05	Plzen	CzRep	50	9	5	14	94	....	....	....	....	....

MAUNU, Mitch (MOW-MOW, MIHTCH) CHI.

Defense. Shoots left. 6'1", 205 lbs. Born, Thunder Bay, Ont., July 30, 1986.
(Chicago's 7th choice, 120th overall, in 2004 Entry Draft).

			Regular Season					Playoffs				
Season	Club	League	GP	G	A	Pts	PIM	GP	G	A	Pts	PIM
2002-03	Windsor Spitfires	OHL	62	4	15	19	25	7	0	1	1	0
2003-04	Windsor Spitfires	OHL	68	11	15	26	91	4	1	0	1	0
2004-05	Windsor Spitfires	OHL	62	6	17	23	84	11	0	2	2	26

MAXIMENKO, Andrei (max-EE-mehn-koh, AWN-dray) **DET.**

Left wing. Shoots right. 5'11", 172 lbs. Born, Moscow, USSR, January 10, 1981.
(Detroit's 2nd choice, 149th overall, in 1999 Entry Draft).

			Regular Season					Playoffs				
Season	Club	League	GP	G	A	Pts	PIM	GP	G	A	Pts	PIM
1997-98	Krylja Sovetov 2	Russia-3	42	2	4	6	12	....	....	....	....	....
1998-99	Krylja Sovetov	Russia	28	1	2	3	24	....	....	....	....	....
99-2000	Krylja Sovetov 2	Russia-3	6	4	2	6	26	....	....	....	....	....
	Krylja Sovetov	Russia-2	39	6	7	13	41	....	....	....	....	....
2000-01	Krylja Sovetov	Russia-2	28	2	5	7	8	....	....	....	....	....
2001-02	THK Tver	Russia-2	20	3	7	10	6	....	....	....	....	....
	Krylja Sovetov 2	Russia-3	7	3	5	8	2	....	....	....	....	....
	Perm	Russia	9	0	1	1	2	....	....	....	....	....
2002-03	Kristall Saratov	Russia-2	47	12	12	24	36	....	....	....	....	....
2003-04	Krylja Sovetov	Russia-2	19	2	3	5	8	....	....	....	....	....
2004-05	Kristall Saratov	Russia-2	16	4	2	6	8	....	....	....	....	....
	Almetjevsk	Russia-2	27	4	8	12	14	3	0	0	0	2

MAY, Jeff (MAY, JEHF) **DET.**

Defense. Shoots left. 6'1", 186 lbs. Born, Richmond, B.C., April 4, 1987.
(Detroit's 7th choice, 151st overall, in 2005 Entry Draft).

			Regular Season					Playoffs				
Season	Club	League	GP	G	A	Pts	PIM	GP	G	A	Pts	PIM
2002-03	Richmond	BCAHA	55	11	26	37	143	....	....	....	....	....
	Prince Albert	WHL	5	0	0	0	2	....	....	....	....	....
2003-04	Prince Albert	WHL	40	0	3	3	19	3	0	0	0	4
2004-05	Prince Albert	WHL	67	3	19	22	66	17	2	3	5	13

McARDLE, Kenndal (mih-KAHR-duhl, KEHN-dahl) **FLA.**

Left wing. Shoots left. 5'11", 190 lbs. Born, Toronto, Ont., January 4, 1987.
(Florida's 1st choice, 20th overall, in 2005 Entry Draft).

			Regular Season					Playoffs				
Season	Club	League	GP	G	A	Pts	PIM	GP	G	A	Pts	PIM
2002-03	Burnaby	BCAHA	30	1	9	10	131	....	....	....	....	....
	Moose Jaw	WHL	2	0	0	0	0	....	....	....	....	....
2003-04	Moose Jaw	WHL	54	8	8	16	57	10	3	2	5	6
2004-05	Moose Jaw	WHL	70	37	37	74	122	5	1	0	1	16

McASLAN, Sean (mihk-AZ-luhn, SHAWN)

Left wing. Shoots right. 6'1", 190 lbs. Born, Okotoks, Alta., January 12, 1980.

			Regular Season					Playoffs				
Season	Club	League	GP	G	A	Pts	PIM	GP	G	A	Pts	PIM
1996-97	Calgary Hitmen	WHL	26	2	3	5	22	....	....	....	....	....
1997-98	Calgary Hitmen	WHL	69	8	16	24	83	....	....	....	....	....
1998-99	Calgary Hitmen	WHL	71	7	16	23	110	21	2	1	3	18
99-2000	Calgary Hitmen	WHL	72	18	16	34	117	13	4	2	6	49
2000-01	Calgary Hitmen	WHL	51	21	32	53	137	12	3	5	8	29
2001-02	Columbus	ECHL	72	16	21	37	139	....	....	....	....	....
2002-03	Columbus	ECHL	53	15	17	32	132	....	....	....	....	....
	Hamilton Bulldogs	AHL	1	0	0	0	0	....	....	....	....	....
2003-04	Toronto	AHL	62	12	15	27	66	3	0	1	1	2
2004-05	Edmonton	AHL	64	6	5	11	61	....	....	....	....	....

Signed as a free agent by **Edmonton**, March 14, 2001.

McCLELLAN, Stephen (muh-KLEHL-uhn, STEE-vehn) **COL.**

Defense. Shoots left. 6'1", 165 lbs. Born, Boston, MA, April 22, 1985.
(Colorado's 9th choice, 281st overall, in 2004 Entry Draft).

			Regular Season					Playoffs				
Season	Club	League	GP	G	A	Pts	PIM	GP	G	A	Pts	PIM
2002-03	Catholic Memorial	High-MA	28	3	9	12	....	....	....	....	....	....
2003-04	Catholic Memorial	High-MA	25	8	18	26	14	....	....	....	....	....
2004-05	Cushing	High-MA	STATISTICS NOT AVAILABLE									

Signed Letter of Intent to attend **Northeastern** (H-East) in fall of 2005.

McCLEMENT, Jay (muh-KLEHM-ehnt, JAY) **ST.L.**

Center. Shoots left. 6'1", 199 lbs. Born, Kingston, Ont., March 2, 1983.
(St. Louis' 1st choice, 57th overall, in 2001 Entry Draft).

			Regular Season					Playoffs				
Season	Club	League	GP	G	A	Pts	PIM	GP	G	A	Pts	PIM
1997-98	Kingston	OPJHL	48	3	8	11	15	....	....	....	....	....
1998-99	Kingston	OPJHL	51	25	28	53	34	....	....	....	....	....
99-2000	Brampton	OHL	63	13	16	29	34	6	0	4	4	8
2000-01	Brampton	OHL	66	30	19	49	61	9	4	2	6	10
2001-02	Brampton	OHL	61	26	29	55	43	....	....	....	....	....
2002-03	Brampton	OHL	45	22	27	49	37	11	3	4	7	11
	Worcester IceCats	AHL	....	....	....	....	....	1	0	0	0	0
2003-04	Worcester IceCats	AHL	69	12	13	25	20	10	0	3	3	0
2004-05	Worcester IceCats	AHL	79	17	34	51	45	....	....	....	....	....

McCULLOCH, Scott (muh-KUHL-uh, SKAWT) **CHI.**

Left wing. Shoots left. 6', 198 lbs. Born, Edmonton, Alta., March 10, 1986.
(Chicago's 11th choice, 165th overall, in 2004 Entry Draft).

			Regular Season					Playoffs				
Season	Club	League	GP	G	A	Pts	PIM	GP	G	A	Pts	PIM
2003-04	Grand Prairie	AJHL	44	23	26	49	85	16	12	8	20	18
2004-05	Colorado College	WCHA	11	4	3	7	6	....	....	....	....	....

McCUTCHEON, Mark (mih-KUH-chuhn, MAHRK) **COL.**

Center. Shoots right. 6', 177 lbs. Born, Ithaca, NY, May 21, 1984.
(Colorado's 3rd choice, 146th overall, in 2003 Entry Draft).

			Regular Season					Playoffs				
Season	Club	League	GP	G	A	Pts	PIM	GP	G	A	Pts	PIM
2001-02	N.E. Jr. Coyotes	EJHL	36	24	26	50	84	....	....	....	....	....
2002-03	N.E. Jr. Coyotes	EJHL	35	27	22	49	76	10	8	5	13	24
2003-04	Cornell Big Red	ECAC	32	0	4	4	12	....	....	....	....	....
2004-05	Cornell Big Red	ECAC	22	0	5	5	12	....	....	....	....	....

McDONALD, Colin (mihk-DAW-nuhld, KAW-lihn) **EDM.**

Right wing. Shoots right. 6'2", 190 lbs. Born, New Haven, CT, September 30, 1984.
(Edmonton's 2nd choice, 51st overall, in 2003 Entry Draft).

			Regular Season					Playoffs				
Season	Club	League	GP	G	A	Pts	PIM	GP	G	A	Pts	PIM
2001-02	N.E. Jr. Coyotes	EJHL	39	16	20	36	50	....	....	....	....	....
2002-03	N.E. Jr. Coyotes	EJHL	44	28	40	*68	59	....	....	....	....	....
2003-04	Providence College	H-East	37	10	6	16	47	....	....	....	....	....
2004-05	Providence College	H-East	26	11	5	16	14	....	....	....	....	....

Hockey East All-Rookie Team (2004)

McGINNIS, Ryan (mih-GIHN-ihs, RIGH-uhn) **L.A.**

Defense. Shoots left. 6'1", 197 lbs. Born, Flint, MI, March 3, 1987.
(Los Angeles' 6th choice, 184th overall, in 2005 Entry Draft).

			Regular Season					Playoffs				
Season	Club	League	GP	G	A	Pts	PIM	GP	G	A	Pts	PIM
2003-04	Plymouth Whalers	OHL	32	2	2	4	31	2	0	0	0	0
2004-05	Plymouth Whalers	OHL	66	0	6	6	93	4	0	1	1	2

McGRATH, Evan (muh-GRATH, EH-vuhn) **DET.**

Center. Shoots left. 5'11", 181 lbs. Born, Oakville, Ont., January 14, 1986.
(Detroit's 2nd choice, 128th overall, in 2004 Entry Draft).

			Regular Season					Playoffs				
Season	Club	League	GP	G	A	Pts	PIM	GP	G	A	Pts	PIM
2001-02	Oakville Blades	OPJHL	49	43	44	87	24	....	....	....	....	....
2002-03	Kitchener Rangers	OHL	64	16	31	47	40	21	6	2	8	6
2003-04	Kitchener Rangers	OHL	68	15	36	51	28	5	2	1	3	2
2004-05	Kitchener Rangers	OHL	67	28	59	87	51	15	7	6	13	6

OHL All-Rookie Team (2003)

McGRATTAN, Brian (muhk-GRA-tuhn, BRIGH-uhn) **OTT.**

Right wing. Shoots right. 6'4", 225 lbs. Born, Hamilton, Ont., September 2, 1981.
(Los Angeles' 5th choice, 104th overall, in 1999 Entry Draft).

			Regular Season					Playoffs				
Season	Club	League	GP	G	A	Pts	PIM	GP	G	A	Pts	PIM
1997-98	Guelph Fire	OHA-B	15	4	3	7	94	....	....	....	....	....
	Guelph Storm	OHL	25	3	2	5	11	....	....	....	....	....
1998-99	Guelph Storm	OHL	6	1	3	4	15	....	....	....	....	....
	Sudbury Wolves	OHL	53	7	10	17	153	4	0	0	0	8
99-2000	Sudbury Wolves	OHL	25	2	8	10	79	....	....	....	....	....
	Mississauga	OHL	42	9	13	22	166	....	....	....	....	....
2000-01	Mississauga	OHL	31	20	9	29	83	....	....	....	....	....
2001-02	Mississauga	OHL	7	2	3	5	16	....	....	....	....	....
	Owen Sound	OHL	2	0	0	0	0	....	....	....	....	....
	Oshawa Generals	OHL	25	10	5	15	72	....	....	....	....	....
	Sault Ste. Marie	OHL	26	8	7	15	71	6	2	0	2	20
2002-03	Binghamton	AHL	59	9	10	19	173	1	0	0	0	0
2003-04	Binghamton	AHL	66	9	11	20	327	1	0	0	0	0
2004-05	Binghamton	AHL	71	7	1	8	*551	6	0	2	2	28

Signed as a free agent by **Ottawa**, June 2, 2002.

McGUIRK, Brian (muh-GUHRK, BRIGH-uhn) **CBJ**

Left wing. Shoots left. 6', 191 lbs. Born, Danvers, MA, July 11, 1985.
(Columbus' 10th choice, 231st overall, in 2004 Entry Draft).

			Regular Season					Playoffs				
Season	Club	League	GP	G	A	Pts	PIM	GP	G	A	Pts	PIM
2003-04	Gov. Dummer	High-MA	25	16	16	32	....	....	....	....	....	....
2004-05	Boston University	H-East	33	0	1	1	18	....	....	....	....	....

McILVANE, Matthew (MAK-uhl-vay-nee, MA-thew) **OTT.**

Center. Shoots right. 6', 202 lbs. Born, Downers Grove, IL, November 2, 1985.
(Ottawa's 10th choice, 251st overall, in 2004 Entry Draft).

			Regular Season					Playoffs				
Season	Club	League	GP	G	A	Pts	PIM	GP	G	A	Pts	PIM
2003-04	Chicago Steel	USHL	59	22	24	46	53	3	1	2	3	0
2004-05	Ohio State	CCHA	42	1	5	6	30	....	....	....	....	....

McIVER, Nathan (mih-KEE-vuhr, NAY-thun) **VAN.**

Defense. Shoots left. 6'2", 195 lbs. Born, Kinkora, P.E.I., January 6, 1985.
(Vancouver's 9th choice, 254th overall, in 2003 Entry Draft).

			Regular Season					Playoffs				
Season	Club	League	GP	G	A	Pts	PIM	GP	G	A	Pts	PIM
2001-02	Summerside	MJrHL	47	4	4	8	91	5	0	0	0	9
2002-03	St. Michael's	OHL	68	5	10	15	121	19	0	4	4	41
2003-04	St. Michael's	OHL	57	4	11	15	183	16	0	1	1	22
2004-05	St. Michael's	OHL	67	4	22	26	160	3	0	1	1	13

McKENZIE, Jim (MIHK-ehn-zee, JIHM) **OTT.**

Right wing. Shoots right. 6'2", 209 lbs. Born, St. Paul, MN, June 10, 1984.
(Ottawa's 7th choice, 141st overall, in 2004 Entry Draft).

			Regular Season					Playoffs				
Season	Club	League	GP	G	A	Pts	PIM	GP	G	A	Pts	PIM
2000-01	Hill-Murray	High-MN	27	9	13	22	....	....	....	....	....	....
2001-02	Green Bay	USHL	17	1	2	3	34	....	....	....	....	....
	USA U-18	USDP	19	7	11	18	23	....	....	....	....	....
2002-03	Sioux Falls	USHL	45	6	18	24	108	....	....	....	....	....
2003-04	Sioux Falls	USHL	59	26	38	64	168	....	....	....	....	....
2004-05	Michigan State	CCHA	34	11	7	18	44	....	....	....	....	....

McKNIGHT, Matt (mihk-NIGHT, MAT) **DAL.**

Forward. Shoots right. 6'2", 190 lbs. Born, Red Deer, Alta., June 14, 1984.
(Dallas' 10th choice, 280th overall, in 2004 Entry Draft).

			Regular Season					Playoffs				
Season	Club	League	GP	G	A	Pts	PIM	GP	G	A	Pts	PIM
2003-04	Camrose Kodiaks	AJHL	42	20	36	56	31	....	....	....	....	....
2004-05	U. Minn-Duluth	WCHA	30	6	13	19	16	....	....	....	....	....

McLACHLAN, Darren (muhk-LAWK-luhn, DAIR-rehn) **PHX.**

Left wing. Shoots left. 6'1", 223 lbs. Born, Penticton, B.C., February 16, 1983.
(Boston's 2nd choice, 77th overall, in 2001 Entry Draft).

			Regular Season					Playoffs				
Season	Club	League	GP	G	A	Pts	PIM	GP	G	A	Pts	PIM
1998-99	Campbell River	VIJHL	31	15	25	40	212	....	....	....	....	....
	Seattle	WHL	2	0	1	1	7	....	....	....	....	....
99-2000	Seattle	WHL	54	5	1	6	175	7	0	0	0	9
2000-01	Seattle	WHL	42	10	9	19	161	9	1	3	4	18
2001-02	Seattle	WHL	51	15	16	31	153	10	1	0	1	20
2002-03	Seattle	WHL	66	17	43	60	195	5	1	0	1	11
2003-04	Springfield Falcons	AHL	11	1	0	1	39	....	....	....	....	....
	Adirondack	UHL	39	3	7	10	166	....	....	....	....	....
2004-05	Idaho Steelheads	ECHL	24	1	1	2	59	....	....	....	....	....

Rights traded to **Phoenix** by **Boston** for Phoenix's 5th round choice (Kris Versteeg) in 2004 Entry Draft, May 30, 2003.

McLEOD, Kiel (muk-KLOWD, KIGHL) PHX.

Center. Shoots right. 6'6", 230 lbs. Born, Ft. Saskatchewan, Alta., December 30, 1982.
(Columbus' 3rd choice, 53rd overall, in 2001 Entry Draft).

				Regular Season					Playoffs			
Season	Club	League	GP	G	A	Pts	PIM	GP	G	A	Pts	PIM
1997-98	North Delta	BCAHA	55	57	55	112	202	....	....	....	....	....
1998-99	Kelowna Rockets	WHL	55	12	15	27	48	6	0	1	1	2
99-2000	Kelowna Rockets	WHL	59	17	13	30	100	5	2	1	3	2
2000-01	Kelowna Rockets	WHL	65	38	28	66	94	4	4	1	5	8
2001-02	Kelowna Rockets	WHL	41	17	31	48	62	15	3	10	13	14
2002-03	Kelowna Rockets	WHL	68	39	51	90	163	8	5	5	10	4
2003-04	Springfield Falcons	AHL	77	7	11	18	71	....	....	....	....	....
2004-05	Utah Grizzlies	AHL	73	13	12	25	107	....	....	....	....	....

WHL West Second All-Star Team (2003)

Signed as a free agent by **Phoenix**, June 9, 2003.

McNEILL, Patrick (muhk-NEEL, PAT-rihk) WSH.

Defense. Shoots left. 6', 195 lbs. Born, Strathroy, Ont., March 17, 1987.
(Washington's 4th choice, 118th overall, in 2005 Entry Draft).

				Regular Season					Playoffs			
Season	Club	League	GP	G	A	Pts	PIM	GP	G	A	Pts	PIM
2002-03	Strathroy Rockets	OHA-B	45	6	13	19	53	....	....	....	....	....
2003-04	Saginaw Spirit	OHL	57	3	11	14	28	....	....	....	....	....
2004-05	Saginaw Spirit	OHL	66	7	26	33	31	....	....	....	....	....

McQUAID, Adam (muhk-WAYD, A-duhm) CBJ

Defense. Shoots right. 6'3", 197 lbs. Born, Charlottetown, P.E.I., October 12, 1986.
(Columbus' 2nd choice, 55th overall, in 2005 Entry Draft).

				Regular Season					Playoffs			
Season	Club	League	GP	G	A	Pts	PIM	GP	G	A	Pts	PIM
2003-04	Sudbury Wolves	OHL	47	3	6	9	25	7	0	1	1	2
2004-05	Sudbury Wolves	OHL	66	3	16	19	98	8	0	2	2	10

MEECH, Derek (MEECH, DAIR-ihk) DET.

Defense. Shoots left. 5'11", 182 lbs. Born, Winnipeg, Man., April 21, 1984.
(Detroit's 7th choice, 229th overall, in 2002 Entry Draft).

				Regular Season					Playoffs			
Season	Club	League	GP	G	A	Pts	PIM	GP	G	A	Pts	PIM
99-2000	Winnipeg Warriors	MMMHL	36	15	40	55	24	....	....	....	....	....
	Red Deer Rebels	WHL	5	1	0	1	2	....	....	....	....	....
2000-01	Red Deer Rebels	WHL	60	2	7	9	40	22	0	0	0	9
2001-02	Red Deer Rebels	WHL	71	8	19	27	33	13	1	1	2	6
2002-03	Red Deer Rebels	WHL	65	6	16	22	53	12	1	1	2	12
2003-04	Red Deer Rebels	WHL	62	10	28	38	40	19	4	7	11	10
2004-05	Grand Rapids	AHL	78	6	8	14	40	....	....	....	....	....

WHL East Second All-Star Team (2004)

MEGALINSKY, Dmitri (meh-gahl-IHN-skee, dih-MEE-tree) OTT.

Defense. Shoots left. 6'2", 212 lbs. Born, Perm, USSR, April 15, 1985.
(Ottawa's 7th choice, 186th overall, in 2005 Entry Draft).

				Regular Season					Playoffs			
Season	Club	League	GP	G	A	Pts	PIM	GP	G	A	Pts	PIM
2003-04	HK Voronezh	Russia-2	42	4	8	12	159	....	....	....	....	....
	Yaroslavl	Russia	1	0	0	0	0	....	....	....	....	....
	Yaroslavl 2	Russia-3	11	0	4	4	16	....	....	....	....	....
2004-05	Yaroslavl	Russia	1	0	0	0	2	....	....	....	....	....
	Yaroslavl 2	Russia-3	30	6	12	18	82	....	....	....	....	....

MEIDL, Vaclav (MY-duhl, VAT-slav) NSH.

Center. Shoots left. 6'4", 215 lbs. Born, Prostejov, Czech., May 27, 1986.
(Nashville's 2nd choice, 81st overall, in 2004 Entry Draft).

				Regular Season					Playoffs			
Season	Club	League	GP	G	A	Pts	PIM	GP	G	A	Pts	PIM
2000-01	HC Zlin U17	CzR-U17	7	1	0	1	2	....	....	....	....	....
2001-02	HC Trinec U17	CzR-U17	36	11	11	22	18	4	1	1	2	2
2002-03	Havirov	CzRep	5	0	1	1	4	....	....	....	....	....
	HC Havirov U17	CzR-U17	13	10	13	23	30	....	....	....	....	....
	HC Havirov Jr.	CzRep-Jr.	28	1	7	8	22	....	....	....	....	....
2003-04	Plymouth Whalers	OHL	67	14	28	42	108	9	0	3	3	4
2004-05	Plymouth Whalers	OHL	66	12	16	28	125	4	0	0	0	8

MELIN, Bjorn (MEH-lihn, b-YOHRN) ANA.

Right wing. Shoots right. 6'1", 178 lbs. Born, Jonkoping, Sweden, July 4, 1981.
(NY Islanders' 11th choice, 163rd overall, in 1999 Entry Draft).

				Regular Season					Playoffs			
Season	Club	League	GP	G	A	Pts	PIM	GP	G	A	Pts	PIM
1997-98	HV 71 Jr.	Swe-Jr.	8	0	3	3	2	....	....	....	....	....
1998-99	HV 71 Jr.	Swe-Jr.	30	12	7	19	50	....	....	....	....	....
99-2000	HV 71 Jr.	Swe-Jr.	24	19	16	35	70	....	....	....	....	....
	HV 71 Jonkoping	Sweden	23	3	0	3	2	5	0	0	0	0
2000-01	HV 71 Jr.	Swe-Jr.	10	6	5	11	66	....	....	....	....	....
	HV 71 Jonkoping	Sweden	43	2	1	3	26	....	....	....	....	....
2001-02	HV 71 Jonkoping	Sweden	50	7	9	16	40	8	0	0	0	6
2002-03	HV 71 Jonkoping	Sweden	48	7	9	16	44	7	0	2	2	6
2003-04	HV 71 Jonkoping	Sweden	47	7	11	18	28	19	4	8	12	10
2004-05	Malmo	Sweden	46	9	10	19	22	....	....	....	....	....
	Malmo	Sweden-Q	10	1	2	3	8	....	....	....	....	....

Rights traded to **Anaheim** by **NY Islanders** with Ben Guite for Dave Roche, March 19, 2002.

MERCIER, Justin (MUHR-see-uhr, JUHS-tihn) COL.

Forward. Shoots left. 5'11", 175 lbs. Born, Erie, PA, June 25, 1987.
(Colorado's 8th choice, 168th overall, in 2005 Entry Draft).

				Regular Season					Playoffs			
Season	Club	League	GP	G	A	Pts	PIM	GP	G	A	Pts	PIM
2003-04	St. Louis	USHL	60	12	9	21	....	....	....	....	....	....
2004-05	USA U-17&U-18	NAHL	16	4	3	7	33	....	....	....	....	....
	USA U-18	USDP	42	5	10	15	64	....	....	....	....	....

Signed Letter of Intent to attend **Miami** (CCHA) in fall of 2005.

MESZAROS, Andrej (MEHT-zahr-ohsh, AWN-dray) OTT.

Defense. Shoots left. 6'1", 200 lbs. Born, Povazska Bystrica, Czech., October 13, 1985.
(Ottawa's 1st choice, 23rd overall, in 2004 Entry Draft).

				Regular Season					Playoffs			
Season	Club	League	GP	G	A	Pts	PIM	GP	G	A	Pts	PIM
2002-03	Dukla Trencin Jr.	Slovak-Jr.	33	6	10	16	12	....	....	....	....	....
	Dukla Trencin	Slovakia	23	0	1	1	4	....	....	....	....	....
2003-04	Dukla Trencin Jr.	Slovak-Jr.	5	2	2	4	0	....	....	....	....	....
	Dukla Trencin	Slovakia	44	3	3	6	8	14	3	1	4	2
2004-05	Vancouver Giants	WHL	59	11	30	41	94	6	1	3	4	14

WHL West Second All-Star Team (2005)

METCALF, Peter (MEHT-kaf, PEE-tuhr)

Defense. Shoots left. 6', 200 lbs. Born, Steamboat Springs, CO, February 25, 1979.
(Toronto's 9th choice, 267th overall, in 1999 Entry Draft).

				Regular Season					Playoffs			
Season	Club	League	GP	G	A	Pts	PIM	GP	G	A	Pts	PIM
1997-98	Cushing	High-MA	25	18	48	66	....	....	....	....	....	....
1998-99	U. of Maine	H-East	33	6	17	23	34	....	....	....	....	....
99-2000	U. of Maine	H-East	40	4	17	21	56	....	....	....	....	....
2000-01	U. of Maine	H-East	31	5	9	14	44	....	....	....	....	....
2001-02	U. of Maine	H-East	44	9	41	50	66	....	....	....	....	....
2002-03	Providence Bruins	AHL	40	0	6	6	24	....	....	....	....	....
	Atlantic City	ECHL	18	2	11	13	48	19	4	6	10	25
2003-04	Providence Bruins	AHL	42	2	13	15	41	1	0	0	0	4
	Trenton Titans	ECHL	25	2	15	17	43	....	....	....	....	....
2004-05	Utah Grizzlies	AHL	31	2	3	5	53	....	....	....	....	....
	Idaho Steelheads	ECHL	38	4	18	22	97	4	1	0	1	4

Hockey East First All-Star Team (2002) • NCAA Championship All-Tournament Team (2002)

Signed as a free agent by **Boston**, June 6, 2002.

METHOT, Francois (meh-TOH, FRAN-swaw)

Center. Shoots right. 6', 203 lbs. Born, Montreal, Que., April 26, 1978.
(Buffalo's 4th choice, 54th overall, in 1996 Entry Draft).

				Regular Season					Playoffs			
Season	Club	League	GP	G	A	Pts	PIM	GP	G	A	Pts	PIM
1993-94	Montreal-Bourassa	QAAA	44	17	38	55	....	4	3	1	4	4
1994-95	St-Hyacinthe Laser	QMJHL	60	14	38	52	22	5	0	1	1	0
1995-96	St-Hyacinthe Laser	QMJHL	68	32	62	94	22	12	6	6	12	4
1996-97	Rouyn-Noranda	QMJHL	47	21	30	51	22	....	....	....	....	....
	Shawinigan	QMJHL	18	8	17	25	2	7	2	6	8	2
1997-98	Shawinigan	QMJHL	36	23	42	65	10	6	1	3	4	5
1998-99	Rochester	AHL	58	5	8	13	8	9	0	1	1	0
99-2000	Rochester	AHL	80	14	18	32	20	21	2	4	6	16
2000-01	Rochester	AHL	79	22	33	55	35	4	1	3	4	0
2001-02	Rochester	AHL	59	17	17	34	28	2	1	0	1	0
2002-03	Rochester	AHL	58	19	34	53	22	3	0	4	4	0
2003-04	Portland Pirates	AHL	53	8	19	27	12	....	....	....	....	....
2004-05	Augsburg	Germany	52	21	23	44	8	5	0	3	3	4

Signed as a free agent by **Washington**, August 19, 2003. Signed as a free agent by **Augsburg** (Germany), August 10, 2004.

METHOT, Marc (meh-TOH, MAHRK) CBJ

Defense. Shoots left. 6'3", 196 lbs. Born, Ottawa, Ont., June 21, 1985.
(Columbus' 7th choice, 168th overall, in 2003 Entry Draft).

				Regular Season					Playoffs			
Season	Club	League	GP	G	A	Pts	PIM	GP	G	A	Pts	PIM
2001-02	Kanata Laser	CJHL	50	3	10	13	22	....	....	....	....	....
2002-03	London Knights	OHL	68	2	13	15	46	14	2	4	6	6
2003-04	London Knights	OHL	63	2	9	11	66	15	0	3	3	18
2004-05	London Knights	OHL	67	4	12	16	88	18	2	1	3	32

MEYER, Stefan (MAY-uhr, steh-FAN) FLA.

Left wing. Shoots left. 6'1", 194 lbs. Born, Medicine Hat, Alta., July 20, 1985.
(Florida's 4th choice, 55th overall, in 2003 Entry Draft).

				Regular Season					Playoffs			
Season	Club	League	GP	G	A	Pts	PIM	GP	G	A	Pts	PIM
2000-01	Notre Dame	SBHL	50	36	52	88	71	....	....	....	....	....
2001-02	Medicine Hat	WHL	67	18	22	40	48	....	....	....	....	....
2002-03	Medicine Hat	WHL	70	36	16	52	90	11	3	3	6	14
2003-04	Medicine Hat	WHL	72	34	41	75	69	19	7	10	17	27
2004-05	Medicine Hat	WHL	69	34	43	77	104	13	2	4	6	8

MEYERS, Josh (MIGH-uhrs, JAWSH) L.A.

Defense. Shoots right. 6'2", 180 lbs. Born, Alexandria, MN, December 7, 1985.
(Los Angeles' 7th choice, 206th overall, in 2005 Entry Draft).

				Regular Season					Playoffs			
Season	Club	League	GP	G	A	Pts	PIM	GP	G	A	Pts	PIM
2003-04	Minnesota Blizzard	NAHL	27	2	12	14	....	....	....	....	....	....
2004-05	Sioux City	USHL	57	8	24	32	92	13	1	9	10	18

Signed Letter of Intent to attend **Minnesota-Duluth** (WCHA) in fall of 2005.

MICKA, Tomas (MIHTSKA, TAW-mas) EDM.

Left wing. Shoots left. 6'2", 180 lbs. Born, Jihlava, Czech., June 7, 1983.
(Edmonton's 13th choice, 245th overall, in 2002 Entry Draft).

				Regular Season					Playoffs			
Season	Club	League	GP	G	A	Pts	PIM	GP	G	A	Pts	PIM
99-2000	HC Slavia Praha Jr.	CzRep-Jr.	42	17	18	35	24	....	....	....	....	....
2000-01	HC Slavia Praha Jr.	CzRep-Jr.	45	2	8	10	65	3	0	1	1	0
2001-02	HC Slavia Praha Jr.	CzRep-Jr.	46	12	16	28	79	....	....	....	....	....
	HC Slavia Praha	CzRep	1	0	0	0	0	....	....	....	....	....
2002-03	Havirov	CzRep	23	1	0	1	12	....	....	....	....	....
	HC Havirov Jr.	CzRep-Jr.	11	4	3	7	12	....	....	....	....	....
	Zdar	CzRep-2	4	1	0	1	2	....	....	....	....	....
2003-04	Columbus	ECHL	67	17	15	32	52	....	....	....	....	....
2004-05	Greenville Grrrowl	ECHL	9	1	3	4	2	....	....	....	....	....
	Toledo Storm	ECHL	40	8	6	14	37	....	....	....	....	....
	Victoria	ECHL	6	0	1	1	10	....	....	....	....	....

MIELONEN, Juho (MEE-eh-loh-nuhn, YEW-ho) DET.

Defense. Shoots right. 6'2", 180 lbs. Born, Savonlinna, Finland, March 1, 1987.
(Detroit's 8th choice, 175th overall, in 2005 Entry Draft).

			Regular Season					Playoffs				
Season	Club	League	GP	G	A	Pts	PIM	GP	G	A	Pts	PIM
2002-03	Ilves Tampere U18	Fin-U18	11	0	1	1	8	....	....	....	....	....
2003-04	Ilves Tampere U18	Fin-U18	15	7	2	9	12	....	....	....	....	....
	Ilves Tampere Jr.	Finland-Jr.	34	1	2	3	30	....	....	....	....	....
2004-05	Ilves Tampere U18	Fin-U18	1	1	0	1	2	....	....	....	....	....
	Ilves Tampere Jr.	Finland-Jr.	37	2	9	11	32	9	0	1	1	6

MIETTINEN, Tommi (mih-EHT-tih-nehn,TAW-mee) ANA.

Center. Shoots left. 5'10", 165 lbs. Born, Kuopio, Finland, December 3, 1975.
(Anaheim's 9th choice, 236th overall, in 1994 Entry Draft).

			Regular Season					Playoffs				
Season	Club	League	GP	G	A	Pts	PIM	GP	G	A	Pts	PIM
1991-92	KalPa Kuopio Jr.	Finland-Jr.	37	9	16	25	12	....	....	....	....	....
1992-93	KalPa Kuopio U18	Fin-U18	7	3	8	11	2	....	....	....	....	....
	KalPa Kuopio Jr.	Finland-Jr.	26	16	27	43	14	....	....	....	....	....
	KalPa Kuopio	Finland	14	0	0	0	0	....	....	....	....	....
1993-94	KalPa Kuopio Jr.	Finland-Jr.	9	5	9	14	10	....	....	....	....	....
	KalPa Kuopio	Finland	47	5	7	12	14	....	....	....	....	....
1994-95	KalPa Kuopio Jr.	Finland-Jr.	2	1	3	4	2	....	....	....	....	....
	KalPa Kuopio	Finland	48	13	16	29	26	3	1	1	2	2
1995-96	TPS Turku	Finland	36	3	10	13	10	10	2	1	3	29
1996-97	TPS Turku	Finland	41	6	15	21	6	12	3	4	7	8
	TPS Turku	EuroHL	6	2	2	4	2	4	1	1	2	0
1997-98	TPS Turku	Finland	42	8	6	14	26	4	0	0	0	0
	TPS Turku	EuroHL	3	0	0	0	2	....	....	....	....	....
1998-99	TPS Turku	Finland	54	10	17	27	26	10	4	4	8	0
99-2000	TPS Turku	Finland	54	13	20	33	24	....	....	....	....	....
2000-01	Ilves Tampere	Finland	55	10	20	30	38	9	0	1	1	4
2001-02	Ilves Tampere	Finland	55	11	31	42	36	3	0	0	0	2
2002-03	Brynas IF Gavle	Sweden	50	9	17	26	76	....	....	....	....	....
2003-04	Brynas IF Gavle	Sweden	50	13	21	34	56	....	....	....	....	....
2004-05	Brynas IF Gavle	Sweden	48	7	17	24	46	....	....	....	....	....
	Brynas IF Gavle	Sweden-Q	10	2	5	7	6	....	....	....	....	....

MIHALIK, Vladimir (mih-HAHL-ihk, vla-DIH-meer) T.B.

Defense. Shoots left. 6'7", 222 lbs. Born, Presov, Czech., January 29, 1987.
(Tampa Bay's 1st choice, 30th overall, in 2005 Entry Draft).

			Regular Season					Playoffs				
Season	Club	League	GP	G	A	Pts	PIM	GP	G	A	Pts	PIM
2003-04	Presov	Svk-U18	6	4	4	8	4	....	....	....	....	....
	Presov Jr.	Slovak-Jr.	23	6	10	16	44	....	....	....	....	....
2004-05	PHK Presov Jr.	Slovak-Jr.	23	6	10	16	44	....	....	....	....	....
	PHK Presov	Slovak-2	32	3	1	4	24	6	0	1	1	2

MIKHAILISHIN, Alexander (mih-khigh-LIHSH-ihn) N.J.

Defense. Shoots left. 6'4", 210 lbs. Born, Neustrelitz, East Germany, February 24, 1986.
(New Jersey's 2nd choice, 155th overall, in 2004 Entry Draft).

			Regular Season					Playoffs				
Season	Club	League	GP	G	A	Pts	PIM	GP	G	A	Pts	PIM
2001-02	Spartak Moscow 2	Russia-3	15	0	0	0	2	....	....	....	....	....
2002-03	Spartak Moscow 2	Russia-3	7	1	1	2	4	....	....	....	....	....
2003-04	Spartak Moscow 2	Russia-3	STATISTICS NOT AVAILABLE									
2004-05	Spartak Moscow	Russia	6	0	1	1	4	....	....	....	....	....

MIKHAILOV, Konstantin (mih-KHIGH-lawv, kawn-stuhn-TEEN) VAN.

Center. Shoots left. 5'11", 180 lbs. Born, Moscow, USSR, February 12, 1983.
(Vancouver's 6th choice, 245th overall, in 2001 Entry Draft).

			Regular Season					Playoffs				
Season	Club	League	GP	G	A	Pts	PIM	GP	G	A	Pts	PIM
99-2000	Dyn'o Moscow 2	Russia-3	14	3	2	5	14	....	....	....	....	....
2000-01	Nizhnekamsk	Russia	24	0	2	2	12	....	....	....	....	....
2001-02	Nizhnekamsk	Russia	38	3	6	9	10	....	....	....	....	....
2002-03	Dynamo Moscow	Russia	14	0	1	1	31	....	....	....	....	....
	Nizhnekamsk	Russia	15	1	1	2	6	....	....	....	....	....
2003-04	Sibir Novosibirsk	Russia	15	0	1	1	2	....	....	....	....	....
2004-05	Cherepovets	Russia	1	0	0	0	2	....	....	....	....	....
	Golden Amur	AsianHL	2	0	0	0	0	....	....	....	....	....
	Yunost-Minsk	BelOpen	3	0	1	1	0	....	....	....	....	....
	HK Gomel	BelOpen	11	2	5	7	6	4	1	2	3	4

MIKHNOV, Alexei (MIHKH-nahf, al-EHX-ay) EDM.

Left wing. Shoots left. 6'5", 200 lbs. Born, Kiev, USSR, August 31, 1982.
(Edmonton's 1st choice, 17th overall, in 2000 Entry Draft).

			Regular Season					Playoffs				
Season	Club	League	GP	G	A	Pts	PIM	GP	G	A	Pts	PIM
1997-98	Torpedo Yaroslavl	Russia	6	0	0	0	0	....	....	....	....	....
1998-99	Yaroslavl 2	Russia-3	14	2	2	4	4	....	....	....	....	....
99-2000	Yaroslavl 2	Russia-3	53	24	17	41	10	....	....	....	....	....
2000-01	HK Moscow	Russia-2	4	0	0	0	2	....	....	....	....	....
	THK Tver	Russia-2	22	5	11	16	6	....	....	....	....	....
2001-02	Dyn'o Moscow 2	Russia-3	8	8	6	14	0	....	....	....	....	....
	Dynamo Moscow	Russia	35	2	1	3	4	3	0	0	0	2
	Ufa	Russia	1	0	0	0	0	....	....	....	....	....
2002-03	Sibir Novosibirsk	Russia	51	7	9	16	10	....	....	....	....	....
2003-04	Sibir Novosibirsk	Russia	58	14	8	22	22	....	....	....	....	....
2004-05	Sibir Novosibirsk	Russia	26	2	3	5	12	....	....	....	....	....
	Yaroslavl 2	Russia-3	2	1	0	1	0	....	....	....	....	....
	Yaroslavl	Russia	18	0	9	9	4	7	0	0	0	4

MIKKELSON, Brendan (MIGHK-ehl-sohn, BREHN-duhn) ANA.

Defense. Shoots left. 6'2", 190 lbs. Born, Regina, Sask., June 22, 1987.
(Anaheim's 2nd choice, 31st overall, in 2005 Entry Draft).

			Regular Season					Playoffs				
Season	Club	League	GP	G	A	Pts	PIM	GP	G	A	Pts	PIM
2003-04	Portland	WHL	65	3	12	15	43	5	1	0	1	0
2004-05	Portland	WHL	70	5	10	15	60	7	1	2	3	0

MIKKOLA, Ilkka (mih-KOHLA, IHL-ka) MTL.

Defense. Shoots left. 6', 189 lbs. Born, Oulu, Finland, January 18, 1979.
(Montreal's 3rd choice, 65th overall, in 1997 Entry Draft).

			Regular Season					Playoffs				
Season	Club	League	GP	G	A	Pts	PIM	GP	G	A	Pts	PIM
1995-96	Karpat Oulu U18	Fin-U18	4	2	0	2	0	....	....	....	....	....
	Karpat Oulu Jr.	Finland-Jr.	21	2	3	5	20	....	....	....	....	....
	Karpat Oulu	Finland-2	10	0	4	4	29	2	0	0	0	2
1996-97	Karpat Oulu Jr.	Finland-Jr.	40	7	12	19	32	6	0	0	0	4
	Karpat Oulu U18	Fin-U18	1	0	1	1	2	....	....	....	....	....
1997-98	Karpat Oulu Jr.	Finland-Jr.	8	4	2	6	10	....	....	....	....	....
	Karpat Oulu	Finland-2	27	7	2	9	34	....	....	....	....	....
1998-99	TPS Turku	Finland	42	1	3	4	41	10	1	0	1	6
99-2000	TPS Turku	Finland	54	2	6	8	48	11	0	0	0	6
	Karpat Oulu	EuroHL	5	0	2	2	4	4	0	0	0	4
2000-01	TPS Turku	Finland	37	3	6	9	22	10	0	1	1	4
2001-02	Jokerit Helsinki	Finland	55	3	2	5	14	12	1	3	4	6
2002-03	Jokerit Helsinki	Finland	38	4	10	14	8	10	0	1	1	10
2003-04	Karpat Oulu	Finland	52	3	13	16	22	15	0	2	2	8
2004-05	Karpat Oulu	Finland	45	4	16	20	44	12	2	4	6	8

MIKKONEN, Tuomas (mih-KOH-nehn, TWOH-muhs) DAL.

Left wing. Shoots left. 6'1", 183 lbs. Born, Jyvaskyla, Finland, March 25, 1983.
(Dallas' 11th choice, 243rd overall, in 2002 Entry Draft).

			Regular Season					Playoffs				
Season	Club	League	GP	G	A	Pts	PIM	GP	G	A	Pts	PIM
99-2000	JyP Jyvaskyla Jr.	Finland-Jr.	3	0	0	0	2	....	....	....	....	....
	JyP Jyvaskyla U18	Fin-U18	21	4	1	5	88	15	3	0	3	10
2000-01	JyP Jyvaskyla Jr.	Finland-Jr.	27	7	8	15	16	....	....	....	....	....
2001-02	JYP Jyvaskyla	Finland	12	1	2	3	12	....	....	....	....	....
	JyP Jyvaskyla Jr.	Finland-Jr.	17	5	9	14	47	4	0	2	2	0
2002-03	JYP Jyvaskyla	Finland	48	5	3	8	41	2	0	1	1	25
2003-04	JYP Jyvaskyla	Finland	43	5	3	8	8	2	0	0	0	0
2004-05	JYP Jyvaskyla	Finland	51	6	5	11	26	3	0	1	1	0

MIKUS, Juraj (MEE-kuhsh, YUHR-ay) MTL.

Right wing. Shoots right. 6'1", 186 lbs. Born, Skalica, Czech., February 22, 1987.
(Montreal's 3rd choice, 121st overall, in 2005 Entry Draft).

			Regular Season					Playoffs				
Season	Club	League	GP	G	A	Pts	PIM	GP	G	A	Pts	PIM
2003-04	HK 36 Skalica U18	Svk-U18	34	18	17	35	26	9	10	5	15	12
	HK 36 Skalica Jr.	Slovak-Jr.	8	3	7	10	16	....	....	....	....	....
	HK 36 Skalica	Slovakia	2	1	0	1	0	4	0	0	0	0
2004-05	HK 36 Skalica U18	Svk-U18	3	1	7	8	2	....	....	....	....	....
	HK 36 Skalica Jr.	Slovak-Jr.	30	17	18	35	40	9	6	8	14	18
	HK 36 Skalica	Slovakia	46	6	6	12	16	....	....	....	....	....

MILLER, Andrew (MIHL-luhr, AN-droo) ANA.

Left wing. Shoots left. 6'2", 165 lbs. Born, Dover, NJ, February 17, 1984.
(Anaheim's 6th choice, 186th overall, in 2003 Entry Draft).

			Regular Season					Playoffs				
Season	Club	League	GP	G	A	Pts	PIM	GP	G	A	Pts	PIM
2000-01	Capital Centre	NAHL	37	4	3	7	22	....	....	....	....	....
2001-02	Capital Centre	NAHL	54	18	16	34	56	....	....	....	....	....
2002-03	Capital Centre	NAHL	11	10	9	19	....	....	....	....	....	....
	River City Lancers	USHL	49	14	11	25	22	11	5	4	9	6
2003-04	Michigan State	CCHA	41	4	6	10	39	....	....	....	....	....
2004-05	Michigan State	CCHA	40	17	16	33	20	....	....	....	....	....

MILLER, Bryan (MIHL-luhr, BRIGH-uhn) N.J.

Defense. Shoots right. 5'10", 180 lbs. Born, Wayne, NJ, February 17, 1983.

			Regular Season					Playoffs				
Season	Club	League	GP	G	A	Pts	PIM	GP	G	A	Pts	PIM
2001-02	Boston University	H-East	34	4	15	19	12	....	....	....	....	....
2002-03	Boston University	H-East	42	5	18	23	48	....	....	....	....	....
2003-04	Boston University	H-East	38	5	15	20	24	....	....	....	....	....
2004-05	Boston University	H-East	39	6	20	26	42	....	....	....	....	....
	Albany River Rats	AHL	8	0	2	2	0	....	....	....	....	....

Signed as a free agent by **New Jersey**, July, 2005.

MILROY, Duncan (MIHL-roi, DUHN-can) MTL.

Right wing. Shoots right. 6', 197 lbs. Born, Edmonton, Alta., February 8, 1983.
(Montreal's 3rd choice, 37th overall, in 2001 Entry Draft).

			Regular Season					Playoffs				
Season	Club	League	GP	G	A	Pts	PIM	GP	G	A	Pts	PIM
1998-99	Edm. Maple Leafs	AMHL	34	34	36	70	73	....	....	....	....	....
	Swift Current	WHL	3	0	0	0	0	....	....	....	....	....
99-2000	Swift Current	WHL	68	15	15	30	20	12	3	5	8	12
2000-01	Swift Current	WHL	68	38	54	92	51	19	9	12	21	6
2001-02	Swift Current	WHL	26	20	11	31	20	....	....	....	....	....
	Kootenay Ice	WHL	38	25	31	56	24	22	*17	*20	*37	26
2002-03	Kootenay Ice	WHL	61	34	44	78	40	11	5	3	8	8
2003-04	Hamilton Bulldogs	AHL	50	4	10	14	14	10	3	1	4	4
2004-05	Hamilton Bulldogs	AHL	76	15	18	33	18	3	0	0	0	2

MIRNOV, Igor (mihr-NAWF, EE-gohr) OTT.

Left wing. Shoots left. 5'11", 191 lbs. Born, Chita, USSR, September 19, 1984.
(Ottawa's 2nd choice, 67th overall, in 2003 Entry Draft).

			Regular Season					Playoffs				
Season	Club	League	GP	G	A	Pts	PIM	GP	G	A	Pts	PIM
2001-02	Dyn'o Moscow 2	Russia-3	30	33	17	50	34	....	....	....	....	....
	Dynamo Moscow	Russia	6	0	0	0	0	....	....	....	....	....
2002-03	Dynamo Moscow	Russia	50	3	7	10	49	5	0	0	0	2
2003-04	Dynamo Moscow	Russia	53	11	10	21	26	3	0	0	0	2
2004-05	Dynamo Moscow	Russia	55	13	13	26	50	9	2	4	6	0

MISHARIN, Grigory (mih-SHAHR-ihn, g'YOHR-gee) MIN.

Defense. Shoots left. 6', 198 lbs. Born, Yekaterinburg, USSR, May 11, 1985.
(Minnesota's 6th choice, 207th overall, in 2003 Entry Draft).

			Regular Season					Playoffs				
Season	Club	League	GP	G	A	Pts	PIM	GP	G	A	Pts	PIM
2001-02	Yekaterinburg 2	Russia-3	STATISTICS NOT AVAILABLE									
	Magnitogorsk 2	Russia-3	STATISTICS NOT AVAILABLE									
2002-03	Yekaterinburg	Russia-2	28	1	3	4	16	....	....	....	....	....
2003-04	Saginaw Spirit	OHL	65	5	22	27	42	....	....	....	....	....
2004-05	Nizhnekamsk	Russia	47	1	3	4	38	3	0	0	0	4

MITCHELL, John (MIH-chuhl, JAWN) **TOR.**

Center. Shoots left. 6'1", 182 lbs. Born, Oakville, Ont., January 22, 1985.
(Toronto's 4th choice, 158th overall, in 2003 Entry Draft).

			Regular Season					Playoffs				
Season	Club	League	GP	G	A	Pts	PIM	GP	G	A	Pts	PIM
2000-01	Waterloo Siskens	OPJHL	47	15	29	44	33	....	....	....	....	....
2001-02	Plymouth Whalers	OHL	62	9	9	18	23	6	1	0	1	4
2002-03	Plymouth Whalers	OHL	68	18	37	55	31	18	2	10	12	8
2003-04	Plymouth Whalers	OHL	65	28	54	82	45	9	6	6	12	6
2004-05	Plymouth Whalers	OHL	63	25	50	75	59	4	1	1	2	0
	St. John's	AHL	2	0	0	0	0	....	....	....	....	....

MITCHELL, Torrey (MIH-chuhl, TOHR-ee) **S.J.**

Center. Shoots right. 5'11", 175 lbs. Born, Montreal, Que., January 30, 1985.
(San Jose's 3rd choice, 126th overall, in 2004 Entry Draft).

			Regular Season					Playoffs				
Season	Club	League	GP	G	A	Pts	PIM	GP	G	A	Pts	PIM
2002-03	Hotchkiss	High-CT	26	19	30	49	33	....	....	....	....	....
2003-04	Hotchkiss	High-CT	25	25	37	62	42	....	....	....	....	....
2004-05	U. of Vermont	ECAC	38	11	19	30	74	....	....	....	....	....

ECAC All-Rookie Team 2005)

MOJZIS, Tomas (MOI-shihsh, TAW-mash) **VAN.**

Defense. Shoots left. 6'1", 192 lbs. Born, Kolin, Czech., May 2, 1982.
(Toronto's 11th choice, 246th overall, in 2001 Entry Draft).

			Regular Season					Playoffs				
Season	Club	League	GP	G	A	Pts	PIM	GP	G	A	Pts	PIM
99-2000	HC Pardubice Jr.	CzRep-Jr.	40	7	1	8	....	....	....	....	....	....
2000-01	Moose Jaw	WHL	72	11	25	36	115	4	0	1	1	8
2001-02	Moose Jaw	WHL	28	2	11	13	43	....	....	....	....	....
	Seattle	WHL	36	8	15	23	66	11	1	3	4	20
2002-03	Seattle	WHL	62	21	49	70	126	15	1	6	7	36
2003-04	Manitoba Moose	AHL	63	5	13	18	50	....	....	....	....	....
2004-05	Manitoba Moose	AHL	80	7	23	30	62	14	0	2	2	28

WHL West First All-Star Team (2003) • Canadian Major Junior First All-Star Team (2003)

Traded to **Vancouver** by **Toronto** for Brad Leeb, September 4, 2002.

MONYCH, Lance (MOH-nihch, LANTS) **PHX.**

Right wing. Shoots right. 6'3", 203 lbs. Born, Red Deer, Alta., July 25, 1984.
(Phoenix's 6th choice, 97th overall, in 2002 Entry Draft).

			Regular Season					Playoffs				
Season	Club	League	GP	G	A	Pts	PIM	GP	G	A	Pts	PIM
99-2000	Brandon Hawks	MBHL	30	32	34	66	98	....	....	....	....	....
	Brandon	WHL	3	0	0	0	0	....	....	....	....	....
2000-01	Brandon	WHL	53	14	8	22	34	6	1	0	1	0
2001-02	Brandon	WHL	71	18	30	48	96	19	4	3	7	20
2002-03	Brandon	WHL	70	19	26	45	111	17	7	3	10	20
2003-04	Brandon	WHL	58	29	26	55	71	11	2	6	8	8
2004-05	Brandon	WHL	64	30	36	66	88	24	*19	7	26	44

MOORE, Greg (MOOR, GREHG) **NYR**

Right wing. Shoots right. 6'1", 215 lbs. Born, Lisbon, ME, March 26, 1984.
(Calgary's 5th choice, 143rd overall, in 2003 Entry Draft).

			Regular Season					Playoffs				
Season	Club	League	GP	G	A	Pts	PIM	GP	G	A	Pts	PIM
99-2000	St. Dominic Saints	High-ME	31	32	40	72	....	....	....	....	....	....
2000-01	USA U-17	USDP	69	12	18	30	23	....	....	....	....	....
2001-02	USA U-18	USDP	53	13	24	37	20	....	....	....	....	....
2002-03	U. of Maine	H-East	33	9	7	16	10	....	....	....	....	....
2003-04	U. of Maine	H-East	39	15	8	23	44	....	....	....	....	....
2004-05	U. of Maine	H-East	40	14	9	23	16	....	....	....	....	....

Traded to **NY Rangers** by **Calgary** with Jamie McLennan and Blair Betts for Chris Simon and NY Rangers' 7th round choice (Matt Schneider) in 2004 Entry Draft, March 6, 2004.

MORIN, Travis (moh-REHN, TRA-vihs) **WSH.**

Center. Shoots left. 6'2", 175 lbs. Born, Minneapolis, MN, January 9, 1984.
(Washington's 13th choice, 263rd overall, in 2004 Entry Draft).

			Regular Season					Playoffs				
Season	Club	League	GP	G	A	Pts	PIM	GP	G	A	Pts	PIM
2001-02	Chicago Steel	USHL	20	5	8	13	....	4	0	0	0	2
2002-03	Chicago Steel	USHL	60	21	26	47	46	....	....	....	....	....
2003-04	Minnesota State	WCHA	38	9	12	21	14	....	....	....	....	....
2004-05	Minnesota State	WCHA	36	12	19	31	20	....	....	....	....	....

MORMINA, Joey (mohr-MEE-nah, JOH-ee) **L.A.**

Defense. Shoots left. 6'6", 220 lbs. Born, Montreal, Que., June 29, 1982.
(Philadelphia's 6th choice, 193rd overall, in 2002 Entry Draft).

			Regular Season					Playoffs				
Season	Club	League	GP	G	A	Pts	PIM	GP	G	A	Pts	PIM
2000-01	Holderness School	High-NH	29	15	15	30	....	....	....	....	....	....
2001-02	Colgate	ECAC	34	2	13	15	28	....	....	....	....	....
2002-03	Colgate	ECAC	40	4	9	13	52	....	....	....	....	....
2003-04	Colgate	ECAC	28	2	10	12	26	....	....	....	....	....
2004-05	Colgate	ECAC	39	8	8	16	50	....	....	....	....	....

Signed as a free agent by **Los Angeles**, August 24, 2005.

MORRIS, Mike (MOHR-his, MIGHK) **S.J.**

Right wing. Shoots right. 6'1", 182 lbs. Born, Dorchester, MA, July 14, 1983.
(San Jose's 1st choice, 27th overall, in 2002 Entry Draft).

			Regular Season					Playoffs				
Season	Club	League	GP	G	A	Pts	PIM	GP	G	A	Pts	PIM
2000-01	St. Sebastian's	High-MA	28	20	28	48	18	....	....	....	....	....
2001-02	St. Sebastian's	High-MA	31	29	29	58	26	....	....	....	....	....
2002-03	Northeastern	H-East	26	9	12	21	16	....	....	....	....	....
2003-04	Northeastern	H-East	34	10	20	30	14	....	....	....	....	....
2004-05	Northeastern	H-East	34	19	20	39	22	....	....	....	....	....

Hockey East Second All-Star Team (2005)

MORRISON, Jordan (MOHR-ih-suhn, JOHN-dan) **PIT.**

Center. Shoots left. 5'11", 167 lbs. Born, Scarborough, Ont., June 4, 1986.
(Pittsburgh's 10th choice, 222nd overall, in 2004 Entry Draft).

			Regular Season					Playoffs				
Season	Club	League	GP	G	A	Pts	PIM	GP	G	A	Pts	PIM
2002-03	Peterborough	OHL	59	6	8	14	14	7	3	1	4	0
2003-04	Peterborough	OHL	66	15	30	45	52	....	....	....	....	....
2004-05	Peterborough	OHL	67	23	41	64	51	14	2	10	12	6

MORRISON, Justin (MOHR-ih-suhn, JUHS-tihn)

Right wing. Shoots right. 6'3", 205 lbs. Born, Los Angeles, CA, September 10, 1979.
(Vancouver's 4th choice, 81st overall, in 1998 Entry Draft).

			Regular Season					Playoffs				
Season	Club	League	GP	G	A	Pts	PIM	GP	G	A	Pts	PIM
1996-97	Omaha Lancers	USHL	62	12	24	36	44	10	2	4	6	8
1997-98	Colorado College	WCHA	42	4	9	13	8	....	....	....	....	....
1998-99	Colorado College	WCHA	38	23	15	38	33	....	....	....	....	....
99-2000	Colorado College	WCHA	38	7	19	26	28	....	....	....	....	....
2000-01	Colorado College	WCHA	41	21	14	35	42	....	....	....	....	....
2001-02	Manitoba Moose	AHL	64	10	9	19	37	7	1	0	1	4
2002-03	Manitoba Moose	AHL	30	10	6	16	13	14	2	3	5	4
	Columbia Inferno	ECHL	40	20	35	55	39	2	0	0	0	4
2003-04	Manitoba Moose	AHL	66	18	18	36	27	....	....	....	....	....
2004-05	Manitoba Moose	AHL	71	11	10	21	33	14	1	5	6	10

MORROW, Thomas (MOHR-roh, TAW-muhs) **BUF.**

Defense. Shoots left. 6'6", 198 lbs. Born, St. Paul, MN, October 21, 1983.
(Buffalo's 6th choice, 150th overall, in 2003 Entry Draft).

			Regular Season					Playoffs				
Season	Club	League	GP	G	A	Pts	PIM	GP	G	A	Pts	PIM
2000-01	Hill-Murray	High-MN	30	2	12	14	....	....	....	....	....	....
2001-02	Hill-Murray	High-MN	31	3	27	39	....	....	....	....	....	....
2002-03	Tri-City Storm	USHL	23	1	3	4	64	....	....	....	....	....
	Des Moines	USHL	34	1	6	7	40	....	....	....	....	....
2003-04	Boston University	H-East	38	0	3	3	34	....	....	....	....	....
2004-05	Boston University	H-East	28	0	1	1	40	....	....	....	....	....

MOSS, David (MAWS, DAY-vihd) **CGY.**

Left wing. Shoots left. 6'3", 203 lbs. Born, Dearborn, MI, December 28, 1981.
(Calgary's 9th choice, 220th overall, in 2001 Entry Draft).

			Regular Season					Playoffs				
Season	Club	League	GP	G	A	Pts	PIM	GP	G	A	Pts	PIM
99-2000	Catholic Central	High-MI	28	18	20	28	20	....	....	....	....	....
2000-01	St. Louis Jr. Blues	CSJHL	9	2	2	4	2	....	....	....	....	....
	Cedar Rapids	USHL	51	20	18	38	14	4	0	1	1	2
2001-02	U. of Michigan	CCHA	43	4	9	13	10	....	....	....	....	....
2002-03	U. of Michigan	CCHA	43	14	17	31	37	....	....	....	....	....
2003-04	U. of Michigan	CCHA	38	8	12	20	18	....	....	....	....	....
2004-05	U. of Michigan	CCHA	38	10	20	30	26	....	....	....	....	....

MOULSON, Matt (MOWL-suhn, MAT) **PIT.**

Left wing. Shoots left. 6'1", 195 lbs. Born, North York, Ont., November 1, 1983.
(Pittsburgh's 11th choice, 263rd overall, in 2003 Entry Draft).

			Regular Season					Playoffs				
Season	Club	League	GP	G	A	Pts	PIM	GP	G	A	Pts	PIM
2001-02	Guelph	OHA-B	42	56	46	102	80	....	....	....	....	....
2002-03	Cornell Big Red	ECAC	33	13	10	23	22	....	....	....	....	....
2003-04	Cornell Big Red	ECAC	32	18	17	35	37	....	....	....	....	....
2004-05	Cornell Big Red	ECAC	34	22	20	42	33	....	....	....	....	....

ECAC First All-Star Team (2005) • NCAA East Second All-American Team (2005)

MOZYAKIN, Sergei (mohz-YA-kihn, SAIR-gay) **CBJ**

Left wing. Shoots right. 5'10", 165 lbs. Born, Yaroslavl, USSR, March 30, 1981.
(Columbus' 13th choice, 263rd overall, in 2002 Entry Draft).

			Regular Season					Playoffs				
Season	Club	League	GP	G	A	Pts	PIM	GP	G	A	Pts	PIM
1998-99	Val-d'Or Foreurs	QMJHL	4	0	1	1	2	....	....	....	....	....
99-2000	HK Moscow 2	Russia-3	6	9	3	12	6	....	....	....	....	....
	HK Moscow	Russia-2	44	23	25	48	10	....	....	....	....	....
2000-01	HK Moscow	Russia-2	37	22	28	50	18	....	....	....	....	....
	CSKA Moscow	Russia	9	0	2	2	0	....	....	....	....	....
2001-02	HK CSKA Moscow	Russia-2	54	34	30	64	10	12	9	12	21	4
2002-03	CSKA Moscow	Russia	33	12	15	27	18	....	....	....	....	....
2003-04	CSKA Moscow	Russia	45	21	19	40	6	....	....	....	....	....
2004-05	CSKA Moscow	Russia	49	11	12	23	22	....	....	....	....	....

MRAZEK, Jaroslav (muh-RA-zehk, YAHR-roh-slav) **NYI**

Defense. Shoots left. 6'3", 198 lbs. Born, Pisek, Czech., January 14, 1986.
(NY Islanders' 6th choice, 179th overall, in 2004 Entry Draft).

			Regular Season					Playoffs				
Season	Club	League	GP	G	A	Pts	PIM	GP	G	A	Pts	PIM
2003-04	Sparta Jr.	CzRep-Jr.	37	3	6	9	36	....	....	....	....	....
	HC Sparta Praha	CzRep	1	0	0	0	0	1	0	0	0	0
2004-05	St. Michael's	OHL	57	0	2	2	54	10	0	3	3	8

MUKHACHEV, Andrei (moo-khah-CHEHV, AWN-dray) **NSH.**

Defense. Shoots left. 6'3", 196 lbs. Born, Sverdlovsk, USSR, July 21, 1980.
(Nashville's 11th choice, 210th overall, in 2003 Entry Draft).

			Regular Season					Playoffs				
Season	Club	League	GP	G	A	Pts	PIM	GP	G	A	Pts	PIM
1998-99	HK CSKA Moscow	Russia-2	38	0	2	2	30	....	....	....	....	....
99-2000	HK Moscow	Russia-2	40	2	9	11	44	....	....	....	....	....
2000-01	CSKA Moscow 2	Russia-3	8	1	5	6	18	....	....	....	....	....
	HK Moscow	Russia-2	40	2	9	11	44	....	....	....	....	....
2001-02	HK CSKA Moscow	Russia-2	39	3	9	12	28	12	2	5	7	10
2002-03	CSKA Moscow	Russia	50	3	7	10	30	....	....	....	....	....
2003-04	CSKA Moscow	Russia	38	2	4	6	28	....	....	....	....	....
2004-05	CSKA Moscow	Russia	21	0	2	2	14	....	....	....	....	....

MURATOV, Yevgeny (muhr-A-tahf, ehv-GEH-nee) **EDM.**

Left wing. Shoots right. 5'10", 178 lbs. Born, Nizhny Tagil, USSR, January 28, 1981.
(Edmonton's 10th choice, 274th overall, in 2000 Entry Draft).

			Regular Season					Playoffs				
Season	Club	League	GP	G	A	Pts	PIM	GP	G	A	Pts	PIM
1997-98	Nizhnekamsk 2	Russia-3	39	7	7	14	2	....	....	....	....	....
1998-99	Nizhnekamsk 2	Russia-4	37	26	9	35	32	....	....	....	....	....
	Nizhnekamsk	Russia	4	0	0	0	0	3	1	0	1	2
99-2000	Nizhnekamsk	Russia	29	9	7	16	2	....	....	....	....	....
	Ak Bars Kazan	Russia	8	2	2	4	2	9	0	0	0	2
2000-01	Nizhnekamsk	Russia	42	9	8	17	14	4	0	0	0	0
2001-02	Nizhnekamsk	Russia	45	5	13	18	4	....	....	....	....	....
2002-03	Nizhnekamsk	Russia	51	10	11	21	41	....	....	....	....	....
2003-04	Nizhnekamsk	Russia	20	1	6	7	8	....	....	....	....	....
2004-05	Novokuznetsk	Russia	58	15	13	28	12	4	1	2	3	0

MURPHY, Colin (MUHR-fee, COHL-ihn)

Left wing. Shoots left. 6', 195 lbs. Born, Fort McMurray, Alta., April 11, 1980.

Season	Club	League	Regular Season GP	G	A	Pts	PIM	Playoffs GP	G	A	Pts	PIM
2001-02	Michigan Tech	WCHA	38	8	19	27	40	....	....	....	....	....
2002-03	Michigan Tech	WCHA	37	20	20	40	42	....	....	....	....	....
2003-04	Michigan Tech	WCHA	33	15	17	32	28	....	....	....	....	....
2004-05	Michigan Tech	WCHA	37	11	*42	53	40	....	....	....	....	....
	St. John's	AHL	12	1	7	8	34	5	1	3	4	17

WCHA First All-Star Team (2005) • NCAA West Second All-American Team (2005)

Signed as a free agent by **Toronto**, March 18, 2005.

MURPHY, Mark (MUHR-fee, MAHRK) PHI.

Left wing. Shoots right. 5'11", 200 lbs. Born, Stoughton, MA, August 6, 1976.
(Toronto's 6th choice, 197th overall, in 1995 Entry Draft).

Season	Club	League	Regular Season GP	G	A	Pts	PIM	Playoffs GP	G	A	Pts	PIM
1994-95	Stratford Cullitons	OHA-B	47	52	56	108	64	....	....	....	....	....
1995-96	Stratford Cullitons	OHA-B	1	0	0	0	0	....	....	....	....	....
	RPI Engineers	ECAC	32	1	1	2	50	....	....	....	....	....
1996-97	RPI Engineers	ECAC	34	9	18	27	56	....	....	....	....	....
1997-98	RPI Engineers	ECAC	35	8	27	35	63	....	....	....	....	....
1998-99	RPI Engineers	ECAC	37	11	30	41	76	....	....	....	....	....
99-2000	Wilkes-Barre	AHL	38	11	22	33	35	....	....	....	....	....
	Trenton Titans	ECHL	37	21	18	39	60	12	2	8	10	17
	Philadelphia	AHL	....	....	....	....	....	2	0	0	0	0
2000-01	Portland Pirates	AHL	76	29	41	70	92	3	2	0	2	2
2001-02	Portland Pirates	AHL	77	20	37	57	56	....	....	....	....	....
2002-03	Portland Pirates	AHL	55	18	24	42	84	3	0	1	1	2
2003-04	Philadelphia	AHL	80	16	22	38	104	12	5	4	9	0
2004-05	Philadelphia	AHL	65	13	30	43	75	6	1	1	2	6

Signed as a free agent by **Washington**, July 13, 2000. Signed as a free agent by **Philadelphia**, July 24, 2003.

MURPHY, Patrick (MUHR-fee, PAT-rihk) EDM.

Left wing. Shoots left. 6'1", 195 lbs. Born, Van Nuys, CA, July 24, 1983.
(Edmonton's 11th choice, 211th overall, in 2002 Entry Draft).

Season	Club	League	Regular Season GP	G	A	Pts	PIM	Playoffs GP	G	A	Pts	PIM
2000-01	Newmarket	OPJHL	40	13	18	31	95	....	....	....	....	....
2001-02	Newmarket	OPJHL	48	11	21	32	99	....	....	....	....	....
2002-03	Northern Mich.	CCHA	22	1	2	3	26	....	....	....	....	....
2003-04	Northern Mich.	CCHA	35	5	3	8	50	....	....	....	....	....
2004-05	Northern Mich.	CCHA	35	2	4	6	50	....	....	....	....	....

MURPHY, Ryan (MUHR-fee, RIGH-yan) N.J.

Left wing. Shoots left. 6'1", 210 lbs. Born, Van Nuys, CA, March 21, 1979.
(Carolina's 4th choice, 113th overall, in 1999 Entry Draft).

Season	Club	League	Regular Season GP	G	A	Pts	PIM	Playoffs GP	G	A	Pts	PIM
1995-96	Thornhill Islanders	MTJHL	32	13	16	29	49	1	0	0	0	0
1996-97	Thornhill Islanders	MTJHL	41	22	32	54	36	12	7	8	15	....
1997-98	Bowling Green	CCHA	36	3	9	12	27	....	....	....	....	....
1998-99	Bowling Green	CCHA	34	10	23	33	38	....	....	....	....	....
99-2000	Bowling Green	CCHA	36	9	10	19	63	....	....	....	....	....
2000-01	Bowling Green	CCHA	38	23	15	38	22	....	....	....	....	....
2001-02	Florida Everblades	ECHL	66	13	18	31	38	6	1	2	3	4
2002-03	Lowell	AHL	12	1	2	3	4	....	....	....	....	....
	Florida Everblades	ECHL	58	28	17	45	47	1	0	0	0	0
2003-04	Albany River Rats	AHL	71	10	9	19	28	....	....	....	....	....
2004-05	Albany River Rats	AHL	75	13	23	36	44	....	....	....	....	....

Signed as a free agent by **New Jersey**, July 30, 2003.

MURRAY, Andrew (MUHR-ree, AN-droo) CBJ

Center. Shoots left. 6'2", 210 lbs. Born, Selkirk, Man., November 6, 1981.
(Columbus' 11th choice, 242nd overall, in 2001 Entry Draft).

Season	Club	League	Regular Season GP	G	A	Pts	PIM	Playoffs GP	G	A	Pts	PIM
99-2000	Selkirk Steelers	MJHL	63	29	48	77	....	....	....	....	....	....
2000-01	Selkirk Steelers	MJHL	64	46	56	102	72	5	3	0	3	6
2001-02	Bemidji State	CHA	35	15	15	30	22	....	....	....	....	....
2002-03	Bemidji State	CHA	36	9	18	27	38	....	....	....	....	....
2003-04	Bemidji State	CHA	25	6	14	20	41	....	....	....	....	....
2004-05	Bemidji State	CHA	32	16	22	38	30	....	....	....	....	....

CHA All-Rookie Team (2002)

MURRAY, Brady (MUHR-ree, BRAY-dee) L.A.

Center. Shoots left. 5'9", 165 lbs. Born, Brandon, Man., August 17, 1984.
(Los Angeles' 6th choice, 152nd overall, in 2003 Entry Draft).

Season	Club	League	Regular Season GP	G	A	Pts	PIM	Playoffs GP	G	A	Pts	PIM
2001-02	Shat.-St. Mary's	High-MN	60	58	92	150	50	....	....	....	....	....
2002-03	Salmon Arm	BCHL	59	42	59	101	30	....	....	....	....	....
2003-04	North Dakota	WCHA	37	19	27	46	32	....	....	....	....	....
2004-05	North Dakota	WCHA	25	8	12	20	22	....	....	....	....	....

WCHA All-Rookie Team (2004) • WCHA Rookie of the Year (2004)

MURRAY, Doug (MUHR-ree, DUHG) S.J.

Defense. Shoots left. 6'3", 245 lbs. Born, Bromma, Sweden, March 12, 1980.
(San Jose's 6th choice, 241st overall, in 1999 Entry Draft).

Season	Club	League	Regular Season GP	G	A	Pts	PIM	Playoffs GP	G	A	Pts	PIM
1998-99	NY Apple Core	MJBHL	60	17	47	64	62	....	....	....	....	....
99-2000	Cornell Big Red	ECAC	32	3	6	9	38	....	....	....	....	....
2000-01	Cornell Big Red	ECAC	25	5	13	18	39	....	....	....	....	....
2001-02	Cornell Big Red	ECAC	35	11	21	32	67	....	....	....	....	....
2002-03	Cornell Big Red	ECAC	35	5	20	25	30	....	....	....	....	....
2003-04	Cleveland Barons	AHL	72	10	12	22	75	9	3	0	3	37
2004-05	Cleveland Barons	AHL	54	6	17	23	56	....	....	....	....	....

ECAC First All-Star Team (2002, 2003) • NCAA East First All-American Team (2003)

NASBY, Bret (NAZ-bee, BREHT) FLA.

Defense. Shoots right. 6'3", 188 lbs. Born, Grimsby, Ont., March 22, 1986.
(Florida's 5th choice, 152nd overall, in 2004 Entry Draft).

Season	Club	League	Regular Season GP	G	A	Pts	PIM	Playoffs GP	G	A	Pts	PIM
2002-03	Grimsby	OHA-C	53	6	14	20	63	....	....	....	....	....
2003-04	Oshawa Generals	OHL	56	0	7	7	41	7	0	3	3	6
2004-05	Oshawa Generals	OHL	66	4	13	17	71	....	....	....	....	....

NASLUND, Fredrik (NAZ-luhnd, FREHD-uhr-ihk) DAL.

Left wing. Shoots right. 6'4", 211 lbs. Born, Bromma, Sweden, February 11, 1986.
(Dallas' 6th choice, 104th overall, in 2004 Entry Draft).

Season	Club	League	Regular Season GP	G	A	Pts	PIM	Playoffs GP	G	A	Pts	PIM
2002-03	Vasteras Jr.	Swe-Jr.	34	12	9	21	8	....	....	....	....	....
2003-04	Vasteras Jr.	Swe-Jr.	17	13	15	28	6	3	0	1	1	4
	Vasteras	Sweden-2	32	2	4	6	0	....	....	....	....	....
2004-05	Vasteras	Sweden-2	3	0	0	0	0	....	....	....	....	....
	Vasteras Jr.	Swe-Jr.	21	7	7	14	2	....	....	....	....	....

NAUROV, Alexander (naw-OO-rawf, ahl-ehx-AN-duhr) DAL.

Right wing. Shoots left. 5'11", 191 lbs. Born, Saratov, USSR, March 4, 1985.
(Dallas' 5th choice, 134th overall, in 2003 Entry Draft).

Season	Club	League	Regular Season GP	G	A	Pts	PIM	Playoffs GP	G	A	Pts	PIM
2001-02	Yaroslavl 2	Russia-3	12	0	0	0	16	....	....	....	....	....
2002-03	Yaroslavl 2	Russia-3	STATISTICS NOT AVAILABLE									
2003-04	Yaroslavl 2	Russia-3	24	9	5	14	73	....	....	....	....	....
2004-05	Yaroslavl	Russia	11	2	2	4	2	....	....	....	....	....
	Yaroslavl 2	Russia-3	35	19	16	35	61	....	....	....	....	....

NEAL, James (NEEL, JAYMS) DAL.

Left wing. Shoots left. 6'2", 185 lbs. Born, Oshawa, Ont., September 3, 1987.
(Dallas' 2nd choice, 33rd overall, in 2005 Entry Draft).

Season	Club	League	Regular Season GP	G	A	Pts	PIM	Playoffs GP	G	A	Pts	PIM
2003-04	Bowmanville	OPJHL	43	28	27	55	....	....	....	....	....	....
	Plymouth Whalers	OHL	9	2	4	6	0	....	....	....	....	....
2004-05	Plymouth Whalers	OHL	67	18	26	44	32	4	1	1	2	6

NEILSON, Eric (NEEHL-sohn, AIR-ihk) L.A.

Right wing. Shoots right. 6'1", 201 lbs. Born, Fredericton, N.B., August 18, 1984.
(Los Angeles' 4th choice, 143rd overall, in 2004 Entry Draft).

Season	Club	League	Regular Season GP	G	A	Pts	PIM	Playoffs GP	G	A	Pts	PIM
2001-02	Rimouski Oceanic	QMJHL	48	0	2	2	130	4	0	0	0	25
2002-03	Rimouski Oceanic	QMJHL	53	2	9	11	341	....	....	....	....	....
2003-04	Rimouski Oceanic	QMJHL	50	4	11	15	194	9	0	0	0	28
2004-05	Rimouski Oceanic	QMJHL	54	13	13	26	157	11	1	3	4	*43

NEMEC, Ondrej (NEH-mehts, AWN-dray) PIT.

Defense. Shoots right. 6'1", 196 lbs. Born, Trebic, Czech., April 18, 1984.
(Pittsburgh's 2nd choice, 35th overall, in 2002 Entry Draft).

Season	Club	League	Regular Season GP	G	A	Pts	PIM	Playoffs GP	G	A	Pts	PIM
99-2000	HC Vsetin Jr.	CzRep-Jr.	5	0	2	2	4	....	....	....	....	....
	HC Vsetin U17	CzR-U17	48	6	18	24	62	....	....	....	....	....
2000-01	HC Vsetin Jr.	CzRep-Jr.	42	10	12	22	77	....	....	....	....	....
	HC Vsetin U17	CzR-U17	8	3	7	10	20	....	....	....	....	....
2001-02	HC Vsetin Jr.	CzRep-Jr.	8	4	7	11	47	....	....	....	....	....
	Trebic	CzRep-2	9	1	0	1	18	....	....	....	....	....
	HC Vsetin	CzRep	44	5	3	8	79	....	....	....	....	....
2002-03	HC Vsetin	CzRep	39	2	7	9	40	4	0	0	0	2
	Trebic	CzRep-2	2	0	0	0	6	....	....	....	....	....
2003-04	HC Vsetin	CzRep	42	2	4	6	30	....	....	....	....	....
	Trebic	CzRep-2	2	0	0	0	2	....	....	....	....	....
	Wilkes-Barre	AHL	7	1	2	3	2	7	0	1	1	6
2004-05	Trebic	CzRep-2	4	0	2	2	4	....	....	....	....	....
	HC Vsetin	CzRep	48	6	9	15	83	....	....	....	....	....

NEPRYAYEV, Ivan (neh-pree-YIGH-ehv, IGH-van) WSH.

Center. Shoots left. 6'1", 180 lbs. Born, Yaroslavl, USSR, February 4, 1982.
(Washington's 5th choice, 163rd overall, in 2000 Entry Draft).

Season	Club	League	Regular Season GP	G	A	Pts	PIM	Playoffs GP	G	A	Pts	PIM
1997-98	Torpedo Yaroslavl	Russia	6	0	0	0	0	....	....	....	....	....
1998-99	Yaroslavl 2	Russia-3	15	1	0	1	0	....	....	....	....	....
99-2000	Yaroslavl 2	Russia-3	40	8	14	22	....	....	....	....	....	....
2000-01	Yaroslavl	Russia	10	0	0	0	2	....	....	....	....	....
2001-02	Yaroslavl 2	Russia-3	2	1	0	1	18	....	....	....	....	....
	Yaroslavl	Russia	36	3	8	11	28	....	....	....	....	....
2002-03	Yaroslavl	Russia	26	3	6	9	12	6	1	0	1	0
2003-04	Yaroslavl 2	Russia-3	13	5	10	15	12	....	....	....	....	....
2004-05	Yaroslavl	Russia	56	10	10	20	73	9	1	0	1	16

NEWBURY, Kris (new-BUHR-ee, KRIHS)

Center. Shoots left. 5'10", 200 lbs. Born, Brampton, Ont., February 19, 1982.
(San Jose's 4th choice, 139th overall, in 2002 Entry Draft).

Season	Club	League	Regular Season GP	G	A	Pts	PIM	Playoffs GP	G	A	Pts	PIM
1996-97	Brampton Capitals	OPJHL	28	9	4	13	36	....	....	....	....	....
1997-98	Brampton Capitals	OPJHL	46	11	21	32	161	....	....	....	....	....
1998-99	Belleville Bulls	OHL	51	6	8	14	89	....	....	....	....	....
99-2000	Belleville Bulls	OHL	34	6	18	24	72	....	....	....	....	....
	Sarnia Sting	OHL	27	6	8	14	44	7	0	3	3	16
2000-01	Sarnia Sting	OHL	64	28	30	58	126	4	1	3	4	20
2001-02	Sarnia Sting	OHL	66	42	62	104	141	5	1	3	4	15
2002-03	Sarnia Sting	OHL	64	34	58	92	149	6	4	4	8	16
2003-04	St. John's	AHL	72	5	15	20	153	....	....	....	....	....
2004-05	St. John's	AHL	55	4	9	13	103	5	0	0	0	36
	Pensacola	ECHL	6	2	4	6	20	....	....	....	....	....

OHL Second All-Star Team (2002)

Signed as a free agent by **St. John's** (AHL), October 2, 2003.

NICKERSON, Matt (NIH-kuhr-suhn, MAT) **DAL.**

Defense. Shoots right. 6'4", 230 lbs. Born, New Haven, CT, January 11, 1985.
(Dallas' 4th choice, 99th overall, in 2003 Entry Draft).

			Regular Season					Playoffs				
Season	**Club**	**League**	**GP**	**G**	**A**	**Pts**	**PIM**	**GP**	**G**	**A**	**Pts**	**PIM**
2000-01	Victoria Salsa	BCHL	....	....	....	....	196	....	....	....	....	....
2001-02	Texas Tornado	NAHL	47	1	12	13	97	6	0	0	0	6
2002-03	Texas Tornado	NAHL	47	6	23	29	277	6	0	1	1	*18
2003-04	Clarkson Knights	ECAC	38	5	9	14	*179	....	....	....	....	....
2004-05	Victoriaville Tigres	QMJHL	48	1	11	12	182	6	0	1	1	27

NIELSEN, Frans (NEEL-sehn, FRAHNS) **NYI**

Center. Shoots left. 5'11", 172 lbs. Born, Herning, Denmark, April 24, 1984.
(NY Islanders' 2nd choice, 87th overall, in 2002 Entry Draft).

			Regular Season					Playoffs				
Season	**Club**	**League**	**GP**	**G**	**A**	**Pts**	**PIM**	**GP**	**G**	**A**	**Pts**	**PIM**
99-2000	Herning IK Jr.	Den-Jr.	36	18	16	34	6	....	....	....	....	....
2000-01	Herning IK	Denmark	38	18	19	37	6	....	....	....	....	....
2001-02	Malmo	Sweden	20	0	1	1	0	....	....	....	....	....
	Malmo Jr.	Swe-Jr.	29	15	27	42	8	7	3	7	10	2
2002-03	Malmo	Sweden	47	3	6	9	10	....	....	....	....	....
	Malmo Jr.	Swe-Jr.	2	1	3	4	0	....	....	....	....	....
2003-04	Malmo	Sweden	50	9	7	16	28	....	....	....	....	....
	Malmo	Sweden-Q	10	3	5	8	2	....	....	....	....	....
2004-05	Malmo	Sweden	49	8	7	15	6	....	....	....	....	....
	Malmo	Sweden-Q	10	7	2	9	0	....	....	....	....	....

NIINIMAKI, Jesse (NIH-nee-ma-kee, JEH-see) **EDM.**

Center. Shoots left. 6'2", 183 lbs. Born, Tampere, Finland, August 19, 1983.
(Edmonton's 1st choice, 15th overall, in 2002 Entry Draft).

			Regular Season					Playoffs				
Season	**Club**	**League**	**GP**	**G**	**A**	**Pts**	**PIM**	**GP**	**G**	**A**	**Pts**	**PIM**
99-2000	Ilves Tampere Jr.	Finland-Jr.	14	0	5	5	6	....	....	....	....	....
2000-01	Ilves Tampere U18	Fin-U18	16	3	5	8	40	....	....	....	....	....
	Ilves Tampere Jr.	Finland-Jr.	18	2	4	6	6	....	....	....	....	....
2001-02	Ilves Tampere Jr.	Finland-Jr.	27	9	23	32	54	....	....	....	....	....
	Ilves Tampere	Finland	16	2	4	6	4	3	0	0	0	0
2002-03	Ilves Tampere	Finland	41	4	13	17	12	....	....	....	....	....
	Ilves Tampere Jr.	Finland-Jr.	9	2	7	9	4	....	....	....	....	....
	Sport Vaasa	Finland-2	2	0	1	1	10	....	....	....	....	....
2003-04	Ilves Tampere	Finland	10	3	3	6	2	....	....	....	....	....
2004-05	Ilves Tampere	Finland	18	4	4	8	8	....	....	....	....	....
	Edmonton	AHL	24	1	0	1	2	....	....	....	....	....

Signed as a fre agent by **Jokerit** (Finkand), August 29, 2005.

NIKITIN, Nikita (nih-KEE-tihn, nih-KEE-tuh) **ST.L.**

Defense. Shoots left. 6'3", 178 lbs. Born, Omsk, USSR, June 16, 1986.
(St. Louis' 5th choice, 136th overall, in 2004 Entry Draft).

			Regular Season					Playoffs				
Season	**Club**	**League**	**GP**	**G**	**A**	**Pts**	**PIM**	**GP**	**G**	**A**	**Pts**	**PIM**
2002-03	Omsk 2	Russia-3	34	3	7	10	4	....	....	....	....	....
2003-04	Omsk 2	Russia-3	34	3	8	11	22	....	....	....	....	....
2004-05	Avangard Omsk	Russia	12	0	0	0	2	3	0	0	0	0
	Omsk 2	Russia-3	31	3	8	11	20	....	....	....	....	....

NIKULIN, Alexander (nih-KOO-lihn, al-EHX-AN-duhr) **OTT.**

Center. Shoots left. 6'1", 195 lbs. Born, Moscow, USSR, August 25, 1985.
(Ottawa's 6th choice, 122nd overall, in 2004 Entry Draft).

			Regular Season					Playoffs				
Season	**Club**	**League**	**GP**	**G**	**A**	**Pts**	**PIM**	**GP**	**G**	**A**	**Pts**	**PIM**
2002-03	CSKA Moscow 2	Russia-3	46	22	14	36	....	....	....	....	....	....
2003-04	CSKA Moscow 2	Russia-3	47	21	20	41	46	....	....	....	....	....
2004-05	CSKA Moscow	Russia	16	3	3	6	0	....	....	....	....	....

NIKULIN, Ilja (nih-KOO-lihn, ihl-YUH) **ATL.**

Defense. Shoots left. 6'3", 210 lbs. Born, Moscow, USSR, March 12, 1982.
(Atlanta's 2nd choice, 31st overall, in 2000 Entry Draft).

			Regular Season					Playoffs				
Season	**Club**	**League**	**GP**	**G**	**A**	**Pts**	**PIM**	**GP**	**G**	**A**	**Pts**	**PIM**
1998-99	Dyn'o Moscow 2	Russia-3	23	0	2	2	18	....	....	....	....	....
99-2000	Dyn'o Moscow 2	Russia-3	4	2	1	3	10	....	....	....	....	....
	THK Tver	Russia-2	39	3	6	9	84	....	....	....	....	....
2000-01	Dynamo Moscow	Russia	44	0	4	4	61	....	....	....	....	....
2001-02	Dyn'o Moscow 2	Russia-3	2	0	1	1	2	....	....	....	....	....
	Dynamo Moscow	Russia	47	2	1	3	44	3	0	0	0	0
2002-03	Dynamo Moscow	Russia	40	1	4	5	46	5	0	1	1	4
2003-04	Dynamo Moscow	Russia	54	1	5	6	56	3	0	0	0	2
2004-05	Dynamo Moscow	Russia	50	1	9	10	65	10	0	3	3	8

NILSON, Patrik (nihl-SUHN, PA-trihk) **CGY.**

Center. Shoots right. 6', 180 lbs. Born, Baltsa, Sweden, May 18, 1981.

			Regular Season					Playoffs				
Season	**Club**	**League**	**GP**	**G**	**A**	**Pts**	**PIM**	**GP**	**G**	**A**	**Pts**	**PIM**
99-2000	Djurgarden	Sweden	6	0	0	0	2	2	0	0	0	0
	Huddinge IK	Sweden-2	25	11	6	17	38	....	....	....	....	....
2000-01	Djurgarden	Sweden	24	1	0	1	4	....	....	....	....	....
	Djurgarden Jr.	Swe-Jr.	10	5	6	11	18	....	....	....	....	....
2001-02	Mora IK	Sweden-2	42	6	19	25	71	....	....	....	....	....
2002-03	Mora IK	Sweden-2	35	9	9	18	12	....	....	....	....	....
2003-04	Laredo Bucks	CHL	60	27	38	65	62	15	*8	2	10	12
	San Antonio	AHL	3	0	0	0	0	....	....	....	....	....
2004-05	Las Vegas	ECHL	30	3	6	9	21	....	....	....	....	....
	Louisiana	ECHL	34	3	8	11	34	....	....	....	....	....

Signed as a free agent by **Calgary**, July 6, 2004.

NILSSON, Mattias (NIHL-suhn, MA-tee-uhs) **NSH.**

Defense. Shoots left. 6'3", 195 lbs. Born, Ornskoldsvik, Sweden, February 6, 1982.
(Nashville's 3rd choice, 72nd overall, in 2000 Entry Draft).

			Regular Season					Playoffs				
Season	**Club**	**League**	**GP**	**G**	**A**	**Pts**	**PIM**	**GP**	**G**	**A**	**Pts**	**PIM**
1997-98	Malmo Jr.	Swe-Jr.	40	20	14	34	34	....	....	....	....	....
1998-99	Malmo Jr.	Swe-Jr.	30	7	7	14	26	....	....	....	....	....
99-2000	Malmo Jr.	Swe-Jr.	33	5	5	10	56	2	0	0	0	0
	MoDo U18	Swe-U18	7	0	2	2	10	....	....	....	....	....
2000-01	Malmo Jr.	Swe-Jr.	18	2	3	5	62	....	....	....	....	....
2001-02	Hammarby Jr.	Swe-Jr.	25	3	8	11	40	....	....	....	....	....
	Hammarby	Sweden-2	20	0	1	1	18	2	1	0	1	0
2002-03	Hammarby	Sweden-2	38	2	6	8	26	....	....	....	....	....
	Hammarby Jr.	Swe-Jr.	2	1	0	1	2	....	....	....	....	....
2003-04	IF Vallentuna BK	Sweden-2	7	0	0	0	16	....	....	....	....	....
	Hammarby Jr.	Swe-Jr.	7	0	0	0	10	....	....	....	....	....
	Hammarby	Sweden-2	25	2	5	7	22	....	....	....	....	....
2004-05	Hammarby Jr.	Swe-Jr.	2	0	0	0	4	....	....	....	....	....
	Hammarby	Sweden-2	40	2	2	4	46	....	....	....	....	....

NILSSON, Robert (NIHL-suhn, RAW-buhrt) **NYI**

Center. Shoots left. 5'11", 176 lbs. Born, Calgary, Alta., January 10, 1985.
(NY Islanders' 1st choice, 15th overall, in 2003 Entry Draft).

			Regular Season					Playoffs				
Season	**Club**	**League**	**GP**	**G**	**A**	**Pts**	**PIM**	**GP**	**G**	**A**	**Pts**	**PIM**
2000-01	Leksands IF Jr.	Swe-Jr.	23	14	28	42	26	2	0	0	0	2
	Leksands IF U18	Swe-U18	4	6	3	9	6	2	0	2	2	2
2001-02	Leksands IF Jr.	Swe-Jr.	21	13	18	31	24	5	0	5	5	8
	Leksands IF	Sweden-2	14	1	4	5	8	....	....	....	....	....
2002-03	Leksands IF	Sweden	41	8	13	21	10	5	0	1	1	2
	Leksands IF Jr.	Swe-Jr.	....	....	....	....	....	2	1	1	2	2
2003-04	Leksands IF Jr.	Swe-Jr.	4	2	8	10	4	....	....	....	....	....
	Leksands IF	Sweden	34	2	4	6	6	....	....	....	....	....
	Fribourg	Swiss	7	1	3	4	2	4	1	0	1	2
2004-05	Almtuna	Sweden-2	3	0	1	1	2	....	....	....	....	....
	Hammarby	Sweden-2	7	0	4	4	4	....	....	....	....	....
	Djurgarden Jr.	Swe-Jr.	8	8	4	12	12	....	....	....	....	....
	Djurgarden	Sweden	23	2	4	6	6	3	0	0	0	0

NISKALA, Janne (NIHS-kah-lah, YAH-nee) **NSH.**

Defense. Shoots left. 5'11", 199 lbs. Born, Rauma, Finland, September 22, 1981.
(Nashville's 5th choice, 147th overall, in 2004 Entry Draft).

			Regular Season					Playoffs				
Season	**Club**	**League**	**GP**	**G**	**A**	**Pts**	**PIM**	**GP**	**G**	**A**	**Pts**	**PIM**
2001-02	Lukko Rauma	Finland	55	7	13	20	81	....	....	....	....	....
2002-03	Lukko Rauma	Finland	46	4	5	9	40	....	....	....	....	....
2003-04	Lukko Rauma	Finland	55	21	15	36	73	4	0	0	0	16
2004-05	Lukko Rauma	Finland	44	9	12	21	63	9	5	2	7	4

NISKANEN, Matt (NIHS-kah-nehn, MAT) **DAL.**

Defense. Shoots right. 6', 194 lbs. Born, Virginia, MN, December 6, 1986.
(Dallas' 1st choice, 28th overall, in 2005 Entry Draft).

			Regular Season					Playoffs				
Season	**Club**	**League**	**GP**	**G**	**A**	**Pts**	**PIM**	**GP**	**G**	**A**	**Pts**	**PIM**
2003-04	Virginia Blue Devils	High-MN	....	24	37	61	....	....	....	....	....	....
2004-05	Virginia Blue Devils	High-MN	29	27	38	65	34	....	....	....	....	....

Signed Letter of Intent to attend **Minnesota-Duluth** (WCHA) in fall of 2005.

NITTEL, Ahren (NIH-tuhl, AH-rehn) **N.J.**

Left wing. Shoots left. 6'3", 225 lbs. Born, Waterloo, Ont., December 6, 1983.
(New Jersey's 5th choice, 85th overall, in 2002 Entry Draft).

			Regular Season					Playoffs				
Season	**Club**	**League**	**GP**	**G**	**A**	**Pts**	**PIM**	**GP**	**G**	**A**	**Pts**	**PIM**
99-2000	Streetsville Derbys	OPJHL	11	1	5	6	10	....	....	....	....	....
2000-01	Windsor Spitfires	OHL	46	6	4	10	56	7	3	1	4	16
2001-02	Windsor Spitfires	OHL	52	19	11	30	100	9	4	1	5	23
2002-03	Windsor Spitfires	OHL	22	5	4	9	30	....	....	....	....	....
	Oshawa Generals	OHL	20	15	7	22	25	13	5	2	7	10
2003-04	Albany River Rats	AHL	42	4	3	7	24	....	....	....	....	....
	Adirondack	UHL	2	1	0	1	0	....	....	....	....	....
2004-05	Albany River Rats	AHL	50	25	11	36	18	....	....	....	....	....

NOKELAINEN, Petteri (noh-kuh-LAY-nehn, PEH-tuh-ree) **NYI**

Center. Shoots right. 6'1", 187 lbs. Born, Imatra, Finland, January 16, 1986.
(NY Islanders' 1st choice, 16th overall, in 2004 Entry Draft).

			Regular Season					Playoffs				
Season	**Club**	**League**	**GP**	**G**	**A**	**Pts**	**PIM**	**GP**	**G**	**A**	**Pts**	**PIM**
2001-02	SaiPa U18	Fin-U18	6	2	1	3	14	....	....	....	....	....
2002-03	SaiPa	Finland	2	1	0	1	2	....	....	....	....	....
	SaiPa U18	Fin-U18	10	3	8	11	18	....	....	....	....	....
	SaiPa Jr.	Finland-Jr.	28	7	4	11	28	3	1	0	1	4
2003-04	SaiPa Jr.	Finland-Jr.	10	5	3	8	4	4	0	1	1	0
	SaiPa	Finland	40	4	4	8	16	....	....	....	....	....
2004-05	SaiPa	Finland	52	15	5	20	34	....	....	....	....	....

NOLAN, Brandon (NOH-lan, BRAN-duhn) **VAN.**

Center. Shoots left. 6'1", 185 lbs. Born, Sault Ste. Marie, Ont., July 18, 1983.
(Vancouver's 3rd choice, 111th overall, in 2003 Entry Draft).

			Regular Season					Playoffs				
Season	**Club**	**League**	**GP**	**G**	**A**	**Pts**	**PIM**	**GP**	**G**	**A**	**Pts**	**PIM**
99-2000	St. Catharines	OHA-B	47	18	13	31	10	....	....	....	....	....
2000-01	Oshawa Generals	OHL	52	15	23	38	21	....	....	....	....	....
2001-02	Oshawa Generals	OHL	57	30	28	58	78	5	2	4	6	4
2002-03	Oshawa Generals	OHL	68	36	52	88	57	13	10	7	17	4
2003-04	Manitoba Moose	AHL	48	7	10	17	18	....	....	....	....	....
	Columbia Inferno	ECHL	19	5	10	15	38	3	0	1	1	17
2004-05	Manitoba Moose	AHL	48	4	8	12	16	....	....	....	....	....

• Re-entered NHL Entry Draft. Originally New Jersey's 6th choice, 72nd overall, in 2001 Entry Draft.

OHL Second All-Star Team (2003)

NORDGREN, Niklas (NORHD-grehn, NIHK-las) CAR.

Left wing. Shoots right. 5'11", 185 lbs. Born, Ornskoldsvik, Sweden, June 28, 1979.
(Carolina's 7th choice, 195th overall, in 1997 Entry Draft).

			Regular Season					Playoffs				
Season	Club	League	GP	G	A	Pts	PIM	GP	G	A	Pts	PIM
1996-97	MoDo	Sweden	5	0	0	0	0	....	....	....	....	....
1997-98	MoDo Jr.	Swe-Jr.	22	14	6	20	....	....	....	....	....	....
	Malmo Jr.	Swe-Jr.	28	15	15	30	52	....	....	....	....	....
1998-99	MoDo	Sweden	7	0	0	0	2	....	....	....	....	....
	Malmo Jr.	Swe-Jr.	22	7	4	11	22	3	2	1	3	0
99-2000	Sundsvall	Sweden-2	27	21	11	32	58	....	....	....	....	....
	MoDo	EuroHL	1	0	0	0	0	1	0	0	0	0
2000-01	Sundsvall	Sweden-2	35	22	19	41	45	....	....	....	....	....
2001-02	Timra IK Jr.	Swe-Jr.	1	1	1	2	0	....	....	....	....	....
	Timra IK	Sweden	49	8	6	14	16	....	....	....	....	....
	Timra IK	Sweden-Q	10	3	3	5	4	....	....	....	....	....
2002-03	Timra IK	Sweden	47	20	23	43	40	10	1	4	5	4
2003-04	Timra IK	Sweden	46	13	15	28	44	10	4	1	5	32
2004-05	Timra IK	Sweden	46	19	17	36	71	7	0	2	2	6

NORDQVIST, Jonas (NAWRD-kvihst, YOH-nuhs) CHI.

Center. Shoots left. 6'3", 202 lbs. Born, Leksand, Sweden, April 26, 1982.
(Chicago's 3rd choice, 49th overall, in 2000 Entry Draft).

			Regular Season					Playoffs				
Season	Club	League	GP	G	A	Pts	PIM	GP	G	A	Pts	PIM
1997-98	Leksands IF Jr.	Swe-Jr.	42	26	35	61	....	....	....	....	....	....
1998-99	Leksands IF Jr.	Swe-Jr.	32	14	25	39	....	....	....	....	....	....
99-2000	Leksands IF Jr.	Swe-Jr.	34	15	24	39	32	2	0	0	0	2
	Leksands IF	Sweden	3	0	0	0	0	....	....	....	....	....
	Leksands IF U18	Swe-U18	2	0	2	2	0	4	3	5	8	0
2000-01	Leksands IF Jr.	Swe-Jr.	10	6	13	19	6	5	1	6	7	2
	Leksands IF	Sweden	42	3	4	7	4	....	....	....	....	....
2001-02	Leksands IF Jr.	Swe-Jr.	8	14	7	21	6	1	0	1	1	0
	Leksands IF	Sweden-2	40	8	7	15	16	....	....	....	....	....
2002-03	Rogle	Sweden-2	27	12	19	32	4	....	....	....	....	....
2003-04	Lulea HF	Sweden	47	13	11	24	18	3	0	0	0	2
2004-05	Lulea HF	Sweden	49	16	16	32	12	4	1	1	2	0

NORTON, Pierce (NOHR-tuhn, PIHRS) TOR.

Right wing. Shoots right. 6'2", 195 lbs. Born, Boston, MA, June 7, 1985.
(Toronto's 6th choice, 285th overall, in 2004 Entry Draft).

			Regular Season					Playoffs				
Season	Club	League	GP	G	A	Pts	PIM	GP	G	A	Pts	PIM
2002-03	Thayer Academy	High-MA	29	16	18	34	....	....	....	....	....	....
2003-04	Thayer Academy	High-MA	34	21	34	55	84	....	....	....	....	....
2004-05	Thayer Academy	High-MA	29	*30	20	50	....	....	....	....	....	....

NOVAK, Filip (NOH-vak, FIH-lihp) FLA.

Defense. Shoots left. 6'1", 185 lbs. Born, Ceske Budejovice, Czech., May 7, 1982.
(NY Rangers' 1st choice, 64th overall, in 2000 Entry Draft).

			Regular Season					Playoffs				
Season	Club	League	GP	G	A	Pts	PIM	GP	G	A	Pts	PIM
1998-99	C. Budejovice Jr.	CzRep-Jr.	68	8	10	18	34	....	....	....	....	....
99-2000	Regina Pats	WHL	47	7	32	39	70	7	1	4	5	5
2000-01	Regina Pats	WHL	64	17	50	67	75	6	1	4	5	6
2001-02	Regina Pats	WHL	60	12	46	58	125	6	2	2	4	19
2002-03	San Antonio	AHL	57	10	17	27	79	1	0	0	0	0
2003-04			DID NOT PLAY – INJURED									
2004-05	San Antonio	AHL	71	1	12	13	84	....	....	....	....	....

WHL East Second All-Star Team (2001) • WHL East First All-Star Team (2002) • AHL All-Rookie Team (2003)

Traded to **Florida** by **NY Rangers** with Igor Ulanov, NY Rangers' 1st (later traded to Calgary – Calgary selected Eric Nystrom) and 2nd (Rob Globke) round choices in 2002 Entry Draft and NY Rangers' 4th round choice (later traded to Atlanta – Atlanta selected Guillaume Desbiens) in 2003 Entry Draft for Pavel Bure and Florida's 2nd round choice (Lee Falardeau) in 2002 Entry Draft, March 18, 2002. • Missed entire 2003-04 season recovering from ankle injury suffered in training camp, September 17, 2003.

NOVAK, Zbynek (NOH-vahk, z'BIHN-nehk) WSH.

Left wing. Shoots left. 6'2", 194 lbs. Born, Kutna Hora, Czech., July 23, 1983.
(Washington's 5th choice, 191st overall, in 2001 Entry Draft).

			Regular Season					Playoffs				
Season	Club	League	GP	G	A	Pts	PIM	GP	G	A	Pts	PIM
99-2000	HC Slavia Praha Jr.	CzRep-Jr.	15	1	2	3	8	2	1	0	1	0
	Slavia U17	CzR-U17	31	14	12	26	12	....	....	....	....	....
2000-01	HC Slavia Praha Jr.	CzRep-Jr.	44	10	8	18	24	3	1	0	1	2
2001-02	Slavia U17	CzR-U17	3	1	0	1	2	....	....	....	....	....
	HC Slavia Praha Jr.	CzRep-Jr.	23	11	12	23	8	....	....	....	....	....
	HC Slavia Praha	CzRep	27	0	1	1	2	....	....	....	....	....
	HC Brod	CzRep-3	5	0	2	2	0	2	1	0	1	2
2002-03	Beroun	CzRep-2	30	4	7	11	14	....	....	....	....	....
	HC Slavia Praha	CzRep	10	1	0	1	0	6	0	0	0	0
	HC Slavia Praha Jr.	CzRep-Jr.	3	1	1	2	2	2	1	0	1	4
2003-04	HC Plzen Jr.	CzRep-Jr.	34	13	18	31	36	....	....	....	....	....
	HC Havirov	CzRep-2	5	0	0	0	4	....	....	....	....	....
	HC Havirov Jr.	CzRep-Jr.	6	0	0	0	6	....	....	....	....	....
2004-05			DID NOT PLAY									

NOVOTNY, Jiri (NOH-vaht-nee, YOO-ree) BUF.

Center. Shoots right. 6'2", 204 lbs. Born, Pelhrimov, Czech., August 12, 1983.
(Buffalo's 1st choice, 22nd overall, in 2001 Entry Draft).

			Regular Season					Playoffs				
Season	Club	League	GP	G	A	Pts	PIM	GP	G	A	Pts	PIM
99-2000	C. Budejovice Jr.	CzRep-Jr.	36	11	10	21	6	....	....	....	....	....
	C. Budejovice U17	CzR-U17	11	5	7	12	4	....	....	....	....	....
	HC Slezan Opava	CzRep-2	17	2	2	4	6	....	....	....	....	....
2000-01	C. Budejovice Jr.	CzRep-Jr.	33	10	10	20	....	....	....	....	....	....
	Havl. Brod	CzRep-3	1	0	0	0	0	....	....	....	....	....
2001-02	C. Budejovice Jr.	CzRep-Jr.	7	4	4	8	4	....	....	....	....	....
	Jind. Hradec	CzRep-3	3	1	3	4	0	....	....	....	....	....
	C. Budejovice	CzRep	41	8	6	14	6	....	....	....	....	....
2002-03	Rochester	AHL	43	2	9	11	14	3	0	1	1	10
2003-04	Rochester	AHL	48	1	14	15	16	13	0	1	1	10
2004-05	Rochester	AHL	61	5	20	25	36	9	2	2	4	4

NUSSLI, Thomas (NEWS-lee, TAW-muhs) VAN.

Right wing. Shoots left. 6'4", 207 lbs. Born, Nesskin, Switz., March 12, 1982.
(Vancouver's 10th choice, 277th overall, in 2002 Entry Draft).

			Regular Season					Playoffs				
Season	Club	League	GP	G	A	Pts	PIM	GP	G	A	Pts	PIM
1998-99	SC Herisau Jr.	Swiss-Jr.	33	30	15	45	24	....	....	....	....	....
	SC Herisau	Swiss-2	5	1	0	1	0	3	1	0	1	0
99-2000	EV Zug	Swiss	2	0	0	0	0	....	....	....	....	....
	EV Zug Jr.	Swiss-Jr.	33	14	18	32	99	2	1	1	2	8
2000-01	Basel	Swiss-2	6	1	2	3	6	....	....	....	....	....
	EV Zug Jr.	Swiss-Jr.	9	7	7	14	30	....	....	....	....	....
	EV Zug	Swiss	34	6	2	8	10	4	0	0	0	2
2001-02	EV Zug Jr.	Swiss-Jr.	1	0	1	1	0	....	....	....	....	....
	EV Zug	Swiss	19	2	2	4	8	....	....	....	....	....
	EHC Basel	Swiss-2	15	3	1	4	70	....	....	....	....	....
	Rapperswil	Swiss	....	....	....	....	....	5	1	1	2	2
2002-03	Rapperswil	Swiss	40	6	5	11	43	6	0	0	0	4
2003-04	Rapperswil	Swiss	37	6	6	12	18	....	....	....	....	....
2004-05	EHC Basel	Swiss-2	42	23	18	41	58	16	8	8	16	10

NYSTROM, Eric (NIGH-stuhm, AIR-ihk) CGY.

Left wing. Shoots left. 6'1", 205 lbs. Born, Syosset, NY, February 14, 1983.
(Calgary's 1st choice, 10th overall, in 2002 Entry Draft).

			Regular Season					Playoffs				
Season	Club	League	GP	G	A	Pts	PIM	GP	G	A	Pts	PIM
99-2000	USA U-17	USDP	55	7	16	23	57	....	....	....	....	....
2000-01	USA U-18	USDP	66	15	17	32	102	....	....	....	....	....
2001-02	U. of Michigan	CCHA	40	18	13	31	42	....	....	....	....	....
2002-03	U. of Michigan	CCHA	39	15	11	26	24	....	....	....	....	....
2003-04	U. of Michigan	CCHA	43	10	12	22	50	....	....	....	....	....
2004-05	U. of Michigan	CCHA	38	13	19	32	33	....	....	....	....	....

CCHA All-Rookie Team (2002)

O'BRIEN, Doug (oh-BRIGH-uhn, DUHG) T.B.

Defense. Shoots left. 6'1", 200 lbs. Born, St. John's, Nfld., February 16, 1984.
(Tampa Bay's 4th choice, 192nd overall, in 2003 Entry Draft).

			Regular Season					Playoffs				
Season	Club	League	GP	G	A	Pts	PIM	GP	G	A	Pts	PIM
2000-01	Hull Olympiques	QMJHL	47	1	6	7	16	5	0	1	1	0
2001-02	Hull Olympiques	QMJHL	46	1	5	6	36	12	0	0	0	14
2002-03	Hull Olympiques	QMJHL	71	10	34	44	102	19	3	12	15	18
2003-04	Gatineau	QMJHL	66	17	46	63	146	15	1	8	9	16
2004-05	Springfield Falcons	AHL	74	4	13	17	76	....	....	....	....	....
	Johnstown Chiefs	ECHL	3	0	0	0	2	....	....	....	....	....

QMJHL First All-Star Team (2004) • Memorial Cup Tournament All-Star Team (2003, 2004) • Ed Chynoweth Trophy (Memorial Cup Tournament Leading Scorer) (2004)

O'BRIEN, Shane (oh-BRIGH-uhn, SHAYN) ANA.

Defense. Shoots left. 6'2", 237 lbs. Born, Port Hope, Ont., August 9, 1983.
(Anaheim's 8th choice, 250th overall, in 2003 Entry Draft).

			Regular Season					Playoffs				
Season	Club	League	GP	G	A	Pts	PIM	GP	G	A	Pts	PIM
99-2000	Port Hope	OPJHL	47	6	27	33	110	....	....	....	....	....
2000-01	Kingston	OHL	61	2	12	14	89	4	0	1	1	6
2001-02	Kingston	OHL	67	10	23	33	132	1	0	0	0	2
2002-03	Kingston	OHL	28	8	15	23	100	....	....	....	....	....
	St. Michael's	OHL	34	8	11	19	108	19	4	10	14	*79
2003-04	Cincinnati	AHL	60	2	8	10	163	9	0	2	2	20
2004-05	Cincinnati	AHL	77	5	20	25	319	12	1	3	4	57

O'BYRNE, Ryan (oh-BUHRN, RIGH-uhn) MTL.

Defense. Shoots right. 6'5", 223 lbs. Born, Victoria, B.C., July 19, 1984.
(Montreal's 4th choice, 79th overall, in 2003 Entry Draft).

			Regular Season					Playoffs				
Season	Club	League	GP	G	A	Pts	PIM	GP	G	A	Pts	PIM
2001-02	Victoria Salsa	BCHL	52	2	9	11	91	....	....	....	....	....
2002-03	Victoria Salsa	BCHL	32	3	6	9	94	....	....	....	....	....
	Nanaimo Clippers	BCHL	9	2	4	6	24	....	....	....	....	....
2003-04	Cornell Big Red	ECAC	31	0	2	2	71	....	....	....	....	....
2004-05	Cornell Big Red	ECAC	33	3	7	10	68	....	....	....	....	....

ODUYA, John (oh-DOO-yuh, JAWN) WSH.

Defense. Shoots left. 6', 200 lbs. Born, Stockholm, Sweden, October 1, 1981.
(Washington's 6th choice, 221st overall, in 2001 Entry Draft).

			Regular Season					Playoffs				
Season	Club	League	GP	G	A	Pts	PIM	GP	G	A	Pts	PIM
1996-97	Hammarby Jr.	Swe-Jr.	13	0	0	0	....	....	....	....	....	....
1997-98	Hammarby Jr.	Swe-Jr.	26	3	11	14	70	....	....	....	....	....
1998-99	Hammarby Jr.	Swe-Jr.	38	14	31	45	45	....	....	....	....	....
99-2000	Hammarby Jr.	Swe-Jr.	32	3	18	21	48	6	1	2	3	4
	Hammarby	Sweden-2	1	0	0	0	0	1	0	0	0	0
2000-01	Moncton Wildcats	QMJHL	44	11	38	49	147	....	....	....	....	....
	Victoriaville Tigres	QMJHL	24	3	16	19	112	13	4	9	13	10
2001-02	Hammarby	Sweden-2	46	11	14	25	66	2	1	0	1	4
2002-03	Hammarby	Sweden-2	48	15	25	40	200	....	....	....	....	....
2003-04	Djurgarden	Sweden	42	4	4	8	*173	4	0	0	0	6
2004-05	Djurgarden	Sweden	49	2	4	6	139	12	0	2	2	39

OGORODNIKOV, Sergei (oh-goh-RAWD-nee-kawf, SAIR-gay) NYI

Center. Shoots left. 6', 178 lbs. Born, Irkutsk, USSR, January 21, 1986.
(NY Islanders' 3rd choice, 82nd overall, in 2004 Entry Draft).

			Regular Season					Playoffs				
Season	Club	League	GP	G	A	Pts	PIM	GP	G	A	Pts	PIM
2002-03	Dyn'o Moscow 2	Russia-3	STATISTICS NOT AVAILABLE									
2003-04	Dyn'o Moscow 2	Russia-3	STATISTICS NOT AVAILABLE									
	THK Tver	Russia-2	21	8	3	11	14	....	....	....	....	....
2004-05	CSKA Moscow	Russia	18	2	4	6	2	....	....	....	....	....

O'HANLEY, Brian (oh-HAN-lee, BRIGH-uhn) S.J.

Defense. Shoots left. 6', 177 lbs. Born, Quincy, MA, December 18, 1984.
(San Jose's 10th choice, 267th overall, in 2003 Entry Draft).

			Regular Season					Playoffs				
Season	Club	League	GP	G	A	Pts	PIM	GP	G	A	Pts	PIM
2001-02	Bos. College High	High-MA	24	22	13	35	20	....	....	....	....	....
2002-03	Bos. College High	High-MA	23	22	21	43	12	....	....	....	....	....
2003-04	Salisbury School	High-CT	26	11	28	39	....	....	....	....	....	....
2004-05	Boston College	H-East	35	2	11	13	18	....	....	....	....	....

OLESZ, Rostislav (OH-lehsh, RAHS-tih-slav) **FLA.**

Center. Shoots left. 6'1", 207 lbs. Born, Bilovec, Czech., October 10, 1985.
(Florida's 1st choice, 7th overall, in 2004 Entry Draft).

			Regular Season					Playoffs				
Season	Club	League	GP	G	A	Pts	PIM	GP	G	A	Pts	PIM
2000-01	HC Vitkovice Jr.	CzRep-Jr.	15	10	3	13	14	....	....	....	....	....
	HC Vitkovice	CzRep	3	0	1	1	0	....	....	....	....	....
2001-02	HC Vitkovice	CzRep	11	1	2	3	0	....	....	....	....	....
	HC Vitkovice Jr.	CzRep-Jr.	34	19	20	39	81	2	0	0	0	2
2002-03	HC Vitkovice	CzRep	40	6	3	9	41	5	0	0	0	2
	HC Vitkovice Jr.	CzRep-Jr.	7	1	1	2	12	....	....	....	....	....
	HC Slezan Opava	CzRep-2	1	0	0	0	0	....	....	....	....	....
2003-04	HC Vitkovice Jr.	CzRep-Jr.	3	2	0	2	0	....	....	....	....	....
	HC Vitkovice	CzRep	35	1	11	12	10	6	2	1	3	4
	HC Dukla Jihlava	CzRep-2	2	1	0	1	0	1	0	0	0	0
2004-05	HC Sparta Praha	CzRep	47	6	7	13	12	5	0	2	2	0
	Sparta Jr.	CzRep-Jr.	....	....	....	....	....	1	0	1	1	0

OLSON, Glenn (OHL-suhn, GLEHN) **S.J.**

Left wing. Shoots left. 6'4", 230 lbs. Born, Fort McNeil, B.C., May 1, 1984.

			Regular Season					Playoffs				
Season	Club	League	GP	G	A	Pts	PIM	GP	G	A	Pts	PIM
2002-03	Cowichan Valley	BCHL	41	1	4	5	168	....	....	....	....	....
2003-04	Kootenay Ice	WHL	41	2	1	3	126	4	0	0	0	8
2004-05	Cleveland Barons	AHL	6	0	1	1	12	....	....	....	....	....
	Fresno Falcons	ECHL	10	0	1	1	105	....	....	....	....	....
	Johnstown Chiefs	ECHL	4	0	0	0	9	....	....	....	....	....

Signed as a free agent by **San Jose**, September 18, 2003.

OLSSON, Kalle (OHL-suhn, KAL-ay) **EDM.**

Right wing. Shoots left. 6', 183 lbs. Born, Munkedal, Sweden, January 31, 1985.
(Edmonton's 6th choice, 147th overall, in 2003 Entry Draft).

			Regular Season					Playoffs				
Season	Club	League	GP	G	A	Pts	PIM	GP	G	A	Pts	PIM
2000-01	Lysekils HK Viking	Sweden-4	30	5	5	10	12	....	....	....	....	....
2001-02	V.Frolunda Jr.	Swe-Jr.	35	10	10	20	10	8	1	5	6	4
2002-03	V.Frolunda Jr.	Swe-Jr.	30	22	13	35	18	6	4	3	7	4
2003-04	V.Frolunda Jr.	Swe-Jr.	30	13	13	26	28	5	2	1	3	2
	V.Frolunda	Sweden	4	1	0	1	0	2	0	0	0	0
2004-05	Frolunda	Sweden	1	0	0	0	2	....	....	....	....	....
	Vaxjo Lakers HC	Sweden-2	2	0	1	1	0	....	....	....	....	....
	Frolunda Jr.	Swe-Jr.	33	15	16	31	50	6	2	2	4	0

OLVECKY, Peter (ohl-VEH-tskee, PEE-tuhr) **MIN.**

Center. Shoots left. 6'2", 195 lbs. Born, Trencin, Czech., October 11, 1985.
(Minnesota's 3rd choice, 78th overall, in 2004 Entry Draft).

			Regular Season					Playoffs				
Season	Club	League	GP	G	A	Pts	PIM	GP	G	A	Pts	PIM
2003-04	Dukla Trencin Jr.	Slovak-Jr.	40	16	20	36	74	2	0	0	0	12
	Dukla Trencin	Slovakia	16	0	0	0	18	....	....	....	....	....
	Dukla Trencin U18	Svk-U18	2	0	0	0	0	....	....	....	....	....
2004-05	SHK 37 Piestany	Slovak-2	1	0	0	0	10	....	....	....	....	....
	Dukla Trencin Jr.	Slovak-Jr.	8	1	3	4	10	2	1	4	5	4
	Dukla Trencin	Slovakia	45	10	9	19	49	12	1	0	1	6

OLVER, Darin (AWL-vuhr, DAIR-uhn) **NYR**

Center. Shoots left. 6', 182 lbs. Born, Burnaby, B.C., March 5, 1985.
(NY Rangers' 3rd choice, 36th overall, in 2004 Entry Draft).

			Regular Season					Playoffs				
Season	Club	League	GP	G	A	Pts	PIM	GP	G	A	Pts	PIM
2002-03	Chilliwack Chiefs	BCHL	59	34	55	89	57	....	....	....	....	....
2003-04	Northern Mich.	CCHA	41	13	21	34	26	....	....	....	....	....
2004-05	Northern Mich.	CCHA	40	9	*34	43	30	....	....	....	....	....

O'MARRA, Ryan (oh-MAHR-ah, RIGH-uhn) **NYI**

Center. Shoots right. 6'1", 193 lbs. Born, Tokyo, Japan, June 9, 1987.
(NY Islanders' 1st choice, 15th overall, in 2005 Entry Draft).

			Regular Season					Playoffs				
Season	Club	League	GP	G	A	Pts	PIM	GP	G	A	Pts	PIM
2002-03	Miss. Senators	GTHL	76	51	60	111	83	....	....	....	....	....
	Georgetown	OPJHL	3	0	2	2	0	....	....	....	....	....
	Streetsville Derbys	OPJHL	6	0	1	1	2	....	....	....	....	....
2003-04	Erie Otters	OHL	63	16	16	32	33	9	5	5	10	6
2004-05	Erie Otters	OHL	64	25	38	63	60	6	4	1	5	0

ONDRUS, Ben (AWN-druhs, BEHN) **TOR.**

Left wing. Shoots right. 6', 185 lbs. Born, Sherwood Park, Alta., June 25, 1982.

			Regular Season					Playoffs				
Season	Club	League	GP	G	A	Pts	PIM	GP	G	A	Pts	PIM
1997-98	Sherwood Park	AMBHL	....	....	....	....	....	....	....	....	....	....
1998-99	Swift Current	WHL	46	4	4	8	58	6	0	1	1	8
99-2000	Swift Current	WHL	67	14	15	29	138	12	1	0	1	22
2000-01	Swift Current	WHL	69	13	17	30	151	....	....	....	....	....
2001-02	Swift Current	WHL	67	30	41	71	153	12	4	3	7	18
2002-03	Swift Current	WHL	67	33	36	69	98	3	0	1	1	11
	Idaho Steelheads	WCHL	4	0	3	3	0	5	0	1	1	6
2003-04	St. John's	AHL	60	6	11	17	102	....	....	....	....	....
2004-05	St. John's	AHL	78	7	11	18	137	5	0	1	1	7

Signed as a free agent by **Idaho** (WCHL), March 23, 2003. Signed as a free agent by **St. John's** (AHL), September 1, 2003. Signed as a fee agent by **Toronto**, May 27, 2004.

O'NEILL, Wes (oh-NEEL, WEHS) **NYI**

Defense. Shoots left. 6'4", 200 lbs. Born, Windsor, Ont., March 3, 1986.
(NY Islanders' 4th choice, 115th overall, in 2004 Entry Draft).

			Regular Season					Playoffs				
Season	Club	League	GP	G	A	Pts	PIM	GP	G	A	Pts	PIM
2000-01	Chatham Maroons	OHA-B	51	6	9	15	50	....	....	....	....	....
2001-02	Chatham Maroons	OHA-B	51	9	36	45	....	....	....	....	....	....
2002-03	Green Bay	USHL	50	2	15	17	79	....	....	....	....	....
2003-04	U. of Notre Dame	CCHA	39	2	10	12	28	....	....	....	....	....
2004-05	U. of Notre Dame	CCHA	38	6	14	20	52	....	....	....	....	....

O'REILLY, Cal (oh-RIGH-lee, KAL) **NSH.**

Center. Shoots left. 5'11", 180 lbs. Born, Toronto, Ont., September 30, 1986.
(Nashville's 4th choice, 150th overall, in 2005 Entry Draft).

			Regular Season					Playoffs				
Season	Club	League	GP	G	A	Pts	PIM	GP	G	A	Pts	PIM
2002-03	St. Mary's Lincolns	OJHL-B	46	11	19	30	2	....	....	....	....	....
2003-04	Windsor Spitfires	OHL	61	3	18	21	2	3	0	1	1	0
2004-05	Windsor Spitfires	OHL	68	24	50	74	16	11	4	5	9	4

ORESKOVIC, Phil (oh-rehs-KOH-vich, FIHL) **TOR.**

Defense. Shoots right. 6'3", 217 lbs. Born, North York, Ont., January 26, 1987.
(Toronto's 2nd choice, 82nd overall, in 2005 Entry Draft).

			Regular Season					Playoffs				
Season	Club	League	GP	G	A	Pts	PIM	GP	G	A	Pts	PIM
2003-04	Brampton	OHL	66	0	7	7	64	12	0	2	2	16
2004-05	Brampton	OHL	61	1	6	7	147	6	0	0	0	4

ORESKOVICH, Victor (oh-rehs-KOH-vihvh, VIHK-tohr) **COL.**

Right wing. Shoots right. 6'2", 216 lbs. Born, Whitby, Ont., August 15, 1986.
(Colorado's 2nd choice, 55th overall, in 2004 Entry Draft).

			Regular Season					Playoffs				
Season	Club	League	GP	G	A	Pts	PIM	GP	G	A	Pts	PIM
2002-03	Milton IceHawks	OPJHL	49	28	46	74	51	....	....	....	....	....
2003-04	Green Bay	USHL	58	11	26	37	33	....	....	....	....	....
2004-05	U. of Notre Dame	CCHA	37	1	2	3	69	....	....	....	....	....

ORLOV, Maxim (ohr-LAHF, max-EEM) **WSH.**

Center. Shoots left. 6', 176 lbs. Born, Moscow, USSR, March 31, 1981.
(Washington's 9th choice, 219th overall, in 1999 Entry Draft).

			Regular Season					Playoffs				
Season	Club	League	GP	G	A	Pts	PIM	GP	G	A	Pts	PIM
1998-99	CSKA Moscow	Russia	2	0	0	0	2	1	0	0	0	0
99-2000	CSKA Moscow	Russia	25	0	0	0	2	2	0	0	0	2
2000-01	CSKA Moscow	Russia	41	5	4	9	14	....	....	....	....	....
2001-02	CSKA Moscow 2	Russia-3	7	7	4	11	4	....	....	....	....	....
	CSKA Moscow	Russia	35	3	5	8	14	....	....	....	....	....
2002-03	MGU Moscow	Russia-3	2	0	0	0	0	....	....	....	....	....
	Leninogorsk	Russia-2	25	3	8	11	24	....	....	....	....	....
2003-04	Leninogorsk	Russia-2	35	5	9	14	39	2	0	0	0	0
2004-05	Kristall Saratov	Russia-2	47	13	23	36	46	4	0	0	0	2

ORPIK, Andrew (OHR-pihk, AN-droo) **BUF.**

Defense. Shoots right. 6'3", 200 lbs. Born, East Amherst, NY, March 12, 1986.
(Buffalo's 9th choice, 227th overall, in 2005 Entry Draft).

			Regular Season					Playoffs				
Season	Club	League	GP	G	A	Pts	PIM	GP	G	A	Pts	PIM
2003-04	Thayer Academy	High-MA	32	9	8	17	18	....	....	....	....	....
2004-05	Thayer Academy	High-MA	31	8	12	20	24	....	....	....	....	....

Signed Letter of Intent to attend **Boston College** (H-East) in fall of 2005.

OSHIE, T.J. (OH-shee, TEE-JAY) **ST.L.**

Center. Shoots right. 5'10", 170 lbs. Born, Mt. Vernon, WA, December 23, 1986.
(St. Louis' 1st choice, 24th overall, in 2005 Entry Draft).

			Regular Season					Playoffs				
Season	Club	League	GP	G	A	Pts	PIM	GP	G	A	Pts	PIM
2004-05	Warroad Warriors	High-MN	31	37	62	99	22	....	....	....	....	....
	Sioux Falls	USHL	11	3	2	5	6	....	....	....	....	....

Signed Letter of Intent to attend **North Dakota** (WCHA) in fall of 2005.

O'SULLIVAN, Patrick (oh-SUHL-ih-van, PAT-rihk) **MIN.**

Center. Shoots left. 5'11", 190 lbs. Born, Winston Salem, NC, February 1, 1985.
(Minnesota's 2nd choice, 56th overall, in 2003 Entry Draft).

			Regular Season					Playoffs				
Season	Club	League	GP	G	A	Pts	PIM	GP	G	A	Pts	PIM
99-2000	Strathroy Rockets	OHA-B	45	6	13	19	53	....	....	....	....	....
2000-01	USA U-18	USDP	64	30	45	75	69	....	....	....	....	....
2001-02	Mississauga	OHL	68	34	58	92	61	....	....	....	....	....
	USA U-18	USDP	1	1	0	1	2	....	....	....	....	....
2002-03	Mississauga	OHL	56	40	41	81	57	5	2	9	11	18
2003-04	Mississauga	OHL	53	43	39	82	32	24	12	11	23	16
2004-05	Mississauga	OHL	57	31	59	90	63	5	0	4	4	6

OTCENAS, Ondrej (AHT-chehn-ash, AWN-dray) **CAR.**

Center. Shoots left. 6'2", 187 lbs. Born, Piestany, Czech., March 6, 1987.
(Carolina's 5th choice, 123rd overall, in 2005 Entry Draft).

			Regular Season					Playoffs				
Season	Club	League	GP	G	A	Pts	PIM	GP	G	A	Pts	PIM
2003-04	Dukla Trencin U18	Svk-U18	25	4	4	8	44	....	....	....	....	....
	Dukla Trencin Jr.	Slovak-Jr.	20	8	5	13	9	2	0	0	0	0
2004-05	Dukla Trencin U18	Svk-U18	7	6	4	10	20	1	0	0	0	10
	Dukla Trencin Jr.	Slovak-Jr.	45	11	22	33	66	8	4	3	7	35

OTTOSSON, Kristofer (AW-toh-suhn, KRIHS-tuh-fuhr) **NYI**

Right wing. Shoots left. 5'10", 187 lbs. Born, Stockholm, Sweden, January 9, 1976.
(NY Islanders' 6th choice, 148th overall, in 2000 Entry Draft).

			Regular Season					Playoffs				
Season	Club	League	GP	G	A	Pts	PIM	GP	G	A	Pts	PIM
1993-94	Djurgarden Jr.	Swe-Jr.	13	3	6	9	4	....	....	....	....	....
1994-95	Djurgarden Jr.	Swe-Jr.	15	8	23	31	2	....	....	....	....	....
	Djurgarden	Sweden	30	0	0	0	2	3	0	0	0	0
1995-96	Djurgarden Jr.	Swe-Jr.	15	5	12	17	4	....	....	....	....	....
	Djurgarden	Sweden	32	1	0	1	2	2	0	0	0	0
1996-97	Djurgarden Jr.	Swe-Jr.	2	1	1	2	0	....	....	....	....	....
	Arlanda HC Marsta	Sweden-2	6	6	0	6	0	....	....	....	....	....
	Djurgarden	Sweden	20	0	0	0	2	....	....	....	....	....
	Huddinge IK	Sweden-2	13	1	3	4	2	2	0	1	1	0
1997-98	Huddinge IK	Sweden-2	16	10	13	23	6	14	7	7	14	8
1998-99	Huddinge IK	Sweden-2	27	12	17	29	14	14	3	2	5	2
	Djurgarden	EuroHL	1	0	0	0	0	....	....	....	....	....
99-2000	Djurgarden	Sweden	47	25	15	40	12	13	7	2	9	2
2000-01	Djurgarden	Sweden	46	17	24	41	14	14	*7	4	11	4
2001-02	Djurgarden	Sweden	41	13	8	21	12	4	0	0	0	0
2002-03	Djurgarden	Sweden	46	19	19	38	30	12	1	4	5	0
2003-04	Djurgarden	Sweden	50	7	12	19	16	4	0	1	1	4
2004-05	Djurgarden	Sweden	34	4	9	13	8	11	1	3	4	6

OUELLET, Michel (oo-LEHT, mee-SHEHL) PIT.

Right wing. Shoots right. 6', 201 lbs. Born, Rimouski, Que., March 5, 1982.
(Pittsburgh's 4th choice, 124th overall, in 2000 Entry Draft).

			Regular Season					Playoffs				
Season	**Club**	**League**	**GP**	**G**	**A**	**Pts**	**PIM**	**GP**	**G**	**A**	**Pts**	**PIM**
1997-98	Jonquiere Elites	QAAA	33	20	32	52	52	....	....	....	....	....
1998-99	Rimouski Oceanic	QMJHL	28	7	13	20	10	11	0	1	1	6
99-2000	Rimouski Oceanic	QMJHL	72	36	53	89	38	14	4	5	9	14
2000-01	Rimouski Oceanic	QMJHL	63	42	50	92	50	11	6	7	13	8
2001-02	Rimouski Oceanic	QMJHL	61	40	58	98	66	7	3	6	9	4
2002-03	Wilkes-Barre	AHL	4	0	2	2	0	....	....	....	....	....
	Wheeling Nailers	ECHL	55	20	26	46	40	....	....	....	....	....
2003-04	Wilkes-Barre	AHL	79	30	19	49	34	22	2	10	12	6
2004-05	Wilkes-Barre	AHL	80	31	32	63	56	11	2	3	5	6

AHL All-Rookie Team (2004)

OULAHEN, Ryan (OO-la-hehn, RIGH-uhn) DET.

Center. Shoots left. 6'1", 180 lbs. Born, Newmarket, Ont., March 26, 1985.
(Detroit's 3rd choice, 164th overall, in 2003 Entry Draft).

			Regular Season					Playoffs				
Season	**Club**	**League**	**GP**	**G**	**A**	**Pts**	**PIM**	**GP**	**G**	**A**	**Pts**	**PIM**
2000-01	Wexford Raiders	OMHA	66	38	58	96	18	....	....	....	....	....
2001-02	Newmarket	OPJHL	48	18	17	35	4	....	....	....	....	....
2002-03	Brampton	OHL	61	21	22	43	6	11	2	1	3	2
2003-04	Brampton	OHL	57	17	18	35	26	12	3	7	10	6
2004-05	Brampton	OHL	64	27	31	58	22	5	1	4	5	4

OVECHKIN, Alexander (oh-VEHCH-kihn, al-EHX-AN-duhr) WSH.

Left wing. Shoots right. 6'2", 212 lbs. Born, Moscow, USSR, September 17, 1985.
(Washington's 1st choice, 1st overall, in 2004 Entry Draft).

			Regular Season					Playoffs				
Season	**Club**	**League**	**GP**	**G**	**A**	**Pts**	**PIM**	**GP**	**G**	**A**	**Pts**	**PIM**
2001-02	Dynamo Moscow	Russia	22	2	2	4	4	3	0	0	0	0
	Dyn'o Moscow 2	Russia-3	19	18	8	26	20	....	....	....	....	....
2002-03	Dynamo Moscow	Russia	40	8	7	15	28	5	0	0	0	2
2003-04	Dynamo Moscow	Russia	53	13	11	24	40	3	0	0	0	2
2004-05	Dynamo Moscow	Russia	37	13	13	26	32	10	2	4	6	31

OYSTRICK, Nathan (OI-strihk, NAY-thun) ATL.

Defense. Shoots left. 6', 195 lbs. Born, Regina, Sask., December 17, 1982.
(Atlanta's 7th choice, 198th overall, in 2002 Entry Draft).

			Regular Season					Playoffs				
Season	**Club**	**League**	**GP**	**G**	**A**	**Pts**	**PIM**	**GP**	**G**	**A**	**Pts**	**PIM**
99-2000	Reg. Pat Cdns.	SMHL	43	6	22	28	214	....	....	....	....	....
2000-01	South Surrey	BCHL	STATISTICS NOT AVAILABLE									
2001-02	South Surrey	BCHL	50	15	42	57	142	....	....	....	....	....
2002-03	Northern Mich.	CCHA	34	2	10	12	26	....	....	....	....	....
2003-04	Northern Mich.	CCHA	39	8	20	28	98	....	....	....	....	....
2004-05	Northern Mich.	CCHA	40	7	13	20	87	....	....	....	....	....

CCHA Second All-Star Team (2004) • CCHA First All-Star Team (2005)

PACKARD, Dennis (PA-kuhrd, DEH-nihs) T.B.

Left wing. Shoots left. 6'4", 234 lbs. Born, St. Catherines, Ont., February 9, 1982.
(Tampa Bay's 8th choice, 219th overall, in 2001 Entry Draft).

			Regular Season					Playoffs				
Season	**Club**	**League**	**GP**	**G**	**A**	**Pts**	**PIM**	**GP**	**G**	**A**	**Pts**	**PIM**
99-2000	USA U-18	USDP	55	11	14	25	85	....	....	....	....	....
2000-01	Harvard Crimson	ECAC	33	4	4	8	28	....	....	....	....	....
2001-02	Harvard Crimson	ECAC	32	9	10	19	34	....	....	....	....	....
2002-03	Harvard Crimson	ECAC	30	8	8	16	32	....	....	....	....	....
2003-04	Harvard Crimson	ECAC	36	11	11	22	16	....	....	....	....	....
2004-05	Springfield Falcons	AHL	47	2	8	10	25	....	....	....	....	....
	Johnstown Chiefs	ECHL	15	3	4	7	6	....	....	....	....	....

PADDOCK, Cam (PA-dawk, KAM) PIT.

Center. Shoots right. 6'1", 191 lbs. Born, Vancouver, B.C., March 22, 1983.
(Pittsburgh's 6th choice, 137th overall, in 2002 Entry Draft).

			Regular Season					Playoffs				
Season	**Club**	**League**	**GP**	**G**	**A**	**Pts**	**PIM**	**GP**	**G**	**A**	**Pts**	**PIM**
99-2000	Kelowna Rockets	WHL	46	5	5	10	42	5	0	0	0	0
2000-01	Kelowna Rockets	WHL	72	14	10	24	110	6	0	0	0	4
2001-02	Kelowna Rockets	WHL	72	38	35	73	122	15	8	6	14	35
2002-03	Kelowna Rockets	WHL	71	33	26	59	107	19	11	8	19	18
2003-04	Kelowna Rockets	WHL	62	17	22	39	86	16	3	4	7	22
	Wilkes-Barre	AHL	1	0	0	0	2	....	....	....	....	....
2004-05	Wilkes-Barre	AHL	16	0	0	0	13	....	....	....	....	....
	Wheeling Nailers	ECHL	53	11	18	29	70	....	....	....	....	....

PAETSCH, Nathan (PASH, NAY-thuhn) BUF.

Defense. Shoots left. 6', 198 lbs. Born, Humboldt, Sask., March 30, 1983.
(Buffalo's 8th choice, 202nd overall, in 2003 Entry Draft).

			Regular Season					Playoffs				
Season	**Club**	**League**	**GP**	**G**	**A**	**Pts**	**PIM**	**GP**	**G**	**A**	**Pts**	**PIM**
1998-99	Tisdale Trojans	SMHL	74	20	55	75	120	....	....	....	....	....
	Moose Jaw	WHL	2	0	0	0	0	....	....	....	....	....
99-2000	Moose Jaw	WHL	68	9	35	44	49	4	0	1	1	0
2000-01	Moose Jaw	WHL	70	8	54	62	118	4	1	2	3	6
2001-02	Moose Jaw	WHL	59	16	36	52	86	12	0	4	4	16
2002-03	Moose Jaw	WHL	59	15	39	54	81	13	3	10	13	6
2003-04	Rochester	AHL	54	5	5	10	49	16	1	1	2	28
2004-05	Rochester	AHL	80	4	19	23	150	9	1	1	2	16

• Re-entered NHL Entry Draft. Originally Washington's 1st choice, 58th overall, in 2001 Entry Draft.

WHL East Second All-Star Team (2003)

PAGE, Rob (PAYJ, RAWB) CBJ

Defense. Shoots right. 6'1", 188 lbs. Born, Edina, MN, July 9, 1985.
(Columbus' 7th choice, 167th overall, in 2004 Entry Draft).

			Regular Season					Playoffs				
Season	**Club**	**League**	**GP**	**G**	**A**	**Pts**	**PIM**	**GP**	**G**	**A**	**Pts**	**PIM**
2003-04	Blake Bears	High-MN	28	8	21	29	18	....	....	....	....	....
2004-05	Yale	ECAC	32	2	9	11	68	....	....	....	....	....

PAIEMENT, Jonathan (PAY-mawnt, JAWN-ah-thuhn) NYR

Defense. Shoots left. 6'1", 222 lbs. Born, Montreal, Que., March 7, 1985.
(NY Rangers' 12th choice, 247th overall, in 2004 Entry Draft).

			Regular Season					Playoffs				
Season	**Club**	**League**	**GP**	**G**	**A**	**Pts**	**PIM**	**GP**	**G**	**A**	**Pts**	**PIM**
2001-02	Sherbrooke Castors	QMJHL	65	5	7	12	61	....	....	....	....	....
2002-03	Sherbrooke	QMJHL	71	4	14	18	118	12	2	5	7	18
2003-04	Lewiston	QMJHL	68	13	52	65	140	7	0	2	2	10
2004-05	Lewiston	QMJHL	67	11	51	62	198	8	2	7	9	34

QMJHL First All-Star Team (2004)

PAILLE, Dan (PIGH-yay, DAN) BUF.

Left wing. Shoots left. 6', 200 lbs. Born, Welland, Ont., April 15, 1984.
(Buffalo's 2nd choice, 20th overall, in 2002 Entry Draft).

			Regular Season					Playoffs				
Season	**Club**	**League**	**GP**	**G**	**A**	**Pts**	**PIM**	**GP**	**G**	**A**	**Pts**	**PIM**
99-2000	Welland Cougars	OHA-B	42	14	17	31	19	16	16	16	32	....
2000-01	Guelph Storm	OHL	64	22	31	53	57	4	2	0	2	2
2001-02	Guelph Storm	OHL	62	27	30	57	54	9	5	2	7	9
2002-03	Guelph Storm	OHL	54	30	27	57	28	11	8	6	14	6
2003-04	Guelph Storm	OHL	59	37	43	80	63	22	9	9	18	14
2004-05	Rochester	AHL	79	14	15	29	54	9	2	2	4	6

PAINCHAUD, Chad (PAYN-show, CHAD) ATL.

Left wing. Shoots left. 5'11", 175 lbs. Born, Mississauga, Ont., May 27, 1986.
(Atlanta's 4th choice, 106th overall, in 2004 Entry Draft).

			Regular Season					Playoffs				
Season	**Club**	**League**	**GP**	**G**	**A**	**Pts**	**PIM**	**GP**	**G**	**A**	**Pts**	**PIM**
2002-03	Mississauga Reps	GTHL	52	47	47	94	....	....	....	....	....	....
2003-04	Mississauga	OHL	68	17	25	42	25	24	4	6	10	23
2004-05	Mississauga	OHL	8	3	3	6	11	....	....	....	....	....
	Sarnia Sting	OHL	49	18	16	34	22	....	....	....	....	....

PALIN, Brett (PAY-lihn, BREHT) CGY.

Defense. Shoots right. 6'2", 204 lbs. Born, Nanaimo, B.C., June 23, 1984.

			Regular Season					Playoffs				
Season	**Club**	**League**	**GP**	**G**	**A**	**Pts**	**PIM**	**GP**	**G**	**A**	**Pts**	**PIM**
2000-01	Kelowna Rockets	WHL	39	0	0	0	25	....	....	....	....	....
2001-02	Kelowna Rockets	WHL	70	0	1	1	88	15	0	0	0	4
2002-03	Kelowna Rockets	WHL	71	1	17	18	118	19	0	4	4	12
2003-04	Kelowna Rockets	WHL	72	1	16	17	106	17	0	5	5	24
2004-05	Kelowna Rockets	WHL	72	4	21	25	71	24	4	6	10	52

Signed as a free agent by **Calgary**, August 5, 2005.

PANOV, Konstantin (PAN-ahv, KAWN-stan-tihn) NSH.

Left wing. Shoots left. 6', 195 lbs. Born, Chelyabinsk, USSR, June 29, 1980.
(Nashville's 10th choice, 131st overall, in 1999 Entry Draft).

			Regular Season					Playoffs				
Season	**Club**	**League**	**GP**	**G**	**A**	**Pts**	**PIM**	**GP**	**G**	**A**	**Pts**	**PIM**
1996-97	Yunior-T Kurgan	Russia-3	25	18	30	48	22	....	....	....	....	....
1997-98	Yunior-T Kurgan	Russia-3	20	7	3	10	6	....	....	....	....	....
	Chelyabinsk	Russia	6	2	0	2	4	2	0	0	0	0
1998-99	Kamloops Blazers	WHL	62	33	30	63	62	13	5	3	8	10
99-2000	Kamloops Blazers	WHL	64	43	30	73	47	....	....	....	....	....
2000-01	Kamloops Blazers	WHL	69	44	56	100	54	4	1	0	1	2
2001-02	Milwaukee	AHL	15	1	5	6	2	....	....	....	....	....
2002-03	Milwaukee	AHL	67	11	20	31	30	2	0	0	0	0
	Toledo Storm	ECHL	2	1	0	1	0	....	....	....	....	....
2003-04	Khabarovsk 2	Russia-3	8	8	6	14	5	....	....	....	....	....
	Amur Khabarovsk	Russia	29	0	1	1	10	....	....	....	....	....
2004-05	Chelyabinsk	Russia-2	51	13	22	35	32	8	2	1	3	12

WHL West Second All-Star Team (2000) • WHL West First All-Star Team (2001)

PANZER, Jeff (PAN-zuhr, JEHF)

Center. Shoots left. 5'7", 160 lbs. Born, Grand Forks, ND, April 7, 1978.

			Regular Season					Playoffs				
Season	**Club**	**League**	**GP**	**G**	**A**	**Pts**	**PIM**	**GP**	**G**	**A**	**Pts**	**PIM**
1996-97	Fargo-Moorhead	USHL	49	30	40	70	52	6	3	7	10	0
1997-98	North Dakota	WCHA	37	14	23	37	18	....	....	....	....	....
1998-99	North Dakota	WCHA	37	21	26	47	14	....	....	....	....	....
99-2000	North Dakota	WCHA	44	19	*44	63	16	....	....	....	....	....
2000-01	North Dakota	WCHA	46	26	*55	*81	28	....	....	....	....	....
2001-02	Worcester IceCats	AHL	70	26	27	53	29	3	0	2	2	0
2002-03	Worcester IceCats	AHL	80	22	32	54	36	3	1	1	2	0
2003-04	Worcester IceCats	AHL	60	14	25	39	20	10	1	4	5	4
2004-05	Syracuse Crunch	AHL	51	8	10	18	19	....	....	....	....	....
	Grand Rapids	AHL	20	6	3	9	11	....	....	....	....	....

WCHA Second All-Star Team (1999) • WCHA First All-Star Team (2000, 2001) • WCHA Player of the Year (2001) • NCAA West First All-American Team (2000, 2001)

Signed as a free agent by **St. Louis**, April 30, 2001. Claimed on waivers by **Columbus** from **St. Louis**, September 7, 2004. Loaned to **Grand Rapids** (AHL) by **Syracuse** (AHL) for loan of Nathan Robinson, March 11, 2005.

PAQUET, Jean-Philippe (pah-KEHT, ZHAWN-fihl-EEP) PIT.

Defense. Shoots left. 6'2", 202 lbs. Born, St-George, Que., January 7, 1987.
(Pittsburgh's 6th choice, 194th overall, in 2005 Entry Draft).

			Regular Season					Playoffs				
Season	**Club**	**League**	**GP**	**G**	**A**	**Pts**	**PIM**	**GP**	**G**	**A**	**Pts**	**PIM**
2003-04	Shawinigan	QMJHL	49	0	8	8	45	10	0	1	1	8
2004-05	Shawinigan	QMJHL	70	5	20	25	96	4	1	2	3	2

PAQUET, Philippe (pah-KEHT, Fihl-EEP) MTL.

Defense. Shoots right. 6'3", 200 lbs. Born, Quebec City, Que., March 12, 1987.
(Montreal's 7th choice, 229th overall, in 2005 Entry Draft).

			Regular Season					Playoffs				
Season	**Club**	**League**	**GP**	**G**	**A**	**Pts**	**PIM**	**GP**	**G**	**A**	**Pts**	**PIM**
2003-04	St-Francois	QAAA	39	6	14	20	136	7	0	3	3	10
2004-05	Salisbury School	High-CT	26	1	4	5	10	....	....	....	....	....

Signed Letter of Intent to attend **Clarkson** (ECAC) in fall of 2005.

PARDY, Adam (PAHR-dee, A-duhm) CGY.

Defense. Shoots left. 6'5", 211 lbs. Born, Bonavista, Nfld., March 29, 1984.
(Calgary's 6th choice, 173rd overall, in 2004 Entry Draft).

			Regular Season					Playoffs				
Season	Club	League	GP	G	A	Pts	PIM	GP	G	A	Pts	PIM
2002-03	Yarmouth	MJrHL	1	0	0	0	2	....	....	....	....	....
	Antigonish	MJrHL	31	5	16	21	42	....	....	....	....	....
	Cape Breton	QMJHL	7	0	1	1	2	2	0	0	0	0
2003-04	Cape Breton	QMJHL	68	4	12	16	137	5	0	1	1	8
2004-05	Cape Breton	QMJHL	69	12	27	39	163	5	2	2	4	8

PARENT, Ryan (PAIR-ehnt, RIGH-uhn) NSH.

Defense. Shoots left. 6'2", 183 lbs. Born, Prince Albert, Sask., March 17, 1987.
(Nashville's 1st choice, 18th overall, in 2005 Entry Draft).

			Regular Season					Playoffs				
Season	Club	League	GP	G	A	Pts	PIM	GP	G	A	Pts	PIM
2002-03	Waterloo Siskins	OHA-B	41	2	8	10	35	....	....	....	....	....
2003-04	Guelph Storm	OHL	58	1	5	6	18	22	0	0	0	2
2004-05	Guelph Storm	OHL	66	2	17	19	36	4	0	1	1	4

PARENTEAU, Pierre (pair-ehn-TOH, PEE-air) ANA.

Center. Shoots right. 5'11", 195 lbs. Born, Hull, Que., March 24, 1983.
(Anaheim's 11th choice, 264th overall, in 2001 Entry Draft).

			Regular Season					Playoffs				
Season	Club	League	GP	G	A	Pts	PIM	GP	G	A	Pts	PIM
99-2000	Charles-Lemoyne	QAAA	40	25	40	65	18	16	4	9	13	8
2000-01	Moncton Wildcats	QMJHL	45	10	19	29	38	....	....	....	....	....
	Chicoutimi	QMJHL	28	10	13	23	14	7	4	7	11	2
2001-02	Chicoutimi	QMJHL	68	51	67	118	120	4	3	1	4	10
2002-03	Chicoutimi	QMJHL	31	20	35	55	56	....	....	....	....	....
	Sherbrooke	QMJHL	28	13	35	48	84	12	8	11	19	6
2003-04	Cincinnati	AHL	66	14	16	30	20	7	1	2	3	6
2004-05	Cincinnati	AHL	76	17	24	41	58	9	2	0	2	8

PARISE, Zach (pah-REE-say, ZAK) N.J.

Center. Shoots left. 5'11", 185 lbs. Born, Minneapolis, MN, July 28, 1984.
(New Jersey's 1st choice, 17th overall, in 2003 Entry Draft).

			Regular Season					Playoffs				
Season	Club	League	GP	G	A	Pts	PIM	GP	G	A	Pts	PIM
2000-01	Shat.-St. Mary's	High-MN	58	69	93	162	....	....	....	....	....	....
2001-02	Shat.-St. Mary's	High-MN	67	77	101	178	58	....	....	....	....	....
	USA U-18	USDP	12	7	7	14	6	....	....	....	....	....
2002-03	North Dakota	WCHA	39	26	35	61	34	....	....	....	....	....
2003-04	North Dakota	WCHA	37	23	32	55	24	....	....	....	....	....
2004-05	Albany River Rats	AHL	73	18	40	58	56	....	....	....	....	....

WCHA All-Rookie Team (2003) • WCHA First All-Star Team (2004) • NCAA West First All-American Team (2004)

PAROULEK, Martin (PAHR-oh-lehk, MAHR-tihn) CBJ

Right wing. Shoots right. 6', 193 lbs. Born, Uherske Hradiste, Czech., November 4, 1979.
(Columbus' 9th choice, 278th overall, in 2000 Entry Draft).

			Regular Season					Playoffs				
Season	Club	League	GP	G	A	Pts	PIM	GP	G	A	Pts	PIM
1998-99	HC Vsetin Jr.	CzRep-Jr.	45	25	19	44	....	....	....	....	....	....
	HC Slovnaft Vsetin	CzRep	11	1	1	2	....	7	0	1	1	0
99-2000	Vsetin	CzRep	48	11	14	25	24	8	1	1	2	4
2000-01	HC Draci Sumperk	CzRep-2	14	0	1	1	27	....	....	....	....	....
	HC Slovnaft Vsetin	CzRep	28	10	4	14	16	14	3	3	6	10
2001-02	Syracuse Crunch	AHL	59	11	14	25	31	9	1	1	2	4
2002-03	Syracuse Crunch	AHL	9	0	1	1	6	....	....	....	....	....
	HC Sparta Praha	CzRep	16	1	4	5	16	9	1	1	2	8
2003-04	HC Sparta Praha	CzRep	17	2	1	3	4	....	....	....	....	....
	Plzen	CzRep	19	7	10	17	16	12	1	3	4	12
2004-05	Beroun	CzRep-2	1	0	0	0	0	....	....	....	....	....
	Plzen	CzRep	38	7	11	18	49	....	....	....	....	....

• Released by **Syracuse** (AHL) and signed as a free agent by **Sparta** (CzRep) with Columbus retaining NHL rights, January 13, 2003.

PARROS, George (PAIR-ohs, JOHRJ) L.A.

Right wing. Shoots right. 6'4", 210 lbs. Born, Washington, PA, December 29, 1979.
(Los Angeles' 9th choice, 222nd overall, in 1999 Entry Draft).

			Regular Season					Playoffs				
Season	Club	League	GP	G	A	Pts	PIM	GP	G	A	Pts	PIM
1996-97	Delbarton	High-NJ	14	15	8	23	....	....	....	....	....	....
1997-98	Delbarton	High-NJ	15	22	17	39	....	....	....	....	....	....
1998-99	Chicago Freeze	NAHL	54	30	20	50	126	....	....	....	....	....
99-2000	Princeton	ECAC	27	4	2	6	14	....	....	....	....	....
2000-01	Princeton	ECAC	31	7	10	17	38	....	....	....	....	....
2001-02	Princeton	ECAC	31	9	13	22	36	....	....	....	....	....
2002-03	Princeton	ECAC	22	0	7	7	29	....	....	....	....	....
	Manchester	AHL	9	0	1	1	7	....	....	....	....	....
2003-04	Manchester	AHL	57	3	6	9	126	5	0	0	0	4
2004-05	Reading Royals	ECHL	3	0	0	0	9	....	....	....	....	....
	Manchester	AHL	67	14	8	22	247	6	1	1	2	27

PARSE, Scott (PARS, SKAWT) L.A.

Forward. Shoots right. 6'1", 185 lbs. Born, Kalamazoo, MI, September 5, 1984.
(Los Angeles' 5th choice, 174th overall, in 2004 Entry Draft).

			Regular Season					Playoffs				
Season	Club	League	GP	G	A	Pts	PIM	GP	G	A	Pts	PIM
2002-03	Tri-City Storm	USHL	48	21	23	44	32	3	2	1	3	8
2003-04	Nebraska-Omaha	CCHA	39	16	19	35	52	....	....	....	....	....
2004-05	Nebraska-Omaha	CCHA	39	19	30	49	32	....	....	....	....	....

USHL All-Rookie Team (2003) • CCHA First All-Star Team (2005)

PARSHIN, Denis (PAHR-shihn, DEH-nihs) COL.

Right wing. Shoots left. 5'9", 146 lbs. Born, Rybinsk, USSR, February 1, 1986.
(Colorado's 3rd choice, 72nd overall, in 2004 Entry Draft).

			Regular Season					Playoffs				
Season	Club	League	GP	G	A	Pts	PIM	GP	G	A	Pts	PIM
2002-03	CSKA Moscow 2	Russia-3	4	1	0	1	2	....	....	....	....	....
2003-04	CSKA Moscow	Russia	27	2	4	6	4	....	....	....	....	....
	CSKA Moscow 2	Russia-3	STATISTICS NOT AVAILABLE									
2004-05	CSKA Moscow	Russia	42	3	4	7	18	....	....	....	....	....

PAUKOVICH, Geoff (paw-KOH-vihch, JEHF) EDM.

Left wing. Shoots left. 6'4", 208 lbs. Born, Englewood, CO, April 24, 1986.
(Edmonton's 4th choice, 57th overall, in 2004 Entry Draft).

			Regular Season					Playoffs				
Season	Club	League	GP	G	A	Pts	PIM	GP	G	A	Pts	PIM
2002-03	Tri-City Storm	USHL	31	1	3	4	29	....	....	....	....	....
2003-04	USA U-18	USDP	55	10	11	21	77	....	....	....	....	....
2004-05	U. of Denver	WCHA	41	12	10	22	120	....	....	....	....	....

PAVELSKI, Joe (pah-VEHL-skee, JOH) S.J.

Center. Shoots left. 5'11", 194 lbs. Born, Plover, WI, July 11, 1984.
(San Jose's 7th choice, 205th overall, in 2003 Entry Draft).

			Regular Season					Playoffs				
Season	Club	League	GP	G	A	Pts	PIM	GP	G	A	Pts	PIM
2002-03	Waterloo	USHL	60	36	33	69	32	7	5	7	12	8
2003-04	Waterloo	USHL	54	21	31	52	58	12	6	6	12	10
2004-05	U. of Wisconsin	WCHA	41	16	29	45	26	....	....	....	....	....

USHL All-Rookie Team (2003) • USHL First All-Star Team (2003) • USHL Rookie of the Year (2003) • WCHA All-Rookie Team (2005)

PECKER, Cory (PEH-kuhr, KOH-ree)

Center. Shoots right. 6', 195 lbs. Born, Montreal, Que., March 20, 1981.
(Calgary's 7th choice, 166th overall, in 1999 Entry Draft).

			Regular Season					Playoffs				
Season	Club	League	GP	G	A	Pts	PIM	GP	G	A	Pts	PIM
1995-96	Lac St-Louis Lions	QAAA	5	0	0	0	0	....	....	....	....	....
1996-97	Lac St-Louis Lions	QAAA	40	30	40	70	....	7	4	2	6	....
1997-98	Sault Ste. Marie	OHL	29	3	4	7	15	....	....	....	....	....
1998-99	Sault Ste. Marie	OHL	68	25	34	59	24	5	1	2	3	2
99-2000	Sault Ste. Marie	OHL	65	33	36	69	38	12	6	8	14	8
2000-01	Sault Ste. Marie	OHL	31	24	16	40	37	....	....	....	....	....
	Erie Otters	OHL	30	17	22	39	32	15	14	9	23	16
2001-02	Erie Otters	OHL	56	*53	46	99	108	21	*25	17	*42	36
2002-03	Cincinnati	AHL	77	20	13	33	66	....	....	....	....	....
2003-04	Cincinnati	AHL	54	6	10	16	32	....	....	....	....	....
	Binghamton	AHL	14	3	5	8	27	1	0	0	0	0
2004-05	Cincinnati	AHL	49	4	8	12	51	....	....	....	....	....
	San Diego Gulls	ECHL	3	1	0	1	0	....	....	....	....	....
	Manitoba Moose	AHL	12	1	1	2	8	5	1	0	1	4

OHL Second All-Star Team (2001) • OHL First All-Star Team (2002) • Memorial Cup Tournament All-Star Team (2002)

• Missed majority of 1997-98 season after being diagnosed with Chron's Disease. Signed as a free agent by **Anaheim**, July 8, 2002. Loaned to **Manitoba** (AHL) by **Anaheim** (Cincinnati-AHL) for cash, March 17, 2005.

PELECH, Matt (PEH-lihk, MAT) CGY.

Defense. Shoots right. 6'3", 227 lbs. Born, Toronto, Ont., September 4, 1987.
(Calgary's 1st choice, 26th overall, in 2005 Entry Draft).

			Regular Season					Playoffs				
Season	Club	League	GP	G	A	Pts	PIM	GP	G	A	Pts	PIM
2002-03	Vaughan	GTHL	44	3	13	16	113	....	....	....	....	....
2003-04	Sarnia Sting	OHL	62	4	6	10	39	5	0	1	1	12
2004-05	Sarnia Sting	OHL	31	1	5	6	74	....	....	....	....	....

PELTIER, Derek (PEHL-tyay, DAIR-ihk) COL.

Defense. Shoots left. 5'11", 190 lbs. Born, Plymounth, MN, March 14, 1985.
(Colorado's 5th choice, 184th overall, in 2004 Entry Draft).

			Regular Season					Playoffs				
Season	Club	League	GP	G	A	Pts	PIM	GP	G	A	Pts	PIM
2003-04	Cedar Rapids	USHL	55	7	26	33	34	4	0	0	0	4
2004-05	U. of Minnesota	WCHA	43	6	13	19	22	....	....	....	....	....

PELUSO, Chris (puh-LOO-soh, KRIHS) PIT.

Defense. Shoots left. 5'11", 180 lbs. Born, Wadena, MN, August 21, 1986.
(Pittsburgh's 9th choice, 194th overall, in 2004 Entry Draft).

			Regular Season					Playoffs				
Season	Club	League	GP	G	A	Pts	PIM	GP	G	A	Pts	PIM
2003-04	Brainerd	High-MN	25	10	33	43	....	....	....	....	....	....
2004-05	Sioux Falls	USHL	53	1	7	8	54	....	....	....	....	....

PEMBERTON, James (PEHM-buhr-tuhn, JAYMZ) FLA.

Defense. Shoots right. 6'4", 215 lbs. Born, Providence, RI, October 2, 1983.
(Florida's 6th choice, 124th overall, in 2003 Entry Draft).

			Regular Season					Playoffs				
Season	Club	League	GP	G	A	Pts	PIM	GP	G	A	Pts	PIM
1998-99	Mount St. Charles	High-RI	15	0	1	1	6	6	0	1	1	4
99-2000	Mount St. Charles	High-RI	18	2	11	13	10	6	0	7	7	0
2000-01	Mount St. Charles	High-RI	18	5	14	19	8	5	1	8	9	6
2001-02	N.E. Jr. Coyotes	EJHL	32	9	13	22	59	13	8	5	13	10
2002-03	Providence College	H-East	33	2	9	11	18	....	....	....	....	....
2003-04	Providence College	H-East	37	0	8	8	30	....	....	....	....	....
2004-05	Providence College	H-East	35	3	9	12	22	....	....	....	....	....

PENNER, Dustin (PEH-nuhr, DUHS-tihn) ANA.

Left wing. Shoots left. 6'4", 245 lbs. Born, Winkler, Man., September 28, 1982.

			Regular Season					Playoffs				
Season	Club	League	GP	G	A	Pts	PIM	GP	G	A	Pts	PIM
2001-02	MSU - Bottineau	NJCAA	23	20	12	32	30	....	....	....	....	....
2002-03	U. of Maine	H-East	DID NOT PLAY – FRESHMAN									
2003-04	U. of Maine	H-East	43	11	12	23	52	....	....	....	....	....
2004-05	Cincinnati	AHL	77	10	18	28	82	9	2	3	5	13

NCAA Championship All-Tournament Team (2004)

Signed as a free agent by **Anaheim**, May 12, 2004.

PEREZHOGIN, Alexander (pehr-eh-ZHO-ghin, al-ehx-AN-duhr) **MTL.**

Left wing. Shoots left. 6', 185 lbs. Born, Ust-Kamenogorsk, USSR, August 10, 1983.
(Montreal's 2nd choice, 25th overall, in 2001 Entry Draft).

			Regular Season					Playoffs				
Season	Club	League	GP	G	A	Pts	PIM	GP	G	A	Pts	PIM
1998-99	Omsk 2	Russia-4	10	3	4	7	0	....	....	....	....	....
99-2000	Omsk 2	Russia-3	22	12	11	23	12	....	....	....	....	....
	Avangard Omsk	Russia	1	0	0	0	0	....	....	....	....	....
2000-01	Omsk 2	Russia-3	41	47	24	71	40	....	....	....	....	....
	Avangard Omsk	Russia	....	....	....	....	....	1	0	0	0	0
2001-02	Avangard Omsk	Russia	4	1	0	1	4	....	....	....	....	....
	Mostovik Kurgan	Russia-2	19	14	10	24	10	....	....	....	....	....
2002-03	Avangard Omsk	Russia	48	15	6	21	28	8	0	2	2	4
2003-04	Hamilton Bulldogs	AHL	77	23	27	50	52	5	3	3	6	16
2004-05	Avangard Omsk	Russia	43	15	18	33	18	11	3	2	5	8

PERIARD, Michel (pair-EE-ahr, mee-SHEHL)

Defense. Shoots left. 5'11", 183 lbs. Born, Montreal, Que., November 10, 1979.
(Ottawa's 8th choice, 188th overall, in 1998 Entry Draft).

			Regular Season					Playoffs				
Season	Club	League	GP	G	A	Pts	PIM	GP	G	A	Pts	PIM
1996-97	Charles-Lemoyne	QAAA	40	8	15	23	64	15	7	20	27	....
1997-98	Shawinigan	QMJHL	68	14	30	44	64	5	0	0	0	18
1998-99	Shawinigan	QMJHL	64	14	40	54	90	6	1	2	3	4
99-2000	Rimouski Oceanic	QMJHL	70	25	75	100	58	14	5	17	22	16
2000-01	Louisville Panthers	AHL	7	0	1	1	0	....	....	....	....	....
	Port Huron	UHL	23	1	8	9	30	....	....	....	....	....
	Rockford IceHogs	UHL	31	3	14	17	20	....	....	....	....	....
2001-02	Macon Whoopee	ECHL	72	4	19	23	26	....	....	....	....	....
2002-03	San Antonio	AHL	10	3	5	8	6	....	....	....	....	....
	Laredo Bucks	CHL	50	18	35	53	26	9	3	5	8	4
2003-04	San Antonio	AHL	77	9	23	32	30	....	....	....	....	....
2004-05	Portland Pirates	AHL	52	2	21	23	8	....	....	....	....	....

QMJHL First All-Star Team (2000) • Canadian Major Junior First All-Star Team (2000) • Memorial Cup Tournament All-Star Team (2000)

Signed as a free agent by **Florida**, August 1, 2000.

PERKOVICH, Nathan (puhr-KOH-vihch, NAY-thun) **N.J.**

Right wing. Shoots right. 6'5", 195 lbs. Born, Canton, MI, October 15, 1985.
(New Jersey's 6th choice, 250th overall, in 2004 Entry Draft).

			Regular Season					Playoffs				
Season	Club	League	GP	G	A	Pts	PIM	GP	G	A	Pts	PIM
2003-04	Cedar Rapids	USHL	35	1	7	8	23	4	1	0	1	0
2004-05	Chicago Steel	USHL	37	6	2	8	55	7	2	2	4	4

PERREAULT, Joel (PAIR-oh, JOHL) **ANA.**

Right wing. Shoots right. 6'1", 197 lbs. Born, Montreal, Que., April 6, 1983.
(Anaheim's 7th choice, 137th overall, in 2001 Entry Draft).

			Regular Season					Playoffs				
Season	Club	League	GP	G	A	Pts	PIM	GP	G	A	Pts	PIM
99-2000	Antoine-Girouard	QAAA	19	4	7	11	6	....	....	....	....	....
2000-01	Baie-Comeau	QMJHL	68	10	14	24	46	11	1	1	2	10
2001-02	Baie-Comeau	QMJHL	57	18	44	62	96	5	2	0	2	6
2002-03	Baie-Comeau	QMJHL	70	51	65	*116	93	12	3	7	10	14
2003-04	Cincinnati	AHL	65	14	14	28	38	9	1	1	2	2
2004-05	Cincinnati	AHL	51	9	19	28	40	....	....	....	....	....

QMJHL First All-Star Team (2003) • Canadian Major Junior First All-Star Team (2003)

PERRY, Corey (PAIR-ee, KOHR-ee) **ANA.**

Right wing. Shoots right. 6'2", 202 lbs. Born, Peterborough, Ont., May 16, 1985.
(Anaheim's 2nd choice, 28th overall, in 2003 Entry Draft).

			Regular Season					Playoffs				
Season	Club	League	GP	G	A	Pts	PIM	GP	G	A	Pts	PIM
2000-01	Peterborough	OMHA	64	69	46	115	20	3	3	0	3	0
2001-02	London Knights	OHL	67	28	31	59	56	12	2	3	5	30
2002-03	London Knights	OHL	67	25	53	78	145	14	7	16	23	27
2003-04	London Knights	OHL	66	40	*73	113	98	15	7	15	22	20
	Cincinnati	AHL	....	....	....	....	....	3	1	1	2	4
2004-05	London Knights	OHL	60	*47	*83	*130	117	18	11	*27	*38	46

OHL First All-Star Team (2004, 2005) • Canadian Major Junior First All-Star Team (2005) • Memorial Cup Tournament All-Star Team (2005) • Stafford Smythe Memorial Trophy (Memorial Cup Tournament MVP) (2005)

PERSSON, Kristofer (PAIR-suhn, KRIHS-toh-fuhr) **CGY.**

Right wing. Shoots left. 6'3", 194 lbs. Born, Umea, Sweden, January 14, 1984.
(Calgary's 8th choice, 159th overall, in 2002 Entry Draft).

			Regular Season					Playoffs				
Season	Club	League	GP	G	A	Pts	PIM	GP	G	A	Pts	PIM
99-2000	Bjorkloven Jr.	Swe-Jr.	8	4	1	5	2	....	....	....	....	....
	Sweden 16	Nat-Tm	3	1	0	1	0	....	....	....	....	....
2000-01	Malmo Jr.	Swe-Jr.	16	8	3	11	4	6	1	0	1	2
2001-02	Malmo Jr.	Swe-Jr.	26	9	7	16	2	3	2	0	2	0
2002-03	Malmo Jr.	Swe-Jr.	24	16	12	28	10	....	....	....	....	....
	Ornskoldsviks SK	Sweden-2	20	4	5	9	8	....	....	....	....	....
2003-04	IF Bjorkloven Umea	Sweden-2	30	5	1	6	12	....	....	....	....	....
2004-05	Skovde IK	Sweden-2	48	10	9	19	14	....	....	....	....	....

PERVYSHIN, Andrei (pair-VIHSH-ihn, AWN-dray) **ST.L.**

Defense. Shoots left. 5'8", 156 lbs. Born, Arkhangelsk, USSR, February 2, 1985.
(St. Louis' 11th choice, 253rd overall, in 2003 Entry Draft).

			Regular Season					Playoffs				
Season	Club	League	GP	G	A	Pts	PIM	GP	G	A	Pts	PIM
2003-04	Spartak Moscow	Russia-2	59	3	6	9	14	13	0	1	1	4
2004-05	Ak Bars Kazan 2	Russia-3	....	0	1	1	....	....	....	....	....	....
	Ak Bars Kazan	Russia	52	0	3	3	10	2	0	0	0	0

PESONEN, Janne (PEHS-oh-nihn, YAH-nee) **ANA.**

Wing. Shoots left. 5'11", 180 lbs. Born, Suomussalmi, Finland, May 11, 1982.
(Anaheim's 8th choice, 269th overall, in 2004 Entry Draft).

			Regular Season					Playoffs				
Season	Club	League	GP	G	A	Pts	PIM	GP	G	A	Pts	PIM
2000-01	Karpat Oulu Jr.	Finland-Jr.	41	9	22	31	18	6	1	1	2	0
2001-02	Karpat Oulu Jr.	Finland-Jr.	42	12	19	31	18	3	2	0	2	2
	Karpat Oulu	Finland	9	2	0	2	0	1	0	0	0	0
2002-03	Hokki Kajaani	Finland-2	40	15	21	36	62	3	2	0	2	4
2003-04	Karpat Oulu	Finland	56	17	13	30	28	15	1	1	2	4
2004-05	Karpat Oulu	Finland	55	11	18	29	42	12	2	0	2	0

PESTUNOV, Dmitri (pehs-too-NAWF, dih-MEE-tree) **PHX.**

Center. Shoots left. 5'9", 196 lbs. Born, Ust-Kamenogorsk, USSR, January 22, 1985.
(Phoenix's 2nd choice, 80th overall, in 2003 Entry Draft).

			Regular Season					Playoffs				
Season	Club	League	GP	G	A	Pts	PIM	GP	G	A	Pts	PIM
2002-03	Magnitogorsk	Russia	32	4	0	4	0	....	....	....	....	....
2003-04	Magnitogorsk	Russia	51	6	7	13	40	14	0	3	3	25
	Magnitogorsk 2	Russia-3	6	3	15	18	2	3	0	2	2	4
2004-05	Magnitogorsk	Russia	37	4	4	8	46	....	....	....	....	....
	Spartak Moscow	Russia	12	1	1	2	14	....	....	....	....	....

Signed as a free agent by **Spartak Moscow** (Russia), February 16, 2005.

PETER, Emanuel (PEE-tuhr, ih-MAN-yew-ehl) **CGY.**

Center. Shoots left. 6', 198 lbs. Born, Nieder Uzwil, Switz., June 9, 1984.
(Calgary's 6th choice, 142nd overall, in 2002 Entry Draft).

			Regular Season					Playoffs				
Season	Club	League	GP	G	A	Pts	PIM	GP	G	A	Pts	PIM
99-2000	SC Herisau Jr.	Swiss-Jr.	18	2	12	14	....	....	....	....	....	....
2000-01	EHC Uzwil Jr.	Swiss-Jr.	26	6	20	26	14	1	0	0	0	0
2001-02	Kloten Flyers	Swiss	39	1	7	8	14	3	0	0	0	0
	Kloten Flyers Jr.	Swiss-Jr.	4	1	2	3	4	3	1	0	1	4
	HC Brod	CzRep-3	18	2	10	12	....	....	....	....	....	....
2002-03	Kloten Flyers	Swiss	43	0	10	10	42	5	0	0	0	4
2003-04	Kloten Flyers	Swiss	45	3	6	9	16	....	....	....	....	....
2004-05	Kloten Flyers	Swiss	6	0	0	0	6	....	....	....	....	....

PETERS, Geoff (PEE-tuhrs, JEHF) **ANA.**

Center. Shoots left. 6'1", 205 lbs. Born, Hamilton, Ont., April 30, 1978.
(Chicago's 3rd choice, 46th overall, in 1996 Entry Draft).

			Regular Season					Playoffs				
Season	Club	League	GP	G	A	Pts	PIM	GP	G	A	Pts	PIM
1993-94	Wexford Raiders	MTHL	34	39	26	65	26	....	....	....	....	....
	Wexford Raiders	MTJHL	1	0	0	0	0	....	....	....	....	....
1994-95	Niagara Falls	OHL	57	11	9	20	37	6	2	0	2	4
1995-96	Niagara Falls	OHL	64	25	34	59	51	10	4	4	8	8
1996-97	Erie Otters	OHL	28	12	10	22	39	5	1	3	4	7
1997-98	Erie Otters	OHL	31	15	11	26	36	....	....	....	....	....
	North Bay	OHL	20	11	14	25	22	....	....	....	....	....
	Indianapolis Ice	IHL	2	0	0	0	10	....	....	....	....	....
1998-99	Canada	Nat-Tm	38	9	4	13	50	....	....	....	....	....
	Portland Pirates	AHL	4	1	1	2	9	....	....	....	....	....
99-2000	Cleveland	IHL	68	10	4	14	87	7	0	3	3	4
2000-01	Norfolk Admirals	AHL	73	11	10	21	48	6	0	1	1	6
2001-02	Trenton Titans	ECHL	43	13	21	34	55	....	....	....	....	....
	Columbus	ECHL	22	5	13	18	7	....	....	....	....	....
	Rochester	AHL	10	1	4	5	18	2	0	1	1	0
2002-03	Manchester	Britain	4	0	1	1	4	....	....	....	....	....
	Reading Royals	ECHL	40	15	13	28	40	....	....	....	....	....
	Milwaukee	AHL	8	0	0	0	7	....	....	....	....	....
2003-04	Rochester	AHL	46	7	4	11	109	16	0	4	4	27
2004-05	Rochester	AHL	57	9	8	17	125	9	0	2	2	18

Traded to **North Bay** (OHL) by **Erie** (OHL) with Brett Gibson for Steve Montador, January 16, 1998. Signed as a free agent by **Manchester** (Britain), August 22, 2002. Signed as a free agent by **Reading** (ECHL) after **Manchester** (Britain) folded, November 11, 2002. Signed as a free agent by **Anaheim**, August 30, 2005.

PETERS, Warren (PEE-tuhrz, WAHR-ihn) **CGY.**

Center. Shoots left. 6', 200 lbs. Born, Saskatoon, Sask., July 10, 1982.

			Regular Season					Playoffs				
Season	Club	League	GP	G	A	Pts	PIM	GP	G	A	Pts	PIM
1998-99	Saskatoon Blades	WHL	53	8	6	14	111	....	....	....	....	....
99-2000	Saskatoon Blades	WHL	70	11	17	28	97	10	1	2	3	13
2000-01	Saskatoon Blades	WHL	63	27	14	41	111	....	....	....	....	....
2001-02	Saskatoon Blades	WHL	72	34	26	60	115	7	1	4	5	13
2002-03	Saskatoon Blades	WHL	71	31	44	75	108	6	1	6	7	6
	Portland Pirates	AHL	1	0	0	0	0	....	....	....	....	....
2003-04	Utah Grizzlies	AHL	55	4	4	8	63	....	....	....	....	....
	Idaho Steelheads	ECHL	21	6	7	13	33	....	....	....	....	....
2004-05	Idaho Steelheads	ECHL	69	23	23	46	131	4	0	1	1	12

Signed as a free agent by **Calgary**, August 5, 2005.

PETIOT, Richard (PEH-tee-awt, RIH-chuhrd) **L.A.**

Defense. Shoots left. 6'2", 190 lbs. Born, Daysland, Alta., August 20, 1982.
(Los Angeles' 6th choice, 116th overall, in 2001 Entry Draft).

			Regular Season					Playoffs				
Season	Club	League	GP	G	A	Pts	PIM	GP	G	A	Pts	PIM
2000-01	Camrose Kodiaks	AJHL	55	8	16	24	81	8	2	1	3	8
2001-02	Colorado College	WCHA	39	4	6	10	35	....	....	....	....	....
2002-03	Colorado College	WCHA	38	1	6	7	86	....	....	....	....	....
2003-04	Colorado College	WCHA	39	3	5	8	61	....	....	....	....	....
2004-05	Colorado College	WCHA	26	3	5	8	42	....	....	....	....	....

AJHL All-Rookie Team (2001) • AJHL South Second All-Star Team (2001)

PETRASEK, David (PEH-truh-sehk, DAY-vihd) **DET.**

Defense. Shoots right. 6', 187 lbs. Born, Jonkoping, Sweden, February 1, 1976.
(Detroit's 10th choice, 226th overall, in 1998 Entry Draft).

			Regular Season					Playoffs				
Season	Club	League	GP	G	A	Pts	PIM	GP	G	A	Pts	PIM
1993-94	HV 71 Jr.	Swe-Jr.	14	3	3	6	26	....	....	....	....	....
1994-95	HV 71 Jr.	Swe-Jr.	19	8	9	17	55	....	....	....	....	....
	HV 71 Jonkoping	Sweden	30	0	1	1	6	11	0	0	0	0
1995-96	HV 71 Jr.	Swe-Jr.	12	1	5	6	16	....	....	....	....	....
	HV 71 Jonkoping	Sweden	36	0	1	1	14	1	0	0	0	0
1996-97	HV 71 Jr.	Swe-Jr.	3	0	0	0	0	....	....	....	....	....
	HV 71 Jonkoping	Sweden	49	2	4	6	14	5	0	0	0	4
1997-98	HV 71 Jonkoping	Sweden	43	6	7	13	80	5	2	2	4	14
1998-99	HV 71 Jonkoping	Sweden	45	3	4	7	48	....	....	....	....	....
99-2000	HV 71 Jonkoping	Sweden	46	4	6	10	54	5	1	1	2	41
2000-01	Malmo	Sweden	47	7	7	14	74	9	1	1	2	8
2001-02	Malmo	Sweden	47	2	9	11	48	2	1	0	1	2
2002-03	Malmo	Sweden	50	7	6	13	72	....	....	....	....	....
2003-04	Malmo	Sweden	49	8	16	24	123	....	....	....	....	....
	Malmo	Sweden-Q	10	2	0	2	16	....	....	....	....	....
2004-05	Malmo	Sweden	49	10	15	25	72	....	....	....	....	....
	Malmo	Sweden-Q	10	4	5	9	14	....	....	....	....	....

PETRE, Henrik (PEH-truh, HEHN-rihk) WSH.

Defense. Shoots left. 6'1", 187 lbs. Born, Stockholm, Sweden, April 9, 1979.
(Washington's 5th choice, 143rd overall, in 1997 Entry Draft).

			Regular Season					Playoffs				
Season	Club	League	GP	G	A	Pts	PIM	GP	G	A	Pts	PIM
1995-96	Djurgarden Jr.	Swe-Jr.	21	6	4	10	8	....	....	....	....	....
1996-97	Djurgarden Jr.	Swe-Jr.	20	7	6	13	....	....	....	....	....	....
1997-98	Huddinge IK	Sweden-2	30	4	4	8	30	....	....	....	....	....
	Djurgarden	Sweden	3	0	0	0	0	....	....	....	....	....
1998-99	Huddinge IK	Sweden-2	14	0	1	1	20	....	....	....	....	....
	Djurgarden	Sweden	9	0	0	0	10	....	....	....	....	....
99-2000	Brynas IF Gavle	Sweden	47	3	3	6	73	11	1	0	1	12
	Brynas IF Gavle	EuroHL	5	0	2	2	4	....	....	....	....	....
2000-01	Brynas IF Gavle	Sweden	27	2	3	5	20	4	0	1	1	27
2001-02	Brynas IF Gavle	Sweden	24	2	1	3	49	4	0	0	0	4
2002-03	Brynas IF Gavle	Sweden	47	1	5	6	32	....	....	....	....	....
	Brynas IF Gavle	Sweden-Q	10	1	1	2	10	....	....	....	....	....
2003-04	Brynas IF Gavle	Sweden	10	0	1	1	6	....	....	....	....	....
	Mora IK	Sweden-2	2	1	0	1	4	....	....	....	....	....
2004-05	Mora IK	Sweden	50	1	5	6	32	....	....	....	....	....

PETRELL, Lennart (peh-TREHL, LEH-nahrt) CBJ

Forward. Shoots left. 6'3", 198 lbs. Born, Helsinki, Finland, April 13, 1984.
(Columbus' 8th choice, 190th overall, in 2004 Entry Draft).

			Regular Season					Playoffs				
Season	Club	League	GP	G	A	Pts	PIM	GP	G	A	Pts	PIM
2002-03	HIFK Helsinki Jr.	Finland-Jr.	28	2	2	4	35	7	3	1	4	29
2003-04	HIFK Helsinki Jr.	Finland-Jr.	33	11	17	28	28	10	6	7	13	2
	HIFK Helsinki	Finland	8	0	0	0	2	1	0	0	0	0
2004-05	HIFK Helsinki Jr.	Finland-Jr.	12	5	5	10	10	2	0	1	1	0
	HIFK Helsinki	Finland	35	3	2	5	35	4	0	1	1	2

PETROCHININ, Evgeny (peht-roh-CHIH-nihn, ehv-GEH-nee) CBJ

Defense. Shoots left. 6'2", 190 lbs. Born, Murmansk, USSR, February 7, 1976.
(Dallas' 5th choice, 150th overall, in 1994 Entry Draft).

			Regular Season					Playoffs				
Season	Club	League	GP	G	A	Pts	PIM	GP	G	A	Pts	PIM
1993-94	Spartak Moscow	CIS	2	0	0	0	0	....	....	....	....	....
1994-95	Spartak Moscow	CIS	45	0	2	2	14	....	....	....	....	....
1995-96	Spartak Moscow	CIS	50	5	17	22	18	5	3	0	3	0
1996-97	Spartak Moscow	Russia	32	5	6	11	52	....	....	....	....	....
1997-98	Spartak Moscow	Russia	46	12	6	18	100	....	....	....	....	....
1998-99	Spartak Moscow	Russia	21	4	6	10	14	....	....	....	....	....
	Ak Bars Kazan	Russia	6	0	2	2	2	9	1	1	2	24
99-2000	Magnitogorsk	Russia	33	7	10	17	38	14	2	1	3	26
2000-01	Cherepovets	Russia	40	8	7	15	38	9	2	0	2	40
2001-02	Cherepovets	Russia	35	35	2	8	10	1	0	0	0	0
2002-03	Cherepovets	Russia	29	3	6	9	14	10	1	0	1	0
2003-04	Cherepovets	Russia	43	4	9	13	85	....	....	....	....	....
	Cherepovets 2	Russia-3	1	0	2	2	0	....	....	....	....	....
2004-05	Magnitogorsk	Russia	48	3	4	7	14	3	0	0	0	2

Rights traded to **Columbus** by **Dallas** for Kirk Muller, September 28, 2001.

PETRUZALEK, Jakub (peh-troo-ZAL-ehk, YA-kuhb) NYR

Right wing. Shoots right. 5'9", 170 lbs. Born, Most, Czech., April 24, 1985.
(NY Rangers' 13th choice, 266th overall, in 2004 Entry Draft).

			Regular Season					Playoffs				
Season	Club	League	GP	G	A	Pts	PIM	GP	G	A	Pts	PIM
2002-03	Litvinov Jr.	CzRep-Jr.	21	17	13	30	10	....	....	....	....	....
	Litvinov	CzRep	5	0	0	0	0	....	....	....	....	....
2003-04	Litvinov Jr.	CzRep-Jr.	53	38	51	89	110	2	0	0	0	2
	Litvinov	CzRep	7	0	0	0	2	....	....	....	....	....
	SK HC Banik Most	CzRep-3	1	0	0	0	0	....	....	....	....	....
2004-05	Ottawa 67's	OHL	59	23	40	63	64	21	8	10	18	30

PETTERSSON, Fredrik (PEH-tuhr-sohn, FREHD-rihk) EDM.

Left wing. Shoots right. 5'10", 183 lbs. Born, Goteborg, Sweden , June 10, 1987.
(Edmonton's 7th choice, 157th overall, in 2005 Entry Draft).

			Regular Season					Playoffs				
Season	Club	League	GP	G	A	Pts	PIM	GP	G	A	Pts	PIM
2002-03	V.Frolunda U18	Swe-U18	12	5	7	12	6	....	....	....	....	....
2003-04	V.Frolunda U18	Swe-U18	14	13	8	21	6	7	6	3	9	8
	V.Frolunda Jr.	Swe-Jr.	6	4	1	5	2	2	0	0	0	0
2004-05	Frolunda U18	Swe-U18	2	1	2	3	10	6	4	5	9	10
	Frolunda Jr.	Swe-Jr.	24	9	8	17	32	6	5	3	8	16

PETTERSTROM, Pontus (PEH-tuhr-stawm, PAWN-tuhs) NYR

Left wing. Shoots left. 6', 174 lbs. Born, Nybro, Sweden, April 21, 1982.
(NY Rangers' 8th choice, 226th overall, in 2001 Entry Draft).

			Regular Season					Playoffs				
Season	Club	League	GP	G	A	Pts	PIM	GP	G	A	Pts	PIM
99-2000	Leksands IF U18	Swe-U18	7	1	2	3	4	....	....	....	....	....
	Leksands IF Jr.	Swe-Jr.	37	13	10	23	26	2	0	0	0	4
2000-01	Tingsryds AIF	Sweden-2	24	6	5	11	24	....	....	....	....	....
2001-02	Tingsryds AIF	Sweden-2	41	8	7	15	0	....	....	....	....	....
2002-03	Skelleftea AIK HK	Sweden-2	26	9	5	14	12	....	....	....	....	....
2003-04	Skelleftea AIK HK	Sweden-2	39	12	17	29	18	....	....	....	....	....
2004-05	Skelleftea AIK HK	Sweden-2	53	6	12	18	26	....	....	....	....	....

PHANEUF, Dion (fah-NOOF, DEE-awn) CGY.

Defense. Shoots left. 6'3", 213 lbs. Born, Edmonton, Alta., April 10, 1985.
(Calgary's 1st choice, 9th overall, in 2003 Entry Draft).

			Regular Season					Playoffs				
Season	Club	League	GP	G	A	Pts	PIM	GP	G	A	Pts	PIM
2000-01	Southgate Lions	AMBHL	35	15	50	65	208	4	3	4	7	15
2001-02	Red Deer Rebels	WHL	67	5	12	17	170	21	0	2	2	14
2002-03	Red Deer Rebels	WHL	71	16	14	30	185	23	7	7	14	34
2003-04	Red Deer Rebels	WHL	62	19	24	43	126	19	2	9	11	30
2004-05	Red Deer Rebels	WHL	55	24	32	56	73	7	1	4	5	12

WHL East First All-Star Team (2004, 2005) • WHL Defenseman of the Year (2004, 2005) • Canadian Major Junior First All-Star Team (2004, 2005)

PICARD, Alexandre (pee-KAR, ahl-ehx-AHN-druh) PHI.

Defense. Shoots left. 6'2", 214 lbs. Born, Gatineau, Que., July 5, 1985.
(Philadelphia's 5th choice, 85th overall, in 2003 Entry Draft).

			Regular Season					Playoffs				
Season	Club	League	GP	G	A	Pts	PIM	GP	G	A	Pts	PIM
2000-01	Gatineau Intrepide	QAAA	42	6	15	21	38	11	0	1	1	8
2001-02	Halifax	QMJHL	59	2	12	14	28	13	2	3	5	6
2002-03	Halifax	QMJHL	71	4	30	34	64	25	1	5	6	14
2003-04	Cape Breton	QMJHL	57	10	26	36	44	5	0	0	0	0
2004-05	Halifax	QMJHL	68	15	23	38	46	13	1	5	6	14
	Philadelphia	AHL	....	....	....	....	....	2	0	0	0	0

QMJHL Second All-Star Team (2005)

PICARD, Alexandre (pee-KAR, ahl-ehx-AHN-druh) CBJ

Left wing. Shoots left. 6'2", 190 lbs. Born, Les Saules, Que., October 9, 1985.
(Columbus' 1st choice, 8th overall, in 2004 Entry Draft).

			Regular Season					Playoffs				
Season	Club	League	GP	G	A	Pts	PIM	GP	G	A	Pts	PIM
2000-01	St-Francois	QAAA	5	1	1	2	0	....	....	....	....	....
2001-02	St-Francois	QAAA	41	21	30	51	48	8	2	7	9	8
	Sherbrooke	QMJHL	6	0	3	3	0	....	....	....	....	....
2002-03	Sherbrooke	QMJHL	66	14	15	29	41	12	4	0	4	10
2003-04	Lewiston	QMJHL	69	39	41	80	88	7	7	4	11	6
2004-05	Lewiston	QMJHL	65	40	45	85	160	8	5	2	7	18

QMJHL Second All-Star Team (2004)

PIISPANEN, Arsi (pihz-PAH-nehn, AHR-see) CBJ

Right wing. Shoots right. 6'3", 163 lbs. Born, Jyvaskyla, Finland, July 23, 1985.
(Columbus' 6th choice, 138th overall, in 2003 Entry Draft).

			Regular Season					Playoffs				
Season	Club	League	GP	G	A	Pts	PIM	GP	G	A	Pts	PIM
2002-03	Jokerit Helsinki Jr.	Finland-Jr.	41	20	15	35	10	13	3	5	8	2
2003-04	Jokerit Helsinki Jr.	Finland-Jr.	36	5	25	30	12	10	3	3	6	2
	Jokerit Helsinki	Finland	5	0	0	0	0	4	0	0	0	0
2004-05	JyP Jyvaskyla Jr.	Finland-Jr.	1	0	0	0	0	....	....	....	....	....
	JYP Jyvaskyla	Finland	52	2	10	12	12	3	0	1	1	0

PIKKARAINEN, Hannu (pih-kar-AY-nihn) NYR

Defense. Shoots left. 5'11", 196 lbs. Born, Helsinki, Finland, October 13, 1983.

			Regular Season					Playoffs				
Season	Club	League	GP	G	A	Pts	PIM	GP	G	A	Pts	PIM
2001-02	HIFK Helsinki Jr.	Finland-Jr.	44	8	14	22	24	4	0	2	2	0
2002-03	HIFK Helsinki	Finland	47	1	3	4	8	4	0	0	0	0
	HIFK Helsinki Jr.	Finland-Jr.	11	3	11	14	16	6	1	4	5	4
2003-04	HIFK Helsinki	Finland	16	0	0	0	6	13	0	0	0	2
	HIFK Helsinki Jr.	Finland-Jr.	12	3	9	12	23	5	1	5	6	0
	Salamat	Finland-2	2	0	1	1	2	....	....	....	....	....
2004-05	HIFK Helsinki	Finland	49	7	13	20	36	5	0	0	0	0

Signed as a free agent by **NY Rangers**, August 18, 2005.

PIKKARAINEN, Ilkka (pih-kar-AY-nihn, IHL-kah) N.J.

Right wing. Shoots left. 6'2", 200 lbs. Born, Sonkajarvi, Finland, April 19, 1981.
(New Jersey's 9th choice, 218th overall, in 2002 Entry Draft).

			Regular Season					Playoffs				
Season	Club	League	GP	G	A	Pts	PIM	GP	G	A	Pts	PIM
1998-99	HIFK Helsinki Jr.	Finland-Jr.	37	12	13	25	38	2	1	0	1	27
99-2000	HIFK Helsinki Jr.	Finland-Jr.	28	3	2	5	14	3	1	1	2	2
2000-01	HIFK Helsinki Jr.	Finland-Jr.	38	27	31	58	186	9	2	5	7	26
	HIFK Helsinki	Finland	4	0	0	0	8	2	0	0	0	0
2001-02	HIFK Helsinki	Finland	54	9	9	18	111	....	....	....	....	....
2002-03	HIFK Helsinki	Finland	47	11	12	23	40	....	....	....	....	....
2003-04	Albany River Rats	AHL	63	8	10	18	118	....	....	....	....	....
2004-05	Albany River Rats	AHL	71	12	12	24	102	....	....	....	....	....

PINEAULT, Adam (pih-NOH, A-duhm) CBJ

Right wing. Shoots right. 6'1", 193 lbs. Born, Holyoke, MA, May 23, 1986.
(Columbus' 2nd choice, 46th overall, in 2004 Entry Draft).

			Regular Season					Playoffs				
Season	Club	League	GP	G	A	Pts	PIM	GP	G	A	Pts	PIM
2000-01	Junior Bruins	EJHL	57	30	35	65	56	....	....	....	....	....
2001-02	USA U-17	USDP	58	16	8	24	25	....	....	....	....	....
2002-03	USA U-17	USDP	52	18	19	37	89	....	....	....	....	....
	USA U-18	USDP	4	4	3	7	6	....	....	....	....	....
2003-04	Boston College	H-East	30	4	4	8	32	....	....	....	....	....
2004-05	Moncton Wildcats	QMJHL	61	26	20	46	64	12	2	6	8	18

PISELLINI, Gino (pih-sehl-EE-nee, JEE-noh) PHI.

Right wing. Shoots right. 6', 210 lbs. Born, Melrose Park, IL, August 5, 1986.
(Philadelphia's 5th choice, 149th overall, in 2004 Entry Draft).

			Regular Season					Playoffs				
Season	Club	League	GP	G	A	Pts	PIM	GP	G	A	Pts	PIM
2003-04	Plymouth Whalers	OHL	68	15	15	30	214	9	0	3	3	23
2004-05	Plymouth Whalers	OHL	59	4	6	10	137	4	0	1	1	9

PITTON, Jason (PIH-tuhn, JAY-suhn) NYI

Left wing. Shoots left. 6'2", 196 lbs. Born, Mississauga, Ont., May 23, 1986.
(NY Islanders' 9th choice, 244th overall, in 2004 Entry Draft).

			Regular Season					Playoffs				
Season	Club	League	GP	G	A	Pts	PIM	GP	G	A	Pts	PIM
2002-03	Brampton Capitals	OPJHL	47	23	18	41	46	....	....	....	....	....
	Sault Ste. Marie	OHL	1	0	0	0	0	....	....	....	....	....
2003-04	Sault Ste. Marie	OHL	67	9	11	20	37	....	....	....	....	....
2004-05	Sault Ste. Marie	OHL	68	23	19	42	35	7	2	2	4	4

PLATIL, Jan (PLA-tihl, YAN) OTT.

Defense. Shoots left. 6'2", 195 lbs. Born, Kladno, Czech., February 9, 1983.
(Ottawa's 8th choice, 218th overall, in 2001 Entry Draft).

			Regular Season					Playoffs				
Season	Club	League	GP	G	A	Pts	PIM	GP	G	A	Pts	PIM
1998-99	HC Kladno Jr.	CzRep-Jr.	46	8	12	20	....	....	....	....	....	....
99-2000	HC Kladno Jr.	CzRep-Jr.	39	5	6	11	....	....	....	....	....	....
2000-01	Barrie Colts	OHL	60	6	18	24	114	5	0	0	0	12
2001-02	Barrie Colts	OHL	68	13	34	47	136	20	1	5	6	51
2002-03	Barrie Colts	OHL	61	15	36	51	163	6	1	5	6	8
2003-04	Binghamton	AHL	66	1	3	4	142	....	....	....	....	....
2004-05	Binghamton	AHL	72	1	3	4	198	6	0	1	1	4

PLATONOV, Denis (PLAH-tah-nahv, DIHN-ihs) NSH.

Right wing. Shoots left. 6'3", 205 lbs. Born, Saratov, USSR, November 6, 1981.
(Nashville's 4th choice, 75th overall, in 2001 Entry Draft).

			Regular Season					Playoffs				
Season	Club	League	GP	G	A	Pts	PIM	GP	G	A	Pts	PIM
1997-98	Kristall Saratov 2	Russia-3	20	4	2	6	34	....	....	....	....	....
1998-99	Kristall Saratov	Russia-2	14	1	0	1	61	....	....	....	....	....
99-2000	Kristall Saratov 2	Russia-3	5	0	0	0	37	....	....	....	....	....
	Kristall Saratov	Russia-2	32	9	4	13	60	....	....	....	....	....
2000-01	Kristall Saratov	Russia-2	51	14	6	20	75	....	....	....	....	....
2001-02	Kristall Saratov	Russia-2	50	18	14	32	96	....	....	....	....	....
2002-03	Ak Bars Kazan	Russia	47	8	9	17	49	5	0	0	0	2
2003-04	Milwaukee	AHL	3	0	0	0	0	....	....	....	....	....
	Ak Bars Kazan	Russia	28	5	3	8	18	8	1	0	1	2
	Ak Bars Kazan 2	Russia-3	STATISTICS NOT AVAILABLE									
2004-05	Ak Bars Kazan	Russia	38	3	7	10	10	....	....	....	....	....
	Nizhnekamsk	Russia	11	3	1	4	34	3	0	1	1	2

Assigned to **Kazan** (Russia) by **Nashville**, October 29, 2003.

PLATT, Jason (PLAT, JAY-suhn) EDM.

Defense. Shoots left. 6'1", 210 lbs. Born, San Francisco, CA, April 29, 1981.
(Edmonton's 9th choice, 247th overall, in 2000 Entry Draft).

			Regular Season					Playoffs				
Season	Club	League	GP	G	A	Pts	PIM	GP	G	A	Pts	PIM
1998-99	Omaha Lancers	USHL	56	2	9	11	65	11	0	0	0	8
99-2000	Omaha Lancers	USHL	49	1	6	7	65	4	0	0	0	9
2000-01	Providence College	H-East	26	0	2	2	12	....	....	....	....	....
2001-02	Providence College	H-East	36	2	5	7	60	....	....	....	....	....
2002-03	Providence College	H-East	30	1	7	8	41	....	....	....	....	....
2003-04	Providence College	H-East	34	2	5	7	36	....	....	....	....	....
	Toronto	AHL	1	0	0	0	0	....	....	....	....	....
2004-05	Edmonton	AHL	44	1	1	2	28	....	....	....	....	....

PLEHANOV, Andrei (pleh-HA-nawf, AWN-dray) CBJ

Defense. Shoots right. 6'1", 187 lbs. Born, Nizhnekamsk, USSR, July 12, 1986.
(Columbus' 5th choice, 96th overall, in 2004 Entry Draft).

			Regular Season					Playoffs				
Season	Club	League	GP	G	A	Pts	PIM	GP	G	A	Pts	PIM
2003-04	Nizhnekamsk 2	Russia-3	STATISTICS NOT AVAILABLE									
2004-05	Nizhnekamsk	Russia	2	0	0	0	2	....	....	....	....	....
	Leninogorsk	Russia-2	1	0	0	0	4	....	....	....	....	....
	Perm 2	Russia-3	2	0	0	0	4	....	....	....	....	....

PLIHAL, Tomas (PLEE-hahl, TAW-mahsh) S.J.

Center. Shoots left. 6'1", 195 lbs. Born, Frydlant v Cechach, Czech., March 28, 1983.
(San Jose's 4th choice, 140th overall, in 2001 Entry Draft).

			Regular Season					Playoffs				
Season	Club	League	GP	G	A	Pts	PIM	GP	G	A	Pts	PIM
99-2000	Liberec U17	CzR-U17	38	22	14	36	....	....	....	....	....	....
	Liberec Jr.	CzRep-Jr.	2	0	0	0	0	....	....	....	....	....
2000-01	HC Liberec U17	CzR-U17	18	3	5	8	....	....	....	....	....	....
	HC Liberec Jr.	CzRep-Jr.	33	16	12	28	....	....	....	....	....	....
2001-02	Kootenay Ice	WHL	72	32	54	86	28	22	4	10	14	14
2002-03	Kootenay Ice	WHL	67	35	42	77	113	11	2	4	6	18
2003-04	Cleveland Barons	AHL	51	4	12	16	16	6	0	3	3	2
2004-05	Cleveland Barons	AHL	62	17	11	28	26	....	....	....	....	....

George Parsons Trophy (Memorial Cup Tournament Most Sportsmanlike Player) (2002)

PODLESAK, Martin (PAWD-leh-shahk, MAHR-tihn) PHX.

Center. Shoots left. 6'6", 219 lbs. Born, Melnik, Czech., September 26, 1982.
(Phoenix's 3rd choice, 45th overall, in 2001 Entry Draft).

			Regular Season					Playoffs				
Season	Club	League	GP	G	A	Pts	PIM	GP	G	A	Pts	PIM
99-2000	Sparta Jr.	CzRep-Jr.	24	6	5	11	....	11	6	2	8	....
2000-01	Tri-City Americans	WHL	39	13	13	26	36	....	....	....	....	....
	Lethbridge	WHL	21	8	6	14	23	3	1	1	2	2
2001-02	Lethbridge	WHL	34	14	20	34	33	....	....	....	....	....
2002-03	Springfield Falcons	AHL	3	0	0	0	4	....	....	....	....	....
2003-04	Springfield Falcons	AHL	57	5	9	14	21	....	....	....	....	....
2004-05	Utah Grizzlies	AHL	10	0	1	1	24	....	....	....	....	....

• Missed majority of 2002-03 season recovering from head injury suffered in game vs. Manchester (AHL), October 23, 2002. Missed majority of 2004-05 season recovering from shoulder injury suffered in game vs. Houston (AHL), November 28, 2004.

POHANKA, Igor (poh-HAHN-kah, EE-gohr) ANA.

Center. Shoots left. 6'2", 210 lbs. Born, Piestany, Czech., July 5, 1983.
(New Jersey's 2nd choice, 44th overall, in 2001 Entry Draft).

			Regular Season					Playoffs				
Season	Club	League	GP	G	A	Pts	PIM	GP	G	A	Pts	PIM
1996-97	HK VTJ Piestany Jr.	Slovak-Jr.	3	1	3	4	4	....	....	....	....	....
1997-98	Bratislava Jr.	Slovak-Jr.	40	19	22	41	6	....	....	....	....	....
1998-99	Bratislava Jr.	Slovak-Jr.	40	14	21	35	36	....	....	....	....	....
99-2000	Bratislava Jr.	Slovak-Jr.	57	36	41	77	62	....	....	....	....	....
2000-01	Prince Albert	WHL	70	16	33	49	24	....	....	....	....	....
2001-02	Prince Albert	WHL	58	25	43	68	18	....	....	....	....	....
2002-03	Prince Albert	WHL	56	25	31	56	28	....	....	....	....	....
2003-04	San Diego Gulls	ECHL	11	1	5	6	10	3	0	2	2	0
	Cincinnati	AHL	42	5	6	11	6	4	0	0	0	0
2004-05	Cincinnati	AHL	35	5	3	8	18	....	....	....	....	....

Traded to **Anaheim** by **New Jersey** with Petr Sykora, Mike Commodore and Jean-Francois Damphousse for Jeff Friesen, Oleg Tverdovsky and Maxim Balmochnykh, July 6, 2002.

POHL, Petr (PAWL, PEE-tuhr) CBJ

Right wing. Shoots right. 5'11", 185 lbs. Born, Prostejov, Czech., August 28, 1986.
(Columbus' 6th choice, 133rd overall, in 2004 Entry Draft).

			Regular Season					Playoffs				
Season	Club	League	GP	G	A	Pts	PIM	GP	G	A	Pts	PIM
2001-02	HC Vitkovice U17	CzR-U17	38	34	19	53	65	2	1	0	1	4
	HC Vitkovice Jr.	CzRep-Jr.	10	0	2	2	2	....	....	....	....	....
2002-03	HC Vitkovice Jr.	CzRep-Jr.	36	13	22	35	30	2	1	0	1	6
2003-04	Gatineau	QMJHL	70	23	27	50	16	8	0	2	2	2
2004-05	Gatineau	QMJHL	62	27	32	59	16	10	6	4	10	4

POKULOK, Sasha (poh-KUH-lawk, SA-shuh) WSH.

Defense. Shoots left. 6'5", 220 lbs. Born, Montreal, Que., May 25, 1986.
(Washington's 1st choice, 14th overall, in 2005 Entry Draft).

			Regular Season					Playoffs				
Season	Club	League	GP	G	A	Pts	PIM	GP	G	A	Pts	PIM
2003-04	Notre Dame	SJHL	39	7	16	23	34	....	....	....	....	....
2004-05	Cornell Big Red	ECAC	26	3	7	10	33	....	....	....	....	....

ECAC All-Rookie Team (2005)

POLAK, Roman (POH-lahk, ROH-muhn) ST.L.

Defense. Shoots right. 6'1", 198 lbs. Born, Ostrava, Czech., April 28, 1986.
(St. Louis' 6th choice, 180th overall, in 2004 Entry Draft).

			Regular Season					Playoffs				
Season	Club	League	GP	G	A	Pts	PIM	GP	G	A	Pts	PIM
2001-02	HC Ostrava Jr.	CzRep-Jr.	46	4	9	13	84	....	....	....	....	....
2002-03	HC Ostrava Jr.	CzRep-Jr.	32	3	12	15	34	....	....	....	....	....
2003-04	HC Vitkovice Jr.	CzRep-Jr.	52	4	8	12	48	....	....	....	....	....
2004-05	Kootenay Ice	WHL	65	5	18	23	85	9	0	0	0	6

POLAK, Vojtech (POH-lahk, VOI-tehk) DAL.

Left wing. Shoots left. 5'11", 180 lbs. Born, Ostrov nad Ohri, Czech., June 27, 1985.
(Dallas' 2nd choice, 36th overall, in 2003 Entry Draft).

			Regular Season					Playoffs				
Season	Club	League	GP	G	A	Pts	PIM	GP	G	A	Pts	PIM
99-2000	Karlovy Vary Jr.	CzRep-Jr.	49	17	23	40	48	....	....	....	....	....
2000-01	Karlovy Vary Jr.	CzRep-Jr.	47	36	33	69	38	....	....	....	....	....
	Karlovy Vary	CzRep	2	0	0	0	0	....	....	....	....	....
2001-02	Karlovy Vary Jr.	CzRep-Jr.	37	11	14	25	26	....	....	....	....	....
	Karlovy Vary	CzRep	9	1	1	2	2	....	....	....	....	....
2002-03	Karlovy Vary	CzRep	41	7	9	16	51	....	....	....	....	....
	Karlovy Vary Jr.	CzRep-Jr.	6	3	7	10	18	....	....	....	....	....
2003-04	HC Sparta Praha	CzRep	1	1	0	1	0	....	....	....	....	....
	Karlovy Vary	CzRep	44	0	8	8	42	....	....	....	....	....
	Karlovy Vary Jr.	CzRep-Jr.	5	8	4	12	2	....	....	....	....	....
2004-05	Jihlava Jr.	CzRep-Jr.	5	4	1	5	6	....	....	....	....	....
	HC Dukla Jihlava	CzRep	16	1	2	3	12	....	....	....	....	....
	Karlovy Vary Jr.	CzRep-Jr.	3	5	5	10	6	....	....	....	....	....
	SK Kadan	CzRep-2	7	1	2	3	39	....	....	....	....	....
	Karlovy Vary	CzRep	26	1	5	6	4	....	....	....	....	....

POLCIK, Peter (POHL-chihk, PEE-tuhr) WSH.

Right wing. Shoots left. 6'4", 190 lbs. Born, Nitra, Czech., July 23, 1983.
(Washington's 8th choice, 254th overall, in 2001 Entry Draft).

			Regular Season					Playoffs				
Season	Club	League	GP	G	A	Pts	PIM	GP	G	A	Pts	PIM
1998-99	Nitra Jr.	Slovak-Jr.	35	13	16	29	14	....	....	....	....	....
99-2000	Nitra Jr.	Slovak-Jr.	40	26	20	46	82	....	....	....	....	....
2000-01	Nitra Jr.	Slovak-Jr.	42	8	10	18	32	....	....	....	....	....
2001-02	Montreal Rocket	QMJHL	70	9	12	21	35	2	0	0	0	0
2002-03	HKM Nitra Jr.	Slovak-Jr.	45	20	21	41	53	2	1	0	1	2
	HKM Nitra	Slovak-2	18	3	1	4	2	....	....	....	....	....
2003-04	HKm Nitra	Slovakia	4	0	0	0	0	....	....	....	....	....
	Usti n. L.	CzRep-2	3	0	0	0	4	....	....	....	....	....
	HK 91 Senica	Slovak-2	10	2	5	7	14	4	0	0	0	2
2004-05	HK Trnava	Slovak-2	12	1	1	2	4	....	....	....	....	....
	HK 91 Senica	Slovak-2	23	5	13	18	6	5	0	2	2	0

POLUSHIN, Alexander (puh-LOOSH-ihn, al-ehx-AN-duhr) T.B.

Center. Shoots left. 6'2", 212 lbs. Born, Kirovo-Chepetsk, USSR, May 8, 1983.
(Tampa Bay's 2nd choice, 47th overall, in 2001 Entry Draft).

			Regular Season					Playoffs				
Season	Club	League	GP	G	A	Pts	PIM	GP	G	A	Pts	PIM
99-2000	Dyn'o Moscow 2	Russia-3	18	4	3	7	14	....	....	....	....	....
	Spartak Moscow	Russia-2	14	1	0	1	2	....	....	....	....	....
2000-01	THK Tver	Russia-2	38	10	5	15	10	....	....	....	....	....
2001-02	HK CSKA Moscow	Russia-2	55	28	21	49	18	....	....	....	....	....
2002-03	CSKA Moscow	Russia	47	5	6	11	22	....	....	....	....	....
2003-04	CSKA Moscow	Russia	13	5	2	7	4	....	....	....	....	....
2004-05	CSKA Moscow	Russia	17	3	4	7	4	....	....	....	....	....

PORTER, Chris (POHR-tuhr, KRIHS) CHI.

Center. Shoots left. 6'1", 203 lbs. Born, Toronto, Ont., May 29, 1984.
(Chicago's 10th choice, 282nd overall, in 2003 Entry Draft).

			Regular Season					Playoffs				
Season	Club	League	GP	G	A	Pts	PIM	GP	G	A	Pts	PIM
2001-02	Shat.-St. Mary's	High-MN	75	10	25	35	32	....	....	....	....	....
2002-03	Lincoln Stars	USHL	59	13	22	35	74	10	4	3	7	10
2003-04	North Dakota	WCHA	41	10	15	25	46	....	....	....	....	....
2004-05	North Dakota	WCHA	45	12	3	15	36	....	....	....	....	....

PORTER, Kevin (POHR-tuhr, KEH-vihn) PHX.

Left wing. Shoots left. 5'11", 194 lbs. Born, Detroit, MI, March 12, 1986.
(Phoenix's 5th choice, 119th overall, in 2004 Entry Draft).

			Regular Season					Playoffs				
Season	Club	League	GP	G	A	Pts	PIM	GP	G	A	Pts	PIM
2002-03	USA U-17	USDP	59	28	20	48	25	....	....	....	....	....
	USA U-18	USDP	13	1	2	3	2	....	....	....	....	....
2003-04	USA U-18	USDP	55	8	29	37	30	....	....	....	....	....
2004-05	U. of Michigan	CCHA	39	11	13	24	51	....	....	....	....	....

POSPISIL, Tomas (PAWS-pih-shihl, TAW-mash) ATL.

Right wing. Shoots right. 6', 185 lbs. Born, Sumperk, Czech., August 25, 1987.
(Atlanta's 6th choice, 135th overall, in 2005 Entry Draft).

			Regular Season					Playoffs				
Season	Club	League	GP	G	A	Pts	PIM	GP	G	A	Pts	PIM
2002-03	HC Trinec U17	CzR-U17	41	24	28	52	44	2	0	1	1	2
	HC Trinec Jr.	CzRep-Jr.	2	0	0	0	0	2	0	0	0	0
2003-04	HC Trinec U17	CzR-U17	3	3	3	6	14	5	5	2	7	26
	HC Trinec Jr.	CzRep-Jr.	45	14	11	25	40	2	1	1	2	0
2004-05	HC Ocelari Trinec	CzRep	14	0	0	0	0	....	....	....	....	....
	HC Trinec Jr.	CzRep-Jr.	38	19	18	37	44	5	4	1	5	27

POTTER, Corey (PAW-tuhr, KOHR-ee) NYR

Defense. Shoots right. 6'2", 191 lbs. Born, Lansing, MI, January 5, 1984.
(NY Rangers' 4th choice, 122nd overall, in 2003 Entry Draft).

			Regular Season					Playoffs				
Season	Club	League	GP	G	A	Pts	PIM	GP	G	A	Pts	PIM
99-2000	Det. Honeybaked	MWEHL	58	10	38	48	....	....	....	....	....	....
2000-01	USA U-17	USDP	66	4	4	8	26	....	....	....	....	....
2001-02	USA U-18	USDP	61	6	11	17	65	....	....	....	....	....
2002-03	Michigan State	CCHA	35	4	4	8	30	....	....	....	....	....
2003-04	Michigan State	CCHA	38	0	8	8	63	....	....	....	....	....
2004-05	Michigan State	CCHA	32	0	6	6	73	....	....	....	....	....

POTULNY, Grant (poh-TUHL-nee, GRANT)

Center. Shoots left. 6'3", 205 lbs. Born, Grand Forks, ND, March 4, 1980.
(Ottawa's 7th choice, 157th overall, in 2000 Entry Draft).

			Regular Season					Playoffs				
Season	Club	League	GP	G	A	Pts	PIM	GP	G	A	Pts	PIM
1998-99	Lincoln Stars	USHL	46	7	11	18	76	10	2	1	3	7
99-2000	Lincoln Stars	USHL	56	25	30	55	85	10	3	4	7	4
2000-01	U. of Minnesota	WCHA	42	22	11	33	38	....	....	....	....	....
2001-02	U. of Minnesota	WCHA	43	15	19	34	38	....	....	....	....	....
2002-03	U. of Minnesota	WCHA	23	15	8	23	12	....	....	....	....	....
2003-04	U. of Minnesota	WCHA	38	16	10	26	28	....	....	....	....	....
	Binghamton	AHL	3	0	1	1	0	2	0	0	0	0
2004-05	Binghamton	AHL	50	4	6	10	104	6	0	0	0	2

NCAA Championship All-Tournament Team (2002) • NCAA Championship Tournament MVP (2002)

POTULNY, Ryan (poh-TUHL-nee, RIGH-uhn) PHI.

Center. Shoots left. 6', 190 lbs. Born, Grand Forks, ND, September 5, 1984.
(Philadelphia's 6th choice, 87th overall, in 2003 Entry Draft).

			Regular Season					Playoffs				
Season	Club	League	GP	G	A	Pts	PIM	GP	G	A	Pts	PIM
2001-02	Lincoln Stars	USHL	60	23	34	57	65	4	0	1	1	2
2002-03	Lincoln Stars	USHL	54	35	*43	*78	18	10	6	*11	*17	8
2003-04	U. of Minnesota	WCHA	15	6	8	14	10	....	....	....	....	....
2004-05	U. of Minnesota	WCHA	44	24	17	41	20	....	....	....	....	....

USHL First All-Star Team (2003) • USHL Player of the Year (2003) • USA Junior Player of the Year (2003)

Missed majority of 2003-04 season recovering from knee injury suffered in game vs. North Dakota (WCHA), November 7, 2003.

POULIOT, Benoit (POO-lee-oh, BEHN-wah) MIN.

Left wing. Shoots left. 6'3", 179 lbs. Born, Alfred, Ont., September 29, 1986.
(Minnesota's 1st choice, 4th overall, in 2005 Entry Draft).

			Regular Season					Playoffs				
Season	Club	League	GP	G	A	Pts	PIM	GP	G	A	Pts	PIM
2002-03	Clarence Beavers	OHA-B	38	13	17	30	86	5	0	2	2	8
	Hawkesbury	CJHL	1	1	0	1	0	....	....	....	....	....
2003-04	Hawkesbury	CJHL	45	21	21	42	85	6	3	7	10	10
	Sudbury Wolves	OHL	4	2	2	4	0	4	2	1	3	0
2004-05	Sudbury Wolves	OHL	67	29	38	67	102	12	6	8	14	20

OHL First All-Star Team (2005) • OHL Rookie of the Year (2005) • Canadian Major Junior All-Rookie Team (2005) • Canadian Major Junior Rookie of the Year (2005)

POULIOT, Marc-Antoine (poo-YOH, MAHRK-AN-twahn) EDM.

Center. Shoots right. 6'1", 195 lbs. Born, Quebec City, Que., May 22, 1985.
(Edmonton's 1st choice, 22nd overall, in 2003 Entry Draft).

			Regular Season					Playoffs				
Season	Club	League	GP	G	A	Pts	PIM	GP	G	A	Pts	PIM
2000-01	Ste-Foy	QAAA	38	16	39	55	52	16	8	12	20	16
2001-02	Rimouski Oceanic	QMJHL	28	9	14	23	32	5	0	0	0	4
2002-03	Rimouski Oceanic	QMJHL	65	32	41	73	100	....	....	....	....	....
2003-04	Rimouski Oceanic	QMJHL	42	25	33	58	62	9	5	7	12	12
2004-05	Rimouski Oceanic	QMJHL	70	45	69	114	83	13	4	15	19	8

QMJHL First All-Star Team (2005) • George Parsons Trophy (Memorial Cup Tournament Most Sportsmanlike Player) (2005)

PRESTBERG, Pelle (PREHST-buhrg, PEHL-lee) ANA.

Left wing. Shoots left. 5'10", 170 lbs. Born, Jonkoping, Sweden, February 5, 1975.
(Anaheim's 7th choice, 233rd overall, in 1998 Entry Draft).

			Regular Season					Playoffs				
Season	Club	League	GP	G	A	Pts	PIM	GP	G	A	Pts	PIM
1990-91	IFK Munkfors	Sweden-3	3	0	3	3	....	....	....	....	....	....
1991-92	IFK Munkfors	Sweden-3	26	6	10	16	18	....	....	....	....	....
1992-93	IFK Munkfors	Sweden-3	36	8	8	16	20	....	....	....	....	....
1993-94	Sunne IK	Sweden-2	32	8	6	14	16	....	....	....	....	....
1994-95	IFK Munkfors	Sweden-2	27	13	9	22	44	....	....	....	....	....
1995-96	IFK Munkfors	Sweden-2	30	20	11	31	32	....	....	....	....	....
1996-97	IFK Munkfors	Sweden-2	32	28	10	38	50	....	....	....	....	....
1997-98	Farjestad	Sweden	45	29	15	44	22	12	*9	2	11	8
1998-99	Farjestad	Sweden	48	18	15	33	28	4	0	1	1	4
99-2000	Farjestad	Sweden	48	13	9	22	26	7	1	1	2	18
2000-01	V.Frolunda	Sweden	50	14	9	23	18	5	0	0	0	8
2001-02	V.Frolunda	Sweden	50	14	11	25	28	10	5	0	5	12
2002-03	Farjestad	Sweden	45	12	6	18	26	14	5	1	6	8
2003-04	Farjestad	Sweden	50	22	23	45	50	12	2	1	3	2
2004-05	Farjestad	Sweden	49	21	14	35	48	15	3	2	5	12

PRINTZ, David (PRIHNTS, DAY-vihd) PHI.

Defense. Shoots left. 6'5", 220 lbs. Born, Stockholm, Sweden, July 24, 1980.
(Philadelphia's 9th choice, 225th overall, in 2001 Entry Draft).

			Regular Season					Playoffs				
Season	Club	League	GP	G	A	Pts	PIM	GP	G	A	Pts	PIM
1996-97	AIK Solna Jr.	Swe-Jr.	1	0	0	0	0	....	....	....	....	....
1997-98	AIK Solna Jr.	Swe-Jr.	8	0	0	0	6	....	....	....	....	....
1998-99	AIK Solna Jr.	Swe-Jr.	23	1	0	1	14	....	....	....	....	....
99-2000	AIK Solna Jr.	Swe-Jr.	36	8	4	12	53	....	....	....	....	....
2000-01	Great Falls	AWHL	54	13	23	36	93	13	3	5	8	16
2001-02	AIK Solna Jr.	Swe-Jr.	8	2	3	5	20	....	....	....	....	....
	AIK Solna	Sweden	37	3	2	5	59	....	....	....	....	....
	AIK Solna	Sweden-Q	10	0	0	0	12	....	....	....	....	....
2002-03	HPK Hameenlinna	Finland	17	1	0	1	10	....	....	....	....	....
	Ilves Tampere	Finland	25	1	2	3	10	....	....	....	....	....
2003-04	AIK Solna	Sweden-2	51	2	9	11	60	5	2	0	2	4
2004-05	Philadelphia	AHL	50	1	5	6	66	1	0	0	0	0
	Trenton Titans	ECHL	2	0	1	1	0	....	....	....	....	....

PRUCHA, Petr (PROO-khah, PEE-tuhr) NYR

Right wing. Shoots right. 5'10", 161 lbs. Born, Chrudim, Czech., September 14, 1982.
(NY Rangers' 8th choice, 240th overall, in 2002 Entry Draft).

			Regular Season					Playoffs				
Season	Club	League	GP	G	A	Pts	PIM	GP	G	A	Pts	PIM
99-2000	HC Chrudim Jr.	CzRep-Jr.	43	35	27	62	62	....	....	....	....	....
2000-01	HC Pardubice Jr.	CzRep-Jr.	54	39	22	61	18	....	....	....	....	....
2001-02	HC Pardubice Jr.	CzRep-Jr.	28	38	28	66	18	3	2	6	8	0
	Sumperk	CzRep-2	8	6	4	10	0	....	....	....	....	....
	Sumperk	CzRep-Q	5	5	3	8	0	....	....	....	....	....
	Pardubice	CzRep	20	1	1	2	2	5	0	0	0	0
2002-03	Pardubice	CzRep	49	7	9	16	12	17	2	6	8	8
	HC Pardubice Jr.	CzRep-Jr.	4	5	4	9	25	....	....	....	....	....
	Hr. Kralove	CzRep-2	11	3	5	8	35	....	....	....	....	....
2003-04	Hr. Kralove	CzRep-2	3	1	0	1	25	....	....	....	....	....
	Pardubice	CzRep	48	11	13	24	24	7	4	3	7	2
2004-05	Pardubice	CzRep	47	7	10	17	24	16	6	7	13	2

PRUDDEN, Josh (PROO-dehn, JAWSH) S.J.

Left wing. Shoots left. 5'11", 190 lbs. Born, Andover, MA, January 10, 1980.

			Regular Season					Playoffs				
Season	Club	League	GP	G	A	Pts	PIM	GP	G	A	Pts	PIM
99-2000	New Hampshire	H-East	16	2	3	5	12	....	....	....	....	....
2000-01	New Hampshire	H-East	37	8	8	16	28	....	....	....	....	....
2001-02	New Hampshire	H-East	36	14	16	30	32	....	....	....	....	....
2002-03	New Hampshire	H-East	42	9	13	22	52	....	....	....	....	....
2003-04	Atlantic City	ECHL	60	18	34	52	54	4	0	0	0	2
2004-05	Cleveland Barons	AHL	73	14	8	22	54	....	....	....	....	....

Signed as a free agent by **San Jose**, August 15, 2005.

PRUST, Brandon (PROOST, BRAN-duhn) CGY.

Center/Left wing. Shoots left. 5'11", 191 lbs. Born, London, Ont., March 16, 1984.
(Calgary's 2nd choice, 70th overall, in 2004 Entry Draft).

			Regular Season					Playoffs				
Season	Club	League	GP	G	A	Pts	PIM	GP	G	A	Pts	PIM
2001-02	London Nationals	OHA-B	52	17	35	52	38	....	....	....	....	....
2002-03	London Knights	OHL	65	12	17	29	94	14	2	1	3	21
2003-04	London Knights	OHL	64	19	33	52	269	15	7	13	20	33
2004-05	London Knights	OHL	48	10	20	30	174	15	3	5	8	*71

PSURNY, Roman (P'SHUHR-nee, ROH-muhn) NYR

Left wing. Shoots left. 6'1", 170 lbs. Born, Gottwaldov, Czech., February 23, 1986.
(NY Rangers' 10th choice, 135th overall, in 2004 Entry Draft).

			Regular Season					Playoffs				
Season	Club	League	GP	G	A	Pts	PIM	GP	G	A	Pts	PIM
2000-01	HC Zlin U17	CzR-U17	42	19	36	55	57	6	3	3	6	6
2002-03	HC Zlin U17	CzR-U17	22	17	27	44	20	3	1	1	2	4
	HC Zlin Jr.	CzRep-Jr.	15	3	7	10	0	....	....	....	....	....
2003-04	HC Zlin Jr.	CzRep-Jr.	52	18	33	51	104	5	0	0	0	2
	HC Hame Zlin	CzRep	9	0	0	0	0	....	....	....	....	....
2004-05	Medicine Hat	WHL	69	21	28	49	64	13	1	4	5	16

PUDLICK, Michael (PUHD-lihk, MIGH-kuhl)

Defense. Shoots left. 6'3", 190 lbs. Born, Blaine, MN, February 24, 1978.

			Regular Season					Playoffs				
Season	Club	League	GP	G	A	Pts	PIM	GP	G	A	Pts	PIM
1995-96	Blaine Bengals	High-MN	25	9	30	39	....	....	....	....	....	....
1996-97	Twin Cities	USHL	49	10	19	29	93	5	0	2	2	4
1997-98	Twin Cities	USHL	50	3	14	17	138	....	....	....	....	....
1998-99	St. Cloud State	WCHA	37	13	12	25	74	....	....	....	....	....
99-2000	St. Cloud State	WCHA	40	8	22	30	65	....	....	....	....	....
2000-01	Lowell	AHL	57	7	13	20	39	4	0	1	1	2
2001-02	Manchester	AHL	64	9	6	15	42	3	0	0	0	6
2002-03	Manchester	AHL	68	7	17	24	52	1	0	0	0	0
2003-04	Portland Pirates	AHL	69	9	15	24	60	3	2	1	3	2
2004-05	Augsburg	Germany	49	8	14	22	64	5	0	1	1	10

WCHA First All-Star Team (2000) • NCAA West Second All-American Team (2000)

Signed as a free agent by **Los Angeles**, April 5, 2000. Signed as a free agent by **Augsburg** (Germany), Septembef 14, 2004.

PULLIAINEN, Tuukka (poo-le-AY-nehn, TOO-kuh) L.A.

Right wing. Shoots left. 5'11", 176 lbs. Born, Turku, Finland, August 25, 1984.
(Los Angeles' 10th choice, 248th overall, in 2002 Entry Draft).

			Regular Season					Playoffs				
Season	Club	League	GP	G	A	Pts	PIM	GP	G	A	Pts	PIM
2000-01	TuTo Turku Jr.	Finland-Jr.	37	3	11	14	8	1	1	1	2	0
2001-02	TuTo Turku	Finland-2	41	11	8	19	8	2	0	1	1	25
	TuTo Turku Jr.	Finland-Jr.	3	0	2	2	0	1	0	0	0	2
2002-03	TuTo Turku	Finland-2	42	15	17	32	12	....	....	....	....	....
2003-04	TPS Turku	Finland	2	0	0	0	0	....	....	....	....	....
	TPS Turku Jr.	Finland-Jr.	1	0	0	0	0	....	....	....	....	....
	TuTo Turku	Finland-2	44	6	25	31	12	....	....	....	....	....
2004-05	TPS Turku Jr.	Finland-Jr.	4	2	2	4	0	....	....	....	....	....
	Jokipojat Joensuu	Finland-2	12	4	4	8	6	....	....	....	....	....
	TuTo Turku	Finland-2	29	4	11	15	4	6	1	1	2	0

PUSHKAREV, Konstantin (puhsh-kar-EHV, kawn-stuhn-TIHN) L.A.

Right wing. Shoots left. 6', 169 lbs. Born, Ust-Kamenogorsk, USSR, February 12, 1985.
(Los Angeles' 4th choice, 44th overall, in 2003 Entry Draft).

			Regular Season					Playoffs				
Season	Club	League	GP	G	A	Pts	PIM	GP	G	A	Pts	PIM
2002-03	Ust-Kam'gorsk 2	Russia-3		STATISTICS NOT AVAILABLE								
	Ust-Kamenogorsk	Russia-2	4	0	0	0	4	....	....	....	....	....
2003-04	Avangard Omsk	Russia	5	1	0	1	0	....	....	....	....	....
	Omsk 2	Russia-3	34	17	11	28	64	....	....	....	....	....
2004-05	Avangard Omsk	Russia	1	0	0	0	0	....	....	....	....	....
	Calgary Hitmen	WHL	69	22	30	52	50	12	2	5	7	4

PYATT, Tom (PEE-yat, TAWM) NYR

Center. Shoots left. 5'11", 181 lbs. Born, Thunder Bay, Ont., February 14, 1987.
(NY Rangers' 6th choice, 107th overall, in 2005 Entry Draft).

			Regular Season					Playoffs				
Season	Club	League	GP	G	A	Pts	PIM	GP	G	A	Pts	PIM
2003-04	Saginaw Spirit	OHL	67	9	9	18	21	....	....	....	....	....
2004-05	Saginaw Spirit	OHL	57	18	30	48	14	....	....	....	....	....

QUINCEY, Kyle (KWIHN-see, KIGHL) DET.

Defense. Shoots left. 6'1", 194 lbs. Born, Kitchener, Ont., August 12, 1985.
(Detroit's 2nd choice, 132nd overall, in 2003 Entry Draft).

			Regular Season					Playoffs				
Season	Club	League	GP	G	A	Pts	PIM	GP	G	A	Pts	PIM
2001-02	Mississauga	OPJHL	27	5	14	19	31	....	....	....	....	....
2002-03	London Knights	OHL	66	6	12	18	77	14	3	4	7	11
2003-04	London Knights	OHL	3	0	2	2	4	....	....	....	....	....
	Mississauga	OHL	61	14	23	37	135	24	3	13	16	32
2004-05	Mississauga	OHL	59	15	31	46	111	5	0	3	3	4

OHL Second All-Star Team (2005)

RABBIT, Wacey (RA-biht, WAY-see) BOS.

Center. Shoots left. 5'9", 169 lbs. Born, Lethbridge, Alta., November 16, 1986.
(Boston's 6th choice, 154th overall, in 2005 Entry Draft).

			Regular Season					Playoffs				
Season	Club	League	GP	G	A	Pts	PIM	GP	G	A	Pts	PIM
2001-02	Cgy. North Stars	AMHL	35	24	28	52	....	....	....	....	....	....
	Saskatoon Blades	WHL	3	0	1	1	0	....	....	....	....	....
2002-03	Saskatoon Blades	WHL	62	21	24	45	33	5	1	3	4	6
2003-04	Saskatoon Blades	WHL	60	9	8	17	51	....	....	....	....	....
2004-05	Saskatoon Blades	WHL	70	22	45	67	70	4	1	2	3	0

RACHUNEK, Ivan (ra-KHOO-nuhk, EE-vahn) T.B.

Left wing. Shoots left. 5'9", 176 lbs. Born, Zlin, Czech., July 6, 1981.
(Tampa Bay's 8th choice, 187th overall, in 1999 Entry Draft).

			Regular Season					Playoffs				
Season	Club	League	GP	G	A	Pts	PIM	GP	G	A	Pts	PIM
1997-98	HC ZPS Zlin Jr.	CzRep-Jr.	48	15	25	40	172	....	....	....	....	....
1998-99	HC ZPS Zlin Jr.	CzRep-Jr.	40	37	22	59	70	....	....	....	....	....
	HC ZPS Barum Zlin	CzRep	5	0	0	0	0	....	....	....	....	....
99-2000	Zlin	CzRep	5	0	1	1	2	....	....	....	....	....
	HC Zlin Jr.	CzRep-Jr.	3	0	7	7	4	....	....	....	....	....
	Windsor Spitfires	OHL	15	2	2	4	21	....	....	....	....	....
2000-01	Zlin	CzRep	50	8	9	17	95	6	1	0	1	8
2001-02	Zlin	CzRep	48	9	11	20	143	11	3	4	7	6
2002-03	HC Hame Zlin	CzRep	48	9	16	25	52	....	....	....	....	....
2003-04	C. Budejovice	CzRep	5	0	2	2	0	....	....	....	....	....
2004-05	Znojmo	CzRep	29	2	4	6	26	....	....	....	....	....

RADULOV, Alexander (rah-DOO-lahf, al-EHX-AN-duhr) NSH.

Left wing. Shoots left. 6'1", 188 lbs. Born, Nizhy Tagil, USSR, July 5, 1986.
(Nashville's 1st choice, 15th overall, in 2004 Entry Draft).

			Regular Season					Playoffs				
Season	Club	League	GP	G	A	Pts	PIM	GP	G	A	Pts	PIM
2002-03	Dyn'o Moscow 2	Russia-3		STATISTICS NOT AVAILABLE								
2003-04	Dyn'o Moscow 2	Russia-3		STATISTICS NOT AVAILABLE								
	Dynamo Moscow	Russia	1	0	0	0	2	....	....	....	....	....
	THK Tver	Russia-2	42	15	16	31	102	....	....	....	....	....
2004-05	Quebec Remparts	QMJHL	65	32	43	75	64	13	6	5	11	15

QMJHL All-Rookie Team (2005)

RADUNSKE, Brock (ra-DOON-skee, BRAWK) EDM.

Left wing. Shoots left. 6'4", 196 lbs. Born, Kitchener, Ont., April 5, 1983.
(Edmonton's 5th choice, 79th overall, in 2002 Entry Draft).

			Regular Season					Playoffs				
Season	Club	League	GP	G	A	Pts	PIM	GP	G	A	Pts	PIM
99-2000	Aurora Tigers	OPJHL	42	6	14	20	23	4	4	8	12	2
2000-01	Newmarket	OPJHL	48	30	39	69	65	....	....	....	....	....
2001-02	Michigan State	CCHA	41	4	9	13	28	....	....	....	....	....
2002-03	Michigan State	CCHA	36	11	18	29	30	....	....	....	....	....
2003-04	Michigan State	CCHA	42	12	10	22	60	....	....	....	....	....
2004-05	Edmonton	AHL	8	1	1	2	2	....	....	....	....	....
	Greenville Grrrowl	ECHL	39	12	17	29	52	....	....	....	....	....

RAJAMAKI, Erkki (righ-ya-MA-kee, UHR-kee) ST.L.

Left wing. Shoots left. 6'2", 205 lbs. Born, Vantaa, Finland, October 30, 1978.
(Tampa Bay's 9th choice, 216th overall, in 1999 Entry Draft).

			Regular Season					Playoffs				
Season	Club	League	GP	G	A	Pts	PIM	GP	G	A	Pts	PIM
1994-95	Kiekko-Vantaa Jr.	Finland-Jr.	2	0	0	0	0	....	....	....	....	....
1995-96	Kiekko-Vantaa Jr.	Finland-Jr.		DID NOT PLAY – INJURED								
1996-97	Kiekko-Vantaa Jr.	Finland-Jr.	33	14	19	33	32	....	....	....	....	....
1997-98	HIFK Helsinki Jr.	Finland-Jr.	14	1	2	3	2	....	....	....	....	....
	Kiekko-Vantaa Jr.	Finland-Jr.	....	....	....	....	....	10	3	0	3	2
1998-99	HIFK Helsinki U18	Fin-U18	14	2	2	4	8	....	....	....	....	....
	HIFK Helsinki	Finland	14	0	0	0	2	....	....	....	....	....
	HIFK Helsinki Jr.	Finland-Jr.	....	....	....	....	....	13	7	3	10	45
99-2000	Colgate	ECAC	31	1	6	7	20	....	....	....	....	....
2000-01	Newcastle Jesters	Britain	11	1	0	1	0	....	....	....	....	....
	FPS Forssa	Finland-2	4	1	3	4	0	....	....	....	....	....
	HIFK Helsinki	Finland	50	1	2	3	10	5	0	0	0	2
2001-02	HPK Hameenlinna	Finland	56	12	7	19	75	8	1	2	3	2
2002-03	HPK Hameenlinna	Finland	40	4	3	7	100	10	1	0	1	36
2003-04	Ilves Tampere	Finland	43	12	6	18	89	5	0	0	0	0
2004-05	Worcester IceCats	AHL	60	5	4	9	67	....	....	....	....	....

Traded to **St. Louis** by **Tampa Bay** for St. Louis' 8th round choice (Justin Keller) in 2004 Entry Draft, October 27, 2003.

RAMHOLT, Tim (RAM-hohlt, TIHM) CGY.

Defense. Shoots left. 6'1", 194 lbs. Born, Zurich, Switz., November 2, 1984.
(Calgary's 2nd choice, 39th overall, in 2003 Entry Draft).

			Regular Season					Playoffs				
Season	Club	League	GP	G	A	Pts	PIM	GP	G	A	Pts	PIM
99-2000	Zurich/Kusn Jr.	Swiss-Jr.	35	2	9	11	26	4	0	2	2	4
	Grasshopper	Swiss-2	2	0	0	0	0	....	....	....	....	....
2000-01	GC Zurich	Swiss-2	37	0	2	2	38	3	0	0	0	4
	GC Zurich Jr.	Swiss-Jr.	17	3	6	9	10	....	....	....	....	....
2001-02	ZSC Lions Zurich	Swiss	37	3	0	3	14	17	0	3	3	2
	GCK/ZSC Zurich Jr.	Swiss-Jr.	5	2	2	4	4	....	....	....	....	....
	GC Zurich	Swiss-2	3	0	0	0	0	....	....	....	....	....
2002-03	ZSC Lions Zurich	Swiss	30	2	0	2	12	9	0	1	1	0
	GC Zurich	Swiss-2	12	0	4	4	6	....	....	....	....	....
2003-04	Cape Breton	QMJHL	51	9	27	36	26	5	0	1	1	4
2004-05	ZSC Lions Zurich	Swiss	41	1	3	4	38	15	0	0	0	10

RAMSAY, Ryan (RAM-zee, RIGH-uhn) ST.L.

Center. Shoots left. 5'11", 200 lbs. Born, Ajax, Ont., May 18, 1983.

			Regular Season					Playoffs				
Season	Club	League	GP	G	A	Pts	PIM	GP	G	A	Pts	PIM
2000-01	Peterborough	OHL	36	16	10	26	67	....	....	....	....	....
	Kitchener Rangers	OHL	22	5	18	23	39	....	....	....	....	....
2001-02	Kitchener Rangers	OHL	54	24	24	48	87	4	1	0	1	4
2002-03	Plymouth Whalers	OHL	59	33	55	88	97	11	2	4	6	18
2003-04	Plymouth Whalers	OHL	61	29	48	77	132	9	1	1	2	18
2004-05	Worcester IceCats	AHL	46	6	12	18	93	....	....	....	....	....
	Peoria Rivermen	ECHL	2	1	2	3	2	....	....	....	....	....

Signed as a free agent by **St. Louis**, August 2, 2005.

RANGER, Paul (RAIN-juhr, PAWL) T.B.

Defense. Shoots left. 6'2", 215 lbs. Born, Whitby, Ont., September 12, 1984.
(Tampa Bay's choice, 183rd overall, in 2002 Entry Draft).

			Regular Season					Playoffs				
Season	Club	League	GP	G	A	Pts	PIM	GP	G	A	Pts	PIM
2000-01	Oshawa Generals	OHL	32	0	1	1	2	....	....	....	....	....
2001-02	Oshawa Generals	OHL	62	0	9	9	49	5	0	0	0	4
2002-03	Oshawa Generals	OHL	68	10	28	38	70	13	0	3	3	10
2003-04	Oshawa Generals	OHL	62	12	31	43	72	7	0	1	1	10
2004-05	Springfield Falcons	AHL	69	3	8	11	46	....	....	....	....	....

RAU, Chad (ROW, CHAD) TOR.

Center. Shoots right. 5'10", 175 lbs. Born, Eden Prairie, MN, January 18, 1987.
(Toronto's 6th choice, 228th overall, in 2005 Entry Draft).

			Regular Season					Playoffs				
Season	Club	League	GP	G	A	Pts	PIM	GP	G	A	Pts	PIM
2004-05	Des Moines	USHL	57	31	40	71	32	....	....	....	....	....

USHL All-Rookie Team (2005) • USHL First All-Star Team (2005) • USHL Rookie of the Year (2005)

Signed Letter of Intent to attend **Colorado College** (WCHA) in fall of 2005.

RAWLYK, Rory (RAW-lihk, ROHR-ee) NYR

Defense. Shoots right. 6'3", 193 lbs. Born, Edmonton, Alta., September 9, 1983.

			Regular Season					Playoffs				
Season	Club	League	GP	G	A	Pts	PIM	GP	G	A	Pts	PIM
1998-99	Edm. Maple Leafs	AMBHL	36	6	18	24	58	....	....	....	....	....
99-2000	Edm. United Cycle	AMHL	28	3	14	17	34	....	....	....	....	....
2000-01	Camrose Kodiaks	AJHL	24	3	6	9	16	16	1	5	6	32
	Medicine Hat	WHL	17	0	1	1	6	....	....	....	....	....
2001-02	Medicine Hat	WHL	40	2	9	11	59	....	....	....	....	....
	Vancouver Giants	WHL	28	3	7	10	21	....	....	....	....	....
2002-03	Vancouver Giants	WHL	4	1	1	2	8	....	....	....	....	....
	Prince Albert	WHL	28	6	9	15	16	....	....	....	....	....
	Red Deer Rebels	WHL	20	4	5	9	16	23	2	9	11	30
2003-04	Hartford Wolf Pack	AHL	5	1	0	1	2	....	....	....	....	....
	Charlotte	ECHL	67	9	23	32	24	....	....	....	....	....
2004-05	Hartford Wolf Pack	AHL	2	0	0	0	0	....	....	....	....	....
	Charlotte	ECHL	68	9	21	30	91	14	1	4	5	12

Signed as a free agent by **NY Rangers**, September 15, 2001.

RAYMOND, Mason (RAY-muhnd, MAY-sohn) VAN.

Left wing. Shoots left. 6', 165 lbs. Born, Calgary, Alta., September 17, 1985.
(Vancouver's 2nd choice, 51st overall, in 2005 Entry Draft).

			Regular Season					Playoffs				
Season	Club	League	GP	G	A	Pts	PIM	GP	G	A	Pts	PIM
2003-04	Camrose Kodiaks	AJHL	....	27	35	62	....	....	....	....	....	....
2004-05	Camrose Kodiaks	AJHL	55	*41	41	82	80	15	8	*12	20	....

AJHL MVP (2005)

Signed Letter of Intent to attend **Minnesota-Duluth** (WCHA) in fall of 2005.

READY, Ryan (REH-dee, RIGH-yan) PHI.

Left wing. Shoots left. 6'2", 195 lbs. Born, Peterborough, Ont., November 7, 1978.
(Calgary's 8th choice, 100th overall, in 1997 Entry Draft).

			Regular Season					Playoffs				
Season	Club	League	GP	G	A	Pts	PIM	GP	G	A	Pts	PIM
1994-95	Peterborough	OPJHL	48	20	33	53	65	....	....	....	....	....
1995-96	Belleville Bulls	OHL	63	5	13	18	54	10	0	2	2	2
1996-97	Belleville Bulls	OHL	66	23	24	47	102	6	1	3	4	4
1997-98	Belleville Bulls	OHL	66	33	39	72	80	10	5	2	7	12
1998-99	Belleville Bulls	OHL	63	33	59	92	73	21	10	28	38	22
99-2000	Syracuse Crunch	AHL	70	4	12	16	59	2	0	0	0	0
2000-01	Kansas City Blades	IHL	67	10	15	25	75	....	....	....	....	....
2001-02	Manitoba Moose	AHL	72	23	32	55	73	7	5	1	6	4
2002-03	Manitoba Moose	AHL	68	24	26	50	52	14	2	5	7	2
2003-04	Manitoba Moose	AHL	64	7	18	25	55	....	....	....	....	....
	Worcester IceCats	AHL	16	2	5	7	10	10	1	2	3	10
2004-05	Philadelphia	AHL	72	7	18	25	104	19	2	11	13	6

OHL First All-Star Team (1999)

Signed as a free agent by **Vancouver**, June 16, 1999. Traded to **St. Louis** by **Vancouver** for Sergei Varlamov, March 9, 2004. Signed as a free agent by **Philadelphia**, August 23, 2004.

REAVES, Ryan (REEVS, RIGH-uhn) ST.L.

Right wing. Shoots right. 6'1", 193 lbs. Born, Winnipeg, Man., January 20, 1987.
(St. Louis' 4th choice, 156th overall, in 2005 Entry Draft).

			Regular Season					Playoffs				
Season	Club	League	GP	G	A	Pts	PIM	GP	G	A	Pts	PIM
2004-05	Brandon	WHL	64	7	9	16	79	23	2	4	6	43

REDDOX, Liam (REH-dawks, LEE-uhm) EDM.

Left wing. Shoots left. 5'9", 179 lbs. Born, East York, Ont., January 27, 1986.
(Edmonton's 5th choice, 112th overall, in 2004 Entry Draft).

			Regular Season					Playoffs				
Season	Club	League	GP	G	A	Pts	PIM	GP	G	A	Pts	PIM
2002-03	Wellington Dukes	OPJHL	45	32	32	64	29	....	....	....	....	....
	Peterborough	OHL	4	0	0	0	0	....	....	....	....	....
2003-04	Peterborough	OHL	68	31	33	64	24	....	....	....	....	....
2004-05	Peterborough	OHL	68	36	46	82	38	14	3	10	13	10

OHL All-Rookie Team (2004)

REDLIHS, Jekabs (REHD-lihs, YEH-kabs) CBJ

Defense. Shoots left. 6'2", 185 lbs. Born, Riga, Latvia, March 29, 1982.
(Columbus' 6th choice, 119th overall, in 2002 Entry Draft).

			Regular Season					Playoffs				
Season	Club	League	GP	G	A	Pts	PIM	GP	G	A	Pts	PIM
1998-99	Dynamo Riga 18	Latvia-Jr.	STATISTICS NOT AVAILABLE									
99-2000	HC Essamika Jr.	EEHL	16	1	4	5	6	....	....	....	....	....
	Metalurgs Liepaja	Latvia	1	0	0	0	0	....	....	....	....	....
	Metalurgs Liepaja	EEHL	11	0	0	0	2	....	....	....	....	....
2000-01	Metalurgs Liepaja	EEHL	31	1	3	4	....	....	....	....	....	....
	Metalurgs Liepaja	Latvia	23	4	5	9	....	....	....	....	....	....
2001-02	NY Apple Core	EJHL	38	3	16	19	24	....	....	....	....	....
2002-03	Boston University	H-East	40	4	12	16	12	....	....	....	....	....
2003-04	Boston University	H-East	23	2	4	6	53	....	....	....	....	....
2004-05	Boston University	H-East	40	1	0	1	32	....	....	....	....	....

Hockey East All-Rookie Team (2003)

REDLIHS, Krisjanis (REHD-lihs, krihs-JA-nihs) N.J.

Defense. Shoots left. 6'3", 190 lbs. Born, Riga, Latvia, January 15, 1981.
(New Jersey's 7th choice, 154th overall, in 2002 Entry Draft).

			Regular Season					Playoffs				
Season	Club	League	GP	G	A	Pts	PIM	GP	G	A	Pts	PIM
1998-99	Dynamo Riga 18	Latvia-Jr.	STATISTICS NOT AVAILABLE									
99-2000	Metalurgs Liepaja	EEHL	12	1	3	4	0	....	....	....	....	....
2000-01	Metalurgs Liepaja	EEHL	27	2	2	4	....	....	....	....	....	....
	Metalurgs Liepaja	Latvia	22	1	6	7	....	....	....	....	....	....
2001-02	Metalurgs Liepaja	EEHL	32	0	2	2	....	11	1	1	2	....
	Metalurgs Liepaja	Latvia	13	0	6	6	4	3	2	2	4	0
2002-03	Albany River Rats	AHL	61	1	9	10	20	....	....	....	....	....
2003-04	Albany River Rats	AHL	66	9	10	19	16	....	....	....	....	....
2004-05	Albany River Rats	AHL	46	0	10	10	12	....	....	....	....	....

REESE, Dylan (REES, DIH-luhn) NYR

Defense. Shoots right. 6', 206 lbs. Born, Pittsburgh, PA, August 29, 1984.
(NY Rangers' 9th choice, 209th overall, in 2003 Entry Draft).

			Regular Season					Playoffs				
Season	Club	League	GP	G	A	Pts	PIM	GP	G	A	Pts	PIM
2000-01	Pittsburgh Hornets	MWEHL	66	14	42	66	....	....	....	....	....	....
2001-02	Pittsburgh Forge	NAHL	48	7	16	23	70	7	0	2	2	4
2002-03	Pittsburgh Forge	NAHL	56	11	30	41	98	5	2	3	5	6
2003-04	Harvard Crimson	ECAC	21	1	4	5	18	....	....	....	....	....
2004-05	Harvard Crimson	ECAC	34	7	12	19	44	....	....	....	....	....

REGEHR, Richie (reh-GEER, RIH-chee) CGY.

Defense. Shoots right. 6', 190 lbs. Born, Rosthern, Sask., January 17, 1983.

			Regular Season					Playoffs				
Season	Club	League	GP	G	A	Pts	PIM	GP	G	A	Pts	PIM
99-2000	Kelowna Rockets	WHL	50	6	8	14	22	5	0	1	1	0
2000-01	Kelowna Rockets	WHL	71	10	27	37	68	6	0	1	1	4
2001-02	Kelowna Rockets	WHL	15	1	9	10	12	....	....	....	....	....
	Portland	WHL	37	7	27	34	50	7	2	5	7	8
2002-03	Portland	WHL	67	16	45	61	115	7	2	2	4	8
2003-04	Portland	WHL	65	9	34	43	88	5	0	1	1	6
2004-05	Lowell	AHL	64	9	16	25	60	11	1	6	7	2

Signed as a free agent by **Calgary**, July 6, 2004.

REGIER, Steve (reh-GEER, STEEV) NYI

Left wing. Shoots left. 6'4", 194 lbs. Born, Edmonton, Alta., August 31, 1984.
(NY Islanders' 5th choice, 148th overall, in 2004 Entry Draft).

			Regular Season					Playoffs				
Season	Club	League	GP	G	A	Pts	PIM	GP	G	A	Pts	PIM
2000-01	Leduc Oil Kings	AMHL	35	22	39	61	135	....	....	....	....	....
2001-02	Medicine Hat	WHL	59	1	4	5	31	....	....	....	....	....
2002-03	Medicine Hat	WHL	61	11	10	21	114	11	2	2	4	20
2003-04	Medicine Hat	WHL	72	25	35	60	111	18	5	11	16	20
2004-05	Bridgeport	AHL	75	7	15	22	43	....	....	....	....	....

REGIN JENSEN, Peter (REE-gihn-JEHN-sehn, PEE-tuhr) OTT.

Center. Shoots left. 6'1", 174 lbs. Born, Herning, Denmark, April 16, 1986.
(Ottawa's 4th choice, 87th overall, in 2004 Entry Draft).

			Regular Season					Playoffs				
Season	Club	League	GP	G	A	Pts	PIM	GP	G	A	Pts	PIM
2002-03	Herning IK	Denmark	24	0	1	1	4	10	1	3	4	4
2003-04	Herning IK	Denmark	33	9	11	20	14	....	....	....	....	....
2004-05	Herning Blue Fox	Denmark	36	19	27	46	43	16	5	8	13	2

REHAK, Denis (REH-hahk, DEH-nihs) NYI

Defense. Shoots left. 6'2", 196 lbs. Born, Trencin, Czech., May 14, 1985.
(NY Islanders' 7th choice, 212th overall, in 2003 Entry Draft).

			Regular Season					Playoffs				
Season	Club	League	GP	G	A	Pts	PIM	GP	G	A	Pts	PIM
2002-03	Dukla Trencin Jr.	Slovak-Jr.	24	0	1	1	8	....	....	....	....	....
2003-04	Prince George	WHL	25	0	3	3	12	....	....	....	....	....
	Dukla Trencin U18	Svk-U18	3	1	0	1	4	....	....	....	....	....
2004-05	VSK Technika Brno	CzRep-3	1	0	0	0	0	....	....	....	....	....
	HC Ytong Brno Jr.	CzRep-Jr.	46	4	15	19	38	....	....	....	....	....

REID, Darren (REED, DAIR-uhn) T.B.

Right wing. Shoots right. 6'2", 205 lbs. Born, Lac La Biche, Alta., May 8, 1983.
(Tampa Bay's 11th choice, 256th overall, in 2002 Entry Draft).

			Regular Season					Playoffs				
Season	Club	League	GP	G	A	Pts	PIM	GP	G	A	Pts	PIM
2000-01	Drayton Valley	AJHL	55	8	18	26	116	....	....	....	....	....
2001-02	Drayton Valley	AJHL	31	9	12	21	195	....	....	....	....	....
	Medicine Hat	WHL	37	8	9	17	70	....	....	....	....	....
2002-03	Medicine Hat	WHL	63	14	30	44	163	11	5	0	5	19
2003-04	Medicine Hat	WHL	67	33	48	81	194	20	*13	8	21	31
2004-05	Springfield Falcons	AHL	56	3	19	22	99	....	....	....	....	....

REINHART, Derek (RIGHN-hart, DEH-rihk) CBJ

Defense. Shoots right. 6'3", 205 lbs. Born, Rosalind, Alta., April 20, 1987.
(Columbus' 6th choice, 177th overall, in 2005 Entry Draft).

			Regular Season					Playoffs				
Season	Club	League	GP	G	A	Pts	PIM	GP	G	A	Pts	PIM
2003-04	Regina Pats	WHL	56	1	2	3	114	2	0	0	0	11
2004-05	Regina Pats	WHL	67	2	9	11	198	....	....	....	....	....

REITZ, Erik (RIGHTZ, AIR-ihk) MIN.

Defense. Shoots right. 6'1", 210 lbs. Born, Detroit, MI, July 29, 1982.
(Minnesota's 5th choice, 170th overall, in 2000 Entry Draft).

			Regular Season					Playoffs				
Season	Club	League	GP	G	A	Pts	PIM	GP	G	A	Pts	PIM
1998-99	Leamington Flyers	OHA-B	50	5	10	15	80	....	....	....	....	....
99-2000	Barrie Colts	OHL	63	2	10	12	85	25	0	5	5	44
2000-01	Barrie Colts	OHL	68	5	21	26	178	5	1	0	1	21
2001-02	Barrie Colts	OHL	61	13	27	40	153	20	4	16	20	40
2002-03	Houston Aeros	AHL	62	6	13	19	112	11	0	3	3	31
2003-04	Houston Aeros	AHL	69	5	19	24	148	2	0	0	0	0
2004-05	Houston Aeros	AHL	38	2	12	14	91	....	....	....	....	....

Memorial Cup Tournament All-Star Team (2000) • OHL First All-Star Team (2002)

Missed majority of 2004-05 season recovering from elbow injury suffered in game vs. Milwaukee (AHL), February 5, 2005.

RIAZANTSEV, Alexander (ree-ZAHNT-sehv, al-ehx-AN-duhr) WSH.

Defense. Shoots right. 6', 210 lbs. Born, Moscow, USSR, March 15, 1980.
(Colorado's 10th choice, 167th overall, in 1998 Entry Draft).

			Regular Season					Playoffs				
Season	Club	League	GP	G	A	Pts	PIM	GP	G	A	Pts	PIM
1996-97	SAK Moscow	Russia-3	18	0	0	0	8	....	....	....	....	....
	Spartak Moscow	Russia	20	1	2	3	4	....	....	....	....	....
1997-98	Spartak Moscow 2	Russia-3	31	3	8	11	26	....	....	....	....	....
	Victoriaville Tigres	QMJHL	22	6	9	15	14	4	0	0	0	0
1998-99	Victoriaville Tigres	QMJHL	64	17	40	57	57	6	0	3	3	10
	Hershey Bears	AHL	2	0	0	0	0	....	....	....	....	....
99-2000	Victoriaville Tigres	QMJHL	48	17	45	62	45	6	2	5	7	20
	Hershey Bears	AHL	2	0	1	1	2	6	1	1	2	0
2000-01	Hershey Bears	AHL	66	5	18	23	26	11	0	0	0	2
2001-02	Hershey Bears	AHL	76	5	19	24	28	5	0	1	1	4
2002-03	Hershey Bears	AHL	57	5	10	15	65	....	....	....	....	....
	Milwaukee	AHL	14	3	4	7	9	5	0	4	4	2
2003-04	Yaroslavl	Russia	41	3	8	11	60	....	....	....	....	....
	Yaroslavl 2	Russia-3	1	0	0	0	0	....	....	....	....	....
2004-05	Yaroslavl	Russia	53	4	15	19	32	4	0	1	1	4

Traded to **Nashville** by **Colorado** for Nashville's 7th round choice (Linus Videll) in 2003 Entry Draft, March 11, 2003. Traded to **Washington** by **Nashville** for Mike Farrell, July 14, 2003.

RICHARDS, Mike (RIH-chahrds, MIGHK) PHI.

Center. Shoots left. 5'11", 185 lbs. Born, Kenora, Ont., February 11, 1985.
(Philadelphia's 2nd choice, 24th overall, in 2003 Entry Draft).

			Regular Season					Playoffs				
Season	Club	League	GP	G	A	Pts	PIM	GP	G	A	Pts	PIM
2000-01	Kenora Stars	NOHA	85	76	73	149	20	....	....	....	....	....
2001-02	Kitchener Rangers	OHL	65	20	38	58	52	4	0	1	1	6
2002-03	Kitchener Rangers	OHL	67	37	50	87	99	21	9	18	27	24
2003-04	Kitchener Rangers	OHL	58	36	53	89	82	1	0	0	0	0
2004-05	Kitchener Rangers	OHL	43	22	36	58	75	15	11	17	28	36
	Philadelphia	AHL	....	....	....	....	....	14	7	8	15	28

Memorial Cup Tournament All-Star Team (2003) • OHL Second All-Star Team (2005)

RICHARDSON, Brad (RIH-chard-suhn, BRAD) COL.

Center. Shoots left. 5'11", 178 lbs. Born, Belleville, Ont., February 4, 1985.
(Colorado's 4th choice, 163rd overall, in 2003 Entry Draft).

			Regular Season					Playoffs				
Season	Club	League	GP	G	A	Pts	PIM	GP	G	A	Pts	PIM
2001-02	Owen Sound	OHL	58	12	21	33	20	....	....	....	....	....
2002-03	Owen Sound	OHL	67	27	40	67	54	4	1	1	2	10
2003-04	Owen Sound	OHL	15	7	9	16	4	....	....	....	....	....
2004-05	Owen Sound	OHL	68	41	56	97	60	8	6	4	10	8

RICHMOND, Danny (RIHCH-muhnd, DA-nee) CAR.

Defense. Shoots left. 6', 190 lbs. Born, Chicago, IL, August 1, 1984.
(Carolina's 2nd choice, 31st overall, in 2003 Entry Draft).

			Regular Season					Playoffs				
Season	Club	League	GP	G	A	Pts	PIM	GP	G	A	Pts	PIM
2000-01	Team Illinois	MWEHL	79	25	40	65	....	....	....	....	....	....
2001-02	Chicago Steel	USHL	56	8	45	53	129	4	0	4	4	20
2002-03	U. of Michigan	CCHA	43	3	19	22	48	....	....	....	....	....
2003-04	London Knights	OHL	59	13	22	35	92	15	5	6	11	10
2004-05	Lowell	AHL	63	4	9	13	139	6	0	2	2	8

USHL All-Rookie Team (2002) • USHL First All-Star Team (2002) • USHL Rookie of the Year (2002) • CCHA All-Rookie Team (2003)

Left **U. of Michigan** (CCHA) and signed with **London** (OHL), June 6, 2003.

RICHTER, Martin (RIHKH-tuhr, MAHR-tihn) NYR

Defense. Shoots right. 6'1", 205 lbs. Born, Prostejov, Czech., June 2, 1977.
(NY Rangers' 9th choice, 269th overall, in 2000 Entry Draft).

			Regular Season					Playoffs				
Season	Club	League	GP	G	A	Pts	PIM	GP	G	A	Pts	PIM
1995-96	HC Olomouc	CzRep	3	0	0	0	0	1	0	0	0	0
1996-97	HC Olomouc	CzRep	27	1	0	1	26	....	....	....	....	....
1997-98	Karlovy Vary	CzRep	42	1	2	3	32	....	....	....	....	....
1998-99	Karlovy Vary	CzRep	51	3	6	9	44	....	....	....	....	....
99-2000	Karlovy Vary	CzRep	24	0	5	5	18	....	....	....	....	....
	SaiPa	Finland	26	1	3	4	54	....	....	....	....	....
2000-01	SaiPa	Finland	41	4	5	9	80	....	....	....	....	....
	Hartford Wolf Pack	AHL	1	0	0	0	0	....	....	....	....	....
2001-02	Hartford Wolf Pack	AHL	29	1	1	2	36	....	....	....	....	....
	HC Sparta Praha	CzRep	8	0	0	0	14	13	0	0	0	10
2002-03	HC Sparta Praha	CzRep	34	2	7	9	77	8	0	0	0	10
2003-04	CSKA Moscow	Russia	14	0	0	0	33	....	....	....	....	....
	HC Sparta Praha	CzRep	16	2	2	4	16	....	....	....	....	....
2004-05	HC Sparta Praha	CzRep	44	4	9	13	32	5	1	1	2	4

RIDDLE, Troy (RIH-duhl, TROI) ST.L.

Center. Shoots right. 5'10", 175 lbs. Born, Minneapolis, MN, August 24, 1981.
(St. Louis' 5th choice, 129th overall, in 2000 Entry Draft).

			Regular Season					Playoffs				
Season	Club	League	GP	G	A	Pts	PIM	GP	G	A	Pts	PIM
1997-98	St. Margaret's	High-MN	29	33	35	68	....	....	....	....	....	....
1998-99	St. Margaret's	High-MN	29	54	45	99	....	....	....	....	....	....
99-2000	Des Moines	USHL	53	36	30	66	95	8	2	2	4	31
2000-01	U. of Minnesota	WCHA	38	16	14	30	49	....	....	....	....	....
2001-02	U. of Minnesota	WCHA	44	16	31	47	46	....	....	....	....	....
2002-03	U. of Minnesota	WCHA	45	26	26	52	50	....	....	....	....	....
2003-04	U. of Minnesota	WCHA	44	24	25	49	52	....	....	....	....	....
2004-05	Worcester IceCats	AHL	42	9	6	15	35	....	....	....	....	....
	Peoria Rivermen	ECHL	14	4	8	12	16	....	....	....	....	....

USHL Second All-Star Team (2000) • USHL Rookie of the Year (2000)

RITOLA, Mattias (RIH-toh-lah, MAT-tee-ahs) DET.

Right wing. Shoots left. 6', 192 lbs. Born, Borlange, Sweden, March 14, 1987.
(Detroit's 4th choice, 103rd overall, in 2005 Entry Draft).

			Regular Season					Playoffs				
Season	Club	League	GP	G	A	Pts	PIM	GP	G	A	Pts	PIM
2003-04	V.Frolunda U18	Swe-U18	11	4	11	15	35	7	2	7	9	12
	V.Frolunda Jr.	Swe-Jr.	24	7	4	11	8	5	0	1	1	0
2004-05	Frolunda Jr.	Swe-Jr.	9	2	6	8	6	....	....	....	....	....
	Leksands IF U18	Swe-U18	STATISTICS NOT AVAILABLE									
	Leksands IF Jr.	Swe-Jr.	18	8	10	18	14	5	1	1	2	2

ROACH, Andy (ROHCH, AN-dee) ST.L.

Defense. Shoots right. 5'11", 181 lbs. Born, Mattawan, MI, August 22, 1973.

			Regular Season					Playoffs				
Season	Club	League	GP	G	A	Pts	PIM	GP	G	A	Pts	PIM
1991-92	Waterloo	USHL	45	12	16	28	6	....	....	....	....	....
1992-93	Waterloo	USHL	42	13	17	30	22	....	....	....	....	....
1993-94	Ferris State	CCHA	32	4	15	19	18	....	....	....	....	....
1994-95	Ferris State	CCHA	36	11	19	30	26	....	....	....	....	....
1995-96	Ferris State	CCHA	33	15	19	34	44	....	....	....	....	....
1996-97	Ferris State	CCHA	37	12	34	46	18	....	....	....	....	....
1997-98	San Antonio	IHL	67	8	16	24	30	....	....	....	....	....
1998-99	Long Beach	IHL	41	5	21	26	34	....	....	....	....	....
	Utah Grizzlies	IHL	44	7	10	17	18	....	....	....	....	....
99-2000	Krefeld Pinguine	Germany	55	19	22	41	40	4	0	0	0	2
2000-01	Adler Mannheim	Germany	59	7	13	20	32	12	2	2	4	6
2001-02	Adler Mannheim	Germany	60	9	21	30	16	12	1	5	6	8
2002-03	Adler Mannheim	Germany	49	18	16	34	16	8	4	5	9	4
2003-04	Adler Mannheim	Germany	46	11	21	32	26	6	2	0	2	6
2004-05	Lausanne HC	Swiss	14	4	5	9	20	10	4	3	7	12
	Lausanne HC	Swiss-Q	7	2	3	5	2	....	....	....	....	....

Signed as a free agent by **St. Louis**, June 30, 2004. Signed as a free agent by **Lausanne** (Swiss), November 18, 2004.

ROBERTSON, Josh (RAW-buhrt-suhn, JAWSH) WSH.

Center. Shoots right. 5'11", 186 lbs. Born, Whitman, MA, August 25, 1984.
(Washington's 4th choice, 155th overall, in 2003 Entry Draft).

			Regular Season					Playoffs				
Season	Club	League	GP	G	A	Pts	PIM	GP	G	A	Pts	PIM
2000-01	Whitman-Hanson	High-MA	28	30	28	58	....	....	....	....	....	....
2001-02	Whitman-Hanson	High-MA	30	50	55	105	....	....	....	....	....	....
2002-03	Proctor Academy	High-NH	34	37	44	81	....	....	....	....	....	....
2003-04	Proctor Academy	High-NH	20	23	37	60	....	....	....	....	....	....
2004-05	Northeastern	H-East	22	4	3	7	0	....	....	....	....	....

ROBINSON, Brent (RAW-bihn-suhn, BREHNT) PHI.

Left wing. Shoots left. 6'1", 195 lbs. Born, Pointe Claire, Que., March 10, 1981.

			Regular Season					Playoffs				
Season	Club	League	GP	G	A	Pts	PIM	GP	G	A	Pts	PIM
1997-98	Lac St-Louis Lions	QAAA	42	23	33	56	....	5	2	4	6	....
1998/00	Hotchkiss	High-CT	52	41	49	90	....	....	....	....	....	....
2000-01	Brown U.	ECAC	23	1	7	8	2	....	....	....	....	....
2001-02	Brown U.	ECAC	31	9	13	22	4	....	....	....	....	....
2002-03	Brown U.	ECAC	35	15	23	38	18	....	....	....	....	....
2003-04	Brown U.	ECAC	31	13	18	31	10	....	....	....	....	....
	Hamilton Bulldogs	AHL	5	0	0	0	0	....	....	....	....	....
2004-05	Philadelphia	AHL	5	0	1	1	0	....	....	....	....	....
	Trenton Titans	ECHL	64	20	38	58	19	20	7	6	13	16

• Statistics for **Hotchkiss** (High-CT) are career totals for 1998-2000 seasons. Signed to a PTO (tryout) contract by **Hamilton** (AHL), March 25, 2004. Signed as a free agent by **Philadelphia**, June 23, 2004.

ROBINSON, Jody (RAW-bihn-suhn, JOH-dee) NYI

Defense. Shoots left. 6'2", 205 lbs. Born, New Haven, CT, September 23, 1978.

			Regular Season					Playoffs				
Season	Club	League	GP	G	A	Pts	PIM	GP	G	A	Pts	PIM
1997-98	Mercyhurst	MAAC	27	3	5	8	0	....	....	....	....	....
1998-99	Mercyhurst	MAAC	25	2	11	13	0	....	....	....	....	....
99-2000	Mercyhurst	MAAC	36	5	14	19	24	....	....	....	....	....
2000-01	Mercyhurst	MAAC	35	3	15	18	28	....	....	....	....	....
2001-02	Elmira Jackals	UHL	72	3	8	11	82	14	0	3	3	6
2002-03	Elmira Jackals	UHL	43	2	9	11	56	....	....	....	....	....
	Rochester	AHL	9	0	1	1	8	....	....	....	....	....
	Bridgeport	AHL	28	0	3	3	24	1	0	0	0	10
2003-04	Bridgeport	AHL	73	1	6	7	86	7	1	1	2	6
2004-05	Bridgeport	AHL	64	0	8	8	63	....	....	....	....	....

Signed as a free agent by **NY Islanders**, July 2, 2003.

ROBITAILLE, Louis (ROH-buh-tigh, LOO-ee) WSH.

Left wing. Shoots left. 6'1", 192 lbs. Born, Montreal, Que., March 16, 1982.

			Regular Season					Playoffs				
Season	Club	League	GP	G	A	Pts	PIM	GP	G	A	Pts	PIM
99-2000	Montreal Rocket	QMJHL	71	3	21	24	266	5	1	1	2	18
2000-01	Montreal Rocket	QMJHL	69	2	10	12	269	....	....	....	....	....
2001-02	Montreal Rocket	QMJHL	71	3	28	31	294	7	3	0	3	241
2002-03	Montreal Rocket	QMJHL	60	7	23	30	191	7	0	10	10	12
2003-04	Portland Pirates	AHL	58	1	5	6	103	5	1	0	1	17
	Quad City	UHL	2	0	1	1	10	....	....	....	....	....
2004-05	Portland Pirates	AHL	59	2	3	5	186	....	....	....	....	....

Signed as a free agent by **Washington**, August 24, 2004.

ROCHE, Ken (ROHCH, KEHN) NYR

Center. Shoots left. 5'11", 202 lbs. Born, Boston, MA, January 2, 1984.
(NY Rangers' 3rd choice, 75th overall, in 2003 Entry Draft).

			Regular Season					Playoffs				
Season	Club	League	GP	G	A	Pts	PIM	GP	G	A	Pts	PIM
2000-01	St. Sebastian's	High-MA	31	20	18	38	....	....	....	....	....	....
2001-02	St. Sebastian's	High-MA	31	27	33	60	....	....	....	....	....	....
2002-03	St. Sebastian's	High-MA	29	25	28	53	16	....	....	....	....	....
2003-04	Boston University	H-East	38	9	9	18	14	....	....	....	....	....
2004-05	Boston University	H-East	39	5	6	11	37	....	....	....	....	....

RODMAN, Marcel (RAWD-muhn, mahr-SEHL) BOS.

Right wing. Shoots right. 6'1", 183 lbs. Born, Jesenice, Yugoslavia, September 25, 1981.
(Boston's 8th choice, 282nd overall, in 2001 Entry Draft).

			Regular Season					Playoffs				
Season	Club	League	GP	G	A	Pts	PIM	GP	G	A	Pts	PIM
1997-98	Jesenice Jr.	Sloven-Jr.	44	29	44	73	14	....	....	....	....	....
1998-99	Pickering Panthers	OPJHL	37	30	21	51	8	....	....	....	....	....
99-2000	Peterborough	OHL	61	17	20	37	16	5	1	2	3	0
2000-01	Peterborough	OHL	61	36	35	71	14	7	4	2	6	2
2001-02	Acroni Jesenice	IEHL	7	4	2	6	4	....	....	....	....	....
	HK Acroni Jesenice	Slovenia	9	12	6	18	4	....	....	....	....	....
2002-03	EHC Linz	Austria	44	22	25	47	22	....	....	....	....	....
2003-04	Krefeld Pinguine	Germany	52	3	9	12	18	....	....	....	....	....
2004-05	HK Acroni Jesenice	Interliga	25	12	24	36	20	....	....	....	....	....
	HK Acroni Jesenice	Slovenia	17	10	18	28	36	....	....	....	....	....

ROGERS, Andy (RAW-juhrs, AN-dee) T.B.

Defense. Shoots left. 6'5", 208 lbs. Born, Calgary, Alta., August 25, 1986.
(Tampa Bay's 1st choice, 30th overall, in 2004 Entry Draft).

			Regular Season					Playoffs				
Season	Club	League	GP	G	A	Pts	PIM	GP	G	A	Pts	PIM
2000-01	Calgary AA Gold	CMHA	32	2	7	9	32	....	....	....	....	....
2001-02	Calgary AAA Gold	CBHL	30	1	13	14	80	....	....	....	....	....
2002-03	Calgary Hitmen	WHL	25	0	3	3	17	....	....	....	....	....
2003-04	Calgary Hitmen	WHL	64	1	3	4	89	7	0	0	0	11
2004-05	Calgary Hitmen	WHL	18	1	4	5	36	....	....	....	....	....
	Prince George	WHL	30	1	5	6	49	....	....	....	....	....

ROHLFS, David (ROHLFS, DAY-vihd) EDM.

Right wing. Shoots right. 6'3", 219 lbs. Born, Ann Arbor, MI, June 4, 1984.
(Edmonton's 7th choice, 154th overall, in 2003 Entry Draft).

			Regular Season					Playoffs				
Season	Club	League	GP	G	A	Pts	PIM	GP	G	A	Pts	PIM
2000-01	Det. Compuware	MWEHL	70	35	21	56	....	....	....	....	....	....
	Det. Compuware	NAHL	4	0	1	1	0	....	....	....	....	....
2001-02	Det. Compuware	NAHL	60	13	10	23	36	....	....	....	....	....
2002-03	Det. Compuware	NAHL	53	30	14	44	36	5	2	1	3	8
2003-04	U. of Michigan	CCHA	43	7	6	13	26	....	....	....	....	....
2004-05	U. of Michigan	CCHA	34	5	5	10	14	....	....	....	....	....

ROME, Aaron (ROHM, AIR-uhn) ANA.

Defense. Shoots left. 6'1", 230 lbs. Born, Nesbitt, Man., September 27, 1983.
(Los Angeles' 4th choice, 104th overall, in 2002 Entry Draft).

			Regular Season					Playoffs				
Season	Club	League	GP	G	A	Pts	PIM	GP	G	A	Pts	PIM
1998-99	Sask. Contacts	SMHL	STATISTICS NOT AVAILABLE									
	Saskatoon Blades	WHL	1	0	0	0	0	....	....	....	....	....
99-2000	Saskatoon Blades	WHL	47	0	6	6	22	1	0	0	0	0
2000-01	Saskatoon Blades	WHL	3	0	0	0	2	....	....	....	....	....
	Kootenay Ice	WHL	53	2	8	10	43	11	1	3	4	6
2001-02	Kootenay Ice	WHL	33	4	13	17	55	....	....	....	....	....
	Swift Current	WHL	37	3	11	14	113	10	1	4	5	23
2002-03	Swift Current	WHL	61	12	44	56	201	4	1	0	1	20
2003-04	Swift Current	WHL	41	7	26	33	122	....	....	....	....	....
	Moose Jaw	WHL	28	3	16	19	88	8	0	6	6	17
2004-05	Cincinnati	AHL	75	2	14	16	130	12	3	3	6	33

WHL East Second All-Star Team (2004)

Signed as a free agent by **Anaheim**, June 7, 2004.

ROME, Ashton (ROHM, ASH-tuhn) BOS.

Right wing. Shoots right. 6'1", 202 lbs. Born, Nesbitt, Man., December 31, 1985.
(Boston's 3rd choice, 108th overall, in 2004 Entry Draft).

			Regular Season					Playoffs				
Season	Club	League	GP	G	A	Pts	PIM	GP	G	A	Pts	PIM
2002-03	Moose Jaw	WHL	61	5	10	15	103	13	1	1	2	6
2003-04	Moose Jaw	WHL	72	15	22	37	139	10	6	2	8	18
2004-05	Moose Jaw	WHL	41	10	17	27	84	....	....	....	....	....
	Red Deer Rebels	WHL	31	9	10	19	39	7	3	1	4	14

ROMY , Kevin (ROH-mee, KEH-vihn) PHI.

Center. Shoots left. 5'11", 180 lbs. Born, La Chaux-de-Fonds, Switz., January 31, 1985.
(Philadelphia's 8th choice, 108th overall, in 2003 Entry Draft).

			Regular Season					Playoffs				
Season	Club	League	GP	G	A	Pts	PIM	GP	G	A	Pts	PIM
2000-01	Chaux-de-Fonds Jr.	Swiss-Jr.	24	28	16	44	42	....	....	....	....	....
	Chaux-de-Fonds	Swiss	17	0	0	0	0	2	0	0	0	0
2001-02	Chaux-de-Fonds	Swiss-2	35	10	13	23	16	10	5	5	10	6
	Chaux-de-Fonds Jr.	Swiss-Jr.	1	0	0	0	0	....	....	....	....	....
2002-03	Geneve	Swiss	35	2	2	4	18	6	0	0	0	2
	Chaux-de-Fonds	Swiss-2	1	0	0	0	0	....	....	....	....	....
2003-04	Geneve	Swiss	39	6	7	13	10	12	1	2	3	6
2004-05	Geneve	Swiss	41	10	12	22	18	4	0	0	0	2

ROONEEM, Mark (ROO-neem, MAHRK) MIN.

Left wing. Shoots left. 6'2", 185 lbs. Born, Hinton, Alta., January 9, 1983.
(Los Angeles' 5th choice, 115th overall, in 2002 Entry Draft).

			Regular Season					Playoffs				
Season	Club	League	GP	G	A	Pts	PIM	GP	G	A	Pts	PIM
1998-99	Spruce Grove	AMBHL	36	32	30	62	183	....	....	....	....	....
99-2000	Kamloops Blazers	WHL	50	3	8	11	39	4	0	0	0	4
2000-01	Kamloops Blazers	WHL	62	8	9	17	77	4	1	0	1	8
2001-02	Kamloops Blazers	WHL	69	18	23	41	77	4	0	0	0	10
2002-03	Kamloops Blazers	WHL	40	9	6	15	60	....	....	....	....	....
	Calgary Hitmen	WHL	31	2	8	10	43	5	0	2	2	0
2003-04	Calgary Hitmen	WHL	52	22	18	40	61	7	1	2	3	4
2004-05	Houston Aeros	AHL	1	0	0	0	0	....	....	....	....	....
	Louisiana	ECHL	57	17	10	27	72	....	....	....	....	....
	Pensacola	ECHL	8	2	7	9	6	4	0	1	1	2

Signed as a free agent by **Minnesota**, June 4, 2004.

ROSEHILL, Jay (ROHZ-hihl, JAY) T.B.

Defense. Shoots left. 6'3", 210 lbs. Born, Olds, Alta., July 16, 1985.
(Tampa Bay's 6th choice, 227th overall, in 2003 Entry Draft).

			Regular Season					Playoffs				
Season	Club	League	GP	G	A	Pts	PIM	GP	G	A	Pts	PIM
2002-03	Olds Grizzlys	AJHL	59	1	4	5	219	....	....	....	....	....
2003-04	Olds Grizzlys	AJHL	42	4	12	16	172	14	2	2	4	....
2004-05	U. Minn-Duluth	WCHA	34	0	5	5	103	....	....	....	....	....

ROULEAU, Alexandre (ROO-loh, al-ehx-AHN-druh) PIT.

Defense. Shoots left. 6'1", 192 lbs. Born, Mont-Laurier, Que., July 29, 1983.
(Pittsburgh's 4th choice, 96th overall, in 2001 Entry Draft).

			Regular Season					Playoffs				
Season	Club	League	GP	G	A	Pts	PIM	GP	G	A	Pts	PIM
1998-99	Amos Forestiers	QAAA	41	7	6	13	144	....	....	....	....	....
99-2000	Amos Forestiers	QAAA	25	5	10	15	114	....	....	....	....	....
	Val-d'Or Foreurs	QMJHL	41	3	3	6	39	....	....	....	....	....
2000-01	Val-d'Or Foreurs	QMJHL	70	8	17	25	124	21	1	0	1	46
2001-02	Val-d'Or Foreurs	QMJHL	69	14	25	39	174	7	0	2	2	16
2002-03	Val-d'Or Foreurs	QMJHL	31	7	12	19	92	....	....	....	....	....
	Quebec Remparts	QMJHL	24	9	17	26	74	11	2	4	6	23
2003-04	Wilkes-Barre	AHL	14	0	2	2	16	....	....	....	....	....
	Wheeling Nailers	ECHL	30	3	1	4	38	5	0	1	1	6
2004-05	Wheeling Nailers	ECHL	70	3	13	16	127	....	....	....	....	....
	Wilkes-Barre	AHL	....	....	....	....	....	2	0	0	0	7

QMJHL Second All-Star Team (2003)

ROUSSIN, Dany (roo-SEH, DA-nee) L.A.

Center. Shoots left. 6'1", 190 lbs. Born, Quebec City, Que., January 9, 1985.
(Los Angeles' 2nd choice, 50th overall, in 2005 Entry Draft).

			Regular Season					Playoffs				
Season	Club	League	GP	G	A	Pts	PIM	GP	G	A	Pts	PIM
2000-01	Ste-Foy	QAAA	38	27	27	54	42	16	8	13	21	16
2001-02	Sherbrooke	QMJHL	66	10	14	24	38	....	....	....	....	....
2002-03	Sherbrooke	QMJHL	33	8	8	16	18	....	....	....	....	....
	Rimouski Oceanic	QMJHL	38	12	26	38	69	....	....	....	....	....
2003-04	Rimouski Oceanic	QMJHL	66	*59	58	117	70	9	2	10	12	12
2004-05	Rimouski Oceanic	QMJHL	69	54	62	116	66	13	11	9	20	8

• Re-entered NHL Entry Draft. Originally Florida's 10th choice, 223rd overall, in 2003 Entry Draft.
QMJHL First All-Star Team (2004) • QMJHL Second All-Star Team (2005)

ROY, Jimmy (ROI, JIHM-mee)

Center. Shoots right. 5'11", 170 lbs. Born, Sioux Lookout, Ont., September 22, 1975.
(Dallas' 7th choice, 254th overall, in 1994 Entry Draft).

			Regular Season					Playoffs				
Season	Club	League	GP	G	A	Pts	PIM	GP	G	A	Pts	PIM
1993-94	Thunder Bay Flyers	USHL	46	21	33	54	101	....	....	....	....	....
1994-95	Michigan Tech	WCHA	38	5	11	16	62	....	....	....	....	....
1995-96	Michigan Tech	WCHA	42	17	17	34	84	....	....	....	....	....
1996-97	Canada	Nat-Tm	55	10	17	27	82	....	....	....	....	....
1997-98	Manitoba Moose	IHL	61	8	10	18	133	3	0	0	0	6
1998-99	Manitoba Moose	IHL	78	10	16	26	185	5	0	1	1	6
99-2000	Manitoba Moose	IHL	74	12	9	21	187	1	0	0	0	16
2000-01	Manitoba Moose	IHL	77	18	13	31	150	12	1	1	2	22
2001-02	Manitoba Moose	AHL	73	16	22	38	167	7	2	0	2	28
2002-03	Manitoba Moose	AHL	50	5	10	15	95	14	4	4	8	27
2003-04	Manitoba Moose	AHL	78	13	16	29	186	....	....	....	....	....
2004-05	Manitoba Moose	AHL	50	10	7	17	187	13	2	1	3	39

ROY, Mathieu (WAH, MA-tyew) EDM.

Defense. Shoots right. 6'2", 214 lbs. Born, St-Georges, Que., August 10, 1983.
(Edmonton's 10th choice, 215th overall, in 2003 Entry Draft).

			Regular Season					Playoffs				
Season	Club	League	GP	G	A	Pts	PIM	GP	G	A	Pts	PIM
1998-99	Levis	QAAA	11	4	1	5	16	....	....	....	....	....
99-2000	Levis	QAAA	24	3	4	7	88	6	1	1	2	22
	Val-d'Or Foreurs	QMJHL	48	1	4	5	66	....	....	....	....	....
2000-01	Val-d'Or Foreurs	QMJHL	30	0	7	7	60	17	0	0	0	4
2001-02	Val-d'Or Foreurs	QMJHL	53	7	26	33	103	7	0	2	2	19
2002-03	Val-d'Or Foreurs	QMJHL	52	11	21	32	164	7	1	0	1	8
2003-04	Toronto	AHL	30	0	2	2	46	....	....	....	....	....
	Columbus	ECHL	10	1	2	3	13	....	....	....	....	....
2004-05	Edmonton	AHL	51	3	22	25	68	....	....	....	....	....

RUDENKO, Konstantin (roo-DEHN-koh, KOHN-stan-tihn) PHI.

Left wing. Shoots right. 5'11", 180 lbs. Born, Ust-Kamenogorsk, USSR, July 23, 1981.
(Philadelphia's 3rd choice, 160th overall, in 1999 Entry Draft).

			Regular Season					Playoffs				
Season	Club	League	GP	G	A	Pts	PIM	GP	G	A	Pts	PIM
1997-98	Omsk 2	Russia-3	22	7	8	15	4	....	....	....	....	....
1998-99	Cherepovets	Russia	28	15	9	24	67	....	....	....	....	....
	Cherepovets 2	Russia-3	3	0	1	1	4	....	....	....	....	....
99-2000	St. Petersburg 2	Russia-3	7	2	4	6	2	....	....	....	....	....
	SKA St. Petersburg	Russia	19	1	1	2	10	1	0	0	0	0
2000-01	Yaroslavl	Russia	18	2	3	5	28	9	2	1	3	8
2001-02	Yaroslavl 2	Russia-3	2	1	1	2	2	....	....	....	....	....
	Yaroslavl	Russia	8	0	2	2	12	1	0	0	0	0
2002-03	Yaroslavl	Russia	20	3	4	7	20	2	0	0	0	0
2003-04	Yaroslavl 2	Russia-3	4	4	2	6	4	....	....	....	....	....
	Yaroslavl	Russia	43	10	12	22	18	3	0	0	0	0
2004-05	Yaroslavl 2	Russia-3	20	13	14	27	42	....	....	....	....	....
	Yaroslavl	Russia	21	1	0	1	8	2	0	0	0	0

RUGGERI, Rosario (ROO-gee-AIR-ee, roh-ZAHR-ee-oh) PHI.

Defense. Shoots left. 6'1", 202 lbs. Born, Montreal, Que., June 8, 1984.
(Philadelphia's 2nd choice, 105th overall, in 2002 Entry Draft).

			Regular Season					Playoffs				
Season	Club	League	GP	G	A	Pts	PIM	GP	G	A	Pts	PIM
99-2000	Lac St-Louis Lions	QAAA	40	0	7	7	70	....	....	....	....	....
2000-01	Lac St-Louis Lions	QAAA	24	6	11	17	117	5	1	3	4	4
	Montreal Rocket	QMJHL	9	0	0	0	8	....	....	....	....	....
2001-02	Chicoutimi	QMJHL	60	2	15	17	131	4	1	1	2	10
2002-03	Chicoutimi	QMJHL	70	10	37	47	64	3	0	0	0	21
2003-04	Chicoutimi	QMJHL	65	12	36	48	98	18	2	2	4	28
2004-05	Philadelphia	AHL	5	0	0	0	0	....	....	....	....	....
	Trenton Titans	ECHL	49	2	12	14	77	20	0	2	2	26

RULLIER, Joe (ROO-yay, JOH) NYR

Defense. Shoots right. 6'3", 230 lbs. Born, Montreal, Que., January 28, 1980.
(Los Angeles' 5th choice, 133rd overall, in 1998 Entry Draft).

			Regular Season					Playoffs				
Season	Club	League	GP	G	A	Pts	PIM	GP	G	A	Pts	PIM
1996-97	Montreal-Bourassa	QAAA	24	5	10	15	....	....	....	....	....	....
	Rimouski Oceanic	QMJHL	23	0	3	3	87	4	0	0	0	11
1997-98	Rimouski Oceanic	QMJHL	55	1	10	11	176	16	1	4	5	34
1998-99	Rimouski Oceanic	QMJHL	54	7	32	39	202	11	2	3	5	26
99-2000	Rimouski Oceanic	QMJHL	49	3	32	35	161	14	1	8	9	34
2000-01	Lowell	AHL	63	1	1	2	162	4	0	1	1	2
2001-02	Manchester	AHL	62	2	2	4	133	3	0	0	0	5
2002-03	Manchester	AHL	62	3	6	9	166	3	0	0	0	2
2003-04	Manchester	AHL	73	3	12	15	186	6	0	0	0	4
2004-05	Manchester	AHL	71	3	13	16	322	6	0	2	2	27

Signed as a free agent by **NY Rangers**, August 10, 2005.

RUMSEY, Myles (RUHM-see, MIGH-uhls) CGY.

Defense. Shoots right. 6'1", 200 lbs. Born, Winnipeg, Man., November 5, 1986.
(Calgary's 8th choice, 221st overall, in 2005 Entry Draft).

			Regular Season					Playoffs				
Season	Club	League	GP	G	A	Pts	PIM	GP	G	A	Pts	PIM
2002-03	Wpg. South Blues	MJHL	56	1	10	11	88	....	....	....	....	....
	Swift Current	WHL	3	0	0	0	0	....	....	....	....	....
2003-04	Swift Current	WHL	66	0	4	4	61	5	0	0	0	5
2004-05	Swift Current	WHL	57	2	4	6	102	....	....	....	....	....

RUSSELL, Kris (RUH-sehl, KRIHS) CBJ

Defense. Shoots left. 5'10", 160 lbs. Born, Caroline, Alta., May 2, 1987.
(Columbus' 3rd choice, 67th overall, in 2005 Entry Draft).

			Regular Season					Playoffs				
Season	Club	League	GP	G	A	Pts	PIM	GP	G	A	Pts	PIM
2003-04	Medicine Hat	WHL	55	4	15	19	30	20	3	2	5	4
2004-05	Medicine Hat	WHL	72	26	35	61	37	10	2	1	3	4

WHL East Second All-Star Team (2005)

RUSSELL, Ryan (RUH-sehl, RIGH-uhn) NYR

Center. Shoots left. 5'9", 165 lbs. Born, Caroline, Alta., May 2, 1987.
(NY Rangers' 9th choice, 211th overall, in 2005 Entry Draft).

			Regular Season					Playoffs				
Season	Club	League	GP	G	A	Pts	PIM	GP	G	A	Pts	PIM
2003-04	Kootenay Ice	WHL	67	3	9	12	27	4	0	0	0	0
2004-05	Kootenay Ice	WHL	66	32	21	53	18	16	6	7	13	12

RUZICKA, Stefan (roo-ZHEECH-kuh, STEH-fan) PHI.

Left wing. Shoots right. 5'11", 189 lbs. Born, Nitra, Czech., February 17, 1985.
(Philadelphia's 4th choice, 81st overall, in 2003 Entry Draft).

			Regular Season					Playoffs				
Season	Club	League	GP	G	A	Pts	PIM	GP	G	A	Pts	PIM
2000-01	Nitra Jr.	Slovak-Jr.	38	30	15	45	....	....	....	....	....	....
2001-02	HKM Nitra Jr.	Slovak-Jr.	29	27	25	52	....	....	....	....	....	....
	HKM Nitra	Slovakia	19	0	5	5	29	....	....	....	....	....
2002-03	HKM Nitra Jr.	Slovak-Jr.	30	18	22	40	64	....	....	....	....	....
	HKM Nitra	Slovak-2	17	5	7	12	4	....	....	....	....	....
2003-04	Owen Sound	OHL	62	34	38	72	63	7	1	6	7	8
	Philadelphia	AHL	2	0	0	0	0	3	1	0	1	2
2004-05	Owen Sound	OHL	62	37	33	70	61	8	3	3	6	14

OHL All-Rookie Team (2004) • OHL Second All-Star Team (2004)

RYABYKIN, Dmitri (ryah-BEE-kihn, dih-MEE-tree) CGY.

Defense. Shoots right. 6'1", 203 lbs. Born, Chirchik, USSR, March 24, 1976.
(Calgary's 2nd choice, 45th overall, in 1994 Entry Draft).

			Regular Season					Playoffs				
Season	Club	League	GP	G	A	Pts	PIM	GP	G	A	Pts	PIM
1994-95	Dynamo Moscow	CIS	48	0	0	0	12	11	0	2	2	0
1995-96	Dynamo Moscow	CIS	47	3	1	4	49	13	1	1	2	6
1996-97	Dynamo Moscow	Russia	34	1	10	11	12	4	0	0	0	8
1997-98	Dynamo Moscow	Russia	34	1	4	5	16	....	....	....	....	....
	Dynamo Moscow	EuroHL	7	1	1	2	6	....	....	....	....	....
1998-99	Avangard Omsk	Russia	40	3	10	13	42	5	0	0	0	42
99-2000	Avangard Omsk	Russia	36	5	10	15	42	8	3	2	5	2
2000-01	Avangard Omsk	Russia	43	3	8	11	101	16	3	4	7	16
2001-02	Avangard Omsk	Russia	17	4	7	11	60	11	4	3	7	6
2002-03	Avangard Omsk	Russia	51	7	18	25	113	12	1	2	3	33
2003-04	Avangard Omsk	Russia	57	8	12	20	94	11	1	4	5	4
2004-05	Omsk 2	Russia-3	1	0	1	1	0	....	....	....	....	....
	Avangard Omsk	Russia	43	5	12	17	109	10	2	2	4	12

RYAN, Billy (RIGH-uhn, BIHL-lee) NYR

Center. Shoots left. 6'1", 175 lbs. Born, Boston, MA, October 23, 1985.
(NY Rangers' 8th choice, 80th overall, in 2004 Entry Draft).

			Regular Season					Playoffs				
Season	Club	League	GP	G	A	Pts	PIM	GP	G	A	Pts	PIM
2002-03	Cushing	High-MA	29	14	33	47	10	....	....	....	....	....
2003-04	Cushing	High-MA	37	35	55	90	40	....	....	....	....	....
2004-05	U. of Maine	H-East	34	6	9	15	30	....	....	....	....	....

RYAN, Bobby (RIGH-uhn, BAW-bee) ANA.

Right wing. Shoots right. 6'2", 213 lbs. Born, Cherry Hill, NJ, March 17, 1987.
(Anaheim's 1st choice, 2nd overall, in 2005 Entry Draft).

			Regular Season					Playoffs				
Season	Club	League	GP	G	A	Pts	PIM	GP	G	A	Pts	PIM
2003-04	Owen Sound	OHL	65	22	17	39	52	7	1	2	3	2
2004-05	Owen Sound	OHL	62	37	52	89	51	8	2	7	9	8

OHL First All-Star Team (2005)

RYAN, Matt (RIGH-uhn, MAT) L.A.

Center. Shoots left. 5'11", 182 lbs. Born, Sharon, Ont., November 12, 1983.

			Regular Season					Playoffs				
Season	Club	League	GP	G	A	Pts	PIM	GP	G	A	Pts	PIM
2001-02	Niagara University	CHA	32	7	12	19	32	....	....	....	....	....
2002-03	Niagara University	CHA	9	6	2	8	14	....	....	....	....	....
	Guelph Storm	OHL	48	14	11	25	34	11	2	7	9	0
2003-04	Guelph Storm	OHL	68	42	35	77	63	22	8	11	19	24
2004-05	Manchester	AHL	77	9	15	24	59	6	0	1	1	4

Signed as a free agent by **Los Angeles**, August 2, 2004.

RYAN, Michael (RIGH-uhn, MIGH-kuhl) BUF.

Center. Shoots left. 6'1", 180 lbs. Born, Boston, MA, May 16, 1980.
(Dallas' 1st choice, 32nd overall, in 1999 Entry Draft).

			Regular Season					Playoffs				
Season	Club	League	GP	G	A	Pts	PIM	GP	G	A	Pts	PIM
1997-98	Bos. College High	High-MA	23	22	14	36	28	....	....	....	....	....
1998-99	Bos. College High	High-MA	21	20	24	44	22	....	....	....	....	....
99-2000	Northeastern	H-East	32	4	9	13	47	....	....	....	....	....
2000-01	Northeastern	H-East	33	17	12	29	52	....	....	....	....	....
2001-02	Northeastern	H-East	36	24	15	39	54	....	....	....	....	....
2002-03	Northeastern	H-East	34	18	14	32	30	....	....	....	....	....
2003-04	Rochester	AHL	45	3	9	12	31	....	....	....	....	....
2004-05	Rochester	AHL	59	11	11	22	20	5	0	1	1	4

Traded to **Buffalo** by **Dallas** with Dallas's 2nd round choice (Branislav Fabry) in 2003 Entry Draft for Stu Barnes, March 10, 2003.

RYAN, Prestin (RIGH-uhn, PREH-stuhn) VAN.

Defense. Shoots left. 6', 190 lbs. Born, Arcola, Sask., June 29, 1980.

			Regular Season					Playoffs				
Season	Club	League	GP	G	A	Pts	PIM	GP	G	A	Pts	PIM
2000-01	U. of Maine	H-East	DID NOT PLAY – FRESHMAN									
2001-02	U. of Maine	H-East	39	6	9	15	*91	....	....	....	....	....
2002-03	U. of Maine	H-East	37	1	8	9	*120	....	....	....	....	....
2003-04	U. of Maine	H-East	43	4	18	22	*148	....	....	....	....	....
	Syracuse Crunch	AHL	....	....	....	....	....	3	0	0	0	2
2004-05	Syracuse Crunch	AHL	59	3	6	9	161	....	....	....	....	....

Hockey East Second All-Star Team (2004) • NCAA East Second All-American Team (2004) • NCAA Championship All-Tournament Team (2004)

Signed as a free agent by **Columbus**, April 12, 2004. Signed as a free agent by **Vancouver**, August 18, 2005.

RYBIN, Maxim (ray-bihn, max-EEM) ANA.

Left wing. Shoots right. 5'8", 182 lbs. Born, Zhukovsky, USSR, June 15, 1981.
(Anaheim's 4th choice, 141st overall, in 1999 Entry Draft).

			Regular Season					Playoffs				
Season	Club	League	GP	G	A	Pts	PIM	GP	G	A	Pts	PIM
1996-97	SAK Moscow	Russia-3	5	0	0	0	4	....	....	....	....	....
	Spartak Moscow	Russia	6	0	0	0	0	....	....	....	....	....
1997-98	Spartak Moscow 2	Russia-3	25	13	5	18	26	....	....	....	....	....
	Spartak Moscow	Russia	5	0	0	0	2	....	....	....	....	....
1998-99	Spartak Moscow	Russia	53	15	12	27	83	....	....	....	....	....
99-2000	Sarnia Sting	OHL	66	29	27	56	47	7	4	1	5	2
2000-01	Sarnia Sting	OHL	67	34	36	70	60	4	0	3	3	2
2001-02	Ufa	Russia	41	6	4	10	30	....	....	....	....	....
2002-03	Cherepovets	Russia	3	0	1	1	2	....	....	....	....	....
	Spartak Moscow	Russia	29	9	4	13	65	....	....	....	....	....
2003-04	Cherepovets	Russia	53	14	14	28	24	....	....	....	....	....
	Cherepovets 2	Russia-3	3	2	2	4	2	....	....	....	....	....
2004-05	Cherepovets	Russia	12	0	1	1	6	....	....	....	....	....
	Spartak Moscow	Russia	30	2	15	17	20	....	....	....	....	....

RYDER, Dan (RIGH-duhr, DAN) CGY.

Center. Shoots right. 5'10", 192 lbs. Born, Bonavista, Nfld., January 12, 1987.
(Calgary's 3rd choice, 74th overall, in 2005 Entry Draft).

			Regular Season					Playoffs				
Season	Club	League	GP	G	A	Pts	PIM	GP	G	A	Pts	PIM
2003-04	Peterborough	OHL	63	20	32	52	16	....	....	....	....	....
2004-05	Peterborough	OHL	68	29	53	82	55	....	....	....	....	....

RYNO, Johan (RYUH-noh, YO-han) DET.

Right wing. Shoots left. 6'4", 198 lbs. Born, Orebro, Sweden, June 5, 1986.
(Detroit's 6th choice, 137th overall, in 2005 Entry Draft).

			Regular Season					Playoffs				
Season	Club	League	GP	G	A	Pts	PIM	GP	G	A	Pts	PIM
2003-04	IFK Hallsberg	Sweden-3	28	9	18	27	30	....	....	....	....	....
2004-05	IFK Arboga IK	Sweden-2	2	0	0	0	0	....	....	....	....	....
	IFK Kumla Jr.	Swe-Jr.	29	20	18	38	14	....	....	....	....	....

RYZNAR, Jason (RIHZ-nuhr, JAY-suhn) N.J.

Left wing. Shoots left. 6'3", 205 lbs. Born, Anchorage, AK, February 19, 1983.
(New Jersey's 3rd choice, 64th overall, in 2002 Entry Draft).

			Regular Season					Playoffs				
Season	Club	League	GP	G	A	Pts	PIM	GP	G	A	Pts	PIM
99-2000	USA U-17	USDP	52	5	10	15	22	....	....	....	....	....
2000-01	USA U-18	USDP	66	15	17	32	102	....	....	....	....	....
2001-02	U. of Michigan	CCHA	40	9	7	16	22	....	....	....	....	....
2002-03	U. of Michigan	CCHA	34	7	9	16	24	....	....	....	....	....
2003-04	U. of Michigan	CCHA	36	6	11	17	28	....	....	....	....	....
2004-05	U. of Michigan	CCHA	36	6	17	23	46	....	....	....	....	....

SAGAT, Martin (SHA-gat, MAHR-tehn) TOR.

Left wing. Shoots right. 6'3", 191 lbs. Born, Handlova, Czech., November 11, 1984.
(Toronto's 2nd choice, 91st overall, in 2003 Entry Draft).

			Regular Season					Playoffs				
Season	Club	League	GP	G	A	Pts	PIM	GP	G	A	Pts	PIM
2002-03	Dukla Trencin Jr.	Slovak-Jr.	37	18	20	38	49	3	1	3	4	4
	Dukla Trencin	Slovakia	17	0	0	0	0	2	0	0	0	0
2003-04	Kootenay Ice	WHL	57	11	32	43	39	4	0	2	2	2
2004-05	Kootenay Ice	WHL	72	17	46	63	51	16	8	14	22	18

ST. JACQUES, Chris (SAINT ZHAWK, KRIHS) TOR.

Center. Shoots right. 5'8", 181 lbs. Born, Edmonton, Alta., January 22, 1983.

			Regular Season					Playoffs				
Season	Club	League	GP	G	A	Pts	PIM	GP	G	A	Pts	PIM
99-2000	Medicine Hat	WHL	61	21	18	39	65	....	....	....	....	....
2000-01	Medicine Hat	WHL	70	37	36	73	84	....	....	....	....	....
2001-02	Medicine Hat	WHL	45	30	38	68	50	....	....	....	....	....
2002-03	Medicine Hat	WHL	70	31	*65	96	78	11	2	14	16	17
2003-04	Medicine Hat	WHL	64	33	59	92	80	20	12	*15	*27	18
2004-05	St. John's	AHL	4	0	0	0	2	....	....	....	....	....
	Pensacola	ECHL	66	18	29	47	74	3	0	1	1	6

Signed as a free agent by **Toronto**, June 2, 2004.

SALCIDO, Brian (sal-SEE-doh, BRIGH-uhn) ANA.

Defense. Shoots left. 6'2", 188 lbs. Born, Los Angeles, CA, April 14, 1985.
(Anaheim's 5th choice, 141st overall, in 2005 Entry Draft).

			Regular Season					Playoffs				
Season	Club	League	GP	G	A	Pts	PIM	GP	G	A	Pts	PIM
2002-03	Shat.-St. Mary's	High-MN	53	8	35	43	....	....	....	....	....	....
2003-04	Colorado College	WCHA	12	1	0	1	48	....	....	....	....	....
2004-05	Colorado College	WCHA	38	7	23	30	52	....	....	....	....	....

SALMONSSON, Johannes (sal-MUHN-suhn, yoh-HA-nuhs) PIT.

Left wing. Shoots left. 6'2", 183 lbs. Born, Uppsala, Sweden, February 7, 1986.
(Pittsburgh's 2nd choice, 31st overall, in 2004 Entry Draft).

			Regular Season					Playoffs				
Season	Club	League	GP	G	A	Pts	PIM	GP	G	A	Pts	PIM
2002-03	Almtuna	Sweden-2	26	10	14	24	4	....	....	....	....	....
2003-04	Djurgarden Jr.	Swe-Jr.	6	4	9	13	6	....	....	....	....	....
	Djurgarden	Sweden	25	0	3	3	4	....	....	....	....	....
	Almtuna	Sweden-2	2	0	0	0	0	....	....	....	....	....
2004-05	Almtuna	Sweden-2	8	0	2	2	6	....	....	....	....	....
	Djurgarden Jr.	Swe-Jr.	4	2	0	2	4	....	....	....	....	....
	Djurgarden	Sweden	30	2	2	4	6	9	0	0	0	0

SALONEN, Pasi (SAH-loh-nehn, PA-see) WSH.

Left wing. Shoots left. 5'11", 187 lbs. Born, Vierumaki, Finland, December 18, 1985.
(Washington's 9th choice, 138th overall, in 2004 Entry Draft).

			Regular Season					Playoffs				
Season	Club	League	GP	G	A	Pts	PIM	GP	G	A	Pts	PIM
2002-03	HIFK Helsinki Jr.	Finland-Jr.	32	16	11	27	10	10	8	3	11	2
2003-04	HIFK Helsinki Jr.	Finland-Jr.	30	12	10	22	60	9	4	4	8	8
	HIFK Helsinki	Finland	3	0	0	0	0	....	....	....	....	....
2004-05			DID NOT PLAY – INJURED									

SANDSTROM, Jan (SAND-struhm, YAN) ANA.

Defense. Shoots left. 6', 190 lbs. Born, Pitea, Sweden, January 24, 1978.
(Anaheim's 5th choice, 173rd overall, in 1999 Entry Draft).

			Regular Season					Playoffs				
Season	Club	League	GP	G	A	Pts	PIM	GP	G	A	Pts	PIM
1994-95	Pitea HC	Sweden-2	12	1	0	1	4	....	....	....	....	....
1995-96	Pitea HC	Sweden-2	29	1	11	12	18	....	....	....	....	....
1996-97	Pitea HC	Sweden-2	28	3	4	7	28	....	....	....	....	....
1997-98	AIK Solna	Sweden	38	0	2	2	16	....	....	....	....	....
1998-99	AIK Solna	Sweden	47	2	7	9	18	....	....	....	....	....
99-2000	AIK Solna	Sweden	49	2	6	8	22	....	....	....	....	....
2000-01	Skelleftea AIK HK	Sweden-2	22	0	5	5	14	....	....	....	....	....
	AIK Solna	Sweden	18	1	3	4	10	....	....	....	....	....
2001-02	Lulea HF	Sweden	41	2	4	6	12	5	0	2	2	2
2002-03	Lulea HF	Sweden	48	3	5	8	36	4	1	0	1	6
2003-04	Lulea HF	Sweden	49	1	10	11	20	5	0	1	1	2
2004-05	Lulea HF	Sweden	41	2	5	7	30	4	0	0	0	0

SANNITZ, Raffaele (ZAH-nihts, ra-FIGH-ehl-lay) CBJ

Center. Shoots left. 6'1", 187 lbs. Born, Mendrisio, Switz., May 18, 1983.
(Columbus' 9th choice, 204th overall, in 2001 Entry Draft).

			Regular Season					Playoffs				
Season	Club	League	GP	G	A	Pts	PIM	GP	G	A	Pts	PIM
1997-98	HC Lugano Jr.	Swiss-Jr.	33	7	12	19	54	....	....	....	....	....
1998-99	HC Lugano Jr.	Swiss-Jr.	38	5	12	17	62	....	....	....	....	....
	HC Lugano	Swiss	8	0	1	1	0	....	....	....	....	....
99-2000	HC Lugano Jr.	Swiss-Jr.	33	13	16	29	47	....	....	....	....	....
	HC Lugano	Swiss	1	0	0	0	2	....	....	....	....	....
2000-01	HC Sierre	Swiss-2	2	0	0	0	0	....	....	....	....	....
	HC Lugano Jr.	Swiss-Jr.	35	22	30	52	152	2	0	0	0	0
	HC Lugano	Swiss	13	1	0	1	0	2	0	0	0	0
2001-02	HC Lugano Jr.	Swiss-Jr.	14	14	13	27	18	3	3	2	5	4
	HC Lugano	Swiss	38	3	4	7	37	12	1	1	2	2
2002-03	HC Lugano	Swiss	14	1	1	2	37	....	....	....	....	....
2003-04	HC Lugano	Swiss	48	7	9	16	20	16	2	1	3	8
	EHC Chur	Swiss-2	2	2	1	3	2	....	....	....	....	....
2004-05	Syracuse Crunch	AHL	53	6	3	9	38	....	....	....	....	....
	Dayton Bombers	ECHL	2	0	3	3	0	....	....	....	....	....

• Missed majority of 2002-03 season recovering from shoulder injury suffered in game vs. Kloten (Swiss), October 12, 2002.

SANTORELLI, Michael (san-toh-REHL-ee, MIGH-kuhl) NSH.

Center. Shoots right. 5'11", 180 lbs. Born, Vancouver, B.C., December 14, 1985.
(Nashville's 6th choice, 178th overall, in 2004 Entry Draft).

			Regular Season					Playoffs				
Season	Club	League	GP	G	A	Pts	PIM	GP	G	A	Pts	PIM
2003-04	Vernon Vipers	BCHL	60	43	53	96	26	5	0	2	2	0
2004-05	Northern Mich.	CCHA	40	16	14	30	22	....	....	....	....	....

CCHA All-Rookie Team (2005)

SARAUER, Andrew (suh-ROW-uhr, AN-droo) **VAN.**

Left wing. Shoots left. 6'4", 194 lbs. Born, Saskatoon, Sask., November 17, 1984.
(Vancouver's 3rd choice, 125th overall, in 2004 Entry Draft).

			Regular Season					Playoffs				
Season	Club	League	GP	G	A	Pts	PIM	GP	G	A	Pts	PIM
2002-03	Victoria Salsa	BCHL	57	11	17	28	73	....	....	....	....	....
2003-04	Langley Hornets	BCHL	57	43	32	75	71	....	....	....	....	....
2004-05	Northern Mich.	CCHA	25	3	4	7	10	....	....	....	....	....

SAUER, Michael (SOW-uhr, MIGHK-uhl) **NYR**

Defense. Shoots right. 6'2", 208 lbs. Born, St. Cloud, MN, August 7, 1987.
(NY Rangers' 2nd choice, 40th overall, in 2005 Entry Draft).

			Regular Season					Playoffs				
Season	Club	League	GP	G	A	Pts	PIM	GP	G	A	Pts	PIM
2003-04	St. Cloud Tech	High-MN	18	12	16	28	34	....	....	....	....	....
2004-05	Portland	WHL	32	2	11	13	10	....	....	....	....	....

• Missed majority of 2004-05 season due to hip injury.

SAUNDERS, Nathan (SAWN-duhrs, NAY-thun) **ANA.**

Defense. Shoots right. 6'4", 216 lbs. Born, Charlottetown, P.E.I., April 25, 1985.
(Anaheim's 5th choice, 119th overall, in 2003 Entry Draft).

			Regular Season					Playoffs				
Season	Club	League	GP	G	A	Pts	PIM	GP	G	A	Pts	PIM
2001-02	Moncton Wildcats	QMJHL	54	4	11	15	88	....	....	....	....	....
2002-03	Moncton Wildcats	QMJHL	69	1	13	14	241	6	2	3	5	12
2003-04	Moncton Wildcats	QMJHL	68	4	26	30	267	20	1	1	2	34
2004-05	Moncton Wildcats	QMJHL	70	5	23	28	198	12	2	2	4	24

SAVIELS, Agris (sah-VEE-ehls, AG-rihs)

Defense. Shoots left. 6'1", 210 lbs. Born, Riga, Latvia, January 15, 1982.
(Colorado's 4th choice, 63rd overall, in 2000 Entry Draft).

			Regular Season					Playoffs				
Season	Club	League	GP	G	A	Pts	PIM	GP	G	A	Pts	PIM
1996-97	Dynamo Riga Jr.	Latvia-Jr.	15	1	2	3	4	....	....	....	....	....
	HK Lido-Nafta	Latvia	40	4	15	19	40	....	....	....	....	....
1997-98	Dynamo Riga Jr.	Latvia-Jr.	15	1	2	3	4	....	....	....	....	....
	HK Lido-Nafta	Latvia	40	7	21	28	30	....	....	....	....	....
1998-99	Notre Dame	SMBHL	18	6	9	15	25	....	....	....	....	....
	Notre Dame	SJHL	30	6	13	19	....	....	....	....	....	....
99-2000	Owen Sound	OHL	65	7	25	32	56	....	....	....	....	....
2000-01	Owen Sound	OHL	68	14	37	51	46	5	0	1	1	2
2001-02	Owen Sound	OHL	60	5	27	32	37	....	....	....	....	....
2002-03	Hershey Bears	AHL	43	0	3	3	33	3	0	0	0	0
	Reading Royals	ECHL	8	1	0	1	4	....	....	....	....	....
2003-04	Hershey Bears	AHL	67	2	5	7	39	....	....	....	....	....
2004-05	Hershey Bears	AHL	47	0	5	5	41	....	....	....	....	....

SAWADA, Raymond (suh-WAW-duh, RAY-mawnd) **DAL.**

Right wing. Shoots right. 6'2", 195 lbs. Born, Richmond, B.C., February 19, 1985.
(Dallas' 3rd choice, 52nd overall, in 2004 Entry Draft).

			Regular Season					Playoffs				
Season	Club	League	GP	G	A	Pts	PIM	GP	G	A	Pts	PIM
2002-03	Richmond	PIJHL	36	7	17	24	155	....	....	....	....	....
2003-04	Nanaimo Clippers	BCHL	54	20	32	52	93	25	6	16	22	22
2004-05	Cornell Big Red	ECAC	35	4	5	9	48	....	....	....	....	....

SCALZO, Mario (SCAL-zoh, MAHR-ee-oh) **DAL.**

Defense. Shoots left. 5'9", 187 lbs. Born, St-Hubert, Que., November 11, 1984.

			Regular Season					Playoffs				
Season	Club	League	GP	G	A	Pts	PIM	GP	G	A	Pts	PIM
2001-02	Antoine-Girouard	QAAA	40	8	27	35	50	....	....	....	....	....
	Victoriaville Tigres	QMJHL	1	0	1	1	0	1	0	0	0	0
2002-03	Victoriaville Tigres	QMJHL	72	10	34	44	134	4	0	3	3	6
2003-04	Victoriaville Tigres	QMJHL	68	16	52	68	113	....	....	....	....	....
2004-05	Victoriaville Tigres	QMJHL	39	11	19	30	73	....	....	....	....	....
	Rimouski Oceanic	QMJHL	23	13	31	44	31	13	7	14	21	10

QMJHL All-Rookie Team (2003) • QMJHL Second All-Star Team (2004) • QMJHL First All-Star Team (2005) • Memorial Cup All-Star Team (2005)

Signed as a free agent by **Dallas**, August 5, 2005.

SCHADILOV, Igor (sha-DEE-lahf, EE-gor) **WSH.**

Defense. Shoots left. 6'2", 189 lbs. Born, Moscow, USSR, June 7, 1980.
(Washington's 10th choice, 249th overall, in 1999 Entry Draft).

			Regular Season					Playoffs				
Season	Club	League	GP	G	A	Pts	PIM	GP	G	A	Pts	PIM
1996-97	Dyn'o Moscow 2	Russia-3	30	3	7	10	30	....	....	....	....	....
1997-98	Dynamo Moscow	Russia	38	1	0	1	6	....	....	....	....	....
1998-99	Dyn'o Moscow 2	Russia-3	28	2	9	11	15	....	....	....	....	....
	Dynamo Moscow	Russia	2	0	0	0	0	....	....	....	....	....
	Krylja Sovetov	Russia	9	0	0	0	0	....	....	....	....	....
99-2000	THK Tver	Russia-2	14	0	3	3	6	....	....	....	....	....
	Dynamo Moscow	Russia	26	0	2	2	8	16	0	0	0	2
2000-01	Dynamo Moscow	Russia	34	1	5	6	12	....	....	....	....	....
2001-02	Cherepovets	Russia	33	7	3	10	10	4	0	0	0	2
2002-03	Cherepovets	Russia	32	3	3	6	28	12	1	3	4	4
2003-04	Dynamo Moscow	Russia	56	4	8	12	16	3	0	1	1	2
2004-05	Dynamo Moscow	Russia	34	0	5	5	12	....	....	....	....	....

SCHAEFFER, Kevin (SHAY-fuhr, KEH-vihn) **NSH.**

Defense. Shoots right. 6'1", 195 lbs. Born, Huntington, NY, October 16, 1984.
(Nashville's 7th choice, 193rd overall, in 2004 Entry Draft).

			Regular Season					Playoffs				
Season	Club	League	GP	G	A	Pts	PIM	GP	G	A	Pts	PIM
2002-03	NY Apple Core	EJHL	65	20	38	58	60	....	....	....	....	....
2003-04	Boston University	H-East	38	5	12	17	20	....	....	....	....	....
2004-05	Boston University	H-East	41	2	12	14	26	....	....	....	....	....

SCHAFER, Evan (SHAY-fuhr, EH-vuhn) **FLA.**

Defense. Shoots right. 6'2", 221 lbs. Born, Mankota, Sask., October 9, 1985.
(Florida's 4th choice, 105th overall, in 2004 Entry Draft).

			Regular Season					Playoffs				
Season	Club	League	GP	G	A	Pts	PIM	GP	G	A	Pts	PIM
2001-02	Sask. Contacts	SMHL	47	9	22	31	49	....	....	....	....	....
2002-03	Prince Albert	WHL	53	0	1	1	76	....	....	....	....	....
2003-04	Prince Albert	WHL	71	3	6	9	190	6	0	0	0	14
2004-05	Prince Albert	WHL	64	1	15	16	124	17	0	1	1	26

SCHAUER, Stefan (SHOW-uhr, SHTEH-fuhn) **OTT.**

Defense. Shoots left. 6'1", 185 lbs. Born, Schongau, West Germany, January 12, 1983.
(Ottawa's 6th choice, 162nd overall, in 2001 Entry Draft).

			Regular Season					Playoffs				
Season	Club	League	GP	G	A	Pts	PIM	GP	G	A	Pts	PIM
2000-01	Riessersee Jr.	Ger-Jr.	11	1	7	8	24	....	....	....	....	....
	Riessersee	German-2	39	1	2	3	12	5	0	1	1	0
2001-02	Riessersee	German-2	46	2	18	20	46	8	0	2	2	18
2002-03	Kolner Haie	Germany	28	0	1	1	12	15	1	0	1	2
	EV Duisburg	German-2	23	1	4	5	10	....	....	....	....	....
2003-04	EV Duisburg	German-2	8	0	0	0	10	....	....	....	....	....
	Kolner Haie	Germany	45	1	1	2	41	5	0	0	0	4
2004-05	Nurnberg	Germany	51	2	6	8	89	6	1	1	2	10

SCHEFFELMAIER, Brett (sch-EHFEHL-mai-uhr, BREHT) **ST.L.**

Defense. Shoots right. 6'5", 220 lbs. Born, Coronation, Alta., March 31, 1981.
(St. Louis' 5th choice, 190th overall, in 2001 Entry Draft).

			Regular Season					Playoffs				
Season	Club	League	GP	G	A	Pts	PIM	GP	G	A	Pts	PIM
1997-98	Red Deer	AMHL	13	0	4	4	36	....	....	....	....	....
	Medicine Hat	WHL	25	0	1	1	69	....	....	....	....	....
1998-99	Medicine Hat	WHL	69	3	10	13	252	....	....	....	....	....
99-2000	Medicine Hat	WHL	71	1	9	10	281	....	....	....	....	....
2000-01	Medicine Hat	WHL	62	3	10	13	279	....	....	....	....	....
2001-02	Medicine Hat	WHL	45	4	6	10	180	....	....	....	....	....
2002-03	Worcester IceCats	AHL	54	0	2	2	143	3	0	0	0	7
2003-04	Worcester IceCats	AHL	23	0	1	1	56	3	0	0	0	0
	Peoria Rivermen	ECHL	10	1	2	3	21	....	....	....	....	....
2004-05	Worcester IceCats	AHL	2	0	0	0	2	....	....	....	....	....
	Peoria Rivermen	ECHL	3	0	1	1	2	....	....	....	....	....

• Re-entered NHL Entry Draft. Originally Tampa Bay's 3rd choice, 75th overall, in 1999 Entry Draft.

• Missed majority of 2003-04 season recovering from hand injury suffered in training camp, September 27, 2003. • Missed majority of 2004-05 season recovering from shoulder injury suffered in training camp, September, 2004.

SCHELL, Brad (SHEHL, BRAD) **ATL.**

Center. Shoots left. 6', 180 lbs. Born, Scott, Sask., August 5, 1984.
(Atlanta's 6th choice, 167th overall, in 2002 Entry Draft).

			Regular Season					Playoffs				
Season	Club	League	GP	G	A	Pts	PIM	GP	G	A	Pts	PIM
99-2000	North Battleford	SMHL	62	38	42	80	28	....	....	....	....	....
	Spokane Chiefs	WHL	1	0	0	0	0	....	....	....	....	....
2000-01	Spokane Chiefs	WHL	60	7	6	13	10	12	0	2	2	2
2001-02	Spokane Chiefs	WHL	70	20	36	56	16	11	0	8	8	6
2002-03	Spokane Chiefs	WHL	37	8	13	21	26	10	0	5	5	2
2003-04	Spokane Chiefs	WHL	71	35	57	92	47	4	1	0	1	0
2004-05	Gwinnett	ECHL	72	14	39	53	28	8	2	4	6	4

WHL West Second All-Star Team (2004)

• Missed majority of 2002-03 season recovering from off-season back surgery.

SCHEVJEV, Maxim (shehv-YAWF-yehv, MAX-ihm) **BUF.**

Center. Shoots left. 6', 178 lbs. Born, Noginsk, USSR, July 5, 1984.
(Buffalo's 7th choice, 178th overall, in 2002 Entry Draft).

			Regular Season					Playoffs				
Season	Club	League	GP	G	A	Pts	PIM	GP	G	A	Pts	PIM
99-2000	Elektrostal 2	Russia-3	11	0	1	1	2	....	....	....	....	....
2000-01	Elektrostal	Russia-2	7	0	0	0	6	....	....	....	....	....
2001-02	Elektrostal 2	Russia-3	6	1	2	3	2	....	....	....	....	....
	Elektrostal	Russia-2	49	6	9	15	34	....	....	....	....	....
2002-03	Amur Khabarovsk	Russia	21	0	0	0	10	....	....	....	....	....
	Khabarovsk 2	Russia-3	5	2	1	3	4	....	....	....	....	....
2003-04	Kristall Elektrostal	Russia-2	26	4	5	9	20	....	....	....	....	....
	Voskresensk	Russia	18	1	0	1	2	....	....	....	....	....
2004-05	Kristall Elektrostal	Russia-2	48	4	7	11	109	....	....	....	....	....

SCHNEIDER, Andy (SHNIGH-duhr, AN-dee) **PIT.**

Defense. Shoots left. 6'1", 215 lbs. Born, Grand Forks, ND, July 31, 1981.
(Pittsburgh's 7th choice, 156th overall, in 2001 Entry Draft).

			Regular Season					Playoffs				
Season	Club	League	GP	G	A	Pts	PIM	GP	G	A	Pts	PIM
1998-99	Lincoln Stars	USHL	9	0	4	4	8	4	0	0	0	2
99-2000	Lincoln Stars	USHL	46	7	10	17	102	10	6	4	10	27
2000-01	Lincoln Stars	USHL	54	12	24	36	134	....	....	....	....	....
2001-02	North Dakota	WCHA	35	3	11	14	65	....	....	....	....	....
2002-03	North Dakota	WCHA	43	11	30	41	52	....	....	....	....	....
2003-04	North Dakota	WCHA	39	2	10	12	54	....	....	....	....	....
2004-05	North Dakota	WCHA	42	2	8	10	58	....	....	....	....	....

SCHNEIDER, Matt (SHNIGH-duhr), MAT) **CGY.**

Center. Shoots right. 6'7", 202 lbs. Born, Vernon, B.C., July 10, 1985.
(Calgary's 8th choice, 200th overall, in 2004 Entry Draft).

			Regular Season					Playoffs				
Season	Club	League	GP	G	A	Pts	PIM	GP	G	A	Pts	PIM
2002-03	Beaver Valley	KIJHL	46	20	36	56	86	....	....	....	....	....
	Tri-City Americans	WHL	1	0	0	0	0	....	....	....	....	....
2003-04	Tri-City Americans	WHL	69	11	12	23	53	11	3	2	5	4
2004-05	Tri-City Americans	WHL	71	16	14	30	42	5	0	0	0	2

SCHREMP, Rob (SHREHMP, RAWB) **EDM.**

Center. Shoots left. 5'11", 197 lbs. Born, Syracuse, NY, July 1, 1986.
(Edmonton's 2nd choice, 25th overall, in 2004 Entry Draft).

			Regular Season					Playoffs				
Season	Club	League	GP	G	A	Pts	PIM	GP	G	A	Pts	PIM
2000-01	Syracuse	OPJHL	49	32	46	78	....	....	....	....	....	....
2001-02	Syracuse	OPJHL	47	41	47	88	93	1	1	2	3	0
2002-03	Mississauga	OHL	65	26	48	74	25	2	1	0	1	0
2003-04	Mississauga	OHL	3	2	4	6	0	....	....	....	....	....
	USA U-18	USDP	2	0	0	0	8	....	....	....	....	....
	London Knights	OHL	60	28	41	69	18	15	7	6	13	2
2004-05	London Knights	OHL	62	41	49	90	54	18	13	16	29	16

OHL All-Rookie Team (2003) • OHL Rookie of the Year (2003)

SCHUBERT, Christoph (SHOO-buhrt, KRIHS-tawf) OTT.

Defense. Shoots left. 6'2", 210 lbs. Born, Munich, West Germany, February 5, 1982.
(Ottawa's 5th choice, 127th overall, in 2001 Entry Draft).

			Regular Season					Playoffs				
Season	**Club**	**League**	**GP**	**G**	**A**	**Pts**	**PIM**	**GP**	**G**	**A**	**Pts**	**PIM**
1998-99	EV Landshut Jr.	Ger-Jr.	28	15	20	35	77	....	....	....	....	....
99-2000	EV Landshut Jr.	Ger-Jr.	11	14	11	25	51	....	....	....	....	....
	EV Landshut	German-3	55	7	5	12	68	....	....	....	....	....
2000-01	Munchen Barons	Germany	55	6	3	9	80	10	0	2	2	27
2001-02	Munchen Barons	Germany	50	5	11	16	125	9	3	4	7	32
2002-03	Binghamton	AHL	70	2	8	10	102	8	0	1	1	2
2003-04	Binghamton	AHL	70	2	10	12	69	1	0	0	0	0
2004-05	Binghamton	AHL	76	10	22	32	110	6	2	2	4	20

SCHULTZ, Jeff (SHUHLTZ, JEHF) WSH.

Defense. Shoots left. 6'6", 212 lbs. Born, Calgary, Alta., February 25, 1986.
(Washington's 2nd choice, 27th overall, in 2004 Entry Draft).

			Regular Season					Playoffs				
Season	**Club**	**League**	**GP**	**G**	**A**	**Pts**	**PIM**	**GP**	**G**	**A**	**Pts**	**PIM**
2000-01	Calgary Hawks	CBHL	27	7	8	15	20	....	....	....	....	....
2001-02	Calgary Rangers	CBHL	27	5	18	23	42	....	....	....	....	....
2002-03	Calgary Hitmen	WHL	50	2	1	3	4	4	0	0	0	0
2003-04	Calgary Hitmen	WHL	72	11	24	35	33	7	1	1	2	0
2004-05	Calgary Hitmen	WHL	72	2	27	29	31	12	2	1	3	6

SCHULTZ, Jesse (SHUHLTZ, JEH-see) VAN.

Right wing. Shoots right. 6', 192 lbs. Born, Strasbourg, Sask., September 28, 1982.

			Regular Season					Playoffs				
Season	**Club**	**League**	**GP**	**G**	**A**	**Pts**	**PIM**	**GP**	**G**	**A**	**Pts**	**PIM**
99-2000	Tri-City Americans	WHL	62	10	6	16	34	4	1	1	2	2
2000-01	Tri-City Americans	WHL	30	5	8	13	16	....	....	....	....	....
	Prince Albert	WHL	35	14	18	32	14	....	....	....	....	....
2001-02	Prince Albert	WHL	45	18	24	42	16	....	....	....	....	....
	Kelowna Rockets	WHL	28	10	12	22	14	....	....	....	....	....
2002-03	Kelowna Rockets	WHL	72	53	51	104	47	19	*12	16	*28	21
2003-04	Manitoba Moose	AHL	2	0	1	1	0	....	....	....	....	....
	Columbia Inferno	ECHL	52	27	21	48	72	4	1	2	3	2
2004-05	Manitoba Moose	AHL	70	9	15	24	33	14	3	2	5	2

WHL West First All-Star Team (2003)

Signed as a free agent by **Vancouver**, August, 2004.

SCHULZ, David (SHUHLZ, DAY-vihd) VAN.

Defense. Shoots right. 6'3", 201 lbs. Born, Winkler, Man., January 3, 1986.
(Vancouver's 6th choice, 254th overall, in 2004 Entry Draft).

			Regular Season					Playoffs				
Season	**Club**	**League**	**GP**	**G**	**A**	**Pts**	**PIM**	**GP**	**G**	**A**	**Pts**	**PIM**
2001-02	Swift Current	WHL	1	0	0	0	0	....	....	....	....	....
2002-03	Swift Current	WHL	48	1	6	7	43	4	0	0	0	0
2003-04	Swift Current	WHL	70	3	14	17	79	5	0	0	0	2
2004-05	Swift Current	WHL	66	8	11	19	138	....	....	....	....	....

SCURKO, Ladislav (SH'CHUHR-koh, LA-dih-slahv) PHI.

Center. Shoots left. 6', 187 lbs. Born, Spisska Nova Ves, Czech., April 4, 1986.
(Philadelphia's 6th choice, 170th overall, in 2004 Entry Draft).

			Regular Season					Playoffs				
Season	**Club**	**League**	**GP**	**G**	**A**	**Pts**	**PIM**	**GP**	**G**	**A**	**Pts**	**PIM**
2001-02	Spis. N. Ves Jr.	Slovak-Jr.	42	15	19	34	....	....	....	....	....	....
2002-03	Spis. N. Ves Jr.	Slovak-Jr.	62	27	21	48	....	....	....	....	....	....
2003-04	Spis. N. Ves Jr.	Slovak-Jr.	37	20	24	44	102	6	6	2	8	8
	Spis. N. Ves	Slovak-2	30	2	3	5	16	2	0	1	1	2
2004-05	Seattle	WHL	67	17	25	42	40	12	5	1	6	10

SEABROOK, Brent (SEE-bruk, BREHNT) CHI.

Defense. Shoots right. 6'3", 215 lbs. Born, Richmond, B.C., April 20, 1985.
(Chicago's 1st choice, 14th overall, in 2003 Entry Draft).

			Regular Season					Playoffs				
Season	**Club**	**League**	**GP**	**G**	**A**	**Pts**	**PIM**	**GP**	**G**	**A**	**Pts**	**PIM**
2000-01	Delta Ice Hawks	PIJHL	54	16	26	42	55	....	....	....	....	....
	Lethbridge	WHL	4	0	0	0	0	....	....	....	....	....
2001-02	Lethbridge	WHL	67	6	33	39	70	4	1	1	2	2
2002-03	Lethbridge	WHL	69	9	33	42	113	....	....	....	....	....
2003-04	Lethbridge	WHL	61	12	29	41	107	....	....	....	....	....
2004-05	Lethbridge	WHL	63	12	42	54	107	5	1	2	3	10
	Norfolk Admirals	AHL	3	0	0	0	2	6	0	1	1	6

WHL East Second All-Star Team (2005)

SEDOV, Pavel (se-DAHF, PAH-vehl) T.B.

Right wing. Shoots left. 6'3", 200 lbs. Born, Voskresensk, USSR, January 12, 1982.
(Tampa Bay's 5th choice, 161st overall, in 2000 Entry Draft).

			Regular Season					Playoffs				
Season	**Club**	**League**	**GP**	**G**	**A**	**Pts**	**PIM**	**GP**	**G**	**A**	**Pts**	**PIM**
99-2000	Voskresensk	Russia-2	10	0	0	0	2	....	....	....	....	....
	Voskresensk 2	Russia-3	21	5	5	-10	26	....	....	....	....	....
2000-01	Voskresensk	Russia-2	38	2	1	3	10	....	....	....	....	....
2001-02	Voskresensk 2	Russia-3	12	4	1	5	0	....	....	....	....	....
	Voskresensk	Russia-2	18	3	1	4	0	....	....	....	....	....
2002-03	Voskresensk	Russia-2	25	1	5	6	6	....	....	....	....	....
	Voskresensk 2	Russia-3	7	2	4	6	4	....	....	....	....	....
2003-04	THK Tver	Russia-2	26	2	6	8	6	....	....	....	....	....
	Voskresensk	Russia	10	1	0	1	2	....	....	....	....	....
	Voskresensk 2	Russia-3	STATISTICS NOT AVAILABLE									
2004-05	HK Tver	Russia-3	STATISTICS NOT AVAILABLE									
	HK Dmitrov	Russia-3	STATISTICS NOT AVAILABLE									
	HK Ryazan	Russia-4	STATISTICS NOT AVAILABLE									

SEELEY, Richard (SEE-lee, RIH-chuhrd)

Defense. Shoots left. 6'2", 205 lbs. Born, Powell River, B.C., April 30, 1979.
(Los Angeles' 6th choice, 137th overall, in 1997 Entry Draft).

			Regular Season					Playoffs				
Season	**Club**	**League**	**GP**	**G**	**A**	**Pts**	**PIM**	**GP**	**G**	**A**	**Pts**	**PIM**
1995-96	Powell River	BCJHL	44	1	8	9	42	....	....	....	....	....
1996-97	Lethbridge	WHL	3	0	0	0	11	....	....	....	....	....
	Prince Albert	WHL	18	0	1	1	9	4	0	0	0	2
1997-98	Prince Albert	WHL	65	8	21	29	114	....	....	....	....	....
1998-99	Prince Albert	WHL	61	10	48	58	110	14	1	11	12	14
99-2000	Lowell	AHL	36	5	1	6	37	....	....	....	....	....
2000-01	Lowell	AHL	55	2	8	10	102	....	....	....	....	....
	Trenton Titans	ECHL	9	0	2	2	18	....	....	....	....	....
2001-02	Manchester	AHL	61	2	10	12	78	5	0	0	0	6
2002-03	Manchester	AHL	69	4	14	18	127	3	0	1	1	0
2003-04	Manchester	AHL	56	2	9	11	80	6	0	0	0	0
2004-05	Bridgeport	AHL	47	2	6	8	108	....	....	....	....	....
	Norfolk Admirals	AHL	12	0	0	0	17	6	1	0	1	8

Signed as a free agent by **NY Islanders**, August 13, 2004.

SEGAL, Brandon (SEE-guhl, BRAN-duhn) NSH.

Right wing. Shoots right. 6'3", 213 lbs. Born, Richmond, B.C., July 12, 1983.
(Nashville's 2nd choice, 102nd overall, in 2002 Entry Draft).

			Regular Season					Playoffs				
Season	**Club**	**League**	**GP**	**G**	**A**	**Pts**	**PIM**	**GP**	**G**	**A**	**Pts**	**PIM**
99-2000	Calgary Hitmen	WHL	44	2	6	8	76	13	1	1	2	13
	Delta Ice Hawks	PIJHL	....	....	....	....	....	3	0	1	1	2
2000-01	Calgary Hitmen	WHL	72	16	11	27	103	12	1	1	2	17
2001-02	Calgary Hitmen	WHL	71	43	40	83	122	7	1	4	5	16
2002-03	Calgary Hitmen	WHL	71	31	27	58	104	5	2	2	4	4
2003-04	Milwaukee	AHL	44	11	10	21	54	13	2	1	3	21
2004-05	Milwaukee	AHL	59	7	8	15	45	3	1	0	1	11
	Rockford IceHogs	UHL	10	5	4	9	27	11	11	5	16	10

SEIKOLA, Markus (SAY-koh-la, MAHR-kuhs) TOR.

Defense. Shoots right. 6'1", 194 lbs. Born, Laitila, Finland, June 5, 1982.
(Toronto's 7th choice, 209th overall, in 2000 Entry Draft).

			Regular Season					Playoffs				
Season	**Club**	**League**	**GP**	**G**	**A**	**Pts**	**PIM**	**GP**	**G**	**A**	**Pts**	**PIM**
1997-98	TPS Turku Jr.	Finland-Jr.	2	0	0	0	0	1	0	0	0	2
1998-99	TPS Turku Jr.	Finland-Jr.	36	2	10	12	24	....	....	....	....	....
99-2000	TPS Turku U18	Fin-U18	9	2	1	3	6	....	....	....	....	....
2000-01	TPS Turku Jr.	Finland-Jr.	26	13	7	20	6	3	1	0	1	0
	TPS Turku	Finland	23	1	0	1	16	....	....	....	....	....
2001-02	TPS Turku	Finland	51	4	4	8	20	7	1	1	2	12
	TPS Turku Jr.	Finland-Jr.	1	0	1	1	2	2	1	0	1	2
2002-03	TPS Turku	Finland	56	5	4	9	36	7	1	0	1	2
2003-04	TPS Turku	Finland	46	3	6	9	12	13	0	1	1	6
2004-05	TPS Turku	Finland	56	5	9	14	14	6	0	1	1	4

SEITSONEN, Aki (SIGHT-soh-nehn, AH-kee) CGY.

Center. Shoots right. 6'3", 206 lbs. Born, Riihimaki, Finland, February 5, 1986.
(Calgary's 4th choice, 118th overall, in 2004 Entry Draft).

			Regular Season					Playoffs				
Season	**Club**	**League**	**GP**	**G**	**A**	**Pts**	**PIM**	**GP**	**G**	**A**	**Pts**	**PIM**
2002-03	HPK Jr.	Finland-Jr.	1	1	0	1	0	....	....	....	....	....
	HPK U18	Fin-U18	28	15	18	33	6	2	1	1	2	0
2003-04	Prince Albert	WHL	71	16	24	40	18	5	0	0	0	0
2004-05	Prince Albert	WHL	67	24	28	52	14	17	5	9	14	10

SEKERA, Andrej (SEH-kuhr-ah, AWN-dray) BUF.

Defense. Shoots left. 6', 191 lbs. Born, Bojnice, Czech., June 8, 1986.
(Buffalo's 3rd choice, 71st overall, in 2004 Entry Draft).

			Regular Season					Playoffs				
Season	**Club**	**League**	**GP**	**G**	**A**	**Pts**	**PIM**	**GP**	**G**	**A**	**Pts**	**PIM**
2001-02	Dukla Trencin Jr.	Slovak-Jr.	52	5	10	15	10	....	....	....	....	....
2002-03	Dukla Trencin Jr.	Slovak-Jr.	48	9	15	24	20	....	....	....	....	....
2003-04	Dukla Trencin Jr.	Slovak-Jr.	42	5	12	17	40	2	0	1	1	4
	Dukla Trencin	Slovakia	3	0	0	0	2	....	....	....	....	....
	Dukla Trencin U18	Svk-U18	5	0	0	0	0	....	....	....	....	....
2004-05	Owen Sound	OHL	51	7	21	28	18	6	0	4	4	4

OHL All-Rookie Team (2005)

SELUYANOV, Alexander (sehl-oo-YA-nahf, al-ehx-AN-duhr) DET.

Defense. Shoots right. 5'11", 172 lbs. Born, Ufa, USSR, March 24, 1982.
(Detroit's 5th choice, 128th overall, in 2000 Entry Draft).

			Regular Season					Playoffs				
Season	**Club**	**League**	**GP**	**G**	**A**	**Pts**	**PIM**	**GP**	**G**	**A**	**Pts**	**PIM**
1997-98	Novoil Ufa	Russia-3	19	0	1	1	8	....	....	....	....	....
1998-99	Novoil Ufa	Russia-3	20	3	3	6	8	....	....	....	....	....
99-2000	Ufa 2	Russia-3	18	3	4	7	10	....	....	....	....	....
	Ufa	Russia	13	1	2	3	4	....	....	....	....	....
2000-01	Ufa	Russia	30	0	3	3	10	....	....	....	....	....
2001-02	CSK VVS Samara	Russia-2	30	2	7	9	58	....	....	....	....	....
	Lada Togliatti	Russia	6	0	0	0	0	....	....	....	....	....
2002-03	Lada Togliatti	Russia	26	2	4	6	12	4	0	0	0	4
	CSK VVS Samara	Russia-2	16	4	4	8	34	....	....	....	....	....
2003-04	Lada Togliatti 2	Russia-3	5	0	1	1	10	4	2	0	2	6
	Lada Togliatti	Russia	43	1	3	4	20	2	0	0	0	0
2004-05	Lada Togliatti	Russia	52	6	5	11	41	8	1	0	1	6

SEMENOV, Dmitri (seh-MEH-nahv, dih-MEE-tree) DET.

Right wing. Shoots left. 5'10", 178 lbs. Born, Moscow, USSR, April 19, 1982.
(Detroit's 4th choice, 127th overall, in 2000 Entry Draft).

			Regular Season					Playoffs				
Season	**Club**	**League**	**GP**	**G**	**A**	**Pts**	**PIM**	**GP**	**G**	**A**	**Pts**	**PIM**
1997-98	Dynamo Moscow	Russia	13	2	1	3	2	....	....	....	....	....
1998-99	Dyn'o Moscow 2	Russia-3	26	14	4	18	16	....	....	....	....	....
99-2000	THK Tver	Russia-2	16	4	2	6	63	....	....	....	....	....
2000-01	Dynamo Moscow	Russia	12	0	0	0	8	....	....	....	....	....
	Yekaterinburg	Russia	24	0	0	0	18	....	....	....	....	....
2001-02	Dyn'o Moscow 2	Russia-3	6	5	2	7	6	....	....	....	....	....
	Yekaterinburg	Russia-2	6	1	2	3	2	....	....	....	....	....
	Dynamo Moscow	Russia	25	2	1	3	8	....	....	....	....	....
2002-03	Spartak Moscow	Russia	6	0	0	0	4	....	....	....	....	....
	THK Tver	Russia-2	16	1	2	3	22	....	....	....	....	....
2003-04	Krylja Sovetov	Russia-2	44	3	4	7	44	....	....	....	....	....
2004-05	Sibir Novosibirsk	Russia	44	4	4	8	28	....	....	....	....	....

SEMENOV, Maxim (seh-MEH-nahv, mahx-EEM) TOR.

Defense. Shoots left. 6', 183 lbs. Born, Kamenogorsk, Kazakhstan, February 9, 1984.
(Los Angeles' 7th choice, 220th overall, in 2004 Entry Draft).

			Regular Season					Playoffs				
Season	Club	League	GP	G	A	Pts	PIM	GP	G	A	Pts	PIM
2002-03	Lada Togliatti 2	Russia-3	18	0	4	4	26	....	....	....	....	....
	Lada Togliatti	Russia	23	0	0	0	16	6	0	1	1	10
2003-04	Lada Togliatti	Russia	59	2	5	7	50	6	0	0	0	0
	Lada Togliatti 2	Russia-3	....	....	....	....	....	4	0	1	1	29
2004-05	Lada Togliatti	Russia	59	2	4	6	79	9	0	0	0	6

SEMIN, Dmitri (SEH-min, dih-MEE-tree) ST.L.

Center. Shoots left. 5'10", 185 lbs. Born, Moscow, USSR, August 14, 1983.
(St. Louis' 4th choice, 159th overall, in 2001 Entry Draft).

			Regular Season					Playoffs				
Season	Club	League	GP	G	A	Pts	PIM	GP	G	A	Pts	PIM
99-2000	Spartak Moscow 2	Russia-3	27	9	10	19	10	....	....	....	....	....
	Spartak Moscow	Russia-2	1	0	0	0	0	....	....	....	....	....
2000-01	Spartak Moscow	Russia	21	6	3	9	4	11	2	3	5	4
2001-02	Spartak Moscow 2	Russia-3	4	5	0	5	4	....	....	....	....	....
	Spartak Moscow	Russia	44	2	6	8	14	....	....	....	....	....
2002-03	Spartak Moscow	Russia	51	9	13	22	30	....	....	....	....	....
2003-04	Spartak Moscow	Russia-2	60	15	23	38	34	13	2	2	4	2
2004-05	Spartak Moscow	Russia	53	7	7	14	34	....	....	....	....	....

SERSEN, Michal (suhr-SEHN, MEE-khahl) PIT.

Defense. Shoots left. 6'1", 200 lbs. Born, Celnica, Czech., December 28, 1985.
(Pittsburgh's 7th choice, 130th overall, in 2004 Entry Draft).

			Regular Season					Playoffs				
Season	Club	League	GP	G	A	Pts	PIM	GP	G	A	Pts	PIM
2002-03	Bratislava Jr.	Slovak-Jr.	33	5	4	9	51	....	....	....	....	....
	Bratislava	Slovakia	17	0	0	0	0	....	....	....	....	....
2003-04	Rimouski Oceanic	QMJHL	45	7	18	25	30	9	1	5	6	6
2004-05	Rimouski Oceanic	QMJHL	67	9	33	42	74	13	0	8	8	18

SERTICH, Andrew (SUHR-tihch, AN-droo) PIT.

Left wing. Shoots left. 6', 175 lbs. Born, Coleraine, MN, May 6, 1983.
(Pittsburgh's 5th choice, 136th overall, in 2002 Entry Draft).

			Regular Season					Playoffs				
Season	Club	League	GP	G	A	Pts	PIM	GP	G	A	Pts	PIM
1998/00	Greenway Raiders	High-MN	47	39	58	97	....	....	....	....	....	....
2000-01	Greenway Raiders	High-MN	31	35	45	80	14	....	....	....	....	....
2001-02	Greenway Raiders	High-MN	26	24	48	72	35	....	....	....	....	....
	Sioux Falls	USHL	13	2	4	6	0	2	0	0	0	2
2002-03	U. of Minnesota	WCHA	44	5	9	14	12	....	....	....	....	....
2003-04	U. of Minnesota	WCHA	43	8	14	22	14	....	....	....	....	....
2004-05	U. of Minnesota	WCHA	44	6	9	15	8	....	....	....	....	....

• Statistics for 1998/00 **Greenway** (High-MN) are totals for 1998-2000 seasons.

SETOGUCHI, Devin (SEHT-oh-GOO-chee, DEH-vihn) S.J.

Right wing. Shoots right. 5'11", 186 lbs. Born, Taber, Alta., January 1, 1987.
(San Jose's 1st choice, 8th overall, in 2005 Entry Draft).

			Regular Season					Playoffs				
Season	Club	League	GP	G	A	Pts	PIM	GP	G	A	Pts	PIM
2003-04	Saskatoon Blades	WHL	66	13	18	31	53	....	....	....	....	....
2004-05	Saskatoon Blades	WHL	69	33	31	64	34	4	0	1	1	0

SETZINGER, Oliver (SEHT-zihn-guhr, AW-lih-vuhr) NSH.

Center. Shoots left. 6', 197 lbs. Born, Horn, Austria, July 11, 1983.
(Nashville's 5th choice, 76th overall, in 2001 Entry Draft).

			Regular Season					Playoffs				
Season	Club	League	GP	G	A	Pts	PIM	GP	G	A	Pts	PIM
1998-99	Wiener EV Jr.	Austria-Jr.	30	25	27	52	30	....	....	....	....	....
99-2000	Ilves Tampere Jr.	Finland-Jr.	35	6	4	10	65	....	....	....	....	....
	Ilves Tampere U18	Fin-U18	18	16	9	25	38	....	....	....	....	....
	Ilves Tampere	Finland	1	0	0	0	2	....	....	....	....	....
2000-01	Ilves Tampere Jr.	Finland-Jr.	31	8	12	20	74	....	....	....	....	....
	Ilves Tampere	Finland	14	0	1	1	10	....	....	....	....	....
2001-02	Ilves Tampere Jr.	Finland-Jr.	1	0	0	0	2	....	....	....	....	....
	Ilves Tampere	Finland	10	1	0	1	4	....	....	....	....	....
	Sport Vaasa	Finland-2	8	5	2	7	6	....	....	....	....	....
	Austria	Olympics	4	1	0	1	2	....	....	....	....	....
	EHC Linz	Austria	8	6	7	13	4	13	4	14	18	14
2002-03	Pelicans Lahti	Finland	56	7	14	21	54	....	....	....	....	....
2003-04	Pelicans Lahti	Finland	20	2	4	6	22	....	....	....	....	....
	KalPa Kuopio	Finland-2	8	4	7	11	20	....	....	....	....	....
	HPK Hameenlinna	Finland	14	6	3	9	10	8	4	2	6	4
2004-05	HPK Hameenlinna	Finland	53	11	17	28	67	10	0	1	1	2

SEYDOUX, Philippe (SAY-doo, fihl-EEP) OTT.

Defense. Shoots left. 6'2", 185 lbs. Born, Bern, Switz., February 23, 1985.
(Ottawa's 3rd choice, 100th overall, in 2003 Entry Draft).

			Regular Season					Playoffs				
Season	Club	League	GP	G	A	Pts	PIM	GP	G	A	Pts	PIM
2000-01	SC Bern Jr.	Swiss-Jr.	30	1	3	4	8	4	1	2	0	6
2001-02	SC Bern Jr.	Swiss-Jr.	35	8	17	25	94	7	3	5	0	24
	SC Bern	Swiss	7	0	0	0	0	2	0	0	0	0
2002-03	Kloten Flyers Jr.	Swiss-Jr.	14	2	10	12	50	....	....	....	....	....
	Kloten Flyers	Swiss	14	0	1	1	4	5	0	0	0	6
2003-04	Kloten Flyers	Swiss	24	2	3	5	20	....	....	....	....	....
2004-05	Kloten Flyers	Swiss	28	1	8	9	22	5	0	0	0	2

SEYMOUR, John (SEE-mohr, JAWN) L.A.

Left wing. Shoots left. 6'3", 176 lbs. Born, Scarborough, Ont., June 16, 1987.
(Los Angeles' 8th choice, 226th overall, in 2005 Entry Draft).

			Regular Season					Playoffs				
Season	Club	League	GP	G	A	Pts	PIM	GP	G	A	Pts	PIM
2002-03	Peterborough	OMHA	48	13	13	26	59	....	....	....	....	....
	Peterborough Bees	OPJHL	1	0	0	0	0	....	....	....	....	....
2003-04	Brampton	OHL	40	0	3	3	16	10	0	0	0	2
2004-05	Brampton	OHL	63	1	4	5	64	6	0	0	0	0

SHAFIGULIN, Grigory (sha-fih-GOO-lihn, grih-GOH-ree) NSH.

Center. Shoots left. 6'2", 185 lbs. Born, Chelyabinsk, USSR, January 13, 1985.
(Nashville's 8th choice, 98th overall, in 2003 Entry Draft).

			Regular Season					Playoffs				
Season	Club	League	GP	G	A	Pts	PIM	GP	G	A	Pts	PIM
2000-01	Chelyabinsk 2	Russia-3	6	3	2	5	8	....	....	....	....	....
2001-02	Yaroslavl 2	Russia-3	19	2	2	4	12	....	....	....	....	....
2002-03	Yaroslavl 2	Russia-3	33	18	12	30	46	7	0	4	4	31
	Yaroslavl	Russia	11	0	1	1	4	8	0	0	0	4
2003-04	Yaroslavl 2	Russia-3	11	3	8	11	22	....	....	....	....	....
	Yaroslavl	Russia	29	3	0	3	4	2	0	0	0	0
2004-05	Yaroslavl 2	Russia-3	1	0	2	2	0	....	....	....	....	....
	Yaroslavl	Russia	46	5	6	11	49	9	0	0	0	10

SHARROW, Jim (SHA-row, JIHM) ATL.

Defense. Shoots right. 6'2", 180 lbs. Born, Framingham, MA, January 31, 1985.
(Atlanta's 2nd choice, 110th overall, in 2003 Entry Draft).

			Regular Season					Playoffs				
Season	Club	League	GP	G	A	Pts	PIM	GP	G	A	Pts	PIM
2001-02	USA U-17	USDP	61	5	16	21	30	....	....	....	....	....
2002-03	Halifax	QMJHL	70	2	14	16	54	25	2	4	6	24
2003-04	Halifax	QMJHL	52	12	26	38	67	....	....	....	....	....
2004-05	Halifax	QMJHL	69	16	31	47	76	13	5	6	11	6

QMJHL All-Rookie Team (2003)

SHASBY, Matt (SHAS-bee, MAT)

Defense. Shoots left. 6'2", 196 lbs. Born, Sioux Falls, SD, July 2, 1980.
(Montreal's 7th choice, 150th overall, in 1999 Entry Draft).

			Regular Season					Playoffs				
Season	Club	League	GP	G	A	Pts	PIM	GP	G	A	Pts	PIM
1997-98	Lincoln Stars	USHL	43	1	15	16	30	8	0	0	0	2
1998-99	Lincoln Stars	USHL	17	1	4	5	10	....	....	....	....	....
	Des Moines	USHL	32	3	18	21	24	11	0	1	1	12
99-2000	Alaska-Anchorage	WCHA	32	1	8	9	36	....	....	....	....	....
2000-01	Alaska-Anchorage	WCHA	35	4	14	18	32	....	....	....	....	....
2001-02	Alaska-Anchorage	WCHA	35	7	20	27	72	....	....	....	....	....
2002-03	Alaska-Anchorage	WCHA	25	0	11	11	18	....	....	....	....	....
2003-04	Columbus	ECHL	66	8	20	28	34	....	....	....	....	....
2004-05	Hamilton Bulldogs	AHL	11	0	0	0	0	....	....	....	....	....
	Long Beach	ECHL	40	4	18	22	52	4	0	0	0	2

WCHA Second All-Star Team (2002)

SHASTIN, Yegor (SHAS-tihn, yeh-GOHR) CGY.

Left wing. Shoots left. 5'9", 172 lbs. Born, Kiev, USSR, September 10, 1982.
(Calgary's 5th choice, 124th overall, in 2001 Entry Draft).

			Regular Season					Playoffs				
Season	Club	League	GP	G	A	Pts	PIM	GP	G	A	Pts	PIM
1997-98	Omsk 2	Russia-3	4	0	1	1	0	....	....	....	....	....
1998-99	Omsk 2	Russia-4	19	11	17	28	30	....	....	....	....	....
	Avangard Omsk	Russia	4	0	0	0	0	4	0	1	1	0
99-2000	Omsk 2	Russia-3	11	6	5	11	20	....	....	....	....	....
	Avangard Omsk	Russia	26	2	4	6	20	7	3	1	4	16
2000-01	Omsk 2	Russia-3	14	13	9	22	62	....	....	....	....	....
	Avangard Omsk	Russia	35	3	11	14	59	9	1	0	1	18
2001-02	Avangard Omsk	Russia	26	2	5	7	10	11	1	0	1	8
2002-03	HC Ambri-Piotta	Swiss	44	2	3	5	18	3	1	0	1	2
	HC Sierre	Swiss-2	2	1	0	1	0	....	....	....	....	....
2003-04	Sibir Novosibirsk	Russia	57	7	5	12	28	....	....	....	....	....
2004-05	Omsk 2	Russia-3	2	1	0	1	0	....	....	....	....	....
	Avangard Omsk	Russia	7	0	0	0	2	....	....	....	....	....
	St. Petersburg 2	Russia-3	2	2	2	4	4	....	....	....	....	....
	SKA St. Petersburg	Russia	21	3	3	6	12	....	....	....	....	....

SHEFER, Andrei (SHEH-fuhr, AN-dray) L.A.

Left wing. Shoots left. 6'1", 194 lbs. Born, Yekaterinburg, USSR, July 26, 1981.
(Los Angeles' 1st choice, 43rd overall, in 1999 Entry Draft).

			Regular Season					Playoffs				
Season	Club	League	GP	G	A	Pts	PIM	GP	G	A	Pts	PIM
1997-98	Yekaterinburg 2	Russia-3	16	3	3	6	18	....	....	....	....	....
1998-99	Cherepovets 3	Russia-4	6	2	2	4	18	....	....	....	....	....
	Cherepovets 2	Russia-3	21	6	5	11	20	....	....	....	....	....
	Cherepovets	Russia	8	1	0	1	4	....	....	....	....	....
99-2000	Halifax	QMJHL	72	34	42	76	30	10	0	5	5	4
2000-01	SKA St. Petersburg	Russia	11	6	1	7	4	....	....	....	....	....
	Cherepovets	Russia	20	1	1	2	10	6	1	0	1	0
2001-02	Cherepovets 2	Russia-3	3	1	2	3	2	....	....	....	....	....
	Cherepovets	Russia	8	0	0	0	6	....	....	....	....	....
	SKA St. Petersburg	Russia	28	4	4	8	10	....	....	....	....	....
2002-03	Cherepovets	Russia	37	2	4	6	10	10	0	0	0	0
	Cherepovets 2	Russia-3	3	1	2	3	2	....	....	....	....	....
2003-04	Cherepovets	Russia	55	4	6	10	46	....	....	....	....	....
2004-05	Cherepovets	Russia	46	1	11	12	18	....	....	....	....	....

SHEMETOV, Sergei (shuh-MEH-tawf, SAIR-gay) COL.

Left wing. Shoots left. 6'1", 185 lbs. Born, Yaroslavl, USSR, September 3, 1984.
(Colorado's 9th choice, 258th overall, in 2002 Entry Draft).

			Regular Season					Playoffs				
Season	Club	League	GP	G	A	Pts	PIM	GP	G	A	Pts	PIM
2000-01	Yaroslavl 2	Russia-3	30	7	0	7	24	....	....	....	....	....
2001-02	Yaroslavl 2	Russia-3	17	3	4	7	42	....	....	....	....	....
	Elektrostal 2	Russia-3	3	0	0	0	8	....	....	....	....	....
	Elektrostal	Russia-2	15	1	1	2	26	....	....	....	....	....
2002-03	HK Voronezh	Russia-2	13	0	1	1	35	....	....	....	....	....
2003-04	Nizhnekamsk	Russia	10	0	0	0	2	....	....	....	....	....
	Gazovik Tyumen	Russia-2	10	0	0	0	8	....	....	....	....	....
	Spartak Moscow	Russia-2	56	16	31	47	71	....	....	....	....	....
2004-05	Gazovik Tyumen	Russia-2	11	0	2	2	2	....	....	....	....	....
	Tyumen 2	Russia-3	28	9	8	17	12	....	....	....	....	....

SHINKAR, Alexander (shihn-KAHR, al-ehx-AN-duhr) **TOR.**

Right wing. Shoots left. 6', 176 lbs. Born, Ufa, USSR, July 3, 1981.
(Toronto's 9th choice, 254th overall, in 2000 Entry Draft).

			Regular Season					Playoffs				
Season	Club	League	GP	G	A	Pts	PIM	GP	G	A	Pts	PIM
1997-98	Novoil Ufa	Russia-3	22	6	2	8	4	....	....	....	....	....
1998-99	Cherepovets 2	Russia-3	25	7	2	9	8	....	....	....	....	....
	Cherepovets 3	Russia-4	8	0	4	4	4	....	....	....	....	....
99-2000	Cherepovets	Russia	18	1	1	2	2	8	0	0	0	0
2000-01	SKA St. Petersburg	Russia	43	7	4	11	50	....	....	....	....	....
2001-02	Ufa	Russia	27	3	3	6	8	....	....	....	....	....
	SKA St. Petersburg	Russia	18	3	4	7	10	....	....	....	....	....
2002-03	Cherepovets	Russia	32	3	1	4	12	11	0	1	1	6
2003-04	Ufa	Russia	15	2	0	2	16	....	....	....	....	....
	SKA St. Petersburg	Russia	12	4	1	5	0	....	....	....	....	....
2004-05	SKA St. Petersburg	Russia	57	16	14	30	22	....	....	....	....	....

SHKOTOV, Alexei (SHKOH-tahv, al-EHX-ay) **ST.L.**

Right wing. Shoots left. 5'10", 175 lbs. Born, Elektrostal, USSR, June 22, 1984.
(St. Louis' 1st choice, 48th overall, in 2002 Entry Draft).

			Regular Season					Playoffs				
Season	Club	League	GP	G	A	Pts	PIM	GP	G	A	Pts	PIM
2000-01	Elektrostal 2	Russia-3	2	0	0	0	0	....	....	....	....	....
2001-02	Elektrostal 2	Russia-3	4	4	5	9	2	....	....	....	....	....
	Elektrostal	Russia-2	52	17	9	26	40	....	....	....	....	....
2002-03	CSKA Moscow	Russia	33	5	1	6	20	....	....	....	....	....
2003-04	Moncton Wildcats	QMJHL	7	2	4	6	2	....	....	....	....	....
	Quebec Remparts	QMJHL	36	25	36	61	24	5	3	1	4	4
2004-05	Worcester IceCats	AHL	23	6	6	12	18	....	....	....	....	....
	Voskresensk	Russia	21	6	1	7	6	....	....	....	....	....

SIDDALL, Matt (sih-DUHL, MAT) **ATL.**

Right wing. Shoots right. 6'1", 205 lbs. Born, North Vancouver, B.C., September 26, 1984.
(Atlanta's 9th choice, 270th overall, in 2004 Entry Draft).

			Regular Season					Playoffs				
Season	Club	League	GP	G	A	Pts	PIM	GP	G	A	Pts	PIM
2003-04	Powell River Kings	BCHL	45	25	36	61	216	7	4	2	6	10
2004-05	Northern Mich.	CCHA	33	4	4	8	62	....	....	....	....	....

SIDORENKO, Kirill (sih-dohr-EHN-koh, KIH-rihl) **DAL.**

Center. Shoots left. 6'3", 187 lbs. Born, Omsk, USSR, March 30, 1983.
(Dallas' 9th choice, 180th overall, in 2002 Entry Draft).

			Regular Season					Playoffs				
Season	Club	League	GP	G	A	Pts	PIM	GP	G	A	Pts	PIM
1998-99	Omsk 2	Russia-4	2	0	0	0	2	....	....	....	....	....
99-2000	Omsk 2	Russia-3	26	2	11	13	14	....	....	....	....	....
2000-01	Omsk 2	Russia-3	30	8	7	15	44	....	....	....	....	....
2001-02	Mostovik Kurgan	Russia-2	50	11	6	17	64	....	....	....	....	....
2002-03	Sibir Novosibirsk	Russia	30	1	1	2	2	....	....	....	....	....
2003-04	Energiya Kemerovo	Russia-2	14	1	1	2	6	....	....	....	....	....
	Zauralje Kurgan	Russia-2	32	3	3	6	6	4	0	0	0	27
2004-05	Omsk 2	Russia-3	18	7	4	11	12	....	....	....	....	....
	CSK VVS Samara	Russia-2	16	2	2	4	0	....	....	....	....	....

SIDYAKIN, Andrei (sihd-YA-kihn, AN-dray) **MTL.**

Right wing. Shoots left. 5'11", 169 lbs. Born, Ufa, USSR, January 20, 1979.
(Montreal's 10th choice, 202nd overall, in 1997 Entry Draft).

			Regular Season					Playoffs				
Season	Club	League	GP	G	A	Pts	PIM	GP	G	A	Pts	PIM
1994-95	Ufa	CIS	7	0	1	1	0	....	....	....	....	....
1995-96	Ufa	CIS	25	1	0	1	4	3	0	0	0	2
1996-97	Ufa	Russia	29	3	5	8	4	....	....	....	....	....
1997-98	Ufa	Russia	42	5	4	9	32	....	....	....	....	....
1998-99	Ufa	Russia	36	6	4	10	14	2	0	0	0	2
99-2000	Ufa	Russia	38	7	2	9	32	....	....	....	....	....
2000-01	Ufa	Russia	44	10	13	23	42	....	....	....	....	....
2001-02	Ufa	Russia	43	9	7	16	20	....	....	....	....	....
2002-03	Cherepovets	Russia	38	8	8	16	20	2	0	0	0	4
2003-04	Cherepovets 2	Russia-3	4	2	3	5	0	....	....	....	....	....
	Cherepovets	Russia	19	1	2	3	12	....	....	....	....	....
	Ufa	Russia	29	8	8	16	28	....	....	....	....	....
2004-05	Ufa	Russia	57	8	20	28	54	....	....	....	....	....

SIGALET, Jonathan (sihg-A-leht, JAWN-ah-thuhn) **BOS.**

Defense. Shoots left. 6'1", 185 lbs. Born, Vancouver, B.C., February 12, 1986.
(Boston's 4th choice, 100th overall, in 2005 Entry Draft).

			Regular Season					Playoffs				
Season	Club	League	GP	G	A	Pts	PIM	GP	G	A	Pts	PIM
2002-03	Salmon Arm	BCHL	52	13	39	52	34	....	....	....	....	....
2003-04	Bowling Green	CCHA	37	3	12	15	26	....	....	....	....	....
2004-05	Bowling Green	CCHA	35	3	13	16	36	....	....	....	....	....

SINDEL, Jakub (SHIHN-dehl, YA-kuhb) **CHI.**

Center. Shoots right. 6', 172 lbs. Born, Jihlava, Czech., January 24, 1986.
(Chicago's 5th choice, 54th overall, in 2004 Entry Draft).

			Regular Season					Playoffs				
Season	Club	League	GP	G	A	Pts	PIM	GP	G	A	Pts	PIM
99-2000	Slavia U17	CzR-U17	32	10	6	16	6	....	....	....	....	....
2000-01	Slavia U17	CzR-U17	26	12	15	27	2	6	1	0	1	0
2001-02	Slavia U17	CzR-U17	34	32	14	46	34	2	0	1	1	2
	HC Slavia Praha Jr.	CzRep-Jr.	14	7	4	11	10	....	....	....	....	....
2002-03	HC Slavia Praha Jr.	CzRep-Jr.	35	12	11	23	39	2	0	1	1	0
2003-04	Sparta Jr.	CzRep-Jr.	13	8	14	22	4	....	....	....	....	....
	HC Sparta Praha	CzRep	34	5	1	6	14	13	1	1	2	2
	HC Dukla Jihlava	CzRep-2	1	0	0	0	0	....	....	....	....	....
2004-05	Sparta Jr.	CzRep-Jr.	9	5	16	21	16	....	....	....	....	....
	HC Sparta Praha	CzRep	10	0	2	2	0	....	....	....	....	....
	Trebic	CzRep-2	5	0	0	0	0	....	....	....	....	....
	Brandon	WHL	35	16	13	29	12	24	7	4	11	22

SIPOTZ, Brian (SIHP-awtz, BRIGH-uhn) **ATL.**

Defense. Shoots right. 6'7", 235 lbs. Born, South Bend, IN, September 16, 1981.
(Atlanta's 3rd choice, 100th overall, in 2001 Entry Draft).

			Regular Season					Playoffs				
Season	Club	League	GP	G	A	Pts	PIM	GP	G	A	Pts	PIM
99-2000	Culver	High-IN	45	14	22	36	56	....	....	....	....	....
2000-01	Miami U.	CCHA	32	0	1	1	48	....	....	....	....	....
2001-02	Miami U.	CCHA	25	0	1	1	28	....	....	....	....	....
2002-03	Miami U.	CCHA	26	0	0	0	24	....	....	....	....	....
2003-04	Miami U.	CCHA	36	0	3	3	39	....	....	....	....	....
2004-05	Chicago Wolves	AHL	75	2	6	8	31	18	1	2	3	6
	Gwinnett	ECHL	2	0	0	0	0	....	....	....	....	....

SKILLE, Jack (SKIH-lee, JAK) **CHI.**

Right wing. Shoots right. 6'1", 198 lbs. Born, Madison, WI, May 19, 1987.
(Chicago's 1st choice, 7th overall, in 2005 Entry Draft).

			Regular Season					Playoffs				
Season	Club	League	GP	G	A	Pts	PIM	GP	G	A	Pts	PIM
2003-04	USA U-17	USDP	61	25	19	44	61	....	....	....	....	....
2004-05	USA U-17&U-18	NAHL	16	6	11	17	20	....	....	....	....	....
	USA U-18	USDP	42	15	22	37	56	....	....	....	....	....

Signed Letter of Intent to attend **Wisconsin** (WCHA) in fall of 2005.

SKINNER, Brett (SKIH-nuhr, BREHT) **VAN.**

Defense. Shoots left. 6'1", 195 lbs. Born, Brandon, Man., June 28, 1983.
(Vancouver's 3rd choice, 68th overall, in 2002 Entry Draft).

			Regular Season					Playoffs				
Season	Club	League	GP	G	A	Pts	PIM	GP	G	A	Pts	PIM
1998-99	Brandon Kings	MMBHL	29	3	18	21	20	....	....	....	....	....
99-2000	Brandon Kings	MMMHL	40	8	27	35	48	....	....	....	....	....
2000-01	Trail Smoke Eaters	BCHL	59	11	24	35	43	....	....	....	....	....
2001-02	Des Moines	USHL	44	9	38	47	25	3	0	1	1	0
2002-03	U. of Denver	WCHA	37	4	13	17	27	....	....	....	....	....
2003-04	U. of Denver	WCHA	44	7	23	30	32	....	....	....	....	....
2004-05	U. of Denver	WCHA	43	4	36	40	30	....	....	....	....	....

USHL First All-Star Team (2002) • USHL Defenseman of the Year (2002) • WCHA First All-Star Team (2005) • NCAA West Second All-American Team (2005) • NCAA Championship All-Tournament Team (2005)

SKLADANY, Frantisek (sklah-DAH-nee, FRAN-tih-shehk) **COL.**

Left wing. Shoots left. 6', 185 lbs. Born, Martin, Czech., April 22, 1982.
(Colorado's 4th choice, 143rd overall, in 2001 Entry Draft).

			Regular Season					Playoffs				
Season	Club	League	GP	G	A	Pts	PIM	GP	G	A	Pts	PIM
1995-96	Martin Jr.	Slovak-Jr.	8	2	1	3	2	....	....	....	....	....
1996-97	Martin Jr.	Slovak-Jr.	46	29	28	57	18	....	....	....	....	....
1997-98	Martin Jr.	Slovak-Jr.	53	46	37	83	18	....	....	....	....	....
1998-99	Martin Jr.	Slovak-Jr.	10	2	4	6	4	....	....	....	....	....
	Martin	Slovakia	1	0	0	0	0	....	....	....	....	....
99-2000	Martin Jr.	Slovak-Jr.	3	2	3	5	0	....	....	....	....	....
	Martin	Slovak-2	13	1	4	5	2	....	....	....	....	....
2000-01	Boston University	H-East	35	4	5	9	4	....	....	....	....	....
2001-02	Boston University	H-East	33	13	13	26	23	....	....	....	....	....
2002-03	Boston University	H-East	41	14	21	35	34	....	....	....	....	....
2003-04	Boston University	H-East	37	3	21	24	16	....	....	....	....	....
2004-05	Hershey Bears	AHL	15	0	0	0	2	....	....	....	....	....
	Quad City	UHL	50	9	11	20	33	7	1	1	2	4

SKLENAR, Jaroslav (SKLEH-nahr, YAHR-oh-slav) **TOR.**

Right wing. Shoots right. 6', 172 lbs. Born, Ivancice, Czech., November 22, 1982.
(Toronto's 8th choice, 183rd overall, in 2001 Entry Draft).

			Regular Season					Playoffs				
Season	Club	League	GP	G	A	Pts	PIM	GP	G	A	Pts	PIM
99-2000	HC Trinec Jr.	CzRep-Jr.	32	5	6	11	2	....	....	....	....	....
2000-01	HC Ytong Brno Jr.	CzRep-Jr.	26	10	11	21	22	....	....	....	....	....
2001-02	Znojmo	CzRep	4	0	0	0	2	....	....	....	....	....
	EV Fussen Jr.	Ger-Jr.	21	4	4	8	6	....	....	....	....	....
	HC Ytong Brno	CzRep-2	5	0	0	0	4	....	....	....	....	....
	Rosice	CzRep-2	8	3	1	4	0	....	....	....	....	....
	Ottawa 67's	OHL	4	1	0	1	0	....	....	....	....	....
2002-03	Znojmo	CzRep	10	0	0	0	0	....	....	....	....	....
	HK 36 Skalica	Slovakia	13	0	0	0	0	....	....	....	....	....
	Trebic	CzRep-2	8	0	1	1	2	....	....	....	....	....
	HC Hvezda Brno	CzRep-2	1	0	0	0	0	....	....	....	....	....
2003-04	HC Velka Bites	CzRep-3	34	9	10	19	49	....	....	....	....	....
2004-05			DID NOT PLAY									

SKOLNEY, Wade (SKOHL-nee, WAYD) **PHI.**

Defense. Shoots right. 6', 197 lbs. Born, Wynyard, Sask., June 24, 1981.

			Regular Season					Playoffs				
Season	Club	League	GP	G	A	Pts	PIM	GP	G	A	Pts	PIM
1996-97	Niacam Bantams	SBHL	54	33	70	103	193	....	....	....	....	....
	Brandon	WHL	1	0	0	0	0	....	....	....	....	....
1997-98	Brandon	WHL	42	1	11	12	49	3	0	0	0	0
1998-99	Brandon	WHL	39	3	10	13	60	5	0	1	1	16
99-2000	Brandon	WHL	13	0	2	2	23	....	....	....	....	....
2000-01	Brandon	WHL	28	2	9	11	37	....	....	....	....	....
2001-02	Brandon	WHL	50	4	12	16	179	19	2	7	9	56
2002-03	Philadelphia	AHL	68	2	7	9	102	....	....	....	....	....
2003-04	Philadelphia	AHL	56	1	8	9	106	12	0	0	0	23
2004-05	Philadelphia	AHL	35	0	8	8	104	21	0	1	1	43

Signed as a free agent by **Philadelphia**, May 20, 2002. • Missed majority of 2004-05 season recovering from head injury suffered in game on November 19, 2004.

SKOOG, Simon (SKOOG, SEE-muhn) **ST.L.**

Defense. Shoots left. 6'2", 218 lbs. Born, Solvesborg, Sweden, February 17, 1983.
(St. Louis' 8th choice, 283rd overall, in 2001 Entry Draft).

			Regular Season					Playoffs				
Season	Club	League	GP	G	A	Pts	PIM	GP	G	A	Pts	PIM
99-2000	Malmo Jr.	Swe-Jr.	4	0	0	0	0	....	....	....	....	....
2000-01	Morrums GoIS IK	Sweden-2	27	0	1	1	12	....	....	....	....	....
2001-02	Morrums GoIS IK	Sweden-2	53	3	8	11	46	....	....	....	....	....
2002-03	Morrums GoIS IK	Sweden-2	39	2	4	6	38	2	0	1	1	4
2003-04	HV 71 Jr.	Swe-Jr.	1	1	0	1	0	....	....	....	....	....
	HV 71 Jonkoping	Sweden	49	6	2	8	47	19	0	1	1	2
2004-05	HV 71 Jr.	Swe-Jr.	2	1	3	4	2	....	....	....	....	....
	Morrums GoIS IK	Sweden-2	4	0	1	1	6	....	....	....	....	....
	HV 71 Jonkoping	Sweden	36	0	3	3	10	....	....	....	....	....

SLATER, Jim (SLAY-tuhr, JIHM) ATL.

Center. Shoots left. 6', 190 lbs. Born, Petoskey, MI, December 9, 1982.
(Atlanta's 2nd choice, 30th overall, in 2002 Entry Draft).

			Regular Season					Playoffs				
Season	Club	League	GP	G	A	Pts	PIM	GP	G	A	Pts	PIM
1998-99	Cleveland Barons	NAHL	50	13	20	33	58	2	0	0	0	2
99-2000	Cleveland Barons	NAHL	56	35	50	85	129	3	1	3	4	4
2000-01	Cleveland Barons	NAHL	48	27	37	64	122	6	6	6	12	6
2001-02	Michigan State	CCHA	37	11	21	32	50	....	....	....	....	....
2002-03	Michigan State	CCHA	37	18	26	44	26	....	....	....	....	....
2003-04	Michigan State	CCHA	42	19	29	*48	38	....	....	....	....	....
2004-05	Michigan State	CCHA	41	16	32	48	30	....	....	....	....	....

CCHA All-Rookie Team (2002) • CCHA First All-Star Team (2003, 2004) • NCAA West Second All-American Team (2004)

SLOVAK, Tomas (SLOHW-vahk, TAW-mawsh) COL.

Defense. Shoots right. 6'1", 203 lbs. Born, Kosice, Czech., April 5, 1983.
(Nashville's 3rd choice, 42nd overall, in 2001 Entry Draft).

			Regular Season					Playoffs				
Season	Club	League	GP	G	A	Pts	PIM	GP	G	A	Pts	PIM
1997-98	HC Kosice Jr.	Slovak-Jr.	47	1	6	7	24	....	....	....	....	....
1998-99	HC VSZ Kosice Jr.	Slovak-Jr.	45	6	14	20	65	....	....	....	....	....
99-2000	HC VSZ Kosice Jr.	Slovak-Jr.	55	16	28	44	117	....	....	....	....	....
	HC VSZ Kosice	Slovakia	2	0	0	0	0	....	....	....	....	....
2000-01	HC VSZ Kosice	Slovakia	43	5	5	10	28	3	1	0	1	2
2001-02	Kelowna Rockets	WHL	53	2	24	26	41	15	0	0	0	8
2002-03	Kelowna Rockets	WHL	65	18	53	71	86	19	2	*20	22	26
2003-04	Hershey Bears	AHL	42	3	8	11	16	....	....	....	....	....
	Reading Royals	ECHL	20	3	7	10	32	....	....	....	....	....
2004-05	Hershey Bears	AHL	1	0	0	0	2	....	....	....	....	....
	HC Kosice	Slovakia	33	3	11	14	42	10	1	2	3	24

WHL West First All-Star Team (2003)

Traded to **Colorado** by **Nashville** for Sergei Soin, June 21, 2003. Assigned to **Kosice** (Slovakia) by **Colorado**, November 2, 2004.

SMABY, Matt (SMA-bee, MAT) T.B.

Defense. Shoots left. 6'5", 211 lbs. Born, Minneapolis, MN, October 14, 1984.
(Tampa Bay's 2nd choice, 41st overall, in 2003 Entry Draft).

			Regular Season					Playoffs				
Season	Club	League	GP	G	A	Pts	PIM	GP	G	A	Pts	PIM
2001-02	Shat.-St. Mary's	High-MN	65	7	18	25	134	....	....	....	....	....
2002-03	Shat.-St. Mary's	High-MN	57	3	20	23	114	....	....	....	....	....
2003-04	North Dakota	WCHA	39	1	6	7	81	....	....	....	....	....
2004-05	North Dakota	WCHA	44	1	2	3	86	....	....	....	....	....

SMID, Ladislav (SHMIHD, LA-dih-slahv) ANA.

Defense. Shoots left. 6'3", 204 lbs. Born, Frydlant V Cechach, Czech., February 1, 1986.
(Anaheim's 1st choice, 9th overall, in 2004 Entry Draft).

			Regular Season					Playoffs				
Season	Club	League	GP	G	A	Pts	PIM	GP	G	A	Pts	PIM
2001-02	HC Liberec Jr.	CzRep-Jr.	17	1	3	3	10	....	....	....	....	....
2002-03	HC Liberec Jr.	CzRep-Jr.	32	1	14	15	12	8	2	1	3	31
	Liberec	CzRep	4	0	0	0	0	....	....	....	....	....
2003-04	Liberec	CzRep	45	1	1	2	51	....	....	....	....	....
	HC Liberec Jr.	CzRep-Jr.	14	4	10	14	38	2	1	0	1	6
	Beroun	CzRep-2	....	....	....	....	....	3	1	1	2	4
2004-05	HC Liberec Jr.	CzRep-Jr.	3	0	1	1	4	....	....	....	....	....
	Liberec	CzRep	39	1	3	4	14	12	0	0	0	6

SMITH, Jeff (SMIHTH, JEHF)

Left wing. Shoots left. 6'6", 212 lbs. Born, Regina, Sask., January 2, 1981.

			Regular Season					Playoffs				
Season	Club	League	GP	G	A	Pts	PIM	GP	G	A	Pts	PIM
1998-99	Reg. Pat Cdns.	SMHL	35	28	19	47	71	....	....	....	....	....
	Red Deer Rebels	WHL	25	0	0	0	0	....	....	....	....	....
99-2000	Red Deer Rebels	WHL	63	9	6	15	74	....	....	....	....	....
2000-01	Red Deer Rebels	WHL	72	22	11	33	187	....	....	....	....	....
2001-02	Red Deer Rebels	WHL	69	9	15	24	236	23	6	6	12	30
2002-03	Philadelphia	AHL	11	1	0	1	22	....	....	....	....	....
	Trenton Titans	ECHL	35	1	7	8	103	1	0	0	0	4
2003-04	Philadelphia	AHL	5	0	0	0	0	....	....	....	....	....
	Trenton Titans	ECHL	47	7	5	12	174	....	....	....	....	....
2004-05	Philadelphia	AHL	41	1	4	5	116	....	....	....	....	....
	Trenton Titans	ECHL	17	4	0	4	19	2	0	0	0	0

Signed as a free agent by **Philadelphia**, August 20, 2002.

SMITH, Jordan (SMIHTH, JOHN-dan) ANA.

Defense. Shoots right. 6'2", 215 lbs. Born, Sault Ste. Marie, Ont., November 4, 1985.
(Anaheim's 2nd choice, 39th overall, in 2004 Entry Draft).

			Regular Season					Playoffs				
Season	Club	League	GP	G	A	Pts	PIM	GP	G	A	Pts	PIM
2001-02	Soo Thunderbirds	NOJHL	8	1	2	3	12	....	....	....	....	....
	Sault Ste. Marie	OHL	19	0	0	0	25	2	0	0	0	2
2002-03	Sault Ste. Marie	OHL	60	2	8	10	107	4	0	0	0	6
2003-04	Sault Ste. Marie	OHL	68	6	20	26	140	....	....	....	....	....
2004-05	Sault Ste. Marie	OHL	64	5	27	32	126	7	1	4	5	7
	Cincinnati	AHL	5	0	1	1	19	9	0	1	1	35

OHL Second All-Star Team (2005)

SMITH, Kenny (SMIHTH, KEHN-nee) EDM.

Defense. Shoots right. 6'2", 209 lbs. Born, Stoneham, MA, December 31, 1981.
(Edmonton's 4th choice, 84th overall, in 2001 Entry Draft).

			Regular Season					Playoffs				
Season	Club	League	GP	G	A	Pts	PIM	GP	G	A	Pts	PIM
1998-99	USA U-17	USDP	29	2	5	7	32	....	....	....	....	....
99-2000	USA U-18	USDP	27	4	6	10	77	....	....	....	....	....
2000-01	Harvard Crimson	ECAC	21	0	2	2	37	....	....	....	....	....
2001-02	Harvard Crimson	ECAC	33	3	10	13	48	....	....	....	....	....
2002-03	Harvard Crimson	ECAC	33	4	11	15	52	....	....	....	....	....
2003-04	Harvard Crimson	ECAC	34	4	7	11	44	....	....	....	....	....
2004-05	Edmonton	AHL	5	0	0	0	4	....	....	....	....	....
	Greenville Grrrowl	ECHL	64	3	6	9	68	4	0	0	0	0

SMITH, Tim (SMIHTH, TIHM)

Center. Shoots left. 5'9", 160 lbs. Born, Whitecourt, Alta., July 21, 1981.
(Vancouver's 7th choice, 272nd overall, in 2000 Entry Draft).

			Regular Season					Playoffs				
Season	Club	League	GP	G	A	Pts	PIM	GP	G	A	Pts	PIM
1997-98	Lebret Eagles	SJHL	36	6	7	13	12	....	....	....	....	....
1998-99	Spokane Chiefs	WHL	57	5	20	25	21	....	....	....	....	....
99-2000	Spokane Chiefs	WHL	71	26	70	96	65	15	7	7	14	32
2000-01	Spokane Chiefs	WHL	38	19	37	56	65	....	....	....	....	....
	Swift Current	WHL	30	12	22	34	38	19	10	14	24	38
2001-02	Swift Current	WHL	67	28	47	75	123	12	7	6	13	20
2002-03	Manitoba Moose	AHL	3	0	0	0	0	....	....	....	....	....
	Columbia Inferno	ECHL	68	22	37	59	44	17	5	11	16	16
2003-04	Manitoba Moose	AHL	1	0	0	0	0	....	....	....	....	....
	Columbia Inferno	ECHL	69	33	*62	*95	112	4	1	3	4	8
2004-05	Manitoba Moose	AHL	29	4	0	4	6	....	....	....	....	....
	Columbia Inferno	ECHL	19	8	11	19	15	5	0	4	4	8

ECHL First All-Star Team (2004)

SMOLENAK, Radek (SMOH-lehn-ahk, RA-dehk) T.B.

Left wing. Shoots left. 6'2", 180 lbs. Born, Prague, Czech., December 3, 1986.
(Tampa Bay's 2nd choice, 73rd overall, in 2005 Entry Draft).

			Regular Season					Playoffs				
Season	Club	League	GP	G	A	Pts	PIM	GP	G	A	Pts	PIM
2001-02	HC Kladno U17	CzR-U17	47	29	20	49	38	....	....	....	....	....
2002-03	HC Kladno U17	CzR-U17	41	39	27	66	50	9	7	3	10	18
	HC Kladno Jr.	CzRep-Jr.	4	2	0	2	6	....	....	....	....	....
2003-04	HC Kladno Jr.	CzRep-Jr.	54	27	25	52	51	7	3	4	7	0
2004-05	Kingston	OHL	67	32	28	60	58	....	....	....	....	....

SMYTH, Adam ATL.

Right wing. Shoots right. 6'1", 215 lbs. Born, Wiarton, Ont., September 8, 1983.

			Regular Season					Playoffs				
Season	Club	League	GP	G	A	Pts	PIM	GP	G	A	Pts	PIM
2000-01	Ottawa 67's	OHL	24	2	2	4	63	....	....	....	....	....
2001-02	Ottawa 67's	OHL	50	4	3	7	205	13	3	1	4	24
2002-03	Ottawa 67's	OHL	48	6	3	9	128	15	5	3	8	29
2003-04	Ottawa 67's	OHL	2	0	2	2	8	....	....	....	....	....
	Owen Sound	OHL	48	11	11	22	152	7	1	0	1	14
	Port Huron	UHL	4	0	0	0	2	7	0	0	0	21
2004-05	Chicago Wolves	AHL	3	0	0	0	2	....	....	....	....	....
	Gwinnett	ECHL	49	6	10	16	217	8	3	2	5	28

Signed as a free agent by **Atlanta**, August 9, 2005.

SOBOTKA, Vladimir (soh-BAWT-kah, vla-DIH-meer) BOS.

Center. Shoots left. 5'10", 183 lbs. Born, Trebic, Czech., July 2, 1987.
(Boston's 5th choice, 106th overall, in 2005 Entry Draft).

			Regular Season					Playoffs				
Season	Club	League	GP	G	A	Pts	PIM	GP	G	A	Pts	PIM
2002-03	Slavia U17	CzR-U17	46	16	24	40	48	8	1	1	2	29
2003-04	Slavia U17	CzR-U17	35	24	41	65	109	7	7	12	19	8
	HC Slavia Praha Jr.	CzRep-Jr.	18	6	6	12	16	....	....	....	....	....
	HC Slavia Praha	CzRep	1	0	0	0	0	....	....	....	....	....
2004-05	HC Slavia Praha Jr.	CzRep-Jr.	27	12	21	33	93	....	....	....	....	....
	HC Slavia Praha	CzRep	18	0	1	1	8	....	....	....	....	....
	Havl. Brod	CzRep-3	7	3	0	3	31	7	1	5	6	0

SOCHOR, Jan (soh-KHAWR, YAN) TOR.

Left wing. Shoots right. 6', 198 lbs. Born, Usti nad Labem, Czech., January 17, 1980.
(Toronto's 6th choice, 161st overall, in 1999 Entry Draft).

			Regular Season					Playoffs				
Season	Club	League	GP	G	A	Pts	PIM	GP	G	A	Pts	PIM
1996-97	HC Slavia Praha Jr.	CzRep-Jr.	26	11	12	23	....	....	....	....	....	....
1997-98	HC Slavia Praha Jr.	CzRep-Jr.	33	26	12	38	....	....	....	....	....	....
	HC Slavia Praha	CzRep	14	1	1	2	2	1	0	0	0	0
1998-99	HC Slavia Praha Jr.	CzRep-Jr.	7	2	1	3	2	....	....	....	....	....
	HC Slavia Praha	CzRep	47	10	10	20	14	....	....	....	....	....
99-2000	HC Slavia Praha Jr.	CzRep-Jr.	12	5	5	10	6	....	....	....	....	....
	HC Slavia Praha	CzRep	39	7	11	18	37	....	....	....	....	....
	Usti n. L.	CzRep-3	6	2	3	5	8	....	....	....	....	....
2000-01	HC Vsetin Jr.	CzRep-Jr.	8	5	3	8	0	....	....	....	....	....
	HC Slovnaft Vsetin	CzRep	41	5	4	9	28	3	0	0	0	0
2001-02	HC Vsetin	CzRep	27	4	0	4	8	....	....	....	....	....
2002-03	HC Vsetin	CzRep	17	2	0	2	10	....	....	....	....	....
	SK Kadan	CzRep-2	18	4	6	10	10	....	....	....	....	....
2003-04	FPS Forssa	Finland-2	26	5	8	13	26	....	....	....	....	....
	Prostejov	CzRep-2	5	1	1	2	2	....	....	....	....	....
	HC Vsetin	CzRep	5	1	0	1	0	....	....	....	....	....
2004-05	Oklahoma City	CHL	4	0	0	0	2	....	....	....	....	....
	Fresno Falcons	ECHL	36	6	9	15	25	....	....	....	....	....
	Victoria	ECHL	4	3	1	4	0	....	....	....	....	....

SODERBERG, Anders (SOH-dehr-buhrg, AN-duhrs) BOS.

Right wing. Shoots right. 5'6", 161 lbs. Born, Ornskoldsvik, Sweden, October 7, 1975.
(Boston's 10th choice, 234th overall, in 1996 Entry Draft).

			Regular Season					Playoffs				
Season	Club	League	GP	G	A	Pts	PIM	GP	G	A	Pts	PIM
1992-93	MoDo Jr.	Swe-Jr.	13	6	12	18	2	....	....	....	....	....
	MoDo	Sweden	1	0	0	0	0	....	....	....	....	....
1993-94	MoDo Jr.	Swe-Jr.	9	8	5	13	10	....	....	....	....	....
	MoDo	Sweden	19	0	0	0	2	9	0	0	0	0
1994-95	MoDo	Sweden	38	9	14	23	2	....	....	....	....	....
1995-96	MoDo	Sweden	40	10	18	28	10	8	3	3	6	0
1996-97	MoDo	Sweden	39	9	13	22	16	....	....	....	....	....
1997-98	MoDo	Sweden	44	15	10	25	4	9	5	1	6	2
1998-99	MoDo	Sweden	49	6	15	21	18	13	3	6	9	4
99-2000	MoDo	Sweden	43	15	10	25	18	9	1	2	3	0
2000-01	MoDo	Sweden	42	11	4	15	12	6	1	6	7	0
2001-02	MODO	Sweden	30	6	9	15	6	11	0	0	0	0
2002-03	MODO	Sweden	49	10	19	29	4	6	0	3	3	0
2003-04	MODO	Sweden	47	6	12	18	8	6	3	2	5	0
2004-05	Skelleftea AIK HK	Sweden-2	48	25	29	54	14	....	....	....	....	....

SODERBERG, Carl (SOH-dehr-buhrg, KARL) ST.L.

Center. Shoots left. 6'3", 198 lbs. Born, Malmo, Sweden, October 12, 1985.
(St. Louis' 2nd choice, 49th overall, in 2004 Entry Draft).

			Regular Season					Playoffs				
Season	Club	League	GP	G	A	Pts	PIM	GP	G	A	Pts	PIM
2000-01	Skane	Exhib.	8	1	2	3	2	....	....	....	....	....
	Malmo U18	Swe-U18	3	1	1	2	0	....	....	....	....	....
2001-02	Malmo U18	Swe-U18	13	9	20	29	18	....	....	....	....	....
	Malmo Jr.	Swe-Jr.	4	0	2	2	2	7	0	2	2	4
2002-03	Malmo U18	Swe-U18	4	6	3	9	25	....	....	....	....	....
	Malmo Jr.	Swe-Jr.	28	17	18	35	22	6	2	4	6	8
2003-04	Malmo	Sweden	24	1	1	2	8	....	....	....	....	....
	Malmo U18	Swe-U18	27	23	25	48	30	6	1	2	3	10
	Malmo	Sweden-Q	8	1	1	2	4	....	....	....	....	....
2004-05	Morrums GoIS IK	Sweden-2	14	5	6	11	8	....	....	....	....	....
	Malmo Jr.	Swe-Jr.	12	13	6	19	43	3	2	1	3	12
	Malmo	Sweden	38	0	5	5	8	....	....	....	....	....
	Malmo	Sweden-Q	7	0	0	0	0	....	....	....	....	....

SODERSTROM, Christian (SAW-duhr-struhm, KRIHS-tyehn) DET.

Left wing. Shoots left. 6'1", 176 lbs. Born, Sundsvall, Sweden, October 13, 1980.
(Detroit's 9th choice, 262nd overall, in 2002 Entry Draft).

			Regular Season					Playoffs				
Season	Club	League	GP	G	A	Pts	PIM	GP	G	A	Pts	PIM
1997-98	Timra IK Jr.	Swe-Jr.	27	7	10	17	22	....	....	....	....	....
1998-99	Timra IK Jr.	Swe-Jr.	STATISTICS NOT AVAILABLE									
	Timra IK	Sweden-2	3	0	1	1	2	....	....	....	....	....
99-2000	Timra IK Jr.	Swe-Jr.	3	4	3	7	0	....	....	....	....	....
	Timra IK	Sweden-2	29	5	3	8	2	....	....	....	....	....
2000-01	Timra IK	Sweden	46	6	6	12	16	....	....	....	....	....
2001-02	Timra IK	Sweden	48	8	8	16	16	....	....	....	....	....
	Timra IK	Sweden-Q	....	....	....	....	....	9	0	1	1	4
2002-03	Timra IK	Sweden	44	5	10	15	6	10	1	2	3	2
2003-04	Timra IK	Sweden	48	7	6	13	62	10	1	1	2	4
2004-05	Timra IK	Sweden	48	9	6	15	22	5	1	1	2	0

SOIN, Sergei (SOY-ihn, SAIR-gay) NSH.

Center/Left wing. Shoots left. 6', 175 lbs. Born, Moscow, USSR, March 31, 1982.
(Colorado's 3rd choice, 50th overall, in 2000 Entry Draft).

			Regular Season					Playoffs				
Season	Club	League	GP	G	A	Pts	PIM	GP	G	A	Pts	PIM
1997-98	Krylja Sovetov 2	Russia-3	2	0	0	0	0	....	....	....	....	....
1998-99	Krylja Sovetov	Russia	34	1	4	5	12	....	....	....	....	....
99-2000	Krylja Sovetov 2	Russia-3	8	2	3	5	12	....	....	....	....	....
	Krylja Sovetov	Russia-2	32	8	8	16	28	14	0	2	2	6
2000-01	Krylja Sovetov 2	Russia-3	8	2	3	5	12	....	....	....	....	....
	Krylja Sovetov	Russia-2	19	6	3	9	8	11	2	2	4	2
2001-02	Krylja Sovetov 2	Russia-3	5	2	6	8	20	....	....	....	....	....
	Krylja Sovetov	Russia	41	5	7	12	8	....	....	....	....	....
2002-03	Krylja Sovetov	Russia	49	8	6	14	40	....	....	....	....	....
2003-04	CSKA Moscow	Russia	49	1	6	7	32	....	....	....	....	....
2004-05	CSKA Moscow	Russia	19	3	3	6	10	....	....	....	....	....

Traded to **Nashville** by **Colorado** for Tomas Slovak, June 21, 2003.

SOMERVUORI, Eero (soh-muhr-VOH-ree, AIR-oh) T.B.

Right wing. Shoots right. 5'10", 190 lbs. Born, Jarvenpaa, Finland, February 7, 1979.
(Tampa Bay's 9th choice, 170th overall, in 1997 Entry Draft).

			Regular Season					Playoffs				
Season	Club	League	GP	G	A	Pts	PIM	GP	G	A	Pts	PIM
1994-95	Jokerit U18	Fin-U18	15	8	10	18	4	....	....	....	....	....
	Jokerit Helsinki Jr.	Finland-Jr.	10	1	1	2	2	1	0	1	1	0
1995-96	Jokerit Helsinki Jr.	Finland-Jr.	28	14	12	26	10	9	4	1	5	4
	Jokerit U18	Fin-U18	13	10	13	23	6	....	....	....	....	....
	Haukat Jarvenpaa	Finland-2	1	0	0	0	0	....	....	....	....	....
	Jokerit Helsinki	Finland	6	1	2	3	0	....	....	....	....	....
1996-97	Jokerit Helsinki Jr.	Finland-Jr.	28	20	19	39	30	5	3	0	3	4
	Jokerit Helsinki	Finland	35	1	1	2	2	5	0	0	0	0
	Jokerit Helsinki	EuroHL	3	0	0	0	0	2	2	0	0	0
1997-98	Jokerit Helsinki	Finland	42	3	7	10	12	8	2	1	3	6
	Jokerit Helsinki	EuroHL	5	0	0	0	0	....	....	....	....	....
	Jokerit Helsinki Jr.	Finland-Jr.	14	4	8	12	2	....	....	....	....	....
1998-99	Jokerit Helsinki	Finland	50	7	8	15	24	3	1	0	1	6
	Jokerit Helsinki	EuroHL	6	0	0	0	0	1	0	0	0	0
	Jokerit Helsinki Jr.	Finland-Jr.	4	1	1	2	2	4	3	0	3	2
99-2000	Jokerit Helsinki	Finland	54	6	6	12	10	11	1	0	1	0
2000-01	HPK Hameenlinna	Finland	56	14	6	20	35	....	....	....	....	....
2001-02	HPK Hameenlinna	Finland	56	25	23	48	34	8	2	2	4	6
2002-03	HPK Hameenlinna	Finland	56	21	24	45	42	13	2	3	5	0
2003-04	Hamilton Bulldogs	AHL	79	19	14	33	14	10	2	3	5	0
2004-05	Karpat Oulu	Finland	56	16	26	42	14	12	2	1	3	4

Signed as a free agent by **Karpat** (Finland), August 1, 2004.

SOUCY, J.F. (SOO-cee, JAY-EHF) T.B.

Center. Shoots left. 6'3", 205 lbs. Born, Riviere Du Loup, Que., March 25, 1983.
(Tampa Bay's 10th choice, 252nd overall, in 2001 Entry Draft).

			Regular Season					Playoffs				
Season	Club	League	GP	G	A	Pts	PIM	GP	G	A	Pts	PIM
1998-99	Levis	QAAA	42	6	17	23	82	....	....	....	....	....
99-2000	Val-d'Or Foreurs	QMJHL	55	1	4	5	9	....	....	....	....	....
2000-01	Val-d'Or Foreurs	QMJHL	38	3	4	7	57	....	....	....	....	....
	Montreal Rocket	QMJHL	27	3	8	11	37	....	....	....	....	....
2001-02	Montreal Rocket	QMJHL	49	8	13	21	94	7	0	2	2	8
2002-03	Montreal Rocket	QMJHL	65	24	31	55	168	7	0	2	2	24
2003-04	Hershey Bears	AHL	12	2	2	4	29	....	....	....	....	....
	Pensacola	ECHL	57	10	10	20	199	5	0	0	0	23
2004-05	Springfield Falcons	AHL	55	1	4	5	203	....	....	....	....	....
	Johnstown Chiefs	ECHL	14	1	2	3	49	....	....	....	....	....

SOUTHERN, Dirk (SUH-thuhrn, DUHRK) ANA.

Center. Shoots right. 6', 177 lbs. Born, Winnipeg, Man., August 9, 1983.
(Anaheim's 7th choice, 218th overall, in 2003 Entry Draft).

			Regular Season					Playoffs				
Season	Club	League	GP	G	A	Pts	PIM	GP	G	A	Pts	PIM
2001-02	Lincoln Stars	USHL	60	22	36	58	46	4	1	1	2	2
2002-03	Northern Mich.	CCHA	41	11	22	33	55	....	....	....	....	....
2003-04	Northern Mich.	CCHA	37	10	15	25	32	....	....	....	....	....
2004-05	Northern Mich.	CCHA	32	11	19	30	28	....	....	....	....	....

CCHA All-Rookie Team (2003)

SPANG, Dan (SPANG, DAN) S.J.

Defense. Shoots left. 6', 205 lbs. Born, Winchester, MA, August 18, 1983.
(San Jose's 2nd choice, 52nd overall, in 2002 Entry Draft).

			Regular Season					Playoffs				
Season	Club	League	GP	G	A	Pts	PIM	GP	G	A	Pts	PIM
2000-01	Winchester High	High-MA	24	8	37	45	14	....	....	....	....	....
2001-02	Winchester High	High-MA	6	9	8	17	14	....	....	....	....	....
2002-03	Boston University	H-East	27	3	6	9	14	....	....	....	....	....
2003-04	Boston University	H-East	38	5	9	14	12	....	....	....	....	....
2004-05	Boston University	H-East	41	3	13	16	22	....	....	....	....	....

• Missed majority of 2001-02 season recovering from head injuries suffered in automobile accident, October, 2001.

SPENCER, Steven (SPEHN-suhr, STEEV) N.J.

Defense. Shoots left. 6'3", 220 lbs. Born, Regina, Sask., June 16, 1982.
(Nashville's 8th choice, 266th overall, in 2002 Entry Draft).

			Regular Season					Playoffs				
Season	Club	League	GP	G	A	Pts	PIM	GP	G	A	Pts	PIM
2000-01	La Ronge	SJHL	48	3	6	9	176	....	....	....	....	....
2001-02	Swift Current	WHL	65	1	4	5	226	11	0	0	0	36
2002-03	Swift Current	WHL	72	2	2	4	187	4	0	0	0	17
2003-04	South Carolina	ECHL	35	0	5	5	119	7	0	0	0	13
2004-05	Albany River Rats	AHL	40	1	1	2	67	....	....	....	....	....
	South Carolina	ECHL	19	1	4	5	68	4	0	0	0	12

• Missed majority of 2003-04 season recovering from wrist injury suffered in game vs. Augusta (ECHL), December 20, 2003. Signed as a free agent by **New Jersey**, July 6, 2004.

SPRUKTS, Janis (SPRUKTS, YAN-ish) FLA.

Center. Shoots left. 6'3", 224 lbs. Born, Riga, Latvia, January 31, 1982.
(Florida's 7th choice, 234th overall, in 2000 Entry Draft).

			Regular Season					Playoffs				
Season	Club	League	GP	G	A	Pts	PIM	GP	G	A	Pts	PIM
99-2000	Lukko Rauma Jr.	Finland-Jr.	26	2	5	7	6	3	0	0	0	0
	HC Essamika Jr.	EEHL-2	2	4	4	8	0	....	....	....	....	....
2000-01	Lukko Rauma Jr.	Finland-Jr.	36	15	22	37	24	3	0	0	0	0
	Lukko Rauma	Finland	9	0	0	0	2	....	....	....	....	....
2001-02	Acadie-Bathurst	QMJHL	63	35	44	79	46	16	14	8	22	12
2002-03	Sport Vaasa	Finland-2	21	5	6	11	8	....	....	....	....	....
	Acadie-Bathurst	QMJHL	30	9	29	38	12	11	3	5	8	0
2003-04	ASK Ogre	Latvia	5	2	4	6	0	....	....	....	....	....
	Odense IK	Denmark	2	0	1	1	2	....	....	....	....	....
2004-05	HK Riga 2000	BelOpen	21	7	9	16	10	3	0	0	0	2
	HK Riga 2000	Latvia	3	2	3	5	0	9	3	4	7	2

• Released by **Vaasa** (Finland-2) and returned to **Acadie-Bathurst** (QMJHL), January 3, 2003.

SPRUNGER, Julien (SRUHN-guhr, JEW-lee-ehn) MIN.

Right wing. Shoots right. 6'4", 197 lbs. Born, Fribourg, Switz., January 4, 1986.
(Minnesota's 7th choice, 117th overall, in 2004 Entry Draft).

			Regular Season					Playoffs				
Season	Club	League	GP	G	A	Pts	PIM	GP	G	A	Pts	PIM
2002-03	Fribourg	Swiss	2	0	0	0	0	....	....	....	....	....
	Fribourg Jr.	Swiss-Jr.	24	21	19	40	32	....	....	....	....	....
	HC Dudingen	Swiss-3	9	7	1	8	....	2	1	1	2	....
2003-04	Fribourg	Swiss	42	2	3	5	14	4	0	0	0	4
2004-05	Fribourg Jr.	Swiss-Jr.	4	3	4	7	4	....	....	....	....	....
	Chaux-de-Fonds	Swiss-2	1	0	0	0	0	....	....	....	....	....
	Fribourg	Swiss	41	9	7	16	35	11	2	1	3	14

SPURGEON, Tyler (SPUHR-juhn, TIGH-luhr) EDM.

Center. Shoots left. 5'11", 188 lbs. Born, Edmonton, Alta., April 10, 1986.
(Edmonton's 9th choice, 242nd overall, in 2004 Entry Draft).

			Regular Season					Playoffs				
Season	Club	League	GP	G	A	Pts	PIM	GP	G	A	Pts	PIM
2001-02	Kelowna Rockets	WHL	2	0	1	1	0	....	....	....	....	....
	Edmonton MLAC	AMHL	35	39	36	75	12	....	....	....	....	....
2002-03	Kelowna Rockets	WHL	50	7	6	13	21	19	2	5	7	6
2003-04	Kelowna Rockets	WHL	49	8	16	24	24	17	4	5	9	9
2004-05	Kelowna Rockets	WHL	72	21	41	62	32	24	11	6	17	12

STAAL, Kim (STAHL, KIHM) MTL.

Center. Shoots right. 6', 185 lbs. Born, Herlev, Denmark, March 10, 1978.
(Montreal's 4th choice, 92nd overall, in 1996 Entry Draft).

			Regular Season					Playoffs				
Season	Club	League	GP	G	A	Pts	PIM	GP	G	A	Pts	PIM
1994-95	Malmo IF Jr.	Swe-Jr.	17	4	2	6	4	....	....	....	....	....
1995-96	Malmo IF Jr.	Swe-Jr.	30	24	20	44	14	....	....	....	....	....
1996-97	Malmo Jr.	Swe-Jr.	3	6	4	10	2	....	....	....	....	....
	Malmo	Sweden	4	0	1	1	2	....	....	....	....	....
1997-98	Malmo Jr.	Swe-Jr.	20	13	11	24	36	....	....	....	....	....
	Malmo	Sweden	13	0	1	1	1	....	....	....	....	....
1998-99	Malmo	Sweden	48	1	5	6	14	4	0	0	0	0
99-2000	Malmo	Sweden	50	14	10	24	24	6	1	1	2	4
2000-01	Malmo	Sweden	48	16	15	31	32	9	4	2	6	4
2001-02	MODO	Sweden	49	14	23	37	16	12	3	7	10	2
2002-03	MODO	Sweden	14	4	5	9	4	6	1	0	1	0
	Ornskoldsviks SK	Sweden-2	2	3	0	3	0	....	....	....	....	....
2003-04	Malmo	Sweden	45	15	8	23	14	....	....	....	....	....
	Malmo	Sweden-Q	10	7	7	14	4	....	....	....	....	....
2004-05	Malmo	Sweden	34	10	11	21	12	....	....	....	....	....
	Malmo	Sweden-Q	9	0	2	2	0	....	....	....	....	....

STAAL, Marc (STAHL, MAHRK) NYR

Defense. Shoots left. 6'3", 196 lbs. Born, Thunder Bay, Ont., January 13, 1987.
(NY Rangers' 1st choice, 12th overall, in 2005 Entry Draft).

			Regular Season					Playoffs				
Season	Club	League	GP	G	A	Pts	PIM	GP	G	A	Pts	PIM
2003-04	Sudbury Wolves	OHL	61	1	13	14	34	7	1	2	3	2
2004-05	Sudbury Wolves	OHL	65	6	20	26	53	12	0	4	4	15

STAFFORD, Drew (STA-fuhrd, DROO) BUF.

Right wing. Shoots right. 6'1", 202 lbs. Born, Milwaukee, WI, October 30, 1985.
(Buffalo's 1st choice, 13th overall, in 2004 Entry Draft).

			Regular Season					Playoffs				
Season	Club	League	GP	G	A	Pts	PIM	GP	G	A	Pts	PIM
2001-02	Shat.-St. Mary's	High-MN	45	35	53	88	30	....	....	....	....	....
2002-03	Shat.-St. Mary's	High-MN	65	49	67	116	....	....	....	....	....	....
2003-04	North Dakota	WCHA	36	11	21	32	30	....	....	....	....	....
2004-05	North Dakota	WCHA	42	13	25	38	34	....	....	....	....	....

STAFFORD, Garrett (STA-fuhrd, GAIR-reht) **S.J.**

Defense. Shoots right. 6', 190 lbs. Born, Los Angeles, CA, January 28, 1980.

			Regular Season					Playoffs				
Season	Club	League	GP	G	A	Pts	PIM	GP	G	A	Pts	PIM
1996-97	Des Moines	USHL	37	1	10	11	40	5	0	0	0	0
1997-98	Des Moines	USHL	53	6	17	23	89	12	1	3	4	42
1998-99	Des Moines	USHL	56	8	33	41	54	13	2	2	4	18
99-2000	New Hampshire	H-East	38	3	9	12	28	....	....	....	....	....
2000-01	New Hampshire	H-East	37	5	21	26	44	....	....	....	....	....
2001-02	New Hampshire	H-East	36	5	22	27	42	....	....	....	....	....
2002-03	New Hampshire	H-East	23	1	15	16	24	....	....	....	....	....
2003-04	Cleveland Barons	AHL	73	12	34	46	71	6	0	0	0	6
2004-05	Cleveland Barons	AHL	68	6	18	24	55	....	....	....	....	....

AHL All-Rookie Team (2004) • AHL Second All-Star Team (2004)

Signed as a free agent by **Cleveland** (AHL), October 10, 2003. Signed as a free agent by **San Jose**, December 9, 2003.

STALS, Juris (STAHLS, YOO-rihs) **NYR**

Left wing. Shoots left. 6'3", 205 lbs. Born, Riga, Latvia, August 4, 1982.
(NY Rangers' 11th choice, 269th overall, in 2001 Entry Draft).

			Regular Season					Playoffs				
Season	Club	League	GP	G	A	Pts	PIM	GP	G	A	Pts	PIM
99-2000	Lukko Rauma Jr.	Finland-Jr.	2	1	0	1	2	....	....	....	....	....
2000-01	Lukko Rauma Jr.	Finland-Jr.	45	23	22	45	26	3	1	0	1	0
2001-02	Sarnia Sting	OHL	60	23	22	45	12	5	0	1	1	2
2002-03	Sport Vaasa	Finland-2	23	3	3	6	16	....	....	....	....	....
	Owen Sound	OHL	25	8	15	23	14	4	0	4	4	4
	Hartford Wolf Pack	AHL	2	0	1	1	0	....	....	....	....	....
2003-04	Hartford Wolf Pack	AHL	62	4	14	18	24	1	0	0	0	0
2004-05	Charlotte	ECHL	54	19	11	30	31	....	....	....	....	....

STAMLER, Bretton (STAM-lehr, BREH-tuhn) **DET.**

Defense. Shoots right. 6'1", 201 lbs. Born, Calgary, Alta., March 10, 1987.
(Detroit's 9th choice, 214th overall, in 2005 Entry Draft).

			Regular Season					Playoffs				
Season	Club	League	GP	G	A	Pts	PIM	GP	G	A	Pts	PIM
2003-04	Seattle	WHL	61	0	9	9	27	....	....	....	....	....
2004-05	Seattle	WHL	72	4	9	13	106	1	0	0	0	0

STARKOV, Kirill (stahr-KAWF, kih-RIHL) **CBJ**

Center. Shoots left. 6', 194 lbs. Born, Yekateringburg, USSR, March 31, 1987.
(Columbus' 7th choice, 189th overall, in 2005 Entry Draft).

			Regular Season					Playoffs				
Season	Club	League	GP	G	A	Pts	PIM	GP	G	A	Pts	PIM
2002-03	Esbjerg Oilers	Denmark	28	2	4	6	6	14	0	0	0	0
2003-04	V.Frolunda U18	Swe-U18	9	6	6	12	2	7	2	3	5	2
	V.Frolunda Jr.	Swe-Jr.	25	3	10	13	4	5	2	0	2	0
2004-05	Frolunda U18	Swe-U18	1	0	0	0	4	3	2	1	3	0
	Frolunda Jr.	Swe-Jr.	34	18	12	30	6	6	2	2	4	2

STASTNY, Paul (STAS-nee, PAWL) **COL.**

Center. Shoots left. 6', 201 lbs. Born, Quebec City, Que., December 27, 1985.
(Colorado's 2nd choice, 44th overall, in 2005 Entry Draft).

			Regular Season					Playoffs				
Season	Club	League	GP	G	A	Pts	PIM	GP	G	A	Pts	PIM
2003-04	River City Lancers	USHL	56	30	*47	77	46	3	1	2	3	0
2004-05	U. of Denver	WCHA	42	17	28	45	30	....	....	....	....	....

WCHA All-Rookie Team (2005) • WCHA Rookie of the Year (2005) • NCAA Championship All-Tournament Team (2005)

STASTNY, Yan (STAS-nee, YAHN) **EDM.**

Center. Shoots left. 5'11", 175 lbs. Born, Quebec City, Que., September 30, 1982.
(Boston's 6th choice, 259th overall, in 2002 Entry Draft).

			Regular Season					Playoffs				
Season	Club	League	GP	G	A	Pts	PIM	GP	G	A	Pts	PIM
99-2000	St. Louis Sting	NAHL	45	12	23	35	77	....	....	....	....	....
2000-01	St. Louis Jr. Blues	CSJHL	6	0	2	2	23	....	....	....	....	....
	Omaha Lancers	USHL	44	17	14	31	101	11	6	6	12	12
2001-02	U. of Notre Dame	CCHA	33	6	11	17	38	....	....	....	....	....
2002-03	U. of Notre Dame	CCHA	39	14	9	23	44	....	....	....	....	....
2003-04	Nurnberg	Germany	44	9	20	29	83	6	0	1	1	6
2004-05	Nurnberg	Germany	51	24	30	54	60	6	2	1	3	8

Signed as a free agent by **Nurnberg** (Germany), September 18, 2003. Traded to **Edmonton** by **Boston** for Boston's 4th round choice (previously acquired) in 2006 Entry Draft, August 30, 2005.

STASYUK, Denis (stah-S'YUHK, DEH-nihs) **FLA.**

Center. Shoots left. 6'1", 165 lbs. Born, Novokuznetsk, USSR, September 2, 1985.
(Florida's 9th choice, 171st overall, in 2003 Entry Draft).

			Regular Season					Playoffs				
Season	Club	League	GP	G	A	Pts	PIM	GP	G	A	Pts	PIM
2002-03	Novokuznetsk 2	Russia-3		STATISTICS NOT AVAILABLE								
	Novokuznetsk	Russia	11	1	0	1	0	....	....	....	....	....
2003-04	Novokuznetsk	Russia	5	0	0	0	0	....	....	....	....	....
	Novokuznetsk 2	Russia-3		STATISTICS NOT AVAILABLE								
2004-05	Amur Khabarovsk	Russia-2	44	11	10	21	12	10	1	2	3	6

STEBER, Jan (STEH-buhr, YAHN) **TOR.**

Left wing. Shoots right. 6'3", 202 lbs. Born, Ostrava, Czech., October 19, 1985.
(Toronto's 5th choice, 252nd overall, in 2004 Entry Draft).

			Regular Season					Playoffs				
Season	Club	League	GP	G	A	Pts	PIM	GP	G	A	Pts	PIM
2000-01	HC Trinec Jr.	CzRep-Jr.	44	16	11	27	12	8	0	1	1	27
2001-02	HC Trinec Jr.	CzRep-Jr.	48	18	14	32	16	6	2	2	4	2
2002-03	HC Trinec Jr.	CzRep-Jr.	31	10	8	18	29	3	1	1	2	2
2003-04	Halifax	QMJHL	69	16	15	31	45	....	....	....	....	....
2004-05	Halifax	QMJHL	63	17	17	34	58	13	3	5	8	8

STECKEL, Dave (STEH-kuhl, DAYV) **WSH.**

Center. Shoots left. 6'5", 215 lbs. Born, Westbend, WI, March 15, 1982.
(Los Angeles' 2nd choice, 30th overall, in 2001 Entry Draft).

			Regular Season					Playoffs				
Season	Club	League	GP	G	A	Pts	PIM	GP	G	A	Pts	PIM
1998-99	USA U-17	USDP	51	3	14	17	18	....	....	....	....	....
	USA U-18	USDP	2	0	0	0	2	....	....	....	....	....
99-2000	USA U-18	USDP	52	13	13	26	94	....	....	....	....	....
2000-01	Ohio State	CCHA	33	17	18	35	80	....	....	....	....	....
2001-02	Ohio State	CCHA	36	6	16	22	75	....	....	....	....	....
2002-03	Ohio State	CCHA	36	10	8	18	50	....	....	....	....	....
2003-04	Ohio State	CCHA	41	17	13	30	44	....	....	....	....	....
2004-05	Manchester	AHL	63	10	7	17	26	6	1	1	2	4

CCHA All-Rookie Team (2001)

Signed as a free agent by **Washington**, August 25, 2005.

STEEN, Alexander (STEEN, al-ehx-AN-duhr) **TOR.**

Center. Shoots left. 5'11", 183 lbs. Born, Winnipeg, Man., March 1, 1984.
(Toronto's 1st choice, 24th overall, in 2002 Entry Draft).

			Regular Season					Playoffs				
Season	Club	League	GP	G	A	Pts	PIM	GP	G	A	Pts	PIM
99-2000	V.Frolunda Jr.	Swe-Jr.	8	5	7	12	0	....	....	....	....	....
	V.Frolunda U18	Swe-U18	14	3	5	8	16	....	....	....	....	....
2000-01	V.Frolunda Jr.	Swe-Jr.	23	11	12	23	15	3	1	0	1	2
	V.Frolunda U18	Swe-U18	6	3	3	6	9	....	....	....	....	....
2001-02	V.Frolunda Jr.	Swe-Jr.	23	21	17	38	47	2	1	1	2	2
	V.Frolunda	Sweden	26	0	3	3	14	10	1	2	3	0
2002-03	V.Frolunda	Sweden	45	5	10	15	18	16	2	3	5	4
	V.Frolunda Jr.	Swe-Jr.	2	0	2	2	0	....	....	....	....	....
2003-04	V.Frolunda	Sweden	48	10	14	24	50	10	4	6	10	14
2004-05	MODO	Sweden	50	9	8	17	26	6	1	0	1	4

STEEN, Calle (STEEN, CAL-lee) **DET.**

Right wing. Shoots left. 5'11", 198 lbs. Born, Stockholm, Sweden, May 16, 1980.
(Detroit's 6th choice, 142nd overall, in 1998 Entry Draft).

			Regular Season					Playoffs				
Season	Club	League	GP	G	A	Pts	PIM	GP	G	A	Pts	PIM
1995-96	Hammarby Jr.	Swe-Jr.	5	0	0	0	0	....	....	....	....	....
1996-97	Hammarby Jr.	Swe-Jr.	24	4	9	13	....	....	....	....	....	....
1997-98	Hammarby	Sweden-2	21	1	3	4	22	....	....	....	....	....
1998-99	Hammarby	Sweden-2	33	4	16	20	28	5	0	2	2	6
99-2000	Mora IK	Sweden-2	32	4	4	8	48	9	0	2	2	10
2000-01	Bofors	Sweden-2	31	4	7	11	69	....	....	....	....	....
	JYP Jyvaskyla	Finland	5	0	0	0	0	....	....	....	....	....
2001-02	Bofors	Sweden-2	53	12	22	34	78	6	2	2	4	12
2002-03	Bofors	Sweden-2	27	12	17	29	71	....	....	....	....	....
	Farjestad	Sweden	11	0	2	2	2	12	1	5	6	12
2003-04	Farjestad	Sweden	43	2	10	12	42	15	2	3	5	41
	Bofors	Sweden-2	4	1	2	3	4	....	....	....	....	....
2004-05	Farjestad	Sweden	47	4	13	17	50	15	0	0	0	18

STEEVES, Ryan (STEEVZ, RIGH-uhn) **COL.**

Center/Left wing. Shoots left. 6', 195 lbs. Born, Ottawa, Ont., December 31, 1982.
(Colorado's 8th choice, 227th overall, in 2002 Entry Draft).

			Regular Season					Playoffs				
Season	Club	League	GP	G	A	Pts	PIM	GP	G	A	Pts	PIM
1998-99	Ott. Jr. Senators	CJHL	51	17	12	29	45	....	....	....	....	....
99-2000	Ott. Jr. Senators	CJHL	55	36	39	75	87	....	....	....	....	....
2000-01	Yale	ECAC	23	3	2	5	10	....	....	....	....	....
2001-02	Yale	ECAC	31	9	13	22	20	....	....	....	....	....
2002-03	Yale	ECAC	32	15	23	38	36	....	....	....	....	....
2003-04	Yale	ECAC	31	10	16	26	44	....	....	....	....	....
2004-05	Hershey Bears	AHL	75	6	5	11	24	....	....	....	....	....

STEHLIK, Richard (SHTEH-lihk, RIH-chuhrd) **NSH.**

Defense. Shoots left. 6'4", 242 lbs. Born, Skalica, Czech., June 22, 1984.
(Nashville's 5th choice, 76th overall, in 2003 Entry Draft).

			Regular Season					Playoffs				
Season	Club	League	GP	G	A	Pts	PIM	GP	G	A	Pts	PIM
99-2000	HK 36 Skalica Jr.	Slovak-Jr.	50	10	5	15	....	....	....	....	....	....
2000-01	HK 36 Skalica	Slovakia	45	1	1	2	14	3	0	0	0	2
2001-02	HK 36 Skalica	Slovakia	35	1	0	1	12	....	....	....	....	....
2002-03	Sherbrooke	QMJHL	43	8	16	24	105	12	1	5	6	20
2003-04	Lewiston	QMJHL	44	11	25	36	109	7	0	1	1	12
2004-05	HK 36 Skalica	Slovakia	40	8	3	11	28	....	....	....	....	....
	Dukla Trencin	Slovakia	13	1	5	6	33	12	3	3	6	62

STEMPNIAK, Lee (STEHMP-nee-ak, LEE) **ST.L.**

Right wing. Shoots right. 6', 190 lbs. Born, Buffalo, NY, February 4, 1983.
(St. Louis' 7th choice, 148th overall, in 2003 Entry Draft).

			Regular Season					Playoffs				
Season	Club	League	GP	G	A	Pts	PIM	GP	G	A	Pts	PIM
2000-01	Buffalo Lightning	OPJHL	48	34	51	86	36	....	....	....	....	....
2001-02	Dartmouth	ECAC	32	12	9	21	8	....	....	....	....	....
2002-03	Dartmouth	ECAC	34	21	28	49	32	....	....	....	....	....
2003-04	Dartmouth	ECAC	34	16	22	38	42	....	....	....	....	....
2004-05	Dartmouth	ECAC	35	14	*29	43	34	....	....	....	....	....

ECAC All-Rookie Team (2002) • ECAC First All-Star Team (2004, 2005) • NCAA East First All-American Team (2004) • NCAA East Second All-American Team (2005)

STEPHENSON, Logan (STEE-vehn-suhn, LOH-guhn) **PHX.**

Defense. Shoots left. 6'2", 189 lbs. Born, Saskatoon, Sask., February 19, 1986.
(Phoenix's 2nd choice, 35th overall, in 2004 Entry Draft).

			Regular Season					Playoffs				
Season	Club	League	GP	G	A	Pts	PIM	GP	G	A	Pts	PIM
2001-02	Notre Dame	SMHL	37	4	2	6	74	....	....	....	....	....
	Tri-City Americans	WHL	....	....	....	....	....	3	0	0	0	0
2002-03	Tri-City Americans	WHL	50	0	6	6	121	....	....	....	....	....
2003-04	Tri-City Americans	WHL	69	3	8	11	112	11	1	1	2	10
2004-05	Tri-City Americans	WHL	59	6	9	15	86	5	0	0	0	2

STEPP, Joel (STEHP, JOHL) ANA.

Center. Shoots left. 6', 215 lbs. Born, Estevan, Sask., February 11, 1983.
(Anaheim's 3rd choice, 69th overall, in 2001 Entry Draft).

			Regular Season					Playoffs				
Season	Club	League	GP	G	A	Pts	PIM	GP	G	A	Pts	PIM
1998-99	Estevan	SMBHL	60	65	70	135	120	....	....	....	....	....
	Red Deer Rebels	WHL	2	0	0	0	0	....	....	....	....	....
99-2000	Red Deer Rebels	WHL	65	11	13	24	59	4	1	0	1	8
2000-01	Red Deer Rebels	WHL	70	24	13	37	89	22	6	3	9	24
2001-02	Red Deer Rebels	WHL	70	27	26	53	59	23	11	11	22	24
2002-03	Red Deer Rebels	WHL	24	4	11	15	18	23	6	7	13	26
2003-04	Cincinnati	AHL	65	7	7	14	28	9	1	1	2	2
2004-05	Cincinnati	AHL	63	3	9	12	23	12	1	0	1	8
	San Diego Gulls	ECHL	12	7	0	7	10	....	....	....	....	....

• Missed majority of 2002-03 season recovering from wrist surgery, September 12, 2002.

STERLING, Brett (STUHR-lihng, BRET) ATL.

Left wing. Shoots left. 5'7", 175 lbs. Born, Los Angeles, CA, April 24, 1984.
(Atlanta's 5th choice, 145th overall, in 2003 Entry Draft).

			Regular Season					Playoffs				
Season	Club	League	GP	G	A	Pts	PIM	GP	G	A	Pts	PIM
99-2000	L.A. Jr. Kings	SCAHA	35	45	25	70	....	....	....	....	....	....
2000-01	USA U-17	USDP	60	26	36	62	66	....	....	....	....	....
2001-02	USA U-18	USDP	50	29	19	48	36	....	....	....	....	....
2002-03	Colorado College	WCHA	36	27	11	38	30	....	....	....	....	....
2003-04	Colorado College	WCHA	30	16	12	28	40	....	....	....	....	....
2004-05	Colorado College	WCHA	43	*34	29	63	74	....	....	....	....	....

WCHA All-Rookie Team (2003) • WCHA First All-Star Team (2005) • NCAA West First All-American Team (2005)

STEVENSON, Grant (STEE-vehn-suhn, GRANT) S.J.

Center. Shoots right. 5'11", 170 lbs. Born, Spruce Grove, Alta., October 15, 1981.

			Regular Season					Playoffs				
Season	Club	League	GP	G	A	Pts	PIM	GP	G	A	Pts	PIM
1998-99	Spruce Grove	RAMHL	26	15	32	47	90	8	10	10	20	30
99-2000	Bonnyville Pontiacs	AJHL	63	20	38	58	....	....	....	....	....	....
2000-01	Grand Prairie	AJHL	53	24	49	73	62	15	7	2	9	38
2001-02	Minnesota State	WCHA	38	8	8	16	36	....	....	....	....	....
2002-03	Minnesota State	WCHA	38	27	36	63	38	....	....	....	....	....
2003-04	Cleveland Barons	AHL	71	13	26	39	45	9	0	7	7	6
2004-05	Cleveland Barons	AHL	77	14	25	39	70	....	....	....	....	....
	Johnstown Chiefs	ECHL	2	1	0	1	2	....	....	....	....	....

WCHA First All-Star Team (2003) • NCAA West Second All-American Team (2003)

Signed as a free agent by **San Jose**, April 18, 2003.

STEWART, Anthony (STEW-ahrt, AN-toh-nee) FLA.

Center. Shoots right. 6'1", 225 lbs. Born, LaSalle, Que., January 5, 1985.
(Florida's 2nd choice, 25th overall, in 2003 Entry Draft).

			Regular Season					Playoffs				
Season	Club	League	GP	G	A	Pts	PIM	GP	G	A	Pts	PIM
2000-01	North York	MTHL	34	30	70	100	....	....	....	....	....	....
2001-02	Kingston	OHL	65	19	24	43	12	1	0	0	0	0
2002-03	Kingston	OHL	68	32	38	70	47	....	....	....	....	....
2003-04	Kingston	OHL	53	35	23	58	76	5	3	4	7	7
2004-05	Kingston	OHL	62	32	35	67	70	....	....	....	....	....
	San Antonio	AHL	10	1	2	3	14	....	....	....	....	....

STEWART, Greg (STEW-ahrt, GREHG) MTL.

Left wing. Shoots left. 6'1", 193 lbs. Born, Kitchener, Ont., May 21, 1986.
(Montreal's 7th choice, 246th overall, in 2004 Entry Draft).

			Regular Season					Playoffs				
Season	Club	League	GP	G	A	Pts	PIM	GP	G	A	Pts	PIM
2003-04	Peterborough	OHL	58	4	6	10	76	....	....	....	....	....
2004-05	Peterborough	OHL	68	16	18	34	111	14	3	3	6	20

STOA, Ryan (STOH-ah, RIGH-uhn) COL.

Center. Shoots left. 6'3", 200 lbs. Born, Bloomington, MN, April 13, 1987.
(Colorado's 1st choice, 34th overall, in 2005 Entry Draft).

			Regular Season					Playoffs				
Season	Club	League	GP	G	A	Pts	PIM	GP	G	A	Pts	PIM
2003-04	USA U-17	USDP	67	26	21	47	23	....	....	....	....	....
2004-05	USA U-18	USDP	38	14	24	38	36	....	....	....	....	....
	USA U-17&U-18	NAHL	15	10	13	23	20	....	....	....	....	....

Signed Letter of Intent to attend **Minnesota** (WCHA), November 18, 2004.

STOESZ, Myles (STOHZ, MIGH-uhls) ATL.

Left wing. Shoots right. 6'1", 197 lbs. Born, Steinbach, Man., February 13, 1987.
(Atlanta's 8th choice, 207th overall, in 2005 Entry Draft).

			Regular Season					Playoffs				
Season	Club	League	GP	G	A	Pts	PIM	GP	G	A	Pts	PIM
2003-04	Spokane Chiefs	WHL	43	1	1	2	133	0	0	0	0	0
2004-05	Spokane Chiefs	WHL	67	1	8	9	238	....	....	....	....	....

STOKES, Ryan (STOHKS, RIGH-uhn) MIN.

Defense. Shoots left. 6'4", 220 lbs. Born, Sarnia, Ont., June 23, 1983.

			Regular Season					Playoffs				
Season	Club	League	GP	G	A	Pts	PIM	GP	G	A	Pts	PIM
2001-02	Barrie Colts	OHL	53	0	5	5	31	20	0	0	0	16
2002-03	Mississauga	OHL	59	2	7	9	139	5	0	1	1	22
2003-04	Mississauga	OHL	66	4	20	24	179	24	2	9	11	74
2004-05	Houston Aeros	AHL	7	0	0	0	7	....	....	....	....	....
	Pensacola	ECHL	59	1	15	16	119	....	....	....	....	....

Signed as a free agent by **Minnesota**, May 25, 2004.

STOLYAROV, Gennady (stohl-yah-RAWF, gehn-AH-dee) DET.

Right wing. Shoots left. 6'4", 187 lbs. Born, Moscow, USSR, August 20, 1986.
(Detroit's 7th choice, 257th overall, in 2004 Entry Draft).

			Regular Season					Playoffs				
Season	Club	League	GP	G	A	Pts	PIM	GP	G	A	Pts	PIM
2003-04	Dyn'o Moscow 2	Russia-3	STATISTICS NOT AVAILABLE									
	THK Tver	Russia-2	24	3	1	4	4	....	....	....	....	....
2004-05	Vityaz Chekhov	Russia-2	25	0	1	1	2	....	....	....	....	....

STONE, Ryan (STOHN, RIGH-uhn) PIT.

Center. Shoots left. 6'2", 200 lbs. Born, Calgary, Alta., March 20, 1985.
(Pittsburgh's 2nd choice, 32nd overall, in 2003 Entry Draft).

			Regular Season					Playoffs				
Season	Club	League	GP	G	A	Pts	PIM	GP	G	A	Pts	PIM
2000-01	Cgy. North Stars	AMHL	34	37	28	55	90	....	....	....	....	....
2001-02	Brandon	WHL	65	11	27	38	128	19	0	3	3	39
2002-03	Brandon	WHL	54	14	31	45	158	12	4	2	6	20
2003-04	Brandon	WHL	50	20	38	58	125	11	1	3	4	24
2004-05	Brandon	WHL	70	33	*66	99	127	24	4	*23	27	48

WHL East First All-Star Team (2005)

STONER, Clayton (STOH-nuhr, KLAY-tuhn) MIN.

Defense. Shoots left. 6'3", 215 lbs. Born, Port McNeill, B.C., February 19, 1985.
(Minnesota's 4th choice, 79th overall, in 2004 Entry Draft).

			Regular Season					Playoffs				
Season	Club	League	GP	G	A	Pts	PIM	GP	G	A	Pts	PIM
2000-01	Campbell River	VIJHL	47	4	16	20	57	....	....	....	....	....
2001-02	Campbell River	VIJHL	42	12	35	47	199	....	....	....	....	....
2002-03	Tri-City Americans	WHL	58	4	12	16	85	....	....	....	....	....
2003-04	Tri-City Americans	WHL	71	7	24	31	109	11	1	1	2	8
2004-05	Tri-City Americans	WHL	60	12	34	46	81	4	0	3	3	2

WHL West Second All-Star Team (2005)

STONKUS, Alexei (STAWN-kuhs, al-EHX-ay) NYI

Defense. Shoots left. 5'11", 175 lbs. Born, Yaroslavl, USSR, May 6, 1984.
(NY Islanders' 4th choice, 189th overall, in 2002 Entry Draft).

			Regular Season					Playoffs				
Season	Club	League	GP	G	A	Pts	PIM	GP	G	A	Pts	PIM
2000-01	Russia Jr.	Exhib.	8	1	1	2	14	....	....	....	....	....
	Yaroslavl 2	Russia-3	....	....	....	....	....	6	0	0	0	2
2001-02	Yaroslavl 2	Russia-3	12	3	3	6	8	....	....	....	....	....
	Elektrostal 2	Russia-3	4	1	0	1	6	....	....	....	....	....
	Elektrostal	Russia-2	31	1	3	4	26	....	....	....	....	....
2002-03	Yaroslavl	Russia	11	0	0	0	2	....	....	....	....	....
2003-04	Yaroslavl	Russia	2	0	0	0	0	....	....	....	....	....
2004-05	Yaroslavl 2	Russia-3	7	0	1	1	6	....	....	....	....	....

STORTINI, Zachery (stohr-TEE-nee, ZA-kuh-ree) EDM.

Right wing. Shoots right. 6'3", 216 lbs. Born, Elliot Lake, Ont., September 11, 1985.
(Edmonton's 5th choice, 94th overall, in 2003 Entry Draft).

			Regular Season					Playoffs				
Season	Club	League	GP	G	A	Pts	PIM	GP	G	A	Pts	PIM
2000-01	Newmarket	OPJHL	34	3	10	13	68	....	....	....	....	....
2001-02	Sudbury Wolves	OHL	65	8	6	14	187	5	1	0	1	24
2002-03	Sudbury Wolves	OHL	62	13	16	29	222	....	....	....	....	....
2003-04	Sudbury Wolves	OHL	62	21	16	37	151	7	1	1	2	14
	Toronto	AHL	2	0	0	0	7	3	0	0	0	4
2004-05	Sudbury Wolves	OHL	58	13	27	40	186	12	2	5	7	27

STRACHAN, Tyson (STRAWN, TIGH-suhn) CAR.

Defense. Shoots right. 6'3", 205 lbs. Born, Melfort, Sask., October 30, 1984.
(Carolina's 6th choice, 137th overall, in 2003 Entry Draft).

			Regular Season					Playoffs				
Season	Club	League	GP	G	A	Pts	PIM	GP	G	A	Pts	PIM
2001-02	Tisdale Trojans	SMHL	42	5	18	23	70	....	....	....	....	....
	Melville	SJHL	2	0	0	0	0	....	....	....	....	....
2002-03	Vernon Vipers	BCHL	56	6	22	28	99	....	....	....	....	....
2003-04	Ohio State	CCHA	30	2	5	7	8	....	....	....	....	....
2004-05	Ohio State	CCHA	31	1	4	5	32	....	....	....	....	....

STRALMAN, Anton (STROHL-muhn, AN-tawn) TOR.

Defense. Shoots right. 6', 176 lbs. Born, Tibro, Sweden , August 1, 1986.
(Toronto's 5th choice, 216th overall, in 2005 Entry Draft).

			Regular Season					Playoffs				
Season	Club	League	GP	G	A	Pts	PIM	GP	G	A	Pts	PIM
2002-03	Skovde IK Jr.	Swe-Jr.	46	20	9	29	38	....	....	....	....	....
2003-04	Skovde IK	Sweden-3	27	4	8	12	18	....	....	....	....	....
2004-05	Skovde IK	Sweden-2	50	10	11	21	40	....	....	....	....	....

STREIT, Mark (STREET, MAHRK) MTL.

Defense. Shoots left. 5'11", 198 lbs. Born, Englisberg, Switz., December 11, 1977.
(Montreal's 8th choice, 262nd overall, in 2004 Entry Draft).

			Regular Season					Playoffs				
Season	Club	League	GP	G	A	Pts	PIM	GP	G	A	Pts	PIM
1995-96	Fribourg	Swiss	34	2	2	4	6	4	0	0	0	2
1996-97	HC Davos	Swiss	46	2	9	11	18	6	0	0	0	0
1997-98	HC Ambri-Piotta	Swiss	2	0	0	0	0	....	....	....	....	....
	HC Davos	Swiss	38	4	10	14	14	18	1	5	6	20
1998-99	HC Davos	Swiss	44	7	18	25	42	6	3	3	6	8
99-2000	Springfield Falcons	AHL	43	3	12	15	18	5	0	0	0	2
	Utah Grizzlies	IHL	1	0	1	1	2	....	....	....	....	....
	Tallahassee	ECHL	14	0	5	5	16	....	....	....	....	....
2000-01	ZSC Lions Zurich	Swiss	44	5	11	16	48	16	2	5	7	37
2001-02	ZSC Lions Zurich	Swiss	28	6	17	23	36	16	0	6	6	14
2002-03	ZSC Lions Zurich	Swiss	37	4	19	23	62	12	1	7	8	2
2003-04	ZSC Lions Zurich	Swiss	48	12	24	36	78	13	5	2	7	14
2004-05	ZSC Lions Zurich	Swiss	44	14	29	43	46	15	4	11	15	20

STREIT, Martin (STREET, MAHR-tihn) CBJ

Right wing. Shoots right. 6'2", 202 lbs. Born, Vyskov, Czech., February 2, 1977.
(Philadelphia's 7th choice, 178th overall, in 1995 Entry Draft).

			Regular Season					Playoffs				
Season	Club	League	GP	G	A	Pts	PIM	GP	G	A	Pts	PIM
1995-96	HC Olomouc Jr.	CzRep-Jr.	19	10	6	16	....	....	....	....	....	....
	HC Olomouc	CzRep	10	0	0	0	....	....	....	....	....	....
1996-97	HC Olomouc	CzRep	18	1	2	3	14	....	....	....	....	....
1997-98	Karlovy Vary	CzRep	48	5	13	18	24	....	....	....	....	....
1998-99	Karlovy Vary	CzRep	48	9	4	13	34	....	....	....	....	....
99-2000	Karlovy Vary	CzRep	18	0	2	2	20	....	....	....	....	....
	HC Vitkovice	CzRep	31	3	6	9	28	....	....	....	....	....
2000-01	HC Femax Havirov	CzRep	11	0	0	0	6	....	....	....	....	....
	Karlovy Vary	CzRep	14	0	1	1	12	....	....	....	....	....
2001-02	HC Vsetin	CzRep	35	3	4	7	65	....	....	....	....	....
2002-03	HC Vsetin	CzRep	47	8	5	13	48	4	0	0	0	2
2003-04	Prostejov	CzRep-2	45	5	7	12	67	....	....	....	....	....
2004-05	HC Unicov	CzRep-3	18	2	6	8	20	....	....	....	....	....

Claimed by **Columbus** from **Philadelphia** in Expansion Draft, June 23, 2000.

STUART, Colin (STEW-ahrt, CAW-lihn) ATL.

Center. Shoots left. 6'1", 195 lbs. Born, Rochester, MN, July 8, 1982.
(Atlanta's 5th choice, 135th overall, in 2001 Entry Draft).

			Regular Season					Playoffs				
Season	Club	League	GP	G	A	Pts	PIM	GP	G	A	Pts	PIM
1998-99	Lourdes	High-MN	23	22	32	54	....	....	....	....	....	....
99-2000	Lincoln Stars	USHL	53	18	19	37	38	9	1	3	4	2
2000-01	Colorado College	WCHA	41	2	7	9	26	....	....	....	....	....
2001-02	Colorado College	WCHA	43	13	9	22	34	....	....	....	....	....
2002-03	Colorado College	WCHA	42	13	11	24	56	....	....	....	....	....
2003-04	Colorado College	WCHA	30	10	12	22	38	....	....	....	....	....
2004-05	Chicago Wolves	AHL	39	3	2	5	12	....	....	....	....	....
	Gwinnett	ECHL	5	1	3	4	4	....	....	....	....	....

STUART, Mark (STEW-ahrt, MAHRK) BOS.

Defense. Shoots left. 6'1", 209 lbs. Born, Rochester, MN, April 27, 1984.
(Boston's 1st choice, 21st overall, in 2003 Entry Draft).

			Regular Season					Playoffs				
Season	Club	League	GP	G	A	Pts	PIM	GP	G	A	Pts	PIM
99-2000	Lourdes	High-MN	28	19	22	41	....	....	....	....	....	....
2000-01	USA U-17	USDP	64	3	16	19	120	....	....	....	....	....
2001-02	USA U-18	USDP	61	9	11	20	25	....	....	....	....	....
	United States	Nat-Tm	15	3	4	7	51	....	....	....	....	....
2002-03	Colorado College	WCHA	38	3	17	20	81	....	....	....	....	....
2003-04	Colorado College	WCHA	37	4	11	15	100	....	....	....	....	....
2004-05	Colorado College	WCHA	43	5	14	19	94	....	....	....	....	....

WCHA All-Rookie Team (2003) • WCHA Second All-Star Team (2005) • NCAA West First All-American Team (2005)

STUSSI, Rene (SHTOO-see, REH-nay) ANA.

Center. Shoots right. 5'11", 183 lbs. Born, Muri, Switz., December 13, 1978.
(Anaheim's 7th choice, 209th overall, in 1997 Entry Draft).

			Regular Season					Playoffs				
Season	Club	League	GP	G	A	Pts	PIM	GP	G	A	Pts	PIM
1995-96	HC Thurgau	Swiss-2	34	2	4	6	10	7	3	0	3	2
1996-97	HC Thurgau	Swiss-2	42	20	31	51	24	8	5	4	9	4
1997-98	EHC Kloten Jr.	Swiss-Jr.	1	5	0	5	0	....	....	....	....	....
	EHC Bulach	Swiss-2	4	3	5	8	20	....	....	....	....	....
	EHC Kloten	Swiss	38	9	8	17	10	7	1	0	1	4
1998-99	EHC Kloten	Swiss	36	5	5	10	14	....	....	....	....	....
	ZSC Lions Zurich	Swiss	7	1	1	2	6	7	1	1	2	4
99-2000	EV Zug	Swiss	45	7	5	12	13	9	0	1	1	0
2000-01	EHC Chur	Swiss	36	7	7	14	26	11	1	1	2	26
2001-02	EHC Chur	Swiss	21	3	2	5	2	....	....	....	....	....
	EHC Basel	Swiss-2	16	11	11	22	2	....	....	....	....	....
	HC Ajoie	Swiss-2	....	....	....	....	....	8	6	4	10	0
2002-03	EHC Basel	Swiss-2	38	22	26	48	8	15	6	12	18	8
2003-04	EHC Basel	Swiss	45	6	10	16	18	....	....	....	....	....
2004-05	HC Thurgau	Swiss-2	33	15	20	35	8	10	5	4	9	8

SUBBOTIN, Dmitri (soo-BOH-tihn, dih-MEE-tree) CBJ

Left wing. Shoots left. 6'1", 183 lbs. Born, Tomsk, USSR, October 20, 1977.
(NY Rangers' 3rd choice, 76th overall, in 1996 Entry Draft).

			Regular Season					Playoffs				
Season	Club	League	GP	G	A	Pts	PIM	GP	G	A	Pts	PIM
1993-94	Yekaterinburg	CIS	12	0	3	3	4	....	....	....	....	....
1994-95	Yekaterinburg	CIS	52	9	6	15	75	2	0	0	0	2
1995-96	CSKA Moscow	CIS	41	6	5	11	62	3	0	0	0	0
1996-97	CSKA Moscow	Russia-2	8	1	0	1	8	....	....	....	....	....
	HK CSKA Moscow	Russia	17	5	3	8	22	2	0	0	0	2
1997-98	HK CSKA Moscow	Russia	16	1	1	2	47	....	....	....	....	....
1998-99	Dynamo Moscow	Russia	1	0	1	1	0	....	....	....	....	....
	Lada Togliatti	Russia	31	8	3	11	47	7	0	0	0	4
99-2000	Lada Togliatti	Russia	27	10	4	14	26	7	1	1	2	4
	Lada Togliatti 2	Russia-3	2	0	1	1	0	....	....	....	....	....
2000-01	Dynamo Moscow	Russia	39	11	15	26	48	....	....	....	....	....
2001-02	Magnitogorsk	Russia	38	8	3	11	18	9	0	2	2	10
2002-03	Cherepovets	Russia	10	0	1	1	31	....	....	....	....	....
	CSKA Moscow	Russia	20	3	9	12	6	....	....	....	....	....
2003-04	CSKA Moscow	Russia	20	0	3	3	14	....	....	....	....	....
	Avangard Omsk	Russia	26	6	6	12	36	11	2	3	5	6
2004-05	Avangard Omsk	Russia	55	5	6	11	66	7	0	0	0	10

Claimed by **Columbus** from **NY Rangers** in Expansion Draft, June 23, 2000.

SUGDEN, Brandon (SUHG-duhn, BRAN-duhn) CBJ

Defense. Shoots right. 6'4", 225 lbs. Born, Toronto, Ont., June 23, 1978.
(Toronto's 8th choice, 111th overall, in 1996 Entry Draft).

			Regular Season					Playoffs				
Season	Club	League	GP	G	A	Pts	PIM	GP	G	A	Pts	PIM
1994-95	Tor. Red Wings	MTHL	53	12	24	36	162	....	....	....	....	....
	St. Mike's B's	MTJHL	15	0	3	3	69	....	....	....	....	....
1995-96	London Knights	OHL	55	2	7	9	*264	....	....	....	....	....
1996-97	London Knights	OHL	31	4	10	14	158	....	....	....	....	....
	Sudbury Wolves	OHL	20	....	4	4	70	....	....	....	....	....
1997-98	Sudbury Wolves	OHL	11	2	3	5	62	....	....	....	....	....
	Barrie Colts	OHL	49	6	21	27	191	6	0	0	0	18
1998-99	Cincinnati	IHL	6	0	2	2	51	....	....	....	....	....
	Dayton Bombers	ECHL	44	0	1	1	233	1	0	0	0	17
99-2000	Dayton Bombers	ECHL	13	0	1	1	110	....	....	....	....	....
2000-01	Worcester IceCats	AHL	11	0	0	0	56	....	....	....	....	....
	Tallahassee	ECHL	12	1	0	1	75	....	....	....	....	....
	Peoria Rivermen	ECHL	1	0	0	0	0	....	....	....	....	....
2001-02			DID NOT PLAY									
2002-03	Verdun Dragons	QSPHL	16	0	2	2	120	7	0	1	1	40
2003-04	Syracuse Crunch	AHL	62	3	5	8	283	3	0	0	0	2
2004-05	Syracuse Crunch	AHL	45	1	0	1	252	....	....	....	....	....

Signed as a free agent by **St. Louis**, June 29, 1998. • Suspended for life by ECHL for throwing his stick into the crowd during game vs. Dayton (ECHL), January 26, 2001. Signed as a free agent by **Columbus**, April 19, 2004.

SULLIVAN, Mike (SUHL-ih-vuhn, MIGHK) L.A.

Center. Shoots left. 6'4", 190 lbs. Born, Scarborough, Ont., September 14, 1984.
(Los Angeles' 9th choice, 244th overall, in 2003 Entry Draft).

			Regular Season					Playoffs				
Season	Club	League	GP	G	A	Pts	PIM	GP	G	A	Pts	PIM
2001-02	Uxbridge Bruins	OHA-C	42	22	27	49	20	....	....	....	....	....
2002-03	Stouffville Spirit	OPJHL	42	24	39	64	14	....	....	....	....	....
2003-04	Clarkson Knights	ECAC	40	8	11	19	14	....	....	....	....	....
2004-05	Clarkson Knights	ECAC	37	8	9	17	20	....	....	....	....	....

SULLIVAN, Sean (SUHL-ih-vuhn, SHAWN) PHX.

Defense. Shoots left. 6', 180 lbs. Born, Boston, MA, March 29, 1984.
(Phoenix's 7th choice, 272nd overall, in 2003 Entry Draft).

			Regular Season					Playoffs				
Season	Club	League	GP	G	A	Pts	PIM	GP	G	A	Pts	PIM
2001-02	St. Sebastian's	High-MA	31	3	11	14	4	....	....	....	....	....
2002-03	St. Sebastian's	High-MA	41	9	30	39	59	....	....	....	....	....
2003-04	Boston University	H-East	36	2	5	7	14	....	....	....	....	....
2004-05	Boston University	H-East	41	1	3	4	10	....	....	....	....	....

SULZER, Alexander (ZUHLT-suhr, ahl-ehx-AN-duhr) NSH.

Defense. Shoots left. 6'1", 207 lbs. Born, Kaufbeuren, West Germany, May 30, 1984.
(Nashville's 7th choice, 92nd overall, in 2003 Entry Draft).

			Regular Season					Playoffs				
Season	Club	League	GP	G	A	Pts	PIM	GP	G	A	Pts	PIM
2000-01	ESV Kaufbeuren	German-3	38	3	6	9	20	....	....	....	....	....
	Kaufbeuren Jr.	Ger-Jr.	1	0	2	2	2	....	....	....	....	....
2001-02	ESV Kaufbeuren	German-3	19	1	9	10	14	....	....	....	....	....
	Kaufbeuren Jr.	Ger-Jr.	1	0	0	0	4	....	....	....	....	....
2002-03	ESV Kaufbeuren	German-2	26	5	3	8	38	1	0	1	1	4
	Hamburg Freezers	Germany	18	0	1	1	18	5	0	0	0	12
2003-04	Dusseldorf	Germany	46	4	1	5	56	4	0	0	0	8
2004-05	Dusseldorf	Germany	42	5	6	11	68	....	....	....	....	....
	EV Duisburg	German-2	....	....	....	....	....	7	0	3	3	6

SUNDIN, Andreas (suhn-DEEN, an-DRAY-uhs) DET.

Left wing. Shoots left. 6', 185 lbs. Born, Linkoping, Sweden, March 15, 1984.
(Detroit's 4th choice, 170th overall, in 2003 Entry Draft).

			Regular Season					Playoffs				
Season	Club	League	GP	G	A	Pts	PIM	GP	G	A	Pts	PIM
2001-02	Linkopings HC Jr.	Swe-Jr.	19	31	13	44	8	....	....	....	....	....
2002-03	Linkopings HC Jr.	Swe-Jr.	4	4	3	7	6	....	....	....	....	....
	Linkopings HC	Sweden	8	0	1	1	0	....	....	....	....	....
	Linkopings HC	Sweden-Q	7	1	0	1	0	....	....	....	....	....
2003-04	Linkopings HC Jr.	Swe-Jr.	22	16	16	32	14	....	....	....	....	....
	Vasteras	Sweden-2	13	4	5	9	0	....	....	....	....	....
	Linkopings HC	Sweden	28	0	0	0	0	5	0	0	0	0
2004-05	Linkopings HC	Sweden	2	0	0	0	0	....	....	....	....	....

SUNDSTROM, Alexander (SUHND-struhm, al-ehx-AN-duhr) N.J.

Center. Shoots left. 5'11", 190 lbs. Born, Vancouver, B.C., March 14, 1987.
(New Jersey's 7th choice, 218th overall, in 2005 Entry Draft).

			Regular Season					Playoffs				
Season	Club	League	GP	G	A	Pts	PIM	GP	G	A	Pts	PIM
2003-04	Bjorkloven U18	Swe-U18	7	2	1	3	4	....	....	....	....	....
	Bjorkloven Jr.	Swe-Jr.	STATISTICS NOT AVAILABLE									
2004-05	Bjorkloven U18	Swe-U18	STATISTICS NOT AVAILABLE									
	Bjorkloven Jr.	Swe-Jr.	STATISTICS NOT AVAILABLE									
	IF Bjorkloven Umea	Sweden-2	9	0	0	0	0	....	....	....	....	....

SUTER, Ryan (SOO-tuhr, RIGH-uhn) NSH.

Defense. Shoots left. 6'1", 196 lbs. Born, Madison, WI, January 21, 1985.
(Nashville's 1st choice, 7th overall, in 2003 Entry Draft).

			Regular Season					Playoffs				
Season	Club	League	GP	G	A	Pts	PIM	GP	G	A	Pts	PIM
2000-01	Culver	High-IN	26	13	32	45	....	....	....	....	....	....
2001-02	USA U-17	USDP	43	4	21	25	96	....	....	....	....	....
	USA U-18	USDP	27	4	10	14	6	....	....	....	....	....
2002-03	USA U-18	USDP	51	9	22	31	136	....	....	....	....	....
2003-04	U. of Wisconsin	WCHA	39	3	16	19	93	....	....	....	....	....
2004-05	Milwaukee	AHL	63	7	16	23	70	7	1	5	6	16

WCHA All-Rookie Team (2004)

SUTTER, Brett (SUH-tuhr, BREHT) CGY.

Center/Left wing. Shoots left. 5'11", 194 lbs. Born, Viking, Alta., June 2, 1987.
(Calgary's 7th choice, 179th overall, in 2005 Entry Draft).

			Regular Season					Playoffs				
Season	Club	League	GP	G	A	Pts	PIM	GP	G	A	Pts	PIM
2003-04	Kootenay Ice	WHL	44	5	7	12	26	4	0	0	0	4
2004-05	Kootenay Ice	WHL	70	8	11	19	70	16	1	2	3	16

SVAGROVSKY, David (shva-GRAWF-skee, DAY-vihd) COL.

Right wing. Shoots right. 6'3", 205 lbs. Born, Prague, Czech., December 21, 1984.
(Colorado's 2nd choice, 131st overall, in 2003 Entry Draft).

			Regular Season					Playoffs				
Season	Club	League	GP	G	A	Pts	PIM	GP	G	A	Pts	PIM
99-2000	HC Slavia Praha Jr.	CzRep-Jr.	31	1	3	4	12	....	....	....	....	....
2000-01	HC Slavia Praha Jr.	CzRep-Jr.	48	20	29	49	82	7	5	1	6	10
2001-02	HC Slavia Praha Jr.	CzRep-Jr.	44	7	6	13	38	....	....	....	....	....
2002-03	Seattle	WHL	68	17	25	42	47	15	4	6	10	12
2003-04	Seattle	WHL	52	6	11	17	42	....	....	....	....	....
2004-05	Colorado Eagles	CHL	35	1	3	4	55	....	....	....	....	....

SVENSK, Mikael (SVEHNSK, mih-KIGH-ehl) EDM.

Defense. Shoots right. 6'2", 191 lbs. Born, Gällstad, Sweden, February 28, 1983.
(Edmonton's 7th choice, 185th overall, in 2001 Entry Draft).

			Regular Season					Playoffs				
Season	Club	League	GP	G	A	Pts	PIM	GP	G	A	Pts	PIM
99-2000	V.Frolunda U18	Swe-U18	18	2	6	8	6	2	0	0	0	2
	V.Frolunda Jr.	Swe-Jr.	10	1	1	2	12	2	0	0	0	0
2000-01	V.Frolunda U18	Swe-U18	6	0	1	1	4	3	0	1	1	2
	V.Frolunda Jr.	Swe-Jr.	15	1	0	1	4	....	....	....	....	....
2001-02	V.Frolunda Jr.	Swe-Jr.	34	4	1	5	16	5	1	0	1	2
2002-03	V.Frolunda	Sweden	17	0	0	0	0	3	0	0	0	0
	V.Frolunda Jr.	Swe-Jr.	25	1	3	4	10	6	1	0	1	4
2003-04	Halmstad	Sweden-2	45	2	2	4	18	....	....	....	....	....
2004-05	Halmstad	Sweden-2	41	3	5	8	26	2	0	0	0	4

SVENSSON, Jimmie (SVEHN-sohn, JIH-mee) DET.

Center. Shoots left. 6'1", 183 lbs. Born, Vasteras, Sweden, February 25, 1982.
(Detroit's 9th choice, 228th overall, in 2000 Entry Draft).

			Regular Season					Playoffs				
Season	**Club**	**League**	**GP**	**G**	**A**	**Pts**	**PIM**	**GP**	**G**	**A**	**Pts**	**PIM**
99-2000	Vasteras IK U18	Swe-U18	5	1	3	4	20	....	....	....	....	....
	Vasteras IK Jr.	Swe-Jr.	29	10	2	12	121	....	....	....	....	....
2000-01	Malmo Jr.	Swe-Jr.	23	3	1	4	74	....	....	....	....	....
2001-02	Malmo Jr.	Swe-Jr.	38	18	10	28	105	5	0	1	1	10
2002-03	IF Troja-Ljungby	Sweden-2	52	13	8	21	139	....	....	....	....	....
2003-04	Malmo	Sweden	31	2	0	2	6	....	....	....	....	....
	Malmo U18	Swe-U18	7	1	2	3	4	....	....	....	....	....
	IF Troja-Ljungby	Sweden-2	14	7	2	9	24	....	....	....	....	....
2004-05	IF Troja-Ljungby	Sweden-2	51	17	14	31	100	....	....	....	....	....

SWANSON, Jeremy (SWAWN-suhn, JAIR-eh-mee) FLA.

Defense. Shoots left. 6', 199 lbs. Born, Nipigon, Ont., June 21, 1984.
(Florida's choice, 169th overall, in 2002 Entry Draft).

			Regular Season					Playoffs				
Season	**Club**	**League**	**GP**	**G**	**A**	**Pts**	**PIM**	**GP**	**G**	**A**	**Pts**	**PIM**
99-2000	Thunder Bay Kings	TBMHL	48	8	16	24	19	....	....	....	....	....
2000-01	Sault Ste. Marie	OHL	54	1	6	7	60	....	....	....	....	....
2001-02	Barrie Colts	OHL	67	8	16	24	78	20	1	4	5	12
2002-03	Barrie Colts	OHL	68	7	34	41	129	....	....	....	....	....
2003-04	Barrie Colts	OHL	66	6	28	34	120	12	0	5	5	16
2004-05	San Antonio	AHL	21	1	3	4	22	....	....	....	....	....
	Texas Wildcatters	ECHL	44	1	6	7	62	....	....	....	....	....

OHL Second All-Star Team (2004)

SWITZER, Craig (SWIHT-zuhr, KRAYG) NSH.

Defense. Shoots left. 6'1", 195 lbs. Born, Calgary, Alta., October 16, 1984.
(Nashville's 11th choice, 275th overall, in 2004 Entry Draft).

			Regular Season					Playoffs				
Season	**Club**	**League**	**GP**	**G**	**A**	**Pts**	**PIM**	**GP**	**G**	**A**	**Pts**	**PIM**
2003-04	Salmon Arm	BCHL	57	14	40	54	117	14	0	12	12	16
2004-05	New Hampshire	H-East	41	1	13	14	22	....	....	....	....	....

SYVRET, Danny (SIHV-reht, DA-nee) EDM.

Defense. Shoots left. 5'11", 203 lbs. Born, Millgrove, Ont., June 13, 1985.
(Edmonton's 3rd choice, 81st overall, in 2005 Entry Draft).

			Regular Season					Playoffs				
Season	**Club**	**League**	**GP**	**G**	**A**	**Pts**	**PIM**	**GP**	**G**	**A**	**Pts**	**PIM**
2001-02	Cambridge	OHA-B	43	6	41	47	23	....	....	....	....	....
	London Knights	OHL	1	0	0	0	0	....	....	....	....	....
2002-03	London Knights	OHL	68	8	14	22	31	14	1	6	7	11
2003-04	London Knights	OHL	68	3	28	31	32	15	1	6	7	4
2004-05	London Knights	OHL	62	23	46	69	33	18	5	15	20	4

OHL First All-Star Team (2005) • Canadian Major Junior Defenseman of the Year (2005) • Canadian Major Junior First All-Star Team (2005) • Memorial Cup All-Star Team (2005)

TALBOT, Maxime (TAL-buht, MAX-eem) PIT.

Center. Shoots left. 5'11", 176 lbs. Born, Lemoyne, Que., February 11, 1984.
(Pittsburgh's 9th choice, 234th overall, in 2002 Entry Draft).

			Regular Season					Playoffs				
Season	**Club**	**League**	**GP**	**G**	**A**	**Pts**	**PIM**	**GP**	**G**	**A**	**Pts**	**PIM**
99-2000	Antoine-Girouard	QAAA	42	19	21	40	32	7	3	6	9	0
2000-01	Rouyn-Noranda	QMJHL	40	9	15	24	78	....	....	....	....	....
	Hull Olympiques	QMJHL	24	6	7	13	60	5	1	0	1	2
2001-02	Hull Olympiques	QMJHL	65	24	36	60	174	12	4	6	10	51
2002-03	Hull Olympiques	QMJHL	69	46	58	104	130	20	14	*30	*44	33
2003-04	Gatineau	QMJHL	51	25	73	98	41	15	*11	*16	*27	0
2004-05	Wilkes-Barre	AHL	75	7	12	19	62	11	0	1	1	22

QMJHL Second All-Star Team (2003, 2004)

TALLACKSON, Barry (TAL-ak-suhn, BAIR-ee) N.J.

Right wing. Shoots right. 6'4", 210 lbs. Born, Grafton, ND, April 14, 1983.
(New Jersey's 2nd choice, 53rd overall, in 2002 Entry Draft).

			Regular Season					Playoffs				
Season	**Club**	**League**	**GP**	**G**	**A**	**Pts**	**PIM**	**GP**	**G**	**A**	**Pts**	**PIM**
99-2000	USA U-17	USDP	53	14	6	20	90	....	....	....	....	....
2000-01	USA U-18	USDP	63	23	24	47	77	....	....	....	....	....
2001-02	U. of Minnesota	WCHA	44	13	10	23	44	....	....	....	....	....
2002-03	U. of Minnesota	WCHA	32	9	14	23	18	....	....	....	....	....
2003-04	U. of Minnesota	WCHA	44	10	15	25	46	....	....	....	....	....
2004-05	U. of Minnesota	WCHA	36	11	8	19	54	....	....	....	....	....
	Albany River Rats	AHL	4	1	1	2	0	....	....	....	....	....

TAMBELLINI, Jeff (tam-buh-LEE-nee, JEHF) L.A.

Left wing. Shoots left. 5'11", 186 lbs. Born, Calgary, Alta., April 13, 1984.
(Los Angeles' 3rd choice, 27th overall, in 2003 Entry Draft).

			Regular Season					Playoffs				
Season	**Club**	**League**	**GP**	**G**	**A**	**Pts**	**PIM**	**GP**	**G**	**A**	**Pts**	**PIM**
99-2000	Poco Buckeroos	PIJHL	41	30	34	64	....	....	....	....	....	....
2000-01	Chilliwack Chiefs	BCHL	54	21	30	51	13	....	....	....	....	....
2001-02	Chilliwack Chiefs	BCHL	34	46	71	117	23	29	27	27	54	....
2002-03	U. of Michigan	CCHA	43	26	19	45	24	....	....	....	....	....
2003-04	U. of Michigan	CCHA	39	15	12	27	18	....	....	....	....	....
2004-05	U. of Michigan	CCHA	42	*24	33	*57	32	....	....	....	....	....

CCHA All-Rookie Team (2003) • CCHA Second All-Star Team (2003) • CCHA Rookie of the Year (2003) • CCHA First All-Star Team (2005) • NCAA West Second All-American Team (2005)

TARATUKHIN, Andrei (tahr-a-TOO-khin, AN-dray) CGY.

Center. Shoots left. 6', 198 lbs. Born, Omsk, USSR, February 22, 1983.
(Calgary's 2nd choice, 41st overall, in 2001 Entry Draft).

			Regular Season					Playoffs				
Season	**Club**	**League**	**GP**	**G**	**A**	**Pts**	**PIM**	**GP**	**G**	**A**	**Pts**	**PIM**
99-2000	Omsk 2	Russia-3	27	10	6	16	16	....	....	....	....	....
	Avangard Omsk	Russia	....	....	....	....	....	1	1	0	1	0
2000-01	Omsk 2	Russia-3	41	19	28	47	69	....	....	....	....	....
2001-02	Mostovik Kurgan	Russia-2	44	13	22	35	30	....	....	....	....	....
	Yaroslavl 2	Russia-3	5	5	2	7	12	....	....	....	....	....
2002-03	Avangard Omsk	Russia	21	0	1	1	4	7	1	0	1	18
	Omsk 2	Russia-3	15	4	13	17	20	....	....	....	....	....
2003-04	Avangard Omsk	Russia	8	0	0	0	4	....	....	....	....	....
	Omsk 2	Russia-3	9	6	5	11	6	....	....	....	....	....
	Mechel	Russia-2	15	3	12	15	12	12	1	4	5	6
2004-05	Ufa 2	Russia-3	1	0	1	1	0	....	....	....	....	....
	Ufa	Russia	54	7	5	12	73	....	....	....	....	....

TARKIR, Zach (TAHR-kihr, ZAK) N.J.

Defense. Shoots right. 6', 180 lbs. Born, Fresno, CA, June 28, 1984.
(New Jersey's 4th choice, 167th overall, in 2003 Entry Draft).

			Regular Season					Playoffs				
Season	**Club**	**League**	**GP**	**G**	**A**	**Pts**	**PIM**	**GP**	**G**	**A**	**Pts**	**PIM**
2001-02	Great Falls	AWHL	24	3	5	8	....	8	0	3	3	....
2002-03	Chilliwack Chiefs	BCHL	53	5	28	33	86	....	....	....	....	....
2003-04	Northern Mich.	CCHA	36	2	3	5	40	....	....	....	....	....
2004-05	Northern Mich.	CCHA	35	2	8	10	51	....	....	....	....	....

TARNASKY, Nick (tahr-NAS-kee, NIHK) T.B.

Center. Shoots left. 6'2", 233 lbs. Born, Rocky Mtn. House, Alta., November 25, 1984.
(Tampa Bay's 11th choice, 287th overall, in 2003 Entry Draft).

			Regular Season					Playoffs				
Season	**Club**	**League**	**GP**	**G**	**A**	**Pts**	**PIM**	**GP**	**G**	**A**	**Pts**	**PIM**
99-2000	Leduc Oil Kings	AMBHL	36	21	11	32	59	....	....	....	....	....
2000-01	Leduc Oil Kings	AMHL	35	39	29	68	95	....	....	....	....	....
2001-02	Drayton Valley	AJHL	20	7	4	11	10	....	....	....	....	....
	Vancouver Giants	WHL	10	1	0	1	5	....	....	....	....	....
2002-03	Kelowna Rockets	WHL	39	4	12	16	39	....	....	....	....	....
	Lethbridge	WHL	30	5	8	13	45	....	....	....	....	....
2003-04	Lethbridge	WHL	71	26	23	49	108	....	....	....	....	....
2004-05	Springfield Falcons	AHL	80	7	10	17	176	....	....	....	....	....

TARVAINEN, Jussi (tahr-VIGH-nehn, YU-see) EDM.

Right wing. Shoots right. 6'3", 215 lbs. Born, Lahti, Finland, May 31, 1976.
(Edmonton's 7th choice, 95th overall, in 1994 Entry Draft).

			Regular Season					Playoffs				
Season	**Club**	**League**	**GP**	**G**	**A**	**Pts**	**PIM**	**GP**	**G**	**A**	**Pts**	**PIM**
1992-93	KalPa Kuopio U18	Fin-U18	18	13	9	22	38	....	....	....	....	....
	KalPa Kuopio Jr.	Finland-Jr.	17	3	6	9	35	....	....	....	....	....
1993-94	KalPa Kuopio Jr.	Finland-Jr.	16	9	14	23	12	....	....	....	....	....
	Junkkarit Kalajoki	Finland-2	1	0	0	0	0	....	....	....	....	....
	KalPa Kuopio	Finland	42	3	4	7	20	....	....	....	....	....
1994-95	KalPa Kuopio Jr.	Finland-Jr.	3	4	0	4	2	....	....	....	....	....
	KalPa Kuopio	Finland	45	10	7	17	34	3	0	0	0	2
1995-96	KalPa Kuopio Jr.	Finland-Jr.	3	2	3	5	10	7	3	4	7	12
	KalPa Kuopio	Finland	47	8	11	19	50	....	....	....	....	....
1996-97	KalPa Kuopio	Finland	49	14	26	40	62	6	4	3	7	4
	KalPa Kuopio Jr.	Finland-Jr.	....	....	....	....	....	1	0	0	0	2
1997-98	JYP Jyvaskyla	Finland	43	12	26	38	59	....	....	....	....	....
1998-99	JYP Jyvaskyla	Finland	54	17	24	41	84	3	0	0	0	8
99-2000	Tappara Tampere	Finland	52	20	27	47	91	4	1	0	1	2
2000-01	Tappara Tampere	Finland	56	23	32	55	36	10	*8	2	10	2
2001-02	Tappara Tampere	Finland	56	24	26	50	42	10	4	3	7	0
2002-03	Tappara Tampere	Finland	56	14	21	35	24	15	*7	2	9	4
2003-04	Linkopings HC	Sweden	48	20	15	35	26	5	0	0	0	10
2004-05	Linkopings HC	Sweden	49	13	13	26	26	6	1	1	2	4

TATARINOV, Alexander (ta-TAHR-ee-nahf, al-ehx-AN-duhr) PHX.

Right wing. Shoots left. 5'11", 176 lbs. Born, Sverdlovsk, USSR, April 14, 1982.
(Phoenix's 2nd choice, 53rd overall, in 2000 Entry Draft).

			Regular Season					Playoffs				
Season	**Club**	**League**	**GP**	**G**	**A**	**Pts**	**PIM**	**GP**	**G**	**A**	**Pts**	**PIM**
1998-99	Yaroslavl 2	Russia-3	32	11	10	21	89	....	....	....	....	....
	Spartak Moscow	Russia	3	0	0	0	0	....	....	....	....	....
99-2000	Yaroslavl 2	Russia-3	35	12	12	24	36	....	....	....	....	....
2000-01	Kristall Saratov	Russia-2	24	3	3	6	8	....	....	....	....	....
	Yaroslavl	Russia	2	0	1	1	0	1	0	0	0	0
2001-02	Yaroslavl	Russia	21	4	3	7	8	....	....	....	....	....
	Amur Khabarovsk	Russia	11	0	0	0	0	....	....	....	....	....
	Yaroslavl 2	Russia-3	5	5	2	7	12	....	....	....	....	....
2002-03	Perm	Russia	31	6	5	11	16	....	....	....	....	....
2003-04	Spartak Moscow	Russia-2	43	8	11	19	14	9	2	5	7	2
2004-05	Mechel 2	Russia-3	1	0	0	0	0	....	....	....	....	....
	Mechel	Russia-2	44	7	17	24	32	7	0	1	1	0

TATICEK, Petr (TA-tih-chehk, PEE-tuhr) FLA.

Center. Shoots left. 6'3", 195 lbs. Born, Rakovnik, Czech., September 22, 1983.
(Florida's 2nd choice, 9th overall, in 2002 Entry Draft).

			Regular Season					Playoffs				
Season	**Club**	**League**	**GP**	**G**	**A**	**Pts**	**PIM**	**GP**	**G**	**A**	**Pts**	**PIM**
1998-99	HC Kladno U17	CzR-U17	42	24	17	41	....	....	....	....	....	....
99-2000	HC Kladno Jr.	CzRep-Jr.	48	11	16	27	26	....	....	....	....	....
	HC Velvana Kladno	CzRep	4	0	0	0	4	....	....	....	....	....
2000-01	HC Kladno Jr.	CzRep-Jr.	30	7	12	19	54	....	....	....	....	....
	Kladno	CzRep	3	0	0	0	0	....	....	....	....	....
2001-02	Sault Ste. Marie	OHL	60	21	42	63	32	6	3	3	6	4
2002-03	Sault Ste. Marie	OHL	54	12	45	57	44	4	1	0	1	0
2003-04	San Antonio	AHL	63	4	15	19	6	....	....	....	....	....
2004-05	San Antonio	AHL	67	7	15	22	21	....	....	....	....	....
	Laredo Bucks	CHL	4	2	5	7	0	....	....	....	....	....

TAYLOR, Jake (TAY-luhr, JAIK) NYR

Defense. Shoots right. 6'4", 220 lbs. Born, Rochester, MN, August 1, 1983.
(NY Rangers' 5th choice, 177th overall, in 2002 Entry Draft).

			Regular Season					Playoffs				
Season	**Club**	**League**	**GP**	**G**	**A**	**Pts**	**PIM**	**GP**	**G**	**A**	**Pts**	**PIM**
2000-01	Rochester	High-MN	29	9	15	24	34	....	....	....	....	....
	Green Bay	USHL	5	0	0	0	8	....	....	....	....	....
2001-02	Green Bay	USHL	56	1	2	3	147	7	0	0	0	11
2002-03	Green Bay	USHL	60	8	8	16	160	....	....	....	....	....
2003-04	U. of Minnesota	WCHA	39	2	6	8	68	....	....	....	....	....
2004-05	Hartford Wolf Pack	AHL	43	0	3	3	156	....	....	....	....	....
	Charlotte	ECHL	11	0	2	2	31	....	....	....	....	....

TAYLOR, Justin (TAY-luhr, JUHS-tihn) CGY.

Left wing. Shoots left. 6'4", 200 lbs. Born, Edmonton, Alta., January 1, 1983.

			Regular Season					Playoffs				
Season	**Club**	**League**	**GP**	**G**	**A**	**Pts**	**PIM**	**GP**	**G**	**A**	**Pts**	**PIM**
99-2000	Medicine Hat	WHL	39	1	5	6	11	....	....	....	....	....
2000-01	Sherwood Park	AJHL	21	6	8	14	19	....	....	....	....	....
2001-02	Sherwood Park	AJHL	55	13	15	28	49	7	2	3	5	14
2002-03	Camrose Kodiaks	AJHL	45	11	24	35	71	17	7	11	18	34
2003-04	Red Deer Rebels	WHL	57	16	22	38	39	19	6	10	16	13
2004-05	Lowell	AHL	62	8	3	11	35	....	....	....	....	....

Signed as a free agent by **Calgary**, July 6, 2004.

TENKANEN, Valtteri (TEHN-kah-nehn, vahl-TEH-ree) L.A.

Forward. Shoots left. 5'11", 183 lbs. Born, Jamsa, Finland, March 27, 1985.
(Los Angeles' 10th choice, 264th overall, in 2004 Entry Draft).

			Regular Season					Playoffs				
Season	Club	League	GP	G	A	Pts	PIM	GP	G	A	Pts	PIM
2002-03	JyP Jyvaskyla Jr.	Finland-Jr.	31	10	8	18	14	4	1	1	2	0
2003-04	JyP Jyvaskyla Jr.	Finland-Jr.	10	3	2	5	2	9	2	3	5	0
	JYP Jyvaskyla	Finland	25	1	3	4	2	2	0	0	0	0
2004-05	JYP Jyvaskyla	Finland	10	0	1	1	0	....	....	....	....	....
	JyP Jyvaskyla Jr.	Finland-Jr.	12	1	5	6	14	6	2	1	3	25

TERESCHENKO, Alexei (teh-REH-shehn-koh, al-EHX-ay) DAL.

Center. Shoots left. 5'11", 176 lbs. Born, Mozhaisk, USSR, December 16, 1980.
(Dallas' 4th choice, 91st overall, in 2000 Entry Draft).

			Regular Season					Playoffs				
Season	Club	League	GP	G	A	Pts	PIM	GP	G	A	Pts	PIM
1996-97	Dyn'o Moscow 2	Russia-3	9	0	0	0	2	....	....	....	....	....
1997-98	Dynamo Moscow	Russia	26	6	7	13	30	....	....	....	....	....
1998-99	Dyn'o Moscow 2	Russia-3	28	4	17	21	20	....	....	....	....	....
	THK Tver	Russia-2	12	3	4	7	4	....	....	....	....	....
	Dynamo Moscow	Russia	1	0	1	1	0	2	0	0	0	0
99-2000	Dynamo Moscow	Russia	27	1	1	2	10	17	1	1	2	8
2000-01	Dynamo Moscow	Russia	39	3	2	5	18	....	....	....	....	....
2001-02	Yaroslavl 2	Russia-3	1	0	0	0	0	....	....	....	....	....
	Dynamo Moscow	Russia	40	3	6	9	20	3	0	0	0	0
2002-03	Dynamo Moscow	Russia	40	7	9	16	14	5	1	0	1	2
2003-04	Dynamo Moscow	Russia	47	8	12	20	26	3	0	0	0	4
2004-05	Dynamo Moscow	Russia	31	3	6	9	8	10	0	1	1	2

TERNAVSKY, Artem (tuhr-NAV-skee, ahr-TEHM) WSH.

Defense. Shoots left. 6'3", 213 lbs. Born, Magnitogorsk, USSR, June 2, 1983.
(Washington's 4th choice, 160th overall, in 2001 Entry Draft).

			Regular Season					Playoffs				
Season	Club	League	GP	G	A	Pts	PIM	GP	G	A	Pts	PIM
99-2000	CSKA Moscow 2	Russia-3	2	0	1	1	0	....	....	....	....	....
	HK Moscow 2	Russia-3	25	0	4	4	42	....	....	....	....	....
2000-01	Sherbrooke	QMJHL	65	3	15	18	143	....	....	....	....	....
2001-02	Mostovik Kurgan	Russia-2	25	0	0	0	46	....	....	....	....	....
2002-03	Sibir Novosibirsk	Russia	42	1	1	2	20	....	....	....	....	....
2003-04	Ufa	Russia	12	0	0	0	4	....	....	....	....	....
	Magnitogorsk 2	Russia-3	7	1	0	1	0	....	....	....	....	....
2004-05	Nizhny Novgorod	Russia-2	16	0	1	1	18	....	....	....	....	....
	Motor Barnaul	Russia-2	8	0	1	1	14	....	....	....	....	....

TESLIUK, Roman (tehs-L'YUHK, ROH-muhn) EDM.

Defense. Shoots right. 6'1", 195 lbs. Born, Severomorsk, USSR, January 21, 1986.
(Edmonton's 3rd choice, 44th overall, in 2004 Entry Draft).

			Regular Season					Playoffs				
Season	Club	League	GP	G	A	Pts	PIM	GP	G	A	Pts	PIM
2002-03	CSKA Moscow 2	Russia-3	6	0	2	2	6	....	....	....	....	....
2003-04	Kamloops Blazers	WHL	70	5	9	14	118	5	0	1	1	2
2004-05	Kamloops Blazers	WHL	70	9	20	29	109	6	4	1	5	6

THELEN, A.J. (THAY-lehn, AY-JAY) MIN.

Defense. Shoots left. 6'3", 210 lbs. Born, Shakopee, Minn., March 11, 1986.
(Minnesota's 1st choice, 12th overall, in 2004 Entry Draft).

			Regular Season					Playoffs				
Season	Club	League	GP	G	A	Pts	PIM	GP	G	A	Pts	PIM
2000-01	Shat.-St. Mary's	High-MN	40	22	17	39	....	....	....	....	....	....
2001-02	Shat.-St. Mary's	High-MN	62	20	33	53	....	....	....	....	....	....
2002-03	USA U-17	USDP	64	6	8	14	80	....	....	....	....	....
	USA U-18	USDP	3	0	0	0	0	....	....	....	....	....
2003-04	Michigan State	CCHA	41	11	18	29	50	....	....	....	....	....
2004-05	Michigan State	CCHA	33	0	11	11	48	....	....	....	....	....

CCHA All-Rookie Team (2004) • CCHA First All-Star Team (2004) • NCAA West Second All-American Team (2004)

THINEL, Marc-Andre (tih-nehl, MAHRK-AWN-dray) MTL.

Right wing. Shoots left. 6', 178 lbs. Born, St-Jerome, Que., March 24, 1981.
(Montreal's 6th choice, 145th overall, in 1999 Entry Draft).

			Regular Season					Playoffs				
Season	Club	League	GP	G	A	Pts	PIM	GP	G	A	Pts	PIM
1996-97	Laval-Laurentides	QAAA	40	12	10	22	....	13	0	5	5	....
1997-98	Victoriaville Tigres	QMJHL	58	7	10	17	20	6	0	3	3	4
1998-99	Victoriaville Tigres	QMJHL	66	45	58	103	16	6	5	3	8	4
99-2000	Victoriaville Tigres	QMJHL	71	59	73	132	55	6	5	6	11	18
2000-01	Victoriaville Tigres	QMJHL	70	62	88	150	101	13	12	13	25	18
2001-02	Quebec Citadelles	AHL	73	6	4	10	8	2	0	0	0	0
2002-03	Utah Grizzlies	AHL	44	5	15	20	10	2	0	0	0	0
	Lexington	ECHL	27	14	14	28	6	....	....	....	....	....
2003-04	Hamilton Bulldogs	AHL	14	1	1	2	2	10	1	0	1	6
	Columbus	ECHL	47	17	25	42	32	....	....	....	....	....
2004-05	Hamilton Bulldogs	AHL	58	8	13	21	8	....	....	....	....	....

QMJHL First All-Star Team (2000) • QMJHL Second All-Star Team (2001)

THOMAS, Andrew (TAW-mas, AN-droo) WSH.

Defense. Shoots right. 6'2", 196 lbs. Born, West Bend, WI, November 14, 1985.
(Washington's 3rd choice, 109th overall, in 2005 Entry Draft).

			Regular Season					Playoffs				
Season	Club	League	GP	G	A	Pts	PIM	GP	G	A	Pts	PIM
2003-04	Waterloo	USHL	57	1	6	7	86	12	0	2	2	28
2004-05	U. of Denver	WCHA	42	2	5	7	78	....	....	....	....	....

THOMPSON, Nate (TAWM-suhn, NAYT) BOS.

Center. Shoots left. 6', 190 lbs. Born, Anchorage, AK, October 5, 1984.
(Boston's 8th choice, 183rd overall, in 2003 Entry Draft).

			Regular Season					Playoffs				
Season	Club	League	GP	G	A	Pts	PIM	GP	G	A	Pts	PIM
2001-02	Seattle	WHL	69	13	26	39	42	11	1	3	4	13
2002-03	Seattle	WHL	61	10	24	34	48	15	5	4	9	6
2003-04	Seattle	WHL	65	13	23	36	24	....	....	....	....	....
2004-05	Seattle	WHL	58	19	15	34	39	12	1	2	3	2
	Providence Bruins	AHL	....	....	....	....	....	11	0	1	1	6

THORBURN, Chris (THOHR-buhrn, KRIHS) BUF.

Center. Shoots right. 6'3", 220 lbs. Born, Sault Ste. Marie, Ont., June 3, 1983.
(Buffalo's 3rd choice, 50th overall, in 2001 Entry Draft).

			Regular Season					Playoffs				
Season	Club	League	GP	G	A	Pts	PIM	GP	G	A	Pts	PIM
1998-99	Elliot Lake Vikings	NOJHA	40	21	12	33	28	....	....	....	....	....
99-2000	North Bay	OHL	56	12	8	20	33	6	0	2	2	0
2000-01	North Bay	OHL	66	22	32	54	64	4	0	1	1	9
2001-02	North Bay	OHL	67	15	43	58	112	5	1	2	3	8
2002-03	Saginaw Spirit	OHL	37	19	19	38	68	....	....	....	....	....
	Plymouth Whalers	OHL	27	11	22	33	56	18	11	9	20	10
2003-04	Rochester	AHL	58	6	16	22	77	16	3	2	5	18
2004-05	Rochester	AHL	73	12	17	29	185	4	0	1	1	2

TIMONEN, Jussi (TEEM-oh-nehn, YU-see) PHI.

Defense. Shoots left. 6', 200 lbs. Born, Kuopio, Finland, June 29, 1983.
(Philadelphia's 3rd choice, 146th overall, in 2001 Entry Draft).

			Regular Season					Playoffs				
Season	Club	League	GP	G	A	Pts	PIM	GP	G	A	Pts	PIM
99-2000	KalPa Kuopio Jr.	Finland-Jr.	33	4	2	6	16	4	0	0	0	4
2000-01	KalPa Kuopio U18	Fin-U18	38	6	7	13	22	....	....	....	....	....
	KalPa Kuopio Jr.	Finland-Jr.	1	0	1	1	0	....	....	....	....	....
2001-02	KalPa Kuopio Jr.	Finland-Jr.	10	1	1	2	10	....	....	....	....	....
	KalPa Kuopio	Finland-2	41	3	8	11	10	8	0	2	2	0
2002-03	TPS Turku	Finland	39	1	0	1	10	7	0	2	2	4
	TuTo Turku	Finland-2	3	0	0	0	0	....	....	....	....	....
2003-04	TPS Turku	Finland	20	0	0	0	4	....	....	....	....	....
	Jukurit Mikkeli	Finland-2	25	7	9	16	10	13	0	4	4	0
2004-05	SaiPa	Finland	54	1	5	6	53	....	....	....	....	....

TKACHENKO, Ivan (t'kuh-CHEHN-koh, ee-VAHN) CBJ

Left wing. Shoots left. 5'10", 183 lbs. Born, Yaroslavl, USSR, November 9, 1979.
(Columbus' 5th choice, 98th overall, in 2002 Entry Draft).

			Regular Season					Playoffs				
Season	Club	League	GP	G	A	Pts	PIM	GP	G	A	Pts	PIM
1997-98	Yaroslavl 2	Russia-2	STATISTICS NOT AVAILABLE									
	Torpedo Yaroslavl	Russia	....	....	....	....	....	1	0	0	0	0
1998-99	Yaroslavl 2	Russia-3	28	15	13	28	26	....	....	....	....	....
99-2000	Yaroslavl 2	Russia-3	1	1	0	1	0	....	....	....	....	....
	Motor Zavolzhje	Russia-2	43	15	14	29	22	....	....	....	....	....
	Nizhnekamsk 2	Russia-3	8	6	3	9	24	....	....	....	....	....
	Nizhnekamsk	Russia	5	1	0	1	0	4	0	1	1	0
2000-01	Nizhnekamsk	Russia	28	2	2	4	14	4	0	1	1	0
2001-02	Yaroslavl 2	Russia-3	1	0	1	1	2	....	....	....	....	....
	Yaroslavl	Russia	44	13	20	33	57	9	5	2	7	4
2002-03	Yaroslavl	Russia	44	11	6	17	57	10	2	3	5	6
2003-04	Yaroslavl	Russia	56	7	11	18	22	3	0	0	0	0
2004-05	Yaroslavl	Russia	59	15	15	30	30	9	2	3	5	8

TOBIN, Mark (TOH-bihn, MAHRK) T.B.

Left wing. Shoots left. 6'3", 211 lbs. Born, St. John's, Nfld., November 26, 1985.
(Tampa Bay's 2nd choice, 65th overall, in 2004 Entry Draft).

			Regular Season					Playoffs				
Season	Club	League	GP	G	A	Pts	PIM	GP	G	A	Pts	PIM
2002-03	Rimouski Oceanic	QMJHL	68	8	8	16	176	....	....	....	....	....
2003-04	Rimouski Oceanic	QMJHL	69	22	16	38	112	9	4	1	5	12
2004-05	Rimouski Oceanic	QMJHL	68	22	28	50	107	13	6	3	9	23

TODD, Scott (TAWD, SKAWT) NSH.

Defense. Shoots left. 6'4", 221 lbs. Born, Kingston, Ont., November 11, 1986.
(Nashville's 6th choice, 213th overall, in 2005 Entry Draft).

			Regular Season					Playoffs				
Season	Club	League	GP	G	A	Pts	PIM	GP	G	A	Pts	PIM
2003-04	Kingston	OPJHL	16	0	4	4	38	....	....	....	....	....
	Oshawa Generals	OHL	44	0	4	4	86	7	0	0	0	16
2004-05	Oshawa Generals	OHL	10	0	1	1	21	....	....	....	....	....
	Windsor Spitfires	OHL	44	0	2	2	134	10	0	2	2	25

TOFFEY, John (TAW-fee, JAWN) T.B.

Center. Shoots left. 6'3", 205 lbs. Born, Barnstable, MA, November 26, 1982.
(Tampa Bay's 13th choice, 287th overall, in 2002 Entry Draft).

			Regular Season					Playoffs				
Season	Club	League	GP	G	A	Pts	PIM	GP	G	A	Pts	PIM
1997/00	St. Sebastian's	High-MA	65	29	27	56	....	....	....	....	....	....
2000-01	St. Sebastian's	High-MA	22	22	24	46	....	....	....	....	....	....
2001-02	Ohio State	CCHA	24	2	3	5	4	....	....	....	....	....
2002-03	Walpole Stars	EJHL	19	7	8	15	10	....	....	....	....	....
2003-04	Massachusetts	H-East	20	2	3	5	16	....	....	....	....	....
2004-05	Massachusetts	H-East	20	0	1	1	14	....	....	....	....	....

• Statistics for 1997/00 **St. Sebastian's** (High-MA) are totals for 1997-2000 seasons.

TOLKUNOV, Dmitri (tohl-ku-NAWF, di-MEE-tree) FLA.

Defense. Shoots right. 6'2", 200 lbs. Born, Kiev, USSR, May 5, 1979.

			Regular Season					Playoffs				
Season	Club	League	GP	G	A	Pts	PIM	GP	G	A	Pts	PIM
1996-97	Hull Olympiques	QMJHL	34	3	8	11	99	....	....	....	....	....
	Beauport Harfangs	QMJHL	27	3	7	10	18	4	0	1	1	4
1997-98	Quebec Remparts	QMJHL	66	10	25	35	81	14	3	9	12	22
1998-99	Quebec Remparts	QMJHL	69	11	57	68	110	13	2	7	9	22
99-2000	Cleveland	IHL	65	3	12	15	54	8	0	0	0	2
2000-01	Norfolk Admirals	AHL	78	5	18	23	93	9	0	1	1	4
2001-02	Norfolk Admirals	AHL	51	1	18	19	20	4	0	0	0	2
2002-03	Norfolk Admirals	AHL	47	1	17	18	39	....	....	....	....	....
2003-04	Yaroslavl 2	Russia-3	14	4	3	7	11	....	....	....	....	....
	Yaroslavl	Russia	6	0	0	0	4	....	....	....	....	....
	Amur Khabarovsk	Russia	27	1	2	3	28	....	....	....	....	....
2004-05	Sibir Novosibirsk	Russia	3	0	0	0	2	....	....	....	....	....
	Amur Khabarovsk	Russia-2	29	2	8	10	32	9	1	0	1	12

QMJHL Second All-Star Team (1999)

Signed as a free agent by **Chicago**, October 8, 1998. Traded to **Florida** by **Chicago** for NY Islanders' 9th round choice (previously acquired – later traded to San Jose – San Jose selected Carter Lee) in 2003 Entry Draft, June 21, 2003. Signed as a free agent by **Yaroslavl** (Russia), September 8, 2003, with **Florida** retaining NHL rights.

TOLLEFSEN, Ole-Kristian (TOHL-uhf-suhn, OH-lay-KRIHS-tyahn) **CBJ**

Defense. Shoots left. 6'2", 200 lbs. Born, Oslo, Norway, March 29, 1984.
(Columbus' 3rd choice, 65th overall, in 2002 Entry Draft).

			Regular Season					Playoffs				
Season	Club	League	GP	G	A	Pts	PIM	GP	G	A	Pts	PIM
2000-01	Lillehammer IK	Norway	4	0	0	0	2	....	....	....	....	....
2001-02	Lillehammer IK	Norway	37	1	5	6	63	6	1	1	2	10
	Lillehammer IK	Nor-Jr.	....	....	....	....	....	1	0	2	2	4
2002-03	Brandon	WHL	43	6	14	20	73	17	0	2	2	38
2003-04	Brandon	WHL	53	3	27	30	94	11	0	4	4	15
2004-05	Dayton Bombers	ECHL	2	0	0	0	0	....	....	....	....	....
	Syracuse Crunch	AHL	64	0	3	3	115	....	....	....	....	....

TOLSA, Jari (TOHL-suh, YA-ree) **DET.**

Center. Shoots left. 6', 172 lbs. Born, Goteborg, Sweden, April 20, 1981.
(Detroit's 1st choice, 120th overall, in 1999 Entry Draft).

			Regular Season					Playoffs				
Season	Club	League	GP	G	A	Pts	PIM	GP	G	A	Pts	PIM
1997-98	V.Frolunda Jr.	Swe-Jr.	26	18	25	43	30	....	....	....	....	....
1998-99	V.Frolunda Jr.	Swe-Jr.	35	16	21	37	51	4	1	3	4	2
99-2000	V.Frolunda Jr.	Swe-Jr.	33	12	47	59	43	6	3	8	11	4
	V.Frolunda	Sweden	10	0	0	0	0	....	....	....	....	....
2000-01	V.Frolunda Jr.	Swe-Jr.	11	4	6	10	8	2	2	4	6	4
	IF Molndal Hockey	Sweden-2	1	0	2	2	0	....	....	....	....	....
	V.Frolunda	Sweden	42	2	5	7	18	5	0	0	0	0
2001-02	V.Frolunda	Sweden	48	8	16	24	18	10	0	0	0	4
2002-03	V.Frolunda	Sweden	43	9	14	23	24	16	4	1	5	8
2003-04	V.Frolunda	Sweden	50	8	20	28	36	10	2	4	6	4
2004-05	Frolunda	Sweden	50	4	13	17	32	14	1	6	7	14

TOMANEK, Roman (toh-MA-nehk, ROH-muhn) **PHX.**

Right wing. Shoots right. 6'1", 176 lbs. Born, Povazka Bystrica, Czech., January 28, 1986.
(Phoenix's 4th choice, 103rd overall, in 2004 Entry Draft).

			Regular Season					Playoffs				
Season	Club	League	GP	G	A	Pts	PIM	GP	G	A	Pts	PIM
2003-04	P. Bystrica U18	Svk-U18	10	14	10	24	31	....	....	....	....	....
	P. Bystrica Jr.	Slovak-Jr.	16	22	13	35	86	....	....	....	....	....
	P. Bystrica	Slovak-2	29	11	9	20	30	....	....	....	....	....
2004-05	Calgary Hitmen	WHL	19	2	4	6	12	....	....	....	....	....

• Missed majority of 2004-05 season recovering from shoulder injury suffered in game vs. Brandon (WHL), November 5, 2004.

TOMICA, Marek (TAW-miht-suh, MAIR-ehk) **DAL.**

Left wing. Shoots left. 6', 178 lbs. Born, Prague, Czech., January 1, 1981.
(Dallas' 10th choice, 285th overall, in 2001 Entry Draft).

			Regular Season					Playoffs				
Season	Club	League	GP	G	A	Pts	PIM	GP	G	A	Pts	PIM
1996-97	Jihlava U17	CzR-U17	22	3	4	7	....	....	....	....	....	....
1997-98	Jihlava U17	CzR-U17	36	24	28	52	....	....	....	....	....	....
1998-99	Jihlava Jr.	CzRep-Jr.	STATISTICS NOT AVAILABLE									
99-2000	HC Slavia Praha Jr.	CzRep-Jr.	41	13	8	21	16	7	2	3	5	0
	HC Slavia Praha	CzRep	13	0	0	0	2	....	....	....	....	....
2000-01	HC Slavia Praha Jr.	CzRep-Jr.	5	2	2	4	4	....	....	....	....	....
	Beroun	CzRep-2	8	0	2	2	2	....	....	....	....	....
	BK Mlada Boleslav	CzRep-3	2	0	0	0	6	....	....	....	....	....
	HC Slavia Praha	CzRep	37	3	9	12	8	11	0	0	0	0
2001-02	HC Slavia Praha	CzRep	49	6	8	14	14	8	0	0	0	4
	HC Slavia Praha Jr.	CzRep-Jr.	5	2	3	5	0	....	....	....	....	....
2002-03	HC Slavia Praha	CzRep	32	1	3	4	14	13	0	1	1	10
2003-04	HC Slavia Praha	CzRep	48	3	9	12	20	19	4	2	6	10
2004-05	HC Slavia Praha	CzRep	42	10	9	19	14	7	1	1	2	0

TOPOL, Sergei (TOH-puhl, SAIR-gay) **VAN.**

Forward. Shoots left. 6'2", 183 lbs. Born, Omsk, USSR, February 15, 1985.
(Vancouver's 8th choice, 252nd overall, in 2003 Entry Draft).

			Regular Season					Playoffs				
Season	Club	League	GP	G	A	Pts	PIM	GP	G	A	Pts	PIM
2002-03	Omsk 2	Russia-3	45	16	5	21	18	....	....	....	....	....
2003-04	Omsk 2	Russia-3	39	25	14	39	10	....	....	....	....	....
	Avangard Omsk	Russia	9	0	0	0	2	....	....	....	....	....
2004-05	Mechel	Russia-2	19	1	0	1	6	....	....	....	....	....
	Mechel 2	Russia-3	5	2	1	3	8	....	....	....	....	....
	Omsk 2	Russia-3	18	6	4	10	4	....	....	....	....	....
	Avangard Omsk	Russia	2	1	0	1	0	....	....	....	....	....

TRATTNIG, Matthias (TRAT-nihg, MAH-tee-uhs)

Center. Shoots left. 6'1", 208 lbs. Born, Graz, Austria, April 22, 1979.
(Chicago's 2nd choice, 94th overall, in 1998 Entry Draft).

			Regular Season					Playoffs				
Season	Club	League	GP	G	A	Pts	PIM	GP	G	A	Pts	PIM
1995-96	EC Graz	Austria	17	0	1	1	0	....	....	....	....	....
1996-97	Capital District	NYJHL	51	30	54	84	64	....	....	....	....	....
1997-98	U. of Maine	H-East	34	8	9	17	30	....	....	....	....	....
1998-99	U. of Maine	H-East	39	5	5	10	32	....	....	....	....	....
99-2000	U. of Maine	H-East	39	8	11	19	26	....	....	....	....	....
2000-01	U. of Maine	H-East	37	11	13	24	51	....	....	....	....	....
2001-02	Djurgarden	Sweden	44	4	5	9	26	5	0	0	0	0
	Austria	Olympics	4	1	1	2	2	....	....	....	....	....
2002-03	Djurgarden	Sweden	48	7	5	12	67	12	3	2	5	16
2003-04	Kassel Huskies	Germany	52	12	19	31	72	....	....	....	....	....
2004-05	Syracuse Crunch	AHL	68	7	11	18	68	....	....	....	....	....

Signed as a free agent by **Columbus**, July 7, 2004.

TRAVIS, Dan (TRA-vihs, DAN) **FLA.**

Right wing. Shoots right. 6'3", 220 lbs. Born, Concord, NH, November 26, 1983.
(Florida's 7th choice, 141st overall, in 2003 Entry Draft).

			Regular Season					Playoffs				
Season	Club	League	GP	G	A	Pts	PIM	GP	G	A	Pts	PIM
2000-01	Bishop Guertin	High-NH	24	29	27	56	....	....	....	....	....	....
2001-02	Deerfield Academy	High-MA	23	14	18	32	30	....	....	....	....	....
2002-03	Deerfield Academy	High-MA	25	16	27	43	30	....	....	....	....	....
2003-04	New Hampshire	H-East	14	2	4	6	2	....	....	....	....	....
2004-05	New Hampshire	H-East	9	0	2	2	6	....	....	....	....	....

TREILLE, Yorick (TRAYL, YOH-rihk)

Right wing. Shoots right. 6'3", 213 lbs. Born, Cannes, France, July 15, 1980.
(Chicago's 7th choice, 195th overall, in 1999 Entry Draft).

			Regular Season					Playoffs				
Season	Club	League	GP	G	A	Pts	PIM	GP	G	A	Pts	PIM
1997-98	Notre Dame	SJHL	54	18	28	46	42	....	....	....	....	....
1998-99	U. Mass-Lowell	H-East	30	6	5	11	24	....	....	....	....	....
99-2000	U. Mass-Lowell	H-East	33	10	12	22	34	....	....	....	....	....
2000-01	U. Mass-Lowell	H-East	31	10	14	24	35	....	....	....	....	....
2001-02	U. Mass-Lowell	H-East	30	10	16	26	24	....	....	....	....	....
2002-03	Norfolk Admirals	AHL	27	3	2	5	25	....	....	....	....	....
	HIFK Helsinki	Finland	5	0	1	1	4	....	....	....	....	....
2003-04	Norfolk Admirals	AHL	74	12	12	24	54	8	2	0	2	4
2004-05	Providence Bruins	AHL	61	5	9	14	35	....	....	....	....	....

Signed as a free agent by **Providence** (AHL), September 22, 2004.

TREMBLAY, Jonathan (TRAHM-blay, JAWN-ah-thuhn) **S.J.**

Right wing. Shoots right. 6'3", 240 lbs. Born, Fauquier, Ont., March 3, 1984.
(San Jose's 6th choice, 201st overall, in 2003 Entry Draft).

			Regular Season					Playoffs				
Season	Club	League	GP	G	A	Pts	PIM	GP	G	A	Pts	PIM
2001-02	Timmins Majors	GNML	STATISTICS NOT AVAILABLE									
	Acadie-Bathurst	QMJHL	2	0	0	0	5	1	0	0	0	0
2002-03	Acadie-Bathurst	QMJHL	62	0	1	1	232	9	0	0	0	45
2003-04	Acadie-Bathurst	QMJHL	60	3	0	3	*316	....	....	....	....	....
2004-05	Cleveland Barons	AHL	1	0	0	0	0	....	....	....	....	....
	Johnstown Chiefs	ECHL	46	2	3	5	136	....	....	....	....	....

TROJOVSKY, Matej (troh-YAWV-skee, MAH-tehzh) **CAR.**

Right wing. Shoots left. 6'5", 220 lbs. Born, Plzen, Czech., October 12, 1984.
(Carolina's 5th choice, 130th overall, in 2003 Entry Draft).

			Regular Season					Playoffs				
Season	Club	League	GP	G	A	Pts	PIM	GP	G	A	Pts	PIM
99-2000	HC Plzen Jr.	CzRep-Jr.	36	2	13	15	58	5	0	1	1	2
2000-01	Lincoln Stars	USHL	17	1	0	1	29	....	....	....	....	....
2001-02	Regina Pats	WHL	67	3	10	13	154	6	0	1	1	18
2002-03	Regina Pats	WHL	70	3	6	9	229	5	0	0	0	6
2003-04	Swift Current	WHL	61	3	6	9	201	3	0	0	0	10
2004-05	Swift Current	WHL	30	3	3	6	119	....	....	....	....	....
	Prince George	WHL	27	2	1	3	80	....	....	....	....	....

TROLIGA, Tomas (TROH-lih-guh, TAW-mash) **ST.L.**

Center. Shoots right. 6'4", 200 lbs. Born, Presov, Czech., April 24, 1984.
(St. Louis' 3rd choice, 89th overall, in 2002 Entry Draft).

			Regular Season					Playoffs				
Season	Club	League	GP	G	A	Pts	PIM	GP	G	A	Pts	PIM
99-2000	Presov Jr.	Slovak-Jr.	39	6	1	7	56	....	....	....	....	....
2000-01	Presov Jr.	Slovak-Jr.	30	14	16	30	108	....	....	....	....	....
	Presov	Slovak-2	7	1	0	1	8	....	....	....	....	....
2001-02	Spis. N. Ves	Slovak-2	11	2	5	7	0	....	....	....	....	....
2002-03	HC Kosice	Slovakia	29	1	1	2	16	....	....	....	....	....
	MHC Martin	Slovakia	11	1	2	3	18	4	0	0	0	6
2003-04	Calgary Hitmen	WHL	59	11	23	34	103	7	0	1	1	16
2004-05	MsHK SKP Zilina	Slovakia	9	0	0	0	6	....	....	....	....	....
	PHK Presov	Slovak-2	2	1	1	2	8	....	....	....	....	....
	Tri-City Storm	USHL	10	26	36	4	3	9	0	2	2	24

TRUBACHEV, Yuri (troo-bah-CHEHV, YOO-ree) **CGY.**

Center. Shoots left. 5'9", 187 lbs. Born, Cherepovets, USSR, March 9, 1983.
(Calgary's 7th choice, 164th overall, in 2001 Entry Draft).

			Regular Season					Playoffs				
Season	Club	League	GP	G	A	Pts	PIM	GP	G	A	Pts	PIM
1997-98	Cherepovets 2	Russia-3	1	0	0	0	0	....	....	....	....	....
1998-99	Cherepovets 3	Russia-4	9	5	1	6	0	....	....	....	....	....
	Cherepovets 2	Russia-3	2	0	0	0	0	....	....	....	....	....
99-2000	Cherepovets 2	Russia-3	42	13	19	32	76	....	....	....	....	....
2000-01	SKA St. Petersburg	Russia	34	6	5	11	24	....	....	....	....	....
2001-02	Cherepovets 2	Russia-3	5	3	3	6	2	....	....	....	....	....
	Cherepovets	Russia	32	2	1	3	6	4	0	2	2	0
2002-03	Cherepovets	Russia	48	5	7	12	26	12	1	2	3	6
2003-04	Cherepovets	Russia	59	8	10	18	50	....	....	....	....	....
2004-05	Cherepovets	Russia	59	12	15	27	44	....	....	....	....	....

TRUKHNO, Vyacheslav (trookh-NOH, VYACH-ih-slav) **EDM.**

Left wing. Shoots left. 6'1", 196 lbs. Born, Khimki, USSR, February 22, 1987.
(Edmonton's 6th choice, 120th overall, in 2005 Entry Draft).

			Regular Season					Playoffs				
Season	Club	League	GP	G	A	Pts	PIM	GP	G	A	Pts	PIM
2002-03	Rungstead IK	Denmark-2	1	2	3	5	0	....	....	....	....	....
	Rungstead	Denmark	27	7	4	11	8	12	0	1	1	8
2003-04	Rungstead	Denmark	35	12	11	23	18	7	0	0	0	8
2004-05	PEI Rocket	QMJHL	64	25	34	59	57	....	....	....	....	....

QMJHL All-Rookie Team (2005) • Canadian Major Junior All-Rookie Team (2005)

TUKIO, Arto (TOO-kee-oh, AHR-toh) **NYI**

Defense. Shoots left. 5'10", 176 lbs. Born, Tampere, Finland, April 4, 1981.
(NY Islanders' 3rd choice, 101st overall, in 2000 Entry Draft).

			Regular Season					Playoffs				
Season	Club	League	GP	G	A	Pts	PIM	GP	G	A	Pts	PIM
1996-97	Ilves Tampere U18	Fin-U18	20	0	2	2	6	1	1	0	1	0
1997-98	Ilves Tampere U18	Fin-U18	39	7	7	14	64	....	....	....	....	....
	Ilves Tampere Jr.	Finland-Jr.	....	....	....	....	....	4	1	0	1	4
1998-99	Ilves Tampere U18	Fin-U18	10	1	5	6	18	....	....	....	....	....
	Ilves Tampere Jr.	Finland-Jr.	18	1	4	5	12	10	0	0	0	2
99-2000	Ilves Tampere Jr.	Finland-Jr.	11	2	1	3	24	....	....	....	....	....
	Hermes Kokkola	Finland-2	1	0	0	0	0	....	....	....	....	....
	Ilves Tampere	Finland	42	2	1	3	20	3	0	0	0	0
2000-01	Ilves Tampere Jr.	Finland-Jr.	3	1	1	2	0	....	....	....	....	....
	Ilves Tampere	Finland	43	5	10	15	26	7	2	1	3	4
2001-02	Ilves Tampere	Finland	47	8	9	17	28	3	0	1	1	0
2002-03	Jokerit Helsinki	Finland	49	6	10	16	26	9	0	1	1	4
2003-04	Jokerit Helsinki	Finland	54	4	12	16	10	....	....	....	....	....
2004-05	Frolunda	Sweden	48	1	7	8	20	13	0	2	2	20

TUKONEN, Lauri (too-KOH-nehn, LOW-ree) L.A.

Right wing. Shoots right. 6'2", 200 lbs. Born, Hyvinkaa, Finland, September 1, 1986.
(Los Angeles' 1st choice, 11th overall, in 2004 Entry Draft).

			Regular Season					Playoffs				
Season	Club	League	GP	G	A	Pts	PIM	GP	G	A	Pts	PIM
2001-02	HC Sunne	Sweden-3	2	4	0	4	2	....	....	....	....	....
	Ahmat Hyvinkaa	Finland-2	24	7	4	11	6	....	....	....	....	....
2002-03	Ahmat Jr.	Finland-Jr.	3	3	1	4	2	1	0	0	0	0
	Ahmat Hyvinkaa	Finland-2	12	2	2	4	2	....	....	....	....	....
	Blues Espoo Jr.	Finland-Jr.	17	6	6	12	18	5	0	0	0	10
2003-04	Blues Espoo	Finland	35	3	3	6	16	7	0	0	0	0
	Blues Espoo Jr.	Finland-Jr.	14	14	9	23	4	....	....	....	....	....
2004-05	Blues Espoo Jr.	Finland-Jr.	2	0	0	0	2	....	....	....	....	....
	Blues Espoo	Finland	43	5	5	10	10	....	....	....	....	....

TUMA, Martin (TOO-ma, MAHR-tehn) FLA.

Defense. Shoots left. 6'4", 209 lbs. Born, Most, Czech., September 14, 1985.
(Florida's 8th choice, 162nd overall, in 2003 Entry Draft).

			Regular Season					Playoffs				
Season	Club	League	GP	G	A	Pts	PIM	GP	G	A	Pts	PIM
2000-01	Litvinov Jr.	CzRep-Jr.	45	4	12	16	62	6	0	3	3	8
2001-02	Litvinov Jr.	CzRep-Jr.	39	2	1	3	104	2	0	0	0	0
	Litvinov	CzRep	1	0	0	0	2	....	....	....	....	....
2002-03	Litvinov Jr.	CzRep-Jr.	34	1	3	4	123	....	....	....	....	....
2003-04	Sault Ste. Marie	OHL	57	0	5	5	48	....	....	....	....	....
2004-05	Sault Ste. Marie	OHL	61	10	13	23	107	7	0	3	3	6
	San Antonio	AHL	5	0	1	1	0	....	....	....	....	....

TUNIK, Yevgeny (TOO-nihk, yehv-GEH-nee) NYI

Center. Shoots left. 6'2", 198 lbs. Born, Kraskovo, USSR, November 17, 1984.
(NY Islanders' 3rd choice, 53rd overall, in 2003 Entry Draft).

			Regular Season					Playoffs				
Season	Club	League	GP	G	A	Pts	PIM	GP	G	A	Pts	PIM
99-2000	Elektrostal 2	Russia-3	3	0	0	0	4	....	....	....	....	....
2000-01	Elektrostal	Russia-2	8	2	0	2	2	....	....	....	....	....
2001-02	Elektrostal 2	Russia-3	14	13	6	19	18	....	....	....	....	....
	Elektrostal	Russia-2	22	5	0	5	8	....	....	....	....	....
2002-03	Elektrostal	Russia-2	42	14	10	24	24	....	....	....	....	....
	Elektrostal 2	Russia-3	1	0	0	0	0	....	....	....	....	....
2003-04	St. Petersburg 2	Russia-3	9	6	5	11	54	1	0	0	0	2
	SKA St. Petersburg	Russia	32	3	1	4	26	....	....	....	....	....
2004-05	St. Petersburg 2	Russia-3	15	8	6	14	64	....	....	....	....	....
	SKA St. Petersburg	Russia	4	0	0	0	8	....	....	....	....	....
	Kristall Elektrostal	Russia-2	12	3	2	5	18	....	....	....	....	....
	Leninogorsk	Russia-2	6	0	0	0	32	1	1	0	1	0

TUOKKO, Marco (too-OH-koh, MAHR-koh) DAL.

Center. Shoots left. 6', 185 lbs. Born, Raisio, Finland, March 27, 1979.
(Dallas' 9th choice, 219th overall, in 2000 Entry Draft).

			Regular Season					Playoffs				
Season	Club	League	GP	G	A	Pts	PIM	GP	G	A	Pts	PIM
1995-96	TPS Turku U18	Fin-U18	31	9	13	22	49	3	1	0	1	0
	Kiekko-67 Turku	Finland-2	1	0	0	0	0	....	....	....	....	....
1996-97	TPS Turku U18	Fin-U18	5	1	3	4	0	6	1	6	7	4
	TPS Turku Jr.	Finland-Jr.	30	8	7	15	32	....	....	....	....	....
	Kiekko-67 Turku	Finland-2	6	3	1	4	31	....	....	....	....	....
1997-98	TPS Turku Jr.	Finland-Jr.	26	5	13	18	77	7	1	4	5	14
1998-99	TPS Turku Jr.	Finland-Jr.	1	0	0	0	0	....	....	....	....	....
	TPS Turku	Finland	48	5	4	9	24	10	0	1	1	10
99-2000	TPS Turku	Finland	54	10	10	20	73	11	2	2	4	6
2000-01	TPS Turku	Finland	53	5	11	16	54	10	2	2	4	16
2001-02	TPS Turku	Finland	42	2	9	11	69	8	1	1	2	4
2002-03	TPS Turku	Finland	41	5	4	9	42	7	1	1	2	2
2003-04	TPS Turku	Finland	54	8	9	17	55	13	4	1	5	4
2004-05	TPS Turku	Finland	37	7	6	13	28	6	0	0	0	18

TUOMAINEN, Miikka (too-oh-MAY-nehn, MEE-kah) ATL.

Left wing. Shoots left. 6'3", 210 lbs. Born, Turku, Finland, May 22, 1986.
(Atlanta's 7th choice, 204th overall, in 2004 Entry Draft).

			Regular Season					Playoffs				
Season	Club	League	GP	G	A	Pts	PIM	GP	G	A	Pts	PIM
2002-03	TuTo Turku Jr.	Finland-Jr.	26	3	4	7	56	4	0	0	0	0
	TuTo Turku	Finland-2	6	0	0	0	0	....	....	....	....	....
2003-04	TuTo Turku Jr.	Finland-Jr.	20	10	7	17	6	....	....	....	....	....
	TuTo Turku	Finland-2	30	4	3	7	2	....	....	....	....	....
2004-05	TuTo Turku	Finland-2	42	4	4	8	22	7	1	0	1	2

TURNER, Brennan (TUHR-nuhr, BREH-nan) CHI.

Defense. Shoots left. 6'3", 220 lbs. Born, Winnipeg, Man., December 5, 1986.
(Chicago's 8th choice, 134th overall, in 2005 Entry Draft).

			Regular Season					Playoffs				
Season	Club	League	GP	G	A	Pts	PIM	GP	G	A	Pts	PIM
2003-04	Notre Dame	SJHL	35	2	8	10	110	....	....	....	....	....
2004-05	Notre Dame	SJHL	41	5	12	17	207	8	0	1	1	25

TURON, David (TUHR-awn, DAY-vihd) TOR.

Defense. Shoots right. 6'3", 202 lbs. Born, Havirov, Czech., October 4, 1983.
(Toronto's 5th choice, 122nd overall, in 2002 Entry Draft).

			Regular Season					Playoffs				
Season	Club	League	GP	G	A	Pts	PIM	GP	G	A	Pts	PIM
99-2000	SK Karvina Jr.	CzRep-Jr.	2	0	0	0	0	....	....	....	....	....
	HC Havirov Jr.	CzRep-Jr.	41	14	11	25	54	....	....	....	....	....
2000-01	HC Havirov Jr.	CzRep-Jr.	43	12	7	19	26	....	....	....	....	....
	HC Femax Havirov	CzRep	4	0	0	0	4	....	....	....	....	....
2001-02	HC Havirov Jr.	CzRep-Jr.	41	5	11	16	75	....	....	....	....	....
	HC Femax Havirov	CzRep	14	0	1	1	10	....	....	....	....	....
2002-03	Portland	WHL	36	3	6	9	38	7	0	2	2	0
2003-04	St. John's	AHL	11	0	1	1	2	....	....	....	....	....
	Memphis	CHL	42	8	7	15	57	....	....	....	....	....
2004-05	St. John's	AHL	1	0	0	0	2	....	....	....	....	....
	Pensacola	ECHL	50	3	9	12	32	....	....	....	....	....
	Louisiana	ECHL	8	0	4	4	4	....	....	....	....	....

• Missed majority of 2002-03 season recovering from shoulder injury suffered in training camp, September 26, 2002.

TUZZOLINO, Nicholas (Tootz-OH-lee-noh, NIHK-o-las) NYI

Defense. Shoots right. 6'5", 225 lbs. Born, Buffalo, NY, January 19, 1986.
(NY Islanders' 6th choice, 196th overall, in 2005 Entry Draft).

			Regular Season					Playoffs				
Season	Club	League	GP	G	A	Pts	PIM	GP	G	A	Pts	PIM
2003-04	Lincoln Stars	USHL	55	2	1	3	55	....	....	....	....	....
2004-05	Sarnia Sting	OHL	67	2	20	22	128	....	....	....	....	....

UCHEVATOV, Victor (oo-cheh-VA-tawf, VIHK-tohr) FLA.

Defense. Shoots left. 6'4", 225 lbs. Born, Angarsk, USSR, February 10, 1983.
(New Jersey's 4th choice, 60th overall, in 2001 Entry Draft).

			Regular Season					Playoffs				
Season	Club	League	GP	G	A	Pts	PIM	GP	G	A	Pts	PIM
2000-01	Yaroslavl 2	Russia-3	28	1	1	2	74	....	....	....	....	....
2001-02	Albany River Rats	AHL	64	0	2	2	50	....	....	....	....	....
2002-03	Albany River Rats	AHL	55	0	2	2	27	....	....	....	....	....
2003-04	Albany River Rats	AHL	52	0	3	3	46	....	....	....	....	....
	San Antonio	AHL	22	3	4	7	6	....	....	....	....	....
2004-05	San Antonio	AHL	48	1	1	2	47	....	....	....	....	....

Traded to **Florida** by **New Jersey** with Christian Berglund for Viktor Kozlov, March 1, 2004.

UJCIK, Viktor (OOY-chehk, VIHK-tohr) MTL.

Right wing. Shoots left. 5'11", 194 lbs. Born, Jihlava, Czech., May 24, 1972.
(Montreal's 8th choice, 266th overall, in 2001 Entry Draft).

			Regular Season					Playoffs				
Season	Club	League	GP	G	A	Pts	PIM	GP	G	A	Pts	PIM
1990-91	Dukla Jihlava	Czech	2	0	0	0	0	....	....	....	....	....
1991-92	Dukla Jihlava	Czech	35	10	9	19	32	8	3	4	7	0
1992-93	Dukla Jihlava	Czech	30	16	16	32	....	....	....	....	....	....
1993-94	HC Dukla Jihlava	CzRep	44	17	30	47	....	4	3	3	6	....
1994-95	HC Dukla Jihlava	CzRep	42	20	16	36	65	2	1	2	3	2
1995-96	HC Slavia Praha	CzRep	39	*37	19	56	59	7	8	4	12	6
1996-97	HC Slavia Praha	CzRep	40	26	21	47	41	3	1	1	2	2
1997-98	HC Slavia Praha	CzRep	17	13	8	21	12	....	....	....	....	....
	Trinec	CzRep	31	21	22	43	63	13	8	10	18	4
1998-99	Trinec	CzRep	44	20	23	43	55	10	4	4	8	18
99-2000	HC Ocelari Trinec	CzRep	42	14	20	34	32	4	1	0	1	28
2000-01	HC Ocelari Trinec	CzRep	31	8	12	20	20	....	....	....	....	....
	HC Slavia Praha	CzRep	19	9	9	18	8	11	8	8	16	10
2001-02	HC Slavia Praha	CzRep	52	25	23	48	51	9	3	0	3	6
2002-03	HC Keramika Plzen	CzRep	23	12	5	17	41	....	....	....	....	....
	HC Sparta Praha	CzRep	26	11	6	17	14	10	3	5	8	6
2003-04	HC Sparta Praha	CzRep	19	11	7	18	6	13	0	2	2	18
	HC Dukla Jihlava	CzRep-2	4	4	0	4	4	....	....	....	....	....
2004-05	Karpat Oulu	Finland	52	20	18	38	36	12	1	4	5	12

UMBERGER, R.J. (UHM-buhr-guhr, AHR-JAY) PHI.

Center. Shoots left. 6'2", 200 lbs. Born, Pittsburgh, PA, May 3, 1982.
(Vancouver's 1st choice, 16th overall, in 2001 Entry Draft).

			Regular Season					Playoffs				
Season	Club	League	GP	G	A	Pts	PIM	GP	G	A	Pts	PIM
1997-98	Plum Mustangs	High-PA	26	*60	*56	*116	....	....	....	....	....	....
1998-99	USA U-17	USDP	50	29	29	58	....	....	....	....	....	....
99-2000	USA U-18	USDP	57	33	35	68	20	....	....	....	....	....
2000-01	Ohio State	CCHA	32	14	23	37	18	....	....	....	....	....
2001-02	Ohio State	CCHA	37	18	21	39	31	....	....	....	....	....
2002-03	Ohio State	CCHA	43	26	27	53	16	....	....	....	....	....
2003-04					DID NOT PLAY							
2004-05	Philadelphia	AHL	80	21	44	65	36	21	3	7	10	12

CCHA All-Rookie Team (2001) • CCHA Rookie of the Year (2001) • CCHA First All-Star Team (2003) • NCAA West Second All-American Team (2003)

• Missed entire 2003-04 season due to a contract dispute. Traded to **NY Rangers** by **Vancouver** with Martin Grenier for Martin Rucinsky, March 9, 2004. Signed as a free agent by **Philadelphia**, June 16, 2004.

UMICEVIC, Dragan (oo-mih-CHAY-vihk, DRA-guhn) EDM.

Left wing. Shoots left. 6', 191 lbs. Born, Köping, Sweden, October 9, 1984.
(Edmonton's 8th choice, 184th overall, in 2003 Entry Draft).

			Regular Season					Playoffs				
Season	Club	League	GP	G	A	Pts	PIM	GP	G	A	Pts	PIM
99-2000	Koping HC	Sweden-3			STATISTICS NOT AVAILABLE							
2000-01	Sodertalje SK U18	Swe-U18	16	8	5	13	49	....	....	....	....	....
	Sodertalje SK Jr.	Swe-Jr.	1	0	0	0	0	....	....	....	....	....
2001-02	Sodertalje SK Jr.	Swe-Jr.	36	20	31	51	41	....	....	....	....	....
	Sodertalje SK	Sweden	3	1	0	1	0	....	....	....	....	....
2002-03	Sodertalje SK	Sweden	22	2	3	5	4	....	....	....	....	....
	Sodertalje SK Jr.	Swe-Jr.	24	19	14	33	28	....	....	....	....	....
2003-04	Sodertalje SK Jr.	Swe-Jr.	9	3	5	8	24	....	....	....	....	....
	IF Bjorkloven Umea	Sweden-2	21	8	8	16	45	....	....	....	....	....
	Sodertalje SK	Sweden	8	0	0	0	0	....	....	....	....	....
2004-05	Sodertalje SK Jr.	Swe-Jr.	4	2	9	11	4	....	....	....	....	....
	Sodertalje SK	Sweden	47	6	13	19	20	10	0	1	1	6

UPPER, Dmitri (OO-puhr, dih-MEE-tree) NYI

Center. Shoots right. 6'1", 185 lbs. Born, Ust-Kamenogorsk, USSR, July 27, 1978.
(NY Islanders' 5th choice, 136th overall, in 2000 Entry Draft).

			Regular Season					Playoffs				
Season	Club	League	GP	G	A	Pts	PIM	GP	G	A	Pts	PIM
1997-98	Ust-Kamenogorsk	Russia-2	47	16	12	28	44	....	....	....	....	....
1998-99	Ust-Kam'gorsk 2	Russia-4	29	10	11	21	44	....	....	....	....	....
	Nizhny Novgorod	Russia-2	11	4	10	14	16	17	6	6	12	49
99-2000	Nizhny Novgorod	Russia	36	14	6	20	50	5	1	1	2	4
2000-01	Nizhny Novgorod	Russia	6	0	2	2	4	....	....	....	....	....
	Ak Bars Kazan	Russia	31	7	4	11	6	1	0	0	0	0
2001-02	Spartak Moscow	Russia	51	16	9	25	74	....	....	....	....	....
2002-03	Spartak Moscow	Russia	43	7	13	20	63	....	....	....	....	....
2003-04	CSKA Moscow	Russia	58	10	9	19	48	....	....	....	....	....
2004-05	CSKA Moscow	Russia	41	7	3	10	30	....	....	....	....	....

URQUHART, Cory (UHRK-hahrt, KOHR-ee) **MTL.**

Center. Shoots left. 6'3", 200 lbs. Born, Halifax, N.S., October 1, 1984.
(Montreal's 2nd choice, 40th overall, in 2003 Entry Draft).

			Regular Season					Playoffs				
Season	**Club**	**League**	**GP**	**G**	**A**	**Pts**	**PIM**	**GP**	**G**	**A**	**Pts**	**PIM**
1997-98	East Hants	NSBHL	60	35	46	81	24	....	....	....	....	....
1998-99	East Hants	NSBHL	62	54	60	114	74	....	....	....	....	....
99-2000	Dalhousie	NSMHL	21	15	14	29	12	....	....	....	....	....
2000-01	Quebec Remparts	QMJHL	60	25	24	49	32	2	0	0	0	2
2001-02	Quebec Remparts	QMJHL	36	8	10	18	4	....	....	....	....	....
	Montreal Rocket	QMJHL	34	9	9	18	6	7	3	2	5	0
2002-03	Montreal Rocket	QMJHL	71	35	43	78	28	7	9	6	15	6
2003-04	PEI Rocket	QMJHL	67	35	44	79	52	10	6	7	13	14
2004-05	Hamilton Bulldogs	AHL	1	0	0	0	0	....	....	....	....	....
	Long Beach	ECHL	63	16	15	31	14	6	0	0	0	2

UTKIN, Dmitri (OOT-kihn, dih-MEE-tree) **BOS.**

Left wing. Shoots left. 6', 169 lbs. Born, Yaroslavl, USSR, June 10, 1984.
(Boston's 5th choice, 228th overall, in 2002 Entry Draft).

			Regular Season					Playoffs				
Season	**Club**	**League**	**GP**	**G**	**A**	**Pts**	**PIM**	**GP**	**G**	**A**	**Pts**	**PIM**
2000-01	Yaroslavl 2	Russia-3	49	12	1	13	10	....	....	....	....	....
2001-02	Yaroslavl 2	Russia-3	32	15	7	22	33	....	....	....	....	....
2002-03	Yaroslavl	Russia	4	0	1	1	0	....	....	....	....	....
2003-04	Spartak Moscow	Russia-2	57	10	10	20	8	13	3	3	6	2
2004-05	Keramin Minsk	BelOpen	8	2	0	2	31	....	....	....	....	....
	HK Brest	BelOpen	20	4	12	16	4	....	....	....	....	....
	HK Riga 2000	BelOpen	....	....	....	....	....	3	0	0	0	0
	HK Riga 2000	Latvia	....	....	....	....	....	6	3	2	5	0

VAGNER, Martin (VAHG-nuhr, MAHR-tihn) **CAR.**

Defense. Shoots left. 6'1", 214 lbs. Born, Jaromer, Czech., March 16, 1984.
(Carolina's 8th choice, 268th overall, in 2004 Entry Draft).

			Regular Season					Playoffs				
Season	**Club**	**League**	**GP**	**G**	**A**	**Pts**	**PIM**	**GP**	**G**	**A**	**Pts**	**PIM**
99-2000	Sparta Jr.	CzRep-Jr.	46	2	8	10	34	....	....	....	....	....
2000-01	HC Pardubice Jr.	CzRep-Jr.	53	2	12	14	46	....	....	....	....	....
2001-02	Hull Olympiques	QMJHL	64	6	28	34	81	8	0	1	1	10
2002-03	Hull Olympiques	QMJHL	53	1	12	13	98	20	1	4	5	38
2003-04	Gatineau	QMJHL	38	6	12	18	85	13	0	3	3	16
2004-05	Acadie-Bathurst	QMJHL	48	3	10	13	84	....	....	....	....	....

• Re-entered NHL Entry Draft. Originally Dallas' 1st choice, 26th overall, in 2002 Entry Draft.

QMJHL All-Rookie Team (2002)

VAINIO, Niko (VAY-nee-oh, NEE-koh) **DAL.**

Defense. Shoots left. 6'1", 180 lbs. Born, Helsinki, Finland, January 24, 1985.
(Dallas' 11th choice, 259th overall, in 2003 Entry Draft).

			Regular Season					Playoffs				
Season	**Club**	**League**	**GP**	**G**	**A**	**Pts**	**PIM**	**GP**	**G**	**A**	**Pts**	**PIM**
2000-01	Jokerit U18	Fin-U18	15	0	1	1	8	....	....	....	....	....
2001-02	Jokerit U18	Fin-U18	26	8	9	17	18	8	0	3	3	6
2002-03	Jokerit U18	Fin-U18	7	2	6	8	8	....	....	....	....	....
	Jokerit Helsinki Jr.	Finland-Jr.	35	1	1	2	8	11	0	0	0	2
2003-04	Jokerit Helsinki Jr.	Finland-Jr.	17	1	0	1	26	....	....	....	....	....
2004-05	Peterborough	OHL	11	1	5	6	10	....	....	....	....	....

VALABIK, Boris (vuh-LA-bihk, BOHR-ihs) **ATL.**

Defense. Shoots left. 6'7", 230 lbs. Born, Nitra, Czech., February 14, 1986.
(Atlanta's 1st choice, 10th overall, in 2004 Entry Draft).

			Regular Season					Playoffs				
Season	**Club**	**League**	**GP**	**G**	**A**	**Pts**	**PIM**	**GP**	**G**	**A**	**Pts**	**PIM**
2002-03	HKM Nitra Jr.	Slovak-Jr.	46	2	12	14	145	....	....	....	....	....
2003-04	Kitchener Rangers	OHL	68	3	13	16	278	5	0	0	0	8
2004-05	Kitchener Rangers	OHL	43	0	4	4	231	15	0	0	0	56

OHL All-Rookie Team (2004) • Canadian Major Junior All-Rookie Team (2004)

VALCAK, Patrik (VAHL-chahk, PAT-rihk) **BOS.**

Center. Shoots left. 6'1", 185 lbs. Born, Ostrava, Czech., December 16, 1984.
(Boston's 6th choice, 129th overall, in 2003 Entry Draft).

			Regular Season					Playoffs				
Season	**Club**	**League**	**GP**	**G**	**A**	**Pts**	**PIM**	**GP**	**G**	**A**	**Pts**	**PIM**
2000-01	HC Ostrava Jr.	CzRep-Jr.	44	13	16	29	34	....	....	....	....	....
2001-02	HC Ostrava Jr.	CzRep-Jr.	45	9	16	25	44	....	....	....	....	....
2002-03	HC Ostrava Jr.	CzRep-Jr.	38	14	18	32	131	....	....	....	....	....
2003-04	Kelowna Rockets	WHL	22	0	1	1	13	11	0	0	0	6
	Lethbridge	WHL	35	2	9	11	28	....	....	....	....	....
2004-05	Lincoln Stars	USHL	4	1	2	3	2	....	....	....	....	....
	HC Havirov	CzRep-2	2	0	1	1	6	....	....	....	....	....
	HC Ostrava Jr.	CzRep-Jr.	5	2	3	5	4	....	....	....	....	....
	HC Sareza Ostrava	CzRep-2	26	1	6	7	32	2	0	0	0	2

VALDIX, Andreas (VAHL-dihx, an-DRAY-uhs) **WSH.**

Left wing. Shoots left. 5'11", 170 lbs. Born, Malmo, Sweden, December 6, 1984.
(Washington's 3rd choice, 109th overall, in 2003 Entry Draft).

			Regular Season					Playoffs				
Season	**Club**	**League**	**GP**	**G**	**A**	**Pts**	**PIM**	**GP**	**G**	**A**	**Pts**	**PIM**
99-2000	Malmo Jr.	Swe-Jr.	14	3	7	10	39	....	....	....	....	....
2000-01	Malmo U18	Swe-U18	6	2	2	4	12	....	....	....	....	....
	Malmo Jr.	Swe-Jr.	19	3	3	6	8	3	2	2	4	4
2001-02	Malmo U18	Swe-U18	39	13	13	26	86	7	0	3	3	6
	Malmo	Sweden	1	0	0	0	0	....	....	....	....	....
2002-03	Malmo U18	Swe-U18	11	10	12	22	16	6	2	5	7	8
	Malmo	Sweden	39	2	0	2	10	....	....	....	....	....
2003-04	Malmo U18	Swe-U18	9	4	3	7	4	....	....	....	....	....
	Malmo	Sweden	47	2	3	5	8	....	....	....	....	....
2004-05	Malmo	Sweden	26	0	1	1	2	....	....	....	....	....
	Halmstad	Sweden-2	24	4	5	9	14	2	0	0	0	6

VALETTE, Craig (va-LEHT, KRAIG) **S.J.**

Center. Shoots left. 6', 190 lbs. Born, Shellbrook, Sask., October 7, 1982.

			Regular Season					Playoffs				
Season	**Club**	**League**	**GP**	**G**	**A**	**Pts**	**PIM**	**GP**	**G**	**A**	**Pts**	**PIM**
1998-99	Sask. Contacts	SMHL	36	19	22	41	....	....	....	....	....	....
99-2000	Saskatoon Blades	WHL	47	2	1	3	25	3	0	0	0	0
2000-01	Saskatoon Blades	WHL	24	2	0	2	19	....	....	....	....	....
	Portland	WHL	39	8	6	14	39	16	0	2	2	27
2001-02	Portland	WHL	67	8	14	22	160	7	2	1	3	6
2002-03	Portland	WHL	71	30	26	56	192	7	5	4	9	18
2003-04	Cleveland Barons	AHL	56	6	10	16	77	5	0	0	0	2
2004-05	Cleveland Barons	AHL	79	6	6	12	94	....	....	....	....	....

Signed as a free agent by **San Jose**, April 4, 2003.

VALTONEN, Tomek (VAL-tuh-nehn, Toh-MEHK) **DET.**

Left wing. Shoots left. 6'1", 198 lbs. Born, Piotrkow Trybunalski, Poland, January 8, 1980.
(Detroit's 3rd choice, 56th overall, in 1998 Entry Draft).

			Regular Season					Playoffs				
Season	**Club**	**League**	**GP**	**G**	**A**	**Pts**	**PIM**	**GP**	**G**	**A**	**Pts**	**PIM**
1995-96	Ilves Tampere U18	Fin-U18	11	7	7	14	28	....	....	....	....	....
	Ilves Tampere Jr.	Finland-Jr.	....	....	....	....	....	1	0	0	0	0
1996-97	Ilves Tampere U18	Fin-U18	26	10	9	19	82	3	0	1	1	6
	Ilves Tampere Jr.	Finland-Jr.	1	0	0	0	0	....	....	....	....	....
1997-98	K-Karhut Jr.	Finland-Jr.	3	0	0	0	12	....	....	....	....	....
	JoKP Joensuu	Finland-2	6	1	2	3	39	....	....	....	....	....
	Ilves Tampere Jr.	Finland-Jr.	13	3	2	5	36	....	....	....	....	....
	Ilves Tampere	Finland	19	1	0	1	14	3	0	0	0	0
	Ilves Tampere U18	Fin-U18	....	....	....	....	....	7	0	2	2	16
1998-99	Plymouth Whalers	OHL	43	8	16	24	53	7	1	0	1	0
99-2000	Jokerit Helsinki	Finland	41	0	3	3	63	9	1	0	1	8
2000-01	Jokerit Helsinki	Finland	45	3	2	5	138	3	0	0	0	0
2001-02	Jokerit Helsinki	Finland	55	4	4	8	65	11	2	1	3	2
2002-03	Jokerit Helsinki	Finland	51	5	9	14	38	10	1	1	2	4
2003-04	Jokerit Helsinki	Finland	53	15	16	31	78	8	1	3	4	8
2004-05	Jokerit Helsinki	Finland	35	6	8	14	59	12	3	0	3	10

VAN DER GULIK, David (VAN-DUHR-GOO-lihk, DAY-vihd) **CGY.**

Right wing. Shoots left. 5'11", 175 lbs. Born, Abbotsford, B.C., April 20, 1983.
(Calgary's 10th choice, 206th overall, in 2002 Entry Draft).

			Regular Season					Playoffs				
Season	**Club**	**League**	**GP**	**G**	**A**	**Pts**	**PIM**	**GP**	**G**	**A**	**Pts**	**PIM**
99-2000	Chilliwack Chiefs	BCHL	41	35	46	81	....	....	....	....	....	....
2000-01	Chilliwack Chiefs	BCHL	60	42	38	80	....	....	....	....	....	....
2001-02	Chilliwack Chiefs	BCHL	56	38	62	100	90	13	8	11	19	....
2002-03	Boston University	H-East	40	10	10	20	56	....	....	....	....	....
2003-04	Boston University	H-East	35	13	7	20	74	....	....	....	....	....
2004-05	Boston University	H-East	41	18	13	31	48	....	....	....	....	....

Hockey East All-Rookie Team (2003)

VANDE VELDE, Chris (VAN-deh-VEHLD, KRIHS) **EDM.**

Center. Shoots left. 6'1", 190 lbs. Born, Moorhead, MN, March 15, 1987.
(Edmonton's 5th choice, 97th overall, in 2005 Entry Draft).

			Regular Season					Playoffs				
Season	**Club**	**League**	**GP**	**G**	**A**	**Pts**	**PIM**	**GP**	**G**	**A**	**Pts**	**PIM**
2003-04	Moorhead Spuds	High-MN	29	19	24	43	....	....	....	....	....	....
2004-05	Moorhead Spuds	High-MN	30	35	32	67	28	....	....	....	....	....
	Lincoln Stars	USHL	7	1	4	5	0	4	0	2	2	0

Signed Letter of Intent to attend **North Dakota** (WCHA), June 8, 2004.

VANDERMEER, Peter (VAN-duhr-meer, PEE-tuhr) **MTL.**

Left wing. Shoots left. 6', 210 lbs. Born, Carolina, Alta., October 14, 1975.

			Regular Season					Playoffs				
Season	**Club**	**League**	**GP**	**G**	**A**	**Pts**	**PIM**	**GP**	**G**	**A**	**Pts**	**PIM**
1992-93	Red Deer	AMHL	34	26	30	56	172	....	....	....	....	....
	Red Deer Rebels	WHL	2	0	0	0	2	....	....	....	....	....
1993-94	Red Deer Rebels	WHL	54	4	9	13	170	....	....	....	....	....
1994-95	Red Deer Rebels	WHL	61	16	16	32	218	....	....	....	....	....
1995-96	Red Deer Rebels	WHL	63	21	40	61	207	....	....	....	....	....
1996-97	Columbus Chill	ECHL	30	6	11	17	195	7	2	1	3	26
1997-98	Columbus Chill	ECHL	20	4	7	11	78	....	....	....	....	....
	Richmond	ECHL	18	2	5	7	165	....	....	....	....	....
	Rochester	AHL	30	4	2	6	140	4	1	0	1	13
1998-99	Rochester	AHL	2	1	0	1	16	16	1	0	1	38
	Binghamton	UHL	62	15	21	36	*390	5	2	2	4	0
99-2000	Wilkes-Barre	AHL	4	0	0	0	7	....	....	....	....	....
	Richmond	ECHL	58	31	25	56	*457	3	0	1	1	20
	Providence Bruins	AHL	....	....	....	....	....	9	0	3	3	2
2000-01	Providence Bruins	AHL	62	19	18	37	240	4	0	0	0	16
2001-02	Trenton Titans	ECHL	2	0	1	1	2	....	....	....	....	....
	Philadelphia	AHL	61	5	1	6	313	5	0	0	0	8
2002-03	Philadelphia	AHL	77	5	8	13	335	....	....	....	....	....
2003-04	Philadelphia	AHL	71	5	8	13	*398	12	1	0	1	29
2004-05	Grand Rapids	AHL	73	4	13	17	310	....	....	....	....	....

Signed as a free agent by **Philadelphia**, July 6, 2001. Signed as a free agent by **Detroit**, August 16, 2004. Signed as a free agent by **Montreal**, August 2, 2005.

VANEK, Thomas (VAH-nehk, TAW-muhs) **BUF.**

Left wing. Shoots right. 6'2", 210 lbs. Born, Vienna, Austria, January 19, 1984.
(Buffalo's 1st choice, 5th overall, in 2003 Entry Draft).

			Regular Season					Playoffs				
Season	**Club**	**League**	**GP**	**G**	**A**	**Pts**	**PIM**	**GP**	**G**	**A**	**Pts**	**PIM**
99-2000	Sioux Falls	USHL	35	15	18	33	12	3	0	1	1	0
2000-01	Sioux Falls	USHL	20	19	10	29	15	8	5	4	9	2
2001-02	Sioux Falls	USHL	53	46	45	91	54	3	0	0	0	9
2002-03	U. of Minnesota	WCHA	45	31	31	62	60	....	....	....	....	....
2003-04	U. of Minnesota	WCHA	38	26	25	51	72	....	....	....	....	....
2004-05	Rochester	AHL	74	42	26	68	62	9	2	3	5	10

USHL First All-Star Team (2002) • USHL MVP (2002) • WCHA All-Rookie Team (2003) • WCHA Second All-Star Team (2003, 2004) • WCHA Rookie of the Year (2003) • NCAA Championship All-Tournament Team (2003) • NCAA Championship Tournament MVP (2003) • NCAA West Second All-American Team (2004) • AHL All-Rookie Team (2005)

VANNELLI, Michael (vuh-NEHL-ee, MIGH-kuhl) ATL.

Defense. Shoots right. 6'2", 190 lbs. Born, St. Paul, MN, October 2, 1983.
(Atlanta's 4th choice, 136th overall, in 2003 Entry Draft).

			Regular Season					Playoffs				
Season	Club	League	GP	G	A	Pts	PIM	GP	G	A	Pts	PIM
2001-02	Cretin-Derham	High-MN	28	0	5	5	16	....	....	....	....	....
	Sioux Falls	USHL	37	0	5	5	24	....	....	....	....	....
2002-03	Sioux Falls	USHL	60	13	34	47	88	....	....	....	....	....
2003-04	U. of Minnesota	WCHA	27	2	9	11	10	....	....	....	....	....
2004-05	U. of Minnesota	WCHA	40	4	12	16	33	....	....	....	....	....

USHL First All-Star Team (2003)

VAN OENE, Darren (van OH-uhn, DAIR-rehn)

Left wing. Shoots left. 6'4", 216 lbs. Born, Edmonton, Alta., January 18, 1978.
(Buffalo's 3rd choice, 33rd overall, in 1996 Entry Draft).

			Regular Season					Playoffs				
Season	Club	League	GP	G	A	Pts	PIM	GP	G	A	Pts	PIM
1993-94	Edmonton SSAC	AMHL	34	15	16	31	121	....	....	....	....	....
1994-95	Brandon	WHL	58	5	13	18	106	18	1	1	2	34
1995-96	Brandon	WHL	47	10	18	28	126	18	1	6	7	*78
1996-97	Brandon	WHL	56	21	27	48	139	6	2	3	5	19
1997-98	Brandon	WHL	51	23	24	47	161	18	6	8	14	51
1998-99	Rochester	AHL	73	11	20	31	143	12	2	4	6	8
99-2000	Rochester	AHL	80	20	18	38	153	21	1	3	4	24
2000-01	Rochester	AHL	64	10	12	22	147	4	1	0	1	4
2001-02	Rochester	AHL	52	8	6	14	73	2	0	0	0	4
2002-03	Providence Bruins	AHL	78	11	17	28	109	4	0	0	0	21
2003-04	Providence Bruins	AHL	72	9	16	25	111	2	0	0	0	0
2004-05	Providence Bruins	AHL	4	0	0	0	7	....	....	....	....	....
	Elmira Jackals	UHL	44	9	15	24	38	....	....	....	....	....
	Manchester	AHL	4	0	0	0	10	....	....	....	....	....
	Worcester IceCats	AHL	14	0	0	0	6	....	....	....	....	....

Signed as a free agent by **Boston**, July 29, 2002. Signed as a free agent by **Elmira** (UHL), October 29, 2004. Signed as a free agent by **Manchester** (AHL), February 20, 2005. Signed as a free agent by **Worcester** (AHL), March 2, 2005.

VANTUCH, Lukas (VAHN-tooh, LEW-kahsh) BOS.

Right wing. Shoots left. 6'3", 200 lbs. Born, Jihlava, Czech., July 20, 1987.
(Boston's 7th choice, 172nd overall, in 2005 Entry Draft).

			Regular Season					Playoffs				
Season	Club	League	GP	G	A	Pts	PIM	GP	G	A	Pts	PIM
2002-03	HC Liberec U17	CzR-U17	38	11	12	23	36	....	....	....	....	....
	HC Liberec Jr.	CzRep-Jr.	1	0	0	0	2	....	....	....	....	....
2003-04	HC Liberec U17	CzR-U17	32	16	19	35	75	....	....	....	....	....
	HC Liberec Jr.	CzRep-Jr.	1	0	0	0	0	....	....	....	....	....
2004-05	HC Liberec Jr.	CzRep-Jr.	45	16	20	36	58	5	0	3	3	12

VAS, Janos (VAHSH, YAH-nohsh) DAL.

Left wing. Shoots left. 6'1", 183 lbs. Born, Dunaujvaros, Hungary, January 29, 1984.
(Dallas' 2nd choice, 32nd overall, in 2002 Entry Draft).

			Regular Season					Playoffs				
Season	Club	League	GP	G	A	Pts	PIM	GP	G	A	Pts	PIM
99-2000	Dunaferr SE	Hungary	2	2	0	0	0	....	....	....	....	....
2000-01	Malmo Jr.	Swe-Jr.	23	4	4	8	12	....	....	....	....	....
	Malmo U18	Swe-U18	3	2	0	2	4	....	....	....	....	....
2001-02	Malmo Jr.	Swe-Jr.	36	15	19	34	52	7	8	2	10	4
2002-03	Malmo Jr.	Swe-Jr.	17	5	12	17	14	....	....	....	....	....
	IK Pantern Malmo	Sweden-3	STATISTICS NOT AVAILABLE									
	IF Troja-Ljungby	Sweden-2	17	2	2	4	20	....	....	....	....	....
	Malmo	Sweden	14	1	0	1	2	....	....	....	....	....
2003-04	Malmo U18	Swe-U18	15	5	3	8	14	8	5	2	7	33
	Malmo	Sweden	6	0	0	0	0	....	....	....	....	....
	IK Pantern Malmo	Sweden-3	3	0	2	2	....	....	....	....	....	....
	Malmo	Sweden-Q	1	0	0	0	0	....	....	....	....	....
2004-05	Halmstad	Sweden-2	39	9	8	17	10	2	0	1	1	2

VENALAINEN, Sami (veh-na-LIGH-nehn, SA-mee) PHX.

Right wing. Shoots right. 5'11", 183 lbs. Born, Kangasala, Finland, October 14, 1981.
(Phoenix's 7th choice, 249th overall, in 2000 Entry Draft).

			Regular Season					Playoffs				
Season	Club	League	GP	G	A	Pts	PIM	GP	G	A	Pts	PIM
1997-98	Tappara U18	Fin-U18	33	18	7	25	12	....	....	....	....	....
1998-99	Tappara U18	Fin-U18	31	27	17	44	45	....	....	....	....	....
	Tappara Jr.	Finland-Jr.	10	3	2	5	29	....	....	....	....	....
99-2000	Tappara Jr.	Finland-Jr.	37	8	9	17	18	....	....	....	....	....
2000-01	Tappara Jr.	Finland-Jr.	21	6	13	19	12	9	3	1	4	0
	Tappara Tampere	Finland	36	0	1	1	2	1	0	0	0	0
2001-02	Tappara Tampere	Finland	56	5	8	13	24	10	0	1	1	8
2002-03	Tappara Tampere	Finland	55	5	9	14	48	13	0	0	0	10
2003-04	Tappara Tampere	Finland	56	18	15	33	22	3	1	0	1	0
2004-05	Tappara Tampere	Finland	55	5	6	11	32	8	1	2	3	6

VERNACE, Michael (vuhr-NA-chee, MIGH-kuhl) S.J.

Defense. Shoots left. 6'2", 200 lbs. Born, Toronto, Ont., May 26, 1986.
(San Jose's 6th choice, 201st overall, in 2004 Entry Draft).

			Regular Season					Playoffs				
Season	Club	League	GP	G	A	Pts	PIM	GP	G	A	Pts	PIM
2003-04	Bramalea Blues	OPJHL	33	3	12	15	16	....	....	....	....	....
	Brampton	OHL	2	1	1	2	0	11	2	3	5	8
2004-05	Brampton	OHL	68	12	38	50	42	6	2	2	4	0

OHL All-Rookie Team (2005)

VERSTEEG, Kris (vuhr-STEEG, KRIHS) BOS.

Right wing. Shoots right. 5'10", 172 lbs. Born, Lethbridge, Alta., May 13, 1986.
(Boston's 4th choice, 134th overall, in 2004 Entry Draft).

			Regular Season					Playoffs				
Season	Club	League	GP	G	A	Pts	PIM	GP	G	A	Pts	PIM
2002-03	Lethbridge	WHL	57	8	10	18	32	....	....	....	....	....
2003-04	Lethbridge	WHL	68	16	33	49	85	....	....	....	....	....
2004-05	Lethbridge	WHL	68	22	30	52	68	5	0	1	1	4

VIDELL, Linus (vih-DEHL, LIH-nuhs) COL.

Left wing. Shoots left. 6'3", 214 lbs. Born, Skarpnack, Sweden, May 5, 1985.
(Colorado's 5th choice, 204th overall, in 2003 Entry Draft).

			Regular Season					Playoffs				
Season	Club	League	GP	G	A	Pts	PIM	GP	G	A	Pts	PIM
2001-02	AIK Solna U18	Swe-U18	14	12	5	17	12	4	7	1	8	....
2002-03	Brynas IF Gavle Jr.	Swe-Jr.	19	4	7	11	4	....	....	....	....	....
	Sodertalje SK U18	Swe-U18	1	0	0	0	2	....	....	....	....	....
	Sodertalje SK Jr.	Swe-Jr.	9	4	2	6	0	3	0	1	1	0
2003-04	Sodertalje SK Jr.	Swe-Jr.	27	20	15	35	6	2	0	0	0	0
	Sodertalje SK	Sweden	23	0	2	2	0	....	....	....	....	....
2004-05	Sodertalje SK	Sweden	5	0	0	0	0	....	....	....	....	....
	Halmstad	Sweden-2	27	6	9	15	6	....	....	....	....	....
	Sodertalje SK Jr.	Swe-Jr.	13	6	4	10	0	3	0	2	2	0

VIENNEAU, Justin (vee-EHN-oo, JUHS-tihn) CBJ

Defense. Shoots left. 6'4", 205 lbs. Born, Saint John, N.B., February 20, 1986.
(Columbus' 9th choice, 198th overall, in 2004 Entry Draft).

			Regular Season					Playoffs				
Season	Club	League	GP	G	A	Pts	PIM	GP	G	A	Pts	PIM
2002-03	Shawinigan	QMJHL	62	0	8	8	150	9	0	1	1	10
2003-04	Shawinigan	QMJHL	53	0	7	7	129	11	0	1	1	19
2004-05	Shawinigan	QMJHL	60	4	11	15	146	4	0	0	0	6

VIHKO, Joonas (VIH-koh, YOO-nuhs) ANA.

Center. Shoots right. 5'9", 172 lbs. Born, Helsinki, Finland, April 6, 1981.
(Anaheim's 4th choice, 103rd overall, in 2002 Entry Draft).

			Regular Season					Playoffs				
Season	Club	League	GP	G	A	Pts	PIM	GP	G	A	Pts	PIM
1998-99	HIFK Helsinki Jr.	Finland-Jr.	32	15	14	29	10	3	1	1	2	0
99-2000	HIFK Helsinki Jr.	Finland-Jr.	38	12	15	27	36	3	0	0	0	0
2000-01	HIFK Helsinki Jr.	Finland-Jr.	27	23	17	40	85	7	5	2	7	18
	HIFK Helsinki	Finland	3	0	0	0	2	....	....	....	....	....
2001-02	HIFK Helsinki	Finland	48	13	11	24	89	....	....	....	....	....
	HIFK Helsinki Jr.	Finland-Jr.	....	....	....	....	....	2	0	2	2	4
2002-03	HIFK Helsinki	Finland	50	14	11	25	20	1	0	0	0	2
2003-04	HIFK Helsinki	Finland	52	9	8	17	56	13	3	5	8	6
2004-05	HIFK Helsinki	Finland	51	5	11	16	24	4	0	0	0	2

VIITANEN, Mikko (vee-EE-tan-ehn, MEE-koh) COL.

Defense. Shoots left. 6'3", 220 lbs. Born, Rajamaki, Finland, February 18, 1982.
(Colorado's 6th choice, 149th overall, in 2001 Entry Draft).

			Regular Season					Playoffs				
Season	Club	League	GP	G	A	Pts	PIM	GP	G	A	Pts	PIM
1998-99	HPK U18	Fin-U18	36	3	6	9	40	....	....	....	....	....
	HPK Jr.	Finland-Jr.	1	0	0	0	0	....	....	....	....	....
99-2000	Chicago Freeze	NAHL	53	4	6	10	126	....	....	....	....	....
2000-01	Ahmat Jr.	Finland-Jr.	9	3	4	7	41	....	....	....	....	....
	Ahmat Hyvinkaa	Finland-2	41	3	9	12	66	3	0	0	0	0
2001-02	Blues Espoo Jr.	Finland-Jr.	10	1	3	4	16	....	....	....	....	....
	Blues Espoo	Finland	3	0	0	0	6	....	....	....	....	....
	Jukurit Mikkeli	Finland-2	21	0	3	3	26	....	....	....	....	....
2002-03	KJT Jarvenpaa	Finland-2	9	0	1	1	56	....	....	....	....	....
	Blues Espoo	Finland	1	0	0	0	0	....	....	....	....	....
2003-04	Hershey Bears	AHL	20	1	1	2	14	....	....	....	....	....
	Reading Royals	ECHL	47	0	4	4	21	13	0	1	1	8
2004-05	Hershey Bears	AHL	22	0	1	1	6	....	....	....	....	....
	Reading Royals	ECHL	52	3	3	6	47	8	0	0	0	8

VIKINGSTAD, Tore (VIH-kihng-stahd, TOO-reh) ST.L.

Left wing. Shoots left. 6'4", 204 lbs. Born, Stavenger, Norway, October 8, 1975.
(St. Louis' 5th choice, 180th overall, in 1999 Entry Draft).

			Regular Season					Playoffs				
Season	Club	League	GP	G	A	Pts	PIM	GP	G	A	Pts	PIM
1993-94	Viking	Norway	2	0	0	0	0	....	....	....	....	....
1994-95	Viking	Norway	28	5	3	8	8	4	1	2	3	2
1995-96	Viking	Norway	27	12	11	23	....	....	....	....	....	....
1996-97	Stjernen	Norway	42	23	35	58	20	....	....	....	....	....
1997-98	Stjernen	Norway	42	26	31	57	18	....	....	....	....	....
1998-99	Farjestad	Sweden	49	9	11	20	18	4	2	3	5	0
	Farjestad	EuroHL	6	1	1	2	10	....	....	....	....	....
99-2000	Farjestad	Sweden	47	8	19	27	26	7	3	0	3	6
2000-01	Leksands IF	Sweden	41	10	15	25	24	....	....	....	....	....
	Leksands IF	Sweden-Q	9	3	3	6	16	....	....	....	....	....
2001-02	Dusseldorf	Germany	58	18	30	48	6	....	....	....	....	....
2002-03	Dusseldorf	Germany	45	13	18	31	40	5	1	0	1	0
2003-04	Dusseldorf	Germany	50	9	21	30	38	4	1	2	3	2
2004-05	Dusseldorf	Germany	28	11	14	25	16	....	....	....	....	....

VISHNYAKOV, Albert (vihsh-nyeh-KAWF, al-BAIRT) T.B.

Wing. Shoots right. 6'1", 178 lbs. Born, Almyetevsk, USSR, December 30, 1983.
(Tampa Bay's 9th choice, 273rd overall, in 2003 Entry Draft).

			Regular Season					Playoffs				
Season	Club	League	GP	G	A	Pts	PIM	GP	G	A	Pts	PIM
99-2000	Almetjevsk 2	Russia-3	41	11	5	16	68	....	....	....	....	....
2000-01	Almetjevsk	Russia-2	29	0	0	0	2	....	....	....	....	....
2001-02	Ak Bars Kazan	Russia	9	0	1	1	2	....	....	....	....	....
	Nizhny Novgorod	Russia	6	1	0	1	0	....	....	....	....	....
	Nizh. Novgorod 2	Russia-3	4	2	2	4	10	....	....	....	....	....
2002-03	Ak Bars Kazan	Russia	47	7	6	13	47	5	1	0	1	0
2003-04	Nizhnekamsk	Russia	10	2	3	5	10	....	....	....	....	....
	Ak Bars Kazan 2	Russia-3	STATISTICS NOT AVAILABLE									
	Ak Bars Kazan	Russia	10	1	1	2	8	....	....	....	....	....
2004-05	Dynamo Moscow	Russia	28	1	2	3	10	....	....	....	....	....

VITALE, Joe (vih-TA-lee, JOH) PIT.

Center. Shoots right. 5'11", 205 lbs. Born, St. Louis, MO, August 20, 1985.
(Pittsburgh's 7th choice, 195th overall, in 2005 Entry Draft).

			Regular Season					Playoffs				
Season	Club	League	GP	G	A	Pts	PIM	GP	G	A	Pts	PIM
2003-04	St. Louis Jr. Blues	CSJHL	43	21	29	50	42	....	....	....	....	....
2004-05	Sioux Falls	USHL	53	11	20	31	62	....	....	....	....	....

Signed Letter of Intent to attend **Northeastern** (H-East), June 27, 2005.

VIUHKOLA, Jari (VEW-koh-lak, YA-ree) **CHI.**

Center. Shoots left. 6', 165 lbs. Born, Oulu, Finland, February 27, 1980.
(Chicago's 4th choice, 158th overall, in 1998 Entry Draft).

			Regular Season					Playoffs				
Season	**Club**	**League**	**GP**	**G**	**A**	**Pts**	**PIM**	**GP**	**G**	**A**	**Pts**	**PIM**
1995-96	Karpat Oulu U18	Fin-U18	11	8	8	16	20	....	....	....	....	....
	Karpat Oulu Jr.	Finland-Jr.	7	2	1	3	4	....	....	....	....	....
1996-97	Karpat Oulu Jr.	Finland-Jr.	32	8	11	19	74	....	....	....	....	....
1997-98	Karpat Oulu Jr.	Finland-Jr.	28	8	18	26	57	....	....	....	....	....
1998-99	Karpat Oulu Jr.	Finland-Jr.	21	8	14	22	6	....	....	....	....	....
	Karpat Oulu	Finland-2	14	5	5	10	6	....	....	....	....	....
99-2000	Karpat Oulu	Finland-2	21	8	14	22	16	9	4	10	14	6
	Karpat Oulu Jr.	Finland-Jr.	5	4	7	11	0	....	....	....	....	....
2000-01	Karpat Oulu	Finland	54	5	8	13	32	9	0	1	1	6
2001-02	Karpat Oulu	Finland	46	8	14	22	24	4	1	0	1	6
2002-03	Karpat Oulu	Finland	49	15	17	32	56	15	4	8	12	10
2003-04	Karpat Oulu	Finland	53	25	31	56	34	14	3	5	8	4
2004-05	Karpat Oulu	Finland	44	15	16	31	30	12	5	*10	*15	6

VLASIC, Marc-Edouard (vih-LASH-ihc, MAHRK-EHD-wahrd) **S.J.**

Defense. Shoots left. 6'1", 190 lbs. Born, Montreal, Que., March 30, 1987.
(San Jose's 2nd choice, 35th overall, in 2005 Entry Draft).

			Regular Season					Playoffs				
Season	**Club**	**League**	**GP**	**G**	**A**	**Pts**	**PIM**	**GP**	**G**	**A**	**Pts**	**PIM**
2003-04	Quebec Remparts	QMJHL	41	1	9	10	4	5	0	1	1	0
2004-05	Quebec Remparts	QMJHL	70	5	25	30	33	13	2	7	9	2

VLCEK, Ladislav (vuhl-CHEHK, LA-dih-slahv) **DAL.**

Right wing. Shoots left. 5'11", 184 lbs. Born, Kladno, Czech., September 26, 1981.
(Dallas' 8th choice, 192nd overall, in 2000 Entry Draft).

			Regular Season					Playoffs				
Season	**Club**	**League**	**GP**	**G**	**A**	**Pts**	**PIM**	**GP**	**G**	**A**	**Pts**	**PIM**
1998-99	HC Kladno Jr.	CzRep-Jr.	46	13	27	40	....	....	....	....	....	....
	HC Velvana Kladno	CzRep	4	0	1	1	0	....	....	....	....	....
99-2000	HC Kladno Jr.	CzRep-Jr.	34	16	15	31	16	....	....	....	....	....
	HC CKD Slany	CzRep-3	4	3	0	3	0	....	....	....	....	....
	Kralupy	CzRep-3	1	0	1	1	0	5	2	2	4	4
	HC Velvana Kladno	CzRep	21	3	2	5	4	....	....	....	....	....
2000-01	Kladno	CzRep	45	6	10	16	22	....	....	....	....	....
2001-02	Kladno	CzRep	20	3	1	4	14	....	....	....	....	....
	HC Ocelari Trinec	CzRep	28	3	6	9	18	6	1	0	1	2
2002-03	HC Hame Zlin	CzRep	13	2	1	3	0	....	....	....	....	....
	Karlovy Vary	CzRep	12	1	0	1	2	....	....	....	....	....
	Beroun	CzRep-2	18	3	5	8	14	....	....	....	....	....
2003-04	IHC Pisek	CzRep-2	5	1	0	1	0	....	....	....	....	....
	HC Rabat Kladno	CzRep	9	1	1	2	2	....	....	....	....	....
	KLH Chomutov	CzRep-2	7	2	0	2	0	2	0	0	0	0
2004-05	Usti n. L.	CzRep-2	8	0	1	1	6	....	....	....	....	....
	HC Olomouc	CzRep-2	30	3	8	11	18	....	....	....	....	....

VOCE, Tony (VOHS, TOH-nee) **PHI.**

Center. Shoots left. 5'8", 185 lbs. Born, Philadelphia, PA, October 30, 1980.

			Regular Season					Playoffs				
Season	**Club**	**League**	**GP**	**G**	**A**	**Pts**	**PIM**	**GP**	**G**	**A**	**Pts**	**PIM**
1998-99	Lawrence	High-MA	....	39	30	*69	....	....	....	....	....	....
99-2000	Lawrence	High-MA	....	26	33	*59	....	....	....	....	....	....
2000-01	Boston College	H-East	42	12	14	26	40	....	....	....	....	....
2001-02	Boston College	H-East	38	26	22	48	65	....	....	....	....	....
2002-03	Boston College	H-East	37	*23	23	46	56	....	....	....	....	....
2003-04	Boston College	H-East	42	*29	18	47	48	....	....	....	....	....
2004-05	Philadelphia	AHL	73	22	17	39	85	4	0	0	0	4

Hockey East First All-Star Team (2002, 2004) • NCAA East First All-American Team (2004)

Signed as a free agent by **Philadelphia**, July 13, 2004.

VOJTA, Jakub (VOI-tah, YA-kuhb) **CAR.**

Defense. Shoots right. 6', 194 lbs. Born, Usti nad Labem, Czech., February 8, 1987.
(Carolina's 4th choice, 94th overall, in 2005 Entry Draft).

			Regular Season					Playoffs				
Season	**Club**	**League**	**GP**	**G**	**A**	**Pts**	**PIM**	**GP**	**G**	**A**	**Pts**	**PIM**
2002-03	Sparta U17	CzR-U17	47	14	24	38	87	1	0	0	0	12
2003-04	Sparta U17	CzR-U17	4	0	2	2	0	3	1	2	3	2
	Sparta Jr.	CzRep-Jr.	39	3	3	6	20	....	....	....	....	....
2004-05	Sparta Jr.	CzRep-Jr.	38	2	7	9	42	8	1	1	2	8

VOLKOV, Igor (VOHL-kawf, EE-gohr) **NYI**

Right wing. Shoots left. 6', 189 lbs. Born, Ufa, USSR, January 24, 1983.
(NY Islanders' 9th choice, 246th overall, in 2003 Entry Draft).

			Regular Season					Playoffs				
Season	**Club**	**League**	**GP**	**G**	**A**	**Pts**	**PIM**	**GP**	**G**	**A**	**Pts**	**PIM**
2000-01	Ufa	Russia	30	1	1	2	4	....	....	....	....	....
2001-02	Ufa	Russia	43	3	1	4	8	....	....	....	....	....
2002-03	Ufa	Russia	41	9	5	14	32	3	1	0	1	4
2003-04	Ufa	Russia	45	11	13	24	38	....	....	....	....	....
2004-05	Ufa	Russia	43	15	12	27	38	....	....	....	....	....
	Dynamo Moscow	Russia	10	0	1	1	0	4	1	0	1	0

VOLKOV, Konstantin (VOHL-kawf, kawn-stuhn-TIHN) **TOR.**

Right wing. Shoots left. 6', 174 lbs. Born, Kolpino, USSR, February 7, 1985.
(Toronto's 3rd choice, 125th overall, in 2003 Entry Draft).

			Regular Season					Playoffs				
Season	**Club**	**League**	**GP**	**G**	**A**	**Pts**	**PIM**	**GP**	**G**	**A**	**Pts**	**PIM**
2000-01	SKA St. Petersburg	Russia	2	0	1	1	0	....	....	....	....	....
2001-02	Dyn'o Moscow 2	Russia-3	21	3	7	10	10	....	....	....	....	....
2002-03	Dyn'o Moscow 2	Russia-3	29	13	17	30	2	....	....	....	....	....
2003-04	THK Tver	Russia-2	18	0	6	6	6	....	....	....	....	....
	CSK VVS Samara	Russia-2	22	6	6	12	16	....	....	....	....	....
	Lada Togliatti 2	Russia-3	10	2	7	9	10	11	0	10	10	4
2004-05	Lada Togliatti	Russia	1	0	0	0	0	....	....	....	....	....

VOLOSHENKO, Roman (voh-loh-SHEHN-koh, ROH-muhn) **MIN.**

Left wing. Shoots right. 6'1", 200 lbs. Born, Brest, USSR, May 12, 1986.
(Minnesota's 2nd choice, 42nd overall, in 2004 Entry Draft).

			Regular Season					Playoffs				
Season	**Club**	**League**	**GP**	**G**	**A**	**Pts**	**PIM**	**GP**	**G**	**A**	**Pts**	**PIM**
2001-02	Krylja Sovetov 2	Russia-3	8	2	3	5	0	....	....	....	....	....
2002-03	Krylja Sovetov	Russia	5	0	1	1	2	....	....	....	....	....
	Krylja Sovetov 2	Russia-3	6	3	1	4	2	....	....	....	....	....
2003-04	Krylja Sovetov	Russia-2	46	7	8	15	40	4	1	1	2	4
2004-05	Krylja Sovetov 2	Russia-3	1	0	0	0	2	....	....	....	....	....
	Krylja Sovetov	Russia-2	38	16	13	29	22	3	0	1	1	2

VOMELA, Lukas (voh-MEH-luh, LOO-kahsh) **DAL.**

Defense. Shoots left. 6'3", 189 lbs. Born, Ceske Budejovice, Czech., September 25, 1985.
(Dallas' 9th choice, 248th overall, in 2004 Entry Draft).

			Regular Season					Playoffs				
Season	**Club**	**League**	**GP**	**G**	**A**	**Pts**	**PIM**	**GP**	**G**	**A**	**Pts**	**PIM**
2000-01	C. Budejovice U17	CzR-U17	39	1	1	2	8	....	....	....	....	....
2001-02	C. Budejovice U17	CzR-U17	47	9	9	18	87	....	....	....	....	....
	C. Budejovice Jr.	CzRep-Jr.	1	0	0	0	0	....	....	....	....	....
2002-03	C. Budejovice Jr.	CzRep-Jr.	36	2	2	4	24	....	....	....	....	....
	C. Budejovice	CzRep	1	0	0	0	4	....	....	....	....	....
2003-04	C. Budejovice	CzRep	15	0	1	1	8	....	....	....	....	....
	C. Budejovice Jr.	CzRep-Jr.	21	1	7	8	45	....	....	....	....	....
2004-05	C. Budejovice	CzRep-2	2	0	0	0	0	....	....	....	....	....
	Jind. Hradec	CzRep-3	5	0	3	3	0	....	....	....	....	....
	C. Budejovice Jr.	CzRep-Jr.	30	3	10	13	68	2	0	1	1	4

VONDRKA, Michal (VOHND-rah-ka, MEE-khahl) **BUF.**

Left wing. Shoots right. 6', 178 lbs. Born, Ceske Budejovice, Czech., May 17, 1983.
(Buffalo's 5th choice, 155th overall, in 2001 Entry Draft).

			Regular Season					Playoffs				
Season	**Club**	**League**	**GP**	**G**	**A**	**Pts**	**PIM**	**GP**	**G**	**A**	**Pts**	**PIM**
1998-99	C. Budejovice U17	CzR-U17	50	28	15	43	....	....	....	....	....	....
99-2000	C. Budejovice Jr.	CzRep-Jr.	31	12	7	19	16	....	....	....	....	....
2000-01	C. Budejovice Jr.	CzRep-Jr.	37	9	14	23	37	....	....	....	....	....
	C. Budejovice	CzRep	8	1	0	1	2	....	....	....	....	....
	Jind. Hradec	CzRep-3	1	0	1	1	2	....	....	....	....	....
2001-02	C. Budejovice Jr.	CzRep-Jr.	14	3	9	12	8	....	....	....	....	....
	IHC Pisek	CzRep-2	2	1	0	1	0	....	....	....	....	....
	C. Budejovice	CzRep	33	1	1	2	2	....	....	....	....	....
2002-03	C. Budejovice	CzRep	27	1	3	4	4	3	0	0	0	0
	C. Budejovice Jr.	CzRep-Jr.	7	4	1	5	4	....	....	....	....	....
	IHC Pisek	CzRep-2	20	4	2	6	39	3	1	0	1	0
2003-04	C. Budejovice	CzRep	8	1	0	1	0	....	....	....	....	....
	HC Slavia Praha	CzRep	37	6	7	13	8	19	2	1	3	4
2004-05	BK Mlada Boleslav	CzRep-2	4	0	0	0	2	....	....	....	....	....
	Hr. Kralove	CzRep-2	5	0	1	1	2	....	....	....	....	....
	HC Slavia Praha	CzRep	25	5	1	6	12	5	0	0	0	2

VOROBIEV, Dmitri (voh-roh-BEE-ehf, dih-MEE-tree) **TOR.**

Defense. Shoots left. 6'1", 211 lbs. Born, Togliatti, USSR, October 18, 1985.
(Toronto's 3rd choice, 157th overall, in 2004 Entry Draft).

			Regular Season					Playoffs				
Season	**Club**	**League**	**GP**	**G**	**A**	**Pts**	**PIM**	**GP**	**G**	**A**	**Pts**	**PIM**
2002-03	Lada Togliatti 2	Russia-3	31	3	5	8	12	....	....	....	....	....
2003-04	Lada Togliatti 2	Russia-3	10	1	1	2	4	....	....	....	....	....
	Lada Togliatti	Russia	23	1	0	1	12	4	0	0	0	4
2004-05	Lada Togliatti	Russia	53	2	6	8	30	10	0	0	0	8

VOROS, Aaron (VOH-ruhs, AIR-uhn) **N.J.**

Center. Shoots left. 6'4", 190 lbs. Born, Vancouver, B.C., July 2, 1981.
(New Jersey's 10th choice, 229th overall, in 2001 Entry Draft).

			Regular Season					Playoffs				
Season	**Club**	**League**	**GP**	**G**	**A**	**Pts**	**PIM**	**GP**	**G**	**A**	**Pts**	**PIM**
99-2000	Victoria Salsa	BCHL	58	14	21	35	285	....	....	....	....	....
2000-01	Victoria Salsa	BCHL	57	34	34	68	196	30	16	15	31	....
2001-02	Alaska-Fairbanks	CCHA	37	18	12	30	*101	....	....	....	....	....
2002-03	Alaska-Fairbanks	CCHA	16	2	5	7	42	....	....	....	....	....
2003-04	Alaska-Fairbanks	CCHA	36	16	8	24	*132	....	....	....	....	....
	Albany River Rats	AHL	9	2	1	3	14	....	....	....	....	....
2004-05	Albany River Rats	AHL	71	11	17	28	220	....	....	....	....	....

CCHA All-Rookie Team (2002)

• Missed majority of 2002-03 season recovering from leg surgery, January 30, 2003.

VOROSHNIN, Pavel (vo-rohsh-NIHN, PAH-vehl) **BUF.**

Defense. Shoots left. 6'3", 175 lbs. Born, Chelyabinsk, USSR, March 23, 1984.
(Buffalo's 7th choice, 172nd overall, in 2003 Entry Draft).

			Regular Season					Playoffs				
Season	**Club**	**League**	**GP**	**G**	**A**	**Pts**	**PIM**	**GP**	**G**	**A**	**Pts**	**PIM**
2001-02	Chelyabinsk	Russia-2	32	0	2	2	10	....	....	....	....	....
2002-03	Mississauga	OHL	68	9	27	36	81	1	0	0	0	2
2003-04	Mississauga	OHL	18	0	4	4	6	....	....	....	....	....
	Owen Sound	OHL	40	3	18	21	36	7	0	2	2	4
2004-05	Metallurg Serov	Russia-2	34	0	1	1	12	....	....	....	....	....

VOSTRIKOV, Artem (VAWS-trih-kawv, ahr-TEHM) **CBJ**

Center. Shoots left. 6'1", 175 lbs. Born, Togliatti, USSR, March 23, 1983.
(Columbus' 8th choice, 187th overall, in 2001 Entry Draft).

			Regular Season					Playoffs				
Season	**Club**	**League**	**GP**	**G**	**A**	**Pts**	**PIM**	**GP**	**G**	**A**	**Pts**	**PIM**
99-2000	Lada Togliatti 2	Russia-3	26	2	1	3	4	....	....	....	....	....
2000-01	Lada Togliatti 2	Russia-3	3	1	0	1	2	1	0	0	0	0
2001-02	Lada Togliatti	Russia	12	1	1	2	0	....	....	....	....	....
	CSK VVS Samara	Russia-2	17	1	4	5	36	6	0	0	0	4
2002-03	Spartak Moscow	Russia	20	2	3	5	0	....	....	....	....	....
2003-04	Krylja Sovetov	Russia-2	49	10	15	25	64	4	1	1	2	4
2004-05	Krylja Sovetov 2	Russia-3	1	1	0	1	0	....	....	....	....	....
	Krylja Sovetov	Russia-2	43	9	14	23	20	3	0	0	0	2

VRANA, Petr (vuh-RA-nuh, PEE-tuhr) N.J.

Center. Shoots left. 5'10", 175 lbs. Born, Sternberk, Czech., March 29, 1985.
(New Jersey's 2nd choice, 42nd overall, in 2003 Entry Draft).

			Regular Season					Playoffs				
Season	Club	League	GP	G	A	Pts	PIM	GP	G	A	Pts	PIM
2001-02	HC Havirov Jr.	CzRep-Jr.	38	11	12	23	....	....	....	....	....	....
	HC Femax Havirov	CzRep	6	0	0	0	4	....	....	....	....	....
2002-03	Halifax	QMJHL	72	37	46	83	32	24	5	15	20	12
2003-04	Halifax	QMJHL	48	13	25	38	56	....	....	....	....	....
2004-05	Halifax	QMJHL	60	16	35	51	77	12	10	4	14	12

QMJHL All-Rookie Team (2003) • QMJHL Rookie of the Year (2003)

VYDARENY, Rene (vih-DAH-reh-nay, REH-nay) MTL.

Defense. Shoots left. 6'1", 198 lbs. Born, Bratislava, Czech., May 6, 1981.
(Vancouver's 3rd choice, 69th overall, in 1999 Entry Draft).

			Regular Season					Playoffs				
Season	Club	League	GP	G	A	Pts	PIM	GP	G	A	Pts	PIM
1997-98	Bratislava Jr.	Slovak-Jr.	50	5	14	19	26	....	....	....	....	....
1998-99	Bratislava Jr.	Slovak-Jr.	42	4	7	11	65	2	0	0	0	2
	HC Trnava	Slovak-2	20	1	6	7	6	....	....	....	....	....
99-2000	Rimouski Oceanic	QMJHL	51	7	23	30	41	14	2	2	4	20
2000-01	Kansas City Blades	IHL	39	0	1	1	25	....	....	....	....	....
2001-02	Manitoba Moose	AHL	61	3	11	14	15	7	0	2	2	4
	Columbia Inferno	ECHL	10	2	1	3	9	....	....	....	....	....
2002-03	Manitoba Moose	AHL	71	2	8	10	46	14	0	2	2	16
2003-04	Manitoba Moose	AHL	50	2	10	12	16	....	....	....	....	....
	Hamilton Bulldogs	AHL	13	0	3	3	2	10	0	1	1	9
2004-05	Bratislava	Slovakia	33	0	4	4	22	19	1	4	5	24

• Missed majority of 2000-01 season due to dispute over ownership of playing rights between **Vancouver** and **Bratislava** (Slovakia), November 28, 2000. Traded to **Montreal** by **Vancouver** for Sylvain Blouin, March 9, 2004. Signed as a free agent by **Bratislava** (Slovakia), November 13, 2004.

WALLIN, Viktor (WAHL-in, VIHK-tohr) ANA.

Defense. Shoots left. 6'3", 200 lbs. Born, Jonkoping, Sweden, January 17, 1980.
(Anaheim's 3rd choice, 112th overall, in 1998 Entry Draft).

			Regular Season					Playoffs				
Season	Club	League	GP	G	A	Pts	PIM	GP	G	A	Pts	PIM
1996-97	HV 71 Jr.	Swe-Jr.	16	1	2	3	....	....	....	....	....	....
1997-98	HV 71 Jr.	Swe-Jr.	28	9	15	24	42	....	....	....	....	....
1998-99	HV 71 Jonkoping	Sweden	23	0	0	0	4	....	....	....	....	....
99-2000	HV 71 Jr.	Swe-Jr.	6	3	1	4	2	....	....	....	....	....
	HV 71 Jonkoping	Sweden	43	2	2	4	16	6	1	1	2	4
2000-01	HV 71 Jonkoping	Sweden	5	0	1	1	2	....	....	....	....	....
2001-02	Timra IK	Sweden	35	0	3	3	18	....	....	....	....	....
	Timra IK	Sweden-Q	10	0	1	1	9	....	....	....	....	....
2002-03	AIK Solna	Sweden-2	50	3	15	18	34	4	0	0	0	4
2003-04	AIK Solna	Sweden-2	46	7	14	21	32	5	1	1	2	2
2004-05	Nybro Vikings IF	Sweden-2	41	2	10	12	34	....	....	....	....	....

WALSH, Brendan (WAHLSH, BREHN-duhn)

Right wing. Shoots right. 5'9", 181 lbs. Born, Dorchester, MA, October 22, 1974.

			Regular Season					Playoffs				
Season	Club	League	GP	G	A	Pts	PIM	GP	G	A	Pts	PIM
1993-94	Omaha Lancers	USHL	31	9	20	29	187	....	....	....	....	....
1994-95	Omaha Lancers	USHL	56	20	36	56	198	....	....	....	....	....
1995-96	Boston University	H-East	38	8	16	24	90	....	....	....	....	....
1996-97	Boston University	H-East	27	5	8	13	83	....	....	....	....	....
1997-98	U. of Maine	H-East	DID NOT PLAY – TRANSFERRED COLLEGES									
1998-99	U. of Maine	H-East	30	7	13	20	58	....	....	....	....	....
99-2000	U. of Maine	H-East	39	9	21	30	*106	....	....	....	....	....
2000-01	Cleveland	IHL	10	1	1	2	45	4	0	0	0	11
	Jackson Bandits	ECHL	25	3	6	9	179	....	....	....	....	....
2001-02	Wilkes-Barre	AHL	29	2	2	4	184	....	....	....	....	....
	Wheeling Nailers	ECHL	29	7	15	22	168	....	....	....	....	....
2002-03	San Antonio	AHL	48	2	5	7	202	3	0	1	1	0
	Atlantic City	ECHL	6	0	2	2	40	....	....	....	....	....
2003-04	Providence Bruins	AHL	52	10	7	17	281	2	0	0	0	14
2004-05	Providence Bruins	AHL	45	1	4	5	274	....	....	....	....	....

Signed as a free agent by **Minnesota**, May 18, 2000. Signed as a free agent by **Providence** (AHL), August 12, 2003.

WALSH, Mike (WAHLSH, MIGHK) NYR

Left wing. Shoots left. 6'2", 220 lbs. Born, Royal Oak, MI, March 4, 1983.
(NY Rangers' 4th choice, 143rd overall, in 2002 Entry Draft).

			Regular Season					Playoffs				
Season	Club	League	GP	G	A	Pts	PIM	GP	G	A	Pts	PIM
2000-01	Det. Compuware	NAHL	50	10	12	22	59	3	1	0	1	4
2001-02	Det. Compuware	NAHL	53	25	25	49	69	6	4	2	6	8
2002-03	U. of Notre Dame	CCHA	23	1	1	2	14	....	....	....	....	....
2003-04	U. of Notre Dame	CCHA	39	12	13	25	46	....	....	....	....	....
2004-05	U. of Notre Dame	CCHA	36	2	8	10	47	....	....	....	....	....

WALSH, Tom (WAHLSH, TAWM) S.J.

Defense. Shoots left. 6', 190 lbs. Born, Arlington, MA, April 22, 1983.
(San Jose's 5th choice, 163rd overall, in 2002 Entry Draft).

			Regular Season					Playoffs				
Season	Club	League	GP	G	A	Pts	PIM	GP	G	A	Pts	PIM
2000-01	Deerfield Academy	High-MA	23	10	26	36	25	....	....	....	....	....
2001-02	Deerfield Academy	High-MA	21	3	18	21	8	....	....	....	....	....
2002-03	Harvard Crimson	ECAC	32	1	6	7	30	....	....	....	....	....
2003-04	Harvard Crimson	ECAC	24	1	4	5	24	....	....	....	....	....
2004-05	Harvard Crimson	ECAC	34	3	9	12	16	....	....	....	....	....

WALTER, Ben (WAHL-tuhr, BEHN) BOS.

Center. Shoots left. 6'1", 195 lbs. Born, Beaconsfield, Que., May 11, 1984.
(Boston's 5th choice, 160th overall, in 2004 Entry Draft).

			Regular Season					Playoffs				
Season	Club	League	GP	G	A	Pts	PIM	GP	G	A	Pts	PIM
2000-01	Langley Hornets	BCHL	50	8	22	30	19	....	....	....	....	....
2001-02	Langley Hornets	BCHL	50	29	47	76	29	....	....	....	....	....
2002-03	U. Mass-Lowell	H-East	35	5	12	17	12	....	....	....	....	....
2003-04	U. Mass-Lowell	H-East	36	18	16	34	18	....	....	....	....	....
2004-05	U. Mass-Lowell	H-East	36	*26	13	39	28	....	....	....	....	....

Hockey East Second All-Star Team (2005)

WANDELL, Tom (VAHN-dehl, TAWM) DAL.

Center. Shoots left. 6'1", 183 lbs. Born, Sodertalje, Sweden, January 29, 1987.
(Dallas' 5th choice, 146th overall, in 2005 Entry Draft).

			Regular Season					Playoffs				
Season	Club	League	GP	G	A	Pts	PIM	GP	G	A	Pts	PIM
2002-03	Sodertalje SK U18	Swe-U18	13	8	7	15	6	....	....	....	....	....
2003-04	Sodertalje SK U18	Swe-U18	6	5	7	12	6	2	0	0	0	0
	Sodertalje SK Jr.	Swe-Jr.	33	7	15	22	14	2	0	0	0	0
2004-05	Sodertalje SK Jr.	Swe-Jr.	5	1	2	3	4	....	....	....	....	....

WATHIER, Francis (waw-TEE-ay, FRAN-sihs) DAL.

Left wing. Shoots left. 6'3", 198 lbs. Born, St Isidore, Ont., December 7, 1984.
(Dallas' 8th choice, 185th overall, in 2003 Entry Draft).

			Regular Season					Playoffs				
Season	Club	League	GP	G	A	Pts	PIM	GP	G	A	Pts	PIM
2001-02	Hull Olympiques	QMJHL	63	1	3	4	68	12	1	2	3	30
2002-03	Hull Olympiques	QMJHL	72	9	18	27	143	20	1	6	7	20
2003-04	Gatineau	QMJHL	51	9	16	25	127	15	0	2	2	23
2004-05	Gatineau	QMJHL	67	15	20	35	96	10	0	2	2	8

WATKINS, Matt (WAHT-kihns, MAT) DAL.

Right wing. Shoots left. 5'10", 180 lbs. Born, Regina, Sask., November 22, 1986.
(Dallas' 6th choice, 160th overall, in 2005 Entry Draft).

			Regular Season					Playoffs				
Season	Club	League	GP	G	A	Pts	PIM	GP	G	A	Pts	PIM
2003-04	Tisdale Trojans	SMHL	44	34	37	71	52	....	....	....	....	....
2004-05	Vernon Vipers	BCHL	60	36	38	74	53	....	....	....	....	....

Signed Letter of Intent to attend **North Dakota** (WCHA), November 19, 2004.

WATSON, Greg (WAWT-suhn, GREHG) OTT.

Center. Shoots left. 6', 205 lbs. Born, Eastend, Sask., March 2, 1983.
(Florida's 3rd choice, 34th overall, in 2001 Entry Draft).

			Regular Season					Playoffs				
Season	Club	League	GP	G	A	Pts	PIM	GP	G	A	Pts	PIM
1998-99	Calgary Buffaloes	AMHL	71	23	23	46	120	....	....	....	....	....
	Prince Albert	WHL	2	0	0	0	5	....	....	....	....	....
99-2000	Prince Albert	WHL	67	10	5	15	63	6	0	2	2	2
2000-01	Prince Albert	WHL	71	22	28	50	72	....	....	....	....	....
2001-02	Prince Albert	WHL	51	22	30	52	88	....	....	....	....	....
2002-03	Prince Albert	WHL	39	11	15	26	58	....	....	....	....	....
	Brandon	WHL	30	6	14	20	37	17	3	8	11	12
2003-04	Binghamton	AHL	69	4	7	11	72	2	0	0	0	2
2004-05	Binghamton	AHL	57	3	4	7	68	1	0	0	0	0

Traded to **Ottawa** by **Florida** with Billy Thompson for Jani Hurme, October 1, 2002.

WATT, J.D. (WHAT , JAY-DEE) CGY.

Right wing. Shoots right. 6'1", 206 lbs. Born, Calgary, Alta., May 25, 1987.
(Calgary's 4th choice, 111th overall, in 2005 Entry Draft).

			Regular Season					Playoffs				
Season	Club	League	GP	G	A	Pts	PIM	GP	G	A	Pts	PIM
2003-04	Drumheller	AJHL	59	20	17	37	245	....	....	....	....	....
	Vancouver Giants	WHL	3	1	0	1	0	10	0	3	3	14
2004-05	Vancouver Giants	WHL	66	6	7	13	213	....	....	....	....	....

WAUGH, Geoff (WAW, JEHF) DAL.

Defense. Shoots right. 6'3", 210 lbs. Born, Winnipeg, Man., August 25, 1983.
(Dallas' 6th choice, 78th overall, in 2002 Entry Draft).

			Regular Season					Playoffs				
Season	Club	League	GP	G	A	Pts	PIM	GP	G	A	Pts	PIM
2000-01	Kindersley Klippers	SJHL	57	2	5	7	74	....	....	....	....	....
2001-02	Kindersley Klippers	SJHL	59	4	21	25	125	18	0	8	8	59
2002-03	Northern Mich.	CCHA	39	0	7	7	41	....	....	....	....	....
2003-04	Northern Mich.	CCHA	41	2	13	15	72	....	....	....	....	....
2004-05	Northern Mich.	CCHA	39	2	8	10	89	....	....	....	....	....

WEBER, Shea (WEH-buhr, SHAY) NSH.

Defense. Shoots right. 6'3", 213 lbs. Born, Sicamous, B.C., August 14, 1985.
(Nashville's 4th choice, 49th overall, in 2003 Entry Draft).

			Regular Season					Playoffs				
Season	Club	League	GP	G	A	Pts	PIM	GP	G	A	Pts	PIM
2001-02	Sicamous Eagles	KIJHL	47	9	33	42	87	....	....	....	....	....
	Kelowna Rockets	WHL	5	0	0	0	0	....	....	....	....	....
2002-03	Kelowna Rockets	WHL	70	2	16	18	167	19	1	4	5	26
2003-04	Kelowna Rockets	WHL	60	12	20	32	126	17	3	14	17	16
2004-05	Kelowna Rockets	WHL	55	12	29	41	95	18	9	8	17	25

WHL West Second All-Star Team (2004) • Memorial Cup Tournament All-Star Team (2004) • WHL West First All-Star Team (2005)

WELCH, Dan (WEHLCH, DAN)

Right wing. Shoots right. 5'10", 199 lbs. Born, Lansing, MI, February 23, 1981.
(Los Angeles' 9th choice, 245th overall, in 2000 Entry Draft).

			Regular Season					Playoffs				
Season	Club	League	GP	G	A	Pts	PIM	GP	G	A	Pts	PIM
1996/99	Hastings Huskies	High-MN	90	76	123	199	....	....	....	....	....	....
99-2000	U. of Minnesota	WCHA	36	6	8	14	31	....	....	....	....	....
2000-01	Omaha Lancers	USHL	52	30	27	57	103	12	9	13	22	20
2001-02	U. of Minnesota	WCHA	19	4	7	11	12	....	....	....	....	....
	Omaha Lancers	USHL	7	4	2	6	8	....	....	....	....	....
2002-03	U. of Minnesota	WCHA	18	5	5	10	12	....	....	....	....	....
	Manchester	AHL	42	3	9	12	22	3	0	0	0	0
2003-04	Manchester	AHL	31	6	6	12	18	1	0	0	0	0
2004-05	Manchester	AHL	59	3	10	13	49	1	0	0	0	0
	Reading Royals	ECHL	11	8	7	15	8	1	0	1	1	2

• Statistics for **Hastings** (High-MN) are career totals for 1996-1999 seasons • Ruled academically ineligible to play 2000-01 WCHA season by U. of Minnesota (WCHA). • Dismissed from U. of Minnesota (WCHA) hockey program for academic violations, January 3, 2003.

WELCH, Noah (WEHLCH, NOH-ah) PIT.

Defense. Shoots left. 6'4", 212 lbs. Born, Brighton, MA, August 26, 1982.
(Pittsburgh's 2nd choice, 54th overall, in 2001 Entry Draft).

			Regular Season					Playoffs				
Season	Club	League	GP	G	A	Pts	PIM	GP	G	A	Pts	PIM
99-2000	St. Sebastian's	High-MA	26	4	11	15	35	....	....	....	....	....
	Eastern-Mass	MBAHL	4	0	3	3	6	....	....	....	....	....
2000-01	St. Sebastian's	High-MA	30	11	20	31	37	....	....	....	....	....
2001-02	Harvard Crimson	ECAC	27	5	6	11	56	....	....	....	....	....
2002-03	Harvard Crimson	ECAC	34	6	22	28	70	....	....	....	....	....
2003-04	Harvard Crimson	ECAC	34	6	13	19	58	....	....	....	....	....
2004-05	Harvard Crimson	ECAC	34	6	12	18	*86	....	....	....	....	....

ECAC All-Rookie Team (2002) • ECAC Second All-Star Team (2002, 2003) • NCAA East Second All-American Team (2003) • ECAC First All-Star Team (2005) • NCAA East First All-American Team (2005)

WELLAR, Patrick (WEHL-uhr, PAT-rihk) ST.L.

Defense. Shoots left. 6'3", 210 lbs. Born, Carrot River, Sask., December 4, 1983.
(Washington's 5th choice, 77th overall, in 2002 Entry Draft).

			Regular Season					Playoffs				
Season	Club	League	GP	G	A	Pts	PIM	GP	G	A	Pts	PIM
99-2000	Sask. Contacts	SMHL	44	5	15	20	120	....	....	....	....	....
	Portland	WHL	1	0	0	0	0	....	....	....	....	....
2000-01	Portland	WHL	57	2	7	9	65	10	0	1	1	13
2001-02	Portland	WHL	61	3	10	13	125	7	0	2	2	4
2002-03	Portland	WHL	11	1	4	5	31	....	....	....	....	....
	Calgary Hitmen	WHL	49	3	11	14	88	5	0	0	0	15
2003-04	Calgary Hitmen	WHL	68	7	10	17	132	7	1	1	2	10
2004-05	Worcester IceCats	AHL	2	0	1	1	0	....	....	....	....	....
	Peoria Rivermen	ECHL	62	2	10	12	91	....	....	....	....	....

Signed as a free agent by **St. Louis**, June 30, 2004.

WELLER, Craig (WEHL-uhr, KRAIG) NYR

Right wing. Shoots right. 6'3", 195 lbs. Born, Calgary, Alta., January 17, 1981.
(St. Louis' 6th choice, 167th overall, in 2000 Entry Draft).

			Regular Season					Playoffs				
Season	Club	League	GP	G	A	Pts	PIM	GP	G	A	Pts	PIM
1997-98	Cgy. AAA Flames	AMHL	33	2	10	12	65	3	0	1	1	2
1998-99	Calgary Canucks	AJHL	49	4	14	18	80	13	0	1	1	10
99-2000	Calgary Canucks	AJHL	53	3	14	17	100	4	0	0	0	4
2000-01	U. Minn-Duluth	WCHA	6	0	1	1	0	....	....	....	....	....
	Kootenay Ice	WHL	30	1	5	6	40	11	0	2	2	26
2001-02	Kootenay Ice	WHL	69	5	13	18	127	22	3	7	10	27
2002-03	Hartford Wolf Pack	AHL	11	0	0	0	8	2	0	0	0	0
	Charlotte	ECHL	48	3	11	14	84	....	....	....	....	....
2003-04	Hartford Wolf Pack	AHL	68	5	9	14	86	16	2	2	4	30
2004-05	Hartford Wolf Pack	AHL	76	10	9	19	182	6	0	1	1	6

WHL West Second All-Star Team (2002)

• Left **Minnesota-Duluth** (WCHA) and signed as a free agent by **Kootenay** (WHL), January 7, 2001. Signed as a free agent by **NY Rangers**, July 11, 2002.

WELLER, Shawn (WEHL-uhr, SHAWN) OTT.

Left wing. Shoots left. 6'1", 188 lbs. Born, Glens Falls, NY, July 8, 1986.
(Ottawa's 3rd choice, 77th overall, in 2004 Entry Draft).

			Regular Season					Playoffs				
Season	Club	League	GP	G	A	Pts	PIM	GP	G	A	Pts	PIM
2001-02	South Glen Falls	High-NY	25	32	21	53	....	....	....	....	....	....
2002-03	Capital District	EJHL	Statistics not available									
2003-04	Capital District	EJHL	37	18	25	43	110	3	3	3	6	6
	Capital District	Exhib.	30	16	19	35	78	....	....	....	....	....
2004-05	Clarkson Knights	ECAC	33	3	11	14	72	....	....	....	....	....

WENNERBERG, Mattias (VEH-nuhr-buhrg, MA-tee-uhs) CHI.

Center. Shoots left. 5'11", 191 lbs. Born, Uma, Sweden, August 6, 1981.
(Chicago's 6th choice, 194th overall, in 1999 Entry Draft).

			Regular Season					Playoffs				
Season	Club	League	GP	G	A	Pts	PIM	GP	G	A	Pts	PIM
1996-97	Vilhelmina HC	Sweden-4	20	7	12	19	14	....	....	....	....	....
1997-98	Malmo Jr.	Swe-Jr.	30	10	17	27	....	....	....	....	....	....
1998-99	Malmo Jr.	Swe-Jr.	43	13	12	25	....	....	....	....	....	....
99-2000	Malmo Jr.	Swe-Jr.	32	14	6	20	102	....	....	....	....	....
2000-01	Bodens IK	Sweden-2	34	9	4	13	36	....	....	....	....	....
2001-02	IF Bjorkloven Umea	Sweden-2	21	8	10	18	43	....	....	....	....	....
	MODO	Sweden	24	2	2	4	16	13	4	4	8	*39
2002-03	MODO	Sweden	50	17	8	25	30	6	0	0	0	2
2003-04	MODO	Sweden	50	4	3	7	34	14	3	5	8	4
2004-05	MODO Jr.	Swe-Jr.	2	5	1	6	0	....	....	....	....	....
	IF Bjorkloven Umea	Sweden-2	12	5	5	10	4	....	....	....	....	....
	MODO	Sweden	34	1	1	2	18	6	0	0	0	6

WERNER, Steve (WUHR-nuhr, STEEV) WSH.

Right wing. Shoots right. 6', 197 lbs. Born, Washington, DC, August 8, 1984.
(Washington's 2nd choice, 83rd overall, in 2003 Entry Draft).

			Regular Season					Playoffs				
Season	Club	League	GP	G	A	Pts	PIM	GP	G	A	Pts	PIM
99-2000	Wsh. Jr. Capitals	MetroHL	42	32	45	77	....	....	....	....	....	....
2000-01	USA U-17	USDP	69	12	23	35	26	....	....	....	....	....
2001-02	USA U-18	USDP	54	16	20	36	42	....	....	....	....	....
2002-03	Massachusetts	H-East	37	16	22	38	4	....	....	....	....	....
2003-04	Massachusetts	H-East	33	7	17	24	18	....	....	....	....	....
2004-05	Massachusetts	H-East	38	14	13	27	12	....	....	....	....	....

Hockey East All-Rookie Team (2003)

WESSBECKER, John (WEHS-beh-kuhr, JAWN) T.B.

Defense. Shoots right. 6'1", 180 lbs. Born, Edina, MN, September 15, 1986.
(Tampa Bay's 9th choice, 225th overall, in 2005 Entry Draft).

			Regular Season					Playoffs				
Season	Club	League	GP	G	A	Pts	PIM	GP	G	A	Pts	PIM
2004-05	Blake Bears	High-MN	16	6	16	22	38	....	....	....	....	....

Signed Letter of Intent to attend **Massachusetts** (H-East) in fall of 2005.

WHARTON, Kyle (WAWR-tuhn, KIGHL) CBJ

Defense. Shoots left. 6'3", 185 lbs. Born, Ottawa, Ont., March 3, 1986.
(Columbus' 3rd choice, 59th overall, in 2004 Entry Draft).

			Regular Season					Playoffs				
Season	Club	League	GP	G	A	Pts	PIM	GP	G	A	Pts	PIM
2001-02	Ottawa Valley	OMHA	34	18	24	42	....	....	....	....	....	....
2002-03	Ottawa 67's	OHL	39	3	5	8	16	....	....	....	....	....
2003-04	Ottawa 67's	OHL	43	4	10	14	50	7	2	3	5	4
2004-05	Ottawa 67's	OHL	29	1	12	13	23	....	....	....	....	....
	Sault Ste. Marie	OHL	28	4	12	16	22	7	1	5	6	4

WHEELER, Blake (WEE-luhr, BLAYK) PHX.

Right wing. Shoots right. 6'5", 200 lbs. Born, Robbinsdale, MN, August 31, 1986.
(Phoenix's 1st choice, 5th overall, in 2004 Entry Draft).

			Regular Season					Playoffs				
Season	Club	League	GP	G	A	Pts	PIM	GP	G	A	Pts	PIM
2002-03	Breck Mustangs	High-MN	26	15	27	42	....	....	....	....	....	....
2003-04	Team Northwest	UMEHL	24	5	6	11	....	....	....	....	....	....
	Breck Mustangs	High-MN	27	39	50	89	34	3	6	5	11	0
2004-05	Green Bay	USHL	58	19	28	47	43	....	....	....	....	....

USHL All-Rookie Team (2005)

Signed Letter of Intent to attend **Minnesota** (WCHA), November 18, 2004.

WHITE, Ian (WIGHT, EE-uhn) TOR.

Defense. Shoots right. 5'10", 185 lbs. Born, Winnipeg, Man., June 4, 1984.
(Toronto's 6th choice, 191st overall, in 2002 Entry Draft).

			Regular Season					Playoffs				
Season	Club	League	GP	G	A	Pts	PIM	GP	G	A	Pts	PIM
99-2000	Eastman Selects	MAHA	32	29	33	62	36	....	....	....	....	....
2000-01	Swift Current	WHL	69	12	31	43	24	....	....	....	....	....
2001-02	Swift Current	WHL	70	32	47	79	40	12	4	5	9	12
2002-03	Swift Current	WHL	64	24	44	68	44	4	0	4	4	0
2003-04	St. John's	AHL	8	0	4	4	2	....	....	....	....	....
	Swift Current	WHL	43	9	23	32	32	5	1	3	4	8
2004-05	St. John's	AHL	78	4	22	26	54	5	0	2	2	2

WHL East Second All-Star Team (2002) • WHL East First All-Star Team (2003)

WHITNEY, Ryan (WIHT-nee, RIGH-uhn) PIT.

Defense. Shoots left. 6'4", 202 lbs. Born, Boston, MA, February 19, 1983.
(Pittsburgh's 1st choice, 5th overall, in 2002 Entry Draft).

			Regular Season					Playoffs				
Season	Club	League	GP	G	A	Pts	PIM	GP	G	A	Pts	PIM
99-2000	Thayer Academy	High-MA	22	5	33	38	....	....	....	....	....	....
2000-01	USA U-18	USDP	60	9	31	40	86	....	....	....	....	....
2001-02	Boston University	H-East	35	4	17	21	46	....	....	....	....	....
2002-03	Boston University	H-East	34	3	10	13	48	....	....	....	....	....
2003-04	Boston University	H-East	38	9	16	25	56	....	....	....	....	....
	Wilkes-Barre	AHL	....	....	....	....	....	20	1	9	10	6
2004-05	Wilkes-Barre	AHL	80	6	35	41	101	11	2	7	9	12

Hockey East All-Rookie Team (2002)

WICHSER, Adrian (WIH-shuhr, A-dree-uhn) FLA.

Center. Shoots left. 6', 180 lbs. Born, Winterthur, Switz., March 18, 1980.
(Florida's 9th choice, 231st overall, in 1998 Entry Draft).

			Regular Season					Playoffs				
Season	Club	League	GP	G	A	Pts	PIM	GP	G	A	Pts	PIM
1997-98	EHC Kloten	Swiss	35	6	5	11	31	7	0	1	1	8
1998-99	EHC Kloten	Swiss	40	11	14	25	14	9	7	0	7	8
	EHC Kloten Jr.	Swiss-Jr.	....	....	....	....	....	1	1	2	3	2
99-2000	EHC Kloten	Swiss	33	8	15	23	12	6	2	1	3	0
2000-01	Kloten Flyers	Swiss	31	9	9	18	12	9	2	3	5	0
2001-02	Kloten Flyers	Swiss	41	18	27	45	16	11	4	4	8	2
2002-03	HC Lugano	Swiss	44	*26	17	43	4	15	2	2	4	2
2003-04	HC Lugano	Swiss	47	17	20	37	16	16	6	7	13	4
2004-05	HC Lugano	Swiss	43	8	17	25	43	5	0	2	2	2

WICK, Roman (WIHK, ROH-muhn) OTT.

Right wing. Shoots left. 6'1", 187 lbs. Born, Kloten, Switz., December 30, 1985.
(Ottawa's 8th choice, 156th overall, in 2004 Entry Draft).

			Regular Season					Playoffs				
Season	Club	League	GP	G	A	Pts	PIM	GP	G	A	Pts	PIM
2000-01	Kloten Flyers Jr.	Swiss-Jr.	26	4	1	5	6	5	1	0	1	2
2001-02	Kloten Flyers Jr.	Swiss-Jr.	34	19	27	46	32	8	1	2	3	4
2002-03	Kloten Flyers	Swiss	9	1	0	1	4	1	0	0	0	0
	Kloten Flyers Jr.	Swiss-Jr.	28	29	22	51	68	2	0	1	1	0
2003-04	Kloten Flyers	Swiss	20	1	1	2	6	....	....	....	....	....
	Kloten Flyers	Swiss-Q	7	3	1	4	0	....	....	....	....	....
	GCK Lions Zurich	Swiss-2	6	4	0	4	6	....	....	....	....	....
2004-05	Red Deer Rebels	WHL	66	32	38	70	25	7	1	2	3	6

WIDEMAN, Dennis (WIGHD-muhn, DEH-nihs) ST.L.

Defense. Shoots right. 6', 200 lbs. Born, Kitchener, Ont., March 20, 1983.
(Buffalo's 9th choice, 241st overall, in 2002 Entry Draft).

			Regular Season					Playoffs				
Season	Club	League	GP	G	A	Pts	PIM	GP	G	A	Pts	PIM
1998-99	Elmira Sugar Kings	OHA-B	47	18	30	48	142	....	....	....	....	....
99-2000	Sudbury Wolves	OHL	63	10	26	36	64	12	1	2	3	22
2000-01	Sudbury Wolves	OHL	25	7	11	18	37	....	....	....	....	....
	London Knights	OHL	24	8	8	16	38	5	0	4	4	6
2001-02	London Knights	OHL	65	27	42	69	141	12	4	9	13	26
2002-03	London Knights	OHL	55	20	27	47	83	14	6	6	12	10
2003-04	London Knights	OHL	60	24	41	65	85	15	7	10	17	17
2004-05	Worcester IceCats	AHL	79	13	30	43	65	....	....	....	....	....

OHL First All-Star Team (2004)

Signed as a free agent by **St. Louis**, June 30, 2004.

WIDING, Daniel (VEE-dihng, DAN-yehl) NSH.

Right wing. Shoots right. 6'1", 202 lbs. Born, Gavle, Sweden, April 13, 1982.
(Nashville's 2nd choice, 36th overall, in 2000 Entry Draft).

			Regular Season					Playoffs				
Season	Club	League	GP	G	A	Pts	PIM	GP	G	A	Pts	PIM
99-2000	Leksands IF U18	Swe-U18	6	2	1	3	20	....	....	....	....	....
	Leksands IF Jr.	Swe-Jr.	34	15	12	27	65	2	1	0	1	4
	Leksands IF	Sweden	3	0	0	0	2	....	....	....	....	....
2000-01	Leksands IF Jr.	Swe-Jr.	6	2	3	5	31	....	....	....	....	....
	Leksands IF	Sweden	40	6	5	11	18	....	....	....	....	....
2001-02	Leksands IF Jr.	Swe-Jr.	3	2	6	8	2	....	....	....	....	....
	Leksands IF	Sweden-2	55	12	12	24	92	....	....	....	....	....
2002-03	Leksands IF	Sweden	47	2	2	4	8	5	0	0	0	2
	Leksands IF Jr.	Swe-Jr.	2	0	1	1	4	....	....	....	....	....
2003-04	Pelicans Lahti	Finland	54	6	7	13	62	....	....	....	....	....
2004-05	Pelicans Lahti	Finland	56	13	15	28	74	....	....	....	....	....

WIKNER, Fred (WIHK-nuhr, FREHD) CGY.

Wing. Shoots left. 6'1", 187 lbs. Born, Molndal, Sweden, January 1, 1986.
(Calgary's 7th choice, 182nd overall, in 2004 Entry Draft).

			Regular Season					Playoffs				
Season	Club	League	GP	G	A	Pts	PIM	GP	G	A	Pts	PIM
2002-03	V.Frolunda Jr.	Swe-Jr.	22	2	5	7	14	7	2	1	3	2
2003-04	V.Frolunda Jr.	Swe-Jr.	36	9	6	15	67	9	2	2	4	8
2004-05	IF Molndal Hockey	Sweden-3	5	1	1	2	10	....	....	....	....	....
	Frolunda Jr.	Swe-Jr.	28	8	11	19	36	6	1	3	4	4

WIKNER, John (WIHK-nuhr, JAWN) OTT.

Left wing. Shoots left. 6'1", 179 lbs. Born, Molndal, Sweden, January 1, 1986.
(Ottawa's 11th choice, 284th overall, in 2004 Entry Draft).

			Regular Season					Playoffs				
Season	Club	League	GP	G	A	Pts	PIM	GP	G	A	Pts	PIM
2002-03	V.Frolunda Jr.	Swe-Jr.	19	3	6	9	41	6	0	0	0	10
2003-04	V.Frolunda Jr.	Swe-Jr.	31	6	3	9	22	9	0	0	0	6
2004-05	IF Molndal Hockey	Sweden-3	5	2	2	4	6	....	....	....	....	....
	Frolunda Jr.	Swe-Jr.	32	10	14	24	56	6	0	2	2	0

WILFORD, Marty (WIHL-fohrd, MAHR-tee) L.A.

Defense. Shoots left. 6'1", 212 lbs. Born, Cobourg, Ont., April 17, 1977.
(Chicago's 7th choice, 149th overall, in 1995 Entry Draft).

			Regular Season					Playoffs				
Season	Club	League	GP	G	A	Pts	PIM	GP	G	A	Pts	PIM
1993-94	Peterborough	OPJHL	40	3	19	22	*107	....	....	....	....	....
1994-95	Oshawa Generals	OHL	63	1	6	7	95	7	1	1	2	4
1995-96	Oshawa Generals	OHL	65	3	24	27	107	5	0	1	1	4
1996-97	Oshawa Generals	OHL	62	19	43	62	126	16	2	18	20	28
1997-98	Indianapolis Ice	IHL	26	0	4	4	16	....	....	....	....	....
	Columbus Chill	ECHL	46	8	27	35	123	....	....	....	....	....
1998-99	Indianapolis Ice	IHL	80	3	13	16	116	7	0	1	1	16
99-2000	Cleveland	IHL	7	0	3	3	24	....	....	....	....	....
	Houston Aeros	IHL	45	0	9	9	30	11	2	2	4	18
2000-01	Norfolk Admirals	AHL	80	7	41	48	102	9	1	5	6	8
2001-02	St. John's	AHL	60	4	21	25	70	....	....	....	....	....
	Milwaukee	AHL	8	1	3	4	12	....	....	....	....	....
	Hartford Wolf Pack	AHL	9	0	2	2	2	10	3	3	6	4
2002-03	Norfolk Admirals	AHL	80	13	35	48	87	9	0	3	3	16
2003-04	Norfolk Admirals	AHL	80	5	35	40	67	8	0	3	3	18
2004-05	Norfolk Admirals	AHL	78	7	30	37	80	6	0	4	4	15

OHL Second All-Star Team (1997)

Traded to **Toronto** by **Chicago** for Shawn Thornton, September 30, 2001. Traded to **Nashville** by **Toronto** with D.J. Smith for Marc Moro, March 1, 2002. Signed as a free agent by **Chicago**, July 8, 2003. Signed as a free agent by **Los Angeles**, August 10, 2005.

WILLIAMS, Jeremy (WIHL-yuhms, JAIR-eh-mee) TOR.

Center. Shoots right. 5'11", 184 lbs. Born, Regina, Sask., January 26, 1984.
(Toronto's 5th choice, 220th overall, in 2003 Entry Draft).

			Regular Season					Playoffs				
Season	Club	League	GP	G	A	Pts	PIM	GP	G	A	Pts	PIM
2001-02	Swift Current	SMMHL	24	18	23	41	64	....	....	....	....	....
	Swift Current	WHL	32	6	7	13	30	12	1	0	1	4
2002-03	Swift Current	WHL	72	41	52	93	117	4	1	0	1	6
2003-04	Swift Current	WHL	68	*52	49	101	82	5	2	1	3	12
	St. John's	AHL	4	0	2	2	0	....	....	....	....	....
2004-05	St. John's	AHL	75	16	20	36	24	5	0	0	0	0

WHL East First All-Star Team (2004) • Canadian Major Junior First All-Star Team (2004)

WILSON, Kyle (WIHL-suhn, KIGHL) MIN.

Center. Shoots right. 6', 200 lbs. Born, Oakville, Ont., December 15, 1984.
(Minnesota's 12th choice, 272nd overall, in 2004 Entry Draft).

			Regular Season					Playoffs				
Season	Club	League	GP	G	A	Pts	PIM	GP	G	A	Pts	PIM
2000-01	Strathroy Rockets	OHA-B	33	12	17	29	15	5	2	2	4	2
2001-02	Strathroy Rockets	OHA-B	53	42	25	67	16	....	....	....	....	....
2002-03	Colgate	ECAC	33	4	2	6	15	....	....	....	....	....
2003-04	Colgate	ECAC	37	14	17	31	23	....	....	....	....	....
2004-05	Colgate	ECAC	30	5	18	23	12	....	....	....	....	....

WINCHESTER, Brad (WIHN-chehst-uhr, BRAD) EDM.

Left wing. Shoots left. 6'5", 215 lbs. Born, Madison, WI, March 1, 1981.
(Edmonton's 2nd choice, 35th overall, in 2000 Entry Draft).

			Regular Season					Playoffs				
Season	Club	League	GP	G	A	Pts	PIM	GP	G	A	Pts	PIM
1997-98	USA U-17	USDP	74	22	23	45	162	....	....	....	....	....
1998-99	USA U-18	USDP	65	21	23	44	103	....	....	....	....	....
99-2000	U. of Wisconsin	WCHA	33	9	9	18	48	....	....	....	....	....
2000-01	U. of Wisconsin	WCHA	41	7	9	16	71	....	....	....	....	....
2001-02	U. of Wisconsin	WCHA	38	14	20	34	38	....	....	....	....	....
2002-03	U. of Wisconsin	WCHA	38	10	6	16	58	....	....	....	....	....
2003-04	Toronto	AHL	65	13	6	19	85	3	0	0	0	2
2004-05	Edmonton	AHL	76	22	18	40	143	....	....	....	....	....

WINNIK, Daniel (WIHN-ihk, DAN-yehl) PHX.

Center/Left wing. Shoots right. 6'2", 210 lbs. Born, Toronto, Ont., March 6, 1985.
(Phoenix's 10th choice, 265th overall, in 2004 Entry Draft).

			Regular Season					Playoffs				
Season	Club	League	GP	G	A	Pts	PIM	GP	G	A	Pts	PIM
2002-03	Wexford	OPJHL	47	20	33	53	70	18	11	11	22	24
2003-04	New Hampshire	H-East	38	4	10	14	12	....	....	....	....	....
2004-05	New Hampshire	H-East	42	18	22	40	26	....	....	....	....	....

WISNIEWSKI, James (wihs-NEHV-skee, JAYMS) CHI.

Defense. Shoots right. 6', 206 lbs. Born, Canton, MI, February 21, 1984.
(Chicago's 5th choice, 156th overall, in 2002 Entry Draft).

			Regular Season					Playoffs				
Season	Club	League	GP	G	A	Pts	PIM	GP	G	A	Pts	PIM
99-2000	Det. Compuware	NAHL	50	5	11	16	67	5	0	3	3	4
2000-01	Plymouth Whalers	OHL	53	6	23	29	72	19	3	10	13	34
2001-02	Plymouth Whalers	OHL	62	11	25	36	100	6	1	2	3	6
2002-03	Plymouth Whalers	OHL	52	18	34	52	60	18	2	10	12	14
2003-04	Plymouth Whalers	OHL	50	17	53	70	63	9	3	7	10	8
2004-05	Norfolk Admirals	AHL	66	7	18	25	110	5	1	3	4	2

OHL First All-Star Team (2004) • OHL Defenseman of the Year (2004) • Canadian Major Junior First All-Star Team (2004) • Canadian Major Junior Defenseman of the Year (2004)

WOLSKI, Wojtek (WOHL-skee, VOI-tehk) COL.

Left wing. Shoots left. 6'3", 200 lbs. Born, Zabrze, Poland, February 24, 1986.
(Colorado's 1st choice, 21st overall, in 2004 Entry Draft).

			Regular Season					Playoffs				
Season	Club	League	GP	G	A	Pts	PIM	GP	G	A	Pts	PIM
2001-02	St. Mike's B's	OPJHL	33	16	33	49	40	....	....	....	....	....
2002-03	Brampton	OHL	64	25	32	57	26	11	5	0	5	6
2003-04	Brampton	OHL	66	29	41	70	30	12	5	3	8	8
2004-05	Brampton	OHL	67	29	44	73	41	6	2	5	7	6

OHL First All-Star Team (2004)

WOOD, Dustin (WUD, DUHS-tihn) MIN.

Defense. Shoots left. 6'1", 208 lbs. Born, Scarborough, Ont., May 21, 1981.

			Regular Season					Playoffs				
Season	Club	League	GP	G	A	Pts	PIM	GP	G	A	Pts	PIM
1998-99	Peterborough	OHL	62	1	8	9	14	5	0	0	0	0
99-2000	Peterborough	OHL	66	2	13	15	29	5	0	1	1	0
2000-01	Peterborough	OHL	64	5	20	25	41	7	0	3	3	11
2001-02	Peterborough	OHL	68	13	38	51	57	6	2	1	3	4
2002-03	Bridgeport	AHL	6	0	0	0	2	....	....	....	....	....
	Trenton Titans	ECHL	63	4	23	27	28	3	0	1	1	2
2003-04	Springfield Falcons	AHL	75	2	6	8	22	....	....	....	....	....
	Adirondack	UHL	1	0	0	0	0	....	....	....	....	....
2004-05	Utah Grizzlies	AHL	80	2	8	10	39	....	....	....	....	....

Signed as a free agent by **Phoenix**, June 2, 2004. Traded to **Minnesota** by **Phoenix** with Erik Westrum for Zbynek Michalek, August 26, 2005.

WOOD, Stephen (WUD, STEE-vehn) PHI.

Defense. Shoots right. 6'3", 210 lbs. Born, Sudbury, MA, August 18, 1981.

			Regular Season					Playoffs				
Season	Club	League	GP	G	A	Pts	PIM	GP	G	A	Pts	PIM
2000-01	Providence College	H-East	36	3	4	7	68	....	....	....	....	....
2001-02	Providence College	H-East	36	5	18	23	78	....	....	....	....	....
2002-03	Providence College	H-East	34	9	20	29	48	....	....	....	....	....
2003-04	Providence College	H-East	37	11	18	29	66	....	....	....	....	....
	Philadelphia	AHL	4	0	0	0	0	....	....	....	....	....
2004-05	Philadelphia	AHL	24	0	2	2	14	....	....	....	....	....
	Trenton Titans	ECHL	42	4	13	17	83	20	4	6	10	39

Hockey East Second All-Star Team (2003) • Hockey East First All-Star Team (2004) • NCAA East Second All-American Team (2004)

Signed as a free agent by **Philadelphia**, March 21, 2004.

WOYWITKA, Jeff (WOI-wiht-ka, JEHF) ST.L.

Defense. Shoots left. 6'2", 209 lbs. Born, Vermilion, Alta., September 1, 1983.
(Philadelphia's 1st choice, 27th overall, in 2001 Entry Draft).

			Regular Season					Playoffs				
Season	Club	League	GP	G	A	Pts	PIM	GP	G	A	Pts	PIM
1998-99	Wainwright	AAHA	26	7	15	22	60	....	....	....	....	....
99-2000	Red Deer Rebels	WHL	67	4	12	16	40	4	0	3	3	2
2000-01	Red Deer Rebels	WHL	72	7	28	35	113	22	2	8	10	25
2001-02	Red Deer Rebels	WHL	72	14	23	37	109	23	2	10	12	22
2002-03	Red Deer Rebels	WHL	57	16	36	52	65	23	1	9	10	25
2003-04	Philadelphia	AHL	29	0	6	6	51	....	....	....	....	....
	Toronto	AHL	53	4	18	22	41	3	0	0	0	2
2004-05	Edmonton	AHL	80	6	20	26	84	....	....	....	....	....

WHL East Second All-Star Team (2002) • WHL East First All-Star Team (2003)

Traded to **Edmonton** by **Philadelphia** with Philadelphia's 1st round choice (Rob Schremp) in 2004 Entry Draft and Philadelphia's 3rd round choice (Danny Syvret) in 2005 Entry Draft for Mike Comrie, December 16, 2003. Traded to **St. Louis** by **Edmonton** with Eric Brewer and Doug Lynch for Chris Pronger, August 2, 2005.

WOZNIEWSKI, Andy (wuhz-NYOO-skee, AN-dee) TOR.

Defense. Shoots left. 6'4", 220 lbs. Born, Buffalo Grove, IL, May 25, 1980.

			Regular Season					Playoffs				
Season	Club	League	GP	G	A	Pts	PIM	GP	G	A	Pts	PIM
99-2000	U. Mass-Lowell	H-East	17	1	1	2	8	....	....	....	....	....
2000-01	Texas Tornado	NAHL	54	10	34	44	98	8	2	7	9	12
2001-02	U. of Wisconsin	WCHA	39	3	13	16	54	....	....	....	....	....
2002-03	U. of Wisconsin	WCHA	33	1	7	8	47	....	....	....	....	....
2003-04	U. of Wisconsin	WCHA	43	6	8	14	*104	....	....	....	....	....
	St. John's	AHL	3	0	1	1	0	....	....	....	....	....
2004-05	St. John's	AHL	28	1	4	5	20	....	....	....	....	....

Signed as a free agent by **Toronto**, May 27, 2004.

WYMAN, James (WIGH-muhn, JAYMZ) MTL.

Right wing. Shoots right. 6'1", 195 lbs. Born, Edina, MN, February 27, 1986.
(Montreal's 3rd choice, 100th overall, in 2004 Entry Draft).

			Regular Season					Playoffs				
Season	Club	League	GP	G	A	Pts	PIM	GP	G	A	Pts	PIM
2001-02	Blake Bears	High-MN	26	7	5	12	....	....	....	....	....	....
2002-03	Blake Bears	High-MN	28	17	23	40	12	....	....	....	....	....
2003-04	Blake Bears	High-MN	27	31	24	55	4	....	....	....	....	....
	Team Southwest	UMEHL	24	8	8	16	....	....	....	....	....	....
2004-05	Dartmouth	ECAC	33	5	6	11	4	....	....	....	....	....

YACHMENEV, Denis (YATCH-muh-nehv, DEH-nihs) FLA.
Left wing. Shoots left. 6'1", 185 lbs. Born, Chelyabinsk, USSR, June 4, 1984.
(Florida's 9th choice, 200th overall, in 2002 Entry Draft).

			Regular Season					Playoffs				
Season	Club	League	GP	G	A	Pts	PIM	GP	G	A	Pts	PIM
2000-01	Chelyabinsk 2	Russia-3	36	40	27	67	....	....	....	....	....	....
2001-02	North Bay	OHL	65	17	12	29	32	5	2	0	2	0
2002-03	Saginaw Spirit	OHL	68	17	28	45	69	....	....	....	....	....
2003-04	Omsk 2	Russia-3	13	12	4	16	10	....	....	....	....	....
	Amur Khabarovsk	Russia	25	0	1	1	4	....	....	....	....	....
2004-05	Amur Khabarovsk	Russia-2	42	7	14	21	28	13	3	1	4	8

YANDLE, Keith (Yan-duhl, KEETH) PHX.
Defense. Shoots left. 6'2", 195 lbs. Born, Boston, MA, September 9, 1986.
(Phoenix's 3rd choice, 105th overall, in 2005 Entry Draft).

			Regular Season					Playoffs				
Season	Club	League	GP	G	A	Pts	PIM	GP	G	A	Pts	PIM
2004-05	Cushing	High-MA	34	14	40	54	52	....	....	....	....	....

Signed Letter of Intent to attend **Maine** (H-East) in fall of 2005.

YEMELIN, Alexei (yeh-MUH-lehn, al-EXH-ay) MTL.
Defense. Shoots left. 6', 187 lbs. Born, Kuibyshev, USSR, April 25, 1986.
(Montreal's 2nd choice, 84th overall, in 2004 Entry Draft).

			Regular Season					Playoffs				
Season	Club	League	GP	G	A	Pts	PIM	GP	G	A	Pts	PIM
2002-03	Lada Togliatti 2	Russia-3	31	1	1	2	20	....	....	....	....	....
2003-04	Lada Togliatti 2	Russia-3	2	0	0	0	10	....	....	....	....	....
	CSK VVS Samara	Russia-2	52	2	4	6	180	1	0	0	0	18
2004-05	Lada Togliatti	Russia	12	0	1	1	24	2	0	0	0	2

YIP, Brandon (YIHP, BRAN-duhn) COL.
Right wing. Shoots right. 6'1", 170 lbs. Born, Vancouver, B.C., April 25, 1985.
(Colorado's 7th choice, 239th overall, in 2004 Entry Draft).

			Regular Season					Playoffs				
Season	Club	League	GP	G	A	Pts	PIM	GP	G	A	Pts	PIM
2003-04	Coquitlam Express	BCHL	56	31	38	69	87	4	1	2	3	14
2004-05	Coquitlam Express	BCHL	43	20	42	62	92	7	6	1	7	12

YOUNG, Bryan (YUHNG, BRIGH-uhn) EDM.
Defense. Shoots left. 6'1", 191 lbs. Born, Ennismore, Ont., August 6, 1986.
(Edmonton's 6th choice, 146th overall, in 2004 Entry Draft).

			Regular Season					Playoffs				
Season	Club	League	GP	G	A	Pts	PIM	GP	G	A	Pts	PIM
2002-03	Lindsay Muskies	OPJHL	47	1	9	10	56	....	....	....	....	....
	Peterborough	OHL	2	0	0	0	0	....	....	....	....	....
2003-04	Peterborough	OHL	60	0	8	8	63	....	....	....	....	....
2004-05	Peterborough	OHL	60	1	11	12	44	14	0	1	1	10

YUNKOV , Mikhail (yuhn-KAWF, mih-kigh-EHL) WSH.
Center. Shoots left. 6', 180 lbs. Born, Voskresensk, USSR, February 16, 1986.
(Washington's 5th choice, 62nd overall, in 2004 Entry Draft).

			Regular Season					Playoffs				
Season	Club	League	GP	G	A	Pts	PIM	GP	G	A	Pts	PIM
2001-02	Krylja Sovetov 2	Russia-3	4	0	1	1	0	....	....	....	....	....
2002-03	Krylja Sovetov	Russia	7	1	0	1	2	....	....	....	....	....
	Krylja Sovetov 2	Russia-3	3	0	1	1	0	....	....	....	....	....
2003-04	Krylja Sovetov	Russia-2	38	5	10	15	12	4	0	1	1	0
	Krylja Sovetov 2	Russia-3	STATISTICS NOT AVAILABLE									
2004-05	Krylja Sovetov 2	Russia-3	1	0	0	0	0	....	....	....	....	....
	Krylja Sovetov	Russia-2	38	9	14	23	22	3	0	1	1	4

ZAGRAPAN, Marek (ZAG-rah-pahn, MAHR-ehk) BUF.
Center. Shoots left. 6'1", 195 lbs. Born, Presov, Czech., December 6, 1986.
(Buffalo's 1st choice, 13th overall, in 2005 Entry Draft).

			Regular Season					Playoffs				
Season	Club	League	GP	G	A	Pts	PIM	GP	G	A	Pts	PIM
2001-02	HC Zlin U17	CzR-U17	48	23	14	37	24	6	1	0	1	2
2002-03	HC Zlin U17	CzR-U17	15	18	16	34	14	3	1	0	1	6
	HC Zlin Jr.	CzRep-Jr.	25	9	13	22	10	....	....	....	....	....
	HC Hame Zlin	CzRep	13	1	1	2	10	....	....	....	....	....
2003-04	HC Zlin Jr.	CzRep-Jr.	42	23	12	35	40	7	1	3	4	4
	HC Hame Zlin	CzRep	5	0	0	0	0	....	....	....	....	....
	HC Kometa Brno	CzRep-2	5	0	1	1	0	....	....	....	....	....
2004-05	Chicoutimi	QMJHL	59	32	50	82	50	17	11	6	17	28

ZAINULLIN, Ruslan (zihj-NOO-luhn, roos-LAHN) CGY.
Right wing. Shoots left. 6'2", 202 lbs. Born, Kazan, USSR, February 14, 1982.
(Tampa Bay's 2nd choice, 34th overall, in 2000 Entry Draft).

			Regular Season					Playoffs				
Season	Club	League	GP	G	A	Pts	PIM	GP	G	A	Pts	PIM
1997-98	Ak Bars Kazan 2	Russia-3	27	0	1	1	2	....	....	....	....	....
1998-99	Ak Bars Kazan 2	Russia-4	36	13	8	21	22	....	....	....	....	....
99-2000	Ak Bars Kazan 2	Russia-3	12	13	6	19	....	....	....	....	....	....
	Ak Bars Kazan	Russia	14	1	1	2	4	....	....	....	....	....
2000-01	Ak Bars Kazan	Russia	29	1	3	4	14	1	0	0	0	0
2001-02	Ak Bars Kazan	Russia	21	0	2	2	8	3	0	0	0	2
2002-03	Ak Bars Kazan	Russia	4	0	1	1	2	....	....	....	....	....
	Nizhnekamsk	Russia	13	1	1	2	8	....	....	....	....	....
2003-04	Dynamo Moscow	Russia	47	3	5	8	30	3	0	0	0	0
2004-05	Spartak Moscow	Russia	45	4	5	9	28	....	....	....	....	....

Traded to **Phoenix** by **Tampa Bay** with Mike Johnson, Paul Mara and NY Islanders' 2nd round choice (previously acquired, Phoenix selected Matthew Spiller) in 2001 Entry Draft for Nikolai Khabibulin and Stan Neckar, March 5, 2001. Rights traded to **Atlanta** by **Phoenix** with Kirill Safronov and Phoenix's 4th round choice (Patrick Dwyer) in 2002 Entry Draft for Darcy Hordichuk and Atlanta's 4th (Lance Monych) and 5th (John Zeiler) round choices in 2002 Entry Draft, March 19, 2002. Traded to **Calgary** by **Atlanta** for Marc Savard, November 15, 2002.

ZAJAC, Travis (ZAY-jak, TRA-vihs) N.J.
Center. Shoots right. 6'2", 205 lbs. Born, Winnipeg, Man., May 13, 1985.
(New Jersey's 1st choice, 20th overall, in 2004 Entry Draft).

			Regular Season					Playoffs				
Season	Club	League	GP	G	A	Pts	PIM	GP	G	A	Pts	PIM
2002-03	Salmon Arm	BCHL	59	16	36	52	27	11	2	4	6	6
2003-04	Salmon Arm	BCHL	59	43	69	112	110	14	10	13	23	10
2004-05	North Dakota	WCHA	45	20	19	39	16	....	....	....	....	....

WCHA All-Rookie Team (2005) • NCAA Championship All-Tournament Team (2005)

ZAKHAROV, Konstantin (za-KHAHR-awv, kawn-stuhn-TIHN) ST.L.
Left wing. Shoots right. 6'1", 190 lbs. Born, Minsk, USSR, May 2, 1985.
(St. Louis' 5th choice, 101st overall, in 2003 Entry Draft).

			Regular Season					Playoffs				
Season	Club	League	GP	G	A	Pts	PIM	GP	G	A	Pts	PIM
2000-01	Yunost Minsk	Belarus	19	11	7	18	40	....	....	....	....	....
2001-02	Yunost Minsk	Belarus	16	7	5	12	39	....	....	....	....	....
2002-03	HK Gomel	Belarus	19	8	19	27	18	....	....	....	....	....
	HK Gomel	EEHL	14	2	4	6	10	....	....	....	....	....
	Yunost Minsk	Belarus	17	18	19	37	34	....	....	....	....	....
2003-04	Moncton Wildcats	QMJHL	55	33	16	49	63	20	7	9	16	18
2004-05	Worcester IceCats	AHL	59	4	10	14	26	....	....	....	....	....

ZALEWSKI, Steven (zuh-LOO-skee, STEE-vehn) S.J.
Center. Shoots left. 6', 185 lbs. Born, Utica, NY, August 20, 1986.
(San Jose's 5th choice, 153rd overall, in 2004 Entry Draft).

			Regular Season					Playoffs				
Season	Club	League	GP	G	A	Pts	PIM	GP	G	A	Pts	PIM
2003-04	Northwood	High-NY	40	32	34	66	22	....	....	....	....	....
2004-05	Clarkson Knights	ECAC	39	12	7	19	60	....	....	....	....	....

ZANON, Greg (ZA-nuhn, GREHG) NSH.
Defense. Shoots left. 5'11", 211 lbs. Born, Burnaby, B.C., June 5, 1980.
(Ottawa's 6th choice, 156th overall, in 2000 Entry Draft).

			Regular Season					Playoffs				
Season	Club	League	GP	G	A	Pts	PIM	GP	G	A	Pts	PIM
1995-96	Burnaby Beavers	BCAHA	49	16	27	43	142	....	....	....	....	....
1996-97	Victoria Salsa	BCHL	53	4	13	17	124	....	....	....	....	....
1997-98	Victoria Salsa	BCHL	59	11	21	32	108	7	0	2	2	10
1998-99	South Surrey	BCHL	59	17	54	71	154	....	....	....	....	....
99-2000	Nebraska-Omaha	CCHA	42	3	26	29	56	....	....	....	....	....
2000-01	Nebraska-Omaha	CCHA	39	12	16	28	64	....	....	....	....	....
2001-02	Nebraska-Omaha	CCHA	41	9	16	25	54	....	....	....	....	....
2002-03	Nebraska-Omaha	CCHA	32	6	19	25	44	....	....	....	....	....
2003-04	Milwaukee	AHL	62	4	12	16	59	22	2	6	8	31
2004-05	Milwaukee	AHL	80	2	17	19	59	7	0	1	1	10

CCHA First All-Star Team (2001) • NCAA West Second All-American Team (2001, 2002) • CCHA Second All-Star Team (2002)

Signed as a free agent by **Nashville**, July 9, 2004.

ZAPLETAL, Jan (ZAH-pleht-tuhl, YAHN) T.B.
Defense. Shoots right. 6'3", 190 lbs. Born, Brno, Czech., August 21, 1986.
(Tampa Bay's 6th choice, 188th overall, in 2004 Entry Draft).

			Regular Season					Playoffs				
Season	Club	League	GP	G	A	Pts	PIM	GP	G	A	Pts	PIM
2001-02	HC Ytong Brno Jr.	CzRep-Jr.	27	3	0	3	8	....	....	....	....	....
2002-03	HC Vsetin Jr.	CzRep-Jr.	27	4	3	7	8	10	0	0	0	2
2003-04	HC Vsetin Jr.	CzRep-Jr.	51	2	4	6	26	4	0	0	0	0
2004-05	Regina Pats	WHL	55	3	2	5	20	....	....	....	....	....

ZARB, Chris (ZAHRB, KRIHS) PHI.
Defense. Shoots right. 6'4", 176 lbs. Born, San Diego, CA, January 11, 1985.
(Philadelphia's 4th choice, 144th overall, in 2004 Entry Draft).

			Regular Season					Playoffs				
Season	Club	League	GP	G	A	Pts	PIM	GP	G	A	Pts	PIM
2002-03	Det. Ceasars	MWEHL	60	15	35	50	60	....	....	....	....	....
2003-04	Tri-City Storm	USHL	43	4	20	24	78	11	0	4	4	17
2004-05	Tri-City Storm	USHL	48	9	14	23	147	....	....	....	....	....

ZAVORAL, Vaclav (ZA-vohr-uhl, VATS-lahf) TOR.
Defense. Shoots left. 6', 216 lbs. Born, Teplice, Czech., May 22, 1981.
(Toronto's 5th choice, 151st overall, in 1999 Entry Draft).

			Regular Season					Playoffs				
Season	Club	League	GP	G	A	Pts	PIM	GP	G	A	Pts	PIM
1997-98	Litvinov Jr.	CzRep-Jr.	46	0	5	5	....	....	....	....	....	....
1998-99	Litvinov Jr.	CzRep-Jr.	43	2	10	12	....	....	....	....	....	....
	Litvinov	CzRep	1	0	1	1	2	....	....	....	....	....
99-2000	Sault Ste. Marie	OHL	57	3	11	14	89	14	0	2	2	28
2000-01	Sault Ste. Marie	OHL	55	4	6	10	116	....	....	....	....	....
2001-02	Flint Generals	UHL	65	2	13	15	123	5	0	0	0	12
2002-03	Memphis	CHL	53	2	2	4	143	....	....	....	....	....
2003-04	Memphis	CHL	12	0	0	0	35	....	....	....	....	....
	Usti n. L.	CzRep-2	1	0	1	1	2	....	....	....	....	....
2004-05	Elmira Jackals	UHL	19	2	1	3	27	....	....	....	....	....
	Kansas City	UHL	31	3	11	14	39	....	....	....	....	....
	Flint Generals	UHL	13	1	0	1	6	....	....	....	....	....

• Placed on suspended list by **Memphis** (CHL), November 14, 2003.

ZEILER, John (ZIGH-luhr, JAWN) PHX.
Right wing. Shoots right. 6', 193 lbs. Born, Pittsburgh, PA, November 21, 1982.
(Phoenix's 7th choice, 132nd overall, in 2002 Entry Draft).

			Regular Season					Playoffs				
Season	Club	League	GP	G	A	Pts	PIM	GP	G	A	Pts	PIM
99-2000	Pittsburgh Hornets	PAHA	27	17	15	32	94	....	....	....	....	....
2000-01	Sioux City	USHL	56	8	20	28	45	2	0	0	0	26
2001-02	Sioux City	USHL	60	23	27	50	116	12	2	3	5	25
2002-03	St. Lawrence	ECAC	37	10	17	27	28	....	....	....	....	....
2003-04	St. Lawrence	ECAC	41	8	*28	36	42	....	....	....	....	....
2004-05	St. Lawrence	ECAC	38	9	23	32	42	....	....	....	....	....

ECAC All-Rookie Team (2003)

ZHVACHKIN, Leonid (ZNVAHCH-kihn, lay-oh-NEED) NYR
Defense. Shoots left. 6'3", 195 lbs. Born, Tula, USSR, February 24, 1983.
(NY Rangers' 9th choice, 230th overall, in 2001 Entry Draft).

			Regular Season					Playoffs				
Season	Club	League	GP	G	A	Pts	PIM	GP	G	A	Pts	PIM
99-2000	HK Moscow 2	Russia-3	9	0	1	1	12	....	....	....	....	....
2000-01	Vityaz Podolsk 2	Russia-3	STATISTICS NOT AVAILABLE									
2001-02	Guelph Storm	OHL	62	2	2	4	58	9	0	0	0	5
2002-03	Guelph Storm	OHL	25	0	2	2	34	....	....	....	....	....
	Barrie Colts	OHL	31	0	1	1	35	6	0	0	0	6
2003-04	Krylja Sovetov	Russia-2	18	0	0	0	36	....	....	....	....	....
	Krylja Sovetov 2	Russia-3	STATISTICS NOT AVAILABLE									
2004-05	Krylja Sovetov	Russia-2	4	1	0	1	4	....	....	....	....	....
	Krylja Sovetov 2	Russia-3	14	0	2	2	45	....	....	....	....	....
	Kristall Elektrostal	Russia-2	27	1	5	6	61	....	....	....	....	....
	Kristall Saratov	Russia-2	6	0	0	0	2	4	1	0	1	4

ZIB, Lukas (ZIHB, LOO-kahsh) **EDM.**

Defense. Shoots right. 6'1", 200 lbs.   Born, Ceske Budejovice, Czech., February 24, 1977.
(Edmonton's 3rd choice, 57th overall, in 1995 Entry Draft).

				Regular Season					Playoffs			
Season	Club	League	GP	G	A	Pts	PIM	GP	G	A	Pts	PIM
1994-95	C. Budejovice	CzRep	13	2	0	2	16	9	1	0	1	6
1995-96	C. Budejovice Jr.	CzRep-Jr.	11	5	1	6	....					
	C. Budejovice	CzRep	10	1	0	1	....	2	0	0	0	....
1996-97	C. Budejovice	CzRep	13	0	0	0	4	2	0	0	0	0
1997-98	C. Budejovice	CzRep	47	5	6	11	22					
1998-99	C. Budejovice	CzRep	24	1	4	5	18					
99-2000	C. Budejovice	CzRep	38	3	6	9	10	1	0	0	0	0
2000-01	C. Budejovice	CzRep	22	2	3	5	16					
	Zlin	CzRep	19	4	3	7	8					
2001-02	Karlovy Vary	CzRep	36	4	10	14	20					
	Blues Espoo	Finland	5	0	0	0	2					
2002-03	Schwenningen	Germany	49	3	11	14	52	6	1	2	3	6
2003-04	Nizhny Novgorod	Russia	47	8	5	13	44					
	Perm	Russia-2	9	5	7	12	20	11	1	2	3	12
2004-05	Perm	Russia	57	0	5	5	36					

ZIMAKOV, Sergei (zih-MAH-kahv, SAIR-gay) **WSH.**

Defense. Shoots left. 6'1", 194 lbs.   Born, Moscow, USSR, January 15, 1978.
(Washington's 4th choice, 58th overall, in 1996 Entry Draft).

				Regular Season					Playoffs			
Season	Club	League	GP	G	A	Pts	PIM	GP	G	A	Pts	PIM
1994-95	Omaha Lancers	USHL	48	14	46	60	22					
1995-96	Krylja Sovetov	CIS	49	2	7	9	36					
1996-97	Krylja Sovetov	Russia	39	4	3	7	57	2	0	0	0	0
1997-98	Krylja Sovetov	Russia	42	4	1	5	48					
1998-99	Ak Bars Kazan	Russia	28	1	0	1	6	8	0	1	1	6
99-2000	Perm	Russia	31	1	2	3	34	3	0	1	1	0
2000-01	CSKA Moscow 2	Russia-3	3	2	2	4	2					
	CSKA Moscow	Russia	26	1	5	6	28					
2001-02	CSKA Moscow	Russia	42	3	10	13	74					
2002-03	Ufa	Russia	11	0	0	0	8					
	Ufa 2	Russia-3	STATISTICS NOT AVAILABLE									
2003-04	Spartak Moscow	Russia-2	60	11	17	28	38	12	0	1	1	10
2004-05	Spartak Moscow	Russia	23	2	2	4	20					

ZIMMERMAN, Sean (ZIH-mehr-man, SHAWN) **N.J.**

Defense. Shoots right. 6'2", 220 lbs.   Born, Denver, CO, May 24, 1987.
(New Jersey's 6th choice, 170th overall, in 2005 Entry Draft).

				Regular Season					Playoffs			
Season	Club	League	GP	G	A	Pts	PIM	GP	G	A	Pts	PIM
2002-03	Spokane Braves	KIJHL	45	3	5	8	70					
2003-04	Spokane Chiefs	WHL	67	4	4	8	16	4	0	0	0	0
2004-05	Spokane Chiefs	WHL	71	2	14	16	36					

ZUBAREV, Andrei (ZOO-bah-rehv, AWN-dray) **ATL.**

Defense. Shoots left. 6'1", 198 lbs.   Born, Ufa, USSR, March 3, 1987.
(Atlanta's 7th choice, 187th overall, in 2005 Entry Draft).

				Regular Season					Playoffs			
Season	Club	League	GP	G	A	Pts	PIM	GP	G	A	Pts	PIM
2003-04	Ufa 2	Russia-3	STATISTICS NOT AVAILABLE									
	Ufa	Russia	6	0	1	1	4					
2004-05	Ufa 2	Russia-3	28	2	4	6	32					
	Ufa	Russia	5	0	0	0	4					

ZUBOV, Ilja (ZOO-bahf, IHL-yah) **OTT.**

Center. Shoots left. 6', 176 lbs.   Born, Chelyabinsk, USSR, February 14, 1987.
(Ottawa's 4th choice, 98th overall, in 2005 Entry Draft).

				Regular Season					Playoffs			
Season	Club	League	GP	G	A	Pts	PIM	GP	G	A	Pts	PIM
2003-04	Chelyabinsk	Russia-2	33	7	7	14	16	8	2	1	3	2
2004-05	Chelyabinsk	Russia-2	40	9	8	17	36					
	Chelyabinsk 2	Russia-3	1	0	0	0	0					

Sidney Crosby, C, 2005 #1

Marc-André Fleury, G, 2003 #1

Kari Lehtonen, G, 2002 #2

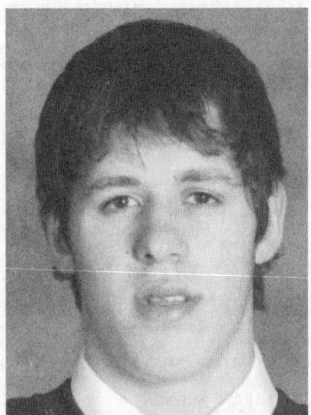

Evgeni Malkin, C, 2004 #2

Rick Nash, LW, 2002 #1

Alexander Ovechkin, LW, 2004 #1

Bobby Ryan, RW, 2005 #2

Eric Staal, C, 2003 #2

A One and A Two...

First and second overall picks from the 2002 to 2005 NHL Entry Drafts.
These fine young players break down as follows: by position: centers 3,
goaltenders 2, left wing 2, right wing 1; by country of origin: Canada 4,
Russia 2, Finland 1, USA 1; by source: Ontario Hockey League 3,
Quebec Major Junior Hockey League 2, Russia 2, Finland 1.

League Abbreviations

AAHA ....Alberta Amateur Hockey Association
AAHL ....Alaska Amateur Hockey League
AASHA.........Alaska All-Stars Hockey Association
ACHA...........American Collegiate Hockey Association
ACHL ....Atlantic Coast Hockey League
AFHL...........American Frontier Hockey League
AHL ....American Hockey League
AJHL ....Alberta Junior Hockey Leagues
Alpenliga .....Alpenliga (Austria, Italy, Slovenia 1994-1999)
AMHA..........Alberta Minor Hockey Association
AMBHL ....Alberta Major Bantam Hockey League
AMHL ....Alberta Midget AAA Hockey League
AUAA...........Atlantic University Athletic Association
AWHL ....American West Hockey League
BCAHA ....British Columbia Amateur Hockey Association
BCHL ....British Columbia (Junior) Hockey League (also BCJHL)
CABHL.........Central Alberta Bantam Hockey League
Cal-Am ....California Amateur Hockey Association
CBHL ....Calgary Bantam Hockey League
CCHA...........Central Collegiate Hockey Association
CEGEP ....Quebec College Prep
CHA.............College Hockey America
CHL..............Central Hockey League
CIS...............Commonwealth of Independent States
CIS...............Canadian Interuniversity Sport
CJHL ....Central Junior A Hockey League
CMHA..........Calgary Minor Hockey Association
ColHL...........Colonial Hockey League
CSHL............Central States Hockey League
CSJHL ....Central States Junior Hockey League
CWUAA ....Canadian Western University Athletic Association
ECAC ....Eastern College Athletic Conference
ECHL............East Coast Hockey League
EEHL ....Eastern European Hockey League
EJHL ....Eastern Junior Hockey League
EMHA ....Edmonton Minor Hockey Association
EuroHL.........European Hockey League
Exhib. ....Exhibition Games, Series or Season
GLHL............Great Lakes Hockey League
GNML..........Greater North Midget League
GPAC ....Great Plains Athletic Conference
GTHL ....Greater Toronto Hockey League
H-East..........Hockey East
HJHL ....Heritage Junior Hockey League
High-(XX).....High School (state/province)
IEHL.............Internationale Eishockey Liga
IHL...............International Hockey League
KIJHL............Kootenay International Junior B Hockey League
LCJHL...........Little Caesar's Junior Hockey League
MAAC..........Metro Atlantic Athletic Conference
MAHA..........Manitoba Amateur Hockey Association
MAHL ....Mid America Hockey League
MBAHL ....Metropolitan Boston Amateur Hockey League
MBHL...........Metropolitan Boston Hockey League
MEHL...........Midwest Elite Hockey League
Metro-HL .....Metro Hockey League
MIAC ....Minnesota Intercollegiate Athletic Conference
MJHL ....Manitoba Junior Hockey League
MJrHL ....Maritime Junior A Hockey League
MMBHL ....Manitoba Major Bantam Hockey League
MMHL.........Manitoba Midget AAA Hockey League
MMHL.........Michigan Minor Hockey League
MMMHL ......Manitoba Minor Midget Hockey League
MNHL ....Michigan National Hockey League
MTJHL..........Metropolitan Toronto Junior Hockey League
MTHL...........Metro Toronto Hockey League
MWEHL ....Midwest Elite Hockey League

NAHL...........North American Hockey League (Tier I Junior)
NAJHL..........North American Junior Hockey League
Nat-Team.......National Team (also Nt.-Team)
NBAHA ....New Brunswick Amateur Hockey Association
NBMHL........New Brunswick Midget Hockey League
NCAA ....National Collegiate Athletic Association
NCHA ....Northern Collegiate Hockey Association
NEJHL..........New England Junior Hockey League
NFAHA.........Newfoundland Amateur Hockey Association
NHL ....National Hockey League
NJCAA ....National Junior Collegiate Athletic Association
NOBHL ....Northern Ontario Bantam Hockey League
NOHA ....Northern Ontario Hockey Association
NOJHA.........Northern Ontario Junior Hockey Association
NOJHL..........Northern Ontario Junior Hockey League
NSBHL ....Nova Scotia Bantam Hockey League
NSMHL ....Nova Scotia Midget AAA Hockey League
NWJHL........Northwest Junior B Hockey League
NYJHL..........New York Junior Hockey League
OCJHL..........Ontario Central Junior A Hockey League
OHA.............Ontario Hockey Association
OHL ....Ontario Hockey League
OJHL-B.........Ontario Junior B Hockey Leagues
OMHA ....Ontario Minor Hockey Association
OMJHL.........Ontario Major Junior Hockey League
OPJHL ....Ontario Provincial Junior A Hockey League
OUAA ....Ontario Universities Athletic Association
PAHA...........Pennsylvania Amateur Hockey Association
PCJHL ....Pacific Coast Junior Hockey League
PEIHA ....Prince Edward Island Hockey Association
PIJHL...........Pacific International Junior Hockey League
QAAA ....Quebec Amateur Athletic Association
QAHA ....Quebec Amateur Hockey Association
QJHL............Quebec Junior Hockey League
QMJHL.........Quebec Major Junior Hockey League
QNAHL ....(Quebec) North American Hockey League
Q-RHL..........(Quebec) Richelieu Elite Hockey League
QSPHL..........Quebec Semi-Pro Hockey League
RAMHL ....Rural Alberta Midget Hockey League
RMJHL ....Rocky Mountain Junior Hockey League
SAHA ....Saskatchewan Amateur Hockey Association
SBHL............Saskatchewan Bantam Hockey League
SCAHA.........Southern California Amateur Hockey Association
SIJHL ....Superior International Junior Hockey League
SJHL.............Saskatchewan Junior Hockey League
SMBHL.........Saskatchewan Major Bantam Hockey League
SMHL...........Saskatchewan Midget AAA Hockey League
SMMHL........Saskatchewan Minor Midget Hockey League
SPHL............Southern Professional Hockey League
SSJHL ....South Saskatchewan Junior B Hockey League
SSMHL ....South Saskatchewan Minor Hockey League
SunHL ....Sunshine Hockey League
TBAHA.........Thunder Bay Amateur Hockey Association
TBJHL...........Thunder Bay Junior Hockey League
TBMHL.........Thunder Bay Midget Hockey League
UHL.............United Hockey League
UMEHL ....Upper Midwest Elite Hockey League
USAHA.........United States Amateur Hockey Association
USDP ....United States National Development Program
USHL............United States (Junior A) Hockey League
VIJHL ....Vancouver Island Junior Hockey League
WCHA..........Western Collegiate Hockey Association
WCHL ....West Coast Hockey League
WHA............World Hockey Association
WHL............Western Hockey League
WNYHA ....Western New York Hockey Association
WPHL..........Western Professional Hockey League
WSJHL ....Western States Junior Hockey League
WMHA.........Winnipeg Minor Hockey Association

Late Additions to Player Register

HACKERT, Michael   (HA-kuhrt, MIGH-kuhl)   DET.

Center. Shoots left. 6', 187 lbs.   Born, Heilbron, West Germany, June 21, 1981.

			Regular Season					Playoffs				
Season	Club	League	GP	G	A	Pts	PIM	GP	G	A	Pts	PIM
1997-98	Heilbronner EC	German-2	9	0	0	0	0	....	....	....	....	....
1998-99	Heilbronner EC	German-2	21	0	2	2	2	....	....	....	....	....
	Iserlohner EC	German-2	16	1	0	1	12	....	....	....	....	....
99-2000	Iserlohner EC Jr.	Ger-Jr.	25	29	26	55	34	....	....	....	....	....
	Iserlohner EC	German-2	33	0	3	3	2	....	....	....	....	....
	Iserlohner EC 1b	German-4	10	18	11	29	10	....	....	....	....	....
2000-01	Heilbronner EC	German-2	50	17	21	38	40	....	....	....	....	....
2001-02	Heilbronner EC	German-2	53	19	9	28	34	....	....	....	....	....
2002-03	Dusseldorf	Germany	20	0	0	0	2	....	....	....	....	....
	ERC Ingolstadt	German-2	27	2	0	2	12	....	....	....	....	....
	EV Duisburg	German-2	4	2	0	2	4	....	....	....	....	....
2003-04	Frankfurt Lions	Germany	51	9	13	22	36	14	2	2	4	31
2004-05	Frankfurt Lions	Germany	49	20	18	38	40	....	....	....	....	....

Signed as a free agent by **Detroit,** August 24, 2005.

REDENBACH, Tyler   (REH-dehn-bak, TIGH-luhr)   BOS.

Center. Shoots left. 5'11", 191 lbs.   Born, Regina, Sask., September 25, 1984.
(Phoenix's 1st choice, 77th overall, in 2003 Entry Draft).

			Regular Season					Playoffs				
Season	Club	League	GP	G	A	Pts	PIM	GP	G	A	Pts	PIM
2000-01	North Kamloops	BCAHA	49	60	66	126	22	...	...	...	...	...
2001-02	Prince George	WHL	65	3	18	21	30	7	0	1	1	2
2002-03	Prince George	WHL	36	8	34	42	29	...	...	...	...	...
	Swift Current	WHL	24	9	17	26	6	4	0	4	4	4
2003-04	Swift Current	WHL	71	31	*74	*105	52	5	1	1	2	14
2004-05	Swift Current	WHL	42	14	23	37	49	...	...	...	...	...
	Lethbridge	WHL	23	5	21	26	14	5	0	2	2	6

Signed as a free agent by **Boston,** September 6, 2005.

TRADES

BEECH, Kris   (Career data panel page 378)   NSH.
Center. Shoots left. 6'2", 208 lbs.   Born, Salmon Arm, B.C., February 5, 1981.
Traded to **Nashville** by **Pittsburgh** for a conditional draft choice, September 9, 2005.

Mark Messier

FREE AGENT SIGNINGS

BELLISSIMO, Vince   (Career data panel page 283)   CAR.
Center. Shoots right. 6', 199 lbs.   Born, Toronto, Ont., December 14, 1982.
Signed as a free agent by **Carolina,** September 15, 2005.

BONDRA, Peter   (Career data panel page 385)   ATL.
Right wing. Shoots left. 6', 200 lbs.   Born, Luck, USSR, February 7, 1968.
Signed as a free agent by **Atlanta,** September 18, 2005.

BROWN, Brad   (Career data panel page 393)   TOR.
Defense. Shoots right. 6'4", 220 lbs.   Born, Baie Verte, Nfld., December 27, 1975.
Signed as a free agent by **Toronto,** September 10, 2005.

CULLEN, Joe   (Career data panel page 292)   OTT.
Cetner. Shoots left. 6'1", 210 lbs.   Born, Virginia, MN, February 14, 1981.
Signed as a free agent by **Ottawa,** September 18, 2005.

CZERKAWSKI, Mariusz   (Career data panel page 407)   TOR.
Right wing. Shoots left. 6', 200 lbs.   Born, Radomsko, Poland, April 13, 1972.
Signed as a free agent by **Toronto,** September 9, 2005.

GAVEY, Aaron   (Career data panel page 429)   ANA.
Center. Shoots left. 6'2", 189 lbs.   Born, Sudbury, Ont., February 22, 1974.
Signed as a free agent by **Anaheim,** September 12, 2005.

LANGFELD, Josh   (Career data panel page 473)   S.J.
Right wing. Shoots right. 6'3", 216 lbs.   Born, Fridley, MN, July 17, 1977.
Signed as a free agent by **San Jose,** September 12, 2005.

SAMUELSSON, Mikael   (Career data panel page 547)   DET.
Right wing. Shoots left. 6'2", 211 lbs.   Born, Mariefred, Sweden, December 23, 1976.
Signed as a free agent by **Detroit,** September 18, 2005.

SAVAGE, BRIAN   (Career data panel page 549)   PHI.
Left wing. Shoots left. 6'1", 200 lbs.   Born, Sudbury, Ont., February 24, 1971.
Signed as a free agent by **Philadelphia,** September 15, 2005.

YOUNG, Scott   (Career data panel page 599)   ST.L.
Right wing. Shoots right. 6'1", 200 lbs.   Born, Clinton, MA, October 1, 1967.
Signed as a free agent by **St. Louis,** September 14, 2005.

RETIREMENTS

FRANCIS, Ron   (Career data panel page 427)
Center. Shoots left. 6'3", 200 lbs.   Born, Sault Ste. Marie, Ont., March 1, 1963.
Announced retirement, September 14, 2005.

KLATT, Trent   (Career data panel page 461)
Right wing. Shoots right. 6'1", 210 lbs.   Born, Robbinsdale, MN, January 30, 1971.
Announced retirement, September 12, 2005.

MacINNIS, Al   (Career data panel page 484)
Defense. Shoots right. 6'2", 204 lbs.   Born, Inverness, N.S., July 11, 1963.
Announced retirement, September 9, 2005.

MESSIER, Mark   (Career data panel page 497)
Center. Shoots left. 6'1", 210 lbs.   Born, Edmonton, Alta., January 18, 1961.
Announced retirement, September 12, 2005.

PATRICK, James   (Career data panel page 521)
Defense. Shoots right. 6'2", 202 lbs.   Born, Winnipeg, Man., June 14, 1963.
Announced retirement, September 8, 2005.

Ron Francis

Trent Klatt

Al MacInnis

James Patrick

Five veteran NHL players announced their retirements just as this edition of the NHL Guide went to press. Mark Messier is a six-time Stanley Cup winner with Edmonton and the New York Rangers. Ron Francis is a three-time winner of the Lady Byng Trophy and won consecutive Stanley Cup titles with Pittsburgh in 1991 and 1992. Trent Klatt starred on an all-Minnesota line with the Flyers in the 1990s and later served as linemate and mentor to the Sedin twins in Vancouver in 2002-03. Al MacInnis was part of Calgary's Cup winner and was named playoff MVP in 1989. James Patrick played 21 NHL seasons and ranks 40th in all-time games played.

2005-06 NHL Player Register

Note: The 2005-06 NHL Player Register lists forwards and defensemen only. Goaltenders are listed separately. The NHL Player Register lists every active skater who played in the NHL in 2003-04 plus additional players with NHL experience. Trades and roster changes are current as of September 6, 2005.

Abbreviations: A – assists; **F%** – faceoff winning percentage; **G** – goals; **GP** – games played; **GW** – game-winning goals scored; **Min** – average time on ice; **PIM** – penalties in minutes; **+/–** – plus/minus rating; **PP** – powerplay goals scored; **Pts** – points; **S** – shots on goal; **S%** – shooting percentage; **SH** – shorthand goal scored; **TF** – Total faceoffs taken; *** – league-leading total; ◆ – member of Stanley Cup-winning team.

Prospect Register begins on page 279.
Goaltender Register begins on page 605.
League abbreviations are listed on page 365.

								Regular Season											Playoffs							
Season	Club	League	GP	G	A	Pts	PIM	PP	SH	GW	S	%	+/-	TF	F%	Min	GP	G	A	Pts	PIM	PP	SH	GW	Min

ABID, Ramzi — (a-BIHD, RAM-zee) — ATL.

Left wing. Shoots left. 6'2", 210 lbs.   Born, Montreal, Que., March 24, 1980. Phoenix's 3rd choice, 85th overall, in 2000 Entry Draft.

Season	Club	League	GP	G	A	Pts	PIM	PP	SH	GW	S	%	+/-	TF	F%	Min	GP	G	A	Pts	PIM	PP	SH	GW	Min
1995-96	Richelieu Riverains	QAAA	42	10	14	24	18	....	....	....	....	....	....	....	....	....	4	1	2	3	2	....	....	....	....
1996-97	Chicoutimi	QMJHL	65	13	24	37	141	....	....	....	....	....	....	....	....	....	21	2	12	14	28	....	....	....	....
1997-98	Chicoutimi	QMJHL	68	50	*85	*135	266	....	....	....	....	....	....	....	....	....	6	3	4	7	10	....	....	....	....
1998-99	Chicoutimi	QMJHL	21	11	15	26	97	....	....	....	....	....	....	....	....	....	....	....	....	....	....	....	....	....	....
	Acadie-Bathurst	QMJHL	24	14	22	36	102	....	....	....	....	....	....	....	....	....	23	14	20	34	*84	....	....	....	....
99-2000	Acadie-Bathurst	QMJHL	13	10	11	21	61	....	....	....	....	....	....	....	....	....	....	....	....	....	....	....	....	....	....
	Halifax	QMJHL	59	57	80	137	148	....	....	....	....	....	....	....	....	....	10	10	13	23	18	....	....	....	....
2000-01	Springfield	AHL	17	6	4	10	38	....	....	....	....	....	....	....	....	....	....	....	....	....	....	....	....	....	....
2001-02	Springfield	AHL	66	18	25	43	214	....	....	....	....	....	....	....	....	....	....	....	....	....	....	....	....	....	....
2002-03	**Phoenix**	**NHL**	30	10	8	18	30	4	0	3	52	19.2	1	1100.0		12:30	....	....	....	....	....	....	....	....	....
	Springfield	AHL	27	15	10	25	50	....	....	....	....	....	....	....	....	....	....	....	....	....	....	....	....	....	....
	Pittsburgh	**NHL**	3	0	0	0	2	0	0	0	7	0.0	-5	1	0.0	17:33	....	....	....	....	....	....	....	....	....
2003-04	**Pittsburgh**	**NHL**	16	3	2	5	27	2	0	1	35	8.6	-5	2	0.0	12:56	....	....	....	....	....	....	....	....	....
2004-05	Wilkes-Barre	AHL	78	26	29	55	119	....	....	....	....	....	....	....	....	....	7	0	2	2	18	....	....	....	....
	NHL Totals		49	13	10	23	59	6	0	4	94	13.8		4	25.0	12:57	....	....	....	....	....	....	....	....	....

• Re-entered NHL Entry Draft. Originally Colorado's 5th choice, 28th overall, in 1998 Entry Draft.
QMJHL First All-Star Team (1998, 2000) • Jean Beliveau Trophy (QMJHL Leading Scorer) (1998) • Michel Briere Trophy (QMJHL MVP) (1998) • Canadian Major Junior First All-Star Team (2000) • Ed Chynoweth Trophy (Memorial Cup Tournament Leading Scorer) (2000)
• Missed majority of 2000-01 season recovering from wrist injury suffered in game vs. Louisville (AHL), October 27, 2000. Traded to **Pittsburgh** by **Phoenix** with Dan Focht and Guillaume Lefebvre for Jan Hrdina and Francois Leroux, March 11, 2003. • Missed majority of 2003-04 season recovering from knee injury suffered in game vs. Edmonton, December 6, 2003. Signed as a free agent by **Atlanta**, August 8, 2005.

ADAMS, Craig — (A-duhms, KRAYG) — ANA.

Right wing. Shoots right. 6', 200 lbs.   Born, Seria, Brunei, April 26, 1977. Hartford's 9th choice, 223rd overall, in 1996 Entry Draft.

Season	Club	League	GP	G	A	Pts	PIM	PP	SH	GW	S	%	+/-	TF	F%	Min	GP	G	A	Pts	PIM	PP	SH	GW	Min
1995-96	Harvard Crimson	ECAC	34	8	9	17	56	....	....	....	....	....	....	....	....	....	....	....	....	....	....	....	....	....	....
1996-97	Harvard Crimson	ECAC	32	6	4	10	36	....	....	....	....	....	....	....	....	....	....	....	....	....	....	....	....	....	....
1997-98	Harvard Crimson	ECAC	12	6	6	12	12	....	....	....	....	....	....	....	....	....	....	....	....	....	....	....	....	....	....
1998-99	Harvard Crimson	ECAC	31	9	14	23	53	....	....	....	....	....	....	....	....	....	....	....	....	....	....	....	....	....	....
99-2000	Cincinnati	IHL	73	12	12	24	124	....	....	....	....	....	....	....	....	....	8	0	1	1	14	....	....	....	....
2000-01	**Carolina**	**NHL**	44	1	0	1	20	0	0	0	15	6.7	-7	4	25.0	4:30	3	0	0	0	0	0	0	0	3:45
	Cincinnati	IHL	4	0	1	1	9	....	....	....	....	....	....	....	....	....	1	0	0	0	2	....	....	....	....
2001-02	**Carolina**	**NHL**	33	0	1	1	38	0	0	0	17	0.0	2	9	33.3	5:54	1	0	0	0	0	0	0	0	7:41
	Lowell	AHL	22	5	4	9	51	....	....	....	....	....	....	....	....	....	....	....	....	....	....	....	....	....	....
2002-03	**Carolina**	**NHL**	81	6	12	18	71	1	0	1	107	5.6	-11	20	35.0	12:12	....	....	....	....	....	....	....	....	....
2003-04	**Carolina**	**NHL**	80	7	10	17	69	0	1	0	110	6.4	-5	20	45.0	13:41	....	....	....	....	....	....	....	....	....
2004-05	Milano	Italy	30	15	14	29	57	....	....	....	....	....	....	....	....	....	15	4	7	11	26	....	....	....	....
	NHL Totals		238	14	23	37	198	1	1	1	249	5.6		53	37.7	10:24	4	0	0	0	0	0	0	0	4:44

Rights transferred to **Carolina** after **Hartford** franchise relocated, June 25, 1997. • Missed majority of 1997-98 season recovering from shoulder injury suffered in game vs. University of Wisconsin (WCHA), December 27, 1997. Signed as a free agent by **Milano**, (Italy), July 28, 2004. Signed as a free agent by **Anaheim**, August 25, 2005.

ADAMS, Kevyn — (A-duhms, KEH-vihn) — CAR.

Center. Shoots right. 6'1", 195 lbs.   Born, Washington, DC, October 8, 1974. Boston's 1st choice, 25th overall, in 1993 Entry Draft.

Season	Club	League	GP	G	A	Pts	PIM	PP	SH	GW	S	%	+/-	TF	F%	Min	GP	G	A	Pts	PIM	PP	SH	GW	Min
1990-91	Niagara Scenics	NAHL	55	17	20	37	24	....	....	....	....	....	....	....	....	....	....	....	....	....	....	....	....	....	....
1991-92	Niagara Scenics	NAHL	40	25	33	58	51	....	....	....	....	....	....	....	....	....	....	....	....	....	....	....	....	....	....
1992-93	Miami-Ohio	CCHA	40	17	15	32	18	....	....	....	....	....	....	....	....	....	....	....	....	....	....	....	....	....	....
1993-94	Miami-Ohio	CCHA	36	15	28	43	24	....	....	....	....	....	....	....	....	....	....	....	....	....	....	....	....	....	....
1994-95	Miami-Ohio	CCHA	38	20	29	49	30	....	....	....	....	....	....	....	....	....	....	....	....	....	....	....	....	....	....
1995-96	Miami-Ohio	CCHA	36	17	30	47	30	....	....	....	....	....	....	....	....	....	....	....	....	....	....	....	....	....	....
1996-97	Grand Rapids	IHL	82	22	25	47	47	....	....	....	....	....	....	....	....	....	5	1	1	2	4	....	....	....	....
1997-98	**Toronto**	**NHL**	5	0	0	0	7	0	0	0	3	0.0	0				....	....	....	....	....	....	....	....	....
	St. John's	AHL	59	17	20	37	99	....	....	....	....	....	....	....	....	....	4	0	0	0	4	....	....	....	....
1998-99	**Toronto**	**NHL**	1	0	0	0	0	0	0	0	1	0.0	0	9	44.4	7:56	7	0	2	2	14	0	0	0	11:18
	St. John's	AHL	80	15	35	50	85	....	....	....	....	....	....	....	....	....	5	2	0	2	14	....	....	....	....
99-2000	**Toronto**	**NHL**	52	5	8	13	39	0	0	0	70	7.1	-7	604	56.5	12:23	12	1	0	1	7	0	1	0	11:06
	St. John's	AHL	23	6	11	17	24	....	....	....	....	....	....	....	....	....	....	....	....	....	....	....	....	....	....
2000-01	**Columbus**	**NHL**	66	8	12	20	52	0	0	1	84	9.5	-4	1152	57.4	15:18	....	....	....	....	....	....	....	....	....
	Florida	**NHL**	12	3	6	9	2	0	0	2	21	14.3	7	198	47.5	17:25	....	....	....	....	....	....	....	....	....
2001-02	**Florida**	**NHL**	44	4	8	12	28	0	0	1	71	5.6	-3	572	57.9	13:21	....	....	....	....	....	....	....	....	....
	Carolina	**NHL**	33	2	3	5	15	0	0	1	37	5.4	-2	187	58.8	9:05	23	1	0	1	4	0	0	0	7:29
2002-03	**Carolina**	**NHL**	77	9	9	18	57	0	0	0	169	5.3	-8	1018	53.1	14:39	....	....	....	....	....	....	....	....	....

			Regular Season														Playoffs								
Season	Club	League	GP	G	A	Pts	PIM	PP	SH	GW	S	%	+/-	TF	F%	Min	GP	G	A	Pts	PIM	PP	SH	GW	Min
2003-04	Carolina	NHL	73	10	12	22	43	0	5	1	141	7.1	6	722	51.9	13:17	....	....	....	....	....	....	....	....	....
2004-05	Dusseldorf	Germany	9	1	2	3	4	....	....	....	....	....	....	....	....	....	....	....	....	....	....	....	....	....	....
	NHL Totals		363	41	58	99	243	0	5	6	597	6.9		4462	55.0	13:34	42	2	2	4	25	0	1	0	9:09

CCHA Second All-Star Team (1995)

Signed as a free agent by **Toronto**, August 7, 1997. Claimed by **Columbus** from **Toronto** in Expansion Draft, June 23, 2000. Traded to **Florida** by **Columbus** with Columbus's 4th round choice (Mike Woodford) in 2001 Entry Draft for Ray Whitney and future considerations, March 13, 2001. Traded to **Carolina** by **Florida** with Bret Hedican and Tomas Malec for Sandis Ozolinsh and Byron Ritchie, January 16, 2002. Signed as a free agent by **Dusseldorf** (Germany), February 13, 2005.

AFANASENKOV, Dmitry
(a-fahn-A-sehn-kahv, dih-MEE-tree) **T.B.**

Left wing. Shoots right. 6'1", 195 lbs. Born, Arkhangelsk, USSR, May 12, 1980. Tampa Bay's 3rd choice, 72nd overall, in 1998 Entry Draft.

1995-96	Yaroslavl 2	CIS-2	25	10	5	15	10	....	....	....	....	....	....	....	....	....	....	....	....	....	....	....	....	....	....
1996-97	Yaroslavl 2	Russia-3	45	20	15	35	14	....	....	....	....	....	....	....	....	....	....	....	....	....	....	....	....	....	....
1997-98	Yaroslavl 2	Russia-2	48	14	7	21	20	....	....	....	....	....	....	....	....	....	....	....	....	....	....	....	....	....	....
1998-99	Moncton Wildcats	QMJHL	15	5	5	10	12	....	....	....	....	....	....	....	....	....	....	....	....	....	....	....	....	....	....
	Sherbrooke	QMJHL	51	23	30	53	22	....	....	....	....	....	....	....	....	....	13	10	6	16	6	....	....	....	....
99-2000	Sherbrooke	QMJHL	60	56	43	99	70	....	....	....	....	....	....	....	....	....	5	3	2	5	4	....	....	....	....
2000-01	Tampa Bay	NHL	9	1	1	2	4	0	0	0	8	12.5	1	7	28.6	11:24	....	....	....	....	....	....	....	....	....
	Detroit Vipers	IHL	65	15	22	37	26	....	....	....	....	....	....	....	....	....	....	....	....	....	....	....	....	....	....
2001-02	Tampa Bay	NHL	5	0	0	0	0	0	0	0	1	0.0	–1	0	0.0	4:54	....	....	....	....	....	....	....	....	....
	Springfield	AHL	28	4	5	9	4	....	....	....	....	....	....	....	....	....	....	....	....	....	....	....	....	....	....
	Grand Rapids	AHL	18	1	2	3	2	....	....	....	....	....	....	....	....	....	....	....	....	....	....	....	....	....	....
2002-03	Springfield	AHL	41	4	9	13	25	....	....	....	....	....	....	....	....	....	....	....	....	....	....	....	....	....	....
	Kloten Flyers	Swiss	....	....	....	....	....	....	....	....	....	....	....	....	....	....	5	1	1	2	0	....	....	....	....
2003-04♦	Tampa Bay	NHL	71	6	10	16	12	0	0	1	98	6.1	–4	2	0.0	12:21	23	1	2	3	6	0	0	0	13:06
2004-05	Lada Togliatti	Russia	30	2	9	11	12	....	....	....	....	....	....	....	....	....	9	0	0	0	4	....	....	....	....
	NHL Totals		85	7	11	18	16	0	0	1	107	6.5		9	22.2	11:49	23	1	2	3	6	0	0	0	13:06

• Assigned to **Kloten** (Swiss) by **Tampa Bay**, February 19, 2003. Signed as a free agent by **Togliatti** (Russia), September 28, 2004.

AFINOGENOV, Maxim
(ah-fihn-ah-GEHN-ahf, mahx-EEM) **BUF.**

Right wing. Shoots left. 6', 190 lbs. Born, Moscow, USSR, September 4, 1979. Buffalo's 3rd choice, 69th overall, in 1997 Entry Draft.

1996-97	Dynamo Moscow	Russia	29	6	5	11	10	....	....	....	....	....	....	....	....	....	4	0	2	2	0	....	....	....	....
	Dynamo Moscow	EuroHL	3	0	0	0	0	....	....	....	....	....	....	....	....	....	3	1	0	1	4	....	....	....	....
1997-98	Dynamo Moscow	Russia	35	10	5	15	53	....	....	....	....	....	....	....	....	....	....	....	....	....	....	....	....	....	....
	Dynamo Moscow	EuroHL	6	3	1	4	27	....	....	....	....	....	....	....	....	....	....	....	....	....	....	....	....	....	....
1998-99	Dynamo Moscow	Russia	38	8	13	21	24	....	....	....	....	....	....	....	....	....	16	*10	6	*16	14	....	....	....	....
	Dynamo Moscow	EuroHL	5	3	5	8	29	....	....	....	....	....	....	....	....	....	4	2	1	3	27	....	....	....	....
99-2000	Buffalo	NHL	65	16	18	34	41	2	0	2	128	12.5	–4	0	0.0	13:09	5	0	1	1	2	0	0	0	12:53
	Rochester	AHL	15	6	12	18	8	....	....	....	....	....	....	....	....	....	8	3	1	4	4	....	....	....	....
2000-01	Buffalo	NHL	78	14	22	36	40	3	0	5	190	7.4	1	2	0.0	14:32	11	2	3	5	4	0	0	0	10:56
2001-02	Buffalo	NHL	81	21	19	40	69	3	1	0	234	9.0	–9	1	100.0	15:22	....	....	....	....	....	....	....	....	....
	Russia	Olympics	6	2	2	4	4	....	....	....	....	....	....	....	....	....	....	....	....	....	....	....	....	....	....
2002-03	Buffalo	NHL	35	5	6	11	21	2	0	2	77	6.5	–12	4	50.0	13:24	....	....	....	....	....	....	....	....	....
2003-04	Buffalo	NHL	73	17	14	31	57	3	0	4	148	11.5	–4	9	22.2	13:46	....	....	....	....	....	....	....	....	....
2004-05	Dynamo Moscow	Russia	36	13	14	27	91	....	....	....	....	....	....	....	....	....	10	4	4	8	8	....	....	....	....
	NHL Totals		332	73	79	152	228	13	1	13	777	9.4		16	31.3	14:11	16	2	4	6	6	0	0	0	11:32

• Missed majority of 2002-03 season recovering from head injury suffered prior to training camp, August, 2002. Signed as a free agent by **Dynamo Moscow** (Russia), June 19, 2004.

AITKEN, Johnathan
(ATE-kin, JAWN-uh-thuhn) **MTL.**

Defense. Shoots left. 6'4", 230 lbs. Born, Edmonton, Alta., May 24, 1978. Boston's 1st choice, 8th overall, in 1996 Entry Draft.

1993-94	Sherwood Park	AMHL	31	4	9	13	54	....	....	....	....	....	....	....	....	....	....	....	....	....	....	....	....	....	....
1994-95	Medicine Hat	WHL	53	0	5	5	71	....	....	....	....	....	....	....	....	....	5	0	0	0	0	....	....	....	....
1995-96	Medicine Hat	WHL	71	6	14	20	131	....	....	....	....	....	....	....	....	....	5	1	0	1	6	....	....	....	....
1996-97	Brandon	WHL	65	4	18	22	211	....	....	....	....	....	....	....	....	....	6	0	0	0	4	....	....	....	....
1997-98	Brandon	WHL	69	9	25	34	183	....	....	....	....	....	....	....	....	....	18	0	8	8	67	....	....	....	....
1998-99	Providence Bruins	AHL	65	2	9	11	92	....	....	....	....	....	....	....	....	....	13	0	0	0	17	....	....	....	....
99-2000	Boston	NHL	3	0	0	0	0	0	0	0	2	0.0	–3	0	0.0	18:57	....	....	....	....	....	....	....	....	....
	Providence Bruins	AHL	70	2	12	14	121	....	....	....	....	....	....	....	....	....	11	1	0	1	26	....	....	....	....
2000-01	HC Sparta Praha	CzRep	24	0	3	3	62	....	....	....	....	....	....	....	....	....	....	....	....	....	....	....	....	....	....
2001-02	Norfolk Admirals	AHL	28	0	1	1	43	....	....	....	....	....	....	....	....	....	4	0	0	0	2	....	....	....	....
	Jackson Bandits	ECHL	43	1	9	10	141	....	....	....	....	....	....	....	....	....	....	....	....	....	....	....	....	....	....
2002-03	Norfolk Admirals	AHL	80	1	7	8	207	....	....	....	....	....	....	....	....	....	9	2	1	3	18	....	....	....	....
2003-04	Chicago	NHL	41	0	1	1	70	0	0	0	37	0.0	–9	0	0.0	17:15	....	....	....	....	....	....	....	....	....
	Norfolk Admirals	AHL	40	1	4	5	97	....	....	....	....	....	....	....	....	....	8	1	4	5	27	....	....	....	....
2004-05	Manitoba Moose	AHL	46	1	6	7	101	....	....	....	....	....	....	....	....	....	1	0	0	0	7	....	....	....	....
	NHL Totals		44	0	1	1	70	0	0	0	39	0.0		0	0.0	17:22	....	....	....	....	....	....	....	....	....

WHL East Second All-Star Team (1998)

Signed as a free agent by **Norfolk** (AHL), September 6, 2001. Signed as a free agent by **Chicago**, May 22, 2002. Signed as a free agent by **Vancouver**, July 7, 2004. Signed as a free agent by **Montreal**, August 16, 2005.

ALEXEEV, Nikita
(uh-LEHX-ee-ehv, nih-KEE-tuh) **T.B.**

Right wing. Shoots left. 6'5", 227 lbs. Born, Murmansk, USSR, December 27, 1981. Tampa Bay's 1st choice, 8th overall, in 2000 Entry Draft.

1996-97	Krylja Sovetov 2	Russia-3	45	4	6	10	8	....	....	....	....	....	....	....	....	....	....	....	....	....	....	....	....	....	....
1997-98	Krylja Sovetov 2	Russia-3	61	11	4	15	36	....	....	....	....	....	....	....	....	....	....	....	....	....	....	....	....	....	....
1998-99	Erie Otters	OHL	61	17	18	35	14	....	....	....	....	....	....	....	....	....	5	1	1	2	4	....	....	....	....
99-2000	Erie Otters	OHL	64	24	29	53	42	....	....	....	....	....	....	....	....	....	13	4	3	7	6	....	....	....	....
2000-01	Erie Otters	OHL	64	31	41	72	45	....	....	....	....	....	....	....	....	....	12	7	7	14	12	....	....	....	....
2001-02	Tampa Bay	NHL	44	4	4	8	8	1	0	1	47	8.5	–9	0	0.0	11:26	....	....	....	....	....	....	....	....	....
	Springfield	AHL	35	5	9	14	16	....	....	....	....	....	....	....	....	....	....	....	....	....	....	....	....	....	....
2002-03	Tampa Bay	NHL	37	4	2	6	8	1	0	1	52	7.7	–6	3	33.3	11:31	11	1	0	1	0	0	0	0	10:12
	Springfield	AHL	36	7	5	12	8	....	....	....	....	....	....	....	....	....	....	....	....	....	....	....	....	....	....
2003-04	Hershey Bears	AHL	14	0	1	1	8	....	....	....	....	....	....	....	....	....	....	....	....	....	....	....	....	....	....
2004-05	Springfield	AHL	72	13	9	22	16	....	....	....	....	....	....	....	....	....	....	....	....	....	....	....	....	....	....
	NHL Totals		81	8	6	14	16	2	0	2	99	8.1		3	33.3	11:28	11	1	0	1	0	0	0	0	10:12

• Missed majority of 2003-04 season recovering from shoulder injury suffered in game vs. Philadelphia (AHL) on November 2, 2003.

ALFREDSSON, Daniel
(AHL-frehd-suhn, DAN-yehl) **OTT.**

Right wing. Shoots right. 5'11", 199 lbs. Born, Goteborg, Sweden, December 11, 1972. Ottawa's 5th choice, 133rd overall, in 1994 Entry Draft.

1990-91	Molndal Hockey	Sweden-2	3	0	0	0	2	....	....	....	....	....	....	....	....	....	8	4	4	8	4	....	....	....	....
1991-92	Molndal	Sweden-2	32	12	8	20	43	....	....	....	....	....	....	....	....	....	....	....	....	....	....	....	....	....	....
1992-93	V.Frolunda	Sweden	20	1	5	6	8	....	....	....	....	....	....	....	....	....	....	....	....	....	....	....	....	....	....
1993-94	V.Frolunda	Sweden	39	20	10	30	18	....	....	....	....	....	....	....	....	....	4	1	1	2	....	....	....	....	....
1994-95	V.Frolunda	Sweden	22	7	11	18	22	....	....	....	....	....	....	....	....	....	....	....	....	....	....	....	....	....	....
1995-96	Ottawa	NHL	82	26	35	61	28	8	2	3	212	12.3	–18	....	....	....	....	....	....	....	....	....	....	....	....
1996-97	Ottawa	NHL	76	24	47	71	30	11	1	1	247	9.7	5	....	....	....	7	5	2	7	6	3	0	2	....
1997-98	Ottawa	NHL	55	17	28	45	18	7	0	7	149	11.4	7	....	....	....	11	7	2	9	20	2	1	1	....
	Sweden	Olympics	4	2	3	5	2	....	....	....	....	....	....	....	....	....	....	....	....	....	....	....	....	....	....
1998-99	Ottawa	NHL	58	11	22	33	14	3	0	5	163	6.7	8	7	57.1	17:22	4	1	2	3	4	1	0	0	22:23
99-2000	Ottawa	NHL	57	21	38	59	28	4	2	0	164	12.8	11	3	66.7	18:45	6	1	3	4	2	1	0	0	20:22
2000-01	Ottawa	NHL	68	24	46	70	30	10	0	3	206	11.7	11	8	50.0	18:47	4	1	0	1	2	0	0	0	21:20
2001-02	Ottawa	NHL	78	37	34	71	45	9	1	4	243	15.2	3	30	30.0	20:19	12	7	6	13	4	3	0	3	21:43
	Sweden	Olympics	4	1	4	5	2	....	....	....	....	....	....	....	....	....	....	....	....	....	....	....	....	....	....
2002-03	Ottawa	NHL	78	27	51	78	42	9	0	6	240	11.3	15	40	40.0	19:32	18	4	4	8	12	4	0	1	18:00

			Regular Season														Playoffs								
Season	Club	League	GP	G	A	Pts	PIM	PP	SH	GW	S	%	+/-	TF	F%	Min	GP	G	A	Pts	PIM	PP	SH	GW	Min
2003-04	**Ottawa**	**NHL**	**77**	**32**	**48**	**80**	**24**	**9**	**0**	**5**	**230**	**13.9**	**12**	**33**	**24.2**	**19:24**	**7**	**1**	**2**	**3**	**2**	**0**	**0**	**0**	**20:03**
2004-05	Frolunda	Sweden	15	8	9	17	10	....	....	....	....	....	....	....	....	....	14	*12	6	*18	8	....	....	....	....
	NHL Totals		**629**	**219**	**349**	**568**	**259**	**70**	**6**	**34**	**1854**	**11.8**		**121**	**35.5**	**19:07**	**69**	**27**	**21**	**48**	**52**	**14**	**1**	**7**	**20:02**

NHL All-Rookie Team (1996) • Calder Memorial Trophy (1996)
Played in NHL All-Star Game (1996, 1997, 1998, 2004)
Signed as a free agent by **Frolunda** (Sweden), November 10, 2004.

ALLEN, Bobby
(AHL-lehn, BAW-bee) **N.J.**

Defense. Shoots left. 6'1", 205 lbs. Born, Braintree, MA, November 14, 1978. Boston's 2nd choice, 52nd overall, in 1998 Entry Draft.

Season	Club	League	GP	G	A	Pts	PIM	PP	SH	GW	S	%	+/-	TF	F%	Min	GP	G	A	Pts	PIM	PP	SH	GW	Min
1996-97	Cushing	High-MA	36	11	33	44	28	....	....	....	....	....	....	....	....	....	....	....	....	....	....	....	....	....	....
1997-98	Boston College	H-East	40	7	21	28	49	....	....	....	....	....	....	....	....	....	....	....	....	....	....	....	....	....	....
1998-99	Boston College	H-East	43	9	23	32	34	....	....	....	....	....	....	....	....	....	....	....	....	....	....	....	....	....	....
99-2000	Boston College	H-East	42	4	23	27	40	....	....	....	....	....	....	....	....	....	....	....	....	....	....	....	....	....	....
2000-01	Boston College	H-East	42	5	18	23	28	....	....	....	....	....	....	....	....	....	....	....	....	....	....	....	....	....	....
2001-02	Providence Bruins	AHL	49	5	10	15	18	....	....	....	....	....	....	....	....	....	....	....	....	....	....	....	....	....	....
	Hamilton	AHL	10	1	6	7	0	....	....	....	....	....	....	....	....	....	14	0	3	3	6	....	....	....	....
2002-03	**Edmonton**	**NHL**	**1**	**0**	**0**	**0**	**0**	**0**	**0**	**0**	**0**	**0.0**	**0**	**0**	**0.0**	**2:53**	....	....	....	....	....	....	....	....	....
	Hamilton	AHL	56	1	12	13	24	....	....	....	....	....	....	....	....	....	23	0	5	5	10	....	....	....	....
2003-04	Toronto	AHL	56	5	10	15	18	....	....	....	....	....	....	....	....	....	3	0	2	2	4	....	....	....	....
2004-05	Albany River Rats	AHL	66	5	11	16	20	....	....	....	....	....	....	....	....	....	....	....	....	....	....	....	....	....	....
	NHL Totals		**1**	**0**	**0**	**0**	**0**	**0**	**0**	**0**	**0**	**0.0**		**0**	**0.0**	**2:53**	....	....	....	....	....	....	....	....	....

Hockey East Second All-Star Team (2000) • Hockey East First All-Star Team (2001) • NCAA East First All-American Team (2001)
Traded to **Edmonton** by **Boston** for Sean Brown, March 19, 2002. Signed as a free agent by **New Jersey**, July 22, 2004.

ALLEN, Bryan
(AHL-lehn, BRIGH-uhn) **VAN.**

Defense. Shoots left. 6'4", 220 lbs. Born, Kingston, Ont., August 21, 1980. Vancouver's 1st choice, 4th overall, in 1998 Entry Draft.

Season	Club	League	GP	G	A	Pts	PIM	PP	SH	GW	S	%	+/-	TF	F%	Min	GP	G	A	Pts	PIM	PP	SH	GW	Min
1995-96	Ernestown Jets	OHA-C	36	1	16	17	71	....	....	....	....	....	....	....	....	....	....	....	....	....	....	....	....	....	....
1996-97	Oshawa Generals	OHL	60	2	4	6	76	....	....	....	....	....	....	....	....	....	18	1	3	4	26	....	....	....	....
1997-98	Oshawa Generals	OHL	48	6	13	19	126	....	....	....	....	....	....	....	....	....	5	0	5	5	18	....	....	....	....
1998-99	Oshawa Generals	OHL	37	7	15	22	77	....	....	....	....	....	....	....	....	....	15	0	3	3	26	....	....	....	....
99-2000	Oshawa Generals	OHL	3	0	2	2	12	....	....	....	....	....	....	....	....	....	3	0	0	0	13	....	....	....	....
	Syracuse Crunch	AHL	9	1	1	2	11	....	....	....	....	....	....	....	....	....	2	0	0	0	2	....	....	....	....
2000-01	**Vancouver**	**NHL**	**6**	**0**	**0**	**0**	**0**	**0**	**0**	**0**	**2**	**0.0**	**0**	**0**	**0.0**	**9:20**	**2**	**0**	**0**	**0**	**2**	**0**	**0**	**0**	**13:47**
	Kansas City	IHL	75	5	20	25	99	....	....	....	....	....	....	....	....	....	....	....	....	....	....	....	....	....	....
2001-02	**Vancouver**	**NHL**	**11**	**0**	**0**	**0**	**6**	**0**	**0**	**0**	**4**	**0.0**	**1**	**0**	**0.0**	**10:47**	....	....	....	....	....	....	....	....	....
	Manitoba Moose	AHL	68	7	18	25	121	....	....	....	....	....	....	....	....	....	5	0	1	1	8	....	....	....	....
2002-03	**Vancouver**	**NHL**	**48**	**5**	**3**	**8**	**73**	**0**	**0**	**1**	**43**	**11.6**	**8**	**0**	**0.0**	**12:56**	**1**	**0**	**0**	**0**	**2**	**0**	**0**	**0**	**10:35**
	Manitoba Moose	AHL	7	0	1	1	4	....	....	....	....	....	....	....	....	....	....	....	....	....	....	....	....	....	....
2003-04	**Vancouver**	**NHL**	**74**	**2**	**5**	**7**	**94**	**0**	**0**	**0**	**70**	**2.9**	**–10**	**0**	**0.0**	**16:51**	**4**	**0**	**0**	**0**	**2**	**0**	**0**	**0**	**14:37**
2004-05	Voskresensk	Russia	19	0	3	3	34	....	....	....	....	....	....	....	....	....	....	....	....	....	....	....	....	....	....
	NHL Totals		**139**	**7**	**8**	**15**	**173**	**0**	**0**	**1**	**119**	**5.9**		**0**	**0.0**	**14:42**	**7**	**0**	**0**	**0**	**6**	**0**	**0**	**0**	**13:48**

OHL First All-Star Team (1999)
• Missed majority of 1999-2000 season recovering from knee injury suffered in training camp, September 21, 1999. Signed as a free agent by **Voskresensk** (Russia), December 20, 2004.

ALLISON, Jamie
(AL-lih-suhn, JAY-mee) **NSH.**

Defense. Shoots left. 6'1", 210 lbs. Born, Lindsay, Ont., May 13, 1975. Calgary's 2nd choice, 44th overall, in 1993 Entry Draft.

Season	Club	League	GP	G	A	Pts	PIM	PP	SH	GW	S	%	+/-	TF	F%	Min	GP	G	A	Pts	PIM	PP	SH	GW	Min
1990-91	Waterloo Siskins	OHA-B	38	3	8	11	91	....	....	....	....	....	....	....	....	....	....	....	....	....	....	....	....	....	....
1991-92	Windsor Spitfires	OHL	59	4	8	12	70	....	....	....	....	....	....	....	....	....	4	1	1	2	2	....	....	....	....
1992-93	Detroit	OHL	61	0	13	13	64	....	....	....	....	....	....	....	....	....	15	2	5	7	23	....	....	....	....
1993-94	Detroit	OHL	40	2	22	24	69	....	....	....	....	....	....	....	....	....	17	2	9	11	35	....	....	....	....
1994-95	Detroit	OHL	50	1	14	15	119	....	....	....	....	....	....	....	....	....	18	2	7	9	35	....	....	....	....
	Calgary	**NHL**	**1**	**0**	**0**	**0**	**0**	**0**	**0**	**0**	**0**	**0.0**	**0**	....	....	....	....	....	....	....	....	....	....	....	....
1995-96	Saint John Flames	AHL	71	3	16	19	223	....	....	....	....	....	....	....	....	....	14	0	2	2	16	....	....	....	....
1996-97	**Calgary**	**NHL**	**20**	**0**	**0**	**0**	**35**	**0**	**0**	**0**	**8**	**0.0**	**–4**	....	....	....	....	....	....	....	....	....	....	....	....
	Saint John Flames	AHL	46	3	6	9	139	....	....	....	....	....	....	....	....	....	5	0	1	1	4	....	....	....	....
1997-98	**Calgary**	**NHL**	**43**	**3**	**8**	**11**	**104**	**0**	**0**	**1**	**27**	**11.1**	**3**	....	....	....	....	....	....	....	....	....	....	....	....
	Saint John Flames	AHL	16	0	5	5	49	....	....	....	....	....	....	....	....	....	....	....	....	....	....	....	....	....	....
1998-99	Saint John Flames	AHL	5	0	0	0	23	....	....	....	....	....	....	....	....	....	....	....	....	....	....	....	....	....	....
	Chicago	**NHL**	**39**	**2**	**2**	**4**	**62**	**0**	**0**	**0**	**24**	**8.3**	**0**	**0**	**0.0**	**14:01**	....	....	....	....	....	....	....	....	....
	Indianapolis Ice	IHL	3	1	0	1	10	....	....	....	....	....	....	....	....	....	....	....	....	....	....	....	....	....	....
99-2000	**Chicago**	**NHL**	**59**	**1**	**3**	**4**	**102**	**0**	**0**	**0**	**24**	**4.2**	**–5**	**0**	**0.0**	**14:14**	....	....	....	....	....	....	....	....	....
2000-01	**Chicago**	**NHL**	**44**	**1**	**3**	**4**	**53**	**0**	**0**	**0**	**16**	**6.3**	**7**	**1**	**100.0**	**14:33**	....	....	....	....	....	....	....	....	....
2001-02	**Calgary**	**NHL**	**37**	**0**	**2**	**2**	**24**	**0**	**0**	**0**	**14**	**0.0**	**–3**	**2**	**0.0**	**7:44**	....	....	....	....	....	....	....	....	....
	Columbus	**NHL**	**7**	**0**	**0**	**0**	**28**	**0**	**0**	**0**	**2**	**0.0**	**–4**	**0**	**0.0**	**11:23**	....	....	....	....	....	....	....	....	....
2002-03	**Columbus**	**NHL**	**48**	**0**	**1**	**1**	**99**	**0**	**0**	**0**	**23**	**0.0**	**–15**	**1**	**100.0**	**11:57**	....	....	....	....	....	....	....	....	....
2003-04	**Nashville**	**NHL**	**47**	**0**	**3**	**3**	**76**	**0**	**0**	**0**	**19**	**0.0**	**–7**	**0**	**0.0**	**13:04**	....	....	....	....	....	....	....	....	....
2004-05	Cambridge	OHA-Sr.	5	0	3	3	4	....	....	....	....	....	....	....	....	....	....	....	....	....	....	....	....	....	....
	NHL Totals		**345**	**7**	**22**	**29**	**583**	**0**	**0**	**1**	**157**	**4.5**		**4**	**50.0**	**12:45**	....	....	....	....	....	....	....	....	....

Traded to **Chicago** by **Calgary** with Marty McInnis and Erik Andersson for Jeff Shantz and Steve Dubinsky, October 27, 1998. Claimed by **Calgary** from **Chicago** in Waiver Draft, September 28, 2001. Traded to **Columbus** by **Calgary** for Blake Sloan, March 19, 2002. Signed as a free agent by **Nashville**, September 10, 2003.

ALLISON, Jason
(AL-lih-suhn, JAY-suhn) **TOR.**

Center. Shoots right. 6'3", 215 lbs. Born, North York, Ont., May 29, 1975. Washington's 2nd choice, 17th overall, in 1993 Entry Draft.

Season	Club	League	GP	G	A	Pts	PIM	PP	SH	GW	S	%	+/-	TF	F%	Min	GP	G	A	Pts	PIM	PP	SH	GW	Min
1990-91	North York	MTJHL	63	53	41	94	....	....	....	....	....	....	....	....	....	....	....	....	....	....	....	....	....	....	....
1991-92	London Knights	OHL	65	11	19	30	15	....	....	....	....	....	....	....	....	....	7	0	0	0	0	....	....	....	....
1992-93	London Knights	OHL	66	42	76	118	50	....	....	....	....	....	....	....	....	....	12	7	13	20	8	....	....	....	....
1993-94	London Knights	OHL	56	55	87	*142	68	....	....	....	....	....	....	....	....	....	5	2	13	15	13	....	....	....	....
	Washington	**NHL**	**2**	**0**	**1**	**1**	**0**	**0**	**0**	**0**	**5**	**0.0**	**1**	....	....	....	....	....	....	....	....	....	....	....	....
	Portland Pirates	AHL	....	....	....	....	....	....	....	....	....	....	....	....	....	....	6	2	1	3	0	....	....	....	....
1994-95	London Knights	OHL	15	15	21	36	43	....	....	....	....	....	....	....	....	....	....	....	....	....	....	....	....	....	....
	Washington	**NHL**	**12**	**2**	**1**	**3**	**6**	**2**	**0**	**0**	**9**	**22.2**	**–3**	....	....	....	....	....	....	....	....	....	....	....	....
	Portland Pirates	AHL	8	5	4	9	2	....	....	....	....	....	....	....	....	....	7	3	8	11	2	....	....	....	....
1995-96	**Washington**	**NHL**	**19**	**0**	**3**	**3**	**2**	**0**	**0**	**0**	**18**	**0.0**	**–3**	....	....	....	....	....	....	....	....	....	....	....	....
	Portland Pirates	AHL	57	28	41	69	42	....	....	....	....	....	....	....	....	....	6	1	6	7	9	....	....	....	....
1996-97	**Washington**	**NHL**	**53**	**5**	**17**	**22**	**25**	**1**	**0**	**1**	**71**	**7.0**	**–3**	....	....	....	....	....	....	....	....	....	....	....	....
	Boston	**NHL**	**19**	**3**	**9**	**12**	**9**	**1**	**0**	**0**	**28**	**10.7**	**–3**	....	....	....	....	....	....	....	....	....	....	....	....
1997-98	**Boston**	**NHL**	**81**	**33**	**50**	**83**	**60**	**5**	**0**	**8**	**158**	**20.9**	**33**	....	....	....	**6**	**2**	**6**	**8**	**4**	**1**	**0**	**0**	....
1998-99	**Boston**	**NHL**	**82**	**23**	**53**	**76**	**68**	**5**	**1**	**3**	**158**	**14.6**	**5**	**1760**	**52.2**	**22:23**	**12**	**2**	**9**	**11**	**6**	**1**	**0**	**0**	**25:36**
99-2000	**Boston**	**NHL**	**37**	**10**	**18**	**28**	**20**	**3**	**0**	**1**	**66**	**15.2**	**5**	**100**	**60.0**	**21:33**	....	....	....	....	....	....	....	....	....
2000-01	**Boston**	**NHL**	**82**	**36**	**59**	**95**	**85**	**11**	**3**	**6**	**185**	**19.5**	**–8**	**1897**	**51.9**	**23:21**	....	....	....	....	....	....	....	....	....
2001-02	**Los Angeles**	**NHL**	**73**	**19**	**55**	**74**	**68**	**5**	**0**	**2**	**139**	**13.7**	**2**	**1698**	**54.5**	**21:47**	**7**	**3**	**3**	**6**	**4**	**0**	**0**	**1**	**22:26**
2002-03	**Los Angeles**	**NHL**	**26**	**6**	**22**	**28**	**22**	**2**	**0**	**3**	**46**	**13.0**	**9**	**538**	**50.9**	**21:36**	....	....	....	....	....	....	....	....	....
2003-04	**Los Angeles**	**NHL**	DID NOT PLAY – INJURED																						
2004-05			DID NOT PLAY																						
	NHL Totals		**486**	**137**	**288**	**425**	**365**	**35**	**4**	**24**	**883**	**15.5**		**5993**	**52.8**	**22:20**	**25**	**7**	**18**	**25**	**14**	**2**	**0**	**1**	**24:26**

OHL First All-Star Team (1994) • OHL MVP (1994) • Canadian Major Junior First All-Star Team (1994) • Canadian Major Junior Player of the Year (1994)
Played in NHL All-Star Game (2001)
Traded to **Boston** by **Washington** with Jim Carey, Anson Carter and Washington's 3rd round choice (Lee Goren) in 1997 Entry Draft for Bill Ranford, Adam Oates and Rick Tocchet, March 1, 1997. • Missed majority of 1999-2000 season recovering from thumb injury suffered in game vs. NY Islanders, January 8, 2000. Traded to **Los Angeles** by **Boston** with Mikko Eloranta for Jozef Stumpel and Glen Murray, October 24, 2001. • Missed majority of 2002-03 season and entire 2003-04 season recovering from knee (October 29, 2002 vs. Atlanta) and hip (January 25, 2003 vs. New Jersey) injuries. Signed as a free agent by **Toronto**, August 5, 2005.

AMONTE, Tony
(uh-MAHN-tee, TOH-nee) **CGY.**

Right wing. Shoots left. 6', 200 lbs. Born, Hingham, MA, August 2, 1970. NY Rangers' 3rd choice, 68th overall, in 1988 Entry Draft.

Season	Club	League	Regular Season GP	G	A	Pts	PIM	PP	SH	GW	S	%	+/-	TF	F%	Min	Playoffs GP	G	A	Pts	PIM	PP	SH	GW	Min
1985-86	Thayer Academy	High-MA	2	0	0	0	0	....	....	....	....	....	....	....	....	....	....	....	....	....	....	....	....	....	....
1986-87	Thayer Academy	High-MA	25	25	32	57	....	....	....	....	....	....	....	....	....	....	....	....	....	....	....	....	....	....	....
1987-88	Thayer Academy	High-MA	28	30	38	68	....	....	....	....	....	....	....	....	....	....	....	....	....	....	....	....	....	....	....
1988-89	Thayer Academy	High-MA	25	35	38	73	....	....	....	....	....	....	....	....	....	....	....	....	....	....	....	....	....	....	....
1989-90	Boston University	H-East	41	25	33	58	52	....	....	....	....	....	....	....	....	....	....	....	....	....	....	....	....	....	....
1990-91	Boston University	H-East	38	31	37	68	82	....	....	....	....	....	....	....	....	....	....	....	....	....	....	....	....	....	....
	NY Rangers	**NHL**	....	....	....	....	....	....	....	....	....	....	....	....	....	....	**2**	**0**	**2**	**2**	**2**	**0**	**0**	**0**	....
1991-92	**NY Rangers**	**NHL**	**79**	**35**	**34**	**69**	**55**	**9**	**0**	**4**	**234**	**15.0**	**12**	....	....	....	**13**	**3**	**6**	**9**	**2**	**2**	**0**	**0**	....
1992-93	**NY Rangers**	**NHL**	**83**	**33**	**43**	**76**	**49**	**13**	**0**	**4**	**270**	**12.2**	**0**	....	....	....	....	....	....	....	....	....	....	....	....
1993-94	**NY Rangers**	**NHL**	**72**	**16**	**22**	**38**	**31**	**3**	**0**	**4**	**179**	**8.9**	**5**	....	....	....	....	....	....	....	....	....	....	....	....
	Chicago	**NHL**	**7**	**1**	**3**	**4**	**6**	**1**	**0**	**0**	**16**	**6.3**	**–5**	....	....	....	**6**	**4**	**2**	**6**	**4**	**1**	**0**	**1**	....
1994-95	HC Fassa	Euroliga	14	22	16	38	10	....	....	....	....	....	....	....	....	....	....	....	....	....	....	....	....	....	....
	HC Fassa	EuroHL	2	5	1	6	0	....	....	....	....	....	....	....	....	....	....	....	....	....	....	....	....	....	....
	Chicago	**NHL**	**48**	**15**	**20**	**35**	**41**	**6**	**1**	**3**	**105**	**14.3**	**7**	....	....	....	**16**	**3**	**3**	**6**	**10**	**0**	**0**	**0**	....
1995-96	**Chicago**	**NHL**	**81**	**31**	**32**	**63**	**62**	**5**	**4**	**5**	**216**	**14.4**	**10**	....	....	....	**7**	**2**	**4**	**6**	**6**	**1**	**0**	**0**	....
1996-97	**Chicago**	**NHL**	**81**	**41**	**36**	**77**	**64**	**9**	**2**	**4**	**266**	**15.4**	**35**	....	....	....	**6**	**4**	**2**	**6**	**8**	**0**	**0**	**0**	....
1997-98	**Chicago**	**NHL**	**82**	**31**	**42**	**73**	**66**	**7**	**3**	**5**	**296**	**10.5**	**21**	....	....	....	....	....	....	....	....	....	....	....	....
	United States	Olympics	4	0	1	1	4	....	....	....	....	....	....	....	....	....	....	....	....	....	....	....	....	....	....
1998-99	**Chicago**	**NHL**	**82**	**44**	**31**	**75**	**60**	**14**	**3**	**8**	**256**	**17.2**	**0**	**8**	**12.5**	**22:12**	....	....	....	....	....	....	....	....	....
99-2000	**Chicago**	**NHL**	**82**	**43**	**41**	**84**	**48**	**11**	**5**	**2**	**260**	**16.5**	**10**	**22**	**22.7**	**21:54**	....	....	....	....	....	....	....	....	....
2000-01	**Chicago**	**NHL**	**82**	**35**	**29**	**64**	**54**	**9**	**1**	**3**	**256**	**13.7**	**–22**	**27**	**40.7**	**22:09**	....	....	....	....	....	....	....	....	....
2001-02	**Chicago**	**NHL**	**82**	**27**	**39**	**66**	**67**	**6**	**1**	**4**	**232**	**11.6**	**11**	**30**	**43.3**	**21:18**	**5**	**0**	**1**	**1**	**4**	**0**	**0**	**0**	**18:43**
	United States	Olympics	6	2	2	4	0	....	....	....	....	....	....	....	....	....	....	....	....	....	....	....	....	....	....
2002-03	**Phoenix**	**NHL**	**59**	**13**	**23**	**36**	**26**	**6**	**0**	**3**	**170**	**7.6**	**–12**	**53**	**35.9**	**19:27**	....	....	....	....	....	....	....	....	....
	Philadelphia	**NHL**	**13**	**7**	**8**	**15**	**2**	**1**	**1**	**2**	**37**	**18.9**	**12**	**3**	**33.3**	**17:39**	**13**	**1**	**6**	**7**	**4**	**0**	**0**	**0**	**19:16**
2003-04	**Philadelphia**	**NHL**	**80**	**20**	**33**	**53**	**38**	**4**	**0**	**3**	**173**	**11.6**	**13**	**8**	**37.5**	**15:14**	**18**	**3**	**5**	**8**	**6**	**2**	**0**	**0**	**14:41**
2004-05			DID NOT PLAY																						
	NHL Totals		**1013**	**392**	**436**	**828**	**669**	**104**	**21**	**54**	**2966**	**13.2**		**151**	**35.1**	**20:22**	**86**	**20**	**31**	**51**	**46**	**6**	**0**	**1**	**16:54**

Hockey East Second All-Star Team (1991) • NCAA Championship All-Tournament Team (1991) • NHL All-Rookie Team (1992)

Played in NHL All-Star Game (1997, 1998, 1999, 2000, 2001)

• Missed majority of 1985-86 season recovering from knee injury, October, 1985. Traded to **Chicago** by **NY Rangers** with the rights to Matt Oates for Stephane Matteau and Brian Noonan, March 21, 1994. Signed as a free agent by **Phoenix**, July 12, 2002. Traded to **Philadelphia** by **Phoenix** for Guillaume Lefebvre, Atlanta's 3rd round choice (previously acquired, Phoenix selected Tyler Redenbach) in 2003 Entry Draft and Philadelphia's 2nd round choice (later traded to NY Rangers – NY Rangers selected Brandon Dubinsky) in 2004 Entry Draft, March 10, 2003. Signed as a free agent by **Calgary**, August 2, 2005.

ANDERSSON, Jonas
(AN-duhr-suhn, JOH-nas) **NSH.**

Right wing. Shoots left. 6'3", 204 lbs. Born, Stockholm, Sweden, February 24, 1981. Nashville's 2nd choice, 33rd overall, in 1999 Entry Draft.

Season	Club	League	Regular Season GP	G	A	Pts	PIM	PP	SH	GW	S	%	+/-	TF	F%	Min	Playoffs GP	G	A	Pts	PIM	PP	SH	GW	Min
1997-98	AIK Solna Jr.	Swe-Jr.	33	14	16	30	32	....	....	....	....	....	....	....	....	....	....	....	....	....	....	....	....	....	....
1998-99	AIK Solna Jr.	Swe-Jr.	16	3	7	10	18	....	....	....	....	....	....	....	....	....	....	....	....	....	....	....	....	....	....
	London Knights	Britain	12	2	3	5	0	....	....	....	....	....	....	....	....	....	....	....	....	....	....	....	....	....	....
99-2000	North Bay	OHL	67	31	36	67	27	....	....	....	....	....	....	....	....	....	6	2	2	4	2	....	....	....	....
	Milwaukee	IHL	2	1	0	1	0	....	....	....	....	....	....	....	....	....	2	0	0	0	2	....	....	....	....
2000-01	Milwaukee	IHL	52	6	7	13	44	....	....	....	....	....	....	....	....	....	5	0	0	0	2	....	....	....	....
2001-02	**Nashville**	**NHL**	**5**	**0**	**0**	**0**	**2**	**0**	**0**	**0**	**4**	**0.0**	**–2**	**0**	**0.0**	**9:06**	....	....	....	....	....	....	....	....	....
	Milwaukee	AHL	71	13	17	30	19	....	....	....	....	....	....	....	....	....	....	....	....	....	....	....	....	....	....
2002-03	Milwaukee	AHL	49	7	4	11	12	....	....	....	....	....	....	....	....	....	5	0	1	1	4	....	....	....	....
2003-04			DID NOT PLAY – INJURED																						
2004-05	Sodertalje SK	Sweden	34	0	4	4	8	....	....	....	....	....	....	....	....	....	....	....	....	....	....	....	....	....	....
	Brynas IF Gavle	Sweden	7	2	0	2	2	....	....	....	....	....	....	....	....	....	....	....	....	....	....	....	....	....	....
	NHL Totals		**5**	**0**	**0**	**0**	**2**	**0**	**0**	**0**	**4**	**0.0**		**0**	**0.0**	**9:06**									

• Missed majority of 2003-04 season recovering from wrist injury suffered in training camp, September 30, 2003. Signed as a free agent by **Sodertalje** (Sweden), April 28, 2004. Signed as a free agent by **Brynas** (Sweden), January 22, 2005.

ANDREYCHUK, Dave
(AN-druh-chuhk, DAYV) **T.B.**

Left wing. Shoots right. 6'4", 220 lbs. Born, Hamilton, Ont., September 29, 1963. Buffalo's 3rd choice, 16th overall, in 1982 Entry Draft.

Season	Club	League	Regular Season GP	G	A	Pts	PIM	PP	SH	GW	S	%	+/-	TF	F%	Min	Playoffs GP	G	A	Pts	PIM	PP	SH	GW	Min
1979-80	Hamilton Hawks	OMHA	21	25	24	49	....	....	....	....	....	....	....	....	....	....	....	....	....	....	....	....	....	....	....
1980-81	Oshawa Generals	OMJHL	67	22	22	44	80	....	....	....	....	....	....	....	....	....	10	3	2	5	20	....	....	....	....
1981-82	Oshawa Generals	OHL	67	57	43	100	71	....	....	....	....	....	....	....	....	....	3	1	4	5	16	....	....	....	....
1982-83	Oshawa Generals	OHL	14	8	24	32	6	....	....	....	....	....	....	....	....	....	....	....	....	....	....	....	....	....	....
	Buffalo	**NHL**	**43**	**14**	**23**	**37**	**16**	**3**	**0**	**1**	**66**	**21.2**	**6**	....	....	....	**4**	**1**	**0**	**1**	**4**	**0**	**0**	**0**	....
1983-84	**Buffalo**	**NHL**	**78**	**38**	**42**	**80**	**42**	**10**	**0**	**7**	**178**	**21.3**	**20**	....	....	....	**2**	**0**	**1**	**1**	**2**	**0**	**0**	**0**	....
1984-85	**Buffalo**	**NHL**	**64**	**31**	**30**	**61**	**54**	**14**	**0**	**2**	**153**	**20.3**	**–4**	....	....	....	**5**	**4**	**2**	**6**	**4**	**0**	**0**	**2**	....
1985-86	**Buffalo**	**NHL**	**80**	**36**	**51**	**87**	**61**	**12**	**0**	**3**	**225**	**16.0**	**3**	....	....	....	....	....	....	....	....	....	....	....	....
1986-87	**Buffalo**	**NHL**	**77**	**25**	**48**	**73**	**46**	**13**	**0**	**2**	**255**	**9.8**	**2**	....	....	....	....	....	....	....	....	....	....	....	....
1987-88	**Buffalo**	**NHL**	**80**	**30**	**48**	**78**	**112**	**15**	**0**	**5**	**253**	**11.9**	**1**	....	....	....	**6**	**2**	**4**	**6**	**0**	**1**	**0**	**0**	....
1988-89	**Buffalo**	**NHL**	**56**	**28**	**24**	**52**	**40**	**7**	**0**	**3**	**145**	**19.3**	**0**	....	....	....	**5**	**0**	**3**	**3**	**0**	**0**	**0**	**0**	....
1989-90	**Buffalo**	**NHL**	**73**	**40**	**42**	**82**	**42**	**18**	**0**	**3**	**206**	**19.4**	**6**	....	....	....	**6**	**2**	**5**	**7**	**2**	**1**	**0**	**0**	....
1990-91	**Buffalo**	**NHL**	**80**	**36**	**33**	**69**	**32**	**13**	**0**	**4**	**234**	**15.4**	**11**	....	....	....	**6**	**2**	**2**	**4**	**8**	**1**	**0**	**0**	....
1991-92	**Buffalo**	**NHL**	**80**	**41**	**50**	**91**	**71**	**28**	**0**	**2**	**337**	**12.2**	**–9**	....	....	....	**7**	**1**	**3**	**4**	**12**	**0**	**0**	**0**	....
1992-93	**Buffalo**	**NHL**	**52**	**29**	**32**	**61**	**48**	**20**	**0**	**2**	**171**	**17.0**	**–8**	....	....	....	....	....	....	....	....	....	....	....	....
	Toronto	**NHL**	**31**	**25**	**13**	**38**	**8**	**12**	**0**	**2**	**139**	**18.0**	**12**	....	....	....	**21**	**12**	**7**	**19**	**35**	**4**	**0**	**3**	....
1993-94	**Toronto**	**NHL**	**83**	**53**	**46**	**99**	**98**	**21**	**5**	**8**	**333**	**15.9**	**22**	....	....	....	**18**	**5**	**5**	**10**	**16**	**3**	**1**	**0**	....
1994-95	**Toronto**	**NHL**	**48**	**22**	**16**	**38**	**34**	**8**	**0**	**2**	**168**	**13.1**	**–7**	....	....	....	**7**	**3**	**2**	**5**	**25**	**2**	**0**	**0**	....
1995-96	**Toronto**	**NHL**	**61**	**20**	**24**	**44**	**54**	**12**	**2**	**3**	**200**	**10.0**	**–11**	....	....	....	....	....	....	....	....	....	....	....	....
	New Jersey	**NHL**	**15**	**8**	**5**	**13**	**10**	**2**	**0**	**0**	**41**	**19.5**	**2**	....	....	....	....	....	....	....	....	....	....	....	....
1996-97	**New Jersey**	**NHL**	**82**	**27**	**34**	**61**	**48**	**4**	**1**	**2**	**233**	**11.6**	**38**	....	....	....	**1**	**0**	**0**	**0**	**0**	**0**	**0**	**0**	....
1997-98	**New Jersey**	**NHL**	**75**	**14**	**34**	**48**	**26**	**4**	**0**	**2**	**180**	**7.8**	**19**	....	....	....	**6**	**1**	**0**	**1**	**4**	**1**	**0**	**0**	....
1998-99	**New Jersey**	**NHL**	**52**	**15**	**13**	**28**	**20**	**4**	**0**	**3**	**110**	**13.6**	**1**	**9**	**44.4**	**15:32**	**4**	**2**	**0**	**2**	**4**	**0**	**0**	**0**	**10:40**
99-2000	**Boston**	**NHL**	**63**	**19**	**14**	**33**	**28**	**7**	**0**	**2**	**192**	**9.9**	**–11**	**446**	**52.0**	**19:50**	....	....	....	....	....	....	....	....	....
	Colorado	**NHL**	**14**	**1**	**2**	**3**	**2**	**1**	**0**	**1**	**41**	**2.4**	**–9**	**15**	**60.0**	**17:16**	**17**	**3**	**2**	**5**	**18**	**2**	**0**	**0**	**16:22**
2000-01	**Buffalo**	**NHL**	**74**	**20**	**13**	**33**	**32**	**8**	**0**	**4**	**119**	**16.8**	**0**	**187**	**49.7**	**12:00**	**13**	**1**	**2**	**3**	**4**	**1**	**0**	**0**	**11:04**
2001-02	**Tampa Bay**	**NHL**	**82**	**21**	**17**	**38**	**109**	**9**	**1**	**5**	**161**	**13.0**	**–12**	**1393**	**53.0**	**16:26**	....	....	....	....	....	....	....	....	....
2002-03	**Tampa Bay**	**NHL**	**72**	**20**	**14**	**34**	**34**	**15**	**0**	**3**	**170**	**11.8**	**–12**	**1117**	**58.4**	**16:27**	**11**	**3**	**3**	**6**	**10**	**1**	**0**	**1**	**21:23**
2003-04♦	**Tampa Bay**	**NHL**	**82**	**21**	**18**	**39**	**42**	**10**	**0**	**5**	**165**	**12.7**	**–9**	**1475**	**57.8**	**17:06**	**23**	**1**	**13**	**14**	**14**	**0**	**0**	**0**	**18:51**
2004-05			DID NOT PLAY																						
	NHL Totals		**1597**	**634**	**686**	**1320**	**1109**	**270**	**9**	**76**	**4475**	**14.2**		**4642**	**55.6**	**16:13**	**162**	**43**	**54**	**97**	**162**	**17**	**1**	**6**	**16:40**

Played in NHL All-Star Game (1990, 1994)

Traded to **Toronto** by **Buffalo** with Daren Puppa and Buffalo's 1st round choice (Kenny Jonsson) in 1993 Entry Draft for Grant Fuhr and Toronto's 5th round choice (Kevin Popp) in 1995 Entry Draft, February 2, 1993. Traded to **New Jersey** by **Toronto** for New Jersey's 2nd round choice (Marek Posmyk) in 1996 Entry Draft and New Jersey's 3rd round choice (later traded back to New Jersey – New Jersey selected Andre Lakos) in 1999 Entry Draft, March 13, 1996. Signed as a free agent by **Boston**, July 29, 1999. Traded to **Colorado** by **Boston** with Raymond Bourque for Brian Rolston, Martin Grenier, Samuel Pahlsson and New Jersey's 1st round choice (previously acquired, Boston selected Martin Samuelsson) in 2000 Entry Draft, March 6, 2000. Signed as a free agent by **Buffalo**, July 13, 2000. Signed as a free agent by **Tampa Bay**, July 13, 2001.

ANGELSTAD, Mel
(AN-gehl-stahd, MEHL)

Left wing. Shoots left. 6'2", 214 lbs. Born, Saskatoon, Sask., October 31, 1972.

Season	Club	League	Regular Season GP	G	A	Pts	PIM	PP	SH	GW	S	%	+/-	TF	F%	Min	Playoffs GP	G	A	Pts	PIM	PP	SH	GW	Min
1988-89	Allan Legionnaires	MAHA	35	15	23	38	256	....	....	....	....	....	....	....	....	....	....	....	....	....	....	....	....	....	....
1989-90	Warman Valley	MJHL	38	1	5	6	411	....	....	....	....	....	....	....	....	....	....	....	....	....	....	....	....	....	....
1990-91	Flin Flon Bombers	MJHL	62	6	11	17	463	....	....	....	....	....	....	....	....	....	....	....	....	....	....	....	....	....	....
1991-92	Dauphin Kings	MJHL	44	8	29	37	*296	....	....	....	....	....	....	....	....	....	....	....	....	....	....	....	....	....	....
1992-93	Thunder Bay	ColHL	45	2	5	7	256	....	....	....	....	....	....	....	....	....	5	0	0	0	10	....	....	....	....
	Nashville Knights	ECHL	1	0	0	0	14	....	....	....	....	....	....	....	....	....	....	....	....	....	....	....	....	....	....
1993-94	Thunder Bay	ColHL	58	1	20	21	374	....	....	....	....	....	....	....	....	....	9	1	2	3	65	....	....	....	....
	P.E.I. Senators	AHL	1	0	0	0	5	....	....	....	....	....	....	....	....	....	....	....	....	....	....	....	....	....	....

			Regular Season														Playoffs								
Season	Club	League	GP	G	A	Pts	PIM	PP	SH	GW	S	%	+/-	TF	F%	Min	GP	G	A	Pts	PIM	PP	SH	GW	Min
1994-95	Thunder Bay	ColHL	46	0	8	8	317	....	....	....	....	....	....	....	....	....	7	0	3	3	62	....	....	....	....
	P.E.I. Senators	AHL	3	0	0	0	16	....	....	....	....	....	....	....	....	....	....	....	....	....	....	....	....	....	....
1995-96	Thunder Bay	ColHL	51	3	3	6	335	....	....	....	....	....	....	....	....	....	16	0	6	6	94	....	....	....	....
	Phoenix	IHL	5	0	0	0	43	....	....	....	....	....	....	....	....	....	....	....	....	....	....	....	....	....	....
1996-97	Thunder Bay	ColHL	66	10	21	31	422	....	....	....	....	....	....	....	....	....	7	0	1	1	21	....	....	....	....
1997-98	Fort Worth Bulls	WPHL	19	1	6	7	102	....	....	....	....	....	....	....	....	....	....	....	....	....	....	....	....	....	....
	Las Vegas	IHL	3	0	0	0	5	....	....	....	....	....	....	....	....	....	....	....	....	....	....	....	....	....	....
	Orlando	IHL	63	1	3	4	321	....	....	....	....	....	....	....	....	....	8	0	0	0	29	....	....	....	....
1998-99	Michigan	IHL	78	3	5	8	421	....	....	....	....	....	....	....	....	....	5	1	0	1	16	....	....	....	....
99-2000	Michigan	IHL	33	3	4	7	144	....	....	....	....	....	....	....	....	....	....	....	....	....	....	....	....	....	....
2000-01	Manitoba Moose	IHL	67	1	5	6	232	....	....	....	....	....	....	....	....	....	8	0	0	0	26	....	....	....	....
2001-02	Portland Pirates	AHL	53	1	7	8	212	....	....	....	....	....	....	....	....	....	....	....	....	....	....	....	....	....	....
2002-03	Portland Pirates	AHL	57	5	2	7	139	....	....	....	....	....	....	....	....	....	3	0	0	0	6	....	....	....	....
2003-04	Portland Pirates	AHL	53	0	1	1	118	....	....	....	....	....	....	....	....	....	....	....	....	....	....	....	....	....	....
	Washington	**NHL**	**2**	**0**	**0**	**0**	**2**	**0**	**0**	**0**	**1**	**0.0**	**0**	**0**	**0.0**	**13:00**	....	....	....	....	....	....	....	....	....
2004-05	Belfast Giants	Britain	30	2	7	9	191	....	....	....	....	....	....	....	....	....	8	0	1	1	42	....	....	....	....
	NHL Totals		**2**	**0**	**0**	**0**	**2**	**0**	**0**	**0**	**1**	**0.0**		**0**	**0.0**	**13:00**	....	....	....	....	....	....	....	....	....

Signed as a free agent by **Dallas**, July 29, 1998. Signed as a free agent by **Portland** (AHL), July 30, 2003. Signed as a free agent by **Washington**, April 3, 2004. Signed as a free agent by **Belfast** (Britain), August 12, 2004.

ANTROPOV, Nik

(an-TROH-pahv, NIHK) **TOR.**

Center. Shoots left. 6'6", 230 lbs. Born, Ust-Kamenogorsk, USSR, February 18, 1980. Toronto's 1st choice, 10th overall, in 1998 Entry Draft.

Season	Club	League	GP	G	A	Pts	PIM	PP	SH	GW	S	%	+/-	TF	F%	Min	GP	G	A	Pts	PIM	PP	SH	GW	Min
1996-97	Ust-Kamenogorsk	Russia-2	8	2	1	3	6	....	....	....	....	....	....	....	....	....	....	....	....	....	....	....	....	....	....
1997-98	Ust-Kamenogorsk	Russia-2	42	15	24	39	62	....	....	....	....	....	....	....	....	....	....	....	....	....	....	....	....	....	....
1998-99	Dynamo Moscow	Russia	30	5	9	14	30	....	....	....	....	....	....	....	....	....	11	0	1	1	4	....	....	....	....
99-2000	**Toronto**	**NHL**	**66**	**12**	**18**	**30**	**41**	**0**	**0**	**2**	**89**	**13.5**	**14**	**501**	**46.3**	**12:48**	**3**	**0**	**0**	**0**	**4**	**0**	**0**	**0**	**10:14**
	St. John's	AHL	2	0	0	0	4	....	....	....	....	....	....	....	....	....	....	....	....	....	....	....	....	....	....
2000-01	**Toronto**	**NHL**	**52**	**6**	**11**	**17**	**30**	**0**	**0**	**1**	**71**	**8.5**	**5**	**431**	**44.3**	**10:02**	**9**	**2**	**1**	**3**	**12**	**1**	**0**	**1**	**11:04**
2001-02	**Toronto**	**NHL**	**11**	**1**	**1**	**2**	**4**	**0**	**0**	**0**	**12**	**8.3**	**−1**	**31**	**38.7**	**8:57**	....	....	....	....	....	....	....	....	....
	St. John's	AHL	34	11	24	35	47	....	....	....	....	....	....	....	....	....	....	....	....	....	....	....	....	....	....
2002-03	**Toronto**	**NHL**	**72**	**16**	**29**	**45**	**124**	**2**	**1**	**6**	**102**	**15.7**	**11**	**621**	**40.1**	**15:00**	**3**	**0**	**0**	**0**	**0**	**0**	**0**	**0**	**19:17**
2003-04	**Toronto**	**NHL**	**62**	**13**	**18**	**31**	**62**	**1**	**1**	**2**	**89**	**14.6**	**7**	**309**	**40.8**	**15:18**	**13**	**0**	**2**	**2**	**18**	**0**	**0**	**0**	**15:56**
2004-05	Ak Bars Kazan	Russia	10	2	3	5	6	....	....	....	....	....	....	....	....	....	....	....	....	....	....	....	....	....	....
	Yaroslavl	Russia	26	4	15	19	44	....	....	....	....	....	....	....	....	....	9	3	4	7	18	....	....	....	....
	NHL Totals		**263**	**48**	**77**	**125**	**261**	**3**	**2**	**11**	**363**	**13.2**		**1893**	**42.8**	**13:17**	**28**	**2**	**3**	**5**	**34**	**1**	**0**	**1**	**14:07**

Signed as a free agent by **Kazan** (Russia), October 27, 2004. Signed as a free agent by **Yaroslavl** (Russia), December 20, 2004.

ARKHIPOV, Denis

(AHR-kih-pahv, DEH-nihs) **NSH.**

Center. Shoots left. 6'3", 206 lbs. Born, Kazan, USSR, May 19, 1979. Nashville's 2nd choice, 60th overall, in 1998 Entry Draft.

Season	Club	League	GP	G	A	Pts	PIM	PP	SH	GW	S	%	+/-	TF	F%	Min	GP	G	A	Pts	PIM	PP	SH	GW	Min
1994-95	Itil Kazan 2	CIS-2	40	20	12	32	10	....	....	....	....	....	....	....	....	....	....	....	....	....	....	....	....	....	....
1995-96	Ak Bars Kazan	CIS	15	10	8	18	10	....	....	....	....	....	....	....	....	....	....	....	....	....	....	....	....	....	....
1996-97	Ak Bars Kazan 2	Russia-3	50	17	23	40	20	....	....	....	....	....	....	....	....	....	....	....	....	....	....	....	....	....	....
	Ak Bars Kazan	Russia	1	1	0	1	0	....	....	....	....	....	....	....	....	....	....	....	....	....	....	....	....	....	....
1997-98	Ak Bars Kazan	Russia	29	2	2	4	2	....	....	....	....	....	....	....	....	....	....	....	....	....	....	....	....	....	....
1998-99	Ak Bars Kazan	Russia	34	12	1	13	22	....	....	....	....	....	....	....	....	....	9	2	3	5	6	....	....	....	....
	Ak Bars Kazan	EuroHL	4	0	0	0	0	....	....	....	....	....	....	....	....	....	1	0	0	0	0	....	....	....	....
99-2000	Ak Bars Kazan	Russia	32	7	9	16	14	....	....	....	....	....	....	....	....	....	18	5	5	10	6	....	....	....	....
2000-01	**Nashville**	**NHL**	**40**	**6**	**7**	**13**	**4**	**0**	**0**	**0**	**42**	**14.3**	**0**	**299**	**43.8**	**9:56**	....	....	....	....	....	....	....	....	....
	Milwaukee	IHL	40	9	8	17	11	....	....	....	....	....	....	....	....	....	....	....	....	....	....	....	....	....	....
2001-02	**Nashville**	**NHL**	**82**	**20**	**22**	**42**	**16**	**7**	**0**	**6**	**118**	**16.9**	**−18**	**1108**	**44.8**	**15:43**	....	....	....	....	....	....	....	....	....
2002-03	**Nashville**	**NHL**	**79**	**11**	**24**	**35**	**32**	**3**	**0**	**1**	**148**	**7.4**	**−18**	**1069**	**46.7**	**15:09**	....	....	....	....	....	....	....	....	....
2003-04	**Nashville**	**NHL**	**72**	**9**	**12**	**21**	**22**	**3**	**0**	**3**	**91**	**9.9**	**−2**	**926**	**44.7**	**13:58**	....	....	....	....	....	....	....	....	....
2004-05	Ak Bars Kazan	Russia	45	9	8	17	28	....	....	....	....	....	....	....	....	....	4	0	0	0	0	....	....	....	....
	NHL Totals		**273**	**46**	**65**	**111**	**74**	**13**	**0**	**10**	**399**	**11.5**		**3402**	**45.3**	**14:15**	....	....	....	....	....	....	....	....	....

Signed as a free agent by **Kazan** (Russia), July 27, 2004.

ARMSTRONG, Chris

(ahrm-STRAWNG, KRIHS)

Defense. Shoots left. 6', 205 lbs. Born, Regina, Sask., June 26, 1975. Florida's 3rd choice, 57th overall, in 1993 Entry Draft.

Season	Club	League	GP	G	A	Pts	PIM	PP	SH	GW	S	%	+/-	TF	F%	Min	GP	G	A	Pts	PIM	PP	SH	GW	Min
1990-91	Whitewood	SMHL	40	25	30	55	40	....	....	....	....	....	....	....	....	....	....	....	....	....	....	....	....	....	....
1991-92	Moose Jaw	WHL	43	2	7	9	19	....	....	....	....	....	....	....	....	....	4	0	0	0	0	....	....	....	....
1992-93	Moose Jaw	WHL	67	9	35	44	104	....	....	....	....	....	....	....	....	....	....	....	....	....	....	....	....	....	....
1993-94	Moose Jaw	WHL	64	13	55	68	54	....	....	....	....	....	....	....	....	....	....	....	....	....	....	....	....	....	....
	Cincinnati	IHL	1	0	0	0	0	....	....	....	....	....	....	....	....	....	10	1	3	4	2	....	....	....	....
1994-95	Moose Jaw	WHL	66	17	54	71	61	....	....	....	....	....	....	....	....	....	10	2	12	14	22	....	....	....	....
	Cincinnati	IHL	....	....	....	....	....	....	....	....	....	....	....	....	....	....	9	1	3	4	10	....	....	....	....
1995-96	Carolina Panthers	AHL	78	9	33	42	65	....	....	....	....	....	....	....	....	....	....	....	....	....	....	....	....	....	....
1996-97	Carolina	AHL	66	9	23	32	38	....	....	....	....	....	....	....	....	....	....	....	....	....	....	....	....	....	....
1997-98	Fort Wayne	IHL	79	8	36	44	66	....	....	....	....	....	....	....	....	....	4	0	2	2	4	....	....	....	....
1998-99	Milwaukee	IHL	5	0	3	3	4	....	....	....	....	....	....	....	....	....	....	....	....	....	....	....	....	....	....
	Hershey Bears	AHL	65	12	32	44	30	....	....	....	....	....	....	....	....	....	5	0	1	1	0	....	....	....	....
99-2000	Kentucky	AHL	78	9	48	57	77	....	....	....	....	....	....	....	....	....	9	1	5	6	4	....	....	....	....
2000-01	**Minnesota**	**NHL**	**3**	**0**	**0**	**0**	**0**	**0**	**0**	**0**	**4**	**0.0**	**−3**	**0**	**0.0**	**18:06**	....	....	....	....	....	....	....	....	....
	Cleveland	IHL	77	9	32	41	42	....	....	....	....	....	....	....	....	....	4	0	2	2	2	....	....	....	....
2001-02	Bridgeport	AHL	80	10	38	48	49	....	....	....	....	....	....	....	....	....	20	3	8	11	4	....	....	....	....
2002-03	EV Zug	Swiss	21	0	7	7	45	....	....	....	....	....	....	....	....	....	....	....	....	....	....	....	....	....	....
	Augsburg	Germany	22	3	16	19	32	....	....	....	....	....	....	....	....	....	....	....	....	....	....	....	....	....	....
2003-04	**Anaheim**	**NHL**	**4**	**0**	**1**	**1**	**0**	**0**	**0**	**0**	**8**	**0.0**	**−1**	**0**	**0.0**	**12:32**	....	....	....	....	....	....	....	....	....
	Cincinnati	AHL	70	9	37	46	48	....	....	....	....	....	....	....	....	....	9	1	3	4	2	....	....	....	....
2004-05	ERC Ingolstadt	Germany	46	5	19	24	36	....	....	....	....	....	....	....	....	....	11	2	6	8	18	....	....	....	....
	NHL Totals		**7**	**0**	**1**	**1**	**0**	**0**	**0**	**0**	**12**	**0.0**		**0**	**0.0**	**14:55**	....	....	....	....	....	....	....	....	....

WHL East First All-Star Team (1994) • Canadian Major Junior Second All-Star Team (1994) • WHL East Second All-Star Team (1995)

Claimed by **Nashville** from **Florida** in Expansion Draft, June 26, 1998. Signed as a free agent by **San Jose**, September 2, 1999. Claimed by **Minnesota** from **San Jose** in Expansion Draft, June 23, 2000. Signed as a free agent by **NY Islanders**, August 8, 2001. Signed as a free agent by **Zug** (Swiss), June 14, 2002. Signed as a free agent by **Anaheim**, June 26, 2003. Signed as a free agent by **Ingolstadt** (Germany), April 4, 2004.

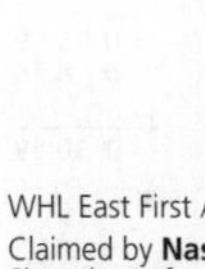

ARMSTRONG, Derek

(ahrm-STRAWNG, DAIR-ihk) **L.A.**

Center. Shoots right. 6', 195 lbs. Born, Ottawa, Ont., April 23, 1973. NY Islanders' 5th choice, 128th overall, in 1992 Entry Draft.

Season	Club	League	GP	G	A	Pts	PIM	PP	SH	GW	S	%	+/-	TF	F%	Min	GP	G	A	Pts	PIM	PP	SH	GW	Min
1989-90	Hawkesbury	CJHL	48	8	10	18	30	....	....	....	....	....	....	....	....	....	....	....	....	....	....	....	....	....	....
1990-91	Hawkesbury	CJHL	54	27	45	72	49	....	....	....	....	....	....	....	....	....	....	....	....	....	....	....	....	....	....
	Sudbury Wolves	OHL	2	0	2	2	0	....	....	....	....	....	....	....	....	....	....	....	....	....	....	....	....	....	....
1991-92	Sudbury Wolves	OHL	66	31	54	85	22	....	....	....	....	....	....	....	....	....	9	2	2	4	2	....	....	....	....
1992-93	Sudbury Wolves	OHL	66	44	62	106	56	....	....	....	....	....	....	....	....	....	14	9	10	19	26	....	....	....	....
1993-94	**NY Islanders**	**NHL**	**1**	**0**	**0**	**0**	**0**	**0**	**0**	**0**	**2**	**0.0**	**0**	....	....	....	....	....	....	....	....	....	....	....	....
	Salt Lake	IHL	76	23	35	58	61	....	....	....	....	....	....	....	....	....	....	....	....	....	....	....	....	....	....
1994-95	Denver Grizzlies	IHL	59	13	18	31	65	....	....	....	....	....	....	....	....	....	6	0	2	2	0	....	....	....	....
1995-96	**NY Islanders**	**NHL**	**19**	**1**	**3**	**4**	**14**	**0**	**0**	**0**	**23**	**4.3**	**−6**	....	....	....	....	....	....	....	....	....	....	....	....
	Worcester IceCats	AHL	51	11	15	26	33	....	....	....	....	....	....	....	....	....	4	2	1	3	0	....	....	....	....
1996-97	**NY Islanders**	**NHL**	**50**	**6**	**7**	**13**	**33**	**0**	**0**	**2**	**36**	**16.7**	**−8**	....	....	....	....	....	....	....	....	....	....	....	....
	Utah Grizzlies	IHL	17	4	8	12	10	....	....	....	....	....	....	....	....	....	6	0	4	4	4	....	....	....	....
1997-98	**Ottawa**	**NHL**	**9**	**2**	**0**	**2**	**9**	**0**	**0**	**1**	**8**	**25.0**	**1**	....	....	....	....	....	....	....	....	....	....	....	....
	Detroit Vipers	IHL	10	0	1	1	2	....	....	....	....	....	....	....	....	....	....	....	....	....	....	....	....	....	....
	Hartford	AHL	54	16	30	46	40	....	....	....	....	....	....	....	....	....	15	2	6	8	22	....	....	....	....
1998-99	**NY Rangers**	**NHL**	**3**	**0**	**0**	**0**	**0**	**0**	**0**	**0**	**1**	**0.0**	**0**	**0**	**0.0**	**2:50**	....	....	....	....	....	....	....	....	....
	Hartford	AHL	59	29	51	80	73	....	....	....	....	....	....	....	....	....	7	5	4	9	10	....	....	....	....
99-2000	**NY Rangers**	**NHL**	**1**	**0**	**0**	**0**	**0**	**0**	**0**	**0**	**1**	**0.0**	**0**	**3**	**33.3**	**3:10**	....	....	....	....	....	....	....	....	....
	Hartford	AHL	77	28	54	82	101	....	....	....	....	....	....	....	....	....	23	7	16	23	24	....	....	....	....

			Regular Season														Playoffs								
Season	Club	League	GP	G	A	Pts	PIM	PP	SH	GW	S	%	+/-	TF	F%	Min	GP	G	A	Pts	PIM	PP	SH	GW	Min
2000-01	NY Rangers	NHL	3	0	0	0	0	0	0	0	6	0.0	0	30	50.0	11:22									
	Hartford	AHL	75	32	*69	*101	73										5	0	6	6	6				
2001-02	SC Bern	Swiss	44	17	36	53	62										6	3	5	8	8				
2002-03	Los Angeles	NHL	66	12	26	38	30	2	0	1	106	11.3	5	708	50.0	15:40									
	Manchester	AHL	2	3	0	3	4																		
2003-04	Los Angeles	NHL	57	14	21	35	33	5	0	1	101	13.9	4	912	52.0	17:00									
2004-05	Geneve	Swiss	9	6	7	13	18																		
	Rapperswil	Swiss	3	1	3	4	4																		
	NHL Totals		209	35	57	92	119	7	0	5	284	12.3		1653	51.1	15:46									

AHL Second All-Star Team (2000) • Jack A. Butterfield Trophy (Playoff MVP – AHL) (2000) • AHL First All-Star Team (2001) • John P. Sollenberger Trophy (Leading Scorer – AHL) (2001) • Les Cunningham Award (MVP – AHL) (2001)

Signed as a free agent by **Ottawa**, July 28, 1997. Loaned to **Hartford** (AHL) by **Ottawa**, October 28, 1997. Signed as a free agent by **NY Rangers**, August 10, 1998. Signed as a free agent by **SC Bern** (Swiss) with NY Rangers retaining NHL rights, July 18, 2001. Traded to **Los Angeles** by **NY Rangers** for Los Angeles' 6th round choice (Chris Holt) in 2003 Entry Draft, July 16, 2002. Signed as a free agent by **Geneve** (Swiss), October 12, 2004. Signed as a free agent by **Rapperswil** (Swiss), February 13, 2005.

ARNASON, Tyler (AHR-na-suhn, TIGH-luhr) CHI.

Center. Shoots left. 5'11", 192 lbs. Born, Oklahoma City, OK, March 16, 1979. Chicago's 6th choice, 183rd overall, in 1998 Entry Draft.

Season	Club	League	GP	G	A	Pts	PIM	PP	SH	GW	S	%	+/-	TF	F%	Min	GP	G	A	Pts	PIM	PP	SH	GW	Min
1996-97	Winnipeg South	MJHL	50	35	50	85	15										6	3	3	6	18				
1997-98	Fargo-Moorhead	USHL	52	37	45	82	16										4	1	1	2	2				
1998-99	St. Cloud State	WCHA	38	14	17	31	16																		
99-2000	St. Cloud State	WCHA	39	19	30	49	18																		
2000-01	St. Cloud State	WCHA	41	28	28	56	14																		
2001-02	Chicago	NHL	21	3	1	4	4	0	0	0	19	15.8	−3	112	41.1	9:28	3	0	0	0	0	0	0	0	7:43
	Norfolk Admirals	AHL	60	26	30	56	42																		
2002-03	Chicago	NHL	82	19	20	39	20	3	0	6	178	10.7	7	626	40.3	14:30									
2003-04	Chicago	NHL	82	22	33	55	16	6	0	2	222	9.9	−13	904	43.1	16:34									
2004-05	Brynas IF Gavle	Sweden	4	0	0	0	0																		
	NHL Totals		185	44	54	98	40	9	0	8	419	10.5		1642	41.9	14:51	3	0	0	0	0	0	0	0	7:43

USHL First All-Star Team (1998) • WCHA All-Rookie Team (1999) • WCHA Second All-Star Team (2000) • AHL All-Rookie Team (2002) • Dudley "Red" Garrett Memorial Award (Rookie of the Year – AHL) (2002) • NHL All-Rookie Team (2003)

Signed as a free agent by **Brynas** (Sweden), October 29, 2004.

ARNOTT, Jason (AHR-niht, JAY-suhn) DAL.

Center. Shoots right. 6'4", 220 lbs. Born, Collingwood, Ont., October 11, 1974. Edmonton's 1st choice, 7th overall, in 1993 Entry Draft.

Season	Club	League	GP	G	A	Pts	PIM	PP	SH	GW	S	%	+/-	TF	F%	Min	GP	G	A	Pts	PIM	PP	SH	GW	Min
1989-90	Stayner Siskins	OHA-C	34	21	31	52	12																		
1990-91	Lindsay Bears	OHA-B	42	17	44	61	10										8	9	8	17	6				
1991-92	Oshawa Generals	OHL	57	9	15	24	12																		
1992-93	Oshawa Generals	OHL	56	41	57	98	74										13	9	9	18	20				
1993-94	Edmonton	NHL	78	33	35	68	104	10	0	4	194	17.0	1												
1994-95	Edmonton	NHL	42	15	22	37	128	7	0	1	156	9.6	−14												
1995-96	Edmonton	NHL	64	28	31	59	87	8	0	5	244	11.5	−6												
1996-97	Edmonton	NHL	67	19	38	57	92	10	1	2	248	7.7	−21				12	3	6	9	18	1	0	0	
1997-98	Edmonton	NHL	35	5	13	18	78	1	0	0	100	5.0	−16												
	New Jersey	NHL	35	5	10	15	21	3	0	2	99	5.1	−8				5	0	2	2	0	0	0	0	
1998-99	New Jersey	NHL	74	27	27	54	79	8	0	3	200	13.5	10	872	49.3	15:24	7	2	2	4	4	1	0	0	16:48
99-2000♦	New Jersey	NHL	76	22	34	56	51	7	0	4	244	9.0	22	1172	46.9	17:05	23	8	12	20	18	3	0	1	16:29
2000-01	New Jersey	NHL	54	21	34	55	75	8	0	3	138	15.2	23	760	49.6	16:12	23	8	7	15	16	5	0	0	15:49
2001-02	New Jersey	NHL	63	22	19	41	59	8	0	1	169	13.0	3	934	47.8	17:13									
	Dallas	NHL	10	3	1	4	6	2	0	2	28	10.7	−1	77	52.0	18:13									
2002-03	Dallas	NHL	72	23	24	47	51	7	0	6	169	13.6	9	1130	53.3	16:12	11	3	2	5	6	1	0	0	15:35
2003-04	Dallas	NHL	73	21	36	57	66	5	0	5	143	14.7	23	1203	53.0	17:00	5	1	1	2	2	1	0	0	17:23
2004-05			DID NOT PLAY																						
	NHL Totals		743	244	324	568	897	84	1	38	2132	11.4		6148	50.1	16:33	86	25	32	57	64	12	0	1	16:13

NHL All-Rookie Team (1994)

Played in NHL All-Star Game (1997)

Traded to **New Jersey** by **Edmonton** with Bryan Muir for Valeri Zelepukin and Bill Guerin, January 4, 1998. Traded to **Dallas** by **New Jersey** with Randy McKay and New Jersey's 1st round choice (later traded to Columbus – later traded to Buffalo – Buffalo selected Dan Paille) in 2002 Entry Draft for Joe Nieuwendyk and Jamie Langenbrunner, March 19, 2002.

ASHAM, Arron (ASH-uhm, AIR-ruhn) NYI

Right wing. Shoots right. 5'11", 209 lbs. Born, Portage La Prairie, Man., April 13, 1978. Montreal's 3rd choice, 71st overall, in 1996 Entry Draft.

Season	Club	League	GP	G	A	Pts	PIM	PP	SH	GW	S	%	+/-	TF	F%	Min	GP	G	A	Pts	PIM	PP	SH	GW	Min
1993-94	Portage	MAHA	21	18	19	37	82																		
1994-95	Red Deer Rebels	WHL	62	11	16	27	126																		
1995-96	Red Deer Rebels	WHL	70	32	45	77	174										10	6	3	9	20				
1996-97	Red Deer Rebels	WHL	67	45	51	96	149										16	12	14	26	36				
1997-98	Red Deer Rebels	WHL	67	43	49	92	153										5	0	2	2	8				
	Fredericton	AHL	2	1	1	2	0										2	0	1	1	0				
1998-99	Montreal	NHL	7	0	0	0	0	0	0	0	5	0.0	−4	0	0.0	7:27									
	Fredericton	AHL	60	16	18	34	118										13	8	6	14	11				
99-2000	Montreal	NHL	33	4	2	6	24	0	1	1	29	13.8	−7	1	0.0	10:14									
	Quebec Citadelles	AHL	13	4	5	9	32										2	0	0	0	2				
2000-01	Montreal	NHL	46	2	3	5	59	0	0	0	32	6.3	−9	3	100.0	8:28									
	Quebec Citadelles	AHL	15	7	9	16	51										7	1	2	3	2				
2001-02	Montreal	NHL	35	5	4	9	55	0	0	0	30	16.7	7	4	25.0	8:13	3	0	1	1	0	0	0	0	5:39
	Quebec Citadelles	AHL	24	9	14	23	35																		
2002-03	NY Islanders	NHL	78	15	19	34	57	4	0	1	114	13.2	1	17	41.2	12:13	5	0	0	0	16	0	0	0	15:09
2003-04	NY Islanders	NHL	79	12	12	24	92	1	0	0	108	11.1	−12	23	34.8	13:13	5	0	1	1	4	0	0	0	8:44
2004-05	EHC Visp	Swiss-2	5	2	4	6	6										4	1	1	2	8				
	NHL Totals		278	38	40	78	287	5	1	2	318	11.9		48	39.6	11:01	13	0	2	2	20	0	0	0	10:29

Traded to **NY Islanders** by **Montreal** with Montreal's 5th round choice (Marcus Paulsson) in 2002 Entry Draft for Mariusz Czerkawski, June 22, 2002. Signed as a free agent by **Visp** (Swiss-2), January 19, 2005.

AUBIN, Serge (oh-BEHN, SAIRZH) ATL.

Left wing. Shoots left. 6'1", 200 lbs. Born, Val-d'Or, Que., February 15, 1975. Pittsburgh's 9th choice, 161st overall, in 1994 Entry Draft.

Season	Club	League	GP	G	A	Pts	PIM	PP	SH	GW	S	%	+/-	TF	F%	Min	GP	G	A	Pts	PIM	PP	SH	GW	Min
1990-91	Abitibi Forestiers	QAAA	27	2	4	6	10																		
1991-92	Abitibi Forestiers	QAAA	42	28	32	60	36										1	0	1	1	0				
1992-93	Drummondville	QMJHL	65	16	34	50	30										8	0	1	1	16				
1993-94	Granby Bisons	QMJHL	63	42	32	74	80										7	2	3	5	8				
1994-95	Granby Bisons	QMJHL	60	37	73	110	55										11	8	15	23	4				
1995-96	Hampton Roads	ECHL	62	24	62	86	74										3	1	4	5	10				
	Cleveland	IHL	2	0	0	0	0										2	0	0	0	0				
1996-97	Cleveland	IHL	57	9	16	25	38										2	0	0	0	0				
1997-98	Syracuse Crunch	AHL	55	6	14	20	57																		
	Hershey Bears	AHL	5	2	1	3	0										7	1	3	4	6				
1998-99	Hershey Bears	AHL	64	30	39	69	58										3	0	1	1	2				
	Colorado	NHL	1	0	0	0	0	0	0	0	1	0.0	0	1	0.0	4:16									
99-2000	Colorado	NHL	15	2	1	3	6	0	0	1	14	14.3	1	79	50.6	6:37	17	0	1	1	6	0	0	0	5:06
	Hershey Bears	AHL	58	42	38	80	56																		
2000-01	Columbus	NHL	81	13	17	30	107	0	0	2	110	11.8	−20	1346	51.3	16:20									
2001-02	Columbus	NHL	71	8	8	16	32	1	0	1	86	9.3	−20	780	50.5	15:30									
2002-03	Colorado	NHL	66	4	6	10	64	0	0	1	62	6.5	−2	613	50.2	11:58	5	0	0	0	4	0	0	0	5:25

			Regular Season														Playoffs								
Season	Club	League	GP	G	A	Pts	PIM	PP	SH	GW	S	%	+/-	TF	F%	Min	GP	G	A	Pts	PIM	PP	SH	GW	Min
2003-04	Atlanta	NHL	66	10	15	25	73	1	0	2	97	10.3	0	668	49.1	16:00	....	....	....	....	....	....	....	....	....
2004-05	Geneve	Swiss	6	2	1	3	8	....	....	....	....	....	....	....	....	....	3	1	2	3	2	....	....	....	....
	NHL Totals		300	37	47	84	282	2	0	7	370	10.0		3487	50.5	14:34	22	0	1	1	10	0	0	0	5:10

AHL First All-Star Team (2000)

Signed as a free agent by **Hershey** (AHL), July 24, 1998. Signed as a free agent by **Colorado**, December 22, 1998. Signed as a free agent by **Columbus**, July 11, 2000. Signed as a free agent by **Colorado**, August 27, 2002. Claimed by **Atlanta** from **Colorado** in Waiver Draft, October 3, 2003. Signed as a free agent by **Geneve** (Swiss), January 5, 2005.

AUCOIN, Adrian

(oh-KOIN, AY-dree-an) **CHI.**

Defense. Shoots right. 6'2", 214 lbs. Born, Ottawa, Ont., July 3, 1973. Vancouver's 7th choice, 117th overall, in 1992 Entry Draft.

Season	Club	League	GP	G	A	Pts	PIM	PP	SH	GW	S	%	+/-	TF	F%	Min	GP	G	A	Pts	PIM	PP	SH	GW	Min
1989-90	Nepean Raiders	CJHL	54	2	14	16	95	....	....	....	....	....	....	....	....	....	4	0	1	1	....	....	....	....	....
1990-91	Nepean Raiders	CJHL	56	17	33	50	125	....	....	....	....	....	....	....	....	....	....	....	....	....	....	....	....	....	....
1991-92	Boston University	H-East	32	2	10	12	60	....	....	....	....	....	....	....	....	....	....	....	....	....	....	....	....	....	....
1992-93	Canada	Nat-Tm	42	8	10	18	71	....	....	....	....	....	....	....	....	....	....	....	....	....	....	....	....	....	....
1993-94	Canada	Nat-Tm	59	5	12	17	80	....	....	....	....	....	....	....	....	....	....	....	....	....	....	....	....	....	....
	Canada	Olympics	4	0	0	0	2	....	....	....	....	....	....	....	....	....	....	....	....	....	....	....	....	....	....
	Hamilton	AHL	13	1	2	3	19	....	....	....	....	....	....	....	....	....	4	0	2	2	6	....	....	....	....
1994-95	Syracuse Crunch	AHL	71	13	18	31	52	....	....	....	....	....	....	....	....	....	....	....	....	....	....	....	....	....	....
	Vancouver	NHL	1	1	0	1	0	0	0	0	2	50.0	1	....	....	....	4	1	0	1	0	1	0	0	....
1995-96	Vancouver	NHL	49	4	14	18	34	2	0	0	85	4.7	8	....	....	....	6	0	0	0	2	0	0	0	....
	Syracuse Crunch	AHL	29	5	13	18	47	....	....	....	....	....	....	....	....	....	....	....	....	....	....	....	....	....	....
1996-97	Vancouver	NHL	70	5	16	21	63	1	0	0	116	4.3	0	....	....	....	....	....	....	....	....	....	....	....	....
1997-98	Vancouver	NHL	35	3	3	6	21	1	0	1	44	6.8	–4	....	....	....	....	....	....	....	....	....	....	....	....
1998-99	Vancouver	NHL	82	23	11	34	77	18	2	3	174	13.2	–14	1	100.0	23:52	....	....	....	....	....	....	....	....	....
99-2000	Vancouver	NHL	57	10	14	24	30	4	0	1	126	7.9	7	0	0.0	23:06	....	....	....	....	....	....	....	....	....
2000-01	Vancouver	NHL	47	3	13	16	20	1	0	0	99	3.0	13	0	0.0	18:21	....	....	....	....	....	....	....	....	....
	Tampa Bay	NHL	26	1	11	12	25	1	0	0	60	1.7	–8	0	0.0	23:34	....	....	....	....	....	....	....	....	....
2001-02	NY Islanders	NHL	81	12	22	34	62	7	0	1	232	5.2	23	0	0.0	28:54	7	2	5	7	4	2	0	0	32:19
2002-03	NY Islanders	NHL	73	8	27	35	70	5	0	1	175	4.6	–5	0	0.0	29:01	5	1	2	3	4	0	0	0	31:43
2003-04	NY Islanders	NHL	81	13	31	44	54	4	0	2	213	6.1	29	0	0.0	26:38	5	0	0	0	6	0	0	0	28:21
2004-05	MODO	Sweden	14	2	4	6	32	....	....	....	....	....	....	....	....	....	6	1	0	1	16	....	....	....	....
	NHL Totals		602	83	162	245	456	44	2	9	1326	6.3		1	100.0	25:25	27	4	7	11	16	3	0	0	30:58

Played in NHL All-Star Game (2004)

• Missed majority of 1997-98 season recovering from ankle (October 4, 1997 vs. Anaheim) and groin (November 1, 1997 vs. Pittsburgh) injuries. Traded to **Tampa Bay** by **Vancouver** with Vancouver's 2nd round choice (Alexander Polushin) in 2001 Entry Draft for Dan Cloutier, February 7, 2001. Traded to **NY Islanders** by **Tampa Bay** with Alexander Kharitonov for Mathieu Biron and NY Islanders' 2nd round choice (later traded to Washington – later traded to Vancouver – Vancouver selected Denis Grot) in 2002 Entry Draft, June 22, 2001. Signed as a free agent by **MODO** (Sweden), December 21, 2004. Signed as a free agent by **Chicago**, August 2, 2005.

AUDETTE, Donald

(aw-DEHT, DAW-nohld)

Right wing. Shoots right. 5'8", 190 lbs. Born, Laval, Que., September 23, 1969. Buffalo's 8th choice, 183rd overall, in 1989 Entry Draft.

Season	Club	League	GP	G	A	Pts	PIM	PP	SH	GW	S	%	+/-	TF	F%	Min	GP	G	A	Pts	PIM	PP	SH	GW	Min
1985-86	Laval-Laurentides	QAAA	41	32	38	70	51	....	....	....	....	....	....	....	....	....	8	5	9	14	10	....	....	....	....
1986-87	Laval Titan	QMJHL	66	17	22	39	36	....	....	....	....	....	....	....	....	....	14	2	6	8	10	....	....	....	....
1987-88	Laval Titan	QMJHL	63	48	61	109	56	....	....	....	....	....	....	....	....	....	14	7	12	19	20	....	....	....	....
1988-89	Laval Titan	QMJHL	70	76	85	161	123	....	....	....	....	....	....	....	....	....	17	17	12	29	43	....	....	....	....
1989-90	Rochester	AHL	70	42	46	88	78	....	....	....	....	....	....	....	....	....	15	9	8	17	29	....	....	....	....
	Buffalo	NHL	....	....	....	....	....	....	....	....	....	....	....	....	....	....	2	0	0	0	0	0	0	0	....
1990-91	Buffalo	NHL	8	4	3	7	4	2	0	1	17	23.5	–1	....	....	....	....	....	....	....	....	....	....	....	....
	Rochester	AHL	5	4	0	4	2	....	....	....	....	....	....	....	....	....	....	....	....	....	....	....	....	....	....
1991-92	Buffalo	NHL	63	31	17	48	75	5	0	6	153	20.3	–1	....	....	....	....	....	....	....	....	....	....	....	....
1992-93	Buffalo	NHL	44	12	7	19	51	2	0	0	92	13.0	–8	....	....	....	8	2	2	4	6	0	0	0	....
	Rochester	AHL	6	8	4	12	10	....	....	....	....	....	....	....	....	....	....	....	....	....	....	....	....	....	....
1993-94	Buffalo	NHL	77	29	30	59	41	16	1	4	207	14.0	2	....	....	....	7	0	1	1	6	0	0	0	....
1994-95	Buffalo	NHL	46	24	13	37	27	13	0	7	124	19.4	–3	....	....	....	5	1	1	2	4	1	0	0	....
1995-96	Buffalo	NHL	23	12	13	25	18	8	0	1	92	13.0	0	....	....	....	....	....	....	....	....	....	....	....	....
1996-97	Buffalo	NHL	73	28	22	50	48	8	0	5	182	15.4	–6	....	....	....	11	4	5	9	6	3	0	0	....
1997-98	Buffalo	NHL	75	24	20	44	59	10	0	5	198	12.1	10	....	....	....	15	5	8	13	10	3	0	2	....
1998-99	Los Angeles	NHL	49	18	18	36	51	6	0	2	152	11.8	7	4	50.0	16:50	....	....	....	....	....	....	....	....	....
99-2000	Los Angeles	NHL	49	12	20	32	45	1	0	3	112	10.7	6	4	50.0	14:56	....	....	....	....	....	....	....	....	....
	Atlanta	NHL	14	7	4	11	12	0	1	1	50	14.0	–4	0	0.0	21:35	....	....	....	....	....	....	....	....	....
2000-01	Atlanta	NHL	64	32	39	71	64	13	1	2	187	17.1	–3	7	57.1	20:18	....	....	....	....	....	....	....	....	....
	Buffalo	NHL	12	2	6	8	12	1	0	1	38	5.3	1	1	0.0	17:25	13	3	6	9	4	0	0	0	17:06
2001-02	Dallas	NHL	20	4	8	12	12	3	0	2	49	8.2	2	2	50.0	12:26	....	....	....	....	....	....	....	....	....
	Montreal	NHL	13	1	5	6	8	0	0	1	33	3.0	1	1	100.0	17:42	12	6	4	10	10	2	0	2	15:32
2002-03	Montreal	NHL	54	11	12	23	19	4	0	4	118	9.3	–7	6	33.3	15:30	....	....	....	....	....	....	....	....	....
	Hamilton	AHL	11	5	5	10	8	....	....	....	....	....	....	....	....	....	....	....	....	....	....	....	....	....	....
2003-04	Montreal	NHL	23	3	5	8	16	0	0	0	41	7.3	–4	4	50.0	13:28	....	....	....	....	....	....	....	....	....
	Florida	NHL	28	6	7	13	22	5	0	0	66	9.1	–9	4	50.0	16:02	....	....	....	....	....	....	....	....	....
2004-05			DID NOT PLAY																						
	NHL Totals		735	260	249	509	584	97	3	45	1911	13.6		33	48.5	16:41	73	21	27	48	46	9	0	4	16:21

QMJHL First All-Star Team (1989) • AHL First All-Star Team (1990) • Dudley "Red" Garret Memorial Award (Rookie of the Year – AHL) (1990)

Played in NHL ALL-Star Game (2001)

• Missed majority of 1990-91 season recovering from knee injury suffered in game vs. Edmonton, November 16, 1990. • Missed majority of 1995-96 season recovering from knee injury suffered in training camp, September 23, 1995. Traded to **Los Angeles** by **Buffalo** for Los Angeles' 2nd round choice (Milan Bartovic) in 1999 Entry Draft, December 18, 1998. Traded to **Atlanta** by **Los Angeles** with Frantisek Kaberle for Kelly Buchberger and Nelson Emerson, March 13, 2000. Traded to **Buffalo** by **Atlanta** for the rights to Kamil Piros and Buffalo's 4th round choice (later traded to St. Louis – St. Louis selected Igor Valeyev) in 2001 Entry Draft, March 13, 2001. Signed as a free agent by **Dallas**, July 2, 2001. Traded to **Montreal** by **Dallas** with Shaun Van Allen for Martin Rucinsky and Benoit Brunet, November 21, 2001. • Missed majority of 2001-02 season recovering from wrist injury suffered in game vs. NY Rangers, December 1, 2001. Signed as a free agent by **Florida**, January 15, 2004, following release by Montreal.

AULIN, Jared

(AW-lihn, JAIR-ehd) **WSH.**

Center/Right wing. Shoots right. 6', 192 lbs. Born, Calgary, Alta., March 15, 1982. Colorado's 2nd choice, 47th overall, in 2000 Entry Draft.

Season	Club	League	GP	G	A	Pts	PIM	PP	SH	GW	S	%	+/-	TF	F%	Min	GP	G	A	Pts	PIM	PP	SH	GW	Min
1997-98	Airdrie Xtreme	AAHA	55	42	61	103	60	....	....	....	....	....	....	....	....	....	....	....	....	....	....	....	....	....	....
	Kamloops Blazers	WHL	2	0	0	0	0	....	....	....	....	....	....	....	....	....	....	....	....	....	....	....	....	....	....
1998-99	Kamloops Blazers	WHL	55	7	19	26	23	....	....	....	....	....	....	....	....	....	13	1	3	4	2	....	....	....	....
99-2000	Kamloops Blazers	WHL	57	17	38	55	70	....	....	....	....	....	....	....	....	....	4	0	1	1	6	....	....	....	....
2000-01	Kamloops Blazers	WHL	70	31	*77	108	62	....	....	....	....	....	....	....	....	....	4	0	2	2	0	....	....	....	....
2001-02	Kamloops Blazers	WHL	46	33	34	67	80	....	....	....	....	....	....	....	....	....	4	1	2	3	2	....	....	....	....
2002-03	Los Angeles	NHL	17	2	2	4	0	1	0	0	21	9.5	–3	92	41.3	9:55	....	....	....	....	....	....	....	....	....
	Manchester	AHL	44	12	32	44	21	....	....	....	....	....	....	....	....	....	3	0	4	4	0	....	....	....	....
2003-04	Portland Pirates	AHL	10	2	1	3	4	....	....	....	....	....	....	....	....	....	6	1	1	2	4	....	....	....	....
2004-05	Portland Pirates	AHL	65	11	28	39	30	....	....	....	....	....	....	....	....	....	....	....	....	....	....	....	....	....	....
	NHL Totals		17	2	2	4	0	1	0	0	21	9.5		92	41.3	9:55	....	....	....	....	....	....	....	....	....

WHL West First All-Star Team (2001, 2002)

Traded to **Los Angeles** by **Colorado** to complete transaction that sent Rob Blake and Steve Reinprecht to Colorado (February 21, 2001), March 22, 2001. • Missed majority of 2003-04 season recovering from shoulder injury suffered in training camp, September 4, 2003. Traded to **Washington** by **Los Angeles** for Anson Carter, March 8, 2004.

AVERY, Sean

(AY-vuhr-ee, SHAWN) **L.A.**

Center. Shoots left. 5'10", 185 lbs. Born, Pickering, Ont., April 10, 1980.

Season	Club	League	GP	G	A	Pts	PIM	PP	SH	GW	S	%	+/-	TF	F%	Min	GP	G	A	Pts	PIM	PP	SH	GW	Min
1995-96	Markham	OMHA	70	34	81	115	180	....	....	....	....	....	....	....	....	....	....	....	....	....	....	....	....	....	....
	Markham Waxers	MTJHL	1	0	0	0	4	....	....	....	....	....	....	....	....	....	....	....	....	....	....	....	....	....	....
1996-97	Owen Sound	OHL	58	10	21	31	86	....	....	....	....	....	....	....	....	....	4	1	0	1	4	....	....	....	....
1997-98	Owen Sound	OHL	47	13	41	54	105	....	....	....	....	....	....	....	....	....	....	....	....	....	....	....	....	....	....
1998-99	Owen Sound	OHL	28	22	23	45	70	....	....	....	....	....	....	....	....	....	....	....	....	....	....	....	....	....	....
	Kingston	OHL	33	14	25	39	88	....	....	....	....	....	....	....	....	....	5	1	3	4	13	....	....	....	....
99-2000	Kingston	OHL	55	28	56	84	215	....	....	....	....	....	....	....	....	....	5	2	2	4	26	....	....	....	....
2000-01	Cincinnati	AHL	58	8	15	23	304	....	....	....	....	....	....	....	....	....	4	1	0	1	19	....	....	....	....

			Regular Season														Playoffs								
Season	Club	League	GP	G	A	Pts	PIM	PP	SH	GW	S	%	+/-	TF	F%	Min	GP	G	A	Pts	PIM	PP	SH	GW	Min
2001-02	**Detroit**	**NHL**	**36**	**2**	**2**	**4**	**68**	**0**	**0**	**1**	**30**	**6.7**	**1**	**299**	**51.8**	**7:51**	....	....	....	....	....	....	....	....	....
	Cincinnati	AHL	36	14	7	21	106	....	....	....	....	....	....	....	....	....	....	....	....	....	....	....	....	....	....
2002-03	**Detroit**	**NHL**	**39**	**5**	**6**	**11**	**120**	**0**	**0**	**2**	**40**	**12.5**	**7**	**224**	**58.0**	**7:03**	....	....	....	....	....	....	....	....	....
	Grand Rapids	AHL	15	6	6	12	82	....	....	....	....	....	....	....	....	....	....	....	....	....	....	....	....	....	....
	Los Angeles	**NHL**	**12**	**1**	**3**	**4**	**33**	**0**	**0**	**0**	**19**	**5.3**	**0**	**49**	**46.9**	**13:50**	....	....	....	....	....	....	....	....	....
	Manchester	AHL	....	....	....	....	....	....	....	....	....	....	....	....	....	....	3	2	1	3	8	....	....	....	....
2003-04	**Los Angeles**	**NHL**	**76**	**9**	**19**	**28**	***261**	**0**	**0**	**2**	**125**	**7.2**	**2**	**124**	**54.8**	**11:41**	....	....	....	....	....	....	....	....	....
2004-05	Pelicans Lahti	Finland	2	3	0	3	26	....	....	....	....	....	....	....	....	....	....	....	....	....	....	....	....	....	....
	Motor City	UHL	16	15	11	26	149	....	....	....	....	....	....	....	....	....	....	....	....	....	....	....	....	....	....
	NHL Totals		**163**	**17**	**30**	**47**	**482**	**0**	**0**	**5**	**214**	**7.9**		**696**	**54.0**	**9:54**	....	....	....	....	....	....	....	....	....

Signed as a free agent by **Detroit**, September 21, 1999. Traded to **Los Angeles** by **Detroit** with Maxim Kuznetsov, Detroit's 1st round choice (Jeff Tambellini) in 2003 Entry Draft and Detroit's 2nd round choice (later traded to Boston – Boston selected Martins Karsums) in 2004 Entry Draft for Mathieu Schneider, March 11, 2003. Signed as a free agent by **Pelicans** (Finland), November 24, 2004. Signed as a free agent by **Motor City** (UHL), February 11, 2005.

AXELSSON, P.J. (AHX-ehl-suhn, PEE-JAY) BOS.

Left wing. Shoots left. 6'1", 184 lbs. Born, Kungalv, Sweden, February 26, 1975. Boston's 7th choice, 177th overall, in 1995 Entry Draft.

Season	Club	League	GP	G	A	Pts	PIM	PP	SH	GW	S	%	+/-	TF	F%	Min	GP	G	A	Pts	PIM	PP	SH	GW	Min
1992-93	V.Frolunda Jr.	Swe-Jr.	16	9	5	14	12	....	....	....	....	....	....	....	....	....	....	....	....	....	....	....	....	....	....
	V.Frolunda	Sweden	1	0	0	0	0	....	....	....	....	....	....	....	....	....	....	....	....	....	....	....	....	....	....
1993-94	V.Frolunda	Sweden	11	0	0	0	4	....	....	....	....	....	....	....	....	....	4	0	0	0	0	....	....	....	....
1994-95	V.Frolunda Jr.	Swe-Jr.	19	16	9	25	22	....	....	....	....	....	....	....	....	....	....	....	....	....	....	....	....	....	....
	V.Frolunda	Sweden	11	2	1	3	6	....	....	....	....	....	....	....	....	....	5	0	0	0	0	....	....	....	....
1995-96	V.Frolunda	Sweden	36	15	5	20	10	....	....	....	....	....	....	....	....	....	13	3	0	3	10	....	....	....	....
1996-97	V.Frolunda	Sweden	50	19	15	34	34	....	....	....	....	....	....	....	....	....	3	0	2	2	0	....	....	....	....
	V.Frolunda	EuroHL	3	1	1	2	0	....	....	....	....	....	....	....	....	....	3	0	0	0	2	....	....	....	....
1997-98	**Boston**	**NHL**	**82**	**8**	**19**	**27**	**38**	**2**	**0**	**1**	**144**	**5.6**	**–14**	....	....	....	**6**	**1**	**0**	**1**	**0**	**0**	**0**	**0**	....
1998-99	**Boston**	**NHL**	**77**	**7**	**10**	**17**	**18**	**0**	**0**	**2**	**146**	**4.8**	**–14**	**8**	**75.0**	**16:38**	**12**	**1**	**1**	**2**	**4**	**0**	**0**	**0**	**15:11**
99-2000	**Boston**	**NHL**	**81**	**10**	**16**	**26**	**24**	**0**	**0**	**4**	**186**	**5.4**	**1**	**22**	**27.3**	**16:43**	....	....	....	....	....	....	....	....	....
2000-01	**Boston**	**NHL**	**81**	**8**	**15**	**23**	**27**	**0**	**0**	**2**	**146**	**5.5**	**–12**	**41**	**36.6**	**12:30**	....	....	....	....	....	....	....	....	....
2001-02	**Boston**	**NHL**	**78**	**7**	**17**	**24**	**16**	**0**	**2**	**0**	**127**	**5.5**	**6**	**17**	**35.3**	**14:42**	**6**	**2**	**1**	**3**	**6**	**0**	**1**	**1**	**16:48**
	Sweden	Olympics	4	0	0	0	2	....	....	....	....	....	....	....	....	....	....	....	....	....	....	....	....	....	....
2002-03	**Boston**	**NHL**	**66**	**17**	**19**	**36**	**24**	**2**	**2**	**1**	**122**	**13.9**	**8**	**17**	**23.5**	**16:37**	**5**	**0**	**0**	**0**	**6**	**0**	**0**	**0**	**13:23**
2003-04	**Boston**	**NHL**	**68**	**6**	**14**	**20**	**42**	**0**	**0**	**1**	**107**	**5.6**	**2**	**13**	**15.4**	**16:19**	**7**	**0**	**0**	**0**	**4**	**0**	**0**	**0**	**14:43**
2004-05	Frolunda	Sweden	45	8	9	17	95	....	....	....	....	....	....	....	....	....	14	1	*10	11	18	....	....	....	....
	NHL Totals		**533**	**63**	**110**	**173**	**189**	**4**	**4**	**11**	**978**	**6.4**		**118**	**33.1**	**15:31**	**36**	**4**	**2**	**6**	**20**	**0**	**1**	**1**	**15:06**

Signed as a free agent by **Frolunda** (Sweden), September 15, 2004.

BABCHUK, Anton (bab-CHUHK, AN-tawn) CHI.

Defense. Shoots right. 6'5", 202 lbs. Born, Kiev, USSR, May 6, 1984. Chicago's 1st choice, 21st overall, in 2002 Entry Draft.

Season	Club	League	GP	G	A	Pts	PIM	PP	SH	GW	S	%	+/-	TF	F%	Min	GP	G	A	Pts	PIM	PP	SH	GW	Min
99-2000	Elektrostal 2	Russia-3	6	0	0	0	8	....	....	....	....	....	....	....	....	....	....	....	....	....	....	....	....	....	....
	Elektrostal 2	Russia-3	18	0	1	1	18	....	....	....	....	....	....	....	....	....	....	....	....	....	....	....	....	....	....
2000-01	Elektrostal	Russia-2	7	0	0	0	12	....	....	....	....	....	....	....	....	....	....	....	....	....	....	....	....	....	....
	Russia 17	Nat-Tm	15	1	3	4	12	....	....	....	....	....	....	....	....	....	....	....	....	....	....	....	....	....	....
2001-02	Elektrostal	Russia-2	40	7	8	15	90	....	....	....	....	....	....	....	....	....	....	....	....	....	....	....	....	....	....
	Elektrostal 2	Russia-3	3	0	0	0	8	....	....	....	....	....	....	....	....	....	....	....	....	....	....	....	....	....	....
2002-03	Ak Bars Kazan	Russia	10	0	0	0	4	....	....	....	....	....	....	....	....	....	....	....	....	....	....	....	....	....	....
	St. Petersburg	Russia	20	3	0	3	10	....	....	....	....	....	....	....	....	....	....	....	....	....	....	....	....	....	....
	Spartak St. Pet.	Russia-2	1	1	0	1	0	....	....	....	....	....	....	....	....	....	....	....	....	....	....	....	....	....	....
2003-04	**Chicago**	**NHL**	**5**	**0**	**2**	**2**	**2**	**0**	**0**	**0**	**11**	**0.0**	**–1**	**0**	**0.0**	**12:43**	....	....	....	....	....	....	....	....	....
	Norfolk Admirals	AHL	73	8	14	22	89	....	....	....	....	....	....	....	....	....	8	0	2	2	6	....	....	....	....
2004-05	Norfolk Admirals	AHL	66	8	16	24	88	....	....	....	....	....	....	....	....	....	2	0	0	0	2	....	....	....	....
	NHL Totals		**5**	**0**	**2**	**2**	**2**	**0**	**0**	**0**	**11**	**0.0**		**0**	**0.0**	**12:43**	....	....	....	....	....	....	....	....	....

BACKMAN, Christian (BAK-man, KRIH-stan) ST.L.

Defense. Shoots left. 6'3", 208 lbs. Born, Alingsas, Sweden, April 28, 1980. St. Louis' 1st choice, 24th overall, in 1998 Entry Draft.

Season	Club	League	GP	G	A	Pts	PIM	PP	SH	GW	S	%	+/-	TF	F%	Min	GP	G	A	Pts	PIM	PP	SH	GW	Min
1996-97	V.Frolunda Jr.	Swe-Jr.	26	2	5	7	16	....	....	....	....	....	....	....	....	....	....	....	....	....	....	....	....	....	....
1997-98	V.Frolunda U18	Swe-U18	4	4	1	5	2	....	....	....	....	....	....	....	....	....	5	2	2	4	2	....	....	....	....
	V.Frolunda Jr.	Swe-Jr.	28	5	14	19	12	....	....	....	....	....	....	....	....	....	2	0	1	1	4	....	....	....	....
1998-99	V.Frolunda Jr.	Swe-Jr.	4	0	2	2	4	....	....	....	....	....	....	....	....	....	....	....	....	....	....	....	....	....	....
	V.Frolunda	Sweden	49	0	4	4	4	....	....	....	....	....	....	....	....	....	4	0	0	0	0	....	....	....	....
99-2000	V.Frolunda Jr.	Swe-Jr.	5	1	1	2	0	....	....	....	....	....	....	....	....	....	3	1	1	2	0	....	....	....	....
	Gislaveds SK	Sweden-2	21	5	2	7	8	....	....	....	....	....	....	....	....	....	....	....	....	....	....	....	....	....	....
	V.Frolunda	Sweden	27	1	0	1	14	....	....	....	....	....	....	....	....	....	5	0	0	0	0	....	....	....	....
2000-01	V.Frolunda	Sweden	50	1	10	11	32	....	....	....	....	....	....	....	....	....	3	0	2	2	2	....	....	....	....
2001-02	V.Frolunda	Sweden	44	7	4	11	38	....	....	....	....	....	....	....	....	....	10	0	0	0	8	....	....	....	....
2002-03	**St. Louis**	**NHL**	**4**	**0**	**0**	**0**	**0**	**0**	**0**	**0**	**4**	**0.0**	**–3**	**0**	**0.0**	**12:22**	....	....	....	....	....	....	....	....	....
	Worcester IceCats	AHL	72	8	19	27	66	....	....	....	....	....	....	....	....	....	3	0	1	1	5	....	....	....	....
2003-04	**St. Louis**	**NHL**	**66**	**5**	**13**	**18**	**16**	**1**	**0**	**0**	**92**	**5.4**	**3**	**0**	**0.0**	**19:20**	**5**	**0**	**2**	**2**	**4**	**0**	**0**	**0**	**23:06**
	Worcester IceCats	AHL	4	1	2	3	2	....	....	....	....	....	....	....	....	....	....	....	....	....	....	....	....	....	....
2004-05	Frolunda	Sweden	50	4	15	19	40	....	....	....	....	....	....	....	....	....	14	2	7	9	10	....	....	....	....
	NHL Totals		**70**	**5**	**13**	**18**	**16**	**1**	**0**	**0**	**96**	**5.2**		**0**	**0.0**	**18:56**	**5**	**0**	**2**	**2**	**4**	**0**	**0**	**0**	**23:06**

Signed as a free agent by **Frolunda** (Sweden), September 15, 2004.

BALA, Chris (BA-la, KRIHS)

Left wing. Shoots left. 6'1", 196 lbs. Born, Alexandria, VA, September 24, 1978. Ottawa's 3rd choice, 58th overall, in 1998 Entry Draft.

Season	Club	League	GP	G	A	Pts	PIM	PP	SH	GW	S	%	+/-	TF	F%	Min	GP	G	A	Pts	PIM	PP	SH	GW	Min
1996-97	The Hill School	High-PA	23	28	33	61	36	....	....	....	....	....	....	....	....	....	....	....	....	....	....	....	....	....	....
1997-98	Harvard Crimson	ECAC	33	16	14	30	23	....	....	....	....	....	....	....	....	....	....	....	....	....	....	....	....	....	....
1998-99	Harvard Crimson	ECAC	28	5	10	15	16	....	....	....	....	....	....	....	....	....	....	....	....	....	....	....	....	....	....
99-2000	Harvard Crimson	ECAC	30	10	14	24	18	....	....	....	....	....	....	....	....	....	....	....	....	....	....	....	....	....	....
2000-01	Harvard Crimson	ECAC	32	14	16	30	24	....	....	....	....	....	....	....	....	....	....	....	....	....	....	....	....	....	....
2001-02	**Ottawa**	**NHL**	**6**	**0**	**1**	**1**	**0**	**0**	**0**	**0**	**2**	**0.0**	**1**	**0**	**0.0**	**5:43**	....	....	....	....	....	....	....	....	....
	Grand Rapids	AHL	70	21	16	37	9	....	....	....	....	....	....	....	....	....	4	0	1	1	0	....	....	....	....
2002-03	Binghamton	AHL	51	6	18	24	20	....	....	....	....	....	....	....	....	....	14	2	5	7	4	....	....	....	....
2003-04	Houston Aeros	AHL	61	11	7	18	18	....	....	....	....	....	....	....	....	....	....	....	....	....	....	....	....	....	....
	Hershey Bears	AHL	13	4	2	6	0	....	....	....	....	....	....	....	....	....	....	....	....	....	....	....	....	....	....
2004-05	Hershey Bears	AHL	58	9	5	14	17	....	....	....	....	....	....	....	....	....	....	....	....	....	....	....	....	....	....
	NHL Totals		**6**	**0**	**1**	**1**	**0**	**0**	**0**	**0**	**2**	**0.0**		**0**	**0.0**	**5:43**	....	....	....	....	....	....	....	....	....

Traded to **Nashville** by **Ottawa** for Peter Smrek, June 26, 2003. Traded to **Minnesota** by **Nashville** for Curtis Murphy, June 26, 2003. Traded to **Colorado** by **Minnesota** for Jordan Krestanovich, March 9, 2004.

BALEJ, Jozef (BAH-lay, YOH-zehf) NYR

Right wing. Shoots right. 6'1", 195 lbs. Born, Myjava, Czech., February 22, 1982. Montreal's 3rd choice, 78th overall, in 2000 Entry Draft.

Season	Club	League	GP	G	A	Pts	PIM	PP	SH	GW	S	%	+/-	TF	F%	Min	GP	G	A	Pts	PIM	PP	SH	GW	Min
1996-97	Dukla Trencin Jr.	Slovak-Jr.	51	31	25	56	36	....	....	....	....	....	....	....	....	....	....	....	....	....	....	....	....	....	....
1997-98	Dukla Trencin Jr.	Slovak-Jr.	52	57	40	97	60	....	....	....	....	....	....	....	....	....	....	....	....	....	....	....	....	....	....
1998-99	Thunder Bay	USHL	38	8	7	15	9	....	....	....	....	....	....	....	....	....	....	....	....	....	....	....	....	....	....
	Rochester	USHL	17	0	1	1	2	....	....	....	....	....	....	....	....	....	....	....	....	....	....	....	....	....	....
99-2000	Portland	WHL	65	22	23	45	33	....	....	....	....	....	....	....	....	....	....	....	....	....	....	....	....	....	....
2000-01	Portland	WHL	46	32	21	53	18	....	....	....	....	....	....	....	....	....	16	9	6	15	6	....	....	....	....
2001-02	Portland	WHL	65	51	41	92	52	....	....	....	....	....	....	....	....	....	7	0	2	2	6	....	....	....	....
2002-03	Hamilton	AHL	56	5	15	20	29	....	....	....	....	....	....	....	....	....	....	....	....	....	....	....	....	....	....

			Regular Season														Playoffs								
Season	Club	League	GP	G	A	Pts	PIM	PP	SH	GW	S	%	+/-	TF	F%	Min	GP	G	A	Pts	PIM	PP	SH	GW	Min
2003-04	**Montreal**	**NHL**	**4**	**0**	**0**	**0**	**0**	**0**	**0**	**0**	**4**	**0.0**	**–1**	**2**	**50.0**	**12:38**									
	Hamilton	AHL	55	25	33	58	32																		
	NY Rangers	**NHL**	**13**	**1**	**4**	**5**	**4**	**0**	**0**	**0**	**25**	**4.0**	**0**	**1**	**0.0**	**13:06**									
	Hartford	AHL	5	1	3	4	21										16	9	7	16	10				
2004-05	Hartford	AHL	69	20	22	42	46										6	0	0	0	4				
	NHL Totals		**17**	**1**	**4**	**5**	**4**	**0**	**0**	**0**	**29**	**3.4**		**3**	**33.3**	**12:59**									

WHL West First All-Star Team (2002)

Traded to **NY Rangers** by **Montreal** with Montreal's 2nd round choice (Bruce Graham) in 2004 Entry Draft for Alex Kovalev, March 2, 2004.

BALMOCHNYKH, Maxim

(bahl-MAWCH-nihky, mahx-EEM)

Left wing. Shoots left. 6'1", 210 lbs. Born, Lipetsk, USSR, March 7, 1979. Anaheim's 2nd choice, 45th overall, in 1997 Entry Draft.

Season	Club	League	GP	G	A	Pts	PIM	PP	SH	GW	S	%	+/-	TF	F%	Min	GP	G	A	Pts	PIM	PP	SH	GW	Min
1994-95	HK Lipetsk	CIS-2	3	0	1	1	4																		
1995-96	HK Lipetsk	CIS-2	40	15	5	20	60																		
1996-97	Lada Togliatti	Russia	18	6	1	7	22																		
1997-98	Lada Togliatti	Russia	37	10	4	14	46																		
	Chelyabinsk	Russia	2	0	0	0	2																		
1998-99	Lada Togliatti	Russia	15	2	1	3	10										4	0	1	1	8				
	Quebec Remparts	QMJHL	21	9	22	31	38																		
99-2000	**Anaheim**	**NHL**	**6**	**0**	**1**	**1**	**2**	**0**	**0**	**0**	**6**	**0.0**	**2**	**0**	**0.0**	**6:44**									
	Cincinnati	AHL	40	9	12	21	82																		
2000-01	Cincinnati	AHL	65	6	9	15	45																		
2001-02	Cincinnati	AHL	23	6	4	10	33																		
2002-03	Cherepovets	Russia	12	1	2	3	31																		
2003-04	Albany River Rats	AHL	42	5	9	14	54																		
2004-05	HK Lipetsk	Russia-2	41	8	7	15	121																		
	NHL Totals		**6**	**0**	**1**	**1**	**2**	**0**	**0**	**0**	**6**	**0.0**		**0**	**0.0**	**6:44**									

Traded to **New Jersey** by **Anaheim** with Jeff Friesen and Oleg Tverdovsky for Petr Sykora, Mike Commodore, Jean-Francois Damphousse and Igor Pohanka, July 6, 2002. Signed as a free agent by **Lipetsk** (Russia-2), September, 2004.

BARINKA, Michal

(ba-RIHN-kuh, MIGH-kuhl) **CHI.**

Defense. Shoots left. 6'3", 217 lbs. Born, Vyskov, Czech., June 12, 1984. Chicago's 3rd choice, 59th overall, in 2003 Entry Draft.

Season	Club	League	GP	G	A	Pts	PIM	PP	SH	GW	S	%	+/-	TF	F%	Min	GP	G	A	Pts	PIM	PP	SH	GW	Min
99-2000	C. Budejovice U17	CzR-U17	48	1	12	13	26										6	0	2	2	4				
2000-01	C. Budejovice Jr.	CzRep-Jr.	26	1	8	9	14										3	0	0	0	0				
	C. Budejovice U17	CzR-U17	7	0	1	1	6																		
2001-02	C. Budejovice Jr.	CzRep-Jr.	31	3	13	16	60										7	3	4	7	35				
	C. Budejovice	CzRep	3	0	0	0	0																		
2002-03	C. Budejovice Jr.	CzRep-Jr.	14	1	5	6	34																		
	C. Budejovice	CzRep	31	0	1	1	14										4	0	0	0	2				
2003-04	**Chicago**	**NHL**	**9**	**0**	**1**	**1**	**6**	**0**	**0**	**0**	**15**	**0.0**	**–5**	**0**	**0.0**	**13:48**									
	Norfolk Admirals	AHL	40	4	2	6	80																		
2004-05	Norfolk Admirals	AHL	59	1	10	11	77																		
	NHL Totals		**9**	**0**	**1**	**1**	**6**	**0**	**0**	**0**	**15**	**0.0**		**0**	**0.0**	**13:48**									

BARNABY, Matthew

(BAHR-na-BEE, MA-thew) **CHI.**

Right wing. Shoots left. 6', 189 lbs. Born, Ottawa, Ont., May 4, 1973. Buffalo's 5th choice, 83rd overall, in 1992 Entry Draft.

Season	Club	League	GP	G	A	Pts	PIM	PP	SH	GW	S	%	+/-	TF	F%	Min	GP	G	A	Pts	PIM	PP	SH	GW	Min
1989-90	Hull Frontaliers	QAHA	50	43	50	93	149																		
	L'Outaouais	QAAA	2	0	0	0	0																		
1990-91	Beauport	QMJHL	52	9	5	14	262																		
1991-92	Beauport	QMJHL	63	29	37	66	*476																		
1992-93	Victoriaville Tigres	QMJHL	65	44	67	111	*448										6	2	4	6	44				
	Buffalo	**NHL**	**2**	**1**	**0**	**1**	**10**	**1**	**0**	**0**	**8**	**12.5**	**0**				**1**	**0**	**1**	**1**	**4**	**0**	**0**	**0**	
1993-94	**Buffalo**	**NHL**	**35**	**2**	**4**	**6**	**106**	**1**	**0**	**0**	**13**	**15.4**	**–7**				**3**	**0**	**0**	**0**	**17**	**0**	**0**	**0**	
	Rochester	AHL	42	10	32	42	153																		
1994-95	Rochester	AHL	56	21	29	50	274																		
	Buffalo	**NHL**	**23**	**1**	**1**	**2**	**116**	**0**	**0**	**0**	**27**	**3.7**	**–2**												
1995-96	**Buffalo**	**NHL**	**73**	**15**	**16**	**31**	***335**	**0**	**0**	**0**	**131**	**11.5**	**–2**												
1996-97	**Buffalo**	**NHL**	**68**	**19**	**24**	**43**	**249**	**2**	**0**	**1**	**121**	**15.7**	**16**				**8**	**0**	**4**	**4**	**36**	**0**	**0**	**0**	
1997-98	**Buffalo**	**NHL**	**72**	**5**	**20**	**25**	**289**	**0**	**0**	**2**	**96**	**5.2**	**8**				**15**	**7**	**6**	**13**	**22**	**3**	**0**	**1**	
1998-99	**Buffalo**	**NHL**	**44**	**4**	**14**	**18**	**143**	**0**	**0**	**3**	**52**	**7.7**	**–2**	**6**	**16.7**	**13:56**									
	Pittsburgh	**NHL**	**18**	**2**	**2**	**4**	**34**	**1**	**0**	**0**	**27**	**7.4**	**–10**	**3**	**66.7**	**13:33**	**13**	**0**	**0**	**0**	**35**	**0**	**0**	**0**	**10:27**
99-2000	**Pittsburgh**	**NHL**	**64**	**12**	**12**	**24**	**197**	**0**	**0**	**3**	**80**	**15.0**	**3**	**75**	**44.0**	**12:38**	**11**	**0**	**2**	**2**	**29**	**0**	**0**	**0**	**13:41**
2000-01	**Pittsburgh**	**NHL**	**47**	**1**	**4**	**5**	***168**	**0**	**0**	**0**	**38**	**2.6**	**–7**	**15**	**33.3**	**7:49**									
	Tampa Bay	**NHL**	**29**	**4**	**4**	**8**	***97**	**1**	**0**	**0**	**29**	**13.8**	**–3**	**1**	**100.0**	**12:34**									
2001-02	**Tampa Bay**	**NHL**	**29**	**0**	**0**	**0**	**70**	**0**	**0**	**0**	**13**	**0.0**	**–7**	**1**	**0.0**	**7:54**									
	NY Rangers	**NHL**	**48**	**8**	**13**	**21**	**144**	**0**	**0**	**1**	**56**	**14.3**	**–3**	**12**	**33.3**	**11:24**									
2002-03	**NY Rangers**	**NHL**	**79**	**14**	**22**	**36**	**142**	**1**	**0**	**1**	**104**	**13.5**	**9**	**5**	**40.0**	**13:00**									
2003-04	**NY Rangers**	**NHL**	**69**	**12**	**20**	**32**	**120**	**0**	**0**	**1**	**80**	**15.0**	**15**	**23**	**43.5**	**11:49**									
	Colorado	**NHL**	**13**	**4**	**5**	**9**	**37**	**1**	**0**	**2**	**24**	**16.7**	**3**	**1**	**100.0**	**15:25**	**11**	**0**	**2**	**2**	**27**	**0**	**0**	**0**	**12:22**
2004-05			DID NOT PLAY																						
	NHL Totals		**713**	**104**	**161**	**265**	**2257**	**8**	**0**	**14**	**899**	**11.6**		**142**	**41.5**	**11:51**	**62**	**7**	**15**	**22**	**170**	**3**	**0**	**1**	**12:04**

Traded to **Pittsburgh** by **Buffalo** for Stu Barnes, March 11, 1999. Traded to **Tampa Bay** by **Pittsburgh** for Wayne Primeau, February 1, 2001. Traded to **NY Rangers** by **Tampa Bay** for Zdeno Ciger, December 12, 2001. Traded to **Colorado** by **NY Rangers** with NY Rangers' 3rd round choice (Denis Parshin) in 2004 Entry Draft for Chris McAllister, David Liffiton and Florida's 2nd round choice (previously acquired, later traded back to Florida – Florida selected David Shantz) in 2004 Entry Draft, March 8, 2004. Signed as a free agent by **Chicago**, July 2, 2004.

BARNES, Ryan

(BAHRNZ, RIGH-uhn)

Left wing. Shoots left. 6'1", 201 lbs. Born, Dunnville, Ont., January 30, 1980. Detroit's 2nd choice, 55th overall, in 1998 Entry Draft.

Season	Club	League	GP	G	A	Pts	PIM	PP	SH	GW	S	%	+/-	TF	F%	Min	GP	G	A	Pts	PIM	PP	SH	GW	Min
1996-97	Quinte Hawks	MTJHL	46	15	19	34	245																		
1997-98	Sudbury Wolves	OHL	46	13	18	31	111										10	0	2	2	24				
1998-99	Sudbury Wolves	OHL	8	2	0	2	23																		
	St. Michael's	OHL	31	11	14	25	*215																		
	Barrie Colts	OHL	24	16	14	30	*161										12	2	4	6	40				
99-2000	Barrie Colts	OHL	31	17	12	29	98										25	7	7	14	49				
2000-01	Cincinnati	AHL	1	0	0	0	7																		
	Toledo Storm	ECHL	16	2	4	6	31																		
2001-02	Toledo Storm	ECHL	1	1	0	1	0																		
	Cincinnati	AHL	46	2	3	5	152																		
2002-03	Grand Rapids	AHL	73	5	6	11	151										15	1	1	2	17				
2003-04	**Detroit**	**NHL**	**2**	**0**	**0**	**0**	**0**	**0**	**0**	**0**	**0**	**0.0**	**0**	**0**	**0.0**	**2:22**									
	Grand Rapids	AHL	69	6	13	19	175										4	0	0	0	7				
2004-05	Grand Rapids	AHL	69	7	8	15	167																		
	Kalamazoo Wings	UHL	11	3	5	8	4																		
	NHL Totals		**2**	**0**	**0**	**0**	**0**	**0**	**0**	**0**	**0**	**0.0**		**0**	**0.0**	**2:22**									

• Missed majority of 2000-01 season recovering from head injury suffered in training camp, September, 2000.

BARNES, Stu

(BAHRNZ, STEW) **DAL.**

Center. Shoots right. 5'11", 180 lbs. Born, Spruce Grove, Alta., December 25, 1970. Winnipeg's 1st choice, 4th overall, in 1989 Entry Draft.

Season	Club	League	GP	G	A	Pts	PIM	PP	SH	GW	S	%	+/-	TF	F%	Min	GP	G	A	Pts	PIM	PP	SH	GW	Min
1986-87	St. Albert Saints	AJHL	53	41	34	*75	103										19	7	15	22					
1987-88	New Westminster	WHL	71	37	64	101	88										5	2	3	5	6				
1988-89	Tri-City	WHL	70	59	82	141	117										7	6	5	11	10				
1989-90	Tri-City	WHL	63	52	92	144	165										7	1	5	6	26				
1990-91	Canada	Nat-Tm	53	22	27	49	68																		
1991-92	**Winnipeg**	**NHL**	**46**	**8**	**9**	**17**	**26**	**4**	**0**	**0**	**75**	**10.7**	**–2**												
	Moncton Hawks	AHL	30	13	19	32	10										11	3	9	12	6				
1992-93	**Winnipeg**	**NHL**	**38**	**12**	**10**	**22**	**10**	**3**	**0**	**3**	**73**	**16.4**	**–3**				**6**	**1**	**3**	**4**	**2**	**0**	**0**	**0**	
	Moncton Hawks	AHL	42	23	31	54	58																		

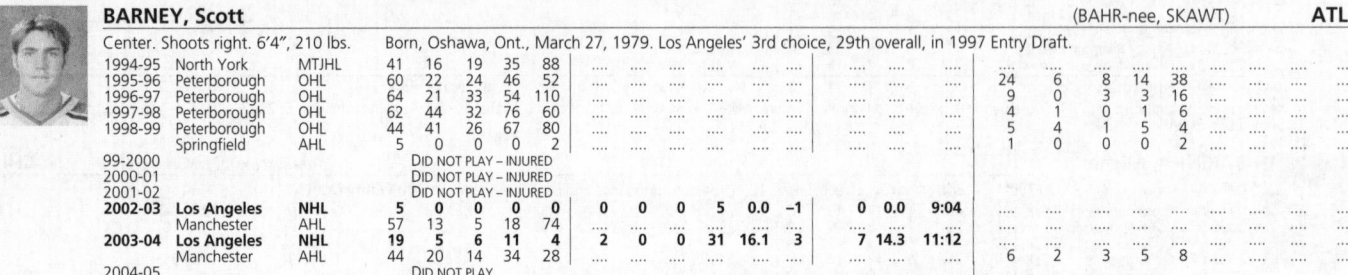

			Regular Season														Playoffs								
Season	Club	League	GP	G	A	Pts	PIM	PP	SH	GW	S	%	+/-	TF	F%	Min	GP	G	A	Pts	PIM	PP	SH	GW	Min
1993-94	**Winnipeg**	**NHL**	**18**	**5**	**4**	**9**	**8**	**2**	**0**	**0**	**24**	**20.8**	**–1**	....	....	....	....	....	....	....	....	....	....	....	....
	Florida	**NHL**	**59**	**18**	**20**	**38**	**30**	**6**	**1**	**3**	**148**	**12.2**	**5**	....	....	....	....	....	....	....	....	....	....	....	....
1994-95	**Florida**	**NHL**	**41**	**10**	**19**	**29**	**8**	**1**	**0**	**2**	**93**	**10.8**	**7**	....	....	....	....	....	....	....	....	....	....	....	....
1995-96	**Florida**	**NHL**	**72**	**19**	**25**	**44**	**46**	**8**	**0**	**5**	**158**	**12.0**	**–12**	....	....	....	**22**	**6**	**10**	**16**	**4**	**2**	**0**	**2**	....
1996-97	**Florida**	**NHL**	**19**	**2**	**8**	**10**	**10**	**1**	**0**	**0**	**44**	**4.5**	**–3**	....	....	....	....	....	....	....	....	....	....	....	....
	Pittsburgh	**NHL**	**62**	**17**	**22**	**39**	**16**	**4**	**0**	**3**	**132**	**12.9**	**–20**	....	....	....	**5**	**0**	**1**	**1**	**0**	**0**	**0**	**0**	....
1997-98	**Pittsburgh**	**NHL**	**78**	**30**	**35**	**65**	**30**	**15**	**1**	**5**	**196**	**15.3**	**15**	....	....	....	**6**	**3**	**3**	**6**	**2**	**0**	**0**	**1**	....
1998-99	**Pittsburgh**	**NHL**	**64**	**20**	**12**	**32**	**20**	**13**	**0**	**3**	**155**	**12.9**	**–12**	**720**	**51.9**	**17:52**	....	....	....	....	....	....	....	....	....
	Buffalo	**NHL**	**17**	**0**	**4**	**4**	**10**	**0**	**0**	**0**	**25**	**0.0**	**1**	**236**	**51.3**	**18:20**	**21**	**7**	**3**	**10**	**6**	**4**	**0**	**1**	**14:40**
99-2000	**Buffalo**	**NHL**	**82**	**20**	**25**	**45**	**16**	**8**	**2**	**2**	**137**	**14.6**	**–3**	**778**	**48.5**	**17:23**	**5**	**3**	**0**	**3**	**2**	**2**	**0**	**1**	**17:02**
2000-01	**Buffalo**	**NHL**	**75**	**19**	**24**	**43**	**26**	**3**	**2**	**5**	**160**	**11.9**	**–2**	**1470**	**48.3**	**19:06**	**13**	**4**	**4**	**8**	**2**	**2**	**0**	**2**	**18:30**
2001-02	**Buffalo**	**NHL**	**68**	**17**	**31**	**48**	**26**	**5**	**0**	**4**	**127**	**13.4**	**6**	**984**	**47.2**	**18:35**	....	....	....	....	....	....	....	....	....
2002-03	**Buffalo**	**NHL**	**68**	**11**	**21**	**32**	**20**	**2**	**1**	**2**	**124**	**8.9**	**–13**	**923**	**49.0**	**18:29**	....	....	....	....	....	....	....	....	....
	Dallas	**NHL**	**13**	**2**	**5**	**7**	**8**	**2**	**0**	**1**	**25**	**8.0**	**2**	**76**	**44.7**	**17:23**	**12**	**2**	**3**	**5**	**0**	**0**	**0**	**2**	**19:06**
2003-04	**Dallas**	**NHL**	**77**	**11**	**18**	**29**	**18**	**0**	**1**	**4**	**135**	**8.1**	**7**	**879**	**52.9**	**18:05**	**5**	**0**	**0**	**0**	**0**	**0**	**0**	**0**	**14:59**
2004-05			DID NOT PLAY																						
	NHL Totals		**897**	**221**	**292**	**513**	**328**	**77**	**8**	**42**	**1831**	**12.1**		**6066**	**49.4**	**18:13**	**95**	**26**	**27**	**53**	**18**	**10**	**0**	**9**	**16:45**

WHL West Second All-Star Team (1988, 1989) • WHL Rookie of the Year (1988) • WHL Player of the Year (1989)

Traded to **Florida** by **Winnipeg** with St. Louis' 6th round choice (previously acquired, later traded to Edmonton – later traded back to Winnipeg – Winnipeg selected Chris Kibermanis) in 1994 Entry Draft for Randy Gilhen, November 25, 1993. Traded to **Pittsburgh** by **Florida** with Jason Woolley for Chris Wells, November 19, 1996. Traded to **Buffalo** by **Pittsburgh** for Matthew Barnaby, March 11, 1999. Traded to **Dallas** by **Buffalo** for Michael Ryan and Dallas's 2nd round choice (Branislav Fabry) in 2003 Entry Draft, March 10, 2003.

BARNEY, Scott

(BAHR-nee, SKAWT) **ATL.**

Center. Shoots right. 6'4", 210 lbs. Born, Oshawa, Ont., March 27, 1979. Los Angeles' 3rd choice, 29th overall, in 1997 Entry Draft.

Season	Club	League	GP	G	A	Pts	PIM	PP	SH	GW	S	%	+/-	TF	F%	Min	GP	G	A	Pts	PIM	PP	SH	GW	Min
1994-95	North York	MTJHL	41	16	19	35	88	....	....	....	....	....	....	....	....	....	....	....	....	....	....	....	....	....	....
1995-96	Peterborough	OHL	60	22	24	46	52	....	....	....	....	....	....	....	....	....	24	6	8	14	38	....	....	....	....
1996-97	Peterborough	OHL	64	21	33	54	110	....	....	....	....	....	....	....	....	....	9	0	3	3	16	....	....	....	....
1997-98	Peterborough	OHL	62	44	32	76	60	....	....	....	....	....	....	....	....	....	4	1	0	1	6	....	....	....	....
1998-99	Peterborough	OHL	44	41	26	67	80	....	....	....	....	....	....	....	....	....	5	4	1	5	4	....	....	....	....
	Springfield	AHL	5	0	0	0	2	....	....	....	....	....	....	....	....	....	1	0	0	0	2	....	....	....	....
99-2000			DID NOT PLAY – INJURED																						
2000-01			DID NOT PLAY – INJURED																						
2001-02			DID NOT PLAY – INJURED																						
2002-03	**Los Angeles**	**NHL**	**5**	**0**	**0**	**0**	**0**	**0**	**0**	**0**	**5**	**0.0**	**–1**	**0**	**0.0**	**9:04**	....	....	....	....	....	....	....	....	....
	Manchester	AHL	57	13	5	18	74	....	....	....	....	....	....	....	....	....	....	....	....	....	....	....	....	....	....
2003-04	**Los Angeles**	**NHL**	**19**	**5**	**6**	**11**	**4**	**2**	**0**	**0**	**31**	**16.1**	**3**	**7**	**14.3**	**11:12**	....	....	....	....	....	....	....	....	....
	Manchester	AHL	44	20	14	34	28	....	....	....	....	....	....	....	....	....	6	2	3	5	8	....	....	....	....
2004-05			DID NOT PLAY																						
	NHL Totals		**24**	**5**	**6**	**11**	**4**	**2**	**0**	**0**	**36**	**13.9**		**7**	**14.3**	**10:46**	....	....	....	....	....	....	....	....	....

• Missed entire 1999-2000, 2000-01 and 2001-02 seasons recovering from back injury suffered in training camp, September 28, 1999. Signed as a free agent by **Atlanta**, August 8, 2005.

BARON, Murray

(BAIR-uhn, MUHR-ray)

Defense. Shoots left. 6'3", 215 lbs. Born, Prince George, B.C., June 1, 1967. Philadelphia's 7th choice, 167th overall, in 1986 Entry Draft.

Season	Club	League	GP	G	A	Pts	PIM	PP	SH	GW	S	%	+/-	TF	F%	Min	GP	G	A	Pts	PIM	PP	SH	GW	Min
1984-85	Vernon Lakers	BCJHL	37	5	9	14	93	....	....	....	....	....	....	....	....	....	13	5	6	11	107	....	....	....	....
1985-86	Vernon Lakers	BCJHL	46	12	32	44	179	....	....	....	....	....	....	....	....	....	7	1	2	3	13	....	....	....	....
1986-87	North Dakota	WCHA	41	4	10	14	62	....	....	....	....	....	....	....	....	....	....	....	....	....	....	....	....	....	....
1987-88	North Dakota	WCHA	41	1	10	11	95	....	....	....	....	....	....	....	....	....	....	....	....	....	....	....	....	....	....
1988-89	North Dakota	WCHA	40	2	6	8	92	....	....	....	....	....	....	....	....	....	....	....	....	....	....	....	....	....	....
	Hershey Bears	AHL	9	0	3	3	8	....	....	....	....	....	....	....	....	....	....	....	....	....	....	....	....	....	....
1989-90	**Philadelphia**	**NHL**	**16**	**2**	**2**	**4**	**12**	**0**	**0**	**0**	**18**	**11.1**	**–1**	....	....	....	....	....	....	....	....	....	....	....	....
	Hershey Bears	AHL	50	0	10	10	101	....	....	....	....	....	....	....	....	....	....	....	....	....	....	....	....	....	....
1990-91	**Philadelphia**	**NHL**	**67**	**8**	**8**	**16**	**74**	**3**	**0**	**1**	**86**	**9.3**	**–3**	....	....	....	....	....	....	....	....	....	....	....	....
	Hershey Bears	AHL	6	2	3	5	0	....	....	....	....	....	....	....	....	....	....	....	....	....	....	....	....	....	....
1991-92	**St. Louis**	**NHL**	**67**	**3**	**8**	**11**	**94**	**0**	**0**	**0**	**55**	**5.5**	**–3**	....	....	....	**2**	**0**	**0**	**0**	**2**	**0**	**0**	**0**	....
1992-93	**St. Louis**	**NHL**	**53**	**2**	**2**	**4**	**59**	**0**	**0**	**1**	**42**	**4.8**	**–5**	....	....	....	**11**	**0**	**0**	**0**	**12**	**0**	**0**	**0**	....
1993-94	**St. Louis**	**NHL**	**77**	**5**	**9**	**14**	**123**	**0**	**0**	**0**	**73**	**6.8**	**–14**	....	....	....	**4**	**0**	**0**	**0**	**10**	**0**	**0**	**0**	....
1994-95	**St. Louis**	**NHL**	**39**	**0**	**5**	**5**	**93**	**0**	**0**	**0**	**28**	**0.0**	**9**	....	....	....	**7**	**1**	**1**	**2**	**2**	**0**	**0**	**0**	....
1995-96	**St. Louis**	**NHL**	**82**	**2**	**9**	**11**	**190**	**0**	**0**	**0**	**86**	**2.3**	**3**	....	....	....	**13**	**1**	**0**	**1**	**20**	**0**	**1**	**0**	....
1996-97	**St. Louis**	**NHL**	**11**	**0**	**2**	**2**	**11**	**0**	**0**	**0**	**7**	**0.0**	**–4**	....	....	....	....	....	....	....	....	....	....	....	....
	Montreal	**NHL**	**60**	**1**	**5**	**6**	**107**	**0**	**0**	**0**	**52**	**1.9**	**–16**	....	....	....	....	....	....	....	....	....	....	....	....
	Phoenix	**NHL**	**8**	**0**	**0**	**0**	**4**	**0**	**0**	**0**	**5**	**0.0**	**0**	....	....	....	**1**	**0**	**0**	**0**	**0**	**0**	**0**	**0**	....
1997-98	**Phoenix**	**NHL**	**45**	**1**	**5**	**6**	**106**	**0**	**0**	**0**	**23**	**4.3**	**–10**	....	....	....	**6**	**0**	**2**	**2**	**6**	**0**	**0**	**0**	....
1998-99	**Vancouver**	**NHL**	**81**	**2**	**6**	**8**	**115**	**0**	**0**	**0**	**53**	**3.8**	**–23**	**0**	**0.0**	**18:14**	....	....	....	....	....	....	....	....	....
99-2000	**Vancouver**	**NHL**	**81**	**2**	**10**	**12**	**67**	**0**	**0**	**0**	**48**	**4.2**	**8**	**2**	**50.0**	**21:36**	....	....	....	....	....	....	....	....	....
2000-01	**Vancouver**	**NHL**	**82**	**3**	**8**	**11**	**63**	**0**	**0**	**1**	**56**	**5.4**	**–13**	**3**	**66.7**	**19:24**	**4**	**0**	**0**	**0**	**0**	**0**	**0**	**0**	**22:16**
2001-02	**Vancouver**	**NHL**	**61**	**1**	**6**	**7**	**68**	**0**	**0**	**0**	**38**	**2.6**	**8**	**2**	**50.0**	**16:57**	**6**	**0**	**1**	**1**	**10**	**0**	**0**	**0**	**12:30**
2002-03	**Vancouver**	**NHL**	**78**	**2**	**4**	**6**	**62**	**0**	**0**	**0**	**34**	**5.9**	**13**	**0**	**0.0**	**17:01**	**14**	**0**	**4**	**4**	**10**	**0**	**0**	**0**	**17:34**
2003-04	**St. Louis**	**NHL**	**80**	**1**	**5**	**6**	**61**	**0**	**0**	**0**	**57**	**1.8**	**–6**	**0**	**0.0**	**19:14**	**5**	**0**	**0**	**0**	**6**	**0**	**0**	**0**	**18:55**
2004-05			DID NOT PLAY																						
	NHL Totals		**988**	**35**	**94**	**129**	**1309**	**3**	**0**	**3**	**761**	**4.6**		**7**	**57.1**	**18:50**	**73**	**2**	**8**	**10**	**78**	**0**	**1**	**0**	**17:24**

Traded to **St. Louis** by **Philadelphia** with Ron Sutter for Dan Quinn and Rod Brind'Amour, September 22, 1991. Traded to **Montreal** by **St. Louis** with Shayne Corson and St. Louis' 5th round choice (Gennady Razin) in 1997 Entry Draft for Pierre Turgeon, Rory Fitzpatrick and Craig Conroy, October 29, 1996. Traded to **Phoenix** by **Montreal** with Chris Murray for Dave Manson, March 18, 1997. Signed as a free agent by **Vancouver**, July 14, 1998. Signed as a free agent by **St. Louis**, September 5, 2003.

BARTECKO, Lubos

(bahr-TESHK-oh, LOO-bohsh)

Left wing. Shoots left. 5'11", 200 lbs. Born, Kezmarok, Czech., July 14, 1976.

Season	Club	League	GP	G	A	Pts	PIM	PP	SH	GW	S	%	+/-	TF	F%	Min	GP	G	A	Pts	PIM	PP	SH	GW	Min
1994-95	HC SKP PS Poprad	Slovakia	3	1	0	1	0	....	....	....	....	....	....	....	....	....	....	....	....	....	....	....	....	....	....
1995-96	Chicoutimi	QMJHL	70	32	41	73	50	....	....	....	....	....	....	....	....	....	17	8	15	23	10	....	....	....	....
1996-97	Drummondville	QMJHL	58	40	51	91	49	....	....	....	....	....	....	....	....	....	8	1	8	9	4	....	....	....	....
1997-98	Worcester IceCats	AHL	34	10	12	22	24	....	....	....	....	....	....	....	....	....	10	4	2	6	2	....	....	....	....
1998-99	HC SKP Poprad	Slovakia	1	1	0	1	0	....	....	....	....	....	....	....	....	....	....	....	....	....	....	....	....	....	....
	St. Louis	**NHL**	**32**	**5**	**11**	**16**	**6**	**0**	**0**	**1**	**37**	**13.5**	**4**	**0**	**0.0**	**13:13**	**5**	**0**	**0**	**0**	**2**	**0**	**0**	**0**	**13:29**
	Worcester IceCats	AHL	49	14	24	38	22	....	....	....	....	....	....	....	....	....	....	....	....	....	....	....	....	....	....
99-2000	**St. Louis**	**NHL**	**67**	**16**	**23**	**39**	**51**	**3**	**0**	**3**	**75**	**21.3**	**24**	**10**	**50.0**	**13:33**	**7**	**1**	**1**	**2**	**0**	**0**	**0**	**0**	**12:02**
	Worcester IceCats	AHL	12	4	7	11	4	....	....	....	....	....	....	....	....	....	....	....	....	....	....	....	....	....	....
2000-01	**St. Louis**	**NHL**	**50**	**5**	**8**	**13**	**12**	**0**	**0**	**3**	**51**	**9.8**	**–1**	**2**	**50.0**	**10:25**	....	....	....	....	....	....	....	....	....
2001-02	**Atlanta**	**NHL**	**71**	**13**	**14**	**27**	**30**	**1**	**0**	**0**	**96**	**13.5**	**–15**	**4**	**25.0**	**14:28**	....	....	....	....	....	....	....	....	....
	Slovakia	Olympics	4	0	1	1	0	....	....	....	....	....	....	....	....	....	....	....	....	....	....	....	....	....	....
2002-03	**Atlanta**	**NHL**	**37**	**7**	**9**	**16**	**8**	**0**	**0**	**1**	**54**	**13.0**	**3**	**6**	**100.0**	**12:31**	....	....	....	....	....	....	....	....	....
2003-04	HC Sparta Praha	CzRep	25	12	8	20	45	....	....	....	....	....	....	....	....	....	13	2	4	6	26	....	....	....	....
2004-05	Dynamo Moscow	Russia	40	6	10	16	28	....	....	....	....	....	....	....	....	....	7	0	1	1	2	....	....	....	....
	NHL Totals		**257**	**46**	**65**	**111**	**107**	**4**	**0**	**8**	**313**	**14.7**		**22**	**59.1**	**13:00**	**12**	**1**	**1**	**2**	**2**	**0**	**0**	**0**	**12:39**

Signed as a free agent by **St. Louis**, October 3, 1997. Traded to **Atlanta** by **St. Louis** for Buffalo's 4th round choice (previously acquired, St. Louis selected Igor Valeyev) in 2001 Entry Draft, June 23, 2001. • Missed majority of 2002-03 season recovering from wrist (November 2, 2002 vs. Florida) and groin (January 13, 2003 vs. Philadelphia) injuries. Signed as a free agent by **Sparta** (CzRep), November 2, 2003. Signed as a free agent by **Dynamo Moscow** (Russia), August 24, 2004.

BARTOVIC, Milan

(BAHR-tuh-vihch, MIH-lan) **BUF.**

Right wing. Shoots left. 5'11", 197 lbs. Born, Trencin, Czech., April 9, 1981. Buffalo's 2nd choice, 35th overall, in 1999 Entry Draft.

Season	Club	League	GP	G	A	Pts	PIM	PP	SH	GW	S	%	+/-	TF	F%	Min	GP	G	A	Pts	PIM	PP	SH	GW	Min
1997-98	Dukla Trencin Jr.	Slovak-Jr.	26	2	6	8	27	....	....	....	....	....	....	....	....	....	....	....	....	....	....	....	....	....	....
1998-99	Dukla Trencin Jr.	Slovak-Jr.	46	36	35	71	62	....	....	....	....	....	....	....	....	....	6	9	3	12	10	....	....	....	....
99-2000	Tri-City	WHL	18	8	9	17	12	....	....	....	....	....	....	....	....	....	....	....	....	....	....	....	....	....	....
	Brandon	WHL	38	18	22	40	28	....	....	....	....	....	....	....	....	....	....	....	....	....	....	....	....	....	....
2000-01	Brandon	WHL	34	15	25	40	40	....	....	....	....	....	....	....	....	....	6	1	2	3	8	....	....	....	....
	Rochester	AHL	2	1	1	2	0	....	....	....	....	....	....	....	....	....	4	0	1	1	2	....	....	....	....
2001-02	Rochester	AHL	73	15	11	26	56	....	....	....	....	....	....	....	....	....	2	0	0	0	0	....	....	....	....
2002-03	**Buffalo**	**NHL**	**3**	**1**	**0**	**1**	**0**	**0**	**0**	**0**	**5**	**20.0**	**0**	**1**	**100.0**	**9:52**	....	....	....	....	....	....	....	....	....
	Rochester	AHL	74	18	10	28	84	....	....	....	....	....	....	....	....	....	3	0	0	0	0	....	....	....	....

Season	Club	League	GP	G	A	Pts	PIM	PP	SH	GW	S	%	+/-	TF	F%	Min	GP	G	A	Pts	PIM	PP	SH	GW	Min
			Regular Season														Playoffs								
2003-04	**Buffalo**	**NHL**	**23**	**1**	**8**	**9**	**18**	**0**	**0**	**0**	**30**	**3.3**	**1**	**2**	**100.0**	**12:53**	....	....	....	....	....	....	....	....	....
	Rochester	AHL	52	18	11	29	52	....	....	....	....	....	....	....	....	....	2	0	0	0	2	....	....	....	....
2004-05	Rochester	AHL	69	10	18	28	83	....	....	....	....	....	....	....	....	....	9	0	3	3	22	....	....	....	....
	NHL Totals		**26**	**2**	**8**	**10**	**18**	**0**	**0**	**0**	**35**	**5.7**		**3**	**100.0**	**12:32**	....	....	....	....	....	....	....	....	....

• Missed majority of 2000-01 season recovering from shoulder injury suffered in game vs. Red Deer (WHL), October 10, 2000.

BATES, Shawn

(BAYTS, SHAWN) **NYI**

Center. Shoots right. 6', 205 lbs. Born, Melrose, MA, April 3, 1975. Boston's 4th choice, 103rd overall, in 1993 Entry Draft.

Season	Club	League	GP	G	A	Pts	PIM	PP	SH	GW	S	%	+/-	TF	F%	Min	GP	G	A	Pts	PIM	PP	SH	GW	Min
1990-91	Medford	High-MA	22	18	43	61	6	....	....	....	....	....	....	....	....	....	....	....	....	....	....	....	....	....	....
1991-92	Medford	High-MA	22	38	41	79	10	....	....	....	....	....	....	....	....	....	....	....	....	....	....	....	....	....	....
1992-93	Medford	High-MA	25	49	46	95	20	....	....	....	....	....	....	....	....	....	....	....	....	....	....	....	....	....	....
1993-94	Boston University	H-East	41	10	19	29	24	....	....	....	....	....	....	....	....	....	....	....	....	....	....	....	....	....	....
1994-95	Boston University	H-East	38	18	12	30	48	....	....	....	....	....	....	....	....	....	....	....	....	....	....	....	....	....	....
1995-96	Boston University	H-East	40	28	22	50	54	....	....	....	....	....	....	....	....	....	....	....	....	....	....	....	....	....	....
1996-97	Boston University	H-East	41	17	18	35	64	....	....	....	....	....	....	....	....	....	....	....	....	....	....	....	....	....	....
1997-98	**Boston**	**NHL**	**13**	**2**	**0**	**2**	**2**	**0**	**0**	**0**	**12**	**16.7**	**-3**	....	....	....	....	....	....	....	....	....	....	....	....
	Providence Bruins	AHL	50	15	19	34	22	....	....	....	....	....	....	....	....	....	....	....	....	....	....	....	....	....	....
1998-99	**Boston**	**NHL**	**33**	**5**	**4**	**9**	**2**	**0**	**0**	**0**	**30**	**16.7**	**3**	**178**	**51.1**	**8:35**	**12**	**0**	**0**	**0**	**4**	**0**	**0**	**0**	**5:12**
	Providence Bruins	AHL	37	25	21	46	39	....	....	....	....	....	....	....	....	....	....	....	....	....	....	....	....	....	....
99-2000	**Boston**	**NHL**	**44**	**5**	**7**	**12**	**14**	**0**	**0**	**1**	**65**	**7.7**	**-17**	**460**	**47.0**	**10:52**	....	....	....	....	....	....	....	....	....
2000-01	**Boston**	**NHL**	**45**	**2**	**3**	**5**	**26**	**0**	**0**	**0**	**59**	**3.4**	**-12**	**413**	**50.6**	**9:19**	....	....	....	....	....	....	....	....	....
	Providence Bruins	AHL	11	5	8	13	12	....	....	....	....	....	....	....	....	....	8	2	6	8	8	....	....	....	....
2001-02	**NY Islanders**	**NHL**	**71**	**17**	**35**	**52**	**30**	**1**	**4**	**4**	**150**	**11.3**	**18**	**306**	**49.4**	**18:45**	**7**	**2**	**4**	**6**	**11**	**1**	**0**	**1**	**20:27**
2002-03	**NY Islanders**	**NHL**	**74**	**13**	**29**	**42**	**52**	**1**	**6**	**1**	**126**	**10.3**	**-9**	**398**	**57.0**	**18:26**	**5**	**1**	**0**	**1**	**0**	**1**	**0**	**0**	**18:36**
2003-04	**NY Islanders**	**NHL**	**69**	**9**	**23**	**32**	**46**	**0**	**1**	**1**	**115**	**7.8**	**-8**	**603**	**55.9**	**18:26**	**5**	**0**	**0**	**0**	**4**	**0**	**0**	**0**	**17:14**
2004-05			DID NOT PLAY																						
	NHL Totals		**349**	**53**	**101**	**154**	**172**	**2**	**11**	**7**	**557**	**9.5**		**2358**	**52.2**	**15:19**	**29**	**3**	**4**	**7**	**19**	**2**	**0**	**1**	**13:16**

NCAA Championship All-Tournament Team (1995)

Signed as a free agent by **NY Islanders**, July 8, 2001.

BATTAGLIA, Bates

(buh-TAG-lee-ah, BAYTS)

Left wing. Shoots left. 6'2", 205 lbs. Born, Chicago, IL, December 13, 1975. Anaheim's 6th choice, 132nd overall, in 1994 Entry Draft.

Season	Club	League	GP	G	A	Pts	PIM	PP	SH	GW	S	%	+/-	TF	F%	Min	GP	G	A	Pts	PIM	PP	SH	GW	Min
1992-93	Team Illinois	MEHL	60	42	42	84	68	....	....	....	....	....	....	....	....	....	....	....	....	....	....	....	....	....	....
1993-94	Caledon	MTJHL	44	15	33	48	104	....	....	....	....	....	....	....	....	....	....	....	....	....	....	....	....	....	....
1994-95	Lake Superior	CCHA	38	6	14	20	34	....	....	....	....	....	....	....	....	....	....	....	....	....	....	....	....	....	....
1995-96	Lake Superior	CCHA	40	13	22	35	48	....	....	....	....	....	....	....	....	....	....	....	....	....	....	....	....	....	....
1996-97	Lake Superior	CCHA	38	12	27	39	80	....	....	....	....	....	....	....	....	....	....	....	....	....	....	....	....	....	....
1997-98	**Carolina**	**NHL**	**33**	**2**	**4**	**6**	**10**	**0**	**0**	**1**	**21**	**9.5**	**-1**	....	....	....	....	....	....	....	....	....	....	....	....
	New Haven	AHL	48	15	21	36	48	....	....	....	....	....	....	....	....	....	1	0	0	0	0	....	....	....	....
1998-99	**Carolina**	**NHL**	**60**	**7**	**11**	**18**	**97**	**0**	**0**	**0**	**52**	**13.5**	**7**	**144**	**39.6**	**9:53**	**6**	**0**	**3**	**3**	**8**	**0**	**0**	**0**	**15:22**
99-2000	**Carolina**	**NHL**	**77**	**16**	**18**	**34**	**39**	**3**	**0**	**3**	**86**	**18.6**	**20**	**23**	**26.1**	**15:12**	....	....	....	....	....	....	....	....	....
2000-01	**Carolina**	**NHL**	**80**	**12**	**15**	**27**	**76**	**2**	**0**	**3**	**133**	**9.0**	**-14**	**5**	**60.0**	**14:28**	**6**	**0**	**2**	**2**	**2**	**0**	**0**	**0**	**11:25**
2001-02	**Carolina**	**NHL**	**82**	**21**	**25**	**46**	**44**	**5**	**1**	**2**	**167**	**12.6**	**-6**	**12**	**33.3**	**19:05**	**23**	**5**	**9**	**14**	**14**	**1**	**0**	**1**	**20:42**
2002-03	**Carolina**	**NHL**	**70**	**5**	**14**	**19**	**90**	**0**	**1**	**1**	**96**	**5.2**	**-17**	**16**	**25.0**	**18:39**	....	....	....	....	....	....	....	....	....
	Colorado	**NHL**	**13**	**1**	**5**	**6**	**10**	**1**	**0**	**1**	**27**	**3.7**	**-2**	**3**	**0.0**	**15:19**	**7**	**0**	**2**	**2**	**4**	**0**	**0**	**0**	**14:39**
2003-04	**Colorado**	**NHL**	**4**	**0**	**1**	**1**	**4**	**0**	**0**	**0**	**1**	**0.0**	**-1**	**1**	**100.0**	**11:04**	....	....	....	....	....	....	....	....	....
	Washington	**NHL**	**66**	**4**	**6**	**10**	**38**	**0**	**0**	**1**	**69**	**5.8**	**-23**	**116**	**32.8**	**13:37**	....	....	....	....	....	....	....	....	....
2004-05	Mississippi	ECHL	25	6	11	17	24	....	....	....	....	....	....	....	....	....	4	0	0	0	10	....	....	....	....
	NHL Totals		**485**	**68**	**99**	**167**	**408**	**11**	**2**	**12**	**652**	**10.4**		**320**	**35.3**	**15:20**	**42**	**5**	**16**	**21**	**28**	**1**	**0**	**1**	**17:36**

Traded to **Hartford** by **Anaheim** with Anaheim's 4th round choice (Josef Vasicek) in 1998 Entry Draft for Mark Janssens, March 18, 1997. Rights transferred to **Carolina** after **Hartford** franchise relocated, June 25, 1997. Traded to **Colorado** by **Carolina** for Radim Vrbata, March 11, 2003. Traded to **Washington** by **Colorado** with Jonas Johansson for Steve Konowalchuk and Washington's 3rd round choice (later traded to Carolina – Carolina selected Casey Borer) in 2004 Entry Draft, October 22, 2003. Signed as a free agent by **Mississippi** (ECHL), February 21, 2005.

BAUMGARTNER, Nolan

(BAWM-gahrt-nuhr, NOH-lan) **VAN.**

Defense. Shoots right. 6'2", 205 lbs. Born, Calgary, Alta., March 23, 1976. Washington's 1st choice, 10th overall, in 1994 Entry Draft.

Season	Club	League	GP	G	A	Pts	PIM	PP	SH	GW	S	%	+/-	TF	F%	Min	GP	G	A	Pts	PIM	PP	SH	GW	Min
1991-92	Cgy. AAA Flames	AMHL	39	11	29	40	40	....	....	....	....	....	....	....	....	....	....	....	....	....	....	....	....	....	....
1992-93	Kamloops Blazers	WHL	43	0	5	5	30	....	....	....	....	....	....	....	....	....	11	1	1	2	0	....	....	....	....
1993-94	Kamloops Blazers	WHL	69	13	42	55	109	....	....	....	....	....	....	....	....	....	19	3	14	17	33	....	....	....	....
1994-95	Kamloops Blazers	WHL	62	8	36	44	71	....	....	....	....	....	....	....	....	....	21	4	13	17	16	....	....	....	....
1995-96	Kamloops Blazers	WHL	28	13	15	28	45	....	....	....	....	....	....	....	....	....	16	1	9	10	26	....	....	....	....
	Washington	**NHL**	**1**	**0**	**0**	**0**	**0**	**0**	**0**	**0**	**0**	**0.0**	**-1**	....	....	....	**1**	**0**	**0**	**0**	**10**	**0**	**0**	**0**	
1996-97	Portland Pirates	AHL	8	2	2	4	4	....	....	....	....	....	....	....	....	....	....	....	....	....	....	....	....	....	....
1997-98	**Washington**	**NHL**	**4**	**0**	**1**	**1**	**0**	**0**	**0**	**0**	**4**	**0.0**	**0**	....	....	....	....	....	....	....	....	....	....	....	....
	Portland Pirates	AHL	70	2	24	26	70	....	....	....	....	....	....	....	....	....	10	1	4	5	10	....	....	....	....
1998-99	**Washington**	**NHL**	**5**	**0**	**0**	**0**	**0**	**0**	**0**	**0**	**1**	**0.0**	**-3**	**0**	**0.0**	**8:41**	....	....	....	....	....	....	....	....	....
	Portland Pirates	AHL	38	5	14	19	62	....	....	....	....	....	....	....	....	....	....	....	....	....	....	....	....	....	....
99-2000	**Washington**	**NHL**	**8**	**0**	**1**	**1**	**2**	**0**	**0**	**0**	**6**	**0.0**	**1**	**0**	**0.0**	**10:31**	....	....	....	....	....	....	....	....	....
	Portland Pirates	AHL	71	5	18	23	56	....	....	....	....	....	....	....	....	....	4	1	2	3	10	....	....	....	....
2000-01	**Chicago**	**NHL**	**8**	**0**	**0**	**0**	**6**	**0**	**0**	**0**	**7**	**0.0**	**-4**	**2**	**50.0**	**12:40**	....	....	....	....	....	....	....	....	....
	Norfolk Admirals	AHL	63	5	28	33	75	....	....	....	....	....	....	....	....	....	9	2	3	5	11	....	....	....	....
2001-02	Norfolk Admirals	AHL	76	10	24	34	72	....	....	....	....	....	....	....	....	....	4	0	1	1	2	....	....	....	....
2002-03	**Vancouver**	**NHL**	**8**	**1**	**2**	**3**	**4**	**1**	**0**	**0**	**7**	**14.3**	**4**	**0**	**0.0**	**11:36**	**2**	**0**	**0**	**0**	**0**	**0**	**0**	**0**	**11:06**
	Manitoba Moose	AHL	59	8	31	39	82	....	....	....	....	....	....	....	....	....	1	0	0	0	4	....	....	....	....
2003-04	**Pittsburgh**	**NHL**	**5**	**0**	**0**	**0**	**2**	**0**	**0**	**0**	**6**	**0.0**	**-7**	**0**	**0.0**	**19:20**	....	....	....	....	....	....	....	....	....
	Vancouver	**NHL**	**9**	**0**	**3**	**3**	**2**	**0**	**0**	**0**	**9**	**0.0**	**3**	**0**	**0.0**	**11:52**	....	....	....	....	....	....	....	....	....
	Manitoba Moose	AHL	55	6	21	27	101	....	....	....	....	....	....	....	....	....	....	....	....	....	....	....	....	....	....
2004-05	Manitoba Moose	AHL	78	9	30	39	51	....	....	....	....	....	....	....	....	....	14	0	4	4	10	....	....	....	....
	NHL Totals		**48**	**1**	**7**	**8**	**16**	**1**	**0**	**0**	**40**	**2.5**		**2**	**50.0**	**12:13**	**3**	**0**	**0**	**0**	**10**	**0**	**0**	**0**	**11:06**

Memorial Cup Tournement All-Star Team (1994, 1995) • WHL West First All-Star Team (1995, 1996) • Canadian Major Junior First All-Star Team (1995) • Canadian Major Junior Defenseman of the Year (1995)

Traded to **Chicago** by **Washington** for Remi Royer, July 20, 2000. Signed as a free agent by **Vancouver**, July 11, 2002. Claimed by **Pittsburgh** from **Vancouver** in Waiver Draft, October 3, 2003. Claimed on waivers by **Vancouver** from **Pittsburgh**, November 1, 2003.

BAYDA, Ryan

(BAY-duh, RIGH-uhn)

Left wing. Shoots left. 5'11", 185 lbs. Born, Saskatoon, Sask., December 9, 1980. Carolina's 2nd choice, 80th overall, in 2000 Entry Draft.

Season	Club	League	GP	G	A	Pts	PIM	PP	SH	GW	S	%	+/-	TF	F%	Min	GP	G	A	Pts	PIM	PP	SH	GW	Min
1995-96	Saskatoon Flyers	SMHL	60	85	74	159	85	....	....	....	....	....	....	....	....	....	....	....	....	....	....	....	....	....	....
1996-97	Sask. Contacts	SMHL	44	22	23	45	18	....	....	....	....	....	....	....	....	....	....	....	....	....	....	....	....	....	....
1997-98	Sask. Contacts	SMHL	41	29	49	78	103	....	....	....	....	....	....	....	....	....	....	....	....	....	....	....	....	....	....
1998-99	Vernon Vipers	BCHL	45	24	58	82	15	....	....	....	....	....	....	....	....	....	....	....	....	....	....	....	....	....	....
99-2000	North Dakota	WCHA	44	17	23	40	30	....	....	....	....	....	....	....	....	....	....	....	....	....	....	....	....	....	....
2000-01	North Dakota	WCHA	46	25	34	59	48	....	....	....	....	....	....	....	....	....	....	....	....	....	....	....	....	....	....
2001-02	North Dakota	WCHA	37	19	28	47	52	....	....	....	....	....	....	....	....	....	....	....	....	....	....	....	....	....	....
	Lowell	AHL	3	1	1	2	0	....	....	....	....	....	....	....	....	....	5	3	0	3	0	....	....	....	....
2002-03	**Carolina**	**NHL**	**25**	**4**	**10**	**14**	**16**	**0**	**0**	**1**	**49**	**8.2**	**-5**	**2**	**100.0**	**17:15**	....	....	....	....	....	....	....	....	....
	Lowell	AHL	53	11	32	43	32	....	....	....	....	....	....	....	....	....	....	....	....	....	....	....	....	....	....
2003-04	**Carolina**	**NHL**	**44**	**3**	**3**	**6**	**22**	**0**	**0**	**1**	**65**	**4.6**	**-14**	**4**	**0.0**	**10:57**	....	....	....	....	....	....	....	....	....
	Lowell	AHL	34	7	15	22	28	....	....	....	....	....	....	....	....	....	....	....	....	....	....	....	....	....	....
2004-05	Lowell	AHL	80	13	27	40	91	....	....	....	....	....	....	....	....	....	9	3	3	6	4	....	....	....	....
	NHL Totals		**69**	**7**	**13**	**20**	**38**	**0**	**0**	**2**	**114**	**6.1**		**6**	**33.3**	**13:14**	....	....	....	....	....	....	....	....	....

BCHL Rookie of the Year (1999) • WCHA All-Rookie Team (2000) • WCHA Second All-Star Team (2001, 2002)

BEAUCHEMIN, Francois
(boh-sheh-MEH, frahn-SWUH) **CBJ**

Defense. Shoots left. 6', 214 lbs. Born, Sorel, Que., June 4, 1980. Montreal's 3rd choice, 75th overall, in 1998 Entry Draft.

			Regular Season														Playoffs								
Season	Club	League	GP	G	A	Pts	PIM	PP	SH	GW	S	%	+/-	TF	F%	Min	GP	G	A	Pts	PIM	PP	SH	GW	Min
1995-96	Richelieu Riverains	QAAA	40	9	23	32	59	....	....	....	....	....	....	....	....	....	....	....	....	....	....	....	....	....	....
1996-97	Laval Titan	QMJHL	66	7	21	28	132	....	....	....	....	....	....	....	....	....	3	0	0	0	2	....	....	....	....
1997-98	Laval Titan	QMJHL	70	12	35	47	132	....	....	....	....	....	....	....	....	....	16	1	3	4	23	....	....	....	....
1998-99	Acadie-Bathurst	QMJHL	31	4	17	21	53	....	....	....	....	....	....	....	....	....	23	2	16	18	55	....	....	....	....
99-2000	Acadie-Bathurst	QMJHL	38	11	36	47	64	....	....	....	....	....	....	....	....	....	....	....	....	....	....	....	....	....	....
	Moncton Wildcats	QMJHL	33	8	31	39	35	....	....	....	....	....	....	....	....	....	16	2	11	13	14	....	....	....	....
2000-01	Quebec Citadelles	AHL	56	3	6	9	44	....	....	....	....	....	....	....	....	....	....	....	....	....	....	....	....	....	....
2001-02	Quebec Citadelles	AHL	56	8	11	19	88	....	....	....	....	....	....	....	....	....	3	0	1	1	0	....	....	....	....
	Mississippi	ECHL	7	1	3	4	2	....	....	....	....	....	....	....	....	....	....	....	....	....	....	....	....	....	....
2002-03	**Montreal**	**NHL**	**1**	**0**	**0**	**0**	**0**	**0**	**0**	**0**	**1**	**0.0**	**–1**	**0**	**0.0**	**17:11**	....	....	....	....	....	....	....	....	....
	Hamilton	AHL	75	7	21	28	92	....	....	....	....	....	....	....	....	....	23	1	9	10	16	....	....	....	....
2003-04	Hamilton	AHL	77	9	27	36	57	....	....	....	....	....	....	....	....	....	10	2	4	6	18	....	....	....	....
2004-05	Syracuse Crunch	AHL	72	3	27	30	55	....	....	....	....	....	....	....	....	....	....	....	....	....	....	....	....	....	....
	NHL Totals		**1**	**0**	**0**	**0**	**0**	**0**	**0**	**0**	**1**	**0.0**		**0**	**0.0**	**17:11**	....	....	....	....	....	....	....	....	....

QMJHL All-Rookie Team (1997) • QMJHL Second All-Star Team (2000)
Claimed on waivers by **Columbus** from **Montreal**, September 15, 2004.

BEAUDOIN, Eric
(boh-DWEH, AIR-ihk)

Left wing. Shoots left. 6'5", 210 lbs. Born, Ottawa, Ont., May 3, 1980. Tampa Bay's 4th choice, 92nd overall, in 1998 Entry Draft.

Season	Club	League	GP	G	A	Pts	PIM	PP	SH	GW	S	%	+/-	TF	F%	Min	GP	G	A	Pts	PIM	PP	SH	GW	Min
1996-97	Ott. Jr. Senators	CJHL	54	12	19	31	55	....	....	....	....	....	....	....	....	....	....	....	....	....	....	....	....	....	....
1997-98	Guelph Storm	OHL	62	9	13	22	43	....	....	....	....	....	....	....	....	....	12	3	2	5	4	....	....	....	....
1998-99	Guelph Storm	OHL	66	28	43	71	79	....	....	....	....	....	....	....	....	....	11	5	3	8	12	....	....	....	....
99-2000	Guelph Storm	OHL	68	38	34	72	126	....	....	....	....	....	....	....	....	....	6	3	0	3	2	....	....	....	....
2000-01	Louisville Panthers	AHL	71	15	10	25	78	....	....	....	....	....	....	....	....	....	....	....	....	....	....	....	....	....	....
2001-02	**Florida**	**NHL**	**8**	**1**	**3**	**4**	**4**	**0**	**0**	**1**	**11**	**9.1**	**–2**	**1**	**0.0**	**17:27**	....	....	....	....	....	....	....	....	....
	Utah Grizzlies	AHL	44	5	16	21	83	....	....	....	....	....	....	....	....	....	....	....	....	....	....	....	....	....	....
2002-03	**Florida**	**NHL**	**15**	**0**	**1**	**1**	**25**	**0**	**0**	**0**	**11**	**0.0**	**–7**	**27**	**29.6**	**9:52**	....	....	....	....	....	....	....	....	....
	San Antonio	AHL	41	14	23	37	36	....	....	....	....	....	....	....	....	....	3	1	0	1	0	....	....	....	....
2003-04	**Florida**	**NHL**	**30**	**2**	**4**	**6**	**12**	**0**	**0**	**0**	**30**	**6.7**	**–6**	**13**	**30.8**	**10:19**	....	....	....	....	....	....	....	....	....
	San Antonio	AHL	38	20	22	42	45	....	....	....	....	....	....	....	....	....	....	....	....	....	....	....	....	....	....
2004-05	San Antonio	AHL	32	6	4	10	21	....	....	....	....	....	....	....	....	....	....	....	....	....	....	....	....	....	....
	Edmonton	AHL	24	3	1	4	9	....	....	....	....	....	....	....	....	....	....	....	....	....	....	....	....	....	....
	NHL Totals		**53**	**3**	**8**	**11**	**41**	**0**	**0**	**1**	**52**	**5.8**		**41**	**29.3**	**11:16**	....	....	....	....	....	....	....	....	....

Traded to **Florida** by **Tampa Bay** for Florida's 7th round choice (Marek Priechodsky) in 2000 Entry Draft, June 1, 2000. • Loaned to **Edmonton** (AHL) by **Florida** (San Antonio-AHL), January 3, 2005.

BEDNAR, Jaroslav
(BEHD-nahr, YA-roh-slahv)

Right wing. Shoots right. 6', 198 lbs. Born, Prague, Czech., November 8, 1976. Los Angeles' 4th choice, 51st overall, in 2001 Entry Draft.

Season	Club	League	GP	G	A	Pts	PIM	PP	SH	GW	S	%	+/-	TF	F%	Min	GP	G	A	Pts	PIM	PP	SH	GW	Min
1994-95	HC Slavia Praha	CzRep	20	6	7	13	4	....	....	....	....	....	....	....	....	....	3	0	0	0	0	....	....	....	....
1995-96	HC Slavia Praha	CzRep	20	3	1	4	6	....	....	....	....	....	....	....	....	....	3	0	0	0	0	....	....	....	....
1996-97	HC Slavia Praha	CzRep	45	18	12	30	18	....	....	....	....	....	....	....	....	....	....	....	....	....	....	....	....	....	....
1997-98	HC Slavia Praha	CzRep	14	2	5	7	6	....	....	....	....	....	....	....	....	....	....	....	....	....	....	....	....	....	....
	Plzen	CzRep	34	26	15	41	16	....	....	....	....	....	....	....	....	....	5	2	4	6	4	....	....	....	....
	Plzen	EuroHL	....	....	....	....	....	....	....	....	....	....	....	....	....	....	5	4	2	6	4	....	....	....	....
1998-99	HC Sparta Praha	CzRep	52	23	14	37	30	....	....	....	....	....	....	....	....	....	8	5	2	7	0	....	....	....	....
99-2000	JYP Jyvaskyla	Finland	53	34	28	62	56	....	....	....	....	....	....	....	....	....	....	....	....	....	....	....	....	....	....
2000-01	HIFK Helsinki	Finland	56	*32	28	60	51	....	....	....	....	....	....	....	....	....	5	3	1	4	0	....	....	....	....
2001-02	**Los Angeles**	**NHL**	**22**	**4**	**2**	**6**	**8**	**1**	**0**	**2**	**20**	**20.0**	**–4**	**2**	**50.0**	**10:42**	**3**	**0**	**0**	**0**	**0**	**0**	**0**	**0**	**11:48**
	Manchester	AHL	48	16	21	37	16	....	....	....	....	....	....	....	....	....	....	....	....	....	....	....	....	....	....
2002-03	**Los Angeles**	**NHL**	**15**	**0**	**9**	**9**	**4**	**0**	**0**	**0**	**29**	**0.0**	**3**	**7**	**57.1**	**14:00**	....	....	....	....	....	....	....	....	....
	Florida	**NHL**	**52**	**5**	**13**	**18**	**14**	**2**	**0**	**1**	**66**	**7.6**	**–2**	**42**	**42.9**	**14:09**	....	....	....	....	....	....	....	....	....
2003-04	**Florida**	**NHL**	**13**	**1**	**1**	**2**	**4**	**0**	**0**	**0**	**19**	**5.3**	**2**	**41**	**43.9**	**13:02**	....	....	....	....	....	....	....	....	....
	San Antonio	AHL	2	2	1	3	0	....	....	....	....	....	....	....	....	....	....	....	....	....	....	....	....	....	....
	Avangard Omsk	Russia	29	10	5	15	34	....	....	....	....	....	....	....	....	....	11	2	0	2	2	....	....	....	....
2004-05	Avangard Omsk	Russia	53	12	16	28	56	....	....	....	....	....	....	....	....	....	10	2	1	3	6	....	....	....	....
	NHL Totals		**102**	**10**	**25**	**35**	**30**	**3**	**0**	**3**	**134**	**7.5**		**92**	**44.6**	**13:15**	**3**	**0**	**0**	**0**	**0**	**0**	**0**	**0**	**11:48**

Traded to **Florida** by **Los Angeles** with Andreas Lilja for Dmitry Yushkevich and NY Islanders' 5th round choice (previously acquired, Los Angeles selected Brady Murray) in 2003 Entry Draft, November 26, 2002. Signed as a free agent by **Omsk** (Russia), December 11, 2003.

BEECH, Kris
(BEECH, KRIHS) **PIT.**

Center. Shoots left. 6'2", 208 lbs. Born, Salmon Arm, B.C., February 5, 1981. Washington's 1st choice, 7th overall, in 1999 Entry Draft.

Season	Club	League	GP	G	A	Pts	PIM	PP	SH	GW	S	%	+/-	TF	F%	Min	GP	G	A	Pts	PIM	PP	SH	GW	Min
1996-97	Sicamous Eagles	KIJHL	49	34	36	70	80	....	....	....	....	....	....	....	....	....	....	....	....	....	....	....	....	....	....
	Calgary Hitmen	WHL	8	1	1	2	0	....	....	....	....	....	....	....	....	....	....	....	....	....	....	....	....	....	....
1997-98	Calgary Hitmen	WHL	58	10	25	35	24	....	....	....	....	....	....	....	....	....	12	4	5	9	32	....	....	....	....
1998-99	Calgary Hitmen	WHL	68	26	41	67	103	....	....	....	....	....	....	....	....	....	6	1	4	5	8	....	....	....	....
99-2000	Calgary Hitmen	WHL	66	32	54	86	99	....	....	....	....	....	....	....	....	....	5	3	5	8	16	....	....	....	....
2000-01	**Washington**	**NHL**	**4**	**0**	**0**	**0**	**2**	**0**	**0**	**0**	**0**	**0.0**	**–2**	**25**	**36.0**	**7:29**	....	....	....	....	....	....	....	....	....
	Calgary Hitmen	WHL	40	22	44	66	103	....	....	....	....	....	....	....	....	....	10	2	8	10	26	....	....	....	....
2001-02	**Pittsburgh**	**NHL**	**79**	**10**	**15**	**25**	**45**	**2**	**0**	**0**	**126**	**7.9**	**–25**	**604**	**45.2**	**13:33**	....	....	....	....	....	....	....	....	....
2002-03	**Pittsburgh**	**NHL**	**12**	**0**	**1**	**1**	**6**	**0**	**0**	**0**	**6**	**0.0**	**–3**	**96**	**42.7**	**10:34**	....	....	....	....	....	....	....	....	....
	Wilkes-Barre	AHL	50	19	24	43	76	....	....	....	....	....	....	....	....	....	5	1	1	2	0	....	....	....	....
2003-04	**Pittsburgh**	**NHL**	**4**	**0**	**1**	**1**	**6**	**0**	**0**	**0**	**6**	**0.0**	**0**	**45**	**40.0**	**12:32**	....	....	....	....	....	....	....	....	....
	Wilkes-Barre	AHL	53	20	25	45	97	....	....	....	....	....	....	....	....	....	22	9	6	15	22	....	....	....	....
2004-05	Wilkes-Barre	AHL	68	14	48	62	146	....	....	....	....	....	....	....	....	....	11	4	6	10	14	....	....	....	....
	NHL Totals		**99**	**10**	**17**	**27**	**59**	**2**	**0**	**0**	**138**	**7.2**		**770**	**44.3**	**12:55**	....	....	....	....	....	....	....	....	....

Traded to **Pittsburgh** by **Washington** with Michal Sivek, Ross Lupaschuk and future considerations for Jaromir Jagr and Frantisek Kucera, July 11, 2001.

BEGIN, Steve
(bay-ZHIN, STEEV) **MTL.**

Center. Shoots left. 5'11", 195 lbs. Born, Trois-Rivieres, Que., June 14, 1978. Calgary's 3rd choice, 40th overall, in 1996 Entry Draft.

Season	Club	League	GP	G	A	Pts	PIM	PP	SH	GW	S	%	+/-	TF	F%	Min	GP	G	A	Pts	PIM	PP	SH	GW	Min
1993-94	Cap-d-Madelaine	QAAA	8	0	1	1	6	....	....	....	....	....	....	....	....	....	2	0	0	0	0	....	....	....	....
1994-95	Cap-d-Madelaine	QAAA	35	9	15	24	48	....	....	....	....	....	....	....	....	....	3	0	0	0	2	....	....	....	....
1995-96	Val-d'Or Foreurs	QMJHL	64	13	23	36	218	....	....	....	....	....	....	....	....	....	13	1	3	4	33	....	....	....	....
1996-97	Val-d'Or Foreurs	QMJHL	58	13	33	46	229	....	....	....	....	....	....	....	....	....	10	0	3	3	8	....	....	....	....
	Saint John Flames	AHL	....	....	....	....	....	....	....	....	....	....	....	....	....	....	4	0	2	2	6	....	....	....	....
1997-98	**Calgary**	**NHL**	**5**	**0**	**0**	**0**	**23**	**0**	**0**	**0**	**2**	**0.0**	**0**	....	....	....	....	....	....	....	....	....	....	....	....
	Val-d'Or Foreurs	QMJHL	35	18	17	35	73	....	....	....	....	....	....	....	....	....	15	2	12	14	34	....	....	....	....
1998-99	Saint John Flames	AHL	73	11	9	20	156	....	....	....	....	....	....	....	....	....	7	2	0	2	18	....	....	....	....
99-2000	**Calgary**	**NHL**	**13**	**1**	**1**	**2**	**18**	**0**	**0**	**0**	**3**	**33.3**	**–3**	**19**	**47.4**	**7:13**	....	....	....	....	....	....	....	....	....
	Saint John Flames	AHL	47	13	12	25	99	....	....	....	....	....	....	....	....	....	....	....	....	....	....	....	....	....	....
2000-01	**Calgary**	**NHL**	**4**	**0**	**0**	**0**	**21**	**0**	**0**	**0**	**3**	**0.0**	**0**	**0**	**0.0**	**6:04**	....	....	....	....	....	....	....	....	....
	Saint John Flames	AHL	58	14	14	28	109	....	....	....	....	....	....	....	....	....	19	10	7	17	18	....	....	....	....
2001-02	**Calgary**	**NHL**	**51**	**7**	**5**	**12**	**79**	**1**	**0**	**0**	**65**	**10.8**	**–3**	**129**	**53.5**	**9:25**	....	....	....	....	....	....	....	....	....
2002-03	**Calgary**	**NHL**	**50**	**3**	**1**	**4**	**51**	**0**	**0**	**1**	**59**	**5.1**	**–7**	**50**	**60.0**	**9:13**	....	....	....	....	....	....	....	....	....
2003-04	**Montreal**	**NHL**	**52**	**10**	**5**	**15**	**41**	**0**	**1**	**1**	**91**	**11.0**	**6**	**436**	**48.6**	**12:32**	**9**	**0**	**1**	**1**	**10**	**0**	**0**	**0**	**12:26**
2004-05	Hamilton	AHL	21	10	3	13	20	....	....	....	....	....	....	....	....	....	4	0	2	2	8	....	....	....	....
	NHL Totals		**175**	**21**	**12**	**33**	**233**	**1**	**1**	**2**	**223**	**9.4**		**634**	**50.5**	**10:04**	**9**	**0**	**1**	**1**	**10**	**0**	**0**	**0**	**12:26**

Jack A. Butterfield Trophy (Playoff MVP – AHL) (2001)
Traded to **Buffalo** by **Calgary** with Chris Drury for Steve Reinprecht and Rhett Warrener, July 3, 2003. Claimed by **Montreal** from **Buffalo** in Waiver Draft, October 3, 2003.

BEKAR, Derek

(BEH-kahr, DAIR-ihk)

Left wing. Shoots left. 6'3", 197 lbs. Born, Burnaby, B.C., September 15, 1975. St. Louis' 7th choice, 205th overall, in 1995 Entry Draft.

Season	Club	League	Regular Season GP	G	A	Pts	PIM	PP	SH	GW	S	%	+/-	TF	F%	Min	Playoffs GP	G	A	Pts	PIM	PP	SH	GW	Min
1992-93	Notre Dame	SMHL	29	25	24	49	68	....	....	....	....	....	....	....	....	....	....	....	....	....	....	....	....	....	....
1993-94	Notre Dame	SJHL	62	20	31	51	77	....	....	....	....	....	....	....	....	....	....	....	....	....	....	....	....	....	....
1994-95	Powell River	BCJHL	46	33	29	62	35	....	....	....	....	....	....	....	....	....	....	....	....	....	....	....	....	....	....
1995-96	New Hampshire	H-East	34	15	18	33	4	....	....	....	....	....	....	....	....	....	....	....	....	....	....	....	....	....	....
1996-97	New Hampshire	H-East	39	18	21	39	34	....	....	....	....	....	....	....	....	....	....	....	....	....	....	....	....	....	....
1997-98	New Hampshire	H-East	35	32	28	60	46	....	....	....	....	....	....	....	....	....	....	....	....	....	....	....	....	....	....
1998-99	Worcester IceCats	AHL	51	16	20	36	6	....	....	....	....	....	....	....	....	....	4	0	0	0	0	....	....	....	....
99-2000	**St. Louis**	**NHL**	**1**	**0**	**0**	**0**	**0**	**0**	**0**	**0**	**0**	**0.0**	**0**	**0**	**0.0**	**5:14**	....	....	....	....	....	....	....	....	....
	Worcester IceCats	AHL	71	21	19	40	26	....	....	....	....	....	....	....	....	....	7	0	3	3	2	....	....	....	....
2000-01	Worcester IceCats	AHL	18	5	2	7	10	....	....	....	....	....	....	....	....	....	....	....	....	....	....	....	....	....	....
	Portland Pirates	AHL	58	19	16	35	49	....	....	....	....	....	....	....	....	....	3	0	0	0	0	....	....	....	....
2001-02	Manchester	AHL	74	27	20	47	42	....	....	....	....	....	....	....	....	....	5	1	4	5	2	....	....	....	....
2002-03	**Los Angeles**	**NHL**	**6**	**0**	**0**	**0**	**4**	**0**	**0**	**0**	**4**	**0.0**	**–1**	**1**	**0.0**	**7:29**	....	....	....	....	....	....	....	....	....
	Manchester	AHL	51	19	19	38	49	....	....	....	....	....	....	....	....	....	3	0	0	0	2	....	....	....	....
2003-04	**NY Islanders**	**NHL**	**4**	**0**	**0**	**0**	**2**	**0**	**0**	**0**	**3**	**0.0**	**0**	**7**	**0.0**	**5:35**	....	....	....	....	....	....	....	....	....
	Bridgeport	AHL	76	24	11	35	57	....	....	....	....	....	....	....	....	....	3	2	2	4	0	....	....	....	....
2004-05	Dundee Stars	Britain-2	3	2	1	3	4	....	....	....	....	....	....	....	....	....	....	....	....	....	....	....	....	....	....
	Springfield	AHL	51	8	14	22	22	....	....	....	....	....	....	....	....	....	....	....	....	....	....	....	....	....	....
	NHL Totals		**11**	**0**	**0**	**0**	**6**	**0**	**0**	**0**	**7**	**0.0**		**8**	**0.0**	**6:35**	....	....	....	....	....	....	....	....	....

Hockey East Second All-Star Team (1998)

Traded to **Washington** by **St. Louis** for Mike Peluso, November 29, 2000. Signed as a free agent by **Los Angeles**, September 25, 2001. Signed as a free agent by **NY Islanders**, September 10, 2003. Signed as a free agent by **Dundee** (Britain-2), November 4, 2004. Signed as a free agent by **Springfield** (AHL), November 22, 2004. Signed as a free agent by **Chur** (Swiss-2), June 30, 2005.

BELAK, Wade

(BEE-lak, WAYD) **TOR.**

Defense/Right wing. Shoots right. 6'5", 221 lbs. Born, Saskatoon, Sask., July 3, 1976. Quebec's 1st choice, 12th overall, in 1994 Entry Draft.

Season	Club	League	Regular Season GP	G	A	Pts	PIM	PP	SH	GW	S	%	+/-	TF	F%	Min	Playoffs GP	G	A	Pts	PIM	PP	SH	GW	Min
1991-92	North Battleford	SMBHL	57	6	20	26	186	....	....	....	....	....	....	....	....	....	....	....	....	....	....	....	....	....	....
1992-93	North Battleford	SJHL	50	5	15	20	146	....	....	....	....	....	....	....	....	....	....	....	....	....	....	....	....	....	....
	Saskatoon Blades	WHL	7	0	0	0	23	....	....	....	....	....	....	....	....	....	7	0	0	0	0	....	....	....	....
1993-94	Saskatoon Blades	WHL	69	4	13	17	226	....	....	....	....	....	....	....	....	....	16	2	2	4	43	....	....	....	....
1994-95	Saskatoon Blades	WHL	72	4	14	18	290	....	....	....	....	....	....	....	....	....	9	0	0	0	36	....	....	....	....
	Cornwall Aces	AHL	....	....	....	....	....	....	....	....	....	....	....	....	....	....	11	1	2	3	40	....	....	....	....
1995-96	Saskatoon Blades	WHL	63	3	15	18	207	....	....	....	....	....	....	....	....	....	4	0	0	0	9	....	....	....	....
	Cornwall Aces	AHL	5	0	0	0	18	....	....	....	....	....	....	....	....	....	2	0	0	0	2	....	....	....	....
1996-97	**Colorado**	**NHL**	**5**	**0**	**0**	**0**	**11**	**0**	**0**	**0**	**1**	**0.0**	**–1**	....	....	....	....	....	....	....	....	....	....	....	....
	Hershey Bears	AHL	65	1	7	8	320	....	....	....	....	....	....	....	....	....	16	0	1	1	61	....	....	....	....
1997-98	**Colorado**	**NHL**	**8**	**1**	**1**	**2**	**27**	**0**	**0**	**1**	**2**	**50.0**	**–3**	....	....	....	....	....	....	....	....	....	....	....	....
	Hershey Bears	AHL	11	0	0	0	30	....	....	....	....	....	....	....	....	....	....	....	....	....	....	....	....	....	....
1998-99	**Colorado**	**NHL**	**22**	**0**	**0**	**0**	**71**	**0**	**0**	**0**	**5**	**0.0**	**–2**	**0**	**0.0**	**6:48**	....	....	....	....	....	....	....	....	....
	Hershey Bears	AHL	17	0	1	1	49	....	....	....	....	....	....	....	....	....	....	....	....	....	....	....	....	....	....
	Calgary	**NHL**	**9**	**0**	**1**	**1**	**23**	**0**	**0**	**0**	**2**	**0.0**	**3**	**0**	**0.0**	**10:46**	....	....	....	....	....	....	....	....	....
	Saint John Flames	AHL	12	0	2	2	43	....	....	....	....	....	....	....	....	....	6	0	1	1	23	....	....	....	....
99-2000	**Calgary**	**NHL**	**40**	**0**	**2**	**2**	**122**	**0**	**0**	**0**	**11**	**0.0**	**–4**	**1**	**0.0**	**7:33**	....	....	....	....	....	....	....	....	....
2000-01	**Calgary**	**NHL**	**23**	**0**	**0**	**0**	**79**	**0**	**0**	**0**	**8**	**0.0**	**–2**	**0**	**0.0**	**6:54**	....	....	....	....	....	....	....	....	....
	Toronto	**NHL**	**16**	**1**	**1**	**2**	**31**	**0**	**0**	**0**	**8**	**12.5**	**–4**	**0**	**0.0**	**13:38**	....	....	....	....	....	....	....	....	....
2001-02	**Toronto**	**NHL**	**63**	**1**	**3**	**4**	**142**	**0**	**0**	**0**	**47**	**2.1**	**2**	**0**	**0.0**	**9:14**	**16**	**1**	**0**	**1**	**18**	**0**	**0**	**0**	**7:28**
2002-03	**Toronto**	**NHL**	**55**	**3**	**6**	**9**	**196**	**0**	**0**	**0**	**33**	**9.1**	**–2**	**0**	**0.0**	**10:50**	**2**	**0**	**0**	**0**	**4**	**0**	**0**	**0**	**8:22**
2003-04	**Toronto**	**NHL**	**34**	**1**	**1**	**2**	**109**	**0**	**0**	**0**	**15**	**6.7**	**0**	**0**	**0.0**	**7:00**	**4**	**0**	**0**	**0**	**14**	**0**	**0**	**0**	**9:59**
2004-05	Coventry Blaze	Britain	20	3	5	8	109	....	....	....	....	....	....	....	....	....	8	1	1	2	16	....	....	....	....
	NHL Totals		**275**	**7**	**15**	**22**	**811**	**0**	**0**	**1**	**132**	**5.3**		**1**	**0.0**	**8:56**	**22**	**1**	**0**	**1**	**36**	**0**	**0**	**0**	**8:00**

Rights transferred to **Colorado** after **Quebec** franchise relocated, June 21, 1995. Traded to **Calgary** by **Colorado** with Rene Corbet, Robyn Regehr and Colorado's 2nd round compensatory choice (Jarret Stoll) in 2000 Entry Draft for Theoren Fleury and Chris Dingman, February 28, 1999. • Missed majority of 1999-2000 and 2000-01 seasons recovering from shoulder injury suffered in game vs. Colorado, February 10, 2000. Claimed on waivers by **Toronto** from **Calgary**, February 16, 2001. • Missed majority of 2003-04 season recovering from abdomen (November 20, 2003 vs. Edmonton) and knee (January 6, 2004 vs. Nashville) injuries. Signed as a free agent by **Coventry** (Britain), November 8, 2004.

BELANGER, Eric

(buh-LAWN-zhay, AIR-ihk) **L.A.**

Center. Shoots left. 6', 185 lbs. Born, Sherbrooke, Que., December 16, 1977. Los Angeles' 5th choice, 96th overall, in 1996 Entry Draft.

Season	Club	League	Regular Season GP	G	A	Pts	PIM	PP	SH	GW	S	%	+/-	TF	F%	Min	Playoffs GP	G	A	Pts	PIM	PP	SH	GW	Min
1993-94	Magog	QAAA	32	19	24	43	24	....	....	....	....	....	....	....	....	....	13	5	6	11	36	....	....	....	....
1994-95	Beauport	QMJHL	71	12	28	40	24	....	....	....	....	....	....	....	....	....	18	5	9	14	25	....	....	....	....
1995-96	Beauport	QMJHL	59	35	48	83	18	....	....	....	....	....	....	....	....	....	20	13	14	27	6	....	....	....	....
1996-97	Beauport	QMJHL	31	13	37	50	30	....	....	....	....	....	....	....	....	....	....	....	....	....	....	....	....	....	....
	Rimouski Oceanic	QMJHL	31	26	41	67	36	....	....	....	....	....	....	....	....	....	4	2	3	5	10	....	....	....	....
1997-98	Fredericton	AHL	56	17	34	51	28	....	....	....	....	....	....	....	....	....	4	2	1	3	2	....	....	....	....
1998-99	Springfield	AHL	33	8	18	26	10	....	....	....	....	....	....	....	....	....	3	0	1	1	2	....	....	....	....
	Long Beach	IHL	1	0	0	0	0	....	....	....	....	....	....	....	....	....	....	....	....	....	....	....	....	....	....
99-2000	Lowell	AHL	65	15	25	40	20	....	....	....	....	....	....	....	....	....	7	3	3	6	2	....	....	....	....
2000-01	**Los Angeles**	**NHL**	**62**	**9**	**12**	**21**	**16**	**1**	**2**	**1**	**80**	**11.3**	**14**	**849**	**56.4**	**13:25**	**13**	**1**	**4**	**5**	**2**	**0**	**0**	**1**	**13:47**
	Lowell	AHL	13	8	10	18	4	....	....	....	....	....	....	....	....	....	....	....	....	....	....	....	....	....	....
2001-02	**Los Angeles**	**NHL**	**53**	**8**	**16**	**24**	**21**	**2**	**1**	**1**	**67**	**11.9**	**2**	**882**	**57.7**	**14:33**	**7**	**0**	**0**	**0**	**4**	**0**	**0**	**0**	**12:57**
2002-03	**Los Angeles**	**NHL**	**62**	**16**	**19**	**35**	**26**	**0**	**3**	**1**	**114**	**14.0**	**–5**	**1143**	**51.8**	**17:42**	....	....	....	....	....	....	....	....	....
2003-04	**Los Angeles**	**NHL**	**81**	**13**	**20**	**33**	**44**	**0**	**1**	**2**	**132**	**9.8**	**–16**	**1418**	**53.7**	**17:01**	....	....	....	....	....	....	....	....	....
2004-05	HC Forst Bolzano	Italy	12	13	10	23	20	....	....	....	....	....	....	....	....	....	9	3	7	10	33	....	....	....	....
	NHL Totals		**258**	**46**	**67**	**113**	**107**	**3**	**7**	**5**	**393**	**11.7**		**4292**	**54.5**	**15:48**	**20**	**1**	**4**	**5**	**6**	**0**	**0**	**1**	**13:30**

Signed as a free agent by **Bolzano** (Italy), December 22, 2004.

BELANGER, Ken

(buh-LAWN-zhay, KEHN)

Left wing. Shoots left. 6'4", 225 lbs. Born, Sault Ste. Marie, Ont., May 14, 1974. Hartford's 7th choice, 153rd overall, in 1992 Entry Draft.

Season	Club	League	Regular Season GP	G	A	Pts	PIM	PP	SH	GW	S	%	+/-	TF	F%	Min	Playoffs GP	G	A	Pts	PIM	PP	SH	GW	Min
1990-91	Soo Legion	NOHA	43	24	29	53	169	....	....	....	....	....	....	....	....	....	....	....	....	....	....	....	....	....	....
1991-92	Ottawa 67's	OHL	51	4	4	8	174	....	....	....	....	....	....	....	....	....	11	0	0	0	24	....	....	....	....
1992-93	Ottawa 67's	OHL	34	6	12	18	139	....	....	....	....	....	....	....	....	....	....	....	....	....	....	....	....	....	....
	Guelph Storm	OHL	29	10	14	24	86	....	....	....	....	....	....	....	....	....	5	2	1	3	14	....	....	....	....
1993-94	Guelph Storm	OHL	55	11	22	33	185	....	....	....	....	....	....	....	....	....	9	2	3	5	30	....	....	....	....
1994-95	St. John's	AHL	47	5	5	10	246	....	....	....	....	....	....	....	....	....	4	0	0	0	30	....	....	....	....
	Toronto	**NHL**	**3**	**0**	**0**	**0**	**9**	**0**	**0**	**0**	**1**	**0.0**	**0**	....	....	....	....	....	....	....	....	....	....	....	....
1995-96	St. John's	AHL	40	16	14	30	222	....	....	....	....	....	....	....	....	....	....	....	....	....	....	....	....	....	....
	NY Islanders	**NHL**	**7**	**0**	**0**	**0**	**27**	**0**	**0**	**0**	**0**	**0.0**	**–2**	....	....	....	....	....	....	....	....	....	....	....	....
1996-97	**NY Islanders**	**NHL**	**18**	**0**	**2**	**2**	**102**	**0**	**0**	**0**	**5**	**0.0**	**–1**	....	....	....	....	....	....	....	....	....	....	....	....
	Kentucky	AHL	38	10	12	22	164	....	....	....	....	....	....	....	....	....	4	0	1	1	27	....	....	....	....
1997-98	**NY Islanders**	**NHL**	**37**	**3**	**1**	**4**	**101**	**0**	**0**	**1**	**10**	**30.0**	**1**	....	....	....	....	....	....	....	....	....	....	....	....
1998-99	**NY Islanders**	**NHL**	**9**	**1**	**1**	**2**	**30**	**0**	**0**	**0**	**3**	**33.3**	**1**	**0**	**0.0**	**5:05**	....	....	....	....	....	....	....	....	....
	Boston	**NHL**	**45**	**1**	**4**	**5**	**152**	**0**	**0**	**0**	**16**	**6.3**	**–2**	**1**	**0.0**	**4:38**	**12**	**1**	**0**	**1**	**16**	**0**	**0**	**0**	**5:11**
99-2000	**Boston**	**NHL**	**37**	**2**	**2**	**4**	**44**	**0**	**0**	**0**	**20**	**10.0**	**–4**	**1**	**0.0**	**5:17**	....	....	....	....	....	....	....	....	....
2000-01	**Boston**	**NHL**	**40**	**2**	**2**	**4**	**121**	**0**	**0**	**1**	**35**	**5.7**	**–6**	**1**	**100.0**	**7:06**	....	....	....	....	....	....	....	....	....
	Providence Bruins	AHL	10	1	4	5	47	....	....	....	....	....	....	....	....	....	2	0	0	0	4	....	....	....	....
2001-02	**Los Angeles**	**NHL**	**43**	**2**	**0**	**2**	**85**	**0**	**0**	**0**	**22**	**9.1**	**–5**	**0**	**0.0**	**4:22**	....	....	....	....	....	....	....	....	....
2002-03	**Los Angeles**	**NHL**	**4**	**0**	**0**	**0**	**17**	**0**	**0**	**0**	**0**	**0.0**	**0**	**0**	**0.0**	**4:03**	....	....	....	....	....	....	....	....	....
2003-04	**Los Angeles**	**NHL**	DID NOT PLAY – INJURED														....	....	....	....	....	....	....	....	....
2004-05	Adirondack	UHL	1	0	0	0	5	....	....	....	....	....	....	....	....	....	....	....	....	....	....	....	....	....	....
	NHL Totals		**243**	**11**	**12**	**23**	**688**	**0**	**0**	**2**	**112**	**9.8**		**3**	**33.3**	**5:16**	**12**	**1**	**0**	**1**	**16**	**0**	**0**	**0**	**5:11**

Traded to **Toronto** by **Hartford** for Toronto's 9th round choice (Matt Ball) in 1994 Entry Draft, March 18, 1994. Traded to **NY Islanders** by **Toronto** with Damian Rhodes for future considerations (Kirk Muller and Don Beaupre, January 23, 1996), January 23, 1996. Traded to **Boston** by **NY Islanders** for Ted Donato, November 7, 1998. • Missed majority of 1999-2000 season recovering from head injury suffered in game vs. Toronto, November 11, 1999. Signed as a free agent by **Los Angeles**, July 2, 2001. • Missed majority of 2002-03 season and entire 2003-04 season recovering from head injury suffered in game vs. San Jose, November 5, 2002. Signed as a free agent by **Adirondack** (UHL), December 30, 2004.

BELL, Mark

(BEHL, MAHRK) **CHI.**

Center. Shoots left. 6'4", 205 lbs. Born, St. Paul's, Ont., August 5, 1980. Chicago's 1st choice, 8th overall, in 1998 Entry Draft.

			Regular Season														Playoffs								
Season	Club	League	GP	G	A	Pts	PIM	PP	SH	GW	S	%	+/-	TF	F%	Min	GP	G	A	Pts	PIM	PP	SH	GW	Min
1995-96	Stratford Cullitons	OHA-B	47	8	15	23	32	....	....	....	....	....	....	....	....	....	....	....	....	....	....	....	....	....	....
1996-97	Ottawa 67's	OHL	65	8	12	20	40	....	....	....	....	....	....	....	....	....	24	4	7	11	13	....	....	....	....
1997-98	Ottawa 67's	OHL	55	34	26	60	87	....	....	....	....	....	....	....	....	....	13	6	5	11	14	....	....	....	....
1998-99	Ottawa 67's	OHL	44	29	26	55	69	....	....	....	....	....	....	....	....	....	9	6	5	11	8	....	....	....	....
99-2000	Ottawa 67's	OHL	48	34	38	72	95	....	....	....	....	....	....	....	....	....	2	0	1	1	0	....	....	....	....
2000-01	**Chicago**	**NHL**	**13**	**0**	**1**	**1**	**4**	**0**	**0**	**0**	**14**	**0.0**	**0**	**141**	**48.9**	**12:00**	....	....	....	....	....	....	....	....	....
	Norfolk Admirals	AHL	61	15	27	42	126	....	....	....	....	....	....	....	....	....	9	4	3	7	10	....	....	....	....
2001-02	**Chicago**	**NHL**	**80**	**12**	**16**	**28**	**124**	**1**	**0**	**1**	**120**	**10.0**	**–6**	**47**	**42.6**	**12:39**	**5**	**0**	**0**	**0**	**8**	**0**	**0**	**0**	**9:18**
2002-03	**Chicago**	**NHL**	**82**	**14**	**15**	**29**	**113**	**0**	**2**	**0**	**127**	**11.0**	**0**	**377**	**52.5**	**14:04**	....	....	....	....	....	....	....	....	....
2003-04	**Chicago**	**NHL**	**82**	**21**	**24**	**45**	**106**	**2**	**0**	**1**	**202**	**10.4**	**–14**	**387**	**48.3**	**17:37**	....	....	....	....	....	....	....	....	....
2004-05	Trondheim IK	Norway	25	10	17	27	87	....	....	....	....	....	....	....	....	....	11	6	6	12	44	....	....	....	....
	NHL Totals		**257**	**47**	**56**	**103**	**347**	**3**	**2**	**2**	**463**	**10.2**		**952**	**49.8**	**14:39**	**5**	**0**	**0**	**0**	**8**	**0**	**0**	**0**	**9:18**

Signed as a free agent by **Trondheim** (Norway), November 6, 2004.

BELLEFEUILLE, Blake

(BEHL-fay, BLAYK)

Center. Shoots right. 5'10", 208 lbs. Born, Framingham, MA, December 27, 1977.

Season	Club	League	GP	G	A	Pts	PIM	PP	SH	GW	S	%	+/-	TF	F%	Min	GP	G	A	Pts	PIM	PP	SH	GW	Min
1994-95	Framingham	High-MA	30	42	50	92	....	....	....	....	....	....	....	....	....	....	....	....	....	....	....	....	....	....	....
1995-96	Framingham	High-MA	30	31	60	91	....	....	....	....	....	....	....	....	....	....	....	....	....	....	....	....	....	....	....
1996-97	Boston College	H-East	34	16	19	35	20	....	....	....	....	....	....	....	....	....	....	....	....	....	....	....	....	....	....
1997-98	Boston College	H-East	41	19	20	39	35	....	....	....	....	....	....	....	....	....	....	....	....	....	....	....	....	....	....
1998-99	Boston College	H-East	43	24	25	49	80	....	....	....	....	....	....	....	....	....	....	....	....	....	....	....	....	....	....
99-2000	Boston College	H-East	39	18	31	49	28	....	....	....	....	....	....	....	....	....	....	....	....	....	....	....	....	....	....
2000-01	Syracuse Crunch	AHL	50	5	5	10	18	....	....	....	....	....	....	....	....	....	5	0	0	0	0	....	....	....	....
2001-02	**Columbus**	**NHL**	**2**	**0**	**1**	**1**	**0**	**0**	**0**	**0**	**2**	**0.0**	**1**	**15**	**60.0**	**8:21**	....	....	....	....	....	....	....	....	....
	Syracuse Crunch	AHL	75	11	19	30	33	....	....	....	....	....	....	....	....	....	4	2	0	2	0	....	....	....	....
2002-03	**Columbus**	**NHL**	**3**	**0**	**0**	**0**	**0**	**0**	**0**	**0**	**0**	**0.0**	**0**	**17**	**64.7**	**7:01**	....	....	....	....	....	....	....	....	....
	Syracuse Crunch	AHL	63	12	19	31	44	....	....	....	....	....	....	....	....	....	....	....	....	....	....	....	....	....	....
2003-04	Providence Bruins	AHL	7	1	0	1	2	....	....	....	....	....	....	....	....	....	....	....	....	....	....	....	....	....	....
	Norfolk Admirals	AHL	59	4	8	12	17	....	....	....	....	....	....	....	....	....	5	1	1	2	0	....	....	....	....
2004-05	Danbury Trashers	UHL	44	16	14	30	14	....	....	....	....	....	....	....	....	....	....	....	....	....	....	....	....	....	....
	Bridgeport	AHL	1	0	0	0	0	....	....	....	....	....	....	....	....	....	....	....	....	....	....	....	....	....	....
	NHL Totals		**5**	**0**	**1**	**1**	**0**	**0**	**0**	**0**	**2**	**0.0**		**32**	**62.5**	**7:33**	....	....	....	....	....	....	....	....	....

Hockey East Second All-Star Team (2000)

Signed as a free agent by **Columbus**, May 26, 2000. Signed to a PTO (tryout) contract by **Providence** (AHL), October 10, 2003. Signed to a PTO (tryout) contract by **Norfolk** (AHL), November 6, 2003, following release by Providence (AHL). Signed as a free agent by **Danbury** (UHL), October 13, 2004. Signed to a PTO (tryout) contract by **Bridgeport** (AHL), November 30, 2004.

BERARD, Bryan

(buh-RAHRD, BRIGH-uhn) **CBJ**

Defense. Shoots left. 6'2", 220 lbs. Born, Woonsocket, RI, March 5, 1977. Ottawa's 1st choice, 1st overall, in 1995 Entry Draft.

Season	Club	League	GP	G	A	Pts	PIM	PP	SH	GW	S	%	+/-	TF	F%	Min	GP	G	A	Pts	PIM	PP	SH	GW	Min
1991-92	Mount St. Charles	High-RI	15	3	15	18	4	....	....	....	....	....	....	....	....	....	....	....	....	....	....	....	....	....	....
1992-93	Mount St. Charles	High-RI	15	8	12	20	18	....	....	....	....	....	....	....	....	....	....	....	....	....	....	....	....	....	....
1993-94	Mount St. Charles	High-RI	15	11	26	37	4.5	....	....	....	....	....	....	....	....	....	4	3	3	6	6	....	....	....	....
1994-95	Detroit	OHL	58	20	55	75	97	....	....	....	....	....	....	....	....	....	21	4	20	24	38	....	....	....	....
1995-96	Detroit	OHL	56	31	58	89	116	....	....	....	....	....	....	....	....	....	17	7	18	25	41	....	....	....	....
1996-97	**NY Islanders**	**NHL**	**82**	**8**	**40**	**48**	**86**	**3**	**0**	**1**	**172**	**4.7**	**1**	....	....	....	....	....	....	....	....	....	....	....	....
1997-98	**NY Islanders**	**NHL**	**75**	**14**	**32**	**46**	**59**	**8**	**1**	**2**	**192**	**7.3**	**–32**	....	....	....	....	....	....	....	....	....	....	....	....
	United States	Olympics	2	0	0	0	0	....	....	....	....	....	....	....	....	....	....	....	....	....	....	....	....	....	....
1998-99	**NY Islanders**	**NHL**	**31**	**4**	**11**	**15**	**26**	**2**	**0**	**3**	**72**	**5.6**	**–6**	**0**	**0.0**	**24:45**	....	....	....	....	....	....	....	....	....
	Toronto	**NHL**	**38**	**5**	**14**	**19**	**22**	**2**	**0**	**2**	**63**	**7.9**	**7**	**0**	**0.0**	**22:38**	**17**	**1**	**8**	**9**	**8**	**1**	**0**	**0**	**21:11**
99-2000	**Toronto**	**NHL**	**64**	**3**	**27**	**30**	**42**	**1**	**0**	**0**	**98**	**3.1**	**11**	**0**	**0.0**	**19:34**	....	....	....	....	....	....	....	....	....
2000-01	**Toronto**	**NHL**	DID NOT PLAY – INJURED																						
2001-02	**NY Rangers**	**NHL**	**82**	**2**	**21**	**23**	**60**	**0**	**0**	**0**	**132**	**1.5**	**–1**	**0**	**0.0**	**19:38**	....	....	....	....	....	....	....	....	....
2002-03	**Boston**	**NHL**	**80**	**10**	**28**	**38**	**64**	**4**	**0**	**1**	**205**	**4.9**	**–4**	**0**	**0.0**	**21:21**	**3**	**1**	**0**	**1**	**2**	**0**	**0**	**0**	**21:50**
2003-04	**Chicago**	**NHL**	**58**	**13**	**34**	**47**	**53**	**6**	**0**	**0**	**203**	**6.4**	**–24**	**0**	**0.0**	**21:46**	....	....	....	....	....	....	....	....	....
2004-05			DID NOT PLAY																						
	NHL Totals		**510**	**59**	**207**	**266**	**412**	**26**	**1**	**9**	**1137**	**5.2**		**0**	**0.0**	**21:08**	**20**	**2**	**8**	**10**	**10**	**1**	**0**	**0**	**21:17**

OHL All-Rookie Team (1995) • OHL First All-Star Team (1995, 1996) • OHL Rookie of the Year (1995) • Canadian Major Junior First All-Star Team (1995, 1996) • Canadian Major Junior Rookie of the Year (1995) • Canadian Major Junior Defenseman of the Year (1996) • NHL All-Rookie Team (1997) • Calder Memorial Trophy (1997) • Bill Masterton Memorial Trophy (2004)

Traded to **NY Islanders** by **Ottawa** with Don Beaupre and Martin Straka for Damian Rhodes and Wade Redden, January 23, 1996. Traded to **Toronto** by **NY Islanders** with NY Islanders' 6th round choice (Jan Sochor) in 1999 Entry Draft for Felix Potvin and Toronto's 6th round choice (later traded to Tampa Bay – Tampa Bay selected Fedor Fedorov) in 1999 Entry Draft, January 9, 1999. • Missed remainder of 1999-2000 season and entire 2000-01 season recovering from eye injury suffered in game vs. Ottawa, March 11, 2000. Signed as a free agent by **NY Rangers**, October 5, 2001. Signed as a free agent by **Boston**, August 13, 2002. Signed as a free agent by **Chicago**, October 31, 2003. Signed as a free agent by **Columbus**, August 3, 2005.

BEREHOWSKY, Drake

(beh-reh-HOW-skee, DRAYK)

Defense. Shoots right. 6'2", 225 lbs. Born, Toronto, Ont., January 3, 1972. Toronto's 1st choice, 10th overall, in 1990 Entry Draft.

Season	Club	League	GP	G	A	Pts	PIM	PP	SH	GW	S	%	+/-	TF	F%	Min	GP	G	A	Pts	PIM	PP	SH	GW	Min
1987-88	Barrie Colts	OHA-B	40	10	36	46	81	....	....	....	....	....	....	....	....	....	....	....	....	....	....	....	....	....	....
1988-89	Kingston Raiders	OHL	63	7	39	46	85	....	....	....	....	....	....	....	....	....	....	....	....	....	....	....	....	....	....
1989-90	Kingston	OHL	9	3	11	14	28	....	....	....	....	....	....	....	....	....	....	....	....	....	....	....	....	....	....
1990-91	**Toronto**	**NHL**	**8**	**0**	**1**	**1**	**25**	**0**	**0**	**0**	**4**	**0.0**	**–6**	....	....	....	....	....	....	....	....	....	....	....	....
	Kingston	OHL	13	5	13	18	38	....	....	....	....	....	....	....	....	....	....	....	....	....	....	....	....	....	....
	North Bay	OHL	26	7	23	30	51	....	....	....	....	....	....	....	....	....	10	2	7	9	21	....	....	....	....
1991-92	**Toronto**	**NHL**	**1**	**0**	**0**	**0**	**0**	**0**	**0**	**0**	**0**	**0.0**	**0**	....	....	....	....	....	....	....	....	....	....	....	....
	North Bay	OHL	62	19	63	82	147	....	....	....	....	....	....	....	....	....	21	7	24	31	22	....	....	....	....
	St. John's	AHL	....	....	....	....	....	....	....	....	....	....	....	....	....	....	6	0	5	5	21	....	....	....	....
1992-93	**Toronto**	**NHL**	**41**	**4**	**15**	**19**	**61**	**1**	**0**	**1**	**41**	**9.8**	**1**	....	....	....	....	....	....	....	....	....	....	....	....
	St. John's	AHL	28	10	17	27	38	....	....	....	....	....	....	....	....	....	....	....	....	....	....	....	....	....	....
1993-94	**Toronto**	**NHL**	**49**	**2**	**8**	**10**	**63**	**2**	**0**	**2**	**29**	**6.9**	**–3**	....	....	....	....	....	....	....	....	....	....	....	....
	St. John's	AHL	18	3	12	15	40	....	....	....	....	....	....	....	....	....	....	....	....	....	....	....	....	....	....
1994-95	**Toronto**	**NHL**	**25**	**0**	**2**	**2**	**15**	**0**	**0**	**0**	**12**	**0.0**	**–10**	....	....	....	....	....	....	....	....	....	....	....	....
	Pittsburgh	**NHL**	**4**	**0**	**0**	**0**	**13**	**0**	**0**	**0**	**2**	**0.0**	**1**	....	....	....	**1**	**0**	**0**	**0**	**0**	**0**	**0**	**0**	....
1995-96	**Pittsburgh**	**NHL**	**1**	**0**	**0**	**0**	**0**	**0**	**0**	**0**	**0**	**0.0**	**1**	....	....	....	....	....	....	....	....	....	....	....	....
	Cleveland	IHL	74	6	28	34	141	....	....	....	....	....	....	....	....	....	3	0	3	3	6	....	....	....	....
1996-97	Carolina	AHL	49	2	15	17	55	....	....	....	....	....	....	....	....	....	....	....	....	....	....	....	....	....	....
	San Antonio	IHL	16	3	4	7	36	....	....	....	....	....	....	....	....	....	....	....	....	....	....	....	....	....	....
1997-98	**Edmonton**	**NHL**	**67**	**1**	**6**	**7**	**169**	**1**	**0**	**1**	**58**	**1.7**	**1**	....	....	....	**12**	**1**	**2**	**3**	**14**	**0**	**0**	**1**	....
	Hamilton	AHL	8	2	0	2	21	....	....	....	....	....	....	....	....	....	....	....	....	....	....	....	....	....	....
1998-99	**Nashville**	**NHL**	**74**	**2**	**15**	**17**	**140**	**0**	**0**	**0**	**79**	**2.5**	**–9**	**1**	**100.0**	**21:43**	....	....	....	....	....	....	....	....	....
99-2000	**Nashville**	**NHL**	**79**	**12**	**20**	**32**	**87**	**5**	**0**	**1**	**102**	**11.8**	**–4**	**0**	**0.0**	**22:39**	....	....	....	....	....	....	....	....	....
2000-01	**Nashville**	**NHL**	**66**	**6**	**18**	**24**	**100**	**3**	**0**	**1**	**94**	**6.4**	**–9**	**1**	**0.0**	**21:38**	....	....	....	....	....	....	....	....	....
	Vancouver	**NHL**	**14**	**1**	**1**	**2**	**21**	**1**	**0**	**0**	**13**	**7.7**	**0**	**0**	**0.0**	**17:10**	**4**	**0**	**0**	**0**	**12**	**0**	**0**	**0**	**14:20**
2001-02	**Vancouver**	**NHL**	**25**	**1**	**2**	**3**	**18**	**0**	**0**	**1**	**15**	**6.7**	**–5**	**1**	**0.0**	**13:28**	....	....	....	....	....	....	....	....	....
	Phoenix	**NHL**	**32**	**1**	**4**	**5**	**42**	**0**	**0**	**0**	**23**	**4.3**	**5**	**0**	**0.0**	**12:20**	**5**	**0**	**1**	**1**	**4**	**0**	**0**	**0**	**13:00**
2002-03	**Phoenix**	**NHL**	**7**	**1**	**2**	**3**	**27**	**0**	**0**	**0**	**8**	**12.5**	**0**	**0**	**0.0**	**10:52**	....	....	....	....	....	....	....	....	....
	Springfield	AHL	2	0	0	0	0	....	....	....	....	....	....	....	....	....	....	....	....	....	....	....	....	....	....
2003-04	**Pittsburgh**	**NHL**	**47**	**5**	**16**	**21**	**50**	**3**	**0**	**0**	**62**	**8.1**	**–16**	**0**	**0.0**	**21:13**	....	....	....	....	....	....	....	....	....
	Toronto	**NHL**	**9**	**1**	**2**	**3**	**17**	**0**	**0**	**0**	**8**	**12.5**	**5**	**0**	**0.0**	**16:17**	....	....	....	....	....	....	....	....	....
2004-05	Skelleftea AIK HK	Sweden-2	18	3	5	8	63	....	....	....	....	....	....	....	....	....	....	....	....	....	....	....	....	....	....
	NHL Totals		**549**	**37**	**112**	**149**	**848**	**16**	**0**	**7**	**550**	**6.7**		**3**	**33.3**	**19:52**	**22**	**1**	**3**	**4**	**30**	**0**	**0**	**1**	**13:36**

OHL First All-Star Team (1992) • Canadian Major Junior Defenseman of the Year (1992)

Traded to **Pittsburgh** by **Toronto** for Grant Jennings, April 7, 1995. Signed as a free agent by **Edmonton**, September 30, 1997. Traded to **Nashville** by **Edmonton** with Eric Fichaud and Greg de Vries for Mikhail Shtalenkov and Jim Dowd, October 1, 1998. Traded to **Vancouver** by **Nashville** for Atlanta's 2nd round choice (previously acquired, Nashville selected Timofei Shishkanov) in 2001 Entry Draft, March 9, 2001. Traded to **Phoenix** by **Vancouver** with Denis Pederson for Todd Warriner, Trevor Letowski, Tyler Bouck and Phoenix's 3rd round choice (later traded back to Phoenix – Phoenix selected Dimitri Pestunov) in 2003 Entry Draft, December 28, 2001. • Missed majority of 2002-03 season recovering from knee injury suffered in training camp, September 24, 2002. Signed as a free agent by **Pittsburgh**, August, 29, 2003. Traded to **Toronto** by **Pittsburgh** for Ric Jackman, February 11, 2004. Signed as a free agent by **Skelleftea** (Sweden-2), December 22, 2004.

			Regular Season															Playoffs							
Season	Club	League	GP	G	A	Pts	PIM	PP	SH	GW	S	%	+/-	TF	F%	Min	GP	G	A	Pts	PIM	PP	SH	GW	Min

BERG, Aki — (BUHRG, AH-kee) — TOR.

Defense. Shoots left. 6'3", 213 lbs. Born, Turku, Finland, July 28, 1977. Los Angeles' 1st choice, 3rd overall, in 1995 Entry Draft.

Season	Club	League	GP	G	A	Pts	PIM	PP	SH	GW	S	%	+/-	TF	F%	Min	GP	G	A	Pts	PIM	PP	SH	GW	Min
1992-93	TPS Turku Jr.	Finland-Jr.	39	18	24	42	24	....	....	....	....	....	....				....	....	....	....	....	....	....	....	....
1993-94	TPS Turku Jr.	Finland-Jr.	21	3	11	14	24	....	....	....	....	....	....				7	0	0	0	10	....	....	....	....
	Kiekko-67 Turku	Finland-2	12	1	1	2	16	....	....	....	....	....	....				....	....	....	....	....	....	....	....	....
	TPS Turku	Finland	6	0	3	3	4	....	....	....	....	....	....				....	....	....	....	....	....	....	....	....
1994-95	TPS Turku Jr.	Finland-Jr.	8	1	0	1	30	....	....	....	....	....	....				....	....	....	....	....	....	....	....	....
	Kiekko-67 Turku	Finland-2	21	3	9	12	24	....	....	....	....	....	....				7	0	0	0	10	....	....	....	....
	TPS Turku	Finland	5	0	0	0	4	....	....	....	....	....	....				....	....	....	....	....	....	....	....	....
1995-96	**Los Angeles**	**NHL**	51	0	7	7	29	0	0	0	56	0.0	–13				....	....	....	....	....	....	....	....	....
	Phoenix	IHL	20	0	3	3	18	....	....	....	....	....	....				2	0	0	0	4	....	....	....	....
1996-97	**Los Angeles**	**NHL**	41	2	6	8	24	2	0	0	65	3.1	–9				....	....	....	....	....	....	....	....	....
	Phoenix	IHL	23	1	3	4	21	....	....	....	....	....	....				....	....	....	....	....	....	....	....	....
1997-98	**Los Angeles**	**NHL**	72	0	8	8	61	0	0	0	58	0.0	3				4	0	3	3	0	0	0	0	
	Finland	Olympics	6	0	0	0	6	....	....	....	....	....	....				....	....	....	....	....	....	....	....	....
1998-99	TPS Turku	Finland	48	8	7	15	137	....	....	....	....	....	....				9	1	1	2	45	....	....	....	....
99-2000	**Los Angeles**	**NHL**	70	3	13	16	45	0	0	0	70	4.3	–1	0	0.0	16:39	2	0	0	0	2	0	0	0	15:03
2000-01	**Los Angeles**	**NHL**	47	0	4	4	43	0	0	0	31	0.0	3	0	0.0	14:54	....	....	....	....	....	....	....	....	....
	Toronto	**NHL**	12	3	0	3	2	3	0	1	12	25.0	–6	0	0.0	18:13	11	0	2	2	4	0	0	0	16:31
2001-02	**Toronto**	**NHL**	81	1	10	11	46	0	0	0	66	1.5	14		1100.0	18:43	20	0	1	1	37	0	0	0	18:25
	Finland	Olympics	4	1	0	1	2	....	....	....	....	....	....				....	....	....	....	....	....	....	....	....
2002-03	**Toronto**	**NHL**	78	4	7	11	28	0	0	2	49	8.2	3	0	0.0	15:02	7	1	1	2	2	0	0	0	19:45
2003-04	**Toronto**	**NHL**	79	2	7	9	40	0	0	0	69	2.9	–1	1	0.0	18:18	10	0	0	0	2	0	0	0	14:52
2004-05	Timra IK	Sweden	47	6	14	20	46	....	....	....	....	....	....				7	0	0	0	6	....	....	....	....
	NHL Totals		531	15	62	77	318	5	0	3	476	3.2		2	50.0	16:57	54	1	7	8	47	0	0	0	17:20

Traded to **Toronto** by **Los Angeles** for Adam Mair and Toronto's 2nd round choice (Mike Cammalleri) in 2001 Entry Draft, March 13, 2001. Signed as a free agent by **Timra** (Sweden), September 22, 2004.

BERGENHEIM, Sean — (BUHR-gehn-highm, SHAWN) — NYI

Center. Shoots left. 5'11", 194 lbs. Born, Helsinki, Finland, February 8, 1984. NY Islanders' 1st choice, 22nd overall, in 2002 Entry Draft.

Season	Club	League	GP	G	A	Pts	PIM	PP	SH	GW	S	%	+/-	TF	F%	Min	GP	G	A	Pts	PIM	PP	SH	GW	Min
99-2000	Jokerit Helsinki Jr.	Finland-Jr.	30	22	11	33	34	....	....	....	....	....	....				3	1	0	1	0	....	....	....	....
	Jokerit U18	Fin-U18	17	10	8	18	14	....	....	....	....	....	....				3	1	0	1	2	....	....	....	....
2000-01	Jokerit Helsinki Jr.	Finland-Jr.	19	7	4	11	30	....	....	....	....	....	....				8	9	5	14	12	....	....	....	....
	Jokerit U18	Fin-U18	1	1	0	1	4	....	....	....	....	....	....				2	0	0	0	2	....	....	....	....
2001-02	Jokerit Helsinki	Finland	28	2	2	4	4	....	....	....	....	....	....				....	....	....	....	....	....	....	....	....
	Jokerit Helsinki Jr.	Finland-Jr.	23	11	19	30	36	....	....	....	....	....	....				6	6	2	8	20	....	....	....	....
	Kiekko-Vantaa	Finland-2	4	0	0	0	52	....	....	....	....	....	....				....	....	....	....	....	....	....	....	....
	Jokerit U18	Fin-U18	....	....	....	....	....	....	....	....	....	....	....				5	6	2	8	18	....	....	....	....
2002-03	Jokerit Helsinki	Finland	38	3	3	6	4	....	....	....	....	....	....				2	0	0	0	0	....	....	....	....
2003-04	Jokerit Helsinki	Finland	20	2	2	4	18	....	....	....	....	....	....				3	1	1	2	0	....	....	....	....
	NY Islanders	**NHL**	18	1	1	2	4	0	1	0	12	8.3	–4	2	50.0	8:55	....	....	....	....	....	....	....	....	....
	Bridgeport	AHL	....	....	....	....	....	....	....	....	....	....	....				7	2	3	5	10	....	....	....	....
2004-05	Bridgeport	AHL	61	15	14	29	69	....	....	....	....	....	....				....	....	....	....	....	....	....	....	....
	NHL Totals		18	1	1	2	4	0	1	0	12	8.3		2	50.0	8:55									

BERGERON, Marc-Andre — (BAIR-zhur-uhn, MAHRK-AWN-dray) — EDM.

Defense. Shoots left. 5'10", 197 lbs. Born, St-Louis-de-France, Que., October 13, 1980.

Season	Club	League	GP	G	A	Pts	PIM	PP	SH	GW	S	%	+/-	TF	F%	Min	GP	G	A	Pts	PIM	PP	SH	GW	Min
1996-97	Cap-d-Madeleine	QAAA	4	0	1	1	0	....	....	....	....	....	....				2	0	0	0	0	....	....	....	....
1997-98	Baie-Comeau	QMJHL	40	6	14	20	48	....	....	....	....	....	....				....	....	....	....	....	....	....	....	....
1998-99	Baie-Comeau	QMJHL	46	8	14	22	57	....	....	....	....	....	....				....	....	....	....	....	....	....	....	....
	Shawinigan	QMJHL	24	6	7	13	66	....	....	....	....	....	....				5	2	2	4	24	....	....	....	....
99-2000	Shawinigan	QMJHL	70	24	50	74	173	....	....	....	....	....	....				13	4	7	11	45	....	....	....	....
2000-01	Shawinigan	QMJHL	69	42	59	101	185	....	....	....	....	....	....				10	4	11	15	24	....	....	....	....
2001-02	Hamilton	AHL	50	2	13	15	61	....	....	....	....	....	....				9	1	4	5	8	....	....	....	....
2002-03	**Edmonton**	**NHL**	5	1	1	2	9	0	0	0	5	20.0	2	0	0.0	16:30	1	0	1	1	0	0	0	0	19:20
	Hamilton	AHL	66	8	31	39	73	....	....	....	....	....	....				20	0	7	7	25	....	....	....	....
2003-04	**Edmonton**	**NHL**	54	9	17	26	26	3	0	0	105	8.6	13	0	0.0	17:39	....	....	....	....	....	....	....	....	....
	Toronto	AHL	17	4	3	7	23	....	....	....	....	....	....				....	....	....	....	....	....	....	....	....
2004-05	Brynas IF Gavle	Sweden	10	3	2	5	72	....	....	....	....	....	....				....	....	....	....	....	....	....	....	....
	Brynas IF Gavle	Sweden-Q	9	1	2	3	8	....	....	....	....	....	....				....	....	....	....	....	....	....	....	....
	NHL Totals		59	10	18	28	35	3	0	0	110	9.1		0	0.0	17:33	1	0	1	1	0	0	0	0	19:20

QMJHL First All-Star Team (2001) • Canadian Major Junior First All-Star Team (2001) • Canadian Major Junior Defenseman of the Year (2001) • AHL Second All-Star Team (2003)
Signed as a free agent by **Edmonton**, July 20, 2001. Signed as a free agent by **Brynas** (Sweden), January 23, 2005.

BERGERON, Patrice — (BAIR-zhur-uhn, pa-TREEZ) — BOS.

Center. Shoots right. 6', 186 lbs. Born, Ancienne-Lorette, Que., July 24, 1985. Boston's 2nd choice, 45th overall, in 2003 Entry Draft.

Season	Club	League	GP	G	A	Pts	PIM	PP	SH	GW	S	%	+/-	TF	F%	Min	GP	G	A	Pts	PIM	PP	SH	GW	Min
2000-01	Ste-Foy	QAAA	5	1	2	3	0	....	....	....	....	....	....				....	....	....	....	....	....	....	....	....
2001-02	St-Francois	QAAA	38	25	37	62	18	....	....	....	....	....	....				8	6	4	10	10	....	....	....	....
	Acadie-Bathurst	QMJHL	4	0	1	1	0	....	....	....	....	....	....				....	....	....	....	....	....	....	....	....
2002-03	Acadie-Bathurst	QMJHL	70	23	50	73	62	....	....	....	....	....	....				11	6	9	15	6	....	....	....	....
2003-04	**Boston**	**NHL**	71	16	23	39	22	7	0	2	133	12.0	5	699	49.4	16:21	7	1	3	4	0	0	0	1	17:13
2004-05	Providence Bruins	AHL	68	21	40	61	59	....	....	....	....	....	....				16	5	7	12	4	....	....	....	....
	NHL Totals		71	16	23	39	22	7	0	2	133	12.0		699	49.4	16:21	7	1	3	4	0	0	0	1	17:13

BERGLUND, Christian — (BUHRG-luhnd, KRIH-stan) — FLA.

Left wing. Shoots left. 5'11", 190 lbs. Born, Orebro, Sweden, March 12, 1980. New Jersey's 3rd choice, 37th overall, in 1998 Entry Draft.

Season	Club	League	GP	G	A	Pts	PIM	PP	SH	GW	S	%	+/-	TF	F%	Min	GP	G	A	Pts	PIM	PP	SH	GW	Min
1994-95	Kariskoga IK	Sweden-4	20	14	13	27	....	....	....	....	....	....	....				....	....	....	....	....	....	....	....	....
1995-96	Kristinehamn SK	Sweden-3	23	8	8	16	12	....	....	....	....	....	....				....	....	....	....	....	....	....	....	....
1996-97	Farjestad Jr.	Swe-Jr.	21	2	3	5	24	....	....	....	....	....	....				....	....	....	....	....	....	....	....	....
1997-98	Farjestad Jr.	Swe-Jr.	29	23	19	42	88	....	....	....	....	....	....				2	0	0	0	0	....	....	....	....
	Farjestad	Sweden	1	0	0	0	0	....	....	....	....	....	....				....	....	....	....	....	....	....	....	....
1998-99	Farjestad Jr.	Swe-Jr.	5	3	4	7	22	....	....	....	....	....	....				....	....	....	....	....	....	....	....	....
	Farjestad	Sweden	37	2	4	6	37	....	....	....	....	....	....				4	1	0	1	4	....	....	....	....
99-2000	Farjestad Jr.	Swe-Jr.	5	3	5	8	8	....	....	....	....	....	....				....	....	....	....	....	....	....	....	....
	Bofors	Sweden-2	6	2	0	2	12	....	....	....	....	....	....				....	....	....	....	....	....	....	....	....
	Farjestad	Sweden	43	8	6	14	44	....	....	....	....	....	....				7	2	1	3	10	....	....	....	....
2000-01	Farjestad	Sweden	49	17	20	37	*142	....	....	....	....	....	....				16	7	7	14	22	....	....	....	....
2001-02	**New Jersey**	**NHL**	15	2	7	9	8	0	0	0	22	9.1	–3	2	50.0	12:26	3	0	0	0	2	0	0	0	11:31
	Albany River Rats	AHL	60	21	26	47	69	....	....	....	....	....	....				....	....	....	....	....	....	....	....	....
2002-03	**New Jersey**	**NHL**	38	4	5	9	20	0	0	0	50	8.0	3	11	9.1	10:11	....	....	....	....	....	....	....	....	....
	Albany River Rats	AHL	26	6	14	20	57	....	....	....	....	....	....				....	....	....	....	....	....	....	....	....
2003-04	**New Jersey**	**NHL**	23	2	3	5	4	0	0	0	33	6.1	–4	2	50.0	11:22	....	....	....	....	....	....	....	....	....
	Florida	**NHL**	10	3	1	4	10	0	0	0	17	17.6	–2	14	28.6	12:01	....	....	....	....	....	....	....	....	....
2004-05	Farjestad	Sweden	48	7	13	20	97	....	....	....	....	....	....				14	2	3	5	56	....	....	....	....
	NHL Totals		86	11	16	27	42	0	0	0	122	9.0		29	24.1	11:06	3	0	0	0	2	0	0	0	11:31

• Missed majority of 2003-04 season recovering from hip injury suffered in game vs. Philadelphia, December 12, 2003. Traded to **Florida** by **New Jersey** with Victor Uchevatov for Viktor Kozlov, March 1, 2004. Signed as a free agent by **Farjestad** (Sweden), September, 2004. Signed as a free agent by **Rapperswil** (Swiss), August 26, 2005.

BERRY, Rick

(BAIR-ree, RIHK)

Defense. Shoots left. 6'2", 210 lbs. Born, Birtle, Man., November 4, 1978. Colorado's 3rd choice, 55th overall, in 1997 Entry Draft.

Season	Club	League	GP	G	A	Pts	PIM	PP	SH	GW	S	%	+/-	TF	F%	Min	Playoffs GP	G	A	Pts	PIM	PP	SH	GW	Min
1994-95	Yellowhead	MMMHL	33	12	19	31	90																		
1995-96	Seattle	WHL	59	4	9	13	103										1	0	0	0	0				
1996-97	Seattle	WHL	72	12	21	33	125										15	3	7	10	23				
1997-98	Seattle	WHL	37	5	12	17	100																		
	Spokane Chiefs	WHL	22	4	9	13	31										17	1	4	5	26				
1998-99	Hershey Bears	AHL	62	2	6	8	153																		
99-2000	Hershey Bears	AHL	64	9	16	25	148										13	2	3	5	24				
2000-01	**Colorado**	**NHL**	**19**	**0**	**4**	**4**	**38**	**0**	**0**	**0**	**10**	**0.0**	**5**	**0**	**0.0**	**12:08**									
	Hershey Bears	AHL	48	6	17	23	87										12	2	2	4	18				
2001-02	**Colorado**	**NHL**	**57**	**0**	**0**	**0**	**60**	**0**	**0**	**0**	**29**	**0.0**	**1**	**0**	**0.0**	**9:29**									
	Pittsburgh	**NHL**	**13**	**0**	**2**	**2**	**21**	**0**	**0**	**0**	**20**	**0.0**	**–4**	**0**	**0.0**	**19:39**									
2002-03	**Washington**	**NHL**	**43**	**2**	**1**	**3**	**87**	**0**	**0**	**1**	**40**	**5.0**	**–3**	**0**	**0.0**	**12:58**									
2003-04	**Washington**	**NHL**	**65**	**0**	**6**	**6**	**108**	**0**	**0**	**0**	**43**	**0.0**	**–5**	**2**	**50.0**	**12:11**									
	Portland Pirates	AHL	10	2	1	3	12																		
2004-05	Utah Grizzlies	AHL	45	2	6	8	83																		
	NHL Totals		**197**	**2**	**13**	**15**	**314**	**0**	**0**	**1**	**142**	**1.4**		**2**	**50.0**	**12:04**									

Traded to **Pittsburgh** by **Colorado** with Ville Nieminen for Darius Kasparaitis, March 19, 2002. Claimed by **Washington** from **Pittsburgh** in Waiver Draft, October 4, 2002. Signed as a free agent by **Phoenix**, September 2, 2004.

BERTUZZI, Todd

(buhr-TOO-zee, TAWD) **VAN.**

Right wing. Shoots left. 6'3", 245 lbs. Born, Sudbury, Ont., February 2, 1975. NY Islanders' 1st choice, 23rd overall, in 1993 Entry Draft.

Season	Club	League	GP	G	A	Pts	PIM	PP	SH	GW	S	%	+/-	TF	F%	Min	Playoffs GP	G	A	Pts	PIM	PP	SH	GW	Min
1990-91	Sudbury Legion	NOHA	48	25	46	71	247																		
	Sudbury Cubs	NOJHA	3	3	2	5	10																		
1991-92	Guelph Storm	OHL	47	7	14	21	145																		
1992-93	Guelph Storm	OHL	59	27	32	59	164										5	2	2	4	6				
1993-94	Guelph Storm	OHL	61	28	54	82	165										9	2	6	8	30				
1994-95	Guelph Storm	OHL	62	54	65	119	58										14	*15	18	33	41				
1995-96	**NY Islanders**	**NHL**	**76**	**18**	**21**	**39**	**83**	**4**	**0**	**2**	**127**	**14.2**	**–14**												
1996-97	**NY Islanders**	**NHL**	**64**	**10**	**13**	**23**	**68**	**3**	**0**	**1**	**79**	**12.7**	**–3**												
	Utah Grizzlies	IHL	13	5	5	10	16																		
1997-98	**NY Islanders**	**NHL**	**52**	**7**	**11**	**18**	**58**	**1**	**0**	**1**	**63**	**11.1**	**–19**												
	Vancouver	**NHL**	**22**	**6**	**9**	**15**	**63**	**1**	**1**	**1**	**39**	**15.4**	**2**												
1998-99	**Vancouver**	**NHL**	**32**	**8**	**8**	**16**	**44**	**1**	**0**	**3**	**72**	**11.1**	**–6**	**191**	**43.5**	**18:28**									
99-2000	**Vancouver**	**NHL**	**80**	**25**	**25**	**50**	**126**	**4**	**0**	**2**	**173**	**14.5**	**–2**	**476**	**46.6**	**15:24**									
2000-01	**Vancouver**	**NHL**	**79**	**25**	**30**	**55**	**93**	**14**	**0**	**3**	**203**	**12.3**	**–18**	**84**	**45.2**	**17:13**	**4**	**2**	**2**	**4**	**8**	**0**	**0**	**0**	**19:01**
2001-02	**Vancouver**	**NHL**	**72**	**36**	**49**	**85**	**110**	**14**	**0**	**3**	**203**	**17.7**	**21**	**151**	**49.0**	**19:40**	**6**	**2**	**2**	**4**	**14**	**1**	**0**	**0**	**21:50**
2002-03	**Vancouver**	**NHL**	**82**	**46**	**51**	**97**	**144**	**25**	**0**	**7**	**243**	**18.9**	**2**	**208**	**47.1**	**20:34**	**14**	**2**	**4**	**6**	***60**	**0**	**0**	**0**	**21:05**
2003-04	**Vancouver**	**NHL**	**69**	**17**	**43**	**60**	**122**	**8**	**0**	**2**	**156**	**10.9**	**21**	**111**	**45.1**	**21:00**									
2004-05			DID NOT PLAY – SUSPENDED																						
	NHL Totals		**628**	**198**	**260**	**458**	**911**	**75**	**1**	**25**	**1358**	**14.6**		**1221**	**46.3**	**18:41**	**24**	**6**	**8**	**14**	**82**	**1**	**0**	**0**	**20:55**

OHL Second All-Star team (1995) • NHL First All-Star Team (2003)

Played in NHL All-Star Game (2003, 2004)

Traded to **Vancouver** by **NY Islanders** with Bryan McCabe and NY Islanders' 3rd round choice (Jarkko Ruutu) in 1998 Entry Draft for Trevor Linden, February 6, 1998. • Missed majority of 1998-99 season recovering from leg injury suffered in game vs. Washington, November 1, 1998. • Suspended indefinitely by NHL for deliberate injury to Steve Moore in game vs. Colorado, March 8, 2004. Reinstated by NHL on August 8, 2005.

BETTS, Blair

(BEHTS, BLAIR) **NYR**

Center. Shoots left. 6'1", 211 lbs. Born, Edmonton, Alta., February 16, 1980. Calgary's 2nd choice, 33rd overall, in 1998 Entry Draft.

Season	Club	League	GP	G	A	Pts	PIM	PP	SH	GW	S	%	+/-	TF	F%	Min	Playoffs GP	G	A	Pts	PIM	PP	SH	GW	Min
1995-96	Sherwood Park	AMHL	34	22	19	41	69																		
1996-97	Prince George	WHL	58	12	18	30	19										15	2	2	4	6				
1997-98	Prince George	WHL	71	35	41	76	38										11	4	6	10	8				
1998-99	Prince George	WHL	42	20	22	42	39										7	3	2	5	8				
99-2000	Prince George	WHL	44	24	35	59	38										13	11	11	22	6				
2000-01	Saint John Flames	AHL	75	13	15	28	28										19	2	3	5	4				
2001-02	**Calgary**	**NHL**	**6**	**1**	**0**	**1**	**2**	**0**	**0**	**1**	**4**	**25.0**	**–1**	**39**	**48.7**	**7:05**									
	Saint John Flames	AHL	67	20	29	49	10																		
2002-03	**Calgary**	**NHL**	**9**	**1**	**3**	**4**	**0**	**0**	**0**	**0**	**16**	**6.3**	**3**	**71**	**53.5**	**11:33**									
	Saint John Flames	AHL	19	6	7	13	6																		
2003-04	**Calgary**	**NHL**	**20**	**1**	**2**	**3**	**10**	**1**	**0**	**1**	**21**	**4.8**	**–1**	**248**	**54.0**	**12:46**									
2004-05	Hartford	AHL	16	5	4	9	4																		
	NHL Totals		**35**	**3**	**5**	**8**	**12**	**1**	**0**	**2**	**41**	**7.3**		**358**	**53.4**	**11:29**									

• Missed majority of 2002-03 season recovering from shoulder injury suffered in training camp, September 27, 2002. • Missed majority of 2003-04 season recovering from shoulder injury suffered in game vs. Chicago, November 22, 2003. • Missed majority of 2003-04 season revovering from shoulder injury suffered in game vs. Colorado, December 31, 2003. Traded to **NY Rangers** by **Calgary** with Jamie McLennan and Greg Moore for Chris Simon and NY Rangers' 7th round choice (Matt Schneider) in 2004 Entry Draft, March 6, 2004.

BEZINA, Goran

(BEH-zee-nuh, GOH-ran)

Defense. Shoots left. 6'2", 215 lbs. Born, Split, Yugoslavia, March 21, 1980. Phoenix's 8th choice, 234th overall, in 1999 Entry Draft.

Season	Club	League	GP	G	A	Pts	PIM	PP	SH	GW	S	%	+/-	TF	F%	Min	Playoffs GP	G	A	Pts	PIM	PP	SH	GW	Min
1998-99	Fribourg Jr.	Swiss-Jr.	22	11	6	17	64																		
	Fribourg	EuroHL	6	0	0	0	0																		
	Fribourg	Swiss	38	0	0	0	14										4	0	0	0	2				
99-2000	Fribourg Jr.	Swiss-Jr.	2	0	1	1	16										2	1	1	2	8				
	Fribourg	Swiss	44	3	6	9	10										4	0	0	0	6				
	EHC Visp	Swiss-2	2	0	0	0	2																		
2000-01	Fribourg	Swiss	44	10	10	20	44										5	1	1	2	12				
2001-02	Springfield	AHL	66	2	11	13	50																		
2002-03	Springfield	AHL	64	3	4	7	27										6	0	1	1	0				
2003-04	**Phoenix**	**NHL**	**3**	**0**	**0**	**0**	**2**	**0**	**0**	**0**	**0**	**0.0**	**–1**	**0**	**0.0**	**5:17**									
	Springfield	AHL	74	11	10	21	65																		
2004-05	Geneve	Swiss	34	7	12	19	51										4	0	0	0	8				
	NHL Totals		**3**	**0**	**0**	**0**	**2**	**0**	**0**	**0**	**0**	**0.0**		**0**	**0.0**	**5:17**									

Signed as a free agent by **Geneve** (Swiss), May 18, 2004.

BICEK, Jiri

(bee-SEHK, YEH-ree)

Right wing. Shoots left. 5'10", 190 lbs. Born, Kosice, Czech., December 3, 1978. New Jersey's 4th choice, 131st overall, in 1997 Entry Draft.

Season	Club	League	GP	G	A	Pts	PIM	PP	SH	GW	S	%	+/-	TF	F%	Min	Playoffs GP	G	A	Pts	PIM	PP	SH	GW	Min
1994-95	HC Kosice Jr.	Slovak-Jr.	42	38	36	74	18																		
1995-96	HC Kosice	Slovakia	30	10	15	25	16										9	2	4	6	0				
1996-97	HC Kosice	Slovakia	44	11	14	25	20										7	1	3	4					
1997-98	Albany River Rats	AHL	50	10	10	20	22										13	1	6	7	4				
1998-99	Albany River Rats	AHL	79	15	45	60	102										5	2	2	4	2				
99-2000	Albany River Rats	AHL	80	7	36	43	51										4	0	2	2	0				
2000-01	**New Jersey**	**NHL**	**5**	**1**	**0**	**1**	**4**	**0**	**0**	**0**	**10**	**10.0**	**0**	**0**	**0.0**	**13:04**									
	Albany River Rats	AHL	73	12	29	41	73																		
2001-02	**New Jersey**	**NHL**	**1**	**0**	**0**	**0**	**0**	**0**	**0**	**0**	**2**	**0.0**	**–1**	**0**	**0.0**	**13:10**									
	Albany River Rats	AHL	62	15	19	34	45																		
2002-03♦	**New Jersey**	**NHL**	**44**	**5**	**6**	**11**	**25**	**1**	**0**	**1**	**63**	**7.9**	**7**	**3**	**0.0**	**11:48**	**5**	**0**	**0**	**0**	**0**	**0**	**0**	**0**	**8:10**
	Albany River Rats	AHL	24	4	10	14	28																		
2003-04	**New Jersey**	**NHL**	**12**	**0**	**1**	**1**	**0**	**0**	**0**	**0**	**10**	**0.0**	**0**	**1**	**0.0**	**9:55**	**2**	**0**	**0**	**0**	**0**	**0**	**0**	**0**	**12:26**
	Albany River Rats	AHL	55	12	18	30	37																		
2004-05	HC Kosice	Slovakia	54	18	23	41	69										10	6	8	14	4				
	NHL Totals		**62**	**6**	**7**	**13**	**29**	**1**	**0**	**1**	**85**	**7.1**		**4**	**0.0**	**11:34**	**7**	**0**	**0**	**0**	**0**	**0**	**0**	**0**	**9:23**

Signed as a free agent by **Kosice** (Slovakia), September 17, 2004.

BIRON, Mathieu

(BEE-rawn, MA-tyew) **WSH.**

Defense. Shoots right. 6'6", 220 lbs. Born, Lac-St-Charles, Que., April 29, 1980. Los Angeles' 1st choice, 21st overall, in 1998 Entry Draft.

			Regular Season														Playoffs								
Season	Club	League	GP	G	A	Pts	PIM	PP	SH	GW	S	%	+/-	TF	F%	Min	GP	G	A	Pts	PIM	PP	SH	GW	Min
1996-97	Ste-Foy	QAAA	40	4	22	26	49	....	....	....	....	....	....	....	....	....	10	3	4	7	....	....	....	....	....
1997-98	Shawinigan	QMJHL	59	8	28	36	60	....	....	....	....	....	....	....	....	....	6	0	1	1	10	....	....	....	....
1998-99	Shawinigan	QMJHL	69	13	32	45	116	....	....	....	....	....	....	....	....	....	6	0	2	2	6	....	....	....	....
99-2000	**NY Islanders**	**NHL**	**60**	**4**	**4**	**8**	**38**	**2**	**0**	**2**	**70**	**5.7**	**–13**	**2**	**0.0**	**15:02**	....	....	....	....	....	....	....	....	....
2000-01	**NY Islanders**	**NHL**	**14**	**0**	**1**	**1**	**12**	**0**	**0**	**0**	**10**	**0.0**	**2**	**0**	**0.0**	**12:21**	....	....	....	....	....	....	....	....	....
	Lowell	AHL	22	1	3	4	17	....	....	....	....	....	....	....	....	....	....	....	....	....	....	....	....	....	....
	Springfield	AHL	34	0	6	6	18	....	....	....	....	....	....	....	....	....	....	....	....	....	....	....	....	....	....
2001-02	**Tampa Bay**	**NHL**	**36**	**0**	**0**	**0**	**12**	**0**	**0**	**0**	**35**	**0.0**	**–16**	**0**	**0.0**	**14:47**	....	....	....	....	....	....	....	....	....
	Springfield	AHL	35	4	9	13	16	....	....	....	....	....	....	....	....	....	....	....	....	....	....	....	....	....	....
2002-03	**Florida**	**NHL**	**34**	**1**	**8**	**9**	**14**	**0**	**1**	**0**	**52**	**1.9**	**–18**	**0**	**0.0**	**21:08**	....	....	....	....	....	....	....	....	....
	San Antonio	AHL	43	3	8	11	58	....	....	....	....	....	....	....	....	....	....	....	....	....	....	....	....	....	....
2003-04	**Florida**	**NHL**	**57**	**3**	**10**	**13**	**51**	**0**	**0**	**1**	**75**	**4.0**	**–13**	**0**	**0.0**	**18:13**	....	....	....	....	....	....	....	....	....
2004-05			DID NOT PLAY																						
	NHL Totals		**201**	**8**	**23**	**31**	**127**	**2**	**1**	**3**	**242**	**3.3**		**2**	**0.0**	**16:44**	....	....	....	....	....	....	....	....	....

Traded to **NY Islanders** by **Los Angeles** with Olli Jokinen, Josh Green and Los Angeles' 1st round choice (Taylor Pyatt) in 1999 Entry Draft for Ziggy Palffy, Brian Smolinski, Marcel Cousineau and New Jersey's 4th round choice (previously acquired, Los Angeles selected Daniel Johansson) in 1999 Entry Draft, June 20, 1999. Traded to **Tampa Bay** by **NY Islanders** with NY Islanders' 2nd round choice (later traded to Washington – later traded to Vancouver – Vancouver selected Denis Grot) in 2002 Entry Draft for Adrian Aucoin and Alexander Kharitonov, June 22, 2001. Claimed by **Columbus** from **Tampa Bay** in Waiver Draft, October 4, 2002. Traded to **Florida** by **Columbus** for Petr Tenkrat, October 4, 2002. Signed as a free agent by **Washington**, August 10, 2005.

BISHAI, Mike

(BIHSH-igh, MIGHK)

Center. Shoots left. 5'11", 185 lbs. Born, Edmonton, Alta., May 30, 1979.

			Regular Season														Playoffs								
Season	Club	League	GP	G	A	Pts	PIM	PP	SH	GW	S	%	+/-	TF	F%	Min	GP	G	A	Pts	PIM	PP	SH	GW	Min
1996-97	South Surrey	BCHL	38	6	13	19	10	....	....	....	....	....	....	....	....	....	....	....	....	....	....	....	....	....	....
1997-98	South Surrey	BCHL	47	48	52	100	36	....	....	....	....	....	....	....	....	....	....	....	....	....	....	....	....	....	....
1998-99	Western Mich.	CCHA	26	0	3	3	20	....	....	....	....	....	....	....	....	....	....	....	....	....	....	....	....	....	....
99-2000	Western Mich.	CCHA	35	18	19	37	52	....	....	....	....	....	....	....	....	....	....	....	....	....	....	....	....	....	....
2000-01	Western Mich.	CCHA	37	23	*45	*68	37	....	....	....	....	....	....	....	....	....	....	....	....	....	....	....	....	....	....
2001-02	Western Mich.	CCHA	34	10	27	37	28	....	....	....	....	....	....	....	....	....	....	....	....	....	....	....	....	....	....
	Hamilton	AHL	3	0	0	0	0	....	....	....	....	....	....	....	....	....	....	....	....	....	....	....	....	....	....
2002-03	Hamilton	AHL	27	7	5	12	11	....	....	....	....	....	....	....	....	....	6	2	1	3	2	....	....	....	....
	Columbus	ECHL	25	12	17	29	24	....	....	....	....	....	....	....	....	....	....	....	....	....	....	....	....	....	....
2003-04	**Edmonton**	**NHL**	**14**	**0**	**2**	**2**	**19**	**0**	**0**	**0**	**14**	**0.0**	**0**	**113**	**41.6**	**9:09**	....	....	....	....	....	....	....	....	....
	Toronto	AHL	48	11	22	33	18	....	....	....	....	....	....	....	....	....	3	0	0	0	4	....	....	....	....
2004-05	Edmonton	AHL	70	10	24	34	36	....	....	....	....	....	....	....	....	....	....	....	....	....	....	....	....	....	....
	NHL Totals		**14**	**0**	**2**	**2**	**19**	**0**	**0**	**0**	**14**	**0.0**		**113**	**41.6**	**9:09**	....	....	....	....	....	....	....	....	....

CCHA Second All-Star Team (2001) • NCAA West Second All-American Team (2001)

Signed as a free agent by **Edmonton**, May 28, 2002.

BLAKE, Jason

(BLAYK, JAY-suhn) **NYI**

Center. Shoots left. 5'10", 180 lbs. Born, Moorhead, MN, September 2, 1973.

			Regular Season														Playoffs								
Season	Club	League	GP	G	A	Pts	PIM	PP	SH	GW	S	%	+/-	TF	F%	Min	GP	G	A	Pts	PIM	PP	SH	GW	Min
1991-92	Moorhead Spuds	High-MN	25	30	30	60	....	....	....	....	....	....	....	....	....	....	....	....	....	....	....	....	....	....	....
1992-93	Waterloo	USHL	45	24	27	51	107	....	....	....	....	....	....	....	....	....	....	....	....	....	....	....	....	....	....
1993-94	Waterloo	USHL	47	50	50	100	76	....	....	....	....	....	....	....	....	....	....	....	....	....	....	....	....	....	....
1994-95	Ferris State	CCHA	36	16	16	32	46	....	....	....	....	....	....	....	....	....	....	....	....	....	....	....	....	....	....
1995-96	North Dakota	WCHA	DID NOT PLAY – TRANSFERRED COLLEGES																						
1996-97	North Dakota	WCHA	43	19	32	51	44	....	....	....	....	....	....	....	....	....	....	....	....	....	....	....	....	....	....
1997-98	North Dakota	WCHA	38	24	27	51	62	....	....	....	....	....	....	....	....	....	....	....	....	....	....	....	....	....	....
1998-99	North Dakota	WCHA	38	*28	*41	*69	49	....	....	....	....	....	....	....	....	....	....	....	....	....	....	....	....	....	....
	Los Angeles	**NHL**	**1**	**1**	**0**	**1**	**0**	**0**	**0**	**0**	**5**	**20.0**	**1**	**14**	**35.7**	**17:13**	....	....	....	....	....	....	....	....	....
	Orlando	IHL	5	3	5	8	6	....	....	....	....	....	....	....	....	....	13	3	4	7	20	....	....	....	....
99-2000	**Los Angeles**	**NHL**	**64**	**5**	**18**	**23**	**26**	**0**	**0**	**1**	**131**	**3.8**	**4**	**269**	**43.9**	**11:17**	**3**	**0**	**0**	**0**	**0**	**0**	**0**	**0**	**9:35**
	Long Beach	IHL	7	3	6	9	2	....	....	....	....	....	....	....	....	....	....	....	....	....	....	....	....	....	....
2000-01	**Los Angeles**	**NHL**	**17**	**1**	**3**	**4**	**10**	**0**	**0**	**0**	**27**	**3.7**	**–8**	**13**	**61.5**	**10:03**	....	....	....	....	....	....	....	....	....
	Lowell	AHL	2	0	1	1	2	....	....	....	....	....	....	....	....	....	....	....	....	....	....	....	....	....	....
	NY Islanders	**NHL**	**30**	**4**	**8**	**12**	**24**	**1**	**1**	**0**	**73**	**5.5**	**–12**	**118**	**44.1**	**15:43**	....	....	....	....	....	....	....	....	....
2001-02	**NY Islanders**	**NHL**	**82**	**8**	**10**	**18**	**36**	**0**	**0**	**1**	**136**	**5.9**	**–11**	**23**	**43.5**	**12:54**	**7**	**0**	**1**	**1**	**13**	**0**	**0**	**0**	**12:13**
2002-03	**NY Islanders**	**NHL**	**81**	**25**	**30**	**55**	**58**	**3**	**1**	**4**	**253**	**9.9**	**16**	**22**	**18.2**	**17:38**	**5**	**0**	**1**	**1**	**2**	**0**	**0**	**0**	**19:39**
2003-04	**NY Islanders**	**NHL**	**75**	**22**	**25**	**47**	**56**	**1**	**4**	**3**	**243**	**9.1**	**11**	**70**	**41.4**	**18:49**	**4**	**2**	**0**	**2**	**2**	**0**	**0**	**0**	**18:09**
2004-05	HC Lugano	Swiss	7	2	2	4	4	....	....	....	....	....	....	....	....	....	....	....	....	....	....	....	....	....	....
	NHL Totals		**350**	**66**	**94**	**160**	**210**	**5**	**6**	**9**	**868**	**7.6**		**529**	**42.7**	**15:05**	**19**	**2**	**2**	**4**	**17**	**0**	**0**	**0**	**15:00**

WCHA First All-Star Team (1997, 1998, 1999) • NCAA West Second All-American Team (1998) • WCHA Player of the Year (1999) • NCAA West First All-American Team (1999)

Signed as a free agent by **Los Angeles**, April 20, 1999. Traded to **NY Islanders** by **Los Angeles** for NY Islanders' 5th round choice (Joel Andresen) in 2002 Entry Draft, January 3, 2001. Signed as a free agent by **Lugano** (Swiss), December 1, 2004.

BLAKE, Rob

(BLAYK, RAWB) **COL.**

Defense. Shoots right. 6'4", 225 lbs. Born, Simcoe, Ont., December 10, 1969. Los Angeles' 4th choice, 70th overall, in 1988 Entry Draft.

			Regular Season														Playoffs								
Season	Club	League	GP	G	A	Pts	PIM	PP	SH	GW	S	%	+/-	TF	F%	Min	GP	G	A	Pts	PIM	PP	SH	GW	Min
1985-86	Brantford Classics	OHA-B	39	3	13	16	43	....	....	....	....	....	....	....	....	....	....	....	....	....	....	....	....	....	....
1986-87	Stratford Cullitons	OHA-B	31	11	20	31	115	....	....	....	....	....	....	....	....	....	....	....	....	....	....	....	....	....	....
1987-88	Bowling Green	CCHA	43	5	8	13	88	....	....	....	....	....	....	....	....	....	....	....	....	....	....	....	....	....	....
1988-89	Bowling Green	CCHA	46	11	21	32	140	....	....	....	....	....	....	....	....	....	....	....	....	....	....	....	....	....	....
1989-90	Bowling Green	CCHA	42	23	36	59	140	....	....	....	....	....	....	....	....	....	....	....	....	....	....	....	....	....	....
	Los Angeles	**NHL**	**4**	**0**	**0**	**0**	**4**	**0**	**0**	**0**	**3**	**0.0**	**0**	....	....	....	**8**	**1**	**3**	**4**	**4**	**1**	**0**	**0**	....
1990-91	**Los Angeles**	**NHL**	**75**	**12**	**34**	**46**	**125**	**9**	**0**	**2**	**150**	**8.0**	**3**	....	....	....	**12**	**1**	**4**	**5**	**26**	**1**	**0**	**0**	....
1991-92	**Los Angeles**	**NHL**	**57**	**7**	**13**	**20**	**102**	**5**	**0**	**0**	**131**	**5.3**	**–5**	....	....	....	**6**	**2**	**1**	**3**	**12**	**0**	**0**	**0**	....
1992-93	**Los Angeles**	**NHL**	**76**	**16**	**43**	**59**	**152**	**10**	**0**	**4**	**243**	**6.6**	**18**	....	....	....	**23**	**4**	**6**	**10**	**46**	**1**	**1**	**0**	....
1993-94	**Los Angeles**	**NHL**	**84**	**20**	**48**	**68**	**137**	**7**	**0**	**6**	**304**	**6.6**	**–7**	....	....	....	....	....	....	....	....	....	....	....	....
1994-95	**Los Angeles**	**NHL**	**24**	**4**	**7**	**11**	**38**	**4**	**0**	**1**	**76**	**5.3**	**–16**	....	....	....	....	....	....	....	....	....	....	....	....
1995-96	**Los Angeles**	**NHL**	**6**	**1**	**2**	**3**	**8**	**0**	**0**	**0**	**13**	**7.7**	**0**	....	....	....	....	....	....	....	....	....	....	....	....
1996-97	**Los Angeles**	**NHL**	**62**	**8**	**23**	**31**	**82**	**4**	**0**	**1**	**169**	**4.7**	**–28**	....	....	....	....	....	....	....	....	....	....	....	....
1997-98	**Los Angeles**	**NHL**	**81**	**23**	**27**	**50**	**94**	**11**	**0**	**4**	**261**	**8.8**	**–3**	....	....	....	**4**	**0**	**0**	**0**	**6**	**0**	**0**	**0**	....
	Canada	Olympics	6	1	1	2	2	....	....	....	....	....	....	....	....	....	....	....	....	....	....	....	....	....	....
1998-99	**Los Angeles**	**NHL**	**62**	**12**	**23**	**35**	**128**	**5**	**1**	**2**	**216**	**5.6**	**–7**	**0**	**0.0**	**24:52**	....	....	....	....	....	....	....	....	....
99-2000	**Los Angeles**	**NHL**	**77**	**18**	**39**	**57**	**112**	**12**	**0**	**5**	**327**	**5.5**	**10**	**0**	**0.0**	**28:30**	**4**	**0**	**2**	**2**	**4**	**0**	**0**	**0**	**30:10**
2000-01	**Los Angeles**	**NHL**	**54**	**17**	**32**	**49**	**69**	**9**	**0**	**1**	**223**	**7.6**	**–8**	**0**	**0.0**	**28:11**	....	....	....	....	....	....	....	....	....
	♦ Colorado	**NHL**	**13**	**2**	**8**	**10**	**8**	**1**	**0**	**1**	**44**	**4.5**	**11**	**0**	**0.0**	**26:03**	**23**	**6**	**13**	**19**	**16**	**3**	**0**	**0**	**29:26**
2001-02	**Colorado**	**NHL**	**75**	**16**	**40**	**56**	**58**	**10**	**0**	**2**	**229**	**7.0**	**16**	**0**	**0.0**	**27:35**	**20**	**6**	**6**	**12**	**16**	**1**	**0**	**0**	**26:38**
	Canada	Olympics	6	1	2	3	2	....	....	....	....	....	....	....	....	....	....	....	....	....	....	....	....	....	....
2002-03	**Colorado**	**NHL**	**79**	**17**	**28**	**45**	**57**	**8**	**2**	**3**	**269**	**6.3**	**20**	**0**	**0.0**	**26:21**	**7**	**1**	**2**	**3**	**8**	**0**	**0**	**0**	**27:28**
2003-04	**Colorado**	**NHL**	**74**	**13**	**33**	**46**	**61**	**8**	**0**	**3**	**242**	**5.4**	**6**	**1**	**0.0**	**24:23**	**9**	**0**	**5**	**5**	**6**	**0**	**0**	**0**	**20:17**
2004-05			DID NOT PLAY																						
	NHL Totals		**903**	**186**	**400**	**586**	**1235**	**103**	**3**	**35**	**2900**	**6.4**		**1**	**0.0**	**26:37**	**116**	**21**	**42**	**63**	**144**	**7**	**1**	**0**	**27:04**

CCHA Second All-Star Team (1989) • CCHA First All-Star Team (1990) • NCAA West First All-American Team (1990) • NHL All-Rookie Team (1991) • NHL First All-Star Team (1998) • James Norris Memorial Trophy (1998) • NHL Second All-Star Team (2000, 2001, 2002)

Played in NHL All-Star Game (1994, 1999, 2000, 2001, 2002, 2003, 2004)

• Missed majority of 1995-96 season recovering from knee injury suffered in game vs. Washington, October 20, 1995. Traded to **Colorado** by **Los Angeles** with Steve Reinprecht for Adam Deadmarsh, Aaron Miller, a player to be named later (Jared Aulin, March 22, 2001) and Colorado's 1st round choices in 2001 (Dave Steckel) and 2003 (Brian Boyle) Entry Drafts, February 21, 2001.

BLATNY, Zdenek

(BLAT-nee, z'DEHN-ehk)

Left wing. Shoots left. 6'1", 190 lbs. Born, Brno, Czech., January 14, 1981. Atlanta's 3rd choice, 68th overall, in 1999 Entry Draft.

			Regular Season														Playoffs								
Season	Club	League	GP	G	A	Pts	PIM	PP	SH	GW	S	%	+/-	TF	F%	Min	GP	G	A	Pts	PIM	PP	SH	GW	Min
1997-98	Brno Jr.	CzRep-Jr.	42	22	21	43	40	....	....	....	....	....	....	....	....	....	....	....	....	....	....	....	....	....	....
1998-99	Seattle	WHL	44	18	15	33	25	....	....	....	....	....	....	....	....	....	11	4	0	4	24	....	....	....	....
99-2000	Seattle	WHL	7	4	5	9	12	....	....	....	....	....	....	....	....	....	....	....	....	....	....	....	....	....	....
	Kootenay Ice	WHL	61	43	39	82	119	....	....	....	....	....	....	....	....	....	21	10	*17	27	46	....	....	....	....
2000-01	Kootenay Ice	WHL	58	37	48	85	120	....	....	....	....	....	....	....	....	....	11	8	10	18	24	....	....	....	....
2001-02	Chicago Wolves	AHL	41	4	3	7	30	....	....	....	....	....	....	....	....	....	3	2	0	2	0	....	....	....	....
	Greenville	ECHL	12	5	5	10	17	....	....	....	....	....	....	....	....	....	9	2	8	10	14	....	....	....	....
2002-03	**Atlanta**	**NHL**	**4**	**0**	**0**	**0**	**0**	**0**	**0**	**0**	**2**	**0.0**	**–1**	**0**	**0.0**	**10:31**	....	....	....	....	....	....	....	....	....
	Chicago Wolves	AHL	72	12	9	21	62	....	....	....	....	....	....	....	....	....	9	0	2	2	20	....	....	....	....
2003-04	**Atlanta**	**NHL**	**16**	**3**	**0**	**3**	**6**	**0**	**0**	**0**	**17**	**17.6**	**0**	**13**	**38.5**	**10:27**	....	....	....	....	....	....	....	....	....
	Chicago Wolves	AHL	61	11	23	34	115	....	....	....	....	....	....	....	....	....	10	0	4	4	24	....	....	....	....
2004-05	Pelicans Lahti	Finland	9	1	1	2	32	....	....	....	....	....	....	....	....	....	....	....	....	....	....	....	....	....	....
	Znojmo	CzRep	15	3	4	7	28	....	....	....	....	....	....	....	....	....	....	....	....	....	....	....	....	....	....
	NHL Totals		**20**	**3**	**0**	**3**	**6**	**0**	**0**	**0**	**19**	**15.8**		**13**	**38.5**	**10:28**	....	....	....	....	....	....	....	....	....

WHL East Second All-Star Team (2000)

Signed as a free agent by **Pelicans** (Finland), November 19, 2004. Signed as a free agent by **Znojmo** (CzRep), January 6, 2005.

BLOUIN, Sylvain

(bluh-WHEN, SIHL-veh)

Left wing. Shoots left. 6'2", 215 lbs. Born, Montreal, Que., May 21, 1974. NY Rangers' 5th choice, 104th overall, in 1994 Entry Draft.

Season	Club	League	GP	G	A	Pts	PIM	PP	SH	GW	S	%	+/-	TF	F%	Min	GP	G	A	Pts	PIM	PP	SH	GW	Min
1991-92	Laval Titan	QMJHL	28	0	0	0	23	....	....	....	....	....	....	....	....	....	9	0	0	0	35	....	....	....	....
1992-93	Laval Titan	QMJHL	68	0	10	10	373	....	....	....	....	....	....	....	....	....	13	1	0	1	*66	....	....	....	....
1993-94	Laval Titan	QMJHL	62	18	22	40	*492	....	....	....	....	....	....	....	....	....	21	4	13	17	*177	....	....	....	....
1994-95	Chicago Wolves	IHL	1	0	0	0	2	....	....	....	....	....	....	....	....	....	....	....	....	....	....	....	....	....	....
	Charlotte	ECHL	50	5	7	12	280	....	....	....	....	....	....	....	....	....	3	0	0	0	6	....	....	....	....
	Binghamton	AHL	10	1	0	1	46	....	....	....	....	....	....	....	....	....	2	0	0	0	24	....	....	....	....
1995-96	Binghamton	AHL	71	5	8	13	*352	....	....	....	....	....	....	....	....	....	4	0	3	3	4	....	....	....	....
1996-97	**NY Rangers**	**NHL**	**6**	**0**	**0**	**0**	**18**	**0**	**0**	**0**	**1**	**0.0**	**–1**	....	....	....	....	....	....	....	....	....	....	....	....
	Binghamton	AHL	62	13	17	30	301	....	....	....	....	....	....	....	....	....	4	2	1	3	16	....	....	....	....
1997-98	**NY Rangers**	**NHL**	**1**	**0**	**0**	**0**	**5**	**0**	**0**	**0**	**0**	**0.0**	**0**	....	....	....	....	....	....	....	....	....	....	....	....
	Hartford	AHL	53	8	9	17	286	....	....	....	....	....	....	....	....	....	9	0	1	1	63	....	....	....	....
1998-99	**Montreal**	**NHL**	**5**	**0**	**0**	**0**	**19**	**0**	**0**	**0**	**1**	**0.0**	**0**	**0**	**0.0**	**3:37**	....	....	....	....	....	....	....	....	....
	Fredericton	AHL	67	6	10	16	333	....	....	....	....	....	....	....	....	....	15	2	0	2	*87	....	....	....	....
99-2000	Worcester IceCats	AHL	70	16	18	34	337	....	....	....	....	....	....	....	....	....	8	3	5	8	30	....	....	....	....
2000-01	**Minnesota**	**NHL**	**41**	**3**	**2**	**5**	**117**	**0**	**0**	**0**	**37**	**8.1**	**–5**	**2**	**100.0**	**9:54**	....	....	....	....	....	....	....	....	....
2001-02	**Minnesota**	**NHL**	**43**	**0**	**2**	**2**	**130**	**0**	**0**	**0**	**28**	**0.0**	**–11**	**0**	**0.0**	**9:51**	....	....	....	....	....	....	....	....	....
2002-03	**Minnesota**	**NHL**	**2**	**0**	**0**	**0**	**4**	**0**	**0**	**0**	**1**	**0.0**	**0**	**1**	**0.0**	**7:38**	....	....	....	....	....	....	....	....	....
	Montreal	**NHL**	**17**	**0**	**0**	**0**	**43**	**0**	**0**	**0**	**3**	**0.0**	**–3**	**0**	**0.0**	**3:36**	....	....	....	....	....	....	....	....	....
	Hamilton	AHL	19	2	4	6	39	....	....	....	....	....	....	....	....	....	11	1	1	2	28	....	....	....	....
2003-04	Hamilton	AHL	29	2	1	3	75	....	....	....	....	....	....	....	....	....	....	....	....	....	....	....	....	....	....
	Manitoba Moose	AHL	11	1	0	1	22	....	....	....	....	....	....	....	....	....	....	....	....	....	....	....	....	....	....
2004-05	Quebec RadioX	QNAHL	35	14	18	32	256	....	....	....	....	....	....	....	....	....	6	2	0	2	34	....	....	....	....
	NHL Totals		**115**	**3**	**4**	**7**	**336**	**0**	**0**	**0**	**71**	**4.2**		**3**	**66.7**	**8:34**	....	....	....	....	....	....	....	....	....

Traded to **Montreal** by **NY Rangers** with NY Rangers' 6th round choice (later traded to Phoenix – Phoenix selected Erik Lewerstrom) in 1999 Entry Draft for Peter Popovic, June 30, 1998. Signed as a free agent by **St. Louis**, August 25, 1999. Signed as a free agent by **Montreal**, July 7, 2000. Claimed by **Minnesota** from **Montreal** in Waiver Draft, September 29, 2000. • Missed majority of 2000-01 season recovering from shoulder injury suffered in game vs. Chicago, December 7, 2000. Traded to **Montreal** by **Minnesota** for Montreal's 7th round choice (Grigory Misharin) in 2003 Entry Draft, October 31, 2002. • Missed majority of 2003-04 season recovering from shoulder injury suffered in pre-season game vs. Toronto, September 23, 2003. Traded to **Vancouver** by **Montreal** for Rene Vydareny, March 9, 2004. Signed as a free agent by **Quebec** (QNAHL), September 21, 2004.

BOGUNIECKI, Eric

(BOH-guhn-ih-kee, AIR-ihk) **ST.L.**

Center. Shoots right. 5'8", 192 lbs. Born, New Haven, CT, May 6, 1975. St. Louis' 6th choice, 193rd overall, in 1993 Entry Draft.

Season	Club	League	GP	G	A	Pts	PIM	PP	SH	GW	S	%	+/-	TF	F%	Min	GP	G	A	Pts	PIM	PP	SH	GW	Min
1992-93	Westminster	High-CT	24	30	24	54	55	....	....	....	....	....	....	....	....	....	....	....	....	....	....	....	....	....	....
1993-94	New Hampshire	H-East	40	17	16	33	66	....	....	....	....	....	....	....	....	....	....	....	....	....	....	....	....	....	....
1994-95	New Hampshire	H-East	34	12	16	28	62	....	....	....	....	....	....	....	....	....	....	....	....	....	....	....	....	....	....
1995-96	New Hampshire	H-East	32	23	28	51	46	....	....	....	....	....	....	....	....	....	....	....	....	....	....	....	....	....	....
1996-97	New Hampshire	H-East	36	26	31	57	58	....	....	....	....	....	....	....	....	....	....	....	....	....	....	....	....	....	....
1997-98	Dayton Bombers	ECHL	26	19	18	37	36	....	....	....	....	....	....	....	....	....	....	....	....	....	....	....	....	....	....
	Fort Wayne	IHL	35	4	8	12	29	....	....	....	....	....	....	....	....	....	4	1	2	3	10	....	....	....	....
1998-99	Fort Wayne	IHL	72	32	34	66	100	....	....	....	....	....	....	....	....	....	2	0	1	1	2	....	....	....	....
99-2000	**Florida**	**NHL**	**4**	**0**	**0**	**0**	**2**	**0**	**0**	**0**	**5**	**0.0**	**–1**	**25**	**36.0**	**8:35**	....	....	....	....	....	....	....	....	....
	Louisville Panthers	AHL	57	33	42	75	148	....	....	....	....	....	....	....	....	....	4	3	2	5	20	....	....	....	....
2000-01	Louisville Panthers	AHL	28	13	12	25	56	....	....	....	....	....	....	....	....	....	....	....	....	....	....	....	....	....	....
	St. Louis	**NHL**	**1**	**0**	**0**	**0**	**0**	**0**	**0**	**0**	**1**	**0.0**	**–1**	**0**	**0.0**	**13:44**	....	....	....	....	....	....	....	....	....
	Worcester IceCats	AHL	45	17	28	45	100	....	....	....	....	....	....	....	....	....	9	3	2	5	10	....	....	....	....
2001-02	**St. Louis**	**NHL**	**8**	**0**	**1**	**1**	**4**	**0**	**0**	**0**	**10**	**0.0**	**–2**	**21**	**38.1**	**11:42**	**1**	**0**	**1**	**1**	**0**	**0**	**0**	**0**	**8:01**
	Worcester IceCats	AHL	63	*38	46	84	181	....	....	....	....	....	....	....	....	....	3	2	0	2	4	....	....	....	....
2002-03	**St. Louis**	**NHL**	**80**	**22**	**27**	**49**	**38**	**3**	**1**	**5**	**117**	**18.8**	**22**	**5**	**40.0**	**14:00**	**7**	**1**	**2**	**3**	**2**	**1**	**0**	**0**	**13:09**
2003-04	**St. Louis**	**NHL**	**27**	**6**	**4**	**10**	**20**	**2**	**0**	**2**	**40**	**15.0**	**–1**	**1**	**0.0**	**14:42**	**1**	**0**	**0**	**0**	**0**	**0**	**0**	**0**	**12:52**
	Worcester IceCats	AHL	3	0	1	1	0	....	....	....	....	....	....	....	....	....	....	....	....	....	....	....	....	....	....
2004-05	SC Langenthal	Swiss-2	10	5	3	8	47	....	....	....	....	....	....	....	....	....	....	....	....	....	....	....	....	....	....
	Worcester IceCats	AHL	30	14	11	25	46	....	....	....	....	....	....	....	....	....	....	....	....	....	....	....	....	....	....
	NHL Totals		**120**	**28**	**32**	**60**	**64**	**5**	**1**	**7**	**173**	**16.2**		**52**	**36.5**	**13:50**	**9**	**1**	**3**	**4**	**2**	**1**	**0**	**0**	**12:33**

Hockey East Second All-Star Team (1997) • AHL First All-Star Team (2002) • Les Cunningham Award (MVP – AHL) (2002)

Signed as a free agent by **Florida**, July 7, 1999. Traded to **St. Louis** by **Florida** for Andrei Podkonicky, December 17, 2000. • Missed majority of 2003-04 season recovering from shoulder (September 23, 2003 in training camp) and head (February 28, 2004 vs. Vancouver) injuries. Signed as a free agent by **Langenthal** (Swiss-2), October 4, 2004.

BOILEAU, Patrick

(BWOI-loh, PAT-rihk)

Defense. Shoots right. 6', 202 lbs. Born, Montreal, Que., February 22, 1975. Washington's 3rd choice, 69th overall, in 1993 Entry Draft.

Season	Club	League	GP	G	A	Pts	PIM	PP	SH	GW	S	%	+/-	TF	F%	Min	GP	G	A	Pts	PIM	PP	SH	GW	Min
1990-91	Laval-Laurentides	QAAA	3	0	1	1	0	....	....	....	....	....	....	....	....	....	....	....	....	....	....	....	....	....	....
1991-92	Laval-Laurentides	QAAA	42	9	36	45	94	....	....	....	....	....	....	....	....	....	12	3	5	8	10	....	....	....	....
1992-93	Laval Titan	QMJHL	69	4	19	23	73	....	....	....	....	....	....	....	....	....	13	1	2	3	10	....	....	....	....
1993-94	Laval Titan	QMJHL	64	13	57	70	56	....	....	....	....	....	....	....	....	....	21	1	7	8	24	....	....	....	....
1994-95	Laval Titan	QMJHL	38	8	25	33	46	....	....	....	....	....	....	....	....	....	20	4	16	20	24	....	....	....	....
1995-96	Portland Pirates	AHL	78	10	28	38	41	....	....	....	....	....	....	....	....	....	19	1	3	4	12	....	....	....	....
1996-97	**Washington**	**NHL**	**1**	**0**	**0**	**0**	**0**	**0**	**0**	**0**	**0**	**0.0**	**0**	....	....	....	....	....	....	....	....	....	....	....	....
	Portland Pirates	AHL	67	16	28	44	63	....	....	....	....	....	....	....	....	....	5	1	1	2	4	....	....	....	....
1997-98	Portland Pirates	AHL	47	6	21	27	53	....	....	....	....	....	....	....	....	....	10	0	1	1	8	....	....	....	....
1998-99	**Washington**	**NHL**	**4**	**0**	**1**	**1**	**2**	**0**	**0**	**0**	**7**	**0.0**	**–4**	**0**	**0.0**	**15:56**	....	....	....	....	....	....	....	....	....
	Portland Pirates	AHL	52	6	18	24	52	....	....	....	....	....	....	....	....	....	....	....	....	....	....	....	....	....	....
	Indianapolis Ice	IHL	29	8	13	21	27	....	....	....	....	....	....	....	....	....	4	0	1	1	2	....	....	....	....
99-2000	Portland Pirates	AHL	63	2	15	17	61	....	....	....	....	....	....	....	....	....	4	0	0	0	4	....	....	....	....
2000-01	Portland Pirates	AHL	77	6	14	20	50	....	....	....	....	....	....	....	....	....	3	0	0	0	8	....	....	....	....
2001-02	**Washington**	**NHL**	**2**	**0**	**0**	**0**	**2**	**0**	**0**	**0**	**0**	**0.0**	**–1**	**0**	**0.0**	**11:52**	....	....	....	....	....	....	....	....	....
	Portland Pirates	AHL	75	17	19	36	43	....	....	....	....	....	....	....	....	....	....	....	....	....	....	....	....	....	....
2002-03	**Detroit**	**NHL**	**25**	**2**	**6**	**8**	**14**	**0**	**0**	**1**	**18**	**11.1**	**8**	**0**	**0.0**	**13:58**	....	....	....	....	....	....	....	....	....
	Grand Rapids	AHL	23	2	11	13	39	....	....	....	....	....	....	....	....	....	....	....	....	....	....	....	....	....	....
2003-04	**Pittsburgh**	**NHL**	**16**	**3**	**4**	**7**	**8**	**3**	**0**	**0**	**41**	**7.3**	**–16**	**0**	**0.0**	**19:52**	....	....	....	....	....	....	....	....	....
	Wilkes-Barre	AHL	51	6	29	35	43	....	....	....	....	....	....	....	....	....	24	3	9	12	24	....	....	....	....
2004-05	Lausanne HC	Swiss	29	7	12	19	34	....	....	....	....	....	....	....	....	....	8	4	4	8	20	....	....	....	....
	Lausanne HC	Swiss-Q	....	....	....	....	....	....	....	....	....	....	....	....	....	....	7	0	1	1	4	....	....	....	....
	NHL Totals		**48**	**5**	**11**	**16**	**26**	**3**	**0**	**1**	**66**	**7.6**		**0**	**0.0**	**16:03**	....	....	....	....	....	....	....	....	....

Canadian Major Junior Scholastic Player of the Year (1994)

Loaned to **Indianapolis** (IHL) by **Washington** (Portland-AHL), February 4, 1999. Signed as a free agent by **Detroit**, August 5, 2002. Signed as a free agent by **Pittsburgh**, August 28, 2003. Signed as a free agent by **Lausanne** (Swiss), May 13, 2004.

BOMBARDIR, Brad

(bawm-bahr-DEER, BRAD)

Defense. Shoots left. 6'1", 205 lbs. Born, Powell River, B.C., May 5, 1972. New Jersey's 5th choice, 56th overall, in 1990 Entry Draft.

			Regular Season														Playoffs								
Season	Club	League	GP	G	A	Pts	PIM	PP	SH	GW	S	%	+/-	TF	F%	Min	GP	G	A	Pts	PIM	PP	SH	GW	Min
1988-89	Powell River	BCJHL	30	6	5	11	24	....	....	....	....	....	....	....	....	....	6	0	0	0	0	....	....	....	....
1989-90	Powell River	BCJHL	60	10	35	45	93	....	....	....	....	....	....	....	....	....	8	2	3	5	4	....	....	....	....
1990-91	North Dakota	WCHA	33	3	6	9	18	....	....	....	....	....	....	....	....	....	....	....	....	....	....	....	....	....	....
1991-92	North Dakota	WCHA	35	3	14	17	54	....	....	....	....	....	....	....	....	....	....	....	....	....	....	....	....	....	....
1992-93	North Dakota	WCHA	38	8	15	23	34	....	....	....	....	....	....	....	....	....	....	....	....	....	....	....	....	....	....
1993-94	North Dakota	WCHA	38	5	17	22	38	....	....	....	....	....	....	....	....	....	....	....	....	....	....	....	....	....	....
1994-95	Albany River Rats	AHL	77	5	22	27	22	....	....	....	....	....	....	....	....	....	14	0	3	3	6	....	....	....	....
1995-96	Albany River Rats	AHL	80	6	25	31	63	....	....	....	....	....	....	....	....	....	3	0	1	1	4	....	....	....	....
1996-97	Albany River Rats	AHL	32	0	8	8	6	....	....	....	....	....	....	....	....	....	16	1	3	4	8	....	....	....	....
1997-98	**New Jersey**	**NHL**	**43**	**1**	**5**	**6**	**8**	**0**	**0**	**0**	**16**	**6.3**	**11**	....	....	....	....	....	....	....	....	....	....	....	....
	Albany River Rats	AHL	5	0	0	0	0	....	....	....	....	....	....	....	....	....	....	....	....	....	....	....	....	....	....
1998-99	**New Jersey**	**NHL**	**56**	**1**	**7**	**8**	**16**	**0**	**0**	**0**	**47**	**2.1**	**–4**	**1**	**0.0**	**15:03**	**5**	**0**	**0**	**0**	**0**	**0**	**0**	**0**	**16:03**
99-2000♦	**New Jersey**	**NHL**	**32**	**3**	**1**	**4**	**6**	**0**	**0**	**0**	**24**	**12.5**	**–6**	**0**	**0.0**	**15:54**	**1**	**0**	**0**	**0**	**0**	**0**	**0**	**0**	**18:55**
2000-01	**Minnesota**	**NHL**	**70**	**0**	**15**	**15**	**42**	**0**	**0**	**0**	**81**	**0.0**	**–6**	**1**	**0.0**	**20:50**	....	....	....	....	....	....	....	....	....
2001-02	**Minnesota**	**NHL**	**28**	**1**	**2**	**3**	**14**	**1**	**0**	**0**	**24**	**4.2**	**–6**	**0**	**0.0**	**20:33**	....	....	....	....	....	....	....	....	....
2002-03	**Minnesota**	**NHL**	**58**	**1**	**14**	**15**	**16**	**1**	**0**	**0**	**55**	**1.8**	**15**	**0**	**0.0**	**22:01**	**4**	**0**	**0**	**0**	**0**	**0**	**0**	**0**	**14:52**
2003-04	**Minnesota**	**NHL**	**56**	**1**	**2**	**3**	**21**	**0**	**0**	**1**	**38**	**2.6**	**–10**	**0**	**0.0**	**20:14**	....	....	....	....	....	....	....	....	....
	Nashville	**NHL**	**13**	**0**	**0**	**0**	**4**	**0**	**0**	**0**	**9**	**0.0**	**1**	**0**	**0.0**	**19:03**	**6**	**0**	**1**	**1**	**2**	**0**	**0**	**0**	**19:38**
2004-05			DID NOT PLAY																						
	NHL Totals		**356**	**8**	**46**	**54**	**127**	**2**	**0**	**1**	**294**	**2.7**		**2**	**0.0**	**19:18**	**16**	**0**	**1**	**1**	**2**	**0**	**0**	**0**	**17:17**

AHL Second All-Star Team (1996)

• Missed majority of 1999-2000 season recovering from esophagus injury suffered in game vs. Philadelphia, October 30, 1999. Traded to **Minnesota** by **New Jersey** for Chris Terreri and Minnesota's 9th round choice (later traded to Tampa Bay – Tampa Bay selected Thomas Ziegler) in 2000 Entry Draft, June 23, 2000. • Missed majority of 2001-02 season recovering from ankle injury suffered in game vs. San Jose, October 16, 2001. Traded to **Nashville** by **Minnesota** with Sergei Zholtok for Buffalo's 3rd round choice (previously acquired, Minnesota selected Clayton Stoner) in 2004 Entry Draft and Nashville's 4th round choice (Patrick Bordeleau) in 2004 Entry Draft, March 5, 2004.

BONDRA, Peter

(BAWN-druh, PEE-tuhr)

Right wing. Shoots left. 6', 200 lbs. Born, Luck, USSR, February 7, 1968. Washington's 9th choice, 156th overall, in 1990 Entry Draft.

Season	Club	League	GP	G	A	Pts	PIM	PP	SH	GW	S	%	+/-	TF	F%	Min	GP	G	A	Pts	PIM	PP	SH	GW	Min
1986-87	VSZ Kosice	Czech	32	4	5	9	24	....	....	....	....	....	....	....	....	....	....	....	....	....	....	....	....	....	....
1987-88	VSZ Kosice	Czech	45	27	11	38	20	....	....	....	....	....	....	....	....	....	....	....	....	....	....	....	....	....	....
1988-89	VSZ Kosice	Czech	40	30	10	40	20	....	....	....	....	....	....	....	....	....	....	....	....	....	....	....	....	....	....
1989-90	VSZ Kosice	Czech	44	29	17	46	....	....	....	....	....	....	....	....	....	....	5	7	2	9	....	....	....	....	....
1990-91	**Washington**	**NHL**	**54**	**12**	**16**	**28**	**47**	**4**	**0**	**1**	**95**	**12.6**	**–10**	....	....	....	**4**	**0**	**1**	**1**	**2**	**0**	**0**	**0**	....
1991-92	**Washington**	**NHL**	**71**	**28**	**28**	**56**	**42**	**4**	**0**	**3**	**158**	**17.7**	**16**	....	....	....	**7**	**6**	**2**	**8**	**4**	**1**	**0**	**0**	....
1992-93	**Washington**	**NHL**	**83**	**37**	**48**	**85**	**70**	**10**	**0**	**7**	**239**	**15.5**	**8**	....	....	....	**6**	**0**	**6**	**6**	**0**	**0**	**0**	**0**	....
1993-94	**Washington**	**NHL**	**69**	**24**	**19**	**43**	**40**	**4**	**0**	**2**	**200**	**12.0**	**22**	....	....	....	**9**	**2**	**4**	**6**	**4**	**0**	**0**	**1**	....
1994-95	HC Kosice	Slovakia	2	1	0	1	0	....	....	....	....	....	....	....	....	....	....	....	....	....	....	....	....	....	....
	Washington	**NHL**	**47**	***34**	**9**	**43**	**24**	**12**	**6**	**3**	**177**	**19.2**	**9**	....	....	....	**7**	**5**	**3**	**8**	**10**	**2**	**0**	**1**	....
1995-96	Detroit Vipers	IHL	7	8	1	9	0	....	....	....	....	....	....	....	....	....	....	....	....	....	....	....	....	....	....
	Washington	**NHL**	**67**	**52**	**28**	**80**	**40**	**11**	**4**	**7**	**322**	**16.1**	**18**	....	....	....	**6**	**3**	**2**	**5**	**8**	**2**	**0**	**1**	....
1996-97	**Washington**	**NHL**	**77**	**46**	**31**	**77**	**72**	**10**	**4**	**3**	**314**	**14.6**	**7**	....	....	....	....	....	....	....	....	....	....	....	....
1997-98	**Washington**	**NHL**	**76**	***52**	**26**	**78**	**44**	**11**	**5**	**13**	**284**	**18.3**	**14**	....	....	....	**17**	**7**	**5**	**12**	**12**	**3**	**0**	**2**	....
	Slovakia	Olympics	2	1	0	1	25	....	....	....	....	....	....	....	....	....	....	....	....	....	....	....	....	....	....
1998-99	**Washington**	**NHL**	**66**	**31**	**24**	**55**	**56**	**6**	**3**	**5**	**284**	**10.9**	**–1**	**1**	**0.0**	**20:35**	....	....	....	....	....	....	....	....	....
99-2000	**Washington**	**NHL**	**62**	**21**	**17**	**38**	**30**	**5**	**3**	**5**	**187**	**11.2**	**5**	**2**	**50.0**	**18:48**	**5**	**1**	**1**	**2**	**4**	**1**	**0**	**0**	**17:30**
2000-01	**Washington**	**NHL**	**82**	**45**	**36**	**81**	**60**	**22**	**4**	**8**	**305**	**14.8**	**8**	**2**	**50.0**	**20:48**	**6**	**2**	**0**	**2**	**2**	**2**	**0**	**1**	**24:55**
2001-02	**Washington**	**NHL**	**77**	**39**	**31**	**70**	**80**	**17**	**1**	**8**	**333**	**11.7**	**–2**	**2**	**50.0**	**21:43**	....	....	....	....	....	....	....	....	....
2002-03	**Washington**	**NHL**	**76**	**30**	**26**	**56**	**52**	**9**	**2**	**4**	**256**	**11.7**	**–3**	**13**	**30.8**	**18:53**	**6**	**4**	**2**	**6**	**8**	**2**	**0**	**0**	**22:39**
2003-04	**Washington**	**NHL**	**54**	**21**	**14**	**35**	**22**	**12**	**0**	**4**	**136**	**15.4**	**–17**	**2**	**50.0**	**18:43**	....	....	....	....	....	....	....	....	....
	Ottawa	**NHL**	**23**	**5**	**9**	**14**	**16**	**2**	**0**	**1**	**52**	**9.6**	**1**	**4**	**0.0**	**18:21**	**7**	**0**	**0**	**0**	**6**	**0**	**0**	**0**	**16:36**
2004-05	HK SKP Poprad	Slovakia	6	4	2	6	4	....	....	....	....	....	....	....	....	....	....	....	....	....	....	....	....	....	....
	NHL Totals		**984**	**477**	**362**	**839**	**695**	**139**	**32**	**74**	**3342**	**14.3**		**26**	**30.8**	**19:56**	**80**	**30**	**26**	**56**	**60**	**13**	**0**	**6**	**20:23**

Played in NHL All-Star Game (1993, 1996, 1997, 1998, 1999)

Traded to **Ottawa** by **Washington** for Brooks Laich and Ottawa's 2nd round choice (later traded to Colorado - Colorado selected Chris Durand) in 2005 Entry Draft, February 18, 2004. Signed as a free agent by **Poprad** (Slovakia), January 17, 2005.

BONK, Radek

(BOHNK, RA-dehk) **MTL.**

Center. Shoots left. 6'3", 220 lbs. Born, Krnov, Czech., January 9, 1976. Ottawa's 1st choice, 3rd overall, in 1994 Entry Draft.

Season	Club	League	GP	G	A	Pts	PIM	PP	SH	GW	S	%	+/-	TF	F%	Min	GP	G	A	Pts	PIM	PP	SH	GW	Min
1990-91	Opava Jr.	Czech-Jr.	35	47	42	89	25	....	....	....	....	....	....	....	....	....	....	....	....	....	....	....	....	....	....
1991-92	AC ZPS Zlin Jr.	Czech-Jr.	45	47	36	83	30	....	....	....	....	....	....	....	....	....	....	....	....	....	....	....	....	....	....
1992-93	AC ZPS Zlin	Czech	30	5	5	10	10	....	....	....	....	....	....	....	....	....	....	....	....	....	....	....	....	....	....
1993-94	Las Vegas	IHL	76	42	45	87	208	....	....	....	....	....	....	....	....	....	5	1	2	3	10	....	....	....	....
1994-95	Las Vegas	IHL	33	7	13	20	62	....	....	....	....	....	....	....	....	....	....	....	....	....	....	....	....	....	....
	Ottawa	**NHL**	**42**	**3**	**8**	**11**	**28**	**1**	**0**	**0**	**40**	**7.5**	**–5**	....	....	....	....	....	....	....	....	....	....	....	....
	P.E.I. Senators	AHL	....	....	....	....	....	....	....	....	....	....	....	....	....	....	1	0	0	0	0	....	....	....	....
1995-96	**Ottawa**	**NHL**	**76**	**16**	**19**	**35**	**36**	**5**	**0**	**1**	**161**	**9.9**	**–5**	....	....	....	....	....	....	....	....	....	....	....	....
1996-97	**Ottawa**	**NHL**	**53**	**5**	**13**	**18**	**14**	**0**	**1**	**0**	**82**	**6.1**	**–4**	....	....	....	**7**	**0**	**1**	**1**	**4**	**0**	**0**	**0**	....
1997-98	**Ottawa**	**NHL**	**65**	**7**	**9**	**16**	**16**	**1**	**0**	**0**	**93**	**7.5**	**–13**	....	....	....	**5**	**0**	**0**	**0**	**2**	**0**	**0**	**0**	....
1998-99	**Ottawa**	**NHL**	**81**	**16**	**16**	**32**	**48**	**0**	**1**	**6**	**110**	**14.5**	**15**	**1184**	**50.1**	**13:44**	**4**	**0**	**0**	**0**	**6**	**0**	**0**	**0**	**16:16**
99-2000	Pardubice	CzRep	3	1	0	1	4	....	....	....	....	....	....	....	....	....	....	....	....	....	....	....	....	....	....
	Ottawa	**NHL**	**80**	**23**	**37**	**60**	**53**	**10**	**0**	**5**	**167**	**13.8**	**–2**	**1654**	**52.0**	**18:14**	**6**	**0**	**0**	**0**	**8**	**0**	**0**	**0**	**15:37**
2000-01	**Ottawa**	**NHL**	**74**	**23**	**36**	**59**	**52**	**5**	**2**	**3**	**139**	**16.5**	**27**	**1506**	**51.2**	**18:16**	**2**	**0**	**0**	**0**	**2**	**0**	**0**	**0**	**14:32**
2001-02	**Ottawa**	**NHL**	**82**	**25**	**45**	**70**	**52**	**6**	**2**	**5**	**170**	**14.7**	**3**	**1530**	**51.0**	**17:57**	**12**	**3**	**7**	**10**	**6**	**2**	**0**	**1**	**18:53**
2002-03	**Ottawa**	**NHL**	**70**	**22**	**32**	**54**	**36**	**11**	**0**	**4**	**146**	**15.1**	**6**	**1218**	**46.2**	**17:32**	**18**	**6**	**5**	**11**	**10**	**2**	**0**	**0**	**17:43**
2003-04	**Ottawa**	**NHL**	**66**	**12**	**32**	**44**	**66**	**6**	**0**	**1**	**98**	**12.2**	**2**	**1184**	**44.9**	**17:38**	**7**	**0**	**2**	**2**	**0**	**0**	**0**	**0**	**18:29**
2004-05	HC Ocelari Trinec	CzRep	27	6	10	16	44	....	....	....	....	....	....	....	....	....	....	....	....	....	....	....	....	....	....
	HC Hame Zlin	CzRep	6	3	2	5	4	....	....	....	....	....	....	....	....	....	6	0	2	2	8	....	....	....	....
	NHL Totals		**689**	**152**	**247**	**399**	**401**	**45**	**6**	**25**	**1206**	**12.6**		**8276**	**49.5**	**17:11**	**61**	**9**	**15**	**24**	**38**	**4**	**0**	**1**	**17:36**

Garry F. Longman Memorial Trophy (Rookie of the Year – IHL) (1994)

Played in NHL All-Star Game (2000, 2001)

Traded to **Los Angeles** by **Ottawa** for Los Angeles' 3rd round choice (Shawn Weller) in 2004 Entry Draft, June 26, 2004. Traded to **Montreal** by **Los Angeles** with Cristobal Huet for Mathieu Garon and San Jose's 3rd round choice (previously acquired, Los Angeles selected Paul Baier) in 2004 Entry Draft, June 26, 2004. Signed as a free agent by **Trinec** (CzRep), September 17, 2004. Signed as a free agent by **Zlin** (CzRep), January 31, 2005.

BONNI, Ryan

(baw-NEE, RIGH-uhn)

Defense. Shoots left. 6'4", 190 lbs. Born, Winnipeg, Man., February 18, 1979. Vancouver's 2nd choice, 34th overall, in 1997 Entry Draft.

Season	Club	League	GP	G	A	Pts	PIM	PP	SH	GW	S	%	+/-	TF	F%	Min	GP	G	A	Pts	PIM	PP	SH	GW	Min
1994-95	Winnipeg Sharks	MMMHL	24	3	19	22	59	....	....	....	....	....	....	....	....	....	....	....	....	....	....	....	....	....	....
1995-96	Saskatoon Blades	WHL	63	1	7	8	78	....	....	....	....	....	....	....	....	....	3	0	0	0	0	....	....	....	....
1996-97	Saskatoon Blades	WHL	69	11	19	30	219	....	....	....	....	....	....	....	....	....	....	....	....	....	....	....	....	....	....
1997-98	Saskatoon Blades	WHL	42	5	14	19	100	....	....	....	....	....	....	....	....	....	....	....	....	....	....	....	....	....	....
1998-99	Saskatoon Blades	WHL	51	6	26	32	211	....	....	....	....	....	....	....	....	....	....	....	....	....	....	....	....	....	....
	Red Deer Rebels	WHL	20	3	10	13	41	....	....	....	....	....	....	....	....	....	9	0	4	4	25	....	....	....	....
99-2000	**Vancouver**	**NHL**	**3**	**0**	**0**	**0**	**0**	**0**	**0**	**0**	**1**	**0.0**	**–1**	**0**	**0.0**	**9:37**	....	....	....	....	....	....	....	....	....
	Syracuse Crunch	AHL	71	5	13	18	125	....	....	....	....	....	....	....	....	....	2	0	1	1	2	....	....	....	....
2000-01	Kansas City	IHL	80	2	9	11	127	....	....	....	....	....	....	....	....	....	....	....	....	....	....	....	....	....	....
2001-02	Manitoba Moose	AHL	11	0	1	1	33	....	....	....	....	....	....	....	....	....	2	0	0	0	2	....	....	....	....
	Columbia Inferno	ECHL	46	3	18	21	128	....	....	....	....	....	....	....	....	....	4	0	4	4	10	....	....	....	....
2002-03	St. John's	AHL	61	1	8	9	86	....	....	....	....	....	....	....	....	....	....	....	....	....	....	....	....	....	....
2003-04	Greensboro	ECHL	15	1	7	8	49	....	....	....	....	....	....	....	....	....	....	....	....	....	....	....	....	....	....
	Grand Rapids	AHL	54	1	6	7	98	....	....	....	....	....	....	....	....	....	4	0	0	0	8	....	....	....	....

			Regular Season														Playoffs								
Season	Club	League	GP	G	A	Pts	PIM	PP	SH	GW	S	%	+/-	TF	F%	Min	GP	G	A	Pts	PIM	PP	SH	GW	Min
2004-05	Rockford IceHogs	UHL	23	3	5	8	41																		
	Milwaukee	AHL	5	0	1	1	11																		
	Landshut Cann.	German-2	17	2	5	7	68										2	0	0	0	27				
	NHL Totals		**3**	**0**	**0**	**0**	**0**	**0**	**0**	**0**	**1**	**0.0**		**0**	**0.0**	**9:37**									

Traded to **Toronto** by **Vancouver** for Toronto's 8th round choice (Sergei Topol) in 2003 Entry Draft, June 25, 2002. Signed as a free agent by **Greensboro** (ECHL), October 28, 2003. Signed as a free agent by **Grand Rapids** (AHL), December 11, 2003. Signed as a free agent by **Rockford** (UHL), October 19, 2004. Signed as a free agent by **Milwaukee** (AHL), December 17, 2004. Signed as a free agent by **Landshut** (German-2), January 9, 2005.

BONVIE, Dennis

(BOHN-vee, DEHN-his)

Right wing. Shoots right. 5'11", 205 lbs. Born, Antigonish, N.S., July 23, 1973.

Season	Club	League	GP	G	A	Pts	PIM	PP	SH	GW	S	%	+/-	TF	F%	Min	GP	G	A	Pts	PIM	PP	SH	GW	Min
1989-90	Antigonish	NSMHL	50	15	30	45	52																		
1990-91	Antigonish	MJrHL	40	1	8	9	347																		
1991-92	Kitchener Rangers	OHL	7	1	1	2	23																		
	North Bay	OHL	49	0	12	12	261										21	0	1	1	91				
1992-93	North Bay	OHL	64	3	21	24	*316										5	0	0	0	34				
1993-94	Cape Breton	AHL	63	1	10	11	278										4	0	0	0	11				
1994-95	Cape Breton	AHL	74	5	15	20	422																		
	Edmonton	**NHL**	**2**	**0**	**0**	**0**	**0**	**0**	**0**	**0**	**0**	**0.0**	**0**												
1995-96	**Edmonton**	**NHL**	**8**	**0**	**0**	**0**	**47**	**0**	**0**	**0**	**0**	**0.0**	**–3**												
	Cape Breton	AHL	38	13	14	27	269																		
1996-97	Hamilton	AHL	73	9	20	29	*522										22	3	11	14	*91				
1997-98	**Edmonton**	**NHL**	**4**	**0**	**0**	**0**	**27**	**0**	**0**	**0**	**0**	**0.0**	**0**												
	Hamilton	AHL	57	11	19	30	295										9	0	5	5	18				
1998-99	**Chicago**	**NHL**	**11**	**0**	**0**	**0**	**44**	**0**	**0**	**0**	**1**	**0.0**	**–4**	**0**	**0.0**	**3:59**									
	Portland Pirates	AHL	3	1	0	1	16																		
	Philadelphia	AHL	37	4	10	14	158										14	3	3	6	26				
99-2000	**Pittsburgh**	**NHL**	**28**	**0**	**0**	**0**	**80**	**0**	**0**	**0**	**6**	**0.0**	**–2**	**0**	**0.0**	**3:14**									
	Wilkes-Barre	AHL	42	5	26	31	243																		
2000-01	**Pittsburgh**	**NHL**	**3**	**0**	**0**	**0**	**0**	**0**	**0**	**0**	**1**	**0.0**	**–1**	**0**	**0.0**	**3:30**									
	Wilkes-Barre	AHL	65	5	18	23	221										21	0	4	4	35				
2001-02	**Boston**	**NHL**	**23**	**1**	**2**	**3**	**84**	**0**	**0**	**0**	**5**	**20.0**	**3**	**0**	**0.0**	**5:05**	**1**	**0**	**0**	**0**	**0**	**0**	**0**	**0**	**3:07**
	Providence Bruins	AHL	55	8	8	16	290																		
2002-03	**Ottawa**	**NHL**	**12**	**0**	**0**	**0**	**29**	**0**	**0**	**0**	**3**	**0.0**	**–1**	**0**	**0.0**	**3:05**									
	Binghamton	AHL	51	7	3	10	311										14	2	4	6	*85				
2003-04	Binghamton	AHL	29	2	4	6	137																		
	Colorado	**NHL**	**1**	**0**	**0**	**0**	**0**	**0**	**0**	**0**	**1**	**0.0**	**0**	**0**	**0.0**	**7:01**									
	Hershey Bears	AHL	30	3	6	9	154																		
2004-05	Hershey Bears	AHL	76	4	14	18	357																		
	NHL Totals		**92**	**1**	**2**	**3**	**311**	**0**	**0**	**0**	**17**	**5.9**		**0**	**0.0**	**3:55**	**1**	**0**	**0**	**0**	**0**	**0**	**0**	**0**	**3:07**

Signed as a free agent by **Edmonton**, August 25, 1994. Claimed by **Chicago** from **Edmonton** in Waiver Draft, October 5, 1998. Traded to **Philadelphia** by **Chicago** for Frank Bialowas, January 8, 1999. Signed as a free agent by **Pittsburgh**, September 20, 1999. Signed as a free agent by **Boston**, October 5, 2001. Signed as a free agent by **Ottawa**, August 26, 2002. Traded to **Colorado** by **Ottawa** for Charlie Stephens, January 23, 2004.

BOOTLAND, Darryl

(BOOT-land, DAIR-ihl) **DET.**

Right wing. Shoots right. 6'1", 194 lbs. Born, Toronto, Ont., November 2, 1981. Colorado's 12th choice, 252nd overall, in 2000 Entry Draft.

Season	Club	League	GP	G	A	Pts	PIM	PP	SH	GW	S	%	+/-	TF	F%	Min	GP	G	A	Pts	PIM	PP	SH	GW	Min
1997-98	Orangeville	OHA-B	44	22	26	48	177																		
1998-99	Barrie Colts	OHL	38	18	11	29	89																		
	St. Michael's	OHL	28	12	6	18	80																		
99-2000	St. Michael's	OHL	65	24	30	54	166																		
2000-01	St. Michael's	OHL	56	32	33	65	136										11	3	1	4	20				
2001-02	St. Michael's	OHL	61	41	56	97	137										15	8	10	18	50				
2002-03	Toledo Storm	ECHL	54	17	19	36	322																		
	Grand Rapids	AHL	16	1	4	5	41										15	3	2	5	46				
2003-04	**Detroit**	**NHL**	**22**	**1**	**1**	**2**	**74**	**0**	**0**	**1**	**13**	**7.7**	**–3**	**1**	**100.0**	**6:07**									
	Grand Rapids	AHL	54	12	2	14	175										4	0	1	1	2				
2004-05	Grand Rapids	AHL	78	14	20	34	336																		
	NHL Totals		**22**	**1**	**1**	**2**	**74**	**0**	**0**	**1**	**13**	**7.7**		**1**	**100.0**	**6:07**									

Signed as a free agent by **Detroit**, July 25, 2002.

BOTTERILL, Jason

(BOH-tuhr-ihl, JAY-suhn)

Left wing. Shoots left. 6'4", 220 lbs. Born, Edmonton, Alta., May 19, 1976. Dallas' 1st choice, 20th overall, in 1994 Entry Draft.

Season	Club	League	GP	G	A	Pts	PIM	PP	SH	GW	S	%	+/-	TF	F%	Min	GP	G	A	Pts	PIM	PP	SH	GW	Min
1992-93	St. Paul's School	High-NH	22	22	26	48																			
1993-94	U. of Michigan	CCHA	36	20	19	39	94																		
1994-95	U. of Michigan	CCHA	34	14	14	28	117																		
1995-96	U. of Michigan	CCHA	37	*32	25	57	*143																		
1996-97	U. of Michigan	CCHA	42	*37	24	61	129																		
1997-98	**Dallas**	**NHL**	**4**	**0**	**0**	**0**	**19**	**0**	**0**	**0**	**2**	**0.0**	**–1**												
	Michigan	IHL	50	11	11	22	82										4	0	0	0	5				
1998-99	**Dallas**	**NHL**	**17**	**0**	**0**	**0**	**23**	**0**	**0**	**0**	**8**	**0.0**	**–2**	**0**	**0.0**	**8:19**									
	Michigan	IHL	56	13	25	38	106										5	2	1	3	4				
99-2000	**Atlanta**	**NHL**	**25**	**1**	**4**	**5**	**17**	**0**	**0**	**1**	**17**	**5.9**	**–7**	**2**	**50.0**	**11:16**									
	Orlando	IHL	17	7	8	15	27																		
	Calgary	**NHL**	**2**	**0**	**0**	**0**	**0**	**0**	**0**	**0**	**2**	**0.0**	**–4**	**0**	**0.0**	**8:00**									
	Saint John Flames	AHL	21	3	4	7	39										3	0	0	0	19				
2000-01	Saint John Flames	AHL	60	13	20	33	101										19	2	7	9	30				
2001-02	**Calgary**	**NHL**	**4**	**1**	**0**	**1**	**2**	**1**	**0**	**1**	**4**	**25.0**	**–3**	**0**	**0.0**	**9:26**									
	Saint John Flames	AHL	71	21	21	42	121																		
2002-03	**Buffalo**	**NHL**	**17**	**1**	**4**	**5**	**14**	**1**	**0**	**0**	**20**	**5.0**	**1**	**5**	**40.0**	**10:48**									
	Rochester	AHL	64	37	22	59	105										3	1	1	2	21				
2003-04	**Buffalo**	**NHL**	**19**	**2**	**1**	**3**	**14**	**1**	**0**	**0**	**20**	**10.0**	**0**	**4**	**25.0**	**11:24**									
	Rochester	AHL	46	16	17	33	68										16	5	10	15	19				
2004-05	Rochester	AHL	8	6	2	8	9																		
	NHL Totals		**88**	**5**	**9**	**14**	**89**	**3**	**0**	**2**	**73**	**6.8**		**11**	**36.4**	**10:27**									

CCHA Second All-Star Team (1996) • NCAA West Second All-American Team (1997)

Traded to **Atlanta** by **Dallas** for Jamie Pushor, July 15, 1999. Traded to **Calgary** by **Atlanta** with Darryl Shannon for Hnat Domenichelli and Dmitri Vlasenkov, February 11, 2000. Signed as a free agent by **Buffalo**, August 12, 2002.

BOUCHARD, Joel

(BOO-shahrd, JOHL) **NYI**

Defense. Shoots left. 6'1", 209 lbs. Born, Montreal, Que., January 23, 1974. Calgary's 7th choice, 129th overall, in 1992 Entry Draft.

Season	Club	League	GP	G	A	Pts	PIM	PP	SH	GW	S	%	+/-	TF	F%	Min	GP	G	A	Pts	PIM	PP	SH	GW	Min
1989-90	Mtl-Bourassa	QAAA	41	7	17	24	10										1	1	0	1	0				
1990-91	Longueuil	QMJHL	53	3	19	22	34										8	1	0	1	11				
1991-92	Verdun	QMJHL	70	9	20	29	55										19	1	7	8	20				
1992-93	Verdun	QMJHL	60	10	49	59	126										4	0	2	2	4				
1993-94	Verdun	QMJHL	60	15	55	70	62										4	1	0	1	6				
	Saint John Flames	AHL	1	0	0	0	0										2	0	0	0	0				
1994-95	Saint John Flames	AHL	77	6	25	31	63										5	1	0	1	4				
	Calgary	**NHL**	**2**	**0**	**0**	**0**	**0**	**0**	**0**	**0**	**0**	**0.0**	**0**												
1995-96	**Calgary**	**NHL**	**4**	**0**	**0**	**0**	**4**	**0**	**0**	**0**	**0**	**0.0**	**0**												
	Saint John Flames	AHL	74	8	25	33	104										16	1	4	5	10				
1996-97	**Calgary**	**NHL**	**76**	**4**	**5**	**9**	**49**	**0**	**1**	**0**	**61**	**6.6**	**–23**												
1997-98	**Calgary**	**NHL**	**44**	**5**	**7**	**12**	**57**	**0**	**1**	**1**	**51**	**9.8**	**0**												
	Saint John Flames	AHL	3	2	1	3	6																		
1998-99	**Nashville**	**NHL**	**64**	**4**	**11**	**15**	**60**	**0**	**0**	**0**	**78**	**5.1**	**–10**	**0**	**0.0**	**22:34**									
99-2000	**Nashville**	**NHL**	**52**	**1**	**4**	**5**	**23**	**0**	**0**	**0**	**60**	**1.7**	**–11**	**0**	**0.0**	**18:41**									
	Dallas	**NHL**	**2**	**0**	**0**	**0**	**2**	**0**	**0**	**0**	**1**	**0.0**	**1**	**0**	**0.0**	**9:45**									

			Regular Season														Playoffs								
Season	Club	League	GP	G	A	Pts	PIM	PP	SH	GW	S	%	+/-	TF	F%	Min	GP	G	A	Pts	PIM	PP	SH	GW	Min
2000-01	**Phoenix**	**NHL**	**32**	**1**	**2**	**3**	**22**	**0**	**0**	**0**	**26**	**3.8**	**–8**	**0**	**0.0**	**14:28**	....	....	....	....	....	....	....	....	....
	Grand Rapids	IHL	19	3	9	12	8	....	....	....	....	....	....	....	....	....	....	....	....	....	....	....	....	....	....
2001-02	**New Jersey**	**NHL**	**1**	**0**	**1**	**1**	**0**	**0**	**0**	**0**	**0**	**0.0**	**1**	**0**	**0.0**	**19:26**	....	....	....	....	....	....	....	....	....
	Albany River Rats	AHL	70	9	22	31	28	....	....	....	....	....	....	....	....	....	....	....	....	....	....	....	....	....	....
2002-03	**NY Rangers**	**NHL**	**27**	**5**	**7**	**12**	**14**	**1**	**0**	**2**	**41**	**12.2**	**6**	**0**	**0.0**	**20:07**	....	....	....	....	....	....	....	....	....
	Hartford	AHL	22	6	14	20	22	....	....	....	....	....	....	....	....	....	....	....	....	....	....	....	....	....	....
	Pittsburgh	**NHL**	**7**	**0**	**1**	**1**	**0**	**0**	**0**	**0**	**6**	**0.0**	**–6**	**0**	**0.0**	**21:49**	....	....	....	....	....	....	....	....	....
2003-04	**NY Rangers**	**NHL**	**28**	**1**	**7**	**8**	**10**	**0**	**0**	**0**	**34**	**2.9**	**2**	**0**	**0.0**	**16:42**	....	....	....	....	....	....	....	....	....
2004-05	Hartford	AHL	7	1	2	3	6	....	....	....	....	....	....	....	....	....	6	0	2	2	20	....	....	....	....
	NHL Totals		**339**	**21**	**45**	**66**	**241**	**1**	**2**	**3**	**358**	**5.9**		**0**	**0.0**	**19:10**	....	....	....	....	....	....	....	....	....

QMJHL First All-Star Team (1994)

Claimed by **Nashville** from **Calgary** in Expansion Draft, June 26, 1998. Claimed on waivers by **Dallas** from **Nashville**, March 14, 2000. Signed as a free agent by **Phoenix**, August 31, 2000. Signed as a free agent by **New Jersey**, October 25, 2001. Signed as a free agent by **NY Rangers**, August 5, 2002. Traded to **Pittsburgh** by **NY Rangers** with Richard Lintner, Rico Fata , Mikael Samuelsson and future considerations for Mike Wilson, Alex Kovalev, Janne Laukkanen and Dan LaCouture, February 10, 2003. Signed as a free agent by **Buffalo**, July 14, 2003. Claimed by **NY Rangers** from **Buffalo** in Waiver Draft, October 3, 2003. • Spent majority of 2003-04 season as a healthy reserve. Signed as a free agent by **Hartford** (AHL), March 17, 2005. Signed as a free agent by **NY Islanders**, August 18, 2005.

BOUCHARD, Pierre-Marc (BOO-shahrd, PEE-air- MAHRK) MIN.

Center. Shoots left. 5'10", 165 lbs. Born, Sherbrooke, Que., April 27, 1984. Minnesota's 1st choice, 8th overall, in 2002 Entry Draft.

Season	Club	League	GP	G	A	Pts	PIM	PP	SH	GW	S	%	+/-	TF	F%	Min	GP	G	A	Pts	PIM	PP	SH	GW	Min
1998-99	Mtl.-Bourassa	QAHA	28	23	41	64	....	....	....	....	....	....	....	....	....	....	....	....	....	....	....	....	....	....	....
99-2000	Charles-Lemoyne	QAAA	42	28	*45	*74	20	....	....	....	....	....	....	....	....	....	9	4	8	12	6	....	....	....	....
2000-01	Chicoutimi	QMJHL	67	38	57	95	20	....	....	....	....	....	....	....	....	....	6	5	8	13	0	....	....	....	....
2001-02	Chicoutimi	QMJHL	69	46	*94	*140	54	....	....	....	....	....	....	....	....	....	4	2	3	5	4	....	....	....	....
2002-03	**Minnesota**	**NHL**	**50**	**7**	**13**	**20**	**18**	**5**	**0**	**1**	**53**	**13.2**	**1**	**474**	**40.7**	**13:16**	**5**	**0**	**1**	**1**	**2**	**0**	**0**	**0**	**13:15**
2003-04	**Minnesota**	**NHL**	**61**	**4**	**18**	**22**	**22**	**2**	**0**	**0**	**60**	**6.7**	**–7**	**60**	**50.0**	**14:00**	....	....	....	....	....	....	....	....	....
2004-05	Houston Aeros	AHL	67	12	42	54	46	....	....	....	....	....	....	....	....	....	5	0	1	1	0	....	....	....	....
	NHL Totals		**111**	**11**	**31**	**42**	**40**	**7**	**0**	**1**	**113**	**9.7**		**534**	**41.8**	**13:40**	**5**	**0**	**1**	**1**	**2**	**0**	**0**	**0**	**13:15**

QMJHL Rookie of the Year (2001) • QMJHL First All-Star Team (2002) • Canadian Major Junior First All-Star Team (2002) • Canadian Major Junior Player of the Year (2002)

BOUCHER, Philippe (boo-SHAY, fihl-EEP) DAL.

Defense. Shoots right. 6'3", 221 lbs. Born, Ste-Apollinaire, Que., March 24, 1973. Buffalo's 1st choice, 13th overall, in 1991 Entry Draft.

Season	Club	League	GP	G	A	Pts	PIM	PP	SH	GW	S	%	+/-	TF	F%	Min	GP	G	A	Pts	PIM	PP	SH	GW	Min
1988-89	Ste-Foy	QAAA	5	0	0	0	2	....	....	....	....	....	....	....	....	....	....	....	....	....	....	....	....	....	....
1989-90	Ste-Foy	QAAA	42	26	60	86	76	....	....	....	....	....	....	....	....	....	12	6	*19	25	16	....	....	....	....
1990-91	Granby Bisons	QMJHL	69	21	46	67	92	....	....	....	....	....	....	....	....	....	....	....	....	....	....	....	....	....	....
1991-92	Granby Bisons	QMJHL	49	22	37	59	47	....	....	....	....	....	....	....	....	....	....	....	....	....	....	....	....	....	....
	Laval Titan	QMJHL	16	7	11	18	36	....	....	....	....	....	....	....	....	....	10	5	6	11	8	....	....	....	....
1992-93	Laval Titan	QMJHL	16	12	15	27	37	....	....	....	....	....	....	....	....	....	13	6	15	21	12	....	....	....	....
	Buffalo	**NHL**	**18**	**0**	**4**	**4**	**14**	**0**	**0**	**0**	**28**	**0.0**	**1**	....	....	....	....	....	....	....	....	....	....	....	....
	Rochester	AHL	5	4	3	7	8	....	....	....	....	....	....	....	....	....	3	0	1	1	2	....	....	....	....
1993-94	**Buffalo**	**NHL**	**38**	**6**	**8**	**14**	**29**	**4**	**0**	**1**	**67**	**9.0**	**–1**	....	....	....	**7**	**1**	**1**	**2**	**2**	**1**	**0**	**0**	....
	Rochester	AHL	31	10	22	32	51	....	....	....	....	....	....	....	....	....	....	....	....	....	....	....	....	....	....
1994-95	Rochester	AHL	43	14	27	41	26	....	....	....	....	....	....	....	....	....	....	....	....	....	....	....	....	....	....
	Buffalo	**NHL**	**9**	**1**	**4**	**5**	**0**	**0**	**0**	**0**	**15**	**6.7**	**6**	....	....	....	....	....	....	....	....	....	....	....	....
	Los Angeles	**NHL**	**6**	**1**	**0**	**1**	**4**	**0**	**0**	**0**	**15**	**6.7**	**–3**	....	....	....	....	....	....	....	....	....	....	....	....
1995-96	**Los Angeles**	**NHL**	**53**	**7**	**16**	**23**	**31**	**5**	**0**	**1**	**145**	**4.8**	**–26**	....	....	....	....	....	....	....	....	....	....	....	....
	Phoenix	IHL	10	4	3	7	4	....	....	....	....	....	....	....	....	....	....	....	....	....	....	....	....	....	....
1996-97	**Los Angeles**	**NHL**	**60**	**7**	**18**	**25**	**25**	**2**	**0**	**1**	**159**	**4.4**	**0**	....	....	....	....	....	....	....	....	....	....	....	....
1997-98	**Los Angeles**	**NHL**	**45**	**6**	**10**	**16**	**49**	**1**	**0**	**0**	**80**	**7.5**	**6**	....	....	....	....	....	....	....	....	....	....	....	....
	Long Beach	IHL	2	0	1	1	4	....	....	....	....	....	....	....	....	....	....	....	....	....	....	....	....	....	....
1998-99	**Los Angeles**	**NHL**	**45**	**2**	**6**	**8**	**32**	**1**	**0**	**0**	**87**	**2.3**	**–12**	**0**	**0.0**	**17:51**	....	....	....	....	....	....	....	....	....
99-2000	**Los Angeles**	**NHL**	**1**	**0**	**0**	**0**	**0**	**0**	**0**	**0**	**3**	**0.0**	**0**	**0**	**0.0**	**17:04**	....	....	....	....	....	....	....	....	....
	Long Beach	IHL	14	4	11	15	8	....	....	....	....	....	....	....	....	....	6	0	9	9	8	....	....	....	....
2000-01	**Los Angeles**	**NHL**	**22**	**2**	**4**	**6**	**20**	**2**	**0**	**0**	**40**	**5.0**	**4**	**0**	**0.0**	**18:25**	**13**	**0**	**1**	**1**	**2**	**0**	**0**	**0**	**15:48**
	Manitoba Moose	IHL	45	10	22	32	39	....	....	....	....	....	....	....	....	....	....	....	....	....	....	....	....	....	....
2001-02	**Los Angeles**	**NHL**	**80**	**7**	**23**	**30**	**94**	**4**	**0**	**2**	**198**	**3.5**	**0**	**0**	**0.0**	**21:36**	**5**	**0**	**1**	**1**	**2**	**0**	**0**	**0**	**19:31**
2002-03	**Dallas**	**NHL**	**80**	**7**	**20**	**27**	**94**	**1**	**1**	**3**	**137**	**5.1**	**28**	**1**	**0.0**	**20:29**	**11**	**1**	**2**	**3**	**11**	**0**	**0**	**0**	**21:28**
2003-04	**Dallas**	**NHL**	**70**	**8**	**16**	**24**	**64**	**2**	**0**	**2**	**134**	**6.0**	**15**	**0**	**0.0**	**22:24**	**5**	**1**	**0**	**1**	**6**	**0**	**0**	**0**	**23:57**
2004-05			DID NOT PLAY																						
	NHL Totals		**527**	**54**	**129**	**183**	**456**	**22**	**1**	**10**	**1108**	**4.9**		**1**	**0.0**	**20:40**	**41**	**3**	**5**	**8**	**23**	**1**	**0**	**0**	**19:23**

QMJHL Second All-Star Team (1991, 1992) • QMJHL Defensive Rookie of the Year (1991) • Canadian Major Junior Rookie of the Year (1991)

Traded to **Los Angeles** by **Buffalo** with Denis Tsygurov and Grant Fuhr for Alexei Zhitnik, Robb Stauber, Charlie Huddy and Los Angeles' 5th round choice (Marian Menhart) in 1995 Entry Draft, February 14, 1995. • Missed majority of 1999-2000 season recovering from foot injury suffered in training camp, September, 1999. Signed as a free agent by **Dallas**, July 2, 2002.

BOUCK, Tyler (BOWK, TIGH-luhr) VAN.

Center. Shoots left. 6', 196 lbs. Born, Camrose, Alta., January 13, 1980. Dallas' 2nd choice, 57th overall, in 1998 Entry Draft.

Season	Club	League	GP	G	A	Pts	PIM	PP	SH	GW	S	%	+/-	TF	F%	Min	GP	G	A	Pts	PIM	PP	SH	GW	Min
1995-96	Sherwood Park	AMHL	22	10	21	31	58	....	....	....	....	....	....	....	....	....	....	....	....	....	....	....	....	....	....
1996-97	Prince George	WHL	12	0	2	2	11	....	....	....	....	....	....	....	....	....	....	....	....	....	....	....	....	....	....
1997-98	Prince George	WHL	65	11	26	37	90	....	....	....	....	....	....	....	....	....	11	1	0	1	21	....	....	....	....
1998-99	Prince George	WHL	56	22	25	47	178	....	....	....	....	....	....	....	....	....	2	0	2	2	10	....	....	....	....
99-2000	Prince George	WHL	57	30	33	63	183	....	....	....	....	....	....	....	....	....	13	6	13	19	36	....	....	....	....
2000-01	**Dallas**	**NHL**	**48**	**2**	**5**	**7**	**29**	**0**	**0**	**1**	**41**	**4.9**	**–3**	**1**	**0.0**	**8:59**	**1**	**0**	**0**	**0**	**0**	**0**	**0**	**0**	**9:02**
	Utah Grizzlies	IHL	24	2	6	8	39	....	....	....	....	....	....	....	....	....	....	....	....	....	....	....	....	....	....
2001-02	**Phoenix**	**NHL**	**7**	**0**	**0**	**0**	**4**	**0**	**0**	**0**	**3**	**0.0**	**–1**	**0**	**0.0**	**6:54**	....	....	....	....	....	....	....	....	....
	Springfield	AHL	21	1	2	3	33	....	....	....	....	....	....	....	....	....	....	....	....	....	....	....	....	....	....
	Manitoba Moose	AHL	20	4	4	8	25	....	....	....	....	....	....	....	....	....	....	....	....	....	....	....	....	....	....
2002-03	Manitoba Moose	AHL	76	10	28	38	103	....	....	....	....	....	....	....	....	....	14	2	2	4	10	....	....	....	....
2003-04	**Vancouver**	**NHL**	**18**	**1**	**2**	**3**	**23**	**0**	**1**	**0**	**12**	**8.3**	**–4**	**0**	**0.0**	**9:18**	**1**	**0**	**0**	**0**	**0**	**0**	**0**	**0**	**5:15**
	Manitoba Moose	AHL	49	11	14	25	100	....	....	....	....	....	....	....	....	....	....	....	....	....	....	....	....	....	....
2004-05	TPS Turku	Finland	40	3	7	10	100	....	....	....	....	....	....	....	....	....	6	1	0	1	12	....	....	....	....
	NHL Totals		**73**	**3**	**7**	**10**	**56**	**0**	**1**	**1**	**56**	**5.4**		**1**	**0.0**	**8:52**	**2**	**0**	**0**	**0**	**0**	**0**	**0**	**0**	**7:08**

WHL West First All-Star Team (2000)

Traded to **Phoenix** by **Dallas** for Jyrki Lumme, June 23, 2001. Traded to **Vancouver** by **Phoenix** with Todd Warriner, Trevor Letowski and Phoenix's 3rd round choice (later traded back to Phoenix – Phoenix selected Dimitri Pestunov) in 2003 Entry Draft for Drake Berehowsky and Denis Pederson, December 28, 2001. Signed as a free agent by **TPS** (Finland), October 22, 2004.

BOUGHNER, Bob (BOOG-nuhr, BAWB) COL.

Defense. Shoots right. 6', 203 lbs. Born, Windsor, Ont., March 8, 1971. Detroit's 2nd choice, 32nd overall, in 1989 Entry Draft.

Season	Club	League	GP	G	A	Pts	PIM	PP	SH	GW	S	%	+/-	TF	F%	Min	GP	G	A	Pts	PIM	PP	SH	GW	Min
1986-87	Belle River	OHA-C	37	3	11	14	88	....	....	....	....	....	....	....	....	....	....	....	....	....	....	....	....	....	....
1987-88	St. Mary's Lincolns	OHA-B	36	4	18	22	177	....	....	....	....	....	....	....	....	....	....	....	....	....	....	....	....	....	....
1988-89	Sault Ste. Marie	OHL	64	6	15	21	182	....	....	....	....	....	....	....	....	....	....	....	....	....	....	....	....	....	....
1989-90	Sault Ste. Marie	OHL	49	7	23	30	122	....	....	....	....	....	....	....	....	....	....	....	....	....	....	....	....	....	....
1990-91	Sault Ste. Marie	OHL	64	13	33	46	156	....	....	....	....	....	....	....	....	....	14	2	9	11	35	....	....	....	....
1991-92	Toledo Storm	ECHL	28	3	10	13	79	....	....	....	....	....	....	....	....	....	5	2	0	2	15	....	....	....	....
	Adirondack	AHL	1	0	0	0	7	....	....	....	....	....	....	....	....	....	....	....	....	....	....	....	....	....	....
1992-93	Adirondack	AHL	69	1	16	17	190	....	....	....	....	....	....	....	....	....	....	....	....	....	....	....	....	....	....
1993-94	Adirondack	AHL	72	8	14	22	292	....	....	....	....	....	....	....	....	....	10	1	1	2	18	....	....	....	....
1994-95	Cincinnati	IHL	81	2	14	16	192	....	....	....	....	....	....	....	....	....	10	0	0	0	18	....	....	....	....
1995-96	Carolina Panthers	AHL	46	2	15	17	127	....	....	....	....	....	....	....	....	....	....	....	....	....	....	....	....	....	....
	Buffalo	**NHL**	**31**	**0**	**1**	**1**	**104**	**0**	**0**	**0**	**14**	**0.0**	**3**	....	....	....	....	....	....	....	....	....	....	....	....
1996-97	**Buffalo**	**NHL**	**77**	**1**	**7**	**8**	**225**	**0**	**0**	**0**	**34**	**2.9**	**12**	....	....	....	**11**	**0**	**1**	**1**	**9**	**0**	**0**	**0**	....
1997-98	**Buffalo**	**NHL**	**69**	**1**	**3**	**4**	**165**	**0**	**0**	**0**	**26**	**3.8**	**5**	....	....	....	**14**	**0**	**4**	**4**	**15**	**0**	**0**	**0**	....
1998-99	**Nashville**	**NHL**	**79**	**3**	**10**	**13**	**137**	**0**	**0**	**1**	**59**	**5.1**	**–6**	**0**	**0.0**	**18:31**	....	....	....	....	....	....	....	....	....
99-2000	**Nashville**	**NHL**	**62**	**2**	**4**	**6**	**97**	**0**	**0**	**0**	**32**	**6.3**	**–13**	**0**	**0.0**	**17:20**	....	....	....	....	....	....	....	....	....
	Pittsburgh	**NHL**	**11**	**1**	**0**	**1**	**69**	**1**	**0**	**1**	**8**	**12.5**	**2**	**0**	**0.0**	**17:05**	**11**	**0**	**2**	**2**	**15**	**0**	**0**	**0**	**18:40**
2000-01	**Pittsburgh**	**NHL**	**58**	**1**	**3**	**4**	**147**	**0**	**0**	**0**	**46**	**2.2**	**18**	**0**	**0.0**	**16:30**	**18**	**0**	**1**	**1**	**22**	**0**	**0**	**0**	**17:08**
2001-02	**Calgary**	**NHL**	**79**	**2**	**4**	**6**	**170**	**0**	**0**	**0**	**58**	**3.4**	**9**	**0**	**0.0**	**18:43**	....	....	....	....	....	....	....	....	....
2002-03	**Calgary**	**NHL**	**69**	**3**	**14**	**17**	**126**	**0**	**0**	**1**	**62**	**4.8**	**5**	**0**	**0.0**	**19:51**	....	....	....	....	....	....	....	....	....

			Regular Season														Playoffs								
Season	Club	League	GP	G	A	Pts	PIM	PP	SH	GW	S	%	+/-	TF	F%	Min	GP	G	A	Pts	PIM	PP	SH	GW	Min
2003-04	**Carolina**	**NHL**	**43**	**0**	**5**	**5**	**80**	**0**	**0**	**0**	**26**	**0.0**	**–9**	**0**	**0.0**	**14:47**	....	....	....	....	....	....	....	....	....
	Colorado	**NHL**	**11**	**0**	**0**	**0**	**8**	**0**	**0**	**0**	**8**	**0.0**	**–1**	**0**	**0.0**	**13:26**	**11**	**0**	**4**	**4**	**6**	**0**	**0**	**0**	**15:39**
2004-05		DID NOT PLAY																							
	NHL Totals		**589**	**14**	**51**	**65**	**1328**	**1**	**0**	**3**	**373**	**3.8**		**0**	**0.0**	**17:45**	**65**	**0**	**12**	**12**	**67**	**0**	**0**	**0**	**17:09**

Signed as a free agent by **Florida**, July 25, 1994. Traded to **Buffalo** by **Florida** for Buffalo's 3rd round choice (Chris Allen) in 1996 Entry Draft, February 1, 1996. Claimed by **Nashville** from **Buffalo** in Expansion Draft, June 26, 1998. Traded to **Pittsburgh** by **Nashville** for Pavel Skrbek, March 13, 2000. Signed as a free agent by **Calgary**, July 2, 2001. Traded to **Carolina** by **Calgary** for New Jersey's 4th round choice (previously acquired, Calgary selected Kristopher Hogg) in 2004 Entry Draft and Carolina's 5th round choice (Kevin Lalande) in 2005 Entry Draft, July 16, 2003. Traded to **Colorado** by **Carolina** for Chris Bahen, Washington's 3rd round choice (previously acquired, Carolina selected Casey Borer) in 2004 Entry Draft and Colorado's 5th round choice (Risto Korhonen) in 2005 Entry Draft, February 20, 2004.

BOUILLON, Francis

(BOO-liawn, FRAN-sihs) **MTL.**

Defense. Shoots left. 5'8", 196 lbs. Born, New York, NY, October 17, 1975.

Season	Club	League	GP	G	A	Pts	PIM	PP	SH	GW	S	%	+/-	TF	F%	Min	GP	G	A	Pts	PIM	PP	SH	GW	Min
1991-92	Mtl-Bourassa	QAAA	42	2	5	7	28	....	....	....	....	....	....	....	....	....	9	1	0	1	6	....	....	....	....
1992-93	Laval Titan	QMJHL	46	0	7	7	45	....	....	....	....	....	....	....	....	....	....	....	....	....	....	....	....	....	....
1993-94	Laval Titan	QMJHL	68	3	15	18	129	....	....	....	....	....	....	....	....	....	19	2	9	11	48	....	....	....	....
1994-95	Laval Titan	QMJHL	72	8	25	33	115	....	....	....	....	....	....	....	....	....	20	3	11	14	21	....	....	....	....
1995-96	Granby	QMJHL	68	11	35	46	156	....	....	....	....	....	....	....	....	....	21	2	12	14	30	....	....	....	....
1996-97	Wheeling Nailers	ECHL	69	10	32	42	77	....	....	....	....	....	....	....	....	....	3	0	2	2	10	....	....	....	....
1997-98	Quebec Rafales	IHL	71	8	27	35	76	....	....	....	....	....	....	....	....	....	....	....	....	....	....	....	....	....	....
1998-99	Fredericton	AHL	79	19	36	55	174	....	....	....	....	....	....	....	....	....	5	2	1	3	0	....	....	....	....
99-2000	**Montreal**	**NHL**	**74**	**3**	**13**	**16**	**38**	**2**	**0**	**1**	**76**	**3.9**	**–7**	**1**	**0.0**	**15:52**	....	....	....	....	....	....	....	....	....
2000-01	**Montreal**	**NHL**	**29**	**0**	**6**	**6**	**26**	**0**	**0**	**0**	**24**	**0.0**	**3**	**0**	**0.0**	**13:24**	....	....	....	....	....	....	....	....	....
	Quebec Citadelles	AHL	4	0	0	0	0	....	....	....	....	....	....	....	....	....	....	....	....	....	....	....	....	....	....
2001-02	**Montreal**	**NHL**	**28**	**0**	**5**	**5**	**33**	**0**	**0**	**0**	**24**	**0.0**	**–5**	**0**	**0.0**	**18:47**	....	....	....	....	....	....	....	....	....
	Quebec Citadelles	AHL	38	8	14	22	30	....	....	....	....	....	....	....	....	....	....	....	....	....	....	....	....	....	....
2002-03	**Nashville**	**NHL**	**4**	**0**	**0**	**0**	**2**	**0**	**0**	**0**	**0**	**0.0**	**–1**	**0**	**0.0**	**12:52**	....	....	....	....	....	....	....	....	....
	Montreal	**NHL**	**20**	**3**	**1**	**4**	**2**	**0**	**1**	**0**	**30**	**10.0**	**–1**	**0**	**0.0**	**20:24**	....	....	....	....	....	....	....	....	....
	Hamilton	AHL	29	1	12	13	31	....	....	....	....	....	....	....	....	....	....	....	....	....	....	....	....	....	....
2003-04	**Montreal**	**NHL**	**73**	**2**	**16**	**18**	**70**	**0**	**0**	**0**	**86**	**2.3**	**1**	**0**	**0.0**	**19:39**	**11**	**0**	**0**	**0**	**7**	**0**	**0**	**0**	**18:00**
2004-05	Leksands IF	Sweden-2	31	10	21	31	46	....	....	....	....	....	....	....	....	....	....	....	....	....	....	....	....	....	....
	NHL Totals		**228**	**8**	**41**	**49**	**171**	**2**	**1**	**1**	**240**	**3.3**		**1**	**0.0**	**17:28**	**11**	**0**	**0**	**0**	**7**	**0**	**0**	**0**	**18:00**

Signed as a free agent by **Montreal**, August 18, 1998. • Missed majority of 2000-01 season recovering from ankle injury suffered in game vs. Calgary, December 31, 2000. Claimed by **Nashville** from **Montreal** in Waiver Draft, October 4, 2002. Claimed on waivers by **Montreal** from **Nashville**, October 25, 2002. Signed as a free agent by **Leksands** (Sweden-2), November 15, 2004.

BOULERICE, Jesse

(BOO-luhr-ighs, JEHS-see) **CAR.**

Right wing. Shoots right. 6'2", 215 lbs. Born, Plattsburgh, NY, August 10, 1978. Philadelphia's 4th choice, 133rd overall, in 1996 Entry Draft.

Season	Club	League	GP	G	A	Pts	PIM	PP	SH	GW	S	%	+/-	TF	F%	Min	GP	G	A	Pts	PIM	PP	SH	GW	Min
1994-95	Hawkesbury	CJHL	46	1	8	9	160	....	....	....	....	....	....	....	....	....	....	....	....	....	....	....	....	....	....
1995-96	Detroit	OHL	64	2	5	7	150	....	....	....	....	....	....	....	....	....	16	0	0	0	12	....	....	....	....
1996-97	Detroit	OHL	33	10	14	24	209	....	....	....	....	....	....	....	....	....	....	....	....	....	....	....	....	....	....
1997-98	Plymouth Whalers	OHL	53	20	23	43	170	....	....	....	....	....	....	....	....	....	13	2	4	6	35	....	....	....	....
1998-99	Philadelphia	AHL	24	1	2	3	82	....	....	....	....	....	....	....	....	....	....	....	....	....	....	....	....	....	....
	New Orleans	ECHL	12	0	1	1	38	....	....	....	....	....	....	....	....	....	....	....	....	....	....	....	....	....	....
99-2000	Philadelphia	AHL	40	3	4	7	85	....	....	....	....	....	....	....	....	....	4	0	2	2	4	....	....	....	....
	Trenton Titans	ECHL	25	8	8	16	90	....	....	....	....	....	....	....	....	....	....	....	....	....	....	....	....	....	....
2000-01	Philadelphia	AHL	60	3	4	7	256	....	....	....	....	....	....	....	....	....	10	1	1	2	28	....	....	....	....
2001-02	**Philadelphia**	**NHL**	**3**	**0**	**0**	**0**	**5**	**0**	**0**	**0**	**1**	**0.0**	**–1**	**0**	**0.0**	**4:18**	....	....	....	....	....	....	....	....	....
	Philadelphia	AHL	41	2	5	7	204	....	....	....	....	....	....	....	....	....	....	....	....	....	....	....	....	....	....
	Lowell	AHL	15	2	4	6	80	....	....	....	....	....	....	....	....	....	5	0	2	2	6	....	....	....	....
2002-03	**Carolina**	**NHL**	**48**	**2**	**1**	**3**	**108**	**0**	**0**	**0**	**12**	**16.7**	**–2**	**0**	**0.0**	**3:54**	....	....	....	....	....	....	....	....	....
2003-04	**Carolina**	**NHL**	**76**	**6**	**1**	**7**	**127**	**0**	**0**	**0**	**46**	**13.0**	**–5**	**0**	**0.0**	**6:32**	....	....	....	....	....	....	....	....	....
2004-05		DID NOT PLAY																							
	NHL Totals		**127**	**8**	**2**	**10**	**240**	**0**	**0**	**0**	**59**	**13.6**		**0**	**0.0**	**5:29**	....	....	....	....	....	....	....	....	....

Traded to **Carolina** by **Philadelphia** for Greg Koehler, February 13, 2002.

BOULTON, Eric

(BOHL-tuhn, AIR-ihk) **ATL.**

Left wing. Shoots left. 6', 225 lbs. Born, Halifax, N.S., August 17, 1976. NY Rangers' 12th choice, 234th overall, in 1994 Entry Draft.

Season	Club	League	GP	G	A	Pts	PIM	PP	SH	GW	S	%	+/-	TF	F%	Min	GP	G	A	Pts	PIM	PP	SH	GW	Min
1992-93	Cole Harbour	MJrHL	44	12	15	27	212	....	....	....	....	....	....	....	....	....	....	....	....	....	....	....	....	....	....
1993-94	Oshawa Generals	OHL	45	4	3	7	149	....	....	....	....	....	....	....	....	....	5	0	0	0	16	....	....	....	....
1994-95	Oshawa Generals	OHL	27	7	5	12	125	....	....	....	....	....	....	....	....	....	....	....	....	....	....	....	....	....	....
	Sarnia Sting	OHL	24	3	7	10	134	....	....	....	....	....	....	....	....	....	4	0	1	1	10	....	....	....	....
1995-96	Sarnia Sting	OHL	66	14	29	43	243	....	....	....	....	....	....	....	....	....	9	0	3	3	29	....	....	....	....
1996-97	Binghamton	AHL	23	2	3	5	67	....	....	....	....	....	....	....	....	....	3	0	0	0	4	....	....	....	....
	Charlotte	ECHL	44	14	11	25	325	....	....	....	....	....	....	....	....	....	3	0	1	1	6	....	....	....	....
1997-98	Charlotte	ECHL	53	11	16	27	202	....	....	....	....	....	....	....	....	....	4	1	0	1	0	....	....	....	....
	Fort Wayne	IHL	8	0	2	2	42	....	....	....	....	....	....	....	....	....	....	....	....	....	....	....	....	....	....
1998-99	Kentucky	AHL	34	3	3	6	154	....	....	....	....	....	....	....	....	....	10	0	1	1	36	....	....	....	....
	Florida Everblades	ECHL	26	9	13	22	143	....	....	....	....	....	....	....	....	....	....	....	....	....	....	....	....	....	....
	Houston Aeros	IHL	7	1	0	1	41	....	....	....	....	....	....	....	....	....	....	....	....	....	....	....	....	....	....
99-2000	Rochester	AHL	76	2	2	4	276	....	....	....	....	....	....	....	....	....	18	2	1	3	53	....	....	....	....
2000-01	**Buffalo**	**NHL**	**35**	**1**	**2**	**3**	**94**	**0**	**0**	**0**	**20**	**5.0**	**–1**	**2**	**0.0**	**5:42**	....	....	....	....	....	....	....	....	....
2001-02	**Buffalo**	**NHL**	**35**	**2**	**3**	**5**	**129**	**0**	**0**	**1**	**21**	**9.5**	**–1**	**0**	**0.0**	**6:08**	....	....	....	....	....	....	....	....	....
2002-03	**Buffalo**	**NHL**	**58**	**1**	**5**	**6**	**178**	**0**	**0**	**0**	**33**	**3.0**	**1**	**6**	**33.3**	**6:35**	....	....	....	....	....	....	....	....	....
2003-04	**Buffalo**	**NHL**	**44**	**1**	**2**	**3**	**110**	**0**	**0**	**0**	**20**	**5.0**	**–2**	**1**	**0.0**	**4:52**	....	....	....	....	....	....	....	....	....
2004-05	Columbia Inferno	ECHL	48	23	16	39	124	....	....	....	....	....	....	....	....	....	4	2	3	5	8	....	....	....	....
	NHL Totals		**172**	**5**	**12**	**17**	**511**	**0**	**0**	**1**	**94**	**5.3**		**9**	**22.2**	**5:52**	....	....	....	....	....	....	....	....	....

Signed as a free agent by **Buffalo**, September 14, 1999. Signed as a free agent by **Columbia** (ECHL), November 24, 2004. Signed as a free agent by **Atlanta**, August 8, 2005.

BOUMEDIENNE, Josef

(BOO-mih-dyehn, JOH-sehf) **WSH.**

Defense. Shoots left. 6'2", 205 lbs. Born, Stockholm, Sweden, January 12, 1978. New Jersey's 7th choice, 91st overall, in 1996 Entry Draft.

Season	Club	League	GP	G	A	Pts	PIM	PP	SH	GW	S	%	+/-	TF	F%	Min	GP	G	A	Pts	PIM	PP	SH	GW	Min
1994-95	Huddinge IK Jr.	Swe-Jr.	10	0	2	2	57	....	....	....	....	....	....	....	....	....	....	....	....	....	....	....	....	....	....
1995-96	Huddinge IK Jr.	Swe-Jr.	25	2	4	6	66	....	....	....	....	....	....	....	....	....	....	....	....	....	....	....	....	....	....
	Huddinge IK	Sweden-2	7	0	0	0	14	....	....	....	....	....	....	....	....	....	....	....	....	....	....	....	....	....	....
1996-97	Sodertalje SK	Sweden	32	1	1	2	32	....	....	....	....	....	....	....	....	....	....	....	....	....	....	....	....	....	....
1997-98	Sodertalje SK	Sweden	26	3	3	6	28	....	....	....	....	....	....	....	....	....	....	....	....	....	....	....	....	....	....
1998-99	Tappara Tampere	Finland	51	6	8	14	119	....	....	....	....	....	....	....	....	....	....	....	....	....	....	....	....	....	....
99-2000	Tappara Tampere	Finland	50	8	24	32	160	....	....	....	....	....	....	....	....	....	4	1	2	3	10	....	....	....	....
2000-01	Albany River Rats	AHL	79	8	28	36	117	....	....	....	....	....	....	....	....	....	....	....	....	....	....	....	....	....	....
2001-02	**New Jersey**	**NHL**	**1**	**1**	**0**	**1**	**2**	**0**	**0**	**0**	**1**	**100.0**	**–1**	**0**	**0.0**	**20:23**	....	....	....	....	....	....	....	....	....
	Albany River Rats	AHL	9	0	3	3	10	....	....	....	....	....	....	....	....	....	....	....	....	....	....	....	....	....	....
	Tampa Bay	**NHL**	**3**	**0**	**0**	**0**	**4**	**0**	**0**	**0**	**0**	**0.0**	**–1**	**0**	**0.0**	**10:58**	....	....	....	....	....	....	....	....	....
	Springfield	AHL	53	7	25	32	57	....	....	....	....	....	....	....	....	....	....	....	....	....	....	....	....	....	....
2002-03	Binghamton	AHL	26	2	15	17	62	....	....	....	....	....	....	....	....	....	....	....	....	....	....	....	....	....	....
	Washington	**NHL**	**6**	**1**	**0**	**1**	**0**	**0**	**0**	**1**	**7**	**14.3**	**–1**	**0**	**0.0**	**19:33**	....	....	....	....	....	....	....	....	....
	Portland Pirates	AHL	44	8	22	30	77	....	....	....	....	....	....	....	....	....	....	....	....	....	....	....	....	....	....
2003-04	**Washington**	**NHL**	**37**	**2**	**12**	**14**	**30**	**2**	**0**	**0**	**44**	**4.5**	**–10**	**0**	**0.0**	**23:02**	....	....	....	....	....	....	....	....	....
	Portland Pirates	AHL	13	1	8	9	10	....	....	....	....	....	....	....	....	....	....	....	....	....	....	....	....	....	....
2004-05	Brynas IF Gavle	Sweden	13	6	0	6	43	....	....	....	....	....	....	....	....	....	....	....	....	....	....	....	....	....	....
	Karpat Oulu	Finland	32	5	10	15	58	....	....	....	....	....	....	....	....	....	12	1	5	6	12	....	....	....	....
	NHL Totals		**47**	**4**	**12**	**16**	**36**	**2**	**0**	**1**	**52**	**7.7**		**0**	**0.0**	**21:46**	....	....	....	....	....	....	....	....	....

Traded to **Tampa Bay** by **New Jersey** with Sascha Goc and the rights to Anton But for Andrei Zyuzin, November 9, 2001. Traded to **Ottawa** by **Tampa Bay** for Ottawa's 7th round choice (Fredrik Norrena) in 2002 Entry Draft, June 23, 2002. Traded to **Washington** by **Ottawa** for Dean Melanson, December 16, 2002. Signed as a free agent by **Brynas** (Sweden), September 25, 2004. Signed as a free agent by **Karpat** (Finland), November 10, 2004.

BOUWMEESTER, Jay

(BOW-mee-stuhr, JAY) **FLA.**

Defense. Shoots left. 6'4", 210 lbs. Born, Edmonton, Alta., September 27, 1983. Florida's 1st choice, 3rd overall, in 2002 Entry Draft.

			Regular Season														Playoffs								
Season	Club	League	GP	G	A	Pts	PIM	PP	SH	GW	S	%	+/-	TF	F%	Min	GP	G	A	Pts	PIM	PP	SH	GW	Min
1998-99	Edmonton SSAC	AMHL	32	14	29	43	36	....	....	....	....	....	....	....	....	....	....	....	....	....	....	....	....	....	....
	Medicine Hat	WHL	8	2	1	3	2	....	....	....	....	....	....	....	....	....	....	....	....	....	....	....	....	....	....
99-2000	Medicine Hat	WHL	64	13	21	34	26	....	....	....	....	....	....	....	....	....	....	....	....	....	....	....	....	....	....
2000-01	Medicine Hat	WHL	61	14	39	53	44	....	....	....	....	....	....	....	....	....	....	....	....	....	....	....	....	....	....
2001-02	Medicine Hat	WHL	61	11	50	61	42	....	....	....	....	....	....	....	....	....	....	....	....	....	....	....	....	....	....
2002-03	**Florida**	**NHL**	**82**	**4**	**12**	**16**	**14**	**2**	**0**	**0**	**110**	**3.6**	**–29**	**0**	**0.0**	**20:09**	....	....	....	....	....	....	....	....	....
2003-04	**Florida**	**NHL**	**61**	**2**	**18**	**20**	**30**	**0**	**0**	**0**	**85**	**2.4**	**–15**	**0**	**0.0**	**23:02**	....	....	....	....	....	....	....	....	....
	San Antonio	AHL	2	0	1	1	2	....	....	....	....	....	....	....	....	....	....	....	....	....	....	....	....	....	....
2004-05	San Antonio	AHL	64	4	13	17	50	....	....	....	....	....	....	....	....	....	....	....	....	....	....	....	....	....	....
	Chicago Wolves	AHL	18	6	3	9	12	....	....	....	....	....	....	....	....	....	18	0	0	0	14	....	....	....	....
	NHL Totals		**143**	**6**	**30**	**36**	**44**	**2**	**0**	**0**	**195**	**3.1**		**0**	**0.0**	**21:23**	....	....	....	....	....	....	....	....	....

WHL East First All-Star Team (2002) • NHL All-Rookie Team (2003)

Loaned to **Chicago** (AHL) by **Florida** (San Antonio-AHL) for cash, March 8, 2005.

BOYES, Brad

(BOIZ, BRAD) **BOS.**

Center. Shoots right. 6'1", 195 lbs. Born, Mississauga, Ont., April 17, 1982. Toronto's 1st choice, 24th overall, in 2000 Entry Draft.

			Regular Season														Playoffs								
Season	Club	League	GP	G	A	Pts	PIM	PP	SH	GW	S	%	+/-	TF	F%	Min	GP	G	A	Pts	PIM	PP	SH	GW	Min
1997-98	Mississauga Reps	MTHL	44	27	50	77	....	....	....	....	....	....	....	....	....	....	....	....	....	....	....	....	....	....	....
1998-99	Erie Otters	OHL	59	24	36	60	30	....	....	....	....	....	....	....	....	....	5	1	2	3	10	....	....	....	....
99-2000	Erie Otters	OHL	68	36	46	82	38	....	....	....	....	....	....	....	....	....	13	6	8	14	10	....	....	....	....
2000-01	Erie Otters	OHL	59	45	45	90	42	....	....	....	....	....	....	....	....	....	15	10	13	23	8	....	....	....	....
2001-02	Erie Otters	OHL	47	36	41	77	42	....	....	....	....	....	....	....	....	....	21	22	*19	41	27	....	....	....	....
2002-03	St. John's	AHL	65	23	28	51	45	....	....	....	....	....	....	....	....	....	....	....	....	....	....	....	....	....	....
	Cleveland Barons	AHL	15	7	6	13	21	....	....	....	....	....	....	....	....	....	....	....	....	....	....	....	....	....	....
2003-04	**San Jose**	**NHL**	**1**	**0**	**0**	**0**	**2**	**0**	**0**	**0**	**0**	**0.0**	**–2**	**0**	**0.0**	**13:03**	....	....	....	....	....	....	....	....	....
	Cleveland Barons	AHL	61	25	35	60	38	....	....	....	....	....	....	....	....	....	....	....	....	....	....	....	....	....	....
	Providence Bruins	AHL	17	6	6	12	13	....	....	....	....	....	....	....	....	....	2	1	0	1	0	....	....	....	....
2004-05	Providence Bruins	AHL	80	33	42	75	58	....	....	....	....	....	....	....	....	....	16	8	7	15	23	....	....	....	....
	NHL Totals		**1**	**0**	**0**	**0**	**2**	**0**	**0**	**0**	**0**	**0.0**		**0**	**0.0**	**13:03**	....	....	....	....	....	....	....	....	....

Canadian Major Junior Scholastic Player of the Year (2000) • OHL Second All-Star Team (2001) • OHL First All-Star Team (2002) • Canadian Major Junior Sportsman of the Year (2002) • AHL All-Rookie Team (2003) • AHL Second All-Star Team (2004)

Traded to **San Jose** by **Toronto** with Alyn McCauley and Toronto's 1st round choice (later traded to Boston – Boston selected Mark Stuart) in 2003 Entry Draft for Owen Nolan, March 5, 2003. Traded to **Boston** by **San Jose** for Jeff Jillson, March 9, 2004.

BOYLE, Dan

(BOIL, DAN) **T.B.**

Defense. Shoots right. 5'11", 190 lbs. Born, Ottawa, Ont., July 12, 1976.

			Regular Season														Playoffs								
Season	Club	League	GP	G	A	Pts	PIM	PP	SH	GW	S	%	+/-	TF	F%	Min	GP	G	A	Pts	PIM	PP	SH	GW	Min
1992-93	Gloucester	CJHL	55	22	51	73	60	....	....	....	....	....	....	....	....	....	....	....	....	....	....	....	....	....	....
1993-94	Gloucester	CJHL	53	27	54	81	155	....	....	....	....	....	....	....	....	....	....	....	....	....	....	....	....	....	....
1994-95	Miami-Ohio	CCHA	35	8	18	26	24	....	....	....	....	....	....	....	....	....	....	....	....	....	....	....	....	....	....
1995-96	Miami-Ohio	CCHA	36	7	20	27	70	....	....	....	....	....	....	....	....	....	....	....	....	....	....	....	....	....	....
1996-97	Miami-Ohio	CCHA	40	11	43	54	52	....	....	....	....	....	....	....	....	....	....	....	....	....	....	....	....	....	....
1997-98	Miami-Ohio	CCHA	37	14	26	40	58	....	....	....	....	....	....	....	....	....	....	....	....	....	....	....	....	....	....
1998-99	**Florida**	**NHL**	**22**	**3**	**5**	**8**	**6**	**1**	**0**	**1**	**31**	**9.7**	**0**	**1**	**100.0**	**18:50**	....	....	....	....	....	....	....	....	....
	Kentucky	AHL	53	8	34	42	87	....	....	....	....	....	....	....	....	....	12	3	5	8	16	....	....	....	....
99-2000	**Florida**	**NHL**	**13**	**0**	**3**	**3**	**4**	**0**	**0**	**0**	**9**	**0.0**	**–2**	**0**	**0.0**	**16:57**	....	....	....	....	....	....	....	....	....
	Louisville Panthers	AHL	58	14	38	52	75	....	....	....	....	....	....	....	....	....	4	0	2	2	8	....	....	....	....
2000-01	**Florida**	**NHL**	**69**	**4**	**18**	**22**	**28**	**1**	**0**	**0**	**83**	**4.8**	**–14**	**0**	**0.0**	**16:56**	....	....	....	....	....	....	....	....	....
	Louisville Panthers	AHL	6	0	5	5	12	....	....	....	....	....	....	....	....	....	....	....	....	....	....	....	....	....	....
2001-02	**Florida**	**NHL**	**25**	**3**	**3**	**6**	**12**	**1**	**0**	**0**	**31**	**9.7**	**–1**	**2**	**50.0**	**15:40**	....	....	....	....	....	....	....	....	....
	Tampa Bay	**NHL**	**41**	**5**	**15**	**20**	**27**	**2**	**0**	**1**	**68**	**7.4**	**–15**	**0**	**0.0**	**22:28**	....	....	....	....	....	....	....	....	....
2002-03	**Tampa Bay**	**NHL**	**77**	**13**	**40**	**53**	**44**	**8**	**0**	**1**	**136**	**9.6**	**9**	**2**	**0.0**	**24:31**	**11**	**0**	**7**	**7**	**6**	**0**	**0**	**0**	**27:45**
2003-04♦	**Tampa Bay**	**NHL**	**78**	**9**	**30**	**39**	**60**	**3**	**0**	**2**	**137**	**6.6**	**23**	**0**	**0.0**	**22:46**	**23**	**2**	**8**	**10**	**16**	**1**	**0**	**0**	**21:27**
2004-05	Djurgarden	Sweden	32	9	9	18	47	....	....	....	....	....	....	....	....	....	12	2	3	5	26	....	....	....	....
	NHL Totals		**325**	**37**	**114**	**151**	**181**	**16**	**0**	**5**	**495**	**7.5**		**5**	**40.0**	**20:52**	**34**	**2**	**15**	**17**	**22**	**1**	**0**	**0**	**23:29**

CCHA First All-Star Team (1997, 1998) • NCAA West First All-American Team (1997, 1998) • AHL All-Rookie Team (1999 • AHL Second All-Star Team (1999, 2000)

Signed as a free agent by **Florida**, March 30, 1998. Traded to **Tampa Bay** by **Florida** for Tampa Bay's 5th round choice (Martin Tuma) in 2003 Entry Draft, January 7, 2002. Signed as a free agent by **Djurgarden** (Sweden), November 14, 2004.

BOYNTON, Nick

(BOIN-tuhn, NIHK) **BOS.**

Defense. Shoots right. 6'2", 211 lbs. Born, Nobleton, Ont., January 14, 1979. Boston's 1st choice, 21st overall, in 1999 Entry Draft.

			Regular Season														Playoffs								
Season	Club	League	GP	G	A	Pts	PIM	PP	SH	GW	S	%	+/-	TF	F%	Min	GP	G	A	Pts	PIM	PP	SH	GW	Min
1993-94	Caledon	MTJHL	4	0	1	1	0	....	....	....	....	....	....	....	....	....	....	....	....	....	....	....	....	....	....
1994-95	Caledon	MTJHL	44	10	35	45	139	....	....	....	....	....	....	....	....	....	....	....	....	....	....	....	....	....	....
1995-96	Ottawa 67's	OHL	64	10	14	24	90	....	....	....	....	....	....	....	....	....	4	0	3	3	10	....	....	....	....
1996-97	Ottawa 67's	OHL	63	13	51	64	143	....	....	....	....	....	....	....	....	....	24	4	*24	28	38	....	....	....	....
1997-98	Ottawa 67's	OHL	40	7	31	38	94	....	....	....	....	....	....	....	....	....	13	0	4	4	24	....	....	....	....
1998-99	Ottawa 67's	OHL	51	11	48	59	83	....	....	....	....	....	....	....	....	....	9	1	9	10	18	....	....	....	....
99-2000	**Boston**	**NHL**	**5**	**0**	**0**	**0**	**0**	**0**	**0**	**0**	**6**	**0.0**	**–5**	**0**	**0.0**	**21:21**	....	....	....	....	....	....	....	....	....
	Providence Bruins	AHL	53	5	14	19	66	....	....	....	....	....	....	....	....	....	12	1	0	1	6	....	....	....	....
2000-01	**Boston**	**NHL**	**1**	**0**	**0**	**0**	**0**	**0**	**0**	**0**	**1**	**0.0**	**–1**	**0**	**0.0**	**14:27**	....	....	....	....	....	....	....	....	....
	Providence Bruins	AHL	78	6	27	33	105	....	....	....	....	....	....	....	....	....	17	0	2	2	35	....	....	....	....
2001-02	**Boston**	**NHL**	**80**	**4**	**14**	**18**	**107**	**0**	**0**	**1**	**136**	**2.9**	**18**	**0**	**0.0**	**18:30**	**6**	**1**	**2**	**3**	**8**	**0**	**0**	**0**	**21:30**
2002-03	**Boston**	**NHL**	**78**	**7**	**17**	**24**	**99**	**0**	**1**	**2**	**160**	**4.4**	**8**	**1**	**0.0**	**22:41**	**5**	**0**	**1**	**1**	**4**	**0**	**0**	**0**	**23:22**
2003-04	**Boston**	**NHL**	**81**	**6**	**24**	**30**	**98**	**1**	**1**	**1**	**178**	**3.4**	**17**	**0**	**0.0**	**22:32**	**7**	**0**	**2**	**2**	**2**	**0**	**0**	**0**	**24:44**
2004-05	Nottingham	Britain	9	1	3	4	4	....	....	....	....	....	....	....	....	....	6	1	2	3	22	....	....	....	....
	NHL Totals		**245**	**17**	**55**	**72**	**304**	**1**	**2**	**4**	**481**	**3.5**		**1**	**0.0**	**21:13**	**18**	**1**	**5**	**6**	**14**	**0**	**0**	**0**	**23:16**

• Re-entered NHL Entry Draft. Originally Washington's 1st choice, 9th overall, in 1997 Entry Draft.

OHL All-Rookie Team (1996) • Memorial Cup Tournament All-Star Team (1999) • Stafford Smythe Memorial Trophy (Memorial Cup Tournament MVP) (1999) • NHL All-Rookie Team (2002)

Played in NHL All-Star Game (2004)

Signed as a free agent by **Nottingham** (Britain), January 26, 2005.

BRADLEY, Matt

(BRAD-lee, MAT) **WSH.**

Right wing. Shoots right. 6'3", 199 lbs. Born, Stittsville, Ont., June 13, 1978. San Jose's 4th choice, 102nd overall, in 1996 Entry Draft.

			Regular Season														Playoffs								
Season	Club	League	GP	G	A	Pts	PIM	PP	SH	GW	S	%	+/-	TF	F%	Min	GP	G	A	Pts	PIM	PP	SH	GW	Min
1994-95	Cumberland	CJHL	49	13	20	33	18	....	....	....	....	....	....	....	....	....	....	....	....	....	....	....	....	....	....
1995-96	Kingston	OHL	55	10	14	24	17	....	....	....	....	....	....	....	....	....	6	0	1	1	6	....	....	....	....
1996-97	Kingston	OHL	65	24	24	48	41	....	....	....	....	....	....	....	....	....	5	0	4	4	2	....	....	....	....
	Kentucky	AHL	1	0	1	1	0	....	....	....	....	....	....	....	....	....	....	....	....	....	....	....	....	....	....
1997-98	Kingston	OHL	55	33	50	83	24	....	....	....	....	....	....	....	....	....	8	3	4	7	7	....	....	....	....
1998-99	Kentucky	AHL	79	23	20	43	57	....	....	....	....	....	....	....	....	....	10	1	4	5	4	....	....	....	....
99-2000	Kentucky	AHL	80	22	19	41	81	....	....	....	....	....	....	....	....	....	9	6	3	9	9	....	....	....	....
2000-01	**San Jose**	**NHL**	**21**	**1**	**1**	**2**	**19**	**0**	**0**	**0**	**16**	**6.3**	**0**	**0**	**0.0**	**6:58**	....	....	....	....	....	....	....	....	....
	Kentucky	AHL	22	5	8	13	16	....	....	....	....	....	....	....	....	....	1	1	0	1	5	....	....	....	....
2001-02	**San Jose**	**NHL**	**54**	**9**	**13**	**22**	**43**	**0**	**0**	**2**	**63**	**14.3**	**22**	**2**	**0.0**	**8:27**	**10**	**0**	**0**	**0**	**0**	**0**	**0**	**0**	**5:16**
2002-03	**San Jose**	**NHL**	**46**	**2**	**3**	**5**	**37**	**0**	**0**	**0**	**21**	**9.5**	**–1**	**1**	**0.0**	**7:54**	....	....	....	....	....	....	....	....	....
2003-04	**Pittsburgh**	**NHL**	**82**	**7**	**9**	**16**	**65**	**0**	**0**	**1**	**85**	**8.2**	**–27**	**29**	**41.4**	**12:48**	....	....	....	....	....	....	....	....	....
2004-05	Bulldogs Dornbirn	Austria-2	6	5	2	7	18	....	....	....	....	....	....	....	....	....	....	....	....	....	....	....	....	....	....
	NHL Totals		**203**	**19**	**26**	**45**	**164**	**0**	**0**	**3**	**185**	**10.3**		**32**	**37.5**	**9:56**	**10**	**0**	**0**	**0**	**0**	**0**	**0**	**0**	**5:16**

Traded to **Pittsburgh** by **San Jose** for Wayne Primeau, March 11, 2003. Signed as a free agent by **Dornbirn** (Austria-2), November 14, 2004. Signed as a free agent by **Washington**, August 18, 2005.

BRANDNER, Christoph

(BRAND-nuhr, KRIH-stahf)

Left wing. Shoots left. 6'4", 224 lbs. Born, Bruck an der Mur, Austria, July 5, 1975. Minnesota's 8th choice, 237th overall, in 2002 Entry Draft.

			Regular Season														Playoffs								
Season	Club	League	GP	G	A	Pts	PIM	PP	SH	GW	S	%	+/-	TF	F%	Min	GP	G	A	Pts	PIM	PP	SH	GW	Min
1997-98	Klagenfurter AC	Austria	27	12	7	19	18	....	....	....	....	....	....	....	....	....	....	....	....	....	....	....	....	....	....
	Klagenfurter AC	Alpenliga	STATISTICS NOT AVAILABLE																						
1998-99	Klagenfurter AC	Austria	21	8	8	16	6	....	....	....	....	....	....	....	....	....	....	....	....	....	....	....	....	....	....
	Klagenfurter AC	Alpenliga	33	23	10	33	16	....	....	....	....	....	....	....	....	....	....	....	....	....	....	....	....	....	....
99-2000	Klagenfurter AC	IEHL	34	29	19	48	30	....	....	....	....	....	....	....	....	....	....	....	....	....	....	....	....	....	....
	Klagenfurter AC	Austria	16	8	3	11	20	....	....	....	....	....	....	....	....	....	....	....	....	....	....	....	....	....	....
2000-01	Klagenfurter AC	Austria	6	6	2	8	4	....	....	....	....	....	....	....	....	....	....	....	....	....	....	....	....	....	....
	Krefeld Pinguine	Germany	59	24	24	48	34	....	....	....	....	....	....	....	....	....	....	....	....	....	....	....	....	....	....
2001-02	Krefeld Pinguine	Germany	50	30	25	55	20	....	....	....	....	....	....	....	....	....	3	1	0	1	4	....	....	....	....
	Austria	Olympics	4	0	1	1	2	....	....	....	....	....	....	....	....	....	....	....	....	....	....	....	....	....	....
2002-03	Krefeld Pinguine	Germany	49	*28	17	45	26	....	....	....	....	....	....	....	....	....	14	9	9	18	8	....	....	....	....
2003-04	**Minnesota**	**NHL**	**35**	**4**	**5**	**9**	**8**	**1**	**0**	**0**	**50**	**8.0**	**–2**	**4**	**50.0**	**13:20**	....	....	....	....	....	....	....	....	....
	Houston Aeros	AHL	37	7	7	14	18	....	....	....	....	....	....	....	....	....	2	1	0	1	0	....	....	....	....
2004-05	Houston Aeros	AHL	26	5	3	8	15	....	....	....	....	....	....	....	....	....	....	....	....	....	....	....	....	....	....
	NHL Totals		**35**	**4**	**5**	**9**	**8**	**1**	**0**	**0**	**50**	**8.0**		**4**	**50.0**	**13:20**	....	....	....	....	....	....	....	....	....

Signed as a free agent by **Sodertalje** (Sweden), April 12, 2005.

BRASHEAR, Donald

(bra-SHEER, DAWN-ohld) **PHI.**

Left wing. Shoots left. 6'2", 235 lbs. Born, Bedford, IN, January 7, 1972.

			Regular Season														Playoffs								
Season	Club	League	GP	G	A	Pts	PIM	PP	SH	GW	S	%	+/-	TF	F%	Min	GP	G	A	Pts	PIM	PP	SH	GW	Min
1988-89	Ste-Foy	QAAA	10	1	2	3	10	....	....	....	....	....	....	....	....	....	....	....	....	....	....	....	....	....	....
1989-90	Longueuil	QMJHL	64	12	14	26	169	....	....	....	....	....	....	....	....	....	7	0	0	0	11	....	....	....	....
1990-91	Longueuil	QMJHL	68	12	26	38	195	....	....	....	....	....	....	....	....	....	8	0	3	3	33	....	....	....	....
1991-92	Verdun	QMJHL	65	18	24	42	283	....	....	....	....	....	....	....	....	....	18	4	2	6	98	....	....	....	....
1992-93	Fredericton	AHL	76	11	3	14	261	....	....	....	....	....	....	....	....	....	5	0	0	0	8	....	....	....	....
1993-94	**Montreal**	**NHL**	**14**	**2**	**2**	**4**	**34**	**0**	**0**	**0**	**15**	**13.3**	**0**	....	....	....	**2**	**0**	**0**	**0**	**0**	**0**	**0**	**0**	....
	Fredericton	AHL	62	38	28	66	250	....	....	....	....	....	....	....	....	....	....	....	....	....	....	....	....	....	....
1994-95	Fredericton	AHL	29	10	9	19	182	....	....	....	....	....	....	....	....	....	17	7	5	12	77	....	....	....	....
	Montreal	**NHL**	**20**	**1**	**1**	**2**	**63**	**0**	**0**	**1**	**10**	**10.0**	**–5**	....	....	....	....	....	....	....	....	....	....	....	....
1995-96	**Montreal**	**NHL**	**67**	**0**	**4**	**4**	**223**	**0**	**0**	**0**	**25**	**0.0**	**–10**	....	....	....	**6**	**0**	**0**	**0**	**2**	**0**	**0**	**0**	....
1996-97	**Montreal**	**NHL**	**10**	**0**	**0**	**0**	**38**	**0**	**0**	**0**	**6**	**0.0**	**–2**	....	....	....	....	....	....	....	....	....	....	....	....
	Vancouver	**NHL**	**59**	**8**	**5**	**13**	**207**	**0**	**0**	**2**	**55**	**14.5**	**–6**	....	....	....	....	....	....	....	....	....	....	....	....
1997-98	**Vancouver**	**NHL**	**77**	**9**	**9**	**18**	***372**	**0**	**0**	**1**	**64**	**14.1**	**–9**	....	....	....	....	....	....	....	....	....	....	....	....
1998-99	**Vancouver**	**NHL**	**82**	**8**	**10**	**18**	**209**	**2**	**0**	**1**	**112**	**7.1**	**–25**	**6**	**16.7**	**13:25**	....	....	....	....	....	....	....	....	....
99-2000	**Vancouver**	**NHL**	**60**	**11**	**2**	**13**	**136**	**1**	**0**	**3**	**83**	**13.3**	**–9**	**11**	**36.4**	**13:07**	....	....	....	....	....	....	....	....	....
2000-01	**Vancouver**	**NHL**	**79**	**9**	**19**	**28**	**145**	**0**	**0**	**1**	**127**	**7.1**	**0**	**6**	**16.7**	**13:27**	**4**	**0**	**0**	**0**	**0**	**0**	**0**	**0**	**14:47**
2001-02	**Vancouver**	**NHL**	**31**	**5**	**8**	**13**	**90**	**1**	**0**	**0**	**45**	**11.1**	**–8**	**4**	**25.0**	**13:58**	....	....	....	....	....	....	....	....	....
	Philadelphia	**NHL**	**50**	**4**	**15**	**19**	**109**	**0**	**0**	**2**	**62**	**6.5**	**0**	**1**	**0.0**	**13:00**	**5**	**0**	**0**	**0**	**19**	**0**	**0**	**0**	**9:55**
2002-03	**Philadelphia**	**NHL**	**80**	**8**	**17**	**25**	**161**	**0**	**0**	**1**	**99**	**8.1**	**5**	**27**	**33.3**	**13:23**	**13**	**1**	**2**	**3**	**21**	**0**	**0**	**0**	**11:09**
2003-04	**Philadelphia**	**NHL**	**64**	**6**	**7**	**13**	**212**	**0**	**0**	**0**	**72**	**8.3**	**–1**	**18**	**38.9**	**11:02**	**18**	**1**	**3**	**4**	**61**	**1**	**0**	**0**	**8:56**
2004-05	Quebec RadioX	QNAHL	47	18	32	50	260	....	....	....	....	....	....	....	....	....	8	4	6	10	42	....	....	....	....
	NHL Totals		**693**	**71**	**99**	**170**	**1999**	**4**	**0**	**12**	**775**	**9.2**		**73**	**31.5**	**13:02**	**48**	**2**	**5**	**7**	**103**	**1**	**0**	**0**	**10:21**

Signed as a free agent by **Montreal**, July 28, 1992. Traded to **Vancouver** by **Montreal** for Jassen Cullimore, November 13, 1996. Traded to **Philadelphia** by **Vancouver** with Vancouver's 6th round choice (later traded to Columbus – Columbus selected Jaroslav Balastik) in 2002 Entry Draft for Jan Hlavac and Tampa Bay's 3rd round choice (previously acquired, Vancouver selected Brett Skinner) in 2002 Entry Draft, December 17, 2001. Signed as a free agent by **Quebec** (QNAHL), September 21, 2004.

BRENDL, Pavel

(BREHN-duhl, PAH-vehl) **CAR.**

Right wing. Shoots right. 6'1", 204 lbs. Born, Opocno, Czech., March 23, 1981. NY Rangers' 1st choice, 4th overall, in 1999 Entry Draft.

			Regular Season														Playoffs								
Season	Club	League	GP	G	A	Pts	PIM	PP	SH	GW	S	%	+/-	TF	F%	Min	GP	G	A	Pts	PIM	PP	SH	GW	Min
1996-97	HC Olomouc Jr.	CzRep-Jr.	40	35	17	52	....	....	....	....	....	....	....	....	....	....	....	....	....	....	....	....	....	....	....
1997-98	HC Olomouc Jr.	CzRep-Jr.	38	29	23	52	....	....	....	....	....	....	....	....	....	....	....	....	....	....	....	....	....	....	....
	HC Olomouc	CzRep-2	12	1	1	2	....	....	....	....	....	....	....	....	....	....	....	....	....	....	....	....	....	....	....
1998-99	Calgary Hitmen	WHL	68	*73	61	*134	40	....	....	....	....	....	....	....	....	....	20	*21	*25	*46	18	....	....	....	....
99-2000	Calgary Hitmen	WHL	61	*59	52	111	94	....	....	....	....	....	....	....	....	....	10	7	12	19	8	....	....	....	....
	Hartford	AHL	....	....	....	....	....	....	....	....	....	....	....	....	....	....	2	0	0	0	0	....	....	....	....
2000-01	Calgary Hitmen	WHL	49	40	35	75	66	....	....	....	....	....	....	....	....	....	10	7	6	13	6	....	....	....	....
2001-02	**Philadelphia**	**NHL**	**8**	**1**	**0**	**1**	**2**	**0**	**0**	**0**	**6**	**16.7**	**–1**	**21**	**19.1**	**8:59**	**2**	**0**	**0**	**0**	**0**	**0**	**0**	**0**	**11:28**
	Philadelphia	AHL	64	15	22	37	22	....	....	....	....	....	....	....	....	....	5	4	1	5	0	....	....	....	....
2002-03	**Philadelphia**	**NHL**	**42**	**5**	**7**	**12**	**4**	**1**	**0**	**1**	**80**	**6.3**	**8**	**9**	**22.2**	**10:19**	....	....	....	....	....	....	....	....	....
	Carolina	**NHL**	**8**	**0**	**1**	**1**	**2**	**0**	**0**	**0**	**14**	**0.0**	**–3**	**2**	**50.0**	**15:05**	....	....	....	....	....	....	....	....	....
2003-04	**Carolina**	**NHL**	**18**	**5**	**3**	**8**	**8**	**1**	**0**	**1**	**27**	**18.5**	**0**	**1**	**0.0**	**14:48**	....	....	....	....	....	....	....	....	....
	Lowell	AHL	33	17	16	33	34	....	....	....	....	....	....	....	....	....	....	....	....	....	....	....	....	....	....
2004-05	HC Ocelari Trinec	CzRep	2	0	0	0	0	....	....	....	....	....	....	....	....	....	....	....	....	....	....	....	....	....	....
	HC Olomouc	CzRep-2	3	0	0	0	12	....	....	....	....	....	....	....	....	....	....	....	....	....	....	....	....	....	....
	Jokipojat Joensuu	Finland-2	21	9	10	19	48	....	....	....	....	....	....	....	....	....	....	....	....	....	....	....	....	....	....
	HC Thurgau	Swiss-2	4	3	0	3	4	....	....	....	....	....	....	....	....	....	....	....	....	....	....	....	....	....	....
	NHL Totals		**76**	**11**	**11**	**22**	**16**	**2**	**0**	**2**	**127**	**8.7**		**33**	**21.2**	**11:45**	**2**	**0**	**0**	**0**	**0**	**0**	**0**	**0**	**11:28**

WHL East First All-Star Team (1999) • WHL Rookie of the Year (1999) • Canadian Major Junior First All-Star Team (1999) • Canadian Major Junior Rookie of the Year (1999) • Memorial Cup Tournament All-Star Team (1999) • WHL East Second All-Star Team (2000)

Traded to **Philadelphia** by **NY Rangers** with Jan Hlavac, Kim Johnsson and NY Rangers' 3rd round choice (Stefan Ruzicka) in 2003 Entry Draft for Eric Lindros, August 20, 2001. Traded to **Carolina** by **Philadelphia** with Bruno St. Jacques for Sami Kapanen and Ryan Bast, February 7, 2003. Signed as a free agent by **Trinec** (CzRep), September 17, 2004. Signed as a free agent by **Olomouc** (CzRep-2), October 14, 2004. Signed as a free agent by **Jokipojat** (Finland-2), November 15, 2004. Signed as a free agent by **Thurgau** (Swiss-2), December 21, 2004. Signed as a free agent by **Jokipojat** (Finland-2), January 13, 2005.

BRENNAN, Kip

(BREHN-nan, KIHP) **ANA.**

Left wing. Shoots left. 6'4", 230 lbs. Born, Kingston, Ont., August 27, 1980. Los Angeles' 4th choice, 103rd overall, in 1998 Entry Draft.

			Regular Season														Playoffs								
Season	Club	League	GP	G	A	Pts	PIM	PP	SH	GW	S	%	+/-	TF	F%	Min	GP	G	A	Pts	PIM	PP	SH	GW	Min
1995-96	St. Mike's B's	OPJHL	40	0	11	11	155	....	....	....	....	....	....	....	....	....	....	....	....	....	....	....	....	....	....
1996-97	Windsor Spitfires	OHL	42	0	10	10	156	....	....	....	....	....	....	....	....	....	5	0	1	1	16	....	....	....	....
1997-98	Windsor Spitfires	OHL	24	0	7	7	103	....	....	....	....	....	....	....	....	....	....	....	....	....	....	....	....	....	....
	Sudbury Wolves	OHL	24	0	3	3	85	....	....	....	....	....	....	....	....	....	....	....	....	....	....	....	....	....	....
1998-99	Sudbury Wolves	OHL	38	9	12	21	160	....	....	....	....	....	....	....	....	....	....	....	....	....	....	....	....	....	....
99-2000	Sudbury Wolves	OHL	55	16	16	32	228	....	....	....	....	....	....	....	....	....	12	3	3	6	67	....	....	....	....
2000-01	Lowell	AHL	23	2	3	5	117	....	....	....	....	....	....	....	....	....	....	....	....	....	....	....	....	....	....
	Sudbury Wolves	OHL	27	7	14	21	94	....	....	....	....	....	....	....	....	....	12	5	6	11	*92	....	....	....	....
2001-02	Manchester	AHL	44	4	1	5	269	....	....	....	....	....	....	....	....	....	4	0	1	1	26	....	....	....	....
	Los Angeles	**NHL**	**4**	**0**	**0**	**0**	**22**	**0**	**0**	**0**	**0**	**0.0**	**1**	**0**	**0.0**	**4:40**	....	....	....	....	....	....	....	....	....
2002-03	**Los Angeles**	**NHL**	**19**	**0**	**0**	**0**	**57**	**0**	**0**	**0**	**6**	**0.0**	**0**	**2**	**0.0**	**4:52**	....	....	....	....	....	....	....	....	....
	Manchester	AHL	35	3	2	5	195	....	....	....	....	....	....	....	....	....	3	0	0	0	0	....	....	....	....
2003-04	**Los Angeles**	**NHL**	**18**	**1**	**0**	**1**	**79**	**0**	**0**	**0**	**6**	**16.7**	**–1**	**0**	**0.0**	**5:01**	....	....	....	....	....	....	....	....	....
	Manchester	AHL	2	0	0	0	6	....	....	....	....	....	....	....	....	....	....	....	....	....	....	....	....	....	....
	Atlanta	**NHL**	**5**	**0**	**0**	**0**	**17**	**0**	**0**	**0**	**2**	**0.0**	**0**	**0**	**0.0**	**3:37**	....	....	....	....	....	....	....	....	....
2004-05	Chicago Wolves	AHL	48	7	6	13	267	....	....	....	....	....	....	....	....	....	18	1	1	2	*105	....	....	....	....
	NHL Totals		**46**	**1**	**0**	**1**	**175**	**0**	**0**	**0**	**14**	**7.1**		**2**	**0.0**	**4:46**	....	....	....	....	....	....	....	....	....

Traded to **Atlanta** by **Los Angeles** for Jeff Cowan, March 9, 2004. • Spent majority 2003-04 season as a healthy reserve. Signed as a free agent by **Chicago** (AHL), September 27, 2004. Traded to **Anaheim** by **Atlanta** for Mark Popovic, August 25, 2005.

BRENNAN, Rich

(BREHN-nan, RIHCH)

Defense. Shoots right. 6'2", 200 lbs. Born, Schenectady, NY, November 26, 1972. Quebec's 3rd choice, 46th overall, in 1991 Entry Draft.

			Regular Season														Playoffs								
Season	Club	League	GP	G	A	Pts	PIM	PP	SH	GW	S	%	+/-	TF	F%	Min	GP	G	A	Pts	PIM	PP	SH	GW	Min
1988-89	Albany	High-NY	25	17	30	47	57	....	....	....	....	....	....	....	....	....	....	....	....	....	....	....	....	....	....
1989-90	Tabor	High-MA	33	12	14	26	68	....	....	....	....	....	....	....	....	....	....	....	....	....	....	....	....	....	....
1990-91	Tabor	High-MA	34	13	37	50	91	....	....	....	....	....	....	....	....	....	....	....	....	....	....	....	....	....	....
1991-92	Boston University	H-East	30	4	13	17	50	....	....	....	....	....	....	....	....	....	....	....	....	....	....	....	....	....	....
1992-93	Boston University	H-East	40	9	11	20	68	....	....	....	....	....	....	....	....	....	....	....	....	....	....	....	....	....	....
1993-94	Boston University	H-East	41	8	27	35	82	....	....	....	....	....	....	....	....	....	....	....	....	....	....	....	....	....	....
1994-95	Boston University	H-East	31	5	22	27	56	....	....	....	....	....	....	....	....	....	....	....	....	....	....	....	....	....	....

			Regular Season														Playoffs								
Season	Club	League	GP	G	A	Pts	PIM	PP	SH	GW	S	%	+/-	TF	F%	Min	GP	G	A	Pts	PIM	PP	SH	GW	Min
1995-96	Brantford Smoke	ColHL	5	1	2	3	2	....	....	....	....	....	....	....	....	....	....	....	....	....	....	....	....	....	....
	Cornwall Aces	AHL	36	4	8	12	61	....	....	....	....	....	....	....	....	....	7	0	0	0	6	....	....	....	....
1996-97	**Colorado**	**NHL**	**2**	**0**	**0**	**0**	**0**	**0**	**0**	**0**	**0**	**0.0**	**0**	....	....	....	....	....	....	....	....	....	....	....	....
	Hershey Bears	AHL	74	11	45	56	88	....	....	....	....	....	....	....	....	....	23	2	*16	18	22	....	....	....	....
1997-98	**San Jose**	**NHL**	**11**	**1**	**2**	**3**	**2**	**1**	**0**	**0**	**24**	**4.2**	**–4**	....	....	....	....	....	....	....	....	....	....	....	....
	Kentucky	AHL	42	11	17	28	71	....	....	....	....	....	....	....	....	....	....	....	....	....	....	....	....	....	....
	Hartford	AHL	9	2	4	6	12	....	....	....	....	....	....	....	....	....	15	4	5	9	14	....	....	....	....
1998-99	**NY Rangers**	**NHL**	**24**	**1**	**3**	**4**	**23**	**0**	**0**	**0**	**36**	**2.8**	**–4**	**0**	**0.0**	**13:02**	....	....	....	....	....	....	....	....	....
	Hartford	AHL	47	4	24	28	42	....	....	....	....	....	....	....	....	....	....	....	....	....	....	....	....	....	....
99-2000	Lowell	AHL	67	15	30	45	110	....	....	....	....	....	....	....	....	....	7	1	5	6	0	....	....	....	....
2000-01	**Los Angeles**	**NHL**	**2**	**0**	**0**	**0**	**0**	**0**	**0**	**0**	**1**	**0.0**	**–3**	**0**	**0.0**	**14:44**	....	....	....	....	....	....	....	....	....
	Lowell	AHL	69	10	31	41	146	....	....	....	....	....	....	....	....	....	....	....	....	....	....	....	....	....	....
2001-02	**Nashville**	**NHL**	**4**	**0**	**0**	**0**	**2**	**0**	**0**	**0**	**0**	**0.0**	**0**	**0**	**0.0**	**14:31**	....	....	....	....	....	....	....	....	....
	Milwaukee	AHL	23	4	8	12	27	....	....	....	....	....	....	....	....	....	....	....	....	....	....	....	....	....	....
	Manchester	AHL	16	2	5	7	6	....	....	....	....	....	....	....	....	....	5	1	1	2	16	....	....	....	....
2002-03	**Boston**	**NHL**	**7**	**0**	**1**	**1**	**6**	**0**	**0**	**0**	**12**	**0.0**	**3**	**0**	**0.0**	**13:37**	....	....	....	....	....	....	....	....	....
	Providence Bruins	AHL	41	3	29	32	51	....	....	....	....	....	....	....	....	....	....	....	....	....	....	....	....	....	....
2003-04	Providence Bruins	AHL	56	12	15	27	47	....	....	....	....	....	....	....	....	....	2	0	1	1	2	....	....	....	....
2004-05	SC Bern	Swiss	23	5	5	10	24	....	....	....	....	....	....	....	....	....	....	....	....	....	....	....	....	....	....
	SC Langenthal	Swiss-2	1	0	2	2	0	....	....	....	....	....	....	....	....	....	....	....	....	....	....	....	....	....	....
	Augsburg	Germany	16	4	5	9	22	....	....	....	....	....	....	....	....	....	5	0	1	1	16	....	....	....	....
	NHL Totals		**50**	**2**	**6**	**8**	**33**	**1**	**0**	**0**	**73**	**2.7**		**0**	**0.0**	**13:24**	....	....	....	....	....	....	....	....	....

Hockey East First All-Star Team (1994) • NCAA East Second All-American Team (1994)

Rights transferred to **Colorado** after **Quebec** franchise relocated, June 21, 1995. Signed as a free agent by **San Jose**, July 9, 1997. Traded to **NY Rangers** by **San Jose** for Jason Muzzatti, March 24, 1998. Signed as a free agent by **Nashville**, September 23, 1999. Claimed by **Los Angeles** from **Nashville** in Waiver Draft, September 27, 1999. Signed as a free agent by **Nashville**, August 8, 2001. Traded to **Los Angeles** by **Nashville** for Brett Hauer, December 19, 2001. Signed as a free agent by **Boston**, July 18, 2002. Signed as a free agent by **Bern** (Swiss), June 30, 2004. Signed as a free agent by **Augsburg** (Germany), January 13, 2005.

BREWER, Eric
(BREW-uhr, AIR-ihk) **ST.L.**

Defense. Shoots left. 6'3", 225 lbs. Born, Vernon, B.C., April 17, 1979. NY Islanders' 2nd choice, 5th overall, in 1997 Entry Draft.

Season	Club	League	GP	G	A	Pts	PIM	PP	SH	GW	S	%	+/-	TF	F%	Min	GP	G	A	Pts	PIM	PP	SH	GW	Min
1994-95	Kamloops	BCAHA	40	19	19	38	62	....	....	....	....	....	....	....	....	....	....	....	....	....	....	....	....	....	....
1995-96	Prince George	WHL	63	4	10	14	25	....	....	....	....	....	....	....	....	....	....	....	....	....	....	....	....	....	....
1996-97	Prince George	WHL	71	5	24	29	81	....	....	....	....	....	....	....	....	....	15	2	4	6	16	....	....	....	....
1997-98	Prince George	WHL	34	5	28	33	45	....	....	....	....	....	....	....	....	....	11	4	2	6	19	....	....	....	....
1998-99	**NY Islanders**	**NHL**	**63**	**5**	**6**	**11**	**32**	**2**	**0**	**0**	**63**	**7.9**	**–14**	**0**	**0.0**	**15:28**	....	....	....	....	....	....	....	....	....
99-2000	**NY Islanders**	**NHL**	**26**	**0**	**2**	**2**	**20**	**0**	**0**	**0**	**30**	**0.0**	**–11**	**0**	**0.0**	**18:33**	....	....	....	....	....	....	....	....	....
	Lowell	AHL	25	2	2	4	26	....	....	....	....	....	....	....	....	....	7	0	0	0	0	....	....	....	....
2000-01	**Edmonton**	**NHL**	**77**	**7**	**14**	**21**	**53**	**2**	**0**	**2**	**91**	**7.7**	**15**	**0**	**0.0**	**18:31**	**6**	**1**	**5**	**6**	**2**	**1**	**0**	**0**	**28:12**
2001-02	**Edmonton**	**NHL**	**81**	**7**	**18**	**25**	**45**	**6**	**0**	**2**	**165**	**4.2**	**–5**	**0**	**0.0**	**23:56**	....	....	....	....	....	....	....	....	....
	Canada	Olympics	6	2	0	2	0	....	....	....	....	....	....	....	....	....	....	....	....	....	....	....	....	....	....
2002-03	**Edmonton**	**NHL**	**80**	**8**	**21**	**29**	**45**	**1**	**0**	**1**	**147**	**5.4**	**–11**	**1**	**100.0**	**24:56**	**6**	**1**	**3**	**4**	**6**	**0**	**0**	**0**	**25:31**
2003-04	**Edmonton**	**NHL**	**77**	**7**	**18**	**25**	**67**	**3**	**0**	**1**	**135**	**5.2**	**–6**	**0**	**0.0**	**24:40**	....	....	....	....	....	....	....	....	....
2004-05			DID NOT PLAY																						
	NHL Totals		**404**	**34**	**79**	**113**	**262**	**14**	**0**	**6**	**631**	**5.4**		**1**	**100.0**	**21:34**	**12**	**2**	**8**	**10**	**8**	**1**	**0**	**0**	**26:51**

WHL West Second All-Star Team (1998)

Played in NHL All-Star Game (2003)

Traded to **Edmonton** by **NY Islanders** with Josh Green and NY Islanders' 2nd round choice (Brad Winchester) in 2000 Entry Draft for Roman Hamrlik, June 24, 2000. Traded to **St. Louis** by **Edmonton** with Doug Lynch and Jeff Woywitka for Chris Pronger, August 2, 2005.

BRIERE, Daniel
(bree-AIR, DAN-yehl) **BUF.**

Center. Shoots right. 5'10", 178 lbs. Born, Gatineau, Que., October 6, 1977. Phoenix's 2nd choice, 24th overall, in 1996 Entry Draft.

Season	Club	League	GP	G	A	Pts	PIM	PP	SH	GW	S	%	+/-	TF	F%	Min	GP	G	A	Pts	PIM	PP	SH	GW	Min
1992-93	Abitibi Regents	QAAA	42	24	30	54	28	....	....	....	....	....	....	....	....	....	3	0	3	3	8	....	....	....	....
1993-94	Gatineau	QAAA	44	56	47	103	56	....	....	....	....	....	....	....	....	....	....	....	....	....	....	....	....	....	....
1994-95	Drummondville	QMJHL	72	51	72	123	54	....	....	....	....	....	....	....	....	....	4	2	3	5	2	....	....	....	....
1995-96	Drummondville	QMJHL	67	*67	*96	*163	84	....	....	....	....	....	....	....	....	....	6	6	12	18	8	....	....	....	....
1996-97	Drummondville	QMJHL	59	52	78	130	94	....	....	....	....	....	....	....	....	....	8	7	7	14	14	....	....	....	....
1997-98	**Phoenix**	**NHL**	**5**	**1**	**0**	**1**	**2**	**0**	**0**	**0**	**4**	**25.0**	**1**	....	....	....	....	....	....	....	....	....	....	....	....
	Springfield	AHL	68	36	56	92	42	....	....	....	....	....	....	....	....	....	4	1	2	3	4	....	....	....	....
1998-99	**Phoenix**	**NHL**	**64**	**8**	**14**	**22**	**30**	**2**	**0**	**2**	**90**	**8.9**	**–3**	**484**	**47.5**	**11:13**	....	....	....	....	....	....	....	....	....
	Las Vegas	IHL	1	1	1	2	0	....	....	....	....	....	....	....	....	....	....	....	....	....	....	....	....	....	....
	Springfield	AHL	13	2	6	8	20	....	....	....	....	....	....	....	....	....	3	0	1	1	2	....	....	....	....
99-2000	**Phoenix**	**NHL**	**13**	**1**	**1**	**2**	**0**	**0**	**0**	**0**	**9**	**11.1**	**0**	**65**	**49.2**	**7:41**	**1**	**0**	**0**	**0**	**0**	**0**	**0**	**0**	**6:16**
	Springfield	AHL	58	29	42	71	56	....	....	....	....	....	....	....	....	....	....	....	....	....	....	....	....	....	....
2000-01	**Phoenix**	**NHL**	**30**	**11**	**4**	**15**	**12**	**9**	**0**	**1**	**43**	**25.6**	**–2**	**210**	**50.0**	**10:50**	....	....	....	....	....	....	....	....	....
	Springfield	AHL	30	21	25	46	30	....	....	....	....	....	....	....	....	....	....	....	....	....	....	....	....	....	....
2001-02	**Phoenix**	**NHL**	**78**	**32**	**28**	**60**	**52**	**12**	**0**	**5**	**149**	**21.5**	**6**	**951**	**51.8**	**15:44**	**5**	**2**	**1**	**3**	**2**	**1**	**0**	**1**	**16:25**
2002-03	**Phoenix**	**NHL**	**68**	**17**	**29**	**46**	**50**	**4**	**0**	**3**	**142**	**12.0**	**–21**	**1108**	**52.5**	**17:02**	....	....	....	....	....	....	....	....	....
	Buffalo	**NHL**	**14**	**7**	**5**	**12**	**12**	**5**	**0**	**1**	**39**	**17.9**	**1**	**206**	**50.0**	**17:49**	....	....	....	....	....	....	....	....	....
2003-04	**Buffalo**	**NHL**	**82**	**28**	**37**	**65**	**70**	**11**	**0**	**3**	**194**	**14.4**	**–7**	**1066**	**47.1**	**18:20**	....	....	....	....	....	....	....	....	....
2004-05	SC Bern	Swiss	36	16	29	45	26	....	....	....	....	....	....	....	....	....	11	1	6	7	2	....	....	....	....
	NHL Totals		**354**	**105**	**118**	**223**	**228**	**43**	**0**	**15**	**670**	**15.7**		**4090**	**50.0**	**15:08**	**6**	**2**	**1**	**3**	**2**	**1**	**0**	**1**	**14:43**

QMJHL All-Rookie Team (1995) • QMJHL Offensive Rookie of the Year (1995) • QMJHL Second All-Star Team (1996, 1997) • AHL All-Rookie Team (1998) • AHL First All-Star Team (1998) • Dudley "Red" Garrett Memorial Award (Rookie of the Year – AHL) (1998)

Traded to **Buffalo** by **Phoenix** with Phoenix's 3rd round choice (Andrej Sekera) in 2004 Entry Draft for Chris Gratton and Buffalo's 4th round choice (later traded to Edmonton – Edmonton selected Liam Reddox) in 2004 Entry Draft, March 10, 2003. Signed as a free agent by **Bern** (Swiss), September 28, 2004.

BRIGLEY, Travis
(BRIH-glee, TRA-vihs)

Left wing. Shoots left. 6', 205 lbs. Born, Coronation, Alta., June 16, 1977. Calgary's 2nd choice, 39th overall, in 1996 Entry Draft.

Season	Club	League	GP	G	A	Pts	PIM	PP	SH	GW	S	%	+/-	TF	F%	Min	GP	G	A	Pts	PIM	PP	SH	GW	Min
1992-93	Leduc Oil Barons	AMHL	32	36	24	60	56	....	....	....	....	....	....	....	....	....	....	....	....	....	....	....	....	....	....
1993-94	Leduc Oil Barons	AMHL	34	29	44	73	141	....	....	....	....	....	....	....	....	....	....	....	....	....	....	....	....	....	....
	Lethbridge	WHL	1	0	0	0	0	....	....	....	....	....	....	....	....	....	....	....	....	....	....	....	....	....	....
1994-95	Lethbridge	WHL	64	14	18	32	14	....	....	....	....	....	....	....	....	....	....	....	....	....	....	....	....	....	....
1995-96	Lethbridge	WHL	69	34	43	77	94	....	....	....	....	....	....	....	....	....	4	2	3	5	8	....	....	....	....
1996-97	Lethbridge	WHL	71	43	47	90	56	....	....	....	....	....	....	....	....	....	19	9	9	18	31	....	....	....	....
1997-98	**Calgary**	**NHL**	**2**	**0**	**0**	**0**	**2**	**0**	**0**	**0**	**1**	**0.0**	**0**	....	....	....	....	....	....	....	....	....	....	....	....
	Saint John Flames	AHL	79	17	15	32	28	....	....	....	....	....	....	....	....	....	8	0	0	0	0	....	....	....	....
1998-99	Saint John Flames	AHL	74	15	35	50	48	....	....	....	....	....	....	....	....	....	7	3	1	4	2	....	....	....	....
99-2000	**Calgary**	**NHL**	**17**	**0**	**2**	**2**	**4**	**0**	**0**	**0**	**17**	**0.0**	**–6**	**2**	**0.0**	**14:14**	....	....	....	....	....	....	....	....	....
	Saint John Flames	AHL	9	3	1	4	4	....	....	....	....	....	....	....	....	....	....	....	....	....	....	....	....	....	....
	Detroit Vipers	IHL	29	6	10	16	24	....	....	....	....	....	....	....	....	....	....	....	....	....	....	....	....	....	....
	Philadelphia	AHL	15	2	2	4	15	....	....	....	....	....	....	....	....	....	5	1	0	1	4	....	....	....	....
2000-01	Knoxville Speed	UHL	4	2	4	6	4	....	....	....	....	....	....	....	....	....	....	....	....	....	....	....	....	....	....
	Cardiff Devils	Britain-2	12	5	9	14	6	....	....	....	....	....	....	....	....	....	....	....	....	....	....	....	....	....	....
	Louisville Panthers	AHL	49	14	21	35	34	....	....	....	....	....	....	....	....	....	....	....	....	....	....	....	....	....	....
2001-02	Macon Whoopee	ECHL	8	4	3	7	2	....	....	....	....	....	....	....	....	....	....	....	....	....	....	....	....	....	....
	Cincinnati	AHL	70	22	21	43	40	....	....	....	....	....	....	....	....	....	3	2	0	2	0	....	....	....	....
2002-03	Cincinnati	AHL	64	18	27	45	58	....	....	....	....	....	....	....	....	....	....	....	....	....	....	....	....	....	....
	Hershey Bears	AHL	13	3	5	8	4	....	....	....	....	....	....	....	....	....	5	1	2	3	2	....	....	....	....
2003-04	**Colorado**	**NHL**	**36**	**3**	**4**	**7**	**10**	**1**	**0**	**0**	**39**	**7.7**	**0**	**198**	**43.4**	**11:52**	....	....	....	....	....	....	....	....	....
	Hershey Bears	AHL	18	6	6	12	8	....	....	....	....	....	....	....	....	....	....	....	....	....	....	....	....	....	....
2004-05	Valerengen IF Oslo	Norway	21	8	11	19	43	....	....	....	....	....	....	....	....	....	10	3	4	7	18	....	....	....	....
	NHL Totals		**55**	**3**	**6**	**9**	**16**	**1**	**0**	**0**	**57**	**5.3**		**200**	**43.0**	**12:38**	....	....	....	....	....	....	....	....	....

Traded to **Philadelphia** by **Calgary** with Calgary's 6th round choice (Andrei Razin) in 2001 Entry Draft for Marc Bureau, March 6, 2000. Signed as a free agent by **Cardiff** (Britain-2), November 3, 2000. Signed as a free agent by **Florida**, December 16, 2000. Signed as a free agent by **Anaheim**, January 22, 2002. Traded to **Colorado** by **Anaheim** for future considerations, August 12, 2003. Signed as a free agent by **Valerengen** (Norway), October 21, 2004.

BRIMANIS, Aris
(brih-MAN-ihs, AR-ihs)

Defense. Shoots right. 6'3", 215 lbs. Born, Cleveland, OH, March 14, 1972. Philadelphia's 3rd choice, 86th overall, in 1991 Entry Draft.

			Regular Season														Playoffs								
Season	Club	League	GP	G	A	Pts	PIM	PP	SH	GW	S	%	+/-	TF	F%	Min	GP	G	A	Pts	PIM	PP	SH	GW	Min
1988-89	Culver	High-IN	38	10	13	23	24	....	....	....	....	....	....	....	....	....	....	....	....	....	....	....	....	....	....
1989-90	Culver	High-IN	37	15	10	25	52	....	....	....	....	....	....	....	....	....	....	....	....	....	....	....	....	....	....
1990-91	Bowling Green	CCHA	38	3	6	9	42	....	....	....	....	....	....	....	....	....	....	....	....	....	....	....	....	....	....
1991-92	Bowling Green	CCHA	32	2	9	11	38	....	....	....	....	....	....	....	....	....	....	....	....	....	....	....	....	....	....
1992-93	Brandon	WHL	71	8	50	58	110	....	....	....	....	....	....	....	....	....	4	2	1	3	7	....	....	....	....
1993-94	**Philadelphia**	**NHL**	**1**	**0**	**0**	**0**	**0**	**0**	**0**	**0**	**1**	**0.0**	**−1**	....	....	....	....	....	....	....	....	....	....	....	....
	Hershey Bears	AHL	75	8	15	23	65	....	....	....	....	....	....	....	....	....	11	2	3	5	12	....	....	....	....
1994-95	Hershey Bears	AHL	76	8	17	25	68	....	....	....	....	....	....	....	....	....	6	1	1	2	14	....	....	....	....
1995-96	**Philadelphia**	**NHL**	**17**	**0**	**2**	**2**	**12**	**0**	**0**	**0**	**11**	**0.0**	**−1**	....	....	....	....	....	....	....	....	....	....	....	....
	Hershey Bears	AHL	54	9	22	31	64	....	....	....	....	....	....	....	....	....	5	1	2	3	4	....	....	....	....
1996-97	**Philadelphia**	**NHL**	**3**	**0**	**1**	**1**	**0**	**0**	**0**	**0**	**1**	**0.0**	**0**	....	....	....	....	....	....	....	....	....	....	....	....
	Philadelphia	AHL	65	14	18	32	69	....	....	....	....	....	....	....	....	....	10	2	2	4	13	....	....	....	....
1997-98	Philadelphia	AHL	30	1	11	12	26	....	....	....	....	....	....	....	....	....	....	....	....	....	....	....	....	....	....
	Michigan	IHL	35	3	9	12	24	....	....	....	....	....	....	....	....	....	4	1	0	1	4	....	....	....	....
1998-99	Grand Rapids	IHL	66	16	21	37	70	....	....	....	....	....	....	....	....	....	....	....	....	....	....	....	....	....	....
	Fredericton	AHL	8	2	4	6	6	....	....	....	....	....	....	....	....	....	15	3	10	13	18	....	....	....	....
99-2000	**NY Islanders**	**NHL**	**18**	**2**	**1**	**3**	**6**	**2**	**0**	**0**	**16**	**12.5**	**−5**	**1**	**0.0**	**20:00**	....	....	....	....	....	....	....	....	....
	Kansas City	IHL	46	5	17	22	28	....	....	....	....	....	....	....	....	....	....	....	....	....	....	....	....	....	....
	Providence Bruins	AHL	7	0	2	2	2	....	....	....	....	....	....	....	....	....	14	3	4	7	10	....	....	....	....
2000-01	**NY Islanders**	**NHL**	**56**	**0**	**8**	**8**	**26**	**0**	**0**	**0**	**66**	**0.0**	**−12**	**0**	**0.0**	**15:36**	....	....	....	....	....	....	....	....	....
	Chicago Wolves	IHL	20	2	2	4	14	....	....	....	....	....	....	....	....	....	16	3	1	4	8	....	....	....	....
2001-02	**Anaheim**	**NHL**	**5**	**0**	**0**	**0**	**9**	**0**	**0**	**0**	**2**	**0.0**	**−1**	**0**	**0.0**	**9:31**	....	....	....	....	....	....	....	....	....
	Cincinnati	AHL	72	2	9	11	44	....	....	....	....	....	....	....	....	....	3	1	0	1	0	....	....	....	....
2002-03	Worcester IceCats	AHL	38	8	13	21	51	....	....	....	....	....	....	....	....	....	3	0	0	0	2	....	....	....	....
2003-04	**St. Louis**	**NHL**	**13**	**0**	**0**	**0**	**4**	**0**	**0**	**0**	**3**	**0.0**	**0**	**1**	**100.0**	**12:02**	....	....	....	....	....	....	....	....	....
	Worcester IceCats	AHL	65	4	15	19	56	....	....	....	....	....	....	....	....	....	10	1	0	1	6	....	....	....	....
2004-05	Worcester IceCats	AHL	69	4	13	17	44	....	....	....	....	....	....	....	....	....	....	....	....	....	....	....	....	....	....
	NHL Totals		**113**	**2**	**12**	**14**	**57**	**2**	**0**	**0**	**100**	**2.0**		**2**	**50.0**	**15:37**	....	....	....	....	....	....	....	....	....

Signed as a free agent by **NY Islanders**, August 16, 1999. Loaned to Providence (AHL) by **NY Islanders**, March 14, 2000. Signed as a free agent by **Anaheim**, August 1, 2001. Signed as a free agent by **St. Louis**, August 15, 2002. • Missed majority of 2002-03 season recovering from leg injury suffered in game vs. Utah (AHL), December 20, 2002.Signed as a free agent by **Kloten**(Swiss), August 29, 2005.

BRIND'AMOUR, Rod
(BRIHND-uh-MOHR, RAWD) **CAR.**

Center. Shoots left. 6'1", 200 lbs. Born, Ottawa, Ont., August 9, 1970. St. Louis' 1st choice, 9th overall, in 1988 Entry Draft.

Season	Club	League	GP	G	A	Pts	PIM	PP	SH	GW	S	%	+/-	TF	F%	Min	GP	G	A	Pts	PIM	PP	SH	GW	Min
1986-87	Notre Dame	SMHL	33	38	50	88	66	....	....	....	....	....	....	....	....	....	....	....	....	....	....	....	....	....	....
1987-88	Notre Dame	SJHL	56	46	61	107	136	....	....	....	....	....	....	....	....	....	....	....	....	....	....	....	....	....	....
1988-89	Michigan State	CCHA	42	27	32	59	63	....	....	....	....	....	....	....	....	....	....	....	....	....	....	....	....	....	....
	St. Louis	**NHL**	....	....	....	....	....	....	....	....	....	....	....	....	....	....	**5**	**2**	**0**	**2**	**4**	**0**	**0**	**0**	....
1989-90	**St. Louis**	**NHL**	**79**	**26**	**35**	**61**	**46**	**10**	**0**	**1**	**160**	**16.3**	**23**	....	....	....	**12**	**5**	**8**	**13**	**6**	**1**	**0**	**0**	....
1990-91	**St. Louis**	**NHL**	**78**	**17**	**32**	**49**	**93**	**4**	**0**	**3**	**169**	**10.1**	**2**	....	....	....	**13**	**2**	**5**	**7**	**10**	**1**	**0**	**0**	....
1991-92	**Philadelphia**	**NHL**	**80**	**33**	**44**	**77**	**100**	**8**	**4**	**5**	**202**	**16.3**	**−3**	....	....	....	....	....	....	....	....	....	....	....	....
1992-93	**Philadelphia**	**NHL**	**81**	**37**	**49**	**86**	**89**	**13**	**4**	**4**	**206**	**18.0**	**−8**	....	....	....	....	....	....	....	....	....	....	....	....
1993-94	**Philadelphia**	**NHL**	**84**	**35**	**62**	**97**	**85**	**14**	**1**	**4**	**230**	**15.2**	**−9**	....	....	....	....	....	....	....	....	....	....	....	....
1994-95	**Philadelphia**	**NHL**	**48**	**12**	**27**	**39**	**33**	**4**	**1**	**2**	**86**	**14.0**	**−4**	....	....	....	**15**	**6**	**9**	**15**	**8**	**2**	**1**	**1**	....
1995-96	**Philadelphia**	**NHL**	**82**	**26**	**61**	**87**	**110**	**4**	**4**	**5**	**213**	**12.2**	**20**	....	....	....	**12**	**2**	**5**	**7**	**6**	**1**	**0**	**0**	....
1996-97	**Philadelphia**	**NHL**	**82**	**27**	**32**	**59**	**41**	**8**	**2**	**3**	**205**	**13.2**	**2**	....	....	....	**19**	***13**	**8**	**21**	**10**	**4**	**2**	**1**	....
1997-98	**Philadelphia**	**NHL**	**82**	**36**	**38**	**74**	**54**	**10**	**2**	**8**	**205**	**17.6**	**−2**	....	....	....	**5**	**2**	**2**	**4**	**7**	**0**	**0**	**0**	....
	Canada	Olympics	6	1	2	3	0	....	....	....	....	....	....	....	....	....	....	....	....	....	....	....	....	....	....
1998-99	**Philadelphia**	**NHL**	**82**	**24**	**50**	**74**	**47**	**10**	**0**	**3**	**191**	**12.6**	**3**	**1773**	**56.5**	**21:29**	**6**	**1**	**3**	**4**	**0**	**0**	**0**	**0**	**25:08**
99-2000	**Philadelphia**	**NHL**	**12**	**5**	**3**	**8**	**4**	**4**	**0**	**0**	**26**	**19.2**	**−1**	**291**	**60.5**	**20:50**	....	....	....	....	....	....	....	....	....
	Carolina	**NHL**	**33**	**4**	**10**	**14**	**22**	**0**	**1**	**1**	**61**	**6.6**	**−12**	**704**	**55.5**	**20:35**	....	....	....	....	....	....	....	....	....
2000-01	**Carolina**	**NHL**	**79**	**20**	**36**	**56**	**47**	**5**	**1**	**5**	**163**	**12.3**	**−7**	**1907**	**60.4**	**22:07**	**6**	**1**	**3**	**4**	**6**	**0**	**0**	**1**	**23:27**
2001-02	**Carolina**	**NHL**	**81**	**23**	**32**	**55**	**40**	**5**	**2**	**5**	**162**	**14.2**	**3**	**2058**	**59.2**	**22:07**	**23**	**4**	**8**	**12**	**16**	**2**	**1**	**1**	**24:52**
2002-03	**Carolina**	**NHL**	**48**	**14**	**23**	**37**	**37**	**7**	**1**	**0**	**110**	**12.7**	**−9**	**1242**	**56.5**	**23:46**	....	....	....	....	....	....	....	....	....
2003-04	**Carolina**	**NHL**	**78**	**12**	**26**	**38**	**28**	**1**	**0**	**1**	**141**	**8.5**	**0**	**1817**	**61.1**	**21:23**	....	....	....	....	....	....	....	....	....
2004-05	Kloten Flyers	Swiss	2	2	1	3	0	....	....	....	....	....	....	....	....	....	5	2	4	6	6	....	....	....	....
	NHL Totals		**1109**	**351**	**560**	**911**	**876**	**107**	**23**	**50**	**2530**	**13.9**		**9792**	**58.7**	**21:53**	**116**	**38**	**51**	**89**	**73**	**11**	**4**	**4**	**24:41**

CCHA Rookie of the Year (1989) • NHL All-Rookie Team (1990)

Played in NHL All-Star Game (1992)

Traded to **Philadelphia** by **St. Louis** with Dan Quinn for Ron Sutter and Murray Baron, September 22, 1991. Traded to **Carolina** by **Philadelphia** with Jean-Marc Pelletier and Philadelphia's 2nd round choice (later traded to Colorado – Colorado selected Agris Saviels) in 2000 Entry Draft for Keith Primeau and Carolina's 5th round choice (later traded to NY Islanders – NY Islanders selected Kristofer Ottosson) in 2000 Entry Draft, January 23, 2000. Signed as a free agent by **Kloten** (Swiss), February 16, 2005.

BRISEBOIS, Patrice
(BREES-bwah, pa-TREEZ) **COL.**

Defense. Shoots right. 6'2", 203 lbs. Born, Montreal, Que., January 27, 1971. Montreal's 2nd choice, 30th overall, in 1989 Entry Draft.

Season	Club	League	GP	G	A	Pts	PIM	PP	SH	GW	S	%	+/-	TF	F%	Min	GP	G	A	Pts	PIM	PP	SH	GW	Min
1986-87	Mtl-Bourassa	QAAA	39	15	19	34	66	....	....	....	....	....	....	....	....	....	....	....	....	....	....	....	....	....	....
1987-88	Laval Titan	QMJHL	48	10	34	44	95	....	....	....	....	....	....	....	....	....	6	0	2	2	2	....	....	....	....
1988-89	Laval Titan	QMJHL	50	20	45	65	95	....	....	....	....	....	....	....	....	....	17	8	14	22	45	....	....	....	....
1989-90	Laval Titan	QMJHL	56	18	70	88	108	....	....	....	....	....	....	....	....	....	13	7	9	16	26	....	....	....	....
1990-91	Drummondville	QMJHL	54	17	44	61	72	....	....	....	....	....	....	....	....	....	14	6	18	24	49	....	....	....	....
	Montreal	**NHL**	**10**	**0**	**2**	**2**	**4**	**0**	**0**	**0**	**11**	**0.0**	**1**	....	....	....	....	....	....	....	....	....	....	....	....
1991-92	**Montreal**	**NHL**	**26**	**2**	**8**	**10**	**20**	**0**	**0**	**1**	**37**	**5.4**	**9**	....	....	....	**11**	**2**	**4**	**6**	**6**	**1**	**0**	**1**	....
	Fredericton	AHL	53	12	27	39	51	....	....	....	....	....	....	....	....	....	....	....	....	....	....	....	....	....	....
1992-93♦	**Montreal**	**NHL**	**70**	**10**	**21**	**31**	**79**	**4**	**0**	**2**	**123**	**8.1**	**6**	....	....	....	**20**	**0**	**4**	**4**	**18**	**0**	**0**	**0**	....
1993-94	**Montreal**	**NHL**	**53**	**2**	**21**	**23**	**63**	**1**	**0**	**0**	**71**	**2.8**	**5**	....	....	....	**7**	**0**	**4**	**4**	**6**	**0**	**0**	**0**	....
1994-95	**Montreal**	**NHL**	**35**	**4**	**8**	**12**	**26**	**0**	**0**	**2**	**67**	**6.0**	**−2**	....	....	....	....	....	....	....	....	....	....	....	....
1995-96	**Montreal**	**NHL**	**69**	**9**	**27**	**36**	**65**	**3**	**0**	**1**	**127**	**7.1**	**10**	....	....	....	**6**	**1**	**2**	**3**	**6**	**0**	**0**	**0**	....
1996-97	**Montreal**	**NHL**	**49**	**2**	**13**	**15**	**24**	**0**	**0**	**1**	**72**	**2.8**	**−7**	....	....	....	**3**	**1**	**1**	**2**	**24**	**0**	**0**	**1**	....
1997-98	**Montreal**	**NHL**	**79**	**10**	**27**	**37**	**67**	**5**	**0**	**1**	**125**	**8.0**	**16**	....	....	....	**10**	**1**	**0**	**1**	**0**	**0**	**0**	**0**	....
1998-99	**Montreal**	**NHL**	**54**	**3**	**9**	**12**	**28**	**1**	**0**	**1**	**90**	**3.3**	**−8**	**0**	**0.0**	**22:26**	....	....	....	....	....	....	....	....	....
99-2000	**Montreal**	**NHL**	**54**	**10**	**25**	**35**	**18**	**5**	**0**	**2**	**88**	**11.4**	**−1**	**0**	**0.0**	**23:14**	....	....	....	....	....	....	....	....	....
2000-01	**Montreal**	**NHL**	**77**	**15**	**21**	**36**	**28**	**11**	**0**	**4**	**178**	**8.4**	**−31**	**1**	**100.0**	**24:43**	....	....	....	....	....	....	....	....	....
2001-02	**Montreal**	**NHL**	**71**	**4**	**29**	**33**	**25**	**2**	**1**	**1**	**95**	**4.2**	**9**	**0**	**0.0**	**23:53**	**10**	**1**	**1**	**2**	**2**	**0**	**0**	**0**	**22:05**
2002-03	**Montreal**	**NHL**	**73**	**4**	**25**	**29**	**32**	**1**	**0**	**1**	**105**	**3.8**	**−14**	**0**	**0.0**	**23:23**	....	....	....	....	....	....	....	....	....
2003-04	**Montreal**	**NHL**	**71**	**4**	**27**	**31**	**22**	**2**	**0**	**0**	**96**	**4.2**	**17**	**0**	**0.0**	**21:20**	**11**	**2**	**1**	**3**	**4**	**1**	**0**	**0**	**22:30**
2004-05	Kloten Flyers	Swiss	10	3	1	4	2	....	....	....	....	....	....	....	....	....	....	....	....	....	....	....	....	....	....
	NHL Totals		**791**	**79**	**263**	**342**	**501**	**35**	**1**	**17**	**1285**	**6.1**		**1**	**100.0**	**23:13**	**78**	**8**	**17**	**25**	**66**	**2**	**0**	**2**	**22:18**

QMJHL Second All-Star Team (1990) • QMJHL First All-Star Team (1991) • Canadian Major Junior Defenseman of the Year (1991) • Memorial Cup Tournament All-Star Team (1991)

Signed as a free agent by **Kloten** (Swiss), October 13, 2004. Signed as a free agent by **Colorado**, August 3, 2005.

BROOKBANK, Wade
(BRUK-bank, WAYD) **VAN.**

Defense. Shoots left. 6'4", 225 lbs. Born, Lanigan, Sask., September 29, 1977.

Season	Club	League	GP	G	A	Pts	PIM	PP	SH	GW	S	%	+/-	TF	F%	Min	GP	G	A	Pts	PIM	PP	SH	GW	Min
1997-98	Melville	SJHL	58	8	21	29	330	....	....	....	....	....	....	....	....	....	....	....	....	....	....	....	....	....	....
	Anchorage Aces	WCHL	7	0	0	0	46	....	....	....	....	....	....	....	....	....	4	0	0	0	20	....	....	....	....
1998-99	Anchorage Aces	WCHL	56	0	4	4	337	....	....	....	....	....	....	....	....	....	....	....	....	....	....	....	....	....	....
99-2000	Oklahoma City	CHL	68	3	9	12	354	....	....	....	....	....	....	....	....	....	7	1	1	2	29	....	....	....	....
2000-01	Orlando	IHL	29	0	1	1	122	....	....	....	....	....	....	....	....	....	4	0	0	0	6	....	....	....	....
	Oklahoma City	CHL	46	1	13	14	267	....	....	....	....	....	....	....	....	....	5	0	0	0	24	....	....	....	....
2001-02	Grand Rapids	AHL	73	1	6	7	337	....	....	....	....	....	....	....	....	....	3	0	1	1	14	....	....	....	....
2002-03	Binghamton	AHL	8	0	0	0	28	....	....	....	....	....	....	....	....	....	....	....	....	....	....	....	....	....	....

			Regular Season														Playoffs								
Season	Club	League	GP	G	A	Pts	PIM	PP	SH	GW	S	%	+/-	TF	F%	Min	GP	G	A	Pts	PIM	PP	SH	GW	Min
2003-04	**Nashville**	**NHL**	**9**	**0**	**0**	**0**	**38**	**0**	**0**	**0**	**1**	**0.0**	**–4**	**0**	**0.0**	**3:28**	....	....	....	....	....	....	....	....	....
	Milwaukee	AHL	6	0	0	0	6	....	....	....	....	....	....	....	....	....	....	....	....	....	....	....	....	....	....
	Binghamton	AHL	4	0	0	0	31	....	....	....	....	....	....	....	....	....	....	....	....	....	....	....	....	....	....
	Vancouver	**NHL**	**20**	**2**	**0**	**2**	**95**	**0**	**0**	**1**	**6**	**33.3**	**3**	**0**	**0.0**	**3:50**	....	....	....	....	....	....	....	....	....
	Manitoba Moose	AHL	4	0	0	0	12	....	....	....	....	....	....	....	....	....	....	....	....	....	....	....	....	....	....
2004-05	Manitoba Moose	AHL	68	0	10	10	285	....	....	....	....	....	....	....	....	....	9	0	0	0	10	....	....	....	....
	NHL Totals		**29**	**2**	**0**	**2**	**133**	**0**	**0**	**1**	**7**	**28.6**		**0**	**0.0**	**3:43**	....	....	....	....	....	....	....	....	....

Signed as a free agent by **Orlando** (IHL), September 1, 2000. Signed as a free agent by **Ottawa**, July 27, 2001. • Missed majority of 2002-03 season recovering from knee injury suffered in game vs. Wilkes-Barre (AHL), November 2, 2002. Claimed by **Nashville** from **Ottawa** in Waiver Draft, October 3, 2003. Traded to **Vancouver** by **Nashville** for future considerations, December 17, 2003. Claimed on waivers by **Ottawa** from **Vancouver**, December 19, 2003. Traded to **Florida** by **Ottawa** for future considerations, December 29, 2003. Claimed on waivers by **Vancouver** from **Florida**, January 3, 2004.

BROWN, Brad

(BROWN, BRAD)

Defense. Shoots right. 6'4", 220 lbs. Born, Baie Verte, Nfld., December 27, 1975. Montreal's 1st choice, 18th overall, in 1994 Entry Draft.

Season	Club	League	GP	G	A	Pts	PIM	PP	SH	GW	S	%	+/-	TF	F%	Min	GP	G	A	Pts	PIM	PP	SH	GW	Min
1990-91	Tor. Red Wings	MTHL	80	15	45	60	105	....	....	....	....	....	....	....	....	....	....	....	....	....	....	....	....	....	....
	St. Mike's B's	OHA-B	2	0	0	0	0	....	....	....	....	....	....	....	....	....	....	....	....	....	....	....	....	....	....
1991-92	North Bay	OHL	49	2	9	11	170	....	....	....	....	....	....	....	....	....	18	0	6	6	43	....	....	....	....
1992-93	North Bay	OHL	61	4	9	13	228	....	....	....	....	....	....	....	....	....	2	0	2	2	13	....	....	....	....
1993-94	North Bay	OHL	66	8	24	32	196	....	....	....	....	....	....	....	....	....	18	3	12	15	33	....	....	....	....
1994-95	North Bay	OHL	64	8	38	46	172	....	....	....	....	....	....	....	....	....	6	1	4	5	8	....	....	....	....
1995-96	Barrie Colts	OHL	27	3	13	16	82	....	....	....	....	....	....	....	....	....	....	....	....	....	....	....	....	....	....
	Fredericton	AHL	38	0	3	3	148	....	....	....	....	....	....	....	....	....	10	2	1	3	6	....	....	....	....
1996-97	**Montreal**	**NHL**	**8**	**0**	**0**	**0**	**22**	**0**	**0**	**0**	**0**	**0.0**	**–1**	....	....	....	....	....	....	....	....	....	....	....	....
	Fredericton	AHL	64	3	7	10	368	....	....	....	....	....	....	....	....	....	....	....	....	....	....	....	....	....	....
1997-98	Fredericton	AHL	64	1	8	9	297	....	....	....	....	....	....	....	....	....	4	0	0	0	29	....	....	....	....
1998-99	**Montreal**	**NHL**	**5**	**0**	**0**	**0**	**21**	**0**	**0**	**0**	**0**	**0.0**	**0**	**0**	**0.0**	**6:02**	....	....	....	....	....	....	....	....	....
	Chicago	**NHL**	**61**	**1**	**7**	**8**	**184**	**0**	**0**	**0**	**26**	**3.8**	**–4**	**0**	**0.0**	**15:08**	....	....	....	....	....	....	....	....	....
99-2000	**Chicago**	**NHL**	**57**	**0**	**9**	**9**	**134**	**0**	**0**	**0**	**15**	**0.0**	**–1**	**0**	**0.0**	**14:12**	....	....	....	....	....	....	....	....	....
2000-01	**NY Rangers**	**NHL**	**48**	**1**	**3**	**4**	**107**	**0**	**0**	**0**	**14**	**7.1**	**0**	**0**	**0.0**	**14:31**	....	....	....	....	....	....	....	....	....
2001-02	**Minnesota**	**NHL**	**51**	**0**	**4**	**4**	**123**	**0**	**0**	**0**	**23**	**0.0**	**–11**	**0**	**0.0**	**15:54**	....	....	....	....	....	....	....	....	....
2002-03	**Minnesota**	**NHL**	**57**	**0**	**1**	**1**	**90**	**0**	**0**	**0**	**10**	**0.0**	**–1**	**0**	**0.0**	**9:14**	**11**	**0**	**0**	**0**	**16**	**0**	**0**	**0**	**8:23**
2003-04	**Minnesota**	**NHL**	**30**	**0**	**1**	**1**	**54**	**0**	**0**	**0**	**14**	**0.0**	**–1**	**0**	**0.0**	**9:41**	....	....	....	....	....	....	....	....	....
	Buffalo	**NHL**	**13**	**0**	**2**	**2**	**12**	**0**	**0**	**0**	**6**	**0.0**	**3**	**0**	**0.0**	**16:33**	....	....	....	....	....	....	....	....	....
2004-05			DID NOT PLAY																						
	NHL Totals		**330**	**2**	**27**	**29**	**747**	**0**	**0**	**0**	**108**	**1.9**		**0**	**0.0**	**13:22**	**11**	**0**	**0**	**0**	**16**	**0**	**0**	**0**	**8:23**

OHL All-Rookie Team (1992)

Traded to **Chicago** by **Montreal** with Jocelyn Thibault and Dave Manson for Jeff Hackett, Eric Weinrich, Alain Nasreddine and Tampa Bay's 4th round choice (previously acquired, Montreal selected Chris Dyment) in 1999 Entry Draft, November 16, 1998. Traded to **NY Rangers** by **Chicago** with Michal Grosek for future considerations, October 5, 2000. Signed as a free agent by **Minnesota**, July 31, 2001. Traded to **Buffalo** by **Minnesota** with Minnesota's 6th round choice (Vjateslav Buravchikov) in 2005 Entry Draft for Buffalo's 4th round choice (Kyle Bailey) in 2005 Entry Draft, March 8, 2004.

BROWN, Curtis

(BROWN, KUHR-tihs) **CHI.**

Center/Left wing. Shoots left. 6', 196 lbs. Born, Unity, Sask., February 12, 1976. Buffalo's 2nd choice, 43rd overall, in 1994 Entry Draft.

Season	Club	League	GP	G	A	Pts	PIM	PP	SH	GW	S	%	+/-	TF	F%	Min	GP	G	A	Pts	PIM	PP	SH	GW	Min
1990-91	Unity Bantams	SBHL	60	93	104	197	55	....	....	....	....	....	....	....	....	....	....	....	....	....	....	....	....	....	....
1991-92	Moose Jaw	SMHL	36	35	30	65	44	....	....	....	....	....	....	....	....	....	....	....	....	....	....	....	....	....	....
1992-93	Moose Jaw	WHL	71	13	16	29	30	....	....	....	....	....	....	....	....	....	....	....	....	....	....	....	....	....	....
1993-94	Moose Jaw	WHL	72	27	38	65	82	....	....	....	....	....	....	....	....	....	....	....	....	....	....	....	....	....	....
1994-95	Moose Jaw	WHL	70	51	53	104	63	....	....	....	....	....	....	....	....	....	10	8	7	15	20	....	....	....	....
	Buffalo	**NHL**	**1**	**1**	**1**	**2**	**2**	**0**	**0**	**0**	**4**	**25.0**	**2**	....	....	....	....	....	....	....	....	....	....	....	....
1995-96	Moose Jaw	WHL	25	20	18	38	30	....	....	....	....	....	....	....	....	....	....	....	....	....	....	....	....	....	....
	Prince Albert	WHL	19	12	21	33	8	....	....	....	....	....	....	....	....	....	18	10	15	25	18	....	....	....	....
	Buffalo	**NHL**	**4**	**0**	**0**	**0**	**0**	**0**	**0**	**0**	**1**	**0.0**	**0**	....	....	....	....	....	....	....	....	....	....	....	....
	Rochester	AHL	....	....	....	....	....	....	....	....	....	....	....	....	....	....	12	0	1	1	2	....	....	....	....
1996-97	**Buffalo**	**NHL**	**28**	**4**	**3**	**7**	**18**	**0**	**0**	**1**	**31**	**12.9**	**4**	....	....	....	....	....	....	....	....	....	....	....	....
	Rochester	AHL	51	22	21	43	30	....	....	....	....	....	....	....	....	....	10	4	6	10	4	....	....	....	....
1997-98	**Buffalo**	**NHL**	**63**	**12**	**12**	**24**	**34**	**1**	**1**	**2**	**91**	**13.2**	**11**	....	....	....	**13**	**1**	**2**	**3**	**10**	**1**	**0**	**0**	....
1998-99	**Buffalo**	**NHL**	**78**	**16**	**31**	**47**	**56**	**5**	**1**	**3**	**128**	**12.5**	**23**	**1198**	**45.0**	**17:30**	**21**	**7**	**6**	**13**	**10**	**3**	**0**	**3**	**18:51**
99-2000	**Buffalo**	**NHL**	**74**	**22**	**29**	**51**	**42**	**5**	**0**	**4**	**149**	**14.8**	**19**	**1318**	**48.6**	**18:11**	**5**	**1**	**3**	**4**	**6**	**1**	**0**	**0**	**17:11**
2000-01	**Buffalo**	**NHL**	**70**	**10**	**22**	**32**	**34**	**2**	**1**	**0**	**105**	**9.5**	**15**	**1159**	**50.4**	**16:34**	**13**	**5**	**0**	**5**	**8**	**0**	**2**	**1**	**18:14**
2001-02	**Buffalo**	**NHL**	**82**	**20**	**17**	**37**	**32**	**4**	**1**	**5**	**171**	**11.7**	**–4**	**1608**	**49.0**	**17:48**	....	....	....	....	....	....	....	....	....
2002-03	**Buffalo**	**NHL**	**74**	**15**	**16**	**31**	**40**	**3**	**4**	**4**	**144**	**10.4**	**4**	**1387**	**49.5**	**16:53**	....	....	....	....	....	....	....	....	....
2003-04	**Buffalo**	**NHL**	**68**	**9**	**12**	**21**	**30**	**2**	**1**	**2**	**117**	**7.7**	**2**	**1182**	**51.5**	**16:36**	....	....	....	....	....	....	....	....	....
	San Jose	**NHL**	**12**	**2**	**2**	**4**	**6**	**0**	**0**	**0**	**21**	**9.5**	**1**	**105**	**47.6**	**16:26**	**17**	**0**	**2**	**2**	**18**	**0**	**0**	**0**	**14:37**
2004-05	San Diego Gulls	ECHL	47	9	29	38	24	....	....	....	....	....	....	....	....	....	....	....	....	....	....	....	....	....	....
	NHL Totals		**554**	**111**	**145**	**256**	**294**	**22**	**9**	**21**	**962**	**11.5**		**7957**	**49.0**	**17:16**	**69**	**14**	**13**	**27**	**52**	**5**	**2**	**4**	**17:16**

WHL East First All-Star Team (1995) • WHL East Second All-Star Team (1996)

Traded to **San Jose** by **Buffalo** with Andy Delmore for Jeff Jillson and a compensatory 7th round choice (Andrew Orpik) in 2005 Entry Draft, March 9, 2004. Signed as a free agent by **Chicago**, July 2, 2004. Signed as a free agent by **San Diego** (ECHL), November 16, 2004.

BROWN, Dustin

(BROWN, DUHS-tihn) **L.A.**

Right wing. Shoots right. 6', 195 lbs. Born, Ithaca, NY, November 4, 1984. Los Angeles' 1st choice, 13th overall, in 2003 Entry Draft.

Season	Club	League	GP	G	A	Pts	PIM	PP	SH	GW	S	%	+/-	TF	F%	Min	GP	G	A	Pts	PIM	PP	SH	GW	Min
1998-99	Ithaca	High-NY	18	4	13	17	....	....	....	....	....	....	....	....	....	....	....	....	....	....	....	....	....	....	....
99-2000	Ithaca	High-NY	24	33	21	53	....	....	....	....	....	....	....	....	....	....	....	....	....	....	....	....	....	....	....
2000-01	Guelph Storm	OHL	53	23	22	45	45	....	....	....	....	....	....	....	....	....	4	0	0	0	10	....	....	....	....
2001-02	Guelph Storm	OHL	63	41	32	73	56	....	....	....	....	....	....	....	....	....	9	8	5	13	14	....	....	....	....
2002-03	Guelph Storm	OHL	58	34	42	76	89	....	....	....	....	....	....	....	....	....	11	7	8	15	6	....	....	....	....
2003-04	**Los Angeles**	**NHL**	**31**	**1**	**4**	**5**	**16**	**0**	**0**	**0**	**40**	**2.5**	**0**	**1**	**0.0**	**10:29**	....	....	....	....	....	....	....	....	....
2004-05	Manchester	AHL	79	29	45	74	96	....	....	....	....	....	....	....	....	....	6	5	2	7	10	....	....	....	....
	NHL Totals		**31**	**1**	**4**	**5**	**16**	**0**	**0**	**0**	**40**	**2.5**		**1**	**0.0**	**10:29**	....	....	....	....	....	....	....	....	....

OHL All-Rookie Team (2001) • Canadian Major Junior Scholastic Player of the Year (2003)

• Missed majority of 2003-04 season recovering from ankle injury suffered in game vs. Chicago, November 29, 2003.

BROWN, Mike

(BROWN, MIGHK)

Left wing. Shoots left. 6'5", 185 lbs. Born, Surrey, B.C., April 27, 1979. Florida's 1st choice, 20th overall, in 1997 Entry Draft.

Season	Club	League	GP	G	A	Pts	PIM	PP	SH	GW	S	%	+/-	TF	F%	Min	GP	G	A	Pts	PIM	PP	SH	GW	Min
1993-94	Penticton	BCJHL	50	52	48	100	100	....	....	....	....	....	....	....	....	....	....	....	....	....	....	....	....	....	....
1994-95	Merritt	BCJHL	45	3	4	7	145	....	....	....	....	....	....	....	....	....	....	....	....	....	....	....	....	....	....
	Red Deer Rebels	WHL	1	0	0	0	0	....	....	....	....	....	....	....	....	....	....	....	....	....	....	....	....	....	....
1995-96	Red Deer Rebels	WHL	62	4	5	9	125	....	....	....	....	....	....	....	....	....	10	0	0	0	18	....	....	....	....
1996-97	Red Deer Rebels	WHL	70	19	13	32	243	....	....	....	....	....	....	....	....	....	16	1	2	3	47	....	....	....	....
1997-98	Kamloops Blazers	WHL	72	23	33	56	305	....	....	....	....	....	....	....	....	....	7	2	1	3	22	....	....	....	....
1998-99	Kamloops Blazers	WHL	69	28	16	44	*285	....	....	....	....	....	....	....	....	....	15	3	7	10	*68	....	....	....	....
99-2000	Syracuse Crunch	AHL	71	13	18	31	284	....	....	....	....	....	....	....	....	....	4	0	0	0	0	....	....	....	....
2000-01	**Vancouver**	**NHL**	**1**	**0**	**0**	**0**	**5**	**0**	**0**	**0**	**1**	**0.0**	**0**	**0**	**0.0**	**4:48**	....	....	....	....	....	....	....	....	....
	Kansas City	IHL	78	14	13	27	214	....	....	....	....	....	....	....	....	....	....	....	....	....	....	....	....	....	....
2001-02	**Vancouver**	**NHL**	**15**	**0**	**0**	**0**	**72**	**0**	**0**	**0**	**2**	**0.0**	**1**	**0**	**0.0**	**3:29**	....	....	....	....	....	....	....	....	....
	Manitoba Moose	AHL	31	7	9	16	155	....	....	....	....	....	....	....	....	....	6	0	1	1	16	....	....	....	....
2002-03	**Anaheim**	**NHL**	**16**	**1**	**1**	**2**	**44**	**0**	**0**	**1**	**8**	**12.5**	**0**	**0**	**0.0**	**0:00**	....	....	....	....	....	....	....	....	....
	Cincinnati	AHL	27	3	3	6	85	....	....	....	....	....	....	....	....	....	....	....	....	....	....	....	....	....	....
2003-04	St. John's	AHL	21	3	3	6	74	....	....	....	....	....	....	....	....	....	....	....	....	....	....	....	....	....	....
	Binghamton	AHL	38	4	7	11	131	....	....	....	....	....	....	....	....	....	....	....	....	....	....	....	....	....	....
2004-05	Norfolk Admirals	AHL	68	7	8	15	284	....	....	....	....	....	....	....	....	....	....	....	....	....	....	....	....	....	....
	NHL Totals		**32**	**1**	**1**	**2**	**121**	**0**	**0**	**1**	**11**	**9.1**		**0**	**0.0**	**1:47**	....	....	....	....	....	....	....	....	....

Traded to **Vancouver** by **Florida** with Ed Jovanovski, Dave Gagner, Kevin Weekes and Florida's 1st round choice (Nathan Smith) in 2000 Entry Draft for Pavel Bure, Bret Hedican, Brad Ference and Vancouver's 3rd round choice (Robert Fried) in 2000 Entry Draft, January 17, 1999. Claimed on waivers by **Anaheim** from **Vancouver**, October 11, 2002. Signed as a free agent by **St. John's** (AHL), October 11, 2003. Signed as a free agent by **Binghamton** (AHL), January 8, 2004. Signed to a PTO (tryout) contract by **Norfolk** (AHL), December 6, 2004.

						Regular Season													Playoffs							
Season	Club	League	GP	G	A	Pts	PIM	PP	SH	GW	S	%	+/-	TF	F%	Min	GP	G	A	Pts	PIM	PP	SH	GW	Min

BROWN, Sean   (BROWN, SHAWN)   **N.J.**

Defense. Shoots left. 6'3", 215 lbs.   Born, Oshawa, Ont., November 5, 1976. Boston's 2nd choice, 21st overall, in 1995 Entry Draft.

Season	Club	League	GP	G	A	Pts	PIM	PP	SH	GW	S	%	+/-	TF	F%	Min	GP	G	A	Pts	PIM	PP	SH	GW	Min
1992-93	Oshawa	MTJHL	15	0	1	1	9	....	....	....	....	....	....	....	....	....	....	....	....	....	....	....	....	....	....
1993-94	Wellington Dukes	MTJHL	32	5	14	19	165	....	....	....	....	....	....	....	....	....	....	....	....	....	....	....	....	....	....
	Belleville Bulls	OHL	28	1	2	3	53	....	....	....	....	....	....	....	....	....	8	0	0	0	17	....	....	....	....
1994-95	Belleville Bulls	OHL	58	2	16	18	200	....	....	....	....	....	....	....	....	....	16	4	2	6	*67	....	....	....	....
1995-96	Belleville Bulls	OHL	37	10	23	33	150	....	....	....	....	....	....	....	....	....	....	....	....	....	....	....	....	....	....
	Sarnia Sting	OHL	26	8	17	25	112	....	....	....	....	....	....	....	....	....	10	1	0	1	38	....	....	....	....
1996-97	**Edmonton**	**NHL**	5	0	0	0	4	0	0	0	2	0.0	–1				....	....	....	....	....	....	....	....	....
	Hamilton	AHL	61	1	7	8	238	....	....	....	....	....	....	....	....	....	19	1	0	1	47	....	....	....	....
1997-98	**Edmonton**	**NHL**	18	0	1	1	43	0	0	0	9	0.0	–1				....	....	....	....	....	....	....	....	....
	Hamilton	AHL	43	4	6	10	166	....	....	....	....	....	....	....	....	....	6	0	2	2	38	....	....	....	....
1998-99	**Edmonton**	**NHL**	51	0	7	7	188	0	0	0	27	0.0	1	0	0.0	12:14	1	0	0	0	10	0	0	0	7:33
99-2000	**Edmonton**	**NHL**	72	4	8	12	192	0	0	2	36	11.1	1	0	0.0	12:41	3	0	0	0	23	0	0	0	6:12
2000-01	**Edmonton**	**NHL**	62	2	3	5	110	0	0	0	30	6.7	2	0	0.0	11:07	....	....	....	....	....	....	....	....	....
2001-02	**Edmonton**	**NHL**	61	6	4	10	127	3	0	1	58	10.3	8	0	0.0	12:36	....	....	....	....	....	....	....	....	....
	Boston	**NHL**	12	0	1	1	47	0	0	0	6	0.0	–1	0	0.0	16:22	4	0	0	0	2	0	0	0	5:49
2002-03	**Boston**	**NHL**	69	1	5	6	117	0	0	0	39	2.6	–6	2	50.0	6:26	....	....	....	....	....	....	....	....	....
2003-04	**New Jersey**	**NHL**	39	0	3	3	44	0	0	0	25	0.0	5	0	0.0	13:56	1	0	0	0	2	0	0	0	11:20
	Albany River Rats	AHL	21	1	6	7	56	....	....	....	....	....	....	....	....	....	....	....	....	....	....	....	....	....	....
2004-05			DID NOT PLAY																						
	NHL Totals		**389**	**13**	**32**	**45**	**872**	**3**	**0**	**3**	**232**	**5.6**		**2**	**50.0**	**11:25**	**9**	**0**	**0**	**0**	**37**	**0**	**0**	**0**	**6:45**

OHL Second All-Star Team (1996)

Rights traded to **Edmonton** by **Boston** with Mariusz Czerkawski and Boston's 1st round choice (Matthieu Descoteaux) in 1996 Entry Draft for Bill Ranford, January 11, 1996. Traded to **Boston** by **Edmonton** for Bobby Allen, March 19, 2002. Signed as a free agent by **New Jersey**, July 24, 2003.

BRULE, Steve   (broo-LAY, STEEV)

Right wing. Shoots right. 6', 200 lbs.   Born, Montreal, Que., January 15, 1975. New Jersey's 6th choice, 143rd overall, in 1993 Entry Draft.

Season	Club	League	GP	G	A	Pts	PIM	PP	SH	GW	S	%	+/-	TF	F%	Min	GP	G	A	Pts	PIM	PP	SH	GW	Min
1990-91	Montreal L'est	QAHA	32	25	30	55	20	....	....	....	....	....	....	....	....	....	....	....	....	....	....	....	....	....	....
1991-92	Mtl-Bourassa	QAAA	40	33	37	70	46	....	....	....	....	....	....	....	....	....	9	9	7	16	10	....	....	....	....
1992-93	St-Jean Lynx	QMJHL	70	33	47	80	46	....	....	....	....	....	....	....	....	....	4	0	0	0	9	....	....	....	....
1993-94	St-Jean Lynx	QMJHL	66	41	64	105	46	....	....	....	....	....	....	....	....	....	5	2	1	3	0	....	....	....	....
1994-95	St-Jean Lynx	QMJHL	69	44	64	108	42	....	....	....	....	....	....	....	....	....	7	3	4	7	8	....	....	....	....
	Albany River Rats	AHL	3	1	4	5	0	....	....	....	....	....	....	....	....	....	14	9	5	14	4	....	....	....	....
1995-96	Albany River Rats	AHL	80	30	21	51	37	....	....	....	....	....	....	....	....	....	4	0	0	0	17	....	....	....	....
1996-97	Albany River Rats	AHL	79	28	48	76	27	....	....	....	....	....	....	....	....	....	16	7	7	14	12	....	....	....	....
1997-98	Albany River Rats	AHL	80	34	43	77	34	....	....	....	....	....	....	....	....	....	13	8	3	11	4	....	....	....	....
1998-99	Albany River Rats	AHL	78	32	52	84	35	....	....	....	....	....	....	....	....	....	5	3	1	4	4	....	....	....	....
99-2000	Albany River Rats	AHL	75	30	46	76	18	....	....	....	....	....	....	....	....	....	5	1	2	3	0	....	....	....	....
	♦ **New Jersey**	**NHL**	....	....	....	....	....	....	....	....	....	....	....	....	....	....	1	0	0	0	0	0	0	0	13:00
2000-01	Manitoba Moose	IHL	78	21	48	69	22	....	....	....	....	....	....	....	....	....	13	3	10	13	12	....	....	....	....
2001-02	Cincinnati	AHL	77	21	42	63	50	....	....	....	....	....	....	....	....	....	3	0	1	1	0	....	....	....	....
2002-03	**Colorado**	**NHL**	2	0	0	0	0	0	0	0	2	0.0	0	0	0.0	9:06	....	....	....	....	....	....	....	....	....
	Hershey Bears	AHL	49	18	19	37	30	....	....	....	....	....	....	....	....	....	5	4	0	4	8	....	....	....	....
2003-04	Hershey Bears	AHL	79	29	29	58	82	....	....	....	....	....	....	....	....	....	....	....	....	....	....	....	....	....	....
2004-05	Krefeld Pinguine	Germany	51	18	29	47	51	....	....	....	....	....	....	....	....	....	....	....	....	....	....	....	....	....	....
	NHL Totals		**2**	**0**	**0**	**0**	**0**	**0**	**0**	**0**	**2**	**0.0**		**0**	**0.0**	**9:06**	**1**	**0**	**0**	**0**	**0**	**0**	**0**	**0**	**13:00**

QMJHL All-Rookie Team (1993) • QMJHL Offensive Rookie of the Year (1993) • QMJHL Second All-Star Team (1995)

Signed as a free agent by **Detroit**, July 20, 2000. Signed as a free agent by **Colorado**, July 22, 2002. Signed as a free agent by **Krefeld** (Germany), July 22, 2004.

BRUNETTE, Andrew   (broo-NEHT, AN-droo)   **COL.**

Left wing. Shoots left. 6'1", 210 lbs.   Born, Sudbury, Ont., August 24, 1973. Washington's 6th choice, 174th overall, in 1993 Entry Draft.

Season	Club	League	GP	G	A	Pts	PIM	PP	SH	GW	S	%	+/-	TF	F%	Min	GP	G	A	Pts	PIM	PP	SH	GW	Min
1989-90	Rayside-Balfour	NOHA	32	38	*65	*103		....	....	....	....	....	....	....	....	....	....	....	....	....	....	....	....	....	....
	Rayside-Balfour	NOJHA	4	1	1	2	0	....	....	....	....	....	....	....	....	....	....	....	....	....	....	....	....	....	....
1990-91	Owen Sound	OHL	63	15	20	35	15	....	....	....	....	....	....	....	....	....	....	....	....	....	....	....	....	....	....
1991-92	Owen Sound	OHL	66	51	47	98	42	....	....	....	....	....	....	....	....	....	5	5	0	5	8	....	....	....	....
1992-93	Owen Sound	OHL	66	*62	*100	*162	91	....	....	....	....	....	....	....	....	....	8	8	6	14	16	....	....	....	....
1993-94	Portland Pirates	AHL	23	9	11	20	10	....	....	....	....	....	....	....	....	....	2	0	1	1	0	....	....	....	....
	Providence Bruins	AHL	3	0	0	0	0	....	....	....	....	....	....	....	....	....	....	....	....	....	....	....	....	....	....
	Hampton Roads	ECHL	20	12	18	30	32	....	....	....	....	....	....	....	....	....	7	7	6	13	18	....	....	....	....
1994-95	Portland Pirates	AHL	79	30	50	80	53	....	....	....	....	....	....	....	....	....	7	3	3	6	10	....	....	....	....
1995-96	**Washington**	**NHL**	11	3	3	6	0	0	0	1	16	18.8	5				6	1	3	4	0	0	0	0	
	Portland Pirates	AHL	69	28	66	94	125	....	....	....	....	....	....	....	....	....	20	11	18	29	15	....	....	....	....
1996-97	**Washington**	**NHL**	23	4	7	11	12	2	0	0	23	17.4	–3				5	1	2	3	0	....	....	....	....
	Portland Pirates	AHL	50	22	51	73	48	....	....	....	....	....	....	....	....	....	....	....	....	....	....	....	....	....	....
1997-98	**Washington**	**NHL**	28	11	12	23	12	4	0	2	42	26.2	2				10	1	11	12	12	....	....	....	....
	Portland Pirates	AHL	43	21	46	67	64	....	....	....	....	....	....	....	....	....	....	....	....	....	....	....	....	....	....
1998-99	**Nashville**	**NHL**	77	11	20	31	26	7	0	1	65	16.9	–10	8	50.0	13:13	....	....	....	....	....	....	....	....	....
99-2000	**Atlanta**	**NHL**	81	23	27	50	30	9	0	2	107	21.5	–32	8	25.0	15:42	....	....	....	....	....	....	....	....	....
2000-01	**Atlanta**	**NHL**	77	15	44	59	26	6	0	4	104	14.4	–5	11	54.6	16:58	....	....	....	....	....	....	....	....	....
2001-02	**Minnesota**	**NHL**	81	21	48	69	18	10	0	2	106	19.8	–4	111	58.6	16:02	....	....	....	....	....	....	....	....	....
2002-03	**Minnesota**	**NHL**	82	18	28	46	30	9	0	2	97	18.6	–10	59	44.1	14:29	18	7	6	13	4	4	0	1	15:00
2003-04	**Minnesota**	**NHL**	82	15	34	49	12	7	0	3	90	16.7	3	49	46.9	15:32	....	....	....	....	....	....	....	....	....
2004-05			DID NOT PLAY																						
	NHL Totals		**542**	**121**	**223**	**344**	**166**	**54**	**0**	**17**	**650**	**18.6**		**246**	**51.2**	**15:19**	**24**	**8**	**9**	**17**	**4**	**4**	**0**	**1**	**15:00**

OHL First All-Star Team (1993) • Canadian Major Junior Second All-Star Team (1993) • AHL Second All-Star Team (1995)

Claimed by **Nashville** from **Washington** in Expansion Draft, June 26, 1998. Traded to **Atlanta** by **Nashville** for Atlanta's 5th round choice (Matt Hendricks) in 2000 Entry Draft, June 21, 1999. Signed as a free agent by **Minnesota**, July 17, 2001. Signed as a free agent by **Colorado**, August 6, 2005.

BRYLIN, Sergei   (BRIH-lin, SAIR-gay)   **N.J.**

Left wing. Shoots left. 5'10", 190 lbs.   Born, Moscow, USSR, January 13, 1974. New Jersey's 2nd choice, 42nd overall, in 1992 Entry Draft.

Season	Club	League	GP	G	A	Pts	PIM	PP	SH	GW	S	%	+/-	TF	F%	Min	GP	G	A	Pts	PIM	PP	SH	GW	Min
1991-92	CSKA Moscow	CIS	44	1	6	7	4	....	....	....	....	....	....	....	....	....	....	....	....	....	....	....	....	....	....
1992-93	CSKA Moscow	CIS	42	5	4	9	36	....	....	....	....	....	....	....	....	....	....	....	....	....	....	....	....	....	....
1993-94	CSKA Moscow	CIS	39	4	6	10	36	....	....	....	....	....	....	....	....	....	3	1	0	1	2	....	....	....	....
	Russian Penguins	IHL	13	4	5	9	18	....	....	....	....	....	....	....	....	....	....	....	....	....	....	....	....	....	....
1994-95	Albany River Rats	AHL	63	19	35	54	78	....	....	....	....	....	....	....	....	....	....	....	....	....	....	....	....	....	....
	♦ **New Jersey**	**NHL**	26	6	8	14	8	0	0	0	41	14.6	12				12	1	2	3	4	0	0	0	
1995-96	**New Jersey**	**NHL**	50	4	5	9	26	0	0	1	51	7.8	–2				....	....	....	....	....	....	....	....	....
1996-97	**New Jersey**	**NHL**	29	2	2	4	20	0	0	0	34	5.9	–13				....	....	....	....	....	....	....	....	....
	Albany River Rats	AHL	43	17	24	41	38	....	....	....	....	....	....	....	....	....	16	4	8	12	12	....	....	....	....
1997-98	**New Jersey**	**NHL**	18	2	3	5	0	0	0	0	20	10.0	4				....	....	....	....	....	....	....	....	....
	Albany River Rats	AHL	44	21	22	43	60	....	....	....	....	....	....	....	....	....	....	....	....	....	....	....	....	....	....
1998-99	**New Jersey**	**NHL**	47	5	10	15	28	3	0	1	51	9.8	8	184	50.5	12:55	5	3	1	4	4	1	0	1	18:21
99-2000 ♦	**New Jersey**	**NHL**	64	9	11	20	20	1	0	1	84	10.7	0	72	41.7	13:23	17	3	5	8	0	0	0	0	13:02
2000-01	**New Jersey**	**NHL**	75	23	29	52	24	3	1	5	130	17.7	25	43	44.2	15:31	20	3	4	7	6	1	0	1	13:07
2001-02	**New Jersey**	**NHL**	76	16	28	44	10	5	0	3	133	12.0	21	17	47.1	17:11	6	0	2	2	2	0	0	0	19:05
2002-03 ♦	**New Jersey**	**NHL**	52	11	9	20	16	3	1	1	86	12.8	–2	90	32.2	16:11	19	1	3	4	8	0	0	1	17:03
2003-04	**New Jersey**	**NHL**	82	14	19	33	20	7	0	1	98	14.3	10	695	46.6	16:25	5	0	0	0	0	0	0	0	15:02
2004-05	Voskresensk	Russia	38	8	19	27	40	....	....	....	....	....	....	....	....	....	....	....	....	....	....	....	....	....	....
	NHL Totals		**519**	**92**	**123**	**215**	**172**	**22**	**2**	**8**	**728**	**12.6**		**1101**	**45.7**	**15:27**	**84**	**11**	**17**	**28**	**24**	**2**	**0**	**3**	**15:08**

Signed as a free agent by **Voskresensk** (Russia), November 4, 2004.

BUCHBERGER, Kelly

(BUK-buhr-guhr, KEHL-lee)

Right wing. Shoots left. 6'2", 210 lbs. Born, Langenburg, Sask., December 2, 1966. Edmonton's 8th choice, 188th overall, in 1985 Entry Draft.

			Regular Season														Playoffs								
Season	Club	League	GP	G	A	Pts	PIM	PP	SH	GW	S	%	+/-	TF	F%	Min	GP	G	A	Pts	PIM	PP	SH	GW	Min
1983-84	Melville	SJHL	60	14	11	25	139	....	....	....	....	....	....	....	....	....	....	....	....	....	....	....	....	....	....
1984-85	Moose Jaw	WHL	51	12	17	29	114	....	....	....	....	....	....	....	....	....	....	....	....	....	....	....	....	....	....
1985-86	Moose Jaw	WHL	72	14	22	36	206	....	....	....	....	....	....	....	....	....	13	11	4	15	37	....	....	....	....
1986-87	Nova Scotia Oilers	AHL	70	12	20	32	257	....	....	....	....	....	....	....	....	....	5	0	1	1	23	....	....	....	....
	♦ **Edmonton**	**NHL**	....	....	....	....	....	....	....	....	....	....	....	....	....	....	**3**	**0**	**1**	**1**	**5**	**0**	**0**	**0**	....
1987-88	**Edmonton**	**NHL**	**19**	**1**	**0**	**1**	**81**	**0**	**0**	**0**	**10**	**10.0**	**–1**	....	....	....	....	....	....	....	....	....	....	....	....
	Nova Scotia Oilers	AHL	49	21	23	44	206	....	....	....	....	....	....	....	....	....	2	0	0	0	11	....	....	....	....
1988-89	**Edmonton**	**NHL**	**66**	**5**	**9**	**14**	**234**	**1**	**0**	**1**	**57**	**8.8**	**–14**	....	....	....	....	....	....	....	....	....	....	....	....
1989-90♦	**Edmonton**	**NHL**	**55**	**2**	**6**	**8**	**168**	**0**	**0**	**2**	**35**	**5.7**	**–8**	....	....	....	**19**	**0**	**5**	**5**	**13**	**0**	**0**	**0**	....
1990-91	**Edmonton**	**NHL**	**64**	**3**	**1**	**4**	**160**	**0**	**0**	**2**	**54**	**5.6**	**–6**	....	....	....	**12**	**2**	**1**	**3**	**25**	**0**	**0**	**0**	....
1991-92	**Edmonton**	**NHL**	**79**	**20**	**24**	**44**	**157**	**0**	**4**	**3**	**90**	**22.2**	**9**	....	....	....	**16**	**1**	**4**	**5**	**32**	**0**	**0**	**0**	....
1992-93	**Edmonton**	**NHL**	**83**	**12**	**18**	**30**	**133**	**1**	**2**	**3**	**92**	**13.0**	**–27**	....	....	....	....	....	....	....	....	....	....	....	....
1993-94	**Edmonton**	**NHL**	**84**	**3**	**18**	**21**	**199**	**0**	**0**	**0**	**93**	**3.2**	**–20**	....	....	....	....	....	....	....	....	....	....	....	....
1994-95	**Edmonton**	**NHL**	**48**	**7**	**17**	**24**	**82**	**2**	**1**	**5**	**73**	**9.6**	**0**	....	....	....	....	....	....	....	....	....	....	....	....
1995-96	**Edmonton**	**NHL**	**82**	**11**	**14**	**25**	**184**	**0**	**2**	**3**	**119**	**9.2**	**–20**	....	....	....	....	....	....	....	....	....	....	....	....
1996-97	**Edmonton**	**NHL**	**81**	**8**	**30**	**38**	**159**	**0**	**0**	**3**	**78**	**10.3**	**4**	....	....	....	**12**	**5**	**2**	**7**	**16**	**0**	**0**	**1**	....
1997-98	**Edmonton**	**NHL**	**82**	**6**	**17**	**23**	**122**	**1**	**1**	**1**	**86**	**7.0**	**–10**	....	....	....	**12**	**1**	**2**	**3**	**25**	**0**	**0**	**0**	....
1998-99	**Edmonton**	**NHL**	**52**	**4**	**4**	**8**	**68**	**0**	**2**	**1**	**29**	**13.8**	**–6**	**23**	**26.1**	**11:49**	**4**	**0**	**0**	**0**	**0**	**0**	**0**	**0**	**10:06**
99-2000	**Atlanta**	**NHL**	**68**	**5**	**12**	**17**	**139**	**0**	**0**	**0**	**56**	**8.9**	**–34**	**577**	**45.6**	**16:21**	....	....	....	....	....	....	....	....	....
	Los Angeles	**NHL**	**13**	**2**	**1**	**3**	**13**	**0**	**0**	**0**	**20**	**10.0**	**–2**	**6**	**16.7**	**14:43**	**4**	**0**	**0**	**0**	**4**	**0**	**0**	**0**	**8:56**
2000-01	**Los Angeles**	**NHL**	**82**	**6**	**14**	**20**	**75**	**0**	**0**	**1**	**66**	**9.1**	**–10**	**155**	**40.7**	**14:26**	**8**	**1**	**0**	**1**	**2**	**0**	**0**	**0**	**9:58**
2001-02	**Los Angeles**	**NHL**	**74**	**6**	**7**	**13**	**105**	**0**	**0**	**1**	**39**	**15.4**	**–13**	**126**	**41.3**	**10:21**	**7**	**0**	**0**	**0**	**7**	**0**	**0**	**0**	**8:48**
2002-03	**Phoenix**	**NHL**	**79**	**3**	**9**	**12**	**109**	**0**	**1**	**0**	**32**	**9.4**	**0**	**784**	**43.1**	**9:59**	....	....	....	....	....	....	....	....	....
2003-04	**Pittsburgh**	**NHL**	**71**	**1**	**3**	**4**	**109**	**0**	**0**	**0**	**34**	**2.9**	**–19**	**64**	**45.3**	**10:21**	....	....	....	....	....	....	....	....	....
2004-05			DID NOT PLAY																						
	NHL Totals		**1182**	**105**	**204**	**309**	**2297**	**5**	**13**	**26**	**1063**	**9.9**		**1735**	**43.3**	**12:17**	**97**	**10**	**15**	**25**	**129**	**0**	**0**	**1**	**9:27**

Claimed by **Atlanta** from **Edmonton** in Expansion Draft, June 25, 1999. Traded to **Los Angeles** by **Atlanta** with Nelson Emerson for Donald Audette and Frantisek Kaberle, March 13, 2000. Signed as a free agent by **Phoenix**, July 7, 2002. Signed as a free agent by **Pittsburgh**, July 31, 2003.

BULIS, Jan

(BOO-lihs, YAHN) **MTL.**

Center. Shoots left. 6'1", 208 lbs. Born, Pardubice, Czech., March 18, 1978. Washington's 3rd choice, 43rd overall, in 1996 Entry Draft.

Season	Club	League	GP	G	A	Pts	PIM	PP	SH	GW	S	%	+/-	TF	F%	Min	GP	G	A	Pts	PIM	PP	SH	GW	Min
1993-94	HC Pardubice Jr.	CzRep-Jr.	25	16	11	27	....	....	....	....	....	....	....	....	....	....	....	....	....	....	....	....	....	....	....
1994-95	Kelowna Spartans	BCJHL	51	23	25	48	36	....	....	....	....	....	....	....	....	....	17	7	9	16	0	....	....	....	....
1995-96	Barrie Colts	OHL	59	29	30	59	22	....	....	....	....	....	....	....	....	....	7	2	3	5	2	....	....	....	....
1996-97	Barrie Colts	OHL	64	42	61	103	42	....	....	....	....	....	....	....	....	....	9	3	7	10	10	....	....	....	....
1997-98	Kingston	OHL	2	0	1	1	0	....	....	....	....	....	....	....	....	....	12	8	10	18	12	....	....	....	....
	Washington	**NHL**	**48**	**5**	**11**	**16**	**18**	**0**	**0**	**0**	**37**	**13.5**	**–5**	....	....	....	....	....	....	....	....	....	....	....	....
	Portland Pirates	AHL	3	1	4	5	12	....	....	....	....	....	....	....	....	....	....	....	....	....	....	....	....	....	....
1998-99	**Washington**	**NHL**	**38**	**7**	**16**	**23**	**6**	**3**	**0**	**3**	**57**	**12.3**	**3**	**599**	**48.9**	**14:27**	....	....	....	....	....	....	....	....	....
	Cincinnati	IHL	10	2	2	4	14	....	....	....	....	....	....	....	....	....	....	....	....	....	....	....	....	....	....
99-2000	**Washington**	**NHL**	**56**	**9**	**22**	**31**	**30**	**0**	**0**	**1**	**92**	**9.8**	**7**	**609**	**45.5**	**13:55**	....	....	....	....	....	....	....	....	....
2000-01	**Washington**	**NHL**	**39**	**5**	**13**	**18**	**26**	**1**	**0**	**0**	**41**	**12.2**	**0**	**224**	**46.9**	**11:53**	....	....	....	....	....	....	....	....	....
	Portland Pirates	AHL	4	0	2	2	0	....	....	....	....	....	....	....	....	....	....	....	....	....	....	....	....	....	....
	Montreal	**NHL**	**12**	**0**	**5**	**5**	**0**	**0**	**0**	**0**	**20**	**0.0**	**–1**	**230**	**48.3**	**18:25**	....	....	....	....	....	....	....	....	....
2001-02	**Montreal**	**NHL**	**53**	**9**	**10**	**19**	**8**	**1**	**0**	**3**	**87**	**10.3**	**–2**	**156**	**43.0**	**13:34**	**6**	**0**	**0**	**0**	**6**	**0**	**0**	**0**	**12:25**
2002-03	**Montreal**	**NHL**	**82**	**16**	**24**	**40**	**30**	**0**	**0**	**2**	**160**	**10.0**	**9**	**153**	**42.5**	**15:42**	....	....	....	....	....	....	....	....	....
2003-04	**Montreal**	**NHL**	**72**	**13**	**17**	**30**	**30**	**1**	**1**	**4**	**147**	**8.8**	**–8**	**103**	**46.6**	**17:07**	**11**	**1**	**1**	**2**	**4**	**0**	**0**	**0**	**17:23**
2004-05	Pardubice	CzRep	45	24	25	49	113	....	....	....	....	....	....	....	....	....	16	7	4	11	43	....	....	....	....
	NHL Totals		**400**	**64**	**118**	**182**	**148**	**6**	**1**	**13**	**641**	**10.0**		**2074**	**46.6**	**14:55**	**17**	**1**	**1**	**2**	**10**	**0**	**0**	**0**	**15:38**

Traded to **Montreal** by **Washington** with Richard Zednik and Washington's 1st round choice (Alexander Perezhogin) in 2001 Entry Draft for Trevor Linden, Dainius Zubrus and New Jersey's 2nd round choice (previously acquired, later traded to Tampa Bay – Tampa Bay selected Andreas Holmqvist) in 2001 Entry Draft, March 13, 2001. Signed as a free agent by **Pardubice** (CzRep), September 17, 2004.

BURE, Valeri

(boo-RAY, VAL-uhr-ee) **L.A.**

Right wing. Shoots right. 5'10", 185 lbs. Born, Moscow, USSR, June 13, 1974. Montreal's 2nd choice, 33rd overall, in 1992 Entry Draft.

Season	Club	League	GP	G	A	Pts	PIM	PP	SH	GW	S	%	+/-	TF	F%	Min	GP	G	A	Pts	PIM	PP	SH	GW	Min
1990-91	CSKA Moscow	USSR	3	0	0	0	0	....	....	....	....	....	....	....	....	....	....	....	....	....	....	....	....	....	....
1991-92	Spokane Chiefs	WHL	53	27	22	49	78	....	....	....	....	....	....	....	....	....	10	11	6	17	10	....	....	....	....
1992-93	Spokane Chiefs	WHL	66	68	79	147	49	....	....	....	....	....	....	....	....	....	9	6	11	17	14	....	....	....	....
1993-94	Spokane Chiefs	WHL	59	40	62	102	48	....	....	....	....	....	....	....	....	....	3	5	3	8	2	....	....	....	....
1994-95	Fredericton	AHL	45	23	25	48	32	....	....	....	....	....	....	....	....	....	....	....	....	....	....	....	....	....	....
	Montreal	**NHL**	**24**	**3**	**1**	**4**	**6**	**0**	**0**	**1**	**39**	**7.7**	**–1**	....	....	....	....	....	....	....	....	....	....	....	....
1995-96	**Montreal**	**NHL**	**77**	**22**	**20**	**42**	**28**	**5**	**0**	**1**	**143**	**15.4**	**10**	....	....	....	**6**	**0**	**1**	**1**	**6**	**0**	**0**	**0**	....
1996-97	**Montreal**	**NHL**	**64**	**14**	**21**	**35**	**6**	**4**	**0**	**2**	**131**	**10.7**	**4**	....	....	....	**5**	**0**	**1**	**1**	**2**	**0**	**0**	**0**	....
1997-98	**Montreal**	**NHL**	**50**	**7**	**22**	**29**	**33**	**2**	**0**	**1**	**134**	**5.2**	**–5**	....	....	....	....	....	....	....	....	....	....	....	....
	Calgary	**NHL**	**16**	**5**	**4**	**9**	**2**	**0**	**0**	**1**	**45**	**11.1**	**0**	....	....	....	....	....	....	....	....	....	....	....	....
	Russia	Olympics	6	1	0	1	0	....	....	....	....	....	....	....	....	....	....	....	....	....	....	....	....	....	....
1998-99	**Calgary**	**NHL**	**80**	**26**	**27**	**53**	**22**	**7**	**0**	**4**	**260**	**10.0**	**0**	**15**	**40.0**	**16:11**	....	....	....	....	....	....	....	....	....
99-2000	**Calgary**	**NHL**	**82**	**35**	**40**	**75**	**50**	**13**	**0**	**6**	**308**	**11.4**	**–7**	**8**	**25.0**	**20:58**	....	....	....	....	....	....	....	....	....
2000-01	**Calgary**	**NHL**	**78**	**27**	**28**	**55**	**26**	**16**	**0**	**2**	**276**	**9.8**	**–21**	**9**	**11.1**	**19:01**	....	....	....	....	....	....	....	....	....
2001-02	**Florida**	**NHL**	**31**	**8**	**10**	**18**	**12**	**2**	**0**	**1**	**100**	**8.0**	**–3**	**30**	**33.3**	**18:36**	....	....	....	....	....	....	....	....	....
	Russia	Olympics	6	1	0	1	2	....	....	....	....	....	....	....	....	....	....	....	....	....	....	....	....	....	....
2002-03	**Florida**	**NHL**	**46**	**5**	**21**	**26**	**10**	**3**	**0**	**2**	**150**	**3.3**	**–11**	**19**	**31.6**	**18:38**	....	....	....	....	....	....	....	....	....
	St. Louis	**NHL**	**5**	**0**	**2**	**2**	**0**	**0**	**0**	**0**	**11**	**0.0**	**–2**	**0**	**0.0**	**15:11**	**6**	**0**	**2**	**2**	**8**	**0**	**0**	**0**	**11:14**
2003-04	**Florida**	**NHL**	**55**	**20**	**25**	**45**	**20**	**8**	**0**	**4**	**175**	**11.4**	**0**	**29**	**41.4**	**19:13**	....	....	....	....	....	....	....	....	....
	Dallas	**NHL**	**13**	**2**	**5**	**7**	**6**	**0**	**0**	**0**	**34**	**5.9**	**3**	**2**	**0.0**	**17:51**	**5**	**0**	**3**	**3**	**0**	**0**	**0**	**0**	**17:13**
2004-05			DID NOT PLAY																						
	NHL Totals		**621**	**174**	**226**	**400**	**221**	**60**	**0**	**25**	**1806**	**9.6**		**112**	**33.0**	**18:42**	**22**	**0**	**7**	**7**	**16**	**0**	**0**	**0**	**13:57**

WHL West First All-Star Team (1993) • WHL West Second All-Star Team (1994)

Played in NHL All-Star Game (2000)

Traded to **Calgary** by **Montreal** with Montreal's 4th round choice (Shaun Sutter) in 1998 Entry Draft for Jonas Hoglund and Zarley Zalapski, February 1, 1998. Traded to **Florida** by **Calgary** with Jason Wiemer for Rob Niedermayer and Philadelphia's 2nd round choice (previously acquired, Calgary selected Andrei Medvedev) in 2001 Entry Draft, June 24, 2001. • Missed majority of 2001-02 season recovering from knee injury suffered in game vs. Vancouver, October 16, 2001. Traded to **St. Louis** by **Florida** with Florida's 5th round choice (Nikita Nikitin) in 2004 Entry Draft for Mike Van Ryn, March 11, 2003. Claimed on waivers by **Florida**, June 25, 2003. Traded to **Dallas** by **Florida** for Drew Bagnall and Dallas' 2nd round compensatory choice (later traded to Phoenix - Phoenix selected Enver Lisin) in 2004 Entry Draft, March 8, 2004. Signed as a free agent by **Los Angeles**, August 12, 2005.

BURNETT, Garrett

(buhr-NEHT, GAIR-eht) **DAL.**

Left wing. Shoots left. 6'3", 225 lbs. Born, Coquitlam, B.C., September 23, 1975.

Season	Club	League	GP	G	A	Pts	PIM	PP	SH	GW	S	%	+/-	TF	F%	Min	GP	G	A	Pts	PIM	PP	SH	GW	Min
1993-94	Trail	RIJHL	26	2	1	3	248	....	....	....	....	....	....	....	....	....	....	....	....	....	....	....	....	....	....
1994-95	Sault Ste. Marie	OHL	14	0	1	1	78	....	....	....	....	....	....	....	....	....	....	....	....	....	....	....	....	....	....
	Kitchener Rangers	OHL	22	0	1	1	74	....	....	....	....	....	....	....	....	....	3	0	1	1	23	....	....	....	....
1995-96	Utica Blizzard	ColHL	15	0	1	1	78	....	....	....	....	....	....	....	....	....	....	....	....	....	....	....	....	....	....
	Oklahoma City	CHL	3	0	0	0	20	....	....	....	....	....	....	....	....	....	....	....	....	....	....	....	....	....	....
	Tulsa Oilers	CHL	6	1	0	1	94	....	....	....	....	....	....	....	....	....	....	....	....	....	....	....	....	....	....
	Nashville Knights	ECHL	3	0	0	0	22	....	....	....	....	....	....	....	....	....	....	....	....	....	....	....	....	....	....
	Jacksonville	ECHL	8	0	1	1	38	....	....	....	....	....	....	....	....	....	1	0	0	0	0	....	....	....	....
1996-97	Knoxville	ECHL	50	5	11	16	321	....	....	....	....	....	....	....	....	....	....	....	....	....	....	....	....	....	....
1997-98	Johnstown Chiefs	ECHL	34	1	1	2	331	....	....	....	....	....	....	....	....	....	....	....	....	....	....	....	....	....	....
	Philadelphia	AHL	14	1	2	3	129	....	....	....	....	....	....	....	....	....	....	....	....	....	....	....	....	....	....
1998-99	Kentucky	AHL	31	1	0	1	186	....	....	....	....	....	....	....	....	....	....	....	....	....	....	....	....	....	....
99-2000	Kentucky	AHL	58	3	3	6	*506	....	....	....	....	....	....	....	....	....	4	0	0	0	31	....	....	....	....
2000-01	Cleveland	IHL	54	2	4	6	250	....	....	....	....	....	....	....	....	....	....	....	....	....	....	....	....	....	....
2001-02	New Haven	UHL	4	1	0	1	40	....	....	....	....	....	....	....	....	....	....	....	....	....	....	....	....	....	....
	Cincinnati	AHL	32	1	0	1	175	....	....	....	....	....	....	....	....	....	....	....	....	....	....	....	....	....	....
2002-03	Hartford	AHL	62	6	1	7	*346	....	....	....	....	....	....	....	....	....	1	0	0	0	2	....	....	....	....

			Regular Season														Playoffs								
Season	Club	League	GP	G	A	Pts	PIM	PP	SH	GW	S	%	+/-	TF	F%	Min	GP	G	A	Pts	PIM	PP	SH	GW	Min
2003-04	**Anaheim**	**NHL**	**39**	**1**	**2**	**3**	**184**	**0**	**0**	**0**	**24**	**4.2**	**0**	**1**	**0.0**	**3:36**	....	....	....	....	....	....	....	....	....
2004-05	Danbury Trashers	UHL	7	0	1	1	48	....	....	....	....	....	....	....	....	....	....	....	....	....	....	....	....	....	....
	NHL Totals		**39**	**1**	**2**	**3**	**184**	**0**	**0**	**0**	**24**	**4.2**		**1**	**0.0**	**3:36**	....	....	....	....	....	....	....	....	....

Signed as a free agent by **San Jose**, July 2, 1998. • Missed majority of 2001-02 season recovering from knee injury suffered in game vs. New Haven (AHL), January 15, 2002. Signed as a free agent by **Hartford** (AHL), August 22, 2002. Signed as a free agent by **Anaheim**, July 25, 2003. • Spent majority of 2003-04 season as a healthy reserve. Signed as a free agent by **Danbury** (UHL), October 8, 2004. Signed as a free agent by **Dallas**, August 15, 2005.

BURNS, Brent (BUHRNZ, BREHNT) MIN.

Defense. Shoots right. 6'4", 200 lbs. Born, Ajax, Ont., March 9, 1985. Minnesota's 1st choice, 20th overall, in 2003 Entry Draft.

2000-01	North York	MTHL	46	4	7	11	16	....	....	....	....	....	....	....	....	....	....	....	....	....	....	....	....	....	....
2001-02	Couchiching	OPJHL	68	15	25	40	14	....	....	....	....	....	....	....	....	....	....	....	....	....	....	....	....	....	....
2002-03	Brampton	OHL	68	15	25	40	14	....	....	....	....	....	....	....	....	....	11	5	6	11	6	....	....	....	....
2003-04	**Minnesota**	**NHL**	**36**	**1**	**5**	**6**	**12**	**0**	**0**	**0**	**34**	**2.9**	**–10**	**7**	**28.6**	**13:29**	....	....	....	....	....	....	....	....	....
	Houston Aeros	AHL	1	0	1	1	2	....	....	....	....	....	....	....	....	....	....	....	....	....	....	....	....	....	....
2004-05	Houston Aeros	AHL	73	11	16	27	57	....	....	....	....	....	....	....	....	....	5	0	0	0	4	....	....	....	....
	NHL Totals		**36**	**1**	**5**	**6**	**12**	**0**	**0**	**0**	**34**	**2.9**		**7**	**28.6**	**13:29**	....	....	....	....	....	....	....	....	....

• Spent majority of 2003-04 season on assignment to Team Canada and as a healthy reserve.

BUTENSCHON, Sven (BUH-tehn-shohn, SVEHN) VAN.

Defense. Shoots left. 6'4", 215 lbs. Born, Itzehoe, West Germany, March 22, 1976. Pittsburgh's 3rd choice, 57th overall, in 1994 Entry Draft.

1991-92	Eastman Selects	MMMHL	36	2	10	12	110	....	....	....	....	....	....	....	....	....	....	....	....	....	....	....	....	....	....
1992-93	Eastman Selects	MMMHL	35	14	22	36	101	....	....	....	....	....	....	....	....	....	....	....	....	....	....	....	....	....	....
1993-94	Brandon	WHL	70	3	19	22	51	....	....	....	....	....	....	....	....	....	4	0	0	0	6	....	....	....	....
1994-95	Brandon	WHL	21	1	5	6	44	....	....	....	....	....	....	....	....	....	18	1	2	3	11	....	....	....	....
1995-96	Brandon	WHL	70	4	37	41	99	....	....	....	....	....	....	....	....	....	19	1	12	13	18	....	....	....	....
1996-97	Cleveland	IHL	75	3	12	15	68	....	....	....	....	....	....	....	....	....	10	0	1	1	4	....	....	....	....
1997-98	**Pittsburgh**	**NHL**	**8**	**0**	**0**	**0**	**6**	**0**	**0**	**0**	**4**	**0.0**	**–1**	....	....	....	....	....	....	....	....	....	....	....	....
	Syracuse Crunch	AHL	65	14	23	37	66	....	....	....	....	....	....	....	....	....	5	1	2	3	0	....	....	....	....
1998-99	**Pittsburgh**	**NHL**	**17**	**0**	**0**	**0**	**6**	**0**	**0**	**0**	**8**	**0.0**	**–7**	**0**	**0.0**	**13:08**	....	....	....	....	....	....	....	....	....
	Houston Aeros	IHL	57	1	4	5	81	....	....	....	....	....	....	....	....	....	....	....	....	....	....	....	....	....	....
99-2000	**Pittsburgh**	**NHL**	**3**	**0**	**0**	**0**	**0**	**0**	**0**	**0**	**2**	**0.0**	**3**	**0**	**0.0**	**16:25**	....	....	....	....	....	....	....	....	....
	Wilkes-Barre	AHL	75	19	21	40	101	....	....	....	....	....	....	....	....	....	....	....	....	....	....	....	....	....	....
2000-01	**Pittsburgh**	**NHL**	**5**	**0**	**1**	**1**	**2**	**0**	**0**	**0**	**6**	**0.0**	**1**	**0**	**0.0**	**17:51**	....	....	....	....	....	....	....	....	....
	Wilkes-Barre	AHL	55	7	28	35	85	....	....	....	....	....	....	....	....	....	....	....	....	....	....	....	....	....	....
	Edmonton	**NHL**	**7**	**1**	**1**	**2**	**2**	**0**	**0**	**0**	**3**	**33.3**	**2**	**0**	**0.0**	**11:07**	....	....	....	....	....	....	....	....	....
2001-02	**Edmonton**	**NHL**	**14**	**0**	**0**	**0**	**4**	**0**	**0**	**0**	**8**	**0.0**	**0**	**0**	**0.0**	**9:39**	....	....	....	....	....	....	....	....	....
	Hamilton	AHL	61	9	35	44	88	....	....	....	....	....	....	....	....	....	....	....	....	....	....	....	....	....	....
2002-03	**NY Islanders**	**NHL**	**37**	**0**	**4**	**4**	**26**	**0**	**0**	**0**	**19**	**0.0**	**–6**	**0**	**0.0**	**12:26**	....	....	....	....	....	....	....	....	....
	Bridgeport	AHL	36	3	13	16	58	....	....	....	....	....	....	....	....	....	9	3	6	9	6	....	....	....	....
2003-04	**NY Islanders**	**NHL**	**41**	**1**	**6**	**7**	**30**	**0**	**0**	**0**	**17**	**5.9**	**–3**	**0**	**0.0**	**11:15**	**4**	**0**	**0**	**0**	**0**	**0**	**0**	**0**	**7:42**
	Bridgeport	AHL	5	0	1	1	4	....	....	....	....	....	....	....	....	....	....	....	....	....	....	....	....	....	....
2004-05	Adler Mannheim	Germany	50	1	5	6	54	....	....	....	....	....	....	....	....	....	14	0	1	1	16	....	....	....	....
	NHL Totals		**132**	**2**	**12**	**14**	**76**	**0**	**0**	**0**	**67**	**3.0**		**0**	**0.0**	**12:04**	**4**	**0**	**0**	**0**	**0**	**0**	**0**	**0**	**7:42**

Traded to **Edmonton** by **Pittsburgh** for Dan LaCouture, March 13, 2001. Signed as a free agent by **Florida**, July 9, 2002. Traded to **NY Islanders** by **Florida** for Juraj Kolnik and NY Islanders' 9th round choice (later traded to San Jose – San Jose selected Carter Lee) in 2003 Entry Draft, October 11, 2003. Signed as a free agent by **Mannheim** (Germany), August 2, 2004. Signed as a free agent by **Vancouver**, August 22, 2005.

BUTSAYEV, Yuri (buht-SIGH-ehv, YOO-ree) ATL.

Left wing. Shoots left. 6', 195 lbs. Born, Togliatti, USSR, October 11, 1978. Detroit's 1st choice, 49th overall, in 1997 Entry Draft.

1995-96	Lada Togliatti 2	CIS-2	35	19	7	26	....	....	....	....	....	....	....	....	....	....	....	....	....	....	....	....	....	....	....
	Lada Togliatti	CIS	1	0	0	0	0	....	....	....	....	....	....	....	....	....	....	....	....	....	....	....	....	....	....
1996-97	Lada Togliatti	Russia	42	13	11	24	38	....	....	....	....	....	....	....	....	....	11	2	2	4	8	....	....	....	....
1997-98	Lada Togliatti	Russia	44	8	9	17	63	....	....	....	....	....	....	....	....	....	....	....	....	....	....	....	....	....	....
	Lada Togliatti	EuroHL	6	2	0	2	8	....	....	....	....	....	....	....	....	....	....	....	....	....	....	....	....	....	....
1998-99	Dynamo Moscow	Russia	1	0	1	1	0	....	....	....	....	....	....	....	....	....	....	....	....	....	....	....	....	....	....
	Lada Togliatti	Russia	39	10	7	17	55	....	....	....	....	....	....	....	....	....	7	1	2	3	14	....	....	....	....
99-2000	**Detroit**	**NHL**	**57**	**5**	**3**	**8**	**12**	**0**	**0**	**0**	**46**	**10.9**	**–6**	**22**	**40.9**	**9:36**	....	....	....	....	....	....	....	....	....
	Cincinnati	AHL	9	0	1	1	0	....	....	....	....	....	....	....	....	....	....	....	....	....	....	....	....	....	....
2000-01	**Detroit**	**NHL**	**15**	**1**	**1**	**2**	**4**	**0**	**0**	**0**	**18**	**5.6**	**–2**	**6**	**33.3**	**9:09**	....	....	....	....	....	....	....	....	....
	Cincinnati	AHL	54	29	17	46	26	....	....	....	....	....	....	....	....	....	4	0	2	2	2	....	....	....	....
2001-02	**Detroit**	**NHL**	**3**	**0**	**0**	**0**	**0**	**0**	**0**	**0**	**4**	**0.0**	**–1**	**0**	**0.0**	**9:44**	....	....	....	....	....	....	....	....	....
	Cincinnati	AHL	61	21	23	44	44	....	....	....	....	....	....	....	....	....	....	....	....	....	....	....	....	....	....
	Atlanta	**NHL**	**8**	**2**	**0**	**2**	**4**	**0**	**0**	**0**	**6**	**33.3**	**1**	**1**	**100.0**	**13:28**	....	....	....	....	....	....	....	....	....
	Chicago Wolves	AHL	4	1	1	2	0	....	....	....	....	....	....	....	....	....	22	7	4	11	20	....	....	....	....
2002-03	**Atlanta**	**NHL**	**16**	**2**	**0**	**2**	**8**	**0**	**0**	**0**	**21**	**9.5**	**–5**	**26**	**30.8**	**12:05**	....	....	....	....	....	....	....	....	....
	Chicago Wolves	AHL	7	6	3	9	0	....	....	....	....	....	....	....	....	....	....	....	....	....	....	....	....	....	....
	Yaroslavl	Russia	19	2	5	7	37	....	....	....	....	....	....	....	....	....	10	2	3	5	4	....	....	....	....
2003-04	CSKA Moscow	Russia	18	1	3	4	6	....	....	....	....	....	....	....	....	....	....	....	....	....	....	....	....	....	....
	Lada Togliatti	Russia	28	7	3	10	30	....	....	....	....	....	....	....	....	....	6	1	0	1	0	....	....	....	....
2004-05	Lada Togliatti	Russia	42	6	6	12	32	....	....	....	....	....	....	....	....	....	9	2	2	4	6	....	....	....	....
	NHL Totals		**99**	**10**	**4**	**14**	**28**	**0**	**0**	**0**	**95**	**10.5**		**55**	**36.4**	**10:15**	....	....	....	....	....	....	....	....	....

Traded to **Atlanta** by **Detroit** with Detroit's 3rd round choice (later traded to Columbus – Columbus selected Jeff Genovy) in 2002 Entry Draft for Jiri Slegr, March 19, 2002. • Assigned to **Yaroslavl** (Russia) by **Atlanta**, November 22, 2002. Signed as a free agent by **CSKA** (Russia), July 1, 2003. Signed as a free agent by **Togliatti**, December, 2003.

BUZEK, Petr (BOO-zehk, PEE-tuhr)

Defense. Shoots left. 6'1", 220 lbs. Born, Jihlava, Czech., April 26, 1977. Dallas' 3rd choice, 63rd overall, in 1995 Entry Draft.

1993-94	Jihlava Jr.	CzRep-Jr.	3	0	0	0	....	....	....	....	....	....	....	....	....	....	....	....	....	....	....	....	....	....	....
1994-95	HC Dukla Jihlava	CzRep	43	2	5	7	47	....	....	....	....	....	....	....	....	....	2	0	0	0	2	....	....	....	....
1995-96	Michigan	IHL	DID NOT PLAY – INJURED																						
1996-97	Michigan	IHL	67	4	6	10	48	....	....	....	....	....	....	....	....	....	....	....	....	....	....	....	....	....	....
1997-98	**Dallas**	**NHL**	**2**	**0**	**0**	**0**	**2**	**0**	**0**	**0**	**0**	**0.0**	**1**	....	....	....	....	....	....	....	....	....	....	....	....
	Michigan	IHL	60	10	15	25	58	....	....	....	....	....	....	....	....	....	2	0	1	1	17	....	....	....	....
1998-99	**Dallas**	**NHL**	**2**	**0**	**0**	**0**	**2**	**0**	**0**	**0**	**0**	**0.0**	**0**	**0**	**0.0**	**13:50**	....	....	....	....	....	....	....	....	....
	Michigan	IHL	74	5	14	19	68	....	....	....	....	....	....	....	....	....	5	0	0	0	10	....	....	....	....
99-2000	**Atlanta**	**NHL**	**63**	**5**	**14**	**19**	**41**	**3**	**0**	**0**	**90**	**5.6**	**–22**	**0**	**0.0**	**18:24**	....	....	....	....	....	....	....	....	....
2000-01	**Atlanta**	**NHL**	**5**	**0**	**0**	**0**	**8**	**0**	**0**	**0**	**11**	**0.0**	**2**	**0**	**0.0**	**17:26**	....	....	....	....	....	....	....	....	....
2001-02	**Atlanta**	**NHL**	**9**	**0**	**0**	**0**	**13**	**0**	**0**	**0**	**2**	**0.0**	**–4**	**0**	**0.0**	**15:58**	....	....	....	....	....	....	....	....	....
	Chicago Wolves	AHL	4	0	1	1	2	....	....	....	....	....	....	....	....	....	....	....	....	....	....	....	....	....	....
	Calgary	**NHL**	**32**	**1**	**3**	**4**	**14**	**0**	**0**	**0**	**34**	**2.9**	**4**	**0**	**0.0**	**17:12**	....	....	....	....	....	....	....	....	....
2002-03	**Calgary**	**NHL**	**44**	**3**	**5**	**8**	**14**	**3**	**0**	**0**	**48**	**6.3**	**–6**	**0**	**0.0**	**14:22**	....	....	....	....	....	....	....	....	....
2003-04	HC Sparta Praha	CzRep	5	0	0	0	10	....	....	....	....	....	....	....	....	....	....	....	....	....	....	....	....	....	....
2004-05	HC Dukla Jihlava	CzRep	34	0	2	2	38	....	....	....	....	....	....	....	....	....	....	....	....	....	....	....	....	....	....
	Litvinov	CzRep	7	0	2	2	6	....	....	....	....	....	....	....	....	....	....	....	....	....	....	....	....	....	....
	NHL Totals		**157**	**9**	**22**	**31**	**94**	**6**	**0**	**0**	**185**	**4.9**		**0**	**0.0**	**16:47**	....	....	....	....	....	....	....	....	....

Played in NHL All-Star Game (2000)

• Missed entire 1995-96 season recovering from injuries suffered in automobile accident, July, 1995. Claimed by **Atlanta** from **Dallas** in Expansion Draft, June 25, 1999. • Missed majority of 2000-01 season recovering from neck injury suffered in game vs. Anaheim, October 17, 2000. Traded to **Calgary** by **Atlanta** with Atlanta's 6th round choice (Adam Pardy) in 2004 Entry Draft for Jeff Cowan and the rights to Kurtis Foster, December 18, 2001. Loaned to **Sparta** (CzRep) by **Calgary**, October 20, 2003. Signed as a free agent by **Jihlava** (CzRep), September, 2004. Signed as a free agent by **Litvinov** (CzRep), January 9, 2005.

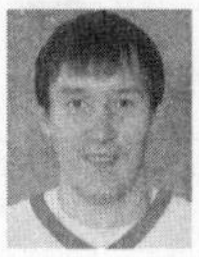

BYKOV, Dmitri

(BEE-kawv, dih-MEE-tree) **DET.**

Defense. Shoots left. 5'10", 169 lbs. Born, Izhevsk, USSR, May 5, 1977. Detroit's 6th choice, 258th overall, in 2001 Entry Draft.

			Regular Season														Playoffs								
Season	Club	League	GP	G	A	Pts	PIM	PP	SH	GW	S	%	+/-	TF	F%	Min	GP	G	A	Pts	PIM	PP	SH	GW	Min
1995-96	CSK VVS Samara	CIS	50	1	2	3	39																		
1996-97	CSK VVS Samara	Russia	44	1	6	7	20										2	0	0	0	2				
1997-98	Lada Togliatti	Russia	9	0	1	1	4																		
	CSK VVS Samara	Russia	27	0	5	5	14																		
	Yaroslavl	Russia	10	1	2	3	6										7	0	1	1	10				
1998-99	Lada Togliatti	Russia	39	0	6	6	24										7	1	0	1	8				
	CSK VVS Samara	Russia	2	0	0	0	0																		
99-2000	Ak Bars Kazan	Russia	35	3	8	11	18										18	0	2	2	8				
	Ak Bars Kazan 2	Russia-3	3	0	1	1	4																		
2000-01	Ak Bars Kazan	Russia	39	3	8	11	28										4	0	1	1	4				
2001-02	Ak Bars Kazan	Russia	44	1	1	2	38										11	0	0	0	4				
2002-03	**Detroit**	**NHL**	**71**	**2**	**10**	**12**	**43**	**1**	**0**	**0**	**58**	**3.4**	**1**	**2**	**100.0**	**18:22**	**4**	**0**	**0**	**0**	**0**	**0**	**0**	**0**	**11:14**
2003-04	Ak Bars Kazan	Russia	55	5	11	16	46										8	2	1	3	10				
2004-05	Ak Bars Kazan	Russia	31	2	2	4	22										4	0	0	0	0				
	NHL Totals		**71**	**2**	**10**	**12**	**43**	**1**	**0**	**0**	**58**	**3.4**		**2**	**100.0**	**18:22**	**4**	**0**	**0**	**0**	**0**	**0**	**0**	**0**	**11:14**

Signed as a free agent by **Kazan** (Russia), June 18, 2003.

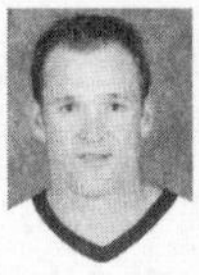

BYLSMA, Dan

(BIGHL-zmah, DAN)

Right wing. Shoots left. 6'2", 212 lbs. Born, Grand Haven, MI, September 19, 1970. Winnipeg's 7th choice, 109th overall, in 1989 Entry Draft.

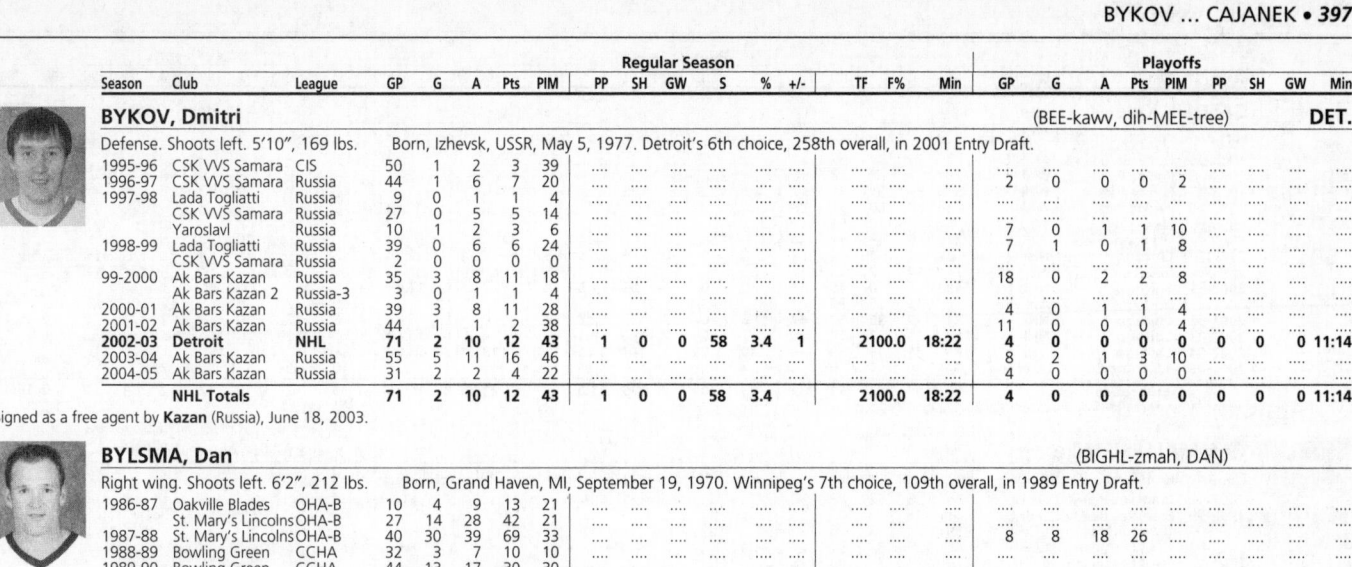

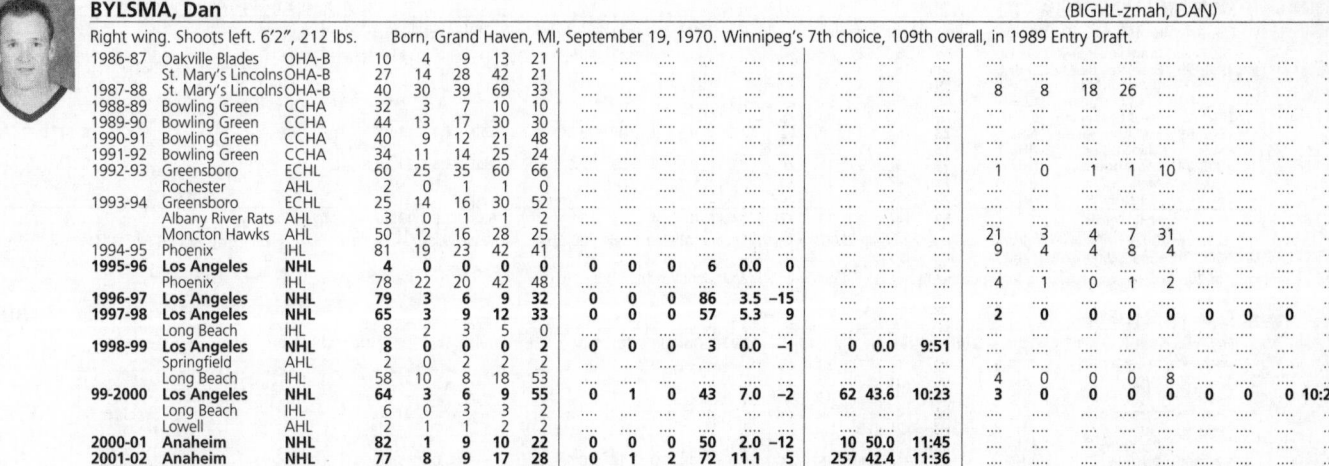

			Regular Season														Playoffs								
Season	Club	League	GP	G	A	Pts	PIM	PP	SH	GW	S	%	+/-	TF	F%	Min	GP	G	A	Pts	PIM	PP	SH	GW	Min
1986-87	Oakville Blades	OHA-B	10	4	9	13	21																		
	St. Mary's Lincolns	OHA-B	27	14	28	42	21																		
1987-88	St. Mary's Lincolns	OHA-B	40	30	39	69	33										8	8	18	26					
1988-89	Bowling Green	CCHA	32	3	7	10	10																		
1989-90	Bowling Green	CCHA	44	13	17	30	30																		
1990-91	Bowling Green	CCHA	40	9	12	21	48																		
1991-92	Bowling Green	CCHA	34	11	14	25	24																		
1992-93	Greensboro	ECHL	60	25	35	60	66										1	0	1	1	10				
	Rochester	AHL	2	0	1	1	0																		
1993-94	Greensboro	ECHL	25	14	16	30	52																		
	Albany River Rats	AHL	3	0	1	1	2																		
	Moncton Hawks	AHL	50	12	16	28	25										21	3	4	7	31				
1994-95	Phoenix	IHL	81	19	23	42	41										9	4	4	8	4				
1995-96	**Los Angeles**	**NHL**	**4**	**0**	**0**	**0**	**0**	**0**	**0**	**0**	**6**	**0.0**	**0**												
	Phoenix	IHL	78	22	20	42	48										4	1	0	1	2				
1996-97	**Los Angeles**	**NHL**	**79**	**3**	**6**	**9**	**32**	**0**	**0**	**0**	**86**	**3.5**	**−15**												
1997-98	**Los Angeles**	**NHL**	**65**	**3**	**9**	**12**	**33**	**0**	**0**	**0**	**57**	**5.3**	**9**				**2**	**0**	**0**	**0**	**0**	**0**	**0**	**0**	
	Long Beach	IHL	8	2	3	5	0																		
1998-99	**Los Angeles**	**NHL**	**8**	**0**	**0**	**0**	**2**	**0**	**0**	**0**	**3**	**0.0**	**−1**	**0**	**0.0**	**9:51**									
	Springfield	AHL	2	0	2	2	2																		
	Long Beach	IHL	58	10	8	18	53										4	0	0	0	8				
99-2000	**Los Angeles**	**NHL**	**64**	**3**	**6**	**9**	**55**	**0**	**1**	**0**	**43**	**7.0**	**−2**	**62**	**43.6**	**10:23**	**3**	**0**	**0**	**0**	**0**	**0**	**0**	**0**	**10:21**
	Long Beach	IHL	6	0	3	3	2																		
	Lowell	AHL	2	1	1	2	2																		
2000-01	**Anaheim**	**NHL**	**82**	**1**	**9**	**10**	**22**	**0**	**0**	**0**	**50**	**2.0**	**−12**	**10**	**50.0**	**11:45**									
2001-02	**Anaheim**	**NHL**	**77**	**8**	**9**	**17**	**28**	**0**	**1**	**2**	**72**	**11.1**	**5**	**257**	**42.4**	**11:36**									
2002-03	**Anaheim**	**NHL**	**39**	**1**	**4**	**5**	**12**	**0**	**0**	**0**	**23**	**4.3**	**−1**	**28**	**53.6**	**9:29**	**11**	**0**	**1**	**1**	**2**	**0**	**0**	**0**	**9:44**
2003-04	**Anaheim**	**NHL**	**11**	**0**	**0**	**0**	**0**	**0**	**0**	**0**	**6**	**0.0**	**−3**	**13**	**53.9**	**7:04**									
	Cincinnati	AHL	36	3	3	6	53										8	1	1	2	4				
2004-05			DID NOT PLAY																						
	NHL Totals		**429**	**19**	**43**	**62**	**184**	**0**	**2**	**2**	**346**	**5.5**		**370**	**44.1**	**10:51**	**16**	**0**	**1**	**1**	**2**	**0**	**0**	**0**	**9:52**

Signed as a free agent by **Los Angeles**, July 7, 1994. Signed as a free agent by **Anaheim**, July 13, 2000. • Missed majority of 2002-03 season recovering from knee (January 28, 2003 vs. San Jose) and head (February 9, 2003 vs. Carolina) injuries.

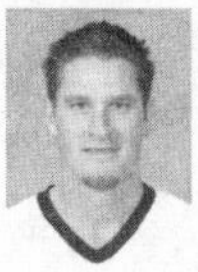

CAIRNS, Eric

(KAIRNZ, AIR-ihk) **FLA.**

Defense. Shoots left. 6'6", 230 lbs. Born, Oakville, Ont., June 27, 1974. NY Rangers' 3rd choice, 72nd overall, in 1992 Entry Draft.

			Regular Season														Playoffs								
Season	Club	League	GP	G	A	Pts	PIM	PP	SH	GW	S	%	+/-	TF	F%	Min	GP	G	A	Pts	PIM	PP	SH	GW	Min
1990-91	Burlington	OHA-B	37	5	16	21	120																		
1991-92	Detroit	OHL	64	1	11	12	237										7	0	0	0	31				
1992-93	Detroit	OHL	64	3	13	16	194										15	0	3	3	24				
1993-94	Detroit	OHL	59	7	35	42	204										17	0	4	4	46				
1994-95	Birmingham Bulls	ECHL	11	1	3	4	49																		
	Binghamton	AHL	27	0	3	3	134										9	1	1	2	28				
1995-96	Binghamton	AHL	46	1	13	14	192										4	0	0	0	37				
	Charlotte	ECHL	6	0	1	1	34																		
1996-97	**NY Rangers**	**NHL**	**40**	**0**	**1**	**1**	**147**	**0**	**0**	**0**	**17**	**0.0**	**−7**				**3**	**0**	**0**	**0**	**0**	**0**	**0**	**0**	
	Binghamton	AHL	10	1	1	2	96																		
1997-98	**NY Rangers**	**NHL**	**39**	**0**	**3**	**3**	**92**	**0**	**0**	**0**	**17**	**0.0**	**−3**												
	Hartford	AHL	7	1	2	3	43																		
1998-99	Hartford	AHL	11	0	2	2	49																		
	NY Islanders	**NHL**	**9**	**0**	**3**	**3**	**23**	**0**	**0**	**0**	**2**	**0.0**	**1**	**0**	**0.0**	**10:15**									
	Lowell	AHL	24	0	0	0	91										3	1	0	1	32				
99-2000	**NY Islanders**	**NHL**	**67**	**2**	**7**	**9**	**196**	**0**	**0**	**0**	**55**	**3.6**	**−5**	**0**	**0.0**	**17:43**									
	Providence Bruins	AHL	4	1	1	2	14																		
2000-01	**NY Islanders**	**NHL**	**45**	**2**	**2**	**4**	**106**	**0**	**0**	**0**	**21**	**9.5**	**−18**	**1**	**0.0**	**16:24**									
2001-02	**NY Islanders**	**NHL**	**74**	**2**	**5**	**7**	**176**	**0**	**0**	**1**	**34**	**5.9**	**−2**	**0**	**0.0**	**11:09**	**7**	**0**	**0**	**0**	**15**	**0**	**0**	**0**	**13:54**
2002-03	**NY Islanders**	**NHL**	**60**	**1**	**4**	**5**	**124**	**0**	**0**	**0**	**31**	**3.2**	**−7**	**0**	**0.0**	**11:50**	**5**	**0**	**0**	**0**	**13**	**0**	**0**	**0**	**6:02**
2003-04	**NY Islanders**	**NHL**	**72**	**2**	**6**	**8**	**189**	**0**	**0**	**0**	**24**	**8.3**	**−5**	**0**	**0.0**	**11:44**	**1**	**0**	**0**	**0**	**0**	**0**	**0**	**0**	**3:53**
2004-05	London Racers	Britain	22	2	6	8	85																		
	NHL Totals		**406**	**9**	**31**	**40**	**1053**	**0**	**0**	**1**	**201**	**4.5**		**1**	**0.0**	**13:27**	**16**	**0**	**0**	**0**	**28**	**0**	**0**	**0**	**10:06**

Claimed on waivers by **NY Islanders** from **NY Rangers**, December 22, 1998. Signed as a free agent by **Florida**, July 5, 2004. Signed as a free agent by **London** (Britain), November 1, 2004.

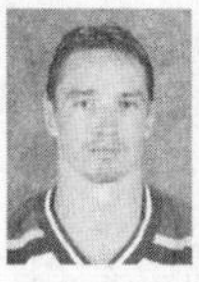

CAJANEK, Petr

(chuh-YA-nihk, PEE-tuhr) **ST.L.**

Right wing. Shoots left. 5'11", 191 lbs. Born, Gottwaldov, Czech., August 18, 1975. St. Louis' 6th choice, 253rd overall, in 2001 Entry Draft.

			Regular Season														Playoffs								
Season	Club	League	GP	G	A	Pts	PIM	PP	SH	GW	S	%	+/-	TF	F%	Min	GP	G	A	Pts	PIM	PP	SH	GW	Min
1993-94	AC ZPS Zlin	CzRep	34	5	4	9											3	0	0	0					
1994-95	AC ZPS Zlin	CzRep	35	7	9	16	8										12	2	6	8	4				
1995-96	AC ZPS Zlin	CzRep	36	8	11	19	32										8	2	6	8	8				
1996-97	AC ZPS Zlin	CzRep	50	9	30	39	46																		
1997-98	Zlin	CzRep	46	19	27	46	117																		
1998-99	Zlin	CzRep	49	15	33	48	123										11	5	7	12	12				
99-2000	Zlin	CzRep	50	23	34	57	66										4	1	0	1	0				
2000-01	Zlin	CzRep	52	18	31	49	105										6	0	4	4	22				
2001-02	Zlin	CzRep	49	20	44	64	64										11	5	7	12	10				
	Czech Republic	Olympics	4	0	0	0	0																		
2002-03	**St. Louis**	**NHL**	**51**	**9**	**29**	**38**	**20**	**2**	**2**	**1**	**90**	**10.0**	**16**	**793**	**48.4**	**15:56**	**2**	**0**	**0**	**0**	**2**	**0**	**0**	**0**	**11:07**
2003-04	**St. Louis**	**NHL**	**70**	**12**	**14**	**26**	**16**	**3**	**0**	**4**	**126**	**9.5**	**12**	**1000**	**47.6**	**17:48**	**5**	**0**	**2**	**2**	**0**	**0**	**0**	**0**	**19:27**
2004-05	HC Hame Zlin	CzRep	49	10	15	25	91										17	5	4	9	24				
	NHL Totals		**121**	**21**	**43**	**64**	**36**	**5**	**2**	**5**	**216**	**9.7**		**1793**	**48.0**	**17:01**	**7**	**0**	**2**	**2**	**4**	**0**	**0**	**0**	**17:04**

Signed as a free agent by **Zlin** (CzRep), September 5, 2004.

			Regular Season														Playoffs								
Season	Club	League	GP	G	A	Pts	PIM	PP	SH	GW	S	%	+/-	TF	F%	Min	GP	G	A	Pts	PIM	PP	SH	GW	Min

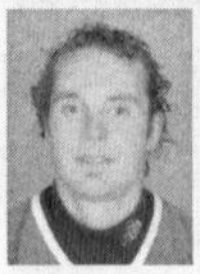

CALDER, Kyle (KAWL-dehr, KIGHL) CHI.

Left wing. Shoots left. 5'11", 176 lbs. Born, Mannville, Alta., January 5, 1979. Chicago's 7th choice, 130th overall, in 1997 Entry Draft.

1994-95	Leduc Oil Barons	AMHL	27	25	32	57	22	....	....	....	....	....	....	....	....	....	....	....	....	....	....	....	....	....	....
1995-96	Regina Pats	WHL	27	1	7	8	10	....	....	....	....	....	....	....	....	....	11	0	0	0	0	....	....	....	....
1996-97	Regina Pats	WHL	62	25	34	59	17	....	....	....	....	....	....	....	....	....	5	3	0	3	6	....	....	....	....
1997-98	Regina Pats	WHL	62	27	50	77	58	....	....	....	....	....	....	....	....	....	2	0	1	1	0	....	....	....	....
1998-99	Regina Pats	WHL	34	23	28	51	29	....	....	....	....	....	....	....	....	....	....	....	....	....	....	....	....	....	....
	Kamloops Blazers	WHL	27	19	18	37	30	....	....	....	....	....	....	....	....	....	15	6	10	16	6	....	....	....	....
99-2000	**Chicago**	**NHL**	**8**	**1**	**1**	**2**	**2**	**0**	**0**	**0**	**5**	**20.0**	**–3**	**2**	**0.0**	**9:59**	....	....	....	....	....	....	....	....	....
	Cleveland	IHL	74	14	22	36	43	....	....	....	....	....	....	....	....	....	9	2	2	4	14	....	....	....	....
2000-01	**Chicago**	**NHL**	**43**	**5**	**10**	**15**	**14**	**0**	**0**	**1**	**63**	**7.9**	**–4**	**2**	**0.0**	**12:43**	....	....	....	....	....	....	....	....	....
	Norfolk Admirals	AHL	37	12	15	27	21	....	....	....	....	....	....	....	....	....	9	2	6	8	2	....	....	....	....
2001-02	**Chicago**	**NHL**	**81**	**17**	**36**	**53**	**47**	**6**	**0**	**3**	**133**	**12.8**	**8**	**0**	**0.0**	**16:33**	**5**	**2**	**0**	**2**	**2**	**1**	**0**	**0**	**16:45**
2002-03	**Chicago**	**NHL**	**82**	**15**	**27**	**42**	**40**	**7**	**0**	**2**	**164**	**9.1**	**–6**	**4**	**25.0**	**16:43**	....	....	....	....	....	....	....	....	....
2003-04	**Chicago**	**NHL**	**66**	**21**	**18**	**39**	**29**	**10**	**0**	**1**	**144**	**14.6**	**–18**	**13**	**30.8**	**17:08**	....	....	....	....	....	....	....	....	....
2004-05	Sodertalje SK	Sweden	12	5	1	6	6	....	....	....	....	....	....	....	....	....	10	5	1	6	2	....	....	....	....
	NHL Totals		**280**	**59**	**92**	**151**	**132**	**23**	**0**	**7**	**509**	**11.6**		**21**	**23.8**	**15:58**	**5**	**2**	**0**	**2**	**2**	**1**	**0**	**0**	**16:45**

Signed as a free agent by **Sodertalje** (Sweden), January 20, 2005.

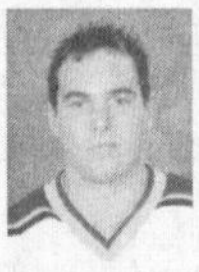

CAMMALLERI, Mike (kam-UH-LAIR-ee, MIGHK) L.A.

Center. Shoots left. 5'9", 180 lbs. Born, Richmond Hill, Ont., June 8, 1982. Los Angeles' 3rd choice, 49th overall, in 2001 Entry Draft.

1997-98	Bramalea Blues	OPJHL	46	36	52	88	30	....	....	....	....	....	....	....	....	....	....	....	....	....	....	....	....	....	....
1998-99	Bramalea Blues	OPJHL	41	31	72	103	51	....	....	....	....	....	....	....	....	....	....	....	....	....	....	....	....	....	....
99-2000	U. of Michigan	CCHA	39	13	13	26	32	....	....	....	....	....	....	....	....	....	....	....	....	....	....	....	....	....	....
2000-01	U. of Michigan	CCHA	42	*29	32	61	24	....	....	....	....	....	....	....	....	....	....	....	....	....	....	....	....	....	....
2001-02	U. of Michigan	CCHA	29	23	21	44	28	....	....	....	....	....	....	....	....	....	....	....	....	....	....	....	....	....	....
2002-03	**Los Angeles**	**NHL**	**28**	**5**	**3**	**8**	**22**	**2**	**0**	**2**	**40**	**12.5**	**–4**	**253**	**51.4**	**14:05**	....	....	....	....	....	....	....	....	....
	Manchester	AHL	13	5	15	20	12	....	....	....	....	....	....	....	....	....	....	....	....	....	....	....	....	....	....
2003-04	**Los Angeles**	**NHL**	**31**	**9**	**6**	**15**	**20**	**2**	**0**	**2**	**53**	**17.0**	**1**	**280**	**53.6**	**13:18**	....	....	....	....	....	....	....	....	....
	Manchester	AHL	41	20	19	39	28	....	....	....	....	....	....	....	....	....	1	0	1	1	0	....	....	....	....
2004-05	Manchester	AHL	79	*46	63	109	60	....	....	....	....	....	....	....	....	....	6	1	5	6	0	....	....	....	....
	NHL Totals		**59**	**14**	**9**	**23**	**42**	**4**	**0**	**4**	**93**	**15.1**		**533**	**52.5**	**13:40**	....	....	....	....	....	....	....	....	....

CCHA First All-Star Team (2001) • NCAA West Second All-American Team (2001) • CCHA Second All-Star Team (2002) • NCAA West First All-American Team (2002) • AHL Second All-Star Team (2005) • Willie Marshall Award (Top Goal-scorer - AHL) (2005)

• Missed majority of 2002-03 season recovering from head injury suffered in game vs. San Jose, January 28, 2003.

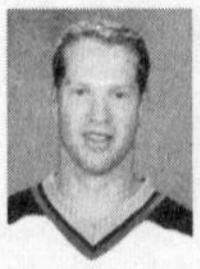

CAMPBELL, Brian (KAM-behl, BRIGH-uhn) BUF.

Defense. Shoots left. 6', 190 lbs. Born, Strathroy, Ont., May 23, 1979. Buffalo's 7th choice, 156th overall, in 1997 Entry Draft.

1994-95	Petrolia Oil Barons	OHA-B	49	11	27	38	43	....	....	....	....	....	....	....	....	....	....	....	....	....	....	....	....	....	....
1995-96	Ottawa 67's	OHL	66	5	22	27	23	....	....	....	....	....	....	....	....	....	4	0	1	1	2	....	....	....	....
1996-97	Ottawa 67's	OHL	66	7	36	43	12	....	....	....	....	....	....	....	....	....	24	2	11	13	8	....	....	....	....
1997-98	Ottawa 67's	OHL	66	14	39	53	31	....	....	....	....	....	....	....	....	....	13	1	14	15	0	....	....	....	....
1998-99	Ottawa 67's	OHL	62	12	75	87	27	....	....	....	....	....	....	....	....	....	9	2	10	12	6	....	....	....	....
	Rochester	AHL	....	....	....	....	....	....	....	....	....	....	....	....	....	....	2	0	0	0	0	....	....	....	....
99-2000	**Buffalo**	**NHL**	**12**	**1**	**4**	**5**	**4**	**0**	**0**	**0**	**10**	**10.0**	**–2**	**0**	**0.0**	**15:48**	....	....	....	....	....	....	....	....	....
	Rochester	AHL	67	2	24	26	22	....	....	....	....	....	....	....	....	....	21	0	3	3	0	....	....	....	....
2000-01	**Buffalo**	**NHL**	**8**	**0**	**0**	**0**	**2**	**0**	**0**	**0**	**7**	**0.0**	**–2**	**0**	**0.0**	**15:40**	....	....	....	....	....	....	....	....	....
	Rochester	AHL	65	7	25	32	24	....	....	....	....	....	....	....	....	....	4	0	1	1	0	....	....	....	....
2001-02	**Buffalo**	**NHL**	**29**	**3**	**3**	**6**	**12**	**0**	**0**	**0**	**30**	**10.0**	**0**	**1**	**0.0**	**15:18**	....	....	....	....	....	....	....	....	....
	Rochester	AHL	45	2	35	37	13	....	....	....	....	....	....	....	....	....	....	....	....	....	....	....	....	....	....
2002-03	**Buffalo**	**NHL**	**65**	**2**	**17**	**19**	**20**	**0**	**0**	**1**	**90**	**2.2**	**–8**	**1**	**0.0**	**18:40**	....	....	....	....	....	....	....	....	....
2003-04	**Buffalo**	**NHL**	**53**	**3**	**8**	**11**	**12**	**0**	**0**	**0**	**45**	**6.7**	**–8**	**0**	**0.0**	**16:02**	....	....	....	....	....	....	....	....	....
2004-05	Jokerit Helsinki	Finland	44	12	13	25	12	....	....	....	....	....	....	....	....	....	12	3	4	7	6	....	....	....	....
	NHL Totals		**167**	**9**	**32**	**41**	**50**	**0**	**0**	**1**	**182**	**4.9**		**2**	**0.0**	**16:54**	....	....	....	....	....	....	....	....	....

OHL First All-Star Team (1999) • OHL MVP (1999) • Canadian Major Junior First All-Star Team (1999) • Canadian Major Junior Player of the Year (1999) • George Parsons Trophy (Memorial Cup Tournament Most Sportsmanlike Player) (1999)

Signed as a free agent by **Jokerit** (Finland), October 19, 2004.

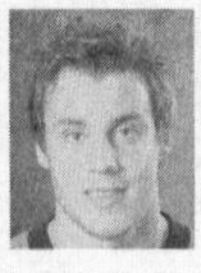

CAMPBELL, Gregory (KAM-behl, GREH-goh-ree) FLA.

Left wing. Shoots left. 6', 191 lbs. Born, London, Ont., December 17, 1983. Florida's 4th choice, 67th overall, in 2002 Entry Draft.

1998-99	Aylmer Aces	OHA-B	49	5	9	14	44	....	....	....	....	....	....	....	....	....	....	....	....	....	....	....	....	....	....
99-2000	St. Thomas Stars	OHA-B	51	12	8	20	51	....	....	....	....	....	....	....	....	....	....	....	....	....	....	....	....	....	....
2000-01	Plymouth Whalers	OHL	65	2	12	14	40	....	....	....	....	....	....	....	....	....	10	0	0	0	7	....	....	....	....
2001-02	Plymouth Whalers	OHL	65	17	36	53	105	....	....	....	....	....	....	....	....	....	6	0	2	2	13	....	....	....	....
2002-03	Kitchener Rangers	OHL	55	23	33	56	116	....	....	....	....	....	....	....	....	....	21	15	4	19	34	....	....	....	....
2003-04	**Florida**	**NHL**	**2**	**0**	**0**	**0**	**5**	**0**	**0**	**0**	**0**	**0.0**	**–1**	**1**	**0.0**	**9:09**	....	....	....	....	....	....	....	....	....
	San Antonio	AHL	76	13	16	29	73	....	....	....	....	....	....	....	....	....	....	....	....	....	....	....	....	....	....
2004-05	San Antonio	AHL	70	12	16	28	113	....	....	....	....	....	....	....	....	....	....	....	....	....	....	....	....	....	....
	NHL Totals		**2**	**0**	**0**	**0**	**5**	**0**	**0**	**0**	**0**	**0.0**		**1**	**0.0**	**9:09**	....	....	....	....	....	....	....	....	....

Memorial Cup Tournament All-Star Team (2003) • George Parsons Trophy (Memorial Cup Tournament Most Sportsmanlike Player) (2003) • Ed Chynoweth Trophy (Memorial Cup Tournament Leading Scorer) (2003)

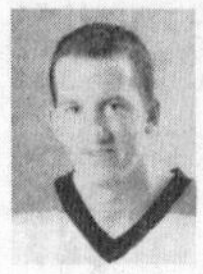

CAMPBELL, Jim (KAM-behl, JIHM) T.B.

Right wing. Shoots right. 6'2", 205 lbs. Born, Worcester, MA, April 3, 1973. Montreal's 2nd choice, 28th overall, in 1991 Entry Draft.

1988-89	Northwood	High-NY	12	12	8	20	6	....	....	....	....	....	....	....	....	....	....	....	....	....	....	....	....	....	....
1989-90	Northwood	High-NY	8	14	7	21	8	....	....	....	....	....	....	....	....	....	....	....	....	....	....	....	....	....	....
1990-91	Lawrence	High-MA	26	36	47	83	26	....	....	....	....	....	....	....	....	....	....	....	....	....	....	....	....	....	....
1991-92	Hull Olympiques	QMJHL	64	41	44	85	51	....	....	....	....	....	....	....	....	....	6	7	3	10	8	....	....	....	....
1992-93	Hull Olympiques	QMJHL	50	42	29	71	66	....	....	....	....	....	....	....	....	....	8	11	4	15	43	....	....	....	....
1993-94	United States	Nat-Tm	56	24	33	57	59	....	....	....	....	....	....	....	....	....	....	....	....	....	....	....	....	....	....
	United States	Olympics	8	0	0	0	6	....	....	....	....	....	....	....	....	....	....	....	....	....	....	....	....	....	....
	Fredericton	AHL	19	6	17	23	6	....	....	....	....	....	....	....	....	....	....	....	....	....	....	....	....	....	....
1994-95	Fredericton	AHL	77	27	24	51	103	....	....	....	....	....	....	....	....	....	12	0	7	7	8	....	....	....	....
1995-96	Fredericton	AHL	44	28	23	51	24	....	....	....	....	....	....	....	....	....	....	....	....	....	....	....	....	....	....
	Anaheim	**NHL**	**16**	**2**	**3**	**5**	**36**	**1**	**0**	**0**	**25**	**8.0**	**0**	....	....	....	....	....	....	....	....	....	....	....	....
	Baltimore Bandits	AHL	16	13	7	20	8	....	....	....	....	....	....	....	....	....	12	7	5	12	10	....	....	....	....
1996-97	**St. Louis**	**NHL**	**68**	**23**	**20**	**43**	**68**	**5**	**0**	**6**	**169**	**13.6**	**3**	....	....	....	**4**	**1**	**0**	**1**	**6**	**1**	**0**	**0**	....
1997-98	**St. Louis**	**NHL**	**76**	**22**	**19**	**41**	**55**	**7**	**0**	**6**	**147**	**15.0**	**0**	....	....	....	**10**	**7**	**3**	**10**	**12**	**4**	**0**	**2**	....
1998-99	**St. Louis**	**NHL**	**55**	**4**	**21**	**25**	**41**	**1**	**0**	**0**	**99**	**4.0**	**–8**	**7**	**42.9**	**13:34**	....	....	....	....	....	....	....	....	....
99-2000	Manitoba Moose	IHL	10	1	3	4	10	....	....	....	....	....	....	....	....	....	....	....	....	....	....	....	....	....	....
	St. Louis	**NHL**	**2**	**0**	**0**	**0**	**9**	**0**	**0**	**0**	**6**	**0.0**	**0**	**0**	**0.0**	**15:17**	....	....	....	....	....	....	....	....	....
	Worcester IceCats	AHL	66	31	34	65	88	....	....	....	....	....	....	....	....	....	9	1	2	3	6	....	....	....	....
2000-01	**Montreal**	**NHL**	**57**	**9**	**11**	**20**	**53**	**6**	**0**	**1**	**81**	**11.1**	**–3**	**14**	**42.9**	**10:19**	....	....	....	....	....	....	....	....	....
	Quebec Citadelles	AHL	3	5	0	5	6	....	....	....	....	....	....	....	....	....	....	....	....	....	....	....	....	....	....
2001-02	**Chicago**	**NHL**	**9**	**1**	**1**	**2**	**4**	**0**	**0**	**0**	**12**	**8.3**	**–3**	**1**	**0.0**	**13:21**	....	....	....	....	....	....	....	....	....
	Norfolk Admirals	AHL	44	11	14	25	26	....	....	....	....	....	....	....	....	....	4	3	1	4	2	....	....	....	....
2002-03	**Florida**	**NHL**	**1**	**0**	**0**	**0**	**0**	**0**	**0**	**0**	**3**	**0.0**	**0**	**1**	**0.0**	**8:56**	....	....	....	....	....	....	....	....	....
	San Antonio	AHL	64	16	37	53	55	....	....	....	....	....	....	....	....	....	1	0	0	0	0	....	....	....	....
2003-04	Chicago Wolves	AHL	41	10	13	23	41	....	....	....	....	....	....	....	....	....	....	....	....	....	....	....	....	....	....
	Nizhnekamsk	Russia	2	0	0	0	2	....	....	....	....	....	....	....	....	....	....	....	....	....	....	....	....	....	....

Season	Club	League	Regular Season														Playoffs								
			GP	G	A	Pts	PIM	PP	SH	GW	S	%	+/-	TF	F%	Min	GP	G	A	Pts	PIM	PP	SH	GW	Min
2004-05	Bridgeport	AHL	46	8	12	20	64																		
	Springfield	AHL	13	2	5	7	8																		
	NHL Totals		**284**	**61**	**75**	**136**	**266**	**20**	**0**	**13**	**542**	**11.3**		**23**	**39.1**	**12:03**	**14**	**8**	**3**	**11**	**18**	**5**	**0**	**2**	

NHL All-Rookie Team (1997)

Traded to **Anaheim** by **Montreal** for Robert Dirk, January 21, 1996. Signed as a free agent by **St. Louis**, July 11, 1996. Loaned to **Manitoba** (IHL) by **St. Louis**, October 4, 1999 and recalled November 1, 1999. Signed as a free agent by **Montreal**, August 21, 2000. Signed as a free agent by **Chicago**, November 19, 2001. Signed as a free agent by **Florida**, July 19, 2002. Signed as a free agent by **Chicago** (AHL), December 10, 2003. Signed as a free agent by **NY Islanders**, August 11, 2004. Signed as a free agent by **Tampa Bay**, August 18, 2005.

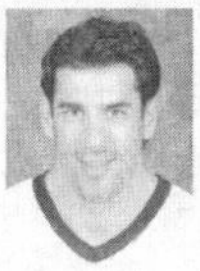

CARNEY, Keith

(KAHRN-nee, KEETH) **ANA.**

Defense. Shoots left. 6'2", 216 lbs. Born, Providence, RI, February 3, 1970. Buffalo's 3rd choice, 76th overall, in 1988 Entry Draft.

1987-88	Mount St. Charles	High-RI	23	12	43	55																			
1988-89	U. of Maine	H-East	40	4	22	26	24																		
1989-90	U. of Maine	H-East	41	3	41	44	43																		
1990-91	U. of Maine	H-East	40	7	49	56	38																		
1991-92	United States	Nat-Tm	49	2	17	19	16																		
	Buffalo	**NHL**	**14**	**1**	**2**	**3**	**18**	**1**	**0**	**0**	**17**	**5.9**	**–3**				**7**	**0**	**3**	**3**	**0**	**0**	**0**	**0**	
	Rochester	AHL	24	1	10	11	2										2	0	2	2	0				
1992-93	**Buffalo**	**NHL**	**30**	**2**	**4**	**6**	**55**	**0**	**0**	**1**	**26**	**7.7**	**3**				**8**	**0**	**3**	**3**	**6**	**0**	**0**	**0**	
	Rochester	AHL	41	5	21	26	32																		
1993-94	**Buffalo**	**NHL**	**7**	**1**	**3**	**4**	**4**	**0**	**0**	**0**	**6**	**16.7**	**–1**												
	Chicago	**NHL**	**30**	**3**	**5**	**8**	**35**	**0**	**0**	**0**	**31**	**9.7**	**15**				**6**	**0**	**1**	**1**	**4**	**0**	**0**	**0**	
	Indianapolis Ice	IHL	28	0	14	14	20																		
1994-95	**Chicago**	**NHL**	**18**	**1**	**0**	**1**	**11**	**0**	**0**	**1**	**14**	**7.1**	**–1**				**4**	**0**	**1**	**1**	**0**	**0**	**0**	**0**	
1995-96	**Chicago**	**NHL**	**82**	**5**	**14**	**19**	**94**	**1**	**0**	**1**	**69**	**7.2**	**31**				**10**	**0**	**3**	**3**	**4**	**0**	**0**	**0**	
1996-97	**Chicago**	**NHL**	**81**	**3**	**15**	**18**	**62**	**0**	**0**	**1**	**77**	**3.9**	**26**				**6**	**1**	**1**	**2**	**2**	**0**	**0**	**0**	
1997-98	**Chicago**	**NHL**	**60**	**2**	**13**	**15**	**73**	**0**	**1**	**0**	**53**	**3.8**	**–7**												
	United States	Olympics	4	0	0	0	2																		
	Phoenix	**NHL**	**20**	**1**	**6**	**7**	**18**	**1**	**0**	**0**	**18**	**5.6**	**5**				**6**	**0**	**0**	**0**	**4**	**0**	**0**	**0**	
1998-99	**Phoenix**	**NHL**	**82**	**2**	**14**	**16**	**62**	**0**	**2**	**0**	**62**	**3.2**	**15**	**0**	**0.0**	**22:46**	**7**	**1**	**2**	**3**	**10**	**0**	**0**	**0**	**23:59**
99-2000	**Phoenix**	**NHL**	**82**	**4**	**20**	**24**	**87**	**0**	**0**	**1**	**73**	**5.5**	**11**	**0**	**0.0**	**21:12**	**5**	**0**	**0**	**0**	**17**	**0**	**0**	**0**	**22:38**
2000-01	**Phoenix**	**NHL**	**82**	**2**	**14**	**16**	**86**	**0**	**0**	**0**	**65**	**3.1**	**15**	**0**	**0.0**	**20:53**									
2001-02	**Anaheim**	**NHL**	**60**	**5**	**9**	**14**	**30**	**0**	**0**	**1**	**66**	**7.6**	**14**	**0**	**0.0**	**20:47**									
2002-03	**Anaheim**	**NHL**	**81**	**4**	**18**	**22**	**65**	**0**	**0**	**1**	**87**	**4.6**	**8**	**0**	**0.0**	**0:00**	**21**	**0**	**4**	**4**	**16**	**0**	**0**	**0**	
2003-04	**Anaheim**	**NHL**	**69**	**2**	**5**	**7**	**42**	**1**	**0**	**0**	**58**	**3.4**	**–5**	**0**	**0.0**	**21:43**									
2004-05			DID NOT PLAY																						
	NHL Totals		**798**	**38**	**142**	**180**	**742**	**4**	**3**	**7**	**722**	**5.3**		**0**	**0.0**	**17:41**	**80**	**2**	**18**	**20**	**63**	**0**	**0**	**0**	**23:25**

Hockey East Second All-Star Team (1990) • NCAA East Second All-American Team (1990) • Hockey East First All-Star Team (1991) • NCAA East First All-American Team (1991)

Traded to **Chicago** by **Buffalo** with Buffalo's 6th round choice (Marc Magliarditi) in 1995 Entry Draft for Craig Muni and Chicago's 5th round choice (Daniel Bienvenue) in 1995 Entry Draft, October 26, 1993. Traded to **Phoenix** by **Chicago** with Jim Cummins for Chad Kilger and Jayson More, March 4, 1998. Traded to **Anaheim** by **Phoenix** for Calgary's 2nd round choice (previously acquired, later traded back to Calgary – Calgary selected Andrei Taratukhin) in 2001 Entry Draft, June 19, 2001.

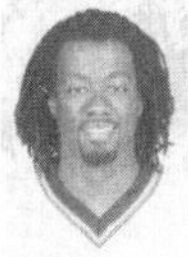

CARTER, Anson

(KAHR-tuhr, AN-sohn) **VAN.**

Right wing. Shoots right. 6'1", 210 lbs. Born, Toronto, Ont., June 6, 1974. Quebec's 11th choice, 220th overall, in 1992 Entry Draft.

1989-90	Don Mills Flyers	MTHL	40	15	47	62	105																		
1990-91	Don Mills Flyers	MTHL	67	69	73	142	43																		
1991-92	Wexford Raiders	MTJHL	42	18	22	40	24																		
1992-93	Michigan State	CCHA	34	15	7	22	20																		
1993-94	Michigan State	CCHA	39	30	24	54	36																		
1994-95	Michigan State	CCHA	39	34	17	51	40																		
1995-96	Michigan State	CCHA	42	23	20	43	36																		
1996-97	**Washington**	**NHL**	**19**	**3**	**2**	**5**	**7**	**1**	**0**	**1**	**28**	**10.7**	**0**												
	Portland Pirates	AHL	27	19	19	38	11																		
	Boston	**NHL**	**19**	**8**	**5**	**13**	**2**	**1**	**1**	**1**	**51**	**15.7**	**–7**												
1997-98	**Boston**	**NHL**	**78**	**16**	**27**	**43**	**31**	**6**	**0**	**4**	**179**	**8.9**	**7**				**6**	**1**	**1**	**2**	**0**	**0**	**0**	**0**	
1998-99	Utah Grizzlies	IHL	6	1	1	2	0																		
	Boston	**NHL**	**55**	**24**	**16**	**40**	**22**	**6**	**0**	**6**	**123**	**19.5**	**7**	**172**	**43.0**	**18:44**	**12**	**4**	**3**	**7**	**0**	**1**	**0**	**1**	**21:31**
99-2000	**Boston**	**NHL**	**59**	**22**	**25**	**47**	**14**	**4**	**0**	**1**	**144**	**15.3**	**8**	**793**	**48.2**	**20:31**									
2000-01	**Edmonton**	**NHL**	**61**	**16**	**26**	**42**	**23**	**7**	**1**	**4**	**102**	**15.7**	**1**	**80**	**47.5**	**18:13**	**6**	**3**	**1**	**4**	**4**	**1**	**0**	**1**	**19:42**
2001-02	**Edmonton**	**NHL**	**82**	**28**	**32**	**60**	**25**	**12**	**0**	**6**	**181**	**15.5**	**3**	**316**	**46.5**	**19:18**									
2002-03	**Edmonton**	**NHL**	**68**	**25**	**30**	**55**	**20**	**10**	**0**	**1**	**176**	**14.2**	**–11**	**217**	**43.8**	**19:39**									
	NY Rangers	**NHL**	**11**	**1**	**4**	**5**	**6**	**0**	**0**	**0**	**17**	**5.9**	**0**	**5**	**20.0**	**17:49**									
2003-04	**NY Rangers**	**NHL**	**43**	**10**	**7**	**17**	**14**	**4**	**1**	**2**	**63**	**15.9**	**–12**	**21**	**28.6**	**15:35**									
	Washington	**NHL**	**19**	**5**	**5**	**10**	**6**	**2**	**0**	**2**	**33**	**15.2**	**2**	**9**	**44.4**	**19:33**									
	Los Angeles	**NHL**	**15**	**0**	**1**	**1**	**0**	**0**	**0**	**0**	**18**	**0.0**	**–5**	**58**	**29.3**	**16:43**									
2004-05			DID NOT PLAY																						
	NHL Totals		**529**	**158**	**180**	**338**	**170**	**53**	**3**	**28**	**1115**	**14.2**		**1671**	**45.7**	**18:47**	**24**	**8**	**5**	**13**	**4**	**2**	**0**	**2**	**20:54**

CCHA First All-Star Team (1994, 1995) • NCAA West Second All-American Team (1995) • CCHA Second All-Star Team (1996)

Rights transferred to **Colorado** after **Quebec** franchise relocated, June 21, 1995. Traded to **Washington** by **Colorado** for Washington's 4th round choice (Ben Storey) in 1996 Entry Draft, April 3, 1996. Traded to **Boston** by **Washington** with Jim Carey, Jason Allison and Washington's 3rd round choice (Lee Goren) in 1997 Entry Draft for Bill Ranford, Adam Oates and Rick Tocchet, March 1, 1997. Signed as a free agent by **Utah** (IHL) with Boston retaining NHL rights, October 20, 1998. Traded to **Edmonton** by **Boston** with Boston's 1st (Ales Hemsky) and 2nd (Doug Lynch) round choices in 2001 Entry Draft for Bill Guerin and future considerations, November 15, 2000. Traded to **NY Rangers** by **Edmonton** with Ales Pisa for Radek Dvorak and Cory Cross, March 11, 2003. Traded to **Washington** by **NY Rangers** for Jaromir Jagr, January 23, 2004. Traded to **Los Angeles** by **Washington** for Jared Aulin, March 8, 2004. Signed as a free agent by **Vancouver**, August 17, 2005.

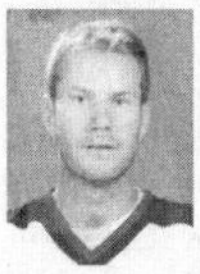

CASSELS, Andrew

(KAS-uhls, AN-droo) **WSH.**

Center. Shoots left. 6'1", 185 lbs. Born, Bramalea, Ont., July 23, 1969. Montreal's 1st choice, 17th overall, in 1987 Entry Draft.

1985-86	Bramalea Blues	OJHL	33	18	25	43	26																		
1986-87	Ottawa 67's	OHL	66	26	66	92	28										11	5	9	14	7				
1987-88	Ottawa 67's	OHL	61	48	*103	*151	39										16	8	*24	*32	13				
1988-89	Ottawa 67's	OHL	56	37	97	134	66										12	5	10	15	10				
1989-90	**Montreal**	**NHL**	**6**	**2**	**0**	**2**	**2**	**0**	**0**	**1**	**5**	**40.0**	**1**												
	Sherbrooke	AHL	55	22	45	67	25										12	2	11	13	6				
1990-91	**Montreal**	**NHL**	**54**	**6**	**19**	**25**	**20**	**1**	**0**	**3**	**55**	**10.9**	**2**				**8**	**0**	**2**	**2**	**2**	**0**	**0**	**0**	
1991-92	**Hartford**	**NHL**	**67**	**11**	**30**	**41**	**18**	**2**	**2**	**3**	**99**	**11.1**	**3**				**7**	**2**	**4**	**6**	**6**	**1**	**0**	**0**	
1992-93	**Hartford**	**NHL**	**84**	**21**	**64**	**85**	**62**	**8**	**3**	**1**	**134**	**15.7**	**–11**												
1993-94	**Hartford**	**NHL**	**79**	**16**	**42**	**58**	**37**	**8**	**1**	**3**	**126**	**12.7**	**–21**												
1994-95	**Hartford**	**NHL**	**46**	**7**	**30**	**37**	**18**	**1**	**0**	**1**	**74**	**9.5**	**–3**												
1995-96	**Hartford**	**NHL**	**81**	**20**	**43**	**63**	**39**	**6**	**0**	**1**	**135**	**14.8**	**8**												
1996-97	**Hartford**	**NHL**	**81**	**22**	**44**	**66**	**46**	**8**	**0**	**2**	**142**	**15.5**	**–16**												
1997-98	**Calgary**	**NHL**	**81**	**17**	**27**	**44**	**32**	**6**	**1**	**2**	**138**	**12.3**	**–7**												
1998-99	**Calgary**	**NHL**	**70**	**12**	**25**	**37**	**18**	**4**	**1**	**3**	**97**	**12.4**	**–12**	**1322**	**51.1**	**18:58**									
99-2000	**Vancouver**	**NHL**	**79**	**17**	**45**	**62**	**16**	**6**	**0**	**1**	**109**	**15.6**	**8**	**1127**	**48.3**	**19:19**									
2000-01	**Vancouver**	**NHL**	**66**	**12**	**44**	**56**	**10**	**2**	**0**	**1**	**104**	**11.5**	**1**	**1164**	**49.9**	**19:22**									
2001-02	**Vancouver**	**NHL**	**53**	**11**	**39**	**50**	**22**	**7**	**0**	**1**	**64**	**17.2**	**5**	**866**	**50.4**	**17:27**	**6**	**2**	**1**	**3**	**0**	**1**	**0**	**0**	**16:55**
2002-03	**Columbus**	**NHL**	**79**	**20**	**48**	**68**	**30**	**9**	**1**	**5**	**113**	**17.7**	**–4**	**1649**	**48.8**	**19:52**									
2003-04	**Columbus**	**NHL**	**58**	**6**	**20**	**26**	**26**	**2**	**0**	**0**	**91**	**6.6**	**–24**	**1205**	**45.1**	**19:18**									
2004-05			DID NOT PLAY																						
	NHL Totals		**984**	**200**	**520**	**720**	**396**	**70**	**9**	**28**	**1486**	**13.5**		**7333**	**48.9**	**19:07**	**21**	**4**	**7**	**11**	**8**	**2**	**0**	**0**	**16:55**

OHL Rookie of the Year (1987) • OHL First All-Star Team (1988,1989) • OHL MVP (1988)

Traded to **Hartford** by **Montreal** for Hartford's 2nd round choice (Valeri Bure) in 1992 Entry Draft, September 17, 1991. Transferred to **Carolina** after **Hartford** franchise relocated, June 25, 1997. Traded to **Calgary** by **Carolina** with Jean-Sebastien Giguere for Gary Roberts and Trevor Kidd, August 25, 1997. Signed as a free agent by **Vancouver**, August 19, 1999. Signed as a free agent by **Columbus**, August 15, 2002. Signed as a free agent by **Washington**, August 9, 2005.

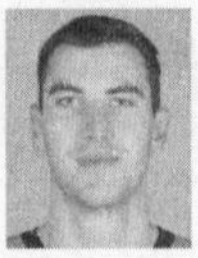

CHARA, Zdeno

(CHAH-rah, ZDEH-noh) **OTT.**

Defense. Shoots left. 6'9", 260 lbs. Born, Trencin, Czech., March 18, 1977. NY Islanders' 3rd choice, 56th overall, in 1996 Entry Draft.

			Regular Season														Playoffs								
Season	Club	League	GP	G	A	Pts	PIM	PP	SH	GW	S	%	+/-	TF	F%	Min	GP	G	A	Pts	PIM	PP	SH	GW	Min
1994-95	Dukla Trencin U18	Svk-U18	30	22	22	44	113	....	....	....	....	....	....	....	....	....	....	....	....	....	....	....	....	....	....
	Dukla Trencin Jr.	Slovak-Jr.	2	0	0	0	0	....	....	....	....	....	....	....	....	....	....	....	....	....	....	....	....	....	....
1995-96	Dukla Trencin Jr.	Slovak-Jr.	22	1	13	14	80	....	....	....	....	....	....	....	....	....	....	....	....	....	....	....	....	....	....
	HK VTJ Piestany	Slovak-2	10	1	3	4	10	....	....	....	....	....	....	....	....	....	....	....	....	....	....	....	....	....	....
	Sparta Jr.	CzRep-Jr.	15	1	2	3	42	....	....	....	....	....	....	....	....	....	....	....	....	....	....	....	....	....	....
	HC Sparta Praha	CzRep	1	0	0	0	0	....	....	....	....	....	....	....	....	....	....	....	....	....	....	....	....	....	....
1996-97	Prince George	WHL	49	3	19	22	120	....	....	....	....	....	....	....	....	....	15	1	7	8	45	....	....	....	....
1997-98	**NY Islanders**	**NHL**	**25**	**0**	**1**	**1**	**50**	**0**	**0**	**0**	**10**	**0.0**	**1**	....	....	....	....	....	....	....	....	....	....	....	....
	Kentucky	AHL	48	4	9	13	125	....	....	....	....	....	....	....	....	....	1	0	0	0	4	....	....	....	....
1998-99	**NY Islanders**	**NHL**	**59**	**2**	**6**	**8**	**83**	**0**	**1**	**0**	**56**	**3.6**	**–8**	**0**	**0.0**	**18:54**	....	....	....	....	....	....	....	....	....
	Lowell	AHL	23	2	2	4	47	....	....	....	....	....	....	....	....	....	....	....	....	....	....	....	....	....	....
99-2000	**NY Islanders**	**NHL**	**65**	**2**	**9**	**11**	**57**	**0**	**0**	**1**	**47**	**4.3**	**–27**	**0**	**0.0**	**22:52**	....	....	....	....	....	....	....	....	....
2000-01	**NY Islanders**	**NHL**	**82**	**2**	**7**	**9**	**157**	**0**	**1**	**0**	**83**	**2.4**	**–27**	**0**	**0.0**	**22:20**	....	....	....	....	....	....	....	....	....
2001-02	Dukla Trencin	Slovakia	8	2	2	4	32	....	....	....	....	....	....	....	....	....	....	....	....	....	....	....	....	....	....
	Ottawa	**NHL**	**75**	**10**	**13**	**23**	**156**	**4**	**1**	**2**	**105**	**9.5**	**30**	**0**	**0.0**	**22:16**	**10**	**0**	**1**	**1**	**12**	**0**	**0**	**0**	**26:07**
2002-03	**Ottawa**	**NHL**	**74**	**9**	**30**	**39**	**116**	**3**	**0**	**2**	**168**	**5.4**	**29**	**0**	**0.0**	**24:57**	**18**	**1**	**6**	**7**	**14**	**0**	**0**	**0**	**25:07**
2003-04	**Ottawa**	**NHL**	**79**	**16**	**25**	**41**	**147**	**7**	**0**	**3**	**185**	**8.6**	**33**	**0**	**0.0**	**24:38**	**7**	**1**	**1**	**2**	**8**	**0**	**0**	**0**	**24:38**
2004-05	Farjestad	Sweden	33	10	15	25	132	....	....	....	....	....	....	....	....	....	13	3	5	8	82	....	....	....	....
	NHL Totals		**459**	**41**	**91**	**132**	**766**	**14**	**3**	**8**	**654**	**6.3**		**0**	**0.0**	**22:48**	**35**	**2**	**8**	**10**	**34**	**0**	**0**	**0**	**25:18**

AHL All-Rookie Team (1998) • NHL First All-Star Team (2004)

Played in NHL All-Star Game (2003)

Traded to **Ottawa** by **NY Islanders** with Bill Muckalt and NY Islanders' 1st round choice (Jason Spezza) in 2001 Entry Draft for Alexei Yashin, June 23, 2001. Signed as a free agent by **Farjestad** (Sweden), September 24, 2004,

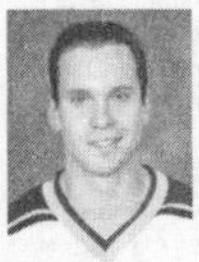

CHARTRAND, Brad

(SHAR-trand, BRAD)

Center. Shoots left. 5'11", 185 lbs. Born, Winnipeg, Man., December 14, 1974.

Season	Club	League	GP	G	A	Pts	PIM	PP	SH	GW	S	%	+/-	TF	F%	Min	GP	G	A	Pts	PIM	PP	SH	GW	Min
1988-89	Winnipeg Hawks	MMMHL	24	30	50	80	40	....	....	....	....	....	....	....	....	....	....	....	....	....	....	....	....	....	....
1989-90	Winnipeg Hawks	MMMHL	24	26	55	81	40	....	....	....	....	....	....	....	....	....	....	....	....	....	....	....	....	....	....
1990-91	Winnipeg Hawks	MMMHL	34	26	45	71	40	....	....	....	....	....	....	....	....	....	....	....	....	....	....	....	....	....	....
1991-92	St. James	MJHL	45	24	25	49	32	....	....	....	....	....	....	....	....	....	....	....	....	....	....	....	....	....	....
1992-93	Cornell Big Red	ECAC	26	10	6	16	16	....	....	....	....	....	....	....	....	....	....	....	....	....	....	....	....	....	....
1993-94	Cornell Big Red	ECAC	30	4	14	18	48	....	....	....	....	....	....	....	....	....	....	....	....	....	....	....	....	....	....
1994-95	Cornell Big Red	ECAC	28	9	9	18	10	....	....	....	....	....	....	....	....	....	....	....	....	....	....	....	....	....	....
1995-96	Cornell Big Red	ECAC	34	24	19	43	16	....	....	....	....	....	....	....	....	....	....	....	....	....	....	....	....	....	....
1996-97	Canada	Nat-Tm	54	10	14	24	42	....	....	....	....	....	....	....	....	....	....	....	....	....	....	....	....	....	....
1997-98	Canada	Nat-Tm	60	24	30	54	47	....	....	....	....	....	....	....	....	....	....	....	....	....	....	....	....	....	....
	Rapperswil	Swiss	8	2	3	5	4	....	....	....	....	....	....	....	....	....	....	....	....	....	....	....	....	....	....
1998-99	St. John's	AHL	64	16	14	30	48	....	....	....	....	....	....	....	....	....	5	0	2	2	2	....	....	....	....
99-2000	**Los Angeles**	**NHL**	**50**	**6**	**6**	**12**	**17**	**0**	**1**	**3**	**51**	**11.8**	**4**	**62**	**53.2**	**11:03**	**4**	**0**	**0**	**0**	**6**	**0**	**0**	**0**	**8:09**
	Lowell	AHL	16	5	10	15	8	....	....	....	....	....	....	....	....	....	....	....	....	....	....	....	....	....	....
	Long Beach	IHL	1	0	0	0	0	....	....	....	....	....	....	....	....	....	3	0	0	0	0	....	....	....	....
2000-01	**Los Angeles**	**NHL**	**4**	**1**	**0**	**1**	**2**	**0**	**0**	**1**	**6**	**16.7**	**–2**	**0**	**0.0**	**11:37**	....	....	....	....	....	....	....	....	....
	Lowell	AHL	72	17	34	51	44	....	....	....	....	....	....	....	....	....	4	0	1	1	8	....	....	....	....
2001-02	**Los Angeles**	**NHL**	**46**	**7**	**9**	**16**	**40**	**0**	**0**	**1**	**49**	**14.3**	**5**	**481**	**53.2**	**12:05**	**7**	**1**	**1**	**2**	**2**	**0**	**0**	**1**	**11:07**
	Manchester	AHL	22	10	12	22	31	....	....	....	....	....	....	....	....	....	....	....	....	....	....	....	....	....	....
2002-03	**Los Angeles**	**NHL**	**62**	**8**	**6**	**14**	**33**	**0**	**1**	**2**	**64**	**12.5**	**–10**	**623**	**51.4**	**12:14**	....	....	....	....	....	....	....	....	....
2003-04	**Los Angeles**	**NHL**	**53**	**3**	**4**	**7**	**30**	**0**	**1**	**0**	**63**	**4.8**	**–3**	**290**	**54.1**	**11:36**	....	....	....	....	....	....	....	....	....
2004-05			DID NOT PLAY																						
	NHL Totals		**215**	**25**	**25**	**50**	**122**	**0**	**3**	**7**	**233**	**10.7**		**1456**	**52.6**	**11:46**	**11**	**1**	**1**	**2**	**8**	**0**	**0**	**1**	**10:03**

Signed as a free agent by **Los Angeles**, July 15, 1999.

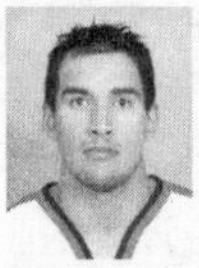

CHEECHOO, Jonathan

(CHEE-choo, JAWN-ah-thuhn) **S.J.**

Right wing. Shoots right. 6'1", 190 lbs. Born, Moose Factory, Ont., July 15, 1980. San Jose's 2nd choice, 29th overall, in 1998 Entry Draft.

Season	Club	League	GP	G	A	Pts	PIM	PP	SH	GW	S	%	+/-	TF	F%	Min	GP	G	A	Pts	PIM	PP	SH	GW	Min
1996-97	Kitchener	OHA-B	43	35	41	76	33	....	....	....	....	....	....	....	....	....	....	....	....	....	....	....	....	....	....
1997-98	Belleville Bulls	OHL	64	31	45	76	62	....	....	....	....	....	....	....	....	....	10	4	2	6	10	....	....	....	....
1998-99	Belleville Bulls	OHL	63	35	47	82	74	....	....	....	....	....	....	....	....	....	21	15	15	30	27	....	....	....	....
99-2000	Belleville Bulls	OHL	66	45	46	91	102	....	....	....	....	....	....	....	....	....	16	5	12	17	16	....	....	....	....
2000-01	Kentucky	AHL	75	32	34	66	63	....	....	....	....	....	....	....	....	....	3	0	0	0	0	....	....	....	....
2001-02	Cleveland Barons	AHL	53	21	25	46	54	....	....	....	....	....	....	....	....	....	....	....	....	....	....	....	....	....	....
2002-03	**San Jose**	**NHL**	**66**	**9**	**7**	**16**	**39**	**0**	**0**	**3**	**94**	**9.6**	**–5**	**8**	**37.5**	**10:43**	....	....	....	....	....	....	....	....	....
	Cleveland Barons	AHL	9	3	4	7	16	....	....	....	....	....	....	....	....	....	....	....	....	....	....	....	....	....	....
2003-04	**San Jose**	**NHL**	**81**	**28**	**19**	**47**	**33**	**8**	**0**	**9**	**175**	**16.0**	**5**	**7**	**14.3**	**16:12**	**17**	**4**	**6**	**10**	**10**	**1**	**0**	**0**	**17:37**
2004-05	HV 71 Jonkoping	Sweden	20	5	0	5	10	....	....	....	....	....	....	....	....	....	....	....	....	....	....	....	....	....	....
	NHL Totals		**147**	**37**	**26**	**63**	**72**	**8**	**0**	**12**	**269**	**13.8**		**15**	**26.7**	**13:44**	**17**	**4**	**6**	**10**	**10**	**1**	**0**	**0**	**17:37**

OHL All-Rookie Team (1998) • AHL All-Rookie Team (2001)

Signed as a free agent by **HV 71** (Sweden), December 21, 2004.

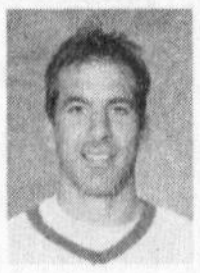

CHELIOS, Chris

(CHELL-EE-ohs, KRIHS) **DET.**

Defense. Shoots right. 6'1", 190 lbs. Born, Chicago, IL, January 25, 1962. Montreal's 5th choice, 40th overall, in 1981 Entry Draft.

Season	Club	League	GP	G	A	Pts	PIM	PP	SH	GW	S	%	+/-	TF	F%	Min	GP	G	A	Pts	PIM	PP	SH	GW	Min
1979-80	Moose Jaw	SJHL	53	12	31	43	118	....	....	....	....	....	....	....	....	....	....	....	....	....	....	....	....	....	....
1980-81	Moose Jaw	SJHL	54	23	64	87	175	....	....	....	....	....	....	....	....	....	....	....	....	....	....	....	....	....	....
1981-82	U. of Wisconsin	WCHA	43	6	43	49	50	....	....	....	....	....	....	....	....	....	....	....	....	....	....	....	....	....	....
1982-83	U. of Wisconsin	WCHA	26	9	17	26	50	....	....	....	....	....	....	....	....	....	....	....	....	....	....	....	....	....	....
1983-84	United States	Nat-Tm	60	14	35	49	58	....	....	....	....	....	....	....	....	....	....	....	....	....	....	....	....	....	....
	United States	Olympics	6	0	4	4	8	....	....	....	....	....	....	....	....	....	....	....	....	....	....	....	....	....	....
	Montreal	**NHL**	**12**	**0**	**2**	**2**	**12**	**0**	**0**	**0**	**23**	**0.0**	**–5**	....	....	....	**15**	**1**	**9**	**10**	**17**	**1**	**0**	**0**	....
1984-85	**Montreal**	**NHL**	**74**	**9**	**55**	**64**	**87**	**2**	**1**	**0**	**199**	**4.5**	**11**	....	....	....	**9**	**2**	**8**	**10**	**17**	**2**	**0**	**0**	....
1985-86♦	**Montreal**	**NHL**	**41**	**8**	**26**	**34**	**67**	**2**	**0**	**0**	**101**	**7.9**	**4**	....	....	....	**20**	**2**	**9**	**11**	**49**	**1**	**0**	**0**	....
1986-87	**Montreal**	**NHL**	**71**	**11**	**33**	**44**	**124**	**6**	**0**	**2**	**141**	**7.8**	**–5**	....	....	....	**17**	**4**	**9**	**13**	**38**	**2**	**1**	**0**	....
1987-88	**Montreal**	**NHL**	**71**	**20**	**41**	**61**	**172**	**10**	**1**	**5**	**199**	**10.1**	**14**	....	....	....	**11**	**3**	**1**	**4**	**29**	**1**	**0**	**0**	....
1988-89	**Montreal**	**NHL**	**80**	**15**	**58**	**73**	**185**	**8**	**0**	**6**	**206**	**7.3**	**35**	....	....	....	**21**	**4**	**15**	**19**	**28**	**1**	**0**	**2**	....
1989-90	**Montreal**	**NHL**	**53**	**9**	**22**	**31**	**136**	**1**	**2**	**1**	**123**	**7.3**	**20**	....	....	....	**5**	**0**	**1**	**1**	**8**	**0**	**0**	**0**	....
1990-91	**Chicago**	**NHL**	**77**	**12**	**52**	**64**	**192**	**5**	**2**	**2**	**187**	**6.4**	**23**	....	....	....	**6**	**1**	**7**	**8**	**46**	**1**	**0**	**0**	....
1991-92	**Chicago**	**NHL**	**80**	**9**	**47**	**56**	**245**	**2**	**2**	**2**	**239**	**3.8**	**24**	....	....	....	**18**	**6**	**15**	**21**	**37**	**3**	**0**	**1**	....
1992-93	**Chicago**	**NHL**	**84**	**15**	**58**	**73**	**282**	**8**	**0**	**2**	**290**	**5.2**	**14**	....	....	....	**4**	**0**	**2**	**2**	**14**	**0**	**0**	**0**	....
1993-94	**Chicago**	**NHL**	**76**	**16**	**44**	**60**	**212**	**7**	**1**	**2**	**219**	**7.3**	**12**	....	....	....	**6**	**1**	**1**	**2**	**8**	**1**	**0**	**0**	....
1994-95	EHC Biel-Bienne	Swiss	3	0	3	3	4	....	....	....	....	....	....	....	....	....	....	....	....	....	....	....	....	....	....
	Chicago	**NHL**	**48**	**5**	**33**	**38**	**72**	**3**	**1**	**0**	**166**	**3.0**	**17**	....	....	....	**16**	**4**	**7**	**11**	**12**	**0**	**1**	**3**	....
1995-96	**Chicago**	**NHL**	**81**	**14**	**58**	**72**	**140**	**7**	**0**	**3**	**219**	**6.4**	**25**	....	....	....	**9**	**0**	**3**	**3**	**8**	**0**	**0**	**0**	....
1996-97	**Chicago**	**NHL**	**72**	**10**	**38**	**48**	**112**	**2**	**0**	**2**	**194**	**5.2**	**16**	....	....	....	**6**	**0**	**1**	**1**	**8**	**0**	**0**	**0**	....
1997-98	**Chicago**	**NHL**	**81**	**3**	**39**	**42**	**151**	**1**	**0**	**0**	**205**	**1.5**	**–7**	....	....	....	....	....	....	....	....	....	....	....	....
	United States	Olympics	4	2	0	2	2	....	....	....	....	....	....	....	....	....	....	....	....	....	....	....	....	....	....
1998-99	**Chicago**	**NHL**	**65**	**8**	**26**	**34**	**89**	**2**	**1**	**0**	**172**	**4.7**	**–4**	**4**	**25.0**	**27:19**	....	....	....	....	....	....	....	....	....
	Detroit	**NHL**	**10**	**1**	**1**	**2**	**4**	**1**	**0**	**1**	**15**	**6.7**	**5**	**0**	**0.0**	**22:21**	**10**	**0**	**4**	**4**	**14**	**0**	**0**	**0**	**27:15**
99-2000	**Detroit**	**NHL**	**81**	**3**	**31**	**34**	**103**	**0**	**0**	**0**	**135**	**2.2**	**48**	**0**	**0.0**	**25:16**	**9**	**0**	**1**	**1**	**8**	**0**	**0**	**0**	**24:06**
2000-01	**Detroit**	**NHL**	**24**	**0**	**3**	**3**	**45**	**0**	**0**	**0**	**26**	**0.0**	**4**	**0**	**0.0**	**22:51**	**5**	**1**	**0**	**1**	**2**	**0**	**0**	**0**	**19:41**
2001-02♦	**Detroit**	**NHL**	**79**	**6**	**33**	**39**	**126**	**1**	**0**	**1**	**128**	**4.7**	**40**	**0**	**0.0**	**25:18**	**23**	**1**	**13**	**14**	**44**	**1**	**0**	**0**	**26:22**
	United States	Olympics	6	1	0	1	4	....	....	....	....	....	....	....	....	....	....	....	....	....	....	....	....	....	....
2002-03	**Detroit**	**NHL**	**66**	**2**	**17**	**19**	**78**	**0**	**1**	**1**	**92**	**2.2**	**4**	**0**	**0.0**	**24:15**	**4**	**0**	**0**	**0**	**2**	**0**	**0**	**0**	**25:43**

			Regular Season														Playoffs								
Season	Club	League	GP	G	A	Pts	PIM	PP	SH	GW	S	%	+/-	TF	F%	Min	GP	G	A	Pts	PIM	PP	SH	GW	Min
2003-04	**Detroit**	**NHL**	**69**	**2**	**19**	**21**	**61**	**0**	**0**	**0**	**113**	**1.8**	**12**	**0**	**0.0**	**21:21**	**8**	**0**	**1**	**1**	**4**	**0**	**0**	**0**	**21:13**
2004-05	Motor City	UHL	23	5	19	24	25	....	....	....	....	....	....	....	....	....	....	....	....	....	....	....	....	....	....
	NHL Totals		**1395**	**178**	**736**	**914**	**2695**	**68**	**12**	**30**	**3392**	**5.2**		**4**	**25.0**	**24:32**	**222**	**30**	**107**	**137**	**393**	**14**	**2**	**6**	**24:52**

WCHA Second All-Star Team (1983) • NCAA Championship All-Tournament Team (1983) • NHL All-Rookie Team (1985) • NHL First All-Star Team (1989, 1993, 1995, 1996, 2002) • James Norris Memorial Trophy (1989, 1993, 1996) • NHL Second All-Star Team (1991, 1997) • Bud Light Plus/Minus Award (2002)

Played in NHL All-Star Game (1985, 1990, 1991, 1992, 1993, 1994, 1996, 1997, 1998, 2000, 2002)

Traded to **Chicago** by **Montreal** with Montreal's 2nd round choice (Michael Pomichter) in 1991 Entry Draft for Denis Savard, June 29, 1990. Traded to **Detroit** by **Chicago** for Anders Eriksson and Detroit's 1st round choices in 1999 (Steve McCarthy) and 2001 (Adam Munro) Entry Drafts, March 23, 1999. • Missed majority of 2000-01 season recovering from knee injury suffered in game vs. Dallas, November 17, 2000. Signed as a free agent by **Motor City** (UHL), February 1, 2005.

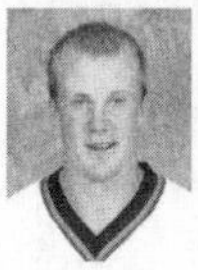

CHIMERA, Jason

(chihm-AIR-a, JAY-suhn) **PHX.**

Left wing. Shoots left. 6'2", 206 lbs. Born, Edmonton, Alta., May 2, 1979. Edmonton's 5th choice, 121st overall, in 1997 Entry Draft.

Season	Club	League	GP	G	A	Pts	PIM	PP	SH	GW	S	%	+/-	TF	F%	Min	GP	G	A	Pts	PIM	PP	SH	GW	Min
1994-95	Edmonton Pats	AMHL	33	27	31	58	42	....	....	....	....	....	....	....	....	....	....	....	....	....	....	....	....	....	....
1995-96	Edmonton Pats	AMHL	34	23	24	47	44	....	....	....	....	....	....	....	....	....	....	....	....	....	....	....	....	....	....
1996-97	Medicine Hat	WHL	71	16	23	39	64	....	....	....	....	....	....	....	....	....	4	0	1	1	4	....	....	....	....
1997-98	Medicine Hat	WHL	72	34	32	66	93	....	....	....	....	....	....	....	....	....	....	....	....	....	....	....	....	....	....
	Hamilton	AHL	4	0	0	0	8	....	....	....	....	....	....	....	....	....	....	....	....	....	....	....	....	....	....
1998-99	Medicine Hat	WHL	37	18	22	40	84	....	....	....	....	....	....	....	....	....	....	....	....	....	....	....	....	....	....
	Brandon	WHL	21	14	12	26	32	....	....	....	....	....	....	....	....	....	5	4	1	5	8	....	....	....	....
99-2000	Hamilton	AHL	78	15	13	28	77	....	....	....	....	....	....	....	....	....	10	0	2	2	12	....	....	....	....
2000-01	**Edmonton**	**NHL**	**1**	**0**	**0**	**0**	**0**	**0**	**0**	**0**	**0**	**0.0**	**0**	**0**	**0.0**	**6:58**	....	....	....	....	....	....	....	....	....
	Hamilton	AHL	78	29	25	54	93	....	....	....	....	....	....	....	....	....	....	....	....	....	....	....	....	....	....
2001-02	**Edmonton**	**NHL**	**3**	**1**	**0**	**1**	**0**	**0**	**0**	**0**	**3**	**33.3**	**-3**	**0**	**0.0**	**12:44**	....	....	....	....	....	....	....	....	....
	Hamilton	AHL	77	26	51	77	158	....	....	....	....	....	....	....	....	....	15	4	6	10	10	....	....	....	....
2002-03	**Edmonton**	**NHL**	**66**	**14**	**9**	**23**	**36**	**0**	**1**	**4**	**90**	**15.6**	**-2**	**11**	**54.6**	**10:46**	**2**	**0**	**2**	**2**	**0**	**0**	**0**	**0**	**10:55**
2003-04	**Edmonton**	**NHL**	**60**	**4**	**8**	**12**	**57**	**0**	**0**	**1**	**79**	**5.1**	**-1**	**22**	**31.8**	**10:07**	....	....	....	....	....	....	....	....	....
2004-05	AS Varese Hockey	Italy	15	7	3	10	34	....	....	....	....	....	....	....	....	....	5	2	1	3	31	....	....	....	....
	NHL Totals		**130**	**19**	**17**	**36**	**93**	**0**	**1**	**5**	**172**	**11.0**		**33**	**39.4**	**10:29**	**2**	**0**	**2**	**2**	**0**	**0**	**0**	**0**	**10:54**

AHL First All-Star Team (2002)

Traded to **Phoenix** by **Edmonton** with Edmonton's 3rd round choice (later transferred to Carolina – later traded to NY Rangers – NY Rangers selected Billy Ryan) in 2004 Entry Draft for New Jersey's 2nd round choice (previously acquired, Edmonton selected Geoff Paukovich) in 2004 Entry Draft and Buffalo's 4th round choice (previously acquired, Edmonton selected Liam Reddox) in 2004 Entry Draft, June 26, 2004. Signed as a free agent by **Varese** (Italy), December 15, 2004.

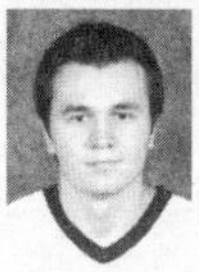

CHISTOV, Stanislav

(chihs-TAHV, STAHN-ihs-lahv) **ANA.**

Left wing. Shoots right. 5'10", 193 lbs. Born, Chelyabinsk, USSR, April 17, 1983. Anaheim's 1st choice, 5th overall, in 2001 Entry Draft.

Season	Club	League	GP	G	A	Pts	PIM	PP	SH	GW	S	%	+/-	TF	F%	Min	GP	G	A	Pts	PIM	PP	SH	GW	Min
1998-99	Chelyabinsk 2	Russia-4	1	0	0	0	0	....	....	....	....	....	....	....	....	....	....	....	....	....	....	....	....	....	....
	Georgetown	OPJHL	14	10	7	17	21	....	....	....	....	....	....	....	....	....	....	....	....	....	....	....	....	....	....
99-2000	Omsk 2	Russia-3	5	4	3	7	8	....	....	....	....	....	....	....	....	....	....	....	....	....	....	....	....	....	....
	Omsk 2	Russia-3	18	12	4	16	24	....	....	....	....	....	....	....	....	....	....	....	....	....	....	....	....	....	....
	Novokuznetsk	Russia	9	7	4	11	18	....	....	....	....	....	....	....	....	....	....	....	....	....	....	....	....	....	....
	Avangard Omsk	Russia	3	1	0	1	2	....	....	....	....	....	....	....	....	....	....	....	....	....	....	....	....	....	....
2000-01	Omsk 2	Russia-3	8	5	4	9	2	....	....	....	....	....	....	....	....	....	....	....	....	....	....	....	....	....	....
	Avangard Omsk	Russia	24	4	8	12	12	....	....	....	....	....	....	....	....	....	5	0	0	0	2	....	....	....	....
2001-02	Avangard Omsk	Russia	9	0	0	0	4	....	....	....	....	....	....	....	....	....	....	....	....	....	....	....	....	....	....
	CSKA Moscow 2	Russia-3	1	1	2	3	0	....	....	....	....	....	....	....	....	....	....	....	....	....	....	....	....	....	....
2002-03	**Anaheim**	**NHL**	**79**	**12**	**18**	**30**	**54**	**3**	**0**	**2**	**114**	**10.5**	**4**	**3**	**0.0**	**13:35**	**21**	**4**	**2**	**6**	**8**	**0**	**0**	**1**	**13:22**
2003-04	**Anaheim**	**NHL**	**56**	**2**	**16**	**18**	**26**	**2**	**0**	**0**	**70**	**2.9**	**-16**	**4**	**0.0**	**12:20**	....	....	....	....	....	....	....	....	....
	Cincinnati	AHL	23	5	8	13	45	....	....	....	....	....	....	....	....	....	9	6	2	8	4	....	....	....	....
2004-05	Cincinnati	AHL	79	15	23	38	141	....	....	....	....	....	....	....	....	....	9	2	1	3	6	....	....	....	....
	NHL Totals		**135**	**14**	**34**	**48**	**80**	**5**	**0**	**2**	**184**	**7.6**		**7**	**0.0**	**13:04**	**21**	**4**	**2**	**6**	**8**	**0**	**0**	**1**	**13:22**

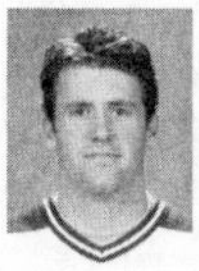

CHOUINARD, Eric

(shwee-NAHR, AIR-ihk) **PHI.**

Left wing. Shoots left. 6'3", 215 lbs. Born, Atlanta, GA, July 8, 1980. Montreal's 1st choice, 16th overall, in 1998 Entry Draft.

Season	Club	League	GP	G	A	Pts	PIM	PP	SH	GW	S	%	+/-	TF	F%	Min	GP	G	A	Pts	PIM	PP	SH	GW	Min
1995-96	Magog	QAHA	22	12	14	26	12	....	....	....	....	....	....	....	....	....	....	....	....	....	....	....	....	....	....
	Ste-Foy	QAAA	17	2	5	7	....	....	....	....	....	....	....	....	....	....	15	7	12	19	12	....	....	....	....
1996-97	Ste-Foy	QAAA	40	29	41	70	40	....	....	....	....	....	....	....	....	....	10	14	9	23	....	....	....	....	....
1997-98	Quebec Remparts	QMJHL	68	41	42	83	18	....	....	....	....	....	....	....	....	....	14	7	10	17	6	....	....	....	....
1998-99	Quebec Remparts	QMJHL	62	50	59	109	56	....	....	....	....	....	....	....	....	....	13	8	10	18	8	....	....	....	....
	Fredericton	AHL	....	....	....	....	....	....	....	....	....	....	....	....	....	....	6	3	2	5	0	....	....	....	....
99-2000	Quebec Remparts	QMJHL	50	57	47	104	105	....	....	....	....	....	....	....	....	....	11	14	4	18	8	....	....	....	....
2000-01	**Montreal**	**NHL**	**13**	**1**	**3**	**4**	**0**	**1**	**0**	**0**	**11**	**9.1**	**0**	**31**	**54.8**	**10:59**	....	....	....	....	....	....	....	....	....
	Quebec Citadelles	AHL	48	12	21	33	6	....	....	....	....	....	....	....	....	....	9	2	0	2	2	....	....	....	....
2001-02	Quebec Citadelles	AHL	65	19	23	42	18	....	....	....	....	....	....	....	....	....	2	0	0	0	0	....	....	....	....
2002-03	Utah Grizzlies	AHL	32	12	12	24	16	....	....	....	....	....	....	....	....	....	....	....	....	....	....	....	....	....	....
	Philadelphia	**NHL**	**28**	**4**	**4**	**8**	**8**	**1**	**0**	**0**	**45**	**8.9**	**2**	**12**	**33.3**	**9:38**	....	....	....	....	....	....	....	....	....
2003-04	**Philadelphia**	**NHL**	**17**	**3**	**0**	**3**	**0**	**0**	**0**	**0**	**15**	**20.0**	**-3**	**24**	**50.0**	**7:59**	....	....	....	....	....	....	....	....	....
	Minnesota	**NHL**	**31**	**3**	**4**	**7**	**6**	**0**	**0**	**1**	**45**	**6.7**	**-7**	**261**	**44.8**	**13:36**	....	....	....	....	....	....	....	....	....
	Philadelphia	AHL	1	0	0	0	0	....	....	....	....	....	....	....	....	....	....	....	....	....	....	....	....	....	....
2004-05	Salzburg	Austria	16	5	5	10	42	....	....	....	....	....	....	....	....	....	....	....	....	....	....	....	....	....	....
	NHL Totals		**89**	**11**	**11**	**22**	**14**	**2**	**0**	**1**	**116**	**9.5**		**328**	**45.7**	**10:54**	....	....	....	....	....	....	....	....	....

Traded to **Philadelphia** by **Montreal** for Philadelphia's 2nd round choice (Maxim Lapierre) in 2003 Entry Draft, January 29, 2003. Traded to **Minnesota** by **Philadelphia** for Minnesota's 5th round choice (Chris Zarb) in 2004 Entry Draft, December 17, 2003. Signed as a free agent by **Salzburg** (Austria), October 14, 2004. Signed as a free agent by **Philadelphia**, August 22, 2005.

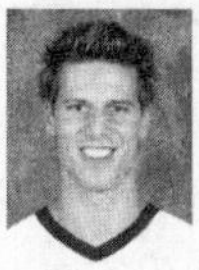

CHOUINARD, Marc

(shwee-NAHR, MAHRK) **MIN.**

Center. Shoots right. 6'5", 218 lbs. Born, Charlesbourg, Que., May 6, 1977. Winnipeg's 2nd choice, 32nd overall, in 1995 Entry Draft.

Season	Club	League	GP	G	A	Pts	PIM	PP	SH	GW	S	%	+/-	TF	F%	Min	GP	G	A	Pts	PIM	PP	SH	GW	Min
1992-93	Ste-Foy	QAAA	3	1	1	2	2	....	....	....	....	....	....	....	....	....	....	....	....	....	....	....	....	....	....
	Beaubourg Selects	QAHA	28	26	45	71	42	....	....	....	....	....	....	....	....	....	....	....	....	....	....	....	....	....	....
1993-94	Beauport	QMJHL	62	11	19	30	23	....	....	....	....	....	....	....	....	....	13	2	5	7	2	....	....	....	....
1994-95	Beauport	QMJHL	68	24	40	64	32	....	....	....	....	....	....	....	....	....	18	1	6	7	4	....	....	....	....
1995-96	Beauport	QMJHL	30	14	21	35	19	....	....	....	....	....	....	....	....	....	....	....	....	....	....	....	....	....	....
	Halifax	QMJHL	24	6	12	18	17	....	....	....	....	....	....	....	....	....	6	2	1	3	2	....	....	....	....
1996-97	Halifax	QMJHL	63	24	49	73	74	....	....	....	....	....	....	....	....	....	18	9	16	25	12	....	....	....	....
1997-98	Cincinnati	AHL	8	1	2	3	4	....	....	....	....	....	....	....	....	....	....	....	....	....	....	....	....	....	....
1998-99	Cincinnati	AHL	69	7	8	15	20	....	....	....	....	....	....	....	....	....	3	0	0	0	4	....	....	....	....
99-2000	Cincinnati	AHL	70	17	16	33	29	....	....	....	....	....	....	....	....	....	....	....	....	....	....	....	....	....	....
2000-01	**Anaheim**	**NHL**	**44**	**3**	**4**	**7**	**12**	**0**	**0**	**1**	**26**	**11.5**	**-5**	**414**	**60.9**	**7:50**	....	....	....	....	....	....	....	....	....
	Cincinnati	AHL	32	10	9	19	4	....	....	....	....	....	....	....	....	....	....	....	....	....	....	....	....	....	....
2001-02	**Anaheim**	**NHL**	**45**	**4**	**5**	**9**	**10**	**0**	**0**	**0**	**40**	**10.0**	**2**	**581**	**54.9**	**10:36**	....	....	....	....	....	....	....	....	....
2002-03	**Anaheim**	**NHL**	**70**	**3**	**4**	**7**	**40**	**0**	**1**	**0**	**52**	**5.8**	**-9**	**662**	**54.5**	**9:25**	**15**	**1**	**0**	**1**	**0**	**0**	**0**	**0**	**7:16**
2003-04	**Minnesota**	**NHL**	**45**	**11**	**10**	**21**	**17**	**3**	**1**	**2**	**70**	**15.7**	**4**	**809**	**53.7**	**15:58**	....	....	....	....	....	....	....	....	....
2004-05	Frisk-Asker IF	Norway	16	9	8	17	26	....	....	....	....	....	....	....	....	....	3	5	2	7	29	....	....	....	....
	NHL Totals		**204**	**21**	**23**	**44**	**79**	**3**	**2**	**3**	**188**	**11.2**		**2466**	**55.4**	**10:47**	**15**	**1**	**0**	**1**	**0**	**0**	**0**	**0**	**7:16**

Traded to **Anaheim** by **Winnipeg** with Teemu Selanne and Winnipeg's 4th round choice (later traded to Toronto – later traded to Montreal – Montreal selected Kim Staal) in 1996 Entry Draft for Chad Kilger, Oleg Tverdovsky and Anaheim's 3rd round choice (Per-Anton Lundstrom) in 1996 Entry Draft, February 7, 1996. Signed as a free agent by **Minnesota**, July 28, 2003. Signed as a free agent by **Frisk-Asker** (Norway), January 1, 2005.

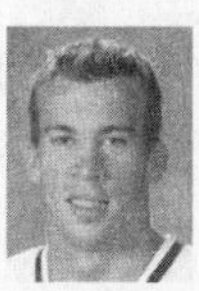

CHRISTIE, Ryan

(KRIHS-tee, RIGH-yuhn)

Left wing. Shoots left. 6'3", 200 lbs. Born, Beamsville, Ont., July 3, 1978. Dallas' 4th choice, 112th overall, in 1996 Entry Draft.

Season	Club	League	GP	G	A	Pts	PIM	PP	SH	GW	S	%	+/-	TF	F%	Min	GP	G	A	Pts	PIM	PP	SH	GW	Min
1994-95	St. Catharines	OHA-B	40	10	11	21	96	....	....	....	....	....	....	....	....	....	....	....	....	....	....	....	....	....	....
1995-96	Owen Sound	OHL	66	29	17	46	93	....	....	....	....	....	....	....	....	....	6	1	1	2	0	....	....	....	....
1996-97	Owen Sound	OHL	66	23	29	52	136	....	....	....	....	....	....	....	....	....	4	1	1	2	8	....	....	....	....
1997-98	Owen Sound	OHL	66	39	41	80	208	....	....	....	....	....	....	....	....	....	11	3	5	8	13	....	....	....	....
1998-99	Michigan	IHL	48	4	5	9	74	....	....	....	....	....	....	....	....	....	3	1	1	2	2	....	....	....	....

			Regular Season														Playoffs								
Season	Club	League	GP	G	A	Pts	PIM	PP	SH	GW	S	%	+/-	TF	F%	Min	GP	G	A	Pts	PIM	PP	SH	GW	Min
99-2000	**Dallas**	**NHL**	**5**	**0**	**0**	**0**	**0**	**0**	**0**	**0**	**1**	**0.0**	**–1**	**0**	**0.0**	**2:29**	....	....	....	....	....	....	....	....	....
	Michigan	IHL	76	24	25	49	140	....	....	....	....	....	....	....	....	....	....	....	....	....	....	....	....	....	....
2000-01	Utah Grizzlies	IHL	69	22	16	38	88	....	....	....	....	....	....	....	....	....	....	....	....	....	....	....	....	....	....
2001-02	**Calgary**	**NHL**	**2**	**0**	**0**	**0**	**0**	**0**	**0**	**0**	**0**	**0.0**	**–1**	**0**	**0.0**	**6:10**	....	....	....	....	....	....	....	....	....
	Saint John Flames	AHL	77	21	18	39	61	....	....	....	....	....	....	....	....	....	....	....	....	....	....	....	....	....	....
2002-03	Saint John Flames	AHL	67	10	14	24	84	....	....	....	....	....	....	....	....	....	....	....	....	....	....	....	....	....	....
2003-04	Las Vegas	ECHL	60	16	11	27	142	....	....	....	....	....	....	....	....	....	4	3	1	4	2	....	....	....	....
	Toronto	AHL	3	0	0	0	0	....	....	....	....	....	....	....	....	....	....	....	....	....	....	....	....	....	....
2004-05	HC Mulhouse	France	25	12	11	23	121	....	....	....	....	....	....	....	....	....	10	3	4	7	18	....	....	....	....
	NHL Totals		**7**	**0**	**0**	**0**	**0**	**0**	**0**	**0**	**1**	**0.0**		**0**	**0.0**	**3:32**	....	....	....	....	....	....	....	....	....

Signed as a free agent by **Calgary**, July 1, 2001. Signed as a free agent by **Las Vegas** (ECHL), October 20, 2003. Signed to a tryout (PTO) contract by **Toronto** (AHL), February 22, 2004. Signed as a free agent by **Mulhouse** (France), July 3, 2004.

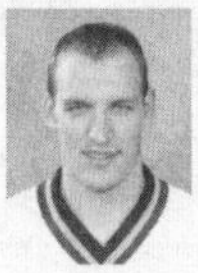

CHUBAROV, Artem (choo-BAH-rahf, AHR-tehm) VAN.

Center. Shoots left. 6'1", 189 lbs. Born, Gorky, USSR, December 12, 1979. Vancouver's 2nd choice, 31st overall, in 1998 Entry Draft.

Season	Club	League	GP	G	A	Pts	PIM	PP	SH	GW	S	%	+/-	TF	F%	Min	GP	G	A	Pts	PIM	PP	SH	GW	Min
1994-95	Nizh. Novgorod 2	CIS-2	60	20	30	50	20	....	....	....	....	....	....	....	....	....	....	....	....	....	....	....	....	....	....
1995-96	Niz. Novgorod Jr.	CIS-Jr.	60	22	25	47	20	....	....	....	....	....	....	....	....	....	....	....	....	....	....	....	....	....	....
1996-97	Nizhny Novgorod	Russia	15	1	1	2	8	....	....	....	....	....	....	....	....	....	....	....	....	....	....	....	....	....	....
1997-98	Dynamo Moscow	Russia	30	1	4	5	4	....	....	....	....	....	....	....	....	....	....	....	....	....	....	....	....	....	....
1998-99	Dynamo Moscow	Russia	34	8	2	10	10	....	....	....	....	....	....	....	....	....	12	0	0	0	4	....	....	....	....
99-2000	**Vancouver**	**NHL**	**49**	**1**	**8**	**9**	**10**	**0**	**0**	**1**	**53**	**1.9**	**–4**	**488**	**48.0**	**11:43**	....	....	....	....	....	....	....	....	....
	Syracuse Crunch	AHL	14	7	6	13	4	....	....	....	....	....	....	....	....	....	1	0	0	0	0	....	....	....	....
2000-01	**Vancouver**	**NHL**	**1**	**0**	**0**	**0**	**0**	**0**	**0**	**0**	**0**	**0.0**	**–1**	**17**	**52.9**	**15:08**	....	....	....	....	....	....	....	....	....
	Kansas City	IHL	10	7	4	11	12	....	....	....	....	....	....	....	....	....	....	....	....	....	....	....	....	....	....
2001-02	**Vancouver**	**NHL**	**51**	**5**	**5**	**10**	**10**	**0**	**0**	**3**	**73**	**6.8**	**–3**	**517**	**53.6**	**12:37**	**6**	**0**	**1**	**1**	**0**	**0**	**0**	**0**	**14:44**
	Manitoba Moose	AHL	19	7	12	19	4	....	....	....	....	....	....	....	....	....	....	....	....	....	....	....	....	....	....
2002-03	**Vancouver**	**NHL**	**62**	**7**	**13**	**20**	**6**	**1**	**0**	**1**	**78**	**9.0**	**4**	**862**	**50.8**	**14:21**	**14**	**0**	**2**	**2**	**4**	**0**	**0**	**0**	**14:56**
2003-04	**Vancouver**	**NHL**	**65**	**12**	**7**	**19**	**14**	**1**	**1**	**3**	**93**	**12.9**	**1**	**963**	**53.3**	**14:05**	**7**	**0**	**1**	**1**	**0**	**0**	**0**	**0**	**19:07**
2004-05	Dynamo Moscow	Russia	27	4	9	13	10	....	....	....	....	....	....	....	....	....	....	....	....	....	....	....	....	....	....
	NHL Totals		**228**	**25**	**33**	**58**	**40**	**2**	**1**	**8**	**297**	**8.4**		**2847**	**51.7**	**13:19**	**27**	**0**	**4**	**4**	**4**	**0**	**0**	**0**	**15:59**

• Missed majority of 2000-01 season recovering from shoulder injury suffered in game vs. Manitoba (IHL), November 15, 2000. Signed as a free agent by **Dynamo Moscow** (Russia), June 19, 2004.

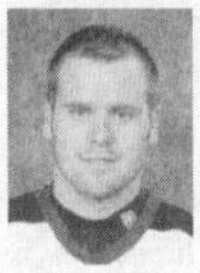

CIBAK, Martin (TSEE-bak, MAHR-tihn) T.B.

Center. Shoots left. 6'1", 196 lbs. Born, Liptovsky Mikulas, Czech., May 17, 1980. Tampa Bay's 11th choice, 252nd overall, in 1998 Entry Draft.

Season	Club	League	GP	G	A	Pts	PIM	PP	SH	GW	S	%	+/-	TF	F%	Min	GP	G	A	Pts	PIM	PP	SH	GW	Min
1995-96	L. Mikulas Jr.	Slovak-Jr.	48	38	35	73	....	....	....	....	....	....	....	....	....	....	....	....	....	....	....	....	....	....	....
1996-97	L. Mikulas Jr.	Slovak-Jr.	45	22	18	40	....	....	....	....	....	....	....	....	....	....	....	....	....	....	....	....	....	....	....
1997-98	L. Mikulas Jr.	Slovak-Jr.	42	31	21	52	....	....	....	....	....	....	....	....	....	....	....	....	....	....	....	....	....	....	....
	L. Mikulas	Slovakia	28	1	3	4	10	....	....	....	....	....	....	....	....	....	....	....	....	....	....	....	....	....	....
1998-99	Medicine Hat	WHL	66	21	26	47	72	....	....	....	....	....	....	....	....	....	....	....	....	....	....	....	....	....	....
99-2000	Medicine Hat	WHL	58	16	29	45	77	....	....	....	....	....	....	....	....	....	....	....	....	....	....	....	....	....	....
2000-01	Detroit Vipers	IHL	79	10	28	38	88	....	....	....	....	....	....	....	....	....	....	....	....	....	....	....	....	....	....
2001-02	**Tampa Bay**	**NHL**	**26**	**1**	**5**	**6**	**8**	**0**	**0**	**0**	**22**	**4.5**	**–6**	**85**	**34.1**	**11:08**	....	....	....	....	....	....	....	....	....
	Springfield	AHL	52	5	9	14	44	....	....	....	....	....	....	....	....	....	....	....	....	....	....	....	....	....	....
2002-03	Springfield	AHL	62	5	15	20	78	....	....	....	....	....	....	....	....	....	6	1	2	3	4	....	....	....	....
2003-04♦	**Tampa Bay**	**NHL**	**63**	**2**	**7**	**9**	**30**	**0**	**0**	**0**	**44**	**4.5**	**–1**	**321**	**45.2**	**7:35**	**6**	**0**	**1**	**1**	**0**	**0**	**0**	**0**	**7:35**
	Hershey Bears	AHL	1	0	0	0	2	....	....	....	....	....	....	....	....	....	....	....	....	....	....	....	....	....	....
2004-05	L. Mikulas	Slovakia	4	0	0	0	6	....	....	....	....	....	....	....	....	....	....	....	....	....	....	....	....	....	....
	Plzen	CzRep	30	4	11	15	52	....	....	....	....	....	....	....	....	....	....	....	....	....	....	....	....	....	....
	HC Kosice	Slovakia	6	1	3	4	8	....	....	....	....	....	....	....	....	....	10	2	5	7	36	....	....	....	....
	NHL Totals		**89**	**3**	**12**	**15**	**38**	**0**	**0**	**0**	**66**	**4.5**		**406**	**42.9**	**8:37**	**6**	**0**	**1**	**1**	**0**	**0**	**0**	**0**	**7:35**

Signed as a free agent by **L. Mikulas** (Slovakia), September 17, 2004. Signed as a free agent by **Plzen** (CzRep), October 18, 2004. Signed as a free agent by **Kosice** (Slovakia), January 31, 2005.

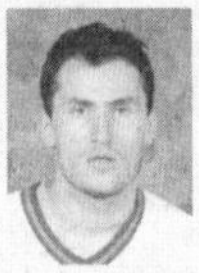

CIERNIK, Ivan (CHAIR-nihk, ee-VAHN)

Right wing. Shoots left. 6'1", 234 lbs. Born, Levice, Czech., October 30, 1977. Ottawa's 6th choice, 216th overall, in 1996 Entry Draft.

Season	Club	League	GP	G	A	Pts	PIM	PP	SH	GW	S	%	+/-	TF	F%	Min	GP	G	A	Pts	PIM	PP	SH	GW	Min
1994-95	HC Nitra Jr.	Slovak-Jr.	30	22	15	37	36	....	....	....	....	....	....	....	....	....	....	....	....	....	....	....	....	....	....
	HC Nitra	Slovakia	7	1	0	1	2	....	....	....	....	....	....	....	....	....	....	....	....	....	....	....	....	....	....
1995-96	HC Nitra	Slovakia	35	9	7	16	36	....	....	....	....	....	....	....	....	....	8	3	3	6	....	....	....	....	....
1996-97	HC Corgon Nitra	Slovakia	41	11	19	30	....	....	....	....	....	....	....	....	....	....	....	....	....	....	....	....	....	....	....
1997-98	**Ottawa**	**NHL**	**2**	**0**	**0**	**0**	**0**	**0**	**0**	**0**	**0**	**0.0**	**0**	....	....	....	....	....	....	....	....	....	....	....	....
	Worcester IceCats	AHL	53	9	12	21	38	....	....	....	....	....	....	....	....	....	1	0	0	0	2	....	....	....	....
1998-99	Adirondack	AHL	21	1	4	5	4	....	....	....	....	....	....	....	....	....	....	....	....	....	....	....	....	....	....
	Cincinnati	AHL	32	10	3	13	10	....	....	....	....	....	....	....	....	....	2	0	0	0	2	....	....	....	....
99-2000	Grand Rapids	IHL	66	13	12	25	64	....	....	....	....	....	....	....	....	....	6	0	6	6	2	....	....	....	....
2000-01	**Ottawa**	**NHL**	**4**	**2**	**0**	**2**	**2**	**0**	**0**	**0**	**7**	**28.6**	**2**	**0**	**0.0**	**7:41**	....	....	....	....	....	....	....	....	....
	Grand Rapids	IHL	66	27	38	65	53	....	....	....	....	....	....	....	....	....	10	5	6	11	26	....	....	....	....
2001-02	**Ottawa**	**NHL**	**23**	**1**	**2**	**3**	**4**	**0**	**0**	**0**	**18**	**5.6**	**0**	**7**	**71.4**	**7:51**	....	....	....	....	....	....	....	....	....
	Grand Rapids	AHL	2	2	1	3	0	....	....	....	....	....	....	....	....	....	....	....	....	....	....	....	....	....	....
	Washington	**NHL**	**6**	**0**	**1**	**1**	**2**	**0**	**0**	**0**	**5**	**0.0**	**0**	**0**	**0.0**	**9:15**	....	....	....	....	....	....	....	....	....
	Portland Pirates	AHL	26	10	5	15	28	....	....	....	....	....	....	....	....	....	....	....	....	....	....	....	....	....	....
2002-03	**Washington**	**NHL**	**47**	**8**	**10**	**18**	**24**	**0**	**0**	**2**	**61**	**13.1**	**6**	**9**	**33.3**	**11:48**	**2**	**0**	**1**	**1**	**6**	**0**	**0**	**0**	**9:09**
	Portland Pirates	AHL	13	4	6	10	6	....	....	....	....	....	....	....	....	....	....	....	....	....	....	....	....	....	....
2003-04	**Washington**	**NHL**	**7**	**1**	**1**	**2**	**0**	**0**	**0**	**0**	**8**	**12.5**	**1**	**0**	**0.0**	**9:38**	....	....	....	....	....	....	....	....	....
	Portland Pirates	AHL	54	10	21	31	43	....	....	....	....	....	....	....	....	....	7	2	1	3	10	....	....	....	....
2004-05	Wolfsburg	Germany	50	26	22	48	91	....	....	....	....	....	....	....	....	....	7	4	2	6	22	....	....	....	....
	NHL Totals		**89**	**12**	**14**	**26**	**32**	**0**	**0**	**2**	**99**	**12.1**		**16**	**50.0**	**10:13**	**2**	**0**	**1**	**1**	**6**	**0**	**0**	**0**	**9:09**

Loaned to **Cincinnati** (AHL) by **Ottawa** with Ratislav Pavlikovsky and Erich Goldmann, January 12, 1999. Claimed on waivers by **Washington** from **Ottawa**, January 19, 2002. Signed as a free agent by **Wolfsburg** (Germany), May 4, 2004.

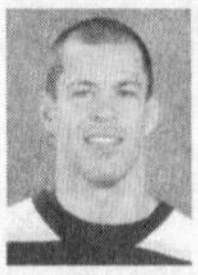

CISAR, Marian (SIH-sahr, MAIR-ee-uhn) NSH.

Right wing. Shoots right. 6', 197 lbs. Born, Bratislava, Czech., February 25, 1978. Los Angeles' 2nd choice, 37th overall, in 1996 Entry Draft.

Season	Club	League	GP	G	A	Pts	PIM	PP	SH	GW	S	%	+/-	TF	F%	Min	GP	G	A	Pts	PIM	PP	SH	GW	Min
1994-95	Bratislava Jr.	Slovak-Jr.	38	42	28	70	16	....	....	....	....	....	....	....	....	....	....	....	....	....	....	....	....	....	....
1995-96	Bratislava Jr.	Slovak-Jr.	16	26	17	43	2	....	....	....	....	....	....	....	....	....	....	....	....	....	....	....	....	....	....
	Bratislava	Slovakia	13	3	3	6	0	....	....	....	....	....	....	....	....	....	6	3	0	3	0	....	....	....	....
1996-97	Spokane Chiefs	WHL	70	31	35	66	52	....	....	....	....	....	....	....	....	....	9	6	2	8	4	....	....	....	....
1997-98	Spokane Chiefs	WHL	52	33	40	73	34	....	....	....	....	....	....	....	....	....	18	8	5	13	8	....	....	....	....
1998-99	Milwaukee	IHL	51	11	17	28	31	....	....	....	....	....	....	....	....	....	2	0	0	0	12	....	....	....	....
99-2000	**Nashville**	**NHL**	**3**	**0**	**0**	**0**	**4**	**0**	**0**	**0**	**2**	**0.0**	**–2**	**0**	**0.0**	**8:18**	....	....	....	....	....	....	....	....	....
	Milwaukee	IHL	78	20	32	52	82	....	....	....	....	....	....	....	....	....	1	0	0	0	0	....	....	....	....
2000-01	**Nashville**	**NHL**	**60**	**12**	**15**	**27**	**45**	**5**	**0**	**1**	**97**	**12.4**	**–7**	**0**	**0.0**	**13:10**	....	....	....	....	....	....	....	....	....
	Milwaukee	IHL	15	4	7	11	4	....	....	....	....	....	....	....	....	....	....	....	....	....	....	....	....	....	....
2001-02	**Nashville**	**NHL**	**10**	**1**	**2**	**3**	**8**	**1**	**0**	**0**	**16**	**6.3**	**–3**	**1**	**100.0**	**12:55**	....	....	....	....	....	....	....	....	....
	Milwaukee	AHL	2	1	0	1	2	....	....	....	....	....	....	....	....	....	....	....	....	....	....	....	....	....	....
2002-03	Znojmo	CzRep	9	2	0	2	4	....	....	....	....	....	....	....	....	....	....	....	....	....	....	....	....	....	....
	Lukko Rauma	Finland	26	6	8	14	6	....	....	....	....	....	....	....	....	....	....	....	....	....	....	....	....	....	....
2003-04	Nurnberg	Germany	43	23	13	36	26	....	....	....	....	....	....	....	....	....	2	0	0	0	2	....	....	....	....
2004-05	Hannover	Germany	14	4	6	10	8	....	....	....	....	....	....	....	....	....	....	....	....	....	....	....	....	....	....
	NHL Totals		**73**	**13**	**17**	**30**	**57**	**6**	**0**	**1**	**115**	**11.3**		**1**	**100.0**	**12:56**	....	....	....	....	....	....	....	....	....

Traded to **Nashville** by **Los Angeles** for future considerations, June 1, 1998. • Missed remainder of 2001-02 season after suffering head iinjury in game vs. Milwaukee (AHL), November 23, 2001. Signed as a free agent by **Znojmo** (CzRep) with Nashville retaining NHL rights, July 22, 2002. Signed as a free agent by **Nurnberg** (Germany), May 21, 2003.

| | | | Regular Season | | | | | | | | | | | | | Playoffs | | | | | | | |
|Season|Club|League|GP|G|A|Pts|PIM|PP|SH|GW|S|%|+/-|TF|F%|Min|GP|G|A|Pts|PIM|PP|SH|GW|Min|

CLARK, Brett (KLAHRK, BREHT) COL.

Defense. Shoots left. 6'1", 195 lbs. Born, Wapella, Sask., December 23, 1976. Montreal's 7th choice, 154th overall, in 1996 Entry Draft.

Season	Club	League	GP	G	A	Pts	PIM	PP	SH	GW	S	%	+/-	TF	F%	Min	GP	G	A	Pts	PIM	PP	SH	GW	Min
1994-95	Melville	SJHL	62	19	32	51	77																		
1995-96	U. of Maine	H-East	39	7	31	38	22																		
1996-97	Canada	Nat-Tm	57	6	21	27	52																		
1997-98	**Montreal**	**NHL**	41	1	0	1	20	0	0	0	26	3.8	-3												
	Fredericton	AHL	20	0	6	6	6										4	0	1	1	17				
1998-99	**Montreal**	**NHL**	61	2	2	4	16	0	0	0	36	5.6	-3	0	0.0	13:11									
	Fredericton	AHL	3	1	0	1	0																		
99-2000	**Atlanta**	**NHL**	14	0	1	1	4	0	0	0	13	0.0	-12	0	0.0	16:51									
	Orlando	IHL	63	9	17	26	31										6	0	1	1	0				
2000-01	**Atlanta**	**NHL**	28	1	2	3	14	0	0	0	35	2.9	-12	0	0.0	18:02									
	Orlando	IHL	43	2	9	11	32										15	1	6	7	2				
2001-02	**Atlanta**	**NHL**	2	0	0	0	0	0	0	0	0	0.0	-3	1	100.0	15:32									
	Chicago Wolves	AHL	42	3	17	20	18																		
	Hershey Bears	AHL	32	7	9	16	12										8	0	2	2	6				
2002-03	Hershey Bears	AHL	80	8	27	35	26										5	0	4	4	4				
2003-04	**Colorado**	**NHL**	12	1	1	2	6	0	0	0	14	7.1	3	0	0.0	10:26									
	Hershey Bears	AHL	64	11	21	32	37																		
2004-05	Hershey Bears	AHL	67	7	37	44	54																		
	NHL Totals		158	5	6	11	60	0	0	0	124	4.0		1	100.0	14:32									

Claimed by **Atlanta** from **Montreal** in Expansion Draft, June 25, 1999. Traded to **Colorado** by **Atlanta** for Frederic Cassivi, January 24, 2002.

CLARK, Chris (KLAHRK, KRIHS) WSH.

Right wing. Shoots right. 6', 200 lbs. Born, South Windsor, CT, March 8, 1976. Calgary's 3rd choice, 77th overall, in 1994 Entry Draft.

Season	Club	League	GP	G	A	Pts	PIM	PP	SH	GW	S	%	+/-	TF	F%	Min	GP	G	A	Pts	PIM	PP	SH	GW	Min
1990-91	South Windsor	High-CT	23	16	15	31	24																		
1991-92	Spring. Olympics	NEJHL	49	21	29	50	56																		
1992-93	Spring. Olympics	NEJHL	43	17	60	77	120																		
1993-94	Spring. Olympics	NEJHL	35	31	26	57	185																		
1994-95	Clarkson Knights	ECAC	32	12	11	23	92																		
1995-96	Clarkson Knights	ECAC	38	10	8	18	108																		
1996-97	Clarkson Knights	ECAC	37	23	25	48	*86																		
1997-98	Clarkson Knights	ECAC	35	18	21	39	*106																		
1998-99	Saint John Flames	AHL	73	13	27	40	123										7	2	4	6	15				
99-2000	**Calgary**	**NHL**	22	0	1	1	14	0	0	0	17	0.0	-3	0	0.0	9:02									
	Saint John Flames	AHL	48	16	17	33	134																		
2000-01	**Calgary**	**NHL**	29	5	1	6	38	1	0	0	43	11.6	0	3	33.3	11:56									
	Saint John Flames	AHL	48	18	17	35	131										18	4	10	14	49				
2001-02	**Calgary**	**NHL**	64	10	7	17	79	2	1	4	109	9.2	-12	21	33.3	13:57									
2002-03	**Calgary**	**NHL**	81	10	12	22	126	2	0	0	156	6.4	-11	40	32.5	14:24									
2003-04	**Calgary**	**NHL**	82	10	15	25	106	4	0	2	137	7.3	-3	97	36.1	14:05	26	3	3	6	30	1	0	0	14:34
2004-05	SC Bern	Swiss	3	0	0	0	6																		
	Storhamar	Norway	15	10	4	14	86										7	4	4	8	14				
	NHL Totals		278	35	36	71	363	9	1	8	462	7.6		161	34.8	13:31	26	3	3	6	30	1	0	0	14:34

ECAC Second All-Star Team (1998)
Signed as a free agent by **Bern** (Swiss), October 3, 2004. Signed as a free agent by **Storhamar** (Norway), December 29, 2004. Traded to **Washington** by **Calgary** for future considerations, August 4, 2005.

CLARKE, Noah (KLAHRK, NOH-uh) L.A.

Left wing. Shoots left. 5'9", 185 lbs. Born, LaVerne, CA, June 11, 1979. Los Angeles' 10th choice, 250th overall, in 1999 Entry Draft.

Season	Club	League	GP	G	A	Pts	PIM	PP	SH	GW	S	%	+/-	TF	F%	Min	GP	G	A	Pts	PIM	PP	SH	GW	Min
1996-97	Shat.-St. Mary's	High-MN	30	33	44	77																			
1997-98	Des Moines	USHL	54	19	30	49	29										12	2	9	11	23				
1998-99	Des Moines	USHL	52	31	32	63	47										13	8	2	10	16				
99-2000	Colorado College	WCHA	39	17	20	37	30																		
2000-01	Colorado College	WCHA	41	12	20	32	22																		
2001-02	Colorado College	WCHA	42	13	24	37	32																		
2002-03	Colorado College	WCHA	42	21	*49	70	15																		
	Manchester	AHL	3	1	1	2	0																		
2003-04	**Los Angeles**	**NHL**	2	0	1	1	0	0	0	0	3	0.0	1	0	0.0	9:39									
	Manchester	AHL	71	26	26	51	24										6	3	1	4	4				
2004-05	Manchester	AHL	61	21	24	45	24										6	1	0	1	4				
	NHL Totals		2	0	1	1	0	0	0	0	3	0.0		0	0.0	9:39									

USHL All-Rookie Team (1998) • USHL First All-Star Team (1999) • Curt Hammer Award (Most Gentlemanly Player – USHL) (1999) • WCHA All-Rookie Team (2000) • WCHA Second All-Star Team (2003) • NCAA West First All-American Team (2003) • AHL All-Rookie Team (2004)

CLASSEN, Greg (KLAW-sihn, GREHG) NSH.

Center. Shoots left. 6'1", 200 lbs. Born, Aylsham, Sask., August 24, 1977.

Season	Club	League	GP	G	A	Pts	PIM	PP	SH	GW	S	%	+/-	TF	F%	Min	GP	G	A	Pts	PIM	PP	SH	GW	Min
1997-98	Nipawin Hawks	SJHL	59	32	50	82	50										14	8	13	21	6				
1998-99	Merrimack	H-East	36	14	11	25	28																		
99-2000	Merrimack	H-East	36	14	16	30	16																		
	Milwaukee	IHL	11	1	0	1	2										2	0	0	0	2				
2000-01	**Nashville**	**NHL**	27	2	4	6	14	1	0	0	18	11.1	-4	195	42.1	10:16									
	Milwaukee	IHL	23	5	10	15	31										5	0	0	0	0				
2001-02	**Nashville**	**NHL**	55	5	6	11	30	0	1	0	32	15.6	1	389	43.2	10:09									
	Milwaukee	AHL	8	2	4	6	12																		
2002-03	**Nashville**	**NHL**	8	0	0	0	4	0	0	0	2	0.0	-3	65	52.3	10:02									
	Milwaukee	AHL	72	20	28	48	61										6	1	1	2	4				
2003-04	Milwaukee	AHL	68	18	29	47	95										20	4	3	7	12				
2004-05	Assat Pori	Finland	42	8	10	18	74										2	0	0	0	0				
	NHL Totals		90	7	10	17	48	1	1	0	52	13.5		649	43.8	10:10									

Hockey East All-Rookie Team (1999)
Signed as a free agent by **Nashville**, March 27, 2000. Signed as a free agent by **Assat** (Finland), July 25, 2004.

CLEARY, Daniel (KLIH-ree, DAN-yehl)

Right wing. Shoots left. 6', 211 lbs. Born, Carbonear, Nfld., December 18, 1978. Chicago's 1st choice, 13th overall, in 1997 Entry Draft.

Season	Club	League	GP	G	A	Pts	PIM	PP	SH	GW	S	%	+/-	TF	F%	Min	GP	G	A	Pts	PIM	PP	SH	GW	Min
1993-94	Kingston	MTJHL	41	18	28	46	33										2	0	1	1	0				
1994-95	Belleville Bulls	OHL	62	26	55	81	62										16	7	10	17	23				
1995-96	Belleville Bulls	OHL	64	53	62	115	74										14	10	17	27	40				
1996-97	Belleville Bulls	OHL	64	32	48	80	88										6	3	4	7	6				
1997-98	**Chicago**	**NHL**	6	0	0	0	0	0	0	0	4	0.0	-2												
	Belleville Bulls	OHL	30	16	31	47	14										10	6	*17	*23	10				
	Indianapolis Ice	IHL	4	2	1	3	6																		
1998-99	**Chicago**	**NHL**	35	4	5	9	24	0	0	0	49	8.2	-1	13	46.2	14:21									
	Portland Pirates	AHL	30	9	17	26	74										3	0	0	0	0				
	Hamilton	AHL	9	0	1	1	7																		
99-2000	**Edmonton**	**NHL**	17	3	2	5	8	0	0	1	18	16.7	-1	1	100.0	9:44	4	0	1	1	2	0	0	0	8:40
	Hamilton	AHL	58	22	52	74	108										5	2	3	5	18				
2000-01	**Edmonton**	**NHL**	81	14	21	35	37	2	0	2	107	13.1	5	13	23.1	12:58	6	1	1	2	8	1	0	0	14:09
2001-02	**Edmonton**	**NHL**	65	10	19	29	51	2	1	1	75	13.3	-1	5	60.0	12:43									
2002-03	**Edmonton**	**NHL**	57	4	13	17	31	0	0	1	89	4.5	5	5	40.0	11:58									

			Regular Season														Playoffs								
Season	Club	League	GP	G	A	Pts	PIM	PP	SH	GW	S	%	+/-	TF	F%	Min	GP	G	A	Pts	PIM	PP	SH	GW	Min
2003-04	Phoenix	NHL	68	6	11	17	42	0	3	0	83	7.2	-8	51	39.2	13:12	....	....	....	....	....	....	....	....	....
2004-05	Mora IK	Sweden	47	11	26	37	138	....	....	....	....	....	....	....	....	....	....	....	....	....	....	....	....	....	....
	NHL Totals		329	41	71	112	193	4	4	5	425	9.6		88	39.8	12:46	10	1	2	3	10	1	0	0	11:57

OHL All-Rookie Team (1995) • OHL First All-Star Team (1996, 1997) • AHL Second All-Star Team (2000)

Traded to **Edmonton** by **Chicago** with Chad Kilger, Ethan Moreau and Christian Laflamme for Boris Mironov, Dean McAmmond and Jonas Elofsson, March 20, 1999. Signed as a free agent by **Phoenix**, July 15, 2003. Signed as a free agent by **Mora** (Sweden), September 6, 2004.

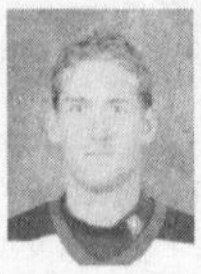

CLYMER, Ben (KLIH-mehr, BEHN) WSH.

Left wing. Shoots right. 6'1", 199 lbs. Born, Bloomington, MN, April 11, 1978. Boston's 3rd choice, 27th overall, in 1997 Entry Draft.

1993-94	Jefferson Jaguars	High-MN	23	3	7	10	20	....	....	....	....	....	....	....	....	....	....	....	....	....	....	....	....	....	....
1994-95	Jefferson Jaguars	High-MN	28	11	22	33	36	....	....	....	....	....	....	....	....	....	....	....	....	....	....	....	....	....	....
1995-96	Jefferson Jaguars	High-MN	18	12	34	46	34	....	....	....	....	....	....	....	....	....	5	0	6	6	6	....	....	....	....
1996-97	U. of Minnesota	WCHA	29	7	13	20	64	....	....	....	....	....	....	....	....	....	....	....	....	....	....	....	....	....	....
1997-98	U. of Minnesota	WCHA	1	0	0	0	2	....	....	....	....	....	....	....	....	....	....	....	....	....	....	....	....	....	....
1998-99	Seattle	WHL	70	12	44	56	93	....	....	....	....	....	....	....	....	....	11	1	5	6	12	....	....	....	....
99-2000	**Tampa Bay**	**NHL**	**60**	**2**	**6**	**8**	**87**	**2**	**0**	**0**	**98**	**2.0**	**-26**	**3**	**66.7**	**19:37**	....	....	....	....	....	....	....	....	....
	Detroit Vipers	IHL	19	1	9	10	30	....	....	....	....	....	....	....	....	....	....	....	....	....	....	....	....	....	....
2000-01	**Tampa Bay**	**NHL**	**23**	**5**	**1**	**6**	**21**	**3**	**0**	**0**	**25**	**20.0**	**-7**	**8**	**25.0**	**13:03**	....	....	....	....	....	....	....	....	....
	Detroit Vipers	IHL	53	5	8	13	88	....	....	....	....	....	....	....	....	....	....	....	....	....	....	....	....	....	....
2001-02	**Tampa Bay**	**NHL**	**81**	**14**	**20**	**34**	**36**	**4**	**0**	**2**	**151**	**9.3**	**-10**	**14**	**28.6**	**17:26**	....	....	....	....	....	....	....	....	....
2002-03	**Tampa Bay**	**NHL**	**65**	**6**	**12**	**18**	**57**	**1**	**0**	**1**	**103**	**5.8**	**-2**	**15**	**0.0**	**13:39**	**11**	**0**	**2**	**2**	**6**	**0**	**0**	**0**	**13:30**
2003-04♦	**Tampa Bay**	**NHL**	**66**	**2**	**8**	**10**	**50**	**0**	**0**	**0**	**96**	**2.1**	**5**	**25**	**28.0**	**9:48**	**5**	**0**	**0**	**0**	**0**	**0**	**0**	**0**	**7:46**
2004-05	EHC Biel-Bienne	Swiss-2	19	11	12	23	30	....	....	....	....	....	....	....	....	....	11	6	11	17	24	....	....	....	....
	NHL Totals		**295**	**29**	**47**	**76**	**251**	**10**	**0**	**3**	**473**	**6.1**		**65**	**23.1**	**15:00**	**16**	**0**	**2**	**2**	**6**	**0**	**0**	**0**	**11:42**

• Missed majority of 1997-98 season recovering from shoulder injury suffered in game vs. U. of Michigan (CCHA), October 10, 1997. Signed as a free agent by **Tampa Bay**, October 2, 1999. Signed as a free agent by **Biel-Bienne** (Swiss-2), December 2, 2004. Signed as a free agent by **Washington**, August 8, 2005.

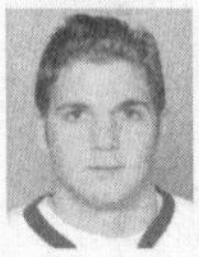

COLAIACOVO, Carlo (koh-lee-A-KOH-voh, KAR-loh) TOR.

Defense. Shoots left. 6'1", 188 lbs. Born, Toronto, Ont., January 27, 1983. Toronto's 1st choice, 17th overall, in 2001 Entry Draft.

1998-99	Mississauga Reps	GTHL	44	10	12	23	28	....	....	....	....	....	....	....	....	....	....	....	....	....	....	....	....	....	....
99-2000	Erie Otters	OHL	52	4	18	22	12	....	....	....	....	....	....	....	....	....	13	2	4	6	9	....	....	....	....
2000-01	Erie Otters	OHL	62	12	27	39	59	....	....	....	....	....	....	....	....	....	14	4	7	11	16	....	....	....	....
2001-02	Erie Otters	OHL	60	13	27	40	49	....	....	....	....	....	....	....	....	....	21	7	10	17	20	....	....	....	....
2002-03	**Toronto**	**NHL**	**2**	**0**	**1**	**1**	**0**	**0**	**0**	**0**	**1**	**0.0**	**0**	**0**	**0.0**	**13:43**	....	....	....	....	....	....	....	....	....
	Erie Otters	OHL	35	14	21	35	12	....	....	....	....	....	....	....	....	....	....	....	....	....	....	....	....	....	....
2003-04	**Toronto**	**NHL**	**2**	**0**	**1**	**1**	**2**	**0**	**0**	**0**	**0**	**0.0**	**1**	**0**	**0.0**	**13:56**	....	....	....	....	....	....	....	....	....
	St. John's	AHL	62	6	25	31	50	....	....	....	....	....	....	....	....	....	....	....	....	....	....	....	....	....	....
2004-05	St. John's	AHL	49	4	20	24	59	....	....	....	....	....	....	....	....	....	5	0	1	1	2	....	....	....	....
	NHL Totals		**4**	**0**	**2**	**2**	**2**	**0**	**0**	**0**	**1**	**0.0**		**0**	**0.0**	**13:49**	....	....	....	....	....	....	....	....	....

OHL Second All-Star Team (2002, 2003)

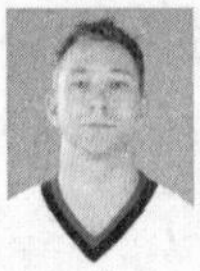

COLE, Erik (KOHL, AIR-ihk) CAR.

Left wing. Shoots left. 6'2", 200 lbs. Born, Oswego, NY, November 6, 1978. Carolina's 3rd choice, 71st overall, in 1998 Entry Draft.

1995-96	Oswego	High-NY	40	49	41	90	....	....	....	....	....	....	....	....	....	....	....	....	....	....	....	....	....	....	....
1996-97	Des Moines	USHL	48	30	34	64	140	....	....	....	....	....	....	....	....	....	5	2	0	2	6	....	....	....	....
1997-98	Clarkson Knights	ECAC	34	11	20	31	55	....	....	....	....	....	....	....	....	....	....	....	....	....	....	....	....	....	....
1998-99	Clarkson Knights	ECAC	36	*22	20	42	50	....	....	....	....	....	....	....	....	....	....	....	....	....	....	....	....	....	....
99-2000	Clarkson Knights	ECAC	33	19	11	30	46	....	....	....	....	....	....	....	....	....	....	....	....	....	....	....	....	....	....
	Cincinnati	IHL	9	4	3	7	2	....	....	....	....	....	....	....	....	....	7	1	1	2	2	....	....	....	....
2000-01	Cincinnati	IHL	69	23	20	43	28	....	....	....	....	....	....	....	....	....	5	1	0	1	2	....	....	....	....
2001-02	**Carolina**	**NHL**	**81**	**16**	**24**	**40**	**35**	**3**	**0**	**2**	**159**	**10.1**	**-10**	**17**	**47.1**	**16:04**	**23**	**6**	**3**	**9**	**30**	**1**	**0**	**1**	**18:27**
2002-03	**Carolina**	**NHL**	**53**	**14**	**13**	**27**	**72**	**6**	**2**	**3**	**125**	**11.2**	**1**	**56**	**39.3**	**17:08**	....	....	....	....	....	....	....	....	....
2003-04	**Carolina**	**NHL**	**80**	**18**	**24**	**42**	**93**	**2**	**2**	**3**	**172**	**10.5**	**-4**	**15**	**46.7**	**18:06**	....	....	....	....	....	....	....	....	....
2004-05	Eisbaren Berlin	Germany	39	6	21	27	76	....	....	....	....	....	....	....	....	....	8	5	1	6	37	....	....	....	....
	NHL Totals		**214**	**48**	**61**	**109**	**200**	**11**	**4**	**8**	**456**	**10.5**		**88**	**42.0**	**17:05**	**23**	**6**	**3**	**9**	**30**	**1**	**0**	**1**	**18:27**

ECAC Rookie of the Year (1998) (co-winner - Willie Mitchell) • ECAC First All-Star Team (1999) • NCAA East Second All-American Team (1999) • ECAC Second All-Star Team (2000)

Signed as a free agent by **Eisbaren Berlin** (Germany), October 24, 2004.

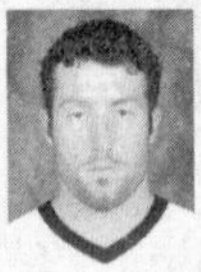

COMMODORE, Mike (KAWM-uh-dohr, MIGHK) CAR.

Defense. Shoots right. 6'4", 230 lbs. Born, Fort Saskatchewan, Alta., November 7, 1979. New Jersey's 2nd choice, 42nd overall, in 1999 Entry Draft.

1996-97	Ft. Saskatchewan	AJHL	51	3	8	11	244	....	....	....	....	....	....	....	....	....	....	....	....	....	....	....	....	....	....
1997-98	North Dakota	WCHA	29	0	5	5	74	....	....	....	....	....	....	....	....	....	....	....	....	....	....	....	....	....	....
1998-99	North Dakota	WCHA	39	5	8	13	154	....	....	....	....	....	....	....	....	....	....	....	....	....	....	....	....	....	....
99-2000	North Dakota	WCHA	38	5	7	12	*154	....	....	....	....	....	....	....	....	....	....	....	....	....	....	....	....	....	....
2000-01	**New Jersey**	**NHL**	**20**	**1**	**4**	**5**	**14**	**0**	**0**	**0**	**11**	**9.1**	**5**	**0**	**0.0**	**12:46**	....	....	....	....	....	....	....	....	....
	Albany River Rats	AHL	41	2	5	7	59	....	....	....	....	....	....	....	....	....	....	....	....	....	....	....	....	....	....
2001-02	**New Jersey**	**NHL**	**37**	**0**	**1**	**1**	**30**	**0**	**0**	**0**	**22**	**0.0**	**-12**	**0**	**0.0**	**12:37**	....	....	....	....	....	....	....	....	....
	Albany River Rats	AHL	14	0	3	3	31	....	....	....	....	....	....	....	....	....	....	....	....	....	....	....	....	....	....
2002-03	Cincinnati	AHL	61	2	9	11	210	....	....	....	....	....	....	....	....	....	....	....	....	....	....	....	....	....	....
	Calgary	**NHL**	**6**	**0**	**1**	**1**	**19**	**0**	**0**	**0**	**5**	**0.0**	**2**	**0**	**0.0**	**11:35**	....	....	....	....	....	....	....	....	....
	Saint John Flames	AHL	7	0	3	3	18	....	....	....	....	....	....	....	....	....	....	....	....	....	....	....	....	....	....
2003-04	**Calgary**	**NHL**	**12**	**0**	**0**	**0**	**25**	**0**	**0**	**0**	**10**	**0.0**	**-4**	**0**	**0.0**	**15:17**	**20**	**0**	**2**	**2**	**19**	**0**	**0**	**0**	**11:34**
	Lowell	AHL	37	5	11	16	75	....	....	....	....	....	....	....	....	....	....	....	....	....	....	....	....	....	....
2004-05	Lowell	AHL	73	6	29	35	175	....	....	....	....	....	....	....	....	....	11	1	2	3	18	....	....	....	....
	NHL Totals		**75**	**1**	**6**	**7**	**88**	**0**	**0**	**0**	**48**	**2.1**		**0**	**0.0**	**13:00**	**20**	**0**	**2**	**2**	**19**	**0**	**0**	**0**	**11:34**

NCAA Championship All-Tournament Team (2000)

Traded to **Anaheim** by **New Jersey** with Petr Sykora, Jean-Francois Damphousse and Igor Pohanka for Jeff Friesen, Oleg Tverdovsky and Maxim Balmochnykh, July 6, 2002. Traded to **Calgary** by **Anaheim** with Jean-Francois Damphousse for Rob Niedermayer, March 11, 2003. Traded to **Carolina** by **Calgary** for Atlanta's 3rd round choice (previously acquired - Calgary selected Gord Baldwin) in 2005 Entry Draft, July 29, 2005.

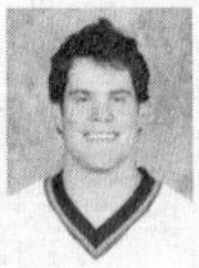

COMRIE, Mike (KAWM-ree, MIGHK) PHX.

Center. Shoots left. 5'10", 185 lbs. Born, Edmonton, Alta., September 11, 1980. Edmonton's 5th choice, 91st overall, in 1999 Entry Draft.

1995-96	Edmonton SSAC	AMHL	33	51	52	103	....	....	....	....	....	....	....	....	....	....	....	....	....	....	....	....	....	....	....
1996-97	St. Albert Saints	AJHL	63	37	41	78	44	....	....	....	....	....	....	....	....	....	....	....	....	....	....	....	....	....	....
1997-98	St. Albert Saints	AJHL	58	*60	*78	*138	134	....	....	....	....	....	....	....	....	....	19	*24	*24	*48	51	....	....	....	....
1998-99	U. of Michigan	CCHA	42	19	25	44	38	....	....	....	....	....	....	....	....	....	....	....	....	....	....	....	....	....	....
99-2000	U. of Michigan	CCHA	40	24	35	59	95	....	....	....	....	....	....	....	....	....	....	....	....	....	....	....	....	....	....
2000-01	Kootenay Ice	WHL	37	39	40	79	79	....	....	....	....	....	....	....	....	....	....	....	....	....	....	....	....	....	....
	Edmonton	**NHL**	**41**	**8**	**14**	**22**	**14**	**3**	**0**	**1**	**62**	**12.9**	**6**	**372**	**43.3**	**11:23**	**6**	**1**	**2**	**3**	**0**	**1**	**0**	**1**	**15:00**
2001-02	**Edmonton**	**NHL**	**82**	**33**	**27**	**60**	**45**	**8**	**0**	**5**	**170**	**19.4**	**16**	**1198**	**47.3**	**17:32**	....	....	....	....	....	....	....	....	....
2002-03	**Edmonton**	**NHL**	**69**	**20**	**31**	**51**	**90**	**8**	**0**	**6**	**170**	**11.8**	**-18**	**1069**	**47.1**	**17:51**	**6**	**1**	**0**	**1**	**10**	**0**	**0**	**0**	**13:07**
2003-04	**Philadelphia**	**NHL**	**21**	**4**	**5**	**9**	**12**	**0**	**0**	**1**	**36**	**11.1**	**2**	**165**	**50.9**	**12:51**	....	....	....	....	....	....	....	....	....
	Phoenix	**NHL**	**28**	**8**	**7**	**15**	**16**	**1**	**1**	**1**	**65**	**12.3**	**-8**	**304**	**50.3**	**17:50**	....	....	....	....	....	....	....	....	....
2004-05	Farjestad	Sweden	10	1	6	7	10	....	....	....	....	....	....	....	....	....	....	....	....	....	....	....	....	....	....
	NHL Totals		**241**	**73**	**84**	**157**	**177**	**20**	**1**	**14**	**503**	**14.5**		**3108**	**47.2**	**16:12**	**12**	**2**	**2**	**4**	**10**	**1**	**0**	**1**	**14:03**

CCHA All-Rookie Team (1999) • CCHA First All-Star Team (1999) • CCHA Rookie of the Year (1999) • CCHA First All-Star Team (2000) • NCAA West Second All-American Team (2000)

• Left **University of Michigan** (CCHA) and signed as a free agent by **Kootenay** (WHL), August 23, 2000. • Left **Kootenay** (WHL) and signed with **Edmonton**, December 30, 2000. Traded to **Philadelphia** by **Edmonton** for Jeff Woywitka, Philadelphia's 1st round choice (Rob Schremp) in 2004 Entry Draft and Philadelphia's 3rd round choice (Danny Syvret) in 2005 Entry Draft, December 16, 2003. Traded to **Phoenix** by **Philadelphia** for Sean Burke, Branko Radivojevic and Ben Eager, February 9, 2004. Signed as a free agent by **Farjestad** (Sweden), October 30, 2004.

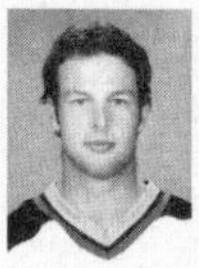

CONNOLLY, Tim
(KAHN-noh-lee, TIHM) **BUF.**

Center. Shoots right. 6'1", 190 lbs. Born, Syracuse, NY, May 7, 1981. NY Islanders' 1st choice, 5th overall, in 1999 Entry Draft.

			Regular Season														Playoffs								
Season	Club	League	GP	G	A	Pts	PIM	PP	SH	GW	S	%	+/-	TF	F%	Min	GP	G	A	Pts	PIM	PP	SH	GW	Min
1996-97	Syracuse	MTJHL	50	42	62	104	34	....	....	....	....	....	....	....	....	....	....	....	....	....	....	....	....	....	....
1997-98	Erie Otters	OHL	59	30	32	62	32	....	....	....	....	....	....	....	....	....	7	1	6	7	6	....	....	....	....
1998-99	Erie Otters	OHL	46	34	34	68	50	....	....	....	....	....	....	....	....	....	....	....	....	....	....	....	....	....	....
99-2000	**NY Islanders**	**NHL**	**81**	**14**	**20**	**34**	**44**	**2**	**1**	**1**	**114**	**12.3**	**–25**	**786**	**36.3**	**16:18**	....	....	....	....	....	....	....	....	....
2000-01	**NY Islanders**	**NHL**	**82**	**10**	**31**	**41**	**42**	**5**	**0**	**0**	**171**	**5.8**	**–14**	**989**	**41.7**	**20:02**	....	....	....	....	....	....	....	....	....
2001-02	**Buffalo**	**NHL**	**82**	**10**	**35**	**45**	**34**	**3**	**0**	**3**	**126**	**7.9**	**4**	**1074**	**39.6**	**16:58**	....	....	....	....	....	....	....	....	....
2002-03	**Buffalo**	**NHL**	**80**	**12**	**13**	**25**	**32**	**6**	**0**	**2**	**159**	**7.5**	**–28**	**845**	**42.8**	**16:00**	....	....	....	....	....	....	....	....	....
2003-04	**Buffalo**	**NHL**	DID NOT PLAY – INJURED																						
2004-05	Langnau	Swiss	16	7	3	10	14	....	....	....	....	....	....	....	....	....	....	....	....	....	....	....	....	....	....
	NHL Totals		**325**	**46**	**99**	**145**	**152**	**16**	**1**	**6**	**570**	**8.1**		**3694**	**40.2**	**17:20**	....	....	....	....	....	....	....	....	....

Traded to **Buffalo** by **NY Islanders** with Taylor Pyatt for Michael Peca, June 24, 2001. • Missed entire 2003-04 season recovering from head injury suffered in pre-season game vs. Chicago, October 2, 2003. Signed as a free agent by **Langnau** (Swiss), October 10, 2004.

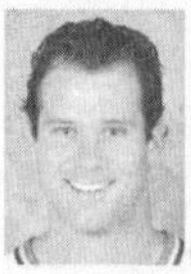

CONROY, Craig
(KAWN-roi, KRAYG) **L.A.**

Center. Shoots right. 6'2", 197 lbs. Born, Potsdam, NY, September 4, 1971. Montreal's 7th choice, 123rd overall, in 1990 Entry Draft.

1989-90	Northwood	High-NY	31	33	43	76		....	....	....	....	....	....	....	....	....	....	....	....	....	....	....	....	....	....
1990-91	Clarkson Knights	ECAC	40	8	21	29	24	....	....	....	....	....	....	....	....	....	....	....	....	....	....	....	....	....	....
1991-92	Clarkson Knights	ECAC	31	19	17	36	36	....	....	....	....	....	....	....	....	....	....	....	....	....	....	....	....	....	....
1992-93	Clarkson Knights	ECAC	35	10	23	33	26	....	....	....	....	....	....	....	....	....	....	....	....	....	....	....	....	....	....
1993-94	Clarkson Knights	ECAC	34	26	*40	*66	46	....	....	....	....	....	....	....	....	....	....	....	....	....	....	....	....	....	....
1994-95	Fredericton	AHL	55	26	18	44	29	....	....	....	....	....	....	....	....	....	11	7	3	10	6	....	....	....	....
	Montreal	**NHL**	**6**	**1**	**0**	**1**	**0**	**0**	**0**	**0**	**4**	**25.0**	**–1**	....	....	....	....	....	....	....	....	....	....	....	....
1995-96	**Montreal**	**NHL**	**7**	**0**	**0**	**0**	**2**	**0**	**0**	**0**	**1**	**0.0**	**–4**	....	....	....	....	....	....	....	....	....	....	....	....
	Fredericton	AHL	67	31	38	69	65	....	....	....	....	....	....	....	....	....	10	5	7	12	6	....	....	....	....
1996-97	Fredericton	AHL	9	10	6	16	10	....	....	....	....	....	....	....	....	....	....	....	....	....	....	....	....	....	....
	St. Louis	**NHL**	**61**	**6**	**11**	**17**	**43**	**0**	**0**	**1**	**74**	**8.1**	**0**	....	....	....	**6**	**0**	**0**	**0**	**8**	**0**	**0**	**0**	....
	Worcester IceCats	AHL	5	5	6	11	2	....	....	....	....	....	....	....	....	....	....	....	....	....	....	....	....	....	....
1997-98	**St. Louis**	**NHL**	**81**	**14**	**29**	**43**	**46**	**0**	**3**	**1**	**118**	**11.9**	**20**	....	....	....	**10**	**1**	**2**	**3**	**8**	**0**	**0**	**1**	....
1998-99	**St. Louis**	**NHL**	**69**	**14**	**25**	**39**	**38**	**0**	**1**	**1**	**134**	**10.4**	**14**	**1190**	**54.6**	**16:39**	**13**	**2**	**1**	**3**	**6**	**0**	**0**	**0**	**15:09**
99-2000	**St. Louis**	**NHL**	**79**	**12**	**15**	**27**	**36**	**1**	**2**	**3**	**98**	**12.2**	**5**	**1339**	**53.6**	**14:48**	**7**	**0**	**2**	**2**	**2**	**0**	**0**	**0**	**13:13**
2000-01	**St. Louis**	**NHL**	**69**	**11**	**14**	**25**	**46**	**0**	**3**	**2**	**101**	**10.9**	**2**	**729**	**55.1**	**14:01**	....	....	....	....	....	....	....	....	....
	Calgary	**NHL**	**14**	**3**	**4**	**7**	**14**	**0**	**1**	**0**	**32**	**9.4**	**0**	**264**	**52.7**	**18:08**	....	....	....	....	....	....	....	....	....
2001-02	**Calgary**	**NHL**	**81**	**27**	**48**	**75**	**32**	**7**	**2**	**4**	**146**	**18.5**	**24**	**1654**	**54.3**	**20:56**	....	....	....	....	....	....	....	....	....
2002-03	**Calgary**	**NHL**	**79**	**22**	**37**	**59**	**36**	**5**	**0**	**2**	**143**	**15.4**	**–4**	**1579**	**57.0**	**19:47**	....	....	....	....	....	....	....	....	....
2003-04	**Calgary**	**NHL**	**63**	**8**	**39**	**47**	**44**	**2**	**0**	**0**	**112**	**7.1**	**13**	**1402**	**53.9**	**19:13**	**26**	**6**	**11**	**17**	**12**	**2**	**0**	**1**	**20:23**
2004-05			DID NOT PLAY																						
	NHL Totals		**609**	**118**	**222**	**340**	**337**	**15**	**12**	**14**	**963**	**12.3**		**8157**	**54.7**	**17:38**	**62**	**9**	**16**	**25**	**36**	**2**	**0**	**2**	**17:48**

ECAC First All-Star Team (1994) • NCAA East First All-American Team (1994) • NCAA Final Four All-Tournament Team (1994)

Traded to **St. Louis** by **Montreal** with Pierre Turgeon and Rory Fitzpatrick for Murray Baron, Shayne Corson and St. Louis' 5th round choice (Gennady Razin) in 1997 Entry Draft, October 29, 1996. Traded to **Calgary** by **St. Louis** with St. Louis' 7th round choice (David Moss) in 2001 Entry Draft for Cory Stillman, March 13, 2001. Signed as a free agent by **Los Angeles**, July 6, 2004.

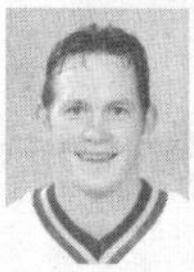

COOKE, Matt
(KUK, MAT) **VAN.**

Center. Shoots left. 6', 205 lbs. Born, Belleville, Ont., September 7, 1978. Vancouver's 8th choice, 144th overall, in 1997 Entry Draft.

1994-95	Wellington Dukes	MTJHL	46	9	23	32	62	....	....	....	....	....	....	....	....	....	....	....	....	....	....	....	....	....	....
1995-96	Windsor Spitfires	OHL	61	8	11	19	102	....	....	....	....	....	....	....	....	....	7	1	3	4	6	....	....	....	....
1996-97	Windsor Spitfires	OHL	65	45	50	95	146	....	....	....	....	....	....	....	....	....	5	5	5	10	10	....	....	....	....
1997-98	Windsor Spitfires	OHL	23	14	19	33	50	....	....	....	....	....	....	....	....	....	....	....	....	....	....	....	....	....	....
	Kingston	OHL	25	8	13	21	49	....	....	....	....	....	....	....	....	....	12	8	8	16	20	....	....	....	....
1998-99	**Vancouver**	**NHL**	**30**	**0**	**2**	**2**	**27**	**0**	**0**	**0**	**22**	**0.0**	**–12**	**189**	**40.2**	**8:07**	....	....	....	....	....	....	....	....	....
	Syracuse Crunch	AHL	37	15	18	33	119	....	....	....	....	....	....	....	....	....	....	....	....	....	....	....	....	....	....
99-2000	**Vancouver**	**NHL**	**51**	**5**	**7**	**12**	**39**	**0**	**1**	**1**	**58**	**8.6**	**3**	**71**	**39.4**	**11:48**	....	....	....	....	....	....	....	....	....
	Syracuse Crunch	AHL	18	5	8	13	27	....	....	....	....	....	....	....	....	....	....	....	....	....	....	....	....	....	....
2000-01	**Vancouver**	**NHL**	**81**	**14**	**13**	**27**	**94**	**0**	**2**	**0**	**121**	**11.6**	**5**	**321**	**43.0**	**14:35**	**4**	**0**	**0**	**0**	**4**	**0**	**0**	**0**	**12:04**
2001-02	**Vancouver**	**NHL**	**82**	**13**	**20**	**33**	**111**	**1**	**0**	**2**	**103**	**12.6**	**4**	**28**	**32.1**	**14:03**	**6**	**3**	**2**	**5**	**0**	**1**	**0**	**0**	**15:09**
2002-03	**Vancouver**	**NHL**	**82**	**15**	**27**	**42**	**82**	**1**	**4**	**0**	**118**	**12.7**	**21**	**31**	**35.5**	**13:24**	**14**	**2**	**1**	**3**	**12**	**0**	**0**	**0**	**14:06**
2003-04	**Vancouver**	**NHL**	**53**	**11**	**12**	**23**	**73**	**1**	**1**	**4**	**79**	**13.9**	**5**	**34**	**52.9**	**14:06**	**7**	**3**	**1**	**4**	**12**	**0**	**0**	**1**	**18:23**
2004-05			DID NOT PLAY																						
	NHL Totals		**379**	**58**	**81**	**139**	**426**	**3**	**8**	**7**	**501**	**11.6**		**674**	**41.5**	**13:15**	**31**	**8**	**4**	**12**	**28**	**1**	**0**	**1**	**15:01**

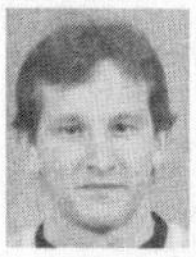

CORAZZINI, Carl
(koh-ra-ZEE-nee, KAHRL)

Center. Shoots right. 5'10", 182 lbs. Born, Framingham, MA, April 21, 1979.

1996-97	St. Sebastian's	High-MA	25	29	31	60	....	....	....	....	....	....	....	....	....	....	....	....	....	....	....	....	....	....	....
1997-98	Boston University	H-East	36	9	6	15	4	....	....	....	....	....	....	....	....	....	....	....	....	....	....	....	....	....	....
1998-99	Boston University	H-East	37	15	9	24	12	....	....	....	....	....	....	....	....	....	....	....	....	....	....	....	....	....	....
99-2000	Boston University	H-East	42	22	20	42	44	....	....	....	....	....	....	....	....	....	....	....	....	....	....	....	....	....	....
2000-01	Boston University	H-East	35	16	20	36	48	....	....	....	....	....	....	....	....	....	....	....	....	....	....	....	....	....	....
2001-02	Providence Bruins	AHL	61	7	8	15	10	....	....	....	....	....	....	....	....	....	....	....	....	....	....	....	....	....	....
2002-03	Providence Bruins	AHL	33	7	6	13	4	....	....	....	....	....	....	....	....	....	4	0	0	0	0	....	....	....	....
	Atlantic City	ECHL	27	13	8	21	14	....	....	....	....	....	....	....	....	....	....	....	....	....	....	....	....	....	....
2003-04	**Boston**	**NHL**	**12**	**2**	**0**	**2**	**0**	**0**	**1**	**0**	**16**	**12.5**	**2**	**6**	**33.3**	**10:41**	....	....	....	....	....	....	....	....	....
	Providence Bruins	AHL	62	16	9	25	6	....	....	....	....	....	....	....	....	....	2	1	0	1	2	....	....	....	....
2004-05	Providence Bruins	AHL	8	0	0	0	0	....	....	....	....	....	....	....	....	....	....	....	....	....	....	....	....	....	....
	Hershey Bears	AHL	52	10	13	23	6	....	....	....	....	....	....	....	....	....	....	....	....	....	....	....	....	....	....
	NHL Totals		**12**	**2**	**0**	**2**	**0**	**0**	**1**	**0**	**16**	**12.5**		**6**	**33.3**	**10:41**	....	....	....	....	....	....	....	....	....

Hockey East All-Rookie Team (1998) • Hockey East First All-Star Team (2001) • NCAA East Second All-American Team (2001)

Signed as a free agent by **Boston**, August 8, 2001. Signed as a free agent by **Providence** (AHL), October 1. 2004. Traded to **Hershey** (AHL) by **Providence** (AHL) for Darrel Scoville, November 15, 2004.

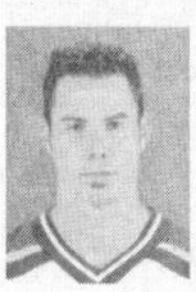

CORSO, Daniel
(KOHR-soh, DAN-yehl)

Center. Shoots left. 5'10", 187 lbs. Born, Montreal, Que., April 3, 1978. St. Louis' 6th choice, 169th overall, in 1996 Entry Draft.

1993-94	Magog	QAAA	36	17	22	39	....	....	....	....	....	....	....	....	....	....	12	10	12	22		....	....	....	....
1994-95	Victoriaville Tigres	QMJHL	65	27	26	53	6	....	....	....	....	....	....	....	....	....	4	2	5	7	2	....	....	....	....
1995-96	Victoriaville Tigres	QMJHL	65	49	65	114	77	....	....	....	....	....	....	....	....	....	12	6	7	13	4	....	....	....	....
1996-97	Victoriaville Tigres	QMJHL	54	51	68	119	50	....	....	....	....	....	....	....	....	....	....	....	....	....	....	....	....	....	....
1997-98	Victoriaville Tigres	QMJHL	35	24	51	75	20	....	....	....	....	....	....	....	....	....	3	1	1	2	2	....	....	....	....
1998-99	Worcester IceCats	AHL	63	14	14	28	26	....	....	....	....	....	....	....	....	....	....	....	....	....	....	....	....	....	....
99-2000	Worcester IceCats	AHL	71	21	34	55	19	....	....	....	....	....	....	....	....	....	9	2	3	5	10	....	....	....	....
2000-01	**St. Louis**	**NHL**	**28**	**10**	**3**	**13**	**14**	**5**	**0**	**4**	**42**	**23.8**	**0**	**296**	**56.1**	**13:56**	**12**	**0**	**1**	**1**	**0**	**0**	**0**	**0**	**8:52**
	Worcester IceCats	AHL	52	19	37	56	47	....	....	....	....	....	....	....	....	....	....	....	....	....	....	....	....	....	....
2001-02	**St. Louis**	**NHL**	**41**	**4**	**7**	**11**	**6**	**1**	**0**	**2**	**25**	**16.0**	**3**	**423**	**54.9**	**11:13**	**2**	**0**	**0**	**0**	**0**	**0**	**0**	**0**	**8:51**
2002-03	**St. Louis**	**NHL**	**1**	**0**	**0**	**0**	**0**	**0**	**0**	**0**	**0**	**0.0**	**–1**	**8**	**50.0**	**7:44**	....	....	....	....	....	....	....	....	....
	Worcester IceCats	AHL	1	0	0	0	0	....	....	....	....	....	....	....	....	....	....	....	....	....	....	....	....	....	....
2003-04	Binghamton	AHL	32	7	11	18	16	....	....	....	....	....	....	....	....	....	....	....	....	....	....	....	....	....	....
	Atlanta	**NHL**	**7**	**0**	**1**	**1**	**0**	**0**	**0**	**0**	**2**	**0.0**	**–2**	**105**	**47.6**	**12:59**	....	....	....	....	....	....	....	....	....
	Chicago Wolves	AHL	29	8	18	26	15	....	....	....	....	....	....	....	....	....	10	1	5	6	0	....	....	....	....
2004-05	Kassel Huskies	Germany	45	8	30	38	32	....	....	....	....	....	....	....	....	....	7	1	5	6	20	....	....	....	....
	NHL Totals		**77**	**14**	**11**	**25**	**20**	**6**	**0**	**6**	**69**	**20.3**		**832**	**54.3**	**12:19**	**14**	**0**	**1**	**1**	**0**	**0**	**0**	**0**	**8:52**

QMJHL All-Rookie Team (1995) • QMJHL First All-Star Team (1997) • QMJHL MVP (1997)

• Spent majority of 2001-02 season on practice roster, October 22, 2001. • Missed majority of 2002-03 season recovering from shoulder injury suffered in game vs. Anaheim, October 10, 2003. Signed as a free agent by **Ottawa**, September 2, 2003. Traded to **Atlanta** by **Ottawa** for Brad Tapper, January 6, 2004. Signed as a free agent by **Kassel** (Germany), August 7, 2004. Signed as a free agent by **Frankfurt** (Germany), June 9, 2005.

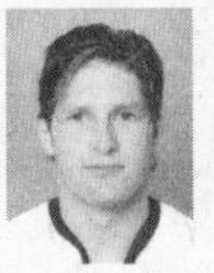

CORSON, Shayne

(KOHR-sohn, SHAYN)

Left wing. Shoots left. 6'1", 202 lbs. Born, Barrie, Ont., August 13, 1966. Montreal's 2nd choice, 8th overall, in 1984 Entry Draft.

Season	Club	League	GP	G	A	Pts	PIM	PP	SH	GW	S	%	+/-	TF	F%	Min	GP	G	A	Pts	PIM	PP	SH	GW	Min
			Regular Season														Playoffs								
1982-83	Barrie Colts	OHA-B	23	13	29	42	87																		
1983-84	Brantford	OHL	66	25	46	71	165										6	4	1	5	26				
1984-85	Hamilton	OHL	54	27	63	90	154										11	3	7	10	19				
1985-86	Hamilton	OHL	47	41	57	98	153																		
	Montreal	**NHL**	**3**	**0**	**0**	**0**	**2**	**0**	**0**	**0**	**1**	**0.0**	**-3**												
1986-87	**Montreal**	**NHL**	**55**	**12**	**11**	**23**	**144**	**0**	**1**	**3**	**69**	**17.4**	**10**				**17**	**6**	**5**	**11**	**30**	**1**	**1**	**1**	
1987-88	**Montreal**	**NHL**	**71**	**12**	**27**	**39**	**152**	**2**	**0**	**2**	**90**	**13.3**	**22**				**3**	**1**	**0**	**1**	**12**	**0**	**0**	**0**	
1988-89	**Montreal**	**NHL**	**80**	**26**	**24**	**50**	**193**	**10**	**0**	**3**	**133**	**19.5**	**-1**				**21**	**4**	**5**	**9**	**65**	**2**	**0**	**2**	
1989-90	**Montreal**	**NHL**	**76**	**31**	**44**	**75**	**144**	**7**	**0**	**6**	**192**	**16.1**	**33**				**11**	**2**	**8**	**10**	**20**	**0**	**0**	**0**	
1990-91	**Montreal**	**NHL**	**71**	**23**	**24**	**47**	**138**	**7**	**0**	**2**	**164**	**14.0**	**9**				**13**	**9**	**6**	**15**	**36**	**4**	**1**	**3**	
1991-92	**Montreal**	**NHL**	**64**	**17**	**36**	**53**	**118**	**3**	**0**	**2**	**165**	**10.3**	**15**				**10**	**2**	**5**	**7**	**15**	**0**	**0**	**0**	
1992-93	**Edmonton**	**NHL**	**80**	**16**	**31**	**47**	**209**	**9**	**2**	**1**	**164**	**9.8**	**-19**												
1993-94	**Edmonton**	**NHL**	**64**	**25**	**29**	**54**	**118**	**11**	**0**	**3**	**171**	**14.6**	**-8**												
1994-95	**Edmonton**	**NHL**	**48**	**12**	**24**	**36**	**86**	**2**	**0**	**1**	**131**	**9.2**	**-17**												
1995-96	**St. Louis**	**NHL**	**77**	**18**	**28**	**46**	**192**	**13**	**0**	**0**	**150**	**12.0**	**3**				**13**	**8**	**6**	**14**	**22**	**6**	**1**	**1**	
1996-97	**St. Louis**	**NHL**	**11**	**2**	**1**	**3**	**24**	**1**	**0**	**0**	**19**	**10.5**	**-4**												
	Montreal	**NHL**	**47**	**6**	**15**	**21**	**80**	**2**	**0**	**2**	**96**	**6.3**	**-5**				**5**	**1**	**0**	**1**	**4**	**0**	**1**	**0**	
1997-98	**Montreal**	**NHL**	**62**	**21**	**34**	**55**	**108**	**14**	**1**	**1**	**142**	**14.8**	**2**				**10**	**3**	**6**	**9**	**26**	**1**	**0**	**1**	
	Canada	Olympics	6	1	1	2	2																		
1998-99	**Montreal**	**NHL**	**63**	**12**	**20**	**32**	**147**	**7**	**0**	**4**	**142**	**8.5**	**-10**	**184**	**45.1**	**20:42**									
99-2000	**Montreal**	**NHL**	**70**	**8**	**20**	**28**	**115**	**2**	**0**	**1**	**121**	**6.6**	**-2**	**445**	**43.4**	**19:05**									
2000-01	**Toronto**	**NHL**	**77**	**8**	**18**	**26**	**189**	**0**	**0**	**2**	**102**	**7.8**	**1**	**602**	**48.8**	**15:50**	**11**	**1**	**1**	**2**	**14**	**0**	**0**	**0**	**18:59**
2001-02	**Toronto**	**NHL**	**74**	**12**	**21**	**33**	**120**	**0**	**1**	**1**	**111**	**10.8**	**11**	**598**	**45.5**	**17:04**	**19**	**1**	**6**	**7**	**33**	**0**	**0**	**0**	**21:04**
2002-03	**Toronto**	**NHL**	**46**	**7**	**8**	**15**	**49**	**0**	**0**	**0**	**69**	**10.1**	**-5**	**202**	**44.6**	**15:02**	**2**	**0**	**0**	**0**	**2**	**0**	**0**	**0**	**9:42**
2003-04	**Dallas**	**NHL**	**17**	**5**	**5**	**10**	**29**	**0**	**1**	**1**	**21**	**23.8**	**12**	**23**	**43.5**	**13:31**	**5**	**0**	**1**	**1**	**12**	**0**	**0**	**0**	**13:56**
2004-05	DID NOT PLAY																								
	NHL Totals		**1156**	**273**	**420**	**693**	**2357**	**90**	**6**	**35**	**2253**	**12.1**		**2054**	**45.9**	**17:25**	**140**	**38**	**49**	**87**	**291**	**14**	**4**	**8**	**18:52**

Played in NHL All-Star Game (1990, 1994, 1998)

Traded to **Edmonton** by **Montreal** with Brent Gilchrist and Vladimir Vujtek for Vincent Damphousse and Edmonton's 4th round choice (Adam Wiesel) in 1993 Entry Draft, August 27, 1992. Signed as a free agent by **St. Louis**, July 28, 1995. Traded to **Montreal** by **St. Louis** with Murray Baron and St. Louis' 5th round choice (Gennady Razin) in 1997 Entry Draft for Pierre Turgeon, Rory Fitzpatrick and Craig Conroy, October 29, 1996. Signed as a free agent by **Toronto**, July 4, 2000. • Officially announced retirement, April 15, 2003. Signed as a free agent by **Dallas**, February 18, 2004.

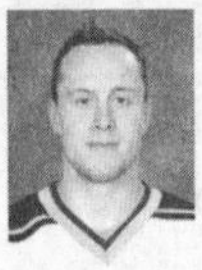

CORVO, Joe

(KOHR-voh, JOH-sehf) **L.A.**

Defense. Shoots right. 6'1", 205 lbs. Born, Oak Park, IL, June 20, 1977. Los Angeles' 4th choice, 83rd overall, in 1997 Entry Draft.

Season	Club	League	GP	G	A	Pts	PIM	PP	SH	GW	S	%	+/-	TF	F%	Min	GP	G	A	Pts	PIM	PP	SH	GW	Min
1995-96	Western Mich.	CCHA	41	5	25	30	38																		
1996-97	Western Mich.	CCHA	32	12	21	33	85																		
1997-98	Western Mich.	CCHA	32	5	12	17	93																		
1998-99	Springfield	AHL	50	5	15	20	32																		
	Hampton Roads	ECHL	5	0	0	0	15										4	0	1	1	0				
99-2000	DID NOT PLAY																								
2000-01	Lowell	AHL	77	10	23	33	31										4	3	1	4	0				
2001-02	Manchester	AHL	80	13	37	50	30										5	0	5	5	0				
2002-03	**Los Angeles**	**NHL**	**50**	**5**	**7**	**12**	**14**	**2**	**0**	**0**	**84**	**6.0**	**2**	**0**	**0.0**	**18:37**									
	Manchester	AHL	26	8	18	26	8										3	0	0	0	0				
2003-04	**Los Angeles**	**NHL**	**72**	**8**	**17**	**25**	**36**	**0**	**0**	**3**	**150**	**5.3**	**7**	**1**	**0.0**	**21:08**									
2004-05	Chicago Wolves	AHL	23	7	7	14	14										18	4	5	9	12				
	NHL Totals		**122**	**13**	**24**	**37**	**50**	**2**	**0**	**3**	**234**	**5.6**		**1**	**0.0**	**20:06**									

CCHA All-Rookie Team (1996) • CCHA Second All-Star Team (1997)

• Missed entire 1999-2000 season after failing to come to contract terms with **Los Angeles.** Signed as a free agent by **Chicago** (AHL), February 24, 2005.

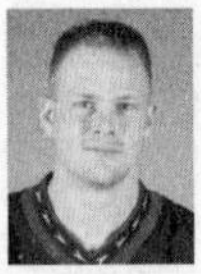

COWAN, Jeff

(KOW-an, JEHF) **L.A.**

Left wing. Shoots left. 6'2", 210 lbs. Born, Scarborough, Ont., September 27, 1976.

Season	Club	League	GP	G	A	Pts	PIM	PP	SH	GW	S	%	+/-	TF	F%	Min	GP	G	A	Pts	PIM	PP	SH	GW	Min
1992-93	Guelph Platers	OHA-B	45	8	8	16	22																		
1993-94	Guelph Platers	OHA-B	43	30	26	56	96																		
	Guelph Storm	OHL	17	1	0	1	5																		
1994-95	Guelph Storm	OHL	51	10	7	17	14										14	1	1	2	0				
1995-96	Barrie Colts	OHL	66	38	14	52	29										5	1	2	3	6				
1996-97	Saint John Flames	AHL	22	5	5	10	8																		
	Roanoke Express	ECHL	47	21	13	34	42																		
1997-98	Saint John Flames	AHL	69	15	13	28	23										13	4	1	5	14				
1998-99	Saint John Flames	AHL	71	7	12	19	117										4	0	1	1	10				
99-2000	**Calgary**	**NHL**	**13**	**4**	**1**	**5**	**16**	**0**	**0**	**0**	**26**	**15.4**	**2**	**0**	**0.0**	**10:22**									
	Saint John Flames	AHL	47	15	10	25	77																		
2000-01	**Calgary**	**NHL**	**51**	**9**	**4**	**13**	**74**	**2**	**0**	**1**	**48**	**18.8**	**-8**	**5**	**20.0**	**9:06**									
2001-02	**Calgary**	**NHL**	**19**	**1**	**0**	**1**	**40**	**0**	**0**	**1**	**13**	**7.7**	**-3**	**2**	**50.0**	**7:44**									
	Atlanta	**NHL**	**38**	**4**	**1**	**5**	**50**	**0**	**0**	**1**	**51**	**7.8**	**-11**	**5**	**20.0**	**12:27**									
2002-03	**Atlanta**	**NHL**	**66**	**3**	**5**	**8**	**115**	**0**	**0**	**0**	**52**	**5.8**	**-15**	**10**	**30.0**	**8:24**									
2003-04	**Atlanta**	**NHL**	**58**	**9**	**15**	**24**	**68**	**1**	**0**	**1**	**74**	**12.2**	**2**	**9**	**22.2**	**10:04**									
	Los Angeles	**NHL**	**13**	**2**	**1**	**3**	**24**	**1**	**0**	**0**	**15**	**13.3**	**-1**	**2**	**50.0**	**11:43**									
2004-05	DID NOT PLAY																								
	NHL Totals		**258**	**32**	**27**	**59**	**387**	**4**	**0**	**4**	**279**	**11.5**		**33**	**27.3**	**9:44**									

Signed as a free agent by **Calgary**, October 2, 1995. Traded to **Atlanta** by **Calgary** with the rights to Kurtis Foster for Petr Buzek and Atlanta's 6th round choice (Adam Pardy) in 2004 Entry Draft, December 18, 2001. Traded to **Los Angeles** by **Atlanta** for Kip Brennan, March 9, 2004.

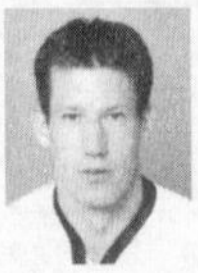

CROSS, Cory

(KRAWS, KOHR-ee) **EDM.**

Defense. Shoots left. 6'5", 225 lbs. Born, Lloydminster, Alta., January 3, 1971. Tampa Bay's 1st choice, 1st overall, in 1992 Supplemental Draft.

Season	Club	League	GP	G	A	Pts	PIM	PP	SH	GW	S	%	+/-	TF	F%	Min	GP	G	A	Pts	PIM	PP	SH	GW	Min
1990-91	U. of Alberta	CWUAA	20	2	5	7	16																		
1991-92	U. of Alberta	CWUAA	41	4	11	15	82																		
1992-93	U. of Alberta	CWUAA	43	11	28	39	107																		
	Atlanta Knights	IHL	7	0	1	1	2										4	0	0	0	6				
1993-94	**Tampa Bay**	**NHL**	**5**	**0**	**0**	**0**	**6**	**0**	**0**	**0**	**5**	**0.0**	**-3**												
	Atlanta Knights	IHL	70	4	14	18	72										9	1	2	3	14				
1994-95	Atlanta Knights	IHL	41	5	10	15	67																		
	Tampa Bay	**NHL**	**43**	**1**	**5**	**6**	**41**	**0**	**0**	**1**	**35**	**2.9**	**-6**												
1995-96	**Tampa Bay**	**NHL**	**75**	**2**	**14**	**16**	**66**	**0**	**0**	**0**	**57**	**3.5**	**4**				**6**	**0**	**0**	**0**	**22**	**0**	**0**	**0**	
1996-97	**Tampa Bay**	**NHL**	**72**	**4**	**5**	**9**	**95**	**0**	**0**	**2**	**75**	**5.3**	**6**												
1997-98	**Tampa Bay**	**NHL**	**74**	**3**	**6**	**9**	**77**	**0**	**1**	**0**	**72**	**4.2**	**-24**												
1998-99	**Tampa Bay**	**NHL**	**67**	**2**	**16**	**18**	**92**	**0**	**0**	**0**	**96**	**2.1**	**-25**	**0**	**0.0**	**22:38**									
99-2000	**Toronto**	**NHL**	**71**	**4**	**11**	**15**	**64**	**0**	**0**	**1**	**60**	**6.7**	**13**	**0**	**0.0**	**15:59**	**12**	**0**	**2**	**2**	**2**	**0**	**0**	**0**	**15:21**
2000-01	**Toronto**	**NHL**	**41**	**3**	**5**	**8**	**50**	**1**	**0**	**1**	**34**	**8.8**	**7**	**0**	**0.0**	**18:00**	**11**	**2**	**1**	**3**	**10**	**0**	**0**	**1**	**16:05**
2001-02	**Toronto**	**NHL**	**50**	**3**	**9**	**12**	**54**	**0**	**0**	**1**	**39**	**7.7**	**11**	**0**	**0.0**	**15:18**	**12**	**0**	**0**	**0**	**8**	**0**	**0**	**0**	**17:00**
2002-03	**NY Rangers**	**NHL**	**26**	**0**	**4**	**4**	**16**	**0**	**0**	**0**	**18**	**0.0**	**13**	**1**	**0.0**	**17:12**									
	Hartford	AHL	2	0	0	0	2																		
	Edmonton	**NHL**	**11**	**2**	**3**	**5**	**8**	**1**	**0**	**1**	**11**	**18.2**	**3**	**0**	**0.0**	**17:51**	**6**	**0**	**1**	**1**	**20**	**0**	**0**	**0**	**20:37**
2003-04	**Edmonton**	**NHL**	**68**	**7**	**14**	**21**	**56**	**1**	**0**	**1**	**83**	**8.4**	**9**	**0**	**0.0**	**19:14**									
2004-05	DID NOT PLAY																								
	NHL Totals		**603**	**31**	**92**	**123**	**625**	**3**	**1**	**8**	**585**	**5.3**		**1**	**0.0**	**18:17**	**47**	**2**	**4**	**6**	**62**	**0**	**0**	**1**	**16:48**

Traded to **Toronto** by **Tampa Bay** with Tampa Bay's 7th round choice (Ivan Kolozvary) in 2001 Entry Draft for Fredrik Modin, October 1, 1999. Signed as a free agent by **NY Rangers**, December 17, 2002. Traded to **Edmonton** by **NY Rangers** with Radek Dvorak for Anson Carter and Ales Pisa, March 11, 2003.

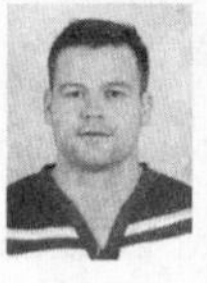

CULLEN, David

(KUH-lehn, DAY-vihd) **BUF.**

Defense. Shoots right. 6'2", 209 lbs. Born, St. Catharines, Ont., December 30, 1976.

Season	Club	League	GP	G	A	Pts	PIM	PP	SH	GW	S	%	+/-	TF	F%	Min	GP	G	A	Pts	PIM	PP	SH	GW	Min
			Regular Season														Playoffs								
1992-93	Thorold Eagles	OHA-B	34	4	6	10	28																		
1993-94	Thorold	OHA-B	40	10	35	45	26																		
1994-95	Thorold	OHA-B	36	16	30	46	12																		
1995-96	U. of Maine	H-East	34	2	4	6	22																		
1996-97	U. of Maine	H-East	35	5	25	30	8																		
1997-98	U. of Maine	H-East	36	10	27	37	24																		
1998-99	U. of Maine	H-East	41	11	33	44	24																		
99-2000	Springfield	AHL	78	10	21	31	57										2	0	0	0	2				
2000-01	**Phoenix**	**NHL**	**2**	**0**	**0**	**0**	**0**	**0**	**0**	**0**	**0**	**0.0**	**1**	**0**	**0.0**	**12:25**									
	Springfield	AHL	69	13	29	42	40																		
2001-02	**Phoenix**	**NHL**	**14**	**0**	**0**	**0**	**6**	**0**	**0**	**0**	**3**	**0.0**	**–5**	**0**	**0.0**	**12:21**									
	Springfield	AHL	15	1	4	5	4																		
	Minnesota	**NHL**	**3**	**0**	**0**	**0**	**0**	**0**	**0**	**0**	**0**	**0.0**	**–3**	**0**	**0.0**	**14:02**									
	Houston Aeros	AHL	38	5	15	20	4										13	0	6	6	6				
2002-03	Houston Aeros	AHL	72	2	27	29	42										23	3	4	7	14				
2003-04	Rochester	AHL	75	12	35	47	26										16	1	4	5	6				
2004-05	Rochester	AHL	43	2	19	21	25										9	2	3	5	4				
	NHL Totals		**19**	**0**	**0**	**0**	**6**	**0**	**0**	**0**	**3**	**0.0**		**0**	**0.0**	**12:37**									

Hockey East First All-Star Team (1999) • NCAA East First All-American Team (1999) • NCAA Championship All-Tournament Team (1999)

Signed as a free agent by **Phoenix**, April 16, 1999. Traded to **Minnesota** by **Phoenix** for Sebastien Bordeleau, January 4, 2002. Signed as a free agent by **Buffalo**, July 28, 2003.

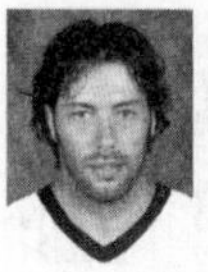

CULLEN, Matt

(KUH-lehn, MAT) **CAR.**

Center. Shoots left. 6'2", 218 lbs. Born, Virginia, MN, November 2, 1976. Anaheim's 2nd choice, 35th overall, in 1996 Entry Draft.

Season	Club	League	GP	G	A	Pts	PIM	PP	SH	GW	S	%	+/-	TF	F%	Min	GP	G	A	Pts	PIM	PP	SH	GW	Min
1994-95	Moorhead Spuds	High-MN	28	47	42	89	78																		
1995-96	St. Cloud State	WCHA	39	12	29	41	28																		
1996-97	St. Cloud State	WCHA	36	15	30	45	70																		
	Baltimore Bandits	AHL	6	3	3	6	7										3	0	2	2	0				
1997-98	**Anaheim**	**NHL**	**61**	**6**	**21**	**27**	**23**	**2**	**0**	**0**	**75**	**8.0**	**–4**												
	Cincinnati	AHL	18	15	12	27	2																		
1998-99	**Anaheim**	**NHL**	**75**	**11**	**14**	**25**	**47**	**5**	**1**	**1**	**112**	**9.8**	**–12**	**1047**	**47.7**	**15:31**	**4**	**0**	**0**	**0**	**0**	**0**	**0**	**0**	**15:30**
	Cincinnati	AHL	3	1	2	3	8																		
99-2000	**Anaheim**	**NHL**	**80**	**13**	**26**	**39**	**24**	**1**	**0**	**1**	**137**	**9.5**	**5**	**1247**	**44.6**	**16:54**									
2000-01	**Anaheim**	**NHL**	**82**	**10**	**30**	**40**	**38**	**4**	**0**	**1**	**159**	**6.3**	**–23**	**1478**	**48.0**	**18:15**									
2001-02	**Anaheim**	**NHL**	**79**	**18**	**30**	**48**	**24**	**3**	**1**	**4**	**164**	**11.0**	**–1**	**1283**	**51.4**	**17:01**									
2002-03	**Anaheim**	**NHL**	**50**	**7**	**14**	**21**	**12**	**1**	**0**	**1**	**77**	**9.1**	**–4**	**271**	**50.6**	**14:18**									
	Florida	**NHL**	**30**	**6**	**6**	**12**	**22**	**2**	**1**	**1**	**54**	**11.1**	**–4**	**423**	**47.3**	**14:43**									
2003-04	**Florida**	**NHL**	**56**	**6**	**13**	**19**	**24**	**1**	**0**	**2**	**75**	**8.0**	**–2**	**735**	**50.6**	**14:12**									
2004-05	SG Cortina	Italy	36	*27	33	60	64										18	8	14	22	32				
	NHL Totals		**513**	**77**	**154**	**231**	**214**	**19**	**3**	**11**	**853**	**9.0**		**6484**	**48.3**	**16:10**	**4**	**0**	**0**	**0**	**0**	**0**	**0**	**0**	**15:30**

WCHA Second All-Star Team (1997)

Traded to **Florida** by **Anaheim** with Pavel Trnka and Anaheim's 4th round choice (James Pemberton) in 2003 Entry Draft for Sandis Ozolinsh and Lance Ward, January 30, 2003. Signed as a free agent by **Carolina**, August 5, 2004. Signed as a free agent by **Cortina** (Italy), September 18, 2004.

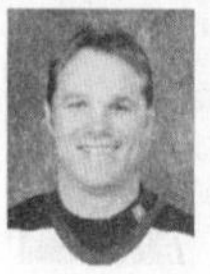

CULLIMORE, Jassen

(KUHL-ih-mohr, JAY-sehn) **CHI.**

Defense. Shoots left. 6'5", 244 lbs. Born, Simcoe, Ont., December 4, 1972. Vancouver's 2nd choice, 29th overall, in 1991 Entry Draft.

Season	Club	League	GP	G	A	Pts	PIM	PP	SH	GW	S	%	+/-	TF	F%	Min	GP	G	A	Pts	PIM	PP	SH	GW	Min
1986-87	Caledonia	OHA-C	18	2	0	2	9																		
1987-88	Simcoe Rams	OHA-C	35	11	14	25	92																		
1988-89	Peterborough	OHA-B	29	11	17	28	88																		
	Peterborough	OHL	20	2	1	3	6																		
1989-90	Peterborough	OHL	59	2	6	8	61										11	0	2	2	8				
1990-91	Peterborough	OHL	62	8	16	24	74										4	1	0	1	7				
1991-92	Peterborough	OHL	54	9	37	46	65										10	3	6	9	8				
1992-93	Hamilton	AHL	56	5	7	12	60																		
1993-94	Hamilton	AHL	71	8	20	28	86										3	0	1	1	2				
1994-95	Syracuse Crunch	AHL	33	2	7	9	66																		
	Vancouver	**NHL**	**34**	**1**	**2**	**3**	**39**	**0**	**0**	**0**	**30**	**3.3**	**–2**				**11**	**0**	**0**	**0**	**12**	**0**	**0**	**0**	
1995-96	**Vancouver**	**NHL**	**27**	**1**	**1**	**2**	**21**	**0**	**0**	**1**	**12**	**8.3**	**4**												
1996-97	**Vancouver**	**NHL**	**3**	**0**	**0**	**0**	**2**	**0**	**0**	**0**	**2**	**0.0**	**–2**												
	Montreal	**NHL**	**49**	**2**	**6**	**8**	**42**	**0**	**1**	**1**	**52**	**3.8**	**4**				**2**	**0**	**0**	**0**	**2**	**0**	**0**	**0**	
1997-98	**Montreal**	**NHL**	**3**	**0**	**0**	**0**	**4**	**0**	**0**	**0**	**1**	**0.0**	**0**												
	Fredericton	AHL	5	1	0	1	8																		
	Tampa Bay	**NHL**	**25**	**1**	**2**	**3**	**22**	**1**	**0**	**0**	**17**	**5.9**	**–4**												
1998-99	**Tampa Bay**	**NHL**	**78**	**5**	**12**	**17**	**81**	**1**	**1**	**1**	**73**	**6.8**	**–22**	**0**	**0.0**	**20:14**									
99-2000	Providence Bruins	AHL	16	5	10	15	31																		
	Tampa Bay	**NHL**	**46**	**1**	**1**	**2**	**66**	**0**	**0**	**0**	**23**	**4.3**	**–12**	**2**	**0.0**	**15:38**									
2000-01	**Tampa Bay**	**NHL**	**74**	**1**	**6**	**7**	**80**	**0**	**0**	**0**	**56**	**1.8**	**–6**	**0**	**0.0**	**19:43**									
2001-02	**Tampa Bay**	**NHL**	**78**	**4**	**9**	**13**	**58**	**0**	**0**	**1**	**84**	**4.8**	**–1**	**0**	**0.0**	**20:07**									
2002-03	**Tampa Bay**	**NHL**	**28**	**1**	**3**	**4**	**31**	**0**	**0**	**0**	**23**	**4.3**	**3**	**0**	**0.0**	**18:25**	**11**	**1**	**1**	**2**	**4**	**0**	**0**	**0**	**22:11**
2003-04♦	**Tampa Bay**	**NHL**	**79**	**2**	**5**	**7**	**58**	**0**	**0**	**1**	**78**	**2.6**	**8**	**0**	**0.0**	**19:02**	**11**	**0**	**2**	**2**	**6**	**0**	**0**	**0**	**15:15**
2004-05			DID NOT PLAY																						
	NHL Totals		**524**	**19**	**47**	**66**	**504**	**2**	**2**	**5**	**451**	**4.2**		**2**	**0.0**	**19:10**	**35**	**1**	**3**	**4**	**24**	**0**	**0**	**0**	**18:43**

OHL Second All-Star Team (1992)

Traded to **Montreal** by **Vancouver** for Donald Brashear, November 13, 1996. Claimed on waivers by **Tampa Bay** from **Montreal**, January 22, 1998. Loaned to **Providence** (AHL) by **Tampa Bay**, October 1, 1999. • Missed majority of 2002-03 season recovering from elbow injury suffered in game vs. Vancouver, November 29, 2002. Signed as a free agent by **Chicago**, July 22, 2004.

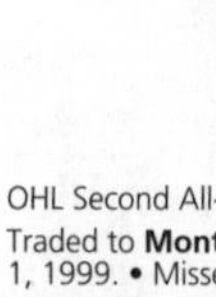

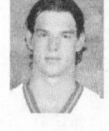

CUTTA, Jakub

(KOO-tuh, YA-kuhb) **WSH.**

Defense. Shoots left. 6'3", 210 lbs. Born, Jablonec nad Nisou, Czech., December 29, 1981. Washington's 3rd choice, 61st overall, in 2000 Entry Draft.

Season	Club	League	GP	G	A	Pts	PIM	PP	SH	GW	S	%	+/-	TF	F%	Min	GP	G	A	Pts	PIM	PP	SH	GW	Min
1997-98	Liberec Jr.	CzRep-Jr.	29	3	13	16	70																		
1998-99	Swift Current	WHL	59	3	3	6	63																		
99-2000	Swift Current	WHL	71	2	12	14	114										12	0	2	2	24				
2000-01	**Washington**	**NHL**	**3**	**0**	**0**	**0**	**0**	**0**	**0**	**0**	**1**	**0.0**	**–1**	**0**	**0.0**	**11:33**									
	Swift Current	WHL	47	5	8	13	102										16	1	3	4	32				
2001-02	**Washington**	**NHL**	**2**	**0**	**0**	**0**	**0**	**0**	**0**	**0**	**2**	**0.0**	**–3**	**0**	**0.0**	**16:02**									
	Portland Pirates	AHL	56	1	3	4	69																		
2002-03	Portland Pirates	AHL	66	3	12	15	106										3	0	0	0	2				
2003-04	**Washington**	**NHL**	**3**	**0**	**0**	**0**	**0**	**0**	**0**	**0**	**1**	**0.0**	**–1**	**0**	**0.0**	**13:54**									
	Portland Pirates	AHL	59	1	5	6	58										7	2	0	2	7				
2004-05	Portland Pirates	AHL	63	0	5	5	100																		
	NHL Totals		**8**	**0**	**0**	**0**	**0**	**0**	**0**	**0**	**4**	**0.0**		**0**	**0.0**	**13:33**									

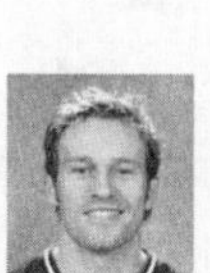

CZERKAWSKI, Mariusz

(chehr-KAWV-skee, MAIR-ee-UHZ)

Right wing. Shoots left. 6', 200 lbs. Born, Radomsko, Poland, April 13, 1972. Boston's 5th choice, 106th overall, in 1991 Entry Draft.

Season	Club	League	GP	G	A	Pts	PIM	PP	SH	GW	S	%	+/-	TF	F%	Min	GP	G	A	Pts	PIM	PP	SH	GW	Min
1990-91	GKS Tychy	Poland	24	25	15	40																			
1991-92	Djurgarden	Sweden	39	8	5	13	4										3	0	0	0	2				
	Poland	Olympics	5	0	1	1	4																		
1992-93	Hammarby	Sweden-2	32	*39	30	*69	74										13	*16	7	*23	34				
1993-94	Djurgarden	Sweden	39	13	21	34	20										6	3	1	4	2				
	Boston	**NHL**	**4**	**2**	**1**	**3**	**0**	**1**	**0**	**0**	**11**	**18.2**	**–2**				**13**	**3**	**3**	**6**	**4**	**1**	**0**	**0**	
1994-95	Kiekko-Espoo	Finland	7	9	3	12	10																		
	Boston	**NHL**	**47**	**12**	**14**	**26**	**31**	**1**	**0**	**2**	**126**	**9.5**	**4**				**5**	**1**	**0**	**1**	**0**	**0**	**0**	**0**	
1995-96	**Boston**	**NHL**	**33**	**5**	**6**	**11**	**10**	**1**	**0**	**0**	**63**	**7.9**	**–11**												
	Edmonton	**NHL**	**37**	**12**	**17**	**29**	**8**	**2**	**0**	**1**	**79**	**15.2**	**7**												
1996-97	**Edmonton**	**NHL**	**76**	**26**	**21**	**47**	**16**	**4**	**0**	**3**	**182**	**14.3**	**0**				**12**	**2**	**1**	**3**	**10**	**0**	**0**	**0**	

			Regular Season														Playoffs								
Season	Club	League	GP	G	A	Pts	PIM	PP	SH	GW	S	%	+/-	TF	F%	Min	GP	G	A	Pts	PIM	PP	SH	GW	Min
1997-98	NY Islanders	NHL	68	12	13	25	23	2	0	1	136	8.8	11	....	....	....	....	....	....	....	....	....	....	....	....
1998-99	NY Islanders	NHL	78	21	17	38	14	4	0	1	205	10.2	–10	2	0.0	14:18	....	....	....	....	....	....	....	....	....
99-2000	NY Islanders	NHL	79	35	35	70	34	16	0	4	276	12.7	–16	4	25.0	17:45	....	....	....	....	....	....	....	....	....
2000-01	NY Islanders	NHL	82	30	32	62	48	10	1	0	287	10.5	–24	8	50.0	18:44	....	....	....	....	....	....	....	....	....
2001-02	NY Islanders	NHL	82	22	29	51	48	6	0	6	169	13.0	–8	10	10.0	15:58	7	2	2	4	4	1	0	0	12:58
2002-03	Montreal	NHL	43	5	9	14	16	1	0	0	77	6.5	–7	2	0.0	13:10	....	....	....	....	....	....	....	....	....
	Hamilton	AHL	20	8	12	20	12	....	....	....	....	....	....	....	....	....	6	1	3	4	6	....	....	....	....
2003-04	NY Islanders	NHL	81	25	24	49	16	9	0	2	157	15.9	8	6	16.7	13:02	5	0	1	1	0	0	0	0	10:43
2004-05	Djurgarden	Sweden	46	15	9	24	20	....	....	....	....	....	....	....	....	....	5	1	0	1	2	....	....	....	....
	NHL Totals		710	207	218	425	264	57	1	20	1768	11.7		32	21.9	15:42	42	8	7	15	18	2	0	0	12:02

Played in NHL All-Star Game (2000)

Traded to **Edmonton** by **Boston** with Sean Brown and Boston's 1st round choice (Matthieu Descoteaux) in 1996 Entry Draft for Bill Ranford, January 11, 1996. Traded to **NY Islanders** by **Edmonton** for Dan LaCouture, August 25, 1997. Traded to **Montreal** by **NY Islanders** for Arron Asham and Montreal's 5th round choice (Marcus Paulsson) in 2002 Entry Draft, June 22, 2002. Signed as a free agent by **NY Islanders**, July 17, 2003. Signed as a free agent by **Djurgarden** (Sweden), September 9, 2004.

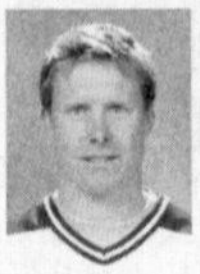

DACKELL, Andreas

(DA-kuhl, an-DRAY-uhs)

Right wing. Shoots right. 5'11", 194 lbs. Born, Gavle, Sweden, December 29, 1972. Ottawa's 3rd choice, 136th overall, in 1996 Entry Draft.

Season	Club	League	GP	G	A	Pts	PIM	PP	SH	GW	S	%	+/-	TF	F%	Min	GP	G	A	Pts	PIM	PP	SH	GW	Min
1990-91	Brynas IF Gavle	Sweden	3	0	1	1	2	....	....	....	....	....	....	....	....	....	....	....	....	....	....	....	....	....	....
1991-92	Brynas IF Gavle Jr.	Swe-Jr.	26	17	24	41	42	....	....	....	....	....	....	....	....	....	2	3	1	4	2	....	....	....	....
	Brynas IF Gavle	Sweden	4	0	0	0	2	....	....	....	....	....	....	....	....	....	2	0	1	1	4	....	....	....	....
1992-93	Brynas IF Gavle	Sweden	40	12	15	27	12	....	....	....	....	....	....	....	....	....	10	4	5	9	2	....	....	....	....
1993-94	Brynas IF Gavle	Sweden	38	12	17	29	47	....	....	....	....	....	....	....	....	....	7	2	2	4	8	....	....	....	....
	Sweden	Olympics	4	0	0	0	0	....	....	....	....	....	....	....	....	....	....	....	....	....	....	....	....	....	....
1994-95	Brynas IF Gavle	Sweden	39	17	16	33	34	....	....	....	....	....	....	....	....	....	14	3	3	6	14	....	....	....	....
1995-96	Brynas IF Gavle	Sweden	40	25	22	47	79	....	....	....	....	....	....	....	....	....	10	9	6	15	12	....	....	....	....
1996-97	Ottawa	NHL	79	12	19	31	8	2	0	3	79	15.2	–6	....	....	....	7	1	0	1	0	0	0	0	....
1997-98	Ottawa	NHL	82	15	18	33	24	3	2	2	130	11.5	–11	....	....	....	11	1	1	2	2	1	0	0	....
1998-99	Ottawa	NHL	77	15	35	50	30	6	0	3	107	14.0	9	5	40.0	17:18	4	0	1	1	0	0	0	0	18:49
99-2000	Ottawa	NHL	82	10	25	35	18	0	0	1	99	10.1	5	1	100.0	16:17	6	2	1	3	2	0	0	1	18:14
2000-01	Ottawa	NHL	81	13	18	31	24	1	0	3	72	18.1	7	13	15.4	14:02	4	0	0	0	0	0	0	0	12:19
2001-02	Montreal	NHL	79	15	18	33	24	2	3	2	83	18.1	–3	16	31.3	17:14	12	1	2	3	6	0	0	0	16:21
2002-03	Montreal	NHL	73	7	18	25	24	0	0	1	74	9.5	–5	18	27.8	14:53	....	....	....	....	....	....	....	....	....
2003-04	Montreal	NHL	60	4	8	12	10	0	0	0	50	8.0	8	16	25.0	15:21	....	....	....	....	....	....	....	....	....
2004-05	Brynas IF Gavle	Sweden	40	9	13	22	48	....	....	....	....	....	....	....	....	....	....	....	....	....	....	....	....	....	....
	Brynas IF Gavle	Sweden-Q	10	2	6	8	8	....	....	....	....	....	....	....	....	....	....	....	....	....	....	....	....	....	....
	NHL Totals		613	91	159	250	162	14	5	15	694	13.1		69	27.5	15:52	44	5	5	10	10	1	0	1	16:33

Traded to **Montreal** by **Ottawa** for Montreal's 8th round choice (Neil Petruic) in 2001 Entry Draft, June 24, 2001. Signed as a free agent by **Brynas** (Sweden), May 14, 2004.

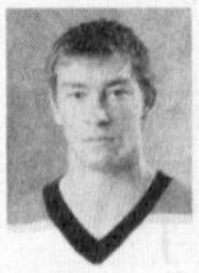

DAGENAIS, Pierre

(da-ZHUH-nay, PEE-air) **MTL.**

Right wing. Shoots left. 6'4", 217 lbs. Born, Blainville, Que., March 4, 1978. New Jersey's 6th choice, 105th overall, in 1998 Entry Draft.

Season	Club	League	GP	G	A	Pts	PIM	PP	SH	GW	S	%	+/-	TF	F%	Min	GP	G	A	Pts	PIM	PP	SH	GW	Min
1994-95	Laval-Laurentides	QAAA	34	28	14	42	68	....	....	....	....	....	....	....	....	....	13	10	9	19	32	....	....	....	....
1995-96	Moncton Alpines	QMJHL	67	43	25	68	59	....	....	....	....	....	....	....	....	....	....	....	....	....	....	....	....	....	....
1996-97	Moncton Wildcats	QMJHL	6	4	2	6	0	....	....	....	....	....	....	....	....	....	....	....	....	....	....	....	....	....	....
	Laval Titan	QMJHL	37	16	14	30	40	....	....	....	....	....	....	....	....	....	....	....	....	....	....	....	....	....	....
	Rouyn-Noranda	QMJHL	27	21	8	29	22	....	....	....	....	....	....	....	....	....	....	....	....	....	....	....	....	....	....
1997-98	Rouyn-Noranda	QMJHL	60	*66	67	133	50	....	....	....	....	....	....	....	....	....	6	6	2	8	2	....	....	....	....
1998-99	Albany River Rats	AHL	69	17	13	30	37	....	....	....	....	....	....	....	....	....	4	0	0	0	0	....	....	....	....
99-2000	Albany River Rats	AHL	80	35	30	65	47	....	....	....	....	....	....	....	....	....	5	1	0	1	14	....	....	....	....
2000-01	New Jersey	NHL	9	3	2	5	6	1	0	1	20	15.0	1	8	37.5	12:22	....	....	....	....	....	....	....	....	....
	Albany River Rats	AHL	69	34	28	62	52	....	....	....	....	....	....	....	....	....	....	....	....	....	....	....	....	....	....
2001-02	New Jersey	NHL	16	3	3	6	4	1	0	1	30	10.0	–5	5	40.0	10:54	....	....	....	....	....	....	....	....	....
	Albany River Rats	AHL	6	0	2	2	2	....	....	....	....	....	....	....	....	....	....	....	....	....	....	....	....	....	....
	Florida	NHL	26	7	1	8	4	2	0	0	47	14.9	–5	4	75.0	11:04	....	....	....	....	....	....	....	....	....
	Utah Grizzlies	AHL	4	1	1	2	2	....	....	....	....	....	....	....	....	....	....	....	....	....	....	....	....	....	....
2002-03	Florida	NHL	9	0	0	0	4	0	0	0	5	0.0	–1	0	0.0	6:01	....	....	....	....	....	....	....	....	....
	San Antonio	AHL	49	21	14	35	28	....	....	....	....	....	....	....	....	....	3	2	0	2	2	....	....	....	....
2003-04	Montreal	NHL	50	17	10	27	24	4	0	3	149	11.4	15	121	42.2	13:53	8	0	1	1	6	0	0	0	12:06
	Hamilton	AHL	20	12	9	21	19	....	....	....	....	....	....	....	....	....	....	....	....	....	....	....	....	....	....
2004-05	HC Ajoie	Swiss-2	7	5	5	10	12	....	....	....	....	....	....	....	....	....	6	7	7	14	6	....	....	....	....
	NHL Totals		110	30	16	46	42	8	0	5	251	12.0		138	42.8	12:01	8	0	1	1	6	0	0	0	12:06

• Re-entered NHL Entry Draft. Originally New Jersey's 4th choice, 47th overall, in 1996 Entry Draft.

QMJHL All-Rookie Team (1996) • QMJHL Second All-Star Team (1998) • AHL Second All-Star Team (2001)

Claimed on waivers by **Florida** from **New Jersey**, January 12, 2002. Signed as a free agent by **Montreal**, July 4, 2003. Signed as a free agent by **Ajoie** (Swiss-2), January 10, 2005.

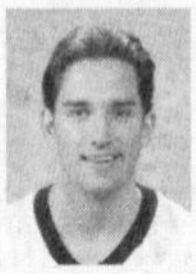

DAIGLE, Alexandre

(DAYG, al-ehx-AHN-druh) **MIN.**

Center. Shoots left. 6', 195 lbs. Born, Montreal, Que., February 7, 1975. Ottawa's 1st choice, 1st overall, in 1993 Entry Draft.

Season	Club	League	GP	G	A	Pts	PIM	PP	SH	GW	S	%	+/-	TF	F%	Min	GP	G	A	Pts	PIM	PP	SH	GW	Min
1990-91	Laval-Laurentides	QAAA	42	*50	*60	*110	98	....	....	....	....	....	....	....	....	....	13	5	9	14	23	....	....	....	....
1991-92	Victoriaville Tigres	QMJHL	66	35	75	110	63	....	....	....	....	....	....	....	....	....	....	....	....	....	....	....	....	....	....
1992-93	Victoriaville Tigres	QMJHL	53	45	92	137	85	....	....	....	....	....	....	....	....	....	6	5	6	11	4	....	....	....	....
1993-94	Ottawa	NHL	84	20	31	51	40	4	0	2	168	11.9	–45	....	....	....	....	....	....	....	....	....	....	....	....
1994-95	Victoriaville Tigres	QMJHL	18	14	20	34	16	....	....	....	....	....	....	....	....	....	....	....	....	....	....	....	....	....	....
	Ottawa	NHL	47	16	21	37	14	4	1	2	105	15.2	–22	....	....	....	....	....	....	....	....	....	....	....	....
1995-96	Ottawa	NHL	50	5	12	17	24	1	0	0	77	6.5	–30	....	....	....	....	....	....	....	....	....	....	....	....
1996-97	Ottawa	NHL	82	26	25	51	33	4	0	5	203	12.8	–33	....	....	....	7	0	0	0	2	0	0	0	....
1997-98	Ottawa	NHL	38	7	9	16	8	4	0	2	68	10.3	–7	....	....	....	....	....	....	....	....	....	....	....	....
	Philadelphia	NHL	37	9	17	26	6	4	0	3	78	11.5	–1	....	....	....	5	0	2	2	0	0	0	0	....
1998-99	Philadelphia	NHL	31	3	2	5	2	1	0	1	26	11.5	–1	53	39.6	7:59	....	....	....	....	....	....	....	....	....
	Tampa Bay	NHL	32	6	6	12	2	3	0	0	56	10.7	–12	4	50.0	13:59	....	....	....	....	....	....	....	....	....
99-2000	NY Rangers	NHL	58	8	18	26	23	1	0	1	52	15.4	–5	339	53.1	10:59	....	....	....	....	....	....	....	....	....
	Hartford	AHL	16	6	13	19	4	....	....	....	....	....	....	....	....	....	....	....	....	....	....	....	....	....	....
2000-01			OUT OF HOCKEY – RETIRED																						
2001-02			OUT OF HOCKEY – RETIRED																						
2002-03	Pittsburgh	NHL	33	4	3	7	8	1	0	0	48	8.3	–10	24	33.3	10:57	....	....	....	....	....	....	....	....	....
	Wilkes-Barre	AHL	40	9	29	38	18	....	....	....	....	....	....	....	....	....	4	0	1	1	0	....	....	....	....
2003-04	Minnesota	NHL	78	20	31	51	14	6	0	3	145	13.8	–4	72	51.4	15:10	....	....	....	....	....	....	....	....	....
2004-05	Morges	Swiss-2	....	....	....	....	....	....	....	....	....	....	....	....	....	....	2	1	1	2	0	....	....	....	....
	NHL Totals		570	124	175	299	174	33	1	19	1026	12.1		492	50.4	12:24	12	0	2	2	2	0	0	0	....

QMJHL Second All-Star Team (1992) • QMJHL Offensive Rookie of the Year (1992) • Canadian Major Junior Rookie of the Year (1992) • QMJHL First All-Star Team (1993)

Traded to **Philadelphia** by **Ottawa** for Vaclav Prospal, Pat Falloon and Dallas' 2nd round choice (previously acquired, Ottawa selected Chris Bala) in 1998 Entry Draft, January 17, 1998. Traded to **Edmonton** by **Philadelphia** for Andrei Kovalenko, January 29, 1999. Traded to **Tampa Bay** by **Edmonton** for Alexander Selivanov, January 29, 1999. Traded to **NY Rangers** by **Tampa Bay** for cash, October 3, 1999. Signed as a free agent by **Pittsburgh**, August 13, 2002. Signed as a free agent by **Minnesota**, September 30, 2003. Signed as a free agent by **Morges** (Swiss-2), February 5, 2005.

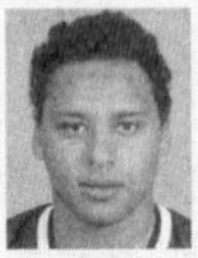

DALEY, Trevor

(DAY-lee, TREH-vuhr) **DAL.**

Defense. Shoots left. 5'9", 197 lbs. Born, Toronto, Ont., October 9, 1983. Dallas' 5th choice, 43rd overall, in 2002 Entry Draft.

Season	Club	League	GP	G	A	Pts	PIM	PP	SH	GW	S	%	+/-	TF	F%	Min	GP	G	A	Pts	PIM	PP	SH	GW	Min
1998-99	Vaughan Vipers	OPJHL	44	10	36	46	79	....	....	....	....	....	....	....	....	....	....	....	....	....	....	....	....	....	....
99-2000	Sault Ste. Marie	OHL	54	16	30	46	77	....	....	....	....	....	....	....	....	....	15	3	7	10	12	....	....	....	....
2000-01	Sault Ste. Marie	OHL	58	14	27	41	105	....	....	....	....	....	....	....	....	....	....	....	....	....	....	....	....	....	....
2001-02	Sault Ste. Marie	OHL	47	9	39	48	38	....	....	....	....	....	....	....	....	....	6	2	2	4	4	....	....	....	....
2002-03	Sault Ste. Marie	OHL	57	20	33	53	128	....	....	....	....	....	....	....	....	....	1	0	0	0	2	....	....	....	....
2003-04	Dallas	NHL	27	1	5	6	14	1	0	0	34	2.9	–6	0	0.0	16:02	1	0	0	0	0	0	0	0	10:21
	Utah Grizzlies	AHL	40	8	6	14	76	....	....	....	....	....	....	....	....	....	....	....	....	....	....	....	....	....	....
2004-05	Hamilton	AHL	78	7	27	34	109	....	....	....	....	....	....	....	....	....	4	0	1	1	2	....	....	....	....
	NHL Totals		27	1	5	6	14	1	0	0	34	2.9		0	0.0	16:02	1	0	0	0	0	0	0	0	10:21

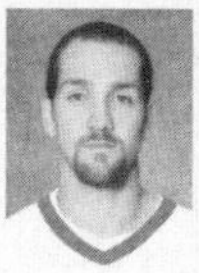

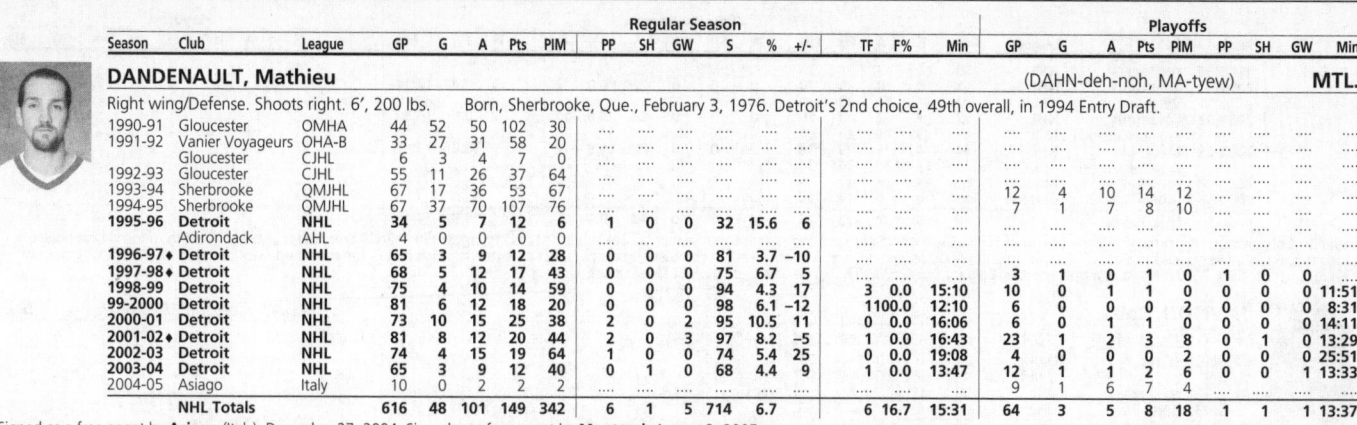

DANDENAULT, Mathieu

(DAHN-deh-noh, MA-tyew) **MTL.**

Right wing/Defense. Shoots right. 6', 200 lbs. Born, Sherbrooke, Que., February 3, 1976. Detroit's 2nd choice, 49th overall, in 1994 Entry Draft.

			Regular Season														Playoffs								
Season	Club	League	GP	G	A	Pts	PIM	PP	SH	GW	S	%	+/-	TF	F%	Min	GP	G	A	Pts	PIM	PP	SH	GW	Min
1990-91	Gloucester	OMHA	44	52	50	102	30	....	....	....	....	....	....	....	....	....	....	....	....	....	....	....	....	....	....
1991-92	Vanier Voyageurs	OHA-B	33	27	31	58	20	....	....	....	....	....	....	....	....	....	....	....	....	....	....	....	....	....	....
	Gloucester	CJHL	6	3	4	7	0	....	....	....	....	....	....	....	....	....	....	....	....	....	....	....	....	....	....
1992-93	Gloucester	CJHL	55	11	26	37	64	....	....	....	....	....	....	....	....	....	....	....	....	....	....	....	....	....	....
1993-94	Sherbrooke	QMJHL	67	17	36	53	67	....	....	....	....	....	....	....	....	....	12	4	10	14	12	....	....	....	....
1994-95	Sherbrooke	QMJHL	67	37	70	107	76	....	....	....	....	....	....	....	....	....	7	1	7	8	10	....	....	....	....
1995-96	**Detroit**	**NHL**	**34**	**5**	**7**	**12**	**6**	**1**	**0**	**0**	**32**	**15.6**	**6**	....	....	....	....	....	....	....	....	....	....	....	....
	Adirondack	AHL	4	0	0	0	0	....	....	....	....	....	....	....	....	....	....	....	....	....	....	....	....	....	....
1996-97 ♦	**Detroit**	**NHL**	**65**	**3**	**9**	**12**	**28**	**0**	**0**	**0**	**81**	**3.7**	**–10**	....	....	....	....	....	....	....	....	....	....	....	....
1997-98 ♦	**Detroit**	**NHL**	**68**	**5**	**12**	**17**	**43**	**0**	**0**	**0**	**75**	**6.7**	**5**	....	....	....	**3**	**1**	**0**	**1**	**0**	**1**	**0**	**0**	....
1998-99	**Detroit**	**NHL**	**75**	**4**	**10**	**14**	**59**	**0**	**0**	**0**	**94**	**4.3**	**17**	**3**	**0.0**	**15:10**	**10**	**0**	**1**	**1**	**0**	**0**	**0**	**0**	**11:51**
99-2000	**Detroit**	**NHL**	**81**	**6**	**12**	**18**	**20**	**0**	**0**	**0**	**98**	**6.1**	**–12**	**1**	**100.0**	**12:10**	**6**	**0**	**0**	**0**	**2**	**0**	**0**	**0**	**8:31**
2000-01	**Detroit**	**NHL**	**73**	**10**	**15**	**25**	**38**	**2**	**0**	**2**	**95**	**10.5**	**11**	**0**	**0.0**	**16:06**	**6**	**0**	**1**	**1**	**0**	**0**	**0**	**0**	**14:11**
2001-02 ♦	**Detroit**	**NHL**	**81**	**8**	**12**	**20**	**44**	**2**	**0**	**3**	**97**	**8.2**	**–5**	**1**	**0.0**	**16:43**	**23**	**1**	**2**	**3**	**8**	**0**	**1**	**0**	**13:29**
2002-03	**Detroit**	**NHL**	**74**	**4**	**15**	**19**	**64**	**1**	**0**	**0**	**74**	**5.4**	**25**	**0**	**0.0**	**19:08**	**4**	**0**	**0**	**0**	**2**	**0**	**0**	**0**	**25:51**
2003-04	**Detroit**	**NHL**	**65**	**3**	**9**	**12**	**40**	**0**	**1**	**0**	**68**	**4.4**	**9**	**1**	**0.0**	**13:47**	**12**	**1**	**1**	**2**	**6**	**0**	**0**	**1**	**13:33**
2004-05	Asiago	Italy	10	0	2	2	2	....	....	....	....	....	....	....	....	....	9	1	6	7	4	....	....	....	....
	NHL Totals		**616**	**48**	**101**	**149**	**342**	**6**	**1**	**5**	**714**	**6.7**		**6**	**16.7**	**15:31**	**64**	**3**	**5**	**8**	**18**	**1**	**1**	**1**	**13:37**

Signed as a free agent by **Asiago** (Italy), December 27, 2004. Signed as a free agent by **Montreal**, August 3, 2005.

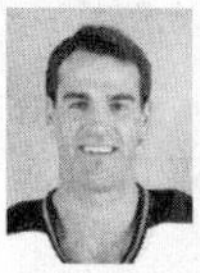

DARBY, Craig

(DAHR-bee, KRAYG) **T.B.**

Center. Shoots right. 6'4", 200 lbs. Born, Oneida, NY, September 26, 1972. Montreal's 3rd choice, 43rd overall, in 1991 Entry Draft.

Season	Club	League	GP	G	A	Pts	PIM	PP	SH	GW	S	%	+/-	TF	F%	Min	GP	G	A	Pts	PIM	PP	SH	GW	Min
1987-88	Albany	High-NY	29	11	27	38	....	....	....	....	....	....	....	....	....	....	....	....	....	....	....	....	....	....	....
1988-89	Albany	High-NY	29	36	40	*76	....	....	....	....	....	....	....	....	....	....	....	....	....	....	....	....	....	....	....
1989-90	Albany	High-NY	29	32	53	85	....	....	....	....	....	....	....	....	....	....	....	....	....	....	....	....	....	....	....
1990-91	Albany	High-NY	29	33	61	*94	....	....	....	....	....	....	....	....	....	....	4	8	1	9	....	....	....	....	....
1991-92	Providence	H-East	35	17	24	41	47	....	....	....	....	....	....	....	....	....	....	....	....	....	....	....	....	....	....
1992-93	Providence	H-East	35	11	21	32	62	....	....	....	....	....	....	....	....	....	....	....	....	....	....	....	....	....	....
1993-94	Fredericton	AHL	66	23	33	56	51	....	....	....	....	....	....	....	....	....	....	....	....	....	....	....	....	....	....
1994-95	Fredericton	AHL	64	21	47	68	82	....	....	....	....	....	....	....	....	....	....	....	....	....	....	....	....	....	....
	Montreal	**NHL**	**10**	**0**	**2**	**2**	**0**	**0**	**0**	**0**	**4**	**0.0**	**–5**	....	....	....	....	....	....	....	....	....	....	....	....
	NY Islanders	**NHL**	**3**	**0**	**0**	**0**	**0**	**0**	**0**	**0**	**1**	**0.0**	**–1**	....	....	....	....	....	....	....	....	....	....	....	....
1995-96	**NY Islanders**	**NHL**	**10**	**0**	**2**	**2**	**0**	**0**	**0**	**0**	**1**	**0.0**	**–1**	....	....	....	....	....	....	....	....	....	....	....	....
	Worcester IceCats	AHL	68	22	28	50	47	....	....	....	....	....	....	....	....	....	4	1	1	2	2	....	....	....	....
1996-97	**Philadelphia**	**NHL**	**9**	**1**	**4**	**5**	**2**	**0**	**1**	**0**	**13**	**7.7**	**2**	....	....	....	....	....	....	....	....	....	....	....	....
	Philadelphia	AHL	59	26	33	59	24	....	....	....	....	....	....	....	....	....	10	3	6	9	0	....	....	....	....
1997-98	**Philadelphia**	**NHL**	**3**	**1**	**0**	**1**	**0**	**0**	**0**	**0**	**3**	**33.3**	**0**	....	....	....	....	....	....	....	....	....	....	....	....
	Philadelphia	AHL	77	*42	45	87	34	....	....	....	....	....	....	....	....	....	20	5	9	14	4	....	....	....	....
1998-99	Milwaukee	IHL	81	32	22	54	33	....	....	....	....	....	....	....	....	....	2	3	0	3	0	....	....	....	....
99-2000	**Montreal**	**NHL**	**76**	**7**	**10**	**17**	**14**	**0**	**1**	**2**	**90**	**7.8**	**–14**	**1068**	**48.3**	**13:45**	....	....	....	....	....	....	....	....	....
2000-01	**Montreal**	**NHL**	**78**	**12**	**16**	**28**	**16**	**0**	**1**	**0**	**97**	**12.4**	**–17**	**1214**	**46.9**	**15:53**	....	....	....	....	....	....	....	....	....
2001-02	**Montreal**	**NHL**	**2**	**0**	**0**	**0**	**0**	**0**	**0**	**0**	**0**	**0.0**	**0**	**10**	**30.0**	**5:20**	....	....	....	....	....	....	....	....	....
	Quebec Citadelles	AHL	66	16	55	71	18	....	....	....	....	....	....	....	....	....	3	2	1	3	0	....	....	....	....
2002-03	**New Jersey**	**NHL**	**3**	**0**	**1**	**1**	**0**	**0**	**0**	**0**	**1**	**0.0**	**–1**	**21**	**47.6**	**10:36**	....	....	....	....	....	....	....	....	....
	Albany River Rats	AHL	76	23	51	74	42	....	....	....	....	....	....	....	....	....	....	....	....	....	....	....	....	....	....
2003-04	**New Jersey**	**NHL**	**2**	**0**	**0**	**0**	**0**	**0**	**0**	**0**	**0**	**0.0**	**–1**	**17**	**58.8**	**7:06**	....	....	....	....	....	....	....	....	....
	Albany River Rats	AHL	77	21	48	69	44	....	....	....	....	....	....	....	....	....	....	....	....	....	....	....	....	....	....
2004-05	Springfield	AHL	70	8	26	34	28	....	....	....	....	....	....	....	....	....	....	....	....	....	....	....	....	....	....
	NHL Totals		**196**	**21**	**35**	**56**	**32**	**0**	**3**	**2**	**210**	**10.0**		**2330**	**47.6**	**14:32**	....	....	....	....	....	....	....	....	....

Hockey East Rookie of the Year (1992) (co-winner - Ian Moran) • AHL First All-Star Team (1998) • AHL Second All-Star Team (2003)

Traded to **NY Islanders** by **Montreal** with Kirk Muller and Mathieu Schneider for Pierre Turgeon and Vladimir Malakhov, April 5, 1995. Claimed on waivers by **Philadelphia** from **NY Islanders**, June 4, 1996. Claimed by **Nashville** from **Philadelphia** in Expansion Draft, June 26, 1998. Signed as a free agent by **Montreal**, August 4, 1999. Signed as a free agent by **New Jersey**, July 12, 2002. Signed as a free agent by **Tampa Bay**, July 19, 2004.

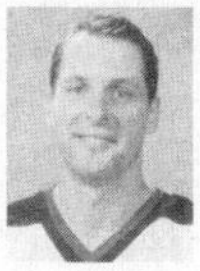

DARCHE, Mathieu

(DAHRSH, MA-thew)

Left wing. Shoots left. 6'1", 210 lbs. Born, St. Laurent, Que., November 26, 1976.

Season	Club	League	GP	G	A	Pts	PIM	PP	SH	GW	S	%	+/-	TF	F%	Min	GP	G	A	Pts	PIM	PP	SH	GW	Min
1995-96	Choate-Rosemary	High-CT	STATISTICS NOT AVAILABLE																						
1996-97	McGill Redmen	OUAA	23	1	2	3	27	....	....	....	....	....	....	....	....	....	....	....	....	....	....	....	....	....	....
1997-98	McGill Redmen	OUAA	40	28	17	45	69	....	....	....	....	....	....	....	....	....	....	....	....	....	....	....	....	....	....
1998-99	McGill Redmen	OUAA	32	16	24	40	60	....	....	....	....	....	....	....	....	....	....	....	....	....	....	....	....	....	....
99-2000	McGill Redmen	OUAA	33	31	41	*72	38	....	....	....	....	....	....	....	....	....	5	2	8	10	16	....	....	....	....
2000-01	**Columbus**	**NHL**	**9**	**0**	**0**	**0**	**0**	**0**	**0**	**0**	**9**	**0.0**	**–4**	**1**	**0.0**	**10:07**	....	....	....	....	....	....	....	....	....
	Syracuse Crunch	AHL	66	16	24	40	21	....	....	....	....	....	....	....	....	....	5	0	1	1	4	....	....	....	....
2001-02	**Columbus**	**NHL**	**14**	**1**	**1**	**2**	**6**	**0**	**0**	**0**	**15**	**6.7**	**–5**	**3**	**33.3**	**9:49**	....	....	....	....	....	....	....	....	....
	Syracuse Crunch	AHL	63	22	23	45	26	....	....	....	....	....	....	....	....	....	10	2	5	7	2	....	....	....	....
2002-03	**Columbus**	**NHL**	**1**	**0**	**0**	**0**	**0**	**0**	**0**	**0**	**0**	**0.0**	**–1**	**0**	**0.0**	**6:57**	....	....	....	....	....	....	....	....	....
	Syracuse Crunch	AHL	76	32	32	64	38	....	....	....	....	....	....	....	....	....	....	....	....	....	....	....	....	....	....
2003-04	**Nashville**	**NHL**	**2**	**0**	**0**	**0**	**0**	**0**	**0**	**0**	**1**	**0.0**	**–1**	**0**	**0.0**	**6:39**	....	....	....	....	....	....	....	....	....
	Milwaukee	AHL	76	28	31	59	41	....	....	....	....	....	....	....	....	....	22	6	8	14	8	....	....	....	....
2004-05	Hershey Bears	AHL	79	29	25	54	49	....	....	....	....	....	....	....	....	....	....	....	....	....	....	....	....	....	....
	NHL Totals		**26**	**1**	**1**	**2**	**6**	**0**	**0**	**0**	**25**	**4.0**		**4**	**25.0**	**9:34**	....	....	....	....	....	....	....	....	....

OUAA East Second All-Star Team (1998) • OUAA East First All-Star Team (1999) • OUAA First All-Star Team (2000) • CIAU All-Canadian Team (2000)

• Played CIAU Football (1996-97). Signed as a free agent by **Columbus**, May 16, 2000. Signed as a free agent by **Nashville**, September 10, 2003. Signed as a free agent by **Colorado**, July 26, 2004.

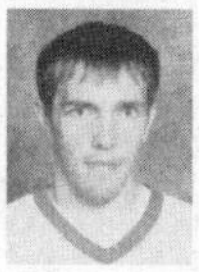

DATSYUK, Pavel

(daht-SOOK, PAH-vehl) **DET.**

Center. Shoots left. 5'11", 180 lbs. Born, Sverdlovsk, USSR, July 20, 1978. Detroit's 8th choice, 171st overall, in 1998 Entry Draft.

Season	Club	League	GP	G	A	Pts	PIM	PP	SH	GW	S	%	+/-	TF	F%	Min	GP	G	A	Pts	PIM	PP	SH	GW	Min
1996-97	Yekaterinburg 2	Russia-3	18	2	2	4	4	....	....	....	....	....	....	....	....	....	....	....	....	....	....	....	....	....	....
	Yekaterinburg	Russia	36	12	10	22	12	....	....	....	....	....	....	....	....	....	....	....	....	....	....	....	....	....	....
1997-98	Yekaterinburg	Russia	24	3	5	8	4	....	....	....	....	....	....	....	....	....	....	....	....	....	....	....	....	....	....
	Yekaterinburg	Russia	22	7	8	15	4	....	....	....	....	....	....	....	....	....	....	....	....	....	....	....	....	....	....
1998-99	Yekaterinburg 2	Russia-4	10	14	14	28	4	....	....	....	....	....	....	....	....	....	....	....	....	....	....	....	....	....	....
	Yekaterinburg	Russia-2	35	21	23	44	14	....	....	....	....	....	....	....	....	....	9	3	7	10	10	....	....	....	....
99-2000	Yekaterinburg	Russia	15	1	3	4	4	....	....	....	....	....	....	....	....	....	....	....	....	....	....	....	....	....	....
2000-01	Ak Bars Kazan	Russia	42	9	18	27	10	....	....	....	....	....	....	....	....	....	4	0	1	1	2	....	....	....	....
2001-02 ♦	**Detroit**	**NHL**	**70**	**11**	**24**	**35**	**4**	**2**	**0**	**1**	**79**	**13.9**	**4**	**794**	**47.7**	**13:39**	**21**	**3**	**3**	**6**	**2**	**1**	**0**	**1**	**10:40**
	Russia	Olympics	6	1	2	3	0	....	....	....	....	....	....	....	....	....	....	....	....	....	....	....	....	....	....
2002-03	**Detroit**	**NHL**	**64**	**12**	**39**	**51**	**16**	**1**	**0**	**1**	**82**	**14.6**	**20**	**778**	**48.2**	**15:28**	**4**	**0**	**0**	**0**	**0**	**0**	**0**	**0**	**18:48**
2003-04	**Detroit**	**NHL**	**75**	**30**	**38**	**68**	**35**	**8**	**1**	**4**	**136**	**22.1**	**–2**	**1314**	**54.0**	**18:16**	**12**	**0**	**6**	**6**	**2**	**0**	**0**	**0**	**17:23**
2004-05	Dynamo Moscow	Russia	47	15	17	32	16	....	....	....	....	....	....	....	....	....	10	*6	3	9	4	....	....	....	....
	NHL Totals		**209**	**53**	**101**	**154**	**55**	**11**	**1**	**6**	**297**	**17.8**		**2886**	**50.7**	**15:52**	**37**	**3**	**9**	**12**	**4**	**1**	**0**	**1**	**13:44**

Played in NHL All-Star Game (2004)

• Spent majority of 1999-2000 season on **Kazan** (Russia) reserve squad. Signed as a free agent by **Dynamo Moscow** (Russia), June 19, 2004. Signed as a free agent by **Omsk**, September 5, 2005.

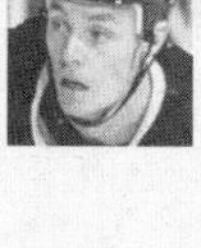

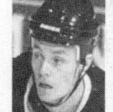

DAVIDSON, Matt

(DAY-vihd-SOHN, MAT)

Right wing. Shoots right. 6'3", 196 lbs. Born, Flin Flon, Man., August 9, 1977. Buffalo's 5th choice, 94th overall, in 1995 Entry Draft.

Season	Club	League	GP	G	A	Pts	PIM	PP	SH	GW	S	%	+/-	TF	F%	Min	GP	G	A	Pts	PIM	PP	SH	GW	Min
1992-93	Sask. Contacts	SMHL	36	14	18	32	36	....	....	....	....	....	....	....	....	....	....	....	....	....	....	....	....	....	....
1993-94	Portland	WHL	59	4	12	16	18	....	....	....	....	....	....	....	....	....	10	0	0	0	4	....	....	....	....
1994-95	Portland	WHL	72	17	20	37	51	....	....	....	....	....	....	....	....	....	9	1	3	4	0	....	....	....	....
1995-96	Portland	WHL	70	24	26	50	96	....	....	....	....	....	....	....	....	....	7	2	2	4	2	....	....	....	....
1996-97	Portland	WHL	72	44	27	71	47	....	....	....	....	....	....	....	....	....	6	0	1	1	2	....	....	....	....
1997-98	Rochester	AHL	72	15	12	27	12	....	....	....	....	....	....	....	....	....	3	1	0	1	2	....	....	....	....
1998-99	Rochester	AHL	80	26	15	41	44	....	....	....	....	....	....	....	....	....	18	2	1	3	6	....	....	....	....

			Regular Season														Playoffs								
Season	Club	League	GP	G	A	Pts	PIM	PP	SH	GW	S	%	+/-	TF	F%	Min	GP	G	A	Pts	PIM	PP	SH	GW	Min
99-2000	Rochester	AHL	80	12	20	32	30	....	....	....	....	....	....	....	....	....	19	4	2	6	8	....	....	....	....
2000-01	**Columbus**	**NHL**	**5**	**0**	**0**	**0**	**0**	**0**	**0**	**0**	**2**	**0.0**	**2**	**0**	**0.0**	**7:14**	....	....	....	....	....	....	....	....	....
	Syracuse Crunch	AHL	72	14	11	25	24	....	....	....	....	....	....	....	....	....	5	1	2	3	2	....	....	....	....
2001-02	**Columbus**	**NHL**	**17**	**1**	**2**	**3**	**10**	**0**	**0**	**0**	**18**	**5.6**	**–11**	**7**	**0.0**	**14:34**	....	....	....	....	....	....	....	....	....
	Syracuse Crunch	AHL	47	9	11	20	64	....	....	....	....	....	....	....	....	....	8	1	3	4	4	....	....	....	....
2002-03	**Columbus**	**NHL**	**34**	**4**	**5**	**9**	**18**	**0**	**0**	**0**	**28**	**14.3**	**–12**	**7**	**28.6**	**11:49**	....	....	....	....	....	....	....	....	....
	Syracuse Crunch	AHL	48	18	16	34	26	....	....	....	....	....	....	....	....	....	....	....	....	....	....	....	....	....	....
2003-04	Lowell	AHL	66	14	28	42	36	....	....	....	....	....	....	....	....	....	....	....	....	....	....	....	....	....	....
2004-05	Dusseldorf	Germany	49	6	8	14	52	....	....	....	....	....	....	....	....	....	....	....	....	....	....	....	....	....	....
	NHL Totals		**56**	**5**	**7**	**12**	**28**	**0**	**0**	**0**	**48**	**10.4**		**14**	**14.3**	**12:14**	....	....	....	....	....	....	....	....	....

Traded to **Columbus** by **Buffalo** with Jean-Luc Grand-Pierre, San Jose's 5th round choice (previously acquired, Columbus selected Tyler Kolarik) in 2000 Entry Draft and Buffalo's 5th round choice (later traded to Calgary – later traded to Detroit – Detroit selected Andreas Jamtin) in 2001 Entry Draft to complete Expansion Draft agreement which had Columbus select Geoff Sanderson and Dwayne Roloson from Buffalo, June 23, 2000. Signed as a free agent by **Calgary**, July 15, 2003. Signed as a free agent by **Dusseldorf** (Germany), March 28, 2004.

DAVISON, Rob

(DAY-vihs-ohn, RAWB) **S.J.**

Defense. Shoots left. 6'2", 225 lbs. Born, St. Catharines, Ont., May 1, 1980. San Jose's 4th choice, 98th overall, in 1998 Entry Draft.

Season	Club	League	GP	G	A	Pts	PIM	PP	SH	GW	S	%	+/-	TF	F%	Min	GP	G	A	Pts	PIM	PP	SH	GW	Min
1995-96	St. Mike's B's	OPJHL	21	0	0	0	21	....	....	....	....	....	....	....	....	....	....	....	....	....	....	....	....	....	....
1996-97	St. Mike's B's	OPJHL	45	2	6	8	93	....	....	....	....	....	....	....	....	....	....	....	....	....	....	....	....	....	....
1997-98	North Bay	OHL	59	0	11	11	200	....	....	....	....	....	....	....	....	....	....	....	....	....	....	....	....	....	....
1998-99	North Bay	OHL	59	2	17	19	150	....	....	....	....	....	....	....	....	....	4	0	1	1	12	....	....	....	....
99-2000	North Bay	OHL	67	4	6	10	194	....	....	....	....	....	....	....	....	....	6	0	1	1	8	....	....	....	....
2000-01	Kentucky	AHL	72	0	4	4	230	....	....	....	....	....	....	....	....	....	3	0	0	0	0	....	....	....	....
2001-02	Cleveland Barons	AHL	70	1	3	4	206	....	....	....	....	....	....	....	....	....	....	....	....	....	....	....	....	....	....
2002-03	**San Jose**	**NHL**	**15**	**1**	**2**	**3**	**22**	**0**	**0**	**0**	**15**	**6.7**	**4**	**0**	**0.0**	**17:53**	....	....	....	....	....	....	....	....	....
	Cleveland Barons	AHL	42	1	3	4	82	....	....	....	....	....	....	....	....	....	....	....	....	....	....	....	....	....	....
2003-04	**San Jose**	**NHL**	**55**	**0**	**3**	**3**	**92**	**0**	**0**	**0**	**33**	**0.0**	**–3**	**0**	**0.0**	**14:22**	**5**	**0**	**2**	**2**	**4**	**0**	**0**	**0**	**9:01**
2004-05	Cardiff Devils	Britain	24	2	3	5	114	....	....	....	....	....	....	....	....	....	8	0	1	1	12	....	....	....	....
	NHL Totals		**70**	**1**	**5**	**6**	**114**	**0**	**0**	**0**	**48**	**2.1**		**0**	**0.0**	**15:08**	**5**	**0**	**2**	**2**	**4**	**0**	**0**	**0**	**9:01**

Signed as a free agent by **Cardiff** (Britain), October 5, 2004.

DAW, Jeff

(DAW, JEHF)

Center. Shoots right. 6'3", 190 lbs. Born, Carlisle, Ont., February 28, 1972.

Season	Club	League	GP	G	A	Pts	PIM	PP	SH	GW	S	%	+/-	TF	F%	Min	GP	G	A	Pts	PIM	PP	SH	GW	Min
1989-90	Milton Merchants	OHA-B	42	19	29	48	2	....	....	....	....	....	....	....	....	....	....	....	....	....	....	....	....	....	....
1990-91	Milton Merchants	OHA-B	34	21	41	62	22	....	....	....	....	....	....	....	....	....	....	....	....	....	....	....	....	....	....
1991-92	Milton Merchants	OHA-B	41	33	33	66	20	....	....	....	....	....	....	....	....	....	....	....	....	....	....	....	....	....	....
1992-93	U. Mass-Lowell	H-East	37	12	18	30	14	....	....	....	....	....	....	....	....	....	....	....	....	....	....	....	....	....	....
1993-94	U. Mass-Lowell	H-East	40	6	12	18	12	....	....	....	....	....	....	....	....	....	....	....	....	....	....	....	....	....	....
1994-95	U. Mass-Lowell	H-East	40	27	15	42	24	....	....	....	....	....	....	....	....	....	....	....	....	....	....	....	....	....	....
1995-96	U. Mass-Lowell	H-East	40	23	28	51	10	....	....	....	....	....	....	....	....	....	....	....	....	....	....	....	....	....	....
1996-97	Wheeling Nailers	ECHL	13	3	8	11	26	....	....	....	....	....	....	....	....	....	....	....	....	....	....	....	....	....	....
	Hamilton	AHL	56	11	8	19	39	....	....	....	....	....	....	....	....	....	19	4	5	9	0	....	....	....	....
1997-98	Hamilton	AHL	79	28	35	63	20	....	....	....	....	....	....	....	....	....	9	6	3	9	0	....	....	....	....
1998-99	Hamilton	AHL	66	18	29	47	10	....	....	....	....	....	....	....	....	....	11	0	3	3	4	....	....	....	....
99-2000	Cleveland	IHL	9	4	1	5	2	....	....	....	....	....	....	....	....	....	....	....	....	....	....	....	....	....	....
	Houston Aeros	IHL	44	9	8	17	12	....	....	....	....	....	....	....	....	....	....	....	....	....	....	....	....	....	....
	Lowell	AHL	10	0	5	5	4	....	....	....	....	....	....	....	....	....	7	1	2	3	6	....	....	....	....
2000-01	Lowell	AHL	65	28	28	56	33	....	....	....	....	....	....	....	....	....	3	0	1	1	2	....	....	....	....
	Cleveland	IHL	8	2	3	5	2	....	....	....	....	....	....	....	....	....	....	....	....	....	....	....	....	....	....
2001-02	**Colorado**	**NHL**	**1**	**0**	**1**	**1**	**0**	**0**	**0**	**0**	**2**	**0.0**	**0**	**0**	**0.0**	**12:34**	....	....	....	....	....	....	....	....	....
	Hershey Bears	AHL	79	26	25	51	22	....	....	....	....	....	....	....	....	....	8	1	1	2	4	....	....	....	....
2002-03	Lowell	AHL	51	14	16	30	18	....	....	....	....	....	....	....	....	....	....	....	....	....	....	....	....	....	....
	Springfield	AHL	12	2	4	6	2	....	....	....	....	....	....	....	....	....	6	0	2	2	2	....	....	....	....
2003-04	St. John's	AHL	67	10	23	33	17	....	....	....	....	....	....	....	....	....	....	....	....	....	....	....	....	....	....
2004-05	Danbury Trashers	UHL	60	29	47	76	12	....	....	....	....	....	....	....	....	....	11	2	8	10	0	....	....	....	....
	Providence Bruins	AHL	....	....	....	....	....	....	....	....	....	....	....	....	....	....	7	0	1	1	2	....	....	....	....
	NHL Totals		**1**	**0**	**1**	**1**	**0**	**0**	**0**	**0**	**2**	**0.0**		**0**	**0.0**	**12:34**	....	....	....	....	....	....	....	....	....

Signed as a free agent by **Edmonton**, August 1, 1996. Signed as a free agent by **Chicago**, July 22, 1999. Traded to **Lowell** (AHL) by **Houston** (IHL) with Chicago retaining NHL rights for David Hymovitz, March 17, 2000. Claimed by **Minnesota** from **Chicago** in Expansion Draft, June 23, 2000. Signed as a free agent by **Colorado**, July 23, 2001. Signed as a free agent by **Carolina**, August 27, 2002. Traded to **Toronto** by **Carolina** for future considerations, May 29, 2003. Signed as a free agent by **Danbury** (UHL), November 24, 2004. Signed as a free agent by **Providence** (AHL), May 11, 2005.

DAZE, Eric

(dah-ZAY, AIR-ihk) **CHI.**

Right wing. Shoots left. 6'6", 235 lbs. Born, Montreal, Que., July 2, 1975. Chicago's 5th choice, 90th overall, in 1993 Entry Draft.

Season	Club	League	GP	G	A	Pts	PIM	PP	SH	GW	S	%	+/-	TF	F%	Min	GP	G	A	Pts	PIM	PP	SH	GW	Min
1990-91	Laval-Laurentides	QAHA	30	25	20	45	30	....	....	....	....	....	....	....	....	....	....	....	....	....	....	....	....	....	....
1991-92	Laval-Laurentides	QAAA	35	30	29	59	40	....	....	....	....	....	....	....	....	....	12	8	10	18	8	....	....	....	....
1992-93	Beauport	QMJHL	68	19	36	55	24	....	....	....	....	....	....	....	....	....	....	....	....	....	....	....	....	....	....
1993-94	Beauport	QMJHL	66	59	48	107	31	....	....	....	....	....	....	....	....	....	15	16	8	24	2	....	....	....	....
1994-95	Beauport	QMJHL	57	54	45	99	20	....	....	....	....	....	....	....	....	....	16	9	12	21	23	....	....	....	....
	Chicago	**NHL**	**4**	**1**	**1**	**2**	**2**	**0**	**0**	**0**	**1**	**100.0**	**2**	....	....	....	**16**	**0**	**1**	**1**	**4**	**0**	**0**	**0**	....
1995-96	**Chicago**	**NHL**	**80**	**30**	**23**	**53**	**18**	**2**	**0**	**2**	**167**	**18.0**	**16**	....	....	....	**10**	**3**	**5**	**8**	**0**	**0**	**0**	**1**	....
1996-97	**Chicago**	**NHL**	**71**	**22**	**19**	**41**	**16**	**11**	**0**	**4**	**176**	**12.5**	**–4**	....	....	....	**6**	**2**	**1**	**3**	**2**	**0**	**0**	**0**	....
1997-98	**Chicago**	**NHL**	**80**	**31**	**11**	**42**	**22**	**10**	**0**	**7**	**216**	**14.4**	**4**	....	....	....	....	....	....	....	....	....	....	....	....
1998-99	**Chicago**	**NHL**	**72**	**22**	**20**	**42**	**22**	**8**	**0**	**2**	**189**	**11.6**	**–13**	**4**	**0.0**	**16:16**	....	....	....	....	....	....	....	....	....
99-2000	**Chicago**	**NHL**	**59**	**23**	**13**	**36**	**28**	**6**	**0**	**1**	**143**	**16.1**	**–16**	**9**	**22.2**	**16:15**	....	....	....	....	....	....	....	....	....
2000-01	**Chicago**	**NHL**	**79**	**33**	**24**	**57**	**16**	**9**	**1**	**8**	**205**	**16.1**	**1**	**3**	**33.3**	**17:45**	....	....	....	....	....	....	....	....	....
2001-02	**Chicago**	**NHL**	**82**	**38**	**32**	**70**	**36**	**12**	**0**	**5**	**264**	**14.4**	**17**	**5**	**0.0**	**17:07**	**5**	**0**	**0**	**0**	**2**	**0**	**0**	**0**	**17:12**
2002-03	**Chicago**	**NHL**	**54**	**22**	**22**	**44**	**14**	**3**	**0**	**5**	**170**	**12.9**	**10**	**4**	**25.0**	**16:17**	....	....	....	....	....	....	....	....	....
2003-04	**Chicago**	**NHL**	**19**	**4**	**7**	**11**	**0**	**1**	**0**	**0**	**76**	**5.3**	**–7**	**1**	**0.0**	**18:56**	....	....	....	....	....	....	....	....	....
2004-05		DID NOT PLAY																							
	NHL Totals		**600**	**226**	**172**	**398**	**174**	**62**	**1**	**34**	**1607**	**14.1**		**26**	**15.4**	**16:55**	**37**	**5**	**7**	**12**	**8**	**0**	**0**	**1**	**17:12**

QMJHL First All-Star Team (1994, 1995) • Canadian Major Junior Most Sportsmanlike Player of the Year (1995) • NHL All-Rookie Team (1996)

Played in NHL All-Star Game (2002)

• Missed majority of 2003-04 season recovering from back injury suffered in game vs. Los Angeles, October 16, 2003.

DEADMARSH, Adam

(DEHD-mahrsh, A-duhm)

Right wing. Shoots right. 6', 205 lbs. Born, Trail, B.C., May 10, 1975. Quebec's 2nd choice, 14th overall, in 1993 Entry Draft.

Season	Club	League	GP	G	A	Pts	PIM	PP	SH	GW	S	%	+/-	TF	F%	Min	GP	G	A	Pts	PIM	PP	SH	GW	Min
1990-91	Beaver Valley	KIJHL	35	28	44	72	95	....	....	....	....	....	....	....	....	....	....	....	....	....	....	....	....	....	....
1991-92	Portland	WHL	68	30	30	60	81	....	....	....	....	....	....	....	....	....	6	3	3	6	13	....	....	....	....
1992-93	Portland	WHL	58	33	36	69	126	....	....	....	....	....	....	....	....	....	16	7	8	15	29	....	....	....	....
1993-94	Portland	WHL	65	43	56	99	212	....	....	....	....	....	....	....	....	....	10	9	8	17	33	....	....	....	....
1994-95	Portland	WHL	29	28	20	48	129	....	....	....	....	....	....	....	....	....	....	....	....	....	....	....	....	....	....
	Quebec	**NHL**	**48**	**9**	**8**	**17**	**56**	**0**	**0**	**0**	**48**	**18.8**	**16**	....	....	....	**6**	**0**	**1**	**1**	**0**	**0**	**0**	**0**	....
1995-96♦	**Colorado**	**NHL**	**78**	**21**	**27**	**48**	**142**	**3**	**0**	**2**	**151**	**13.9**	**20**	....	....	....	**22**	**5**	**12**	**17**	**25**	**1**	**0**	**0**	....
1996-97	**Colorado**	**NHL**	**78**	**33**	**27**	**60**	**136**	**10**	**3**	**4**	**198**	**16.7**	**8**	....	....	....	**17**	**3**	**6**	**9**	**24**	**1**	**0**	**1**	....
1997-98	**Colorado**	**NHL**	**73**	**22**	**21**	**43**	**125**	**10**	**0**	**6**	**187**	**11.8**	**0**	....	....	....	**7**	**2**	**0**	**2**	**4**	**1**	**0**	**0**	....
	United States	Olympics	4	1	0	1	2	....	....	....	....	....	....	....	....	....	....	....	....	....	....	....	....	....	....
1998-99	**Colorado**	**NHL**	**66**	**22**	**27**	**49**	**99**	**10**	**0**	**3**	**152**	**14.5**	**–2**	**621**	**45.9**	**20:46**	**19**	**8**	**4**	**12**	**20**	**3**	**0**	**0**	**18:51**
99-2000	**Colorado**	**NHL**	**71**	**18**	**27**	**45**	**106**	**5**	**0**	**4**	**153**	**11.8**	**–10**	**430**	**46.5**	**20:27**	**17**	**4**	**11**	**15**	**21**	**1**	**0**	**1**	**18:47**
2000-01	**Colorado**	**NHL**	**39**	**13**	**13**	**26**	**59**	**7**	**0**	**2**	**86**	**15.1**	**–2**	**56**	**55.4**	**17:38**	....	....	....	....	....	....	....	....	....
	Los Angeles	**NHL**	**18**	**4**	**2**	**6**	**4**	**0**	**0**	**0**	**40**	**10.0**	**3**	**21**	**57.1**	**18:47**	**13**	**3**	**3**	**6**	**4**	**0**	**0**	**2**	**20:09**
2001-02	**Los Angeles**	**NHL**	**76**	**29**	**33**	**62**	**71**	**12**	**0**	**5**	**139**	**20.9**	**8**	**60**	**38.3**	**19:17**	**4**	**1**	**3**	**4**	**2**	**0**	**0**	**0**	**18:51**
	United States	Olympics	6	1	1	2	2	....	....	....	....	....	....	....	....	....	....	....	....	....	....	....	....	....	....
2002-03	**Los Angeles**	**NHL**	**20**	**13**	**4**	**17**	**21**	**4**	**0**	**1**	**55**	**23.6**	**2**	**26**	**46.2**	**19:18**	....	....	....	....	....	....	....	....	....

			Regular Season														Playoffs								
Season	Club	League	GP	G	A	Pts	PIM	PP	SH	GW	S	%	+/-	TF	F%	Min	GP	G	A	Pts	PIM	PP	SH	GW	Min
2003-04	**Los Angeles**	**NHL**	DID NOT PLAY – INJURED																						
2004-05			DID NOT PLAY																						
	NHL Totals		**567**	**184**	**189**	**373**	**819**	**61**	**3**	**27**	**1209**	**15.2**		**1214**	**46.4**	**19:39**	**105**	**26**	**40**	**66**	**100**	**7**	**0**	**4**	**19:09**

Transferred to **Colorado** after **Quebec** franchise relocated, June 21, 1995. Traded to **Los Angeles** by **Colorado** with Aaron Miller, a player to be named later (Jared Aulin, March 22, 2001) and Colorado's 1st round choices in 2001 (Dave Steckel) and 2003 (Brian Boyle) Entry Drafts for Rob Blake and Steve Reinprecht, February 21, 2001. • Missed majority of 2002-03 season and entire 2003-04 season recovering from head injury suffered in game vs. Phoenix, December 15, 2002.

DELMORE, Andy

(DEHL-mohr, AN-dee) **DET.**

Defense. Shoots right. 6'1", 200 lbs. Born, LaSalle, Ont., December 26, 1976.

			Regular Season														Playoffs								
Season	Club	League	GP	G	A	Pts	PIM	PP	SH	GW	S	%	+/-	TF	F%	Min	GP	G	A	Pts	PIM	PP	SH	GW	Min
1992-93	Chatham	OHA-B	47	4	21	25	38	....	....	....	....	....	....	....	....	....	....	....	....	....	....	....	....	....	....
1993-94	North Bay	OHL	45	2	7	9	33	....	....	....	....	....	....	....	....	....	17	0	0	0	2	....	....	....	....
1994-95	North Bay	OHL	40	2	14	16	21	....	....	....	....	....	....	....	....	....	....	....	....	....	....	....	....	....	....
	Sarnia Sting	OHL	27	5	13	18	27	....	....	....	....	....	....	....	....	....	3	0	0	0	2	....	....	....	....
1995-96	Sarnia Sting	OHL	64	21	38	59	45	....	....	....	....	....	....	....	....	....	10	3	7	10	2	....	....	....	....
1996-97	Sarnia Sting	OHL	64	18	60	78	39	....	....	....	....	....	....	....	....	....	12	2	10	12	10	....	....	....	....
	Fredericton	AHL	4	0	1	1	0	....	....	....	....	....	....	....	....	....	....	....	....	....	....	....	....	....	....
1997-98	Philadelphia	AHL	73	9	30	39	46	....	....	....	....	....	....	....	....	....	18	4	4	8	21	....	....	....	....
1998-99	**Philadelphia**	**NHL**	**2**	**0**	**1**	**1**	**0**	**0**	**0**	**0**	**2**	**0.0**	**–1**	**0**	**0.0**	**20:42**	....	....	....	....	....	....	....	....	....
	Philadelphia	AHL	70	5	18	23	51	....	....	....	....	....	....	....	....	....	15	1	4	5	6	....	....	....	....
99-2000	**Philadelphia**	**NHL**	**27**	**2**	**5**	**7**	**8**	**0**	**0**	**1**	**55**	**3.6**	**–1**	**0**	**0.0**	**17:17**	**18**	**5**	**2**	**7**	**14**	**1**	**0**	**1**	**17:33**
	Philadelphia	AHL	39	12	14	26	31	....	....	....	....	....	....	....	....	....	....	....	....	....	....	....	....	....	....
2000-01	**Philadelphia**	**NHL**	**66**	**5**	**9**	**14**	**16**	**2**	**0**	**0**	**119**	**4.2**	**2**	**0**	**0.0**	**17:39**	**2**	**1**	**0**	**1**	**2**	**0**	**0**	**1**	**15:20**
2001-02	**Nashville**	**NHL**	**73**	**16**	**22**	**38**	**22**	**11**	**0**	**3**	**175**	**9.1**	**–13**	**0**	**0.0**	**19:40**	....	....	....	....	....	....	....	....	....
2002-03	**Nashville**	**NHL**	**71**	**18**	**16**	**34**	**28**	**14**	**0**	**6**	**149**	**12.1**	**–17**	**0**	**0.0**	**17:05**	....	....	....	....	....	....	....	....	....
2003-04	**Buffalo**	**NHL**	**37**	**2**	**5**	**7**	**29**	**2**	**0**	**0**	**40**	**5.0**	**–5**	**0**	**0.0**	**15:11**	....	....	....	....	....	....	....	....	....
	Rochester	AHL	8	0	2	2	2	....	....	....	....	....	....	....	....	....	....	....	....	....	....	....	....	....	....
2004-05	Adler Mannheim	Germany	50	7	16	23	59	....	....	....	....	....	....	....	....	....	14	1	6	7	12	....	....	....	....
	NHL Totals		**276**	**43**	**58**	**101**	**103**	**29**	**0**	**10**	**540**	**8.0**		**0**	**0.0**	**17:41**	**20**	**6**	**2**	**8**	**16**	**1**	**0**	**2**	**17:19**

OHL First All-Star Team (1997)

Signed as a free agent by **Philadelphia**, June 9, 1997. Traded to **Nashville** by **Philadelphia** for Nashville's 3rd round choice (later traded to Phoenix – Phoenix selected Joe Callahan) in 2002 Entry Draft, July 31, 2001. Traded to **Buffalo** by **Nashville** for Buffalo's 3rd round choice (later traded to Minnesota – Minnesota selected Clayton Stoner) in 2004 Entry Draft, June 27, 2003. Traded to **San Jose** by **Buffalo** with Curtis Brown for Jeff Jillson and a compensatory 7th round choice (Andrew Orpik) in 2005 Entry Draft, March 9, 2004. Traded to **Boston** by **San Jose** for future considerations, March 9, 2004. Signed as a free agent by **Mannheim** (Germany), July 21, 2004. Signed as a free agent by **Detroit**, August 16, 2005.

DEMITRA, Pavol

(deh-MEET-rah, PAH-vohl) **L.A.**

Left wing. Shoots left. 6', 206 lbs. Born, Dubnica, Czech., November 29, 1974. Ottawa's 9th choice, 227th overall, in 1993 Entry Draft.

			Regular Season														Playoffs								
Season	Club	League	GP	G	A	Pts	PIM	PP	SH	GW	S	%	+/-	TF	F%	Min	GP	G	A	Pts	PIM	PP	SH	GW	Min
1991-92	Dubnica	Czech-2	28	13	10	23	12	....	....	....	....	....	....	....	....	....	....	....	....	....	....	....	....	....	....
1992-93	Dubnica	Czech-2	4	3	0	3	....	....	....	....	....	....	....	....	....	....	....	....	....	....	....	....	....	....	....
	Dukla Trencin	Czech	46	11	17	28	0	....	....	....	....	....	....	....	....	....	....	....	....	....	....	....	....	....	....
1993-94	**Ottawa**	**NHL**	**12**	**1**	**1**	**2**	**4**	**1**	**0**	**0**	**10**	**10.0**	**–7**	....	....	....	....	....	....	....	....	....	....	....	....
	P.E.I. Senators	AHL	41	18	23	41	8	....	....	....	....	....	....	....	....	....	....	....	....	....	....	....	....	....	....
1994-95	P.E.I. Senators	AHL	61	26	48	74	23	....	....	....	....	....	....	....	....	....	5	0	7	7	0	....	....	....	....
	Ottawa	**NHL**	**16**	**4**	**3**	**7**	**0**	**1**	**0**	**0**	**21**	**19.0**	**–4**	....	....	....	....	....	....	....	....	....	....	....	....
1995-96	**Ottawa**	**NHL**	**31**	**7**	**10**	**17**	**6**	**2**	**0**	**1**	**66**	**10.6**	**–3**	....	....	....	....	....	....	....	....	....	....	....	....
	P.E.I. Senators	AHL	48	28	53	81	44	....	....	....	....	....	....	....	....	....	....	....	....	....	....	....	....	....	....
1996-97	Dukla Trencin	Slovakia	1	1	1	2	....	....	....	....	....	....	....	....	....	....	....	....	....	....	....	....	....	....	....
	Las Vegas	IHL	22	8	13	21	10	....	....	....	....	....	....	....	....	....	....	....	....	....	....	....	....	....	....
	St. Louis	**NHL**	**8**	**3**	**0**	**3**	**2**	**2**	**0**	**1**	**15**	**20.0**	**0**	....	....	....	**6**	**1**	**3**	**4**	**6**	**0**	**0**	**0**	....
	Grand Rapids	IHL	42	20	30	50	24	....	....	....	....	....	....	....	....	....	....	....	....	....	....	....	....	....	....
1997-98	**St. Louis**	**NHL**	**61**	**22**	**30**	**52**	**22**	**4**	**4**	**6**	**147**	**15.0**	**11**	....	....	....	**10**	**3**	**3**	**6**	**2**	**0**	**0**	**0**	....
1998-99	**St. Louis**	**NHL**	**82**	**37**	**52**	**89**	**16**	**14**	**0**	**10**	**259**	**14.3**	**13**	**250**	**44.0**	**20:10**	**13**	**5**	**4**	**9**	**4**	**3**	**0**	**1**	**19:10**
99-2000	**St. Louis**	**NHL**	**71**	**28**	**47**	**75**	**8**	**8**	**0**	**4**	**241**	**11.6**	**34**	**41**	**39.0**	**19:13**	....	....	....	....	....	....	....	....	....
2000-01	**St. Louis**	**NHL**	**44**	**20**	**25**	**45**	**16**	**5**	**0**	**5**	**124**	**16.1**	**27**	**8**	**37.5**	**18:03**	**15**	**2**	**4**	**6**	**2**	**0**	**0**	**1**	**18:13**
2001-02	**St. Louis**	**NHL**	**82**	**35**	**43**	**78**	**46**	**11**	**0**	**10**	**212**	**16.5**	**13**	**1224**	**48.1**	**19:11**	**10**	**4**	**7**	**11**	**6**	**2**	**1**	**1**	**19:45**
	Slovakia	Olympics	2	1	2	3	2	....	....	....	....	....	....	....	....	....	....	....	....	....	....	....	....	....	....
2002-03	**St. Louis**	**NHL**	**78**	**36**	**57**	**93**	**32**	**11**	**0**	**4**	**205**	**17.6**	**0**	**1253**	**46.1**	**19:47**	**7**	**2**	**4**	**6**	**2**	**1**	**0**	**0**	**18:20**
2003-04	**St. Louis**	**NHL**	**68**	**23**	**35**	**58**	**18**	**8**	**0**	**5**	**179**	**12.8**	**1**	**770**	**47.3**	**20:30**	**5**	**1**	**0**	**1**	**4**	**0**	**0**	**0**	**18:07**
2004-05	Dukla Trencin	Slovakia	54	*28	*54	*82	39	....	....	....	....	....	....	....	....	....	12	4	13	17	14	....	....	....	....
	NHL Totals		**553**	**216**	**303**	**519**	**170**	**67**	**4**	**46**	**1479**	**14.6**		**3546**	**46.8**	**19:35**	**66**	**18**	**25**	**43**	**26**	**6**	**1**	**3**	**18:47**

Lady Byng Trophy (2000)

Played in NHL All-Star Game (1999, 2000, 2002)

Traded to **St. Louis** by **Ottawa** for Christer Olsson, November 27, 1996. Signed as a free agent by **Trencin** (Slovakia), September 17, 2004. Signed as a free agent by **Los Angeles**, August 2, 2005.

DEMPSEY, Nathan

(DEHMP-see, NAY-thun) **L.A.**

Defense. Shoots right. 6', 190 lbs. Born, Spruce Grove, Alta., July 14, 1974. Toronto's 12th choice, 245th overall, in 1992 Entry Draft.

			Regular Season														Playoffs								
Season	Club	League	GP	G	A	Pts	PIM	PP	SH	GW	S	%	+/-	TF	F%	Min	GP	G	A	Pts	PIM	PP	SH	GW	Min
1990-91	St. Albert Saints	AMHL	34	11	20	31	73	....	....	....	....	....	....	....	....	....	....	....	....	....	....	....	....	....	....
1991-92	Regina Pats	WHL	70	4	22	26	72	....	....	....	....	....	....	....	....	....	....	....	....	....	....	....	....	....	....
1992-93	Regina Pats	WHL	72	12	29	41	95	....	....	....	....	....	....	....	....	....	13	3	8	11	14	....	....	....	....
	St. John's	AHL	....	....	....	....	....	....	....	....	....	....	....	....	....	....	2	0	0	0	0	....	....	....	....
1993-94	Regina Pats	WHL	56	14	36	50	100	....	....	....	....	....	....	....	....	....	4	0	0	0	4	....	....	....	....
1994-95	St. John's	AHL	74	7	30	37	91	....	....	....	....	....	....	....	....	....	5	1	0	1	11	....	....	....	....
1995-96	St. John's	AHL	73	5	15	20	103	....	....	....	....	....	....	....	....	....	4	1	0	1	9	....	....	....	....
1996-97	**Toronto**	**NHL**	**14**	**1**	**1**	**2**	**2**	**0**	**0**	**0**	**11**	**9.1**	**–2**	....	....	....	....	....	....	....	....	....	....	....	....
	St. John's	AHL	52	8	18	26	108	....	....	....	....	....	....	....	....	....	6	1	0	1	4	....	....	....	....
1997-98	St. John's	AHL	68	12	16	28	85	....	....	....	....	....	....	....	....	....	4	0	0	0	0	....	....	....	....
1998-99	St. John's	AHL	67	2	29	31	70	....	....	....	....	....	....	....	....	....	5	0	1	1	2	....	....	....	....
99-2000	**Toronto**	**NHL**	**6**	**0**	**2**	**2**	**2**	**0**	**0**	**0**	**3**	**0.0**	**2**	**1**	**0.0**	**13:40**	....	....	....	....	....	....	....	....	....
	St. John's	AHL	44	15	12	27	40	....	....	....	....	....	....	....	....	....	....	....	....	....	....	....	....	....	....
2000-01	**Toronto**	**NHL**	**25**	**1**	**9**	**10**	**4**	**1**	**0**	**0**	**31**	**3.2**	**13**	**0**	**0.0**	**15:53**	....	....	....	....	....	....	....	....	....
	St. John's	AHL	55	11	28	39	60	....	....	....	....	....	....	....	....	....	4	0	4	4	8	....	....	....	....
2001-02	**Toronto**	**NHL**	**3**	**0**	**0**	**0**	**0**	**0**	**0**	**0**	**3**	**0.0**	**1**	**0**	**0.0**	**14:00**	**6**	**0**	**2**	**2**	**0**	**0**	**0**	**0**	**14:31**
	St. John's	AHL	75	13	48	61	66	....	....	....	....	....	....	....	....	....	11	1	5	6	8	....	....	....	....
2002-03	**Chicago**	**NHL**	**67**	**5**	**23**	**28**	**26**	**1**	**0**	**2**	**124**	**4.0**	**–7**	**0**	**0.0**	**20:55**	....	....	....	....	....	....	....	....	....
2003-04	**Chicago**	**NHL**	**58**	**8**	**17**	**25**	**30**	**2**	**0**	**1**	**155**	**5.2**	**–5**	**1**	**0.0**	**23:48**	....	....	....	....	....	....	....	....	....
	Los Angeles	**NHL**	**17**	**4**	**3**	**7**	**2**	**1**	**0**	**0**	**28**	**14.3**	**–7**	**0**	**0.0**	**20:23**	....	....	....	....	....	....	....	....	....
2004-05	Eisbaren Berlin	Germany	10	2	3	5	26	....	....	....	....	....	....	....	....	....	12	0	3	3	14	....	....	....	....
	NHL Totals		**190**	**19**	**55**	**74**	**66**	**5**	**0**	**3**	**355**	**5.4**		**2**	**0.0**	**20:44**	**6**	**0**	**2**	**2**	**0**	**0**	**0**	**0**	**14:30**

WHL East Second All-Star Team (1994) • AHL Second All-Star Team (2002) • Fred T. Hunt Memorial Award (Sportsmanship – AHL) (2002)

Signed as a free agent by **Chicago**, July 12, 2002. Traded to **Los Angeles** by **Chicago** for Los Angeles' 4th round choice (Nathan Davis) in 2005 Entry Draft, March 2, 2004. Signed as a free agent by **Eisbaren Berlin** (Germany), February 9, 2005.

DESJARDINS, Eric

(deh-ZHAHR-dai, AIR-ihk) **PHI.**

Defense. Shoots right. 6'1", 205 lbs. Born, Rouyn, Que., June 14, 1969. Montreal's 3rd choice, 38th overall, in 1987 Entry Draft.

			Regular Season														Playoffs								
Season	Club	League	GP	G	A	Pts	PIM	PP	SH	GW	S	%	+/-	TF	F%	Min	GP	G	A	Pts	PIM	PP	SH	GW	Min
1985-86	Laval-Laurentides	QAAA	42	6	30	36	54	....	....	....	....	....	....	....	....	....	8	2	10	12	14	....	....	....	....
1986-87	Granby Bisons	QMJHL	66	14	24	38	178	....	....	....	....	....	....	....	....	....	8	3	2	5	10	....	....	....	....
1987-88	Granby Bisons	QMJHL	62	18	49	67	138	....	....	....	....	....	....	....	....	....	5	0	3	3	10	....	....	....	....
	Sherbrooke	AHL	3	0	0	0	6	....	....	....	....	....	....	....	....	....	4	0	2	2	2	....	....	....	....
1988-89	**Montreal**	**NHL**	**36**	**2**	**12**	**14**	**26**	**1**	**0**	**0**	**39**	**5.1**	**9**	....	....	....	**14**	**1**	**1**	**2**	**6**	**1**	**0**	**0**	....
1989-90	**Montreal**	**NHL**	**55**	**3**	**13**	**16**	**51**	**1**	**0**	**0**	**48**	**6.3**	**1**	....	....	....	**6**	**0**	**0**	**0**	**10**	**0**	**0**	**0**	....
1990-91	**Montreal**	**NHL**	**62**	**7**	**18**	**25**	**27**	**0**	**0**	**1**	**114**	**6.1**	**7**	....	....	....	**13**	**1**	**4**	**5**	**8**	**1**	**0**	**0**	....
1991-92	**Montreal**	**NHL**	**77**	**6**	**32**	**38**	**50**	**4**	**0**	**2**	**141**	**4.3**	**17**	....	....	....	**11**	**3**	**3**	**6**	**4**	**1**	**0**	**0**	....
1992-93♦	**Montreal**	**NHL**	**82**	**13**	**32**	**45**	**98**	**7**	**0**	**1**	**163**	**8.0**	**20**	....	....	....	**20**	**4**	**10**	**14**	**23**	**1**	**0**	**1**	....
1993-94	**Montreal**	**NHL**	**84**	**12**	**23**	**35**	**97**	**6**	**1**	**3**	**193**	**6.2**	**–1**	....	....	....	**7**	**0**	**2**	**2**	**4**	**0**	**0**	**0**	....
1994-95	**Montreal**	**NHL**	**9**	**0**	**6**	**6**	**2**	**0**	**0**	**0**	**14**	**0.0**	**2**	....	....	....	....	....	....	....	....	....	....	....	....
	Philadelphia	**NHL**	**34**	**5**	**18**	**23**	**12**	**1**	**0**	**1**	**79**	**6.3**	**10**	....	....	....	**15**	**4**	**4**	**8**	**10**	**1**	**0**	**2**	....

			Regular Season														Playoffs								
Season	Club	League	GP	G	A	Pts	PIM	PP	SH	GW	S	%	+/-	TF	F%	Min	GP	G	A	Pts	PIM	PP	SH	GW	Min
1995-96	**Philadelphia**	**NHL**	**80**	**7**	**40**	**47**	**45**	**5**	**0**	**2**	**184**	**3.8**	**19**	....	....	....	**12**	**0**	**6**	**6**	**2**	**0**	**0**	**0**	....
1996-97	**Philadelphia**	**NHL**	**82**	**12**	**34**	**46**	**50**	**5**	**1**	**1**	**183**	**6.6**	**25**	....	....	....	**19**	**2**	**8**	**10**	**12**	**0**	**0**	**0**	....
1997-98	**Philadelphia**	**NHL**	**77**	**6**	**27**	**33**	**36**	**2**	**1**	**0**	**150**	**4.0**	**11**	....	....	....	**5**	**0**	**1**	**1**	**0**	**0**	**0**	**0**	....
	Canada	Olympics	6	0	0	0	2	....	....	....	....	....	....	....	....	....	....	....	....	....	....	....	....	....	....
1998-99	**Philadelphia**	**NHL**	**68**	**15**	**36**	**51**	**38**	**6**	**0**	**2**	**190**	**7.9**	**18**	**0**	**0.0**	**25:48**	**6**	**2**	**2**	**4**	**4**	**1**	**0**	**1**	**26:40**
99-2000	**Philadelphia**	**NHL**	**81**	**14**	**41**	**55**	**32**	**8**	**0**	**4**	**207**	**6.8**	**20**	**1**	**0.0**	**27:01**	**18**	**2**	**10**	**12**	**2**	**1**	**0**	**1**	**28:00**
2000-01	**Philadelphia**	**NHL**	**79**	**15**	**33**	**48**	**50**	**6**	**1**	**4**	**187**	**8.0**	**–3**	**3**	**100.0**	**26:27**	**6**	**1**	**1**	**2**	**0**	**0**	**0**	**0**	**27:49**
2001-02	**Philadelphia**	**NHL**	**65**	**6**	**19**	**25**	**24**	**2**	**1**	**0**	**117**	**5.1**	**–1**	**2**	**0.0**	**22:12**	**5**	**0**	**1**	**1**	**2**	**0**	**0**	**0**	**22:30**
2002-03	**Philadelphia**	**NHL**	**79**	**8**	**24**	**32**	**35**	**1**	**0**	**2**	**197**	**4.1**	**30**	**0**	**0.0**	**22:55**	**5**	**2**	**1**	**3**	**0**	**0**	**0**	**0**	**27:38**
2003-04	**Philadelphia**	**NHL**	**48**	**1**	**11**	**12**	**28**	**0**	**0**	**0**	**92**	**1.1**	**11**	**1**	**0.0**	**22:29**	....	....	....	....	....	....	....	....	....
2004-05			DID NOT PLAY																						
	NHL Totals		**1098**	**132**	**419**	**551**	**701**	**55**	**5**	**23**	**2298**	**5.7**		**7**	**42.9**	**24:41**	**162**	**22**	**54**	**76**	**87**	**7**	**0**	**5**	**27:02**

QMJHL Second All-Star Team (1987) • QMJHL First All-Star Team (1988) • NHL Second All-Star Team (1999, 2000)

Played in NHL All-Star Game (1992, 1996, 2000)

Traded to **Philadelphia** by **Montreal** with Gilbert Dionne and John LeClair for Mark Recchi and Philadelphia's 3rd round choice (Martin Hohenberger) in 1995 Entry Draft, February 9, 1995.

DEVEREAUX, Boyd
(DEH-vuhr-oh, BOID) **PHX.**

Center. Shoots left. 6'2", 195 lbs. Born, Seaforth, Ont., April 16, 1978. Edmonton's 1st choice, 6th overall, in 1996 Entry Draft.

Season	Club	League	GP	G	A	Pts	PIM	PP	SH	GW	S	%	+/-	TF	F%	Min	GP	G	A	Pts	PIM	PP	SH	GW	Min
1992-93	Seaforth Sailors	OHA-D	34	7	20	27	13	....	....	....	....	....	....	....	....	....	....	....	....	....	....	....	....	....	....
1993-94	Stratford Cullitons	OHA-B	46	12	27	39	8	....	....	....	....	....	....	....	....	....	....	....	....	....	....	....	....	....	....
1994-95	Stratford Cullitons	OHA-B	45	31	74	105	21	....	....	....	....	....	....	....	....	....	....	....	....	....	....	....	....	....	....
1995-96	Kitchener Rangers	OHL	66	20	38	58	35	....	....	....	....	....	....	....	....	....	12	3	7	10	4	....	....	....	....
1996-97	Kitchener Rangers	OHL	54	28	41	69	37	....	....	....	....	....	....	....	....	....	13	4	11	15	8	....	....	....	....
	Hamilton	AHL	....	....	....	....	....	....	....	....	....	....	....	....	....	....	1	0	1	1	0	....	....	....	....
1997-98	**Edmonton**	**NHL**	**38**	**1**	**4**	**5**	**6**	**0**	**0**	**0**	**27**	**3.7**	**–5**	....	....	....	....	....	....	....	....	....	....	....	....
	Hamilton	AHL	14	5	6	11	6	....	....	....	....	....	....	....	....	....	9	1	1	2	8	....	....	....	....
1998-99	**Edmonton**	**NHL**	**61**	**6**	**8**	**14**	**23**	**0**	**1**	**4**	**39**	**15.4**	**2**	**409**	**42.8**	**10:09**	**1**	**0**	**0**	**0**	**0**	**0**	**0**	**0**	**32:46**
	Hamilton	AHL	7	4	6	10	2	....	....	....	....	....	....	....	....	....	8	0	3	3	4	....	....	....	....
99-2000	**Edmonton**	**NHL**	**76**	**8**	**19**	**27**	**20**	**0**	**1**	**2**	**108**	**7.4**	**7**	**241**	**34.9**	**12:36**	....	....	....	....	....	....	....	....	....
2000-01	**Detroit**	**NHL**	**55**	**5**	**6**	**11**	**14**	**0**	**0**	**0**	**66**	**7.6**	**1**	**124**	**37.1**	**10:08**	**2**	**0**	**0**	**0**	**0**	**0**	**0**	**0**	**10:39**
2001-02 ♦	**Detroit**	**NHL**	**79**	**9**	**16**	**25**	**24**	**0**	**0**	**2**	**116**	**7.8**	**9**	**12**	**33.3**	**11:30**	**21**	**2**	**4**	**6**	**4**	**0**	**0**	**0**	**10:58**
2002-03	**Detroit**	**NHL**	**61**	**3**	**9**	**12**	**16**	**0**	**0**	**1**	**72**	**4.2**	**4**	**7**	**42.9**	**9:26**	....	....	....	....	....	....	....	....	....
2003-04	**Detroit**	**NHL**	**61**	**6**	**9**	**15**	**20**	**0**	**0**	**2**	**62**	**9.7**	**–1**	**14**	**50.0**	**9:58**	**3**	**1**	**0**	**1**	**0**	**0**	**0**	**0**	**6:36**
2004-05			DID NOT PLAY																						
	NHL Totals		**431**	**38**	**71**	**109**	**123**	**0**	**2**	**11**	**490**	**7.8**		**807**	**39.5**	**10:45**	**27**	**3**	**4**	**7**	**4**	**0**	**0**	**0**	**11:16**

Canadian Major Junior Scholastic Player of the Year (1996)

Signed as a free agent by **Detroit**, August 23, 2000. Signed as a free agent by **Phoenix**, July 5, 2004.

de VRIES, Greg
(deh-VREES, GREHG) **ATL.**

Defense. Shoots left. 6'3", 215 lbs. Born, Sundridge, Ont., January 4, 1973.

Season	Club	League	GP	G	A	Pts	PIM	PP	SH	GW	S	%	+/-	TF	F%	Min	GP	G	A	Pts	PIM	PP	SH	GW	Min
1988-89	Cortina Astros	OMHA	35	28	40	68	....	....	....	....	....	....	....	....	....	....	....	....	....	....	....	....	....	....	....
1989-90	Aurora Eagles	OHA-B	42	1	16	17	32	....	....	....	....	....	....	....	....	....	....	....	....	....	....	....	....	....	....
1990-91	Stratford Cullitons	OHA-B	40	8	32	40	120	....	....	....	....	....	....	....	....	....	3	2	1	3	20	....	....	....	....
1991-92	Thorold	OHA-B	3	0	0	0	0	....	....	....	....	....	....	....	....	....	....	....	....	....	....	....	....	....	....
	Bowling Green	CCHA	24	0	3	3	20	....	....	....	....	....	....	....	....	....	....	....	....	....	....	....	....	....	....
1992-93	Niagara Falls	OHL	62	3	23	26	86	....	....	....	....	....	....	....	....	....	4	0	1	1	6	....	....	....	....
1993-94	Niagara Falls	OHL	64	5	40	45	135	....	....	....	....	....	....	....	....	....	....	....	....	....	....	....	....	....	....
	Cape Breton	AHL	9	0	0	0	11	....	....	....	....	....	....	....	....	....	1	0	0	0	0	....	....	....	....
1994-95	Cape Breton	AHL	77	5	19	24	68	....	....	....	....	....	....	....	....	....	....	....	....	....	....	....	....	....	....
1995-96	**Edmonton**	**NHL**	**13**	**1**	**1**	**2**	**12**	**0**	**0**	**0**	**8**	**12.5**	**–2**	....	....	....	....	....	....	....	....	....	....	....	....
	Cape Breton	AHL	58	9	30	39	174	....	....	....	....	....	....	....	....	....	....	....	....	....	....	....	....	....	....
1996-97	**Edmonton**	**NHL**	**37**	**0**	**4**	**4**	**52**	**0**	**0**	**0**	**31**	**0.0**	**–2**	....	....	....	**12**	**0**	**1**	**1**	**8**	**0**	**0**	**0**	....
	Hamilton	AHL	34	4	14	18	26	....	....	....	....	....	....	....	....	....	....	....	....	....	....	....	....	....	....
1997-98	**Edmonton**	**NHL**	**65**	**7**	**4**	**11**	**80**	**1**	**0**	**0**	**53**	**13.2**	**–17**	....	....	....	**7**	**0**	**0**	**0**	**21**	**0**	**0**	**0**	....
1998-99	**Nashville**	**NHL**	**6**	**0**	**0**	**0**	**4**	**0**	**0**	**0**	**1**	**1.0**	**–4**	**0**	**0.0**	**18:11**	....	....	....	....	....	....	....	....	....
	Colorado	**NHL**	**67**	**1**	**3**	**4**	**60**	**0**	**0**	**0**	**56**	**56.0**	**–3**	**1**	**100.0**	**16:23**	**19**	**0**	**2**	**2**	**22**	**0**	**0**	**0**	**12:09**
99-2000	**Colorado**	**NHL**	**69**	**2**	**7**	**9**	**73**	**0**	**0**	**0**	**40**	**5.0**	**–7**	**0**	**0.0**	**14:59**	**5**	**0**	**0**	**0**	**4**	**0**	**0**	**0**	**8:09**
2000-01 ♦	**Colorado**	**NHL**	**79**	**5**	**12**	**17**	**51**	**0**	**0**	**0**	**76**	**6.6**	**23**	**0**	**0.0**	**17:06**	**23**	**0**	**1**	**1**	**20**	**0**	**0**	**0**	**14:17**
2001-02	**Colorado**	**NHL**	**82**	**8**	**12**	**20**	**57**	**1**	**1**	**3**	**148**	**5.4**	**18**	**1**	**0.0**	**23:03**	**21**	**4**	**9**	**13**	**2**	**0**	**0**	**1**	**24:12**
2002-03	**Colorado**	**NHL**	**82**	**6**	**26**	**32**	**70**	**0**	**0**	**2**	**112**	**5.4**	**15**	**1**	**100.0**	**22:15**	**7**	**2**	**0**	**2**	**0**	**0**	**0**	**0**	**22:11**
2003-04	**NY Rangers**	**NHL**	**53**	**3**	**12**	**15**	**37**	**0**	**0**	**0**	**58**	**5.2**	**12**	**0**	**0.0**	**19:01**	....	....	....	....	....	....	....	....	....
	Ottawa	**NHL**	**13**	**0**	**1**	**1**	**6**	**0**	**0**	**0**	**12**	**0.0**	**0**	**0**	**0.0**	**17:51**	**7**	**0**	**1**	**1**	**8**	**0**	**0**	**0**	**17:51**
2004-05			DID NOT PLAY																						
	NHL Totals		**566**	**33**	**82**	**115**	**502**	**2**	**1**	**5**	**595**	**5.5**		**3**	**66.7**	**18:57**	**101**	**6**	**14**	**20**	**85**	**0**	**0**	**1**	**16:56**

Signed as a free agent by **Edmonton**, March 20, 1994. Traded to **Nashville** by **Edmonton** with Eric Fichaud and Drake Berehowsky for Mikhail Shtalenkov and Jim Dowd, October 1, 1998. Traded to **Colorado** by **Nashville** for Colorado's 2nd round choice (Ed Hill) in 1999 Entry Draft, October 24, 1998. Signed as a free agent by **NY Rangers**, July 14, 2003. Traded to **Ottawa** by **NY Rangers** for Karel Rachunek and Alexandre Giroux, March 9, 2004. Traded to **Atlanta** by **Ottawa** with Marian Hossa for Dany Heatley, August 23, 2005.

DiMAIO, Rob
(duh-MIGH-oh, RAWB) **T.B.**

Right wing. Shoots right. 5'10", 190 lbs. Born, Calgary, Alta., February 19, 1968. NY Islanders' 6th choice, 118th overall, in 1987 Entry Draft.

Season	Club	League	GP	G	A	Pts	PIM	PP	SH	GW	S	%	+/-	TF	F%	Min	GP	G	A	Pts	PIM	PP	SH	GW	Min
1984-85	Kamloops Blazers	WHL	55	9	18	27	29	....	....	....	....	....	....	....	....	....	7	1	3	4	2	....	....	....	....
1985-86	Kamloops Blazers	WHL	6	1	0	1	0	....	....	....	....	....	....	....	....	....	....	....	....	....	....	....	....	....	....
	Medicine Hat	WHL	55	20	30	50	82	....	....	....	....	....	....	....	....	....	22	6	6	12	39	....	....	....	....
1986-87	Medicine Hat	WHL	70	27	43	70	130	....	....	....	....	....	....	....	....	....	20	7	11	18	46	....	....	....	....
1987-88	Medicine Hat	WHL	54	47	43	90	120	....	....	....	....	....	....	....	....	....	14	12	19	*31	59	....	....	....	....
1988-89	**NY Islanders**	**NHL**	**16**	**1**	**0**	**1**	**30**	**0**	**0**	**1**	**16**	**6.3**	**–6**	....	....	....	....	....	....	....	....	....	....	....	....
	Springfield	AHL	40	13	18	31	67	....	....	....	....	....	....	....	....	....	....	....	....	....	....	....	....	....	....
1989-90	**NY Islanders**	**NHL**	**7**	**0**	**0**	**0**	**2**	**0**	**0**	**0**	**2**	**0.0**	**0**	....	....	....	**1**	**1**	**0**	**1**	**4**	**0**	**0**	**0**	....
	Springfield	AHL	54	25	27	52	69	....	....	....	....	....	....	....	....	....	16	4	7	11	45	....	....	....	....
1990-91	**NY Islanders**	**NHL**	**1**	**0**	**0**	**0**	**0**	**0**	**0**	**0**	**0**	**0.0**	**0**	....	....	....	....	....	....	....	....	....	....	....	....
	Capital District	AHL	12	3	4	7	22	....	....	....	....	....	....	....	....	....	....	....	....	....	....	....	....	....	....
1991-92	**NY Islanders**	**NHL**	**50**	**5**	**2**	**7**	**43**	**0**	**2**	**0**	**43**	**11.6**	**–23**	....	....	....	....	....	....	....	....	....	....	....	....
1992-93	**Tampa Bay**	**NHL**	**54**	**9**	**15**	**24**	**62**	**2**	**0**	**0**	**75**	**12.0**	**0**	....	....	....	....	....	....	....	....	....	....	....	....
1993-94	**Tampa Bay**	**NHL**	**39**	**8**	**7**	**15**	**40**	**2**	**0**	**1**	**51**	**15.7**	**–5**	....	....	....	....	....	....	....	....	....	....	....	....
	Philadelphia	**NHL**	**14**	**3**	**5**	**8**	**6**	**0**	**0**	**1**	**30**	**10.0**	**1**	....	....	....	....	....	....	....	....	....	....	....	....
1994-95	**Philadelphia**	**NHL**	**36**	**3**	**1**	**4**	**53**	**0**	**0**	**0**	**34**	**8.8**	**8**	....	....	....	**15**	**2**	**4**	**6**	**4**	**0**	**1**	**1**	....
1995-96	**Philadelphia**	**NHL**	**59**	**6**	**15**	**21**	**58**	**1**	**1**	**0**	**49**	**12.2**	**0**	....	....	....	**3**	**0**	**0**	**0**	**0**	**0**	**0**	**0**	....
1996-97	**Boston**	**NHL**	**72**	**13**	**15**	**28**	**82**	**0**	**3**	**2**	**152**	**8.6**	**–21**	....	....	....	....	....	....	....	....	....	....	....	....
1997-98	**Boston**	**NHL**	**79**	**10**	**17**	**27**	**82**	**0**	**0**	**4**	**112**	**8.9**	**–13**	....	....	....	**6**	**1**	**0**	**1**	**8**	**0**	**0**	**0**	....
1998-99	**Boston**	**NHL**	**71**	**7**	**14**	**21**	**95**	**1**	**0**	**0**	**121**	**5.8**	**–14**	**83**	**45.8**	**16:41**	**12**	**2**	**0**	**2**	**8**	**0**	**0**	**1**	**16:50**
99-2000	**Boston**	**NHL**	**50**	**5**	**16**	**21**	**42**	**0**	**0**	**0**	**93**	**5.4**	**–1**	**278**	**44.2**	**16:47**	....	....	....	....	....	....	....	....	....
	NY Rangers	**NHL**	**12**	**1**	**3**	**4**	**8**	**0**	**0**	**0**	**18**	**5.6**	**–8**	**1**	**0.0**	**15:30**	....	....	....	....	....	....	....	....	....
2000-01	**Carolina**	**NHL**	**74**	**6**	**18**	**24**	**54**	**0**	**2**	**1**	**99**	**6.1**	**–14**	**46**	**43.5**	**14:58**	**6**	**0**	**0**	**0**	**4**	**0**	**0**	**0**	**14:30**
2001-02	**Dallas**	**NHL**	**61**	**6**	**6**	**12**	**25**	**0**	**2**	**2**	**63**	**9.5**	**–2**	**76**	**44.7**	**10:52**	....	....	....	....	....	....	....	....	....
	Utah Grizzlies	AHL	3	1	1	2	0	....	....	....	....	....	....	....	....	....	....	....	....	....	....	....	....	....	....
2002-03	**Dallas**	**NHL**	**69**	**10**	**9**	**19**	**76**	**0**	**0**	**2**	**81**	**12.3**	**18**	**49**	**44.9**	**12:58**	**12**	**1**	**4**	**5**	**10**	**0**	**0**	**0**	**15:50**
2003-04	**Dallas**	**NHL**	**69**	**9**	**15**	**24**	**52**	**0**	**1**	**1**	**76**	**11.8**	**2**	**21**	**38.1**	**12:58**	**5**	**0**	**1**	**1**	**2**	**0**	**0**	**0**	**10:28**
2004-05	Langnau	Swiss	9	2	3	5	8	....	....	....	....	....	....	....	....	....	....	....	....	....	....	....	....	....	....
	Milano	Italy	9	4	8	12	4	....	....	....	....	....	....	....	....	....	15	9	11	20	20	....	....	....	....
	NHL Totals		**833**	**102**	**158**	**260**	**810**	**6**	**11**	**15**	**1115**	**9.1**		**554**	**44.2**	**14:13**	**60**	**7**	**9**	**16**	**40**	**0**	**1**	**2**	**15:11**

Memorial Cup Tournament All-Star Team (1988) • Stafford Smythe Memorial Trophy (Memorial Cup Tournament MVP) (1988)

Claimed by **Tampa Bay** from **NY Islanders** in Expansion Draft, June 18, 1992. Traded to **Philadelphia** by **Tampa Bay** for Jim Cummins and Philadelphia's 4th round choice (later traded back to Philadelphia – Philadelphia selected Radovan Somik) in 1995 Entry Draft, March 18, 1994. Claimed by **San Jose** from **Philadelphia** in Waiver Draft, September 30, 1996. Traded to **Boston** by **San Jose** for Boston's 5th round choice (Adam Nittel) in 1997 Entry Draft, September 30, 1996. Traded to **NY Rangers** by **Boston** for Mike Knuble, March 10, 2000. Traded to **Carolina** by **NY Rangers** with Darren Langdon for Sandy McCarthy and Carolina's 4th round choice (Bryce Lampman) in 2001 Entry Draft, August 4, 2000. Signed as a free agent by **Dallas**, July 1, 2001. Signed as a free agent by **Langnau** (Swiss), November 20, 2004. Signed as a free agent by **Milano** (Italy), December 20, 2004. Signed as a free agent by **Tampa Bay**, August 9, 2005.

			Regular Season														Playoffs								
Season	Club	League	GP	G	A	Pts	PIM	PP	SH	GW	S	%	+/-	TF	F%	Min	GP	G	A	Pts	PIM	PP	SH	GW	Min

DIMITRAKOS, Niko

(DIH-mih-tra-kohs, NEEK-oh) **S.J.**

Right wing. Shoots right. 5'10", 205 lbs. Born, Sommerville, MA, May 21, 1979. San Jose's 4th choice, 155th overall, in 1999 Entry Draft.

Season	Club	League	GP	G	A	Pts	PIM	PP	SH	GW	S	%	+/-	TF	F%	Min	GP	G	A	Pts	PIM	PP	SH	GW	Min
1994-95	Matignon	High-MA	23	10	12	22	....	....	....	....	....	....	....	....	....	....	....	....	....	....	....	....	....	....	....
1995-96	Matignon	High-MA	25	12	28	40	....	....	....	....	....	....	....	....	....	....	....	....	....	....	....	....	....	....	....
1996-97	Matignon	High-MA	25	23	32	55	....	....	....	....	....	....	....	....	....	....	....	....	....	....	....	....	....	....	....
1997-98	Avon Old Farms	High-CT	26	27	28	55	....	....	....	....	....	....	....	....	....	....	....	....	....	....	....	....	....	....	....
1998-99	U. of Maine	H-East	35	8	19	27	33	....	....	....	....	....	....	....	....	....	....	....	....	....	....	....	....	....	....
99-2000	U. of Maine	H-East	32	11	16	27	16	....	....	....	....	....	....	....	....	....	....	....	....	....	....	....	....	....	....
2000-01	U. of Maine	H-East	29	11	14	25	43	....	....	....	....	....	....	....	....	....	....	....	....	....	....	....	....	....	....
2001-02	U. of Maine	H-East	43	20	31	51	44	....	....	....	....	....	....	....	....	....	....	....	....	....	....	....	....	....	....
2002-03	**San Jose**	**NHL**	**21**	**6**	**7**	**13**	**8**	**3**	**0**	**0**	**34**	**17.6**	**-7**	**2**	**50.0**	**14:15**	....	....	....	....	....	....	....	....	....
	Cleveland Barons	AHL	55	15	29	44	30	....	....	....	....	....	....	....	....	....	....	....	....	....	....	....	....	....	....
2003-04	**San Jose**	**NHL**	**68**	**9**	**15**	**24**	**49**	**2**	**0**	**4**	**116**	**7.8**	**6**	**4**	**50.0**	**13:20**	**15**	**1**	**8**	**9**	**8**	**0**	**0**	**1**	**14:31**
	Cleveland Barons	AHL	7	4	4	8	4	....	....	....	....	....	....	....	....	....	....	....	....	....	....	....	....	....	....
2004-05	Langnau	Swiss	3	0	1	1	2	....	....	....	....	....	....	....	....	....	6	3	3	6	16	....	....	....	....
	NHL Totals		**89**	**15**	**22**	**37**	**57**	**5**	**0**	**4**	**150**	**10.0**		**6**	**50.0**	**13:33**	**15**	**1**	**8**	**9**	**8**	**0**	**0**	**1**	**14:31**

NCAA Championship All-Tournament Team (1999) • Hockey East Second All-Star Team (2002)

Signed as a free agent by **Langnau** (Swiss), February 2, 2005.

DINGMAN, Chris

(DIHNG-man, KRIHS) **T.B.**

Left wing. Shoots left. 6'4", 235 lbs. Born, Edmonton, Alta., July 6, 1976. Calgary's 1st choice, 19th overall, in 1994 Entry Draft.

Season	Club	League	GP	G	A	Pts	PIM	PP	SH	GW	S	%	+/-	TF	F%	Min	GP	G	A	Pts	PIM	PP	SH	GW	Min
1991-92	Edm. Mercurys	AMHL	36	23	18	41	72	....	....	....	....	....	....	....	....	....	....	....	....	....	....	....	....	....	....
1992-93	Brandon	WHL	50	10	17	27	64	....	....	....	....	....	....	....	....	....	4	0	0	0	0	....	....	....	....
1993-94	Brandon	WHL	45	21	20	41	77	....	....	....	....	....	....	....	....	....	13	1	7	8	39	....	....	....	....
1994-95	Brandon	WHL	66	40	43	83	201	....	....	....	....	....	....	....	....	....	3	1	0	1	9	....	....	....	....
1995-96	Brandon	WHL	40	16	29	45	109	....	....	....	....	....	....	....	....	....	19	12	11	23	60	....	....	....	....
	Saint John Flames	AHL	....	....	....	....	....	....	....	....	....	....	....	....	....	....	1	0	0	0	0	....	....	....	....
1996-97	Saint John Flames	AHL	71	5	6	11	195	....	....	....	....	....	....	....	....	....	....	....	....	....	....	....	....	....	....
1997-98	**Calgary**	**NHL**	**70**	**3**	**3**	**6**	**149**	**1**	**0**	**0**	**47**	**6.4**	**-11**	....	....	....	....	....	....	....	....	....	....	....	....
1998-99	**Calgary**	**NHL**	**2**	**0**	**0**	**0**	**17**	**0**	**0**	**0**	**1**	**0.0**	**-2**	**0**	**0.0**	**8:11**	....	....	....	....	....	....	....	....	....
	Saint John Flames	AHL	50	5	7	12	140	....	....	....	....	....	....	....	....	....	....	....	....	....	....	....	....	....	....
	Colorado	**NHL**	**1**	**0**	**0**	**0**	**7**	**0**	**0**	**0**	**0**	**0.0**	**0**	**0**	**0.0**	**0:30**	....	....	....	....	....	....	....	....	....
	Hershey Bears	AHL	17	1	3	4	102	....	....	....	....	....	....	....	....	....	5	0	2	2	6	....	....	....	....
99-2000	**Colorado**	**NHL**	**68**	**8**	**3**	**11**	**132**	**2**	**0**	**1**	**54**	**14.8**	**-2**	**2**	**0.0**	**6:29**	....	....	....	....	....	....	....	....	....
2000-01♦	**Colorado**	**NHL**	**41**	**1**	**1**	**2**	**108**	**0**	**0**	**0**	**33**	**3.0**	**-3**	**0**	**0.0**	**6:26**	**16**	**0**	**4**	**4**	**14**	**0**	**0**	**0**	**6:18**
2001-02	**Carolina**	**NHL**	**30**	**0**	**1**	**1**	**77**	**0**	**0**	**0**	**17**	**0.0**	**-2**	**2**	**100.0**	**6:54**	....	....	....	....	....	....	....	....	....
	Tampa Bay	**NHL**	**14**	**0**	**4**	**4**	**26**	**0**	**0**	**0**	**24**	**0.0**	**-8**	**0**	**0.0**	**10:43**	....	....	....	....	....	....	....	....	....
2002-03	**Tampa Bay**	**NHL**	**51**	**2**	**1**	**3**	**91**	**0**	**0**	**0**	**41**	**4.9**	**-11**	**3**	**33.3**	**9:34**	**10**	**1**	**0**	**1**	**4**	**0**	**0**	**0**	**12:45**
2003-04♦	**Tampa Bay**	**NHL**	**74**	**1**	**5**	**6**	**140**	**0**	**0**	**0**	**65**	**1.5**	**-9**	**20**	**30.0**	**8:16**	**23**	**1**	**1**	**2**	**63**	**0**	**0**	**0**	**5:58**
2004-05			DID NOT PLAY																						
	NHL Totals		**351**	**15**	**18**	**33**	**747**	**3**	**0**	**1**	**282**	**5.3**		**27**	**33.3**	**7:45**	**49**	**2**	**5**	**7**	**81**	**0**	**0**	**0**	**7:28**

Traded to **Colorado** by **Calgary** with Theoren Fleury for Rene Corbet, Wade Belak, Robyn Regehr and Colorado's 2nd round compensatory choice (Jarret Stoll) in 2000 Entry Draft, February 28, 1999. • Missed majority of 2000-01 season recovering from knee injury suffered in game vs. Ottawa, November 15, 2000. Traded to **Carolina** by **Colorado** for Carolina's 5th round choice (Mikko Viitanen) in 2001 Entry Draft, June 24, 2001. Traded to **Tampa Bay** by **Carolina** with Shane Willis for Kevin Weekes, March 5, 2002.

DiPENTA, Joe

(DIH-pehn-tah, JOH) **ANA.**

Defense. Shoots left. 6'2", 235 lbs. Born, Barrie, Ont., February 25, 1979. Florida's 2nd choice, 61st overall, in 1998 Entry Draft.

Season	Club	League	GP	G	A	Pts	PIM	PP	SH	GW	S	%	+/-	TF	F%	Min	GP	G	A	Pts	PIM	PP	SH	GW	Min
1996-97	Smiths Falls Bears	CJHL	54	13	22	35	92	....	....	....	....	....	....	....	....	....	....	....	....	....	....	....	....	....	....
1997-98	Boston University	H-East	38	2	16	18	50	....	....	....	....	....	....	....	....	....	....	....	....	....	....	....	....	....	....
1998-99	Boston University	H-East	36	2	15	17	72	....	....	....	....	....	....	....	....	....	....	....	....	....	....	....	....	....	....
99-2000	Halifax	QMJHL	63	13	43	56	83	....	....	....	....	....	....	....	....	....	10	3	4	7	26	....	....	....	....
2000-01	Philadelphia	AHL	71	3	5	8	65	....	....	....	....	....	....	....	....	....	10	1	2	3	15	....	....	....	....
2001-02	Philadelphia	AHL	61	2	4	6	71	....	....	....	....	....	....	....	....	....	....	....	....	....	....	....	....	....	....
	Chicago Wolves	AHL	15	0	2	2	15	....	....	....	....	....	....	....	....	....	25	1	3	4	22	....	....	....	....
2002-03	**Atlanta**	**NHL**	**3**	**1**	**1**	**2**	**0**	**0**	**0**	**0**	**2**	**50.0**	**3**	**0**	**0.0**	**15:47**	....	....	....	....	....	....	....	....	....
	Chicago Wolves	AHL	76	2	17	19	107	....	....	....	....	....	....	....	....	....	9	0	1	1	7	....	....	....	....
2003-04	Chicago Wolves	AHL	73	0	6	6	105	....	....	....	....	....	....	....	....	....	10	1	0	1	13	....	....	....	....
2004-05	Manitoba Moose	AHL	73	2	10	12	48	....	....	....	....	....	....	....	....	....	14	0	5	5	2	....	....	....	....
	NHL Totals		**3**	**1**	**1**	**2**	**0**	**0**	**0**	**0**	**2**	**50.0**		**0**	**0.0**	**15:47**									

• Left **Boston U.** (H-East) and signed with **Halifax** (QMJHL), May 2, 1999. Signed as a free agent by **Philadelphia**, July 12, 2000. Traded to **Atlanta** by **Philadelphia** for Jarrod Skalde, March 5, 2002. Signed as a free agent by **Vancouver**, August 19, 2004. Signed as a free agent by **Anaheim**, August 11, 2005.

DOAN, Shane

(DOHN, SHAYN) **PHX.**

Right wing. Shoots right. 6'2", 216 lbs. Born, Halkirk, Alta., October 10, 1976. Winnipeg's 1st choice, 7th overall, in 1995 Entry Draft.

Season	Club	League	GP	G	A	Pts	PIM	PP	SH	GW	S	%	+/-	TF	F%	Min	GP	G	A	Pts	PIM	PP	SH	GW	Min
1991-92	Killam Selects	AAHA	56	80	84	164	74	....	....	....	....	....	....	....	....	....	....	....	....	....	....	....	....	....	....
1992-93	Kamloops Blazers	WHL	51	7	12	19	65	....	....	....	....	....	....	....	....	....	13	0	1	1	8	....	....	....	....
1993-94	Kamloops Blazers	WHL	52	24	24	48	88	....	....	....	....	....	....	....	....	....	....	....	....	....	....	....	....	....	....
1994-95	Kamloops Blazers	WHL	71	37	57	94	106	....	....	....	....	....	....	....	....	....	21	6	10	16	16	....	....	....	....
1995-96	**Winnipeg**	**NHL**	**74**	**7**	**10**	**17**	**101**	**1**	**0**	**3**	**106**	**6.6**	**-9**	....	....	....	**6**	**0**	**0**	**0**	**6**	**0**	**0**	**0**	....
1996-97	**Phoenix**	**NHL**	**63**	**4**	**8**	**12**	**49**	**0**	**0**	**0**	**100**	**4.0**	**-3**	....	....	....	**4**	**0**	**0**	**0**	**2**	**0**	**0**	**0**	....
1997-98	**Phoenix**	**NHL**	**33**	**5**	**6**	**11**	**35**	**0**	**0**	**3**	**42**	**11.9**	**-3**	....	....	....	**6**	**1**	**0**	**1**	**6**	**0**	**0**	**0**	....
	Springfield	AHL	39	21	21	42	64	....	....	....	....	....	....	....	....	....	....	....	....	....	....	....	....	....	....
1998-99	**Phoenix**	**NHL**	**79**	**6**	**16**	**22**	**54**	**0**	**0**	**0**	**156**	**3.8**	**-5**	**6**	**16.7**	**12:42**	**7**	**2**	**2**	**4**	**6**	**0**	**0**	**2**	**17:58**
99-2000	**Phoenix**	**NHL**	**81**	**26**	**25**	**51**	**66**	**1**	**1**	**4**	**221**	**11.8**	**6**	**25**	**36.0**	**16:51**	**4**	**1**	**2**	**3**	**8**	**1**	**0**	**0**	**18:11**
2000-01	**Phoenix**	**NHL**	**76**	**26**	**37**	**63**	**89**	**6**	**1**	**6**	**220**	**11.8**	**0**	**15**	**40.0**	**19:32**	....	....	....	....	....	....	....	....	....
2001-02	**Phoenix**	**NHL**	**81**	**20**	**29**	**49**	**61**	**6**	**0**	**2**	**205**	**9.8**	**11**	**52**	**44.2**	**18:10**	**5**	**2**	**2**	**4**	**6**	**0**	**0**	**0**	**17:21**
2002-03	**Phoenix**	**NHL**	**82**	**21**	**37**	**58**	**86**	**7**	**0**	**2**	**225**	**9.3**	**3**	**623**	**39.8**	**18:47**	....	....	....	....	....	....	....	....	....
2003-04	**Phoenix**	**NHL**	**79**	**27**	**41**	**68**	**47**	**9**	**2**	**1**	**254**	**10.6**	**-11**	**55**	**40.0**	**21:46**	....	....	....	....	....	....	....	....	....
2004-05			DID NOT PLAY																						
	NHL Totals		**648**	**142**	**209**	**351**	**588**	**30**	**4**	**21**	**1529**	**9.3**		**776**	**39.8**	**17:58**	**32**	**6**	**6**	**12**	**34**	**1**	**0**	**2**	**17:49**

Memorial Cup Tournament All-Star Team (1995) • Stafford Smythe Memorial Trophy (Memorial Cup Tournament MVP) (1995)

Played in NHL All-Star Game (2004)

Transferred to **Phoenix** after **Winnipeg** franchise relocated, July 1, 1996.

DOIG, Jason

(DOIG, JAY-suhn)

Defense. Shoots right. 6'3", 230 lbs. Born, Montreal, Que., January 29, 1977. Winnipeg's 3rd choice, 34th overall, in 1995 Entry Draft.

Season	Club	League	GP	G	A	Pts	PIM	PP	SH	GW	S	%	+/-	TF	F%	Min	GP	G	A	Pts	PIM	PP	SH	GW	Min
1990-91	North Shore	QAHA	31	30	33	63	53	....	....	....	....	....	....	....	....	....	....	....	....	....	....	....	....	....	....
1991-92	North Shore	QAHA	29	11	11	22	20	....	....	....	....	....	....	....	....	....	....	....	....	....	....	....	....	....	....
1992-93	Lac St-Louis Lions	QAAA	35	11	16	27	40	....	....	....	....	....	....	....	....	....	7	5	5	10	16	....	....	....	....
1993-94	St-Jean Lynx	QMJHL	63	8	17	25	65	....	....	....	....	....	....	....	....	....	5	0	2	2	2	....	....	....	....
1994-95	Laval Titan	QMJHL	55	13	42	55	259	....	....	....	....	....	....	....	....	....	20	4	13	17	39	....	....	....	....
1995-96	Laval Titan	QMJHL	5	3	6	9	20	....	....	....	....	....	....	....	....	....	....	....	....	....	....	....	....	....	....
	Granby	QMJHL	24	4	30	34	91	....	....	....	....	....	....	....	....	....	20	10	22	32	*110	....	....	....	....
	Winnipeg	**NHL**	**15**	**1**	**1**	**2**	**28**	**0**	**0**	**0**	**7**	**14.3**	**-2**	....	....	....	....	....	....	....	....	....	....	....	....
	Springfield	AHL	5	0	0	0	28	....	....	....	....	....	....	....	....	....	....	....	....	....	....	....	....	....	....
1996-97	Granby	QMJHL	39	14	33	47	211	....	....	....	....	....	....	....	....	....	5	0	4	4	27	....	....	....	....
	Las Vegas	IHL	6	0	1	1	19	....	....	....	....	....	....	....	....	....	....	....	....	....	....	....	....	....	....
	Springfield	AHL	5	0	3	3	2	....	....	....	....	....	....	....	....	....	17	1	4	5	37	....	....	....	....
1997-98	**Phoenix**	**NHL**	**4**	**0**	**1**	**1**	**12**	**0**	**0**	**0**	**1**	**0.0**	**-4**	....	....	....	....	....	....	....	....	....	....	....	....
	Springfield	AHL	46	2	25	27	153	....	....	....	....	....	....	....	....	....	3	0	0	0	2	....	....	....	....
1998-99	**Phoenix**	**NHL**	**9**	**0**	**1**	**1**	**10**	**0**	**0**	**0**	**0**	**0.0**	**2**	**0**	**0.0**	**5:08**	....	....	....	....	....	....	....	....	....
	Springfield	AHL	32	3	5	8	67	....	....	....	....	....	....	....	....	....	....	....	....	....	....	....	....	....	....
	Hartford	AHL	8	1	4	5	40	....	....	....	....	....	....	....	....	....	7	1	1	2	39	....	....	....	....

			Regular Season														Playoffs								
Season	Club	League	GP	G	A	Pts	PIM	PP	SH	GW	S	%	+/-	TF	F%	Min	GP	G	A	Pts	PIM	PP	SH	GW	Min
99-2000	NY Rangers	NHL	7	0	1	1	22	0	0	0	3	0.0	–2	0	0.0	8:50									
	Hartford	AHL	27	3	11	14	70										21	1	5	6	20				
2000-01	NY Rangers	NHL	3	0	0	0	0	0	0	0	1	0.0	0	0	0.0	6:35									
	Hartford	AHL	52	4	20	24	178										5	0	1	1	4				
2001-02	Grand Rapids	AHL	57	1	17	18	103										5	0	0	0	18				
2002-03	Washington	NHL	55	3	5	8	108	0	0	1	41	7.3	–3	1	0.0	14:11	6	0	1	1	6	0	0	0	16:52
	Portland Pirates	AHL	21	1	4	5	66																		
2003-04	Washington	NHL	65	2	9	11	105	0	0	0	59	3.4	–12	0	0.0	19:09									
2004-05		DID NOT PLAY																							
	NHL Totals		158	6	18	24	285	0	0	1	112	5.4		1	0.0	15:29	6	0	1	1	6	0	0	0	16:52

QMJHL All-Rookie Team (1994) • Memorial Cup Tournament All-Star Team (1996)

Transferred to **Phoenix** after **Winnipeg** franchise relocated, July 1, 1996. Traded to **NY Rangers** by **Phoenix** with Phoenix's 6th round choice (Jay Dardis) in 1999 Entry Draft for Stan Neckar, March 23, 1999. Traded to **Ottawa** by **NY Rangers** with Jeff Ulmer for Sean Gagnon, June 29, 2001. Signed as free agent by **Washington**, September 12, 2002.

DOME, Robert
(doh-MAY, RAW-buhrt)

Right wing. Shoots left. 6', 210 lbs. Born, Skalica, Czech., January 29, 1979. Pittsburgh's 1st choice, 17th overall, in 1997 Entry Draft.

Season	Club	League	GP	G	A	Pts	PIM	PP	SH	GW	S	%	+/-	TF	F%	Min	GP	G	A	Pts	PIM	PP	SH	GW	Min
1994-95	Dukla Trencin Jr.	Slovak-Jr.	36	36	43	79	39																		
1995-96	Utah Grizzlies	IHL	56	10	9	19	28																		
1996-97	Long Beach	IHL	13	4	6	10	14																		
	Las Vegas	IHL	43	10	7	17	22																		
1997-98	Pittsburgh	NHL	30	5	2	7	12	1	0	0	29	17.2	–1												
	Syracuse Crunch	AHL	36	21	25	46	77																		
1998-99	Syracuse Crunch	AHL	48	18	17	35	70																		
	Houston Aeros	IHL	20	2	4	6	24																		
99-2000	Pittsburgh	NHL	22	2	5	7	0	0	0	0	27	7.4	1	5	40.0	9:51									
	Wilkes-Barre	AHL	51	12	26	38	83																		
2000-01	Kladno	CzRep	29	9	12	21	57																		
	HC Ocelari Trinec	CzRep	5	0	3	3	4																		
2001-02	Wilkes-Barre	AHL	39	9	8	17	53																		
2002-03	Calgary	NHL	1	0	0	0	0	0	0	0	1	0.0	0	0	0.0	8:16									
	Saint John Flames	AHL	56	27	29	56	41																		
2003-04	Lowell	AHL	13	5	7	12	19																		
	Sodertalje SK	Sweden	28	10	19	29	8																		
2004-05	Sodertalje SK	Sweden	50	12	10	22	92										10	0	1	1	8				
	NHL Totals		53	7	7	14	12	1	0	0	57	12.3		5	40.0	9:47									

• Missed majority of 2001-02 season recovering from heel injury suffered during off-season training, July 10, 2001. Signed as a free agent by **Calgary**, July 17, 2002. Assigned to **Sodertalje** (Sweden) by **Calgary**, November 19, 2003.

DOMI, Tie
(DOH-mee, TIGH) **TOR.**

Right wing. Shoots right. 5'10", 213 lbs. Born, Windsor, Ont., November 1, 1969. Toronto's 2nd choice, 27th overall, in 1988 Entry Draft.

Season	Club	League	GP	G	A	Pts	PIM	PP	SH	GW	S	%	+/-	TF	F%	Min	GP	G	A	Pts	PIM	PP	SH	GW	Min
1984-85	Belle River	OHA-C	28	7	5	12	98																		
1985-86	Windsor Bulldogs	OHA-B	42	8	17	25	*346																		
1986-87	Peterborough	OHA-B	2	0	0	0	10																		
	Peterborough	OHL	18	1	1	2	79																		
1987-88	Peterborough	OHL	60	22	21	43	*292										12	3	9	12	24				
1988-89	Peterborough	OHL	43	14	16	30	175										17	10	9	19	*70				
1989-90	Toronto	NHL	2	0	0	0	42	0	0	0	0	0.0	0												
	Newmarket Saints	AHL	57	14	11	25	285																		
1990-91	NY Rangers	NHL	28	1	0	1	185	0	0	0	5	20.0	–5												
	Binghamton	AHL	25	11	6	17	219										7	3	2	5	16				
1991-92	NY Rangers	NHL	42	2	4	6	246	0	0	1	20	10.0	–4				6	1	1	2	32	0	0	0	
1992-93	NY Rangers	NHL	12	2	0	2	95	0	0	0	11	18.2	–1												
	Winnipeg	NHL	49	3	10	13	249	0	0	0	29	10.3	2				6	1	0	1	23	0	0	0	
1993-94	Winnipeg	NHL	81	8	11	19	*347	0	0	1	98	8.2	–8												
1994-95	Winnipeg	NHL	31	4	4	8	128	0	0	0	34	11.8	–6												
	Toronto	NHL	9	0	1	1	31	0	0	0	12	0.0	1				7	1	0	1	0	0	0	0	
1995-96	Toronto	NHL	72	7	6	13	297	0	0	1	61	11.5	–3				6	0	2	2	4	0	0	0	
1996-97	Toronto	NHL	80	11	17	28	275	2	0	1	98	11.2	–17												
1997-98	Toronto	NHL	80	4	10	14	365	0	0	0	72	5.6	–5												
1998-99	Toronto	NHL	72	8	14	22	198	0	0	1	65	12.3	5	9	44.4	9:42	14	0	2	2	24	0	0	0	6:58
99-2000	Toronto	NHL	70	5	9	14	198	0	0	2	64	7.8	–5	4	25.0	9:58	12	0	1	1	20	0	0	0	6:40
2000-01	Toronto	NHL	82	13	7	20	214	1	0	1	60	21.7	2	5	80.0	8:23	8	0	1	1	20	0	0	0	8:27
2001-02	Toronto	NHL	74	9	10	19	157	0	0	2	93	9.7	3	22	45.5	10:20	19	1	3	4	*61	0	0	1	11:15
2002-03	Toronto	NHL	79	15	14	29	171	4	0	0	91	16.5	–1	21	19.1	10:56	7	1	0	1	13	0	0	0	14:47
2003-04	Toronto	NHL	80	7	13	20	208	1	0	0	84	8.3	–2	7	0.0	11:12	13	2	2	4	41	0	0	1	11:49
2004-05		DID NOT PLAY																							
	NHL Totals		943	99	130	229	3406	8	0	10	897	11.0		68	33.8	10:05	98	7	12	19	238	0	0	2	9:49

Traded to **NY Rangers** by **Toronto** with Mark LaForest for Greg Johnston, June 28, 1990. Traded to **Winnipeg** by **NY Rangers** with Kris King for Ed Olczyk, December 28, 1992. Traded to **Toronto** by **Winnipeg** for Mike Eastwood and Toronto's 3rd round choice (Brad Isbister) in 1995 Entry Draft, April 7, 1995. Traded to **Nashville** by **Toronto** for Nashville's 8th round choice (Shaun Landolt) in 2003 Entry Draft, June 30, 2002. Signed as a free agent by **Toronto**, July 14, 2002.

DONOVAN, Shean
(DAW-nuh-vuhn, SHAWN) **CGY.**

Right wing. Shoots right. 6'2", 200 lbs. Born, Timmins, Ont., January 22, 1975. San Jose's 2nd choice, 28th overall, in 1993 Entry Draft.

Season	Club	League	GP	G	A	Pts	PIM	PP	SH	GW	S	%	+/-	TF	F%	Min	GP	G	A	Pts	PIM	PP	SH	GW	Min
1990-91	Kanata Valley	CJHL	44	8	5	13	8																		
1991-92	Ottawa 67's	OHL	58	11	8	19	14										11	1	0	1	5				
1992-93	Ottawa 67's	OHL	66	29	23	52	33																		
1993-94	Ottawa 67's	OHL	62	35	49	84	63										17	10	11	21	14				
1994-95	Ottawa 67's	OHL	29	22	19	41	41																		
	San Jose	NHL	14	0	0	0	6	0	0	0	13	0.0	–6				7	0	1	1	6	0	0	0	
	Kansas City	IHL	5	0	2	2	7										14	5	3	8	23				
1995-96	San Jose	NHL	74	13	8	21	39	0	1	2	73	17.8	–17												
	Kansas City	IHL	4	0	0	0	8										5	0	0	0	8				
1996-97	San Jose	NHL	73	9	6	15	42	0	1	0	115	7.8	–18												
	Kentucky	AHL	3	1	3	4	18																		
1997-98	San Jose	NHL	20	3	3	6	22	0	0	0	24	12.5	3												
	Colorado	NHL	47	5	7	12	48	0	0	0	57	8.8	3												
1998-99	Colorado	NHL	68	7	12	19	37	1	0	1	81	8.6	4	9	22.2	8:46	5	0	0	0	2	0	0	0	4:55
99-2000	Colorado	NHL	18	1	0	1	8	0	0	0	13	7.7	–4	1	0.0	5:20									
	Atlanta	NHL	33	4	7	11	18	1	0	1	53	7.5	–13	22	31.8	14:19									
2000-01	Atlanta	NHL	63	12	11	23	47	1	3	1	93	12.9	–14	218	45.9	14:03									
2001-02	Atlanta	NHL	48	6	6	12	40	1	0	2	64	9.4	–16	12	50.0	13:30									
	Pittsburgh	NHL	13	2	1	3	4	0	0	0	18	11.1	–5	4	0.0	14:34									
2002-03	Pittsburgh	NHL	52	4	5	9	30	0	1	0	66	6.1	–6	37	24.3	13:01									
	Calgary	NHL	13	1	2	3	7	0	0	1	22	4.5	–2	3	66.7	15:39									
2003-04	Calgary	NHL	82	18	24	42	72	3	3	8	138	13.0	14	53	39.6	14:55	24	5	5	10	23	0	0	2	15:27
2004-05	Geneve	Swiss	12	5	3	8	30																		
	NHL Totals		618	85	92	177	420	7	9	16	830	10.2		359	40.9	12:48	36	5	6	11	31	0	0	2	13:38

Traded to **Colorado** by **San Jose** with San Jose's 1st round choice (Alex Tanguay) in 1998 Entry Draft for Mike Ricci and Colorado's 2nd round choice (later traded to Buffalo – Buffalo selected Jaroslav Kristek), in 1998 Entry Draft, November 21, 1997. Traded to **Atlanta** by **Colorado** for Rick Tabaracci, December 8, 1999. Claimed on waivers by **Pittsburgh** from **Atlanta**, March 15, 2002. Traded to **Calgary** by **Pittsburgh** for Micki Dupont and Mathias Johansson, March 11, 2003. Signed as a free agent by **Geneve** (Swiss), November 13, 2004.

DOULL, Doug

(DOOL, DUHG) **PHX.**

Left wing. Shoots left. 6'2", 216 lbs. Born, Green Bay, N.S., May 31, 1974.

			Regular Season														Playoffs								
Season	Club	League	GP	G	A	Pts	PIM	PP	SH	GW	S	%	+/-	TF	F%	Min	GP	G	A	Pts	PIM	PP	SH	GW	Min
1990-91	Wexford Raiders	MTHL	39	22	36	58	141	....	....	....	....	....	....	....	....	....	....	....	....	....	....	....	....	....	....
1991-92	Belleville Bulls	OHL	62	6	11	17	123	....	....	....	....	....	....	....	....	....	....	....	....	....	....	....	....	....	....
1992-93	Belleville Bulls	OHL	65	19	37	56	143	....	....	....	....	....	....	....	....	....	....	....	....	....	....	....	....	....	....
1993-94	Belleville Bulls	OHL	62	13	24	37	143	....	....	....	....	....	....	....	....	....	....	....	....	....	....	....	....	....	....
1994-95	Belleville Bulls	OHL	29	7	12	19	71	....	....	....	....	....	....	....	....	....	16	2	13	15	39	....	....	....	....
1995-96	St. Mary's Huskies	AUAA	11	4	4	8	54	....	....	....	....	....	....	....	....	....	....	....	....	....	....	....	....	....	....
1996-97	St. Mary's Huskies	AUAA	18	3	10	13	138	....	....	....	....	....	....	....	....	....	....	....	....	....	....	....	....	....	....
1997-98	St. Mary's Huskies	AUAA	25	4	11	15	227	....	....	....	....	....	....	....	....	....	....	....	....	....	....	....	....	....	....
1998-99	Michigan	IHL	55	4	11	15	227	....	....	....	....	....	....	....	....	....	3	1	1	2	4	....	....	....	....
99-2000	Detroit Vipers	IHL	17	0	2	2	69	....	....	....	....	....	....	....	....	....	....	....	....	....	....	....	....	....	....
	Manitoba Moose	IHL	45	4	4	8	184	....	....	....	....	....	....	....	....	....	2	0	0	0	2	....	....	....	....
2000-01	Manchester Storm	Britain	15	1	6	7	51	....	....	....	....	....	....	....	....	....	....	....	....	....	....	....	....	....	....
	Saint John Flames	AHL	49	3	10	13	167	....	....	....	....	....	....	....	....	....	16	0	1	1	32	....	....	....	....
2001-02	St. John's	AHL	36	5	8	13	166	....	....	....	....	....	....	....	....	....	9	0	1	1	17	....	....	....	....
2002-03	St. John's	AHL	70	15	10	25	257	....	....	....	....	....	....	....	....	....	....	....	....	....	....	....	....	....	....
2003-04	**Boston**	**NHL**	**35**	**0**	**1**	**1**	**132**	**0**	**0**	**0**	**4**	**0.0**	**2**	**0**	**0.0**	**2:50**	....	....	....	....	....	....	....	....	....
	Providence Bruins	AHL	22	1	0	1	98	....	....	....	....	....	....	....	....	....	....	....	....	....	....	....	....	....	....
2004-05	Utah Grizzlies	AHL	40	1	1	2	232	....	....	....	....	....	....	....	....	....	....	....	....	....	....	....	....	....	....
	NHL Totals		**35**	**0**	**1**	**1**	**132**	**0**	**0**	**0**	**4**	**0.0**		**0**	**0.0**	**2:50**	....	....	....	....	....	....	....	....	....

Signed as a free agent by **Manchester** (Britain), August 15, 2000. Signed to a 25-game tryout contract by **Saint John** (AHL) after securing release from **Manchester** (Britain), December 19, 2000. Signed as a free agent by **Saint John** (AHL), February 18, 2001. Signed as a free agent by **Toronto**, July 25, 2001. • Missed majority of 2001-02 season recovering from ankle injury suffered in game vs. Manitoba (AHL), October 19, 2001. Signed as a free agent by **Boston**, July 28, 2003. Signed as a free agent by **Phoenix**, September 2, 2004.

DOWD, Jim

(DOWD, JIHM) **CHI.**

Center. Shoots right. 6'1", 190 lbs. Born, Brick, NJ, December 25, 1968. New Jersey's 7th choice, 149th overall, in 1987 Entry Draft.

Season	Club	League	GP	G	A	Pts	PIM	PP	SH	GW	S	%	+/-	TF	F%	Min	GP	G	A	Pts	PIM	PP	SH	GW	Min
1983-84	Brick	High-NJ	20	19	30	49	....	....	....	....	....	....	....	....	....	....	....	....	....	....	....	....	....	....	....
1984-85	Brick	High-NJ	24	58	55	113	....	....	....	....	....	....	....	....	....	....	....	....	....	....	....	....	....	....	....
1985-86	Brick	High-NJ	24	47	51	98	....	....	....	....	....	....	....	....	....	....	....	....	....	....	....	....	....	....	....
1986-87	Brick	High-NJ	24	22	33	55	....	....	....	....	....	....	....	....	....	....	....	....	....	....	....	....	....	....	....
1987-88	Lake Superior	CCHA	45	18	27	45	16	....	....	....	....	....	....	....	....	....	....	....	....	....	....	....	....	....	....
1988-89	Lake Superior	CCHA	46	24	35	59	40	....	....	....	....	....	....	....	....	....	....	....	....	....	....	....	....	....	....
1989-90	Lake Superior	CCHA	46	25	*67	92	30	....	....	....	....	....	....	....	....	....	....	....	....	....	....	....	....	....	....
1990-91	Lake Superior	CCHA	44	24	*54	*78	53	....	....	....	....	....	....	....	....	....	....	....	....	....	....	....	....	....	....
1991-92	**New Jersey**	**NHL**	**1**	**0**	**0**	**0**	**0**	**0**	**0**	**0**	**0**	**0.0**	**0**	....	....	....	....	....	....	....	....	....	....	....	....
	Utica Devils	AHL	78	17	42	59	47	....	....	....	....	....	....	....	....	....	4	2	2	4	4	....	....	....	....
1992-93	**New Jersey**	**NHL**	**1**	**0**	**0**	**0**	**0**	**0**	**0**	**0**	**1**	**0.0**	**–1**	....	....	....	....	....	....	....	....	....	....	....	....
	Utica Devils	AHL	78	27	45	72	62	....	....	....	....	....	....	....	....	....	5	1	7	8	10	....	....	....	....
1993-94	**New Jersey**	**NHL**	**15**	**5**	**10**	**15**	**0**	**2**	**0**	**0**	**26**	**19.2**	**8**	....	....	....	**19**	**2**	**6**	**8**	**8**	**0**	**0**	**0**	....
	Albany River Rats	AHL	58	26	37	63	76	....	....	....	....	....	....	....	....	....	....	....	....	....	....	....	....	....	....
1994-95♦	**New Jersey**	**NHL**	**10**	**1**	**4**	**5**	**0**	**1**	**0**	**0**	**14**	**7.1**	**–5**	....	....	....	**11**	**2**	**1**	**3**	**8**	**0**	**0**	**1**	....
1995-96	**New Jersey**	**NHL**	**28**	**4**	**9**	**13**	**17**	**0**	**0**	**0**	**41**	**9.8**	**–1**	....	....	....	....	....	....	....	....	....	....	....	....
	Vancouver	**NHL**	**38**	**1**	**6**	**7**	**6**	**0**	**0**	**0**	**35**	**2.9**	**–8**	....	....	....	**1**	**0**	**0**	**0**	**0**	**0**	**0**	**0**	....
1996-97	**NY Islanders**	**NHL**	**3**	**0**	**0**	**0**	**0**	**0**	**0**	**0**	**0**	**0.0**	**–1**	....	....	....	....	....	....	....	....	....	....	....	....
	Utah Grizzlies	IHL	48	10	21	31	27	....	....	....	....	....	....	....	....	....	....	....	....	....	....	....	....	....	....
	Saint John Flames	AHL	24	5	11	16	18	....	....	....	....	....	....	....	....	....	5	1	2	3	0	....	....	....	....
1997-98	**Calgary**	**NHL**	**48**	**6**	**8**	**14**	**12**	**0**	**1**	**0**	**58**	**10.3**	**10**	....	....	....	....	....	....	....	....	....	....	....	....
	Saint John Flames	AHL	35	8	30	38	20	....	....	....	....	....	....	....	....	....	19	3	13	16	10	....	....	....	....
1998-99	**Edmonton**	**NHL**	**1**	**0**	**0**	**0**	**0**	**0**	**0**	**0**	**1**	**0.0**	**0**	**7**	**14.3**	**9:47**	....	....	....	....	....	....	....	....	....
	Hamilton	AHL	51	15	29	44	82	....	....	....	....	....	....	....	....	....	11	3	6	9	8	....	....	....	....
99-2000	**Edmonton**	**NHL**	**69**	**5**	**18**	**23**	**45**	**2**	**0**	**1**	**103**	**4.9**	**10**	**720**	**54.0**	**13:08**	**5**	**2**	**1**	**3**	**4**	**0**	**0**	**0**	**15:22**
2000-01	**Minnesota**	**NHL**	**68**	**7**	**22**	**29**	**80**	**0**	**0**	**0**	**92**	**7.6**	**–6**	**1154**	**50.7**	**17:50**	....	....	....	....	....	....	....	....	....
2001-02	**Minnesota**	**NHL**	**82**	**13**	**30**	**43**	**54**	**5**	**0**	**1**	**111**	**11.7**	**–14**	**1243**	**52.9**	**15:34**	....	....	....	....	....	....	....	....	....
2002-03	**Minnesota**	**NHL**	**78**	**8**	**17**	**25**	**31**	**3**	**1**	**2**	**78**	**10.3**	**–1**	**930**	**47.9**	**13:03**	**15**	**0**	**2**	**2**	**0**	**0**	**0**	**0**	**12:58**
2003-04	**Minnesota**	**NHL**	**55**	**4**	**20**	**24**	**38**	**2**	**0**	**2**	**41**	**9.8**	**6**	**712**	**48.5**	**14:07**	....	....	....	....	....	....	....	....	....
	Montreal	**NHL**	**14**	**3**	**2**	**5**	**6**	**0**	**1**	**0**	**13**	**23.1**	**6**	**167**	**47.3**	**13:30**	**11**	**0**	**2**	**2**	**2**	**0**	**0**	**0**	**15:34**
2004-05	Hamburg Freezers	Germany	20	4	9	13	12	....	....	....	....	....	....	....	....	....	....	....	....	....	....	....	....	....	....
	NHL Totals		**511**	**57**	**146**	**203**	**289**	**15**	**3**	**6**	**614**	**9.3**		**4933**	**50.7**	**14:41**	**62**	**6**	**12**	**18**	**22**	**0**	**0**	**1**	**14:17**

CCHA Second All-Star Team (1990) • NCAA West Second All-American Team (1990) • CCHA First All-Star Team (1991) • CCHA Player of the Year (1991) • NCAA West First All-American Team (1991)

• Missed majority of 1994-95 season recovering from shoulder injury suffered in game vs. Quebec, February 2, 1995. Traded to **Hartford** by **New Jersey** with New Jersey's 2nd round choice (later traded to Calgary – Calgary selected Dmitri Kokorev) in 1997 Entry Draft for Jocelyn Lemieux and Hartford's 2nd round choice (later traded to Dallas – Dallas selected John Erskine) in 1998 Entry Draft, December 19, 1995. Traded to **Vancouver** by **Hartford** with Frantisek Kucera and Hartford's 2nd round choice (Ryan Bonni) in 1997 Entry Draft for Jeff Brown and Vancouver's 3rd round choice (later traded to Calgary – Calgary selected Paul Manning) in 1998 Entry Draft, December 19, 1995. Claimed by **NY Islanders** from **Vancouver** in Waiver Draft, September 30, 1996. Signed as a free agent by **Calgary**, August, 1997. Traded to **Nashville** by **Calgary** for future considerations, June 26, 1998. Traded to **Edmonton** by **Nashville** with Mikhail Shtalenkov for Eric Fichaud, Drake Berehowsky and Greg de Vries, October 1, 1998. Claimed by **Minnesota** from **Edmonton** in Expansion Draft, June 23, 2000. Traded to **Montreal** by **Minnesota** for Montreal's 4th round choice (Julien Sprunger) in 2004 Entry Draft, March 4, 2004. Signed as a free agent by **Hamburg** (Germany), October 1, 2004. Signed as a free agent by **Chicago**, August 5, 2005.

DOWNEY, Aaron

(DOW-nee, AIR-ruhn) **ST.L.**

Right wing. Shoots right. 6'1", 220 lbs. Born, Shelburne, Ont., August 27, 1974.

Season	Club	League	GP	G	A	Pts	PIM	PP	SH	GW	S	%	+/-	TF	F%	Min	GP	G	A	Pts	PIM	PP	SH	GW	Min
1990-91	Grand Valley	OHA-C	27	6	8	14	57	....	....	....	....	....	....	....	....	....	....	....	....	....	....	....	....	....	....
1991-92	Collingwood	OHA-B	40	9	8	17	111	....	....	....	....	....	....	....	....	....	....	....	....	....	....	....	....	....	....
1992-93	Guelph Storm	OHL	53	3	3	6	88	....	....	....	....	....	....	....	....	....	5	1	0	1	0	....	....	....	....
1993-94	Cole Harbour	NSMHL	35	8	20	28	210	....	....	....	....	....	....	....	....	....	....	....	....	....	....	....	....	....	....
1994-95	Cole Harbour	NSMHL	40	10	31	41	320	....	....	....	....	....	....	....	....	....	....	....	....	....	....	....	....	....	....
1995-96	Hampton Roads	ECHL	65	12	11	23	354	....	....	....	....	....	....	....	....	....	....	....	....	....	....	....	....	....	....
1996-97	Manitoba Moose	IHL	2	0	0	0	17	....	....	....	....	....	....	....	....	....	....	....	....	....	....	....	....	....	....
	Portland Pirates	AHL	3	0	0	0	19	....	....	....	....	....	....	....	....	....	....	....	....	....	....	....	....	....	....
	Hampton Roads	ECHL	64	8	8	16	338	....	....	....	....	....	....	....	....	....	9	0	3	3	26	....	....	....	....
1997-98	Providence Bruins	AHL	78	5	10	15	*407	....	....	....	....	....	....	....	....	....	....	....	....	....	....	....	....	....	....
1998-99	Providence Bruins	AHL	75	10	12	22	*401	....	....	....	....	....	....	....	....	....	19	1	1	2	46	....	....	....	....
99-2000	**Boston**	**NHL**	**1**	**0**	**0**	**0**	**0**	**0**	**0**	**0**	**0**	**0.0**	**0**	**0**	**0.0**	**8:31**	....	....	....	....	....	....	....	....	....
	Providence Bruins	AHL	47	6	4	10	221	....	....	....	....	....	....	....	....	....	14	1	0	1	24	....	....	....	....
2000-01	**Chicago**	**NHL**	**3**	**0**	**0**	**0**	**6**	**0**	**0**	**0**	**2**	**0.0**	**–1**	**0**	**0.0**	**5:30**	....	....	....	....	....	....	....	....	....
	Norfolk Admirals	AHL	67	6	15	21	234	....	....	....	....	....	....	....	....	....	9	0	0	0	4	....	....	....	....
2001-02	**Chicago**	**NHL**	**36**	**1**	**0**	**1**	**76**	**0**	**0**	**1**	**10**	**10.0**	**–2**	**0**	**0.0**	**5:06**	**4**	**0**	**0**	**0**	**8**	**0**	**0**	**0**	**6:29**
	Norfolk Admirals	AHL	12	0	2	2	21	....	....	....	....	....	....	....	....	....	....	....	....	....	....	....	....	....	....
2002-03	**Dallas**	**NHL**	**43**	**1**	**1**	**2**	**69**	**0**	**0**	**0**	**14**	**7.1**	**1**	**0**	**0.0**	**4:47**	....	....	....	....	....	....	....	....	....
2003-04	**Dallas**	**NHL**	**37**	**1**	**1**	**2**	**77**	**0**	**0**	**1**	**11**	**9.1**	**2**	**0**	**0.0**	**4:30**	....	....	....	....	....	....	....	....	....
2004-05			DID NOT PLAY																						
	NHL Totals		**120**	**3**	**2**	**5**	**228**	**0**	**0**	**2**	**37**	**8.1**		**0**	**0.0**	**4:50**	**4**	**0**	**0**	**0**	**8**	**0**	**0**	**0**	**6:29**

Signed as a free agent by **Boston**, January 20, 1998. Signed as a free agent by **Chicago**, August 13, 2000. Signed as a free agent by **Dallas**, July 3, 2002. • Spent majority of 2003-04 season as a healthy reserve. Signed as a free agent by **St. Louis**, August 1, 2005.

DRAKE, Dallas

(DRAYK, DAL-uhs) **ST.L.**

Right wing. Shoots left. 6'1", 195 lbs. Born, Trail, B.C., February 4, 1969. Detroit's 6th choice, 116th overall, in 1989 Entry Draft.

Season	Club	League	GP	G	A	Pts	PIM	PP	SH	GW	S	%	+/-	TF	F%	Min	GP	G	A	Pts	PIM	PP	SH	GW	Min
1984-85	Rossland	KIJHL	30	13	37	50	....	....	....	....	....	....	....	....	....	....	....	....	....	....	....	....	....	....	....
1985-86	Rossland	KIJHL	41	53	73	126	....	....	....	....	....	....	....	....	....	....	....	....	....	....	....	....	....	....	....
1986-87	Rossland	KIJHL	40	55	80	135	....	....	....	....	....	....	....	....	....	....	....	....	....	....	....	....	....	....	....
1987-88	Vernon Lakers	BCJHL	47	39	85	124	50	....	....	....	....	....	....	....	....	....	11	9	17	26	30	....	....	....	....
1988-89	Northern Mich.	WCHA	38	17	22	39	22	....	....	....	....	....	....	....	....	....	7	1	2	3	4	....	....	....	....
1989-90	Northern Mich.	WCHA	36	13	24	37	42	....	....	....	....	....	....	....	....	....	....	....	....	....	....	....	....	....	....
1990-91	Northern Mich.	WCHA	44	22	36	58	89	....	....	....	....	....	....	....	....	....	....	....	....	....	....	....	....	....	....
1991-92	Northern Mich.	WCHA	38	*39	41	*80	46	....	....	....	....	....	....	....	....	....	....	....	....	....	....	....	....	....	....
1992-93	**Detroit**	**NHL**	**72**	**18**	**26**	**44**	**93**	**3**	**2**	**5**	**89**	**20.2**	**15**	....	....	....	**7**	**3**	**3**	**6**	**6**	**1**	**0**	**0**	....

			Regular Season														Playoffs								
Season	Club	League	GP	G	A	Pts	PIM	PP	SH	GW	S	%	+/-	TF	F%	Min	GP	G	A	Pts	PIM	PP	SH	GW	Min
1993-94	Detroit	NHL	47	10	22	32	37	0	1	2	78	12.8	5	....	....	....	....	....	....	....	....	....	....	....	....
	Adirondack	AHL	1	2	0	2	0	....	....	....	....	....	....	....	....	....	....	....	....	....	....	....	....	....	....
	Winnipeg	NHL	15	3	5	8	12	1	1	1	34	8.8	–6	....	....	....	....	....	....	....	....	....	....	....	....
1994-95	Winnipeg	NHL	43	8	18	26	30	0	0	1	66	12.1	–6	....	....	....	....	....	....	....	....	....	....	....	....
1995-96	Winnipeg	NHL	69	19	20	39	36	4	4	2	121	15.7	–7	....	....	....	3	0	0	0	0	0	0	0	....
1996-97	Phoenix	NHL	63	17	19	36	52	5	1	1	113	15.0	–11	....	....	....	7	0	1	1	2	0	0	0	....
1997-98	Phoenix	NHL	60	11	29	40	71	3	0	2	112	9.8	17	....	....	....	4	0	1	1	2	0	0	0	....
1998-99	Phoenix	NHL	53	9	22	31	65	0	0	3	105	8.6	17	5	60.0	15:38	7	4	3	7	4	2	0	1	19:51
99-2000	Phoenix	NHL	79	15	30	45	62	0	2	5	127	11.8	11	4	25.0	15:48	5	0	1	1	4	0	0	0	15:30
2000-01	St. Louis	NHL	82	12	29	41	71	2	0	3	142	8.5	18	11	45.5	14:44	15	4	2	6	16	0	1	1	14:08
2001-02	St. Louis	NHL	80	11	15	26	87	1	3	2	116	9.5	8	92	32.6	13:26	8	0	0	0	8	0	0	0	11:59
2002-03	St. Louis	NHL	80	20	10	30	66	4	1	2	113	17.7	–7	56	39.3	14:48	7	1	4	5	23	0	0	1	13:04
2003-04	St. Louis	NHL	79	13	22	35	65	3	2	1	121	10.7	10	92	45.7	16:57	5	1	1	2	2	0	0	1	16:45
2004-05			DID NOT PLAY																						
	NHL Totals		822	166	267	433	747	26	17	30	1337	12.4		260	39.6	15:12	68	13	16	29	67	3	1	4	14:53

WCHA First All-Star Team (1992) • NCAA West First All-American Team (1992)

Traded to **Winnipeg** by **Detroit** with Tim Cheveldae for Bob Essensa and Sergei Bautin, March 8, 1994. Transferred to **Phoenix** after **Winnipeg** franchise relocated, July 1, 1996. Claimed by **Minnesota** from **Phoenix** in Expansion Draft, June 23, 2000. Signed as a free agent by **St. Louis**, July 1, 2000.

DRAPER, Kris

(DRAY-puhr, KRIHS) **DET.**

Center. Shoots left. 5'11", 190 lbs. Born, Toronto, Ont., May 24, 1971. Winnipeg's 4th choice, 62nd overall, in 1989 Entry Draft.

Season	Club	League	GP	G	A	Pts	PIM	PP	SH	GW	S	%	+/-	TF	F%	Min	GP	G	A	Pts	PIM	PP	SH	GW	Min
1987-88	Don Mills Flyers	MTHL	40	35	32	67	46	....	....	....	....	....	....	....	....	....	....	....	....	....	....	....	....	....	....
1988-89	Canada	Nat-Tm	60	11	15	26	16	....	....	....	....	....	....	....	....	....	....	....	....	....	....	....	....	....	....
1989-90	Canada	Nat-Tm	61	12	22	34	44	....	....	....	....	....	....	....	....	....	....	....	....	....	....	....	....	....	....
1990-91	Ottawa 67's	OHL	39	19	42	61	35	....	....	....	....	....	....	....	....	....	17	8	11	19	20	....	....	....	....
	Winnipeg	NHL	3	1	0	1	5	0	0	0	1	100.0	0	....	....	....	....	....	....	....	....	....	....	....	....
	Moncton Hawks	AHL	7	2	1	3	2	....	....	....	....	....	....	....	....	....	....	....	....	....	....	....	....	....	....
1991-92	Winnipeg	NHL	10	2	0	2	2	0	0	0	19	10.5	0	....	....	....	2	0	0	0	0	0	0	0	....
	Moncton Hawks	AHL	61	11	18	29	113	....	....	....	....	....	....	....	....	....	4	0	1	1	6	....	....	....	....
1992-93	Winnipeg	NHL	7	0	0	0	2	0	0	0	5	0.0	–6	....	....	....	....	....	....	....	....	....	....	....	....
	Moncton Hawks	AHL	67	12	23	35	40	....	....	....	....	....	....	....	....	....	5	2	2	4	18	....	....	....	....
1993-94	Detroit	NHL	39	5	8	13	31	0	1	0	55	9.1	11	....	....	....	7	2	2	4	4	0	1	0	....
	Adirondack	AHL	46	20	23	43	49	....	....	....	....	....	....	....	....	....	....	....	....	....	....	....	....	....	....
1994-95	Detroit	NHL	36	2	6	8	22	0	0	0	44	4.5	1	....	....	....	18	4	1	5	12	0	1	1	....
1995-96	Detroit	NHL	52	7	9	16	32	0	1	0	51	13.7	2	....	....	....	18	4	2	6	18	0	1	0	....
1996-97♦	Detroit	NHL	76	8	5	13	73	1	0	1	85	9.4	–11	....	....	....	20	2	4	6	12	0	1	0	....
1997-98♦	Detroit	NHL	64	13	10	23	45	1	0	4	96	13.5	5	....	....	....	19	1	3	4	12	0	0	1	....
1998-99	Detroit	NHL	80	4	14	18	79	0	1	1	78	5.1	2	887	54.6	12:43	10	0	1	1	6	0	0	0	11:35
99-2000	Detroit	NHL	51	5	7	12	28	0	0	3	76	6.6	3	380	57.6	13:33	9	2	0	2	6	0	0	0	12:26
2000-01	Detroit	NHL	75	8	17	25	38	0	1	1	123	6.5	17	997	56.5	13:26	6	0	1	1	2	0	0	0	16:08
2001-02♦	Detroit	NHL	82	15	15	30	56	0	2	3	137	10.9	26	756	53.2	15:35	23	2	3	5	20	0	0	0	17:00
2002-03	Detroit	NHL	82	14	21	35	82	0	1	2	142	9.9	6	1059	56.9	16:12	4	0	0	0	4	0	0	0	17:29
2003-04	Detroit	NHL	67	24	16	40	31	2	5	1	149	16.1	22	1058	56.9	17:44	12	1	3	4	6	0	0	0	18:29
2004-05			DID NOT PLAY																						
	NHL Totals		724	108	128	236	526	4	12	16	1061	10.2		5137	55.9	14:54	148	18	20	38	102	0	4	2	15:44

Frank J. Selke Trophy (2004)

Traded to **Detroit** by **Winnipeg** for future considerations, June 30, 1993.

DRUKEN, Harold

(DROO-kehn, HAIR-ohld)

Center. Shoots left. 6', 200 lbs. Born, St. John's, Nfld., January 26, 1979. Vancouver's 3rd choice, 36th overall, in 1997 Entry Draft.

Season	Club	League	GP	G	A	Pts	PIM	PP	SH	GW	S	%	+/-	TF	F%	Min	GP	G	A	Pts	PIM	PP	SH	GW	Min
1995-96	Nobles	High-MA	30	37	28	65	28	....	....	....	....	....	....	....	....	....	....	....	....	....	....	....	....	....	....
1996-97	Detroit	OHL	63	27	31	58	14	....	....	....	....	....	....	....	....	....	5	3	2	5	0	....	....	....	....
1997-98	Plymouth Whalers	OHL	64	38	44	82	12	....	....	....	....	....	....	....	....	....	15	9	11	20	4	....	....	....	....
1998-99	Plymouth Whalers	OHL	60	*58	45	103	34	....	....	....	....	....	....	....	....	....	11	9	12	21	14	....	....	....	....
99-2000	Vancouver	NHL	33	7	9	16	10	2	0	0	69	10.1	14	307	47.9	13:01	....	....	....	....	....	....	....	....	....
	Syracuse Crunch	AHL	47	20	25	45	32	....	....	....	....	....	....	....	....	....	4	1	2	3	6	....	....	....	....
2000-01	Vancouver	NHL	55	15	15	30	14	6	0	3	82	18.3	2	598	43.8	11:59	4	0	1	1	0	0	0	0	13:44
	Kansas City	IHL	15	5	9	14	20	....	....	....	....	....	....	....	....	....	....	....	....	....	....	....	....	....	....
2001-02	Vancouver	NHL	27	4	4	8	6	1	0	2	33	12.1	–1	269	54.7	11:09	....	....	....	....	....	....	....	....	....
	Manitoba Moose	AHL	11	2	9	11	4	....	....	....	....	....	....	....	....	....	....	....	....	....	....	....	....	....	....
2002-03	Vancouver	NHL	3	1	1	2	0	0	0	0	3	33.3	–1	21	47.6	8:48	....	....	....	....	....	....	....	....	....
	Carolina	NHL	10	0	1	1	2	0	0	0	3	0.0	–1	31	41.9	4:03	....	....	....	....	....	....	....	....	....
	Toronto	NHL	5	0	2	2	2	0	0	0	8	0.0	1	25	44.0	12:50	....	....	....	....	....	....	....	....	....
	St. John's	AHL	6	0	3	3	2	....	....	....	....	....	....	....	....	....	....	....	....	....	....	....	....	....	....
	Carolina	NHL	4	0	0	0	0	0	0	0	2	0.0	0	8	75.0	3:52	....	....	....	....	....	....	....	....	....
	Lowell	AHL	24	8	10	18	8	....	....	....	....	....	....	....	....	....	....	....	....	....	....	....	....	....	....
2003-04	Toronto	NHL	9	0	4	4	2	0	0	0	19	0.0	4	3	33.3	10:48	....	....	....	....	....	....	....	....	....
	St. John's	AHL	57	26	25	51	31	....	....	....	....	....	....	....	....	....	....	....	....	....	....	....	....	....	....
2004-05	St. John's	AHL	48	18	20	38	28	....	....	....	....	....	....	....	....	....	....	....	....	....	....	....	....	....	....
	NHL Totals		146	27	36	63	36	9	0	5	219	12.3		1262	47.3	11:11	4	0	1	1	0	0	0	0	13:43

OHL All-Rookie Team (1997) • OHL Second All-Star Team (1999) • AHL All-Rookie Team (2000)

Missed majority of 2001-02 season recovering from ankle injury suffered in game vs. Dallas, December 2, 2001. Traded to **Carolina** by **Vancouver** with Jan Hlavac for Darren Langdon and Marek Malik, November 1, 2002. Claimed on waivers by **Toronto** from **Carolina**, December 11, 2002. Claimed on waivers by **Carolina** from **Toronto**, January 17, 2003. Traded to **Toronto** by **Carolina** for Allan Rourke, May 29, 2003. Signed as a free agent by **Basel** (Swiss), August, 2005.

DRURY, Chris

(DROO-ree, KRIHS) **BUF.**

Center. Shoots right. 5'10", 200 lbs. Born, Trumbull, CT, August 20, 1976. Quebec's 5th choice, 72nd overall, in 1994 Entry Draft.

Season	Club	League	GP	G	A	Pts	PIM	PP	SH	GW	S	%	+/-	TF	F%	Min	GP	G	A	Pts	PIM	PP	SH	GW	Min
1991-92	Fairfield Prep	High-CT	25	22	27	49	....	....	....	....	....	....	....	....	....	....	....	....	....	....	....	....	....	....	....
1992-93	Fairfield Prep	High-CT	24	25	32	57	15	....	....	....	....	....	....	....	....	....	....	....	....	....	....	....	....	....	....
1993-94	Fairfield Prep	High-CT	24	37	18	55	....	....	....	....	....	....	....	....	....	....	....	....	....	....	....	....	....	....	....
1994-95	Boston University	H-East	39	12	15	27	38	....	....	....	....	....	....	....	....	....	....	....	....	....	....	....	....	....	....
1995-96	Boston University	H-East	37	35	33	*68	46	....	....	....	....	....	....	....	....	....	....	....	....	....	....	....	....	....	....
1996-97	Boston University	H-East	41	*38	24	62	64	....	....	....	....	....	....	....	....	....	....	....	....	....	....	....	....	....	....
1997-98	Boston University	H-East	38	28	29	57	88	....	....	....	....	....	....	....	....	....	....	....	....	....	....	....	....	....	....
1998-99	Colorado	NHL	79	20	24	44	62	6	0	3	138	14.5	9	418	46.9	13:15	19	6	2	8	4	0	0	4	11:28
99-2000	Colorado	NHL	82	20	47	67	42	7	0	2	213	9.4	8	1321	53.1	18:33	17	4	10	14	4	1	0	2	18:30
2000-01♦	Colorado	NHL	71	24	41	65	47	11	0	5	204	11.8	6	552	55.1	18:03	23	11	5	16	4	2	0	2	19:06
2001-02	Colorado	NHL	82	21	25	46	38	5	0	6	236	8.9	1	1139	53.2	17:57	21	5	7	12	10	1	0	3	17:01
	United States	Olympics	6	0	0	0	0	....	....	....	....	....	....	....	....	....	....	....	....	....	....	....	....	....	....
2002-03	Calgary	NHL	80	23	30	53	33	5	1	5	224	10.3	–9	942	53.8	18:33	....	....	....	....	....	....	....	....	....
2003-04	Buffalo	NHL	76	18	35	53	68	5	1	2	152	11.8	8	1491	54.9	18:04	....	....	....	....	....	....	....	....	....
2004-05			DID NOT PLAY																						
	NHL Totals		470	126	202	328	290	39	2	23	1167	10.8		5863	53.4	17:24	80	26	24	50	22	4	0	11	16:37

Hockey East Second All-Star Team (1996, 1997) • NCAA East Second All-American Team (1996) • Hockey East Player of the Year (1997, 1998) • NCAA East First All-American Team (1997, 1998) • NCAA Championship All-Tournament Team (1997) • Hockey East First All-Star Team (1998) • Hobey Baker Memorial Award (Top U.S. Collegiate Player) (1998) • NHL All-Rookie Team (1999) • Calder Memorial Trophy (1999)

Rights transferred to **Colorado** after **Quebec** franchise relocated, June 21, 1995. Traded to **Calgary** by **Colorado** with Stephane Yelle for Derek Morris, Jeff Shantz and Dean McAmmond, October 1, 2002. Traded to **Buffalo** by **Calgary** with Steve Begin for Steve Reinprecht and Rhett Warrener, July 3, 2003.

			Regular Season														Playoffs								
Season	Club	League	GP	G	A	Pts	PIM	PP	SH	GW	S	%	+/-	TF	F%	Min	GP	G	A	Pts	PIM	PP	SH	GW	Min

DUMONT, J.P.

(DOO-mawnt, JAY-pee) **BUF.**

Right wing. Shoots left. 6'1", 205 lbs. Born, Montreal, Que., April 1, 1978. NY Islanders' 1st choice, 3rd overall, in 1996 Entry Draft.

Season	Club	League	GP	G	A	Pts	PIM	PP	SH	GW	S	%	+/-	TF	F%	Min	GP	G	A	Pts	PIM	PP	SH	GW	Min
1993-94	Mtl-Bourassa	QAAA	44	27	20	47	44	....	....	....	....	....	....	....	....	....	4	2	3	5	4	....	....	....	....
1994-95	Mtl-Bourassa	QAAA	10	2	7	9	12	....	....	....	....	....	....	....	....	....	....	....	....	....	....	....	....	....	....
	Val-d'Or Foreurs	QMJHL	48	5	14	19	24	....	....	....	....	....	....	....	....	....	....	....	....	....	....	....	....	....	....
1995-96	Val-d'Or Foreurs	QMJHL	66	48	57	105	109	....	....	....	....	....	....	....	....	....	13	12	8	20	22	....	....	....	....
1996-97	Val-d'Or Foreurs	QMJHL	62	44	64	108	86	....	....	....	....	....	....	....	....	....	13	9	7	16	12	....	....	....	....
1997-98	Val-d'Or Foreurs	QMJHL	55	57	42	99	63	....	....	....	....	....	....	....	....	....	19	31	15	46	18	....	....	....	....
1998-99	**Chicago**	**NHL**	**25**	**9**	**6**	**15**	**10**	**0**	**0**	**2**	**42**	**21.4**	**7**	**10**	**50.0**	**14:14**	....	....	....	....	....	....	....	....	....
	Portland Pirates	AHL	50	32	14	46	39	....	....	....	....	....	....	....	....	....	....	....	....	....	....	....	....	....	....
	Chicago Wolves	IHL	....	....	....	....	....	....	....	....	....	....	....	....	....	....	10	4	1	5	6	....	....	....	....
99-2000	**Chicago**	**NHL**	**47**	**10**	**8**	**18**	**18**	**0**	**0**	**1**	**86**	**11.6**	**–6**	**12**	**33.3**	**12:54**	....	....	....	....	....	....	....	....	....
	Cleveland	IHL	7	5	2	7	8	....	....	....	....	....	....	....	....	....	....	....	....	....	....	....	....	....	....
	Rochester	AHL	13	7	10	17	18	....	....	....	....	....	....	....	....	....	21	14	7	21	32	....	....	....	....
2000-01	**Buffalo**	**NHL**	**79**	**23**	**28**	**51**	**54**	**9**	**0**	**5**	**156**	**14.7**	**1**	**3**	**33.3**	**15:01**	**13**	**4**	**3**	**7**	**8**	**0**	**0**	**0**	**14:32**
2001-02	**Buffalo**	**NHL**	**76**	**23**	**21**	**44**	**42**	**7**	**0**	**3**	**154**	**14.9**	**–10**	**4**	**50.0**	**15:14**	....	....	....	....	....	....	....	....	....
2002-03	**Buffalo**	**NHL**	**76**	**14**	**21**	**35**	**44**	**2**	**0**	**2**	**135**	**10.4**	**–14**	**15**	**20.0**	**15:04**	....	....	....	....	....	....	....	....	....
2003-04	**Buffalo**	**NHL**	**77**	**22**	**31**	**53**	**40**	**10**	**0**	**1**	**156**	**14.1**	**–9**	**32**	**43.8**	**17:00**	....	....	....	....	....	....	....	....	....
2004-05	SC Bern	Swiss	3	2	2	4	6	....	....	....	....	....	....	....	....	....	10	4	1	5	16	....	....	....	....
	NHL Totals		**380**	**101**	**115**	**216**	**208**	**28**	**0**	**14**	**729**	**13.9**		**76**	**38.2**	**15:09**	**13**	**4**	**3**	**7**	**8**	**0**	**0**	**0**	**14:32**

QMJHL Second All-Star Team (1997) • AHL All-Rookie Team (1999)

Rights traded to **Chicago** by **NY Islanders** with NY Islanders' 5th round choice (later traded to Philadelphia – Philadelphia selected Francis Belanger) in 1998 Entry Draft for Dmitri Nabokov, May 30, 1998. Traded to **Buffalo** by **Chicago** with Doug Gilmour for Michal Grosek, March 10, 2000. Signed as a free agent by **Bern** (Swiss), February 9, 2005.

DUPUIS, Pascal

(doo-PWEE, pas-KAL) **MIN.**

Left wing. Shoots left. 6', 196 lbs. Born, Laval, Que., April 7, 1979.

Season	Club	League	GP	G	A	Pts	PIM	PP	SH	GW	S	%	+/-	TF	F%	Min	GP	G	A	Pts	PIM	PP	SH	GW	Min
1995-96	Laval-Laurentides	QAAA	41	10	15	25	....	....	....	....	....	....	....	....	....	....	14	11	11	22	....	....	....	....	....
1996-97	Rouyn-Noranda	QMJHL	44	9	15	24	20	....	....	....	....	....	....	....	....	....	....	....	....	....	....	....	....	....	....
1997-98	Rouyn-Noranda	QMJHL	39	9	17	26	36	....	....	....	....	....	....	....	....	....	....	....	....	....	....	....	....	....	....
	Shawinigan	QMJHL	28	7	13	20	10	....	....	....	....	....	....	....	....	....	6	2	0	2	4	....	....	....	....
1998-99	Shawinigan	QMJHL	57	30	42	72	118	....	....	....	....	....	....	....	....	....	6	1	8	9	18	....	....	....	....
99-2000	Shawinigan	QMJHL	61	50	55	105	99	....	....	....	....	....	....	....	....	....	13	*15	7	22	4	....	....	....	....
2000-01	**Minnesota**	**NHL**	**4**	**1**	**0**	**1**	**4**	**1**	**0**	**0**	**8**	**12.5**	**0**	**0**	**0.0**	**15:36**	....	....	....	....	....	....	....	....	....
	Cleveland	IHL	70	19	24	43	37	....	....	....	....	....	....	....	....	....	4	0	0	0	0	....	....	....	....
2001-02	**Minnesota**	**NHL**	**76**	**15**	**12**	**27**	**16**	**3**	**2**	**0**	**154**	**9.7**	**–10**	**40**	**32.5**	**15:08**	....	....	....	....	....	....	....	....	....
2002-03	**Minnesota**	**NHL**	**80**	**20**	**28**	**48**	**44**	**6**	**0**	**4**	**183**	**10.9**	**17**	**186**	**40.9**	**17:30**	**16**	**4**	**4**	**8**	**8**	**2**	**0**	**1**	**16:58**
2003-04	**Minnesota**	**NHL**	**59**	**11**	**15**	**26**	**20**	**2**	**0**	**1**	**127**	**8.7**	**5**	**129**	**45.7**	**15:48**	....	....	....	....	....	....	....	....	....
2004-05	HC Ajoie	Swiss-2	8	5	5	10	26	....	....	....	....	....	....	....	....	....	6	6	8	14	8	....	....	....	....
	NHL Totals		**219**	**47**	**55**	**102**	**84**	**12**	**2**	**5**	**472**	**10.0**		**355**	**41.7**	**16:11**	**16**	**4**	**4**	**8**	**8**	**2**	**0**	**1**	**16:58**

Signed as a free agent by **Minnesota**, August 18, 2000. Signed as a free agent by **Ajoie** (Swiss-2), January 14, 2005.

DVORAK, Radek

(duh-VOHR-ak, RA-dehk) **EDM.**

Right wing. Shoots right. 6'2", 200 lbs. Born, Tabor, Czech., March 9, 1977. Florida's 1st choice, 10th overall, in 1995 Entry Draft.

Season	Club	League	GP	G	A	Pts	PIM	PP	SH	GW	S	%	+/-	TF	F%	Min	GP	G	A	Pts	PIM	PP	SH	GW	Min
1992-93	C. Budejovice Jr.	Czech-Jr.	35	44	46	90	....	....	....	....	....	....	....	....	....	....	....	....	....	....	....	....	....	....	....
1993-94	C. Budejovice Jr.	CzRep-Jr.	20	17	18	35	....	....	....	....	....	....	....	....	....	....	....	....	....	....	....	....	....	....	....
	C. Budejovice	CzRep	8	0	0	0	0	....	....	....	....	....	....	....	....	....	....	....	....	....	....	....	....	....	....
1994-95	C. Budejovice	CzRep	10	3	5	8	2	....	....	....	....	....	....	....	....	....	9	5	1	6	....	....	....	....	....
1995-96	**Florida**	**NHL**	**77**	**13**	**14**	**27**	**20**	**0**	**0**	**4**	**126**	**10.3**	**5**	....	....	....	**16**	**1**	**3**	**4**	**0**	**0**	**0**	**0**	....
1996-97	**Florida**	**NHL**	**78**	**18**	**21**	**39**	**30**	**2**	**0**	**1**	**139**	**12.9**	**–2**	....	....	....	**3**	**0**	**0**	**0**	**0**	**0**	**0**	**0**	....
1997-98	**Florida**	**NHL**	**64**	**12**	**24**	**36**	**33**	**2**	**3**	**0**	**112**	**10.7**	**–1**	....	....	....	....	....	....	....	....	....	....	....	....
1998-99	**Florida**	**NHL**	**82**	**19**	**24**	**43**	**29**	**0**	**4**	**0**	**182**	**10.4**	**7**	**98**	**46.9**	**16:13**	....	....	....	....	....	....	....	....	....
99-2000	**Florida**	**NHL**	**35**	**7**	**10**	**17**	**6**	**0**	**0**	**1**	**67**	**10.4**	**5**	**16**	**37.5**	**15:25**	....	....	....	....	....	....	....	....	....
	NY Rangers	**NHL**	**46**	**11**	**22**	**33**	**10**	**2**	**1**	**0**	**90**	**12.2**	**0**	**34**	**35.3**	**18:24**	....	....	....	....	....	....	....	....	....
2000-01	**NY Rangers**	**NHL**	**82**	**31**	**36**	**67**	**20**	**5**	**2**	**3**	**230**	**13.5**	**9**	**20**	**30.0**	**19:04**	....	....	....	....	....	....	....	....	....
2001-02	**NY Rangers**	**NHL**	**65**	**17**	**20**	**37**	**14**	**3**	**3**	**1**	**210**	**8.1**	**–20**	**5**	**0.0**	**19:44**	....	....	....	....	....	....	....	....	....
	Czech Republic	Olympics	4	0	0	0	0	....	....	....	....	....	....	....	....	....	....	....	....	....	....	....	....	....	....
2002-03	**NY Rangers**	**NHL**	**63**	**6**	**21**	**27**	**16**	**2**	**0**	**0**	**134**	**4.5**	**–3**	**9**	**44.4**	**15:42**	....	....	....	....	....	....	....	....	....
	Edmonton	**NHL**	**12**	**4**	**4**	**8**	**14**	**1**	**0**	**0**	**32**	**12.5**	**–3**	**1**	**0.0**	**16:07**	**4**	**1**	**0**	**1**	**0**	**0**	**0**	**1**	**15:05**
2003-04	**Edmonton**	**NHL**	**78**	**15**	**35**	**50**	**26**	**6**	**0**	**0**	**188**	**8.0**	**18**	**24**	**29.2**	**16:56**	....	....	....	....	....	....	....	....	....
2004-05	C. Budejovice	CzRep-2	32	23	35	58	18	....	....	....	....	....	....	....	....	....	16	5	13	18	20	....	....	....	....
	NHL Totals		**682**	**153**	**231**	**384**	**218**	**23**	**13**	**10**	**1510**	**10.1**		**207**	**39.1**	**17:25**	**23**	**2**	**3**	**5**	**0**	**0**	**0**	**1**	**15:05**

Traded to **San Jose** by **Florida** for Mike Vernon and San Jose's 3rd round choice (Sean O'Connor) in 2000 Entry Draft, December 30, 1999. Traded to **NY Rangers** by **San Jose** for Todd Harvey and NY Rangers' 4th round choice (Dimitri Patzold) in 2001 Entry Draft, December 30, 1999. Traded to **Edmonton** by **NY Rangers** with Cory Cross for Anson Carter and Ales Pisa, March 11, 2003. Signed as a free agent by **Budejovice** (CzRep-2), September 15, 2004.

DWYER, Gordie

(DWIGH-uhr, GOHR-dee) **CAR.**

Left wing. Shoots left. 6'3", 215 lbs. Born, Dalhousie, N.B., January 25, 1978. Montreal's 5th choice, 152nd overall, in 1998 Entry Draft.

Season	Club	League	GP	G	A	Pts	PIM	PP	SH	GW	S	%	+/-	TF	F%	Min	GP	G	A	Pts	PIM	PP	SH	GW	Min
1993-94	Magog	QAAA	42	7	15	22	62	....	....	....	....	....	....	....	....	....	4	2	1	3	0	....	....	....	....
1994-95	Hull Olympiques	QMJHL	57	3	7	10	204	....	....	....	....	....	....	....	....	....	17	1	3	4	54	....	....	....	....
1995-96	Hull Olympiques	QMJHL	25	5	9	14	199	....	....	....	....	....	....	....	....	....	....	....	....	....	....	....	....	....	....
	Laval Titan	QMJHL	22	5	17	22	72	....	....	....	....	....	....	....	....	....	....	....	....	....	....	....	....	....	....
	Beauport	QMJHL	22	4	9	13	87	....	....	....	....	....	....	....	....	....	20	3	5	8	104	....	....	....	....
1996-97	Drummondville	QMJHL	66	21	48	69	393	....	....	....	....	....	....	....	....	....	8	6	1	7	39	....	....	....	....
1997-98	Quebec Remparts	QMJHL	59	18	27	45	365	....	....	....	....	....	....	....	....	....	14	4	9	13	67	....	....	....	....
1998-99	Fredericton	AHL	14	0	0	0	46	....	....	....	....	....	....	....	....	....	....	....	....	....	....	....	....	....	....
	New Orleans	ECHL	36	1	3	4	163	....	....	....	....	....	....	....	....	....	11	0	0	0	27	....	....	....	....
99-2000	Quebec Citadelles	AHL	7	0	0	0	37	....	....	....	....	....	....	....	....	....	....	....	....	....	....	....	....	....	....
	Tampa Bay	**NHL**	**24**	**0**	**1**	**1**	**135**	**0**	**0**	**0**	**7**	**0.0**	**–6**	**0**	**0.0**	**4:57**	....	....	....	....	....	....	....	....	....
	Detroit Vipers	IHL	27	0	2	2	147	....	....	....	....	....	....	....	....	....	....	....	....	....	....	....	....	....	....
2000-01	**Tampa Bay**	**NHL**	**28**	**0**	**1**	**1**	**96**	**0**	**0**	**0**	**12**	**0.0**	**–7**	**2**	**50.0**	**5:47**	....	....	....	....	....	....	....	....	....
	Detroit Vipers	IHL	24	2	3	5	169	....	....	....	....	....	....	....	....	....	....	....	....	....	....	....	....	....	....
2001-02	**Tampa Bay**	**NHL**	**26**	**0**	**2**	**2**	**60**	**0**	**0**	**0**	**6**	**0.0**	**–4**	**0**	**0.0**	**5:05**	....	....	....	....	....	....	....	....	....
	Springfield	AHL	17	1	3	4	80	....	....	....	....	....	....	....	....	....	....	....	....	....	....	....	....	....	....
2002-03	**NY Rangers**	**NHL**	**17**	**0**	**1**	**1**	**50**	**0**	**0**	**0**	**8**	**0.0**	**–1**	**1**	**0.0**	**6:28**	....	....	....	....	....	....	....	....	....
	Hartford	AHL	15	3	2	5	117	....	....	....	....	....	....	....	....	....	....	....	....	....	....	....	....	....	....
	Montreal	**NHL**	**11**	**0**	**0**	**0**	**46**	**0**	**0**	**0**	**2**	**0.0**	**–2**	**2**	**50.0**	**7:33**	....	....	....	....	....	....	....	....	....
2003-04	**Montreal**	**NHL**	**2**	**0**	**0**	**0**	**7**	**0**	**0**	**0**	**0**	**0.0**	**0**	**0**	**0.0**	**5:55**	....	....	....	....	....	....	....	....	....
	Hamilton	AHL	55	6	6	12	110	....	....	....	....	....	....	....	....	....	6	0	0	0	15	....	....	....	....
2004-05	Lowell	AHL	56	2	7	9	183	....	....	....	....	....	....	....	....	....	11	1	0	1	54	....	....	....	....
	NHL Totals		**108**	**0**	**5**	**5**	**394**	**0**	**0**	**0**	**35**	**0.0**		**5**	**40.0**	**5:43**	....	....	....	....	....	....	....	....	....

• Re-entered NHL Entry Draft. Originally St. Louis' 2nd choice, 67th overall, in 1996 Entry Draft.

Traded to **Tampa Bay** by **Montreal** for Mike McBain, November 26, 1999. Traded to **NY Rangers** by **Tampa Bay** for Boyd Kane, October 10, 2002. Claimed on waivers by **Montreal** from **NY Rangers**, February 21, 2003. Signed as a free agent by **Carolina**, August 11, 2004.

DYKHUIS, Karl

(DIGH-kowz, KAHRL)

Defense. Shoots left. 6'3", 209 lbs. Born, Sept-Iles, Que., July 8, 1972. Chicago's 1st choice, 16th overall, in 1990 Entry Draft.

Season	Club	League	GP	G	A	Pts	PIM	PP	SH	GW	S	%	+/-	TF	F%	Min	GP	G	A	Pts	PIM	PP	SH	GW	Min
1987-88	Lac St-Jean	QAAA	37	2	12	14	....	....	....	....	....	....	....	....	....	....	2	0	1	1	2	....	....	....	....
1988-89	Hull Olympiques	QMJHL	63	2	29	31	59	....	....	....	....	....	....	....	....	....	9	1	9	10	6	....	....	....	....
1989-90	Hull Olympiques	QMJHL	69	10	46	56	119	....	....	....	....	....	....	....	....	....	11	2	5	7	2	....	....	....	....
1990-91	Canada	Nat-Tm	37	2	9	11	16	....	....	....	....	....	....	....	....	....	....	....	....	....	....	....	....	....	....
	Longueuil	QMJHL	3	1	4	5	6	....	....	....	....	....	....	....	....	....	8	2	5	7	6	....	....	....	....
1991-92	Canada	Nat-Tm	19	1	2	3	16	....	....	....	....	....	....	....	....	....	....	....	....	....	....	....	....	....	....
	Verdun	QMJHL	29	5	19	24	55	....	....	....	....	....	....	....	....	....	17	0	12	12	14	....	....	....	....
	Chicago	**NHL**	**6**	**1**	**3**	**4**	**4**	**1**	**0**	**0**	**12**	**8.3**	**–1**	....	....	....	....	....	....	....	....	....	....	....	....

			Regular Season														Playoffs								
Season	Club	League	GP	G	A	Pts	PIM	PP	SH	GW	S	%	+/-	TF	F%	Min	GP	G	A	Pts	PIM	PP	SH	GW	Min
1992-93	**Chicago**	**NHL**	**12**	**0**	**5**	**5**	**0**	**0**	**0**	**0**	**10**	**0.0**	**2**	....	....	....	....	....	....	....	....	....	....	....	....
	Indianapolis Ice	IHL	59	5	18	23	76	....	....	....	....	....	....	....	....	....	5	1	1	2	8	....	....	....	....
1993-94	Indianapolis Ice	IHL	73	7	25	32	132	....	....	....	....	....	....	....	....	....	....	....	....	....	....	....	....	....	....
1994-95	Indianapolis Ice	IHL	52	2	21	23	63	....	....	....	....	....	....	....	....	....	....	....	....	....	....	....	....	....	....
	Philadelphia	**NHL**	**33**	**2**	**6**	**8**	**37**	**1**	**0**	**1**	**46**	**4.3**	**7**	....	....	....	**15**	**4**	**4**	**8**	**14**	**2**	**0**	**2**	....
	Hershey Bears	AHL	1	0	0	0	0	....	....	....	....	....	....	....	....	....	....	....	....	....	....	....	....	....	....
1995-96	**Philadelphia**	**NHL**	**82**	**5**	**15**	**20**	**101**	**1**	**0**	**0**	**104**	**4.8**	**12**	....	....	....	**12**	**2**	**2**	**4**	**22**	**1**	**0**	**0**	....
1996-97	**Philadelphia**	**NHL**	**62**	**4**	**15**	**19**	**35**	**2**	**0**	**1**	**101**	**4.0**	**6**	....	....	....	**18**	**0**	**3**	**3**	**2**	**0**	**0**	**0**	....
1997-98	**Tampa Bay**	**NHL**	**78**	**5**	**9**	**14**	**110**	**0**	**1**	**0**	**91**	**5.5**	**–8**	....	....	....	....	....	....	....	....	....	....	....	....
1998-99	**Tampa Bay**	**NHL**	**33**	**2**	**1**	**3**	**18**	**0**	**0**	**0**	**27**	**7.4**	**–21**	**0**	**0.0**	**20:14**	....	....	....	....	....	....	....	....	....
	Philadelphia	**NHL**	**45**	**2**	**4**	**6**	**32**	**1**	**0**	**0**	**61**	**3.3**	**–2**	**0**	**0.0**	**18:15**	**5**	**1**	**0**	**1**	**4**	**0**	**0**	**0**	**18:05**
99-2000	**Philadelphia**	**NHL**	**5**	**0**	**1**	**1**	**6**	**0**	**0**	**0**	**5**	**0.0**	**–2**	**0**	**0.0**	**14:54**	....	....	....	....	....	....	....	....	....
	Montreal	**NHL**	**67**	**7**	**12**	**19**	**40**	**3**	**1**	**0**	**64**	**10.9**	**–3**	**0**	**0.0**	**19:53**	....	....	....	....	....	....	....	....	....
2000-01	**Montreal**	**NHL**	**67**	**8**	**9**	**17**	**44**	**2**	**0**	**1**	**66**	**12.1**	**9**	**4**	**100.0**	**15:40**	....	....	....	....	....	....	....	....	....
2001-02	**Montreal**	**NHL**	**80**	**5**	**7**	**12**	**32**	**0**	**0**	**1**	**85**	**5.9**	**16**	**0**	**0.0**	**19:54**	**12**	**1**	**1**	**2**	**8**	**0**	**0**	**0**	**18:39**
2002-03	**Montreal**	**NHL**	**65**	**1**	**4**	**5**	**34**	**0**	**0**	**0**	**24**	**4.2**	**–5**	**1**	**0.0**	**15:00**	....	....	....	....	....	....	....	....	....
2003-04	**Montreal**	**NHL**	**9**	**0**	**0**	**0**	**2**	**0**	**0**	**0**	**6**	**0.0**	**–2**	**1**	**0.0**	**13:02**	....	....	....	....	....	....	....	....	....
	Hamilton	AHL	54	5	17	22	61	....	....	....	....	....	....	....	....	....	5	1	0	1	8	....	....	....	....
2004-05	Amsterdam	Nether.	5	1	1	2	36	....	....	....	....	....	....	....	....	....	7	1	3	4	39	....	....	....	....
	NHL Totals		**644**	**42**	**91**	**133**	**495**	**11**	**2**	**4**	**702**	**6.0**		**6**	**66.7**	**17:52**	**62**	**8**	**10**	**18**	**50**	**3**	**0**	**2**	**18:29**

QMJHL All-Rookie Team (1989) • QMJHL Defensive Rookie of the Year (1989) • QMJHL First All-Star Team (1990)

Traded to **Philadelphia** by **Chicago** for Bob Wilkie and Philadelphia's 5th round choice (Kyle Calder) in 1997 Entry Draft, February 16, 1995. Traded to **Tampa Bay** by **Philadelphia** with Mikael Renberg for Philadelphia's 1st round choices (previously acquired) in 1998 (Simon Gagne), 1999 (Maxime Ouellet), 2000 (Justin Williams) and 2001 (later traded to Ottawa – Ottawa selected Tim Gleason) Entry Drafts, August 20, 1997. Traded to **Philadelphia** by **Tampa Bay** for Petr Svoboda, December 28, 1998. Traded to **Montreal** by **Philadelphia** for cash, October 20, 1999. Signed as a free agent by **Amsterdam** (Netherlands), January 3, 2005. Signed as a free agent by **Mannheim** (Germany), August 25, 2005.

EASTWOOD, Mike

(EEST-wuhd, MIGHK)

Center. Shoots right. 6'3", 216 lbs. Born, Ottawa, Ont., July 1, 1967. Toronto's 5th choice, 91st overall, in 1987 Entry Draft.

1984-85	Nepean Raiders	CJHL	46	10	13	23	18	....	....	....	....	....	....	....	....	....	....	....	....	....	....	....	....	....	....
1985-86	Nepean Raiders	CJHL	7	4	2	6	6	....	....	....	....	....	....	....	....	....	....	....	....	....	....	....	....	....	....
1986-87	Pembroke	CJHL	54	58	45	103	62	....	....	....	....	....	....	....	....	....	23	36	11	47	32	....	....	....	....
1987-88	Western Mich.	CCHA	42	5	8	13	14	....	....	....	....	....	....	....	....	....	....	....	....	....	....	....	....	....	....
1988-89	Western Mich.	CCHA	40	10	13	23	87	....	....	....	....	....	....	....	....	....	....	....	....	....	....	....	....	....	....
1989-90	Western Mich.	CCHA	40	25	27	52	36	....	....	....	....	....	....	....	....	....	....	....	....	....	....	....	....	....	....
1990-91	Western Mich.	CCHA	42	29	32	61	84	....	....	....	....	....	....	....	....	....	....	....	....	....	....	....	....	....	....
1991-92	**Toronto**	**NHL**	**9**	**0**	**2**	**2**	**4**	**0**	**0**	**0**	**6**	**0.0**	**–4**	....	....	....	....	....	....	....	....	....	....	....	....
	St. John's	AHL	61	18	25	43	28	....	....	....	....	....	....	....	....	....	16	9	10	19	16	....	....	....	....
1992-93	**Toronto**	**NHL**	**12**	**1**	**6**	**7**	**21**	**0**	**0**	**0**	**11**	**9.1**	**–2**	....	....	....	**10**	**1**	**2**	**3**	**8**	**0**	**0**	**0**	....
	St. John's	AHL	60	24	35	59	32	....	....	....	....	....	....	....	....	....	....	....	....	....	....	....	....	....	....
1993-94	**Toronto**	**NHL**	**54**	**8**	**10**	**18**	**28**	**1**	**0**	**2**	**41**	**19.5**	**2**	....	....	....	**18**	**3**	**2**	**5**	**12**	**1**	**0**	**1**	....
1994-95	**Toronto**	**NHL**	**36**	**5**	**5**	**10**	**32**	**0**	**0**	**0**	**38**	**13.2**	**–12**	....	....	....	....	....	....	....	....	....	....	....	....
	Winnipeg	**NHL**	**13**	**3**	**6**	**9**	**4**	**0**	**0**	**0**	**17**	**17.6**	**3**	....	....	....	....	....	....	....	....	....	....	....	....
1995-96	**Winnipeg**	**NHL**	**80**	**14**	**14**	**28**	**20**	**2**	**0**	**3**	**94**	**14.9**	**–14**	....	....	....	**6**	**0**	**1**	**1**	**2**	**0**	**0**	**0**	....
1996-97	**Phoenix**	**NHL**	**33**	**1**	**3**	**4**	**4**	**0**	**0**	**0**	**22**	**4.5**	**–3**	....	....	....	....	....	....	....	....	....	....	....	....
	NY Rangers	**NHL**	**27**	**1**	**7**	**8**	**10**	**0**	**0**	**0**	**22**	**4.5**	**2**	....	....	....	**15**	**1**	**2**	**3**	**22**	**0**	**0**	**0**	....
1997-98	**NY Rangers**	**NHL**	**48**	**5**	**5**	**10**	**16**	**0**	**0**	**0**	**34**	**14.7**	**–2**	....	....	....	....	....	....	....	....	....	....	....	....
	St. Louis	**NHL**	**10**	**1**	**0**	**1**	**6**	**0**	**0**	**1**	**4**	**25.0**	**0**	....	....	....	**3**	**1**	**0**	**1**	**0**	**0**	**0**	**1**	....
1998-99	**St. Louis**	**NHL**	**82**	**9**	**21**	**30**	**36**	**0**	**0**	**0**	**76**	**11.8**	**6**	**1235**	**56.6**	**14:59**	**13**	**1**	**1**	**2**	**6**	**0**	**0**	**0**	**16:02**
99-2000	**St. Louis**	**NHL**	**79**	**19**	**15**	**34**	**32**	**1**	**3**	**3**	**83**	**22.9**	**5**	**872**	**52.2**	**15:08**	**7**	**1**	**1**	**2**	**6**	**0**	**0**	**0**	**13:28**
2000-01	**St. Louis**	**NHL**	**77**	**6**	**17**	**23**	**28**	**0**	**2**	**1**	**51**	**11.8**	**4**	**1230**	**53.4**	**14:08**	**15**	**0**	**2**	**2**	**2**	**0**	**0**	**0**	**15:13**
2001-02	**St. Louis**	**NHL**	**71**	**7**	**10**	**17**	**41**	**0**	**0**	**2**	**60**	**11.7**	**–2**	**1110**	**53.8**	**12:55**	**10**	**0**	**0**	**0**	**6**	**0**	**0**	**0**	**15:32**
2002-03	**St. Louis**	**NHL**	**17**	**1**	**3**	**4**	**8**	**1**	**0**	**0**	**7**	**14.3**	**1**	**203**	**42.9**	**10:44**	....	....	....	....	....	....	....	....	....
	Chicago	**NHL**	**53**	**2**	**10**	**12**	**24**	**0**	**0**	**0**	**32**	**6.3**	**–6**	**713**	**53.3**	**12:54**	....	....	....	....	....	....	....	....	....
2003-04	**Pittsburgh**	**NHL**	**82**	**4**	**15**	**19**	**40**	**0**	**0**	**1**	**55**	**7.3**	**–18**	**1401**	**51.5**	**14:09**	....	....	....	....	....	....	....	....	....
2004-05			DID NOT PLAY																						
	NHL Totals		**783**	**87**	**149**	**236**	**354**	**5**	**5**	**13**	**653**	**13.3**		**6764**	**53.2**	**14:00**	**97**	**8**	**11**	**19**	**64**	**1**	**0**	**2**	**15:15**

CCHA Second All-Star Team (1991)

Traded to **Winnipeg** by **Toronto** with Toronto's 3rd round choice (Brad Isbister) in 1995 Entry Draft for Tie Domi, April 7, 1995. Transferred to **Phoenix** after **Winnipeg** franchise relocated, July 1, 1996. Traded to **NY Rangers** by **Phoenix** with Dallas Eakins for Jayson More, February 6, 1997. Traded to **St. Louis** by **NY Rangers** for Harry York, March 24, 1998. Claimed on waivers by **Chicago** from **St. Louis**, December 11, 2002. Signed as a free agent by **Pittsburgh**, July 31, 2003.

EATON, Mark

(EE-tohn, MAHRK) **NSH.**

Defense. Shoots left. 6'2", 212 lbs. Born, Wilmington, DE, May 6, 1977.

1995-96	Waterloo	USHL	50	4	21	25	....	....	....	....	....	....	....	....	....	....	....	....	....	....	....	....	....	....	....
1996-97	Waterloo	USHL	50	6	32	38	62	....	....	....	....	....	....	....	....	....	....	....	....	....	....	....	....	....	....
1997-98	U. of Notre Dame	CCHA	41	12	17	29	32	....	....	....	....	....	....	....	....	....	....	....	....	....	....	....	....	....	....
1998-99	Philadelphia	AHL	74	9	27	36	38	....	....	....	....	....	....	....	....	....	16	4	8	12	0	....	....	....	....
99-2000	**Philadelphia**	**NHL**	**27**	**1**	**1**	**2**	**8**	**0**	**0**	**1**	**25**	**4.0**	**1**	**0**	**0.0**	**18:17**	**7**	**0**	**0**	**0**	**0**	**0**	**0**	**0**	**13:36**
	Philadelphia	AHL	47	9	17	26	6	....	....	....	....	....	....	....	....	....	....	....	....	....	....	....	....	....	....
2000-01	**Nashville**	**NHL**	**34**	**3**	**8**	**11**	**14**	**1**	**0**	**1**	**32**	**9.4**	**7**	**0**	**0.0**	**17:13**	....	....	....	....	....	....	....	....	....
	Milwaukee	IHL	34	3	12	15	27	....	....	....	....	....	....	....	....	....	....	....	....	....	....	....	....	....	....
2001-02	**Nashville**	**NHL**	**58**	**3**	**5**	**8**	**24**	**0**	**0**	**0**	**52**	**5.8**	**–12**	**0**	**0.0**	**17:12**	....	....	....	....	....	....	....	....	....
2002-03	**Nashville**	**NHL**	**50**	**2**	**7**	**9**	**22**	**0**	**0**	**0**	**52**	**3.8**	**1**	**0**	**0.0**	**15:45**	....	....	....	....	....	....	....	....	....
	Milwaukee	AHL	3	1	0	1	2	....	....	....	....	....	....	....	....	....	....	....	....	....	....	....	....	....	....
2003-04	**Nashville**	**NHL**	**75**	**4**	**9**	**13**	**26**	**0**	**0**	**1**	**82**	**4.9**	**16**	**0**	**0.0**	**20:56**	**6**	**0**	**0**	**0**	**2**	**0**	**0**	**0**	**19:51**
2004-05	Grand Rapids	AHL	29	3	3	6	21	....	....	....	....	....	....	....	....	....	....	....	....	....	....	....	....	....	....
	NHL Totals		**244**	**13**	**30**	**43**	**94**	**1**	**0**	**3**	**243**	**5.3**		**0**	**0.0**	**18:10**	**13**	**0**	**0**	**0**	**2**	**0**	**0**	**0**	**16:29**

USHL Second All-Star Team (1997) • Curt Hammer Award (Most Gentlemanly Player – USHL) (1997) • CCHA Rookie of the Year (1998)

Signed as a free agent by **Philadelphia**, August 4, 1998. Traded to **Nashville** by **Philadelphia** for Detroit's 3rd round choice (previously acquired, Philadelphia selected Patrick Sharp) in 2001 Entry Draft, September 29, 2000. Signed as a free agent by **Grand Rapids** (AHL), February 16, 2005.

EHRHOFF, Christian

(AIR-hawf, KRIHS-tyehn) **S.J.**

Defense. Shoots left. 6'2", 195 lbs. Born, Moers, West Germany, July 6, 1982. San Jose's 2nd choice, 106th overall, in 2001 Entry Draft.

1998-99	Krefelder EV Jr.	Ger-Jr.	22	10	14	24	46	....	....	....	....	....	....	....	....	....	....	....	....	....	....	....	....	....	....
99-2000	EV Duisburg	German-3	41	3	12	15	50	....	....	....	....	....	....	....	....	....	....	....	....	....	....	....	....	....	....
	Krefeld Pinguine	Germany	9	1	0	1	6	....	....	....	....	....	....	....	....	....	3	0	0	0	0	....	....	....	....
2000-01	EV Duisburg	German-3	6	1	2	3	12	....	....	....	....	....	....	....	....	....	....	....	....	....	....	....	....	....	....
	Krefeld Pinguine	Germany	58	3	11	14	73	....	....	....	....	....	....	....	....	....	....	....	....	....	....	....	....	....	....
2001-02	Krefeld Pinguine	Germany	46	7	17	24	81	....	....	....	....	....	....	....	....	....	3	0	0	0	2	....	....	....	....
	Germany	Olympics	7	0	0	0	8	....	....	....	....	....	....	....	....	....	....	....	....	....	....	....	....	....	....
2002-03	Krefeld Pinguine	Germany	48	10	17	27	54	....	....	....	....	....	....	....	....	....	14	3	6	9	24	....	....	....	....
2003-04	**San Jose**	**NHL**	**41**	**1**	**11**	**12**	**14**	**0**	**0**	**1**	**58**	**1.7**	**4**	**0**	**0.0**	**15:23**	....	....	....	....	....	....	....	....	....
	Cleveland Barons	AHL	27	4	10	14	43	....	....	....	....	....	....	....	....	....	9	2	6	8	11	....	....	....	....
2004-05	Cleveland Barons	AHL	79	12	23	35	103	....	....	....	....	....	....	....	....	....	....	....	....	....	....	....	....	....	....
	NHL Totals		**41**	**1**	**11**	**12**	**14**	**0**	**0**	**1**	**58**	**1.7**		**0**	**0.0**	**15:23**	....	....	....	....	....	....	....	....	....

EKMAN, Nils

(EHK-mahn, NIHLS) **S.J.**

Left wing. Shoots left. 6', 185 lbs. Born, Stockholm, Sweden, March 11, 1976. Calgary's 6th choice, 107th overall, in 1994 Entry Draft.

1993-94	Hammarby Jr.	Swe-Jr.	11	4	5	9	14	....	....	....	....	....	....	....	....	....	....	....	....	....	....	....	....	....	....
	Hammarby	Sweden-2	18	7	2	9	4	....	....	....	....	....	....	....	....	....	....	....	....	....	....	....	....	....	....
1994-95	Hammarby Jr.	Swe-Jr.	2	2	1	3	0	....	....	....	....	....	....	....	....	....	....	....	....	....	....	....	....	....	....
	Hammarby	Sweden-2	32	10	8	18	18	....	....	....	....	....	....	....	....	....	....	....	....	....	....	....	....	....	....
1995-96	Hammarby	Sweden-2	26	9	7	16	53	....	....	....	....	....	....	....	....	....	1	0	0	0	0	....	....	....	....
1996-97	Kiekko-Espoo	Finland	50	24	19	43	60	....	....	....	....	....	....	....	....	....	4	2	0	2	4	....	....	....	....
1997-98	Kiekko-Espoo	Finland	43	14	14	28	86	....	....	....	....	....	....	....	....	....	7	2	2	4	27	....	....	....	....
	Saint John Flames	AHL	....	....	....	....	....	....	....	....	....	....	....	....	....	....	1	0	0	0	2	....	....	....	....

Season	Club	League	Regular Season GP	G	A	Pts	PIM	PP	SH	GW	S	%	+/-	TF	F%	Min	Playoffs GP	G	A	Pts	PIM	PP	SH	GW	Min
1998-99	Blues Espoo	Finland	52	20	14	34	96	....	....	....	....	....	....	....	....	....	3	1	1	2	6	....	....	....	....
99-2000	Detroit Vipers	IHL	10	7	2	9	8	....	....	....	....	....	....	....	....	....	....	....	....	....	....	....	....	....	....
	Tampa Bay	**NHL**	**28**	**2**	**2**	**4**	**36**	**1**	**0**	**0**	**42**	**4.8**	**–8**	**3**	**0.0**	**11:12**	....	....	....	....	....	....	....	....	....
	Long Beach	IHL	27	11	12	23	26	....	....	....	....	....	....	....	....	....	5	3	3	6	4	....	....	....	....
2000-01	**Tampa Bay**	**NHL**	**43**	**9**	**11**	**20**	**40**	**2**	**1**	**1**	**72**	**12.5**	**–15**	**16**	**37.5**	**15:45**	....	....	....	....	....	....	....	....	....
	Detroit Vipers	IHL	33	22	14	36	63	....	....	....	....	....	....	....	....	....	....	....	....	....	....	....	....	....	....
2001-02	Djurgarden	Sweden	38	16	15	31	57	....	....	....	....	....	....	....	....	....	4	1	0	1	32	....	....	....	....
2002-03	Hartford	AHL	57	30	36	66	73	....	....	....	....	....	....	....	....	....	2	0	2	2	4	....	....	....	....
2003-04	**San Jose**	**NHL**	**82**	**22**	**33**	**55**	**34**	**1**	**4**	**5**	**147**	**15.0**	**30**	**23**	**21.7**	**14:54**	**16**	**0**	**3**	**3**	**8**	**0**	**0**	**0**	**13:02**
2004-05	Djurgarden	Sweden	44	18	27	45	106	....	....	....	....	....	....	....	....	....	12	4	5	9	20	....	....	....	....
	NHL Totals		**153**	**33**	**46**	**79**	**110**	**4**	**5**	**6**	**261**	**12.6**		**42**	**26.2**	**14:28**	**16**	**0**	**3**	**3**	**8**	**0**	**0**	**0**	**13:02**

Garry F. Longman Memorial Trophy (Rookie of the Year – IHL) (2000)

Traded to **Tampa Bay** by **Calgary** with Calgary's 4th round choice (later traded to NY Islanders – NY Islanders selected Vladimir Gorbunov) in 2000 Entry Draft for Andreas Johansson, November 20, 1999. Traded to **NY Rangers** by **Tampa Bay** with Kyle Freadrich for Tim Taylor, June 30, 2001. Traded to **San Jose** by **NY Rangers** for Chad Wiseman, August 12, 2003. Signed as a free agent by **Djurgarden** (Sweden), September 16, 2004.

ELIAS, Patrik (ehl-EE-ahsh, PA-trihk) N.J.

Left wing. Shoots left. 6'1", 195 lbs. Born, Trebic, Czech., April 13, 1976. New Jersey's 2nd choice, 51st overall, in 1994 Entry Draft.

Season	Club	League	GP	G	A	Pts	PIM	PP	SH	GW	S	%	+/-	TF	F%	Min	GP	G	A	Pts	PIM	PP	SH	GW	Min
1992-93	Poldi Kladno	Czech	2	0	0	0	....	....	....	....	....	....	....	....	....	....	....	....	....	....	....	....	....	....	....
1993-94	HC Kladno	CzRep	15	1	2	3	....	....	....	....	....	....	....	....	....	....	11	2	2	4	....	....	....	....	....
1994-95	HC Kladno	CzRep	28	4	3	7	37	....	....	....	....	....	....	....	....	....	7	1	2	3	12	....	....	....	....
1995-96	**New Jersey**	**NHL**	**1**	**0**	**0**	**0**	**0**	**0**	**0**	**0**	**2**	**0.0**	**–1**	....	....	....	....	....	....	....	....	....	....	....	....
	Albany River Rats	AHL	74	27	36	63	83	....	....	....	....	....	....	....	....	....	4	1	1	2	2	....	....	....	....
1996-97	**New Jersey**	**NHL**	**17**	**2**	**3**	**5**	**2**	**0**	**0**	**0**	**23**	**8.7**	**–4**	....	....	....	**8**	**2**	**3**	**5**	**4**	**1**	**0**	**0**	....
	Albany River Rats	AHL	57	24	43	67	76	....	....	....	....	....	....	....	....	....	6	1	2	3	8	....	....	....	....
1997-98	**New Jersey**	**NHL**	**74**	**18**	**19**	**37**	**28**	**5**	**0**	**6**	**147**	**12.2**	**18**	....	....	....	**4**	**0**	**1**	**1**	**0**	**0**	**0**	**0**	....
	Albany River Rats	AHL	3	3	0	3	2	....	....	....	....	....	....	....	....	....	....	....	....	....	....	....	....	....	....
1998-99	**New Jersey**	**NHL**	**74**	**17**	**33**	**50**	**34**	**3**	**0**	**2**	**157**	**10.8**	**19**	**99**	**38.4**	**15:50**	**7**	**0**	**5**	**5**	**6**	**0**	**0**	**0**	**18:07**
99-2000	Trebic	CzRep-2	2	2	1	3	2	....	....	....	....	....	....	....	....	....	....	....	....	....	....	....	....	....	....
	Pardubice	CzRep	5	1	4	5	31	....	....	....	....	....	....	....	....	....	....	....	....	....	....	....	....	....	....
	♦ **New Jersey**	**NHL**	**72**	**35**	**37**	**72**	**58**	**9**	**0**	**9**	**183**	**19.1**	**16**	**134**	**45.5**	**17:28**	**23**	**7**	***13**	**20**	**9**	**2**	**1**	**1**	**17:44**
2000-01	**New Jersey**	**NHL**	**82**	**40**	**56**	**96**	**51**	**8**	**3**	**6**	**220**	**18.2**	**45**	**155**	**41.3**	**18:44**	**25**	**9**	**14**	**23**	**10**	**3**	**1**	**2**	**18:14**
2001-02	**New Jersey**	**NHL**	**75**	**29**	**32**	**61**	**36**	**8**	**1**	**8**	**199**	**14.6**	**4**	**128**	**45.3**	**18:57**	**6**	**2**	**4**	**6**	**6**	**2**	**0**	**0**	**20:33**
	Czech Republic	Olympics	4	1	1	2	0	....	....	....	....	....	....	....	....	....	....	....	....	....	....	....	....	....	....
2002-03♦	**New Jersey**	**NHL**	**81**	**28**	**29**	**57**	**22**	**6**	**0**	**4**	**255**	**11.0**	**17**	**427**	**43.8**	**18:05**	**24**	**5**	**8**	**13**	**26**	**2**	**0**	**2**	**17:14**
2003-04	**New Jersey**	**NHL**	**82**	**38**	**43**	**81**	**44**	**9**	**3**	**9**	**300**	**12.7**	**26**	**49**	**36.7**	**18:46**	**5**	**3**	**2**	**5**	**2**	**1**	**0**	**1**	**18:59**
2004-05	Znojmo	CzRep	28	8	20	28	65	....	....	....	....	....	....	....	....	....	....	....	....	....	....	....	....	....	....
	Magnitogorsk	Russia	17	5	9	14	28	....	....	....	....	....	....	....	....	....	....	....	....	....	....	....	....	....	....
	NHL Totals		**558**	**207**	**252**	**459**	**275**	**48**	**7**	**44**	**1486**	**13.9**		**992**	**42.9**	**18:00**	**102**	**28**	**50**	**78**	**63**	**11**	**2**	**6**	**18:02**

NHL All-Rookie Team (1998) • NHL First All-Star Team (2001) • Bud Light Plus/Minus Award (2001) (tied with Joe Sakic)

Played in NHL All-Star Game (2000, 2002)

Signed as a free agent by **Znojmo** (CzRep), September 6, 2004. Signed as a free agent by **Magnitogorsk** (Russia), December 9, 2004.

ELLISON, Matt (EHL-ih-suhn, MAT) CHI.

Right wing. Shoots right. 6', 192 lbs. Born, Duncan, B.C., December 8, 1983. Chicago's 4th choice, 128th overall, in 2002 Entry Draft.

Season	Club	League	GP	G	A	Pts	PIM	PP	SH	GW	S	%	+/-	TF	F%	Min	GP	G	A	Pts	PIM	PP	SH	GW	Min
1997-98	Cowichan Valley	BCAHA	24	27	31	58	10	....	....	....	....	....	....	....	....	....	....	....	....	....	....	....	....	....	....
1998-99	Kerry Park	VIJHL	38	40	47	87	110	....	....	....	....	....	....	....	....	....	....	....	....	....	....	....	....	....	....
99-2000	Cowichan Valley	BCHL	60	11	23	34	95	....	....	....	....	....	....	....	....	....	....	....	....	....	....	....	....	....	....
2000-01	Cowichan Valley	BCHL	60	22	44	66	102	....	....	....	....	....	....	....	....	....	....	....	....	....	....	....	....	....	....
2001-02	Cowichan Valley	BCHL	60	42	*75	*117	76	....	....	....	....	....	....	....	....	....	10	5	6	11	8	....	....	....	....
2002-03	Red Deer Rebels	WHL	72	40	56	96	80	....	....	....	....	....	....	....	....	....	22	7	13	20	28	....	....	....	....
2003-04	**Chicago**	**NHL**	**10**	**0**	**1**	**1**	**0**	**0**	**0**	**0**	**4**	**0.0**	**–3**	**46**	**39.1**	**12:40**	....	....	....	....	....	....	....	....	....
	Norfolk Admirals	AHL	71	14	21	35	115	....	....	....	....	....	....	....	....	....	7	0	1	1	4	....	....	....	....
2004-05	Norfolk Admirals	AHL	71	14	37	51	44	....	....	....	....	....	....	....	....	....	5	0	1	1	2	....	....	....	....
	NHL Totals		**10**	**0**	**1**	**1**	**0**	**0**	**0**	**0**	**4**	**0.0**		**46**	**39.1**	**12:40**	....	....	....	....	....	....	....	....	....

WHL East Second All-Star Team (2003) • WHL Rookie of the Year (2003) • Canadian Major Junior Rookie of the Year (2003)

EMINGER, Steve (EH-mihn-juhr, STEEV) WSH.

Defense. Shoots right. 6'2", 203 lbs. Born, Woodbridge, Ont., October 31, 1983. Washington's 1st choice, 12th overall, in 2002 Entry Draft.

Season	Club	League	GP	G	A	Pts	PIM	PP	SH	GW	S	%	+/-	TF	F%	Min	GP	G	A	Pts	PIM	PP	SH	GW	Min
1998-99	Bramalea Blues	OPJHL	47	6	9	15	81	....	....	....	....	....	....	....	....	....	....	....	....	....	....	....	....	....	....
99-2000	Kitchener Rangers	OHL	50	2	14	16	74	....	....	....	....	....	....	....	....	....	5	0	0	0	0	....	....	....	....
2000-01	Kitchener Rangers	OHL	54	6	26	32	66	....	....	....	....	....	....	....	....	....	....	....	....	....	....	....	....	....	....
2001-02	Kitchener Rangers	OHL	64	19	39	58	93	....	....	....	....	....	....	....	....	....	4	0	2	2	10	....	....	....	....
2002-03	**Washington**	**NHL**	**17**	**0**	**2**	**2**	**24**	**0**	**0**	**0**	**6**	**0.0**	**–3**	**0**	**0.0**	**10:08**	....	....	....	....	....	....	....	....	....
	Kitchener Rangers	OHL	23	2	27	29	40	....	....	....	....	....	....	....	....	....	21	3	8	11	44	....	....	....	....
2003-04	**Washington**	**NHL**	**41**	**0**	**4**	**4**	**45**	**0**	**0**	**0**	**12**	**0.0**	**–11**	**0**	**0.0**	**17:32**	....	....	....	....	....	....	....	....	....
	Portland Pirates	AHL	41	0	4	4	40	....	....	....	....	....	....	....	....	....	7	0	1	1	2	....	....	....	....
2004-05	Portland Pirates	AHL	62	3	17	20	40	....	....	....	....	....	....	....	....	....	....	....	....	....	....	....	....	....	....
	NHL Totals		**58**	**0**	**6**	**6**	**69**	**0**	**0**	**0**	**18**	**0.0**		**0**	**0.0**	**15:22**	....	....	....	....	....	....	....	....	....

OHL Second All-Star Team (2002, 2003) • Memorial Cup Tournament All-Star Team (2003)

ENDICOTT, Shane (ehn-DIH-kawt, SHAYN) PIT.

Center. Shoots left. 6'3", 214 lbs. Born, Saskatoon, Sask., December 21, 1981. Pittsburgh's 2nd choice, 52nd overall, in 2000 Entry Draft.

Season	Club	League	GP	G	A	Pts	PIM	PP	SH	GW	S	%	+/-	TF	F%	Min	GP	G	A	Pts	PIM	PP	SH	GW	Min
1997-98	Sask. Contacts	SMHL	43	31	32	63	42	....	....	....	....	....	....	....	....	....	....	....	....	....	....	....	....	....	....
	Seattle	WHL	....	....	....	....	....	....	....	....	....	....	....	....	....	....	5	0	0	0	0	....	....	....	....
1998-99	Seattle	WHL	72	13	26	39	27	....	....	....	....	....	....	....	....	....	11	0	1	1	0	....	....	....	....
99-2000	Seattle	WHL	70	23	32	55	62	....	....	....	....	....	....	....	....	....	7	1	6	7	6	....	....	....	....
2000-01	Seattle	WHL	72	36	43	79	86	....	....	....	....	....	....	....	....	....	9	4	5	9	12	....	....	....	....
2001-02	**Pittsburgh**	**NHL**	**4**	**0**	**1**	**1**	**4**	**0**	**0**	**0**	**2**	**0.0**	**–1**	**18**	**33.3**	**8:28**	....	....	....	....	....	....	....	....	....
	Wilkes-Barre	AHL	63	19	20	39	46	....	....	....	....	....	....	....	....	....	....	....	....	....	....	....	....	....	....
2002-03	Wilkes-Barre	AHL	74	13	26	39	68	....	....	....	....	....	....	....	....	....	6	0	2	2	4	....	....	....	....
2003-04	Wilkes-Barre	AHL	79	17	22	39	68	....	....	....	....	....	....	....	....	....	24	8	4	12	26	....	....	....	....
2004-05	Wilkes-Barre	AHL	68	24	23	47	89	....	....	....	....	....	....	....	....	....	11	2	2	4	31	....	....	....	....
	NHL Totals		**4**	**0**	**1**	**1**	**4**	**0**	**0**	**0**	**2**	**0.0**		**18**	**33.3**	**8:28**	....	....	....	....	....	....	....	....	....

ERAT, Martin (EE-rat, mahr-TIHN) NSH.

Left wing. Shoots left. 6', 195 lbs. Born, Trebic, Czech., August 29, 1981. Nashville's 12th choice, 191st overall, in 1999 Entry Draft.

Season	Club	League	GP	G	A	Pts	PIM	PP	SH	GW	S	%	+/-	TF	F%	Min	GP	G	A	Pts	PIM	PP	SH	GW	Min
1997-98	HC ZPS Zlin Jr.	CzRep-Jr.	46	35	30	65	....	....	....	....	....	....	....	....	....	....	....	....	....	....	....	....	....	....	....
1998-99	HC ZPS Zlin Jr.	CzRep-Jr.	35	21	23	44	....	....	....	....	....	....	....	....	....	....	....	....	....	....	....	....	....	....	....
	Zlin	CzRep	5	0	0	0	2	....	....	....	....	....	....	....	....	....	....	....	....	....	....	....	....	....	....
99-2000	Saskatoon Blades	WHL	66	27	26	53	82	....	....	....	....	....	....	....	....	....	11	4	8	12	16	....	....	....	....
2000-01	Saskatoon Blades	WHL	31	19	35	54	48	....	....	....	....	....	....	....	....	....	....	....	....	....	....	....	....	....	....
	Red Deer Rebels	WHL	17	4	24	28	24	....	....	....	....	....	....	....	....	....	22	*15	*21	*36	32	....	....	....	....
2001-02	**Nashville**	**NHL**	**80**	**9**	**24**	**33**	**32**	**2**	**0**	**2**	**84**	**10.7**	**–11**	**3**	**66.7**	**13:10**	....	....	....	....	....	....	....	....	....
2002-03	**Nashville**	**NHL**	**27**	**1**	**7**	**8**	**14**	**1**	**0**	**0**	**39**	**2.6**	**–9**	**1**	**0.0**	**12:47**	....	....	....	....	....	....	....	....	....
	Milwaukee	AHL	45	10	22	32	41	....	....	....	....	....	....	....	....	....	6	5	4	9	4	....	....	....	....
2003-04	**Nashville**	**NHL**	**76**	**16**	**33**	**49**	**38**	**4**	**0**	**2**	**137**	**11.7**	**10**	**31**	**29.0**	**15:00**	**6**	**0**	**1**	**1**	**6**	**0**	**0**	**0**	**14:09**
2004-05	HC Hame Zlin	CzRep	48	20	23	43	129	....	....	....	....	....	....	....	....	....	16	*7	5	12	12	....	....	....	....
	NHL Totals		**183**	**26**	**64**	**90**	**84**	**7**	**0**	**4**	**260**	**10.0**		**35**	**31.4**	**13:52**	**6**	**0**	**1**	**1**	**6**	**0**	**0**	**0**	**14:09**

Signed as a free agent by **Zlin** (CzRep), September 5, 2004.

ERIKSSON, Anders

(AIR-ihk-suhn, AND-uhrs)

Defense. Shoots left. 6'2", 220 lbs. Born, Bollnas, Sweden, January 9, 1975. Detroit's 1st choice, 22nd overall, in 1993 Entry Draft.

			Regular Season														Playoffs								
Season	Club	League	GP	G	A	Pts	PIM	PP	SH	GW	S	%	+/-	TF	F%	Min	GP	G	A	Pts	PIM	PP	SH	GW	Min
1992-93	MoDo Jr.	Swe-Jr.	10	5	3	8	14																		
	MoDo	Sweden	20	0	2	2	2										1	0	0	0	0				
1993-94	MoDo Jr.	Swe-Jr.	3	1	2	3	34																		
	MoDo	Sweden	38	2	8	10	42										11	0	0	0	8				
1994-95	MoDo	Sweden	39	3	6	9	54																		
1995-96	**Detroit**	**NHL**	**1**	**0**	**0**	**0**	**2**	**0**	**0**	**0**	**0**	**0.0**	**1**				**3**	**0**	**0**	**0**	**0**	**0**	**0**	**0**	
	Adirondack	AHL	75	6	36	42	64										3	0	0	0	0				
1996-97	**Detroit**	**NHL**	**23**	**0**	**6**	**6**	**10**	**0**	**0**	**0**	**27**	**0.0**	**5**												
	Adirondack	AHL	44	3	25	28	36										4	0	1	1	4				
1997-98 ♦	**Detroit**	**NHL**	**66**	**7**	**14**	**21**	**32**	**1**	**0**	**2**	**91**	**7.7**	**21**				**18**	**0**	**5**	**5**	**16**	**0**	**0**	**0**	
1998-99	**Detroit**	**NHL**	**61**	**2**	**10**	**12**	**34**	**0**	**0**	**1**	**67**	**3.0**	**5**	**0**	**0.0**	**15:54**									
	Chicago	**NHL**	**11**	**0**	**8**	**8**	**0**	**0**	**0**	**0**	**12**	**0.0**	**6**	**0**	**0.0**	**22:51**									
99-2000	**Chicago**	**NHL**	**73**	**3**	**25**	**28**	**20**	**0**	**0**	**1**	**86**	**3.5**	**4**	**1**	**100.0**	**21:03**									
2000-01	**Chicago**	**NHL**	**13**	**2**	**3**	**5**	**2**	**1**	**0**	**0**	**19**	**10.5**	**–4**	**0**	**0.0**	**21:20**									
	Florida	**NHL**	**60**	**0**	**21**	**21**	**28**	**0**	**0**	**0**	**80**	**0.0**	**2**	**1**	**0.0**	**21:02**									
2001-02	**Toronto**	**NHL**	**34**	**0**	**2**	**2**	**12**	**0**	**0**	**0**	**31**	**0.0**	**–1**	**0**	**0.0**	**15:55**	**10**	**0**	**0**	**0**	**0**	**0**	**0**	**0**	**17:24**
	St. John's	AHL	25	4	6	10	14										11	0	5	5	6				
2002-03	**Toronto**	**NHL**	**4**	**0**	**0**	**0**	**0**	**0**	**0**	**0**	**7**	**0.0**	**1**	**0**	**0.0**	**19:02**									
	St. John's	AHL	72	5	34	39	133																		
2003-04	**Columbus**	**NHL**	**66**	**7**	**20**	**27**	**18**	**2**	**0**	**1**	**84**	**8.3**	**–6**	**0**	**0.0**	**20:42**									
	Syracuse Crunch	AHL	9	1	3	4	12																		
2004-05	HV 71 Jonkoping	Sweden	32	1	9	10	54																		
	NHL Totals		**412**	**21**	**109**	**130**	**158**	**4**	**0**	**5**	**504**	**4.2**		**2**	**50.0**	**19:30**	**31**	**0**	**5**	**5**	**16**	**0**	**0**	**0**	**17:24**

Traded to **Chicago** by **Detroit** with Detroit's 1st round choices in 1999 (Steve McCarthy) and 2001 (Adam Munro) Entry Drafts for Chris Chelios, March 23, 1999. Traded to **Florida** by **Chicago** for Jaroslav Spacek, November 6, 2000. Signed as a free agent by **Toronto**, July 9, 2001. Signed as a free agent by **Columbus**, October 10, 2003. Signed as a free agent by **Calgary**, September 16, 2004. Signed as a free agent by **HV 71** (Sweden), October 29, 2004

ERSKINE, John

(AIR-skign, JAWN) **DAL.**

Defense. Shoots left. 6'4", 215 lbs. Born, Kingston, Ont., June 26, 1980. Dallas' 1st choice, 39th overall, in 1998 Entry Draft.

Season	Club	League	GP	G	A	Pts	PIM	PP	SH	GW	S	%	+/-	TF	F%	Min	GP	G	A	Pts	PIM	PP	SH	GW	Min
1996-97	Quinte Hawks	MTJHL	48	4	16	20	241																		
1997-98	London Knights	OHL	55	0	9	9	205										16	0	5	5	25				
1998-99	London Knights	OHL	57	8	12	20	208										25	5	10	15	38				
99-2000	London Knights	OHL	58	12	31	43	177																		
2000-01	Utah Grizzlies	IHL	77	1	8	9	284																		
2001-02	**Dallas**	**NHL**	**33**	**0**	**1**	**1**	**62**	**0**	**0**	**0**	**16**	**0.0**	**–8**	**0**	**0.0**	**10:44**									
	Utah Grizzlies	AHL	39	2	6	8	118										3	0	0	0	10				
2002-03	**Dallas**	**NHL**	**16**	**2**	**0**	**2**	**29**	**0**	**0**	**0**	**12**	**16.7**	**1**	**0**	**0.0**	**10:45**									
	Utah Grizzlies	AHL	52	2	8	10	274										1	0	1	1	15				
2003-04	**Dallas**	**NHL**	**32**	**0**	**1**	**1**	**84**	**0**	**0**	**0**	**23**	**0.0**	**–9**	**0**	**0.0**	**12:36**									
	Utah Grizzlies	AHL	5	0	0	0	18																		
2004-05	Houston Aeros	AHL	61	3	7	10	238										5	0	1	1	20				
	NHL Totals		**81**	**2**	**2**	**4**	**175**	**0**	**0**	**0**	**51**	**3.9**		**0**	**0.0**	**11:29**									

OHL First All-Star Team (2000)

• Missed majority of 2003-04 season recovering from ankle (December 27, 2003 vs. Columbus) and hernia (January 24, 2004 vs. St. Louis) injuries.

EVANS, Brennan

(EH-vans, BREHN-nan)

Defense. Shoots left. 6'3", 205 lbs. Born, North Battleford, Sask., January 6, 1982.

Season	Club	League	GP	G	A	Pts	PIM	PP	SH	GW	S	%	+/-	TF	F%	Min	GP	G	A	Pts	PIM	PP	SH	GW	Min
1998-99	Camrose Kodiaks	AJHL	47	1	6	7	98										5	0	2	2	0				
	Seattle	WHL															1	0	0	0	0				
99-2000	Seattle	WHL	52	1	2	3	40										1	0	0	0	0				
2000-01	Seattle	WHL	11	1	0	1	25																		
	Kootenay Ice	WHL	55	2	7	9	105										11	0	0	0	25				
2001-02	Kootenay Ice	WHL	72	2	3	5	121										22	0	6	6	38				
2002-03	Kootenay Ice	WHL	67	6	17	23	182										11	1	1	2	24				
2003-04	Lowell	AHL	64	1	9	10	65																		
	Calgary	**NHL**															**2**	**0**	**0**	**0**	**0**	**0**	**0**	**0**	**2:52**
2004-05	Lowell	AHL	51	0	7	7	79										5	0	0	0	2				
	NHL Totals																**2**	**0**	**0**	**0**	**0**	**0**	**0**	**0**	**2:52**

Signed as a free agent by **Calgary**, September 30, 2003.

EXELBY, Garnet

(EHX-uhl-bee, GAHR-neht) **ATL.**

Defense. Shoots left. 6'1", 215 lbs. Born, Ste. Anne, Man., August 16, 1981. Atlanta's 9th choice, 217th overall, in 1999 Entry Draft.

Season	Club	League	GP	G	A	Pts	PIM	PP	SH	GW	S	%	+/-	TF	F%	Min	GP	G	A	Pts	PIM	PP	SH	GW	Min
1997-98	Winnipeg South	MJHL	46	5	11	16	110																		
1998-99	Saskatoon Blades	WHL	61	5	3	8	91																		
99-2000	Saskatoon Blades	WHL	63	1	8	9	79										11	0	2	2	21				
2000-01	Saskatoon Blades	WHL	43	5	10	15	110																		
	Regina Pats	WHL	22	2	8	10	51										6	0	2	2	2				
2001-02	Chicago Wolves	AHL	75	3	4	7	257										25	0	4	4	49				
2002-03	**Atlanta**	**NHL**	**15**	**0**	**2**	**2**	**41**	**0**	**0**	**0**	**9**	**0.0**	**0**	**0**	**0.0**	**18:04**									
	Chicago Wolves	AHL	53	3	6	9	140										9	0	1	1	27				
2003-04	**Atlanta**	**NHL**	**71**	**1**	**9**	**10**	**134**	**0**	**0**	**0**	**42**	**2.4**	**–10**	**0**	**0.0**	**19:32**									
2004-05			DID NOT PLAY																						
	NHL Totals		**86**	**1**	**11**	**12**	**175**	**0**	**0**	**0**	**51**	**2.0**		**0**	**0.0**	**19:17**									

FAHEY, Jim

(FA-hee, JIHM) **S.J.**

Defense. Shoots right. 6', 205 lbs. Born, Boston, MA, May 11, 1979. San Jose's 9th choice, 212th overall, in 1998 Entry Draft.

Season	Club	League	GP	G	A	Pts	PIM	PP	SH	GW	S	%	+/-	TF	F%	Min	GP	G	A	Pts	PIM	PP	SH	GW	Min
1997-98	Catholic Memorial	High-MA	24	12	32	44	28																		
1998-99	Northeastern	H-East	32	5	13	18	34																		
99-2000	Northeastern	H-East	36	3	17	20	62																		
2000-01	Northeastern	H-East	36	4	23	27	48																		
2001-02	Northeastern	H-East	39	14	32	46	50																		
2002-03	**San Jose**	**NHL**	**43**	**1**	**19**	**20**	**33**	**0**	**0**	**0**	**66**	**1.5**	**–3**	**1**	**100.0**	**18:20**									
	Cleveland Barons	AHL	25	3	14	17	42																		
2003-04	**San Jose**	**NHL**	**15**	**0**	**2**	**2**	**18**	**0**	**0**	**0**	**19**	**0.0**	**–2**	**0**	**0.0**	**16:54**	**2**	**0**	**0**	**0**	**0**	**0**	**0**	**0**	**4:41**
	Cleveland Barons	AHL	32	1	18	19	64																		
2004-05	Cleveland Barons	AHL	69	4	22	26	146																		
	NHL Totals		**58**	**1**	**21**	**22**	**51**	**0**	**0**	**0**	**85**	**1.2**		**1**	**100.0**	**17:58**	**2**	**0**	**0**	**0**	**0**	**0**	**0**	**0**	**4:41**

Hockey East Second All-Star Team (2001) • Hockey East First All-Star Team (2002)

FARRELL, Mike

(FAIR-uhl, MIGHK)

Right wing. Shoots right. 6', 222 lbs. Born, Edina, MN, October 20, 1978. Washington's 9th choice, 220th overall, in 1998 Entry Draft.

Season	Club	League	GP	G	A	Pts	PIM	PP	SH	GW	S	%	+/-	TF	F%	Min	GP	G	A	Pts	PIM	PP	SH	GW	Min
1997-98	Providence	H-East	33	5	8	13	32																		
1998-99	Providence	H-East	29	3	12	15	51																		
99-2000	Providence	H-East	36	3	6	9	71																		
	Portland Pirates	AHL	7	2	0	2	0										4	0	1	1	0				
2000-01	Portland Pirates	AHL	79	6	18	24	61										3	0	2	2	2				
2001-02	**Washington**	**NHL**	**8**	**0**	**0**	**0**	**0**	**0**	**0**	**0**	**1**	**0.0**	**–1**	**0**	**0.0**	**5:35**									
	Portland Pirates	AHL	61	12	15	27	62																		
2002-03	**Washington**	**NHL**	**4**	**0**	**0**	**0**	**2**	**0**	**0**	**0**	**2**	**0.0**	**1**	**0**	**0.0**	**2:48**									
	Portland Pirates	AHL	68	12	12	24	107										3	0	1	1	0				

			Regular Season														Playoffs								
Season	Club	League	GP	G	A	Pts	PIM	PP	SH	GW	S	%	+/-	TF	F%	Min	GP	G	A	Pts	PIM	PP	SH	GW	Min
2003-04	**Nashville**	**NHL**	1	0	0	0	0	0	0	0	0	0.0	0	0	0.0	5:08	....	....	....	....	....	....	....	....	....
	Milwaukee	AHL	49	10	8	18	66	....	....	....	....	....	....	....	....	....	19	1	1	2	13	....	....	....	....
2004-05			DID NOT PLAY																						
	NHL Totals		13	0	0	0	2	0	0	0	3	0.0		0	0.0	4:42	....	....	....	....	....	....	....	....	....

Traded to **Nashville** by **Washington** for Alexander Riazantsev, July 14, 2003.

FAST, Brad

(FAST, BRAD) **L.A.**

Defense. Shoots left. 6', 195 lbs. Born, Fort St. John, B.C., February 21, 1980. Carolina's 2nd choice, 84th overall, in 1999 Entry Draft.

Season	Club	League	GP	G	A	Pts	PIM	PP	SH	GW	S	%	+/-	TF	F%	Min	GP	G	A	Pts	PIM	PP	SH	GW	Min
1994-95	Fort St. John	BCAHA	40	9	26	35	40	....	....	....	....	....	....	....	....	....	....	....	....	....	....	....	....	....	....
1995-96	Fort St. John	BCAHA	60	53	52	105	70	....	....	....	....	....	....	....	....	....	....	....	....	....	....	....	....	....	....
1996-97	Prince George	BCHL	49	3	7	10	19	....	....	....	....	....	....	....	....	....	....	....	....	....	....	....	....	....	....
1997-98	Prince George	BCJHL	59	10	33	43	22	....	....	....	....	....	....	....	....	....	....	....	....	....	....	....	....	....	....
1998-99	Prince George	BCHL	59	27	46	73	....	....	....	....	....	....	....	....	....	....	....	....	....	....	....	....	....	....	....
99-2000	Michigan State	CCHA	42	5	9	14	20	....	....	....	....	....	....	....	....	....	....	....	....	....	....	....	....	....	....
2000-01	Michigan State	CCHA	42	4	24	28	16	....	....	....	....	....	....	....	....	....	....	....	....	....	....	....	....	....	....
2001-02	Michigan State	CCHA	41	10	16	26	26	....	....	....	....	....	....	....	....	....	....	....	....	....	....	....	....	....	....
2002-03	Michigan State	CCHA	39	11	35	46	28	....	....	....	....	....	....	....	....	....	....	....	....	....	....	....	....	....	....
	Lowell	AHL	7	0	1	1	12	....	....	....	....	....	....	....	....	....	....	....	....	....	....	....	....	....	....
2003-04	**Carolina**	**NHL**	1	1	0	1	0	0	0	0	4	25.0	1	0	0.0	21:24	....	....	....	....	....	....	....	....	....
	Lowell	AHL	79	10	25	35	35	....	....	....	....	....	....	....	....	....	....	....	....	....	....	....	....	....	....
2004-05	Lowell	AHL	32	1	5	6	23	....	....	....	....	....	....	....	....	....	....	....	....	....	....	....	....	....	....
	Florida Everblades	ECHL	14	2	5	7	0	....	....	....	....	....	....	....	....	....	18	1	3	4	6	....	....	....	....
	NHL Totals		1	1	0	1	0	0	0	0	4	25.0		0	0.0	21:24	....	....	....	....	....	....	....	....	....

CCHA First All-Star Team (2003) • NCAA West Second All-American Team (2003)

• One of only three players (Rolly Huard, Dean Morton) to score a goal in his only NHL game. Signed as a free agent by **Los Angeles**, August 15, 2005.

FATA, Rico

(FA-tuh, REE-koh) **PIT.**

Right wing. Shoots left. 6', 205 lbs. Born, Sault Ste. Marie, Ont., February 12, 1980. Calgary's 1st choice, 6th overall, in 1998 Entry Draft.

Season	Club	League	GP	G	A	Pts	PIM	PP	SH	GW	S	%	+/-	TF	F%	Min	GP	G	A	Pts	PIM	PP	SH	GW	Min
1994-95	Soo Legion	NOHA	51	52	51	103	....	....	....	....	....	....	....	....	....	....	....	....	....	....	....	....	....	....	....
1995-96	Sault Ste. Marie	OHL	62	11	15	26	52	....	....	....	....	....	....	....	....	....	4	0	0	0	0	....	....	....	....
1996-97	London Knights	OHL	59	19	34	53	76	....	....	....	....	....	....	....	....	....	....	....	....	....	....	....	....	....	....
1997-98	London Knights	OHL	64	43	33	76	110	....	....	....	....	....	....	....	....	....	16	9	5	14	*49	....	....	....	....
1998-99	**Calgary**	**NHL**	20	0	1	1	4	0	0	0	13	0.0	0	2	50.0	7:36	....	....	....	....	....	....	....	....	....
	London Knights	OHL	23	15	18	33	41	....	....	....	....	....	....	....	....	....	25	10	12	22	42	....	....	....	....
99-2000	**Calgary**	**NHL**	2	0	0	0	0	0	0	0	0	0.0	−1	0	0.0	10:06	....	....	....	....	....	....	....	....	....
	Saint John Flames	AHL	76	29	29	58	65	....	....	....	....	....	....	....	....	....	3	0	0	0	4	....	....	....	....
2000-01	**Calgary**	**NHL**	5	0	0	0	6	0	0	0	6	0.0	−3	0	0.0	9:25	....	....	....	....	....	....	....	....	....
	Saint John Flames	AHL	70	23	29	52	129	....	....	....	....	....	....	....	....	....	19	2	3	5	22	....	....	....	....
2001-02	**NY Rangers**	**NHL**	10	0	0	0	0	0	0	0	8	0.0	−2	55	47.3	8:31	....	....	....	....	....	....	....	....	....
	Hartford	AHL	61	35	36	71	36	....	....	....	....	....	....	....	....	....	10	2	5	7	4	....	....	....	....
2002-03	**NY Rangers**	**NHL**	36	2	4	6	6	0	0	0	30	6.7	−1	30	50.0	7:16	....	....	....	....	....	....	....	....	....
	Hartford	AHL	9	8	6	14	6	....	....	....	....	....	....	....	....	....	....	....	....	....	....	....	....	....	....
	Pittsburgh	**NHL**	27	5	8	13	10	0	0	0	49	10.2	−6	87	49.4	17:46	....	....	....	....	....	....	....	....	....
2003-04	**Pittsburgh**	**NHL**	73	16	18	34	54	6	2	1	163	9.8	−46	1205	47.1	17:58	....	....	....	....	....	....	....	....	....
2004-05	Asiago	Italy	35	18	20	38	36	....	....	....	....	....	....	....	....	....	9	7	5	12	10	....	....	....	....
	NHL Totals		173	23	31	54	80	6	2	1	269	8.6		1379	47.4	13:38	....	....	....	....	....	....	....	....	....

AHL All-Rookie Team (2000) • AHL Second All-Star Team (2002)

Claimed on waivers by **NY Rangers** from **Calgary**, October 3, 2001. Traded to **Pittsburgh** by **NY Rangers** with Joel Bouchard, Richard Lintner, Mikael Samuelsson and future considerations for Mike Wilson, Alex Kovalev, Janne Laukkanen and Dan LaCouture, February 10, 2003. Signed as a free agent by **Asiago** (Italy), August 15, 2004.

FEDOROV, Fedor

(FEH-duh-rahf, feh-DUHR) **VAN.**

Center. Shoots left. 6'3", 230 lbs. Born, Appatity, USSR, June 11, 1981. Vancouver's 2nd choice, 66th overall, in 2001 Entry Draft.

Season	Club	League	GP	G	A	Pts	PIM	PP	SH	GW	S	%	+/-	TF	F%	Min	GP	G	A	Pts	PIM	PP	SH	GW	Min
1997-98	Det. Caesars	MNHL	13	3	7	10	18	....	....	....	....	....	....	....	....	....	....	....	....	....	....	....	....	....	....
1998-99	Port Huron	UHL	42	2	5	7	20	....	....	....	....	....	....	....	....	....	....	....	....	....	....	....	....	....	....
99-2000	Windsor Spitfires	OHL	60	7	10	17	115	....	....	....	....	....	....	....	....	....	12	1	0	1	4	....	....	....	....
2000-01	Sudbury Wolves	OHL	67	33	45	78	88	....	....	....	....	....	....	....	....	....	12	4	6	10	36	....	....	....	....
2001-02	Manitoba Moose	AHL	8	2	1	3	6	....	....	....	....	....	....	....	....	....	....	....	....	....	....	....	....	....	....
	Columbia Inferno	ECHL	2	0	2	2	0	....	....	....	....	....	....	....	....	....	....	....	....	....	....	....	....	....	....
2002-03	**Vancouver**	**NHL**	7	0	1	1	4	0	0	0	2	0.0	0	26	46.2	9:10	....	....	....	....	....	....	....	....	....
	Manitoba Moose	AHL	50	10	13	23	61	....	....	....	....	....	....	....	....	....	3	1	2	3	0	....	....	....	....
2003-04	**Vancouver**	**NHL**	8	0	1	1	4	0	0	0	10	0.0	0	4	50.0	10:59	....	....	....	....	....	....	....	....	....
	Manitoba Moose	AHL	58	23	16	39	52	....	....	....	....	....	....	....	....	....	....	....	....	....	....	....	....	....	....
2004-05	Spartak Moscow	Russia	19	4	7	11	52	....	....	....	....	....	....	....	....	....	....	....	....	....	....	....	....	....	....
	Magnitogorsk	Russia	10	3	0	3	22	....	....	....	....	....	....	....	....	....	5	2	0	2	30	....	....	....	....
	NHL Totals		15	0	2	2	8	0	0	0	12	0.0		30	46.7	10:08	....	....	....	....	....	....	....	....	....

• Re-entered NHL Entry Draft. Originally Tampa Bay's 7th choice, 182nd overall, in 1999 Entry Draft.

Signed as an underage free agent by **Detroit** (IHL), August 5, 1998. Released by **Detroit** (IHL), September 30, 1998. Signed as an underage free agent by **Port Huron** (UHL), October 1, 1998. • Missed majority of 2001-02 season recovering from eye injury suffered in game vs. Macon (ECHL), November 17, 2001. Signed as a free agent by **Spartak** (Russia), November 15, 2004. Signed as a free agent by **Magnitogorsk** (Russia), February 16, 2005.

FEDOROV, Sergei

(FEH-duh-rahf, SAIR-gay) **ANA.**

Center. Shoots left. 6'2", 205 lbs. Born, Pskov, USSR, December 13, 1969. Detroit's 4th choice, 74th overall, in 1989 Entry Draft.

Season	Club	League	GP	G	A	Pts	PIM	PP	SH	GW	S	%	+/-	TF	F%	Min	GP	G	A	Pts	PIM	PP	SH	GW	Min
1985-86	Dynamo Minsk	USSR-2	15	6	1	7	10	....	....	....	....	....	....	....	....	....	....	....	....	....	....	....	....	....	....
1986-87	CSKA Moscow	USSR	29	6	6	12	12	....	....	....	....	....	....	....	....	....	....	....	....	....	....	....	....	....	....
1987-88	CSKA Moscow	USSR	48	7	9	16	20	....	....	....	....	....	....	....	....	....	....	....	....	....	....	....	....	....	....
1988-89	CSKA Moscow	USSR	44	9	8	17	35	....	....	....	....	....	....	....	....	....	....	....	....	....	....	....	....	....	....
1989-90	CSKA Moscow	USSR	48	19	10	29	22	....	....	....	....	....	....	....	....	....	....	....	....	....	....	....	....	....	....
1990-91	**Detroit**	**NHL**	77	31	48	79	66	11	3	5	259	12.0	11	....	....	....	7	1	5	6	4	0	0	1	....
1991-92	**Detroit**	**NHL**	80	32	54	86	72	7	2	5	249	12.9	26	....	....	....	11	5	5	10	8	1	2	1	....
1992-93	**Detroit**	**NHL**	73	34	53	87	72	13	4	3	217	15.7	33	....	....	....	7	3	6	9	23	1	1	0	....
1993-94	**Detroit**	**NHL**	82	56	64	120	34	13	4	10	337	16.6	48	....	....	....	7	1	7	8	6	0	0	0	....
1994-95	**Detroit**	**NHL**	42	20	30	50	24	7	3	5	147	13.6	6	....	....	....	17	7	*17	*24	6	3	0	0	....
1995-96	**Detroit**	**NHL**	78	39	68	107	48	11	3	11	306	12.7	49	....	....	....	19	2	*18	20	10	0	0	2	....
1996-97♦	**Detroit**	**NHL**	74	30	33	63	30	9	2	4	273	11.0	29	....	....	....	20	8	12	20	12	3	0	4	....
1997-98	Russia	Olympics	6	1	5	6	8	....	....	....	....	....	....	....	....	....	....	....	....	....	....	....	....	....	....
	♦ **Detroit**	**NHL**	21	6	11	17	25	2	0	2	68	8.8	10	....	....	....	22	*10	10	20	12	2	1	1	....
1998-99	**Detroit**	**NHL**	77	26	37	63	66	6	2	3	224	11.6	9	1414	51.7	19:21	10	1	8	9	8	0	0	0	19:54
99-2000	**Detroit**	**NHL**	68	27	35	62	22	4	4	7	263	10.3	8	1274	53.8	20:05	9	4	4	8	4	2	0	1	20:48
2000-01	**Detroit**	**NHL**	75	32	37	69	40	14	2	7	268	11.9	12	1601	55.8	21:05	6	2	5	7	0	1	0	1	22:19
2001-02♦	**Detroit**	**NHL**	81	31	37	68	36	10	0	6	256	12.1	20	1160	51.7	19:33	23	5	14	19	20	2	1	0	22:20
	Russia	Olympics	6	2	2	4	4	....	....	....	....	....	....	....	....	....	....	....	....	....	....	....	....	....	....
2002-03	**Detroit**	**NHL**	80	36	47	83	52	10	2	11	281	12.8	15	1580	53.4	21:11	4	1	2	3	0	0	0	0	22:07
2003-04	**Anaheim**	**NHL**	80	31	34	65	42	9	2	6	268	11.6	−5	1558	56.6	21:05	....	....	....	....	....	....	....	....	....
2004-05			DID NOT PLAY																						
	NHL Totals		988	431	588	1019	629	126	33	85	3416	12.6		8587	54.0	20:24	162	50	113	163	113	15	5	11	21:35

NHL All-Rookie Team (1991) • NHL First All-Star Team (1994) • Frank J. Selke Trophy (1994, 1996) • Lester B. Pearson Award (1994) • Hart Trophy (1994)

Played in NHL All-Star Game (1992, 1994, 1996, 2001, 2002, 2003)

• Missed majority of 1997-98 season after failing to come to contract terms with **Detroit**. Signed as a free agent by **Anaheim**, July 19, 2003.

			Regular Season														Playoffs								
Season	Club	League	GP	G	A	Pts	PIM	PP	SH	GW	S	%	+/-	TF	F%	Min	GP	G	A	Pts	PIM	PP	SH	GW	Min

FEDORUK, Todd

(FEH-duh-ruhk, TAWD) **ANA.**

Left wing. Shoots left. 6'2", 235 lbs. Born, Redwater, Alta., February 13, 1979. Philadelphia's 6th choice, 164th overall, in 1997 Entry Draft.

1994-95	Ft. Saskatchewan	AMHL	STATISTICS NOT AVAILABLE																						
1995-96	Kelowna Rockets	WHL	44	1	1	2	83	....	....	....	....	....	....	....	....	....	4	0	0	0	6	....	....	....	....
1996-97	Kelowna Rockets	WHL	31	1	5	6	87	....	....	....	....	....	....	....	....	....	6	0	0	0	13	....	....	....	....
1997-98	Kelowna Rockets	WHL	31	3	5	8	120	....	....	....	....	....	....	....	....	....	....	....	....	....	....	....	....	....	....
	Regina Pats	WHL	21	4	3	7	80	....	....	....	....	....	....	....	....	....	9	1	2	3	23	....	....	....	....
1998-99	Regina Pats	WHL	39	12	12	24	107	....	....	....	....	....	....	....	....	....	....	....	....	....	....	....	....	....	....
	Prince Albert	WHL	28	6	4	10	75	....	....	....	....	....	....	....	....	....	13	1	6	7	49	....	....	....	....
99-2000	Trenton Titans	ECHL	18	2	5	7	118	....	....	....	....	....	....	....	....	....	....	....	....	....	....	....	....	....	....
	Philadelphia	AHL	19	1	2	3	40	....	....	....	....	....	....	....	....	....	5	0	1	1	2	....	....	....	....
2000-01	**Philadelphia**	**NHL**	**53**	**5**	**5**	**10**	**109**	**0**	**0**	**0**	**28**	**17.9**	**0**	**0**	**0.0**	**7:02**	**2**	**0**	**0**	**0**	**20**	**0**	**0**	**0**	**5:57**
	Philadelphia	AHL	14	0	1	1	49	....	....	....	....	....	....	....	....	....	....	....	....	....	....	....	....	....	....
2001-02	**Philadelphia**	**NHL**	**55**	**3**	**4**	**7**	**141**	**0**	**0**	**0**	**21**	**14.3**	**–2**	**5**	**0.0**	**6:21**	**3**	**0**	**0**	**0**	**0**	**0**	**0**	**0**	**2:46**
	Philadelphia	AHL	7	0	1	1	54	....	....	....	....	....	....	....	....	....	....	....	....	....	....	....	....	....	....
2002-03	**Philadelphia**	**NHL**	**63**	**1**	**5**	**6**	**105**	**0**	**0**	**0**	**33**	**3.0**	**1**	**1**	**0.0**	**6:30**	**1**	**0**	**0**	**0**	**0**	**0**	**0**	**0**	**4:52**
2003-04	**Philadelphia**	**NHL**	**49**	**1**	**4**	**5**	**136**	**0**	**0**	**1**	**33**	**3.0**	**–4**	**0**	**0.0**	**6:47**	**1**	**0**	**0**	**0**	**2**	**0**	**0**	**0**	**6:42**
	Philadelphia	AHL	2	0	2	2	2	....	....	....	....	....	....	....	....	....	....	....	....	....	....	....	....	....	....
2004-05	Philadelphia	AHL	42	4	12	16	142	....	....	....	....	....	....	....	....	....	16	2	2	4	33	....	....	....	....
	NHL Totals		**220**	**10**	**18**	**28**	**491**	**0**	**0**	**1**	**115**	**8.7**		**6**	**0.0**	**6:39**	**7**	**0**	**0**	**0**	**22**	**0**	**0**	**0**	**4:32**

Traded to **Anaheim** by **Philadelphia** for Anaheim's 2nd round choice (later traded to Phoenix - Phoenix selected Pier-Olivier Pelletier) in 2005 Entry Draft, July 29, 2005.

FEDOTENKO, Ruslan

(feh-doh-TEHN-koh, roos-LAHN) **T.B.**

Left wing. Shoots left. 6'2", 195 lbs. Born, Kiev, Ukraine, January 18, 1979.

1995-96	Kiev 2	EEHL	33	9	11	20	12	....	....	....	....	....	....	....	....	....	....	....	....	....	....	....	....	....	....
	Sokol Kiev	CIS	2	0	0	0	0	....	....	....	....	....	....	....	....	....	....	....	....	....	....	....	....	....	....
1996-97	TPS Turku U18	Fin-U18	3	3	2	5	2	....	....	....	....	....	....	....	....	....	....	....	....	....	....	....	....	....	....
	TPS Turku Jr.	Finland-Jr.	11	1	1	2	2	....	....	....	....	....	....	....	....	....	....	....	....	....	....	....	....	....	....
	Kiekko-67 Turku	Finland-2	22	4	3	7	16	....	....	....	....	....	....	....	....	....	....	....	....	....	....	....	....	....	....
	Kiekko Turku	Finland-3	....	....	....	....	....	....	....	....	....	....	....	....	....	....	3	1	0	1	2	....	....	....	....
1997-98	Melfort Mustangs	SJHL	68	35	31	66	55	....	....	....	....	....	....	....	....	....	....	....	....	....	....	....	....	....	....
1998-99	Sioux City	USHL	55	43	34	77	139	....	....	....	....	....	....	....	....	....	5	5	1	6	9	....	....	....	....
99-2000	Trenton Titans	ECHL	8	5	3	8	9	....	....	....	....	....	....	....	....	....	....	....	....	....	....	....	....	....	....
	Philadelphia	AHL	67	16	34	50	42	....	....	....	....	....	....	....	....	....	2	0	0	0	0	....	....	....	....
2000-01	**Philadelphia**	**NHL**	**74**	**16**	**20**	**36**	**72**	**3**	**0**	**4**	**119**	**13.4**	**8**	**7**	**71.4**	**14:38**	**6**	**0**	**1**	**1**	**4**	**0**	**0**	**0**	**11:18**
	Philadelphia	AHL	8	1	0	1	8	....	....	....	....	....	....	....	....	....	....	....	....	....	....	....	....	....	....
2001-02	**Philadelphia**	**NHL**	**78**	**17**	**9**	**26**	**43**	**0**	**1**	**3**	**121**	**14.0**	**15**	**41**	**43.9**	**13:56**	**5**	**1**	**0**	**1**	**2**	**0**	**0**	**1**	**14:11**
	Ukraine	Olympics	1	1	0	1	4	....	....	....	....	....	....	....	....	....	....	....	....	....	....	....	....	....	....
2002-03	**Tampa Bay**	**NHL**	**76**	**19**	**13**	**32**	**44**	**6**	**0**	**6**	**114**	**16.7**	**–7**	**90**	**48.9**	**16:01**	**11**	**0**	**1**	**1**	**2**	**0**	**0**	**0**	**13:58**
2003-04♦	**Tampa Bay**	**NHL**	**77**	**17**	**22**	**39**	**30**	**0**	**0**	**3**	**116**	**14.7**	**14**	**58**	**55.2**	**14:39**	**22**	**12**	**2**	**14**	**14**	**5**	**0**	**3**	**16:40**
2004-05			DID NOT PLAY																						
	NHL Totals		**305**	**69**	**64**	**133**	**189**	**9**	**1**	**16**	**470**	**14.7**		**196**	**50.5**	**14:48**	**44**	**13**	**4**	**17**	**22**	**5**	**0**	**4**	**14:59**

Signed as a free agent by **Philadelphia**, August 3, 1999. Traded to **Tampa Bay** by **Philadelphia** with Tampa Bay's 2nd round choice (previously acquired, later traded to Dallas – Dallas selected Tobias Stephan) in 2002 Entry Draft and Phoenix's 2nd round choice (previously acquired, later traded to San Jose – San Jose selected Dan Spang) in 2002 Entry Draft for Tampa Bay's 1st round choice (Joni Pitkanen) in 2002 Entry Draft, June 21, 2002.

FERENCE, Andrew

(FAIR-ehns, AN-droo) **CGY.**

Defense. Shoots left. 5'10", 196 lbs. Born, Edmonton, Alta., March 17, 1979. Pittsburgh's 8th choice, 208th overall, in 1997 Entry Draft.

1994-95	Sherwood Park	AMHL	31	4	14	18	74	....	....	....	....	....	....	....	....	....	....	....	....	....	....	....	....	....	....
	Portland	WHL	2	0	0	0	4	....	....	....	....	....	....	....	....	....	....	....	....	....	....	....	....	....	....
1995-96	Portland	WHL	72	9	31	40	159	....	....	....	....	....	....	....	....	....	7	1	3	4	12	....	....	....	....
1996-97	Portland	WHL	72	12	32	44	163	....	....	....	....	....	....	....	....	....	6	1	2	3	12	....	....	....	....
1997-98	Portland	WHL	72	11	57	68	142	....	....	....	....	....	....	....	....	....	16	2	18	20	28	....	....	....	....
1998-99	Portland	WHL	40	11	21	32	104	....	....	....	....	....	....	....	....	....	4	1	4	5	10	....	....	....	....
	Kansas City	IHL	5	1	2	3	4	....	....	....	....	....	....	....	....	....	3	0	0	0	9	....	....	....	....
99-2000	**Pittsburgh**	**NHL**	**30**	**2**	**4**	**6**	**20**	**0**	**0**	**1**	**26**	**7.7**	**3**	**0**	**0.0**	**16:19**	....	....	....	....	....	....	....	....	....
	Wilkes-Barre	AHL	44	8	20	28	58	....	....	....	....	....	....	....	....	....	....	....	....	....	....	....	....	....	....
2000-01	Wilkes-Barre	AHL	43	6	18	24	95	....	....	....	....	....	....	....	....	....	3	1	0	1	12	....	....	....	....
	Pittsburgh	**NHL**	**36**	**4**	**11**	**15**	**28**	**1**	**0**	**1**	**47**	**8.5**	**6**	**0**	**0.0**	**18:51**	**18**	**3**	**7**	**10**	**16**	**1**	**0**	**1**	**22:02**
2001-02	**Pittsburgh**	**NHL**	**75**	**4**	**7**	**11**	**73**	**1**	**0**	**0**	**82**	**4.9**	**–12**	**2**	**0.0**	**18:34**	....	....	....	....	....	....	....	....	....
2002-03	**Pittsburgh**	**NHL**	**22**	**1**	**3**	**4**	**36**	**1**	**0**	**0**	**22**	**4.5**	**–16**	**1**	**100.0**	**19:33**	....	....	....	....	....	....	....	....	....
	Wilkes-Barre	AHL	1	0	0	0	2	....	....	....	....	....	....	....	....	....	....	....	....	....	....	....	....	....	....
	Calgary	**NHL**	**16**	**0**	**4**	**4**	**6**	**0**	**0**	**0**	**17**	**0.0**	**1**	**0**	**0.0**	**17:38**	....	....	....	....	....	....	....	....	....
2003-04	**Calgary**	**NHL**	**72**	**4**	**12**	**16**	**53**	**1**	**0**	**0**	**86**	**4.7**	**5**	**0**	**0.0**	**18:40**	**26**	**0**	**3**	**3**	**25**	**0**	**0**	**0**	**24:13**
2004-05	C. Budejovice	CzRep-2	19	5	6	11	45	....	....	....	....	....	....	....	....	....	12	2	7	9	10	....	....	....	....
	NHL Totals		**251**	**15**	**41**	**56**	**216**	**4**	**0**	**2**	**280**	**5.4**		**3**	**33.3**	**18:24**	**44**	**3**	**10**	**13**	**41**	**1**	**0**	**1**	**23:19**

WHL West First All-Star Team (1998) • WHL West Second All-Star Team (1999)

• Missed majority of 2002-03 season recovering from groin (November 18, 2002 vs. Montreal) and ankle (March 20, 2003 vs. Los Angeles) injuries. Traded to **Calgary** by **Pittsburgh** for Calgary's 3rd round choice (Brian Gifford) in 2004 Entry Draft, February 9, 2003. Signed as a free agent by **Budejovice** (CzRep-2), December 1, 2004.

FERENCE, Brad

(FAIR-ehns, BRAD) **PHX.**

Defense. Shoots right. 6'3", 218 lbs. Born, Calgary, Alta., April 2, 1979. Vancouver's 1st choice, 10th overall, in 1997 Entry Draft.

1994-95	Calgary Royals	ABHL	60	19	47	66	220	....	....	....	....	....	....	....	....	....	....	....	....	....	....	....	....	....	....
1995-96	Calgary Royals	ABHL	22	7	21	28	140	....	....	....	....	....	....	....	....	....	....	....	....	....	....	....	....	....	....
	Spokane Chiefs	WHL	5	0	2	2	18	....	....	....	....	....	....	....	....	....	....	....	....	....	....	....	....	....	....
1996-97	Spokane Chiefs	WHL	67	6	20	26	324	....	....	....	....	....	....	....	....	....	9	0	4	4	21	....	....	....	....
1997-98	Spokane Chiefs	WHL	54	9	30	39	213	....	....	....	....	....	....	....	....	....	18	0	7	7	59	....	....	....	....
1998-99	Spokane Chiefs	WHL	31	3	22	25	125	....	....	....	....	....	....	....	....	....	....	....	....	....	....	....	....	....	....
	Tri-City	WHL	20	6	15	21	116	....	....	....	....	....	....	....	....	....	12	1	9	10	63	....	....	....	....
99-2000	**Florida**	**NHL**	**13**	**0**	**2**	**2**	**46**	**0**	**0**	**0**	**10**	**0.0**	**2**	**0**	**0.0**	**13:40**	....	....	....	....	....	....	....	....	....
	Louisville Panthers	AHL	58	2	7	9	231	....	....	....	....	....	....	....	....	....	2	0	0	0	2	....	....	....	....
2000-01	**Florida**	**NHL**	**14**	**0**	**1**	**1**	**14**	**0**	**0**	**0**	**5**	**0.0**	**–10**	**0**	**0.0**	**13:03**	....	....	....	....	....	....	....	....	....
	Louisville Panthers	AHL	52	3	21	24	200	....	....	....	....	....	....	....	....	....	....	....	....	....	....	....	....	....	....
2001-02	**Florida**	**NHL**	**80**	**2**	**15**	**17**	**254**	**0**	**0**	**0**	**65**	**3.1**	**–13**	**1**	**0.0**	**19:44**	....	....	....	....	....	....	....	....	....
2002-03	**Florida**	**NHL**	**60**	**2**	**6**	**8**	**118**	**0**	**0**	**0**	**41**	**4.9**	**2**	**0**	**0.0**	**15:58**	....	....	....	....	....	....	....	....	....
	Phoenix	**NHL**	**15**	**0**	**1**	**1**	**28**	**0**	**0**	**0**	**8**	**0.0**	**–5**	**0**	**0.0**	**16:33**	....	....	....	....	....	....	....	....	....
2003-04	**Phoenix**	**NHL**	**63**	**0**	**5**	**5**	**103**	**0**	**0**	**0**	**39**	**0.0**	**–19**	**0**	**0.0**	**14:03**	....	....	....	....	....	....	....	....	....
2004-05	Morzine-Avoriaz	France	17	2	10	12	138	....	....	....	....	....	....	....	....	....	4	1	4	5	10	....	....	....	....
	NHL Totals		**245**	**4**	**30**	**34**	**563**	**0**	**0**	**0**	**168**	**2.4**		**1**	**0.0**	**16:27**	....	....	....	....	....	....	....	....	....

Memorial Cup Tournament All-Star Team (1998)

Traded to **Florida** by **Vancouver** with Pavel Bure, Bret Hedican and Vancouver's 3rd round choice (Robert Fried) in 2000 Entry Draft for Ed Jovanovski, Dave Gagner, Mike Brown, Kevin Weekes and Florida's 1st round choice (Nathan Smith) in 2000 Entry Draft, January 17, 1999. Traded to **Phoenix** by **Florida** for Darcy Hordichuk and Phoenix's 2nd round choice (later traded to Tampa Bay – Tampa Bay selected Matt Smaby) in 2003 Entry Draft, March 8, 2003. Signed as a free agent by **Morzine-Avoriaz** (France), October 28, 2004.

FERGUSON, Scott

(fuhr-GUH-sohn, SKAWT) **MIN.**

Defense. Shoots left. 6'1", 195 lbs. Born, Camrose, Alta., January 6, 1973.

1990-91	Sherwood Park	AJHL	32	2	9	11	91	....	....	....	....	....	....	....	....	....	....	....	....	....	....	....	....	....	....
	Kamloops Blazers	WHL	4	0	0	0	0	....	....	....	....	....	....	....	....	....	....	....	....	....	....	....	....	....	....
1991-92	Kamloops Blazers	WHL	62	4	10	14	138	....	....	....	....	....	....	....	....	....	12	0	2	2	21	....	....	....	....
1992-93	Kamloops Blazers	WHL	71	4	19	23	206	....	....	....	....	....	....	....	....	....	13	0	2	2	24	....	....	....	....
1993-94	Kamloops Blazers	WHL	68	5	49	54	180	....	....	....	....	....	....	....	....	....	19	5	11	16	48	....	....	....	....
1994-95	Cape Breton	AHL	58	4	6	10	103	....	....	....	....	....	....	....	....	....	....	....	....	....	....	....	....	....	....
	Wheeling	ECHL	5	1	5	6	16	....	....	....	....	....	....	....	....	....	....	....	....	....	....	....	....	....	....
1995-96	Cape Breton	AHL	80	5	16	21	196	....	....	....	....	....	....	....	....	....	....	....	....	....	....	....	....	....	....
1996-97	Hamilton	AHL	74	6	14	20	115	....	....	....	....	....	....	....	....	....	21	5	7	12	59	....	....	....	....

Season	Club	League	GP	G	A	Pts	PIM	PP	SH	GW	S	%	+/-	TF	F%	Min	GP	G	A	Pts	PIM	PP	SH	GW	Min
			Regular Season														Playoffs								
1997-98	**Edmonton**	**NHL**	**1**	**0**	**0**	**0**	**0**	**0**	**0**	**0**	**0**	**0.0**	**1**	....	....	....	....	....	....	....	....	....	....	....	....
	Hamilton	AHL	77	7	17	24	150	....	....	....	....	....	....	....	....	....	9	0	3	3	16	....	....	....	....
1998-99	**Anaheim**	**NHL**	**2**	**0**	**1**	**1**	**0**	**0**	**0**	**0**	**1**	**0.0**	**0**	**0**	**0.0**	**15:09**	....	....	....	....	....	....	....	....	....
	Cincinnati	AHL	78	4	31	35	59	....	....	....	....	....	....	....	....	....	3	0	0	0	4	....	....	....	....
99-2000	Cincinnati	AHL	77	7	25	32	166	....	....	....	....	....	....	....	....	....	....	....	....	....	....	....	....	....	....
2000-01	**Edmonton**	**NHL**	**20**	**0**	**1**	**1**	**13**	**0**	**0**	**0**	**8**	**0.0**	**2**	**0**	**0.0**	**10:55**	**6**	**0**	**0**	**0**	**0**	**0**	**0**	**0**	**8:21**
	Hamilton	AHL	42	3	18	21	79	....	....	....	....	....	....	....	....	....	....	....	....	....	....	....	....	....	....
2001-02	**Edmonton**	**NHL**	**50**	**3**	**2**	**5**	**75**	**0**	**0**	**0**	**27**	**11.1**	**11**	**0**	**0.0**	**13:40**	....	....	....	....	....	....	....	....	....
2002-03	**Edmonton**	**NHL**	**78**	**3**	**5**	**8**	**120**	**0**	**0**	**0**	**45**	**6.7**	**11**	**1**	**100.0**	**0:00**	**5**	**0**	**0**	**0**	**8**	**0**	**0**	**0**	....
2003-04	**Edmonton**	**NHL**	**52**	**1**	**5**	**6**	**80**	**0**	**0**	**1**	**38**	**2.6**	**-5**	**0**	**0.0**	**13:21**	....	....	....	....	....	....	....	....	....
2004-05			DID NOT PLAY																						
	NHL Totals		**203**	**7**	**14**	**21**	**288**	**0**	**0**	**1**	**119**	**5.9**		**1**	**0.0**	**8:03**	**11**	**0**	**0**	**0**	**8**	**0**	**0**	**0**	**8:21**

WHL West Second All-Star Team (1994)

Signed as a free agent by **Edmonton**, June 2, 1994. Traded to **Ottawa** by **Edmonton** for Frantisek Musil, March 9, 1998. Signed as a free agent by **Anaheim**, July 27, 1998. Signed as a free agent by **Edmonton**, July 5, 2000. Signed as a free agent by **Minnesota**, August 4, 2005.

FERRARO, Chris

(fuh-RAHR-oh, KRIHS)

Center. Shoots right. 5'9", 175 lbs. Born, Port Jefferson, NY, January 24, 1973. NY Rangers' 4th choice, 85th overall, in 1992 Entry Draft.

Season	Club	League	GP	G	A	Pts	PIM	PP	SH	GW	S	%	+/-	TF	F%	Min	GP	G	A	Pts	PIM	PP	SH	GW	Min
1990-91	Dubuque	USHL	45	53	44	97	84	....	....	....	....	....	....	....	....	....	8	3	9	12	12	....	....	....	....
1991-92	Dubuque	USHL	20	30	19	49	52	....	....	....	....	....	....	....	....	....	....	....	....	....	....	....	....	....	....
	Waterloo	USHL	18	19	31	50	54	....	....	....	....	....	....	....	....	....	4	5	6	11	14	....	....	....	....
1992-93	U. of Maine	H-East	39	25	26	51	46	....	....	....	....	....	....	....	....	....	....	....	....	....	....	....	....	....	....
1993-94	U. of Maine	H-East	4	0	1	1	8	....	....	....	....	....	....	....	....	....	....	....	....	....	....	....	....	....	....
	United States	Nat-Tm	48	8	34	42	58	....	....	....	....	....	....	....	....	....	....	....	....	....	....	....	....	....	....
1994-95	Atlanta Knights	IHL	54	13	14	27	72	....	....	....	....	....	....	....	....	....	....	....	....	....	....	....	....	....	....
	Binghamton	AHL	13	6	4	10	38	....	....	....	....	....	....	....	....	....	10	2	3	5	16	....	....	....	....
1995-96	**NY Rangers**	**NHL**	**2**	**1**	**0**	**1**	**0**	**1**	**0**	**0**	**4**	**25.0**	**-3**	....	....	....	....	....	....	....	....	....	....	....	....
	Binghamton	AHL	77	32	67	99	208	....	....	....	....	....	....	....	....	....	4	4	2	6	13	....	....	....	....
1996-97	**NY Rangers**	**NHL**	**12**	**1**	**1**	**2**	**6**	**0**	**0**	**0**	**23**	**4.3**	**1**	....	....	....	....	....	....	....	....	....	....	....	....
	Binghamton	AHL	53	29	34	63	94	....	....	....	....	....	....	....	....	....	....	....	....	....	....	....	....	....	....
1997-98	**Pittsburgh**	**NHL**	**46**	**3**	**4**	**7**	**43**	**0**	**0**	**0**	**42**	**7.1**	**-2**	....	....	....	....	....	....	....	....	....	....	....	....
1998-99	**Edmonton**	**NHL**	**2**	**1**	**0**	**1**	**0**	**0**	**0**	**0**	**1**	**100.0**	**1**	**19**	**52.6**	**8:33**	....	....	....	....	....	....	....	....	....
	Hamilton	AHL	72	35	41	76	104	....	....	....	....	....	....	....	....	....	11	8	5	13	20	....	....	....	....
99-2000	**NY Islanders**	**NHL**	**11**	**1**	**3**	**4**	**8**	**0**	**0**	**0**	**15**	**6.7**	**1**	**92**	**50.0**	**9:30**	....	....	....	....	....	....	....	....	....
	Providence Bruins	AHL	21	9	9	18	32	....	....	....	....	....	....	....	....	....	....	....	....	....	....	....	....	....	....
	Chicago Wolves	IHL	25	7	18	25	40	....	....	....	....	....	....	....	....	....	16	5	8	13	14	....	....	....	....
2000-01	Albany River Rats	AHL	74	24	42	66	111	....	....	....	....	....	....	....	....	....	....	....	....	....	....	....	....	....	....
2001-02	**Washington**	**NHL**	**1**	**0**	**1**	**1**	**0**	**0**	**0**	**0**	**4**	**0.0**	**0**	**2**	**0.0**	**15:17**	....	....	....	....	....	....	....	....	....
	Portland Pirates	AHL	2	1	1	2	6	....	....	....	....	....	....	....	....	....	....	....	....	....	....	....	....	....	....
2002-03	Portland Pirates	AHL	57	19	32	51	121	....	....	....	....	....	....	....	....	....	3	0	1	1	6	....	....	....	....
2003-04	Springfield	AHL	64	14	24	38	137	....	....	....	....	....	....	....	....	....	....	....	....	....	....	....	....	....	....
2004-05	Sodertalje SK	Sweden	12	1	4	5	26	....	....	....	....	....	....	....	....	....	....	....	....	....	....	....	....	....	....
	Syracuse Crunch	AHL	24	7	7	14	50	....	....	....	....	....	....	....	....	....	....	....	....	....	....	....	....	....	....
	NHL Totals		**74**	**7**	**9**	**16**	**57**	**1**	**0**	**0**	**89**	**7.9**		**113**	**49.6**	**9:47**	....	....	....	....	....	....	....	....	....

Fred T. Hunt Memorial Award (Sportsmanship – AHL) (2003) (co-winner - Eric Healey)

Claimed on waivers by **Pittsburgh** from **NY Rangers**, October 1, 1997. Signed as a free agent by **Edmonton**, August 13, 1998. Signed as a free agent by **NY Islanders**, July 22, 1999. Signed as a free agent by **New Jersey**, July 20, 2000. Traded to **Washington** by **New Jersey** for future considerations, August 22, 2001. • Missed majority of 2001-02 season after being granted personal leave of absence by Washington, October 15, 2001. Signed as a free agent by **Phoenix**, July 17, 2003. Signed as a free agent by **Sodertalje** (Sweden), September 10, 2004. Signed as a free agent by **Syracuse** (AHL), December 13, 2004.

FERRARO, Peter

(fuh-RAHR-oh, PEE-tuhr)

Left wing. Shoots right. 5'10", 180 lbs. Born, Port Jefferson, NY, January 24, 1973. NY Rangers' 1st choice, 24th overall, in 1992 Entry Draft.

Season	Club	League	GP	G	A	Pts	PIM	PP	SH	GW	S	%	+/-	TF	F%	Min	GP	G	A	Pts	PIM	PP	SH	GW	Min
1990-91	Dubuque	USHL	29	21	31	52	83	....	....	....	....	....	....	....	....	....	8	7	5	12	10	....	....	....	....
1991-92	Dubuque	USHL	21	25	25	50	92	....	....	....	....	....	....	....	....	....	....	....	....	....	....	....	....	....	....
	Waterloo	USHL	21	23	28	51	76	....	....	....	....	....	....	....	....	....	4	8	5	13	16	....	....	....	....
1992-93	U. of Maine	H-East	36	18	32	50	106	....	....	....	....	....	....	....	....	....	....	....	....	....	....	....	....	....	....
1993-94	U. of Maine	H-East	4	3	6	9	16	....	....	....	....	....	....	....	....	....	....	....	....	....	....	....	....	....	....
	United States	Nat-Tm	60	30	34	64	87	....	....	....	....	....	....	....	....	....	....	....	....	....	....	....	....	....	....
	United States	Olympics	8	6	0	6	6	....	....	....	....	....	....	....	....	....	....	....	....	....	....	....	....	....	....
1994-95	Atlanta Knights	IHL	61	15	24	39	118	....	....	....	....	....	....	....	....	....	....	....	....	....	....	....	....	....	....
	Binghamton	AHL	12	2	6	8	67	....	....	....	....	....	....	....	....	....	11	4	3	7	51	....	....	....	....
1995-96	**NY Rangers**	**NHL**	**5**	**0**	**1**	**1**	**0**	**0**	**0**	**0**	**6**	**0.0**	**-5**	....	....	....	....	....	....	....	....	....	....	....	....
	Binghamton	AHL	68	48	53	101	157	....	....	....	....	....	....	....	....	....	4	1	6	7	22	....	....	....	....
1996-97	**NY Rangers**	**NHL**	**2**	**0**	**0**	**0**	**0**	**0**	**0**	**0**	**3**	**0.0**	**0**	....	....	....	**2**	**0**	**0**	**0**	**0**	**0**	**0**	**0**	....
	Binghamton	AHL	75	38	39	77	171	....	....	....	....	....	....	....	....	....	4	3	1	4	18	....	....	....	....
1997-98	**Pittsburgh**	**NHL**	**29**	**3**	**4**	**7**	**12**	**0**	**0**	**0**	**34**	**8.8**	**-2**	....	....	....	....	....	....	....	....	....	....	....	....
	NY Rangers	**NHL**	**1**	**0**	**0**	**0**	**2**	**0**	**0**	**0**	**3**	**0.0**	**-2**	....	....	....	....	....	....	....	....	....	....	....	....
	Hartford	AHL	36	17	23	40	54	....	....	....	....	....	....	....	....	....	15	8	6	14	59	....	....	....	....
1998-99	**Boston**	**NHL**	**46**	**6**	**8**	**14**	**44**	**1**	**0**	**1**	**61**	**9.8**	**10**	**70**	**37.1**	**10:12**	....	....	....	....	....	....	....	....	....
	Providence Bruins	AHL	16	15	10	25	14	....	....	....	....	....	....	....	....	....	19	9	12	21	38	....	....	....	....
99-2000	**Boston**	**NHL**	**5**	**0**	**1**	**1**	**0**	**0**	**0**	**0**	**3**	**0.0**	**-1**	**19**	**47.4**	**8:11**	....	....	....	....	....	....	....	....	....
	Providence Bruins	AHL	48	21	25	46	98	....	....	....	....	....	....	....	....	....	13	5	7	12	14	....	....	....	....
2000-01	Providence Bruins	AHL	78	26	45	71	109	....	....	....	....	....	....	....	....	....	17	4	5	9	34	....	....	....	....
2001-02	**Washington**	**NHL**	**4**	**0**	**1**	**1**	**0**	**0**	**0**	**0**	**3**	**0.0**	**-1**	**0**	**0.0**	**12:54**	....	....	....	....	....	....	....	....	....
	Portland Pirates	AHL	67	21	37	58	119	....	....	....	....	....	....	....	....	....	....	....	....	....	....	....	....	....	....
2002-03	Portland Pirates	AHL	59	22	41	63	123	....	....	....	....	....	....	....	....	....	3	0	2	2	16	....	....	....	....
2003-04	Springfield	AHL	64	19	31	50	100	....	....	....	....	....	....	....	....	....	....	....	....	....	....	....	....	....	....
2004-05	Sodertalje SK	Sweden	12	2	1	3	6	....	....	....	....	....	....	....	....	....	....	....	....	....	....	....	....	....	....
	Syracuse Crunch	AHL	48	9	17	26	75	....	....	....	....	....	....	....	....	....	....	....	....	....	....	....	....	....	....
	NHL Totals		**92**	**9**	**15**	**24**	**58**	**1**	**0**	**1**	**113**	**8.0**		**89**	**39.3**	**10:13**	**2**	**0**	**0**	**0**	**0**	**0**	**0**	**0**	....

AHL First All-Star Team (1996) • Jack A. Butterfield Trophy (Playoff MVP – AHL) (1999)

Claimed on waivers by **Pittsburgh** from **NY Rangers**, October 1, 1997. Claimed on waivers by **NY Rangers** from **Pittsburgh**, January 9, 1998. Signed as a free agent by **Boston**, August 5, 1998. Claimed by **Atlanta** from **Boston** in Expansion Draft, June 25, 1999. Traded to **Boston** by **Atlanta** for Randy Robitaille, June 25, 1999. Signed as a free agent by **Washington**, August 1, 2001. Signed as a free agent by **Phoenix**, July 17, 2003. Signed as a free agent by **Sodertalje** (Sweden), September 10, 2004. Signed as a free agent by **Syracuse** (AHL), December 13, 2004.

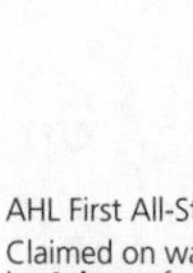

FIBIGER, Jesse

(feh-BEH-gehr, JEH-see)

Defense. Shoots left. 6'3", 210 lbs. Born, Victoria, B.C., April 4, 1978. Anaheim's 5th choice, 178th overall, in 1998 Entry Draft.

Season	Club	League	GP	G	A	Pts	PIM	PP	SH	GW	S	%	+/-	TF	F%	Min	GP	G	A	Pts	PIM	PP	SH	GW	Min
1996-97	Victoria Salsa	BCHL	53	6	18	24	88	....	....	....	....	....	....	....	....	....	....	....	....	....	....	....	....	....	....
1997-98	U. Minn-Duluth	WCHA	40	3	6	9	82	....	....	....	....	....	....	....	....	....	....	....	....	....	....	....	....	....	....
1998-99	U. Minn-Duluth	WCHA	36	4	16	20	61	....	....	....	....	....	....	....	....	....	....	....	....	....	....	....	....	....	....
99-2000	U. Minn-Duluth	WCHA	37	4	6	10	83	....	....	....	....	....	....	....	....	....	....	....	....	....	....	....	....	....	....
2000-01	U. Minn-Duluth	WCHA	37	0	8	8	56	....	....	....	....	....	....	....	....	....	....	....	....	....	....	....	....	....	....
2001-02	Cleveland Barons	AHL	79	6	12	18	94	....	....	....	....	....	....	....	....	....	....	....	....	....	....	....	....	....	....
2002-03	**San Jose**	**NHL**	**16**	**0**	**0**	**0**	**2**	**0**	**0**	**0**	**2**	**0.0**	**-5**	**0**	**0.0**	**6:05**	....	....	....	....	....	....	....	....	....
	Cleveland Barons	AHL	59	3	11	14	63	....	....	....	....	....	....	....	....	....	....	....	....	....	....	....	....	....	....
2003-04	Cleveland Barons	AHL	55	5	12	17	39	....	....	....	....	....	....	....	....	....	9	0	2	2	8	....	....	....	....
2004-05	Binghamton	AHL	79	3	19	22	79	....	....	....	....	....	....	....	....	....	6	1	0	1	6	....	....	....	....
	NHL Totals		**16**	**0**	**0**	**0**	**2**	**0**	**0**	**0**	**2**	**0.0**		**0**	**0.0**	**6:05**	....	....	....	....	....	....	....	....	....

Signed as a free agent by **San Jose**, August 15, 2001. Signed as a free agent by **Ottawa**, August 11, 2004.

FIDDLER, Vern

(FIHD-luhr, VUHRN) **NSH.**

Center. Shoots left. 5'11", 204 lbs. Born, Edmonton, Alta., May 9, 1980.

			Regular Season														Playoffs								
Season	Club	League	GP	G	A	Pts	PIM	PP	SH	GW	S	%	+/-	TF	F%	Min	GP	G	A	Pts	PIM	PP	SH	GW	Min
1997-98	Kelowna Rockets	WHL	65	10	11	21	31	....	....	....	....	....	....	....	....	....	7	0	1	1	4	....	....	....	....
1998-99	Kelowna Rockets	WHL	68	22	21	43	82	....	....	....	....	....	....	....	....	....	6	2	0	2	8	....	....	....	....
99-2000	Kelowna Rockets	WHL	64	20	28	48	60	....	....	....	....	....	....	....	....	....	5	1	3	4	4	....	....	....	....
2000-01	Kelowna Rockets	WHL	3	0	2	2	0	....	....	....	....	....	....	....	....	....	....	....	....	....	....	....	....	....	....
	Medicine Hat	WHL	67	33	38	71	100	....	....	....	....	....	....	....	....	....	....	....	....	....	....	....	....	....	....
	Arkansas	ECHL	3	0	1	1	2	....	....	....	....	....	....	....	....	....	5	3	0	3	5	....	....	....	....
2001-02	Roanoke Express	ECHL	44	27	28	55	71	....	....	....	....	....	....	....	....	....	....	....	....	....	....	....	....	....	....
	Norfolk Admirals	AHL	38	8	5	13	28	....	....	....	....	....	....	....	....	....	4	1	3	4	2	....	....	....	....
2002-03	**Nashville**	**NHL**	**19**	**4**	**2**	**6**	**14**	**0**	**0**	**1**	**20**	**20.0**	**2**	**171**	**53.8**	**9:40**	....	....	....	....	....	....	....	....	....
	Milwaukee	AHL	54	8	16	24	70	....	....	....	....	....	....	....	....	....	6	1	2	3	14	....	....	....	....
2003-04	**Nashville**	**NHL**	**17**	**0**	**0**	**0**	**23**	**0**	**0**	**0**	**8**	**0.0**	**–6**	**123**	**49.6**	**8:06**	....	....	....	....	....	....	....	....	....
	Milwaukee	AHL	47	9	15	24	72	....	....	....	....	....	....	....	....	....	22	5	3	8	36	....	....	....	....
2004-05	Milwaukee	AHL	73	20	22	42	70	....	....	....	....	....	....	....	....	....	7	0	0	0	18	....	....	....	....
	NHL Totals		**36**	**4**	**2**	**6**	**37**	**0**	**0**	**1**	**28**	**14.3**		**294**	**52.0**	**8:56**	....	....	....	....	....	....	....	....	....

ECHL All-Rookie Team (2002)

Signed as a free agent by **Arkansas** (ECHL), March 31, 2001. Traded to **Roanoke** (ECHL) by **Arkansas** (ECHL) for Calvin Elfring, August 11, 2001. Signed as a free agent by **Nashville**, May 6, 2002.

FINLEY, Jeff

(FIHN-lee, JEHF)

Defense. Shoots left. 6'2", 205 lbs. Born, Edmonton, Alta., April 14, 1967. NY Islanders' 4th choice, 55th overall, in 1985 Entry Draft.

Season	Club	League	GP	G	A	Pts	PIM	PP	SH	GW	S	%	+/-	TF	F%	Min	GP	G	A	Pts	PIM	PP	SH	GW	Min
1983-84	Summerland	BCJHL	49	0	21	21	14	....	....	....	....	....	....	....	....	....	....	....	....	....	....	....	....	....	....
	Portland	WHL	5	0	0	0	5	....	....	....	....	....	....	....	....	....	5	0	1	1	4	....	....	....	....
1984-85	Portland	WHL	69	6	44	50	57	....	....	....	....	....	....	....	....	....	6	1	2	3	2	....	....	....	....
1985-86	Portland	WHL	70	11	59	70	83	....	....	....	....	....	....	....	....	....	15	1	7	8	16	....	....	....	....
1986-87	Portland	WHL	72	13	53	66	113	....	....	....	....	....	....	....	....	....	20	1	*21	22	27	....	....	....	....
1987-88	**NY Islanders**	**NHL**	**10**	**0**	**5**	**5**	**15**	**0**	**0**	**0**	**9**	**0.0**	**5**	....	....	....	**1**	**0**	**0**	**0**	**2**	**0**	**0**	**0**	....
	Springfield	AHL	52	5	18	23	50	....	....	....	....	....	....	....	....	....	....	....	....	....	....	....	....	....	....
1988-89	**NY Islanders**	**NHL**	**4**	**0**	**0**	**0**	**6**	**0**	**0**	**0**	**1**	**0.0**	**1**	....	....	....	....	....	....	....	....	....	....	....	....
	Springfield	AHL	65	3	16	19	55	....	....	....	....	....	....	....	....	....	....	....	....	....	....	....	....	....	....
1989-90	**NY Islanders**	**NHL**	**11**	**0**	**1**	**1**	**0**	**0**	**0**	**0**	**7**	**0.0**	**0**	....	....	....	**5**	**0**	**2**	**2**	**2**	**0**	**0**	**0**	....
	Springfield	AHL	57	1	15	16	41	....	....	....	....	....	....	....	....	....	13	1	4	5	23	....	....	....	....
1990-91	**NY Islanders**	**NHL**	**11**	**0**	**0**	**0**	**4**	**0**	**0**	**0**	**0**	**0.0**	**–1**	....	....	....	....	....	....	....	....	....	....	....	....
	Capital District	AHL	67	10	34	44	34	....	....	....	....	....	....	....	....	....	....	....	....	....	....	....	....	....	....
1991-92	**NY Islanders**	**NHL**	**51**	**1**	**10**	**11**	**26**	**0**	**0**	**0**	**25**	**4.0**	**–6**	....	....	....	....	....	....	....	....	....	....	....	....
	Capital District	AHL	20	1	9	10	6	....	....	....	....	....	....	....	....	....	....	....	....	....	....	....	....	....	....
1992-93	Capital District	AHL	61	6	29	35	34	....	....	....	....	....	....	....	....	....	4	0	1	1	0	....	....	....	....
1993-94	**Philadelphia**	**NHL**	**55**	**1**	**8**	**9**	**24**	**0**	**0**	**0**	**43**	**2.3**	**16**	....	....	....	....	....	....	....	....	....	....	....	....
1994-95	Hershey Bears	AHL	36	2	9	11	33	....	....	....	....	....	....	....	....	....	6	0	1	1	8	....	....	....	....
1995-96	**Winnipeg**	**NHL**	**65**	**1**	**5**	**6**	**81**	**0**	**0**	**0**	**27**	**3.7**	**–2**	....	....	....	**6**	**0**	**0**	**0**	**4**	**0**	**0**	**0**	....
	Springfield	AHL	14	3	12	15	22	....	....	....	....	....	....	....	....	....	....	....	....	....	....	....	....	....	....
1996-97	**Phoenix**	**NHL**	**65**	**3**	**7**	**10**	**40**	**1**	**0**	**1**	**38**	**7.9**	**–8**	....	....	....	**1**	**0**	**0**	**0**	**2**	**0**	**0**	**0**	....
1997-98	**NY Rangers**	**NHL**	**63**	**1**	**6**	**7**	**55**	**0**	**0**	**0**	**32**	**3.1**	**–3**	....	....	....	....	....	....	....	....	....	....	....	....
1998-99	**NY Rangers**	**NHL**	**2**	**0**	**0**	**0**	**0**	**0**	**0**	**0**	**0**	**0.0**	**–1**	**0**	**0.0**	**11:40**	....	....	....	....	....	....	....	....	....
	Hartford	AHL	42	2	10	12	28	....	....	....	....	....	....	....	....	....	....	....	....	....	....	....	....	....	....
	St. Louis	**NHL**	**30**	**1**	**2**	**3**	**20**	**0**	**0**	**0**	**16**	**6.3**	**12**	**0**	**0.0**	**17:36**	**13**	**1**	**2**	**3**	**8**	**0**	**0**	**1**	**20:10**
99-2000	**St. Louis**	**NHL**	**74**	**2**	**8**	**10**	**38**	**0**	**0**	**2**	**31**	**6.5**	**26**	**1**	**100.0**	**17:49**	**7**	**0**	**2**	**2**	**4**	**0**	**0**	**0**	**17:21**
2000-01	**St. Louis**	**NHL**	**72**	**2**	**8**	**10**	**38**	**0**	**0**	**0**	**35**	**5.7**	**7**	**1**	**0.0**	**18:53**	**2**	**0**	**0**	**0**	**0**	**0**	**0**	**0**	**3:25**
2001-02	**St. Louis**	**NHL**	**78**	**0**	**6**	**6**	**30**	**0**	**0**	**0**	**39**	**0.0**	**12**	**0**	**0.0**	**18:31**	**10**	**0**	**0**	**0**	**8**	**0**	**0**	**0**	**18:02**
2002-03	**St. Louis**	**NHL**	**64**	**1**	**3**	**4**	**46**	**0**	**0**	**1**	**30**	**3.3**	**–2**	**0**	**0.0**	**15:37**	**6**	**0**	**0**	**0**	**6**	**0**	**0**	**0**	**15:11**
2003-04	**St. Louis**	**NHL**	**53**	**0**	**1**	**1**	**34**	**0**	**0**	**0**	**25**	**0.0**	**–9**	**0**	**0.0**	**17:05**	**1**	**0**	**0**	**0**	**2**	**0**	**0**	**0**	**12:14**
2004-05			DID NOT PLAY																						
	NHL Totals		**708**	**13**	**70**	**83**	**457**	**1**	**0**	**4**	**358**	**3.6**		**2**	**50.0**	**17:38**	**52**	**1**	**6**	**7**	**38**	**0**	**0**	**1**	**17:17**

Rights traded to **Ottawa** by **NY Islanders** for Chris Luongo, June 30, 1993. Signed as a free agent by **Philadelphia**, July 30, 1993. Traded to **Winnipeg** by **Philadelphia** for Russ Romaniuk, June 27, 1995. Transferred to **Phoenix** after **Winnipeg** franchise relocated, July 1, 1996. Signed as a free agent by **NY Rangers**, August 18, 1997. Traded to **St. Louis** by **NY Rangers** with Geoff Smith for future considerations (Chris Kenady, February 22, 1999), February 13, 1999.

FISCHER, Jiri

(FIH-shuhr, YIH-ree) **DET.**

Defense. Shoots left. 6'5", 225 lbs. Born, Horovice, Czech., July 31, 1980. Detroit's 1st choice, 25th overall, in 1998 Entry Draft.

Season	Club	League	GP	G	A	Pts	PIM	PP	SH	GW	S	%	+/-	TF	F%	Min	GP	G	A	Pts	PIM	PP	SH	GW	Min
1995-96	Kladno Jr.	CzRep-Jr.	39	6	10	16	....	....	....	....	....	....	....	....	....	....	....	....	....	....	....	....	....	....	....
1996-97	Kladno Jr.	CzRep-Jr.	38	7	21	28	....	....	....	....	....	....	....	....	....	....	....	....	....	....	....	....	....	....	....
1997-98	Hull Olympiques	QMJHL	70	3	19	22	112	....	....	....	....	....	....	....	....	....	11	1	4	5	16	....	....	....	....
1998-99	Hull Olympiques	QMJHL	65	22	56	78	141	....	....	....	....	....	....	....	....	....	23	6	17	23	44	....	....	....	....
99-2000	**Detroit**	**NHL**	**52**	**0**	**8**	**8**	**45**	**0**	**0**	**0**	**41**	**0.0**	**1**	**0**	**0.0**	**10:51**	....	....	....	....	....	....	....	....	....
	Cincinnati	AHL	7	0	2	2	10	....	....	....	....	....	....	....	....	....	....	....	....	....	....	....	....	....	....
2000-01	**Detroit**	**NHL**	**55**	**1**	**8**	**9**	**59**	**0**	**0**	**0**	**64**	**1.6**	**3**	**0**	**0.0**	**16:46**	**5**	**0**	**0**	**0**	**9**	**0**	**0**	**0**	**16:25**
	Cincinnati	AHL	18	2	6	8	22	....	....	....	....	....	....	....	....	....	....	....	....	....	....	....	....	....	....
2001-02♦	**Detroit**	**NHL**	**80**	**2**	**8**	**10**	**67**	**0**	**0**	**1**	**103**	**1.9**	**17**	**0**	**0.0**	**17:10**	**22**	**3**	**3**	**6**	**30**	**0**	**0**	**1**	**19:41**
2002-03	**Detroit**	**NHL**	**15**	**1**	**5**	**6**	**16**	**0**	**0**	**0**	**19**	**5.3**	**0**	**0**	**0.0**	**21:24**	....	....	....	....	....	....	....	....	....
2003-04	**Detroit**	**NHL**	**81**	**4**	**15**	**19**	**75**	**1**	**0**	**0**	**115**	**3.5**	**0**	**0**	**0.0**	**18:30**	**11**	**1**	**0**	**1**	**16**	**0**	**0**	**0**	**11:29**
2004-05	Liberec	CzRep	27	6	12	18	52	....	....	....	....	....	....	....	....	....	11	1	4	5	22	....	....	....	....
	Beroun	CzRep-2	1	0	1	1	25	....	....	....	....	....	....	....	....	....	....	....	....	....	....	....	....	....	....
	NHL Totals		**283**	**8**	**44**	**52**	**262**	**1**	**0**	**1**	**342**	**2.3**		**0**	**0.0**	**16:32**	**38**	**4**	**3**	**7**	**55**	**0**	**0**	**1**	**16:53**

QMJHL First All-Star Team (1999)

• Missed majority of 2002-03 season recovering from knee injury suffered in game vs. Nashville, November 12, 2002. Signed as a free agent by **Liberec** (CzRep), September 4, 2004.

FISHER, Mike

(FIH-shuhr, MIGHK) **OTT.**

Center. Shoots right. 6'1", 200 lbs. Born, Peterborough, Ont., June 5, 1980. Ottawa's 2nd choice, 44th overall, in 1998 Entry Draft.

Season	Club	League	GP	G	A	Pts	PIM	PP	SH	GW	S	%	+/-	TF	F%	Min	GP	G	A	Pts	PIM	PP	SH	GW	Min
1996-97	Peterborough	OPJHL	51	26	30	56	35	....	....	....	....	....	....	....	....	....	....	....	....	....	....	....	....	....	....
1997-98	Sudbury Wolves	OHL	66	24	25	49	65	....	....	....	....	....	....	....	....	....	9	2	2	4	13	....	....	....	....
1998-99	Sudbury Wolves	OHL	68	41	65	106	55	....	....	....	....	....	....	....	....	....	4	2	1	3	4	....	....	....	....
99-2000	**Ottawa**	**NHL**	**32**	**4**	**5**	**9**	**15**	**0**	**0**	**1**	**49**	**8.2**	**–6**	**356**	**47.8**	**12:57**	....	....	....	....	....	....	....	....	....
2000-01	**Ottawa**	**NHL**	**60**	**7**	**12**	**19**	**46**	**0**	**0**	**3**	**83**	**8.4**	**–1**	**709**	**50.2**	**11:38**	**4**	**0**	**1**	**1**	**4**	**0**	**0**	**0**	**13:41**
2001-02	**Ottawa**	**NHL**	**58**	**15**	**9**	**24**	**55**	**0**	**3**	**4**	**123**	**12.2**	**8**	**848**	**48.7**	**14:05**	**10**	**2**	**1**	**3**	**0**	**0**	**0**	**0**	**16:17**
2002-03	**Ottawa**	**NHL**	**74**	**18**	**20**	**38**	**54**	**5**	**1**	**3**	**142**	**12.7**	**13**	**1077**	**48.1**	**15:59**	**18**	**2**	**2**	**4**	**16**	**0**	**1**	**1**	**16:58**
2003-04	**Ottawa**	**NHL**	**24**	**4**	**6**	**10**	**39**	**1**	**0**	**0**	**47**	**8.5**	**–3**	**357**	**42.0**	**17:26**	**7**	**1**	**0**	**1**	**4**	**0**	**0**	**1**	**16:11**
2004-05	EV Zug	Swiss	21	9	18	27	34	....	....	....	....	....	....	....	....	....	9	2	3	5	10	....	....	....	....
	NHL Totals		**248**	**48**	**52**	**100**	**209**	**6**	**4**	**11**	**444**	**10.8**		**3347**	**48.0**	**14:14**	**39**	**5**	**4**	**9**	**24**	**0**	**1**	**2**	**16:19**

• Missed majority of 1999-2000 season recovering from knee injury suffered in game vs. Boston, December 30, 1999. • Missed majority of 2003-04 season recovering from elbow injury suffered in practice, October 4, 2003. Signed as a free agent by **Zug** (Swiss), November 1, 2004.

FITZGERALD, Tom

(fihtz-JAIR-uhld, TAWM) **BOS.**

Right wing. Shoots right. 6', 190 lbs. Born, Billerica, MA, August 28, 1968. NY Islanders' 1st choice, 17th overall, in 1986 Entry Draft.

Season	Club	League	GP	G	A	Pts	PIM	PP	SH	GW	S	%	+/-	TF	F%	Min	GP	G	A	Pts	PIM	PP	SH	GW	Min
1984-85	Austin Mustangs	High-MA	18	20	21	41	....	....	....	....	....	....	....	....	....	....	....	....	....	....	....	....	....	....	....
1985-86	Austin Mustangs	High-MA	24	35	38	73	....	....	....	....	....	....	....	....	....	....	....	....	....	....	....	....	....	....	....
1986-87	Providence	H-East	27	8	14	22	22	....	....	....	....	....	....	....	....	....	....	....	....	....	....	....	....	....	....
1987-88	Providence	H-East	36	19	15	34	50	....	....	....	....	....	....	....	....	....	....	....	....	....	....	....	....	....	....
1988-89	**NY Islanders**	**NHL**	**23**	**3**	**5**	**8**	**10**	**0**	**0**	**1**	**24**	**12.5**	**1**	....	....	....	....	....	....	....	....	....	....	....	....
	Springfield	AHL	61	24	18	42	43	....	....	....	....	....	....	....	....	....	....	....	....	....	....	....	....	....	....
1989-90	**NY Islanders**	**NHL**	**19**	**2**	**5**	**7**	**4**	**0**	**0**	**1**	**24**	**8.3**	**–3**	....	....	....	**4**	**1**	**0**	**1**	**4**	**0**	**0**	**0**	....
	Springfield	AHL	53	30	23	53	32	....	....	....	....	....	....	....	....	....	14	2	9	11	13	....	....	....	....
1990-91	**NY Islanders**	**NHL**	**41**	**5**	**5**	**10**	**24**	**0**	**0**	**2**	**60**	**8.3**	**–9**	....	....	....	....	....	....	....	....	....	....	....	....
	Capital District	AHL	27	7	7	14	50	....	....	....	....	....	....	....	....	....	....	....	....	....	....	....	....	....	....
1991-92	**NY Islanders**	**NHL**	**45**	**6**	**11**	**17**	**28**	**0**	**2**	**2**	**71**	**8.5**	**–3**	....	....	....	....	....	....	....	....	....	....	....	....
	Capital District	AHL	4	1	1	2	4	....	....	....	....	....	....	....	....	....	....	....	....	....	....	....	....	....	....

						Regular Season														Playoffs					
Season	Club	League	GP	G	A	Pts	PIM	PP	SH	GW	S	%	+/-	TF	F%	Min	GP	G	A	Pts	PIM	PP	SH	GW	Min
1992-93	NY Islanders	NHL	77	9	18	27	34	0	3	1	83	10.8	–2	....	....	....	18	2	5	7	18	0	0	0	....
1993-94	Florida	NHL	83	18	14	32	54	0	3	1	144	12.5	–3	....	....	....	....	....	....	....	....	....	....	....	....
1994-95	Florida	NHL	48	3	13	16	31	0	0	0	78	3.8	–3	....	....	....	....	....	....	....	....	....	....	....	....
1995-96	Florida	NHL	82	13	21	34	75	1	6	2	141	9.2	–3	....	....	....	22	4	4	8	34	0	0	2	....
1996-97	Florida	NHL	71	10	14	24	64	0	2	1	135	7.4	7	....	....	....	5	0	1	1	0	0	0	0	....
1997-98	Florida	NHL	69	10	5	15	57	0	1	1	105	9.5	–4	....	....	....	....	....	....	....	....	....	....	....	....
	Colorado	NHL	11	2	1	3	22	0	1	0	14	14.3	0	....	....	....	7	0	1	1	20	0	0	0	....
1998-99	Nashville	NHL	80	13	19	32	48	0	0	1	180	7.2	–18	155	52.3	17:17	....	....	....	....	....	....	....	....	....
99-2000	Nashville	NHL	82	13	9	22	66	0	3	1	119	10.9	–18	264	51.9	13:57	....	....	....	....	....	....	....	....	....
2000-01	Nashville	NHL	82	9	9	18	71	0	2	2	135	6.7	–5	458	54.6	14:58	....	....	....	....	....	....	....	....	....
2001-02	Nashville	NHL	63	7	9	16	33	0	1	0	101	6.9	–4	525	48.4	14:15	....	....	....	....	....	....	....	....	....
	Chicago	NHL	15	1	3	4	6	0	1	0	24	4.2	–3	110	50.0	16:16	5	0	0	0	4	0	0	0	15:15
2002-03	Toronto	NHL	66	4	13	17	57	0	0	0	89	4.5	10	90	50.0	12:07	7	0	1	1	4	0	0	0	18:11
2003-04	Toronto	NHL	69	7	10	17	52	1	0	1	81	8.6	–2	300	53.0	12:23	10	0	0	0	6	0	0	0	13:26
2004-05			DID NOT PLAY																						
	NHL Totals		1026	135	184	319	736	2	25	17	1608	8.4		1902	51.6	14:20	78	7	12	19	90	0	0	2	15:22

Claimed by **Florida** from **NY Islanders** in Expansion Draft, June 24, 1993. Traded to **Colorado** by **Florida** for the rights to Mark Parrish and Anaheim's 3rd round choice (previously acquired, Florida selected Lance Ward) in 1998 Entry Draft, March 24, 1998. Signed as a free agent by **Nashville**, July 6, 1998. Traded to **Chicago** by **Nashville** for Chicago's 4th round choice (later traded to Anaheim – Anaheim selected Nathan Saunders) in 2003 Entry Draft and future considerations, March 13, 2002. Signed as a free agent by **Toronto**, July 17, 2002. Signed as a free agent by **Boston**, July 28, 2004.

FITZPATRICK, Rory

(FIHTZ-pa-trihk, ROHR-ee) **BUF.**

Defense. Shoots right. 6'2", 208 lbs. Born, Rochester, NY, January 11, 1975. Montreal's 2nd choice, 47th overall, in 1993 Entry Draft.

1990-91	Rochester	EmJHL	40	0	5	5	....	....	....	....	....	....	....	....	....	....	....	....	....	....	....	....	....	....	....
1991-92	Rochester	EmJHL	28	8	28	36	141	....	....	....	....	....	....	....	....	....	....	....	....	....	....	....	....	....	....
1992-93	Sudbury Wolves	OHL	58	4	20	24	68	....	....	....	....	....	....	....	....	....	14	0	0	0	17	....	....	....	....
1993-94	Sudbury Wolves	OHL	65	12	34	46	112	....	....	....	....	....	....	....	....	....	10	2	5	7	10	....	....	....	....
1994-95	Sudbury Wolves	OHL	56	12	36	48	72	....	....	....	....	....	....	....	....	....	18	3	15	18	21	....	....	....	....
	Fredericton	AHL	....	....	....	....	....	....	....	....	....	....	....	....	....	....	10	1	2	3	5	....	....	....	....
1995-96	Montreal	NHL	42	0	2	2	18	0	0	0	31	0.0	–7	....	....	....	6	1	1	2	0	0	0	0	....
	Fredericton	AHL	18	4	6	10	36	....	....	....	....	....	....	....	....	....	....	....	....	....	....	....	....	....	....
1996-97	Montreal	NHL	6	0	1	1	6	0	0	0	5	0.0	–2	....	....	....	....	....	....	....	....	....	....	....	....
	St. Louis	NHL	2	0	0	0	2	0	0	0	1	0.0	–2	....	....	....	....	....	....	....	....	....	....	....	....
	Worcester IceCats	AHL	49	4	13	17	78	....	....	....	....	....	....	....	....	....	5	1	2	3	0	....	....	....	....
1997-98	Worcester IceCats	AHL	62	8	22	30	111	....	....	....	....	....	....	....	....	....	11	0	3	3	26	....	....	....	....
1998-99	St. Louis	NHL	1	0	0	0	2	0	0	0	0	0.0	–3	0	0.0	4:49	....	....	....	....	....	....	....	....	....
	Worcester IceCats	AHL	53	5	16	21	82	....	....	....	....	....	....	....	....	....	4	0	1	1	17	....	....	....	....
99-2000	Worcester IceCats	AHL	28	0	5	5	48	....	....	....	....	....	....	....	....	....	....	....	....	....	....	....	....	....	....
	Milwaukee	IHL	27	2	1	3	27	....	....	....	....	....	....	....	....	....	3	0	2	2	2	....	....	....	....
2000-01	Nashville	NHL	2	0	0	0	2	0	0	0	0	0.0	–2	0	0.0	9:47	....	....	....	....	....	....	....	....	....
	Milwaukee	IHL	22	0	2	2	32	....	....	....	....	....	....	....	....	....	....	....	....	....	....	....	....	....	....
	Hamilton	AHL	34	3	17	20	29	....	....	....	....	....	....	....	....	....	....	....	....	....	....	....	....	....	....
2001-02	Buffalo	NHL	5	0	0	0	4	0	0	0	2	0.0	–2	0	0.0	11:54	....	....	....	....	....	....	....	....	....
	Rochester	AHL	60	4	8	12	83	....	....	....	....	....	....	....	....	....	2	0	1	1	0	....	....	....	....
2002-03	Buffalo	NHL	36	1	3	4	16	0	0	0	29	3.4	–7	0	0.0	17:02	....	....	....	....	....	....	....	....	....
	Rochester	AHL	41	5	11	16	65	....	....	....	....	....	....	....	....	....	....	....	....	....	....	....	....	....	....
2003-04	Buffalo	NHL	60	4	7	11	44	2	0	2	78	5.1	–5	1	100.0	19:02	....	....	....	....	....	....	....	....	....
2004-05	Rochester	AHL	20	1	1	2	18	....	....	....	....	....	....	....	....	....	9	0	1	1	12	....	....	....	....
	NHL Totals		154	5	13	18	94	2	0	2	146	3.4		1	100.0	17:41	6	1	1	2	0	0	0	0	....

OHL All-Rookie Team (1993)

Traded to **St. Louis** by **Montreal** with Pierre Turgeon and Craig Conroy for Murray Baron, Shayne Corson and St. Louis' 5th round choice (Gennady Razin) in 1997 Entry Draft, October 29, 1996. Claimed by **Boston** from **St. Louis** in Waiver Draft, October 5, 1998. Claimed on waivers by **St. Louis** from **Boston**, October 7, 1998. Traded to **Nashville** by **St. Louis** for Dan Keczmer, February 9, 2000. Traded to **Edmonton** by **Nashville** for future considerations, January 12, 2001. Signed as a free agent by **Buffalo**, August 14, 2001. Signed as a free agent by **Rochester** (AHL), March 2, 2005.

FLINN, Ryan

(FLIHN, RIGH-yan) **L.A.**

Left wing. Shoots left. 6'5", 248 lbs. Born, Halifax, N.S., April 20, 1980. New Jersey's 8th choice, 143rd overall, in 1998 Entry Draft.

1996-97	Laval Titan	QMJHL	23	3	2	5	56	....	....	....	....	....	....	....	....	....	2	0	0	0	0	....	....	....	....
1997-98	Laval Titan	QMJHL	59	4	12	16	217	....	....	....	....	....	....	....	....	....	15	1	0	1	63	....	....	....	....
1998-99	Acadie-Bathurst	QMJHL	44	3	4	7	195	....	....	....	....	....	....	....	....	....	23	2	0	2	37	....	....	....	....
99-2000	Halifax	QMJHL	67	14	19	33	365	....	....	....	....	....	....	....	....	....	....	....	....	....	....	....	....	....	....
2000-01	Cape Breton	QMJHL	57	16	17	33	280	....	....	....	....	....	....	....	....	....	9	1	1	2	43	....	....	....	....
2001-02	Reading Royals	ECHL	20	1	3	4	130	....	....	....	....	....	....	....	....	....	....	....	....	....	....	....	....	....	....
	Los Angeles	NHL	10	0	0	0	51	0	0	0	2	0.0	0	0	0.0	3:29	....	....	....	....	....	....	....	....	....
	Manchester	AHL	37	0	1	1	113	....	....	....	....	....	....	....	....	....	1	0	0	0	0	....	....	....	....
2002-03	Los Angeles	NHL	19	1	0	1	28	0	0	0	13	7.7	0	0	0.0	5:28	....	....	....	....	....	....	....	....	....
	Manchester	AHL	27	2	2	4	95	....	....	....	....	....	....	....	....	....	....	....	....	....	....	....	....	....	....
2003-04	Manchester	AHL	59	3	5	8	164	....	....	....	....	....	....	....	....	....	6	0	0	0	4	....	....	....	....
2004-05	Manchester	AHL	14	1	1	2	112	....	....	....	....	....	....	....	....	....	....	....	....	....	....	....	....	....	....
	NHL Totals		29	1	0	1	79	0	0	0	15	6.7		0	0.0	4:47	....	....	....	....	....	....	....	....	....

Signed as a free agent by **Los Angeles**, January 8, 2002.

FOCHT, Dan

(FOHKT, DAN) **FLA.**

Defense. Shoots left. 6'6", 234 lbs. Born, Regina, Sask., December 31, 1977. Phoenix's 1st choice, 11th overall, in 1996 Entry Draft.

1994-95	Saskatoon Blazers	SMHL	33	6	12	18	98	....	....	....	....	....	....	....	....	....	....	....	....	....	....	....	....	....	....
1995-96	Tri-City	WHL	63	6	12	18	161	....	....	....	....	....	....	....	....	....	11	1	1	2	23	....	....	....	....
1996-97	Tri-City	WHL	28	0	5	5	92	....	....	....	....	....	....	....	....	....	....	....	....	....	....	....	....	....	....
	Regina Pats	WHL	22	2	2	4	59	....	....	....	....	....	....	....	....	....	5	0	2	2	8	....	....	....	....
	Springfield	AHL	1	0	0	0	2	....	....	....	....	....	....	....	....	....	....	....	....	....	....	....	....	....	....
1997-98	Springfield	AHL	61	2	5	7	125	....	....	....	....	....	....	....	....	....	3	0	0	0	4	....	....	....	....
1998-99	Mississippi	ECHL	2	0	0	0	6	....	....	....	....	....	....	....	....	....	....	....	....	....	....	....	....	....	....
	Springfield	AHL	30	0	2	2	58	....	....	....	....	....	....	....	....	....	3	1	0	1	10	....	....	....	....
99-2000	Jokerit Helsinki	Finland	2	0	0	0	0	....	....	....	....	....	....	....	....	....	....	....	....	....	....	....	....	....	....
	Mississippi	ECHL	4	0	1	1	0	....	....	....	....	....	....	....	....	....	....	....	....	....	....	....	....	....	....
	Springfield	AHL	44	2	9	11	86	....	....	....	....	....	....	....	....	....	5	0	1	1	2	....	....	....	....
2000-01	Springfield	AHL	69	0	6	6	156	....	....	....	....	....	....	....	....	....	....	....	....	....	....	....	....	....	....
2001-02	Phoenix	NHL	8	0	0	0	11	0	0	0	5	0.0	0	0	0.0	12:25	1	0	1	1	0	0	0	0	8:20
	Springfield	AHL	56	2	8	10	134	....	....	....	....	....	....	....	....	....	....	....	....	....	....	....	....	....	....
2002-03	Phoenix	NHL	10	0	0	0	10	0	0	0	1	0.0	–2	0	0.0	8:40	....	....	....	....	....	....	....	....	....
	Springfield	AHL	37	2	7	9	80	....	....	....	....	....	....	....	....	....	....	....	....	....	....	....	....	....	....
	Pittsburgh	NHL	12	0	3	3	19	0	0	0	11	0.0	–7	1	0.0	18:14	....	....	....	....	....	....	....	....	....
2003-04	Pittsburgh	NHL	52	2	3	5	105	0	0	0	56	3.6	–23	0	0.0	16:36	....	....	....	....	....	....	....	....	....
2004-05	Hamilton	AHL	26	2	3	5	84	....	....	....	....	....	....	....	....	....	....	....	....	....	....	....	....	....	....
	NHL Totals		82	2	6	8	145	0	0	0	73	2.7		1	0.0	15:28	1	0	1	1	0	0	0	0	8:20

Traded to **Pittsburgh** by **Phoenix** with Ramzi Abid and Guillaume Lefebvre for Jan Hrdina and Francois Leroux, March 11, 2003. Signed as a free agent by **Hamilton** (AHL), October 25, 2004. Signed as a free agent by **Florida**, August 26, 2005.

FOOTE, Adam

(FUT, A-duhm) **CBJ**

Defense. Shoots right. 6'2", 215 lbs. Born, Toronto, Ont., July 10, 1971. Quebec's 2nd choice, 22nd overall, in 1989 Entry Draft.

1987-88	Whitby Midgets	OMHA	65	25	43	68	108	....	....	....	....	....	....	....	....	....	....	....	....	....	....	....	....	....	....
1988-89	Sault Ste. Marie	OHL	66	7	32	39	120	....	....	....	....	....	....	....	....	....	....	....	....	....	....	....	....	....	....
1989-90	Sault Ste. Marie	OHL	61	12	43	55	199	....	....	....	....	....	....	....	....	....	....	....	....	....	....	....	....	....	....
1990-91	Sault Ste. Marie	OHL	59	18	51	69	93	....	....	....	....	....	....	....	....	....	14	5	12	17	28	....	....	....	....
1991-92	Quebec	NHL	46	2	5	7	44	0	0	0	55	3.6	–4	....	....	....	....	....	....	....	....	....	....	....	....
	Halifax Citadels	AHL	6	0	1	1	2	....	....	....	....	....	....	....	....	....	....	....	....	....	....	....	....	....	....
1992-93	Quebec	NHL	81	4	12	16	168	0	1	0	54	7.4	6	....	....	....	6	0	1	1	2	0	0	0	....
1993-94	Quebec	NHL	45	2	6	8	67	0	0	0	42	4.8	3	....	....	....	....	....	....	....	....	....	....	....	....
1994-95	Quebec	NHL	35	0	7	7	52	0	0	0	24	0.0	17	....	....	....	6	0	1	1	14	0	0	0	....

Season	Club	League	Regular Season														Playoffs								
Season	Club	League	GP	G	A	Pts	PIM	PP	SH	GW	S	%	+/-	TF	F%	Min	GP	G	A	Pts	PIM	PP	SH	GW	Min
1995-96♦	Colorado	NHL	73	5	11	16	88	1	0	1	49	10.2	27	....	....	....	22	1	3	4	36	0	0	0	....
1996-97	Colorado	NHL	78	2	19	21	135	0	0	0	60	3.3	16	....	....	....	17	0	4	4	62	0	0	0	....
1997-98	Colorado	NHL	77	3	14	17	124	0	0	1	64	4.7	–3	....	....	....	7	0	0	0	23	0	0	0	....
	Canada	Olympics	6	0	1	1	4	....	....	....	....	....	....	....	....	....	....	....	....	....	....	....	....	....	....
1998-99	Colorado	NHL	64	5	16	21	92	3	0	0	83	6.0	20	0	0.0	24:50	19	2	3	5	24	1	0	0	28:34
99-2000	Colorado	NHL	59	5	13	18	98	1	0	2	63	7.9	5	0	0.0	25:51	16	0	7	7	28	0	0	0	26:05
2000-01♦	Colorado	NHL	35	3	12	15	42	1	1	1	59	5.1	6	0	0.0	25:22	23	3	4	7	*47	1	0	1	28:22
2001-02	Colorado	NHL	55	5	22	27	55	1	1	0	85	5.9	7	0	0.0	25:59	21	1	6	7	28	0	0	0	27:46
	Canada	Olympics	6	1	0	1	2	....	....	....	....	....	....	....	....	....	....	....	....	....	....	....	....	....	....
2002-03	Colorado	NHL	78	11	20	31	88	3	0	2	106	10.4	30	0	0.0	25:43	6	0	1	1	8	0	0	0	24:12
2003-04	Colorado	NHL	73	8	22	30	87	5	0	1	105	7.6	13	0	0.0	24:03	11	0	4	4	10	0	0	0	25:06
2004-05		DID NOT PLAY																							
	NHL Totals		799	55	179	234	1140	15	3	8	849	6.5		0	0.0	25:15	154	7	34	41	282	2	0	1	27:15

OHL First All-Star Team (1991)

Transferred to **Colorado** after **Quebec** franchise relocated, June 21, 1995. • Missed majority of 2000-01 season recovering from shoulder injury suffered in game vs. Carolina, January 6, 2001. Signed as a free agent by **Columbus**, August 2, 2005.

FORBES, Colin

(FOHRBS, COHL-ihn) **CAR.**

Center. Shoots left. 6'3", 215 lbs. Born, New Westminster, B.C., February 16, 1976. Philadelphia's 5th choice, 166th overall, in 1994 Entry Draft.

Season	Club	League	GP	G	A	Pts	PIM	PP	SH	GW	S	%	+/-	TF	F%	Min	GP	G	A	Pts	PIM	PP	SH	GW	Min
1993-94	Sherwood Park	AJHL	47	18	22	40	76	....	....	....	....	....	....	....	....	....	....	....	....	....	....	....	....	....	....
1994-95	Portland	WHL	72	24	31	55	108	....	....	....	....	....	....	....	....	....	9	1	3	4	10	....	....	....	....
1995-96	Portland	WHL	72	33	44	77	137	....	....	....	....	....	....	....	....	....	7	2	5	7	14	....	....	....	....
	Hershey Bears	AHL	2	1	0	1	2	....	....	....	....	....	....	....	....	....	4	0	2	2	2	....	....	....	....
1996-97	Philadelphia	NHL	3	1	0	1	0	0	0	0	3	33.3	0	....	....	....	3	0	0	0	0	0	0	0	....
	Philadelphia	AHL	74	21	28	49	108	....	....	....	....	....	....	....	....	....	10	5	5	10	33	....	....	....	....
1997-98	Philadelphia	NHL	63	12	7	19	59	2	0	2	93	12.9	2	....	....	....	5	0	0	0	2	0	0	0	....
	Philadelphia	AHL	13	7	4	11	22	....	....	....	....	....	....	....	....	....	....	....	....	....	....	....	....	....	....
1998-99	Philadelphia	NHL	66	9	7	16	51	0	0	4	92	9.8	0	2	50.0	12:35	....	....	....	....	....	....	....	....	....
	Tampa Bay	NHL	14	3	1	4	10	0	1	0	25	12.0	–5	0	0.0	17:30	....	....	....	....	....	....	....	....	....
99-2000	Tampa Bay	NHL	8	0	0	0	18	0	0	0	3	0.0	–4	1	0.0	8:53	....	....	....	....	....	....	....	....	....
	Ottawa	NHL	45	2	5	7	12	0	0	0	54	3.7	–1	82	47.6	8:34	5	1	0	1	14	0	0	0	6:48
2000-01	Ottawa	NHL	39	0	1	1	31	0	0	0	26	0.0	–3	10	40.0	6:10	....	....	....	....	....	....	....	....	....
	NY Rangers	NHL	19	1	4	5	15	0	0	0	20	5.0	–3	1	0.0	7:52	....	....	....	....	....	....	....	....	....
2001-02	Utah Grizzlies	AHL	4	0	0	0	21	....	....	....	....	....	....	....	....	....	....	....	....	....	....	....	....	....	....
	Washington	NHL	38	5	3	8	15	0	1	1	49	10.2	–2	253	44.7	11:01	....	....	....	....	....	....	....	....	....
	Portland Pirates	AHL	14	4	5	9	18	....	....	....	....	....	....	....	....	....	....	....	....	....	....	....	....	....	....
2002-03	Washington	NHL	5	0	0	0	0	0	0	0	3	0.0	–2	12	50.0	9:38	....	....	....	....	....	....	....	....	....
	Portland Pirates	AHL	69	22	38	60	73	....	....	....	....	....	....	....	....	....	3	2	2	4	4	....	....	....	....
2003-04	Washington	NHL	2	0	0	0	0	0	0	0	2	0.0	0	3	33.3	8:53	....	....	....	....	....	....	....	....	....
	Portland Pirates	AHL	69	16	32	48	59	....	....	....	....	....	....	....	....	....	7	0	6	6	16	....	....	....	....
2004-05	Lowell	AHL	76	27	37	64	80	....	....	....	....	....	....	....	....	....	11	3	1	4	20	....	....	....	....
	NHL Totals		302	33	28	61	211	2	2	7	370	8.9		364	45.1	10:12	13	1	0	1	16	0	0	0	6:48

Traded to **Tampa Bay** by **Philadelphia** with Philadelphia's 4th round choice (Michal Lanicek) in 1999 Entry Draft for Mikael Andersson and Sandy McCarthy, March 20, 1999. Traded to **Ottawa** by **Tampa Bay** for Bruce Gardiner, November 11, 1999. Traded to **NY Rangers** by **Ottawa** for Eric Lacroix, March 1, 2001. Signed as a free agent by **Washington**, January 8, 2002. Signed as a free agent by **Hershey** (AHL), September 11, 2003. Signed as a free agent by **Portland** (AHL), October 14, 2003. Signed as a free agent by **Washington**, November 4, 2003. Signed as a free agent by **Carolina**, August 11, 2004.

FORSBERG, Peter

(FOHRS-buhrg, PEE-tuhr) **PHI.**

Center. Shoots left. 6', 205 lbs. Born, Ornskoldsvik, Sweden, July 20, 1973. Philadelphia's 1st choice, 6th overall, in 1991 Entry Draft.

Season	Club	League	GP	G	A	Pts	PIM	PP	SH	GW	S	%	+/-	TF	F%	Min	GP	G	A	Pts	PIM	PP	SH	GW	Min
1989-90	MoDo Jr.	Swe-Jr.	30	15	12	27	42	....	....	....	....	....	....	....	....	....	....	....	....	....	....	....	....	....	....
	MoDo	Sweden	1	0	1	1	4	....	....	....	....	....	....	....	....	....	....	....	....	....	....	....	....	....	....
1990-91	MoDo Jr.	Swe-Jr.	39	38	64	102	56	....	....	....	....	....	....	....	....	....	....	....	....	....	....	....	....	....	....
	MoDo	Sweden	23	7	10	17	22	....	....	....	....	....	....	....	....	....	....	....	....	....	....	....	....	....	....
1991-92	MoDo	Sweden	39	9	18	27	78	....	....	....	....	....	....	....	....	....	....	....	....	....	....	....	....	....	....
1992-93	MoDo Jr.	Swe-Jr.	2	0	3	3	4	....	....	....	....	....	....	....	....	....	....	....	....	....	....	....	....	....	....
	MoDo	Sweden	39	23	24	47	92	....	....	....	....	....	....	....	....	....	3	4	1	5	0	....	....	....	....
1993-94	MoDo	Sweden	39	18	26	44	82	....	....	....	....	....	....	....	....	....	11	9	7	16	14	....	....	....	....
	Sweden	Olympics	8	2	6	8	6	....	....	....	....	....	....	....	....	....	....	....	....	....	....	....	....	....	....
1994-95	MoDo	Sweden	11	5	9	14	20	....	....	....	....	....	....	....	....	....	....	....	....	....	....	....	....	....	....
	Quebec	NHL	47	15	35	50	16	3	0	3	86	17.4	17	....	....	....	6	2	4	6	4	1	0	0	....
1995-96♦	Colorado	NHL	82	30	86	116	47	7	3	3	217	13.8	26	....	....	....	22	10	11	21	18	3	0	1	....
1996-97	Colorado	NHL	65	28	58	86	73	5	4	4	188	14.9	31	....	....	....	14	5	12	17	10	3	0	0	....
1997-98	Colorado	NHL	72	25	66	91	94	7	3	7	202	12.4	6	....	....	....	7	6	5	11	12	2	0	0	....
	Sweden	Olympics	4	1	4	5	6	....	....	....	....	....	....	....	....	....	....	....	....	....	....	....	....	....	....
1998-99	Colorado	NHL	78	30	67	97	108	9	2	7	217	13.8	27	895	54.4	23:29	19	8	16	*24	31	1	1	0	21:39
99-2000	Colorado	NHL	49	14	37	51	52	3	0	2	105	13.3	9	519	46.6	20:55	16	7	8	15	12	2	1	4	20:59
2000-01♦	Colorado	NHL	73	27	62	89	54	12	2	5	178	15.2	23	755	46.6	20:48	11	4	10	14	6	1	0	2	21:55
2001-02	Colorado	NHL	....	....	....	....	....	....	....	....	....	....	....	....	....	....	20	9	*18	*27	20	0	0	4	18:10
2002-03	Colorado	NHL	75	29	*77	*106	70	8	0	2	166	17.5	52	709	47.0	19:20	7	2	6	8	6	1	0	0	20:01
2003-04	Colorado	NHL	39	18	37	55	30	3	1	5	85	21.2	16	549	42.3	19:12	11	4	7	11	12	1	0	1	19:02
2004-05	MODO	Sweden	33	13	26	39	88	....	....	....	....	....	....	....	....	....	1	0	0	0	2	....	....	....	....
	NHL Totals		580	216	525	741	544	57	15	38	1444	15.0		3427	48.0	20:56	133	57	97	154	131	15	2	12	20:15

NHL All-Rookie Team (1995) • Calder Memorial Trophy (1995) • NHL First All-Star Team (1998, 1999, 2003) • Bud Light Plus/Minus Award (2003) (tied with Milan Hejduk) • Art Ross Trophy (2003) • Hart Trophy (2003)

Played in NHL All-Star Game (1996, 1998, 1999, 2001, 2003)

Traded to **Quebec** by **Philadelphia** with Steve Duchesne, Kerry Huffman, Mike Ricci, Ron Hextall, Philadelphia's 1st round choice (Jocelyn Thibault) in 1993 Entry Draft, $15,000,000 and future considerations (Chris Simon and Philadelphia's 1st round choice (later traded to Toronto – later traded to Washington – Washington selected Nolan Baumgartner) in 1994 Entry Draft, July 21, 1992) for Eric Lindros, June 30, 1992. Transferred to **Colorado** after **Quebec** franchise relocated, June 21, 1995. • Missed entire 2001-02 regular season recovering from spleen injury suffered in game vs. Los Angeles, May 9, 2001 and ankle injury suffered in practice, January 10, 2002. • Missed majority of 2003-04 season recovering from groin (October 28, 2003 vs. Calgary) and hip (February 16, 2004 vs. Vancouver) injuries. Signed as a free agent by **MODO** (Sweden), September 18, 2004. Signed as a free agent by **Philadelphia**, August 3, 2005.

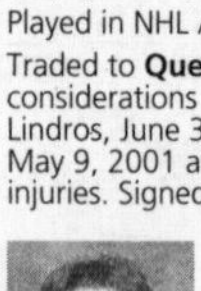

FORTIN, Jean-Francois

(fohr-TEHN, ZHAWN-fran-SWUH) **WSH.**

Defense. Shoots right. 6'2", 205 lbs. Born, Laval, Que., March 15, 1979. Washington's 2nd choice, 35th overall, in 1997 Entry Draft.

Season	Club	League	GP	G	A	Pts	PIM	PP	SH	GW	S	%	+/-	TF	F%	Min	GP	G	A	Pts	PIM	PP	SH	GW	Min
1993-94	Laval-Laurentides	QAHA	31	8	20	28	32	....	....	....	....	....	....	....	....	....	....	....	....	....	....	....	....	....	....
1994-95	Abitibi Forestiers	QAAA	44	2	14	16	34	....	....	....	....	....	....	....	....	....	10	2	2	4		....	....	....	....
1995-96	Sherbrooke	QMJHL	69	7	15	22	40	....	....	....	....	....	....	....	....	....	7	2	6	8	2	....	....	....	....
1996-97	Sherbrooke	QMJHL	59	7	30	37	89	....	....	....	....	....	....	....	....	....	2	0	1	1	14	....	....	....	....
1997-98	Sherbrooke	QMJHL	55	12	25	37	37	....	....	....	....	....	....	....	....	....	....	....	....	....	....	....	....	....	....
1998-99	Sherbrooke	QMJHL	64	17	33	50	78	....	....	....	....	....	....	....	....	....	12	5	13	18	20	....	....	....	....
99-2000	Portland Pirates	AHL	43	3	5	8	44	....	....	....	....	....	....	....	....	....	2	0	0	0	0	....	....	....	....
	Hampton Roads	ECHL	7	0	2	2	0	....	....	....	....	....	....	....	....	....	....	....	....	....	....	....	....	....	....
2000-01	Portland Pirates	AHL	32	1	7	8	22	....	....	....	....	....	....	....	....	....	1	0	0	0	0	....	....	....	....
	Richmond	ECHL	15	0	4	4	2	....	....	....	....	....	....	....	....	....	....	....	....	....	....	....	....	....	....
2001-02	Washington	NHL	36	1	3	4	20	0	0	0	24	4.2	–1	1	100.0	19:25	....	....	....	....	....	....	....	....	....
	Portland Pirates	AHL	44	4	9	13	20	....	....	....	....	....	....	....	....	....	....	....	....	....	....	....	....	....	....
2002-03	Washington	NHL	33	0	1	1	22	0	0	0	20	0.0	–3	0	0.0	15:14	....	....	....	....	....	....	....	....	....
	Portland Pirates	AHL	10	2	1	3	17	....	....	....	....	....	....	....	....	....	....	....	....	....	....	....	....	....	....
2003-04	Washington	NHL	2	0	0	0	0	0	0	0	0	0.0	0	0	0.0	7:57	....	....	....	....	....	....	....	....	....
	Portland Pirates	AHL	4	0	1	1	6	....	....	....	....	....	....	....	....	....	....	....	....	....	....	....	....	....	....
2004-05	Portland Pirates	AHL	39	1	8	9	50	....	....	....	....	....	....	....	....	....	....	....	....	....	....	....	....	....	....
	NHL Totals		71	1	4	5	42	0	0	0	44	2.3		1	100.0	17:09	....	....	....	....	....	....	....	....	....

• Missed majority of 2003-04 season recovering from back injury suffered in game vs.St. John's (AHL), October 24, 2003. Signed as a free agent by **Portland** (AHL), February 3, 2005.

FOSTER, Kurtis (FAW-stuhr, KUHR-this) MIN.

Defense. Shoots right. 6'5", 235 lbs. Born, Carp, Ont., November 24, 1981. Calgary's 2nd choice, 40th overall, in 2000 Entry Draft.

			Regular Season														Playoffs								
Season	Club	League	GP	G	A	Pts	PIM	PP	SH	GW	S	%	+/-	TF	F%	Min	GP	G	A	Pts	PIM	PP	SH	GW	Min
1996-97	Ottawa Valley	ODMHA	36	7	18	25	88																		
1997-98	Peterborough	OHL	39	1	1	2	45										4	0	0	0	2				
1998-99	Peterborough	OHL	54	2	13	15	59										5	0	0	0	6				
99-2000	Peterborough	OHL	68	6	18	24	116										5	1	2	3	4				
2000-01	Peterborough	OHL	62	17	24	41	78										7	1	1	2	10				
2001-02	Peterborough	OHL	33	10	4	14	58																		
	Chicago Wolves	AHL	39	6	9	15	59										14	1	1	2	21				
2002-03	**Atlanta**	**NHL**	**2**	**0**	**0**	**0**	**0**	**0**	**0**	**0**	**1**	**0.0**	**–2**	**0**	**0.0**	**11:06**									
	Chicago Wolves	AHL	75	15	27	42	159										9	1	3	4	14				
2003-04	**Atlanta**	**NHL**	**3**	**0**	**1**	**1**	**0**	**0**	**0**	**0**	**1**	**0.0**	**0**	**0**	**0.0**	**6:58**									
	Chicago Wolves	AHL	67	11	19	30	95										10	0	3	3	12				
2004-05	Cincinnati	AHL	78	17	25	42	71										9	2	3	5	28				
	NHL Totals		**5**	**0**	**1**	**1**	**0**	**0**	**0**	**0**	**2**	**0.0**		**0**	**0.0**	**8:37**									

Rights traded to **Atlanta** by **Calgary** with Jeff Cowan for Petr Buzek and Atlanta's 6th round choice (Adam Pardy) in 2004 Entry Draft, December 18, 2001. Traded to **Anaheim** by **Atlanta** for Niclas Havelid, June 26, 2004.

FRANCIS, Ron (FRAN-sihs, RAWN)

Center. Shoots left. 6'3", 200 lbs. Born, Sault Ste. Marie, Ont., March 1, 1963. Hartford's 1st choice, 4th overall, in 1981 Entry Draft.

Season	Club	League	GP	G	A	Pts	PIM	PP	SH	GW	S	%	+/-	TF	F%	Min	GP	G	A	Pts	PIM	PP	SH	GW	Min
1979-80	Soo Legion	NOHA	45	57	92	149																			
1980-81	Sault Ste. Marie	OMJHL	64	26	43	69	33										19	7	8	15	34				
1981-82	Sault Ste. Marie	OHL	25	18	30	48	46																		
	Hartford	**NHL**	**59**	**25**	**43**	**68**	**51**	**12**	**0**	**1**	**163**	**15.3**	**–13**												
1982-83	**Hartford**	**NHL**	**79**	**31**	**59**	**90**	**60**	**4**	**2**	**4**	**212**	**14.6**	**–25**												
1983-84	**Hartford**	**NHL**	**72**	**23**	**60**	**83**	**45**	**5**	**0**	**5**	**202**	**11.4**	**–10**												
1984-85	**Hartford**	**NHL**	**80**	**24**	**57**	**81**	**66**	**4**	**0**	**1**	**195**	**12.3**	**–23**												
1985-86	**Hartford**	**NHL**	**53**	**24**	**53**	**77**	**24**	**7**	**1**	**4**	**120**	**20.0**	**8**				**10**	**1**	**2**	**3**	**4**	**0**	**0**	**0**	
1986-87	**Hartford**	**NHL**	**75**	**30**	**63**	**93**	**45**	**7**	**0**	**7**	**189**	**15.9**	**10**				**6**	**2**	**2**	**4**	**6**	**1**	**0**	**0**	
1987-88	**Hartford**	**NHL**	**80**	**25**	**50**	**75**	**87**	**11**	**1**	**3**	**172**	**14.5**	**–8**				**6**	**2**	**5**	**7**	**2**	**1**	**0**	**0**	
1988-89	**Hartford**	**NHL**	**69**	**29**	**48**	**77**	**36**	**8**	**0**	**4**	**156**	**18.6**	**4**				**4**	**0**	**2**	**2**	**0**	**0**	**0**	**0**	
1989-90	**Hartford**	**NHL**	**80**	**32**	**69**	**101**	**73**	**15**	**1**	**5**	**170**	**18.8**	**13**				**7**	**3**	**3**	**6**	**8**	**1**	**0**	**0**	
1990-91	**Hartford**	**NHL**	**67**	**21**	**55**	**76**	**51**	**10**	**1**	**6**	**149**	**14.1**	**–2**												
	♦ Pittsburgh	**NHL**	**14**	**2**	**9**	**11**	**21**	**0**	**0**	**1**	**25**	**8.0**	**0**				**24**	**7**	**10**	**17**	**24**	**0**	**0**	**4**	
1991-92 ♦	**Pittsburgh**	**NHL**	**70**	**21**	**33**	**54**	**30**	**5**	**1**	**2**	**121**	**17.4**	**–7**				**21**	**8**	***19**	**27**	**6**	**2**	**0**	**2**	
1992-93	**Pittsburgh**	**NHL**	**84**	**24**	**76**	**100**	**68**	**9**	**2**	**4**	**215**	**11.2**	**6**				**12**	**6**	**11**	**17**	**19**	**1**	**0**	**1**	
1993-94	**Pittsburgh**	**NHL**	**82**	**27**	**66**	**93**	**62**	**8**	**0**	**2**	**216**	**12.5**	**–3**				**6**	**0**	**2**	**2**	**6**	**0**	**0**	**0**	
1994-95	**Pittsburgh**	**NHL**	**44**	**11**	***48**	**59**	**18**	**3**	**0**	**1**	**94**	**11.7**	**30**				**12**	**6**	**13**	**19**	**4**	**2**	**0**	**0**	
1995-96	**Pittsburgh**	**NHL**	**77**	**27**	***92**	**119**	**56**	**12**	**1**	**4**	**158**	**17.1**	**25**				**11**	**3**	**6**	**9**	**4**	**2**	**0**	**1**	
1996-97	**Pittsburgh**	**NHL**	**81**	**27**	**63**	**90**	**20**	**10**	**1**	**2**	**183**	**14.8**	**7**				**5**	**1**	**2**	**3**	**2**	**1**	**0**	**0**	
1997-98	**Pittsburgh**	**NHL**	**81**	**25**	**62**	**87**	**20**	**7**	**0**	**5**	**189**	**13.2**	**12**				**6**	**1**	**5**	**6**	**2**	**0**	**0**	**0**	
1998-99	**Carolina**	**NHL**	**82**	**21**	**31**	**52**	**34**	**8**	**0**	**2**	**133**	**15.8**	**–2**	**1589**	**51.5**	**21:55**	**3**	**0**	**1**	**1**	**0**	**0**	**0**	**0**	**16:27**
99-2000	**Carolina**	**NHL**	**78**	**23**	**50**	**73**	**18**	**7**	**0**	**4**	**150**	**15.3**	**10**	**1566**	**53.3**	**21:58**									
2000-01	**Carolina**	**NHL**	**82**	**15**	**50**	**65**	**32**	**7**	**0**	**4**	**130**	**11.5**	**–15**	**1271**	**57.5**	**20:15**	**3**	**0**	**0**	**0**	**0**	**0**	**0**	**0**	**13:21**
2001-02	**Carolina**	**NHL**	**80**	**27**	**50**	**77**	**18**	**14**	**0**	**5**	**165**	**16.4**	**4**	**1136**	**58.9**	**20:41**	**23**	**6**	**10**	**16**	**6**	**4**	**0**	**3**	**21:03**
2002-03	**Carolina**	**NHL**	**82**	**22**	**35**	**57**	**30**	**8**	**1**	**1**	**156**	**14.1**	**–22**	**880**	**52.5**	**19:56**									
2003-04	**Carolina**	**NHL**	**68**	**10**	**20**	**30**	**14**	**5**	**0**	**1**	**79**	**12.7**	**–12**	**773**	**56.1**	**16:12**									
	Toronto	**NHL**	**12**	**3**	**7**	**10**	**0**	**2**	**0**	**1**	**12**	**25.0**	**3**	**131**	**56.5**	**13:44**	**12**	**0**	**4**	**4**	**2**	**0**	**0**	**0**	**15:28**
2004-05			Did not play																						
	NHL Totals		**1731**	**549**	**1249**	**1798**	**979**	**188**	**12**	**79**	**3754**	**14.6**		**7346**	**54.8**	**20:06**	**171**	**46**	**97**	**143**	**95**	**15**	**0**	**11**	**18:31**

Alka-Seltzer Plus Award (1995) • Frank J. Selke Trophy (1995) • Lady Byng Trophy (1995, 1998, 2002) • King Clancy Memorial Trophy (2002)

Played in NHL All-Star Game (1983, 1985, 1990, 1996)

Traded to **Pittsburgh** by **Hartford** with Grant Jennings and Ulf Samuelsson for John Cullen, Jeff Parker and Zarley Zalapski, March 4, 1991. Signed as a free agent by **Carolina**, July 13, 1998. Traded to **Toronto** by **Carolina** for Toronto's 4th round choice (later traded to Columbus - Columbus selected Jared Boll) in 2005 Entry Draft, March 9, 2004.

FRIESEN, Jeff (FREE-zuhn, JEHF) N.J.

Left wing. Shoots left. 6'1", 205 lbs. Born, Meadow Lake, Sask., August 5, 1976. San Jose's 1st choice, 11th overall, in 1994 Entry Draft.

Season	Club	League	GP	G	A	Pts	PIM	PP	SH	GW	S	%	+/-	TF	F%	Min	GP	G	A	Pts	PIM	PP	SH	GW	Min
1991-92	Sask. Contacts	SMHL	35	37	51	88	75																		
	Regina Pats	WHL	4	3	1	4	2																		
1992-93	Regina Pats	WHL	70	45	38	83	23										13	7	10	17	8				
1993-94	Regina Pats	WHL	66	51	67	118	48										4	3	2	5	2				
1994-95	Regina Pats	WHL	25	21	23	44	22																		
	San Jose	**NHL**	**48**	**15**	**10**	**25**	**14**	**5**	**1**	**2**	**86**	**17.4**	**–8**				**11**	**1**	**5**	**6**	**4**	**0**	**0**	**0**	
1995-96	**San Jose**	**NHL**	**79**	**15**	**31**	**46**	**42**	**2**	**0**	**0**	**123**	**12.2**	**–19**												
1996-97	**San Jose**	**NHL**	**82**	**28**	**34**	**62**	**75**	**6**	**2**	**5**	**200**	**14.0**	**–8**												
1997-98	**San Jose**	**NHL**	**79**	**31**	**32**	**63**	**40**	**7**	**6**	**7**	**186**	**16.7**	**8**				**6**	**0**	**1**	**1**	**2**	**0**	**0**	**0**	
1998-99	**San Jose**	**NHL**	**78**	**22**	**35**	**57**	**42**	**10**	**1**	**3**	**215**	**10.2**	**3**	**24**	**33.3**	**19:25**	**6**	**2**	**2**	**4**	**14**	**1**	**0**	**0**	**22:22**
99-2000	**San Jose**	**NHL**	**82**	**26**	**35**	**61**	**47**	**11**	**3**	**7**	**191**	**13.6**	**–2**	**3**	**66.7**	**19:48**	**11**	**2**	**2**	**4**	**10**	**0**	**0**	**0**	**17:21**
2000-01	**San Jose**	**NHL**	**64**	**12**	**24**	**36**	**56**	**2**	**0**	**1**	**120**	**10.0**	**7**	**7**	**28.6**	**18:51**									
	Anaheim	**NHL**	**15**	**2**	**10**	**12**	**10**	**2**	**0**	**0**	**29**	**6.9**	**–2**	**43**	**55.8**	**21:28**									
2001-02	**Anaheim**	**NHL**	**81**	**17**	**26**	**43**	**44**	**1**	**1**	**0**	**161**	**10.6**	**–1**	**45**	**48.9**	**17:59**									
2002-03 ♦	**New Jersey**	**NHL**	**81**	**23**	**28**	**51**	**26**	**3**	**0**	**4**	**179**	**12.8**	**23**	**11**	**45.5**	**15:33**	**24**	**10**	**4**	**14**	**6**	**1**	**0**	**4**	**16:02**
2003-04	**New Jersey**	**NHL**	**81**	**17**	**20**	**37**	**26**	**5**	**0**	**4**	**177**	**9.6**	**8**	**31**	**45.2**	**15:08**	**5**	**0**	**0**	**0**	**4**	**0**	**0**	**0**	**12:55**
2004-05			Did not play																						
	NHL Totals		**770**	**208**	**285**	**493**	**422**	**54**	**14**	**33**	**1667**	**12.5**		**164**	**47.0**	**17:52**	**63**	**15**	**14**	**29**	**40**	**2**	**0**	**4**	**16:50**

WHL Rookie of the Year (1993) • Canadian Major Junior Rookie of the Year (1993) • NHL All-Rookie Team (1995)

Traded to **Anaheim** by **San Jose** with Steve Shields and San Jose's 2nd round choice (later traded to Dallas – Dallas selected Vojtech Polak) in 2003 Entry Draft for Teemu Selanne, March 5, 2001. Traded to **New Jersey** by **Anaheim** with Oleg Tverdovsky and Maxim Balmochnykh for Petr Sykora, Mike Commodore, Jean-Francois Damphousse and Igor Pohanka, July 6, 2002.

FRITSCHE, Dan (FRIHCH, DAN) CBJ

Center. Shoots right. 6'1", 198 lbs. Born, Parma, OH, July 13, 1985. Columbus' 2nd choice, 46th overall, in 2003 Entry Draft.

Season	Club	League	GP	G	A	Pts	PIM	PP	SH	GW	S	%	+/-	TF	F%	Min	GP	G	A	Pts	PIM	PP	SH	GW	Min
2000-01	Cleveland Barons	NAHL	49	23	29	52	47										1	1	1	2	0				
2001-02	Sarnia Sting	OHL	17	5	13	18	20																		
2002-03	Sarnia Sting	OHL	61	32	39	71	79										5	2	2	4	4				
2003-04	**Columbus**	**NHL**	**19**	**1**	**0**	**1**	**12**	**0**	**0**	**0**	**19**	**5.3**	**–5**	**139**	**38.1**	**8:24**									
	Sarnia Sting	OHL	27	16	13	29	26										5	1	5	6	0				
	Syracuse Crunch	AHL	4	2	0	2	0										4	0	1	1	4				
2004-05	Sarnia Sting	OHL	2	1	1	2	0																		
	London Knights	OHL	28	17	18	35	18										17	9	13	22	12				
	NHL Totals		**19**	**1**	**0**	**1**	**12**	**0**	**0**	**0**	**19**	**5.3**		**139**	**38.1**	**8:24**									

Memorial Cup Tournament All-Star Team (2005)

• Missed majority of 2001-02 season recovering from shoulder surgery, December 12, 2001. • Returned to **Sarnia** (OHL) by **Columbus**, January 7, 2004.

FROLOV, Alexander (froh-LAHF, al-ehx-AN-duhr) L.A.

Left wing. Shoots right. 6'3", 210 lbs. Born, Moscow, USSR, June 19, 1982. Los Angeles' 1st choice, 20th overall, in 2000 Entry Draft.

Season	Club	League	GP	G	A	Pts	PIM	PP	SH	GW	S	%	+/-	TF	F%	Min	GP	G	A	Pts	PIM	PP	SH	GW	Min
1998-99	Spartak Moscow	Russia	1	0	0	0	0																		
99-2000	Yaroslavl 2	Russia-3	36	27	13	40	30																		
2001-02	Spartak Moscow	Russia	44	20	19	39	8																		
	Krylja Sovetov 2	Russia-3	2	0	0	0	4																		
	Krylja Sovetov	Russia	43	18	12	30	16										3	1	0	1	0				
2002-03	**Los Angeles**	**NHL**	**79**	**14**	**17**	**31**	**34**	**1**	**0**	**3**	**141**	**9.9**	**12**	**9**	**22.2**	**14:23**									
2003-04	**Los Angeles**	**NHL**	**77**	**24**	**24**	**48**	**24**	**5**	**2**	**3**	**168**	**14.3**	**8**	**34**	**32.4**	**17:13**									
	Nizhny Novgorod	Russia	1	0	0	0	0																		

			Regular Season														Playoffs								
Season	Club	League	GP	G	A	Pts	PIM	PP	SH	GW	S	%	+/-	TF	F%	Min	GP	G	A	Pts	PIM	PP	SH	GW	Min
2004-05	CSKA Moscow	Russia	42	20	17	37	10	....	....	....	....	....	....	....	....	....	....	....	....	....	....	....	....	....	....
	Dynamo Moscow	Russia	6	2	1	3	2	....	....	....	....	....	....	....	....	....	6	2	1	3	0	....	....	....	....
	NHL Totals		**156**	**38**	**41**	**79**	**58**	**6**	**2**	**6**	**309**	**12.3**		**43**	**30.2**	**15:47**	....	....	....	....	....	....	....	....	....

Signed as a free agent by **CSKA** (Russia), July 14, 2004. Signed as a free agent by **Dynamo Moscow** (Russia), February 17, 2005.

FUSSEY, Owen (FOO-see, OH-when) WSH.

Right wing. Shoots left. 6', 195 lbs. Born, Winnipeg, Man., April 2, 1983. Washington's 2nd choice, 90th overall, in 2001 Entry Draft.

Season	Club	League	GP	G	A	Pts	PIM	PP	SH	GW	S	%	+/-	TF	F%	Min	GP	G	A	Pts	PIM	PP	SH	GW	Min
1998-99	Wpg. Warriors	MMMHL	40	38	33	71	24	....	....	....	....	....	....	....	....	....	....	....	....	....	....	....	....	....	....
99-2000	Calgary Hitmen	WHL	51	7	6	13	35	....	....	....	....	....	....	....	....	....	12	3	4	7	2	....	....	....	....
2000-01	Calgary Hitmen	WHL	48	15	10	25	33	....	....	....	....	....	....	....	....	....	12	2	1	3	6	....	....	....	....
2001-02	Calgary Hitmen	WHL	72	43	27	70	61	....	....	....	....	....	....	....	....	....	7	3	1	4	4	....	....	....	....
2002-03	Calgary Hitmen	WHL	39	17	18	35	31	....	....	....	....	....	....	....	....	....	....	....	....	....	....	....	....	....	....
	Moose Jaw	WHL	27	24	12	36	20	....	....	....	....	....	....	....	....	....	13	6	6	12	10	....	....	....	....
2003-04	**Washington**	**NHL**	**4**	**0**	**1**	**1**	**0**	**0**	**0**	**0**	**6**	**0.0**	**–1**	**0**	**0.0**	**8:16**	....	....	....	....	....	....	....	....	....
	Portland Pirates	AHL	69	6	7	13	23	....	....	....	....	....	....	....	....	....	7	0	0	0	5	....	....	....	....
2004-05	Portland Pirates	AHL	71	14	12	26	26	....	....	....	....	....	....	....	....	....	....	....	....	....	....	....	....	....	....
	NHL Totals		**4**	**0**	**1**	**1**	**0**	**0**	**0**	**0**	**6**	**0.0**		**0**	**0.0**	**8:16**	....	....	....	....	....	....	....	....	....

GABORIK, Marian (GA-bohr-ihk, MAIR-ee-uhn) MIN.

Right wing. Shoots left. 6'1", 190 lbs. Born, Trencin, Czech., February 14, 1982. Minnesota's 1st choice, 3rd overall, in 2000 Entry Draft.

Season	Club	League	GP	G	A	Pts	PIM	PP	SH	GW	S	%	+/-	TF	F%	Min	GP	G	A	Pts	PIM	PP	SH	GW	Min
1997-98	Dukla Trencin Jr.	Slovak-Jr.	36	37	22	59	28	....	....	....	....	....	....	....	....	....	....	....	....	....	....	....	....	....	....
	Dukla Trencin	Slovakia	1	1	0	1	0	....	....	....	....	....	....	....	....	....	....	....	....	....	....	....	....	....	....
1998-99	Dukla Trencin	Slovakia	33	11	9	20	6	....	....	....	....	....	....	....	....	....	3	1	0	1	2	....	....	....	....
99-2000	Dukla Trencin	Slovakia	50	25	21	46	34	....	....	....	....	....	....	....	....	....	5	1	2	3	2	....	....	....	....
2000-01	**Minnesota**	**NHL**	**71**	**18**	**18**	**36**	**32**	**6**	**0**	**3**	**179**	**10.1**	**–6**	**3**	**33.3**	**15:26**	....	....	....	....	....	....	....	....	....
2001-02	**Minnesota**	**NHL**	**78**	**30**	**37**	**67**	**34**	**10**	**0**	**4**	**221**	**13.6**	**0**	**4**	**25.0**	**16:47**	....	....	....	....	....	....	....	....	....
2002-03	**Minnesota**	**NHL**	**81**	**30**	**35**	**65**	**46**	**5**	**1**	**8**	**280**	**10.7**	**12**	**16**	**25.0**	**17:24**	**18**	**9**	**8**	**17**	**6**	**4**	**0**	**0**	**18:12**
2003-04	Dukla Trencin	Slovakia	9	10	3	13	10	....	....	....	....	....	....	....	....	....	....	....	....	....	....	....	....	....	....
	Minnesota	**NHL**	**65**	**18**	**22**	**40**	**20**	**3**	**0**	**4**	**220**	**8.2**	**10**	**11**	**45.5**	**18:17**	....	....	....	....	....	....	....	....	....
2004-05	Farjestad	Sweden	12	6	4	10	45	....	....	....	....	....	....	....	....	....	....	....	....	....	....	....	....	....	....
	Dukla Trencin	Slovakia	29	25	27	52	46	....	....	....	....	....	....	....	....	....	12	8	9	17	26	....	....	....	....
	NHL Totals		**295**	**96**	**112**	**208**	**132**	**24**	**1**	**19**	**900**	**10.7**		**34**	**32.4**	**16:57**	**18**	**9**	**8**	**17**	**6**	**4**	**0**	**0**	**18:12**

Played in NHL All-Star Game (2003)

Signed as a free agent by **Trencin** (Slovakia), July 5, 2004. Signed as a free agent by **Farjestad** (Sweden), December 21, 2004. Signed as a free agent by **Trencin** (Slovakia), January 31, 2005.

GAGNE, Simon (GAH-nyay, see-MOHN) PHI.

Left wing. Shoots left. 6', 190 lbs. Born, Ste-Foy, Que., February 29, 1980. Philadelphia's 1st choice, 22nd overall, in 1998 Entry Draft.

Season	Club	League	GP	G	A	Pts	PIM	PP	SH	GW	S	%	+/-	TF	F%	Min	GP	G	A	Pts	PIM	PP	SH	GW	Min
1995-96	Ste-Foy	QAAA	27	13	9	22	18	....	....	....	....	....	....	....	....	....	15	7	8	15	8	....	....	....	....
1996-97	Beauport	QMJHL	51	9	22	31	49	....	....	....	....	....	....	....	....	....	....	....	....	....	....	....	....	....	....
1997-98	Quebec Remparts	QMJHL	53	30	39	69	26	....	....	....	....	....	....	....	....	....	12	11	5	16	23	....	....	....	....
1998-99	Quebec Remparts	QMJHL	61	50	*70	*120	42	....	....	....	....	....	....	....	....	....	13	9	8	17	4	....	....	....	....
99-2000	**Philadelphia**	**NHL**	**80**	**20**	**28**	**48**	**22**	**8**	**1**	**4**	**159**	**12.6**	**11**	**443**	**42.2**	**14:59**	**17**	**5**	**5**	**10**	**2**	**2**	**0**	**1**	**16:46**
2000-01	**Philadelphia**	**NHL**	**69**	**27**	**32**	**59**	**18**	**6**	**0**	**7**	**191**	**14.1**	**24**	**21**	**28.6**	**18:05**	**6**	**3**	**0**	**3**	**0**	**2**	**0**	**0**	**19:09**
2001-02	**Philadelphia**	**NHL**	**79**	**33**	**33**	**66**	**32**	**4**	**1**	**7**	**199**	**16.6**	**31**	**6**	**83.3**	**18:09**	**5**	**0**	**0**	**0**	**2**	**0**	**0**	**0**	**19:16**
	Canada	Olympics	6	1	3	4	0	....	....	....	....	....	....	....	....	....	....	....	....	....	....	....	....	....	....
2002-03	**Philadelphia**	**NHL**	**46**	**9**	**18**	**27**	**16**	**1**	**1**	**3**	**115**	**7.8**	**20**	**70**	**42.9**	**17:24**	**13**	**4**	**1**	**5**	**6**	**0**	**1**	**1**	**18:13**
2003-04	**Philadelphia**	**NHL**	**80**	**24**	**21**	**45**	**29**	**6**	**0**	**6**	**211**	**11.4**	**12**	**104**	**39.4**	**16:27**	**18**	**5**	**4**	**9**	**12**	**0**	**0**	**1**	**16:48**
2004-05			DID NOT PLAY																						
	NHL Totals		**354**	**113**	**132**	**245**	**117**	**25**	**3**	**27**	**875**	**12.9**		**644**	**41.8**	**16:56**	**59**	**17**	**10**	**27**	**22**	**4**	**1**	**3**	**17:33**

QMJHL Second All-Star Team (1999) • NHL All-Rookie Team (2000)

Played in NHL ALL-Star Game (2001)

GAINEY, Steve (GAY-nee, STEEV)

Left wing. Shoots left. 6'1", 192 lbs. Born, Montreal, Que., January 26, 1979. Dallas' 3rd choice, 77th overall, in 1997 Entry Draft.

Season	Club	League	GP	G	A	Pts	PIM	PP	SH	GW	S	%	+/-	TF	F%	Min	GP	G	A	Pts	PIM	PP	SH	GW	Min
1995-96	Kamloops Blazers	WHL	49	1	4	5	40	....	....	....	....	....	....	....	....	....	3	0	0	0	0	....	....	....	....
1996-97	Kamloops Blazers	WHL	60	9	18	27	60	....	....	....	....	....	....	....	....	....	2	0	0	0	9	....	....	....	....
1997-98	Kamloops Blazers	WHL	68	21	34	55	93	....	....	....	....	....	....	....	....	....	7	1	7	8	15	....	....	....	....
1998-99	Kamloops Blazers	WHL	68	30	34	64	155	....	....	....	....	....	....	....	....	....	15	5	4	9	38	....	....	....	....
99-2000	Fort Wayne	UHL	1	0	0	0	0	....	....	....	....	....	....	....	....	....	....	....	....	....	....	....	....	....	....
	Michigan	IHL	58	8	10	18	41	....	....	....	....	....	....	....	....	....	....	....	....	....	....	....	....	....	....
2000-01	**Dallas**	**NHL**	**1**	**0**	**0**	**0**	**0**	**0**	**0**	**0**	**0**	**0.0**	**0**	**0**	**0.0**	**2:21**	....	....	....	....	....	....	....	....	....
	Utah Grizzlies	IHL	61	7	7	14	167	....	....	....	....	....	....	....	....	....	....	....	....	....	....	....	....	....	....
2001-02	**Dallas**	**NHL**	**5**	**0**	**1**	**1**	**7**	**0**	**0**	**0**	**1**	**0.0**	**–1**	**0**	**0.0**	**7:24**	....	....	....	....	....	....	....	....	....
	Utah Grizzlies	AHL	58	16	18	34	87	....	....	....	....	....	....	....	....	....	....	....	....	....	....	....	....	....	....
2002-03	Utah Grizzlies	AHL	68	9	17	26	106	....	....	....	....	....	....	....	....	....	2	0	0	0	11	....	....	....	....
2003-04	**Dallas**	**NHL**	**7**	**0**	**0**	**0**	**7**	**0**	**0**	**0**	**0**	**0.0**	**1**	**0**	**0.0**	**5:27**	....	....	....	....	....	....	....	....	....
	Utah Grizzlies	AHL	45	7	8	15	74	....	....	....	....	....	....	....	....	....	....	....	....	....	....	....	....	....	....
	Philadelphia	AHL	27	2	7	9	27	....	....	....	....	....	....	....	....	....	11	0	1	1	14	....	....	....	....
2004-05	HC d'Epinal	France	30	10	13	23	97	....	....	....	....	....	....	....	....	....	....	....	....	....	....	....	....	....	....
	NHL Totals		**13**	**0**	**1**	**1**	**14**	**0**	**0**	**0**	**1**	**0.0**		**0**	**0.0**	**5:58**	....	....	....	....	....	....	....	....	....

Traded to **Philadelphia** by **Dallas** for Mike Siklenka, February 16, 2004. Signed as a free agent by **Epinal** (France), September 17, 2004.

GAMACHE, Simon (ga-MOHSH, see-MOHN) NSH.

Center. Shoots left. 5'10", 186 lbs. Born, Thetford Mines, Que., January 3, 1981. Atlanta's 14th choice, 290th overall, in 2000 Entry Draft.

Season	Club	League	GP	G	A	Pts	PIM	PP	SH	GW	S	%	+/-	TF	F%	Min	GP	G	A	Pts	PIM	PP	SH	GW	Min
1997-98	Levis-Lauzon	QAAA	42	28	26	54	....	....	....	....	....	....	....	....	....	....	4	1	1	2	....	....	....	....	....
1998-99	Val-d'Or Foreurs	QMJHL	70	19	43	62	54	....	....	....	....	....	....	....	....	....	6	1	2	3	4	....	....	....	....
99-2000	Val-d'Or Foreurs	QMJHL	72	64	79	143	74	....	....	....	....	....	....	....	....	....	....	....	....	....	....	....	....	....	....
2000-01	Val-d'Or Foreurs	QMJHL	72	*74	*110	*184	70	....	....	....	....	....	....	....	....	....	21	*22	*35	*57	18	....	....	....	....
2001-02	Chicago Wolves	AHL	26	2	4	6	11	....	....	....	....	....	....	....	....	....	....	....	....	....	....	....	....	....	....
	Greenville	ECHL	31	19	19	38	35	....	....	....	....	....	....	....	....	....	17	*15	9	*24	22	....	....	....	....
2002-03	**Atlanta**	**NHL**	**2**	**0**	**0**	**0**	**2**	**0**	**0**	**0**	**3**	**0.0**	**–1**	**0**	**0.0**	**12:37**	....	....	....	....	....	....	....	....	....
	Chicago Wolves	AHL	76	35	42	77	37	....	....	....	....	....	....	....	....	....	9	7	2	9	4	....	....	....	....
2003-04	**Atlanta**	**NHL**	**2**	**0**	**1**	**1**	**0**	**0**	**0**	**0**	**1**	**0.0**	**0**	**0**	**0.0**	**6:39**	....	....	....	....	....	....	....	....	....
	Chicago Wolves	AHL	16	5	6	11	4	....	....	....	....	....	....	....	....	....	....	....	....	....	....	....	....	....	....
	Nashville	**NHL**	**7**	**1**	**0**	**1**	**0**	**1**	**0**	**0**	**4**	**25.0**	**–3**	**18**	**55.6**	**7:35**	....	....	....	....	....	....	....	....	....
	Milwaukee	AHL	52	18	27	45	26	....	....	....	....	....	....	....	....	....	22	6	*18	24	14	....	....	....	....
2004-05	Milwaukee	AHL	80	29	57	86	93	....	....	....	....	....	....	....	....	....	7	6	4	10	18	....	....	....	....
	NHL Totals		**11**	**1**	**1**	**2**	**2**	**1**	**0**	**0**	**8**	**12.5**		**18**	**55.6**	**8:20**	....	....	....	....	....	....	....	....	....

Canadian Major Junior Second All-Star Team (2000) • QMJHL First All-Star Team (2001) • Michel Briere Trophy (MVP – QMJHL) (2001) • Canadian Major Junior First All-Star Team (2001) • Canadian Major Junior Player of the Year (2001) • Memorial Cup Tournament All-Star Team (2001) • Ed Chynoweth Trophy (Memorial Cup Tournament Leading Scorer) (2001) • ECHL All-Rookie Team (2002) • ECHL Playoff MVP (2002) (co-winner - Tyrone Garner) • AHL First All-Star Team (2005)

Traded to **Nashville** by **Atlanta** with Kirill Safronov for Ben Simon and Tomas Kloucek, December 2, 2003.

GAUSTAD, Paul (GAW-stad, PAWL) BUF.

Center. Shoots left. 6'4", 220 lbs. Born, Fargo, ND, February 3, 1982. Buffalo's 6th choice, 220th overall, in 2000 Entry Draft.

Season	Club	League	GP	G	A	Pts	PIM	PP	SH	GW	S	%	+/-	TF	F%	Min	GP	G	A	Pts	PIM	PP	SH	GW	Min
1998-99	Portland Hawks	USAHA	45	47	53	100	81	....	....	....	....	....	....	....	....	....	....	....	....	....	....	....	....	....	....
99-2000	Portland	WHL	56	6	8	14	110	....	....	....	....	....	....	....	....	....	....	....	....	....	....	....	....	....	....
2000-01	Portland	WHL	70	11	30	41	168	....	....	....	....	....	....	....	....	....	16	10	6	16	59	....	....	....	....
2001-02	Portland	WHL	72	36	44	80	202	....	....	....	....	....	....	....	....	....	6	3	1	4	16	....	....	....	....
2002-03	**Buffalo**	**NHL**	**1**	**0**	**0**	**0**	**0**	**0**	**0**	**0**	**0**	**0.0**	**0**	**7**	**42.9**	**5:48**	....	....	....	....	....	....	....	....	....
	Rochester	AHL	80	14	39	53	137	....	....	....	....	....	....	....	....	....	3	0	0	0	4	....	....	....	....

			Regular Season														Playoffs								
Season	Club	League	GP	G	A	Pts	PIM	PP	SH	GW	S	%	+/-	TF	F%	Min	GP	G	A	Pts	PIM	PP	SH	GW	Min
2003-04	Rochester	AHL	78	9	22	31	169	....	....	....	....	....	....	....	....	....	16	3	10	13	30	....	....	....	....
2004-05	Rochester	AHL	76	18	25	43	192	....	....	....	....	....	....	....	....	....	9	6	5	11	16	....	....	....	....
	NHL Totals		**1**	**0**	**0**	**0**	**0**	**0**	**0**	**0**	**0**	**0.0**		**7**	**42.9**	**5:48**	....	....	....	....	....	....	....	....	....

GAUTHIER, Denis

(GOH-tyay, DEH-nihs) **PHX.**

Defense. Shoots left. 6'3", 224 lbs. Born, Montreal, Que., October 1, 1976. Calgary's 1st choice, 20th overall, in 1995 Entry Draft.

Season	Club	League	GP	G	A	Pts	PIM	PP	SH	GW	S	%	+/-	TF	F%	Min	GP	G	A	Pts	PIM	PP	SH	GW	Min
1991-92	Richelieu AA	QAHA	STATISTICS NOT AVAILABLE																						
1992-93	Drummondville	QMJHL	61	1	7	8	136	....	....	....	....	....	....	....	....	....	10	0	5	5	40	....	....	....	....
1993-94	Drummondville	QMJHL	60	0	7	7	176	....	....	....	....	....	....	....	....	....	9	2	0	2	41	....	....	....	....
1994-95	Drummondville	QMJHL	64	9	31	40	190	....	....	....	....	....	....	....	....	....	4	0	5	5	12	....	....	....	....
1995-96	Drummondville	QMJHL	53	25	49	74	140	....	....	....	....	....	....	....	....	....	6	4	4	8	32	....	....	....	....
	Saint John Flames	AHL	5	2	0	2	8	....	....	....	....	....	....	....	....	....	16	1	6	7	20	....	....	....	....
1996-97	Saint John Flames	AHL	73	3	28	31	74	....	....	....	....	....	....	....	....	....	5	0	0	0	6	....	....	....	....
1997-98	**Calgary**	**NHL**	**10**	**0**	**0**	**0**	**16**	**0**	**0**	**0**	**3**	**0.0**	**-5**	....	....	....	....	....	....	....	....	....	....	....	....
	Saint John Flames	AHL	68	4	20	24	154	....	....	....	....	....	....	....	....	....	21	0	4	4	83	....	....	....	....
1998-99	**Calgary**	**NHL**	**55**	**3**	**4**	**7**	**68**	**0**	**0**	**0**	**40**	**7.5**	**3**	**0**	**0.0**	**12:41**	....	....	....	....	....	....	....	....	....
	Saint John Flames	AHL	16	0	3	3	31	....	....	....	....	....	....	....	....	....	....	....	....	....	....	....	....	....	....
99-2000	**Calgary**	**NHL**	**39**	**1**	**1**	**2**	**50**	**0**	**0**	**0**	**29**	**3.4**	**-4**	**0**	**0.0**	**19:21**	....	....	....	....	....	....	....	....	....
2000-01	**Calgary**	**NHL**	**62**	**2**	**6**	**8**	**78**	**0**	**0**	**0**	**33**	**6.1**	**3**	**0**	**0.0**	**16:37**	....	....	....	....	....	....	....	....	....
2001-02	**Calgary**	**NHL**	**66**	**5**	**8**	**13**	**91**	**0**	**1**	**2**	**76**	**6.6**	**9**	**0**	**0.0**	**19:19**	....	....	....	....	....	....	....	....	....
2002-03	**Calgary**	**NHL**	**72**	**1**	**11**	**12**	**99**	**0**	**0**	**1**	**50**	**2.0**	**5**	**0**	**0.0**	**19:52**	....	....	....	....	....	....	....	....	....
2003-04	**Calgary**	**NHL**	**80**	**1**	**15**	**16**	**113**	**0**	**0**	**0**	**90**	**1.1**	**4**	**0**	**0.0**	**18:43**	**6**	**0**	**1**	**1**	**4**	**0**	**0**	**0**	**18:33**
2004-05			DID NOT PLAY																						
	NHL Totals		**384**	**13**	**45**	**58**	**515**	**0**	**1**	**3**	**321**	**4.0**		**0**	**0.0**	**17:53**	**6**	**0**	**1**	**1**	**4**	**0**	**0**	**0**	**18:33**

QMJHL First All-Star Team (1996) • Canadian Major Junior First All-Star Team (1996)

• Missed majority of 1999-2000 season recovering from hip injury suffered in game vs. St. Louis, February 1, 2000. Traded to **Phoenix** by **Calgary** with Oleg Saprykin for Daymond Langkow, August 26, 2004.

GAVEY, Aaron

(GAY-vee, AIR-ruhn) **PHX.**

Center. Shoots left. 6'2", 189 lbs. Born, Sudbury, Ont., February 22, 1974. Tampa Bay's 4th choice, 74th overall, in 1992 Entry Draft.

Season	Club	League	GP	G	A	Pts	PIM	PP	SH	GW	S	%	+/-	TF	F%	Min	GP	G	A	Pts	PIM	PP	SH	GW	Min
1990-91	Peterborough	OHA-B	42	26	30	56	68	....	....	....	....	....	....	....	....	....	....	....	....	....	....	....	....	....	....
1991-92	Sault Ste. Marie	OHL	48	7	11	18	27	....	....	....	....	....	....	....	....	....	19	5	1	6	10	....	....	....	....
1992-93	Sault Ste. Marie	OHL	62	45	39	84	116	....	....	....	....	....	....	....	....	....	18	5	9	14	36	....	....	....	....
1993-94	Sault Ste. Marie	OHL	60	42	60	102	116	....	....	....	....	....	....	....	....	....	14	11	10	21	22	....	....	....	....
1994-95	Atlanta Knights	IHL	66	18	17	35	85	....	....	....	....	....	....	....	....	....	5	0	1	1	9	....	....	....	....
1995-96	**Tampa Bay**	**NHL**	**73**	**8**	**4**	**12**	**56**	**1**	**1**	**2**	**65**	**12.3**	**-6**	....	....	....	**6**	**0**	**0**	**0**	**4**	**0**	**0**	**0**	....
1996-97	**Tampa Bay**	**NHL**	**16**	**1**	**2**	**3**	**12**	**0**	**0**	**0**	**8**	**12.5**	**-1**	....	....	....	....	....	....	....	....	....	....	....	....
	Calgary	**NHL**	**41**	**7**	**9**	**16**	**34**	**3**	**0**	**1**	**54**	**13.0**	**-11**	....	....	....	....	....	....	....	....	....	....	....	....
1997-98	**Calgary**	**NHL**	**26**	**2**	**3**	**5**	**24**	**0**	**0**	**1**	**27**	**7.4**	**-5**	....	....	....	....	....	....	....	....	....	....	....	....
	Saint John Flames	AHL	8	4	3	7	28	....	....	....	....	....	....	....	....	....	....	....	....	....	....	....	....	....	....
1998-99	**Dallas**	**NHL**	**7**	**0**	**0**	**0**	**10**	**0**	**0**	**0**	**4**	**0.0**	**-1**	**43**	**48.8**	**8:09**	....	....	....	....	....	....	....	....	....
	Michigan	IHL	67	24	33	57	128	....	....	....	....	....	....	....	....	....	5	2	3	5	4	....	....	....	....
99-2000	**Dallas**	**NHL**	**41**	**7**	**6**	**13**	**44**	**1**	**0**	**2**	**39**	**17.9**	**0**	**263**	**51.7**	**9:55**	**13**	**1**	**2**	**3**	**10**	**0**	**0**	**1**	**6:09**
	Michigan	IHL	28	14	15	29	73	....	....	....	....	....	....	....	....	....	....	....	....	....	....	....	....	....	....
2000-01	**Minnesota**	**NHL**	**75**	**10**	**14**	**24**	**52**	**1**	**0**	**2**	**100**	**10.0**	**-8**	**584**	**43.5**	**14:00**	....	....	....	....	....	....	....	....	....
2001-02	**Minnesota**	**NHL**	**71**	**6**	**11**	**17**	**38**	**1**	**0**	**0**	**75**	**8.0**	**-21**	**254**	**42.5**	**11:55**	....	....	....	....	....	....	....	....	....
2002-03	**Toronto**	**NHL**	**5**	**0**	**1**	**1**	**0**	**0**	**0**	**0**	**8**	**0.0**	**1**	**31**	**48.4**	**11:19**	....	....	....	....	....	....	....	....	....
	St. John's	AHL	70	14	29	43	83	....	....	....	....	....	....	....	....	....	....	....	....	....	....	....	....	....	....
2003-04	St. John's	AHL	75	22	45	67	100	....	....	....	....	....	....	....	....	....	....	....	....	....	....	....	....	....	....
2004-05	Storhamar	Norway	1	0	0	0	0	....	....	....	....	....	....	....	....	....	....	....	....	....	....	....	....	....	....
	Utah Grizzlies	AHL	60	5	14	19	58	....	....	....	....	....	....	....	....	....	....	....	....	....	....	....	....	....	....
	NHL Totals		**355**	**41**	**50**	**91**	**270**	**7**	**1**	**8**	**380**	**10.8**		**1175**	**45.4**	**12:08**	**19**	**1**	**2**	**3**	**14**	**0**	**0**	**1**	**6:09**

Traded to **Calgary** by **Tampa Bay** for Rick Tabaracci, November 19, 1996. Traded to **Dallas** by **Calgary** for Bob Bassen, July 14, 1998. Traded to **Minnesota** by **Dallas** with Pavel Patera, Dallas' 8th round choice (Eric Johansson) in 2000 Entry Draft and Minnesota's 4th round choice (previously acquired, later traded to Los Angeles – Los Angeles selected Aaron Rome) in 2002 Entry Draft for Brad Lukowich and Minnesota's 3rd (Yared Hagos) and 9th (Dale Sullivan) round choices in 2001 Entry Draft, June 25, 2000. Signed as a free agent by **Toronto**, July 24, 2002. Signed as a free agent by **Storhamar** (Norway), November 2, 2004. Signed as a free agent by **Phoenix**, November 29, 2004.

GELINAS, Martin

(ZHEHL-in-nuh, MAHR-tihn) **FLA.**

Left wing. Shoots left. 5'11", 195 lbs. Born, Shawinigan, Que., June 5, 1970. Los Angeles' 1st choice, 7th overall, in 1988 Entry Draft.

Season	Club	League	GP	G	A	Pts	PIM	PP	SH	GW	S	%	+/-	TF	F%	Min	GP	G	A	Pts	PIM	PP	SH	GW	Min
1985-86	Noranda Aces	NOHA	5	1	1	2	0	....	....	....	....	....	....	....	....	....	....	....	....	....	....	....	....	....	....
1986-87	Montreal L'est	QAAA	41	36	42	78	36	....	....	....	....	....	....	....	....	....	7	7	5	12	2	....	....	....	....
1987-88	Hull Olympiques	QMJHL	65	63	68	131	74	....	....	....	....	....	....	....	....	....	17	15	18	33	32	....	....	....	....
1988-89	Hull Olympiques	QMJHL	41	38	39	77	31	....	....	....	....	....	....	....	....	....	9	5	4	9	14	....	....	....	....
	Edmonton	**NHL**	**6**	**1**	**2**	**3**	**0**	**0**	**0**	**0**	**14**	**7.1**	**-1**	....	....	....	....	....	....	....	....	....	....	....	....
1989-90♦	**Edmonton**	**NHL**	**46**	**17**	**8**	**25**	**30**	**5**	**0**	**2**	**71**	**23.9**	**0**	....	....	....	**20**	**2**	**3**	**5**	**6**	**0**	**0**	**0**	....
1990-91	**Edmonton**	**NHL**	**73**	**20**	**20**	**40**	**34**	**4**	**0**	**2**	**124**	**16.1**	**-7**	....	....	....	**18**	**3**	**6**	**9**	**25**	**0**	**0**	**1**	....
1991-92	**Edmonton**	**NHL**	**68**	**11**	**18**	**29**	**62**	**1**	**0**	**0**	**94**	**11.7**	**14**	....	....	....	**15**	**1**	**3**	**4**	**10**	**0**	**0**	**0**	....
1992-93	**Edmonton**	**NHL**	**65**	**11**	**12**	**23**	**30**	**0**	**0**	**1**	**93**	**11.8**	**3**	....	....	....	....	....	....	....	....	....	....	....	....
1993-94	**Quebec**	**NHL**	**31**	**6**	**6**	**12**	**8**	**0**	**0**	**0**	**53**	**11.3**	**-2**	....	....	....	....	....	....	....	....	....	....	....	....
	Vancouver	**NHL**	**33**	**8**	**8**	**16**	**26**	**3**	**0**	**1**	**54**	**14.8**	**-6**	....	....	....	**24**	**5**	**4**	**9**	**14**	**2**	**0**	**1**	....
1994-95	**Vancouver**	**NHL**	**46**	**13**	**10**	**23**	**36**	**1**	**0**	**4**	**75**	**17.3**	**8**	....	....	....	**3**	**0**	**1**	**1**	**0**	**0**	**0**	**0**	....
1995-96	**Vancouver**	**NHL**	**81**	**30**	**26**	**56**	**59**	**3**	**4**	**5**	**181**	**16.6**	**8**	....	....	....	**6**	**1**	**1**	**2**	**12**	**1**	**0**	**0**	....
1996-97	**Vancouver**	**NHL**	**74**	**35**	**33**	**68**	**42**	**6**	**1**	**3**	**177**	**19.8**	**6**	....	....	....	....	....	....	....	....	....	....	....	....
1997-98	**Vancouver**	**NHL**	**24**	**4**	**4**	**8**	**10**	**1**	**1**	**1**	**49**	**8.2**	**-6**	....	....	....	....	....	....	....	....	....	....	....	....
	Carolina	**NHL**	**40**	**12**	**14**	**26**	**30**	**2**	**1**	**4**	**98**	**12.2**	**1**	....	....	....	....	....	....	....	....	....	....	....	....
1998-99	**Carolina**	**NHL**	**76**	**13**	**15**	**28**	**67**	**0**	**0**	**2**	**111**	**11.7**	**3**	**6**	**50.0**	**13:13**	**6**	**0**	**3**	**3**	**2**	**0**	**0**	**0**	**19:33**
99-2000	**Carolina**	**NHL**	**81**	**14**	**16**	**30**	**40**	**3**	**0**	**0**	**139**	**10.1**	**-10**	**5**	**40.0**	**13:39**	....	....	....	....	....	....	....	....	....
2000-01	**Carolina**	**NHL**	**79**	**23**	**29**	**52**	**59**	**6**	**1**	**4**	**170**	**13.5**	**-4**	**6**	**0.0**	**17:54**	**6**	**0**	**1**	**1**	**6**	**0**	**0**	**0**	**17:51**
2001-02	**Carolina**	**NHL**	**72**	**13**	**16**	**29**	**30**	**3**	**0**	**1**	**121**	**10.7**	**-1**	**13**	**23.1**	**16:05**	**23**	**3**	**4**	**7**	**10**	**0**	**0**	**1**	**14:16**
2002-03	**Calgary**	**NHL**	**81**	**21**	**31**	**52**	**51**	**6**	**0**	**3**	**152**	**13.8**	**-3**	**96**	**51.0**	**16:33**	....	....	....	....	....	....	....	....	....
2003-04	**Calgary**	**NHL**	**76**	**17**	**18**	**35**	**70**	**5**	**0**	**3**	**139**	**12.2**	**10**	**27**	**48.2**	**14:50**	**26**	**8**	**7**	**15**	**35**	**2**	**0**	**3**	**15:58**
2004-05	Morges	Swiss-2	41	37	21	58	81	....	....	....	....	....	....	....	....	....	4	2	2	4	24	....	....	....	....
	HC Lugano	Swiss	1	0	0	0	0	....	....	....	....	....	....	....	....	....	5	0	1	1	2	....	....	....	....
	NHL Totals		**1052**	**269**	**286**	**555**	**684**	**49**	**8**	**36**	**1915**	**14.0**		**153**	**45.8**	**15:23**	**147**	**23**	**33**	**56**	**120**	**5**	**0**	**6**	**15:51**

QMJHL First All-Star Team (1988) • QMJHL Offensive Rookie of the Year (1988) • Canadian Major Junior Rookie of the Year (1988) • George Parsons Trophy (Memorial Cup Tournament Most Sportsmanlike Player) (1988)

Traded to **Edmonton** by **Los Angeles** with Jimmy Carson and Los Angeles' 1st round choices in 1989 (later traded to New Jersey – New Jersey selected Jason Miller), 1991 (Martin Rucinsky) and 1993 (Nick Stajduhar) Entry Drafts and cash for Wayne Gretzky, Mike Krushelnyski and Marty McSorley, August 9, 1988. Traded to **Quebec** by **Edmonton** with Edmonton's 6th round choice (Nicholas Checco) in 1993 Entry Draft for Scott Pearson, June 20, 1993. Claimed on waivers by **Vancouver** from **Quebec**, January 15, 1994. Traded to **Carolina** by **Vancouver** with Kirk McLean for Sean Burke, Geoff Sanderson and Enrico Ciccone, January 3, 1998. Signed as a free agent by **Calgary**, July 2, 2002. Signed as a free agent by **Morges** (Swiss-2), September 23, 2004. Signed as a free agent by **Lugano** (Swiss), February 17, 2005. Signed as a free agent by **Florida**, August 2, 2005.

GILL, Hal

(GIHL, HAL) **BOS.**

Defense. Shoots left. 6'7", 250 lbs. Born, Concord, MA, April 6, 1975. Boston's 8th choice, 207th overall, in 1993 Entry Draft.

Season	Club	League	GP	G	A	Pts	PIM	PP	SH	GW	S	%	+/-	TF	F%	Min	GP	G	A	Pts	PIM	PP	SH	GW	Min
1992-93	Nashoba	High-MA	20	25	25	50	....	....	....	....	....	....	....	....	....	....	....	....	....	....	....	....	....	....	....
1993-94	Providence	H-East	31	1	2	3	26	....	....	....	....	....	....	....	....	....	....	....	....	....	....	....	....	....	....
1994-95	Providence	H-East	26	1	3	4	22	....	....	....	....	....	....	....	....	....	....	....	....	....	....	....	....	....	....
1995-96	Providence	H-East	39	5	12	17	54	....	....	....	....	....	....	....	....	....	....	....	....	....	....	....	....	....	....
1996-97	Providence	H-East	35	5	16	21	52	....	....	....	....	....	....	....	....	....	....	....	....	....	....	....	....	....	....
1997-98	**Boston**	**NHL**	**68**	**2**	**4**	**6**	**47**	**0**	**0**	**0**	**56**	**3.6**	**4**	....	....	....	**6**	**0**	**0**	**0**	**4**	**0**	**0**	**0**	....
	Providence Bruins	AHL	4	1	0	1	23	....	....	....	....	....	....	....	....	....	....	....	....	....	....	....	....	....	....
1998-99	**Boston**	**NHL**	**80**	**3**	**7**	**10**	**63**	**0**	**0**	**2**	**102**	**2.9**	**-10**	**1**	**100.0**	**20:54**	**12**	**0**	**0**	**0**	**14**	**0**	**0**	**0**	**20:41**
99-2000	**Boston**	**NHL**	**81**	**3**	**9**	**12**	**51**	**0**	**0**	**0**	**120**	**2.5**	**0**	**0**	**0.0**	**17:15**	....	....	....	....	....	....	....	....	....
2000-01	**Boston**	**NHL**	**80**	**1**	**10**	**11**	**71**	**0**	**0**	**0**	**79**	**1.3**	**-2**	**0**	**0.0**	**18:21**	....	....	....	....	....	....	....	....	....
2001-02	**Boston**	**NHL**	**79**	**4**	**18**	**22**	**77**	**0**	**0**	**0**	**137**	**2.9**	**16**	**0**	**0.0**	**24:13**	**6**	**0**	**1**	**1**	**2**	**0**	**0**	**0**	**23:04**
2002-03	**Boston**	**NHL**	**76**	**4**	**13**	**17**	**56**	**0**	**0**	**0**	**114**	**3.5**	**21**	**0**	**0.0**	**20:42**	**5**	**0**	**0**	**0**	**4**	**0**	**0**	**0**	**20:19**

			Regular Season														Playoffs								
Season	Club	League	GP	G	A	Pts	PIM	PP	SH	GW	S	%	+/-	TF	F%	Min	GP	G	A	Pts	PIM	PP	SH	GW	Min
2003-04	**Boston**	**NHL**	**82**	**2**	**7**	**9**	**99**	**0**	**0**	**0**	**104**	**1.9**	**16**	**0**	**0.0**	**18:24**	**7**	**0**	**1**	**1**	**4**	**0**	**0**	**0**	**19:03**
2004-05	Lukko Rauma	Finland	31	2	8	10	110	....	....	....	....	....	....	....	....	....	8	0	0	0	*57	....	....	....	....
	NHL Totals		**546**	**19**	**68**	**87**	**464**	**0**	**0**	**2**	**712**	**2.7**		**1**	**100.0**	**19:57**	**36**	**0**	**2**	**2**	**28**	**0**	**0**	**0**	**20:43**

Signed as a free agent by **Lukko** (Finland), November 25, 2004.

GIONTA, Brian (jee-OHN-tuh, BRIGH-uhn) N.J.

Right wing. Shoots right. 5'7", 175 lbs. Born, Rochester, NY, January 18, 1979. New Jersey's 4th choice, 82nd overall, in 1998 Entry Draft.

Season	Club	League	GP	G	A	Pts	PIM	PP	SH	GW	S	%	+/-	TF	F%	Min	GP	G	A	Pts	PIM	PP	SH	GW	Min
1994-95	Rochester	EmJHL	28	*52	37	*89	....	....	....	....	....	....	....	....	....	....	....	....	....	....	....	....	....	....	....
1995-96	Niagara Scenic	MTJHL	51	47	44	91	59	....	....	....	....	....	....	....	....	....	....	....	....	....	....	....	....	....	....
1996-97	Niagara Scenic	MTJHL	50	57	70	127	101	....	....	....	....	....	....	....	....	....	6	6	11	17	21	....	....	....	....
1997-98	Boston College	H-East	40	30	32	62	44	....	....	....	....	....	....	....	....	....	....	....	....	....	....	....	....	....	....
1998-99	Boston College	H-East	39	27	33	60	46	....	....	....	....	....	....	....	....	....	....	....	....	....	....	....	....	....	....
99-2000	Boston College	H-East	42	*33	23	56	66	....	....	....	....	....	....	....	....	....	....	....	....	....	....	....	....	....	....
2000-01	Boston College	H-East	43	*33	21	*54	47	....	....	....	....	....	....	....	....	....	....	....	....	....	....	....	....	....	....
2001-02	**New Jersey**	**NHL**	**33**	**4**	**7**	**11**	**8**	**0**	**0**	**0**	**58**	**6.9**	**10**	**36**	**44.4**	**13:25**	**6**	**2**	**2**	**4**	**0**	**0**	**1**	**2**	**17:08**
	Albany River Rats	AHL	37	9	16	25	18	....	....	....	....	....	....	....	....	....	....	....	....	....	....	....	....	....	....
2002-03♦	**New Jersey**	**NHL**	**58**	**12**	**13**	**25**	**23**	**2**	**0**	**3**	**129**	**9.3**	**5**	**14**	**57.1**	**14:48**	**24**	**1**	**8**	**9**	**6**	**0**	**0**	**0**	**14:31**
2003-04	**New Jersey**	**NHL**	**75**	**21**	**8**	**29**	**36**	**0**	**0**	**8**	**174**	**12.1**	**19**	**60**	**58.3**	**14:44**	**5**	**2**	**3**	**5**	**0**	**1**	**0**	**0**	**15:41**
2004-05	Albany River Rats	AHL	15	5	7	12	10	....	....	....	....	....	....	....	....	....	....	....	....	....	....	....	....	....	....
	NHL Totals		**166**	**37**	**28**	**65**	**67**	**2**	**0**	**11**	**361**	**10.2**		**110**	**53.6**	**14:29**	**35**	**5**	**13**	**18**	**6**	**1**	**1**	**2**	**15:08**

Hockey East Rookie of the Year (1998) • Hockey East Second All-Star Team (1998) • NCAA East Second All-American Team (1998) • Hockey East First All-Star Team (1999, 2000, 2001) • NCAA East First All-American Team (1999, 2000, 2001) • Hockey East Player of the Year (2001) • Walter Brown Award (New England's Outstanding American-born College player) (2001) (co-winner - Ty Conklin)

GIRARD, Jonathan (zhih-RAHR, JAWN-ah-thuhn) BOS.

Defense. Shoots right. 5'11", 201 lbs. Born, Rawdon, Que., May 27, 1980. Boston's 1st choice, 48th overall, in 1998 Entry Draft.

Season	Club	League	GP	G	A	Pts	PIM	PP	SH	GW	S	%	+/-	TF	F%	Min	GP	G	A	Pts	PIM	PP	SH	GW	Min
1995-96	Laval-Laurentides	QAAA	39	11	22	33	44	....	....	....	....	....	....	....	....	....	16	4	11	15	16	....	....	....	....
1996-97	Laval Titan	QMJHL	39	11	23	34	13	....	....	....	....	....	....	....	....	....	3	0	3	3	0	....	....	....	....
1997-98	Laval Titan	QMJHL	64	20	47	67	44	....	....	....	....	....	....	....	....	....	16	2	16	18	13	....	....	....	....
1998-99	**Boston**	**NHL**	**3**	**0**	**0**	**0**	**0**	**0**	**0**	**0**	**3**	**0.0**	**1**	**0**	**0.0**	**9:28**	....	....	....	....	....	....	....	....	....
	Acadie-Bathurst	QMJHL	50	9	58	67	60	....	....	....	....	....	....	....	....	....	23	13	18	31	22	....	....	....	....
99-2000	**Boston**	**NHL**	**23**	**1**	**2**	**3**	**2**	**0**	**0**	**0**	**17**	**5.9**	**–1**	**0**	**0.0**	**9:32**	....	....	....	....	....	....	....	....	....
	Moncton Wildcats	QMJHL	26	10	25	35	36	....	....	....	....	....	....	....	....	....	16	3	15	18	36	....	....	....	....
	Providence Bruins	AHL	5	0	1	1	0	....	....	....	....	....	....	....	....	....	....	....	....	....	....	....	....	....	....
2000-01	**Boston**	**NHL**	**31**	**3**	**13**	**16**	**14**	**2**	**0**	**1**	**42**	**7.1**	**2**	**0**	**0.0**	**16:32**	....	....	....	....	....	....	....	....	....
	Providence Bruins	AHL	39	3	21	24	6	....	....	....	....	....	....	....	....	....	17	0	5	5	4	....	....	....	....
2001-02	**Boston**	**NHL**	**20**	**0**	**3**	**3**	**9**	**0**	**0**	**0**	**28**	**0.0**	**0**	**0**	**0.0**	**14:43**	**1**	**0**	**0**	**0**	**2**	**0**	**0**	**0**	**10:06**
	Providence Bruins	AHL	59	6	31	37	36	....	....	....	....	....	....	....	....	....	2	0	0	0	2	....	....	....	....
2002-03	**Boston**	**NHL**	**73**	**6**	**16**	**22**	**21**	**2**	**0**	**2**	**123**	**4.9**	**4**	**0**	**0.0**	**20:50**	**2**	**0**	**1**	**1**	**0**	**0**	**0**	**0**	**16:40**
2003-04			DID NOT PLAY – INJURED																						
2004-05			DID NOT PLAY – INJURED																						
	NHL Totals		**150**	**10**	**34**	**44**	**46**	**4**	**0**	**3**	**213**	**4.7**		**0**	**0.0**	**17:10**	**3**	**0**	**1**	**1**	**2**	**0**	**0**	**0**	**14:28**

QMJHL All-Rookie Team (1997) • QMJHL Second All-Star Team (1998) • QMJHL First All-Star Team (1999, 2000)

• Missed entire 2003-04 and 2004-05 seasons recovering from pelvis injury suffered in automobile accident, July 24, 2003.

GIROUX, Raymond (zhih-ROO, ray-MAWN)

Defense. Shoots left. 6'1", 190 lbs. Born, North Bay, Ont., July 20, 1976. Philadelphia's 7th choice, 202nd overall, in 1994 Entry Draft.

Season	Club	League	GP	G	A	Pts	PIM	PP	SH	GW	S	%	+/-	TF	F%	Min	GP	G	A	Pts	PIM	PP	SH	GW	Min
1992-93	Powassan Hawks	NOHA	45	8	18	26	117	....	....	....	....	....	....	....	....	....	....	....	....	....	....	....	....	....	....
1993-94	Powassan Hawks	NOJHA	36	10	40	50	42	....	....	....	....	....	....	....	....	....	....	....	....	....	....	....	....	....	....
1994-95	Yale	ECAC	27	1	3	4	8	....	....	....	....	....	....	....	....	....	....	....	....	....	....	....	....	....	....
1995-96	Yale	ECAC	30	3	16	19	36	....	....	....	....	....	....	....	....	....	....	....	....	....	....	....	....	....	....
1996-97	Yale	ECAC	32	9	12	21	38	....	....	....	....	....	....	....	....	....	....	....	....	....	....	....	....	....	....
1997-98	Yale	ECAC	35	9	*30	39	62	....	....	....	....	....	....	....	....	....	....	....	....	....	....	....	....	....	....
1998-99	Lowell	AHL	59	13	19	32	92	....	....	....	....	....	....	....	....	....	3	1	1	2	0	....	....	....	....
99-2000	**NY Islanders**	**NHL**	**14**	**0**	**9**	**9**	**10**	**0**	**0**	**0**	**24**	**0.0**	**0**	**9**	**22.2**	**14:40**	....	....	....	....	....	....	....	....	....
	Lowell	AHL	49	12	21	33	34	....	....	....	....	....	....	....	....	....	7	0	0	0	2	....	....	....	....
2000-01	HIFK Helsinki	Finland	22	3	9	12	34	....	....	....	....	....	....	....	....	....	....	....	....	....	....	....	....	....	....
	AIK Solna	Sweden	9	0	1	1	16	....	....	....	....	....	....	....	....	....	....	....	....	....	....	....	....	....	....
	Jokerit Helsinki	Finland	24	4	9	13	16	....	....	....	....	....	....	....	....	....	5	0	0	0	0	....	....	....	....
2001-02	**NY Islanders**	**NHL**	**2**	**0**	**0**	**0**	**2**	**0**	**0**	**0**	**2**	**0.0**	**–1**	**0**	**0.0**	**12:18**	....	....	....	....	....	....	....	....	....
	Bridgeport	AHL	79	13	40	53	73	....	....	....	....	....	....	....	....	....	19	1	7	8	20	....	....	....	....
2002-03	**New Jersey**	**NHL**	**11**	**0**	**1**	**1**	**6**	**0**	**0**	**0**	**20**	**0.0**	**–2**	**0**	**0.0**	**18:18**	....	....	....	....	....	....	....	....	....
	Albany River Rats	AHL	67	11	38	49	49	....	....	....	....	....	....	....	....	....	....	....	....	....	....	....	....	....	....
2003-04	**New Jersey**	**NHL**	**11**	**0**	**3**	**3**	**4**	**0**	**0**	**0**	**17**	**0.0**	**–3**	**0**	**0.0**	**20:55**	**4**	**0**	**0**	**0**	**0**	**0**	**0**	**0**	**15:15**
	Albany River Rats	AHL	65	11	17	28	34	....	....	....	....	....	....	....	....	....	....	....	....	....	....	....	....	....	....
2004-05	Houston Aeros	AHL	70	13	20	33	54	....	....	....	....	....	....	....	....	....	5	0	0	0	13	....	....	....	....
	NHL Totals		**38**	**0**	**13**	**13**	**22**	**0**	**0**	**0**	**63**	**0.0**		**9**	**22.2**	**17:24**	**4**	**0**	**0**	**0**	**0**	**0**	**0**	**0**	**15:15**

ECAC First All-Star Team (1998) • ECAC Player of the Year (1998) • NCAA East First All-American Team (1998) • AHL First All-Star Team (2003)

Rights traded to **NY Islanders** by **Philadelphia** for NY Islanders' 6th round choice (later traded to Montreal – Montreal selected Scott Selig) in 2000 Entry Draft, August 25, 1998. Signed as a free agent by **New Jersey**, July 12, 2002. Signed as a free agent by **Minnesota**, July 7, 2004.

GLEASON, Tim (GLEE-suhn, TIHM) L.A.

Defense. Shoots left. 6'1", 202 lbs. Born, Southfield, MI, January 29, 1983. Ottawa's 2nd choice, 23rd overall, in 2001 Entry Draft.

Season	Club	League	GP	G	A	Pts	PIM	PP	SH	GW	S	%	+/-	TF	F%	Min	GP	G	A	Pts	PIM	PP	SH	GW	Min
1998-99	Leamington Flyers	OHA-B	52	5	26	31	76	....	....	....	....	....	....	....	....	....	....	....	....	....	....	....	....	....	....
99-2000	Windsor Spitfires	OHL	55	5	13	18	101	....	....	....	....	....	....	....	....	....	12	2	4	6	14	....	....	....	....
2000-01	Windsor Spitfires	OHL	47	8	28	36	124	....	....	....	....	....	....	....	....	....	9	1	2	3	23	....	....	....	....
2001-02	Windsor Spitfires	OHL	67	17	42	59	109	....	....	....	....	....	....	....	....	....	16	7	13	20	40	....	....	....	....
2002-03	Windsor Spitfires	OHL	45	7	31	38	75	....	....	....	....	....	....	....	....	....	7	5	2	7	17	....	....	....	....
2003-04	**Los Angeles**	**NHL**	**47**	**0**	**7**	**7**	**21**	**0**	**0**	**0**	**45**	**0.0**	**1**	**0**	**0.0**	**14:59**	....	....	....	....	....	....	....	....	....
	Manchester	AHL	22	0	8	8	19	....	....	....	....	....	....	....	....	....	6	0	1	1	4	....	....	....	....
2004-05	Manchester	AHL	67	10	14	24	112	....	....	....	....	....	....	....	....	....	5	0	0	0	4	....	....	....	....
	NHL Totals		**47**	**0**	**7**	**7**	**21**	**0**	**0**	**0**	**45**	**0.0**		**0**	**0.0**	**14:59**	....	....	....	....	....	....	....	....	....

Rights traded to **Los Angeles** by **Ottawa** with future considerations for Bryan Smolinski, March 11, 2003.

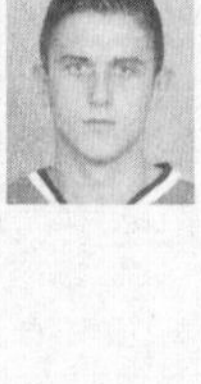

GOC, Marcel (GAWCH, mahr-SEHL) S.J.

Center. Shoots left. 6', 195 lbs. Born, Calw, West Germany, August 24, 1983. San Jose's 1st choice, 20th overall, in 2001 Entry Draft.

Season	Club	League	GP	G	A	Pts	PIM	PP	SH	GW	S	%	+/-	TF	F%	Min	GP	G	A	Pts	PIM	PP	SH	GW	Min
1998-99	Schwenningen Jr.	Ger-Jr.	12	23	10	33	12	....	....	....	....	....	....	....	....	....	....	....	....	....	....	....	....	....	....
99-2000	Schwenningen	Germany	51	0	3	3	4	....	....	....	....	....	....	....	....	....	11	1	1	2	2	....	....	....	....
2000-01	Schwenningen	Germany	58	13	28	41	12	....	....	....	....	....	....	....	....	....	....	....	....	....	....	....	....	....	....
2001-02	Schwenningen	Germany	45	8	9	17	24	....	....	....	....	....	....	....	....	....	....	....	....	....	....	....	....	....	....
	Adler Mannheim	Germany	8	0	2	2	0	....	....	....	....	....	....	....	....	....	....	....	....	....	....	....	....	....	....
2002-03	Adler Mannheim	Germany	36	6	14	20	16	....	....	....	....	....	....	....	....	....	8	1	2	3	0	....	....	....	....
2003-04	Cleveland Barons	AHL	78	16	21	37	24	....	....	....	....	....	....	....	....	....	....	....	....	....	....	....	....	....	....
	San Jose	**NHL**	....	....	....	....	....	....	....	....	....	....	....	....	....	....	**5**	**1**	**1**	**2**	**0**	**0**	**0**	**1**	**7:08**
2004-05	Cleveland Barons	AHL	76	16	34	50	28	....	....	....	....	....	....	....	....	....	....	....	....	....	....	....	....	....	....
	NHL Totals		....	....	....	....	....	....	....	....	....	....		....	....	....	**5**	**1**	**1**	**2**	**0**	**0**	**0**	**1**	**7:08**

GOC, Sascha
(GAWCH, SA-shah) **T.B.**

Defense. Shoots right. 6'6", 220 lbs. Born, Calw, West Germany, April 14, 1979. New Jersey's 5th choice, 159th overall, in 1997 Entry Draft.

			Regular Season														Playoffs								
Season	Club	League	GP	G	A	Pts	PIM	PP	SH	GW	S	%	+/-	TF	F%	Min	GP	G	A	Pts	PIM	PP	SH	GW	Min
1994-95	Schwenningen	Germany	14	5	1	6	10	....	....	....	....	....	....	....	....	....	....	....	....	....	....	....	....	....	....
1995-96	Schwenningen Jr.	Ger-Jr.	11	3	6	9	77	....	....	....	....	....	....	....	....	....	....	....	....	....	....	....	....	....	....
	Schwenningen	Germany	1	0	0	0	0	....	....	....	....	....	....	....	....	....	....	....	....	....	....	....	....	....	....
1996-97	Schwenningen Jr.	Ger-Jr.	1	1	1	2	2	....	....	....	....	....	....	....	....	....	....	....	....	....	....	....	....	....	....
	Schwenningen	Germany	41	3	1	4	28	....	....	....	....	....	....	....	....	....	5	0	0	0	0	....	....	....	....
1997-98	Schwenningen	Germany	49	5	5	10	45	....	....	....	....	....	....	....	....	....	....	....	....	....	....	....	....	....	....
	Schwenningen Jr.	Ger-Jr.	4	1	3	4	8	....	....	....	....	....	....	....	....	....	....	....	....	....	....	....	....	....	....
1998-99	Albany River Rats	AHL	55	1	12	13	24	....	....	....	....	....	....	....	....	....	2	0	0	0	0	....	....	....	....
99-2000	Albany River Rats	AHL	64	9	22	31	35	....	....	....	....	....	....	....	....	....	5	2	0	2	6	....	....	....	....
2000-01	**New Jersey**	**NHL**	**11**	**0**	**0**	**0**	**4**	**0**	**0**	**0**	**7**	**0.0**	**7**	**0**	**0.0**	**13:37**	....	....	....	....	....	....	....	....	....
	Albany River Rats	AHL	55	10	29	39	49	....	....	....	....	....	....	....	....	....	....	....	....	....	....	....	....	....	....
2001-02	**New Jersey**	**NHL**	**2**	**0**	**0**	**0**	**0**	**0**	**0**	**0**	**2**	**0.0**	**-2**	**0**	**0.0**	**19:21**	....	....	....	....	....	....	....	....	....
	Albany River Rats	AHL	10	0	5	5	12	....	....	....	....	....	....	....	....	....	....	....	....	....	....	....	....	....	....
	Tampa Bay	**NHL**	**9**	**0**	**0**	**0**	**0**	**0**	**0**	**0**	**2**	**0.0**	**0**	**0**	**0.0**	**5:32**	....	....	....	....	....	....	....	....	....
	Springfield	AHL	36	3	9	12	30	....	....	....	....	....	....	....	....	....	....	....	....	....	....	....	....	....	....
2002-03	Adler Mannheim	Germany	49	1	3	4	87	....	....	....	....	....	....	....	....	....	7	1	0	1	*41	....	....	....	....
2003-04	Adler Mannheim	Germany	46	5	12	17	58	....	....	....	....	....	....	....	....	....	3	0	0	0	0	....	....	....	....
2004-05	Adler Mannheim	Germany	39	1	4	5	67	....	....	....	....	....	....	....	....	....	4	0	0	0	0	....	....	....	....
	NHL Totals		**22**	**0**	**0**	**0**	**4**	**0**	**0**	**0**	**11**	**0.0**		**0**	**0.0**	**10:50**	....	....	....	....	....	....	....	....	....

Traded to **Tampa Bay** by **New Jersey** with Josef Boumedienne and the rights to Anton But for Andrei Zyuzin, November 9, 2001. Signed as a free agent by **Mannheim** (Germany), April 23, 2002.

GODARD, Eric
(GAW-duhrd, AIR-ihk) **NYI**

Right wing. Shoots right. 6'4", 227 lbs. Born, Vernon, B.C., March 7, 1980.

Season	Club	League	GP	G	A	Pts	PIM	PP	SH	GW	S	%	+/-	TF	F%	Min	GP	G	A	Pts	PIM	PP	SH	GW	Min
1997-98	Lethbridge	WHL	7	0	0	0	26	....	....	....	....	....	....	....	....	....	2	0	0	0	0	....	....	....	....
1998-99	Lethbridge	WHL	66	2	5	7	213	....	....	....	....	....	....	....	....	....	4	0	0	0	14	....	....	....	....
99-2000	Lethbridge	WHL	60	3	5	8	*310	....	....	....	....	....	....	....	....	....	....	....	....	....	....	....	....	....	....
	Louisville Panthers	AHL	4	0	1	1	16	....	....	....	....	....	....	....	....	....	....	....	....	....	....	....	....	....	....
2000-01	Louisville Panthers	AHL	45	0	0	0	132	....	....	....	....	....	....	....	....	....	....	....	....	....	....	....	....	....	....
2001-02	Bridgeport	AHL	67	1	4	5	198	....	....	....	....	....	....	....	....	....	20	0	4	4	30	....	....	....	....
2002-03	**NY Islanders**	**NHL**	**19**	**0**	**0**	**0**	**48**	**0**	**0**	**0**	**6**	**0.0**	**-3**	**0**	**0.0**	**4:32**	**2**	**0**	**1**	**1**	**4**	**0**	**0**	**0**	**1:09**
	Bridgeport	AHL	46	2	2	4	199	....	....	....	....	....	....	....	....	....	6	0	0	0	16	....	....	....	....
2003-04	**NY Islanders**	**NHL**	**31**	**0**	**1**	**1**	**97**	**0**	**0**	**0**	**5**	**0.0**	**-2**	**1**	**0.0**	**3:46**	....	....	....	....	....	....	....	....	....
	Bridgeport	AHL	7	0	0	0	13	....	....	....	....	....	....	....	....	....	....	....	....	....	....	....	....	....	....
2004-05	Bridgeport	AHL	75	7	11	18	295	....	....	....	....	....	....	....	....	....	....	....	....	....	....	....	....	....	....
	NHL Totals		**50**	**0**	**1**	**1**	**145**	**0**	**0**	**0**	**11**	**0.0**		**1**	**0.0**	**4:03**	**2**	**0**	**1**	**1**	**4**	**0**	**0**	**0**	**1:09**

Signed as a free agent by **Florida**, September 24, 1999. Traded to **NY Islanders** by **Florida** for Florida's 3rd round choice (previously acquired, Florida selected Gregory Campbell) in 2002 Entry Draft, June 22, 2002. • Spent majority of 2003-04 season as a healthy reserve.

GOMEZ, Scott
(GOH-mehz, SKAWT) **N.J.**

Center. Shoots left. 5'11", 200 lbs. Born, Anchorage, AK, December 23, 1979. New Jersey's 2nd choice, 27th overall, in 1998 Entry Draft.

Season	Club	League	GP	G	A	Pts	PIM	PP	SH	GW	S	%	+/-	TF	F%	Min	GP	G	A	Pts	PIM	PP	SH	GW	Min
1994-95	East	High-AK	28	30	48	78	....	....	....	....	....	....	....	....	....	....	....	....	....	....	....	....	....	....	....
1995-96	East	High-AK	27	*56	49	*101	....	....	....	....	....	....	....	....	....	....	....	....	....	....	....	....	....	....	....
	Anchorage	AAHL	40	*70	*67	*137	44	....	....	....	....	....	....	....	....	....	....	....	....	....	....	....	....	....	....
1996-97	South Surrey	BCHL	56	48	76	124	94	....	....	....	....	....	....	....	....	....	21	18	23	41	57	....	....	....	....
1997-98	Tri-City	WHL	45	12	37	49	57	....	....	....	....	....	....	....	....	....	....	....	....	....	....	....	....	....	....
1998-99	Tri-City	WHL	58	30	*78	108	55	....	....	....	....	....	....	....	....	....	10	6	13	19	31	....	....	....	....
99-2000♦	**New Jersey**	**NHL**	**82**	**19**	**51**	**70**	**78**	**7**	**0**	**1**	**204**	**9.3**	**14**	**341**	**44.6**	**16:21**	**23**	**4**	**6**	**10**	**4**	**1**	**0**	**2**	**14:08**
2000-01	**New Jersey**	**NHL**	**76**	**14**	**49**	**63**	**46**	**2**	**0**	**4**	**155**	**9.0**	**-1**	**1010**	**44.6**	**15:46**	**25**	**5**	**9**	**14**	**24**	**0**	**0**	**0**	**16:06**
2001-02	**New Jersey**	**NHL**	**76**	**10**	**38**	**48**	**36**	**1**	**0**	**1**	**156**	**6.4**	**-4**	**628**	**48.7**	**16:46**	....	....	....	....	....	....	....	....	....
2002-03♦	**New Jersey**	**NHL**	**80**	**13**	**42**	**55**	**48**	**2**	**0**	**4**	**205**	**6.3**	**17**	**864**	**47.5**	**16:01**	**24**	**3**	**9**	**12**	**2**	**0**	**0**	**0**	**13:45**
2003-04	**New Jersey**	**NHL**	**80**	**14**	***56**	**70**	**70**	**3**	**0**	**1**	**189**	**7.4**	**18**	**1129**	**46.2**	**16:00**	**5**	**0**	**6**	**6**	**0**	**0**	**0**	**0**	**17:14**
2004-05	Alaska Aces	ECHL	61	13	*73	*86	69	....	....	....	....	....	....	....	....	....	4	1	3	4	4	....	....	....	....
	NHL Totals		**394**	**70**	**236**	**306**	**278**	**15**	**0**	**11**	**909**	**7.7**		**3972**	**46.3**	**16:11**	**77**	**12**	**30**	**42**	**30**	**1**	**0**	**2**	**14:51**

WHL West First All-Star Team (1999) • NHL All-Rookie Team (2000) • Calder Memorial Trophy (2000) • ECHL First All-Star Team (2005) • ECHL MVP (2005)

Played in NHL All-Star Game (2000)

Signed as a free agent by **Alaska** (ECHL), October 25, 2004.

GONCHAR, Sergei
(gohn-CHAR, SAIR-gay) **PIT.**

Defense. Shoots left. 6'2", 215 lbs. Born, Chelyabinsk, USSR, April 13, 1974. Washington's 1st choice, 14th overall, in 1992 Entry Draft.

Season	Club	League	GP	G	A	Pts	PIM	PP	SH	GW	S	%	+/-	TF	F%	Min	GP	G	A	Pts	PIM	PP	SH	GW	Min
1991-92	Chelyabinsk	CIS	31	1	0	1	6	....	....	....	....	....	....	....	....	....	....	....	....	....	....	....	....	....	....
1992-93	Dynamo Moscow	CIS	31	1	3	4	70	....	....	....	....	....	....	....	....	....	10	0	0	0	12	....	....	....	....
1993-94	Dynamo Moscow	CIS	44	4	5	9	36	....	....	....	....	....	....	....	....	....	10	0	3	3	14	....	....	....	....
	Portland Pirates	AHL	....	....	....	....	....	....	....	....	....	....	....	....	....	....	2	0	0	0	0	....	....	....	....
1994-95	Portland Pirates	AHL	61	10	32	42	67	....	....	....	....	....	....	....	....	....	....	....	....	....	....	....	....	....	....
	Washington	**NHL**	**31**	**2**	**5**	**7**	**22**	**0**	**0**	**0**	**38**	**5.3**	**4**	....	....	....	**7**	**2**	**2**	**4**	**2**	**0**	**0**	**1**	....
1995-96	**Washington**	**NHL**	**78**	**15**	**26**	**41**	**60**	**4**	**0**	**4**	**139**	**10.8**	**25**	....	....	....	**6**	**2**	**4**	**6**	**4**	**1**	**0**	**0**	....
1996-97	**Washington**	**NHL**	**57**	**13**	**17**	**30**	**36**	**3**	**0**	**3**	**129**	**10.1**	**-11**	....	....	....	....	....	....	....	....	....	....	....	....
1997-98	Lada Togliatti	Russia	7	3	2	5	4	....	....	....	....	....	....	....	....	....	....	....	....	....	....	....	....	....	....
	Lada Togliatti	EuroHL	1	1	0	1	2	....	....	....	....	....	....	....	....	....	....	....	....	....	....	....	....	....	....
	Washington	**NHL**	**72**	**5**	**16**	**21**	**66**	**2**	**0**	**0**	**134**	**3.7**	**2**	....	....	....	**21**	**7**	**4**	**11**	**30**	**3**	**1**	**2**	....
	Russia	Olympics	6	0	2	2	0	....	....	....	....	....	....	....	....	....	....	....	....	....	....	....	....	....	....
1998-99	**Washington**	**NHL**	**53**	**21**	**10**	**31**	**57**	**13**	**1**	**3**	**180**	**11.7**	**1**	**0**	**0.0**	**23:55**	....	....	....	....	....	....	....	....	....
99-2000	**Washington**	**NHL**	**73**	**18**	**36**	**54**	**52**	**5**	**0**	**3**	**181**	**9.9**	**26**	**0**	**0.0**	**21:46**	**5**	**1**	**0**	**1**	**6**	**0**	**0**	**0**	**19:58**
2000-01	**Washington**	**NHL**	**76**	**19**	**38**	**57**	**70**	**8**	**0**	**2**	**241**	**7.9**	**12**	**1**	**100.0**	**22:26**	**6**	**1**	**3**	**4**	**2**	**1**	**0**	**0**	**19:45**
2001-02	**Washington**	**NHL**	**76**	**26**	**33**	**59**	**58**	**7**	**0**	**2**	**216**	**12.0**	**-1**	**1**	**100.0**	**23:51**	....	....	....	....	....	....	....	....	....
	Russia	Olympics	6	0	0	0	2	....	....	....	....	....	....	....	....	....	....	....	....	....	....	....	....	....	....
2002-03	**Washington**	**NHL**	**82**	**18**	**49**	**67**	**52**	**7**	**0**	**2**	**224**	**8.0**	**13**	**0**	**0.0**	**26:35**	**6**	**0**	**5**	**5**	**4**	**0**	**0**	**0**	**29:00**
2003-04	**Washington**	**NHL**	**56**	**7**	**42**	**49**	**44**	**4**	**0**	**0**	**127**	**5.5**	**-20**	**0**	**0.0**	**27:57**	....	....	....	....	....	....	....	....	....
	Boston	**NHL**	**15**	**4**	**5**	**9**	**12**	**2**	**0**	**0**	**34**	**11.8**	**6**	**0**	**0.0**	**25:32**	**7**	**1**	**4**	**5**	**4**	**1**	**0**	**1**	**27:51**
2004-05	Magnitogorsk	Russia	40	2	17	19	54	....	....	....	....	....	....	....	....	....	4	1	1	2	6	....	....	....	....
	NHL Totals		**669**	**148**	**277**	**425**	**529**	**55**	**1**	**19**	**1643**	**9.0**		**2**	**100.0**	**24:22**	**58**	**14**	**22**	**36**	**52**	**6**	**1**	**4**	**24:28**

NHL Second All-Star Team (2002, 2003)

Played in NHL All-Star Game (2001, 2002, 2003)

Traded to **Boston** by **Washington** for Shaonne Morrisonn and Boston's 1st (Jeff Schultz) and 2nd (Michail Yunkov) round choices in 2004 Entry Draft, March 3, 2004. Signed as a free agent by **Magnitogorsk** (Russia), September 21, 2004. Signed as a free agent by **Pittsburgh**, August 3, 2005.

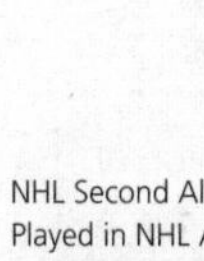

GORDON, Boyd
(GOHR-duhn, BOYD) **WSH.**

Right wing. Shoots right. 6', 198 lbs. Born, Unity, Sask., October 19, 1983. Washington's 3rd choice, 17th overall, in 2002 Entry Draft.

Season	Club	League	GP	G	A	Pts	PIM	PP	SH	GW	S	%	+/-	TF	F%	Min	GP	G	A	Pts	PIM	PP	SH	GW	Min
1997-98	Regina Flyers	SMHA	60	70	102	172	53	....	....	....	....	....	....	....	....	....	....	....	....	....	....	....	....	....	....
1998-99	Regina Rangers	SMBHL	60	70	102	172	53	....	....	....	....	....	....	....	....	....	....	....	....	....	....	....	....	....	....
99-2000	Red Deer Rebels	WHL	66	10	26	36	24	....	....	....	....	....	....	....	....	....	4	0	1	1	16	....	....	....	....
2000-01	Red Deer Rebels	WHL	72	12	27	39	39	....	....	....	....	....	....	....	....	....	22	3	6	9	2	....	....	....	....
2001-02	Red Deer Rebels	WHL	66	22	29	51	19	....	....	....	....	....	....	....	....	....	23	10	12	22	8	....	....	....	....
2002-03	Red Deer Rebels	WHL	56	33	48	81	28	....	....	....	....	....	....	....	....	....	23	8	12	20	14	....	....	....	....
2003-04	**Washington**	**NHL**	**41**	**1**	**5**	**6**	**8**	**0**	**0**	**0**	**42**	**2.4**	**-9**	**328**	**43.0**	**13:11**	....	....	....	....	....	....	....	....	....
	Portland Pirates	AHL	43	5	17	22	16	....	....	....	....	....	....	....	....	....	7	2	1	3	0	....	....	....	....
2004-05	Portland Pirates	AHL	80	17	22	39	35	....	....	....	....	....	....	....	....	....	....	....	....	....	....	....	....	....	....
	NHL Totals		**41**	**1**	**5**	**6**	**8**	**0**	**0**	**0**	**42**	**2.4**		**328**	**43.0**	**13:11**	....	....	....	....	....	....	....	....	....

WHL East First All-Star Team (2003)

GOREN, Lee

(GOH-rehn, LEE) **VAN.**

Right wing. Shoots right. 6'3", 205 lbs. Born, Winnipeg, Man., December 26, 1977. Boston's 5th choice, 63rd overall, in 1997 Entry Draft.

			Regular Season														Playoffs								
Season	Club	League	GP	G	A	Pts	PIM	PP	SH	GW	S	%	+/-	TF	F%	Min	GP	G	A	Pts	PIM	PP	SH	GW	Min
1994-95	Wpg. Warriors	MMMHL	31	19	31	50	50	....	....	....	....	....	....	....	....	....	....	....	....	....	....	....	....	....	....
1995-96	Minot Top Guns	SJHL	56	25	35	61	....	....	....	....	....	....	....	....	....	....	12	5	20	25	....	....	....	....	....
	Saskatoon Blades	WHL	2	0	0	0	2	....	....	....	....	....	....	....	....	....	....	....	....	....	....	....	....	....	....
1996-97	North Dakota	WCHA	DID NOT PLAY																						
1997-98	North Dakota	WCHA	29	3	13	16	26	....	....	....	....	....	....	....	....	....	....	....	....	....	....	....	....	....	....
1998-99	North Dakota	WCHA	38	26	19	45	20	....	....	....	....	....	....	....	....	....	....	....	....	....	....	....	....	....	....
99-2000	North Dakota	WCHA	44	*34	29	63	42	....	....	....	....	....	....	....	....	....	....	....	....	....	....	....	....	....	....
2000-01	**Boston**	**NHL**	**21**	**2**	**0**	**2**	**7**	**1**	**0**	**0**	**9**	**22.2**	**–3**	**21**	**38.1**	**4:24**	....	....	....	....	....	....	....	....	....
	Providence Bruins	AHL	54	15	18	33	72	....	....	....	....	....	....	....	....	....	17	5	2	7	11	....	....	....	....
2001-02	Providence Bruins	AHL	71	11	26	37	121	....	....	....	....	....	....	....	....	....	2	0	0	0	0	....	....	....	....
2002-03	Providence Bruins	AHL	65	32	37	69	106	....	....	....	....	....	....	....	....	....	3	0	1	1	0	....	....	....	....
	Boston	**NHL**	**14**	**2**	**1**	**3**	**7**	**2**	**0**	**0**	**15**	**13.3**	**–2**	**0**	**0.0**	**8:15**	**5**	**0**	**0**	**0**	**5**	**0**	**0**	**0**	**6:29**
2003-04	**Florida**	**NHL**	**2**	**0**	**1**	**1**	**0**	**0**	**0**	**0**	**1**	**0.0**	**–4**	**1**	**100.0**	**13:20**	....	....	....	....	....	....	....	....	....
	San Antonio	AHL	65	27	22	49	72	....	....	....	....	....	....	....	....	....	....	....	....	....	....	....	....	....	....
2004-05	Manitoba Moose	AHL	79	32	30	62	117	....	....	....	....	....	....	....	....	....	14	*10	3	13	23	....	....	....	....
	NHL Totals		**37**	**4**	**2**	**6**	**14**	**3**	**0**	**0**	**25**	**16.0**		**22**	**40.9**	**6:20**	**5**	**0**	**0**	**0**	**5**	**0**	**0**	**0**	**6:29**

WCHA Second All-Star Team (2000) • NCAA West Second All-American Team (2000) • NCAA Championship All-Tournament Team (2000) • NCAA Championship Tournament MVP (2000)

• Ruled ineligible to play during 1996-97 season by NCAA due to appearance with **Saskatoon** (WHL) in 1995-96 season. Signed as a free agent by **Florida**, July 24, 2003. Signed as a free agent by **Vancouver**, July 7, 2004.

GRAND-PIERRE, Jean-Luc

(GRAHN pee-AIR, ZHAHN-LOOK)

Defense. Shoots right. 6'3", 223 lbs. Born, Montreal, Que., February 2, 1977. St. Louis' 6th choice, 179th overall, in 1995 Entry Draft.

Season	Club	League	GP	G	A	Pts	PIM	PP	SH	GW	S	%	+/-	TF	F%	Min	GP	G	A	Pts	PIM	PP	SH	GW	Min
1992-93	Lac St-Louis Lions	QAAA	1	0	0	0	2	....	....	....	....	....	....	....	....	....	....	....	....	....	....	....	....	....	....
1993-94	Beauport	QMJHL	46	1	4	5	27	....	....	....	....	....	....	....	....	....	1	0	0	0	0	....	....	....	....
1994-95	Val-d'Or Foreurs	QMJHL	59	10	13	23	126	....	....	....	....	....	....	....	....	....	....	....	....	....	....	....	....	....	....
1995-96	Val-d'Or Foreurs	QMJHL	67	13	21	34	209	....	....	....	....	....	....	....	....	....	13	1	4	5	47	....	....	....	....
1996-97	Val-d'Or Foreurs	QMJHL	58	9	24	33	186	....	....	....	....	....	....	....	....	....	13	5	8	13	46	....	....	....	....
1997-98	Rochester	AHL	75	4	6	10	211	....	....	....	....	....	....	....	....	....	4	0	0	0	2	....	....	....	....
1998-99	**Buffalo**	**NHL**	**16**	**0**	**1**	**1**	**17**	**0**	**0**	**0**	**11**	**0.0**	**0**	**0**	**0.0**	**13:36**	....	....	....	....	....	....	....	....	....
	Rochester	AHL	55	5	4	9	90	....	....	....	....	....	....	....	....	....	....	....	....	....	....	....	....	....	....
99-2000	**Buffalo**	**NHL**	**11**	**0**	**0**	**0**	**15**	**0**	**0**	**0**	**11**	**0.0**	**–1**	**0**	**0.0**	**15:11**	**4**	**0**	**0**	**0**	**4**	**0**	**0**	**0**	**17:34**
	Rochester	AHL	62	5	8	13	124	....	....	....	....	....	....	....	....	....	17	0	1	1	40	....	....	....	....
2000-01	**Columbus**	**NHL**	**64**	**1**	**4**	**5**	**73**	**0**	**0**	**0**	**33**	**3.0**	**–6**	**0**	**0.0**	**12:51**	....	....	....	....	....	....	....	....	....
2001-02	**Columbus**	**NHL**	**81**	**2**	**6**	**8**	**90**	**0**	**0**	**0**	**62**	**3.2**	**–28**	**3**	**0.0**	**15:20**	....	....	....	....	....	....	....	....	....
2002-03	**Columbus**	**NHL**	**41**	**1**	**0**	**1**	**64**	**0**	**0**	**0**	**32**	**3.1**	**–6**	**0**	**0.0**	**13:38**	....	....	....	....	....	....	....	....	....
	Syracuse Crunch	AHL	2	1	0	1	6	....	....	....	....	....	....	....	....	....	....	....	....	....	....	....	....	....	....
2003-04	**Columbus**	**NHL**	**16**	**0**	**0**	**0**	**12**	**0**	**0**	**0**	**15**	**0.0**	**–3**	**2**	**100.0**	**7:25**	....	....	....	....	....	....	....	....	....
	Atlanta	**NHL**	**27**	**2**	**2**	**4**	**26**	**0**	**1**	**0**	**19**	**10.5**	**–7**	**1**	**0.0**	**15:25**	....	....	....	....	....	....	....	....	....
	Washington	**NHL**	**13**	**1**	**0**	**1**	**14**	**0**	**0**	**0**	**19**	**5.3**	**–2**	**2**	**0.0**	**11:34**	....	....	....	....	....	....	....	....	....
2004-05	IF Troja-Ljungby	Sweden-2	21	2	3	5	69	....	....	....	....	....	....	....	....	....	....	....	....	....	....	....	....	....	....
	NHL Totals		**269**	**7**	**13**	**20**	**311**	**0**	**1**	**0**	**202**	**3.5**		**8**	**25.0**	**13:44**	**4**	**0**	**0**	**0**	**4**	**0**	**0**	**0**	**17:34**

Traded to **Buffalo** by **St. Louis** with Ottawa's 2nd round choice (previously acquired, Buffalo selected Cory Sarich) in 1996 Entry Draft and St. Louis' 3rd round choice (Maxim Afinogenov) in 1997 Entry Draft for Yuri Khmylev and Buffalo's 8th round choice (Andrei Podkonicky) in 1996 Entry Draft, March 20, 1996. Traded to **Columbus** by **Buffalo** with Matt Davidson, San Jose's 5th round choice (previously acquired, Columbus selected Tyler Kolarik) in 2000 Entry Draft and Buffalo's 5th round choice (later traded to Calgary – later traded to Detroit – Detroit selected Andreas Jamtin) in 2001 Entry Draft to complete Expansion Draft agreement which had Columbus select Geoff Sanderson and Dwayne Roloson from Buffalo, June 23, 2000. Traded to **Atlanta** by **Columbus** for future considerations, December 31, 2003. Claimed on waivers by **Washington** from **Atlanta**, March 9, 2004. Signed as a free agent by **Troja-Ljungby** (Sweden-2), December 10, 2004.

GRATTON, Benoit

(grah-TOHN, BEHN-wah)

Center. Shoots left. 5'11", 194 lbs. Born, Montreal, Que., December 28, 1976. Washington's 6th choice, 105th overall, in 1995 Entry Draft.

Season	Club	League	GP	G	A	Pts	PIM	PP	SH	GW	S	%	+/-	TF	F%	Min	GP	G	A	Pts	PIM	PP	SH	GW	Min
1992-93	Laval-Laurentides	QAAA	40	19	38	57	74	....	....	....	....	....	....	....	....	....	13	1	9	10	27	....	....	....	....
1993-94	Laval Titan	QMJHL	51	9	14	23	70	....	....	....	....	....	....	....	....	....	20	2	1	3	19	....	....	....	....
1994-95	Laval Titan	QMJHL	71	30	58	88	199	....	....	....	....	....	....	....	....	....	20	8	*21	29	42	....	....	....	....
1995-96	Laval Titan	QMJHL	38	21	39	60	130	....	....	....	....	....	....	....	....	....	....	....	....	....	....	....	....	....	....
	Granby	QMJHL	27	12	46	58	97	....	....	....	....	....	....	....	....	....	21	13	26	39	68	....	....	....	....
1996-97	Portland Pirates	AHL	76	6	40	46	140	....	....	....	....	....	....	....	....	....	5	2	1	3	14	....	....	....	....
1997-98	**Washington**	**NHL**	**6**	**0**	**1**	**1**	**6**	**0**	**0**	**0**	**5**	**0.0**	**1**	....	....	....	....	....	....	....	....	....	....	....	....
	Portland Pirates	AHL	58	19	31	50	137	....	....	....	....	....	....	....	....	....	8	4	2	6	24	....	....	....	....
1998-99	**Washington**	**NHL**	**16**	**4**	**3**	**7**	**16**	**0**	**0**	**0**	**24**	**16.7**	**–1**	**136**	**54.4**	**13:28**	....	....	....	....	....	....	....	....	....
	Portland Pirates	AHL	64	18	42	60	135	....	....	....	....	....	....	....	....	....	....	....	....	....	....	....	....	....	....
99-2000	**Calgary**	**NHL**	**10**	**0**	**2**	**2**	**10**	**0**	**0**	**0**	**4**	**0.0**	**1**	**68**	**63.2**	**8:15**	....	....	....	....	....	....	....	....	....
	Saint John Flames	AHL	65	17	49	66	137	....	....	....	....	....	....	....	....	....	3	0	1	1	4	....	....	....	....
2000-01	**Calgary**	**NHL**	**14**	**1**	**3**	**4**	**14**	**0**	**0**	**0**	**13**	**7.7**	**0**	**105**	**63.8**	**9:11**	....	....	....	....	....	....	....	....	....
	Saint John Flames	AHL	53	10	36	46	153	....	....	....	....	....	....	....	....	....	....	....	....	....	....	....	....	....	....
2001-02	**Montreal**	**NHL**	**8**	**1**	**0**	**1**	**8**	**0**	**0**	**0**	**8**	**12.5**	**–1**	**98**	**63.3**	**9:51**	....	....	....	....	....	....	....	....	....
	Quebec Citadelles	AHL	35	10	19	29	70	....	....	....	....	....	....	....	....	....	3	2	3	5	10	....	....	....	....
2002-03	Hamilton	AHL	43	21	39	60	78	....	....	....	....	....	....	....	....	....	22	2	*15	17	73	....	....	....	....
2003-04	**Montreal**	**NHL**	**4**	**0**	**1**	**1**	**4**	**0**	**0**	**0**	**3**	**0.0**	**0**	**31**	**54.8**	**9:44**	....	....	....	....	....	....	....	....	....
	Hamilton	AHL	50	18	33	51	119	....	....	....	....	....	....	....	....	....	10	1	2	3	*67	....	....	....	....
2004-05	HC Lugano	Swiss	32	6	12	18	81	....	....	....	....	....	....	....	....	....	....	....	....	....	....	....	....	....	....
	NHL Totals		**58**	**6**	**10**	**16**	**58**	**0**	**0**	**0**	**57**	**10.5**		**438**	**60.0**	**10:28**	....	....	....	....	....	....	....	....	....

Traded to **Calgary** by **Washington** for Steve Shirreffs, August 18, 1999. Claimed on waivers by **Montreal** from **Calgary**, April 11, 2001. Signed as a free agent by **Lugano** (Swiss), June 9, 2004. Signed as a free agent by **Hamburg** (Germany), April 22, 2005.

GRATTON, Chris

(grah-TOHN, KRIHS) **FLA.**

Center. Shoots left. 6'4", 220 lbs. Born, Brantford, Ont., July 5, 1975. Tampa Bay's 1st choice, 3rd overall, in 1993 Entry Draft.

Season	Club	League	GP	G	A	Pts	PIM	PP	SH	GW	S	%	+/-	TF	F%	Min	GP	G	A	Pts	PIM	PP	SH	GW	Min
1989-90	Brantford Classics	OHA-B	1	0	2	2	2	....	....	....	....	....	....	....	....	....	....	....	....	....	....	....	....	....	....
1990-91	Brantford Classics	OHA-B	31	30	30	60	28	....	....	....	....	....	....	....	....	....	....	....	....	....	....	....	....	....	....
1991-92	Kingston	OHL	62	27	39	66	37	....	....	....	....	....	....	....	....	....	....	....	....	....	....	....	....	....	....
1992-93	Kingston	OHL	58	55	54	109	125	....	....	....	....	....	....	....	....	....	16	11	18	29	42	....	....	....	....
1993-94	**Tampa Bay**	**NHL**	**84**	**13**	**29**	**42**	**123**	**5**	**1**	**2**	**161**	**8.1**	**–25**	....	....	....	....	....	....	....	....	....	....	....	....
1994-95	**Tampa Bay**	**NHL**	**46**	**7**	**20**	**27**	**89**	**2**	**0**	**0**	**91**	**7.7**	**–2**	....	....	....	....	....	....	....	....	....	....	....	....
1995-96	**Tampa Bay**	**NHL**	**82**	**17**	**21**	**38**	**105**	**7**	**0**	**3**	**183**	**9.3**	**–13**	....	....	....	**6**	**0**	**2**	**2**	**27**	**0**	**0**	**0**	....
1996-97	**Tampa Bay**	**NHL**	**82**	**30**	**32**	**62**	**201**	**9**	**0**	**4**	**230**	**13.0**	**–28**	....	....	....	....	....	....	....	....	....	....	....	....
1997-98	**Philadelphia**	**NHL**	**82**	**22**	**40**	**62**	**159**	**5**	**0**	**2**	**182**	**12.1**	**11**	....	....	....	**5**	**2**	**0**	**2**	**10**	**0**	**0**	**0**	....
1998-99	**Philadelphia**	**NHL**	**26**	**1**	**7**	**8**	**41**	**0**	**0**	**0**	**54**	**1.9**	**–8**	**38**	**42.1**	**14:25**	....	....	....	....	....	....	....	....	....
	Tampa Bay	**NHL**	**52**	**7**	**19**	**26**	**102**	**1**	**0**	**1**	**127**	**5.5**	**–20**	**1032**	**53.9**	**18:20**	....	....	....	....	....	....	....	....	....
99-2000	**Tampa Bay**	**NHL**	**58**	**14**	**27**	**41**	**121**	**4**	**0**	**1**	**168**	**8.3**	**–24**	**1341**	**55.9**	**20:03**	....	....	....	....	....	....	....	....	....
	Buffalo	**NHL**	**14**	**1**	**7**	**8**	**15**	**0**	**0**	**0**	**34**	**2.9**	**1**	**256**	**54.3**	**16:40**	**5**	**0**	**1**	**1**	**4**	**0**	**0**	**0**	**14:56**
2000-01	**Buffalo**	**NHL**	**82**	**19**	**21**	**40**	**102**	**5**	**0**	**5**	**156**	**12.2**	**0**	**1161**	**57.3**	**14:37**	**13**	**6**	**4**	**10**	**14**	**2**	**0**	**1**	**12:33**
2001-02	**Buffalo**	**NHL**	**82**	**15**	**24**	**39**	**75**	**1**	**0**	**5**	**139**	**10.8**	**0**	**1297**	**53.8**	**14:57**	....	....	....	....	....	....	....	....	....
2002-03	**Buffalo**	**NHL**	**66**	**15**	**29**	**44**	**86**	**4**	**0**	**2**	**187**	**8.0**	**–5**	**1099**	**58.9**	**16:26**	....	....	....	....	....	....	....	....	....
	Phoenix	**NHL**	**14**	**0**	**1**	**1**	**21**	**0**	**0**	**0**	**28**	**0.0**	**–11**	**231**	**57.1**	**17:12**	....	....	....	....	....	....	....	....	....
2003-04	**Phoenix**	**NHL**	**68**	**11**	**18**	**29**	**93**	**3**	**0**	**1**	**122**	**9.0**	**–19**	**1090**	**55.3**	**14:40**	....	....	....	....	....	....	....	....	....
	Colorado	**NHL**	**13**	**2**	**1**	**3**	**18**	**0**	**0**	**0**	**28**	**7.1**	**1**	**252**	**57.5**	**16:55**	**11**	**0**	**0**	**0**	**27**	**0**	**0**	**0**	**12:14**
2004-05			DID NOT PLAY																						
	NHL Totals		**851**	**174**	**296**	**470**	**1351**	**46**	**1**	**26**	**1890**	**9.2**		**7797**	**55.8**	**16:12**	**40**	**8**	**7**	**15**	**82**	**2**	**0**	**1**	**12:50**

OHL All-Rookie Team (1992) • OHL Rookie of the Year (1992)

Signed as a free agent by **Philadelphia**, August 14, 1997. Traded to **Tampa Bay** by **Philadelphia** with Mike Sillinger for Mikael Renberg and Daymond Langkow, December 12, 1998. Traded to **Buffalo** by **Tampa Bay** with Tampa Bay's 2nd round choice (Derek Roy) in 2001 Entry Draft for Cory Sarich, Wayne Primeau, Brian Holzinger and Buffalo's 3rd round choice (Alexander Kharitonov) in 2000 Entry Draft, March 9, 2000. Traded to **Phoenix** by **Buffalo** with Buffalo's 4th round choice (later traded to Edmonton – Edmonton selected Liam Reddox) in 2004 Entry Draft for Daniel Briere and Phoenix's 3rd round choice (Andrej Sekera) in 2004 Entry Draft, March 10, 2003. Traded to **Colorado** by **Phoenix** with Ossi Vaananen and Phoenix's 2nd round choice (Paul Stastny) in 2005 Entry Draft for Derek Morris and Keith Ballard, March 8, 2004. Signed as a free agent by **Florida**, August 12, 2005.

GREBESHKOV, Denis (greh-behsh-KAHV, DEH-nihs) L.A.

Defense. Shoots left. 6'1", 200 lbs. Born, Yaroslavl, USSR, October 11, 1983. Los Angeles' 1st choice, 18th overall, in 2002 Entry Draft.

			Regular Season														Playoffs								
Season	Club	League	GP	G	A	Pts	PIM	PP	SH	GW	S	%	+/-	TF	F%	Min	GP	G	A	Pts	PIM	PP	SH	GW	Min
99-2000	Yaroslavl 2	Russia-3	42	2	1	3	12	....	....	....	....	....	....	....	....	....	6	0	0	0	2	....	....	....	....
2000-01	Yaroslavl 2	Russia-3	34	7	2	9	20	....	....	....	....	....	....	....	....	....	....	....	....	....	....	....	....	....	....
2001-02	Yaroslavl 2	Russia-3	7	1	1	2	2	....	....	....	....	....	....	....	....	....	....	....	....	....	....	....	....	....	....
	Yaroslavl	Russia	27	1	2	3	10	....	....	....	....	....	....	....	....	....	....	....	....	....	....	....	....	....	....
2002-03	Yaroslavl	Russia	48	0	7	7	26	....	....	....	....	....	....	....	....	....	10	0	1	1	2	....	....	....	....
2003-04	**Los Angeles**	**NHL**	**4**	**0**	**1**	**1**	**0**	**0**	**0**	**0**	**5**	**0.0**	**–4**	**0**	**0.0**	**18:29**	....	....	....	....	....	....	....	....	....
	Manchester	AHL	43	2	7	9	34	....	....	....	....	....	....	....	....	....	6	0	1	1	6	....	....	....	....
2004-05	Manchester	AHL	75	5	44	49	87	....	....	....	....	....	....	....	....	....	6	0	4	4	2	....	....	....	....
	NHL Totals		**4**	**0**	**1**	**1**	**0**	**0**	**0**	**0**	**5**	**0.0**		**0**	**0.0**	**18:29**	....	....	....	....	....	....	....	....	....

GREEN, Josh (GREEN, JAWSH) VAN.

Left wing. Shoots left. 6'3", 215 lbs. Born, Camrose, Alta., November 16, 1977. Los Angeles' 1st choice, 30th overall, in 1996 Entry Draft.

Season	Club	League	GP	G	A	Pts	PIM	PP	SH	GW	S	%	+/-	TF	F%	Min	GP	G	A	Pts	PIM	PP	SH	GW	Min
1992-93	Camrose Kodiacs	ABHL	60	55	45	100	80	....	....	....	....	....	....	....	....	....	....	....	....	....	....	....	....	....	....
1993-94	Medicine Hat	WHL	63	22	22	44	43	....	....	....	....	....	....	....	....	....	3	0	0	0	4	....	....	....	....
1994-95	Medicine Hat	WHL	68	32	23	55	64	....	....	....	....	....	....	....	....	....	5	5	1	6	2	....	....	....	....
1995-96	Medicine Hat	WHL	46	18	25	43	55	....	....	....	....	....	....	....	....	....	5	2	2	4	4	....	....	....	....
1996-97	Medicine Hat	WHL	51	25	32	57	61	....	....	....	....	....	....	....	....	....	....	....	....	....	....	....	....	....	....
	Swift Current	WHL	23	10	15	25	33	....	....	....	....	....	....	....	....	....	10	9	7	16	19	....	....	....	....
1997-98	Swift Current	WHL	5	9	1	10	9	....	....	....	....	....	....	....	....	....	....	....	....	....	....	....	....	....	....
	Portland	WHL	26	26	18	44	27	....	....	....	....	....	....	....	....	....	....	....	....	....	....	....	....	....	....
	Fredericton	AHL	43	16	15	31	14	....	....	....	....	....	....	....	....	....	4	1	3	4	6	....	....	....	....
1998-99	**Los Angeles**	**NHL**	**27**	**1**	**3**	**4**	**8**	**1**	**0**	**0**	**35**	**2.9**	**–5**	**2**	**50.0**	**11:44**	....	....	....	....	....	....	....	....	....
	Springfield	AHL	41	15	15	30	29	....	....	....	....	....	....	....	....	....	....	....	....	....	....	....	....	....	....
99-2000	**NY Islanders**	**NHL**	**49**	**12**	**14**	**26**	**41**	**2**	**0**	**3**	**109**	**11.0**	**–7**	**12**	**50.0**	**13:36**	....	....	....	....	....	....	....	....	....
	Lowell	AHL	17	6	2	8	19	....	....	....	....	....	....	....	....	....	....	....	....	....	....	....	....	....	....
2000-01	Hamilton	AHL	2	2	0	2	2	....	....	....	....	....	....	....	....	....	....	....	....	....	....	....	....	....	....
	Edmonton	**NHL**	....	....	....	....	....	....	....	....	....	....	....	....	....	....	**3**	**0**	**0**	**0**	**0**	**0**	**0**	**0**	**7:55**
2001-02	**Edmonton**	**NHL**	**61**	**10**	**5**	**15**	**52**	**1**	**0**	**1**	**78**	**12.8**	**9**	**18**	**38.9**	**10:05**	....	....	....	....	....	....	....	....	....
2002-03	**Edmonton**	**NHL**	**20**	**0**	**2**	**2**	**12**	**0**	**0**	**0**	**20**	**0.0**	**–3**	**5**	**0.0**	**10:22**	....	....	....	....	....	....	....	....	....
	NY Rangers	**NHL**	**4**	**0**	**0**	**0**	**2**	**0**	**0**	**0**	**3**	**0.0**	**–1**	**0**	**0.0**	**9:06**	....	....	....	....	....	....	....	....	....
	Washington	**NHL**	**21**	**1**	**2**	**3**	**7**	**0**	**0**	**0**	**20**	**5.0**	**1**	**3**	**0.0**	**8:07**	....	....	....	....	....	....	....	....	....
2003-04	**Calgary**	**NHL**	**36**	**2**	**4**	**6**	**24**	**0**	**0**	**0**	**47**	**4.3**	**–3**	**39**	**30.8**	**11:18**	....	....	....	....	....	....	....	....	....
	Lowell	AHL	22	6	9	15	46	....	....	....	....	....	....	....	....	....	....	....	....	....	....	....	....	....	....
	NY Rangers	**NHL**	**14**	**3**	**2**	**5**	**8**	**0**	**0**	**1**	**29**	**10.3**	**0**	**9**	**55.6**	**14:16**	....	....	....	....	....	....	....	....	....
2004-05	Manitoba Moose	AHL	67	21	19	40	72	....	....	....	....	....	....	....	....	....	14	9	5	14	26	....	....	....	....
	NHL Totals		**232**	**29**	**32**	**61**	**154**	**4**	**0**	**5**	**341**	**8.5**		**88**	**35.2**	**11:17**	**3**	**0**	**0**	**0**	**0**	**0**	**0**	**0**	**7:55**

Traded to **NY Islanders** by **Los Angeles** with Olli Jokinen, Mathieu Biron and Los Angeles' 1st round choice (Taylor Pyatt) in 1999 Entry Draft for Ziggy Palffy, Brian Smolinski, Marcel Cousineau and New Jersey's 4th round choice (previously acquired, Los Angeles selected Daniel Johansson) in 1999 Entry Draft, June 20, 1999. Traded to **Edmonton** by **NY Islanders** with Eric Brewer and NY Islanders' 2nd round choice (Brad Winchester) in 2000 Entry Draft for Roman Hamrlik, June 24, 2000. • Missed majority of 2000-01 season recovering from shoulder injury suffered in game vs. Detroit, October 10, 2000. Traded to **NY Rangers** by **Edmonton** for future considerations, December 12, 2002. Claimed on waivers by **Washington** from **NY Rangers**, January 15, 2003. Signed as a free agent by **Calgary**, July 17, 2003. Claimed on waivers by **NY Rangers** from **Calgary**, March 6, 2004. Signed to a PTO (tryout) contract by **Manitoba** (AHL), September 27, 2004. Signed as a free agent by **Vancouver**, August 23, 2005.

GREEN, Mike (GREEN, MIGHK)

Center. Shoots right. 5'11", 192 lbs. Born, Calgary, Alta., August 23, 1979.

Season	Club	League	GP	G	A	Pts	PIM	PP	SH	GW	S	%	+/-	TF	F%	Min	GP	G	A	Pts	PIM	PP	SH	GW	Min
1996-97	Cgy. North Stars	AMHL	35	34	27	61	78	....	....	....	....	....	....	....	....	....	....	....	....	....	....	....	....	....	....
	Edmonton Ice	WHL	7	0	2	2	0	....	....	....	....	....	....	....	....	....	....	....	....	....	....	....	....	....	....
1997-98	Edmonton Ice	WHL	71	15	26	41	16	....	....	....	....	....	....	....	....	....	....	....	....	....	....	....	....	....	....
1998-99	Kootenay Ice	WHL	71	35	45	80	37	....	....	....	....	....	....	....	....	....	7	2	2	4	4	....	....	....	....
99-2000	Kootenay Ice	WHL	69	43	49	92	63	....	....	....	....	....	....	....	....	....	21	9	16	25	20	....	....	....	....
2000-01	Port Huron	UHL	11	1	5	6	6	....	....	....	....	....	....	....	....	....	....	....	....	....	....	....	....	....	....
	Louisville Panthers	AHL	24	2	1	3	4	....	....	....	....	....	....	....	....	....	....	....	....	....	....	....	....	....	....
	Knoxville Speed	UHL	48	18	24	42	35	....	....	....	....	....	....	....	....	....	1	0	0	0	0	....	....	....	....
2001-02	Macon Whoopee	ECHL	54	27	35	62	18	....	....	....	....	....	....	....	....	....	....	....	....	....	....	....	....	....	....
	Cincinnati	AHL	22	2	9	11	4	....	....	....	....	....	....	....	....	....	3	0	0	0	0	....	....	....	....
2002-03	San Antonio	AHL	80	26	34	60	25	....	....	....	....	....	....	....	....	....	3	0	2	2	0	....	....	....	....
2003-04	**Florida**	**NHL**	**11**	**0**	**1**	**1**	**2**	**0**	**0**	**0**	**7**	**0.0**	**0**	**42**	**47.6**	**8:16**	....	....	....	....	....	....	....	....	....
	San Antonio	AHL	45	12	23	35	16	....	....	....	....	....	....	....	....	....	....	....	....	....	....	....	....	....	....
	NY Rangers	**NHL**	**13**	**1**	**2**	**3**	**2**	**0**	**0**	**0**	**13**	**7.7**	**0**	**98**	**39.8**	**9:53**	....	....	....	....	....	....	....	....	....
2004-05	Nurnberg	Germany	44	11	17	28	38	....	....	....	....	....	....	....	....	....	6	1	3	4	0	....	....	....	....
	NHL Totals		**24**	**1**	**3**	**4**	**4**	**0**	**0**	**0**	**20**	**5.0**		**140**	**42.1**	**9:08**	....	....	....	....	....	....	....	....	....

WHL East Second All-Star Team (2000)

Signed as a free agent by **Florida**, April 7, 2000. Claimed on waivers by **NY Rangers** from **Florida**, March 9, 2004. Signed as a free agent by **Nurnberg** (Germany), August 2, 2004.

GREEN, Travis (GREEN, TRA-vihs) BOS.

Center. Shoots right. 6'2", 200 lbs. Born, Castlegar, B.C., December 20, 1970. NY Islanders' 2nd choice, 23rd overall, in 1989 Entry Draft.

Season	Club	League	GP	G	A	Pts	PIM	PP	SH	GW	S	%	+/-	TF	F%	Min	GP	G	A	Pts	PIM	PP	SH	GW	Min
1985-86	Castlegar Rebels	KIJHL	35	30	40	70	41	....	....	....	....	....	....	....	....	....	....	....	....	....	....	....	....	....	....
1986-87	Spokane Chiefs	WHL	64	8	17	25	27	....	....	....	....	....	....	....	....	....	3	0	0	0	0	....	....	....	....
1987-88	Spokane Chiefs	WHL	72	33	54	87	42	....	....	....	....	....	....	....	....	....	15	10	10	20	13	....	....	....	....
1988-89	Spokane Chiefs	WHL	75	51	51	102	79	....	....	....	....	....	....	....	....	....	....	....	....	....	....	....	....	....	....
1989-90	Spokane Chiefs	WHL	50	45	44	89	80	....	....	....	....	....	....	....	....	....	....	....	....	....	....	....	....	....	....
	Medicine Hat	WHL	25	15	24	39	19	....	....	....	....	....	....	....	....	....	3	0	0	0	2	....	....	....	....
1990-91	Capital District	AHL	73	21	34	55	26	....	....	....	....	....	....	....	....	....	....	....	....	....	....	....	....	....	....
1991-92	Capital District	AHL	71	23	27	50	10	....	....	....	....	....	....	....	....	....	7	0	4	4	21	....	....	....	....
1992-93	**NY Islanders**	**NHL**	**61**	**7**	**18**	**25**	**43**	**1**	**0**	**0**	**115**	**6.1**	**4**	....	....	....	**12**	**3**	**1**	**4**	**6**	**0**	**0**	**0**	....
	Capital District	AHL	20	12	11	23	39	....	....	....	....	....	....	....	....	....	....	....	....	....	....	....	....	....	....
1993-94	**NY Islanders**	**NHL**	**83**	**18**	**22**	**40**	**44**	**1**	**0**	**2**	**164**	**11.0**	**16**	....	....	....	**4**	**0**	**0**	**0**	**2**	**0**	**0**	**0**	....
1994-95	**NY Islanders**	**NHL**	**42**	**5**	**7**	**12**	**25**	**0**	**0**	**0**	**59**	**8.5**	**–10**	....	....	....	....	....	....	....	....	....	....	....	....
1995-96	**NY Islanders**	**NHL**	**69**	**25**	**45**	**70**	**42**	**14**	**1**	**2**	**186**	**13.4**	**–20**	....	....	....	....	....	....	....	....	....	....	....	....
1996-97	**NY Islanders**	**NHL**	**79**	**23**	**41**	**64**	**38**	**10**	**0**	**3**	**177**	**13.0**	**–5**	....	....	....	....	....	....	....	....	....	....	....	....
1997-98	**NY Islanders**	**NHL**	**54**	**14**	**12**	**26**	**66**	**8**	**0**	**2**	**99**	**14.1**	**–19**	....	....	....	....	....	....	....	....	....	....	....	....
	Anaheim	**NHL**	**22**	**5**	**11**	**16**	**16**	**1**	**0**	**0**	**42**	**11.9**	**–10**	....	....	....	....	....	....	....	....	....	....	....	....
1998-99	**Anaheim**	**NHL**	**79**	**13**	**17**	**30**	**81**	**3**	**1**	**2**	**165**	**7.9**	**–7**	**1325**	**52.8**	**17:17**	**4**	**0**	**1**	**1**	**4**	**0**	**0**	**0**	**15:02**
99-2000	**Phoenix**	**NHL**	**78**	**25**	**21**	**46**	**45**	**6**	**0**	**2**	**157**	**15.9**	**–4**	**1322**	**55.6**	**16:36**	**5**	**2**	**1**	**3**	**2**	**0**	**0**	**0**	**17:23**
2000-01	**Phoenix**	**NHL**	**69**	**13**	**15**	**28**	**63**	**3**	**0**	**0**	**113**	**11.5**	**–11**	**1135**	**54.9**	**16:05**	....	....	....	....	....	....	....	....	....
2001-02	**Toronto**	**NHL**	**82**	**11**	**23**	**34**	**61**	**3**	**0**	**2**	**119**	**9.2**	**13**	**647**	**54.1**	**14:32**	**20**	**3**	**6**	**9**	**34**	**0**	**0**	**1**	**20:34**
2002-03	**Toronto**	**NHL**	**75**	**12**	**12**	**24**	**67**	**2**	**1**	**3**	**86**	**14.0**	**2**	**802**	**53.5**	**12:57**	**4**	**2**	**1**	**3**	**4**	**0**	**1**	**1**	**18:08**
2003-04	**Boston**	**NHL**	**64**	**11**	**5**	**16**	**67**	**2**	**0**	**2**	**104**	**10.6**	**–6**	**845**	**55.6**	**15:17**	**7**	**0**	**1**	**1**	**8**	**0**	**0**	**0**	**15:37**
2004-05			DID NOT PLAY																						
	NHL Totals		**857**	**182**	**249**	**431**	**658**	**54**	**3**	**20**	**1586**	**11.5**		**6076**	**54.4**	**15:28**	**56**	**10**	**11**	**21**	**60**	**0**	**1**	**2**	**18:30**

Traded to **Anaheim** by **NY Islanders** with Doug Houda and Tony Tuzzolino for Joe Sacco, J.J. Daigneault and Mark Janssens, February 6, 1998. Traded to **Phoenix** by **Anaheim** with Anaheim's 1st round choice (Scott Kelman) in 1999 Entry Draft for Oleg Tverdovsky, June 26, 1999. Traded to **Toronto** by **Phoenix** with Robert Reichel and Craig Mills for Danny Markov, June 12, 2001. Claimed by **Columbus** from **Toronto** in Waiver Draft, October 3, 2003. Traded to **Boston** by **Columbus** for Boston's 6th round choice (Lennart Petrell) in 2004 Entry Draft, October 3, 2003.

GRENIER, Martin (GREH-nyay, MAHR-tihn) NYR

Defense. Shoots left. 6'5", 255 lbs. Born, Laval, Que., November 2, 1980. Colorado's 2nd choice, 45th overall, in 1999 Entry Draft.

Season	Club	League	GP	G	A	Pts	PIM	PP	SH	GW	S	%	+/-	TF	F%	Min	GP	G	A	Pts	PIM	PP	SH	GW	Min
1996-97	Laval-Laurentides	QAAA	34	3	16	19	117	....	....	....	....	....	....	....	....	....	13	0	4	4	....	....	....	....	....
1997-98	Quebec Remparts	QMJHL	61	4	11	15	202	....	....	....	....	....	....	....	....	....	14	0	2	2	36	....	....	....	....
1998-99	Quebec Remparts	QMJHL	60	7	18	25	*479	....	....	....	....	....	....	....	....	....	13	0	4	4	29	....	....	....	....
99-2000	Quebec Remparts	QMJHL	67	11	35	46	302	....	....	....	....	....	....	....	....	....	7	1	4	5	27	....	....	....	....
2000-01	Quebec Remparts	QMJHL	26	5	16	21	82	....	....	....	....	....	....	....	....	....	....	....	....	....	....	....	....	....	....
	Victoriaville Tigres	QMJHL	28	9	19	28	108	....	....	....	....	....	....	....	....	....	13	2	8	10	51	....	....	....	....

			Regular Season														Playoffs								
Season	Club	League	GP	G	A	Pts	PIM	PP	SH	GW	S	%	+/-	TF	F%	Min	GP	G	A	Pts	PIM	PP	SH	GW	Min
2001-02	Phoenix	NHL	5	0	0	0	5	0	0	0	1	0.0	0	1	100.0	5:56	....	....	....	....	....	....	....	....	....
	Springfield	AHL	69	2	6	8	241	....	....	....	....	....	....	....	....	....	....	....	....	....	....	....	....	....	....
2002-03	Phoenix	NHL	3	0	0	0	0	0	0	0	0	0.0	−1	0	0.0	6:11	....	....	....	....	....	....	....	....	....
	Springfield	AHL	73	2	10	12	232	....	....	....	....	....	....	....	....	....	6	0	1	1	12	....	....	....	....
2003-04	Vancouver	NHL	7	1	0	1	9	0	0	0	6	16.7	3	0	0.0	6:50	....	....	....	....	....	....	....	....	....
	Manitoba Moose	AHL	38	5	4	9	145	....	....	....	....	....	....	....	....	....	....	....	....	....	....	....	....	....	....
	Hartford	AHL	12	0	2	2	105	....	....	....	....	....	....	....	....	....	9	0	1	1	32	....	....	....	....
2004-05	Charlotte	ECHL	4	0	2	2	10	....	....	....	....	....	....	....	....	....	....	....	....	....	....	....	....	....	....
	Hartford	AHL	23	2	5	7	136	....	....	....	....	....	....	....	....	....	5	0	0	0	32	....	....	....	....
	NHL Totals		15	1	0	1	14	0	0	0	7	14.3		1	100.0	6:24	....	....	....	....	....	....	....	....	....

Traded to **Boston** by **Colorado** with Brian Rolston, Samuel Pahlsson and New Jersey's 1st round choice (previously acquired, Boston selected Martin Samuelsson) in 2000 Entry Draft for Raymond Bourque and Dave Andreychuk, March 6, 2000. Signed as a free agent by **Phoenix**, June 27, 2001. Traded to **Vancouver** by **Phoenix** for Bryan Helmer, July 25, 2003. Traded to **NY Rangers** by **Vancouver** with R.J. Umberger for Martin Rucinsky, March 9, 2004.

GRIER, Mike

(GREER, MIGHK) **BUF.**

Right wing. Shoots right. 6'1", 227 lbs. Born, Detroit, MI, January 5, 1975. St. Louis' 7th choice, 219th overall, in 1993 Entry Draft.

Season	Club	League	GP	G	A	Pts	PIM	PP	SH	GW	S	%	+/-	TF	F%	Min	GP	G	A	Pts	PIM	PP	SH	GW	Min
1992-93	St. Sebastian's	High-MA	22	16	27	43	32	....	....	....	....	....	....	....	....	....	....	....	....	....	....	....	....	....	....
1993-94	Boston University	H-East	39	9	9	18	56	....	....	....	....	....	....	....	....	....	....	....	....	....	....	....	....	....	....
1994-95	Boston University	H-East	37	*29	26	55	85	....	....	....	....	....	....	....	....	....	....	....	....	....	....	....	....	....	....
1995-96	Boston University	H-East	38	21	25	46	82	....	....	....	....	....	....	....	....	....	....	....	....	....	....	....	....	....	....
1996-97	Edmonton	NHL	79	15	17	32	45	4	0	2	89	16.9	7	....	....	....	12	3	1	4	4	1	0	1	....
1997-98	Edmonton	NHL	66	9	6	15	73	1	0	1	90	10.0	−3	....	....	....	12	2	2	4	13	0	0	1	....
1998-99	Edmonton	NHL	82	20	24	44	54	3	2	1	143	14.0	5	34	20.6	15:57	4	1	1	2	6	0	0	0	23:26
99-2000	Edmonton	NHL	65	9	22	31	68	0	3	2	115	7.8	9	32	46.8	15:45	....	....	....	....	....	....	....	....	....
2000-01	Edmonton	NHL	74	20	16	36	20	2	3	2	124	16.1	11	36	38.9	16:44	6	0	0	0	8	0	0	0	21:23
2001-02	Edmonton	NHL	82	8	17	25	32	0	2	3	112	7.1	1	38	47.4	15:01	....	....	....	....	....	....	....	....	....
2002-03	Washington	NHL	82	15	17	32	36	2	2	2	133	11.3	−14	98	43.9	17:48	6	1	1	2	2	0	0	0	17:59
2003-04	Washington	NHL	68	8	12	20	32	1	1	0	115	7.0	−19	54	44.4	17:25	....	....	....	....	....	....	....	....	....
	Buffalo	NHL	14	1	8	9	4	0	0	0	18	5.6	10	11	63.6	17:29	....	....	....	....	....	....	....	....	....
2004-05			DID NOT PLAY																						
	NHL Totals		612	105	139	244	364	13	13	13	939	11.2		303	42.2	16:28	40	7	5	12	33	1	0	2	20:37

Hockey East First All-Star Team (1995) • NCAA East First All-American Team (1995)

Rights traded to **Edmonton** by **St. Louis** with Curtis Joseph for St. Louis' 1st round choices in 1996 (previously acquired, St. Louis selected Marty Reasoner) and 1997 (previously acquired, later traded to Los Angeles – Los Angeles selected Matt Zultek) Entry Drafts, August 4, 1995. Traded to **Washington** by **Edmonton** for Washington's 2nd round choice (later traded to NY Islanders – NY Islanders selected Evgeni Tunik) in 2003 Entry Draft and Vancouver's 3rd round choice (previously acquired, Edmonton selected Zachery Stortini) in 2003 Entry Draft, October 7, 2002. Traded to **Buffalo** by **Washington** for Jakub Klepis, March 9, 2004.

GROSEK, Michal

(GROH-shehk, MIGH-kuhl)

Left wing. Shoots right. 6'2", 207 lbs. Born, Vyskov, Czech., June 1, 1975. Winnipeg's 7th choice, 145th overall, in 1993 Entry Draft.

Season	Club	League	GP	G	A	Pts	PIM	PP	SH	GW	S	%	+/-	TF	F%	Min	GP	G	A	Pts	PIM	PP	SH	GW	Min
1992-93	AC ZPS Zlin	Czech	17	1	3	4	....	....	....	....	....	....	....	....	....	....	....	....	....	....	....	....	....	....	....
1993-94	Tacoma Rockets	WHL	30	25	20	45	106	....	....	....	....	....	....	....	....	....	7	2	2	4	30	....	....	....	....
	Winnipeg	NHL	3	1	0	1	0	0	0	0	4	25.0	−1	....	....	....	....	....	....	....	....	....	....	....	....
	Moncton Hawks	AHL	20	1	2	3	47	....	....	....	....	....	....	....	....	....	2	0	0	0	0	....	....	....	....
1994-95	Springfield	AHL	45	10	22	32	98	....	....	....	....	....	....	....	....	....	....	....	....	....	....	....	....	....	....
	Winnipeg	NHL	24	2	2	4	21	0	0	1	27	7.4	−3	....	....	....	....	....	....	....	....	....	....	....	....
1995-96	Winnipeg	NHL	1	0	0	0	0	0	0	0	1	0.0	−1	....	....	....	....	....	....	....	....	....	....	....	....
	Springfield	AHL	39	16	19	35	68	....	....	....	....	....	....	....	....	....	....	....	....	....	....	....	....	....	....
	Buffalo	NHL	22	6	4	10	31	2	0	1	33	18.2	0	....	....	....	....	....	....	....	....	....	....	....	....
1996-97	Buffalo	NHL	82	15	21	36	71	1	0	2	117	12.8	25	....	....	....	12	3	3	6	8	0	0	0	....
1997-98	Buffalo	NHL	67	10	20	30	60	2	0	1	114	8.8	9	....	....	....	15	6	4	10	28	2	0	3	....
1998-99	Buffalo	NHL	76	20	30	50	102	4	0	3	140	14.3	21	5	60.0	17:14	13	0	4	4	28	0	0	0	11:51
99-2000	Buffalo	NHL	61	11	23	34	35	2	0	2	96	11.5	12	8	25.0	16:17	....	....	....	....	....	....	....	....	....
	Chicago	NHL	14	2	4	6	12	1	0	0	18	11.1	−1	1	0.0	13:06	....	....	....	....	....	....	....	....	....
2000-01	NY Rangers	NHL	65	9	11	20	61	2	0	0	84	10.7	−10	14	28.6	11:05	....	....	....	....	....	....	....	....	....
	Hartford	AHL	12	8	7	15	12	....	....	....	....	....	....	....	....	....	....	....	....	....	....	....	....	....	....
2001-02	NY Rangers	NHL	15	3	2	5	12	0	0	0	23	13.0	−3	2	0.0	12:24	....	....	....	....	....	....	....	....	....
	Hartford	AHL	48	14	30	44	167	....	....	....	....	....	....	....	....	....	....	....	....	....	....	....	....	....	....
2002-03	Boston	NHL	63	2	18	20	71	0	0	1	74	2.7	2	95	43.2	10:43	5	0	0	0	13	0	0	0	6:12
2003-04	Boston	NHL	33	3	2	5	33	0	0	0	24	12.5	1	82	51.2	6:14	....	....	....	....	....	....	....	....	....
2004-05	Geneve	Swiss	41	15	21	36	149	....	....	....	....	....	....	....	....	....	....	....	....	....	....	....	....	....	....
	NHL Totals		526	84	137	221	509	14	0	11	755	11.1		207	44.4	13:04	45	9	11	20	77	2	0	3	10:17

Traded to **Buffalo** by **Winnipeg** with Darryl Shannon for Craig Muni, February 15, 1996. Traded to **Chicago** by **Buffalo** for Doug Gilmour, J.P. Dumont and future considerations, March 10, 2000. Traded to **NY Rangers** by **Chicago** with Brad Brown for future considerations, October 5, 2000. Signed as a free agent by **Boston**, July 16, 2002. • Missed majority of 2003-04 season recovering from head injury suffered in game vs. Detroit, January 10, 2004. Signed as a free agent by **Geneve** (Swiss), August 9, 2004.

GRUDEN, John

(GROO-duhn, JAWN)

Defense. Shoots left. 6', 203 lbs. Born, Virginia, MN, June 4, 1970. Boston's 7th choice, 168th overall, in 1990 Entry Draft.

Season	Club	League	GP	G	A	Pts	PIM	PP	SH	GW	S	%	+/-	TF	F%	Min	GP	G	A	Pts	PIM	PP	SH	GW	Min
1989-90	Waterloo	USHL	47	7	39	46	35	....	....	....	....	....	....	....	....	....	....	....	....	....	....	....	....	....	....
1990-91	Ferris State	CCHA	37	4	11	15	27	....	....	....	....	....	....	....	....	....	....	....	....	....	....	....	....	....	....
1991-92	Ferris State	CCHA	37	9	14	23	24	....	....	....	....	....	....	....	....	....	....	....	....	....	....	....	....	....	....
1992-93	Ferris State	CCHA	41	16	14	30	58	....	....	....	....	....	....	....	....	....	....	....	....	....	....	....	....	....	....
1993-94	Ferris State	CCHA	38	11	25	36	52	....	....	....	....	....	....	....	....	....	....	....	....	....	....	....	....	....	....
	Boston	NHL	7	0	1	1	2	0	0	0	8	0.0	−3	....	....	....	....	....	....	....	....	....	....	....	....
1994-95	Boston	NHL	38	0	6	6	22	0	0	0	30	0.0	3	....	....	....	....	....	....	....	....	....	....	....	....
	Providence Bruins	AHL	1	0	1	1	0	....	....	....	....	....	....	....	....	....	....	....	....	....	....	....	....	....	....
1995-96	Boston	NHL	14	0	0	0	4	0	0	0	12	0.0	−3	....	....	....	3	0	1	1	0	0	0	0	....
	Providence Bruins	AHL	39	5	19	24	29	....	....	....	....	....	....	....	....	....	....	....	....	....	....	....	....	....	....
1996-97	Providence Bruins	AHL	78	18	27	45	52	....	....	....	....	....	....	....	....	....	10	3	6	9	4	....	....	....	....
1997-98	Detroit Vipers	IHL	76	13	42	55	74	....	....	....	....	....	....	....	....	....	21	1	8	9	14	....	....	....	....
1998-99	Ottawa	NHL	13	0	1	1	8	0	0	0	10	0.0	0	0	0.0	13:07	....	....	....	....	....	....	....	....	....
	Detroit Vipers	IHL	59	10	28	38	52	....	....	....	....	....	....	....	....	....	10	0	1	1	6	....	....	....	....
99-2000	Ottawa	NHL	9	0	0	0	4	0	0	0	3	0.0	0	0	0.0	16:29	....	....	....	....	....	....	....	....	....
	Grand Rapids	IHL	50	5	17	22	24	....	....	....	....	....	....	....	....	....	12	1	4	5	8	....	....	....	....
2000-01	Grand Rapids	IHL	34	2	6	8	18	....	....	....	....	....	....	....	....	....	10	1	4	5	8	....	....	....	....
2001-02	Grand Rapids	AHL	57	3	14	17	48	....	....	....	....	....	....	....	....	....	5	1	0	1	2	....	....	....	....
2002-03	Eisbaren Berlin	Germany	38	6	25	31	34	....	....	....	....	....	....	....	....	....	9	2	6	8	4	....	....	....	....
2003-04	Washington	NHL	11	1	0	1	6	0	0	1	7	14.3	−1	0	0.0	13:18	....	....	....	....	....	....	....	....	....
2004-05			DID NOT PLAY																						
	NHL Totals		92	1	8	9	46	0	0	1	70	1.4		0	0.0	14:06	3	0	1	1	0	0	0	0	....

CCHA First All-Star Team (1994) • NCAA West First All-American Team (1994) • IHL Second All-Star Team (1998) • AHL First All-Star Team (2002)

Signed as a free agent by **Ottawa**, August 7, 1998. • Missed majority of 2000-01 season recovering from shoulder injury suffered in training camp, October 1, 2000. Signed as a free agent by **Eisbaren Berlin** (Germany), May 3, 2002. Signed as a free agent by **Washington**, July 18, 2003. • Missed majority of 2003-04 season recovering from head injury suffered in game vs. Los Angeles, November 10, 2003.

GUERIN, Bill

(GAIR-ihn, BIHL) **DAL.**

Right wing. Shoots right. 6'2", 210 lbs. Born, Worcester, MA, November 9, 1970. New Jersey's 1st choice, 5th overall, in 1989 Entry Draft.

Season	Club	League	GP	G	A	Pts	PIM	PP	SH	GW	S	%	+/-	TF	F%	Min	GP	G	A	Pts	PIM	PP	SH	GW	Min
1985-86	Spring. Olympics	NEJHL	48	26	19	45	71	....	....	....	....	....	....	....	....	....	....	....	....	....	....	....	....	....	....
1986-87	Spring. Olympics	NEJHL	32	34	20	54	40	....	....	....	....	....	....	....	....	....	....	....	....	....	....	....	....	....	....
1987-88	Spring. Olympics	NEJHL	38	31	44	75	146	....	....	....	....	....	....	....	....	....	....	....	....	....	....	....	....	....	....
1988-89	Spring. Olympics	NEJHL	31	32	35	67	90	....	....	....	....	....	....	....	....	....	....	....	....	....	....	....	....	....	....
1989-90	Boston College	H-East	39	14	11	25	54	....	....	....	....	....	....	....	....	....	....	....	....	....	....	....	....	....	....
1990-91	Boston College	H-East	38	26	19	45	102	....	....	....	....	....	....	....	....	....	....	....	....	....	....	....	....	....	....
1991-92	United States	Nat-Tm	46	12	15	27	67	....	....	....	....	....	....	....	....	....	....	....	....	....	....	....	....	....	....
	New Jersey	NHL	5	0	1	1	9	0	0	0	8	0.0	1	....	....	....	6	3	0	3	4	0	0	0	....
	Utica Devils	AHL	22	13	10	23	6	....	....	....	....	....	....	....	....	....	4	1	3	4	14	....	....	....	....

			Regular Season														Playoffs								
Season	Club	League	GP	G	A	Pts	PIM	PP	SH	GW	S	%	+/-	TF	F%	Min	GP	G	A	Pts	PIM	PP	SH	GW	Min
1992-93	**New Jersey**	**NHL**	**65**	**14**	**20**	**34**	**63**	**0**	**0**	**2**	**123**	**11.4**	**14**	....	....	....	**5**	**1**	**1**	**2**	**4**	**0**	**0**	**0**	....
	Utica Devils	AHL	18	10	7	17	47	....	....	....	....	....	....	....	....	....	....	....	....	....	....	....	....	....	....
1993-94	**New Jersey**	**NHL**	**81**	**25**	**19**	**44**	**101**	**2**	**0**	**3**	**195**	**12.8**	**14**	....	....	....	**17**	**2**	**1**	**3**	**35**	**0**	**0**	**1**	....
1994-95♦	**New Jersey**	**NHL**	**48**	**12**	**13**	**25**	**72**	**4**	**0**	**3**	**96**	**12.5**	**6**	....	....	....	**20**	**3**	**8**	**11**	**30**	**1**	**0**	**0**	....
1995-96	**New Jersey**	**NHL**	**80**	**23**	**30**	**53**	**116**	**8**	**0**	**6**	**216**	**10.6**	**7**	....	....	....	....	....	....	....	....	....	....	....	....
1996-97	**New Jersey**	**NHL**	**82**	**29**	**18**	**47**	**95**	**7**	**0**	**9**	**177**	**16.4**	**–2**	....	....	....	**8**	**2**	**1**	**3**	**18**	**1**	**0**	**1**	....
1997-98	**New Jersey**	**NHL**	**19**	**5**	**5**	**10**	**13**	**1**	**0**	**2**	**48**	**10.4**	**0**	....	....	....	....	....	....	....	....	....	....	....	....
	Edmonton	**NHL**	**40**	**13**	**16**	**29**	**80**	**8**	**0**	**2**	**130**	**10.0**	**1**	....	....	....	**12**	**7**	**1**	**8**	**17**	**4**	**0**	**0**	....
	United States	Olympics	4	0	3	3	2	....	....	....	....	....	....	....	....	....	....	....	....	....	....	....	....	....	....
1998-99	**Edmonton**	**NHL**	**80**	**30**	**34**	**64**	**133**	**13**	**0**	**2**	**261**	**11.5**	**7**	**74**	**40.5**	**19:42**	**3**	**0**	**2**	**2**	**2**	**0**	**0**	**0**	**26:14**
99-2000	**Edmonton**	**NHL**	**70**	**24**	**22**	**46**	**123**	**11**	**0**	**2**	**188**	**12.8**	**4**	**13**	**46.2**	**18:01**	**5**	**3**	**2**	**5**	**9**	**1**	**0**	**0**	**17:55**
2000-01	**Edmonton**	**NHL**	**21**	**12**	**10**	**22**	**18**	**4**	**0**	**1**	**64**	**18.8**	**11**	**0**	**0.0**	**19:49**	....	....	....	....	....	....	....	....	....
	Boston	**NHL**	**64**	**28**	**35**	**63**	**122**	**7**	**1**	**4**	**225**	**12.4**	**–4**	**36**	**41.7**	**22:43**	....	....	....	....	....	....	....	....	....
2001-02	**Boston**	**NHL**	**78**	**41**	**25**	**66**	**91**	**10**	**1**	**7**	**355**	**11.5**	**–1**	**17**	**52.9**	**20:45**	**6**	**4**	**2**	**6**	**6**	**3**	**0**	**0**	**21:17**
	United States	Olympics	6	4	0	4	4	....	....	....	....	....	....	....	....	....	....	....	....	....	....	....	....	....	....
2002-03	**Dallas**	**NHL**	**64**	**25**	**25**	**50**	**113**	**11**	**0**	**2**	**229**	**10.9**	**5**	**20**	**25.0**	**18:33**	**4**	**0**	**0**	**0**	**4**	**0**	**0**	**0**	**8:34**
2003-04	**Dallas**	**NHL**	**82**	**34**	**35**	**69**	**109**	**9**	**0**	**10**	**263**	**12.9**	**14**	**16**	**18.8**	**18:42**	**5**	**0**	**1**	**1**	**4**	**0**	**0**	**0**	**20:09**
2004-05		DID NOT PLAY																							
	NHL Totals		**879**	**315**	**308**	**623**	**1258**	**95**	**2**	**55**	**2578**	**12.2**		**176**	**38.6**	**19:42**	**91**	**25**	**19**	**44**	**133**	**10**	**0**	**2**	**18:44**

NHL Second All-Star Team (2002)

Played in NHL All-Star Game (2001, 2003, 2004)

Traded to **Edmonton** by **New Jersey** with Valeri Zelepukin for Jason Arnott and Bryan Muir, January 4, 1998. Traded to **Boston** by **Edmonton** for Anson Carter, Boston's 1st (Ales Hemsky) and 2nd (Doug Lynch) round choices in 2001 Entry Draft and future considerations, November 15, 2000. Signed as a free agent by **Dallas**, July 3, 2002.

GUOLLA, Steve

(GUH-wah-lah, STEEV)

Center. Shoots left. 6', 190 lbs. Born, Scarborough, Ont., March 15, 1973. Ottawa's 1st choice, 3rd overall, in 1994 Supplemental Draft.

Season	Club	League	GP	G	A	Pts	PIM	PP	SH	GW	S	%	+/-	TF	F%	Min	GP	G	A	Pts	PIM	PP	SH	GW	Min
1988-89	Tor. Red Wings	MTHL	25	14	20	34	....	....	....	....	....	....	....	....	....	....	....	....	....	....	....	....	....	....	....
1989-90	Tor. Red Wings	MTHL	40	42	47	89	....	....	....	....	....	....	....	....	....	....	....	....	....	....	....	....	....	....	....
1990-91	Wexford Raiders	OHA-B	44	34	44	78	34	....	....	....	....	....	....	....	....	....	12	12	16	28	....	....	....	....	....
1991-92	Michigan State	CCHA	33	4	9	13	8	....	....	....	....	....	....	....	....	....	....	....	....	....	....	....	....	....	....
1992-93	Michigan State	CCHA	39	19	35	54	6	....	....	....	....	....	....	....	....	....	....	....	....	....	....	....	....	....	....
1993-94	Michigan State	CCHA	41	23	46	69	16	....	....	....	....	....	....	....	....	....	....	....	....	....	....	....	....	....	....
1994-95	Michigan State	CCHA	40	16	35	51	16	....	....	....	....	....	....	....	....	....	....	....	....	....	....	....	....	....	....
1995-96	P.E.I. Senators	AHL	72	32	48	80	28	....	....	....	....	....	....	....	....	....	3	0	0	0	0	....	....	....	....
1996-97	**San Jose**	**NHL**	**43**	**13**	**8**	**21**	**14**	**2**	**0**	**1**	**81**	**16.0**	**–10**	....	....	....	....	....	....	....	....	....	....	....	....
	Kentucky	AHL	34	22	22	44	10	....	....	....	....	....	....	....	....	....	4	2	1	3	0	....	....	....	....
1997-98	**San Jose**	**NHL**	**7**	**1**	**1**	**2**	**0**	**0**	**0**	**0**	**9**	**11.1**	**–2**	....	....	....	....	....	....	....	....	....	....	....	....
	Kentucky	AHL	69	37	63	100	45	....	....	....	....	....	....	....	....	....	3	0	0	0	0	....	....	....	....
1998-99	**San Jose**	**NHL**	**14**	**2**	**2**	**4**	**6**	**0**	**0**	**1**	**22**	**9.1**	**3**	**172**	**36.6**	**13:54**	....	....	....	....	....	....	....	....	....
	Kentucky	AHL	53	29	47	76	33	....	....	....	....	....	....	....	....	....	....	....	....	....	....	....	....	....	....
99-2000	**Tampa Bay**	**NHL**	**46**	**6**	**10**	**16**	**11**	**2**	**0**	**0**	**52**	**11.5**	**2**	**155**	**45.8**	**11:26**	....	....	....	....	....	....	....	....	....
	Atlanta	**NHL**	**20**	**4**	**9**	**13**	**4**	**2**	**0**	**0**	**34**	**11.8**	**–13**	**345**	**42.6**	**17:47**	....	....	....	....	....	....	....	....	....
2000-01	**Atlanta**	**NHL**	**63**	**12**	**16**	**28**	**23**	**2**	**0**	**3**	**96**	**12.5**	**–6**	**859**	**47.7**	**14:41**	....	....	....	....	....	....	....	....	....
2001-02	Albany River Rats	AHL	68	25	35	60	27	....	....	....	....	....	....	....	....	....	....	....	....	....	....	....	....	....	....
2002-03	**New Jersey**	**NHL**	**12**	**2**	**0**	**2**	**2**	**0**	**0**	**0**	**6**	**33.3**	**1**	**61**	**41.0**	**8:00**	....	....	....	....	....	....	....	....	....
	Albany River Rats	AHL	22	11	17	28	4	....	....	....	....	....	....	....	....	....	....	....	....	....	....	....	....	....	....
2003-04	Albany River Rats	AHL	7	2	3	5	0	....	....	....	....	....	....	....	....	....	....	....	....	....	....	....	....	....	....
2004-05	Kloten Flyers	Swiss	12	4	9	13	4	....	....	....	....	....	....	....	....	....	....	....	....	....	....	....	....	....	....
	NHL Totals		**205**	**40**	**46**	**86**	**60**	**8**	**0**	**5**	**300**	**13.3**		**1592**	**45.0**	**13:32**	....	....	....	....	....	....	....	....	....

CCHA Second All-Star Team (1994) • NCAA West Second All-American Team (1994) • AHL Second All-Star Team (1998, 1999) • Les Cunningham Award (MVP – AHL) (1998)

Signed as a free agent by **San Jose**, August 22, 1996. Traded to **Tampa Bay** by **San Jose** with Bill Houlder, Shawn Burr and Andrei Zyuzin for Niklas Sundstrom and NY Rangers' 3rd round choice (previously acquired, later traded to Chicago – Chicago selected Igor Radulov) in 2000 Entry Draft, August 4, 1999. Claimed on waivers by **Atlanta** from **Tampa Bay**, March 1, 2000. Signed as a free agent by **New Jersey**, October 21, 2001. • Missed majority of 2002-03 and 2003-04 seasons recovering from back injury suffered in game vs. NY Islanders, November 27, 2002. Signed as a free agent by **Kloten** (Swiss), April 22, 2004.

GUREN, Miloslav

(GOO-rihn, MEER-oh-slahf) **MTL.**

Defense. Shoots left. 6'2", 215 lbs. Born, Uherske Hradiste, Czech., September 24, 1976. Montreal's 2nd choice, 60th overall, in 1995 Entry Draft.

Season	Club	League	GP	G	A	Pts	PIM	PP	SH	GW	S	%	+/-	TF	F%	Min	GP	G	A	Pts	PIM	PP	SH	GW	Min
1993-94	AC ZPS Zlin	CzRep	22	1	5	6	....	....	....	....	....	....	....	....	....	....	3	0	0	0	....	....	....	....	....
1994-95	AC ZPS Zlin	CzRep	32	3	7	10	10	....	....	....	....	....	....	....	....	....	12	1	0	1	6	....	....	....	....
1995-96	AC ZPS Zlin	CzRep	28	1	2	3	....	....	....	....	....	....	....	....	....	....	7	1	0	1	....	....	....	....	....
1996-97	Fredericton	AHL	79	6	26	32	26	....	....	....	....	....	....	....	....	....	....	....	....	....	....	....	....	....	....
1997-98	Fredericton	AHL	78	15	36	51	36	....	....	....	....	....	....	....	....	....	4	1	2	3	0	....	....	....	....
1998-99	**Montreal**	**NHL**	**12**	**0**	**1**	**1**	**4**	**0**	**0**	**0**	**11**	**0.0**	**–1**	**0**	**0.0**	**12:02**	....	....	....	....	....	....	....	....	....
	Fredericton	AHL	63	5	16	21	24	....	....	....	....	....	....	....	....	....	15	4	7	11	10	....	....	....	....
99-2000	**Montreal**	**NHL**	**24**	**1**	**2**	**3**	**12**	**1**	**0**	**0**	**20**	**5.0**	**–5**	**0**	**0.0**	**15:14**	....	....	....	....	....	....	....	....	....
	Quebec Citadelles	AHL	29	5	12	17	16	....	....	....	....	....	....	....	....	....	3	0	0	0	2	....	....	....	....
2000-01	Quebec Citadelles	AHL	75	11	40	51	24	....	....	....	....	....	....	....	....	....	8	4	2	6	6	....	....	....	....
2001-02	HC Ocelari Trinec	CzRep	52	2	9	11	44	....	....	....	....	....	....	....	....	....	6	1	2	3	9	....	....	....	....
2002-03	CSKA Moscow	Russia	39	2	7	9	14	....	....	....	....	....	....	....	....	....	....	....	....	....	....	....	....	....	....
2003-04	Sibir Novosibirsk	Russia	55	7	8	15	26	....	....	....	....	....	....	....	....	....	....	....	....	....	....	....	....	....	....
2004-05	Sibir Novosibirsk	Russia	30	5	2	7	22	....	....	....	....	....	....	....	....	....	....	....	....	....	....	....	....	....	....
	NHL Totals		**36**	**1**	**3**	**4**	**16**	**1**	**0**	**0**	**31**	**3.2**		**0**	**0.0**	**14:10**	....	....	....	....	....	....	....	....	....

HAAKANA, Kari

(HA-kuh-nuh, KAH-ree) **EDM.**

Defense. Shoots left. 6'1", 222 lbs. Born, Outokumpu, Finland, November 8, 1973. Edmonton's 9th choice, 248th overall, in 2001 Entry Draft.

Season	Club	League	GP	G	A	Pts	PIM	PP	SH	GW	S	%	+/-	TF	F%	Min	GP	G	A	Pts	PIM	PP	SH	GW	Min
1990-91	Kiekko-Espoo Jr.	Finland-Jr.	36	3	3	6	34	....	....	....	....	....	....	....	....	....	....	....	....	....	....	....	....	....	....
	Kiekko-Espoo	Finland-2	4	0	1	1	0	....	....	....	....	....	....	....	....	....	....	....	....	....	....	....	....	....	....
1991-92	Kiekko-Espoo Jr.	Finland-Jr.	26	0	4	4	34	....	....	....	....	....	....	....	....	....	....	....	....	....	....	....	....	....	....
1992-93	Lukko Rauma Jr.	Finland-Jr.	36	4	16	20	60	....	....	....	....	....	....	....	....	....	....	....	....	....	....	....	....	....	....
	Lukko Rauma	Finland	4	0	0	0	0	....	....	....	....	....	....	....	....	....	....	....	....	....	....	....	....	....	....
1993-94	Kiekko-Espoo Jr.	Finland-Jr.	5	0	2	2	2	....	....	....	....	....	....	....	....	....	....	....	....	....	....	....	....	....	....
	Kiekko-Espoo	Finland	47	3	2	5	40	....	....	....	....	....	....	....	....	....	....	....	....	....	....	....	....	....	....
1994-95	Kiekko-Espoo	Finland	48	4	3	7	54	....	....	....	....	....	....	....	....	....	4	0	0	0	0	....	....	....	....
1995-96	Kiekko-Espoo	Finland	45	1	7	8	48	....	....	....	....	....	....	....	....	....	....	....	....	....	....	....	....	....	....
1996-97	Kiekko-Espoo	Finland	48	0	12	12	69	....	....	....	....	....	....	....	....	....	....	....	....	....	....	....	....	....	....
1997-98	Kiekko-Espoo	Finland	47	4	1	5	59	....	....	....	....	....	....	....	....	....	8	0	1	1	6	....	....	....	....
1998-99	Rosenheim	Germany	51	1	9	10	58	....	....	....	....	....	....	....	....	....	....	....	....	....	....	....	....	....	....
99-2000	Rosenheim	Germany	51	3	5	8	46	....	....	....	....	....	....	....	....	....	10	1	4	5	28	....	....	....	....
2000-01	Jokerit Helsinki	Finland	52	2	8	10	98	....	....	....	....	....	....	....	....	....	5	0	0	0	2	....	....	....	....
2001-02	Hamilton	AHL	6	0	2	2	25	....	....	....	....	....	....	....	....	....	....	....	....	....	....	....	....	....	....
	Jokerit Helsinki	Finland	36	0	3	3	40	....	....	....	....	....	....	....	....	....	12	2	2	4	2	....	....	....	....
2002-03	**Edmonton**	**NHL**	**13**	**0**	**0**	**0**	**4**	**0**	**0**	**0**	**2**	**0.0**	**–2**	**0**	**0.0**	**7:55**	....	....	....	....	....	....	....	....	....
	Hamilton	AHL	12	0	4	4	12	....	....	....	....	....	....	....	....	....	14	1	2	3	6	....	....	....	....
2003-04	MODO	Sweden	31	1	3	4	50	....	....	....	....	....	....	....	....	....	6	0	0	0	12	....	....	....	....
2004-05	Blues Espoo	Finland	47	1	9	10	52	....	....	....	....	....	....	....	....	....	....	....	....	....	....	....	....	....	....
	NHL Totals		**13**	**0**	**0**	**0**	**4**	**0**	**0**	**0**	**2**	**0.0**		**0**	**0.0**	**7:55**	....	....	....	....	....	....	....	....	....

• Missed majority of 2002-03 season recovering from rib injury suffered in game vs. Vancouver, December 26, 2002. Signed as a free agent by **MODO** (Sweden), August 25, 2003. Signed as a free agent by **Blues** (Finland), April 13, 2004.

HAGMAN, Niklas

(HAG-muhn, NIHK-las) **FLA.**

Left wing. Shoots left. 6', 200 lbs. Born, Espoo, Finland, December 5, 1979. Florida's 3rd choice, 70th overall, in 1999 Entry Draft.

			Regular Season														Playoffs								
Season	Club	League	GP	G	A	Pts	PIM	PP	SH	GW	S	%	+/-	TF	F%	Min	GP	G	A	Pts	PIM	PP	SH	GW	Min
1995-96	HIFK Helsinki U18	Fin-U18	26	12	21	33	32	....	....	....	....	....	....	....	....	....	4	3	0	3	2	....	....	....	....
	HIFK Helsinki Jr.	Finland-Jr.	12	3	1	4	0	....	....	....	....	....	....	....	....	....	....	....	....	....	....	....	....	....	....
1996-97	HIFK Helsinki Jr.	Finland-Jr.	30	13	12	25	30	....	....	....	....	....	....	....	....	....	4	1	1	2	0	....	....	....	....
1997-98	HIFK Helsinki Jr.	Finland-Jr.	26	9	5	14	16	....	....	....	....	....	....	....	....	....	....	....	....	....	....	....	....	....	....
	HIFK Helsinki	Finland	8	1	0	1	0	....	....	....	....	....	....	....	....	....	....	....	....	....	....	....	....	....	....
	HIFK Helsinki U18	Fin-U18	1	0	1	1	0	....	....	....	....	....	....	....	....	....	....	....	....	....	....	....	....	....	....
1998-99	HIFK Helsinki Jr.	Finland-Jr.	14	4	9	13	43	....	....	....	....	....	....	....	....	....	....	....	....	....	....	....	....	....	....
	HIFK Helsinki	Finland	17	1	1	2	14	....	....	....	....	....	....	....	....	....	....	....	....	....	....	....	....	....	....
	HIFK Helsinki	EuroHL	1	0	1	1	0	....	....	....	....	....	....	....	....	....	....	....	....	....	....	....	....	....	....
	Blues Espoo	Finland	14	1	1	2	2	....	....	....	....	....	....	....	....	....	4	1	0	1	0	....	....	....	....
99-2000	Karpat Oulu	Finland-2	41	17	18	35	12	....	....	....	....	....	....	....	....	....	7	4	2	6	....	....	....	....	....
2000-01	Karpat Oulu	Finland	56	28	18	46	32	....	....	....	....	....	....	....	....	....	8	3	1	4	0	....	....	....	....
2001-02	**Florida**	**NHL**	**78**	**10**	**18**	**28**	**8**	**0**	**1**	**2**	**134**	**7.5**	**-6**	**32**	**28.1**	**13:50**	....	....	....	....	....	....	....	....	....
	Finland	Olympics	4	1	2	3	0	....	....	....	....	....	....	....	....	....	....	....	....	....	....	....	....	....	....
2002-03	**Florida**	**NHL**	**80**	**8**	**15**	**23**	**20**	**2**	**0**	**0**	**132**	**6.1**	**-8**	**17**	**11.8**	**13:31**	....	....	....	....	....	....	....	....	....
2003-04	**Florida**	**NHL**	**75**	**10**	**13**	**23**	**22**	**0**	**1**	**2**	**122**	**8.2**	**-5**	**19**	**21.1**	**14:47**	....	....	....	....	....	....	....	....	....
2004-05	HC Davos	Swiss	44	17	22	39	20	....	....	....	....	....	....	....	....	....	15	10	7	17	6	....	....	....	....
	NHL Totals		**233**	**28**	**46**	**74**	**50**	**2**	**2**	**4**	**388**	**7.2**		**68**	**22.1**	**14:02**	....	....	....	....	....	....	....	....	....

Signed as a free agent by **Davos** (Swiss), July 23, 2004.

HAHL, Riku

(HAHL, REE-koo) **COL.**

Center. Shoots left. 6'1", 205 lbs. Born, Hameenlinna, Finland, November 1, 1980. Colorado's 9th choice, 183rd overall, in 1999 Entry Draft.

Season	Club	League	GP	G	A	Pts	PIM	PP	SH	GW	S	%	+/-	TF	F%	Min	GP	G	A	Pts	PIM	PP	SH	GW	Min
1996-97	HPK U18	Fin-U18	32	19	24	43	22	....	....	....	....	....	....	....	....	....	....	....	....	....	....	....	....	....	....
	HPK Jr.	Finland-Jr.	2	0	1	1	2	....	....	....	....	....	....	....	....	....	6	2	0	2	2	....	....	....	....
1997-98	HPK U18	Fin-U18	10	5	14	19	6	....	....	....	....	....	....	....	....	....	....	....	....	....	....	....	....	....	....
	HPK Jr.	Finland-Jr.	35	13	6	19	12	....	....	....	....	....	....	....	....	....	....	....	....	....	....	....	....	....	....
1998-99	HPK Jr.	Finland-Jr.	6	0	2	2	6	....	....	....	....	....	....	....	....	....	....	....	....	....	....	....	....	....	....
	HPK Hameenlinna	Finland	28	0	1	1	0	....	....	....	....	....	....	....	....	....	8	0	0	0	2	....	....	....	....
99-2000	HPK Jr.	Finland-Jr.	12	1	6	7	8	....	....	....	....	....	....	....	....	....	9	5	4	9	16	....	....	....	....
	HPK Hameenlinna	Finland	50	4	3	7	18	....	....	....	....	....	....	....	....	....	8	0	0	0	2	....	....	....	....
2000-01	HPK Jr.	Finland-Jr.	2	1	3	4	0	....	....	....	....	....	....	....	....	....	....	....	....	....	....	....	....	....	....
	HPK Hameenlinna	Finland	55	3	9	12	32	....	....	....	....	....	....	....	....	....	....	....	....	....	....	....	....	....	....
2001-02	**Colorado**	**NHL**	**22**	**2**	**3**	**5**	**14**	**0**	**0**	**1**	**17**	**11.8**	**1**	**94**	**35.1**	**9:26**	**21**	**1**	**2**	**3**	**0**	**0**	**0**	**0**	**7:31**
	Hershey Bears	AHL	52	6	17	23	16	....	....	....	....	....	....	....	....	....	....	....	....	....	....	....	....	....	....
2002-03	**Colorado**	**NHL**	**42**	**3**	**4**	**7**	**12**	**0**	**0**	**0**	**61**	**4.9**	**3**	**69**	**37.7**	**11:03**	**6**	**0**	**2**	**2**	**2**	**0**	**0**	**0**	**13:49**
	Hershey Bears	AHL	28	7	7	14	17	....	....	....	....	....	....	....	....	....	....	....	....	....	....	....	....	....	....
2003-04	**Colorado**	**NHL**	**28**	**0**	**1**	**1**	**12**	**0**	**0**	**0**	**40**	**0.0**	**-7**	**107**	**41.1**	**12:17**	**7**	**1**	**0**	**1**	**2**	**0**	**0**	**0**	**12:08**
2004-05	HPK Hameenlinna	Finland	44	8	13	21	12	....	....	....	....	....	....	....	....	....	10	2	6	8	2	....	....	....	....
	NHL Totals		**92**	**5**	**8**	**13**	**38**	**0**	**0**	**1**	**118**	**4.2**		**270**	**38.1**	**11:02**	**34**	**2**	**4**	**6**	**4**	**0**	**0**	**0**	**9:35**

• Missed majority of 2003-04 season recovering from shoulder injury suffered in game vs. Edmonton, October 23, 2003. Signed as a free agent by **HPK** (Finland), September 15, 2004.

HAINSEY, Ron

(HAYN-zee, RAWN) **MTL.**

Defense. Shoots left. 6'3", 211 lbs. Born, Bolton, CT, March 24, 1981. Montreal's 1st choice, 13th overall, in 2000 Entry Draft.

Season	Club	League	GP	G	A	Pts	PIM	PP	SH	GW	S	%	+/-	TF	F%	Min	GP	G	A	Pts	PIM	PP	SH	GW	Min
1997-98	USA U-18	USDP	66	6	15	21	44	....	....	....	....	....	....	....	....	....	....	....	....	....	....	....	....	....	....
1998-99	USA U-18	USDP	48	5	12	17	45	....	....	....	....	....	....	....	....	....	....	....	....	....	....	....	....	....	....
99-2000	U. Mass-Lowell	H-East	30	3	8	11	20	....	....	....	....	....	....	....	....	....	....	....	....	....	....	....	....	....	....
2000-01	U. Mass-Lowell	H-East	33	10	26	36	51	....	....	....	....	....	....	....	....	....	....	....	....	....	....	....	....	....	....
	Quebec Citadelles	AHL	4	1	0	1	0	....	....	....	....	....	....	....	....	....	1	0	0	0	0	....	....	....	....
2001-02	Quebec Citadelles	AHL	63	7	24	31	26	....	....	....	....	....	....	....	....	....	3	0	0	0	0	....	....	....	....
2002-03	**Montreal**	**NHL**	**21**	**0**	**0**	**0**	**2**	**0**	**0**	**0**	**12**	**0.0**	**-1**	**0**	**0.0**	**12:25**	....	....	....	....	....	....	....	....	....
	Hamilton	AHL	33	2	11	13	26	....	....	....	....	....	....	....	....	....	23	1	10	11	20	....	....	....	....
2003-04	**Montreal**	**NHL**	**11**	**1**	**1**	**2**	**4**	**0**	**0**	**0**	**11**	**9.1**	**3**	**0**	**0.0**	**13:15**	....	....	....	....	....	....	....	....	....
	Hamilton	AHL	54	7	24	31	35	....	....	....	....	....	....	....	....	....	10	0	5	5	6	....	....	....	....
2004-05	Hamilton	AHL	68	9	14	23	45	....	....	....	....	....	....	....	....	....	4	1	1	2	0	....	....	....	....
	NHL Totals		**32**	**1**	**1**	**2**	**6**	**0**	**0**	**0**	**23**	**4.3**		**0**	**0.0**	**12:42**	....	....	....	....	....	....	....	....	....

Hockey East First All-Star Team (2001) • NCAA East Second All-American Team (2001) • AHL All-Rookie Team (2002)

HAJT, Chris

(HIGHT, KRIHS) **CAR.**

Defense. Shoots left. 6'3", 206 lbs. Born, Saskatoon, Sask., July 5, 1978. Edmonton's 3rd choice, 32nd overall, in 1996 Entry Draft.

Season	Club	League	GP	G	A	Pts	PIM	PP	SH	GW	S	%	+/-	TF	F%	Min	GP	G	A	Pts	PIM	PP	SH	GW	Min
1993-94	Amherst Knights	WNYHA	38	8	20	28	16	....	....	....	....	....	....	....	....	....	....	....	....	....	....	....	....	....	....
1994-95	Guelph Storm	OHL	57	1	7	8	35	....	....	....	....	....	....	....	....	....	14	0	2	2	9	....	....	....	....
1995-96	Guelph Storm	OHL	63	8	27	35	69	....	....	....	....	....	....	....	....	....	16	0	6	6	13	....	....	....	....
1996-97	Guelph Storm	OHL	58	11	15	26	62	....	....	....	....	....	....	....	....	....	18	0	8	8	25	....	....	....	....
1997-98	Guelph Storm	OHL	44	2	21	23	46	....	....	....	....	....	....	....	....	....	12	1	5	6	11	....	....	....	....
1998-99	Hamilton	AHL	64	0	4	4	36	....	....	....	....	....	....	....	....	....	....	....	....	....	....	....	....	....	....
99-2000	Hamilton	AHL	54	0	8	8	30	....	....	....	....	....	....	....	....	....	10	0	2	2	0	....	....	....	....
2000-01	**Edmonton**	**NHL**	**1**	**0**	**0**	**0**	**0**	**0**	**0**	**0**	**0**	**0.0**	**-1**	**0**	**0.0**	**7:38**	....	....	....	....	....	....	....	....	....
	Hamilton	AHL	70	0	10	10	48	....	....	....	....	....	....	....	....	....	....	....	....	....	....	....	....	....	....
2001-02	Hamilton	AHL	39	2	3	5	34	....	....	....	....	....	....	....	....	....	15	1	2	3	8	....	....	....	....
2002-03	Portland Pirates	AHL	71	11	15	26	61	....	....	....	....	....	....	....	....	....	1	0	0	0	2	....	....	....	....
2003-04	**Washington**	**NHL**	**5**	**0**	**0**	**0**	**2**	**0**	**0**	**0**	**1**	**0.0**	**0**	**0**	**0.0**	**10:44**	....	....	....	....	....	....	....	....	....
	Portland Pirates	AHL	66	3	13	16	53	....	....	....	....	....	....	....	....	....	7	1	2	3	8	....	....	....	....
2004-05	Portland Pirates	AHL	53	3	6	9	16	....	....	....	....	....	....	....	....	....	....	....	....	....	....	....	....	....	....
	Augusta Lynx	ECHL	13	1	4	5	8	....	....	....	....	....	....	....	....	....	....	....	....	....	....	....	....	....	....
	NHL Totals		**6**	**0**	**0**	**0**	**2**	**0**	**0**	**0**	**1**	**0.0**		**0**	**0.0**	**10:13**	....	....	....	....	....	....	....	....	....

OHL Second All-Star Team (1998)

Signed as a free agent by **Washington**, July 23, 2002. Signed as a free agent by **Carolina**, August 16, 2005.

HALE, David

(HAYL, DAY-vihd) **N.J.**

Defense. Shoots left. 6'1", 215 lbs. Born, Colorado Springs, CO, June 18, 1981. New Jersey's 1st choice, 22nd overall, in 2000 Entry Draft.

Season	Club	League	GP	G	A	Pts	PIM	PP	SH	GW	S	%	+/-	TF	F%	Min	GP	G	A	Pts	PIM	PP	SH	GW	Min
1997-98	Colorado North	High-CO	25	11	33	44	154	....	....	....	....	....	....	....	....	....	....	....	....	....	....	....	....	....	....
1998-99	Sioux City	USHL	56	3	15	18	127	....	....	....	....	....	....	....	....	....	5	0	0	0	18	....	....	....	....
99-2000	Sioux City	USHL	54	6	18	24	187	....	....	....	....	....	....	....	....	....	5	0	2	2	6	....	....	....	....
2000-01	North Dakota	WCHA	44	4	5	9	79	....	....	....	....	....	....	....	....	....	....	....	....	....	....	....	....	....	....
2001-02	North Dakota	WCHA	34	4	5	9	63	....	....	....	....	....	....	....	....	....	....	....	....	....	....	....	....	....	....
2002-03	North Dakota	WCHA	26	2	6	8	49	....	....	....	....	....	....	....	....	....	....	....	....	....	....	....	....	....	....
2003-04	**New Jersey**	**NHL**	**65**	**0**	**4**	**4**	**72**	**0**	**0**	**0**	**45**	**0.0**	**12**	**0**	**0.0**	**15:01**	**1**	**0**	**0**	**0**	**0**	**0**	**0**	**0**	**8:59**
2004-05	Albany River Rats	AHL	30	2	3	5	39	....	....	....	....	....	....	....	....	....	....	....	....	....	....	....	....	....	....
	NHL Totals		**65**	**0**	**4**	**4**	**72**	**0**	**0**	**0**	**45**	**0.0**		**0**	**0.0**	**15:01**	**1**	**0**	**0**	**0**	**0**	**0**	**0**	**0**	**8:59**

USHL First All-Star Team (2000)

HALL, Adam

(HAWL, A-duhm) **NSH.**

Right wing. Shoots right. 6'3", 208 lbs. Born, Kalamazoo, MI, August 14, 1980. Nashville's 3rd choice, 52nd overall, in 1999 Entry Draft.

Season	Club	League	GP	G	A	Pts	PIM	PP	SH	GW	S	%	+/-	TF	F%	Min	GP	G	A	Pts	PIM	PP	SH	GW	Min
1996-97	Bramalea Blues	OPJHL	43	9	14	23	92	....	....	....	....	....	....	....	....	....	....	....	....	....	....	....	....	....	....
1997-98	USA U-18	USDP	71	42	23	65	63	....	....	....	....	....	....	....	....	....	....	....	....	....	....	....	....	....	....
1998-99	Michigan State	CCHA	36	16	7	23	74	....	....	....	....	....	....	....	....	....	....	....	....	....	....	....	....	....	....
99-2000	Michigan State	CCHA	40	*26	13	39	38	....	....	....	....	....	....	....	....	....	....	....	....	....	....	....	....	....	....
2000-01	Michigan State	CCHA	42	18	12	30	42	....	....	....	....	....	....	....	....	....	....	....	....	....	....	....	....	....	....
2001-02	Michigan State	CCHA	41	19	15	34	36	....	....	....	....	....	....	....	....	....	....	....	....	....	....	....	....	....	....
	Nashville	**NHL**	**1**	**0**	**1**	**1**	**0**	**0**	**0**	**0**	**2**	**0.0**	**0**	**0**	**0.0**	**14:04**	....	....	....	....	....	....	....	....	....
	Milwaukee	AHL	6	2	2	4	4	....	....	....	....	....	....	....	....	....	....	....	....	....	....	....	....	....	....

			Regular Season														Playoffs								
Season	Club	League	GP	G	A	Pts	PIM	PP	SH	GW	S	%	+/-	TF	F%	Min	GP	G	A	Pts	PIM	PP	SH	GW	Min
2002-03	Nashville	NHL	79	16	12	28	31	8	0	2	146	11.0	-8	17	52.9	14:09	....	....	....	....	....	....	....	....	....
	Milwaukee	AHL	1	0	0	0	2	....	....	....	....	....	....	....	....	....	....	....	....	....	....	....	....	....	....
2003-04	Nashville	NHL	79	13	14	27	37	6	0	1	151	8.6	-8	348	56.3	16:14	6	2	1	3	2	0	0	1	18:29
2004-05	KalPa Kuopio	Finland-2	36	23	17	40	28	....	....	....	....	....	....	....	....	....	9	2	3	5	4	....	....	....	....
	NHL Totals		159	29	27	56	68	14	0	3	299	9.7		365	56.2	15:11	6	2	1	3	2	0	0	1	18:29

CCHA Second All-Star Team (2000)

Signed as a free agent by **KalPa** (Finland-2), October 11, 2004.

HALPERN, Jeff

(HAL-pehrn, JEHF) **WSH.**

Center. Shoots right. 6', 198 lbs. Born, Potomac, MD, May 3, 1976.

1994-95	Stratford Cullitons	OHA-B	44	29	54	83	43	....	....	....	....	....	....	....	....	....	....	....	....	....	....	....	....	....	....
1995-96	Princeton	ECAC	29	3	11	14	30	....	....	....	....	....	....	....	....	....	....	....	....	....	....	....	....	....	....
1996-97	Princeton	ECAC	33	7	24	31	35	....	....	....	....	....	....	....	....	....	....	....	....	....	....	....	....	....	....
1997-98	Princeton	ECAC	36	*28	25	*53	46	....	....	....	....	....	....	....	....	....	....	....	....	....	....	....	....	....	....
1998-99	Princeton	ECAC	33	*22	22	44	32	....	....	....	....	....	....	....	....	....	....	....	....	....	....	....	....	....	....
	Portland Pirates	AHL	6	2	1	3	4	....	....	....	....	....	....	....	....	....	....	....	....	....	....	....	....	....	....
99-2000	Washington	NHL	79	18	11	29	39	4	4	1	108	16.7	21	812	51.1	13:14	5	2	1	3	0	1	0	1	15:16
2000-01	Washington	NHL	80	21	21	42	60	2	1	5	110	19.1	13	1293	52.4	16:08	6	2	3	5	17	1	0	1	20:01
2001-02	Washington	NHL	48	5	14	19	29	0	0	4	74	6.8	-9	661	56.0	15:19	....	....	....	....	....	....	....	....	....
2002-03	Washington	NHL	82	13	21	34	88	1	2	2	126	10.3	6	1492	54.1	17:25	6	0	1	1	2	0	0	0	19:59
2003-04	Washington	NHL	79	19	27	46	56	7	0	2	114	16.7	-21	1509	54.3	19:03	....	....	....	....	....	....	....	....	....
2004-05	HC Ajoie	Swiss-2	15	5	12	17	52	....	....	....	....	....	....	....	....	....	....	....	....	....	....	....	....	....	....
	Kloten Flyers	Swiss	9	7	4	11	6	....	....	....	....	....	....	....	....	....	....	....	....	....	....	....	....	....	....
	NHL Totals		368	76	94	170	272	14	7	14	532	14.3		5767	53.5	16:19	17	4	5	9	19	2	0	2	18:37

ECAC Second All-Star Team (1998, 1999)

Signed as a free agent by **Washington**, March 29, 1999. Signed as a free agent by **Ajoie** (Swiss-2), October 8, 2004. Signed as a free agent by **Kloten** (Swiss), December 30, 2004.

HAMEL, Denis

(ha-MEHL, deh-NEE) **OTT.**

Left wing. Shoots left. 6'1", 201 lbs. Born, Lachute, Que., May 10, 1977. St. Louis' 5th choice, 153rd overall, in 1995 Entry Draft.

1992-93	Lachute Regents	QAAA	32	18	24	42	....	....	....	....	....	....	....	....	....	....	....	....	....	....	....	....	....	....	....
1993-94	Lac St-Louis Lions	QAAA	28	10	11	21	50	....	....	....	....	....	....	....	....	....	....	....	....	....	....	....	....	....	....
	Abitibi Forestiers	QAAA	15	5	7	12	29	....	....	....	....	....	....	....	....	....	5	0	3	3	16	....	....	....	....
1994-95	Chicoutimi	QMJHL	66	15	12	27	155	....	....	....	....	....	....	....	....	....	12	2	0	2	27	....	....	....	....
1995-96	Chicoutimi	QMJHL	65	40	49	89	199	....	....	....	....	....	....	....	....	....	17	10	14	24	64	....	....	....	....
1996-97	Chicoutimi	QMJHL	70	50	50	100	357	....	....	....	....	....	....	....	....	....	20	15	10	25	58	....	....	....	....
1997-98	Rochester	AHL	74	10	15	25	98	....	....	....	....	....	....	....	....	....	4	1	2	3	0	....	....	....	....
1998-99	Rochester	AHL	74	16	17	33	121	....	....	....	....	....	....	....	....	....	20	3	4	7	10	....	....	....	....
99-2000	Buffalo	NHL	3	1	0	1	0	0	0	0	3	33.3	-1	0	0.0	9:45	....	....	....	....	....	....	....	....	....
	Rochester	AHL	76	34	24	58	122	....	....	....	....	....	....	....	....	....	21	6	7	13	49	....	....	....	....
2000-01	Buffalo	NHL	41	8	3	11	22	1	1	3	55	14.5	-2	171	33.9	10:58	....	....	....	....	....	....	....	....	....
2001-02	Buffalo	NHL	61	2	6	8	28	0	0	0	80	2.5	-1	94	39.4	11:00	....	....	....	....	....	....	....	....	....
2002-03	Buffalo	NHL	25	2	0	2	17	0	0	1	41	4.9	-4	4	25.0	12:40	....	....	....	....	....	....	....	....	....
	Rochester	AHL	48	27	20	47	64	....	....	....	....	....	....	....	....	....	3	3	2	5	4	....	....	....	....
2003-04	Ottawa	NHL	5	0	0	0	0	0	0	0	6	0.0	-3	1	100.0	6:16	....	....	....	....	....	....	....	....	....
	Binghamton	AHL	78	29	38	67	116	....	....	....	....	....	....	....	....	....	2	0	0	0	2	....	....	....	....
2004-05	Binghamton	AHL	80	39	39	78	75	....	....	....	....	....	....	....	....	....	5	1	0	1	4	....	....	....	....
	NHL Totals		135	13	9	22	67	1	1	4	185	7.0		270	35.9	11:06	....	....	....	....	....	....	....	....	....

QMJHL All-Rookie Team (1995) • AHL First All-Star Team (2004)

Traded to **Buffalo** by **St. Louis** for Charlie Huddy and Buffalo's 7th round choice (Daniel Corso) in 1996 Entry Draft, March 19, 1996. • Missed majority of 2000-01 season recovering from knee injury suffered in game vs. NY Islanders, January 27, 2001. Signed as a free agent by **Ottawa**, July 5, 2003. Claimed by **Washington** from **Ottawa** in Waiver Draft, October 3, 2003. Traded to **Ottawa** by **Washington** for future considerations, October 5, 2003.

HAMHUIS, Dan

(HAM-yoos, DAN) **NSH.**

Defense. Shoots left. 6'1", 200 lbs. Born, Smithers, B.C., December 13, 1982. Nashville's 1st choice, 12th overall, in 2001 Entry Draft.

1997-98	Smithers A's	BCAHA	59	59	72	131	59	....	....	....	....	....	....	....	....	....	....	....	....	....	....	....	....	....	....
1998-99	Prince George	WHL	56	1	3	4	45	....	....	....	....	....	....	....	....	....	7	1	2	3	8	....	....	....	....
99-2000	Prince George	WHL	70	10	23	33	140	....	....	....	....	....	....	....	....	....	13	2	3	5	35	....	....	....	....
2000-01	Prince George	WHL	62	13	47	60	125	....	....	....	....	....	....	....	....	....	6	2	3	5	15	....	....	....	....
2001-02	Prince George	WHL	59	10	50	60	135	....	....	....	....	....	....	....	....	....	7	0	5	5	16	....	....	....	....
2002-03	Milwaukee	AHL	68	6	21	27	81	....	....	....	....	....	....	....	....	....	6	0	3	3	2	....	....	....	....
2003-04	Nashville	NHL	80	7	19	26	57	2	0	4	115	6.1	-12	0	0.0	22:08	6	0	2	2	6	0	0	0	20:29
2004-05	Milwaukee	AHL	76	13	38	51	85	....	....	....	....	....	....	....	....	....	7	0	2	2	10	....	....	....	....
	NHL Totals		80	7	19	26	57	2	0	4	115	6.1		0	0.0	22:08	6	0	2	2	6	0	0	0	20:29

WHL West First All-Star Team (2001, 2002) • WHL Player of the Year (2002) • Canadian Major Junior First All-Star Team (2002) • Canadian Major Junior Defenseman of the Year (2002) • AHL Second All-Star Team (2005)

HAMILTON, Jeff

(HAM-ihl-tuhn, JEHF) **NYI**

Center. Shoots right. 5'10", 180 lbs. Born, Englewood, OH, September 4, 1977.

1995-96	Avon Old Farms	High-CT	24	29	23	52	....	....	....	....	....	....	....	....	....	....	....	....	....	....	....	....	....	....	....
1996-97	Yale	ECAC	31	10	13	23	26	....	....	....	....	....	....	....	....	....	....	....	....	....	....	....	....	....	....
1997-98	Yale	ECAC	33	27	20	47	28	....	....	....	....	....	....	....	....	....	....	....	....	....	....	....	....	....	....
1998-99	Yale	ECAC	30	20	28	48	51	....	....	....	....	....	....	....	....	....	....	....	....	....	....	....	....	....	....
99-2000	Yale	ECAC	2	0	1	1	0	....	....	....	....	....	....	....	....	....	....	....	....	....	....	....	....	....	....
2000-01	Yale	ECAC	31	23	32	55	39	....	....	....	....	....	....	....	....	....	....	....	....	....	....	....	....	....	....
2001-02	Karpat Oulu	Finland	39	18	15	33	16	....	....	....	....	....	....	....	....	....	3	0	0	0	0	....	....	....	....
2002-03	Bridgeport	AHL	67	22	16	38	35	....	....	....	....	....	....	....	....	....	9	3	3	6	0	....	....	....	....
2003-04	NY Islanders	NHL	1	0	0	0	0	0	0	0	1	0.0	0	0	0.0	10:00	....	....	....	....	....	....	....	....	....
	Bridgeport	AHL	67	*43	25	68	26	....	....	....	....	....	....	....	....	....	7	4	0	4	4	....	....	....	....
2004-05	Hartford	AHL	60	23	30	53	32	....	....	....	....	....	....	....	....	....	6	4	3	7	0	....	....	....	....
	NHL Totals		1	0	0	0	0	0	0	0	1	0.0		0	0.0	10:00	....	....	....	....	....	....	....	....	....

ECAC All-Rookie Team (1997) • ECAC First All-Star Team (1998, 1999, 2001) • NCAA East Second All-American Team (1998, 1999) • NCAA East First All-American Team (2001) • AHL First All-Star Team (2004) • Willie Marshall Award (Top Goal-scorer - AHL) (2004)

• Missed majority of 1999-2000 season recovering from abdominal injury originally suffered in game vs. U. of Michigan (CCHA), October 30, 1999. Signed as a free agent by **Karpat** (Finland), October 4, 2001. Signed as a free agent by **NY Islanders**, August 6, 2002. Signed as a free agent by **Hartford** (AHL), October 10, 2004.

HAMRLIK, Roman

(HAHM-reh-lik, ROH-muhn) **CGY.**

Defense. Shoots left. 6'2", 210 lbs. Born, Zlin, Czech., April 12, 1974. Tampa Bay's 1st choice, 1st overall, in 1992 Entry Draft.

1990-91	AC ZPS Zlin	Czech	14	2	2	4	18	....	....	....	....	....	....	....	....	....	....	....	....	....	....	....	....	....	....
1991-92	AC ZPS Zlin	Czech	34	5	5	10	50	....	....	....	....	....	....	....	....	....	....	....	....	....	....	....	....	....	....
1992-93	Tampa Bay	NHL	67	6	15	21	71	1	0	1	113	5.3	-21	....	....	....	....	....	....	....	....	....	....	....	....
	Atlanta Knights	IHL	2	1	1	2	2	....	....	....	....	....	....	....	....	....	....	....	....	....	....	....	....	....	....
1993-94	Tampa Bay	NHL	64	3	18	21	135	0	0	0	158	1.9	-14	....	....	....	....	....	....	....	....	....	....	....	....
1994-95	AC ZPS Zlin	CzRep	2	1	0	1	10	....	....	....	....	....	....	....	....	....	....	....	....	....	....	....	....	....	....
	Tampa Bay	NHL	48	12	11	23	86	7	1	2	134	9.0	-18	....	....	....	....	....	....	....	....	....	....	....	....
1995-96	Tampa Bay	NHL	82	16	49	65	103	12	0	2	281	5.7	-24	....	....	....	5	0	1	1	4	0	0	0	....
1996-97	Tampa Bay	NHL	79	12	28	40	57	6	0	0	238	5.0	-29	....	....	....	....	....	....	....	....	....	....	....	....
1997-98	Tampa Bay	NHL	37	3	12	15	22	1	0	0	86	3.5	-18	....	....	....	....	....	....	....	....	....	....	....	....
	Edmonton	NHL	41	6	20	26	48	4	1	3	112	5.4	3	....	....	....	12	0	6	6	12	0	0	0	....
	Czech Republic	Olympics	6	1	0	1	2	....	....	....	....	....	....	....	....	....	....	....	....	....	....	....	....	....	....
1998-99	Edmonton	NHL	75	8	24	32	70	3	0	0	172	4.7	9	0	0.0	23:49	3	0	0	0	2	0	0	0	16:23
99-2000	Zlin	CzRep	6	0	3	3	4	....	....	....	....	....	....	....	....	....	....	....	....	....	....	....	....	....	....
	Edmonton	NHL	80	8	37	45	68	5	0	0	180	4.4	1	0	0.0	25:18	5	0	1	1	4	0	0	0	24:44
2000-01	NY Islanders	NHL	76	16	30	46	92	5	1	4	232	6.9	-20	1	100.0	25:12	....	....	....	....	....	....	....	....	....

			Regular Season														Playoffs								
Season	Club	League	GP	G	A	Pts	PIM	PP	SH	GW	S	%	+/-	TF	F%	Min	GP	G	A	Pts	PIM	PP	SH	GW	Min
2001-02	NY Islanders	NHL	70	11	26	37	78	4	1	1	169	6.5	7	1	0.0	25:32	7	1	6	7	6	0	0	0	29:09
	Czech Republic	Olympics	4	0	1	1	2	....	....	....	....	....	....	....	....	....	....	....	....	....	....	....	....	....	....
2002-03	NY Islanders	NHL	73	9	32	41	87	3	0	2	151	6.0	21	0	0.0	26:34	5	0	2	2	2	0	0	0	29:24
2003-04	NY Islanders	NHL	81	7	22	29	68	2	0	2	182	3.8	2	0	0.0	24:35	5	0	1	1	2	0	0	0	25:30
2004-05	HC Hame Zlin	CzRep	45	2	14	16	70	....	....	....	....	....	....	....	....	....	17	1	3	4	24	....	....	....	....
	NHL Totals		873	117	324	441	985	53	4	17	2208	5.3		2	50.0	25:09	42	1	17	18	32	0	0	0	26:03

Played in NHL All-Star Game (1996, 1999, 2003)

Traded to **Edmonton** by **Tampa Bay** with Paul Comrie for Bryan Marchment, Steve Kelly and Jason Bonsignore, December 30, 1997. Traded to **NY Islanders** by **Edmonton** for Eric Brewer, Josh Green and NY Islanders' 2nd round choice (Brad Winchester) in 2000 Entry Draft, June 24, 2000. Signed as a free agent by **Zlin** (CzRep), August 4, 2004. Signed as a free agent by **Calgary**, August 14, 2005.

HANDZUS, Michal

(HAHND-zuhs, MIGH-kuhl) **PHI.**

Center. Shoots left. 6'5", 217 lbs. Born, Banska Bystrica, Czech., March 11, 1977. St. Louis' 3rd choice, 101st overall, in 1995 Entry Draft.

Season	Club	League	GP	G	A	Pts	PIM	PP	SH	GW	S	%	+/-	TF	F%	Min	GP	G	A	Pts	PIM	PP	SH	GW	Min
1993-94	B. Bystrica Jr.	Slovak-Jr.	40	23	36	59	....	....	....	....	....	....	....	....	....	....	....	....	....	....	....	....	....	....	....
1994-95	B. Bystrica	Slovak-2	22	15	14	29	10	....	....	....	....	....	....	....	....	....	....	....	....	....	....	....	....	....	....
1995-96	B. Bystrica	Slovakia	19	3	1	4	8	....	....	....	....	....	....	....	....	....	....	....	....	....	....	....	....	....	....
1996-97	HC SKP PS Poprad	Slovakia	44	15	18	33	....	....	....	....	....	....	....	....	....	....	....	....	....	....	....	....	....	....	....
1997-98	Worcester IceCats	AHL	69	27	36	63	54	....	....	....	....	....	....	....	....	....	11	2	6	8	10	....	....	....	....
1998-99	St. Louis	NHL	66	4	12	16	30	0	0	0	78	5.1	-9	794	49.9	14:48	11	0	2	2	8	0	0	0	16:52
99-2000	St. Louis	NHL	81	25	28	53	44	3	4	5	166	15.1	19	1243	51.5	17:43	7	0	3	3	6	0	0	0	16:35
2000-01	St. Louis	NHL	36	10	14	24	12	3	2	2	58	17.2	11	581	50.6	18:00	....	....	....	....	....	....	....	....	....
	Phoenix	NHL	10	4	4	8	21	0	1	0	14	28.6	5	111	60.4	15:26	....	....	....	....	....	....	....	....	....
2001-02	Phoenix	NHL	79	15	30	45	34	3	1	1	94	16.0	-8	1227	48.7	16:09	5	0	0	0	2	0	0	0	15:01
	Slovakia	Olympics	2	1	0	1	6	....	....	....	....	....	....	....	....	....	....	....	....	....	....	....	....	....	....
2002-03	Philadelphia	NHL	82	23	21	44	46	1	1	9	133	17.3	13	1350	52.3	17:33	13	2	6	8	6	0	0	1	18:23
2003-04	Philadelphia	NHL	82	20	38	58	82	7	1	2	135	14.8	18	1457	49.9	18:43	18	5	5	10	10	0	0	0	18:33
2004-05	HKm Zvolen	Slovakia	33	14	24	38	34	....	....	....	....	....	....	....	....	....	17	5	10	15	6	....	....	....	....
	NHL Totals		436	101	147	248	269	17	10	19	678	14.9		6763	50.7	17:07	54	7	16	23	32	0	0	1	17:35

Traded to **Phoenix** by **St. Louis** with Ladislav Nagy, the rights to Jeff Taffe and St. Louis' 1st round choice (Ben Eager) in 2002 Entry Draft for Keith Tkachuk, March 13, 2001. Traded to **Philadelphia** by **Phoenix** with Robert Esche for Brian Boucher and Nashville's 3rd round choice (previously acquired, Phoenix selected Joe Callahan) in 2002 Entry Draft, June 12, 2002. Signed as a free agent by **Zvolen** (Slovakia), October 27, 2004.

HANKINSON, Casey

(HAN-kihn-suhn, KAY-see)

Left wing. Shoots left. 6'1", 187 lbs. Born, Edina, MN, May 8, 1976. Chicago's 9th choice, 201st overall, in 1995 Entry Draft.

Season	Club	League	GP	G	A	Pts	PIM	PP	SH	GW	S	%	+/-	TF	F%	Min	GP	G	A	Pts	PIM	PP	SH	GW	Min
1992-93	Edina Hornets	High-MN	25	20	26	46	....	....	....	....	....	....	....	....	....	....	....	....	....	....	....	....	....	....	....
1993-94	Edina Hornets	High-MN	24	21	20	41	50	....	....	....	....	....	....	....	....	....	....	....	....	....	....	....	....	....	....
1994-95	U. of Minnesota	WCHA	33	7	1	8	86	....	....	....	....	....	....	....	....	....	....	....	....	....	....	....	....	....	....
1995-96	U. of Minnesota	WCHA	39	16	19	35	101	....	....	....	....	....	....	....	....	....	....	....	....	....	....	....	....	....	....
1996-97	U. of Minnesota	WCHA	42	17	24	41	79	....	....	....	....	....	....	....	....	....	....	....	....	....	....	....	....	....	....
1997-98	U. of Minnesota	WCHA	35	10	12	22	81	....	....	....	....	....	....	....	....	....	....	....	....	....	....	....	....	....	....
1998-99	Portland Pirates	AHL	72	10	13	23	106	....	....	....	....	....	....	....	....	....	....	....	....	....	....	....	....	....	....
99-2000	Cleveland	IHL	82	7	22	29	140	....	....	....	....	....	....	....	....	....	2	0	0	0	2	....	....	....	....
2000-01	Chicago	NHL	11	0	1	1	9	0	0	0	15	0.0	-3	0	0.0	9:46	....	....	....	....	....	....	....	....	....
	Norfolk Admirals	AHL	69	30	21	51	74	....	....	....	....	....	....	....	....	....	9	5	4	9	2	....	....	....	....
2001-02	Chicago	NHL	3	0	0	0	0	0	0	0	1	0.0	-2	6	33.3	8:38	....	....	....	....	....	....	....	....	....
	Norfolk Admirals	AHL	72	19	30	49	85	....	....	....	....	....	....	....	....	....	4	1	2	3	0	....	....	....	....
2002-03	Norfolk Admirals	AHL	78	27	28	55	59	....	....	....	....	....	....	....	....	....	9	4	3	7	10	....	....	....	....
2003-04	Anaheim	NHL	4	0	0	0	4	0	0	0	0	0.0	0	1	100.0	6:20	....	....	....	....	....	....	....	....	....
	Cincinnati	AHL	78	15	23	38	123	....	....	....	....	....	....	....	....	....	9	4	1	5	10	....	....	....	....
2004-05	Chaux-de-Fonds	Swiss-2	4	2	1	3	6	....	....	....	....	....	....	....	....	....	....	....	....	....	....	....	....	....	....
	Cincinnati	AHL	54	4	7	11	92	....	....	....	....	....	....	....	....	....	12	2	4	6	36	....	....	....	....
	NHL Totals		18	0	1	1	13	0	0	0	16	0.0		7	42.9	8:49	....	....	....	....	....	....	....	....	....

Signed as a free agent by **Anaheim**, July 25, 2003. Signed as a free agent by **Chaux-de-Fonds** (Swiss-2), October 7, 2004. Signed as a free agent by **Cincinnati** (AHL), December 3, 2004.

HANNAN, Scott

(HAN-nan, SKAWT) **S.J.**

Defense. Shoots left. 6'1", 220 lbs. Born, Richmond, B.C., January 23, 1979. San Jose's 2nd choice, 23rd overall, in 1997 Entry Draft.

Season	Club	League	GP	G	A	Pts	PIM	PP	SH	GW	S	%	+/-	TF	F%	Min	GP	G	A	Pts	PIM	PP	SH	GW	Min
1994-95	Surrey Wolves	BCAHA	70	54	54	108	200	....	....	....	....	....	....	....	....	....	....	....	....	....	....	....	....	....	....
	Tacoma Rockets	WHL	2	0	0	0	0	....	....	....	....	....	....	....	....	....	....	....	....	....	....	....	....	....	....
1995-96	Kelowna Rockets	WHL	69	4	5	9	76	....	....	....	....	....	....	....	....	....	6	0	1	1	4	....	....	....	....
1996-97	Kelowna Rockets	WHL	70	17	26	43	101	....	....	....	....	....	....	....	....	....	6	0	0	0	8	....	....	....	....
1997-98	Kelowna Rockets	WHL	47	10	30	40	70	....	....	....	....	....	....	....	....	....	7	2	7	9	14	....	....	....	....
1998-99	San Jose	NHL	5	0	2	2	6	0	0	0	4	0.0	0	0	0.0	7:15	....	....	....	....	....	....	....	....	....
	Kelowna Rockets	WHL	47	15	30	45	92	....	....	....	....	....	....	....	....	....	6	1	2	3	14	....	....	....	....
	Kentucky	AHL	2	0	0	0	2	....	....	....	....	....	....	....	....	....	12	0	2	2	10	....	....	....	....
99-2000	San Jose	NHL	30	1	2	3	10	0	0	0	28	3.6	7	1	0.0	17:09	1	0	1	1	0	0	0	0	18:14
	Kentucky	AHL	41	5	12	17	40	....	....	....	....	....	....	....	....	....	....	....	....	....	....	....	....	....	....
2000-01	San Jose	NHL	75	3	14	17	51	0	0	1	96	3.1	10	0	0.0	19:02	6	0	1	1	6	0	0	0	25:10
2001-02	San Jose	NHL	75	2	12	14	57	0	0	1	68	2.9	10	1	100.0	20:19	12	0	2	2	12	0	0	0	20:46
2002-03	San Jose	NHL	81	3	19	22	61	1	0	0	103	2.9	0	3	33.3	24:16	....	....	....	....	....	....	....	....	....
2003-04	San Jose	NHL	82	6	15	21	48	0	0	0	114	5.3	10	0	0.0	23:41	17	1	5	6	22	1	0	1	26:38
2004-05			DID NOT PLAY																						
	NHL Totals		348	15	64	79	233	1	0	2	413	3.6		5	40.0	21:17	36	1	9	10	40	1	0	1	24:12

WHL West First All-Star Team (1999)

HANSEN, Tavis

(HAN-suhn, TA-vihs)

Right wing. Shoots right. 6'1", 205 lbs. Born, Prince Albert, Sask., June 17, 1975. Winnipeg's 3rd choice, 58th overall, in 1994 Entry Draft.

Season	Club	League	GP	G	A	Pts	PIM	PP	SH	GW	S	%	+/-	TF	F%	Min	GP	G	A	Pts	PIM	PP	SH	GW	Min
1992-93	Shellbrook	SMHL	42	42	63	105	107	....	....	....	....	....	....	....	....	....	....	....	....	....	....	....	....	....	....
1993-94	Tacoma Rockets	WHL	71	23	31	54	122	....	....	....	....	....	....	....	....	....	8	1	3	4	17	....	....	....	....
1994-95	Tacoma Rockets	WHL	71	32	41	73	142	....	....	....	....	....	....	....	....	....	4	1	1	2	8	....	....	....	....
	Winnipeg	NHL	1	0	0	0	0	0	0	0	0	0.0	0	....	....	....	....	....	....	....	....	....	....	....	....
1995-96	Springfield	AHL	67	6	16	22	85	....	....	....	....	....	....	....	....	....	5	1	2	3	2	....	....	....	....
1996-97	Phoenix	NHL	1	0	0	0	0	0	0	0	0	0.0	0	....	....	....	....	....	....	....	....	....	....	....	....
	Springfield	AHL	12	3	1	4	23	....	....	....	....	....	....	....	....	....	....	....	....	....	....	....	....	....	....
1997-98	Springfield	AHL	73	20	14	34	70	....	....	....	....	....	....	....	....	....	4	1	2	3	18	....	....	....	....
1998-99	Phoenix	NHL	20	2	1	3	12	0	0	0	14	14.3	-4	5	80.0	8:07	2	0	0	0	0	0	0	0	3:45
	Springfield	AHL	63	23	11	34	85	....	....	....	....	....	....	....	....	....	3	0	1	1	5	....	....	....	....
99-2000	Phoenix	NHL	5	0	0	0	0	0	0	0	2	0.0	0	0	0.0	4:17	....	....	....	....	....	....	....	....	....
	Springfield	AHL	59	21	27	48	164	....	....	....	....	....	....	....	....	....	5	2	1	3	4	....	....	....	....
2000-01	Phoenix	NHL	7	0	0	0	4	0	0	0	2	0.0	-1	1	100.0	5:05	....	....	....	....	....	....	....	....	....
	Springfield	AHL	24	6	10	16	81	....	....	....	....	....	....	....	....	....	....	....	....	....	....	....	....	....	....
2001-02	Hershey Bears	AHL	35	9	6	15	50	....	....	....	....	....	....	....	....	....	8	0	3	3	8	....	....	....	....
2002-03	Cleveland Barons	AHL	80	23	21	44	81	....	....	....	....	....	....	....	....	....	....	....	....	....	....	....	....	....	....
2003-04	Cleveland Barons	AHL	77	17	17	34	118	....	....	....	....	....	....	....	....	....	9	5	2	7	13	....	....	....	....
2004-05	Oji Eagles	AsianHL	STATISTICS NOT AVAILABLE																						
	NHL Totals		34	2	1	3	16	0	0	0	18	11.1		6	83.3	6:51	2	0	0	0	0	0	0	0	3:45

Transferred to **Phoenix** after **Winnipeg** franchise relocated, July 1, 1996. • Missed majority of 2000-01 and 2001-02 seasons recovering from arm injury suffered in game vs. Hershey (AHL), February 3, 2001. Signed as a free agent by **Hershey** (AHL), January 16, 2002. Signed as a free agent by **San Jose**, September 5, 2002.

HARTIGAN, Mark

(HAHR-tih-guhn, MAHRK) **CBJ**

Center. Shoots left. 6'1", 205 lbs. Born, Fort St. John, B.C., October 15, 1977.

Season	Club	League	GP	G	A	Pts	PIM	PP	SH	GW	S	%	+/-	TF	F%	Min	GP	G	A	Pts	PIM	PP	SH	GW	Min
			Regular Season														Playoffs								
1996-97	Weyburn	SJHL	52	44	32	76	....	....	....	....	....	....	....	....	....	....	....	....	....	....	....	....	....	....	....
1997-98	Weyburn	SJHL	62	*59	46	*105	81	....	....	....	....	....	....	....	....	....	23	17	21	38	10	....	....	....	....
1998-99	St. Cloud State	WCHA	DID NOT PLAY – FRESHMAN					....	....	....	....	....	....	....	....	....	....	....	....	....	....	....	....	....	....
99-2000	St. Cloud State	WCHA	37	22	20	42	24	....	....	....	....	....	....	....	....	....	....	....	....	....	....	....	....	....	....
2000-01	St. Cloud State	WCHA	40	27	21	48	20	....	....	....	....	....	....	....	....	....	....	....	....	....	....	....	....	....	....
2001-02	St. Cloud State	WCHA	42	*37	38	75	42	....	....	....	....	....	....	....	....	....	....	....	....	....	....	....	....	....	....
	Atlanta	NHL	2	0	0	0	2	0	0	0	3	0.0	-2	18	38.9	13:16	....	....	....	....	....	....	....	....	....
2002-03	Atlanta	NHL	23	5	2	7	6	1	0	0	25	20.0	-8	220	47.3	10:52	....	....	....	....	....	....	....	....	....
	Chicago Wolves	AHL	55	15	31	46	43	....	....	....	....	....	....	....	....	....	9	1	2	3	10	....	....	....	....
2003-04	Columbus	NHL	9	1	3	4	6	1	0	0	15	6.7	-2	138	40.6	16:19	....	....	....	....	....	....	....	....	....
	Syracuse Crunch	AHL	69	23	23	46	86	....	....	....	....	....	....	....	....	....	7	1	4	5	8	....	....	....	....
2004-05	Syracuse Crunch	AHL	69	31	28	59	105	....	....	....	....	....	....	....	....	....	....	....	....	....	....	....	....	....	....
	NHL Totals		34	6	5	11	14	2	0	0	43	14.0		376	44.4	12:27	....	....	....	....	....	....	....	....	....

WCHA First All-Star Team (2002) • WCHA Player of the Year (2002)

Signed as a free agent by **Atlanta**, March 27, 2002. Signed as a free agent by **Columbus**, July 15, 2003.

HARTNELL, Scott

(HAHRT-nuhl, SKAWT) **NSH.**

Left wing. Shoots left. 6'2", 210 lbs. Born, Regina, Sask., April 18, 1982. Nashville's 1st choice, 6th overall, in 2000 Entry Draft.

Season	Club	League	GP	G	A	Pts	PIM	PP	SH	GW	S	%	+/-	TF	F%	Min	GP	G	A	Pts	PIM	PP	SH	GW	Min
1997-98	Lloydminster	AJHL	56	9	25	34	82	....	....	....	....	....	....	....	....	....	4	2	1	3	8	....	....	....	....
	Prince Albert	WHL	1	0	1	1	2	....	....	....	....	....	....	....	....	....	....	....	....	....	....	....	....	....	....
1998-99	Prince Albert	WHL	65	10	34	44	104	....	....	....	....	....	....	....	....	....	14	0	5	5	22	....	....	....	....
99-2000	Prince Albert	WHL	62	27	55	82	124	....	....	....	....	....	....	....	....	....	6	3	2	5	6	....	....	....	....
2000-01	Nashville	NHL	75	2	14	16	48	0	0	0	92	2.2	-8	3	33.3	10:54	....	....	....	....	....	....	....	....	....
2001-02	Nashville	NHL	75	14	27	41	111	3	0	4	162	8.6	5	12	25.0	16:58	....	....	....	....	....	....	....	....	....
2002-03	Nashville	NHL	82	12	22	34	101	2	0	2	221	5.4	-3	23	30.4	15:17	....	....	....	....	....	....	....	....	....
2003-04	Nashville	NHL	59	18	15	33	87	5	0	3	154	11.7	-5	48	37.5	16:16	6	1	2	3	2	0	0	0	15:37
2004-05	Valerengen IF Oslo	Norway	28	17	12	29	103	....	....	....	....	....	....	....	....	....	11	12	7	19	24	....	....	....	....
	NHL Totals		291	46	78	124	347	10	0	9	629	7.3		86	33.7	14:47	6	1	2	3	2	0	0	0	15:37

Signed as a free agent by **Valerengen** (Norway), October 21, 2004.

HARVEY, Todd

(HAHR-vee, TAWD) **EDM.**

Right wing/Center. Shoots right. 6', 210 lbs. Born, Hamilton, Ont., February 17, 1975. Dallas' 1st choice, 9th overall, in 1993 Entry Draft.

Season	Club	League	GP	G	A	Pts	PIM	PP	SH	GW	S	%	+/-	TF	F%	Min	GP	G	A	Pts	PIM	PP	SH	GW	Min
1989-90	Cambridge	OHA-B	41	35	27	62	213	....	....	....	....	....	....	....	....	....	....	....	....	....	....	....	....	....	....
1990-91	Cambridge	OHA-B	35	32	39	71	174	....	....	....	....	....	....	....	....	....	....	....	....	....	....	....	....	....	....
1991-92	Detroit	OHL	58	21	43	64	141	....	....	....	....	....	....	....	....	....	7	3	5	8	30	....	....	....	....
1992-93	Detroit	OHL	55	50	50	100	83	....	....	....	....	....	....	....	....	....	15	9	12	21	39	....	....	....	....
1993-94	Detroit	OHL	49	34	51	85	75	....	....	....	....	....	....	....	....	....	17	10	12	22	26	....	....	....	....
1994-95	Detroit	OHL	11	8	14	22	12	....	....	....	....	....	....	....	....	....	....	....	....	....	....	....	....	....	....
	Dallas	NHL	40	11	9	20	67	2	0	1	64	17.2	-3	....	....	....	5	0	0	0	8	0	0	0	....
1995-96	Dallas	NHL	69	9	20	29	136	3	0	1	101	8.9	-13	....	....	....	....	....	....	....	....	....	....	....	....
	Michigan	IHL	5	1	3	4	8	....	....	....	....	....	....	....	....	....	....	....	....	....	....	....	....	....	....
1996-97	Dallas	NHL	71	9	22	31	142	1	0	2	99	9.1	19	....	....	....	7	0	1	1	10	0	0	0	....
1997-98	Dallas	NHL	59	9	10	19	104	0	0	1	88	10.2	5	....	....	....	....	....	....	....	....	....	....	....	....
1998-99	NY Rangers	NHL	37	11	17	28	72	6	0	2	58	19.0	-1	175	50.3	17:19	....	....	....	....	....	....	....	....	....
99-2000	NY Rangers	NHL	31	3	3	6	62	0	0	0	31	9.7	-9	173	49.1	12:21	....	....	....	....	....	....	....	....	....
	San Jose	NHL	40	8	4	12	78	2	0	0	59	13.6	-2	44	43.2	12:55	12	1	0	1	8	1	0	0	10:47
2000-01	San Jose	NHL	68	10	11	21	72	1	0	2	66	15.2	6	98	40.8	11:05	6	0	0	0	8	0	0	0	6:59
2001-02	San Jose	NHL	69	9	13	22	73	1	0	1	66	13.6	16	223	48.4	9:47	12	0	2	2	12	0	0	0	7:32
2002-03	San Jose	NHL	76	3	16	19	74	0	0	0	64	4.7	5	119	44.5	9:57	....	....	....	....	....	....	....	....	....
2003-04	San Jose	NHL	47	4	5	9	38	0	0	0	51	7.8	3	29	44.8	9:46	16	1	2	3	2	0	0	0	10:30
	Cleveland Barons	AHL	13	6	1	7	29	....	....	....	....	....	....	....	....	....	....	....	....	....	....	....	....	....	....
2004-05	Cambridge	OHA-Sr.	16	9	15	24	31	....	....	....	....	....	....	....	....	....	....	....	....	....	....	....	....	....	....
	NHL Totals		608	86	130	216	918	15	0	10	747	11.5		861	47.2	11:22	58	2	5	7	48	1	0	0	9:21

OHL All-Rookie Team (1992)

Traded to **NY Rangers** by **Dallas** with Bob Errey and Dallas' 4th round choice (Boyd Kane) in 1998 Entry Draft for Brian Skrudland, Mike Keane and NY Rangers' 6th round choice (Pavel Patera) in 1998 Entry Draft, March 24, 1998. Traded to **San Jose** by **NY Rangers** with NY Rangers' 4th round choice (Dimitri Patzold) in 2001 Entry Draft for Radek Dvorak, December 30, 1999. Signed as a free agent by **Cambridge** (OHA-Sr.), October 21, 2004.

HATCHER, Derian

(HAT-chuhr, DAIR-ee-an) **PHI.**

Defense. Shoots left. 6'5", 235 lbs. Born, Sterling Hts., MI, June 4, 1972. Minnesota's 1st choice, 8th overall, in 1990 Entry Draft.

Season	Club	League	GP	G	A	Pts	PIM	PP	SH	GW	S	%	+/-	TF	F%	Min	GP	G	A	Pts	PIM	PP	SH	GW	Min
1987-88	Detroit GPD	MNHL	25	5	13	18	52	....	....	....	....	....	....	....	....	....	....	....	....	....	....	....	....	....	....
1988-89	Detroit GPD	MNHL	51	19	35	54	100	....	....	....	....	....	....	....	....	....	....	....	....	....	....	....	....	....	....
1989-90	North Bay	OHL	64	14	38	52	81	....	....	....	....	....	....	....	....	....	5	2	3	5	8	....	....	....	....
1990-91	North Bay	OHL	64	13	49	62	163	....	....	....	....	....	....	....	....	....	10	2	10	12	28	....	....	....	....
1991-92	Minnesota	NHL	43	8	4	12	88	0	0	2	51	15.7	7	....	....	....	5	0	2	2	8	0	0	0	....
1992-93	Minnesota	NHL	67	4	15	19	178	0	0	1	73	5.5	-27	....	....	....	....	....	....	....	....	....	....	....	....
	Kalamazoo Wings	IHL	2	1	2	3	21	....	....	....	....	....	....	....	....	....	....	....	....	....	....	....	....	....	....
1993-94	Dallas	NHL	83	12	19	31	211	2	1	2	132	9.1	19	....	....	....	9	0	2	2	14	0	0	0	....
1994-95	Dallas	NHL	43	5	11	16	105	2	0	2	74	6.8	3	....	....	....	....	....	....	....	....	....	....	....	....
1995-96	Dallas	NHL	79	8	23	31	129	2	0	1	125	6.4	-12	....	....	....	....	....	....	....	....	....	....	....	....
1996-97	Dallas	NHL	63	3	19	22	97	0	0	0	96	3.1	8	....	....	....	7	0	2	2	20	0	0	0	....
1997-98	Dallas	NHL	70	6	25	31	132	3	0	2	74	8.1	9	....	....	....	17	3	3	6	39	2	0	0	....
	United States	Olympics	4	0	0	0	0	....	....	....	....	....	....	....	....	....	....	....	....	....	....	....	....	....	....
1998-99♦	Dallas	NHL	80	9	21	30	102	3	0	2	125	7.2	21	0	0.0	24:44	18	1	6	7	24	0	0	0	29:06
99-2000	Dallas	NHL	57	2	22	24	68	0	0	0	90	2.2	6	0	0.0	27:33	23	1	3	4	29	0	0	0	27:40
2000-01	Dallas	NHL	80	2	21	23	77	1	0	2	97	2.1	5	0	0.0	25:53	10	0	1	1	16	0	0	0	28:53
2001-02	Dallas	NHL	80	4	21	25	87	1	0	0	111	3.6	12	0	0.0	26:40	....	....	....	....	....	....	....	....	....
2002-03	Dallas	NHL	82	8	22	30	106	1	1	2	159	5.0	37	0	0.0	25:51	11	1	2	3	33	0	0	0	30:02
2003-04	Detroit	NHL	15	0	4	4	8	0	0	0	18	0.0	4	0	0.0	19:38	12	0	1	1	15	0	0	0	22:54
2004-05	Motor City	UHL	24	5	12	17	27	....	....	....	....	....	....	....	....	....	....	....	....	....	....	....	....	....	....
	NHL Totals		842	71	227	298	1388	15	2	16	1225	5.8		0	0.0	25:48	112	6	22	28	198	2	0	0	27:45

NHL Second All-Star Team (2003)

Played in NHL All-Star Game (1997)

Transferred to **Dallas** after **Minnesota** franchise relocated, June 9, 1993. Signed as a free agent by **Detroit**, July 3, 2003. • Missed majority of 2003-04 season recovering from knee injury suffered in game vs. Vancouver, October 16, 2003. Signed as a free agent by **Motor City** (UHL), February 1, 2005. Signed as a free agent by **Philadelphia**, August 2, 2005.

HAVELID, Niclas

(HAHV-lihd, NIH-kluhs) **ATL.**

Defense. Shoots left. 6', 200 lbs. Born, Stockholm, Sweden, April 12, 1973. Anaheim's 2nd choice, 83rd overall, in 1999 Entry Draft.

Season	Club	League	GP	G	A	Pts	PIM	PP	SH	GW	S	%	+/-	TF	F%	Min	GP	G	A	Pts	PIM	PP	SH	GW	Min
1988-89	Enkopings SK	Sweden-3	7	0	1	1	0	....	....	....	....	....	....	....	....	....	....	....	....	....	....	....	....	....	....
1989-90	Enkopings SK	Sweden-3	24	1	2	3	28	....	....	....	....	....	....	....	....	....	....	....	....	....	....	....	....	....	....
1990-91	Arlanda	Sweden-2	30	2	3	5	22	....	....	....	....	....	....	....	....	....	....	....	....	....	....	....	....	....	....
1991-92	AIK Solna	Sweden	10	0	0	0	2	....	....	....	....	....	....	....	....	....	....	....	....	....	....	....	....	....	....
1992-93	AIK Solna	Sweden	30	1	2	3	22	....	....	....	....	....	....	....	....	....	3	0	0	0	2	....	....	....	....
1993-94	AIK Solna	Sweden-2	22	3	9	12	14	....	....	....	....	....	....	....	....	....	....	....	....	....	....	....	....	....	....
1994-95	AIK Solna	Sweden	40	3	7	10	38	....	....	....	....	....	....	....	....	....	....	....	....	....	....	....	....	....	....
1995-96	AIK Solna	Sweden	40	5	6	11	30	....	....	....	....	....	....	....	....	....	....	....	....	....	....	....	....	....	....
1996-97	AIK Solna	Sweden	49	3	6	9	42	....	....	....	....	....	....	....	....	....	7	1	2	3	8	....	....	....	....
1997-98	AIK Solna	Sweden	43	8	4	12	42	....	....	....	....	....	....	....	....	....	10	1	3	4	39	....	....	....	....
1998-99	Malmo	Sweden	50	10	12	22	42	....	....	....	....	....	....	....	....	....	8	0	4	4	10	....	....	....	....
99-2000	Anaheim	NHL	50	2	7	9	20	0	0	2	70	2.9	0	1	0.0	19:10	....	....	....	....	....	....	....	....	....
	Cincinnati	AHL	2	0	0	0	0	....	....	....	....	....	....	....	....	....	....	....	....	....	....	....	....	....	....
2000-01	Anaheim	NHL	47	4	10	14	34	2	0	1	69	5.8	-6	4	0.0	21:51	....	....	....	....	....	....	....	....	....

			Regular Season														Playoffs								
Season	Club	League	GP	G	A	Pts	PIM	PP	SH	GW	S	%	+/-	TF	F%	Min	GP	G	A	Pts	PIM	PP	SH	GW	Min
2001-02	**Anaheim**	**NHL**	**52**	**1**	**2**	**3**	**40**	**0**	**0**	**0**	**45**	**2.2**	**–13**	**1**	**0.0**	**17:01**	....	....	....	....	....	....	....	....	....
2002-03	**Anaheim**	**NHL**	**82**	**11**	**22**	**33**	**30**	**4**	**0**	**5**	**169**	**6.5**	**5**	**3**	**0.0**	**22:30**	**21**	**0**	**4**	**4**	**2**	**0**	**0**	**0**	**25:41**
2003-04	**Anaheim**	**NHL**	**79**	**6**	**20**	**26**	**28**	**5**	**0**	**3**	**122**	**4.9**	**–28**	**0**	**0.0**	**22:39**	....	....	....	....	....	....	....	....	....
2004-05	Sodertalje SK	Sweden	46	2	2	4	60	....	....	....	....	....	....	....	....	....	10	1	1	2	18	....	....	....	....
	NHL Totals		**310**	**24**	**61**	**85**	**152**	**11**	**0**	**11**	**475**	**5.1**		**9**	**0.0**	**20:59**	**21**	**0**	**4**	**4**	**2**	**0**	**0**	**0**	**25:41**

Traded to **Atlanta** by **Anaheim** for Kurtis Foster, June 26, 2004. Signed as a free agent by **Sodertalje** (Sweden), August 9, 2004.

HAVLAT, Martin (HAHV-lat, MAHR-tihn) OTT.

Left wing. Shoots left. 6'1", 190 lbs. Born, Mlada Boleslav, Czech., April 19, 1981. Ottawa's 1st choice, 26th overall, in 1999 Entry Draft.

Season	Club	League	GP	G	A	Pts	PIM	PP	SH	GW	S	%	+/-	TF	F%	Min	GP	G	A	Pts	PIM	PP	SH	GW	Min
1997-98	Ytong Brno Jr.	CzRep-Jr.	32	38	29	67	....	....	....	....	....	....	....	....	....	....	....	....	....	....	....	....	....	....	....
1998-99	HC Trinec Jr.	CzRep-Jr.	31	28	23	51	....	....	....	....	....	....	....	....	....	....	....	....	....	....	....	....	....	....	....
	Trinec	CzRep	24	2	3	5	4	....	....	....	....	....	....	....	....	....	8	0	0	0	....	....	....	....	....
99-2000	HC Ocelari Trinec	CzRep	46	13	29	42	42	....	....	....	....	....	....	....	....	....	4	0	2	2	8	....	....	....	....
2000-01	**Ottawa**	**NHL**	**73**	**19**	**23**	**42**	**20**	**7**	**0**	**5**	**133**	**14.3**	**8**	**40**	**30.0**	**13:47**	**4**	**0**	**0**	**0**	**2**	**0**	**0**	**0**	**14:04**
2001-02	**Ottawa**	**NHL**	**72**	**22**	**28**	**50**	**66**	**9**	**0**	**6**	**145**	**15.2**	**–7**	**15**	**40.0**	**14:46**	**12**	**2**	**5**	**7**	**14**	**2**	**0**	**2**	**16:19**
	Czech Republic	Olympics	4	3	1	4	27	....	....	....	....	....	....	....	....	....	....	....	....	....	....	....	....	....	....
2002-03	**Ottawa**	**NHL**	**67**	**24**	**35**	**59**	**30**	**9**	**0**	**4**	**179**	**13.4**	**20**	**7**	**14.3**	**16:27**	**18**	**5**	**6**	**11**	**14**	**1**	**0**	**2**	**16:27**
2003-04	HC Sparta Praha	CzRep	5	1	3	4	8	....	....	....	....	....	....	....	....	....	....	....	....	....	....	....	....	....	....
	Ottawa	**NHL**	**68**	**31**	**37**	**68**	**46**	**13**	**0**	**7**	**175**	**17.7**	**12**	**11**	**36.4**	**16:44**	**7**	**0**	**3**	**3**	**2**	**0**	**0**	**0**	**16:10**
2004-05	Znojmo	CzRep	12	10	4	14	16	....	....	....	....	....	....	....	....	....	....	....	....	....	....	....	....	....	....
	Dynamo Moscow	Russia	10	2	0	2	14	....	....	....	....	....	....	....	....	....	....	....	....	....	....	....	....	....	....
	HC Sparta Praha	CzRep	9	5	4	9	37	....	....	....	....	....	....	....	....	....	5	0	0	0	20	....	....	....	....
	NHL Totals		**280**	**96**	**123**	**219**	**162**	**38**	**0**	**22**	**632**	**15.2**		**73**	**31.5**	**15:23**	**41**	**7**	**14**	**21**	**32**	**3**	**0**	**4**	**16:08**

NHL All-Rookie Team (2001)

Signed as a free agent by **Znojmo** (CzRep), September 24, 2004. Signed as a free agent by **Dynamo Moscow** (Russia), November 10, 2004. Signed as a free agent by **Znojmo** (CzRep), January 18, 2005. Signed as a free agent by **Sparta** (CzRep), January 31, 2005.

HAY, Dwayne (HAY, DWAYN)

Left wing. Shoots left. 6'1", 203 lbs. Born, London, Ont., February 11, 1977. Washington's 3rd choice, 43rd overall, in 1995 Entry Draft.

Season	Club	League	GP	G	A	Pts	PIM	PP	SH	GW	S	%	+/-	TF	F%	Min	GP	G	A	Pts	PIM	PP	SH	GW	Min
1991-92	London Travellers	OMHA	86	70	56	126	104	....	....	....	....	....	....	....	....	....	....	....	....	....	....	....	....	....	....
1992-93	Listowel Cyclones	OHA-B	50	19	33	52	40	....	....	....	....	....	....	....	....	....	....	....	....	....	....	....	....	....	....
1993-94	Listowel Cyclones	OHA-B	48	10	24	34	56	....	....	....	....	....	....	....	....	....	....	....	....	....	....	....	....	....	....
1994-95	Guelph Storm	OHL	65	26	28	54	37	....	....	....	....	....	....	....	....	....	14	5	7	12	6	....	....	....	....
1995-96	Guelph Storm	OHL	60	28	30	58	49	....	....	....	....	....	....	....	....	....	16	4	9	13	18	....	....	....	....
1996-97	Guelph Storm	OHL	32	17	17	34	21	....	....	....	....	....	....	....	....	....	11	4	6	10	0	....	....	....	....
1997-98	**Washington**	**NHL**	**2**	**0**	**0**	**0**	**2**	**0**	**0**	**0**	**1**	**0.0**	**0**	....	....	....	....	....	....	....	....	....	....	....	....
	Portland Pirates	AHL	58	6	7	13	35	....	....	....	....	....	....	....	....	....	....	....	....	....	....	....	....	....	....
	New Haven	AHL	10	3	2	5	4	....	....	....	....	....	....	....	....	....	2	0	0	0	0	....	....	....	....
1998-99	**Florida**	**NHL**	**9**	**0**	**0**	**0**	**0**	**0**	**0**	**0**	**3**	**0.0**	**–1**	**1**	**0.0**	**6:35**	....	....	....	....	....	....	....	....	....
	New Haven	AHL	46	18	17	35	22	....	....	....	....	....	....	....	....	....	....	....	....	....	....	....	....	....	....
99-2000	**Florida**	**NHL**	**6**	**0**	**0**	**0**	**2**	**0**	**0**	**0**	**3**	**0.0**	**–2**	**0**	**0.0**	**6:36**	....	....	....	....	....	....	....	....	....
	Louisville Panthers	AHL	41	11	20	31	18	....	....	....	....	....	....	....	....	....	....	....	....	....	....	....	....	....	....
	Tampa Bay	**NHL**	**13**	**1**	**1**	**2**	**2**	**0**	**0**	**0**	**11**	**9.1**	**0**	**1**	**0.0**	**6:04**	....	....	....	....	....	....	....	....	....
2000-01	**Calgary**	**NHL**	**49**	**1**	**3**	**4**	**16**	**0**	**0**	**0**	**39**	**2.6**	**–4**	**6**	**16.7**	**8:24**	....	....	....	....	....	....	....	....	....
2001-02	Saint John Flames	AHL	70	5	12	17	39	....	....	....	....	....	....	....	....	....	....	....	....	....	....	....	....	....	....
2002-03	St. John's	AHL	51	10	19	29	31	....	....	....	....	....	....	....	....	....	....	....	....	....	....	....	....	....	....
2003-04	Pensacola	ECHL	62	29	30	59	40	....	....	....	....	....	....	....	....	....	5	1	3	4	2	....	....	....	....
	Hershey Bears	AHL	4	0	1	1	0	....	....	....	....	....	....	....	....	....	....	....	....	....	....	....	....	....	....
2004-05	Pensacola	ECHL	72	24	33	57	68	....	....	....	....	....	....	....	....	....	4	2	0	2	8	....	....	....	....
	NHL Totals		**79**	**2**	**4**	**6**	**22**	**0**	**0**	**0**	**57**	**3.5**		**8**	**12.5**	**7:39**	....	....	....	....	....	....	....	....	....

Traded to **Florida** by **Washington** with future considerations for Esa Tikkanen, March 9, 1998. Traded to **Tampa Bay** by **Florida** with Ryan Johnson for Mike Sillinger, March 14, 2000. Claimed on waivers by **Calgary** from **Tampa Bay**, October 3, 2000. Signed as a free agent by **Toronto**, November 30, 2002. Signed as a free agent by **Tampa Bay**, October 21, 2003.

HAYDAR, Darren (HAY-duhr, DAIR-ehn) NSH.

Right wing. Shoots left. 5'9", 166 lbs. Born, Toronto, Ont., October 22, 1979. Nashville's 14th choice, 248th overall, in 1999 Entry Draft.

Season	Club	League	GP	G	A	Pts	PIM	PP	SH	GW	S	%	+/-	TF	F%	Min	GP	G	A	Pts	PIM	PP	SH	GW	Min
1995-96	Milton Merchants	OPJHL	6	1	2	3	4	....	....	....	....	....	....	....	....	....	....	....	....	....	....	....	....	....	....
1996-97	Milton Merchants	OPJHL	51	32	68	100	68	....	....	....	....	....	....	....	....	....	....	....	....	....	....	....	....	....	....
1997-98	Milton Merchants	OPJHL	51	*71	*69	*140	65	....	....	....	....	....	....	....	....	....	....	....	....	....	....	....	....	....	....
1998-99	New Hampshire	H-East	41	31	30	61	34	....	....	....	....	....	....	....	....	....	....	....	....	....	....	....	....	....	....
99-2000	New Hampshire	H-East	38	22	19	41	42	....	....	....	....	....	....	....	....	....	....	....	....	....	....	....	....	....	....
2000-01	New Hampshire	H-East	39	18	23	41	38	....	....	....	....	....	....	....	....	....	....	....	....	....	....	....	....	....	....
2001-02	New Hampshire	H-East	40	31	*45	*76	28	....	....	....	....	....	....	....	....	....	....	....	....	....	....	....	....	....	....
2002-03	**Nashville**	**NHL**	**2**	**0**	**0**	**0**	**0**	**0**	**0**	**0**	**1**	**0.0**	**–1**	**0**	**0.0**	**8:54**	....	....	....	....	....	....	....	....	....
	Milwaukee	AHL	75	29	46	75	36	....	....	....	....	....	....	....	....	....	6	1	4	5	2	....	....	....	....
2003-04	Milwaukee	AHL	79	22	37	59	35	....	....	....	....	....	....	....	....	....	22	11	15	26	10	....	....	....	....
2004-05	Milwaukee	AHL	59	24	26	50	42	....	....	....	....	....	....	....	....	....	7	3	4	7	14	....	....	....	....
	NHL Totals		**2**	**0**	**0**	**0**	**0**	**0**	**0**	**0**	**1**	**0.0**		**0**	**0.0**	**8:54**	....	....	....	....	....	....	....	....	....

Hockey East Second All-Star Team (1999, 2000) • Hockey East Rookie of the Year (1999) • Hockey East First All-Star Team (2002) • Hockey East Player of the Year (2002) • AHL All-Rookie Team (2003) • Dudley "Red" Garrett Memorial Award (Rookie of the Year – AHL) (2003)

HEALEY, Paul (HEE-lee, PAWL) COL.

Left wing. Shoots right. 6'2", 198 lbs. Born, Edmonton, Alta., March 20, 1975. Philadelphia's 7th choice, 192nd overall, in 1993 Entry Draft.

Season	Club	League	GP	G	A	Pts	PIM	PP	SH	GW	S	%	+/-	TF	F%	Min	GP	G	A	Pts	PIM	PP	SH	GW	Min
1991-92	Ft. Saskatchewan	AJHL	52	11	19	30	40	....	....	....	....	....	....	....	....	....	....	....	....	....	....	....	....	....	....
1992-93	Prince Albert	WHL	72	12	20	32	66	....	....	....	....	....	....	....	....	....	....	....	....	....	....	....	....	....	....
1993-94	Prince Albert	WHL	63	23	26	49	70	....	....	....	....	....	....	....	....	....	....	....	....	....	....	....	....	....	....
1994-95	Prince Albert	WHL	71	43	50	93	67	....	....	....	....	....	....	....	....	....	12	3	4	7	2	....	....	....	....
1995-96	Hershey Bears	AHL	60	7	15	22	35	....	....	....	....	....	....	....	....	....	....	....	....	....	....	....	....	....	....
1996-97	**Philadelphia**	**NHL**	**2**	**0**	**0**	**0**	**0**	**0**	**0**	**0**	**0**	**0.0**	**0**	....	....	....	....	....	....	....	....	....	....	....	....
	Philadelphia	AHL	64	21	19	40	56	....	....	....	....	....	....	....	....	....	10	4	1	5	10	....	....	....	....
1997-98	**Philadelphia**	**NHL**	**4**	**0**	**0**	**0**	**12**	**0**	**0**	**0**	**0**	**0.0**	**0**	....	....	....	....	....	....	....	....	....	....	....	....
	Philadelphia	AHL	71	34	18	52	48	....	....	....	....	....	....	....	....	....	20	6	2	8	4	....	....	....	....
1998-99	Philadelphia	AHL	72	26	20	46	39	....	....	....	....	....	....	....	....	....	15	4	6	10	11	....	....	....	....
99-2000	Milwaukee	IHL	76	21	18	39	28	....	....	....	....	....	....	....	....	....	3	1	2	3	0	....	....	....	....
2000-01	Hamilton	AHL	79	39	32	71	34	....	....	....	....	....	....	....	....	....	....	....	....	....	....	....	....	....	....
2001-02	**Toronto**	**NHL**	**21**	**3**	**7**	**10**	**2**	**0**	**0**	**0**	**29**	**10.3**	**7**	**5**	**60.0**	**11:03**	**18**	**0**	**1**	**1**	**2**	**0**	**0**	**0**	**9:01**
	St. John's	AHL	58	27	29	56	30	....	....	....	....	....	....	....	....	....	2	1	1	2	8	....	....	....	....
2002-03	**Toronto**	**NHL**	**44**	**3**	**7**	**10**	**16**	**1**	**0**	**0**	**43**	**7.0**	**8**	**13**	**38.5**	**12:00**	**4**	**0**	**1**	**1**	**2**	**0**	**0**	**0**	**9:14**
	St. John's	AHL	17	6	10	16	12	....	....	....	....	....	....	....	....	....	....	....	....	....	....	....	....	....	....
2003-04	**NY Rangers**	**NHL**	**4**	**0**	**0**	**0**	**0**	**0**	**0**	**0**	**0**	**0.0**	**0**	**1**	**0.0**	**4:50**	....	....	....	....	....	....	....	....	....
	Hartford	AHL	50	11	10	21	37	....	....	....	....	....	....	....	....	....	....	....	....	....	....	....	....	....	....
	San Antonio	AHL	18	5	5	10	20	....	....	....	....	....	....	....	....	....	....	....	....	....	....	....	....	....	....
2004-05	San Antonio	AHL	62	6	17	23	50	....	....	....	....	....	....	....	....	....	....	....	....	....	....	....	....	....	....
	Edmonton	AHL	17	3	6	9	29	....	....	....	....	....	....	....	....	....	....	....	....	....	....	....	....	....	....
	NHL Totals		**75**	**6**	**14**	**20**	**30**	**1**	**0**	**0**	**72**	**8.3**		**19**	**42.1**	**11:18**	**22**	**0**	**2**	**2**	**4**	**0**	**0**	**0**	**9:03**

WHL East Second All-Star Team (1995)

Traded to **Nashville** by **Philadelphia** for Matt Henderson, September 27, 1999. Signed as a free agent by **Edmonton**, August 31, 2000. Signed as a free agent by **Toronto**, July 24, 2001. Signed as a free agent by **NY Rangers**, July 28, 2003. Traded to **Florida** by **NY Rangers** for Jeff Paul, March 9, 2004. Loaned to **Edmonton** (AHL) by **Florida** (San Antonio-AHL) for cash, March 12, 2005. Signed as a free agent by **Colorado**, August 16, 2005.

HEATLEY, Dany

(HEET-lee, DA-nee) **OTT.**

Right wing. Shoots left. 6'3", 215 lbs. Born, Freiburg, West Germany, January 21, 1981. Atlanta's 1st choice, 2nd overall, in 2000 Entry Draft.

			Regular Season														Playoffs								
Season	Club	League	GP	G	A	Pts	PIM	PP	SH	GW	S	%	+/-	TF	F%	Min	GP	G	A	Pts	PIM	PP	SH	GW	Min
1996-97	Calgary Blazers	AMHL	25	30	42	72	26																		
1997-98	Calgary Buffaloes	AMHL	36	39	42	*81	34										10	10	12	*22	30				
1998-99	Calgary Canucks	AJHL	60	*70	56	*126	91										13	*22	13	*35	6				
99-2000	U. of Wisconsin	WCHA	38	28	28	56	32																		
2000-01	U. of Wisconsin	WCHA	39	24	33	57	74																		
2001-02	**Atlanta**	**NHL**	**82**	**26**	**41**	**67**	**56**	**7**	**0**	**4**	**202**	**12.9**	**–19**	**116**	**32.8**	**19:53**									
2002-03	**Atlanta**	**NHL**	**77**	**41**	**48**	**89**	**58**	**19**	**1**	**6**	**252**	**16.3**	**–8**	**49**	**36.7**	**21:57**									
2003-04	**Atlanta**	**NHL**	**31**	**13**	**12**	**25**	**18**	**5**	**0**	**3**	**83**	**15.7**	**–8**	**41**	**24.4**	**19:53**									
2004-05	SC Bern	Swiss	16	14	10	24	58																		
	Ak Bars Kazan	Russia	11	3	1	4	22										4	2	1	3	4				
	NHL Totals		**190**	**80**	**101**	**181**	**132**	**31**	**1**	**13**	**537**	**14.9**		**206**	**32.0**	**20:43**									

WCHA First All-Star Team (2000) • WCHA Rookie of the Year (2000) • NCAA West Second All-American Team (2000) • WCHA Second All-Star Team (2001) • NCAA West First All-American Team (2001) • NHL All-Rookie Team (2002) • Calder Memorial Trophy (2002)

Played in NHL All-Star Game (2003)

• Missed majority of 2003-04 season recovering from injuries suffered in automobile accident, September 29, 2003. Signed as a free agent by **Bern** (Swiss), October 13, 2004. Signed as a free agent by **Kazan** (Russia), February 9, 2005. Traded to **Ottawa** by **Atlanta** for Marian Hossa and Greg de Vries, August 23, 2005.

HECHT, Jochen

(HEHKHT, YOH-khehn) **BUF.**

Left wing. Shoots left. 6'1", 200 lbs. Born, Mannheim, West Germany, June 21, 1977. St. Louis' 1st choice, 49th overall, in 1995 Entry Draft.

			Regular Season														Playoffs								
Season	Club	League	GP	G	A	Pts	PIM	PP	SH	GW	S	%	+/-	TF	F%	Min	GP	G	A	Pts	PIM	PP	SH	GW	Min
1993-94	Mannheim Jr.	Ger-Jr.	28	27	13	40	103																		
1994-95	Adler Mannheim	Germany	43	11	12	23	68										10	5	4	9	12				
1995-96	Adler Mannheim	Germany	44	12	16	28	68										8	3	2	5	6				
1996-97	Adler Mannheim	Germany	46	21	21	42	36										9	3	3	6	4				
1997-98	Adler Mannheim	Germany	44	7	19	26	42										10	1	1	2	14				
	Adler Mannheim	EuroHL	5	0	4	4	8																		
	Germany	Olympics	4	1	0	1	6																		
1998-99	**St. Louis**	**NHL**	**3**	**0**	**0**	**0**	**0**	**0**	**0**	**0**	**4**	**0.0**	**–2**	**19**	**21.1**	**13:16**	**5**	**2**	**0**	**2**	**0**	**0**	**0**	**0**	**16:40**
	Worcester IceCats	AHL	74	21	35	56	48										4	1	1	2	2				
99-2000	**St. Louis**	**NHL**	**63**	**13**	**21**	**34**	**28**	**5**	**0**	**1**	**140**	**9.3**	**20**	**75**	**49.3**	**15:25**	**7**	**4**	**6**	**10**	**2**	**1**	**0**	**1**	**17:02**
2000-01	**St. Louis**	**NHL**	**72**	**19**	**25**	**44**	**48**	**8**	**3**	**1**	**208**	**9.1**	**11**	**160**	**43.8**	**17:56**	**15**	**2**	**4**	**6**	**4**	**0**	**0**	**0**	**17:19**
2001-02	**Edmonton**	**NHL**	**82**	**16**	**24**	**40**	**60**	**5**	**0**	**3**	**211**	**7.6**	**4**	**26**	**53.9**	**15:00**									
	Germany	Olympics	4	1	1	2	2																		
2002-03	**Buffalo**	**NHL**	**49**	**10**	**16**	**26**	**30**	**2**	**0**	**2**	**145**	**6.9**	**4**	**33**	**30.3**	**17:55**									
2003-04	**Buffalo**	**NHL**	**64**	**15**	**37**	**52**	**49**	**2**	**1**	**0**	**174**	**8.6**	**17**	**141**	**43.3**	**19:00**									
2004-05	Adler Mannheim	Germany	48	16	34	50	151										14	10	10	*20	14				
	NHL Totals		**333**	**73**	**123**	**196**	**215**	**22**	**4**	**7**	**882**	**8.3**		**454**	**43.2**	**16:54**	**27**	**8**	**10**	**18**	**6**	**1**	**0**	**1**	**17:07**

Traded to **Edmonton** by **St. Louis** with Marty Reasoner and Jan Horacek for Doug Weight and Michel Riesen, July 1, 2001. Traded to **Buffalo** by **Edmonton** for Atlanta's 2nd round choice (previously acquired, Edmonton selected Jeff Deslauriers) in 2002 Entry Draft and Nashville's 2nd round choice (previously acquired, Edmonton selected Jarret Stoll) in 2002 Entry Draft, June 22, 2002. Signed as a free agent by **Mannheim** (Germany), August 2, 2004.

HEDICAN, Bret

(HEH-dih-kan, BREHT) **CAR.**

Defense. Shoots left. 6'2", 205 lbs. Born, St. Paul, MN, August 10, 1970. St. Louis' 10th choice, 198th overall, in 1988 Entry Draft.

			Regular Season														Playoffs								
Season	Club	League	GP	G	A	Pts	PIM	PP	SH	GW	S	%	+/-	TF	F%	Min	GP	G	A	Pts	PIM	PP	SH	GW	Min
1987-88	North St. Paul	High-MN	23	15	19	34	16																		
1988-89	St. Cloud State	NCAA-3	28	5	3	8	28																		
1989-90	St. Cloud State	NCAA-3	36	4	17	21	37																		
1990-91	St. Cloud State	WCHA	41	21	26	47	26																		
1991-92	United States	Nat-Tm	54	1	8	9	59																		
	United States	Olympics	8	0	0	0	4																		
	St. Louis	**NHL**	**4**	**1**	**0**	**1**	**0**	**0**	**0**	**0**	**1**	**100.0**	**1**				**5**	**0**	**0**	**0**	**0**	**0**	**0**	**0**	
1992-93	**St. Louis**	**NHL**	**42**	**0**	**8**	**8**	**30**	**0**	**0**	**0**	**40**	**0.0**	**–2**				**10**	**0**	**0**	**0**	**14**	**0**	**0**	**0**	
	Peoria Rivermen	IHL	19	0	8	8	10																		
1993-94	**St. Louis**	**NHL**	**61**	**0**	**11**	**11**	**64**	**0**	**0**	**0**	**78**	**0.0**	**–8**												
	Vancouver	**NHL**	**8**	**0**	**1**	**1**	**0**	**0**	**0**	**0**	**10**	**0.0**	**1**				**24**	**1**	**6**	**7**	**16**	**0**	**0**	**0**	
1994-95	**Vancouver**	**NHL**	**45**	**2**	**11**	**13**	**34**	**0**	**0**	**0**	**56**	**3.6**	**–3**				**11**	**0**	**2**	**2**	**6**	**0**	**0**	**0**	
1995-96	**Vancouver**	**NHL**	**77**	**6**	**23**	**29**	**83**	**1**	**0**	**0**	**113**	**5.3**	**8**				**6**	**0**	**1**	**1**	**10**	**0**	**0**	**0**	
1996-97	**Vancouver**	**NHL**	**67**	**4**	**15**	**19**	**51**	**2**	**0**	**1**	**93**	**4.3**	**–3**												
1997-98	**Vancouver**	**NHL**	**71**	**3**	**24**	**27**	**79**	**1**	**0**	**0**	**84**	**3.6**	**3**												
1998-99	**Vancouver**	**NHL**	**42**	**2**	**11**	**13**	**34**	**0**	**2**	**0**	**52**	**3.8**	**7**	**0**	**0.0**	**18:40**									
	Florida	**NHL**	**25**	**3**	**7**	**10**	**17**	**0**	**0**	**1**	**38**	**7.9**	**–2**	**0**	**0.0**	**22:24**									
99-2000	**Florida**	**NHL**	**76**	**6**	**19**	**25**	**68**	**2**	**0**	**1**	**58**	**10.3**	**4**	**0**	**0.0**	**19:36**	**4**	**0**	**0**	**0**	**0**	**0**	**0**	**0**	**20:42**
2000-01	**Florida**	**NHL**	**70**	**5**	**15**	**20**	**72**	**4**	**0**	**1**	**104**	**4.8**	**–7**	**0**	**0.0**	**21:49**									
2001-02	**Florida**	**NHL**	**31**	**3**	**7**	**10**	**12**	**0**	**0**	**0**	**46**	**6.5**	**–4**	**0**	**0.0**	**24:27**									
	Carolina	**NHL**	**26**	**2**	**4**	**6**	**10**	**0**	**0**	**1**	**39**	**5.1**	**3**	**0**	**0.0**	**22:56**	**23**	**1**	**4**	**5**	**20**	**0**	**0**	**0**	**23:52**
2002-03	**Carolina**	**NHL**	**72**	**3**	**14**	**17**	**75**	**1**	**0**	**1**	**113**	**2.7**	**–24**	**0**	**0.0**	**23:02**									
2003-04	**Carolina**	**NHL**	**81**	**7**	**17**	**24**	**64**	**2**	**0**	**3**	**112**	**6.3**	**–10**	**0**	**0.0**	**22:35**									
2004-05			DID NOT PLAY																						
	NHL Totals		**798**	**47**	**187**	**234**	**693**	**13**	**2**	**9**	**1037**	**4.5**		**0**	**0.0**	**21:45**	**83**	**2**	**13**	**15**	**66**	**0**	**0**	**0**	**23:24**

WCHA First All-Star Team (1991)

Traded to **Vancouver** by **St. Louis** with Jeff Brown and Nathan LaFayette for Craig Janney, March 21, 1994. Traded to **Florida** by **Vancouver** with Pavel Bure, Brad Ference and Vancouver's 3rd round choice (Robert Fried) in 2000 Entry Draft for Ed Jovanovski, Dave Gagner, Mike Brown, Kevin Weekes and Florida's 1st round choice (Nathan Smith) in 2000 Entry Draft, January 17, 1999. Traded to **Carolina** by **Florida** with Kevyn Adams, Tomas Malec for Sandis Ozolinsh and Byron Ritchie, January 16, 2002.

HEDIN, Pierre

(heh-DEEN, PEE-air) **TOR.**

Defense. Shoots left. 6'1", 198 lbs. Born, Ornskoldsvik, Sweden, February 19, 1978. Toronto's 8th choice, 239th overall, in 1999 Entry Draft.

			Regular Season														Playoffs								
Season	Club	League	GP	G	A	Pts	PIM	PP	SH	GW	S	%	+/-	TF	F%	Min	GP	G	A	Pts	PIM	PP	SH	GW	Min
1995-96	MoDo Jr.	Swe-Jr.	21	0	3	3	20																		
1996-97	MoDo Jr.	Swe-Jr.	29	6	8	14	34																		
	MoDo	Sweden	19	1	2	3	6																		
1997-98	Malmo Jr.	Swe-Jr.	7	1	6	7	10																		
	MoDo	Sweden	29	2	1	3	26										9	1	1	2	4				
1998-99	MoDo	Sweden	41	6	5	11	28										13	1	1	2	12				
99-2000	MoDo	Sweden	48	9	5	14	36										13	0	2	2	8				
2000-01	MoDo	Sweden	46	5	8	13	59										7	3	0	3	4				
2001-02	MODO	Sweden	39	7	9	16	20										14	*8	2	10	10				
2002-03	MODO	Sweden	46	8	14	22	32										6	0	1	1	4				
2003-04	**Toronto**	**NHL**	**3**	**0**	**1**	**1**	**0**	**0**	**0**	**0**	**4**	**0.0**	**–1**	**0**	**0.0**	**19:20**									
	St. John's	AHL	62	5	19	24	52																		
2004-05	MODO	Sweden	31	3	4	7	28										6	1	0	1	6				
	NHL Totals		**3**	**0**	**1**	**1**	**0**	**0**	**0**	**0**	**4**	**0.0**		**0**	**0.0**	**19:20**									

Signed as a free agent by **MODO** (Sweden), September 18, 2004. Signed as a free agent by **Mannheim** (Germany), August 23, 2005.

HEDSTROM, Jonathan

(HEHD-struhm, JAWN-ah-thuhn) **ANA.**

Right wing. Shoots left. 6', 200 lbs. Born, Skelleftea, Sweden, December 27, 1977. Toronto's 8th choice, 221st overall, in 1997 Entry Draft.

			Regular Season														Playoffs								
Season	Club	League	GP	G	A	Pts	PIM	PP	SH	GW	S	%	+/-	TF	F%	Min	GP	G	A	Pts	PIM	PP	SH	GW	Min
1995-96	Skelleftea AIK HK	Sweden-2	7	0	0	0	0																		
1996-97	Skelleftea Jr.	Swe-Jr.	9	4	4	8																			
	Skelleftea AIK HK	Sweden-2	12	1	1	2	10										6	0	0	0	2				
1997-98	Skelleftea Jr.	Swe-Jr.	1	0	0	0	2																		
	Skelleftea AIK HK	Sweden-2	16	2	3	5																			
1998-99	Skelleftea AIK HK	Sweden-2	36	15	28	43	74																		
99-2000	Lulea HF	Sweden	48	9	17	26	46										9	2	1	3	12				
2000-01	Lulea HF	Sweden	46	9	19	28	68										12	1	6	7	16				
2001-02	Lulea HF	Sweden	47	11	7	18	38										4	2	1	3	6				

			Regular Season														Playoffs								
Season	Club	League	GP	G	A	Pts	PIM	PP	SH	GW	S	%	+/-	TF	F%	Min	GP	G	A	Pts	PIM	PP	SH	GW	Min
2002-03	**Anaheim**	**NHL**	**4**	**0**	**0**	**0**	**0**	**0**	**0**	**0**	**3**	**0.0**	**–1**	**1**	**0.0**	**7:51**	....	....	....	....	....	....	....	....	....
	Cincinnati	AHL	50	14	21	35	62	....	....	....	....	....	....	....	....	....	....	....	....	....	....	....	....	....	....
2003-04	Djurgarden	Sweden	48	12	22	34	94	....	....	....	....	....	....	....	....	....	3	0	2	2	12	....	....	....	....
2004-05	Timra IK	Sweden	46	14	21	35	92	....	....	....	....	....	....	....	....	....	7	3	5	8	16	....	....	....	....
	NHL Totals		**4**	**0**	**0**	**0**	**0**	**0**	**0**	**0**	**3**	**0.0**		**1**	**0.0**	**7:51**	....	....	....	....	....	....	....	....	....

Rights traded to **Anaheim** by **Toronto** for Anaheim's 6th (Vadim Sozinov) and 7th (Markus Seikola) round choices in 2000 Entry Draft, June 25, 2000. Signed as a free agent by **Djurgarden** (Sweden), September 1, 2003. Signed as a free agent by **Timra** (Sweden), September, 2004.

HEEREMA, Jeff

(HEER-eh-muh, JEHF) **OTT.**

Right wing. Shoots right. 6'1", 190 lbs. Born, Thunder Bay, Ont., January 17, 1980. Carolina's 1st choice, 11th overall, in 1998 Entry Draft.

1996-97	T. Bay Kings	TBMHL	54	42	29	71	112	....	....	....	....	....	....	....	....	....	....	....	....	....	....	....	....	....	....
1997-98	Sarnia Sting	OHL	63	32	40	72	88	....	....	....	....	....	....	....	....	....	5	4	1	5	10	....	....	....	....
1998-99	Sarnia Sting	OHL	62	31	39	70	113	....	....	....	....	....	....	....	....	....	6	5	1	6	0	....	....	....	....
99-2000	Sarnia Sting	OHL	67	36	41	77	62	....	....	....	....	....	....	....	....	....	7	4	2	6	10	....	....	....	....
2000-01	Cincinnati	IHL	73	17	16	33	42	....	....	....	....	....	....	....	....	....	4	0	0	0	0	....	....	....	....
2001-02	Lowell	AHL	76	33	37	70	90	....	....	....	....	....	....	....	....	....	5	2	3	5	2	....	....	....	....
2002-03	**Carolina**	**NHL**	**10**	**3**	**0**	**3**	**2**	**1**	**0**	**0**	**16**	**18.8**	**–2**	**0**	**0.0**	**9:37**	....	....	....	....	....	....	....	....	....
	Lowell	AHL	36	15	17	32	25	....	....	....	....	....	....	....	....	....	....	....	....	....	....	....	....	....	....
2003-04	**St. Louis**	**NHL**	**22**	**1**	**2**	**3**	**4**	**0**	**0**	**1**	**28**	**3.6**	**–5**	**2**	**50.0**	**10:26**	....	....	....	....	....	....	....	....	....
	Worcester IceCats	AHL	1	0	0	0	2	....	....	....	....	....	....	....	....	....	....	....	....	....	....	....	....	....	....
	Hartford	AHL	41	12	15	27	25	....	....	....	....	....	....	....	....	....	4	0	0	0	9	....	....	....	....
2004-05	Manitoba Moose	AHL	80	14	31	45	67	....	....	....	....	....	....	....	....	....	14	4	6	10	12	....	....	....	....
	NHL Totals		**32**	**4**	**2**	**6**	**6**	**1**	**0**	**1**	**44**	**9.1**		**2**	**50.0**	**10:11**	....	....	....	....	....	....	....	....	....

Claimed on waivers by **NY Rangers** from **Carolina**, September 30, 2003. Claimed by **St. Louis** from **NY Rangers** in Waiver Draft, October 3, 2003. Claimed on waivers by **NY Rangers** from **St. Louis**, January 10, 2004. Signed as a free agent by **Vancouver**, August 19, 2004. Signed as a free agent by **Ottawa**, August 26, 2005.

HEINS, Shawn

(HIGHNS, SHAWN)

Defense. Shoots left. 6'4", 210 lbs. Born, Eganville, Ont., December 24, 1973.

1991-92	Peterborough	OHL	49	1	1	2	73	....	....	....	....	....	....	....	....	....	7	0	0	0	5	....	....	....	....
1992-93	Peterborough	OHL	5	0	0	0	10	....	....	....	....	....	....	....	....	....	....	....	....	....	....	....	....	....	....
	Windsor Spitfires	OHL	53	7	10	17	107	....	....	....	....	....	....	....	....	....	....	....	....	....	....	....	....	....	....
1993-94	Renfrew	OHA-B	32	16	34	50	250	....	....	....	....	....	....	....	....	....	....	....	....	....	....	....	....	....	....
1994-95	Renfrew	OHA-B	35	30	49	79	188	....	....	....	....	....	....	....	....	....	....	....	....	....	....	....	....	....	....
1995-96	Mobile Mysticks	ECHL	62	7	20	27	152	....	....	....	....	....	....	....	....	....	....	....	....	....	....	....	....	....	....
	Cape Breton	AHL	1	0	0	0	0	....	....	....	....	....	....	....	....	....	....	....	....	....	....	....	....	....	....
1996-97	Mobile Mysticks	ECHL	56	6	17	23	253	....	....	....	....	....	....	....	....	....	3	0	2	2	2	....	....	....	....
	Kansas City	IHL	6	0	0	0	9	....	....	....	....	....	....	....	....	....	....	....	....	....	....	....	....	....	....
1997-98	Kansas City	IHL	82	22	28	50	303	....	....	....	....	....	....	....	....	....	11	1	0	1	49	....	....	....	....
1998-99	Canada	Nat-Tm	36	5	16	21	66	....	....	....	....	....	....	....	....	....	....	....	....	....	....	....	....	....	....
	San Jose	**NHL**	**5**	**0**	**0**	**0**	**13**	**0**	**0**	**0**	**4**	**0.0**	**0**	**0**	**0.0**	**13:38**	....	....	....	....	....	....	....	....	....
	Kentucky	AHL	18	2	2	4	108	....	....	....	....	....	....	....	....	....	12	2	7	9	10	....	....	....	....
99-2000	**San Jose**	**NHL**	**1**	**0**	**0**	**0**	**2**	**0**	**0**	**0**	**1**	**0.0**	**–1**	**0**	**0.0**	**10:57**	....	....	....	....	....	....	....	....	....
	Kentucky	AHL	69	11	52	63	238	....	....	....	....	....	....	....	....	....	9	3	3	6	44	....	....	....	....
2000-01	**San Jose**	**NHL**	**38**	**3**	**4**	**7**	**57**	**2**	**0**	**0**	**45**	**6.7**	**2**	**0**	**0.0**	**10:15**	**2**	**0**	**0**	**0**	**0**	**0**	**0**	**0**	**7:31**
2001-02	**San Jose**	**NHL**	**17**	**0**	**2**	**2**	**24**	**0**	**0**	**0**	**20**	**0.0**	**1**	**0**	**0.0**	**9:46**	....	....	....	....	....	....	....	....	....
2002-03	**San Jose**	**NHL**	**20**	**0**	**1**	**1**	**9**	**0**	**0**	**0**	**10**	**0.0**	**–2**	**0**	**0.0**	**8:32**	....	....	....	....	....	....	....	....	....
	Pittsburgh	**NHL**	**27**	**1**	**1**	**2**	**33**	**0**	**0**	**1**	**28**	**3.6**	**–2**	**0**	**0.0**	**19:11**	....	....	....	....	....	....	....	....	....
2003-04	**Atlanta**	**NHL**	**17**	**0**	**4**	**4**	**16**	**0**	**0**	**0**	**17**	**0.0**	**–1**	**0**	**0.0**	**13:53**	....	....	....	....	....	....	....	....	....
	Chicago Wolves	AHL	58	12	19	31	120	....	....	....	....	....	....	....	....	....	10	1	5	6	44	....	....	....	....
2004-05	Eisbaren Berlin	Germany	49	6	21	27	142	....	....	....	....	....	....	....	....	....	11	3	4	7	24	....	....	....	....
	NHL Totals		**125**	**4**	**12**	**16**	**154**	**2**	**0**	**1**	**125**	**3.2**		**0**	**0.0**	**12:28**	**2**	**0**	**0**	**0**	**0**	**0**	**0**	**0**	**7:31**

AHL First All-Star Team (2000)

Signed as a free agent by **San Jose**, January 5, 1997. • Missed majority of 2000-01 season recovering from head injury suffered in game vs. Chicago, February 14, 2001. • Missed majority of 2001-02 season recovering from knee (December 4, 2001 vs. Calgary) and jaw (January 19, 2002 vs. Colorado) injuries. Traded to **Pittsburgh** by **San Jose** for Pittsburgh's 5th round choice (Patrick Ehelechner) in 2003 Entry Draft, February 9, 2003. Signed as a free agent by **Atlanta**, September 10, 2003. Claimed on waivers by **NY Rangers** from **Atlanta**, September 30, 2003. Claimed by **Atlanta** from **NY Rangers** in Waiver Draft, October 3, 2003. Signed as a free agent by **Eisbaren Berlin** (Germany), July 15, 2004.

HEISTEN, Barrett

(HIGH-stehn, BAIR-reht)

Left wing. Shoots left. 6'1", 200 lbs. Born, Anchorage, AK, March 19, 1980. Buffalo's 1st choice, 20th overall, in 1999 Entry Draft.

1996-97	Anchorage	AAHL	39	35	29	64	....	....	....	....	....	....	....	....	....	....	....	....	....	....	....	....	....	....	....
1997-98	USA U-18	USDP	50	11	26	37	245	....	....	....	....	....	....	....	....	....	....	....	....	....	....	....	....	....	....
1998-99	U. of Maine	H-East	34	12	16	28	72	....	....	....	....	....	....	....	....	....	....	....	....	....	....	....	....	....	....
99-2000	U. of Maine	H-East	37	13	24	37	86	....	....	....	....	....	....	....	....	....	....	....	....	....	....	....	....	....	....
2000-01	Seattle	WHL	58	20	57	77	61	....	....	....	....	....	....	....	....	....	9	2	6	8	20	....	....	....	....
2001-02	**NY Rangers**	**NHL**	**10**	**0**	**0**	**0**	**2**	**0**	**0**	**0**	**7**	**0.0**	**–4**	**7**	**28.6**	**7:36**	....	....	....	....	....	....	....	....	....
	Hartford	AHL	49	9	9	18	60	....	....	....	....	....	....	....	....	....	....	....	....	....	....	....	....	....	....
	Utah Grizzlies	AHL	12	5	1	6	14	....	....	....	....	....	....	....	....	....	5	1	0	1	4	....	....	....	....
2002-03	Utah Grizzlies	AHL	58	10	10	20	47	....	....	....	....	....	....	....	....	....	2	0	0	0	4	....	....	....	....
2003-04	Utah Grizzlies	AHL	73	4	13	17	98	....	....	....	....	....	....	....	....	....	....	....	....	....	....	....	....	....	....
2004-05	Bridgeport	AHL	64	7	13	20	59	....	....	....	....	....	....	....	....	....	....	....	....	....	....	....	....	....	....
	NHL Totals		**10**	**0**	**0**	**0**	**2**	**0**	**0**	**0**	**7**	**0.0**		**7**	**28.6**	**7:36**	....	....	....	....	....	....	....	....	....

• Left **University of Maine** (H-East) and signed with **Seattle** (WHL), August 7, 2000. Signed as a free agent by **NY Rangers**, June 16, 2001. Traded to **Dallas** by **NY Rangers** with Manny Malhotra for Martin Rucinsky and Roman Lyashenko, March 12, 2002. Signed as a free agent by **NY Islanders**, August 25, 2004.

HEJDUK, Milan

(HAY-dook, MEE-lan) **COL.**

Right wing. Shoots right. 5'11", 185 lbs. Born, Usti-nad-Labem, Czech., February 14, 1976. Quebec's 6th choice, 87th overall, in 1994 Entry Draft.

1993-94	HC Pardubice	CzRep	22	6	3	9	....	....	....	....	....	....	....	....	....	....	10	5	1	6	....	....	....	....	....
1994-95	HC Pardubice	CzRep	43	11	13	24	6	....	....	....	....	....	....	....	....	....	6	3	1	4	0	....	....	....	....
1995-96	Pardubice	CzRep	37	13	7	20	....	....	....	....	....	....	....	....	....	....	....	....	....	....	....	....	....	....	....
1996-97	Pardubice	CzRep	51	27	11	38	10	....	....	....	....	....	....	....	....	....	10	6	0	6	27	....	....	....	....
1997-98	Pardubice	CzRep	48	26	19	45	20	....	....	....	....	....	....	....	....	....	3	0	0	0	2	....	....	....	....
	Czech Republic	Olympics	4	0	0	0	2	....	....	....	....	....	....	....	....	....	....	....	....	....	....	....	....	....	....
1998-99	**Colorado**	**NHL**	**82**	**14**	**34**	**48**	**26**	**4**	**0**	**5**	**178**	**7.9**	**8**	**2**	**50.0**	**15:45**	**16**	**6**	**6**	**12**	**4**	**1**	**0**	**3**	**15:53**
99-2000	**Colorado**	**NHL**	**82**	**36**	**36**	**72**	**16**	**13**	**0**	**9**	**228**	**15.8**	**14**	**3**	**100.0**	**19:58**	**17**	**5**	**4**	**9**	**6**	**3**	**0**	**1**	**19:56**
2000-01♦	**Colorado**	**NHL**	**80**	**41**	**38**	**79**	**36**	**12**	**1**	**9**	**213**	**19.2**	**32**	**3**	**33.3**	**19:52**	**23**	**7**	***16**	**23**	**6**	**4**	**0**	**1**	**21:33**
2001-02	**Colorado**	**NHL**	**62**	**21**	**23**	**44**	**24**	**7**	**1**	**5**	**139**	**15.1**	**0**	**5**	**40.0**	**20:11**	**16**	**3**	**3**	**6**	**4**	**1**	**0**	**0**	**18:24**
	Czech Republic	Olympics	4	1	0	1	0	....	....	....	....	....	....	....	....	....	....	....	....	....	....	....	....	....	....
2002-03	**Colorado**	**NHL**	**82**	***50**	**48**	**98**	**32**	**18**	**0**	**4**	**244**	**20.5**	**52**	**43**	**44.2**	**19:50**	**7**	**2**	**2**	**4**	**2**	**1**	**0**	**0**	**20:42**
2003-04	**Colorado**	**NHL**	**82**	**35**	**40**	**75**	**20**	**16**	**0**	**6**	**237**	**14.8**	**19**	**69**	**47.8**	**18:46**	**11**	**5**	**2**	**7**	**0**	**2**	**0**	**0**	**18:40**
2004-05	Pardubice	CzRep	48	25	26	51	14	....	....	....	....	....	....	....	....	....	16	6	2	8	6	....	....	....	....
	NHL Totals		**470**	**197**	**219**	**416**	**154**	**70**	**2**	**38**	**1239**	**15.9**		**125**	**47.2**	**19:01**	**90**	**28**	**33**	**61**	**22**	**12**	**0**	**5**	**19:16**

NHL All-Rookie Team (1999) • NHL Second All-Star Team (2003) • Bud Light Plus/Minus Award (2003) (tied with Peter Forsberg) • Maurice "Rocket" Richard Trophy (2003)

Played in NHL All-Star Game (2000, 2001)

Rights transferred to **Colorado** after **Quebec** franchise relocated, June 21, 1995. Signed as a free agent by **Pardubice** (CzRep), September 18, 2004.

HELMER, Bryan

(HEHL-muhr, BRIGH-uhn) **DET.**

Defense. Shoots right. 6'1", 200 lbs. Born, Sault Ste. Marie, Ont., July 15, 1972.

1989-90	Wellington Dukes	OHA-B	44	4	20	24	204	....	....	....	....	....	....	....	....	....	....	....	....	....	....	....	....	....	....
	Belleville Bulls	OHL	6	0	1	1	0	....	....	....	....	....	....	....	....	....	....	....	....	....	....	....	....	....	....
1990-91	Wellington Dukes	OHA-B	50	11	14	25	109	....	....	....	....	....	....	....	....	....	....	....	....	....	....	....	....	....	....
1991-92	Wellington Dukes	MTJHL	42	17	31	48	66	....	....	....	....	....	....	....	....	....	3	2	1	3	0	....	....	....	....
1992-93	Wellington Dukes	MTJHL	48	21	54	75	84	....	....	....	....	....	....	....	....	....	9	4	8	12	22	....	....	....	....
1993-94	Albany River Rats	AHL	65	4	19	23	79	....	....	....	....	....	....	....	....	....	5	0	0	0	9	....	....	....	....
1994-95	Albany River Rats	AHL	77	7	36	43	101	....	....	....	....	....	....	....	....	....	7	1	0	1	0	....	....	....	....

			Regular Season															Playoffs								
Season	Club	League	GP	G	A	Pts	PIM	PP	SH	GW	S	%	+/-	TF	F%	Min	GP	G	A	Pts	PIM	PP	SH	GW	Min
1995-96	Albany River Rats	AHL	80	14	30	44	107	....	....	....	....	....	....	....	....	....	4	2	0	2	6	....	....	....	....
1996-97	Albany River Rats	AHL	77	12	27	39	113	....	....	....	....	....	....	....	....	....	16	1	7	8	10	....	....	....	....
1997-98	Albany River Rats	AHL	80	14	49	63	101	....	....	....	....	....	....	....	....	....	13	4	9	13	18	....	....	....	....
1998-99	**Phoenix**	**NHL**	**11**	**0**	**0**	**0**	**23**	**0**	**0**	**0**	**11**	**0.0**	**2**	**0**	**0.0**	**7:43**	....	....	....	....	....	....	....	....	....
	Las Vegas	IHL	8	1	3	4	28	....	....	....	....	....	....	....	....	....	....	....	....	....	....	....	....	....	....
	St. Louis	**NHL**	**29**	**0**	**4**	**4**	**19**	**0**	**0**	**0**	**38**	**0.0**	**3**	**1**	**100.0**	**19:08**	....	....	....	....	....	....	....	....	....
	Worcester IceCats	AHL	16	7	8	15	18	....	....	....	....	....	....	....	....	....	4	0	0	0	12	....	....	....	....
99-2000	**St. Louis**	**NHL**	**15**	**1**	**1**	**2**	**10**	**1**	**0**	**1**	**19**	**5.3**	**−3**	**0**	**0.0**	**16:15**	....	....	....	....	....	....	....	....	....
	Worcester IceCats	AHL	54	10	25	35	124	....	....	....	....	....	....	....	....	....	9	1	4	5	10	....	....	....	....
2000-01	**Vancouver**	**NHL**	**20**	**2**	**4**	**6**	**18**	**0**	**0**	**0**	**28**	**7.1**	**0**	**0**	**0.0**	**16:51**	....	....	....	....	....	....	....	....	....
	Kansas City	IHL	42	4	15	19	76	....	....	....	....	....	....	....	....	....	....	....	....	....	....	....	....	....	....
2001-02	**Vancouver**	**NHL**	**40**	**5**	**5**	**10**	**53**	**2**	**0**	**1**	**43**	**11.6**	**10**	**0**	**0.0**	**12:04**	**6**	**0**	**0**	**0**	**0**	**0**	**0**	**0**	**9:09**
	Manitoba Moose	AHL	34	6	18	24	69	....	....	....	....	....	....	....	....	....	....	....	....	....	....	....	....	....	....
2002-03	**Vancouver**	**NHL**	**2**	**0**	**0**	**0**	**0**	**0**	**0**	**0**	**2**	**0.0**	**1**	**0**	**0.0**	**13:24**	....	....	....	....	....	....	....	....	....
	Manitoba Moose	AHL	60	7	24	31	82	....	....	....	....	....	....	....	....	....	14	0	4	4	20	....	....	....	....
2003-04	**Phoenix**	**NHL**	**17**	**0**	**1**	**1**	**10**	**0**	**0**	**0**	**10**	**0.0**	**−5**	**0**	**0.0**	**12:46**	....	....	....	....	....	....	....	....	....
	Springfield	AHL	9	1	6	7	6	....	....	....	....	....	....	....	....	....	....	....	....	....	....	....	....	....	....
2004-05	Grand Rapids	AHL	80	7	18	25	64	....	....	....	....	....	....	....	....	....	....	....	....	....	....	....	....	....	....
	NHL Totals		**134**	**8**	**15**	**23**	**133**	**3**	**0**	**2**	**151**	**5.3**		**1**	**100.0**	**14:32**	**6**	**0**	**0**	**0**	**0**	**0**	**0**	**0**	**9:09**

AHL First All-Star Team (1998)

Signed as a free agent by **New Jersey**, July 10, 1994. Signed as a free agent by **Phoenix**, July 17, 1998. Claimed on waivers by **St. Louis** from **Phoenix**, December 19, 1998. Signed as a free agent by **Vancouver**, August 21, 2000. Traded to **Phoenix** by **Vancouver** for Martin Grenier, July 25, 2003. • Missed majority of 2003-04 season recovering from shoulder injury suffered in training camp, September 29, 2003. Signed as a free agent by **Detroit**, July 21, 2004.

HEMSKY, Ales

(HEHM-skee, ahl-EHSH) **EDM.**

Right wing. Shoots right. 6', 192 lbs. Born, Pardubice, Czech., August 13, 1983. Edmonton's 1st choice, 13th overall, in 2001 Entry Draft.

99-2000	HC Pardubice Jr.	CzRep-Jr.	45	20	36	56	54	....	....	....	....	....	....	....	....	....	7	4	14	18	36	....	....	....	....
	Pardubice	CzRep	4	0	1	1	0	....	....	....	....	....	....	....	....	....	....	....	....	....	....	....	....	....	....
2000-01	Hull Olympiques	QMJHL	68	36	64	100	67	....	....	....	....	....	....	....	....	....	5	2	3	5	2	....	....	....	....
2001-02	Hull Olympiques	QMJHL	53	27	70	97	86	....	....	....	....	....	....	....	....	....	10	6	10	16	6	....	....	....	....
2002-03	**Edmonton**	**NHL**	**59**	**6**	**24**	**30**	**14**	**0**	**0**	**1**	**50**	**12.0**	**5**	**3**	**33.3**	**12:04**	**6**	**0**	**0**	**0**	**0**	**0**	**0**	**0**	**12:46**
2003-04	**Edmonton**	**NHL**	**71**	**12**	**22**	**34**	**14**	**4**	**0**	**3**	**87**	**13.8**	**−7**	**3**	**33.3**	**14:26**	....	....	....	....	....	....	....	....	....
2004-05	Pardubice	CzRep	47	13	18	31	28	....	....	....	....	....	....	....	....	....	16	4	*10	*14	26	....	....	....	....
	NHL Totals		**130**	**18**	**46**	**64**	**28**	**4**	**0**	**4**	**137**	**13.1**		**6**	**33.3**	**13:22**	**6**	**0**	**0**	**0**	**0**	**0**	**0**	**0**	**12:46**

QMJHL Second All-Star Team (2002)

Signed as a free agent by **Pardubice** (CzRep), September 18, 2004.

HENDERSON, Jay

(HEHN-duhr-SOHN, JAY)

Left wing. Shoots left. 5'11", 190 lbs. Born, Edmonton, Alta., September 17, 1978. Boston's 12th choice, 246th overall, in 1997 Entry Draft.

1993-94	Sherwood Park	AMBHL	31	12	21	33	36	....	....	....	....	....	....	....	....	....	....	....	....	....	....	....	....	....	....
1994-95	Red Deer Rebels	WHL	54	3	9	12	80	....	....	....	....	....	....	....	....	....	....	....	....	....	....	....	....	....	....
1995-96	Red Deer Rebels	WHL	71	15	13	28	139	....	....	....	....	....	....	....	....	....	10	1	1	2	11	....	....	....	....
1996-97	Edmonton Ice	WHL	66	28	32	60	127	....	....	....	....	....	....	....	....	....	....	....	....	....	....	....	....	....	....
1997-98	Edmonton Ice	WHL	72	49	45	94	130	....	....	....	....	....	....	....	....	....	....	....	....	....	....	....	....	....	....
	Providence Bruins	AHL	11	3	1	4	11	....	....	....	....	....	....	....	....	....	....	....	....	....	....	....	....	....	....
1998-99	**Boston**	**NHL**	**4**	**0**	**0**	**0**	**2**	**0**	**0**	**0**	**4**	**0.0**	**−1**	**0**	**0.0**	**5:39**	....	....	....	....	....	....	....	....	....
	Providence Bruins	AHL	55	7	9	16	172	....	....	....	....	....	....	....	....	....	2	0	0	0	2	....	....	....	....
99-2000	**Boston**	**NHL**	**16**	**1**	**3**	**4**	**9**	**0**	**0**	**0**	**18**	**5.6**	**1**	**2**	**0.0**	**5:22**	....	....	....	....	....	....	....	....	....
	Providence Bruins	AHL	60	18	27	45	200	....	....	....	....	....	....	....	....	....	14	1	2	3	16	....	....	....	....
2000-01	**Boston**	**NHL**	**13**	**0**	**0**	**0**	**26**	**0**	**0**	**0**	**12**	**0.0**	**−1**	**3**	**100.0**	**6:58**	....	....	....	....	....	....	....	....	....
	Providence Bruins	AHL	41	9	7	16	121	....	....	....	....	....	....	....	....	....	1	0	0	0	2	....	....	....	....
2001-02	**Boston**	**NHL**	DID NOT PLAY – INJURED																						
2002-03	Providence Bruins	AHL	39	7	13	20	152	....	....	....	....	....	....	....	....	....	....	....	....	....	....	....	....	....	....
	Hartford	AHL	14	3	4	7	27	....	....	....	....	....	....	....	....	....	....	....	....	....	....	....	....	....	....
	Houston Aeros	AHL	22	7	4	11	65	....	....	....	....	....	....	....	....	....	23	2	2	4	25	....	....	....	....
2003-04	Milwaukee	AHL	70	15	16	31	122	....	....	....	....	....	....	....	....	....	18	1	3	4	55	....	....	....	....
2004-05	Providence Bruins	AHL	72	8	10	18	235	....	....	....	....	....	....	....	....	....	17	1	4	5	56	....	....	....	....
	NHL Totals		**33**	**1**	**3**	**4**	**37**	**0**	**0**	**0**	**34**	**2.9**		**5**	**60.0**	**6:02**									

• Missed entire 2001-02 season recovering from knee injury suffered in pre-season game vs. Detroit, September 21, 2001. Traded to **NY Rangers** by **Boston** for Boston's 9th round choice (later traded to San Jose - San Jose selected Brian Mahoney-Wilson) in 2004 Entry Draft, January 17, 2003. Traded to **Minnesota** by **NY Rangers** for Cory Larose, February 20, 2003. Signed as a free agent by **Milwaukee** (AHL), September 3, 2003. Signed as a free agent by **Providence** (AHL), September 7, 2004.

HENDRICKSON, Darby

(HEHN-drihk-SOHN, DAHR-bee)

Center. Shoots left. 6'1", 195 lbs. Born, Richfield, MN, August 28, 1972. Toronto's 3rd choice, 73rd overall, in 1990 Entry Draft.

1987-88	Richfield Spartans	High-MN	22	12	9	21	10	....	....	....	....	....	....	....	....	....	....	....	....	....	....	....	....	....	....
1988-89	Richfield Spartans	High-MN	22	22	20	42	12	....	....	....	....	....	....	....	....	....	....	....	....	....	....	....	....	....	....
1989-90	Richfield Spartans	High-MN	24	23	27	50	49	....	....	....	....	....	....	....	....	....	....	....	....	....	....	....	....	....	....
1990-91	Richfield Spartans	High-MN	27	32	29	61	....	....	....	....	....	....	....	....	....	....	....	....	....	....	....	....	....	....	....
1991-92	U. of Minnesota	WCHA	41	25	28	53	61	....	....	....	....	....	....	....	....	....	....	....	....	....	....	....	....	....	....
1992-93	U. of Minnesota	WCHA	31	12	15	27	35	....	....	....	....	....	....	....	....	....	....	....	....	....	....	....	....	....	....
1993-94	United States	Nat-Tm	59	12	16	28	30	....	....	....	....	....	....	....	....	....	....	....	....	....	....	....	....	....	....
	United States	Olympics	8	0	0	0	6	....	....	....	....	....	....	....	....	....	....	....	....	....	....	....	....	....	....
	Toronto	**NHL**	....	....	....	....	....	....	....	....	....	....	....	....	....	....	**2**	**0**	**0**	**0**	**0**	**0**	**0**	**0**	
	St. John's	AHL	6	4	1	5	4	....	....	....	....	....	....	....	....	....	3	1	1	2	0	....	....	....	....
1994-95	St. John's	AHL	59	16	20	36	48	....	....	....	....	....	....	....	....	....	....	....	....	....	....	....	....	....	....
	Toronto	**NHL**	**8**	**0**	**1**	**1**	**4**	**0**	**0**	**0**	**4**	**0.0**	**0**	....	....	....	....	....	....	....	....	....	....	....	....
1995-96	**Toronto**	**NHL**	**46**	**6**	**6**	**12**	**47**	**0**	**0**	**0**	**43**	**14.0**	**−2**	....	....	....	....	....	....	....	....	....	....	....	....
	NY Islanders	**NHL**	**16**	**1**	**4**	**5**	**33**	**0**	**0**	**1**	**30**	**3.3**	**−6**	....	....	....	....	....	....	....	....	....	....	....	....
1996-97	**Toronto**	**NHL**	**64**	**11**	**6**	**17**	**47**	**0**	**1**	**0**	**105**	**10.5**	**−20**	....	....	....	....	....	....	....	....	....	....	....	....
	St. John's	AHL	12	5	4	9	21	....	....	....	....	....	....	....	....	....	....	....	....	....	....	....	....	....	....
1997-98	**Toronto**	**NHL**	**80**	**8**	**4**	**12**	**67**	**0**	**0**	**0**	**115**	**7.0**	**−20**	....	....	....	....	....	....	....	....	....	....	....	....
1998-99	**Toronto**	**NHL**	**35**	**2**	**3**	**5**	**30**	**0**	**0**	**0**	**34**	**5.9**	**−4**	**278**	**46.0**	**10:16**	....	....	....	....	....	....	....	....	....
	Vancouver	**NHL**	**27**	**2**	**2**	**4**	**22**	**1**	**0**	**0**	**36**	**5.6**	**−15**	**427**	**46.8**	**17:15**	....	....	....	....	....	....	....	....	....
99-2000	**Vancouver**	**NHL**	**40**	**5**	**4**	**9**	**14**	**0**	**1**	**1**	**39**	**12.8**	**−3**	**407**	**46.2**	**11:32**	....	....	....	....	....	....	....	....	....
	Syracuse Crunch	AHL	20	5	8	13	16	....	....	....	....	....	....	....	....	....	....	....	....	....	....	....	....	....	....
2000-01	**Minnesota**	**NHL**	**72**	**18**	**11**	**29**	**36**	**3**	**1**	**1**	**114**	**15.8**	**1**	**1119**	**45.2**	**15:50**	....	....	....	....	....	....	....	....	....
2001-02	**Minnesota**	**NHL**	**68**	**9**	**15**	**24**	**50**	**2**	**2**	**1**	**79**	**11.4**	**−22**	**1206**	**47.7**	**16:43**	....	....	....	....	....	....	....	....	....
2002-03	**Minnesota**	**NHL**	**28**	**1**	**5**	**6**	**8**	**0**	**0**	**0**	**34**	**2.9**	**−3**	**413**	**48.4**	**15:16**	**17**	**2**	**3**	**5**	**4**	**0**	**0**	**1**	**16:58**
2003-04	**Minnesota**	**NHL**	**14**	**1**	**0**	**1**	**6**	**0**	**0**	**0**	**14**	**7.1**	**−7**	**170**	**47.1**	**14:12**	....	....	....	....	....	....	....	....	....
	Houston Aeros	AHL	31	4	5	9	19	....	....	....	....	....	....	....	....	....	....	....	....	....	....	....	....	....	....
	Colorado	**NHL**	**20**	**1**	**3**	**4**	**6**	**0**	**0**	**0**	**21**	**4.8**	**−8**	**255**	**57.7**	**12:51**	**6**	**1**	**0**	**1**	**2**	**0**	**0**	**0**	**11:51**
2004-05	HK Riga 2000	Latvia	1	1	1	2	0	....	....	....	....	....	....	....	....	....	....	....	....	....	....	....	....	....	....
	HK Riga 2000	BelOpen	6	2	2	4	26	....	....	....	....	....	....	....	....	....	....	....	....	....	....	....	....	....	....
	NHL Totals		**518**	**65**	**64**	**129**	**370**	**6**	**5**	**4**	**668**	**9.7**		**4275**	**47.3**	**14:38**	**25**	**3**	**3**	**6**	**6**	**0**	**0**	**1**	**15:38**

WCHA Rookie of the Year (1992)

Traded to **NY Islanders** by **Toronto** with Sean Haggerty, Kenny Jonsson and Toronto's 1st round choice (Roberto Luongo) in 1997 Entry Draft for Wendel Clark, Mathieu Schneider and D.J. Smith, March 13, 1996. Traded to **Toronto** by **NY Islanders** for Toronto's 5th round choice (Jiri Dopita) in 1998 Entry Draft, October 11, 1996. Traded to **Vancouver** by **Toronto** for Chris McAllister, February 16, 1999. Claimed by **Minnesota** from **Vancouver** in Expansion Draft, June 23, 2000. • Missed majority of 2002-03 season recovering from arm injury suffered in training camp, September 24, 2002. Traded to **Colorado** by **Minnesota** with Minnesota's 8th round choice (Brandon Yip) in 2004 Entry Draft for Colorado's 4th round choice (later traded to Ottawa - Ottawa selected Cody Bass) in 2005 Entry Draft, February 25, 2004. Signed as a free agent by **Riga** (Latvia), October 2, 2004.

HENRY, Alex (HEHN-ree, AL-ehx) MIN.

Defense. Shoots left. 6'5", 220 lbs. Born, Elliot Lake, Ont., October 18, 1979. Edmonton's 2nd choice, 67th overall, in 1998 Entry Draft.

			Regular Season														Playoffs								
Season	Club	League	GP	G	A	Pts	PIM	PP	SH	GW	S	%	+/-	TF	F%	Min	GP	G	A	Pts	PIM	PP	SH	GW	Min
1995-96	Timmins Majors	NOHA	30	4	11	15	6	....	....	....	....	....	....	....	....	....	....	....	....	....	....	....	....	....	....
	Timmins	NOJHA	2	0	0	0	0	....	....	....	....	....	....	....	....	....	....	....	....	....	....	....	....	....	....
1996-97	London Knights	OHL	61	1	10	11	65	....	....	....	....	....	....	....	....	....	....	....	....	....	....	....	....	....	....
1997-98	London Knights	OHL	62	5	9	14	97	....	....	....	....	....	....	....	....	....	16	0	3	3	14	....	....	....	....
1998-99	London Knights	OHL	68	5	23	28	105	....	....	....	....	....	....	....	....	....	25	3	10	13	22	....	....	....	....
99-2000	Hamilton	AHL	60	1	0	1	69	....	....	....	....	....	....	....	....	....	....	....	....	....	....	....	....	....	....
2000-01	Hamilton	AHL	56	2	3	5	87	....	....	....	....	....	....	....	....	....	....	....	....	....	....	....	....	....	....
2001-02	Hamilton	AHL	69	4	8	12	143	....	....	....	....	....	....	....	....	....	15	1	2	3	16	....	....	....	....
2002-03	**Edmonton**	**NHL**	**3**	**0**	**0**	**0**	**0**	**0**	**0**	**0**	**0**	**0.0**	**–1**	**0**	**0.0**	**7:02**	....	....	....	....	....	....	....	....	....
	Washington	**NHL**	**38**	**0**	**0**	**0**	**80**	**0**	**0**	**0**	**8**	**0.0**	**–4**	**1**	**0.0**	**3:39**	....	....	....	....	....	....	....	....	....
	Portland Pirates	AHL	3	0	1	1	0	....	....	....	....	....	....	....	....	....	....	....	....	....	....	....	....	....	....
2003-04	**Minnesota**	**NHL**	**71**	**2**	**4**	**6**	**106**	**0**	**0**	**0**	**37**	**5.4**	**4**	**2**	**0.0**	**14:53**	....	....	....	....	....	....	....	....	....
2004-05	ESV Kaufbeuren	German-2	26	6	6	12	32	....	....	....	....	....	....	....	....	....	....	....	....	....	....	....	....	....	....
	NHL Totals		**112**	**2**	**4**	**6**	**186**	**0**	**0**	**0**	**45**	**4.4**		**3**	**0.0**	**10:52**	....	....	....	....	....	....	....	....	....

Claimed on waivers by **Washington** from **Edmonton**, October 24, 2002. Claimed on waivers by **Minnesota** from **Washington**, October 9, 2003. Signed as a free agent by **Kaufbeuren** (German-2), January 15, 2005.

HENRY, Burke (HEHN-ree, BUHRK)

Defense. Shoots left. 6'3", 206 lbs. Born, Ste. Rose, Man., January 21, 1979. NY Rangers' 3rd choice, 73rd overall, in 1997 Entry Draft.

1995-96	Brandon	WHL	50	6	11	17	58	....	....	....	....	....	....	....	....	....	19	0	4	4	19	....	....	....	....
1996-97	Brandon	WHL	55	6	25	31	81	....	....	....	....	....	....	....	....	....	6	1	3	4	4	....	....	....	....
1997-98	Brandon	WHL	72	18	65	83	153	....	....	....	....	....	....	....	....	....	18	3	16	19	37	....	....	....	....
1998-99	Brandon	WHL	68	18	58	76	151	....	....	....	....	....	....	....	....	....	5	1	6	7	9	....	....	....	....
99-2000	Hartford	AHL	64	3	12	15	47	....	....	....	....	....	....	....	....	....	5	0	0	0	2	....	....	....	....
2000-01	Hartford	AHL	80	8	30	38	133	....	....	....	....	....	....	....	....	....	5	0	0	0	2	....	....	....	....
2001-02	Saint John Flames	AHL	58	0	17	17	92	....	....	....	....	....	....	....	....	....	....	....	....	....	....	....	....	....	....
2002-03	Norfolk Admirals	AHL	60	6	22	28	121	....	....	....	....	....	....	....	....	....	9	1	2	3	9	....	....	....	....
	Chicago	**NHL**	**16**	**0**	**2**	**2**	**9**	**0**	**0**	**0**	**25**	**0.0**	**–13**	**0**	**0.0**	**18:32**	....	....	....	....	....	....	....	....	....
2003-04	**Chicago**	**NHL**	**23**	**2**	**4**	**6**	**24**	**0**	**0**	**0**	**31**	**6.5**	**0**	**0**	**0.0**	**17:02**	....	....	....	....	....	....	....	....	....
	Norfolk Admirals	AHL	53	1	8	9	70	....	....	....	....	....	....	....	....	....	8	0	1	1	4	....	....	....	....
2004-05	San Antonio	AHL	24	0	2	2	44	....	....	....	....	....	....	....	....	....	....	....	....	....	....	....	....	....	....
	Milwaukee	AHL	16	0	3	3	28	....	....	....	....	....	....	....	....	....	1	0	0	0	0	....	....	....	....
	NHL Totals		**39**	**2**	**6**	**8**	**33**	**0**	**0**	**0**	**56**	**3.6**		**0**	**0.0**	**17:39**	....	....	....	....	....	....	....	....	....

WHL East First All-Star Team (1998) • WHL East Second All-Star Team (1999)

Traded to **Calgary** by **NY Rangers** for Chris St. Croix, June 23, 2001. Signed to a PTO (tryout) contract by **Norfolk** (AHL), October 9, 2002. Signed as a free agent by **Norfolk** (AHL), October 23, 2002. Signed as a free agent by **Chicago**, December 11, 2002. Signed as a free agent by **Florida**, July 23, 2004. Loaned to **Milwaukee** (AHL) by **Florida** (San Antonio-AHL) for cash, January 13, 2005.

HENTUNEN, Jukka (HEHN-too-nehn, YOO-kuh) NSH.

Right wing. Shoots right. 5'10", 194 lbs. Born, Joroinen, Finland, May 3, 1974. Calgary's 7th choice, 176th overall, in 2000 Entry Draft.

1993-94	K-Warkaus	Finland-3	16	7	6	13	10	....	....	....	....	....	....	....	....	....	8	4	1	5	2	....	....	....	....
1994-95	K-Warkaus	Finland-3	29	23	23	46	28	....	....	....	....	....	....	....	....	....	....	....	....	....	....	....	....	....	....
1995-96	Diskos Jyvaskyla	Finland-2	43	23	18	41	14	....	....	....	....	....	....	....	....	....	10	5	6	11	4	....	....	....	....
1996-97	Hermes Kokkola	Finland-2	35	10	13	23	43	....	....	....	....	....	....	....	....	....	3	1	0	1	0	....	....	....	....
1997-98	Hermes Kokkola	Finland-2	49	19	16	35	36	....	....	....	....	....	....	....	....	....	3	3	3	6	0	....	....	....	....
1998-99	Hermes Kokkola	Finland-2	1	0	0	0	0	....	....	....	....	....	....	....	....	....	....	....	....	....	....	....	....	....	....
	HPK Hameenlinna	Finland	41	13	21	34	32	....	....	....	....	....	....	....	....	....	8	1	4	5	12	....	....	....	....
99-2000	HPK Hameenlinna	Finland	53	17	28	45	76	....	....	....	....	....	....	....	....	....	8	4	2	6	12	....	....	....	....
2000-01	Jokerit Helsinki	Finland	56	27	28	55	24	....	....	....	....	....	....	....	....	....	5	1	0	1	4	....	....	....	....
2001-02	**Calgary**	**NHL**	**28**	**2**	**3**	**5**	**4**	**1**	**0**	**0**	**38**	**5.3**	**–9**	**0**	**0.0**	**11:09**	....	....	....	....	....	....	....	....	....
	Saint John Flames	AHL	9	3	3	6	0	....	....	....	....	....	....	....	....	....	....	....	....	....	....	....	....	....	....
	Nashville	**NHL**	**10**	**2**	**2**	**4**	**0**	**0**	**0**	**1**	**12**	**16.7**	**0**	**0**	**0.0**	**12:46**	....	....	....	....	....	....	....	....	....
2002-03	Jokerit Helsinki	Finland	48	11	11	22	28	....	....	....	....	....	....	....	....	....	10	4	2	6	0	....	....	....	....
2003-04	Fribourg	Swiss	47	25	28	53	22	....	....	....	....	....	....	....	....	....	4	2	4	6	6	....	....	....	....
2004-05	Fribourg	Swiss	44	24	20	44	46	....	....	....	....	....	....	....	....	....	8	5	6	11	6	....	....	....	....
	NHL Totals		**38**	**4**	**5**	**9**	**4**	**1**	**0**	**1**	**50**	**8.0**		**0**	**0.0**	**11:35**	....	....	....	....	....	....	....	....	....

Traded to **Nashville** by **Calgary** for future considerations, March 17, 2002. Signed as a free agent by **Jokerit** (Finland), August 13, 2002.

HERR, Matt (HUHR, MAT)

Center. Shoots left. 6'2", 204 lbs. Born, Hackensack, NJ, May 26, 1976. Washington's 4th choice, 93rd overall, in 1994 Entry Draft.

1990-91	Hotchkiss	High-CT	26	9	5	14	....	....	....	....	....	....	....	....	....	....	....	....	....	....	....	....	....	....	....
1991-92	Hotchkiss	High-CT	25	17	16	33	....	....	....	....	....	....	....	....	....	....	....	....	....	....	....	....	....	....	....
1992-93	Hotchkiss	High-CT	24	48	30	78	....	....	....	....	....	....	....	....	....	....	....	....	....	....	....	....	....	....	....
1993-94	Hotchkiss	High-CT	24	28	19	47	....	....	....	....	....	....	....	....	....	....	....	....	....	....	....	....	....	....	....
1994-95	U. of Michigan	CCHA	37	11	8	19	51	....	....	....	....	....	....	....	....	....	3	1	0	1	4	....	....	....	....
1995-96	U. of Michigan	CCHA	40	18	13	31	55	....	....	....	....	....	....	....	....	....	7	0	4	4	0	....	....	....	....
1996-97	U. of Michigan	CCHA	43	29	23	52	67	....	....	....	....	....	....	....	....	....	6	2	2	4	8	....	....	....	....
1997-98	U. of Michigan	CCHA	31	14	17	31	62	....	....	....	....	....	....	....	....	....	....	....	....	....	....	....	....	....	....
1998-99	**Washington**	**NHL**	**30**	**2**	**2**	**4**	**8**	**1**	**0**	**0**	**40**	**5.0**	**–7**	**176**	**52.8**	**11:05**	....	....	....	....	....	....	....	....	....
	Portland Pirates	AHL	46	15	14	29	29	....	....	....	....	....	....	....	....	....	....	....	....	....	....	....	....	....	....
99-2000	Portland Pirates	AHL	77	22	21	43	51	....	....	....	....	....	....	....	....	....	4	1	1	2	4	....	....	....	....
2000-01	**Washington**	**NHL**	**22**	**2**	**3**	**5**	**17**	**0**	**0**	**1**	**20**	**10.0**	**3**	**2**	**100.0**	**8:09**	....	....	....	....	....	....	....	....	....
	Portland Pirates	AHL	40	21	13	34	58	....	....	....	....	....	....	....	....	....	....	....	....	....	....	....	....	....	....
	Philadelphia	AHL	11	2	4	6	18	....	....	....	....	....	....	....	....	....	9	2	1	3	8	....	....	....	....
2001-02	**Florida**	**NHL**	**3**	**0**	**0**	**0**	**0**	**0**	**0**	**0**	**1**	**0.0**	**–2**	**15**	**53.3**	**6:27**	....	....	....	....	....	....	....	....	....
	Hershey Bears	AHL	61	18	16	34	68	....	....	....	....	....	....	....	....	....	7	1	2	3	15	....	....	....	....
2002-03	**Boston**	**NHL**	**3**	**0**	**0**	**0**	**0**	**0**	**0**	**0**	**1**	**0.0**	**0**	**8**	**50.0**	**8:17**	....	....	....	....	....	....	....	....	....
	Providence Bruins	AHL	77	34	38	72	146	....	....	....	....	....	....	....	....	....	4	0	1	1	12	....	....	....	....
2003-04	Providence Bruins	AHL	71	18	26	44	108	....	....	....	....	....	....	....	....	....	2	0	1	1	0	....	....	....	....
2004-05	Dusseldorf	Germany	44	13	7	20	96	....	....	....	....	....	....	....	....	....	....	....	....	....	....	....	....	....	....
	NHL Totals		**58**	**4**	**5**	**9**	**25**	**1**	**0**	**1**	**62**	**6.5**		**201**	**53.2**	**9:35**	....	....	....	....	....	....	....	....	....

AHL First All-Star Team (2003)

Traded to **Philadelphia** by **Washington** for Dean Melanson, March 13, 2001. Signed as a free agent by **Florida**, August 21, 2001. Signed as a free agent by **Boston**, July 18, 2002. Signed as a free agent by **Dusseldorf** (Germany), July 22, 2004.

HEWARD, Jamie (HEW-uhrd, JAY-mee) WSH.

Defense. Shoots right. 6'2", 207 lbs. Born, Regina, Sask., March 30, 1971. Pittsburgh's 1st choice, 16th overall, in 1989 Entry Draft.

1987-88	Regina Pats	WHL	68	10	17	27	17	....	....	....	....	....	....	....	....	....	4	1	1	2	2	....	....	....	....
1988-89	Regina Pats	WHL	52	31	28	59	29	....	....	....	....	....	....	....	....	....	....	....	....	....	....	....	....	....	....
1989-90	Regina Pats	WHL	72	14	44	58	42	....	....	....	....	....	....	....	....	....	11	2	2	4	10	....	....	....	....
1990-91	Regina Pats	WHL	71	23	61	84	41	....	....	....	....	....	....	....	....	....	8	2	9	11	6	....	....	....	....
1991-92	Muskegon	IHL	54	6	21	27	37	....	....	....	....	....	....	....	....	....	14	1	4	5	4	....	....	....	....
1992-93	Cleveland	IHL	58	9	18	27	64	....	....	....	....	....	....	....	....	....	....	....	....	....	....	....	....	....	....
1993-94	Cleveland	IHL	73	8	16	24	72	....	....	....	....	....	....	....	....	....	....	....	....	....	....	....	....	....	....
1994-95	Canada	Nat-Tm	51	11	35	46	32	....	....	....	....	....	....	....	....	....	....	....	....	....	....	....	....	....	....
1995-96	**Toronto**	**NHL**	**5**	**0**	**0**	**0**	**0**	**0**	**0**	**0**	**8**	**0.0**	**–1**	....	....	....	....	....	....	....	....	....	....	....	....
	St. John's	AHL	73	22	34	56	33	....	....	....	....	....	....	....	....	....	3	1	1	2	6	....	....	....	....
1996-97	**Toronto**	**NHL**	**20**	**1**	**4**	**5**	**6**	**0**	**0**	**0**	**23**	**4.3**	**–6**	....	....	....	....	....	....	....	....	....	....	....	....
	St. John's	AHL	27	8	19	27	26	....	....	....	....	....	....	....	....	....	9	1	3	4	6	....	....	....	....
1997-98	Philadelphia	AHL	72	17	48	65	54	....	....	....	....	....	....	....	....	....	20	3	16	19	10	....	....	....	....
1998-99	**Nashville**	**NHL**	**63**	**6**	**12**	**18**	**44**	**4**	**0**	**1**	**124**	**4.8**	**–24**	**0**	**0.0**	**16:12**	....	....	....	....	....	....	....	....	....
99-2000	**NY Islanders**	**NHL**	**54**	**6**	**11**	**17**	**26**	**2**	**0**	**1**	**92**	**6.5**	**–9**	**0**	**0.0**	**19:58**	....	....	....	....	....	....	....	....	....
2000-01	**Columbus**	**NHL**	**69**	**11**	**16**	**27**	**33**	**9**	**0**	**1**	**108**	**10.2**	**3**	**0**	**0.0**	**14:21**	....	....	....	....	....	....	....	....	....

			Regular Season														Playoffs								
Season	Club	League	GP	G	A	Pts	PIM	PP	SH	GW	S	%	+/-	TF	F%	Min	GP	G	A	Pts	PIM	PP	SH	GW	Min
2001-02	**Columbus**	**NHL**	**28**	**1**	**2**	**3**	**7**	**0**	**0**	**0**	**38**	**2.6**	**-9**	**1**	**100.0**	**14:04**	....	....	....	....	....	....	....	....	....
	Syracuse Crunch	AHL	14	3	10	13	6	....	....	....	....	....	....	....	....	....	10	0	4	4	6	....	....	....	....
2002-03	Geneve	Swiss	40	8	23	31	60	....	....	....	....	....	....	....	....	....	6	1	1	2	22	....	....	....	....
2003-04	ZSC Lions Zurich	Swiss	25	5	9	14	57	....	....	....	....	....	....	....	....	....	6	0	1	1	24	....	....	....	....
2004-05	Langnau	Swiss	44	3	14	17	91	....	....	....	....	....	....	....	....	....	5	0	0	0	40	....	....	....	....
	NHL Totals		**239**	**25**	**45**	**70**	**116**	**15**	**0**	**3**	**393**	**6.4**		**1**	**100.0**	**16:17**	....	....	....	....	....	....	....	....	....

WHL East First All-Star Team (1991) • AHL First All-Star Team (1996, 1998) • Eddie Shore Award (Outstanding Defenseman – AHL) (1998)

Signed as a free agent by **Toronto**, May 4, 1995. Signed as a free agent by **Philadelphia**, July 31, 1997. Signed as a free agent by **Nashville**, August 10, 1998. Signed as a free agent by **NY Islanders**, July 27, 1999. Claimed on waivers by **Columbus** from **NY Islanders**, May 26, 2000. Signed as a free agent by **Geneve** (Swiss), April 17, 2002. Signed as a free agent by **Washington**, August 12, 2005.

HIGGINS, Christopher

(HIH-gihns, KRIHS-toh-fuhr) **MTL.**

Center. Shoots left. 5'11", 192 lbs. Born, Smithtown, NY, June 2, 1983. Montreal's 1st choice, 14th overall, in 2002 Entry Draft.

Season	Club	League	GP	G	A	Pts	PIM	PP	SH	GW	S	%	+/-	TF	F%	Min	GP	G	A	Pts	PIM	PP	SH	GW	Min
99-2000	Avon Old Farms	High-CT	27	19	20	39	10	....	....	....	....	....	....	....	....	....	....	....	....	....	....	....	....	....	....
2000-01	Avon Old Farms	High-CT	24	22	14	36	29	....	....	....	....	....	....	....	....	....	....	....	....	....	....	....	....	....	....
2001-02	Yale	ECAC	27	14	17	31	32	....	....	....	....	....	....	....	....	....	....	....	....	....	....	....	....	....	....
2002-03	Yale	ECAC	28	20	21	41	41	....	....	....	....	....	....	....	....	....	....	....	....	....	....	....	....	....	....
2003-04	**Montreal**	**NHL**	**2**	**0**	**0**	**0**	**0**	**0**	**0**	**0**	**0**	**0.0**	**0**	**9**	**22.2**	**6:18**	....	....	....	....	....	....	....	....	....
	Hamilton	AHL	67	21	27	48	18	....	....	....	....	....	....	....	....	....	10	3	2	5	0	....	....	....	....
2004-05	Hamilton	AHL	76	28	23	51	33	....	....	....	....	....	....	....	....	....	4	3	3	6	4	....	....	....	....
	NHL Totals		**2**	**0**	**0**	**0**	**0**	**0**	**0**	**0**	**0**	**0.0**		**9**	**22.2**	**6:18**	....	....	....	....	....	....	....	....	....

ECAC All-Rookie Team (2002) • ECAC Second All-Star Team (2002) • ECAC Rookie of the Year (2002) • ECAC First All-Star Team (2003) • ECAC Player of the Year (2003) (co-winner - David LeNeveu) • NCAA East First All-American Team (2003)

HILBERT, Andy

(HIHL-buhrt, AN-dee) **BOS.**

Center/Left wing. Shoots left. 5'11", 194 lbs. Born, Lansing, MI, February 6, 1981. Boston's 3rd choice, 37th overall, in 2000 Entry Draft.

Season	Club	League	GP	G	A	Pts	PIM	PP	SH	GW	S	%	+/-	TF	F%	Min	GP	G	A	Pts	PIM	PP	SH	GW	Min
1997-98	USA U-18	USDP	75	34	30	64	148	....	....	....	....	....	....	....	....	....	....	....	....	....	....	....	....	....	....
1998-99	USA U-18	USDP	46	23	35	58	140	....	....	....	....	....	....	....	....	....	....	....	....	....	....	....	....	....	....
99-2000	U. of Michigan	CCHA	35	17	15	32	39	....	....	....	....	....	....	....	....	....	....	....	....	....	....	....	....	....	....
2000-01	U. of Michigan	CCHA	42	26	38	64	72	....	....	....	....	....	....	....	....	....	....	....	....	....	....	....	....	....	....
2001-02	**Boston**	**NHL**	**6**	**1**	**0**	**1**	**2**	**0**	**0**	**0**	**11**	**9.1**	**-2**	**4**	**50.0**	**11:34**	....	....	....	....	....	....	....	....	....
	Providence Bruins	AHL	72	26	27	53	74	....	....	....	....	....	....	....	....	....	2	0	0	0	2	....	....	....	....
2002-03	**Boston**	**NHL**	**14**	**0**	**3**	**3**	**7**	**0**	**0**	**0**	**22**	**0.0**	**-1**	**34**	**44.1**	**11:30**	....	....	....	....	....	....	....	....	....
	Providence Bruins	AHL	64	35	35	70	119	....	....	....	....	....	....	....	....	....	4	0	1	1	4	....	....	....	....
2003-04	**Boston**	**NHL**	**18**	**2**	**0**	**2**	**9**	**0**	**0**	**0**	**27**	**7.4**	**1**	**11**	**54.6**	**8:57**	**5**	**1**	**0**	**1**	**0**	**0**	**0**	**0**	**5:32**
	Providence Bruins	AHL	19	3	5	8	20	....	....	....	....	....	....	....	....	....	....	....	....	....	....	....	....	....	....
2004-05	Providence Bruins	AHL	79	37	42	79	83	....	....	....	....	....	....	....	....	....	17	7	*14	*21	27	....	....	....	....
	NHL Totals		**38**	**3**	**3**	**6**	**18**	**0**	**0**	**0**	**60**	**5.0**		**49**	**46.9**	**10:18**	**5**	**1**	**0**	**1**	**0**	**0**	**0**	**0**	**5:32**

CCHA First All-Star Team (2001) • NCAA West First All-American Team (2001) • AHL All-Rookie Team (2002) • AHL Second All-Star Team (2005)

• Missed majority of 2003-04 season recovering from groin injury suffered in pre-season game vs. Detroit, September 15, 2003.

HILL, Sean

(HIHL, SHAWN) **FLA.**

Defense. Shoots right. 6', 205 lbs. Born, Duluth, MN, February 14, 1970. Montreal's 9th choice, 167th overall, in 1988 Entry Draft.

Season	Club	League	GP	G	A	Pts	PIM	PP	SH	GW	S	%	+/-	TF	F%	Min	GP	G	A	Pts	PIM	PP	SH	GW	Min
1986-87	Lakefield Chiefs	OHA-C	3	1	1	2	14	....	....	....	....	....	....	....	....	....	....	....	....	....	....	....	....	....	....
1987-88	Duluth East	High-MN	24	10	17	27	....	....	....	....	....	....	....	....	....	....	....	....	....	....	....	....	....	....	....
1988-89	U. of Wisconsin	WCHA	45	2	23	25	69	....	....	....	....	....	....	....	....	....	....	....	....	....	....	....	....	....	....
1989-90	U. of Wisconsin	WCHA	42	14	39	53	78	....	....	....	....	....	....	....	....	....	....	....	....	....	....	....	....	....	....
1990-91	U. of Wisconsin	WCHA	37	19	32	51	122	....	....	....	....	....	....	....	....	....	....	....	....	....	....	....	....	....	....
	Montreal	**NHL**	....	....	....	....	....	....	....	....	....	....	....	....	....	....	**1**	**0**	**0**	**0**	**0**	**0**	**0**	**0**	....
	Fredericton	AHL	....	....	....	....	....	....	....	....	....	....	....	....	....	....	3	0	2	2	2	....	....	....	....
1991-92	Fredericton	AHL	42	7	20	27	65	....	....	....	....	....	....	....	....	....	7	1	3	4	6	....	....	....	....
	United States	Nat-Tm	12	4	3	7	16	....	....	....	....	....	....	....	....	....	....	....	....	....	....	....	....	....	....
	United States	Olympics	8	2	0	2	6	....	....	....	....	....	....	....	....	....	....	....	....	....	....	....	....	....	....
	Montreal	**NHL**	....	....	....	....	....	....	....	....	....	....	....	....	....	....	**4**	**1**	**0**	**1**	**2**	**0**	**0**	**0**	....
1992-93♦	**Montreal**	**NHL**	**31**	**2**	**6**	**8**	**54**	**1**	**0**	**1**	**37**	**5.4**	**-5**	....	....	....	**3**	**0**	**0**	**0**	**4**	**0**	**0**	**0**	....
	Fredericton	AHL	6	1	3	4	10	....	....	....	....	....	....	....	....	....	....	....	....	....	....	....	....	....	....
1993-94	**Anaheim**	**NHL**	**68**	**7**	**20**	**27**	**78**	**2**	**1**	**1**	**165**	**4.2**	**-12**	....	....	....	....	....	....	....	....	....	....	....	....
1994-95	**Ottawa**	**NHL**	**45**	**1**	**14**	**15**	**30**	**0**	**0**	**0**	**107**	**0.9**	**-11**	....	....	....	....	....	....	....	....	....	....	....	....
1995-96	**Ottawa**	**NHL**	**80**	**7**	**14**	**21**	**94**	**2**	**0**	**2**	**157**	**4.5**	**-26**	....	....	....	....	....	....	....	....	....	....	....	....
1996-97	**Ottawa**	**NHL**	**5**	**0**	**0**	**0**	**4**	**0**	**0**	**0**	**9**	**0.0**	**1**	....	....	....	....	....	....	....	....	....	....	....	....
1997-98	**Ottawa**	**NHL**	**13**	**1**	**1**	**2**	**6**	**0**	**0**	**0**	**16**	**6.3**	**-3**	....	....	....	....	....	....	....	....	....	....	....	....
	Carolina	**NHL**	**42**	**0**	**5**	**5**	**48**	**0**	**0**	**0**	**37**	**0.0**	**-2**	....	....	....	....	....	....	....	....	....	....	....	....
1998-99	**Carolina**	**NHL**	**54**	**0**	**10**	**10**	**48**	**0**	**0**	**0**	**44**	**0.0**	**9**	**0**	**0.0**	**19:02**	....	....	....	....	....	....	....	....	....
99-2000	**Carolina**	**NHL**	**62**	**13**	**31**	**44**	**59**	**8**	**0**	**2**	**150**	**8.7**	**3**	**1**	**0.0**	**24:31**	....	....	....	....	....	....	....	....	....
2000-01	**St. Louis**	**NHL**	**48**	**1**	**10**	**11**	**51**	**0**	**0**	**0**	**47**	**2.1**	**5**	**1**	**0.0**	**17:23**	**15**	**0**	**1**	**1**	**12**	**0**	**0**	**0**	**13:46**
2001-02	**St. Louis**	**NHL**	**23**	**0**	**3**	**3**	**28**	**0**	**0**	**0**	**29**	**0.0**	**1**	**0**	**0.0**	**15:56**	....	....	....	....	....	....	....	....	....
	Carolina	**NHL**	**49**	**7**	**23**	**30**	**61**	**4**	**0**	**2**	**116**	**6.0**	**-1**	**1**	**0.0**	**23:58**	**23**	**4**	**4**	**8**	**20**	**4**	**0**	**1**	**25:55**
2002-03	**Carolina**	**NHL**	**82**	**5**	**24**	**29**	**141**	**1**	**0**	**0**	**188**	**2.7**	**4**	**1**	**0.0**	**24:21**	....	....	....	....	....	....	....	....	....
2003-04	**Carolina**	**NHL**	**80**	**13**	**26**	**39**	**84**	**6**	**0**	**1**	**228**	**5.7**	**-2**	**2**	**50.0**	**25:24**	....	....	....	....	....	....	....	....	....
2004-05			DID NOT PLAY																						
	NHL Totals		**682**	**57**	**187**	**244**	**786**	**24**	**1**	**9**	**1330**	**4.3**		**6**	**16.7**	**22:30**	**46**	**5**	**5**	**10**	**38**	**4**	**0**	**1**	**21:07**

WCHA Second All-Star Team (1990, 1991) • NCAA West Second All-American Team (1991)

Claimed by **Anaheim** from **Montreal** in Expansion Draft, June 24, 1993. Traded to **Ottawa** by **Anaheim** with Anaheim's 9th round choice (Frederic Cassivi) in 1994 Entry Draft for Ottawa's 3rd round choice (later traded to Tampa Bay – Tampa Bay selected Vadim Epanchintsev) in 1994 Entry Draft, June 29, 1994. • Missed remainder of 1996-97 season recovering from knee injury suffered in game vs. New Jersey, October 18, 1996. Traded to **Carolina** by **Ottawa** for Chris Murray, November 18, 1997. Signed as a free agent by **St. Louis**, July 1, 2000. Traded to **Carolina** by **St. Louis** for Steve Halko and Carolina's 4th round choice (later traded to Atlanta – Atlanta selected Lane Manson) in 2002 Entry Draft, December 5, 2001. Signed as a free agent by **Florida**, July 15, 2004.

HINOTE, Dan

(HIGH-noht, DAN) **COL.**

Right wing. Shoots right. 6', 190 lbs. Born, Leesburg, FL, January 30, 1977. Colorado's 9th choice, 167th overall, in 1996 Entry Draft.

Season	Club	League	GP	G	A	Pts	PIM	PP	SH	GW	S	%	+/-	TF	F%	Min	GP	G	A	Pts	PIM	PP	SH	GW	Min
1993-94	Elk River Elks	High-MN	STATISTICS NOT AVAILABLE																						
1994-95	Army	NCAA	33	20	24	44	20	....	....	....	....	....	....	....	....	....	....	....	....	....	....	....	....	....	....
1995-96	Army	NCAA	34	21	24	45	22	....	....	....	....	....	....	....	....	....	....	....	....	....	....	....	....	....	....
1996-97	Oshawa Generals	OHL	60	15	13	28	58	....	....	....	....	....	....	....	....	....	18	4	5	9	8	....	....	....	....
1997-98	Oshawa Generals	OHL	35	12	15	27	39	....	....	....	....	....	....	....	....	....	5	2	2	4	7	....	....	....	....
	Hershey Bears	AHL	24	1	4	5	25	....	....	....	....	....	....	....	....	....	....	....	....	....	....	....	....	....	....
1998-99	Hershey Bears	AHL	65	4	16	20	95	....	....	....	....	....	....	....	....	....	5	3	1	4	6	....	....	....	....
99-2000	**Colorado**	**NHL**	**27**	**1**	**3**	**4**	**10**	**0**	**0**	**0**	**14**	**7.1**	**0**	**132**	**51.5**	**7:51**	....	....	....	....	....	....	....	....	....
	Hershey Bears	AHL	55	28	31	59	96	....	....	....	....	....	....	....	....	....	14	4	5	9	19	....	....	....	....
2000-01♦	**Colorado**	**NHL**	**76**	**5**	**10**	**15**	**51**	**1**	**0**	**1**	**69**	**7.2**	**1**	**506**	**49.8**	**10:21**	**23**	**2**	**4**	**6**	**21**	**0**	**0**	**0**	**8:22**
2001-02	**Colorado**	**NHL**	**58**	**6**	**6**	**12**	**39**	**0**	**1**	**3**	**75**	**8.0**	**8**	**267**	**51.3**	**12:27**	**19**	**1**	**2**	**3**	**9**	**0**	**0**	**0**	**10:46**
2002-03	**Colorado**	**NHL**	**60**	**6**	**4**	**10**	**49**	**0**	**0**	**3**	**65**	**9.2**	**4**	**218**	**46.8**	**10:36**	**7**	**1**	**2**	**3**	**2**	**0**	**0**	**0**	**14:19**
2003-04	**Colorado**	**NHL**	**59**	**4**	**7**	**11**	**57**	**0**	**2**	**0**	**53**	**7.5**	**-6**	**151**	**48.3**	**12:42**	**11**	**1**	**0**	**1**	**0**	**0**	**1**	**0**	**13:04**
2004-05	MODO	Sweden	18	2	1	3	106	....	....	....	....	....	....	....	....	....	5	0	0	0	56	....	....	....	....
	NHL Totals		**280**	**22**	**30**	**52**	**206**	**1**	**3**	**7**	**276**	**8.0**		**1274**	**49.6**	**11:06**	**60**	**5**	**8**	**13**	**32**	**0**	**1**	**0**	**10:41**

Signed as a free agent by **MODO** (Sweden), December 22, 2004.

HLAVAC, Jan

(huh-LAH-vahch, YAHN)

Left wing. Shoots left. 6', 185 lbs. Born, Prague, Czech., September 20, 1976. NY Islanders' 2nd choice, 28th overall, in 1995 Entry Draft.

Season	Club	League	GP	G	A	Pts	PIM	PP	SH	GW	S	%	+/-	TF	F%	Min	GP	G	A	Pts	PIM	PP	SH	GW	Min
1993-94	Sparta Jr.	CzRep-Jr.	27	12	15	27	....	....	....	....	....	....	....	....	....	....	....	....	....	....	....	....	....	....	....
	HC Sparta Praha	CzRep	9	1	1	2	....	....	....	....	....	....	....	....	....	....	....	....	....	....	....	....	....	....	....
1994-95	HC Sparta Praha	CzRep	38	7	6	13	18	....	....	....	....	....	....	....	....	....	5	0	2	2	0	....	....	....	....
1995-96	HC Sparta Praha	CzRep	34	8	5	13	....	....	....	....	....	....	....	....	....	....	12	1	2	3	....	....	....	....	....
1996-97	HC Sparta Praha	CzRep	38	8	13	21	24	....	....	....	....	....	....	....	....	....	10	5	2	7	2	....	....	....	....
	HC Sparta Praha	EuroHL	3	4	0	4	6	....	....	....	....	....	....	....	....	....	....	....	....	....	....	....	....	....	....

			Regular Season														Playoffs								
Season	Club	League	GP	G	A	Pts	PIM	PP	SH	GW	S	%	+/-	TF	F%	Min	GP	G	A	Pts	PIM	PP	SH	GW	Min
1997-98	HC Sparta Praha	CzRep	48	17	30	47	40	....	....	....	....	....	....	....	....	....	5	1	0	1	2	....	....	....	....
	HC Sparta Praha	EuroHL	5	0	3	3	4	....	....	....	....	....	....	....	....	....	....	....	....	....	....	....	....	....	....
1998-99	HC Sparta Praha	CzRep	49	*33	20	53	52	....	....	....	....	....	....	....	....	....	6	1	3	4	....	....	....	....	....
	HC Sparta Praha	EuroHL	5	4	2	6	0	....	....	....	....	....	....	....	....	....	1	1	1	2	0	....	....	....	....
99-2000	**NY Rangers**	**NHL**	67	19	23	42	16	6	0	2	134	14.2	3	6	33.3	15:09	....	....	....	....	....	....	....	....	....
	Hartford	AHL	3	1	0	1	0	....	....	....	....	....	....	....	....	....	....	....	....	....	....	....	....	....	....
2000-01	**NY Rangers**	**NHL**	79	28	36	64	20	5	0	6	195	14.4	3	0	0.0	16:38	....	....	....	....	....	....	....	....	....
2001-02	**Philadelphia**	**NHL**	31	7	3	10	8	0	0	1	62	11.3	5	0	0.0	12:36	....	....	....	....	....	....	....	....	....
	Vancouver	**NHL**	46	9	12	21	10	1	0	2	70	12.9	4	2	100.0	14:46	5	0	1	1	0	0	0	0	9:38
2002-03	**Vancouver**	**NHL**	9	1	1	2	6	0	0	0	7	14.3	−1	0	0.0	10:51	....	....	....	....	....	....	....	....	....
	Carolina	**NHL**	52	9	15	24	22	6	0	1	116	7.8	−9	21	38.1	17:10	....	....	....	....	....	....	....	....	....
2003-04	**NY Rangers**	**NHL**	72	5	21	26	16	2	0	0	125	4.0	−8	7	42.9	13:52	....	....	....	....	....	....	....	....	....
2004-05	HC Sparta Praha	CzRep	48	10	28	38	34	....	....	....	....	....	....	....	....	....	5	2	0	2	6	....	....	....	....
	NHL Totals		356	78	111	189	98	20	0	12	709	11.0		36	41.7	15:08	5	0	1	1	0	0	0	0	9:38

Traded to **Calgary** by **NY Islanders** for Jorgen Jonsson, July 14, 1998. Rights traded to **NY Rangers** by **Calgary** with Calgary's 1st (Jamie Lundmark) and 3rd (later traded back to Calgary – Calgary selected Craig Andersson) round choices in 1999 Entry Draft for Marc Savard and NY Rangers' 1st round choice (Oleg Saprykin) in 1999 Entry Draft, June 26, 1999. Traded to **Philadelphia** by **NY Rangers** with Kim Johnsson, Pavel Brendl and NY Rangers' 3rd round choice (Stefan Ruzicka) in 2003 Entry Draft for Eric Lindros, August 20, 2001. Traded to **Vancouver** by **Philadelphia** with Tampa Bay's 3rd round choice (previously acquired, Vancouver selected Brett Skinner) in 2002 Entry Draft for Donald Brashear and Vancouver's 6th round choice (later traded to Columbus – Columbus selected Jaroslav Balastik) in 2002 Entry Draft, December 17, 2001. Traded to **Carolina** by **Vancouver** with Harold Druken for Darren Langdon and Marek Malik, November 1, 2002. Signed as a free agent by **NY Rangers**, August 28, 2003. Signed as a free agent by **Sparta** (CzRep), August 9, 2004.

HNIDY, Shane

(NIGH-dee, SHAYN) **ATL.**

Defense. Shoots right. 6'1", 210 lbs. Born, Neepawa, Man., November 8, 1975. Buffalo's 7th choice, 173rd overall, in 1994 Entry Draft.

Season	Club	League	GP	G	A	Pts	PIM	PP	SH	GW	S	%	+/-	TF	F%	Min	GP	G	A	Pts	PIM	PP	SH	GW	Min
1990-91	Yellowhead	MMMHL	36	9	11	20	92	....	....	....	....	....	....	....	....	....	....	....	....	....	....	....	....	....	....
1991-92	Swift Current	WHL	56	1	3	4	11	....	....	....	....	....	....	....	....	....	4	0	0	0	0	....	....	....	....
1992-93	Swift Current	WHL	45	5	12	17	62	....	....	....	....	....	....	....	....	....	....	....	....	....	....	....	....	....	....
	Prince Albert	WHL	27	2	10	12	43	....	....	....	....	....	....	....	....	....	....	....	....	....	....	....	....	....	....
1993-94	Prince Albert	WHL	69	7	26	33	113	....	....	....	....	....	....	....	....	....	....	....	....	....	....	....	....	....	....
1994-95	Prince Albert	WHL	72	5	29	34	169	....	....	....	....	....	....	....	....	....	15	4	7	11	29	....	....	....	....
1995-96	Prince Albert	WHL	58	11	42	53	100	....	....	....	....	....	....	....	....	....	18	4	11	15	34	....	....	....	....
1996-97	Baton Rouge	ECHL	21	3	10	13	50	....	....	....	....	....	....	....	....	....	....	....	....	....	....	....	....	....	....
	Saint John Flames	AHL	44	2	12	14	112	....	....	....	....	....	....	....	....	....	....	....	....	....	....	....	....	....	....
1997-98	Grand Rapids	IHL	77	6	12	18	210	....	....	....	....	....	....	....	....	....	3	0	2	2	23	....	....	....	....
1998-99	Adirondack	AHL	68	9	20	29	121	....	....	....	....	....	....	....	....	....	3	0	1	1	0	....	....	....	....
99-2000	Cincinnati	AHL	68	9	19	28	153	....	....	....	....	....	....	....	....	....	....	....	....	....	....	....	....	....	....
2000-01	**Ottawa**	**NHL**	52	3	2	5	84	0	0	1	47	6.4	8	0	0.0	13:05	1	0	0	0	0	0	0	0	13:23
	Grand Rapids	IHL	2	0	0	0	2	....	....	....	....	....	....	....	....	....	....	....	....	....	....	....	....	....	....
2001-02	**Ottawa**	**NHL**	33	1	1	2	57	0	0	0	34	2.9	−10	0	0.0	16:56	12	1	1	2	12	0	0	0	16:00
2002-03	**Ottawa**	**NHL**	67	0	8	8	130	0	0	0	58	0.0	−1	1	0.0	13:55	1	0	0	0	0	0	0	0	9:38
2003-04	**Ottawa**	**NHL**	37	0	5	5	72	0	0	0	16	0.0	2	0	0.0	11:19	....	....	....	....	....	....	....	....	....
	Nashville	**NHL**	9	0	2	2	10	0	0	0	12	0.0	3	0	0.0	18:11	5	0	0	0	6	0	0	0	12:31
2004-05	Florida Everblades	ECHL	19	1	4	5	56	....	....	....	....	....	....	....	....	....	17	0	4	4	6	....	....	....	....
	NHL Totals		198	4	18	22	353	0	0	1	167	2.4		1	0.0	13:54	19	1	1	2	18	0	0	0	14:37

Signed as a free agent by **Detroit**, August 6, 1998. Traded to **Ottawa** by **Detroit** for Ottawa's 8th round choice (Todd Jackson) in 2000 Entry Draft, June 25, 2000. • Missed majority of 2001-02 season recovering from ankle injury suffered in game vs. Boston, December 26, 2001. Traded to **Nashville** by **Ottawa** for Colorado's 3rd round choice (previously acquired, Ottawa selected Peter Regin) in 2004 Entry Draft, March 9, 2004. Signed as a free agent by **Florida** (ECHL), December 6, 2004. Traded to **Atlanta** by **Nashville** for Atlanta's 4th round choice in 2006 Entry Draft, July 30, 2005.

HOLDEN, Josh

(HOHL-dehn, JAWSH)

Center. Shoots left. 6', 190 lbs. Born, Calgary, Alta., January 18, 1978. Vancouver's 1st choice, 12th overall, in 1996 Entry Draft.

Season	Club	League	GP	G	A	Pts	PIM	PP	SH	GW	S	%	+/-	TF	F%	Min	GP	G	A	Pts	PIM	PP	SH	GW	Min
1993-94	Calgary Buffaloes	AMHL	34	14	15	29	82	....	....	....	....	....	....	....	....	....	....	....	....	....	....	....	....	....	....
1994-95	Regina Pats	WHL	62	20	23	43	45	....	....	....	....	....	....	....	....	....	4	3	1	4	0	....	....	....	....
1995-96	Regina Pats	WHL	70	57	55	112	105	....	....	....	....	....	....	....	....	....	11	4	5	9	23	....	....	....	....
1996-97	Regina Pats	WHL	58	49	49	98	148	....	....	....	....	....	....	....	....	....	5	3	2	5	10	....	....	....	....
1997-98	Regina Pats	WHL	56	41	58	99	134	....	....	....	....	....	....	....	....	....	2	2	2	4	10	....	....	....	....
1998-99	**Vancouver**	**NHL**	30	2	4	6	10	1	0	0	44	4.5	−10	269	39.0	12:44	....	....	....	....	....	....	....	....	....
	Syracuse Crunch	AHL	38	14	15	29	48	....	....	....	....	....	....	....	....	....	....	....	....	....	....	....	....	....	....
99-2000	**Vancouver**	**NHL**	6	1	5	6	2	0	0	0	5	20.0	2	42	42.9	10:25	....	....	....	....	....	....	....	....	....
	Syracuse Crunch	AHL	45	19	32	51	113	....	....	....	....	....	....	....	....	....	4	1	0	1	10	....	....	....	....
2000-01	**Vancouver**	**NHL**	10	1	0	1	0	0	0	0	12	8.3	0	85	35.3	9:27	....	....	....	....	....	....	....	....	....
	Kansas City	IHL	60	27	26	53	136	....	....	....	....	....	....	....	....	....	....	....	....	....	....	....	....	....	....
2001-02	**Carolina**	**NHL**	8	0	0	0	2	0	0	0	3	0.0	0	41	41.5	5:17	....	....	....	....	....	....	....	....	....
	Manitoba Moose	AHL	68	16	17	33	187	....	....	....	....	....	....	....	....	....	7	1	1	2	4	....	....	....	....
2002-03	**Toronto**	**NHL**	5	1	0	1	2	0	0	0	6	16.7	−2	0	0.0	8:06	....	....	....	....	....	....	....	....	....
	St. John's	AHL	65	24	29	53	123	....	....	....	....	....	....	....	....	....	....	....	....	....	....	....	....	....	....
2003-04	**Toronto**	**NHL**	1	0	0	0	0	0	0	0	0	0.0	0	0	0.0	10:32	....	....	....	....	....	....	....	....	....
	St. John's	AHL	52	22	33	55	106	....	....	....	....	....	....	....	....	....	....	....	....	....	....	....	....	....	....
2004-05	HPK Hameenlinna	Finland	51	21	15	36	94	....	....	....	....	....	....	....	....	....	10	6	1	7	12	....	....	....	....
	NHL Totals		60	5	9	14	16	1	0	0	70	7.1		437	38.9	10:32	....	....	....	....	....	....	....	....	....

WHL East Second All-Star Team (1998)

Claimed by **Carolina** from **Vancouver** in Waiver Draft, September 28, 2001. Claimed on waivers by **Vancouver** from **Carolina**, October 25, 2001. Traded to **Toronto** by **Vancouver** for Jeff Farkas, June 23, 2002. Signed as a free agent by **HPK** (Finland), September 19, 2004. Signed as a free agent by **Fribourg** (Swiss), March 6, 2005.

HOLIK, Bobby

(HOH-leek, BAWB-ee) **ATL.**

Center. Shoots right. 6'4", 235 lbs. Born, Jihlava, Czech., January 1, 1971. Hartford's 1st choice, 10th overall, in 1989 Entry Draft.

Season	Club	League	GP	G	A	Pts	PIM	PP	SH	GW	S	%	+/-	TF	F%	Min	GP	G	A	Pts	PIM	PP	SH	GW	Min
1987-88	Dukla Jihlava	Czech	31	5	9	14	16	....	....	....	....	....	....	....	....	....	....	....	....	....	....	....	....	....	....
1988-89	Dukla Jihlava	Czech	24	7	10	17	32	....	....	....	....	....	....	....	....	....	....	....	....	....	....	....	....	....	....
1989-90	Dukla Jihlava	Czech	42	15	26	41	....	....	....	....	....	....	....	....	....	....	....	....	....	....	....	....	....	....	....
1990-91	**Hartford**	**NHL**	78	21	22	43	113	8	0	3	173	12.1	−3	....	....	....	6	0	0	0	7	0	0	0	....
1991-92	**Hartford**	**NHL**	76	21	24	45	44	1	0	2	207	10.1	4	....	....	....	7	0	1	1	6	0	0	0	....
1992-93	**New Jersey**	**NHL**	61	20	19	39	76	7	0	4	180	11.1	−6	....	....	....	5	1	1	2	6	0	0	0	....
	Utica Devils	AHL	1	0	0	0	2	....	....	....	....	....	....	....	....	....	....	....	....	....	....	....	....	....	....
1993-94	**New Jersey**	**NHL**	70	13	20	33	72	2	0	3	130	10.0	28	....	....	....	20	0	3	3	6	0	0	0	....
1994-95♦	**New Jersey**	**NHL**	48	10	10	20	18	0	0	2	84	11.9	9	....	....	....	20	4	4	8	22	2	0	1	....
1995-96	**New Jersey**	**NHL**	63	13	17	30	58	1	0	1	157	8.3	9	....	....	....	....	....	....	....	....	....	....	....	....
1996-97	**New Jersey**	**NHL**	82	23	39	62	54	5	0	6	192	12.0	24	....	....	....	10	2	3	5	4	1	0	0	....
1997-98	**New Jersey**	**NHL**	82	29	36	65	100	8	0	8	238	12.2	23	....	....	....	5	0	0	0	8	0	0	0	....
1998-99	**New Jersey**	**NHL**	78	27	37	64	119	5	0	8	253	10.7	16	1350	53.6	17:34	7	0	7	7	6	0	0	0	18:14
99-2000♦	**New Jersey**	**NHL**	79	23	23	46	106	7	0	4	257	8.9	7	1390	55.6	16:53	23	3	7	10	14	0	0	1	17:29
2000-01	**New Jersey**	**NHL**	80	15	35	50	97	3	0	3	206	7.3	19	1365	56.0	15:49	25	6	10	16	37	1	0	3	16:05
2001-02	**New Jersey**	**NHL**	81	25	29	54	97	6	0	3	270	9.3	7	1594	54.5	17:42	6	4	1	5	2	1	0	0	17:53
2002-03	**NY Rangers**	**NHL**	64	16	19	35	52	3	0	2	213	7.5	−1	1390	58.2	18:07	....	....	....	....	....	....	....	....	....
2003-04	**NY Rangers**	**NHL**	82	25	31	56	96	8	0	4	225	11.1	4	1664	54.2	18:34	....	....	....	....	....	....	....	....	....
2004-05			DID NOT PLAY																						
	NHL Totals		1024	281	361	642	1102	64	0	53	2785	10.1		8753	55.3	17:25	134	20	37	57	118	5	0	5	17:02

Played in NHL All-Star Game (1998, 1999)

Traded to **New Jersey** by **Hartford** with Hartford's 2nd round choice (Jay Pandolfo) in 1993 Entry Draft for Sean Burke and Eric Weinrich, August 28, 1992. Signed as a free agent by **NY Rangers**, July 1, 2002. Signed as a free agent by **Atlanta**, August 2, 2005.

HOLLAND, Jason

(HAWL-land, JAY-suhn)

Defense. Shoots right. 6'3", 219 lbs. Born, Morinville, Alta., April 30, 1976. NY Islanders' 2nd choice, 38th overall, in 1994 Entry Draft.

Season	Club	League	GP	G	A	Pts	PIM	PP	SH	GW	S	%	+/-	TF	F%	Min	GP	G	A	Pts	PIM	PP	SH	GW	Min
1991-92	St. Albert Raiders	AMHL	38	9	29	38	94	....	....	....	....	....	....	....	....	....	....	....	....	....	....	....	....	....	....
1992-93	St. Albert Raiders	AMHL	31	11	25	36	36	....	....	....	....	....	....	....	....	....	....	....	....	....	....	....	....	....	....
	Kamloops Blazers	WHL	4	0	0	0	2	....	....	....	....	....	....	....	....	....	....	....	....	....	....	....	....	....	....
1993-94	Kamloops Blazers	WHL	59	14	15	29	80	....	....	....	....	....	....	....	....	....	18	2	3	5	4	....	....	....	....
1994-95	Kamloops Blazers	WHL	71	9	32	41	65	....	....	....	....	....	....	....	....	....	21	2	7	9	9	....	....	....	....
1995-96	Kamloops Blazers	WHL	63	24	33	57	98	....	....	....	....	....	....	....	....	....	16	4	9	13	22	....	....	....	....

			Regular Season														Playoffs								
Season	Club	League	GP	G	A	Pts	PIM	PP	SH	GW	S	%	+/-	TF	F%	Min	GP	G	A	Pts	PIM	PP	SH	GW	Min
1996-97	NY Islanders	NHL	4	1	0	1	0	0	0	0	3	33.3	1	....	....	....	....	....	....	....	....	....	....	....	....
	Kentucky	AHL	72	14	25	39	46	....	....	....	....	....	....	....	....	....	4	0	2	2	0	....	....	....	....
1997-98	NY Islanders	NHL	8	0	0	0	4	0	0	0	6	0.0	–4	....	....	....	....	....	....	....	....	....	....	....	....
	Kentucky	AHL	50	10	16	26	29	....	....	....	....	....	....	....	....	....	....	....	....	....	....	....	....	....	....
	Rochester	AHL	9	0	4	4	10	....	....	....	....	....	....	....	....	....	4	0	3	3	4	....	....	....	....
1998-99	Buffalo	NHL	3	0	0	0	8	0	0	0	2	0.0	–1	0	0.0	10:58	....	....	....	....	....	....	....	....	....
	Rochester	AHL	74	4	25	29	36	....	....	....	....	....	....	....	....	....	20	2	5	7	8	....	....	....	....
99-2000	Buffalo	NHL	9	0	1	1	0	0	0	0	8	0.0	0	0	0.0	15:31	1	0	0	0	0	0	0	0	15:41
	Rochester	AHL	54	3	15	18	24	....	....	....	....	....	....	....	....	....	12	1	0	1	2	....	....	....	....
2000-01	Rochester	AHL	63	4	19	23	45	....	....	....	....	....	....	....	....	....	4	1	0	1	0	....	....	....	....
2001-02	Los Angeles	NHL	3	0	0	0	0	0	0	0	1	0.0	–1	0	0.0	15:50	....	....	....	....	....	....	....	....	....
	Manchester	AHL	65	9	18	27	39	....	....	....	....	....	....	....	....	....	5	1	0	1	5	....	....	....	....
2002-03	Los Angeles	NHL	2	0	1	1	0	0	0	0	0	0.0	1	0	0.0	13:31	....	....	....	....	....	....	....	....	....
	Manchester	AHL	67	4	27	31	53	....	....	....	....	....	....	....	....	....	3	0	0	0	0	....	....	....	....
2003-04	Los Angeles	NHL	52	3	3	6	24	0	0	1	64	4.7	5	0	0.0	17:41	....	....	....	....	....	....	....	....	....
2004-05	HC Alleghe	Italy	13	3	4	7	6	....	....	....	....	....	....	....	....	....	....	....	....	....	....	....	....	....	....
	Manchester	AHL	53	1	9	10	64	....	....	....	....	....	....	....	....	....	6	1	1	2	0	....	....	....	....
	NHL Totals		81	4	5	9	36	0	0	1	84	4.8		0	0.0	16:54	1	0	0	0	0	0	0	0	15:41

WHL West First All-Star Team (1996) • AHL All-Rookie Team (1997)

Traded to **Buffalo** by **NY Islanders** with Paul Kruse for Jason Dawe, March 24, 1998. Signed as a free agent by **Los Angeles**, August 23, 2001. Signed as a free agent by **Alleghe** (Italy), October 24, 2004. Signed as a free agent by **Manchester** (AHL), December 12, 2004.

HOLMQVIST, Mikael

(HOHLM-kvihst, MIGH-kuhl) **CHI.**

Center. Shoots left. 6'3", 205 lbs. Born, Stockholm, Sweden, June 8, 1979. Anaheim's 1st choice, 18th overall, in 1997 Entry Draft.

Season	Club	League	GP	G	A	Pts	PIM	PP	SH	GW	S	%	+/-	TF	F%	Min	GP	G	A	Pts	PIM	PP	SH	GW	Min
1995-96	Djurgarden Jr.	Swe-Jr.	24	7	2	9	4	....	....	....	....	....	....	....	....	....	....	....	....	....	....	....	....	....	....
1996-97	Djurgarden Jr.	Swe-Jr.	39	29	35	64	110	....	....	....	....	....	....	....	....	....	....	....	....	....	....	....	....	....	....
	Djurgarden	Sweden	9	0	0	0	0	....	....	....	....	....	....	....	....	....	....	....	....	....	....	....	....	....	....
1997-98	Farjestad	Sweden	41	2	3	5	6	....	....	....	....	....	....	....	....	....	7	0	0	0	0	....	....	....	....
	Farjestad	EuroHL	5	2	2	4	2	....	....	....	....	....	....	....	....	....	....	....	....	....	....	....	....	....	....
1998-99	Farjestad Jr.	Swe-Jr.	2	2	2	4	2	....	....	....	....	....	....	....	....	....	....	....	....	....	....	....	....	....	....
	Farjestad	EuroHL	3	0	0	0	0	....	....	....	....	....	....	....	....	....	1	0	0	0	0	....	....	....	....
	Farjestad	Sweden	15	0	0	0	6	....	....	....	....	....	....	....	....	....	....	....	....	....	....	....	....	....	....
	Hammarby	Sweden-2	3	2	0	2	0	....	....	....	....	....	....	....	....	....	....	....	....	....	....	....	....	....	....
99-2000	TPS Turku	Finland	54	12	3	15	14	....	....	....	....	....	....	....	....	....	11	2	3	5	4	....	....	....	....
2000-01	TPS Turku	Finland	46	4	5	9	8	....	....	....	....	....	....	....	....	....	10	1	3	4	2	....	....	....	....
2001-02	TPS Turku	Finland	56	9	13	22	16	....	....	....	....	....	....	....	....	....	8	1	0	1	12	....	....	....	....
2002-03	TPS Turku	Finland	56	15	25	40	36	....	....	....	....	....	....	....	....	....	7	0	0	0	4	....	....	....	....
2003-04	Anaheim	NHL	21	2	0	2	25	0	0	0	18	11.1	–6	16	31.3	8:24	....	....	....	....	....	....	....	....	....
	Cincinnati	AHL	24	7	7	14	20	....	....	....	....	....	....	....	....	....	....	....	....	....	....	....	....	....	....
2004-05	Cincinnati	AHL	79	14	32	46	111	....	....	....	....	....	....	....	....	....	11	2	2	4	10	....	....	....	....
	NHL Totals		21	2	0	2	25	0	0	0	18	11.1		16	31.3	8:24	....	....	....	....	....	....	....	....	....

Traded to **Chicago** by **Anaheim** for Travis Moen, July 30, 2005.

HOLMSTROM, Tomas

(HOHLM-struhm, TAW-mas) **DET.**

Left wing. Shoots left. 6', 200 lbs. Born, Pitea, Sweden, January 23, 1973. Detroit's 9th choice, 257th overall, in 1994 Entry Draft.

Season	Club	League	GP	G	A	Pts	PIM	PP	SH	GW	S	%	+/-	TF	F%	Min	GP	G	A	Pts	PIM	PP	SH	GW	Min
1989-90	Pitea HC	Sweden-2	9	1	0	1	4	....	....	....	....	....	....	....	....	....	....	....	....	....	....	....	....	....	....
1990-91	Pitea HC	Sweden-2	26	5	4	9	16	....	....	....	....	....	....	....	....	....	....	....	....	....	....	....	....	....	....
1991-92	Pitea HC	Sweden-2	31	15	12	27	44	....	....	....	....	....	....	....	....	....	....	....	....	....	....	....	....	....	....
1992-93	Pitea HC	Sweden-2	32	17	15	32	30	....	....	....	....	....	....	....	....	....	....	....	....	....	....	....	....	....	....
1993-94	Bodens IK	Sweden-2	34	23	16	39	86	....	....	....	....	....	....	....	....	....	9	3	3	6	24	....	....	....	....
1994-95	Lulea HF	Sweden	40	14	14	28	56	....	....	....	....	....	....	....	....	....	8	1	2	3	20	....	....	....	....
1995-96	Lulea HF	Sweden	34	12	11	23	78	....	....	....	....	....	....	....	....	....	11	6	2	8	22	....	....	....	....
1996-97♦	Detroit	NHL	47	6	3	9	33	3	0	0	53	11.3	–10	....	....	....	1	0	0	0	0	0	0	0	....
	Adirondack	AHL	6	3	1	4	7	....	....	....	....	....	....	....	....	....	....	....	....	....	....	....	....	....	....
1997-98♦	Detroit	NHL	57	5	17	22	44	1	0	1	48	10.4	6	....	....	....	22	7	12	19	16	2	0	0	....
1998-99	Detroit	NHL	82	13	21	34	69	5	0	4	100	13.0	–11	0	0.0	12:22	10	4	3	7	4	2	0	1	12:32
99-2000	Detroit	NHL	72	13	22	35	43	4	0	1	71	18.3	4	0	0.0	12:06	9	3	1	4	16	1	0	1	11:42
2000-01	Detroit	NHL	73	16	24	40	40	9	0	2	74	21.6	–12	2	50.0	11:41	6	1	3	4	8	1	0	0	14:23
2001-02♦	Detroit	NHL	69	8	18	26	58	6	0	1	79	10.1	–12	2	0.0	12:23	23	8	3	11	8	3	0	2	11:31
	Sweden	Olympics	4	1	0	1	0	....	....	....	....	....	....	....	....	....	....	....	....	....	....	....	....	....	....
2002-03	Detroit	NHL	74	20	20	40	62	12	0	2	109	18.3	11	2	0.0	12:28	4	1	1	2	4	1	0	0	14:37
2003-04	Detroit	NHL	67	15	15	30	38	6	0	0	74	20.3	8	3	0.0	12:23	12	2	2	4	10	1	0	1	11:27
2004-05	Lulea HF	Sweden	47	14	16	30	50	....	....	....	....	....	....	....	....	....	4	0	0	0	18	....	....	....	....
	NHL Totals		541	96	140	236	387	46	0	11	608	15.8		9	11.1	12:14	87	26	25	51	66	11	0	5	12:09

Signed as a free agent by **Lulea** (Sweden), September 16, 2004.

HOLZINGER, Brian

(HOHL-zihn-guhr, BRIGH-uhn)

Center. Shoots right. 5'11", 186 lbs. Born, Parma, OH, October 10, 1972. Buffalo's 7th choice, 124th overall, in 1991 Entry Draft.

Season	Club	League	GP	G	A	Pts	PIM	PP	SH	GW	S	%	+/-	TF	F%	Min	GP	G	A	Pts	PIM	PP	SH	GW	Min
1988-89	Padua	High-OH	35	73	65	138	....	....	....	....	....	....	....	....	....	....	....	....	....	....	....	....	....	....	....
1989-90	Det. Compuware	NAHL	44	36	37	73	....	....	....	....	....	....	....	....	....	....	....	....	....	....	....	....	....	....	....
1990-91	Det. Compuware	NAHL	37	45	41	86	16	....	....	....	....	....	....	....	....	....	....	....	....	....	....	....	....	....	....
1991-92	Bowling Green	CCHA	30	14	8	22	36	....	....	....	....	....	....	....	....	....	....	....	....	....	....	....	....	....	....
1992-93	Bowling Green	CCHA	41	31	26	57	44	....	....	....	....	....	....	....	....	....	....	....	....	....	....	....	....	....	....
1993-94	Bowling Green	CCHA	38	22	15	37	24	....	....	....	....	....	....	....	....	....	....	....	....	....	....	....	....	....	....
1994-95	Bowling Green	CCHA	38	35	33	68	42	....	....	....	....	....	....	....	....	....	....	....	....	....	....	....	....	....	....
	Buffalo	NHL	4	0	3	3	0	0	0	0	3	0.0	2	....	....	....	4	2	1	3	2	1	0	0	....
1995-96	Buffalo	NHL	58	10	10	20	37	5	0	1	71	14.1	–21	....	....	....	....	....	....	....	....	....	....	....	....
	Rochester	AHL	17	10	11	21	14	....	....	....	....	....	....	....	....	....	19	10	14	24	10	....	....	....	....
1996-97	Buffalo	NHL	81	22	29	51	54	2	2	6	142	15.5	9	....	....	....	12	2	5	7	8	0	1	0	....
1997-98	Buffalo	NHL	69	14	21	35	36	4	2	1	116	12.1	–2	....	....	....	15	4	7	11	18	1	1	0	....
1998-99	Buffalo	NHL	81	17	17	34	45	5	0	2	143	11.9	2	852	50.4	16:31	21	3	5	8	33	1	0	0	15:50
99-2000	Buffalo	NHL	59	7	17	24	30	0	1	2	81	8.6	4	839	45.7	14:38	....	....	....	....	....	....	....	....	....
	Tampa Bay	NHL	14	3	3	6	21	1	1	0	23	13.0	–7	119	46.2	16:10	....	....	....	....	....	....	....	....	....
2000-01	Tampa Bay	NHL	70	11	25	36	64	3	0	2	87	12.6	–9	775	47.4	16:03	....	....	....	....	....	....	....	....	....
2001-02	Tampa Bay	NHL	23	1	2	3	4	0	0	0	20	5.0	–4	54	55.6	9:19	....	....	....	....	....	....	....	....	....
2002-03	Tampa Bay	NHL	5	0	1	1	2	0	0	0	3	0.0	1	26	34.6	9:08	....	....	....	....	....	....	....	....	....
	Springfield	AHL	28	6	20	26	16	....	....	....	....	....	....	....	....	....	....	....	....	....	....	....	....	....	....
	Pittsburgh	NHL	9	1	2	3	6	0	0	0	20	5.0	–6	161	47.8	16:24	....	....	....	....	....	....	....	....	....
2003-04	Pittsburgh	NHL	61	6	15	21	38	1	1	1	82	7.3	–27	994	47.7	16:50	....	....	....	....	....	....	....	....	....
	Columbus	NHL	13	1	0	1	2	0	0	0	14	7.1	–4	155	54.8	15:17	....	....	....	....	....	....	....	....	....
2004-05			DID NOT PLAY																						
	NHL Totals		547	93	145	238	339	21	7	15	805	11.6		3975	48.0	15:29	52	11	18	29	61	3	2	0	15:50

CCHA Second All-Star Team (1993) • CCHA First All-Star Team (1995) • CCHA Player of the Year (1995) • NCAA West First All-American Team (1995) • Hobey Baker Memorial Award (Top U.S. Collegiate Player) (1995)

Traded to **Tampa Bay** by **Buffalo** with Cory Sarich, Wayne Primeau and Buffalo's 3rd round choice (Alexander Kharitonov) in 2000 Entry Draft for Chris Gratton and Tampa Bay's 2nd round choice (Derek Roy) in 2001 Entry Draft, March 9, 2000. • Missed majority of 2001-02 season recovering from shoulder injury suffered in game vs. Florida, October 7, 2001. Traded to **Pittsburgh** by **Tampa Bay** for Marc Bergevin, March 11, 2003. Traded to **Columbus** by **Pittsburgh** for Lasse Pirjeta, March 9, 2004.

HORCOFF, Shawn

(HOHR-cuhf, SHAWN) **EDM.**

Center. Shoots left. 6'1", 204 lbs. Born, Trail, B.C., September 17, 1978. Edmonton's 3rd choice, 99th overall, in 1998 Entry Draft.

Season	Club	League	GP	G	A	Pts	PIM	PP	SH	GW	S	%	+/-	TF	F%	Min	GP	G	A	Pts	PIM	PP	SH	GW	Min
1994-95	Trail Smokies	RMJHL	47	50	46	96	26	....	....	....	....	....	....	....	....	....	....	....	....	....	....	....	....	....	....
1995-96	Chilliwack Chiefs	BCHL	58	49	96	*145	44	....	....	....	....	....	....	....	....	....	9	5	19	24	12	....	....	....	....
1996-97	Michigan State	CCHA	40	10	13	23	20	....	....	....	....	....	....	....	....	....	....	....	....	....	....	....	....	....	....
1997-98	Michigan State	CCHA	34	14	13	27	50	....	....	....	....	....	....	....	....	....	....	....	....	....	....	....	....	....	....
1998-99	Michigan State	CCHA	39	12	25	37	70	....	....	....	....	....	....	....	....	....	....	....	....	....	....	....	....	....	....
99-2000	Michigan State	CCHA	42	14	*51	*65	50	....	....	....	....	....	....	....	....	....	....	....	....	....	....	....	....	....	....

			Regular Season														Playoffs								
Season	Club	League	GP	G	A	Pts	PIM	PP	SH	GW	S	%	+/-	TF	F%	Min	GP	G	A	Pts	PIM	PP	SH	GW	Min
2000-01	Edmonton	NHL	49	9	7	16	10	0	0	2	42	21.4	8	122	41.8	9:14	5	0	0	0	0	0	0	0	6:31
	Hamilton	AHL	24	10	18	28	19	....	....	....	....	....	....	....	....	....	....	....	....	....	....	....	....	....	....
2001-02	Edmonton	NHL	61	8	14	22	18	0	0	0	57	14.0	3	454	46.3	11:20	....	....	....	....	....	....	....	....	....
	Hamilton	AHL	2	1	2	3	6	....	....	....	....	....	....	....	....	....	....	....	....	....	....	....	....	....	....
2002-03	Edmonton	NHL	78	12	21	33	55	2	0	3	98	12.2	10	301	42.9	13:30	6	3	1	4	6	0	0	1	15:27
2003-04	Edmonton	NHL	80	15	25	40	73	0	2	3	110	13.6	0	1378	50.7	17:31	....	....	....	....	....	....	....	....	....
2004-05	Mora IK	Sweden	50	19	27	46	117	....	....	....	....	....	....	....	....	....	....	....	....	....	....	....	....	....	....
	NHL Totals		268	44	67	111	156	2	2	8	307	14.3		2255	48.2	13:25	11	3	1	4	6	0	0	1	11:23

CCHA First All-Star Team (2000) • CCHA Player of the Year (2000) • NCAA West First All-American Team (2000)

Signed as a free agent by **Mora** (Sweden), September 6, 2004.

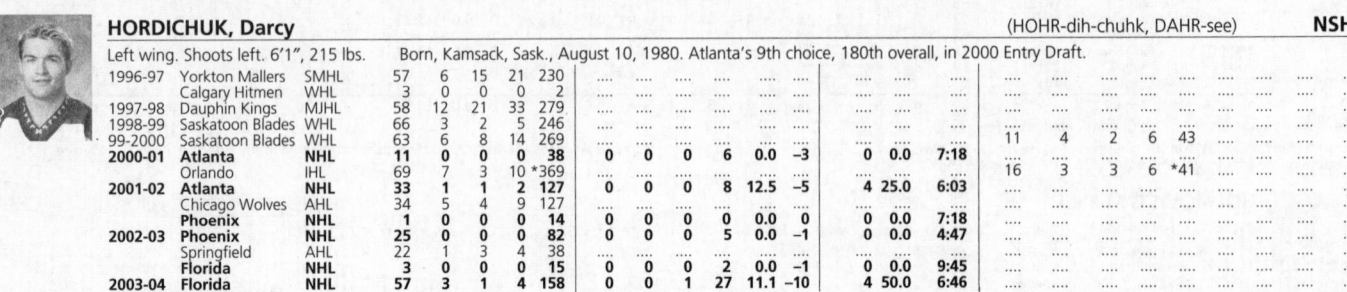

HORDICHUK, Darcy
(HOHR-dih-chuhk, DAHR-see) **NSH.**

Left wing. Shoots left. 6'1", 215 lbs. Born, Kamsack, Sask., August 10, 1980. Atlanta's 9th choice, 180th overall, in 2000 Entry Draft.

1996-97	Yorkton Mallers	SMHL	57	6	15	21	230	....	....	....	....	....	....	....	....	....	....	....	....	....	....	....	....	....	....
	Calgary Hitmen	WHL	3	0	0	0	2	....	....	....	....	....	....	....	....	....	....	....	....	....	....	....	....	....	....
1997-98	Dauphin Kings	MJHL	58	12	21	33	279	....	....	....	....	....	....	....	....	....	....	....	....	....	....	....	....	....	....
1998-99	Saskatoon Blades	WHL	66	3	2	5	246	....	....	....	....	....	....	....	....	....	....	....	....	....	....	....	....	....	....
99-2000	Saskatoon Blades	WHL	63	6	8	14	269	....	....	....	....	....	....	....	....	....	11	4	2	6	43	....	....	....	....
2000-01	Atlanta	NHL	11	0	0	0	38	0	0	0	6	0.0	–3	0	0.0	7:18	....	....	....	....	....	....	....	....	....
	Orlando	IHL	69	7	3	10	*369	....	....	....	....	....	....	....	....	....	16	3	3	6	*41	....	....	....	....
2001-02	Atlanta	NHL	33	1	1	2	127	0	0	0	8	12.5	–5	4	25.0	6:03	....	....	....	....	....	....	....	....	....
	Chicago Wolves	AHL	34	5	4	9	127	....	....	....	....	....	....	....	....	....	....	....	....	....	....	....	....	....	....
	Phoenix	NHL	1	0	0	0	14	0	0	0	0	0.0	0	0	0.0	7:18	....	....	....	....	....	....	....	....	....
2002-03	Phoenix	NHL	25	0	0	0	82	0	0	0	5	0.0	–1	0	0.0	4:47	....	....	....	....	....	....	....	....	....
	Springfield	AHL	22	1	3	4	38	....	....	....	....	....	....	....	....	....	....	....	....	....	....	....	....	....	....
	Florida	NHL	3	0	0	0	15	0	0	0	2	0.0	–1	0	0.0	9:45	....	....	....	....	....	....	....	....	....
2003-04	Florida	NHL	57	3	1	4	158	0	0	1	27	11.1	–10	4	50.0	6:46	....	....	....	....	....	....	....	....	....
2004-05			DID NOT PLAY																						
	NHL Totals		130	4	2	6	434	0	0	1	48	8.3		8	37.5	6:19	....	....	....	....	....	....	....	....	....

Traded to **Phoenix** by **Atlanta** with Atlanta's 4th (Lance Monych) and 5th (John Zeiler) round choices in 2002 Entry Draft for Kiril Safronov, the rights to Ruslan Zainullin and Phoenix's 4th round choice (Patrick Dwyer) in 2002 Entry Draft, March 19, 2002. Traded to **Florida** by **Phoenix** with Phoenix's 2nd round choice (later traded to Tampa Bay – Tampa Bay selected Matt Smaby) in 2003 Entry Draft for Brad Ference, March 8, 2003. Traded to **Nashville** by **Florida** for Nashville's 4th round choice (Matt Duffy) in 2005 Entry Draft, July 27, 2005.

HORTON, Nathan
(HOHR-tohn, NAY-thun) **FLA.**

Center. Shoots right. 6'2", 201 lbs. Born, Welland, Ont., May 29, 1985. Florida's 1st choice, 3rd overall, in 2003 Entry Draft.

2000-01	Thorold	OHA-B	41	16	31	47	75	....	....	....	....	....	....	....	....	....	....	....	....	....	....	....	....	....	....
2001-02	Oshawa Generals	OHL	64	31	36	67	84	....	....	....	....	....	....	....	....	....	5	1	2	3	10	....	....	....	....
2002-03	Oshawa Generals	OHL	54	33	35	68	111	....	....	....	....	....	....	....	....	....	13	9	6	15	10	....	....	....	....
2003-04	Florida	NHL	55	14	8	22	57	6	1	0	81	17.3	–5	270	41.9	13:20	....	....	....	....	....	....	....	....	....
2004-05	San Antonio	AHL	21	5	4	9	21	....	....	....	....	....	....	....	....	....	....	....	....	....	....	....	....	....	....
	NHL Totals		55	14	8	22	57	6	1	0	81	17.3		270	41.9	13:20	....	....	....	....	....	....	....	....	....

OHL All-Rookie Team (2002)

Signed as a free agent by **San Antonio** (AHL), October 28, 2004.

HOSSA, Marcel
(HOH-sah, MAHR-sehl) **MTL.**

Left wing. Shoots left. 6'2", 215 lbs. Born, Ilava, Czech., October 12, 1981. Montreal's 2nd choice, 16th overall, in 2000 Entry Draft.

1996-97	Dukla Trencin Jr.	Slovak-Jr.	45	30	21	51	30	....	....	....	....	....	....	....	....	....	....	....	....	....	....	....	....	....	....
1997-98	Dukla Trencin Jr.	Slovak-Jr.	39	11	38	49	44	....	....	....	....	....	....	....	....	....	....	....	....	....	....	....	....	....	....
1998-99	Portland	WHL	70	7	14	21	66	....	....	....	....	....	....	....	....	....	2	0	0	0	2	....	....	....	....
99-2000	Portland	WHL	60	24	29	53	58	....	....	....	....	....	....	....	....	....	....	....	....	....	....	....	....	....	....
2000-01	Portland	WHL	58	34	56	90	58	....	....	....	....	....	....	....	....	....	16	5	7	12	14	....	....	....	....
2001-02	Montreal	NHL	10	3	1	4	2	0	0	0	20	15.0	2	0	0.0	11:09	....	....	....	....	....	....	....	....	....
	Quebec Citadelles	AHL	50	17	15	32	24	....	....	....	....	....	....	....	....	....	3	0	0	0	4	....	....	....	....
2002-03	Montreal	NHL	34	6	7	13	14	2	0	1	51	11.8	3	4	50.0	13:58	....	....	....	....	....	....	....	....	....
	Hamilton	AHL	37	19	13	32	18	....	....	....	....	....	....	....	....	....	21	4	7	11	12	....	....	....	....
2003-04	Montreal	NHL	15	1	1	2	8	0	0	0	19	5.3	–3	5	40.0	14:50	....	....	....	....	....	....	....	....	....
	Hamilton	AHL	57	18	22	40	45	....	....	....	....	....	....	....	....	....	10	2	3	5	8	....	....	....	....
2004-05	Mora IK	Sweden	48	18	6	24	69	....	....	....	....	....	....	....	....	....	....	....	....	....	....	....	....	....	....
	NHL Totals		59	10	9	19	24	2	0	1	90	11.1		9	44.4	13:43	....	....	....	....	....	....	....	....	....

WHL West Second All-Star Team (2001)

Signed as a free agent by **Mora** (Sweden), September 25, 2004.

HOSSA, Marian
(HOH-sah, MAIR-ee-uhn) **ATL.**

Right wing. Shoots left. 6'1", 208 lbs. Born, Stara Lubovna, Czech., January 12, 1979. Ottawa's 1st choice, 12th overall, in 1997 Entry Draft.

1995-96	Dukla Trencin Jr.	Slovak-Jr.	53	42	49	91	26	....	....	....	....	....	....	....	....	....	....	....	....	....	....	....	....	....	....
1996-97	Dukla Trencin	Slovakia	46	25	19	44	33	....	....	....	....	....	....	....	....	....	7	5	5	10	....	....	....	....	....
1997-98	Portland	WHL	53	45	40	85	50	....	....	....	....	....	....	....	....	....	16	13	6	19	6	....	....	....	....
	Ottawa	NHL	7	0	1	1	0	0	0	0	10	0.0	–1	....	....	....	....	....	....	....	....	....	....	....	....
1998-99	Ottawa	NHL	60	15	15	30	37	1	0	2	124	12.1	18	4	25.0	13:59	4	0	2	2	4	0	0	0	16:46
99-2000	Ottawa	NHL	78	29	27	56	32	5	0	4	240	12.1	5	7	57.1	17:12	6	0	0	0	2	0	0	0	15:22
2000-01	Ottawa	NHL	81	32	43	75	44	11	2	7	249	12.9	19	14	42.9	18:01	4	1	1	2	4	0	0	0	19:01
2001-02	Dukla Trencin	Slovakia	8	3	4	7	16	....	....	....	....	....	....	....	....	....	....	....	....	....	....	....	....	....	....
	Ottawa	NHL	80	31	35	66	50	9	1	4	278	11.2	11	12	33.3	18:29	12	4	6	10	2	1	0	0	19:04
	Slovakia	Olympics	2	4	2	6	0	....	....	....	....	....	....	....	....	....	....	....	....	....	....	....	....	....	....
2002-03	Ottawa	NHL	80	45	35	80	34	14	0	10	229	19.7	8	19	36.8	18:31	18	5	11	16	6	3	0	1	18:41
2003-04	Ottawa	NHL	81	36	46	82	46	14	1	5	233	15.5	4	25	40.0	18:37	7	3	1	4	0	1	0	2	21:24
2004-05	Mora IK	Sweden	24	18	14	32	22	....	....	....	....	....	....	....	....	....	....	....	....	....	....	....	....	....	....
	Dukla Trencin	Slovakia	25	22	20	42	38	....	....	....	....	....	....	....	....	....	5	4	5	9	14	....	....	....	....
	NHL Totals		467	188	202	390	243	54	4	32	1363	13.8		81	39.5	17:38	51	13	21	34	18	5	0	3	18:38

WHL West First All-Star Team (1998) • WHL Rookie of the Year (1998) • Canadian Major Junior First All-Star Team (1998) • Memorial Cup Tournament All-Star Team (1998) • NHL All-Rookie Team (1999)

Played in NHL All-Star Game (2001, 2003)

Signed as a free agent by **Trencin** (Slovakia), September 16, 2004. Signed as a free agent by **Mora** (Sweden), November 11, 2004. Signed as a free agent by **Trencin** (Slovakia), January 31, 2005. Traded to **Atlanta** by **Ottawa** with Greg de Vries for Dany Heatley, August 23, 2005.

HRDINA, Jan
(huhr-DEE-nah, YAN) **CBJ**

Center. Shoots right. 6', 205 lbs. Born, Hradec Kralove, Czech., February 5, 1976. Pittsburgh's 4th choice, 128th overall, in 1995 Entry Draft.

1993-94	Hr. Kralove Jr.	CzRep-Jr.	10	1	6	7	0	....	....	....	....	....	....	....	....	....	....	....	....	....	....	....	....	....	....
	Hr. Kralove	CzRep	23	1	5	6	....	....	....	....	....	....	....	....	....	....	4	0	1	1	....	....	....	....	....
1994-95	Seattle	WHL	69	41	59	100	79	....	....	....	....	....	....	....	....	....	4	0	1	1	8	....	....	....	....
1995-96	Seattle	WHL	30	19	28	47	37	....	....	....	....	....	....	....	....	....	....	....	....	....	....	....	....	....	....
	Spokane Chiefs	WHL	18	10	16	26	25	....	....	....	....	....	....	....	....	....	18	5	14	19	49	....	....	....	....
1996-97	Cleveland	IHL	68	23	31	54	82	....	....	....	....	....	....	....	....	....	13	1	2	3	8	....	....	....	....
1997-98	Syracuse Crunch	AHL	72	20	24	44	82	....	....	....	....	....	....	....	....	....	5	1	3	4	10	....	....	....	....
1998-99	Pittsburgh	NHL	82	13	29	42	40	3	0	2	94	13.8	–2	1461	56.7	16:26	13	4	1	5	12	1	0	1	21:03
99-2000	Pittsburgh	NHL	70	13	33	46	43	3	0	1	84	15.5	13	1392	53.7	18:47	9	4	8	12	2	1	0	0	22:04
2000-01	Pittsburgh	NHL	78	15	28	43	48	3	0	1	89	16.9	19	1067	53.8	15:56	18	2	5	7	8	0	0	0	15:04
2001-02	Pittsburgh	NHL	79	24	33	57	50	6	0	6	115	20.9	–7	667	50.4	19:51	....	....	....	....	....	....	....	....	....
	Czech Republic	Olympics	4	0	0	0	0	....	....	....	....	....	....	....	....	....	....	....	....	....	....	....	....	....	....
2002-03	Pittsburgh	NHL	57	14	25	39	34	11	0	4	84	16.7	1	984	56.0	19:45	....	....	....	....	....	....	....	....	....
	Phoenix	NHL	4	0	4	4	8	0	0	0	2	0.0	3	70	60.0	18:12	....	....	....	....	....	....	....	....	....

Season	Club	League	GP	G	A	Pts	PIM	PP	SH	GW	S	%	+/-	TF	F%	Min	GP	G	A	Pts	PIM	PP	SH	GW	Min
			Regular Season														Playoffs								
2003-04	**Phoenix**	**NHL**	**55**	**11**	**15**	**26**	**30**	**5**	**0**	**1**	**62**	**17.7**	**–10**	**677**	**50.7**	**17:57**									
	New Jersey	**NHL**	**13**	**1**	**6**	**7**	**10**	**0**	**0**	**0**	**11**	**9.1**	**4**	**148**	**55.4**	**12:51**	**5**	**2**	**0**	**2**	**2**	**0**	**0**	**0**	**13:22**
2004-05	HC Rabat Kladno	CzRep	23	4	3	7	38										7	3	3	6	4				
	NHL Totals		**438**	**91**	**173**	**264**	**263**	**31**	**0**	**15**	**541**	**16.8**		**6466**	**54.2**	**17:52**	**45**	**12**	**14**	**26**	**24**	**2**	**0**	**1**	**18:00**

Traded to **Phoenix** by **Pittsburgh** with Francois Leroux for Ramzi Abid, Dan Focht and Guillaume Lefebvre, March 11, 2003. Traded to **New Jersey** by **Phoenix** for Mike Rupp and New Jersey's 2nd round choice (later traded to Edmonton – Edmonton selected Geoff Paukovich) in 2004 Entry Draft, March 5, 2004. Signed as a free agent by **Kladno** (CzRep), October 4, 2004. Signed as a free agent by **Columbus**, August 10, 2005.

HRKAC, Tony

(HUHR-kuhz, TOH-nee)

Center. Shoots left. 5'10", 190 lbs. Born, Thunder Bay, Ont., July 7, 1966. St. Louis' 2nd choice, 32nd overall, in 1984 Entry Draft.

Season	Club	League	GP	G	A	Pts	PIM	PP	SH	GW	S	%	+/-	TF	F%	Min	GP	G	A	Pts	PIM	PP	SH	GW	Min
1983-84	Orillia Travelways	OJHL	42	*52	54	*106	20																		
1984-85	North Dakota	WCHA	36	18	36	54	16																		
1985-86	Canada	Nat-Tm	62	19	30	49	36																		
1986-87	North Dakota	WCHA	48	46	70	116	48																		
	St. Louis	**NHL**															**3**	**0**	**0**	**0**	**0**	**0**	**0**	**0**	
1987-88	**St. Louis**	**NHL**	**67**	**11**	**37**	**48**	**22**	**2**	**1**	**3**	**86**	**12.8**	**5**				**10**	**6**	**1**	**7**	**4**	**3**	**1**	**1**	
1988-89	**St. Louis**	**NHL**	**70**	**17**	**28**	**45**	**8**	**5**	**0**	**1**	**133**	**12.8**	**–10**				**4**	**1**	**1**	**2**	**0**	**0**	**0**	**1**	
1989-90	**St. Louis**	**NHL**	**28**	**5**	**12**	**17**	**8**	**1**	**0**	**0**	**41**	**12.2**	**1**												
	Quebec	**NHL**	**22**	**4**	**8**	**12**	**2**	**2**	**0**	**0**	**29**	**13.8**	**–5**												
	Halifax Citadels	AHL	20	12	21	33	4										6	5	9	14	4				
1990-91	**Quebec**	**NHL**	**70**	**16**	**32**	**48**	**16**	**6**	**0**	**0**	**122**	**13.1**	**–22**												
	Halifax Citadels	AHL	3	4	1	5	2																		
1991-92	**San Jose**	**NHL**	**22**	**2**	**10**	**12**	**4**	**0**	**0**	**0**	**31**	**6.5**	**–2**												
	Chicago	**NHL**	**18**	**1**	**2**	**3**	**6**	**0**	**0**	**0**	**22**	**4.5**	**4**				**3**	**0**	**0**	**0**	**2**	**0**	**0**	**0**	
1992-93	Indianapolis Ice	IHL	80	45	*87	*132	70										5	0	2	2	2				
1993-94	**St. Louis**	**NHL**	**36**	**6**	**5**	**11**	**8**	**1**	**1**	**1**	**43**	**14.0**	**–11**				**4**	**0**	**0**	**0**	**0**	**0**	**0**	**0**	
	Peoria Rivermen	IHL	45	30	51	81	25										1	1	2	3	0				
1994-95	Milwaukee	IHL	71	24	67	91	26										15	4	9	13	16				
1995-96	Milwaukee	IHL	43	14	28	42	18										5	1	3	4	4				
1996-97	Milwaukee	IHL	81	27	61	88	20										3	1	1	2	2				
1997-98	**Dallas**	**NHL**	**13**	**5**	**3**	**8**	**0**	**3**	**0**	**0**	**14**	**35.7**	**0**												
	Michigan	IHL	20	7	15	22	6																		
	Edmonton	**NHL**	**36**	**8**	**11**	**19**	**10**	**4**	**0**	**1**	**43**	**18.6**	**3**				**12**	**0**	**3**	**3**	**2**	**0**	**0**	**0**	
1998-99 ♦	**Dallas**	**NHL**	**69**	**13**	**14**	**27**	**26**	**2**	**0**	**2**	**67**	**19.4**	**2**	**666**	**48.0**	**12:02**	**5**	**0**	**2**	**2**	**4**	**0**	**0**	**0**	**9:15**
99-2000	**NY Islanders**	**NHL**	**7**	**0**	**2**	**2**	**0**	**0**	**0**	**0**	**2**	**0.0**	**–1**	**34**	**35.3**	**11:22**									
	Anaheim	**NHL**	**60**	**4**	**7**	**11**	**8**	**1**	**0**	**0**	**37**	**10.8**	**–2**	**536**	**50.8**	**9:04**									
2000-01	**Anaheim**	**NHL**	**80**	**13**	**25**	**38**	**29**	**0**	**0**	**1**	**88**	**14.8**	**0**	**1072**	**50.7**	**13:46**									
2001-02	**Atlanta**	**NHL**	**80**	**18**	**26**	**44**	**12**	**5**	**1**	**2**	**101**	**17.8**	**–12**	**935**	**47.5**	**17:29**									
2002-03	**Atlanta**	**NHL**	**80**	**9**	**17**	**26**	**14**	**2**	**0**	**2**	**86**	**10.5**	**–16**	**1125**	**44.6**	**16:06**									
2003-04	Milwaukee	AHL	68	20	39	59	20										22	8	12	20	8				
2004-05	Milwaukee	AHL	77	12	28	40	14										6	0	1	1	8				
	NHL Totals		**758**	**132**	**239**	**371**	**173**	**34**	**3**	**13**	**945**	**14.0**		**4368**	**47.9**	**13:56**	**41**	**7**	**7**	**14**	**12**	**3**	**1**	**2**	**9:15**

WCHA First All-Star Team (1987) • WCHA Most Valuable Player (1987) • NCAA West First All-American Team (1987) • NCAA Championship All-Tournament Team (1987) • NCAA Championship Tournament MVP (1987) • Hobey Baker Memorial Award (Top U.S. Collegiate Player) (1987) • IHL First All-Star Team (1993) • Leo P. Lamoureux Memorial Trophy (Leading Scorer – IHL) (1993) • James Gatschene Memorial Trophy (MVP – IHL) (1993)

Traded to **Quebec** by **St. Louis** with Greg Millen for Jeff Brown, December 13, 1989. Traded to **San Jose** by **Quebec** for Greg Paslawski, May 31, 1991. Traded to **Chicago** by **San Jose** for Chicago's 6th round choice (Fredrik Oduya) in 1993 Entry Draft, February 7, 1992. Signed as a free agent by **St. Louis**, July 30, 1993. Signed as a free agent by **Dallas**, August 12, 1997. Claimed on waivers by **Edmonton** from **Dallas**, January 6, 1998. Traded to **Pittsburgh** by **Edmonton** with Bobby Dollas for Josef Beranek, June 16, 1998. Claimed by **Nashville** from **Pittsburgh** in Expansion Draft, June 26, 1998. Traded to **Dallas** by **Nashville** for future considerations, July 9, 1998. Signed as a free agent by **NY Islanders**, July 29, 1999. Traded to **Anaheim** by **NY Islanders** with Dean Malkoc for Ted Drury, October 29, 1999. Signed as a free agent by **Atlanta**, July 25, 2001. Signed as a free agent by **Nashville**, November 4, 2003.

HUBACEK, Petr

(HOO-buh-chehk, PEE-tuhr) **NSH.**

Center. Shoots right. 6'2", 183 lbs. Born, Brno, Czech., September 2, 1979. Philadelphia's 11th choice, 243rd overall, in 1998 Entry Draft.

Season	Club	League	GP	G	A	Pts	PIM	PP	SH	GW	S	%	+/-	TF	F%	Min	GP	G	A	Pts	PIM	PP	SH	GW	Min
1997-98	Brno Jr.	CzRep-Jr.	17	9	5	14																			
	Brno	CzRep-2	48	6	10	16																			
1998-99	HC Vitkovice	CzRep	25	0	4	4	2										4	0	0	0					
99-2000	HC Vitkovice	CzRep	48	11	12	23	81																		
2000-01	**Philadelphia**	**NHL**	**6**	**1**	**0**	**1**	**2**	**0**	**0**	**0**	**5**	**20.0**	**–1**	**39**	**25.6**	**11:20**									
	Philadelphia	AHL	62	3	9	12	29										9	0	1	1	6				
2001-02	Philadelphia	AHL	22	1	6	7	8																		
	Milwaukee	AHL	14	2	0	2	0																		
2002-03	HC Hame Zlin	CzRep	44	4	15	19	14																		
	HC Vitkovice	CzRep	7	1	4	5	10										6	1	0	1	16				
2003-04	HC Vitkovice	CzRep	46	7	14	21	26										6	1	0	1	*53				
2004-05	Vitkovice	CzRep	51	13	11	24	38										9	0	1	1	33				
	NHL Totals		**6**	**1**	**0**	**1**	**2**	**0**	**0**	**0**	**5**	**20.0**		**39**	**25.6**	**11:20**									

Traded to **Nashville** by **Philadelphia** with Jason Beckett for Yves Sarault, January 11, 2002. Signed as a free agent by **Zlin** (CzRep) with Nashville retaining NHL rights, August 4, 2002.

HUDLER, Jiri

(HUHD-luhr, YIH-ree) **DET.**

Center. Shoots left. 5'9", 178 lbs. Born, Olomouc, Czech., January 4, 1984. Detroit's 1st choice, 58th overall, in 2002 Entry Draft.

Season	Club	League	GP	G	A	Pts	PIM	PP	SH	GW	S	%	+/-	TF	F%	Min	GP	G	A	Pts	PIM	PP	SH	GW	Min
1998-99	HC Vsetin U17	CzR-U17	46	57	57	114																			
99-2000	HC Vsetin Jr.	CzRep-Jr.	53	29	31	60	75																		
	Vsetin	CzRep	2	0	1	1	0																		
2000-01	HC Vsetin Jr.	CzRep-Jr.	16	8	14	22	16																		
	HC Slovnaft Vsetin	CzRep	22	1	4	5	10																		
	HC Femax Havirov	CzRep	15	5	1	6	12																		
2001-02	HC Vsetin	CzRep	46	15	31	46	54																		
	Liberec	CzRep-2	13	9	7	16	10																		
	HC Olomouc	CzRep-3	1	0	2	2	4																		
2002-03	HC Vsetin	CzRep	30	19	27	46	22																		
	Ak Bars Kazan	Russia	11	1	5	6	12										1	0	0	0	0				
2003-04	**Detroit**	**NHL**	**12**	**1**	**2**	**3**	**10**	**1**	**0**	**0**	**8**	**12.5**	**–1**	**50**	**30.0**	**8:09**									
	Grand Rapids	AHL	57	17	32	49	46										4	1	5	6	2				
2004-05	HC Vsetin	CzRep	7	5	2	7	10																		
	Grand Rapids	AHL	52	12	22	34	10																		
	NHL Totals		**12**	**1**	**2**	**3**	**10**	**1**	**0**	**0**	**8**	**12.5**		**50**	**30.0**	**8:09**									

Signed as a free agent by **Vsetin** (CzRep), December 2, 2004.

HULL, Brett

(HUHL, BREHT) **PHX.**

Right wing. Shoots right. 5'11", 203 lbs. Born, Belleville, Ont., August 9, 1964. Calgary's 6th choice, 117th overall, in 1984 Entry Draft.

Season	Club	League	GP	G	A	Pts	PIM	PP	SH	GW	S	%	+/-	TF	F%	Min	GP	G	A	Pts	PIM	PP	SH	GW	Min
1982-83	Penticton Knights	BCJHL	50	48	56	104	27																		
1983-84	Penticton Knights	BCJHL	56	*105	83	*188	20																		
1984-85	U. Minn-Duluth	WCHA	48	32	28	60	24																		
1985-86	U. Minn-Duluth	WCHA	42	52	32	84	46																		
	Calgary	**NHL**															**2**	**0**	**0**	**0**	**0**	**0**	**0**	**0**	
1986-87	**Calgary**	**NHL**	**5**	**1**	**0**	**1**	**0**	**0**	**0**	**1**	**5**	**20.0**	**–1**				**4**	**2**	**1**	**3**	**0**	**0**	**0**	**0**	
	Moncton	AHL	67	50	42	92	16										3	2	2	4	2				
1987-88	**Calgary**	**NHL**	**52**	**26**	**24**	**50**	**12**	**4**	**0**	**3**	**153**	**17.0**	**10**												
	St. Louis	**NHL**	**13**	**6**	**8**	**14**	**4**	**2**	**0**	**0**	**58**	**10.3**	**4**				**10**	**7**	**2**	**9**	**4**	**4**	**0**	**3**	
1988-89	**St. Louis**	**NHL**	**78**	**41**	**43**	**84**	**33**	**16**	**0**	**6**	**305**	**13.4**	**–17**				**10**	**5**	**5**	**10**	**6**	**1**	**0**	**2**	
1989-90	**St. Louis**	**NHL**	**80**	***72**	**41**	**113**	**24**	**27**	**0**	**12**	**385**	**18.7**	**–1**				**12**	**13**	**8**	**21**	**17**	**7**	**0**	**3**	
1990-91	**St. Louis**	**NHL**	**78**	***86**	**45**	**131**	**22**	**29**	**0**	**11**	**389**	**22.1**	**23**				**13**	**11**	**8**	**19**	**4**	**3**	**0**	**2**	
1991-92	**St. Louis**	**NHL**	**73**	***70**	**39**	**109**	**48**	**20**	**5**	**9**	**408**	**17.2**	**–2**				**6**	**4**	**4**	**8**	**4**	**1**	**1**	**1**	
1992-93	**St. Louis**	**NHL**	**80**	**54**	**47**	**101**	**41**	**29**	**0**	**2**	**390**	**13.8**	**–27**				**11**	**8**	**5**	**13**	**2**	**5**	**0**	**2**	
1993-94	**St. Louis**	**NHL**	**81**	**57**	**40**	**97**	**38**	**25**	**3**	**6**	**392**	**14.5**	**–3**				**4**	**2**	**1**	**3**	**0**	**1**	**0**	**0**	
1994-95	**St. Louis**	**NHL**	**48**	**29**	**21**	**50**	**10**	**9**	**3**	**6**	**200**	**14.5**	**13**				**7**	**6**	**2**	**8**	**0**	**2**	**0**	**0**	

			Regular Season														Playoffs								
Season	Club	League	GP	G	A	Pts	PIM	PP	SH	GW	S	%	+/-	TF	F%	Min	GP	G	A	Pts	PIM	PP	SH	GW	Min
1995-96	**St. Louis**	**NHL**	70	43	40	83	30	16	5	6	327	13.1	4	....	....	....	13	6	5	11	10	2	1	1	....
1996-97	**St. Louis**	**NHL**	77	42	40	82	10	12	2	6	302	13.9	–9	....	....	....	6	2	7	9	2	0	0	0	....
1997-98	**St. Louis**	**NHL**	66	27	45	72	26	10	0	6	211	12.8	–1	....	....	....	10	3	3	6	2	1	0	1	....
	United States	Olympics	4	2	1	3	0	....	....	....	....	....	....	....	....	....	....	....	....	....	....	....	....	....	....
1998-99♦	**Dallas**	**NHL**	60	32	26	58	30	15	0	11	192	16.7	19	12	50.0	17:24	22	8	7	15	4	3	0	2	18:29
99-2000	**Dallas**	**NHL**	79	24	35	59	43	11	0	3	223	10.8	–21	10	40.0	18:37	23	*11	*13	*24	4	3	0	4	19:59
2000-01	**Dallas**	**NHL**	79	39	40	79	18	11	0	8	219	17.8	10	10	30.0	17:53	10	2	5	7	6	1	0	0	20:10
2001-02♦	**Detroit**	**NHL**	82	30	33	63	35	7	1	4	247	12.1	18	5	20.0	18:49	23	*10	8	18	4	3	2	2	17:54
	United States	Olympics	6	3	5	8	6	....	....	....	....	....	....	....	....	....	....	....	....	....	....	....	....	....	....
2002-03	**Detroit**	**NHL**	82	37	39	76	22	12	1	4	262	14.1	11	18	38.9	18:07	4	0	1	1	0	0	0	0	20:17
2003-04	**Detroit**	**NHL**	81	25	43	68	12	10	0	6	200	12.5	–4	7	42.9	16:54	12	3	2	5	4	1	0	1	15:15
2004-05			DID NOT PLAY																						
	NHL Totals		**1264**	**741**	**649**	**1390**	**458**	**265**	**20**	**110**	**4868**	**15.2**		**62**	**38.7**	**17:59**	**202**	**103**	**87**	**190**	**73**	**38**	**4**	**24**	**18:33**

WCHA Freshman of the Year (1985) • WCHA First All-Star Team (1986) • AHL First All-Star Team (1987) • Dudley "Red" Garrett Memorial Award (Rookie of the Year – AHL) (1987) • NHL First All-Star Team (1990, 1991, 1992) • Dodge Ram Tough Award (1990, 1991) • Lady Byng Trophy (1990) • ProSet/NHL Player of the Year Award (1991) • Lester B. Pearson Award (1991) • Hart Memorial Trophy (1991)

Played in NHL All-Star Game (1989, 1990, 1992, 1993, 1994, 1996, 1997, 2001)

Traded to **St. Louis** by **Calgary** with Steve Bozek for Rob Ramage and Rick Wamsley, March 7, 1988. Signed as a free agent by **Dallas**, July 3, 1998. Signed as a free agent by **Detroit**, August 22, 2001. Signed as a free agent by **Phoenix**, August 6, 2004.

HULSE, Cale (HUHLS, KAYL) PHX.

Defense. Shoots right. 6'3", 220 lbs. Born, Edmonton, Alta., November 10, 1973. New Jersey's 3rd choice, 66th overall, in 1992 Entry Draft.

Season	Club	League	GP	G	A	Pts	PIM	PP	SH	GW	S	%	+/-	TF	F%	Min	GP	G	A	Pts	PIM	PP	SH	GW	Min
1990-91	Calgary Royals	AJHL	49	3	23	26	220	....	....	....	....	....	....	....	....	....	....	....	....	....	....	....	....	....	....
1991-92	Portland	WHL	70	4	18	22	230	....	....	....	....	....	....	....	....	....	6	0	2	2	27	....	....	....	....
1992-93	Portland	WHL	72	10	26	36	284	....	....	....	....	....	....	....	....	....	16	4	4	8	65	....	....	....	....
1993-94	Albany River Rats	AHL	79	7	14	21	186	....	....	....	....	....	....	....	....	....	5	0	3	3	11	....	....	....	....
1994-95	Albany River Rats	AHL	77	5	13	18	215	....	....	....	....	....	....	....	....	....	12	1	1	2	17	....	....	....	....
1995-96	**New Jersey**	**NHL**	8	0	0	0	15	0	0	0	5	0.0	–2	....	....	....	....	....	....	....	....	....	....	....	....
	Albany River Rats	AHL	42	4	23	27	107	....	....	....	....	....	....	....	....	....	....	....	....	....	....	....	....	....	....
	Calgary	**NHL**	3	0	0	0	5	0	0	0	4	0.0	3	....	....	....	1	0	0	0	0	0	0	0	....
	Saint John Flames	AHL	13	2	7	9	39	....	....	....	....	....	....	....	....	....	....	....	....	....	....	....	....	....	....
1996-97	**Calgary**	**NHL**	63	1	6	7	91	0	1	0	58	1.7	–2	....	....	....	....	....	....	....	....	....	....	....	....
1997-98	**Calgary**	**NHL**	79	5	22	27	169	1	1	0	117	4.3	1	....	....	....	....	....	....	....	....	....	....	....	....
1998-99	**Calgary**	**NHL**	73	3	9	12	117	0	0	0	83	3.6	–8	1	0.0	16:38	....	....	....	....	....	....	....	....	....
99-2000	**Calgary**	**NHL**	47	1	6	7	47	0	0	0	41	2.4	–11	1	100.0	12:38	....	....	....	....	....	....	....	....	....
2000-01	**Nashville**	**NHL**	82	1	7	8	128	0	0	1	93	1.1	–5	0	0.0	20:05	....	....	....	....	....	....	....	....	....
2001-02	**Nashville**	**NHL**	63	0	2	2	121	0	0	0	70	0.0	–18	0	0.0	18:51	....	....	....	....	....	....	....	....	....
2002-03	**Nashville**	**NHL**	80	2	6	8	121	0	0	1	82	2.4	–11	0	0.0	19:05	....	....	....	....	....	....	....	....	....
2003-04	**Phoenix**	**NHL**	82	3	17	20	123	1	0	0	115	2.6	–4	0	0.0	21:28	....	....	....	....	....	....	....	....	....
2004-05			DID NOT PLAY																						
	NHL Totals		**580**	**16**	**75**	**91**	**937**	**2**	**2**	**2**	**668**	**2.4**		**2**	**50.0**	**18:34**	**1**	**0**	**0**	**0**	**0**	**0**	**0**	**0**	....

Traded to **Calgary** by **New Jersey** with Tommy Albelin and Jocelyn Lemieux for Phil Housley and Dan Keczmer, February 26, 1996. Traded to **Nashville** by **Calgary** with Calgary's 3rd round choice (Denis Platonov) in 2001 Entry Draft for Sergei Krivokrasov, March 14, 2000. Signed as a free agent by **Phoenix**, July 10, 2003.

HUML, Ivan (HUH-muhl, ee-VAHN) BOS.

Left wing. Shoots left. 6'2", 194 lbs. Born, Kladno, Czech., September 6, 1981. Boston's 4th choice, 59th overall, in 2000 Entry Draft.

Season	Club	League	GP	G	A	Pts	PIM	PP	SH	GW	S	%	+/-	TF	F%	Min	GP	G	A	Pts	PIM	PP	SH	GW	Min
1996-97	Kladno Jr.	CzRep-Jr.	37	16	3	19	....	....	....	....	....	....	....	....	....	....	....	....	....	....	....	....	....	....	....
1997-98	HC Kladno Jr.	CzRep-Jr.	46	37	24	61	....	....	....	....	....	....	....	....	....	....	....	....	....	....	....	....	....	....	....
	Kladno	CzRep	1	0	0	0	0	....	....	....	....	....	....	....	....	....	....	....	....	....	....	....	....	....	....
1998-99	HC Kladno Jr.	CzRep-Jr.	18	6	6	12	....	....	....	....	....	....	....	....	....	....	....	....	....	....	....	....	....	....	....
	Langley Hornets	BCHL	33	23	17	40	41	....	....	....	....	....	....	....	....	....	....	....	....	....	....	....	....	....	....
99-2000	Langley Hornets	BCHL	49	53	51	104	72	....	....	....	....	....	....	....	....	....	....	....	....	....	....	....	....	....	....
2000-01	Providence Bruins	AHL	79	13	6	19	28	....	....	....	....	....	....	....	....	....	17	0	0	0	2	....	....	....	....
2001-02	**Boston**	**NHL**	1	0	1	1	0	0	0	0	2	0.0	2	0	0.0	15:43	....	....	....	....	....	....	....	....	....
	Providence Bruins	AHL	76	28	19	47	75	....	....	....	....	....	....	....	....	....	2	0	0	0	0	....	....	....	....
2002-03	**Boston**	**NHL**	41	6	11	17	30	0	0	2	75	8.0	3	22	45.5	12:46	....	....	....	....	....	....	....	....	....
	Providence Bruins	AHL	30	10	16	26	42	....	....	....	....	....	....	....	....	....	4	2	0	2	0	....	....	....	....
2003-04	**Boston**	**NHL**	7	0	0	0	6	0	0	0	11	0.0	–3	0	0.0	9:13	....	....	....	....	....	....	....	....	....
	Providence Bruins	AHL	62	15	16	31	51	....	....	....	....	....	....	....	....	....	1	0	0	0	0	....	....	....	....
2004-05	HC Rabat Kladno	CzRep	3	0	0	0	2	....	....	....	....	....	....	....	....	....	1	0	0	0	0	....	....	....	....
	NHL Totals		**49**	**6**	**12**	**18**	**36**	**0**	**0**	**2**	**88**	**6.8**		**22**	**45.5**	**12:19**	....	....	....	....	....	....	....	....	....

Signed as a free agent by **Kladno** (CzRep), September 5, 2004.

HUNTER, Trent (HUHN-tuhr, TREHNT) NYI

Right wing. Shoots right. 6'3", 191 lbs. Born, Red Deer, Alta., July 5, 1980. Anaheim's 4th choice, 150th overall, in 1998 Entry Draft.

Season	Club	League	GP	G	A	Pts	PIM	PP	SH	GW	S	%	+/-	TF	F%	Min	GP	G	A	Pts	PIM	PP	SH	GW	Min
1996-97	Red Deer	AMHL	42	30	25	55	50	....	....	....	....	....	....	....	....	....	....	....	....	....	....	....	....	....	....
1997-98	Prince George	WHL	60	13	14	27	34	....	....	....	....	....	....	....	....	....	8	1	0	1	4	....	....	....	....
1998-99	Prince George	WHL	50	18	20	38	34	....	....	....	....	....	....	....	....	....	7	2	5	7	2	....	....	....	....
99-2000	Prince George	WHL	67	46	49	95	47	....	....	....	....	....	....	....	....	....	13	7	15	22	6	....	....	....	....
2000-01	Springfield	AHL	57	18	17	35	14	....	....	....	....	....	....	....	....	....	....	....	....	....	....	....	....	....	....
2001-02	Bridgeport	AHL	80	30	35	65	30	....	....	....	....	....	....	....	....	....	17	8	11	19	6	....	....	....	....
	NY Islanders	**NHL**	....	....	....	....	....	....	....	....	....	....	....	....	....	....	4	1	1	2	2	0	0	0	11:13
2002-03	**NY Islanders**	**NHL**	8	0	4	4	4	0	0	0	19	0.0	5	1	0.0	12:13	....	....	....	....	....	....	....	....	....
	Bridgeport	AHL	70	30	41	71	39	....	....	....	....	....	....	....	....	....	9	7	4	11	10	....	....	....	....
2003-04	**NY Islanders**	**NHL**	77	25	26	51	16	4	0	7	187	13.4	23	19	36.8	15:39	5	0	0	0	4	0	0	0	11:38
2004-05	Nykoping	Sweden-2	33	13	12	25	73	....	....	....	....	....	....	....	....	....	4	5	3	8	2	....	....	....	....
	NHL Totals		**85**	**25**	**30**	**55**	**20**	**4**	**0**	**7**	**206**	**12.1**		**20**	**35.0**	**15:19**	**9**	**1**	**1**	**2**	**6**	**0**	**0**	**0**	**11:27**

WHL West First All-Star Team (2000) • NHL All-Rookie Team (2004)

Traded to **NY Islanders** by **Anaheim** for Columbus' 4th round choice (previously acquired, Anaheim selected Jonas Ronnqvist) in 2000 Entry Draft, May 23, 2000. Signed as a free agent by **Nykoping** (Sweden-2), November 8, 2004.

HUSELIUS, Kristian (hoo-SAY-lee-oos, KRIHST-yan) FLA.

Left wing. Shoots left. 6'1", 190 lbs. Born, Osterhaninge, Sweden, November 10, 1978. Florida's 2nd choice, 47th overall, in 1997 Entry Draft.

Season	Club	League	GP	G	A	Pts	PIM	PP	SH	GW	S	%	+/-	TF	F%	Min	GP	G	A	Pts	PIM	PP	SH	GW	Min
1994-95	Hammarby Jr.	Swe-Jr.	17	6	2	8	2	....	....	....	....	....	....	....	....	....	....	....	....	....	....	....	....	....	....
1995-96	Hammarby Jr.	Swe-Jr.	25	13	8	21	14	....	....	....	....	....	....	....	....	....	....	....	....	....	....	....	....	....	....
	Hammarby	Sweden-2	6	1	0	1	0	....	....	....	....	....	....	....	....	....	....	....	....	....	....	....	....	....	....
1996-97	Farjestad	Sweden	13	2	0	2	4	....	....	....	....	....	....	....	....	....	5	1	0	1	0	....	....	....	....
1997-98	Farjestad	Sweden	34	2	1	3	2	....	....	....	....	....	....	....	....	....	11	0	0	0	0	....	....	....	....
	Farjestad	EuroHL	5	2	3	5	0	....	....	....	....	....	....	....	....	....	....	....	....	....	....	....	....	....	....
1998-99	Farjestad	Sweden	28	4	4	8	4	....	....	....	....	....	....	....	....	....	....	....	....	....	....	....	....	....	....
	Farjestad	EuroHL	6	2	2	4	8	....	....	....	....	....	....	....	....	....	1	0	0	0	0	....	....	....	....
	V.Frolunda	Sweden	20	2	2	4	2	....	....	....	....	....	....	....	....	....	4	1	0	1	0	....	....	....	....
99-2000	V.Frolunda	Sweden	50	21	23	44	20	....	....	....	....	....	....	....	....	....	5	2	2	4	8	....	....	....	....
2000-01	V.Frolunda	Sweden	49	*32	*35	*67	26	....	....	....	....	....	....	....	....	....	5	4	5	9	14	....	....	....	....
2001-02	**Florida**	**NHL**	79	23	22	45	14	6	1	3	169	13.6	–4	14	21.4	16:55	....	....	....	....	....	....	....	....	....
2002-03	**Florida**	**NHL**	78	20	23	43	20	3	0	3	187	10.7	–6	6	33.3	17:20	....	....	....	....	....	....	....	....	....
2003-04	**Florida**	**NHL**	76	10	21	31	24	2	0	2	168	6.0	–6	185	37.8	14:14	....	....	....	....	....	....	....	....	....
2004-05	Rapperswil	Swiss	....	....	....	....	....	....	....	....	....	....	....	....	....	....	4	1	3	4	2	....	....	....	....
	Linkopings HC	Sweden	34	14	*35	49	10	....	....	....	....	....	....	....	....	....	....	....	....	....	....	....	....	....	....
	NHL Totals		**233**	**53**	**66**	**119**	**58**	**11**	**1**	**8**	**524**	**10.1**		**205**	**36.6**	**16:11**	....	....	....	....	....	....	....	....	....

NHL All-Rookie Team (2002)

Signed as a free agent by **Linkopings** (Sweden), July 29, 2004. Signed as a free agent by **Rapperswil** (Swiss), February 23, 2005.

			Regular Season														Playoffs								
Season	Club	League	GP	G	A	Pts	PIM	PP	SH	GW	S	%	+/-	TF	F%	Min	GP	G	A	Pts	PIM	PP	SH	GW	Min

HUSSEY, Matt
(HUH-see, MAT) **PIT.**

Center. Shoots left. 6'2", 215 lbs. Born, New Haven, CT, May 28, 1979. Pittsburgh's 10th choice, 254th overall, in 1998 Entry Draft.

Season	Club	League	GP	G	A	Pts	PIM	PP	SH	GW	S	%	+/-	TF	F%	Min	GP	G	A	Pts	PIM	PP	SH	GW	Min
1996-97	Wayzata	High-MN	48	34	31	65	....	....	....	....	....	....	....	....	....	....	....	....	....	....	....	....	....	....	....
1997-98	Avon Old Farms	High-CT	26	26	23	49	20	....	....	....	....	....	....	....	....	....	....	....	....	....	....	....	....	....	....
1998-99	U. of Wisconsin	WCHA	37	10	5	15	18	....	....	....	....	....	....	....	....	....	....	....	....	....	....	....	....	....	....
99-2000	U. of Wisconsin	WCHA	35	5	11	16	8	....	....	....	....	....	....	....	....	....	....	....	....	....	....	....	....	....	....
2000-01	U. of Wisconsin	WCHA	40	9	11	20	24	....	....	....	....	....	....	....	....	....	....	....	....	....	....	....	....	....	....
2001-02	U. of Wisconsin	WCHA	39	18	15	33	16	....	....	....	....	....	....	....	....	....	....	....	....	....	....	....	....	....	....
2002-03	Wilkes-Barre	AHL	69	12	11	23	28	....	....	....	....	....	....	....	....	....	2	0	0	0	0	....	....	....	....
2003-04	**Pittsburgh**	**NHL**	**3**	**2**	**1**	**3**	**0**	**2**	**0**	**0**	**8**	**25.0**	**–1**	**0**	**0.0**	**13:35**	....	....	....	....	....	....	....	....	....
	Wilkes-Barre	AHL	55	2	1	3	6	....	....	....	....	....	....	....	....	....	6	2	2	4	0	....	....	....	....
2004-05	Wilkes-Barre	AHL	80	16	14	30	19	....	....	....	....	....	....	....	....	....	10	1	2	3	2	....	....	....	....
	NHL Totals		**3**	**2**	**1**	**3**	**0**	**2**	**0**	**0**	**8**	**25.0**		**0**	**0.0**	**13:35**	....	....	....	....	....	....	....	....	....

HUTCHINSON, Andrew
(HUHT-chihn-suhn, AN-droo) **CAR.**

Defense. Shoots right. 6'2", 204 lbs. Born, Evanston, IL, March 24, 1980. Nashville's 4th choice, 54th overall, in 1999 Entry Draft.

Season	Club	League	GP	G	A	Pts	PIM	PP	SH	GW	S	%	+/-	TF	F%	Min	GP	G	A	Pts	PIM	PP	SH	GW	Min
1996-97	Det. Caesars	MNHL	82	15	41	56	....	....	....	....	....	....	....	....	....	....	....	....	....	....	....	....	....	....	....
1997-98	USA U-18	USDP	59	7	21	28	53	....	....	....	....	....	....	....	....	....	....	....	....	....	....	....	....	....	....
1998-99	Michigan State	CCHA	37	3	12	15	26	....	....	....	....	....	....	....	....	....	....	....	....	....	....	....	....	....	....
99-2000	Michigan State	CCHA	42	5	12	17	64	....	....	....	....	....	....	....	....	....	....	....	....	....	....	....	....	....	....
2000-01	Michigan State	CCHA	42	5	19	24	46	....	....	....	....	....	....	....	....	....	....	....	....	....	....	....	....	....	....
2001-02	Michigan State	CCHA	39	6	16	22	24	....	....	....	....	....	....	....	....	....	....	....	....	....	....	....	....	....	....
	Milwaukee	AHL	5	0	1	1	0	....	....	....	....	....	....	....	....	....	....	....	....	....	....	....	....	....	....
2002-03	Toledo Storm	ECHL	10	2	5	7	4	....	....	....	....	....	....	....	....	....	....	....	....	....	....	....	....	....	....
	Milwaukee	AHL	63	9	17	26	40	....	....	....	....	....	....	....	....	....	3	1	0	1	0	....	....	....	....
2003-04	**Nashville**	**NHL**	**18**	**4**	**4**	**8**	**4**	**2**	**0**	**1**	**24**	**16.7**	**1**	**0**	**0.0**	**16:43**	....	....	....	....	....	....	....	....	....
	Milwaukee	AHL	46	12	12	24	39	....	....	....	....	....	....	....	....	....	22	5	11	16	33	....	....	....	....
2004-05	Milwaukee	AHL	76	10	35	45	79	....	....	....	....	....	....	....	....	....	7	1	3	4	8	....	....	....	....
	NHL Totals		**18**	**4**	**4**	**8**	**4**	**2**	**0**	**1**	**24**	**16.7**		**0**	**0.0**	**16:43**	....	....	....	....	....	....	....	....	....

CCHA Second All-Star Team (2001, 2002) • NCAA West Second All-American Team (2002)

Traded to **Carolina** by **Nashville** for Phoenix's 3rd round choice (previously acquired, Nashville selected Teemu Laakso) in 2005 Entry Draft, July 29, 2005.

HYVONEN, Hannes
(HOO-voh-nuhn, HAH-nuhs) **CBJ**

Right wing. Shoots right. 6'2", 200 lbs. Born, Oulu, Finland, August 29, 1975. San Jose's 7th choice, 257th overall, in 1999 Entry Draft.

Season	Club	League	GP	G	A	Pts	PIM	PP	SH	GW	S	%	+/-	TF	F%	Min	GP	G	A	Pts	PIM	PP	SH	GW	Min
1993-94	Karpat Oulu Jr.	Finland-Jr.	35	15	13	28	26	....	....	....	....	....	....	....	....	....	3	0	0	0	0	....	....	....	....
	Karpat Oulu	Finland-2	3	3	1	4	2	....	....	....	....	....	....	....	....	....	....	....	....	....	....	....	....	....	....
1994-95	TPS Turku Jr.	Finland-Jr.	10	8	2	10	64	....	....	....	....	....	....	....	....	....	....	....	....	....	....	....	....	....	....
	Kiekko-67 Jr.	Finland-Jr.	1	1	0	1	0	....	....	....	....	....	....	....	....	....	....	....	....	....	....	....	....	....	....
	Kiekko-67 Turku	Finland-2	16	4	2	6	10	....	....	....	....	....	....	....	....	....	....	....	....	....	....	....	....	....	....
	TPS Turku	Finland	9	4	3	7	16	....	....	....	....	....	....	....	....	....	5	0	0	0	7	....	....	....	....
1995-96	Kiekko-67 Turku	Finland-2	2	1	0	1	8	....	....	....	....	....	....	....	....	....	....	....	....	....	....	....	....	....	....
	TPS Turku	Finland	30	11	5	16	49	....	....	....	....	....	....	....	....	....	7	0	1	1	28	....	....	....	....
1996-97	TPS Turku	Finland	41	10	5	15	48	....	....	....	....	....	....	....	....	....	10	4	2	6	14	....	....	....	....
1997-98	TPS Turku	Finland	29	2	6	8	71	....	....	....	....	....	....	....	....	....	2	0	0	0	0	....	....	....	....
1998-99	Blues Espoo	Finland	52	23	18	41	74	....	....	....	....	....	....	....	....	....	4	2	1	3	2	....	....	....	....
99-2000	Blues Espoo	Finland	18	5	2	7	*89	....	....	....	....	....	....	....	....	....	....	....	....	....	....	....	....	....	....
	HIFK Helsinki	Finland	22	2	2	4	*100	....	....	....	....	....	....	....	....	....	9	4	0	4	8	....	....	....	....
2000-01	HIFK Helsinki	Finland	56	14	12	26	34	....	....	....	....	....	....	....	....	....	5	0	0	0	8	....	....	....	....
2001-02	**San Jose**	**NHL**	**6**	**0**	**0**	**0**	**0**	**0**	**0**	**0**	**4**	**0.0**	**–2**	**0**	**0.0**	**5:40**	....	....	....	....	....	....	....	....	....
	Cleveland Barons	AHL	67	24	18	42	136	....	....	....	....	....	....	....	....	....	....	....	....	....	....	....	....	....	....
2002-03	**Columbus**	**NHL**	**36**	**4**	**5**	**9**	**22**	**0**	**0**	**0**	**48**	**8.3**	**–11**	**8**	**25.0**	**10:02**	....	....	....	....	....	....	....	....	....
	Farjestad	Sweden	10	11	0	11	12	....	....	....	....	....	....	....	....	....	14	5	0	5	41	....	....	....	....
2003-04	Farjestad	Sweden	47	15	13	28	98	....	....	....	....	....	....	....	....	....	17	7	5	12	43	....	....	....	....
2004-05	Farjestad	Sweden	8	1	0	1	10	....	....	....	....	....	....	....	....	....	....	....	....	....	....	....	....	....	....
	Ilves Tampere	Finland	36	27	18	45	51	....	....	....	....	....	....	....	....	....	7	4	1	5	6	....	....	....	....
	NHL Totals		**42**	**4**	**5**	**9**	**22**	**0**	**0**	**0**	**52**	**7.7**		**8**	**25.0**	**9:25**	....	....	....	....	....	....	....	....	....

Traded to **Florida** by **San Jose** for Florida's 7th round choice (Jonathon Tremblay) in 2003 Entry Draft, July 16, 2002. Claimed on waivers by **Columbus** from **Florida**, October 5, 2002. • Loaned to **Farjestad** (Sweden) by **Columbus**, January 25, 2003. Signed as a free agent by **Ilves** (Finland), November 7, 2004.

IGINLA, Jarome
(ih-GIHN-lah, jah-ROHM) **CGY.**

Right wing. Shoots right. 6'1", 208 lbs. Born, Edmonton, Alta., July 1, 1977. Dallas' 1st choice, 11th overall, in 1995 Entry Draft.

Season	Club	League	GP	G	A	Pts	PIM	PP	SH	GW	S	%	+/-	TF	F%	Min	GP	G	A	Pts	PIM	PP	SH	GW	Min
1991-92	St. Albert Raiders	AMHL	36	26	30	56	22	....	....	....	....	....	....	....	....	....	....	....	....	....	....	....	....	....	....
1992-93	St. Albert Raiders	AMHL	36	34	53	*87	20	....	....	....	....	....	....	....	....	....	....	....	....	....	....	....	....	....	....
1993-94	Kamloops Blazers	WHL	48	6	23	29	33	....	....	....	....	....	....	....	....	....	19	3	6	9	10	....	....	....	....
1994-95	Kamloops Blazers	WHL	72	33	38	71	111	....	....	....	....	....	....	....	....	....	21	7	11	18	34	....	....	....	....
1995-96	Kamloops Blazers	WHL	63	63	73	136	120	....	....	....	....	....	....	....	....	....	16	16	13	29	44	....	....	....	....
	Calgary	**NHL**	....	....	....	....	....	....	....	....	....	....	....	....	....	....	**2**	**1**	**1**	**2**	**0**	**0**	**0**	**0**	....
1996-97	**Calgary**	**NHL**	**82**	**21**	**29**	**50**	**37**	**8**	**1**	**3**	**169**	**12.4**	**–4**	....	....	....	....	....	....	....	....	....	....	....	....
1997-98	**Calgary**	**NHL**	**70**	**13**	**19**	**32**	**29**	**0**	**2**	**1**	**154**	**8.4**	**–10**	....	....	....	....	....	....	....	....	....	....	....	....
1998-99	**Calgary**	**NHL**	**82**	**28**	**23**	**51**	**58**	**7**	**0**	**4**	**211**	**13.3**	**1**	**111**	**51.4**	**16:30**	....	....	....	....	....	....	....	....	....
99-2000	**Calgary**	**NHL**	**77**	**29**	**34**	**63**	**26**	**12**	**0**	**4**	**256**	**11.3**	**0**	**278**	**52.9**	**18:24**	....	....	....	....	....	....	....	....	....
2000-01	**Calgary**	**NHL**	**77**	**31**	**40**	**71**	**62**	**10**	**0**	**4**	**229**	**13.5**	**–2**	**638**	**51.7**	**19:58**	....	....	....	....	....	....	....	....	....
2001-02	**Calgary**	**NHL**	**82**	***52**	**44**	***96**	**77**	**16**	**1**	**7**	**311**	**16.7**	**27**	**308**	**55.2**	**22:22**	....	....	....	....	....	....	....	....	....
	Canada	Olympics	6	3	1	4	0	....	....	....	....	....	....	....	....	....	....	....	....	....	....	....	....	....	....
2002-03	**Calgary**	**NHL**	**75**	**35**	**32**	**67**	**49**	**11**	**3**	**6**	**316**	**11.1**	**–10**	**90**	**43.3**	**21:26**	....	....	....	....	....	....	....	....	....
2003-04	**Calgary**	**NHL**	**81**	***41**	**32**	**73**	**84**	**8**	**4**	**10**	**265**	**15.5**	**21**	**305**	**54.4**	**21:18**	**26**	***13**	**9**	**22**	**45**	**4**	**2**	**3**	**23:18**
2004-05			DID NOT PLAY																						
	NHL Totals		**626**	**250**	**253**	**503**	**422**	**72**	**11**	**39**	**1911**	**13.1**		**1730**	**52.5**	**19:59**	**28**	**14**	**10**	**24**	**45**	**4**	**2**	**3**	**23:18**

George Parsons Trophy (Memorial Cup Tournament Most Sportsmanlike Player) (1995) • WHL West First All-Star Team (1996) • WHL Player of the Year (1996) • Canadian Major Junior First All-Star Team (1996) • NHL All-Rookie Team (1997) • NHL First All-Star Team (2002) • Maurice "Rocket" Richard Trophy (2002) • Art Ross Trophy (2002) • Lester B. Pearson Award (2002) • NHL Second All-Star Team (2004) • King Clancy Memorial Trophy (2004) • Maurice "Rocket" Richard Trophy (2004) (tied with Ilya Kovalchuk and Rick Nash)

Played in NHL All-Star Game (2002, 2003, 2004)

Traded to **Calgary** by **Dallas** with Corey Millen for Joe Nieuwendyk, December 19, 1995.

ISBISTER, Brad
(IHZ-bihs-tuhr, BRAD) **BOS.**

Left wing. Shoots right. 6'4", 231 lbs. Born, Edmonton, Alta., May 7, 1977. Winnipeg's 4th choice, 67th overall, in 1995 Entry Draft.

Season	Club	League	GP	G	A	Pts	PIM	PP	SH	GW	S	%	+/-	TF	F%	Min	GP	G	A	Pts	PIM	PP	SH	GW	Min
1992-93	Calgary Canucks	ABHL	35	24	25	49	74	....	....	....	....	....	....	....	....	....	....	....	....	....	....	....	....	....	....
1993-94	Portland	WHL	64	7	10	17	45	....	....	....	....	....	....	....	....	....	10	0	2	2	0	....	....	....	....
1994-95	Portland	WHL	67	16	20	36	123	....	....	....	....	....	....	....	....	....	....	....	....	....	....	....	....	....	....
1995-96	Portland	WHL	71	45	44	89	184	....	....	....	....	....	....	....	....	....	7	2	4	6	20	....	....	....	....
1996-97	Portland	WHL	24	15	18	33	45	....	....	....	....	....	....	....	....	....	6	2	1	3	16	....	....	....	....
	Springfield	AHL	7	3	1	4	14	....	....	....	....	....	....	....	....	....	9	1	2	3	10	....	....	....	....
1997-98	**Phoenix**	**NHL**	**66**	**9**	**8**	**17**	**102**	**1**	**0**	**1**	**115**	**7.8**	**4**	....	....	....	**5**	**0**	**0**	**0**	**2**	**0**	**0**	**0**	....
	Springfield	AHL	9	8	2	10	36	....	....	....	....	....	....	....	....	....	....	....	....	....	....	....	....	....	....
1998-99	**Phoenix**	**NHL**	**32**	**4**	**4**	**8**	**46**	**0**	**0**	**2**	**48**	**8.3**	**1**	**3**	**0.0**	**11:33**	....	....	....	....	....	....	....	....	....
	Springfield	AHL	4	1	1	2	12	....	....	....	....	....	....	....	....	....	....	....	....	....	....	....	....	....	....
	Las Vegas	IHL	2	0	0	0	9	....	....	....	....	....	....	....	....	....	....	....	....	....	....	....	....	....	....
99-2000	**NY Islanders**	**NHL**	**64**	**22**	**20**	**42**	**100**	**9**	**0**	**1**	**135**	**16.3**	**–18**	**55**	**54.6**	**16:58**	....	....	....	....	....	....	....	....	....
2000-01	**NY Islanders**	**NHL**	**51**	**18**	**14**	**32**	**59**	**7**	**1**	**4**	**129**	**14.0**	**–19**	**255**	**45.9**	**19:26**	....	....	....	....	....	....	....	....	....
2001-02	**NY Islanders**	**NHL**	**79**	**17**	**21**	**38**	**113**	**4**	**0**	**2**	**142**	**12.0**	**1**	**71**	**45.1**	**15:18**	**3**	**1**	**1**	**2**	**17**	**1**	**0**	**1**	**12:33**
2002-03	**NY Islanders**	**NHL**	**53**	**10**	**13**	**23**	**34**	**2**	**0**	**2**	**90**	**11.1**	**–9**	**13**	**46.2**	**13:54**	....	....	....	....	....	....	....	....	....
	Edmonton	**NHL**	**13**	**3**	**2**	**5**	**9**	**0**	**0**	**1**	**29**	**10.3**	**0**	**10**	**50.0**	**13:14**	**6**	**0**	**1**	**1**	**12**	**0**	**0**	**0**	**10:04**

			Regular Season														Playoffs								
Season	Club	League	GP	G	A	Pts	PIM	PP	SH	GW	S	%	+/-	TF	F%	Min	GP	G	A	Pts	PIM	PP	SH	GW	Min
2003-04	Edmonton	NHL	51	10	8	18	54	1	0	2	80	12.5	–2	55	56.4	12:46	....	....	....	....	....	....	....	....	....
2004-05	Innsbruck	Austria	11	7	4	11	41	....	....	....	....	....	....	....	....	....	5	3	1	4	6	....	....	....	....
	NHL Totals		409	93	90	183	517	24	1	15	768	12.1		462	47.8	15:12	14	1	2	3	31	1	0	1	10:54

WHL West Second All-Star Team (1997)

Rights transferred to **Phoenix** after **Winnipeg** franchise relocated, July 1, 1996. Traded to **NY Islanders** by **Phoenix** with Phoenix's 3rd round choice (Brian Collins) in 1999 Entry Draft for Robert Reichel, NY Islanders' 3rd round choice (Jason Jaspers) in 1999 Entry Draft and Ottawa's 4th round choice (previously acquired, Phoenix selected Preston Mizzi) in 1999 Entry Draft, March 20, 1999. Traded to **Edmonton** by **NY Islanders** with Raffi Torres for Janne Niinimaa and Washington's 2nd round choice (previously acquired, NY Islanders selected Evgeni Tunik) in 2003 Entry Draft , March 11, 2003. Signed as a free agent by **Innsbuck** (Austria), February 12, 2005. Traded to **Boston** by **Edmonton** for Boston's 4th round choice (later traded back to Boston) in 2006 Entry Draft, August 1, 2005.

JACKMAN, Barret

(JAK-man, BAIR-reht) **ST.L.**

Defense. Shoots left. 6', 209 lbs. Born, Trail, B.C., March 5, 1981. St. Louis' 1st choice, 17th overall, in 1999 Entry Draft.

1996-97	Beaver Valley	VIJHL	32	22	25	47	180	....	....	....	....	....	....	....	....	....	....	....	....	....	....	....	....	....	....
1997-98	Regina Pats	WHL	68	2	11	13	224	....	....	....	....	....	....	....	....	....	9	0	3	3	32	....	....	....	....
1998-99	Regina Pats	WHL	70	8	36	44	259	....	....	....	....	....	....	....	....	....	....	....	....	....	....	....	....	....	....
99-2000	Regina Pats	WHL	53	9	37	46	175	....	....	....	....	....	....	....	....	....	6	1	1	2	19	....	....	....	....
	Worcester IceCats	AHL	....	....	....	....	....	....	....	....	....	....	....	....	....	....	2	0	0	0	13	....	....	....	....
2000-01	Regina Pats	WHL	43	9	27	36	138	....	....	....	....	....	....	....	....	....	6	0	3	3	8	....	....	....	....
2001-02	St. Louis	NHL	1	0	0	0	0	0	0	0	1	0.0	0	0	0.0	18:56	1	0	0	0	2	0	0	0	18:24
	Worcester IceCats	AHL	75	2	12	14	266	....	....	....	....	....	....	....	....	....	3	0	1	1	4	....	....	....	....
2002-03	St. Louis	NHL	82	3	16	19	190	0	0	0	66	4.5	23	0	0.0	20:03	7	0	0	0	14	0	0	0	21:59
2003-04	St. Louis	NHL	15	1	2	3	41	0	0	0	11	9.1	–1	0	0.0	18:16	....	....	....	....	....	....	....	....	....
2004-05	Missouri	UHL	28	3	17	20	61	....	....	....	....	....	....	....	....	....	3	0	0	0	4	....	....	....	....
	NHL Totals		98	4	18	22	231	0	0	0	78	5.1		0	0.0	19:46	8	0	0	0	16	0	0	0	21:32

WHL East Second All-Star Team (2000) • AHL All-Rookie Team (2002) • NHL All-Rookie Team (2003) • Calder Memorial Trophy (2003)

• Missed majority of 2003-04 season recovering from shoulder injury suffered in game vs. Vancouver, October 22, 2003. Signed as a free agent by **Missouri** (UHL), February 3, 2005.

JACKMAN, Ric

(JAK-man, RIHK) **PIT.**

Defense. Shoots right. 6'2", 197 lbs. Born, Toronto, Ont., June 28, 1978. Dallas' 1st choice, 5th overall, in 1996 Entry Draft.

1993-94	Mississauga Sens	MTHL	81	35	53	88	156	....	....	....	....	....	....	....	....	....	....	....	....	....	....	....	....	....	....
1994-95	Mississauga Sens	MTHL	53	20	37	57	120	....	....	....	....	....	....	....	....	....	....	....	....	....	....	....	....	....	....
	Richmond Hill	MTJHL	10	2	9	11	16	....	....	....	....	....	....	....	....	....	....	....	....	....	....	....	....	....	....
1995-96	Sault Ste. Marie	OHL	66	13	29	42	97	....	....	....	....	....	....	....	....	....	4	1	0	1	15	....	....	....	....
1996-97	Sault Ste. Marie	OHL	53	13	34	47	116	....	....	....	....	....	....	....	....	....	10	2	6	8	24	....	....	....	....
1997-98	Sault Ste. Marie	OHL	60	33	40	73	111	....	....	....	....	....	....	....	....	....	....	....	....	....	....	....	....	....	....
	Michigan	IHL	14	1	5	6	10	....	....	....	....	....	....	....	....	....	4	0	0	0	10	....	....	....	....
1998-99	Michigan	IHL	71	13	17	30	106	....	....	....	....	....	....	....	....	....	5	0	4	4	6	....	....	....	....
99-2000	Dallas	NHL	22	1	2	3	6	1	0	0	16	6.3	–1	0	0.0	8:06	....	....	....	....	....	....	....	....	....
	Michigan	IHL	50	3	16	19	51	....	....	....	....	....	....	....	....	....	....	....	....	....	....	....	....	....	....
2000-01	Dallas	NHL	16	0	0	0	18	0	0	0	10	0.0	–6	0	0.0	8:51	....	....	....	....	....	....	....	....	....
	Utah Grizzlies	IHL	57	9	19	28	24	....	....	....	....	....	....	....	....	....	....	....	....	....	....	....	....	....	....
2001-02	Boston	NHL	2	0	0	0	2	0	0	0	4	0.0	–1	0	0.0	13:26	....	....	....	....	....	....	....	....	....
	Providence Bruins	AHL	9	0	1	1	8	....	....	....	....	....	....	....	....	....	2	0	0	0	2	....	....	....	....
2002-03	Toronto	NHL	42	0	2	2	41	0	0	0	35	0.0	–10	0	0.0	13:59	....	....	....	....	....	....	....	....	....
	St. John's	AHL	8	2	6	8	24	....	....	....	....	....	....	....	....	....	....	....	....	....	....	....	....	....	....
2003-04	Toronto	NHL	29	2	4	6	13	1	0	1	35	5.7	–11	0	0.0	18:00	....	....	....	....	....	....	....	....	....
	Pittsburgh	NHL	25	7	17	24	14	6	0	1	56	12.5	–5	0	0.0	24:14	....	....	....	....	....	....	....	....	....
2004-05	Bjorkloven	Sweden-2	46	13	26	39	209	....	....	....	....	....	....	....	....	....	....	....	....	....	....	....	....	....	....
	NHL Totals		136	10	25	35	94	8	0	2	156	6.4		0	0.0	15:10	....	....	....	....	....	....	....	....	....

OHL All-Rookie Team (1996) • OHL Second All-Star Team (1998)

Traded to **Boston** by **Dallas** for Cameron Mann, June 23, 2001. • Missed majority of 2001-02 season recovering from shoulder injury suffered in game vs. St. Louis, October 21, 2001. Traded to **Toronto** by **Boston** for the rights to Kris Vernarsky, May 13, 2002. Traded to **Pittsburgh** by **Toronto** for Drake Berehowsky, February 11, 2004. Signed as a free agent by **Bjorkloven** (Sweden-2), September 17, 2004.

JACKMAN, Tim

(JAK-man, TIHM) **CBJ**

Right wing. Shoots right. 6'4", 210 lbs. Born, Minot, ND, November 14, 1981. Columbus' 2nd choice, 38th overall, in 2001 Entry Draft.

1998-99	Park Center	High-MN	22	22	22	44	....	....	....	....	....	....	....	....	....	....	....	....	....	....	....	....	....	....	....
99-2000	Park Center	High-MN	19	34	22	56	....	....	....	....	....	....	....	....	....	....	....	....	....	....	....	....	....	....	....
	Twin Cities	USHL	25	11	9	20	58	....	....	....	....	....	....	....	....	....	13	8	5	13	12	....	....	....	....
2000-01	Minnesota State	WCHA	37	11	14	25	92	....	....	....	....	....	....	....	....	....	....	....	....	....	....	....	....	....	....
2001-02	Minnesota State	WCHA	36	14	14	28	86	....	....	....	....	....	....	....	....	....	....	....	....	....	....	....	....	....	....
2002-03	Syracuse Crunch	AHL	77	9	7	16	48	....	....	....	....	....	....	....	....	....	....	....	....	....	....	....	....	....	....
2003-04	Columbus	NHL	19	1	2	3	16	0	0	0	18	5.6	–7	1	100.0	9:56	....	....	....	....	....	....	....	....	....
	Syracuse Crunch	AHL	64	23	13	36	61	....	....	....	....	....	....	....	....	....	7	2	3	5	12	....	....	....	....
2004-05	Syracuse Crunch	AHL	73	14	21	35	98	....	....	....	....	....	....	....	....	....	....	....	....	....	....	....	....	....	....
	NHL Totals		19	1	2	3	16	0	0	0	18	5.6		1	100.0	9:56	....	....	....	....	....	....	....	....	....

JAGR, Jaromir

(YAH-guhr, YAIR-oh-MEER) **NYR**

Right wing. Shoots left. 6'2", 224 lbs. Born, Kladno, Czech., February 15, 1972. Pittsburgh's 1st choice, 5th overall, in 1990 Entry Draft.

1984-85	Kladno Jr.	Czech-Jr.	34	24	17	41	....	....	....	....	....	....	....	....	....	....	....	....	....	....	....	....	....	....	....
1985-86	Kladno Jr.	Czech-Jr.	36	41	29	70	....	....	....	....	....	....	....	....	....	....	....	....	....	....	....	....	....	....	....
1986-87	Kladno Jr.	Czech-Jr.	30	35	35	70	....	....	....	....	....	....	....	....	....	....	....	....	....	....	....	....	....	....	....
1987-88	Kladno Jr.	Czech-Jr.	35	57	27	84	....	....	....	....	....	....	....	....	....	....	....	....	....	....	....	....	....	....	....
1988-89	Kladno	Czech	29	3	3	6	4	....	....	....	....	....	....	....	....	....	10	5	7	12	0	....	....	....	....
1989-90	Poldi Kladno	Czech	42	22	28	50	....	....	....	....	....	....	....	....	....	....	9	*8	2	10	....	....	....	....	....
1990-91 ♦	Pittsburgh	NHL	80	27	30	57	42	7	0	4	136	19.9	–4	....	....	....	24	3	10	13	6	1	0	1	....
1991-92 ♦	Pittsburgh	NHL	70	32	37	69	34	4	0	4	194	16.5	12	....	....	....	21	11	13	24	6	2	0	4	....
1992-93	Pittsburgh	NHL	81	34	60	94	61	10	1	9	242	14.0	30	....	....	....	12	5	4	9	23	1	0	1	....
1993-94	Pittsburgh	NHL	80	32	67	99	61	9	0	6	298	10.7	15	....	....	....	6	2	4	6	16	0	0	1	....
1994-95	HC Kladno	CzRep	11	8	14	22	10	....	....	....	....	....	....	....	....	....	....	....	....	....	....	....	....	....	....
	HC Bolzano	Euroliga	5	8	8	16	4	....	....	....	....	....	....	....	....	....	....	....	....	....	....	....	....	....	....
	HC Bolzano	Italy	1	0	0	0	0	....	....	....	....	....	....	....	....	....	....	....	....	....	....	....	....	....	....
	Schalke	German-2	1	1	10	11	0	....	....	....	....	....	....	....	....	....	....	....	....	....	....	....	....	....	....
	Pittsburgh	NHL	48	32	38	*70	37	8	3	7	192	16.7	23	....	....	....	12	10	5	15	6	2	1	1	....
1995-96	Pittsburgh	NHL	82	62	87	149	96	20	1	12	403	15.4	31	....	....	....	18	11	12	23	18	5	1	1	....
1996-97	Pittsburgh	NHL	63	47	48	95	40	11	2	6	234	20.1	22	....	....	....	5	4	4	8	4	2	0	0	....
1997-98	Pittsburgh	NHL	77	35	*67	*102	64	7	0	8	262	13.4	17	....	....	....	6	4	5	9	2	1	0	0	....
	Czech Republic	Olympics	6	1	4	5	2	....	....	....	....	....	....	....	....	....	....	....	....	....	....	....	....	....	....
1998-99	Pittsburgh	NHL	81	44	*83	*127	66	10	1	7	343	12.8	17	4	50.0	25:51	9	5	7	12	16	1	0	1	25:32
99-2000	Pittsburgh	NHL	63	42	54	*96	50	10	0	5	290	14.5	25	9	22.2	23:12	11	8	8	16	6	2	0	4	24:32
2000-01	Pittsburgh	NHL	81	52	*69	*121	42	14	1	10	317	16.4	19	2	0.0	23:19	16	2	10	12	18	2	0	0	22:15
2001-02	Washington	NHL	69	31	48	79	30	10	0	3	197	15.7	0	2	50.0	21:43	....	....	....	....	....	....	....	....	....
	Czech Republic	Olympics	4	2	3	5	4	....	....	....	....	....	....	....	....	....	....	....	....	....	....	....	....	....	....
2002-03	Washington	NHL	75	36	41	77	38	13	2	9	290	12.4	5	5	20.0	21:18	6	2	5	7	2	1	0	0	25:13
2003-04	Washington	NHL	46	16	29	45	26	6	0	1	159	10.1	–4	1	0.0	21:05	....	....	....	....	....	....	....	....	....
	NY Rangers	NHL	31	15	14	29	12	4	0	2	98	15.3	–1	0	0.0	20:45	....	....	....	....	....	....	....	....	....
2004-05	HC Rabat Kladno	CzRep	17	11	17	28	16	....	....	....	....	....	....	....	....	....	....	....	....	....	....	....	....	....	....
	Avangard Omsk	Russia	32	16	22	38	63	....	....	....	....	....	....	....	....	....	11	4	*10	*14	22	....	....	....	....
	NHL Totals		1027	537	772	1309	699	143	11	93	3655	14.7		23	26.1	22:46	146	67	87	154	123	20	2	14	23:59

NHL All-Rookie Team (1991) • NHL First All-Star Team (1995, 1996, 1998, 1999, 2000, 2001) • Art Ross Trophy (1995, 1998, 1999, 2000, 2001) • NHL Second All-Star Team (1997) • Lester B. Pearson Award (1999, 2000) • Hart Trophy (1999)

Played in NHL All-Star Game (1992, 1993, 1996, 1998, 1999, 2000, 2002, 2003, 2004)

Traded to **Washington** by **Pittsburgh** with Frantisek Kucera for Kris Beech, Michal Sivek, Ross Lupaschuk and future considerations, July 11, 2001. Traded to **NY Rangers** by **Washington** for Anson Carter, January 23, 2003. Signed as a free agent by **Kladno** (CzRep), September 17, 2004. Signed as a free agent by **Omsk** (Russia), November 7, 2004.

JANIK, Doug

(JAN-nihk, DUHG) **BUF.**

Defense. Shoots left. 6'2", 209 lbs. Born, Agawam, MA, March 26, 1980. Buffalo's 3rd choice, 55th overall, in 1999 Entry Draft.

			Regular Season														Playoffs								
Season	Club	League	GP	G	A	Pts	PIM	PP	SH	GW	S	%	+/-	TF	F%	Min	GP	G	A	Pts	PIM	PP	SH	GW	Min
1995-96	N.E. Jr. Whalers	EJHL	48	16	38	54																			
1996-97	N.E. Jr. Whalers	EJHL	39	12	24	36	22										11	5	9	14	10				
1997-98	USA U-18	USDP	65	8	26	34	105																		
1998-99	U. of Maine	H-East	35	3	13	16	44																		
99-2000	U. of Maine	H-East	36	6	14	20	54																		
2000-01	U. of Maine	H-East	39	3	15	18	52																		
2001-02	Rochester	AHL	80	6	17	23	100										2	0	0	0	0				
2002-03	**Buffalo**	**NHL**	**6**	**0**	**0**	**0**	**2**	**0**	**0**	**0**	**1**	**0.0**	**1**	**0**	**0.0**	**7:42**									
	Rochester	AHL	75	3	13	16	120										3	0	0	0	6				
2003-04	**Buffalo**	**NHL**	**4**	**0**	**0**	**0**	**19**	**0**	**0**	**0**	**3**	**0.0**	**0**	**0**	**0.0**	**8:26**									
	Rochester	AHL	74	2	14	16	109										16	1	2	3	22				
2004-05	Rochester	AHL	76	2	10	12	196										9	0	2	2	10				
	NHL Totals		**10**	**0**	**0**	**0**	**21**	**0**	**0**	**0**	**4**	**0.0**		**0**	**0.0**	**8:00**									

JARDINE, Ryan

(JAHR-dighn, RIGH-yan)

Left wing. Shoots left. 6', 210 lbs. Born, Ottawa, Ont., March 15, 1980. Florida's 4th choice, 89th overall, in 1998 Entry Draft.

Season	Club	League	GP	G	A	Pts	PIM	PP	SH	GW	S	%	+/-	TF	F%	Min	GP	G	A	Pts	PIM	PP	SH	GW	Min
1996-97	Kanata Valley	CJHL	52	30	27	57	76																		
1997-98	Sault Ste. Marie	OHL	65	28	32	60	16																		
1998-99	Sault Ste. Marie	OHL	68	27	34	61	56										5	0	1	1	6				
99-2000	Sault Ste. Marie	OHL	65	43	34	77	58										17	11	8	19	16				
2000-01	Louisville Panthers	AHL	77	12	14	26	38																		
2001-02	**Florida**	**NHL**	**8**	**0**	**2**	**2**	**2**	**0**	**0**	**0**	**6**	**0.0**	**0**	**2**	**100.0**	**8:55**									
	Utah Grizzlies	AHL	64	16	16	32	56										4	1	1	2	0				
2002-03	San Antonio	AHL	64	14	17	31	37										3	1	0	1	0				
2003-04	San Antonio	AHL	22	6	1	7	12																		
2004-05	San Antonio	AHL	77	14	20	34	72																		
	NHL Totals		**8**	**0**	**2**	**2**	**2**	**0**	**0**	**0**	**6**	**0.0**		**2**	**100.0**	**8:55**									

OHL All-Rookie Team (1998)

• Missed majority of 2003-04 season recovering from knee injury suffered in game vs. Milwaukee (AHL), November 7, 2003.

JASPERS, Jason

(JAS-puhrs, JAY-suhn) **T.B.**

Center. Shoots left. 5'11", 207 lbs. Born, Thunder Bay, Ont., April 8, 1981. Phoenix's 4th choice, 71st overall, in 1999 Entry Draft.

Season	Club	League	GP	G	A	Pts	PIM	PP	SH	GW	S	%	+/-	TF	F%	Min	GP	G	A	Pts	PIM	PP	SH	GW	Min
1996-97	Thunder Bay	TBAHA	70	51	69	120	67																		
1997-98	Thunder Bay	TBAHA	72	45	75	120	90																		
1998-99	Sudbury Wolves	OHL	68	28	33	61	81										4	2	1	3	13				
99-2000	Sudbury Wolves	OHL	68	46	61	107	107										12	4	6	10	27				
2000-01	Sudbury Wolves	OHL	63	42	42	84	77										12	3	16	19	18				
2001-02	**Phoenix**	**NHL**	**4**	**0**	**1**	**1**	**4**	**0**	**0**	**0**	**1**	**0.0**	**–1**	**14**	**35.7**	**8:07**									
	Springfield	AHL	71	25	23	48	55																		
2002-03	**Phoenix**	**NHL**	**2**	**0**	**0**	**0**	**0**	**0**	**0**	**0**	**0**	**0.0**	**–1**	**14**	**57.1**	**7:17**									
	Springfield	AHL	63	4	15	19	57										6	0	0	0	4				
2003-04	**Phoenix**	**NHL**	**3**	**0**	**0**	**0**	**2**	**0**	**0**	**0**	**3**	**0.0**	**–1**	**19**	**57.9**	**11:24**									
	Springfield	AHL	58	16	22	38	56																		
2004-05	Utah Grizzlies	AHL	11	0	3	3	6																		
	Springfield	AHL	48	12	17	29	45																		
	NHL Totals		**9**	**0**	**1**	**1**	**6**	**0**	**0**	**0**	**4**	**0.0**		**47**	**51.1**	**9:01**									

OHL Second All-Star Team (2000)

Loaned to **Springfield** (AHL) by **Utah** (AHL) for cash, November 20, 2004. Signed as a free agent by **Tampa Bay**, August 18, 2005.

JILLSON, Jeff

(JIHL-sohn, JEHF) **BUF.**

Defense. Shoots right. 6'3", 215 lbs. Born, North Smithfield, RI, July 24, 1980. San Jose's 1st choice, 14th overall, in 1999 Entry Draft.

Season	Club	League	GP	G	A	Pts	PIM	PP	SH	GW	S	%	+/-	TF	F%	Min	GP	G	A	Pts	PIM	PP	SH	GW	Min
1995-96	Mount St. Charles	High-RI	15	8	7	15	15										5	1	1	2	4				
1996-97	Mount St. Charles	High-RI	15	16	14	30	20										4	0	4	4	6				
1997-98	Mount St. Charles	High-RI	15	10	13	23	32										5	4	5	9	6				
1998-99	U. of Michigan	CCHA	38	5	19	24	71																		
99-2000	U. of Michigan	CCHA	38	8	26	34	115																		
2000-01	U. of Michigan	CCHA	43	10	20	30	74																		
2001-02	**San Jose**	**NHL**	**48**	**5**	**13**	**18**	**29**	**3**	**0**	**2**	**47**	**10.6**	**2**	**0**	**0.0**	**14:36**	**4**	**0**	**0**	**0**	**0**	**0**	**0**	**0**	**5:45**
	Cleveland Barons	AHL	27	2	13	15	45																		
2002-03	**San Jose**	**NHL**	**26**	**0**	**6**	**6**	**9**	**0**	**0**	**0**	**22**	**0.0**	**–7**	**0**	**0.0**	**13:45**									
	Cleveland Barons	AHL	19	3	5	8	12																		
	Providence Bruins	AHL	30	4	11	15	26										4	0	2	2	8				
2003-04	**Boston**	**NHL**	**50**	**4**	**10**	**14**	**35**	**1**	**0**	**1**	**80**	**5.0**	**–1**	**0**	**0.0**	**17:53**									
	Buffalo	**NHL**	**14**	**0**	**3**	**3**	**19**	**0**	**0**	**0**	**35**	**0.0**	**–3**	**0**	**0.0**	**18:21**									
2004-05	Rochester	AHL	78	12	17	29	46										9	1	1	2	12				
	NHL Totals		**138**	**9**	**32**	**41**	**92**	**4**	**0**	**3**	**184**	**4.9**		**0**	**0.0**	**16:01**	**4**	**0**	**0**	**0**	**0**	**0**	**0**	**0**	**5:45**

CCHA All-Rookie Team (1999) • CCHA First All-Star Team (2000, 2001) • NCAA West First All-American Team (2000) • NCAA West Second All-American Team (2001)

Traded to **Boston** by **San Jose** with Jeff Hackett for Kyle McLaren and Boston's 4th round choice (Torrey Mitchell) in 2004 Entry Draft, January 23, 2003. Traded to **San Jose** by **Boston** for Brad Boyes, March 9, 2004. Traded to **Buffalo** by **San Jose** with a compensatory 7th round choice (Andrew Orpik) in 2005 Entry Draft for Curtis Brown and Andy Delmore, March 9, 2004.

JOHANSSON, Andreas

(yoh-HAHN-suhn, ahn-DRAY-uhs)

Center. Shoots left. 6', 202 lbs. Born, Hofors, Sweden, May 19, 1973. NY Islanders' 7th choice, 136th overall, in 1991 Entry Draft.

Season	Club	League	GP	G	A	Pts	PIM	PP	SH	GW	S	%	+/-	TF	F%	Min	GP	G	A	Pts	PIM	PP	SH	GW	Min
1987-88	Bofors	Sweden-3	1	0	0	0	0																		
1988-89	Bofors	Sweden-3	28	19	11	30																			
1989-90	Falu IF	Sweden-2	21	3	1	4	14																		
1990-91	Falu IF	Sweden-2	31	12	10	22	38																		
1991-92	Farjestad	Sweden	30	3	1	4	10										6	0	0	0	4				
1992-93	Farjestad	Sweden	38	4	7	11	38										2	0	0	0	0				
1993-94	Farjestad	Sweden	37	11	16	27	24										3	1	4	5	2				
1994-95	Farjestad	Sweden	36	9	10	19	42										4	0	0	0	10				
1995-96	**NY Islanders**	**NHL**	**3**	**0**	**1**	**1**	**0**	**0**	**0**	**0**	**6**	**0.0**	**1**												
	Worcester IceCats	AHL	29	5	5	10	32																		
	Utah Grizzlies	IHL	22	4	13	17	28										12	0	5	5	6				
1996-97	**NY Islanders**	**NHL**	**15**	**2**	**2**	**4**	**0**	**1**	**0**	**0**	**21**	**9.5**	**–6**												
	Pittsburgh	**NHL**	**27**	**2**	**7**	**9**	**20**	**0**	**0**	**0**	**38**	**5.3**	**–6**												
	Cleveland	IHL	10	2	4	6	42										11	1	5	6	8				
1997-98	**Pittsburgh**	**NHL**	**50**	**5**	**10**	**15**	**20**	**0**	**1**	**0**	**49**	**10.2**	**4**				**1**	**0**	**0**	**0**	**0**	**0**	**0**	**0**	
	Sweden	Olympics	3	0	0	0	2																		
1998-99	**Ottawa**	**NHL**	**69**	**21**	**16**	**37**	**34**	**7**	**0**	**6**	**144**	**14.6**	**1**	**9**	**22.2**	**14:39**	**2**	**0**	**0**	**0**	**0**	**0**	**0**	**0**	**14:13**
99-2000	**Tampa Bay**	**NHL**	**12**	**2**	**3**	**5**	**8**	**0**	**0**	**0**	**11**	**18.2**	**1**	**0**	**0.0**	**10:50**									
	Calgary	**NHL**	**28**	**3**	**7**	**10**	**14**	**1**	**0**	**0**	**47**	**6.4**	**–3**	**5**	**20.0**	**13:33**									
2000-01	SC Bern	Swiss	40	15	29	44	94										7	5	4	9	0				
2001-02	**NY Rangers**	**NHL**	**70**	**14**	**10**	**24**	**46**	**3**	**0**	**1**	**108**	**13.0**	**6**	**299**	**43.1**	**16:19**									
2002-03	**Nashville**	**NHL**	**56**	**20**	**17**	**37**	**22**	**10**	**0**	**0**	**124**	**16.1**	**–4**	**14**	**50.0**	**16:46**									

			Regular Season														Playoffs								
Season	Club	League	GP	G	A	Pts	PIM	PP	SH	GW	S	%	+/-	TF	F%	Min	GP	G	A	Pts	PIM	PP	SH	GW	Min
2003-04	**Nashville**	**NHL**	**47**	**12**	**15**	**27**	**26**	**3**	**1**	**1**	**108**	**11.1**	**–2**	**140**	**38.6**	**15:48**	**6**	**0**	**0**	**0**	**0**	**0**	**0**	**0**	**15:17**
	Milwaukee	AHL	1	0	0	0	2	....	....	....	....	....	....	....	....	....	....	....	....	....	....	....	....	....	....
2004-05	Geneve	Swiss	40	12	26	38	60	....	....	....	....	....	....	....	....	....	4	0	6	6	24	....	....	....	....
	NHL Totals		**377**	**81**	**88**	**169**	**190**	**25**	**2**	**8**	**656**	**12.3**		**467**	**41.3**	**15:24**	**9**	**0**	**0**	**0**	**0**	**0**	**0**	**0**	**15:01**

Traded to **Pittsburgh** by **NY Islanders** with Darius Kasparaitis for Bryan Smolinski, November 17, 1996. Signed as a free agent by **Ottawa**, September 29, 1998. Traded to **Tampa Bay** by **Ottawa** for Rob Zamuner and Tampa Bay's 2nd round choice (later traded to Philadelphia – later traded back to Tampa Bay – later traded to Dallas – Dallas selected Tobias Stephan) in 2002 Entry Draft, June 29, 1999. Traded to **Calgary** by **Tampa Bay** for Nils Ekman and Calgary's 4th round choice (later traded to NY Islanders – NY Islanders selected Vladimir Gorbunov) in 2000 Entry Draft, November 13, 1999. • Missed majority of 1999-2000 season recovering from back injury suffered in game vs. Vancouver, January 2, 2000. Claimed by **NY Rangers** from **Calgary** in Waiver Draft, September 29, 2000. Signed as a free agent by **Nashville**, September 6, 2002. Signed as a free agent by **Geneve** (Swiss), August 19, 2004.

JOHNSON, Aaron

(JAWN-suhn, AIR-ruhn) **CBJ**

Defense. Shoots left. 6', 197 lbs. Born, Port Hawkesbury, N.S., April 30, 1983. Columbus' 4th choice, 85th overall, in 2001 Entry Draft.

Season	Club	League	GP	G	A	Pts	PIM	PP	SH	GW	S	%	+/-	TF	F%	Min	GP	G	A	Pts	PIM	PP	SH	GW	Min
1998-99	Cape Breton	NSAHA	56	28	42	70	98	....	....	....	....	....	....	....	....	....	....	....	....	....	....	....	....	....	....
99-2000	Rimouski Oceanic	QMJHL	63	1	14	15	57	....	....	....	....	....	....	....	....	....	8	0	0	0	0	....	....	....	....
2000-01	Rimouski Oceanic	QMJHL	64	12	41	53	128	....	....	....	....	....	....	....	....	....	11	2	4	6	35	....	....	....	....
2001-02	Rimouski Oceanic	QMJHL	68	17	49	66	172	....	....	....	....	....	....	....	....	....	7	1	2	3	12	....	....	....	....
2002-03	Rimouski Oceanic	QMJHL	25	4	20	24	41	....	....	....	....	....	....	....	....	....	....	....	....	....	....	....	....	....	....
	Quebec Remparts	QMJHL	32	6	31	37	41	....	....	....	....	....	....	....	....	....	11	4	4	8	25	....	....	....	....
2003-04	**Columbus**	**NHL**	**29**	**2**	**6**	**8**	**32**	**0**	**0**	**1**	**33**	**6.1**	**–2**	**0**	**0.0**	**15:02**	....	....	....	....	....	....	....	....	....
	Syracuse Crunch	AHL	49	6	15	21	83	....	....	....	....	....	....	....	....	....	7	2	3	5	27	....	....	....	....
2004-05	Syracuse Crunch	AHL	77	6	17	23	140	....	....	....	....	....	....	....	....	....	....	....	....	....	....	....	....	....	....
	NHL Totals		**29**	**2**	**6**	**8**	**32**	**0**	**0**	**1**	**33**	**6.1**		**0**	**0.0**	**15:02**	....	....	....	....	....	....	....	....	....

JOHNSON, Craig

(JAWN-suhn, KRAYG)

Left wing. Shoots left. 6'2", 200 lbs. Born, St. Paul, MN, March 18, 1972. St. Louis' 1st choice, 33rd overall, in 1990 Entry Draft.

Season	Club	League	GP	G	A	Pts	PIM	PP	SH	GW	S	%	+/-	TF	F%	Min	GP	G	A	Pts	PIM	PP	SH	GW	Min
1987-88	Hill-Murray	High-MN	28	14	20	34	4	....	....	....	....	....	....	....	....	....	....	....	....	....	....	....	....	....	....
1988-89	Hill-Murray	High-MN	24	22	30	52	10	....	....	....	....	....	....	....	....	....	....	....	....	....	....	....	....	....	....
1989-90	Hill-Murray	High-MN	23	15	36	51	0	....	....	....	....	....	....	....	....	....	....	....	....	....	....	....	....	....	....
1990-91	U. of Minnesota	WCHA	33	13	18	31	34	....	....	....	....	....	....	....	....	....	....	....	....	....	....	....	....	....	....
1991-92	U. of Minnesota	WCHA	41	17	38	55	66	....	....	....	....	....	....	....	....	....	....	....	....	....	....	....	....	....	....
1992-93	U. of Minnesota	WCHA	42	22	24	46	70	....	....	....	....	....	....	....	....	....	....	....	....	....	....	....	....	....	....
	Jacksonville	SunHL	23	2	9	11	38	....	....	....	....	....	....	....	....	....	....	....	....	....	....	....	....	....	....
1993-94	United States	Nat-Tm	54	25	26	51	64	....	....	....	....	....	....	....	....	....	....	....	....	....	....	....	....	....	....
	United States	Olympics	8	0	4	4	4	....	....	....	....	....	....	....	....	....	....	....	....	....	....	....	....	....	....
1994-95	**St. Louis**	**NHL**	**15**	**3**	**3**	**6**	**6**	**0**	**0**	**0**	**19**	**15.8**	**4**	....	....	....	**1**	**0**	**0**	**0**	**2**	**0**	**0**	**0**	....
	Peoria Rivermen	IHL	16	2	6	8	25	....	....	....	....	....	....	....	....	....	9	0	4	4	10	....	....	....	....
1995-96	**St. Louis**	**NHL**	**49**	**8**	**7**	**15**	**30**	**1**	**0**	**0**	**69**	**11.6**	**–4**	....	....	....	....	....	....	....	....	....	....	....	....
	Worcester IceCats	AHL	5	3	0	3	2	....	....	....	....	....	....	....	....	....	....	....	....	....	....	....	....	....	....
	Los Angeles	**NHL**	**11**	**5**	**4**	**9**	**6**	**3**	**0**	**0**	**28**	**17.9**	**–4**	....	....	....	....	....	....	....	....	....	....	....	....
1996-97	**Los Angeles**	**NHL**	**31**	**4**	**3**	**7**	**26**	**1**	**0**	**0**	**30**	**13.3**	**–7**	....	....	....	....	....	....	....	....	....	....	....	....
1997-98	**Los Angeles**	**NHL**	**74**	**17**	**21**	**38**	**42**	**6**	**0**	**2**	**125**	**13.6**	**9**	....	....	....	**4**	**1**	**0**	**1**	**4**	**0**	**0**	**0**	....
1998-99	**Los Angeles**	**NHL**	**69**	**7**	**12**	**19**	**32**	**2**	**0**	**2**	**94**	**7.4**	**–12**	**2**	**50.0**	**12:02**	....	....	....	....	....	....	....	....	....
99-2000	**Los Angeles**	**NHL**	**76**	**9**	**14**	**23**	**28**	**1**	**0**	**1**	**106**	**8.5**	**–10**	**9**	**55.6**	**13:56**	**4**	**1**	**0**	**1**	**2**	**0**	**0**	**0**	**11:28**
2000-01	**Los Angeles**	**NHL**	**26**	**4**	**5**	**9**	**16**	**0**	**0**	**0**	**36**	**11.1**	**0**	**2**	**100.0**	**10:40**	....	....	....	....	....	....	....	....	....
2001-02	**Los Angeles**	**NHL**	**72**	**13**	**14**	**27**	**24**	**4**	**1**	**3**	**102**	**12.7**	**14**	**11**	**36.4**	**14:15**	**7**	**1**	**2**	**3**	**2**	**0**	**0**	**1**	**14:00**
2002-03	**Los Angeles**	**NHL**	**70**	**3**	**6**	**9**	**22**	**0**	**0**	**0**	**87**	**3.4**	**–13**	**28**	**32.1**	**14:05**	....	....	....	....	....	....	....	....	....
2003-04	**Anaheim**	**NHL**	**39**	**1**	**2**	**3**	**14**	**0**	**0**	**0**	**45**	**2.2**	**–4**	**62**	**62.9**	**10:43**	....	....	....	....	....	....	....	....	....
	Toronto	**NHL**	**10**	**1**	**1**	**2**	**6**	**0**	**0**	**0**	**12**	**8.3**	**0**	**16**	**56.3**	**13:03**	....	....	....	....	....	....	....	....	....
	Washington	**NHL**	**15**	**0**	**6**	**6**	**8**	**0**	**0**	**0**	**20**	**0.0**	**–6**	**26**	**34.6**	**16:53**	....	....	....	....	....	....	....	....	....
2004-05	Hamburg Freezers	Germany	42	19	25	44	56	....	....	....	....	....	....	....	....	....	....	....	....	....	....	....	....	....	....
	NHL Totals		**557**	**75**	**98**	**173**	**260**	**18**	**1**	**8**	**773**	**9.7**		**156**	**50.0**	**13:13**	**16**	**3**	**2**	**5**	**10**	**0**	**0**	**1**	**13:05**

Traded to **Los Angeles** by **St. Louis** with Patrice Tardif, Roman Vopat, St. Louis' 5th round choice (Peter Hogan) in 1996 Entry Draft and St. Louis' 1st round choice (Matt Zultek) in 1997 Entry Draft for Wayne Gretzky, February 27, 1996. • Missed majority of 2000-01 season recovering from ankle injury suffered in game vs. San Jose, December 26, 2000. Signed as a free agent by **Anaheim**, September 9, 2003. Claimed on waivers by **Toronto** from **Anaheim**, January 10, 2004. Claimed on waivers by **Washington** from **Toronto**, March 5, 2004. Signed as a free agent by **Hamburg** (Germany), August 5, 2004. Signed as a free agent by **Dusseldorf** (Germany), May 14, 2005.

JOHNSON, Greg

(JAWN-suhn, GREHG) **NSH.**

Center. Shoots left. 5'11", 200 lbs. Born, Thunder Bay, Ont., March 16, 1971. Philadelphia's 1st choice, 33rd overall, in 1989 Entry Draft.

Season	Club	League	GP	G	A	Pts	PIM	PP	SH	GW	S	%	+/-	TF	F%	Min	GP	G	A	Pts	PIM	PP	SH	GW	Min
1988-89	Thunder Bay	USHL	47	32	64	96	4	....	....	....	....	....	....	....	....	....	12	5	13	18	0	....	....	....	....
1989-90	North Dakota	WCHA	44	17	38	55	11	....	....	....	....	....	....	....	....	....	....	....	....	....	....	....	....	....	....
1990-91	North Dakota	WCHA	38	18	*61	79	6	....	....	....	....	....	....	....	....	....	....	....	....	....	....	....	....	....	....
1991-92	North Dakota	WCHA	39	20	*54	74	8	....	....	....	....	....	....	....	....	....	....	....	....	....	....	....	....	....	....
1992-93	North Dakota	WCHA	34	19	45	64	18	....	....	....	....	....	....	....	....	....	....	....	....	....	....	....	....	....	....
	Canada	Nat-Tm	23	6	14	20	2	....	....	....	....	....	....	....	....	....	....	....	....	....	....	....	....	....	....
1993-94	**Detroit**	**NHL**	**52**	**6**	**11**	**17**	**22**	**1**	**1**	**0**	**48**	**12.5**	**–7**	....	....	....	**7**	**2**	**2**	**4**	**2**	**1**	**0**	**0**	....
	Adirondack	AHL	3	2	4	6	0	....	....	....	....	....	....	....	....	....	4	0	4	4	2	....	....	....	....
	Canada	Olympics	8	0	3	3	0	....	....	....	....	....	....	....	....	....	....	....	....	....	....	....	....	....	....
1994-95	**Detroit**	**NHL**	**22**	**3**	**5**	**8**	**14**	**2**	**0**	**0**	**32**	**9.4**	**1**	....	....	....	**1**	**0**	**0**	**0**	**0**	**0**	**0**	**0**	....
1995-96	**Detroit**	**NHL**	**60**	**18**	**22**	**40**	**30**	**5**	**0**	**2**	**87**	**20.7**	**6**	....	....	....	**13**	**3**	**1**	**4**	**8**	**0**	**0**	**0**	....
1996-97	**Detroit**	**NHL**	**43**	**6**	**10**	**16**	**12**	**0**	**0**	**0**	**56**	**10.7**	**–5**	....	....	....	....	....	....	....	....	....	....	....	....
	Pittsburgh	**NHL**	**32**	**7**	**9**	**16**	**14**	**1**	**0**	**0**	**52**	**13.5**	**–13**	....	....	....	**5**	**1**	**0**	**1**	**2**	**0**	**0**	**0**	....
1997-98	**Pittsburgh**	**NHL**	**5**	**1**	**0**	**1**	**2**	**0**	**0**	**0**	**4**	**25.0**	**0**	....	....	....	....	....	....	....	....	....	....	....	....
	Chicago	**NHL**	**69**	**11**	**22**	**33**	**38**	**4**	**0**	**3**	**85**	**12.9**	**–2**	....	....	....	....	....	....	....	....	....	....	....	....
1998-99	**Nashville**	**NHL**	**68**	**16**	**34**	**50**	**24**	**2**	**3**	**0**	**120**	**13.3**	**–8**	**1441**	**53.6**	**19:26**	....	....	....	....	....	....	....	....	....
99-2000	**Nashville**	**NHL**	**82**	**11**	**33**	**44**	**40**	**2**	**0**	**1**	**133**	**8.3**	**–15**	**1684**	**50.8**	**19:13**	....	....	....	....	....	....	....	....	....
2000-01	**Nashville**	**NHL**	**82**	**15**	**17**	**32**	**46**	**1**	**0**	**4**	**97**	**15.5**	**–6**	**1583**	**51.8**	**17:49**	....	....	....	....	....	....	....	....	....
2001-02	**Nashville**	**NHL**	**82**	**18**	**26**	**44**	**38**	**3**	**0**	**2**	**145**	**12.4**	**–14**	**1764**	**51.8**	**19:34**	....	....	....	....	....	....	....	....	....
2002-03	**Nashville**	**NHL**	**38**	**8**	**9**	**17**	**22**	**0**	**0**	**0**	**55**	**14.5**	**7**	**753**	**52.1**	**17:11**	....	....	....	....	....	....	....	....	....
2003-04	**Nashville**	**NHL**	**82**	**14**	**18**	**32**	**33**	**1**	**4**	**4**	**100**	**14.0**	**–21**	**1607**	**55.1**	**17:38**	**6**	**1**	**2**	**3**	**0**	**0**	**0**	**0**	**17:48**
2004-05				DID NOT PLAY																					
	NHL Totals		**717**	**134**	**216**	**350**	**335**	**22**	**8**	**16**	**1014**	**13.2**		**8832**	**52.5**	**18:35**	**32**	**7**	**5**	**12**	**12**	**1**	**0**	**0**	**17:48**

WCHA First All-Star Team (1991, 1992, 1993) • NCAA West First All-American Team (1991, 1993) • NCAA West Second All-American Team (1992)

Traded to **Detroit** by **Philadelphia** with Philadelphia's 5th round choice (Frederic Deschenes) in 1994 Entry Draft for Jim Cummins and Philadelphia's 4th round choice (previously acquired, later traded to Boston – Boston selected Charles Paquette) in 1993 Entry Draft, June 20, 1993. Traded to **Pittsburgh** by **Detroit** for Tomas Sandstrom, January 27, 1997. Traded to **Chicago** by **Pittsburgh** for Tuomas Gronman, October 27, 1997. Claimed by **Nashville** from **Chicago** in Expansion Draft, June 26, 1998. • Missed majority of 2002-03 season recovering from head injury suffered in game vs. Vancouver, October 21, 2002.

JOHNSON, Matt

(JAWN-suhn, MAT)

Left wing. Shoots left. 6'5", 235 lbs. Born, Welland, Ont., November 23, 1975. Los Angeles' 2nd choice, 33rd overall, in 1994 Entry Draft.

Season	Club	League	GP	G	A	Pts	PIM	PP	SH	GW	S	%	+/-	TF	F%	Min	GP	G	A	Pts	PIM	PP	SH	GW	Min
1991-92	Welland Aerostars	OHA-B	38	6	19	25	214	....	....	....	....	....	....	....	....	....	....	....	....	....	....	....	....	....	....
	Ajax Axemen	OHA-B	1	0	0	0	0	....	....	....	....	....	....	....	....	....	....	....	....	....	....	....	....	....	....
1992-93	Peterborough	OHL	66	8	17	25	211	....	....	....	....	....	....	....	....	....	16	1	1	2	56	....	....	....	....
1993-94	Peterborough	OHL	50	13	24	37	233	....	....	....	....	....	....	....	....	....	....	....	....	....	....	....	....	....	....
1994-95	Peterborough	OHL	14	1	2	3	43	....	....	....	....	....	....	....	....	....	....	....	....	....	....	....	....	....	....
	Los Angeles	**NHL**	**14**	**1**	**0**	**1**	**102**	**0**	**0**	**0**	**4**	**25.0**	**0**	....	....	....	....	....	....	....	....	....	....	....	....
1995-96	**Los Angeles**	**NHL**	**1**	**0**	**0**	**0**	**5**	**0**	**0**	**0**	**1**	**0.0**	**0**	....	....	....	....	....	....	....	....	....	....	....	....
	Phoenix	IHL	29	4	4	8	87	....	....	....	....	....	....	....	....	....	....	....	....	....	....	....	....	....	....
1996-97	**Los Angeles**	**NHL**	**52**	**1**	**3**	**4**	**194**	**0**	**0**	**0**	**20**	**5.0**	**–4**	....	....	....	....	....	....	....	....	....	....	....	....
1997-98	**Los Angeles**	**NHL**	**66**	**2**	**4**	**6**	**249**	**0**	**0**	**0**	**18**	**11.1**	**–8**	....	....	....	**4**	**0**	**0**	**0**	**6**	**0**	**0**	**0**	....
1998-99	**Los Angeles**	**NHL**	**49**	**2**	**1**	**3**	**131**	**0**	**0**	**0**	**14**	**14.3**	**–5**	**1**	**0.0**	**5:55**	....	....	....	....	....	....	....	....	....
99-2000	**Atlanta**	**NHL**	**64**	**2**	**5**	**7**	**144**	**0**	**0**	**0**	**54**	**3.7**	**–11**	**1**	**100.0**	**8:25**	....	....	....	....	....	....	....	....	....
2000-01	**Minnesota**	**NHL**	**50**	**1**	**1**	**2**	**137**	**0**	**0**	**0**	**21**	**4.8**	**–6**	**1**	**100.0**	**7:43**	....	....	....	....	....	....	....	....	....
2001-02	**Minnesota**	**NHL**	**60**	**4**	**0**	**4**	**183**	**0**	**0**	**1**	**23**	**17.4**	**–13**	**1**	**100.0**	**7:23**	....	....	....	....	....	....	....	....	....
2002-03	**Minnesota**	**NHL**	**60**	**3**	**5**	**8**	**201**	**0**	**0**	**1**	**24**	**12.5**	**–8**	**5**	**40.0**	**7:24**	**12**	**0**	**0**	**0**	**25**	**0**	**0**	**0**	**6:39**
2003-04	**Minnesota**	**NHL**	**57**	**7**	**1**	**8**	**177**	**0**	**0**	**1**	**21**	**33.3**	**4**	**3**	**33.3**	**6:27**	....	....	....	....	....	....	....	....	....

			Regular Season														Playoffs								
Season	Club	League	GP	G	A	Pts	PIM	PP	SH	GW	S	%	+/-	TF	F%	Min	GP	G	A	Pts	PIM	PP	SH	GW	Min
2004-05			DID NOT PLAY																						
	NHL Totals		**473**	**23**	**20**	**43**	**1523**	**0**	**0**	**3**	**200**	**11.5**		**12**	**50.0**	**7:16**	**16**	**0**	**0**	**0**	**31**	**0**	**0**	**0**	**6:39**

OHL All-Rookie Team (1993)

Claimed by **Atlanta** from **Los Angeles** in Expansion Draft, June 25, 1999. Traded to **Minnesota** by **Atlanta** for San Jose's 3rd round choice (previously acquired, later traded to Pittsburgh – later traded to Columbus – Columbus selected Aaron Johnson) in 2001 Entry Draft, September 29, 2000.

JOHNSON, Mike

(JAWN-suhn, MIGHK) **PHX.**

Right wing. Shoots right. 6'2", 201 lbs. Born, Scarborough, Ont., October 3, 1974.

1991-92	Hillcrest Summits	MTHL	45	43	66	109	....	....	....	....	....	....	....	....	....	....	20	10	19	29	....	....	....	....	....
1992-93	Aurora Eagles	MTJHL	48	25	40	65	18	....	....	....	....	....	....	....	....	....	7	7	15	22	....	....	....	....	....
1993-94	Bowling Green	CCHA	38	6	14	20	18	....	....	....	....	....	....	....	....	....	....	....	....	....	....	....	....	....	....
1994-95	Bowling Green	CCHA	37	16	33	49	35	....	....	....	....	....	....	....	....	....	....	....	....	....	....	....	....	....	....
1995-96	Bowling Green	CCHA	30	12	19	31	22	....	....	....	....	....	....	....	....	....	....	....	....	....	....	....	....	....	....
1996-97	Bowling Green	CCHA	38	30	32	62	46	....	....	....	....	....	....	....	....	....	....	....	....	....	....	....	....	....	....
	Toronto	**NHL**	**13**	**2**	**2**	**4**	**4**	**0**	**1**	**1**	**27**	**7.4**	**–2**	....	....	....	....	....	....	....	....	....	....	....	....
1997-98	**Toronto**	**NHL**	**82**	**15**	**32**	**47**	**24**	**5**	**0**	**0**	**143**	**10.5**	**–4**	....	....	....	....	....	....	....	....	....	....	....	....
1998-99	**Toronto**	**NHL**	**79**	**20**	**24**	**44**	**35**	**5**	**3**	**2**	**149**	**13.4**	**13**	**15**	**53.3**	**16:16**	**17**	**3**	**2**	**5**	**4**	**0**	**0**	**1**	**16:28**
99-2000	**Toronto**	**NHL**	**52**	**11**	**14**	**25**	**23**	**2**	**1**	**3**	**89**	**12.4**	**8**	**2**	**50.0**	**15:22**	....	....	....	....	....	....	....	....	....
	Tampa Bay	**NHL**	**28**	**10**	**12**	**22**	**4**	**4**	**0**	**0**	**43**	**23.3**	**–2**	**5**	**60.0**	**20:33**	....	....	....	....	....	....	....	....	....
2000-01	**Tampa Bay**	**NHL**	**64**	**11**	**27**	**38**	**38**	**3**	**1**	**0**	**107**	**10.3**	**–10**	**2**	**0.0**	**18:13**	....	....	....	....	....	....	....	....	....
	Phoenix	**NHL**	**12**	**2**	**3**	**5**	**4**	**1**	**0**	**0**	**17**	**11.8**	**0**	**0**	**0.0**	**12:12**	....	....	....	....	....	....	....	....	....
2001-02	**Phoenix**	**NHL**	**57**	**5**	**22**	**27**	**28**	**1**	**2**	**0**	**73**	**6.8**	**14**	**13**	**30.8**	**15:49**	**5**	**1**	**1**	**2**	**6**	**0**	**0**	**0**	**14:45**
2002-03	**Phoenix**	**NHL**	**82**	**23**	**40**	**63**	**47**	**8**	**0**	**3**	**178**	**12.9**	**9**	**34**	**50.0**	**19:39**	....	....	....	....	....	....	....	....	....
2003-04	**Phoenix**	**NHL**	**11**	**1**	**9**	**10**	**10**	**1**	**0**	**0**	**17**	**5.9**	**–1**	**2**	**50.0**	**19:50**	....	....	....	....	....	....	....	....	....
2004-05	Farjestad	Sweden	8	1	2	3	4	....	....	....	....	....	....	....	....	....	6	0	2	2	4	....	....	....	....
	NHL Totals		**480**	**100**	**185**	**285**	**217**	**30**	**8**	**9**	**843**	**11.9**		**73**	**46.6**	**17:25**	**22**	**4**	**3**	**7**	**10**	**0**	**0**	**1**	**16:05**

NHL All-Rookie Team (1998)

Signed as a free agent by **Toronto**, March 16, 1997. Traded to **Tampa Bay** by **Toronto** with Marek Posmyk and Toronto's 5th (Pavel Sedov) and 6th (Aaron Gionet) round choices in 2000 Entry Draft for Darcy Tucker and Tampa Bay's 4th round choice (Miguel Delisle) in 2000 Entry Draft, February 9, 2000. Traded to **Phoenix** by **Tampa Bay** with Paul Mara, Ruslan Zainullin and NY Islanders' 2nd round choice (previously acquired, Phoenix selected Matthew Spiller) in 2001 Entry Draft for Nikolai Khabibulin and Stan Neckar, March 5, 2001. • Missed majority of 2003-04 season recovering from shoulder injury suffered in game vs. Los Angeles, Novembeer 1, 2003. Signed as a free agent by **Farjestad** (Sweden), January 31, 2005.

JOHNSON, Ryan

(JAWN-suhn, RIGH-yuhn) **ST.L.**

Center. Shoots left. 6'1", 205 lbs. Born, Thunder Bay, Ont., June 14, 1976. Florida's 4th choice, 36th overall, in 1994 Entry Draft.

1992-93	Thunder Bay	TBAHA	60	25	33	58	....	....	....	....	....	....	....	....	....	....	....	....	....	....	....	....	....	....	....
1993-94	Thunder Bay	USHL	48	14	36	50	28	....	....	....	....	....	....	....	....	....	....	....	....	....	....	....	....	....	....
1994-95	North Dakota	WCHA	38	6	22	28	39	....	....	....	....	....	....	....	....	....	....	....	....	....	....	....	....	....	....
1995-96	North Dakota	WCHA	21	2	17	19	14	....	....	....	....	....	....	....	....	....	....	....	....	....	....	....	....	....	....
	Canada	Nat-Tm	28	5	12	17	14	....	....	....	....	....	....	....	....	....	....	....	....	....	....	....	....	....	....
1996-97	Carolina	AHL	79	18	24	42	28	....	....	....	....	....	....	....	....	....	....	....	....	....	....	....	....	....	....
1997-98	**Florida**	**NHL**	**10**	**0**	**2**	**2**	**0**	**0**	**0**	**0**	**6**	**0.0**	**–4**	....	....	....	....	....	....	....	....	....	....	....	....
	New Haven	AHL	64	19	48	67	12	....	....	....	....	....	....	....	....	....	3	0	1	1	0	....	....	....	....
1998-99	**Florida**	**NHL**	**1**	**1**	**0**	**1**	**0**	**0**	**0**	**0**	**1**	**100.0**	**0**	**16**	**37.5**	**15:26**	....	....	....	....	....	....	....	....	....
	New Haven	AHL	37	8	19	27	18	....	....	....	....	....	....	....	....	....	....	....	....	....	....	....	....	....	....
99-2000	**Florida**	**NHL**	**66**	**4**	**12**	**16**	**14**	**0**	**0**	**0**	**44**	**9.1**	**1**	**684**	**51.8**	**11:47**	....	....	....	....	....	....	....	....	....
	Tampa Bay	**NHL**	**14**	**0**	**2**	**2**	**2**	**0**	**0**	**0**	**5**	**0.0**	**–9**	**117**	**53.0**	**11:02**	....	....	....	....	....	....	....	....	....
2000-01	**Tampa Bay**	**NHL**	**80**	**7**	**14**	**21**	**44**	**1**	**0**	**0**	**71**	**9.9**	**–20**	**951**	**48.9**	**15:47**	....	....	....	....	....	....	....	....	....
2001-02	**Florida**	**NHL**	**29**	**1**	**3**	**4**	**10**	**0**	**0**	**0**	**24**	**4.2**	**–5**	**336**	**47.9**	**13:00**	....	....	....	....	....	....	....	....	....
2002-03	**Florida**	**NHL**	**58**	**2**	**5**	**7**	**26**	**0**	**0**	**0**	**54**	**3.7**	**–13**	**689**	**48.0**	**10:40**	....	....	....	....	....	....	....	....	....
	St. Louis	**NHL**	**17**	**0**	**0**	**0**	**12**	**0**	**0**	**0**	**13**	**0.0**	**0**	**180**	**51.7**	**10:34**	**6**	**0**	**2**	**2**	**6**	**0**	**0**	**0**	**8:14**
2003-04	**St. Louis**	**NHL**	**69**	**4**	**7**	**11**	**8**	**0**	**1**	**1**	**36**	**11.1**	**–2**	**537**	**53.6**	**9:54**	**3**	**0**	**0**	**0**	**0**	**0**	**0**	**0**	**6:11**
2004-05	Missouri	UHL	29	7	14	21	12	....	....	....	....	....	....	....	....	....	6	1	0	1	13	....	....	....	....
	NHL Totals		**344**	**19**	**45**	**64**	**116**	**1**	**1**	**1**	**254**	**7.5**		**3510**	**50.1**	**12:11**	**9**	**0**	**2**	**2**	**6**	**0**	**0**	**0**	**7:33**

Traded to **Tampa Bay** by **Florida** with Dwayne Hay for Mike Sillinger, March 14, 2000. Traded to **Florida** by **Tampa Bay** with Tampa Bay's 6th round choice (later traded back to Tampa Bay – Tampa Bay selected Doug O'Brien) in 2003 Entry Draft for Vaclav Prospal, July 10, 2001. • Missed majority of 2001-02 season recovering from head injury suffered in game vs. St. Louis, December 22, 2001. Claimed on waivers by **St. Louis** from **Florida**, February 19, 2003. Signed as a free agent by **Missouri** (UHL), February 3, 2005.

JOHNSSON, Kim

(YAWN-suhn, KIHM) **PHI.**

Defense. Shoots left. 6'1", 205 lbs. Born, Malmo, Sweden, March 16, 1976. NY Rangers' 15th choice, 286th overall, in 1994 Entry Draft.

1993-94	Malmo IF Jr.	Swe-Jr.	14	5	3	8	14	....	....	....	....	....	....	....	....	....	....	....	....	....	....	....	....	....	....
	Malmo IF	Sweden	2	0	0	0	0	....	....	....	....	....	....	....	....	....	....	....	....	....	....	....	....	....	....
1994-95	Malmo IF Jr.	Swe-Jr.	29	6	15	21	40	....	....	....	....	....	....	....	....	....	....	....	....	....	....	....	....	....	....
	Malmo IF	Sweden	13	0	0	0	4	....	....	....	....	....	....	....	....	....	1	0	0	0	0	....	....	....	....
1995-96	Malmo IF	Sweden	38	2	0	2	30	....	....	....	....	....	....	....	....	....	4	0	1	1	8	....	....	....	....
1996-97	Malmo	Sweden	49	4	9	13	42	....	....	....	....	....	....	....	....	....	4	0	0	0	2	....	....	....	....
1997-98	Malmo	Sweden	45	5	9	14	29	....	....	....	....	....	....	....	....	....	....	....	....	....	....	....	....	....	....
1998-99	Malmo	Sweden	49	9	8	17	76	....	....	....	....	....	....	....	....	....	8	2	3	5	12	....	....	....	....
99-2000	**NY Rangers**	**NHL**	**76**	**6**	**15**	**21**	**46**	**1**	**0**	**1**	**101**	**5.9**	**–13**	**0**	**0.0**	**18:06**	....	....	....	....	....	....	....	....	....
2000-01	**NY Rangers**	**NHL**	**75**	**5**	**21**	**26**	**40**	**4**	**0**	**0**	**104**	**4.8**	**–3**	**0**	**0.0**	**21:16**	....	....	....	....	....	....	....	....	....
2001-02	**Philadelphia**	**NHL**	**82**	**11**	**30**	**41**	**42**	**5**	**0**	**1**	**150**	**7.3**	**12**	**0**	**0.0**	**23:02**	**5**	**0**	**0**	**0**	**2**	**0**	**0**	**0**	**22:48**
	Sweden	Olympics	4	1	1	2	0	....	....	....	....	....	....	....	....	....	....	....	....	....	....	....	....	....	....
2002-03	**Philadelphia**	**NHL**	**82**	**10**	**29**	**39**	**38**	**5**	**0**	**2**	**159**	**6.3**	**11**	**0**	**0.0**	**24:05**	**13**	**0**	**3**	**3**	**8**	**0**	**0**	**0**	**26:07**
2003-04	**Philadelphia**	**NHL**	**80**	**13**	**29**	**42**	**26**	**4**	**0**	**3**	**189**	**6.9**	**16**	**0**	**0.0**	**24:27**	**15**	**2**	**6**	**8**	**8**	**0**	**0**	**1**	**26:11**
2004-05	HC Ambri-Piotta	Swiss	24	4	10	14	61	....	....	....	....	....	....	....	....	....	....	....	....	....	....	....	....	....	....
	NHL Totals		**395**	**45**	**124**	**169**	**192**	**19**	**0**	**7**	**703**	**6.4**		**0**	**0.0**	**22:15**	**33**	**2**	**9**	**11**	**18**	**0**	**0**	**1**	**25:39**

Traded to **Philadelphia** by **NY Rangers** with Jan Hlavac, Pavel Brendl and NY Rangers' 3rd round choice (Stefan Ruzicka) in 2003 Entry Draft for Eric Lindros, August 20, 2001. Signed as a free agent by **Ambri** (Swiss), September 18, 2004.

JOKELA, Mikko

(YOH-kih-lah, MIH-koh) **VAN.**

Defense. Shoots right. 6'1", 210 lbs. Born, Lappeenranta, Finland, March 4, 1980. New Jersey's 5th choice, 96th overall, in 1998 Entry Draft.

1995-96	KalPa Kuopio U18	Fin-U18	9	2	1	3	20	....	....	....	....	....	....	....	....	....	....	....	....	....	....	....	....	....	....
	KalPa Kuopio Jr.	Finland-Jr.	11	2	1	3	20	....	....	....	....	....	....	....	....	....	....	....	....	....	....	....	....	....	....
1996-97	KalPa Kuopio Jr.	Finland-Jr.	45	5	7	12	26	....	....	....	....	....	....	....	....	....	5	1	1	2	4	....	....	....	....
1997-98	HIFK Helsinki Jr.	Finland-Jr.	22	2	5	7	14	....	....	....	....	....	....	....	....	....	....	....	....	....	....	....	....	....	....
	Hermes Kokkola	Finland-2	6	0	1	1	2	....	....	....	....	....	....	....	....	....	....	....	....	....	....	....	....	....	....
	HIFK Helsinki	Finland	16	0	0	0	0	....	....	....	....	....	....	....	....	....	....	....	....	....	....	....	....	....	....
1998-99	KalPa Kuopio Jr.	Finland-Jr.	1	0	1	1	2	....	....	....	....	....	....	....	....	....	....	....	....	....	....	....	....	....	....
	KalPa Kuopio	Finland	42	1	2	3	18	....	....	....	....	....	....	....	....	....	....	....	....	....	....	....	....	....	....
	HIFK Helsinki	Finland	3	0	0	0	2	....	....	....	....	....	....	....	....	....	....	....	....	....	....	....	....	....	....
	KalPa Kuopio	Finland	....	....	....	....	....	....	....	....	....	....	....	....	....	....	6	0	0	0	2	....	....	....	....
99-2000	SaiPa	Finland	48	0	5	5	50	....	....	....	....	....	....	....	....	....	....	....	....	....	....	....	....	....	....
	SaiPa Jr.	Finland-Jr.	....	....	....	....	....	....	....	....	....	....	....	....	....	....	1	0	0	0	0	....	....	....	....
2000-01	SaiPa Jr.	Finland-Jr.	4	2	2	4	2	....	....	....	....	....	....	....	....	....	3	0	0	0	2	....	....	....	....
	KooKoo Kouvola	Finland-2	5	3	0	3	0	....	....	....	....	....	....	....	....	....	....	....	....	....	....	....	....	....	....
	SaiPa	Finland	50	1	0	1	24	....	....	....	....	....	....	....	....	....	....	....	....	....	....	....	....	....	....
2001-02	Albany River Rats	AHL	56	5	13	18	28	....	....	....	....	....	....	....	....	....	....	....	....	....	....	....	....	....	....
2002-03	Albany River Rats	AHL	44	8	11	19	35	....	....	....	....	....	....	....	....	....	....	....	....	....	....	....	....	....	....
	Vancouver	**NHL**	**1**	**0**	**0**	**0**	**0**	**0**	**0**	**0**	**3**	**0.0**	**0**	**0**	**0.0**	**5:09**	....	....	....	....	....	....	....	....	....
	Manitoba Moose	AHL	32	3	7	10	17	....	....	....	....	....	....	....	....	....	14	1	4	5	2	....	....	....	....
2003-04	Manitoba Moose	AHL	78	5	10	15	52	....	....	....	....	....	....	....	....	....	....	....	....	....	....	....	....	....	....
2004-05	HPK Hameenlinna	Finland	55	4	12	16	102	....	....	....	....	....	....	....	....	....	10	2	1	3	12	....	....	....	....
	NHL Totals		**1**	**0**	**0**	**0**	**0**	**0**	**0**	**0**	**3**	**0.0**		**0**	**0.0**	**5:09**	....	....	....	....	....	....	....	....	....

Traded to **Vancouver** by **New Jersey** for Steve Kariya, January 24, 2003. Signed as a free agent by **HPK** (Finland), April 17, 2004.

			Regular Season														Playoffs								
Season	Club	League	GP	G	A	Pts	PIM	PP	SH	GW	S	%	+/-	TF	F%	Min	GP	G	A	Pts	PIM	PP	SH	GW	Min

JOKINEN, Olli

(YOH-kih-nihn, OH-lee) **FLA.**

Center. Shoots left. 6'3", 205 lbs. Born, Kuopio, Finland, December 5, 1978. Los Angeles' 1st choice, 3rd overall, in 1997 Entry Draft.

Season	Club	League	GP	G	A	Pts	PIM	PP	SH	GW	S	%	+/-	TF	F%	Min	GP	G	A	Pts	PIM	PP	SH	GW	Min
1994-95	KalPa Kuopio U18	Fin-U18	12	9	14	23	46	....	....	....	....	....	....	....	....	....	....	....	....	....	....	....	....	....	....
	KalPa Kuopio Jr.	Finland-Jr.	6	0	1	1	6	....	....	....	....	....	....	....	....	....	....	....	....	....	....	....	....	....	....
1995-96	KalPa Kuopio Jr.	Finland-Jr.	25	20	14	34	47	....	....	....	....	....	....	....	....	....	7	4	4	8	20	....	....	....	....
	KalPa Kuopio	Finland	15	1	1	2	2	....	....	....	....	....	....	....	....	....	....	....	....	....	....	....	....	....	....
1996-97	HIFK Helsinki Jr.	Finland-Jr.	2	1	0	1	6	....	....	....	....	....	....	....	....	....	....	....	....	....	....	....	....	....	....
	HIFK Helsinki	Finland	50	14	27	41	88	....	....	....	....	....	....	....	....	....	....	....	....	....	....	....	....	....	....
1997-98	**Los Angeles**	**NHL**	**8**	**0**	**0**	**0**	**6**	**0**	**0**	**0**	**12**	**0.0**	**–5**	....	....	....	....	....	....	....	....	....	....	....	....
	HIFK Helsinki	Finland	30	11	28	39	8	....	....	....	....	....	....	....	....	....	9	*7	2	9	2	....	....	....	....
1998-99	**Los Angeles**	**NHL**	**66**	**9**	**12**	**21**	**44**	**3**	**1**	**1**	**87**	**10.3**	**–10**	**779**	**43.9**	**14:42**	....	....	....	....	....	....	....	....	....
	Springfield	AHL	9	3	6	9	6	....	....	....	....	....	....	....	....	....	....	....	....	....	....	....	....	....	....
99-2000	**NY Islanders**	**NHL**	**82**	**11**	**10**	**21**	**80**	**1**	**2**	**3**	**138**	**8.0**	**0**	**841**	**46.1**	**16:15**	....	....	....	....	....	....	....	....	....
2000-01	**Florida**	**NHL**	**78**	**6**	**10**	**16**	**106**	**0**	**0**	**0**	**121**	**5.0**	**–22**	**638**	**42.3**	**13:23**	....	....	....	....	....	....	....	....	....
2001-02	**Florida**	**NHL**	**80**	**9**	**20**	**29**	**98**	**3**	**1**	**0**	**153**	**5.9**	**–16**	**1222**	**45.2**	**18:05**	....	....	....	....	....	....	....	....	....
	Finland	Olympics	4	2	1	3	0	....	....	....	....	....	....	....	....	....	....	....	....	....	....	....	....	....	....
2002-03	**Florida**	**NHL**	**81**	**36**	**29**	**65**	**79**	**13**	**3**	**6**	**240**	**15.0**	**–17**	**1925**	**46.7**	**22:02**	....	....	....	....	....	....	....	....	....
2003-04	**Florida**	**NHL**	**82**	**26**	**32**	**58**	**81**	**8**	**2**	**8**	**280**	**9.3**	**–16**	**1986**	**47.1**	**22:35**	....	....	....	....	....	....	....	....	....
2004-05	Kloten Flyers	Swiss	8	6	1	7	14	....	....	....	....	....	....	....	....	....	....	....	....	....	....	....	....	....	....
	Sodertalje SK	Sweden	23	13	9	22	52	....	....	....	....	....	....	....	....	....	....	....	....	....	....	....	....	....	....
	HIFK Helsinki	Finland	14	9	8	17	10	....	....	....	....	....	....	....	....	....	5	2	0	2	24	....	....	....	....
	NHL Totals		**477**	**97**	**113**	**210**	**494**	**28**	**9**	**18**	**1031**	**9.4**		**7391**	**45.8**	**17:58**	....	....	....	....	....	....	....	....	....

Played in NHL All-Star Game (2003)

Traded to **NY Islanders** by **Los Angeles** with Josh Green, Mathieu Biron and Los Angeles' 1st round choice (Taylor Pyatt) in 1999 Entry Draft for Ziggy Palffy, Bryan Smolinski, Marcel Cousineau and New Jersey's 4th round choice (previously acquired, Los Angeles selected Daniel Johansson) in 1999 Entry Draft, June 20, 1999. Traded to **Florida** by **NY Islanders** with Roberto Luongo for Mark Parrish and Oleg Kvasha, June 24, 2000. Signed as a free agent by **Kloten** (Swiss), September 15, 2004. Signed as a free agent by **Sodertalje** (Sweden), November, 2004. Signed as a free agent by **HIFK** (Finland), January 30, 2005.

JONES, Randy

(JOHNZ, RAN-dee) **PHI.**

Defense. Shoots left. 6'2", 200 lbs. Born, Quispamsis, N.B., July 23, 1981.

Season	Club	League	GP	G	A	Pts	PIM	PP	SH	GW	S	%	+/-	TF	F%	Min	GP	G	A	Pts	PIM	PP	SH	GW	Min
99-2000	Cobourg Cougars	OPJHL	44	20	36	56	51	....	....	....	....	....	....	....	....	....	....	....	....	....	....	....	....	....	....
2000-01	Cobourg Cougars	OPJHL	28	15	21	36	46	....	....	....	....	....	....	....	....	....	....	....	....	....	....	....	....	....	....
2001-02	Clarkson Knights	ECAC	34	9	11	20	32	....	....	....	....	....	....	....	....	....	....	....	....	....	....	....	....	....	....
2002-03	Clarkson Knights	ECAC	33	13	20	33	65	....	....	....	....	....	....	....	....	....	....	....	....	....	....	....	....	....	....
2003-04	**Philadelphia**	**NHL**	**5**	**0**	**0**	**0**	**0**	**0**	**0**	**0**	**5**	**0.0**	**1**	**0**	**0.0**	**12:00**	....	....	....	....	....	....	....	....	....
	Philadelphia	AHL	55	8	24	32	63	....	....	....	....	....	....	....	....	....	12	0	1	1	17	....	....	....	....
2004-05	Philadelphia	AHL	69	5	19	24	32	....	....	....	....	....	....	....	....	....	18	0	5	5	10	....	....	....	....
	NHL Totals		**5**	**0**	**0**	**0**	**0**	**0**	**0**	**0**	**5**	**0.0**		**0**	**0.0**	**12:00**	....	....	....	....	....	....	....	....	....

ECAC First All-Star Team (2003)

Signed as a free agent by **Philadelphia**, July 24, 2003.

JONES, Ty

(JOHNZ, TIGH)

Right wing. Shoots right. 6'3", 218 lbs. Born, Richland, WA, February 22, 1979. Chicago's 2nd choice, 16th overall, in 1997 Entry Draft.

Season	Club	League	GP	G	A	Pts	PIM	PP	SH	GW	S	%	+/-	TF	F%	Min	GP	G	A	Pts	PIM	PP	SH	GW	Min
1993-94	Alaska Arctic Ice	AAHL	64	84	104	188	126	....	....	....	....	....	....	....	....	....	....	....	....	....	....	....	....	....	....
1994-95	Alaska All-Stars	AAHL	42	33	35	68	98	....	....	....	....	....	....	....	....	....	....	....	....	....	....	....	....	....	....
1995-96	Spokane Chiefs	WHL	34	1	0	1	77	....	....	....	....	....	....	....	....	....	3	0	0	0	6	....	....	....	....
1996-97	Spokane Chiefs	WHL	67	20	34	54	202	....	....	....	....	....	....	....	....	....	9	2	4	6	10	....	....	....	....
1997-98	Spokane Chiefs	WHL	60	36	48	84	161	....	....	....	....	....	....	....	....	....	18	2	14	16	35	....	....	....	....
1998-99	Spokane Chiefs	WHL	26	15	12	27	98	....	....	....	....	....	....	....	....	....	....	....	....	....	....	....	....	....	....
	Kamloops Blazers	WHL	20	3	16	19	84	....	....	....	....	....	....	....	....	....	14	5	3	8	22	....	....	....	....
	Chicago	**NHL**	**8**	**0**	**0**	**0**	**12**	**0**	**0**	**0**	**3**	**0.0**	**–1**	**0**	**0.0**	**7:53**	....	....	....	....	....	....	....	....	....
99-2000	Cleveland	IHL	10	1	1	2	34	....	....	....	....	....	....	....	....	....	....	....	....	....	....	....	....	....	....
	Florida Everblades	ECHL	48	11	26	37	81	....	....	....	....	....	....	....	....	....	5	1	1	2	17	....	....	....	....
2000-01	Norfolk Admirals	AHL	64	11	17	28	114	....	....	....	....	....	....	....	....	....	....	....	....	....	....	....	....	....	....
2001-02	Norfolk Admirals	AHL	55	6	14	20	172	....	....	....	....	....	....	....	....	....	4	0	0	0	2	....	....	....	....
2002-03	Anchorage Aces	WCHL	12	1	7	8	49	....	....	....	....	....	....	....	....	....	....	....	....	....	....	....	....	....	....
2003-04	Norfolk Admirals	AHL	37	4	5	9	93	....	....	....	....	....	....	....	....	....	....	....	....	....	....	....	....	....	....
	Florida	**NHL**	**6**	**0**	**0**	**0**	**7**	**0**	**0**	**0**	**1**	**0.0**	**0**	**0**	**0.0**	**3:05**	....	....	....	....	....	....	....	....	....
	San Antonio	AHL	2	0	0	0	2	....	....	....	....	....	....	....	....	....	....	....	....	....	....	....	....	....	....
2004-05			DID NOT PLAY																						
	NHL Totals		**14**	**0**	**0**	**0**	**19**	**0**	**0**	**0**	**4**	**0.0**		**0**	**0.0**	**5:50**	....	....	....	....	....	....	....	....	....

• Missed majority of 2002-03 season recovering from shoulder injury suffered during off-season training, July 15, 2002. Signed as a free agent by **Anchorage** (WCHL), February 21, 2003 with Chicago retaining NHL rights. Traded to **Florida** by **Chicago** for future considerations, March 2, 2004.

JONSSON, Hans

(YAWN-suhn, HANS)

Defense. Shoots left. 6'1", 205 lbs. Born, Jarved, Sweden, August 2, 1973. Pittsburgh's 11th choice, 286th overall, in 1993 Entry Draft.

Season	Club	League	GP	G	A	Pts	PIM	PP	SH	GW	S	%	+/-	TF	F%	Min	GP	G	A	Pts	PIM	PP	SH	GW	Min
1991-92	Husums IF	Sweden-2	13	4	6	10	10	....	....	....	....	....	....	....	....	....	....	....	....	....	....	....	....	....	....
	MoDo	Sweden	6	0	1	1	4	....	....	....	....	....	....	....	....	....	....	....	....	....	....	....	....	....	....
1992-93	MoDo	Sweden	40	2	2	4	24	....	....	....	....	....	....	....	....	....	3	0	1	1	2	....	....	....	....
1993-94	MoDo	Sweden	23	4	1	5	18	....	....	....	....	....	....	....	....	....	10	0	1	1	12	....	....	....	....
1994-95	MoDo	Sweden	39	4	6	10	30	....	....	....	....	....	....	....	....	....	....	....	....	....	....	....	....	....	....
1995-96	MoDo	Sweden	36	10	6	16	30	....	....	....	....	....	....	....	....	....	8	2	1	3	24	....	....	....	....
1996-97	MoDo	Sweden	27	7	5	12	18	....	....	....	....	....	....	....	....	....	....	....	....	....	....	....	....	....	....
1997-98	MoDo	Sweden	40	8	6	14	40	....	....	....	....	....	....	....	....	....	8	1	1	2	12	....	....	....	....
1998-99	MoDo	Sweden	41	3	4	7	40	....	....	....	....	....	....	....	....	....	13	2	4	6	22	....	....	....	....
99-2000	**Pittsburgh**	**NHL**	**68**	**3**	**11**	**14**	**12**	**0**	**1**	**1**	**49**	**6.1**	**–5**	**0**	**0.0**	**18:34**	**11**	**0**	**1**	**1**	**6**	**0**	**0**	**0**	**23:16**
2000-01	**Pittsburgh**	**NHL**	**58**	**4**	**18**	**22**	**22**	**2**	**0**	**0**	**44**	**9.1**	**11**	**0**	**0.0**	**18:27**	**16**	**0**	**0**	**0**	**8**	**0**	**0**	**0**	**17:11**
2001-02	**Pittsburgh**	**NHL**	**53**	**2**	**5**	**7**	**22**	**2**	**0**	**0**	**37**	**5.4**	**–12**	**0**	**0.0**	**18:12**	....	....	....	....	....	....	....	....	....
2002-03	**Pittsburgh**	**NHL**	**63**	**1**	**4**	**5**	**36**	**0**	**0**	**0**	**40**	**2.5**	**–23**	**2**	**0.0**	**17:04**	....	....	....	....	....	....	....	....	....
2003-04	MODO	Sweden	28	4	5	9	38	....	....	....	....	....	....	....	....	....	6	0	1	1	24	....	....	....	....
2004-05	MODO	Sweden	49	6	7	13	46	....	....	....	....	....	....	....	....	....	6	4	0	4	8	....	....	....	....
	NHL Totals		**242**	**10**	**38**	**48**	**92**	**4**	**1**	**1**	**170**	**5.9**		**2**	**0.0**	**18:04**	**27**	**0**	**1**	**1**	**14**	**0**	**0**	**0**	**19:39**

Signed as a free agent by **MODO** (Sweden), Septermber 26, 2003.

JONSSON, Kenny

(YAWN-suhn, KEHN-nee) **NYI**

Defense. Shoots left. 6'3", 217 lbs. Born, Angelholm, Sweden, October 6, 1974. Toronto's 1st choice, 12th overall, in 1993 Entry Draft.

Season	Club	League	GP	G	A	Pts	PIM	PP	SH	GW	S	%	+/-	TF	F%	Min	GP	G	A	Pts	PIM	PP	SH	GW	Min
1991-92	Rogle	Sweden-2	30	4	11	15	24	....	....	....	....	....	....	....	....	....	5	0	0	0	0	....	....	....	....
1992-93	Rogle Jr.	Swe-Jr.	2	1	2	3	25	....	....	....	....	....	....	....	....	....	....	....	....	....	....	....	....	....	....
	Rogle	Sweden	39	3	10	13	42	....	....	....	....	....	....	....	....	....	....	....	....	....	....	....	....	....	....
1993-94	Rogle	Sweden	36	4	13	17	40	....	....	....	....	....	....	....	....	....	3	1	1	2	2	....	....	....	....
	Sweden	Olympics	3	1	0	1	0	....	....	....	....	....	....	....	....	....	....	....	....	....	....	....	....	....	....
1994-95	Rogle	Sweden	8	3	1	4	20	....	....	....	....	....	....	....	....	....	....	....	....	....	....	....	....	....	....
	St. John's	AHL	10	2	5	7	2	....	....	....	....	....	....	....	....	....	....	....	....	....	....	....	....	....	....
	Toronto	**NHL**	**39**	**2**	**7**	**9**	**16**	**0**	**0**	**1**	**50**	**4.0**	**–8**	....	....	....	**4**	**0**	**0**	**0**	**0**	**0**	**0**	**0**	....
1995-96	**Toronto**	**NHL**	**50**	**4**	**22**	**26**	**22**	**3**	**0**	**1**	**90**	**4.4**	**12**	....	....	....	....	....	....	....	....	....	....	....	....
	NY Islanders	**NHL**	**16**	**0**	**4**	**4**	**10**	**0**	**0**	**0**	**40**	**0.0**	**–5**	....	....	....	....	....	....	....	....	....	....	....	....
1996-97	**NY Islanders**	**NHL**	**81**	**3**	**18**	**21**	**24**	**1**	**0**	**0**	**92**	**3.3**	**10**	....	....	....	....	....	....	....	....	....	....	....	....
1997-98	**NY Islanders**	**NHL**	**81**	**14**	**26**	**40**	**58**	**6**	**0**	**2**	**108**	**13.0**	**–2**	....	....	....	....	....	....	....	....	....	....	....	....
1998-99	**NY Islanders**	**NHL**	**63**	**8**	**18**	**26**	**34**	**6**	**0**	**0**	**91**	**8.8**	**–18**	**0**	**0.0**	**24:59**	....	....	....	....	....	....	....	....	....
99-2000	**NY Islanders**	**NHL**	**65**	**1**	**24**	**25**	**32**	**1**	**0**	**0**	**84**	**1.2**	**–15**	**0**	**0.0**	**24:29**	....	....	....	....	....	....	....	....	....
2000-01	**NY Islanders**	**NHL**	**65**	**8**	**21**	**29**	**30**	**5**	**0**	**0**	**91**	**8.8**	**–22**	**0**	**0.0**	**24:04**	....	....	....	....	....	....	....	....	....
2001-02	**NY Islanders**	**NHL**	**76**	**10**	**22**	**32**	**26**	**2**	**1**	**0**	**107**	**9.3**	**15**	**2**	**0.0**	**25:34**	**5**	**1**	**2**	**3**	**4**	**1**	**0**	**0**	**23:48**
	Sweden	Olympics	3	1	0	1	2	....	....	....	....	....	....	....	....	....	....	....	....	....	....	....	....	....	....
2002-03	**NY Islanders**	**NHL**	**71**	**8**	**18**	**26**	**24**	**3**	**1**	**0**	**108**	**7.4**	**–8**	**6**	**50.0**	**23:12**	**5**	**0**	**1**	**1**	**0**	**0**	**0**	**0**	**28:46**

			Regular Season														Playoffs								
Season	Club	League	GP	G	A	Pts	PIM	PP	SH	GW	S	%	+/-	TF	F%	Min	GP	G	A	Pts	PIM	PP	SH	GW	Min
2003-04	**NY Islanders**	**NHL**	**79**	**5**	**24**	**29**	**22**	**3**	**0**	**2**	**106**	**4.7**	**25**	**0**	**0.0**	**22:56**	**5**	**0**	**0**	**0**	**2**	**0**	**0**	**0**	**21:58**
2004-05	Rogle	Sweden-2	11	3	7	10	12	....	....	....	....	....	....	....	....	....	2	0	0	0	2	....	....	....	....
	NHL Totals		**686**	**63**	**204**	**267**	**298**	**30**	**2**	**6**	**967**	**6.5**		**8**	**37.5**	**24:11**	**19**	**1**	**3**	**4**	**6**	**1**	**0**	**0**	**24:51**

NHL All-Rookie Team (1995)

Traded to **NY Islanders** by **Toronto** with Sean Haggerty, Darby Hendrickson and Toronto's 1st round choice (Roberto Luongo) in 1997 Entry Draft for Wendel Clark, Mathieu Schneider and D.J. Smith, March 13, 1996. Signed as a free agent by **Rogle** (Sweden-2), December 20, 2004.

JOVANOVSKI, Ed
(joh-van-OHV-skee, EHD) **VAN.**

Defense. Shoots left. 6'2", 210 lbs. Born, Windsor, Ont., June 26, 1976. Florida's 1st choice, 1st overall, in 1994 Entry Draft.

Season	Club	League	GP	G	A	Pts	PIM	PP	SH	GW	S	%	+/-	TF	F%	Min	GP	G	A	Pts	PIM	PP	SH	GW	Min
1991-92	Windsor	OMHA	50	25	40	65	88	....	....	....	....	....	....	....	....	....	....	....	....	....	....	....	....	....	....
1992-93	Windsor Bulldogs	OHA-B	48	7	46	53	88	....	....	....	....	....	....	....	....	....	....	....	....	....	....	....	....	....	....
1993-94	Windsor Spitfires	OHL	62	15	36	51	221	....	....	....	....	....	....	....	....	....	4	0	0	0	15	....	....	....	....
1994-95	Windsor Spitfires	OHL	50	23	42	65	198	....	....	....	....	....	....	....	....	....	9	2	7	9	39	....	....	....	....
1995-96	**Florida**	**NHL**	**70**	**10**	**11**	**21**	**137**	**2**	**0**	**2**	**116**	**8.6**	**–3**	....	....	....	**22**	**1**	**8**	**9**	**52**	**0**	**0**	**0**	....
1996-97	**Florida**	**NHL**	**61**	**7**	**16**	**23**	**172**	**3**	**0**	**1**	**80**	**8.8**	**–1**	....	....	....	**5**	**0**	**0**	**0**	**4**	**0**	**0**	**0**	....
1997-98	**Florida**	**NHL**	**81**	**9**	**14**	**23**	**158**	**2**	**1**	**3**	**142**	**6.3**	**–12**	....	....	....	....	....	....	....	....	....	....	....	....
1998-99	**Florida**	**NHL**	**41**	**3**	**13**	**16**	**82**	**1**	**0**	**1**	**68**	**4.4**	**–4**	**0**	**0.0**	**22:35**	....	....	....	....	....	....	....	....	....
	Vancouver	**NHL**	**31**	**2**	**9**	**11**	**44**	**0**	**0**	**0**	**41**	**4.9**	**–5**	**0**	**0.0**	**21:16**	....	....	....	....	....	....	....	....	....
99-2000	**Vancouver**	**NHL**	**75**	**5**	**21**	**26**	**54**	**1**	**0**	**1**	**109**	**4.6**	**–3**	**0**	**0.0**	**24:03**	....	....	....	....	....	....	....	....	....
2000-01	**Vancouver**	**NHL**	**79**	**12**	**35**	**47**	**102**	**4**	**0**	**2**	**193**	**6.2**	**–1**	**0**	**0.0**	**24:57**	**4**	**1**	**1**	**2**	**0**	**0**	**0**	**0**	**25:54**
2001-02	**Vancouver**	**NHL**	**82**	**17**	**31**	**48**	**101**	**7**	**1**	**3**	**202**	**8.4**	**–7**	**0**	**0.0**	**25:11**	**6**	**1**	**4**	**5**	**8**	**1**	**0**	**0**	**25:48**
	Canada	Olympics	6	0	3	3	4	....	....	....	....	....	....	....	....	....	....	....	....	....	....	....	....	....	....
2002-03	**Vancouver**	**NHL**	**67**	**6**	**40**	**46**	**113**	**2**	**0**	**1**	**145**	**4.1**	**19**	**0**	**0.0**	**24:15**	**14**	**7**	**1**	**8**	**22**	**4**	**1**	**2**	**23:40**
2003-04	**Vancouver**	**NHL**	**56**	**7**	**16**	**23**	**64**	**2**	**0**	**1**	**143**	**4.9**	**2**	**0**	**0.0**	**23:11**	**7**	**0**	**4**	**4**	**6**	**0**	**0**	**0**	**26:36**
2004-05			DID NOT PLAY																						
	NHL Totals		**643**	**78**	**206**	**284**	**1027**	**24**	**2**	**15**	**1239**	**6.3**		**0**	**0.0**	**24:01**	**58**	**10**	**18**	**28**	**92**	**5**	**1**	**2**	**25:02**

OHL All-Rookie Team (1994) • OHL Second All-Star Team (1994) • OHL First All-Star Team (1995) • NHL All-Rookie Team (1996)

Played in NHL All-Star Game (2001, 2002, 2003)

Traded to **Vancouver** by **Florida** with Dave Gagner, Mike Brown, Kevin Weekes and Florida's 1st round choice (Nathan Smith) in 2000 Entry Draft for Pavel Bure, Bret Hedican, Brad Ference and Vancouver's 3rd round choice (Robert Fried) in 2000 Entry Draft, January 17, 1999.

KABERLE, Frantisek
(KA-buhr-lay, FRAN-tih-sehk) **CAR.**

Defense. Shoots left. 6'1", 190 lbs. Born, Kladno, Czech., November 8, 1973. Los Angeles' 3rd choice, 76th overall, in 1999 Entry Draft.

Season	Club	League	GP	G	A	Pts	PIM	PP	SH	GW	S	%	+/-	TF	F%	Min	GP	G	A	Pts	PIM	PP	SH	GW	Min
1991-92	Poldi Kladno	Czech	37	1	4	5	8	....	....	....	....	....	....	....	....	....	8	0	1	1	0	....	....	....	....
1992-93	Poldi Kladno	Czech	40	4	5	9	....	....	....	....	....	....	....	....	....	....	9	2	4	6	....	....	....	....	....
1993-94	HC Kladno	CzRep	41	4	16	20	....	....	....	....	....	....	....	....	....	....	11	1	1	2	....	....	....	....	....
1994-95	HC Kladno	CzRep	40	7	17	24	20	....	....	....	....	....	....	....	....	....	8	0	3	3	12	....	....	....	....
1995-96	MoDo	Sweden	40	5	7	12	34	....	....	....	....	....	....	....	....	....	8	0	1	1	0	....	....	....	....
1996-97	MoDo	Sweden	50	3	11	14	28	....	....	....	....	....	....	....	....	....	....	....	....	....	....	....	....	....	....
1997-98	MoDo	Sweden	46	5	4	9	22	....	....	....	....	....	....	....	....	....	9	1	1	2	4	....	....	....	....
1998-99	MoDo	Sweden	45	15	18	33	4	....	....	....	....	....	....	....	....	....	13	2	5	7	8	....	....	....	....
99-2000	**Los Angeles**	**NHL**	**37**	**0**	**9**	**9**	**4**	**0**	**0**	**0**	**41**	**0.0**	**3**	**0**	**0.0**	**17:04**	....	....	....	....	....	....	....	....	....
	Long Beach	IHL	18	2	8	10	8	....	....	....	....	....	....	....	....	....	....	....	....	....	....	....	....	....	....
	Atlanta	**NHL**	**14**	**1**	**6**	**7**	**6**	**0**	**1**	**0**	**35**	**2.9**	**–13**	**0**	**0.0**	**24:39**	....	....	....	....	....	....	....	....	....
	Lowell	AHL	4	0	2	2	0	....	....	....	....	....	....	....	....	....	....	....	....	....	....	....	....	....	....
2000-01	**Atlanta**	**NHL**	**51**	**4**	**11**	**15**	**18**	**1**	**0**	**1**	**99**	**4.0**	**11**	**1**	**0.0**	**22:17**	....	....	....	....	....	....	....	....	....
2001-02	**Atlanta**	**NHL**	**61**	**5**	**20**	**25**	**24**	**1**	**0**	**0**	**82**	**6.1**	**–11**	**0**	**0.0**	**21:35**	....	....	....	....	....	....	....	....	....
2002-03	**Atlanta**	**NHL**	**79**	**7**	**19**	**26**	**32**	**3**	**1**	**2**	**105**	**6.7**	**–19**	**0**	**0.0**	**21:57**	....	....	....	....	....	....	....	....	....
2003-04	**Atlanta**	**NHL**	**67**	**3**	**26**	**29**	**30**	**2**	**0**	**1**	**94**	**3.2**	**2**	**2**	**50.0**	**23:20**	....	....	....	....	....	....	....	....	....
2004-05	HC Rabat Kladno	CzRep	22	5	11	16	34	....	....	....	....	....	....	....	....	....	....	....	....	....	....	....	....	....	....
	MODO	Sweden	8	2	2	4	0	....	....	....	....	....	....	....	....	....	6	1	0	1	27	....	....	....	....
	NHL Totals		**309**	**20**	**91**	**111**	**114**	**7**	**2**	**4**	**456**	**4.4**		**3**	**33.3**	**21:46**	....	....	....	....	....	....	....	....	....

Traded to **Atlanta** by **Los Angeles** with Donald Audette for Kelly Buchberger and Nelson Emerson, March 13, 2000. Signed as a free agent by **Carolina**, July 15, 2004. Signed as a free agent by **Kladno** (CzRep), September 17, 2004. Signed as a free agent by **MODO** (Sweden), January 31, 2005.

KABERLE, Tomas
(KA-buhr-lay, TAW-mas) **TOR.**

Defense. Shoots left. 6'1", 198 lbs. Born, Rakovnik, Czech., March 2, 1978. Toronto's 13th choice, 204th overall, in 1996 Entry Draft.

Season	Club	League	GP	G	A	Pts	PIM	PP	SH	GW	S	%	+/-	TF	F%	Min	GP	G	A	Pts	PIM	PP	SH	GW	Min
1994-95	HC Kladno Jr.	CzRep-Jr.	37	7	10	17	....	....	....	....	....	....	....	....	....	....	....	....	....	....	....	....	....	....	....
	HC Kladno	CzRep	4	0	1	1	0	....	....	....	....	....	....	....	....	....	....	....	....	....	....	....	....	....	....
1995-96	Kladno Jr.	CzRep-Jr.	23	6	13	19	....	....	....	....	....	....	....	....	....	....	....	....	....	....	....	....	....	....	....
	HC Poldi Kladno	CzRep	23	0	1	1	2	....	....	....	....	....	....	....	....	....	2	0	0	0	0	....	....	....	....
1996-97	HC Poldi Kladno	CzRep	49	0	5	5	26	....	....	....	....	....	....	....	....	....	3	0	0	0	0	....	....	....	....
1997-98	Kladno	CzRep	47	4	19	23	12	....	....	....	....	....	....	....	....	....	....	....	....	....	....	....	....	....	....
	St. John's	AHL	2	0	0	0	0	....	....	....	....	....	....	....	....	....	....	....	....	....	....	....	....	....	....
1998-99	**Toronto**	**NHL**	**57**	**4**	**18**	**22**	**12**	**0**	**0**	**2**	**71**	**5.6**	**3**	**0**	**0.0**	**18:42**	**14**	**0**	**3**	**3**	**2**	**0**	**0**	**0**	**17:10**
99-2000	**Toronto**	**NHL**	**82**	**7**	**33**	**40**	**24**	**2**	**0**	**0**	**82**	**8.5**	**3**	**0**	**0.0**	**22:55**	**12**	**1**	**4**	**5**	**0**	**0**	**0**	**1**	**23:01**
2000-01	**Toronto**	**NHL**	**82**	**6**	**39**	**45**	**24**	**0**	**0**	**1**	**96**	**6.3**	**10**	**2**	**0.0**	**22:41**	**11**	**1**	**3**	**4**	**0**	**0**	**0**	**1**	**21:33**
2001-02	Kladno	CzRep	9	1	7	8	4	....	....	....	....	....	....	....	....	....	....	....	....	....	....	....	....	....	....
	Toronto	**NHL**	**69**	**10**	**29**	**39**	**2**	**5**	**0**	**3**	**85**	**11.8**	**5**	**2**	**100.0**	**25:00**	**20**	**2**	**8**	**10**	**16**	**0**	**0**	**0**	**28:40**
	Czech Republic	Olympics	4	0	1	1	2	....	....	....	....	....	....	....	....	....	....	....	....	....	....	....	....	....	....
2002-03	**Toronto**	**NHL**	**82**	**11**	**36**	**47**	**30**	**4**	**1**	**2**	**119**	**9.2**	**20**	**3**	**66.7**	**24:50**	**7**	**2**	**1**	**3**	**0**	**1**	**0**	**1**	**30:04**
2003-04	**Toronto**	**NHL**	**71**	**3**	**28**	**31**	**18**	**0**	**0**	**1**	**88**	**3.4**	**16**	**2**	**0.0**	**23:12**	**13**	**0**	**3**	**3**	**6**	**0**	**0**	**0**	**20:16**
2004-05	HC Rabat Kladno	CzRep	49	8	31	39	38	....	....	....	....	....	....	....	....	....	7	1	0	1	0	....	....	....	....
	NHL Totals		**443**	**41**	**183**	**224**	**110**	**11**	**1**	**9**	**541**	**7.6**		**9**	**44.4**	**23:03**	**77**	**6**	**22**	**28**	**24**	**1**	**0**	**3**	**23:23**

Played in NHL All-Star Game (2002)

Signed as a restricted free agent by **Kladno** (CzRep) with **Toronto** retaining NHL rights, September 29, 2001. Signed as a free agent by **Kladno** (CzRep), September 17, 2004.

KALININ, Dmitri
(kah-LIHN-ihn, DIH-mih-TREE) **BUF.**

Defense. Shoots left. 6'3", 206 lbs. Born, Chelyabinsk, USSR, July 22, 1980. Buffalo's 1st choice, 18th overall, in 1998 Entry Draft.

Season	Club	League	GP	G	A	Pts	PIM	PP	SH	GW	S	%	+/-	TF	F%	Min	GP	G	A	Pts	PIM	PP	SH	GW	Min
1995-96	Chelyabinsk	CIS	20	0	3	3	10	....	....	....	....	....	....	....	....	....	....	....	....	....	....	....	....	....	....
1996-97	Yunior-T Kurgan	Russia-3	20	0	0	0	10	....	....	....	....	....	....	....	....	....	....	....	....	....	....	....	....	....	....
	Chelyabinsk	Russia	2	0	0	0	0	....	....	....	....	....	....	....	....	....	2	0	0	0	0	....	....	....	....
1997-98	Chelyabinsk	Russia	26	0	2	2	24	....	....	....	....	....	....	....	....	....	....	....	....	....	....	....	....	....	....
1998-99	Moncton Wildcats	QMJHL	39	7	18	25	44	....	....	....	....	....	....	....	....	....	4	1	1	2	0	....	....	....	....
	Rochester	AHL	3	0	1	1	14	....	....	....	....	....	....	....	....	....	7	0	0	0	6	....	....	....	....
99-2000	**Buffalo**	**NHL**	**4**	**0**	**0**	**0**	**4**	**0**	**0**	**0**	**3**	**0.0**	**0**	**0**	**0.0**	**16:53**	....	....	....	....	....	....	....	....	....
	Rochester	AHL	75	2	19	21	52	....	....	....	....	....	....	....	....	....	21	2	9	11	8	....	....	....	....
2000-01	**Buffalo**	**NHL**	**79**	**4**	**18**	**22**	**38**	**2**	**0**	**0**	**88**	**4.5**	**–2**	**1**	**100.0**	**19:50**	**13**	**0**	**2**	**2**	**4**	**0**	**0**	**0**	**20:05**
2001-02	**Buffalo**	**NHL**	**58**	**2**	**11**	**13**	**26**	**0**	**0**	**0**	**67**	**3.0**	**–6**	**0**	**0.0**	**18:03**	....	....	....	....	....	....	....	....	....
2002-03	Rochester	AHL	1	0	0	0	0	....	....	....	....	....	....	....	....	....	....	....	....	....	....	....	....	....	....
	Buffalo	**NHL**	**65**	**8**	**13**	**21**	**57**	**3**	**1**	**0**	**83**	**9.6**	**–7**	**0**	**0.0**	**21:41**	....	....	....	....	....	....	....	....	....
2003-04	**Buffalo**	**NHL**	**77**	**10**	**24**	**34**	**42**	**2**	**1**	**4**	**118**	**8.5**	**0**	**0**	**0.0**	**23:06**	....	....	....	....	....	....	....	....	....
2004-05	Magnitogorsk	Russia	48	2	8	10	14	....	....	....	....	....	....	....	....	....	5	0	0	0	2	....	....	....	....
	NHL Totals		**283**	**24**	**66**	**90**	**167**	**7**	**2**	**4**	**359**	**6.7**		**1**	**100.0**	**20:44**	**13**	**0**	**2**	**2**	**4**	**0**	**0**	**0**	**20:05**

AHL All-Rookie Team (2000)

Signed as a free agent by **Magnitogorsk** (Russia), September 25, 2004.

KANE, Boyd

(KAYN, BOIYD) **WSH.**

Left wing. Shoots left. 6'2", 218 lbs. Born, Swift Current, Sask., April 18, 1978. NY Rangers' 4th choice, 114th overall, in 1998 Entry Draft.

			Regular Season														Playoffs								
Season	Club	League	GP	G	A	Pts	PIM	PP	SH	GW	S	%	+/-	TF	F%	Min	GP	G	A	Pts	PIM	PP	SH	GW	Min
1994-95	Regina Pats	WHL	25	6	5	11	6										4	0	0	0	0				
1995-96	Regina Pats	WHL	72	21	42	63	155										11	5	7	12	12				
1996-97	Regina Pats	WHL	66	25	50	75	154										5	1	1	2	15				
1997-98	Regina Pats	WHL	68	48	45	93	133										9	5	7	12	29				
1998-99	Hartford	AHL	56	3	5	8	23																		
	Charlotte	ECHL	12	5	6	11	14																		
99-2000	Charlotte	ECHL	47	10	19	29	110																		
	Hartford	AHL	8	0	0	0	9																		
	Binghamton	UHL	3	0	2	2	4										1	0	0	0	0				
2000-01	Charlotte	ECHL	12	9	8	17	6																		
	Hartford	AHL	56	11	17	28	81										5	2	0	2	2				
2001-02	Hartford	AHL	78	17	22	39	193										10	1	2	3	50				
2002-03	Springfield	AHL	72	15	22	37	121										6	3	1	4	8				
2003-04	**Philadelphia**	**NHL**	**7**	**0**	**0**	**0**	**7**	**0**	**0**	**0**	**6**	**0.0**	**–4**	**3**	**33.3**	**9:56**									
	Philadelphia	AHL	73	13	22	35	177										12	0	1	1	39				
2004-05	Philadelphia	AHL	58	9	15	24	112										21	0	7	7	28				
	NHL Totals		**7**	**0**	**0**	**0**	**7**	**0**	**0**	**0**	**6**	**0.0**		**3**	**33.3**	**9:56**									

• Re-entered NHL Entry Draft. Originally Pittsburgh's 3rd choice, 72nd overall, in 1996 Entry Draft.
Traded to **Tampa Bay** by **NY Rangers** for Gordie Dwyer, October 10, 2002. Signed as a free agent by **Philadelphia**, July 14, 2003.

KAPANEN, Niko

(KA-pah-nehn, NEE-KOH) **DAL.**

Center. Shoots left. 5'9", 180 lbs. Born, Hameenlinna, Finland, April 29, 1978. Dallas' 5th choice, 173rd overall, in 1998 Entry Draft.

1993-94	HPK Jr.	Finland-Jr.	31	17	33	50	34																		
1994-95	HPK U18	Fin-U18	37	19	44	63	40																		
1995-96	HPK U18	Fin-U18	10	6	6	12	8																		
	HPK Jr.	Finland-Jr.	26	15	22	37	34																		
	HPK Hameenlinna	Finland	7	1	0	1	0																		
1996-97	HPK Jr.	Finland-Jr.	5	1	7	8	2										2	0	1	1	2				
	HPK Hameenlinna	Finland	41	6	9	15	12										10	4	5	9	2				
	HPK Hameenlinna	EuroHL	6	3	0	3	4										1	0	0	0	0				
1997-98	HPK Jr.	Finland-Jr.	2	1	1	2	0																		
	HPK Hameenlinna	Finland	48	8	18	26	44																		
1998-99	HPK Hameenlinna	Finland	53	14	29	43	49										8	3	4	7	4				
99-2000	HPK Hameenlinna	Finland	53	20	28	48	40										8	1	9	10	4				
2000-01	TPS Turku	Finland	56	11	21	32	20										10	2	1	3	4				
2001-02	**Dallas**	**NHL**	**9**	**0**	**1**	**1**	**2**	**0**	**0**	**0**	**3**	**0.0**	**–1**	**59**	**40.7**	**9:44**									
	Utah Grizzlies	AHL	59	13	28	41	40										5	2	1	3	0				
2002-03	**Dallas**	**NHL**	**82**	**5**	**29**	**34**	**44**	**0**	**1**	**1**	**80**	**6.3**	**25**	**1111**	**47.5**	**14:39**	**12**	**4**	**3**	**7**	**12**	**0**	**1**	**0**	**16:03**
2003-04	**Dallas**	**NHL**	**67**	**1**	**5**	**6**	**16**	**0**	**0**	**0**	**57**	**1.8**	**–15**	**619**	**47.7**	**11:30**	**1**	**1**	**0**	**1**	**0**	**0**	**0**	**0**	**6:51**
2004-05	EV Zug	Swiss	44	10	33	43	24										9	2	5	7	35				
	NHL Totals		**158**	**6**	**35**	**41**	**62**	**0**	**1**	**1**	**140**	**4.3**		**1789**	**47.3**	**13:02**	**13**	**5**	**3**	**8**	**12**	**0**	**1**	**0**	**15:21**

Signed as a free agent by **Zug** (Swiss), June 9, 2004.

KAPANEN, Sami

(KA-pah-nehn, SA-mee) **PHI.**

Right wing. Shoots left. 5'10", 185 lbs. Born, Vantaa, Finland, June 14, 1973. Hartford's 4th choice, 87th overall, in 1995 Entry Draft.

1989-90	KalPa Kuopio Jr.	Finland-Jr.	30	14	13	27	4																		
1990-91	KalPa Kuopio Jr.	Finland-Jr.	31	9	27	36	10																		
	KalPa Kuopio	Finland	14	1	2	3	2										8	2	1	3	2				
1991-92	KalPa Kuopio Jr.	Finland-Jr.	8	1	3	4	12																		
	KalPa Kuopio	Finland	42	15	10	25	8																		
1992-93	KalPa Kuopio Jr.	Finland-Jr.	7	11	14	25	2																		
	KalPa Kuopio	Finland	37	4	17	21	12																		
1993-94	KalPa Kuopio	Finland	48	23	32	55	16																		
	Finland	Olympics	8	1	0	1	2																		
1994-95	HIFK Helsinki	Finland	49	14	28	42	42										3	0	0	0	0				
1995-96	**Hartford**	**NHL**	**35**	**5**	**4**	**9**	**6**	**0**	**0**	**0**	**46**	**10.9**	**0**												
	Springfield	AHL	28	14	17	31	4										3	1	2	3	0				
1996-97	**Hartford**	**NHL**	**45**	**13**	**12**	**25**	**2**	**3**	**0**	**2**	**82**	**15.9**	**6**												
1997-98	**Carolina**	**NHL**	**81**	**26**	**37**	**63**	**16**	**4**	**0**	**5**	**190**	**13.7**	**9**												
	Finland	Olympics	6	0	1	1	0																		
1998-99	**Carolina**	**NHL**	**81**	**24**	**35**	**59**	**10**	**5**	**0**	**7**	**254**	**9.4**	**–1**	**10**	**50.0**	**19:25**	**5**	**1**	**1**	**2**	**0**	**0**	**0**	**0**	**19:09**
99-2000	**Carolina**	**NHL**	**76**	**24**	**24**	**48**	**12**	**7**	**0**	**5**	**229**	**10.5**	**10**	**2**	**50.0**	**19:53**									
2000-01	**Carolina**	**NHL**	**82**	**20**	**37**	**57**	**24**	**7**	**0**	**4**	**223**	**9.0**	**–12**	**6**	**16.7**	**18:56**	**6**	**2**	**3**	**5**	**0**	**1**	**0**	**0**	**20:13**
2001-02	**Carolina**	**NHL**	**77**	**27**	**42**	**69**	**23**	**11**	**0**	**4**	**248**	**10.9**	**9**	**7**	**14.3**	**20:38**	**23**	**1**	**8**	**9**	**6**	**0**	**0**	**0**	**20:03**
	Finland	Olympics	4	1	2	3	4																		
2002-03	**Carolina**	**NHL**	**43**	**6**	**12**	**18**	**12**	**3**	**0**	**1**	**108**	**5.6**	**–17**	**16**	**31.3**	**18:37**									
	Philadelphia	**NHL**	**28**	**4**	**9**	**13**	**6**	**2**	**0**	**1**	**81**	**4.9**	**–1**	**5**	**40.0**	**19:21**	**13**	**4**	**3**	**7**	**6**	**2**	**0**	**0**	**20:12**
2003-04	**Philadelphia**	**NHL**	**74**	**12**	**18**	**30**	**14**	**0**	**1**	**2**	**149**	**8.1**	**9**	**18**	**44.4**	**16:31**	**18**	**3**	**7**	**10**	**6**	**0**	**1**	**1**	**17:41**
2004-05	KalPa Kuopio	Finland-2	10	6	3	9	2										9	5	3	8	4				
	NHL Totals		**622**	**161**	**230**	**391**	**125**	**42**	**1**	**31**	**1610**	**10.0**		**64**	**35.9**	**19:04**	**65**	**11**	**22**	**33**	**18**	**3**	**1**	**1**	**19:22**

Played in NHL All-Star Game (2000, 2002)

Transferred to **Carolina** after **Hartford** franchise relocated, June 25, 1997. Traded to **Philadelphia** by **Carolina** with Ryan Bast for Pavel Brendl and Bruno St. Jacques, February 7, 2003. Signed as a free agent by **KalPa** (Finland-2), November 17, 2004.

KARIYA, Paul

(kah-REE-ah, PAWL) **NSH.**

Left wing. Shoots left. 5'10", 176 lbs. Born, Vancouver, B.C., October 16, 1974. Anaheim's 1st choice, 4th overall, in 1993 Entry Draft.

1990-91	Penticton	BCJHL	54	45	67	112	8																		
1991-92	Penticton	BCJHL	40	46	86	132	18																		
1992-93	U. of Maine	H-East	39	25	*75	*100	12																		
1993-94	U. of Maine	H-East	12	8	16	24	4																		
	Canada	Nat-Tm	23	7	34	41	2																		
	Canada	Olympics	8	3	4	7	2																		
1994-95	**Anaheim**	**NHL**	**47**	**18**	**21**	**39**	**4**	**7**	**1**	**3**	**134**	**13.4**	**–17**												
1995-96	**Anaheim**	**NHL**	**82**	**50**	**58**	**108**	**20**	**20**	**3**	**9**	**349**	**14.3**	**9**												
1996-97	**Anaheim**	**NHL**	**69**	**44**	**55**	**99**	**6**	**15**	**3**	**10**	**340**	**12.9**	**36**				**11**	**7**	**6**	**13**	**4**	**4**	**0**	**1**	
1997-98	**Anaheim**	**NHL**	**22**	**17**	**14**	**31**	**23**	**3**	**0**	**2**	**103**	**16.5**	**12**												
1998-99	**Anaheim**	**NHL**	**82**	**39**	**62**	**101**	**40**	**11**	**2**	**4**	**429**	**9.1**	**17**	**91**	**48.4**	**25:32**	**3**	**1**	**3**	**4**	**0**	**0**	**0**	**0**	**26:03**
99-2000	**Anaheim**	**NHL**	**74**	**42**	**44**	**86**	**24**	**11**	**3**	**3**	**324**	**13.0**	**22**	**99**	**39.4**	**24:22**									
2000-01	**Anaheim**	**NHL**	**66**	**33**	**34**	**67**	**20**	**18**	**3**	**3**	**230**	**14.3**	**–9**	**149**	**44.3**	**23:02**									
2001-02	**Anaheim**	**NHL**	**82**	**32**	**25**	**57**	**28**	**11**	**0**	**8**	**289**	**11.1**	**–15**	**94**	**41.5**	**22:13**									
	Canada	Olympics	6	3	1	4	0																		
2002-03	**Anaheim**	**NHL**	**82**	**25**	**56**	**81**	**48**	**11**	**1**	**2**	**257**	**9.7**	**–3**	**39**	**30.8**	**20:17**	**21**	**6**	**6**	**12**	**6**	**0**	**0**	**1**	**21:15**
2003-04	**Colorado**	**NHL**	**51**	**11**	**25**	**36**	**22**	**5**	**1**	**1**	**110**	**10.0**	**–5**	**18**	**27.8**	**18:37**	**1**	**0**	**1**	**1**	**0**	**0**	**0**	**0**	**16:00**
2004-05		DID NOT PLAY																							
	NHL Totals		**657**	**311**	**394**	**705**	**235**	**112**	**17**	**45**	**2565**	**12.1**		**490**	**41.8**	**22:33**	**36**	**14**	**16**	**30**	**10**	**4**	**0**	**2**	**21:37**

Hockey East First All-Star Team (1993) • Hockey East Rookie of the Year (1993) • Hockey East Player of the Year (1993) • NCAA East First All-American Team (1993) • NCAA Championship All-Tournament Team (1993) • Hobey Baker Memorial Award (Top U.S. Collegiate Player) (1993) • NHL All-Rookie Team (1995) • Lady Byng Trophy (1996, 1997) • NHL First All-Star Team (1996, 1997, 1999) • NHL Second All-Star Team (2000, 2003)

Played in NHL All-Star Game (1996, 1997, 1999, 2000, 2001, 2002, 2003)

• Missed majority of 1997-98 season after failing to come to contract terms with **Anaheim** and recovering from head injury suffered in game vs. San Jose, February 1, 1998. Signed as a free agent by **Colorado**, July 3, 2003. Signed as a free agent by **Nashville**, August 5, 2005.

KARIYA, Steve

(kah-REE-ah, STEEV)

Left wing. Shoots right. 5'8", 170 lbs. Born, North Vancouver, B.C., December 22, 1977.

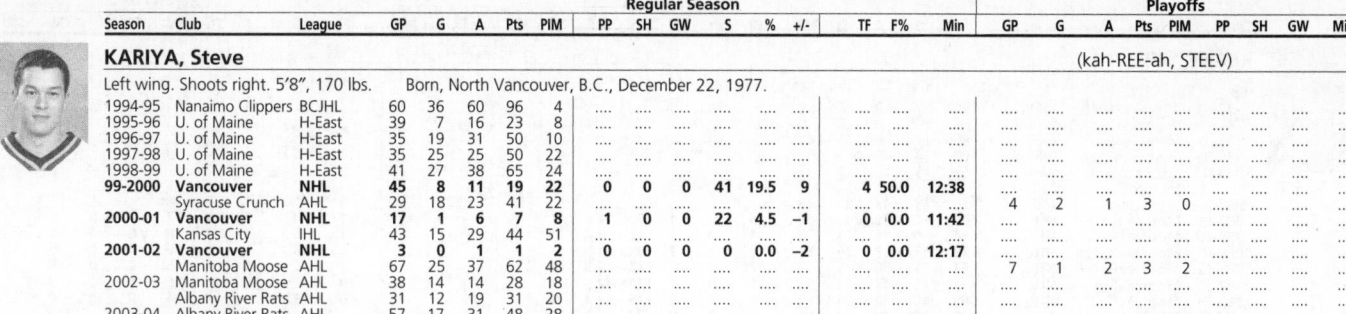

			Regular Season														Playoffs								
Season	Club	League	GP	G	A	Pts	PIM	PP	SH	GW	S	%	+/-	TF	F%	Min	GP	G	A	Pts	PIM	PP	SH	GW	Min
1994-95	Nanaimo Clippers	BCJHL	60	36	60	96	4	....	....	....	....	....	....	....	....	....	....	....	....	....	....	....	....	....	....
1995-96	U. of Maine	H-East	39	7	16	23	8	....	....	....	....	....	....	....	....	....	....	....	....	....	....	....	....	....	....
1996-97	U. of Maine	H-East	35	19	31	50	10	....	....	....	....	....	....	....	....	....	....	....	....	....	....	....	....	....	....
1997-98	U. of Maine	H-East	35	25	25	50	22	....	....	....	....	....	....	....	....	....	....	....	....	....	....	....	....	....	....
1998-99	U. of Maine	H-East	41	27	38	65	24	....	....	....	....	....	....	....	....	....	....	....	....	....	....	....	....	....	....
99-2000	**Vancouver**	**NHL**	**45**	**8**	**11**	**19**	**22**	**0**	**0**	**0**	**41**	**19.5**	**9**	**4**	**50.0**	**12:38**	....	....	....	....	....	....	....	....	....
	Syracuse Crunch	AHL	29	18	23	41	22	....	....	....	....	....	....	....	....	....	4	2	1	3	0	....	....	....	....
2000-01	**Vancouver**	**NHL**	**17**	**1**	**6**	**7**	**8**	**1**	**0**	**0**	**22**	**4.5**	**–1**	**0**	**0.0**	**11:42**	....	....	....	....	....	....	....	....	....
	Kansas City	IHL	43	15	29	44	51	....	....	....	....	....	....	....	....	....	....	....	....	....	....	....	....	....	....
2001-02	**Vancouver**	**NHL**	**3**	**0**	**1**	**1**	**2**	**0**	**0**	**0**	**0**	**0.0**	**–2**	**0**	**0.0**	**12:17**	....	....	....	....	....	....	....	....	....
	Manitoba Moose	AHL	67	25	37	62	48	....	....	....	....	....	....	....	....	....	7	1	2	3	2	....	....	....	....
2002-03	Manitoba Moose	AHL	38	14	14	28	18	....	....	....	....	....	....	....	....	....	....	....	....	....	....	....	....	....	....
	Albany River Rats	AHL	31	12	19	31	20	....	....	....	....	....	....	....	....	....	....	....	....	....	....	....	....	....	....
2003-04	Albany River Rats	AHL	57	17	31	48	28	....	....	....	....	....	....	....	....	....	....	....	....	....	....	....	....	....	....
2004-05	Ilves Tampere	Finland	55	24	*35	*59	32	....	....	....	....	....	....	....	....	....	7	3	2	5	4	....	....	....	....
	NHL Totals		**65**	**9**	**18**	**27**	**32**	**1**	**0**	**0**	**63**	**14.3**		**4**	**50.0**	**12:23**	....	....	....	....	....	....	....	....	....

Hockey East First All-Star Team (1999) • NCAA East First All-American Team (1999)

Signed as a free agent by **Vancouver**, April 21, 1999. Traded to **New Jersey** by **Vancouver** for Mikko Jokela, January 24, 2003. Signed as a free agent by **Ilves** (Finland), August 9, 2004.

KARPOVTSEV, Alexander

(kar-POHV-tzehv, al-ehx-AN-duhr) **FLA.**

Defense. Shoots right. 6'3", 221 lbs. Born, Moscow, USSR, April 7, 1970. Quebec's 7th choice, 158th overall, in 1990 Entry Draft.

Season	Club	League	GP	G	A	Pts	PIM	PP	SH	GW	S	%	+/-	TF	F%	Min	GP	G	A	Pts	PIM	PP	SH	GW	Min
1989-90	Dynamo Moscow	USSR	35	1	1	2	27	....	....	....	....	....	....	....	....	....	....	....	....	....	....	....	....	....	....
1990-91	Dynamo Moscow	USSR	40	0	5	5	15	....	....	....	....	....	....	....	....	....	....	....	....	....	....	....	....	....	....
1991-92	Dynamo Moscow	CIS	35	4	2	6	26	....	....	....	....	....	....	....	....	....	....	....	....	....	....	....	....	....	....
1992-93	Dynamo Moscow	CIS	36	3	11	14	100	....	....	....	....	....	....	....	....	....	7	2	1	3	0	....	....	....	....
1993-94♦	**NY Rangers**	**NHL**	**67**	**3**	**15**	**18**	**58**	**1**	**0**	**1**	**78**	**3.8**	**12**	....	....	....	**17**	**0**	**4**	**4**	**12**	**0**	**0**	**0**	....
1994-95	Dynamo Moscow	CIS	13	0	2	2	10	....	....	....	....	....	....	....	....	....	....	....	....	....	....	....	....	....	....
	NY Rangers	**NHL**	**47**	**4**	**8**	**12**	**30**	**1**	**0**	**1**	**82**	**4.9**	**–4**	....	....	....	**8**	**1**	**0**	**1**	**0**	**0**	**0**	**0**	....
1995-96	**NY Rangers**	**NHL**	**40**	**2**	**16**	**18**	**26**	**1**	**0**	**1**	**71**	**2.8**	**12**	....	....	....	**6**	**0**	**1**	**1**	**4**	**0**	**0**	**0**	....
1996-97	**NY Rangers**	**NHL**	**77**	**9**	**29**	**38**	**59**	**6**	**1**	**0**	**84**	**10.7**	**1**	....	....	....	**13**	**1**	**3**	**4**	**20**	**1**	**0**	**0**	....
1997-98	**NY Rangers**	**NHL**	**47**	**3**	**7**	**10**	**38**	**1**	**0**	**1**	**46**	**6.5**	**–1**	....	....	....	....	....	....	....	....	....	....	....	....
1998-99	**NY Rangers**	**NHL**	**2**	**1**	**0**	**1**	**0**	**0**	**0**	**0**	**4**	**25.0**	**1**	**0**	**0.0**	**22:38**	....	....	....	....	....	....	....	....	....
	Toronto	**NHL**	**56**	**2**	**25**	**27**	**52**	**1**	**0**	**1**	**61**	**3.3**	**38**	**0**	**0.0**	**20:58**	**14**	**1**	**3**	**4**	**12**	**1**	**0**	**0**	**19:44**
99-2000	**Toronto**	**NHL**	**69**	**3**	**14**	**17**	**54**	**3**	**0**	**0**	**51**	**5.9**	**9**	**2**	**0.0**	**20:14**	**11**	**0**	**3**	**3**	**4**	**0**	**0**	**0**	**21:04**
2000-01	Dynamo Moscow	Russia	5	0	1	1	0	....	....	....	....	....	....	....	....	....	....	....	....	....	....	....	....	....	....
	Chicago	**NHL**	**53**	**2**	**13**	**15**	**39**	**1**	**0**	**0**	**52**	**3.8**	**–4**	**0**	**0.0**	**20:28**	....	....	....	....	....	....	....	....	....
2001-02	**Chicago**	**NHL**	**65**	**1**	**9**	**10**	**40**	**0**	**1**	**0**	**40**	**2.5**	**10**	**3**	**33.3**	**20:40**	**5**	**1**	**0**	**1**	**0**	**0**	**0**	**1**	**20:53**
2002-03	**Chicago**	**NHL**	**40**	**4**	**10**	**14**	**12**	**3**	**0**	**1**	**36**	**11.1**	**–8**	**0**	**0.0**	**21:40**	....	....	....	....	....	....	....	....	....
2003-04	**Chicago**	**NHL**	**24**	**0**	**7**	**7**	**14**	**0**	**0**	**0**	**31**	**0.0**	**–17**	**0**	**0.0**	**19:56**	....	....	....	....	....	....	....	....	....
	NY Islanders	**NHL**	**3**	**0**	**1**	**1**	**4**	**0**	**0**	**0**	**3**	**0.0**	**1**	**0**	**0.0**	**10:54**	....	....	....	....	....	....	....	....	....
2004-05	Sibir Novosibirsk	Russia	5	0	1	1	16	....	....	....	....	....	....	....	....	....	....	....	....	....	....	....	....	....	....
	Yaroslavl	Russia	33	2	5	7	45	....	....	....	....	....	....	....	....	....	9	0	0	0	0	....	....	....	....
	NHL Totals		**590**	**34**	**154**	**188**	**426**	**18**	**2**	**6**	**639**	**5.3**		**5**	**20.0**	**20:35**	**74**	**4**	**14**	**18**	**52**	**2**	**0**	**1**	**20:25**

Traded to **NY Rangers** by **Quebec** for Mike Hurlbut, September 7, 1993. Traded to **Toronto** by **NY Rangers** with NY Rangers' 4th round choice (Mirko Murovic) in 1999 Entry Draft for Mathieu Schneider, October 14, 1998. Traded to **Chicago** by **Toronto** with Toronto's 4th round choice (Vladimir Gusev) in 2001 Entry Draft for Bryan McCabe, October 2, 2000. • Missed majority of 2002-03 season recovering from ankle (November 5, 2002 vs. Detroit) and cheekbone (February 20, 2003 vs. Phoenix) injuries. • Missed majority of 2003-04 season recovering from ankle injury suffered in game vs. San Jose, November 26, 2003. Traded to **NY Islanders** by **Chicago** for NY Islanders' 4th round choice (Niklas Hjalmarsson) in 2005 Entry Draft, March 9, 2004. Signed as a free agent by **Florida**, July 14, 2004. Signed as a free agent by **Novosibirsk** (Russia), August 21, 2004. Signed as a free agent by **Yaroslavl** (Russia), November, 2004.

KASPARAITIS, Darius

(KAZ-puhr-IGH-tihz, DAIR-ee-uhs) **NYR**

Defense. Shoots left. 5'11", 215 lbs. Born, Elektrenai, USSR, October 16, 1972. NY Islanders' 1st choice, 5th overall, in 1992 Entry Draft.

Season	Club	League	GP	G	A	Pts	PIM	PP	SH	GW	S	%	+/-	TF	F%	Min	GP	G	A	Pts	PIM	PP	SH	GW	Min
1988-89	Dynamo Moscow	USSR	3	0	0	0	0	....	....	....	....	....	....	....	....	....	....	....	....	....	....	....	....	....	....
1989-90	Dynamo Moscow	USSR	1	0	0	0	0	....	....	....	....	....	....	....	....	....	....	....	....	....	....	....	....	....	....
1990-91	Dynamo Moscow	USSR	17	0	1	1	10	....	....	....	....	....	....	....	....	....	....	....	....	....	....	....	....	....	....
1991-92	Dynamo Moscow	CIS	31	2	10	12	14	....	....	....	....	....	....	....	....	....	....	....	....	....	....	....	....	....	....
	Russia	Olympics	8	0	2	2	2	....	....	....	....	....	....	....	....	....	....	....	....	....	....	....	....	....	....
1992-93	Dynamo Moscow	CIS	7	1	3	4	8	....	....	....	....	....	....	....	....	....	....	....	....	....	....	....	....	....	....
	NY Islanders	**NHL**	**79**	**4**	**17**	**21**	**166**	**0**	**0**	**0**	**92**	**4.3**	**15**	....	....	....	**18**	**0**	**5**	**5**	**31**	**0**	**0**	**0**	....
1993-94	**NY Islanders**	**NHL**	**76**	**1**	**10**	**11**	**142**	**0**	**0**	**0**	**81**	**1.2**	**–6**	....	....	....	**4**	**0**	**0**	**0**	**8**	**0**	**0**	**0**	....
1994-95	**NY Islanders**	**NHL**	**13**	**0**	**1**	**1**	**22**	**0**	**0**	**0**	**8**	**0.0**	**–11**	....	....	....	....	....	....	....	....	....	....	....	....
1995-96	**NY Islanders**	**NHL**	**46**	**1**	**7**	**8**	**93**	**0**	**0**	**0**	**34**	**2.9**	**–12**	....	....	....	....	....	....	....	....	....	....	....	....
1996-97	**NY Islanders**	**NHL**	**18**	**0**	**5**	**5**	**16**	**0**	**0**	**0**	**12**	**0.0**	**–7**	....	....	....	....	....	....	....	....	....	....	....	....
	Pittsburgh	**NHL**	**57**	**2**	**16**	**18**	**84**	**0**	**0**	**0**	**46**	**4.3**	**24**	....	....	....	**5**	**0**	**0**	**0**	**6**	**0**	**0**	**0**	....
1997-98	**Pittsburgh**	**NHL**	**81**	**4**	**8**	**12**	**127**	**0**	**2**	**0**	**71**	**5.6**	**3**	....	....	....	**5**	**0**	**0**	**0**	**8**	**0**	**0**	**0**	....
	Russia	Olympics	6	0	2	2	6	....	....	....	....	....	....	....	....	....	....	....	....	....	....	....	....	....	....
1998-99	**Pittsburgh**	**NHL**	**48**	**1**	**4**	**5**	**70**	**0**	**0**	**0**	**32**	**3.1**	**12**	**0**	**0.0**	**16:01**	....	....	....	....	....	....	....	....	....
99-2000	**Pittsburgh**	**NHL**	**73**	**3**	**12**	**15**	**146**	**1**	**0**	**1**	**76**	**3.9**	**–12**	**0**	**0.0**	**18:07**	**11**	**1**	**1**	**2**	**10**	**0**	**0**	**0**	**21:39**
2000-01	**Pittsburgh**	**NHL**	**77**	**3**	**16**	**19**	**111**	**1**	**0**	**0**	**81**	**3.7**	**11**	**0**	**0.0**	**19:14**	**17**	**1**	**1**	**2**	**26**	**0**	**0**	**1**	**19:52**
2001-02	**Pittsburgh**	**NHL**	**69**	**2**	**12**	**14**	**123**	**0**	**0**	**0**	**75**	**2.7**	**–1**	**1**	**0.0**	**20:32**	....	....	....	....	....	....	....	....	....
	Russia	Olympics	6	1	0	1	4	....	....	....	....	....	....	....	....	....	....	....	....	....	....	....	....	....	....
	Colorado	**NHL**	**11**	**0**	**0**	**0**	**19**	**0**	**0**	**0**	**6**	**0.0**	**1**	**0**	**0.0**	**19:44**	**21**	**0**	**3**	**3**	**18**	**0**	**0**	**0**	**20:46**
2002-03	**NY Rangers**	**NHL**	**80**	**3**	**11**	**14**	**85**	**0**	**0**	**1**	**84**	**3.6**	**5**	**0**	**0.0**	**18:54**	....	....	....	....	....	....	....	....	....
2003-04	**NY Rangers**	**NHL**	**44**	**1**	**9**	**10**	**48**	**0**	**0**	**0**	**29**	**3.4**	**11**	**0**	**0.0**	**16:23**	....	....	....	....	....	....	....	....	....
2004-05	Ak Bars Kazan	Russia	28	1	3	4	118	....	....	....	....	....	....	....	....	....	3	0	0	0	6	....	....	....	....
	NHL Totals		**772**	**25**	**128**	**153**	**1252**	**2**	**2**	**2**	**727**	**3.4**		**1**	**0.0**	**18:30**	**81**	**2**	**10**	**12**	**107**	**0**	**0**	**1**	**20:39**

Traded to **Pittsburgh** by **NY Islanders** with Andreas Johansson for Bryan Smolinski, November 17, 1996. Traded to **Colorado** by **Pittsburgh** for Ville Niemenen and Rick Berry, March 19, 2002. Signed as a free agent by **NY Rangers**, July 2, 2002. Signed as a free aget by **Kazan** (Russia), October 22, 2004.

KAVANAGH, Pat

(KA-vuh-naw, PAT) **PHI.**

Right wing. Shoots right. 6'3", 192 lbs. Born, Ottawa, Ont., March 14, 1979. Philadelphia's 2nd choice, 50th overall, in 1997 Entry Draft.

Season	Club	League	GP	G	A	Pts	PIM	PP	SH	GW	S	%	+/-	TF	F%	Min	GP	G	A	Pts	PIM	PP	SH	GW	Min
1995-96	Kanata Valley	CJHL	54	19	16	35	99	....	....	....	....	....	....	....	....	....	....	....	....	....	....	....	....	....	....
1996-97	Peterborough	OHL	43	6	8	14	53	....	....	....	....	....	....	....	....	....	11	1	1	2	12	....	....	....	....
1997-98	Peterborough	OHL	66	10	16	26	85	....	....	....	....	....	....	....	....	....	4	1	0	1	6	....	....	....	....
1998-99	Peterborough	OHL	68	26	43	69	118	....	....	....	....	....	....	....	....	....	5	0	5	5	10	....	....	....	....
99-2000	Syracuse Crunch	AHL	68	12	8	20	56	....	....	....	....	....	....	....	....	....	4	0	0	0	0	....	....	....	....
2000-01	Kansas City	IHL	78	26	15	41	86	....	....	....	....	....	....	....	....	....	....	....	....	....	....	....	....	....	....
	Vancouver	**NHL**	....	....	....	....	....	....	....	....	....	....	....	....	....	....	**3**	**0**	**0**	**0**	**2**	**0**	**0**	**0**	**8:27**
2001-02	Manitoba Moose	AHL	70	13	19	32	100	....	....	....	....	....	....	....	....	....	7	1	0	1	6	....	....	....	....
2002-03	**Vancouver**	**NHL**	**3**	**1**	**0**	**1**	**2**	**0**	**0**	**1**	**4**	**25.0**	**2**	**27**	**37.0**	**10:23**	....	....	....	....	....	....	....	....	....
	Manitoba Moose	AHL	63	15	15	30	96	....	....	....	....	....	....	....	....	....	14	7	4	11	20	....	....	....	....
2003-04	**Vancouver**	**NHL**	**3**	**1**	**0**	**1**	**0**	**0**	**0**	**0**	**1**	**100.0**	**0**	**21**	**52.4**	**7:58**	....	....	....	....	....	....	....	....	....
	Manitoba Moose	AHL	73	23	22	45	69	....	....	....	....	....	....	....	....	....	....	....	....	....	....	....	....	....	....
2004-05	Binghamton	AHL	80	14	17	31	87	....	....	....	....	....	....	....	....	....	6	0	1	1	10	....	....	....	....
	NHL Totals		**6**	**2**	**0**	**2**	**2**	**0**	**0**	**1**	**5**	**40.0**		**48**	**43.8**	**9:11**	**3**	**0**	**0**	**0**	**2**	**0**	**0**	**0**	**8:27**

Traded to **Vancouver** by **Philadelphia** for Vancouver's 6th round choice (Konstantin Rudenko) in 1999 Entry Draft, June 1, 1999. Signed as a free agent by **Ottawa**, July 27, 2004. Signed as a free agent by **Philadelphia**, August 22, 2005.

Season	Club	League	Regular Season GP	G	A	Pts	PIM	PP	SH	GW	S	%	+/-	TF	F%	Min	Playoffs GP	G	A	Pts	PIM	PP	SH	GW	Min

KEANE, Mike

(KEEN, MIGHK)

Right wing. Shoots right. 5'10", 185 lbs. Born, Winnipeg, Man., May 29, 1967.

Season	Club	League	GP	G	A	Pts	PIM	PP	SH	GW	S	%	+/-	TF	F%	Min	GP	G	A	Pts	PIM	PP	SH	GW	Min
1983-84	Wpg. Monarchs	MMMHL	21	17	19	36	59	....	....	....	....	....	....	....	....	....	....	....	....	....	....	....	....	....	....
	Winnipeg	WHL	1	0	0	0	0	....	....	....	....	....	....	....	....	....	....	....	....	....	....	....	....	....	....
1984-85	Moose Jaw	WHL	65	17	26	43	141	....	....	....	....	....	....	....	....	....	....	....	....	....	....	....	....	....	....
1985-86	Moose Jaw	WHL	67	34	49	83	162	....	....	....	....	....	....	....	....	....	13	6	8	14	9	....	....	....	....
1986-87	Moose Jaw	WHL	53	25	45	70	107	....	....	....	....	....	....	....	....	....	9	3	9	12	11	....	....	....	....
	Sherbrooke	AHL	....	....	....	....	....	....	....	....	....	....	....	....	....	....	9	2	2	4	16	....	....	....	....
1987-88	Sherbrooke	AHL	78	25	43	68	70	....	....	....	....	....	....	....	....	....	6	1	1	2	18	....	....	....	....
1988-89	**Montreal**	**NHL**	**69**	**16**	**19**	**35**	**69**	**5**	**0**	**1**	**90**	**17.8**	**9**	....	....	....	**21**	**4**	**3**	**7**	**17**	**2**	**0**	**0**	....
1989-90	**Montreal**	**NHL**	**74**	**9**	**15**	**24**	**78**	**1**	**0**	**1**	**92**	**9.8**	**0**	....	....	....	**11**	**0**	**1**	**1**	**8**	**0**	**0**	**0**	....
1990-91	**Montreal**	**NHL**	**73**	**13**	**23**	**36**	**50**	**2**	**1**	**2**	**109**	**11.9**	**6**	....	....	....	**12**	**3**	**2**	**5**	**6**	**0**	**0**	**0**	....
1991-92	**Montreal**	**NHL**	**67**	**11**	**30**	**41**	**64**	**2**	**0**	**2**	**116**	**9.5**	**16**	....	....	....	**8**	**1**	**1**	**2**	**16**	**0**	**0**	**0**	....
1992-93♦	**Montreal**	**NHL**	**77**	**15**	**45**	**60**	**95**	**0**	**0**	**1**	**120**	**12.5**	**29**	....	....	....	**19**	**2**	**13**	**15**	**6**	**0**	**0**	**0**	....
1993-94	**Montreal**	**NHL**	**80**	**16**	**30**	**46**	**119**	**6**	**2**	**2**	**129**	**12.4**	**6**	....	....	....	**6**	**3**	**1**	**4**	**4**	**0**	**0**	**0**	....
1994-95	**Montreal**	**NHL**	**48**	**10**	**10**	**20**	**15**	**1**	**0**	**0**	**75**	**13.3**	**5**	....	....	....	....	....	....	....	....	....	....	....	....
1995-96	**Montreal**	**NHL**	**18**	**0**	**7**	**7**	**6**	**0**	**0**	**0**	**17**	**0.0**	**-6**	....	....	....	....	....	....	....	....	....	....	....	....
	♦ Colorado	**NHL**	**55**	**10**	**10**	**20**	**40**	**0**	**2**	**2**	**67**	**14.9**	**1**	....	....	....	**22**	**3**	**2**	**5**	**16**	**0**	**0**	**1**	....
1996-97	**Colorado**	**NHL**	**81**	**10**	**17**	**27**	**63**	**0**	**1**	**1**	**91**	**11.0**	**2**	....	....	....	**17**	**3**	**1**	**4**	**24**	**0**	**0**	**1**	....
1997-98	**NY Rangers**	**NHL**	**70**	**8**	**10**	**18**	**47**	**2**	**0**	**0**	**113**	**7.1**	**-12**	....	....	....	....	....	....	....	....	....	....	....	....
	Dallas	**NHL**	**13**	**2**	**3**	**5**	**5**	**0**	**0**	**1**	**15**	**13.3**	**0**	....	....	....	**17**	**4**	**4**	**8**	**0**	**0**	**1**	**1**	....
1998-99♦	**Dallas**	**NHL**	**81**	**6**	**23**	**29**	**62**	**1**	**1**	**1**	**106**	**5.7**	**-2**	**11**	**27.3**	**13:57**	**23**	**5**	**2**	**7**	**6**	**0**	**1**	**1**	**18:02**
99-2000	**Dallas**	**NHL**	**81**	**13**	**21**	**34**	**41**	**0**	**4**	**3**	**85**	**15.3**	**9**	**10**	**50.0**	**16:10**	**23**	**2**	**4**	**6**	**14**	**0**	**0**	**0**	**16:20**
2000-01	**Dallas**	**NHL**	**67**	**10**	**14**	**24**	**35**	**1**	**0**	**1**	**64**	**15.6**	**4**	**25**	**60.0**	**15:28**	**10**	**3**	**2**	**5**	**4**	**0**	**0**	**0**	**16:08**
2001-02	**St. Louis**	**NHL**	**56**	**4**	**6**	**10**	**22**	**1**	**0**	**0**	**47**	**8.5**	**-2**	**49**	**30.6**	**14:19**	....	....	....	....	....	....	....	....	....
	Colorado	**NHL**	**22**	**2**	**5**	**7**	**16**	**0**	**0**	**0**	**26**	**7.7**	**-2**	**42**	**31.0**	**16:55**	**18**	**1**	**4**	**5**	**8**	**0**	**0**	**0**	**16:18**
2002-03	**Colorado**	**NHL**	**65**	**5**	**5**	**10**	**34**	**0**	**1**	**1**	**35**	**14.3**	**0**	**102**	**19.6**	**12:15**	**6**	**0**	**0**	**0**	**2**	**0**	**0**	**0**	**7:57**
2003-04	**Vancouver**	**NHL**	**64**	**8**	**9**	**17**	**20**	**0**	**0**	**2**	**41**	**19.5**	**7**	**72**	**34.7**	**11:11**	**7**	**0**	**0**	**0**	**4**	**0**	**0**	**0**	**12:18**
2004-05			DID NOT PLAY																						
	NHL Totals		**1161**	**168**	**302**	**470**	**881**	**22**	**12**	**21**	**1438**	**11.7**		**311**	**30.9**	**14:08**	**220**	**34**	**40**	**74**	**135**	**2**	**2**	**4**	**15:51**

Signed as a free agent by **Montreal**, September 25, 1985. Traded to **Colorado** by **Montreal** with Patrick Roy for Andrei Kovalenko, Martin Rucinsky and Jocelyn Thibault, December 6, 1995. Signed as a free agent by **NY Rangers**, July 30, 1997. Traded to **Dallas** by **NY Rangers** with Brian Skrudland and NY Rangers' 6th round choice (Pavel Patera) in 1998 Entry Draft for Todd Harvey, Bob Errey and Dallas' 4th round choice (Boyd Kane) in 1998 Entry Draft, March 24, 1998. Signed as a free agent by **St. Louis**, July 10, 2001. Traded to **Colorado** by **St. Louis** for Shjon Podein, February 11, 2002. Signed as a free agent by **Vancouver**, October 10, 2003.

KEEFE, Sheldon

(KEEF, SHEHL-duhn) **PHX.**

Right wing. Shoots right. 5'11", 185 lbs. Born, Brampton, Ont., September 17, 1980. Tampa Bay's 1st choice, 47th overall, in 1999 Entry Draft.

Season	Club	League	GP	G	A	Pts	PIM	PP	SH	GW	S	%	+/-	TF	F%	Min	GP	G	A	Pts	PIM	PP	SH	GW	Min
1995-96	Tor. Young Nats	MTHL	45	66	71	137	....	....	....	....	....	....	....	....	....	....	....	....	....	....	....	....	....	....	....
1996-97	Quinte Hawks	MTJHL	44	21	23	44	41	....	....	....	....	....	....	....	....	....	....	....	....	....	....	....	....	....	....
	Bramalea Blues	OPJHL	8	0	3	3	4	....	....	....	....	....	....	....	....	....	....	....	....	....	....	....	....	....	....
1997-98	Caledon	MTJHL	43	41	40	81	117	....	....	....	....	....	....	....	....	....	13	15	8	23	....	....	....	....	....
1998-99	St. Michael's	OHL	38	37	37	74	80	....	....	....	....	....	....	....	....	....	....	....	....	....	....	....	....	....	....
	Barrie Colts	OHL	28	14	28	42	60	....	....	....	....	....	....	....	....	....	10	5	5	10	31	....	....	....	....
99-2000	Barrie Colts	OHL	66	48	*73	*121	95	....	....	....	....	....	....	....	....	....	25	10	13	23	41	....	....	....	....
2000-01	**Tampa Bay**	**NHL**	**49**	**4**	**0**	**4**	**38**	**0**	**0**	**0**	**32**	**12.5**	**-13**	**1**	**0.0**	**8:00**	....	....	....	....	....	....	....	....	....
	Detroit Vipers	IHL	13	7	5	12	23	....	....	....	....	....	....	....	....	....	....	....	....	....	....	....	....	....	....
2001-02	**Tampa Bay**	**NHL**	**39**	**6**	**7**	**13**	**16**	**0**	**0**	**1**	**52**	**11.5**	**-11**	**70**	**45.7**	**13:00**	....	....	....	....	....	....	....	....	....
	Springfield	AHL	24	9	9	18	26	....	....	....	....	....	....	....	....	....	....	....	....	....	....	....	....	....	....
2002-03	**Tampa Bay**	**NHL**	**37**	**2**	**5**	**7**	**24**	**0**	**0**	**0**	**51**	**3.9**	**-1**	**32**	**43.8**	**10:15**	....	....	....	....	....	....	....	....	....
	Springfield	AHL	33	16	15	31	28	....	....	....	....	....	....	....	....	....	6	0	0	0	4	....	....	....	....
2003-04	Hershey Bears	AHL	59	16	16	32	82	....	....	....	....	....	....	....	....	....	....	....	....	....	....	....	....	....	....
2004-05	Utah Grizzlies	AHL	4	0	1	1	0	....	....	....	....	....	....	....	....	....	....	....	....	....	....	....	....	....	....
	NHL Totals		**125**	**12**	**12**	**24**	**78**	**0**	**0**	**1**	**135**	**8.9**		**103**	**44.7**	**10:14**	....	....	....	....	....	....	....	....	....

OHL All-Rookie Team (1999) • OHL Rookie of the Year (1999) • OHL Second All-Star Team (2000) • Eddie Powers Memorial Trophy (Top Scorer – OHL) (2000) • Canadian Major Junior First All-Star Team (2000) • Memorial Cup Tournament All-Star Team (2000)

Claimed by **NY Rangers** from **Tampa Bay** in Waiver Draft, October 3, 2003. Claimed on waivers by **Tampa Bay** from **NY Rangers**, October 24, 2003. Signed as a free agent by **Phoenix**, July 12, 2004.

KEITH, Matt

(KEETH, MAT) **CHI.**

Right wing. Shoots right. 6'2", 200 lbs. Born, Edmonton, Alta., April 11, 1983. Chicago's 3rd choice, 59th overall, in 2001 Entry Draft.

Season	Club	League	GP	G	A	Pts	PIM	PP	SH	GW	S	%	+/-	TF	F%	Min	GP	G	A	Pts	PIM	PP	SH	GW	Min
1998-99	Banff Icemen	HJHL	STATISTICS NOT AVAILABLE																						
	Spokane Chiefs	WHL	7	1	0	1	4	....	....	....	....	....	....	....	....	....	....	....	....	....	....	....	....	....	....
99-2000	Spokane Chiefs	WHL	39	1	3	4	37	....	....	....	....	....	....	....	....	....	15	1	2	3	11	....	....	....	....
2000-01	Spokane Chiefs	WHL	33	13	14	27	63	....	....	....	....	....	....	....	....	....	12	1	3	4	14	....	....	....	....
2001-02	Spokane Chiefs	WHL	68	34	33	67	71	....	....	....	....	....	....	....	....	....	11	5	5	10	16	....	....	....	....
2002-03	Spokane Chiefs	WHL	7	2	2	4	11	....	....	....	....	....	....	....	....	....	....	....	....	....	....	....	....	....	....
	Red Deer Rebels	WHL	49	25	26	51	32	....	....	....	....	....	....	....	....	....	23	6	7	13	30	....	....	....	....
2003-04	**Chicago**	**NHL**	**20**	**2**	**3**	**5**	**10**	**1**	**0**	**0**	**21**	**9.5**	**-5**	**2**	**100.0**	**11:58**	....	....	....	....	....	....	....	....	....
	Norfolk Admirals	AHL	66	13	13	26	57	....	....	....	....	....	....	....	....	....	8	1	2	3	10	....	....	....	....
2004-05	Norfolk Admirals	AHL	80	18	31	49	74	....	....	....	....	....	....	....	....	....	6	0	1	1	0	....	....	....	....
	NHL Totals		**20**	**2**	**3**	**5**	**10**	**1**	**0**	**0**	**21**	**9.5**		**2**	**100.0**	**11:58**	....	....	....	....	....	....	....	....	....

• Missed majority of 2000-01 season recovering from shoulder injury suffered in game vs. Tri-City (WHL), September 22, 2000.

KELLY, Chris

(KEHL-lee, KRIHS) **OTT.**

Center/Left wing. Shoots left. 6', 190 lbs. Born, Toronto, Ont., November 11, 1980. Ottawa's 4th choice, 94th overall, in 1999 Entry Draft.

Season	Club	League	GP	G	A	Pts	PIM	PP	SH	GW	S	%	+/-	TF	F%	Min	GP	G	A	Pts	PIM	PP	SH	GW	Min
1995-96	Toronto Marlies	MTHL	42	25	45	70	25	....	....	....	....	....	....	....	....	....	....	....	....	....	....	....	....	....	....
1996-97	Aurora Tigers	MTJHL	49	14	20	34	11	....	....	....	....	....	....	....	....	....	....	....	....	....	....	....	....	....	....
1997-98	London Knights	OHL	54	15	14	29	4	....	....	....	....	....	....	....	....	....	16	4	5	9	12	....	....	....	....
1998-99	London Knights	OHL	68	36	41	77	60	....	....	....	....	....	....	....	....	....	25	9	17	26	22	....	....	....	....
99-2000	London Knights	OHL	63	29	43	72	57	....	....	....	....	....	....	....	....	....	....	....	....	....	....	....	....	....	....
2000-01	London Knights	OHL	31	21	34	55	46	....	....	....	....	....	....	....	....	....	....	....	....	....	....	....	....	....	....
	Sudbury Wolves	OHL	19	5	16	21	17	....	....	....	....	....	....	....	....	....	12	11	5	16	14	....	....	....	....
2001-02	Muskegon Fury	UHL	4	1	2	3	0	....	....	....	....	....	....	....	....	....	....	....	....	....	....	....	....	....	....
	Grand Rapids	AHL	31	3	3	6	20	....	....	....	....	....	....	....	....	....	5	1	1	2	5	....	....	....	....
2002-03	Binghamton	AHL	77	17	14	31	73	....	....	....	....	....	....	....	....	....	14	2	3	5	8	....	....	....	....
2003-04	**Ottawa**	**NHL**	**4**	**0**	**0**	**0**	**0**	**0**	**0**	**0**	**4**	**0.0**	**-2**	**5**	**40.0**	**9:29**	....	....	....	....	....	....	....	....	....
	Binghamton	AHL	54	15	19	34	40	....	....	....	....	....	....	....	....	....	2	0	0	0	4	....	....	....	....
2004-05	Binghamton	AHL	77	24	36	60	57	....	....	....	....	....	....	....	....	....	6	1	2	3	11	....	....	....	....
	NHL Totals		**4**	**0**	**0**	**0**	**0**	**0**	**0**	**0**	**4**	**0.0**		**5**	**40.0**	**9:29**	....	....	....	....	....	....	....	....	....

KELLY, Steve

(KEHL-lee, STEEV) **L.A.**

Center. Shoots left. 6'2", 205 lbs. Born, Vancouver, B.C., October 26, 1976. Edmonton's 1st choice, 6th overall, in 1995 Entry Draft.

Season	Club	League	GP	G	A	Pts	PIM	PP	SH	GW	S	%	+/-	TF	F%	Min	GP	G	A	Pts	PIM	PP	SH	GW	Min
1991-92	Westbank	BCAHA	30	25	60	85	75	....	....	....	....	....	....	....	....	....	....	....	....	....	....	....	....	....	....
1992-93	Prince Albert	WHL	65	11	9	20	75	....	....	....	....	....	....	....	....	....	....	....	....	....	....	....	....	....	....
1993-94	Prince Albert	WHL	65	19	42	61	106	....	....	....	....	....	....	....	....	....	....	....	....	....	....	....	....	....	....
1994-95	Prince Albert	WHL	68	31	41	72	153	....	....	....	....	....	....	....	....	....	15	7	9	16	35	....	....	....	....
1995-96	Prince Albert	WHL	70	27	74	101	203	....	....	....	....	....	....	....	....	....	18	13	18	31	47	....	....	....	....
1996-97	**Edmonton**	**NHL**	**8**	**1**	**0**	**1**	**6**	**0**	**0**	**1**	**6**	**16.7**	**-1**	....	....	....	**6**	**0**	**0**	**0**	**2**	**0**	**0**	**0**	....
	Hamilton	AHL	48	9	29	38	111	....	....	....	....	....	....	....	....	....	11	3	3	6	24	....	....	....	....
1997-98	**Edmonton**	**NHL**	**19**	**0**	**2**	**2**	**8**	**0**	**0**	**0**	**5**	**0.0**	**-4**	....	....	....	....	....	....	....	....	....	....	....	....
	Hamilton	AHL	11	2	8	10	18	....	....	....	....	....	....	....	....	....	....	....	....	....	....	....	....	....	....
	Tampa Bay	**NHL**	**24**	**2**	**1**	**3**	**15**	**1**	**0**	**0**	**17**	**11.8**	**-9**	....	....	....	....	....	....	....	....	....	....	....	....
	Milwaukee	IHL	5	0	1	1	19	....	....	....	....	....	....	....	....	....	....	....	....	....	....	....	....	....	....
	Cleveland	IHL	5	1	1	2	29	....	....	....	....	....	....	....	....	....	1	0	1	1	0	....	....	....	....
1998-99	**Tampa Bay**	**NHL**	**34**	**1**	**3**	**4**	**27**	**0**	**0**	**1**	**15**	**6.7**	**-15**	**11**	**54.5**	**10:51**	....	....	....	....	....	....	....	....	....
	Cleveland	IHL	18	6	7	13	36	....	....	....	....	....	....	....	....	....	....	....	....	....	....	....	....	....	....

Season	Club	League	Regular Season GP	G	A	Pts	PIM	PP	SH	GW	S	%	+/-	TF	F%	Min	Playoffs GP	G	A	Pts	PIM	PP	SH	GW	Min
99-2000	Detroit Vipers	IHL	1	0	0	0	4	....	....	....	....	....	....	....	....	....	....	....	....	....	....	....	....	....	....
	♦ New Jersey	NHL	1	0	0	0	0	0	0	0	0	0.0	0	0	0.0	4:28	10	0	0	0	4	0	0	0	11:32
	Albany River Rats	AHL	76	21	36	57	131	....	....	....	....	....	....	....	....	....	3	1	1	2	2	....	....	....	....
2000-01	New Jersey	NHL	24	2	2	4	21	0	0	0	18	11.1	0	87	48.3	9:58	....	....	....	....	....	....	....	....	....
	Los Angeles	NHL	11	1	0	1	4	0	0	0	4	25.0	0	51	39.2	6:44	8	0	0	0	2	0	0	0	5:23
2001-02	Los Angeles	NHL	8	0	1	1	2	0	0	0	0	0.0	-1	44	36.4	6:52	1	0	0	0	0	0	0	0	5:54
	Manchester	AHL	49	10	21	31	88	....	....	....	....	....	....	....	....	....	5	1	8	9	4	....	....	....	....
2002-03	Manchester	AHL	54	19	44	63	144	....	....	....	....	....	....	....	....	....	3	0	1	1	0	....	....	....	....
	Los Angeles	NHL	15	2	3	5	0	0	0	1	14	14.3	-6	133	42.9	12:29	....	....	....	....	....	....	....	....	....
2003-04	Los Angeles	NHL	3	0	0	0	0	0	0	0	5	0.0	0	30	43.3	10:30	....	....	....	....	....	....	....	....	....
	Manchester	AHL	59	21	49	70	117	....	....	....	....	....	....	....	....	....	1	0	0	0	2	....	....	....	....
2004-05	Adler Mannheim	Germany	46	11	22	33	*210	....	....	....	....	....	....	....	....	....	12	1	4	5	*72	....	....	....	....
	NHL Totals		147	9	12	21	83	1	0	3	84	10.7		356	43.3	10:00	25	0	0	0	8	0	0	0	8:39

Traded to **Tampa Bay** by **Edmonton** with Bryan Marchment and Jason Bonsignore for Roman Hamrlik and Paul Comrie, December 30, 1997. Traded to **New Jersey** by **Tampa Bay** for New Jersey's 7th round choice (Brian Eklund) in 2000 Entry Draft, October 7, 1999. Traded to **Los Angeles** by **New Jersey** to complete transaction that sent Bob Corkum to New Jersey (February 23, 2001), February 27, 2001. • Spent majority of 2000-01 season with New Jersey and Los Angeles as a healthy reserve. Signed as a free agent by **Mannheim** (Germany), May 4, 2004.

KESLER, Ryan

(KEHZ-luhr, RIGH-uhn) **VAN.**

Center. Shoots right. 6'2", 195 lbs. Born, Detroit, MI, August 31, 1984. Vancouver's 1st choice, 23rd overall, in 2003 Entry Draft.

Season	Club	League	GP	G	A	Pts	PIM	PP	SH	GW	S	%	+/-	TF	F%	Min	GP	G	A	Pts	PIM	PP	SH	GW	Min
99-2000	Det. Honeybaked	MWEHL	72	44	73	117	....	....	....	....	....	....	....	....	....	....	....	....	....	....	....	....	....	....	....
2000-01	USA U-18	USDP	82	15	41	56	64	....	....	....	....	....	....	....	....	....	....	....	....	....	....	....	....	....	....
2001-02	USA U-18	USDP	69	21	44	65	37	....	....	....	....	....	....	....	....	....	....	....	....	....	....	....	....	....	....
2002-03	Ohio State	CCHA	40	11	20	31	44	....	....	....	....	....	....	....	....	....	....	....	....	....	....	....	....	....	....
2003-04	Vancouver	NHL	28	2	3	5	16	0	0	0	23	8.7	-2	194	40.2	10:42	....	....	....	....	....	....	....	....	....
	Manitoba Moose	AHL	33	3	8	11	29	....	....	....	....	....	....	....	....	....	....	....	....	....	....	....	....	....	....
2004-05	Manitoba Moose	AHL	78	30	27	57	105	....	....	....	....	....	....	....	....	....	14	4	5	9	8	....	....	....	....
	NHL Totals		28	2	3	5	16	0	0	0	23	8.7		194	40.2	10:42	....	....	....	....	....	....	....	....	....

KHAVANOV, Alexander

(khuh-VAN-ahf, al-ehx-AN-duhr) **TOR.**

Defense. Shoots left. 6'2", 205 lbs. Born, Moscow, USSR, January 30, 1972. St. Louis' 8th choice, 232nd overall, in 1999 Entry Draft.

Season	Club	League	GP	G	A	Pts	PIM	PP	SH	GW	S	%	+/-	TF	F%	Min	GP	G	A	Pts	PIM	PP	SH	GW	Min
1992-93	Birmingham Bulls	ECHL	19	0	3	3	14	....	....	....	....	....	....	....	....	....	....	....	....	....	....	....	....	....	....
	Raleigh IceCaps	ECHL	17	0	6	6	8	....	....	....	....	....	....	....	....	....	....	....	....	....	....	....	....	....	....
1993-94	St. Petersburg	CIS	41	1	2	3	24	....	....	....	....	....	....	....	....	....	....	....	....	....	....	....	....	....	....
1994-95	St. Petersburg	CIS	49	7	0	7	32	....	....	....	....	....	....	....	....	....	3	0	0	0	0	....	....	....	....
1995-96	St. Petersburg	CIS	32	1	5	6	41	....	....	....	....	....	....	....	....	....	....	....	....	....	....	....	....	....	....
	HPK Hameenlinna	Finland	16	0	2	2	4	....	....	....	....	....	....	....	....	....	....	....	....	....	....	....	....	....	....
1996-97	Cherepovets	Russia	39	3	8	11	56	....	....	....	....	....	....	....	....	....	9	0	0	0	0	....	....	....	....
1997-98	Cherepovets	Russia	44	3	5	8	46	....	....	....	....	....	....	....	....	....	3	1	0	1	4	....	....	....	....
1998-99	Dynamo Moscow	Russia	40	2	7	9	14	....	....	....	....	....	....	....	....	....	16	1	5	6	35	....	....	....	....
	Dynamo Moscow	EuroHL	5	0	1	1	2	....	....	....	....	....	....	....	....	....	6	0	0	0	4	....	....	....	....
99-2000	Dynamo Moscow	Russia	38	5	12	17	49	....	....	....	....	....	....	....	....	....	17	0	3	3	4	....	....	....	....
	Dynamo Moscow	EuroHL	6	2	0	2	0	....	....	....	....	....	....	....	....	....	....	....	....	....	....	....	....	....	....
2000-01	St. Louis	NHL	74	7	16	23	52	2	0	0	92	7.6	16	0	0.0	20:54	15	3	2	5	14	1	0	0	21:16
2001-02	St. Louis	NHL	81	3	21	24	55	0	0	0	87	3.4	9	0	0.0	17:13	4	0	0	0	2	0	0	0	15:08
2002-03	St. Louis	NHL	81	8	25	33	48	2	1	2	90	8.9	-1	2	50.0	21:57	7	2	3	5	2	1	0	0	19:05
2003-04	St. Louis	NHL	48	3	7	10	18	2	0	2	62	4.8	2	1	0.0	19:20	....	....	....	....	....	....	....	....	....
2004-05	St. Petersburg	Russia	3	0	0	0	27	....	....	....	....	....	....	....	....	....	....	....	....	....	....	....	....	....	....
	NHL Totals		284	21	69	90	173	6	1	2	331	6.3		3	33.3	19:53	26	5	5	10	18	2	0	0	19:44

Signed as a free agent by **St. Petersburg** (Russia), September 25, 2004. Signed as a free agent by **Toronto**, August 9, 2005.

KILGER, Chad

(KIHL-guhr, CHAD) **TOR.**

Left wing. Shoots left. 6'4", 224 lbs. Born, Cornwall, Ont., November 27, 1976. Anaheim's 1st choice, 4th overall, in 1995 Entry Draft.

Season	Club	League	GP	G	A	Pts	PIM	PP	SH	GW	S	%	+/-	TF	F%	Min	GP	G	A	Pts	PIM	PP	SH	GW	Min
1992-93	Cornwall Colts	CJHL	55	30	36	66	26	....	....	....	....	....	....	....	....	....	6	0	0	0	0	....	....	....	....
1993-94	Kingston	OHL	66	17	35	52	23	....	....	....	....	....	....	....	....	....	6	7	2	9	8	....	....	....	....
1994-95	Kingston	OHL	65	42	53	95	95	....	....	....	....	....	....	....	....	....	6	5	2	7	10	....	....	....	....
1995-96	Anaheim	NHL	45	5	7	12	22	0	0	1	38	13.2	-2	....	....	....	....	....	....	....	....	....	....	....	....
	Winnipeg	NHL	29	2	3	5	12	0	0	0	19	10.5	-2	....	....	....	4	1	0	1	0	0	0	1	....
1996-97	Phoenix	NHL	24	4	3	7	13	1	0	0	30	13.3	-5	....	....	....	....	....	....	....	....	....	....	....	....
	Springfield	AHL	52	17	28	45	36	....	....	....	....	....	....	....	....	....	16	5	7	12	56	....	....	....	....
1997-98	Phoenix	NHL	10	0	1	1	4	0	0	0	9	0.0	-2	....	....	....	....	....	....	....	....	....	....	....	....
	Springfield	AHL	35	14	14	28	33	....	....	....	....	....	....	....	....	....	....	....	....	....	....	....	....	....	....
	Chicago	NHL	22	3	8	11	6	2	0	1	23	13.0	2	....	....	....	....	....	....	....	....	....	....	....	....
1998-99	Chicago	NHL	64	14	11	25	30	2	1	1	68	20.6	-1	488	56.6	14:03	....	....	....	....	....	....	....	....	....
	Edmonton	NHL	13	1	1	2	4	0	0	0	13	7.7	-3	82	53.7	11:22	4	0	0	0	4	0	0	0	12:59
99-2000	Edmonton	NHL	40	3	2	5	18	0	0	0	32	9.4	-6	269	48.0	8:33	3	0	0	0	0	0	0	0	8:01
	Hamilton	AHL	7	4	2	6	4	....	....	....	....	....	....	....	....	....	....	....	....	....	....	....	....	....	....
2000-01	Edmonton	NHL	34	5	2	7	17	1	0	0	28	17.9	-7	391	53.5	8:18	....	....	....	....	....	....	....	....	....
	Montreal	NHL	43	9	16	25	34	1	1	1	75	12.0	-1	319	52.4	17:57	....	....	....	....	....	....	....	....	....
2001-02	Montreal	NHL	75	8	15	23	27	0	1	2	87	9.2	-7	357	53.8	13:14	12	0	1	1	9	0	0	0	14:00
2002-03	Montreal	NHL	60	9	7	16	21	0	0	1	60	15.0	-4	208	46.6	10:42	....	....	....	....	....	....	....	....	....
2003-04	Montreal	NHL	36	2	2	4	14	0	0	0	29	6.9	2	95	48.4	10:26	....	....	....	....	....	....	....	....	....
	Hamilton	AHL	2	1	0	1	0	....	....	....	....	....	....	....	....	....	....	....	....	....	....	....	....	....	....
	Toronto	NHL	5	1	1	2	2	0	0	1	6	16.7	2	2	0.0	12:14	13	2	1	3	0	0	0	0	11:41
2004-05		DID NOT PLAY																							
	NHL Totals		500	66	79	145	224	7	3	8	517	12.8		2211	52.5	12:12	36	3	2	5	13	0	0	1	12:22

Traded to **Winnipeg** by **Anaheim** with Oleg Tverdovsky and Anaheim's 3rd round choice (Per-Anton Lundstrom) in 1996 Entry Draft for Teemu Selanne, Marc Chouinard and Winnipeg's 4th round choice (later traded to Toronto – later traded to Montreal – Montreal selected Kim Staal) in 1996 Entry Draft, February 7, 1996. Transferred to **Phoenix** after **Winnipeg** franchise relocated, July 1, 1996. Traded to **Chicago** by **Phoenix** with Jayson More for Keith Carney and Jim Cummins, March 4, 1998. Traded to **Edmonton** by **Chicago** with Daniel Cleary, Ethan Moreau and Christian Laflamme for Boris Mironov, Dean McAmmond and Jonas Elofsson, March 20, 1999. Traded to **Montreal** by **Edmonton** for Sergei Zholtok, December 18, 2000. Claimed on waivers by **Toronto** from **Montreal**, March 9, 2004.

KING, Jason

(KIHNG, JAY-suhn) **VAN.**

Center. Shoots left. 6'1", 195 lbs. Born, Corner Brook, Nfld., September 14, 1981. Vancouver's 5th choice, 212th overall, in 2001 Entry Draft.

Season	Club	League	GP	G	A	Pts	PIM	PP	SH	GW	S	%	+/-	TF	F%	Min	GP	G	A	Pts	PIM	PP	SH	GW	Min
99-2000	Halifax	QMJHL	53	3	7	10	8	....	....	....	....	....	....	....	....	....	10	0	0	0	2	....	....	....	....
2000-01	Halifax	QMJHL	72	48	41	89	78	....	....	....	....	....	....	....	....	....	6	3	2	5	16	....	....	....	....
2001-02	Halifax	QMJHL	61	*63	36	99	39	....	....	....	....	....	....	....	....	....	13	9	8	17	13	....	....	....	....
2002-03	Vancouver	NHL	8	0	2	2	0	0	0	0	12	0.0	0	0	0.0	11:17	....	....	....	....	....	....	....	....	....
	Manitoba Moose	AHL	67	20	20	40	15	....	....	....	....	....	....	....	....	....	14	4	3	7	14	....	....	....	....
2003-04	Vancouver	NHL	47	12	9	21	8	6	0	1	107	11.2	0	3	66.7	12:43	1	0	0	0	0	0	0	0	6:21
	Manitoba Moose	AHL	29	12	11	23	6	....	....	....	....	....	....	....	....	....	....	....	....	....	....	....	....	....	....
2004-05	Manitoba Moose	AHL	59	26	27	53	22	....	....	....	....	....	....	....	....	....	....	....	....	....	....	....	....	....	....
	NHL Totals		55	12	11	23	8	6	0	1	119	10.1		3	66.7	12:30	1	0	0	0	0	0	0	0	6:21

QMJHL Second All-Star Team (2001)

KLATT, Trent

(KLAT, TREHNT) **L.A.**

Right wing. Shoots right. 6'1", 210 lbs. Born, Robbinsdale, MN, January 30, 1971. Washington's 5th choice, 82nd overall, in 1989 Entry Draft.

Season	Club	League	GP	G	A	Pts	PIM	PP	SH	GW	S	%	+/-	TF	F%	Min	GP	G	A	Pts	PIM	PP	SH	GW	Min
1986-87	Osseo Orioles	High-MN	22	9	27	36	....	....	....	....	....	....	....	....	....	....	....	....	....	....	....	....	....	....	....
1987-88	Osseo Orioles	High-MN	22	19	17	36	....	....	....	....	....	....	....	....	....	....	....	....	....	....	....	....	....	....	....
1988-89	Osseo Orioles	High-MN	22	24	39	63	....	....	....	....	....	....	....	....	....	....	....	....	....	....	....	....	....	....	....
1989-90	U. of Minnesota	WCHA	38	22	14	36	16	....	....	....	....	....	....	....	....	....	....	....	....	....	....	....	....	....	....
1990-91	U. of Minnesota	WCHA	39	16	28	44	58	....	....	....	....	....	....	....	....	....	....	....	....	....	....	....	....	....	....
1991-92	U. of Minnesota	WCHA	41	27	36	63	76	....	....	....	....	....	....	....	....	....	....	....	....	....	....	....	....	....	....
	Minnesota	NHL	1	0	0	0	0	0	0	0	1	0.0	0	....	....	....	6	0	0	0	2	0	0	0	....
1992-93	Minnesota	NHL	47	4	19	23	38	1	0	0	69	5.8	2	....	....	....	....	....	....	....	....	....	....	....	....
	Kalamazoo Wings	IHL	31	8	11	19	18	....	....	....	....	....	....	....	....	....	....	....	....	....	....	....	....	....	....

			Regular Season														Playoffs								
Season	Club	League	GP	G	A	Pts	PIM	PP	SH	GW	S	%	+/-	TF	F%	Min	GP	G	A	Pts	PIM	PP	SH	GW	Min
1993-94	**Dallas**	**NHL**	**61**	**14**	**24**	**38**	**30**	**3**	**0**	**2**	**86**	**16.3**	**13**				**9**	**2**	**1**	**3**	**4**	**1**	**0**	**0**	
	Kalamazoo Wings	IHL	6	3	2	5	4																		
1994-95	**Dallas**	**NHL**	**47**	**12**	**10**	**22**	**26**	**5**	**0**	**3**	**91**	**13.2**	**–2**				**5**	**1**	**0**	**1**	**0**	**1**	**0**	**0**	
1995-96	**Dallas**	**NHL**	**22**	**4**	**4**	**8**	**23**	**0**	**0**	**1**	**37**	**10.8**	**0**												
	Michigan	IHL	2	1	2	3	5																		
	Philadelphia	**NHL**	**49**	**3**	**8**	**11**	**21**	**0**	**0**	**1**	**64**	**4.7**	**2**				**12**	**4**	**1**	**5**	**0**	**0**	**0**	**0**	
1996-97	**Philadelphia**	**NHL**	**76**	**24**	**21**	**45**	**20**	**5**	**5**	**5**	**131**	**18.3**	**9**				**19**	**4**	**3**	**7**	**12**	**0**	**0**	**2**	
1997-98	**Philadelphia**	**NHL**	**82**	**14**	**28**	**42**	**16**	**5**	**0**	**3**	**143**	**9.8**	**2**				**5**	**0**	**0**	**0**	**0**	**0**	**0**	**0**	
1998-99	**Philadelphia**	**NHL**	**2**	**0**	**0**	**0**	**0**	**0**	**0**	**0**	**2**	**0.0**	**0**	**0**	**0.0**	**11:11**									
	Vancouver	**NHL**	**73**	**4**	**10**	**14**	**12**	**0**	**0**	**0**	**58**	**6.9**	**–3**	**37**	**32.4**	**11:21**									
99-2000	**Vancouver**	**NHL**	**47**	**10**	**10**	**20**	**26**	**8**	**0**	**0**	**100**	**10.0**	**–8**	**19**	**63.2**	**16:04**									
	Syracuse Crunch	AHL	24	13	10	23	6																		
2000-01	**Vancouver**	**NHL**	**77**	**13**	**20**	**33**	**31**	**3**	**0**	**1**	**140**	**9.3**	**8**	**75**	**50.7**	**13:33**	**4**	**3**	**0**	**3**	**0**	**2**	**0**	**0**	**15:54**
2001-02	**Vancouver**	**NHL**	**34**	**8**	**7**	**15**	**10**	**2**	**1**	**3**	**67**	**11.9**	**9**	**101**	**54.5**	**15:27**									
2002-03	**Vancouver**	**NHL**	**82**	**16**	**13**	**29**	**8**	**3**	**0**	**2**	**127**	**12.6**	**10**	**47**	**40.4**	**12:25**	**14**	**2**	**4**	**6**	**2**	**2**	**0**	**1**	**12:42**
2003-04	**Los Angeles**	**NHL**	**82**	**17**	**26**	**43**	**46**	**6**	**0**	**2**	**160**	**10.6**	**2**	**96**	**46.9**	**16:15**									
2004-05		DID NOT PLAY																							
	NHL Totals		**782**	**143**	**200**	**343**	**307**	**41**	**6**	**23**	**1276**	**11.2**		**375**	**48.3**	**13:55**	**74**	**16**	**9**	**25**	**20**	**6**	**0**	**3**	**13:25**

Minnesota High School Player of the Year (1989)

Traded to **Minnesota** by **Washington** with Steve Maltais for Shawn Chambers, June 21, 1991. Transferred to **Dallas** after **Minnesota** franchise relocated, June 9, 1993. Traded to **Philadelphia** by **Dallas** for Brent Fedyk, December 13, 1995. Traded to **Vancouver** by **Philadelphia** for Vancouver's 6th round choice (later traded to Atlanta – Atlanta selected Jeff Dwyer) in 2000 Entry Draft, October 19, 1998. • Missed majority of 2001-02 season recovering from abdominal injury suffered in game vs. Ottawa, November 20, 2001. Signed as a free agent by **Los Angeles**, July 7, 2003.

KLEE, Ken — (KLEE, KEHN) — TOR.

Defense. Shoots right. 6', 210 lbs. Born, Indianapolis, IN, April 24, 1971. Washington's 11th choice, 177th overall, in 1990 Entry Draft.

Season	Club	League	GP	G	A	Pts	PIM	PP	SH	GW	S	%	+/-	TF	F%	Min	GP	G	A	Pts	PIM	PP	SH	GW	Min
1988-89	St. Mike's B's	OHA-B	40	9	23	32	64										27	5	12	17	54				
1989-90	Bowling Green	CCHA	39	0	5	5	52																		
1990-91	Bowling Green	CCHA	37	7	28	35	50																		
1991-92	Bowling Green	CCHA	10	0	1	1	14																		
1992-93	Baltimore	AHL	77	4	14	18	93										7	0	1	1	15				
1993-94	Portland Pirates	AHL	65	2	9	11	87										17	1	2	3	14				
1994-95	Portland Pirates	AHL	49	5	7	12	89																		
	Washington	**NHL**	**23**	**3**	**1**	**4**	**41**	**0**	**0**	**0**	**18**	**16.7**	**2**				**7**	**0**	**0**	**0**	**4**	**0**	**0**	**0**	
1995-96	**Washington**	**NHL**	**66**	**8**	**3**	**11**	**60**	**0**	**1**	**2**	**76**	**10.5**	**–1**				**1**	**0**	**0**	**0**	**0**	**0**	**0**	**0**	
1996-97	**Washington**	**NHL**	**80**	**3**	**8**	**11**	**115**	**0**	**0**	**2**	**108**	**2.8**	**–5**												
1997-98	**Washington**	**NHL**	**51**	**4**	**2**	**6**	**46**	**0**	**0**	**1**	**44**	**9.1**	**–3**				**9**	**1**	**0**	**1**	**10**	**0**	**0**	**0**	
1998-99	**Washington**	**NHL**	**78**	**7**	**13**	**20**	**80**	**0**	**0**	**1**	**132**	**5.3**	**–9**	**0**	**0.0**	**19:07**									
99-2000	**Washington**	**NHL**	**80**	**7**	**13**	**20**	**79**	**0**	**0**	**2**	**113**	**6.2**	**8**	**0**	**0.0**	**20:29**	**5**	**0**	**1**	**1**	**10**	**0**	**0**	**0**	**21:38**
2000-01	**Washington**	**NHL**	**54**	**2**	**4**	**6**	**60**	**0**	**0**	**0**	**58**	**3.4**	**–5**	**0**	**0.0**	**17:15**	**6**	**0**	**1**	**1**	**8**	**0**	**0**	**0**	**13:47**
2001-02	**Washington**	**NHL**	**68**	**8**	**8**	**16**	**38**	**2**	**0**	**3**	**85**	**9.4**	**4**	**2**	**0.0**	**19:24**									
2002-03	**Washington**	**NHL**	**70**	**1**	**16**	**17**	**89**	**0**	**0**	**0**	**67**	**1.5**	**22**	**0**	**0.0**	**21:49**	**6**	**0**	**0**	**0**	**6**	**0**	**0**	**0**	**23:11**
2003-04	**Toronto**	**NHL**	**66**	**4**	**25**	**29**	**36**	**3**	**0**	**1**	**85**	**4.7**	**–1**	**1**	**100.0**	**22:08**	**11**	**0**	**0**	**0**	**6**	**0**	**0**	**0**	**18:45**
2004-05		DID NOT PLAY																							
	NHL Totals		**636**	**47**	**93**	**140**	**644**	**5**	**1**	**12**	**786**	**6.0**		**3**	**33.3**	**20:07**	**45**	**1**	**2**	**3**	**44**	**0**	**0**	**0**	**19:09**

Signed as a free agent by **Toronto**, September 27, 2003.

KLEMM, Jon — (KLEHM, JAWN) — DAL.

Defense. Shoots right. 6'2", 200 lbs. Born, Cranbrook, B.C., January 8, 1970.

Season	Club	League	GP	G	A	Pts	PIM	PP	SH	GW	S	%	+/-	TF	F%	Min	GP	G	A	Pts	PIM	PP	SH	GW	Min
1986-87	Cranbrook Colts	KIJHL	59	20	51	71	54																		
1987-88	Seattle	WHL	68	6	7	13	24																		
1988-89	Seattle	WHL	2	1	1	2	0																		
	Spokane Chiefs	WHL	66	6	34	40	42																		
1989-90	Spokane Chiefs	WHL	66	3	28	31	100										6	1	1	2	5				
1990-91	Spokane Chiefs	WHL	72	7	58	65	65										15	3	6	9	8				
1991-92	**Quebec**	**NHL**	**4**	**0**	**1**	**1**	**0**	**0**	**0**	**0**	**2**	**0.0**	**2**												
	Halifax Citadels	AHL	70	6	13	19	40																		
1992-93	Halifax Citadels	AHL	80	3	20	23	32																		
1993-94	**Quebec**	**NHL**	**7**	**0**	**0**	**0**	**4**	**0**	**0**	**0**	**11**	**0.0**	**–1**												
	Cornwall Aces	AHL	66	4	26	30	78										13	1	2	3	6				
1994-95	Cornwall Aces	AHL	65	6	13	19	84																		
	Quebec	**NHL**	**4**	**1**	**0**	**1**	**2**	**0**	**0**	**0**	**5**	**20.0**	**3**												
1995-96♦	**Colorado**	**NHL**	**56**	**3**	**12**	**15**	**20**	**0**	**1**	**1**	**61**	**4.9**	**12**				**15**	**2**	**1**	**3**	**0**	**1**	**0**	**0**	
1996-97	**Colorado**	**NHL**	**80**	**9**	**15**	**24**	**37**	**1**	**2**	**1**	**103**	**8.7**	**12**				**17**	**1**	**1**	**2**	**6**	**0**	**0**	**0**	
1997-98	**Colorado**	**NHL**	**67**	**6**	**8**	**14**	**30**	**0**	**0**	**0**	**60**	**10.0**	**–3**				**4**	**0**	**0**	**0**	**0**	**0**	**0**	**0**	
1998-99	**Colorado**	**NHL**	**39**	**1**	**2**	**3**	**31**	**0**	**0**	**0**	**28**	**3.6**	**4**	**14**	**35.7**	**13:43**	**19**	**0**	**1**	**1**	**10**	**0**	**0**	**0**	**8:32**
99-2000	**Colorado**	**NHL**	**73**	**5**	**7**	**12**	**34**	**0**	**0**	**0**	**64**	**7.8**	**26**	**17**	**47.1**	**17:22**	**17**	**2**	**1**	**3**	**9**	**0**	**0**	**0**	**14:25**
2000-01♦	**Colorado**	**NHL**	**78**	**4**	**11**	**15**	**54**	**2**	**0**	**2**	**97**	**4.1**	**22**	**1**	**100.0**	**19:56**	**22**	**1**	**2**	**3**	**16**	**0**	**0**	**1**	**16:15**
2001-02	**Chicago**	**NHL**	**82**	**4**	**16**	**20**	**42**	**2**	**0**	**1**	**111**	**3.6**	**–3**	**1**	**0.0**	**23:50**	**5**	**0**	**1**	**1**	**4**	**0**	**0**	**0**	**21:58**
2002-03	**Chicago**	**NHL**	**70**	**2**	**14**	**16**	**44**	**1**	**0**	**1**	**74**	**2.7**	**–9**	**2**	**0.0**	**21:57**									
2003-04	**Chicago**	**NHL**	**19**	**0**	**1**	**1**	**20**	**0**	**0**	**0**	**19**	**0.0**	**6**	**0**	**0.0**	**21:21**									
	Dallas	**NHL**	**58**	**2**	**4**	**6**	**24**	**0**	**0**	**1**	**52**	**3.8**	**10**	**1**	**0.0**	**16:00**									
2004-05		DID NOT PLAY																							
	NHL Totals		**637**	**37**	**91**	**128**	**342**	**6**	**3**	**7**	**687**	**5.4**		**36**	**38.9**	**19:32**	**99**	**6**	**7**	**13**	**45**	**1**	**0**	**1**	**13:53**

WHL West Second All-Star Team (1991)

Signed as a free agent by **Quebec**, May 14, 1991. Transferred to **Colorado** after **Quebec** franchise relocated, June 21, 1995. • Missed majority of 1998-99 season recovering from knee injury suffered in game vs. Phoenix, November 10, 1998. Signed as a free agent by **Chicago**, July 1, 2001. Traded to **Dallas** by **Chicago** with NY Rangers' 4th round choice (previously acquired, Dallas selected Fredrik Naslund) in 2004 Entry Draft for Stephane Robidas and Dallas' 2nd round choice (Jakub Sindel) in 2004 Entry Draft, November 17, 2003.

KLESLA, Rostislav — (KLEHS-luh, RAHS-tih-slav) — CBJ

Defense. Shoots left. 6'3", 208 lbs. Born, Novy Jicin, Czech., March 21, 1982. Columbus' 1st choice, 4th overall, in 2000 Entry Draft.

Season	Club	League	GP	G	A	Pts	PIM	PP	SH	GW	S	%	+/-	TF	F%	Min	GP	G	A	Pts	PIM	PP	SH	GW	Min
1997-98	HC Opava Jr.	CzRep-Jr.	38	11	18	29	87										8	2	2	4	0				
1998-99	Sioux City	USHL	54	4	12	16	100										5	2	0	2	2				
99-2000	Brampton	OHL	67	16	29	45	174										6	1	1	2	21				
2000-01	**Columbus**	**NHL**	**8**	**2**	**0**	**2**	**6**	**0**	**0**	**0**	**10**	**20.0**	**–1**	**0**	**0.0**	**18:25**									
	Brampton	OHL	45	18	36	54	59										9	2	9	11	26				
2001-02	**Columbus**	**NHL**	**75**	**8**	**8**	**16**	**74**	**1**	**0**	**0**	**102**	**7.8**	**–6**	**0**	**0.0**	**18:52**									
2002-03	**Columbus**	**NHL**	**72**	**2**	**14**	**16**	**71**	**0**	**0**	**0**	**89**	**2.2**	**–22**	**0**	**0.0**	**18:45**									
2003-04	**Columbus**	**NHL**	**47**	**2**	**11**	**13**	**27**	**0**	**0**	**1**	**74**	**2.7**	**–16**	**0**	**0.0**	**18:19**									
2004-05	HC Vsetin	CzRep	41	7	17	24	136																		
	HPK Hameenlinna	Finland	9	1	2	3	12										10	0	2	2	12				
	NHL Totals		**202**	**14**	**33**	**47**	**178**	**1**	**0**	**1**	**275**	**5.1**		**0**	**0.0**	**18:41**									

OHL All-Rookie Team (2000) • Canadian Major Junior All-Rookie Team (2000) • OHL First All-Star Team (2001) • NHL All-Rookie Team (2002)

Returned to **Brampton** (OHL) by **Columbus**, October 28, 2000. Signed as a free agent by **Vsetin** (CzRep), September 17, 2004. Signed as a free agent by **HPK** (Finland), January 29, 2005.

KLOUCEK, Tomas — (KLOH-chehk, TAW-mahsh) — ATL.

Defense. Shoots left. 6'3", 225 lbs. Born, Prague, Czech., March 7, 1980. NY Rangers' 6th choice, 131st overall, in 1998 Entry Draft.

Season	Club	League	GP	G	A	Pts	PIM	PP	SH	GW	S	%	+/-	TF	F%	Min	GP	G	A	Pts	PIM	PP	SH	GW	Min
1995-96	Slavia Jr.	CzRep-Jr.	40	2	8	10																			
1996-97	Slavia Jr.	CzRep-Jr.	43	4	14	18	44																		
1997-98	Slavia Jr.	CzRep-Jr.	43	1	9	10																			
1998-99	Cape Breton	QMJHL	59	4	17	21	162										2	0	0	0	4				
99-2000	Hartford	AHL	73	2	8	10	113										23	0	4	4	18				
2000-01	**NY Rangers**	**NHL**	**43**	**1**	**4**	**5**	**74**	**0**	**0**	**0**	**22**	**4.5**	**–3**	**0**	**0.0**	**16:43**									
	Hartford	AHL	21	0	2	2	44																		
2001-02	**NY Rangers**	**NHL**	**52**	**1**	**3**	**4**	**137**	**0**	**0**	**0**	**21**	**4.8**	**–2**	**1**	**0.0**	**11:58**									
	Hartford	AHL	9	0	2	2	27										10	1	1	2	8				

			Regular Season														Playoffs								
Season	Club	League	GP	G	A	Pts	PIM	PP	SH	GW	S	%	+/-	TF	F%	Min	GP	G	A	Pts	PIM	PP	SH	GW	Min
2002-03	Hartford	AHL	20	3	4	7	102	....	....	....	....	....	....	....	....	....	....	....	....	....	....	....	....	....	....
	Nashville	**NHL**	**3**	**0**	**0**	**0**	**2**	**0**	**0**	**0**	**1**	**0.0**	**1**	**0**	**0.0**	**9:45**	....	....	....	....	....	....	....	....	....
	Milwaukee	AHL	34	0	6	6	80	....	....	....	....	....	....	....	....	....	....	....	....	....	....	....	....	....	....
2003-04	**Nashville**	**NHL**	**5**	**0**	**1**	**1**	**10**	**0**	**0**	**0**	**0**	**0.0**	**3**	**0**	**0.0**	**11:34**	....	....	....	....	....	....	....	....	....
	Atlanta	**NHL**	**37**	**0**	**0**	**0**	**25**	**0**	**0**	**0**	**12**	**0.0**	**–8**	**0**	**0.0**	**8:00**	....	....	....	....	....	....	....	....	....
2004-05	HC Slavia Praha	CzRep	29	1	1	2	28	....	....	....	....	....	....	....	....	....	....	....	....	....	....	....	....	....	....
	HC Ocelari Trinec	CzRep	11	1	2	3	24	....	....	....	....	....	....	....	....	....	....	....	....	....	....	....	....	....	....
	Liberec	CzRep	8	1	0	1	12	....	....	....	....	....	....	....	....	....	9	0	1	1	35	....	....	....	....
	NHL Totals		**140**	**2**	**8**	**10**	**248**	**0**	**0**	**0**	**56**	**3.6**		**1**	**0.0**	**12:19**	....	....	....	....	....	....	....	....	....

AHL All-Rookie Team (2000)

Traded to **Nashville** by **NY Rangers** with Rem Murray and Marek Zidlicky for Mike Dunham, December 12, 2002. Traded to **Atlanta** by **Nashville** with Ben Simon for Simon Gamache and Kirill Safronov, December 2, 2003. Signed as a free agent by **Slavia** (CzRep), September 17, 2004. Signed as a free agent by **Trinec** (CzRep), December, 2004. Signed as a free agent by **Liberec** (CzRep), January 31, 2005.

KNUBLE, Mike (kuh-NOO-buhl, MIGHK) PHI.

Right wing. Shoots right. 6'3", 228 lbs. Born, Toronto, Ont., July 4, 1972. Detroit's 4th choice, 76th overall, in 1991 Entry Draft.

Season	Club	League	GP	G	A	Pts	PIM	PP	SH	GW	S	%	+/-	TF	F%	Min	GP	G	A	Pts	PIM	PP	SH	GW	Min
1988-89	East Kentwood	High-MI	28	52	37	89	60	....	....	....	....	....	....	....	....	....	....	....	....	....	....	....	....	....	....
1989-90	East Kentwood	High-MI	29	63	40	103	40	....	....	....	....	....	....	....	....	....	....	....	....	....	....	....	....	....	....
1990-91	Kalamazoo	NAHL	36	18	24	42	30	....	....	....	....	....	....	....	....	....	....	....	....	....	....	....	....	....	....
1991-92	U. of Michigan	CCHA	43	7	8	15	48	....	....	....	....	....	....	....	....	....	....	....	....	....	....	....	....	....	....
1992-93	U. of Michigan	CCHA	39	26	16	42	57	....	....	....	....	....	....	....	....	....	....	....	....	....	....	....	....	....	....
1993-94	U. of Michigan	CCHA	41	32	26	58	71	....	....	....	....	....	....	....	....	....	....	....	....	....	....	....	....	....	....
1994-95	U. of Michigan	CCHA	34	*38	22	60	62	....	....	....	....	....	....	....	....	....	....	....	....	....	....	....	....	....	....
	Adirondack	AHL	....	....	....	....	....	....	....	....	....	....	....	....	....	....	3	0	0	0	0	....	....	....	....
1995-96	Adirondack	AHL	80	22	23	45	59	....	....	....	....	....	....	....	....	....	3	1	0	1	0	....	....	....	....
1996-97	**Detroit**	**NHL**	**9**	**1**	**0**	**1**	**0**	**0**	**0**	**0**	**10**	**10.0**	**–1**	....	....	....	....	....	....	....	....	....	....	....	....
	Adirondack	AHL	68	28	35	63	54	....	....	....	....	....	....	....	....	....	....	....	....	....	....	....	....	....	....
1997-98♦	**Detroit**	**NHL**	**53**	**7**	**6**	**13**	**16**	**0**	**0**	**0**	**54**	**13.0**	**2**	....	....	....	**3**	**0**	**1**	**1**	**0**	**0**	**0**	**0**	....
1998-99	**NY Rangers**	**NHL**	**82**	**15**	**20**	**35**	**26**	**3**	**0**	**1**	**113**	**13.3**	**–7**	**1**	**100.0**	**14:52**	....	....	....	....	....	....	....	....	....
99-2000	**NY Rangers**	**NHL**	**59**	**9**	**5**	**14**	**18**	**1**	**0**	**1**	**50**	**18.0**	**–5**	**9**	**55.6**	**10:39**	....	....	....	....	....	....	....	....	....
	Boston	**NHL**	**14**	**3**	**3**	**6**	**8**	**1**	**0**	**1**	**28**	**10.7**	**–2**	**3**	**0.0**	**19:29**	....	....	....	....	....	....	....	....	....
2000-01	**Boston**	**NHL**	**82**	**7**	**13**	**20**	**37**	**0**	**1**	**1**	**92**	**7.6**	**0**	**115**	**31.3**	**10:34**	....	....	....	....	....	....	....	....	....
2001-02	**Boston**	**NHL**	**54**	**8**	**6**	**14**	**42**	**0**	**0**	**2**	**77**	**10.4**	**9**	**27**	**44.4**	**9:45**	**2**	**0**	**0**	**0**	**0**	**0**	**0**	**0**	**3:30**
2002-03	**Boston**	**NHL**	**75**	**30**	**29**	**59**	**45**	**9**	**0**	**4**	**185**	**16.2**	**18**	**34**	**44.1**	**17:24**	**5**	**0**	**2**	**2**	**2**	**0**	**0**	**0**	**17:35**
2003-04	**Boston**	**NHL**	**82**	**21**	**25**	**46**	**32**	**4**	**0**	**3**	**192**	**10.9**	**19**	**54**	**31.5**	**18:47**	**7**	**2**	**0**	**2**	**0**	**1**	**0**	**0**	**19:45**
2004-05	Linkopings HC	Sweden	49	*26	13	39	40	....	....	....	....	....	....	....	....	....	6	0	1	1	2	....	....	....	....
	NHL Totals		**510**	**101**	**107**	**208**	**224**	**18**	**1**	**13**	**801**	**12.6**		**243**	**35.4**	**14:12**	**17**	**2**	**3**	**5**	**2**	**1**	**0**	**0**	**16:39**

CCHA Second All-Star Team (1994, 1995) • NCAA West Second All-American Team (1995)

Traded to **NY Rangers** by **Detroit** for NY Rangers' 2nd round choice (Tomas Kopecky) in 2000 Entry Draft, October 1, 1998. Traded to **Boston** by **NY Rangers** for Rob DiMaio, March 10, 2000. Signed as a free agent by **Philadelphia**, July 3, 2004. Signed as a free agent by **Linkopings** (Sweden), August 2, 2004.

KOBASEW, Chuck (KOH-buh-soo, CHUK) CGY.

Center. Shoots left. 6'1", 195 lbs. Born, Osoyoos, B.C., April 17, 1982. Calgary's 1st choice, 14th overall, in 2001 Entry Draft.

Season	Club	League	GP	G	A	Pts	PIM	PP	SH	GW	S	%	+/-	TF	F%	Min	GP	G	A	Pts	PIM	PP	SH	GW	Min
1997-98	Osoyoos Heat	KIJHL	6	2	2	4	2	....	....	....	....	....	....	....	....	....	....	....	....	....	....	....	....	....	....
1998-99	Osoyoos Heat	KIJHL	23	25	24	49	....	....	....	....	....	....	....	....	....	....	....	....	....	....	....	....	....	....	....
	Penticton	BCHL	30	11	17	28	18	....	....	....	....	....	....	....	....	....	....	....	....	....	....	....	....	....	....
99-2000	Penticton	BCHL	58	*54	52	106	83	....	....	....	....	....	....	....	....	....	....	....	....	....	....	....	....	....	....
2000-01	Boston College	H-East	43	27	22	49	38	....	....	....	....	....	....	....	....	....	....	....	....	....	....	....	....	....	....
2001-02	Kelowna Rockets	WHL	55	41	21	62	114	....	....	....	....	....	....	....	....	....	15	10	5	15	22	....	....	....	....
2002-03	**Calgary**	**NHL**	**23**	**4**	**2**	**6**	**8**	**1**	**0**	**1**	**29**	**13.8**	**–3**	**5**	**0.0**	**11:48**	....	....	....	....	....	....	....	....	....
	Saint John Flames	AHL	48	21	12	33	61	....	....	....	....	....	....	....	....	....	....	....	....	....	....	....	....	....	....
2003-04	**Calgary**	**NHL**	**70**	**6**	**11**	**17**	**51**	**3**	**0**	**0**	**78**	**7.7**	**–12**	**91**	**42.9**	**10:22**	**26**	**0**	**1**	**1**	**24**	**0**	**0**	**0**	**9:02**
2004-05	Lowell	AHL	79	38	37	75	110	....	....	....	....	....	....	....	....	....	11	6	3	9	27	....	....	....	....
	NHL Totals		**93**	**10**	**13**	**23**	**59**	**4**	**0**	**1**	**107**	**9.3**		**96**	**40.6**	**10:44**	**26**	**0**	**1**	**1**	**24**	**0**	**0**	**0**	**9:02**

Hockey East Second All-Star Team (2001) • Hockey East Rookie of the Year (2001) • NCAA Championship All-Tournament Team (2001) • NCAA Championship Tournament MVP (2001) • AHL First All-Star Team (2005)

• Left **Boston College** (H-East) and signed with **Kelowna** (WHL), August 13, 2001.

KOIVISTO, Tom (KOI-vihs-toh, TAWM)

Defense. Shoots right. 5'10", 194 lbs. Born, Turku, Finland, June 4, 1974. St. Louis' 8th choice, 253rd overall, in 2002 Entry Draft.

Season	Club	League	GP	G	A	Pts	PIM	PP	SH	GW	S	%	+/-	TF	F%	Min	GP	G	A	Pts	PIM	PP	SH	GW	Min
1991-92	TPS Turku Jr.	Finland-Jr.	36	4	9	13	40	....	....	....	....	....	....	....	....	....	8	1	3	4	12	....	....	....	....
1992-93	TPS Turku Jr.	Finland-Jr.	21	10	8	18	30	....	....	....	....	....	....	....	....	....	5	1	1	2	6	....	....	....	....
	Kiekko-67 Turku	Finland-2	16	0	4	4	4	....	....	....	....	....	....	....	....	....	....	....	....	....	....	....	....	....	....
	TPS Turku	Finland	1	0	0	0	0	....	....	....	....	....	....	....	....	....	1	0	0	0	0	....	....	....	....
1993-94	TPS Turku Jr.	Finland-Jr.	10	4	5	9	16	....	....	....	....	....	....	....	....	....	7	0	5	5	8	....	....	....	....
	Kiekko-67 Turku	Finland-2	16	4	12	16	2	....	....	....	....	....	....	....	....	....	....	....	....	....	....	....	....	....	....
	TPS Turku	Finland	18	2	5	7	4	....	....	....	....	....	....	....	....	....	1	0	1	1	2	....	....	....	....
1994-95	TPS Turku Jr.	Finland-Jr.	5	0	2	2	8	....	....	....	....	....	....	....	....	....	....	....	....	....	....	....	....	....	....
	Kiekko-67 Turku	Finland-2	14	7	3	10	6	....	....	....	....	....	....	....	....	....	....	....	....	....	....	....	....	....	....
	TPS Turku	Finland	4	0	0	0	4	....	....	....	....	....	....	....	....	....	....	....	....	....	....	....	....	....	....
	HPK Hameenlinna	Finland	25	3	3	6	16	....	....	....	....	....	....	....	....	....	....	....	....	....	....	....	....	....	....
1995-96	HPK Hameenlinna	Finland	50	8	11	19	52	....	....	....	....	....	....	....	....	....	9	1	2	3	6	....	....	....	....
1996-97	HPK Hameenlinna	Finland	46	18	17	35	50	....	....	....	....	....	....	....	....	....	10	4	2	6	6	....	....	....	....
1997-98	HPK Hameenlinna	Finland	23	6	6	12	28	....	....	....	....	....	....	....	....	....	....	....	....	....	....	....	....	....	....
	HPK Hameenlinna	EuroHL	3	1	0	1	0	....	....	....	....	....	....	....	....	....	....	....	....	....	....	....	....	....	....
1998-99	HPK Hameenlinna	Finland	52	13	26	39	91	....	....	....	....	....	....	....	....	....	8	5	1	6	14	....	....	....	....
99-2000	Jokerit Helsinki	Finland	43	8	20	28	58	....	....	....	....	....	....	....	....	....	11	2	1	3	2	....	....	....	....
2000-01	Jokerit Helsinki	Finland	47	8	15	23	36	....	....	....	....	....	....	....	....	....	5	0	0	0	2	....	....	....	....
2001-02	Jokerit Helsinki	Finland	43	8	14	22	30	....	....	....	....	....	....	....	....	....	12	3	*8	11	2	....	....	....	....
2002-03	**St. Louis**	**NHL**	**22**	**2**	**4**	**6**	**10**	**0**	**0**	**1**	**26**	**7.7**	**1**	**0**	**0.0**	**16:44**	....	....	....	....	....	....	....	....	....
	Worcester IceCats	AHL	47	4	13	17	32	....	....	....	....	....	....	....	....	....	3	0	0	0	0	....	....	....	....
2003-04	Worcester IceCats	AHL	28	4	13	17	16	....	....	....	....	....	....	....	....	....	....	....	....	....	....	....	....	....	....
	Springfield	AHL	17	0	8	8	12	....	....	....	....	....	....	....	....	....	....	....	....	....	....	....	....	....	....
2004-05	Frolunda	Sweden	50	9	19	28	66	....	....	....	....	....	....	....	....	....	14	1	1	2	14	....	....	....	....
	NHL Totals		**22**	**2**	**4**	**6**	**10**	**0**	**0**	**1**	**26**	**7.7**		**0**	**0.0**	**16:44**	....	....	....	....	....	....	....	....	....

Finnish Elite League All-Star Team (2002) • Finnish Elite League Best Defenseman (2002)

Traded to **Phoenix** by **St. Louis** for future considerations, March 9, 2004. Signed as a free agent by **Frolunda** (Sweden), April 15, 2004.

KOIVU, Saku (KOI-voo, SA-koo) MTL.

Center. Shoots left. 5'10", 181 lbs. Born, Turku, Finland, November 23, 1974. Montreal's 1st choice, 21st overall, in 1993 Entry Draft.

Season	Club	League	GP	G	A	Pts	PIM	PP	SH	GW	S	%	+/-	TF	F%	Min	GP	G	A	Pts	PIM	PP	SH	GW	Min
1990-91	TPS Turku U18	Fin-U18	24	20	28	48	26	....	....	....	....	....	....	....	....	....	....	....	....	....	....	....	....	....	....
1991-92	TPS Turku U18	Fin-U18	12	3	7	10	6	....	....	....	....	....	....	....	....	....	....	....	....	....	....	....	....	....	....
	TPS Turku Jr.	Finland-Jr.	34	25	28	53	57	....	....	....	....	....	....	....	....	....	8	5	*9	*14	6	....	....	....	....
1992-93	TPS Turku	Finland	46	3	7	10	28	....	....	....	....	....	....	....	....	....	11	3	2	5	2	....	....	....	....
1993-94	TPS Turku	Finland	47	23	30	53	42	....	....	....	....	....	....	....	....	....	11	4	8	12	16	....	....	....	....
	Finland	Olympics	8	4	3	7	12	....	....	....	....	....	....	....	....	....	....	....	....	....	....	....	....	....	....
1994-95	TPS Turku	Finland	45	27	*47	*74	73	....	....	....	....	....	....	....	....	....	13	*7	10	17	16	....	....	....	....
1995-96	**Montreal**	**NHL**	**82**	**20**	**25**	**45**	**40**	**8**	**3**	**2**	**136**	**14.7**	**–7**	....	....	....	**6**	**3**	**1**	**4**	**8**	**0**	**0**	**0**	....
1996-97	**Montreal**	**NHL**	**50**	**17**	**39**	**56**	**38**	**5**	**0**	**3**	**135**	**12.6**	**7**	....	....	....	**5**	**1**	**3**	**4**	**10**	**0**	**0**	**0**	....
1997-98	**Montreal**	**NHL**	**69**	**14**	**43**	**57**	**48**	**2**	**2**	**3**	**145**	**9.7**	**8**	....	....	....	**6**	**2**	**3**	**5**	**2**	**1**	**0**	**0**	....
	Finland	Olympics	6	2	*8	*10	4	....	....	....	....	....	....	....	....	....	....	....	....	....	....	....	....	....	....
1998-99	**Montreal**	**NHL**	**65**	**14**	**30**	**44**	**38**	**4**	**2**	**0**	**145**	**9.7**	**–7**	**1427**	**52.6**	**20:02**	....	....	....	....	....	....	....	....	....
99-2000	**Montreal**	**NHL**	**24**	**3**	**18**	**21**	**14**	**1**	**0**	**0**	**53**	**5.7**	**7**	**495**	**52.9**	**19:13**	....	....	....	....	....	....	....	....	....
2000-01	**Montreal**	**NHL**	**54**	**17**	**30**	**47**	**40**	**7**	**0**	**3**	**113**	**15.0**	**2**	**1092**	**47.6**	**21:23**	....	....	....	....	....	....	....	....	....
2001-02	**Montreal**	**NHL**	**3**	**0**	**2**	**2**	**0**	**0**	**0**	**0**	**2**	**0.0**	**0**	**13**	**61.5**	**13:57**	**12**	**4**	**6**	**10**	**4**	**1**	**0**	**1**	**15:54**
2002-03	**Montreal**	**NHL**	**82**	**21**	**50**	**71**	**72**	**5**	**1**	**5**	**147**	**14.3**	**5**	**1566**	**49.6**	**19:14**	....	....	....	....	....	....	....	....	....

			Regular Season														Playoffs								
Season	Club	League	GP	G	A	Pts	PIM	PP	SH	GW	S	%	+/-	TF	F%	Min	GP	G	A	Pts	PIM	PP	SH	GW	Min
2003-04	**Montreal**	**NHL**	**68**	**14**	**41**	**55**	**52**	**5**	**0**	**3**	**112**	**12.5**	**-5**	**1194**	**53.9**	**19:18**	**11**	**3**	**8**	**11**	**10**	**2**	**0**	**0**	**20:34**
2004-05	TPS Turku	Finland	20	8	8	16	28	....	....	....	....	....	....	....	....	....	6	3	2	5	30	....	....	....	....
	NHL Totals		**497**	**120**	**278**	**398**	**342**	**37**	**8**	**19**	**988**	**12.1**		**5787**	**51.2**	**19:46**	**40**	**13**	**21**	**34**	**34**	**4**	**0**	**1**	**18:08**

Bill Masterton Memorial Trophy (2002)
Played in NHL All-Star Game (1998)
Missed majority of 1999-2000 season recovering from shoulder injury suffered in game vs. NY Rangers, October 30, 1999. • Missed majority of 2001-02 season recovering from non-Hodgkin's lymphoma, September 6, 2001. Signed as a free agent by **TPS** (Finland), October 21, 2004.

KOLANOS, Krystofer (koh-LA-nohs, KRIHS) PHX.

Center. Shoots right. 6'3", 206 lbs. Born, Calgary, Alta., July 27, 1981. Phoenix's 1st choice, 19th overall, in 2000 Entry Draft.

Season	Club	League	GP	G	A	Pts	PIM	PP	SH	GW	S	%	+/-	TF	F%	Min	GP	G	A	Pts	PIM	PP	SH	GW	Min
1996-97	Calgary Flames	AAHA	24	24	35	59	....	....	....	....	....	....	....	....	....	....	....	....	....	....	....	....	....	....	....
1997-98	Calgary Buffaloes	AMHL	34	34	43	77	29	....	....	....	....	....	....	....	....	....	....	....	....	....	....	....	....	....	....
1998-99	Calgary Royals	AJHL	58	43	67	110	98	....	....	....	....	....	....	....	....	....	....	....	....	....	....	....	....	....	....
99-2000	Boston College	H-East	42	16	16	32	48	....	....	....	....	....	....	....	....	....	....	....	....	....	....	....	....	....	....
2000-01	Boston College	H-East	41	25	25	50	54	....	....	....	....	....	....	....	....	....	....	....	....	....	....	....	....	....	....
2001-02	**Phoenix**	**NHL**	**57**	**11**	**11**	**22**	**48**	**0**	**0**	**5**	**81**	**13.6**	**6**	**703**	**46.4**	**13:05**	**2**	**0**	**0**	**0**	**6**	**0**	**0**	**0**	**11:12**
2002-03	**Phoenix**	**NHL**	**2**	**0**	**0**	**0**	**0**	**0**	**0**	**0**	**8**	**0.0**	**0**	**16**	**31.3**	**14:06**	....	....	....	....	....	....	....	....	....
2003-04	**Phoenix**	**NHL**	**41**	**4**	**6**	**10**	**24**	**1**	**0**	**1**	**61**	**6.6**	**-9**	**283**	**43.8**	**13:31**	....	....	....	....	....	....	....	....	....
	Springfield	AHL	32	10	11	21	38	....	....	....	....	....	....	....	....	....	....	....	....	....	....	....	....	....	....
2004-05	Blues Espoo	Finland	15	7	9	16	40	....	....	....	....	....	....	....	....	....	....	....	....	....	....	....	....	....	....
	Krefeld Pinguine	Germany	7	3	2	5	16	....	....	....	....	....	....	....	....	....	....	....	....	....	....	....	....	....	....
	NHL Totals		**100**	**15**	**17**	**32**	**72**	**1**	**0**	**6**	**150**	**10.0**		**1002**	**45.4**	**13:17**	**2**	**0**	**0**	**0**	**6**	**0**	**0**	**0**	**11:12**

Hockey East All-Rookie Team (2000) • Hockey East Second All-Star Team (2001) • NCAA East Second All-American Team (2001) • NCAA Championship All-Tournament Team (2001)
• Missed majority of 2002-03 season recovering from head injury suffered in game vs. Pittsburgh, March 20, 2002. Signed as a free agent by **Blues** (Finland), October 25, 2004. Signed as a free agent by **Krefeld** (Germany), February 16, 2005.

KOLNIK, Juraj (KOHL-nihk, YEW-igh) FLA.

Right wing. Shoots right. 5'10", 190 lbs. Born, Nitra, Czech., November 13, 1980. NY Islanders' 7th choice, 101st overall, in 1999 Entry Draft.

Season	Club	League	GP	G	A	Pts	PIM	PP	SH	GW	S	%	+/-	TF	F%	Min	GP	G	A	Pts	PIM	PP	SH	GW	Min
1997-98	Nitra Jr.	Slovak-Jr.	26	28	16	44	50	....	....	....	....	....	....	....	....	....	....	....	....	....	....	....	....	....	....
	Nitra	Slovakia	28	1	3	4	6	....	....	....	....	....	....	....	....	....	....	....	....	....	....	....	....	....	....
1998-99	Quebec Remparts	QMJHL	12	6	5	11	6	....	....	....	....	....	....	....	....	....	....	....	....	....	....	....	....	....	....
	Rimouski Oceanic	QMJHL	50	36	37	73	34	....	....	....	....	....	....	....	....	....	11	9	6	15	6	....	....	....	....
99-2000	Rimouski Oceanic	QMJHL	47	53	53	106	53	....	....	....	....	....	....	....	....	....	14	10	17	27	16	....	....	....	....
2000-01	**NY Islanders**	**NHL**	**29**	**4**	**3**	**7**	**12**	**0**	**0**	**0**	**38**	**10.5**	**-8**	**1**	**100.0**	**10:28**	....	....	....	....	....	....	....	....	....
	Lowell	AHL	25	2	6	8	18	....	....	....	....	....	....	....	....	....	....	....	....	....	....	....	....	....	....
	Springfield	AHL	29	15	20	35	20	....	....	....	....	....	....	....	....	....	....	....	....	....	....	....	....	....	....
2001-02	**NY Islanders**	**NHL**	**7**	**2**	**0**	**2**	**0**	**1**	**0**	**0**	**10**	**20.0**	**-2**	**1**	**0.0**	**7:57**	....	....	....	....	....	....	....	....	....
	Bridgeport	AHL	67	18	30	48	40	....	....	....	....	....	....	....	....	....	20	7	14	21	17	....	....	....	....
2002-03	**Florida**	**NHL**	**10**	**0**	**1**	**1**	**0**	**0**	**0**	**0**	**14**	**0.0**	**1**	**1**	**0.0**	**10:33**	....	....	....	....	....	....	....	....	....
	San Antonio	AHL	65	25	15	40	36	....	....	....	....	....	....	....	....	....	3	0	1	1	4	....	....	....	....
2003-04	**Florida**	**NHL**	**53**	**14**	**11**	**25**	**14**	**2**	**0**	**1**	**100**	**14.0**	**-7**	**25**	**64.0**	**16:05**	....	....	....	....	....	....	....	....	....
	San Antonio	AHL	15	2	14	16	21	....	....	....	....	....	....	....	....	....	....	....	....	....	....	....	....	....	....
2004-05	San Antonio	AHL	74	13	16	29	24	....	....	....	....	....	....	....	....	....	....	....	....	....	....	....	....	....	....
	NHL Totals		**99**	**20**	**15**	**35**	**26**	**3**	**0**	**1**	**162**	**12.3**		**28**	**60.7**	**13:18**	....	....	....	....	....	....	....	....	....

Memorial Cup Tournament All-Star Team (2000)
Traded to **Florida** by **NY Islanders** with NY Islanders' 9th round choice (later traded to San Jose – San Jose selected Carter Lee) in 2003 Entry Draft for Sven Butenschon, October 11, 2002.

KOLTSOV, Konstantin (kohlt-SAHV, kawn-stuhn-TEEN) PIT.

Right wing. Shoots left. 6', 206 lbs. Born, Minsk, USSR, April 17, 1981. Pittsburgh's 1st choice, 18th overall, in 1999 Entry Draft.

Season	Club	League	GP	G	A	Pts	PIM	PP	SH	GW	S	%	+/-	TF	F%	Min	GP	G	A	Pts	PIM	PP	SH	GW	Min
1997-98	Cherepovets 2	Russia-3	44	11	12	23	16	....	....	....	....	....	....	....	....	....	....	....	....	....	....	....	....	....	....
	Cherepovets	Russia	2	0	0	0	2	....	....	....	....	....	....	....	....	....	....	....	....	....	....	....	....	....	....
1998-99	Cherepovets 3	Russia-4	2	0	1	1	2	....	....	....	....	....	....	....	....	....	....	....	....	....	....	....	....	....	....
	Cherepovets 2	Russia-3	11	1	4	5	18	....	....	....	....	....	....	....	....	....	....	....	....	....	....	....	....	....	....
	Cherepovets	Russia	33	3	0	3	8	....	....	....	....	....	....	....	....	....	1	0	0	0	2	....	....	....	....
99-2000	Magnitogorsk	Russia	30	3	4	7	12	....	....	....	....	....	....	....	....	....	11	1	1	2	6	....	....	....	....
2000-01	Ak Bars Kazan	Russia	24	7	8	15	10	....	....	....	....	....	....	....	....	....	2	0	0	0	4	....	....	....	....
	Spartak 2	Russia-3	2	0	1	1	0	....	....	....	....	....	....	....	....	....	....	....	....	....	....	....	....	....	....
2001-02	Ak Bars Kazan	Russia	10	1	2	3	2	....	....	....	....	....	....	....	....	....	....	....	....	....	....	....	....	....	....
	Spartak Moscow	Russia	23	1	0	1	12	....	....	....	....	....	....	....	....	....	....	....	....	....	....	....	....	....	....
	Belarus	Olympics	2	0	0	0	0	....	....	....	....	....	....	....	....	....	....	....	....	....	....	....	....	....	....
2002-03	**Pittsburgh**	**NHL**	**2**	**0**	**0**	**0**	**0**	**0**	**0**	**0**	**4**	**0.0**	**-2**	**0**	**0.0**	**13:06**	....	....	....	....	....	....	....	....	....
	Wilkes-Barre	AHL	65	9	21	30	41	....	....	....	....	....	....	....	....	....	6	2	4	6	4	....	....	....	....
2003-04	**Pittsburgh**	**NHL**	**82**	**9**	**20**	**29**	**30**	**2**	**0**	**3**	**123**	**7.3**	**-30**	**12**	**33.3**	**15:21**	....	....	....	....	....	....	....	....	....
	Wilkes-Barre	AHL	....	....	....	....	....	....	....	....	....	....	....	....	....	....	24	6	11	17	18	....	....	....	....
2004-05	Dynamo Minsk	BelOpen	11	6	2	8	38	....	....	....	....	....	....	....	....	....	....	....	....	....	....	....	....	....	....
	Spartak Moscow	Russia	31	6	10	16	48	....	....	....	....	....	....	....	....	....	....	....	....	....	....	....	....	....	....
	NHL Totals		**84**	**9**	**20**	**29**	**30**	**2**	**0**	**3**	**127**	**7.1**		**12**	**33.3**	**15:18**	....	....	....	....	....	....	....	....	....

Signed as a free agent by **Dynamo Minsk** (BelOpen), September 15, 2004. Signed as a free agent by **Spartak** (Russia), November, 2004.

KOMARNISKI, Zenith (KOH-mahr-NIHS-kee, ZEE-nihth) CGY.

Defense. Shoots left. 6', 200 lbs. Born, Edmonton, Alta., August 13, 1978. Vancouver's 2nd choice, 75th overall, in 1996 Entry Draft.

Season	Club	League	GP	G	A	Pts	PIM	PP	SH	GW	S	%	+/-	TF	F%	Min	GP	G	A	Pts	PIM	PP	SH	GW	Min
1993-94	Ft. Saskatchewan	AMHL	32	14	32	46	42	....	....	....	....	....	....	....	....	....	....	....	....	....	....	....	....	....	....
1994-95	Tri-City	WHL	66	5	19	24	110	....	....	....	....	....	....	....	....	....	17	1	2	3	47	....	....	....	....
1995-96	Tri-City	WHL	42	5	21	26	85	....	....	....	....	....	....	....	....	....	....	....	....	....	....	....	....	....	....
1996-97	Tri-City	WHL	58	12	44	56	112	....	....	....	....	....	....	....	....	....	....	....	....	....	....	....	....	....	....
1997-98	Tri-City	WHL	3	0	4	4	18	....	....	....	....	....	....	....	....	....	....	....	....	....	....	....	....	....	....
	Spokane Chiefs	WHL	43	7	20	27	90	....	....	....	....	....	....	....	....	....	18	4	6	10	49	....	....	....	....
1998-99	Syracuse Crunch	AHL	58	9	19	28	89	....	....	....	....	....	....	....	....	....	....	....	....	....	....	....	....	....	....
99-2000	**Vancouver**	**NHL**	**18**	**1**	**1**	**2**	**8**	**0**	**0**	**0**	**21**	**4.8**	**-1**	**0**	**0.0**	**16:11**	....	....	....	....	....	....	....	....	....
	Syracuse Crunch	AHL	42	4	12	16	130	....	....	....	....	....	....	....	....	....	4	2	0	2	6	....	....	....	....
2000-01	Kansas City	IHL	70	7	22	29	191	....	....	....	....	....	....	....	....	....	....	....	....	....	....	....	....	....	....
2001-02	Manitoba Moose	AHL	77	5	20	25	153	....	....	....	....	....	....	....	....	....	7	0	2	2	13	....	....	....	....
2002-03	**Vancouver**	**NHL**	**1**	**0**	**0**	**0**	**2**	**0**	**0**	**0**	**0**	**0.0**	**0**	**0**	**0.0**	**6:25**	....	....	....	....	....	....	....	....	....
	Manitoba Moose	AHL	53	15	8	23	94	....	....	....	....	....	....	....	....	....	13	2	2	4	30	....	....	....	....
2003-04	Manitoba Moose	AHL	10	0	0	0	35	....	....	....	....	....	....	....	....	....	....	....	....	....	....	....	....	....	....
	Columbus	**NHL**	**2**	**0**	**0**	**0**	**0**	**0**	**0**	**0**	**1**	**0.0**	**0**	**0**	**0.0**	**14:48**	....	....	....	....	....	....	....	....	....
	Syracuse Crunch	AHL	54	2	22	24	84	....	....	....	....	....	....	....	....	....	7	0	1	1	4	....	....	....	....
2004-05	Syracuse Crunch	AHL	62	3	11	14	99	....	....	....	....	....	....	....	....	....	....	....	....	....	....	....	....	....	....
	NHL Totals		**21**	**1**	**1**	**2**	**10**	**0**	**0**	**0**	**22**	**4.5**		**0**	**0.0**	**15:35**	....	....	....	....	....	....	....	....	....

WHL West First All-Star Team (1997)
Traded to **Columbus** by **Vancouver** for Sean Pronger, October 30, 2003. Signed as a free agent by **Calgary**, August 11, 2005.

KOMISAREK, Mike (koh-mih-SAIR-ehk, MIGHK) MTL.

Defense. Shoots right. 6'4", 237 lbs. Born, Islip Terrace, NY, January 19, 1982. Montreal's 1st choice, 7th overall, in 2001 Entry Draft.

Season	Club	League	GP	G	A	Pts	PIM	PP	SH	GW	S	%	+/-	TF	F%	Min	GP	G	A	Pts	PIM	PP	SH	GW	Min
1998-99	N.E. Jr. Coyotes	EJHL	53	17	24	51	....	....	....	....	....	....	....	....	....	....	....	....	....	....	....	....	....	....	....
99-2000	USA U-18	USDP	51	5	8	13	124	....	....	....	....	....	....	....	....	....	....	....	....	....	....	....	....	....	....
2000-01	U. of Michigan	CCHA	41	4	12	16	77	....	....	....	....	....	....	....	....	....	....	....	....	....	....	....	....	....	....
2001-02	U. of Michigan	CCHA	40	11	19	30	70	....	....	....	....	....	....	....	....	....	....	....	....	....	....	....	....	....	....
2002-03	**Montreal**	**NHL**	**21**	**0**	**1**	**1**	**28**	**0**	**0**	**0**	**26**	**0.0**	**-6**	**0**	**0.0**	**16:42**	....	....	....	....	....	....	....	....	....
	Hamilton	AHL	56	5	25	30	79	....	....	....	....	....	....	....	....	....	23	1	5	6	60	....	....	....	....

			Regular Season														Playoffs								
Season	Club	League	GP	G	A	Pts	PIM	PP	SH	GW	S	%	+/-	TF	F%	Min	GP	G	A	Pts	PIM	PP	SH	GW	Min
2003-04	**Montreal**	**NHL**	**46**	**0**	**4**	**4**	**34**	**0**	**0**	**0**	**40**	**0.0**	**4**	**0**	**0.0**	**12:00**	**7**	**0**	**0**	**0**	**8**	**0**	**0**	**0**	**14:09**
	Hamilton	AHL	18	2	7	9	47	....	....	....	....	....	....	....	....	....	....	....	....	....	....	....	....	....	....
2004-05	Hamilton	AHL	20	1	4	5	49	....	....	....	....	....	....	....	....	....	4	0	1	1	8	....	....	....	....
	NHL Totals		**67**	**0**	**5**	**5**	**62**	**0**	**0**	**0**	**66**	**0.0**		**0**	**0.0**	**13:28**	**7**	**0**	**0**	**0**	**8**	**0**	**0**	**0**	**14:09**

CCHA First All-Star Team (2002) • NCAA West First All-American Team (2002) • AHL All-Rookie Team (2003)

KONDRATIEV, Maxim

(kohn-DRAT-yehv, mahx-EEM) **NYR**

Defense. Shoots left. 6'1", 192 lbs. Born, Togliatti, USSR, January 20, 1983. Toronto's 7th choice, 168th overall, in 2001 Entry Draft.

Season	Club	League	GP	G	A	Pts	PIM	PP	SH	GW	S	%	+/-	TF	F%	Min	GP	G	A	Pts	PIM	PP	SH	GW	Min
99-2000	Lada Togliatti 2	Russia-3	16	0	2	2	6	....	....	....	....	....	....	....	....	....	....	....	....	....	....	....	....	....	....
	Lada Togliatti	Russia	20	1	1	2	....	....	....	....	....	....	....	....	....	....	....	....	....	....	....	....	....	....	....
2000-01	Lada Togliatti 2	Russia-3	STATISTICS NOT AVAILABLE																						
	CSK VVS Samara	Russia-2	18	2	1	3	24	....	....	....	....	....	....	....	....	....	....	....	....	....	....	....	....	....	....
2001-02	Lada Togliatti	Russia	43	3	3	6	32	....	....	....	....	....	....	....	....	....	4	0	0	0	0	....	....	....	....
2002-03	Lada Togliatti	Russia	47	2	3	5	56	....	....	....	....	....	....	....	....	....	10	0	0	0	6	....	....	....	....
2003-04	**Toronto**	**NHL**	**7**	**0**	**0**	**0**	**2**	**0**	**0**	**0**	**6**	**0.0**	**0**	**0**	**0.0**	**15:36**	....	....	....	....	....	....	....	....	....
	St. John's	AHL	18	3	5	8	10	....	....	....	....	....	....	....	....	....	....	....	....	....	....	....	....	....	....
	Lada Togliatti	Russia	29	2	3	5	85	....	....	....	....	....	....	....	....	....	6	0	0	0	16	....	....	....	....
2004-05	Hartford	AHL	13	1	4	5	8	....	....	....	....	....	....	....	....	....	....	....	....	....	....	....	....	....	....
	Lada Togliatti	Russia	32	2	4	6	65	....	....	....	....	....	....	....	....	....	5	0	2	2	0	....	....	....	....
	NHL Totals		**7**	**0**	**0**	**0**	**2**	**0**	**0**	**0**	**6**	**0.0**		**0**	**0.0**	**15:36**									

Assigned to **Togliatti** (Russia) by **Toronto**, December 16, 2003. Traded to **NY Rangers** by **Toronto** with Jarkko Immonen, Toronto's 1st round choice (later traded to Calgary - Calgary selected Kris Chucko) in 2004 Entry Draft and Toronto's 2nd round choice (Michael Sauer) in 2005 Entry Draft for Brian Leetch and Edmonton's 4th round choice (previously acquired, Toronto selected Roman Kukumberg) in 2004 Entry Draft, March 3, 2004. Signed as a free agent by **Togliatti** (Russia), November 11, 2004.

KONOWALCHUK, Steve

(kahn-uh-WAHL-chuhk, STEEV) **COL.**

Left wing. Shoots left. 6'2", 207 lbs. Born, Salt Lake City, UT, November 11, 1972. Washington's 5th choice, 58th overall, in 1991 Entry Draft.

Season	Club	League	GP	G	A	Pts	PIM	PP	SH	GW	S	%	+/-	TF	F%	Min	GP	G	A	Pts	PIM	PP	SH	GW	Min
1989-90	Prince Albert	SMHL	36	30	28	58	22	....	....	....	....	....	....	....	....	....	....	....	....	....	....	....	....	....	....
1990-91	Portland	WHL	72	43	49	92	78	....	....	....	....	....	....	....	....	....	....	....	....	....	....	....	....	....	....
1991-92	Portland	WHL	64	51	53	104	95	....	....	....	....	....	....	....	....	....	6	3	6	9	12	....	....	....	....
	Washington	**NHL**	**1**	**0**	**0**	**0**	**0**	**0**	**0**	**0**	**1**	**0.0**	**0**	....	....	....	....	....	....	....	....	....	....	....	....
	Baltimore	AHL	3	1	1	2	0	....	....	....	....	....	....	....	....	....	....	....	....	....	....	....	....	....	....
1992-93	**Washington**	**NHL**	**36**	**4**	**7**	**11**	**16**	**1**	**0**	**1**	**34**	**11.8**	**4**	....	....	....	**2**	**0**	**1**	**1**	**0**	**0**	**0**	**0**	....
	Baltimore	AHL	37	18	28	46	74	....	....	....	....	....	....	....	....	....	....	....	....	....	....	....	....	....	....
1993-94	**Washington**	**NHL**	**62**	**12**	**14**	**26**	**33**	**0**	**0**	**0**	**63**	**19.0**	**9**	....	....	....	**11**	**0**	**1**	**1**	**10**	**0**	**0**	**0**	....
	Portland Pirates	AHL	8	11	4	15	4	....	....	....	....	....	....	....	....	....	....	....	....	....	....	....	....	....	....
1994-95	**Washington**	**NHL**	**46**	**11**	**14**	**25**	**44**	**3**	**3**	**3**	**88**	**12.5**	**7**	....	....	....	**7**	**2**	**5**	**7**	**12**	**0**	**1**	**0**	....
1995-96	**Washington**	**NHL**	**70**	**23**	**22**	**45**	**92**	**7**	**1**	**3**	**197**	**11.7**	**13**	....	....	....	**2**	**0**	**2**	**2**	**0**	**0**	**0**	**0**	....
1996-97	**Washington**	**NHL**	**78**	**17**	**25**	**42**	**67**	**2**	**1**	**3**	**155**	**11.0**	**−3**	....	....	....	....	....	....	....	....	....	....	....	....
1997-98	**Washington**	**NHL**	**80**	**10**	**24**	**34**	**80**	**2**	**0**	**2**	**131**	**7.6**	**9**	....	....	....	....	....	....	....	....	....	....	....	....
1998-99	**Washington**	**NHL**	**45**	**12**	**12**	**24**	**26**	**4**	**1**	**2**	**98**	**12.2**	**0**	**124**	**51.6**	**17:50**	....	....	....	....	....	....	....	....	....
99-2000	**Washington**	**NHL**	**82**	**16**	**27**	**43**	**80**	**3**	**0**	**1**	**146**	**11.0**	**19**	**147**	**49.7**	**17:36**	**5**	**1**	**0**	**1**	**2**	**0**	**1**	**0**	**17:25**
2000-01	**Washington**	**NHL**	**82**	**24**	**23**	**47**	**87**	**6**	**0**	**5**	**163**	**14.7**	**8**	**91**	**55.0**	**17:04**	**6**	**2**	**3**	**5**	**14**	**2**	**0**	**0**	**19:39**
2001-02	**Washington**	**NHL**	**28**	**2**	**12**	**14**	**23**	**0**	**0**	**0**	**36**	**5.6**	**−2**	**64**	**56.3**	**16:29**	....	....	....	....	....	....	....	....	....
2002-03	**Washington**	**NHL**	**77**	**15**	**15**	**30**	**71**	**2**	**0**	**3**	**119**	**12.6**	**3**	**92**	**44.6**	**16:42**	**6**	**0**	**0**	**0**	**6**	**0**	**0**	**0**	**16:07**
2003-04	**Washington**	**NHL**	**6**	**0**	**1**	**1**	**0**	**0**	**0**	**0**	**7**	**0.0**	**−5**	**7**	**57.1**	**14:38**	....	....	....	....	....	....	....	....	....
	Colorado	**NHL**	**76**	**19**	**20**	**39**	**70**	**3**	**0**	**3**	**145**	**13.1**	**2**	**338**	**47.0**	**18:20**	**11**	**4**	**0**	**4**	**12**	**4**	**0**	**1**	**18:15**
2004-05			DID NOT PLAY																						
	NHL Totals		**769**	**165**	**216**	**381**	**689**	**33**	**6**	**26**	**1383**	**11.9**		**863**	**49.5**	**17:22**	**50**	**9**	**12**	**21**	**56**	**6**	**2**	**1**	**17:57**

WHL West First All-Star Team (1992) • WHL Player of the Year (1992)

• Missed majority of 2001-02 season recovering from shoulder injury suffered in game vs. Los Angeles, October 16, 2001. Traded to **Colorado** by **Washington** with Washington's 3rd round choice (later traded to Carolina – Carolina selected Casey Borer) in 2004 Entry Draft for Bates Battaglia and Jonas Johansson, October 22, 2003.

KOROLEV, Evgeny

(KOH-roh-lehv, ehv-GEHN-ee) **NYI**

Defense. Shoots left. 6'1", 214 lbs. Born, Moscow, USSR, July 24, 1978. NY Islanders' 6th choice, 182nd overall, in 1998 Entry Draft.

Season	Club	League	GP	G	A	Pts	PIM	PP	SH	GW	S	%	+/-	TF	F%	Min	GP	G	A	Pts	PIM	PP	SH	GW	Min
1995-96	Peterborough	OHL	60	2	12	14	60	....	....	....	....	....	....	....	....	....	6	0	0	0	2	....	....	....	....
1996-97	Peterborough	OHL	64	5	17	22	60	....	....	....	....	....	....	....	....	....	11	1	1	2	8	....	....	....	....
1997-98	Peterborough	OHL	37	5	21	26	39	....	....	....	....	....	....	....	....	....									
	London Knights	OHL	27	4	10	14	36	....	....	....	....	....	....	....	....	....	15	2	7	9	29	....	....	....	....
1998-99	Roanoke Express	ECHL	2	0	1	1	0	....	....	....	....	....	....	....	....	....	....	....	....	....	....	....	....	....	....
	Lowell	AHL	54	2	6	8	48	....	....	....	....	....	....	....	....	....	2	0	1	1	0	....	....	....	....
99-2000	**NY Islanders**	**NHL**	**17**	**1**	**2**	**3**	**8**	**0**	**0**	**0**	**7**	**14.3**	**−10**	**0**	**0.0**	**16:12**	....	....	....	....	....	....	....	....	....
	Lowell	AHL	57	1	10	11	61	....	....	....	....	....	....	....	....	....	6	0	0	0	4	....	....	....	....
2000-01	**NY Islanders**	**NHL**	**8**	**0**	**0**	**0**	**6**	**0**	**0**	**0**	**11**	**0.0**	**0**	**0**	**0.0**	**16:40**	....	....	....	....	....	....	....	....	....
	Chicago Wolves	IHL	4	0	1	1	0	....	....	....	....	....	....	....	....	....	....	....	....	....	....	....	....	....	....
	Louisville Panthers	AHL	36	2	14	16	68	....	....	....	....	....	....	....	....	....	....	....	....	....	....	....	....	....	....
2001-02	**NY Islanders**	**NHL**	**17**	**0**	**2**	**2**	**6**	**0**	**0**	**0**	**9**	**0.0**	**0**	**0**	**0.0**	**10:22**	**2**	**0**	**0**	**0**	**0**	**0**	**0**	**0**	**5:35**
	Bridgeport	AHL	53	5	8	13	30	....	....	....	....	....	....	....	....	....	....	....	....	....	....	....	....	....	....
2002-03	Yaroslavl	Russia	16	1	2	3	22	....	....	....	....	....	....	....	....	....	8	0	0	0	6	....	....	....	....
2003-04	Yaroslavl 2	Russia-3	3	0	1	1	0	....	....	....	....	....	....	....	....	....	....	....	....	....	....	....	....	....	....
	Yaroslavl	Russia	25	1	1	2	39	....	....	....	....	....	....	....	....	....	....	....	....	....	....	....	....	....	....
	Cherepovets	Russia	22	1	5	6	20	....	....	....	....	....	....	....	....	....	....	....	....	....	....	....	....	....	....
2004-05	Cherepovets	Russia	58	5	14	19	72	....	....	....	....	....	....	....	....	....	....	....	....	....	....	....	....	....	....
	NHL Totals		**42**	**1**	**4**	**5**	**20**	**0**	**0**	**0**	**27**	**3.7**		**0**	**0.0**	**13:56**	**2**	**0**	**0**	**0**	**0**	**0**	**0**	**0**	**5:35**

• Re-entered NHL Entry Draft. Originally NY Islanders' 9th choice, 192nd overall, in 1996 Entry Draft.
Signed as a free agent by **Yaroslavl** (Russia), October 14, 2002. Signed as a free agent by **Dynamo Moscow** (Russia), May 30, 2005.

KOROLEV, Igor

(KOH-roh-lehv, EE-gohr)

Center. Shoots left. 6'1", 190 lbs. Born, Moscow, USSR, September 6, 1970. St. Louis' 1st choice, 38th overall, in 1992 Entry Draft.

Season	Club	League	GP	G	A	Pts	PIM	PP	SH	GW	S	%	+/-	TF	F%	Min	GP	G	A	Pts	PIM	PP	SH	GW	Min
1988-89	Dynamo Moscow	USSR	1	0	0	0	2	....	....	....	....	....	....	....	....	....	....	....	....	....	....	....	....	....	....
1989-90	Dynamo Moscow	USSR	17	3	2	5	2	....	....	....	....	....	....	....	....	....	....	....	....	....	....	....	....	....	....
1990-91	Dynamo Moscow	USSR	38	12	4	16	12	....	....	....	....	....	....	....	....	....	....	....	....	....	....	....	....	....	....
1991-92	Dynamo Moscow	CIS	39	15	12	27	16	....	....	....	....	....	....	....	....	....	....	....	....	....	....	....	....	....	....
1992-93	Dynamo Moscow	CIS	5	1	2	3	4	....	....	....	....	....	....	....	....	....	....	....	....	....	....	....	....	....	....
	St. Louis	**NHL**	**74**	**4**	**23**	**27**	**20**	**2**	**0**	**0**	**76**	**5.3**	**−1**	....	....	....	**3**	**0**	**0**	**0**	**0**	**0**	**0**	**0**	....
1993-94	**St. Louis**	**NHL**	**73**	**6**	**10**	**16**	**40**	**0**	**0**	**1**	**93**	**6.5**	**−12**	....	....	....	**2**	**0**	**0**	**0**	**0**	**0**	**0**	**0**	....
1994-95	Dynamo Moscow	CIS	13	4	6	10	18	....	....	....	....	....	....	....	....	....	....	....	....	....	....	....	....	....	....
	Winnipeg	**NHL**	**45**	**8**	**22**	**30**	**10**	**1**	**0**	**1**	**85**	**9.4**	**1**	....	....	....	....	....	....	....	....	....	....	....	....
1995-96	**Winnipeg**	**NHL**	**73**	**22**	**29**	**51**	**42**	**8**	**0**	**5**	**165**	**13.3**	**1**	....	....	....	**6**	**0**	**3**	**3**	**0**	**0**	**0**	**0**	....
1996-97	**Phoenix**	**NHL**	**41**	**3**	**7**	**10**	**28**	**2**	**0**	**0**	**41**	**7.3**	**−5**	....	....	....	**1**	**0**	**0**	**0**	**0**	**0**	**0**	**0**	....
	Michigan	IHL	4	2	2	4	0	....	....	....	....	....	....	....	....	....	....	....	....	....	....	....	....	....	....
	Phoenix	IHL	4	2	6	8	4	....	....	....	....	....	....	....	....	....	....	....	....	....	....	....	....	....	....
1997-98	**Toronto**	**NHL**	**78**	**17**	**22**	**39**	**22**	**6**	**3**	**5**	**97**	**17.5**	**−18**	....	....	....	....	....	....	....	....	....	....	....	....
1998-99	**Toronto**	**NHL**	**66**	**13**	**34**	**47**	**46**	**1**	**0**	**2**	**99**	**13.1**	**11**	**973**	**42.0**	**18:06**	**1**	**0**	**0**	**0**	**0**	**0**	**0**	**0**	**7:42**
99-2000	**Toronto**	**NHL**	**80**	**20**	**26**	**46**	**22**	**5**	**3**	**4**	**101**	**19.8**	**12**	**964**	**41.3**	**17:56**	**12**	**0**	**4**	**4**	**6**	**0**	**0**	**0**	**18:56**
2000-01	**Toronto**	**NHL**	**73**	**10**	**19**	**29**	**28**	**2**	**0**	**0**	**78**	**12.8**	**3**	**569**	**42.5**	**15:41**	**11**	**0**	**0**	**0**	**4**	**0**	**0**	**0**	**17:43**
2001-02	**Chicago**	**NHL**	**82**	**9**	**20**	**29**	**20**	**0**	**1**	**1**	**78**	**11.5**	**−5**	**1166**	**41.1**	**16:49**	**5**	**0**	**1**	**1**	**0**	**0**	**0**	**0**	**15:50**
2002-03	**Chicago**	**NHL**	**48**	**4**	**5**	**9**	**30**	**1**	**0**	**1**	**32**	**12.5**	**−1**	**375**	**42.4**	**13:39**	....	....	....	....	....	....	....	....	....
	Norfolk Admirals	AHL	14	4	3	7	0	....	....	....	....	....	....	....	....	....	9	2	4	6	4	....	....	....	....
2003-04	**Chicago**	**NHL**	**62**	**3**	**10**	**13**	**22**	**0**	**0**	**1**	**38**	**7.9**	**−15**	**462**	**47.2**	**11:11**	....	....	....	....	....	....	....	....	....
	Norfolk Admirals	AHL	10	1	4	5	4	....	....	....	....	....	....	....	....	....	....	....	....	....	....	....	....	....	....
2004-05	Yaroslavl	Russia	60	8	20	28	28	....	....	....	....	....	....	....	....	....	9	1	6	7	2	....	....	....	....
	NHL Totals		**795**	**119**	**227**	**346**	**330**	**28**	**7**	**21**	**983**	**12.1**		**4509**	**42.2**	**15:49**	**41**	**0**	**8**	**8**	**6**	**0**	**0**	**0**	**17:33**

Claimed by **Winnipeg** from **St. Louis** in Waiver Draft, January 18, 1995. Transferred to **Phoenix** after **Winnipeg** franchise relocated, July 1, 1996. Signed as a free agent by **Toronto**, September 29, 1997. Traded to **Chicago** by **Toronto** for Philadelphia's 3rd round choice (previously acquired, Toronto selected Nicolas Corbeil) in 2001 Entry Draft, June 23, 2001. Signed as a free agent by **Yaroslavl** (Russia), July 13, 2004.

			Regular Season														Playoffs								
Season	Club	League	GP	G	A	Pts	PIM	PP	SH	GW	S	%	+/-	TF	F%	Min	GP	G	A	Pts	PIM	PP	SH	GW	Min

KOROLYUK, Alexander

(koh-roh-LYUHK, al-ehx-AN-duhr) **S.J.**

Left wing. Shoots left. 5'9", 190 lbs. Born, Moscow, USSR, January 15, 1976. San Jose's 6th choice, 141st overall, in 1994 Entry Draft.

Season	Club	League	GP	G	A	Pts	PIM	PP	SH	GW	S	%	+/-	TF	F%	Min	GP	G	A	Pts	PIM	PP	SH	GW	Min
1993-94	Krylja Sovetov	CIS	22	4	4	8	20										3	1	0	1	4				
1994-95	Krylja Sovetov	CIS	52	16	13	29	62										4	1	2	3	4				
1995-96	Krylja Sovetov	CIS	50	30	19	49	77																		
1996-97	Krylja Sovetov	Russia	17	8	5	13	46																		
	Manitoba Moose	IHL	42	20	16	36	71																		
1997-98	**San Jose**	**NHL**	**19**	**2**	**3**	**5**	**6**	**1**	**0**	**0**	**23**	**8.7**	**–5**												
	Kentucky	AHL	44	16	23	39	96										3	0	0	0	0				
1998-99	**San Jose**	**NHL**	**55**	**12**	**18**	**30**	**26**	**2**	**0**	**0**	**96**	**12.5**	**3**	**4**	**50.0**	**13:53**	**6**	**1**	**3**	**4**	**2**	**0**	**0**	**1**	**11:01**
	Kentucky	AHL	23	9	13	22	16																		
99-2000	**San Jose**	**NHL**	**57**	**14**	**21**	**35**	**35**	**3**	**0**	**1**	**124**	**11.3**	**4**	**1**	**100.0**	**13:36**	**9**	**0**	**3**	**3**	**6**	**0**	**0**	**0**	**11:37**
2000-01	Ak Bars Kazan	Russia	6	0	5	5	4																		
	San Jose	**NHL**	**70**	**12**	**13**	**25**	**41**	**3**	**0**	**1**	**140**	**8.6**	**2**	**30**	**33.3**	**11:56**	**2**	**0**	**0**	**0**	**0**	**0**	**0**	**0**	**8:11**
2001-02	**San Jose**	**NHL**	**32**	**3**	**7**	**10**	**14**	**0**	**0**	**1**	**49**	**6.1**	**2**	**10**	**30.0**	**12:16**									
2002-03	Ak Bars Kazan	Russia	45	14	17	31	46										4	0	0	0	0				
2003-04	**San Jose**	**NHL**	**63**	**19**	**18**	**37**	**18**	**4**	**0**	**2**	**108**	**17.6**	**20**	**14**	**50.0**	**14:55**	**17**	**5**	**2**	**7**	**10**	**2**	**0**	**1**	**16:40**
2004-05	Vityaz Chekhov	Russia-2	42	24	28	52	54																		
	Voskresensk	Russia	10	4	3	7	14																		
	NHL Totals		**296**	**62**	**80**	**142**	**140**	**13**	**0**	**5**	**540**	**11.5**		**59**	**39.0**	**13:23**	**34**	**6**	**8**	**14**	**18**	**2**	**0**	**2**	**13:50**

• Spent majority of 2001-02 season on practice roster. Signed as a free agent by **Kazan** (Russia), July 9, 2002. Signed as a free agent by **Vityaz** (Russia-2), September 25, 2004. Signed as a free agent by **Voskresensk** (Russia), February 14, 2005.

KOSTOPOULOS, Tom

(kaw-STAWP-oh-lihs, TAWM) **L.A.**

Right wing. Shoots right. 6', 200 lbs. Born, Mississauga, Ont., January 24, 1979. Pittsburgh's 9th choice, 204th overall, in 1999 Entry Draft.

Season	Club	League	GP	G	A	Pts	PIM	PP	SH	GW	S	%	+/-	TF	F%	Min	GP	G	A	Pts	PIM	PP	SH	GW	Min
1995-96	Brampton	OPJHL	24	9	9	18	28																		
1996-97	London Knights	OHL	64	13	12	25	67																		
1997-98	London Knights	OHL	66	24	26	50	108										16	6	4	10	26				
1998-99	London Knights	OHL	66	27	60	87	114										25	19	16	35	32				
99-2000	Wilkes-Barre	AHL	76	26	32	58	121																		
2000-01	Wilkes-Barre	AHL	80	16	36	52	120										21	3	9	12	6				
2001-02	**Pittsburgh**	**NHL**	**11**	**1**	**2**	**3**	**9**	**0**	**0**	**0**	**8**	**12.5**	**–1**	**0**	**0.0**	**12:03**									
	Wilkes-Barre	AHL	70	27	26	53	112																		
2002-03	**Pittsburgh**	**NHL**	**8**	**0**	**1**	**1**	**0**	**0**	**0**	**0**	**6**	**0.0**	**–4**	**2**	**0.0**	**4:33**									
	Wilkes-Barre	AHL	71	21	42	63	131										6	1	2	3	7				
2003-04	**Pittsburgh**	**NHL**	**60**	**9**	**13**	**22**	**67**	**2**	**1**	**1**	**101**	**8.9**	**–14**	**10**	**30.0**	**14:26**									
	Wilkes-Barre	AHL	21	7	13	20	43										24	7	16	23	32				
2004-05	Manchester	AHL	64	25	46	71	99										6	0	7	7	10				
	NHL Totals		**79**	**10**	**16**	**26**	**76**	**2**	**1**	**1**	**115**	**8.7**		**12**	**25.0**	**13:06**									

Signed as a free agent by **Manchester** (AHL), July 12, 2004. Signed as a free agent by **Los Angeles**, August 1, 2005.

KOTALIK, Ales

(KOH-tahl-eek, ALehsh) **BUF.**

Right wing. Shoots right. 6'1", 227 lbs. Born, Jindrichuv Hradec, Czech., December 23, 1978. Buffalo's 7th choice, 164th overall, in 1998 Entry Draft.

Season	Club	League	GP	G	A	Pts	PIM	PP	SH	GW	S	%	+/-	TF	F%	Min	GP	G	A	Pts	PIM	PP	SH	GW	Min
1993-94	C. Budejovice Jr.	CzRep-Jr.	28	12	12	24																			
1994-95	C. Budejovice Jr.	CzRep-Jr.	36	26	17	43																			
1995-96	C. Budejovice Jr.	CzRep-Jr.	28	6	7	13																			
1996-97	C. Budejovice Jr.	CzRep-Jr.	36	15	16	31	24																		
1997-98	C. Budejovice	CzRep	47	9	7	16	14																		
1998-99	C. Budejovice	CzRep	41	8	13	21	16										3	0	0	0					
99-2000	C. Budejovice	CzRep	43	7	12	19	34										3	0	1	1	6				
2000-01	C. Budejovice	CzRep	52	19	29	48	54																		
2001-02	Rochester	AHL	68	18	25	43	55										1	0	0	0	0				
	Buffalo	**NHL**	**13**	**1**	**3**	**4**	**2**	**0**	**0**	**0**	**21**	**4.8**	**–1**	**11**	**27.3**	**12:35**									
2002-03	**Buffalo**	**NHL**	**68**	**21**	**14**	**35**	**30**	**4**	**0**	**2**	**138**	**15.2**	**–2**	**37**	**51.4**	**15:15**									
	Rochester	AHL	8	0	2	2	4																		
2003-04	**Buffalo**	**NHL**	**62**	**15**	**11**	**26**	**41**	**2**	**0**	**3**	**142**	**10.6**	**–1**	**14**	**50.0**	**15:11**									
2004-05	Liberec	CzRep	25	8	8	16	46										12	2	5	7	12				
	NHL Totals		**143**	**37**	**28**	**65**	**73**	**6**	**0**	**5**	**301**	**12.3**		**62**	**46.8**	**14:59**									

Signed as a free agent by **Liberec** (CzRep), September 6, 2004.

KOVALCHUK, Ilya

(koh-vuhl-CHOOK, IHL-yah) **ATL.**

Left wing. Shoots right. 6'2", 220 lbs. Born, Tver, USSR, April 15, 1983. Atlanta's 1st choice, 1st overall, in 2001 Entry Draft.

Season	Club	League	GP	G	A	Pts	PIM	PP	SH	GW	S	%	+/-	TF	F%	Min	GP	G	A	Pts	PIM	PP	SH	GW	Min
99-2000	Spartak Moscow	Russia-2	49	12	5	17	75																		
	Spartak 2	Russia-3	2	2	1	3	14																		
2001-02	**Atlanta**	**NHL**	**65**	**29**	**22**	**51**	**28**	**7**	**0**	**4**	**184**	**15.8**	**–19**	**6**	**16.7**	**18:32**									
	Spartak Moscow	Russia	51	42	22	64	112																		
	Russia	Olympics	6	1	2	3	14																		
2002-03	**Atlanta**	**NHL**	**81**	**38**	**29**	**67**	**57**	**9**	**0**	**3**	**257**	**14.8**	**–24**	**15**	**40.0**	**19:27**									
2003-04	**Atlanta**	**NHL**	**81**	***41**	**46**	**87**	**63**	**16**	**1**	**6**	**341**	**12.0**	**–10**	**28**	**32.1**	**23:41**									
2004-05	Ak Bars Kazan	Russia	53	19	23	42	72										4	0	1	1	0				
	NHL Totals		**227**	**108**	**97**	**205**	**148**	**32**	**1**	**13**	**782**	**13.8**		**49**	**32.7**	**20:42**									

NHL All-Rookie Team (2002) • NHL Second All-Star Team (2004) • Maurice "Rocket" Richard Trophy (2004) (tied with Jarome Iginla and Rick Nash)
Played in NHL All-Star Game (2004)
Signed as a free agent by **Kazan** (Russia) August 22, 2004.

KOVALEV, Alex

(koh-VAH-lehv, al-EHX) **MTL.**

Right wing. Shoots left. 6'1", 220 lbs. Born, Togliatti, USSR, February 24, 1973. NY Rangers' 1st choice, 15th overall, in 1991 Entry Draft.

Season	Club	League	GP	G	A	Pts	PIM	PP	SH	GW	S	%	+/-	TF	F%	Min	GP	G	A	Pts	PIM	PP	SH	GW	Min
1989-90	Dynamo Moscow	USSR	1	0	0	0	0																		
1990-91	Dynamo Moscow	USSR	18	1	2	3	4																		
1991-92	Dynamo Moscow	CIS	33	16	9	25	20																		
	Russia	Olympics	8	1	2	3	14																		
1992-93	**NY Rangers**	**NHL**	**65**	**20**	**18**	**38**	**79**	**3**	**0**	**3**	**134**	**14.9**	**–10**												
	Binghamton	AHL	13	13	11	24	35										9	3	5	8	14				
1993-94♦	**NY Rangers**	**NHL**	**76**	**23**	**33**	**56**	**154**	**7**	**0**	**3**	**184**	**12.5**	**18**				**23**	**9**	**12**	**21**	**18**	**5**	**0**	**2**	
1994-95	Lada Togliatti	CIS	12	8	8	16	49																		
	NY Rangers	**NHL**	**48**	**13**	**15**	**28**	**30**	**1**	**1**	**1**	**103**	**12.6**	**–6**				**10**	**4**	**7**	**11**	**10**	**0**	**0**	**0**	
1995-96	**NY Rangers**	**NHL**	**81**	**24**	**34**	**58**	**98**	**8**	**1**	**7**	**206**	**11.7**	**5**				**11**	**3**	**4**	**7**	**14**	**0**	**0**	**1**	
1996-97	**NY Rangers**	**NHL**	**45**	**13**	**22**	**35**	**42**	**1**	**0**	**0**	**110**	**11.8**	**11**												
1997-98	**NY Rangers**	**NHL**	**73**	**23**	**30**	**53**	**44**	**8**	**0**	**3**	**173**	**13.3**	**–22**												
1998-99	**NY Rangers**	**NHL**	**14**	**3**	**4**	**7**	**12**	**1**	**0**	**1**	**35**	**8.6**	**–6**	**18**	**44.4**	**19:53**									
	Pittsburgh	**NHL**	**63**	**20**	**26**	**46**	**37**	**5**	**1**	**4**	**156**	**12.8**	**8**	**226**	**43.4**	**20:30**	**10**	**5**	**7**	**12**	**14**	**0**	**0**	**1**	**20:24**
99-2000	**Pittsburgh**	**NHL**	**82**	**26**	**40**	**66**	**94**	**9**	**2**	**4**	**254**	**10.2**	**–3**	**306**	**47.4**	**22:53**	**11**	**1**	**5**	**6**	**10**	**0**	**0**	**0**	**26:35**
2000-01	**Pittsburgh**	**NHL**	**79**	**44**	**51**	**95**	**96**	**12**	**2**	**9**	**307**	**14.3**	**12**	**255**	**40.0**	**23:35**	**18**	**5**	**5**	**10**	**16**	**1**	**0**	**0**	**20:57**
2001-02	**Pittsburgh**	**NHL**	**67**	**32**	**44**	**76**	**80**	**8**	**1**	**3**	**266**	**12.0**	**2**	**179**	**45.3**	**24:03**									
	Russia	Olympics	6	3	1	4	4																		
2002-03	**Pittsburgh**	**NHL**	**54**	**27**	**37**	**64**	**50**	**8**	**0**	**1**	**212**	**12.7**	**–11**	**19**	**31.6**	**24:03**									
	NY Rangers	**NHL**	**24**	**10**	**3**	**13**	**20**	**3**	**0**	**2**	**59**	**16.9**	**2**	**19**	**42.1**	**20:09**									

							Regular Season										Playoffs								
Season	Club	League	GP	G	A	Pts	PIM	PP	SH	GW	S	%	+/-	TF	F%	Min	GP	G	A	Pts	PIM	PP	SH	GW	Min
2003-04	NY Rangers	NHL	66	13	29	42	54	3	0	0	178	7.3	–5	29	48.3	19:37	....	....	....	....	....	....	....	....	....
	Montreal	NHL	12	1	2	3	12	0	0	1	29	3.4	–4	2	50.0	15:36	11	6	4	10	8	1	0	1	20:11
2004-05	Ak Bars Kazan	Russia	35	10	12	22	80	....	....	....	....	....	....	....	....	....	4	0	0	0	8	....	....	....	....
	NHL Totals		**849**	**292**	**388**	**680**	**902**	**77**	**8**	**42**	**2406**	**12.1**		**1053**	**44.0**	**22:06**	**94**	**33**	**44**	**77**	**90**	**7**	**0**	**5**	**21:54**

Played in NHL All-Star Game (2001, 2003)

Traded to **Pittsburgh** by **NY Rangers** with Harry York for Petr Nedved, Chris Tamer and Sean Pronger, November 25, 1998. Traded to **NY Rangers** by **Pittsburgh** with Mike Wilson, Janne Laukkanen and Dan LaCouture for Joel Bouchard, Richard Lintner, Rico Fata, Mikael Samuelsson and future considerations, February 10, 2003. Traded to **Montreal** by **NY Rangers** for Jozef Balej and Montreal's 2nd round choice (Bruce Graham) in 2004 Entry Draft, March 2, 2004. Signed as a free agent by **Kazan** (Russia), November 3, 2004.

KOZLOV, Viktor

(KAHS-lahf, VIHK-tohr) **N.J.**

Center. Shoots right. 6'5", 235 lbs. Born, Togliatti, USSR, February 14, 1975. San Jose's 1st choice, 6th overall, in 1993 Entry Draft.

Season	Club	League	GP	G	A	Pts	PIM	PP	SH	GW	S	%	+/-	TF	F%	Min	GP	G	A	Pts	PIM	PP	SH	GW	Min
1990-91	Lada Togliatti	USSR-2	2	2	0	2	0	....	....	....	....	....	....	....	....	....	....	....	....	....	....	....	....	....	....
1991-92	Lada Togliatti	CIS	3	0	0	0	0	....	....	....	....	....	....	....	....	....	....	....	....	....	....	....	....	....	....
1992-93	Dynamo Moscow	CIS	30	6	5	11	4	....	....	....	....	....	....	....	....	....	10	3	0	3	0	....	....	....	....
1993-94	Dynamo Moscow	CIS	42	16	9	25	14	....	....	....	....	....	....	....	....	....	7	3	2	5	0	....	....	....	....
1994-95	Dynamo Moscow	CIS	3	1	1	2	2	....	....	....	....	....	....	....	....	....	....	....	....	....	....	....	....	....	....
	San Jose	NHL	16	2	0	2	2	0	0	0	23	8.7	–5	....	....	....	....	....	....	....	....	....	....	....	....
	Kansas City	IHL	4	1	1	2	0	....	....	....	....	....	....	....	....	....	13	4	5	9	12	....	....	....	....
1995-96	San Jose	NHL	62	6	13	19	6	1	0	0	107	5.6	–15	....	....	....	....	....	....	....	....	....	....	....	....
	Kansas City	IHL	15	4	7	11	12	....	....	....	....	....	....	....	....	....	....	....	....	....	....	....	....	....	....
1996-97	San Jose	NHL	78	16	25	41	40	4	0	4	184	8.7	–16	....	....	....	....	....	....	....	....	....	....	....	....
1997-98	San Jose	NHL	18	5	2	7	2	2	0	0	51	9.8	–2	....	....	....	....	....	....	....	....	....	....	....	....
	Florida	NHL	46	12	11	23	14	3	2	0	114	10.5	–1	....	....	....	....	....	....	....	....	....	....	....	....
1998-99	Florida	NHL	65	16	35	51	24	5	1	1	209	7.7	13	985	41.2	19:03	....	....	....	....	....	....	....	....	....
99-2000	Florida	NHL	80	17	53	70	16	6	0	2	223	7.6	24	1616	42.9	19:27	4	0	1	1	0	0	0	0	16:05
2000-01	Florida	NHL	51	14	23	37	10	6	0	2	139	10.1	–4	817	41.6	18:23	....	....	....	....	....	....	....	....	....
2001-02	Florida	NHL	50	9	18	27	20	6	0	1	143	6.3	–16	840	43.1	19:54	....	....	....	....	....	....	....	....	....
2002-03	Florida	NHL	74	22	34	56	18	7	1	1	232	9.5	–8	404	42.8	22:35	....	....	....	....	....	....	....	....	....
2003-04	Florida	NHL	48	11	16	27	16	3	1	1	117	9.4	–4	200	49.0	19:30	....	....	....	....	....	....	....	....	....
	New Jersey	NHL	11	2	4	6	2	0	0	0	26	7.7	0	112	56.3	13:26	2	0	0	0	0	0	0	0	8:55
2004-05	Lada Togliatti	Russia	52	15	22	37	22	....	....	....	....	....	....	....	....	....	10	3	3	6	6	....	....	....	....
	NHL Totals		**599**	**132**	**234**	**366**	**170**	**43**	**5**	**12**	**1568**	**8.4**		**4974**	**42.9**	**19:45**	**6**	**0**	**1**	**1**	**0**	**0**	**0**	**0**	**13:42**

Played in NHL All-Star Game (2000)

Traded to **Florida** by **San Jose** with Florida's 5th round choice (previously acquired, Florida selected Jaroslav Spacek) in 1998 Entry Draft for Dave Lowry and Florida's 1st round choice (later traded to Tampa Bay – Tampa Bay selected Vincent Lecavalier) in 1998 Entry Draft, November 13, 1997. Traded to **New Jersey** by **Florida** for Christian Berglund and Victor Uchevatov, March 1, 2004. Signed as a free agent by **Togliatti** (Russia), July 11, 2004.

KOZLOV, Vyacheslav

(KAHS-lahf, VYACH-ih-slav) **ATL.**

Right wing. Shoots left. 5'10", 185 lbs. Born, Voskresensk, USSR, May 3, 1972. Detroit's 2nd choice, 45th overall, in 1990 Entry Draft.

Season	Club	League	GP	G	A	Pts	PIM	PP	SH	GW	S	%	+/-	TF	F%	Min	GP	G	A	Pts	PIM	PP	SH	GW	Min
1987-88	Voskresensk	USSR	2	0	0	0	0	....	....	....	....	....	....	....	....	....	....	....	....	....	....	....	....	....	....
1988-89	Voskresensk	USSR	14	0	1	1	2	....	....	....	....	....	....	....	....	....	....	....	....	....	....	....	....	....	....
1989-90	Voskresensk	USSR	45	14	12	26	38	....	....	....	....	....	....	....	....	....	....	....	....	....	....	....	....	....	....
1990-91	Voskresensk	USSR	45	11	13	24	46	....	....	....	....	....	....	....	....	....	....	....	....	....	....	....	....	....	....
1991-92	CSKA Moscow	CIS	11	6	5	11	12	....	....	....	....	....	....	....	....	....	....	....	....	....	....	....	....	....	....
	Detroit	NHL	7	0	2	2	2	0	0	0	9	0.0	–2	....	....	....	....	....	....	....	....	....	....	....	....
1992-93	Detroit	NHL	17	4	1	5	14	0	0	0	26	15.4	–1	....	....	....	4	0	2	2	2	0	0	0	....
	Adirondack	AHL	45	23	36	59	54	....	....	....	....	....	....	....	....	....	4	1	1	2	4	....	....	....	....
1993-94	Detroit	NHL	77	34	39	73	50	8	2	6	202	16.8	27	....	....	....	7	2	5	7	12	0	0	0	....
	Adirondack	AHL	3	0	1	1	15	....	....	....	....	....	....	....	....	....	....	....	....	....	....	....	....	....	....
1994-95	CSKA Moscow	CIS	10	3	4	7	14	....	....	....	....	....	....	....	....	....	....	....	....	....	....	....	....	....	....
	Detroit	NHL	46	13	20	33	45	5	0	3	97	13.4	12	....	....	....	18	9	7	16	10	1	0	4	....
1995-96	Detroit	NHL	82	36	37	73	70	9	0	7	237	15.2	33	....	....	....	19	5	7	12	10	2	0	1	....
1996-97♦	Detroit	NHL	75	23	22	45	46	3	0	6	211	10.9	21	....	....	....	20	8	5	13	14	4	0	2	....
1997-98♦	Detroit	NHL	80	25	27	52	46	6	0	1	221	11.3	14	....	....	....	22	6	8	14	10	1	0	4	....
1998-99	Detroit	NHL	79	29	29	58	45	6	1	4	209	13.9	10	38	36.8	16:02	10	6	1	7	4	3	0	0	14:44
99-2000	Detroit	NHL	72	18	18	36	28	4	0	3	165	10.9	11	28	35.7	15:30	8	2	1	3	12	1	0	1	12:20
2000-01	Detroit	NHL	72	20	18	38	30	4	0	5	187	10.7	9	51	47.1	14:43	6	4	1	5	2	2	0	0	16:27
2001-02	Buffalo	NHL	38	9	13	22	16	3	0	1	68	13.2	0	24	41.7	16:31	....	....	....	....	....	....	....	....	....
2002-03	Atlanta	NHL	79	21	49	70	66	9	1	2	185	11.4	–10	67	34.3	20:01	....	....	....	....	....	....	....	....	....
2003-04	Atlanta	NHL	76	20	32	52	74	6	0	1	191	10.5	–12	164	32.3	20:20	....	....	....	....	....	....	....	....	....
2004-05	Voskresensk	Russia	38	12	18	30	69	....	....	....	....	....	....	....	....	....	....	....	....	....	....	....	....	....	....
	Ak Bars Kazan	Russia	8	2	4	6	0	....	....	....	....	....	....	....	....	....	4	1	0	1	8	....	....	....	....
	NHL Totals		**800**	**252**	**307**	**559**	**532**	**63**	**4**	**39**	**2008**	**12.5**		**372**	**36.0**	**17:18**	**114**	**42**	**37**	**79**	**76**	**14**	**0**	**12**	**14:22**

Traded to **Buffalo** by **Detroit** with Detroit's 1st round choice (later traded to Columbus – later traded to Atlanta – Atlanta selected Jim Slater) in 2002 Entry Draft and future considerations for Dominik Hasek, July 1, 2001. • Missed majority of 2001-02 season recovering from Achilles tendon injury suffered in game vs. Columbus, December 31, 2001. Traded to **Atlanta** by **Buffalo** with Buffalo's 2nd round choice (later traded to Nashville – Nashville selected Konstantin Glazachev) in 2003 Entry Draft for Atlanta's 2nd (later traded to Florida – Florida selected Kamil Kreps) and 3rd (later traded to Phoenix – Phoenix selected Tyler Redenbach) round choices in 2003 Entry Draft, June 22, 2002. Signed as a free agent by **Voskresensk** (Russia), September 15, 2004. Signed as a free agent by **Kazan** (Russia), February 17, 2005.

KRAFT, Milan

(KRAFT, MIH-lan) **PIT.**

Center. Shoots right. 6'4", 212 lbs. Born, Plzen, Czech., January 17, 1980. Pittsburgh's 1st choice, 23rd overall, in 1998 Entry Draft.

Season	Club	League	GP	G	A	Pts	PIM	PP	SH	GW	S	%	+/-	TF	F%	Min	GP	G	A	Pts	PIM	PP	SH	GW	Min
1995-96	HC Plzen Jr.	CzRep-Jr.	49	54	41	95	....	....	....	....	....	....	....	....	....	....	....	....	....	....	....	....	....	....	....
1996-97	HC Plzen Jr.	CzRep-Jr.	29	24	12	36	....	....	....	....	....	....	....	....	....	....	....	....	....	....	....	....	....	....	....
	HC ZKZ Plzen	CzRep	9	0	1	1	2	....	....	....	....	....	....	....	....	....	....	....	....	....	....	....	....	....	....
1997-98	HC Plzen Jr.	CzRep-Jr.	24	22	21	43	12	....	....	....	....	....	....	....	....	....	....	....	....	....	....	....	....	....	....
	Plzen	CzRep	16	0	5	5	0	....	....	....	....	....	....	....	....	....	1	0	0	0	0	....	....	....	....
1998-99	Prince Albert	WHL	68	40	46	86	32	....	....	....	....	....	....	....	....	....	14	7	13	20	6	....	....	....	....
99-2000	Prince Albert	WHL	56	34	35	69	42	....	....	....	....	....	....	....	....	....	6	4	1	5	4	....	....	....	....
2000-01	Pittsburgh	NHL	42	7	7	14	8	1	1	1	63	11.1	–6	427	37.9	11:41	8	0	0	0	2	0	0	0	12:13
	Wilkes-Barre	AHL	40	21	23	44	27	....	....	....	....	....	....	....	....	....	14	12	7	19	6	....	....	....	....
2001-02	Pittsburgh	NHL	68	8	8	16	16	1	0	2	103	7.8	–9	766	44.7	12:29	....	....	....	....	....	....	....	....	....
	Wilkes-Barre	AHL	8	4	4	8	10	....	....	....	....	....	....	....	....	....	....	....	....	....	....	....	....	....	....
2002-03	Pittsburgh	NHL	31	7	5	12	10	0	0	1	50	14.0	–8	392	43.1	13:56	....	....	....	....	....	....	....	....	....
	Wilkes-Barre	AHL	40	13	24	37	28	....	....	....	....	....	....	....	....	....	6	2	4	6	4	....	....	....	....
2003-04	Pittsburgh	NHL	66	19	21	40	18	6	0	1	134	14.2	–22	970	47.4	15:16	....	....	....	....	....	....	....	....	....
2004-05	Plzen	CzRep	17	2	4	6	6	....	....	....	....	....	....	....	....	....	....	....	....	....	....	....	....	....	....
	Karlovy Vary	CzRep	35	9	10	19	20	....	....	....	....	....	....	....	....	....	....	....	....	....	....	....	....	....	....
	NHL Totals		**207**	**41**	**41**	**82**	**52**	**8**	**1**	**5**	**350**	**11.7**		**2555**	**44.3**	**13:26**	**8**	**0**	**0**	**0**	**2**	**0**	**0**	**0**	**12:13**

Signed as a free agent by **Plzen** (CzRep), September 17, 2004. Signed as a free agent by **Karlovy Vary** (CzRep), October 27, 2004. Signed as a free agent by **Omsk** (Russia), August 26, 2005.

KRAFT, Ryan

(KRAFT, RIGH-uhn)

Center. Shoots left. 5'9", 181 lbs. Born, Bottineau, ND, November 7, 1975. San Jose's 11th choice, 194th overall, in 1995 Entry Draft.

Season	Club	League	GP	G	A	Pts	PIM	PP	SH	GW	S	%	+/-	TF	F%	Min	GP	G	A	Pts	PIM	PP	SH	GW	Min
1993-94	Moorhead Spuds	High-MN	25	40	45	85	....	....	....	....	....	....	....	....	....	....	....	....	....	....	....	....	....	....	....
1994-95	U. of Minnesota	WCHA	44	13	33	46	44	....	....	....	....	....	....	....	....	....	....	....	....	....	....	....	....	....	....
1995-96	U. of Minnesota	WCHA	41	13	24	37	24	....	....	....	....	....	....	....	....	....	....	....	....	....	....	....	....	....	....
1996-97	U. of Minnesota	WCHA	42	25	21	46	37	....	....	....	....	....	....	....	....	....	....	....	....	....	....	....	....	....	....
1997-98	U. of Minnesota	WCHA	32	11	26	37	16	....	....	....	....	....	....	....	....	....	....	....	....	....	....	....	....	....	....
1998-99	Richmond	ECHL	63	28	36	64	35	....	....	....	....	....	....	....	....	....	18	10	10	20	4	....	....	....	....
99-2000	Richmond	ECHL	44	32	35	67	32	....	....	....	....	....	....	....	....	....	....	....	....	....	....	....	....	....	....
	Cleveland	IHL	1	0	1	1	0	....	....	....	....	....	....	....	....	....	....	....	....	....	....	....	....	....	....
	Kentucky	AHL	15	7	6	13	2	....	....	....	....	....	....	....	....	....	5	3	1	4	0	....	....	....	....
2000-01	Kentucky	AHL	77	38	50	88	36	....	....	....	....	....	....	....	....	....	3	2	0	2	0	....	....	....	....
2001-02	Cleveland Barons	AHL	63	19	41	60	42	....	....	....	....	....	....	....	....	....	....	....	....	....	....	....	....	....	....
2002-03	San Jose	NHL	7	0	1	1	0	0	0	0	1	0.0	2	41	34.2	8:33	....	....	....	....	....	....	....	....	....
	Cleveland Barons	AHL	53	14	27	41	12	....	....	....	....	....	....	....	....	....	....	....	....	....	....	....	....	....	....

			Regular Season														Playoffs								
Season	Club	League	GP	G	A	Pts	PIM	PP	SH	GW	S	%	+/-	TF	F%	Min	GP	G	A	Pts	PIM	PP	SH	GW	Min
2003-04	Bridgeport	AHL	74	15	21	36	20	....	....	....	....	....	....	....	....	....	6	2	2	4	0	....	....	....	....
2004-05	Bridgeport	AHL	38	9	9	18	12	....	....	....	....	....	....	....	....	....	....	....	....	....	....	....	....	....	....
	NHL Totals		**7**	**0**	**1**	**1**	**0**	**0**	**0**	**0**	**1**	**0.0**		**41**	**34.1**	**8:33**									

WCHA All-Rookie Team (1995) • WCHA All-Academic Team (1996) • AHL All-Rookie Team (2001) • AHL Second All-Star Team (2001) • Dudley "Red" Garrett Memorial Award (Rookie of the Year – AHL) (2001)

Signed as a free agent by **NY Islanders**, July 8, 2003.

KRAJICEK, Lukas (KRIGH-ee-chehk, LOO-kahsh) FLA.

Defense. Shoots left. 6'2", 185 lbs. Born, Prostejov, Czech., March 11, 1983. Florida's 2nd choice, 24th overall, in 2001 Entry Draft.

Season	Club	League	GP	G	A	Pts	PIM	PP	SH	GW	S	%	+/-	TF	F%	Min	GP	G	A	Pts	PIM	PP	SH	GW	Min
1998-99	HC ZPS Zlin Jr.	CzRep-Jr.	48	8	18	26	40	....	....	....	....	....	....	....	....	....	....	....	....	....	....	....	....	....	....
99-2000	Det. Compuware	NAHL	53	5	22	27	61	....	....	....	....	....	....	....	....	....	5	0	1	1	18	....	....	....	....
2000-01	Peterborough	OHL	61	8	27	35	53	....	....	....	....	....	....	....	....	....	7	0	5	5	0	....	....	....	....
2001-02	**Florida**	**NHL**	**5**	**0**	**0**	**0**	**0**	**0**	**0**	**0**	**3**	**0.0**	**0**	**0**	**0.0**	**13:23**	....	....	....	....	....	....	....	....	....
	Peterborough	OHL	55	10	32	42	56	....	....	....	....	....	....	....	....	....	6	0	5	5	6	....	....	....	....
2002-03	Peterborough	OHL	52	11	42	53	42	....	....	....	....	....	....	....	....	....	7	0	3	3	0	....	....	....	....
	San Antonio	AHL	3	0	1	1	0	....	....	....	....	....	....	....	....	....	3	0	0	0	0	....	....	....	....
2003-04	**Florida**	**NHL**	**18**	**1**	**6**	**7**	**12**	**1**	**0**	**0**	**16**	**6.3**	**–2**	**0**	**0.0**	**13:32**	....	....	....	....	....	....	....	....	....
	San Antonio	AHL	54	5	12	17	24	....	....	....	....	....	....	....	....	....	....	....	....	....	....	....	....	....	....
2004-05	San Antonio	AHL	78	2	22	24	57	....	....	....	....	....	....	....	....	....	....	....	....	....	....	....	....	....	....
	NHL Totals		**23**	**1**	**6**	**7**	**12**	**1**	**0**	**0**	**19**	**5.3**		**0**	**0.0**	**13:30**	....	....	....	....	....	....	....	....	....

OHL All-Rookie Team (2001) • OHL First All-Star Team (2003)

• Returned to **Peterborough** (OHL) by **Florida**, October 28, 2001.

KRESTANOVICH, Jordan (KREH-sta-noh-vihtch, JOHR-dan)

Left wing. Shoots left. 6'1", 180 lbs. Born, Langley, B.C., June 14, 1981. Colorado's 7th choice, 152nd overall, in 1999 Entry Draft.

Season	Club	League	GP	G	A	Pts	PIM	PP	SH	GW	S	%	+/-	TF	F%	Min	GP	G	A	Pts	PIM	PP	SH	GW	Min
1996-97	Surrey Chiefs	BCAHA	55	79	81	160	....	....	....	....	....	....	....	....	....	....	....	....	....	....	....	....	....	....	....
1997-98	Calgary Hitmen	WHL	22	1	0	1	0	....	....	....	....	....	....	....	....	....	13	0	0	0	0	....	....	....	....
1998-99	Calgary Hitmen	WHL	62	6	13	19	10	....	....	....	....	....	....	....	....	....	20	3	8	11	4	....	....	....	....
99-2000	Calgary Hitmen	WHL	72	19	24	43	22	....	....	....	....	....	....	....	....	....	13	7	7	14	4	....	....	....	....
	Hershey Bears	AHL	....	....	....	....	....	....	....	....	....	....	....	....	....	....	1	0	0	0	0	....	....	....	....
2000-01	Calgary Hitmen	WHL	70	40	60	100	32	....	....	....	....	....	....	....	....	....	12	8	4	12	8	....	....	....	....
	Hershey Bears	AHL	....	....	....	....	....	....	....	....	....	....	....	....	....	....	2	0	0	0	0	....	....	....	....
2001-02	**Colorado**	**NHL**	**8**	**0**	**2**	**2**	**0**	**0**	**0**	**0**	**6**	**0.0**	**1**	**0**	**0.0**	**8:34**	....	....	....	....	....	....	....	....	....
	Hershey Bears	AHL	68	12	22	34	18	....	....	....	....	....	....	....	....	....	8	1	0	1	0	....	....	....	....
2002-03	Hershey Bears	AHL	70	13	21	34	24	....	....	....	....	....	....	....	....	....	4	0	1	1	2	....	....	....	....
2003-04	**Colorado**	**NHL**	**14**	**0**	**0**	**0**	**6**	**0**	**0**	**0**	**25**	**0.0**	**0**	**21**	**23.8**	**10:08**	....	....	....	....	....	....	....	....	....
	Hershey Bears	AHL	38	4	15	19	11	....	....	....	....	....	....	....	....	....	....	....	....	....	....	....	....	....	....
	Houston Aeros	AHL	12	2	1	3	0	....	....	....	....	....	....	....	....	....	2	0	0	0	0	....	....	....	....
2004-05	Pensacola	ECHL	69	27	41	68	22	....	....	....	....	....	....	....	....	....	3	1	1	2	0	....	....	....	....
	NHL Totals		**22**	**0**	**2**	**2**	**6**	**0**	**0**	**0**	**31**	**0.0**		**21**	**23.8**	**9:34**	....	....	....	....	....	....	....	....	....

Traded to **Minnesota** by **Colorado** for Chris Bala, March 9, 2004. Signed as a free agent by **Houston** (AHL), September 24, 2004. • Assigned to **Pensacola** (ECHL) by **Houston** (AHL), October 4, 2004.

KROG, Jason (KROHG, JAY-suhn)

Center. Shoots right. 5'11", 191 lbs. Born, Fernie, B.C., October 9, 1975.

Season	Club	League	GP	G	A	Pts	PIM	PP	SH	GW	S	%	+/-	TF	F%	Min	GP	G	A	Pts	PIM	PP	SH	GW	Min
1992-93	Chilliwack Chiefs	BCJHL	52	30	27	57	52	....	....	....	....	....	....	....	....	....	....	....	....	....	....	....	....	....	....
1993-94	Chilliwack Chiefs	BCJHL	42	19	36	55	20	....	....	....	....	....	....	....	....	....	....	....	....	....	....	....	....	....	....
1994-95	Chilliwack Chiefs	BCJHL	60	47	81	128	36	....	....	....	....	....	....	....	....	....	....	....	....	....	....	....	....	....	....
1995-96	New Hampshire	H-East	34	4	16	20	20	....	....	....	....	....	....	....	....	....	....	....	....	....	....	....	....	....	....
1996-97	New Hampshire	H-East	39	23	*44	*67	28	....	....	....	....	....	....	....	....	....	....	....	....	....	....	....	....	....	....
1997-98	New Hampshire	H-East	38	*33	33	66	44	....	....	....	....	....	....	....	....	....	....	....	....	....	....	....	....	....	....
1998-99	New Hampshire	H-East	41	*34	*51	*85	38	....	....	....	....	....	....	....	....	....	....	....	....	....	....	....	....	....	....
99-2000	**NY Islanders**	**NHL**	**17**	**2**	**4**	**6**	**6**	**1**	**0**	**0**	**22**	**9.1**	**–1**	**81**	**53.1**	**10:03**	....	....	....	....	....	....	....	....	....
	Lowell	AHL	45	6	21	27	22	....	....	....	....	....	....	....	....	....	....	....	....	....	....	....	....	....	....
	Providence Bruins	AHL	11	9	8	17	4	....	....	....	....	....	....	....	....	....	6	2	2	4	0	....	....	....	....
2000-01	**NY Islanders**	**NHL**	**9**	**0**	**3**	**3**	**0**	**0**	**0**	**0**	**7**	**0.0**	**4**	**60**	**48.3**	**10:32**	....	....	....	....	....	....	....	....	....
	Lowell	AHL	26	11	16	27	6	....	....	....	....	....	....	....	....	....	....	....	....	....	....	....	....	....	....
	Springfield	AHL	24	7	23	30	4	....	....	....	....	....	....	....	....	....	....	....	....	....	....	....	....	....	....
2001-02	**NY Islanders**	**NHL**	**2**	**0**	**0**	**0**	**0**	**0**	**0**	**0**	**0**	**0.0**	**0**	**13**	**46.2**	**6:40**	....	....	....	....	....	....	....	....	....
	Bridgeport	AHL	64	26	36	62	13	....	....	....	....	....	....	....	....	....	20	10	13	23	8	....	....	....	....
2002-03	Cincinnati	AHL	9	3	4	7	6	....	....	....	....	....	....	....	....	....	....	....	....	....	....	....	....	....	....
	Anaheim	**NHL**	**67**	**10**	**15**	**25**	**12**	**0**	**1**	**1**	**92**	**10.9**	**1**	**634**	**60.4**	**13:47**	**21**	**3**	**1**	**4**	**4**	**0**	**0**	**0**	**12:10**
2003-04	**Anaheim**	**NHL**	**80**	**6**	**12**	**18**	**16**	**1**	**0**	**1**	**111**	**5.4**	**–4**	**769**	**58.5**	**11:58**	....	....	....	....	....	....	....	....	....
2004-05	EC Villacher SV	Austria	48	27	33	60	38	....	....	....	....	....	....	....	....	....	3	0	1	1	4	....	....	....	....
	NHL Totals		**175**	**18**	**34**	**52**	**34**	**2**	**1**	**2**	**232**	**7.8**		**1557**	**58.5**	**12:21**	**21**	**3**	**1**	**4**	**4**	**0**	**0**	**0**	**12:10**

Hockey East First All-Star Team (1997, 1998, 1999) • NCAA East Second All-American Team (1997) • Hockey East Player of the Year (1999) • NCAA East First All-American Team (1999) • NCAA Championship All-Tournament Team (1999) • Hobey Baker Memorial Award (Top U.S. Collegiate Player) (1999)

Signed as a free agent by **NY Islanders**, May 14, 1999. Loaned to **Providence** (AHL) by **NY Islanders**, March 1, 2000. Signed as a free agent by **Anaheim**, July 17, 2002. Signed as a free agent by **Villacher** (Austria), August 24, 2004. Signed as a free agent by **Geneve** (Swiss), May 19, 2005.

KRONWALL, Niklas (KRAHN-wuhl, NIHK-las) DET.

Defense. Shoots left. 5'11", 165 lbs. Born, Stockholm, Sweden, January 12, 1981. Detroit's 1st choice, 29th overall, in 2000 Entry Draft.

Season	Club	League	GP	G	A	Pts	PIM	PP	SH	GW	S	%	+/-	TF	F%	Min	GP	G	A	Pts	PIM	PP	SH	GW	Min
1996-97	Djurgarden Jr.	Swe-Jr.	1	0	0	0	0	....	....	....	....	....	....	....	....	....	....	....	....	....	....	....	....	....	....
1997-98	Djurgarden Jr.	Swe-Jr.	27	4	3	7	71	....	....	....	....	....	....	....	....	....	2	0	0	0	2	....	....	....	....
1998-99	Huddinge IK	Sweden-2	14	0	1	1	10	....	....	....	....	....	....	....	....	....	....	....	....	....	....	....	....	....	....
	Huddinge IK Jr.	Swe-Jr.	2	0	0	0	6	....	....	....	....	....	....	....	....	....	....	....	....	....	....	....	....	....	....
99-2000	Djurgarden	Sweden	37	1	4	5	16	....	....	....	....	....	....	....	....	....	8	0	0	0	8	....	....	....	....
2000-01	Djurgarden	Sweden	31	1	9	10	32	....	....	....	....	....	....	....	....	....	15	0	1	1	8	....	....	....	....
2001-02	Djurgarden	Sweden	48	5	7	12	34	....	....	....	....	....	....	....	....	....	5	0	0	0	0	....	....	....	....
2002-03	Djurgarden	Sweden	50	5	13	18	46	....	....	....	....	....	....	....	....	....	12	3	2	5	18	....	....	....	....
2003-04	**Detroit**	**NHL**	**20**	**1**	**4**	**5**	**16**	**0**	**0**	**1**	**18**	**5.6**	**5**	**0**	**0.0**	**13:51**	....	....	....	....	....	....	....	....	....
	Grand Rapids	AHL	25	2	11	13	20	....	....	....	....	....	....	....	....	....	....	....	....	....	....	....	....	....	....
2004-05	Grand Rapids	AHL	76	13	40	53	53	....	....	....	....	....	....	....	....	....	....	....	....	....	....	....	....	....	....
	NHL Totals		**20**	**1**	**4**	**5**	**16**	**0**	**0**	**1**	**18**	**5.6**		**0**	**0.0**	**13:51**	....	....	....	....	....	....	....	....	....

AHL First All-Star Team (2005) • Eddie Shore Award (Outstanding Defenseman – AHL) (2005)

KUBA, Filip (KOO-bah, FIHL-ihp) MIN.

Defense. Shoots left. 6'3", 205 lbs. Born, Ostrava, Czech., December 29, 1976. Florida's 8th choice, 192nd overall, in 1995 Entry Draft.

Season	Club	League	GP	G	A	Pts	PIM	PP	SH	GW	S	%	+/-	TF	F%	Min	GP	G	A	Pts	PIM	PP	SH	GW	Min
1994-95	HC Vitkovice Jr.	CzRep-Jr.	35	10	15	25	....	....	....	....	....	....	....	....	....	....	....	....	....	....	....	....	....	....	....
	HC Vitkovice	CzRep	....	....	....	....	....	....	....	....	....	....	....	....	....	....	4	0	0	0	2	....	....	....	....
1995-96	HC Vitkovice	CzRep	19	0	1	1	....	....	....	....	....	....	....	....	....	....	....	....	....	....	....	....	....	....	....
1996-97	Carolina	AHL	51	0	12	12	38	....	....	....	....	....	....	....	....	....	....	....	....	....	....	....	....	....	....
1997-98	New Haven	AHL	77	4	13	17	58	....	....	....	....	....	....	....	....	....	3	1	1	2	0	....	....	....	....
1998-99	**Florida**	**NHL**	**5**	**0**	**1**	**1**	**0**	**0**	**0**	**0**	**5**	**0.0**	**2**	**0**	**0.0**	**22:29**	....	....	....	....	....	....	....	....	....
	Kentucky	AHL	45	2	8	10	33	....	....	....	....	....	....	....	....	....	10	0	1	1	4	....	....	....	....
99-2000	**Florida**	**NHL**	**13**	**1**	**5**	**6**	**2**	**1**	**0**	**1**	**16**	**6.3**	**–3**	**0**	**0.0**	**13:52**	....	....	....	....	....	....	....	....	....
	Houston Aeros	IHL	27	3	6	9	13	....	....	....	....	....	....	....	....	....	11	1	2	3	4	....	....	....	....
2000-01	**Minnesota**	**NHL**	**75**	**9**	**21**	**30**	**28**	**4**	**0**	**4**	**141**	**6.4**	**–6**	**1**	**0.0**	**24:16**	....	....	....	....	....	....	....	....	....
2001-02	**Minnesota**	**NHL**	**62**	**5**	**19**	**24**	**32**	**3**	**0**	**1**	**101**	**5.0**	**–6**	**0**	**0.0**	**25:30**	....	....	....	....	....	....	....	....	....
2002-03	**Minnesota**	**NHL**	**78**	**8**	**21**	**29**	**29**	**4**	**2**	**1**	**129**	**6.2**	**0**	**1**	**0.0**	**23:56**	**18**	**3**	**5**	**8**	**24**	**3**	**0**	**0**	**26:46**
2003-04	**Minnesota**	**NHL**	**77**	**5**	**19**	**24**	**28**	**2**	**1**	**2**	**114**	**4.4**	**–7**	**2**	**0.0**	**24:06**	....	....	....	....	....	....	....	....	....

			Regular Season														Playoffs								
Season	Club	League	GP	G	A	Pts	PIM	PP	SH	GW	S	%	+/-	TF	F%	Min	GP	G	A	Pts	PIM	PP	SH	GW	Min
2004-05			DID NOT PLAY																						
	NHL Totals		**310**	**28**	**86**	**114**	**119**	**14**	**3**	**9**	**506**	**5.5**		**4**	**0.0**	**23:55**	**18**	**3**	**5**	**8**	**24**	**3**	**0**	**0**	**26:46**

Played in NHL All-Star Game (2004)

Traded to **Calgary** by **Florida** for Rocky Thompson, March 16, 2000. Claimed by **Minnesota** from **Calgary** in Expansion Draft, June 23, 2000.

KUBINA, Pavel (koo-BEE-nuh, PAH-vehl) T.B.

Defense. Shoots right. 6'4", 230 lbs. Born, Celadna, Czech., April 15, 1977. Tampa Bay's 6th choice, 179th overall, in 1996 Entry Draft.

Season	Club	League	GP	G	A	Pts	PIM	PP	SH	GW	S	%	+/-	TF	F%	Min	GP	G	A	Pts	PIM	PP	SH	GW	Min
1993-94	HC Vitkovice Jr.	CzRep-Jr.	35	4	3	7	....	....	....	....	....	....	....	....	....	....	....	....	....	....	....	....	....	....	....
	HC Vitkovice	CzRep	1	0	0	0	....	....	....	....	....	....	....	....	....	....	....	....	....	....	....	....	....	....	....
1994-95	HC Vitkovice Jr.	CzRep-Jr.	20	6	10	16	....	....	....	....	....	....	....	....	....	....	....	....	....	....	....	....	....	....	....
	HC Vitkovice	CzRep	8	2	0	2	10	....	....	....	....	....	....	....	....	....	4	0	0	0	0	....	....	....	....
1995-96	HC Vitkovice Jr.	CzRep-Jr.	16	5	10	15	....	....	....	....	....	....	....	....	....	....	....	....	....	....	....	....	....	....	....
	HC Vitkovice	CzRep	33	3	4	7	32	....	....	....	....	....	....	....	....	....	4	0	0	0	0	....	....	....	....
1996-97	HC Vitkovice	CzRep	1	0	0	0	0	....	....	....	....	....	....	....	....	....	....	....	....	....	....	....	....	....	....
	Moose Jaw	WHL	61	12	32	44	116	....	....	....	....	....	....	....	....	....	11	2	5	7	27	....	....	....	....
1997-98	**Tampa Bay**	**NHL**	**10**	**1**	**2**	**3**	**22**	**0**	**0**	**0**	**8**	**12.5**	**–1**	....	....	....	....	....	....	....	....	....	....	....	....
	Adirondack	AHL	55	4	8	12	86	....	....	....	....	....	....	....	....	....	1	1	0	1	14	....	....	....	....
1998-99	**Tampa Bay**	**NHL**	**68**	**9**	**12**	**21**	**80**	**3**	**1**	**1**	**119**	**7.6**	**–33**	**2**	**0.0**	**22:47**	....	....	....	....	....	....	....	....	....
	Cleveland	IHL	6	2	2	4	16	....	....	....	....	....	....	....	....	....	....	....	....	....	....	....	....	....	....
99-2000	**Tampa Bay**	**NHL**	**69**	**8**	**18**	**26**	**93**	**6**	**0**	**3**	**128**	**6.3**	**–19**	**0**	**0.0**	**22:32**	....	....	....	....	....	....	....	....	....
2000-01	**Tampa Bay**	**NHL**	**70**	**11**	**19**	**30**	**103**	**6**	**1**	**1**	**128**	**8.6**	**–14**	**2**	**0.0**	**24:06**	....	....	....	....	....	....	....	....	....
2001-02	**Tampa Bay**	**NHL**	**82**	**11**	**23**	**34**	**106**	**5**	**2**	**3**	**189**	**5.8**	**–22**	**1**	**100.0**	**23:39**	....	....	....	....	....	....	....	....	....
	Czech Republic	Olympics	4	0	1	1	0	....	....	....	....	....	....	....	....	....	....	....	....	....	....	....	....	....	....
2002-03	**Tampa Bay**	**NHL**	**75**	**3**	**19**	**22**	**78**	**0**	**0**	**0**	**139**	**2.2**	**–7**	**1**	**0.0**	**21:24**	**11**	**0**	**0**	**0**	**12**	**0**	**0**	**0**	**24:52**
2003-04♦	**Tampa Bay**	**NHL**	**81**	**17**	**18**	**35**	**85**	**8**	**1**	**4**	**153**	**11.1**	**9**	**1**	**0.0**	**21:09**	**22**	**0**	**4**	**4**	**50**	**0**	**0**	**0**	**22:54**
2004-05	Vitkovice	CzRep	28	6	5	11	46	....	....	....	....	....	....	....	....	....	12	4	6	10	34	....	....	....	....
	NHL Totals		**455**	**60**	**111**	**171**	**567**	**28**	**5**	**12**	**864**	**6.9**		**7**	**14.3**	**22:35**	**33**	**0**	**4**	**4**	**62**	**0**	**0**	**0**	**23:33**

Played in NHL All-Star Game (2004)

Signed as a free agent by **Vitkovice** (CzRep), September 17, 2004.

KUDROC, Kristian (KOO-drawch, KRIHS-tan)

Defense. Shoots right. 6'7", 255 lbs. Born, Michalovce, Czech., May 21, 1981. NY Islanders' 4th choice, 28th overall, in 1999 Entry Draft.

Season	Club	League	GP	G	A	Pts	PIM	PP	SH	GW	S	%	+/-	TF	F%	Min	GP	G	A	Pts	PIM	PP	SH	GW	Min
1997-98	Michalovce Jr.	Slovak-Jr.	47	7	4	11	66	....	....	....	....	....	....	....	....	....	....	....	....	....	....	....	....	....	....
	Michalovce	Slovak-2	4	0	0	0	0	....	....	....	....	....	....	....	....	....	....	....	....	....	....	....	....	....	....
1998-99	Michalovce	Slovak-2	17	0	3	3	12	....	....	....	....	....	....	....	....	....	....	....	....	....	....	....	....	....	....
99-2000	Quebec Remparts	QMJHL	57	9	22	31	172	....	....	....	....	....	....	....	....	....	11	2	5	7	29	....	....	....	....
2000-01	**Tampa Bay**	**NHL**	**22**	**2**	**2**	**4**	**36**	**0**	**0**	**1**	**12**	**16.7**	**0**	**0**	**0.0**	**9:09**	....	....	....	....	....	....	....	....	....
	Detroit Vipers	IHL	44	4	3	7	80	....	....	....	....	....	....	....	....	....	....	....	....	....	....	....	....	....	....
2001-02	**Tampa Bay**	**NHL**	**2**	**0**	**0**	**0**	**0**	**0**	**0**	**0**	**0**	**0.0**	**0**	**0**	**0.0**	**7:49**	....	....	....	....	....	....	....	....	....
	Springfield	AHL	55	0	8	8	126	....	....	....	....	....	....	....	....	....	....	....	....	....	....	....	....	....	....
	Philadelphia	AHL	10	0	3	3	14	....	....	....	....	....	....	....	....	....	5	1	1	2	21	....	....	....	....
2002-03	Springfield	AHL	35	0	4	4	58	....	....	....	....	....	....	....	....	....	....	....	....	....	....	....	....	....	....
2003-04	**Florida**	**NHL**	**2**	**0**	**0**	**0**	**2**	**0**	**0**	**0**	**0**	**0.0**	**0**	**0**	**0.0**	**7:15**	....	....	....	....	....	....	....	....	....
	San Antonio	AHL	47	1	4	5	120	....	....	....	....	....	....	....	....	....	....	....	....	....	....	....	....	....	....
2004-05	Hammarby	Sweden-2	6	0	2	2	65	....	....	....	....	....	....	....	....	....	....	....	....	....	....	....	....	....	....
	NHL Totals		**26**	**2**	**2**	**4**	**38**	**0**	**0**	**1**	**12**	**16.7**		**0**	**0.0**	**8:54**	....	....	....	....	....	....	....	....	....

Traded to **Tampa Bay** by **NY Islanders** with Kevin Weekes and NY Islanders' 2nd round choice (later traded to Phoenix – Phoenix selected Matthew Spiller) in 2001 Entry Draft for Tampa Bay's 1st round choice (Raffi Torres) in 2000 Entry Draft, Calgary's 4th round choice (previously acquired, NY Islanders selected Vladimir Gorbunov) in 2000 Entry Draft and NY Islanders' 7th round choice (previously acquired, NY Islanders selected Ryan Caldwell) in 2000 Entry Draft, June 24, 2000. • Missed majority of 2002-03 season recovering from head injury suffered in game vs. Providence (AHL), October 2, 2002. Signed as a free agent by **Florida**, July 3, 2003. Signed as a free agent by **Hammarby** (Sweden-2), December 20, 2004.

KUKKONEN, Lasse (koo-KOH-nuhn, LA-she) CHI.

Defense. Shoots left. 6', 187 lbs. Born, Oulu, Finland, September 18, 1981. Chicago's 4th choice, 151st overall, in 2003 Entry Draft.

Season	Club	League	GP	G	A	Pts	PIM	PP	SH	GW	S	%	+/-	TF	F%	Min	GP	G	A	Pts	PIM	PP	SH	GW	Min
1997-98	Karpat Oulu Jr.	Finland-Jr.	36	5	16	21	46	....	....	....	....	....	....	....	....	....	....	....	....	....	....	....	....	....	....
1998-99	Karpat Oulu Jr.	Finland-Jr.	34	2	13	15	24	....	....	....	....	....	....	....	....	....	....	....	....	....	....	....	....	....	....
99-2000	Karpat Oulu Jr.	Finland-Jr.	27	9	11	20	26	....	....	....	....	....	....	....	....	....	....	....	....	....	....	....	....	....	....
	Karpat Oulu	Finland-2	22	0	4	4	14	....	....	....	....	....	....	....	....	....	....	....	....	....	....	....	....	....	....
2000-01	Karpat Oulu	Finland	47	1	5	6	46	....	....	....	....	....	....	....	....	....	9	0	2	2	4	....	....	....	....
2001-02	Karpat Oulu	Finland	55	2	6	8	42	....	....	....	....	....	....	....	....	....	4	0	3	3	4	....	....	....	....
	Karpat Oulu Jr.	Finland-Jr.	....	....	....	....	....	....	....	....	....	....	....	....	....	....	1	1	0	1	0	....	....	....	....
2002-03	Karpat Oulu	Finland	56	6	12	18	67	....	....	....	....	....	....	....	....	....	15	1	4	5	16	....	....	....	....
2003-04	**Chicago**	**NHL**	**10**	**0**	**1**	**1**	**4**	**0**	**0**	**0**	**9**	**0.0**	**–2**	**0**	**0.0**	**13:37**	....	....	....	....	....	....	....	....	....
	Norfolk Admirals	AHL	59	3	11	14	58	....	....	....	....	....	....	....	....	....	8	0	0	0	8	....	....	....	....
2004-05	Karpat Oulu	Finland	55	5	13	18	68	....	....	....	....	....	....	....	....	....	12	0	2	2	6	....	....	....	....
	NHL Totals		**10**	**0**	**1**	**1**	**4**	**0**	**0**	**0**	**9**	**0.0**		**0**	**0.0**	**13:37**	....	....	....	....	....	....	....	....	....

Signed as a free agent by **Karpat** (Finland), September 11, 2004.

KULESHOV, Mikhail (koo-leh-SHAWV, mih-kigh-EHL)

Left wing. Shoots right. 6'2", 205 lbs. Born, Perm, USSR, January 7, 1981. Colorado's 1st choice, 25th overall, in 1999 Entry Draft.

Season	Club	League	GP	G	A	Pts	PIM	PP	SH	GW	S	%	+/-	TF	F%	Min	GP	G	A	Pts	PIM	PP	SH	GW	Min
1997-98	Omsk 2	Russia-3	12	12	3	15	12	....	....	....	....	....	....	....	....	....	....	....	....	....	....	....	....	....	....
	Avangard Omsk	Russia	4	1	0	1	4	....	....	....	....	....	....	....	....	....	....	....	....	....	....	....	....	....	....
1998-99	Cherepovets 3	Russia-4	3	2	1	3	32	....	....	....	....	....	....	....	....	....	....	....	....	....	....	....	....	....	....
	Cherepovets 2	Russia-3	25	7	5	12	12	....	....	....	....	....	....	....	....	....	....	....	....	....	....	....	....	....	....
	Cherepovets	Russia	15	2	0	2	8	....	....	....	....	....	....	....	....	....	3	0	0	0	4	....	....	....	....
99-2000	Cherepovets	Russia	8	0	0	0	4	....	....	....	....	....	....	....	....	....	3	0	0	0	2	....	....	....	....
2000-01	St. Petersburg	Russia	7	0	0	0	8	....	....	....	....	....	....	....	....	....	....	....	....	....	....	....	....	....	....
	Hershey Bears	AHL	3	0	0	0	4	....	....	....	....	....	....	....	....	....	11	1	0	1	0	....	....	....	....
2001-02	Hershey Bears	AHL	60	8	11	19	43	....	....	....	....	....	....	....	....	....	7	0	1	1	4	....	....	....	....
2002-03	Hershey Bears	AHL	77	7	13	20	76	....	....	....	....	....	....	....	....	....	5	0	0	0	6	....	....	....	....
2003-04	**Colorado**	**NHL**	**3**	**0**	**0**	**0**	**0**	**0**	**0**	**0**	**4**	**0.0**	**–1**	**0**	**0.0**	**11:19**	....	....	....	....	....	....	....	....	....
	Hershey Bears	AHL	55	4	6	10	38	....	....	....	....	....	....	....	....	....	....	....	....	....	....	....	....	....	....
2004-05	St. Petersburg	Russia	11	0	0	0	6	....	....	....	....	....	....	....	....	....	....	....	....	....	....	....	....	....	....
	Perm	Russia	23	0	3	3	16	....	....	....	....	....	....	....	....	....	....	....	....	....	....	....	....	....	....
	NHL Totals		**3**	**0**	**0**	**0**	**0**	**0**	**0**	**0**	**4**	**0.0**		**0**	**0.0**	**11:19**	....	....	....	....	....	....	....	....	....

Signed as a free agent by **St. Petersburg** (Russia), September, 2004. Signed as a free agent by **Perm** (Russia), November 15, 2004.

KULTANEN, Jarno (kuhl-TAH-nuhn, YAR-noh) BOS.

Defense. Shoots left. 6'2", 198 lbs. Born, Luumaki, Finland, January 8, 1973. Boston's 8th choice, 174th overall, in 2000 Entry Draft.

Season	Club	League	GP	G	A	Pts	PIM	PP	SH	GW	S	%	+/-	TF	F%	Min	GP	G	A	Pts	PIM	PP	SH	GW	Min
1991-92	KooKoo Jr.	Finland-Jr.	22	7	17	24	28	....	....	....	....	....	....	....	....	....	....	....	....	....	....	....	....	....	....
	KooKoo Kouvola	Finland-2	1	0	0	0	0	....	....	....	....	....	....	....	....	....	....	....	....	....	....	....	....	....	....
1992-93	KooKoo Jr.	Finland-Jr.	11	6	5	11	8	....	....	....	....	....	....	....	....	....	....	....	....	....	....	....	....	....	....
	KooKoo Kouvola	Finland-2	27	1	1	2	33	....	....	....	....	....	....	....	....	....	....	....	....	....	....	....	....	....	....
	Centers	Finland-2	1	1	0	1	0	....	....	....	....	....	....	....	....	....	....	....	....	....	....	....	....	....	....
1993-94	KooKoo Jr.	Finland-Jr.	3	1	0	1	2	....	....	....	....	....	....	....	....	....	....	....	....	....	....	....	....	....	....
	KooKoo Kouvola	Finland-2	45	7	10	17	42	....	....	....	....	....	....	....	....	....	....	....	....	....	....	....	....	....	....
1994-95	KalPa Kuopio	Finland	47	5	12	17	26	....	....	....	....	....	....	....	....	....	3	0	0	0	8	....	....	....	....
1995-96	KalPa Kuopio	Finland	49	4	10	14	42	....	....	....	....	....	....	....	....	....	....	....	....	....	....	....	....	....	....
1996-97	HIFK Helsinki	Finland	24	1	3	4	6	....	....	....	....	....	....	....	....	....	....	....	....	....	....	....	....	....	....
1997-98	HIFK Helsinki	Finland	25	0	1	1	20	....	....	....	....	....	....	....	....	....	8	0	1	1	2	....	....	....	....
1998-99	HIFK Helsinki	Finland	51	6	6	12	53	....	....	....	....	....	....	....	....	....	10	1	0	1	27	....	....	....	....
	HIFK Helsinki	EuroHL	5	1	0	1	4	....	....	....	....	....	....	....	....	....	4	0	1	1	2	....	....	....	....
99-2000	HIFK Helsinki	Finland	46	6	8	14	51	....	....	....	....	....	....	....	....	....	9	0	0	0	6	....	....	....	....
	HIFK Helsinki	EuroHL	5	2	2	4	31	....	....	....	....	....	....	....	....	....	2	0	0	0	2	....	....	....	....
2000-01	**Boston**	**NHL**	**62**	**2**	**8**	**10**	**26**	**0**	**0**	**1**	**76**	**2.6**	**–3**	**0**	**0.0**	**19:29**	....	....	....	....	....	....	....	....	....

Season	Club	League	GP	G	A	Pts	PIM	PP	SH	GW	S	%	+/-	TF	F%	Min	GP	G	A	Pts	PIM	PP	SH	GW	Min
			Regular Season														Playoffs								
2001-02	**Boston**	**NHL**	**38**	**0**	**3**	**3**	**33**	**0**	**0**	**0**	**31**	**0.0**	**–1**	**0**	**0.0**	**12:58**	....	....	....	....	....	....	....	....	....
2002-03	**Boston**	**NHL**	**2**	**0**	**0**	**0**	**0**	**0**	**0**	**0**	**3**	**0.0**	**1**	**0**	**0.0**	**10:16**	....	....	....	....	....	....	....	....	....
	Providence Bruins	AHL	59	9	25	34	35	....	....	....	....	....	....	....	....	....	4	0	0	0	6	....	....	....	....
2003-04	HIFK Helsinki	Finland	44	3	5	8	40	....	....	....	....	....	....	....	....	....	13	1	1	2	0	....	....	....	....
2004-05	HIFK Helsinki	Finland	56	6	3	9	45	....	....	....	....	....	....	....	....	....	5	1	0	1	25	....	....	....	....
	NHL Totals		**102**	**2**	**11**	**13**	**59**	**0**	**0**	**1**	**110**	**1.8**		**0**	**0.0**	**16:52**	....	....	....	....	....	....	....	....	....

• Missed majority of 2001-02 season recovering from knee injury suffered in game vs. Minnesota, October 8, 2001. Signed as a free agent by **HIFK** (Finland), May 19, 2003.

KUNITZ, Chris
(KOO-hihtz, KRIHS) **ANA.**

Left wing. Shoots left. 6', 194 lbs. Born, Regina, Sask., September 26, 1979.

Season	Club	League	GP	G	A	Pts	PIM	PP	SH	GW	S	%	+/-	TF	F%	Min	GP	G	A	Pts	PIM	PP	SH	GW	Min
1996-97	Yorkton Mallers	SMHL	64	38	38	76	233	....	....	....	....	....	....	....	....	....	....	....	....	....	....	....	....	....	....
1997-98	Melville	SJHL	STATISTICS NOT AVAILABLE					....	....	....	....	....	....	....	....	....	....	....	....	....	....	....	....	....	....
1998-99	Melville	SJHL	63	57	32	89	222	....	....	....	....	....	....	....	....	....	....	....	....	....	....	....	....	....	....
99-2000	Ferris State	CCHA	38	20	9	29	70	....	....	....	....	....	....	....	....	....	....	....	....	....	....	....	....	....	....
2000-01	Ferris State	CCHA	37	16	13	29	81	....	....	....	....	....	....	....	....	....	....	....	....	....	....	....	....	....	....
2001-02	Ferris State	CCHA	35	*28	10	38	68	....	....	....	....	....	....	....	....	....	....	....	....	....	....	....	....	....	....
2002-03	Ferris State	CCHA	42	*35	*44	*79	56	....	....	....	....	....	....	....	....	....	....	....	....	....	....	....	....	....	....
2003-04	**Anaheim**	**NHL**	**21**	**0**	**6**	**6**	**12**	**0**	**0**	**0**	**31**	**0.0**	**1**	**7**	**14.3**	**9:07**	....	....	....	....	....	....	....	....	....
	Cincinnati	AHL	59	19	25	44	101	....	....	....	....	....	....	....	....	....	9	3	2	5	24	....	....	....	....
2004-05	Cincinnati	AHL	54	22	17	39	71	....	....	....	....	....	....	....	....	....	12	1	7	8	20	....	....	....	....
	NHL Totals		**21**	**0**	**6**	**6**	**12**	**0**	**0**	**0**	**31**	**0.0**		**7**	**14.3**	**9:07**	....	....	....	....	....	....	....	....	....

CCHA First All-Star Team (2002, 2003) • CCHA Player of the Year (2003) • NCAA West First All-American Team (2003)
Signed as a free agent by **Anaheim**, April 1, 2003.

KURKA, Tomas
(KUHR-kuh, TAW-mahsh)

Left wing. Shoots left. 5'11", 190 lbs. Born, Most, Czech., December 14, 1981. Carolina's 1st choice, 32nd overall, in 2000 Entry Draft.

Season	Club	League	GP	G	A	Pts	PIM	PP	SH	GW	S	%	+/-	TF	F%	Min	GP	G	A	Pts	PIM	PP	SH	GW	Min
1996-97	Litvinov Jr.	CzRep-Jr.	38	25	20	45	20	....	....	....	....	....	....	....	....	....	....	....	....	....	....	....	....	....	....
1997-98	Litvinov Jr.	CzRep-Jr.	44	38	23	61	90	....	....	....	....	....	....	....	....	....	....	....	....	....	....	....	....	....	....
1998-99	Litvinov Jr.	CzRep-Jr.	42	23	16	39	47	....	....	....	....	....	....	....	....	....	....	....	....	....	....	....	....	....	....
	Litvinov	CzRep	6	0	0	0	0	....	....	....	....	....	....	....	....	....	....	....	....	....	....	....	....	....	....
99-2000	Plymouth Whalers	OHL	64	36	28	64	37	....	....	....	....	....	....	....	....	....	17	7	6	13	6	....	....	....	....
2000-01	Plymouth Whalers	OHL	47	15	29	44	20	....	....	....	....	....	....	....	....	....	16	8	13	21	13	....	....	....	....
2001-02	Lowell	AHL	71	13	15	28	24	....	....	....	....	....	....	....	....	....	5	1	1	2	2	....	....	....	....
2002-03	**Carolina**	**NHL**	**14**	**3**	**2**	**5**	**2**	**0**	**0**	**0**	**22**	**13.6**	**1**	**4**	**50.0**	**14:59**	....	....	....	....	....	....	....	....	....
	Lowell	AHL	61	17	12	29	10	....	....	....	....	....	....	....	....	....	....	....	....	....	....	....	....	....	....
2003-04	**Carolina**	**NHL**	**3**	**0**	**0**	**0**	**0**	**0**	**0**	**0**	**3**	**0.0**	**0**	**0**	**0.0**	**8:45**	....	....	....	....	....	....	....	....	....
	Lowell	AHL	55	6	26	32	14	....	....	....	....	....	....	....	....	....	....	....	....	....	....	....	....	....	....
2004-05	Litvinov	CzRep	29	1	5	6	6	....	....	....	....	....	....	....	....	....	....	....	....	....	....	....	....	....	....
	Providence Bruins	AHL	40	8	3	11	4	....	....	....	....	....	....	....	....	....	17	4	4	8	13	....	....	....	....
	NHL Totals		**17**	**3**	**2**	**5**	**2**	**0**	**0**	**0**	**25**	**12.0**		**4**	**50.0**	**13:53**	....	....	....	....	....	....	....	....	....

Signed as a free agent by **Litvinov** (CzRep), September 25, 2004. Signed as a free agent by **Providence** (AHL), December 13, 2004. Signed as a free agent by **KalPa** (Finland-2), August 27, 2005.

KUTLAK, Zdenek
(KUHT-lak, z'DEHN-ehk) **BOS.**

Defense. Shoots left. 6'3", 221 lbs. Born, Ceske Budejovice, Czech., February 13, 1980. Boston's 10th choice, 237th overall, in 2000 Entry Draft.

Season	Club	League	GP	G	A	Pts	PIM	PP	SH	GW	S	%	+/-	TF	F%	Min	GP	G	A	Pts	PIM	PP	SH	GW	Min
1996-97	C. Budejovice Jr.	CzRep-Jr.	45	8	11	19	20	....	....	....	....	....	....	....	....	....	....	....	....	....	....	....	....	....	....
1997-98	C. Budejovice Jr.	CzRep-Jr.	43	1	6	7	30	....	....	....	....	....	....	....	....	....	....	....	....	....	....	....	....	....	....
1998-99	C. Budejovice Jr.	CzRep-Jr.	31	6	14	20	20	....	....	....	....	....	....	....	....	....	....	....	....	....	....	....	....	....	....
	C. Budejovice	CzRep	22	1	3	4	4	....	....	....	....	....	....	....	....	....	3	0	0	0	0	....	....	....	....
99-2000	C. Budejovice Jr.	CzRep-Jr.	8	4	2	6	26	....	....	....	....	....	....	....	....	....	....	....	....	....	....	....	....	....	....
	Jind. Hradec	CzRep-3	4	1	1	2	0	....	....	....	....	....	....	....	....	....	....	....	....	....	....	....	....	....	....
	IHC Pisek	CzRep-2	3	1	0	1	0	....	....	....	....	....	....	....	....	....	2	0	0	0	2	....	....	....	....
	C. Budejovice	CzRep	28	1	0	1	2	....	....	....	....	....	....	....	....	....	1	0	0	0	0	....	....	....	....
2000-01	**Boston**	**NHL**	**10**	**0**	**2**	**2**	**4**	**0**	**0**	**0**	**7**	**0.0**	**–3**	**0**	**0.0**	**16:05**	....	....	....	....	....	....	....	....	....
	Providence Bruins	AHL	62	4	5	9	16	....	....	....	....	....	....	....	....	....	....	....	....	....	....	....	....	....	....
2001-02	Providence Bruins	AHL	80	5	15	20	73	....	....	....	....	....	....	....	....	....	2	0	0	0	0	....	....	....	....
2002-03	**Boston**	**NHL**	**4**	**1**	**0**	**1**	**0**	**0**	**0**	**0**	**1**	**100.0**	**0**	**0**	**0.0**	**5:16**	....	....	....	....	....	....	....	....	....
	Providence Bruins	AHL	68	4	12	16	52	....	....	....	....	....	....	....	....	....	4	1	0	1	2	....	....	....	....
2003-04	**Boston**	**NHL**	**2**	**0**	**0**	**0**	**0**	**0**	**0**	**0**	**0**	**0.0**	**–1**	**0**	**0.0**	**11:33**	....	....	....	....	....	....	....	....	....
	Providence Bruins	AHL	47	7	12	19	22	....	....	....	....	....	....	....	....	....	2	0	0	0	2	....	....	....	....
2004-05	Karlovy Vary	CzRep	52	5	9	14	26	....	....	....	....	....	....	....	....	....	....	....	....	....	....	....	....	....	....
	NHL Totals		**16**	**1**	**2**	**3**	**4**	**0**	**0**	**0**	**8**	**12.5**		**0**	**0.0**	**12:49**	....	....	....	....	....	....	....	....	....

Signed as a free agent by **Karlovy Vary** (CzRep), May 16, 2004.

KUZNETSOV, Maxim
(kooz-NEHT-zahv, MAX-ihm)

Defense. Shoots left. 6'5", 230 lbs. Born, Pavlodar, USSR, March 24, 1977. Detroit's 1st choice, 26th overall, in 1995 Entry Draft.

Season	Club	League	GP	G	A	Pts	PIM	PP	SH	GW	S	%	+/-	TF	F%	Min	GP	G	A	Pts	PIM	PP	SH	GW	Min
1994-95	Dynamo Moscow	CIS	11	0	0	0	8	....	....	....	....	....	....	....	....	....	....	....	....	....	....	....	....	....	....
1995-96	Dynamo Moscow	CIS	9	1	1	2	22	....	....	....	....	....	....	....	....	....	4	0	0	0	0	....	....	....	....
1996-97	Dynamo Moscow	Russia	23	0	2	2	16	....	....	....	....	....	....	....	....	....	....	....	....	....	....	....	....	....	....
	Adirondack	AHL	2	0	1	1	6	....	....	....	....	....	....	....	....	....	2	0	0	0	0	....	....	....	....
1997-98	Adirondack	AHL	51	5	5	10	43	....	....	....	....	....	....	....	....	....	3	0	1	1	4	....	....	....	....
1998-99	Adirondack	AHL	60	0	4	4	30	....	....	....	....	....	....	....	....	....	3	0	0	0	0	....	....	....	....
99-2000	Cincinnati	AHL	47	2	9	11	36	....	....	....	....	....	....	....	....	....	....	....	....	....	....	....	....	....	....
2000-01	**Detroit**	**NHL**	**25**	**1**	**2**	**3**	**23**	**0**	**0**	**0**	**17**	**5.9**	**–1**	**1**	**0.0**	**9:28**	....	....	....	....	....	....	....	....	....
2001-02	**Detroit**	**NHL**	**39**	**1**	**2**	**3**	**40**	**0**	**0**	**0**	**27**	**3.7**	**0**	**0**	**0.0**	**11:51**	....	....	....	....	....	....	....	....	....
	Cincinnati	AHL	7	1	0	1	4	....	....	....	....	....	....	....	....	....	....	....	....	....	....	....	....	....	....
2002-03	**Detroit**	**NHL**	**53**	**0**	**3**	**3**	**54**	**0**	**0**	**0**	**32**	**0.0**	**0**	**1**	**100.0**	**13:10**	....	....	....	....	....	....	....	....	....
	Los Angeles	**NHL**	**3**	**0**	**0**	**0**	**0**	**0**	**0**	**0**	**1**	**0.0**	**1**	**0**	**0.0**	**16:37**	....	....	....	....	....	....	....	....	....
2003-04	**Los Angeles**	**NHL**	**16**	**0**	**1**	**1**	**20**	**0**	**0**	**0**	**11**	**0.0**	**–5**	**0**	**0.0**	**15:11**	....	....	....	....	....	....	....	....	....
	Manchester	AHL	39	2	8	10	57	....	....	....	....	....	....	....	....	....	2	0	0	0	4	....	....	....	....
2004-05	Dynamo Moscow	Russia	10	0	0	0	24	....	....	....	....	....	....	....	....	....	....	....	....	....	....	....	....	....	....
	St. Petersburg	Russia	34	4	6	10	72	....	....	....	....	....	....	....	....	....	....	....	....	....	....	....	....	....	....
	NHL Totals		**136**	**2**	**8**	**10**	**137**	**0**	**0**	**0**	**88**	**2.3**		**2**	**50.0**	**12:25**	....	....	....	....	....	....	....	....	....

• Missed majority of 2000-01 season recovering from knee injury suffered in game vs. Vancouver, November 24, 2000. Traded to **Los Angeles** by **Detroit** with Sean Avery, Detroit's 1st round choice (Jeff Tambellini) in 2003 Entry Draft and Detroit's 2nd round choice (later traded to Boston - Boston selected Martins Karsums) in 2004 Entry Draft for Mathieu Schneider, March 11, 2003. Signed as a free agent by **Dynamo Moscow** (Russia), June 7, 2004. Signed as a free agent by **St. Petersburg** (Russia), November, 2004

KVASHA, Oleg
(kuh-VAH-shah, OH-lehg) **NYI**

Left wing/Center. Shoots right. 6'5", 230 lbs. Born, Moscow, USSR, July 26, 1978. Florida's 3rd choice, 65th overall, in 1996 Entry Draft.

Season	Club	League	GP	G	A	Pts	PIM	PP	SH	GW	S	%	+/-	TF	F%	Min	GP	G	A	Pts	PIM	PP	SH	GW	Min
1995-96	CSKA Moscow	CIS	38	2	3	5	14	....	....	....	....	....	....	....	....	....	2	0	0	0	0	....	....	....	....
1996-97	CSKA Moscow	Russia-2	44	20	22	42	115	....	....	....	....	....	....	....	....	....	....	....	....	....	....	....	....	....	....
1997-98	New Haven	AHL	57	13	16	29	46	....	....	....	....	....	....	....	....	....	3	2	1	3	0	....	....	....	....
1998-99	**Florida**	**NHL**	**68**	**12**	**13**	**25**	**45**	**4**	**0**	**2**	**138**	**8.7**	**5**	**373**	**28.4**	**12:48**	....	....	....	....	....	....	....	....	....
99-2000	**Florida**	**NHL**	**78**	**5**	**20**	**25**	**34**	**2**	**0**	**0**	**110**	**4.5**	**3**	**553**	**34.9**	**11:24**	**4**	**0**	**0**	**0**	**0**	**0**	**0**	**0**	**10:18**
2000-01	**NY Islanders**	**NHL**	**62**	**11**	**9**	**20**	**46**	**0**	**0**	**0**	**118**	**9.3**	**–15**	**627**	**43.7**	**14:56**	....	....	....	....	....	....	....	....	....
2001-02	**NY Islanders**	**NHL**	**71**	**13**	**25**	**38**	**80**	**2**	**0**	**3**	**119**	**10.9**	**–4**	**456**	**47.4**	**14:12**	**7**	**0**	**1**	**1**	**6**	**0**	**0**	**0**	**15:17**
	Russia	Olympics	5	0	0	0	0	....	....	....	....	....	....	....	....	....	....	....	....	....	....	....	....	....	....
2002-03	**NY Islanders**	**NHL**	**69**	**12**	**14**	**26**	**44**	**0**	**1**	**2**	**121**	**9.9**	**4**	**256**	**43.0**	**13:03**	**5**	**0**	**1**	**1**	**2**	**0**	**0**	**0**	**16:26**
2003-04	**NY Islanders**	**NHL**	**81**	**15**	**36**	**51**	**48**	**5**	**3**	**3**	**147**	**10.2**	**4**	**656**	**38.3**	**17:52**	**5**	**1**	**0**	**1**	**0**	**1**	**0**	**0**	**16:05**
2004-05	Cherepovets	Russia	22	6	5	11	24	....	....	....	....	....	....	....	....	....	....	....	....	....	....	....	....	....	....
	CSKA Moscow	Russia	26	3	6	9	20	....	....	....	....	....	....	....	....	....	....	....	....	....	....	....	....	....	....
	NHL Totals		**429**	**68**	**117**	**185**	**297**	**13**	**4**	**10**	**753**	**9.0**		**2921**	**39.4**	**14:05**	**21**	**1**	**2**	**3**	**8**	**1**	**0**	**0**	**14:48**

Traded to **NY Islanders** by **Florida** with Mark Parrish for Roberto Luongo and Olli Jokinen, June 24, 2000. Signed as a free agent by **Cherepovets** (Russia), September 25, 2004. Loaned to **CSKA** (Russia), December 20, 2004.

			Regular Season														Playoffs								
Season	Club	League	GP	G	A	Pts	PIM	PP	SH	GW	S	%	+/-	TF	F%	Min	GP	G	A	Pts	PIM	PP	SH	GW	Min

KWIATKOWSKI, Joel (KWEE-at-KOW-skee, JOHL) FLA.

Defense. Shoots left. 6'2", 210 lbs. Born, Kindersley, Sask., March 22, 1977. Dallas' 7th choice, 194th overall, in 1996 Entry Draft.

1994-95	Tacoma Rockets	WHL	70	4	13	17	66	....	....	....	....	....	....	....	....	....	4	0	0	0	2	....	....	....	....
1995-96	Kelowna Rockets	WHL	40	6	17	23	85	....	....	....	....	....	....	....	....	....	....	....	....	....	....	....	....	....	....
	Prince George	WHL	32	6	11	17	48	....	....	....	....	....	....	....	....	....	....	....	....	....	....	....	....	....	....
1996-97	Prince George	WHL	72	15	37	52	94	....	....	....	....	....	....	....	....	....	15	4	2	6	24	....	....	....	....
1997-98	Prince George	WHL	62	21	43	64	65	....	....	....	....	....	....	....	....	....	11	3	6	9	6	....	....	....	....
1998-99	Cincinnati	AHL	80	12	21	33	48	....	....	....	....	....	....	....	....	....	3	2	0	2	0	....	....	....	....
99-2000	Cincinnati	AHL	70	4	22	26	28	....	....	....	....	....	....	....	....	....	....	....	....	....	....	....	....	....	....
2000-01	**Ottawa**	**NHL**	4	1	0	1	0	0	0	0	2	50.0	1	0	0.0	12:04	....	....	....	....	....	....	....	....	....
	Grand Rapids	IHL	77	4	17	21	58	....	....	....	....	....	....	....	....	....	10	1	0	1	4	....	....	....	....
2001-02	**Ottawa**	**NHL**	11	0	0	0	12	0	0	0	9	0.0	5	0	0.0	13:41	....	....	....	....	....	....	....	....	....
	Grand Rapids	AHL	65	8	21	29	94	....	....	....	....	....	....	....	....	....	5	1	2	3	12	....	....	....	....
2002-03	**Ottawa**	**NHL**	20	0	2	2	6	0	0	0	28	0.0	2	2	0.0	12:13	....	....	....	....	....	....	....	....	....
	Binghamton	AHL	1	0	0	0	2	....	....	....	....	....	....	....	....	....	....	....	....	....	....	....	....	....	....
	Washington	**NHL**	34	0	3	3	12	0	0	0	28	0.0	1	2	0.0	15:32	6	0	0	0	2	0	0	0	17:48
2003-04	**Washington**	**NHL**	80	6	6	12	89	2	0	0	90	6.7	–28	0	0.0	21:16	....	....	....	....	....	....	....	....	....
2004-05	San Antonio	AHL	64	13	19	32	76	....	....	....	....	....	....	....	....	....	....	....	....	....	....	....	....	....	....
	St. John's	AHL	17	7	6	13	16	....	....	....	....	....	....	....	....	....	5	0	4	4	23	....	....	....	....
	NHL Totals		**149**	**7**	**11**	**18**	**119**	**2**	**0**	**0**	**157**	**4.5**		**4**	**0.0**	**17:56**	**6**	**0**	**0**	**0**	**2**	**0**	**0**	**0**	**17:48**

WHL West Second All-Star Team (1997) • WHL West First All-Star Team (1998)

Signed as a free agent by **Anaheim**, June 18, 1998. Traded to **Ottawa** by **Anaheim** for Patrick Traverse, June 12, 2000. Traded to **Washington** by **Ottawa** for Washington's 9th round choice (later traded back to Washington – Washington selected Mark Olafson) in 2003 Entry Draft, January 15, 2003. Signed as a free agent by **Florida**, July 16, 2004. Loaned to **St. John's** by **Florida** (San Antonio-AHL) for cash, March 11, 2005.

LAAKSONEN, Antti (lah-AHK-soh-nehn, AHN-tee) COL.

Left wing. Shoots left. 6', 180 lbs. Born, Tammela, Finland, October 3, 1973. Boston's 10th choice, 191st overall, in 1997 Entry Draft.

1991-92	FoPS Forssa Jr.	Finland-Jr.	24	19	23	42	22	....	....	....	....	....	....	....	....	....	....	....	....	....	....	....	....	....	....
	FoPS Forssa	Finland-2	41	16	15	31	8	....	....	....	....	....	....	....	....	....	....	....	....	....	....	....	....	....	....
1992-93	FoPS Forssa Jr.	Finland-Jr.	9	5	3	8	10	....	....	....	....	....	....	....	....	....	....	....	....	....	....	....	....	....	....
	FoPS Forssa	Finland-2	34	11	19	30	36	....	....	....	....	....	....	....	....	....	....	....	....	....	....	....	....	....	....
	HPK Jr.	Finland-Jr.	1	1	1	2	0	....	....	....	....	....	....	....	....	....	....	....	....	....	....	....	....	....	....
	HPK Hameenlinna	Finland	2	0	0	0	0	....	....	....	....	....	....	....	....	....	....	....	....	....	....	....	....	....	....
1993-94	U. of Denver	WCHA	36	12	9	21	38	....	....	....	....	....	....	....	....	....	....	....	....	....	....	....	....	....	....
1994-95	U. of Denver	WCHA	40	17	18	35	42	....	....	....	....	....	....	....	....	....	....	....	....	....	....	....	....	....	....
1995-96	U. of Denver	WCHA	39	25	28	53	71	....	....	....	....	....	....	....	....	....	....	....	....	....	....	....	....	....	....
1996-97	U. of Denver	WCHA	39	21	17	38	63	....	....	....	....	....	....	....	....	....	....	....	....	....	....	....	....	....	....
1997-98	Providence Bruins	AHL	38	3	2	5	14	....	....	....	....	....	....	....	....	....	....	....	....	....	....	....	....	....	....
	Charlotte	ECHL	15	4	3	7	12	....	....	....	....	....	....	....	....	....	6	0	3	3	0	....	....	....	....
1998-99	**Boston**	**NHL**	11	1	2	3	2	0	0	0	8	12.5	–1	0	0.0	9:20	....	....	....	....	....	....	....	....	....
	Providence Bruins	AHL	66	25	33	58	52	....	....	....	....	....	....	....	....	....	19	7	2	9	28	....	....	....	....
99-2000	**Boston**	**NHL**	27	6	3	9	2	0	0	1	23	26.1	3	3	66.7	7:50	....	....	....	....	....	....	....	....	....
	Providence Bruins	AHL	40	10	12	22	57	....	....	....	....	....	....	....	....	....	14	5	4	9	4	....	....	....	....
2000-01	**Minnesota**	**NHL**	82	12	16	28	24	0	2	1	129	9.3	–7	15	26.7	16:27	....	....	....	....	....	....	....	....	....
2001-02	**Minnesota**	**NHL**	82	16	17	33	22	0	0	1	104	15.4	–5	19	42.1	16:20	....	....	....	....	....	....	....	....	....
2002-03	**Minnesota**	**NHL**	82	15	16	31	26	1	2	4	106	14.2	4	51	29.4	15:55	16	1	3	4	4	0	0	0	16:34
2003-04	**Minnesota**	**NHL**	77	12	14	26	20	0	1	1	100	12.0	0	144	36.1	16:03	....	....	....	....	....	....	....	....	....
2004-05			Did not play														....	....	....	....	....	....	....	....	....
	NHL Totals		**361**	**62**	**68**	**130**	**96**	**1**	**5**	**8**	**470**	**13.2**		**232**	**34.9**	**15:21**	**16**	**1**	**3**	**4**	**4**	**0**	**0**	**0**	**16:34**

WCHA Second All-Star Team (1996)

Signed as a free agent by **Minnesota**, July 14, 2000. Signed as a free agent by **Colorado**, July 2, 2004.

LACHANCE, Scott (lah-CHANTS, SKAWT)

Defense. Shoots left. 6'1", 215 lbs. Born, Charlottesville, VA, October 22, 1972. NY Islanders' 1st choice, 4th overall, in 1991 Entry Draft.

1988-89	Spring. Olympics	NEJHL	36	8	28	36	20	....	....	....	....	....	....	....	....	....	....	....	....	....	....	....	....	....	....
1989-90	Spring. Olympics	NEJHL	34	25	41	66	62	....	....	....	....	....	....	....	....	....	....	....	....	....	....	....	....	....	....
1990-91	Boston University	H-East	31	5	19	24	48	....	....	....	....	....	....	....	....	....	....	....	....	....	....	....	....	....	....
1991-92	United States	Nat-Tm	36	1	10	11	34	....	....	....	....	....	....	....	....	....	....	....	....	....	....	....	....	....	....
	United States	Olympics	8	0	1	1	6	....	....	....	....	....	....	....	....	....	....	....	....	....	....	....	....	....	....
	NY Islanders	**NHL**	17	1	4	5	9	0	0	0	20	5.0	13	....	....	....	....	....	....	....	....	....	....	....	....
1992-93	**NY Islanders**	**NHL**	75	7	17	24	67	0	1	2	62	11.3	–1	....	....	....	....	....	....	....	....	....	....	....	....
1993-94	**NY Islanders**	**NHL**	74	3	11	14	70	0	0	1	59	5.1	–5	....	....	....	3	0	0	0	0	0	0	0	....
1994-95	**NY Islanders**	**NHL**	26	6	7	13	26	3	0	0	56	10.7	2	....	....	....	....	....	....	....	....	....	....	....	....
1995-96	**NY Islanders**	**NHL**	55	3	10	13	54	1	0	0	81	3.7	–19	....	....	....	....	....	....	....	....	....	....	....	....
1996-97	**NY Islanders**	**NHL**	81	3	11	14	47	1	0	0	97	3.1	–7	....	....	....	....	....	....	....	....	....	....	....	....
1997-98	**NY Islanders**	**NHL**	63	2	11	13	45	1	0	0	62	3.2	–11	....	....	....	....	....	....	....	....	....	....	....	....
1998-99	**NY Islanders**	**NHL**	59	1	8	9	30	1	0	0	37	2.7	–19	0	0.0	21:34	....	....	....	....	....	....	....	....	....
	Montreal	**NHL**	17	1	1	2	11	0	0	0	22	4.5	–2	0	0.0	22:29	....	....	....	....	....	....	....	....	....
99-2000	**Montreal**	**NHL**	57	0	6	6	22	0	0	0	41	0.0	–4	0	0.0	17:47	....	....	....	....	....	....	....	....	....
2000-01	**Vancouver**	**NHL**	76	3	11	14	46	0	0	0	55	5.5	5	0	0.0	19:26	2	0	1	1	2	0	0	0	13:09
2001-02	**Vancouver**	**NHL**	81	1	10	11	50	0	0	0	48	2.1	15	2	100.0	20:02	6	1	1	2	4	0	0	1	20:33
2002-03	**Columbus**	**NHL**	61	0	1	1	46	0	0	0	35	0.0	–20	0	0.0	20:01	....	....	....	....	....	....	....	....	....
2003-04	**Columbus**	**NHL**	77	0	4	4	44	0	0	0	35	0.0	–23	1	0.0	18:59	....	....	....	....	....	....	....	....	....
2004-05			Did not play														....	....	....	....	....	....	....	....	....
	NHL Totals		**819**	**31**	**112**	**143**	**567**	**7**	**1**	**3**	**710**	**4.4**		**3**	**66.7**	**19:45**	**11**	**1**	**2**	**3**	**6**	**0**	**0**	**1**	**18:41**

Played in NHL All-Star Game (1997)

Traded to **Montreal** by **NY Islanders** for Montreal's 3rd round choice (Mattias Weinhandl) in 1999 Entry Draft, March 9, 1999. Signed as a free agent by **Vancouver**, August 13, 2000. Signed as a free agent by **Columbus**, July 4, 2002.

LaCOUTURE, Dan (LA-koo-TUHR, DAN)

Left wing. Shoots left. 6'2", 208 lbs. Born, Hyannis, MA, April 18, 1977. NY Islanders' 2nd choice, 29th overall, in 1996 Entry Draft.

1992-93	Natick Redmen	High-MA	20	38	34	72	46	....	....	....	....	....	....	....	....	....	....	....	....	....	....	....	....	....	....
1993-94	Natick Redmen	High-MA	21	52	49	101	58	....	....	....	....	....	....	....	....	....	....	....	....	....	....	....	....	....	....
1994-95	Spring. Olympics	NEJHL	52	44	56	100	98	....	....	....	....	....	....	....	....	....	....	....	....	....	....	....	....	....	....
1995-96	Spring. Olympics	NEJHL	29	24	35	59	79	....	....	....	....	....	....	....	....	....	13	12	13	25	23	....	....	....	....
1996-97	Boston University	H-East	31	13	12	25	18	....	....	....	....	....	....	....	....	....	....	....	....	....	....	....	....	....	....
1997-98	Hamilton	AHL	77	15	10	25	31	....	....	....	....	....	....	....	....	....	5	1	0	1	0	....	....	....	....
1998-99	**Edmonton**	**NHL**	3	0	0	0	0	0	0	0	0	0.0	1	0	0.0	6:30	....	....	....	....	....	....	....	....	....
	Hamilton	AHL	72	17	14	31	73	....	....	....	....	....	....	....	....	....	9	2	1	3	2	....	....	....	....
99-2000	**Edmonton**	**NHL**	5	0	0	0	10	0	0	0	2	0.0	0	0	0.0	7:02	1	0	0	0	0	0	0	0	2:05
	Hamilton	AHL	70	23	17	40	85	....	....	....	....	....	....	....	....	....	6	2	1	3	0	....	....	....	....
2000-01	**Edmonton**	**NHL**	37	2	4	6	29	0	0	1	22	9.1	–2	5	20.0	7:06	....	....	....	....	....	....	....	....	....
	Pittsburgh	**NHL**	11	0	0	0	14	0	0	0	1	0.0	0	1	100.0	5:57	5	0	0	0	2	0	0	0	5:46
2001-02	**Pittsburgh**	**NHL**	82	6	11	17	71	0	1	0	77	7.8	–19	21	38.1	13:16	....	....	....	....	....	....	....	....	....
2002-03	**Pittsburgh**	**NHL**	44	2	2	4	72	0	0	0	30	6.7	–8	5	80.0	9:13	....	....	....	....	....	....	....	....	....
	NY Rangers	**NHL**	24	1	4	5	0	0	0	0	17	5.9	4	1	0.0	10:18	....	....	....	....	....	....	....	....	....
2003-04	**NY Rangers**	**NHL**	59	5	2	7	82	1	0	1	39	12.8	–13	8	50.0	9:29	....	....	....	....	....	....	....	....	....
2004-05	Providence Bruins	AHL	64	12	15	27	52	....	....	....	....	....	....	....	....	....	6	1	1	2	4	....	....	....	....
	NHL Totals		**265**	**16**	**23**	**39**	**278**	**1**	**1**	**2**	**188**	**8.5**		**41**	**43.9**	**10:08**	**6**	**0**	**0**	**0**	**2**	**0**	**0**	**0**	**5:09**

Traded to **Edmonton** by **NY Islanders** for Mariusz Czerkawski, August 25, 1997. Traded to **Pittsburgh** by **Edmonton** for Sven Butenschon, March 13, 2001. Traded to **NY Rangers** by **Pittsburgh** with Mike Wilson, Alex Kovalev and Janne Laukkanen for Joel Bouchard, Richard Lintner, Rico Fata, Mikael Samuelsson and future considerations, February 10, 2003. Signed to a PTO (tryout) contract by **Providence** (AHL), November 2, 2004,

LAFLAMME, Christian

(lah-FLAM, KRIHS-tan)

Defense. Shoots right. 6'1", 206 lbs. Born, St-Charles, Que., November 24, 1976. Chicago's 2nd choice, 45th overall, in 1995 Entry Draft.

			Regular Season														Playoffs								
Season	Club	League	GP	G	A	Pts	PIM	PP	SH	GW	S	%	+/-	TF	F%	Min	GP	G	A	Pts	PIM	PP	SH	GW	Min
1991-92	Ste-Foy	QAAA	42	5	27	32	100										8	1	2	3	14				
1992-93	Verdun	QMJHL	69	2	17	19	85										3	0	2	2	6				
1993-94	Verdun	QMJHL	72	4	34	38	85										4	0	3	3	4				
1994-95	Beauport	QMJHL	67	6	41	47	82										8	1	4	5	6				
1995-96	Beauport	QMJHL	41	13	23	36	63										20	7	17	24	32				
1996-97	**Chicago**	**NHL**	**4**	**0**	**1**	**1**	**2**	**0**	**0**	**0**	**3**	**0.0**	**3**												
	Indianapolis Ice	IHL	62	5	15	20	60										4	1	1	2	16				
1997-98	**Chicago**	**NHL**	**72**	**0**	**11**	**11**	**59**	**0**	**0**	**0**	**75**	**0.0**	**14**												
1998-99	**Chicago**	**NHL**	**62**	**2**	**11**	**13**	**70**	**0**	**0**	**0**	**53**	**3.8**	**0**	**0**	**0.0**	**18:51**									
	Portland Pirates	AHL	2	0	1	1	2																		
	Edmonton	**NHL**	**11**	**0**	**1**	**1**	**0**	**0**	**0**	**0**	**15**	**0.0**	**–3**	**0**	**0.0**	**16:33**	**4**	**0**	**1**	**1**	**2**	**0**	**0**	**0**	**21:51**
99-2000	**Edmonton**	**NHL**	**50**	**0**	**5**	**5**	**32**	**0**	**0**	**0**	**18**	**0.0**	**–4**	**5**	**40.0**	**13:40**									
	Montreal	**NHL**	**15**	**0**	**2**	**2**	**8**	**0**	**0**	**0**	**6**	**0.0**	**–5**	**0**	**0.0**	**14:32**									
2000-01	**Montreal**	**NHL**	**39**	**0**	**3**	**3**	**42**	**0**	**0**	**0**	**16**	**0.0**	**–11**	**1**	**0.0**	**12:04**									
2001-02	**St. Louis**	**NHL**	**8**	**0**	**1**	**1**	**4**	**0**	**0**	**0**	**6**	**0.0**	**3**	**0**	**0.0**	**13:54**									
	Worcester IceCats	AHL	62	2	17	19	52																		
2002-03	**St. Louis**	**NHL**	**47**	**0**	**9**	**9**	**45**	**0**	**0**	**0**	**44**	**0.0**	**1**	**0**	**0.0**	**15:10**	**5**	**0**	**0**	**0**	**4**	**0**	**0**	**0**	**12:28**
	Worcester IceCats	AHL	8	0	4	4	6																		
2003-04	**St. Louis**	**NHL**	**16**	**0**	**1**	**1**	**20**	**0**	**0**	**0**	**9**	**0.0**	**–3**	**0**	**0.0**	**13:00**									
	Worcester IceCats	AHL	28	1	4	5	25										7	0	0	0	6				
2004-05	Kassel Huskies	Germany	43	4	12	16	96										7	0	1	1	12				
	NHL Totals		**324**	**2**	**45**	**47**	**282**	**0**	**0**	**0**	**245**	**0.8**		**6**	**33.3**	**15:08**	**9**	**0**	**1**	**1**	**6**	**0**	**0**	**0**	**16:38**

QMJHL All-Rookie Team (1993) • QMJHL Second All-Star Team (1995)

Traded to **Edmonton** by **Chicago** with Daniel Cleary, Ethan Moreau and Chad Kilger for Boris Mironov, Dean McAmmond and Jonas Elofsson, March 20, 1999. Traded to **Montreal** by **Edmonton** with Matthieu Descoteaux for Igor Ulanov and Alain Nasreddine, March 9, 2000. • Missed majority of 2000-01 season recovering from groin injury suffered in game vs. Calgary, December 13, 2000. Signed as a free agent by **St. Louis**, August 21, 2001. Signed as a free agent by **Kassel** (Germany), May 16, 2004.

LAICH, Brooks

(LAYCH, BROOKS) **WSH.**

Center. Shoots left. 6'2", 199 lbs. Born, Wawota, Sask., June 23, 1983. Ottawa's 7th choice, 193rd overall, in 2001 Entry Draft.

			Regular Season														Playoffs								
Season	Club	League	GP	G	A	Pts	PIM	PP	SH	GW	S	%	+/-	TF	F%	Min	GP	G	A	Pts	PIM	PP	SH	GW	Min
99-2000	Tisdale Trojans	SMHL	57	51	52	103																			
2000-01	Moose Jaw	WHL	71	9	21	30	28										4	0	0	0	5				
2001-02	Moose Jaw	WHL	28	6	14	20	12																		
	Seattle	WHL	47	22	36	58	42										11	5	3	8	11				
2002-03	Seattle	WHL	60	41	53	94	65										15	5	14	19	24				
2003-04	**Ottawa**	**NHL**	**1**	**0**	**0**	**0**	**2**	**0**	**0**	**0**	**1**	**0.0**	**0**	**7**	**42.9**	**9:34**									
	Binghamton	AHL	44	15	18	33	16																		
	Washington	**NHL**	**4**	**0**	**1**	**1**	**0**	**0**	**0**	**0**	**2**	**0.0**	**–1**	**49**	**51.0**	**10:50**									
	Portland Pirates	AHL	22	1	3	4	12										6	0	0	0	0				
2004-05	Portland Pirates	AHL	68	16	10	26	33																		
	NHL Totals		**5**	**0**	**1**	**1**	**2**	**0**	**0**	**0**	**3**	**0.0**		**56**	**50.0**	**10:35**									

WHL West First All-Star Team (2003)

Traded to **Washington** by **Ottawa** with Ottawa's 2nd round choice (later traded to Colorado - Colorado selected Chris Durand) in 2005 Entry Draft for Peter Bondra, February 18, 2004.

LAING, Quintin

(LAY-ihng, QUIHN-tihn) **CHI.**

Left wing. Shoots left. 6'2", 175 lbs. Born, Rosetown, Sask., June 8, 1979. Detroit's 3rd choice, 102nd overall, in 1997 Entry Draft.

			Regular Season														Playoffs								
Season	Club	League	GP	G	A	Pts	PIM	PP	SH	GW	S	%	+/-	TF	F%	Min	GP	G	A	Pts	PIM	PP	SH	GW	Min
1993-94	Delisle Contacts	SAHA	30	25	50	75	25																		
1994-95	Delisle Contacts	SAHA	30	30	45	75	15																		
1995-96	Sask. Contacts	SMHL	44	18	12	30	20																		
1996-97	Kelowna Rockets	WHL	63	13	24	37	54										1	0	0	0	0				
1997-98	Kelowna Rockets	WHL	59	11	24	35	47										7	0	1	1	8				
1998-99	Kelowna Rockets	WHL	70	11	10	21	107										6	3	0	3	0				
99-2000	Kelowna Rockets	WHL	68	22	30	52	61										5	1	1	2	8				
2000-01	Norfolk Admirals	AHL	10	0	1	1	10																		
	Jackson Bandits	ECHL	60	13	24	37	39										5	0	0	0	0				
2001-02	Jackson Bandits	ECHL	16	4	6	10	12																		
	Norfolk Admirals	AHL	61	6	15	21	32										4	0	0	0	2				
2002-03	Norfolk Admirals	AHL	69	5	12	17	33										8	2	2	4	0				
2003-04	**Chicago**	**NHL**	**3**	**0**	**1**	**1**	**0**	**0**	**0**	**0**	**3**	**0.0**	**1**	**0**	**0.0**	**11:57**									
	Norfolk Admirals	AHL	78	12	10	22	74										8	5	1	6	4				
2004-05	Norfolk Admirals	AHL	66	10	13	23	54										4	0	0	0	0				
	NHL Totals		**3**	**0**	**1**	**1**	**0**	**0**	**0**	**0**	**3**	**0.0**		**0**	**0.0**	**11:57**									

Signed as a free agent by **Chicago**, June 4, 2003.

LAMPMAN, Bryce

(LAMP-man, BRIGHS) **NYR**

Defense. Shoots left. 6'1", 200 lbs. Born, Rochester, MN, August 31, 1982. NY Rangers' 4th choice, 113th overall, in 2001 Entry Draft.

			Regular Season														Playoffs								
Season	Club	League	GP	G	A	Pts	PIM	PP	SH	GW	S	%	+/-	TF	F%	Min	GP	G	A	Pts	PIM	PP	SH	GW	Min
1998-99	Rochester	USHL	53	3	8	11	33																		
99-2000	Rochester	USHL	10	0	0	0	14																		
	Omaha Lancers	USHL	11	1	2	3	38										4	0	0	0	0				
2000-01	Omaha Lancers	USHL	55	10	11	21	77										12	1	4	5	12				
2001-02	Nebraska-Omaha	CCHA	26	0	4	4	28																		
2002-03	Kamloops Blazers	WHL	29	1	17	18	32																		
	Hartford	AHL	45	0	6	6	32										2	0	1	1	0				
2003-04	**NY Rangers**	**NHL**	**8**	**0**	**0**	**0**	**0**	**0**	**0**	**0**	**7**	**0.0**	**–4**	**0**	**0.0**	**19:34**									
	Hartford	AHL	68	4	11	15	50										16	1	3	4	14				
2004-05	Hartford	AHL	74	7	18	25	74										4	0	0	0	4				
	NHL Totals		**8**	**0**	**0**	**0**	**0**	**0**	**0**	**0**	**7**	**0.0**		**0**	**0.0**	**19:34**									

• Left **Nebraska-Omaha** (CCHA) and signed as a free agent by **Kamloops** (WHL), August 1, 2002.

LANG, Robert

(LANG, RAW-buhrt) **DET.**

Center. Shoots right. 6'2", 216 lbs. Born, Teplice, Czech., December 19, 1970. Los Angeles' 6th choice, 133rd overall, in 1990 Entry Draft.

			Regular Season														Playoffs								
Season	Club	League	GP	G	A	Pts	PIM	PP	SH	GW	S	%	+/-	TF	F%	Min	GP	G	A	Pts	PIM	PP	SH	GW	Min
1988-89	CHZ Litvinov	Czech	7	3	2	5	0																		
1989-90	CHZ Litvinov	Czech	32	8	7	15											8	3	3	6					
1990-91	HC CHZ Litvinov	Czech	56	26	26	52	38																		
1991-92	Litvinov	Czech	43	12	31	43	34																		
	Czechoslovakia	Olympics	8	5	8	13	8																		
1992-93	**Los Angeles**	**NHL**	**11**	**0**	**5**	**5**	**2**	**0**	**0**	**0**	**3**	**0.0**	**–3**												
	Phoenix	IHL	38	9	21	30	20																		
1993-94	**Los Angeles**	**NHL**	**32**	**9**	**10**	**19**	**10**	**0**	**0**	**0**	**41**	**22.0**	**7**												
	Phoenix	IHL	44	11	24	35	34																		
1994-95	Litvinov	CzRep	16	4	19	23	28																		
	Los Angeles	**NHL**	**36**	**4**	**8**	**12**	**4**	**0**	**0**	**0**	**38**	**10.5**	**–7**												
1995-96	**Los Angeles**	**NHL**	**68**	**6**	**16**	**22**	**10**	**0**	**2**	**0**	**71**	**8.5**	**–15**												
1996-97	HC Sparta Praha	CzRep	38	14	27	41	30										5	1	2	3	4				
	HC Sparta Praha	EuroHL	4	2	2	4	0										4	2	1	3	2				
1997-98	**Boston**	**NHL**	**3**	**0**	**0**	**0**	**2**	**0**	**0**	**0**	**2**	**0.0**	**1**												
	Pittsburgh	**NHL**	**51**	**9**	**13**	**22**	**14**	**1**	**1**	**2**	**64**	**14.1**	**6**				**6**	**0**	**3**	**3**	**2**	**0**	**0**	**0**	
	Czech Republic	Olympics	6	0	3	3	0																		
	Houston Aeros	IHL	9	1	7	8	4																		
1998-99	**Pittsburgh**	**NHL**	**72**	**21**	**23**	**44**	**24**	**7**	**0**	**3**	**137**	**15.3**	**–10**	**964**	**44.8**	**16:24**	**12**	**0**	**2**	**2**	**0**	**0**	**0**	**0**	**13:58**
99-2000	**Pittsburgh**	**NHL**	**78**	**23**	**42**	**65**	**14**	**13**	**0**	**5**	**142**	**16.2**	**–9**	**1433**	**50.7**	**19:22**	**11**	**3**	**3**	**6**	**0**	**2**	**0**	**0**	**21:42**
2000-01	**Pittsburgh**	**NHL**	**82**	**32**	**48**	**80**	**28**	**10**	**0**	**2**	**177**	**18.1**	**20**	**1348**	**43.9**	**20:24**	**16**	**4**	**4**	**8**	**4**	**0**	**0**	**0**	**19:21**
2001-02	**Pittsburgh**	**NHL**	**62**	**18**	**32**	**50**	**16**	**5**	**1**	**3**	**175**	**10.3**	**9**	**1172**	**46.3**	**22:56**									
	Czech Republic	Olympics	4	1	2	3	2																		

Season	Club	League	GP	G	A	Pts	PIM	PP	SH	GW	S	%	+/-	TF	F%	Min	GP	G	A	Pts	PIM	PP	SH	GW	Min
			Regular Season														Playoffs								
2002-03	Washington	NHL	82	22	47	69	22	10	0	2	146	15.1	12	1069	45.9	18:47	6	2	1	3	2	0	0	1	21:55
2003-04	Washington	NHL	63	29	45	74	24	10	0	2	149	19.5	2	744	44.1	21:46	....	....	....	....	....	....	....	....	....
	Detroit	NHL	6	1	4	5	0	0	0	1	14	7.1	2	96	57.3	16:20	12	4	5	9	6	0	0	0	18:10
2004-05			DID NOT PLAY																						
	NHL Totals		646	174	293	467	170	56	4	20	1159	15.0		6826	46.4	19:46	63	13	18	31	14	2	0	1	18:42

Played in NHL All-Star Game (2004)

Signed as a free agent by **Pittsburgh**, September 2, 1997. Claimed by **Boston** from **Pittsburgh** in Waiver Draft, September 28, 1997. Claimed on waivers by **Pittsburgh** from **Boston**, October 25, 1997. Signed as a free agent by **Washington**, July 1, 2002. Traded to **Detroit** by **Washington** for Tomas Fleischmann, Detroit's 1st round choice (Mike Green) in 2004 Entry Draft and Detroit's 4th round choice in 2006 Entry Draft, February 27, 2004.

LANGDON, Darren

(LAING-duhn, DAIR-uhn) **N.J.**

Left wing. Shoots left. 6'1", 205 lbs. Born, Deer Lake, Nfld., January 8, 1971.

Season	Club	League	GP	G	A	Pts	PIM	PP	SH	GW	S	%	+/-	TF	F%	Min	GP	G	A	Pts	PIM	PP	SH	GW	Min
1991-92	Summerside	MJrHL	44	34	49	83	441	....	....	....	....	....	....	....	....	....	....	....	....	....	....	....	....	....	....
1992-93	Binghamton	AHL	18	3	4	7	115	....	....	....	....	....	....	....	....	....	8	0	1	1	14	....	....	....	....
	Dayton Bombers	ECHL	54	23	22	45	429	....	....	....	....	....	....	....	....	....	3	0	1	1	40	....	....	....	....
1993-94	Binghamton	AHL	54	2	7	9	327	....	....	....	....	....	....	....	....	....	....	....	....	....	....	....	....	....	....
1994-95	Binghamton	AHL	55	6	14	20	296	....	....	....	....	....	....	....	....	....	11	1	3	4	*84	....	....	....	....
	NY Rangers	**NHL**	**18**	**1**	**1**	**2**	**62**	**0**	**0**	**0**	**6**	**16.7**	**0**	....	....	....	....	....	....	....	....	....	....	....	....
1995-96	**NY Rangers**	**NHL**	**64**	**7**	**4**	**11**	**175**	**0**	**0**	**1**	**29**	**24.1**	**2**	....	....	....	**2**	**0**	**0**	**0**	**0**	**0**	**0**	**0**	....
	Binghamton	AHL	1	0	0	0	12	....	....	....	....	....	....	....	....	....	....	....	....	....	....	....	....	....	....
1996-97	**NY Rangers**	**NHL**	**60**	**3**	**6**	**9**	**195**	**0**	**0**	**1**	**24**	**12.5**	**–1**	....	....	....	**10**	**0**	**0**	**0**	**2**	**0**	**0**	**0**	....
1997-98	**NY Rangers**	**NHL**	**70**	**3**	**3**	**6**	**197**	**0**	**0**	**0**	**15**	**20.0**	**0**	....	....	....	....	....	....	....	....	....	....	....	....
1998-99	**NY Rangers**	**NHL**	**44**	**0**	**0**	**0**	**80**	**0**	**0**	**0**	**8**	**0.0**	**–3**	**0**	**0.0**	**3:33**	....	....	....	....	....	....	....	....	....
99-2000	**NY Rangers**	**NHL**	**21**	**0**	**1**	**1**	**26**	**0**	**0**	**0**	**13**	**0.0**	**–2**	**0**	**0.0**	**5:36**	....	....	....	....	....	....	....	....	....
2000-01	**Carolina**	**NHL**	**54**	**0**	**2**	**2**	**94**	**0**	**0**	**0**	**6**	**0.0**	**–4**	**2**	**100.0**	**3:21**	**4**	**0**	**0**	**0**	**12**	**0**	**0**	**0**	**3:32**
2001-02	**Carolina**	**NHL**	**58**	**2**	**1**	**3**	**106**	**0**	**0**	**1**	**12**	**16.7**	**2**	**1**	**100.0**	**4:11**	....	....	....	....	....	....	....	....	....
2002-03	**Carolina**	**NHL**	**9**	**0**	**0**	**0**	**16**	**0**	**0**	**0**	**4**	**0.0**	**0**	**0**	**0.0**	**2:45**	....	....	....	....	....	....	....	....	....
	Vancouver	**NHL**	**45**	**0**	**1**	**1**	**143**	**0**	**0**	**0**	**15**	**0.0**	**–2**	**1**	**0.0**	**5:26**	....	....	....	....	....	....	....	....	....
2003-04	**Montreal**	**NHL**	**64**	**0**	**3**	**3**	**135**	**0**	**0**	**0**	**22**	**0.0**	**–2**	**1**	**0.0**	**6:16**	**9**	**1**	**0**	**1**	**6**	**0**	**0**	**0**	**3:15**
2004-05			DID NOT PLAY																						
	NHL Totals		**507**	**16**	**22**	**38**	**1229**	**0**	**0**	**3**	**154**	**10.4**		**5**	**60.0**	**4:38**	**25**	**1**	**0**	**1**	**20**	**0**	**0**	**0**	**3:20**

Signed as a free agent by **NY Rangers**, August 16, 1993. • Missed majority of 1999-2000 season recovering from hernia injury suffered in game vs. New Jersey, December 1, 1999. Traded to **Carolina** by **NY Rangers** with Rob DiMaio for Sandy McCarthy and Carolina's 4th round choice (Bryce Lampman) in 2001 Entry Draft, August 4, 2000. Traded to **Vancouver** by **Carolina** with Marek Malik for Jan Hlavac and Harold Druken, November 1, 2002. Claimed by **Montreal** from **Vancouver** in Waiver Draft, October 3, 2003. Signed as a free agent by **New Jersey**, July 3, 2004.

LANGENBRUNNER, Jamie

(lan-gehn-BRUH-nuhr, JAY-mee) **N.J.**

Right wing. Shoots right. 6'1", 200 lbs. Born, Cloquet, MN, July 24, 1975. Dallas' 2nd choice, 35th overall, in 1993 Entry Draft.

Season	Club	League	GP	G	A	Pts	PIM	PP	SH	GW	S	%	+/-	TF	F%	Min	GP	G	A	Pts	PIM	PP	SH	GW	Min
1990-91	Cloquet	High-MN	20	6	16	22	8	....	....	....	....	....	....	....	....	....	....	....	....	....	....	....	....	....	....
1991-92	Cloquet	High-MN	23	16	23	39	24	....	....	....	....	....	....	....	....	....	....	....	....	....	....	....	....	....	....
1992-93	Cloquet	High-MN	27	27	62	89	18	....	....	....	....	....	....	....	....	....	....	....	....	....	....	....	....	....	....
1993-94	Peterborough	OHL	62	33	58	91	53	....	....	....	....	....	....	....	....	....	7	4	6	10	2	....	....	....	....
1994-95	Peterborough	OHL	62	42	57	99	84	....	....	....	....	....	....	....	....	....	11	8	14	22	12	....	....	....	....
	Dallas	**NHL**	**2**	**0**	**0**	**0**	**2**	**0**	**0**	**0**	**1**	**0.0**	**0**	....	....	....	....	....	....	....	....	....	....	....	....
	Kalamazoo Wings	IHL	....	....	....	....	....	....	....	....	....	....	....	....	....	....	11	1	3	4	2	....	....	....	....
1995-96	**Dallas**	**NHL**	**12**	**2**	**2**	**4**	**6**	**1**	**0**	**0**	**15**	**13.3**	**–2**	....	....	....	....	....	....	....	....	....	....	....	....
	Michigan	IHL	59	25	40	65	129	....	....	....	....	....	....	....	....	....	10	3	10	13	8	....	....	....	....
1996-97	**Dallas**	**NHL**	**76**	**13**	**26**	**39**	**51**	**3**	**0**	**3**	**112**	**11.6**	**–2**	....	....	....	**5**	**1**	**1**	**2**	**14**	**0**	**0**	**1**	....
1997-98	**Dallas**	**NHL**	**81**	**23**	**29**	**52**	**61**	**8**	**0**	**6**	**159**	**14.5**	**9**	....	....	....	**16**	**1**	**4**	**5**	**14**	**0**	**0**	**1**	....
	United States	Olympics	3	0	0	0	4	....	....	....	....	....	....	....	....	....	....	....	....	....	....	....	....	....	....
1998-99♦	**Dallas**	**NHL**	**75**	**12**	**33**	**45**	**62**	**4**	**0**	**1**	**145**	**8.3**	**10**	**217**	**46.1**	**15:51**	**23**	**10**	**7**	**17**	**16**	**4**	**0**	**3**	**17:43**
99-2000	**Dallas**	**NHL**	**65**	**18**	**21**	**39**	**68**	**4**	**2**	**6**	**153**	**11.8**	**16**	**40**	**50.0**	**17:33**	**15**	**1**	**7**	**8**	**18**	**1**	**0**	**0**	**15:28**
2000-01	**Dallas**	**NHL**	**53**	**12**	**18**	**30**	**57**	**3**	**2**	**4**	**104**	**11.5**	**4**	**316**	**45.3**	**16:30**	**10**	**2**	**2**	**4**	**6**	**0**	**0**	**1**	**19:26**
2001-02	**Dallas**	**NHL**	**68**	**10**	**16**	**26**	**54**	**0**	**1**	**2**	**132**	**7.6**	**–11**	**120**	**45.0**	**15:45**	....	....	....	....	....	....	....	....	....
	New Jersey	**NHL**	**14**	**3**	**3**	**6**	**23**	**0**	**0**	**2**	**31**	**9.7**	**2**	**2**	**50.0**	**15:27**	**5**	**0**	**1**	**1**	**8**	**0**	**0**	**0**	**14:57**
2002-03♦	**New Jersey**	**NHL**	**78**	**22**	**33**	**55**	**65**	**5**	**1**	**5**	**197**	**11.2**	**17**	**72**	**47.2**	**17:48**	**24**	***11**	**7**	***18**	**16**	**1**	**0**	**4**	**17:34**
2003-04	**New Jersey**	**NHL**	**53**	**10**	**16**	**26**	**43**	**1**	**2**	**2**	**130**	**7.7**	**9**	**31**	**51.6**	**16:01**	**5**	**0**	**2**	**2**	**2**	**0**	**0**	**0**	**15:04**
2004-05	ERC Ingolstadt	Germany	11	2	2	4	22	....	....	....	....	....	....	....	....	....	11	1	6	7	6	....	....	....	....
	NHL Totals		**577**	**125**	**197**	**322**	**492**	**29**	**8**	**31**	**1179**	**10.6**		**798**	**46.1**	**16:34**	**103**	**26**	**31**	**57**	**94**	**6**	**0**	**10**	**17:08**

Traded to **New Jersey** by **Dallas** with Joe Nieuwendyk for Jason Arnott, Randy McKay and New Jersey's 1st round choice (later traded to Columbus – later traded to Buffalo – Buffalo selected Dan Paille) in 2002 Entry Draft, March 19, 2002. Signed as a free agent by **Ingolstadt** (Germany), January 24, 2005.

LANGFELD, Josh

(LANG-fehld, JAWSH)

Right wing. Shoots right. 6'3", 216 lbs. Born, Fridley, MN, July 17, 1977. Ottawa's 3rd choice, 66th overall, in 1997 Entry Draft.

Season	Club	League	GP	G	A	Pts	PIM	PP	SH	GW	S	%	+/-	TF	F%	Min	GP	G	A	Pts	PIM	PP	SH	GW	Min
1995-96	Great Falls	AFHL	45	45	40	85	105	....	....	....	....	....	....	....	....	....	....	....	....	....	....	....	....	....	....
1996-97	Lincoln Stars	USHL	38	35	23	58	100	....	....	....	....	....	....	....	....	....	14	8	*13	*21	42	....	....	....	....
1997-98	U. of Michigan	CCHA	46	19	17	36	66	....	....	....	....	....	....	....	....	....	....	....	....	....	....	....	....	....	....
1998-99	U. of Michigan	CCHA	41	21	14	35	84	....	....	....	....	....	....	....	....	....	....	....	....	....	....	....	....	....	....
99-2000	U. of Michigan	CCHA	39	9	21	30	56	....	....	....	....	....	....	....	....	....	....	....	....	....	....	....	....	....	....
2000-01	U. of Michigan	CCHA	42	16	12	28	44	....	....	....	....	....	....	....	....	....	....	....	....	....	....	....	....	....	....
2001-02	**Ottawa**	**NHL**	**1**	**0**	**0**	**0**	**2**	**0**	**0**	**0**	**5**	**0.0**	**0**	**0**	**0.0**	**8:15**	....	....	....	....	....	....	....	....	....
	Grand Rapids	AHL	68	21	16	37	29	....	....	....	....	....	....	....	....	....	5	2	0	2	0	....	....	....	....
2002-03	**Ottawa**	**NHL**	**12**	**0**	**1**	**1**	**4**	**0**	**0**	**0**	**16**	**0.0**	**2**	**0**	**0.0**	**11:11**	....	....	....	....	....	....	....	....	....
	Binghamton	AHL	59	14	21	35	38	....	....	....	....	....	....	....	....	....	13	5	3	8	8	....	....	....	....
2003-04	**Ottawa**	**NHL**	**38**	**7**	**10**	**17**	**16**	**2**	**0**	**2**	**59**	**11.9**	**6**	**5**	**80.0**	**10:53**	....	....	....	....	....	....	....	....	....
	Binghamton	AHL	30	13	14	27	25	....	....	....	....	....	....	....	....	....	2	0	0	0	0	....	....	....	....
2004-05	Binghamton	AHL	74	32	25	57	75	....	....	....	....	....	....	....	....	....	6	2	2	4	2	....	....	....	....
	NHL Totals		**51**	**7**	**11**	**18**	**22**	**2**	**0**	**2**	**80**	**8.8**		**5**	**80.0**	**10:54**	....	....	....	....	....	....	....	....	....

NCAA Championship All-Tournament Team (1998)

LANGKOW, Daymond

(LAING-kow, DAY-muhn) **CGY.**

Center. Shoots left. 5'11", 192 lbs. Born, Edmonton, Alta., September 27, 1976. Tampa Bay's 1st choice, 5th overall, in 1995 Entry Draft.

Season	Club	League	GP	G	A	Pts	PIM	PP	SH	GW	S	%	+/-	TF	F%	Min	GP	G	A	Pts	PIM	PP	SH	GW	Min
1991-92	Edmonton Pats	AMHL	35	36	45	81	100	....	....	....	....	....	....	....	....	....	....	....	....	....	....	....	....	....	....
	Tri-City	WHL	1	0	0	0	0	....	....	....	....	....	....	....	....	....	....	....	....	....	....	....	....	....	....
1992-93	Tri-City	WHL	64	22	42	64	100	....	....	....	....	....	....	....	....	....	4	1	0	1	4	....	....	....	....
1993-94	Tri-City	WHL	61	40	43	83	174	....	....	....	....	....	....	....	....	....	4	2	2	4	15	....	....	....	....
1994-95	Tri-City	WHL	72	*67	73	*140	142	....	....	....	....	....	....	....	....	....	17	12	15	27	52	....	....	....	....
1995-96	Tri-City	WHL	48	30	61	91	103	....	....	....	....	....	....	....	....	....	11	14	13	27	20	....	....	....	....
	Tampa Bay	**NHL**	**4**	**0**	**1**	**1**	**0**	**0**	**0**	**0**	**4**	**0.0**	**–1**	....	....	....	....	....	....	....	....	....	....	....	....
1996-97	**Tampa Bay**	**NHL**	**79**	**15**	**13**	**28**	**35**	**3**	**1**	**1**	**170**	**8.8**	**1**	....	....	....	....	....	....	....	....	....	....	....	....
	Adirondack	AHL	2	1	1	2	0	....	....	....	....	....	....	....	....	....	....	....	....	....	....	....	....	....	....
1997-98	**Tampa Bay**	**NHL**	**68**	**8**	**14**	**22**	**62**	**2**	**0**	**1**	**156**	**5.1**	**–9**	....	....	....	....	....	....	....	....	....	....	....	....
1998-99	**Tampa Bay**	**NHL**	**22**	**4**	**6**	**10**	**15**	**1**	**0**	**1**	**40**	**10.0**	**0**	**399**	**48.4**	**17:10**	....	....	....	....	....	....	....	....	....
	Cleveland	IHL	4	1	1	2	18	....	....	....	....	....	....	....	....	....	....	....	....	....	....	....	....	....	....
	Philadelphia	**NHL**	**56**	**10**	**13**	**23**	**24**	**3**	**1**	**1**	**109**	**9.2**	**–8**	**738**	**48.0**	**15:12**	**6**	**0**	**2**	**2**	**2**	**0**	**0**	**0**	**16:50**
99-2000	**Philadelphia**	**NHL**	**82**	**18**	**32**	**50**	**56**	**5**	**0**	**7**	**222**	**8.1**	**1**	**1263**	**45.1**	**16:57**	**16**	**5**	**5**	**10**	**23**	**1**	**1**	**2**	**20:03**
2000-01	**Philadelphia**	**NHL**	**71**	**13**	**41**	**54**	**50**	**3**	**0**	**2**	**190**	**6.8**	**12**	**1181**	**47.2**	**18:38**	**6**	**2**	**4**	**6**	**2**	**1**	**0**	**0**	**20:17**
2001-02	**Phoenix**	**NHL**	**80**	**27**	**35**	**62**	**36**	**6**	**3**	**2**	**171**	**15.8**	**18**	**1379**	**46.2**	**19:11**	**5**	**1**	**0**	**1**	**0**	**0**	**0**	**0**	**21:06**
2002-03	**Phoenix**	**NHL**	**81**	**20**	**32**	**52**	**56**	**4**	**2**	**2**	**196**	**10.2**	**20**	**1972**	**46.5**	**21:00**	....	....	....	....	....	....	....	....	....
2003-04	**Phoenix**	**NHL**	**81**	**21**	**31**	**52**	**40**	**4**	**1**	**2**	**174**	**12.1**	**4**	**1472**	**43.1**	**21:07**	....	....	....	....	....	....	....	....	....
2004-05			DID NOT PLAY																						
	NHL Totals		**625**	**136**	**218**	**354**	**374**	**31**	**8**	**19**	**1432**	**9.5**		**8404**	**46.0**	**18:48**	**33**	**8**	**11**	**19**	**27**	**2**	**1**	**2**	**19:40**

WHL West First All-Star Team (1995) • Canadian Major Junior First All-Star Team (1995) • WHL West Second All-Star Team (1996)

Traded to **Philadelphia** by **Tampa Bay** with Mikael Renberg for Chris Gratton and Mike Sillinger, December 12, 1998. Traded to **Phoenix** by **Philadelphia** for Phoenix's 2nd round choice (later traded to Tampa Bay – later traded to San Jose – San Jose selected Dan Spang) in 2002 Entry Draft and Phoenix's 1st round choice (Jeff Carter) in 2003 Entry Draft, July 2, 2001. Traded to **Calgary** by **Phoenix** for Denis Gauthier and Oleg Saprykin, August 26, 2004.

LAPERRIERE, Ian
(luh-PAIR-ee-YAIR, EE-an) **COL.**

Right wing. Shoots right. 6'1", 201 lbs. Born, Montreal, Que., January 19, 1974. St. Louis' 6th choice, 158th overall, in 1992 Entry Draft.

Season	Club	League	GP	G	A	Pts	PIM	PP	SH	GW	S	%	+/-	TF	F%	Min	Playoffs GP	G	A	Pts	PIM	PP	SH	GW	Min
1989-90	Mtl-Bourassa	QAAA	22	4	10	14	10										3	0	1	1	6				
1990-91	Drummondville	QMJHL	65	19	29	48	117										14	2	9	11	48				
1991-92	Drummondville	QMJHL	70	28	49	77	160										4	2	2	4	9				
1992-93	Drummondville	QMJHL	60	44	*96	140	188										10	6	13	19	20				
1993-94	Drummondville	QMJHL	62	41	72	113	150										9	4	6	10	35				
	St. Louis	NHL	1	0	0	0	0	0	0	0	1	0.0	0												
	Peoria Rivermen	IHL															5	1	3	4	2				
1994-95	Peoria Rivermen	IHL	51	16	32	48	111																		
	St. Louis	NHL	37	13	14	27	85	1	0	1	53	24.5	12				7	0	4	4	21	0	0	0	
1995-96	St. Louis	NHL	33	3	6	9	87	1	0	1	31	9.7	–4												
	Worcester IceCats	AHL	3	2	1	3	22																		
	NY Rangers	NHL	28	1	2	3	53	0	0	0	21	4.8	–5												
	Los Angeles	NHL	10	2	3	5	15	0	0	0	18	11.1	–2												
1996-97	Los Angeles	NHL	62	8	15	23	102	0	1	2	84	9.5	–25												
1997-98	Los Angeles	NHL	77	6	15	21	131	0	1	1	74	8.1	0				4	1	0	1	6	0	0	0	
1998-99	Los Angeles	NHL	72	3	10	13	138	0	0	1	62	4.8	–5	643	47.3	11:47									
99-2000	Los Angeles	NHL	79	9	13	22	185	0	0	1	87	10.3	–14	1111	53.7	13:15	4	0	0	0	2	0	0	0	10:22
2000-01	Los Angeles	NHL	79	8	10	18	141	0	0	0	60	13.3	5	297	51.9	12:02	13	1	2	3	12	0	0	0	14:01
2001-02	Los Angeles	NHL	81	8	14	22	125	0	0	3	89	9.0	5	134	49.3	13:45	7	0	1	1	9	0	0	0	14:18
2002-03	Los Angeles	NHL	73	7	12	19	122	1	1	1	85	8.2	–9	317	49.2	15:46									
2003-04	Los Angeles	NHL	62	10	12	22	58	1	0	3	59	16.9	–4	446	54.0	15:50									
2004-05		DID NOT PLAY																							
	NHL Totals		694	78	126	204	1242	4	3	14	724	10.8		2948	51.5	13:40	35	2	7	9	50	0	0	0	13:29

QMJHL Second All-Star Team (1993)

Traded to **NY Rangers** by **St. Louis** for Stephane Matteau, December 28, 1995. Traded to **Los Angeles** by **NY Rangers** with Ray Ferraro, Mattias Norstrom, Nathan LaFayette and NY Rangers' 4th round choice (Sean Blanchard) in 1997 Entry Draft for Marty McSorley, Jari Kurri and Shane Churla, March 14, 1996. Signed as a free agent by **Colorado**, July 2, 2004.

LAPOINTE, Claude
(luh-POYNT, KLOHD)

Left wing/Center. Shoots left. 5'9", 188 lbs. Born, Lachine, Que., October 11, 1968. Quebec's 12th choice, 234th overall, in 1988 Entry Draft.

Season	Club	League	GP	G	A	Pts	PIM	PP	SH	GW	S	%	+/-	TF	F%	Min	Playoffs GP	G	A	Pts	PIM	PP	SH	GW	Min
1983-84	Lac St-Louis Lions	QAAA	42	28	29	57	42										8	3	7	10	8				
1984-85	Lac St-Louis Lions	QAAA	42	20	32	52	66										11	4	8	12	16				
1985-86	Trois-Rivieres	QMJHL	63	14	32	46	70										9	5	6	11	4				
1986-87	Trois-Rivieres	QMJHL	70	47	57	104	123																		
1987-88	Laval Titan	QMJHL	69	37	83	120	143										13	2	17	19	53				
1988-89	Laval Titan	QMJHL	63	32	72	104	158										17	5	14	19	66				
1989-90	Halifax Citadels	AHL	63	18	19	37	51										6	1	1	2	34				
1990-91	Quebec	NHL	13	2	2	4	4	0	0	0	7	28.6	3												
	Halifax Citadels	AHL	43	17	17	34	46																		
1991-92	Quebec	NHL	78	13	20	33	86	0	2	2	95	13.7	–8												
1992-93	Quebec	NHL	74	10	26	36	98	0	0	1	91	11.0	5				6	2	4	6	8	0	0	0	
1993-94	Quebec	NHL	59	11	17	28	70	1	1	1	73	15.1	2												
1994-95	Quebec	NHL	29	4	8	12	41	0	0	0	40	10.0	5				5	0	0	0	8	0	0	0	
1995-96	Colorado	NHL	3	0	0	0	0	0	0	0	0	0.0	–1												
	Calgary	NHL	32	4	5	9	20	0	2	1	44	9.1	2				2	0	0	0	0	0	0	0	
	Saint John Flames	AHL	12	5	3	8	10																		
1996-97	NY Islanders	NHL	73	13	5	18	49	0	3	3	80	16.3	–12												
	Utah Grizzlies	IHL	9	7	6	13	14																		
1997-98	NY Islanders	NHL	78	10	10	20	47	0	1	3	82	12.2	–9												
1998-99	NY Islanders	NHL	82	14	23	37	62	2	2	1	134	10.4	–19	1218	56.6	19:21									
99-2000	NY Islanders	NHL	76	15	16	31	60	2	1	3	129	11.6	–22	1284	54.0	19:39									
2000-01	NY Islanders	NHL	80	9	23	32	56	1	1	1	94	9.6	–2	1074	50.4	18:40									
2001-02	NY Islanders	NHL	80	9	12	21	60	0	3	0	74	12.2	–9	907	54.6	13:05	7	0	0	0	14	0	0	0	13:20
2002-03	NY Islanders	NHL	66	6	6	12	20	0	0	1	67	9.0	–3	686	55.0	12:16									
	Philadelphia	NHL	14	2	2	4	16	0	0	0	20	10.0	5	107	63.6	11:05	13	2	3	5	14	0	0	0	13:15
2003-04	Philadelphia	NHL	42	5	3	8	32	0	1	1	26	19.2	2	402	51.7	11:04	1	0	0	0	0	0	0	0	9:38
	Philadelphia	AHL	2	1	1	2	0																		
2004-05		DID NOT PLAY																							
	NHL Totals		879	127	178	305	721	6	17	18	1056	12.0		5678	54.1	16:01	34	4	7	11	44	0	0	0	13:06

Transferred to **Colorado** after **Quebec** franchise relocated, June 21, 1995. Traded to **Calgary** by **Colorado** for Calgary's 7th round choice (Samuel Pahlsson) in 1996 Entry Draft, November 1, 1995. Signed as a free agent by **NY Islanders**, August 14, 1996. Traded to **Philadelphia** by **NY Islanders** for Philadelphia's 5th round choice (later traded to Pittsburgh – Pittsburgh selected Evgeni Isakov) in 2003 Entry Draft, March 9, 2003.

LAPOINTE, Martin
(luh-POYNT, MAHR-tihn) **CHI.**

Right wing. Shoots right. 5'11", 215 lbs. Born, Ville St-Pierre, Que., September 12, 1973. Detroit's 1st choice, 10th overall, in 1991 Entry Draft.

Season	Club	League	GP	G	A	Pts	PIM	PP	SH	GW	S	%	+/-	TF	F%	Min	Playoffs GP	G	A	Pts	PIM	PP	SH	GW	Min
1988-89	Lac St-Louis Lions	QAAA	42	39	45	84	46										3	6	2	8	4				
1989-90	Laval Titan	QMJHL	65	42	54	96	77										14	8	17	25	54				
1990-91	Laval Titan	QMJHL	64	44	54	98	66										13	7	14	21	26				
1991-92	Laval Titan	QMJHL	31	25	30	55	84										10	4	10	14	32				
	Detroit	NHL	4	0	1	1	5	0	0	0	2	0.0	2				3	0	1	1	4	0	0	0	
	Adirondack	AHL															8	2	2	4	4				
1992-93	Laval Titan	QMJHL	35	38	51	89	41										13	*13	*17	*30	22				
	Detroit	NHL	3	0	0	0	0	0	0	0	2	0.0	–2												
	Adirondack	AHL	8	1	2	3	9																		
1993-94	Detroit	NHL	50	8	8	16	55	2	0	0	45	17.8	7				4	0	0	0	6	0	0	0	
	Adirondack	AHL	28	25	21	46	47										4	1	1	2	8				
1994-95	Adirondack	AHL	39	29	16	45	80																		
	Detroit	NHL	39	4	6	10	73	0	0	1	46	8.7	1				2	0	1	1	8	0	0	0	
1995-96	Detroit	NHL	58	6	3	9	93	1	0	0	76	7.9	0				11	1	2	3	12	0	0	0	
1996-97♦	Detroit	NHL	78	16	17	33	167	5	1	1	149	10.7	–14				20	4	8	12	60	1	0	1	
1997-98♦	Detroit	NHL	79	15	19	34	106	4	0	3	154	9.7	0				21	9	6	15	20	2	1	1	
1998-99	Detroit	NHL	77	16	13	29	141	7	1	4	153	10.5	7	217	47.9	15:06	10	0	2	2	20	0	0	0	11:43
99-2000	Detroit	NHL	82	16	25	41	121	1	1	2	127	12.6	17	287	54.4	14:43	9	3	1	4	20	2	0	1	14:28
2000-01	Detroit	NHL	82	27	30	57	127	13	0	8	181	14.9	3	461	53.2	16:06	6	0	1	1	8	0	0	0	16:53
2001-02	Boston	NHL	68	17	23	40	101	4	0	2	141	12.1	12	222	53.6	17:22	6	1	2	3	12	1	0	1	16:58
2002-03	Boston	NHL	59	8	10	18	87	1	0	1	110	7.3	–19	52	48.1	15:22	5	1	0	1	14	0	0	0	14:39
2003-04	Boston	NHL	78	15	10	25	67	9	0	2	136	11.0	–5	101	51.5	14:26	7	0	0	0	14	0	0	0	15:21
2004-05		DID NOT PLAY																							
	NHL Totals		757	148	165	313	1143	47	3	24	1322	11.2		1340	52.3	15:29	104	19	24	43	198	6	1	4	14:41

QMJHL First All-Star Team (1990, 1993) • QMJHL Offensive Rookie of the Year (1990) • QMJHL Second All-Star Team (1991) • Memorial Cup Tournament All-Star Team (1993)

Signed as a free agent by **Boston**, July 2, 2001. Signed as a free agent by **Chicago**, August 3, 2005.

LARAQUE, Georges
(luh-RAK, zhawrzh) **EDM.**

Right wing. Shoots right. 6'3", 243 lbs. Born, Montreal, Que., December 7, 1976. Edmonton's 2nd choice, 31st overall, in 1995 Entry Draft.

Season	Club	League	GP	G	A	Pts	PIM	PP	SH	GW	S	%	+/-	TF	F%	Min	Playoffs GP	G	A	Pts	PIM	PP	SH	GW	Min
1991-92	Mtl-Bourassa	QAHA	28	20	20	40	30																		
1992-93	Mtl-Bourassa	QAAA	37	8	20	28	50										3	1	2	3	2				
1993-94	St-Jean Lynx	QMJHL	70	11	11	22	142										4	0	0	0	7				
1994-95	St-Jean Lynx	QMJHL	62	19	22	41	259										7	1	1	2	42				
1995-96	Laval Titan	QMJHL	11	8	13	21	76																		
	St-Hyacinthe	QMJHL	8	3	4	7	59																		
	Granby	QMJHL	22	9	7	16	125										18	7	6	13	104				
1996-97	Hamilton	AHL	73	14	20	34	179										15	1	3	4	12				
1997-98	Edmonton	NHL	11	0	0	0	59	0	0	0	4	0.0	–4												
	Hamilton	AHL	46	10	20	30	154										3	0	0	0	11				
1998-99	Edmonton	NHL	39	3	2	5	57	0	0	0	17	17.6	–1	0	0.0	5:31	4	0	0	0	2	0	0	0	7:35
	Hamilton	AHL	25	6	8	14	93																		

Season	Club	League	GP	G	A	Pts	PIM	PP	SH	GW	S	%	+/-	TF	F%	Min	GP	G	A	Pts	PIM	PP	SH	GW	Min
			Regular Season														Playoffs								
99-2000	Edmonton	NHL	76	8	8	16	123	0	0	0	56	14.3	5	0	0.0	8:28	5	0	1	1	6	0	0	0	9:14
2000-01	Edmonton	NHL	82	13	16	29	148	1	0	1	73	17.8	5	0	0.0	9:03	6	1	1	2	8	0	0	0	9:54
2001-02	Edmonton	NHL	80	5	14	19	157	1	0	1	95	5.3	6	0	0.0	9:48	....	....	....	....	....	....	....	....	....
2002-03	Edmonton	NHL	64	6	7	13	110	0	0	2	46	13.0	–4	0	0.0	9:15	6	1	3	4	4	0	0	0	12:11
2003-04	Edmonton	NHL	66	6	11	17	99	1	0	1	54	11.1	7	0	0.0	9:22	....	....	....	....	....	....	....	....	....
2004-05	AIK Solna	Sweden-3	16	11	5	16	24	....	....	....	....	....	....	....	....	....	....	....	....	....	....	....	....	....	....
	NHL Totals		418	41	58	99	753	3	0	5	345	11.9		0	0.0	8:50	21	2	5	7	20	0	0	0	9:57

Signed as a free agent by **AIK Solna** (Sweden-3), January 31, 2005.

LAROSE, Cory

(la-ROHZ, KOH-ree)

Center. Shoots left. 6', 191 lbs. Born, Campbellton, N.B., May 14, 1975.

Season	Club	League	GP	G	A	Pts	PIM	PP	SH	GW	S	%	+/-	TF	F%	Min	GP	G	A	Pts	PIM	PP	SH	GW	Min
1993-94	Kimball Union	High-NH	21	18	11	29	14	....	....	....	....	....	....	....	....	....	....	....	....	....	....	....	....	....	....
1994-95	Langley Thunder	BCJHL	STATISTICS NOT AVAILABLE					....	....	....	....	....	....	....	....	....	....	....	....	....	....	....	....	....	....
1995-96	Langley Thunder	BCJHL	54	28	46	74	61	....	....	....	....	....	....	....	....	....	....	....	....	....	....	....	....	....	....
1996-97	U. of Maine	H-East	35	10	27	37	32	....	....	....	....	....	....	....	....	....	....	....	....	....	....	....	....	....	....
1997-98	U. of Maine	H-East	34	15	25	40	22	....	....	....	....	....	....	....	....	....	....	....	....	....	....	....	....	....	....
1998-99	U. of Maine	H-East	38	21	31	52	34	....	....	....	....	....	....	....	....	....	....	....	....	....	....	....	....	....	....
99-2000	U. of Maine	H-East	39	15	*36	51	45	....	....	....	....	....	....	....	....	....	....	....	....	....	....	....	....	....	....
2000-01	Cleveland	IHL	4	1	1	2	6	....	....	....	....	....	....	....	....	....	....	....	....	....	....	....	....	....	....
	Jackson Bandits	ECHL	63	21	32	53	73	....	....	....	....	....	....	....	....	....	5	2	2	4	12	....	....	....	....
2001-02	Houston Aeros	AHL	78	32	32	64	73	....	....	....	....	....	....	....	....	....	14	6	8	14	15	....	....	....	....
2002-03	Houston Aeros	AHL	58	18	38	56	57	....	....	....	....	....	....	....	....	....	....	....	....	....	....	....	....	....	....
	Hartford	AHL	24	9	10	19	20	....	....	....	....	....	....	....	....	....	2	0	1	1	0	....	....	....	....
2003-04	NY Rangers	NHL	7	0	1	1	4	0	0	0	10	0.0	–2	40	47.5	11:27	....	....	....	....	....	....	....	....	....
	Hartford	AHL	69	13	36	49	66	....	....	....	....	....	....	....	....	....	14	4	6	10	24	....	....	....	....
2004-05	Chicago Wolves	AHL	80	26	37	63	44	....	....	....	....	....	....	....	....	....	18	6	6	12	29	....	....	....	....
	NHL Totals		7	0	1	1	4	0	0	0	10	0.0		40	47.5	11:27	....	....	....	....	....	....	....	....	....

Hockey East First All-Star Team (2000) • NCAA East Second All-American Team (2000) • AHL All-Rookie Team (2002)

Signed as a free agent by **Minnesota**, May 10, 2000. Traded to **NY Rangers** by **Minnesota** for Jay Henderson, February 20, 2003. Signed as a free agent by **Atlanta**, July 14, 2004. Signed as a free agent by **Langnau** (Swiss), May 5, 2005.

LARSEN, Brad

(LARH-sehn, BRAD) **ATL.**

Left wing. Shoots left. 6', 200 lbs. Born, Nakusp, B.C., June 28, 1977. Colorado's 5th choice, 87th overall, in 1997 Entry Draft.

Season	Club	League	GP	G	A	Pts	PIM	PP	SH	GW	S	%	+/-	TF	F%	Min	GP	G	A	Pts	PIM	PP	SH	GW	Min
1992-93	Nelson	RMJHL	42	31	37	68	164	....	....	....	....	....	....	....	....	....	....	....	....	....	....	....	....	....	....
1993-94	Swift Current	WHL	64	15	18	33	32	....	....	....	....	....	....	....	....	....	7	1	2	3	4	....	....	....	....
1994-95	Swift Current	WHL	62	24	33	57	73	....	....	....	....	....	....	....	....	....	6	0	1	1	2	....	....	....	....
1995-96	Swift Current	WHL	51	30	47	77	67	....	....	....	....	....	....	....	....	....	6	3	2	5	13	....	....	....	....
1996-97	Swift Current	WHL	61	36	46	82	61	....	....	....	....	....	....	....	....	....	....	....	....	....	....	....	....	....	....
1997-98	Colorado	NHL	1	0	0	0	0	0	0	0	0	0.0	0	....	....	....	....	....	....	....	....	....	....	....	....
	Hershey Bears	AHL	65	12	10	22	80	....	....	....	....	....	....	....	....	....	7	3	2	5	2	....	....	....	....
1998-99	Hershey Bears	AHL	18	3	4	7	11	....	....	....	....	....	....	....	....	....	5	0	1	1	6	....	....	....	....
99-2000	Hershey Bears	AHL	52	13	26	39	66	....	....	....	....	....	....	....	....	....	14	5	2	7	29	....	....	....	....
2000-01	Colorado	NHL	9	0	0	0	0	0	0	0	3	0.0	1	14	57.1	9:17	....	....	....	....	....	....	....	....	....
	Hershey Bears	AHL	67	21	25	46	93	....	....	....	....	....	....	....	....	....	10	1	3	4	6	....	....	....	....
2001-02	Colorado	NHL	50	2	7	9	47	1	0	0	38	5.3	4	71	54.9	8:07	21	1	1	2	13	0	0	0	7:07
2002-03	Colorado	NHL	6	0	3	3	2	0	0	0	6	0.0	3	31	41.9	8:17	....	....	....	....	....	....	....	....	....
	Hershey Bears	AHL	25	3	6	9	25	....	....	....	....	....	....	....	....	....	4	1	1	2	8	....	....	....	....
2003-04	Colorado	NHL	26	2	2	4	11	0	0	0	17	11.8	2	9	44.4	7:41	....	....	....	....	....	....	....	....	....
	Hershey Bears	AHL	21	4	13	17	40	....	....	....	....	....	....	....	....	....	....	....	....	....	....	....	....	....	....
	Atlanta	NHL	6	0	0	0	2	0	0	0	6	0.0	–2	6	66.7	13:39	....	....	....	....	....	....	....	....	....
2004-05	Chicago Wolves	AHL	75	26	23	49	112	....	....	....	....	....	....	....	....	....	18	4	7	11	22	....	....	....	....
	NHL Totals		98	4	12	16	62	1	0	0	70	5.7		131	51.9	8:28	21	1	1	2	13	0	0	0	7:07

• Re-entered NHL Entry Draft. Originally Ottawa's 3rd choice, 53rd overall, in 1995 Entry Draft.

WHL East Second All-Star Team (1997)

Rights traded to **Colorado** by **Ottawa** for Janne Laukkanen, January 26, 1996. • Missed majority of 1998-99 season recovering from abdominal injury suffered in game vs. Albany (AHL), November 20, 1998. • Missed majority of 2002-03 season recovering from groin (October 27, 2002 vs. Minnesota) and back (December 11, 2002 vs. Vancouver) injuries. Claimed on waivers by **Atlanta** from **Colorado**, February 25, 2004.

LAW, Kirby

(LAW, KUHR-bee) **MIN.**

Right wing. Shoots right. 6'1", 185 lbs. Born, McCreary, Man., March 11, 1977.

Season	Club	League	GP	G	A	Pts	PIM	PP	SH	GW	S	%	+/-	TF	F%	Min	GP	G	A	Pts	PIM	PP	SH	GW	Min
1991-92	McCreary	MAHA	60	89	103	192	60	....	....	....	....	....	....	....	....	....	....	....	....	....	....	....	....	....	....
1992-93	Dauphin Kings	MJHL	48	20	15	35	8	....	....	....	....	....	....	....	....	....	....	....	....	....	....	....	....	....	....
1993-94	Saskatoon Blades	WHL	66	9	11	20	39	....	....	....	....	....	....	....	....	....	16	0	0	0	6	....	....	....	....
1994-95	Saskatoon Blades	WHL	46	10	15	25	44	....	....	....	....	....	....	....	....	....	....	....	....	....	....	....	....	....	....
	Lethbridge	WHL	24	4	10	14	38	....	....	....	....	....	....	....	....	....	....	....	....	....	....	....	....	....	....
1995-96	Lethbridge	WHL	71	17	45	62	133	....	....	....	....	....	....	....	....	....	4	0	0	0	12	....	....	....	....
1996-97	Lethbridge	WHL	72	39	52	91	200	....	....	....	....	....	....	....	....	....	19	4	14	18	60	....	....	....	....
1997-98	Brandon	WHL	49	34	44	78	153	....	....	....	....	....	....	....	....	....	9	3	3	6	41	....	....	....	....
1998-99	Orlando	IHL	67	18	13	31	136	....	....	....	....	....	....	....	....	....	....	....	....	....	....	....	....	....	....
	Adirondack	AHL	11	2	3	5	40	....	....	....	....	....	....	....	....	....	3	1	0	1	2	....	....	....	....
99-2000	Louisville Panthers	AHL	66	31	21	52	173	....	....	....	....	....	....	....	....	....	....	....	....	....	....	....	....	....	....
	Orlando	IHL	1	1	0	1	0	....	....	....	....	....	....	....	....	....	....	....	....	....	....	....	....	....	....
	Philadelphia	AHL	12	1	4	5	6	....	....	....	....	....	....	....	....	....	5	2	0	2	2	....	....	....	....
2000-01	Philadelphia	NHL	1	0	0	0	0	0	0	0	0	0.0	–1	0	0.0	3:23	....	....	....	....	....	....	....	....	....
	Philadelphia	AHL	78	27	34	61	150	....	....	....	....	....	....	....	....	....	10	1	6	7	16	....	....	....	....
2001-02	Philadelphia	AHL	71	18	24	42	102	....	....	....	....	....	....	....	....	....	5	0	0	0	0	....	....	....	....
2002-03	Philadelphia	NHL	2	0	0	0	2	0	0	0	0	0.0	0	0	0.0	1:41	....	....	....	....	....	....	....	....	....
	Philadelphia	AHL	74	22	19	41	166	....	....	....	....	....	....	....	....	....	....	....	....	....	....	....	....	....	....
2003-04	Philadelphia	NHL	6	0	1	1	2	0	0	0	1	0.0	0	0	0.0	8:09	....	....	....	....	....	....	....	....	....
	Philadelphia	AHL	74	32	41	73	139	....	....	....	....	....	....	....	....	....	12	0	5	5	12	....	....	....	....
2004-05	Houston Aeros	AHL	80	25	24	49	134	....	....	....	....	....	....	....	....	....	5	0	1	1	4	....	....	....	....
	NHL Totals		9	0	1	1	4	0	0	0	1	0.0		0	0.0	6:11	....	....	....	....	....	....	....	....	....

Signed as a free agent by **Atlanta**, July 27, 1999. Traded to **Philadelphia** by **Atlanta** for Vancouver's 6th round choice (previously acquired, Atlanta selected Jeff Dwyer) in 2000 Entry Draft and Philadelphia's 6th round choice (Pasi Nurminen) in 2001 Entry Draft, March 14, 2000. Signed as a free agent by **Minnesota**, July 6, 2004.

LEAHY, Patrick

(LEH-hey, PAT-rihk) **BOS.**

Right wing. Shoots right. 6'3", 200 lbs. Born, Brighton, MA, June 9, 1979. NY Rangers' 5th choice, 122nd overall, in 1998 Entry Draft.

Season	Club	League	GP	G	A	Pts	PIM	PP	SH	GW	S	%	+/-	TF	F%	Min	GP	G	A	Pts	PIM	PP	SH	GW	Min
1996-97	Bos. College High	High-MA	25	24	24	48		....	....	....	....	....	....	....	....	....	....	....	....	....	....	....	....	....	....
1997-98	Miami U.	CCHA	28	0	1	1	24	....	....	....	....	....	....	....	....	....	....	....	....	....	....	....	....	....	....
1998-99	Miami U.	CCHA	34	10	20	30	40	....	....	....	....	....	....	....	....	....	....	....	....	....	....	....	....	....	....
99-2000	Miami U.	CCHA	36	16	22	38	89	....	....	....	....	....	....	....	....	....	....	....	....	....	....	....	....	....	....
2000-01	Miami U.	CCHA	37	13	19	32	14	....	....	....	....	....	....	....	....	....	....	....	....	....	....	....	....	....	....
2001-02	Trenton Titans	ECHL	41	20	21	41	64	....	....	....	....	....	....	....	....	....	....	....	....	....	....	....	....	....	....
	Hershey Bears	AHL	9	1	2	3	8	....	....	....	....	....	....	....	....	....	....	....	....	....	....	....	....	....	....
	Portland Pirates	AHL	9	1	1	2	8	....	....	....	....	....	....	....	....	....	....	....	....	....	....	....	....	....	....
	Bridgeport	AHL	14	2	2	4	2	....	....	....	....	....	....	....	....	....	20	3	4	7	4	....	....	....	....
2002-03	Providence Bruins	AHL	66	20	23	43	63	....	....	....	....	....	....	....	....	....	4	1	0	1	18	....	....	....	....
2003-04	Boston	NHL	6	0	0	0	0	0	0	0	2	0.0	1	0	0.0	5:27	....	....	....	....	....	....	....	....	....
	Providence Bruins	AHL	55	14	16	30	37	....	....	....	....	....	....	....	....	....	2	0	0	0	0	....	....	....	....
2004-05	Providence Bruins	AHL	38	1	14	15	18	....	....	....	....	....	....	....	....	....	17	4	6	10	20	....	....	....	....
	NHL Totals		6	0	0	0	0	0	0	0	2	0.0		0	0.0	5:27	....	....	....	....	....	....	....	....	....

Signed as a free agent by **Boston**, July 28, 2003.

LECAVALIER, Vincent

(luh-KAV-uhl-YAY, VIHN-sihnt) **T.B.**

Center. Shoots left. 6'4", 207 lbs. Born, Ile Bizard, Que., April 21, 1980. Tampa Bay's 1st choice, 1st overall, in 1998 Entry Draft.

			Regular Season														Playoffs								
Season	Club	League	GP	G	A	Pts	PIM	PP	SH	GW	S	%	+/-	TF	F%	Min	GP	G	A	Pts	PIM	PP	SH	GW	Min
1995-96	Notre Dame	SMHL	22	52	52	104	....	....	....	....	....	....	....	....	....	....	....	....	....	....	....	....	....	....	....
1996-97	Rimouski Oceanic	QMJHL	64	42	61	103	38	....	....	....	....	....	....	....	....	....	4	4	3	7	2	....	....	....	....
1997-98	Rimouski Oceanic	QMJHL	58	44	71	115	117	....	....	....	....	....	....	....	....	....	18	*15	*26	*41	46	....	....	....	....
1998-99	**Tampa Bay**	**NHL**	82	13	15	28	23	2	0	2	125	10.4	–19	953	40.3	13:40	....	....	....	....	....	....	....	....	....
99-2000	**Tampa Bay**	**NHL**	80	25	42	67	43	6	0	3	166	15.1	–25	1288	44.4	19:18	....	....	....	....	....	....	....	....	....
2000-01	**Tampa Bay**	**NHL**	68	23	28	51	66	7	0	3	165	13.9	–26	1278	44.9	19:57	....	....	....	....	....	....	....	....	....
2001-02	**Tampa Bay**	**NHL**	76	20	17	37	61	5	0	3	164	12.2	–18	931	41.5	17:09	....	....	....	....	....	....	....	....	....
2002-03	**Tampa Bay**	**NHL**	80	33	45	78	39	11	2	3	274	12.0	0	1200	43.9	19:33	11	3	3	6	22	1	0	1	22:36
2003-04♦	**Tampa Bay**	**NHL**	81	32	34	66	52	5	2	6	242	13.2	23	1119	41.4	18:04	23	9	7	16	25	2	0	0	19:39
2004-05	Ak Bars Kazan	Russia	30	7	9	16	78	....	....	....	....	....	....	....	....	....	4	1	0	1	6	....	....	....	....
	NHL Totals		**467**	**146**	**181**	**327**	**284**	**36**	**4**	**20**	**1136**	**12.9**		**6769**	**42.9**	**17:53**	**34**	**12**	**10**	**22**	**47**	**3**	**0**	**1**	**20:36**

QMJHL All-Rookie Team (1997) • QMJHL Offensive Rookie of the Year (1997) • Canadian Major Junior Rookie of the Year (1997) • QMJHL First All-Star Team (1998) • Canadian Major Junior First All-Star Team (1998)

Played in NHL All-Star Game (2003)

Signed as a free agent by **Kazan** (Russia), November 4, 2004.

LeCLAIR, John

(luh-KLAIR, JAWN) **PIT.**

Left wing. Shoots left. 6'3", 226 lbs. Born, St. Albans, VT, July 5, 1969. Montreal's 2nd choice, 33rd overall, in 1987 Entry Draft.

			Regular Season														Playoffs								
Season	Club	League	GP	G	A	Pts	PIM	PP	SH	GW	S	%	+/-	TF	F%	Min	GP	G	A	Pts	PIM	PP	SH	GW	Min
1985-86	Bellows	High-VT	22	41	28	69	14	....	....	....	....	....	....	....	....	....	....	....	....	....	....	....	....	....	....
1986-87	Bellows	High-VT	23	44	40	84	14	....	....	....	....	....	....	....	....	....	....	....	....	....	....	....	....	....	....
1987-88	U. of Vermont	ECAC	31	12	22	34	62	....	....	....	....	....	....	....	....	....	....	....	....	....	....	....	....	....	....
1988-89	U. of Vermont	ECAC	18	9	12	21	40	....	....	....	....	....	....	....	....	....	....	....	....	....	....	....	....	....	....
1989-90	U. of Vermont	ECAC	10	10	6	16	38	....	....	....	....	....	....	....	....	....	....	....	....	....	....	....	....	....	....
1990-91	U. of Vermont	ECAC	33	25	20	45	58	....	....	....	....	....	....	....	....	....	....	....	....	....	....	....	....	....	....
	Montreal	**NHL**	10	2	5	7	2	0	0	1	12	16.7	1	....	....	....	3	0	0	0	0	0	0	0	....
1991-92	**Montreal**	**NHL**	59	8	11	19	14	3	0	0	73	11.0	5	....	....	....	8	1	1	2	4	0	0	0	....
	Fredericton	AHL	8	7	7	14	10	....	....	....	....	....	....	....	....	....	2	0	0	0	4	....	....	....	....
1992-93♦	**Montreal**	**NHL**	72	19	25	44	33	2	0	2	139	13.7	11	....	....	....	20	4	6	10	14	0	0	3	....
1993-94	**Montreal**	**NHL**	74	19	24	43	32	1	0	1	153	12.4	17	....	....	....	7	2	1	3	8	1	0	0	....
1994-95	**Montreal**	**NHL**	9	1	4	5	10	1	0	0	18	5.6	–1	....	....	....	....	....	....	....	....	....	....	....	....
	Philadelphia	**NHL**	37	25	24	49	20	5	0	7	113	22.1	21	....	....	....	15	5	7	12	4	1	0	1	....
1995-96	**Philadelphia**	**NHL**	82	51	46	97	64	19	0	10	270	18.9	21	....	....	....	11	6	5	11	6	4	0	1	....
1996-97	**Philadelphia**	**NHL**	82	50	47	97	58	10	0	5	324	15.4	44	....	....	....	19	9	12	21	10	4	0	3	....
1997-98	**Philadelphia**	**NHL**	82	51	36	87	32	16	0	9	303	16.8	30	....	....	....	5	1	1	2	8	1	0	1	....
	United States	Olympics	4	0	1	1	0	....	....	....	....	....	....	....	....	....	....	....	....	....	....	....	....	....	....
1998-99	**Philadelphia**	**NHL**	76	43	47	90	30	16	0	7	246	17.5	36	7	14.3	21:03	6	3	0	3	12	2	0	0	20:14
99-2000	**Philadelphia**	**NHL**	82	40	37	77	36	13	0	7	249	16.1	8	7	28.6	20:18	18	6	7	13	6	4	0	2	21:16
2000-01	**Philadelphia**	**NHL**	16	7	5	12	0	3	0	2	48	14.6	2	0	0.0	19:06	6	1	2	3	2	0	0	0	19:34
2001-02	**Philadelphia**	**NHL**	82	25	26	51	30	4	0	6	220	11.4	5	4	75.0	17:30	5	0	0	0	2	0	0	0	17:18
	United States	Olympics	6	*6	1	7	2	....	....	....	....	....	....	....	....	....	....	....	....	....	....	....	....	....	....
2002-03	**Philadelphia**	**NHL**	35	18	10	28	16	8	0	4	99	18.2	10	3	66.7	16:09	13	2	3	5	10	1	0	0	17:09
2003-04	**Philadelphia**	**NHL**	75	23	32	55	51	8	0	4	182	12.6	20	9	33.3	16:06	18	2	2	4	8	0	0	0	15:57
2004-05			DID NOT PLAY																						
	NHL Totals		**873**	**382**	**379**	**761**	**428**	**109**	**0**	**65**	**2449**	**15.6**		**30**	**36.7**	**18:31**	**154**	**42**	**47**	**89**	**94**	**18**	**0**	**11**	**18:28**

ECAC Second All-Star Team (1991) • NHL First All-Star Team (1995, 1998) • NHL Second All-Star Team (1996, 1997, 1999) • Bud Ice Plus/Minus Award (1997) • Bud Light Plus/Minus Award (1999)

Played in NHL All-Star Game (1996, 1997, 1998, 1999, 2000)

• Missed majority of 1989-90 season recovering from knee surgery, January 20, 1990. Traded to **Philadelphia** by **Montreal** with Eric Desjardins and Gilbert Dionne for Mark Recchi and Philadelphia's 3rd round choice (Martin Hohenberger) in 1995 Entry Draft, February 9, 1995. • Missed majority of 2000-01 season recovering from back injury suffered in game vs. Boston, October 7, 2000. • Missed majority of 2002-03 season recovering from shoulder injury suffered in game vs. St. Louis, November 27, 2002. Signed as a free agent by **Pittsburgh**, August 15, 2005.

LECLERC, Mike

(luh-KLAIR, MIGHK) **PHX.**

Left wing. Shoots left. 6'2", 208 lbs. Born, Winnipeg, Man., November 10, 1976. Anaheim's 3rd choice, 55th overall, in 1995 Entry Draft.

			Regular Season														Playoffs								
Season	Club	League	GP	G	A	Pts	PIM	PP	SH	GW	S	%	+/-	TF	F%	Min	GP	G	A	Pts	PIM	PP	SH	GW	Min
1991-92	St. Boniface	MJHL	43	16	12	28	25	....	....	....	....	....	....	....	....	....	....	....	....	....	....	....	....	....	....
	Victoria Cougars	WHL	2	0	0	0	0	....	....	....	....	....	....	....	....	....	....	....	....	....	....	....	....	....	....
1992-93	Victoria Cougars	WHL	70	4	11	15	118	....	....	....	....	....	....	....	....	....	....	....	....	....	....	....	....	....	....
1993-94	Victoria Cougars	WHL	68	29	11	40	112	....	....	....	....	....	....	....	....	....	....	....	....	....	....	....	....	....	....
1994-95	Prince George	WHL	43	20	36	56	78	....	....	....	....	....	....	....	....	....	....	....	....	....	....	....	....	....	....
	Brandon	WHL	23	5	8	13	50	....	....	....	....	....	....	....	....	....	18	10	6	16	33	....	....	....	....
1995-96	Brandon	WHL	71	58	53	111	161	....	....	....	....	....	....	....	....	....	19	6	19	25	25	....	....	....	....
1996-97	**Anaheim**	**NHL**	5	1	1	2	0	0	0	1	3	33.3	2	....	....	....	1	0	0	0	0	0	0	0	....
	Baltimore Bandits	AHL	71	29	27	56	134	....	....	....	....	....	....	....	....	....	....	....	....	....	....	....	....	....	....
1997-98	**Anaheim**	**NHL**	7	0	0	0	6	0	0	0	11	0.0	–6	....	....	....	....	....	....	....	....	....	....	....	....
	Cincinnati	AHL	48	18	22	40	83	....	....	....	....	....	....	....	....	....	....	....	....	....	....	....	....	....	....
1998-99	**Anaheim**	**NHL**	7	0	0	0	4	0	0	0	1	0.0	–2	0	0.0	5:52	1	0	0	0	0	0	0	0	15:02
	Cincinnati	AHL	65	25	28	53	153	....	....	....	....	....	....	....	....	....	3	0	1	1	19	....	....	....	....
99-2000	**Anaheim**	**NHL**	69	8	11	19	70	0	0	2	105	7.6	–15	1	0.0	12:08	....	....	....	....	....	....	....	....	....
2000-01	**Anaheim**	**NHL**	54	15	20	35	26	3	0	3	130	11.5	–1	5	20.0	17:35	....	....	....	....	....	....	....	....	....
2001-02	**Anaheim**	**NHL**	82	20	24	44	107	8	0	4	178	11.2	–12	10	50.0	17:23	....	....	....	....	....	....	....	....	....
2002-03	**Anaheim**	**NHL**	57	9	19	28	34	1	0	4	122	7.4	–8	17	29.4	16:56	21	2	9	11	12	1	0	2	19:02
2003-04	**Anaheim**	**NHL**	10	1	3	4	4	0	0	0	19	5.3	–1	4	75.0	15:37	....	....	....	....	....	....	....	....	....
2004-05			DID NOT PLAY																						
	NHL Totals		**291**	**54**	**78**	**132**	**251**	**12**	**0**	**14**	**569**	**9.5**		**37**	**37.8**	**15:41**	**23**	**2**	**9**	**11**	**12**	**1**	**0**	**2**	**18:51**

WHL East Second All-Star Team (1996) • AHL All-Rookie Team (1997)

• Missed majority of 2003-04 season recovering from knee surgery, July 15, 2003. Traded to **Phoenix** by **Anaheim** for a conditional choice in 2007 Entry Draft, August 23, 2005.

LEEB, Brad

(LEEB, BRAD) **TOR.**

Right wing. Shoots right. 5'11", 187 lbs. Born, Red Deer, Alta., August 27, 1979.

			Regular Season														Playoffs								
Season	Club	League	GP	G	A	Pts	PIM	PP	SH	GW	S	%	+/-	TF	F%	Min	GP	G	A	Pts	PIM	PP	SH	GW	Min
1994-95	Red Deer Vipers	AMHL	36	31	14	45	93	....	....	....	....	....	....	....	....	....	....	....	....	....	....	....	....	....	....
	Red Deer Rebels	WHL	3	0	0	0	4	....	....	....	....	....	....	....	....	....	....	....	....	....	....	....	....	....	....
1995-96	Red Deer Rebels	WHL	38	3	6	9	30	....	....	....	....	....	....	....	....	....	10	2	0	2	11	....	....	....	....
1996-97	Red Deer Rebels	WHL	70	15	20	35	76	....	....	....	....	....	....	....	....	....	16	3	3	6	6	....	....	....	....
1997-98	Red Deer Rebels	WHL	63	23	23	46	88	....	....	....	....	....	....	....	....	....	3	2	0	2	2	....	....	....	....
1998-99	Red Deer Rebels	WHL	64	32	47	79	84	....	....	....	....	....	....	....	....	....	9	5	9	14	10	....	....	....	....
99-2000	**Vancouver**	**NHL**	2	0	0	0	2	0	0	0	3	0.0	–2	0	0.0	12:07	....	....	....	....	....	....	....	....	....
	Syracuse Crunch	AHL	61	19	18	37	50	....	....	....	....	....	....	....	....	....	4	0	0	0	6	....	....	....	....
2000-01	Kansas City	IHL	53	18	16	34	53	....	....	....	....	....	....	....	....	....	....	....	....	....	....	....	....	....	....
2001-02	**Vancouver**	**NHL**	2	0	0	0	0	0	0	0	1	0.0	1	0	0.0	9:35	....	....	....	....	....	....	....	....	....
	Manitoba Moose	AHL	60	17	15	32	45	....	....	....	....	....	....	....	....	....	....	....	....	....	....	....	....	....	....
2002-03	St. John's	AHL	79	35	26	61	78	....	....	....	....	....	....	....	....	....	....	....	....	....	....	....	....	....	....
2003-04	**Toronto**	**NHL**	1	0	0	0	0	0	0	0	1	0.0	–1	0	0.0	10:31	....	....	....	....	....	....	....	....	....
	St. John's	AHL	77	24	25	49	116	....	....	....	....	....	....	....	....	....	....	....	....	....	....	....	....	....	....
2004-05	St. John's	AHL	48	16	13	29	43	....	....	....	....	....	....	....	....	....	3	2	1	3	0	....	....	....	....
	NHL Totals		**5**	**0**	**0**	**0**	**2**	**0**	**0**	**0**	**5**	**0.0**		**0**	**0.0**	**10:47**	....	....	....	....	....	....	....	....	....

WHL East Second All-Star Team (1999)

Signed as a free agent by **Vancouver**, October 8, 1999. Traded to **Toronto** by **Vancouver** for Tomas Mojzis, September 4, 2002.

			Regular Season														Playoffs								
Season	Club	League	GP	G	A	Pts	PIM	PP	SH	GW	S	%	+/-	TF	F%	Min	GP	G	A	Pts	PIM	PP	SH	GW	Min

LEETCH, Brian

(LEECH, BRIGH-uhn) **BOS.**

Defense. Shoots left. 6', 185 lbs. Born, Corpus Christi, TX, March 3, 1968. NY Rangers' 1st choice, 9th overall, in 1986 Entry Draft.

Season	Club	League	GP	G	A	Pts	PIM	PP	SH	GW	S	%	+/-	TF	F%	Min	GP	G	A	Pts	PIM	PP	SH	GW	Min
1983-84	Cheshire	High-CT	28	52	49	101	24	....	....	....	....	....	....	....	....	....	....	....	....	....	....	....	....	....	....
1984-85	Avon Old Farms	High-CT	26	30	46	76	15	....	....	....	....	....	....	....	....	....	....	....	....	....	....	....	....	....	....
1985-86	Avon Old Farms	High-CT	28	40	44	84	18	....	....	....	....	....	....	....	....	....	....	....	....	....	....	....	....	....	....
1986-87	Boston College	H-East	37	9	38	47	10	....	....	....	....	....	....	....	....	....	....	....	....	....	....	....	....	....	....
1987-88	United States	Nat-Tm	50	13	61	74	38	....	....	....	....	....	....	....	....	....	....	....	....	....	....	....	....	....	....
	United States	Olympics	6	1	5	6	4	....	....	....	....	....	....	....	....	....	....	....	....	....	....	....	....	....	....
	NY Rangers	**NHL**	**17**	**2**	**12**	**14**	**0**	**1**	**0**	**1**	**40**	**5.0**	**5**	....	....	....	....	....	....	....	....	....	....	....	....
1988-89	**NY Rangers**	**NHL**	**68**	**23**	**48**	**71**	**50**	**8**	**3**	**1**	**268**	**8.6**	**8**	....	....	....	**4**	**3**	**2**	**5**	**2**	**2**	**0**	**0**	....
1989-90	**NY Rangers**	**NHL**	**72**	**11**	**45**	**56**	**26**	**5**	**0**	**2**	**222**	**5.0**	**–18**	....	....	....	....	....	....	....	....	....	....	....	....
1990-91	**NY Rangers**	**NHL**	**80**	**16**	**72**	**88**	**42**	**6**	**0**	**4**	**206**	**7.8**	**2**	....	....	....	**6**	**1**	**3**	**4**	**0**	**0**	**0**	**0**	....
1991-92	**NY Rangers**	**NHL**	**80**	**22**	**80**	**102**	**26**	**10**	**1**	**3**	**245**	**9.0**	**25**	....	....	....	**13**	**4**	**11**	**15**	**4**	**1**	**1**	**0**	....
1992-93	**NY Rangers**	**NHL**	**36**	**6**	**30**	**36**	**26**	**2**	**1**	**1**	**150**	**4.0**	**2**	....	....	....	....	....	....	....	....	....	....	....	....
1993-94♦	**NY Rangers**	**NHL**	**84**	**23**	**56**	**79**	**67**	**17**	**1**	**4**	**328**	**7.0**	**28**	....	....	....	**23**	**11**	***23**	***34**	**6**	**4**	**0**	**4**	....
1994-95	**NY Rangers**	**NHL**	**48**	**9**	**32**	**41**	**18**	**3**	**0**	**2**	**182**	**4.9**	**0**	....	....	....	**10**	**6**	**8**	**14**	**8**	**3**	**0**	**1**	....
1995-96	**NY Rangers**	**NHL**	**82**	**15**	**70**	**85**	**30**	**7**	**0**	**3**	**276**	**5.4**	**12**	....	....	....	**11**	**1**	**6**	**7**	**4**	**1**	**0**	**0**	....
1996-97	**NY Rangers**	**NHL**	**82**	**20**	**58**	**78**	**40**	**9**	**0**	**2**	**256**	**7.8**	**31**	....	....	....	**15**	**2**	**8**	**10**	**6**	**1**	**0**	**1**	....
1997-98	**NY Rangers**	**NHL**	**76**	**17**	**33**	**50**	**32**	**11**	**0**	**2**	**230**	**7.4**	**–36**	....	....	....	....	....	....	....	....	....	....	....	....
	United States	Olympics	4	1	1	2	0	....	....	....	....	....	....	....	....	....	....	....	....	....	....	....	....	....	....
1998-99	**NY Rangers**	**NHL**	**82**	**13**	**42**	**55**	**42**	**4**	**0**	**1**	**184**	**7.1**	**–7**	**0**	**0.0**	**29:52**	....	....	....	....	....	....	....	....	....
99-2000	**NY Rangers**	**NHL**	**50**	**7**	**19**	**26**	**20**	**3**	**0**	**2**	**124**	**5.6**	**–16**	**0**	**0.0**	**26:57**	....	....	....	....	....	....	....	....	....
2000-01	**NY Rangers**	**NHL**	**82**	**21**	**58**	**79**	**34**	**10**	**1**	**3**	**241**	**8.7**	**–18**	**0**	**0.0**	**29:21**	....	....	....	....	....	....	....	....	....
2001-02	**NY Rangers**	**NHL**	**82**	**10**	**45**	**55**	**28**	**1**	**0**	**3**	**202**	**5.0**	**14**	**0**	**0.0**	**25:52**	....	....	....	....	....	....	....	....	....
	United States	Olympics	6	0	5	5	0	....	....	....	....	....	....	....	....	....	....	....	....	....	....	....	....	....	....
2002-03	**NY Rangers**	**NHL**	**51**	**12**	**18**	**30**	**20**	**5**	**0**	**2**	**150**	**8.0**	**–3**	**0**	**0.0**	**26:06**	....	....	....	....	....	....	....	....	....
2003-04	**NY Rangers**	**NHL**	**57**	**13**	**23**	**36**	**24**	**4**	**1**	**1**	**165**	**7.9**	**–5**	**0**	**0.0**	**26:15**	....	....	....	....	....	....	....	....	....
	Toronto	**NHL**	**15**	**2**	**13**	**15**	**10**	**1**	**0**	**1**	**41**	**4.9**	**11**	**0**	**0.0**	**26:26**	**13**	**0**	**8**	**8**	**6**	**0**	**0**	**0**	**28:29**
2004-05		DID NOT PLAY																							
	NHL Totals		**1144**	**242**	**754**	**996**	**535**	**107**	**8**	**38**	**3510**	**6.9**		**0**	**0.0**	**27:34**	**95**	**28**	**69**	**97**	**36**	**12**	**1**	**6**	**28:29**

Hockey East First All-Star Team (1987) • Hockey East Rookie of the Year (1987) • Hockey East Player of the Year (1987) • NCAA East First All-American Team (1987) • NHL All-Rookie Team (1989) • Calder Memorial Trophy (1989) • NHL Second All-Star Team (1991, 1994, 1996) • NHL First All-Star Team (1992, 1997) • James Norris Memorial Trophy (1992, 1997) • Conn Smythe Trophy (1994)

Played in NHL All-Star Game (1990, 1991, 1992, 1994, 1996, 1997, 1998, 2001, 2002)

Traded to **Edmonton** by **NY Rangers** for Jussi Markkanen and Edmonton's 4th round choice (later traded to Toronto – Toronto selected Roman Kukumberg), June 30, 2003. Signed as a free agent by **NY Rangers**, July 30, 2003. Traded to **Toronto** by **NY Rangers** with Edmonton's 4th round choice (previously acquired, Toronto selected Roman Kukumberg) in 2004 Entry Draft for Maxim Kondratiev, Jarkko Immonen, Toronto's 1st round choice (later traded to Calgary – Calgary selected Kris Chucko) in 2004 Entry Draft and Toronto's 2nd round choice (Michael Sauer) in 2005 Entry Draft, March 3, 2004. Signed as a free agent by **Boston**, August 3, 2005.

LEFEBVRE, Guillaume

(luh-FAYV, GEE-ohm) **PIT.**

Left wing. Shoots left. 6'1", 202 lbs. Born, Amos, Que., May 7, 1981. Philadelphia's 6th choice, 227th overall, in 2000 Entry Draft.

Season	Club	League	GP	G	A	Pts	PIM	PP	SH	GW	S	%	+/-	TF	F%	Min	GP	G	A	Pts	PIM	PP	SH	GW	Min
1996-97	Amos Forestiers	QAAA	40	7	12	19	14	....	....	....	....	....	....	....	....	....	....	....	....	....	....	....	....	....	....
1997-98	Amos Forestiers	QAAA	42	12	16	28	100	....	....	....	....	....	....	....	....	....	6	4	5	9	....	....	....	....	....
1998-99	Shawinigan	QMJHL	40	3	1	4	49	....	....	....	....	....	....	....	....	....	....	....	....	....	....	....	....	....	....
	Cape Breton	QMJHL	24	2	7	9	13	....	....	....	....	....	....	....	....	....	5	0	1	1	0	....	....	....	....
99-2000	Cape Breton	QMJHL	44	26	28	54	82	....	....	....	....	....	....	....	....	....	....	....	....	....	....	....	....	....	....
	Quebec Remparts	QMJHL	2	3	1	4	0	....	....	....	....	....	....	....	....	....	....	....	....	....	....	....	....	....	....
	Rouyn-Noranda	QMJHL	25	4	11	15	39	....	....	....	....	....	....	....	....	....	11	4	0	4	25	....	....	....	....
2000-01	Rouyn-Noranda	QMJHL	61	24	43	67	160	....	....	....	....	....	....	....	....	....	9	3	1	4	22	....	....	....	....
	Philadelphia	AHL	....	....	....	....	....	....	....	....	....	....	....	....	....	....	9	0	1	1	2	....	....	....	....
2001-02	**Philadelphia**	**NHL**	**3**	**0**	**0**	**0**	**0**	**0**	**0**	**0**	**3**	**0.0**	**–1**	**0**	**0.0**	**5:55**	....	....	....	....	....	....	....	....	....
	Philadelphia	AHL	78	19	15	34	111	....	....	....	....	....	....	....	....	....	5	0	0	0	4	....	....	....	....
2002-03	**Philadelphia**	**NHL**	**14**	**0**	**0**	**0**	**4**	**0**	**0**	**0**	**5**	**0.0**	**1**	**0**	**0.0**	**7:27**	....	....	....	....	....	....	....	....	....
	Philadelphia	AHL	47	7	6	13	113	....	....	....	....	....	....	....	....	....	....	....	....	....	....	....	....	....	....
	Pittsburgh	**NHL**	**12**	**2**	**4**	**6**	**0**	**0**	**0**	**0**	**14**	**14.3**	**1**	**1**	**100.0**	**17:30**	....	....	....	....	....	....	....	....	....
	Wilkes-Barre	AHL	1	1	0	1	0	....	....	....	....	....	....	....	....	....	5	0	0	0	6	....	....	....	....
2003-04	Wilkes-Barre	AHL	64	4	12	16	78	....	....	....	....	....	....	....	....	....	14	1	0	1	19	....	....	....	....
2004-05	Wilkes-Barre	AHL	34	3	3	6	76	....	....	....	....	....	....	....	....	....	11	1	0	1	23	....	....	....	....
	NHL Totals		**29**	**2**	**4**	**6**	**4**	**0**	**0**	**0**	**22**	**9.1**		**1**	**100.0**	**11:27**	....	....	....	....	....	....	....	....	....

Traded to **Phoenix** by **Philadelphia** with Atlanta's 3rd round choice (previously acquired, Phoenix selected Tyler Redenbach) in 2003 Entry Draft and Philadelphia's 2nd round choice (later traded to NY Rangers – NY Rangers selected Brandon Dubinsky) in 2004 Entry Draft for Tony Amonte, March 10, 2003. Traded to **Pittsburgh** by **Phoenix** with Ramzi Abid and Dan Focht for Jan Hrdina and Francois Leroux, March 11, 2003.

LEGWAND, David

(LEHG-wuhnd, DAY-vihd) **NSH.**

Center. Shoots left. 6'2", 190 lbs. Born, Detroit, MI, August 17, 1980. Nashville's 1st choice, 2nd overall, in 1998 Entry Draft.

Season	Club	League	GP	G	A	Pts	PIM	PP	SH	GW	S	%	+/-	TF	F%	Min	GP	G	A	Pts	PIM	PP	SH	GW	Min
1996-97	Det. Compuware	MNHL	44	21	41	62	58	....	....	....	....	....	....	....	....	....	....	....	....	....	....	....	....	....	....
1997-98	Plymouth Whalers	OHL	59	54	51	105	56	....	....	....	....	....	....	....	....	....	15	8	12	20	24	....	....	....	....
1998-99	Plymouth Whalers	OHL	55	31	49	80	65	....	....	....	....	....	....	....	....	....	11	3	8	11	8	....	....	....	....
	Nashville	**NHL**	**1**	**0**	**0**	**0**	**0**	**0**	**0**	**0**	**2**	**0.0**	**0**	**9**	**55.6**	**12:50**	....	....	....	....	....	....	....	....	....
99-2000	**Nashville**	**NHL**	**71**	**13**	**15**	**28**	**30**	**4**	**0**	**2**	**111**	**11.7**	**–6**	**637**	**41.6**	**14:43**	....	....	....	....	....	....	....	....	....
2000-01	**Nashville**	**NHL**	**81**	**13**	**28**	**41**	**38**	**3**	**0**	**3**	**172**	**7.6**	**1**	**888**	**40.3**	**15:14**	....	....	....	....	....	....	....	....	....
2001-02	**Nashville**	**NHL**	**63**	**11**	**19**	**30**	**54**	**1**	**1**	**1**	**121**	**9.1**	**1**	**843**	**40.5**	**16:25**	....	....	....	....	....	....	....	....	....
2002-03	**Nashville**	**NHL**	**64**	**17**	**31**	**48**	**34**	**3**	**1**	**4**	**167**	**10.2**	**–2**	**1095**	**46.6**	**19:14**	....	....	....	....	....	....	....	....	....
2003-04	**Nashville**	**NHL**	**82**	**18**	**29**	**47**	**46**	**5**	**1**	**5**	**165**	**10.9**	**9**	**1109**	**45.1**	**17:16**	**6**	**1**	**0**	**1**	**8**	**0**	**1**	**0**	**15:41**
2004-05	EHC Basel	Swiss-2	3	6	2	8	2	....	....	....	....	....	....	....	....	....	19	16	23	39	20	....	....	....	....
	NHL Totals		**362**	**72**	**122**	**194**	**202**	**16**	**3**	**15**	**738**	**9.8**		**4581**	**43.2**	**16:30**	**6**	**1**	**0**	**1**	**8**	**0**	**1**	**0**	**15:41**

OHL All-Rookie Team (1998) • OHL First All-Star Team (1998) • OHL Rookie of the Year (1998) • OHL MVP (1998) • Canadian Major Junior Rookie of the Year (1998)

Signed as a free agent by **Basel** (Swiss-2), January 27, 2005.

LEHTINEN, Jere

(LEH-tih-nehn, YUH-ree) **DAL.**

Right wing. Shoots right. 6', 200 lbs. Born, Espoo, Finland, June 24, 1973. Minnesota's 3rd choice, 88th overall, in 1992 Entry Draft.

Season	Club	League	GP	G	A	Pts	PIM	PP	SH	GW	S	%	+/-	TF	F%	Min	GP	G	A	Pts	PIM	PP	SH	GW	Min
1989-90	Kiekko-67 Jr.	Finland-Jr.	32	23	23	46	6	....	....	....	....	....	....	....	....	....	5	0	3	3	0	....	....	....	....
1990-91	Kiekko-Espoo Jr.	Finland-Jr.	3	3	1	4	0	....	....	....	....	....	....	....	....	....	....	....	....	....	....	....	....	....	....
	Kiekko-Espoo	Finland-2	32	15	9	24	12	....	....	....	....	....	....	....	....	....	....	....	....	....	....	....	....	....	....
1991-92	Kiekko-67 Jr.	Finland-Jr.	8	5	4	9	2	....	....	....	....	....	....	....	....	....	....	....	....	....	....	....	....	....	....
	Kiekko-Espoo	Finland-2	43	32	17	49	6	....	....	....	....	....	....	....	....	....	....	....	....	....	....	....	....	....	....
1992-93	Kiekko-67 Jr.	Finland-Jr.	4	5	3	8	8	....	....	....	....	....	....	....	....	....	....	....	....	....	....	....	....	....	....
	Kiekko-Espoo	Finland	45	13	14	27	6	....	....	....	....	....	....	....	....	....	....	....	....	....	....	....	....	....	....
1993-94	TPS Turku	Finland	42	19	20	39	6	....	....	....	....	....	....	....	....	....	11	*11	2	13	*2	....	....	....	....
	Finland	Olympics	8	3	0	3	0	....	....	....	....	....	....	....	....	....	....	....	....	....	....	....	....	....	....
1994-95	TPS Turku	Finland	39	19	23	42	33	....	....	....	....	....	....	....	....	....	13	*8	6	14	4	....	....	....	....
1995-96	**Dallas**	**NHL**	**57**	**6**	**22**	**28**	**16**	**0**	**0**	**1**	**109**	**5.5**	**5**	....	....	....	....	....	....	....	....	....	....	....	....
	Michigan	IHL	1	1	0	1	0	....	....	....	....	....	....	....	....	....	....	....	....	....	....	....	....	....	....
1996-97	**Dallas**	**NHL**	**63**	**16**	**27**	**43**	**2**	**3**	**1**	**2**	**134**	**11.9**	**26**	....	....	....	**7**	**2**	**2**	**4**	**0**	**0**	**0**	**0**	....
1997-98	**Dallas**	**NHL**	**72**	**23**	**19**	**42**	**20**	**7**	**2**	**6**	**201**	**11.4**	**19**	....	....	....	**12**	**3**	**5**	**8**	**2**	**1**	**0**	**0**	....
	Finland	Olympics	6	4	2	6	2	....	....	....	....	....	....	....	....	....	....	....	....	....	....	....	....	....	....
1998-99♦	**Dallas**	**NHL**	**74**	**20**	**32**	**52**	**18**	**7**	**1**	**2**	**173**	**11.6**	**29**	**9**	**33.3**	**19:36**	**23**	**10**	**3**	**13**	**2**	**1**	**1**	**0**	**21:09**
99-2000	**Dallas**	**NHL**	**17**	**3**	**5**	**8**	**0**	**0**	**0**	**1**	**29**	**10.3**	**1**	**0**	**0.0**	**17:31**	**13**	**1**	**5**	**6**	**2**	**0**	**0**	**0**	**21:15**
2000-01	**Dallas**	**NHL**	**74**	**20**	**25**	**45**	**24**	**7**	**0**	**1**	**148**	**13.5**	**14**	**7**	**28.6**	**19:17**	**10**	**1**	**0**	**1**	**2**	**0**	**0**	**0**	**20:13**
2001-02	**Dallas**	**NHL**	**73**	**25**	**24**	**49**	**14**	**7**	**1**	**4**	**198**	**12.6**	**27**	**18**	**22.2**	**19:50**	....	....	....	....	....	....	....	....	....
	Finland	Olympics	4	1	2	3	2	....	....	....	....	....	....	....	....	....	....	....	....	....	....	....	....	....	....
2002-03	**Dallas**	**NHL**	**80**	**31**	**17**	**48**	**20**	**5**	**0**	**3**	**238**	**13.0**	**39**	**36**	**22.2**	**18:47**	**12**	**3**	**2**	**5**	**0**	**1**	**0**	**1**	**21:12**
2003-04	**Dallas**	**NHL**	**58**	**13**	**13**	**26**	**20**	**4**	**1**	**4**	**138**	**9.4**	**0**	**10**	**40.0**	**19:27**	**5**	**0**	**0**	**0**	**0**	**0**	**0**	**0**	**19:19**

			Regular Season														Playoffs								
Season	Club	League	GP	G	A	Pts	PIM	PP	SH	GW	S	%	+/-	TF	F%	Min	GP	G	A	Pts	PIM	PP	SH	GW	Min
2004-05			DID NOT PLAY																						
	NHL Totals		**568**	**157**	**184**	**341**	**134**	**40**	**6**	**24**	**1368**	**11.5**		**80**	**26.3**	**19:18**	**82**	**20**	**17**	**37**	**8**	**3**	**1**	**1**	**20:53**

Frank J. Selke Trophy (1998, 1999, 2003)

Played in NHL All-Star Game (1998)

Rights transferred to **Dallas** after **Minnesota** franchise relocated, June 9, 1993. • Missed majority of 1999-2000 season recovering from leg injury suffered in game vs. Nashville, October 16, 1999.

LEMIEUX, Mario (lehm-YOO, MAHR-ee-oh) PIT.

Center. Shoots right. 6'4", 230 lbs. Born, Montreal, Que., October 5, 1965. Pittsburgh's 1st choice, 1st overall, in 1984 Entry Draft.

			Regular Season														Playoffs								
Season	Club	League	GP	G	A	Pts	PIM	PP	SH	GW	S	%	+/-	TF	F%	Min	GP	G	A	Pts	PIM	PP	SH	GW	Min
1980-81	Mtl-Concordia	QAAA	47	62	62	124	127	....	....	....	....	....	....	....	....	....	3	2	5	7	8	....	....	....	....
1981-82	Laval Voisins	QMJHL	64	30	66	96	22	....	....	....	....	....	....	....	....	....	18	5	9	14	31	....	....	....	....
1982-83	Laval Voisins	QMJHL	66	84	100	184	76	....	....	....	....	....	....	....	....	....	12	14	18	32	18	....	....	....	....
1983-84	Laval Voisins	QMJHL	70	*133	*149	*282	92	....	....	....	....	....	....	....	....	....	14	*29	*23	*52	29	....	....	....	....
1984-85	**Pittsburgh**	**NHL**	**73**	**43**	**57**	**100**	**54**	**11**	**0**	**2**	**209**	**20.6**	**–35**	....	....	....	....	....	....	....	....	....	....	....	....
1985-86	**Pittsburgh**	**NHL**	**79**	**48**	**93**	**141**	**43**	**17**	**0**	**4**	**276**	**17.4**	**–6**	....	....	....	....	....	....	....	....	....	....	....	....
1986-87	**Pittsburgh**	**NHL**	**63**	**54**	**53**	**107**	**57**	**19**	**0**	**4**	**267**	**20.2**	**13**	....	....	....	....	....	....	....	....	....	....	....	....
1987-88	**Pittsburgh**	**NHL**	**77**	***70**	**98**	***168**	**92**	**22**	**10**	**7**	**382**	**18.3**	**23**	....	....	....	....	....	....	....	....	....	....	....	....
1988-89	**Pittsburgh**	**NHL**	**76**	***85**	***114**	***199**	**100**	**31**	**13**	**8**	**313**	**27.2**	**41**	....	....	....	**11**	**12**	**7**	**19**	**16**	**7**	**1**	**0**	....
1989-90	**Pittsburgh**	**NHL**	**59**	**45**	**78**	**123**	**78**	**14**	**3**	**4**	**226**	**19.9**	**–18**	....	....	....	....	....	....	....	....	....	....	....	....
1990-91♦	**Pittsburgh**	**NHL**	**26**	**19**	**26**	**45**	**30**	**6**	**1**	**2**	**89**	**21.3**	**8**	....	....	....	**23**	**16**	***28**	***44**	**16**	**6**	**2**	**0**	....
1991-92♦	**Pittsburgh**	**NHL**	**64**	**44**	**87**	***131**	**94**	**12**	**4**	**5**	**249**	**17.7**	**27**	....	....	....	**15**	***16**	**18**	***34**	**2**	**8**	**2**	**5**	....
1992-93	**Pittsburgh**	**NHL**	**60**	**69**	**91**	***160**	**38**	**16**	**6**	**10**	**286**	**24.1**	**55**	....	....	....	**11**	**8**	**10**	**18**	**10**	**3**	**1**	**1**	....
1993-94	**Pittsburgh**	**NHL**	**22**	**17**	**20**	**37**	**32**	**7**	**0**	**4**	**92**	**18.5**	**–2**	....	....	....	**6**	**4**	**3**	**7**	**2**	**1**	**0**	**0**	....
1994-95	**Pittsburgh**	**NHL**	DID NOT PLAY																						
1995-96	**Pittsburgh**	**NHL**	**70**	***69**	***92**	***161**	**54**	**31**	**8**	**8**	**338**	**20.4**	**10**	....	....	....	**18**	**11**	**16**	**27**	**33**	**3**	**1**	**2**	....
1996-97	**Pittsburgh**	**NHL**	**76**	**50**	***72**	***122**	**65**	**15**	**3**	**7**	**327**	**15.3**	**27**	....	....	....	**5**	**3**	**3**	**6**	**4**	**0**	**0**	**0**	....
1997-98			OUT OF HOCKEY – RETIRED																						
1998-99			OUT OF HOCKEY – RETIRED																						
99-2000			OUT OF HOCKEY – RETIRED																						
2000-01	**Pittsburgh**	**NHL**	**43**	**35**	**41**	**76**	**18**	**16**	**1**	**5**	**171**	**20.5**	**15**	**852**	**52.1**	**24:20**	**18**	**6**	**11**	**17**	**4**	**1**	**0**	**3**	**24:35**
2001-02	**Pittsburgh**	**NHL**	**24**	**6**	**25**	**31**	**14**	**2**	**0**	**0**	**75**	**8.0**	**0**	**354**	**44.6**	**22:16**	....	....	....	....	....	....	....	....	....
	Canada	Olympics	5	2	4	6	0	....	....	....	....	....	....	....	....	....	....	....	....	....	....	....	....	....	....
2002-03	**Pittsburgh**	**NHL**	**67**	**28**	**63**	**91**	**43**	**14**	**0**	**4**	**235**	**11.9**	**–25**	**1029**	**46.1**	**23:05**	....	....	....	....	....	....	....	....	....
2003-04	**Pittsburgh**	**NHL**	**10**	**1**	**8**	**9**	**6**	**0**	**0**	**0**	**21**	**4.8**	**–2**	**173**	**49.1**	**22:24**	....	....	....	....	....	....	....	....	....
2004-05			DID NOT PLAY																						
	NHL Totals		**889**	**683**	**1018**	**1701**	**818**	**233**	**49**	**74**	**3556**	**19.2**		**2408**	**48.2**	**23:16**	**107**	**76**	**96**	**172**	**87**	**29**	**7**	**11**	**24:35**

QMJHL Second All-Star Team (1983) • QMJHL First All-Star Team (1984) • QMJHL MVP (1984) • Canadian Major Junior Player of the Year (1984) • NHL All-Rookie Team (1985) • Calder Memorial Trophy (1985) • NHL Second All-Star Team (1986, 1987, 1992, 2001) • Lester B. Pearson Award (1986, 1988, 1993, 1996) • Canada Cup All-Star Team (1987) • NHL First All-Star Team (1988, 1989, 1993, 1996, 1997) • Dodge Performance of the Year Award (1988) • Dodge Performer of the Year Award (1988, 1989) • Art Ross Trophy (1988, 1989, 1992, 1993, 1996, 1997) • Hart Trophy (1988, 1993, 1996) • Dodge Ram Tough Award (1989) • Conn Smythe Trophy (1991, 1992) • ProSet/NHL Player of the Year Award (1992) • Alka-Seltzer Plus Award (1993) • Bill Masterton Memorial Trophy (1993) • Lester Patrick Trophy (2000)

Played in NHL All-Star Game (1985, 1986, 1988, 1989, 1990, 1992, 1996, 1997, 2001, 2002)

• Missed remainder of 1989-90 and majority of 1990-91 seasons recovering from back injury suffered in game vs. NY Rangers, February 14, 1989. • Missed remainder of 1992-93 season after being diagnosed with Hodgkin's Disease, January 12, 1993. • Missed majority of 1993-94 season recovering from back injury suffered in game vs. Chicago, November 11, 1993. • Missed entire 1994-95 season recovering from effects of treatment for Hodgkin's Disease and back injury suffered in game vs. NY Rangers, March 12, 1994. • Became third player (Gordie Howe, Guy Lafleur) to appear in NHL game after being inducted into Hockey Hall of Fame, December 27, 2000. • Missed majority of 2001-02 season recovering from hip injury suffered in game vs. Anaheim, October 6, 2001. • Missed majority of 2003-04 season recovering from hip injury suffered in game vs. Boston, November 1, 2003.

LEOPOLD, Jordan (LEE-oh-pohld, JOHR-dan) CGY.

Defense. Shoots left. 6', 193 lbs. Born, Golden Valley, MN, August 3, 1980. Anaheim's 1st choice, 44th overall, in 1999 Entry Draft.

			Regular Season														Playoffs								
Season	Club	League	GP	G	A	Pts	PIM	PP	SH	GW	S	%	+/-	TF	F%	Min	GP	G	A	Pts	PIM	PP	SH	GW	Min
1995-96	Armstrong	High-MN	19	11	14	25	30	....	....	....	....	....	....	....	....	....	....	....	....	....	....	....	....	....	....
1996-97	Armstrong	High-MN	30	24	36	60	....	....	....	....	....	....	....	....	....	....	....	....	....	....	....	....	....	....	....
1997-98	USA U-18	USDP	60	11	12	23	16	....	....	....	....	....	....	....	....	....	....	....	....	....	....	....	....	....	....
1998-99	U. of Minnesota	WCHA	39	7	16	23	20	....	....	....	....	....	....	....	....	....	....	....	....	....	....	....	....	....	....
99-2000	U. of Minnesota	WCHA	39	6	18	24	20	....	....	....	....	....	....	....	....	....	....	....	....	....	....	....	....	....	....
2000-01	U. of Minnesota	WCHA	42	12	37	49	38	....	....	....	....	....	....	....	....	....	....	....	....	....	....	....	....	....	....
2001-02	U. of Minnesota	WCHA	44	20	28	48	28	....	....	....	....	....	....	....	....	....	....	....	....	....	....	....	....	....	....
2002-03	**Calgary**	**NHL**	**58**	**4**	**10**	**14**	**12**	**3**	**0**	**0**	**78**	**5.1**	**–15**	**0**	**0.0**	**20:36**	....	....	....	....	....	....	....	....	....
	Saint John Flames	AHL	3	1	2	3	0	....	....	....	....	....	....	....	....	....	....	....	....	....	....	....	....	....	....
2003-04	**Calgary**	**NHL**	**82**	**9**	**24**	**33**	**24**	**6**	**0**	**1**	**138**	**6.5**	**8**	**0**	**0.0**	**22:14**	**26**	**0**	**10**	**10**	**6**	**0**	**0**	**0**	**25:41**
2004-05			DID NOT PLAY																						
	NHL Totals		**140**	**13**	**34**	**47**	**36**	**9**	**0**	**1**	**216**	**6.0**		**0**	**0.0**	**21:33**	**26**	**0**	**10**	**10**	**6**	**0**	**0**	**0**	**25:41**

WCHA All-Rookie Team (1999) • WCHA Second All-Star Team (2000) • WCHA First All-Star Team (2001, 2002) • NCAA West First All-American Team (2001) • Hobey Baker Memorial Award (Top U.S. Collegiate Player) (2002)

Traded to **Calgary** by **Anaheim** for Andrei Nazarov and Calgary's 2nd round choice (later traded to Phoenix – later traded back to Calgary – Calgary selected Andrei Taratukhin) in 2001 Entry Draft, September 26, 2000.

LESCHYSHYN, Curtis (luh-SIH-shuhn, KUHR-tihs) COL.

Defense. Shoots left. 6'1", 207 lbs. Born, Thompson, Man., September 21, 1969. Quebec's 1st choice, 3rd overall, in 1988 Entry Draft.

			Regular Season														Playoffs								
Season	Club	League	GP	G	A	Pts	PIM	PP	SH	GW	S	%	+/-	TF	F%	Min	GP	G	A	Pts	PIM	PP	SH	GW	Min
1985-86	Saskatoon Blazers	SMHL	34	9	34	43	52	....	....	....	....	....	....	....	....	....	....	....	....	....	....	....	....	....	....
	Saskatoon Blades	WHL	1	0	0	0	0	....	....	....	....	....	....	....	....	....	....	....	....	....	....	....	....	....	....
1986-87	Saskatoon Blades	WHL	70	14	26	40	107	....	....	....	....	....	....	....	....	....	11	1	5	6	14	....	....	....	....
1987-88	Saskatoon Blades	WHL	56	14	41	55	86	....	....	....	....	....	....	....	....	....	10	2	5	7	16	....	....	....	....
1988-89	**Quebec**	**NHL**	**71**	**4**	**9**	**13**	**71**	**1**	**1**	**0**	**58**	**6.9**	**–32**	....	....	....	....	....	....	....	....	....	....	....	....
1989-90	**Quebec**	**NHL**	**68**	**2**	**6**	**8**	**44**	**1**	**0**	**0**	**42**	**4.8**	**–41**	....	....	....	....	....	....	....	....	....	....	....	....
1990-91	**Quebec**	**NHL**	**55**	**3**	**7**	**10**	**49**	**2**	**0**	**1**	**57**	**5.3**	**–19**	....	....	....	....	....	....	....	....	....	....	....	....
1991-92	**Quebec**	**NHL**	**42**	**5**	**12**	**17**	**42**	**3**	**0**	**1**	**61**	**8.2**	**–28**	....	....	....	....	....	....	....	....	....	....	....	....
	Halifax Citadels	AHL	6	0	2	2	4	....	....	....	....	....	....	....	....	....	....	....	....	....	....	....	....	....	....
1992-93	**Quebec**	**NHL**	**82**	**9**	**23**	**32**	**61**	**4**	**0**	**2**	**73**	**12.3**	**25**	....	....	....	**6**	**1**	**1**	**2**	**6**	**1**	**0**	**0**	....
1993-94	**Quebec**	**NHL**	**72**	**5**	**17**	**22**	**65**	**3**	**0**	**2**	**97**	**5.2**	**–2**	....	....	....	....	....	....	....	....	....	....	....	....
1994-95	**Quebec**	**NHL**	**44**	**2**	**13**	**15**	**20**	**0**	**0**	**0**	**43**	**4.7**	**29**	....	....	....	**3**	**0**	**1**	**1**	**4**	**0**	**0**	**0**	....
1995-96♦	**Colorado**	**NHL**	**77**	**4**	**15**	**19**	**73**	**0**	**0**	**1**	**76**	**5.3**	**32**	....	....	....	**17**	**1**	**2**	**3**	**8**	**0**	**0**	**0**	....
1996-97	**Colorado**	**NHL**	**11**	**0**	**5**	**5**	**6**	**0**	**0**	**0**	**8**	**0.0**	**1**	....	....	....	....	....	....	....	....	....	....	....	....
	Washington	**NHL**	**2**	**0**	**0**	**0**	**2**	**0**	**0**	**0**	**0**	**0.0**	**0**	....	....	....	....	....	....	....	....	....	....	....	....
	Hartford	**NHL**	**64**	**4**	**13**	**17**	**30**	**1**	**1**	**1**	**94**	**4.3**	**–19**	....	....	....	....	....	....	....	....	....	....	....	....
1997-98	**Carolina**	**NHL**	**73**	**2**	**10**	**12**	**45**	**1**	**0**	**1**	**53**	**3.8**	**–2**	....	....	....	....	....	....	....	....	....	....	....	....
1998-99	**Carolina**	**NHL**	**65**	**2**	**7**	**9**	**50**	**0**	**0**	**0**	**35**	**5.7**	**–1**	**0**	**0.0**	**19:18**	**6**	**0**	**0**	**0**	**6**	**0**	**0**	**0**	**24:07**
99-2000	**Carolina**	**NHL**	**53**	**0**	**2**	**2**	**14**	**0**	**0**	**0**	**31**	**0.0**	**–19**	**0**	**0.0**	**17:47**	....	....	....	....	....	....	....	....	....
2000-01	**Minnesota**	**NHL**	**54**	**2**	**3**	**5**	**19**	**1**	**0**	**1**	**43**	**4.7**	**–2**	**0**	**0.0**	**19:31**	....	....	....	....	....	....	....	....	....
	Ottawa	**NHL**	**11**	**0**	**4**	**4**	**0**	**0**	**0**	**0**	**8**	**0.0**	**7**	**0**	**0.0**	**19:04**	**4**	**0**	**0**	**0**	**0**	**0**	**0**	**0**	**21:05**
2001-02	**Ottawa**	**NHL**	**79**	**1**	**9**	**10**	**44**	**0**	**0**	**0**	**59**	**1.7**	**–5**	**0**	**0.0**	**18:28**	**12**	**0**	**1**	**1**	**0**	**0**	**0**	**0**	**16:49**
2002-03	**Ottawa**	**NHL**	**54**	**1**	**6**	**7**	**18**	**0**	**0**	**0**	**30**	**3.3**	**11**	**0**	**0.0**	**15:13**	**18**	**0**	**1**	**1**	**10**	**0**	**0**	**0**	**14:11**
2003-04	**Ottawa**	**NHL**	**56**	**1**	**4**	**5**	**16**	**0**	**0**	**0**	**30**	**3.3**	**13**	**2**	**0.0**	**13:54**	**2**	**0**	**0**	**0**	**0**	**0**	**0**	**0**	**15:37**
2004-05			DID NOT PLAY																						
	NHL Totals		**1033**	**47**	**165**	**212**	**669**	**17**	**2**	**10**	**898**	**5.2**		**2**	**0.0**	**17:32**	**68**	**2**	**6**	**8**	**34**	**1**	**0**	**0**	**17:05**

WHL East First All-Star Team (1988)

Transferred to **Colorado** after **Quebec** franchise relcoated, June 21, 1995. Traded to **Washington** by **Colorado** with Chris Simon for Keith Jones, Washington's 1st (Scott Parker) and 4th (later traded back to Washington – Washington selected Krys Barch) round choices in 1998 Entry Draft, November 2, 1996. Traded to **Hartford** by **Washington** for Andrei Nikolishin, November 9, 1996. Transferred to **Carolina** after **Hartford** franchise relocated, June 25, 1997. Claimed by **Minnesota** from **Carolina** in Expansion Draft, June 23, 2000. Traded to **Ottawa** by **Minnesota** for Ottawa's 3rd round choice (Stephane Veilleux) in 2001 Entry Draft and future considerations, March 13, 2001. Signed as a free agent by **Colorado**, August 17, 2005.

LESSARD, Francis
(leh-SAHR, FRAN-sihs) **ATL.**

Right wing. Shoots right. 6'3", 225 lbs. Born, Montreal, Que., May 30, 1979. Carolina's 3rd choice, 80th overall, in 1997 Entry Draft.

			Regular Season														Playoffs								
Season	Club	League	GP	G	A	Pts	PIM	PP	SH	GW	S	%	+/-	TF	F%	Min	GP	G	A	Pts	PIM	PP	SH	GW	Min
1994-95	Laval-Laurentides	QAAA	1	0	0	0	0	....	....	....	....	....	....	....	....	....	....	....	....	....	....	....	....	....	....
1995-96	Laval-Laurentides	QAAA	41	5	7	12	73	....	....	....	....	....	....	....	....	....	13	1	3	4	....	....	....	....	....
1996-97	Val-d'Or Foreurs	QMJHL	66	1	9	10	287	....	....	....	....	....	....	....	....	....	....	....	....	....	....	....	....	....	....
1997-98	Val-d'Or Foreurs	QMJHL	63	3	20	23	338	....	....	....	....	....	....	....	....	....	19	1	6	7	*101	....	....	....	....
1998-99	Drummondville	QMJHL	53	12	36	48	295	....	....	....	....	....	....	....	....	....	....	....	....	....	....	....	....	....	....
99-2000	Philadelphia	AHL	78	4	8	12	416	....	....	....	....	....	....	....	....	....	5	0	1	1	7	....	....	....	....
2000-01	Philadelphia	AHL	64	3	7	10	330	....	....	....	....	....	....	....	....	....	10	0	0	0	33	....	....	....	....
2001-02	Philadelphia	AHL	60	0	6	6	251	....	....	....	....	....	....	....	....	....	....	....	....	....	....	....	....	....	....
	Atlanta	**NHL**	**5**	**0**	**0**	**0**	**26**	**0**	**0**	**0**	**2**	**0.0**	**0**	**0**	**0.0**	**12:45**	....	....	....	....	....	....	....	....	....
	Chicago Wolves	AHL	7	2	1	3	34	....	....	....	....	....	....	....	....	....	15	0	1	1	40	....	....	....	....
2002-03	**Atlanta**	**NHL**	**18**	**0**	**2**	**2**	**61**	**0**	**0**	**0**	**7**	**0.0**	**1**	**0**	**0.0**	**5:40**	....	....	....	....	....	....	....	....	....
	Chicago Wolves	AHL	50	2	5	7	194	....	....	....	....	....	....	....	....	....	1	0	0	0	0	....	....	....	....
2003-04	**Atlanta**	**NHL**	**62**	**1**	**1**	**2**	**181**	**0**	**0**	**0**	**19**	**5.3**	**–5**	**1**	**0.0**	**4:28**	....	....	....	....	....	....	....	....	....
2004-05			DID NOT PLAY																						
	NHL Totals		**85**	**1**	**3**	**4**	**268**	**0**	**0**	**0**	**28**	**3.6**		**1**	**0.0**	**5:12**	....	....	....	....	....	....	....	....	....

Memorial Cup Tournament All-Star Team (1998)

Traded to **Philadelphia** by **Carolina** for Philadelphia's 8th round choice (Antti Jokella) in 1999 Entry Draft, May 25, 1999. Traded to **Atlanta** by **Philadelphia** for David Harlock and Atlanta's 3rd (later traded to Phoenix – Phoenix selected Tyler Redenbach) and 7th (later traded to San Jose – San Jose selected Joe Pavelski) round choices in 2003 Entry Draft, March 15, 2002.

LETANG, Alan
(leh-TANG, A-luhn)

Defense. Shoots left. 6'1", 201 lbs. Born, Renfrew, Ont., September 4, 1975. Montreal's 10th choice, 203rd overall, in 1993 Entry Draft.

			Regular Season														Playoffs								
Season	Club	League	GP	G	A	Pts	PIM	PP	SH	GW	S	%	+/-	TF	F%	Min	GP	G	A	Pts	PIM	PP	SH	GW	Min
1990-91	Ottawa Valley	ODMHA	32	3	26	29	16	....	....	....	....	....	....	....	....	....	....	....	....	....	....	....	....	....	....
1991-92	Cornwall Royals	OHL	47	1	4	5	16	....	....	....	....	....	....	....	....	....	6	0	0	0	2	....	....	....	....
1992-93	Newmarket	OHL	66	1	25	26	14	....	....	....	....	....	....	....	....	....	6	0	3	3	2	....	....	....	....
1993-94	Newmarket	OHL	58	3	21	24	30	....	....	....	....	....	....	....	....	....	....	....	....	....	....	....	....	....	....
1994-95	Sarnia Sting	OHL	62	5	36	41	35	....	....	....	....	....	....	....	....	....	4	2	2	4	6	....	....	....	....
1995-96	Fredericton	AHL	71	0	26	26	40	....	....	....	....	....	....	....	....	....	10	0	3	3	4	....	....	....	....
1996-97	Fredericton	AHL	60	2	9	11	8	....	....	....	....	....	....	....	....	....	....	....	....	....	....	....	....	....	....
1997-98	Kaufbeurer Adler	Germany	15	1	5	6	8	....	....	....	....	....	....	....	....	....	....	....	....	....	....	....	....	....	....
	SC Langnau	Swiss-2	11	4	3	7	6	....	....	....	....	....	....	....	....	....	....	....	....	....	....	....	....	....	....
	Augsburg	Germany	17	0	1	1	4	....	....	....	....	....	....	....	....	....	....	....	....	....	....	....	....	....	....
1998-99	Canada	Nat-Tm	41	3	9	12	20	....	....	....	....	....	....	....	....	....	....	....	....	....	....	....	....	....	....
	EV Zug	Swiss	....	....	....	....	....	....	....	....	....	....	....	....	....	....	9	0	4	4	4	....	....	....	....
	Michigan	IHL	12	3	3	6	0	....	....	....	....	....	....	....	....	....	5	0	2	2	0	....	....	....	....
99-2000	**Dallas**	**NHL**	**8**	**0**	**0**	**0**	**2**	**0**	**0**	**0**	**1**	**0.0**	**–5**	**0**	**0.0**	**9:57**	....	....	....	....	....	....	....	....	....
	Michigan	IHL	51	1	12	13	30	....	....	....	....	....	....	....	....	....	....	....	....	....	....	....	....	....	....
2000-01	Utah Grizzlies	IHL	79	6	24	30	26	....	....	....	....	....	....	....	....	....	....	....	....	....	....	....	....	....	....
2001-02	**Calgary**	**NHL**	**2**	**0**	**0**	**0**	**0**	**0**	**0**	**0**	**0**	**0.0**	**–2**	**0**	**0.0**	**11:06**	....	....	....	....	....	....	....	....	....
	Saint John Flames	AHL	61	4	24	28	33	....	....	....	....	....	....	....	....	....	....	....	....	....	....	....	....	....	....
2002-03	**NY Islanders**	**NHL**	**4**	**0**	**0**	**0**	**0**	**0**	**0**	**0**	**2**	**0.0**	**–1**	**0**	**0.0**	**13:28**	....	....	....	....	....	....	....	....	....
	Bridgeport	AHL	70	3	21	24	21	....	....	....	....	....	....	....	....	....	8	1	0	1	0	....	....	....	....
2003-04	Bridgeport	AHL	76	1	13	14	18	....	....	....	....	....	....	....	....	....	7	1	1	2	4	....	....	....	....
2004-05	Hamburg Freezers	Germany	42	1	9	10	20	....	....	....	....	....	....	....	....	....	5	0	1	1	4	....	....	....	....
	NHL Totals		**14**	**0**	**0**	**0**	**2**	**0**	**0**	**0**	**3**	**0.0**		**0**	**0.0**	**11:07**	....	....	....	....	....	....	....	....	....

Signed as a free agent by **Dallas**, March 22, 1999. Signed as a free agent by **Calgary**, August 22, 2001. Signed as a free agent by **NY Islanders**, July 18, 2002. Signed as a free agent by **Hamburg** (Germany), May 27, 2004.

LETOWSKI, Trevor
(leh-TOW-skee, TREH-vuhr) **CBJ**

Right wing. Shoots right. 5'10", 180 lbs. Born, Thunder Bay, Ont., April 5, 1977. Phoenix's 6th choice, 174th overall, in 1996 Entry Draft.

			Regular Season														Playoffs								
Season	Club	League	GP	G	A	Pts	PIM	PP	SH	GW	S	%	+/-	TF	F%	Min	GP	G	A	Pts	PIM	PP	SH	GW	Min
1993-94	T. Bay Kings	TBMHL	64	41	60	101	48	....	....	....	....	....	....	....	....	....	....	....	....	....	....	....	....	....	....
1994-95	Sarnia Sting	OHL	66	22	19	41	33	....	....	....	....	....	....	....	....	....	4	0	1	1	9	....	....	....	....
1995-96	Sarnia Sting	OHL	66	36	63	99	66	....	....	....	....	....	....	....	....	....	10	9	5	14	10	....	....	....	....
1996-97	Sarnia Sting	OHL	55	35	73	108	51	....	....	....	....	....	....	....	....	....	12	9	12	21	20	....	....	....	....
1997-98	Springfield	AHL	75	11	20	31	26	....	....	....	....	....	....	....	....	....	4	1	0	1	2	....	....	....	....
1998-99	**Phoenix**	**NHL**	**14**	**2**	**2**	**4**	**2**	**0**	**0**	**0**	**8**	**25.0**	**1**	**49**	**55.1**	**6:01**	....	....	....	....	....	....	....	....	....
	Springfield	AHL	67	32	35	67	46	....	....	....	....	....	....	....	....	....	3	1	0	1	2	....	....	....	....
99-2000	**Phoenix**	**NHL**	**82**	**19**	**20**	**39**	**20**	**3**	**4**	**3**	**125**	**15.2**	**2**	**692**	**47.7**	**16:03**	**5**	**1**	**1**	**2**	**4**	**0**	**0**	**0**	**15:52**
2000-01	**Phoenix**	**NHL**	**77**	**7**	**15**	**22**	**32**	**0**	**1**	**3**	**110**	**6.4**	**–2**	**726**	**46.1**	**16:20**	....	....	....	....	....	....	....	....	....
2001-02	**Phoenix**	**NHL**	**33**	**2**	**6**	**8**	**4**	**0**	**0**	**0**	**43**	**4.7**	**2**	**250**	**52.4**	**14:27**	....	....	....	....	....	....	....	....	....
	Vancouver	**NHL**	**42**	**7**	**10**	**17**	**15**	**1**	**0**	**0**	**65**	**10.8**	**2**	**111**	**44.1**	**12:47**	**6**	**0**	**1**	**1**	**8**	**0**	**0**	**0**	**11:50**
2002-03	**Vancouver**	**NHL**	**78**	**11**	**14**	**25**	**36**	**1**	**1**	**2**	**136**	**8.1**	**8**	**70**	**41.4**	**12:26**	**6**	**0**	**1**	**1**	**0**	**0**	**0**	**0**	**9:40**
2003-04	**Columbus**	**NHL**	**73**	**15**	**17**	**32**	**16**	**4**	**0**	**1**	**126**	**11.9**	**–12**	**146**	**43.8**	**16:19**	....	....	....	....	....	....	....	....	....
2004-05	Fribourg	Swiss	9	4	5	9	6	....	....	....	....	....	....	....	....	....	11	7	9	16	8	....	....	....	....
	NHL Totals		**399**	**63**	**84**	**147**	**125**	**9**	**6**	**9**	**613**	**10.3**		**2044**	**47.2**	**14:37**	**17**	**1**	**3**	**4**	**12**	**0**	**0**	**0**	**12:15**

Traded to **Vancouver** by **Phoenix** with Todd Warriner, Tyler Bouck and Phoenix's 3rd round choice (later traded back to Phoenix – Phoenix selected Dimitri Pestunov) in 2003 Entry Draft for Drake Berehowsky and Denis Pederson, December 28, 2001. Signed as a free agent by **Columbus**, July 3, 2003. Signed as a free agent by **Fribourg** (Swiss), January 7, 2005.

LIDSTROM, Nicklas
(LID-struhm, NIHK-las) **DET.**

Defense. Shoots left. 6'2", 185 lbs. Born, Vasteras, Sweden, April 28, 1970. Detroit's 3rd choice, 53rd overall, in 1989 Entry Draft.

			Regular Season														Playoffs								
Season	Club	League	GP	G	A	Pts	PIM	PP	SH	GW	S	%	+/-	TF	F%	Min	GP	G	A	Pts	PIM	PP	SH	GW	Min
1987-88	Vasteras	Sweden-2	3	0	0	0	0	....	....	....	....	....	....	....	....	....	5	0	0	0	6	....	....	....	....
1988-89	Vasteras IK	Sweden	34	1	6	7	4	....	....	....	....	....	....	....	....	....	5	0	2	2	0	....	....	....	....
1989-90	Vasteras IK	Sweden	39	8	8	16	14	....	....	....	....	....	....	....	....	....	2	0	1	1	2	....	....	....	....
1990-91	Vasteras IK	Sweden	38	4	19	23	2	....	....	....	....	....	....	....	....	....	4	0	0	0	4	....	....	....	....
1991-92	**Detroit**	**NHL**	**80**	**11**	**49**	**60**	**22**	**5**	**0**	**1**	**168**	**6.5**	**36**	....	....	....	**11**	**1**	**2**	**3**	**0**	**1**	**0**	**0**	....
1992-93	**Detroit**	**NHL**	**84**	**7**	**34**	**41**	**28**	**3**	**0**	**2**	**156**	**4.5**	**7**	....	....	....	**7**	**1**	**0**	**1**	**0**	**1**	**0**	**0**	....
1993-94	**Detroit**	**NHL**	**84**	**10**	**46**	**56**	**26**	**4**	**0**	**3**	**200**	**5.0**	**43**	....	....	....	**7**	**3**	**2**	**5**	**0**	**1**	**1**	**0**	....
1994-95	Vasteras IK	Sweden	13	2	10	12	4	....	....	....	....	....	....	....	....	....	....	....	....	....	....	....	....	....	....
	Detroit	**NHL**	**43**	**10**	**16**	**26**	**6**	**7**	**0**	**0**	**90**	**11.1**	**15**	....	....	....	**18**	**4**	**12**	**16**	**8**	**3**	**0**	**2**	....
1995-96	**Detroit**	**NHL**	**81**	**17**	**50**	**67**	**20**	**8**	**1**	**1**	**211**	**8.1**	**29**	....	....	....	**19**	**5**	**9**	**14**	**10**	**1**	**0**	**0**	....
1996-97♦	**Detroit**	**NHL**	**79**	**15**	**42**	**57**	**30**	**8**	**0**	**1**	**214**	**7.0**	**11**	....	....	....	**20**	**2**	**6**	**8**	**2**	**0**	**0**	**0**	....
1997-98♦	**Detroit**	**NHL**	**80**	**17**	**42**	**59**	**18**	**7**	**1**	**1**	**205**	**8.3**	**22**	....	....	....	**22**	**6**	**13**	**19**	**8**	**2**	**0**	**2**	....
	Sweden	Olympics	4	1	1	2	2	....	....	....	....	....	....	....	....	....	....	....	....	....	....	....	....	....	....
1998-99	**Detroit**	**NHL**	**81**	**14**	**43**	**57**	**14**	**6**	**2**	**3**	**205**	**6.8**	**14**	**0**	**0.0**	**26:31**	**10**	**2**	**9**	**11**	**4**	**2**	**0**	**0**	**30:21**
99-2000	**Detroit**	**NHL**	**81**	**20**	**53**	**73**	**18**	**9**	**4**	**3**	**218**	**9.2**	**19**	**0**	**0.0**	**28:45**	**9**	**2**	**4**	**6**	**4**	**1**	**0**	**0**	**30:28**
2000-01	**Detroit**	**NHL**	**82**	**15**	**56**	**71**	**18**	**8**	**1**	**0**	**272**	**5.5**	**9**	**0**	**0.0**	**28:27**	**6**	**1**	**7**	**8**	**0**	**0**	**0**	**0**	**29:17**
2001-02♦	**Detroit**	**NHL**	**78**	**9**	**50**	**59**	**20**	**6**	**0**	**0**	**215**	**4.2**	**13**	**0**	**0.0**	**28:49**	**23**	**5**	**11**	**16**	**2**	**2**	**1**	**2**	**31:10**
	Sweden	Olympics	4	1	5	6	0	....	....	....	....	....	....	....	....	....	....	....	....	....	....	....	....	....	....
2002-03	**Detroit**	**NHL**	**82**	**18**	**44**	**62**	**38**	**8**	**1**	**4**	**175**	**10.3**	**40**	**0**	**0.0**	**29:20**	**4**	**0**	**2**	**2**	**0**	**0**	**0**	**0**	**33:35**
2003-04	**Detroit**	**NHL**	**81**	**10**	**28**	**38**	**18**	**3**	**1**	**3**	**194**	**5.2**	**19**	**0**	**0.0**	**27:39**	**12**	**2**	**5**	**7**	**4**	**2**	**0**	**0**	**27:01**
2004-05			DID NOT PLAY																						
	NHL Totals		**1016**	**173**	**553**	**726**	**276**	**82**	**10**	**22**	**2523**	**6.9**		**0**	**0.0**	**28:15**	**168**	**34**	**82**	**116**	**42**	**16**	**2**	**6**	**30:08**

NHL All-Rookie Team (1992) • NHL First All-Star Team (1998, 1999, 2000, 2001, 2002, 2003) • James Norris Memorial Trophy (2001, 2002, 2003) • Conn Smythe Trophy (2002)

Played in NHL All-Star Game (1996, 1998, 1999, 2000, 2001, 2002, 2003, 2004)

LILES, John-Michael
(LIGH-uhls, JAWN-MIGHK-uhl) **COL.**

Defense. Shoots left. 5'10", 185 lbs. Born, Zionsville, IN, November 25, 1980. Colorado's 8th choice, 159th overall, in 2000 Entry Draft.

			Regular Season														Playoffs								
Season	Club	League	GP	G	A	Pts	PIM	PP	SH	GW	S	%	+/-	TF	F%	Min	GP	G	A	Pts	PIM	PP	SH	GW	Min
1997-98	USA U-17	USDP	67	6	14	20	44	....	....	....	....	....	....	....	....	....	....	....	....	....	....	....	....	....	....
1998-99	USA U-17	USDP	13	2	5	7	6	....	....	....	....	....	....	....	....	....	....	....	....	....	....	....	....	....	....
	USA U-18	USDP	46	4	14	18	47	....	....	....	....	....	....	....	....	....	....	....	....	....	....	....	....	....	....
99-2000	Michigan State	CCHA	40	8	20	28	26	....	....	....	....	....	....	....	....	....	....	....	....	....	....	....	....	....	....
2000-01	Michigan State	CCHA	42	7	18	25	28	....	....	....	....	....	....	....	....	....	....	....	....	....	....	....	....	....	....
2001-02	Michigan State	CCHA	41	13	22	35	18	....	....	....	....	....	....	....	....	....	....	....	....	....	....	....	....	....	....

			Regular Season														Playoffs								
Season	Club	League	GP	G	A	Pts	PIM	PP	SH	GW	S	%	+/-	TF	F%	Min	GP	G	A	Pts	PIM	PP	SH	GW	Min
2002-03	Michigan State	CCHA	39	16	34	50	46	....	....	....	....	....	....	....	....	....	....	....	....	....	....	....	....	....	....
	Hershey Bears	AHL	5	0	1	1	4	....	....	....	....	....	....	....	....	....	5	0	0	0	2	....	....	....	....
2003-04	**Colorado**	**NHL**	**79**	**10**	**24**	**34**	**28**	**2**	**0**	**1**	**115**	**8.7**	**7**	**0**	**0.0**	**16:14**	**11**	**0**	**1**	**1**	**4**	**0**	**0**	**0**	**16:41**
2004-05	Iserlohn Roosters	Germany	17	5	6	11	24	....	....	....	....	....	....	....	....	....	....	....	....	....	....	....	....	....	....
	NHL Totals		**79**	**10**	**24**	**34**	**28**	**2**	**0**	**1**	**115**	**8.7**		**0**	**0.0**	**16:14**	**11**	**0**	**1**	**1**	**4**	**0**	**0**	**0**	**16:41**

CCHA Second All-Star Team (2001) • CCHA First All-Star Team (2002, 2003) • NCAA West Second All-American Team (2002) • NCAA West First All-American Team (2003) • NHL All-Rookie Team (2004)

Signed as a free agent by **Iserlohn** (Germany), December 29, 2004.

LILJA, Andreas

(LIHL-yuh, an-DRAY-uhs) **DET.**

Defense. Shoots left. 6'3", 228 lbs. Born, Helsingborg, Sweden, July 13, 1975. Los Angeles' 2nd choice, 54th overall, in 2000 Entry Draft.

Season	Club	League	GP	G	A	Pts	PIM	PP	SH	GW	S	%	+/-	TF	F%	Min	GP	G	A	Pts	PIM	PP	SH	GW	Min
1993-94	Malmo IF Jr.	Swe-Jr.	14	3	7	10	38	....	....	....	....	....	....	....	....	....	....	....	....	....	....	....	....	....	....
1994-95	Malmo IF Jr.	Swe-Jr.	30	7	13	20	82	....	....	....	....	....	....	....	....	....	....	....	....	....	....	....	....	....	....
	Malmo IF	Sweden	3	0	0	0	2	....	....	....	....	....	....	....	....	....	....	....	....	....	....	....	....	....	....
1995-96	Malmo IF Jr.	Swe-Jr.	3	0	1	1	6	....	....	....	....	....	....	....	....	....	....	....	....	....	....	....	....	....	....
	Malmo IF	Sweden	40	1	5	6	63	....	....	....	....	....	....	....	....	....	5	0	1	1	2	....	....	....	....
1996-97	Malmo	Sweden	47	1	0	1	22	....	....	....	....	....	....	....	....	....	4	0	0	0	10	....	....	....	....
1997-98	Malmo	Sweden	10	0	0	0	0	....	....	....	....	....	....	....	....	....	....	....	....	....	....	....	....	....	....
	Mora IK	Sweden-2	13	1	4	5	30	....	....	....	....	....	....	....	....	....	4	1	0	1	14	....	....	....	....
1998-99	Malmo	Sweden	41	0	3	3	44	....	....	....	....	....	....	....	....	....	1	0	0	0	4	....	....	....	....
99-2000	Malmo	Sweden	49	8	11	19	88	....	....	....	....	....	....	....	....	....	6	0	0	0	8	....	....	....	....
2000-01	**Los Angeles**	**NHL**	**2**	**0**	**0**	**0**	**4**	**0**	**0**	**0**	**1**	**0.0**	**–2**	**0**	**0.0**	**12:22**	**1**	**0**	**0**	**0**	**0**	**0**	**0**	**0**	**6:56**
	Lowell	AHL	61	7	29	36	149	....	....	....	....	....	....	....	....	....	4	0	6	6	6	....	....	....	....
2001-02	**Los Angeles**	**NHL**	**26**	**1**	**4**	**5**	**22**	**1**	**0**	**0**	**12**	**8.3**	**3**	**0**	**0.0**	**11:27**	**5**	**0**	**0**	**0**	**6**	**0**	**0**	**0**	**10:26**
	Manchester	AHL	4	0	1	1	4	....	....	....	....	....	....	....	....	....	....	....	....	....	....	....	....	....	....
2002-03	**Los Angeles**	**NHL**	**17**	**0**	**3**	**3**	**14**	**0**	**0**	**0**	**13**	**0.0**	**5**	**0**	**0.0**	**20:04**	....	....	....	....	....	....	....	....	....
	Florida	**NHL**	**56**	**4**	**8**	**12**	**56**	**0**	**0**	**0**	**59**	**6.8**	**8**	**0**	**0.0**	**19:11**	....	....	....	....	....	....	....	....	....
2003-04	**Florida**	**NHL**	**79**	**3**	**4**	**7**	**90**	**0**	**0**	**0**	**79**	**3.8**	**–8**	**1**	**0.0**	**19:34**	....	....	....	....	....	....	....	....	....
2004-05	Mora IK	Sweden	44	3	8	11	67	....	....	....	....	....	....	....	....	....	....	....	....	....	....	....	....	....	....
	HC Ambri-Piotta	Swiss	....	....	....	....	....	....	....	....	....	....	....	....	....	....	5	0	2	2	6	....	....	....	....
	NHL Totals		**180**	**8**	**19**	**27**	**186**	**1**	**0**	**0**	**164**	**4.9**		**1**	**0.0**	**18:14**	**6**	**0**	**0**	**0**	**6**	**0**	**0**	**0**	**9:51**

• Spent majority of 2001-02 season as a healthy reserve. Traded to **Florida** by **Los Angeles** with Jaroslav Bednar for Dmitry Yushkevich and Florida's 5th round choice (previously acquired, Los Angeles selected Brady Murray) in 2003 Entry Draft, November 26, 2002. Signed as a free agent by **Nashville**, July 26, 2004. Signed as a free agent by **Mora** (Sweden), September 15, 2004. Signed as a free agent by **Ambri** (Swiss), February 25, 2005. Signed as a free agent by **Detroit**, August 24, 2005.

LINDEN, Trevor

(LIHND-dehn, TREH-vuhr) **VAN.**

Right wing. Shoots right. 6'4", 215 lbs. Born, Medicine Hat, Alta., April 11, 1970. Vancouver's 1st choice, 2nd overall, in 1988 Entry Draft.

Season	Club	League	GP	G	A	Pts	PIM	PP	SH	GW	S	%	+/-	TF	F%	Min	GP	G	A	Pts	PIM	PP	SH	GW	Min
1985-86	Medicine Hat	AMHL	40	14	22	36	14	....	....	....	....	....	....	....	....	....	....	....	....	....	....	....	....	....	....
	Medicine Hat	WHL	5	2	0	2	0	....	....	....	....	....	....	....	....	....	....	....	....	....	....	....	....	....	....
1986-87	Medicine Hat	WHL	72	14	22	36	59	....	....	....	....	....	....	....	....	....	20	5	4	9	17	....	....	....	....
1987-88	Medicine Hat	WHL	67	46	64	110	76	....	....	....	....	....	....	....	....	....	16	*13	12	25	19	....	....	....	....
1988-89	**Vancouver**	**NHL**	**80**	**30**	**29**	**59**	**41**	**10**	**1**	**2**	**186**	**16.1**	**–10**	....	....	....	**7**	**3**	**4**	**7**	**8**	**2**	**1**	**0**	....
1989-90	**Vancouver**	**NHL**	**73**	**21**	**30**	**51**	**43**	**6**	**2**	**3**	**171**	**12.3**	**–17**	....	....	....	....	....	....	....	....	....	....	....	....
1990-91	**Vancouver**	**NHL**	**80**	**33**	**37**	**70**	**65**	**16**	**2**	**4**	**229**	**14.4**	**–25**	....	....	....	**6**	**0**	**7**	**7**	**2**	**0**	**0**	**0**	....
1991-92	**Vancouver**	**NHL**	**80**	**31**	**44**	**75**	**101**	**6**	**1**	**6**	**201**	**15.4**	**3**	....	....	....	**13**	**4**	**8**	**12**	**6**	**2**	**0**	**1**	....
1992-93	**Vancouver**	**NHL**	**84**	**33**	**39**	**72**	**64**	**8**	**0**	**3**	**209**	**15.8**	**19**	....	....	....	**12**	**5**	**8**	**13**	**16**	**2**	**0**	**1**	....
1993-94	**Vancouver**	**NHL**	**84**	**32**	**29**	**61**	**73**	**10**	**2**	**3**	**234**	**13.7**	**6**	....	....	....	**24**	**12**	**13**	**25**	**18**	**5**	**1**	**1**	....
1994-95	**Vancouver**	**NHL**	**48**	**18**	**22**	**40**	**40**	**9**	**0**	**1**	**129**	**14.0**	**–5**	....	....	....	**11**	**2**	**6**	**8**	**12**	**1**	**0**	**0**	....
1995-96	**Vancouver**	**NHL**	**82**	**33**	**47**	**80**	**42**	**12**	**1**	**2**	**202**	**16.3**	**6**	....	....	....	**6**	**4**	**4**	**8**	**6**	**2**	**0**	**0**	....
1996-97	**Vancouver**	**NHL**	**49**	**9**	**31**	**40**	**27**	**2**	**2**	**2**	**84**	**10.7**	**5**	....	....	....	....	....	....	....	....	....	....	....	....
1997-98	**Vancouver**	**NHL**	**42**	**7**	**14**	**21**	**49**	**2**	**0**	**1**	**74**	**9.5**	**–13**	....	....	....	....	....	....	....	....	....	....	....	....
	NY Islanders	**NHL**	**25**	**10**	**7**	**17**	**33**	**3**	**2**	**1**	**59**	**16.9**	**–1**	....	....	....	....	....	....	....	....	....	....	....	....
	Canada	Olympics	6	1	0	1	10	....	....	....	....	....	....	....	....	....	....	....	....	....	....	....	....	....	....
1998-99	**NY Islanders**	**NHL**	**82**	**18**	**29**	**47**	**32**	**8**	**1**	**1**	**167**	**10.8**	**–14**	**261**	**50.2**	**21:29**	....	....	....	....	....	....	....	....	....
99-2000	**Montreal**	**NHL**	**50**	**13**	**17**	**30**	**34**	**4**	**0**	**3**	**87**	**14.9**	**–3**	**860**	**56.3**	**17:51**	....	....	....	....	....	....	....	....	....
2000-01	**Montreal**	**NHL**	**57**	**12**	**21**	**33**	**52**	**6**	**0**	**3**	**96**	**12.5**	**–2**	**1142**	**52.7**	**20:47**	....	....	....	....	....	....	....	....	....
	Washington	**NHL**	**12**	**3**	**1**	**4**	**8**	**0**	**0**	**0**	**30**	**10.0**	**2**	**75**	**60.0**	**18:03**	**6**	**0**	**4**	**4**	**14**	**0**	**0**	**0**	**22:41**
2001-02	**Washington**	**NHL**	**16**	**1**	**2**	**3**	**6**	**1**	**0**	**0**	**19**	**5.3**	**–2**	**71**	**49.3**	**16:06**	....	....	....	....	....	....	....	....	....
	Vancouver	**NHL**	**64**	**12**	**22**	**34**	**65**	**2**	**0**	**2**	**122**	**9.8**	**–3**	**1190**	**53.4**	**19:23**	**6**	**1**	**4**	**5**	**0**	**0**	**0**	**0**	**19:36**
2002-03	**Vancouver**	**NHL**	**71**	**19**	**22**	**41**	**30**	**4**	**1**	**1**	**116**	**16.4**	**–1**	**568**	**54.4**	**15:52**	**14**	**1**	**2**	**3**	**10**	**0**	**1**	**0**	**17:38**
2003-04	**Vancouver**	**NHL**	**82**	**14**	**22**	**36**	**26**	**4**	**0**	**1**	**97**	**14.4**	**–6**	**1285**	**55.8**	**16:17**	**7**	**0**	**0**	**0**	**6**	**0**	**0**	**0**	**18:29**
2004-05			DID NOT PLAY																						
	NHL Totals		**1161**	**349**	**465**	**814**	**831**	**113**	**15**	**39**	**2512**	**13.9**		**5452**	**54.3**	**18:28**	**112**	**32**	**60**	**92**	**98**	**14**	**3**	**3**	**19:05**

WHL East Second All-Star Team (1988) • Memorial Cup Tournament All-Star Team (1988) • NHL All-Rookie Team (1989) • King Clancy Memorial Trophy (1997)

Played in NHL All-Star Game (1991, 1992)

Traded to **NY Islanders** by **Vancouver** for Todd Bertuzzi, Bryan McCabe and NY Islanders' 3rd round choice (Jarkko Ruutu) in 1998 Entry Draft, February 6, 1998. Traded to **Montreal** by **NY Islanders** for Montreal's 1st round choice (Branislav Mezei) in 1999 Entry Draft, May 29, 1999. Traded to **Washington** by **Montreal** with Dainius Zubrus and New Jersey's 2nd round choice (previously acquired, later traded to Tampa Bay – Tampa Bay selected Andreas Holmqvist) in 2001 Entry Draft for Richard Zednik, Jan Bulis and Washington's 1st round choice (Alexander Perezhogin) in 2001 Entry Draft, March 13, 2001. Traded to **Vancouver** by **Washington** with NY Islanders' 2nd round choice (previously acquired, Vancouver selected Denis Grot) in 2002 Entry Draft for Vancouver's 1st round choice (Boyd Gordon) in 2002 Entry Draft and Vancouver's 3rd round choice (later traded to Edmonton – Edmonton selected Zachery Stortini) in 2003 Entry Draft, November 10, 2001.

LINDROS, Eric

(LIHND-rahz, AIR-ihk) **TOR.**

Center. Shoots right. 6'4", 240 lbs. Born, London, Ont., February 28, 1973. Quebec's 1st choice, 1st overall, in 1991 Entry Draft.

Season	Club	League	GP	G	A	Pts	PIM	PP	SH	GW	S	%	+/-	TF	F%	Min	GP	G	A	Pts	PIM	PP	SH	GW	Min
1988-89	St. Mike's B's	OHA-B	37	24	43	67	193	....	....	....	....	....	....	....	....	....	27	23	25	48	155	....	....	....	....
1989-90	Det. Compuware	NAHL	14	23	29	52	123	....	....	....	....	....	....	....	....	....	....	....	....	....	....	....	....	....	....
	Oshawa Generals	OHL	25	17	19	36	61	....	....	....	....	....	....	....	....	....	17	18	18	36	76	....	....	....	....
1990-91	Oshawa Generals	OHL	57	*71	78	*149	189	....	....	....	....	....	....	....	....	....	16	*18	20	*38	*93	....	....	....	....
1991-92	Oshawa Generals	OHL	13	9	22	31	54	....	....	....	....	....	....	....	....	....	....	....	....	....	....	....	....	....	....
	Canada	Nat-Tm	24	19	16	35	34	....	....	....	....	....	....	....	....	....	....	....	....	....	....	....	....	....	....
	Canada	Olympics	8	5	6	11	5	....	....	....	....	....	....	....	....	....	....	....	....	....	....	....	....	....	....
1992-93	**Philadelphia**	**NHL**	**61**	**41**	**34**	**75**	**147**	**8**	**1**	**5**	**180**	**22.8**	**28**	....	....	....	....	....	....	....	....	....	....	....	....
1993-94	**Philadelphia**	**NHL**	**65**	**44**	**53**	**97**	**103**	**13**	**2**	**9**	**197**	**22.3**	**16**	....	....	....	....	....	....	....	....	....	....	....	....
1994-95	**Philadelphia**	**NHL**	**46**	**29**	**41**	***70**	**60**	**7**	**0**	**4**	**144**	**20.1**	**27**	....	....	....	**12**	**4**	**11**	**15**	**18**	**0**	**0**	**1**	....
1995-96	**Philadelphia**	**NHL**	**73**	**47**	**68**	**115**	**163**	**15**	**0**	**4**	**294**	**16.0**	**26**	....	....	....	**12**	**6**	**6**	**12**	**43**	**3**	**0**	**2**	....
1996-97	**Philadelphia**	**NHL**	**52**	**32**	**47**	**79**	**136**	**9**	**0**	**7**	**198**	**16.2**	**31**	....	....	....	**19**	**12**	**14**	***26**	**40**	**4**	**0**	**1**	....
1997-98	**Philadelphia**	**NHL**	**63**	**30**	**41**	**71**	**134**	**10**	**1**	**4**	**202**	**14.9**	**14**	....	....	....	**5**	**1**	**2**	**3**	**17**	**0**	**0**	**0**	....
	Canada	Olympics	6	2	3	5	2	....	....	....	....	....	....	....	....	....	....	....	....	....	....	....	....	....	....
1998-99	**Philadelphia**	**NHL**	**71**	**40**	**53**	**93**	**120**	**10**	**1**	**2**	**242**	**16.5**	**35**	**1529**	**60.0**	**22:56**	....	....	....	....	....	....	....	....	....
99-2000	**Philadelphia**	**NHL**	**55**	**27**	**32**	**59**	**83**	**10**	**1**	**2**	**187**	**14.4**	**11**	**1318**	**57.8**	**22:02**	**2**	**1**	**0**	**1**	**0**	**0**	**0**	**0**	**8:26**
2000-01	**Philadelphia**	**NHL**	DID NOT PLAY – INJURED																						
2001-02	**NY Rangers**	**NHL**	**72**	**37**	**36**	**73**	**138**	**12**	**1**	**4**	**196**	**18.9**	**19**	**1707**	**54.4**	**21:03**	....	....	....	....	....	....	....	....	....
	Canada	Olympics	6	1	0	1	8	....	....	....	....	....	....	....	....	....	....	....	....	....	....	....	....	....	....
2002-03	**NY Rangers**	**NHL**	**81**	**19**	**34**	**53**	**141**	**9**	**0**	**3**	**235**	**8.1**	**5**	**778**	**53.0**	**20:15**	....	....	....	....	....	....	....	....	....
2003-04	**NY Rangers**	**NHL**	**39**	**10**	**22**	**32**	**60**	**3**	**0**	**0**	**83**	**12.0**	**7**	**492**	**54.5**	**15:59**	....	....	....	....	....	....	....	....	....
2004-05			DID NOT PLAY																						
	NHL Totals		**678**	**356**	**461**	**817**	**1285**	**106**	**7**	**44**	**2158**	**16.5**		**5824**	**56.5**	**20:49**	**50**	**24**	**33**	**57**	**118**	**7**	**0**	**4**	**8:26**

Memorial Cup Tournament All-Star Team (1990) • OHL First All-Star Team (1991) • OHL MVP (1991) • Canadian Major Junior Player of the Year (1991) • NHL All-Rookie Team (1993) • NHL First All-Star Team (1995) • Lester B. Pearson Award (1995) • Hart Trophy (1995) • NHL Second All-Star Team (1996)

Played in NHL All-Star Game (1994, 1996, 1997, 1998, 1999, 2000)

Traded to **Philadelphia** by **Quebec** for Peter Forsberg, Steve Duchesne, Kerry Huffman, Mike Ricci, Ron Hextall, Philadelphia's 1st round choice (Jocelyn Thibault) in 1993 Entry Draft, $15,000,000 and future considerations (Chris Simon and Philadelphia's 1st round choice (later traded to Toronto – later traded to Washington – Washington selected Nolan Baumgartner) in 1994 Entry Draft, July 21, 1992), June 30, 1992. • Missed entire 2000-01 season recovering from head injury suffered in game vs. New Jersey, May 26, 2000 and due to contract dispute with Philadelphia Flyers. Traded to **NY Rangers** by **Philadelphia** for Kim Johnsson, Jan Havac, Pavel Brendl and NY Rangers' 3rd round choice (Stefan Ruzicka) in 2003 Entry Draft, August 20, 2001. • Missed majority of 2003-04 season recovering from shoulder (October 23, 2003 vs. Florida) and head (January 28, 2004 vs. Washington) injuries. Signed as a free agent by **Toronto**, August 11, 2005.

LINDSAY, Bill

(LIHND-see, BIHL)

Right wing. Shoots left. 6', 195 lbs. Born, Fernie, B.C., May 17, 1971. Quebec's 6th choice, 103rd overall, in 1991 Entry Draft.

			Regular Season														Playoffs								
Season	Club	League	GP	G	A	Pts	PIM	PP	SH	GW	S	%	+/-	TF	F%	Min	GP	G	A	Pts	PIM	PP	SH	GW	Min
1988-89	Vernon Lakers	BCJHL	56	24	29	53	166	....	....	....	....	....	....	....	....	....	....	....	....	....	....	....	....	....	....
1989-90	Tri-City	WHL	72	40	45	85	84	....	....	....	....	....	....	....	....	....	7	3	0	3	17	....	....	....	....
1990-91	Tri-City	WHL	63	46	47	93	151	....	....	....	....	....	....	....	....	....	5	3	6	9	10	....	....	....	....
1991-92	Tri-City	WHL	42	34	59	93	81	....	....	....	....	....	....	....	....	....	3	2	3	5	16	....	....	....	....
	Quebec	**NHL**	**23**	**2**	**4**	**6**	**14**	**0**	**0**	**1**	**35**	**5.7**	**–6**	....	....	....	....	....	....	....	....	....	....	....	....
1992-93	**Quebec**	**NHL**	**44**	**4**	**9**	**13**	**16**	**0**	**0**	**0**	**58**	**6.9**	**0**	....	....	....	....	....	....	....	....	....	....	....	....
	Halifax Citadels	AHL	20	11	13	24	18	....	....	....	....	....	....	....	....	....	....	....	....	....	....	....	....	....	....
1993-94	**Florida**	**NHL**	**84**	**6**	**6**	**12**	**97**	**0**	**0**	**0**	**90**	**6.7**	**–2**	....	....	....	....	....	....	....	....	....	....	....	....
1994-95	**Florida**	**NHL**	**48**	**10**	**9**	**19**	**46**	**0**	**1**	**0**	**63**	**15.9**	**1**	....	....	....	....	....	....	....	....	....	....	....	....
1995-96	**Florida**	**NHL**	**73**	**12**	**22**	**34**	**57**	**0**	**3**	**2**	**118**	**10.2**	**13**	....	....	....	**22**	**5**	**5**	**10**	**18**	**0**	**1**	**1**	....
1996-97	**Florida**	**NHL**	**81**	**11**	**23**	**34**	**120**	**0**	**1**	**3**	**168**	**6.5**	**1**	....	....	....	**3**	**0**	**1**	**1**	**8**	**0**	**0**	**0**	....
1997-98	**Florida**	**NHL**	**82**	**12**	**16**	**28**	**80**	**0**	**2**	**5**	**150**	**8.0**	**–2**	....	....	....	....	....	....	....	....	....	....	....	....
1998-99	**Florida**	**NHL**	**75**	**12**	**15**	**27**	**92**	**0**	**1**	**2**	**135**	**8.9**	**–1**	**57**	**40.4**	**13:37**	....	....	....	....	....	....	....	....	....
99-2000	**Calgary**	**NHL**	**80**	**8**	**12**	**20**	**86**	**0**	**0**	**2**	**147**	**5.4**	**–7**	**28**	**39.3**	**12:55**	....	....	....	....	....	....	....	....	....
2000-01	**Calgary**	**NHL**	**52**	**1**	**9**	**10**	**97**	**0**	**0**	**0**	**57**	**1.8**	**–8**	**9**	**55.6**	**10:32**	....	....	....	....	....	....	....	....	....
	San Jose	**NHL**	**16**	**0**	**4**	**4**	**29**	**0**	**0**	**0**	**14**	**0.0**	**2**	**2**	**0.0**	**9:16**	**6**	**0**	**0**	**0**	**16**	**0**	**0**	**0**	**6:40**
2001-02	**Florida**	**NHL**	**63**	**4**	**7**	**11**	**117**	**0**	**0**	**1**	**63**	**6.3**	**–11**	**124**	**44.4**	**9:40**	....	....	....	....	....	....	....	....	....
	Montreal	**NHL**	**13**	**1**	**3**	**4**	**23**	**0**	**0**	**0**	**14**	**7.1**	**0**	**26**	**53.9**	**10:10**	**11**	**2**	**2**	**4**	**2**	**0**	**0**	**0**	**6:58**
2002-03	**Montreal**	**NHL**	**19**	**0**	**2**	**2**	**23**	**0**	**0**	**0**	**7**	**0.0**	**–1**	**21**	**42.9**	**5:20**	....	....	....	....	....	....	....	....	....
	Hamilton	AHL	28	6	12	18	89	....	....	....	....	....	....	....	....	....	23	10	3	13	31	....	....	....	....
2003-04	**Atlanta**	**NHL**	**24**	**0**	**0**	**0**	**25**	**0**	**0**	**0**	**10**	**0.0**	**–6**	**8**	**50.0**	**5:55**	....	....	....	....	....	....	....	....	....
	Chicago Wolves	AHL	13	3	5	8	8	....	....	....	....	....	....	....	....	....	....	....	....	....	....	....	....	....	....
2004-05	Long Beach	ECHL	32	9	14	23	78	....	....	....	....	....	....	....	....	....	7	2	2	4	12	....	....	....	....
	NHL Totals		**777**	**83**	**141**	**224**	**922**	**0**	**8**	**16**	**1129**	**7.4**		**275**	**44.0**	**10:55**	**42**	**7**	**8**	**15**	**44**	**0**	**1**	**1**	**6:52**

WHL West Second All-Star Team (1992)

Claimed by **Florida** from **Quebec** in Expansion Draft, June 24, 1993. Traded to **Calgary** by **Florida** for Todd Simpson, September 30, 1999. Traded to **San Jose** by **Calgary** for Minnesota's 8th round choice (previously acquired, Calgary selected Joe Campbell) in 2001 Entry Draft, March 6, 2001. Signed as a free agent by **Florida**, August 23, 2001. Claimed on waivers by **Montreal** from **Florida**, March 19, 2002. Signed as a free agent by **Atlanta**, August 25, 2003. Claimed on waivers by **Washington** from **Atlanta**, March 9, 2004. • Missed majority of 2003-04 season recovering from throat injury suffered in game vs. Montreal, January 3, 2004. Signed as a free agent by **Long Beach** (ECHL), December 10, 2004.

LING, David

(LIHNG, DAY-vihd)

Right wing. Shoots right. 5'10", 204 lbs. Born, Halifax, N.S., January 9, 1975. Quebec's 9th choice, 179th overall, in 1993 Entry Draft.

			Regular Season														Playoffs								
Season	Club	League	GP	G	A	Pts	PIM	PP	SH	GW	S	%	+/-	TF	F%	Min	GP	G	A	Pts	PIM	PP	SH	GW	Min
1991-92	Charlotwn Abbies	MJrHL	30	33	42	75	270	....	....	....	....	....	....	....	....	....	....	....	....	....	....	....	....	....	....
	St. Mike's B's	OHA-B	8	5	14	19	25	....	....	....	....	....	....	....	....	....	....	....	....	....	....	....	....	....	....
1992-93	Kingston	OHL	64	17	46	63	275	....	....	....	....	....	....	....	....	....	16	3	12	15	*72	....	....	....	....
1993-94	Kingston	OHL	61	37	40	77	*254	....	....	....	....	....	....	....	....	....	6	4	2	6	16	....	....	....	....
1994-95	Kingston	OHL	62	*61	74	135	136	....	....	....	....	....	....	....	....	....	6	7	8	15	12	....	....	....	....
1995-96	Saint John Flames	AHL	75	24	32	56	179	....	....	....	....	....	....	....	....	....	9	0	5	5	12	....	....	....	....
1996-97	Saint John Flames	AHL	5	0	2	2	19	....	....	....	....	....	....	....	....	....	....	....	....	....	....	....	....	....	....
	Montreal	**NHL**	**2**	**0**	**0**	**0**	**0**	**0**	**0**	**0**	**0**	**0.0**	**0**	....	....	....	....	....	....	....	....	....	....	....	....
	Fredericton	AHL	48	22	36	58	229	....	....	....	....	....	....	....	....	....	....	....	....	....	....	....	....	....	....
1997-98	**Montreal**	**NHL**	**1**	**0**	**0**	**0**	**0**	**0**	**0**	**0**	**1**	**0.0**	**–1**	....	....	....	....	....	....	....	....	....	....	....	....
	Fredericton	AHL	67	25	41	66	148	....	....	....	....	....	....	....	....	....	....	....	....	....	....	....	....	....	....
	Indianapolis Ice	IHL	12	8	6	14	30	....	....	....	....	....	....	....	....	....	5	4	1	5	31	....	....	....	....
1998-99	Kansas City	IHL	82	30	42	72	112	....	....	....	....	....	....	....	....	....	3	1	0	1	20	....	....	....	....
99-2000	Kansas City	IHL	82	35	48	83	210	....	....	....	....	....	....	....	....	....	....	....	....	....	....	....	....	....	....
2000-01	Utah Grizzlies	IHL	79	15	28	43	202	....	....	....	....	....	....	....	....	....	....	....	....	....	....	....	....	....	....
2001-02	**Columbus**	**NHL**	**5**	**0**	**0**	**0**	**7**	**0**	**0**	**0**	**5**	**0.0**	**–1**	**1**	**0.0**	**9:47**	....	....	....	....	....	....	....	....	....
	Syracuse Crunch	AHL	71	19	41	60	240	....	....	....	....	....	....	....	....	....	10	5	5	10	16	....	....	....	....
2002-03	**Columbus**	**NHL**	**35**	**3**	**2**	**5**	**86**	**0**	**0**	**0**	**37**	**8.1**	**–6**	**15**	**40.0**	**7:56**	....	....	....	....	....	....	....	....	....
	Syracuse Crunch	AHL	46	7	34	41	129	....	....	....	....	....	....	....	....	....	....	....	....	....	....	....	....	....	....
2003-04	**Columbus**	**NHL**	**50**	**1**	**2**	**3**	**98**	**0**	**0**	**0**	**45**	**2.2**	**–3**	**8**	**37.5**	**7:45**	....	....	....	....	....	....	....	....	....
	Syracuse Crunch	AHL	14	7	10	17	25	....	....	....	....	....	....	....	....	....	7	0	1	1	36	....	....	....	....
2004-05	St. John's	AHL	80	28	60	88	152	....	....	....	....	....	....	....	....	....	5	1	1	2	43	....	....	....	....
	NHL Totals		**93**	**4**	**4**	**8**	**191**	**0**	**0**	**0**	**88**	**4.5**		**24**	**37.5**	**7:56**	....	....	....	....	....	....	....	....	....

OHL First All-Star Team (1995) • OHL MVP (1995) • Canadian Major Junior First All-Star Team (1995) • Canadian Major Junior Player of the Year (1995) • IHL First All-Star Team (2000)

Rights transferred to **Colorado** after **Quebec** franchise relocated, June 21, 1995. Traded to **Calgary** by **Colorado** with Colorado's 9th round choice (Steve Shirreffs) in 1995 Entry Draft for Calgary's 9th round choice (Chris George) in 1995 Entry Draft, July 7, 1995. Traded to **Montreal** by **Calgary** with Calgary's 6th round choice (Gordie Dwyer) in 1998 Entry Draft for Scott Fraser, October 24, 1996. Traded to **Chicago** by **Montreal** for Martin Gendron, March 14, 1998. Signed as a free agent by **Kansas City** (IHL) with Chicago retaining NHL rights, September 3, 1998. Traded to **Dallas** by **Chicago** for future considerations, August 11, 2000. Signed as a free agent by **Columbus**, July 7, 2001. Signed as a free agent by **Toronto**, July 29, 2004.

LOMBARDI, Matthew

(lawm-BAHR-dee, MA-thew) **CGY.**

Center. Shoots left. 6', 195 lbs. Born, Montreal, Que., March 18, 1982. Calgary's 3rd choice, 90th overall, in 2002 Entry Draft.

			Regular Season														Playoffs								
Season	Club	League	GP	G	A	Pts	PIM	PP	SH	GW	S	%	+/-	TF	F%	Min	GP	G	A	Pts	PIM	PP	SH	GW	Min
1997-98	Gatineau	QAAA	42	10	13	23	....	....	....	....	....	....	....	....	....	....	13	4	7	11	....	....	....	....	....
1998-99	Victoriaville Tigres	QMJHL	47	6	10	16	8	....	....	....	....	....	....	....	....	....	5	0	0	0	0	....	....	....	....
99-2000	Victoriaville Tigres	QMJHL	65	18	26	44	28	....	....	....	....	....	....	....	....	....	6	0	0	0	6	....	....	....	....
2000-01	Victoriaville Tigres	QMJHL	72	28	39	67	66	....	....	....	....	....	....	....	....	....	13	12	6	18	10	....	....	....	....
2001-02	Victoriaville Tigres	QMJHL	66	57	73	130	70	....	....	....	....	....	....	....	....	....	22	*17	18	35	18	....	....	....	....
2002-03	Saint John Flames	AHL	76	25	21	46	41	....	....	....	....	....	....	....	....	....	....	....	....	....	....	....	....	....	....
2003-04	**Calgary**	**NHL**	**79**	**16**	**13**	**29**	**32**	**3**	**2**	**4**	**130**	**12.3**	**4**	**992**	**47.9**	**14:26**	**13**	**1**	**5**	**6**	**4**	**0**	**0**	**1**	**14:46**
2004-05	Lowell	AHL	9	3	1	4	9	....	....	....	....	....	....	....	....	....	11	0	3	3	16	....	....	....	....
	NHL Totals		**79**	**16**	**13**	**29**	**32**	**3**	**2**	**4**	**130**	**12.3**		**992**	**47.9**	**14:26**	**13**	**1**	**5**	**6**	**4**	**0**	**0**	**1**	**14:46**

• Re-entered NHL Entry Draft. Originally Edmonton's 7th choice, 215th overall, in 2000 Entry Draft.

Memorial Cup Tournament All-Star Team (2002) • Ed Chynoweth Trophy (Memorial Cup Tournament Leading Scorer) (2002)

LOW, Reed

(LOH, REED) **ST.L.**

Right wing. Shoots right. 6'4", 227 lbs. Born, Moose Jaw, Sask., June 21, 1976. St. Louis' 7th choice, 177th overall, in 1996 Entry Draft.

			Regular Season														Playoffs								
Season	Club	League	GP	G	A	Pts	PIM	PP	SH	GW	S	%	+/-	TF	F%	Min	GP	G	A	Pts	PIM	PP	SH	GW	Min
1994-95	Minot Top Guns	SJHL	STATISTICS NOT AVAILABLE																						
	Regina Pats	WHL	2	0	0	0	5	....	....	....	....	....	....	....	....	....	....	....	....	....	....	....	....	....	....
1995-96	Moose Jaw	WHL	61	12	7	19	221	....	....	....	....	....	....	....	....	....	....	....	....	....	....	....	....	....	....
1996-97	Moose Jaw	WHL	62	16	11	27	228	....	....	....	....	....	....	....	....	....	12	2	1	3	50	....	....	....	....
1997-98	Worcester IceCats	AHL	17	1	1	2	75	....	....	....	....	....	....	....	....	....	3	0	0	0	0	....	....	....	....
	Baton Rouge	ECHL	39	4	2	6	145	....	....	....	....	....	....	....	....	....	....	....	....	....	....	....	....	....	....
1998-99	Worcester IceCats	AHL	77	5	6	11	239	....	....	....	....	....	....	....	....	....	4	0	0	0	2	....	....	....	....
99-2000	Worcester IceCats	AHL	80	12	16	28	203	....	....	....	....	....	....	....	....	....	9	1	3	4	16	....	....	....	....
2000-01	**St. Louis**	**NHL**	**56**	**1**	**5**	**6**	**159**	**0**	**0**	**0**	**31**	**3.2**	**4**	**2**	**50.0**	**6:17**	....	....	....	....	....	....	....	....	....
2001-02	**St. Louis**	**NHL**	**58**	**0**	**5**	**5**	**160**	**0**	**0**	**0**	**25**	**0.0**	**–3**	**0**	**0.0**	**5:22**	....	....	....	....	....	....	....	....	....
2002-03	**St. Louis**	**NHL**	**79**	**2**	**4**	**6**	**234**	**0**	**0**	**1**	**48**	**4.2**	**3**	**14**	**71.4**	**6:19**	....	....	....	....	....	....	....	....	....
2003-04	**St. Louis**	**NHL**	**57**	**0**	**2**	**2**	**141**	**0**	**0**	**0**	**28**	**0.0**	**–6**	**0**	**0.0**	**5:42**	....	....	....	....	....	....	....	....	....
2004-05			DID NOT PLAY																						
	NHL Totals		**250**	**3**	**16**	**19**	**694**	**0**	**0**	**1**	**132**	**2.3**		**16**	**68.8**	**5:57**	....	....	....	....	....	....	....	....	....

LOYNS, Lynn

(LOINZ, LIHN) **CGY.**

Left wing. Shoots left. 5'11", 205 lbs. Born, Naicam, Sask., February 21, 1981.

			Regular Season														Playoffs								
Season	Club	League	GP	G	A	Pts	PIM	PP	SH	GW	S	%	+/-	TF	F%	Min	GP	G	A	Pts	PIM	PP	SH	GW	Min
1996-97	Naicam Vikings	SAHA	41	90	70	160	58	....	....	....	....	....	....	....	....	....	....	....	....	....	....	....	....	....	....
1997-98	Spokane Chiefs	WHL	49	1	12	13	8	....	....	....	....	....	....	....	....	....	13	1	4	5	2	....	....	....	....
1998-99	Spokane Chiefs	WHL	72	20	30	50	43	....	....	....	....	....	....	....	....	....	....	....	....	....	....	....	....	....	....
99-2000	Spokane Chiefs	WHL	71	20	29	49	47	....	....	....	....	....	....	....	....	....	14	3	2	5	12	....	....	....	....
2000-01	Spokane Chiefs	WHL	66	31	42	73	81	....	....	....	....	....	....	....	....	....	....	....	....	....	....	....	....	....	....
2001-02	Cleveland Barons	AHL	76	9	9	18	81	....	....	....	....	....	....	....	....	....	....	....	....	....	....	....	....	....	....
2002-03	**San Jose**	**NHL**	**19**	**3**	**0**	**3**	**19**	**0**	**0**	**0**	**12**	**25.0**	**–4**	**1**	**0.0**	**7:50**	....	....	....	....	....	....	....	....	....
	Cleveland Barons	AHL	36	7	8	15	39	....	....	....	....	....	....	....	....	....	....	....	....	....	....	....	....	....	....

			Regular Season														Playoffs								
Season	Club	League	GP	G	A	Pts	PIM	PP	SH	GW	S	%	+/-	TF	F%	Min	GP	G	A	Pts	PIM	PP	SH	GW	Min
2003-04	**San Jose**	**NHL**	**2**	**0**	**0**	**0**	**0**	**0**	**0**	**0**	**0**	**0.0**	**–1**	**0**	**0.0**	**7:33**	....	....	....	....	....	....	....	....	....
	Cleveland Barons	AHL	30	5	9	14	40	....	....	....	....	....	....	....	....	....	....	....	....	....	....	....	....	....	....
	Calgary	**NHL**	**12**	**0**	**2**	**2**	**2**	**0**	**0**	**0**	**6**	**0.0**	**–2**	**86**	**44.2**	**11:13**	....	....	....	....	....	....	....	....	....
	Lowell	AHL	18	6	6	12	9	....	....	....	....	....	....	....	....	....	....	....	....	....	....	....	....	....	....
2004-05	Lowell	AHL	77	7	8	15	42	....	....	....	....	....	....	....	....	....	11	0	0	0	0	....	....	....	....
	NHL Totals		**33**	**3**	**2**	**5**	**21**	**0**	**0**	**0**	**18**	**16.7**		**87**	**43.7**	**9:03**	....	....	....	....	....	....	....	....	....

Signed as a free agent by **San Jose**, October 3, 2001. Traded to **Calgary** by **San Jose** for Calgary's 5th round choice (later traded to Florida – Florida selected Bret Nasby) in 2004 Entry Draft, January 9, 2004.

LUKOWICH, Brad

(loo-KUH-which, BRAD) **NYI**

Defense. Shoots left. 6'1", 200 lbs. Born, Cranbrook, B.C., August 12, 1976. NY Islanders' 4th choice, 90th overall, in 1994 Entry Draft.

Season	Club	League	GP	G	A	Pts	PIM	PP	SH	GW	S	%	+/-	TF	F%	Min	GP	G	A	Pts	PIM	PP	SH	GW	Min
1992-93	Cranbrook Colts	RMJHL	54	21	41	62	162	....	....	....	....	....	....	....	....	....	....	....	....	....	....	....	....	....	....
	Kamloops Blazers	WHL	1	0	0	0	0	....	....	....	....	....	....	....	....	....	....	....	....	....	....	....	....	....	....
1993-94	Kamloops Blazers	WHL	42	5	11	16	166	....	....	....	....	....	....	....	....	....	16	0	1	1	35	....	....	....	....
1994-95	Kamloops Blazers	WHL	63	10	35	45	125	....	....	....	....	....	....	....	....	....	18	0	7	7	21	....	....	....	....
1995-96	Kamloops Blazers	WHL	65	14	55	69	114	....	....	....	....	....	....	....	....	....	13	2	10	12	29	....	....	....	....
1996-97	Michigan	IHL	69	2	6	8	77	....	....	....	....	....	....	....	....	....	4	0	1	1	2	....	....	....	....
1997-98	**Dallas**	**NHL**	**4**	**0**	**1**	**1**	**2**	**0**	**0**	**0**	**2**	**0.0**	**–2**	....	....	....	....	....	....	....	....	....	....	....	....
	Michigan	IHL	60	6	27	33	104	....	....	....	....	....	....	....	....	....	4	0	4	4	14	....	....	....	....
1998-99	**Dallas**	**NHL**	**14**	**1**	**2**	**3**	**19**	**0**	**0**	**0**	**8**	**12.5**	**3**	**0**	**0.0**	**16:18**	**8**	**0**	**1**	**1**	**4**	**0**	**0**	**0**	**10:00**
	Michigan	IHL	67	8	21	29	95	....	....	....	....	....	....	....	....	....	....	....	....	....	....	....	....	....	....
99-2000	**Dallas**	**NHL**	**60**	**3**	**1**	**4**	**50**	**0**	**0**	**1**	**33**	**9.1**	**–14**	**1**	**0.0**	**11:44**	....	....	....	....	....	....	....	....	....
2000-01	**Dallas**	**NHL**	**80**	**4**	**10**	**14**	**76**	**0**	**0**	**2**	**43**	**9.3**	**28**	**1**	**100.0**	**14:48**	**10**	**1**	**0**	**1**	**4**	**0**	**0**	**0**	**17:28**
2001-02	**Dallas**	**NHL**	**66**	**1**	**6**	**7**	**40**	**0**	**0**	**0**	**56**	**1.8**	**–1**	**0**	**0.0**	**13:14**	....	....	....	....	....	....	....	....	....
2002-03	**Tampa Bay**	**NHL**	**70**	**1**	**14**	**15**	**46**	**0**	**0**	**0**	**52**	**1.9**	**4**	**1**	**0.0**	**17:34**	**9**	**0**	**1**	**1**	**2**	**0**	**0**	**0**	**17:48**
2003-04♦	**Tampa Bay**	**NHL**	**79**	**5**	**14**	**19**	**24**	**0**	**0**	**1**	**86**	**5.8**	**29**	**3**	**0.0**	**18:45**	**18**	**0**	**2**	**2**	**6**	**0**	**0**	**0**	**15:51**
2004-05	Fort Worth	CHL	16	3	5	8	33	....	....	....	....	....	....	....	....	....	....	....	....	....	....	....	....	....	....
	NHL Totals		**373**	**15**	**48**	**63**	**257**	**0**	**0**	**4**	**280**	**5.4**		**6**	**16.7**	**15:27**	**45**	**1**	**4**	**5**	**16**	**0**	**0**	**0**	**15:34**

Traded to **Dallas** by **NY Islanders** for Dallas' 3rd round choice (Robert Schnabel) in 1997 Entry Draft, June 1, 1996. Traded to **Minnesota** by **Dallas** with Manny Fernandez for Minnesota's 3rd round choice (Joel Lundqvist) in 2000 Entry Draft and Minnesota's 4th round choice (later traded back to Minnesota – later traded to Los Angeles – Los Angeles selected Aaron Rome) in 2002 Entry Draft, June 12, 2000. Traded to **Dallas** by **Minnesota** with Minnesota's 3rd (Yared Hagos) and 9th (Dale Sullivan) round choices in 2001 Entry Draft for Aaron Gavey, Pavel Patera, Dallas' 8th round choice (Eric Johansson) in 2000 Entry Draft and Minnesota's 4th round choice (previously acquired, later traded to Los Angeles – Los Angeles selected Aaron Rome) in 2002 Entry Draft, June 25, 2000. Traded to **Tampa Bay** by **Dallas** with Dallas' 7th round choice (Jay Rosehill) in 2003 Entry Draft for Tampa Bay's 2nd round choice (previously acquired, later traded back to Tampa Bay – later traded to Dallas – Dallas selected Tobias Stephan) in 2002 Entry Draft, June 22, 2002. Signed as a free agent by **Fort Worth** (CHL), September 21, 2004. Signed as a free agent by **NY Islanders**, August 11, 2005.

LUNDMARK, Jamie

(LUHND-mahrk, JAY-mee) **NYR**

Center. Shoots right. 6', 200 lbs. Born, Edmonton, Alta., January 16, 1981. NY Rangers' 2nd choice, 9th overall, in 1999 Entry Draft.

Season	Club	League	GP	G	A	Pts	PIM	PP	SH	GW	S	%	+/-	TF	F%	Min	GP	G	A	Pts	PIM	PP	SH	GW	Min
1996-97	St. Albert Saints	AJHL	35	10	9	19	8	....	....	....	....	....	....	....	....	....	....	....	....	....	....	....	....	....	....
1997-98	St. Albert Saints	AJHL	57	33	58	91	171	....	....	....	....	....	....	....	....	....	19	13	18	31	5	....	....	....	....
1998-99	Moose Jaw	WHL	70	40	51	91	121	....	....	....	....	....	....	....	....	....	11	5	4	9	24	....	....	....	....
99-2000	Moose Jaw	WHL	37	21	27	48	33	....	....	....	....	....	....	....	....	....	....	....	....	....	....	....	....	....	....
2000-01	Seattle	WHL	52	35	42	77	49	....	....	....	....	....	....	....	....	....	9	4	4	8	16	....	....	....	....
2001-02	Hartford	AHL	79	27	32	59	56	....	....	....	....	....	....	....	....	....	10	3	4	7	16	....	....	....	....
2002-03	**NY Rangers**	**NHL**	**55**	**8**	**11**	**19**	**16**	**0**	**0**	**0**	**78**	**10.3**	**–3**	**62**	**43.6**	**12:04**	....	....	....	....	....	....	....	....	....
	Hartford	AHL	22	9	9	18	18	....	....	....	....	....	....	....	....	....	2	0	0	0	0	....	....	....	....
2003-04	**NY Rangers**	**NHL**	**56**	**2**	**8**	**10**	**33**	**0**	**0**	**1**	**68**	**2.9**	**–8**	**379**	**40.4**	**12:46**	....	....	....	....	....	....	....	....	....
2004-05	HC Forst Bolzano	Italy	14	9	9	18	22	....	....	....	....	....	....	....	....	....	....	....	....	....	....	....	....	....	....
	Hartford	AHL	64	14	27	41	146	....	....	....	....	....	....	....	....	....	6	2	4	6	8	....	....	....	....
	NHL Totals		**111**	**10**	**19**	**29**	**49**	**0**	**0**	**1**	**146**	**6.8**		**441**	**40.8**	**12:25**	....	....	....	....	....	....	....	....	....

WHL All-Rookie Team (1999) • WHL East Second All-Star Team (1999) • WHL West First All-Star Team (2001)

Signed as a free agent by **Bolzano** (Italy), September 21, 2004. Signed as a free agent by **Hartford** (AHL), November 16, 2004.

LUOMA, Mikko

(loo-OH-mah, MEE-koh) **EDM.**

Defense. Shoots left. 6'3", 207 lbs. Born, Jyvaskyla, Finland, June 22, 1976. Edmonton's 9th choice, 181st overall, in 2002 Entry Draft.

Season	Club	League	GP	G	A	Pts	PIM	PP	SH	GW	S	%	+/-	TF	F%	Min	GP	G	A	Pts	PIM	PP	SH	GW	Min
1993-94	JyP HT Jr.	Finland-Jr.	13	1	3	4	6	....	....	....	....	....	....	....	....	....	....	....	....	....	....	....	....	....	....
1994-95	JyP HT Jr.	Finland-Jr.	23	8	17	25	34	....	....	....	....	....	....	....	....	....	....	....	....	....	....	....	....	....	....
	JYP HT Jyvaskyla	Finland	....	....	....	....	....	....	....	....	....	....	....	....	....	....	7	1	2	3	2	....	....	....	....
1995-96	JyP HT Jr.	Finland-Jr.	27	4	10	14	56	....	....	....	....	....	....	....	....	....	....	....	....	....	....	....	....	....	....
	JYP HT Jyvaskyla	Finland	5	0	0	0	0	....	....	....	....	....	....	....	....	....	6	0	0	0	0	....	....	....	....
1996-97	JyP HT Jr.	Finland-Jr.	3	0	2	2	6	....	....	....	....	....	....	....	....	....	4	2	2	4	4	....	....	....	....
	JYP HT Jyvaskyla	Finland	34	15	52	67	34	....	....	....	....	....	....	....	....	....	....	....	....	....	....	....	....	....	....
1997-98	JYP Jyvaskyla	Finland	44	2	18	20	60	....	....	....	....	....	....	....	....	....	5	1	0	1	10	....	....	....	....
1998-99	JYP Jyvaskyla	Finland	53	2	8	10	60	....	....	....	....	....	....	....	....	....	3	0	0	0	4	....	....	....	....
99-2000	JYP Jyvaskyla	Finland	51	2	6	8	58	....	....	....	....	....	....	....	....	....	....	....	....	....	....	....	....	....	....
2000-01	Tappara Tampere	Finland	56	10	11	21	72	....	....	....	....	....	....	....	....	....	10	0	2	2	10	....	....	....	....
2001-02	Tappara Tampere	Finland	56	11	18	29	74	....	....	....	....	....	....	....	....	....	10	1	2	3	10	....	....	....	....
2002-03	Tappara Tampere	Finland	55	4	13	17	52	....	....	....	....	....	....	....	....	....	14	2	1	3	12	....	....	....	....
2003-04	**Edmonton**	**NHL**	**3**	**0**	**1**	**1**	**0**	**0**	**0**	**0**	**4**	**0.0**	**0**	**0**	**0.0**	**17:32**	....	....	....	....	....	....	....	....	....
	Toronto	AHL	65	4	22	26	54	....	....	....	....	....	....	....	....	....	3	1	0	1	8	....	....	....	....
2004-05	Malmo	Sweden	50	9	9	18	72	....	....	....	....	....	....	....	....	....	....	....	....	....	....	....	....	....	....
	NHL Totals		**3**	**0**	**1**	**1**	**0**	**0**	**0**	**0**	**4**	**0.0**		**0**	**0.0**	**17:32**	....	....	....	....	....	....	....	....	....

Signed as a free agent by **Malmo** (Sweden), June 9, 2004. Signed as a free agent by **Linkoping** (Sweden), April 19, 2005.

LUPASCHUK, Ross

(LOO-puhs-chuhk, RAWS) **PIT.**

Defense. Shoots right. 6'1", 210 lbs. Born, Edmonton, Alta., January 19, 1981. Washington's 4th choice, 34th overall, in 1999 Entry Draft.

Season	Club	League	GP	G	A	Pts	PIM	PP	SH	GW	S	%	+/-	TF	F%	Min	GP	G	A	Pts	PIM	PP	SH	GW	Min
1996-97	Edmonton Mets	AJHL	65	5	22	27	87	....	....	....	....	....	....	....	....	....	....	....	....	....	....	....	....	....	....
1997-98	Prince Albert	WHL	67	6	12	18	170	....	....	....	....	....	....	....	....	....	....	....	....	....	....	....	....	....	....
1998-99	Prince Albert	WHL	67	8	20	28	127	....	....	....	....	....	....	....	....	....	14	4	9	13	16	....	....	....	....
99-2000	Prince Albert	WHL	22	8	8	16	42	....	....	....	....	....	....	....	....	....	....	....	....	....	....	....	....	....	....
	Red Deer Rebels	WHL	46	13	27	40	116	....	....	....	....	....	....	....	....	....	4	0	1	1	10	....	....	....	....
2000-01	Red Deer Rebels	WHL	65	28	37	65	135	....	....	....	....	....	....	....	....	....	22	5	10	15	54	....	....	....	....
2001-02	Wilkes-Barre	AHL	72	9	20	29	91	....	....	....	....	....	....	....	....	....	....	....	....	....	....	....	....	....	....
2002-03	**Pittsburgh**	**NHL**	**3**	**0**	**0**	**0**	**4**	**0**	**0**	**0**	**3**	**0.0**	**–3**	**0**	**0.0**	**16:20**	....	....	....	....	....	....	....	....	....
	Wilkes-Barre	AHL	74	18	18	36	101	....	....	....	....	....	....	....	....	....	4	0	2	2	20	....	....	....	....
2003-04	Wilkes-Barre	AHL	58	4	17	21	96	....	....	....	....	....	....	....	....	....	8	0	2	2	37	....	....	....	....
2004-05	Wilkes-Barre	AHL	67	11	19	30	145	....	....	....	....	....	....	....	....	....	5	0	0	0	2	....	....	....	....
	NHL Totals		**3**	**0**	**0**	**0**	**4**	**0**	**0**	**0**	**3**	**0.0**		**0**	**0.0**	**16:20**	....	....	....	....	....	....	....	....	....

WHL East Second All-Star Team (2001) • Memorial Cup Tournament All-Star Team (2001)

Traded to **Pittsburgh** by **Washington** with Kris Beech, Michal Sivek and future considerations for Jaromir Jagr and Frantisek Kucera, July 11, 2001.

LUPUL, Joffrey

(LOO-puhl, JAWF-ree) **ANA.**

Center. Shoots right. 6'1", 205 lbs. Born, Edmonton, Alta., September 23, 1983. Anaheim's 1st choice, 7th overall, in 2002 Entry Draft.

Season	Club	League	GP	G	A	Pts	PIM	PP	SH	GW	S	%	+/-	TF	F%	Min	GP	G	A	Pts	PIM	PP	SH	GW	Min
1998-99	Ft. Saskatchewan	ABHL	36	40	50	90	40	....	....	....	....	....	....	....	....	....	....	....	....	....	....	....	....	....	....
99-2000	Ft. Saskatchewan	AMHL	34	43	30	*73	47	....	....	....	....	....	....	....	....	....	4	0	1	1	2	....	....	....	....
2000-01	Medicine Hat	WHL	69	30	26	56	39	....	....	....	....	....	....	....	....	....	22	3	6	9	2	....	....	....	....
2001-02	Medicine Hat	WHL	72	*56	50	106	95	....	....	....	....	....	....	....	....	....	....	....	....	....	....	....	....	....	....
2002-03	Medicine Hat	WHL	50	41	37	78	82	....	....	....	....	....	....	....	....	....	11	4	11	15	20	....	....	....	....
2003-04	**Anaheim**	**NHL**	**75**	**13**	**21**	**34**	**28**	**4**	**0**	**2**	**137**	**9.5**	**–6**	**11**	**9.1**	**13:37**	....	....	....	....	....	....	....	....	....
	Cincinnati	AHL	3	3	2	5	2	....	....	....	....	....	....	....	....	....	....	....	....	....	....	....	....	....	....
2004-05	Cincinnati	AHL	65	30	26	56	58	....	....	....	....	....	....	....	....	....	12	3	9	12	27	....	....	....	....
	NHL Totals		**75**	**13**	**21**	**34**	**28**	**4**	**0**	**2**	**137**	**9.5**		**11**	**9.1**	**13:37**	....	....	....	....	....	....	....	....	....

WHL East First All-Star Team (2002) • Canadian Major Junior First All-Star Team (2002)

LYDMAN, Toni

(LEED-man, TOH-nee) **BUF.**

Defense. Shoots left. 6'1", 202 lbs. Born, Lahti, Finland, September 25, 1977. Calgary's 5th choice, 89th overall, in 1996 Entry Draft.

			Regular Season														Playoffs								
Season	Club	League	GP	G	A	Pts	PIM	PP	SH	GW	S	%	+/-	TF	F%	Min	GP	G	A	Pts	PIM	PP	SH	GW	Min
1993-94	K-Reipas U18	Fin-U18	9	3	1	4	4	....	....	....	....	....	....	....	....	....	....	....	....	....	....	....	....	....	....
	K-Reipas Jr.	Finland-Jr.	1	0	0	0	0	....	....	....	....	....	....	....	....	....	....	....	....	....	....	....	....	....	....
1994-95	K-Reipas U18	Fin-U18	9	7	4	11	12	....	....	....	....	....	....	....	....	....	....	....	....	....	....	....	....	....	....
	K-Reipas Jr.	Finland-Jr.	26	6	4	10	10	....	....	....	....	....	....	....	....	....	....	....	....	....	....	....	....	....	....
1995-96	K-Reipas Jr.	Finland-Jr.	9	2	2	4	6	....	....	....	....	....	....	....	....	....	....	....	....	....	....	....	....	....	....
	Kiekko-67 Turku	Finland-2	39	5	2	7	30	....	....	....	....	....	....	....	....	....	3	0	1	1	0	....	....	....	....
1996-97	Tappara Tampere	Finland	49	1	2	3	65	....	....	....	....	....	....	....	....	....	3	0	0	0	6	....	....	....	....
1997-98	Tappara Tampere	Finland	48	4	10	14	48	....	....	....	....	....	....	....	....	....	4	0	2	2	0	....	....	....	....
1998-99	HIFK Helsinki	Finland	42	4	7	11	36	....	....	....	....	....	....	....	....	....	11	0	3	3	2	....	....	....	....
	HIFK Helsinki	EuroHL	6	0	2	2	29	....	....	....	....	....	....	....	....	....	4	1	....	....	....	....	....	....	....
99-2000	HIFK Helsinki	Finland	46	4	18	22	36	....	....	....	....	....	....	....	....	....	9	0	4	4	6	....	....	....	....
2000-01	**Calgary**	**NHL**	**62**	**3**	**16**	**19**	**30**	**1**	**0**	**0**	**80**	**3.8**	**–7**	**0**	**0.0**	**20:36**	....	....	....	....	....	....	....	....	....
2001-02	**Calgary**	**NHL**	**79**	**6**	**22**	**28**	**52**	**1**	**0**	**0**	**126**	**4.8**	**–8**	**0**	**0.0**	**21:10**	....	....	....	....	....	....	....	....	....
2002-03	**Calgary**	**NHL**	**81**	**6**	**20**	**26**	**28**	**3**	**0**	**0**	**143**	**4.2**	**–7**	**0**	**0.0**	**25:47**	....	....	....	....	....	....	....	....	....
2003-04	**Calgary**	**NHL**	**67**	**4**	**16**	**20**	**30**	**2**	**0**	**1**	**93**	**4.3**	**6**	**0**	**0.0**	**21:13**	**6**	**0**	**1**	**1**	**2**	**0**	**0**	**0**	**14:30**
2004-05	HIFK Helsinki	Finland	8	1	2	3	2	....	....	....	....	....	....	....	....	....	5	0	3	3	0	....	....	....	....
	NHL Totals		**289**	**19**	**74**	**93**	**140**	**7**	**0**	**1**	**442**	**4.3**		**0**	**0.0**	**22:21**	**6**	**0**	**1**	**1**	**2**	**0**	**0**	**0**	**14:30**

Signed as a free agent by **HIFK** (Finland), January 31, 2005. Traded to **Buffalo** by **Calgary** for Buffalo's 3rd round choice in 2006 Entry Draft, August 25, 2005.

LYNCH, Doug

(LIHNCH, DUHG) **ST.L.**

Defense. Shoots left. 6'3", 214 lbs. Born, North Vancouver, B.C., April 4, 1983. Edmonton's 2nd choice, 43rd overall, in 2001 Entry Draft.

			Regular Season														Playoffs								
Season	Club	League	GP	G	A	Pts	PIM	PP	SH	GW	S	%	+/-	TF	F%	Min	GP	G	A	Pts	PIM	PP	SH	GW	Min
1998-99	Port Coquitlam	BCAHA	45	47	48	95	120	....	....	....	....	....	....	....	....	....	....	....	....	....	....	....	....	....	....
	Red Deer Rebels	WHL	2	0	1	1	2	....	....	....	....	....	....	....	....	....	....	....	....	....	....	....	....	....	....
99-2000	Red Deer Rebels	WHL	65	9	5	14	57	....	....	....	....	....	....	....	....	....	4	0	0	0	5	....	....	....	....
2000-01	Red Deer Rebels	WHL	72	12	37	49	181	....	....	....	....	....	....	....	....	....	21	1	9	10	30	....	....	....	....
2001-02	Red Deer Rebels	WHL	71	21	27	48	202	....	....	....	....	....	....	....	....	....	22	5	4	9	12	....	....	....	....
2002-03	Red Deer Rebels	WHL	13	7	5	12	27	....	....	....	....	....	....	....	....	....	....	....	....	....	....	....	....	....	....
	Spokane Chiefs	WHL	42	6	12	18	129	....	....	....	....	....	....	....	....	....	4	1	0	1	16	....	....	....	....
2003-04	**Edmonton**	**NHL**	**2**	**0**	**0**	**0**	**0**	**0**	**0**	**0**	**2**	**0.0**	**0**	**0**	**0.0**	**10:16**	....	....	....	....	....	....	....	....	....
	Toronto	AHL	74	11	25	36	77	....	....	....	....	....	....	....	....	....	3	0	1	1	2	....	....	....	....
2004-05	Edmonton	AHL	74	1	13	14	109	....	....	....	....	....	....	....	....	....	....	....	....	....	....	....	....	....	....
	NHL Totals		**2**	**0**	**0**	**0**	**0**	**0**	**0**	**0**	**2**	**0.0**		**0**	**0.0**	**10:16**	....	....	....	....	....	....	....	....	....

AHL All-Rookie Team (2004)

Traded to **St. Louis** by **Edmonton** with Eric Brewer and Jeff Woywitka for Chris Pronger, August 2, 2005.

LYSAK, Brett

(LIGH-sak, BREHT)

Center. Shoots left. 6', 190 lbs. Born, Edmonton, Alta., December 30, 1980. Carolina's 2nd choice, 49th overall, in 1999 Entry Draft.

			Regular Season														Playoffs								
Season	Club	League	GP	G	A	Pts	PIM	PP	SH	GW	S	%	+/-	TF	F%	Min	GP	G	A	Pts	PIM	PP	SH	GW	Min
1994-95	St. Albert Sabres	AMBHL	STATISTICS NOT AVAILABLE																						
1995-96	St. Albert Raiders	AMHL	35	20	23	43	68	....	....	....	....	....	....	....	....	....	....	....	....	....	....	....	....	....	....
1996-97	Regina Pats	WHL	66	11	14	25	41	....	....	....	....	....	....	....	....	....	5	0	1	1	5	....	....	....	....
1997-98	Regina Pats	WHL	70	22	38	60	82	....	....	....	....	....	....	....	....	....	9	6	2	8	8	....	....	....	....
1998-99	Regina Pats	WHL	71	39	49	88	84	....	....	....	....	....	....	....	....	....	....	....	....	....	....	....	....	....	....
99-2000	Regina Pats	WHL	70	38	40	78	24	....	....	....	....	....	....	....	....	....	7	5	4	9	2	....	....	....	....
2000-01	Regina Pats	WHL	64	35	48	83	44	....	....	....	....	....	....	....	....	....	6	5	1	6	4	....	....	....	....
2001-02	Lowell	AHL	53	6	8	14	26	....	....	....	....	....	....	....	....	....	3	0	0	0	0	....	....	....	....
	Florida Everblades	ECHL	16	2	7	9	14	....	....	....	....	....	....	....	....	....	6	3	1	4	6	....	....	....	....
2002-03	Lowell	AHL	49	6	9	15	59	....	....	....	....	....	....	....	....	....	....	....	....	....	....	....	....	....	....
2003-04	**Carolina**	**NHL**	**2**	**0**	**0**	**0**	**2**	**0**	**0**	**0**	**0**	**0.0**	**0**	**1**	**0.0**	**3:24**	....	....	....	....	....	....	....	....	....
	Lowell	AHL	71	17	18	35	104	....	....	....	....	....	....	....	....	....	....	....	....	....	....	....	....	....	....
2004-05	Iserlohn Roosters	Germany	49	9	9	18	151	....	....	....	....	....	....	....	....	....	....	....	....	....	....	....	....	....	....
	NHL Totals		**2**	**0**	**0**	**0**	**2**	**0**	**0**	**0**	**0**	**0.0**		**1**	**0.0**	**3:24**	....	....	....	....	....	....	....	....	....

WHL East Second All-Star Team (1999) • Memorial Cup Tournament All-Star Team (2001)

Signed as a free agent by **Iserlohn** (Germany), September, 2004.

MacDONALD, Craig

(MAK-DAWN-uhld, KRAYG) **CGY.**

Left wing. Shoots left. 6'1", 195 lbs. Born, Antigonish, N.S., April 7, 1977. Hartford's 3rd choice, 88th overall, in 1996 Entry Draft.

			Regular Season														Playoffs								
Season	Club	League	GP	G	A	Pts	PIM	PP	SH	GW	S	%	+/-	TF	F%	Min	GP	G	A	Pts	PIM	PP	SH	GW	Min
1994-95	Lawrence	High-MA	30	25	52	77	10	....	....	....	....	....	....	....	....	....	....	....	....	....	....	....	....	....	....
1995-96	Harvard Crimson	ECAC	34	7	10	17	10	....	....	....	....	....	....	....	....	....	....	....	....	....	....	....	....	....	....
1996-97	Harvard Crimson	ECAC	32	6	10	16	20	....	....	....	....	....	....	....	....	....	....	....	....	....	....	....	....	....	....
1997-98	Canada	Nat-Tm	58	18	29	47	38	....	....	....	....	....	....	....	....	....	....	....	....	....	....	....	....	....	....
1998-99	**Carolina**	**NHL**	**11**	**0**	**0**	**0**	**0**	**0**	**0**	**0**	**5**	**0.0**	**0**	**2**	**100.0**	**2:29**	**1**	**0**	**0**	**0**	**0**	**0**	**0**	**0**	**2:46**
	New Haven	AHL	62	17	31	48	77	....	....	....	....	....	....	....	....	....	....	....	....	....	....	....	....	....	....
99-2000	Cincinnati	IHL	78	12	24	36	76	....	....	....	....	....	....	....	....	....	11	4	1	5	8	....	....	....	....
2000-01	Cincinnati	IHL	82	20	28	48	104	....	....	....	....	....	....	....	....	....	5	0	1	1	6	....	....	....	....
2001-02	**Carolina**	**NHL**	**12**	**1**	**1**	**2**	**0**	**0**	**0**	**0**	**15**	**6.7**	**–1**	**19**	**47.4**	**10:11**	**4**	**0**	**0**	**0**	**2**	**0**	**0**	**0**	**4:42**
	Lowell	AHL	64	19	22	41	61	....	....	....	....	....	....	....	....	....	....	....	....	....	....	....	....	....	....
2002-03	**Carolina**	**NHL**	**35**	**1**	**3**	**4**	**20**	**0**	**0**	**0**	**43**	**2.3**	**–3**	**72**	**55.6**	**9:21**	....	....	....	....	....	....	....	....	....
	Lowell	AHL	27	7	20	27	38	....	....	....	....	....	....	....	....	....	....	....	....	....	....	....	....	....	....
2003-04	**Florida**	**NHL**	**34**	**0**	**3**	**3**	**25**	**0**	**0**	**0**	**42**	**0.0**	**–5**	**398**	**45.7**	**12:31**	....	....	....	....	....	....	....	....	....
	San Antonio	AHL	2	0	0	0	4	....	....	....	....	....	....	....	....	....	....	....	....	....	....	....	....	....	....
	Boston	**NHL**	**18**	**0**	**3**	**3**	**8**	**0**	**0**	**0**	**17**	**0.0**	**0**	**155**	**47.1**	**8:42**	**1**	**0**	**0**	**0**	**0**	**0**	**0**	**0**	**2:11**
2004-05	Lowell	AHL	71	10	18	28	104	....	....	....	....	....	....	....	....	....	2	0	0	0	0	....	....	....	....
	NHL Totals		**110**	**2**	**10**	**12**	**53**	**0**	**0**	**0**	**122**	**1.6**		**646**	**47.4**	**9:38**	**6**	**0**	**0**	**0**	**2**	**0**	**0**	**0**	**3:58**

Rights transferred to **Carolina** after **Hartford** franchise relocated, June 25, 1997. Signed as a free agent by **Florida**, August 14, 2003. Claimed on waivers by **Boston** from **Florida**, January 20, 2004. Signed as a free agent by **Calgary**, August 11, 2005.

MacDONALD, Jason

(MAK-DAWN-uhld, JAY-suhn) **BOS.**

Right wing. Shoots right. 5'11", 210 lbs. Born, Charlottetown, P.E.I., April 1, 1974. Detroit's 5th choice, 142nd overall, in 1992 Entry Draft.

			Regular Season														Playoffs								
Season	Club	League	GP	G	A	Pts	PIM	PP	SH	GW	S	%	+/-	TF	F%	Min	GP	G	A	Pts	PIM	PP	SH	GW	Min
1989-90	Charlottown Abbies	MJrHL	29	11	29	40	206	....	....	....	....	....	....	....	....	....	....	....	....	....	....	....	....	....	....
1990-91	North Bay	OHL	57	12	15	27	126	....	....	....	....	....	....	....	....	....	10	3	3	6	15	....	....	....	....
1991-92	North Bay	OHL	17	5	8	13	50	....	....	....	....	....	....	....	....	....	....	....	....	....	....	....	....	....	....
	Owen Sound	OHL	42	17	19	36	129	....	....	....	....	....	....	....	....	....	5	0	3	3	16	....	....	....	....
1992-93	Owen Sound	OHL	56	46	43	89	197	....	....	....	....	....	....	....	....	....	8	6	5	11	28	....	....	....	....
1993-94	Owen Sound	OHL	66	55	61	116	177	....	....	....	....	....	....	....	....	....	9	7	11	18	36	....	....	....	....
	Adirondack	AHL	....	....	....	....	....	....	....	....	....	....	....	....	....	....	1	0	0	0	0	....	....	....	....
1994-95	Adirondack	AHL	68	14	21	35	238	....	....	....	....	....	....	....	....	....	4	0	0	0	2	....	....	....	....
1995-96	Adirondack	AHL	43	9	13	22	99	....	....	....	....	....	....	....	....	....	....	....	....	....	....	....	....	....	....
	Toledo Storm	ECHL	9	5	5	10	26	....	....	....	....	....	....	....	....	....	9	3	1	4	39	....	....	....	....
1996-97	Adirondack	AHL	1	0	0	0	2	....	....	....	....	....	....	....	....	....	....	....	....	....	....	....	....	....	....
	Fredericton	AHL	63	22	25	47	189	....	....	....	....	....	....	....	....	....	....	....	....	....	....	....	....	....	....
1997-98	Canada	Nat-Tm	51	15	20	35	133	....	....	....	....	....	....	....	....	....	....	....	....	....	....	....	....	....	....
	Saint John Flames	AHL	6	2	0	2	27	....	....	....	....	....	....	....	....	....	11	1	3	4	17	....	....	....	....
1998-99	Manitoba Moose	IHL	82	25	27	52	283	....	....	....	....	....	....	....	....	....	5	2	2	4	13	....	....	....	....
99-2000	Manitoba Moose	IHL	30	5	10	15	77	....	....	....	....	....	....	....	....	....	....	....	....	....	....	....	....	....	....
	Orlando	IHL	29	7	7	14	113	....	....	....	....	....	....	....	....	....	4	0	0	0	19	....	....	....	....
2000-01	Wilkes-Barre	AHL	74	17	16	33	290	....	....	....	....	....	....	....	....	....	17	1	3	4	*66	....	....	....	....
2001-02	Wilkes-Barre	AHL	57	8	13	21	330	....	....	....	....	....	....	....	....	....	....	....	....	....	....	....	....	....	....
2002-03	Wilkes-Barre	AHL	56	4	7	11	137	....	....	....	....	....	....	....	....	....	1	0	0	0	0	....	....	....	....

			Regular Season														Playoffs								
Season	Club	League	GP	G	A	Pts	PIM	PP	SH	GW	S	%	+/-	TF	F%	Min	GP	G	A	Pts	PIM	PP	SH	GW	Min
2003-04	Hartford	AHL	41	11	11	22	101	....	....	....	....	....	....	....	....	....	10	4	0	4	50	....	....	....	....
	NY Rangers	NHL	4	0	0	0	19	0	0	0	3	0.0	–1	0	0.0	8:11	....	....	....	....	....	....	....	....	....
2004-05	St. John's	AHL	29	4	8	12	152	....	....	....	....	....	....	....	....	....	5	2	0	2	27	....	....	....	....
	NHL Totals		4	0	0	0	19	0	0	0	3	0.0		0	0.0	8:11	....	....	....	....	....	....	....	....	....

OHL Second All-Star Team (1994)

Traded to **Montreal** by **Detroit** for cash, November 8, 1996. Signed as a free agent by **Pittsburgh**, July 18, 2001. Signed as a free agent by **Hartford** (AHL), September 9, 2003. Signed as a free agent by **NY Rangers**, December 11, 2003. Signed as a free agent by **Toronto**, July 29, 2004. Signed as a free agent by **Boston**, August 15, 2005.

MacINNIS, Al

(MAK-IHN-his, AL)

Defense. Shoots right. 6'2", 204 lbs. Born, Inverness, N.S., July 11, 1963. Calgary's 1st choice, 15th overall, in 1981 Entry Draft.

Season	Club	League	GP	G	A	Pts	PIM	PP	SH	GW	S	%	+/-	TF	F%	Min	GP	G	A	Pts	PIM	PP	SH	GW	Min
1979-80	Regina Blues	SJHL	59	20	28	48	110	....	....	....	....	....	....	....	....	....	....	....	....	....	....	....	....	....	....
1980-81	Kitchener Rangers	OMJHL	47	11	28	39	59	....	....	....	....	....	....	....	....	....	18	4	12	16	20	....	....	....	....
1981-82	Kitchener Rangers	OHL	59	25	50	75	145	....	....	....	....	....	....	....	....	....	15	5	10	15	44	....	....	....	....
	Calgary	NHL	2	0	0	0	0	0	0	0	2	0.0	0	....	....	....	....	....	....	....	....	....	....	....	....
1982-83	Kitchener Rangers	OHL	51	38	46	84	67	....	....	....	....	....	....	....	....	....	8	3	8	11	9	....	....	....	....
	Calgary	NHL	14	1	3	4	9	0	0	0	7	14.3	0	....	....	....	....	....	....	....	....	....	....	....	....
1983-84	Calgary	NHL	51	11	34	45	42	7	0	2	160	6.9	0	....	....	....	11	2	12	14	13	2	0	1	....
	Colorado Flames	CHL	19	5	14	19	22	....	....	....	....	....	....	....	....	....	....	....	....	....	....	....	....	....	....
1984-85	Calgary	NHL	67	14	52	66	75	8	0	0	259	5.4	7	....	....	....	4	1	2	3	8	1	0	0	....
1985-86	Calgary	NHL	77	11	57	68	76	4	0	0	241	4.6	38	....	....	....	21	4	*15	19	30	2	0	0	....
1986-87	Calgary	NHL	79	20	56	76	97	7	0	2	262	7.6	20	....	....	....	4	1	0	1	0	1	0	0	....
1987-88	Calgary	NHL	80	25	58	83	114	7	2	2	245	10.2	13	....	....	....	7	3	6	9	18	2	0	0	....
1988-89♦	Calgary	NHL	79	16	58	74	136	8	0	3	277	5.8	38	....	....	....	22	7	*24	*31	46	5	0	4	....
1989-90	Calgary	NHL	79	28	62	90	82	14	1	3	304	9.2	20	....	....	....	6	2	3	5	8	1	0	0	....
1990-91	Calgary	NHL	78	28	75	103	90	17	0	1	305	9.2	42	....	....	....	7	2	3	5	8	2	0	0	....
1991-92	Calgary	NHL	72	20	57	77	83	11	0	0	304	6.6	13	....	....	....	....	....	....	....	....	....	....	....	....
1992-93	Calgary	NHL	50	11	43	54	61	7	0	4	201	5.5	15	....	....	....	6	1	6	7	10	1	0	0	....
1993-94	Calgary	NHL	75	28	54	82	95	12	1	5	324	8.6	35	....	....	....	7	2	6	8	12	1	0	0	....
1994-95	St. Louis	NHL	32	8	20	28	43	2	0	0	110	7.3	19	....	....	....	7	1	5	6	10	0	0	0	....
1995-96	St. Louis	NHL	82	17	44	61	88	9	1	1	317	5.4	5	....	....	....	13	3	4	7	20	1	0	0	....
1996-97	St. Louis	NHL	72	13	30	43	65	6	1	1	296	4.4	2	....	....	....	6	1	2	3	4	1	0	0	....
1997-98	St. Louis	NHL	71	19	30	49	80	9	1	2	227	8.4	6	....	....	....	8	2	6	8	12	1	0	0	....
	Canada	Olympics	6	2	0	2	2	....	....	....	....	....	....	....	....	....	....	....	....	....	....	....	....	....	....
1998-99	St. Louis	NHL	82	20	42	62	70	11	1	2	314	6.4	33	0	0.0	29:07	13	4	8	12	20	2	0	0	35:14
99-2000	St. Louis	NHL	61	11	28	39	34	6	0	7	245	4.5	20	0	0.0	26:07	7	1	3	4	14	1	0	0	28:52
2000-01	St. Louis	NHL	59	12	42	54	52	6	1	3	218	5.5	23	0	0.0	26:32	15	2	8	10	18	2	0	0	30:46
2001-02	St. Louis	NHL	71	11	35	46	52	6	0	4	231	4.8	3	0	0.0	26:56	10	0	7	7	4	0	0	0	29:03
	Canada	Olympics	6	0	0	0	8	....	....	....	....	....	....	....	....	....	....	....	....	....	....	....	....	....	....
2002-03	St. Louis	NHL	80	16	52	68	61	9	1	2	299	5.4	22	2	100.0	26:55	3	0	1	1	0	0	0	0	12:41
2003-04	St. Louis	NHL	3	0	2	2	6	0	0	0	9	0.0	–1	0	0.0	24:59	....	....	....	....	....	....	....	....	....
2004-05			DID NOT PLAY																						
	NHL Totals		1416	340	934	1274	1511	166	10	44	5157	6.6		2	100.0	27:13	177	39	121	160	255	26	0	5	30:13

OHL First All-Star Team (1982, 1983) • Memorial Cup Tournament All-Star Team (1982) • NHL Second All-Star Team (1987, 1989, 1994) • Conn Smythe Trophy (1989) • NHL First All-Star Team (1990, 1991, 1999, 2003) • James Norris Memorial Trophy (1999)

Played in NHL All-Star Game (1985, 1988, 1990, 1991, 1992, 1994, 1996, 1997, 1998, 1999, 2000, 2003)

Traded to **St. Louis** by **Calgary** with Calgary's 4th round choice (Didier Tremblay) in 1997 Entry Draft for Phil Housley and St. Louis' 2nd round choices in 1996 (Steve Begin) and 1997 (John Tripp) Entry Drafts, July 4, 1994. • Missed majority of 2003-04 season recovering from eye injury suffered in game vs. Nashville, October 16, 2003.

MacKENZIE, Derek

(muh-KEHN-zee, DAIR-ihk) **ATL.**

Center. Shoots left. 5'11", 180 lbs. Born, Sudbury, Ont., June 11, 1981. Atlanta's 6th choice, 128th overall, in 1999 Entry Draft.

Season	Club	League	GP	G	A	Pts	PIM	PP	SH	GW	S	%	+/-	TF	F%	Min	GP	G	A	Pts	PIM	PP	SH	GW	Min
1996-97	Rayside-Balfour	NOJHA	40	23	32	55	40	....	....	....	....	....	....	....	....	....	....	....	....	....	....	....	....	....	....
1997-98	Sudbury Wolves	OHL	59	9	11	20	26	....	....	....	....	....	....	....	....	....	....	....	....	....	....	....	....	....	....
1998-99	Sudbury Wolves	OHL	68	22	65	87	74	....	....	....	....	....	....	....	....	....	4	2	4	6	2	....	....	....	....
99-2000	Sudbury Wolves	OHL	68	24	33	57	110	....	....	....	....	....	....	....	....	....	12	5	9	14	16	....	....	....	....
2000-01	Sudbury Wolves	OHL	62	40	49	89	89	....	....	....	....	....	....	....	....	....	12	6	8	14	16	....	....	....	....
2001-02	Atlanta	NHL	1	0	0	0	2	0	0	0	1	0.0	–1	16	56.3	13:51	....	....	....	....	....	....	....	....	....
	Chicago Wolves	AHL	68	13	12	25	80	....	....	....	....	....	....	....	....	....	25	4	2	6	20	....	....	....	....
2002-03	Chicago Wolves	AHL	80	14	18	32	97	....	....	....	....	....	....	....	....	....	9	0	0	0	4	....	....	....	....
2003-04	Atlanta	NHL	12	0	1	1	10	0	0	0	7	0.0	0	63	46.0	6:38	....	....	....	....	....	....	....	....	....
	Chicago Wolves	AHL	63	19	16	35	67	....	....	....	....	....	....	....	....	....	10	7	1	8	13	....	....	....	....
2004-05	Chicago Wolves	AHL	78	13	20	33	87	....	....	....	....	....	....	....	....	....	18	5	6	11	33	....	....	....	....
	NHL Totals		13	0	1	1	12	0	0	0	8	0.0		79	48.1	7:12	....	....	....	....	....	....	....	....	....

MacLEAN, Don

(mihk-LAYN, DAWN) **DET.**

Center. Shoots left. 6'2", 199 lbs. Born, Sydney, N.S., January 14, 1977. Los Angeles' 2nd choice, 33rd overall, in 1995 Entry Draft.

Season	Club	League	GP	G	A	Pts	PIM	PP	SH	GW	S	%	+/-	TF	F%	Min	GP	G	A	Pts	PIM	PP	SH	GW	Min
1992-93	Halifax Hawks	NSMHL	27	15	25	40	34	....	....	....	....	....	....	....	....	....	....	....	....	....	....	....	....	....	....
1993-94	Halifax Hawks	NSMHL	25	35	35	70	151	....	....	....	....	....	....	....	....	....	....	....	....	....	....	....	....	....	....
1994-95	Beauport	QMJHL	64	15	27	42	37	....	....	....	....	....	....	....	....	....	17	4	4	8	6	....	....	....	....
1995-96	Beauport	QMJHL	1	0	1	1	0	....	....	....	....	....	....	....	....	....	....	....	....	....	....	....	....	....	....
	Laval Titan	QMJHL	21	17	11	28	29	....	....	....	....	....	....	....	....	....	....	....	....	....	....	....	....	....	....
	Hull Olympiques	QMJHL	39	26	34	60	44	....	....	....	....	....	....	....	....	....	17	6	7	13	14	....	....	....	....
1996-97	Hull Olympiques	QMJHL	69	34	47	81	67	....	....	....	....	....	....	....	....	....	14	11	10	21	39	....	....	....	....
1997-98	Los Angeles	NHL	22	5	2	7	4	2	0	0	25	20.0	–1	....	....	....	....	....	....	....	....	....	....	....	....
	Fredericton	AHL	39	9	5	14	32	....	....	....	....	....	....	....	....	....	4	1	3	4	2	....	....	....	....
1998-99	Springfield	AHL	41	5	14	19	31	....	....	....	....	....	....	....	....	....	....	....	....	....	....	....	....	....	....
	Grand Rapids	IHL	28	6	13	19	8	....	....	....	....	....	....	....	....	....	....	....	....	....	....	....	....	....	....
99-2000	Lowell	AHL	40	11	17	28	18	....	....	....	....	....	....	....	....	....	....	....	....	....	....	....	....	....	....
	St. John's	AHL	21	14	12	26	8	....	....	....	....	....	....	....	....	....	....	....	....	....	....	....	....	....	....
2000-01	Toronto	NHL	3	0	1	1	2	0	0	0	2	0.0	–2	33	54.6	9:48	....	....	....	....	....	....	....	....	....
	St. John's	AHL	61	26	34	60	48	....	....	....	....	....	....	....	....	....	4	2	1	3	2	....	....	....	....
2001-02	St. John's	AHL	75	33	*54	*87	49	....	....	....	....	....	....	....	....	....	9	5	5	10	6	....	....	....	....
	Toronto	NHL	....	....	....	....	....	....	....	....	....	....	....	....	....	....	3	0	0	0	0	0	0	0	1:39
2002-03	Syracuse Crunch	AHL	17	9	9	18	6	....	....	....	....	....	....	....	....	....	....	....	....	....	....	....	....	....	....
2003-04	Columbus	NHL	4	1	0	1	0	0	0	0	10	10.0	–1	31	58.1	11:41	....	....	....	....	....	....	....	....	....
	Syracuse Crunch	AHL	77	27	41	68	45	....	....	....	....	....	....	....	....	....	7	0	3	3	4	....	....	....	....
2004-05	Blues Espoo	Finland	51	22	21	43	46	....	....	....	....	....	....	....	....	....	....	....	....	....	....	....	....	....	....
	NHL Totals		29	6	3	9	6	2	0	0	37	16.2		64	56.3	10:52	3	0	0	0	0	0	0	0	1:39

John P. Sollenberger Trophy (Leading Scorer – AHL) (2002)

Traded to **Toronto** by **Los Angeles** for Craig Charron, February 23, 2000. Signed as a free agent by **Columbus**, July 17, 2002. • Missed majority of 2002-03 season recovering from neck surgery, September 16, 2002. Signed as a free agent by **Blues** (Finland), July 2, 2004. Signed as a free agent by **Detroit**, August 24, 2005.

MacMILLAN, Jeff

(muhk-MIHL-uhn, JEHF) **CBJ**

Defense. Shoots left. 6'3", 210 lbs. Born, Durham, Ont., March 30, 1979. Dallas' 8th choice, 215th overall, in 1999 Entry Draft.

Season	Club	League	GP	G	A	Pts	PIM	PP	SH	GW	S	%	+/-	TF	F%	Min	GP	G	A	Pts	PIM	PP	SH	GW	Min
1995-96	Hanover Barons	OHA-C	29	7	13	20	26	....	....	....	....	....	....	....	....	....	....	....	....	....	....	....	....	....	....
1996-97	Oshawa Generals	OHL	39	0	4	4	15	....	....	....	....	....	....	....	....	....	15	0	0	0	4	....	....	....	....
1997-98	Oshawa Generals	OHL	64	3	12	15	72	....	....	....	....	....	....	....	....	....	7	0	3	3	11	....	....	....	....
1998-99	Oshawa Generals	OHL	65	3	18	21	109	....	....	....	....	....	....	....	....	....	15	3	6	9	28	....	....	....	....
99-2000	Michigan	IHL	53	0	3	3	54	....	....	....	....	....	....	....	....	....	....	....	....	....	....	....	....	....	....
	Fort Wayne	UHL	7	1	1	2	25	....	....	....	....	....	....	....	....	....	9	0	2	2	10	....	....	....	....
2000-01	Utah Grizzlies	IHL	81	5	15	20	105	....	....	....	....	....	....	....	....	....	....	....	....	....	....	....	....	....	....
2001-02	Utah Grizzlies	AHL	77	6	9	15	146	....	....	....	....	....	....	....	....	....	5	1	0	1	17	....	....	....	....
2002-03	Utah Grizzlies	AHL	78	8	7	15	132	....	....	....	....	....	....	....	....	....	2	0	0	0	6	....	....	....	....

			Regular Season														Playoffs								
Season	Club	League	GP	G	A	Pts	PIM	PP	SH	GW	S	%	+/-	TF	F%	Min	GP	G	A	Pts	PIM	PP	SH	GW	Min
2003-04	**Dallas**	**NHL**	4	0	0	0	0	0	0	0	3	0.0	−2	0	0.0	8:19	....	....	....	....	....	....	....	....	....
	Utah Grizzlies	AHL	73	4	6	10	108	....	....	....	....	....	....	....	....	....	....	....	....	....	....	....	....	....	....
2004-05	Hartford	AHL	71	2	5	7	136	....	....	....	....	....	....	....	....	....	6	0	0	0	4	....	....	....	....
	NHL Totals		**4**	**0**	**0**	**0**	**0**	**0**	**0**	**0**	**3**	**0.0**		**0**	**0.0**	**8:19**	....	....	....	....	....	....	....	....	....

Signed as a free agent by **NY Rangers**, July 22, 2004. Signed as a free agent by **Columbus**, August 12, 2005.

MacNEIL, Ian

(muhk-NEEL, EE-an)

Center. Shoots left. 6'2", 190 lbs. Born, Halifax, N.S., April 27, 1977. Hartford's 3rd choice, 85th overall, in 1995 Entry Draft.

Season	Club	League	GP	G	A	Pts	PIM	PP	SH	GW	S	%	+/-	TF	F%	Min	GP	G	A	Pts	PIM	PP	SH	GW	Min
1993-94	Whitby Lions	OMHA	50	30	22	52	102	....	....	....	....	....	....	....	....	....	....	....	....	....	....	....	....	....	....
1994-95	Oshawa Generals	OHL	60	7	21	28	62	....	....	....	....	....	....	....	....	....	7	0	2	2	0	....	....	....	....
1995-96	Oshawa Generals	OHL	49	15	17	32	54	....	....	....	....	....	....	....	....	....	5	1	2	3	8	....	....	....	....
1996-97	Oshawa Generals	OHL	64	23	20	43	96	....	....	....	....	....	....	....	....	....	18	2	3	5	37	....	....	....	....
1997-98	New Haven	AHL	68	12	21	33	67	....	....	....	....	....	....	....	....	....	3	1	0	1	10	....	....	....	....
1998-99	New Haven	AHL	47	6	4	10	62	....	....	....	....	....	....	....	....	....	....	....	....	....	....	....	....	....	....
99-2000	Cincinnati	IHL	81	19	18	37	100	....	....	....	....	....	....	....	....	....	11	3	2	5	25	....	....	....	....
2000-01	Cincinnati	IHL	82	17	22	39	139	....	....	....	....	....	....	....	....	....	5	0	1	1	4	....	....	....	....
2001-02	Lowell	AHL	79	14	20	34	128	....	....	....	....	....	....	....	....	....	2	0	1	1	4	....	....	....	....
2002-03	**Philadelphia**	**NHL**	2	0	0	0	0	0	0	0	2	0.0	1	0	0.0	10:08	....	....	....	....	....	....	....	....	....
	Philadelphia	AHL	71	10	13	23	132	....	....	....	....	....	....	....	....	....	....	....	....	....	....	....	....	....	....
2003-04	Philadelphia	AHL	71	13	15	28	151	....	....	....	....	....	....	....	....	....	12	2	6	8	34	....	....	....	....
2004-05	Schwenningen	German-2	48	21	31	52	175	....	....	....	....	....	....	....	....	....	7	2	2	4	12	....	....	....	....
	NHL Totals		**2**	**0**	**0**	**0**	**0**	**0**	**0**	**0**	**2**	**0.0**		**0**	**0.0**	**10:08**	....	....	....	....	....	....	....	....	....

Rights transferred to **Carolina** after **Hartford** franchise relocated, June 25, 1997. Signed as a free agent by **Philadelphia**, July 2, 2002. Signed as a free agent by **Schwenningen** (German-2), September 8, 2004.

MADDEN, John

(MA-dehn, JAWN) **N.J.**

Center. Shoots left. 5'11", 190 lbs. Born, Barrie, Ont., May 4, 1973.

Season	Club	League	GP	G	A	Pts	PIM	PP	SH	GW	S	%	+/-	TF	F%	Min	GP	G	A	Pts	PIM	PP	SH	GW	Min
1989-90	Alliston Hornets	OHA-C	31	24	25	49	26	....	....	....	....	....	....	....	....	....	....	....	....	....	....	....	....	....	....
1990-91	Alliston Hornets	OHA-C	14	15	21	36	10	....	....	....	....	....	....	....	....	....	....	....	....	....	....	....	....	....	....
	Barrie Colts	OHA-B	1	0	0	0	0	....	....	....	....	....	....	....	....	....	....	....	....	....	....	....	....	....	....
1991-92	Barrie Colts	OHA-B	42	50	54	104	46	....	....	....	....	....	....	....	....	....	13	10	9	19	14	....	....	....	....
1992-93	Barrie Colts	COJHL	43	49	75	124	62	....	....	....	....	....	....	....	....	....	....	....	....	....	....	....	....	....	....
1993-94	U. of Michigan	CCHA	36	6	11	17	14	....	....	....	....	....	....	....	....	....	....	....	....	....	....	....	....	....	....
1994-95	U. of Michigan	CCHA	39	21	22	43	8	....	....	....	....	....	....	....	....	....	....	....	....	....	....	....	....	....	....
1995-96	U. of Michigan	CCHA	43	27	30	57	45	....	....	....	....	....	....	....	....	....	....	....	....	....	....	....	....	....	....
1996-97	U. of Michigan	CCHA	42	26	37	63	56	....	....	....	....	....	....	....	....	....	....	....	....	....	....	....	....	....	....
1997-98	Albany River Rats	AHL	74	20	36	56	40	....	....	....	....	....	....	....	....	....	13	3	13	16	14	....	....	....	....
1998-99	**New Jersey**	**NHL**	4	0	1	1	0	0	0	0	4	0.0	−2	0	0.0	9:13	....	....	....	....	....	....	....	....	....
	Albany River Rats	AHL	75	38	60	98	44	....	....	....	....	....	....	....	....	....	5	2	2	4	6	....	....	....	....
99-2000♦	**New Jersey**	**NHL**	74	16	9	25	6	0	6	3	115	13.9	7	770	47.5	11:40	20	3	4	7	0	0	1	2	15:30
2000-01	**New Jersey**	**NHL**	80	23	15	38	12	0	3	4	163	14.1	24	974	46.6	15:35	25	4	3	7	6	0	0	0	15:15
2001-02	**New Jersey**	**NHL**	82	15	8	23	25	0	0	2	170	8.8	6	1001	47.0	15:36	6	0	0	0	0	0	0	0	17:25
2002-03♦	**New Jersey**	**NHL**	80	19	22	41	26	2	2	3	207	9.2	13	1502	50.9	18:18	24	6	10	16	2	2	1	1	19:38
2003-04	**New Jersey**	**NHL**	80	12	23	35	22	1	1	1	210	5.7	7	1377	53.3	17:17	5	0	0	0	0	0	0	0	14:51
2004-05	HIFK Helsinki	Finland	3	0	0	0	0	....	....	....	....	....	....	....	....	....	....	....	....	....	....	....	....	....	....
	NHL Totals		**400**	**85**	**78**	**163**	**91**	**3**	**12**	**13**	**869**	**9.8**		**5624**	**49.6**	**15:41**	**80**	**13**	**17**	**30**	**8**	**2**	**2**	**3**	**16:46**

CCHA First All-Star Team (1997) • NCAA West First All-American Team (1997) • Frank J. Selke Trophy (2001)
Signed as a free agent by **New Jersey**, June 26, 1997. Signed as a free agent by **HIFK** (Finland), November 29, 2004.

MAIR, Adam

(MAIR, A-duhm) **BUF.**

Center. Shoots right. 6'2", 208 lbs. Born, Hamilton, Ont., February 15, 1979. Toronto's 2nd choice, 84th overall, in 1997 Entry Draft.

Season	Club	League	GP	G	A	Pts	PIM	PP	SH	GW	S	%	+/-	TF	F%	Min	GP	G	A	Pts	PIM	PP	SH	GW	Min
1994-95	Ohsweken	OHA-B	39	21	23	44	91	....	....	....	....	....	....	....	....	....	....	....	....	....	....	....	....	....	....
1995-96	Owen Sound	OHL	62	12	15	27	63	....	....	....	....	....	....	....	....	....	6	0	0	0	2	....	....	....	....
1996-97	Owen Sound	OHL	65	16	35	51	113	....	....	....	....	....	....	....	....	....	4	1	0	1	2	....	....	....	....
1997-98	Owen Sound	OHL	56	25	27	52	179	....	....	....	....	....	....	....	....	....	11	6	3	9	31	....	....	....	....
1998-99	Owen Sound	OHL	43	23	41	64	109	....	....	....	....	....	....	....	....	....	16	10	10	20	*47	....	....	....	....
	Toronto	**NHL**	....	....	....	....	....	....	....	....	....	....	....	....	....	....	5	1	0	1	14	0	0	0	5:37
	St. John's	AHL	....	....	....	....	....	....	....	....	....	....	....	....	....	....	3	1	0	1	6	....	....	....	....
99-2000	**Toronto**	**NHL**	8	1	0	1	6	0	0	0	7	14.3	−1	9	33.3	11:33	5	0	0	0	8	0	0	0	10:15
	St. John's	AHL	66	22	27	49	124	....	....	....	....	....	....	....	....	....	....	....	....	....	....	....	....	....	....
2000-01	**Toronto**	**NHL**	16	0	2	2	14	0	0	0	17	0.0	3	56	51.8	9:00	....	....	....	....	....	....	....	....	....
	St. John's	AHL	47	18	27	45	69	....	....	....	....	....	....	....	....	....	....	....	....	....	....	....	....	....	....
	Los Angeles	**NHL**	10	0	0	0	6	0	0	0	5	0.0	−3	21	61.9	6:14	....	....	....	....	....	....	....	....	....
2001-02	**Los Angeles**	**NHL**	18	1	1	2	57	0	0	0	10	10.0	1	31	58.1	7:11	....	....	....	....	....	....	....	....	....
	Manchester	AHL	27	10	9	19	48	....	....	....	....	....	....	....	....	....	5	5	1	6	10	....	....	....	....
2002-03	**Buffalo**	**NHL**	79	6	11	17	146	0	1	1	83	7.2	−4	572	51.2	10:37	....	....	....	....	....	....	....	....	....
2003-04	**Buffalo**	**NHL**	81	6	14	20	146	1	0	1	82	7.3	−3	340	45.9	9:38	....	....	....	....	....	....	....	....	....
2004-05			DID NOT PLAY																						
	NHL Totals		**212**	**14**	**28**	**42**	**375**	**1**	**1**	**2**	**204**	**6.9**		**1029**	**49.8**	**9:39**	**10**	**1**	**0**	**1**	**22**	**0**	**0**	**0**	**7:56**

Traded to **Los Angeles** by **Toronto** with Toronto's 2nd round choice (Mike Cammalleri) in 2001 Entry Draft for Aki Berg, March 13, 2001. Traded to **Buffalo** by **Los Angeles** with Los Angeles' 5th round choice (Thomas Morrow) in 2003 Entry Draft for Erik Rasmussen, July 24, 2002.

MAJESKY, Ivan

(migh-EHV-skee, ee-VAHN) **WSH.**

Defense. Shoots right. 6'5", 230 lbs. Born, Banska Bystrica, Czech., September 2, 1976. Florida's 12th choice, 267th overall, in 2001 Entry Draft.

Season	Club	League	GP	G	A	Pts	PIM	PP	SH	GW	S	%	+/-	TF	F%	Min	GP	G	A	Pts	PIM	PP	SH	GW	Min
1995-96	B. Bystrica	Slovakia	17	0	0	0	18	....	....	....	....	....	....	....	....	....	....	....	....	....	....	....	....	....	....
1996-97	B. Bystrica	Slovakia	49	2	4	6		....	....	....	....	....	....	....	....	....	....	....	....	....	....	....	....	....	....
1997-98	B. Bystrica	Slovak-2	43	6	7	13	50	....	....	....	....	....	....	....	....	....	....	....	....	....	....	....	....	....	....
1998-99	B. Bystrica	Slovakia	48	7	7	14	68	....	....	....	....	....	....	....	....	....	....	....	....	....	....	....	....	....	....
	HKm Zvolen	Slovakia	....	....	....	....	....	....	....	....	....	....	....	....	....	....	6	0	2	2	2	....	....	....	....
99-2000	HKm Zvolen	Slovakia	51	7	9	16	68	....	....	....	....	....	....	....	....	....	10	0	4	4	2	....	....	....	....
2000-01	Ilves Tampere	Finland	54	2	14	16	99	....	....	....	....	....	....	....	....	....	9	0	1	1	6	....	....	....	....
2001-02	Ilves Tampere	Finland	44	6	6	12	84	....	....	....	....	....	....	....	....	....	....	....	....	....	....	....	....	....	....
	Slovakia	Olympics	4	0	1	1	4	....	....	....	....	....	....	....	....	....	....	....	....	....	....	....	....	....	....
2002-03	**Florida**	**NHL**	82	4	8	12	92	0	0	2	52	7.7	−18	0	0.0	20:53	....	....	....	....	....	....	....	....	....
2003-04	**Atlanta**	**NHL**	63	3	7	10	76	0	0	0	35	8.6	−7	2	50.0	14:28	....	....	....	....	....	....	....	....	....
2004-05	HC Sparta Praha	CzRep	28	2	6	8	40	....	....	....	....	....	....	....	....	....	5	2	1	3	6	....	....	....	....
	NHL Totals		**145**	**7**	**15**	**22**	**168**	**0**	**0**	**2**	**87**	**8.0**		**2**	**50.0**	**18:06**	....	....	....	....	....	....	....	....	....

Traded to **Atlanta** by **Florida** for Atlanta's 2nd round choice (Kamil Kreps) in 2003 Entry Draft, June 21, 2003. Signed as a free agent by **Sparta** (CzRep), November 12, 2004. Signed as a free agent by **Washington**, August 10, 2005.

MALAKHOV, Vladimir

(mah-LAH-kahf, vla-DIH-meer) **N.J.**

Defense. Shoots left. 6'4", 230 lbs. Born, Sverdlovsk, USSR, August 30, 1968. NY Islanders' 12th choice, 191st overall, in 1989 Entry Draft.

Season	Club	League	GP	G	A	Pts	PIM	PP	SH	GW	S	%	+/-	TF	F%	Min	GP	G	A	Pts	PIM	PP	SH	GW	Min
1986-87	Spartak Moscow	USSR	22	0	1	1	12	....	....	....	....	....	....	....	....	....	....	....	....	....	....	....	....	....	....
1987-88	Spartak Moscow	USSR	28	2	2	4	26	....	....	....	....	....	....	....	....	....	....	....	....	....	....	....	....	....	....
1988-89	CSKA Moscow	USSR	34	6	2	8	16	....	....	....	....	....	....	....	....	....	....	....	....	....	....	....	....	....	....
1989-90	CSKA Moscow	USSR	48	2	10	12	34	....	....	....	....	....	....	....	....	....	....	....	....	....	....	....	....	....	....
1990-91	CSKA Moscow	USSR	46	5	13	18	22	....	....	....	....	....	....	....	....	....	....	....	....	....	....	....	....	....	....
1991-92	CSKA Moscow	CIS	40	1	9	10	12	....	....	....	....	....	....	....	....	....	....	....	....	....	....	....	....	....	....
	Russia	Olympics	8	3	0	3	4	....	....	....	....	....	....	....	....	....	....	....	....	....	....	....	....	....	....
1992-93	**NY Islanders**	**NHL**	64	14	38	52	59	7	0	0	178	7.9	14	....	....	....	17	3	6	9	12	0	0	0	....
	Capital District	AHL	3	2	1	3	11	....	....	....	....	....	....	....	....	....	....	....	....	....	....	....	....	....	....
1993-94	**NY Islanders**	**NHL**	76	10	47	57	80	4	0	2	235	4.3	29	....	....	....	4	0	0	0	6	0	0	0	....
1994-95	**NY Islanders**	**NHL**	26	3	13	16	32	1	0	0	61	4.9	−1	....	....	....	....	....	....	....	....	....	....	....	....
	Montreal	**NHL**	14	1	4	5	14	0	0	0	30	3.3	−2	....	....	....	....	....	....	....	....	....	....	....	....

			Regular Season														Playoffs								
Season	Club	League	GP	G	A	Pts	PIM	PP	SH	GW	S	%	+/-	TF	F%	Min	GP	G	A	Pts	PIM	PP	SH	GW	Min
1995-96	Montreal	NHL	61	5	23	28	79	2	0	0	122	4.1	7	....	....	....	....	....	....	....	....	....	....	....	....
1996-97	Montreal	NHL	65	10	20	30	43	5	0	1	177	5.6	3	....	....	....	5	0	0	0	6	0	0	0	....
1997-98	Montreal	NHL	74	13	31	44	70	8	0	2	166	7.8	16	....	....	....	9	3	4	7	10	2	0	0	....
1998-99	Montreal	NHL	62	13	21	34	77	8	0	3	143	9.1	−7	0	0.0	23:29	....	....	....	....	....	....	....	....	....
99-2000	Montreal	NHL	7	0	0	0	4	0	0	0	7	0.0	0	0	0.0	21:20	....	....	....	....	....	....	....	....	....
	♦ New Jersey	NHL	17	1	4	5	19	1	0	1	11	9.1	1	0	0.0	20:18	23	1	4	5	18	1	0	0	19:31
2000-01	NY Rangers	NHL	3	0	2	2	4	0	0	0	6	0.0	0	0	0.0	19:07	....	....	....	....	....	....	....	....	....
2001-02	NY Rangers	NHL	81	6	22	28	83	1	0	0	145	4.1	10	1	100.0	22:48	....	....	....	....	....	....	....	....	....
	Russia	Olympics	6	1	3	4	4	....	....	....	....	....	....	....	....	....	....	....	....	....	....	....	....	....	....
2002-03	NY Rangers	NHL	71	3	14	17	52	1	0	0	131	2.3	−7	0	0.0	21:24	....	....	....	....	....	....	....	....	....
2003-04	NY Rangers	NHL	56	3	15	18	53	1	0	0	83	3.6	−5	1	100.0	19:37	....	....	....	....	....	....	....	....	....
	Philadelphia	NHL	6	0	1	1	2	0	0	0	12	0.0	−1	0	0.0	22:57	17	1	5	6	12	0	0	0	24:56
2004-05		DID NOT PLAY																							
	NHL Totals		683	82	255	337	671	39	0	9	1507	5.4		2	100.0	21:49	75	8	19	27	64	3	0	0	21:49

NHL All-Rookie Team (1993)

Traded to **Montreal** by **NY Islanders** with Pierre Turgeon for Kirk Muller, Mathieu Schneider and Craig Darby, April 5, 1995. • Missed majority of 1999-2000 season recovering from knee injury suffered in exhibition game vs. Boston, September 27, 1999. Traded to **New Jersey** by **Montreal** for Sheldon Souray, Josh DeWolf and New Jersey's 2nd round choice (later traded to Washington – later traded to Tampa Bay – Tampa Bay selected Andreas Holmqvist) in 2001 Entry Draft, March 1, 2000. Signed as a free agent by **NY Rangers**, July 10, 2000. • Missed majority of 2000-01 season recovering from knee injury suffered in game vs. Montreal, November 11, 2000. Traded to **Philadelphia** by **NY Rangers** for Rick Kozak and Philadelphia's 2nd round choice (later traded to Atlanta - Atlanta selected Ondrej Pavelec) in 2005 Entry Draft, March 8, 2004. Signed as a free agent by **New Jersey**, August 4, 2005.

MALEC, Tomas

(MA-lehts, TAW-mahsh) **OTT.**

Defense. Shoots left. 6'2", 193 lbs. Born, Skalica, Czech., May 13, 1982. Florida's 4th choice, 64th overall, in 2001 Entry Draft.

Season	Club	League	GP	G	A	Pts	PIM	PP	SH	GW	S	%	+/-	TF	F%	Min	GP	G	A	Pts	PIM	PP	SH	GW	Min
99-2000	HK 36 Skalica Jr.	Slovak-Jr.	46	6	5	11	150	....	....	....	....	....	....	....	....	....	....	....	....	....	....	....	....	....	....
2000-01	Rimouski Oceanic	QMJHL	64	13	50	63	198	....	....	....	....	....	....	....	....	....	11	0	11	11	26	....	....	....	....
2001-02	Rimouski Oceanic	QMJHL	51	14	32	46	164	....	....	....	....	....	....	....	....	....	7	3	1	4	10	....	....	....	....
	Lowell	AHL	....	....	....	....	....	....	....	....	....	....	....	....	....	....	4	0	0	0	4	....	....	....	....
2002-03	Carolina	NHL	41	0	2	2	43	0	0	0	30	0.0	−5	1	100.0	11:13	....	....	....	....	....	....	....	....	....
	Lowell	AHL	30	0	4	4	50	....	....	....	....	....	....	....	....	....	....	....	....	....	....	....	....	....	....
2003-04	Carolina	NHL	2	0	0	0	2	0	0	0	1	0.0	−1	0	0.0	9:32	....	....	....	....	....	....	....	....	....
	Lowell	AHL	74	7	13	20	101	....	....	....	....	....	....	....	....	....	....	....	....	....	....	....	....	....	....
2004-05	Cincinnati	AHL	66	4	14	18	104	....	....	....	....	....	....	....	....	....	6	0	2	2	10	....	....	....	....
	NHL Totals		43	0	2	2	45	0	0	0	31	0.0		1	100.0	11:09	....	....	....	....	....	....	....	....	....

Traded to **Carolina** by **Florida** with Bret Hedican and Kevyn Adams for Sandis Ozolinsh and Byron Ritchie, January 16, 2002. Traded to **Anaheim** by **Carolina** with Carolina's 3rd round choice (Kyle Klubertanz) in 2004 Entry Draft for Martin Gerber, June 18, 2004. Signed as a free agent by **Ottawa**, August 19, 2005.

MALHOTRA, Manny

(mal-HOH-truh, MAHN-ee) **CBJ**

Center. Shoots left. 6'2", 215 lbs. Born, Mississauga, Ont., May 18, 1980. NY Rangers' 1st choice, 7th overall, in 1998 Entry Draft.

Season	Club	League	GP	G	A	Pts	PIM	PP	SH	GW	S	%	+/-	TF	F%	Min	GP	G	A	Pts	PIM	PP	SH	GW	Min
1995-96	Mississauga Reps	MTHL	54	27	44	71	62	....	....	....	....	....	....	....	....	....	....	....	....	....	....	....	....	....	....
1996-97	Guelph Storm	OHL	61	16	28	44	26	....	....	....	....	....	....	....	....	....	18	7	7	14	11	....	....	....	....
1997-98	Guelph Storm	OHL	57	16	35	51	29	....	....	....	....	....	....	....	....	....	12	7	6	13	8	....	....	....	....
1998-99	NY Rangers	NHL	73	8	8	16	13	1	0	2	61	13.1	−2	588	43.9	8:36	....	....	....	....	....	....	....	....	....
99-2000	NY Rangers	NHL	27	0	0	0	4	0	0	0	18	0.0	−6	132	44.7	6:42	....	....	....	....	....	....	....	....	....
	Guelph Storm	OHL	5	2	2	4	4	....	....	....	....	....	....	....	....	....	6	0	2	2	4	....	....	....	....
	Hartford	AHL	12	1	5	6	2	....	....	....	....	....	....	....	....	....	23	1	2	3	10	....	....	....	....
2000-01	NY Rangers	NHL	50	4	8	12	31	0	0	2	46	8.7	−10	248	44.4	9:03	....	....	....	....	....	....	....	....	....
	Hartford	AHL	28	5	6	11	69	....	....	....	....	....	....	....	....	....	5	0	0	0	0	....	....	....	....
2001-02	NY Rangers	NHL	56	7	6	13	42	0	1	1	41	17.1	−1	310	42.9	10:14	....	....	....	....	....	....	....	....	....
	Dallas	NHL	16	1	0	1	5	0	0	0	19	5.3	−3	121	48.8	10:37	....	....	....	....	....	....	....	....	....
2002-03	Dallas	NHL	59	3	7	10	42	0	0	1	62	4.8	−2	447	47.0	9:22	5	1	0	1	0	0	0	0	8:13
2003-04	Dallas	NHL	9	0	0	0	4	0	0	0	4	0.0	−2	13	61.5	7:48	....	....	....	....	....	....	....	....	....
	Columbus	NHL	56	12	13	25	24	1	0	2	103	11.7	−5	840	53.8	14:47	....	....	....	....	....	....	....	....	....
2004-05	Ljubljana	Slovenia	13	6	7	13	20	....	....	....	....	....	....	....	....	....	....	....	....	....	....	....	....	....	....
	Ljubljana	Interliga	13	7	7	14	16	....	....	....	....	....	....	....	....	....	....	....	....	....	....	....	....	....	....
	HV 71 Jonkoping	Sweden	20	5	2	7	16	....	....	....	....	....	....	....	....	....	....	....	....	....	....	....	....	....	....
	NHL Totals		346	35	42	77	165	2	1	8	354	9.9		2699	47.8	9:59	5	1	0	1	0	0	0	0	8:13

Memorial Cup Tournament All-Star Team (1998) • George Parsons Trophy (Memorial Cup Tournament Most Sportsmanlike Player) (1998)

Traded to **Dallas** by **NY Rangers** with Barrett Heisten for Martin Rucinsky and Roman Lyashenko, March 12, 2002. Claimed on waivers by **Columbus** from **Dallas**, November 21, 2003. Signed as a free agent by **Ljubljana** (Slovenia), October 8, 2004. Signed as a free agent by **HV 71** (Sweden), December 20, 2004.

MALIK, Marek

(MAW-leck, MAIR-ehk) **NYR**

Defense. Shoots left. 6'5", 215 lbs. Born, Ostrava, Czech., June 24, 1975. Hartford's 2nd choice, 72nd overall, in 1993 Entry Draft.

Season	Club	League	GP	G	A	Pts	PIM	PP	SH	GW	S	%	+/-	TF	F%	Min	GP	G	A	Pts	PIM	PP	SH	GW	Min
1992-93	TJ Vitkovice Jr.	Czech-Jr.	20	5	10	15	16	....	....	....	....	....	....	....	....	....	....	....	....	....	....	....	....	....	....
1993-94	HC Vitkovice	CzRep	38	3	3	6	0	....	....	....	....	....	....	....	....	....	3	0	1	1	0	....	....	....	....
1994-95	Springfield	AHL	58	11	30	41	91	....	....	....	....	....	....	....	....	....	....	....	....	....	....	....	....	....	....
	Hartford	NHL	1	0	1	1	0	0	0	0	0	0.0	1	....	....	....	....	....	....	....	....	....	....	....	....
1995-96	Hartford	NHL	7	0	0	0	4	0	0	0	2	0.0	−3	....	....	....	....	....	....	....	....	....	....	....	....
	Springfield	AHL	68	8	14	22	135	....	....	....	....	....	....	....	....	....	8	1	3	4	20	....	....	....	....
1996-97	Hartford	NHL	47	1	5	6	50	0	0	1	33	3.0	5	....	....	....	....	....	....	....	....	....	....	....	....
	Springfield	AHL	3	0	3	3	4	....	....	....	....	....	....	....	....	....	....	....	....	....	....	....	....	....	....
1997-98	Malmo	Sweden	37	1	5	6	21	....	....	....	....	....	....	....	....	....	....	....	....	....	....	....	....	....	....
1998-99	HC Vitkovice	CzRep	1	1	0	1	6	....	....	....	....	....	....	....	....	....	....	....	....	....	....	....	....	....	....
	Carolina	NHL	52	2	9	11	36	1	0	0	36	5.6	−6	0	0.0	21:14	4	0	0	0	4	0	0	0	11:26
	New Haven	AHL	21	2	8	10	28	....	....	....	....	....	....	....	....	....	....	....	....	....	....	....	....	....	....
99-2000	Carolina	NHL	57	4	10	14	63	0	0	1	57	7.0	13	0	0.0	18:00	....	....	....	....	....	....	....	....	....
2000-01	Carolina	NHL	61	6	14	20	34	1	0	1	72	8.3	−4	0	0.0	19:36	3	0	0	0	6	0	0	0	19:37
2001-02	Carolina	NHL	82	4	19	23	88	0	0	0	91	4.4	8	0	0.0	20:29	23	0	3	3	18	0	0	0	18:09
2002-03	Carolina	NHL	10	0	2	2	16	0	0	0	9	0.0	−3	0	0.0	17:02	....	....	....	....	....	....	....	....	....
	Vancouver	NHL	69	7	11	18	52	1	1	2	68	10.3	23	1	0.0	18:06	14	1	1	2	10	1	0	0	16:06
2003-04	Vancouver	NHL	78	3	16	19	45	0	0	0	61	4.9	35	1	0.0	18:05	7	0	0	0	10	0	0	0	20:03
2004-05	Vitkovice	CzRep	42	1	9	10	50	....	....	....	....	....	....	....	....	....	7	0	0	0	37	....	....	....	....
	NHL Totals		464	27	87	114	388	3	1	5	429	6.3		2	0.0	19:09	51	1	4	5	48	1	0	0	17:24

Transferred to **Carolina** after **Hartford** franchise relocated, June 25, 1997. Traded to **Vancouver** by **Carolina** with Darren Langdon for Jan Hlavac and Harold Druken, November 1, 2002. Signed as a free agent by **Vitkovice** (CzRep), September 17, 2004. Signed as a free agent by **NY Rangers**, August 2, 2005.

MALONE, Ryan

(MA-lohn, RIGH-yan) **PIT.**

Left wing. Shoots left. 6'4", 216 lbs. Born, Pittsburgh, PA, December 1, 1979. Pittsburgh's 5th choice, 115th overall, in 1999 Entry Draft.

Season	Club	League	GP	G	A	Pts	PIM	PP	SH	GW	S	%	+/-	TF	F%	Min	GP	G	A	Pts	PIM	PP	SH	GW	Min
1997-98	Shat.-St. Mary's	High-MN	50	41	44	85	69	....	....	....	....	....	....	....	....	....	....	....	....	....	....	....	....	....	....
1998-99	Omaha Lancers	USHL	51	14	22	36	81	....	....	....	....	....	....	....	....	....	12	2	4	6	23	....	....	....	....
99-2000	St. Cloud State	WCHA	38	9	21	30	68	....	....	....	....	....	....	....	....	....	....	....	....	....	....	....	....	....	....
2000-01	St. Cloud State	WCHA	36	7	18	25	52	....	....	....	....	....	....	....	....	....	....	....	....	....	....	....	....	....	....
2001-02	St. Cloud State	WCHA	41	24	25	49	76	....	....	....	....	....	....	....	....	....	....	....	....	....	....	....	....	....	....
2002-03	St. Cloud State	WCHA	27	16	20	36	85	....	....	....	....	....	....	....	....	....	....	....	....	....	....	....	....	....	....
	Wilkes-Barre	AHL	3	0	1	1	2	....	....	....	....	....	....	....	....	....	....	....	....	....	....	....	....	....	....
2003-04	Pittsburgh	NHL	81	22	21	43	64	5	3	4	139	15.8	−23	230	27.4	18:54	....	....	....	....	....	....	....	....	....
2004-05	Blues Espoo	Finland	9	2	1	3	36	....	....	....	....	....	....	....	....	....	....	....	....	....	....	....	....	....	....
	SV Renon	Italy	10	6	2	8	20	....	....	....	....	....	....	....	....	....	6	4	4	8	36	....	....	....	....
	HC Ambri-Piotta	Swiss	....	....	....	....	....	....	....	....	....	....	....	....	....	....	1	0	0	0	2	....	....	....	....
	NHL Totals		81	22	21	43	64	5	3	4	139	15.8		230	27.4	18:54	....	....	....	....	....	....	....	....	....

NHL All-Rookie Team (2004)

Signed as a free agent by **Blues** (Finland), September 29, 2004. Signed as a free agent by **Renon** (Italy), January 3, 2005. Signed as a free agent by **Ambri** (Swiss), February 25, 2005.

			Regular Season															Playoffs							
Season	Club	League	GP	G	A	Pts	PIM	PP	SH	GW	S	%	+/-	TF	F%	Min	GP	G	A	Pts	PIM	PP	SH	GW	Min

MALTBY, Kirk (MAHLT-bee, KUHRK) **DET.**

Right wing. Shoots right. 6', 180 lbs.   Born, Guelph, Ont., December 22, 1972. Edmonton's 4th choice, 65th overall, in 1992 Entry Draft.

Season	Club	League	GP	G	A	Pts	PIM	PP	SH	GW	S	%	+/-	TF	F%	Min	GP	G	A	Pts	PIM	PP	SH	GW	Min
1988-89	Cambridge	OHA-B	48	28	18	46	138	....	....	....	....	....	....	....	....	....	....	....	....	....	....	....	....	....	....
1989-90	Owen Sound	OHL	61	12	15	27	90	....	....	....	....	....	....	....	....	....	12	1	6	7	15	....	....	....	....
1990-91	Owen Sound	OHL	66	34	32	66	100	....	....	....	....	....	....	....	....	....	....	....	....	....	....	....	....	....	....
1991-92	Owen Sound	OHL	66	50	41	91	99	....	....	....	....	....	....	....	....	....	5	3	3	6	18	....	....	....	....
1992-93	Cape Breton	AHL	73	22	23	45	130	....	....	....	....	....	....	....	....	....	16	3	3	6	45	....	....	....	....
1993-94	Edmonton	NHL	68	11	8	19	74	0	1	1	89	12.4	–2	....	....	....	....	....	....	....	....	....	....	....	....
1994-95	Edmonton	NHL	47	8	3	11	49	0	2	1	73	11.0	–11	....	....	....	....	....	....	....	....	....	....	....	....
1995-96	Edmonton	NHL	49	2	6	8	61	0	0	1	51	3.9	–16	....	....	....	....	....	....	....	....	....	....	....	....
	Cape Breton	AHL	4	1	2	3	6	....	....	....	....	....	....	....	....	....	....	....	....	....	....	....	....	....	....
	Detroit	NHL	6	1	0	1	6	0	0	0	4	25.0	0	....	....	....	8	0	1	1	4	0	0	0	
1996-97♦	Detroit	NHL	66	3	5	8	75	0	0	0	62	4.8	3	....	....	....	20	5	2	7	24	0	1	1	
1997-98♦	Detroit	NHL	65	14	9	23	89	2	1	3	106	13.2	11	....	....	....	22	3	1	4	30	0	1	0	
1998-99	Detroit	NHL	53	8	6	14	34	0	1	2	76	10.5	–6	10	40.0	13:13	10	1	0	1	8	0	0	1	11:32
99-2000	Detroit	NHL	41	6	8	14	24	0	2	1	71	8.5	1	2	50.0	13:30	8	0	1	1	4	0	0	0	13:45
2000-01	Detroit	NHL	79	12	7	19	22	1	3	3	119	10.1	16	14	35.7	14:17	6	0	0	0	6	0	0	0	15:23
2001-02♦	Detroit	NHL	82	9	15	24	40	0	1	5	108	8.3	15	38	47.4	13:23	23	3	3	6	32	0	2	0	16:34
2002-03	Detroit	NHL	82	14	23	37	91	0	4	1	116	12.1	17	43	37.2	16:10	4	0	0	0	4	0	0	0	17:18
2003-04	Detroit	NHL	79	14	19	33	80	1	4	4	123	11.4	24	30	43.3	16:16	12	1	3	4	11	0	0	0	17:34
2004-05			DID NOT PLAY																						
	NHL Totals		**717**	**102**	**109**	**211**	**645**	**4**	**19**	**22**	**998**	**10.2**		**137**	**41.6**	**14:38**	**113**	**13**	**11**	**24**	**123**	**0**	**4**	**2**	**15:32**

Traded to **Detroit** by **Edmonton** for Dan McGillis, March 20, 1996. • Missed majority of 1999-2000 season recovering from hernia injury suffered in game vs. Dallas, October 5, 1999.

MANLOW, Eric (MAN-low, AIR-ihk) **DET.**

Center. Shoots left. 6', 180 lbs.   Born, Belleville, Ont., April 7, 1975. Chicago's 2nd choice, 50th overall, in 1993 Entry Draft.

Season	Club	League	GP	G	A	Pts	PIM	PP	SH	GW	S	%	+/-	TF	F%	Min	GP	G	A	Pts	PIM	PP	SH	GW	Min
1990-91	Peterborough	OMHA	59	67	51	118	90	....	....	....	....	....	....	....	....	....	....	....	....	....	....	....	....	....	....
	Peterborough	OHA-B	1	0	0	0	0	....	....	....	....	....	....	....	....	....	....	....	....	....	....	....	....	....	....
1991-92	Kitchener Rangers	OHL	59	12	20	32	17	....	....	....	....	....	....	....	....	....	14	2	5	7	10	....	....	....	....
1992-93	Kitchener Rangers	OHL	53	26	21	47	31	....	....	....	....	....	....	....	....	....	4	0	1	1	2	....	....	....	....
1993-94	Kitchener Rangers	OHL	49	28	32	60	25	....	....	....	....	....	....	....	....	....	3	0	1	1	4	....	....	....	....
1994-95	Kitchener Rangers	OHL	44	25	29	54	26	....	....	....	....	....	....	....	....	....	....	....	....	....	....	....	....	....	....
	Detroit	OHL	16	4	16	20	11	....	....	....	....	....	....	....	....	....	21	11	10	21	18	....	....	....	....
1995-96	Indianapolis Ice	IHL	75	6	11	17	32	....	....	....	....	....	....	....	....	....	4	0	1	1	4	....	....	....	....
1996-97	Baltimore Bandits	AHL	36	6	6	12	13	....	....	....	....	....	....	....	....	....	3	0	0	0	0	....	....	....	....
	Columbus Chill	ECHL	32	18	18	36	20	....	....	....	....	....	....	....	....	....	....	....	....	....	....	....	....	....	....
1997-98	Indianapolis Ice	IHL	60	8	11	19	25	....	....	....	....	....	....	....	....	....	3	1	0	1	0	....	....	....	....
1998-99	Long Beach	IHL	51	9	19	28	30	....	....	....	....	....	....	....	....	....	8	0	0	0	8	....	....	....	....
	Florida Everblades	ECHL	18	8	15	23	11	....	....	....	....	....	....	....	....	....	....	....	....	....	....	....	....	....	....
99-2000	Florida Everblades	ECHL	26	14	24	38	24	....	....	....	....	....	....	....	....	....	14	6	8	14	8	....	....	....	....
	Providence Bruins	AHL	46	17	16	33	14	....	....	....	....	....	....	....	....	....	....	....	....	....	....	....	....	....	....
2000-01	**Boston**	NHL	8	0	1	1	2	0	0	0	3	0.0	0	61	50.8	7:26	....	....	....	....	....	....	....	....	....
	Providence Bruins	AHL	60	16	51	67	18	....	....	....	....	....	....	....	....	....	17	6	7	13	6	....	....	....	....
2001-02	**Boston**	NHL	3	0	0	0	0	0	0	0	2	0.0	0	16	31.3	6:05	....	....	....	....	....	....	....	....	....
	Providence Bruins	AHL	70	13	35	48	30	....	....	....	....	....	....	....	....	....	2	0	0	0	2	....	....	....	....
2002-03	**NY Islanders**	NHL	8	2	1	3	4	1	0	0	7	28.6	2	84	54.8	12:27	....	....	....	....	....	....	....	....	....
	Bridgeport	AHL	62	19	40	59	58	....	....	....	....	....	....	....	....	....	9	0	6	6	2	....	....	....	....
2003-04	**NY Islanders**	NHL	18	0	2	2	2	0	0	0	10	0.0	–2	178	53.9	10:13	....	....	....	....	....	....	....	....	....
	Bridgeport	AHL	40	8	27	35	16	....	....	....	....	....	....	....	....	....	1	0	0	0	2	....	....	....	....
2004-05	Grand Rapids	AHL	61	21	20	41	24	....	....	....	....	....	....	....	....	....	....	....	....	....	....	....	....	....	....
	NHL Totals		**37**	**2**	**4**	**6**	**8**	**1**	**0**	**0**	**22**	**9.1**		**339**	**52.5**	**9:46**									

Signed as a free agent by **Providence** (AHL), January 24, 2000. Signed as a free agent by **Boston**, July 11, 2000. Signed as a free agent by **NY Islanders**, July 21, 2002. Signed as a free agent by **Detroit**, July 21, 2004.

MANNING, Paul (MAN-nihng, PAWL) **CBJ**

Defense. Shoots left. 6'4", 205 lbs.   Born, Red Deer, Alta., April 15, 1979. Calgary's 3rd choice, 62nd overall, in 1998 Entry Draft.

Season	Club	League	GP	G	A	Pts	PIM	PP	SH	GW	S	%	+/-	TF	F%	Min	GP	G	A	Pts	PIM	PP	SH	GW	Min
1995-96	Red Deer	AMHL	32	8	32	40	....	....	....	....	....	....	....	....	....	....	....	....	....	....	....	....	....	....	....
1996-97	Red Deer Vipers	HJHL	36	9	33	42	....	....	....	....	....	....	....	....	....	....	....	....	....	....	....	....	....	....	....
1997-98	Colorado College	WCHA	30	1	5	6	16	....	....	....	....	....	....	....	....	....	....	....	....	....	....	....	....	....	....
1998-99	Colorado College	WCHA	41	3	10	13	75	....	....	....	....	....	....	....	....	....	....	....	....	....	....	....	....	....	....
99-2000	Colorado College	WCHA	39	6	17	23	26	....	....	....	....	....	....	....	....	....	....	....	....	....	....	....	....	....	....
2000-01	Colorado College	WCHA	34	2	28	30	48	....	....	....	....	....	....	....	....	....	....	....	....	....	....	....	....	....	....
2001-02	Syracuse Crunch	AHL	35	1	4	5	16	....	....	....	....	....	....	....	....	....	....	....	....	....	....	....	....	....	....
	Elmira Jackals	UHL	1	1	0	1	0	....	....	....	....	....	....	....	....	....	....	....	....	....	....	....	....	....	....
2002-03	**Columbus**	NHL	8	0	0	0	2	0	0	0	4	0.0	0	0	0.0	13:02	....	....	....	....	....	....	....	....	....
	Syracuse Crunch	AHL	52	2	5	7	37	....	....	....	....	....	....	....	....	....	11	0	3	3	6	....	....	....	....
2003-04	Hamburg Freezers	Germany	50	2	2	4	67	....	....	....	....	....	....	....	....	....	6	1	0	1	10	....	....	....	....
2004-05	Hamburg Freezers	Germany	36	4	6	10	90	....	....	....	....	....	....	....	....	....	....	....	....	....	....	....	....	....	....
	NHL Totals		**8**	**0**	**0**	**0**	**2**	**0**	**0**	**0**	**4**	**0.0**		**0**	**0.0**	**13:02**									

WCHA Second All-Star Team (2001)

Rights traded to **Columbus** by **Calgary** for Buffalo's 5th round choice (previously acquired, later traded to Detroit – Detroit selected Andreas Jamtin) in 2001 Entry Draft, June 24, 2001. Signed as a free agent by **Hamburg** (Germany), August 9, 2003.

MAPLETOFT, Justin (MAPLE-tawft, JUHS-tihn) **NYI**

Center. Shoots left. 6'1", 180 lbs.   Born, Lloydminster, Sask., January 11, 1981. NY Islanders' 9th choice, 130th overall, in 1999 Entry Draft.

Season	Club	League	GP	G	A	Pts	PIM	PP	SH	GW	S	%	+/-	TF	F%	Min	GP	G	A	Pts	PIM	PP	SH	GW	Min
1996-97	Calgary Royals	AMHL	36	25	36	51	....	....	....	....	....	....	....	....	....	....	....	....	....	....	....	....	....	....	....
	Red Deer Rebels	WHL	2	0	0	0	0	....	....	....	....	....	....	....	....	....	....	....	....	....	....	....	....	....	....
1997-98	Red Deer Rebels	WHL	65	9	4	13	41	....	....	....	....	....	....	....	....	....	....	....	....	....	....	....	....	....	....
1998-99	Red Deer Rebels	WHL	72	24	22	46	81	....	....	....	....	....	....	....	....	....	....	....	....	....	....	....	....	....	....
99-2000	Red Deer Rebels	WHL	72	39	57	96	135	....	....	....	....	....	....	....	....	....	4	2	1	3	28	....	....	....	....
2000-01	Red Deer Rebels	WHL	70	43	*77	*120	111	....	....	....	....	....	....	....	....	....	22	13	*21	34	59	....	....	....	....
2001-02	Bridgeport	AHL	80	13	20	33	60	....	....	....	....	....	....	....	....	....	20	7	10	17	23	....	....	....	....
2002-03	**NY Islanders**	NHL	11	2	2	4	2	1	0	0	12	16.7	–1	138	41.3	12:17	2	0	0	0	0	0	0	0	7:23
	Bridgeport	AHL	63	13	26	39	47	....	....	....	....	....	....	....	....	....	7	1	2	3	6	....	....	....	....
2003-04	**NY Islanders**	NHL	27	1	4	5	6	0	0	0	15	6.7	–1	134	48.5	6:09	....	....	....	....	....	....	....	....	....
	Bridgeport	AHL	36	10	13	23	59	....	....	....	....	....	....	....	....	....	....	....	....	....	....	....	....	....	....
2004-05	Bridgeport	AHL	61	11	24	35	51	....	....	....	....	....	....	....	....	....	....	....	....	....	....	....	....	....	....
	NHL Totals		**38**	**3**	**6**	**9**	**8**	**1**	**0**	**0**	**27**	**11.1**		**272**	**44.9**	**7:56**	**2**	**0**	**0**	**0**	**0**	**0**	**0**	**0**	**7:23**

WHL East First All-Star Team (2000, 2001) • WHL Player of the Year (2001) • Canadian Major Junior First All-Star Team (2001)

MARA, Paul (MAIR-uh, PAWL) **PHX.**

Defense. Shoots left. 6'4", 219 lbs.   Born, Ridgewood, NJ, September 7, 1979. Tampa Bay's 1st choice, 7th overall, in 1997 Entry Draft.

Season	Club	League	GP	G	A	Pts	PIM	PP	SH	GW	S	%	+/-	TF	F%	Min	GP	G	A	Pts	PIM	PP	SH	GW	Min
1994-95	Belmont Hill	High-MA	28	5	17	22	28	....	....	....	....	....	....	....	....	....	....	....	....	....	....	....	....	....	....
1995-96	Belmont Hill	High-MA	28	18	20	38	40	....	....	....	....	....	....	....	....	....	....	....	....	....	....	....	....	....	....
1996-97	Sudbury Wolves	OHL	44	9	34	43	61	....	....	....	....	....	....	....	....	....	....	....	....	....	....	....	....	....	....
1997-98	Sudbury Wolves	OHL	25	8	18	26	79	....	....	....	....	....	....	....	....	....	15	3	14	17	30	....	....	....	....
	Plymouth Whalers	OHL	25	8	15	23	30	....	....	....	....	....	....	....	....	....	....	....	....	....	....	....	....	....	....
1998-99	Plymouth Whalers	OHL	52	13	41	54	95	....	....	....	....	....	....	....	....	....	11	5	7	12	28	....	....	....	....
	Tampa Bay	NHL	1	1	1	2	0	1	0	0	1	100.0	–3	0	0.0	19:34	....	....	....	....	....	....	....	....	....
99-2000	**Tampa Bay**	NHL	54	7	11	18	73	4	0	1	78	9.0	–27	0	0.0	22:13	....	....	....	....	....	....	....	....	....
	Detroit Vipers	IHL	15	3	5	8	22	....	....	....	....	....	....	....	....	....	....	....	....	....	....	....	....	....	....
2000-01	**Tampa Bay**	NHL	46	6	10	16	40	2	0	1	58	10.3	–17	0	0.0	23:06	....	....	....	....	....	....	....	....	....
	Detroit Vipers	IHL	10	3	3	6	22	....	....	....	....	....	....	....	....	....	....	....	....	....	....	....	....	....	....
	Phoenix	NHL	16	0	4	4	14	0	0	0	20	0.0	1	0	0.0	19:22	....	....	....	....	....	....	....	....	....
2001-02	**Phoenix**	NHL	75	7	17	24	58	2	0	0	112	6.3	–6	2100.0	21:34	5	0	0	0	4	0	0	0	22:57

			Regular Season														Playoffs								
Season	Club	League	GP	G	A	Pts	PIM	PP	SH	GW	S	%	+/-	TF	F%	Min	GP	G	A	Pts	PIM	PP	SH	GW	Min
2002-03	**Phoenix**	**NHL**	73	10	15	25	78	1	0	0	95	10.5	–7	1	0.0	21:06	....	....	....	....	....	....	....	....	....
2003-04	**Phoenix**	**NHL**	81	6	36	42	48	1	0	0	140	4.3	–11	2	0.0	23:37	....	....	....	....	....	....	....	....	....
2004-05	Hannover	Germany	35	5	13	18	89	....	....	....	....	....	....	....	....	....	....	....	....	....	....	....	....	....	....
	NHL Totals		346	37	94	131	311	11	0	2	504	7.3		5	40.0	22:09	5	0	0	0	4	0	0	0	22:57

Traded to **Phoenix** by **Tampa Bay** with Mike Johnson, Ruslan Zainullin and NY Islanders' 2nd round choice (previously acquired, Phoenix selected Matthew Spiller) in 2001 Entry Draft for Nikolai Khabibulin and Stan Neckar, March 5, 2001. Signed as a free agent by **Hannover** (Germany), October 29, 2004.

MARCHANT, Todd

(mahr-SHAHNT, TAWD) **CBJ**

Center. Shoots left. 5'10", 180 lbs. Born, Buffalo, NY, August 12, 1973. NY Rangers' 8th choice, 164th overall, in 1993 Entry Draft.

1990-91	Niagara Scenics	NAHL	37	31	47	78	....	....	....	....	....	....	....	....	....	....	....	....	....	....	....	....	....	....	....
1991-92	Clarkson Knights	ECAC	32	20	12	32	32	....	....	....	....	....	....	....	....	....	....	....	....	....	....	....	....	....	....
1992-93	Clarkson Knights	ECAC	33	18	28	46	38	....	....	....	....	....	....	....	....	....	....	....	....	....	....	....	....	....	....
1993-94	United States	Nat-Tm	59	28	39	67	48	....	....	....	....	....	....	....	....	....	....	....	....	....	....	....	....	....	....
	United States	Olympics	8	1	1	2	6	....	....	....	....	....	....	....	....	....	....	....	....	....	....	....	....	....	....
	NY Rangers	**NHL**	1	0	0	0	0	0	0	0	1	0.0	–1	....	....	....	....	....	....	....	....	....	....	....	....
	Binghamton	AHL	8	2	7	9	6	....	....	....	....	....	....	....	....	....	....	....	....	....	....	....	....	....	....
	Edmonton	**NHL**	3	0	1	1	2	0	0	0	5	0.0	–1	....	....	....	....	....	....	....	....	....	....	....	....
	Cape Breton	AHL	3	1	4	5	2	....	....	....	....	....	....	....	....	....	5	1	1	2	0	....	....	....	....
1994-95	Cape Breton	AHL	38	22	25	47	25	....	....	....	....	....	....	....	....	....	....	....	....	....	....	....	....	....	....
	Edmonton	**NHL**	45	13	14	27	32	3	2	2	95	13.7	–3	....	....	....	....	....	....	....	....	....	....	....	....
1995-96	**Edmonton**	**NHL**	81	19	19	38	66	2	3	2	221	8.6	–19	....	....	....	....	....	....	....	....	....	....	....	....
1996-97	**Edmonton**	**NHL**	79	14	19	33	44	0	4	3	202	6.9	11	....	....	....	12	4	2	6	12	0	3	1	....
1997-98	**Edmonton**	**NHL**	76	14	21	35	71	2	1	3	194	7.2	9	....	....	....	12	1	1	2	10	0	0	0	....
1998-99	**Edmonton**	**NHL**	82	14	22	36	65	3	1	2	183	7.7	3	1449	50.0	16:47	4	1	1	2	12	0	0	0	24:21
99-2000	**Edmonton**	**NHL**	82	17	23	40	70	0	1	0	170	10.0	7	1593	52.9	17:08	3	1	0	1	2	0	0	0	18:07
2000-01	**Edmonton**	**NHL**	71	13	26	39	51	0	4	2	113	11.5	1	1549	53.8	17:54	6	0	0	0	4	0	0	0	22:57
2001-02	**Edmonton**	**NHL**	82	12	22	34	41	0	3	1	124	9.7	7	1523	52.4	16:58	....	....	....	....	....	....	....	....	....
2002-03	**Edmonton**	**NHL**	77	20	40	60	48	7	1	3	146	13.7	13	1336	58.0	19:54	6	0	2	2	2	0	0	0	20:03
2003-04	**Columbus**	**NHL**	77	9	25	34	34	4	0	2	163	5.5	–17	1412	50.9	20:39	....	....	....	....	....	....	....	....	....
2004-05			DID NOT PLAY																						
	NHL Totals		756	145	232	377	524	21	20	20	1617	9.0		8862	53.0	18:11	43	7	6	13	42	0	3	1	21:34

ECAC Second All-Star Team (1993)

Traded to **Edmonton** by **NY Rangers** for Craig MacTavish, March 21, 1994. Signed as a free agent by **Columbus**, July 3, 2003.

MARCHMENT, Bryan

(MAHRCH-mehnt, BRIGH-uhn)

Defense. Shoots left. 6'1", 200 lbs. Born, Scarborough, Ont., May 1, 1969. Winnipeg's 1st choice, 16th overall, in 1987 Entry Draft.

1984-85	Tor. Young Nats	MTHL	69	14	35	49	229	....	....	....	....	....	....	....	....	....	....	....	....	....	....	....	....	....	....
1985-86	Belleville Bulls	OHL	57	5	15	20	225	....	....	....	....	....	....	....	....	....	21	0	7	7	83	....	....	....	....
1986-87	Belleville Bulls	OHL	52	6	38	44	238	....	....	....	....	....	....	....	....	....	6	0	4	4	17	....	....	....	....
1987-88	Belleville Bulls	OHL	56	7	51	58	200	....	....	....	....	....	....	....	....	....	6	1	3	4	19	....	....	....	....
1988-89	Belleville Bulls	OHL	43	14	36	50	118	....	....	....	....	....	....	....	....	....	5	0	1	1	12	....	....	....	....
	Winnipeg	**NHL**	2	0	0	0	2	0	0	0	1	0.0	0	....	....	....	....	....	....	....	....	....	....	....	....
1989-90	**Winnipeg**	**NHL**	7	0	2	2	28	0	0	0	5	0.0	0	....	....	....	....	....	....	....	....	....	....	....	....
	Moncton Hawks	AHL	56	4	19	23	217	....	....	....	....	....	....	....	....	....	....	....	....	....	....	....	....	....	....
1990-91	**Winnipeg**	**NHL**	28	2	2	4	91	0	0	0	24	8.3	–5	....	....	....	....	....	....	....	....	....	....	....	....
	Moncton Hawks	AHL	33	2	11	13	101	....	....	....	....	....	....	....	....	....	....	....	....	....	....	....	....	....	....
1991-92	**Chicago**	**NHL**	58	5	10	15	168	2	0	0	55	9.1	–4	....	....	....	16	1	0	1	36	0	0	0	....
1992-93	**Chicago**	**NHL**	78	5	15	20	313	1	0	1	75	6.7	15	....	....	....	4	0	0	0	12	0	0	0	....
1993-94	**Chicago**	**NHL**	13	1	4	5	42	0	0	0	18	5.6	–2	....	....	....	....	....	....	....	....	....	....	....	....
	Hartford	**NHL**	42	3	7	10	124	0	1	1	74	4.1	–12	....	....	....	....	....	....	....	....	....	....	....	....
1994-95	**Edmonton**	**NHL**	40	1	5	6	184	0	0	0	57	1.8	–11	....	....	....	....	....	....	....	....	....	....	....	....
1995-96	**Edmonton**	**NHL**	78	3	15	18	202	0	0	0	96	3.1	–7	....	....	....	....	....	....	....	....	....	....	....	....
1996-97	**Edmonton**	**NHL**	71	3	13	16	132	1	0	0	89	3.4	13	....	....	....	3	0	0	0	4	0	0	0	....
1997-98	**Edmonton**	**NHL**	27	0	4	4	58	0	0	0	23	0.0	–2	....	....	....	....	....	....	....	....	....	....	....	....
	Tampa Bay	**NHL**	22	2	4	6	43	0	0	0	20	10.0	–3	....	....	....	....	....	....	....	....	....	....	....	....
	San Jose	**NHL**	12	0	3	3	43	0	0	0	13	0.0	2	....	....	....	6	0	0	0	10	0	0	0	....
1998-99	**San Jose**	**NHL**	59	2	6	8	101	0	0	0	49	4.1	–7	0	0.0	17:43	6	0	0	0	4	0	0	0	16:41
99-2000	**San Jose**	**NHL**	49	0	4	4	72	0	0	0	51	0.0	3	0	0.0	18:55	11	2	1	3	12	0	0	0	18:40
2000-01	**San Jose**	**NHL**	75	7	11	18	204	0	1	3	73	9.6	15	1	100.0	18:12	5	0	1	1	2	0	0	0	17:00
2001-02	**San Jose**	**NHL**	72	2	20	22	178	0	0	0	68	2.9	22	0	0.0	18:47	12	1	1	2	10	0	0	0	15:29
2002-03	**San Jose**	**NHL**	67	2	9	11	108	0	0	0	66	3.0	–2	0	0.0	19:19	....	....	....	....	....	....	....	....	....
	Colorado	**NHL**	14	0	3	3	33	0	0	0	18	0.0	4	0	0.0	16:42	7	0	0	0	4	0	0	0	16:02
2003-04	**Toronto**	**NHL**	75	1	3	4	106	0	0	0	56	1.8	4	0	0.0	15:13	13	0	0	0	8	0	0	0	14:31
2004-05			DID NOT PLAY																						
	NHL Totals		889	39	140	179	2232	4	2	5	931	4.2		1	100.0	17:54	83	4	3	7	102	0	0	0	16:15

OHL Second All-Star Team (1989)

Traded to **Chicago** by **Winnipeg** with Chris Norton for Troy Murray and Warren Rychel, July 22, 1991. Traded to **Hartford** by **Chicago** with Steve Larmer for Eric Weinrich and Patrick Poulin, November 2, 1993. Transferred to **Edmonton** from **Hartford** as compensation for Hartford's signing of free agent Steven Rice, August 30, 1994. Traded to **Tampa Bay** by **Edmonton** with Steve Kelly and Jason Bonsignore for Roman Hamrlik and Paul Comrie, December 30, 1997. Traded to **San Jose** by **Tampa Bay** with David Shaw and Tampa Bay's 1st round choice (later traded to Nashville – Nashville selected David Legwand) in 1998 Entry Draft for Andrei Nazarov and Florida's 1st round choice (previously acquired, Tampa Bay selected Vincent Lecavallier) in 1998 Entry Draft, March 24, 1998. Traded to **Colorado** by **San Jose** for Colorado's 3rd (later traded to Calgary – Calgary selected Ryan Donally) and 5th (later traded back to Colorado – Colorado selected Brad Richardson) round choices in 2003 Entry Draft, March 8, 2003. Signed as a free agent by **Toronto**, July 11, 2003.

MARKOV, Andrei

(MAHR-kahf, AHN-dray) **MTL.**

Defense. Shoots left. 6', 208 lbs. Born, Voskresensk, USSR, December 20, 1978. Montreal's 6th choice, 162nd overall, in 1998 Entry Draft.

1995-96	Voskresensk	CIS	38	0	0	0	14	....	....	....	....	....	....	....	....	....	....	....	....	....	....	....	....	....	....
1996-97	Voskresensk	Russia	43	8	4	12	32	....	....	....	....	....	....	....	....	....	2	1	1	2	0	....	....	....	....
1997-98	Voskresensk	Russia	43	10	5	15	83	....	....	....	....	....	....	....	....	....	....	....	....	....	....	....	....	....	....
1998-99	Dynamo Moscow	Russia	38	10	11	21	32	....	....	....	....	....	....	....	....	....	16	3	6	9	6	....	....	....	....
	Dynamo Moscow	EuroHL	12	7	5	12	12	....	....	....	....	....	....	....	....	....	6	2	2	4	4	....	....	....	....
99-2000	Dynamo Moscow	Russia	29	11	12	23	28	....	....	....	....	....	....	....	....	....	17	4	3	7	8	....	....	....	....
2000-01	**Montreal**	**NHL**	63	6	17	23	18	2	0	0	82	7.3	–6	2	50.0	16:53	....	....	....	....	....	....	....	....	....
	Quebec Citadelles	AHL	14	0	5	5	4	....	....	....	....	....	....	....	....	....	7	1	1	2	2	....	....	....	....
2001-02	**Montreal**	**NHL**	56	5	19	24	24	2	0	1	73	6.8	–1	0	0.0	17:15	12	1	3	4	8	0	0	1	15:53
	Quebec Citadelles	AHL	12	4	6	10	7	....	....	....	....	....	....	....	....	....	....	....	....	....	....	....	....	....	....
2002-03	**Montreal**	**NHL**	79	13	24	37	34	3	0	2	159	8.2	13	1	0.0	23:17	....	....	....	....	....	....	....	....	....
2003-04	**Montreal**	**NHL**	69	6	22	28	20	2	0	0	105	5.7	–2	2	50.0	21:29	11	1	4	5	8	0	0	1	22:52
2004-05	Dynamo Moscow	Russia	42	7	16	23	76	....	....	....	....	....	....	....	....	....	10	2	0	2	22	....	....	....	....
	NHL Totals		267	30	82	112	96	9	0	3	419	7.2		5	40.0	20:03	23	2	7	9	16	0	0	2	19:14

Signed as a free agent by **Dynamo Moscow** (Russia), June 19, 2004.

MARKOV, Danny

(MAHR-kahf, DA-nee) **NSH.**

Defense. Shoots left. 6'1", 190 lbs. Born, Moscow, USSR, July 30, 1976. Toronto's 7th choice, 223rd overall, in 1995 Entry Draft.

1993-94	Spartak Moscow	CIS	13	1	0	1	6	....	....	....	....	....	....	....	....	....	1	0	0	0	0	....	....	....	....
1994-95	Spartak Moscow	CIS	39	0	1	1	36	....	....	....	....	....	....	....	....	....	....	....	....	....	....	....	....	....	....
1995-96	Spartak Moscow	CIS	38	2	0	2	12	....	....	....	....	....	....	....	....	....	2	0	0	0	2	....	....	....	....
1996-97	Spartak Moscow	Russia	39	3	6	9	41	....	....	....	....	....	....	....	....	....	....	....	....	....	....	....	....	....	....
	St. John's	AHL	10	2	4	6	18	....	....	....	....	....	....	....	....	....	11	2	6	8	14	....	....	....	....
1997-98	**Toronto**	**NHL**	25	2	5	7	28	1	0	0	15	13.3	0	....	....	....	....	....	....	....	....	....	....	....	....
	St. John's	AHL	52	3	23	26	124	....	....	....	....	....	....	....	....	....	2	0	1	1	0	....	....	....	....
1998-99	**Toronto**	**NHL**	57	4	8	12	47	0	0	0	34	11.8	5	0	0.0	18:41	17	0	6	6	18	0	0	0	22:24
99-2000	**Toronto**	**NHL**	59	0	10	10	28	0	0	0	38	0.0	13	1	0.0	20:08	12	0	3	3	10	0	0	0	21:05
2000-01	**Toronto**	**NHL**	59	3	13	16	34	1	0	2	49	6.1	6	0	0.0	19:02	11	1	1	2	12	0	0	0	21:30
2001-02	**Phoenix**	**NHL**	72	6	30	36	67	4	0	1	103	5.8	–7	0	0.0	22:55	....	....	....	....	....	....	....	....	....
	Russia	Olympics	5	0	1	1	0	....	....	....	....	....	....	....	....	....	....	....	....	....	....	....	....	....	....
2002-03	**Phoenix**	**NHL**	64	4	16	20	36	2	0	0	105	3.8	2	0	0.0	23:16	....	....	....	....	....	....	....	....	....

Season	Club	League	GP	G	A	Pts	PIM	PP	SH	GW	S	%	+/-	TF	F%	Min	GP	G	A	Pts	PIM	PP	SH	GW	Min
			Regular Season														Playoffs								
2003-04	Carolina	NHL	44	4	10	14	37	2	0	1	73	5.5	–6	0	0.0	23:39	....	....	....	....	....	....	....	....	....
	Philadelphia	NHL	34	2	3	5	58	1	0	1	27	7.4	0	0	0.0	21:16	18	1	2	3	25	0	0	1	23:03
2004-05	Vityaz Chekhov	Russia-2	26	5	7	12	16	....	....	....	....	....	....	....	....	....	12	0	3	3	6	....	....	....	....
	NHL Totals		414	25	95	120	335	11	0	5	444	5.6		1	0.0	21:17	58	2	12	14	65	0	0	1	22:09

Traded to **Phoenix** by **Toronto** for Robert Reichel, Travis Green and Craig Mills, June 12, 2001. Traded to **Carolina** by **Phoenix** with future considerations (Edmonton's 3rd round choice (previously acquired, later traded to NY Rangers - NY Rangers selected Billy Ryan) in 2004 Entry Draft, June 26, 2004) for David Tanabe and Igor Knyazev, June 21, 2003. Traded to **Philadelphia** by **Carolina** for Justin Williams, January 20, 2004. Signed as a free agent by **Vityaz Chekhov** (Russia-2), November 15, 2004. Traded to **Nashville** by **Philadelphia** for Nashville's 3rd round choice (later traded to Los Angeles) in 2006 Entry Draft, August 2, 2005.

MARLEAU, Patrick

(mahr-LOH, PAT-rihk) **S.J.**

Center. Shoots left. 6'2", 220 lbs. Born, Aneroid, Sask., September 15, 1979. San Jose's 1st choice, 2nd overall, in 1997 Entry Draft.

Season	Club	League	GP	G	A	Pts	PIM	PP	SH	GW	S	%	+/-	TF	F%	Min	GP	G	A	Pts	PIM	PP	SH	GW	Min
1993-94	Swift Current	SMHL	53	72	95	167	....	....	....	....	....	....	....	....	....	....	....	....	....	....	....	....	....	....	....
1994-95	Swift Current	SMHL	31	30	22	52	18	....	....	....	....	....	....	....	....	....	....	....	....	....	....	....	....	....	....
1995-96	Seattle	WHL	72	32	42	74	22	....	....	....	....	....	....	....	....	....	5	3	4	7	4	....	....	....	....
1996-97	Seattle	WHL	71	51	74	125	37	....	....	....	....	....	....	....	....	....	15	7	16	23	12	....	....	....	....
1997-98	**San Jose**	**NHL**	74	13	19	32	14	1	0	2	90	14.4	5	....	....	....	5	0	1	1	0	0	0	0	....
1998-99	**San Jose**	**NHL**	81	21	24	45	24	4	0	4	134	15.7	10	1121	43.4	15:11	6	2	1	3	4	2	0	0	11:08
99-2000	**San Jose**	**NHL**	81	17	23	40	36	3	0	3	161	10.6	–9	851	42.0	14:11	5	1	1	2	2	1	0	0	11:51
2000-01	**San Jose**	**NHL**	81	25	27	52	22	5	0	6	146	17.1	7	1088	44.8	16:17	6	2	0	2	4	0	0	0	14:50
2001-02	**San Jose**	**NHL**	79	21	23	44	40	3	0	5	121	17.4	9	897	47.3	14:04	12	6	5	11	6	1	0	3	15:50
2002-03	**San Jose**	**NHL**	82	28	29	57	33	8	1	3	172	16.3	–10	1403	47.3	18:31	....	....	....	....	....	....	....	....	....
2003-04	**San Jose**	**NHL**	80	28	29	57	24	9	0	5	220	12.7	–5	1014	41.6	18:12	17	8	4	12	6	4	1	2	19:16
2004-05			DID NOT PLAY																						
	NHL Totals		558	153	174	327	193	33	1	28	1044	14.7		6374	44.6	16:05	51	19	12	31	22	8	1	5	15:56

WHL West First All-Star Team (1997)
Played in NHL All-Star Game (2004)

MARSHALL, Grant

(MAHR-shahl, GRANT) **N.J.**

Right wing. Shoots right. 6'1", 200 lbs. Born, Mississauga, Ont., June 9, 1973. Toronto's 2nd choice, 23rd overall, in 1992 Entry Draft.

Season	Club	League	GP	G	A	Pts	PIM	PP	SH	GW	S	%	+/-	TF	F%	Min	GP	G	A	Pts	PIM	PP	SH	GW	Min
1989-90	Tor. Young Nats	MTHL	39	15	28	43	56	....	....	....	....	....	....	....	....	....	....	....	....	....	....	....	....	....	....
1990-91	Ottawa 67's	OHL	26	6	11	17	25	....	....	....	....	....	....	....	....	....	1	0	0	0	0	....	....	....	....
1991-92	Ottawa 67's	OHL	61	32	51	83	132	....	....	....	....	....	....	....	....	....	11	6	11	17	11	....	....	....	....
1992-93	Ottawa 67's	OHL	30	14	29	43	83	....	....	....	....	....	....	....	....	....	....	....	....	....	....	....	....	....	....
	Newmarket	OHL	31	11	25	36	89	....	....	....	....	....	....	....	....	....	7	4	7	11	20	....	....	....	....
	St. John's	AHL	2	0	0	0	0	....	....	....	....	....	....	....	....	....	2	0	0	0	2	....	....	....	....
1993-94	St. John's	AHL	67	11	29	40	155	....	....	....	....	....	....	....	....	....	11	1	5	6	17	....	....	....	....
1994-95	Kalamazoo Wings	IHL	61	17	29	46	96	....	....	....	....	....	....	....	....	....	16	9	3	12	27	....	....	....	....
	Dallas	**NHL**	2	0	1	1	0	0	0	0	0	0.0	1	....	....	....	....	....	....	....	....	....	....	....	....
1995-96	**Dallas**	**NHL**	70	9	19	28	111	0	0	0	62	14.5	0	....	....	....	....	....	....	....	....	....	....	....	....
1996-97	**Dallas**	**NHL**	56	6	4	10	98	0	0	0	0	0.0	5	....	....	....	5	0	2	2	8	0	0	0	....
1997-98	**Dallas**	**NHL**	72	9	10	19	96	3	0	1	91	9.9	–2	....	....	....	17	0	2	2	*47	0	0	0	....
1998-99 ♦	**Dallas**	**NHL**	82	13	18	31	85	2	0	4	112	11.6	1	2	50.0	12:39	14	0	3	3	20	0	0	0	11:42
99-2000	**Dallas**	**NHL**	45	2	6	8	38	1	0	0	43	4.7	–5	3	0.0	11:19	14	0	1	1	4	0	0	0	10:08
2000-01	**Dallas**	**NHL**	75	13	24	37	64	4	0	1	93	14.0	1	16	56.3	11:05	9	0	0	0	0	0	0	0	11:15
2001-02	**Columbus**	**NHL**	81	15	18	33	86	6	0	4	152	9.9	–20	28	39.3	15:27	....	....	....	....	....	....	....	....	....
2002-03	**Columbus**	**NHL**	66	8	20	28	71	3	0	2	96	8.3	–8	26	46.2	13:56	....	....	....	....	....	....	....	....	....
	♦ **New Jersey**	**NHL**	10	1	3	4	7	0	0	0	17	5.9	–3	1	100.0	11:38	24	6	2	8	8	2	0	1	14:30
2003-04	**New Jersey**	**NHL**	65	8	7	15	67	5	0	2	76	10.5	–9	5	40.0	12:53	....	....	....	....	....	....	....	....	....
2004-05			DID NOT PLAY																						
	NHL Totals		624	84	130	214	723	24	0	14	742	11.3		81	44.4	12:59	83	6	10	16	87	2	0	1	12:23

• Missed majority of 1990-91 season recovering from neck injury suffered in game vs. Sudbury (OHL), December 4, 1990. Transferred to **Dallas** from **Toronto** with Peter Zezel as compensation for Toronto's signing of free agent Mike Craig, August 10, 1994. Traded to **Columbus** by **Dallas** for Columbus' 2nd round choice (Loui Eriksson) in 2003 Entry Draft, August 29, 2001. Traded to **New Jersey** by **Columbus** for New Jersey's 4th round choice (later traded to Carolina – later traded to Calgary – Calgary selected Kristopher Hogg) in 2004 Entry Draft, March 10, 2003.

MARSHALL, Jason

(MAHR-shahl, JAY-suhn) **ANA.**

Defense. Shoots right. 6'2", 200 lbs. Born, Cranbrook, B.C., February 22, 1971. St. Louis' 1st choice, 9th overall, in 1989 Entry Draft.

Season	Club	League	GP	G	A	Pts	PIM	PP	SH	GW	S	%	+/-	TF	F%	Min	GP	G	A	Pts	PIM	PP	SH	GW	Min
1987-88	Columbia Valley	RMJHL	40	4	28	32	150	....	....	....	....	....	....	....	....	....	....	....	....	....	....	....	....	....	....
1988-89	Vernon Lakers	BCJHL	48	10	30	40	197	....	....	....	....	....	....	....	....	....	31	6	6	12	14	....	....	....	....
1989-90	Canada	Nat-Tm	73	1	11	12	57	....	....	....	....	....	....	....	....	....	....	....	....	....	....	....	....	....	....
1990-91	Tri-City	WHL	59	10	34	44	236	....	....	....	....	....	....	....	....	....	7	1	2	3	20	....	....	....	....
	Peoria Rivermen	IHL	....	....	....	....	....	....	....	....	....	....	....	....	....	....	18	0	1	1	48	....	....	....	....
1991-92	**St. Louis**	**NHL**	2	1	0	1	4	0	0	0	2	50.0	0	....	....	....	....	....	....	....	....	....	....	....	....
	Peoria Rivermen	IHL	78	4	18	22	178	....	....	....	....	....	....	....	....	....	10	0	1	1	16	....	....	....	....
1992-93	Peoria Rivermen	IHL	77	4	16	20	229	....	....	....	....	....	....	....	....	....	4	0	0	0	20	....	....	....	....
1993-94	Canada	Nat-Tm	41	3	10	13	60	....	....	....	....	....	....	....	....	....	....	....	....	....	....	....	....	....	....
	Peoria Rivermen	IHL	20	1	1	2	72	....	....	....	....	....	....	....	....	....	3	2	0	2	2	....	....	....	....
1994-95	San Diego Gulls	IHL	80	7	18	25	218	....	....	....	....	....	....	....	....	....	5	0	1	1	8	....	....	....	....
	Anaheim	**NHL**	1	0	0	0	0	0	0	0	1	0.0	–2	....	....	....	....	....	....	....	....	....	....	....	....
1995-96	**Anaheim**	**NHL**	24	0	1	1	42	0	0	0	9	0.0	3	....	....	....	....	....	....	....	....	....	....	....	....
	Baltimore Bandits	AHL	57	1	13	14	150	....	....	....	....	....	....	....	....	....	....	....	....	....	....	....	....	....	....
1996-97	**Anaheim**	**NHL**	73	1	9	10	140	0	0	0	34	2.9	6	....	....	....	7	0	1	1	4	0	0	0	....
1997-98	**Anaheim**	**NHL**	72	3	6	9	189	1	0	0	68	4.4	–8	....	....	....	....	....	....	....	....	....	....	....	....
1998-99	**Anaheim**	**NHL**	72	1	7	8	142	0	0	0	63	1.6	–5	0	0.0	19:06	4	1	0	1	10	1	0	0	21:29
99-2000	**Anaheim**	**NHL**	55	0	3	3	88	0	0	0	41	0.0	–10	2	50.0	16:33	....	....	....	....	....	....	....	....	....
2000-01	**Anaheim**	**NHL**	50	3	4	7	105	2	1	1	38	7.9	–12	1	0.0	14:36	....	....	....	....	....	....	....	....	....
	Washington	**NHL**	5	0	0	0	17	0	0	0	5	0.0	–1	0	0.0	11:48	....	....	....	....	....	....	....	....	....
2001-02	**Minnesota**	**NHL**	80	5	6	11	148	1	0	0	73	6.8	–8	0	0.0	16:18	....	....	....	....	....	....	....	....	....
2002-03	**Minnesota**	**NHL**	45	1	5	6	69	0	0	0	40	2.5	4	7	28.6	11:24	15	1	1	2	16	0	0	1	10:50
2003-04	**Minnesota**	**NHL**	12	1	4	5	18	1	0	0	16	6.3	–1	0	0.0	15:36	....	....	....	....	....	....	....	....	....
	Houston Aeros	AHL	49	7	12	19	87	....	....	....	....	....	....	....	....	....	....	....	....	....	....	....	....	....	....
	San Jose	**NHL**	12	0	2	2	8	0	0	0	14	0.0	–2	0	0.0	16:00	17	0	1	1	25	0	0	0	14:44
2004-05	Plzen	CzRep	11	1	3	4	53	....	....	....	....	....	....	....	....	....	....	....	....	....	....	....	....	....	....
	NHL Totals		503	16	47	63	970	5	1	1	404	4.0		10	30.0	15:56	43	2	3	5	55	1	0	1	13:52

Traded to **Anaheim** by **St. Louis** for Bill Houlder, August 29, 1994. Traded to **Washington** by **Anaheim** for Alexei Tezikov and Edmonton's 4th round choice (previously acquired, Anaheim selected Brandon Rogers) in 2001 Entry Draft, March 13, 2001. Signed as a free agent by **Minnesota**, July 2, 2001. Traded to **San Jose** by **Minnesota** for San Jose's 5th round choice (Jean-Claude Sawyer) in 2004 Entry Draft, March 3, 2004. Signed as a free agent by **NY Rangers**, August 25, 2004. Signed as a free agent by **Plzen** (CzRep), January 22, 2005. Signed as a free agent by **Anaheim**, August 8, 2005.

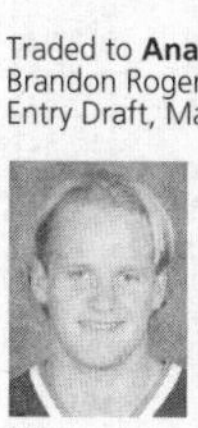

MARTENSSON, Tony

(MOHR-tehn-suhn, TOH-nee) **ANA.**

Center. Shoots left. 6', 189 lbs. Born, Upplands Vasby, Sweden, June 23, 1980. Anaheim's 9th choice, 224th overall, in 2001 Entry Draft.

Season	Club	League	GP	G	A	Pts	PIM	PP	SH	GW	S	%	+/-	TF	F%	Min	GP	G	A	Pts	PIM	PP	SH	GW	Min
1997-98	Arlanda	Sweden-2	12	2	4	6	0	....	....	....	....	....	....	....	....	....	2	0	0	0	0	....	....	....	....
1998-99	Arlanda	Sweden-2	37	8	22	30	8	....	....	....	....	....	....	....	....	....	2	0	0	0	0	....	....	....	....
99-2000	Arlanda	Sweden-2	44	21	28	49	14	....	....	....	....	....	....	....	....	....	....	....	....	....	....	....	....	....	....
2000-01	Brynas IF Gavle	Sweden	50	15	11	26	20	....	....	....	....	....	....	....	....	....	4	0	1	1	2	....	....	....	....
	Brynas IF Gavle Jr.	Swe-Jr.	1	1	0	1	0	....	....	....	....	....	....	....	....	....	....	....	....	....	....	....	....	....	....
2001-02	Brynas IF Gavle	Sweden	50	9	17	26	14	....	....	....	....	....	....	....	....	....	4	1	3	4	0	....	....	....	....
2002-03	Cincinnati	AHL	79	17	36	53	20	....	....	....	....	....	....	....	....	....	....	....	....	....	....	....	....	....	....
2003-04	**Anaheim**	**NHL**	6	1	1	2	0	0	0	0	4	25.0	–2	18	44.4	6:58	....	....	....	....	....	....	....	....	....
	Cincinnati	AHL	67	16	34	50	20	....	....	....	....	....	....	....	....	....	9	3	10	13	4	....	....	....	....
2004-05	Linkopings HC	Sweden	50	13	21	34	12	....	....	....	....	....	....	....	....	....	5	0	1	1	0	....	....	....	....
	NHL Totals		6	1	1	2	0	0	0	0	4	25.0		18	44.4	6:58	....	....	....	....	....	....	....	....	....

Signed as a free agent by **Linkopings** (Sweden), May 17, 2004.

			Regular Season																Playoffs							
Season	Club	League	GP	G	A	Pts	PIM	PP	SH	GW	S	%	+/-	TF	F%	Min	GP	G	A	Pts	PIM	PP	SH	GW	Min

MARTIN, Paul (MAHR-tihn, PAWL) **N.J.**

Defense. Shoots left. 6'1", 190 lbs. Born, Minneapolis, MN, March 5, 1981. New Jersey's 5th choice, 62nd overall, in 2000 Entry Draft.

Season	Club	League	GP	G	A	Pts	PIM	PP	SH	GW	S	%	+/-	TF	F%	Min	GP	G	A	Pts	PIM	PP	SH	GW	Min
1998-99	Elk River Elks	High-MN	24	9	11	20		....	....	....	....	....	....	....	....	....	....	....	....	....	....	....	....	....	....
99-2000	Elk River Elks	High-MN	24	15	35	50	26	....	....	....	....	....	....	....	....	....	....	....	....	....	....	....	....	....	....
2000-01	U. of Minnesota	WCHA	38	3	17	20	8	....	....	....	....	....	....	....	....	....	....	....	....	....	....	....	....	....	....
2001-02	U. of Minnesota	WCHA	44	8	30	38	22	....	....	....	....	....	....	....	....	....	....	....	....	....	....	....	....	....	....
2002-03	U. of Minnesota	WCHA	45	9	30	39	32	....	....	....	....	....	....	....	....	....	....	....	....	....	....	....	....	....	....
2003-04	**New Jersey**	**NHL**	70	6	18	24	4	2	0	2	82	7.3	12	0	0.0	20:08	5	1	1	2	4	1	0	0	23:40
2004-05	Fribourg	Swiss	11	3	4	7	2	....	....	....	....	....	....	....	....	....	....	....	....	....	....	....	....	....	....
	NHL Totals		70	6	18	24	4	2	0	2	82	7.3		0	0.0	20:08	5	1	1	2	4	1	0	0	23:40

Minnesota High School Player of the Year (1999) • WCHA All-Rookie Team (2001) • WCHA Second All-Star Team (2002, 2003) • NCAA West Second All-American Team (2003) • NCAA Championship All-Tournament Team (2003)
Signed as a free agent by **Fribourg** (Swiss), November 4, 2004.

MARTINEK, Radek (MAHR-tih-nehk, RA-dehk) **NYI**

Defense. Shoots right. 6'1", 200 lbs. Born, Havlickuv Brod, Czech., August 31, 1976. NY Islanders' 12th choice, 228th overall, in 1999 Entry Draft.

Season	Club	League	GP	G	A	Pts	PIM	PP	SH	GW	S	%	+/-	TF	F%	Min	GP	G	A	Pts	PIM	PP	SH	GW	Min
1996-97	C. Budejovice	CzRep	52	3	5	8	40	....	....	....	....	....	....	....	....	....	5	0	1	1	2	....	....	....	....
	C. Budejovice	EuroHL	6	0	0	0	0	....	....	....	....	....	....	....	....	....	2	0	0	0	0	....	....	....	....
1997-98	C. Budejovice	CzRep	42	2	7	9	36	....	....	....	....	....	....	....	....	....	....	....	....	....	....	....	....	....	....
1998-99	C. Budejovice	CzRep	52	12	13	25	50	....	....	....	....	....	....	....	....	....	3	0	2	2	....	....	....	....	....
99-2000	C. Budejovice	CzRep	45	5	18	23	24	....	....	....	....	....	....	....	....	....	3	0	0	0	6	....	....	....	....
2000-01	C. Budejovice	CzRep	44	8	10	18	45	....	....	....	....	....	....	....	....	....	....	....	....	....	....	....	....	....	....
2001-02	**NY Islanders**	**NHL**	23	1	4	5	16	0	0	1	25	4.0	5	0	0.0	21:07	4	0	0	0	4	0	0	0	10:16
2002-03	**NY Islanders**	**NHL**	66	2	11	13	26	0	0	1	67	3.0	15	0	0.0	17:15	....	....	....	....	....	....	....	....	....
	Bridgeport	AHL	3	0	3	3	2	....	....	....	....	....	....	....	....	....	....	....	....	....	....	....	....	....	....
2003-04	**NY Islanders**	**NHL**	47	4	3	7	43	0	0	1	48	8.3	–9	0	0.0	13:03	5	0	1	1	0	0	0	0	12:12
2004-05	C. Budejovice	CzRep-2	30	12	18	30	80	....	....	....	....	....	....	....	....	....	12	2	3	5	6	....	....	....	....
	NHL Totals		136	7	18	25	85	0	0	3	140	5.0		0	0.0	16:27	9	0	1	1	4	0	0	0	11:20

• Missed majority of 2001-02 season recovering from knee injury suffered in game vs. NY Rangers, November 11, 2001. Signed as a free agent by **Budejovice** (CzRep-2), September 17, 2004.

MARTINS, Steve (MAHR-tihns, STEEV) **OTT.**

Center. Shoots left. 5'9", 185 lbs. Born, Gatineau, Que., April 13, 1972. Hartford's 1st choice, 5th overall, in 1994 Supplemental Draft.

Season	Club	League	GP	G	A	Pts	PIM	PP	SH	GW	S	%	+/-	TF	F%	Min	GP	G	A	Pts	PIM	PP	SH	GW	Min
1988-89	L'Outaouais	QAAA	38	18	33	51	70	....	....	....	....	....	....	....	....	....	....	....	....	....	....	....	....	....	....
1989-90	Choate-Rosemary	High-CT	STATISTICS NOT AVAILABLE																						
1990-91	Choate-Rosemary	High-CT	STATISTICS NOT AVAILABLE																						
1991-92	Harvard Crimson	ECAC	20	13	14	27	26	....	....	....	....	....	....	....	....	....	....	....	....	....	....	....	....	....	....
1992-93	Harvard Crimson	ECAC	18	6	8	14	40	....	....	....	....	....	....	....	....	....	....	....	....	....	....	....	....	....	....
1993-94	Harvard Crimson	ECAC	32	25	35	60	*93	....	....	....	....	....	....	....	....	....	....	....	....	....	....	....	....	....	....
1994-95	Harvard Crimson	ECAC	28	15	23	38	93	....	....	....	....	....	....	....	....	....	....	....	....	....	....	....	....	....	....
1995-96	**Hartford**	**NHL**	23	1	3	4	8	0	0	0	27	3.7	–3				....	....	....	....	....	....	....	....	....
	Springfield	AHL	30	9	20	29	10	....	....	....	....	....	....	....	....	....	....	....	....	....	....	....	....	....	....
1996-97	**Hartford**	**NHL**	2	0	1	1	0	0	0	0	2	0.0	0				....	....	....	....	....	....	....	....	....
	Springfield	AHL	63	12	31	43	78	....	....	....	....	....	....	....	....	....	17	1	3	4	26	....	....	....	....
1997-98	**Carolina**	**NHL**	3	0	0	0	0	0	0	0	0	0.0	0				....	....	....	....	....	....	....	....	....
	Chicago Wolves	IHL	78	20	41	61	122	....	....	....	....	....	....	....	....	....	21	6	14	20	28	....	....	....	....
1998-99	**Ottawa**	**NHL**	36	4	3	7	10	1	0	1	27	14.8	4	191	56.0	8:28	....	....	....	....	....	....	....	....	....
	Detroit Vipers	IHL	4	1	6	7	16	....	....	....	....	....	....	....	....	....	....	....	....	....	....	....	....	....	....
99-2000	**Ottawa**	**NHL**	2	1	0	1	0	0	0	0	3	33.3	–1	3	0.0	11:10	....	....	....	....	....	....	....	....	....
	Tampa Bay	**NHL**	57	5	7	12	37	0	1	1	62	8.1	–11	806	50.9	13:27	....	....	....	....	....	....	....	....	....
2000-01	**Tampa Bay**	**NHL**	20	1	1	2	13	0	0	0	18	5.6	–9	184	52.2	9:35	....	....	....	....	....	....	....	....	....
	Detroit Vipers	IHL	8	5	4	9	4	....	....	....	....	....	....	....	....	....	....	....	....	....	....	....	....	....	....
	NY Islanders	**NHL**	39	1	3	4	20	0	1	0	28	3.6	–7	302	58.0	9:41	....	....	....	....	....	....	....	....	....
	Chicago Wolves	IHL	5	1	2	3	0	....	....	....	....	....	....	....	....	....	16	1	6	7	22	....	....	....	....
2001-02	**Ottawa**	**NHL**	14	1	0	1	4	0	0	0	11	9.1	1	121	55.4	9:33	2	0	0	0	0	0	0	0	7:13
	Grand Rapids	AHL	51	10	21	31	66	....	....	....	....	....	....	....	....	....	3	0	0	0	0	....	....	....	....
2002-03	**Ottawa**	**NHL**	14	2	3	5	10	0	0	0	13	15.4	3	111	55.9	9:45	....	....	....	....	....	....	....	....	....
	Binghamton	AHL	26	5	11	16	31	....	....	....	....	....	....	....	....	....	....	....	....	....	....	....	....	....	....
	St. Louis	**NHL**	28	3	3	6	18	0	1	0	25	12.0	–8	369	54.7	13:38	2	0	1	1	0	0	0	0	9:23
2003-04	**St. Louis**	**NHL**	25	1	0	1	22	0	1	0	27	3.7	–7	172	61.1	10:29	1	0	0	0	0	0	0	0	5:29
	Worcester IceCats	AHL	22	4	9	13	16	....	....	....	....	....	....	....	....	....	....	....	....	....	....	....	....	....	....
2004-05	JYP Jyvaskyla	Finland	54	13	12	25	66	....	....	....	....	....	....	....	....	....	3	0	0	0	4	....	....	....	....
	NHL Totals		263	20	24	44	142	1	4	2	243	8.2		2259	54.2	10:58	5	0	1	1	0	0	0	0	7:44

ECAC First All-Star Team (1994) • ECAC Player of the Year (1994) • NCAA East First All-American Team (1994) • NCAA Final Four All-Tournament Team (1994)
Transferred to **Carolina** after **Hartford** franchise relocated, June 25, 1997. Signed as a free agent by **Ottawa**, July 20, 1998. Claimed on waivers by **Tampa Bay** from **Ottawa**, October 29, 1999. Traded to **NY Islanders** by **Tampa Bay** for future considerations, January 3, 2001. Signed as a free agent by **Ottawa**, August 30, 2001. Claimed on waivers by **St. Louis** from **Ottawa**, January 15, 2003. Signed as a free agent by **JYP** (Finland), September 7, 2004. Signed as a free agent by **Ottawa**, August 19, 2005.

MATVICHUK, Richard (MAT-vih-chuhk, RIH-chuhrd) **N.J.**

Defense. Shoots left. 6'2", 215 lbs. Born, Edmonton, Alta., February 5, 1973. Minnesota's 1st choice, 8th overall, in 1991 Entry Draft.

Season	Club	League	GP	G	A	Pts	PIM	PP	SH	GW	S	%	+/-	TF	F%	Min	GP	G	A	Pts	PIM	PP	SH	GW	Min
1988-89	Ft. Saskatchewan	AJHL	58	7	36	43	147	....	....	....	....	....	....	....	....	....	....	....	....	....	....	....	....	....	....
1989-90	Saskatoon Blades	WHL	56	8	24	32	126	....	....	....	....	....	....	....	....	....	10	2	8	10	16	....	....	....	....
1990-91	Saskatoon Blades	WHL	68	13	36	49	117	....	....	....	....	....	....	....	....	....	....	....	....	....	....	....	....	....	....
1991-92	Saskatoon Blades	WHL	58	14	40	54	126	....	....	....	....	....	....	....	....	....	22	1	9	10	61	....	....	....	....
1992-93	**Minnesota**	**NHL**	53	2	3	5	26	1	0	0	51	3.9	–8				....	....	....	....	....	....	....	....	....
	Kalamazoo Wings	IHL	3	0	1	1	6	....	....	....	....	....	....	....	....	....	....	....	....	....	....	....	....	....	....
1993-94	**Dallas**	**NHL**	25	0	3	3	22	0	0	0	18	0.0	1				7	1	1	2	12	1	0	0	
	Kalamazoo Wings	IHL	43	8	17	25	84	....	....	....	....	....	....	....	....	....	....	....	....	....	....	....	....	....	....
1994-95	**Dallas**	**NHL**	14	0	2	2	14	0	0	0	21	0.0	–7				5	0	2	2	4	0	0	0	
	Kalamazoo Wings	IHL	17	0	6	6	16	....	....	....	....	....	....	....	....	....	....	....	....	....	....	....	....	....	....
1995-96	**Dallas**	**NHL**	73	6	16	22	71	0	0	1	81	7.4	4				....	....	....	....	....	....	....	....	....
1996-97	**Dallas**	**NHL**	57	5	7	12	87	0	2	0	83	6.0	1				7	0	1	1	20	0	0	0	
1997-98	**Dallas**	**NHL**	74	3	15	18	63	0	0	0	71	4.2	7				16	1	1	2	14	0	0	0	
1998-99♦	**Dallas**	**NHL**	64	3	9	12	51	1	0	0	54	5.6	23	0	0.0	21:19	22	1	5	6	20	0	0	0	22:40
99-2000	**Dallas**	**NHL**	70	4	21	25	42	0	0	1	73	5.5	7	0	0.0	24:27	23	2	5	7	14	0	0	0	25:51
2000-01	**Dallas**	**NHL**	78	4	16	20	62	2	0	1	85	4.7	5	1100	0.0	22:53	10	0	0	0	14	0	0	0	22:43
2001-02	**Dallas**	**NHL**	82	9	12	21	52	4	0	2	109	8.3	11	1	0.0	23:47	....	....	....	....	....	....	....	....	....
2002-03	**Dallas**	**NHL**	68	1	5	6	58	0	0	1	59	1.7	1	3	0.0	19:23	12	0	3	3	8	0	0	0	19:55
2003-04	**Dallas**	**NHL**	75	1	20	21	36	0	0	0	85	1.2	0	2	50.0	21:50	5	0	1	1	8	0	0	0	22:15
2004-05			DID NOT PLAY																						
	NHL Totals		733	38	129	167	584	8	2	7	790	4.8		7	28.6	22:21	107	5	19	24	114	1	0	0	23:12

WHL East First All-Star Team (1992)
Transferred to **Dallas** after **Minnesota** franchise relocated, June 9, 1993. Signed as a free agent by **New Jersey**, July 12, 2004.

MAULDIN, Greg (MAWL-dihn, GREHG) **CBJ**

Center. Shoots right. 5'11", 180 lbs. Born, Boston, MA, June 10, 1982. Columbus' 10th choice, 199th overall, in 2002 Entry Draft.

Season	Club	League	GP	G	A	Pts	PIM	PP	SH	GW	S	%	+/-	TF	F%	Min	GP	G	A	Pts	PIM	PP	SH	GW	Min
99-2000	Junior Bruins	EJHL	58	45	42	87	14	....	....	....	....	....	....	....	....	....	....	....	....	....	....	....	....	....	....
2000-01	Junior Bruins	EJHL	53	48	58	106	73	....	....	....	....	....	....	....	....	....	....	....	....	....	....	....	....	....	....
2001-02	Massachusetts	H-East	33	12	12	24	10	....	....	....	....	....	....	....	....	....	....	....	....	....	....	....	....	....	....
2002-03	Massachusetts	H-East	36	21	20	41	26	....	....	....	....	....	....	....	....	....	....	....	....	....	....	....	....	....	....

Season	Club	League	Regular Season GP	G	A	Pts	PIM	PP	SH	GW	S	%	+/-	TF	F%	Min	Playoffs GP	G	A	Pts	PIM	PP	SH	GW	Min
2003-04	Massachusetts	H-East	29	15	14	29	15	....	....	....	....	....	....	....	....	....	....	....	....	....	....	....	....	....	....
	Columbus	**NHL**	**6**	**0**	**0**	**0**	**4**	**0**	**0**	**0**	**6**	**0.0**	**–2**	**0**	**0.0**	**8:47**	....	....	....	....	....	....	....	....	....
	Syracuse Crunch	AHL	2	0	0	0	0	....	....	....	....	....	....	....	....	....	1	0	0	0	0	....	....	....	....
2004-05	Syracuse Crunch	AHL	66	7	20	27	49	....	....	....	....	....	....	....	....	....	....	....	....	....	....	....	....	....	....
	NHL Totals		**6**	**0**	**0**	**0**	**4**	**0**	**0**	**0**	**6**	**0.0**		**0**	**0.0**	**8:47**	....	....	....	....	....	....	....	....	....

EJHL First All-Star Team (2000, 2001) • EJHL MVP (2000)

MAY, Brad
(MAY, BRAD) **COL.**

Left wing. Shoots left. 6'1", 217 lbs. Born, Toronto, Ont., November 29, 1971. Buffalo's 1st choice, 14th overall, in 1990 Entry Draft.

Season	Club	League	GP	G	A	Pts	PIM	PP	SH	GW	S	%	+/-	TF	F%	Min	GP	G	A	Pts	PIM	PP	SH	GW	Min
1987-88	Markham	OMHA	31	22	37	59	58	....	....	....	....	....	....	....	....	....	....	....	....	....	....	....	....	....	....
	Markham	OHA-B	6	1	1	2	21	....	....	....	....	....	....	....	....	....	....	....	....	....	....	....	....	....	....
1988-89	Niagara Falls	OHL	65	8	14	22	304	....	....	....	....	....	....	....	....	....	17	0	1	1	55	....	....	....	....
1989-90	Niagara Falls	OHL	61	32	58	90	223	....	....	....	....	....	....	....	....	....	16	9	13	22	64	....	....	....	....
1990-91	Niagara Falls	OHL	34	37	32	69	93	....	....	....	....	....	....	....	....	....	14	11	14	25	53	....	....	....	....
1991-92	**Buffalo**	**NHL**	**69**	**11**	**6**	**17**	**309**	**1**	**0**	**3**	**82**	**13.4**	**–12**	....	....	....	**7**	**1**	**4**	**5**	**2**	**0**	**0**	**1**	....
1992-93	**Buffalo**	**NHL**	**82**	**13**	**13**	**26**	**242**	**0**	**0**	**1**	**114**	**11.4**	**3**	....	....	....	**8**	**1**	**1**	**2**	**14**	**0**	**0**	**1**	....
1993-94	**Buffalo**	**NHL**	**84**	**18**	**27**	**45**	**171**	**3**	**0**	**3**	**166**	**10.8**	**–6**	....	....	....	**7**	**0**	**2**	**2**	**9**	**0**	**0**	**0**	....
1994-95	**Buffalo**	**NHL**	**33**	**3**	**3**	**6**	**87**	**1**	**0**	**0**	**42**	**7.1**	**5**	....	....	....	**4**	**0**	**0**	**0**	**2**	**0**	**0**	**0**	....
1995-96	**Buffalo**	**NHL**	**79**	**15**	**29**	**44**	**295**	**3**	**0**	**4**	**168**	**8.9**	**6**	....	....	....	....	....	....	....	....	....	....	....	....
1996-97	**Buffalo**	**NHL**	**42**	**3**	**4**	**7**	**106**	**1**	**0**	**1**	**75**	**4.0**	**–8**	....	....	....	**10**	**1**	**1**	**2**	**32**	**0**	**0**	**0**	....
1997-98	**Buffalo**	**NHL**	**36**	**4**	**7**	**11**	**113**	**0**	**0**	**0**	**41**	**9.8**	**2**	....	....	....	....	....	....	....	....	....	....	....	....
	Vancouver	**NHL**	**27**	**9**	**3**	**12**	**41**	**4**	**0**	**2**	**56**	**16.1**	**0**	....	....	....	....	....	....	....	....	....	....	....	....
1998-99	**Vancouver**	**NHL**	**66**	**6**	**11**	**17**	**102**	**1**	**0**	**1**	**91**	**6.6**	**–14**	**8**	**12.5**	**13:04**	....	....	....	....	....	....	....	....	....
99-2000	**Vancouver**	**NHL**	**59**	**9**	**7**	**16**	**90**	**0**	**0**	**3**	**66**	**13.6**	**–2**	**3**	**0.0**	**10:24**	....	....	....	....	....	....	....	....	....
2000-01	**Phoenix**	**NHL**	**62**	**11**	**14**	**25**	**107**	**0**	**0**	**0**	**83**	**13.3**	**10**	**3**	**33.3**	**11:11**	....	....	....	....	....	....	....	....	....
2001-02	**Phoenix**	**NHL**	**72**	**10**	**12**	**22**	**95**	**1**	**0**	**3**	**105**	**9.5**	**11**	**3**	**0.0**	**12:04**	**5**	**0**	**0**	**0**	**0**	**0**	**0**	**0**	**10:19**
2002-03	**Phoenix**	**NHL**	**20**	**3**	**4**	**7**	**32**	**0**	**0**	**0**	**24**	**12.5**	**3**	**0**	**0.0**	**9:56**	....	....	....	....	....	....	....	....	....
	Vancouver	**NHL**	**3**	**0**	**0**	**0**	**10**	**0**	**0**	**0**	**1**	**0.0**	**1**	**0**	**0.0**	**7:48**	**14**	**0**	**0**	**0**	**15**	**0**	**0**	**0**	**7:25**
2003-04	**Vancouver**	**NHL**	**70**	**5**	**6**	**11**	**137**	**0**	**0**	**0**	**75**	**6.7**	**–2**	**8**	**50.0**	**8:56**	**6**	**1**	**0**	**1**	**6**	**0**	**0**	**0**	**7:07**
2004-05			DID NOT PLAY																						
	NHL Totals		**804**	**120**	**146**	**266**	**1937**	**15**	**0**	**21**	**1189**	**10.1**		**25**	**24.0**	**11:02**	**61**	**4**	**8**	**12**	**80**	**0**	**0**	**2**	**7:55**

OHL Second All-Star Team (1990, 1991)

• Missed majority of 1990-91 season recovering from knee injury suffered at Team Canada Juniors evaluation camp, August 21, 1990. Traded to **Vancouver** by **Buffalo** with Buffalo's 3rd round choice (later traded to Tampa Bay – Tampa Bay selected Jimmie Olvestad) in 1999 Entry Draft for Geoff Sanderson, February 4, 1998. Traded to **Phoenix** by **Vancouver** for future considerations, June 24, 2000. • Missed majority of 2002-03 season recovering from shoulder injury suffered in pre-season game vs. Detroit, October 6, 2002. Traded to **Vancouver** by **Phoenix** for Phoenix's 3rd round choice (previously acquired, Phoenix selected Dimitri Pestunov) in 2003 Entry Draft, March 11, 2003. Signed as a free agent by **Colorado**, August 5, 2005.

MAYERS, Jamal
(MAI-uhrz, JUH-MAHL) **ST.L.**

Right wing. Shoots right. 6'1", 212 lbs. Born, Toronto, Ont., October 24, 1974. St. Louis' 3rd choice, 89th overall, in 1993 Entry Draft.

Season	Club	League	GP	G	A	Pts	PIM	PP	SH	GW	S	%	+/-	TF	F%	Min	GP	G	A	Pts	PIM	PP	SH	GW	Min
1990-91	Thornhill	MTJHL	44	12	24	36	78	....	....	....	....	....	....	....	....	....	....	....	....	....	....	....	....	....	....
1991-92	Thornhill	MTJHL	56	38	69	107	36	....	....	....	....	....	....	....	....	....	....	....	....	....	....	....	....	....	....
1992-93	Western Mich.	CCHA	38	8	17	25	26	....	....	....	....	....	....	....	....	....	....	....	....	....	....	....	....	....	....
1993-94	Western Mich.	CCHA	40	17	32	49	40	....	....	....	....	....	....	....	....	....	....	....	....	....	....	....	....	....	....
1994-95	Western Mich.	CCHA	39	13	32	45	40	....	....	....	....	....	....	....	....	....	....	....	....	....	....	....	....	....	....
1995-96	Western Mich.	CCHA	38	17	22	39	75	....	....	....	....	....	....	....	....	....	....	....	....	....	....	....	....	....	....
1996-97	**St. Louis**	**NHL**	**6**	**0**	**1**	**1**	**2**	**0**	**0**	**0**	**7**	**0.0**	**–3**	....	....	....	....	....	....	....	....	....	....	....	....
	Worcester IceCats	AHL	62	12	14	26	104	....	....	....	....	....	....	....	....	....	5	4	5	9	4	....	....	....	....
1997-98	Worcester IceCats	AHL	61	19	24	43	117	....	....	....	....	....	....	....	....	....	11	3	4	7	10	....	....	....	....
1998-99	**St. Louis**	**NHL**	**34**	**4**	**5**	**9**	**40**	**0**	**0**	**0**	**48**	**8.3**	**–3**	**2**	**50.0**	**8:08**	**11**	**0**	**1**	**1**	**8**	**0**	**0**	**0**	**8:34**
	Worcester IceCats	AHL	20	9	7	16	34	....	....	....	....	....	....	....	....	....	....	....	....	....	....	....	....	....	....
99-2000	**St. Louis**	**NHL**	**79**	**7**	**10**	**17**	**90**	**0**	**0**	**0**	**99**	**7.1**	**0**	**77**	**52.0**	**9:46**	**7**	**0**	**4**	**4**	**2**	**0**	**0**	**0**	**10:42**
2000-01	**St. Louis**	**NHL**	**77**	**8**	**13**	**21**	**117**	**0**	**0**	**0**	**132**	**6.1**	**–3**	**273**	**51.3**	**11:04**	**15**	**2**	**3**	**5**	**8**	**0**	**0**	**0**	**11:28**
2001-02	**St. Louis**	**NHL**	**77**	**9**	**8**	**17**	**99**	**0**	**1**	**0**	**105**	**8.6**	**9**	**761**	**52.6**	**11:36**	**10**	**3**	**0**	**3**	**2**	**0**	**0**	**2**	**11:14**
2002-03	**St. Louis**	**NHL**	**15**	**2**	**5**	**7**	**8**	**0**	**0**	**0**	**26**	**7.7**	**1**	**111**	**51.4**	**14:21**	....	....	....	....	....	....	....	....	....
2003-04	**St. Louis**	**NHL**	**80**	**6**	**5**	**11**	**91**	**0**	**1**	**3**	**130**	**4.6**	**–19**	**681**	**48.6**	**13:01**	**5**	**0**	**0**	**0**	**0**	**0**	**0**	**0**	**12:55**
2004-05	Hammarby	Sweden-2	19	9	13	22	36	....	....	....	....	....	....	....	....	....	....	....	....	....	....	....	....	....	....
	Missouri	UHL	13	5	2	7	68	....	....	....	....	....	....	....	....	....	....	....	....	....	....	....	....	....	....
	NHL Totals		**368**	**36**	**47**	**83**	**447**	**0**	**2**	**3**	**547**	**6.6**		**1905**	**50.9**	**11:11**	**48**	**5**	**8**	**13**	**20**	**0**	**0**	**2**	**10:47**

• Missed majority of 2002-03 season recovering from knee injury suffered in game vs. Calgary, November 16, 2002. Signed as a free agent by **Hammarby** (Sweden-2), November 16, 2004. Signed as a free agent by **Missouri** (UHL), March 11, 2005.

McALLISTER, Chris
(mih-KAL-ihs-tuhr, KRIHS) **PHX.**

Defense. Shoots left. 6'8", 250 lbs. Born, Saskatoon, Sask., June 16, 1975. Vancouver's 1st choice, 40th overall, in 1995 Entry Draft.

Season	Club	League	GP	G	A	Pts	PIM	PP	SH	GW	S	%	+/-	TF	F%	Min	GP	G	A	Pts	PIM	PP	SH	GW	Min
1992-93	Saskatoon Royals	NSJHL	40	14	14	28	224	....	....	....	....	....	....	....	....	....	....	....	....	....	....	....	....	....	....
	Saskatoon Blades	WHL	4	0	0	0	2	....	....	....	....	....	....	....	....	....	....	....	....	....	....	....	....	....	....
1993-94	Humboldt	SJHL	50	3	5	8	150	....	....	....	....	....	....	....	....	....	....	....	....	....	....	....	....	....	....
	Saskatoon Blades	WHL	2	0	0	0	5	....	....	....	....	....	....	....	....	....	....	....	....	....	....	....	....	....	....
1994-95	Saskatoon Blades	WHL	65	2	8	10	134	....	....	....	....	....	....	....	....	....	10	0	0	0	28	....	....	....	....
1995-96	Syracuse Crunch	AHL	68	0	2	2	142	....	....	....	....	....	....	....	....	....	16	0	0	0	34	....	....	....	....
1996-97	Syracuse Crunch	AHL	43	3	1	4	108	....	....	....	....	....	....	....	....	....	3	0	0	0	6	....	....	....	....
1997-98	**Vancouver**	**NHL**	**36**	**1**	**2**	**3**	**106**	**0**	**0**	**0**	**15**	**6.7**	**–12**	....	....	....	....	....	....	....	....	....	....	....	....
	Syracuse Crunch	AHL	23	0	1	1	71	....	....	....	....	....	....	....	....	....	5	0	0	0	21	....	....	....	....
1998-99	**Vancouver**	**NHL**	**28**	**1**	**1**	**2**	**63**	**0**	**0**	**0**	**6**	**16.7**	**–7**	**0**	**0.0**	**5:53**	....	....	....	....	....	....	....	....	....
	Syracuse Crunch	AHL	5	0	0	0	24	....	....	....	....	....	....	....	....	....	....	....	....	....	....	....	....	....	....
	Toronto	**NHL**	**20**	**0**	**2**	**2**	**39**	**0**	**0**	**0**	**12**	**0.0**	**4**	**0**	**0.0**	**13:59**	**6**	**0**	**1**	**1**	**4**	**0**	**0**	**0**	**13:00**
99-2000	**Toronto**	**NHL**	**36**	**0**	**3**	**3**	**68**	**0**	**0**	**0**	**12**	**0.0**	**–4**	**0**	**0.0**	**12:02**	....	....	....	....	....	....	....	....	....
2000-01	**Philadelphia**	**NHL**	**60**	**2**	**2**	**4**	**124**	**0**	**0**	**0**	**33**	**6.1**	**1**	**0**	**0.0**	**11:36**	**2**	**0**	**0**	**0**	**0**	**0**	**0**	**0**	**8:00**
2001-02	**Philadelphia**	**NHL**	**42**	**0**	**5**	**5**	**113**	**0**	**0**	**0**	**26**	**0.0**	**–7**	**0**	**0.0**	**9:12**	....	....	....	....	....	....	....	....	....
2002-03	**Philadelphia**	**NHL**	**19**	**0**	**0**	**0**	**21**	**0**	**0**	**0**	**9**	**0.0**	**–2**	**0**	**0.0**	**9:32**	....	....	....	....	....	....	....	....	....
	Philadelphia	AHL	4	0	0	0	12	....	....	....	....	....	....	....	....	....	....	....	....	....	....	....	....	....	....
	Colorado	**NHL**	**14**	**0**	**1**	**1**	**26**	**0**	**0**	**0**	**4**	**0.0**	**6**	**0**	**0.0**	**8:02**	**1**	**0**	**0**	**0**	**0**	**0**	**0**	**0**	**2:34**
2003-04	**Colorado**	**NHL**	**34**	**0**	**0**	**0**	**62**	**0**	**0**	**0**	**11**	**0.0**	**–2**	**0**	**0.0**	**5:34**	....	....	....	....	....	....	....	....	....
	NY Rangers	**NHL**	**12**	**0**	**1**	**1**	**12**	**0**	**0**	**0**	**8**	**0.0**	**–4**	**4**	**50.0**	**12:49**	....	....	....	....	....	....	....	....	....
2004-05	Newcastle Vipers	Britain-2	14	0	3	3	40	....	....	....	....	....	....	....	....	....	....	....	....	....	....	....	....	....	....
	NHL Totals		**301**	**4**	**17**	**21**	**634**	**0**	**0**	**0**	**136**	**2.9**		**4**	**50.0**	**9:48**	**9**	**0**	**1**	**1**	**4**	**0**	**0**	**0**	**10:43**

Traded to **Toronto** by **Vancouver** for Darby Hendrickson, February 16, 1999. Traded to **Philadelphia** by **Toronto** for the rights to Regan Kelly, September 26, 2000. Traded to **Colorado** by **Philadelphia** for Colorado's 6th round choice (Ville Hostikka) in 2003 Entry Draft, February 5, 2003. Traded to **NY Rangers** by **Colorado** with David Liffiton and Florida's 2nd round choice (previously acquired, later traded back to Florida – Florida selected David Shantz) in 2004 Entry Draft for Matthew Barnaby and NY Rangers' 3rd round choice (Denis Parshin) in 2004 Entry Draft, March 8, 2004. Signed as a free agent by **Newcastle** (Britain-2), January 7, 2005. Signed as a free agent by **Phoenix**, August 11, 2005.

McAMMOND, Dean
(MIHK-AM-uhnd, DEEN) **ST.L.**

Left wing. Shoots left. 5'11", 200 lbs. Born, Grand Cache, Alta., June 15, 1973. Chicago's 1st choice, 22nd overall, in 1991 Entry Draft.

Season	Club	League	GP	G	A	Pts	PIM	PP	SH	GW	S	%	+/-	TF	F%	Min	GP	G	A	Pts	PIM	PP	SH	GW	Min
1988-89	St. Albert Raiders	AMHL	36	33	44	77	132	....	....	....	....	....	....	....	....	....	....	....	....	....	....	....	....	....	....
1989-90	Prince Albert	WHL	53	11	11	22	49	....	....	....	....	....	....	....	....	....	14	2	3	5	18	....	....	....	....
1990-91	Prince Albert	WHL	71	33	35	68	108	....	....	....	....	....	....	....	....	....	2	0	1	1	6	....	....	....	....
1991-92	Prince Albert	WHL	63	37	54	91	189	....	....	....	....	....	....	....	....	....	10	12	11	23	26	....	....	....	....
	Chicago	**NHL**	**5**	**0**	**2**	**2**	**0**	**0**	**0**	**0**	**4**	**0.0**	**–2**	....	....	....	**3**	**0**	**0**	**0**	**2**	**0**	**0**	**0**	....
1992-93	Prince Albert	WHL	30	19	29	48	44	....	....	....	....	....	....	....	....	....	....	....	....	....	....	....	....	....	....
	Swift Current	WHL	18	10	13	23	24	....	....	....	....	....	....	....	....	....	17	*16	19	35	20	....	....	....	....
1993-94	**Edmonton**	**NHL**	**45**	**6**	**21**	**27**	**16**	**2**	**0**	**0**	**52**	**11.5**	**12**	....	....	....	....	....	....	....	....	....	....	....	....
	Cape Breton	AHL	28	9	12	21	38	....	....	....	....	....	....	....	....	....	....	....	....	....	....	....	....	....	....
1994-95	**Edmonton**	**NHL**	**6**	**0**	**0**	**0**	**0**	**0**	**0**	**0**	**3**	**0.0**	**–1**	....	....	....	....	....	....	....	....	....	....	....	....
1995-96	**Edmonton**	**NHL**	**53**	**15**	**15**	**30**	**23**	**4**	**0**	**0**	**79**	**19.0**	**6**	....	....	....	....	....	....	....	....	....	....	....	....
	Cape Breton	AHL	22	9	15	24	55	....	....	....	....	....	....	....	....	....	....	....	....	....	....	....	....	....	....
1996-97	**Edmonton**	**NHL**	**57**	**12**	**17**	**29**	**28**	**4**	**0**	**6**	**106**	**11.3**	**–15**	....	....	....	....	....	....	....	....	....	....	....	....
1997-98	**Edmonton**	**NHL**	**77**	**19**	**31**	**50**	**46**	**8**	**0**	**3**	**128**	**14.8**	**9**	....	....	....	**12**	**1**	**4**	**5**	**12**	**0**	**0**	**0**	....

Season	Club	League	GP	G	A	Pts	PIM	PP	SH	GW	S	%	+/-	TF	F%	Min	GP	G	A	Pts	PIM	PP	SH	GW	Min
			Regular Season														Playoffs								
1998-99	**Edmonton**	**NHL**	**65**	**9**	**16**	**25**	**36**	**1**	**0**	**0**	**122**	**7.4**	**5**	**26**	**38.5**	**14:15**	....	....	....	....	....	....	....	....	....
	Chicago	**NHL**	**12**	**1**	**4**	**5**	**2**	**0**	**0**	**1**	**16**	**6.3**	**3**	**37**	**48.6**	**15:43**	....	....	....	....	....	....	....	....	....
99-2000	**Chicago**	**NHL**	**76**	**14**	**18**	**32**	**72**	**1**	**0**	**1**	**118**	**11.9**	**11**	**257**	**39.7**	**16:25**	....	....	....	....	....	....	....	....	....
2000-01	**Chicago**	**NHL**	**61**	**10**	**16**	**26**	**43**	**1**	**0**	**1**	**95**	**10.5**	**4**	**23**	**43.5**	**15:30**	....	....	....	....	....	....	....	....	....
	Philadelphia	**NHL**	**10**	**1**	**1**	**2**	**0**	**1**	**0**	**0**	**17**	**5.9**	**–1**	**65**	**46.2**	**12:00**	**4**	**0**	**0**	**0**	**2**	**0**	**0**	**0**	**9:25**
2001-02	**Calgary**	**NHL**	**73**	**21**	**30**	**51**	**60**	**7**	**0**	**4**	**152**	**13.8**	**2**	**143**	**55.2**	**18:56**	....	....	....	....	....	....	....	....	....
2002-03	**Colorado**	**NHL**	**41**	**10**	**8**	**18**	**10**	**2**	**0**	**2**	**72**	**13.9**	**1**	**9**	**55.6**	**14:24**	....	....	....	....	....	....	....	....	....
2003-04	**Calgary**	**NHL**	**64**	**17**	**13**	**30**	**18**	**4**	**1**	**5**	**101**	**16.8**	**9**	**768**	**49.1**	**16:52**	....	....	....	....	....	....	....	....	....
2004-05	Albany River Rats	AHL	79	19	42	61	72	....	....	....	....	....	....	....	....	....	....	....	....	....	....	....	....	....	....
	NHL Totals		**645**	**135**	**192**	**327**	**354**	**35**	**1**	**23**	**1065**	**12.7**		**1328**	**47.5**	**16:07**	**19**	**1**	**4**	**5**	**16**	**0**	**0**	**0**	**9:25**

Traded to **Edmonton** by **Chicago** with Igor Kravchuk for Joe Murphy, February 24, 1993. Traded to **Chicago** by **Edmonton** with Boris Mironov and Jonas Elofsson for Chad Kilger, Daniel Cleary, Ethan Moreau and Christian Laflamme, March 20, 1999. Traded to **Philadelphia** by **Chicago** for Philadelphia's 3rd round choice (later traded to Toronto – Toronto selected Nicolas Corbeil) in 2001 Entry Draft, March 13, 2001. Traded to **Calgary** by **Philadelphia** for Calgary's 4th round choice (Rosario Ruggeri) in 2002 Entry Draft, June 24, 2001. Traded to **Colorado** by **Calgary** with Derek Morris and Jeff Shantz for Chris Drury and Stephane Yelle, October 1, 2002. Traded to **Calgary** by **Colorado** for Calgary's 5th round choice (Mark McCutcheon) in 2003 Entry Draft, March 11, 2003. • Ruled ineligible to play remainder of 2002-03 season by NHL due to transaction violation by Calgary, March 15, 2003. Signed as a free agent by **New Jersey**, October 5, 2004. Signed as a free agent by **St. Louis**, August 9, 2005.

McCABE, Bryan

(mih-KAYB, BRIGH-uhn) **TOR.**

Defense. Shoots left. 6'2", 220 lbs. Born, St. Catharines, Ont., June 8, 1975. NY Islanders' 2nd choice, 40th overall, in 1993 Entry Draft.

Season	Club	League	GP	G	A	Pts	PIM	PP	SH	GW	S	%	+/-	TF	F%	Min	GP	G	A	Pts	PIM	PP	SH	GW	Min
1990-91	Calgary Canucks	AMHL	33	14	34	48	55	....	....	....	....	....	....	....	....	....	....	....	....	....	....	....	....	....	....
1991-92	Medicine Hat	WHL	68	6	24	30	157	....	....	....	....	....	....	....	....	....	4	0	0	0	6	....	....	....	....
1992-93	Medicine Hat	WHL	14	0	13	13	83	....	....	....	....	....	....	....	....	....	....	....	....	....	....	....	....	....	....
	Spokane Chiefs	WHL	46	3	44	47	134	....	....	....	....	....	....	....	....	....	6	1	5	6	28	....	....	....	....
1993-94	Spokane Chiefs	WHL	64	22	62	84	218	....	....	....	....	....	....	....	....	....	3	0	4	4	4	....	....	....	....
1994-95	Spokane Chiefs	WHL	42	14	39	53	115	....	....	....	....	....	....	....	....	....	....	....	....	....	....	....	....	....	....
	Brandon	WHL	20	6	10	16	38	....	....	....	....	....	....	....	....	....	18	4	13	17	59	....	....	....	....
1995-96	**NY Islanders**	**NHL**	**82**	**7**	**16**	**23**	**156**	**3**	**0**	**1**	**130**	**5.4**	**–24**	....	....	....	....	....	....	....	....	....	....	....	....
1996-97	**NY Islanders**	**NHL**	**82**	**8**	**20**	**28**	**165**	**2**	**1**	**2**	**117**	**6.8**	**–2**	....	....	....	....	....	....	....	....	....	....	....	....
1997-98	**NY Islanders**	**NHL**	**56**	**3**	**9**	**12**	**145**	**1**	**0**	**0**	**81**	**3.7**	**9**	....	....	....	....	....	....	....	....	....	....	....	....
	Vancouver	**NHL**	**26**	**1**	**11**	**12**	**64**	**0**	**1**	**0**	**42**	**2.4**	**10**	....	....	....	....	....	....	....	....	....	....	....	....
1998-99	**Vancouver**	**NHL**	**69**	**7**	**14**	**21**	**120**	**1**	**2**	**0**	**98**	**7.1**	**–11**	**1**	**0.0**	**24:13**	....	....	....	....	....	....	....	....	....
99-2000	**Chicago**	**NHL**	**79**	**6**	**19**	**25**	**139**	**2**	**0**	**2**	**119**	**5.0**	**–8**	**1**	**0.0**	**23:23**	....	....	....	....	....	....	....	....	....
2000-01	**Toronto**	**NHL**	**82**	**5**	**24**	**29**	**123**	**3**	**0**	**2**	**159**	**3.1**	**16**	**0**	**0.0**	**23:49**	**11**	**2**	**3**	**5**	**16**	**1**	**0**	**0**	**23:56**
2001-02	**Toronto**	**NHL**	**82**	**17**	**26**	**43**	**129**	**8**	**0**	**1**	**157**	**10.8**	**16**	**1**	**0.0**	**24:34**	**20**	**5**	**5**	**10**	**30**	**3**	**0**	**1**	**29:33**
2002-03	**Toronto**	**NHL**	**75**	**6**	**18**	**24**	**135**	**3**	**0**	**1**	**149**	**4.0**	**9**	**1**	**0.0**	**23:39**	**7**	**0**	**3**	**3**	**10**	**0**	**0**	**0**	**27:28**
2003-04	**Toronto**	**NHL**	**75**	**16**	**37**	**53**	**86**	**8**	**0**	**2**	**168**	**9.5**	**22**	**2**	**50.0**	**25:44**	**13**	**3**	**5**	**8**	**14**	**2**	**0**	**0**	**28:47**
2004-05	HV 71 Jonkoping	Sweden	10	1	0	1	30	....	....	....	....	....	....	....	....	....	....	....	....	....	....	....	....	....	....
	NHL Totals		**708**	**76**	**194**	**270**	**1262**	**31**	**4**	**11**	**1220**	**6.2**		**6**	**16.7**	**24:13**	**51**	**10**	**16**	**26**	**70**	**6**	**0**	**1**	**27:51**

WHL West Second All-Star Team (1993) • WHL West First All-Star Team (1994) • WHL East First All-Star Team (1995) • Memorial Cup Tournament All-Star Team (1995) • NHL Second All-Star Team (2004)

Traded to **Vancouver** by **NY Islanders** with Todd Bertuzzi and NY Islanders' 3rd round choice (Jarkko Ruutu) in 1998 Entry Draft for Trevor Linden, February 6, 1998. Traded to **Chicago** by **Vancouver** with Vancouver's 1st round choice (Pavel Vorobiev) in 2000 Entry Draft for Chicago's 1st round choice (later traded to Tampa Bay – later traded to NY Rangers – NY Rangers selected Pavel Brendl) in 1999 Entry Draft, June 25, 1999. Traded to **Toronto** by **Chicago** for Alexander Karpovtsev and Toronto's 4th round choice (Vladimir Gusev) in 2001 Entry Draft, October 2, 2000. Signed as a free agent by **HV 71** (Sweden), October 29, 2004.

McCARTHY, Sandy

(mih-KAHR-thee, SAN-dee)

Right wing. Shoots right. 6'3", 222 lbs. Born, Toronto, Ont., June 15, 1972. Calgary's 3rd choice, 52nd overall, in 1991 Entry Draft.

Season	Club	League	GP	G	A	Pts	PIM	PP	SH	GW	S	%	+/-	TF	F%	Min	GP	G	A	Pts	PIM	PP	SH	GW	Min
1987-88	Midland	OHA-C	18	2	1	3	70	....	....	....	....	....	....	....	....	....	....	....	....	....	....	....	....	....	....
1988-89	Hawkesbury	CJHL	42	4	11	15	139	....	....	....	....	....	....	....	....	....	....	....	....	....	....	....	....	....	....
1989-90	Laval Titan	QMJHL	65	10	11	21	269	....	....	....	....	....	....	....	....	....	14	3	3	6	60	....	....	....	....
1990-91	Laval Titan	QMJHL	68	21	19	40	297	....	....	....	....	....	....	....	....	....	13	6	5	11	67	....	....	....	....
1991-92	Laval Titan	QMJHL	62	39	51	90	326	....	....	....	....	....	....	....	....	....	8	4	5	9	81	....	....	....	....
1992-93	Salt Lake	IHL	77	18	20	38	220	....	....	....	....	....	....	....	....	....	....	....	....	....	....	....	....	....	....
1993-94	**Calgary**	**NHL**	**79**	**5**	**5**	**10**	**173**	**0**	**0**	**0**	**39**	**12.8**	**–3**	....	....	....	**7**	**0**	**0**	**0**	**34**	**0**	**0**	**0**	....
1994-95	**Calgary**	**NHL**	**37**	**5**	**3**	**8**	**101**	**0**	**0**	**2**	**29**	**17.2**	**1**	....	....	....	**6**	**0**	**1**	**1**	**17**	**0**	**0**	**0**	....
1995-96	**Calgary**	**NHL**	**75**	**9**	**7**	**16**	**173**	**3**	**0**	**1**	**98**	**9.2**	**–8**	....	....	....	**4**	**0**	**0**	**0**	**10**	**0**	**0**	**0**	....
1996-97	**Calgary**	**NHL**	**33**	**3**	**5**	**8**	**113**	**1**	**0**	**1**	**38**	**7.9**	**–8**	....	....	....	....	....	....	....	....	....	....	....	....
1997-98	**Calgary**	**NHL**	**52**	**8**	**5**	**13**	**170**	**1**	**0**	**1**	**68**	**11.8**	**–18**	....	....	....	....	....	....	....	....	....	....	....	....
	Tampa Bay	**NHL**	**14**	**0**	**5**	**5**	**71**	**0**	**0**	**0**	**26**	**0.0**	**–1**	....	....	....	....	....	....	....	....	....	....	....	....
1998-99	**Tampa Bay**	**NHL**	**67**	**5**	**7**	**12**	**135**	**1**	**0**	**0**	**89**	**5.6**	**–22**	**0**	**0.0**	**11:02**	....	....	....	....	....	....	....	....	....
	Philadelphia	**NHL**	**13**	**0**	**1**	**1**	**25**	**0**	**0**	**0**	**18**	**0.0**	**–2**	**2**	**50.0**	**11:09**	**6**	**0**	**1**	**1**	**0**	**0**	**0**	**0**	**6:33**
99-2000	**Philadelphia**	**NHL**	**58**	**6**	**5**	**11**	**111**	**1**	**0**	**0**	**68**	**8.8**	**–5**	**4**	**0.0**	**10:27**	....	....	....	....	....	....	....	....	....
	Carolina	**NHL**	**13**	**0**	**0**	**0**	**9**	**0**	**0**	**0**	**12**	**0.0**	**2**	**0**	**0.0**	**7:24**	....	....	....	....	....	....	....	....	....
2000-01	**NY Rangers**	**NHL**	**81**	**11**	**10**	**21**	**171**	**0**	**0**	**2**	**95**	**11.6**	**3**	**4**	**0.0**	**10:25**	....	....	....	....	....	....	....	....	....
2001-02	**NY Rangers**	**NHL**	**82**	**10**	**13**	**23**	**171**	**1**	**0**	**3**	**90**	**11.1**	**–8**	**6**	**50.0**	**8:29**	....	....	....	....	....	....	....	....	....
2002-03	**NY Rangers**	**NHL**	**82**	**6**	**9**	**15**	**81**	**0**	**0**	**1**	**81**	**7.4**	**–4**	**11**	**9.1**	**7:26**	....	....	....	....	....	....	....	....	....
2003-04	**Boston**	**NHL**	**37**	**3**	**1**	**4**	**28**	**0**	**0**	**1**	**27**	**11.1**	**0**	**1**	**0.0**	**6:22**	....	....	....	....	....	....	....	....	....
	NY Rangers	**NHL**	**13**	**1**	**0**	**1**	**2**	**1**	**0**	**0**	**11**	**9.1**	**–8**	**1**	**0.0**	**9:58**	....	....	....	....	....	....	....	....	....
2004-05			DID NOT PLAY																						
	NHL Totals		**736**	**72**	**76**	**148**	**1534**	**9**	**0**	**12**	**789**	**9.1**		**29**	**17.2**	**9:12**	**23**	**0**	**2**	**2**	**61**	**0**	**0**	**0**	**6:33**

Traded to **Tampa Bay** by **Calgary** with Calgary's 3rd (Brad Richards) and 5th (Curtis Rich) round choices in 1998 Entry Draft for Jason Wiemer, March 24, 1998. Traded to **Philadelphia** by **Tampa Bay** with Mikael Andersson for Colin Forbes and Philadelphia's 4th round choice (Michal Lanicek) in 1999 Entry Draft, March 20, 1999. Traded to **Carolina** by **Philadelphia** for Kent Manderville, March 14, 2000. Traded to **NY Rangers** by **Carolina** with Carolina's' 4th round choice (Bryce Lampman) in 2001 Entry Draft for Darren Langdon and Rob DiMaio, August 4, 2000. Signed as a free agent by **Boston**, August 12, 2003. Claimed on waivers by **NY Rangers** from **Boston**, March 9, 2004.

McCARTHY, Steve

(mih-KAHR-thee, STEEV) **VAN.**

Defense. Shoots left. 6'1", 198 lbs. Born, Trail, B.C., February 3, 1981. Chicago's 1st choice, 23rd overall, in 1999 Entry Draft.

Season	Club	League	GP	G	A	Pts	PIM	PP	SH	GW	S	%	+/-	TF	F%	Min	GP	G	A	Pts	PIM	PP	SH	GW	Min
1996-97	Trail	BCHL	57	25	52	77	81	....	....	....	....	....	....	....	....	....	....	....	....	....	....	....	....	....	....
	Edmonton Ice	WHL	2	0	0	0	0	....	....	....	....	....	....	....	....	....	....	....	....	....	....	....	....	....	....
1997-98	Edmonton Ice	WHL	58	11	29	40	59	....	....	....	....	....	....	....	....	....	....	....	....	....	....	....	....	....	....
1998-99	Kootenay Ice	WHL	57	19	33	52	79	....	....	....	....	....	....	....	....	....	6	0	5	5	8	....	....	....	....
99-2000	**Chicago**	**NHL**	**5**	**1**	**1**	**2**	**4**	**1**	**0**	**0**	**4**	**25.0**	**0**	**0**	**0.0**	**15:09**	....	....	....	....	....	....	....	....	....
	Kootenay Ice	WHL	37	13	23	36	36	....	....	....	....	....	....	....	....	....	....	....	....	....	....	....	....	....	....
2000-01	**Chicago**	**NHL**	**44**	**0**	**5**	**5**	**8**	**0**	**0**	**0**	**32**	**0.0**	**–7**	**0**	**0.0**	**14:47**	....	....	....	....	....	....	....	....	....
	Norfolk Admirals	AHL	7	0	4	4	2	....	....	....	....	....	....	....	....	....	....	....	....	....	....	....	....	....	....
2001-02	**Chicago**	**NHL**	**3**	**0**	**0**	**0**	**2**	**0**	**0**	**0**	**2**	**0.0**	**–1**	**0**	**0.0**	**11:48**	....	....	....	....	....	....	....	....	....
	Norfolk Admirals	AHL	77	7	21	28	37	....	....	....	....	....	....	....	....	....	2	0	3	3	2	....	....	....	....
2002-03	**Chicago**	**NHL**	**57**	**1**	**4**	**5**	**23**	**0**	**0**	**0**	**55**	**1.8**	**–1**	**0**	**0.0**	**16:25**	....	....	....	....	....	....	....	....	....
	Norfolk Admirals	AHL	19	1	6	7	14	....	....	....	....	....	....	....	....	....	9	0	4	4	0	....	....	....	....
2003-04	**Chicago**	**NHL**	**25**	**1**	**3**	**4**	**8**	**0**	**0**	**0**	**29**	**3.4**	**–9**	**0**	**0.0**	**19:21**	....	....	....	....	....	....	....	....	....
2004-05			DID NOT PLAY																						
	NHL Totals		**134**	**3**	**13**	**16**	**45**	**1**	**0**	**0**	**122**	**2.5**		**0**	**0.0**	**16:16**	....	....	....	....	....	....	....	....	....

• Missed majority of 2003-04 season recovering from groin injury suffered in game vs. Calgary, November 22, 2003. Traded to **Vancouver** by **Chicago** for Vancouver's 3rd round choice in 2007 Entry Draft, August 22, 2005.

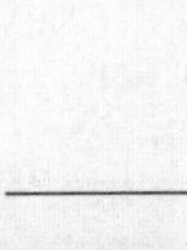

McCARTY, Darren

(mih-KAHR-tee, DAIR-ehn) **CGY.**

Right wing. Shoots right. 6'1", 210 lbs. Born, Burnaby, B.C., April 1, 1972. Detroit's 2nd choice, 46th overall, in 1992 Entry Draft.

Season	Club	League	GP	G	A	Pts	PIM	PP	SH	GW	S	%	+/-	TF	F%	Min	GP	G	A	Pts	PIM	PP	SH	GW	Min
1988-89	Peterborough	OHA-B	34	18	17	35	135	....	....	....	....	....	....	....	....	....	....	....	....	....	....	....	....	....	....
1989-90	Belleville Bulls	OHL	63	12	15	27	142	....	....	....	....	....	....	....	....	....	11	1	1	2	21	....	....	....	....
1990-91	Belleville Bulls	OHL	60	30	37	67	151	....	....	....	....	....	....	....	....	....	6	2	2	4	13	....	....	....	....
1991-92	Belleville Bulls	OHL	65	*55	72	127	177	....	....	....	....	....	....	....	....	....	5	1	4	5	13	....	....	....	....
1992-93	Adirondack	AHL	73	17	19	36	278	....	....	....	....	....	....	....	....	....	11	0	1	1	33	....	....	....	....
1993-94	**Detroit**	**NHL**	**67**	**9**	**17**	**26**	**181**	**0**	**0**	**2**	**81**	**11.1**	**12**	....	....	....	**7**	**2**	**2**	**4**	**8**	**0**	**0**	**0**	....
1994-95	**Detroit**	**NHL**	**31**	**5**	**8**	**13**	**88**	**1**	**0**	**2**	**27**	**18.5**	**5**	....	....	....	**18**	**3**	**2**	**5**	**14**	**0**	**0**	**0**	....
1995-96	**Detroit**	**NHL**	**63**	**15**	**14**	**29**	**158**	**8**	**0**	**1**	**102**	**14.7**	**14**	....	....	....	**19**	**3**	**2**	**5**	**20**	**0**	**0**	**1**	....
1996-97 ♦	**Detroit**	**NHL**	**68**	**19**	**30**	**49**	**126**	**5**	**0**	**6**	**171**	**11.1**	**14**	....	....	....	**20**	**3**	**4**	**7**	**34**	**0**	**0**	**2**	....
1997-98 ♦	**Detroit**	**NHL**	**71**	**15**	**22**	**37**	**157**	**5**	**1**	**2**	**166**	**9.0**	**0**	....	....	....	**22**	**3**	**8**	**11**	**34**	**0**	**0**	**1**	....
1998-99	**Detroit**	**NHL**	**69**	**14**	**26**	**40**	**108**	**6**	**0**	**1**	**140**	**10.0**	**10**	**15**	**33.3**	**17:04**	**10**	**1**	**1**	**2**	**23**	**0**	**0**	**0**	**13:04**

			Regular Season														Playoffs								
Season	Club	League	GP	G	A	Pts	PIM	PP	SH	GW	S	%	+/-	TF	F%	Min	GP	G	A	Pts	PIM	PP	SH	GW	Min
99-2000	**Detroit**	**NHL**	**24**	**6**	**6**	**12**	**48**	**0**	**0**	**1**	**40**	**15.0**	**1**	**1**	**0.0**	**13:40**	**9**	**0**	**1**	**1**	**12**	**0**	**0**	**0**	**14:09**
2000-01	**Detroit**	**NHL**	**72**	**12**	**10**	**22**	**123**	**1**	**1**	**3**	**118**	**10.2**	**–5**	**26**	**53.9**	**13:26**	**6**	**1**	**0**	**1**	**2**	**0**	**0**	**0**	**13:11**
2001-02 ♦	**Detroit**	**NHL**	**62**	**5**	**7**	**12**	**98**	**0**	**0**	**1**	**74**	**6.8**	**2**	**26**	**38.5**	**11:47**	**23**	**4**	**4**	**8**	**34**	**0**	**0**	**1**	**13:33**
2002-03	**Detroit**	**NHL**	**73**	**13**	**9**	**22**	**138**	**1**	**0**	**2**	**129**	**10.1**	**10**	**320**	**57.8**	**13:18**	**4**	**0**	**0**	**0**	**6**	**0**	**0**	**0**	**15:45**
2003-04	**Detroit**	**NHL**	**43**	**6**	**5**	**11**	**50**	**1**	**0**	**0**	**61**	**9.8**	**2**	**141**	**50.4**	**12:20**	**12**	**0**	**1**	**1**	**7**	**0**	**0**	**0**	**11:30**
2004-05		DID NOT PLAY																							
	NHL Totals		**643**	**119**	**154**	**273**	**1275**	**28**	**2**	**21**	**1109**	**10.7**		**529**	**53.9**	**13:43**	**150**	**20**	**25**	**45**	**194**	**0**	**0**	**5**	**13:17**

OHL First All-Star Team (1992)

• Missed majority of 1999-2000 season recovering from hernia injury suffered in game vs. Dallas, November 10, 1999. Signed as a free agent by **Calgary**, August 2, 2005.

McCAULEY, Alyn

(mih-KAW-lee, AL-ihn) **S.J.**

Center. Shoots left. 5'11", 200 lbs. Born, Brockville, Ont., May 29, 1977. New Jersey's 5th choice, 79th overall, in 1995 Entry Draft.

1991-92	Kingston	MTJHL	37	5	17	22	6	....	....	....	....	....	....	....	....	....	....	....	....	....	....	....	....	....	....
1992-93	Kingston	MTJHL	38	31	29	60	18	....	....	....	....	....	....	....	....	....	....	....	....	....	....	....	....	....	....
1993-94	Ottawa 67's	OHL	38	13	23	36	10	....	....	....	....	....	....	....	....	....	13	5	14	19	4	....	....	....	....
1994-95	Ottawa 67's	OHL	65	16	38	54	20	....	....	....	....	....	....	....	....	....	....	....	....	....	....	....	....	....	....
1995-96	Ottawa 67's	OHL	55	34	48	82	24	....	....	....	....	....	....	....	....	....	2	0	0	0	0	....	....	....	....
1996-97	Ottawa 67's	OHL	50	*56	56	112	16	....	....	....	....	....	....	....	....	....	22	14	22	36	14	....	....	....	....
	St. John's	AHL	....	....	....	....	....	....	....	....	....	....	....	....	....	....	3	0	1	1	0	....	....	....	....
1997-98	**Toronto**	**NHL**	**60**	**6**	**10**	**16**	**6**	**0**	**0**	**1**	**77**	**7.8**	**–7**	....	....	....	....	....	....	....	....	....	....	....	....
1998-99	**Toronto**	**NHL**	**39**	**9**	**15**	**24**	**2**	**1**	**0**	**1**	**76**	**11.8**	**7**	**591**	**46.4**	**15:10**	....	....	....	....	....	....	....	....	....
99-2000	**Toronto**	**NHL**	**45**	**5**	**5**	**10**	**10**	**1**	**0**	**0**	**41**	**12.2**	**–6**	**450**	**47.8**	**10:46**	**5**	**0**	**0**	**0**	**6**	**0**	**0**	**0**	**7:51**
	St. John's	AHL	5	1	1	2	0	....	....	....	....	....	....	....	....	....	....	....	....	....	....	....	....	....	....
2000-01	**Toronto**	**NHL**	**14**	**1**	**0**	**1**	**0**	**0**	**0**	**0**	**13**	**7.7**	**0**	**139**	**46.8**	**10:28**	**10**	**0**	**0**	**0**	**2**	**0**	**0**	**0**	**9:34**
	St. John's	AHL	47	16	28	44	12	....	....	....	....	....	....	....	....	....	....	....	....	....	....	....	....	....	....
2001-02	**Toronto**	**NHL**	**82**	**6**	**10**	**16**	**18**	**0**	**1**	**1**	**95**	**6.3**	**10**	**951**	**48.1**	**11:24**	**20**	**5**	**10**	**15**	**4**	**1**	**0**	**2**	**19:12**
2002-03	**Toronto**	**NHL**	**64**	**6**	**9**	**15**	**16**	**0**	**0**	**0**	**79**	**7.6**	**3**	**515**	**44.5**	**12:54**	....	....	....	....	....	....	....	....	....
	San Jose	**NHL**	**16**	**3**	**7**	**10**	**4**	**3**	**0**	**0**	**29**	**10.3**	**–2**	**81**	**50.6**	**17:29**	....	....	....	....	....	....	....	....	....
2003-04	**San Jose**	**NHL**	**82**	**20**	**27**	**47**	**28**	**5**	**0**	**4**	**146**	**13.7**	**23**	**1216**	**47.7**	**16:51**	**11**	**2**	**1**	**3**	**2**	**0**	**0**	**0**	**14:17**
2004-05		DID NOT PLAY																							
	NHL Totals		**402**	**56**	**83**	**139**	**84**	**10**	**1**	**7**	**556**	**10.1**		**3943**	**47.2**	**13:35**	**46**	**7**	**11**	**18**	**14**	**1**	**0**	**2**	**14:42**

OHL First All-Star Team (1996, 1997) • OHL MVP (1996, 1997) • Canadian Major Junior First All-Star Team (1997) • Canadian Major Junior Player of the Year (1997)

Rights traded to **Toronto** by **New Jersey** with Jason Smith and Steve Sullivan for Doug Gilmour, Dave Ellett and New Jersey's 3rd round choice (previously acquired, New Jersey selected Andre Lakos) in 1999 Entry Draft, February 25, 1997. Traded to **San Jose** by **Toronto** with Brad Boyes and Toronto's 1st round choice (later traded to Boston – Boston selected Mark Stuart) in 2003 Entry Draft for Owen Nolan, March 5, 2003.

McCORMICK, Cody

(muh-KOHR-mihk, KOH-dee) **COL.**

Center/Right wing. Shoots right. 6'2", 200 lbs. Born, London, Ont., April 18, 1983. Colorado's 5th choice, 144th overall, in 2001 Entry Draft.

1998-99	Elgin-Middlesex	MHAO	58	22	40	62	81	....	....	....	....	....	....	....	....	....	....	....	....	....	....	....	....	....	....
99-2000	Belleville Bulls	OHL	45	3	4	7	42	....	....	....	....	....	....	....	....	....	9	1	0	1	10	....	....	....	....
2000-01	Belleville Bulls	OHL	66	7	16	23	135	....	....	....	....	....	....	....	....	....	10	1	1	2	23	....	....	....	....
2001-02	Belleville Bulls	OHL	63	10	17	27	118	....	....	....	....	....	....	....	....	....	11	2	4	6	24	....	....	....	....
2002-03	Belleville Bulls	OHL	61	36	33	69	166	....	....	....	....	....	....	....	....	....	7	4	7	11	11	....	....	....	....
2003-04	**Colorado**	**NHL**	**44**	**2**	**3**	**5**	**73**	**0**	**0**	**1**	**33**	**6.1**	**–4**	**110**	**32.7**	**8:07**	....	....	....	....	....	....	....	....	....
	Hershey Bears	AHL	32	3	6	9	60	....	....	....	....	....	....	....	....	....	....	....	....	....	....	....	....	....	....
2004-05	Hershey Bears	AHL	40	5	6	11	68	....	....	....	....	....	....	....	....	....	....	....	....	....	....	....	....	....	....
	NHL Totals		**44**	**2**	**3**	**5**	**73**	**0**	**0**	**1**	**33**	**6.1**		**110**	**32.7**	**8:07**	....	....	....	....	....	....	....	....	....

OHL First All-Star Team (2003)

McDONALD, Andy

(mihk-DAW-nuhld, AN-dee) **ANA.**

Center. Shoots left. 5'10", 186 lbs. Born, Strathroy, Ont., August 25, 1977.

1993-94	Strathroy Rockets	OHA-B	7	2	2	4	0	....	....	....	....	....	....	....	....	....	....	....	....	....	....	....	....	....	....
1994-95	Strathroy Rockets	OHA-B	50	32	41	73	24	....	....	....	....	....	....	....	....	....	....	....	....	....	....	....	....	....	....
1995-96	Strathroy Rockets	OHA-B	52	31	56	87	103	....	....	....	....	....	....	....	....	....	....	....	....	....	....	....	....	....	....
1996-97	Colgate	ECAC	33	9	10	19	16	....	....	....	....	....	....	....	....	....	....	....	....	....	....	....	....	....	....
1997-98	Colgate	ECAC	35	13	19	32	26	....	....	....	....	....	....	....	....	....	....	....	....	....	....	....	....	....	....
1998-99	Colgate	ECAC	35	20	26	46	42	....	....	....	....	....	....	....	....	....	....	....	....	....	....	....	....	....	....
99-2000	Colgate	ECAC	34	25	*33	*58	49	....	....	....	....	....	....	....	....	....	....	....	....	....	....	....	....	....	....
2000-01	**Anaheim**	**NHL**	**16**	**1**	**0**	**1**	**6**	**0**	**0**	**0**	**21**	**4.8**	**0**	**139**	**48.9**	**11:11**	....	....	....	....	....	....	....	....	....
	Cincinnati	AHL	46	15	25	40	21	....	....	....	....	....	....	....	....	....	3	0	1	1	2	....	....	....	....
2001-02	**Anaheim**	**NHL**	**53**	**7**	**21**	**28**	**10**	**2**	**0**	**3**	**79**	**8.9**	**2**	**818**	**53.7**	**15:59**	....	....	....	....	....	....	....	....	....
	Cincinnati	AHL	21	7	25	32	6	....	....	....	....	....	....	....	....	....	....	....	....	....	....	....	....	....	....
2002-03	**Anaheim**	**NHL**	**46**	**10**	**11**	**21**	**14**	**3**	**0**	**1**	**92**	**10.9**	**–1**	**604**	**56.0**	**18:31**	....	....	....	....	....	....	....	....	....
2003-04	**Anaheim**	**NHL**	**79**	**9**	**21**	**30**	**24**	**2**	**1**	**1**	**162**	**5.6**	**–13**	**282**	**54.3**	**16:34**	....	....	....	....	....	....	....	....	....
2004-05	ERC Ingolstadt	Germany	36	13	17	30	26	....	....	....	....	....	....	....	....	....	10	5	2	7	35	....	....	....	....
	NHL Totals		**194**	**27**	**53**	**80**	**54**	**7**	**1**	**5**	**354**	**7.6**		**1843**	**54.2**	**16:25**	....	....	....	....	....	....	....	....	....

ECAC Second All-Star Team (1999) • ECAC First All-Star Team (2000) • ECAC Player of the Year (2000) • NCAA East First All-American Team (2000)

Signed as a free agent by **Anaheim**, April 3, 2000. Signed as a free agent by **Ingolstadt** (Germany), September 17, 2004.

McDONELL, Kent

(MAHK-dah-NEHL, KEHNT) **DET.**

Right wing. Shoots right. 6'2", 205 lbs. Born, Williamstown, Ont., March 1, 1979. Detroit's 3rd choice, 181st overall, in 1999 Entry Draft.

1995-96	Cornwall Colts	CJHL	33	21	14	35	64	....	....	....	....	....	....	....	....	....	....	....	....	....	....	....	....	....	....
1996-97	Guelph Storm	OHL	56	7	5	12	57	....	....	....	....	....	....	....	....	....	16	0	2	2	4	....	....	....	....
1997-98	Guelph Storm	OHL	64	28	23	51	76	....	....	....	....	....	....	....	....	....	12	7	4	11	18	....	....	....	....
1998-99	Guelph Storm	OHL	60	31	38	69	110	....	....	....	....	....	....	....	....	....	11	4	3	7	36	....	....	....	....
99-2000	Guelph Storm	OHL	56	35	35	70	100	....	....	....	....	....	....	....	....	....	6	1	4	5	6	....	....	....	....
2000-01	Dayton Bombers	ECHL	28	16	9	25	94	....	....	....	....	....	....	....	....	....	3	0	0	0	4	....	....	....	....
	Syracuse Crunch	AHL	32	3	3	6	36	....	....	....	....	....	....	....	....	....	3	1	0	1	0	....	....	....	....
2001-02	Syracuse Crunch	AHL	72	18	13	31	122	....	....	....	....	....	....	....	....	....	3	0	2	2	0	....	....	....	....
2002-03	**Columbus**	**NHL**	**3**	**0**	**0**	**0**	**0**	**0**	**0**	**0**	**4**	**0.0**	**–1**	**0**	**0.0**	**8:40**	....	....	....	....	....	....	....	....	....
	Syracuse Crunch	AHL	72	14	24	38	93	....	....	....	....	....	....	....	....	....	....	....	....	....	....	....	....	....	....
2003-04	**Columbus**	**NHL**	**29**	**1**	**2**	**3**	**36**	**0**	**0**	**0**	**23**	**4.3**	**–7**	**5**	**60.0**	**10:18**	....	....	....	....	....	....	....	....	....
	Syracuse Crunch	AHL	51	17	31	48	102	....	....	....	....	....	....	....	....	....	5	0	1	1	10	....	....	....	....
2004-05	Aylmer Blues	OHA-Sr.	5	2	4	6	21	....	....	....	....	....	....	....	....	....	....	....	....	....	....	....	....	....	....
	Bergen Flyers	Norway	11	12	3	15	75	....	....	....	....	....	....	....	....	....	....	....	....	....	....	....	....	....	....
	EV Duisburg	German-2	19	4	9	13	57	....	....	....	....	....	....	....	....	....	10	3	3	6	37	....	....	....	....
	NHL Totals		**32**	**1**	**2**	**3**	**36**	**0**	**0**	**0**	**27**	**3.7**		**5**	**60.0**	**10:09**	....	....	....	....	....	....	....	....	....

• Re-entered NHL Entry Draft. Originally Carolina's 9th choice, 225th overall, in 1997 Entry Draft.

Traded to **Columbus** by **Detroit** for Columbus's 6th round choice (Andreas Sundin) in 2003 Entry Draft, August 14, 2000. Signed as a free agent by **Aylmer** (OHA-Sr.), October, 2004. Signed as a free agent by **Bergen** (Norway), October 22, 2004. Signed as a free agent by **Duisburg** (German-2), December 30, 2004. Signed as a free agent by **Detroit**, August 12, 2005.

McEACHERN, Shawn

(muh-GEH-kruhn, SHAWN) **BOS.**

Right wing. Shoots left. 5'11", 200 lbs. Born, Waltham, MA, February 28, 1969. Pittsburgh's 6th choice, 110th overall, in 1987 Entry Draft.

1985-86	Matignon	High-MA	20	32	20	52	....	....	....	....	....	....	....	....	....	....	....	....	....	....	....	....	....	....	....
1986-87	Matignon	High-MA	16	29	28	57	....	....	....	....	....	....	....	....	....	....	....	....	....	....	....	....	....	....	....
1987-88	Matignon	High-MA	22	52	40	92	....	....	....	....	....	....	....	....	....	....	....	....	....	....	....	....	....	....	....
1988-89	Boston University	H-East	36	20	28	48	32	....	....	....	....	....	....	....	....	....	....	....	....	....	....	....	....	....	....
1989-90	Boston University	H-East	43	25	31	56	78	....	....	....	....	....	....	....	....	....	....	....	....	....	....	....	....	....	....
1990-91	Boston University	H-East	41	34	48	82	43	....	....	....	....	....	....	....	....	....	....	....	....	....	....	....	....	....	....
1991-92	United States	Nat-Tm	57	26	23	49	38	....	....	....	....	....	....	....	....	....	....	....	....	....	....	....	....	....	....
	United States	Olympics	8	1	0	1	10	....	....	....	....	....	....	....	....	....	....	....	....	....	....	....	....	....	....
	♦ **Pittsburgh**	**NHL**	**15**	**0**	**4**	**4**	**0**	**0**	**0**	**0**	**14**	**0.0**	**1**	....	....	....	**19**	**2**	**7**	**9**	**4**	**0**	**0**	**0**	....
1992-93	**Pittsburgh**	**NHL**	**84**	**28**	**33**	**61**	**46**	**7**	**0**	**6**	**196**	**14.3**	**21**	....	....	....	**12**	**3**	**2**	**5**	**10**	**0**	**0**	**1**	....

			Regular Season														Playoffs								
Season	Club	League	GP	G	A	Pts	PIM	PP	SH	GW	S	%	+/-	TF	F%	Min	GP	G	A	Pts	PIM	PP	SH	GW	Min
1993-94	Los Angeles	NHL	49	8	13	21	24	0	3	0	81	9.9	1	....	....	....	....	....	....	....	....	....	....	....	....
	Pittsburgh	NHL	27	12	9	21	10	0	2	1	78	15.4	13	....	....	....	6	1	0	1	2	0	0	0	....
1994-95	Kiekko-Espoo	Finland	8	1	3	4	6	....	....	....	....	....	....	....	....	....	....	....	....	....	....	....	....	....	....
	Pittsburgh	NHL	44	13	13	26	22	1	2	1	97	13.4	4	....	....	....	11	0	2	2	8	0	0	0	....
1995-96	Boston	NHL	82	24	29	53	34	3	2	3	238	10.1	–5	....	....	....	5	2	1	3	8	0	0	0	....
1996-97	Ottawa	NHL	65	11	20	31	18	0	1	2	150	7.3	–5	....	....	....	7	2	0	2	8	1	0	0	....
1997-98	Ottawa	NHL	81	24	24	48	42	8	2	4	229	10.5	1	....	....	....	11	0	4	4	8	0	0	0	....
1998-99	Ottawa	NHL	77	31	25	56	46	7	0	4	223	13.9	8	441	48.5	18:45	4	2	0	2	6	1	0	0	21:51
99-2000	Ottawa	NHL	69	29	22	51	24	10	0	4	219	13.2	2	54	50.0	17:50	6	0	3	3	4	0	0	0	18:08
2000-01	Ottawa	NHL	82	32	40	72	62	9	0	1	231	13.9	10	420	48.8	18:25	4	0	2	2	2	0	0	0	20:49
2001-02	Ottawa	NHL	80	15	31	46	52	5	0	3	196	7.7	9	210	52.4	17:40	12	0	4	4	2	0	0	0	16:59
2002-03	Atlanta	NHL	46	10	16	26	28	4	1	1	120	8.3	–27	154	43.5	19:18	....	....	....	....	....	....	....	....	....
2003-04	Atlanta	NHL	82	17	38	55	76	5	1	3	176	9.7	5	181	44.2	20:14	....	....	....	....	....	....	....	....	....
2004-05	Malmo	Sweden	6	0	1	1	14	....	....	....	....	....	....	....	....	....	....	....	....	....	....	....	....	....	....
	Malmo	Sweden-Q	10	1	1	2	12	....	....	....	....	....	....	....	....	....	....	....	....	....	....	....	....	....	....
	NHL Totals		883	254	317	571	484	59	14	33	2248	11.3		1460	48.2	18:41	97	12	25	37	62	2	0	1	18:35

Hockey East Second All-Star Team (1990) • Hockey East First All-Star Team (1991) • NCAA East First All-American Team (1991)

Traded to **Los Angeles** by **Pittsburgh** for Marty McSorley, August 27, 1993. Traded to **Pittsburgh** by **Los Angeles** with Tomas Sandstrom for Marty McSorley and Jim Paek, February 16, 1994. Traded to **Boston** by **Pittsburgh** with Kevin Stevens for Glen Murray, Bryan Smolinski and Boston's 3rd round choice (Boyd Kane) in 1996 Entry Draft, August 2, 1995. Traded to **Ottawa** by **Boston** for Trent McCleary and Ottawa's 3rd round choice (Eric Naud) in 1996 Entry Draft, June 22, 1996. Traded to **Atlanta** by **Ottawa** with Ottawa's 6th round choice (Dan Turple) in 2004 Entry Draft for Brian Pothier, June 29, 2002. Signed as a free agent by **Malmo** (Sweden), January 24, 2005. Signed as a free agent by **Boston**, August 2, 2005.

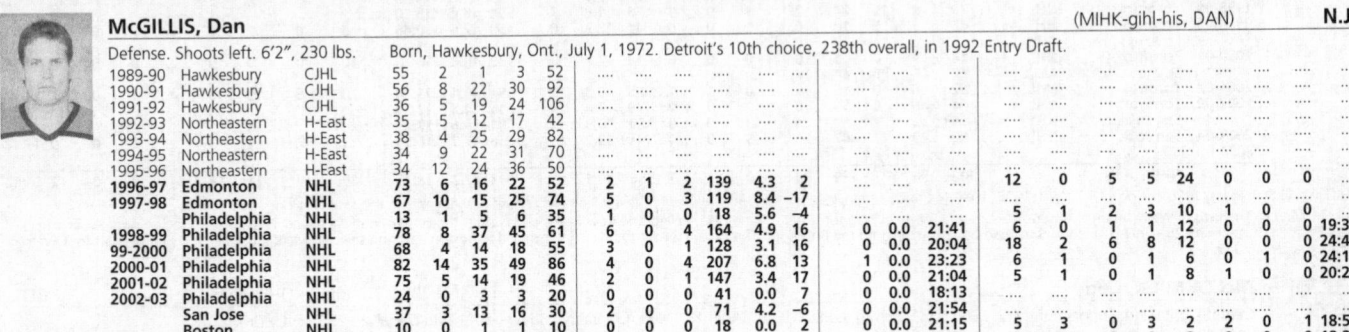

McGILLIS, Dan

(MIHK-gihl-his, DAN) **N.J.**

Defense. Shoots left. 6'2", 230 lbs. Born, Hawkesbury, Ont., July 1, 1972. Detroit's 10th choice, 238th overall, in 1992 Entry Draft.

Season	Club	League	GP	G	A	Pts	PIM	PP	SH	GW	S	%	+/-	TF	F%	Min	GP	G	A	Pts	PIM	PP	SH	GW	Min
1989-90	Hawkesbury	CJHL	55	2	1	3	52	....	....	....	....	....	....	....	....	....	....	....	....	....	....	....	....	....	....
1990-91	Hawkesbury	CJHL	56	8	22	30	92	....	....	....	....	....	....	....	....	....	....	....	....	....	....	....	....	....	....
1991-92	Hawkesbury	CJHL	36	5	19	24	106	....	....	....	....	....	....	....	....	....	....	....	....	....	....	....	....	....	....
1992-93	Northeastern	H-East	35	5	12	17	42	....	....	....	....	....	....	....	....	....	....	....	....	....	....	....	....	....	....
1993-94	Northeastern	H-East	38	4	25	29	82	....	....	....	....	....	....	....	....	....	....	....	....	....	....	....	....	....	....
1994-95	Northeastern	H-East	34	9	22	31	70	....	....	....	....	....	....	....	....	....	....	....	....	....	....	....	....	....	....
1995-96	Northeastern	H-East	34	12	24	36	50	....	....	....	....	....	....	....	....	....	....	....	....	....	....	....	....	....	....
1996-97	Edmonton	NHL	73	6	16	22	52	2	1	2	139	4.3	2	....	....	....	12	0	5	5	24	0	0	0	....
1997-98	Edmonton	NHL	67	10	15	25	74	5	0	3	119	8.4	–17	....	....	....	....	....	....	....	....	....	....	....	....
	Philadelphia	NHL	13	1	5	6	35	1	0	0	18	5.6	–4	....	....	....	5	1	2	3	10	1	0	0	....
1998-99	Philadelphia	NHL	78	8	37	45	61	6	0	4	164	4.9	16	0	0.0	21:41	6	0	1	1	12	0	0	0	19:36
99-2000	Philadelphia	NHL	68	4	14	18	55	3	0	1	128	3.1	16	0	0.0	20:04	18	2	6	8	12	0	0	0	24:42
2000-01	Philadelphia	NHL	82	14	35	49	86	4	0	4	207	6.8	13	1	0.0	23:23	6	1	0	1	6	0	1	0	24:12
2001-02	Philadelphia	NHL	75	5	14	19	46	2	0	1	147	3.4	17	0	0.0	21:04	5	1	0	1	8	1	0	0	20:27
2002-03	Philadelphia	NHL	24	0	3	3	20	0	0	0	41	0.0	7	0	0.0	18:13	....	....	....	....	....	....	....	....	....
	San Jose	NHL	37	3	13	16	30	2	0	0	71	4.2	–6	0	0.0	21:54	....	....	....	....	....	....	....	....	....
	Boston	NHL	10	0	1	1	10	0	0	0	18	0.0	2	0	0.0	21:15	5	3	0	3	2	2	0	1	18:54
2003-04	Boston	NHL	80	5	23	28	65	1	0	2	117	4.3	–1	1	0.0	19:43	7	0	0	0	2	0	0	0	18:38
2004-05			DID NOT PLAY																						
	NHL Totals		607	56	176	232	534	26	1	17	1169	4.8		2	0.0	21:08	64	8	14	22	76	4	1	1	22:01

Hockey East First All-Star Team (1995, 1996) • NCAA East First All-American Team (1996)

Traded to **Edmonton** by **Detroit** for Kirk Maltby, March 20, 1996. Traded to **Philadelphia** by **Edmonton** with Edmonton's 2nd round choice (Jason Beckett) in 1998 Entry Draft for Janne Niinimaa, March 24, 1998. Traded to **San Jose** by **Philadelphia** for Marcus Ragnarsson, December 6, 2002. Traded to **Boston** by **San Jose** for Boston's 2nd round choice (later traded to NY Rangers – NY Rangers selected Ivan Baranka) in 2003 Entry Draft, March 11, 2003. Signed as a free agent by **New Jersey**, August 4, 2005.

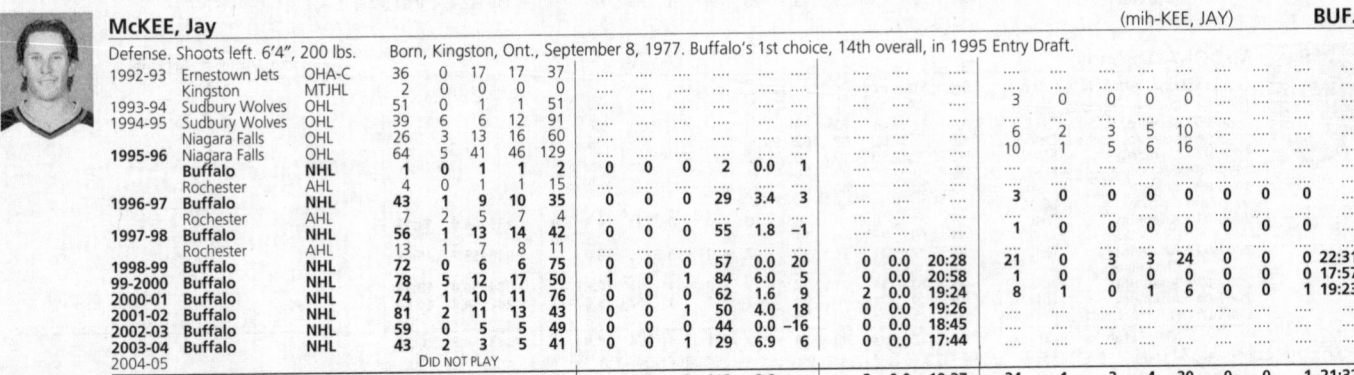

McKEE, Jay

(mih-KEE, JAY) **BUF.**

Defense. Shoots left. 6'4", 200 lbs. Born, Kingston, Ont., September 8, 1977. Buffalo's 1st choice, 14th overall, in 1995 Entry Draft.

Season	Club	League	GP	G	A	Pts	PIM	PP	SH	GW	S	%	+/-	TF	F%	Min	GP	G	A	Pts	PIM	PP	SH	GW	Min
1992-93	Ernestown Jets	OHA-C	36	0	17	17	37	....	....	....	....	....	....	....	....	....	....	....	....	....	....	....	....	....	....
	Kingston	MTJHL	2	0	0	0	0	....	....	....	....	....	....	....	....	....	....	....	....	....	....	....	....	....	....
1993-94	Sudbury Wolves	OHL	51	0	1	1	51	....	....	....	....	....	....	....	....	....	3	0	0	0	0	....	....	....	....
1994-95	Sudbury Wolves	OHL	39	6	6	12	91	....	....	....	....	....	....	....	....	....	....	....	....	....	....	....	....	....	....
	Niagara Falls	OHL	26	3	13	16	60	....	....	....	....	....	....	....	....	....	6	2	3	5	10	....	....	....	....
1995-96	Niagara Falls	OHL	64	5	41	46	129	....	....	....	....	....	....	....	....	....	10	1	5	6	16	....	....	....	....
	Buffalo	NHL	1	0	1	1	2	0	0	0	2	0.0	1	....	....	....	....	....	....	....	....	....	....	....	....
	Rochester	AHL	4	0	1	1	15	....	....	....	....	....	....	....	....	....	....	....	....	....	....	....	....	....	....
1996-97	Buffalo	NHL	43	1	9	10	35	0	0	0	29	3.4	3	....	....	....	3	0	0	0	0	0	0	0	....
	Rochester	AHL	7	2	5	7	4	....	....	....	....	....	....	....	....	....	....	....	....	....	....	....	....	....	....
1997-98	Buffalo	NHL	56	1	13	14	42	0	0	0	55	1.8	–1	....	....	....	1	0	0	0	0	0	0	0	....
	Rochester	AHL	13	1	7	8	11	....	....	....	....	....	....	....	....	....	....	....	....	....	....	....	....	....	....
1998-99	Buffalo	NHL	72	0	6	6	75	0	0	0	57	0.0	20	0	0.0	20:28	21	0	3	3	24	0	0	0	22:31
99-2000	Buffalo	NHL	78	5	12	17	50	1	0	1	84	6.0	5	0	0.0	20:58	1	0	0	0	0	0	0	0	17:57
2000-01	Buffalo	NHL	74	1	10	11	76	0	0	0	62	1.6	9	2	0.0	19:24	8	1	0	1	6	0	0	1	19:23
2001-02	Buffalo	NHL	81	2	11	13	43	0	0	1	50	4.0	18	0	0.0	19:26	....	....	....	....	....	....	....	....	....
2002-03	Buffalo	NHL	59	0	5	5	49	0	0	0	44	0.0	–16	0	0.0	18:45	....	....	....	....	....	....	....	....	....
2003-04	Buffalo	NHL	43	2	3	5	41	0	0	1	29	6.9	6	0	0.0	17:44	....	....	....	....	....	....	....	....	....
2004-05			DID NOT PLAY																						
	NHL Totals		507	12	70	82	413	1	0	3	412	2.9		2	0.0	19:37	34	1	3	4	30	0	0	1	21:32

OHL Second All-Star Team (1996)

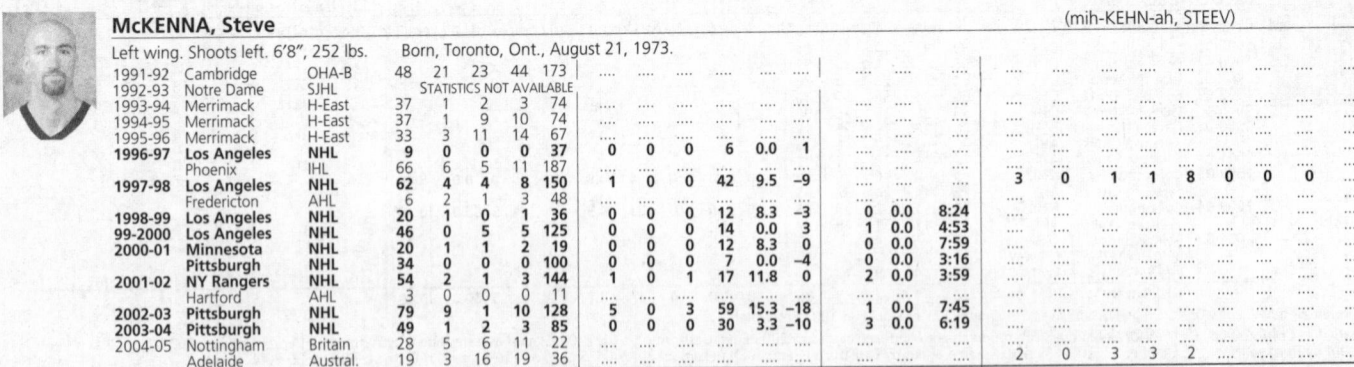

McKENNA, Steve

(mih-KEHN-ah, STEEV)

Left wing. Shoots left. 6'8", 252 lbs. Born, Toronto, Ont., August 21, 1973.

Season	Club	League	GP	G	A	Pts	PIM	PP	SH	GW	S	%	+/-	TF	F%	Min	GP	G	A	Pts	PIM	PP	SH	GW	Min
1991-92	Cambridge	OHA-B	48	21	23	44	173	....	....	....	....	....	....	....	....	....	....	....	....	....	....	....	....	....	....
1992-93	Notre Dame	SJHL	STATISTICS NOT AVAILABLE																						
1993-94	Merrimack	H-East	37	1	2	3	74	....	....	....	....	....	....	....	....	....	....	....	....	....	....	....	....	....	....
1994-95	Merrimack	H-East	37	1	9	10	74	....	....	....	....	....	....	....	....	....	....	....	....	....	....	....	....	....	....
1995-96	Merrimack	H-East	33	3	11	14	67	....	....	....	....	....	....	....	....	....	....	....	....	....	....	....	....	....	....
1996-97	Los Angeles	NHL	9	0	0	0	37	0	0	0	6	0.0	1	....	....	....	....	....	....	....	....	....	....	....	....
	Phoenix	IHL	66	6	5	11	187	....	....	....	....	....	....	....	....	....	....	....	....	....	....	....	....	....	....
1997-98	Los Angeles	NHL	62	4	4	8	150	1	0	0	42	9.5	–9	....	....	....	3	0	1	1	8	0	0	0	....
	Fredericton	AHL	6	2	1	3	48	....	....	....	....	....	....	....	....	....	....	....	....	....	....	....	....	....	....
1998-99	Los Angeles	NHL	20	1	0	1	36	0	0	0	12	8.3	–3	0	0.0	8:24	....	....	....	....	....	....	....	....	....
99-2000	Los Angeles	NHL	46	0	5	5	125	0	0	0	14	0.0	3	1	0.0	4:53	....	....	....	....	....	....	....	....	....
2000-01	Minnesota	NHL	20	1	1	2	19	0	0	0	12	8.3	0	0	0.0	7:59	....	....	....	....	....	....	....	....	....
	Pittsburgh	NHL	34	0	0	0	100	0	0	0	7	0.0	–4	0	0.0	3:16	....	....	....	....	....	....	....	....	....
2001-02	NY Rangers	NHL	54	2	1	3	144	1	0	1	17	11.8	0	2	0.0	3:59	....	....	....	....	....	....	....	....	....
	Hartford	AHL	3	0	0	0	11	....	....	....	....	....	....	....	....	....	....	....	....	....	....	....	....	....	....
2002-03	Pittsburgh	NHL	79	9	1	10	128	5	0	3	59	15.3	–18	1	0.0	7:45	....	....	....	....	....	....	....	....	....
2003-04	Pittsburgh	NHL	49	1	2	3	85	0	0	0	30	3.3	–10	3	0.0	6:19	....	....	....	....	....	....	....	....	....
2004-05	Nottingham	Britain	28	5	6	11	22	....	....	....	....	....	....	....	....	....	....	....	....	....	....	....	....	....	....
	Adelaide	Austral.	19	3	16	19	36	....	....	....	....	....	....	....	....	....	2	0	3	3	2	....	....	....	....
	NHL Totals		373	18	14	32	824	7	0	4	199	9.0		7	0.0	5:58	3	0	1	1	8	0	0	0	....

Signed as a free agent by **Los Angeles**, May 23, 1996. Claimed by **Minnesota** from **Los Angeles** in Expansion Draft, June 23, 2000. Traded to **Pittsburgh** by **Minnesota** for Roman Simicek, January 13, 2001. Signed as a free agent by **NY Rangers**, August 28, 2001. Signed as a free agent by **Pittsburgh**, July 12, 2002. Signed as a free agent by **Nottingham** (Britain), October 26, 2004. Signed as a free agent by **Adelaide** (Australia), May 5, 2005.

McKENZIE, Jim

(MIHK-ehn-zee, JIHM)

Left wing. Shoots left. 6'4", 230 lbs. Born, Gull Lake, Sask., November 3, 1969. Hartford's 3rd choice, 73rd overall, in 1989 Entry Draft.

Season	Club	League	Regular Season GP	G	A	Pts	PIM	PP	SH	GW	S	%	+/-	TF	F%	Min	Playoffs GP	G	A	Pts	PIM	PP	SH	GW	Min
1985-86	Moose Jaw	SMHL	36	18	26	44	89	....	....	....	....	....	....	....	....	....	....	....	....	....	....	....	....	....	....
	Moose Jaw	WHL	3	0	2	2	0	....	....	....	....	....	....	....	....	....	....	....	....	....	....	....	....	....	....
1986-87	Moose Jaw	WHL	65	5	3	8	125	....	....	....	....	....	....	....	....	....	9	0	0	0	7	....	....	....	....
1987-88	Moose Jaw	WHL	62	1	17	18	134	....	....	....	....	....	....	....	....	....	....	....	....	....	....	....	....	....	....
1988-89	Victoria Cougars	WHL	67	15	27	42	176	....	....	....	....	....	....	....	....	....	8	1	4	5	30	....	....	....	....
1989-90	**Hartford**	**NHL**	**5**	**0**	**0**	**0**	**4**	**0**	**0**	**0**	**0**	**0.0**	**0**	....	....	....	....	....	....	....	....	....	....	....	....
	Binghamton	AHL	56	4	12	16	149	....	....	....	....	....	....	....	....	....	....	....	....	....	....	....	....	....	....
1990-91	**Hartford**	**NHL**	**41**	**4**	**3**	**7**	**108**	**0**	**0**	**0**	**16**	**25.0**	**–7**	....	....	....	**6**	**0**	**0**	**0**	**8**	**0**	**0**	**0**	....
	Springfield	AHL	24	3	4	7	102	....	....	....	....	....	....	....	....	....	....	....	....	....	....	....	....	....	....
1991-92	**Hartford**	**NHL**	**67**	**5**	**1**	**6**	**87**	**0**	**0**	**0**	**34**	**14.7**	**–6**	....	....	....	....	....	....	....	....	....	....	....	....
1992-93	**Hartford**	**NHL**	**64**	**3**	**6**	**9**	**202**	**0**	**0**	**0**	**36**	**8.3**	**–10**	....	....	....	....	....	....	....	....	....	....	....	....
1993-94	**Hartford**	**NHL**	**26**	**1**	**2**	**3**	**67**	**0**	**0**	**0**	**9**	**11.1**	**–6**	....	....	....	....	....	....	....	....	....	....	....	....
	Dallas	**NHL**	**34**	**2**	**3**	**5**	**63**	**0**	**0**	**1**	**18**	**11.1**	**4**	....	....	....	....	....	....	....	....	....	....	....	....
	Pittsburgh	**NHL**	**11**	**0**	**0**	**0**	**16**	**0**	**0**	**0**	**6**	**0.0**	**–5**	....	....	....	**3**	**0**	**0**	**0**	**0**	**0**	**0**	**0**	....
1994-95	**Pittsburgh**	**NHL**	**39**	**2**	**1**	**3**	**63**	**0**	**0**	**1**	**16**	**12.5**	**–7**	....	....	....	**5**	**0**	**0**	**0**	**4**	**0**	**0**	**0**	....
1995-96	**Winnipeg**	**NHL**	**73**	**4**	**2**	**6**	**202**	**0**	**0**	**0**	**28**	**14.3**	**–4**	....	....	....	**1**	**0**	**0**	**0**	**2**	**0**	**0**	**0**	....
1996-97	**Phoenix**	**NHL**	**65**	**5**	**3**	**8**	**200**	**0**	**0**	**1**	**38**	**13.2**	**–5**	....	....	....	**7**	**0**	**0**	**0**	**2**	**0**	**0**	**0**	....
1997-98	**Phoenix**	**NHL**	**64**	**3**	**4**	**7**	**146**	**0**	**0**	**0**	**35**	**8.6**	**–7**	....	....	....	**1**	**0**	**0**	**0**	**0**	**0**	**0**	**0**	....
1998-99	**Anaheim**	**NHL**	**73**	**5**	**4**	**9**	**99**	**1**	**0**	**1**	**59**	**8.5**	**–18**	**8**	**50.0**	**10:22**	**4**	**0**	**0**	**0**	**4**	**0**	**0**	**0**	**6:58**
99-2000	**Anaheim**	**NHL**	**31**	**3**	**3**	**6**	**48**	**0**	**0**	**0**	**22**	**13.6**	**–5**	**2**	**0.0**	**10:26**	....	....	....	....	....	....	....	....	....
	Washington	**NHL**	**30**	**1**	**2**	**3**	**16**	**0**	**0**	**0**	**10**	**10.0**	**0**	**0**	**0.0**	**6:22**	**1**	**0**	**0**	**0**	**0**	**0**	**0**	**0**	**0:17**
2000-01	**New Jersey**	**NHL**	**53**	**2**	**2**	**4**	**119**	**0**	**0**	**0**	**32**	**6.3**	**0**	**0**	**0.0**	**7:56**	**3**	**0**	**0**	**0**	**2**	**0**	**0**	**0**	**5:42**
2001-02	**New Jersey**	**NHL**	**67**	**3**	**5**	**8**	**123**	**1**	**0**	**0**	**33**	**9.1**	**0**	**3**	**0.0**	**7:19**	**6**	**0**	**0**	**0**	**2**	**0**	**0**	**0**	**9:47**
2002-03♦	**New Jersey**	**NHL**	**76**	**4**	**8**	**12**	**88**	**0**	**0**	**2**	**42**	**9.5**	**3**	**5**	**60.0**	**7:42**	**13**	**0**	**0**	**0**	**14**	**0**	**0**	**0**	**8:00**
2003-04	**Nashville**	**NHL**	**61**	**1**	**3**	**4**	**88**	**0**	**0**	**0**	**10**	**10.0**	**–13**	**3**	**66.7**	**6:14**	**1**	**0**	**0**	**0**	**0**	**0**	**0**	**0**	**3:32**
2004-05			Did not play																						
	NHL Totals		**880**	**48**	**52**	**100**	**1739**	**2**	**0**	**6**	**444**	**10.8**		**21**	**42.9**	**8:03**	**51**	**0**	**0**	**0**	**38**	**0**	**0**	**0**	**7:33**

Traded to **Florida** by **Hartford** for Alexander Godynyuk, December 16, 1993. Traded to **Dallas** by **Florida** for Dallas' 4th round choice (later traded to Ottawa – Ottawa selected Kevin Bolibruck) in 1995 Entry Draft, December 16, 1993. Traded to **Pittsburgh** by **Dallas** for Mike Needham, March 21, 1994. Signed as a free agent by **NY Islanders**, August 2, 1995. Claimed by **Winnipeg** from **NY Islanders** in Waiver Draft, October 2, 1995. Transferred to **Phoenix** after **Winnipeg** franchise relocated, July 1, 1996. Traded to **Anaheim** by **Phoenix** for Jean-Francois Jomphe, June 18, 1998. Claimed on waivers by **Washington** from **Anaheim**, January 20, 2000. Signed as a free agent by **New Jersey**, July 3, 2000. Signed as a free agent by **Nashville**, July 22, 2003.

McLAREN, Kyle

(mih-KLAIR-uhn, KIGHL) **S.J.**

Defense. Shoots left. 6'4", 225 lbs. Born, Humboldt, Sask., June 18, 1977. Boston's 1st choice, 9th overall, in 1995 Entry Draft.

Season	Club	League	Regular Season GP	G	A	Pts	PIM	PP	SH	GW	S	%	+/-	TF	F%	Min	Playoffs GP	G	A	Pts	PIM	PP	SH	GW	Min
1992-93	Lethbridge	AMHL	60	28	28	56	84	....	....	....	....	....	....	....	....	....	....	....	....	....	....	....	....	....	....
1993-94	Tacoma Rockets	WHL	62	1	9	10	53	....	....	....	....	....	....	....	....	....	6	1	4	5	6	....	....	....	....
1994-95	Tacoma Rockets	WHL	47	13	19	32	68	....	....	....	....	....	....	....	....	....	4	1	1	2	4	....	....	....	....
1995-96	**Boston**	**NHL**	**74**	**5**	**12**	**17**	**73**	**0**	**0**	**0**	**74**	**6.8**	**16**	....	....	....	**5**	**0**	**0**	**0**	**14**	**0**	**0**	**0**	....
1996-97	**Boston**	**NHL**	**58**	**5**	**9**	**14**	**54**	**0**	**0**	**1**	**68**	**7.4**	**–9**	....	....	....	....	....	....	....	....	....	....	....	....
1997-98	**Boston**	**NHL**	**66**	**5**	**20**	**25**	**56**	**2**	**0**	**0**	**101**	**5.0**	**13**	....	....	....	**6**	**1**	**0**	**1**	**4**	**1**	**0**	**0**	....
1998-99	**Boston**	**NHL**	**52**	**6**	**18**	**24**	**48**	**3**	**0**	**0**	**97**	**6.2**	**1**	**0**	**0.0**	**23:25**	**12**	**0**	**3**	**3**	**10**	**0**	**0**	**0**	**26:45**
99-2000	**Boston**	**NHL**	**71**	**8**	**11**	**19**	**67**	**2**	**0**	**3**	**142**	**5.6**	**–4**	**5**	**40.0**	**23:18**	....	....	....	....	....	....	....	....	....
2000-01	**Boston**	**NHL**	**58**	**5**	**12**	**17**	**53**	**2**	**0**	**0**	**91**	**5.5**	**–5**	**4**	**50.0**	**24:14**	....	....	....	....	....	....	....	....	....
2001-02	**Boston**	**NHL**	**38**	**0**	**8**	**8**	**19**	**0**	**0**	**0**	**57**	**0.0**	**–4**	**1**	**0.0**	**19:21**	**4**	**0**	**0**	**0**	**20**	**0**	**0**	**0**	**18:37**
2002-03	**San Jose**	**NHL**	**33**	**0**	**8**	**8**	**30**	**0**	**0**	**0**	**43**	**0.0**	**–10**	**0**	**0.0**	**22:40**	....	....	....	....	....	....	....	....	....
2003-04	**San Jose**	**NHL**	**64**	**2**	**22**	**24**	**60**	**0**	**1**	**0**	**67**	**3.0**	**10**	**1**	**0.0**	**21:01**	**16**	**0**	**3**	**3**	**10**	**0**	**0**	**0**	**24:09**
2004-05			Did not play																						
	NHL Totals		**514**	**36**	**120**	**156**	**460**	**9**	**1**	**4**	**740**	**4.9**		**11**	**36.4**	**22:29**	**43**	**1**	**6**	**7**	**58**	**1**	**0**	**0**	**24:26**

NHL All-Rookie Team (1996)

• Missed majority of 2001-02 season recovering from chest (October 10, 2001 vs. Minnesota) and wrist (December 26, 2001 vs. Ottawa) injuries. • Missed majority of 2002-03 season in contract dispute with Boston. Traded to **San Jose** by **Boston** with Boston's 4th round choice (Torrey Mitchell) in 2004 Entry Draft for Jeff Hackett and Jeff Jillson, January 23, 2003.

McLAREN, Steve

(muh-KLAIR-uhn, STEEV) **T.B.**

Defense. Shoots left. 6', 227 lbs. Born, Owen Sound, Ont., February 3, 1975. Chicago's 3rd choice, 85th overall, in 1994 Entry Draft.

Season	Club	League	Regular Season GP	G	A	Pts	PIM	PP	SH	GW	S	%	+/-	TF	F%	Min	Playoffs GP	G	A	Pts	PIM	PP	SH	GW	Min
1992-93	N. Bay Trappers	NOJHA	30	15	18	33	110	....	....	....	....	....	....	....	....	....	....	....	....	....	....	....	....	....	....
1993-94	North Bay	OHL	55	2	15	17	130	....	....	....	....	....	....	....	....	....	18	0	3	3	50	....	....	....	....
1994-95	North Bay	OHL	27	3	10	13	119	....	....	....	....	....	....	....	....	....	6	2	1	3	23	....	....	....	....
1995-96	Indianapolis Ice	IHL	54	1	2	3	170	....	....	....	....	....	....	....	....	....	3	0	0	0	2	....	....	....	....
1996-97	Indianapolis Ice	IHL	63	2	5	7	309	....	....	....	....	....	....	....	....	....	4	0	0	0	10	....	....	....	....
1997-98	Indianapolis Ice	IHL	61	3	5	8	208	....	....	....	....	....	....	....	....	....	5	0	0	0	24	....	....	....	....
1998-99	Philadelphia	AHL	52	4	3	7	216	....	....	....	....	....	....	....	....	....	7	0	0	0	2	....	....	....	....
99-2000	Philadelphia	AHL	64	1	2	3	247	....	....	....	....	....	....	....	....	....	....	....	....	....	....	....	....	....	....
2000-01	Philadelphia	AHL	48	3	1	4	177	....	....	....	....	....	....	....	....	....	8	0	0	0	38	....	....	....	....
2001-02	Worcester IceCats	AHL	58	0	4	4	251	....	....	....	....	....	....	....	....	....	1	0	0	0	2	....	....	....	....
2002-03	Worcester IceCats	AHL	40	0	0	0	80	....	....	....	....	....	....	....	....	....	3	0	0	0	4	....	....	....	....
2003-04	**St. Louis**	**NHL**	**6**	**0**	**0**	**0**	**25**	**0**	**0**	**0**	**2**	**0.0**	**0**	**0**	**0.0**	**2:47**	....	....	....	....	....	....	....	....	....
	Worcester IceCats	AHL	35	2	1	3	146	....	....	....	....	....	....	....	....	....	6	0	0	0	2	....	....	....	....
2004-05	Springfield	AHL	26	1	0	1	78	....	....	....	....	....	....	....	....	....	....	....	....	....	....	....	....	....	....
	NHL Totals		**6**	**0**	**0**	**0**	**25**	**0**	**0**	**0**	**2**	**0.0**		**0**	**0.0**	**2:47**	....	....	....	....	....	....	....	....	....

Signed as a free agent by **Philadelphia**, August 24, 1998. Signed as a free agent by **St. Louis**, July 16, 2001. • Missed majority of 2003-04 season recovering from head injury suffered in game vs. Columbus, December 29, 2003. Signed as a free agent by **Tampa Bay**, July 28, 2004.

McLEAN, Brett

(mihk-LAYN, BREHT) **COL.**

Center. Shoots left. 5'11", 194 lbs. Born, Comox, B.C., August 14, 1978. Dallas' 9th choice, 242nd overall, in 1997 Entry Draft.

Season	Club	League	Regular Season GP	G	A	Pts	PIM	PP	SH	GW	S	%	+/-	TF	F%	Min	Playoffs GP	G	A	Pts	PIM	PP	SH	GW	Min
1993-94	Notre Dame	SMBHL	71	109	124	233	70	....	....	....	....	....	....	....	....	....	....	....	....	....	....	....	....	....	....
1994-95	Tacoma Rockets	WHL	67	11	23	34	33	....	....	....	....	....	....	....	....	....	4	0	1	1	0	....	....	....	....
1995-96	Kelowna Rockets	WHL	71	37	42	79	60	....	....	....	....	....	....	....	....	....	6	2	2	4	6	....	....	....	....
1996-97	Kelowna Rockets	WHL	72	44	60	104	98	....	....	....	....	....	....	....	....	....	6	4	2	6	12	....	....	....	....
1997-98	Kelowna Rockets	WHL	54	42	45	87	91	....	....	....	....	....	....	....	....	....	7	4	5	9	17	....	....	....	....
1998-99	Kelowna Rockets	WHL	44	32	38	70	46	....	....	....	....	....	....	....	....	....	....	....	....	....	....	....	....	....	....
	Brandon	WHL	21	15	16	31	20	....	....	....	....	....	....	....	....	....	5	1	6	7	8	....	....	....	....
	Cincinnati	AHL	7	0	3	3	6	....	....	....	....	....	....	....	....	....	....	....	....	....	....	....	....	....	....
99-2000	Johnstown Chiefs	ECHL	8	4	7	11	6	....	....	....	....	....	....	....	....	....	....	....	....	....	....	....	....	....	....
	Saint John Flames	AHL	72	15	23	38	115	....	....	....	....	....	....	....	....	....	3	0	1	1	2	....	....	....	....
2000-01	Cleveland	IHL	74	20	24	44	54	....	....	....	....	....	....	....	....	....	4	0	0	0	18	....	....	....	....
2001-02	Houston Aeros	AHL	78	24	21	45	71	....	....	....	....	....	....	....	....	....	14	1	6	7	12	....	....	....	....
2002-03	**Chicago**	**NHL**	**2**	**0**	**0**	**0**	**0**	**0**	**0**	**0**	**1**	**0.0**	**–1**	**19**	**26.3**	**10:47**	....	....	....	....	....	....	....	....	....
	Norfolk Admirals	AHL	77	23	38	61	60	....	....	....	....	....	....	....	....	....	9	2	6	8	9	....	....	....	....
2003-04	**Chicago**	**NHL**	**76**	**11**	**20**	**31**	**54**	**5**	**1**	**0**	**125**	**8.8**	**–11**	**1135**	**51.1**	**17:33**	....	....	....	....	....	....	....	....	....
	Norfolk Admirals	AHL	4	3	3	6	6	....	....	....	....	....	....	....	....	....	....	....	....	....	....	....	....	....	....
2004-05	Malmo	Sweden	38	7	6	13	102	....	....	....	....	....	....	....	....	....	....	....	....	....	....	....	....	....	....
	Malmo	Sweden-Q	9	1	1	2	16	....	....	....	....	....	....	....	....	....	....	....	....	....	....	....	....	....	....
	NHL Totals		**78**	**11**	**20**	**31**	**54**	**5**	**1**	**0**	**126**	**8.7**		**1154**	**50.7**	**17:23**	....	....	....	....	....	....	....	....	....

WHL West Second All-Star Team (1998)

Signed as a free agent by **Calgary**, September, 1999. Signed as a free agent by **Minnesota**, July 13, 2000. Signed as a free agent by **Chicago**, July 23, 2002. Signed as a free agent by **Colorado**, July 22, 2004. Signed as a free agent by **Malmo** (Sweden), September 24, 2004.

			Regular Season														Playoffs								
Season	Club	League	GP	G	A	Pts	PIM	PP	SH	GW	S	%	+/-	TF	F%	Min	GP	G	A	Pts	PIM	PP	SH	GW	Min

McMORROW, Sean

(muhk-MOHR-roh, SHAWN) **BUF.**

Left wing. Shoots right. 6'4", 235 lbs. Born, Vancouver, B.C., January 19, 1982. Buffalo's 7th choice, 258th overall, in 2000 Entry Draft.

Season	Club	League	GP	G	A	Pts	PIM	PP	SH	GW	S	%	+/-	TF	F%	Min	GP	G	A	Pts	PIM	PP	SH	GW	Min
1998-99	Pickering Panthers	OPJHL	35	2	10	12	175	....	....	....	....	....	....	....	....	....	....	....	....	....	....	....	....	....	....
99-2000	Sarnia Sting	OHL	31	0	1	1	75	....	....	....	....	....	....	....	....	....	....	....	....	....	....	....	....	....	....
	Kitchener Rangers	OHL	31	0	1	1	67	....	....	....	....	....	....	....	....	....	4	0	0	0	12	....	....	....	....
2000-01	Mississauga	OHL	13	0	0	0	34	....	....	....	....	....	....	....	....	....	....	....	....	....	....	....	....	....	....
	Kingston	OHL	7	0	1	1	22	....	....	....	....	....	....	....	....	....	....	....	....	....	....	....	....	....	....
	London Knights	OHL	29	0	3	3	75	....	....	....	....	....	....	....	....	....	5	0	0	0	0	....	....	....	....
2001-02	London Knights	OHL	38	0	1	1	107	....	....	....	....	....	....	....	....	....	....	....	....	....	....	....	....	....	....
	Oshawa Generals	OHL	27	6	1	7	63	....	....	....	....	....	....	....	....	....	5	1	0	1	12	....	....	....	....
2002-03	**Buffalo**	**NHL**	**1**	**0**	**0**	**0**	**0**	**0**	**0**	**0**	**0**	**0.0**	**0**	**0**	**0.0**	**1:27**	....	....	....	....	....	....	....	....	....
	Rochester	AHL	64	0	1	1	315	....	....	....	....	....	....	....	....	....	3	0	0	0	17	....	....	....	....
2003-04	Rochester	AHL	57	0	0	0	287	....	....	....	....	....	....	....	....	....	14	1	0	1	15	....	....	....	....
2004-05	Rochester	AHL	59	3	3	6	288	....	....	....	....	....	....	....	....	....	4	0	0	0	16	....	....	....	....
	NHL Totals		**1**	**0**	**0**	**0**	**0**	**0**	**0**	**0**	**0**	**0.0**		**0**	**0.0**	**1:27**	....	....	....	....	....	....	....	....	....

McNEILL, Grant

(muhk-NEEL, GRANT) **FLA.**

Defense. Shoots left. 6'2", 210 lbs. Born, Vermillion, Alta., June 8, 1983. Florida's 5th choice, 68th overall, in 2001 Entry Draft.

Season	Club	League	GP	G	A	Pts	PIM	PP	SH	GW	S	%	+/-	TF	F%	Min	GP	G	A	Pts	PIM	PP	SH	GW	Min
1998-99	Wainwright	AAHL	26	2	11	13	83	....	....	....	....	....	....	....	....	....	6	0	6	6	14	....	....	....	....
99-2000	Prince Albert	WHL	58	1	1	2	43	....	....	....	....	....	....	....	....	....	6	0	1	1	0	....	....	....	....
2000-01	Prince Albert	WHL	61	2	6	8	280	....	....	....	....	....	....	....	....	....	....	....	....	....	....	....	....	....	....
2001-02	Prince Albert	WHL	70	7	6	13	*326	....	....	....	....	....	....	....	....	....	....	....	....	....	....	....	....	....	....
2002-03	Prince Albert	WHL	71	1	8	9	280	....	....	....	....	....	....	....	....	....	....	....	....	....	....	....	....	....	....
2003-04	**Florida**	**NHL**	**3**	**0**	**0**	**0**	**5**	**0**	**0**	**0**	**0**	**0.0**	**0**	**0**	**0.0**	**2:43**	....	....	....	....	....	....	....	....	....
	San Antonio	AHL	33	0	0	0	110	....	....	....	....	....	....	....	....	....	....	....	....	....	....	....	....	....	....
2004-05	San Antonio	AHL	40	0	2	2	231	....	....	....	....	....	....	....	....	....	....	....	....	....	....	....	....	....	....
	Texas Wildcatters	ECHL	24	0	3	3	111	....	....	....	....	....	....	....	....	....	....	....	....	....	....	....	....	....	....
	NHL Totals		**3**	**0**	**0**	**0**	**5**	**0**	**0**	**0**	**0**	**0.0**		**0**	**0.0**	**2:43**	....	....	....	....	....	....	....	....	....

• Missed majority of 2003-04 season recovering from jaw injury suffered in game vs. Cincinnati (AHL), January 21, 2004.

MELICHAR, Josef

(mehl-ee-KHAHR, YOH-sehf) **PIT.**

Defense. Shoots left. 6'2", 220 lbs. Born, Ceske Budejovice, Czech., January 20, 1979. Pittsburgh's 3rd choice, 71st overall, in 1997 Entry Draft.

Season	Club	League	GP	G	A	Pts	PIM	PP	SH	GW	S	%	+/-	TF	F%	Min	GP	G	A	Pts	PIM	PP	SH	GW	Min
1995-96	C. Budejovice Jr.	CzRep-Jr.	38	3	4	7		....	....	....	....	....	....	....	....	....	....	....	....	....	....	....	....	....	....
1996-97	C. Budejovice Jr.	CzRep-Jr.	41	2	3	5	10	....	....	....	....	....	....	....	....	....	....	....	....	....	....	....	....	....	....
1997-98	Tri-City	WHL	67	9	24	33	154	....	....	....	....	....	....	....	....	....	....	....	....	....	....	....	....	....	....
1998-99	Tri-City	WHL	65	8	28	36	125	....	....	....	....	....	....	....	....	....	11	1	0	1	15	....	....	....	....
99-2000	Wilkes-Barre	AHL	80	3	9	12	126	....	....	....	....	....	....	....	....	....	....	....	....	....	....	....	....	....	....
2000-01	**Pittsburgh**	**NHL**	**18**	**0**	**2**	**2**	**21**	**0**	**0**	**0**	**9**	**0.0**	**-5**	**0**	**0.0**	**14:54**	....	....	....	....	....	....	....	....	....
	Wilkes-Barre	AHL	46	2	5	7	69	....	....	....	....	....	....	....	....	....	21	0	5	5	6	....	....	....	....
2001-02	**Pittsburgh**	**NHL**	**60**	**0**	**3**	**3**	**68**	**0**	**0**	**0**	**46**	**0.0**	**-1**	**0**	**0.0**	**16:46**	....	....	....	....	....	....	....	....	....
2002-03	**Pittsburgh**	**NHL**	**8**	**0**	**0**	**0**	**2**	**0**	**0**	**0**	**6**	**0.0**	**-2**	**0**	**0.0**	**15:19**	....	....	....	....	....	....	....	....	....
2003-04	**Pittsburgh**	**NHL**	**82**	**3**	**5**	**8**	**62**	**0**	**0**	**0**	**78**	**3.8**	**-17**	**0**	**0.0**	**19:01**	....	....	....	....	....	....	....	....	....
2004-05	HC Sparta Praha	CzRep	13	0	4	4	8	....	....	....	....	....	....	....	....	....	5	0	0	0	6	....	....	....	....
	NHL Totals		**168**	**3**	**10**	**13**	**153**	**0**	**0**	**0**	**139**	**2.2**		**0**	**0.0**	**17:36**	....	....	....	....	....	....	....	....	....

• Missed majority of 2002-03 season recovering from shoulder injury suffered in game vs. Boston, October 13, 2002. Signed as a free agent by **Sparta** (CzRep), September 17, 2004.

MELLANBY, Scott

(MEH-lihn-bee, SKAWT) **ATL.**

Right wing. Shoots right. 6'1", 210 lbs. Born, Montreal, Que., June 11, 1966. Philadelphia's 2nd choice, 27th overall, in 1984 Entry Draft.

Season	Club	League	GP	G	A	Pts	PIM	PP	SH	GW	S	%	+/-	TF	F%	Min	GP	G	A	Pts	PIM	PP	SH	GW	Min
1982-83	Don Mills Flyers	MTHL	72	66	52	118	38	....	....	....	....	....	....	....	....	....	....	....	....	....	....	....	....	....	....
1983-84	Henry Carr	OHA-B	39	37	37	74	97	....	....	....	....	....	....	....	....	....	....	....	....	....	....	....	....	....	....
1984-85	U. of Wisconsin	WCHA	40	14	24	38	60	....	....	....	....	....	....	....	....	....	....	....	....	....	....	....	....	....	....
1985-86	U. of Wisconsin	WCHA	32	21	23	44	89	....	....	....	....	....	....	....	....	....	....	....	....	....	....	....	....	....	....
	Philadelphia	**NHL**	**2**	**0**	**0**	**0**	**0**	**0**	**0**	**0**	**0**	**0.0**	**-1**	....	....	....	....	....	....	....	....	....	....	....	....
1986-87	**Philadelphia**	**NHL**	**71**	**11**	**21**	**32**	**94**	**1**	**0**	**0**	**118**	**9.3**	**8**	....	....	....	**24**	**5**	**5**	**10**	**46**	**0**	**0**	**1**	....
1987-88	**Philadelphia**	**NHL**	**75**	**25**	**26**	**51**	**185**	**7**	**0**	**2**	**190**	**13.2**	**-7**	....	....	....	**7**	**0**	**1**	**1**	**16**	**0**	**0**	**0**	....
1988-89	**Philadelphia**	**NHL**	**76**	**21**	**29**	**50**	**183**	**11**	**0**	**3**	**202**	**10.4**	**-13**	....	....	....	**19**	**4**	**5**	**9**	**28**	**0**	**0**	**0**	....
1989-90	**Philadelphia**	**NHL**	**57**	**6**	**17**	**23**	**77**	**0**	**0**	**1**	**104**	**5.8**	**-4**	....	....	....	....	....	....	....	....	....	....	....	....
1990-91	**Philadelphia**	**NHL**	**74**	**20**	**21**	**41**	**155**	**5**	**0**	**6**	**165**	**12.1**	**8**	....	....	....	....	....	....	....	....	....	....	....	....
1991-92	**Edmonton**	**NHL**	**80**	**23**	**27**	**50**	**197**	**7**	**0**	**5**	**159**	**14.5**	**5**	....	....	....	**16**	**2**	**1**	**3**	**29**	**1**	**0**	**1**	....
1992-93	**Edmonton**	**NHL**	**69**	**15**	**17**	**32**	**147**	**6**	**0**	**3**	**114**	**13.2**	**-4**	....	....	....	....	....	....	....	....	....	....	....	....
1993-94	**Florida**	**NHL**	**80**	**30**	**30**	**60**	**149**	**17**	**0**	**4**	**204**	**14.7**	**0**	....	....	....	....	....	....	....	....	....	....	....	....
1994-95	**Florida**	**NHL**	**48**	**13**	**12**	**25**	**90**	**4**	**0**	**5**	**130**	**10.0**	**-16**	....	....	....	....	....	....	....	....	....	....	....	....
1995-96	**Florida**	**NHL**	**79**	**32**	**38**	**70**	**160**	**19**	**0**	**3**	**225**	**14.2**	**4**	....	....	....	**22**	**3**	**6**	**9**	**44**	**2**	**0**	**0**	....
1996-97	**Florida**	**NHL**	**82**	**27**	**29**	**56**	**170**	**9**	**1**	**4**	**221**	**12.2**	**7**	....	....	....	**5**	**0**	**2**	**2**	**4**	**0**	**0**	**0**	....
1997-98	**Florida**	**NHL**	**79**	**15**	**24**	**39**	**127**	**6**	**0**	**1**	**188**	**8.0**	**-14**	....	....	....	....	....	....	....	....	....	....	....	....
1998-99	**Florida**	**NHL**	**67**	**18**	**27**	**45**	**85**	**4**	**0**	**3**	**136**	**13.2**	**5**	**11**	**27.3**	**16:14**	....	....	....	....	....	....	....	....	....
99-2000	**Florida**	**NHL**	**77**	**18**	**28**	**46**	**126**	**6**	**0**	**2**	**134**	**13.4**	**14**	**20**	**60.0**	**14:51**	**4**	**0**	**1**	**1**	**2**	**0**	**0**	**0**	**13:09**
2000-01	**Florida**	**NHL**	**40**	**4**	**9**	**13**	**46**	**1**	**0**	**0**	**58**	**6.9**	**-13**	**4**	**50.0**	**14:59**	....	....	....	....	....	....	....	....	....
	St. Louis	**NHL**	**23**	**7**	**1**	**8**	**25**	**2**	**0**	**0**	**37**	**18.9**	**0**	**1**	**0.0**	**15:00**	**15**	**3**	**3**	**6**	**17**	**2**	**0**	**0**	**14:43**
2001-02	**St. Louis**	**NHL**	**64**	**15**	**26**	**41**	**93**	**8**	**0**	**2**	**137**	**10.9**	**-5**	**3**	**0.0**	**15:40**	**10**	**7**	**3**	**10**	**18**	**4**	**0**	**1**	**17:54**
2002-03	**St. Louis**	**NHL**	**80**	**26**	**31**	**57**	**176**	**13**	**0**	**4**	**132**	**19.7**	**1**	**11**	**45.5**	**16:39**	**6**	**0**	**1**	**1**	**10**	**0**	**0**	**0**	**16:18**
2003-04	**St. Louis**	**NHL**	**68**	**14**	**17**	**31**	**76**	**6**	**0**	**3**	**103**	**13.6**	**-7**	**4**	**50.0**	**15:29**	**4**	**0**	**1**	**1**	**2**	**0**	**0**	**0**	**14:16**
2004-05			DID NOT PLAY																						
	NHL Totals		**1291**	**340**	**430**	**770**	**2361**	**132**	**1**	**51**	**2757**	**12.3**		**54**	**44.4**	**15:40**	**132**	**24**	**29**	**53**	**216**	**9**	**0**	**3**	**15:34**

Played in NHL All-Star Game (1996)

Traded to **Edmonton** by **Philadelphia** with Craig Fisher and Craig Berube for Dave Brown, Corey Foster and Jari Kurri, May 30, 1991. Claimed by **Florida** from **Edmonton** in Expansion Draft, June 24, 1993. Traded to **St. Louis** by **Florida** for the rights to Dave Morisset and St. Louis' 5th round choice (Vince Bellissimo) in 2002 Entry Draft, February 9, 2001. Signed as a free agent by **Atlanta**, July 26, 2004.

MELOCHE, Eric

(muh-LAWSH, AIR-ihk) **PHI.**

Right wing. Shoots right. 5'10", 197 lbs. Born, Montreal, Que., May 1, 1976. Pittsburgh's 7th choice, 186th overall, in 1996 Entry Draft.

Season	Club	League	GP	G	A	Pts	PIM	PP	SH	GW	S	%	+/-	TF	F%	Min	GP	G	A	Pts	PIM	PP	SH	GW	Min
1994-95	Cornwall Colts	CJHL	40	7	15	22	51	....	....	....	....	....	....	....	....	....	....	....	....	....	....	....	....	....	....
1995-96	Cornwall Colts	CJHL	64	68	53	121	162	....	....	....	....	....	....	....	....	....	....	....	....	....	....	....	....	....	....
1996-97	Ohio State	CCHA	39	12	11	23	78	....	....	....	....	....	....	....	....	....	....	....	....	....	....	....	....	....	....
1997-98	Ohio State	CCHA	42	26	22	48	86	....	....	....	....	....	....	....	....	....	....	....	....	....	....	....	....	....	....
1998-99	Ohio State	CCHA	35	11	16	27	87	....	....	....	....	....	....	....	....	....	....	....	....	....	....	....	....	....	....
99-2000	Ohio State	CCHA	36	20	11	31	*138	....	....	....	....	....	....	....	....	....	....	....	....	....	....	....	....	....	....
2000-01	Wilkes-Barre	AHL	79	20	20	40	72	....	....	....	....	....	....	....	....	....	21	6	10	16	17	....	....	....	....
2001-02	**Pittsburgh**	**NHL**	**23**	**0**	**1**	**1**	**8**	**0**	**0**	**0**	**29**	**0.0**	**-7**	**4**	**0.0**	**10:10**	....	....	....	....	....	....	....	....	....
	Wilkes-Barre	AHL	55	13	14	27	91	....	....	....	....	....	....	....	....	....	....	....	....	....	....	....	....	....	....
2002-03	**Pittsburgh**	**NHL**	**13**	**5**	**1**	**6**	**4**	**2**	**0**	**1**	**34**	**14.7**	**-2**	**27**	**55.6**	**0:00**	....	....	....	....	....	....	....	....	....
	Wilkes-Barre	AHL	59	12	17	29	95	....	....	....	....	....	....	....	....	....	6	1	0	1	20	....	....	....	....
2003-04	**Pittsburgh**	**NHL**	**25**	**3**	**7**	**10**	**20**	**0**	**0**	**0**	**28**	**10.7**	**-6**	**92**	**39.1**	**14:47**	....	....	....	....	....	....	....	....	....
	Wilkes-Barre	AHL	56	16	26	42	49	....	....	....	....	....	....	....	....	....	23	9	6	15	14	....	....	....	....
2004-05	Philadelphia	AHL	63	6	11	17	102	....	....	....	....	....	....	....	....	....	17	3	2	5	18	....	....	....	....
	NHL Totals		**61**	**8**	**9**	**17**	**32**	**2**	**0**	**1**	**91**	**8.8**		**123**	**29.3**	**9:54**	....	....	....	....	....	....	....	....	....

Signed as a free agent by **Philadelphia**, July 14, 2004.

MESSIER, Eric

(MEHS-see-ay, AIR-ihk)

Left wing. Shoots left. 6'2", 195 lbs. Born, Drummondville, Que., October 29, 1973.

Season	Club	League	Regular Season GP	G	A	Pts	PIM	PP	SH	GW	S	%	+/-	TF	F%	Min	Playoffs GP	G	A	Pts	PIM	PP	SH	GW	Min
1990-91	Swift Textile	QAHA	STATISTICS NOT AVAILABLE																						
	Mtl-Bourassa	QAAA	3	0	1	1	0	....	....	....	....	....	....	....	....	....	2	0	0	0	0	....	....	....	....
1991-92	Trois-Rivieres	QMJHL	58	2	10	12	28	....	....	....	....	....	....	....	....	....	15	2	2	4	13	....	....	....	....
1992-93	Sherbrooke	QMJHL	51	4	17	21	82	....	....	....	....	....	....	....	....	....	15	0	4	4	18	....	....	....	....
1993-94	Sherbrooke	QMJHL	67	4	24	28	69	....	....	....	....	....	....	....	....	....	12	1	7	8	14	....	....	....	....
1994-95	U. Quebec T-R	OUAA	13	8	5	13	20	....	....	....	....	....	....	....	....	....	4	0	3	3	8	....	....	....	....
1995-96	Cornwall Aces	AHL	72	5	9	14	111	....	....	....	....	....	....	....	....	....	8	1	1	2	20	....	....	....	....
1996-97	**Colorado**	**NHL**	**21**	**0**	**0**	**0**	**4**	**0**	**0**	**0**	**11**	**0.0**	**7**	....	....	....	**6**	**0**	**0**	**0**	**4**	**0**	**0**	**0**	....
	Hershey Bears	AHL	55	16	26	42	69	....	....	....	....	....	....	....	....	....	9	3	8	11	14	....	....	....	....
1997-98	**Colorado**	**NHL**	**62**	**4**	**12**	**16**	**20**	**0**	**0**	**0**	**66**	**6.1**	**4**	....	....	....	....	....	....	....	....	....	....	....	....
1998-99	**Colorado**	**NHL**	**31**	**4**	**2**	**6**	**14**	**1**	**0**	**1**	**30**	**13.3**	**0**	**0**	**0.0**	**13:43**	**3**	**0**	**0**	**0**	**0**	**0**	**0**	**0**	**4:40**
	Hershey Bears	AHL	6	1	3	4	4	....	....	....	....	....	....	....	....	....	....	....	....	....	....	....	....	....	....
99-2000	**Colorado**	**NHL**	**61**	**3**	**6**	**9**	**24**	**1**	**0**	**0**	**28**	**10.7**	**0**	**4**	**25.0**	**10:27**	**14**	**0**	**1**	**1**	**4**	**0**	**0**	**0**	**4:55**
2000-01 ♦	**Colorado**	**NHL**	**64**	**5**	**7**	**12**	**26**	**0**	**0**	**1**	**60**	**8.3**	**–3**	**9**	**44.4**	**12:16**	**23**	**2**	**2**	**4**	**14**	**0**	**0**	**0**	**16:16**
2001-02	**Colorado**	**NHL**	**74**	**5**	**10**	**15**	**26**	**0**	**0**	**3**	**84**	**6.0**	**–5**	**8**	**25.0**	**15:15**	**21**	**1**	**2**	**3**	**0**	**0**	**0**	**0**	**16:34**
2002-03	**Colorado**	**NHL**	**72**	**4**	**10**	**14**	**16**	**0**	**1**	**1**	**52**	**7.7**	**–2**	**17**	**17.7**	**12:20**	**5**	**0**	**0**	**0**	**0**	**0**	**0**	**0**	**6:57**
2003-04	**Florida**	**NHL**	**21**	**0**	**3**	**3**	**16**	**0**	**0**	**0**	**13**	**0.0**	**–2**	**19**	**10.5**	**11:16**	....	....	....	....	....	....	....	....	....
2004-05			DID NOT PLAY																						
	NHL Totals		**406**	**25**	**50**	**75**	**146**	**2**	**1**	**6**	**344**	**7.3**		**57**	**21.1**	**12:42**	**72**	**3**	**5**	**8**	**22**	**0**	**0**	**0**	**12:43**

QMJHL Second All-Star Team (1994)

Signed as a free agent by **Colorado**, June 14, 1995. • Missed majority of 1998-99 season recovering from elbow injury suffered in game vs. Ottawa, October 10, 1998. Traded to **Florida** by **Colorado** with Vaclav Nedorost for Peter Worrell and Florida's 2nd round choice (later traded to NY Rangers – later traded back to Florida – Florida selected David Shantz) in 2004 Entry Draft, July 18, 2003. • Missed majority of 2003-04 season recovering from wrist injury suffered in game vs. Atlanta, November 21, 2003.

MESSIER, Mark

(MEHS-see-ay, MAHRK)

Center. Shoots left. 6'1", 210 lbs. Born, Edmonton, Alta., January 18, 1961. Edmonton's 2nd choice, 48th overall, in 1979 Entry Draft.

Season	Club	League	Regular Season GP	G	A	Pts	PIM	PP	SH	GW	S	%	+/-	TF	F%	Min	Playoffs GP	G	A	Pts	PIM	PP	SH	GW	Min
1976-77	Spruce Grove	AJHL	57	27	39	66	91																		
1977-78	St. Albert Saints	AJHL	54	25	49	74	194	....	....	....	....	....	....	....	....	....	....	....	....	....	....	....	....	....	....
	Portland	WHL	....	....	....	....	....	....	....	....	....	....	....	....	....	....	7	4	1	5	2	....	....	....	....
1978-79	St. Albert Saints	AJHL	17	15	18	33	64	....	....	....	....	....	....	....	....	....	....	....	....	....	....	....	....	....	....
	Indianapolis	WHA	5	0	0	0	0	....	....	....	....	....	....	....	....	....	....	....	....	....	....	....	....	....	....
	Cincinnati	WHA	47	1	10	11	58	....	....	....	....	....	....	....	....	....	....	....	....	....	....	....	....	....	....
1979-80	**Edmonton**	**NHL**	**75**	**12**	**21**	**33**	**120**	**1**	**1**	**1**	**113**	**10.6**	**–10**	....	....	....	**3**	**1**	**2**	**3**	**2**	**0**	**1**	**0**	....
	Houston Apollos	CHL	4	0	3	3	4	....	....	....	....	....	....	....	....	....	....	....	....	....	....	....	....	....	....
1980-81	**Edmonton**	**NHL**	**72**	**23**	**40**	**63**	**102**	**4**	**0**	**1**	**179**	**12.8**	**–12**	....	....	....	**9**	**2**	**5**	**7**	**13**	**0**	**0**	**0**	....
1981-82	**Edmonton**	**NHL**	**78**	**50**	**38**	**88**	**119**	**10**	**0**	**3**	**235**	**21.3**	**21**	....	....	....	**5**	**1**	**2**	**3**	**8**	**0**	**0**	**0**	....
1982-83	**Edmonton**	**NHL**	**77**	**48**	**58**	**106**	**72**	**12**	**1**	**2**	**237**	**20.3**	**19**	....	....	....	**15**	**15**	**6**	**21**	**14**	**4**	**2**	**0**	....
1983-84 ♦	**Edmonton**	**NHL**	**73**	**37**	**64**	**101**	**165**	**7**	**4**	**7**	**219**	**16.9**	**40**	....	....	....	**19**	**8**	**18**	**26**	**19**	**1**	**1**	**2**	....
1984-85 ♦	**Edmonton**	**NHL**	**55**	**23**	**31**	**54**	**57**	**4**	**5**	**1**	**136**	**16.9**	**8**	....	....	....	**18**	**12**	**13**	**25**	**12**	**1**	**1**	**1**	....
1985-86	**Edmonton**	**NHL**	**63**	**35**	**49**	**84**	**68**	**10**	**5**	**7**	**201**	**17.4**	**36**	....	....	....	**10**	**4**	**6**	**10**	**18**	**0**	**2**	**0**	....
1986-87 ♦	**Edmonton**	**NHL**	**77**	**37**	**70**	**107**	**73**	**7**	**4**	**5**	**208**	**17.8**	**21**	....	....	....	**21**	**12**	**16**	**28**	**16**	**1**	**2**	**1**	....
1987-88 ♦	**Edmonton**	**NHL**	**77**	**37**	**74**	**111**	**103**	**12**	**3**	**7**	**182**	**20.3**	**21**	....	....	....	**19**	**11**	**23**	**34**	**29**	**7**	**1**	**0**	....
1988-89	**Edmonton**	**NHL**	**72**	**33**	**61**	**94**	**130**	**6**	**6**	**4**	**164**	**20.1**	**–5**	....	....	....	**7**	**1**	**11**	**12**	**8**	**0**	**0**	**0**	....
1989-90 ♦	**Edmonton**	**NHL**	**79**	**45**	**84**	**129**	**79**	**13**	**6**	**3**	**211**	**21.3**	**19**	....	....	....	**22**	**9**	***22**	***31**	**20**	**1**	**1**	**1**	....
1990-91	**Edmonton**	**NHL**	**53**	**12**	**52**	**64**	**34**	**3**	**1**	**2**	**109**	**11.0**	**15**	....	....	....	**18**	**4**	**11**	**15**	**16**	**1**	**0**	**0**	....
1991-92	**NY Rangers**	**NHL**	**79**	**35**	**72**	**107**	**76**	**12**	**4**	**6**	**212**	**16.5**	**31**	....	....	....	**11**	**7**	**7**	**14**	**6**	**2**	**2**	**0**	....
1992-93	**NY Rangers**	**NHL**	**75**	**25**	**66**	**91**	**72**	**7**	**2**	**2**	**215**	**11.6**	**–6**	....	....	....	....	....	....	....	....	....	....	....	....
1993-94 ♦	**NY Rangers**	**NHL**	**76**	**26**	**58**	**84**	**76**	**6**	**2**	**5**	**216**	**12.0**	**25**	....	....	....	**23**	**12**	**18**	**30**	**33**	**2**	**1**	**4**	....
1994-95	**NY Rangers**	**NHL**	**46**	**14**	**39**	**53**	**40**	**3**	**3**	**2**	**126**	**11.1**	**8**	....	....	....	**10**	**3**	**10**	**13**	**8**	**2**	**0**	**1**	....
1995-96	**NY Rangers**	**NHL**	**74**	**47**	**52**	**99**	**122**	**14**	**1**	**5**	**241**	**19.5**	**29**	....	....	....	**11**	**4**	**7**	**11**	**16**	**2**	**0**	**1**	....
1996-97	**NY Rangers**	**NHL**	**71**	**36**	**48**	**84**	**88**	**7**	**5**	**9**	**227**	**15.9**	**12**	....	....	....	**15**	**3**	**9**	**12**	**6**	**0**	**0**	**1**	....
1997-98	**Vancouver**	**NHL**	**82**	**22**	**38**	**60**	**58**	**8**	**2**	**2**	**139**	**15.8**	**–10**	....	....	....	....	....	....	....	....	....	....	....	....
1998-99	**Vancouver**	**NHL**	**59**	**13**	**35**	**48**	**33**	**4**	**2**	**2**	**97**	**13.4**	**–12**	**1536**	**53.9**	**22:36**	....	....	....	....	....	....	....	....	....
99-2000	**Vancouver**	**NHL**	**66**	**17**	**37**	**54**	**30**	**6**	**0**	**4**	**131**	**13.0**	**–15**	**1684**	**56.8**	**21:12**	....	....	....	....	....	....	....	....	....
2000-01	**NY Rangers**	**NHL**	**82**	**24**	**43**	**67**	**89**	**12**	**3**	**2**	**131**	**18.3**	**–25**	**1879**	**55.5**	**19:14**	....	....	....	....	....	....	....	....	....
2001-02	**NY Rangers**	**NHL**	**41**	**7**	**16**	**23**	**32**	**2**	**0**	**2**	**69**	**10.1**	**–1**	**787**	**53.6**	**18:31**	....	....	....	....	....	....	....	....	....
2002-03	**NY Rangers**	**NHL**	**78**	**18**	**22**	**40**	**30**	**8**	**1**	**5**	**117**	**15.4**	**–2**	**1280**	**52.9**	**18:38**	....	....	....	....	....	....	....	....	....
2003-04	**NY Rangers**	**NHL**	**76**	**18**	**25**	**43**	**42**	**1**	**2**	**3**	**104**	**17.3**	**3**	**1241**	**55.0**	**16:29**	....	....	....	....	....	....	....	....	....
2004-05			DID NOT PLAY																						
	NHL Totals		**1756**	**694**	**1193**	**1887**	**1910**	**179**	**63**	**92**	**4219**	**16.4**		**8407**	**54.8**	**19:20**	**236**	**109**	**186**	**295**	**244**	**24**	**14**	**12**	....

NHL First All-Star Team (1982, 1983, 1990, 1992) • NHL Second All-Star Team (1984) • Conn Smythe Trophy (1984) • Lester B. Pearson Award (1990, 1992) • Hart Trophy (1990, 1992)

Played in NHL All-Star Game (1982, 1983, 1984, 1986, 1988, 1989, 1990, 1991, 1992, 1994, 1996, 1997, 1998, 2000, 2004)

Signed as an underage free agent by **Indianapolis** (WHA) to a 10-game tryout contract, November 5, 1978. Signed as a free agent by **Cincinnati** (WHA) after **Indianapolis** (WHA) franchise folded, December, 1978. Traded to **NY Rangers** by **Edmonton** with future considerations (Jeff Beukeboom for David Shaw, November 12, 1991) for Bernie Nicholls, Steven Rice and Louie DeBrusk, October 4, 1991. Signed as a free agent by **Vancouver**, July 30, 1997. Signed as a free agent by **NY Rangers**, July 13, 2000. • Missed majority of 2001-02 season recovering from back injury suffered in game vs. Toronto, December 8, 2001. Traded to **San Jose** by **NY Rangers** for San Jose's 4th round choice (Ryan Callahan) in 2004 Entry Draft, June 30, 2003. Signed as a free agent by **NY Rangers**, September 5, 2003.

MEYER, Freddy

(MAY-uhr, FREHD) **PHI.**

Defense. Shoots left. 5'10", 192 lbs. Born, Sanbornville, NH, January 4, 1981.

Season	Club	League	Regular Season GP	G	A	Pts	PIM	PP	SH	GW	S	%	+/-	TF	F%	Min	Playoffs GP	G	A	Pts	PIM	PP	SH	GW	Min
1996-97	Cardigan Mtn.	High-NH	STATISTICS NOT AVAILABLE																						
1997-98	USA U-17	USDP	STATISTICS NOT AVAILABLE																						
1998-99	USA U-17	USDP	3	0	2	2	0	....	....	....	....	....	....	....	....	....	....	....	....	....	....	....	....	....	....
	USA U-18	USDP	54	10	23	33	151	....	....	....	....	....	....	....	....	....	....	....	....	....	....	....	....	....	....
99-2000	USA U-18	USDP	28	3	8	11	60	....	....	....	....	....	....	....	....	....	....	....	....	....	....	....	....	....	....
	Boston University	H-East	25	1	11	12	52	....	....	....	....	....	....	....	....	....	....	....	....	....	....	....	....	....	....
2000-01	Boston University	H-East	28	6	13	19	82	....	....	....	....	....	....	....	....	....	....	....	....	....	....	....	....	....	....
2001-02	Boston University	H-East	37	5	15	20	78	....	....	....	....	....	....	....	....	....	....	....	....	....	....	....	....	....	....
2002-03	Boston University	H-East	36	5	16	21	76	....	....	....	....	....	....	....	....	....	....	....	....	....	....	....	....	....	....
2003-04	**Philadelphia**	**NHL**	**1**	**0**	**0**	**0**	**0**	**0**	**0**	**0**	**1**	**0.0**	**0**	**0**	**0.0**	**15:24**	....	....	....	....	....	....	....	....	....
	Philadelphia	AHL	59	14	14	28	50	....	....	....	....	....	....	....	....	....	12	0	3	3	8	....	....	....	....
2004-05	Philadelphia	AHL	59	6	9	15	71	....	....	....	....	....	....	....	....	....	21	3	9	12	34	....	....	....	....
	NHL Totals		**1**	**0**	**0**	**0**	**0**	**0**	**0**	**0**	**1**	**0.0**		**0**	**0.0**	**15:24**	....	....	....	....	....	....	....	....	....

Hockey East All-Rookie Team (2000) • Hockey East First All-Star Team (2003) • NCAA East First All-American Team (2003)

Signed as a free agent by **Philadelphia**, May 21, 2003.

MEZEI, Branislav

(MEH-tzay, BRAN-ih-slav) **FLA.**

Defense. Shoots left. 6'5", 236 lbs. Born, Nitra, Czech., October 8, 1980. NY Islanders' 3rd choice, 10th overall, in 1999 Entry Draft.

Season	Club	League	Regular Season GP	G	A	Pts	PIM	PP	SH	GW	S	%	+/-	TF	F%	Min	Playoffs GP	G	A	Pts	PIM	PP	SH	GW	Min
1996-97	Nitra Jr.	Slovak-Jr.	40	8	17	25	42	....	....	....	....	....	....	....	....	....	....	....	....	....	....	....	....	....	....
1997-98	Belleville Bulls	OHL	53	3	5	8	58	....	....	....	....	....	....	....	....	....	8	0	2	2	8	....	....	....	....
1998-99	Belleville Bulls	OHL	60	5	18	23	90	....	....	....	....	....	....	....	....	....	18	0	4	4	29	....	....	....	....
99-2000	Belleville Bulls	OHL	58	7	21	28	99	....	....	....	....	....	....	....	....	....	6	0	3	3	10	....	....	....	....
2000-01	**NY Islanders**	**NHL**	**42**	**1**	**4**	**5**	**53**	**0**	**0**	**0**	**29**	**3.4**	**–5**	**0**	**0.0**	**14:48**	....	....	....	....	....	....	....	....	....
	Lowell	AHL	20	0	3	3	28	....	....	....	....	....	....	....	....	....	....	....	....	....	....	....	....	....	....
2001-02	**NY Islanders**	**NHL**	**24**	**0**	**2**	**2**	**12**	**0**	**0**	**0**	**4**	**0.0**	**2**	**0**	**0.0**	**8:28**	....	....	....	....	....	....	....	....	....
	Bridgeport	AHL	59	1	9	10	137	....	....	....	....	....	....	....	....	....	20	0	1	1	48	....	....	....	....
2002-03	**Florida**	**NHL**	**11**	**2**	**0**	**2**	**10**	**0**	**0**	**1**	**10**	**20.0**	**–2**	**0**	**0.0**	**18:22**	....	....	....	....	....	....	....	....	....
	San Antonio	AHL	1	0	0	0	0	....	....	....	....	....	....	....	....	....	3	0	0	0	0	....	....	....	....
2003-04	**Florida**	**NHL**	**45**	**0**	**7**	**7**	**80**	**0**	**0**	**0**	**26**	**0.0**	**–4**	**0**	**0.0**	**17:43**	....	....	....	....	....	....	....	....	....

Season	Club	League	GP	G	A	Pts	PIM	PP	SH	GW	S	%	+/-	TF	F%	Min	GP	G	A	Pts	PIM	PP	SH	GW	Min
			Regular Season														Playoffs								
2004-05	HC Ocelari Trinec	CzRep	41	1	2	3	68																		
	Dukla Trencin	Slovakia	10	1	1	2	16										12	1	2	3	38				
	NHL Totals		122	3	13	16	155	0	0	1	69	4.3		0	0.0	14:57									

OHL First All-Star Team (2000)

Traded to **Florida** by **NY Islanders** for Jason Wiemer, July 3, 2002. • Missed majority of 2002-03 season recovering from ankle (October 12, 2002 vs. Atlanta) and foot (January 1, 2003 vs. New Jersey) injuries. Signed as a free agent by **Trinec** (CzRep), September 25, 2004. Signed as a free agent by **Trencin** (Slovakia), January 30, 2005.

MICHALEK, Milan

(mih-KHAL-ihk, MEE-lahn) **S.J.**

Right wing. Shoots left. 6'2", 220 lbs. Born, Jindrichuv Hradec, Czech., December 7, 1984. San Jose's 1st choice, 6th overall, in 2003 Entry Draft.

Season	Club	League	GP	G	A	Pts	PIM	PP	SH	GW	S	%	+/-	TF	F%	Min	GP	G	A	Pts	PIM	PP	SH	GW	Min
99-2000	C. Budejovice Jr.	CzRep-Jr.	48	16	26	42	42										6	3	1	4	4				
2000-01	C. Budejovice Jr.	CzRep-Jr.	30	10	13	23	30										4	1	3	4	2				
	C. Budejovice	CzRep	5	0	0	0	0																		
2001-02	C. Budejovice	CzRep	47	6	11	17	12																		
	C. Budejovice Jr.	CzRep-Jr.	5	3	2	5	4										7	5	4	9	14				
2002-03	C. Budejovice	CzRep	46	3	5	8	14										4	1	0	1	2				
	Kladno	CzRep-2															6	2	2	4	16				
2003-04	San Jose	NHL	2	1	0	1	4	0	0	0	1	100.0	1	0	0.0	9:05									
	Cleveland Barons	AHL	7	2	2	4	4																		
2004-05			DID NOT PLAY																						
	NHL Totals		2	1	0	1	4	0	0	0	1	100.0		0	0.0	9:05									

• Missed majority of 2003-04 season recovering from knee injury suffered in game vs. Calgary, October 11, 2003.

MICHALEK, Zbynek

(mih-KHAL-ihk, ZBIGH-nehk) **PHX.**

Defense. Shoots right. 6'1", 199 lbs. Born, Jindrichuv Hradec, Czech., December 23, 1982.

Season	Club	League	GP	G	A	Pts	PIM	PP	SH	GW	S	%	+/-	TF	F%	Min	GP	G	A	Pts	PIM	PP	SH	GW	Min
99-2000	Karlovy Vary Jr.	CzRep-Jr.	40	2	10	12	20																		
2000-01	Shawinigan	QMJHL	69	10	29	39	52										3	0	0	0	0				
2001-02	Shawinigan	QMJHL	68	16	35	51	54										12	8	9	17	17				
2002-03	Houston Aeros	AHL	62	4	10	14	26										23	1	1	2	6				
2003-04	Minnesota	NHL	22	1	1	2	4	0	0	0	17	5.9	–7	0	0.0	14:13									
	Houston Aeros	AHL	55	5	16	21	32										2	1	0	1	0				
2004-05	Houston Aeros	AHL	76	7	17	24	48										5	1	2	3	4				
	NHL Totals		22	1	1	2	4	0	0	0	17	5.9		0	0.0	14:13									

Signed as a free agent by **Minnesota**, September 29, 2001. Traded to **Phoenix** by **Minnesota** for Erik Westrum and Dustin Wood, August 26, 2005.

MIETTINEN, Antti

(mih-EHT-tih-nehn, AN-tee) **DAL.**

Center. Shoots right. 5'11", 180 lbs. Born, Hameenlinna, Finland, July 3, 1980. Dallas' 10th choice, 224th overall, in 2000 Entry Draft.

Season	Club	League	GP	G	A	Pts	PIM	PP	SH	GW	S	%	+/-	TF	F%	Min	GP	G	A	Pts	PIM	PP	SH	GW	Min
1996-97	HPK U18	Fin-U18	36	24	29	53	34																		
1997-98	HPK U18	Fin-U18	34	13	28	41	63										8	1	0	1	2				
	HPK Jr.	Finland-Jr.	8	1	0	1	2																		
1998-99	HPK Jr.	Finland-Jr.	35	17	22	39	28																		
	FPS Forssa	Finland-2	4	3	1	4	6																		
	HPK Hameenlinna	Finland	13	0	0	0	2										4	0	0	0	0				
99-2000	HPK Jr.	Finland-Jr.	16	11	13	24	16																		
	HPK Hameenlinna	Finland	39	2	1	3	8										7	1	0	1	0				
2000-01	HPK Jr.	Finland-Jr.	4	3	10	13	2																		
	HPK Hameenlinna	Finland	55	13	11	24	20																		
2001-02	HPK Hameenlinna	Finland	56	19	37	56	50										8	2	4	6	8				
2002-03	HPK Hameenlinna	Finland	53	25	25	50	54										10	1	7	8	29				
2003-04	Dallas	NHL	16	1	0	1	0	0	0	1	17	5.9	–9	1	0.0	9:51									
	Utah Grizzlies	AHL	48	7	23	30	20																		
2004-05	Hamilton	AHL	35	8	20	28	21										4	1	1	2	6				
	NHL Totals		16	1	0	1	0	0	0	1	17	5.9		1	0.0	9:51									

MILLER, Aaron

(MIHL-luhr, AIR-ruhn) **L.A.**

Defense. Shoots right. 6'4", 200 lbs. Born, Buffalo, NY, August 11, 1971. NY Rangers' 6th choice, 88th overall, in 1989 Entry Draft.

Season	Club	League	GP	G	A	Pts	PIM	PP	SH	GW	S	%	+/-	TF	F%	Min	GP	G	A	Pts	PIM	PP	SH	GW	Min
1987-88	Niagara Scenics	NAHL	30	4	9	13	2																		
1988-89	Niagara Scenics	NAHL	59	24	38	62	60																		
1989-90	U. of Vermont	ECAC	31	1	15	16	24																		
1990-91	U. of Vermont	ECAC	30	3	7	10	22																		
1991-92	U. of Vermont	ECAC	31	3	16	19	28																		
1992-93	U. of Vermont	ECAC	30	4	13	17	16																		
1993-94	Quebec	NHL	1	0	0	0	0	0	0	0	0	0.0	–1												
	Cornwall Aces	AHL	64	4	10	14	49										13	0	2	2	10				
1994-95	Cornwall Aces	AHL	76	4	18	22	69																		
	Quebec	NHL	9	0	3	3	6	0	0	0	12	0.0	2												
1995-96	Colorado	NHL	5	0	0	0	0	0	0	0	2	0.0	0												
	Cornwall Aces	AHL	62	4	23	27	77										8	0	1	1	6				
1996-97	Colorado	NHL	56	5	12	17	15	0	0	3	47	10.6	15				17	1	2	3	10	0	0	0	
1997-98	Colorado	NHL	55	2	2	4	51	0	0	0	29	6.9	0				7	0	0	0	8	0	0	0	
1998-99	Colorado	NHL	76	5	13	18	42	1	0	2	87	5.7	3	0	0.0	21:49	19	1	5	6	10	0	0	0	21:13
99-2000	Colorado	NHL	53	1	7	8	36	0	0	0	44	2.3	3	0	0.0	19:05	17	1	1	2	6	0	0	0	19:12
2000-01	Colorado	NHL	56	4	9	13	29	0	0	0	49	8.2	19	0	0.0	18:25									
	Los Angeles	NHL	13	0	5	5	14	0	0	0	10	0.0	3	1	0.0	22:44	13	0	1	1	6	0	0	0	22:02
2001-02	Los Angeles	NHL	74	5	12	17	54	0	1	3	75	6.7	14	0	0.0	22:21	7	0	0	0	0	0	0	0	26:28
	United States	Olympics	6	0	0	0	4																		
2002-03	Los Angeles	NHL	49	1	5	6	24	0	0	0	34	2.9	–7	1	100.0	21:30									
2003-04	Los Angeles	NHL	35	1	2	3	32	0	0	0	26	3.8	–3	0	0.0	19:00									
2004-05			DID NOT PLAY																						
	NHL Totals		482	24	70	94	303	1	1	8	415	5.8		2	50.0	20:42	80	3	9	12	40	0	0	0	21:27

ECAC First All-Star Team (1993) • NCAA East Second All-American Team (1993)

Traded to **Quebec** by **NY Rangers** with NY Rangers' 5th round choice (Bill Lindsay) in 1991 Entry Draft for Joe Cirella, January 17, 1991. Transferred to **Colorado** after **Quebec** franchise relocated, June 21, 1995. Traded to **Los Angeles** by **Colorado** with Adam Deadmarsh, a player to be named later (Jared Aulin, March 22, 2001) and Colorado's 1st round choices in 2001 (Dave Steckel) and 2003 (Brian Boyle) Entry Drafts for Rob Blake and Steve Reinprecht, February 21, 2001. • Missed majority of 2003-04 season recovering from cervical injury suffered in game vs. Atlanta, December 10, 2003.

MILLER, Kevin

(MIHL-luhr, KEH-vihn)

Center. Shoots right. 5'11", 190 lbs. Born, Lansing, MI, September 2, 1965. NY Rangers' 10th choice, 202nd overall, in 1984 Entry Draft.

Season	Club	League	GP	G	A	Pts	PIM	PP	SH	GW	S	%	+/-	TF	F%	Min	GP	G	A	Pts	PIM	PP	SH	GW	Min
1983-84	Redford Royals	GLJHL	44	28	57	85																			
1984-85	Michigan State	CCHA	44	11	29	40	84																		
1985-86	Michigan State	CCHA	45	19	52	71	112																		
1986-87	Michigan State	CCHA	42	25	56	81	63																		
1987-88	Michigan State	CCHA	9	6	3	9	18																		
	United States	Nat-Tm	48	31	32	63	33																		
	United States	Olympics	5	1	3	4	4																		
1988-89	NY Rangers	NHL	24	3	5	8	2	0	0	1	40	7.5	–1												
	Denver Rangers	IHL	55	29	47	76	19										4	2	1	3	2				
1989-90	NY Rangers	NHL	16	0	5	5	2	0	0	0	9	0.0	–1				1	0	0	0	0	0	0	0	
	Flint Spirits	IHL	48	19	23	42	41																		
1990-91	NY Rangers	NHL	63	17	27	44	63	1	2	3	113	15.0	1												
	Detroit	NHL	11	5	2	7	4	0	1	0	23	21.7	–4				7	3	2	5	20	0	1	0	
1991-92	Detroit	NHL	80	20	26	46	53	3	1	4	130	15.4	6				9	0	2	2	4	0	0	0	
1992-93	Washington	NHL	10	0	3	3	35	0	0	0	10	0.0	–4												
	St. Louis	NHL	72	24	22	46	65	8	3	4	153	15.7	6				10	0	3	3	11	0	0	0	
1993-94	St. Louis	NHL	75	23	25	48	83	6	3	5	154	14.9	6				3	1	0	1	4	0	1	0	

			Regular Season														Playoffs								
Season	Club	League	GP	G	A	Pts	PIM	PP	SH	GW	S	%	+/-	TF	F%	Min	GP	G	A	Pts	PIM	PP	SH	GW	Min
1994-95	St. Louis	NHL	15	2	5	7	0	0	0	0	19	10.5	4												
	San Jose	NHL	21	6	7	13	13	1	1	2	41	14.6	0				6	0	0	0	2	0	0	0	
1995-96	San Jose	NHL	68	22	20	42	41	2	2	2	146	15.1	–8												
	Pittsburgh	NHL	13	6	5	11	4	1	0	0	33	18.2	4				18	3	2	5	8	0	0	0	
1996-97	Chicago	NHL	69	14	17	31	41	5	1	2	139	10.1	–10				6	0	1	1	0	0	0	0	
1997-98	Chicago	NHL	37	4	7	11	8	0	0	1	37	10.8	–4												
	Indianapolis Ice	IHL	26	11	11	22	41										2	1	1	2	0				
1998-99	NY Islanders	NHL	33	1	5	6	13	0	0	0	37	2.7	–5	114	49.1	10:19									
	Chicago Wolves	IHL	30	11	20	31	8										10	2	7	9	22				
99-2000	Ottawa	NHL	9	3	2	5	2	1	0	2	11	27.3	1	34	41.2	8:10	1	0	0	0	0	0	0	0	4:33
	Grand Rapids	IHL	63	20	34	54	51										17	*11	7	*18	30				
2000-01	HC Davos	Swiss	36	*29	27	56	61										4	3	0	3	2				
2001-02	HC Davos	Swiss	43	23	18	41	78										16	4	10	14	12				
2002-03	HC Davos	Swiss	44	14	24	38	40										17	8	3	11	4				
2003-04	Detroit	NHL	4	0	2	2	0	0	0	0	2	0.0	2	4	75.0	7:21									
	Grand Rapids	AHL	74	27	21	48	22										4	3	0	3	5				
2004-05	Flint Generals	UHL	7	1	4	5	10																		
	NHL Totals		**620**	**150**	**185**	**335**	**429**	**28**	**14**	**26**	**1097**	**13.7**		**152**	**48.0**	**9:38**	**61**	**7**	**10**	**17**	**49**	**0**	**2**	**0**	**4:33**

Traded to **Detroit** by **NY Rangers** with Jim Cummins and Dennis Vial for Joe Kocur and Per Djoos, March 5, 1991. Traded to **Washington** by **Detroit** for Dino Ciccarelli, June 20, 1992. Traded to **St. Louis** by **Washington** for Paul Cavallini, November 2, 1992. Traded to **San Jose** by **St. Louis** for Todd Elik, March 23, 1995. Traded to **Pittsburgh** by **San Jose** for Pittsburgh's 5th round choice (later traded to Boston – Boston selected Elias Abrahamsson) in 1996 Entry Draft , March 20, 1996. Signed as a free agent by **Chicago**, July 18, 1996. Signed as a free agent by **NY Islanders**, October 9, 1998. Signed as a free agent by **Ottawa**, August 24, 1999. Signed as a free agent by **Davos** (Swiss), July 26, 2000. Signed as a free agent by **Detroit**, August 27, 2003. Signed as a free agent by **Flint** (UHL), March 3, 2005.

MILLER, Kip

(MIHL-luhr, KIHP)

Center. Shoots left. 5'10", 190 lbs. Born, Lansing, MI, June 11, 1969. Quebec's 4th choice, 72nd overall, in 1987 Entry Draft.

Season	Club	League	GP	G	A	Pts	PIM	PP	SH	GW	S	%	+/-	TF	F%	Min	GP	G	A	Pts	PIM	PP	SH	GW	Min
1984-85	Det. Compuware	MNHL	65	69	63	132																			
1985-86	Det. Compuware	GLJHL	30	25	28	53																			
1986-87	Michigan State	CCHA	41	20	19	39	92																		
1987-88	Michigan State	CCHA	39	16	25	41	51																		
1988-89	Michigan State	CCHA	47	32	45	77	94																		
1989-90	Michigan State	CCHA	45	*48	53	*101	60																		
1990-91	Quebec	NHL	13	4	3	7	7	0	0	0	16	25.0	–1												
	Halifax Citadels	AHL	66	36	33	69	40																		
1991-92	Quebec	NHL	36	5	10	15	12	1	0	2	46	10.9	–21												
	Halifax Citadels	AHL	24	9	17	26	8																		
	Minnesota	NHL	3	1	2	3	2	1	0	0	3	33.3	–1												
	Kalamazoo Wings	IHL	6	1	8	9	4										12	3	9	12	12				
1992-93	Kalamazoo Wings	IHL	61	17	39	56	59																		
1993-94	San Jose	NHL	11	2	2	4	6	0	0	0	21	9.5	–1												
	Kansas City	IHL	71	38	54	92	51																		
1994-95	Denver Grizzlies	IHL	71	46	60	106	54										17	*15	14	29	8				
	NY Islanders	NHL	8	0	1	1	0	0	0	0	11	0.0	1												
1995-96	Chicago	NHL	10	1	4	5	2	0	0	0	12	8.3	1												
	Indianapolis Ice	IHL	73	32	59	91	46										5	2	6	8	2				
1996-97	Chicago Wolves	IHL	43	11	41	52	32																		
	Indianapolis Ice	IHL	37	17	24	41	18										4	2	2	4	2				
1997-98	Utah Grizzlies	IHL	72	38	59	97	30										4	3	2	5	10				
	NY Islanders	NHL	9	1	3	4	2	0	0	0	11	9.1	–2												
1998-99	Pittsburgh	NHL	77	19	23	42	22	1	0	4	125	15.2	1	150	44.7	16:55	13	2	7	9	19	1	0	0	18:56
99-2000	Pittsburgh	NHL	44	4	15	19	10	0	0	1	50	8.0	–1	132	40.2	14:18									
	Anaheim	NHL	30	6	17	23	4	2	0	1	32	18.8	1	7	42.9	13:44									
2000-01	Pittsburgh	NHL	33	3	8	11	6	1	0	0	38	7.9	0	61	50.8	9:46									
	Grand Rapids	IHL	34	16	19	35	12										10	5	8	13	2				
2001-02	Grand Rapids	AHL	41	21	35	56	27																		
	NY Islanders	NHL	37	7	17	24	6	2	0	1	52	13.5	2	119	58.8	14:07	7	4	2	6	2	2	0	1	11:14
2002-03	Washington	NHL	72	12	38	50	18	3	0	4	89	13.5	–1	171	49.7	14:58	5	0	2	2	2	0	0	0	10:36
2003-04	Washington	NHL	66	9	22	31	8	6	0	2	74	12.2	–10	297	47.5	14:03									
2004-05	Grand Rapids	AHL	50	13	32	45	17																		
	NHL Totals		**449**	**74**	**165**	**239**	**105**	**17**	**0**	**15**	**580**	**12.8**		**937**	**48.0**	**14:28**	**25**	**6**	**11**	**17**	**23**	**3**	**0**	**1**	**15:07**

CCHA First All-Star Team (1989, 1990) • CCHA Player of the Year (1990) • NCAA West First All-American Team (1989, 1990) • Hobey Baker Memorial Award (Top U.S. Collegiate Player) (1990) • N.R. "Bud" Poile Trophy (Playoff MVP – IHL) (1995)

Traded to **Minnesota** by **Quebec** for Steve Maltais, March 8, 1992. Signed as a free agent by **San Jose**, August 10, 1993. Signed as a free agent by **NY Islanders**, July 7, 1994. Signed as a free agent by **Chicago**, July 21, 1995. Signed as a free agent by **NY Islanders**, November 26, 1997. Claimed by **Pittsburgh** from **NY Islanders** in Waiver Draft, October 5, 1998. Traded to **Anaheim** by **Pittsburgh** for Anaheim's 9th round choice (Roman Simicek) in 2000 Entry Draft, January 29, 2000. Signed as a free agent by **Pittsburgh**, September 24, 2000. Signed as a free agent by **Grand Rapids** (AHL), May 31, 2001. Signed as a free agent by **NY Islanders**, January 16, 2002. Signed as a free agent by **Washington**, July 9, 2002. Signed as a free agent by **Grand Rapids** (AHL), December 26, 2004.

MILLEY, Norm

(MIHL-lee, NOHR-man) **T.B.**

Right wing. Shoots right. 6', 211 lbs. Born, Toronto, Ont., February 14, 1980. Buffalo's 3rd choice, 47th overall, in 1998 Entry Draft.

Season	Club	League	GP	G	A	Pts	PIM	PP	SH	GW	S	%	+/-	TF	F%	Min	GP	G	A	Pts	PIM	PP	SH	GW	Min
1995-96	Tor. Red Wings	MTHL	42	42	36	78																			
	St. Mike's B's	OPJHL	5	2	1	3	0																		
1996-97	Sudbury Wolves	OHL	61	30	32	62	15																		
1997-98	Sudbury Wolves	OHL	62	33	41	74	48										10	0	1	1	4				
1998-99	Sudbury Wolves	OHL	68	52	68	120	47										4	2	3	5	4				
99-2000	Sudbury Wolves	OHL	68	*52	60	112	47										12	8	11	19	6				
2000-01	Rochester	AHL	77	20	27	47	56										4	0	0	0	2				
2001-02	Buffalo	NHL	5	0	1	1	0	0	0	0	10	0.0	0	1	0.0	13:12									
	Rochester	AHL	74	20	18	38	20										2	0	3	3	6				
2002-03	Buffalo	NHL	8	0	2	2	6	0	0	0	8	0.0	–2	2	50.0	10:41									
	Rochester	AHL	67	16	32	48	39										3	2	0	2	2				
2003-04	Buffalo	NHL	2	0	0	0	2	0	0	0	2	0.0	0	0	0.0	8:20									
	Rochester	AHL	77	18	19	37	60										16	7	6	13	10				
2004-05	Rochester	AHL	72	12	21	33	46										9	1	2	3	4				
	NHL Totals		**15**	**0**	**3**	**3**	**8**	**0**	**0**	**0**	**20**	**0.0**		**3**	**33.3**	**11:12**									

OHL All-Rookie Team (1997) • OHL Second All-Star Team (1999) • OHL First All-Star Team (2000) • Canadian Major Junior First All-Star Team (2000)

Signed as a free agent by **Tampa Bay**, August 18, 2005.

MINK, Graham

(MIHNK, GRAY-uhm) **WSH.**

Center. Shoots right. 6'3", 217 lbs. Born, Stowe, VT, May 21, 1979.

Season	Club	League	GP	G	A	Pts	PIM	PP	SH	GW	S	%	+/-	TF	F%	Min	GP	G	A	Pts	PIM	PP	SH	GW	Min
1997-98	Northfield Mt.H.	High-MA	25	17	25	42																			
1998-99	U. of Vermont	ECAC	27	4	2	6	34																		
99-2000	U. of Vermont	ECAC	17	7	4	11	14																		
2000-01	U. of Vermont	ECAC	32	17	12	29	52																		
2001-02	Richmond	ECHL	29	8	9	17	78																		
	Portland Pirates	AHL	56	17	17	34	50																		
2002-03	Portland Pirates	AHL	71	22	15	37	115																		
2003-04	Washington	NHL	2	0	0	0	2	0	0	0	0	0.0	–1	1	0.0	5:32									
	Portland Pirates	AHL	68	18	19	37	74										3	0	1	1	4				
2004-05	Portland Pirates	AHL	63	18	21	39	86																		
	NHL Totals		**2**	**0**	**0**	**0**	**2**	**0**	**0**	**0**	**0**	**0.0**		**1**	**0.0**	**5:32**									

Signed as a free agent by **Portland** (AHL), September 30, 2001. Signed as a free agent by **Washington**, April 9, 2002.

			Regular Season														Playoffs								
Season	Club	League	GP	G	A	Pts	PIM	PP	SH	GW	S	%	+/-	TF	F%	Min	GP	G	A	Pts	PIM	PP	SH	GW	Min

MIRONOV, Boris
(mih-RAWN-ohv, BOHR-ihs)

Defense. Shoots right. 6'3", 223 lbs. Born, Moscow, USSR, March 21, 1972. Winnipeg's 2nd choice, 27th overall, in 1992 Entry Draft.

Season	Club	League	GP	G	A	Pts	PIM	PP	SH	GW	S	%	+/-	TF	F%	Min	GP	G	A	Pts	PIM	PP	SH	GW	Min
1988-89	CSKA Moscow	USSR	1	0	0	0	0	....	....	....	....	....	....	....	....	....	....	....	....	....	....	....	....	....	....
1989-90	CSKA Moscow	USSR	7	0	0	0	0	....	....	....	....	....	....	....	....	....	....	....	....	....	....	....	....	....	....
1990-91	CSKA Moscow	USSR	36	1	5	6	16	....	....	....	....	....	....	....	....	....	....	....	....	....	....	....	....	....	....
1991-92	CSKA Moscow	CIS	36	2	1	3	22	....	....	....	....	....	....	....	....	....	....	....	....	....	....	....	....	....	....
1992-93	CSKA Moscow	CIS	19	0	5	5	20	....	....	....	....	....	....	....	....	....	....	....	....	....	....	....	....	....	....
1993-94	**Winnipeg**	**NHL**	65	7	22	29	96	5	0	0	122	5.7	–29	....	....	....	....	....	....	....	....	....	....	....	....
	Edmonton	**NHL**	14	0	2	2	14	0	0	0	23	0.0	–4	....	....	....	....	....	....	....	....	....	....	....	....
1994-95	**Edmonton**	**NHL**	29	1	7	8	40	0	0	0	48	2.1	–9	....	....	....	....	....	....	....	....	....	....	....	....
	Cape Breton	AHL	4	2	5	7	23	....	....	....	....	....	....	....	....	....	....	....	....	....	....	....	....	....	....
1995-96	**Edmonton**	**NHL**	78	8	24	32	101	7	0	1	158	5.1	–23	....	....	....	....	....	....	....	....	....	....	....	....
1996-97	**Edmonton**	**NHL**	55	6	26	32	85	2	0	1	147	4.1	2	....	....	....	12	2	8	10	16	2	0	0	....
1997-98	**Edmonton**	**NHL**	81	16	30	46	100	10	1	1	203	7.9	–8	....	....	....	12	3	3	6	27	1	0	1	....
	Russia	Olympics	6	0	2	2	2	....	....	....	....	....	....	....	....	....	....	....	....	....	....	....	....	....	....
1998-99	**Edmonton**	**NHL**	63	11	29	40	104	5	0	4	138	8.0	6	0	0.0	25:55	....	....	....	....	....	....	....	....	....
	Chicago	**NHL**	12	0	9	9	27	0	0	0	35	0.0	7	0	0.0	24:17	....	....	....	....	....	....	....	....	....
99-2000	**Chicago**	**NHL**	58	9	28	37	72	4	2	1	144	6.3	–3	1	100.0	24:53	....	....	....	....	....	....	....	....	....
2000-01	**Chicago**	**NHL**	66	5	17	22	42	3	0	0	143	3.5	–14	0	0.0	22:05	....	....	....	....	....	....	....	....	....
2001-02	**Chicago**	**NHL**	64	4	14	18	68	0	0	1	129	3.1	15	0	0.0	22:43	1	0	0	0	2	0	0	0	5:41
	Russia	Olympics	6	1	0	1	2	....	....	....	....	....	....	....	....	....	....	....	....	....	....	....	....	....	....
2002-03	**Chicago**	**NHL**	20	3	1	4	22	1	0	0	14	21.4	–1	0	0.0	19:12	....	....	....	....	....	....	....	....	....
	NY Rangers	**NHL**	36	3	9	12	34	1	0	0	56	5.4	3	0	0.0	20:35	....	....	....	....	....	....	....	....	....
2003-04	**NY Rangers**	**NHL**	75	3	13	16	86	1	0	1	129	2.3	1	1	0.0	20:37	....	....	....	....	....	....	....	....	....
2004-05			DID NOT PLAY																						
	NHL Totals		**716**	**76**	**231**	**307**	**891**	**39**	**3**	**10**	**1489**	**5.1**		**2**	**50.0**	**22:43**	**25**	**5**	**11**	**16**	**45**	**3**	**0**	**1**	**5:41**

NHL All-Rookie Team (1994)

Traded to **Edmonton** by **Winnipeg** with Mats Lindgren, Winnipeg's 1st round choice (Jason Bonsignore) in 1994 Entry Draft and Florida's 4th round choice (previously acquired, Edmonton selected Adam Copeland) in 1994 Entry Draft for Dave Manson and St. Louis' 6th round choice (previously acquired, Winnipeg selected Chris Kibermanis) in 1994 Entry Draft, March 15, 1994. Traded to **Chicago** by **Edmonton** with Dean McAmmond and Jonas Elofsson for Chad Kilger, Daniel Cleary, Ethan Moreau and Christian Laflamme, March 20, 1999. Traded to **NY Rangers** by **Chicago** for NY Rangers' 4th round choice (later traded to Dallas – Dallas selected Fredrik Naslund) in 2004 Entry Draft, January 8, 2003.

MITCHELL, Willie
(MIH-chuhl, WIHL-lee) **MIN.**

Defense. Shoots left. 6'3", 205 lbs. Born, Port McNeill, B.C., April 23, 1977. New Jersey's 12th choice, 199th overall, in 1996 Entry Draft.

1993-94	Notre Dame	SMHL	31	4	11	15	81	....	....	....	....	....	....	....	....	....	....	....	....	....	....	....	....	....	....
1994-95	Kelowna Spartans	BCHL	42	3	8	11	71	....	....	....	....	....	....	....	....	....	....	....	....	....	....	....	....	....	....
1995-96	Melfort Mustangs	SJHL	19	2	6	8	....	....	....	....	....	....	....	....	....	....	14	0	2	2	12	....	....	....	....
1996-97	Melfort Mustangs	SJHL	64	14	42	56	227	....	....	....	....	....	....	....	....	....	4	0	1	1	23	....	....	....	....
1997-98	Clarkson Knights	ECAC	34	9	17	26	105	....	....	....	....	....	....	....	....	....	....	....	....	....	....	....	....	....	....
1998-99	Clarkson Knights	ECAC	34	10	19	29	40	....	....	....	....	....	....	....	....	....	....	....	....	....	....	....	....	....	....
	Albany River Rats	AHL	6	1	3	4	29	....	....	....	....	....	....	....	....	....	....	....	....	....	....	....	....	....	....
99-2000	**New Jersey**	**NHL**	2	0	0	0	0	0	0	0	2	0.0	1	0	0.0	16:04	....	....	....	....	....	....	....	....	....
	Albany River Rats	AHL	63	5	14	19	71	....	....	....	....	....	....	....	....	....	5	1	2	3	4	....	....	....	....
2000-01	**New Jersey**	**NHL**	16	0	2	2	29	0	0	0	14	0.0	0	0	0.0	14:52	....	....	....	....	....	....	....	....	....
	Albany River Rats	AHL	41	3	13	16	94	....	....	....	....	....	....	....	....	....	....	....	....	....	....	....	....	....	....
	Minnesota	**NHL**	17	1	7	8	11	0	0	0	16	6.3	4	0	0.0	20:49	....	....	....	....	....	....	....	....	....
2001-02	**Minnesota**	**NHL**	68	3	10	13	68	0	0	1	67	4.5	–16	0	0.0	21:25	....	....	....	....	....	....	....	....	....
2002-03	**Minnesota**	**NHL**	69	2	12	14	84	0	1	1	67	3.0	13	0	0.0	21:28	18	1	3	4	14	0	0	0	24:48
2003-04	**Minnesota**	**NHL**	70	1	13	14	83	0	0	0	58	1.7	12	2	50.0	22:36	....	....	....	....	....	....	....	....	....
2004-05			DID NOT PLAY																						
	NHL Totals		**242**	**7**	**44**	**51**	**275**	**0**	**1**	**2**	**224**	**3.1**		**2**	**50.0**	**21:15**	**18**	**1**	**3**	**4**	**14**	**0**	**0**	**0**	**24:48**

SJHL First All-Star Team (1997) • SJHL Top Defenseman Award (1997) • ECAC Second All-Star Team (1998) • ECAC Rookie of the Year (1998) (co-winner - Erik Cole) • ECAC First All-Star Team (1999) • NCAA East Second All-American Team (1999)

Traded to **Minnesota** by **New Jersey** for Sean O'Donnell, March 4, 2001.

MODANO, Mike
(moh-DA-noh, MIGHK) **DAL.**

Center. Shoots left. 6'3", 205 lbs. Born, Livonia, MI, June 7, 1970. Minnesota's 1st choice, 1st overall, in 1988 Entry Draft.

1985-86	Det. Compuware	MNHL	69	66	65	131	32	....	....	....	....	....	....	....	....	....	....	....	....	....	....	....	....	....	....
1986-87	Prince Albert	WHL	70	32	30	62	96	....	....	....	....	....	....	....	....	....	8	1	4	5	4	....	....	....	....
1987-88	Prince Albert	WHL	65	47	80	127	80	....	....	....	....	....	....	....	....	....	9	7	11	18	18	....	....	....	....
1988-89	Prince Albert	WHL	41	39	66	105	74	....	....	....	....	....	....	....	....	....	....	....	....	....	....	....	....	....	....
	Minnesota	**NHL**	....	....	....	....	....	....	....	....	....	....	....	....	....	....	2	0	0	0	0	0	0	0	....
1989-90	**Minnesota**	**NHL**	80	29	46	75	63	12	0	2	172	16.9	–7	....	....	....	7	1	1	2	12	0	0	0	....
1990-91	**Minnesota**	**NHL**	79	28	36	64	65	9	0	2	232	12.1	2	....	....	....	23	8	12	20	16	3	0	1	....
1991-92	**Minnesota**	**NHL**	76	33	44	77	46	5	0	8	256	12.9	–9	....	....	....	7	3	2	5	4	1	0	0	....
1992-93	**Minnesota**	**NHL**	82	33	60	93	83	9	0	7	307	10.7	–7	....	....	....	....	....	....	....	....	....	....	....	....
1993-94	**Dallas**	**NHL**	76	50	43	93	54	18	0	4	281	17.8	–8	....	....	....	9	7	3	10	16	2	0	2	....
1994-95	**Dallas**	**NHL**	30	12	17	29	8	4	1	0	100	12.0	7	....	....	....	....	....	....	....	....	....	....	....	....
1995-96	**Dallas**	**NHL**	78	36	45	81	63	8	4	4	320	11.3	–12	....	....	....	....	....	....	....	....	....	....	....	....
1996-97	**Dallas**	**NHL**	80	35	48	83	42	9	5	9	291	12.0	43	....	....	....	7	4	1	5	0	1	1	2	....
1997-98	**Dallas**	**NHL**	52	21	38	59	32	7	5	2	191	11.0	25	....	....	....	17	4	10	14	12	1	0	1	....
	United States	Olympics	4	2	0	2	0	....	....	....	....	....	....	....	....	....	....	....	....	....	....	....	....	....	....
1998-99♦	**Dallas**	**NHL**	77	34	47	81	44	6	4	7	224	15.2	29	1572	51.1	20:50	23	5	*18	23	16	1	1	1	24:40
99-2000	**Dallas**	**NHL**	77	38	43	81	48	11	1	8	188	20.2	0	1763	51.4	22:55	23	10	*13	23	10	4	0	2	25:26
2000-01	**Dallas**	**NHL**	81	33	51	84	52	8	3	7	208	15.9	26	1791	52.0	22:24	9	3	4	7	0	2	0	0	25:43
2001-02	**Dallas**	**NHL**	78	34	43	77	38	6	2	5	219	15.5	14	1710	53.7	22:27	....	....	....	....	....	....	....	....	....
	United States	Olympics	6	0	*6	6	4	....	....	....	....	....	....	....	....	....	....	....	....	....	....	....	....	....	....
2002-03	**Dallas**	**NHL**	79	28	57	85	30	5	2	6	193	14.5	34	1808	51.4	20:53	12	5	10	15	4	1	0	2	23:53
2003-04	**Dallas**	**NHL**	76	14	30	44	46	6	0	0	152	9.2	–21	1523	52.6	20:27	5	1	2	3	8	1	0	0	23:17
2004-05			DID NOT PLAY																						
	NHL Totals		**1101**	**458**	**648**	**1106**	**714**	**123**	**27**	**71**	**3334**	**13.7**		**10167**	**52.0**	**21:40**	**144**	**51**	**76**	**127**	**98**	**17**	**2**	**11**	**24:49**

WHL East First All-Star Team (1989) • NHL All-Rookie Team (1990) • NHL Second All-Star Team (2000)

Played in NHL All-Star Game (1993, 1998, 1999, 2000, 2003, 2004)

Transferred to **Dallas** after **Minnesota** franchise relocated, June 9, 1993.

MODIN, Fredrik
(moh-DEEN, FREHD-rihk) **T.B.**

Left wing. Shoots left. 6'4", 220 lbs. Born, Sundsvall, Sweden, October 8, 1974. Toronto's 3rd choice, 64th overall, in 1994 Entry Draft.

1991-92	Sundsvall/Timra	Sweden-2	11	1	0	1	0	....	....	....	....	....	....	....	....	....	....	....	....	....	....	....	....	....	....
1992-93	Sundsvall/Timra	Sweden-2	30	5	7	12	12	....	....	....	....	....	....	....	....	....	5	1	0	1	0	....	....	....	....
1993-94	Sundsvall/Timra	Sweden-2	30	16	15	31	36	....	....	....	....	....	....	....	....	....	2	0	1	1	6	....	....	....	....
1994-95	Brynas IF Gavle	Sweden	38	9	10	19	33	....	....	....	....	....	....	....	....	....	14	4	4	8	6	....	....	....	....
1995-96	Brynas IF Gavle	Sweden	22	4	8	12	22	....	....	....	....	....	....	....	....	....	....	....	....	....	....	....	....	....	....
1996-97	**Toronto**	**NHL**	76	6	7	13	24	0	0	0	85	7.1	–14	....	....	....	....	....	....	....	....	....	....	....	....
1997-98	**Toronto**	**NHL**	74	16	16	32	32	1	0	4	137	11.7	–5	....	....	....	....	....	....	....	....	....	....	....	....
1998-99	**Toronto**	**NHL**	67	16	15	31	35	1	0	3	108	14.8	14	2	50.0	13:34	8	0	0	0	6	0	0	0	9:50
99-2000	**Tampa Bay**	**NHL**	80	22	26	48	18	3	0	5	167	13.2	–26	6	50.0	15:32	....	....	....	....	....	....	....	....	....
2000-01	**Tampa Bay**	**NHL**	76	32	24	56	48	8	0	4	217	14.7	–1	21	42.9	17:15	....	....	....	....	....	....	....	....	....
2001-02	**Tampa Bay**	**NHL**	54	14	17	31	27	2	0	4	141	9.9	0	25	40.0	19:05	....	....	....	....	....	....	....	....	....
2002-03	**Tampa Bay**	**NHL**	76	17	23	40	43	2	1	4	179	9.5	7	35	28.6	17:35	11	2	0	2	18	0	0	0	19:18
2003-04♦	**Tampa Bay**	**NHL**	82	29	28	57	32	5	1	2	206	14.1	31	138	38.4	18:12	23	8	11	19	10	3	0	2	20:47
2004-05	Timra IK	Sweden	43	12	24	36	58	....	....	....	....	....	....	....	....	....	7	1	1	2	8	....	....	....	....
	NHL Totals		**585**	**152**	**156**	**308**	**259**	**22**	**2**	**26**	**1240**	**12.3**		**227**	**37.9**	**16:50**	**42**	**10**	**11**	**21**	**34**	**3**	**0**	**2**	**18:18**

Played in NHL All-Star Game (2001)

Traded to **Tampa Bay** by **Toronto** for Cory Cross and Tampa Bay's 7th round choice (Ivan Kolozvary) in 2001 Entry Draft, October 1, 1999. Signed as a free agent by **Timra** (Sweden), October 5, 2004.

MODRY, Jaroslav

(MOH-dree, YAHRO-slahv) **ATL.**

Defense. Shoots left. 6'2", 225 lbs. Born, Ceske Budejovice, Czech., February 27, 1971. New Jersey's 11th choice, 179th overall, in 1990 Entry Draft.

			Regular Season														Playoffs								
Season	Club	League	GP	G	A	Pts	PIM	PP	SH	GW	S	%	+/-	TF	F%	Min	GP	G	A	Pts	PIM	PP	SH	GW	Min
1987-88	C. Budejovice	Czech	3	0	0	0	0	....	....	....	....	....	....	....	....	....	....	....	....	....	....	....	....	....	....
1988-89	C. Budejovice	Czech	28	0	1	1	8	....	....	....	....	....	....	....	....	....	....	....	....	....	....	....	....	....	....
1989-90	C. Budejovice	Czech	41	2	2	4	....	....	....	....	....	....	....	....	....	....	....	....	....	....	....	....	....	....	....
1990-91	Dukla Trencin	Czech	33	1	9	10	6	....	....	....	....	....	....	....	....	....	....	....	....	....	....	....	....	....	....
1991-92	C. Budejovice	Czech-2	14	4	10	14	....	....	....	....	....	....	....	....	....	....	....	....	....	....	....	....	....	....	....
	Dukla Trencin	Czech	18	0	4	4	6	....	....	....	....	....	....	....	....	....	....	....	....	....	....	....	....	....	....
1992-93	Utica Devils	AHL	80	7	35	42	62	....	....	....	....	....	....	....	....	....	5	0	2	2	2	....	....	....	....
1993-94	**New Jersey**	**NHL**	**41**	**2**	**15**	**17**	**18**	**2**	**0**	**0**	**35**	**5.7**	**10**	....	....	....	....	....	....	....	....	....	....	....	....
	Albany River Rats	AHL	19	1	5	6	25	....	....	....	....	....	....	....	....	....	....	....	....	....	....	....	....	....	....
1994-95	C. Budejovice	CzRep	19	1	3	4	30	....	....	....	....	....	....	....	....	....	....	....	....	....	....	....	....	....	....
	New Jersey	**NHL**	**11**	**0**	**0**	**0**	**0**	**0**	**0**	**0**	**10**	**0.0**	**–1**	....	....	....	....	....	....	....	....	....	....	....	....
	Albany River Rats	AHL	18	5	6	11	14	....	....	....	....	....	....	....	....	....	14	3	3	6	4	....	....	....	....
1995-96	**Ottawa**	**NHL**	**64**	**4**	**14**	**18**	**38**	**1**	**0**	**1**	**89**	**4.5**	**–17**	....	....	....	....	....	....	....	....	....	....	....	....
	Los Angeles	**NHL**	**9**	**0**	**3**	**3**	**6**	**0**	**0**	**0**	**17**	**0.0**	**–4**	....	....	....	....	....	....	....	....	....	....	....	....
1996-97	**Los Angeles**	**NHL**	**30**	**3**	**3**	**6**	**25**	**1**	**1**	**0**	**32**	**9.4**	**–13**	....	....	....	....	....	....	....	....	....	....	....	....
	Phoenix	IHL	23	3	12	15	17	....	....	....	....	....	....	....	....	....	....	....	....	....	....	....	....	....	....
	Utah Grizzlies	IHL	11	1	4	5	20	....	....	....	....	....	....	....	....	....	7	0	1	1	6	....	....	....	....
1997-98	Utah Grizzlies	IHL	74	12	21	33	72	....	....	....	....	....	....	....	....	....	4	0	2	2	6	....	....	....	....
1998-99	**Los Angeles**	**NHL**	**5**	**0**	**1**	**1**	**0**	**0**	**0**	**0**	**11**	**0.0**	**1**	**0**	**0.0**	**26:00**	....	....	....	....	....	....	....	....	....
	Long Beach	IHL	64	6	29	35	44	....	....	....	....	....	....	....	....	....	8	4	2	6	4	....	....	....	....
99-2000	**Los Angeles**	**NHL**	**26**	**5**	**4**	**9**	**18**	**5**	**0**	**1**	**32**	**15.6**	**–2**	**0**	**0.0**	**19:13**	**2**	**0**	**0**	**0**	**2**	**0**	**0**	**0**	**16:48**
	Long Beach	IHL	11	2	4	6	8	....	....	....	....	....	....	....	....	....	....	....	....	....	....	....	....	....	....
2000-01	**Los Angeles**	**NHL**	**63**	**4**	**15**	**19**	**48**	**0**	**0**	**0**	**72**	**5.6**	**16**	**0**	**0.0**	**18:22**	**10**	**1**	**0**	**1**	**4**	**1**	**0**	**1**	**16:08**
2001-02	**Los Angeles**	**NHL**	**80**	**4**	**38**	**42**	**65**	**4**	**0**	**0**	**119**	**3.4**	**–4**	**0**	**0.0**	**19:31**	**7**	**0**	**2**	**2**	**0**	**0**	**0**	**0**	**21:26**
2002-03	**Los Angeles**	**NHL**	**82**	**13**	**25**	**38**	**68**	**8**	**0**	**1**	**205**	**6.3**	**–13**	**1**	**0.0**	**22:39**	....	....	....	....	....	....	....	....	....
2003-04	**Los Angeles**	**NHL**	**79**	**5**	**27**	**32**	**44**	**1**	**0**	**1**	**196**	**2.6**	**11**	**1**	**0.0**	**24:24**	....	....	....	....	....	....	....	....	....
2004-05	Liberec	CzRep	19	3	7	10	24	....	....	....	....	....	....	....	....	....	12	0	4	4	22	....	....	....	....
	NHL Totals		**490**	**40**	**145**	**185**	**330**	**22**	**1**	**4**	**818**	**4.9**		**2**	**0.0**	**21:18**	**19**	**1**	**2**	**3**	**6**	**1**	**0**	**1**	**18:09**

Played in NHL All-Star Game (2002)

Traded to **Ottawa** by **New Jersey** for Ottawa's 4th round choice (Alyn McCauley) in 1995 Entry Draft, July 8, 1995. Traded to **Los Angeles** by **Ottawa** with Ottawa's 8th round choice (Stephen Valiquette) in 1996 Entry Draft for Kevin Brown, March 20, 1996. Signed as a free agent by **Atlanta**, July 1, 2004. Signed as a free agent by **Liberec** (CzRep), October 20, 2004.

MOEN, Travis

(MOH-ehn, TRA-vihs) **ANA.**

Left wing. Shoots left. 6'2", 210 lbs. Born, Stewart Valley, Sask., April 6, 1982. Calgary's 6th choice, 155th overall, in 2000 Entry Draft.

Season	Club	League	GP	G	A	Pts	PIM	PP	SH	GW	S	%	+/-	TF	F%	Min	GP	G	A	Pts	PIM	PP	SH	GW	Min
1998-99	Swift Current	SMHL	STATISTICS NOT AVAILABLE																						
	Kelowna Rockets	WHL	4	0	0	0	0	....	....	....	....	....	....	....	....	....	....	....	....	....	....	....	....	....	....
99-2000	Kelowna Rockets	WHL	66	9	6	15	96	....	....	....	....	....	....	....	....	....	5	1	1	2	2	....	....	....	....
2000-01	Kelowna Rockets	WHL	40	8	8	16	106	....	....	....	....	....	....	....	....	....	....	....	....	....	....	....	....	....	....
2001-02	Kelowna Rockets	WHL	71	10	17	27	197	....	....	....	....	....	....	....	....	....	13	1	0	1	28	....	....	....	....
2002-03	Norfolk Admirals	AHL	42	1	2	3	62	....	....	....	....	....	....	....	....	....	9	0	0	0	20	....	....	....	....
2003-04	**Chicago**	**NHL**	**82**	**4**	**2**	**6**	**142**	**0**	**0**	**2**	**51**	**7.8**	**–17**	**19**	**15.8**	**10:57**	....	....	....	....	....	....	....	....	....
2004-05	Norfolk Admirals	AHL	79	8	12	20	187	....	....	....	....	....	....	....	....	....	6	0	1	1	6	....	....	....	....
	NHL Totals		**82**	**4**	**2**	**6**	**142**	**0**	**0**	**2**	**51**	**7.8**		**19**	**15.8**	**10:57**	....	....	....	....	....	....	....	....	....

Signed as a free agent by **Chicago**, October 21, 2002. Traded to **Anaheim** by **Chicago** for Michael Holmqvist, July 30, 2005.

MOGILNY, Alexander

(moh-GIHL-nee, al-ehx-AN-duhr) **N.J.**

Right wing. Shoots left. 6', 210 lbs. Born, Khabarovsk, USSR, February 18, 1969. Buffalo's 4th choice, 89th overall, in 1988 Entry Draft.

Season	Club	League	GP	G	A	Pts	PIM	PP	SH	GW	S	%	+/-	TF	F%	Min	GP	G	A	Pts	PIM	PP	SH	GW	Min
1986-87	CSKA Moscow	USSR	28	15	1	16	4	....	....	....	....	....	....	....	....	....	....	....	....	....	....	....	....	....	....
1987-88	CSKA Moscow	USSR	39	12	8	20	14	....	....	....	....	....	....	....	....	....	....	....	....	....	....	....	....	....	....
	Soviet Union	Olympics	6	3	2	5	2	....	....	....	....	....	....	....	....	....	....	....	....	....	....	....	....	....	....
1988-89	CSKA Moscow	USSR	31	11	11	22	24	....	....	....	....	....	....	....	....	....	....	....	....	....	....	....	....	....	....
1989-90	**Buffalo**	**NHL**	**65**	**15**	**28**	**43**	**16**	**4**	**0**	**2**	**130**	**11.5**	**8**	....	....	....	**4**	**0**	**1**	**1**	**2**	**0**	**0**	**0**	....
1990-91	**Buffalo**	**NHL**	**62**	**30**	**34**	**64**	**16**	**3**	**3**	**5**	**201**	**14.9**	**14**	....	....	....	**6**	**0**	**6**	**6**	**2**	**0**	**0**	**0**	....
1991-92	**Buffalo**	**NHL**	**67**	**39**	**45**	**84**	**73**	**15**	**0**	**2**	**236**	**16.5**	**7**	....	....	....	**2**	**0**	**2**	**2**	**0**	**0**	**0**	**0**	....
1992-93	**Buffalo**	**NHL**	**77**	***76**	**51**	**127**	**40**	**27**	**0**	**11**	**360**	**21.1**	**7**	....	....	....	**7**	**7**	**3**	**10**	**6**	**2**	**0**	**0**	....
1993-94	**Buffalo**	**NHL**	**66**	**32**	**47**	**79**	**22**	**17**	**0**	**7**	**258**	**12.4**	**8**	....	....	....	**7**	**4**	**2**	**6**	**6**	**1**	**0**	**0**	....
1994-95	Spartak Moscow	CIS	1	0	1	1	0	....	....	....	....	....	....	....	....	....	....	....	....	....	....	....	....	....	....
	Buffalo	**NHL**	**44**	**19**	**28**	**47**	**36**	**12**	**0**	**2**	**148**	**12.8**	**0**	....	....	....	**5**	**3**	**2**	**5**	**2**	**0**	**0**	**0**	....
1995-96	**Vancouver**	**NHL**	**79**	**55**	**52**	**107**	**16**	**10**	**5**	**6**	**292**	**18.8**	**14**	....	....	....	**6**	**1**	**8**	**9**	**8**	**0**	**0**	**0**	....
1996-97	**Vancouver**	**NHL**	**76**	**31**	**42**	**73**	**18**	**7**	**1**	**4**	**174**	**17.8**	**9**	....	....	....	....	....	....	....	....	....	....	....	....
1997-98	**Vancouver**	**NHL**	**51**	**18**	**27**	**45**	**36**	**5**	**4**	**1**	**118**	**15.3**	**–6**	....	....	....	....	....	....	....	....	....	....	....	....
1998-99	**Vancouver**	**NHL**	**59**	**14**	**31**	**45**	**58**	**3**	**2**	**1**	**110**	**12.7**	**0**	**47**	**23.4**	**20:35**	....	....	....	....	....	....	....	....	....
99-2000	**Vancouver**	**NHL**	**47**	**21**	**17**	**38**	**16**	**3**	**1**	**1**	**126**	**16.7**	**7**	**9**	**11.1**	**19:34**	....	....	....	....	....	....	....	....	....
	♦ New Jersey	**NHL**	**12**	**3**	**3**	**6**	**4**	**2**	**0**	**0**	**35**	**8.6**	**–4**	**0**	**0.0**	**17:04**	**23**	**4**	**3**	**7**	**4**	**2**	**0**	**1**	**16:06**
2000-01	**New Jersey**	**NHL**	**75**	**43**	**40**	**83**	**43**	**12**	**0**	**7**	**240**	**17.9**	**10**	**11**	**36.4**	**16:53**	**25**	**5**	**11**	**16**	**8**	**1**	**0**	**2**	**16:42**
2001-02	**Toronto**	**NHL**	**66**	**24**	**33**	**57**	**8**	**5**	**0**	**4**	**188**	**12.8**	**1**	**5**	**40.0**	**17:38**	**20**	**8**	**3**	**11**	**8**	**2**	**0**	**2**	**19:23**
2002-03	**Toronto**	**NHL**	**73**	**33**	**46**	**79**	**12**	**5**	**3**	**9**	**165**	**20.0**	**4**	**18**	**33.3**	**20:03**	**6**	**5**	**2**	**7**	**4**	**0**	**1**	**0**	**21:43**
2003-04	**Toronto**	**NHL**	**37**	**8**	**22**	**30**	**12**	**4**	**1**	**1**	**92**	**8.7**	**9**	**10**	**60.0**	**18:29**	**13**	**2**	**4**	**6**	**8**	**0**	**0**	**0**	**16:28**
2004-05			DID NOT PLAY																						
	NHL Totals		**956**	**461**	**546**	**1007**	**426**	**134**	**20**	**63**	**2873**	**16.0**		**100**	**30.0**	**18:45**	**124**	**39**	**47**	**86**	**58**	**8**	**1**	**5**	**17:28**

NHL Second All-Star Team (1993, 1996) • Lady Byng Trophy (2003)

Played in NHL All-Star Game (1992, 1993, 1994, 1996)

Traded to **Vancouver** by **Buffalo** with Buffalo's 5th round choice (Todd Norman) in 1995 Entry Draft for Michael Peca, Mike Wilson and Vancouver's 1st round choice (Jay McKee) in 1995 Entry Draft, July 8, 1995. Traded to **New Jersey** by **Vancouver** for Brendan Morrison and Denis Pederson, March 14, 2000. Signed as a free agent by **Toronto**, July 3, 2001. • Missed majority of 2003-04 season recovering from hip injury suffered in game vs. Edmonton, November 20, 2003. Signed as a free agent by **New Jersey**, August 17, 2005.

MONTADOR, Steve

(MAWN-tuh-dohr, STEEV) **CGY.**

Defense. Shoots right. 6', 210 lbs. Born, Vancouver, B.C., December 21, 1979.

Season	Club	League	GP	G	A	Pts	PIM	PP	SH	GW	S	%	+/-	TF	F%	Min	GP	G	A	Pts	PIM	PP	SH	GW	Min
1995-96	St. Mike's B's	OPJHL	46	3	16	19	145	....	....	....	....	....	....	....	....	....	....	....	....	....	....	....	....	....	....
1996-97	North Bay	OHL	63	7	28	35	129	....	....	....	....	....	....	....	....	....	....	....	....	....	....	....	....	....	....
1997-98	North Bay	OHL	37	5	16	21	54	....	....	....	....	....	....	....	....	....	....	....	....	....	....	....	....	....	....
	Erie Otters	OHL	26	3	17	20	35	....	....	....	....	....	....	....	....	....	7	1	1	2	9	....	....	....	....
1998-99	Erie Otters	OHL	61	9	33	42	114	....	....	....	....	....	....	....	....	....	5	0	2	2	4	....	....	....	....
99-2000	Peterborough	OHL	64	14	42	56	97	....	....	....	....	....	....	....	....	....	5	0	2	2	4	....	....	....	....
	Saint John Flames	AHL	....	....	....	....	....	....	....	....	....	....	....	....	....	....	2	0	0	0	0	....	....	....	....
2000-01	Saint John Flames	AHL	58	1	6	7	95	....	....	....	....	....	....	....	....	....	19	0	8	8	13	....	....	....	....
2001-02	**Calgary**	**NHL**	**11**	**1**	**2**	**3**	**26**	**0**	**0**	**0**	**10**	**10.0**	**–2**	**0**	**0.0**	**12:12**	....	....	....	....	....	....	....	....	....
	Saint John Flames	AHL	67	9	16	25	107	....	....	....	....	....	....	....	....	....	....	....	....	....	....	....	....	....	....
2002-03	**Calgary**	**NHL**	**50**	**1**	**1**	**2**	**114**	**0**	**0**	**0**	**64**	**1.6**	**–9**	**0**	**0.0**	**15:11**	....	....	....	....	....	....	....	....	....
	Saint John Flames	AHL	11	1	7	8	20	....	....	....	....	....	....	....	....	....	....	....	....	....	....	....	....	....	....
2003-04	**Calgary**	**NHL**	**26**	**1**	**2**	**3**	**50**	**0**	**0**	**1**	**31**	**3.2**	**–1**	**1**	**0.0**	**11:46**	**20**	**1**	**2**	**3**	**6**	**0**	**0**	**1**	**17:43**
2004-05	HC Mulhouse	France	15	1	7	8	69	....	....	....	....	....	....	....	....	....	....	....	....	....	....	....	....	....	....
	NHL Totals		**87**	**3**	**5**	**8**	**190**	**0**	**0**	**1**	**105**	**2.9**		**1**	**0.0**	**13:47**	**20**	**1**	**2**	**3**	**6**	**0**	**0**	**1**	**17:43**

Signed as a free agent by **Calgary**, April 10, 2000. • Spent majority of 2003-04 season as a healthy reserve. Signed as a free agent by **Mulhouse** (France), September 17, 2004.

MOORE, Dominic

(MOOR, DOHM-ih-nihk) **NYR**

Center. Shoots left. 6', 195 lbs. Born, Thornhill, Ont., August 3, 1980. NY Rangers' 2nd choice, 95th overall, in 2000 Entry Draft.

			Regular Season														Playoffs								
Season	Club	League	GP	G	A	Pts	PIM	PP	SH	GW	S	%	+/-	TF	F%	Min	GP	G	A	Pts	PIM	PP	SH	GW	Min
1996-97	Thornhill Islanders	MTJHL	29	4	6	10	48	....	....	....	....	....	....	....	....	....	1	0	1	1	0	....	....	....	....
1997-98	Aurora Tigers	OPJHL	51	10	15	25	16	....	....	....	....	....	....	....	....	....	....	....	....	....	....	....	....	....	....
1998-99	Aurora Tigers	OPJHL	51	34	53	87	70	....	....	....	....	....	....	....	....	....	....	....	....	....	....	....	....	....	....
99-2000	Harvard Crimson	ECAC	30	12	24	28	16	....	....	....	....	....	....	....	....	....	....	....	....	....	....	....	....	....	....
2000-01	Harvard Crimson	ECAC	32	15	28	43	40	....	....	....	....	....	....	....	....	....	....	....	....	....	....	....	....	....	....
2001-02	Harvard Crimson	ECAC	32	13	16	29	37	....	....	....	....	....	....	....	....	....	....	....	....	....	....	....	....	....	....
2002-03	Harvard Crimson	ECAC	34	*24	27	*51	30	....	....	....	....	....	....	....	....	....	....	....	....	....	....	....	....	....	....
2003-04	**NY Rangers**	**NHL**	**5**	**0**	**3**	**3**	**0**	**0**	**0**	**0**	**3**	**0.0**	**0**	**36**	**30.6**	**9:18**	....	....	....	....	....	....	....	....	....
	Hartford	AHL	70	14	25	39	60	....	....	....	....	....	....	....	....	....	16	3	3	6	8	....	....	....	....
2004-05	Hartford	AHL	78	19	31	50	78	....	....	....	....	....	....	....	....	....	6	1	1	2	4	....	....	....	....
	NHL Totals		**5**	**0**	**3**	**3**	**0**	**0**	**0**	**0**	**3**	**0.0**		**36**	**30.6**	**9:18**	....	....	....	....	....	....	....	....	....

ECAC All-Rookie Team (2000) • ECAC Second All-Star Team (2001) • ECAC First All-Star Team (2003) • NCAA East First All-American Team (2003)

MOORE, Steve

(MOOR, STEEV)

Center. Shoots right. 6'2", 205 lbs. Born, Windsor, Ont., September 22, 1978. Colorado's 7th choice, 53rd overall, in 1998 Entry Draft.

Season	Club	League	GP	G	A	Pts	PIM	PP	SH	GW	S	%	+/-	TF	F%	Min	GP	G	A	Pts	PIM	PP	SH	GW	Min
1995-96	Thornhill Islanders	MTJHL	50	25	27	52	57	....	....	....	....	....	....	....	....	....	18	4	5	9	....	....	....	....	....
1996-97	Thornhill Islanders	MTJHL	50	34	52	86	52	....	....	....	....	....	....	....	....	....	13	10	11	21	2	....	....	....	....
1997-98	Harvard Crimson	ECAC	33	10	23	33	46	....	....	....	....	....	....	....	....	....	....	....	....	....	....	....	....	....	....
1998-99	Harvard Crimson	ECAC	30	18	13	31	34	....	....	....	....	....	....	....	....	....	....	....	....	....	....	....	....	....	....
99-2000	Harvard Crimson	ECAC	27	10	16	26	53	....	....	....	....	....	....	....	....	....	....	....	....	....	....	....	....	....	....
2000-01	Harvard Crimson	ECAC	32	7	26	33	43	....	....	....	....	....	....	....	....	....	....	....	....	....	....	....	....	....	....
2001-02	**Colorado**	**NHL**	**8**	**0**	**0**	**0**	**4**	**0**	**0**	**0**	**5**	**0.0**	**–4**	**33**	**51.5**	**7:05**	....	....	....	....	....	....	....	....	....
	Hershey Bears	AHL	68	10	17	27	31	....	....	....	....	....	....	....	....	....	8	0	1	1	6	....	....	....	....
2002-03	**Colorado**	**NHL**	**4**	**0**	**0**	**0**	**0**	**0**	**0**	**0**	**0**	**0.0**	**0**	**23**	**30.4**	**8:56**	....	....	....	....	....	....	....	....	....
	Hershey Bears	AHL	58	10	13	23	41	....	....	....	....	....	....	....	....	....	5	0	1	1	4	....	....	....	....
2003-04	**Colorado**	**NHL**	**57**	**5**	**7**	**12**	**37**	**0**	**0**	**1**	**52**	**9.6**	**–5**	**387**	**40.3**	**13:06**	....	....	....	....	....	....	....	....	....
	Hershey Bears	AHL	13	4	4	8	6	....	....	....	....	....	....	....	....	....	....	....	....	....	....	....	....	....	....
2004-05			DID NOT PLAY – INJURED																						
	NHL Totals		**69**	**5**	**7**	**12**	**41**	**0**	**0**	**1**	**57**	**8.8**		**443**	**40.6**	**12:10**	....	....	....	....	....	....	....	....	....

• Missed remainder of 2003-04 season and entire 2004-05 season recovering from head and neck injuries sustained in game vs. Vancouver, March 8, 2004.

MORAN, Brad

(moh-RAN, BRAD)

Center. Shoots left. 5'11", 187 lbs. Born, Abbotsford, B.C., March 20, 1979. Buffalo's 8th choice, 191st overall, in 1998 Entry Draft.

Season	Club	League	GP	G	A	Pts	PIM	PP	SH	GW	S	%	+/-	TF	F%	Min	GP	G	A	Pts	PIM	PP	SH	GW	Min
1994-95	Abbotsford	BCAHA	56	66	93	159	40	....	....	....	....	....	....	....	....	....	....	....	....	....	....	....	....	....	....
1995-96	Calgary Hitmen	WHL	70	13	31	44	28	....	....	....	....	....	....	....	....	....	....	....	....	....	....	....	....	....	....
1996-97	Calgary Hitmen	WHL	72	30	36	66	61	....	....	....	....	....	....	....	....	....	....	....	....	....	....	....	....	....	....
1997-98	Calgary Hitmen	WHL	72	53	49	102	64	....	....	....	....	....	....	....	....	....	18	10	8	18	20	....	....	....	....
1998-99	Calgary Hitmen	WHL	71	60	58	118	96	....	....	....	....	....	....	....	....	....	21	17	*25	42	26	....	....	....	....
99-2000	Calgary Hitmen	WHL	72	48	*72	*120	84	....	....	....	....	....	....	....	....	....	13	7	15	22	18	....	....	....	....
2000-01	Syracuse Crunch	AHL	71	11	19	30	30	....	....	....	....	....	....	....	....	....	5	3	4	7	2	....	....	....	....
2001-02	**Columbus**	**NHL**	**3**	**0**	**0**	**0**	**0**	**0**	**0**	**0**	**2**	**0.0**	**0**	**22**	**40.9**	**7:39**	....	....	....	....	....	....	....	....	....
	Syracuse Crunch	AHL	64	25	24	49	51	....	....	....	....	....	....	....	....	....	10	5	8	13	2	....	....	....	....
2002-03	Syracuse Crunch	AHL	47	12	19	31	22	....	....	....	....	....	....	....	....	....	....	....	....	....	....	....	....	....	....
2003-04	**Columbus**	**NHL**	**2**	**1**	**1**	**2**	**2**	**0**	**0**	**0**	**4**	**25.0**	**–1**	**25**	**64.0**	**10:03**	....	....	....	....	....	....	....	....	....
	Syracuse Crunch	AHL	72	24	35	59	44	....	....	....	....	....	....	....	....	....	7	5	3	8	2	....	....	....	....
2004-05	Syracuse Crunch	AHL	80	26	46	72	70	....	....	....	....	....	....	....	....	....	....	....	....	....	....	....	....	....	....
	NHL Totals		**5**	**1**	**1**	**2**	**2**	**0**	**0**	**0**	**6**	**16.7**		**47**	**53.2**	**8:36**	....	....	....	....	....	....	....	....	....

WHL East First All-Star Team (1999, 2000) • WHL Player of the Year (2000)

Signed as a free agent by **Columbus**, June 5, 2000.

MORAN, Ian

(moh-RAN, EE-an) **BOS.**

Defense. Shoots right. 6', 200 lbs. Born, Cleveland, OH, August 24, 1972. Pittsburgh's 5th choice, 107th overall, in 1990 Entry Draft.

Season	Club	League	GP	G	A	Pts	PIM	PP	SH	GW	S	%	+/-	TF	F%	Min	GP	G	A	Pts	PIM	PP	SH	GW	Min
1987-88	Belmont Hill	High-MA	25	3	13	16	15	....	....	....	....	....	....	....	....	....	....	....	....	....	....	....	....	....	....
1988-89	Belmont Hill	High-MA	23	7	25	32	8	....	....	....	....	....	....	....	....	....	....	....	....	....	....	....	....	....	....
1989-90	Belmont Hill	High-MA	23	10	36	46	....	....	....	....	....	....	....	....	....	....	....	....	....	....	....	....	....	....	....
1990-91	Belmont Hill	High-MA	23	7	44	51	12	....	....	....	....	....	....	....	....	....	....	....	....	....	....	....	....	....	....
1991-92	Boston College	H-East	30	2	16	18	44	....	....	....	....	....	....	....	....	....	....	....	....	....	....	....	....	....	....
1992-93	Boston College	H-East	31	8	12	20	32	....	....	....	....	....	....	....	....	....	....	....	....	....	....	....	....	....	....
1993-94	United States	Nat-Tm	50	8	15	23	69	....	....	....	....	....	....	....	....	....	....	....	....	....	....	....	....	....	....
	Cleveland	IHL	33	5	13	18	39	....	....	....	....	....	....	....	....	....	....	....	....	....	....	....	....	....	....
1994-95	Cleveland	IHL	64	7	31	38	94	....	....	....	....	....	....	....	....	....	4	0	1	1	2	....	....	....	....
	Pittsburgh	**NHL**	....	....	....	....	....	....	....	....	....	....	....	....	....	....	**8**	**0**	**0**	**0**	**0**	**0**	**0**	**0**	....
1995-96	**Pittsburgh**	**NHL**	**51**	**1**	**1**	**2**	**47**	**0**	**0**	**0**	**44**	**2.3**	**–1**	....	....	....	....	....	....	....	....	....	....	....	....
1996-97	**Pittsburgh**	**NHL**	**36**	**4**	**5**	**9**	**22**	**0**	**0**	**0**	**50**	**8.0**	**–11**	....	....	....	**5**	**1**	**2**	**3**	**4**	**0**	**0**	**0**	....
	Cleveland	IHL	36	6	23	29	26	....	....	....	....	....	....	....	....	....	....	....	....	....	....	....	....	....	....
1997-98	**Pittsburgh**	**NHL**	**37**	**1**	**6**	**7**	**19**	**0**	**0**	**1**	**33**	**3.0**	**0**	....	....	....	**6**	**0**	**0**	**0**	**2**	**0**	**0**	**0**	....
1998-99	**Pittsburgh**	**NHL**	**62**	**4**	**5**	**9**	**37**	**0**	**1**	**0**	**65**	**6.2**	**1**	**32**	**34.4**	**16:34**	**13**	**0**	**2**	**2**	**8**	**0**	**0**	**0**	**21:10**
99-2000	**Pittsburgh**	**NHL**	**73**	**4**	**8**	**12**	**28**	**0**	**0**	**0**	**58**	**6.9**	**–10**	**210**	**33.8**	**11:21**	**11**	**0**	**1**	**1**	**2**	**0**	**0**	**0**	**8:52**
2000-01	**Pittsburgh**	**NHL**	**40**	**3**	**4**	**7**	**28**	**0**	**0**	**1**	**73**	**4.1**	**5**	**4**	**25.0**	**17:42**	**18**	**0**	**1**	**1**	**4**	**0**	**0**	**0**	**15:54**
2001-02	**Pittsburgh**	**NHL**	**64**	**2**	**8**	**10**	**54**	**0**	**0**	**1**	**94**	**2.1**	**–11**	**2**	**100.0**	**20:00**	....	....	....	....	....	....	....	....	....
2002-03	**Pittsburgh**	**NHL**	**70**	**0**	**7**	**7**	**46**	**0**	**0**	**0**	**85**	**0.0**	**–17**	**4**	**75.0**	**18:37**	....	....	....	....	....	....	....	....	....
	Boston	**NHL**	**8**	**0**	**1**	**1**	**2**	**0**	**0**	**0**	**11**	**0.0**	**–1**	**1**	**100.0**	**16:22**	**5**	**0**	**1**	**1**	**4**	**0**	**0**	**0**	**18:24**
2003-04	**Boston**	**NHL**	**35**	**1**	**4**	**5**	**28**	**0**	**0**	**0**	**54**	**1.9**	**3**	**1**	**100.0**	**18:45**	....	....	....	....	....	....	....	....	....
2004-05	Bofors	Sweden-2	7	0	4	4	22	....	....	....	....	....	....	....	....	....	....	....	....	....	....	....	....	....	....
	Nottingham	Britain	9	0	4	4	8	....	....	....	....	....	....	....	....	....	5	0	1	1	2	....	....	....	....
	NHL Totals		**476**	**20**	**49**	**69**	**311**	**0**	**1**	**3**	**567**	**3.5**		**254**	**35.4**	**16:52**	**66**	**1**	**7**	**8**	**24**	**0**	**0**	**0**	**15:59**

Hockey East All-Rookie Team (1992) • Hockey East Rookie of the Year (1992) (co-winner - Craig Darby)

• Missed majority of 1997-98 season recovering from knee injury suffered in training camp, September 30, 1997. • Missed majority of 2000-01 season recovering from hand injury suffered in game vs. Edmonton, November 11, 2000. Traded to **Boston** by **Pittsburgh** for Boston's 4th round choice (Paul Bissonnette) in 2003 Entry Draft, March 11, 2003. • Missed majority of 2003-04 season recovering from ankle injury suffered in game vs. Tampa Bay, December 23, 2003. Signed as a free agent by **Bofors** (Sweden-2), November 3, 2004. Signed as a free agent by **Nottingham** (Britain), January 22, 2005.

MOREAU, Ethan

(moh-ROH, EE-than) **EDM.**

Left wing. Shoots left. 6'2", 220 lbs. Born, Huntsville, Ont., September 22, 1975. Chicago's 1st choice, 14th overall, in 1994 Entry Draft.

Season	Club	League	GP	G	A	Pts	PIM	PP	SH	GW	S	%	+/-	TF	F%	Min	GP	G	A	Pts	PIM	PP	SH	GW	Min
1990-91	Orillia Terriers	OHA-B	42	17	22	39	26	....	....	....	....	....	....	....	....	....	12	6	6	12	18	....	....	....	....
1991-92	Niagara Falls	OHL	62	20	35	55	39	....	....	....	....	....	....	....	....	....	17	4	6	10	4	....	....	....	....
1992-93	Niagara Falls	OHL	65	32	41	73	69	....	....	....	....	....	....	....	....	....	4	0	3	3	4	....	....	....	....
1993-94	Niagara Falls	OHL	59	44	54	98	100	....	....	....	....	....	....	....	....	....	....	....	....	....	....	....	....	....	....
1994-95	Niagara Falls	OHL	39	25	41	66	69	....	....	....	....	....	....	....	....	....	....	....	....	....	....	....	....	....	....
	Sudbury Wolves	OHL	23	13	17	30	22	....	....	....	....	....	....	....	....	....	18	6	12	18	26	....	....	....	....
1995-96	**Chicago**	**NHL**	**8**	**0**	**1**	**1**	**4**	**0**	**0**	**0**	**1**	**0.0**	**1**	....	....	....	....	....	....	....	....	....	....	....	....
	Indianapolis Ice	IHL	71	21	20	41	126	....	....	....	....	....	....	....	....	....	5	4	0	4	8	....	....	....	....
1996-97	**Chicago**	**NHL**	**82**	**15**	**16**	**31**	**123**	**0**	**0**	**1**	**114**	**13.2**	**13**	....	....	....	**6**	**1**	**0**	**1**	**9**	**0**	**0**	**0**	....
1997-98	**Chicago**	**NHL**	**54**	**9**	**9**	**18**	**73**	**2**	**0**	**0**	**87**	**10.3**	**0**	....	....	....	....	....	....	....	....	....	....	....	....
1998-99	**Chicago**	**NHL**	**66**	**9**	**6**	**15**	**84**	**0**	**0**	**1**	**80**	**11.3**	**–5**	**3**	**33.3**	**12:30**	....	....	....	....	....	....	....	....	....
	Edmonton	**NHL**	**14**	**1**	**5**	**6**	**8**	**0**	**0**	**1**	**16**	**6.3**	**2**	**1**	**0.0**	**11:47**	**4**	**0**	**3**	**3**	**6**	**0**	**0**	**0**	**17:26**
99-2000	**Edmonton**	**NHL**	**73**	**17**	**10**	**27**	**62**	**1**	**0**	**3**	**106**	**16.0**	**8**	**8**	**62.5**	**15:07**	**5**	**0**	**1**	**1**	**0**	**0**	**0**	**0**	**15:46**
2000-01	**Edmonton**	**NHL**	**68**	**9**	**10**	**19**	**90**	**0**	**1**	**3**	**97**	**9.3**	**–6**	**2**	**0.0**	**14:11**	**4**	**0**	**0**	**0**	**2**	**0**	**0**	**0**	**10:35**
2001-02	**Edmonton**	**NHL**	**80**	**11**	**5**	**16**	**81**	**0**	**2**	**1**	**129**	**8.5**	**4**	**11**	**54.6**	**12:43**	....	....	....	....	....	....	....	....	....
2002-03	**Edmonton**	**NHL**	**78**	**14**	**17**	**31**	**112**	**2**	**3**	**2**	**137**	**10.2**	**–7**	**25**	**12.0**	**13:30**	**6**	**0**	**1**	**1**	**16**	**0**	**0**	**0**	**12:23**

			Regular Season													Playoffs								
Season	Club	League	GP	G	A	Pts	PIM	PP	SH	GW	S	%	+/-	TF	F%	Min	GP	G	A	Pts	PIM	PP	SH	GW	Min
2003-04	**Edmonton**	**NHL**	81	20	12	32	96	0	3	5	180	11.1	7	59	44.1	15:04									
2004-05	EC Villacher SV	Austria	16	10	6	16	73										3	4	0	4	0				
	NHL Totals		604	105	91	196	733	5	9	17	947	11.1		109	37.6	13:48	25	1	5	6	33	0	0	0	13:57

OHL All-Rookie Team (1992)

Traded to **Edmonton** by **Chicago** with Daniel Cleary, Chad Kilger and Christian Laflamme for Boris Mironov, Dean McAmmond and Jonas Elofsson, March 20, 1999. Signed as a free agent by **Villacher** (Austria), December 20, 2004.

MORGAN, Gavin

(MOHR-guhn, GA-vign)

Center. Shoots right. 5'11", 191 lbs. Born, Scarborough, Ont., July 9, 1976.

Season	Club	League	GP	G	A	Pts	PIM	PP	SH	GW	S	%	+/-	TF	F%	Min	GP	G	A	Pts	PIM	PP	SH	GW	Min
1992-93	Wexford Raiders	MTJHL	3	0	1	1	0																		
1993-94	Wexford Raiders	MTJHL	49	18	32	50	91																		
1994-95	Wexford Raiders	MTJHL	49	26	39	65	170																		
1995-96	U. of Denver	WCHA	28	2	9	11	47																		
1996-97	U. of Denver	WCHA	41	8	15	23	46																		
1997-98	U. of Denver	WCHA	37	9	8	17	42																		
1998-99	U. of Denver	WCHA	40	13	16	29	85																		
99-2000	Idaho Steelheads	WCHL	54	17	33	50	150										3	0	3	3	4				
	Long Beach	IHL	7	0	1	1	10																		
	Utah Grizzlies	IHL	10	0	2	2	4										2	1	0	1	2				
2000-01	Utah Grizzlies	IHL	79	7	14	21	187																		
2001-02	Utah Grizzlies	AHL	76	8	24	32	249										5	0	1	1	2				
2002-03	Utah Grizzlies	AHL	73	15	24	39	244										2	0	1	1	17				
2003-04	**Dallas**	**NHL**	6	0	0	0	21	0	0	0	7	0.0	0	20	70.0	5:49									
	Hershey Bears	AHL	67	10	23	33	152																		
2004-05	Hamilton	AHL	76	10	23	33	147										4	0	0	0	6				
	NHL Totals		6	0	0	0	21	0	0	0	7	0.0		20	70.0	5:49									

Signed as a free agent by **Idaho** (WCHL), August 25, 1999. Signed as a free agent by **Utah** (IHL), June 26, 2000. Signed as a free agent by **Dallas**, July 17, 2001. Signed as a free agent by **Montreal**, July 26, 2004. Signed as a free agent by **Basel** (Swiss), August 29, 2005.

MORGAN, Jason

(MOHR-gan, JAY-son) **CHI.**

Center. Shoots left. 6'1", 200 lbs. Born, St. John's, Nfld., October 9, 1976. Los Angeles' 5th choice, 118th overall, in 1995 Entry Draft.

Season	Club	League	GP	G	A	Pts	PIM	PP	SH	GW	S	%	+/-	TF	F%	Min	GP	G	A	Pts	PIM	PP	SH	GW	Min
1992-93	Kitchener AA	OMHA	69	44	40	84	85																		
1993-94	Kitchener Rangers	OHL	65	6	15	21	16										5	1	0	1	0				
1994-95	Kitchener Rangers	OHL	35	3	15	18	25																		
	Kingston	OHL	20	0	3	3	14										6	0	2	2	0				
1995-96	Kingston	OHL	66	16	38	54	50										6	1	2	3	0				
1996-97	**Los Angeles**	**NHL**	3	0	0	0	0	0	0	0	4	0.0	–3												
	Phoenix	IHL	57	3	6	9	29																		
	Mississippi	ECHL	6	3	0	3	0										3	1	1	2	6				
1997-98	**Los Angeles**	**NHL**	11	1	0	1	4	0	0	0	5	20.0	–7												
	Springfield	AHL	58	13	22	35	66										3	1	0	1	18				
1998-99	Long Beach	IHL	13	4	6	10	18																		
	Springfield	AHL	46	6	16	22	51										3	0	0	0	6				
99-2000	Cincinnati	IHL	15	1	3	4	14																		
	Florida Everblades	ECHL	48	14	25	39	79										5	2	2	4	16				
2000-01	Florida Everblades	ECHL	37	15	22	37	41										5	2	3	5	17				
	Hamilton	AHL	11	2	0	2	10																		
	Springfield	AHL	16	1	4	5	19																		
	Saint John Flames	AHL															6	0	1	1	2				
2001-02	Saint John Flames	AHL	76	17	20	37	69																		
2002-03	Saint John Flames	AHL	80	13	40	53	63																		
2003-04	**Calgary**	**NHL**	13	0	2	2	2	0	0	0	14	0.0	1	98	44.9	9:45									
	Lowell	AHL	21	6	13	19	16																		
	Nashville	**NHL**	6	0	2	2	2	0	0	0	6	0.0	0	15	73.3	10:06									
	Norfolk Admirals	AHL	19	6	8	14	16										8	0	1	1	10				
2004-05	Norfolk Admirals	AHL	71	9	20	29	116										6	2	2	4	8				
	NHL Totals		33	1	4	5	8	0	0	0	29	3.4		113	48.7	9:51									

Signed to a PTO (tryout) contract by **Saint John** (AHL), April 22, 2001. Signed as a free agent by **Saint John** (AHL), August 28, 2001. Signed as a free agent by **Calgary**, July 11, 2002. Claimed on waivers by **Nashville** from **Calgary**, December 31, 2003. Claimed on waivers by **Calgary** from **Nashville**, February 19, 2004. Traded to **Chicago** by **Calgary** with Calgary's 6th round choice (Joseph Fallon) in 2005 Entry Draft for Ville Nieminen, February 24, 2004.

MORO, Marc

(MOH-roh, MAHRK) **TOR.**

Defense. Shoots left. 6'1", 218 lbs. Born, Toronto, Ont., July 17, 1977. Ottawa's 2nd choice, 27th overall, in 1995 Entry Draft.

Season	Club	League	GP	G	A	Pts	PIM	PP	SH	GW	S	%	+/-	TF	F%	Min	GP	G	A	Pts	PIM	PP	SH	GW	Min
1992-93	Mississauga Sens	MTHL	42	9	18	27	56																		
	Mississauga Sens	MTJHL	2	0	0	0	0																		
1993-94	Kingston	MTJHL	12	0	2	2	10																		
	Kingston	OHL	43	0	3	3	81																		
1994-95	Kingston	OHL	64	4	12	16	255										6	0	0	0	23				
1995-96	Kingston	OHL	66	4	17	21	261										6	0	0	0	12				
	P.E.I. Senators	AHL	2	0	0	0	7										2	0	0	0	4				
1996-97	Kingston	OHL	37	4	8	12	97																		
	Sault Ste. Marie	OHL	26	0	5	5	74										11	1	6	7	38				
1997-98	**Anaheim**	**NHL**	1	0	0	0	0	0	0	0	0	0.0	0												
	Cincinnati	AHL	74	1	6	7	181																		
1998-99	Milwaukee	IHL	80	0	5	5	264										2	0	0	0	4				
99-2000	**Nashville**	**NHL**	8	0	0	0	40	0	0	0	3	0.0	–3	0	0.0	10:55									
	Milwaukee	IHL	64	5	5	10	203																		
2000-01	**Nashville**	**NHL**	6	0	0	0	12	0	0	0	1	0.0	1	0	0.0	3:34									
	Milwaukee	IHL	68	2	9	11	190										5	1	0	1	10				
2001-02	**Nashville**	**NHL**	13	0	0	0	23	0	0	0	7	0.0	–3	0	0.0	12:02									
	Milwaukee	AHL	41	1	8	9	81																		
	Toronto	**NHL**	2	0	0	0	2	0	0	0	0	0.0	0	0	0.0	11:23									
	St. John's	AHL	7	1	0	1	21																		
2002-03	St. John's	AHL	68	3	8	11	128																		
2003-04	St. John's	AHL	76	1	9	10	144																		
2004-05	St. John's	AHL	78	2	6	8	202										5	0	1	1	4				
	NHL Totals		30	0	0	0	77	0	0	0	11	0.0		0	0.0	9:56									

Rights traded to **Anaheim** by **Ottawa** with Ted Drury for Jason York and Shaun Van Allen, October 1, 1996. Traded to **Nashville** by **Anaheim** with Chris Mason for Dominic Roussel, October 5, 1998. Traded to **Toronto** by **Nashville** for D.J. Smith and Marty Wilford, March 1, 2002.

MOROZOV, Aleksey

(moh-ROH-zohv, ah-LEHK-see) **PIT.**

Right wing. Shoots left. 6'1", 204 lbs. Born, Moscow, USSR, February 16, 1977. Pittsburgh's 1st choice, 24th overall, in 1995 Entry Draft.

Season	Club	League	GP	G	A	Pts	PIM	PP	SH	GW	S	%	+/-	TF	F%	Min	GP	G	A	Pts	PIM	PP	SH	GW	Min
1993-94	Krylja Sovetov	CIS	7	0	0	0	0										3	0	0	0	2				
1994-95	Krylja Sovetov	CIS	48	15	12	27	53										4	0	3	3	0				
1995-96	Krylja Sovetov	CIS	47	13	9	22	26																		
1996-97	Krylja Sovetov	Russia	44	21	11	32	32										2	0	1	1	2				
1997-98	Krylja Sovetov	Russia	6	2	1	3	4																		
	Pittsburgh	**NHL**	76	13	13	26	8	2	0	3	80	16.3	–4				6	0	1	1	2	0	0	0	
	Russia	Olympics	6	2	2	4	0																		
1998-99	**Pittsburgh**	**NHL**	67	9	10	19	14	0	0	0	75	12.0	5	7	42.9	11:50	10	1	1	2	0	0	0	0	12:01
99-2000	**Pittsburgh**	**NHL**	68	12	19	31	14	0	1	0	101	11.9	12	27	33.3	13:51	5	0	0	0	0	0	0	0	11:48
2000-01	**Pittsburgh**	**NHL**	66	5	14	19	6	0	0	1	72	6.9	–8	19	42.1	10:41	18	3	3	6	6	0	1	0	14:59
2001-02	**Pittsburgh**	**NHL**	72	20	29	49	16	7	0	3	162	12.3	–7	1	100.0	16:42									
2002-03	**Pittsburgh**	**NHL**	27	9	16	25	16	6	0	2	46	19.6	–3	0	0.0	18:42									

			Regular Season														Playoffs								
Season	Club	League	GP	G	A	Pts	PIM	PP	SH	GW	S	%	+/-	TF	F%	Min	GP	G	A	Pts	PIM	PP	SH	GW	Min
2003-04	**Pittsburgh**	**NHL**	**75**	**16**	**34**	**50**	**24**	**8**	**0**	**5**	**132**	**12.1**	**–24**	**0**	**0.0**	**16:34**	....	....	....	....	....	....	....	....	....
2004-05	Ak Bars Kazan	Russia	58	20	27	47	30	....	....	....	....	....	....	....	....	....	4	0	1	1	2	....	....	....	....
	NHL Totals		**451**	**84**	**135**	**219**	**98**	**23**	**1**	**14**	**668**	**12.6**		**54**	**38.9**	**14:22**	**39**	**4**	**5**	**9**	**8**	**0**	**1**	**0**	**13:36**

• Missed majority of 2002-03 season recovering from wrist injury suffered in game vs. Toronto, December 10, 2002. Signed as a free agent by **Kazan** (Russia), September 25, 2004.

MORRIS, Derek

(MOH-rihs, DAIR-ihk) **PHX.**

Defense. Shoots right. 6', 220 lbs. Born, Edmonton, Alta., August 24, 1978. Calgary's 1st choice, 13th overall, in 1996 Entry Draft.

1994-95	Red Deer Vipers	AMHL	31	6	35	41	74	....	....	....	....	....	....	....	....	....	....	....	....	....	....	....	....	....	....
1995-96	Regina Pats	WHL	67	8	44	52	70	....	....	....	....	....	....	....	....	....	11	1	7	8	26	....	....	....	....
1996-97	Regina Pats	WHL	67	18	57	75	180	....	....	....	....	....	....	....	....	....	5	0	3	3	9	....	....	....	....
	Saint John Flames	AHL	7	0	3	3	7	....	....	....	....	....	....	....	....	....	5	0	3	3	7	....	....	....	....
1997-98	**Calgary**	**NHL**	**82**	**9**	**20**	**29**	**88**	**5**	**1**	**1**	**120**	**7.5**	**1**	....	....	....	....	....	....	....	....	....	....	....	....
1998-99	**Calgary**	**NHL**	**71**	**7**	**27**	**34**	**73**	**3**	**0**	**2**	**150**	**4.7**	**4**	**0**	**0.0**	**20:44**	....	....	....	....	....	....	....	....	....
99-2000	**Calgary**	**NHL**	**78**	**9**	**29**	**38**	**80**	**3**	**0**	**2**	**193**	**4.7**	**2**	**0**	**0.0**	**24:51**	....	....	....	....	....	....	....	....	....
2000-01	**Calgary**	**NHL**	**51**	**5**	**23**	**28**	**56**	**3**	**1**	**4**	**142**	**3.5**	**–15**	**0**	**0.0**	**25:51**	....	....	....	....	....	....	....	....	....
	Saint John Flames	AHL	3	1	2	3	2	....	....	....	....	....	....	....	....	....	....	....	....	....	....	....	....	....	....
2001-02	**Calgary**	**NHL**	**61**	**4**	**30**	**34**	**88**	**2**	**0**	**1**	**166**	**2.4**	**–4**	**1**	**100.0**	**24:40**	....	....	....	....	....	....	....	....	....
2002-03	**Colorado**	**NHL**	**75**	**11**	**37**	**48**	**68**	**9**	**0**	**7**	**191**	**5.8**	**16**	**0**	**0.0**	**23:49**	**7**	**0**	**3**	**3**	**6**	**0**	**0**	**0**	**22:44**
2003-04	**Colorado**	**NHL**	**69**	**6**	**22**	**28**	**47**	**2**	**0**	**1**	**139**	**4.3**	**4**	**0**	**0.0**	**20:53**	....	....	....	....	....	....	....	....	....
	Phoenix	**NHL**	**14**	**0**	**4**	**4**	**2**	**0**	**0**	**0**	**28**	**0.0**	**–5**	**0**	**0.0**	**25:02**	....	....	....	....	....	....	....	....	....
2004-05			DID NOT PLAY																						
	NHL Totals		**501**	**51**	**192**	**243**	**502**	**27**	**2**	**18**	**1129**	**4.5**		**1**	**100.0**	**23:25**	**7**	**0**	**3**	**3**	**6**	**0**	**0**	**0**	**22:44**

WHL East First All-Star Team (1997) • NHL All-Rookie Team (1998)

Traded to **Colorado** by **Calgary** with Jeff Shantz and Dean McAmmond for Chris Drury and Stephane Yelle, October 1, 2002. Traded to **Phoenix** by **Colorado** with Keith Ballard for Ossi Vaananen, Chris Gratton and Phoenix's 2nd round choice (Paul Stastny) in 2005 Entry Draft, March 8, 2004.

MORRISON, Brendan

(MOHR-ih-suhn, BREHN-duhn) **VAN.**

Center. Shoots left. 5'11", 190 lbs. Born, Pitt Meadows, B.C., August 15, 1975. New Jersey's 3rd choice, 39th overall, in 1993 Entry Draft.

1990-91	Ridge Meadows	BCAHA	77	126	127	253	88	....	....	....	....	....	....	....	....	....	....	....	....	....	....	....	....	....	....
1991-92	Ridge Meadows	BCAHA	55	56	111	167	56	....	....	....	....	....	....	....	....	....	....	....	....	....	....	....	....	....	....
1992-93	Penticton	BCJHL	56	35	59	94	45	....	....	....	....	....	....	....	....	....	....	....	....	....	....	....	....	....	....
1993-94	U. of Michigan	CCHA	38	20	28	48	24	....	....	....	....	....	....	....	....	....	5	2	7	9	2	....	....	....	....
1994-95	U. of Michigan	CCHA	39	23	*53	*76	42	....	....	....	....	....	....	....	....	....	5	1	11	12	6	....	....	....	....
1995-96	U. of Michigan	CCHA	35	28	44	*72	41	....	....	....	....	....	....	....	....	....	7	6	9	15	4	....	....	....	....
1996-97	U. of Michigan	CCHA	43	31	*57	*88	52	....	....	....	....	....	....	....	....	....	6	6	8	14	8	....	....	....	....
1997-98	**New Jersey**	**NHL**	**11**	**5**	**4**	**9**	**0**	**0**	**0**	**1**	**19**	**26.3**	**3**	....	....	....	**3**	**0**	**1**	**1**	**0**	**0**	**0**	**0**	....
	Albany River Rats	AHL	72	35	49	84	44	....	....	....	....	....	....	....	....	....	8	3	4	7	19	....	....	....	....
1998-99	**New Jersey**	**NHL**	**76**	**13**	**33**	**46**	**18**	**5**	**0**	**2**	**111**	**11.7**	**–4**	**920**	**51.1**	**13:55**	**7**	**0**	**2**	**2**	**0**	**0**	**0**	**0**	**13:04**
99-2000	Trebic	CzRep-2	2	0	0	0	0	....	....	....	....	....	....	....	....	....	....	....	....	....	....	....	....	....	....
	Pardubice	CzRep	6	5	2	7	2	....	....	....	....	....	....	....	....	....	....	....	....	....	....	....	....	....	....
	New Jersey	**NHL**	**44**	**5**	**21**	**26**	**8**	**2**	**0**	**1**	**79**	**6.3**	**8**	**572**	**51.1**	**16:09**	....	....	....	....	....	....	....	....	....
	Vancouver	**NHL**	**12**	**2**	**7**	**9**	**10**	**0**	**0**	**0**	**17**	**11.8**	**4**	**48**	**54.2**	**14:41**	....	....	....	....	....	....	....	....	....
2000-01	**Vancouver**	**NHL**	**82**	**16**	**38**	**54**	**42**	**3**	**2**	**3**	**179**	**8.9**	**2**	**1685**	**50.1**	**18:22**	**4**	**1**	**2**	**3**	**0**	**1**	**0**	**0**	**20:50**
2001-02	**Vancouver**	**NHL**	**82**	**23**	**44**	**67**	**26**	**6**	**0**	**4**	**183**	**12.6**	**18**	**1307**	**49.9**	**19:21**	**6**	**0**	**2**	**2**	**6**	**0**	**0**	**0**	**19:44**
2002-03	**Vancouver**	**NHL**	**82**	**25**	**46**	**71**	**36**	**6**	**2**	**8**	**167**	**15.0**	**18**	**1585**	**48.3**	**21:13**	**14**	**4**	**7**	**11**	**18**	**1**	**0**	**1**	**20:18**
2003-04	**Vancouver**	**NHL**	**82**	**22**	**38**	**60**	**50**	**5**	**1**	**4**	**161**	**13.7**	**16**	**1486**	**51.0**	**20:08**	**7**	**2**	**3**	**5**	**8**	**1**	**0**	**1**	**22:00**
2004-05	Linkopings HC	Sweden	45	16	28	44	50	....	....	....	....	....	....	....	....	....	6	0	2	2	10	....	....	....	....
	NHL Totals		**471**	**111**	**231**	**342**	**190**	**27**	**5**	**23**	**916**	**12.1**		**7603**	**50.1**	**18:19**	**41**	**7**	**17**	**24**	**32**	**3**	**0**	**2**	**19:15**

CCHA Rookie of the Year (1994) • CCHA First All-Star Team (1995, 1996, 1997) • NCAA West First All-American Team (1995, 1996, 1997) • CCHA Player of the Year (1996, 1997) • NCAA Championship All-Tournament Team (1996) • NCAA Championship Tournament MVP (1996) • Hobey Baker Memorial Award (Top U.S. Collegiate Player) (1997) • AHL All-Rookie Team (1998)

Traded to **Vancouver** by **New Jersey** with Denis Pederson for Alexander Mogilny, March 14, 2000. Signed as a free agent by **Linkopings** (Sweden), September, 2004.

MORRISONN, Shaone

(MOHR-ih-suhn, SHAWN) **WSH.**

Defense. Shoots left. 6'3", 205 lbs. Born, Vancouver, B.C., December 23, 1982. Boston's 1st choice, 19th overall, in 2001 Entry Draft.

1997-98	Vancouver T-Birds	BCAHA	45	16	44	60	75	....	....	....	....	....	....	....	....	....	....	....	....	....	....	....	....	....	....
1998-99	South Surrey	BCHL	19	0	2	2	13	....	....	....	....	....	....	....	....	....	....	....	....	....	....	....	....	....	....
99-2000	Kamloops Blazers	WHL	57	1	6	7	80	....	....	....	....	....	....	....	....	....	4	0	0	0	6	....	....	....	....
2000-01	Kamloops Blazers	WHL	61	13	25	38	132	....	....	....	....	....	....	....	....	....	4	0	0	0	6	....	....	....	....
2001-02	Kamloops Blazers	WHL	61	11	26	37	106	....	....	....	....	....	....	....	....	....	4	0	2	2	2	....	....	....	....
2002-03	**Boston**	**NHL**	**11**	**0**	**0**	**0**	**8**	**0**	**0**	**0**	**4**	**0.0**	**0**	**0**	**0.0**	**8:57**	....	....	....	....	....	....	....	....	....
	Providence Bruins	AHL	60	5	16	21	103	....	....	....	....	....	....	....	....	....	4	0	0	0	6	....	....	....	....
2003-04	**Boston**	**NHL**	**30**	**1**	**7**	**8**	**10**	**0**	**0**	**0**	**13**	**7.7**	**10**	**0**	**0.0**	**18:11**	....	....	....	....	....	....	....	....	....
	Providence Bruins	AHL	18	0	2	2	16	....	....	....	....	....	....	....	....	....	....	....	....	....	....	....	....	....	....
	Washington	**NHL**	**3**	**0**	**0**	**0**	**0**	**0**	**0**	**0**	**1**	**0.0**	**0**	**0**	**0.0**	**18:52**	....	....	....	....	....	....	....	....	....
	Portland Pirates	AHL	13	1	4	5	10	....	....	....	....	....	....	....	....	....	7	0	1	1	4	....	....	....	....
2004-05	Portland Pirates	AHL	71	4	14	18	63	....	....	....	....	....	....	....	....	....	....	....	....	....	....	....	....	....	....
	NHL Totals		**44**	**1**	**7**	**8**	**18**	**0**	**0**	**0**	**18**	**5.6**		**0**	**0.0**	**15:55**	....	....	....	....	....	....	....	....	....

Traded to **Washington** by **Boston** with Boston's 1st (Jeff Schultz) and 2nd (Michail Yunkov) round choices in 2004 Entry Draft for Sergei Gonchar, March 3, 2004.

MORROW, Brenden

(MOHR-roh, BREHN-duhn) **DAL.**

Left wing. Shoots left. 5'11", 210 lbs. Born, Carlyle, Sask., January 16, 1979. Dallas' 1st choice, 25th overall, in 1997 Entry Draft.

1994-95	Estevan	SMBHL	60	117	72	189	45	....	....	....	....	....	....	....	....	....	....	....	....	....	....	....	....	....	....
1995-96	Portland	WHL	65	13	12	25	61	....	....	....	....	....	....	....	....	....	7	0	0	0	8	....	....	....	....
1996-97	Portland	WHL	71	39	49	88	178	....	....	....	....	....	....	....	....	....	6	2	1	3	4	....	....	....	....
1997-98	Portland	WHL	68	34	52	86	184	....	....	....	....	....	....	....	....	....	16	10	8	18	65	....	....	....	....
1998-99	Portland	WHL	61	41	44	85	248	....	....	....	....	....	....	....	....	....	4	0	4	4	18	....	....	....	....
99-2000	**Dallas**	**NHL**	**64**	**14**	**19**	**33**	**81**	**3**	**0**	**3**	**113**	**12.4**	**8**	**25**	**48.0**	**15:51**	**21**	**2**	**4**	**6**	**22**	**1**	**0**	**0**	**15:04**
	Michigan	IHL	9	2	0	2	18	....	....	....	....	....	....	....	....	....	....	....	....	....	....	....	....	....	....
2000-01	**Dallas**	**NHL**	**82**	**20**	**24**	**44**	**128**	**7**	**0**	**6**	**121**	**16.5**	**18**	**22**	**45.5**	**15:29**	**10**	**0**	**3**	**3**	**12**	**0**	**0**	**0**	**17:00**
2001-02	**Dallas**	**NHL**	**72**	**17**	**18**	**35**	**109**	**4**	**0**	**3**	**102**	**16.7**	**12**	**39**	**41.0**	**16:52**	....	....	....	....	....	....	....	....	....
2002-03	**Dallas**	**NHL**	**71**	**21**	**22**	**43**	**134**	**2**	**3**	**4**	**105**	**20.0**	**20**	**29**	**27.6**	**15:43**	**12**	**3**	**5**	**8**	**16**	**2**	**0**	**0**	**21:03**
2003-04	**Dallas**	**NHL**	**81**	**25**	**24**	**49**	**121**	**9**	**0**	**3**	**132**	**18.9**	**10**	**38**	**47.4**	**19:24**	**5**	**0**	**1**	**1**	**4**	**0**	**0**	**0**	**21:29**
2004-05	Oklahoma City	CHL	19	8	14	22	31	....	....	....	....	....	....	....	....	....	....	....	....	....	....	....	....	....	....
	NHL Totals		**370**	**97**	**107**	**204**	**573**	**25**	**3**	**19**	**573**	**16.9**		**153**	**41.8**	**16:43**	**48**	**5**	**13**	**18**	**54**	**3**	**0**	**0**	**17:38**

WHL West First All-Star Team (1999)

Signed as a free agent by **Oklahoma City** (CHL), October 19, 2004.

MOTTAU, Mike

(MAW-tuh, MIGHK)

Defense. Shoots left. 6', 192 lbs. Born, Quincy, MA, March 19, 1978. NY Rangers' 10th choice, 182nd overall, in 1997 Entry Draft.

1994-95	Thayer Academy	High-MA	29	7	19	26	....	....	....	....	....	....	....	....	....	....	....	....	....	....	....	....	....	....	....
1995-96	Thayer Academy	High-MA	31	6	20	26	14	....	....	....	....	....	....	....	....	....	....	....	....	....	....	....	....	....	....
1996-97	Boston College	H-East	38	5	18	23	77	....	....	....	....	....	....	....	....	....	....	....	....	....	....	....	....	....	....
1997-98	Boston College	H-East	40	13	36	49	50	....	....	....	....	....	....	....	....	....	....	....	....	....	....	....	....	....	....
1998-99	Boston College	H-East	43	3	39	42	44	....	....	....	....	....	....	....	....	....	....	....	....	....	....	....	....	....	....
99-2000	Boston College	H-East	42	6	37	43	61	....	....	....	....	....	....	....	....	....	....	....	....	....	....	....	....	....	....
2000-01	**NY Rangers**	**NHL**	**18**	**0**	**3**	**3**	**13**	**0**	**0**	**0**	**17**	**0.0**	**–6**	**0**	**0.0**	**15:18**	....	....	....	....	....	....	....	....	....
	Hartford	AHL	61	10	33	43	45	....	....	....	....	....	....	....	....	....	5	0	1	1	19	....	....	....	....
2001-02	**NY Rangers**	**NHL**	**1**	**0**	**0**	**0**	**0**	**0**	**0**	**0**	**0**	**0.0**	**0**	**0**	**0.0**	**6:20**	....	....	....	....	....	....	....	....	....
	Hartford	AHL	80	9	42	51	56	....	....	....	....	....	....	....	....	....	10	0	5	5	4	....	....	....	....
2002-03	Hartford	AHL	29	1	18	19	24	....	....	....	....	....	....	....	....	....	....	....	....	....	....	....	....	....	....
	Calgary	**NHL**	**4**	**0**	**0**	**0**	**0**	**0**	**0**	**0**	**0**	**0.0**	**–1**	**0**	**0.0**	**9:50**	....	....	....	....	....	....	....	....	....
	Saint John Flames	AHL	32	5	12	17	14	....	....	....	....	....	....	....	....	....	....	....	....	....	....	....	....	....	....

			Regular Season														Playoffs								
Season	Club	League	GP	G	A	Pts	PIM	PP	SH	GW	S	%	+/-	TF	F%	Min	GP	G	A	Pts	PIM	PP	SH	GW	Min
2003-04	Cincinnati	AHL	69	9	22	31	79										9	1	2	3	8				
2004-05	Worcester IceCats	AHL	73	4	31	35	23																		
	NHL Totals		**23**	**0**	**3**	**3**	**13**	**0**	**0**	**0**	**17**	**0.0**		**0**	**0.0**	**13:57**									

Hockey East First All-Star Team (1998, 2000) • NCAA East Second All-American Team (1998) • NCAA Championship All-Tournament Team (1998, 2000) • Hockey East Second All-Star Team (1999) • NCAA East First All-American Team (1999, 2000) • Hockey East Player of the Year (2000) (co-winner - Ty Conklin) • Hobey Baker Memorial Award (Top U.S. Collegiate Player) (2000) • AHL All-Rookie Team (2001)

Traded to **Calgary** by **NY Rangers** for Calgary's 6th round choice (Ivan Dornic) in 2003 Entry Draft and future considerations, January 22, 2003. Signed as a free agent by **Anaheim**, July 25, 2003. Signed as a free agent by **Worcester** (AHL), September 30, 2004.

MOTZKO, Joe

(MAWTS-koh, JOH) **CBJ**

Right wing. Shoots right. 6', 190 lbs. Born, Bemidji, MN, March 14, 1980.

Season	Club	League	GP	G	A	Pts	PIM	PP	SH	GW	S	%	+/-	TF	F%	Min	GP	G	A	Pts	PIM	PP	SH	GW	Min
1997-98	Bemidji Jacks	High-MN	25	24	28	52																			
1998-99	Omaha Lancers	USHL	51	15	21	36	60										12	7	3	10	12				
99-2000	St. Cloud State	WCHA	36	9	15	24	52																		
2000-01	St. Cloud State	WCHA	41	17	20	37	54																		
2001-02	St. Cloud State	WCHA	39	9	30	39	34																		
2002-03	St. Cloud State	WCHA	38	17	25	42	59																		
	Syracuse Crunch	AHL	2	0	0	0	0																		
2003-04	**Columbus**	**NHL**	**2**	**0**	**0**	**0**	**0**	**0**	**0**	**0**	**1**	**0.0**	**0**	**0**	**0.0**	**7:16**									
	Syracuse Crunch	AHL	70	17	24	41	38										7	2	2	4	6				
2004-05	Syracuse Crunch	AHL	79	28	38	66	72																		
	NHL Totals		**2**	**0**	**0**	**0**	**0**	**0**	**0**	**0**	**1**	**0.0**		**0**	**0.0**	**7:16**									

Signed as a free agent by **Columbus**, May 15, 2003.

MOWERS, Mark

(MAHW-uhrs, MAHRK) **DET.**

Center. Shoots right. 5'11", 187 lbs. Born, Whitesboro, NY, February 16, 1974.

Season	Club	League	GP	G	A	Pts	PIM	PP	SH	GW	S	%	+/-	TF	F%	Min	GP	G	A	Pts	PIM	PP	SH	GW	Min
1992-93	Saginaw Jr. Gears	NAHL	39	31	39	70																			
1993-94	Dubuque	USHL	47	51	31	82	80																		
1994-95	New Hampshire	H-East	36	13	23	36	16																		
1995-96	New Hampshire	H-East	34	21	26	47	18																		
1996-97	New Hampshire	H-East	39	26	32	58	52																		
1997-98	New Hampshire	H-East	35	25	31	56	32																		
1998-99	**Nashville**	**NHL**	**30**	**0**	**6**	**6**	**4**	**0**	**0**	**0**	**24**	**0.0**	**–4**	**241**	**49.0**	**9:22**									
	Milwaukee	IHL	51	14	22	36	24										1	0	0	0	0				
99-2000	**Nashville**	**NHL**	**41**	**4**	**5**	**9**	**10**	**0**	**0**	**0**	**50**	**8.0**	**0**	**312**	**45.2**	**10:58**									
	Milwaukee	IHL	23	11	15	26	34																		
2000-01	Milwaukee	IHL	63	25	25	50	54										5	1	2	3	2				
2001-02	**Nashville**	**NHL**	**14**	**1**	**2**	**3**	**2**	**0**	**0**	**0**	**5**	**20.0**	**–2**	**24**	**33.3**	**8:31**									
	Milwaukee	AHL	45	19	20	39	34																		
2002-03	Grand Rapids	AHL	78	34	47	81	47										15	3	4	7	4				
2003-04	**Detroit**	**NHL**	**52**	**3**	**8**	**11**	**4**	**1**	**0**	**1**	**48**	**6.3**	**3**	**400**	**47.8**	**10:27**									
	Grand Rapids	AHL	16	8	6	14	4																		
2004-05	Malmo	Sweden	9	2	0	2	0																		
	Fribourg	Swiss	3	2	0	2	0										9	9	8	17	12				
	NHL Totals		**137**	**8**	**21**	**29**	**20**	**1**	**0**	**1**	**127**	**6.3**		**977**	**46.9**	**10:10**									

Hockey East Rookie of the Year (1995) • Hockey East Second All-Star Team (1998) • NCAA East First All-American Team (1998) • Ken McKenzie Trophy (U.S. - Born Rookie of the Year – IHL) (1999) • AHL Second All-Star Team (2003)

Signed as a free agent by **Nashville**, June 11, 1998. Signed as a free agent by **Detroit**, August 5, 2002. Signed as a free agent by **Malmo** (Sweden), December 21, 2004. Signed as a free agent by **Fribourg** (Swiss), February 4, 2005.

MROZIK, Rick

(muh-ROH-zihk, RIHK)

Center. Shoots left. 6'2", 185 lbs. Born, Duluth, MN, January 2, 1975. Dallas' 4th choice, 136th overall, in 1993 Entry Draft.

Season	Club	League	GP	G	A	Pts	PIM	PP	SH	GW	S	%	+/-	TF	F%	Min	GP	G	A	Pts	PIM	PP	SH	GW	Min
1992-93	Cloquet	High-MN	28	9	38	47	12																		
1993-94	U. Minn-Duluth	WCHA	38	2	9	11	38																		
1994-95	U. Minn-Duluth	WCHA	3	0	0	0	2																		
1995-96	U. Minn-Duluth	WCHA	35	3	19	22	63																		
1996-97	U. Minn-Duluth	WCHA	38	11	23	34	56																		
1997-98	Portland Pirates	AHL	75	2	15	17	52										10	1	3	4	2				
1998-99	Portland Pirates	AHL	70	4	8	12	63																		
99-2000	Pee Dee Pride	ECHL	60	9	19	28	44										5	2	0	2	6				
	Worcester IceCats	AHL	3	0	0	0	0																		
	Syracuse Crunch	AHL	1	0	0	0	0																		
2000-01	Saint John Flames	AHL	76	5	11	16	26										19	1	1	2	6				
2001-02	Saint John Flames	AHL	55	2	5	7	27																		
2002-03	**Calgary**	**NHL**	**2**	**0**	**0**	**0**	**0**	**0**	**0**	**0**	**2**	**0.0**	**0**	**0**	**0.0**	**10:02**									
	Saint John Flames	AHL	68	2	10	12	46																		
2003-04	Rochester	AHL	72	4	10	14	47										15	1	4	5	4				
2004-05	Edmonton	AHL	68	3	18	21	61																		
	NHL Totals		**2**	**0**	**0**	**0**	**0**	**0**	**0**	**0**	**2**	**0.0**		**0**	**0.0**	**10:02**									

WCHA Second All-Star Team (1997)

Traded to **Washington** by **Dallas** with Mark Tinordi for Kevin Hatcher, January 18, 1995. Signed as a free agent by **Calgary**, August 6, 2001. Signed as a free agent by **Buffalo**, August 21, 2003. Signed as a free agent by **Edmonton**, August 24, 2004.

MUCKALT, Bill

(MUH-kawlt, BIHL)

Right wing. Shoots right. 6'1", 200 lbs. Born, Surrey, B.C., July 15, 1974. Vancouver's 9th choice, 221st overall, in 1994 Entry Draft.

Season	Club	League	GP	G	A	Pts	PIM	PP	SH	GW	S	%	+/-	TF	F%	Min	GP	G	A	Pts	PIM	PP	SH	GW	Min
1991-92	Merritt	BCJHL	55	14	11	25	75																		
1992-93	Merritt	BCJHL	59	31	43	74	80																		
1993-94	Merritt	BCJHL	43	58	51	109	99																		
	Kelowna Spartans	BCJHL	15	12	10	22	20																		
1994-95	U. of Michigan	CCHA	39	19	18	37	42										5	1	1	2	6				
1995-96	U. of Michigan	CCHA	41	28	30	58	34										7	5	6	11	6				
1996-97	U. of Michigan	CCHA	36	26	38	64	69										6	5	9	14	2				
1997-98	U. of Michigan	CCHA	46	32	*35	*67	94																		
1998-99	**Vancouver**	**NHL**	**73**	**16**	**20**	**36**	**98**	**4**	**2**	**1**	**119**	**13.4**	**–9**	**68**	**55.9**	**15:24**									
99-2000	**Vancouver**	**NHL**	**33**	**4**	**8**	**12**	**17**	**1**	**0**	**1**	**53**	**7.5**	**6**	**6**	**50.0**	**14:34**									
	NY Islanders	**NHL**	**12**	**4**	**3**	**7**	**4**	**0**	**0**	**0**	**26**	**15.4**	**5**	**8**	**50.0**	**12:23**									
2000-01	**NY Islanders**	**NHL**	**60**	**11**	**15**	**26**	**33**	**1**	**0**	**2**	**90**	**12.2**	**–4**	**7**	**14.3**	**13:43**									
2001-02	**Ottawa**	**NHL**	**70**	**0**	**8**	**8**	**46**	**0**	**0**	**0**	**73**	**0.0**	**–3**	**13**	**69.2**	**9:46**									
2002-03	**Minnesota**	**NHL**	**8**	**5**	**3**	**8**	**6**	**0**	**0**	**0**	**13**	**38.5**	**5**	**6**	**50.0**	**13:00**	**5**	**0**	**0**	**0**	**0**	**0**	**0**	**0**	**11:15**
2003-04	Houston Aeros	AHL	9	0	3	3	6																		
2004-05			DID NOT PLAY																						
	NHL Totals		**256**	**40**	**57**	**97**	**204**	**6**	**2**	**4**	**374**	**10.7**		**108**	**53.7**	**13:08**	**5**	**0**	**0**	**0**	**0**	**0**	**0**	**0**	**11:15**

CCHA First All-Star Team (1998) • NCAA West First All-American Team (1998)

Traded to **NY Islanders** by **Vancouver** with Kevin Weekes and Dave Scatchard for Felix Potvin, NY Islanders' 2nd round compensatory choice (later traded to New Jersey – New Jersey selected Teemu Laine) in 2000 Entry Draft and NY Islanders' 3rd round choice (Thatcher Bell) in 2000 Entry Draft, December 19, 1999. • Missed majority of 1999-2000 season recovering from shoulder injury suffered in game vs. Tampa Bay, January 13, 2000. Traded to **Ottawa** by **NY Islanders** with Zdeno Chara and NY Islanders' 1st round choice (Jason Spezza) in 2001 Entry Draft for Alexei Yashin, June 23, 2001. Signed as a free agent by **Minnesota**, July 3, 2002. • Missed majority of 2002-03 and 2003-04 seasons recovering from shoulder injury suffered in game vs. Calgary, October 22, 2002.

MUIR, Bryan — (MEWR, BRIGH-uhn) — WSH.

Defense. Shoots left. 6'4", 220 lbs. Born, Winnipeg, Man., June 8, 1973.

Season	Club	League	GP	G	A	Pts	PIM	PP	SH	GW	S	%	+/-	TF	F%	Min	GP	G	A	Pts	PIM	PP	SH	GW	Min
			Regular Season														Playoffs								
1991-92	Wexford Raiders	MTJHL	44	3	19	22	35																		
1992-93	New Hampshire	H-East	26	1	2	3	24																		
1993-94	New Hampshire	H-East	40	0	4	4	48																		
1994-95	New Hampshire	H-East	28	9	9	18	46																		
1995-96	Canada	Nat-Tm	42	6	12	18	38																		
	Edmonton	**NHL**	**5**	**0**	**0**	**0**	**6**	**0**	**0**	**0**	**4**	**0.0**	**-4**												
1996-97	Hamilton	AHL	75	8	16	24	80										14	0	5	5	12				
	Edmonton	**NHL**															**5**	**0**	**0**	**0**	**4**	**0**	**0**	**0**	
1997-98	**Edmonton**	**NHL**	**7**	**0**	**0**	**0**	**17**	**0**	**0**	**0**	**6**	**0.0**	**0**												
	Hamilton	AHL	28	3	10	13	62																		
	Albany River Rats	AHL	41	3	10	13	67										13	3	0	3	12				
1998-99	**New Jersey**	**NHL**	**1**	**0**	**0**	**0**	**0**	**0**	**0**	**0**	**4**	**0.0**	**0**	**0**	**0.0**	**9:54**									
	Albany River Rats	AHL	10	0	0	0	29																		
	Chicago	**NHL**	**53**	**1**	**4**	**5**	**50**	**0**	**0**	**0**	**78**	**1.3**	**1**	**0**	**0.0**	**18:49**									
	Portland Pirates	AHL	2	1	1	2	2																		
99-2000	**Chicago**	**NHL**	**11**	**2**	**3**	**5**	**13**	**0**	**1**	**0**	**19**	**10.5**	**-1**	**0**	**0.0**	**17:54**									
	Tampa Bay	**NHL**	**30**	**1**	**1**	**2**	**32**	**0**	**0**	**0**	**32**	**3.1**	**-8**	**1**	**100.0**	**19:29**									
2000-01	**Tampa Bay**	**NHL**	**10**	**0**	**3**	**3**	**15**	**0**	**0**	**0**	**14**	**0.0**	**-7**	**1**	**0.0**	**18:34**									
	Detroit Vipers	IHL	21	5	7	12	36																		
	Colorado	**NHL**	**8**	**0**	**0**	**0**	**4**	**0**	**0**	**0**	**3**	**0.0**	**0**	**0**	**0.0**	**8:14**	**3**	**0**	**0**	**0**	**0**	**0**	**0**	**0**	**3:15**
	Hershey Bears	AHL	26	5	8	13	50																		
2001-02	**Colorado**	**NHL**	**22**	**1**	**1**	**2**	**9**	**0**	**0**	**0**	**26**	**3.8**	**1**	**0**	**0.0**	**10:20**	**21**	**0**	**0**	**0**	**2**	**0**	**0**	**0**	**5:39**
	Hershey Bears	AHL	59	10	16	26	133																		
2002-03	**Colorado**	**NHL**	**32**	**0**	**2**	**2**	**19**	**0**	**0**	**0**	**9**	**0.0**	**3**	**0**	**0.0**	**6:33**									
	Hershey Bears	AHL	36	9	12	21	75										5	2	6	8	6				
2003-04	**Los Angeles**	**NHL**	**2**	**0**	**1**	**1**	**2**	**0**	**0**	**0**	**2**	**0.0**	**1**	**0**	**0.0**	**17:56**									
	Manchester	AHL	73	13	37	50	141										6	2	3	5	12				
2004-05	MODO	Sweden	26	1	5	6	36																		
	Blues Espoo	Finland	11	1	0	1	30																		
	NHL Totals		**181**	**5**	**15**	**20**	**167**	**0**	**1**	**0**	**197**	**2.5**		**2**	**50.0**	**14:52**	**29**	**0**	**0**	**0**	**6**	**0**	**0**	**0**	**5:21**

AHL First All-Star Team (2004)

Signed to five-game amateur tryout contract by **Edmonton**, February 29, 1996. Signed as a free agent by **Edmonton**, April 30, 1996. Traded to **New Jersey** by **Edmonton** with Jason Arnott for Valeri Zelepukin and Bill Guerin, January 4, 1998. Traded to **Chicago** by **New Jersey** for Chicago's 3rd round choice (Mike Rupp) in 2000 Entry Draft. November 13, 1998. Traded to **Tampa Bay** by **Chicago** with Reid Simpson for Michael Nylander, November 12, 1999. • Missed majority of 1999-2000 season recovering from leg injury suffered in game vs. Atlanta, November 17, 1999. Traded to **Colorado** by **Tampa Bay** for Colorado's 8th round choice (Dmitri Bezrukov) in 2001 Entry Draft, January 23, 2001. Signed as a free agent by **Los Angeles**, July 31, 2003. Signed as a free agent by **MODO** (Sweden), July 26, 2004. Signed as a free agent by **Blues** (Finland), January 31, 2005. Signed as a free agent by **Washington**, August 30, 2005.

MURLEY, Matt — (MUHR-lee, MAT) — PIT.

Left wing. Shoots left. 6'1", 206 lbs. Born, Troy, NY, December 17, 1979. Pittsburgh's 2nd choice, 51st overall, in 1999 Entry Draft.

Season	Club	League	GP	G	A	Pts	PIM	PP	SH	GW	S	%	+/-	TF	F%	Min	GP	G	A	Pts	PIM	PP	SH	GW	Min
1996-97	Syracuse	MTJHL	48	52	58	110	111																		
1997-98	Syracuse	MTJHL	49	56	70	126	103																		
1998-99	RPI Engineers	ECAC	36	17	32	49	32																		
99-2000	RPI Engineers	ECAC	35	9	29	38	42																		
2000-01	RPI Engineers	ECAC	34	*24	18	42	34																		
2001-02	RPI Engineers	ECAC	32	*24	22	46	26																		
2002-03	Wilkes-Barre	AHL	73	21	37	58	45										6	0	2	2	15				
2003-04	**Pittsburgh**	**NHL**	**18**	**1**	**1**	**2**	**14**	**0**	**0**	**0**	**20**	**5.0**	**-6**	**2**	**50.0**	**11:49**									
	Wilkes-Barre	AHL	63	10	26	36	69										24	7	6	13	17				
2004-05	Wilkes-Barre	AHL	80	17	24	41	55										11	3	0	3	0				
	NHL Totals		**18**	**1**	**1**	**2**	**14**	**0**	**0**	**0**	**20**	**5.0**		**2**	**50.0**	**11:49**									

ECAC First All-Star Team (2002)

MURPHY, Curtis — (MUHR-fee, KUHR-this)

Defense. Shoots right. 5'8", 185 lbs. Born, Kerrobert, Sask., December 3, 1975.

Season	Club	League	GP	G	A	Pts	PIM	PP	SH	GW	S	%	+/-	TF	F%	Min	GP	G	A	Pts	PIM	PP	SH	GW	Min
1993-94	Nipawin Hawks	SJHL	60	21	33	54																			
1994-95	North Dakota	WCHA	33	6	10	16	28																		
1995-96	North Dakota	WCHA	38	6	12	18	58																		
1996-97	North Dakota	WCHA	43	12	30	42	36																		
1997-98	North Dakota	WCHA	39	8	34	42	78																		
1998-99	Orlando	IHL	80	22	35	57	60										17	4	5	9	16				
99-2000	Orlando	IHL	81	8	43	51	59										6	0	2	2	6				
2000-01	Orlando	IHL	51	19	30	49	55										10	2	9	11	12				
2001-02	Houston Aeros	AHL	80	12	35	47	75										14	2	4	6	10				
2002-03	**Minnesota**	**NHL**	**1**	**0**	**0**	**0**	**0**	**0**	**0**	**0**	**0**	**0.0**	**0**	**0**	**0.0**	**8:56**									
	Houston Aeros	AHL	80	23	31	54	63										23	2	7	9	22				
2003-04	Milwaukee	AHL	79	17	36	53	51										22	4	8	12	12				
2004-05	Yaroslavl	Russia	60	6	6	12	50										9	1	1	2	6				
	NHL Totals		**1**	**0**	**0**	**0**	**0**	**0**	**0**	**0**	**0**	**0.0**		**0**	**0.0**	**8:56**									

WCHA First All-Star Team (1997, 1998) • NCAA West Second All-American Team (1997) • WCHA Player of the Year (1998) • NCAA West First All-American Team (1998) • IHL First All-Star Team (2001) • AHL First All-Star Team (2003, 2004) • Eddie Shore Award (Outstanding Defenseman – AHL) (2003, 2004)

Signed as a free agent by **Minnesota**, June 18, 2001. Traded to **Nashville** by **Minnesota** for Chris Bala, June 26, 2003. Signed as a free agent by **Yaroslavl** (Russia), May 28, 2004.

MURRAY, Garth — (MUHR-ree, GARTH) — NYR

Center. Shoots left. 6'1", 215 lbs. Born, Regina, Sask., September 17, 1982. NY Rangers' 3rd choice, 79th overall, in 2001 Entry Draft.

Season	Club	League	GP	G	A	Pts	PIM	PP	SH	GW	S	%	+/-	TF	F%	Min	GP	G	A	Pts	PIM	PP	SH	GW	Min
1997-98	Calgary Buffaloes	AMHL	56	26	34	60	110																		
	Regina Pats	WHL	4	0	0	0	2										2	0	0	0	0				
1998-99	Regina Pats	WHL	60	3	5	8	101																		
99-2000	Regina Pats	WHL	68	14	26	40	155										7	1	1	2	7				
2000-01	Regina Pats	WHL	72	28	16	44	183										6	1	1	2	10				
2001-02	Regina Pats	WHL	62	33	30	63	154										6	2	3	5	9				
	Hartford	AHL	4	0	0	0	0										9	1	3	4	6				
2002-03	Hartford	AHL	64	10	14	24	121										2	0	0	0	6				
2003-04	**NY Rangers**	**NHL**	**20**	**1**	**0**	**1**	**24**	**0**	**0**	**0**	**18**	**5.6**	**-5**	**5**	**20.0**	**9:16**									
	Hartford	AHL	63	11	11	22	159										16	0	4	4	29				
2004-05	Hartford	AHL	55	4	5	9	182										5	1	0	1	8				
	NHL Totals		**20**	**1**	**0**	**1**	**24**	**0**	**0**	**0**	**18**	**5.6**		**5**	**20.0**	**9:16**									

MURRAY, Glen — (MUHR-ree, GLEHN) — BOS.

Right wing. Shoots right. 6'3", 225 lbs. Born, Halifax, N.S., November 1, 1972. Boston's 1st choice, 18th overall, in 1991 Entry Draft.

Season	Club	League	GP	G	A	Pts	PIM	PP	SH	GW	S	%	+/-	TF	F%	Min	GP	G	A	Pts	PIM	PP	SH	GW	Min
1988-89	Bridgewater	NSMHL	45	50	56	106	62																		
1989-90	Sudbury Wolves	OHL	62	8	28	36	17										7	0	0	0	4				
1990-91	Sudbury Wolves	OHL	66	27	38	65	82										5	8	4	12	10				
1991-92	Sudbury Wolves	OHL	54	37	47	84	93										11	7	4	11	18				
	Boston	**NHL**	**5**	**3**	**1**	**4**	**0**	**1**	**0**	**0**	**20**	**15.0**	**2**				**15**	**4**	**2**	**6**	**10**	**1**	**0**	**0**	
1992-93	**Boston**	**NHL**	**27**	**3**	**4**	**7**	**8**	**2**	**0**	**1**	**28**	**10.7**	**-6**												
	Providence Bruins	AHL	48	30	26	56	42										6	1	4	5	4				
1993-94	**Boston**	**NHL**	**81**	**18**	**13**	**31**	**48**	**0**	**0**	**4**	**114**	**15.8**	**-1**				**13**	**4**	**5**	**9**	**14**	**0**	**0**	**0**	
1994-95	**Boston**	**NHL**	**35**	**5**	**2**	**7**	**46**	**0**	**0**	**2**	**64**	**7.8**	**-11**				**2**	**0**	**0**	**0**	**2**	**0**	**0**	**0**	
1995-96	**Pittsburgh**	**NHL**	**69**	**14**	**15**	**29**	**57**	**0**	**0**	**2**	**100**	**14.0**	**4**				**18**	**2**	**6**	**8**	**10**	**0**	**0**	**1**	
1996-97	**Pittsburgh**	**NHL**	**66**	**11**	**11**	**22**	**24**	**3**	**0**	**1**	**127**	**8.7**	**-19**												
	Los Angeles	**NHL**	**11**	**5**	**3**	**8**	**8**	**0**	**0**	**0**	**26**	**19.2**	**-2**												
1997-98	**Los Angeles**	**NHL**	**81**	**29**	**31**	**60**	**54**	**7**	**3**	**7**	**193**	**15.0**	**6**				**4**	**2**	**0**	**2**	**6**	**0**	**0**	**0**	
1998-99	**Los Angeles**	**NHL**	**61**	**16**	**15**	**31**	**36**	**3**	**3**	**3**	**173**	**9.2**	**-14**	**12**	**25.0**	**20:33**									

			Regular Season														Playoffs								
Season	Club	League	GP	G	A	Pts	PIM	PP	SH	GW	S	%	+/-	TF	F%	Min	GP	G	A	Pts	PIM	PP	SH	GW	Min
99-2000	**Los Angeles**	**NHL**	**78**	**29**	**33**	**62**	**60**	**10**	**1**	**2**	**202**	**14.4**	**13**	**15**	**80.0**	**18:30**	**4**	**0**	**0**	**0**	**2**	**0**	**0**	**0**	**19:04**
2000-01	**Los Angeles**	**NHL**	**64**	**18**	**21**	**39**	**32**	**3**	**1**	**1**	**138**	**13.0**	**9**	**7**	**42.9**	**18:12**	**13**	**4**	**3**	**7**	**4**	**1**	**0**	**1**	**19:51**
2001-02	**Los Angeles**	**NHL**	**9**	**6**	**5**	**11**	**0**	**4**	**0**	**2**	**34**	**17.6**	**5**	**1**	**100.0**	**19:08**	....	....	....	....	....	....	....	....	....
	Boston	**NHL**	**73**	**35**	**25**	**60**	**40**	**5**	**0**	**7**	**212**	**16.5**	**26**	**39**	**23.1**	**19:50**	**6**	**1**	**4**	**5**	**4**	**0**	**0**	**0**	**18:02**
2002-03	**Boston**	**NHL**	**82**	**44**	**48**	**92**	**64**	**12**	**0**	**5**	**331**	**13.3**	**9**	**32**	**37.5**	**22:36**	**5**	**1**	**1**	**2**	**4**	**0**	**0**	**0**	**19:36**
2003-04	**Boston**	**NHL**	**81**	**32**	**28**	**60**	**56**	**11**	**0**	**9**	**260**	**12.3**	**17**	**53**	**35.9**	**20:56**	**7**	**2**	**1**	**3**	**8**	**0**	**0**	**1**	**19:57**
2004-05				DID NOT PLAY																					
	NHL Totals		**823**	**268**	**255**	**523**	**533**	**61**	**8**	**46**	**2022**	**13.3**		**159**	**37.1**	**20:10**	**87**	**20**	**22**	**42**	**64**	**2**	**0**	**3**	**19:26**

Played in NHL All-Star Game (2003, 2004)

Traded to **Pittsburgh** by **Boston** with Bryan Smolinski and Boston's 3rd round choice (Boyd Kane) in 1996 Entry Draft for Kevin Stevens and Shawn McEachern, August 2, 1995. Traded to **Los Angeles** by **Pittsburgh** for Ed Olczyk, March 18, 1997. Traded to **Boston** by **Los Angeles** with Jozef Stumpel for Jason Allison and Mikko Eloranta, October 24, 2001.

MURRAY, Marty

(MUHR-ree, MAHR-tee)

Center. Shoots left. 5'9", 180 lbs. Born, Lylton, Man., February 16, 1975. Calgary's 5th choice, 96th overall, in 1993 Entry Draft.

Season	Club	League	GP	G	A	Pts	PIM	PP	SH	GW	S	%	+/-	TF	F%	Min	GP	G	A	Pts	PIM	PP	SH	GW	Min
1990-91	S-W Cougars	MMMHL	36	46	47	93	50	....	....	....	....	....	....	....	....	....	....	....	....	....	....	....	....	....	....
1991-92	Brandon	WHL	68	20	36	56	22	....	....	....	....	....	....	....	....	....	....	....	....	....	....	....	....	....	....
1992-93	Brandon	WHL	67	29	65	94	50	....	....	....	....	....	....	....	....	....	4	1	3	4	0	....	....	....	....
1993-94	Brandon	WHL	64	43	71	114	33	....	....	....	....	....	....	....	....	....	14	6	14	20	14	....	....	....	....
1994-95	Brandon	WHL	65	40	*88	128	53	....	....	....	....	....	....	....	....	....	18	9	*20	29	16	....	....	....	....
1995-96	**Calgary**	**NHL**	**15**	**3**	**3**	**6**	**0**	**2**	**0**	**0**	**22**	**13.6**	**–4**	....	....	....	....	....	....	....	....	....	....	....	....
	Saint John Flames	AHL	58	25	31	56	20	....	....	....	....	....	....	....	....	....	14	2	4	6	4	....	....	....	....
1996-97	**Calgary**	**NHL**	**2**	**0**	**0**	**0**	**4**	**0**	**0**	**0**	**2**	**0.0**	**0**	....	....	....	....	....	....	....	....	....	....	....	....
	Saint John Flames	AHL	67	19	39	58	40	....	....	....	....	....	....	....	....	....	5	2	3	5	4	....	....	....	....
1997-98	**Calgary**	**NHL**	**2**	**0**	**0**	**0**	**2**	**0**	**0**	**0**	**2**	**0.0**	**1**	....	....	....	....	....	....	....	....	....	....	....	....
	Saint John Flames	AHL	41	10	30	40	16	....	....	....	....	....	....	....	....	....	21	10	10	20	12	....	....	....	....
1998-99	EC Villacher SV	Alpenliga	33	26	41	67	12	....	....	....	....	....	....	....	....	....	....	....	....	....	....	....	....	....	....
	EC Villacher SV	Austria	17	13	17	30	6	....	....	....	....	....	....	....	....	....	6	1	4	5	0	....	....	....	....
99-2000	Kolner Haie	Germany	56	12	47	59	28	....	....	....	....	....	....	....	....	....	10	4	3	7	2	....	....	....	....
2000-01	**Calgary**	**NHL**	**7**	**0**	**0**	**0**	**0**	**0**	**0**	**0**	**6**	**0.0**	**–2**	**88**	**55.7**	**14:28**	....	....	....	....	....	....	....	....	....
	Saint John Flames	AHL	56	24	52	76	36	....	....	....	....	....	....	....	....	....	19	4	16	20	18	....	....	....	....
2001-02	**Philadelphia**	**NHL**	**74**	**12**	**15**	**27**	**10**	**1**	**1**	**2**	**109**	**11.0**	**10**	**913**	**50.7**	**13:56**	**5**	**0**	**1**	**1**	**0**	**0**	**0**	**0**	**13:14**
	Philadelphia	AHL	3	0	3	3	2	....	....	....	....	....	....	....	....	....	....	....	....	....	....	....	....	....	....
2002-03	**Philadelphia**	**NHL**	**76**	**11**	**15**	**26**	**13**	**1**	**1**	**0**	**105**	**10.5**	**–1**	**472**	**55.1**	**12:22**	**4**	**0**	**0**	**0**	**4**	**0**	**0**	**0**	**11:00**
2003-04	**Carolina**	**NHL**	**66**	**5**	**7**	**12**	**8**	**0**	**0**	**0**	**56**	**8.9**	**6**	**229**	**52.8**	**11:49**	....	....	....	....	....	....	....	....	....
2004-05				DID NOT PLAY																					
	NHL Totals		**242**	**31**	**40**	**71**	**37**	**4**	**2**	**2**	**302**	**10.3**		**1702**	**52.5**	**12:47**	**9**	**0**	**1**	**1**	**4**	**0**	**0**	**0**	**12:15**

WHL East First All-Star Team (1994, 1995) • Canadian Major Junior Second All-Star Team (1994) • WHL Player of the Year (1995)

Signed as a free agent by **Philadelphia**, July 9, 2001. Traded to **Carolina** by **Philadelphia** for Carolina's 6th round choice (Frederik Cabana) in 2004 Entry Draft, June 22, 2003.

MURRAY, Rem

(MUHR-ree, REHM)

Center/left wing. Shoots left. 6'2", 200 lbs. Born, Stratford, Ont., October 9, 1972. Los Angeles' 5th choice, 135th overall, in 1992 Entry Draft.

Season	Club	League	GP	G	A	Pts	PIM	PP	SH	GW	S	%	+/-	TF	F%	Min	GP	G	A	Pts	PIM	PP	SH	GW	Min
1989-90	Stratford Cullitons	OHA-B	46	19	32	51	48	....	....	....	....	....	....	....	....	....	....	....	....	....	....	....	....	....	....
1990-91	Stratford Cullitons	OHA-B	48	39	59	98	39	....	....	....	....	....	....	....	....	....	....	....	....	....	....	....	....	....	....
1991-92	Michigan State	CCHA	41	12	36	48	16	....	....	....	....	....	....	....	....	....	....	....	....	....	....	....	....	....	....
1992-93	Michigan State	CCHA	40	22	35	57	24	....	....	....	....	....	....	....	....	....	....	....	....	....	....	....	....	....	....
1993-94	Michigan State	CCHA	41	16	38	54	18	....	....	....	....	....	....	....	....	....	....	....	....	....	....	....	....	....	....
1994-95	Michigan State	CCHA	40	20	36	56	21	....	....	....	....	....	....	....	....	....	....	....	....	....	....	....	....	....	....
1995-96	Cape Breton	AHL	79	31	59	90	40	....	....	....	....	....	....	....	....	....	....	....	....	....	....	....	....	....	....
1996-97	**Edmonton**	**NHL**	**82**	**11**	**20**	**31**	**16**	**1**	**0**	**2**	**85**	**12.9**	**9**	....	....	....	**12**	**1**	**2**	**3**	**4**	**0**	**0**	**0**	....
1997-98	**Edmonton**	**NHL**	**61**	**9**	**9**	**18**	**39**	**2**	**2**	**0**	**59**	**15.3**	**–9**	....	....	....	**11**	**1**	**4**	**5**	**2**	**0**	**0**	**0**	....
1998-99	**Edmonton**	**NHL**	**78**	**21**	**18**	**39**	**20**	**4**	**1**	**4**	**116**	**18.1**	**4**	**1013**	**48.1**	**15:50**	**4**	**1**	**1**	**2**	**2**	**0**	**0**	**0**	**22:40**
99-2000	**Edmonton**	**NHL**	**44**	**9**	**5**	**14**	**8**	**2**	**0**	**3**	**65**	**13.8**	**–2**	**303**	**50.5**	**14:16**	**5**	**0**	**1**	**1**	**2**	**0**	**0**	**0**	**15:19**
2000-01	**Edmonton**	**NHL**	**82**	**15**	**21**	**36**	**24**	**1**	**3**	**3**	**122**	**12.3**	**5**	**694**	**49.3**	**15:21**	**6**	**2**	**0**	**2**	**6**	**1**	**0**	**0**	**18:10**
2001-02	**Edmonton**	**NHL**	**69**	**7**	**17**	**24**	**14**	**0**	**2**	**1**	**84**	**8.3**	**5**	**825**	**50.9**	**14:27**	....	....	....	....	....	....	....	....	....
	NY Rangers	**NHL**	**11**	**1**	**2**	**3**	**4**	**0**	**0**	**0**	**14**	**7.1**	**–9**	**151**	**51.7**	**15:51**	....	....	....	....	....	....	....	....	....
2002-03	**NY Rangers**	**NHL**	**32**	**6**	**6**	**12**	**4**	**1**	**1**	**1**	**62**	**9.7**	**–3**	**118**	**53.4**	**15:39**	....	....	....	....	....	....	....	....	....
	Nashville	**NHL**	**53**	**6**	**13**	**19**	**18**	**1**	**0**	**0**	**81**	**7.4**	**1**	**720**	**49.2**	**17:16**	....	....	....	....	....	....	....	....	....
2003-04	**Nashville**	**NHL**	**39**	**8**	**9**	**17**	**12**	**0**	**2**	**1**	**58**	**13.8**	**–1**	**169**	**46.2**	**16:37**	....	....	....	....	....	....	....	....	....
2004-05				DID NOT PLAY																					
	NHL Totals		**551**	**93**	**120**	**213**	**159**	**12**	**11**	**15**	**746**	**12.5**		**3993**	**49.5**	**15:35**	**38**	**5**	**8**	**13**	**16**	**1**	**0**	**0**	**18:25**

CCHA Second All-Star Team (1995)

Signed as a free agent by **Edmonton**, September 19, 1995. Traded to **NY Rangers** by **Edmonton** with Tom Poti for Mike York and NY Rangers' 4th round choice (Ivan Koltsov) in 2002 Entry Draft, March 19, 2002. Traded to **Nashville** by **NY Rangers** with Tomas Kloucek and Marek Zidlicky for Mike Dunham, December 12, 2002. • Missed majority of 2003-04 season recovering from neck injury suffered in game vs. Detroit, January 5, 2004.

MYHRES, Brantt

(MIGH-uhrs, BRANT) **CGY.**

Right wing. Shoots right. 6'3", 220 lbs. Born, Edmonton, Alta., March 18, 1974. Tampa Bay's 5th choice, 97th overall, in 1992 Entry Draft.

Season	Club	League	GP	G	A	Pts	PIM	PP	SH	GW	S	%	+/-	TF	F%	Min	GP	G	A	Pts	PIM	PP	SH	GW	Min
1989-90	Bonnyville Barons	AAHA	60	40	62	102	195	....	....	....	....	....	....	....	....	....	....	....	....	....	....	....	....	....	....
1990-91	Portland	WHL	59	2	7	9	125	....	....	....	....	....	....	....	....	....	....	....	....	....	....	....	....	....	....
1991-92	Portland	WHL	4	0	2	2	22	....	....	....	....	....	....	....	....	....	....	....	....	....	....	....	....	....	....
	Lethbridge	WHL	53	4	11	15	359	....	....	....	....	....	....	....	....	....	5	0	0	0	36	....	....	....	....
1992-93	Lethbridge	WHL	64	13	35	48	277	....	....	....	....	....	....	....	....	....	3	0	0	0	11	....	....	....	....
1993-94	Lethbridge	WHL	34	10	21	31	103	....	....	....	....	....	....	....	....	....	....	....	....	....	....	....	....	....	....
	Spokane Chiefs	WHL	27	10	22	32	139	....	....	....	....	....	....	....	....	....	3	1	4	5	7	....	....	....	....
	Atlanta Knights	IHL	2	0	0	0	17	....	....	....	....	....	....	....	....	....	....	....	....	....	....	....	....	....	....
1994-95	Atlanta Knights	IHL	40	5	5	10	213	....	....	....	....	....	....	....	....	....	....	....	....	....	....	....	....	....	....
	Tampa Bay	**NHL**	**15**	**2**	**0**	**2**	**81**	**0**	**0**	**1**	**4**	**50.0**	**–2**	....	....	....	....	....	....	....	....	....	....	....	....
1995-96	Atlanta Knights	IHL	12	0	2	2	58	....	....	....	....	....	....	....	....	....	....	....	....	....	....	....	....	....	....
1996-97	**Tampa Bay**	**NHL**	**47**	**3**	**1**	**4**	**136**	**0**	**0**	**1**	**13**	**23.1**	**1**	....	....	....	....	....	....	....	....	....	....	....	....
	San Antonio	IHL	12	0	0	0	98	....	....	....	....	....	....	....	....	....	....	....	....	....	....	....	....	....	....
1997-98	**Philadelphia**	**NHL**	**23**	**0**	**0**	**0**	**169**	**0**	**0**	**0**	**0**	**0.0**	**–1**	....	....	....	....	....	....	....	....	....	....	....	....
	Philadelphia	AHL	18	4	4	8	67	....	....	....	....	....	....	....	....	....	....	....	....	....	....	....	....	....	....
1998-99	**San Jose**	**NHL**	**30**	**1**	**0**	**1**	**116**	**0**	**0**	**0**	**7**	**14.3**	**–2**	**1**	**0.0**	**4:47**	....	....	....	....	....	....	....	....	....
	Kentucky	AHL	4	0	0	0	16	....	....	....	....	....	....	....	....	....	....	....	....	....	....	....	....	....	....
99-2000	**San Jose**	**NHL**	**13**	**0**	**1**	**1**	**97**	**0**	**0**	**0**	**2**	**0.0**	**0**	**1**	**0.0**	**3:03**	....	....	....	....	....	....	....	....	....
	Kentucky	AHL	10	1	5	6	18	....	....	....	....	....	....	....	....	....	7	0	1	1	21	....	....	....	....
2000-01	**Nashville**	**NHL**	**20**	**0**	**0**	**0**	**28**	**0**	**0**	**0**	**1**	**0.0**	**–5**	**0**	**0.0**	**3:48**	....	....	....	....	....	....	....	....	....
	Milwaukee	IHL	6	0	1	1	10	....	....	....	....	....	....	....	....	....	....	....	....	....	....	....	....	....	....
	Washington	**NHL**	**5**	**0**	**0**	**0**	**29**	**0**	**0**	**0**	**0**	**0.0**	**0**	**0**	**0.0**	**3:36**	....	....	....	....	....	....	....	....	....
	Portland Pirates	AHL	9	1	0	1	53	....	....	....	....	....	....	....	....	....	....	....	....	....	....	....	....	....	....
2001-02				DID NOT PLAY																					
2002-03	**Boston**	**NHL**	**1**	**0**	**0**	**0**	**31**	**0**	**0**	**0**	**0**	**0.0**	**0**	**0**	**0.0**	**5:26**	....	....	....	....	....	....	....	....	....
	Providence Bruins	AHL	63	3	10	13	185	....	....	....	....	....	....	....	....	....	4	0	0	0	2	....	....	....	....
2003-04				DID NOT PLAY																					
2004-05	Lowell	AHL	29	1	1	2	77	....	....	....	....	....	....	....	....	....	4	0	0	0	9	....	....	....	....
	NHL Totals		**154**	**6**	**2**	**8**	**687**	**0**	**0**	**2**	**27**	**22.2**		**2**	**0.0**	**4:06**	....	....	....	....	....	....	....	....	....

Traded to **Edmonton** by **Tampa Bay** with Toronto's 3rd round choice (previously acquired, Edmonton selected Alex Henry) in 1998 Entry Draft for Vladimir Vujtek and Edmonton's 3rd round choice (Dmitry Afanasenkov) in 1998 Entry Draft, July 16, 1997. Traded to **Philadelphia** by **Edmonton** for Jason Bowen, October 15, 1997. Signed as a free agent by **San Jose**, September 11, 1998. Signed as a free agent by **Nashville**, August 15, 2000. Traded to **Washington** by **Nashville** for future considerations, February 1, 2001. Signed as a free agent by **Boston**, September 19, 2002. Signed as a free agent by **Lowell** (AHL), October 3, 2004. Signed as a free agent by **Calgary**, August 11, 2005.

MYRVOLD, Anders
(MYOOR-vohld, AN-duhrs)

Defense. Shoots left. 6'2", 200 lbs. Born, Lorenskog, Norway, August 12, 1975. Quebec's 6th choice, 127th overall, in 1993 Entry Draft.

			Regular Season														Playoffs								
Season	Club	League	GP	G	A	Pts	PIM	PP	SH	GW	S	%	+/-	TF	F%	Min	GP	G	A	Pts	PIM	PP	SH	GW	Min
1991-92	Storhamar IL	Norway	1	0	0	0	4	....	....	....	....	....	....	....	....	....	....	....	....	....	....	....	....	....	....
1992-93	Farjestad	Sweden	2	0	0	0	0	....	....	....	....	....	....	....	....	....	....	....	....	....	....	....	....	....	....
1993-94	Grums IK	Sweden-2	24	1	0	1	59	....	....	....	....	....	....	....	....	....	2	1	0	1	5	....	....	....	....
1994-95	Laval Titan	QMJHL	64	14	50	64	173	....	....	....	....	....	....	....	....	....	20	4	10	14	68	....	....	....	....
	Cornwall Aces	AHL	....	....	....	....	....	....	....	....	....	....	....	....	....	....	3	0	1	1	2	....	....	....	....
1995-96	**Colorado**	**NHL**	**4**	**0**	**1**	**1**	**6**	**0**	**0**	**0**	**4**	**0.0**	**–2**	....	....	....	....	....	....	....	....	....	....	....	....
	Cornwall Aces	AHL	70	5	24	29	125	....	....	....	....	....	....	....	....	....	5	1	0	1	19	....	....	....	....
1996-97	Hershey Bears	AHL	20	0	3	3	16	....	....	....	....	....	....	....	....	....	....	....	....	....	....	....	....	....	....
	Boston	**NHL**	**9**	**0**	**2**	**2**	**4**	**0**	**0**	**0**	**8**	**0.0**	**–1**	....	....	....	....	....	....	....	....	....	....	....	....
	Providence Bruins	AHL	53	6	15	21	107	....	....	....	....	....	....	....	....	....	10	0	1	1	6	....	....	....	....
1997-98	Providence Bruins	AHL	75	4	21	25	91	....	....	....	....	....	....	....	....	....	....	....	....	....	....	....	....	....	....
1998-99	Djurgarden	Sweden	29	3	4	7	52	....	....	....	....	....	....	....	....	....	....	....	....	....	....	....	....	....	....
	Djurgarden	EuroHL	3	0	1	1	4	....	....	....	....	....	....	....	....	....	....	....	....	....	....	....	....	....	....
	AIK Solna	Sweden	19	1	3	4	24	....	....	....	....	....	....	....	....	....	....	....	....	....	....	....	....	....	....
99-2000	AIK Solna	Sweden	49	1	3	4	87	....	....	....	....	....	....	....	....	....	....	....	....	....	....	....	....	....	....
2000-01	**NY Islanders**	**NHL**	**12**	**0**	**1**	**1**	**0**	**0**	**0**	**0**	**8**	**0.0**	**–2**	**0**	**0.0**	**9:26**	....	....	....	....	....	....	....	....	....
	Springfield	AHL	69	5	25	30	129	....	....	....	....	....	....	....	....	....	....	....	....	....	....	....	....	....	....
2001-02	Hartford	AHL	19	3	3	6	28	....	....	....	....	....	....	....	....	....	....	....	....	....	....	....	....	....	....
	Fribourg	Swiss	6	0	0	0	16	....	....	....	....	....	....	....	....	....	4	0	1	1	6	....	....	....	....
2002-03	Adler Mannheim	Germany	45	0	3	3	82	....	....	....	....	....	....	....	....	....	7	0	0	0	4	....	....	....	....
2003-04	**Detroit**	**NHL**	**8**	**0**	**1**	**1**	**2**	**0**	**0**	**0**	**6**	**0.0**	**–1**	**0**	**0.0**	**12:12**	....	....	....	....	....	....	....	....	....
	Grand Rapids	AHL	71	0	21	21	94	....	....	....	....	....	....	....	....	....	4	0	1	1	2	....	....	....	....
2004-05	Valerengen IF Oslo	Norway	40	8	24	32	108	....	....	....	....	....	....	....	....	....	11	2	1	3	24	....	....	....	....
	NHL Totals		**33**	**0**	**5**	**5**	**12**	**0**	**0**	**0**	**26**	**0.0**		**0**	**0.0**	**10:32**	....	....	....	....	....	....	....	....	....

QMJHL All-Rookie Team (1995)

Rights transferred to **Colorado** after **Quebec** franchise relocated, June 21, 1995. Traded to **Boston** by **Colorado** with Landon Wilson for Boston's 1st round choice (Robyn Regehr) in 1998 Entry Draft, November 22, 1996. Signed as a free agent by **NY Islanders**, August 28, 2000. Signed as a free agent by **Fribourg** (Swiss), January 10, 2002. Signed as a free agent by **Florida**, July 28, 2002. Signed as a free agent by **Detroit**, September 1, 2003. Signed as a free agent by **Valerengen** (Norway), September 15, 2004.

NAGY, Ladislav
(NA-gee, LA-dih-slahv) **PHX.**

Left wing. Shoots left. 5'11", 192 lbs. Born, Saca, Czech., June 1, 1979. St. Louis' 6th choice, 177th overall, in 1997 Entry Draft.

Season	Club	League	GP	G	A	Pts	PIM	PP	SH	GW	S	%	+/-	TF	F%	Min	GP	G	A	Pts	PIM	PP	SH	GW	Min
1995-96	HK Dragon Presov	Slovakia	11	6	5	11	....	....	....	....	....	....	....	....	....	....	....	....	....	....	....	....	....	....	....
1996-97	HC Kosice Jr.	Slovak-Jr.	45	29	30	59	105	....	....	....	....	....	....	....	....	....	....	....	....	....	....	....	....	....	....
1997-98	HC Kosice	Slovakia	29	19	15	34	41	....	....	....	....	....	....	....	....	....	11	2	4	6	6	....	....	....	....
1998-99	Halifax	QMJHL	63	71	55	126	148	....	....	....	....	....	....	....	....	....	5	3	3	6	18	....	....	....	....
	Worcester IceCats	AHL	....	....	....	....	....	....	....	....	....	....	....	....	....	....	3	2	2	4	0	....	....	....	....
99-2000	**St. Louis**	**NHL**	**11**	**2**	**4**	**6**	**2**	**1**	**0**	**0**	**15**	**13.3**	**2**	**6**	**33.3**	**12:19**	**6**	**1**	**1**	**2**	**0**	**0**	**0**	**0**	**13:29**
	Worcester IceCats	AHL	69	23	28	51	67	....	....	....	....	....	....	....	....	....	2	1	0	1	0	....	....	....	....
2000-01	**St. Louis**	**NHL**	**40**	**8**	**8**	**16**	**20**	**2**	**0**	**2**	**59**	**13.6**	**–2**	**28**	**50.0**	**13:03**	....	....	....	....	....	....	....	....	....
	Worcester IceCats	AHL	20	6	14	20	36	....	....	....	....	....	....	....	....	....	....	....	....	....	....	....	....	....	....
	Phoenix	**NHL**	**6**	**0**	**1**	**1**	**2**	**0**	**0**	**0**	**5**	**0.0**	**0**	**0**	**0.0**	**12:38**	....	....	....	....	....	....	....	....	....
2001-02	**Phoenix**	**NHL**	**74**	**23**	**19**	**42**	**50**	**5**	**0**	**5**	**187**	**12.3**	**6**	**17**	**47.1**	**15:04**	**5**	**0**	**0**	**0**	**21**	**0**	**0**	**0**	**15:45**
2002-03	HC Kosice	Slovakia	1	2	1	3	0	....	....	....	....	....	....	....	....	....	....	....	....	....	....	....	....	....	....
	Phoenix	**NHL**	**80**	**22**	**35**	**57**	**92**	**8**	**0**	**6**	**209**	**10.5**	**17**	**41**	**34.2**	**17:28**	....	....	....	....	....	....	....	....	....
2003-04	**Phoenix**	**NHL**	**55**	**24**	**28**	**52**	**46**	**11**	**0**	**6**	**160**	**15.0**	**11**	**33**	**42.4**	**18:10**	....	....	....	....	....	....	....	....	....
2004-05	HC Kosice	Slovakia	18	9	7	16	40	....	....	....	....	....	....	....	....	....	....	....	....	....	....	....	....	....	....
	Mora IK	Sweden	19	4	4	8	22	....	....	....	....	....	....	....	....	....	....	....	....	....	....	....	....	....	....
	NHL Totals		**266**	**79**	**95**	**174**	**212**	**27**	**0**	**19**	**635**	**12.4**		**125**	**41.6**	**15:57**	**11**	**1**	**1**	**2**	**21**	**0**	**0**	**0**	**14:30**

Traded to **Phoenix** by **St. Louis** with Michal Handzus, the rights to Jeff Taffe and St. Louis' 1st round choice (Ben Eager) in 2002 Entry Draft for Keith Tkachuk, March 13, 2001. Signed as a free agent by **Kosice** (Slovakia), September 17, 2004. Signed as a free agent by **Mora** (Sweden), December 17, 2004.

NASH, Rick
(NASH, RIHK) **CBJ**

Left wing. Shoots left. 6'4", 206 lbs. Born, Brampton, Ont., June 16, 1984. Columbus' 1st choice, 1st overall, in 2002 Entry Draft.

Season	Club	League	GP	G	A	Pts	PIM	PP	SH	GW	S	%	+/-	TF	F%	Min	GP	G	A	Pts	PIM	PP	SH	GW	Min
99-2000	Tor. Marlboros	GTHL	34	61	54	115	34	....	....	....	....	....	....	....	....	....	....	....	....	....	....	....	....	....	....
2000-01	London Knights	OHL	58	31	35	66	56	....	....	....	....	....	....	....	....	....	4	3	3	6	8	....	....	....	....
2001-02	London Knights	OHL	54	32	40	72	88	....	....	....	....	....	....	....	....	....	12	10	9	19	21	....	....	....	....
2002-03	**Columbus**	**NHL**	**74**	**17**	**22**	**39**	**78**	**6**	**0**	**2**	**154**	**11.0**	**–27**	**14**	**35.7**	**13:57**	....	....	....	....	....	....	....	....	....
2003-04	**Columbus**	**NHL**	**80**	***41**	**16**	**57**	**87**	**19**	**0**	**7**	**269**	**15.2**	**–35**	**21**	**28.6**	**17:38**	....	....	....	....	....	....	....	....	....
2004-05	HC Davos	Swiss	44	26	20	46	83	....	....	....	....	....	....	....	....	....	15	9	2	11	26	....	....	....	....
	NHL Totals		**154**	**58**	**38**	**96**	**165**	**25**	**0**	**9**	**423**	**13.7**		**35**	**31.4**	**15:52**	....	....	....	....	....	....	....	....	....

OHL All-Rookie Team (2001) • OHL Rookie of the Year (2001) • CHL All-Rookie Team (2001) • NHL All-Rookie Team (2003) • Maurice "Rocket" Richard Trophy (2004) (tied with Jarome Iginla and Ilya Kovalchuk)

Played in NHL All-Star Game (2004)

Signed as a free agent by **Davos** (Swiss), August 3, 2004.

NASH, Tyson
(NASH, TIGH-sohn) **PHX.**

Left wing. Shoots left. 5'11", 191 lbs. Born, Edmonton, Alta., March 11, 1975. Vancouver's 10th choice, 247th overall, in 1994 Entry Draft.

Season	Club	League	GP	G	A	Pts	PIM	PP	SH	GW	S	%	+/-	TF	F%	Min	GP	G	A	Pts	PIM	PP	SH	GW	Min
1990-91	Sherwood Park	AMHL	40	17	28	43	63	....	....	....	....	....	....	....	....	....	....	....	....	....	....	....	....	....	....
1991-92	Kamloops Blazers	WHL	33	1	6	7	62	....	....	....	....	....	....	....	....	....	4	0	0	0	0	....	....	....	....
1992-93	Kamloops Blazers	WHL	61	10	16	26	78	....	....	....	....	....	....	....	....	....	13	3	2	5	32	....	....	....	....
1993-94	Kamloops Blazers	WHL	65	20	36	56	135	....	....	....	....	....	....	....	....	....	16	3	4	7	12	....	....	....	....
1994-95	Kamloops Blazers	WHL	63	34	41	75	70	....	....	....	....	....	....	....	....	....	21	10	7	17	30	....	....	....	....
1995-96	Syracuse Crunch	AHL	50	4	7	11	58	....	....	....	....	....	....	....	....	....	4	0	0	0	11	....	....	....	....
	Raleigh IceCaps	ECHL	6	1	1	2	8	....	....	....	....	....	....	....	....	....	....	....	....	....	....	....	....	....	....
1996-97	Syracuse Crunch	AHL	77	17	17	34	105	....	....	....	....	....	....	....	....	....	3	0	2	2	0	....	....	....	....
1997-98	Syracuse Crunch	AHL	74	20	20	40	184	....	....	....	....	....	....	....	....	....	5	0	2	2	28	....	....	....	....
1998-99	**St. Louis**	**NHL**	**2**	**0**	**0**	**0**	**5**	**0**	**0**	**0**	**1**	**0.0**	**–1**	**0**	**0.0**	**7:44**	**1**	**0**	**0**	**0**	**2**	**0**	**0**	**0**	**6:25**
	Worcester IceCats	AHL	55	14	22	36	143	....	....	....	....	....	....	....	....	....	4	4	1	5	27	....	....	....	....
99-2000	**St. Louis**	**NHL**	**66**	**4**	**9**	**13**	**150**	**0**	**1**	**1**	**68**	**5.9**	**6**	**0**	**0.0**	**8:35**	**6**	**1**	**0**	**1**	**24**	**0**	**0**	**0**	**8:36**
2000-01	**St. Louis**	**NHL**	**57**	**8**	**7**	**15**	**110**	**0**	**1**	**0**	**113**	**7.1**	**8**	**2**	**50.0**	**12:29**	....	....	....	....	....	....	....	....	....
2001-02	**St. Louis**	**NHL**	**64**	**6**	**7**	**13**	**100**	**0**	**0**	**1**	**66**	**9.1**	**2**	**14**	**35.7**	**10:02**	**9**	**0**	**1**	**1**	**20**	**0**	**0**	**0**	**8:03**
2002-03	**St. Louis**	**NHL**	**66**	**6**	**3**	**9**	**114**	**1**	**0**	**2**	**77**	**7.8**	**0**	**9**	**11.1**	**9:53**	**7**	**2**	**1**	**3**	**6**	**0**	**0**	**0**	**9:05**
2003-04	**Phoenix**	**NHL**	**69**	**3**	**5**	**8**	**110**	**0**	**0**	**0**	**83**	**3.6**	**–6**	**13**	**38.5**	**11:53**	....	....	....	....	....	....	....	....	....
2004-05			DID NOT PLAY																						
	NHL Totals		**324**	**27**	**31**	**58**	**589**	**1**	**2**	**4**	**408**	**6.6**		**38**	**31.6**	**10:31**	**23**	**3**	**2**	**5**	**52**	**0**	**0**	**0**	**8:26**

Signed as a free agent by **St. Louis**, July 14, 1998. Traded to **Phoenix** by **St. Louis** for Phoenix's 5th round choice (Lee Stempniak) in 2003 Enrey Draft, June 21, 2003.

NASLUND, Markus
(NAZ-luhnd, MAHR-kuhs)

Left wing. Shoots left. 5'11", 195 lbs. Born, Ornskoldsvik, Sweden, July 30, 1973. Pittsburgh's 1st choice, 16th overall, in 1991 Entry Draft.

Season	Club	League	GP	G	A	Pts	PIM	PP	SH	GW	S	%	+/-	TF	F%	Min	GP	G	A	Pts	PIM	PP	SH	GW	Min
1988-89	Ornskoldsviks IF	Sweden-3	14	7	6	13	....	....	....	....	....	....	....	....	....	....	....	....	....	....	....	....	....	....	....
1989-90	MoDo Jr.	Swe-Jr.	33	43	35	78	20	....	....	....	....	....	....	....	....	....	....	....	....	....	....	....	....	....	....
1990-91	MoDo	Sweden	32	10	9	19	14	....	....	....	....	....	....	....	....	....	....	....	....	....	....	....	....	....	....
1991-92	MoDo	Sweden	39	22	18	40	54	....	....	....	....	....	....	....	....	....	....	....	....	....	....	....	....	....	....
1992-93	MoDo Jr.	Swe-Jr.	2	4	1	5	2	....	....	....	....	....	....	....	....	....	....	....	....	....	....	....	....	....	....
	MoDo	Sweden	39	22	17	39	67	....	....	....	....	....	....	....	....	....	3	3	2	5	0	....	....	....	....
1993-94	**Pittsburgh**	**NHL**	**71**	**4**	**7**	**11**	**27**	**1**	**0**	**0**	**80**	**5.0**	**–3**	....	....	....	....	....	....	....	....	....	....	....	....
	Cleveland	IHL	5	1	6	7	4	....	....	....	....	....	....	....	....	....	....	....	....	....	....	....	....	....	....
1994-95	**Pittsburgh**	**NHL**	**14**	**2**	**2**	**4**	**2**	**0**	**0**	**0**	**13**	**15.4**	**0**	....	....	....	....	....	....	....	....	....	....	....	....
	Cleveland	IHL	7	3	4	7	6	....	....	....	....	....	....	....	....	....	4	1	3	4	8	....	....	....	....
1995-96	**Pittsburgh**	**NHL**	**66**	**19**	**33**	**52**	**36**	**3**	**0**	**4**	**125**	**15.2**	**17**	....	....	....	....	....	....	....	....	....	....	....	....
	Vancouver	**NHL**	**10**	**3**	**0**	**3**	**6**	**1**	**0**	**1**	**19**	**15.8**	**3**	....	....	....	**6**	**1**	**2**	**3**	**8**	**1**	**0**	**0**	....
1996-97	**Vancouver**	**NHL**	**78**	**21**	**20**	**41**	**30**	**4**	**0**	**4**	**120**	**17.5**	**–15**	....	....	....	....	....	....	....	....	....	....	....	....

			Regular Season														Playoffs								
Season	Club	League	GP	G	A	Pts	PIM	PP	SH	GW	S	%	+/-	TF	F%	Min	GP	G	A	Pts	PIM	PP	SH	GW	Min
1997-98	Vancouver	NHL	76	14	20	34	56	2	1	0	106	13.2	5	....	....	....	....	....	....	....	....	....	....	....	....
1998-99	Vancouver	NHL	80	36	30	66	74	15	2	3	205	17.6	–13	14	57.1	19:57	....	....	....	....	....	....	....	....	....
99-2000	Vancouver	NHL	82	27	38	65	64	6	2	3	271	10.0	–5	13	46.2	20:13	....	....	....	....	....	....	....	....	....
2000-01	Vancouver	NHL	72	41	34	75	58	18	1	5	277	14.8	–2	6	50.0	19:03	....	....	....	....	....	....	....	....	....
2001-02	Vancouver	NHL	81	40	50	90	50	8	0	6	302	13.2	22	5	20.0	19:31	6	1	1	2	2	0	0	0	18:54
	Sweden	Olympics	4	2	1	3	0	....	....	....	....	....	....	....	....	....	....	....	....	....	....	....	....	....	....
2002-03	Vancouver	NHL	82	48	56	104	52	24	0	12	294	16.3	6	6	33.3	19:54	14	5	9	14	18	2	0	1	18:14
2003-04	Vancouver	NHL	78	35	49	84	58	5	0	6	296	11.8	24	14	35.7	19:23	7	2	7	9	2	2	0	0	19:21
2004-05	MODO	Sweden	13	8	9	17	8	....	....	....	....	....	....	....	....	....	6	0	1	1	10	....	....	....	....
	NHL Totals		790	290	339	629	513	87	6	44	2108	13.8		58	43.1	19:41	33	9	19	28	30	5	0	1	18:40

NHL First All-Star Team (2002, 2003, 2004) • Lester B. Pearson Award (2003)
Played in NHL All-Star Game (1999, 2001, 2002, 2003, 2004)
Traded to **Vancouver** by **Pittsburgh** for Alek Stojanov, March 20, 1996. Signed as a free agent by **MODO** (Sweden), December 20, 2004.

NASREDDINE, Alain

(NAS-ruh-deen, AL-eh) **PIT.**

Defense. Shoots left. 6'1", 201 lbs. Born, Montreal, Que., July 10, 1975. Florida's 8th choice, 135th overall, in 1993 Entry Draft.

Season	Club	League	GP	G	A	Pts	PIM	PP	SH	GW	S	%	+/-	TF	F%	Min	GP	G	A	Pts	PIM	PP	SH	GW	Min
1990-91	Mtl-Bourassa	QAAA	35	10	25	35	50	....	....	....	....	....	....	....	....	....	....	....	....	....	....	....	....	....	....
1991-92	Drummondville	QMJHL	61	1	9	10	78	....	....	....	....	....	....	....	....	....	4	0	0	0	17	....	....	....	....
1992-93	Drummondville	QMJHL	64	0	14	14	137	....	....	....	....	....	....	....	....	....	10	0	1	1	36	....	....	....	....
1993-94	Chicoutimi	QMJHL	60	3	24	27	218	....	....	....	....	....	....	....	....	....	26	2	10	12	118	....	....	....	....
1994-95	Chicoutimi	QMJHL	67	8	31	39	342	....	....	....	....	....	....	....	....	....	13	3	5	8	40	....	....	....	....
1995-96	Carolina Panthers	AHL	63	0	5	5	245	....	....	....	....	....	....	....	....	....	....	....	....	....	....	....	....	....	....
1996-97	Carolina	AHL	26	0	4	4	109	....	....	....	....	....	....	....	....	....	....	....	....	....	....	....	....	....	....
	Indianapolis Ice	IHL	49	0	2	2	248	....	....	....	....	....	....	....	....	....	4	1	1	2	27	....	....	....	....
1997-98	Indianapolis Ice	IHL	75	1	12	13	258	....	....	....	....	....	....	....	....	....	5	0	2	2	12	....	....	....	....
1998-99	Chicago	NHL	7	0	0	0	19	0	0	0	2	0.0	–2	0	0.0	12:11	....	....	....	....	....	....	....	....	....
	Portland Pirates	AHL	7	0	1	1	36	....	....	....	....	....	....	....	....	....	....	....	....	....	....	....	....	....	....
	Montreal	NHL	8	0	0	0	33	0	0	0	1	0.0	1	0	0.0	8:12	....	....	....	....	....	....	....	....	....
	Fredericton	AHL	38	0	10	10	108	....	....	....	....	....	....	....	....	....	15	0	3	3	39	....	....	....	....
99-2000	Quebec Citadelles	AHL	59	1	6	7	178	....	....	....	....	....	....	....	....	....	....	....	....	....	....	....	....	....	....
	Hamilton	AHL	11	0	0	0	12	....	....	....	....	....	....	....	....	....	10	1	1	2	14	....	....	....	....
2000-01	Hamilton	AHL	74	4	14	18	164	....	....	....	....	....	....	....	....	....	....	....	....	....	....	....	....	....	....
2001-02	Hamilton	AHL	79	7	10	17	154	....	....	....	....	....	....	....	....	....	12	1	3	4	22	....	....	....	....
2002-03	NY Islanders	NHL	3	0	0	0	2	0	0	0	0	0.0	0	0	0.0	12:11	....	....	....	....	....	....	....	....	....
	Bridgeport	AHL	67	3	9	12	114	....	....	....	....	....	....	....	....	....	9	0	0	0	27	....	....	....	....
2003-04	Bridgeport	AHL	53	1	6	7	70	....	....	....	....	....	....	....	....	....	....	....	....	....	....	....	....	....	....
	Wilkes-Barre	AHL	17	1	1	2	16	....	....	....	....	....	....	....	....	....	24	1	0	1	48	....	....	....	....
2004-05	Wilkes-Barre	AHL	75	3	15	18	129	....	....	....	....	....	....	....	....	....	11	0	1	1	18	....	....	....	....
	NHL Totals		18	0	0	0	54	0	0	0	3	0.0		0	0.0	10:25	....	....	....	....	....	....	....	....	....

QMJHL Second All-Star Team (1995)
Traded to **Chicago** by **Florida** for Ivan Droppa, December 18, 1996. Traded to **Montreal** by **Chicago** with Jeff Hackett, Eric Weinrich and Tampa Bay's 4th round choice (previously acquired, Montreal selected Chris Dyment) in 1999 Entry Draft for Jocelyn Thibault, Dave Manson and Brad Brown, November 16, 1998. Traded to **Edmonton** by **Montreal** with Igor Ulanov for Christian Laflamme and Matthieu Descoteaux, March 9, 2000. Signed as a free agent by **NY Islanders**, September 6, 2002. Traded to **Pittsburgh** by **NY Islanders** for Steve Webb, March 8, 2004.

NAZAROV, Andrei

(nah-ZAH-rohv, AWN-dray) **MIN.**

Left wing. Shoots right. 6'5", 242 lbs. Born, Chelyabinsk, USSR, May 22, 1974. San Jose's 2nd choice, 10th overall, in 1992 Entry Draft.

Season	Club	League	GP	G	A	Pts	PIM	PP	SH	GW	S	%	+/-	TF	F%	Min	GP	G	A	Pts	PIM	PP	SH	GW	Min
1991-92	Dynamo Moscow	CIS	2	1	0	1	2	....	....	....	....	....	....	....	....	....	....	....	....	....	....	....	....	....	....
1992-93	Dynamo Moscow	CIS	42	8	2	10	79	....	....	....	....	....	....	....	....	....	10	1	1	2	8	....	....	....	....
1993-94	Dynamo Moscow	CIS	6	2	2	4	0	....	....	....	....	....	....	....	....	....	....	....	....	....	....	....	....	....	....
	San Jose	NHL	1	0	0	0	0	0	0	0	0	0.0	0	....	....	....	....	....	....	....	....	....	....	....	....
	Kansas City	IHL	71	15	18	33	64	....	....	....	....	....	....	....	....	....	....	....	....	....	....	....	....	....	....
1994-95	Kansas City	IHL	43	15	10	25	55	....	....	....	....	....	....	....	....	....	....	....	....	....	....	....	....	....	....
	San Jose	NHL	26	3	5	8	94	0	0	0	19	15.8	–1	....	....	....	6	0	0	0	9	0	0	0	....
1995-96	San Jose	NHL	42	7	7	14	62	2	0	1	55	12.7	–15	....	....	....	....	....	....	....	....	....	....	....	....
	Kansas City	IHL	27	4	6	10	118	....	....	....	....	....	....	....	....	....	2	0	0	0	2	....	....	....	....
1996-97	San Jose	NHL	60	12	15	27	222	1	0	1	116	10.3	–4	....	....	....	....	....	....	....	....	....	....	....	....
	Kentucky	AHL	3	1	2	3	4	....	....	....	....	....	....	....	....	....	....	....	....	....	....	....	....	....	....
1997-98	San Jose	NHL	40	1	1	2	112	0	0	0	31	3.2	–4	....	....	....	....	....	....	....	....	....	....	....	....
	Tampa Bay	NHL	14	1	1	2	58	0	0	0	19	5.3	–9	....	....	....	....	....	....	....	....	....	....	....	....
1998-99	Tampa Bay	NHL	26	2	0	2	43	0	0	0	18	11.1	–5	4	50.0	8:13	....	....	....	....	....	....	....	....	....
	Calgary	NHL	36	5	9	14	30	0	0	2	53	9.4	1	0	0.0	14:31	....	....	....	....	....	....	....	....	....
99-2000	Calgary	NHL	76	10	22	32	78	1	0	1	110	9.1	3	2	100.0	11:44	....	....	....	....	....	....	....	....	....
2000-01	Anaheim	NHL	16	1	0	1	29	0	0	0	13	7.7	–9	2	50.0	8:42	....	....	....	....	....	....	....	....	....
	Boston	NHL	63	1	4	5	200	0	0	0	50	2.0	–14	14	21.4	8:12	....	....	....	....	....	....	....	....	....
2001-02	Boston	NHL	47	0	2	2	164	0	0	0	18	0.0	–2	1	100.0	3:10	....	....	....	....	....	....	....	....	....
	Phoenix	NHL	30	6	3	9	51	0	0	0	38	15.8	7	1	100.0	7:35	3	0	0	0	2	0	0	0	9:34
2002-03	Phoenix	NHL	59	3	0	3	135	2	0	0	35	8.6	–9	6	33.3	6:34	....	....	....	....	....	....	....	....	....
2003-04	Phoenix	NHL	33	1	2	3	125	0	0	0	17	5.9	–7	0	0.0	5:28	....	....	....	....	....	....	....	....	....
2004-05	Novokuznetsk	Russia	9	0	0	0	*20	....	....	....	....	....	....	....	....	....	....	....	....	....	....	....	....	....	....
	Avangard Omsk	Russia	23	0	2	2	*153	....	....	....	....	....	....	....	....	....	7	0	0	0	6	....	....	....	....
	NHL Totals		569	53	71	124	1403	6	0	5	592	9.0		30	40.0	8:22	9	0	0	0	11	0	0	0	9:34

Traded to **Tampa Bay** by **San Jose** with Florida's 1st round choice (previously acquired, Tampa Bay selected Vincent Lecavalier) in 1998 Entry Draft for Bryan Marchment, David Shaw and Tampa Bay's 1st round choice (later traded to Nashville – Nashville selected David Legwand) in 1998 Entry Draft, March 24, 1998. Traded to **Calgary** by **Tampa Bay** for Michael Nylander, January 19, 1999. Traded to **Anaheim** by **Calgary** with Calgary's 2nd round choice (later traded to Phoenix – later traded back to Calgary – Calgary selected Andrei Taratukhin) in 2001 Entry Draft for Jordan Leopold, September 26, 2000. Traded to **Boston** by **Anaheim** with Patrick Traverse for Samuel Pahlsson, November 18, 2000. Traded to **Phoenix** by **Boston** for Phoenix's 5th round choice (Peter Hamerlik) in 2002 Entry Draft, January 25, 2002. • Spent majority of 2003-04 season as a healthy reserve. Signed as a free agent by **Novokuznetsk** (Russia), September 25, 2004. Signed as a free agent by **Omsk** (Russia), November, 2004. Signed as a free agent by **Minnesota**, August 1, 2005.

NECKAR, Stan

(NEHTS-kahzh, STAN)

Defense. Shoots left. 6'1", 214 lbs. Born, Ceske Budejovice, Czech., December 22, 1975. Ottawa's 2nd choice, 29th overall, in 1994 Entry Draft.

Season	Club	League	GP	G	A	Pts	PIM	PP	SH	GW	S	%	+/-	TF	F%	Min	GP	G	A	Pts	PIM	PP	SH	GW	Min
1991-92	C. Budejovice Jr.	Czech-Jr.	18	1	3	4	....	....	....	....	....	....	....	....	....	....	....	....	....	....	....	....	....	....	....
1992-93	C. Budejovice	Czech	42	2	9	11	12	....	....	....	....	....	....	....	....	....	....	....	....	....	....	....	....	....	....
1993-94	C. Budejovice	CzRep	12	3	2	5	2	....	....	....	....	....	....	....	....	....	3	0	0	0	....	....	....	....	....
1994-95	Detroit Vipers	IHL	15	2	2	4	15	....	....	....	....	....	....	....	....	....	....	....	....	....	....	....	....	....	....
	Ottawa	NHL	48	1	3	4	37	0	0	0	34	2.9	–20	....	....	....	....	....	....	....	....	....	....	....	....
1995-96	Ottawa	NHL	82	3	9	12	54	1	0	0	57	5.3	–16	....	....	....	....	....	....	....	....	....	....	....	....
1996-97	Ottawa	NHL	5	0	0	0	2	0	0	0	3	0.0	2	....	....	....	....	....	....	....	....	....	....	....	....
1997-98	Ottawa	NHL	60	2	2	4	31	0	0	0	43	4.7	–14	....	....	....	9	0	0	0	2	0	0	0	....
1998-99	Ottawa	NHL	3	0	2	2	0	0	0	0	2	0.0	–1	0	0.0	15:53	....	....	....	....	....	....	....	....	....
	NY Rangers	NHL	18	0	0	0	8	0	0	0	8	0.0	–1	0	0.0	13:46	....	....	....	....	....	....	....	....	....
	Phoenix	NHL	11	0	1	1	10	0	0	0	6	0.0	3	0	0.0	15:08	6	0	1	1	4	0	0	0	10:20
99-2000	Phoenix	NHL	66	2	8	10	36	0	0	0	34	5.9	1	0	0.0	14:27	5	0	0	0	0	0	0	0	11:28
2000-01	Phoenix	NHL	53	2	2	4	63	0	0	1	16	12.5	–2	0	0.0	15:26	....	....	....	....	....	....	....	....	....
	Tampa Bay	NHL	16	0	2	2	8	0	0	0	10	0.0	–1	0	0.0	18:33	....	....	....	....	....	....	....	....	....
2001-02	Tampa Bay	NHL	77	1	7	8	24	0	1	0	38	2.6	–18	0	0.0	20:31	....	....	....	....	....	....	....	....	....
2002-03	Tampa Bay	NHL	70	1	4	5	43	0	0	1	38	2.6	–6	0	0.0	18:42	7	0	2	2	2	0	0	0	18:35
2003-04	Nashville	NHL	1	0	1	1	0	0	0	0	0	0.0	2	0	0.0	14:59	....	....	....	....	....	....	....	....	....
	Milwaukee	AHL	3	0	3	3	2	....	....	....	....	....	....	....	....	....	....	....	....	....	....	....	....	....	....
	Tampa Bay	NHL	....	....	....	....	....	....	....	....	....	....	....	....	....	....	2	0	0	0	0	0	0	0	13:48
2004-05	C. Budejovice	CzRep-2	16	2	6	8	8	....	....	....	....	....	....	....	....	....	16	0	1	1	18	....	....	....	....
	NHL Totals		510	12	41	53	316	1	1	2	289	4.2		0	0.0	17:15	29	0	3	3	8	0	0	0	13:51

Traded to **NY Rangers** by **Ottawa** for Bill Berg and NY Rangers' 2nd round choice (later traded to Anaheim – Anaheim selected Jordan Leopold) in 1999 Entry Draft, November 27, 1998. Traded to **Phoenix** by **NY Rangers** for Jason Doig and Phoenix's 6th round choice (Jay Dardis) in 1999 Entry Draft, March 23, 1999. Traded to **Tampa Bay** by **Phoenix** with Nikolai Khabibulin for Mike Johnson, Paul Mara, Ruslan Zainullin and NY Islanders' 2nd round choice (previously acquired, Phoenix selected Matthew Spiller) in 2001 Entry Draft, March 5, 2001. Signed as a free agent by **Nashville**, November 26, 2003. • Missed majority of 2003-04 season recovering from groin injury suffered in practice, November 29, 2003. Traded to **Tampa Bay** by **Nashville** for Tampa Bay's 6th round choice (Kevin Schaeffer) in 2004 Entry Draft, March 9, 2004. Signed as a free agent by **Budejovice** (CzRep-2), December 16, 2004.

			Regular Season														Playoffs								
Season	Club	League	GP	G	A	Pts	PIM	PP	SH	GW	S	%	+/-	TF	F%	Min	GP	G	A	Pts	PIM	PP	SH	GW	Min

NEDOROST, Andrej

(NEHD-ohr-ohst, AWN-dray) **CBJ**

Left wing. Shoots left. 6'1", 198 lbs. Born, Trencin, Czech., April 30, 1980. Columbus' 10th choice, 286th overall, in 2000 Entry Draft.

Season	Club	League	GP	G	A	Pts	PIM	PP	SH	GW	S	%	+/-	TF	F%	Min	GP	G	A	Pts	PIM	PP	SH	GW	Min
1995-96	Dukla Trencin Jr.	Slovak-Jr.	40	50	35	85	....	....	....	....	....	....	....	....	....	....	....	....	....	....	....	....	....	....	....
1996-97	Dukla Trencin Jr.	Slovak-Jr.	45	15	16	31	....	....	....	....	....	....	....	....	....	....	....	....	....	....	....	....	....	....	....
1997-98	Dukla Trencin Jr.	Slovak-Jr.	45	27	22	49	61	....	....	....	....	....	....	....	....	....	....	....	....	....	....	....	....	....	....
	Dukla Trencin	Slovakia	1	0	0	0	0	....	....	....	....	....	....	....	....	....	....	....	....	....	....	....	....	....	....
1998-99	Essen Jr.	Ger-Jr.	17	37	18	55	43	....	....	....	....	....	....	....	....	....	....	....	....	....	....	....	....	....	....
	Essen	German-2	30	3	5	8	22	....	....	....	....	....	....	....	....	....	....	....	....	....	....	....	....	....	....
99-2000	Essen	Germany	66	7	5	12	44	....	....	....	....	....	....	....	....	....	....	....	....	....	....	....	....	....	....
2000-01	Plzen	CzRep	33	10	8	18	22	....	....	....	....	....	....	....	....	....	....	....	....	....	....	....	....	....	....
2001-02	**Columbus**	**NHL**	**7**	**0**	**2**	**2**	**2**	**0**	**0**	**0**	**12**	**0.0**	**–3**	**1**	**100.0**	**12:56**	....	....	....	....	....	....	....	....	....
	Syracuse Crunch	AHL	37	5	13	18	28	....	....	....	....	....	....	....	....	....	10	1	3	4	4	....	....	....	....
2002-03	**Columbus**	**NHL**	**12**	**0**	**1**	**1**	**4**	**0**	**0**	**0**	**10**	**0.0**	**–6**	**30**	**36.7**	**9:15**	....	....	....	....	....	....	....	....	....
	Syracuse Crunch	AHL	63	14	19	33	85	....	....	....	....	....	....	....	....	....	....	....	....	....	....	....	....	....	....
2003-04	**Columbus**	**NHL**	**9**	**2**	**0**	**2**	**6**	**0**	**0**	**0**	**16**	**12.5**	**0**	**13**	**69.2**	**13:02**	....	....	....	....	....	....	....	....	....
	Syracuse Crunch	AHL	8	0	2	2	6	....	....	....	....	....	....	....	....	....	....	....	....	....	....	....	....	....	....
	Magnitogorsk	Russia	16	3	4	7	12	....	....	....	....	....	....	....	....	....	7	0	3	3	4	....	....	....	....
2004-05	Magnitogorsk	Russia	12	1	0	1	4	....	....	....	....	....	....	....	....	....	....	....	....	....	....	....	....	....	....
	Nizhnekamsk	Russia	7	0	0	0	4	....	....	....	....	....	....	....	....	....	....	....	....	....	....	....	....	....	....
	Karlovy Vary	CzRep	20	6	5	11	16	....	....	....	....	....	....	....	....	....	....	....	....	....	....	....	....	....	....
	NHL Totals		**28**	**2**	**3**	**5**	**12**	**0**	**0**	**0**	**38**	**5.3**		**44**	**47.7**	**11:23**	....	....	....	....	....	....	....	....	....

Assigned to **Magnitogorsk** (Russia) by **Columbus**, December 17, 2003. Signed as a free agent by **Karlovy Vary** (CzRep), January 22, 2005.

NEDOROST, Vaclav

(neh-DOHR-uhst, VAT-slav) **FLA.**

Center. Shoots left. 6'1", 190 lbs. Born, Budejovice, Czech., March 16, 1982. Colorado's 1st choice, 14th overall, in 2000 Entry Draft.

Season	Club	League	GP	G	A	Pts	PIM	PP	SH	GW	S	%	+/-	TF	F%	Min	GP	G	A	Pts	PIM	PP	SH	GW	Min
1997-98	C. Budejovice Jr.	CzRep-Jr.	43	30	23	53	20	....	....	....	....	....	....	....	....	....	....	....	....	....	....	....	....	....	....
1998-99	C. Budejovice Jr.	CzRep-Jr.	39	6	15	21	20	....	....	....	....	....	....	....	....	....	....	....	....	....	....	....	....	....	....
	C. Budejovice	CzRep	7	0	2	2	0	....	....	....	....	....	....	....	....	....	....	....	....	....	....	....	....	....	....
99-2000	C. Budejovice Jr.	CzRep-Jr.	14	4	7	11	4	....	....	....	....	....	....	....	....	....	....	....	....	....	....	....	....	....	....
	C. Budejovice	CzRep	38	8	6	14	6	....	....	....	....	....	....	....	....	....	3	0	0	0	0	....	....	....	....
2000-01	C. Budejovice	CzRep	36	3	12	15	14	....	....	....	....	....	....	....	....	....	....	....	....	....	....	....	....	....	....
2001-02	**Colorado**	**NHL**	**25**	**2**	**2**	**4**	**2**	**1**	**0**	**0**	**22**	**9.1**	**–4**	**62**	**45.2**	**10:15**	....	....	....	....	....	....	....	....	....
	Hershey Bears	AHL	49	12	22	34	16	....	....	....	....	....	....	....	....	....	7	2	3	5	2	....	....	....	....
2002-03	**Colorado**	**NHL**	**42**	**4**	**5**	**9**	**20**	**1**	**0**	**0**	**35**	**11.4**	**8**	**151**	**44.4**	**10:29**	....	....	....	....	....	....	....	....	....
	Hershey Bears	AHL	5	3	2	5	0	....	....	....	....	....	....	....	....	....	5	2	2	4	0	....	....	....	....
2003-04	**Florida**	**NHL**	**32**	**4**	**3**	**7**	**12**	**2**	**0**	**0**	**38**	**10.5**	**–6**	**121**	**42.2**	**11:32**	....	....	....	....	....	....	....	....	....
	San Antonio	AHL	21	9	6	15	2	....	....	....	....	....	....	....	....	....	....	....	....	....	....	....	....	....	....
2004-05	Liberec	CzRep	48	15	18	33	20	....	....	....	....	....	....	....	....	....	6	0	1	1	12	....	....	....	....
	NHL Totals		**99**	**10**	**10**	**20**	**34**	**4**	**0**	**0**	**95**	**10.5**		**334**	**43.7**	**10:46**	....	....	....	....	....	....	....	....	....

Traded to **Florida** by **Colorado** with Eric Messier for Peter Worrell and Florida's 2nd round choice (later traded to NY Rangers – later traded back to Florida – Florida selected David Shantz) in 2004 Entry Draft, July 18, 2003. Signed as a free agent by **Liberec** (CzRep), September 4, 2004. Signed as a free agent by **Budejovice** (CzRep), April 28, 2005.

NEDVED, Petr

(NEHD-VEHD, PEE-tuhr) **PHX.**

Center. Shoots left. 6'3", 196 lbs. Born, Liberec, Czech., December 9, 1971. Vancouver's 1st choice, 2nd overall, in 1990 Entry Draft.

Season	Club	League	GP	G	A	Pts	PIM	PP	SH	GW	S	%	+/-	TF	F%	Min	GP	G	A	Pts	PIM	PP	SH	GW	Min
1988-89	CHZ Litvinov Jr.	Czech-Jr.	20	32	19	51	12	....	....	....	....	....	....	....	....	....	....	....	....	....	....	....	....	....	....
1989-90	Seattle	WHL	71	65	80	145	80	....	....	....	....	....	....	....	....	....	11	4	9	13	2	....	....	....	....
1990-91	**Vancouver**	**NHL**	**61**	**10**	**6**	**16**	**20**	**1**	**0**	**0**	**97**	**10.3**	**–21**	....	....	....	**6**	**0**	**1**	**1**	**0**	**0**	**0**	**0**	....
1991-92	**Vancouver**	**NHL**	**77**	**15**	**22**	**37**	**36**	**5**	**0**	**1**	**99**	**15.2**	**–3**	....	....	....	**10**	**1**	**4**	**5**	**16**	**0**	**0**	**0**	....
1992-93	**Vancouver**	**NHL**	**84**	**38**	**33**	**71**	**96**	**2**	**1**	**3**	**149**	**25.5**	**20**	....	....	....	**12**	**2**	**3**	**5**	**2**	**0**	**0**	**0**	....
1993-94	Canada	Nat-Tm	17	19	12	31	16	....	....	....	....	....	....	....	....	....	....	....	....	....	....	....	....	....	....
	Canada	Olympics	8	5	1	6	6	....	....	....	....	....	....	....	....	....	....	....	....	....	....	....	....	....	....
	St. Louis	**NHL**	**19**	**6**	**14**	**20**	**8**	**2**	**0**	**0**	**63**	**9.5**	**2**	....	....	....	**4**	**0**	**1**	**1**	**4**	**0**	**0**	**0**	....
1994-95	**NY Rangers**	**NHL**	**46**	**11**	**12**	**23**	**26**	**1**	**0**	**3**	**123**	**8.9**	**–1**	....	....	....	**10**	**3**	**2**	**5**	**6**	**2**	**0**	**0**	....
1995-96	**Pittsburgh**	**NHL**	**80**	**45**	**54**	**99**	**68**	**8**	**1**	**5**	**204**	**22.1**	**37**	....	....	....	**18**	**10**	**10**	**20**	**16**	**4**	**0**	**2**	....
1996-97	**Pittsburgh**	**NHL**	**74**	**33**	**38**	**71**	**66**	**12**	**3**	**4**	**189**	**17.5**	**–2**	....	....	....	**5**	**1**	**2**	**3**	**12**	**0**	**1**	**0**	....
1997-98	Stadion Liberec	CzRep-2	2	0	3	3	....	....	....	....	....	....	....	....	....	....	....	....	....	....	....	....	....	....	....
	TJ Novy Jicin	CzRep-3	7	9	16	25	....	....	....	....	....	....	....	....	....	....	....	....	....	....	....	....	....	....	....
	HC Sparta Praha	CzRep	5	2	3	5	8	....	....	....	....	....	....	....	....	....	6	0	2	2	52	....	....	....	....
	Las Vegas	IHL	3	3	3	6	4	....	....	....	....	....	....	....	....	....	....	....	....	....	....	....	....	....	....
1998-99	Las Vegas	IHL	13	8	10	18	32	....	....	....	....	....	....	....	....	....	....	....	....	....	....	....	....	....	....
	NY Rangers	**NHL**	**56**	**20**	**27**	**47**	**50**	**9**	**1**	**3**	**153**	**13.1**	**–6**	**1069**	**52.5**	**20:31**	....	....	....	....	....	....	....	....	....
99-2000	**NY Rangers**	**NHL**	**76**	**24**	**44**	**68**	**40**	**6**	**2**	**4**	**201**	**11.9**	**2**	**1354**	**54.0**	**19:54**	....	....	....	....	....	....	....	....	....
2000-01	**NY Rangers**	**NHL**	**79**	**32**	**46**	**78**	**54**	**9**	**1**	**5**	**230**	**13.9**	**10**	**1349**	**49.7**	**20:16**	....	....	....	....	....	....	....	....	....
2001-02	Liberec	CzRep-2	1	3	0	3	2	....	....	....	....	....	....	....	....	....	....	....	....	....	....	....	....	....	....
	NY Rangers	**NHL**	**78**	**21**	**25**	**46**	**36**	**6**	**1**	**3**	**175**	**12.0**	**–8**	**1402**	**52.1**	**19:22**	....	....	....	....	....	....	....	....	....
2002-03	**NY Rangers**	**NHL**	**78**	**27**	**31**	**58**	**64**	**8**	**3**	**4**	**205**	**13.2**	**–4**	**1142**	**53.0**	**20:21**	....	....	....	....	....	....	....	....	....
2003-04	**NY Rangers**	**NHL**	**65**	**14**	**17**	**31**	**42**	**5**	**0**	**3**	**153**	**9.2**	**–9**	**929**	**48.6**	**18:51**	....	....	....	....	....	....	....	....	....
	Edmonton	**NHL**	**16**	**5**	**10**	**15**	**4**	**2**	**0**	**0**	**37**	**13.5**	**1**	**226**	**46.9**	**18:11**	....	....	....	....	....	....	....	....	....
2004-05	HC Sparta Praha	CzRep	46	22	13	35	44	....	....	....	....	....	....	....	....	....	5	2	3	5	10	....	....	....	....
	NHL Totals		**889**	**301**	**379**	**680**	**610**	**76**	**13**	**38**	**2078**	**14.5**		**7471**	**51.6**	**19:49**	**65**	**17**	**23**	**40**	**56**	**6**	**1**	**2**	....

WHL Rookie of the Year (1990) • Canadian Major Junior Rookie of the Year (1990)

Signed as a free agent by **St. Louis**, March 5, 1994. Traded to **NY Rangers** by **St. Louis** for Esa Tikkanen and Doug Lidster, July 24, 1994. Traded to **Pittsburgh** by **NY Rangers** with Sergei Zubov for Luc Robitaille and Ulf Samuelsson, August 31, 1995. Traded to **NY Rangers** by **Pittsburgh** with Chris Tamer and Sean Pronger for Alex Kovalev and Harry York, November 25, 1998. Traded to **Edmonton** by **NY Rangers** with Jussi Markkanen for Stephen Valiquette, Dwight Helminen, Edmonton's 2nd round compensatory choice (Dane Byers) in 2004 Entry Draft and future considerations, March 3, 2004. Signed as a free agent by **Phoenix**, August 26, 2004. Signed as a free agent by **Sparta** (CzRep), September 17, 2004.

NEIL, Chris

(NEEL, KRIHS) **OTT.**

Right wing. Shoots right. 6', 213 lbs. Born, Markdale, Ont., June 18, 1979. Ottawa's 7th choice, 161st overall, in 1998 Entry Draft.

Season	Club	League	GP	G	A	Pts	PIM	PP	SH	GW	S	%	+/-	TF	F%	Min	GP	G	A	Pts	PIM	PP	SH	GW	Min
1995-96	Orangeville	OHA-B	43	15	15	30	50	....	....	....	....	....	....	....	....	....	....	....	....	....	....	....	....	....	....
1996-97	North Bay	OHL	65	13	16	29	150	....	....	....	....	....	....	....	....	....	....	....	....	....	....	....	....	....	....
1997-98	North Bay	OHL	59	26	29	55	231	....	....	....	....	....	....	....	....	....	....	....	....	....	....	....	....	....	....
1998-99	North Bay	OHL	66	26	46	72	215	....	....	....	....	....	....	....	....	....	4	1	0	1	15	....	....	....	....
99-2000	Mobile Mysticks	ECHL	4	0	2	2	39	....	....	....	....	....	....	....	....	....	....	....	....	....	....	....	....	....	....
	Grand Rapids	IHL	51	9	10	19	301	....	....	....	....	....	....	....	....	....	8	0	2	2	24	....	....	....	....
2000-01	Grand Rapids	IHL	78	15	21	36	354	....	....	....	....	....	....	....	....	....	10	2	2	4	22	....	....	....	....
2001-02	**Ottawa**	**NHL**	**72**	**10**	**7**	**17**	**231**	**1**	**0**	**0**	**56**	**17.9**	**5**	**0**	**0.0**	**8:22**	**12**	**0**	**0**	**0**	**12**	**0**	**0**	**0**	**7:12**
2002-03	**Ottawa**	**NHL**	**68**	**6**	**4**	**10**	**147**	**0**	**0**	**0**	**62**	**9.7**	**8**	**5**	**60.0**	**7:40**	**15**	**1**	**0**	**1**	**24**	**0**	**0**	**0**	**7:57**
2003-04	**Ottawa**	**NHL**	**82**	**8**	**8**	**16**	**194**	**0**	**0**	**1**	**76**	**10.5**	**13**	**14**	**42.9**	**8:51**	**7**	**0**	**1**	**1**	**19**	**0**	**0**	**0**	**6:45**
2004-05	Binghamton	AHL	22	4	6	10	132	....	....	....	....	....	....	....	....	....	6	1	1	2	26	....	....	....	....
	NHL Totals		**222**	**24**	**19**	**43**	**572**	**1**	**0**	**1**	**194**	**12.4**		**19**	**47.4**	**8:20**	**34**	**1**	**1**	**2**	**55**	**0**	**0**	**0**	**7:27**

Signed as a free agent by **Binghamton** (AHL), March 2, 2005.

NEMECEK, Jan

(NEHM-eh-chehk, YAHN) **L.A.**

Defense. Shoots Left. 6'1", 220 lbs. Born, Pisek, Czech., February 14, 1976. Los Angeles' 7th choice, 215th overall, in 1994 Entry Draft.

Season	Club	League	GP	G	A	Pts	PIM	PP	SH	GW	S	%	+/-	TF	F%	Min	GP	G	A	Pts	PIM	PP	SH	GW	Min
1992-93	C. Budejovice	Czech	15	0	0	0	....	....	....	....	....	....	....	....	....	....	....	....	....	....	....	....	....	....	....
1993-94	C. Budejovice	CzRep	16	0	1	1	16	....	....	....	....	....	....	....	....	....	....	....	....	....	....	....	....	....	....
1994-95	Hull Olympiques	QMJHL	49	10	16	26	48	....	....	....	....	....	....	....	....	....	21	5	9	14	10	....	....	....	....
1995-96	Hull Olympiques	QMJHL	57	17	49	66	58	....	....	....	....	....	....	....	....	....	17	2	13	15	10	....	....	....	....
1996-97	Mississippi	ECHL	20	3	9	12	16	....	....	....	....	....	....	....	....	....	3	0	0	0	4	....	....	....	....
	Phoenix	IHL	24	1	1	2	2	....	....	....	....	....	....	....	....	....	....	....	....	....	....	....	....	....	....
1997-98	Fredericton	AHL	65	7	24	31	43	....	....	....	....	....	....	....	....	....	2	0	0	0	0	....	....	....	....
1998-99	**Los Angeles**	**NHL**	**6**	**1**	**0**	**1**	**4**	**0**	**0**	**1**	**8**	**12.5**	**–1**	**0**	**0.0**	**16:42**	....	....	....	....	....	....	....	....	....
	Long Beach	IHL	66	5	16	21	42	....	....	....	....	....	....	....	....	....	....	....	....	....	....	....	....	....	....
99-2000	**Los Angeles**	**NHL**	**1**	**0**	**0**	**0**	**0**	**0**	**0**	**0**	**0**	**0.0**	**0**	**0**	**0.0**	**9:36**	....	....	....	....	....	....	....	....	....
	Long Beach	IHL	71	9	15	24	22	....	....	....	....	....	....	....	....	....	6	1	0	1	4	....	....	....	....

			Regular Season														Playoffs								
Season	**Club**	**League**	**GP**	**G**	**A**	**Pts**	**PIM**	**PP**	**SH**	**GW**	**S**	**%**	**+/-**	**TF**	**F%**	**Min**	**GP**	**G**	**A**	**Pts**	**PIM**	**PP**	**SH**	**GW**	**Min**
2000-01	Nurnberg	Germany	60	5	16	21	18	....	....	....	....	....	....	....	....	....	4	1	0	1	0	....	....	....	....
2001-02	Nurnberg	Germany	60	6	18	24	18	....	....	....	....	....	....	....	....	....	4	0	3	3	2	....	....	....	....
2002-03	Karlovy Vary	CzRep	30	1	9	10	16	....	....	....	....	....	....	....	....	....	....	....	....	....	....	....	....	....	....
	KLH Chomutov	CzRep-2	2	0	0	0	0	....	....	....	....	....	....	....	....	....	....	....	....	....	....	....	....	....	....
2003-04	Timra IK	Sweden	50	4	8	12	18	....	....	....	....	....	....	....	....	....	9	0	1	1	2	....	....	....	....
2004-05	Leksands IF	Sweden-2	46	4	13	17	18	....	....	....	....	....	....	....	....	....	....	....	....	....	....	....	....	....	....
	NHL Totals		**7**	**1**	**0**	**1**	**4**	**0**	**0**	**1**	**8**	**12.5**		**0**	**0.0**	**15:41**	....	....	....	....	....	....	....	....	....

QMJHL Second All-Star Team (1996)

NICHOL, Scott (NIH-KOHL, SKAWT) NSH.

Center. Shoots right. 5'8", 173 lbs. Born, Edmonton, Alta., December 31, 1974. Buffalo's 9th choice, 272nd overall, in 1993 Entry Draft.

1991-92	Cgy. AAA Flames	AMHL	23	26	16	42	132	....	....	....	....	....	....	....	....	....	....	....	....	....	....	....	....	....	....
1992-93	Portland	WHL	67	31	33	64	146	....	....	....	....	....	....	....	....	....	16	8	8	16	41	....	....	....	....
1993-94	Portland	WHL	65	40	53	93	144	....	....	....	....	....	....	....	....	....	10	3	8	11	16	....	....	....	....
1994-95	Rochester	AHL	71	11	16	27	136	....	....	....	....	....	....	....	....	....	5	0	3	3	14	....	....	....	....
1995-96	**Buffalo**	**NHL**	**2**	**0**	**0**	**0**	**10**	**0**	**0**	**0**	**4**	**0.0**	**0**	....	....	....	....	....	....	....	....	....	....	....	....
	Rochester	AHL	62	14	18	32	170	....	....	....	....	....	....	....	....	....	19	7	6	13	36	....	....	....	....
1996-97	Rochester	AHL	68	22	21	43	133	....	....	....	....	....	....	....	....	....	10	2	1	3	26	....	....	....	....
1997-98	**Buffalo**	**NHL**	**3**	**0**	**0**	**0**	**4**	**0**	**0**	**0**	**5**	**0.0**	**0**	....	....	....	....	....	....	....	....	....	....	....	....
	Rochester	AHL	35	13	7	20	113	....	....	....	....	....	....	....	....	....	....	....	....	....	....	....	....	....	....
1998-99	Rochester	AHL	52	13	20	33	120	....	....	....	....	....	....	....	....	....	....	....	....	....	....	....	....	....	....
99-2000	Rochester	AHL	37	7	11	18	141	....	....	....	....	....	....	....	....	....	....	....	....	....	....	....	....	....	....
2000-01	Detroit Vipers	IHL	67	7	24	31	198	....	....	....	....	....	....	....	....	....	....	....	....	....	....	....	....	....	....
2001-02	**Calgary**	**NHL**	**60**	**8**	**9**	**17**	**107**	**2**	**1**	**0**	**49**	**16.3**	**–9**	**458**	**53.1**	**12:41**	....	....	....	....	....	....	....	....	....
2002-03	**Calgary**	**NHL**	**68**	**5**	**5**	**10**	**149**	**0**	**1**	**0**	**66**	**7.6**	**–7**	**357**	**58.3**	**10:47**	....	....	....	....	....	....	....	....	....
2003-04	**Chicago**	**NHL**	**75**	**7**	**11**	**18**	**145**	**0**	**0**	**1**	**112**	**6.3**	**–16**	**1178**	**57.4**	**15:46**	....	....	....	....	....	....	....	....	....
2004-05	London Racers	Britain	10	1	7	8	70	....	....	....	....	....	....	....	....	....	....	....	....	....	....	....	....	....	....
	NHL Totals		**208**	**20**	**25**	**45**	**415**	**2**	**2**	**1**	**236**	**8.5**		**1993**	**56.5**	**13:11**	....	....	....	....	....	....	....	....	....

• Missed majority of 1999-2000 season recovering from knee injury suffered in game vs. Saint John (AHL), February 16, 2000. Signed as a free agent by **Calgary**, July 1, 2001. Signed as a free agent by **Chicago**, July 1, 2003. Signed as a free agent by **London** (Britain), October 26, 2004. Signed as a free agent by **Nashville**, August 6, 2005.

NICKULAS, Eric (NICK-luhs, AIR-ihk) BOS.

Right wing. Shoots right. 5'11", 206 lbs. Born, Hyannis, MA, March 25, 1975. Boston's 3rd choice, 99th overall, in 1994 Entry Draft.

1991-92	Barnstable	High-MA	24	30	25	55	....	....	....	....	....	....	....	....	....	....	....	....	....	....	....	....	....	....	....
1992-93	Tabor	High-MA	28	25	25	50	....	....	....	....	....	....	....	....	....	....	....	....	....	....	....	....	....	....	....
1993-94	Cushing	High-MA	25	46	36	82	....	....	....	....	....	....	....	....	....	....	....	....	....	....	....	....	....	....	....
1994-95	New Hampshire	H-East	33	15	9	24	32	....	....	....	....	....	....	....	....	....	....	....	....	....	....	....	....	....	....
1995-96	New Hampshire	H-East	34	26	12	38	66	....	....	....	....	....	....	....	....	....	....	....	....	....	....	....	....	....	....
1996-97	New Hampshire	H-East	39	29	22	51	80	....	....	....	....	....	....	....	....	....	....	....	....	....	....	....	....	....	....
1997-98	Orlando	IHL	76	22	9	31	77	....	....	....	....	....	....	....	....	....	6	0	0	0	10	....	....	....	....
1998-99	**Boston**	**NHL**	**2**	**0**	**0**	**0**	**0**	**0**	**0**	**0**	**0**	**0.0**	**0**	**0**	**0.0**	**3:27**	**1**	**0**	**0**	**0**	**2**	**0**	**0**	**0**	**4:35**
	Providence Bruins	AHL	75	31	27	58	83	....	....	....	....	....	....	....	....	....	18	8	12	20	33	....	....	....	....
99-2000	**Boston**	**NHL**	**20**	**5**	**6**	**11**	**12**	**1**	**0**	**0**	**28**	**17.9**	**–1**	**4**	**50.0**	**11:13**	....	....	....	....	....	....	....	....	....
	Providence Bruins	AHL	40	6	6	12	37	....	....	....	....	....	....	....	....	....	12	2	3	5	20	....	....	....	....
2000-01	**Boston**	**NHL**	**7**	**0**	**0**	**0**	**4**	**0**	**0**	**0**	**6**	**0.0**	**–2**	**1**	**100.0**	**7:07**	....	....	....	....	....	....	....	....	....
	Providence Bruins	AHL	62	20	23	43	100	....	....	....	....	....	....	....	....	....	12	4	4	8	24	....	....	....	....
2001-02	Worcester IceCats	AHL	54	11	25	36	48	....	....	....	....	....	....	....	....	....	3	0	1	1	2	....	....	....	....
2002-03	**St. Louis**	**NHL**	**8**	**0**	**1**	**1**	**6**	**0**	**0**	**0**	**3**	**0.0**	**–2**	**0**	**0.0**	**9:31**	....	....	....	....	....	....	....	....	....
	Worcester IceCats	AHL	39	17	16	33	40	....	....	....	....	....	....	....	....	....	3	0	0	0	2	....	....	....	....
2003-04	**St. Louis**	**NHL**	**44**	**7**	**11**	**18**	**44**	**1**	**0**	**1**	**80**	**8.8**	**–2**	**10**	**30.0**	**12:50**	....	....	....	....	....	....	....	....	....
	Chicago	**NHL**	**21**	**1**	**1**	**2**	**8**	**0**	**0**	**0**	**41**	**2.4**	**–6**	**11**	**45.5**	**13:46**	....	....	....	....	....	....	....	....	....
2004-05	Norfolk Admirals	AHL	53	11	11	22	32	....	....	....	....	....	....	....	....	....	6	0	3	3	8	....	....	....	....
	NHL Totals		**102**	**13**	**19**	**32**	**74**	**2**	**0**	**1**	**158**	**8.2**		**26**	**42.3**	**11:52**	**1**	**0**	**0**	**0**	**2**	**0**	**0**	**0**	**4:35**

Ken McKenzie Trophy (U.S.- Born Rookie of the Year – IHL) (1998)

Signed as a free agent by **Worcester** (AHL), November 10, 2001. Signed as a free agent by **St. Louis**, July 16, 2002. Claimed on waivers by **Chicago** from **St. Louis**, February 24, 2004. Signed as a free agent by **Boston**, August 23, 2005.

NIEDERMAYER, Rob (NEE-duhr-MIGH-uhr, RAWB) ANA.

Center. Shoots left. 6'2", 204 lbs. Born, Cassiar, B.C., December 28, 1974. Florida's 1st choice, 5th overall, in 1993 Entry Draft.

1989-90	Cranbrook Blazers	BCAHA	35	42	40	82	30	....	....	....	....	....	....	....	....	....	....	....	....	....	....	....	....	....	....
1990-91	Medicine Hat	WHL	71	24	26	50	8	....	....	....	....	....	....	....	....	....	12	3	7	10	2	....	....	....	....
1991-92	Medicine Hat	WHL	71	32	46	78	77	....	....	....	....	....	....	....	....	....	4	2	3	5	2	....	....	....	....
1992-93	Medicine Hat	WHL	52	43	34	77	67	....	....	....	....	....	....	....	....	....	....	....	....	....	....	....	....	....	....
1993-94	**Florida**	**NHL**	**65**	**9**	**17**	**26**	**51**	**3**	**0**	**2**	**67**	**13.4**	**–11**	....	....	....	....	....	....	....	....	....	....	....	....
1994-95	Medicine Hat	WHL	13	9	15	24	14	....	....	....	....	....	....	....	....	....	....	....	....	....	....	....	....	....	....
	Florida	**NHL**	**48**	**4**	**6**	**10**	**36**	**1**	**0**	**0**	**58**	**6.9**	**–13**	....	....	....	....	....	....	....	....	....	....	....	....
1995-96	**Florida**	**NHL**	**82**	**26**	**35**	**61**	**107**	**11**	**0**	**6**	**155**	**16.8**	**1**	....	....	....	**22**	**5**	**3**	**8**	**12**	**2**	**0**	**2**	....
1996-97	**Florida**	**NHL**	**60**	**14**	**24**	**38**	**54**	**3**	**0**	**2**	**136**	**10.3**	**4**	....	....	....	**5**	**2**	**1**	**3**	**6**	**1**	**0**	**0**	....
1997-98	**Florida**	**NHL**	**33**	**8**	**7**	**15**	**41**	**5**	**0**	**2**	**64**	**12.5**	**–9**	....	....	....	....	....	....	....	....	....	....	....	....
1998-99	**Florida**	**NHL**	**82**	**18**	**33**	**51**	**50**	**6**	**1**	**3**	**142**	**12.7**	**–13**	**1895**	**47.1**	**21:17**	....	....	....	....	....	....	....	....	....
99-2000	**Florida**	**NHL**	**81**	**10**	**23**	**33**	**46**	**1**	**0**	**4**	**135**	**7.4**	**–5**	**1632**	**47.9**	**19:04**	**4**	**1**	**0**	**1**	**6**	**0**	**0**	**0**	**15:55**
2000-01	**Florida**	**NHL**	**67**	**12**	**20**	**32**	**50**	**3**	**1**	**0**	**115**	**10.4**	**–12**	**997**	**45.0**	**20:30**	....	....	....	....	....	....	....	....	....
2001-02	**Calgary**	**NHL**	**57**	**6**	**14**	**20**	**49**	**1**	**2**	**1**	**87**	**6.9**	**–15**	**777**	**48.4**	**18:01**	....	....	....	....	....	....	....	....	....
2002-03	**Calgary**	**NHL**	**54**	**8**	**10**	**18**	**42**	**2**	**0**	**1**	**104**	**7.7**	**–13**	**139**	**48.9**	**17:29**	....	....	....	....	....	....	....	....	....
	Anaheim	**NHL**	**12**	**2**	**2**	**4**	**15**	**1**	**0**	**0**	**21**	**9.5**	**3**	**14**	**42.9**	**15:21**	**21**	**3**	**7**	**10**	**18**	**0**	**2**	**0**	**23:35**
2003-04	**Anaheim**	**NHL**	**55**	**12**	**16**	**28**	**34**	**6**	**0**	**2**	**111**	**10.8**	**–6**	**45**	**64.4**	**19:28**	....	....	....	....	....	....	....	....	....
2004-05	Ferencvaros	Hungary	5	2	1	3	14	....	....	....	....	....	....	....	....	....	....	....	....	....	....	....	....	....	....
	NHL Totals		**696**	**129**	**207**	**336**	**575**	**43**	**4**	**23**	**1195**	**10.8**		**5499**	**47.3**	**19:20**	**52**	**11**	**11**	**22**	**42**	**3**	**2**	**2**	**22:21**

WHL East First All-Star Team (1993)

• Missed majority of 1997-98 season recovering from thumb (November 26, 1997 vs. Boston) and head (March 19, 1998 vs. Buffalo) injuries. Traded to **Calgary** by **Florida** with Philadelphia's 2nd round choice (previously acquired, Calgary selected Andrei Medvedev) in 2001 Entry Draft for Valeri Bure and Jason Wiemer, June 23, 2001. Traded to **Anaheim** by **Calgary** for Mike Commodore and Jean-Francois Damphousse, March 11, 2003. Signed as a free agent by **Ferencvaros** (Hungary), January 17, 2005.

NIEDERMAYER, Scott (NEE-duhr-MIGH-uhr, SKAWT) ANA.

Defense. Shoots left. 6'1", 200 lbs. Born, Edmonton, Alta., August 31, 1973. New Jersey's 1st choice, 3rd overall, in 1991 Entry Draft.

1988-89	Cranbrook Blazers	BCAHA	62	55	37	92	100	....	....	....	....	....	....	....	....	....	....	....	....	....	....	....	....	....	....
1989-90	Kamloops Blazers	WHL	64	14	55	69	64	....	....	....	....	....	....	....	....	....	17	2	14	16	35	....	....	....	....
1990-91	Kamloops Blazers	WHL	57	26	56	82	52	....	....	....	....	....	....	....	....	....	....	....	....	....	....	....	....	....	....
1991-92	Kamloops Blazers	WHL	35	7	32	39	61	....	....	....	....	....	....	....	....	....	17	9	14	23	28	....	....	....	....
	New Jersey	**NHL**	**4**	**0**	**1**	**1**	**2**	**0**	**0**	**0**	**4**	**0.0**	**1**	....	....	....	....	....	....	....	....	....	....	....	....
1992-93	**New Jersey**	**NHL**	**80**	**11**	**29**	**40**	**47**	**5**	**0**	**0**	**131**	**8.4**	**8**	....	....	....	**5**	**0**	**3**	**3**	**2**	**0**	**0**	**0**	....
1993-94	**New Jersey**	**NHL**	**81**	**10**	**36**	**46**	**42**	**5**	**0**	**2**	**135**	**7.4**	**34**	....	....	....	**20**	**2**	**2**	**4**	**8**	**1**	**0**	**0**	....
1994-95♦	**New Jersey**	**NHL**	**48**	**4**	**15**	**19**	**18**	**4**	**0**	**0**	**52**	**7.7**	**19**	....	....	....	**20**	**4**	**7**	**11**	**10**	**2**	**0**	**1**	....
1995-96	**New Jersey**	**NHL**	**79**	**8**	**25**	**33**	**46**	**6**	**0**	**0**	**179**	**4.5**	**5**	....	....	....	....	....	....	....	....	....	....	....	....
1996-97	**New Jersey**	**NHL**	**81**	**5**	**30**	**35**	**64**	**3**	**0**	**3**	**159**	**3.1**	**–4**	....	....	....	**10**	**2**	**4**	**6**	**6**	**2**	**0**	**1**	....
1997-98	**New Jersey**	**NHL**	**81**	**14**	**43**	**57**	**27**	**11**	**0**	**1**	**175**	**8.0**	**5**	....	....	....	**6**	**0**	**2**	**2**	**4**	**0**	**0**	**0**	....
1998-99	Utah Grizzlies	IHL	5	0	2	2	0	....	....	....	....	....	....	....	....	....	....	....	....	....	....	....	....	....	....
	New Jersey	**NHL**	**72**	**11**	**35**	**46**	**26**	**1**	**1**	**3**	**161**	**6.8**	**16**	**13**	**15.4**	**24:40**	**7**	**1**	**3**	**4**	**18**	**1**	**0**	**0**	**25:30**
99-2000♦	**New Jersey**	**NHL**	**71**	**7**	**31**	**38**	**48**	**1**	**0**	**0**	**109**	**6.4**	**19**	**8**	**37.5**	**24:21**	**22**	**5**	**2**	**7**	**10**	**0**	**2**	**1**	**25:28**
2000-01	**New Jersey**	**NHL**	**57**	**6**	**29**	**35**	**22**	**1**	**0**	**5**	**87**	**6.9**	**14**	**5**	**0.0**	**23:19**	**21**	**0**	**6**	**6**	**14**	**0**	**0**	**0**	**23:53**
2001-02	**New Jersey**	**NHL**	**76**	**11**	**22**	**33**	**30**	**2**	**0**	**6**	**129**	**8.5**	**12**	**1**	**100.0**	**24:17**	**6**	**0**	**2**	**2**	**6**	**0**	**0**	**0**	**26:37**
	Canada	Olympics	6	1	1	2	4	....	....	....	....	....	....	....	....	....	....	....	....	....	....	....	....	....	....
2002-03♦	**New Jersey**	**NHL**	**81**	**11**	**28**	**39**	**62**	**3**	**0**	**3**	**164**	**6.7**	**23**	**1**	**0.0**	**24:30**	**24**	**2**	***16**	***18**	**16**	**1**	**0**	**0**	**26:07**
2003-04	**New Jersey**	**NHL**	**81**	**14**	**40**	**54**	**44**	**9**	**0**	**3**	**165**	**8.5**	**20**	**1**	**0.0**	**25:56**	**5**	**1**	**0**	**1**	**6**	**0**	**0**	**0**	**27:21**

Season	Club	League	GP	G	A	Pts	PIM	PP	SH	GW	S	%	+/-	TF	F%	Min	GP	G	A	Pts	PIM	PP	SH	GW	Min
			Regular Season														Playoffs								
2004-05			DID NOT PLAY																						
	NHL Totals		892	112	364	476	478	51	1	26	1650	6.8		29	20.7	24:35	146	17	47	64	100	7	2	3	25:27

WHL West First All-Star Team (1991, 1992) • Canadian Major Junior Scholastic Player of the Year (1991) • Memorial Cup Tournament All-Star Team (1992) • Stafford Smythe Memorial Trophy (Memorial Cup Tournament MVP) (1992) • NHL All-Rookie Team (1993) • NHL Second All-Star Team (1998) • NHL First All-Star Team (2004) • James Norris Trophy (2004)

Played in NHL All-Star Game (1998, 2001, 2004)

Signed to tryout (PTO) contract by **Utah** (IHL) with **New Jersey** retaining NHL rights, October 19, 1998. Signed as a free agent by **Anaheim**, August 3, 2005.

NIELSEN, Chris

(NEEL-sehn, KRIHS)

Right wing. Shoots right. 6'2", 204 lbs. Born, Moshi, Tanzania, February 16, 1980. NY Islanders' 2nd choice, 36th overall, in 1998 Entry Draft.

Season	Club	League	GP	G	A	Pts	PIM	PP	SH	GW	S	%	+/-	TF	F%	Min	GP	G	A	Pts	PIM	PP	SH	GW	Min
1995-96	S-W Cougars	MMMHL	39	37	35	72	59	....	....	....	....	....	....	....	....	....	....	....	....	....	....	....	....	....	....
	Calgary Hitmen	WHL	6	0	0	0	0	....	....	....	....	....	....	....	....	....	....	....	....	....	....	....	....	....	....
1996-97	Calgary Hitmen	WHL	62	11	19	30	39	....	....	....	....	....	....	....	....	....	....	....	....	....	....	....	....	....	....
1997-98	Calgary Hitmen	WHL	68	22	29	51	31	....	....	....	....	....	....	....	....	....	18	2	4	6	10	....	....	....	....
1998-99	Calgary Hitmen	WHL	70	22	24	46	45	....	....	....	....	....	....	....	....	....	21	11	5	16	28	....	....	....	....
99-2000	Calgary Hitmen	WHL	62	38	31	69	86	....	....	....	....	....	....	....	....	....	13	14	9	23	20	....	....	....	....
2000-01	**Columbus**	**NHL**	**29**	**4**	**5**	**9**	**4**	**0**	**0**	**1**	**36**	**11.1**	**4**	**18**	**55.6**	**10:30**	....	....	....	....	....	....	....	....	....
	Syracuse Crunch	AHL	47	10	11	21	24	....	....	....	....	....	....	....	....	....	5	2	2	4	4	....	....	....	....
2001-02	**Columbus**	**NHL**	**23**	**2**	**3**	**5**	**4**	**0**	**0**	**1**	**28**	**7.1**	**–3**	**6**	**33.3**	**10:47**	....	....	....	....	....	....	....	....	....
	Syracuse Crunch	AHL	47	12	12	24	18	....	....	....	....	....	....	....	....	....	10	2	2	4	2	....	....	....	....
2002-03	Syracuse Crunch	AHL	19	1	3	4	8	....	....	....	....	....	....	....	....	....	....	....	....	....	....	....	....	....	....
	Chicago Wolves	AHL	18	3	4	7	4	....	....	....	....	....	....	....	....	....	....	....	....	....	....	....	....	....	....
	Manitoba Moose	AHL	33	3	10	13	13	....	....	....	....	....	....	....	....	....	14	1	2	3	16	....	....	....	....
2003-04	Manitoba Moose	AHL	72	4	7	11	21	....	....	....	....	....	....	....	....	....	....	....	....	....	....	....	....	....	....
2004-05	San Antonio	AHL	54	8	8	16	20	....	....	....	....	....	....	....	....	....	....	....	....	....	....	....	....	....	....
	Laredo Bucks	CHL	7	0	4	4	4	....	....	....	....	....	....	....	....	....	....	....	....	....	....	....	....	....	....
	NHL Totals		**52**	**6**	**8**	**14**	**8**	**0**	**0**	**2**	**64**	**9.4**		**24**	**50.0**	**10:38**									

Traded to **Columbus** by **NY Islanders** for Columbus' 4th (later traded to Anaheim – Anaheim selected Jonas Ronnqvist) and 9th (Dmitri Altarev) round choices in 2000 Entry Draft, May 11, 2000. Traded to **Atlanta** by **Columbus** with Petteri Nummelin for Tomi Kallio and Pauli Levokari, December 2, 2002. Traded to **Vancouver** by **Atlanta** with Chris Herperger for Jeff Farkas, January 20, 2003. Signed as a free agent by **San Antonio** (AHL), October 21, 2004.

NIEMINEN, Ville

(nee-EHM-ih-nehn, VIHL-ee) **NYR**

Left wing. Shoots left. 6', 200 lbs. Born, Tampere, Finland, April 6, 1977. Colorado's 4th choice, 78th overall, in 1997 Entry Draft.

Season	Club	League	GP	G	A	Pts	PIM	PP	SH	GW	S	%	+/-	TF	F%	Min	GP	G	A	Pts	PIM	PP	SH	GW	Min
1994-95	Tappara Jr.	Finland-Jr.	16	11	21	32	47	....	....	....	....	....	....	....	....	....	....	....	....	....	....	....	....	....	....
	Tappara Tampere	Finland	16	0	0	0	0	....	....	....	....	....	....	....	....	....	....	....	....	....	....	....	....	....	....
1995-96	Tappara Jr.	Finland-Jr.	20	20	23	43	63	....	....	....	....	....	....	....	....	....	....	....	....	....	....	....	....	....	....
	KooKoo Kouvola	Finland-2	7	2	1	3	4	....	....	....	....	....	....	....	....	....	....	....	....	....	....	....	....	....	....
	Tappara Tampere	Finland	4	0	1	1	8	....	....	....	....	....	....	....	....	....	....	....	....	....	....	....	....	....	....
1996-97	Tappara Tampere	Finland	49	10	13	23	120	....	....	....	....	....	....	....	....	....	3	1	0	1	8	....	....	....	....
1997-98	Hershey Bears	AHL	74	14	22	36	85	....	....	....	....	....	....	....	....	....	....	....	....	....	....	....	....	....	....
1998-99	Hershey Bears	AHL	67	24	19	43	127	....	....	....	....	....	....	....	....	....	3	0	1	1	0	....	....	....	....
99-2000	**Colorado**	**NHL**	**1**	**0**	**0**	**0**	**0**	**0**	**0**	**0**	**2**	**0.0**	**0**	**0**	**0.0**	**10:12**	....	....	....	....	....	....	....	....	....
	Hershey Bears	AHL	74	21	30	51	54	....	....	....	....	....	....	....	....	....	9	2	4	6	6	....	....	....	....
2000-01♦	**Colorado**	**NHL**	**50**	**14**	**8**	**22**	**38**	**2**	**0**	**3**	**68**	**20.6**	**8**	**3**	**33.3**	**12:26**	**23**	**4**	**6**	**10**	**20**	**3**	**0**	**1**	**14:10**
	Hershey Bears	AHL	28	10	11	21	48	....	....	....	....	....	....	....	....	....	....	....	....	....	....	....	....	....	....
2001-02	**Colorado**	**NHL**	**53**	**10**	**14**	**24**	**30**	**1**	**0**	**5**	**72**	**13.9**	**1**	**8**	**62.5**	**12:41**	....	....	....	....	....	....	....	....	....
	Finland	Olympics	4	0	1	1	2	....	....	....	....	....	....	....	....	....	....	....	....	....	....	....	....	....	....
	Pittsburgh	**NHL**	**13**	**1**	**2**	**3**	**8**	**0**	**0**	**0**	**11**	**9.1**	**–2**	**0**	**0.0**	**16:10**	....	....	....	....	....	....	....	....	....
2002-03	**Pittsburgh**	**NHL**	**75**	**9**	**12**	**21**	**93**	**0**	**2**	**1**	**86**	**10.5**	**–25**	**46**	**52.2**	**14:08**	....	....	....	....	....	....	....	....	....
2003-04	**Chicago**	**NHL**	**60**	**2**	**11**	**13**	**40**	**1**	**0**	**0**	**56**	**3.6**	**–15**	**4**	**25.0**	**11:46**	....	....	....	....	....	....	....	....	....
	Calgary	**NHL**	**19**	**3**	**5**	**8**	**18**	**0**	**0**	**1**	**27**	**11.1**	**6**	**5**	**0.0**	**14:36**	**24**	**4**	**4**	**8**	**55**	**1**	**0**	**0**	**16:17**
2004-05	Tappara Tampere	Finland	26	14	13	27	32	....	....	....	....	....	....	....	....	....	8	2	4	6	12	....	....	....	....
	NHL Totals		**271**	**39**	**52**	**91**	**227**	**4**	**2**	**10**	**322**	**12.1**		**66**	**47.0**	**13:08**	**47**	**8**	**10**	**18**	**75**	**4**	**0**	**1**	**15:15**

Traded to **Pittsburgh** by **Colorado** with Rick Berry for Darius Kasparaitis, March 19, 2002. Signed as a free agent by **Chicago**, July 29, 2003. Traded to **Calgary** by **Chicago** for Jason Morgan and Calgary's 6th round choice (Joseph Fallon) in 2005 Entry Draft, February 24, 2004. Signed as a free agent by **Tappara** (Finland), July 22, 2004. Signed as a free agent by **NY Rangers**, August 4, 2005.

NIEUWENDYK, Joe

(NOO-ihn-DIGHK, JOH) **FLA.**

Center. Shoots left. 6'2", 205 lbs. Born, Oshawa, Ont., September 10, 1966. Calgary's 2nd choice, 27th overall, in 1985 Entry Draft.

Season	Club	League	GP	G	A	Pts	PIM	PP	SH	GW	S	%	+/-	TF	F%	Min	GP	G	A	Pts	PIM	PP	SH	GW	Min
1983-84	Pickering Panthers	OHA-B	38	30	28	58	35	....	....	....	....	....	....	....	....	....	....	....	....	....	....	....	....	....	....
1984-85	Cornell Big Red	ECAC	29	21	24	45	30	....	....	....	....	....	....	....	....	....	....	....	....	....	....	....	....	....	....
1985-86	Cornell Big Red	ECAC	29	26	28	54	67	....	....	....	....	....	....	....	....	....	....	....	....	....	....	....	....	....	....
1986-87	Cornell Big Red	ECAC	23	26	26	52	26	....	....	....	....	....	....	....	....	....	....	....	....	....	....	....	....	....	....
	Calgary	**NHL**	**9**	**5**	**1**	**6**	**0**	**2**	**0**	**1**	**16**	**31.3**	**0**	....	....	....	**6**	**2**	**2**	**4**	**0**	**0**	**0**	**0**	....
1987-88	**Calgary**	**NHL**	**75**	**51**	**41**	**92**	**23**	**31**	**3**	**8**	**212**	**24.1**	**20**	....	....	....	**8**	**3**	**4**	**7**	**2**	**1**	**0**	**0**	....
1988-89♦	**Calgary**	**NHL**	**77**	**51**	**31**	**82**	**40**	**19**	**3**	**11**	**215**	**23.7**	**26**	....	....	....	**22**	**10**	**4**	**14**	**10**	**6**	**0**	**1**	....
1989-90	**Calgary**	**NHL**	**79**	**45**	**50**	**95**	**40**	**18**	**0**	**3**	**226**	**19.9**	**32**	....	....	....	**6**	**4**	**6**	**10**	**4**	**1**	**0**	**0**	....
1990-91	**Calgary**	**NHL**	**79**	**45**	**40**	**85**	**36**	**22**	**4**	**1**	**222**	**20.3**	**19**	....	....	....	**7**	**4**	**1**	**5**	**10**	**2**	**0**	**0**	....
1991-92	**Calgary**	**NHL**	**69**	**22**	**34**	**56**	**55**	**7**	**0**	**2**	**137**	**16.1**	**–1**	....	....	....	....	....	....	....	....	....	....	....	....
1992-93	**Calgary**	**NHL**	**79**	**38**	**37**	**75**	**52**	**14**	**0**	**6**	**208**	**18.3**	**9**	....	....	....	**6**	**3**	**6**	**9**	**10**	**1**	**0**	**0**	....
1993-94	**Calgary**	**NHL**	**64**	**36**	**39**	**75**	**51**	**14**	**1**	**7**	**191**	**18.8**	**19**	....	....	....	**6**	**2**	**2**	**4**	**0**	**1**	**0**	**0**	....
1994-95	**Calgary**	**NHL**	**46**	**21**	**29**	**50**	**33**	**3**	**0**	**4**	**122**	**17.2**	**11**	....	....	....	**5**	**4**	**3**	**7**	**0**	**2**	**0**	**1**	....
1995-96	**Dallas**	**NHL**	**52**	**14**	**18**	**32**	**41**	**8**	**0**	**3**	**138**	**10.1**	**–17**	....	....	....	....	....	....	....	....	....	....	....	....
1996-97	**Dallas**	**NHL**	**66**	**30**	**21**	**51**	**32**	**8**	**0**	**2**	**173**	**17.3**	**–5**	....	....	....	**7**	**2**	**2**	**4**	**6**	**0**	**0**	**0**	....
1997-98	**Dallas**	**NHL**	**73**	**39**	**30**	**69**	**30**	**14**	**0**	**11**	**203**	**19.2**	**16**	....	....	....	**1**	**1**	**0**	**1**	**0**	**0**	**0**	**0**	....
	Canada	Olympics	6	2	3	5	2	....	....	....	....	....	....	....	....	....	....	....	....	....	....	....	....	....	....
1998-99♦	**Dallas**	**NHL**	**67**	**28**	**27**	**55**	**34**	**8**	**0**	**8**	**157**	**17.8**	**11**	**1170**	**63.2**	**15:33**	**23**	***11**	**10**	**21**	**19**	**3**	**0**	**6**	**18:27**
99-2000	**Dallas**	**NHL**	**48**	**15**	**19**	**34**	**26**	**7**	**0**	**2**	**110**	**13.6**	**–1**	**924**	**59.1**	**16:15**	**23**	**7**	**3**	**10**	**18**	**3**	**0**	**2**	**16:41**
2000-01	**Dallas**	**NHL**	**69**	**29**	**23**	**52**	**30**	**12**	**0**	**4**	**166**	**17.5**	**5**	**1262**	**57.2**	**16:11**	**7**	**4**	**0**	**4**	**4**	**1**	**0**	**1**	**15:50**
2001-02	**Dallas**	**NHL**	**67**	**23**	**24**	**47**	**18**	**6**	**0**	**5**	**157**	**14.6**	**–2**	**1345**	**59.6**	**16:59**	....	....	....	....	....	....	....	....	....
	Canada	Olympics	6	1	1	2	0	....	....	....	....	....	....	....	....	....	....	....	....	....	....	....	....	....	....
	New Jersey	**NHL**	**14**	**2**	**9**	**11**	**4**	**0**	**0**	**1**	**32**	**6.3**	**2**	**275**	**55.3**	**16:22**	**5**	**0**	**1**	**1**	**0**	**0**	**0**	**0**	**19:22**
2002-03♦	**New Jersey**	**NHL**	**80**	**17**	**28**	**45**	**56**	**3**	**0**	**4**	**201**	**8.5**	**10**	**1383**	**58.5**	**16:45**	**17**	**3**	**6**	**9**	**4**	**1**	**0**	**0**	**15:03**
2003-04	**Toronto**	**NHL**	**64**	**22**	**28**	**50**	**26**	**10**	**1**	**5**	**131**	**16.8**	**7**	**970**	**60.4**	**15:38**	**9**	**6**	**0**	**6**	**4**	**1**	**0**	**2**	**15:24**
2004-05			DID NOT PLAY																						
	NHL Totals		**1177**	**533**	**529**	**1062**	**627**	**206**	**12**	**88**	**3017**	**17.7**		**7329**	**59.4**	**16:15**	**158**	**66**	**50**	**116**	**91**	**23**	**0**	**13**	**16:47**

ECAC Rookie of the Year (1985) • ECAC First All-Star Team (1986, 1987) • NCAA East First All-American Team (1986, 1987) • ECAC Player of the Year (1987) • Calder Memorial Trophy (1988) • NHL All-Rookie Team (1988) • Dodge Ram Tough Award (1988) • King Clancy Memorial Trophy (1995) • Conn Smythe Trophy (1999)

Played in NHL All-Star Game (1988, 1989, 1990, 1994)

Traded to **Dallas** by **Calgary** for Corey Millen and Jarome Iginla, December 19, 1995. Traded to **New Jersey** by **Dallas** with Jamie Langenbrunner for Jason Arnott, Randy McKay and New Jersey's 1st round choice (later traded to Columbus – later traded to Buffalo – Buffalo selected Dan Paille) in 2002 Entry Draft, March 19, 2002. Signed as a free agent by **Toronto**, September 9, 2003. Signed as a free agent by **Florida**, August 1, 2005.

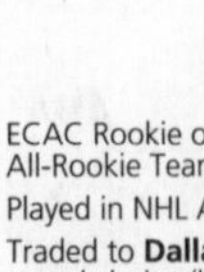

NIINIMAA, Janne

(nihn-EE-mah, YAH-nee) **NYI**

Defense. Shoots left. 6'1", 220 lbs. Born, Raahe, Finland, May 22, 1975. Philadelphia's 1st choice, 36th overall, in 1993 Entry Draft.

Season	Club	League	GP	G	A	Pts	PIM	PP	SH	GW	S	%	+/-	TF	F%	Min	GP	G	A	Pts	PIM	PP	SH	GW	Min
1990-91	Karpat Oulu Jr.	Finland-Jr.	3	1	0	1	2	....	....	....	....	....	....	....	....	....	....	....	....	....	....	....	....	....	....
1991-92	Karpat Oulu Jr.	Finland-Jr.	3	0	0	0	4	....	....	....	....	....	....	....	....	....	....	....	....	....	....	....	....	....	....
	Karpat Oulu	Finland-2	41	2	11	13	49	....	....	....	....	....	....	....	....	....	....	....	....	....	....	....	....	....	....
1992-93	Karpat Oulu Jr.	Finland-Jr.	10	3	9	12	16	....	....	....	....	....	....	....	....	....	....	....	....	....	....	....	....	....	....
	KKP Kiiminki	Finland-4	1	0	2	2	4	....	....	....	....	....	....	....	....	....	....	....	....	....	....	....	....	....	....
	Karpat Oulu	Finland-2	29	2	3	5	14	....	....	....	....	....	....	....	....	....	....	....	....	....	....	....	....	....	....
1993-94	Jokerit Helsinki Jr.	Finland-Jr.	10	2	6	8	41	....	....	....	....	....	....	....	....	....	....	....	....	....	....	....	....	....	....
	Jokerit Helsinki	Finland	45	3	8	11	24	....	....	....	....	....	....	....	....	....	12	1	1	2	4	....	....	....	....
1994-95	Jokerit Helsinki Jr.	Finland-Jr.	3	1	2	3	4	....	....	....	....	....	....	....	....	....	....	....	....	....	....	....	....	....	....
	Jokerit Helsinki	Finland	42	7	10	17	36	....	....	....	....	....	....	....	....	....	10	1	4	5	35	....	....	....	....
1995-96	Jokerit Helsinki	Finland	49	5	15	20	79	....	....	....	....	....	....	....	....	....	11	0	2	2	12	....	....	....	....
	Jokerit Helsinki Jr.	Finland-Jr.	....	....	....	....	....	....	....	....	....	....	....	....	....	....	2	3	4	7	6	....	....	....	....

			Regular Season														Playoffs								
Season	Club	League	GP	G	A	Pts	PIM	PP	SH	GW	S	%	+/-	TF	F%	Min	GP	G	A	Pts	PIM	PP	SH	GW	Min
1996-97	**Philadelphia**	**NHL**	**77**	**4**	**40**	**44**	**58**	**1**	**0**	**2**	**141**	**2.8**	**12**	....	....	....	**19**	**1**	**12**	**13**	**16**	**1**	**0**	**1**	....
1997-98	**Philadelphia**	**NHL**	**66**	**3**	**31**	**34**	**56**	**2**	**0**	**1**	**115**	**2.6**	**6**	....	....	....	....	....	....	....	....	....	....	....	....
	Edmonton	**NHL**	**11**	**1**	**8**	**9**	**6**	**1**	**0**	**0**	**19**	**5.3**	**7**	....	....	....	**11**	**1**	**1**	**2**	**12**	**0**	**0**	**1**	....
	Finland	Olympics	6	0	3	3	8	....	....	....	....	....	....	....	....	....	....	....	....	....	....	....	....	....	....
1998-99	**Edmonton**	**NHL**	**81**	**4**	**24**	**28**	**88**	**2**	**0**	**1**	**142**	**2.8**	**7**	**1**	**0.0**	**23:54**	**4**	**0**	**0**	**0**	**2**	**0**	**0**	**0**	**28:16**
99-2000	**Edmonton**	**NHL**	**81**	**8**	**25**	**33**	**89**	**2**	**2**	**0**	**133**	**6.0**	**14**	**0**	**0.0**	**24:28**	**5**	**0**	**2**	**2**	**2**	**0**	**0**	**0**	**21:39**
2000-01	**Edmonton**	**NHL**	**82**	**12**	**34**	**46**	**90**	**8**	**0**	**1**	**122**	**9.8**	**6**	**0**	**0.0**	**25:20**	**6**	**0**	**2**	**2**	**6**	**0**	**0**	**0**	**28:33**
2001-02	**Edmonton**	**NHL**	**81**	**5**	**39**	**44**	**80**	**1**	**0**	**2**	**119**	**4.2**	**13**	**0**	**0.0**	**26:02**	....	....	....	....	....	....	....	....	....
	Finland	Olympics	4	0	3	3	2	....	....	....	....	....	....	....	....	....	....	....	....	....	....	....	....	....	....
2002-03	**Edmonton**	**NHL**	**63**	**4**	**24**	**28**	**66**	**2**	**0**	**0**	**90**	**4.4**	**–7**	**1**	**0.0**	**26:48**	....	....	....	....	....	....	....	....	....
	NY Islanders	**NHL**	**13**	**1**	**5**	**6**	**14**	**1**	**0**	**0**	**11**	**9.1**	**–2**	**0**	**0.0**	**23:02**	**5**	**0**	**1**	**1**	**12**	**0**	**0**	**0**	**23:32**
2003-04	**NY Islanders**	**NHL**	**82**	**9**	**19**	**28**	**64**	**4**	**0**	**2**	**97**	**9.3**	**12**	**0**	**0.0**	**23:15**	**5**	**1**	**2**	**3**	**2**	**1**	**0**	**1**	**24:31**
2004-05	Karpat Oulu	Finland	26	3	10	13	30	....	....	....	....	....	....	....	....	....	12	0	5	5	8	....	....	....	....
	Malmo	Sweden	10	0	3	3	34	....	....	....	....	....	....	....	....	....	....	....	....	....	....	....	....	....	....
	NHL Totals		**637**	**51**	**249**	**300**	**611**	**24**	**2**	**9**	**989**	**5.2**		**2**	**0.0**	**24:50**	**55**	**3**	**20**	**23**	**52**	**2**	**0**	**3**	**25:19**

NHL All-Rookie Team (1997)

Played in NHL All-Star Game (2001)

Traded to **Edmonton** by **Philadelphia** for Dan McGillis and Edmonton's 2nd round choice (Jason Beckett) in 1998 Entry Draft, March 24, 1998. Traded to **NY Islanders** by **Edmonton** with Washington's 2nd round choice (previously acquired, NY Islanders selected Evgeni Tunik) in 2003 Entry Draft for Brad Isbister and Raffi Torres, March 11, 2003. Signed as a free agent by **Karpat** (Finland), October 6, 2004. Signed as a free agent by **Malmo** (Sweden), November 17, 2004. Signed as a free agent by **Karpat** (Finland), January 3, 2005.

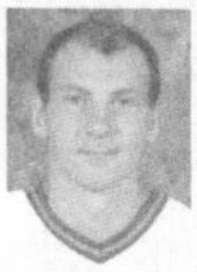

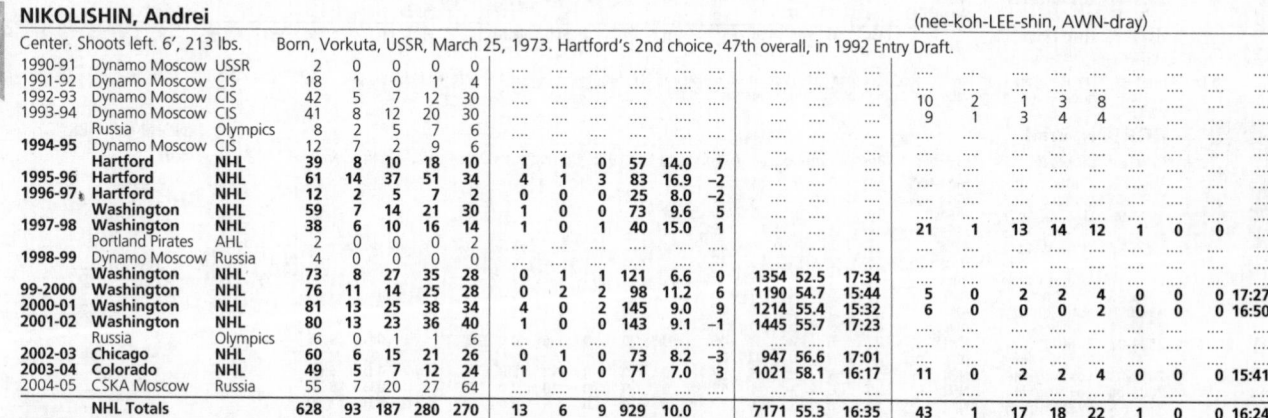

NIKOLISHIN, Andrei

(nee-koh-LEE-shin, AWN-dray)

Center. Shoots left. 6', 213 lbs. Born, Vorkuta, USSR, March 25, 1973. Hartford's 2nd choice, 47th overall, in 1992 Entry Draft.

Season	Club	League	GP	G	A	Pts	PIM	PP	SH	GW	S	%	+/-	TF	F%	Min	GP	G	A	Pts	PIM	PP	SH	GW	Min
1990-91	Dynamo Moscow	USSR	2	0	0	0	0	....	....	....	....	....	....	....	....	....	....	....	....	....	....	....	....	....	....
1991-92	Dynamo Moscow	CIS	18	1	0	1	4	....	....	....	....	....	....	....	....	....	....	....	....	....	....	....	....	....	....
1992-93	Dynamo Moscow	CIS	42	5	7	12	30	....	....	....	....	....	....	....	....	....	10	2	1	3	8	....	....	....	....
1993-94	Dynamo Moscow	CIS	41	8	12	20	30	....	....	....	....	....	....	....	....	....	9	1	3	4	4	....	....	....	....
	Russia	Olympics	8	2	5	7	6	....	....	....	....	....	....	....	....	....	....	....	....	....	....	....	....	....	....
1994-95	Dynamo Moscow	CIS	12	7	2	9	6	....	....	....	....	....	....	....	....	....	....	....	....	....	....	....	....	....	....
	Hartford	**NHL**	**39**	**8**	**10**	**18**	**10**	**1**	**1**	**0**	**57**	**14.0**	**7**	....	....	....	....	....	....	....	....	....	....	....	....
1995-96	**Hartford**	**NHL**	**61**	**14**	**37**	**51**	**34**	**4**	**1**	**3**	**83**	**16.9**	**–2**	....	....	....	....	....	....	....	....	....	....	....	....
1996-97	**Hartford**	**NHL**	**12**	**2**	**5**	**7**	**2**	**0**	**0**	**0**	**25**	**8.0**	**–2**	....	....	....	....	....	....	....	....	....	....	....	....
	Washington	**NHL**	**59**	**7**	**14**	**21**	**30**	**1**	**0**	**0**	**73**	**9.6**	**5**	....	....	....	....	....	....	....	....	....	....	....	....
1997-98	**Washington**	**NHL**	**38**	**6**	**10**	**16**	**14**	**1**	**0**	**1**	**40**	**15.0**	**1**	....	....	....	**21**	**1**	**13**	**14**	**12**	**1**	**0**	**0**	....
	Portland Pirates	AHL	2	0	0	0	2	....	....	....	....	....	....	....	....	....	....	....	....	....	....	....	....	....	....
1998-99	Dynamo Moscow	Russia	4	0	0	0	0	....	....	....	....	....	....	....	....	....	....	....	....	....	....	....	....	....	....
	Washington	**NHL**	**73**	**8**	**27**	**35**	**28**	**0**	**1**	**1**	**121**	**6.6**	**0**	**1354**	**52.5**	**17:34**	....	....	....	....	....	....	....	....	....
99-2000	**Washington**	**NHL**	**76**	**11**	**14**	**25**	**28**	**0**	**2**	**2**	**98**	**11.2**	**6**	**1190**	**54.7**	**15:44**	**5**	**0**	**2**	**2**	**4**	**0**	**0**	**0**	**17:27**
2000-01	**Washington**	**NHL**	**81**	**13**	**25**	**38**	**34**	**4**	**0**	**2**	**145**	**9.0**	**9**	**1214**	**55.4**	**15:32**	**6**	**0**	**0**	**0**	**2**	**0**	**0**	**0**	**16:50**
2001-02	**Washington**	**NHL**	**80**	**13**	**23**	**36**	**40**	**1**	**0**	**0**	**143**	**9.1**	**–1**	**1445**	**55.7**	**17:23**	....	....	....	....	....	....	....	....	....
	Russia	Olympics	6	0	1	1	6	....	....	....	....	....	....	....	....	....	....	....	....	....	....	....	....	....	....
2002-03	**Chicago**	**NHL**	**60**	**6**	**15**	**21**	**26**	**0**	**1**	**0**	**73**	**8.2**	**–3**	**947**	**56.6**	**17:01**	....	....	....	....	....	....	....	....	....
2003-04	**Colorado**	**NHL**	**49**	**5**	**7**	**12**	**24**	**1**	**0**	**0**	**71**	**7.0**	**3**	**1021**	**58.1**	**16:17**	**11**	**0**	**2**	**2**	**4**	**0**	**0**	**0**	**15:41**
2004-05	CSKA Moscow	Russia	55	7	20	27	64	....	....	....	....	....	....	....	....	....	....	....	....	....	....	....	....	....	....
	NHL Totals		**628**	**93**	**187**	**280**	**270**	**13**	**6**	**9**	**929**	**10.0**		**7171**	**55.3**	**16:35**	**43**	**1**	**17**	**18**	**22**	**1**	**0**	**0**	**16:24**

Traded to **Washington** by **Hartford** for Curtis Leschyshyn, November 9, 1996. Traded to **Chicago** by **Washington** with Chris Simon for Michael Nylander, Chicago's 3rd round choice (Stephen Werner) in 2003 Entry Draft and future considerations, November 1, 2002. Traded to **Colorado** by **Chicago** for Colorado's 4th round choice (Mitch Maunu) in 2004 Entry Draft, June 21, 2003. Signed as a free agent by **CSKA** (Russia), June 4, 2004.

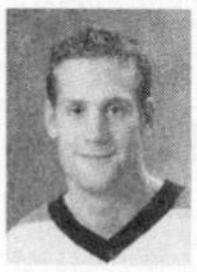

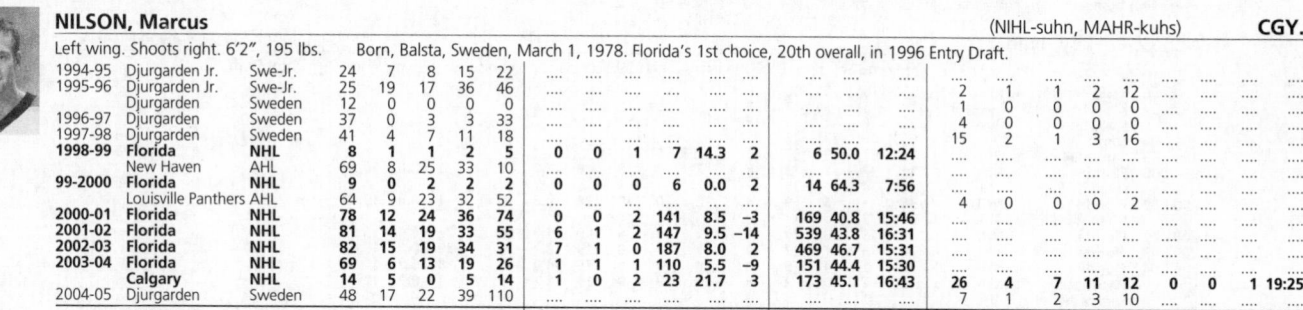

NILSON, Marcus

(NIHL-suhn, MAHR-kuhs) **CGY.**

Left wing. Shoots right. 6'2", 195 lbs. Born, Balsta, Sweden, March 1, 1978. Florida's 1st choice, 20th overall, in 1996 Entry Draft.

Season	Club	League	GP	G	A	Pts	PIM	PP	SH	GW	S	%	+/-	TF	F%	Min	GP	G	A	Pts	PIM	PP	SH	GW	Min
1994-95	Djurgarden Jr.	Swe-Jr.	24	7	8	15	22	....	....	....	....	....	....	....	....	....	....	....	....	....	....	....	....	....	....
1995-96	Djurgarden Jr.	Swe-Jr.	25	19	17	36	46	....	....	....	....	....	....	....	....	....	2	1	1	2	12	....	....	....	....
	Djurgarden	Sweden	12	0	0	0	0	....	....	....	....	....	....	....	....	....	1	0	0	0	0	....	....	....	....
1996-97	Djurgarden	Sweden	37	0	3	3	33	....	....	....	....	....	....	....	....	....	4	0	0	0	0	....	....	....	....
1997-98	Djurgarden	Sweden	41	4	7	11	18	....	....	....	....	....	....	....	....	....	15	2	1	3	16	....	....	....	....
1998-99	**Florida**	**NHL**	**8**	**1**	**1**	**2**	**5**	**0**	**0**	**1**	**7**	**14.3**	**2**	**6**	**50.0**	**12:24**	....	....	....	....	....	....	....	....	....
	New Haven	AHL	69	8	25	33	10	....	....	....	....	....	....	....	....	....	....	....	....	....	....	....	....	....	....
99-2000	**Florida**	**NHL**	**9**	**0**	**2**	**2**	**2**	**0**	**0**	**0**	**6**	**0.0**	**2**	**14**	**64.3**	**7:56**	....	....	....	....	....	....	....	....	....
	Louisville Panthers	AHL	64	9	23	32	52	....	....	....	....	....	....	....	....	....	4	0	0	0	2	....	....	....	....
2000-01	**Florida**	**NHL**	**78**	**12**	**24**	**36**	**74**	**0**	**0**	**2**	**141**	**8.5**	**–3**	**169**	**40.8**	**15:46**	....	....	....	....	....	....	....	....	....
2001-02	**Florida**	**NHL**	**81**	**14**	**19**	**33**	**55**	**6**	**1**	**2**	**147**	**9.5**	**–14**	**539**	**43.8**	**16:31**	....	....	....	....	....	....	....	....	....
2002-03	**Florida**	**NHL**	**82**	**15**	**19**	**34**	**31**	**7**	**1**	**0**	**187**	**8.0**	**2**	**469**	**46.7**	**15:31**	....	....	....	....	....	....	....	....	....
2003-04	**Florida**	**NHL**	**69**	**6**	**13**	**19**	**26**	**1**	**1**	**1**	**110**	**5.5**	**–9**	**151**	**44.4**	**15:30**	....	....	....	....	....	....	....	....	....
	Calgary	**NHL**	**14**	**5**	**0**	**5**	**14**	**1**	**0**	**2**	**23**	**21.7**	**3**	**173**	**45.1**	**16:43**	**26**	**4**	**7**	**11**	**12**	**0**	**0**	**1**	**19:25**
2004-05	Djurgarden	Sweden	48	17	22	39	110	....	....	....	....	....	....	....	....	....	7	1	2	3	10	....	....	....	....
	NHL Totals		**341**	**53**	**78**	**131**	**207**	**15**	**3**	**8**	**621**	**8.5**		**1521**	**44.8**	**15:35**	**26**	**4**	**7**	**11**	**12**	**0**	**0**	**1**	**19:25**

Traded to **Calgary** by **Florida** for Calgary's 2nd round choice (David Booth) in 2004 Entry Draft, March 8, 2004. Signed as a free agent by **Djurgarden** (Sweden), September 16, 2004.

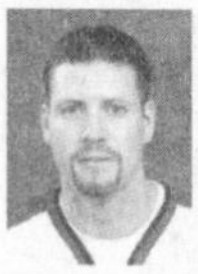

NOLAN, Owen

(NOH-lan, OH-wehn)

Right wing. Shoots right. 6'1", 215 lbs. Born, Belfast, Ireland, February 12, 1972. Quebec's 1st choice, 1st overall, in 1990 Entry Draft.

Season	Club	League	GP	G	A	Pts	PIM	PP	SH	GW	S	%	+/-	TF	F%	Min	GP	G	A	Pts	PIM	PP	SH	GW	Min
1987-88	Thorold	OMHA	28	53	32	85	24	....	....	....	....	....	....	....	....	....	....	....	....	....	....	....	....	....	....
	Thorold	OHA-B	3	1	0	1	2	....	....	....	....	....	....	....	....	....	....	....	....	....	....	....	....	....	....
1988-89	Cornwall Royals	OHL	62	34	25	59	213	....	....	....	....	....	....	....	....	....	18	5	11	16	41	....	....	....	....
1989-90	Cornwall Royals	OHL	58	51	59	110	240	....	....	....	....	....	....	....	....	....	6	7	5	12	26	....	....	....	....
1990-91	**Quebec**	**NHL**	**59**	**3**	**10**	**13**	**109**	**0**	**0**	**0**	**54**	**5.6**	**–19**	....	....	....	....	....	....	....	....	....	....	....	....
	Halifax Citadels	AHL	6	4	4	8	11	....	....	....	....	....	....	....	....	....	....	....	....	....	....	....	....	....	....
1991-92	**Quebec**	**NHL**	**75**	**42**	**31**	**73**	**183**	**17**	**0**	**0**	**190**	**22.1**	**–9**	....	....	....	....	....	....	....	....	....	....	....	....
1992-93	**Quebec**	**NHL**	**73**	**36**	**41**	**77**	**185**	**15**	**0**	**4**	**241**	**14.9**	**–1**	....	....	....	**5**	**1**	**0**	**1**	**2**	**0**	**0**	**0**	....
1993-94	**Quebec**	**NHL**	**6**	**2**	**2**	**4**	**8**	**0**	**0**	**0**	**15**	**13.3**	**2**	....	....	....	....	....	....	....	....	....	....	....	....
1994-95	**Quebec**	**NHL**	**46**	**30**	**19**	**49**	**46**	**13**	**2**	**8**	**137**	**21.9**	**21**	....	....	....	**6**	**2**	**3**	**5**	**6**	**0**	**0**	**0**	....
1995-96	**Colorado**	**NHL**	**9**	**4**	**4**	**8**	**9**	**4**	**0**	**0**	**23**	**17.4**	**–3**	....	....	....	....	....	....	....	....	....	....	....	....
	San Jose	**NHL**	**72**	**29**	**32**	**61**	**137**	**12**	**1**	**2**	**184**	**15.8**	**–30**	....	....	....	....	....	....	....	....	....	....	....	....
1996-97	**San Jose**	**NHL**	**72**	**31**	**32**	**63**	**155**	**10**	**0**	**3**	**225**	**13.8**	**–19**	....	....	....	....	....	....	....	....	....	....	....	....
1997-98	**San Jose**	**NHL**	**75**	**14**	**27**	**41**	**144**	**3**	**1**	**1**	**192**	**7.3**	**–2**	....	....	....	**6**	**2**	**2**	**4**	**26**	**2**	**0**	**1**	....
1998-99	**San Jose**	**NHL**	**78**	**19**	**26**	**45**	**129**	**6**	**2**	**3**	**207**	**9.2**	**16**	**657**	**49.3**	**19:09**	**6**	**1**	**1**	**2**	**6**	**0**	**0**	**0**	**20:15**
99-2000	**San Jose**	**NHL**	**78**	**44**	**40**	**84**	**110**	**18**	**4**	**6**	**261**	**16.9**	**–1**	**357**	**50.7**	**21:07**	**10**	**8**	**2**	**10**	**6**	**2**	**2**	**3**	**22:14**
2000-01	**San Jose**	**NHL**	**57**	**24**	**25**	**49**	**75**	**10**	**1**	**4**	**191**	**12.6**	**0**	**407**	**46.9**	**21:49**	**6**	**1**	**1**	**2**	**8**	**0**	**0**	**1**	**22:45**
2001-02	**San Jose**	**NHL**	**75**	**23**	**43**	**66**	**93**	**8**	**2**	**2**	**217**	**10.6**	**7**	**545**	**47.0**	**19:23**	**12**	**3**	**6**	**9**	**8**	**0**	**0**	**0**	**19:46**
	Canada	Olympics	6	0	3	3	2	....	....	....	....	....	....	....	....	....	....	....	....	....	....	....	....	....	....
2002-03	**San Jose**	**NHL**	**61**	**22**	**20**	**42**	**91**	**8**	**3**	**4**	**192**	**11.5**	**–5**	**226**	**50.4**	**18:08**	....	....	....	....	....	....	....	....	....
	Toronto	**NHL**	**14**	**7**	**5**	**12**	**16**	**5**	**0**	**1**	**29**	**24.1**	**2**	**56**	**48.2**	**17:00**	**7**	**0**	**2**	**2**	**2**	**0**	**0**	**0**	**23:19**
2003-04	**Toronto**	**NHL**	**65**	**19**	**29**	**48**	**110**	**7**	**2**	**3**	**154**	**12.3**	**4**	**242**	**53.3**	**17:57**	....	....	....	....	....	....	....	....	....
2004-05			DID NOT PLAY																						
	NHL Totals		**915**	**349**	**386**	**735**	**1600**	**136**	**18**	**41**	**2512**	**13.9**		**2490**	**49.1**	**19:30**	**58**	**18**	**17**	**35**	**64**	**4**	**2**	**5**	**21:29**

OHL Rookie of the Year (1989) • OHL First All-Star Team (1990)

Played in NHL All-Star Game (1992, 1996, 1997, 2000, 2002)

• Missed majority of 1993-94 season recovering from shoulder injury suffered in game vs. Tampa Bay, November 13, 1993. Transferred to **Colorado** after **Quebec** franchise relocated, June 21, 1995. Traded to **San Jose** by **Colorado** for Sandis Ozolinsh, October 26, 1995. Traded to **Toronto** by **San Jose** for Alyn McCauley, Brad Boyes and Toronto's 1st round choice (later traded to Boston – Boston selected Mark Stuart) in 2003 Entry Draft, March 5, 2003.

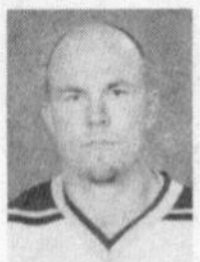

NORSTROM, Mattias

(NOHR-struhm, MAT-tee-ahs) **L.A.**

Defense. Shoots left. 6'2", 210 lbs. Born, Stockholm, Sweden, January 2, 1972. NY Rangers' 2nd choice, 48th overall, in 1992 Entry Draft.

			Regular Season														Playoffs								
Season	Club	League	GP	G	A	Pts	PIM	PP	SH	GW	S	%	+/-	TF	F%	Min	GP	G	A	Pts	PIM	PP	SH	GW	Min
1990-91	Mora IK	Sweden-2	9	1	1	2	6	....	....	....	....	....	....	....	....	....	1	0	0	0	2	....	....	....	....
1991-92	AIK Solna	Sweden	39	4	3	7	28	....	....	....	....	....	....	....	....	....	3	0	2	2	2	....	....	....	....
1992-93	AIK Solna	Sweden	22	0	1	1	16	....	....	....	....	....	....	....	....	....	....	....	....	....	....	....	....	....	....
1993-94	**NY Rangers**	**NHL**	**9**	**0**	**2**	**2**	**6**	**0**	**0**	**0**	**3**	**0.0**	**0**	....	....	....	....	....	....	....	....	....	....	....	....
	Binghamton	AHL	55	1	9	10	70	....	....	....	....	....	....	....	....	....	....	....	....	....	....	....	....	....	....
1994-95	Binghamton	AHL	63	9	10	19	91	....	....	....	....	....	....	....	....	....	....	....	....	....	....	....	....	....	....
	NY Rangers	**NHL**	**9**	**0**	**3**	**3**	**2**	**0**	**0**	**0**	**4**	**0.0**	**2**	....	....	....	**3**	**0**	**0**	**0**	**0**	**0**	**0**	**0**	....
1995-96	**NY Rangers**	**NHL**	**25**	**2**	**1**	**3**	**22**	**0**	**0**	**0**	**17**	**11.8**	**5**	....	....	....	....	....	....	....	....	....	....	....	....
	Los Angeles	**NHL**	**11**	**0**	**1**	**1**	**18**	**0**	**0**	**0**	**17**	**0.0**	**–8**	....	....	....	....	....	....	....	....	....	....	....	....
1996-97	**Los Angeles**	**NHL**	**80**	**1**	**21**	**22**	**84**	**0**	**0**	**0**	**106**	**0.9**	**–4**	....	....	....	....	....	....	....	....	....	....	....	....
1997-98	**Los Angeles**	**NHL**	**73**	**1**	**12**	**13**	**90**	**0**	**0**	**0**	**61**	**1.6**	**14**	....	....	....	**4**	**0**	**0**	**0**	**2**	**0**	**0**	**0**	....
	Sweden	Olympics	4	0	1	1	2	....	....	....	....	....	....	....	....	....	....	....	....	....	....	....	....	....	....
1998-99	**Los Angeles**	**NHL**	**78**	**2**	**5**	**7**	**36**	**0**	**1**	**0**	**61**	**3.3**	**–10**	**1**	**0.0**	**20:20**	....	....	....	....	....	....	....	....	....
99-2000	**Los Angeles**	**NHL**	**82**	**1**	**13**	**14**	**66**	**0**	**0**	**0**	**62**	**1.6**	**22**	**0**	**0.0**	**21:49**	**4**	**0**	**0**	**0**	**6**	**0**	**0**	**0**	**21:35**
2000-01	**Los Angeles**	**NHL**	**82**	**0**	**18**	**18**	**60**	**0**	**0**	**0**	**59**	**0.0**	**10**	**2**	**0.0**	**21:50**	**13**	**0**	**2**	**2**	**18**	**0**	**0**	**0**	**23:16**
2001-02	**Los Angeles**	**NHL**	**79**	**2**	**9**	**11**	**38**	**0**	**0**	**0**	**42**	**4.8**	**–2**	**0**	**0.0**	**23:01**	**7**	**0**	**0**	**0**	**4**	**0**	**0**	**0**	**23:24**
	Sweden	Olympics	4	0	0	0	0	....	....	....	....	....	....	....	....	....	....	....	....	....	....	....	....	....	....
2002-03	**Los Angeles**	**NHL**	**82**	**0**	**6**	**6**	**49**	**0**	**0**	**0**	**63**	**0.0**	**0**	**1**	**100.0**	**21:30**	....	....	....	....	....	....	....	....	....
2003-04	**Los Angeles**	**NHL**	**74**	**1**	**13**	**14**	**44**	**0**	**0**	**0**	**65**	**1.5**	**–3**	**1**	**100.0**	**22:26**	....	....	....	....	....	....	....	....	....
2004-05	AIK Solna	Sweden-3	8	1	0	1	4	....	....	....	....	....	....	....	....	....	....	....	....	....	....	....	....	....	....
	NHL Totals		**684**	**10**	**104**	**114**	**515**	**0**	**1**	**0**	**560**	**1.8**		**5**	**40.0**	**21:49**	**31**	**0**	**2**	**2**	**30**	**0**	**0**	**0**	**23:02**

Played in NHL All-Star Game (1999, 2004)

Traded to **Los Angeles** by **NY Rangers** with Ray Ferraro, Ian Laperriere, Nathan Lafayette and NY Rangers' 4th round choice (Sean Blanchard) in 1997 Entry Draft for Marty McSorley, Jari Kurri and Shane Churla, March 14, 1996. Signed as a free agent by **AIK Solna** (Sweden-3), January 11, 2005.

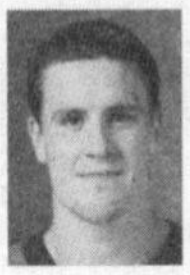

NORTON, Brad

(NOHR-tuhn, BRAD)

Defense. Shoots left. 6'4", 235 lbs. Born, Cambridge, MA, February 13, 1975. Edmonton's 9th choice, 215th overall, in 1993 Entry Draft.

1992-93	Cushing	High-MA	31	10	26	36	....	....	....	....	....	....	....	....	....	....	....	....	....	....	....	....	....	....	....
1993-94	Cushing	High-MA	STATISTICS NOT AVAILABLE																						
1994-95	U. Mass-Amherst	H-East	30	0	6	6	89	....	....	....	....	....	....	....	....	....	....	....	....	....	....	....	....	....	....
1995-96	U. Mass-Amherst	H-East	34	4	12	16	99	....	....	....	....	....	....	....	....	....	....	....	....	....	....	....	....	....	....
1996-97	U. Mass-Amherst	H-East	35	2	16	18	88	....	....	....	....	....	....	....	....	....	....	....	....	....	....	....	....	....	....
1997-98	U. Mass-Amherst	H-East	20	2	13	15	28	....	....	....	....	....	....	....	....	....	....	....	....	....	....	....	....	....	....
	Detroit Vipers	IHL	33	1	4	5	56	....	....	....	....	....	....	....	....	....	22	0	2	2	87	....	....	....	....
1998-99	Hamilton	AHL	58	1	8	9	134	....	....	....	....	....	....	....	....	....	11	0	1	1	6	....	....	....	....
99-2000	Hamilton	AHL	40	5	12	17	104	....	....	....	....	....	....	....	....	....	10	1	4	5	26	....	....	....	....
2000-01	Hamilton	AHL	46	3	15	18	114	....	....	....	....	....	....	....	....	....	....	....	....	....	....	....	....	....	....
2001-02	**Florida**	**NHL**	**22**	**0**	**2**	**2**	**45**	**0**	**0**	**0**	**6**	**0.0**	**–2**	**1**	**0.0**	**9:15**	....	....	....	....	....	....	....	....	....
	Hershey Bears	AHL	40	0	10	10	62	....	....	....	....	....	....	....	....	....	2	0	0	0	6	....	....	....	....
2002-03	**Los Angeles**	**NHL**	**53**	**3**	**3**	**6**	**97**	**0**	**0**	**0**	**19**	**15.8**	**1**	**2**	**0.0**	**6:04**	....	....	....	....	....	....	....	....	....
2003-04	**Los Angeles**	**NHL**	**20**	**0**	**1**	**1**	**77**	**0**	**0**	**0**	**10**	**0.0**	**–1**	**0**	**0.0**	**8:34**	....	....	....	....	....	....	....	....	....
	Washington	**NHL**	**16**	**0**	**1**	**1**	**17**	**0**	**0**	**0**	**6**	**0.0**	**–4**	**0**	**0.0**	**12:50**	....	....	....	....	....	....	....	....	....
2004-05			DID NOT PLAY																						
	NHL Totals		**111**	**3**	**7**	**10**	**236**	**0**	**0**	**0**	**41**	**7.3**		**3**	**0.0**	**8:08**	....	....	....	....	....	....	....	....	....

Signed as a free agent by **Florida**, July 27, 2001. Signed as a free agent by **Los Angeles**, October, 8, 2002. Claimed on waivers by **Washington** from **Los Angeles**, March 4, 2004. • Missed majority of 2003-04 season recovering from arm injury suffered in pre-season game vs. Phoenix, September 20, 2003.

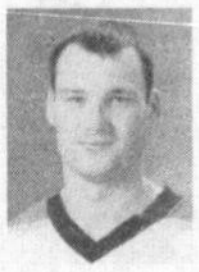

NOVOSELTSEV, Ivan

(noh-voh-SEHLT-sehv, ee-VAHN)

Right wing. Shoots left. 6'1", 210 lbs. Born, Golitsino, USSR, January 23, 1979. Florida's 5th choice, 95th overall, in 1997 Entry Draft.

1995-96	Krylja Sovetov	CIS	1	0	0	0	2	....	....	....	....	....	....	....	....	....	....	....	....	....	....	....	....	....	....
1996-97	Krylja Sovetov 2	Russia-3	19	5	3	8	39	....	....	....	....	....	....	....	....	....	....	....	....	....	....	....	....	....	....
	Krylja Sovetov	Russia	30	0	3	3	18	....	....	....	....	....	....	....	....	....	2	0	0	0	4	....	....	....	....
1997-98	Sarnia Sting	OHL	53	26	22	48	41	....	....	....	....	....	....	....	....	....	5	1	1	2	8	....	....	....	....
1998-99	Sarnia Sting	OHL	68	57	39	96	45	....	....	....	....	....	....	....	....	....	5	2	4	6	6	....	....	....	....
99-2000	**Florida**	**NHL**	**14**	**2**	**1**	**3**	**8**	**2**	**0**	**0**	**8**	**25.0**	**–3**	**1**	**100.0**	**10:29**	....	....	....	....	....	....	....	....	....
	Louisville Panthers	AHL	47	14	21	35	22	....	....	....	....	....	....	....	....	....	4	1	0	1	6	....	....	....	....
2000-01	**Florida**	**NHL**	**38**	**3**	**6**	**9**	**16**	**0**	**0**	**0**	**34**	**8.8**	**–5**	**1**	**0.0**	**10:44**	....	....	....	....	....	....	....	....	....
	Louisville Panthers	AHL	34	2	10	12	8	....	....	....	....	....	....	....	....	....	....	....	....	....	....	....	....	....	....
2001-02	**Florida**	**NHL**	**70**	**13**	**16**	**29**	**44**	**1**	**1**	**5**	**109**	**11.9**	**–10**	**27**	**44.4**	**14:53**	....	....	....	....	....	....	....	....	....
2002-03	**Florida**	**NHL**	**78**	**10**	**17**	**27**	**30**	**1**	**0**	**0**	**115**	**8.7**	**–16**	**39**	**30.8**	**15:02**	....	....	....	....	....	....	....	....	....
2003-04	**Florida**	**NHL**	**17**	**1**	**4**	**5**	**8**	**0**	**0**	**0**	**25**	**4.0**	**–6**	**8**	**75.0**	**11:55**	....	....	....	....	....	....	....	....	....
	Phoenix	**NHL**	**17**	**2**	**0**	**2**	**6**	**0**	**0**	**0**	**23**	**8.7**	**–7**	**1**	**0.0**	**10:11**	....	....	....	....	....	....	....	....	....
	Springfield	AHL	2	1	0	1	2	....	....	....	....	....	....	....	....	....	....	....	....	....	....	....	....	....	....
2004-05	Lada Togliatti	Russia	13	0	2	2	8	....	....	....	....	....	....	....	....	....	....	....	....	....	....	....	....	....	....
	Spartak Moscow	Russia	26	5	1	6	47	....	....	....	....	....	....	....	....	....	....	....	....	....	....	....	....	....	....
	NHL Totals		**234**	**31**	**44**	**75**	**112**	**4**	**1**	**5**	**314**	**9.9**		**77**	**40.3**	**13:26**	....	....	....	....	....	....	....	....	....

OHL First All-Star Team (1999)

Traded to **Phoenix** by **Florida** for future considerations, December 30, 2003. • Missed majority of 2003-04 season recovering from head injury suffered in game vs. Detroit, January 16, 2004. Signed as a free agent by **Togliatti** (Russia), July 28, 2004. Signed as a free agent by **Spartak** (Russia), December 20, 2004.

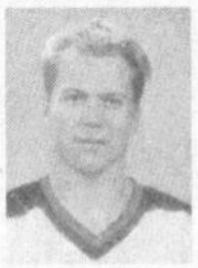

NUMMELIN, Petteri

(NOO-muh-lihn, PEH-tuh-ree) **ATL.**

Defense. Shoots left. 5'10", 200 lbs. Born, Turku, Finland, November 25, 1972. Columbus' 3rd choice, 133rd overall, in 2000 Entry Draft.

1988-89	TPS Turku Jr.	Finland-Jr.	11	2	3	5	2	....	....	....	....	....	....	....	....	....	....	....	....	....	....	....	....	....	....
1989-90	TPS Turku Jr.	Finland-Jr.	33	6	14	20	45	....	....	....	....	....	....	....	....	....	....	....	....	....	....	....	....	....	....
1990-91	TPS Turku Jr.	Finland-Jr.	35	20	16	36	28	....	....	....	....	....	....	....	....	....	....	....	....	....	....	....	....	....	....
	Kiekko-67 Turku	Finland-2	2	0	2	2	4	....	....	....	....	....	....	....	....	....	....	....	....	....	....	....	....	....	....
1991-92	Kiekko-67 Jr.	Finland-Jr.	13	16	15	31	28	....	....	....	....	....	....	....	....	....	....	....	....	....	....	....	....	....	....
	Kiekko-67 Turku	Finland-2	41	12	24	36	36	....	....	....	....	....	....	....	....	....	....	....	....	....	....	....	....	....	....
1992-93	TPS Turku Jr.	Finland-Jr.	1	1	0	1	0	....	....	....	....	....	....	....	....	....	....	....	....	....	....	....	....	....	....
	TPS Turku	Finland	3	0	0	0	8	....	....	....	....	....	....	....	....	....	....	....	....	....	....	....	....	....	....
	Reipas Lahti	Finland	20	5	8	13	20	....	....	....	....	....	....	....	....	....	....	....	....	....	....	....	....	....	....
	Kiekko-67 Turku	Finland-2	28	14	15	29	18	....	....	....	....	....	....	....	....	....	....	....	....	....	....	....	....	....	....
1993-94	TPS Turku	Finland	44	14	24	38	20	....	....	....	....	....	....	....	....	....	11	0	3	3	4	....	....	....	....
1994-95	TPS Turku	Finland	48	10	17	27	32	....	....	....	....	....	....	....	....	....	11	4	3	7	0	....	....	....	....
1995-96	V.Frolunda	Sweden	32	7	11	18	26	....	....	....	....	....	....	....	....	....	12	2	7	9	4	....	....	....	....
1996-97	V.Frolunda	Sweden	44	20	14	34	39	....	....	....	....	....	....	....	....	....	2	0	1	1	0	....	....	....	....
1997-98	HC Davos	Swiss	33	13	17	30	24	....	....	....	....	....	....	....	....	....	17	8	14	22	2	....	....	....	....
1998-99	HC Davos	Swiss	44	11	42	53	22	....	....	....	....	....	....	....	....	....	4	0	2	2	2	....	....	....	....
99-2000	HC Davos	Swiss	40	15	23	38	20	....	....	....	....	....	....	....	....	....	5	0	3	3	0	....	....	....	....
2000-01	**Columbus**	**NHL**	**61**	**4**	**12**	**16**	**10**	**2**	**0**	**0**	**99**	**4.0**	**–11**	**1**	**0.0**	**17:14**	....	....	....	....	....	....	....	....	....
2001-02	HC Lugano	Swiss	35	4	18	22	6	....	....	....	....	....	....	....	....	....	13	6	9	15	2	....	....	....	....
2002-03	HC Lugano	Swiss	43	18	*39	*57	12	....	....	....	....	....	....	....	....	....	8	3	6	9	2	....	....	....	....
2003-04	HC Lugano	Swiss	48	20	39	59	59	....	....	....	....	....	....	....	....	....	16	6	*19	*25	4	....	....	....	....
2004-05	HC Lugano	Swiss	36	13	34	47	18	....	....	....	....	....	....	....	....	....	3	1	0	1	2	....	....	....	....
	NHL Totals		**61**	**4**	**12**	**16**	**10**	**2**	**0**	**0**	**99**	**4.0**		**1**	**0.0**	**17:14**									

Traded to **Atlanta** by **Columbus** with Chris Nielsen for Tomi Kallio and Pauli Levokari, December 2, 2002.

			Regular Season														Playoffs								
Season	Club	League	GP	G	A	Pts	PIM	PP	SH	GW	S	%	+/-	TF	F%	Min	GP	G	A	Pts	PIM	PP	SH	GW	Min

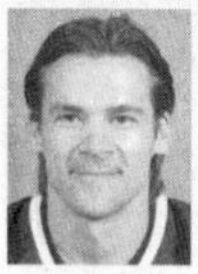

NUMMINEN, Teppo

(NOO-mih-nehn, TEH-poh) **BUF.**

Defense. Shoots right. 6'2", 197 lbs. Born, Tampere, Finland, July 3, 1968. Winnipeg's 2nd choice, 29th overall, in 1986 Entry Draft.

Season	Club	League	GP	G	A	Pts	PIM	PP	SH	GW	S	%	+/-	TF	F%	Min	GP	G	A	Pts	PIM	PP	SH	GW	Min
1984-85	Tappara Jr.	Finland-Jr.	30	14	17	31	10																		
	Whitby Lawmen	OJHL	16	3	9	12	0																		
1985-86	Tappara Jr.	Finland-Jr.	2	0	0	0	0										3	0	1	1	2				
	Tappara Tampere	Finland	31	2	4	6	6										8	0	0	0	0				
1986-87	Tappara Tampere	Finland	44	9	9	18	16										9	4	1	5	4				
1987-88	Tappara Tampere	Finland	40	10	10	20	29										10	6	6	12	6				
	Finland	Olympics	6	1	4	5	0																		
1988-89	**Winnipeg**	**NHL**	**69**	**1**	**14**	**15**	**36**	**0**	**1**	**0**	**85**	**1.2**	**-11**												
1989-90	**Winnipeg**	**NHL**	**79**	**11**	**32**	**43**	**20**	**1**	**0**	**1**	**105**	**10.5**	**-4**				**7**	**1**	**2**	**3**	**10**	**0**	**0**	**0**	
1990-91	**Winnipeg**	**NHL**	**80**	**8**	**25**	**33**	**28**	**3**	**0**	**0**	**151**	**5.3**	**-15**												
1991-92	**Winnipeg**	**NHL**	**80**	**5**	**34**	**39**	**32**	**4**	**0**	**1**	**143**	**3.5**	**15**				**7**	**0**	**0**	**0**	**0**	**0**	**0**	**0**	
1992-93	**Winnipeg**	**NHL**	**66**	**7**	**30**	**37**	**33**	**3**	**1**	**0**	**103**	**6.8**	**4**				**6**	**1**	**1**	**2**	**2**	**1**	**0**	**0**	
1993-94	**Winnipeg**	**NHL**	**57**	**5**	**18**	**23**	**28**	**4**	**0**	**1**	**89**	**5.6**	**-23**												
1994-95	TuTo Turku	Finland	12	3	8	11	4																		
	Winnipeg	**NHL**	**42**	**5**	**16**	**21**	**16**	**2**	**0**	**0**	**86**	**5.8**	**12**												
1995-96	**Winnipeg**	**NHL**	**74**	**11**	**43**	**54**	**22**	**6**	**0**	**3**	**165**	**6.7**	**-4**				**6**	**0**	**0**	**0**	**2**	**0**	**0**	**0**	
1996-97	**Phoenix**	**NHL**	**82**	**2**	**25**	**27**	**28**	**0**	**0**	**0**	**135**	**1.5**	**-3**				**7**	**3**	**3**	**6**	**0**	**1**	**0**	**1**	
1997-98	**Phoenix**	**NHL**	**82**	**11**	**40**	**51**	**30**	**6**	**0**	**2**	**126**	**8.7**	**25**				**1**	**0**	**0**	**0**	**0**	**0**	**0**	**0**	
	Finland	Olympics	6	1	1	2	2																		
1998-99	**Phoenix**	**NHL**	**82**	**10**	**30**	**40**	**30**	**1**	**0**	**0**	**156**	**6.4**	**3**	**2**	**0.0**	**24:26**	**7**	**2**	**1**	**3**	**4**	**2**	**0**	**0**	**26:09**
99-2000	**Phoenix**	**NHL**	**79**	**8**	**34**	**42**	**16**	**2**	**0**	**2**	**126**	**6.3**	**21**	**1**	**0.0**	**23:37**	**5**	**1**	**1**	**2**	**0**	**0**	**0**	**0**	**23:11**
2000-01	**Phoenix**	**NHL**	**72**	**5**	**26**	**31**	**36**	**1**	**0**	**2**	**109**	**4.6**	**9**	**0**	**0.0**	**24:28**									
2001-02	**Phoenix**	**NHL**	**76**	**13**	**35**	**48**	**20**	**4**	**0**	**6**	**117**	**11.1**	**13**	**0**	**0.0**	**23:51**	**4**	**0**	**0**	**0**	**2**	**0**	**0**	**0**	**25:33**
	Finland	Olympics	4	0	1	1	0																		
2002-03	**Phoenix**	**NHL**	**78**	**6**	**24**	**30**	**30**	**2**	**0**	**1**	**108**	**5.6**	**0**	**0**	**0.0**	**23:51**									
2003-04	**Dallas**	**NHL**	**62**	**3**	**14**	**17**	**18**	**0**	**0**	**0**	**83**	**3.6**	**-5**	**1**	**100.0**	**21:40**	**4**	**0**	**1**	**1**	**0**	**0**	**0**	**0**	**19:12**
2004-05		DID NOT PLAY																							
	NHL Totals		**1160**	**111**	**440**	**551**	**423**	**39**	**2**	**19**	**1887**	**5.9**		**4**	**25.0**	**23:43**	**54**	**8**	**9**	**17**	**20**	**4**	**0**	**1**	**23:54**

Played in NHL All-Star Game (1999, 2000, 2001)

Transferred to **Phoenix** after **Winnipeg** franchise relocated, July 1, 1996. Traded to **Dallas** by **Phoenix** for Mike Sillinger, July 22, 2003. Signed as a free agent by **Buffalo**, August 4, 2005.

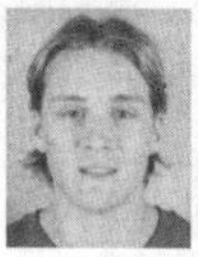

NYCHOLAT, Lawrence

(NIH-coh-lat, LAW-rehnts) **WSH.**

Defense. Shoots left. 6', 192 lbs. Born, Calgary, Alta., May 7, 1979.

Season	Club	League	GP	G	A	Pts	PIM	PP	SH	GW	S	%	+/-	TF	F%	Min	GP	G	A	Pts	PIM	PP	SH	GW	Min
1995-96	Notre Dame	SMHL	42	10	36	46	66																		
1996-97	Swift Current	WHL	67	8	13	21	82										10	0	0	0	24				
1997-98	Swift Current	WHL	71	13	35	48	108										1	0	0	0	0				
1998-99	Swift Current	WHL	72	16	44	60	125										6	2	2	4	12				
99-2000	Swift Current	WHL	70	22	58	80	92										2	0	0	0	0				
2000-01	Jackson Bandits	ECHL	5	1	2	3	5																		
	Cleveland	IHL	42	3	7	10	69										4	0	0	0	2				
2001-02	Houston Aeros	AHL	72	3	11	14	92										14	1	0	1	23				
2002-03	Houston Aeros	AHL	66	11	28	39	155																		
	Hartford	AHL	15	2	9	11	6										2	2	0	2	0				
2003-04	**NY Rangers**	**NHL**	**9**	**0**	**0**	**0**	**6**	**0**	**0**	**0**	**6**	**0.0**	**-2**	**0**	**0.0**	**17:09**									
	Hartford	AHL	72	6	26	32	130										16	0	5	5	28				
2004-05	Hartford	AHL	79	5	38	43	132										6	0	3	3	11				
	NHL Totals		**9**	**0**	**0**	**0**	**6**	**0**	**0**	**0**	**6**	**0.0**		**0**	**0.0**	**17:09**									

Signed as a free agent by **Minnesota**, August 31, 2000. Traded to **NY Rangers** by **Minnesota** for Johan Holmqvist, March 11, 2003. Signed as a free agent by **Washington**, August 9, 2005.

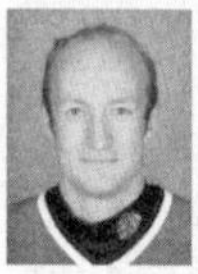

NYLANDER, Michael

(NEE-lan-duhr, MIGH-kuhl) **NYR**

Center. Shoots left. 6'1", 195 lbs. Born, Stockholm, Sweden, October 3, 1972. Hartford's 4th choice, 59th overall, in 1991 Entry Draft.

Season	Club	League	GP	G	A	Pts	PIM	PP	SH	GW	S	%	+/-	TF	F%	Min	GP	G	A	Pts	PIM	PP	SH	GW	Min
1989-90	Huddinge IK	Sweden-2	31	7	15	22	4										5	3	0	3	0				
1990-91	Huddinge IK	Sweden-2	33	14	20	34	10										2	0	0	0	0				
1991-92	AIK Solna	Sweden	40	11	17	28	30										3	1	4	5	4				
1992-93	**Hartford**	**NHL**	**59**	**11**	**22**	**33**	**36**	**3**	**0**	**1**	**85**	**12.9**	**-7**												
	Springfield	AHL															3	3	3	6	2				
1993-94	**Hartford**	**NHL**	**58**	**11**	**33**	**44**	**24**	**4**	**0**	**1**	**74**	**14.9**	**-2**												
	Springfield	AHL	4	0	9	9	0																		
	Calgary	**NHL**	**15**	**2**	**9**	**11**	**6**	**0**	**0**	**0**	**21**	**9.5**	**10**				**3**	**0**	**0**	**0**	**0**	**0**	**0**	**0**	
1994-95	JYP HT Jyvaskyla	Finland	16	11	19	30	63																		
	Calgary	**NHL**	**6**	**0**	**1**	**1**	**2**	**0**	**0**	**0**	**2**	**0.0**	**1**				**6**	**0**	**6**	**6**	**2**	**0**	**0**	**0**	
1995-96	**Calgary**	**NHL**	**73**	**17**	**38**	**55**	**20**	**4**	**0**	**6**	**163**	**10.4**	**0**				**4**	**0**	**0**	**0**	**0**	**0**	**0**	**0**	
1996-97	HC Lugano	Swiss	36	12	43	55	28										8	3	8	11	8				
1997-98	**Calgary**	**NHL**	**65**	**13**	**23**	**36**	**24**	**0**	**0**	**2**	**117**	**11.1**	**10**												
	Sweden	Olympics	4	0	0	0	6																		
1998-99	**Calgary**	**NHL**	**9**	**2**	**3**	**5**	**2**	**1**	**0**	**0**	**7**	**28.6**	**1**	**25**	**60.0**	**11:10**									
	Tampa Bay	**NHL**	**24**	**2**	**7**	**9**	**6**	**0**	**0**	**0**	**26**	**7.7**	**-10**	**75**	**44.0**	**13:29**									
99-2000	**Tampa Bay**	**NHL**	**11**	**1**	**2**	**3**	**4**	**1**	**0**	**0**	**10**	**10.0**	**-3**	**35**	**57.1**	**10:32**									
	Chicago	**NHL**	**66**	**23**	**28**	**51**	**26**	**4**	**0**	**2**	**112**	**20.5**	**9**	**561**	**46.9**	**16:39**									
2000-01	**Chicago**	**NHL**	**82**	**25**	**39**	**64**	**32**	**4**	**0**	**5**	**176**	**14.2**	**7**	**1036**	**48.3**	**18:52**									
2001-02	**Chicago**	**NHL**	**82**	**15**	**46**	**61**	**50**	**6**	**0**	**2**	**158**	**9.5**	**28**	**974**	**50.2**	**15:33**	**5**	**0**	**3**	**3**	**2**	**0**	**0**	**0**	**15:20**
	Sweden	Olympics	4	1	2	3	0																		
2002-03	**Chicago**	**NHL**	**9**	**0**	**4**	**4**	**4**	**0**	**0**	**0**	**20**	**0.0**	**0**	**86**	**48.8**	**15:19**									
	Washington	**NHL**	**71**	**17**	**39**	**56**	**36**	**7**	**0**	**2**	**141**	**12.1**	**3**	**1005**	**47.4**	**18:41**	**6**	**3**	**2**	**5**	**8**	**1**	**0**	**1**	**16:45**
2003-04	**Washington**	**NHL**	**3**	**0**	**2**	**2**	**8**	**0**	**0**	**0**	**1**	**0.0**	**1**	**22**	**54.6**	**14:57**									
	Boston	**NHL**	**15**	**1**	**11**	**12**	**14**	**0**	**0**	**1**	**29**	**3.4**	**3**	**128**	**46.1**	**15:43**	**6**	**3**	**3**	**6**	**0**	**0**	**0**	**0**	**18:57**
2004-05	Karpat Oulu	Finland	23	5	15	20	22																		
	St. Petersburg	Russia	8	2	5	7	0																		
	Ak Bars Kazan	Russia	5	0	1	1	2																		
	NHL Totals		**648**	**140**	**307**	**447**	**294**	**34**	**0**	**22**	**1142**	**12.3**		**3947**	**48.4**	**16:41**	**30**	**6**	**14**	**20**	**12**	**1**	**0**	**1**	**17:06**

Traded to **Calgary** by **Hartford** with James Patrick and Zarley Zalapski for Gary Suter, Paul Ranheim and Ted Drury, March 10, 1994. • Missed majority of 1994-95 season recovering from wrist injury suffered in game vs. St. Louis, January 24, 1995. Traded to **Tampa Bay** by **Calgary** for Andrei Nazarov, January 19, 1999. Traded to **Chicago** by **Tampa Bay** for Bryan Muir and Reid Simpson, November 12, 1999. Traded to **Washington** by **Chicago** with Chicago's 3rd round choice (Stephen Werner) in 2003 Entry Draft and future considerations for Chris Simon and Andrei Nikolishin, November 1, 2002. • Missed majority of 2003-04 season recovering from leg injury suffered in practice, October 2, 2003. Traded to **Boston** by **Washington** for Boston's 4th round compensatory choice (Patrick McNeill) in 2005 Entry Draft and Boston's 2nd round choice in 2006 Entry Draft, March 4, 2004. Signed as a free agent by **NY Rangers**, August 10, 2004. Signed as a free agent by **Karpat** (Finland), September 25, 2004. Signed as a free agent by **St. Petersburg** (Russia), December 20, 2004. Signed as a free agent by **Kazan** (Russia), February 14, 2005.

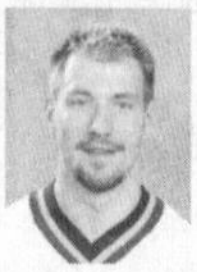

OBSUT, Jaroslav

(OHB-suht, YAHR-oh-slahv)

Defense. Shoots left. 6'1", 200 lbs. Born, Presov, Czech., September 3, 1976. Winnipeg's 9th choice, 188th overall, in 1995 Entry Draft.

Season	Club	League	GP	G	A	Pts	PIM	PP	SH	GW	S	%	+/-	TF	F%	Min	GP	G	A	Pts	PIM	PP	SH	GW	Min
1994-95	North Battleford	SJHL	55	21	30	51	126																		
1995-96	Swift Current	WHL	72	10	11	21	57										6	0	0	0	2				
1996-97	Edmonton Ice	WHL	13	2	9	11	4																		
	Medicine Hat	WHL	50	8	26	34	42										4	0	2	2	2				
	Toledo Storm	ECHL	3	1	0	1	0										5	0	1	1	6				
1997-98	Raleigh IceCaps	ECHL	60	6	26	32	46																		
	Syracuse Crunch	AHL	4	0	1	1	4																		
1998-99	Augusta Lynx	ECHL	41	11	25	36	42																		
	Manitoba Moose	IHL	2	0	0	0	0																		
	Worcester IceCats	AHL	31	2	8	10	14										4	0	1	1	2				
99-2000	Worcester IceCats	AHL	7	0	2	2	4																		
2000-01	**St. Louis**	**NHL**	**4**	**0**	**0**	**0**	**2**	**0**	**0**	**0**	**3**	**0.0**	**1**	**0**	**0.0**	**18:31**									
	Peoria Rivermen	ECHL	3	0	4	4	2																		
	Worcester IceCats	AHL	47	9	12	21	20										7	0	1	1	4				

			Regular Season														Playoffs								
Season	Club	League	GP	G	A	Pts	PIM	PP	SH	GW	S	%	+/-	TF	F%	Min	GP	G	A	Pts	PIM	PP	SH	GW	Min
2001-02	Colorado	NHL	3	0	0	0	0	0	0	0	3	0.0	0	0	0.0	9:47	....	....	....	....	....	....	....	....	....
	Hershey Bears	AHL	58	3	22	25	48	....	....	....	....	....	....	....	....	....	8	0	2	2	2	....	....	....	....
	Slovakia	Olympics	4	0	0	0	2	....	....	....	....	....	....	....	....	....	....	....	....	....	....	....	....	....	....
2002-03	Manitoba Moose	AHL	60	6	13	19	59	....	....	....	....	....	....	....	....	....	14	0	4	4	8	....	....	....	....
2003-04	Manitoba Moose	AHL	65	11	26	37	42	....	....	....	....	....	....	....	....	....	....	....	....	....	....	....	....	....	....
2004-05	Lulea HF	Sweden	49	11	19	30	50	....	....	....	....	....	....	....	....	....	2	0	0	0	50	....	....	....	....
	NHL Totals		7	0	0	0	2	0	0	0	6	0.0		0	0.0	14:46	....	....	....	....	....	....	....	....	....

Signed as a free agent by **St. Louis**, April 26, 1999. • Missed majority of 1999-2000 season recovering from knee injury suffered in practice, October, 1999. Signed as a free agent by **Colorado**, August 11, 2001. Signed as a free agent by **Vancouver**, July 10, 2002. Signed as a free agent by **Lulea** (Sweden), April 28, 2004.

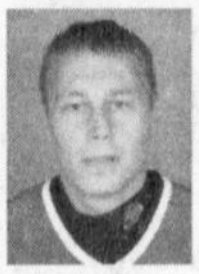

ODELEIN, Lyle
(OH-duh-LIGHN, LIGHL) **PIT.**

Defense. Shoots right. 6', 210 lbs. Born, Quill Lake, Sask., July 21, 1968. Montreal's 8th choice, 141st overall, in 1986 Entry Draft.

1984-85	Reg. Pat Cdns.	SMHL	26	12	13	25	30	....	....	....	....	....	....	....	....	....	....	....	....	....	....	....	....	....	....
1985-86	Moose Jaw	WHL	67	9	37	46	117	....	....	....	....	....	....	....	....	....	13	1	6	7	34	....	....	....	....
1986-87	Moose Jaw	WHL	59	9	50	59	70	....	....	....	....	....	....	....	....	....	9	2	5	7	26	....	....	....	....
1987-88	Moose Jaw	WHL	63	15	43	58	166	....	....	....	....	....	....	....	....	....	....	....	....	....	....	....	....	....	....
1988-89	Sherbrooke	AHL	33	3	4	7	120	....	....	....	....	....	....	....	....	....	3	0	2	2	5	....	....	....	....
	Peoria Rivermen	IHL	36	2	8	10	116	....	....	....	....	....	....	....	....	....	....	....	....	....	....	....	....	....	....
1989-90	Montreal	NHL	8	0	2	2	33	0	0	0	1	0.0	-1	....	....	....	....	....	....	....	....	....	....	....	....
	Sherbrooke	AHL	68	7	24	31	265	....	....	....	....	....	....	....	....	....	12	6	5	11	79	....	....	....	....
1990-91	Montreal	NHL	52	0	2	2	259	0	0	0	25	0.0	7	....	....	....	12	0	0	0	54	0	0	0	....
1991-92	Montreal	NHL	71	1	7	8	212	0	0	0	43	2.3	15	....	....	....	7	0	0	0	11	0	0	0	....
1992-93♦	Montreal	NHL	83	2	14	16	205	0	0	0	79	2.5	35	....	....	....	20	1	5	6	30	0	0	0	....
1993-94	Montreal	NHL	79	11	29	40	276	6	0	2	116	9.5	8	....	....	....	7	0	0	0	17	0	0	0	....
1994-95	Montreal	NHL	48	3	7	10	152	0	0	0	74	4.1	-13	....	....	....	....	....	....	....	....	....	....	....	....
1995-96	Montreal	NHL	79	3	14	17	230	0	1	0	74	4.1	8	....	....	....	6	1	1	2	6	0	1	0	....
1996-97	New Jersey	NHL	79	3	13	16	110	1	0	2	93	3.2	16	....	....	....	10	2	2	4	19	1	0	0	....
1997-98	New Jersey	NHL	79	4	19	23	171	1	0	0	76	5.3	11	....	....	....	6	1	1	2	21	1	0	1	....
1998-99	New Jersey	NHL	70	5	26	31	114	1	0	0	101	5.0	6	0	0.0	19:53	7	0	3	3	10	0	0	0	18:28
99-2000	New Jersey	NHL	57	1	15	16	104	0	0	1	59	1.7	-10	0	0.0	16:42	....	....	....	....	....	....	....	....	....
	Phoenix	NHL	16	1	7	8	19	1	0	0	30	3.3	1	0	0.0	21:45	5	0	0	0	16	0	0	0	16:38
2000-01	Columbus	NHL	81	3	14	17	118	1	0	0	104	2.9	-16	0	0.0	21:31	....	....	....	....	....	....	....	....	....
2001-02	Columbus	NHL	65	2	14	16	89	1	0	0	76	2.6	-28	0	0.0	22:12	....	....	....	....	....	....	....	....	....
	Chicago	NHL	12	0	2	2	4	0	0	0	10	0.0	0	0	0.0	24:23	4	0	1	1	25	0	0	0	24:08
2002-03	Chicago	NHL	65	7	4	11	76	0	0	0	77	9.1	7	1	100.0	19:05	....	....	....	....	....	....	....	....	....
	Dallas	NHL	3	0	0	0	6	0	0	0	1	0.0	0	0	0.0	17:49	2	0	0	0	0	0	0	0	12:52
2003-04	Florida	NHL	82	4	12	16	88	2	0	0	67	6.0	-7	1	100.0	18:53	....	....	....	....	....	....	....	....	....
2004-05			DID NOT PLAY																						
	NHL Totals		1029	50	201	251	2266	13	1	5	1106	4.5		2	100.0	19:59	86	5	13	18	209	2	1	1	18:36

Traded to **New Jersey** by **Montreal** for Stephane Richer, August 22, 1996. Traded to **Phoenix** by **New Jersey** for Deron Quint and Phoenix's 3rd round choice (later traded back to Phoenix – Phoenix selected Beat Forster) in 2001 Entry Draft, March 7, 2000. Claimed by **Columbus** from **Phoenix** in Expansion Draft, June 23, 2000. Traded to **Chicago** by **Columbus** for Jaroslav Spacek and Chicago's 2nd round choice (Dan Fritsche) in 2003 Entry Draft, March 19, 2002. Traded to **Dallas** by **Chicago** for Sami Helenius and Dallas's 7th round choice (Troy Brouwer) in 2004 Entry Draft, March 10, 2003. Signed as a free agent by **Florida**, September 9, 2003. Signed as a free agent by **Pittsburgh**, September 2, 2005.

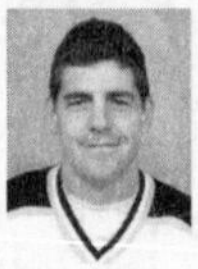

O'DONNELL, Sean
(oh-DOHN-ehl, SHAWN) **PHX.**

Defense. Shoots left. 6'3", 227 lbs. Born, Ottawa, Ont., October 13, 1971. Buffalo's 6th choice, 123rd overall, in 1991 Entry Draft.

1987-88	Kanata Valley	CJHL	54	4	25	29	96	....	....	....	....	....	....	....	....	....	....	....	....	....	....	....	....	....	....
1988-89	Sudbury Wolves	OHL	56	1	9	10	49	....	....	....	....	....	....	....	....	....	....	....	....	....	....	....	....	....	....
1989-90	Sudbury Wolves	OHL	64	7	19	26	84	....	....	....	....	....	....	....	....	....	7	1	2	3	8	....	....	....	....
1990-91	Sudbury Wolves	OHL	66	8	23	31	114	....	....	....	....	....	....	....	....	....	5	1	4	5	10	....	....	....	....
1991-92	Rochester	AHL	73	4	9	13	193	....	....	....	....	....	....	....	....	....	16	1	2	3	21	....	....	....	....
1992-93	Rochester	AHL	74	3	18	21	203	....	....	....	....	....	....	....	....	....	17	1	6	7	38	....	....	....	....
1993-94	Rochester	AHL	64	2	10	12	242	....	....	....	....	....	....	....	....	....	4	0	1	1	21	....	....	....	....
1994-95	Phoenix	IHL	61	2	18	20	132	....	....	....	....	....	....	....	....	....	9	0	1	1	21	....	....	....	....
	Los Angeles	NHL	15	0	2	2	49	0	0	0	12	0.0	-2	....	....	....	....	....	....	....	....	....	....	....	....
1995-96	Los Angeles	NHL	71	2	5	7	127	0	0	0	65	3.1	3	....	....	....	....	....	....	....	....	....	....	....	....
1996-97	Los Angeles	NHL	55	5	12	17	144	2	0	0	68	7.4	-13	....	....	....	....	....	....	....	....	....	....	....	....
1997-98	Los Angeles	NHL	80	2	15	17	179	0	0	1	71	2.8	7	....	....	....	4	1	0	1	36	0	0	0	....
1998-99	Los Angeles	NHL	80	1	13	14	186	0	0	0	64	1.6	1	0	0.0	19:10	....	....	....	....	....	....	....	....	....
99-2000	Los Angeles	NHL	80	2	12	14	114	0	0	1	51	3.9	4	0	0.0	17:41	4	1	0	1	4	0	0	0	16:26
2000-01	Minnesota	NHL	63	4	12	16	128	1	0	2	58	6.9	-2	12	50.0	23:00	....	....	....	....	....	....	....	....	....
	New Jersey	NHL	17	0	1	1	33	0	0	0	9	0.0	2	0	0.0	16:27	23	1	2	3	41	0	0	0	16:21
2001-02	Boston	NHL	80	3	22	25	89	1	0	2	112	2.7	27	0	0.0	24:50	6	0	2	2	4	0	0	0	24:57
2002-03	Boston	NHL	70	1	15	16	76	0	0	1	61	1.6	8	1	0.0	22:05	....	....	....	....	....	....	....	....	....
2003-04	Boston	NHL	82	1	10	11	110	1	0	0	72	1.4	10	3	33.3	20:36	7	0	0	0	0	0	0	0	19:53
2004-05			DID NOT PLAY																						
	NHL Totals		693	21	119	140	1235	4	0	7	643	3.3		16	43.8	20:58	44	3	4	7	85	0	0	0	18:16

Traded to **Los Angeles** by **Buffalo** for Doug Houda, July 26, 1994. Claimed by **Minnesota** from **Los Angeles** in Expansion Draft, June 23, 2000. Traded to **New Jersey** by **Minnesota** for Willie Mitchell, March 4, 2001. Signed as a free agent by **Boston**, July 2, 2001. Signed as a free agent by **Phoenix**, July 6, 2004.

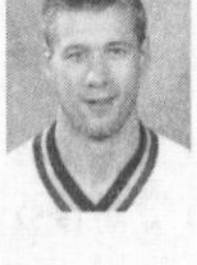

OHLUND, Mattias
(OH-luhnd, MAT-tee-ahs) **VAN.**

Defense. Shoots left. 6'2", 220 lbs. Born, Pitea, Sweden, September 9, 1976. Vancouver's 1st choice, 13th overall, in 1994 Entry Draft.

1992-93	Pitea HC	Sweden-2	22	0	6	6	16	....	....	....	....	....	....	....	....	....	....	....	....	....	....	....	....	....	....
1993-94	Pitea HC	Sweden-2	28	7	10	17	62	....	....	....	....	....	....	....	....	....	....	....	....	....	....	....	....	....	....
1994-95	Lulea HF	Sweden	34	6	10	16	34	....	....	....	....	....	....	....	....	....	9	4	0	4	16	....	....	....	....
1995-96	Lulea HF	Sweden	38	4	10	14	26	....	....	....	....	....	....	....	....	....	13	1	0	1	47	....	....	....	....
1996-97	Lulea HF	Sweden	47	7	9	16	38	....	....	....	....	....	....	....	....	....	10	1	2	3	8	....	....	....	....
	Lulea HF	EuroHL	6	0	3	3	0	....	....	....	....	....	....	....	....	....	....	....	....	....	....	....	....	....	....
1997-98	Vancouver	NHL	77	7	23	30	76	1	0	0	172	4.1	3	....	....	....	....	....	....	....	....	....	....	....	....
	Sweden	Olympics	4	0	1	1	4	....	....	....	....	....	....	....	....	....	....	....	....	....	....	....	....	....	....
1998-99	Vancouver	NHL	74	9	26	35	83	2	1	1	129	7.0	-19	0	0.0	26:04	....	....	....	....	....	....	....	....	....
99-2000	Vancouver	NHL	42	4	16	20	24	2	1	1	63	6.3	6	0	0.0	27:41	....	....	....	....	....	....	....	....	....
2000-01	Vancouver	NHL	65	8	20	28	46	1	1	4	136	5.9	-16	0	0.0	25:00	4	1	3	4	6	1	0	0	26:32
2001-02	Vancouver	NHL	81	10	26	36	56	4	1	3	193	5.2	16	0	0.0	25:17	6	1	1	2	6	0	0	0	28:48
	Sweden	Olympics	4	0	2	2	2	....	....	....	....	....	....	....	....	....	....	....	....	....	....	....	....	....	....
2002-03	Vancouver	NHL	59	2	27	29	42	0	0	0	100	2.0	1	0	0.0	25:23	13	3	4	7	12	0	0	0	24:01
2003-04	Vancouver	NHL	82	14	20	34	73	5	0	3	129	10.9	14	0	0.0	25:47	7	1	4	5	13	0	0	1	27:25
2004-05	Lulea HF	Sweden	2	1	0	1	4	....	....	....	....	....	....	....	....	....	....	....	....	....	....	....	....	....	....
	NHL Totals		480	54	158	212	400	15	4	12	922	5.9		0	0.0	25:45	30	6	12	18	37	1	0	1	26:06

NHL All-Rookie Team (1998)

Played in NHL All-Star Game (1999)

Signed as a free agent by **Lulea** (Sweden), December 21, 2004.

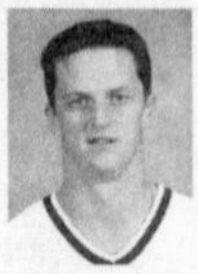

OLIVER, David
(AWL-ih-vuhr, DAY-vihd) **DAL.**

Right wing. Shoots right. 6', 190 lbs. Born, Sechelt, B.C., April 17, 1971. Edmonton's 7th choice, 144th overall, in 1991 Entry Draft.

1988-89	Vernon Lakers	BCJHL	58	41	38	79	38	....	....	....	....	....	....	....	....	....	....	....	....	....	....	....	....	....	....
1989-90	Vernon Lakers	BCJHL	58	51	48	99	22	....	....	....	....	....	....	....	....	....	....	....	....	....	....	....	....	....	....
1990-91	U. of Michigan	CCHA	27	13	11	24	34	....	....	....	....	....	....	....	....	....	....	....	....	....	....	....	....	....	....
1991-92	U. of Michigan	CCHA	44	31	27	58	32	....	....	....	....	....	....	....	....	....	....	....	....	....	....	....	....	....	....
1992-93	U. of Michigan	CCHA	40	35	20	55	18	....	....	....	....	....	....	....	....	....	....	....	....	....	....	....	....	....	....
1993-94	U. of Michigan	CCHA	41	28	40	68	16	....	....	....	....	....	....	....	....	....	....	....	....	....	....	....	....	....	....
1994-95	Cape Breton	AHL	32	11	18	29	8	....	....	....	....	....	....	....	....	....	....	....	....	....	....	....	....	....	....
	Edmonton	NHL	44	16	14	30	20	10	0	0	79	20.3	-11	....	....	....	....	....	....	....	....	....	....	....	....
1995-96	Edmonton	NHL	80	20	19	39	34	14	0	0	131	15.3	-22	....	....	....	....	....	....	....	....	....	....	....	....
1996-97	Edmonton	NHL	17	1	2	3	4	0	0	0	22	4.5	-8	....	....	....	....	....	....	....	....	....	....	....	....
	NY Rangers	NHL	14	2	1	3	4	0	0	0	13	15.4	3	....	....	....	3	0	0	0	0	0	0	0	....

			Regular Season														Playoffs								
Season	Club	League	GP	G	A	Pts	PIM	PP	SH	GW	S	%	+/-	TF	F%	Min	GP	G	A	Pts	PIM	PP	SH	GW	Min
1997-98	Houston Aeros	IHL	78	38	27	65	60	....	....	....	....	....	....	....	....	....	4	3	0	3	4	....	....	....	....
1998-99	**Ottawa**	**NHL**	**17**	**2**	**5**	**7**	**4**	**0**	**0**	**0**	**18**	**11.1**	**1**	**3**	**33.3**	**10:34**	....	....	....	....	....	....	....	....	....
	Houston Aeros	IHL	37	18	17	35	30	....	....	....	....	....	....	....	....	....	19	10	6	16	22	....	....	....	....
99-2000	**Phoenix**	**NHL**	**9**	**1**	**0**	**1**	**2**	**1**	**0**	**0**	**6**	**16.7**	**0**	**0**	**0.0**	**7:38**	....	....	....	....	....	....	....	....	....
	Houston Aeros	IHL	45	16	11	27	40	....	....	....	....	....	....	....	....	....	11	3	4	7	8	....	....	....	....
2000-01	**Ottawa**	**NHL**	**7**	**0**	**0**	**0**	**2**	**0**	**0**	**0**	**2**	**0.0**	**0**	**0**	**0.0**	**5:37**	....	....	....	....	....	....	....	....	....
	Grand Rapids	IHL	51	14	17	31	35	....	....	....	....	....	....	....	....	....	10	6	2	8	8	....	....	....	....
2001-02	Munchen Barons	Germany	59	20	14	34	30	....	....	....	....	....	....	....	....	....	9	2	2	4	6	....	....	....	....
2002-03	**Dallas**	**NHL**	**6**	**0**	**3**	**3**	**2**	**0**	**0**	**0**	**5**	**0.0**	**1**	**0**	**0.0**	**9:13**	**6**	**0**	**0**	**0**	**2**	**0**	**0**	**0**	**6:33**
	Utah Grizzlies	AHL	37	11	14	25	14	....	....	....	....	....	....	....	....	....	....	....	....	....	....	....	....	....	....
2003-04	**Dallas**	**NHL**	**36**	**7**	**5**	**12**	**12**	**3**	**0**	**1**	**30**	**23.3**	**6**	**1**	**100.0**	**9:51**	**1**	**0**	**0**	**0**	**0**	**0**	**0**	**0**	**7:31**
	Utah Grizzlies	AHL	31	5	12	17	12	....	....	....	....	....	....	....	....	....	....	....	....	....	....	....	....	....	....
2004-05	Guildford Flames	Britain-2	16	8	14	22	4	....	....	....	....	....	....	....	....	....	15	3	5	8	31	....	....	....	....
	NHL Totals		**230**	**49**	**49**	**98**	**84**	**28**	**0**	**1**	**306**	**16.0**		**4**	**50.0**	**9:18**	**10**	**0**	**0**	**0**	**2**	**0**	**0**	**0**	**6:41**

CCHA Second All-Star Team (1993) • CCHA First All-Star Team (1994) • CCHA Player of the Year (1994) • NCAA West First All-American Team (1994)

Claimed on waivers by **NY Rangers** from **Edmonton**, February 21, 1997. Signed as a free agent by **Ottawa**, July 2, 1998. Signed as a free agent by **Phoenix**, July 20, 1999. Signed as a free agent by **Ottawa**, August 2, 2000. Signed as a free agent by **Dallas**, July 30, 2002. Signed as a free agent by **Guildford** (Britain-2), January 13, 2005.

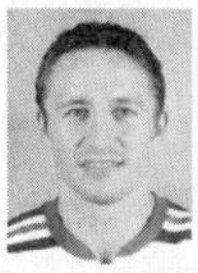

OLIWA, Krzysztof

(oh-LEE-vuh, KHRIH-stahf) **N.J.**

Left wing. Shoots left. 6'5", 245 lbs. Born, Tychy, Poland, April 12, 1973. New Jersey's 4th choice, 65th overall, in 1993 Entry Draft.

Season	Club	League	GP	G	A	Pts	PIM	PP	SH	GW	S	%	+/-	TF	F%	Min	GP	G	A	Pts	PIM	PP	SH	GW	Min
1990-91	GKS Katowski Jr.	Poland-Jr.	5	4	4	8	10	....	....	....	....	....	....	....	....	....	....	....	....	....	....	....	....	....	....
1991-92	GKS Tychy	Poland	10	3	7	10	6	....	....	....	....	....	....	....	....	....	....	....	....	....	....	....	....	....	....
1992-93	Welland Cougars	OHA-B	30	13	21	34	127	....	....	....	....	....	....	....	....	....	....	....	....	....	....	....	....	....	....
1993-94	Albany River Rats	AHL	33	2	4	6	151	....	....	....	....	....	....	....	....	....	....	....	....	....	....	....	....	....	....
	Raleigh IceCaps	ECHL	15	0	2	2	65	....	....	....	....	....	....	....	....	....	9	0	0	0	35	....	....	....	....
1994-95	Albany River Rats	AHL	20	1	1	2	77	....	....	....	....	....	....	....	....	....	....	....	....	....	....	....	....	....	....
	Saint John Flames	AHL	14	1	4	5	79	....	....	....	....	....	....	....	....	....	....	....	....	....	....	....	....	....	....
	Raleigh IceCaps	ECHL	5	0	2	2	32	....	....	....	....	....	....	....	....	....	....	....	....	....	....	....	....	....	....
	Detroit Vipers	IHL	4	0	1	1	24	....	....	....	....	....	....	....	....	....	....	....	....	....	....	....	....	....	....
1995-96	Albany River Rats	AHL	51	5	11	16	217	....	....	....	....	....	....	....	....	....	....	....	....	....	....	....	....	....	....
	Raleigh IceCaps	ECHL	9	1	0	1	53	....	....	....	....	....	....	....	....	....	....	....	....	....	....	....	....	....	....
1996-97	**New Jersey**	**NHL**	**1**	**0**	**0**	**0**	**5**	**0**	**0**	**0**	**0**	**0.0**	**–1**	....	....	....	....	....	....	....	....	....	....	....	....
	Albany River Rats	AHL	60	13	14	27	322	....	....	....	....	....	....	....	....	....	15	7	1	8	49	....	....	....	....
1997-98	**New Jersey**	**NHL**	**73**	**2**	**3**	**5**	**295**	**0**	**0**	**2**	**53**	**3.8**	**3**	....	....	....	**6**	**0**	**0**	**0**	**23**	**0**	**0**	**0**	....
1998-99	**New Jersey**	**NHL**	**64**	**5**	**7**	**12**	**240**	**0**	**0**	**1**	**59**	**8.5**	**4**	**1**	**0.0**	**7:02**	**1**	**0**	**0**	**0**	**2**	**0**	**0**	**0**	**2:35**
99-2000♦	**New Jersey**	**NHL**	**69**	**6**	**10**	**16**	**184**	**1**	**0**	**2**	**61**	**9.8**	**–2**	**3**	**66.7**	**6:45**	....	....	....	....	....	....	....	....	....
2000-01	**Columbus**	**NHL**	**10**	**0**	**2**	**2**	**34**	**0**	**0**	**0**	**5**	**0.0**	**1**	**0**	**0.0**	**5:17**	....	....	....	....	....	....	....	....	....
	Pittsburgh	**NHL**	**26**	**1**	**2**	**3**	**131**	**0**	**0**	**0**	**17**	**5.9**	**–4**	**1**	**100.0**	**4:58**	**5**	**0**	**0**	**0**	**16**	**0**	**0**	**0**	**2:14**
2001-02	**Pittsburgh**	**NHL**	**57**	**0**	**2**	**2**	**150**	**0**	**0**	**0**	**31**	**0.0**	**–5**	**0**	**0.0**	**5:35**	....	....	....	....	....	....	....	....	....
2002-03	**NY Rangers**	**NHL**	**9**	**0**	**0**	**0**	**51**	**0**	**0**	**0**	**3**	**0.0**	**1**	**1**	**0.0**	**3:45**	....	....	....	....	....	....	....	....	....
	Hartford	AHL	15	0	1	1	30	....	....	....	....	....	....	....	....	....	....	....	....	....	....	....	....	....	....
	Boston	**NHL**	**33**	**0**	**0**	**0**	**110**	**0**	**0**	**0**	**11**	**0.0**	**–4**	**1**	**0.0**	**3:58**	....	....	....	....	....	....	....	....	....
2003-04	**Calgary**	**NHL**	**65**	**3**	**2**	**5**	**247**	**0**	**0**	**0**	**32**	**9.4**	**–8**	**5**	**20.0**	**4:56**	**20**	**2**	**0**	**2**	**6**	**0**	**0**	**0**	**3:44**
2004-05	Nowy Targ	Poland	....	....	....	....	....	....	....	....	....	....	....	....	....	....	2	0	0	0	12	....	....	....	....
	NHL Totals		**407**	**17**	**28**	**45**	**1447**	**1**	**0**	**5**	**272**	**6.3**		**12**	**33.3**	**5:42**	**32**	**2**	**0**	**2**	**47**	**0**	**0**	**0**	**3:24**

Traded to **Columbus** by **New Jersey** with future considerations (Deron Quint, June 23, 2000) for Columbus' 3rd round choice (Brandon Nolan) in 2001 Entry Draft and future considerations (Turner Stevenson, June 23, 2000), June 12, 2000. • Missed majority of 2000-2001 season recovering from arm injury suffered in game vs. Detroit, October 28, 2000. Traded to **Pittsburgh** by **Columbus** for San Jose's 3rd round choice (previously acquired, Columbus selected Aaron Johnson) in 2001 Entry Draft, January 14, 2001. Traded to **NY Rangers** by **Pittsburgh** for NY Rangers' 9th round choice (later traded to Tampa Bay – Tampa Bay selected Albert Vishnyakov) in 2003 Entry Draft, June 23, 2002. Traded to **Boston** by **NY Rangers** for Boston's 9th round choice (later traded to San Jose - San Jose selected Brian Mahoney-Wilson) in 2004 Entry Draft, January 6, 2003. Signed as a free agent by **Calgary**, July 30, 2003. Signed as a free agent by **New Jersey**, July 15, 2004. Signed as a free agent by **Nowy Targ** (Poland), October 1, 2004.

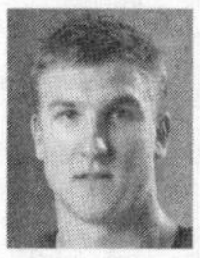

OLSON, Josh

(OHL-suhn, JAWSH)

Left wing. Shoots left. 6'5", 225 lbs. Born, Grand Forks, ND, July 13, 1981. Florida's 6th choice, 190th overall, in 2000 Entry Draft.

Season	Club	League	GP	G	A	Pts	PIM	PP	SH	GW	S	%	+/-	TF	F%	Min	GP	G	A	Pts	PIM	PP	SH	GW	Min
1998-99	Fargo-Moorhead	USHL	11	2	2	4	8	....	....	....	....	....	....	....	....	....	....	....	....	....	....	....	....	....	....
99-2000	Fargo-Moorhead	USHL	18	2	5	7	37	....	....	....	....	....	....	....	....	....	....	....	....	....	....	....	....	....	....
	Omaha Lancers	USHL	43	6	7	13	44	....	....	....	....	....	....	....	....	....	4	0	0	0	4	....	....	....	....
2000-01	Portland	WHL	72	22	38	60	86	....	....	....	....	....	....	....	....	....	16	5	4	9	17	....	....	....	....
2001-02	Portland	WHL	72	40	48	88	85	....	....	....	....	....	....	....	....	....	7	4	3	7	8	....	....	....	....
	Utah Grizzlies	AHL	1	0	0	0	0	....	....	....	....	....	....	....	....	....	1	0	0	0	0	....	....	....	....
2002-03	San Antonio	AHL	23	0	1	1	14	....	....	....	....	....	....	....	....	....	....	....	....	....	....	....	....	....	....
	Jackson Bandits	ECHL	39	10	17	27	13	....	....	....	....	....	....	....	....	....	1	0	1	1	0	....	....	....	....
2003-04	**Florida**	**NHL**	**5**	**1**	**0**	**1**	**0**	**0**	**0**	**0**	**6**	**16.7**	**1**	**0**	**0.0**	**8:17**	....	....	....	....	....	....	....	....	....
	San Antonio	AHL	73	22	16	38	33	....	....	....	....	....	....	....	....	....	....	....	....	....	....	....	....	....	....
2004-05	San Antonio	AHL	53	9	7	16	17	....	....	....	....	....	....	....	....	....	....	....	....	....	....	....	....	....	....
	Hershey Bears	AHL	23	1	2	3	4	....	....	....	....	....	....	....	....	....	....	....	....	....	....	....	....	....	....
	NHL Totals		**5**	**1**	**0**	**1**	**0**	**0**	**0**	**0**	**6**	**16.7**		**0**	**0.0**	**8:17**	....	....	....	....	....	....	....	....	....

Loaned to **Hershey** (AHL) by **San Antonio** (AHL) for the loan of Andre Savage, February 25, 2005.

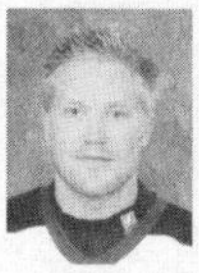

OLVESTAD, Jimmie

(OHL-vuh-stahd, JIHM-mee) **T.B.**

Left wing. Shoots left. 6'1", 194 lbs. Born, Stockholm, Sweden, February 16, 1980. Tampa Bay's 4th choice, 88th overall, in 1999 Entry Draft.

Season	Club	League	GP	G	A	Pts	PIM	PP	SH	GW	S	%	+/-	TF	F%	Min	GP	G	A	Pts	PIM	PP	SH	GW	Min
1996-97	Huddinge IK Jr.	Swe-Jr.	40	15	16	31	....	....	....	....	....	....	....	....	....	....	....	....	....	....	....	....	....	....	....
1997-98	Djurgarden Jr.	Swe-Jr.	10	3	3	6	10	....	....	....	....	....	....	....	....	....	....	....	....	....	....	....	....	....	....
	Huddinge IK	Sweden-2	11	0	0	0	6	....	....	....	....	....	....	....	....	....	....	....	....	....	....	....	....	....	....
1998-99	Djurgarden	Sweden	44	2	4	6	18	....	....	....	....	....	....	....	....	....	4	0	0	0	8	....	....	....	....
99-2000	Djurgarden	Sweden	50	6	3	9	34	....	....	....	....	....	....	....	....	....	13	1	2	3	12	....	....	....	....
2000-01	Djurgarden	Sweden	50	7	8	15	79	....	....	....	....	....	....	....	....	....	16	7	2	9	14	....	....	....	....
2001-02	**Tampa Bay**	**NHL**	**74**	**3**	**11**	**14**	**24**	**0**	**0**	**0**	**99**	**3.0**	**3**	**14**	**28.6**	**14:00**	....	....	....	....	....	....	....	....	....
2002-03	**Tampa Bay**	**NHL**	**37**	**0**	**3**	**3**	**16**	**0**	**0**	**0**	**30**	**0.0**	**–2**	**12**	**33.3**	**10:28**	....	....	....	....	....	....	....	....	....
	Springfield	AHL	6	0	1	1	13	....	....	....	....	....	....	....	....	....	....	....	....	....	....	....	....	....	....
2003-04	Hamilton	AHL	76	7	14	21	56	....	....	....	....	....	....	....	....	....	4	2	0	2	4	....	....	....	....
2004-05	Djurgarden	Sweden	46	4	8	12	89	....	....	....	....	....	....	....	....	....	12	0	1	1	47	....	....	....	....
	NHL Totals		**111**	**3**	**14**	**17**	**40**	**0**	**0**	**0**	**129**	**2.3**		**26**	**30.8**	**12:49**	....	....	....	....	....	....	....	....	....

Signed as a free agent by **Djurgarden** (Sweden), April 27, 2004.

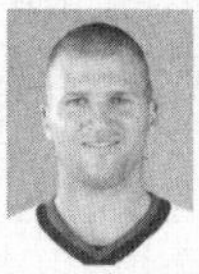

O'NEILL, Jeff

(oh-NEEL, JEHF) **TOR.**

Right wing. Shoots right. 6'1", 195 lbs. Born, Richmond Hill, Ont., February 23, 1976. Hartford's 1st choice, 5th overall, in 1994 Entry Draft.

Season	Club	League	GP	G	A	Pts	PIM	PP	SH	GW	S	%	+/-	TF	F%	Min	GP	G	A	Pts	PIM	PP	SH	GW	Min
1990-91	Richmond Hill	OMHA	78	56	134	190	....	....	....	....	....	....	....	....	....	....	....	....	....	....	....	....	....	....	....
1991-92	Thornhill	MTJHL	43	27	*53	80	48	....	....	....	....	....	....	....	....	....	....	....	....	....	....	....	....	....	....
1992-93	Guelph Storm	OHL	65	32	47	79	88	....	....	....	....	....	....	....	....	....	5	2	2	4	6	....	....	....	....
1993-94	Guelph Storm	OHL	66	45	81	126	95	....	....	....	....	....	....	....	....	....	9	2	11	13	31	....	....	....	....
1994-95	Guelph Storm	OHL	57	43	81	124	56	....	....	....	....	....	....	....	....	....	14	8	18	26	34	....	....	....	....
1995-96	**Hartford**	**NHL**	**65**	**8**	**19**	**27**	**40**	**1**	**0**	**1**	**65**	**12.3**	**–3**	....	....	....	....	....	....	....	....	....	....	....	....
1996-97	**Hartford**	**NHL**	**72**	**14**	**16**	**30**	**40**	**2**	**1**	**2**	**101**	**13.9**	**–24**	....	....	....	....	....	....	....	....	....	....	....	....
	Springfield	AHL	1	0	0	0	0	....	....	....	....	....	....	....	....	....	....	....	....	....	....	....	....	....	....
1997-98	**Carolina**	**NHL**	**74**	**19**	**20**	**39**	**67**	**7**	**1**	**4**	**114**	**16.7**	**–8**	....	....	....	....	....	....	....	....	....	....	....	....
1998-99	**Carolina**	**NHL**	**75**	**16**	**15**	**31**	**66**	**4**	**0**	**2**	**121**	**13.2**	**3**	**941**	**45.6**	**16:44**	**6**	**0**	**1**	**1**	**0**	**0**	**0**	**0**	**19:25**
99-2000	**Carolina**	**NHL**	**80**	**25**	**38**	**63**	**72**	**4**	**0**	**7**	**189**	**13.2**	**–9**	**1337**	**49.5**	**19:20**	....	....	....	....	....	....	....	....	....
2000-01	**Carolina**	**NHL**	**82**	**41**	**26**	**67**	**106**	**17**	**0**	**5**	**242**	**16.9**	**–18**	**726**	**50.0**	**18:20**	**6**	**1**	**2**	**3**	**10**	**0**	**0**	**1**	**17:33**
2001-02	**Carolina**	**NHL**	**76**	**31**	**33**	**64**	**63**	**11**	**0**	**6**	**272**	**11.4**	**–5**	**831**	**56.7**	**19:44**	**22**	**8**	**5**	**13**	**27**	**3**	**0**	**1**	**19:00**
2002-03	**Carolina**	**NHL**	**82**	**30**	**31**	**61**	**38**	**11**	**0**	**7**	**316**	**9.5**	**–21**	**986**	**54.1**	**19:09**	....	....	....	....	....	....	....	....	....
2003-04	**Carolina**	**NHL**	**67**	**14**	**20**	**34**	**60**	**7**	**0**	**4**	**207**	**6.8**	**–12**	**660**	**57.6**	**17:29**	....	....	....	....	....	....	....	....	....

					Regular Season														Playoffs						
Season	Club	League	GP	G	A	Pts	PIM	PP	SH	GW	S	%	+/-	TF	F%	Min	GP	G	A	Pts	PIM	PP	SH	GW	Min
2004-05			DID NOT PLAY																						
	NHL Totals		673	198	218	416	552	64	2	38	1627	12.2		5481	51.8	18:30	34	9	8	17	37	3	0	2	18:49

OHL All-Rookie Team (1993) • OHL Rookie of the Year (1993) • OHL First All-Star Team (1995)
Played in NHL All-Star Game (2003)
Transferred to **Carolina** after **Hartford** franchise relocated, June 25, 1997. Traded to **Toronto** by **Carolina** for a conditional choice in 2006 Entry Draft, July 30, 2005.

ORPIK, Brooks
(OHR-pihk, BRUKS)   **PIT.**

Defense. Shoots left. 6'2", 228 lbs.   Born, San Francisco, CA, September 26, 1980. Pittsburgh's 1st choice, 18th overall, in 2000 Entry Draft.

Season	Club	League	GP	G	A	Pts	PIM	PP	SH	GW	S	%	+/-	TF	F%	Min	GP	G	A	Pts	PIM	PP	SH	GW	Min
1996-97	Thayer Academy	High-MA	20	4	1	5	....																		
1997-98	Thayer Academy	High-MA	22	0	7	7	....																		
1998-99	Boston College	H-East	41	1	10	11	*96																		
99-2000	Boston College	H-East	38	1	9	10	102																		
2000-01	Boston College	H-East	40	0	20	20	*124																		
2001-02	Wilkes-Barre	AHL	78	2	18	20	99																		
2002-03	**Pittsburgh**	**NHL**	6	0	0	0	2	0	0	0	2	0.0	-5	0	0.0	18:19									
	Wilkes-Barre	AHL	71	4	14	18	105										6	0	0	0	14				
2003-04	**Pittsburgh**	**NHL**	79	1	9	10	127	0	0	0	56	1.8	-36	0	0.0	18:25									
	Wilkes-Barre	AHL	3	0	0	0	2										24	0	4	4	53				
2004-05			DID NOT PLAY																						
	NHL Totals		85	1	9	10	129	0	0	0	58	1.7		0	0.0	18:25									

ORR, Colton
(OHR, KOHL-tuhn)   **BOS.**

Right wing. Shoots right. 6'3", 210 lbs.   Born, Winnipeg, Man., March 3, 1982.

Season	Club	League	GP	G	A	Pts	PIM	PP	SH	GW	S	%	+/-	TF	F%	Min	GP	G	A	Pts	PIM	PP	SH	GW	Min
1998-99	St. Boniface	MJHL	STATISTICS NOT AVAILABLE																						
	Swift Current	WHL	2	0	0	0	0																		
99-2000	Swift Current	WHL	61	3	2	5	130										12	1	0	1	25				
2000-01	Swift Current	WHL	19	0	4	4	67																		
	Kamloops Blazers	WHL	41	8	1	9	179										3	0	0	0	20				
2001-02	Kamloops Blazers	WHL	1	0	0	0	7										2	0	0	0	2				
2002-03	Kamloops Blazers	WHL	3	2	0	2	17																		
	Regina Pats	WHL	37	6	2	8	170										3	0	0	0	19				
	Providence Bruins	AHL	1	0	0	0	7																		
2003-04	**Boston**	**NHL**	1	0	0	0	0	0	0	0	0	0.0	-1	0	0.0	2:13									
	Providence Bruins	AHL	64	1	4	5	257										2	0	0	0	9				
2004-05	Providence Bruins	AHL	61	1	6	7	279										17	1	0	1	44				
	NHL Totals		1	0	0	0	0	0	0	0	0	0.0		0	0.0	2:13									

Signed as a free agent by **Boston**, September 19, 2001. • Missed majority of 2001-02 season recovering from wrist injury suffered in game vs. Red Deer (WHL), October 20, 2001.

ORSZAGH, Vladimir
(OHR-sahg, vla-DIH-meer)

Right wing. Shoots left. 5'11", 195 lbs.   Born, Banska Bystrica, Czech., May 24, 1977. NY Islanders' 4th choice, 106th overall, in 1995 Entry Draft.

Season	Club	League	GP	G	A	Pts	PIM	PP	SH	GW	S	%	+/-	TF	F%	Min	GP	G	A	Pts	PIM	PP	SH	GW	Min
1993-94	B. Bystrica Jr.	Slovak-Jr.	38	38	27	65	....																		
1994-95	B. Bystrica	Slovak-2	38	18	12	30	....																		
1995-96	B. Bystrica	Slovakia	31	9	5	14	22																		
1996-97	Utah Grizzlies	IHL	68	12	15	27	30										3	0	1	1	4				
1997-98	**NY Islanders**	**NHL**	11	0	1	1	2	0	0	0	9	0.0	-3												
	Utah Grizzlies	IHL	62	13	10	23	60										4	2	0	2	0				
1998-99	**NY Islanders**	**NHL**	12	1	0	1	6	0	0	0	4	20.0	2	0	0.0	6:36									
	Lowell	AHL	68	18	23	41	57										3	2	2	4	2				
99-2000	**NY Islanders**	**NHL**	11	2	1	3	4	0	0	0	16	12.5	1	0	0.0	11:55	7	3	3	6	2				
	Lowell	AHL	55	8	12	20	22										16	*7	3	10	20				
2000-01	Djurgarden	Sweden	50	23	13	36	62																		
2001-02	**Nashville**	**NHL**	79	15	21	36	56	5	0	3	113	13.3	-15	10	20.0	16:04									
2002-03	**Nashville**	**NHL**	78	16	16	32	38	3	0	3	152	10.5	-1	17	29.4	17:34									
2003-04	**Nashville**	**NHL**	82	16	21	37	74	2	2	3	124	12.9	-4	39	25.6	17:00	6	2	0	2	4	0	0	0	16:08
2004-05	HKm Zvolen	Slovakia	37	16	14	30	50										17	5	2	7	24				
	B. Bystrica	Slovak-2	2	2	0	2	4																		
	NHL Totals		273	50	60	110	180	10	2	9	418	12.0		66	25.8	16:12	6	2	0	2	4	0	0	0	16:08

Signed as a free agent by **Nashville**, May 30, 2001.Signed as a free agent by **Zvolen** (Slovakia), October 6, 2004.

ORTMEYER, Jed
(OHRT-migh-uhr, JEHD)   **NYR**

Center. Shoots right. 6'1", 191 lbs.   Born, Omaha, NE, September 3, 1978.

Season	Club	League	GP	G	A	Pts	PIM	PP	SH	GW	S	%	+/-	TF	F%	Min	GP	G	A	Pts	PIM	PP	SH	GW	Min
1997-98	Omaha Lancers	USHL	54	23	25	48	52										14	3	4	7	31				
1998-99	Omaha Lancers	USHL	52	23	36	59	81										12	5	6	11	16				
99-2000	U. of Michigan	CCHA	41	8	16	24	40																		
2000-01	U. of Michigan	CCHA	27	10	11	21	52																		
2001-02	U. of Michigan	CCHA	41	15	23	38	40																		
2002-03	U. of Michigan	CCHA	36	18	16	34	48																		
2003-04	**NY Rangers**	**NHL**	58	2	4	6	16	0	0	0	48	4.2	-10	16	31.3	9:52									
	Hartford	AHL	13	2	8	10	4										16	5	2	7	6				
2004-05	Hartford	AHL	61	7	20	27	63										6	0	1	1	4				
	NHL Totals		58	2	4	6	16	0	0	0	48	4.2		16	31.3	9:52									

Signed as a free agent by **NY Rangers**, May 10, 2003.

OTT, Steve
(AWT, STEEV)   **DAL.**

Center. Shoots left. 6', 185 lbs.   Born, Summerside, P.E.I., August 19, 1982. Dallas' 1st choice, 25th overall, in 2000 Entry Draft.

Season	Club	League	GP	G	A	Pts	PIM	PP	SH	GW	S	%	+/-	TF	F%	Min	GP	G	A	Pts	PIM	PP	SH	GW	Min
1998-99	Leamington Flyers	OHA-B	48	14	30	44	110																		
99-2000	Windsor Spitfires	OHL	66	23	39	62	131										12	3	5	8	21				
2000-01	Windsor Spitfires	OHL	55	50	37	87	164										9	3	8	11	27				
2001-02	Windsor Spitfires	OHL	53	43	45	88	178										14	6	10	16	49				
2002-03	**Dallas**	**NHL**	26	3	4	7	31	0	0	0	25	12.0	6	4	50.0	8:46	1	0	0	0	0	0	0	0	6:57
	Utah Grizzlies	AHL	40	9	11	20	98																		
2003-04	**Dallas**	**NHL**	73	2	10	12	152	0	0	1	74	2.7	-2	59	49.2	10:14	4	1	0	1	0	0	0	1	6:55
2004-05	Hamilton	AHL	67	18	21	39	279										4	0	0	0	20				
	NHL Totals		99	5	14	19	183	0	0	1	99	5.1		63	49.2	9:51	5	1	0	1	0	0	0	1	6:55

OHL Second All-Star Team (2002)

OZOLINSH, Sandis
(OH-zoh-LIHNCH, SAN-dihz)   **ANA.**

Defense. Shoots left. 6'3", 217 lbs.   Born, Riga, Latvia, August 3, 1972. San Jose's 3rd choice, 30th overall, in 1991 Entry Draft.

Season	Club	League	GP	G	A	Pts	PIM	PP	SH	GW	S	%	+/-	TF	F%	Min	GP	G	A	Pts	PIM	PP	SH	GW	Min
1990-91	Dynamo Riga	USSR	44	0	3	3	51																		
1991-92	Rigas Stars	CIS	30	6	0	6	42																		
	Kansas City	IHL	34	6	9	15	20										15	2	5	7	22				
1992-93	**San Jose**	**NHL**	37	7	16	23	40	2	0	0	83	8.4	-9												
1993-94	**San Jose**	**NHL**	81	26	38	64	24	4	0	3	157	16.6	16				14	0	10	10	8	0	0	0	
1994-95	**San Jose**	**NHL**	48	9	16	25	30	3	1	2	83	10.8	-6				11	3	2	5	6	1	0	0	
1995-96	San Francisco	IHL	2	1	0	1	0																		
	♦ Colorado	**NHL**	66	13	37	50	50	1	0	0	21	4.8	2				22	5	14	19	16	2	0	1	
1996-97	**Colorado**	**NHL**	80	23	45	68	88	13	0	4	232	9.9	4				14	4	13	17	24	2	0	1	
1997-98	**Colorado**	**NHL**	66	13	38	51	65	9	0	2	135	9.6	-12				7	0	7	7	14	0	0	0	
1998-99	**Colorado**	**NHL**	39	17	25	32	22	4	0	3	81	8.6	10	0	0.0	22:06	19	4	8	12	22	3	0	1	22:14
99-2000	**Colorado**	**NHL**	82	16	36	52	46	6	0	1	210	7.6	17	0	0.0	22:41	17	5	5	10	20	3	0	1	18:35
2000-01	**Carolina**	**NHL**	72	12	32	44	71	4	2	2	145	8.3	-25	0	0.0	22:12	6	0	2	2	5	0	0	0	19:04

Season	Club	League	GP	G	A	Pts	PIM	PP	SH	GW	S	%	+/-	TF	F%	Min	GP	G	A	Pts	PIM	PP	SH	GW	Min
			Regular Season														Playoffs								
2001-02	Carolina	NHL	46	4	19	23	34	1	0	0	71	5.6	-4	0	0.0	19:30									
	Florida	NHL	37	10	19	29	24	2	0	1	101	9.9	-3	0	0.0	30:30									
	Latvia	Olympics	1	0	4	4	0																		
2002-03	Florida	NHL	51	7	19	26	40	5	0	2	83	8.4	-16	0	0.0	28:23									
	Anaheim	NHL	31	5	13	18	16	1	0	1	54	9.3	10	0	0.0	22:08	21	2	6	8	10	0	0	1	23:37
2003-04	Anaheim	NHL	36	5	11	16	24	1	0	2	58	8.6	-7	0	0.0	19:57									
2004-05		DID NOT PLAY																							
	NHL Totals		779	158	367	525	578	63	4	24	1659	9.5		0	0.0	23:21	134	23	67	90	125	11	0	5	21:28

NHL First All-Star Team (1997)

Played in NHL All-Star Game (1994, 1997, 1998, 2000, 2001, 2002, 2003)

• Missed majority of 1992-93 season recovering from knee injury suffered in game vs. Philadelphia, December 30, 1992. Traded to **Colorado** by **San Jose** for Owen Nolan, October 26, 1995. Traded to **Carolina** by **Colorado** with Columbus' 2nd round choice (previously acquired, Carolina selected Tomas Kurka) in 2000 Entry Draft for Nolan Pratt, Carolina's 1st (Vaclav Nedorost) and 2nd (Jared Aulin) round choices in 2000 Entry Draft and Philadelphia's 2nd round choice (previously acquired, Colorado selected Agris Saviels) in 2000 Entry Draft, June 24, 2000. Traded to **Florida** by **Carolina** with Byron Ritchie for Bret Hedican, Kevyn Adams and Tomas Malec, January 16, 2002. Traded to **Anaheim** by **Florida** with Lance Ward for Pavel Trnka, Matt Cullen and Anaheim's 4th round choice (James Pemberton) in 2003 Entry Draft, January 30, 2003. • Missed majority of 2003-04 season recovering from shoulder injury suffered in game vs. Colorado, December 19, 2003.

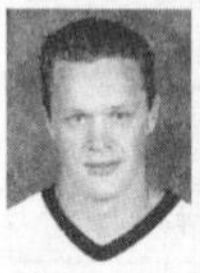

PAHLSSON, Samuel (PAWL-suhn, SAM-ew-l) ANA.

Center. Shoots left. 5'11", 212 lbs. Born, Ornskoldsvik, Sweden, December 17, 1977. Colorado's 10th choice, 176th overall, in 1996 Entry Draft.

Season	Club	League	GP	G	A	Pts	PIM	PP	SH	GW	S	%	+/-	TF	F%	Min	GP	G	A	Pts	PIM	PP	SH	GW	Min
1992-93	Ange IK	Sweden-4	9	0	0	0	0																		
1993-94	Ange IK	Sweden-4	STATISTICS NOT AVAILABLE																						
1994-95	MoDo	Sweden	1	0	0	0	0																		
1995-96	MoDo Jr.	Swe-Jr.	30	10	11	21	26																		
	MoDo	Sweden	36	1	3	4	8										4	0	0	0	0				
1996-97	MoDo Jr.	Swe-Jr.	5	2	6	8	2																		
	MoDo	Sweden	49	8	9	17	83																		
1997-98	MoDo	Sweden	23	6	11	17	24										9	3	0	3	6				
1998-99	MoDo	Sweden	50	17	17	34	44										13	3	3	6	10				
99-2000	MoDo	Sweden	47	16	11	27	67										13	3	3	6	8				
	MoDo	EuroHL	4	1	0	1	0										3	1	1	2	2				
2000-01	Boston	NHL	17	1	1	2	6	0	0	0	13	7.7	-5	239	40.2	14:19									
	Anaheim	NHL	59	3	4	7	14	1	1	1	46	6.5	-9	867	45.1	14:14									
2001-02	Anaheim	NHL	80	6	14	20	26	1	1	0	99	6.1	-16	1201	49.8	16:24									
2002-03	Anaheim	NHL	34	4	11	15	18	0	1	2	28	14.3	10	118	52.5	13:20	21	2	4	6	12	0	0	0	16:41
	Cincinnati	AHL	13	1	7	8	24																		
2003-04	Anaheim	NHL	82	8	14	22	52	1	0	2	134	6.0	-2	908	55.3	16:51									
2004-05	Frolunda	Sweden	48	6	18	24	56										14	4	7	11	24				
	NHL Totals		272	22	44	66	116	3	3	5	320	6.9		3333	49.5	15:33	21	2	4	6	12	0	0	0	16:41

Traded to **Boston** by **Colorado** with Brian Rolston, Martin Grenier and New Jersey's 1st round choice (previously acquired, Boston selected Martin Samuelsson) in 2000 Entry Draft for Raymond Bourque and Dave Andreychuk, March 6, 2000. Traded to **Anaheim** by **Boston** for Patrick Traverse and Andrei Nazarov, November 18, 2000. Signed as a free agent by **Frolunda** (Sweden), September, 2004.

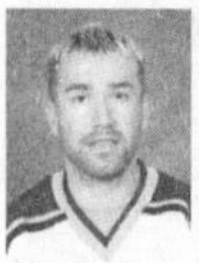

PALFFY, Ziggy (PAHL-fee, ZIHG-gee) PIT.

Right wing. Shoots left. 5'10", 183 lbs. Born, Skalica, Czech., May 5, 1972. NY Islanders' 2nd choice, 26th overall, in 1991 Entry Draft.

Season	Club	League	GP	G	A	Pts	PIM	PP	SH	GW	S	%	+/-	TF	F%	Min	GP	G	A	Pts	PIM	PP	SH	GW	Min
1990-91	AC Nitra	Czech	50	34	16	50	18																		
1991-92	Dukla Trencin	Czech	45	41	33	74	36																		
1992-93	Dukla Trencin	Czech	43	38	41	79																			
1993-94	NY Islanders	NHL	5	0	0	0	0	0	0	0	5	0.0	-6												
	Salt Lake	IHL	57	25	32	57	83																		
	Slovakia	Olympics	8	3	*7	*10	8																		
1994-95	Denver Grizzlies	IHL	33	20	23	43	40																		
	NY Islanders	NHL	33	10	7	17	6	1	0	1	75	13.3	3												
1995-96	NY Islanders	NHL	81	43	44	87	56	17	1	6	257	16.7	-17												
1996-97	Dukla Trencin	Slovakia	1	0	0	0																			
	NY Islanders	NHL	80	48	42	90	43	6	4	6	292	16.4	21												
1997-98	NY Islanders	NHL	82	45	42	87	34	17	2	5	277	16.2	-2												
1998-99	HK 36 Skalica	Slovakia	9	11	8	19	6																		
	NY Islanders	NHL	50	22	28	50	34	5	2	1	168	13.1	-6	1	100.0	22:04									
99-2000	Los Angeles	NHL	64	27	39	66	32	4	0	3	186	14.5	18	7	42.9	19:39	4	2	0	2	0	0	0	0	21:21
2000-01	Los Angeles	NHL	73	38	51	89	20	12	4	8	217	17.5	22	5	80.0	19:46	13	3	5	8	8	0	0	0	22:27
2001-02	Los Angeles	NHL	63	32	27	59	26	15	1	6	161	19.9	5	3	66.7	20:18	7	4	5	9	0	0	0	0	22:23
	Slovakia	Olympics	1	0	0	0	0																		
2002-03	Los Angeles	NHL	76	37	48	85	47	10	2	5	277	13.4	22	10	30.0	22:27									
2003-04	Los Angeles	NHL	35	16	25	41	12	3	3	2	109	14.7	18	7	0.0	21:32									
2004-05	HK 36 Skalica	Slovakia	8	10	3	13	6																		
	HC Slavia Praha	CzRep	41	21	19	40	30										7	5	2	7	2				
	NHL Totals		642	318	353	671	310	90	19	43	2024	15.7		33	39.4	20:54	24	9	10	19	8	0	0	0	22:15

Played in NHL All-Star Game (1998, 2001, 2002)

Traded to **Los Angeles** by **NY Islanders** with Brian Smolinski, Marcel Cousineau and New Jersey's 4th round choice (previously acquired, Los Angeles selected Daniel Johansson) in 1999 Entry Draft for Olli Jokinen, Josh Green, Mathieu Biron and Los Angeles' 1st round choice (Taylor Pyatt) in 1999 Entry Draft, June 20, 1999. • Missed majority of 2003-04 season recovering from shoulder injury suffered in game vs. Anaheim, January 7, 2004. Signed as a free agent by **Slavia** (CzRep), September 15, 2004. Signed as a free agent by **Skalica** (Slovakia), October 7, 2004. Signed as a free agent by **Slavia** (CzRep), November 16, 2004. Signed as a free agent by **Pittsburgh**, August 6, 2005.

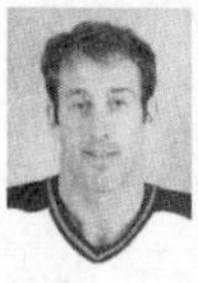

PANDOLFO, Jay (pan-DAHL-foh, JAY) N.J.

Left wing. Shoots left. 6'1", 190 lbs. Born, Winchester, MA, December 27, 1974. New Jersey's 2nd choice, 32nd overall, in 1993 Entry Draft.

Season	Club	League	GP	G	A	Pts	PIM	PP	SH	GW	S	%	+/-	TF	F%	Min	GP	G	A	Pts	PIM	PP	SH	GW	Min
1989-90	Burlington	High-MA	23	33	30	63	18																		
1990-91	Burlington	High-MA	20	19	27	46	10																		
1991-92	Burlington	High-MA	20	35	34	69	14																		
1992-93	Boston University	H-East	37	16	22	38	16																		
1993-94	Boston University	H-East	37	17	25	42	27																		
1994-95	Boston University	H-East	20	7	13	20	6																		
1995-96	Boston University	H-East	39	*38	29	67	6																		
	Albany River Rats	AHL	5	3	1	4	0										3	0	0	0	0				
1996-97	New Jersey	NHL	46	6	8	14	6	0	0	1	61	9.8	-1				6	0	1	1	0	0	0	0	
	Albany River Rats	AHL	12	3	9	12	0																		
1997-98	New Jersey	NHL	23	1	3	4	4	0	0	0	23	4.3	-4				3	0	2	2	0	0	0	0	
	Albany River Rats	AHL	51	18	19	37	24																		
1998-99	New Jersey	NHL	70	14	13	27	10	1	1	4	100	14.0	3	10	40.0	15:13	7	1	0	1	0	0	0	0	13:19
99-2000♦	New Jersey	NHL	71	7	8	15	4	1	0	0	86	8.1	0	19	47.4	13:25	23	0	5	5	0	0	0	0	15:35
2000-01	New Jersey	NHL	63	4	12	16	16	0	0	0	57	7.0	3	15	53.3	14:05	25	1	4	5	4	0	0	0	12:38
2001-02	New Jersey	NHL	65	4	10	14	15	0	1	0	72	5.6	12	12	41.7	13:59	6	0	0	0	0	0	0	0	16:11
2002-03♦	New Jersey	NHL	68	6	11	17	23	0	1	4	92	6.5	12	13	23.1	16:08	24	6	6	12	2	0	0	1	16:34
2003-04	New Jersey	NHL	82	13	13	26	14	1	2	4	140	9.3	5	25	44.0	16:00	5	0	0	0	0	0	0	0	13:41
2004-05	Salzburg	Austria	19	5	7	12	0																		
	NHL Totals		488	55	78	133	92	2	5	13	631	8.7		94	42.6	14:51	99	8	18	26	6	0	0	1	14:47

Hockey East First All-Star Team (1996) • Hockey East Player of the Year (1996) • NCAA East First All-American Team (1996)

Signed as a free agent by **Salzburg** (Austria), December 27, 2004.

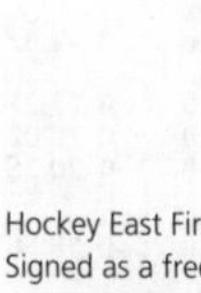

PANDOLFO, Mike (pan-DAHL-foh, MIGHK)

Left wing. Shoots left. 6'3", 221 lbs. Born, Winchester, MA, September 15, 1979. Buffalo's 5th choice, 77th overall, in 1998 Entry Draft.

Season	Club	League	GP	G	A	Pts	PIM	PP	SH	GW	S	%	+/-	TF	F%	Min	GP	G	A	Pts	PIM	PP	SH	GW	Min
1996-97	St. Sebastian's	High-MA	32	27	28	55	30																		
1997-98	St. Sebastian's	High-MA	28	29	23	52	18																		
1998-99	Boston University	H-East	34	13	4	17	26																		
99-2000	Boston University	H-East	41	13	10	23	37																		
2000-01	Boston University	H-East	37	16	13	29	30																		
2001-02	Boston University	H-East	38	22	18	40	22																		
2002-03	Syracuse Crunch	AHL	74	9	9	18	31																		

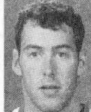

			Regular Season														Playoffs								
Season	Club	League	GP	G	A	Pts	PIM	PP	SH	GW	S	%	+/-	TF	F%	Min	GP	G	A	Pts	PIM	PP	SH	GW	Min
2003-04	**Columbus**	**NHL**	**3**	**0**	**0**	**0**	**0**	**0**	**0**	**0**	**3**	**0.0**	**–2**	**0**	**0.0**	**8:18**	....	....	....	....	....	....	....	....	....
	Syracuse Crunch	AHL	77	18	19	37	29	....	....	....	....	....	....	....	....	....	7	1	0	1	2	....	....	....	....
2004-05	Syracuse Crunch	AHL	62	8	8	16	18	....	....	....	....	....	....	....	....	....	....	....	....	....	....	....	....	....	....
	NHL Totals		**3**	**0**	**0**	**0**	**0**	**0**	**0**	**0**	**3**	**0.0**		**0**	**0.0**	**8:18**	....	....	....	....	....	....	....	....	....

Rights traded to **Columbus** by **Buffalo** with Detroit's 1st round choice (previously acquired, later traded to Atlanta – Atlanta selected Jim Slater) in 2002 Entry Draft for New Jersey's 1st round choice (previously acquired, Buffalo selected Dan Paille) in 2002 Entry Draft, June 22, 2002.

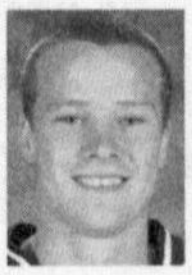

PAPINEAU, Justin

(PA-pee-noh, JUHS-tihn) **NYI**

Center. Shoots left. 5'10", 178 lbs. Born, Ottawa, Ont., January 15, 1980. St. Louis' 3rd choice, 75th overall, in 2000 Entry Draft.

Season	Club	League	GP	G	A	Pts	PIM	PP	SH	GW	S	%	+/-	TF	F%	Min	GP	G	A	Pts	PIM	PP	SH	GW	Min
1995-96	Ott. Jr. Senators	CJHL	52	31	19	50	51	....	....	....	....	....	....	....	....	....	....	....	....	....	....	....	....	....	....
1996-97	Belleville Bulls	OHL	50	10	32	42	32	....	....	....	....	....	....	....	....	....	....	....	....	....	....	....	....	....	....
1997-98	Belleville Bulls	OHL	66	41	53	94	34	....	....	....	....	....	....	....	....	....	10	5	9	14	6	....	....	....	....
1998-99	Belleville Bulls	OHL	68	52	47	99	28	....	....	....	....	....	....	....	....	....	21	*21	*30	*51	20	....	....	....	....
99-2000	Belleville Bulls	OHL	60	40	36	76	52	....	....	....	....	....	....	....	....	....	16	4	12	16	16	....	....	....	....
2000-01	Worcester IceCats	AHL	43	7	22	29	33	....	....	....	....	....	....	....	....	....	11	7	3	10	8	....	....	....	....
2001-02	**St. Louis**	**NHL**	**1**	**0**	**0**	**0**	**0**	**0**	**0**	**0**	**0**	**0.0**	**–2**	**7**	**42.9**	**8:40**	....	....	....	....	....	....	....	....	....
	Worcester IceCats	AHL	75	*38	38	76	86	....	....	....	....	....	....	....	....	....	3	1	2	3	4	....	....	....	....
2002-03	**St. Louis**	**NHL**	**11**	**2**	**1**	**3**	**0**	**0**	**0**	**1**	**15**	**13.3**	**–1**	**99**	**44.4**	**10:59**	....	....	....	....	....	....	....	....	....
	Worcester IceCats	AHL	44	21	17	38	42	....	....	....	....	....	....	....	....	....	....	....	....	....	....	....	....	....	....
	NY Islanders	**NHL**	**5**	**1**	**2**	**3**	**4**	**0**	**0**	**1**	**8**	**12.5**	**1**	**15**	**53.3**	**14:50**	**1**	**0**	**0**	**0**	**0**	**0**	**0**	**0**	**5:12**
	Bridgeport	AHL	5	7	1	8	4	....	....	....	....	....	....	....	....	....	7	1	3	4	7	....	....	....	....
2003-04	**NY Islanders**	**NHL**	**64**	**8**	**5**	**13**	**8**	**5**	**0**	**2**	**44**	**18.2**	**4**	**49**	**38.8**	**7:42**	....	....	....	....	....	....	....	....	....
2004-05	Bridgeport	AHL	59	18	15	33	52	....	....	....	....	....	....	....	....	....	....	....	....	....	....	....	....	....	....
	NHL Totals		**81**	**11**	**8**	**19**	**12**	**5**	**0**	**4**	**67**	**16.4**		**170**	**43.5**	**8:36**	**1**	**0**	**0**	**0**	**0**	**0**	**0**	**0**	**5:12**

• Re-entered NHL Entry Draft. Originally Los Angeles' 2nd choice, 46th overall, in 1998 Entry Draft.

Traded to **NY Islanders** by **St. Louis** with St. Louis' 2nd round choice (Jeremy Colliton) in 2003 Entry Draft for Chris Osgood and NY Islanders' 3rd round choice (Konstantin Barulin) in 2003 Entry Draft, March 11, 2003.

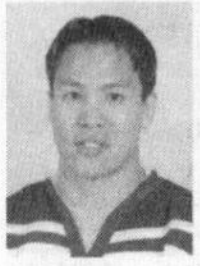

PARK, Richard

(PAHRK, RIH-chuhrd) **VAN.**

Right wing. Shoots right. 5'11", 190 lbs. Born, Seoul, South Korea, May 27, 1976. Pittsburgh's 2nd choice, 50th overall, in 1994 Entry Draft.

Season	Club	League	GP	G	A	Pts	PIM	PP	SH	GW	S	%	+/-	TF	F%	Min	GP	G	A	Pts	PIM	PP	SH	GW	Min
1991-92	Tor. Young Nats	MTHL	76	49	58	107	91	....	....	....	....	....	....	....	....	....	....	....	....	....	....	....	....	....	....
1992-93	Belleville Bulls	OHL	66	23	38	61	38	....	....	....	....	....	....	....	....	....	5	0	0	0	14	....	....	....	....
1993-94	Belleville Bulls	OHL	59	27	49	76	70	....	....	....	....	....	....	....	....	....	12	3	5	8	18	....	....	....	....
1994-95	Belleville Bulls	OHL	45	28	51	79	35	....	....	....	....	....	....	....	....	....	16	9	18	27	12	....	....	....	....
	Pittsburgh	**NHL**	**1**	**0**	**1**	**1**	**2**	**0**	**0**	**0**	**4**	**0.0**	**1**	....	....	....	**3**	**0**	**0**	**0**	**2**	**0**	**0**	**0**	....
1995-96	Belleville Bulls	OHL	6	7	6	13	2	....	....	....	....	....	....	....	....	....	14	18	12	30	10	....	....	....	....
	Pittsburgh	**NHL**	**56**	**4**	**6**	**10**	**36**	**0**	**1**	**1**	**62**	**6.5**	**3**	....	....	....	**1**	**0**	**0**	**0**	**0**	**0**	**0**	**0**	....
1996-97	**Pittsburgh**	**NHL**	**1**	**0**	**0**	**0**	**0**	**0**	**0**	**0**	**1**	**0.0**	**–1**	....	....	....	....	....	....	....	....	....	....	....	....
	Cleveland	IHL	50	12	15	27	30	....	....	....	....	....	....	....	....	....	....	....	....	....	....	....	....	....	....
	Anaheim	**NHL**	**11**	**1**	**1**	**2**	**10**	**0**	**0**	**0**	**9**	**11.1**	**0**	....	....	....	**11**	**0**	**1**	**1**	**2**	**0**	**0**	**0**	....
1997-98	**Anaheim**	**NHL**	**15**	**0**	**2**	**2**	**8**	**0**	**0**	**0**	**14**	**0.0**	**–3**	....	....	....	....	....	....	....	....	....	....	....	....
	Cincinnati	AHL	56	17	26	43	36	....	....	....	....	....	....	....	....	....	....	....	....	....	....	....	....	....	....
1998-99	**Philadelphia**	**NHL**	**7**	**0**	**0**	**0**	**0**	**0**	**0**	**0**	**5**	**0.0**	**–1**	**15**	**53.3**	**9:21**	....	....	....	....	....	....	....	....	....
	Philadelphia	AHL	75	41	42	83	33	....	....	....	....	....	....	....	....	....	16	9	6	15	4	....	....	....	....
99-2000	Utah Grizzlies	IHL	82	28	32	60	36	....	....	....	....	....	....	....	....	....	5	1	0	1	0	....	....	....	....
2000-01	Cleveland	IHL	75	27	21	48	29	....	....	....	....	....	....	....	....	....	4	0	2	2	4	....	....	....	....
2001-02	**Minnesota**	**NHL**	**63**	**10**	**15**	**25**	**10**	**2**	**1**	**2**	**115**	**8.7**	**–1**	**79**	**41.8**	**16:28**	....	....	....	....	....	....	....	....	....
	Houston Aeros	AHL	13	4	10	14	6	....	....	....	....	....	....	....	....	....	....	....	....	....	....	....	....	....	....
2002-03	**Minnesota**	**NHL**	**81**	**14**	**10**	**24**	**16**	**2**	**2**	**3**	**149**	**9.4**	**–3**	**178**	**48.9**	**16:36**	**18**	**3**	**3**	**6**	**4**	**0**	**0**	**1**	**17:03**
2003-04	**Minnesota**	**NHL**	**73**	**13**	**12**	**25**	**28**	**4**	**0**	**1**	**142**	**9.2**	**0**	**379**	**40.1**	**16:30**	....	....	....	....	....	....	....	....	....
2004-05	Malmo	Sweden	9	1	3	4	4	....	....	....	....	....	....	....	....	....	....	....	....	....	....	....	....	....	....
	Langnau	Swiss	10	3	0	3	8	....	....	....	....	....	....	....	....	....	6	4	1	5	6	....	....	....	....
	NHL Totals		**308**	**42**	**47**	**89**	**110**	**8**	**4**	**7**	**501**	**8.4**		**651**	**43.0**	**16:18**	**33**	**3**	**4**	**7**	**8**	**0**	**0**	**1**	**17:03**

OHL All-Rookie Team (1993) • AHL Second All-Star Team (1999)

Traded to **Anaheim** by **Pittsburgh** for Roman Oksiuta, March 18, 1997. Signed as a free agent by **Philadelphia**, August 24, 1998. Signed as a free agent by **Utah** (IHL), September 22, 1999. Signed as a free agent by **Minnesota**, June 6, 2000. Signed as a free agent by **Malmo** (Sweden), November 8, 2004. Signed as a free agent by **Langnau** (Swiss), January 4, 2005. Signed as a free agent by **Vancouver**, August 8, 2005.

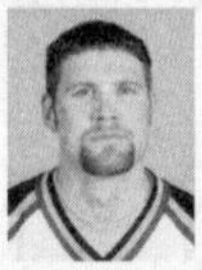

PARKER, Scott

(PAR-kuhr, SKAWT) **S.J.**

Right wing. Shoots right. 6'5", 230 lbs. Born, Hanford, CA, January 29, 1978. Colorado's 4th choice, 20th overall, in 1998 Entry Draft.

Season	Club	League	GP	G	A	Pts	PIM	PP	SH	GW	S	%	+/-	TF	F%	Min	GP	G	A	Pts	PIM	PP	SH	GW	Min
1993-94	Alaska Arctic Ice	AAHL	34	8	12	20	86	....	....	....	....	....	....	....	....	....	....	....	....	....	....	....	....	....	....
1994-95	Spokane Braves	KIJHL	43	7	21	28	128	....	....	....	....	....	....	....	....	....	....	....	....	....	....	....	....	....	....
1995-96	Kelowna Rockets	WHL	64	3	4	7	159	....	....	....	....	....	....	....	....	....	6	0	0	0	12	....	....	....	....
1996-97	Kelowna Rockets	WHL	68	18	8	26	*330	....	....	....	....	....	....	....	....	....	6	0	2	2	4	....	....	....	....
1997-98	Kelowna Rockets	WHL	71	30	22	52	243	....	....	....	....	....	....	....	....	....	7	6	0	6	23	....	....	....	....
1998-99	**Colorado**	**NHL**	**27**	**0**	**0**	**0**	**71**	**0**	**0**	**0**	**3**	**0.0**	**–3**	**1**	**0.0**	**1:37**	....	....	....	....	....	....	....	....	....
	Hershey Bears	AHL	32	4	3	7	143	....	....	....	....	....	....	....	....	....	4	0	0	0	6	....	....	....	....
99-2000	Hershey Bears	AHL	68	12	7	19	206	....	....	....	....	....	....	....	....	....	11	1	1	2	56	....	....	....	....
2000-01 ♦	**Colorado**	**NHL**	**69**	**2**	**3**	**5**	**155**	**0**	**0**	**1**	**35**	**5.7**	**–2**	**2**	**0.0**	**5:42**	**4**	**0**	**0**	**0**	**2**	**0**	**0**	**0**	**2:12**
2001-02	**Colorado**	**NHL**	**63**	**1**	**4**	**5**	**154**	**0**	**0**	**0**	**32**	**3.1**	**0**	**0**	**0.0**	**5:50**	....	....	....	....	....	....	....	....	....
2002-03	**Colorado**	**NHL**	**43**	**1**	**3**	**4**	**82**	**0**	**0**	**0**	**20**	**5.0**	**6**	**0**	**0.0**	**6:15**	**1**	**0**	**0**	**0**	**2**	**0**	**0**	**0**	**1:44**
2003-04	**San Jose**	**NHL**	**50**	**1**	**3**	**4**	**101**	**0**	**0**	**0**	**20**	**5.0**	**0**	**5**	**40.0**	**6:37**	....	....	....	....	....	....	....	....	....
2004-05		DID NOT PLAY																							
	NHL Totals		**252**	**5**	**13**	**18**	**563**	**0**	**0**	**1**	**110**	**4.5**		**8**	**25.0**	**5:34**	**5**	**0**	**0**	**0**	**4**	**0**	**0**	**0**	**2:06**

• Re-entered NHL Entry Draft. Originally New Jersey's 6th choice, 63rd overall, in 1996 Entry Draft.

Traded to **San Jose** by **Colorado** for Colorado's 5th round choice (previously acquired, Colorado selected Brad Richardson) in 2003 Entry Draft, June 21, 2003.

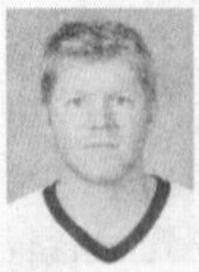

PARRISH, Mark

(PAIR-ihsh, MAHRK) **NYI**

Right wing. Shoots right. 5'11", 200 lbs. Born, Bloomington, MN, February 2, 1977. Colorado's 3rd choice, 79th overall, in 1996 Entry Draft.

Season	Club	League	GP	G	A	Pts	PIM	PP	SH	GW	S	%	+/-	TF	F%	Min	GP	G	A	Pts	PIM	PP	SH	GW	Min
1994-95	Jefferson Jaguars	High-MN	27	40	20	60	42	....	....	....	....	....	....	....	....	....	....	....	....	....	....	....	....	....	....
1995-96	St. Cloud State	WCHA	39	15	13	28	30	....	....	....	....	....	....	....	....	....	....	....	....	....	....	....	....	....	....
1996-97	St. Cloud State	WCHA	35	*27	15	42	60	....	....	....	....	....	....	....	....	....	....	....	....	....	....	....	....	....	....
1997-98	Seattle	WHL	54	54	38	92	29	....	....	....	....	....	....	....	....	....	5	2	3	5	2	....	....	....	....
	New Haven	AHL	1	1	0	1	2	....	....	....	....	....	....	....	....	....	....	....	....	....	....	....	....	....	....
1998-99	**Florida**	**NHL**	**73**	**24**	**13**	**37**	**25**	**5**	**0**	**5**	**129**	**18.6**	**–6**	**1**	**0.0**	**13:59**	....	....	....	....	....	....	....	....	....
	New Haven	AHL	2	1	0	1	0	....	....	....	....	....	....	....	....	....	....	....	....	....	....	....	....	....	....
99-2000	**Florida**	**NHL**	**81**	**26**	**18**	**44**	**39**	**6**	**0**	**3**	**152**	**17.1**	**1**	**8**	**75.0**	**14:04**	**4**	**0**	**1**	**1**	**0**	**0**	**0**	**0**	**12:37**
2000-01	**NY Islanders**	**NHL**	**70**	**17**	**13**	**30**	**28**	**6**	**0**	**3**	**123**	**13.8**	**–27**	**3**	**33.3**	**15:27**	....	....	....	....	....	....	....	....	....
2001-02	**NY Islanders**	**NHL**	**78**	**30**	**30**	**60**	**32**	**9**	**1**	**6**	**162**	**18.5**	**10**	**10**	**40.0**	**16:48**	**7**	**2**	**1**	**3**	**6**	**2**	**0**	**0**	**17:27**
2002-03	**NY Islanders**	**NHL**	**81**	**23**	**25**	**48**	**28**	**9**	**0**	**5**	**147**	**15.6**	**–11**	**9**	**44.4**	**16:12**	**5**	**1**	**0**	**1**	**4**	**1**	**0**	**0**	**16:02**
2003-04	**NY Islanders**	**NHL**	**59**	**24**	**11**	**35**	**18**	**6**	**0**	**6**	**105**	**22.9**	**8**	**5**	**20.0**	**17:20**	**5**	**1**	**2**	**3**	**0**	**0**	**0**	**0**	**20:35**
2004-05		DID NOT PLAY																							
	NHL Totals		**442**	**144**	**110**	**254**	**170**	**41**	**1**	**28**	**818**	**17.6**		**36**	**44.4**	**15:35**	**21**	**4**	**4**	**8**	**10**	**3**	**0**	**0**	**16:56**

NCAA West Second All-American Team (1997) • WHL West First All-Star Team (1998)

Played in NHL All-Star Game (2002)

Rights traded to **Florida** by **Colorado** with Anaheim's 3rd round choice (previously acquired, Florida selected Lance Ward) in 1998 Entry Draft for Tom Fitzgerald, March 24, 1998. Traded to **NY Islanders** by **Florida** with Oleg Kvasha for Roberto Luongo and Olli Jokinen, June 24, 2000.

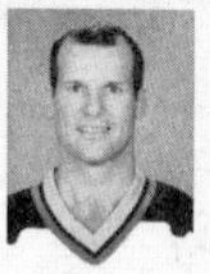

PATRICK, James
(PAT-rihk, JAYMS)

Defense. Shoots right. 6'2", 202 lbs. Born, Winnipeg, Man., June 14, 1963. NY Rangers' 1st choice, 9th overall, in 1981 Entry Draft.

			Regular Season													Playoffs								
Season	Club	League	GP	G	A	Pts	PIM	PP	SH	GW	S	%	+/-	TF	F%	Min	GP	G	A	Pts	PIM	PP	SH	GW	Min
1980-81	Prince Albert	SJHL	59	21	61	82	162	....	....	....	....	....	....	....	....	....	....	....	....	....	....	....	....	....	....
1981-82	North Dakota	WCHA	42	5	24	29	26	....	....	....	....	....	....	....	....	....	....	....	....	....	....	....	....	....	....
1982-83	North Dakota	WCHA	36	12	36	48	29	....	....	....	....	....	....	....	....	....	....	....	....	....	....	....	....	....	....
1983-84	Canada	Nat-Tm	63	7	24	31	52	....	....	....	....	....	....	....	....	....	....	....	....	....	....	....	....	....	....
	Canada	Olympics	7	0	3	3	4	....	....	....	....	....	....	....	....	....	....	....	....	....	....	....	....	....	....
	NY Rangers	**NHL**	12	1	7	8	2	0	0	0	15	6.7	6	....	....	....	5	0	3	3	2	0	0	0	....
1984-85	**NY Rangers**	**NHL**	75	8	28	36	71	4	1	1	101	7.9	−17	....	....	....	3	0	0	0	4	0	0	0	....
1985-86	**NY Rangers**	**NHL**	75	14	29	43	88	2	1	1	131	10.7	14	....	....	....	16	1	5	6	34	0	0	0	....
1986-87	**NY Rangers**	**NHL**	78	10	45	55	62	5	0	0	143	7.0	13	....	....	....	6	1	2	3	2	1	0	1	....
1987-88	**NY Rangers**	**NHL**	70	17	45	62	52	9	0	1	187	9.1	16	....	....	....	....	....	....	....	....	....	....	....	....
1988-89	**NY Rangers**	**NHL**	68	11	36	47	41	6	0	2	147	7.5	3	....	....	....	4	0	1	1	2	0	0	0	....
1989-90	**NY Rangers**	**NHL**	73	14	43	57	50	9	0	0	136	10.3	4	....	....	....	10	3	8	11	0	2	0	1	....
1990-91	**NY Rangers**	**NHL**	74	10	49	59	58	6	0	2	138	7.2	−5	....	....	....	6	0	0	0	6	0	0	0	....
1991-92	**NY Rangers**	**NHL**	80	14	57	71	54	6	0	1	148	9.5	34	....	....	....	13	0	7	7	12	0	0	0	....
1992-93	**NY Rangers**	**NHL**	60	5	21	26	61	3	0	0	99	5.1	1	....	....	....	....	....	....	....	....	....	....	....	....
1993-94	**NY Rangers**	**NHL**	6	0	3	3	2	0	0	0	6	0.0	1	....	....	....	....	....	....	....	....	....	....	....	....
	Hartford	**NHL**	47	8	20	28	32	4	1	2	65	12.3	−12	....	....	....	....	....	....	....	....	....	....	....	....
	Calgary	**NHL**	15	2	2	4	6	1	0	0	20	10.0	6	....	....	....	7	0	1	1	6	0	0	0	....
1994-95	**Calgary**	**NHL**	43	0	10	10	14	0	0	0	43	0.0	−3	....	....	....	5	0	1	1	0	0	0	0	....
1995-96	**Calgary**	**NHL**	80	3	32	35	30	1	0	0	116	2.6	3	....	....	....	4	0	0	0	2	0	0	0	....
1996-97	**Calgary**	**NHL**	19	3	1	4	6	1	0	0	22	13.6	2	....	....	....	....	....	....	....	....	....	....	....	....
1997-98	**Calgary**	**NHL**	60	6	11	17	26	1	0	1	57	10.5	−2	....	....	....	....	....	....	....	....	....	....	....	....
1998-99	**Buffalo**	**NHL**	45	1	7	8	16	0	0	0	31	3.2	12	0	0.0	14:45	20	0	1	1	12	0	0	0	13:57
99-2000	**Buffalo**	**NHL**	66	5	8	13	22	0	0	3	40	12.5	8	0	0.0	15:59	5	0	1	1	2	0	0	0	15:23
2000-01	**Buffalo**	**NHL**	54	4	9	13	12	1	0	0	48	8.3	9	0	0.0	17:16	13	1	2	3	2	0	0	0	20:10
2001-02	**Buffalo**	**NHL**	56	5	8	13	16	1	0	0	45	11.1	3	0	0.0	16:27	....	....	....	....	....	....	....	....	....
2002-03	**Buffalo**	**NHL**	69	4	12	16	26	2	0	1	63	6.3	−3	2	100.0	18:55	....	....	....	....	....	....	....	....	....
2003-04	**Buffalo**	**NHL**	55	4	7	11	12	0	0	1	44	9.1	11	0	0.0	18:59	....	....	....	....	....	....	....	....	....
2004-05			DID NOT PLAY																						
	NHL Totals		1280	149	490	639	759	62	3	16	1845	8.1		2	100.0	17:10	117	6	32	38	86	3	0	2	16:16

WCHA Second All-Star Team (1982) • WCHA Freshman of the Year (1982) • NCAA Chamionship All-Tournament Team (1982) • WCHA First All-Star Team (1983) • NCAA West All American Team (1983)

Traded to **Hartford** by **NY Rangers** with Darren Turcotte for Steve Larmer, Nick Kypreos, Barry Richter and Hartford's 6th round choice (Yuri Litvinov) in 1994 Entry Draft, November 2, 1993. Traded to **Calgary** by **Hartford** with Zarley Zalapski and Michael Nylander for Gary Suter, Paul Ranheim and Ted Drury, March 10, 1994. • Missed majority of 1996-97 season recovering from knee injury suffered in game vs. Pittsburgh, October 24, 1996. Signed as a free agent by **Buffalo**, October 7, 1998.

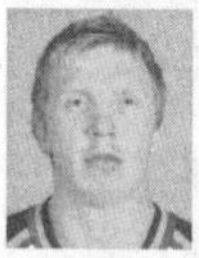

PAUL, Jeff
(PAWL, JEHF) **MTL.**

Defense. Shoots right. 6'4", 225 lbs. Born, London, Ont., March 1, 1978. Chicago's 2nd choice, 42nd overall, in 1996 Entry Draft.

Season	Club	League	GP	G	A	Pts	PIM	PP	SH	GW	S	%	+/-	TF	F%	Min	GP	G	A	Pts	PIM	PP	SH	GW	Min
1993-94	Woodstock	OHA-C	36	1	6	7	73	....	....	....	....	....	....	....	....	....	....	....	....	....	....	....	....	....	....
1994-95	Niagara Falls	OHL	57	3	10	13	64	....	....	....	....	....	....	....	....	....	6	0	2	2	0	....	....	....	....
1995-96	Niagara Falls	OHL	48	1	7	8	81	....	....	....	....	....	....	....	....	....	10	0	4	4	37	....	....	....	....
1996-97	Erie Otters	OHL	60	4	23	27	152	....	....	....	....	....	....	....	....	....	5	2	0	2	12	....	....	....	....
1997-98	Erie Otters	OHL	48	3	17	20	108	....	....	....	....	....	....	....	....	....	7	0	2	2	13	....	....	....	....
1998-99	Portland Pirates	AHL	6	0	0	0	4	....	....	....	....	....	....	....	....	....	....	....	....	....	....	....	....	....	....
	Indianapolis Ice	IHL	55	0	7	7	120	....	....	....	....	....	....	....	....	....	7	0	2	2	12	....	....	....	....
99-2000	Cleveland	IHL	69	6	6	12	210	....	....	....	....	....	....	....	....	....	9	1	0	1	12	....	....	....	....
2000-01	Norfolk Admirals	AHL	59	5	6	11	171	....	....	....	....	....	....	....	....	....	9	0	2	2	12	....	....	....	....
2001-02	Hershey Bears	AHL	58	1	13	14	201	....	....	....	....	....	....	....	....	....	7	0	1	1	6	....	....	....	....
2002-03	**Colorado**	**NHL**	2	0	0	0	7	0	0	0	0	0.0	0	0	0.0	3:32	....	....	....	....	....	....	....	....	....
	Hershey Bears	AHL	50	2	3	5	123	....	....	....	....	....	....	....	....	....	....	....	....	....	....	....	....	....	....
2003-04	San Antonio	AHL	57	2	6	8	174	....	....	....	....	....	....	....	....	....	....	....	....	....	....	....	....	....	....
	Hartford	AHL	17	0	5	5	38	....	....	....	....	....	....	....	....	....	15	1	2	3	31	....	....	....	....
2004-05	Portland Pirates	AHL	54	1	2	3	137	....	....	....	....	....	....	....	....	....	....	....	....	....	....	....	....	....	....
	NHL Totals		2	0	0	0	7	0	0	0	0	0.0		0	0.0	3:32	....	....	....	....	....	....	....	....	....

Signed as a free agent by **Colorado**, August 8, 2001. Signed as a free agent by **Florida**, August 19, 2003. Traded to **NY Rangers** by **Florida** for Paul Healey, March 9, 2004. Signed as a free agent by **Washington**, August 2, 2004. Signed as a free agent by **Montreal**, September 1, 2005.

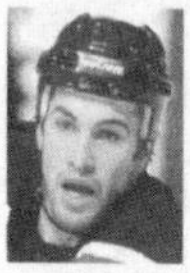

PAYER, Serge
(pie-YAY, SAIRZH) **FLA.**

Center. Shoots left. 6', 192 lbs. Born, Rockland, Ont., May 7, 1979.

Season	Club	League	GP	G	A	Pts	PIM	PP	SH	GW	S	%	+/-	TF	F%	Min	GP	G	A	Pts	PIM	PP	SH	GW	Min
1994-95	Cumberland Colts	ODMHA	42	37	46	83	55	....	....	....	....	....	....	....	....	....	....	....	....	....	....	....	....	....	....
1995-96	Kitchener Rangers	OHL	66	8	16	24	18	....	....	....	....	....	....	....	....	....	12	0	2	2	2	....	....	....	....
1996-97	Kitchener Rangers	OHL	63	7	16	23	27	....	....	....	....	....	....	....	....	....	13	1	3	4	2	....	....	....	....
1997-98	Kitchener Rangers	OHL	44	20	21	41	51	....	....	....	....	....	....	....	....	....	6	3	0	3	7	....	....	....	....
1998-99	Kitchener Rangers	OHL	40	18	19	37	22	....	....	....	....	....	....	....	....	....	....	....	....	....	....	....	....	....	....
99-2000	Kitchener Rangers	OHL	44	10	26	36	53	....	....	....	....	....	....	....	....	....	5	0	3	3	6	....	....	....	....
2000-01	**Florida**	**NHL**	43	5	1	6	21	0	1	0	34	14.7	0	97	42.3	7:27	....	....	....	....	....	....	....	....	....
	Louisville Panthers	AHL	32	6	6	12	15	....	....	....	....	....	....	....	....	....	....	....	....	....	....	....	....	....	....
2001-02	Utah Grizzlies	AHL	20	6	2	8	9	....	....	....	....	....	....	....	....	....	....	....	....	....	....	....	....	....	....
2002-03	San Antonio	AHL	78	10	31	41	30	....	....	....	....	....	....	....	....	....	1	0	0	0	2	....	....	....	....
2003-04	**Ottawa**	**NHL**	5	0	1	1	2	0	0	0	2	0.0	1	43	46.5	10:30	....	....	....	....	....	....	....	....	....
	Binghamton	AHL	67	14	20	34	91	....	....	....	....	....	....	....	....	....	2	0	0	0	0	....	....	....	....
2004-05	San Antonio	AHL	3	1	1	2	4	....	....	....	....	....	....	....	....	....	....	....	....	....	....	....	....	....	....
	NHL Totals		48	5	2	7	23	0	1	0	36	13.9		140	43.6	7:46	....	....	....	....	....	....	....	....	....

Signed as a free agent by **Florida**, September 30, 1997. • Missed majority of 2001-02 season recovering from back injury suffered in training camp, September, 2001. Traded to **Ottawa** by **Florida** for Ottawa's 9th round choice (Luke Beaverson) in 2004 Entry Draft, September 10, 2003. Signed as a free agent by **Florida**, July 23, 2004.

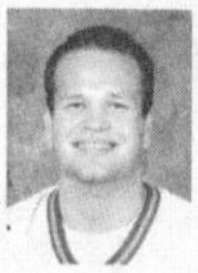

PEAT, Stephen
(PEET, STEE-vehn) **WSH.**

Right wing. Shoots right. 6'3", 230 lbs. Born, Princeton, B.C., March 10, 1980. Anaheim's 2nd choice, 32nd overall, in 1998 Entry Draft.

Season	Club	League	GP	G	A	Pts	PIM	PP	SH	GW	S	%	+/-	TF	F%	Min	GP	G	A	Pts	PIM	PP	SH	GW	Min
1995-96	Langley Thunder	BCJHL	59	5	15	20	112	....	....	....	....	....	....	....	....	....	....	....	....	....	....	....	....	....	....
	Red Deer Rebels	WHL	1	0	0	0	0	....	....	....	....	....	....	....	....	....	....	....	....	....	....	....	....	....	....
1996-97	Red Deer Rebels	WHL	68	3	14	17	161	....	....	....	....	....	....	....	....	....	16	0	2	2	22	....	....	....	....
1997-98	Red Deer Rebels	WHL	63	6	12	18	189	....	....	....	....	....	....	....	....	....	5	0	0	0	8	....	....	....	....
1998-99	Red Deer Rebels	WHL	31	2	6	8	98	....	....	....	....	....	....	....	....	....	....	....	....	....	....	....	....	....	....
	Tri-City	WHL	5	0	0	0	19	....	....	....	....	....	....	....	....	....	....	....	....	....	....	....	....	....	....
99-2000	Tri-City	WHL	12	0	2	2	48	....	....	....	....	....	....	....	....	....	....	....	....	....	....	....	....	....	....
	Calgary Hitmen	WHL	23	0	8	8	100	....	....	....	....	....	....	....	....	....	13	0	1	1	33	....	....	....	....
2000-01	Portland Pirates	AHL	6	0	0	0	16	....	....	....	....	....	....	....	....	....	....	....	....	....	....	....	....	....	....
2001-02	**Washington**	**NHL**	38	2	2	4	85	0	0	0	11	18.2	−1	0	0.0	5:04	....	....	....	....	....	....	....	....	....
	Portland Pirates	AHL	17	2	2	4	57	....	....	....	....	....	....	....	....	....	....	....	....	....	....	....	....	....	....
2002-03	**Washington**	**NHL**	27	1	0	1	57	0	0	0	7	14.3	−3	0	0.0	4:09	....	....	....	....	....	....	....	....	....
	Portland Pirates	AHL	18	0	0	0	52	....	....	....	....	....	....	....	....	....	....	....	....	....	....	....	....	....	....
2003-04	**Washington**	**NHL**	64	5	0	5	90	0	0	0	21	23.8	−10	4	0.0	6:38	....	....	....	....	....	....	....	....	....
2004-05	Danbury Trashers	UHL	7	0	1	1	45	....	....	....	....	....	....	....	....	....	....	....	....	....	....	....	....	....	....
	NHL Totals		129	8	2	10	232	0	0	0	39	20.5		4	0.0	5:39	....	....	....	....	....	....	....	....	....

• Missed majority of 1999-2000 season recovering from injuries sustained off-ice, February 8, 2000. Rights traded to **Washington** by **Anaheim** for Washington's 4th round choice (later traded to Montreal – later traded to Pittsburgh – Pittsburgh selected Michel Ouellet) in 2000 Entry Draft, June 1, 2000. • Missed majority of 2000-01 season recovering from groin injury suffered in training camp, September 29, 2000. Signed as a free agent by **Danbury** (UHL), December 16, 2004.

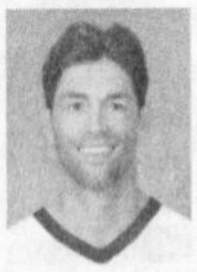

PECA, Michael

(PEH-kuh, MIGH-kuhl) **EDM.**

Center. Shoots right. 5'11", 190 lbs. Born, Toronto, Ont., March 26, 1974. Vancouver's 2nd choice, 40th overall, in 1992 Entry Draft.

Season	Club	League	GP	G	A	Pts	PIM	PP	SH	GW	S	%	+/-	TF	F%	Min	Playoffs GP	G	A	Pts	PIM	PP	SH	GW	Min
1989-90	Tor. Red Wings	MTHL	39	42	53	95	40	....	....	....	....	....	....	....	....	....	....	....	....	....	....	....	....	....	....
1990-91	Sudbury Wolves	OHL	62	14	27	41	24	....	....	....	....	....	....	....	....	....	5	1	0	1	7	....	....	....	....
1991-92	Sudbury Wolves	OHL	39	16	34	50	61	....	....	....	....	....	....	....	....	....	....	....	....	....	....	....	....	....	....
	Ottawa 67's	OHL	27	8	17	25	32	....	....	....	....	....	....	....	....	....	11	6	10	16	6	....	....	....	....
1992-93	Ottawa 67's	OHL	55	38	64	102	80	....	....	....	....	....	....	....	....	....	....	....	....	....	....	....	....	....	....
	Hamilton	AHL	9	6	3	9	11	....	....	....	....	....	....	....	....	....	....	....	....	....	....	....	....	....	....
1993-94	Ottawa 67's	OHL	55	50	63	113	101	....	....	....	....	....	....	....	....	....	17	7	22	29	30	....	....	....	....
	Vancouver	NHL	4	0	0	0	2	0	0	0	5	0.0	–1	....	....	....	....	....	....	....	....	....	....	....	....
1994-95	Syracuse Crunch	AHL	35	10	24	34	75	....	....	....	....	....	....	....	....	....	....	....	....	....	....	....	....	....	....
	Vancouver	NHL	33	6	6	12	30	2	0	1	46	13.0	–6	....	....	....	5	0	1	1	8	0	0	0	....
1995-96	Buffalo	NHL	68	11	20	31	67	4	3	1	109	10.1	–1	....	....	....	....	....	....	....	....	....	....	....	....
1996-97	Buffalo	NHL	79	20	29	49	80	5	6	4	137	14.6	26	....	....	....	10	0	2	2	8	0	0	0	....
1997-98	Buffalo	NHL	61	18	22	40	57	6	5	1	132	13.6	12	....	....	....	13	3	2	5	8	0	0	1	....
1998-99	Buffalo	NHL	82	27	29	56	81	10	0	8	199	13.6	7	1855	49.4	20:44	21	5	8	13	18	2	1	0	22:28
99-2000	Buffalo	NHL	73	20	21	41	67	2	0	3	144	13.9	6	1604	48.6	19:57	5	0	1	1	4	0	0	0	18:42
2000-01			DID NOT PLAY																						
2001-02	NY Islanders	NHL	80	25	35	60	62	3	6	5	168	14.9	19	1804	52.4	20:14	5	1	0	1	2	0	0	0	16:15
	Canada	Olympics	6	0	2	2	2	....	....	....	....	....	....	....	....	....	....	....	....	....	....	....	....	....	....
2002-03	NY Islanders	NHL	66	13	29	42	43	4	2	2	117	11.1	–4	1315	53.0	18:57	5	0	0	0	4	0	0	0	20:10
2003-04	NY Islanders	NHL	76	11	29	40	71	0	1	0	117	9.4	17	1674	53.1	19:02	5	0	0	0	6	0	0	0	23:01
2004-05			DID NOT PLAY																						
	NHL Totals		622	151	220	371	560	36	23	25	1174	12.9		8252	51.2	19:49	69	9	14	23	58	2	1	1	21:02

Frank J. Selke Trophy (1997, 2002)

Traded to **Buffalo** by **Vancouver** with Mike Wilson and Vancouver's 1st round choice (Jay McKee) in 1995 Entry Draft for Alexander Mogilny and Buffalo's 5th round choice (Todd Norman) in 1995 Entry Draft, July 8, 1995. • Missed entire 2000-01 season after failing to come to contract terms with **Buffalo**. Rights traded to **NY Islanders** by **Buffalo** for Tim Connolly and Taylor Pyatt, June 24, 2001. Traded to **Edmonton** by **NY Islanders** for Mike York and a conditional choice in 2006 Entry Draft, August 3, 2005.

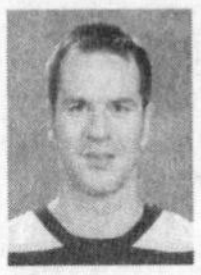

PEDERSON, Denis

(PEE-duhr-suhn, DEH-nihs)

Center/Right wing. Shoots right. 6'2", 205 lbs. Born, Prince Albert, Sask., September 10, 1975. New Jersey's 1st choice, 13th overall, in 1993 Entry Draft.

Season	Club	League	GP	G	A	Pts	PIM	PP	SH	GW	S	%	+/-	TF	F%	Min	Playoffs GP	G	A	Pts	PIM	PP	SH	GW	Min
1990-91	Prince Albert	SMHL	30	25	17	42	84	....	....	....	....	....	....	....	....	....	....	....	....	....	....	....	....	....	....
1991-92	Prince Albert	SMHL	21	33	25	58	40	....	....	....	....	....	....	....	....	....	....	....	....	....	....	....	....	....	....
	Prince Albert	WHL	10	0	0	0	6	....	....	....	....	....	....	....	....	....	7	0	1	1	13	....	....	....	....
1992-93	Prince Albert	WHL	72	33	40	73	134	....	....	....	....	....	....	....	....	....	....	....	....	....	....	....	....	....	....
1993-94	Prince Albert	WHL	71	53	45	98	157	....	....	....	....	....	....	....	....	....	....	....	....	....	....	....	....	....	....
1994-95	Prince Albert	WHL	63	30	38	68	122	....	....	....	....	....	....	....	....	....	15	11	14	25	14	....	....	....	....
	Albany River Rats	AHL	....	....	....	....	....	....	....	....	....	....	....	....	....	....	3	0	0	0	2	....	....	....	....
1995-96	New Jersey	NHL	10	3	1	4	0	1	0	2	6	50.0	–1	....	....	....	....	....	....	....	....	....	....	....	....
	Albany River Rats	AHL	68	28	43	71	104	....	....	....	....	....	....	....	....	....	4	1	2	3	0	....	....	....	....
1996-97	New Jersey	NHL	70	12	20	32	62	3	0	3	106	11.3	7	....	....	....	9	0	0	0	2	0	0	0	....
	Albany River Rats	AHL	3	1	3	4	7	....	....	....	....	....	....	....	....	....	....	....	....	....	....	....	....	....	....
1997-98	New Jersey	NHL	80	15	13	28	97	7	0	1	135	11.1	–6	....	....	....	6	1	1	2	2	0	1	0	....
1998-99	New Jersey	NHL	76	11	12	23	66	3	0	1	145	7.6	–10	540	42.8	15:19	3	0	1	1	0	0	0	0	9:36
99-2000	New Jersey	NHL	35	3	3	6	16	0	0	0	41	7.3	–7	125	48.8	10:42	....	....	....	....	....	....	....	....	....
	Vancouver	NHL	12	3	2	5	2	0	0	1	15	20.0	1	70	45.7	12:41	....	....	....	....	....	....	....	....	....
2000-01	Vancouver	NHL	61	4	8	12	65	0	1	3	70	5.7	0	351	42.7	11:42	4	0	1	1	4	0	0	0	15:53
2001-02	Vancouver	NHL	29	1	5	6	31	0	0	0	24	4.2	–2	142	47.2	8:18	....	....	....	....	....	....	....	....	....
	Phoenix	NHL	19	1	1	2	20	0	0	0	18	5.6	–2	202	49.0	10:32	5	0	2	2	0	0	0	0	10:36
2002-03	Nashville	NHL	43	4	6	10	39	0	0	0	64	6.3	2	440	50.2	12:48	....	....	....	....	....	....	....	....	....
2003-04	Eisbaren Berlin	Germany	41	15	21	36	40	....	....	....	....	....	....	....	....	....	11	5	6	11	8	....	....	....	....
2004-05	Eisbaren Berlin	Germany	49	19	19	38	75	....	....	....	....	....	....	....	....	....	12	7	4	11	20	....	....	....	....
	NHL Totals		435	57	71	128	398	14	1	11	624	9.1		1870	46.0	12:21	27	1	5	6	8	0	1	0	12:07

WHL East Second All-Star Team (1994)

Traded to **Vancouver** by **New Jersey** with Brendan Morrison for Alexander Mogilny, March 14, 2000. Traded to **Phoenix** by **Vancouver** with Drake Berehowsky for Todd Warriner, Trevor Letowski, Tyler Bouck and Phoenix's 3rd round choice (later traded back to Phoenix – Phoenix selected Dimitri Pestunov) in 2003 Entry Draft, December 28, 2001. Signed as a free agent by **Nashville**, July 24, 2002. Signed as a free agent by **Eisbaren Berlin** (Germany), September 9, 2003.

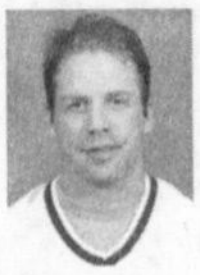

PELLERIN, Scott

(PEHL-ih-rihn, SKAWT)

Left wing. Shoots left. 5'11", 190 lbs. Born, Shediac, N.B., January 9, 1970. New Jersey's 4th choice, 47th overall, in 1989 Entry Draft.

Season	Club	League	GP	G	A	Pts	PIM	PP	SH	GW	S	%	+/-	TF	F%	Min	Playoffs GP	G	A	Pts	PIM	PP	SH	GW	Min
1985-86	Moncton Flyers	NBAHA	45	65	34	99	34	....	....	....	....	....	....	....	....	....	....	....	....	....	....	....	....	....	....
1986-87	Notre Dame	SMHL	72	62	68	130	98	....	....	....	....	....	....	....	....	....	....	....	....	....	....	....	....	....	....
1987-88	Notre Dame	SJHL	57	37	49	86	139	....	....	....	....	....	....	....	....	....	....	....	....	....	....	....	....	....	....
1988-89	U. of Maine	H-East	45	29	33	62	92	....	....	....	....	....	....	....	....	....	....	....	....	....	....	....	....	....	....
1989-90	U. of Maine	H-East	42	22	34	56	68	....	....	....	....	....	....	....	....	....	....	....	....	....	....	....	....	....	....
1990-91	U. of Maine	H-East	43	23	25	48	60	....	....	....	....	....	....	....	....	....	....	....	....	....	....	....	....	....	....
1991-92	U. of Maine	H-East	37	*32	25	57	54	....	....	....	....	....	....	....	....	....	....	....	....	....	....	....	....	....	....
	Utica Devils	AHL	....	....	....	....	....	....	....	....	....	....	....	....	....	....	3	1	0	1	0	....	....	....	....
1992-93	New Jersey	NHL	45	10	11	21	41	1	2	0	60	16.7	–1	....	....	....	....	....	....	....	....	....	....	....	....
	Utica Devils	AHL	27	15	18	33	33	....	....	....	....	....	....	....	....	....	2	0	1	1	0	....	....	....	....
1993-94	New Jersey	NHL	1	0	0	0	2	0	0	0	0	0.0	0	....	....	....	....	....	....	....	....	....	....	....	....
	Albany River Rats	AHL	73	28	46	74	84	....	....	....	....	....	....	....	....	....	5	2	1	3	11	....	....	....	....
1994-95	Albany River Rats	AHL	74	23	33	56	95	....	....	....	....	....	....	....	....	....	14	6	4	10	8	....	....	....	....
1995-96	New Jersey	NHL	6	2	1	3	0	0	0	0	9	22.2	1	....	....	....	....	....	....	....	....	....	....	....	....
	Albany River Rats	AHL	75	35	47	82	142	....	....	....	....	....	....	....	....	....	4	0	3	3	10	....	....	....	....
1996-97	St. Louis	NHL	54	8	10	18	35	0	2	2	76	10.5	12	....	....	....	6	0	0	0	6	0	0	0	....
	Worcester IceCats	AHL	24	10	16	26	37	....	....	....	....	....	....	....	....	....	....	....	....	....	....	....	....	....	....
1997-98	St. Louis	NHL	80	8	21	29	62	1	1	0	96	8.3	14	....	....	....	10	0	2	2	10	0	0	0	....
1998-99	St. Louis	NHL	80	20	21	41	42	0	5	4	138	14.5	1	6	66.7	17:18	8	1	0	1	4	0	0	0	13:50
99-2000	St. Louis	NHL	80	8	15	23	48	0	2	2	120	6.7	9	6	16.7	14:47	7	0	0	0	2	0	0	0	14:55
2000-01	Minnesota	NHL	58	11	28	39	45	2	2	2	117	9.4	6	47	31.9	18:40	....	....	....	....	....	....	....	....	....
	Carolina	NHL	19	0	5	5	6	0	0	0	21	0.0	–4	52	44.2	14:14	6	0	0	0	4	0	0	0	11:10
2001-02	Boston	NHL	35	1	5	6	6	0	0	0	41	2.4	–6	24	37.5	11:38	....	....	....	....	....	....	....	....	....
	Dallas	NHL	33	3	5	8	15	0	0	0	22	13.6	–5	8	25.0	9:13	....	....	....	....	....	....	....	....	....
2002-03	Dallas	NHL	20	1	3	4	8	1	0	0	20	5.0	–3	5	20.0	10:43	....	....	....	....	....	....	....	....	....
	Phoenix	NHL	23	0	1	1	8	0	0	0	17	0.0	–5	12	58.3	9:32	....	....	....	....	....	....	....	....	....
2003-04	Portland Pirates	AHL	6	0	3	3	0	....	....	....	....	....	....	....	....	....	....	....	....	....	....	....	....	....	....
	Worcester IceCats	AHL	49	9	21	30	38	....	....	....	....	....	....	....	....	....	10	3	1	4	19	....	....	....	....
	St. Louis	NHL	2	0	0	0	2	0	0	0	1	0.0	–3	2	0.0	14:05	....	....	....	....	....	....	....	....	....
2004-05			DID NOT PLAY																						
	NHL Totals		536	72	126	198	320	5	14	10	738	9.8		162	38.3	14:33	37	1	2	3	26	0	0	0	13:26

Hockey East Rookie of the Year (1989) (co-winner - Rob Gaudreau) • Hockey East First All-Star Team (1992) • Hockey East Player of the Year (1992) • NCAA East First All-American Team (1992) • Hobey Baker Memorial Award (Top U.S. Collegiate Player) (1992)

Signed as a free agent by **St. Louis**, July 10, 1996. Claimed by **Minnesota** from **St. Louis** in Expansion Draft, June 23, 2000. Traded to **Carolina** by **Minnesota** for Askhat Rakhmatullin, Carolina's 3rd round choice (later traded to NY Rangers – NY Rangers selected Garth Murray) in 2001 Entry Draft and Carolina's 5th round compensatory choice (Armands Berzins) in 2002 Entry Draft, March 1, 2001. Signed as a free agent by **Boston**, July 26, 2001. Claimed on waivers by **Dallas** from **Boston**, January 12, 2002. Traded to **Phoenix** by **Dallas** with Dallas' 4th round choice (Kevin Porter) in 2004 Entry Draft for Claude Lemieux, January 16, 2003. Signed as a free agent by **Portland** (AHL), September 12, 2003. Signed as a free agent by **Worcester** (AHL), November 5, 2003. Signed as a free agent by **St. Louis**, December 22, 2003.

Season	Club	League	Regular Season														Playoffs								
Season	Club	League	GP	G	A	Pts	PIM	PP	SH	GW	S	%	+/-	TF	F%	Min	GP	G	A	Pts	PIM	PP	SH	GW	Min

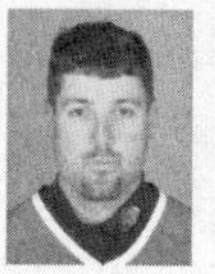

PELUSO, Mike

(puh-LOO-soh, MIGHK)

Right wing. Shoots right. 6'1", 208 lbs. Born, Bismarck, ND, September 2, 1974. Calgary's 12th choice, 253rd overall, in 1994 Entry Draft.

1992-93	Omaha Lancers	USHL	45	21	12	33	31	....	....	....	....	....	....	....	....	....	....	....	....	....	....	....	....	....	....
1993-94	Omaha Lancers	USHL	48	36	29	65	77	....	....	....	....	....	....	....	....	....	....	....	....	....	....	....	....	....	....
1994-95	U. Minn-Duluth	WCHA	38	11	23	34	38	....	....	....	....	....	....	....	....	....	....	....	....	....	....	....	....	....	....
1995-96	U. Minn-Duluth	WCHA	38	25	19	44	64	....	....	....	....	....	....	....	....	....	....	....	....	....	....	....	....	....	....
1996-97	U. Minn-Duluth	WCHA	37	20	20	40	53	....	....	....	....	....	....	....	....	....	....	....	....	....	....	....	....	....	....
1997-98	U. Minn-Duluth	WCHA	40	24	21	45	100	....	....	....	....	....	....	....	....	....	....	....	....	....	....	....	....	....	....
1998-99	Portland Pirates	AHL	26	7	6	13	6	....	....	....	....	....	....	....	....	....	....	....	....	....	....	....	....	....	....
99-2000	Portland Pirates	AHL	71	25	29	54	86	....	....	....	....	....	....	....	....	....	4	2	0	2	0	....	....	....	....
2000-01	Portland Pirates	AHL	19	12	10	22	17	....	....	....	....	....	....	....	....	....	....	....	....	....	....	....	....	....	....
	Worcester IceCats	AHL	44	17	23	40	22	....	....	....	....	....	....	....	....	....	11	3	3	6	4	....	....	....	....
2001-02	**Chicago**	**NHL**	**37**	**4**	**2**	**6**	**19**	**0**	**0**	**1**	**45**	**8.9**	**–3**	**1**	**0.0**	**9:17**	....	....	....	....	....	....	....	....	....
	Norfolk Admirals	AHL	29	18	9	27	4	....	....	....	....	....	....	....	....	....	4	1	0	1	0	....	....	....	....
2002-03	Norfolk Admirals	AHL	74	24	31	55	35	....	....	....	....	....	....	....	....	....	9	1	2	3	4	....	....	....	....
2003-04	**Philadelphia**	**NHL**	**1**	**0**	**0**	**0**	**0**	**0**	**0**	**0**	**2**	**0.0**	**0**	**0**	**0.0**	**9:34**	....	....	....	....	....	....	....	....	....
	Philadelphia	AHL	72	13	18	31	87	....	....	....	....	....	....	....	....	....	5	0	1	1	4	....	....	....	....
2004-05			DID NOT PLAY																						
	NHL Totals		**38**	**4**	**2**	**6**	**19**	**0**	**0**	**1**	**47**	**8.5**		**1**	**0.0**	**9:17**	....	....	....	....	....	....	....	....	....

WCHA Second All-Star Team (1997)

Signed as a free agent by **Washington**, October 9, 1998. Traded to **St. Louis** by **Washington** for Derek Bekar, November 29, 2000. Signed as a free agent by **Chicago**, August 1, 2001. Signed as a free agent by **Philadelphia**, July 24, 2003.

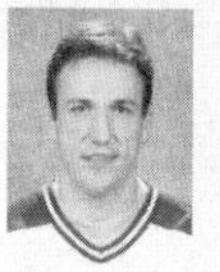

PERREAULT, Yanic

(puh-ROH, YAH-nihk)

Center. Shoots left. 5'11", 185 lbs. Born, Sherbrooke, Que., April 4, 1971. Toronto's 1st choice, 47th overall, in 1991 Entry Draft.

1987-88	Montreal L'est	QAAA	42	*70	57	*127	14	....	....	....	....	....	....	....	....	....	8	12	10	22	6	....	....	....	....
1988-89	Trois-Rivieres	QMJHL	70	53	55	108	48	....	....	....	....	....	....	....	....	....	....	....	....	....	....	....	....	....	....
1989-90	Trois-Rivieres	QMJHL	63	51	63	114	75	....	....	....	....	....	....	....	....	....	7	6	5	11	19	....	....	....	....
1990-91	Trois-Rivieres	QMJHL	67	*87	98	*185	103	....	....	....	....	....	....	....	....	....	6	4	7	11	6	....	....	....	....
1991-92	St. John's	AHL	62	38	38	76	19	....	....	....	....	....	....	....	....	....	16	7	8	15	4	....	....	....	....
1992-93	St. John's	AHL	79	49	46	95	56	....	....	....	....	....	....	....	....	....	9	4	5	9	2	....	....	....	....
1993-94	**Toronto**	**NHL**	**13**	**3**	**3**	**6**	**0**	**2**	**0**	**0**	**24**	**12.5**	**1**	....	....	....	....	....	....	....	....	....	....	....	....
	St. John's	AHL	62	45	60	105	38	....	....	....	....	....	....	....	....	....	11	*12	6	18	14	....	....	....	....
1994-95	Phoenix	IHL	68	51	48	99	52	....	....	....	....	....	....	....	....	....	....	....	....	....	....	....	....	....	....
	Los Angeles	**NHL**	**26**	**2**	**5**	**7**	**20**	**0**	**0**	**1**	**43**	**4.7**	**3**	....	....	....	....	....	....	....	....	....	....	....	....
1995-96	**Los Angeles**	**NHL**	**78**	**25**	**24**	**49**	**16**	**8**	**3**	**7**	**175**	**14.3**	**–11**	....	....	....	....	....	....	....	....	....	....	....	....
1996-97	**Los Angeles**	**NHL**	**41**	**11**	**14**	**25**	**20**	**1**	**1**	**0**	**98**	**11.2**	**0**	....	....	....	....	....	....	....	....	....	....	....	....
1997-98	**Los Angeles**	**NHL**	**79**	**28**	**20**	**48**	**32**	**3**	**2**	**3**	**206**	**13.6**	**6**	....	....	....	**4**	**1**	**2**	**3**	**6**	**1**	**0**	**0**	....
1998-99	**Los Angeles**	**NHL**	**64**	**10**	**17**	**27**	**30**	**2**	**2**	**1**	**113**	**8.8**	**–3**	**1024**	**56.5**	**15:24**	....	....	....	....	....	....	....	....	....
	Toronto	**NHL**	**12**	**7**	**8**	**15**	**12**	**2**	**1**	**2**	**28**	**25.0**	**10**	**164**	**62.8**	**13:20**	**17**	**3**	**6**	**9**	**6**	**0**	**0**	**2**	**15:55**
99-2000	**Toronto**	**NHL**	**58**	**18**	**27**	**45**	**22**	**5**	**0**	**4**	**114**	**15.8**	**3**	**987**	**61.8**	**15:18**	**1**	**0**	**1**	**1**	**0**	**0**	**0**	**0**	**12:56**
2000-01	**Toronto**	**NHL**	**76**	**24**	**28**	**52**	**52**	**5**	**0**	**2**	**134**	**17.9**	**0**	**1055**	**62.7**	**14:01**	**11**	**2**	**3**	**5**	**4**	**1**	**0**	**1**	**12:20**
2001-02	**Montreal**	**NHL**	**82**	**27**	**29**	**56**	**40**	**6**	**0**	**7**	**156**	**17.3**	**–3**	**1485**	**61.3**	**16:47**	**11**	**3**	**5**	**8**	**0**	**2**	**0**	**1**	**13:05**
2002-03	**Montreal**	**NHL**	**73**	**24**	**22**	**46**	**30**	**7**	**0**	**4**	**145**	**16.6**	**–11**	**1156**	**62.9**	**16:05**	....	....	....	....	....	....	....	....	....
2003-04	**Montreal**	**NHL**	**69**	**16**	**15**	**31**	**40**	**5**	**0**	**3**	**114**	**14.0**	**–10**	**861**	**65.2**	**13:46**	**9**	**2**	**2**	**4**	**0**	**0**	**0**	**1**	**12:29**
2004-05			DID NOT PLAY																						
	NHL Totals		**671**	**195**	**212**	**407**	**314**	**46**	**9**	**34**	**1350**	**14.4**		**6732**	**61.7**	**15:12**	**53**	**11**	**19**	**30**	**16**	**4**	**0**	**5**	**13:47**

QMJHL All-Rookie Team (1989) • QMJHL Offensive Rookie of the Year (1989) • Canadian Major Junior Rookie of the Year (1989) • QMJHL First All-Star Team (1991) • QMJHL MVP (1991)

Traded to **Los Angeles** by **Toronto** for Los Angeles' 4th round choice (later traded to Philadelphia – later traded back to Los Angeles – Los Angeles selected Mikael Simons) in 1996 Entry Draft, July 11, 1994. Traded to **Toronto** by **Los Angeles** for Jason Podollan and Toronto's 3rd round choice (Cory Campbell) in 1999 Entry Draft, March 23, 1999. Signed as a free agent by **Montreal**, July 4, 2001.

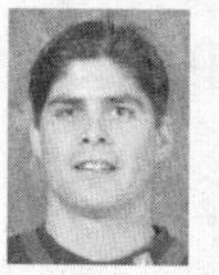

PERRIN, Eric

(peh-REHN, AIR-ihk) **T.B.**

Center. Shoots left. 5'9", 176 lbs. Born, Laval, Que., November 1, 1975.

1991-92	Laval-Laurentides	QAAA	42	41	50	91	....	....	....	....	....	....	....	....	....	....	12	7	16	23	....	....	....	....	....
1992-93	Laval College	CEGEP	STATISTICS NOT AVAILABLE																						
1993-94	U. of Vermont	ECAC	32	24	21	45	34	....	....	....	....	....	....	....	....	....	....	....	....	....	....	....	....	....	....
1994-95	U. of Vermont	ECAC	35	28	39	67	38	....	....	....	....	....	....	....	....	....	....	....	....	....	....	....	....	....	....
1995-96	U. of Vermont	ECAC	38	29	56	85	38	....	....	....	....	....	....	....	....	....	....	....	....	....	....	....	....	....	....
1996-97	U. of Vermont	ECAC	36	26	33	59	40	....	....	....	....	....	....	....	....	....	....	....	....	....	....	....	....	....	....
1997-98	Cleveland	IHL	69	12	31	43	34	....	....	....	....	....	....	....	....	....	....	....	....	....	....	....	....	....	....
	Quebec Rafales	IHL	13	2	12	14	4	....	....	....	....	....	....	....	....	....	....	....	....	....	....	....	....	....	....
1998-99	Kansas City	IHL	82	24	37	61	71	....	....	....	....	....	....	....	....	....	3	0	0	0	0	....	....	....	....
99-2000	Kansas City	IHL	21	3	15	18	16	....	....	....	....	....	....	....	....	....	....	....	....	....	....	....	....	....	....
2000-01	Jokerit Helsinki	Finland	6	1	1	2	4	....	....	....	....	....	....	....	....	....	....	....	....	....	....	....	....	....	....
	Assat Pori	Finland	43	15	23	38	70	....	....	....	....	....	....	....	....	....	....	....	....	....	....	....	....	....	....
2001-02	Assat Pori	Finland	45	13	13	26	16	....	....	....	....	....	....	....	....	....	....	....	....	....	....	....	....	....	....
	HPK Hameenlinna	Finland	12	5	10	15	4	....	....	....	....	....	....	....	....	....	8	2	4	6	6	....	....	....	....
2002-03	JYP Jyvaskyla	Finland	56	18	28	46	36	....	....	....	....	....	....	....	....	....	7	4	6	10	8	....	....	....	....
2003-04♦	**Tampa Bay**	**NHL**	**4**	**0**	**0**	**0**	**0**	**0**	**0**	**0**	**3**	**0.0**	**–1**	**30**	**60.0**	**8:32**	**12**	**0**	**1**	**1**	**6**	**0**	**0**	**0**	**5:20**
	Hershey Bears	AHL	71	21	54	75	49	....	....	....	....	....	....	....	....	....	....	....	....	....	....	....	....	....	....
2004-05	Hershey Bears	AHL	80	24	49	73	46	....	....	....	....	....	....	....	....	....	....	....	....	....	....	....	....	....	....
	NHL Totals		**4**	**0**	**0**	**0**	**0**	**0**	**0**	**0**	**3**	**0.0**		**30**	**60.0**	**8:32**	**12**	**0**	**1**	**1**	**6**	**0**	**0**	**0**	**5:20**

ECAC All-Rookie Team (1994) • ECAC Rookie of the Year (1994) • ECAC First All-Star Team (1995, 1996) • ECAC Player of the Year (1996) • NCAA East First All-American Team (1996) • AHL First All-Star Team (2004)

Signed as a free agent by **Tampa Bay**, June 19, 2003.

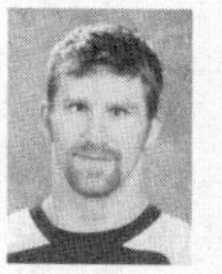

PERROTT, Nathan

(PEHR-roht, NAY-than) **TOR.**

Right wing. Shoots right. 6', 225 lbs. Born, Owen Sound, Ont., December 8, 1976. New Jersey's 2nd choice, 44th overall, in 1995 Entry Draft.

1992-93	Walkerton	OHA-C	25	6	13	19	45	....	....	....	....	....	....	....	....	....	....	....	....	....	....	....	....	....	....
1993-94	St. Mary's Lincolns	OHA-B	41	11	26	37	249	....	....	....	....	....	....	....	....	....	....	....	....	....	....	....	....	....	....
1994-95	Oshawa Generals	OHL	63	18	28	46	233	....	....	....	....	....	....	....	....	....	2	1	1	2	9	....	....	....	....
1995-96	Oshawa Generals	OHL	59	30	32	62	158	....	....	....	....	....	....	....	....	....	5	2	3	5	8	....	....	....	....
	Albany River Rats	AHL	4	0	0	0	12	....	....	....	....	....	....	....	....	....	....	....	....	....	....	....	....	....	....
1996-97	Oshawa Generals	OHL	5	1	0	1	17	....	....	....	....	....	....	....	....	....	....	....	....	....	....	....	....	....	....
	Sault Ste. Marie	OHL	37	18	23	41	120	....	....	....	....	....	....	....	....	....	11	5	5	10	60	....	....	....	....
1997-98	Indianapolis Ice	IHL	31	4	3	7	76	....	....	....	....	....	....	....	....	....	....	....	....	....	....	....	....	....	....
	Jacksonville	ECHL	30	6	8	14	135	....	....	....	....	....	....	....	....	....	....	....	....	....	....	....	....	....	....
1998-99	Indianapolis Ice	IHL	72	14	11	25	307	....	....	....	....	....	....	....	....	....	7	3	1	4	45	....	....	....	....
99-2000	Cleveland	IHL	65	12	9	21	248	....	....	....	....	....	....	....	....	....	9	2	1	3	19	....	....	....	....
2000-01	Norfolk Admirals	AHL	73	11	17	28	268	....	....	....	....	....	....	....	....	....	9	2	0	2	18	....	....	....	....
2001-02	Norfolk Admirals	AHL	2	0	0	0	5	....	....	....	....	....	....	....	....	....	....	....	....	....	....	....	....	....	....
	Nashville	**NHL**	**22**	**1**	**2**	**3**	**74**	**0**	**0**	**1**	**7**	**14.3**	**–1**	**1**	**0.0**	**4:55**	....	....	....	....	....	....	....	....	....
	Milwaukee	AHL	56	6	10	16	190	....	....	....	....	....	....	....	....	....	....	....	....	....	....	....	....	....	....
2002-03	**Nashville**	**NHL**	**1**	**0**	**0**	**0**	**5**	**0**	**0**	**0**	**0**	**0.0**	**0**	**0**	**0.0**	**4:13**	....	....	....	....	....	....	....	....	....
	Milwaukee	AHL	27	1	2	3	106	....	....	....	....	....	....	....	....	....	....	....	....	....	....	....	....	....	....
	St. John's	AHL	36	7	8	15	97	....	....	....	....	....	....	....	....	....	....	....	....	....	....	....	....	....	....
2003-04	**Toronto**	**NHL**	**40**	**1**	**2**	**3**	**116**	**0**	**0**	**0**	**47**	**2.1**	**–1**	**5**	**20.0**	**7:40**	....	....	....	....	....	....	....	....	....
2004-05	St. John's	AHL	60	16	12	28	276	....	....	....	....	....	....	....	....	....	2	0	0	0	6	....	....	....	....
	NHL Totals		**63**	**2**	**4**	**6**	**195**	**0**	**0**	**1**	**54**	**3.7**		**6**	**16.7**	**6:39**	....	....	....	....	....	....	....	....	....

Signed as a free agent by **Chicago**, August 27, 1997. Traded to **Nashville** by **Chicago** for future considerations, October 9, 2001. Traded to **Toronto** by **Nashville** for Bob Wren, Deceber 31, 2002.
• Spent majority of 2003-04 season as a healthy reserve.

			Regular Season														Playoffs								
Season	Club	League	GP	G	A	Pts	PIM	PP	SH	GW	S	%	+/-	TF	F%	Min	GP	G	A	Pts	PIM	PP	SH	GW	Min

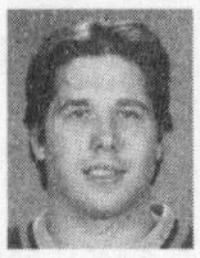

PETERS, Andrew

(PEE-tuhrs, AN-droo) **BUF.**

Left wing. Shoots left. 6'4", 240 lbs. Born, St. Catharines, Ont., May 5, 1980. Buffalo's 2nd choice, 34th overall, in 1998 Entry Draft.

Season	Club	League	GP	G	A	Pts	PIM	PP	SH	GW	S	%	+/-	TF	F%	Min	GP	G	A	Pts	PIM	PP	SH	GW	Min
1996-97	Georgetown	OPJHL	46	11	16	27	65																		
1997-98	Oshawa Generals	OHL	60	11	7	18	220										7	2	0	2	19				
1998-99	Oshawa Generals	OHL	54	14	10	24	137										15	2	7	9	36				
99-2000	Kitchener Rangers	OHL	42	6	13	19	95										4	0	1	1	14				
2000-01	Rochester	AHL	49	0	4	4	118																		
2001-02	Rochester	AHL	67	4	1	5	*388																		
2002-03	Rochester	AHL	57	3	0	3	223										3	0	0	0	24				
2003-04	**Buffalo**	**NHL**	**42**	**2**	**0**	**2**	**151**	**0**	**0**	**0**	**19**	**10.5**	**–3**	**2**	**0.0**	**4:10**									
2004-05	Bodens IK	Sweden-2	22	2	4	6	195																		
	NHL Totals		**42**	**2**	**0**	**2**	**151**	**0**	**0**	**0**	**19**	**10.5**		**2**	**0.0**	**4:10**									

Signed as a free agent by **Bodens** (Sweden-2), August 20, 2004.

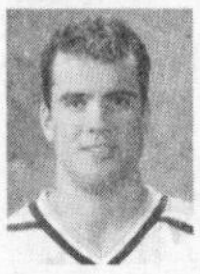

PETERSEN, Toby

(PEE-tuhr-sohn, TOH-bee) **EDM.**

Center. Shoots left. 5'10", 197 lbs. Born, Minneapolis, MN, October 27, 1978. Pittsburgh's 9th choice, 244th overall, in 1998 Entry Draft.

Season	Club	League	GP	G	A	Pts	PIM	PP	SH	GW	S	%	+/-	TF	F%	Min	GP	G	A	Pts	PIM	PP	SH	GW	Min
1995-96	Jefferson Jaguars	High-MN	25	29	30	59																			
1996-97	Colorado College	WCHA	40	17	21	38	18																		
1997-98	Colorado College	WCHA	40	16	17	33	34																		
1998-99	Colorado College	WCHA	21	12	12	24	2																		
99-2000	Colorado College	WCHA	37	14	19	33	8																		
2000-01	**Pittsburgh**	**NHL**	**12**	**2**	**6**	**8**	**4**	**0**	**0**	**1**	**25**	**8.0**	**3**	**39**	**35.9**	**13:22**									
	Wilkes-Barre	AHL	73	26	41	67	22										21	7	6	13	4				
2001-02	**Pittsburgh**	**NHL**	**79**	**8**	**10**	**18**	**4**	**1**	**1**	**0**	**116**	**6.9**	**–15**	**338**	**45.6**	**12:16**									
2002-03	Wilkes-Barre	AHL	80	31	35	66	24										6	1	3	4	4				
2003-04	Wilkes-Barre	AHL	62	15	29	44	4										21	2	10	12	12				
2004-05	Edmonton	AHL	78	14	15	29	21																		
	NHL Totals		**91**	**10**	**16**	**26**	**8**	**1**	**1**	**1**	**141**	**7.1**		**377**	**44.6**	**12:25**									

WCHA All-Rookie Team (1997) • AHL All-Rookie Team (2001)

Signed as a free agent by **Edmonton**, July 30, 2004.

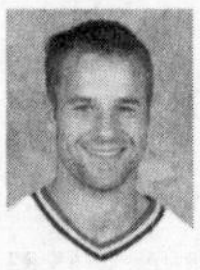

PETROVICKY, Ronald

(PEHT-roh-vih-kee, RAW-nohld) **ATL.**

Right wing. Shoots right. 6', 190 lbs. Born, Zilina, Czechoslovakia, February 15, 1977. Calgary's 9th choice, 228th overall, in 1996 Entry Draft.

Season	Club	League	GP	G	A	Pts	PIM	PP	SH	GW	S	%	+/-	TF	F%	Min	GP	G	A	Pts	PIM	PP	SH	GW	Min
1993-94	Dukla Trencin Jr.	Slovak-Jr.	36	28	27	55	42																		
	Dukla Trencin	Slovakia	1	0	0	0	0																		
1994-95	Tri-City	WHL	39	4	11	15	86																		
	Prince George	WHL	21	4	6	10	37																		
1995-96	Prince George	WHL	39	19	21	40	61																		
1996-97	Prince George	WHL	72	32	37	69	119										15	4	9	13	31				
1997-98	Regina Pats	WHL	71	64	49	113	168										9	2	4	6	11				
1998-99	Saint John Flames	AHL	78	12	21	33	114										7	1	2	3	19				
99-2000	Saint John Flames	AHL	67	23	33	56	131										3	1	1	2	6				
2000-01	**Calgary**	**NHL**	**30**	**4**	**5**	**9**	**54**	**1**	**0**	**1**	**30**	**13.3**	**0**	**7**	**42.9**	**11:33**									
2001-02	**Calgary**	**NHL**	**77**	**5**	**7**	**12**	**85**	**1**	**0**	**1**	**78**	**6.4**	**0**	**28**	**46.4**	**11:42**									
2002-03	**NY Rangers**	**NHL**	**66**	**5**	**9**	**14**	**77**	**2**	**1**	**1**	**65**	**7.7**	**–12**	**52**	**42.3**	**12:25**									
2003-04	**Atlanta**	**NHL**	**78**	**16**	**15**	**31**	**123**	**0**	**0**	**1**	**102**	**15.7**	**–9**	**27**	**40.7**	**14:16**									
2004-05	MsHK SKP Zilina	Slovakia	34	10	9	19	34																		
	Brynas IF Gavle	Sweden	10	0	5	5	27																		
	Brynas IF Gavle	Sweden-Q	9	0	2	2	0																		
	NHL Totals		**251**	**30**	**36**	**66**	**339**	**4**	**1**	**4**	**275**	**10.9**		**114**	**43.0**	**12:40**									

WHL East Second All-Star Team (1998)

• Missed majority of 2000-01 season recovering from wrist injury suffered in game vs. Detroit, October 5, 2000. Claimed by **NY Rangers** from **Calgary** in Waiver Draft, October 4, 2002. Claimed by **Atlanta** from **NY Rangers** in Waiver Draft, October 3, 2003. Signed as a free agent by **Zilina** (Slovakia), September 17, 2004. Signed as a free agent by **Brynas** (Sweden), January 23, 2005.

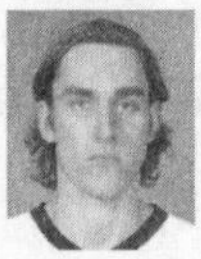

PETTINEN, Tomi

(peh-TIHN-ehn, TAW-mee) **NYI**

Defense. Shoots left. 6'3", 220 lbs. Born, Ylojarvi, Finland, June 17, 1977. NY Islanders' 9th choice, 267th overall, in 2000 Entry Draft.

Season	Club	League	GP	G	A	Pts	PIM	PP	SH	GW	S	%	+/-	TF	F%	Min	GP	G	A	Pts	PIM	PP	SH	GW	Min
1994-95	Ilves Tampere U18	Fin-U18	31	1	6	7	46										4	0	0	0	2				
	Ilves Tampere Jr.	Finland-Jr.	1	0	0	0	0																		
1995-96	KooVee Jr.	Finland-Jr.	21	0	0	0	64																		
	Ilves Tampere Jr.	Finland-Jr.	12	1	1	2	18																		
1996-97	Ilves Tampere	Finland	16	1	0	1	12																		
	Ilves Tampere Jr.	Finland-Jr.	26	3	8	11	44																		
1997-98	Ilves Tampere	Finland	3	0	0	0	0																		
	Ilves Tampere Jr.	Finland-Jr.	14	1	4	5	24																		
	Lukko Rauma	Finland	27	0	2	2	16																		
	Lukko Rauma Jr.	Finland-Jr.	11	2	6	8	14																		
1998-99	HIFK Helsinki	Finland	4	0	0	0	2																		
	Hermes Kokkola	Finland-2	42	8	6	14	76										3	0	0	0	6				
99-2000	Ilves Tampere	Finland	51	1	6	7	78										3	1	2	3	2				
2000-01	Ilves Tampere	Finland	56	2	2	4	86										9	0	0	0	4				
2001-02	Ilves Tampere	Finland	48	5	4	9	51										3	0	0	0	4				
	Bridgeport	AHL															9	0	1	1	0				
2002-03	**NY Islanders**	**NHL**	**2**	**0**	**0**	**0**	**0**	**0**	**0**	**0**	**0**	**0.0**	**1**	**0**	**0.0**	**11:34**									
	Bridgeport	AHL	75	1	8	9	56										9	0	0	0	17				
2003-04	**NY Islanders**	**NHL**	**4**	**0**	**0**	**0**	**2**	**0**	**0**	**0**	**2**	**0.0**	**–2**	**0**	**0.0**	**10:24**									
	Bridgeport	AHL	71	1	8	9	37										7	1	0	1	0				
2004-05	Lukko Rauma	Finland	56	6	14	20	49										9	0	2	2	33				
	NHL Totals		**6**	**0**	**0**	**0**	**2**	**0**	**0**	**0**	**2**	**0.0**		**0**	**0.0**	**10:47**									

Signed as a free agent by **Lukko** (Finland), June 7, 2004.

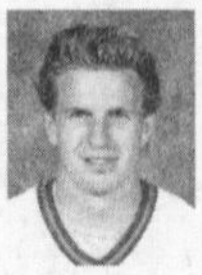

PETTINGER, Matt

(PEH-tihn-juhr, MAT) **WSH.**

Left wing. Shoots left. 6'1", 205 lbs. Born, Edmonton, Alta., October 22, 1980. Washington's 2nd choice, 43rd overall, in 2000 Entry Draft.

Season	Club	League	GP	G	A	Pts	PIM	PP	SH	GW	S	%	+/-	TF	F%	Min	GP	G	A	Pts	PIM	PP	SH	GW	Min
1994-95	Victoria Racquet	BCAHA	55	52	48	100	41																		
1995-96	Victoria Racquet	BCAHA	60	80	65	145	45																		
1996-97	Victoria Salsa	BCHL	49	22	14	36	31																		
1997-98	Victoria Salsa	BCHL	55	22	20	42	56										7	5	1	6	8				
1998-99	U. of Denver	WCHA	33	6	14	20	44																		
99-2000	U. of Denver	WCHA	19	2	6	8	49																		
	Calgary Hitmen	WHL	27	14	6	20	41										11	2	6	8	30				
2000-01	**Washington**	**NHL**	**10**	**0**	**0**	**0**	**2**	**0**	**0**	**0**	**6**	**0.0**	**–1**	**2**	**50.0**	**7:47**									
	Portland Pirates	AHL	64	19	17	36	92										2	0	0	0	4				
2001-02	**Washington**	**NHL**	**61**	**7**	**3**	**10**	**44**	**1**	**0**	**1**	**73**	**9.6**	**–8**	**5**	**20.0**	**9:39**									
	Portland Pirates	AHL	9	3	3	6	24																		
2002-03	**Washington**	**NHL**	**1**	**0**	**0**	**0**	**0**	**0**	**0**	**0**	**0**	**0.0**	**0**	**1**	**0.0**	**3:30**									
	Portland Pirates	AHL	69	14	13	27	72										3	0	2	2	2				
2003-04	**Washington**	**NHL**	**71**	**7**	**5**	**12**	**37**	**1**	**0**	**1**	**92**	**7.6**	**–9**	**18**	**44.4**	**11:25**									
2004-05	Ljubljana	Slovenia	1	0	1	1	0																		
	Ljubljana	Interliga	7	2	4	6	41																		
	NHL Totals		**143**	**14**	**8**	**22**	**83**	**2**	**0**	**2**	**171**	**8.2**		**26**	**38.5**	**10:21**									

Left **U. of Denver** (WCHA) and signed as a free agent with **Calgary** (WHL), January 10, 2000. Signed as a free agent by **Ljubljana** (Slovenia). December 6, 2004.

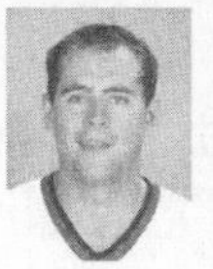

PHILLIPS, Chris

(FIHL-ihps, KRIHS) **OTT.**

Defense. Shoots left. 6'3", 215 lbs. Born, Calgary, Alta., March 9, 1978. Ottawa's 1st choice, 1st overall, in 1996 Entry Draft.

Season	Club	League	GP	G	A	Pts	PIM	PP	SH	GW	S	%	+/-	TF	F%	Min	GP	G	A	Pts	PIM	PP	SH	GW	Min
			Regular Season														**Playoffs**								
1993-94	Fort McMurray	AJHL	56	6	16	22	72	....	....	....	....	....	....	....	....	....	10	0	3	3	16	....	....	....	....
1994-95	Fort McMurray	AJHL	48	16	32	48	127	....	....	....	....	....	....	....	....	....	11	4	2	6	10	....	....	....	....
1995-96	Prince Albert	WHL	61	10	30	40	97	....	....	....	....	....	....	....	....	....	18	2	12	14	30	....	....	....	....
1996-97	Prince Albert	WHL	32	3	23	26	58	....	....	....	....	....	....	....	....	....	....	....	....	....	....	....	....	....	....
	Lethbridge	WHL	26	4	18	22	28	....	....	....	....	....	....	....	....	....	19	4	*21	25	20	....	....	....	....
1997-98	**Ottawa**	**NHL**	**72**	**5**	**11**	**16**	**38**	**2**	**0**	**2**	**107**	**4.7**	**2**	....	....	....	**11**	**0**	**2**	**2**	**2**	**0**	**0**	**0**	....
1998-99	**Ottawa**	**NHL**	**34**	**3**	**3**	**6**	**32**	**2**	**0**	**0**	**51**	**5.9**	**–5**	**0**	**0.0**	**18:06**	**3**	**0**	**0**	**0**	**0**	**0**	**0**	**0**	**13:50**
99-2000	**Ottawa**	**NHL**	**65**	**5**	**14**	**19**	**39**	**0**	**0**	**1**	**96**	**5.2**	**12**	**0**	**0.0**	**16:50**	**6**	**0**	**1**	**1**	**4**	**0**	**0**	**0**	**18:17**
2000-01	**Ottawa**	**NHL**	**73**	**2**	**12**	**14**	**31**	**2**	**0**	**0**	**77**	**2.6**	**8**	**1**	**0.0**	**21:28**	**1**	**1**	**0**	**1**	**0**	**0**	**0**	**0**	**20:52**
2001-02	**Ottawa**	**NHL**	**63**	**6**	**16**	**22**	**29**	**1**	**0**	**1**	**103**	**5.8**	**5**	**0**	**0.0**	**19:31**	**12**	**0**	**0**	**0**	**12**	**0**	**0**	**0**	**21:44**
2002-03	**Ottawa**	**NHL**	**78**	**3**	**16**	**19**	**71**	**2**	**0**	**1**	**97**	**3.1**	**7**	**0**	**0.0**	**20:13**	**18**	**2**	**4**	**6**	**12**	**0**	**0**	**1**	**21:36**
2003-04	**Ottawa**	**NHL**	**82**	**7**	**16**	**23**	**46**	**0**	**0**	**1**	**93**	**7.5**	**15**	**1**	**100.0**	**20:50**	**7**	**1**	**0**	**1**	**12**	**1**	**0**	**0**	**20:26**
2004-05	Brynas IF Gavle	Sweden	27	5	3	8	45	....	....	....	....	....	....	....	....	....	....	....	....	....	....	....	....	....	....
	Brynas IF Gavle	Sweden-Q	9	1	2	3	2	....	....	....	....	....	....	....	....	....	....	....	....	....	....	....	....	....	....
	NHL Totals		**467**	**31**	**88**	**119**	**286**	**9**	**0**	**6**	**624**	**5.0**		**2**	**50.0**	**19:44**	**58**	**4**	**7**	**11**	**42**	**1**	**0**	**1**	**20:32**

WHL Rookie of the Year (1996) • WHL East First All-Star Team (1997) • Canadian Major Junior First All-Star Team (1997) • Memorial Cup Tournament All-Star Team (1997)

• Missed majority of 1998-99 season recovering from ankle injury suffered in game vs. Buffalo, December 30, 1998. Signed as a free agent by **Brynas** (Sweden), November 2, 2004.

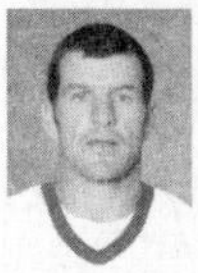

PICARD, Michel

(PEE-cahr, mee-SHEHL)

Left wing. Shoots left. 5'11", 190 lbs. Born, Beauport, Que., November 7, 1969. Hartford's 8th choice, 178th overall, in 1989 Entry Draft.

Season	Club	League	GP	G	A	Pts	PIM	PP	SH	GW	S	%	+/-	TF	F%	Min	GP	G	A	Pts	PIM	PP	SH	GW	Min
1985-86	Ste-Foy	QAAA	42	53	34	87	....	....	....	....	....	....	....	....	....	....	....	....	....	....	....	....	....	....	....
1986-87	Trois-Rivieres	QMJHL	66	33	35	68	53	....	....	....	....	....	....	....	....	....	....	....	....	....	....	....	....	....	....
1987-88	Trois-Rivieres	QMJHL	69	40	55	95	71	....	....	....	....	....	....	....	....	....	....	....	....	....	....	....	....	....	....
1988-89	Trois-Rivieres	QMJHL	66	59	81	140	170	....	....	....	....	....	....	....	....	....	4	1	3	4	2	....	....	....	....
1989-90	Binghamton	AHL	67	16	24	40	98	....	....	....	....	....	....	....	....	....	....	....	....	....	....	....	....	....	....
1990-91	**Hartford**	**NHL**	**5**	**1**	**0**	**1**	**2**	**0**	**0**	**0**	**7**	**14.3**	**–2**	....	....	....	....	....	....	....	....	....	....	....	....
	Springfield	AHL	77	*56	40	96	61	....	....	....	....	....	....	....	....	....	18	8	13	21	18	....	....	....	....
1991-92	**Hartford**	**NHL**	**25**	**3**	**5**	**8**	**6**	**1**	**0**	**0**	**41**	**7.3**	**–2**	....	....	....	....	....	....	....	....	....	....	....	....
	Springfield	AHL	40	21	17	38	44	....	....	....	....	....	....	....	....	....	11	2	0	2	34	....	....	....	....
1992-93	**San Jose**	**NHL**	**25**	**4**	**0**	**4**	**24**	**2**	**0**	**0**	**32**	**12.5**	**–17**	....	....	....	....	....	....	....	....	....	....	....	....
	Kansas City	IHL	33	7	10	17	51	....	....	....	....	....	....	....	....	....	12	3	2	5	20	....	....	....	....
1993-94	Portland Pirates	AHL	61	41	44	85	99	....	....	....	....	....	....	....	....	....	17	11	10	21	22	....	....	....	....
1994-95	P.E.I. Senators	AHL	57	32	57	89	58	....	....	....	....	....	....	....	....	....	8	4	4	8	6	....	....	....	....
	Ottawa	**NHL**	**24**	**5**	**8**	**13**	**14**	**1**	**0**	**0**	**33**	**15.2**	**–1**	....	....	....	....	....	....	....	....	....	....	....	....
1995-96	**Ottawa**	**NHL**	**17**	**2**	**6**	**8**	**10**	**0**	**0**	**1**	**21**	**9.5**	**–1**	....	....	....	....	....	....	....	....	....	....	....	....
	P.E.I. Senators	AHL	55	37	45	82	79	....	....	....	....	....	....	....	....	....	5	5	1	6	2	....	....	....	....
1996-97	V.Frolunda	Sweden	3	0	1	1	0	....	....	....	....	....	....	....	....	....	....	....	....	....	....	....	....	....	....
	Grand Rapids	IHL	82	46	55	101	58	....	....	....	....	....	....	....	....	....	5	2	0	2	10	....	....	....	....
1997-98	Grand Rapids	IHL	58	28	41	69	42	....	....	....	....	....	....	....	....	....	....	....	....	....	....	....	....	....	....
	St. Louis	**NHL**	**16**	**1**	**8**	**9**	**29**	**0**	**0**	**0**	**19**	**5.3**	**3**	....	....	....	....	....	....	....	....	....	....	....	....
1998-99	**St. Louis**	**NHL**	**45**	**11**	**11**	**22**	**16**	**0**	**0**	**2**	**69**	**15.9**	**5**	**1**	**100.0**	**14:20**	**5**	**0**	**0**	**0**	**2**	**0**	**0**	**0**	**13:54**
	Grand Rapids	IHL	6	2	2	4	2	....	....	....	....	....	....	....	....	....	....	....	....	....	....	....	....	....	....
99-2000	Grand Rapids	IHL	65	33	35	68	50	....	....	....	....	....	....	....	....	....	17	8	10	*18	4	....	....	....	....
	Edmonton	**NHL**	**2**	**0**	**0**	**0**	**2**	**0**	**0**	**0**	**2**	**0.0**	**0**	**0**	**0.0**	**9:56**	....	....	....	....	....	....	....	....	....
2000-01	**Philadelphia**	**NHL**	**7**	**1**	**4**	**5**	**0**	**1**	**0**	**0**	**12**	**8.3**	**6**	**0**	**0.0**	**14:14**	....	....	....	....	....	....	....	....	....
	Philadelphia	AHL	72	31	39	70	22	....	....	....	....	....	....	....	....	....	10	4	5	9	4	....	....	....	....
2001-02	Adler Mannheim	Germany	60	24	28	52	30	....	....	....	....	....	....	....	....	....	12	*7	6	13	4	....	....	....	....
2002-03	Grand Rapids	AHL	78	32	52	84	34	....	....	....	....	....	....	....	....	....	15	3	1	4	8	....	....	....	....
2003-04	Grand Rapids	AHL	75	17	37	54	35	....	....	....	....	....	....	....	....	....	4	0	0	0	2	....	....	....	....
2004-05	Thetford Mines	QNAHL	60	36	55	91	22	....	....	....	....	....	....	....	....	....	17	6	11	17	8	....	....	....	....
	NHL Totals		**166**	**28**	**42**	**70**	**103**	**5**	**0**	**3**	**236**	**11.9**		**1**	**100.0**	**14:09**	**5**	**0**	**0**	**0**	**2**	**0**	**0**	**0**	**13:54**

QMJHL Second All-Star Team (1989) • AHL First All-Star Team (1991, 1995) • AHL Second All-Star Team (1994, 2003) • IHL First All-Star Team (1997)

Traded to **San Jose** by **Hartford** for future considerations (Yvon Corriveau, January 21, 1993), October 9, 1992. Signed as a free agent by **Portland** (AHL), September, 1993. Signed as a free agent by **Ottawa**, June 16, 1994. Traded to **Washington** by **Ottawa** for cash, May 21, 1996. Signed as a free agent by **St. Louis**, January 5, 1998. Signed as a free agent by **Edmonton**, December 2, 1999. Signed as a free agent by **Philadelphia**, August 14, 2000. Signed as a free agent by **Detroit**, July 15, 2002. Signed as a free agent by **Thetford Mines** (QNAHL), September, 2004.

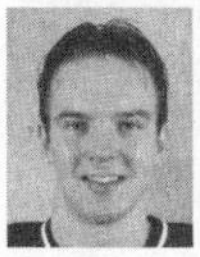

PIHLMAN, Tuomas

(PIHL-mahn, TAWH-muhs) **N.J.**

Left wing. Shoots left. 6'3", 210 lbs. Born, Espoo, Finland, November 13, 1982. New Jersey's 3rd choice, 48th overall, in 2001 Entry Draft.

Season	Club	League	GP	G	A	Pts	PIM	PP	SH	GW	S	%	+/-	TF	F%	Min	GP	G	A	Pts	PIM	PP	SH	GW	Min
1997-98	JyP Jyvaskyla U18	Fin-U18	30	2	5	7	18	....	....	....	....	....	....	....	....	....	4	1	3	4	6	....	....	....	....
1998-99	JyP Jyvaskyla U18	Fin-U18	35	21	20	41	64	....	....	....	....	....	....	....	....	....	6	1	1	2	12	....	....	....	....
99-2000	JyP Jyvaskyla Jr.	Finland-Jr.	20	4	4	8	54	....	....	....	....	....	....	....	....	....	4	0	0	0	8	....	....	....	....
	JYP Jyvaskyla	Finland	17	0	0	0	18	....	....	....	....	....	....	....	....	....	....	....	....	....	....	....	....	....	....
2000-01	JyP Jyvaskyla Jr.	Finland-Jr.	1	1	0	1	0	....	....	....	....	....	....	....	....	....	....	....	....	....	....	....	....	....	....
	JYP Jyvaskyla	Finland	47	3	6	9	59	....	....	....	....	....	....	....	....	....	....	....	....	....	....	....	....	....	....
2001-02	JyP Jyvaskyla Jr.	Finland-Jr.	3	1	1	2	4	....	....	....	....	....	....	....	....	....	....	....	....	....	....	....	....	....	....
	JYP Jyvaskyla	Finland	44	9	2	11	93	....	....	....	....	....	....	....	....	....	....	....	....	....	....	....	....	....	....
2002-03	JYP Jyvaskyla	Finland	53	19	15	34	58	....	....	....	....	....	....	....	....	....	1	0	0	0	0	....	....	....	....
2003-04	**New Jersey**	**NHL**	**2**	**0**	**0**	**0**	**2**	**0**	**0**	**0**	**1**	**0.0**	**0**	**0**	**0.0**	**6:56**	....	....	....	....	....	....	....	....	....
	Albany River Rats	AHL	73	10	19	29	59	....	....	....	....	....	....	....	....	....	....	....	....	....	....	....	....	....	....
2004-05	Albany River Rats	AHL	68	9	13	22	48	....	....	....	....	....	....	....	....	....	....	....	....	....	....	....	....	....	....
	NHL Totals		**2**	**0**	**0**	**0**	**2**	**0**	**0**	**0**	**1**	**0.0**		**0**	**0.0**	**6:56**	....	....	....	....	....	....	....	....	....

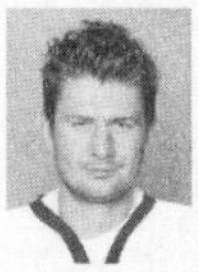

PILAR, Karel

(PEE-lahr, KAH-rehl) **TOR.**

Defense. Shoots right. 6'3", 207 lbs. Born, Prague, Czech., December 23, 1977. Toronto's 2nd choice, 39th overall, in 2001 Entry Draft.

Season	Club	League	GP	G	A	Pts	PIM	PP	SH	GW	S	%	+/-	TF	F%	Min	GP	G	A	Pts	PIM	PP	SH	GW	Min
99-2000	Litvinov	CzRep	49	2	12	14	61	....	....	....	....	....	....	....	....	....	7	0	0	0	4	....	....	....	....
2000-01	Litvinov	CzRep	52	12	26	38	52	....	....	....	....	....	....	....	....	....	4	1	1	2	25	....	....	....	....
2001-02	**Toronto**	**NHL**	**23**	**1**	**3**	**4**	**8**	**0**	**0**	**0**	**32**	**3.1**	**3**	**0**	**0.0**	**16:03**	**11**	**0**	**4**	**4**	**12**	**0**	**0**	**0**	**17:47**
	St. John's	AHL	52	10	14	24	26	....	....	....	....	....	....	....	....	....	....	....	....	....	....	....	....	....	....
2002-03	**Toronto**	**NHL**	**17**	**3**	**4**	**7**	**12**	**1**	**0**	**1**	**22**	**13.6**	**–7**	**0**	**0.0**	**18:29**	....	....	....	....	....	....	....	....	....
	St. John's	AHL	7	2	5	7	28	....	....	....	....	....	....	....	....	....	....	....	....	....	....	....	....	....	....
2003-04	**Toronto**	**NHL**	**50**	**2**	**17**	**19**	**22**	**1**	**0**	**1**	**74**	**2.7**	**2**	**0**	**0.0**	**18:03**	**1**	**1**	**0**	**1**	**0**	**0**	**0**	**0**	**20:48**
	St. John's	AHL	6	3	4	7	6	....	....	....	....	....	....	....	....	....	....	....	....	....	....	....	....	....	....
2004-05	HC Sparta Praha	CzRep	52	13	15	28	70	....	....	....	....	....	....	....	....	....	....	....	....	....	....	....	....	....	....
	NHL Totals		**90**	**6**	**24**	**30**	**42**	**2**	**0**	**2**	**128**	**4.7**		**0**	**0.0**	**17:38**	**12**	**1**	**4**	**5**	**12**	**0**	**0**	**0**	**18:02**

• Missed remainder of 2002-03 season and start of 2003-04 season after being diagnosed with a heart condition, January, 2003. Signed as a free agent by **Sparta** (CzRep), August 9, 2004.

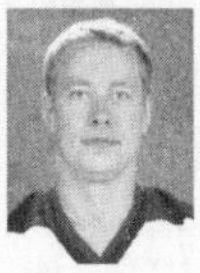

PIRJETA, Lasse

(PEER-yeh-tuh, LAH-see) **PIT.**

Left wing. Shoots left. 6'4", 225 lbs. Born, Oulu, Finland, April 4, 1974. Columbus' 7th choice, 133rd overall, in 2002 Entry Draft.

Season	Club	League	GP	G	A	Pts	PIM	PP	SH	GW	S	%	+/-	TF	F%	Min	GP	G	A	Pts	PIM	PP	SH	GW	Min
1990-91	Karpat Oulu Jr.	Finland-Jr.	21	5	6	11	10	....	....	....	....	....	....	....	....	....	....	....	....	....	....	....	....	....	....
1991-92	Tacoma Rockets	WHL	16	5	2	7	4	....	....	....	....	....	....	....	....	....	....	....	....	....	....	....	....	....	....
	Karpat Oulu Jr.	Finland-Jr.	7	1	4	5	8	....	....	....	....	....	....	....	....	....	....	....	....	....	....	....	....	....	....
	Karpat Oulu	Finland-2	2	0	0	0	0	....	....	....	....	....	....	....	....	....	....	....	....	....	....	....	....	....	....
1992-93	Karpat Oulu Jr.	Finland-Jr.	24	13	19	32	34	....	....	....	....	....	....	....	....	....	....	....	....	....	....	....	....	....	....
	Karpat Oulu	Finland-2	20	4	3	7	6	....	....	....	....	....	....	....	....	....	....	....	....	....	....	....	....	....	....
1993-94	TPS Turku Jr.	Finland-Jr.	6	2	2	4	2	....	....	....	....	....	....	....	....	....	4	6	2	8	2	....	....	....	....
	Kiekko-67 Turku	Finland-2	2	2	1	3	0	....	....	....	....	....	....	....	....	....	....	....	....	....	....	....	....	....	....
	TPS Turku	Finland	43	9	9	18	14	....	....	....	....	....	....	....	....	....	11	4	0	4	2	....	....	....	....
1994-95	TPS Turku Jr.	Finland-Jr.	1	0	0	0	0	....	....	....	....	....	....	....	....	....	....	....	....	....	....	....	....	....	....
	TPS Turku	Finland	49	7	13	20	64	....	....	....	....	....	....	....	....	....	8	0	1	1	29	....	....	....	....
1995-96	TPS Turku	Finland	45	13	14	27	34	....	....	....	....	....	....	....	....	....	11	6	3	9	4	....	....	....	....
1996-97	V.Frolunda	Sweden	50	14	8	22	36	....	....	....	....	....	....	....	....	....	3	0	1	1	4	....	....	....	....
	V.Frolunda	EuroHL	5	2	6	8	4	....	....	....	....	....	....	....	....	....	....	....	....	....	....	....	....	....	....
1997-98	Tappara Tampere	Finland	48	24	22	46	20	....	....	....	....	....	....	....	....	....	4	1	1	2	2	....	....	....	....

Season	Club	League	GP	G	A	Pts	PIM	PP	SH	GW	S	%	+/-	TF	F%	Min	GP	G	A	Pts	PIM	PP	SH	GW	Min
		Regular Season															Playoffs								
1998-99	Tappara Tampere	Finland	54	22	19	41	32	....	....	....	....	....	....	....	....	....	....	....	....	....	....	....	....	....	....
99-2000	HIFK Helsinki	Finland	54	18	25	43	24	....	....	....	....	....	....	....	....	....	9	2	3	5	10	....	....	....	....
	HIFK Helsinki	EuroHL	6	1	3	4	6	....	....	....	....	....	....	....	....	....	2	1	1	2	0	....	....	....	....
2000-01	HIFK Helsinki	Finland	55	15	18	33	24	....	....	....	....	....	....	....	....	....	....	....	....	....	....	....	....	....	....
2001-02	Karpat Oulu	Finland	55	15	26	41	24	....	....	....	....	....	....	....	....	....	4	2	2	4	2	....	....	....	....
2002-03	**Columbus**	**NHL**	**51**	**11**	**10**	**21**	**12**	**2**	**0**	**2**	**80**	**13.8**	**–4**	**327**	**43.1**	**11:28**	....	....	....	....	....	....	....	....	....
2003-04	**Columbus**	**NHL**	**57**	**2**	**8**	**10**	**20**	**0**	**0**	**0**	**78**	**2.6**	**–6**	**465**	**49.5**	**10:46**	....	....	....	....	....	....	....	....	....
	Syracuse Crunch	AHL	5	1	2	3	2	....	....	....	....	....	....	....	....	....	....	....	....	....	....	....	....	....	....
	Pittsburgh	**NHL**	**13**	**6**	**6**	**12**	**0**	**1**	**0**	**1**	**33**	**18.2**	**3**	**187**	**51.9**	**14:22**	....	....	....	....	....	....	....	....	....
2004-05	HIFK Helsinki	Finland	45	16	20	36	26	....	....	....	....	....	....	....	....	....	5	2	0	2	2	....	....	....	....
	NHL Totals		**121**	**19**	**24**	**43**	**32**	**3**	**0**	**3**	**191**	**9.9**		**979**	**47.8**	**11:27**	....	....	....	....	....	....	....	....	....

Traded to **Pittsburgh** by **Columbus** for Brian Holzinger, March 9, 2004. Signed as a free agent by **HIFK** (Finland), September 30, 2004.

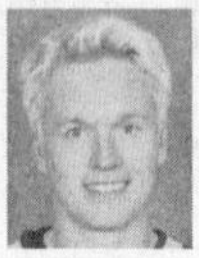

PIRNES, Esa

(PEER-nehz, EH-sah)

Center. Shoots left. 6', 189 lbs. Born, Oulu, Finland, April 1, 1977. Los Angeles' 7th choice, 174th overall, in 2003 Entry Draft.

Season	Club	League	GP	G	A	Pts	PIM	PP	SH	GW	S	%	+/-	TF	F%	Min	GP	G	A	Pts	PIM	PP	SH	GW	Min
1994-95	Karpat Oulu Jr.	Finland-Jr.	18	3	3	6	10	....	....	....	....	....	....	....	....	....	14	5	6	11	6	....	....	....	....
1995-96	Karpat Oulu Jr.	Finland-Jr.	24	19	13	32	8	....	....	....	....	....	....	....	....	....	....	....	....	....	....	....	....	....	....
	Karpat Oulu	Finland-2	20	8	4	12	12	....	....	....	....	....	....	....	....	....	3	0	0	0	0	....	....	....	....
1996-97	Karpat Oulu Jr.	Finland-Jr.	9	5	5	10	6	....	....	....	....	....	....	....	....	....	....	....	....	....	....	....	....	....	....
	Karpat Oulu	Finland-2	36	17	16	33	20	....	....	....	....	....	....	....	....	....	3	0	0	0	12	....	....	....	....
1997-98	Karpat Oulu Jr.	Finland-Jr.	15	9	23	32	4	....	....	....	....	....	....	....	....	....	....	....	....	....	....	....	....	....	....
	Karpat Oulu	Finland-2	32	6	15	21	12	....	....	....	....	....	....	....	....	....	....	....	....	....	....	....	....	....	....
1998-99	Karpat Oulu	Finland-2	47	26	26	52	16	....	....	....	....	....	....	....	....	....	5	0	3	3	2	....	....	....	....
99-2000	Blues Espoo	Finland	51	15	24	39	12	....	....	....	....	....	....	....	....	....	4	0	1	1	2	....	....	....	....
2000-01	Blues Espoo	Finland	54	10	8	18	51	....	....	....	....	....	....	....	....	....	....	....	....	....	....	....	....	....	....
2001-02	Tappara Tampere	Finland	49	8	16	24	30	....	....	....	....	....	....	....	....	....	10	0	1	1	2	....	....	....	....
2002-03	Tappara Tampere	Finland	56	23	14	37	6	....	....	....	....	....	....	....	....	....	15	5	*9	*14	2	....	....	....	....
2003-04	**Los Angeles**	**NHL**	**57**	**3**	**8**	**11**	**12**	**0**	**1**	**0**	**57**	**5.3**	**–9**	**549**	**45.4**	**11:45**	....	....	....	....	....	....	....	....	....
	Manchester	AHL	4	3	1	4	2	....	....	....	....	....	....	....	....	....	....	....	....	....	....	....	....	....	....
2004-05	Lukko Rauma	Finland	47	9	29	38	31	....	....	....	....	....	....	....	....	....	9	1	3	4	2	....	....	....	....
	NHL Totals		**57**	**3**	**8**	**11**	**12**	**0**	**1**	**0**	**57**	**5.3**		**549**	**45.4**	**11:45**	....	....	....	....	....	....	....	....	....

Signed as a free agent by **Lukko** (Finland), July 30, 2004. Signed as a free agent by **Blues** (Finland), April 28, 2005.

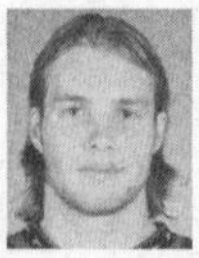

PIROS, Kamil

(PIH-ruhsh, KA-mihl)

Center. Shoots left. 6', 200 lbs. Born, Most, Czech., November 20, 1978. Buffalo's 9th choice, 212th overall, in 1997 Entry Draft.

Season	Club	League	GP	G	A	Pts	PIM	PP	SH	GW	S	%	+/-	TF	F%	Min	GP	G	A	Pts	PIM	PP	SH	GW	Min
1993-94	Banik Most Jr.	CzRep-Jr.	16	12	10	22	....	....	....	....	....	....	....	....	....	....	....	....	....	....	....	....	....	....	....
	Litvinov Jr.	CzRep-Jr.	22	6	13	19	....	....	....	....	....	....	....	....	....	....	....	....	....	....	....	....	....	....	....
1994-95	Litvinov Jr.	CzRep-Jr.	40	27	16	43	....	....	....	....	....	....	....	....	....	....	....	....	....	....	....	....	....	....	....
1995-96	Litvinov Jr.	CzRep-Jr.	42	16	13	29	....	....	....	....	....	....	....	....	....	....	....	....	....	....	....	....	....	....	....
1996-97	Litvinov Jr.	CzRep-Jr.	3	2	1	3	....	....	....	....	....	....	....	....	....	....	....	....	....	....	....	....	....	....	....
	Litvinov	CzRep	38	4	9	13	10	....	....	....	....	....	....	....	....	....	....	....	....	....	....	....	....	....	....
1997-98	Litvinov	CzRep	14	0	1	1	2	....	....	....	....	....	....	....	....	....	....	....	....	....	....	....	....	....	....
	HC Vitkovice	CzRep	26	2	9	11	14	....	....	....	....	....	....	....	....	....	....	....	....	....	....	....	....	....	....
1998-99	Litvinov	CzRep	41	7	9	16	10	....	....	....	....	....	....	....	....	....	....	....	....	....	....	....	....	....	....
99-2000	Litvinov	CzRep	40	8	8	16	18	....	....	....	....	....	....	....	....	....	7	0	3	3	2	....	....	....	....
2000-01	Litvinov	CzRep	48	11	13	24	28	....	....	....	....	....	....	....	....	....	6	1	1	2	2	....	....	....	....
2001-02	**Atlanta**	**NHL**	**8**	**0**	**1**	**1**	**4**	**0**	**0**	**0**	**4**	**0.0**	**–2**	**81**	**32.1**	**12:12**	....	....	....	....	....	....	....	....	....
	Chicago Wolves	AHL	64	19	30	49	16	....	....	....	....	....	....	....	....	....	25	6	11	17	6	....	....	....	....
2002-03	**Atlanta**	**NHL**	**3**	**3**	**2**	**5**	**2**	**0**	**0**	**1**	**8**	**37.5**	**4**	**47**	**40.4**	**17:05**	....	....	....	....	....	....	....	....	....
	Chicago Wolves	AHL	51	10	9	19	16	....	....	....	....	....	....	....	....	....	9	1	0	1	4	....	....	....	....
2003-04	**Atlanta**	**NHL**	**14**	**0**	**1**	**1**	**4**	**0**	**0**	**0**	**10**	**0.0**	**–3**	**3**	**33.3**	**9:57**	....	....	....	....	....	....	....	....	....
	Chicago Wolves	AHL	50	10	20	30	20	....	....	....	....	....	....	....	....	....	....	....	....	....	....	....	....	....	....
	Florida	**NHL**	**3**	**1**	**0**	**1**	**0**	**1**	**0**	**0**	**1**	**100.0**	**–1**	**19**	**26.3**	**6:59**	....	....	....	....	....	....	....	....	....
	San Antonio	AHL	14	2	5	7	6	....	....	....	....	....	....	....	....	....	....	....	....	....	....	....	....	....	....
2004-05	Voskresensk	Russia	27	2	6	8	8	....	....	....	....	....	....	....	....	....	....	....	....	....	....	....	....	....	....
	NHL Totals		**28**	**4**	**4**	**8**	**10**	**1**	**0**	**1**	**23**	**17.4**		**150**	**34.0**	**11:02**	....	....	....	....	....	....	....	....	....

Rights traded to **Atlanta** by **Buffalo** with Buffalo's 4th round choice (later traded to St. Louis – St. Louis selected Igor Valeyev) in 2001 Entry Draft for Donald Audette, March 13, 2001. Traded to **Florida** by **Atlanta** for Kyle Rossiter, March 8, 2004. Signed as a free agent by **Voskresensk** (Russia), November 15, 2004.

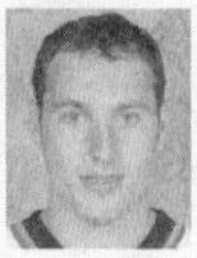

PISANI, Fernando

(pih-ZAN-ee, FUHR-nan-DOH) **EDM.**

Right wing. Shoots left. 6'1", 205 lbs. Born, Edmonton, Alta., December 27, 1976. Edmonton's 9th choice, 195th overall, in 1996 Entry Draft.

Season	Club	League	GP	G	A	Pts	PIM	PP	SH	GW	S	%	+/-	TF	F%	Min	GP	G	A	Pts	PIM	PP	SH	GW	Min
1993-94	St. Albert Saints	AJHL	50	6	21	27	24	....	....	....	....	....	....	....	....	....	....	....	....	....	....	....	....	....	....
1994-95	Bonnyville	AJHL	16	4	34	37	97	....	....	....	....	....	....	....	....	....	....	....	....	....	....	....	....	....	....
	St. Albert Saints	AJHL	40	26	21	47	16	....	....	....	....	....	....	....	....	....	....	....	....	....	....	....	....	....	....
1995-96	St. Albert Saints	AJHL	58	40	63	103	134	....	....	....	....	....	....	....	....	....	18	7	22	29	28	....	....	....	....
1996-97	Providence	H-East	35	12	18	30	36	....	....	....	....	....	....	....	....	....	....	....	....	....	....	....	....	....	....
1997-98	Providence	H-East	36	16	18	34	20	....	....	....	....	....	....	....	....	....	....	....	....	....	....	....	....	....	....
1998-99	Providence	H-East	38	14	37	51	42	....	....	....	....	....	....	....	....	....	....	....	....	....	....	....	....	....	....
99-2000	Providence	H-East	38	14	24	38	56	....	....	....	....	....	....	....	....	....	....	....	....	....	....	....	....	....	....
2000-01	Hamilton	AHL	52	12	13	25	28	....	....	....	....	....	....	....	....	....	....	....	....	....	....	....	....	....	....
2001-02	Hamilton	AHL	79	26	34	60	60	....	....	....	....	....	....	....	....	....	15	4	6	10	4	....	....	....	....
2002-03	**Edmonton**	**NHL**	**35**	**8**	**5**	**13**	**10**	**0**	**1**	**0**	**32**	**25.0**	**9**	**1**	**100.0**	**10:43**	**6**	**1**	**0**	**1**	**2**	**0**	**0**	**0**	**13:48**
	Hamilton	AHL	41	17	15	32	24	....	....	....	....	....	....	....	....	....	....	....	....	....	....	....	....	....	....
2003-04	**Edmonton**	**NHL**	**76**	**16**	**14**	**30**	**46**	**4**	**1**	**1**	**99**	**16.2**	**14**	**10**	**20.0**	**12:46**	....	....	....	....	....	....	....	....	....
2004-05	Langnau	Swiss	7	1	3	4	0	....	....	....	....	....	....	....	....	....	....	....	....	....	....	....	....	....	....
	Asiago	Italy	12	1	5	6	6	....	....	....	....	....	....	....	....	....	9	4	6	10	0	....	....	....	....
	NHL Totals		**111**	**24**	**19**	**43**	**56**	**4**	**2**	**1**	**131**	**18.3**		**11**	**27.3**	**12:07**	**6**	**1**	**0**	**1**	**2**	**0**	**0**	**0**	**13:48**

Signed as a free agent by **Langnau** (Swiss), October 24, 2004. Signed as a free agent by **Asiago** (Italy), December 23, 2004.

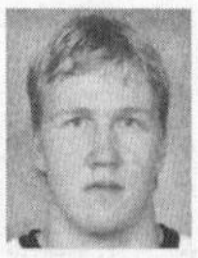

PITKANEN, Joni

(PIHT-ka-nuhn, YOH-nee) **PHI.**

Defense. Shoots left. 6'3", 200 lbs. Born, Oulu, Finland, September 19, 1983. Philadelphia's 1st choice, 4th overall, in 2002 Entry Draft.

Season	Club	League	GP	G	A	Pts	PIM	PP	SH	GW	S	%	+/-	TF	F%	Min	GP	G	A	Pts	PIM	PP	SH	GW	Min
1998-99	Karpat Oulu Jr.	Finland-Jr.	30	1	5	6	12	....	....	....	....	....	....	....	....	....	....	....	....	....	....	....	....	....	....
99-2000	Karpat Oulu Jr.	Finland-Jr.	38	12	14	26	26	....	....	....	....	....	....	....	....	....	6	1	4	5	2	....	....	....	....
2000-01	Karpat Oulu Jr.	Finland-Jr.	24	6	11	17	77	....	....	....	....	....	....	....	....	....	....	....	....	....	....	....	....	....	....
	Karpat Oulu	Finland	21	0	0	0	10	....	....	....	....	....	....	....	....	....	2	0	0	0	2	....	....	....	....
2001-02	Karpat Oulu	Finland	49	4	15	19	65	....	....	....	....	....	....	....	....	....	4	0	0	0	12	....	....	....	....
	Karpat Oulu Jr.	Finland-Jr.	....	....	....	....	....	....	....	....	....	....	....	....	....	....	1	0	0	0	0	....	....	....	....
2002-03	Karpat Oulu	Finland	35	5	15	20	38	....	....	....	....	....	....	....	....	....	....	....	....	....	....	....	....	....	....
2003-04	**Philadelphia**	**NHL**	**71**	**8**	**19**	**27**	**44**	**5**	**0**	**2**	**133**	**6.0**	**15**	**0**	**0.0**	**16:35**	**15**	**0**	**3**	**3**	**6**	**0**	**0**	**0**	**12:13**
2004-05	Philadelphia	AHL	76	6	35	41	105	....	....	....	....	....	....	....	....	....	21	3	4	7	16	....	....	....	....
	NHL Totals		**71**	**8**	**19**	**27**	**44**	**5**	**0**	**2**	**133**	**6.0**		**0**	**0.0**	**16:35**	**15**	**0**	**3**	**3**	**6**	**0**	**0**	**0**	**12:13**

NHL All-Rookie Team (2004)

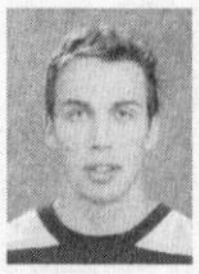

PITTIS, Domenic

(PIH-THIS, DOHM-ihn-ihk)

Center. Shoots left. 5'11", 190 lbs. Born, Calgary, Alta., October 1, 1974. Pittsburgh's 2nd choice, 52nd overall, in 1993 Entry Draft.

Season	Club	League	GP	G	A	Pts	PIM	PP	SH	GW	S	%	+/-	TF	F%	Min	GP	G	A	Pts	PIM	PP	SH	GW	Min
1990-91	Cgy. AAA Flames	AMHL	35	23	54	77	43	....	....	....	....	....	....	....	....	....	....	....	....	....	....	....	....	....	....
1991-92	Lethbridge	WHL	65	6	17	23	18	....	....	....	....	....	....	....	....	....	5	0	2	2	4	....	....	....	....
1992-93	Lethbridge	WHL	66	46	73	119	69	....	....	....	....	....	....	....	....	....	4	3	3	6	8	....	....	....	....
1993-94	Lethbridge	WHL	72	58	69	127	93	....	....	....	....	....	....	....	....	....	8	4	11	15	16	....	....	....	....
1994-95	Cleveland	IHL	62	18	32	50	66	....	....	....	....	....	....	....	....	....	3	0	2	2	2	....	....	....	....
1995-96	Cleveland	IHL	74	10	28	38	100	....	....	....	....	....	....	....	....	....	3	0	0	0	2	....	....	....	....
1996-97	**Pittsburgh**	**NHL**	**1**	**0**	**0**	**0**	**0**	**0**	**0**	**0**	**0**	**0.0**	**–1**	....	....	....	....	....	....	....	....	....	....	....	....
	Long Beach	IHL	65	23	43	66	91	....	....	....	....	....	....	....	....	....	18	5	9	14	26	....	....	....	....
1997-98	Syracuse Crunch	AHL	75	23	41	64	90	....	....	....	....	....	....	....	....	....	5	1	3	4	4	....	....	....	....

			Regular Season														Playoffs								
Season	Club	League	GP	G	A	Pts	PIM	PP	SH	GW	S	%	+/-	TF	F%	Min	GP	G	A	Pts	PIM	PP	SH	GW	Min
1998-99	**Buffalo**	**NHL**	**3**	**0**	**0**	**0**	**2**	**0**	**0**	**0**	**1**	**0.0**	**0**	**19**	**42.1**	**8:35**	....	....	....	....	....	....	....	....	....
	Rochester	AHL	76	38	66	*104	108	....	....	....	....	....	....	....	....	....	20	7	*14	*21	40	....	....	....	....
99-2000	**Buffalo**	**NHL**	**7**	**1**	**0**	**1**	**6**	**0**	**0**	**0**	**6**	**16.7**	**1**	**65**	**44.6**	**11:27**	....	....	....	....	....	....	....	....	....
	Rochester	AHL	53	17	48	65	85	....	....	....	....	....	....	....	....	....	21	4	*26	*30	28	....	....	....	....
2000-01	**Edmonton**	**NHL**	**47**	**4**	**5**	**9**	**49**	**0**	**0**	**2**	**42**	**9.5**	**–5**	**367**	**54.8**	**10:46**	**3**	**0**	**0**	**0**	**2**	**0**	**0**	**0**	**8:00**
2001-02	**Edmonton**	**NHL**	**22**	**0**	**6**	**6**	**8**	**0**	**0**	**0**	**18**	**0.0**	**–2**	**52**	**55.8**	**11:23**	....	....	....	....	....	....	....	....	....
2002-03	**Nashville**	**NHL**	**2**	**0**	**0**	**0**	**2**	**0**	**0**	**0**	**1**	**0.0**	**0**	**6**	**16.7**	**5:00**	....	....	....	....	....	....	....	....	....
	Milwaukee	AHL	30	11	21	32	65	....	....	....	....	....	....	....	....	....	6	2	4	6	8	....	....	....	....
2003-04	**Buffalo**	**NHL**	**4**	**0**	**0**	**0**	**4**	**0**	**0**	**0**	**3**	**0.0**	**–1**	**47**	**53.2**	**11:37**	....	....	....	....	....	....	....	....	....
	Rochester	AHL	75	20	*57	77	137	....	....	....	....	....	....	....	....	....	16	5	14	19	30	....	....	....	....
2004-05	Kloten Flyers	Swiss	43	17	29	46	110	....	....	....	....	....	....	....	....	....	3	2	2	4	4	....	....	....	....
	NHL Totals		**86**	**5**	**11**	**16**	**71**	**0**	**0**	**2**	**71**	**7.0**		**556**	**52.7**	**10:49**	**3**	**0**	**0**	**0**	**2**	**0**	**0**	**0**	**8:00**

WHL East Second All-Star Team (1994) • John P. Sollenberger Trophy (Leading Scorer – AHL) (1999)

Signed as a free agent by **Buffalo**, August 10, 1998. Signed as a free agent by **Edmonton**, July 25, 2000. • Missed majority of 2001-02 season recovering from head injury suffered in game vs. Nashvile, February 28, 2002. Signed as a free agent by **Nashville**, July 24, 2002. • Missed majority of 2002-03 season recovering from head injury suffered in game vs. San Jose, November 7, 2002. Signed as a free agent by **Buffalo**, July 26, 2003. Signed as a free agent by **Kloten** (Swiss), April 4, 2004.

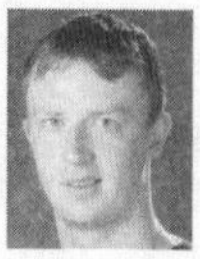

PIVKO, Libor
(PIHV-koh, LEE-bohr) **NSH.**

Left wing. Shoots left. 6'3", 214 lbs. Born, Novy Vicin, Czech., March 29, 1980. Nashville's 4th choice, 89th overall, in 2000 Entry Draft.

1995-96	Opava Jr.	CzRep-Jr.	37	19	14	33	30	....	....	....	....	....	....	....	....	....	....	....	....	....	....	....	....	....	....
1996-97	Opava Jr.	CzRep-Jr.	16	12	9	21	22	....	....	....	....	....	....	....	....	....	....	....	....	....	....	....	....	....	....
1997-98	HC Opava Jr.	CzRep-Jr.	37	15	11	26	36	....	....	....	....	....	....	....	....	....	....	....	....	....	....	....	....	....	....
1998-99	HC Opava Jr.	CzRep-Jr.	38	21	14	35	....	....	....	....	....	....	....	....	....	....	....	....	....	....	....	....	....	....	....
	Opava	CzRep	5	0	1	1	0	....	....	....	....	....	....	....	....	....	....	....	....	....	....	....	....	....	....
99-2000	HC Havirov Jr.	CzRep-Jr.	5	1	3	4	4	....	....	....	....	....	....	....	....	....	....	....	....	....	....	....	....	....	....
	HC Femax Havirov	CzRep	40	11	11	22	41	....	....	....	....	....	....	....	....	....	....	....	....	....	....	....	....	....	....
	HC Ytong Brno	CzRep-3	....	....	....	....	....	....	....	....	....	....	....	....	....	....	4	3	4	7	0	....	....	....	....
2000-01	HC Femax Havirov	CzRep	45	7	12	19	58	....	....	....	....	....	....	....	....	....	....	....	....	....	....	....	....	....	....
2001-02	Zlin	CzRep	46	8	20	28	36	....	....	....	....	....	....	....	....	....	9	5	3	8	8	....	....	....	....
2002-03	HC Hame Zlin	CzRep	52	13	12	25	60	....	....	....	....	....	....	....	....	....	....	....	....	....	....	....	....	....	....
2003-04	**Nashville**	**NHL**	**1**	**0**	**0**	**0**	**0**	**0**	**0**	**0**	**2**	**0.0**	**0**	**0**	**0.0**	**6:50**	....	....	....	....	....	....	....	....	....
	Milwaukee	AHL	67	11	20	31	50	....	....	....	....	....	....	....	....	....	21	7	6	13	22	....	....	....	....
2004-05	Milwaukee	AHL	56	5	15	20	59	....	....	....	....	....	....	....	....	....	6	0	1	1	2	....	....	....	....
	NHL Totals		**1**	**0**	**0**	**0**	**0**	**0**	**0**	**0**	**2**	**0.0**		**0**	**0.0**	**6:50**	....	....	....	....	....	....	....	....	....

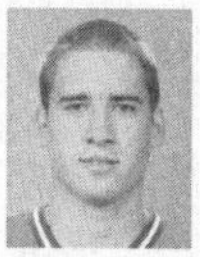

PLEKANEC, Tomas
(pleh-KA-nyehts, TAW-mahsh) **MTL.**

Left wing. Shoots left. 5'10", 200 lbs. Born, Kladno, Czech., October 31, 1982. Montreal's 4th choice, 71st overall, in 2001 Entry Draft.

1996-97	Kladno U17	CzR-U17	13	1	3	4	....	....	....	....	....	....	....	....	....	....	....	....	....	....	....	....	....	....	....
1997-98	HC Kladno U17	CzR-U17	45	38	26	64	....	....	....	....	....	....	....	....	....	....	....	....	....	....	....	....	....	....	....
1998-99	HC Kladno Jr.	CzRep-Jr.	53	22	20	42	....	....	....	....	....	....	....	....	....	....	....	....	....	....	....	....	....	....	....
99-2000	HC Kladno Jr.	CzRep-Jr.	43	14	16	30	....	....	....	....	....	....	....	....	....	....	....	....	....	....	....	....	....	....	....
	Kralupy	CzRep-3	6	2	2	4	2	....	....	....	....	....	....	....	....	....	....	....	....	....	....	....	....	....	....
	HC CKD Slany	CzRep-3	3	0	1	1	6	....	....	....	....	....	....	....	....	....	....	....	....	....	....	....	....	....	....
2000-01	Kladno	CzRep	47	9	9	18	24	....	....	....	....	....	....	....	....	....	....	....	....	....	....	....	....	....	....
	HC Kladno Jr.	CzRep-Jr.	9	6	4	10	4	....	....	....	....	....	....	....	....	....	....	....	....	....	....	....	....	....	....
2001-02	Kladno	CzRep	48	7	16	23	28	....	....	....	....	....	....	....	....	....	....	....	....	....	....	....	....	....	....
	BK Mlada Boleslav	CzRep-3	6	6	3	9	14	....	....	....	....	....	....	....	....	....	....	....	....	....	....	....	....	....	....
	Kladno	CzRep-Q	5	0	1	1	0	....	....	....	....	....	....	....	....	....	....	....	....	....	....	....	....	....	....
2002-03	Hamilton	AHL	77	19	27	46	74	....	....	....	....	....	....	....	....	....	13	3	2	5	8	....	....	....	....
2003-04	**Montreal**	**NHL**	**2**	**0**	**0**	**0**	**0**	**0**	**0**	**0**	**0**	**0.0**	**0**	**11**	**45.5**	**9:02**	....	....	....	....	....	....	....	....	....
	Hamilton	AHL	74	23	43	66	90	....	....	....	....	....	....	....	....	....	10	2	5	7	6	....	....	....	....
2004-05	Hamilton	AHL	80	29	35	64	68	....	....	....	....	....	....	....	....	....	4	2	4	6	6	....	....	....	....
	NHL Totals		**2**	**0**	**0**	**0**	**0**	**0**	**0**	**0**	**0**	**0.0**		**11**	**45.5**	**9:02**	....	....	....	....	....	....	....	....	....

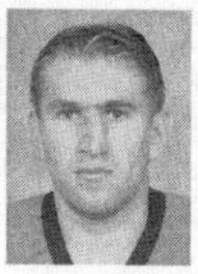

PLETKA, Vaclav
(PLEHT-kuh, VAT-slav) **PHI.**

Right wing. Shoots left. 5'11", 182 lbs. Born, Mlada Boleslav, Czech., June 8, 1979. Philadelphia's 5th choice, 208th overall, in 1999 Entry Draft.

1995-96	Ml. Boleslav Jr.	CzRep-Jr.	35	22	17	39	....	....	....	....	....	....	....	....	....	....	....	....	....	....	....	....	....	....	....
1996-97	Ml. Boleslav Jr.	CzRep-Jr.	37	28	13	41	....	....	....	....	....	....	....	....	....	....	....	....	....	....	....	....	....	....	....
1997-98	Ml. Boleslav Jr.	CzRep-Jr.	36	23	25	48	....	....	....	....	....	....	....	....	....	....	....	....	....	....	....	....	....	....	....
1998-99	HC Trinec Jr.	CzRep-Jr.	20	11	5	16	....	....	....	....	....	....	....	....	....	....	....	....	....	....	....	....	....	....	....
	Trinec	CzRep	50	15	11	26	20	....	....	....	....	....	....	....	....	....	10	2	1	3	....	....	....	....	....
99-2000	HC Ocelari Trinec	CzRep	51	28	21	49	62	....	....	....	....	....	....	....	....	....	4	2	2	4	2	....	....	....	....
2000-01	Philadelphia	AHL	71	20	21	41	51	....	....	....	....	....	....	....	....	....	10	1	3	4	4	....	....	....	....
2001-02	**Philadelphia**	**NHL**	**1**	**0**	**0**	**0**	**0**	**0**	**0**	**0**	**2**	**0.0**	**0**	**0**	**0.0**	**11:34**	....	....	....	....	....	....	....	....	....
	Philadelphia	AHL	61	20	19	39	43	....	....	....	....	....	....	....	....	....	....	....	....	....	....	....	....	....	....
2002-03	HC Ocelari Trinec	CzRep	47	20	24	44	58	....	....	....	....	....	....	....	....	....	12	3	2	5	18	....	....	....	....
2003-04	HC Ocelari Trinec	CzRep	47	12	17	29	104	....	....	....	....	....	....	....	....	....	5	0	0	0	2	....	....	....	....
2004-05	HC Ocelari Trinec	CzRep	16	2	2	4	14	....	....	....	....	....	....	....	....	....	....	....	....	....	....	....	....	....	....
	NHL Totals		**1**	**0**	**0**	**0**	**0**	**0**	**0**	**0**	**2**	**0.0**		**0**	**0.0**	**11:34**	....	....	....	....	....	....	....	....	....

Signed as a free agent by **Trinec** (CzRep), July 27, 2002.

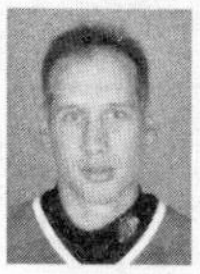

POAPST, Steve
(POHPST, STEEV)

Defense. Shoots left. 6', 199 lbs. Born, Cornwall, Ont., January 3, 1969.

1986-87	Smiths Falls Bears	CJHL	54	10	27	37	94	....	....	....	....	....	....	....	....	....	....	....	....	....	....	....	....	....	....
1987-88	Colgate	ECAC	32	3	13	16	22	....	....	....	....	....	....	....	....	....	....	....	....	....	....	....	....	....	....
1988-89	Colgate	ECAC	30	0	5	5	38	....	....	....	....	....	....	....	....	....	....	....	....	....	....	....	....	....	....
1989-90	Colgate	ECAC	38	4	15	19	54	....	....	....	....	....	....	....	....	....	....	....	....	....	....	....	....	....	....
1990-91	Colgate	ECAC	32	6	15	21	43	....	....	....	....	....	....	....	....	....	....	....	....	....	....	....	....	....	....
1991-92	Hampton Roads	ECHL	55	8	20	28	29	....	....	....	....	....	....	....	....	....	14	1	4	5	12	....	....	....	....
1992-93	Hampton Roads	ECHL	63	10	35	45	57	....	....	....	....	....	....	....	....	....	4	0	1	1	4	....	....	....	....
	Baltimore	AHL	7	0	1	1	4	....	....	....	....	....	....	....	....	....	7	0	3	3	6	....	....	....	....
1993-94	Portland Pirates	AHL	78	14	21	35	47	....	....	....	....	....	....	....	....	....	12	0	3	3	8	....	....	....	....
1994-95	Portland Pirates	AHL	71	8	22	30	60	....	....	....	....	....	....	....	....	....	7	0	1	1	16	....	....	....	....
1995-96	**Washington**	**NHL**	**3**	**1**	**0**	**1**	**0**	**0**	**0**	**1**	**2**	**50.0**	**–1**	....	....	....	**6**	**0**	**0**	**0**	**0**	**0**	**0**	**0**	....
	Portland Pirates	AHL	70	10	24	34	79	....	....	....	....	....	....	....	....	....	20	2	6	8	16	....	....	....	....
1996-97	Portland Pirates	AHL	47	1	20	21	34	....	....	....	....	....	....	....	....	....	5	0	1	1	6	....	....	....	....
1997-98	Portland Pirates	AHL	76	8	29	37	46	....	....	....	....	....	....	....	....	....	10	2	3	5	8	....	....	....	....
1998-99	**Washington**	**NHL**	**22**	**0**	**0**	**0**	**8**	**0**	**0**	**0**	**11**	**0.0**	**–8**	**0**	**0.0**	**12:26**	....	....	....	....	....	....	....	....	....
	Portland Pirates	AHL	54	3	21	24	36	....	....	....	....	....	....	....	....	....	....	....	....	....	....	....	....	....	....
99-2000	Portland Pirates	AHL	58	0	14	14	20	....	....	....	....	....	....	....	....	....	3	1	0	1	2	....	....	....	....
2000-01	**Chicago**	**NHL**	**36**	**2**	**3**	**5**	**12**	**0**	**0**	**0**	**27**	**7.4**	**3**	**0**	**0.0**	**17:03**	....	....	....	....	....	....	....	....	....
	Norfolk Admirals	AHL	37	1	8	9	14	....	....	....	....	....	....	....	....	....	....	....	....	....	....	....	....	....	....
2001-02	**Chicago**	**NHL**	**56**	**1**	**7**	**8**	**30**	**0**	**0**	**0**	**48**	**2.1**	**6**	**0**	**0.0**	**14:52**	**5**	**0**	**0**	**0**	**0**	**0**	**0**	**0**	**23:14**
2002-03	**Chicago**	**NHL**	**75**	**2**	**11**	**13**	**50**	**0**	**0**	**0**	**49**	**4.1**	**14**	**0**	**0.0**	**22:51**	....	....	....	....	....	....	....	....	....
2003-04	**Chicago**	**NHL**	**53**	**2**	**2**	**4**	**26**	**0**	**0**	**1**	**55**	**3.6**	**–16**	**1**	**0.0**	**22:15**	....	....	....	....	....	....	....	....	....
2004-05			DID NOT PLAY																						
	NHL Totals		**245**	**8**	**23**	**31**	**126**	**0**	**0**	**2**	**192**	**4.2**		**1**	**0.0**	**19:04**	**11**	**0**	**0**	**0**	**0**	**0**	**0**	**0**	**23:14**

ECHL First All-Star Team (1993)

Signed as a free agent by **Washington**, February 4, 1995. Signed as a free agent by **Chicago**, July 27, 2000.

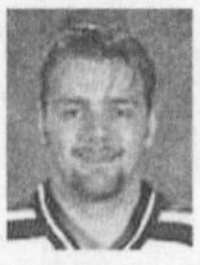

PODKONICKY, Andrej
(pohd-koh-NIHTZ-kee, AWN-dray)

Center. Shoots left. 6'2", 202 lbs. Born, Zvolen, Czech., May 9, 1978. St. Louis' 8th choice, 196th overall, in 1996 Entry Draft.

			Regular Season														Playoffs								
Season	Club	League	GP	G	A	Pts	PIM	PP	SH	GW	S	%	+/-	TF	F%	Min	GP	G	A	Pts	PIM	PP	SH	GW	Min
1994-95	HK Hell Zvolen	Slovak-2	17	0	4	4	6	....	....	....	....	....	....	....	....	....	....	....	....	....	....	....	....	....	....
1995-96	HK Hell Zvolen	Slovak-2	38	18	12	30	18	....	....	....	....	....	....	....	....	....	....	....	....	....	....	....	....	....	....
1996-97	Portland	WHL	71	25	46	71	127	....	....	....	....	....	....	....	....	....	6	1	1	2	8	....	....	....	....
1997-98	Portland	WHL	64	30	44	74	81	....	....	....	....	....	....	....	....	....	16	4	12	16	20	....	....	....	....
1998-99	Worcester IceCats	AHL	61	19	24	43	52	....	....	....	....	....	....	....	....	....	4	0	0	0	4	....	....	....	....
99-2000	Worcester IceCats	AHL	77	16	25	41	68	....	....	....	....	....	....	....	....	....	9	2	5	7	6	....	....	....	....
2000-01	Worcester IceCats	AHL	16	2	3	5	15	....	....	....	....	....	....	....	....	....	....	....	....	....	....	....	....	....	....
	Florida	**NHL**	**6**	**1**	**0**	**1**	**2**	**0**	**0**	**0**	**5**	**20.0**	**0**	**34**	**55.9**	**6:04**	....	....	....	....	....	....	....	....	....
	Louisville Panthers	AHL	41	6	10	16	31	....	....	....	....	....	....	....	....	....	....	....	....	....	....	....	....	....	....
2001-02	HIFK Helsinki	Finland	23	3	6	9	41	....	....	....	....	....	....	....	....	....	....	....	....	....	....	....	....	....	....
	Bratislava	Slovakia	16	11	2	13	2	....	....	....	....	....	....	....	....	....	19	4	7	11	49	....	....	....	....
2002-03	Iserlohn Roosters	Germany	52	18	15	33	54	....	....	....	....	....	....	....	....	....	....	....	....	....	....	....	....	....	....
2003-04	**Washington**	**NHL**	**2**	**0**	**0**	**0**	**0**	**0**	**0**	**0**	**1**	**0.0**	**–1**	**0**	**0.0**	**3:34**	....	....	....	....	....	....	....	....	....
	Portland Pirates	AHL	56	12	14	26	31	....	....	....	....	....	....	....	....	....	7	0	2	2	16	....	....	....	....
2004-05	Liberec	CzRep	24	9	4	13	16	....	....	....	....	....	....	....	....	....	10	3	4	7	4	....	....	....	....
	NHL Totals		**8**	**1**	**0**	**1**	**2**	**0**	**0**	**0**	**6**	**16.7**		**34**	**55.9**	**5:27**	....	....	....	....	....	....	....	....	....

Memorial Cup Tournament All-Star Team (1998) • Ed Chynoweth Award (Memorial Cup Tournament Top Scorer) (1998)

Traded to **Florida** by **St. Louis** for Eric Boguniecki, December 17, 2000. Signed as a free agent by **HIFK** (Finland), August 14, 2001. Signed as a free agent by **Iserlohn** (Germany), August 3, 2002. Signed as a free agent by **Washington**, July 14, 2003. Signed as a free agent by **Liberec** (CzRep), May 2, 2004.

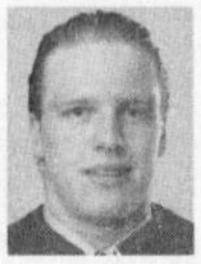

POECK, Thomas
(PAWK, TAW-muhs) **NYR**

Defense. Shoots left. 6'1", 208 lbs. Born, Klagenfurt, Austria, December 2, 1981.

1998-99	Klagenfurt Jr.	Austria-Jr.	31	0	0	0	2	....	....	....	....	....	....	....	....	....	....	....	....	....	....	....	....	....	....
99-2000	Klagenfurter AC	Austria	15	3	8	11	14	....	....	....	....	....	....	....	....	....	....	....	....	....	....	....	....	....	....
	Klagenfurt	Alpenliga	33	4	11	15	48	....	....	....	....	....	....	....	....	....	....	....	....	....	....	....	....	....	....
2000-01	Massachusetts	H-East	33	6	6	12	59	....	....	....	....	....	....	....	....	....	....	....	....	....	....	....	....	....	....
2001-02	Massachusetts	H-East	23	5	7	12	26	....	....	....	....	....	....	....	....	....	....	....	....	....	....	....	....	....	....
	Austria	Nat-Tm	10	1	2	3	4	....	....	....	....	....	....	....	....	....	....	....	....	....	....	....	....	....	....
	Austria	Olympics	4	0	0	0	2	....	....	....	....	....	....	....	....	....	....	....	....	....	....	....	....	....	....
2002-03	Massachusetts	H-East	37	17	20	37	46	....	....	....	....	....	....	....	....	....	....	....	....	....	....	....	....	....	....
2003-04	Massachusetts	H-East	37	16	25	41	48	....	....	....	....	....	....	....	....	....	....	....	....	....	....	....	....	....	....
	NY Rangers	**NHL**	**6**	**2**	**2**	**4**	**0**	**0**	**0**	**0**	**8**	**25.0**	**–4**	**0**	**0.0**	**18:38**	....	....	....	....	....	....	....	....	....
2004-05	Hartford	AHL	50	1	5	6	55	....	....	....	....	....	....	....	....	....	6	0	1	1	8	....	....	....	....
	Charlotte	ECHL	3	0	2	2	2	....	....	....	....	....	....	....	....	....	....	....	....	....	....	....	....	....	....
	NHL Totals		**6**	**2**	**2**	**4**	**0**	**0**	**0**	**0**	**8**	**25.0**		**0**	**0.0**	**18:38**	....	....	....	....	....	....	....	....	....

Hockey East Second All-Star Team (2003) • Hockey East First All-Star Team (2004) • NCAA East First All-American Team (2004)

Signed as a free agent by **NY Rangers**, March 23, 2004.

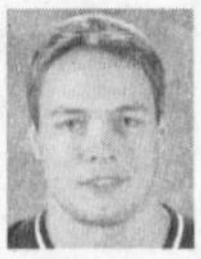

POHL, John
(PAWL, JAWN) **TOR.**

Center. Shoots right. 6', 186 lbs. Born, Rochester, MN, June 29, 1979. St. Louis' 8th choice, 255th overall, in 1998 Entry Draft.

1997-98	Red Wing	High-MN	28	30	77	107	18	....	....	....	....	....	....	....	....	....	....	....	....	....	....	....	....	....	....
	Twin Cities	USHL	10	5	3	8	10	....	....	....	....	....	....	....	....	....	....	....	....	....	....	....	....	....	....
1998-99	U. of Minnesota	WCHA	42	7	10	17	18	....	....	....	....	....	....	....	....	....	....	....	....	....	....	....	....	....	....
99-2000	U. of Minnesota	WCHA	41	18	41	59	26	....	....	....	....	....	....	....	....	....	....	....	....	....	....	....	....	....	....
2000-01	U. of Minnesota	WCHA	38	19	26	45	24	....	....	....	....	....	....	....	....	....	....	....	....	....	....	....	....	....	....
2001-02	U. of Minnesota	WCHA	44	27	*52	*79	26	....	....	....	....	....	....	....	....	....	....	....	....	....	....	....	....	....	....
2002-03	Worcester IceCats	AHL	58	26	32	58	34	....	....	....	....	....	....	....	....	....	3	0	1	1	6	....	....	....	....
2003-04	**St. Louis**	**NHL**	**1**	**0**	**0**	**0**	**0**	**0**	**0**	**0**	**1**	**0.0**	**–2**	**9**	**55.6**	**8:18**	....	....	....	....	....	....	....	....	....
	Worcester IceCats	AHL	65	16	25	41	65	....	....	....	....	....	....	....	....	....	3	0	1	1	2	....	....	....	....
2004-05	Worcester IceCats	AHL	13	3	6	9	2	....	....	....	....	....	....	....	....	....	....	....	....	....	....	....	....	....	....
	NHL Totals		**1**	**0**	**0**	**0**	**0**	**0**	**0**	**0**	**1**	**0.0**		**9**	**55.6**	**8:18**	....	....	....	....	....	....	....	....	....

WCHA Second All-Star Team (2000) • WCHA First All-Star Team (2002) • NCAA Championship All-Tournament Team (2002)

Traded to **Toronto** by **St. Louis** for future considerations, August 24, 2005.

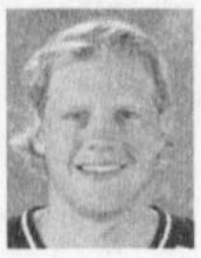

POLLOCK, Jame
(PAWL-lawk, JAYM)

Defense. Shoots right. 6'1", 210 lbs. Born, Quebec City, Que., June 16, 1979. St. Louis' 4th choice, 106th overall, in 1997 Entry Draft.

1994-95	Victoria Legion	BCAHA	43	22	56	78	96	....	....	....	....	....	....	....	....	....	....	....	....	....	....	....	....	....	....
1995-96	Seattle	WHL	32	0	1	1	15	....	....	....	....	....	....	....	....	....	....	....	....	....	....	....	....	....	....
1996-97	Seattle	WHL	66	15	19	34	94	....	....	....	....	....	....	....	....	....	15	3	5	8	16	....	....	....	....
1997-98	Seattle	WHL	66	11	36	47	78	....	....	....	....	....	....	....	....	....	5	0	1	1	17	....	....	....	....
1998-99	Seattle	WHL	59	10	32	42	78	....	....	....	....	....	....	....	....	....	11	3	4	7	8	....	....	....	....
99-2000	Worcester IceCats	AHL	56	12	12	24	50	....	....	....	....	....	....	....	....	....	9	5	3	8	6	....	....	....	....
2000-01	Worcester IceCats	AHL	55	15	8	23	36	....	....	....	....	....	....	....	....	....	11	1	7	8	10	....	....	....	....
2001-02	Worcester IceCats	AHL	71	23	43	66	89	....	....	....	....	....	....	....	....	....	3	1	0	1	2	....	....	....	....
2002-03	Worcester IceCats	AHL	44	5	17	22	50	....	....	....	....	....	....	....	....	....	3	1	0	1	2	....	....	....	....
2003-04	**St. Louis**	**NHL**	**9**	**0**	**0**	**0**	**6**	**0**	**0**	**0**	**19**	**0.0**	**–1**	**0**	**0.0**	**15:25**	....	....	....	....	....	....	....	....	....
	Worcester IceCats	AHL	44	8	24	32	52	....	....	....	....	....	....	....	....	....	7	1	4	5	14	....	....	....	....
2004-05	Kloten Flyers	Swiss	26	4	8	12	34	....	....	....	....	....	....	....	....	....	....	....	....	....	....	....	....	....	....
	HC Lugano	Swiss	....	....	....	....	....	....	....	....	....	....	....	....	....	....	2	0	1	1	8	....	....	....	....
	NHL Totals		**9**	**0**	**0**	**0**	**6**	**0**	**0**	**0**	**19**	**0.0**		**0**	**0.0**	**15:25**	....	....	....	....	....	....	....	....	....

Signed as a free agent by **Kloten** (Swiss), April 6, 2004. Signed as a free agent by **Lugano** (Swiss), February 22, 2005.

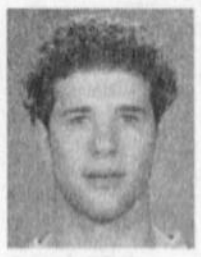

POMINVILLE, Jason
(paw-MIHN-vihl, JAY-suhn) **BUF.**

Right wing. Shoots right. 6', 186 lbs. Born, Repentigny, Que., November 30, 1982. Buffalo's 4th choice, 55th overall, in 2001 Entry Draft.

1997-98	Cap-d-Madeleine	QAAA	13	3	7	10	....	....	....	....	....	....	....	....	....	....	....	....	....	....	....	....	....	....	....
1998-99	Cap-d-Madeleine	QAAA	41	18	38	56	16	....	....	....	....	....	....	....	....	....	7	2	7	9	0	....	....	....	....
	Shawinigan	QMJHL	2	0	0	0	0	....	....	....	....	....	....	....	....	....	....	....	....	....	....	....	....	....	....
99-2000	Shawinigan	QMJHL	60	4	17	21	12	....	....	....	....	....	....	....	....	....	13	2	3	5	0	....	....	....	....
2000-01	Shawinigan	QMJHL	71	46	67	113	24	....	....	....	....	....	....	....	....	....	10	6	6	12	0	....	....	....	....
2001-02	Shawinigan	QMJHL	66	57	64	121	32	....	....	....	....	....	....	....	....	....	2	0	0	0	0	....	....	....	....
2002-03	Rochester	AHL	73	13	21	34	16	....	....	....	....	....	....	....	....	....	3	1	1	2	0	....	....	....	....
2003-04	**Buffalo**	**NHL**	**1**	**0**	**0**	**0**	**0**	**0**	**0**	**0**	**3**	**0.0**	**0**	**0**	**0.0**	**14:22**	....	....	....	....	....	....	....	....	....
	Rochester	AHL	66	34	30	64	30	....	....	....	....	....	....	....	....	....	16	9	10	19	6	....	....	....	....
2004-05	Rochester	AHL	78	30	38	68	43	....	....	....	....	....	....	....	....	....	....	....	....	....	....	....	....	....	....
	NHL Totals		**1**	**0**	**0**	**0**	**0**	**0**	**0**	**0**	**3**	**0.0**		**0**	**0.0**	**14:22**	....	....	....	....	....	....	....	....	....

QMJHL First All-Star Team (2002)

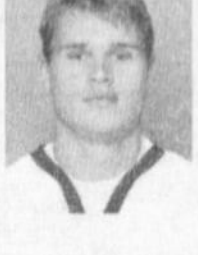

PONIKAROVSKY, Alexei
(poh-NIH-kahr-ohv-skee, al-EHX-ay) **TOR.**

Left wing. Shoots left. 6'4", 220 lbs. Born, Kiev, USSR, April 9, 1980. Toronto's 4th choice, 87th overall, in 1998 Entry Draft.

1996-97	Dyn'o Moscow 2	Russia-3	60	12	15	27	30	....	....	....	....	....	....	....	....	....	....	....	....	....	....	....	....	....	....
	Dyn'o Moscow 2	Russia-3	2	0	0	0	2	....	....	....	....	....	....	....	....	....	....	....	....	....	....	....	....	....	....
1997-98	Dynamo Moscow	Russia	24	1	2	3	30	....	....	....	....	....	....	....	....	....	....	....	....	....	....	....	....	....	....
1998-99	Krylja Sovetov	Russia	13	2	1	3	2	....	....	....	....	....	....	....	....	....	....	....	....	....	....	....	....	....	....
	Dynamo Moscow	Russia	....	....	....	....	....	....	....	....	....	....	....	....	....	....	3	0	0	0	2	....	....	....	....
99-2000	THK Tver	Russia-2	29	8	14	22	26	....	....	....	....	....	....	....	....	....	....	....	....	....	....	....	....	....	....
	Dynamo Moscow	Russia	19	1	0	1	8	....	....	....	....	....	....	....	....	....	1	0	0	0	0	....	....	....	....
	Dynamo Moscow	EuroHL	2	0	2	2	0	....	....	....	....	....	....	....	....	....	....	....	....	....	....	....	....	....	....
2000-01	**Toronto**	**NHL**	**22**	**1**	**3**	**4**	**14**	**0**	**0**	**0**	**21**	**4.8**	**–1**	**7**	**28.6**	**8:32**	....	....	....	....	....	....	....	....	....
	St. John's	AHL	49	12	24	36	44	....	....	....	....	....	....	....	....	....	4	0	0	0	4	....	....	....	....

			Regular Season														Playoffs								
Season	Club	League	GP	G	A	Pts	PIM	PP	SH	GW	S	%	+/-	TF	F%	Min	GP	G	A	Pts	PIM	PP	SH	GW	Min
2001-02	**Toronto**	**NHL**	**8**	**2**	**0**	**2**	**0**	**0**	**0**	**1**	**8**	**25.0**	**2**	**2**	**50.0**	**8:03**	**10**	**0**	**0**	**0**	**4**	**0**	**0**	**0**	**8:15**
	St. John's	AHL	72	21	27	48	74	....	....	....	....	....	....	....	....	....	5	2	1	3	8	....	....	....	....
	Ukraine	Olympics	4	1	1	2	6	....	....	....	....	....	....	....	....	....	....	....	....	....	....	....	....	....	....
2002-03	St. John's	AHL	63	24	22	46	68	....	....	....	....	....	....	....	....	....	....	....	....	....	....	....	....	....	....
	Toronto	**NHL**	**13**	**0**	**3**	**3**	**11**	**0**	**0**	**0**	**13**	**0.0**	**4**	**4**	**25.0**	**10:43**	....	....	....	....	....	....	....	....	....
2003-04	**Toronto**	**NHL**	**73**	**9**	**19**	**28**	**44**	**1**	**0**	**2**	**110**	**8.2**	**14**	**20**	**30.0**	**11:36**	**13**	**1**	**3**	**4**	**8**	**0**	**0**	**1**	**14:20**
2004-05	Voskresensk	Russia	19	1	5	6	16	....	....	....	....	....	....	....	....	....	....	....	....	....	....	....	....	....	....
	NHL Totals		**116**	**12**	**25**	**37**	**69**	**1**	**0**	**3**	**152**	**7.9**		**33**	**30.3**	**10:41**	**23**	**1**	**3**	**4**	**12**	**0**	**0**	**1**	**11:42**

Signed as a free agent by **Voskresensk** (Russia), November 13, 2004.

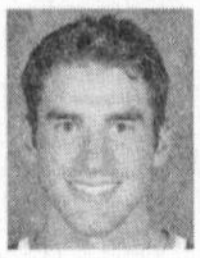

POPOVIC, Mark

(poh-PUH-vihk, MAHRK) **ATL.**

Defense. Shoots left. 6'1", 207 lbs. Born, Stoney Creek, Ont., October 11, 1982. Anaheim's 2nd choice, 35th overall, in 2001 Entry Draft.

Season	Club	League	GP	G	A	Pts	PIM	PP	SH	GW	S	%	+/-	TF	F%	Min	GP	G	A	Pts	PIM	PP	SH	GW	Min
1997-98	Mississauga	OPJHL	51	10	16	26	32	....	....	....	....	....	....	....	....	....	....	....	....	....	....	....	....	....	....
1998-99	St. Michael's	OHL	60	6	26	32	46	....	....	....	....	....	....	....	....	....	....	....	....	....	....	....	....	....	....
99-2000	St. Michael's	OHL	68	11	29	40	68	....	....	....	....	....	....	....	....	....	....	....	....	....	....	....	....	....	....
2000-01	St. Michael's	OHL	61	7	35	42	54	....	....	....	....	....	....	....	....	....	18	3	5	8	22	....	....	....	....
2001-02	St. Michael's	OHL	58	12	29	41	42	....	....	....	....	....	....	....	....	....	15	1	11	12	10	....	....	....	....
2002-03	Cincinnati	AHL	73	3	21	24	46	....	....	....	....	....	....	....	....	....	....	....	....	....	....	....	....	....	....
2003-04	**Anaheim**	**NHL**	**1**	**0**	**0**	**0**	**0**	**0**	**0**	**0**	**1**	**0.0**	**0**	**0**	**0.0**	**13:48**	....	....	....	....	....	....	....	....	....
	Cincinnati	AHL	74	4	10	14	63	....	....	....	....	....	....	....	....	....	9	1	2	3	4	....	....	....	....
2004-05	Cincinnati	AHL	74	1	17	18	47	....	....	....	....	....	....	....	....	....	11	2	3	5	6	....	....	....	....
	NHL Totals		**1**	**0**	**0**	**0**	**0**	**0**	**0**	**0**	**1**	**0.0**		**0**	**0.0**	**13:48**	....	....	....	....	....	....	....	....	....

OHL First All-Star Team (2002)

Traded to **Atlanta** by **Anaheim** for Kip Brennan, August 25, 2005.

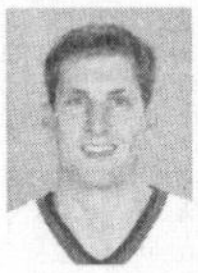

POTHIER, Brian

(POH-thee-uhr, BRIGH-uhn) **OTT.**

Defense. Shoots right. 6', 195 lbs. Born, New Bedford, MA, April 15, 1977.

Season	Club	League	GP	G	A	Pts	PIM	PP	SH	GW	S	%	+/-	TF	F%	Min	GP	G	A	Pts	PIM	PP	SH	GW	Min
1995-96	Northfield Mt.H.	High-MA	27	11	22	33	36	....	....	....	....	....	....	....	....	....	....	....	....	....	....	....	....	....	....
1996-97	RPI Engineers	ECAC	34	1	11	12	42	....	....	....	....	....	....	....	....	....	....	....	....	....	....	....	....	....	....
1997-98	RPI Engineers	ECAC	35	2	9	11	28	....	....	....	....	....	....	....	....	....	....	....	....	....	....	....	....	....	....
1998-99	RPI Engineers	ECAC	37	5	13	18	36	....	....	....	....	....	....	....	....	....	....	....	....	....	....	....	....	....	....
99-2000	RPI Engineers	ECAC	36	9	24	33	44	....	....	....	....	....	....	....	....	....	....	....	....	....	....	....	....	....	....
2000-01	**Atlanta**	**NHL**	**3**	**0**	**0**	**0**	**2**	**0**	**0**	**0**	**0**	**0.0**	**4**	**0**	**0.0**	**20:38**	....	....	....	....	....	....	....	....	....
	Orlando	IHL	76	12	29	41	69	....	....	....	....	....	....	....	....	....	16	3	5	8	11	....	....	....	....
2001-02	**Atlanta**	**NHL**	**33**	**3**	**6**	**9**	**22**	**1**	**0**	**1**	**65**	**4.6**	**–19**	**0**	**0.0**	**21:41**	....	....	....	....	....	....	....	....	....
	Chicago Wolves	AHL	39	6	13	19	30	....	....	....	....	....	....	....	....	....	....	....	....	....	....	....	....	....	....
2002-03	**Ottawa**	**NHL**	**14**	**2**	**4**	**6**	**6**	**0**	**0**	**1**	**23**	**8.7**	**11**	**0**	**0.0**	**15:23**	**1**	**0**	**0**	**0**	**2**	**0**	**0**	**0**	**13:11**
	Binghamton	AHL	68	7	40	47	58	....	....	....	....	....	....	....	....	....	8	2	8	10	4	....	....	....	....
2003-04	**Ottawa**	**NHL**	**55**	**2**	**6**	**8**	**24**	**1**	**0**	**1**	**78**	**2.6**	**6**	**0**	**0.0**	**16:43**	**7**	**0**	**0**	**0**	**6**	**0**	**0**	**0**	**17:15**
2004-05	Binghamton	AHL	77	12	36	48	64	....	....	....	....	....	....	....	....	....	6	0	1	1	6	....	....	....	....
	NHL Totals		**105**	**7**	**16**	**23**	**54**	**2**	**0**	**3**	**166**	**4.2**		**0**	**0.0**	**18:13**	**8**	**0**	**0**	**0**	**8**	**0**	**0**	**0**	**16:44**

ECAC Second All-Star Team (2000) • ECAC All-Tournament Team (2000) • NCAA East Second All-American Team (2000) • Ken McKenzie Trophy (U.S. - Born Rookie of the Year – IHL) (2001) • Garry F. Longman Memorial Trophy (Rookie of the Year – IHL) (2001) • AHL Second All-Star Team (2003, 2005)

Signed as a free agent by **Atlanta**, March 27, 2000. Traded to **Ottawa** by **Atlanta** for Shawn McEachern and Ottawa's 6th round choice (Dan Turple) in 2004 Entry Draft, June 29, 2002.

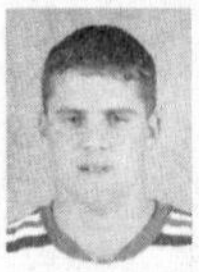

POTI, Tom

(POH-tee, TAWM) **NYR**

Defense. Shoots left. 6'3", 210 lbs. Born, Worcester, MA, March 22, 1977. Edmonton's 4th choice, 59th overall, in 1996 Entry Draft.

Season	Club	League	GP	G	A	Pts	PIM	PP	SH	GW	S	%	+/-	TF	F%	Min	GP	G	A	Pts	PIM	PP	SH	GW	Min
1992-93	St. Peter's Marian	High-MA	55	25	46	71	....	....	....	....	....	....	....	....	....	....	....	....	....	....	....	....	....	....	....
1993-94	Cushing	High-MA	30	10	35	45	....	....	....	....	....	....	....	....	....	....	....	....	....	....	....	....	....	....	....
1994-95	Cushing	High-MA	36	17	54	71	35	....	....	....	....	....	....	....	....	....	....	....	....	....	....	....	....	....	....
	Central-Mass	MBAHL	8	8	10	18	....	....	....	....	....	....	....	....	....	....	....	....	....	....	....	....	....	....	....
1995-96	Cushing	High-MA	29	14	59	73	18	....	....	....	....	....	....	....	....	....	....	....	....	....	....	....	....	....	....
1996-97	Boston University	H-East	38	4	17	21	54	....	....	....	....	....	....	....	....	....	....	....	....	....	....	....	....	....	....
1997-98	Boston University	H-East	38	13	29	42	60	....	....	....	....	....	....	....	....	....	....	....	....	....	....	....	....	....	....
1998-99	**Edmonton**	**NHL**	**73**	**5**	**16**	**21**	**42**	**2**	**0**	**3**	**94**	**5.3**	**10**	**0**	**0.0**	**19:33**	**4**	**0**	**1**	**1**	**2**	**0**	**0**	**0**	**28:02**
99-2000	**Edmonton**	**NHL**	**76**	**9**	**26**	**35**	**65**	**2**	**1**	**1**	**125**	**7.2**	**8**	**0**	**0.0**	**24:10**	**5**	**0**	**1**	**1**	**0**	**0**	**0**	**0**	**23:53**
2000-01	**Edmonton**	**NHL**	**81**	**12**	**20**	**32**	**60**	**6**	**0**	**3**	**161**	**7.5**	**–4**	**0**	**0.0**	**22:44**	**6**	**0**	**2**	**2**	**2**	**0**	**0**	**0**	**20:25**
2001-02	**Edmonton**	**NHL**	**55**	**1**	**16**	**17**	**42**	**1**	**0**	**0**	**100**	**1.0**	**–6**	**0**	**0.0**	**24:32**	....	....	....	....	....	....	....	....	....
	United States	Olympics	6	0	1	1	4	....	....	....	....	....	....	....	....	....	....	....	....	....	....	....	....	....	....
	NY Rangers	**NHL**	**11**	**1**	**7**	**8**	**2**	**1**	**0**	**1**	**9**	**11.1**	**–4**	**0**	**0.0**	**21:45**	....	....	....	....	....	....	....	....	....
2002-03	**NY Rangers**	**NHL**	**80**	**11**	**37**	**48**	**58**	**3**	**0**	**2**	**148**	**7.4**	**–6**	**0**	**0.0**	**24:43**	....	....	....	....	....	....	....	....	....
2003-04	**NY Rangers**	**NHL**	**67**	**10**	**14**	**24**	**47**	**4**	**0**	**5**	**124**	**8.1**	**–1**	**0**	**0.0**	**22:28**	....	....	....	....	....	....	....	....	....
2004-05			DID NOT PLAY																						
	NHL Totals		**443**	**49**	**136**	**185**	**316**	**19**	**1**	**15**	**761**	**6.4**		**0**	**0.0**	**22:58**	**15**	**0**	**4**	**4**	**4**	**0**	**0**	**0**	**23:36**

NCAA Championship All-Tournament Team (1997) • Hockey East First All-Star Team (1998) • NCAA East First All-American Team (1998) • NHL All-Rookie Team (1999)

Played in NHL All-Star Game (2003)

Traded to **NY Rangers** by **Edmonton** with Rem Murray for Mike York and NY Rangers' 4th round choice (Ivan Koltsov) in 2002 Entry Draft, March 19, 2002.

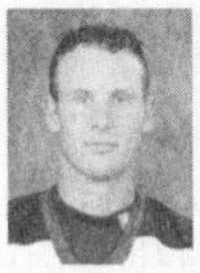

PRATT, Nolan

(PRAT, NOH-lan) **T.B.**

Defense. Shoots left. 6'3", 203 lbs. Born, Fort McMurray, Alta., August 14, 1975. Hartford's 4th choice, 115th overall, in 1993 Entry Draft.

Season	Club	League	GP	G	A	Pts	PIM	PP	SH	GW	S	%	+/-	TF	F%	Min	GP	G	A	Pts	PIM	PP	SH	GW	Min
1991-92	Bonnyville	AJHL	33	3	7	10	57	....	....	....	....	....	....	....	....	....	....	....	....	....	....	....	....	....	....
	Portland	WHL	22	2	9	11	13	....	....	....	....	....	....	....	....	....	6	1	3	4	12	....	....	....	....
1992-93	Portland	WHL	70	4	19	23	97	....	....	....	....	....	....	....	....	....	16	2	7	9	31	....	....	....	....
1993-94	Portland	WHL	72	4	32	36	105	....	....	....	....	....	....	....	....	....	10	1	2	3	14	....	....	....	....
1994-95	Portland	WHL	72	6	37	43	196	....	....	....	....	....	....	....	....	....	9	1	6	7	10	....	....	....	....
1995-96	Springfield	AHL	62	2	6	8	72	....	....	....	....	....	....	....	....	....	2	0	0	0	0	....	....	....	....
	Richmond	ECHL	4	1	0	1	2	....	....	....	....	....	....	....	....	....	....	....	....	....	....	....	....	....	....
1996-97	**Hartford**	**NHL**	**9**	**0**	**2**	**2**	**6**	**0**	**0**	**0**	**4**	**0.0**	**0**	....	....	....	....	....	....	....	....	....	....	....	....
	Springfield	AHL	66	1	18	19	127	....	....	....	....	....	....	....	....	....	17	0	3	3	18	....	....	....	....
1997-98	**Carolina**	**NHL**	**23**	**0**	**2**	**2**	**44**	**0**	**0**	**0**	**11**	**0.0**	**–2**	....	....	....	....	....	....	....	....	....	....	....	....
	New Haven	AHL	54	3	15	18	135	....	....	....	....	....	....	....	....	....	....	....	....	....	....	....	....	....	....
1998-99	**Carolina**	**NHL**	**61**	**1**	**14**	**15**	**95**	**0**	**0**	**1**	**46**	**2.2**	**15**	**0**	**0.0**	**16:45**	**3**	**0**	**0**	**0**	**2**	**0**	**0**	**0**	**19:58**
99-2000	**Carolina**	**NHL**	**64**	**3**	**1**	**4**	**90**	**0**	**0**	**1**	**47**	**6.4**	**–22**	**0**	**0.0**	**19:10**	....	....	....	....	....	....	....	....	....
2000-01	**Colorado**	**NHL**	**46**	**1**	**2**	**3**	**40**	**0**	**0**	**1**	**26**	**3.8**	**2**	**1**	**0.0**	**9:50**	....	....	....	....	....	....	....	....	....
2001-02	**Tampa Bay**	**NHL**	**46**	**0**	**3**	**3**	**51**	**0**	**0**	**0**	**38**	**0.0**	**–4**	**1**	**0.0**	**18:25**	....	....	....	....	....	....	....	....	....
2002-03	**Tampa Bay**	**NHL**	**67**	**1**	**7**	**8**	**35**	**0**	**0**	**0**	**38**	**2.6**	**–6**	**0**	**0.0**	**17:34**	**4**	**0**	**1**	**1**	**0**	**0**	**0**	**0**	**21:01**
2003-04♦	**Tampa Bay**	**NHL**	**58**	**1**	**3**	**4**	**42**	**0**	**0**	**0**	**35**	**2.9**	**11**	**0**	**0.0**	**16:25**	**20**	**0**	**0**	**0**	**8**	**0**	**0**	**0**	**18:06**
2004-05	EV Duisburg	German-2	10	2	2	4	14	....	....	....	....	....	....	....	....	....	12	0	3	3	10	....	....	....	....
	NHL Totals		**374**	**7**	**34**	**41**	**403**	**0**	**0**	**3**	**245**	**2.9**		**2**	**0.0**	**16:36**	**27**	**0**	**1**	**1**	**10**	**0**	**0**	**0**	**18:44**

Transferred to **Carolina** after **Hartford** franchise relocated, June 25, 1997. Traded to **Colorado** by **Carolina** with Carolina's 1st (Vaclav Nedorost) and 2nd (Jared Aulin) round choices in 2000 Entry Draft and Philadelphia's 2nd round choice (previously acquired, Colorado selected Agris Saviels) in 2000 Entry Draft for Sandis Ozolinsh and Columbus' 2nd round choice (previously acquired, Carolina selected Tomas Kurka) in 2000 Entry Draft, June 24, 2000. Traded to **Tampa Bay** by **Colorado** for Los Angeles' 6th round choice (previously acquired, Colorado selected Scott Horvath) in 2001 Entry Draft, June 24, 2001. Signed as a free agent by **Duisburg** (German-2), January 15, 2005.

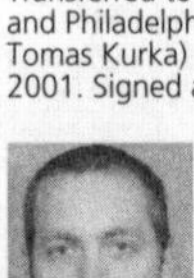

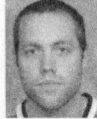

PREISSING, Tom

(PREH-sihng, TAWM) **S.J.**

Defense. Shoots right. 6', 205 lbs. Born, Rosemount, MN, December 3, 1978.

Season	Club	League	GP	G	A	Pts	PIM	PP	SH	GW	S	%	+/-	TF	F%	Min	GP	G	A	Pts	PIM	PP	SH	GW	Min
1997-98	Green Bay	USHL	56	8	13	21	30	....	....	....	....	....	....	....	....	....	4	0	2	2	2	....	....	....	....
1998-99	Green Bay	USHL	53	18	37	55	40	....	....	....	....	....	....	....	....	....	6	3	6	9	2	....	....	....	....
99-2000	Colorado College	WCHA	36	4	14	18	20	....	....	....	....	....	....	....	....	....	....	....	....	....	....	....	....	....	....
2000-01	Colorado College	WCHA	33	6	18	24	26	....	....	....	....	....	....	....	....	....	....	....	....	....	....	....	....	....	....
2001-02	Colorado College	WCHA	43	6	26	32	42	....	....	....	....	....	....	....	....	....	....	....	....	....	....	....	....	....	....
2002-03	Colorado College	WCHA	42	23	29	52	16	....	....	....	....	....	....	....	....	....	....	....	....	....	....	....	....	....	....

			Regular Season														Playoffs								
Season	Club	League	GP	G	A	Pts	PIM	PP	SH	GW	S	%	+/-	TF	F%	Min	GP	G	A	Pts	PIM	PP	SH	GW	Min
2003-04	San Jose	NHL	69	2	17	19	12	2	0	1	89	2.2	8	0	0.0	18:12	11	0	1	1	0	0	0	0	12:49
2004-05	Krefeld Pinguine	Germany	33	1	6	7	32	....	....	....	....	....	....	....	....	....	....	....	....	....	....	....	....	....	....
	NHL Totals		69	2	17	19	12	2	0	1	89	2.2		0	0.0	18:12	11	0	1	1	0	0	0	0	12:49

WCHA First All-Star Team (2003) • NCAA West First All-American Team (2003)

Signed as a free agent by **San Jose**, April 4, 2003. Signed as a free agent by **Krefeld** (Germany), November 15, 2004.

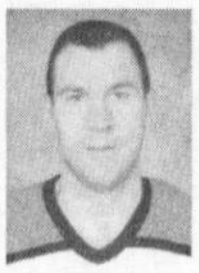

PRIMEAU, Keith (PREE-moh, KEETH) PHI.

Center. Shoots left. 6'5", 220 lbs. Born, Toronto, Ont., November 24, 1971. Detroit's 1st choice, 3rd overall, in 1990 Entry Draft.

Season	Club	League	GP	G	A	Pts	PIM	PP	SH	GW	S	%	+/-	TF	F%	Min	GP	G	A	Pts	PIM	PP	SH	GW	Min
1986-87	Whitby Flyers	OMHA	65	69	80	149	116	....	....	....	....	....	....	....	....	....	....	....	....	....	....	....	....	....	....
1987-88	Hamilton Kilty B's	OHA-B	19	19	17	36	16	....	....	....	....	....	....	....	....	....	....	....	....	....	....	....	....	....	....
	Hamilton	OHL	47	6	6	12	69	....	....	....	....	....	....	....	....	....	11	0	2	2	2	....	....	....	....
1988-89	Niagara Falls	OHL	48	20	35	55	56	....	....	....	....	....	....	....	....	....	17	9	16	25	12	....	....	....	....
1989-90	Niagara Falls	OHL	65	*57	70	*127	97	....	....	....	....	....	....	....	....	....	16	*16	17	*33	49	....	....	....	....
1990-91	Detroit	NHL	58	3	12	15	106	0	0	1	33	9.1	-12	....	....	....	5	1	1	2	25	0	0	0	....
	Adirondack	AHL	6	3	5	8	8	....	....	....	....	....	....	....	....	....	....	....	....	....	....	....	....	....	....
1991-92	Detroit	NHL	35	6	10	16	83	0	0	0	27	22.2	9	....	....	....	11	0	0	0	14	0	0	0	....
	Adirondack	AHL	42	21	24	45	89	....	....	....	....	....	....	....	....	....	9	1	7	8	27	....	....	....	....
1992-93	Detroit	NHL	73	15	17	32	152	4	1	2	75	20.0	-6	....	....	....	7	0	2	2	26	0	0	0	....
1993-94	Detroit	NHL	78	31	42	73	173	7	3	4	155	20.0	34	....	....	....	7	0	2	2	6	0	0	0	....
1994-95	Detroit	NHL	45	15	27	42	99	1	0	3	96	15.6	17	....	....	....	17	4	5	9	45	2	0	0	....
1995-96	Detroit	NHL	74	27	25	52	168	6	2	7	150	18.0	19	....	....	....	17	1	4	5	28	0	0	0	....
1996-97	Hartford	NHL	75	26	25	51	161	6	3	2	169	15.4	-3	....	....	....	....	....	....	....	....	....	....	....	....
1997-98	Carolina	NHL	81	26	37	63	110	7	3	2	180	14.4	19	....	....	....	....	....	....	....	....	....	....	....	....
	Canada	Olympics	6	2	1	3	4	....	....	....	....	....	....	....	....	....	....	....	....	....	....	....	....	....	....
1998-99	Carolina	NHL	78	30	32	62	75	9	1	5	178	16.9	8	1823	53.5	21:21	6	0	3	3	6	0	0	0	24:35
99-2000	Philadelphia	NHL	23	7	10	17	31	1	0	1	51	13.7	10	478	54.2	17:38	18	2	11	13	13	0	0	1	20:25
2000-01	Philadelphia	NHL	71	34	39	73	76	11	0	4	165	20.6	17	1811	53.5	19:58	4	0	3	3	8	0	0	0	19:44
2001-02	Philadelphia	NHL	75	19	29	48	128	5	0	3	151	12.6	-3	1595	51.3	18:00	5	0	0	0	6	0	0	0	17:20
2002-03	Philadelphia	NHL	80	19	27	46	93	6	0	4	171	11.1	4	1613	51.4	19:16	13	1	1	2	14	0	0	0	20:21
2003-04	Philadelphia	NHL	54	7	15	22	80	0	1	2	86	8.1	11	1010	53.3	16:36	18	9	7	16	22	0	2	3	18:58
2004-05		DID NOT PLAY																							
	NHL Totals		900	265	347	612	1535	63	14	40	1687	15.7		8330	52.7	19:06	128	18	39	57	213	2	2	4	20:06

OHL Second All-Star Team (1990)

Played in NHL All-Star Game (1999, 2004)

Traded to **Hartford** by **Detroit** with Paul Coffey and Detroit's 1st round choice (Nikos Tselios) in 1997 Entry Draft for Brendan Shanahan and Brian Glynn, October 9, 1996. Transferred to **Carolina** after **Hartford** franchise relocated, June 25, 1997. • Missed majority of 1999-2000 season after failing to come to contract terms with **Carolina**. Traded to **Philadelphia** by **Carolina** with Carolina's 5th round choice (later traded to NY Islanders – NY Islanders selected Kristofer Ottosson) in 2000 Entry Draft for Rod Brind'Amour, Jean-Marc Pelletier and Philadelphia's 2nd round choice (later traded to Colorado – Colorado selected Agris Saviels) in 2000 Entry Draft, January 23, 2000.

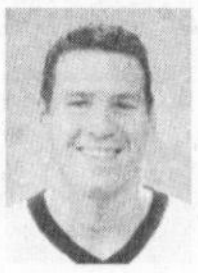

PRIMEAU, Wayne (PREE-moh, WAYN) S.J.

Center. Shoots left. 6'4", 230 lbs. Born, Scarborough, Ont., June 4, 1976. Buffalo's 1st choice, 17th overall, in 1994 Entry Draft.

Season	Club	League	GP	G	A	Pts	PIM	PP	SH	GW	S	%	+/-	TF	F%	Min	GP	G	A	Pts	PIM	PP	SH	GW	Min
1991-92	Whitby Flyers	OMHA	63	36	50	86	96	....	....	....	....	....	....	....	....	....	....	....	....	....	....	....	....	....	....
1992-93	Owen Sound	OHL	66	10	27	37	108	....	....	....	....	....	....	....	....	....	8	1	4	5	0	....	....	....	....
1993-94	Owen Sound	OHL	65	25	50	75	75	....	....	....	....	....	....	....	....	....	9	1	6	7	8	....	....	....	....
1994-95	Owen Sound	OHL	66	34	62	96	84	....	....	....	....	....	....	....	....	....	10	4	9	13	15	....	....	....	....
	Buffalo	NHL	1	1	0	1	0	0	0	1	2	50.0	-2	....	....	....	....	....	....	....	....	....	....	....	....
1995-96	Owen Sound	OHL	28	15	29	44	52	....	....	....	....	....	....	....	....	....	....	....	....	....	....	....	....	....	....
	Oshawa Generals	OHL	24	12	13	25	33	....	....	....	....	....	....	....	....	....	3	2	3	5	2	....	....	....	....
	Buffalo	NHL	2	0	0	0	0	0	0	0	0	0.0	0	....	....	....	....	....	....	....	....	....	....	....	....
	Rochester	AHL	8	2	3	5	6	....	....	....	....	....	....	....	....	....	17	3	1	4	11	....	....	....	....
1996-97	Buffalo	NHL	45	2	4	6	64	1	0	0	25	8.0	-2	....	....	....	9	0	0	0	6	0	0	0	....
	Rochester	AHL	24	9	5	14	27	....	....	....	....	....	....	....	....	....	1	0	0	0	0	....	....	....	....
1997-98	Buffalo	NHL	69	6	6	12	87	2	0	1	51	11.8	9	....	....	....	14	1	3	4	6	0	0	0	....
1998-99	Buffalo	NHL	67	5	8	13	38	0	0	0	55	9.1	-6	529	48.6	10:19	19	3	4	7	6	1	0	0	13:29
99-2000	Buffalo	NHL	41	5	7	12	38	2	0	1	40	12.5	-8	430	45.6	11:03	....	....	....	....	....	....	....	....	....
	Tampa Bay	NHL	17	2	3	5	25	0	0	0	35	5.7	-4	290	45.5	14:21	....	....	....	....	....	....	....	....	....
2000-01	Tampa Bay	NHL	47	2	13	15	77	0	0	0	47	4.3	-17	630	52.2	14:11	....	....	....	....	....	....	....	....	....
	Pittsburgh	NHL	28	1	6	7	54	0	0	0	30	3.3	0	318	51.3	12:45	18	1	3	4	2	0	0	0	15:06
2001-02	Pittsburgh	NHL	33	3	7	10	18	0	1	0	28	10.7	-1	519	53.2	12:38	....	....	....	....	....	....	....	....	....
2002-03	Pittsburgh	NHL	70	5	11	16	55	1	0	0	101	5.0	-30	1240	50.4	16:17	....	....	....	....	....	....	....	....	....
	San Jose	NHL	7	1	1	2	0	0	0	0	13	7.7	2	98	45.9	15:59	....	....	....	....	....	....	....	....	....
2003-04	San Jose	NHL	72	9	20	29	90	0	1	1	142	6.3	4	867	46.6	15:28	17	1	2	3	4	0	0	0	15:41
2004-05		DID NOT PLAY																							
	NHL Totals		499	42	86	128	546	6	2	4	569	7.4		4921	49.3	13:36	77	6	12	18	24	1	0	0	14:43

Traded to **Tampa Bay** by **Buffalo** with Cory Sarich, Brian Holzinger and Buffalo's 3rd round choice (Alexander Kharitonov) in 2000 Entry Draft for Chris Gratton and Tampa Bay's 2nd round choice (Derek Roy) in 2001 Entry Draft, March 9, 2000. Traded to **Pittsburgh** by **Tampa Bay** for Matthew Barnaby, February 1, 2001. • Missed majority of 2001-02 season recovering from knee injury suffered in game vs. Buffalo, January 8, 2002. Traded to **San Jose** by **Pittsburgh** for Matt Bradley, March 11, 2003.

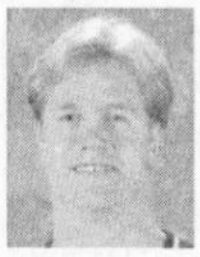

PRONGER, Chris (PRAHN-guhr, KRIHS) EDM.

Defense. Shoots left. 6'6", 220 lbs. Born, Dryden, Ont., October 10, 1974. Hartford's 1st choice, 2nd overall, in 1993 Entry Draft.

Season	Club	League	GP	G	A	Pts	PIM	PP	SH	GW	S	%	+/-	TF	F%	Min	GP	G	A	Pts	PIM	PP	SH	GW	Min
1990-91	Stratford Cullitons	OHA-B	48	15	37	52	132	....	....	....	....	....	....	....	....	....	....	....	....	....	....	....	....	....	....
1991-92	Peterborough	OHL	63	17	45	62	90	....	....	....	....	....	....	....	....	....	10	1	8	9	28	....	....	....	....
1992-93	Peterborough	OHL	61	15	62	77	108	....	....	....	....	....	....	....	....	....	21	15	25	40	51	....	....	....	....
1993-94	Hartford	NHL	81	5	25	30	113	2	0	0	174	2.9	-3	....	....	....	....	....	....	....	....	....	....	....	....
1994-95	Hartford	NHL	43	5	9	14	54	3	0	1	94	5.3	-12	....	....	....	....	....	....	....	....	....	....	....	....
1995-96	St. Louis	NHL	78	7	18	25	110	3	1	1	138	5.1	-18	....	....	....	13	1	5	6	16	0	0	0	....
1996-97	St. Louis	NHL	79	11	24	35	143	4	0	0	147	7.5	15	....	....	....	6	1	1	2	22	0	0	0	....
1997-98	St. Louis	NHL	81	9	27	36	180	1	0	2	145	6.2	47	....	....	....	10	1	9	10	26	0	0	0	....
	Canada	Olympics	6	0	0	0	4	....	....	....	....	....	....	....	....	....	....	....	....	....	....	....	....	....	....
1998-99	St. Louis	NHL	67	13	33	46	113	8	0	0	172	7.6	3	0	0.0	30:36	13	1	4	5	28	1	0	0	35:53
99-2000	St. Louis	NHL	79	14	48	62	92	8	0	3	192	7.3	52	1	0.0	30:14	7	3	4	7	32	2	0	2	30:14
2000-01	St. Louis	NHL	51	8	39	47	75	4	0	0	121	6.6	21	0	0.0	27:45	15	1	7	8	32	0	0	0	33:50
2001-02	St. Louis	NHL	78	7	40	47	120	4	1	3	204	3.4	23	0	0.0	29:28	9	1	7	8	24	0	0	0	27:51
	Canada	Olympics	6	0	1	1	2	....	....	....	....	....	....	....	....	....	....	....	....	....	....	....	....	....	....
2002-03	St. Louis	NHL	5	1	3	4	10	0	0	0	11	9.1	-2	1	0.0	21:39	7	1	3	4	14	0	0	0	24:36
2003-04	St. Louis	NHL	80	14	40	54	88	7	0	3	203	6.9	-1	2	0.0	27:28	5	0	1	1	16	0	0	0	27:54
2004-05		DID NOT PLAY																							
	NHL Totals		722	94	306	400	1098	44	2	13	1601	5.9		4	0.0	29:03	85	10	41	51	210	3	0	2	31:13

OHL All-Rookie Team (1992) • OHL First All-Star Team (1993) • Canadian Major Junior First All-Star Team (1993) • Canadian Major Junior Defenseman of the Year (1993) • NHL All-Rookie Team (1994) • NHL Second All-Star Team (1998, 2004) • Bud Ice Plus/Minus Award (1998) • NHL First All-Star Team (2000) • Bud Light Plus/Minus Award (2000) • James Norris Memorial Trophy (2000) • Hart Trophy (2000)

Played in NHL All-Star Game (1999, 2000, 2002, 2004)

Traded to **St. Louis** by **Hartford** for Brendan Shanahan, July 27, 1995. • Missed majority of 2002-03 season recovering from wrist and knee surgery, September 10, 2002. Traded to **Edmonton** by **St. Louis** for Eric Brewer, Doug Lynch and Jeff Woywitka, August 2, 2005.

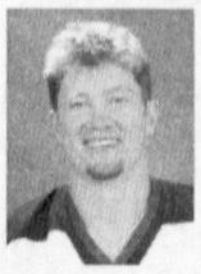

PRONGER, Sean (PRAHN-guhr, SHAWN)

Center. Shoots left. 6'3", 209 lbs. Born, Thunder Bay, Ont., November 30, 1972. Vancouver's 3rd choice, 51st overall, in 1991 Entry Draft.

Season	Club	League	GP	G	A	Pts	PIM	PP	SH	GW	S	%	+/-	TF	F%	Min	GP	G	A	Pts	PIM	PP	SH	GW	Min
1988-89	Kenora Boise	NOHA	33	38	30	68	....	....	....	....	....	....	....	....	....	....	....	....	....	....	....	....	....	....	....
1989-90	Thunder Bay	USHL	48	18	34	52	61	....	....	....	....	....	....	....	....	....	....	....	....	....	....	....	....	....	....
1990-91	Bowling Green	CCHA	40	3	7	10	30	....	....	....	....	....	....	....	....	....	....	....	....	....	....	....	....	....	....
1991-92	Bowling Green	CCHA	34	9	7	16	28	....	....	....	....	....	....	....	....	....	....	....	....	....	....	....	....	....	....
1992-93	Bowling Green	CCHA	39	23	23	46	35	....	....	....	....	....	....	....	....	....	....	....	....	....	....	....	....	....	....
1993-94	Bowling Green	CCHA	38	17	17	34	38	....	....	....	....	....	....	....	....	....	....	....	....	....	....	....	....	....	....

			Regular Season														Playoffs								
Season	Club	League	GP	G	A	Pts	PIM	PP	SH	GW	S	%	+/-	TF	F%	Min	GP	G	A	Pts	PIM	PP	SH	GW	Min
1994-95	Knoxville	ECHL	34	18	23	41	55	....	....	....	....	....	....	....	....	....	....	....	....	....	....	....	....	....	....
	Greensboro	ECHL	2	0	2	2	0	....	....	....	....	....	....	....	....	....	....	....	....	....	....	....	....	....	....
	San Diego Gulls	IHL	8	0	0	0	2	....	....	....	....	....	....	....	....	....	....	....	....	....	....	....	....	....	....
1995-96	**Anaheim**	**NHL**	**7**	**0**	**1**	**1**	**6**	**0**	**0**	**0**	**3**	**0.0**	**0**	....	....	....	....	....	....	....	....	....	....	....	....
	Baltimore Bandits	AHL	72	16	17	33	61	....	....	....	....	....	....	....	....	....	12	3	7	10	16	....	....	....	....
1996-97	**Anaheim**	**NHL**	**39**	**7**	**7**	**14**	**20**	**1**	**0**	**1**	**43**	**16.3**	**6**	....	....	....	**9**	**0**	**2**	**2**	**4**	**0**	**0**	**0**	....
	Baltimore Bandits	AHL	41	26	17	43	17	....	....	....	....	....	....	....	....	....	....	....	....	....	....	....	....	....	....
1997-98	**Anaheim**	**NHL**	**62**	**5**	**15**	**20**	**30**	**1**	**0**	**2**	**68**	**7.4**	**–9**	....	....	....	....	....	....	....	....	....	....	....	....
	Pittsburgh	**NHL**	**5**	**1**	**0**	**1**	**2**	**0**	**0**	**1**	**5**	**20.0**	**–1**	....	....	....	**5**	**0**	**0**	**0**	**4**	**0**	**0**	**0**	....
1998-99	**Pittsburgh**	**NHL**	**2**	**0**	**0**	**0**	**0**	**0**	**0**	**0**	**3**	**0.0**	**0**	**4**	**75.0**	**8:48**	....	....	....	....	....	....	....	....	....
	Houston Aeros	IHL	16	11	7	18	32	....	....	....	....	....	....	....	....	....	....	....	....	....	....	....	....	....	....
	NY Rangers	**NHL**	**14**	**0**	**3**	**3**	**4**	**0**	**0**	**0**	**3**	**0.0**	**–3**	**15**	**20.0**	**6:28**	....	....	....	....	....	....	....	....	....
	Los Angeles	**NHL**	**13**	**0**	**1**	**1**	**4**	**0**	**0**	**0**	**8**	**0.0**	**2**	**20**	**35.0**	**11:00**	....	....	....	....	....	....	....	....	....
99-2000	**Boston**	**NHL**	**11**	**0**	**1**	**1**	**13**	**0**	**0**	**0**	**7**	**0.0**	**–4**	**116**	**46.6**	**10:47**	....	....	....	....	....	....	....	....	....
	Providence Bruins	AHL	51	11	18	29	26	....	....	....	....	....	....	....	....	....	....	....	....	....	....	....	....	....	....
	Manitoba Moose	IHL	14	3	5	8	21	....	....	....	....	....	....	....	....	....	2	0	1	1	2	....	....	....	....
2000-01	Manitoba Moose	IHL	82	18	21	39	85	....	....	....	....	....	....	....	....	....	13	3	6	9	2	....	....	....	....
2001-02	**Columbus**	**NHL**	**26**	**3**	**1**	**4**	**4**	**0**	**0**	**0**	**25**	**12.0**	**–4**	**167**	**52.1**	**11:26**	....	....	....	....	....	....	....	....	....
	Syracuse Crunch	AHL	54	23	26	49	53	....	....	....	....	....	....	....	....	....	8	4	1	5	10	....	....	....	....
2002-03	**Columbus**	**NHL**	**78**	**7**	**6**	**13**	**72**	**1**	**0**	**0**	**67**	**10.4**	**–26**	**655**	**49.5**	**11:32**	....	....	....	....	....	....	....	....	....
2003-04	Syracuse Crunch	AHL	7	2	0	2	7	....	....	....	....	....	....	....	....	....	....	....	....	....	....	....	....	....	....
	Vancouver	**NHL**	**3**	**0**	**1**	**1**	**4**	**0**	**0**	**0**	**6**	**0.0**	**–1**	**35**	**42.9**	**10:17**	....	....	....	....	....	....	....	....	....
	Manitoba Moose	AHL	68	17	15	32	68	....	....	....	....	....	....	....	....	....	....	....	....	....	....	....	....	....	....
2004-05	Frankfurt Lions	Germany	51	6	10	16	78	....	....	....	....	....	....	....	....	....	4	0	0	0	6	....	....	....	....
	NHL Totals		**260**	**23**	**36**	**59**	**159**	**3**	**0**	**4**	**238**	**9.7**		**1012**	**48.7**	**10:52**	**14**	**0**	**2**	**2**	**8**	**0**	**0**	**0**	....

Signed as a free agent by **Anaheim**, February 14, 1995. Traded to **Pittsburgh** by **Anaheim** for the rights to Patrick Lalime, March 24, 1998. Traded to **NY Rangers** by **Pittsburgh** with Chris Tamer and Petr Nedved for Alex Kovalev and Harry York, November 25, 1998. Traded to **Los Angeles** by **NY Rangers** for Eric Lacroix, February 12, 1999. Signed as a free agent by **Boston**, August 25, 1999. Traded to **Manitoba** (IHL) by **Providence** (AHL) with Keith McCambridge for Terry Hollinger, March 16, 2000 with Boston retaining Pronger's NHL rights. Traded to **NY Islanders** by **Boston** for future considerations, December 5, 2000. Claimed on waivers by **Columbus** from **NY Islanders**, May 18, 2001. Traded to **Vancouver** by **Columbus** for Zenith Komarniski, October 30, 2003. Signed as a free agent by **Frankfurt** (Germany), June 2, 2004.

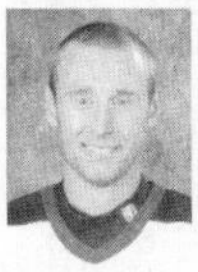

PROSPAL, Vaclav

(PRAWS-pahl, VAT-slav) **T.B.**

Center. Shoots left. 6'2", 195 lbs. Born, Ceske Budejovice, Czech., February 17, 1975. Philadelphia's 2nd choice, 71st overall, in 1993 Entry Draft.

Season	Club	League	GP	G	A	Pts	PIM	PP	SH	GW	S	%	+/-	TF	F%	Min	GP	G	A	Pts	PIM	PP	SH	GW	Min
1991-92	C. Budejovice Jr.	Czech-Jr.	36	16	16	32	12	....	....	....	....	....	....	....	....	....	....	....	....	....	....	....	....	....	....
1992-93	C. Budejovice Jr.	Czech-Jr.	32	26	31	57	24	....	....	....	....	....	....	....	....	....	....	....	....	....	....	....	....	....	....
1993-94	Hershey Bears	AHL	55	14	21	35	38	....	....	....	....	....	....	....	....	....	2	0	0	0	2	....	....	....	....
1994-95	Hershey Bears	AHL	69	13	32	45	36	....	....	....	....	....	....	....	....	....	2	1	0	1	4	....	....	....	....
1995-96	Hershey Bears	AHL	68	15	36	51	59	....	....	....	....	....	....	....	....	....	5	2	4	6	2	....	....	....	....
1996-97	**Philadelphia**	**NHL**	**18**	**5**	**10**	**15**	**4**	**0**	**0**	**0**	**35**	**14.3**	**3**	....	....	....	**5**	**1**	**3**	**4**	**4**	**0**	**0**	**0**	....
	Philadelphia	AHL	63	32	63	95	70	....	....	....	....	....	....	....	....	....	....	....	....	....	....	....	....	....	....
1997-98	**Philadelphia**	**NHL**	**41**	**5**	**13**	**18**	**17**	**4**	**0**	**0**	**60**	**8.3**	**–10**	....	....	....	....	....	....	....	....	....	....	....	....
	Ottawa	**NHL**	**15**	**1**	**6**	**7**	**4**	**0**	**0**	**0**	**28**	**3.6**	**–1**	....	....	....	**6**	**0**	**0**	**0**	**0**	**0**	**0**	**0**	....
1998-99	**Ottawa**	**NHL**	**79**	**10**	**26**	**36**	**58**	**2**	**0**	**3**	**114**	**8.8**	**8**	**997**	**56.2**	**13:03**	**4**	**0**	**0**	**0**	**0**	**0**	**0**	**0**	**12:37**
99-2000	**Ottawa**	**NHL**	**79**	**22**	**33**	**55**	**40**	**5**	**0**	**4**	**204**	**10.8**	**–2**	**1331**	**49.6**	**16:26**	**6**	**0**	**4**	**4**	**4**	**0**	**0**	**0**	**17:40**
2000-01	**Ottawa**	**NHL**	**40**	**1**	**12**	**13**	**12**	**0**	**0**	**0**	**68**	**1.5**	**1**	**501**	**50.1**	**12:57**	....	....	....	....	....	....	....	....	....
	Florida	**NHL**	**34**	**4**	**12**	**16**	**10**	**1**	**0**	**0**	**68**	**5.9**	**–2**	**487**	**54.6**	**16:36**	....	....	....	....	....	....	....	....	....
2001-02	**Tampa Bay**	**NHL**	**81**	**18**	**37**	**55**	**38**	**7**	**0**	**2**	**166**	**10.8**	**–11**	**555**	**52.8**	**17:31**	....	....	....	....	....	....	....	....	....
2002-03	**Tampa Bay**	**NHL**	**80**	**22**	**57**	**79**	**53**	**9**	**0**	**4**	**134**	**16.4**	**9**	**161**	**51.6**	**18:39**	**11**	**4**	**2**	**6**	**8**	**2**	**0**	**0**	**21:15**
2003-04	**Anaheim**	**NHL**	**82**	**19**	**35**	**54**	**54**	**7**	**0**	**4**	**185**	**10.3**	**–9**	**45**	**46.7**	**18:37**	....	....	....	....	....	....	....	....	....
2004-05	C. Budejovice	CzRep-2	39	28	60	88	82	....	....	....	....	....	....	....	....	....	16	15	15	30	32	....	....	....	....
	NHL Totals		**549**	**107**	**241**	**348**	**290**	**35**	**0**	**17**	**1062**	**10.1**		**4077**	**52.3**	**16:32**	**32**	**5**	**9**	**14**	**16**	**2**	**0**	**0**	**18:35**

AHL First All-Star Team (1997)

Traded to **Ottawa** by **Philadelphia** with Pat Falloon and Dallas' 2nd round choice (previously acquired, Ottawa selected Chris Bala) in 1998 Entry Draft for Alexandre Daigle, January 17, 1998. Traded to **Florida** by **Ottawa** for future considerations, January 20, 2001. Traded to **Tampa Bay** by **Florida** for Ryan Johnson and Tampa Bay's 6th round choice (later traded back to Tampa Bay – Tampa Bay selected Doug O'Brien) in 2003 Entry Draft, July 10, 2001. Signed as a free agent by **Anaheim**, July 17, 2003. Traded to **Tampa Bay** by **Anaheim** for Tampa Bay's 2nd round choice (Brendan Mikkelson) in 2005 Entry Draft, August 16, 2004. Signed as a free agent by **Budejovice** (CzRep-2), September 17, 2004.

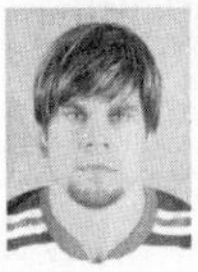

PURINTON, Dale

(PUHR-ihn-TOHN, DAYL) **NYR**

Defense. Shoots left. 6'3", 228 lbs. Born, Fort Wayne, IN, October 11, 1976. NY Rangers' 5th choice, 117th overall, in 1995 Entry Draft.

Season	Club	League	GP	G	A	Pts	PIM	PP	SH	GW	S	%	+/-	TF	F%	Min	GP	G	A	Pts	PIM	PP	SH	GW	Min
1992-93	Moose Jaw	SMHL	34	1	16	17	107	....	....	....	....	....	....	....	....	....	....	....	....	....	....	....	....	....	....
	Moose Jaw	WHL	2	0	0	0	2	....	....	....	....	....	....	....	....	....	....	....	....	....	....	....	....	....	....
1993-94	Vernon Vipers	BCJHL	42	1	6	7	194	....	....	....	....	....	....	....	....	....	....	....	....	....	....	....	....	....	....
1994-95	Tacoma Rockets	WHL	65	0	8	8	291	....	....	....	....	....	....	....	....	....	3	0	0	0	13	....	....	....	....
1995-96	Kelowna Rockets	WHL	22	1	4	5	88	....	....	....	....	....	....	....	....	....	....	....	....	....	....	....	....	....	....
	Lethbridge	WHL	37	3	6	9	144	....	....	....	....	....	....	....	....	....	4	1	1	2	25	....	....	....	....
1996-97	Lethbridge	WHL	51	6	26	32	254	....	....	....	....	....	....	....	....	....	18	3	5	8	*88	....	....	....	....
1997-98	Hartford	AHL	17	0	0	0	95	....	....	....	....	....	....	....	....	....	....	....	....	....	....	....	....	....	....
	Charlotte	ECHL	34	3	5	8	186	....	....	....	....	....	....	....	....	....	....	....	....	....	....	....	....	....	....
1998-99	Hartford	AHL	45	1	3	4	306	....	....	....	....	....	....	....	....	....	7	0	2	2	24	....	....	....	....
99-2000	**NY Rangers**	**NHL**	**1**	**0**	**0**	**0**	**7**	**0**	**0**	**0**	**1**	**0.0**	**–1**	**0**	**0.0**	**12:45**	....	....	....	....	....	....	....	....	....
	Hartford	AHL	62	4	4	8	415	....	....	....	....	....	....	....	....	....	23	0	3	3	*87	....	....	....	....
2000-01	**NY Rangers**	**NHL**	**42**	**0**	**2**	**2**	**180**	**0**	**0**	**0**	**13**	**0.0**	**5**	**0**	**0.0**	**9:33**	....	....	....	....	....	....	....	....	....
	Hartford	AHL	11	0	1	1	75	....	....	....	....	....	....	....	....	....	....	....	....	....	....	....	....	....	....
2001-02	**NY Rangers**	**NHL**	**40**	**0**	**4**	**4**	**113**	**0**	**0**	**0**	**11**	**0.0**	**4**	**0**	**0.0**	**7:37**	....	....	....	....	....	....	....	....	....
2002-03	**NY Rangers**	**NHL**	**58**	**3**	**9**	**12**	**161**	**0**	**0**	**0**	**50**	**6.0**	**–2**	**0**	**0.0**	**15:02**	....	....	....	....	....	....	....	....	....
2003-04	**NY Rangers**	**NHL**	**40**	**1**	**1**	**2**	**117**	**0**	**0**	**0**	**31**	**3.2**	**–9**	**0**	**0.0**	**12:47**	....	....	....	....	....	....	....	....	....
2004-05	Victoria	ECHL	25	3	9	12	192	....	....	....	....	....	....	....	....	....	....	....	....	....	....	....	....	....	....
	NHL Totals		**181**	**4**	**16**	**20**	**578**	**0**	**0**	**0**	**106**	**3.8**		**0**	**0.0**	**11:37**	....	....	....	....	....	....	....	....	....

• Spent majority of 2003-04 season as a healthy reserve. Signed as a free agent by **Victoria** (ECHL), December 3, 2004.

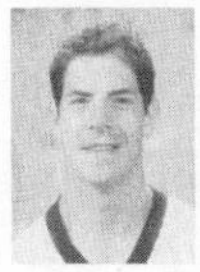

PUSHOR, Jamie

(PUH-shohr, JAY-mee)

Defense. Shoots right. 6'3", 218 lbs. Born, Lethbridge, Alta., February 11, 1973. Detroit's 2nd choice, 32nd overall, in 1991 Entry Draft.

Season	Club	League	GP	G	A	Pts	PIM	PP	SH	GW	S	%	+/-	TF	F%	Min	GP	G	A	Pts	PIM	PP	SH	GW	Min
1988-89	Lethbridge	AMHL	37	1	8	9	20	....	....	....	....	....	....	....	....	....	....	....	....	....	....	....	....	....	....
	Lethbridge	WHL	2	0	0	0	0	....	....	....	....	....	....	....	....	....	....	....	....	....	....	....	....	....	....
1989-90	Lethbridge	AMHL	35	6	27	33	92	....	....	....	....	....	....	....	....	....	....	....	....	....	....	....	....	....	....
	Lethbridge	WHL	10	0	2	2	2	....	....	....	....	....	....	....	....	....	16	0	0	0	63	....	....	....	....
1990-91	Lethbridge	WHL	71	1	13	14	202	....	....	....	....	....	....	....	....	....	....	....	....	....	....	....	....	....	....
1991-92	Lethbridge	WHL	49	2	15	17	232	....	....	....	....	....	....	....	....	....	5	0	0	0	33	....	....	....	....
1992-93	Lethbridge	WHL	72	6	22	28	200	....	....	....	....	....	....	....	....	....	4	0	1	1	9	....	....	....	....
1993-94	Adirondack	AHL	73	1	17	18	124	....	....	....	....	....	....	....	....	....	12	0	0	0	22	....	....	....	....
1994-95	Adirondack	AHL	58	2	11	13	129	....	....	....	....	....	....	....	....	....	4	0	1	1	0	....	....	....	....
1995-96	**Detroit**	**NHL**	**5**	**0**	**1**	**1**	**17**	**0**	**0**	**0**	**6**	**0.0**	**2**	....	....	....	....	....	....	....	....	....	....	....	....
	Adirondack	AHL	65	2	16	18	126	....	....	....	....	....	....	....	....	....	3	0	0	0	5	....	....	....	....
1996-97♦	**Detroit**	**NHL**	**75**	**4**	**7**	**11**	**129**	**0**	**0**	**0**	**63**	**6.3**	**1**	....	....	....	**5**	**0**	**1**	**1**	**5**	**0**	**0**	**0**	....
1997-98	**Detroit**	**NHL**	**54**	**2**	**5**	**7**	**71**	**0**	**0**	**0**	**43**	**4.7**	**2**	....	....	....	....	....	....	....	....	....	....	....	....
	Anaheim	**NHL**	**10**	**0**	**2**	**2**	**10**	**0**	**0**	**0**	**8**	**0.0**	**1**	....	....	....	....	....	....	....	....	....	....	....	....
1998-99	**Anaheim**	**NHL**	**70**	**1**	**2**	**3**	**112**	**0**	**0**	**0**	**75**	**1.3**	**–20**	**0**	**0.0**	**19:16**	**4**	**0**	**0**	**0**	**6**	**0**	**0**	**0**	**14:08**
99-2000	**Dallas**	**NHL**	**62**	**0**	**8**	**8**	**53**	**0**	**0**	**0**	**27**	**0.0**	**0**	**0**	**0.0**	**11:36**	**5**	**0**	**0**	**0**	**5**	**0**	**0**	**0**	**10:06**
2000-01	**Columbus**	**NHL**	**75**	**3**	**10**	**13**	**94**	**0**	**1**	**0**	**64**	**4.7**	**7**	**0**	**0.0**	**20:48**	....	....	....	....	....	....	....	....	....
2001-02	**Columbus**	**NHL**	**61**	**0**	**6**	**6**	**54**	**0**	**0**	**0**	**46**	**0.0**	**–10**	**0**	**0.0**	**17:06**	....	....	....	....	....	....	....	....	....
	Pittsburgh	**NHL**	**15**	**0**	**2**	**2**	**30**	**0**	**0**	**0**	**14**	**0.0**	**–3**	**0**	**0.0**	**19:03**	....	....	....	....	....	....	....	....	....
2002-03	**Pittsburgh**	**NHL**	**76**	**3**	**1**	**4**	**76**	**0**	**0**	**0**	**54**	**5.6**	**–28**	**0**	**0.0**	**16:58**	....	....	....	....	....	....	....	....	....

			Regular Season														Playoffs								
Season	Club	League	GP	G	A	Pts	PIM	PP	SH	GW	S	%	+/-	TF	F%	Min	GP	G	A	Pts	PIM	PP	SH	GW	Min
2003-04	Syracuse Crunch	AHL	17	1	4	5	24																		
	Columbus	**NHL**	**7**	**0**	**0**	**0**	**2**	**0**	**0**	**0**	**6**	**0.0**	**−2**	**0**	**0.0**	**13:12**									
	NY Rangers	**NHL**	**7**	**0**	**0**	**0**	**0**	**0**	**0**	**0**	**4**	**0.0**	**−3**	**0**	**0.0**	**13:08**									
	Hartford	AHL	14	0	2	2	21										16	1	1	2	18				
2004-05	Syracuse Crunch	AHL	68	1	9	10	85																		
	NHL Totals		**517**	**13**	**44**	**57**	**648**	**0**	**1**	**0**	**410**	**3.2**		**0**	**0.0**	**17:15**	**14**	**0**	**1**	**1**	**16**	**0**	**0**	**0**	**11:53**

Traded to **Anaheim** by **Detroit** with Detroit's 4th round choice (Viktor Wallin) in 1998 Entry Draft for Dmitri Mironov, March 24, 1998. Claimed by **Atlanta** from **Anaheim** in Expansion Draft, June 25, 1999. Traded to **Dallas** by **Atlanta** for Jason Botterill, July 15, 1999. Claimed by **Columbus** from **Dallas** in Expansion Draft, June 23, 2000. Traded to **Pittsburgh** by **Columbus** for Pittsburgh's 4th round choice (Kevin Jarman) in 2003 Entry Draft, March 15, 2002. Signed as a free agent by **Syracuse** (AHL), November 18, 2003. Signed as a free agent by **Columbus**, December 10, 2003. Traded to **NY Rangers** by **Columbus** for NY Rangers' 8th round choice (Matt Greer) in 2004 Entry Draft, January 23, 2004. Signed as a free agent by **Syracuse** (AHL), August 9, 2004.

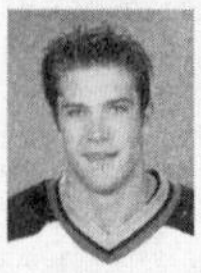

PYATT, Taylor
(PIGH-at, TAY-luhr) **BUF.**

Left wing. Shoots left. 6'4", 227 lbs. Born, Thunder Bay, Ont., August 19, 1981. NY Islanders' 2nd choice, 8th overall, in 1999 Entry Draft.

Season	Club	League	GP	G	A	Pts	PIM	PP	SH	GW	S	%	+/-	TF	F%	Min	GP	G	A	Pts	PIM	PP	SH	GW	Min
1996-97	Thunder Bay	TBAHA	60	52	61	113	72																		
1997-98	Sudbury Wolves	OHL	58	14	17	31	104										10	3	1	4	8				
1998-99	Sudbury Wolves	OHL	68	37	38	75	95										4	0	4	4	6				
99-2000	Sudbury Wolves	OHL	68	40	49	89	98										12	8	7	15	25				
2000-01	**NY Islanders**	**NHL**	**78**	**4**	**14**	**18**	**39**	**1**	**0**	**2**	**86**	**4.7**	**−17**	**1**	**0.0**	**12:14**									
2001-02	Rochester	AHL	27	6	4	10	36																		
	Buffalo	**NHL**	**48**	**10**	**10**	**20**	**35**	**0**	**0**	**0**	**61**	**16.4**	**4**	**0**	**0.0**	**13:30**									
2002-03	**Buffalo**	**NHL**	**78**	**14**	**14**	**28**	**38**	**2**	**0**	**0**	**110**	**12.7**	**−8**	**8**	**25.0**	**14:06**									
2003-04	**Buffalo**	**NHL**	**63**	**8**	**12**	**20**	**25**	**1**	**2**	**4**	**98**	**8.2**	**−7**	**19**	**26.3**	**15:36**									
2004-05	Hammarby	Sweden-2	24	11	9	20	20																		
	NHL Totals		**267**	**36**	**50**	**86**	**137**	**4**	**2**	**6**	**355**	**10.1**		**28**	**25.0**	**13:48**									

OHL First All-Star Team (2000)

Traded to **Buffalo** by **NY Islanders** with Tim Connolly for Michael Peca, June 24, 2001. Signed as a free agent by **Hammarby** (Sweden-2), November 16, 2004.

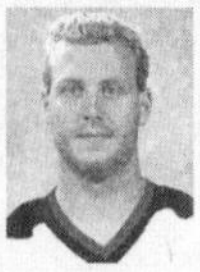

QUINT, Deron
(KWIHNT, DAIR-ohn)

Defense. Shoots left. 6'2", 219 lbs. Born, Durham, NH, March 12, 1976. Winnipeg's 1st choice, 30th overall, in 1994 Entry Draft.

Season	Club	League	GP	G	A	Pts	PIM	PP	SH	GW	S	%	+/-	TF	F%	Min	GP	G	A	Pts	PIM	PP	SH	GW	Min
1990-91	Cardigan Mtn.	High-NH	31	67	54	121																			
1991-92	Cardigan Mtn.	High-NH	21	111	58	169																			
1992-93	Tabor	High-MA	28	15	26	41	30										1	0	2	2	0				
1993-94	Seattle	WHL	63	15	29	44	47										9	4	12	16	8				
1994-95	Seattle	WHL	65	29	60	89	82										3	1	2	3	6				
1995-96	**Winnipeg**	**NHL**	**51**	**5**	**13**	**18**	**22**	**2**	**0**	**0**	**97**	**5.2**	**−2**												
	Springfield	AHL	11	2	3	5	4										10	2	3	5	6				
	Seattle	WHL															5	4	1	5	6				
1996-97	**Phoenix**	**NHL**	**27**	**3**	**11**	**14**	**4**	**1**	**0**	**0**	**63**	**4.8**	**−4**				**7**	**0**	**2**	**2**	**0**	**0**	**0**	**0**	
	Springfield	AHL	43	6	18	24	20										12	2	7	9	4				
1997-98	**Phoenix**	**NHL**	**32**	**4**	**7**	**11**	**16**	**1**	**0**	**1**	**61**	**6.6**	**−6**												
	Springfield	AHL	8	1	7	8	10										1	0	0	0	0				
1998-99	**Phoenix**	**NHL**	**60**	**5**	**8**	**13**	**20**	**2**	**0**	**0**	**94**	**5.3**	**−10**	**0**	**0.0**	**16:12**									
99-2000	**Phoenix**	**NHL**	**50**	**3**	**7**	**10**	**22**	**0**	**0**	**1**	**88**	**3.4**	**0**	**0**	**0.0**	**16:39**									
	New Jersey	**NHL**	**4**	**1**	**0**	**1**	**2**	**0**	**0**	**0**	**6**	**16.7**	**−2**	**0**	**0.0**	**16:26**									
2000-01	**Columbus**	**NHL**	**57**	**7**	**16**	**23**	**16**	**3**	**0**	**0**	**148**	**4.7**	**−19**	**1**	**100.0**	**24:06**									
	Syracuse Crunch	AHL	21	5	15	20	30																		
2001-02	**Columbus**	**NHL**	**75**	**7**	**18**	**25**	**26**	**3**	**0**	**1**	**169**	**4.1**	**−34**	**0**	**0.0**	**22:01**									
2002-03	Springfield	AHL	4	1	2	3	4																		
	Phoenix	**NHL**	**51**	**7**	**10**	**17**	**20**	**2**	**0**	**0**	**85**	**8.2**	**−5**	**0**	**0.0**	**15:51**									
2003-04	**Chicago**	**NHL**	**51**	**4**	**7**	**11**	**18**	**2**	**0**	**0**	**72**	**5.6**	**−26**	**0**	**0.0**	**18:08**									
2004-05	HC Forst Bolzano	Italy	14	5	11	16	10										9	4	5	9	12				
	NHL Totals		**458**	**46**	**97**	**143**	**166**	**16**	**0**	**3**	**883**	**5.2**		**1**	**100.0**	**19:03**	**7**	**0**	**2**	**2**	**0**	**0**	**0**	**0**	

WHL West First All-Star Team (1995)

Transferred to **Phoenix** after **Winnipeg** franchise relocated, July 1, 1996. Traded to **New Jersey** by **Phoenix** with Phoenix's 3rd round choice (later traded back to Phoenix – Phoenix selected Beat Forster) in 2001 Entry Draft for Lyle Odelein, March 7, 2000. Traded to **Columbus** by **New Jersey** to complete transaction that sent Krzysztof Oliwa to Columbus (June 12, 2000) and Turner Stevenson to New Jersey (June 23, 2000), June 23, 2000. Signed to a PTO (tryout) contract by **Springfield** (AHL), October 16, 2002. Signed as a free agent by **Phoenix**, October 26, 2002. Signed as a free agent by **Chicago**, August 5, 2003. Signed as a free agent by **Bolzano** (Italy), December 20, 2004. Signed as a free agent by **Kloten** (Swiss), May 21, 2005.

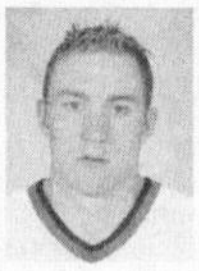

RACHUNEK, Karel
(ra-KHOO-nehk, KAH-rehl) **NYR**

Defense. Shoots right. 6'2", 211 lbs. Born, Zlin, Czech., August 27, 1979. Ottawa's 8th choice, 229th overall, in 1997 Entry Draft.

Season	Club	League	GP	G	A	Pts	PIM	PP	SH	GW	S	%	+/-	TF	F%	Min	GP	G	A	Pts	PIM	PP	SH	GW	Min
1995-96	AC ZPS Zlin Jr.	CzRep-Jr.	38	8	11	19																			
1996-97	AC ZPS Zlin Jr.	CzRep-Jr.	27	2	11	13																			
1997-98	Zlin	CzRep	27	1	2	3	16																		
1998-99	Zlin	CzRep	39	3	9	12	88										6	0	0	0					
99-2000	**Ottawa**	**NHL**	**6**	**0**	**0**	**0**	**2**	**0**	**0**	**0**	**3**	**0.0**	**0**	**0**	**0.0**	**8:03**									
	Grand Rapids	IHL	62	6	20	26	64										9	0	5	5	6				
2000-01	**Ottawa**	**NHL**	**71**	**3**	**30**	**33**	**60**	**3**	**0**	**0**	**77**	**3.9**	**17**	**0**	**0.0**	**20:54**	**3**	**0**	**0**	**0**	**0**	**0**	**0**	**0**	**22:38**
2001-02	**Ottawa**	**NHL**	**51**	**3**	**15**	**18**	**24**	**1**	**0**	**2**	**55**	**5.5**	**7**	**2**	**0.0**	**19:19**									
2002-03	Yaroslavl	Russia	9	3	0	3	8																		
	Ottawa	**NHL**	**58**	**4**	**25**	**29**	**30**	**3**	**0**	**1**	**110**	**3.6**	**23**	**3**	**33.3**	**21:46**	**17**	**1**	**3**	**4**	**14**	**0**	**0**	**0**	**23:14**
	Binghamton	AHL	6	0	2	2	10																		
2003-04	**Ottawa**	**NHL**	**60**	**1**	**16**	**17**	**29**	**0**	**0**	**0**	**99**	**1.0**	**17**	**0**	**0.0**	**19:43**									
	NY Rangers	**NHL**	**12**	**1**	**3**	**4**	**4**	**1**	**0**	**0**	**21**	**4.8**	**−9**	**0**	**0.0**	**19:04**									
2004-05	Znojmo	CzRep	21	5	6	11	55																		
	Yaroslavl	Russia	27	6	8	14	69										9	2	0	2	6				
	NHL Totals		**258**	**12**	**89**	**101**	**149**	**8**	**0**	**3**	**365**	**3.3**		**5**	**20.0**	**20:07**	**20**	**1**	**3**	**4**	**14**	**0**	**0**	**0**	**23:09**

Traded to **NY Rangers** by **Ottawa** with Alexandre Giroux for Greg De Vries, March 9, 2004. Signed as a free agent by **Znojmo** (CzRep), September 6, 2004. Signed as a free agent by **Yaroslavl** (Russia), November 1, 2004.

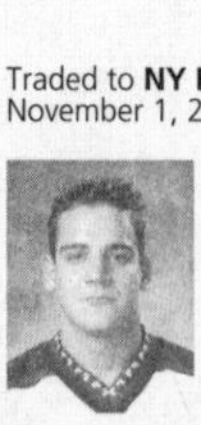

RADIVOJEVIC, Branko
(ra-dih-VOI-uh-vihch, BRAN-koh) **PHI.**

Right wing. Shoots right. 6'1", 209 lbs. Born, Piestany, Czech., November 24, 1980. Colorado's 3rd choice, 93rd overall, in 1999 Entry Draft.

Season	Club	League	GP	G	A	Pts	PIM	PP	SH	GW	S	%	+/-	TF	F%	Min	GP	G	A	Pts	PIM	PP	SH	GW	Min
1997-98	Dukla Trencin Jr.	Slovak-Jr.	52	30	31	61	50																		
	Dukla Trencin	Slovakia	1	0	0	0	2																		
1998-99	Belleville Bulls	OHL	68	20	38	58	61										21	7	17	24	18				
99-2000	Belleville Bulls	OHL	59	23	49	72	86										16	5	8	13	32				
2000-01	Belleville Bulls	OHL	61	34	70	104	77										10	6	10	16	18				
2001-02	**Phoenix**	**NHL**	**18**	**4**	**2**	**6**	**4**	**0**	**0**	**1**	**19**	**21.1**	**1**	**0**	**0.0**	**9:22**	**1**	**0**	**0**	**0**	**2**	**0**	**0**	**0**	**8:07**
	Springfield	AHL	62	18	21	39	64																		
2002-03	**Phoenix**	**NHL**	**79**	**12**	**15**	**27**	**63**	**1**	**0**	**3**	**109**	**11.0**	**−2**	**20**	**40.0**	**13:18**									
2003-04	**Phoenix**	**NHL**	**53**	**9**	**14**	**23**	**36**	**2**	**1**	**2**	**83**	**10.8**	**−5**	**30**	**30.0**	**16:27**									
	Philadelphia	**NHL**	**24**	**1**	**8**	**9**	**36**	**0**	**0**	**0**	**24**	**4.2**	**0**	**11**	**54.6**	**10:28**	**18**	**1**	**1**	**2**	**32**	**0**	**0**	**0**	**9:56**
2004-05	HC Vsetin	CzRep	31	7	11	18	114																		
	Lulea HF	Sweden	10	6	5	11	8										4	0	0	0	44				
	NHL Totals		**174**	**26**	**39**	**65**	**139**	**3**	**1**	**6**	**235**	**11.1**		**61**	**37.7**	**13:28**	**19**	**1**	**1**	**2**	**34**	**0**	**0**	**0**	**9:51**

OHL First All-Star Team (2001)

Signed as a free agent by **Phoenix**, June 19, 2001. Traded to **Philadelphia** by **Phoenix** with Sean Burke and Ben Eager for Mike Comrie, February 9, 2004. Signed as a free agent by **Vsetin** (CzRep), September 17, 2004. Signed as a free agent by **Lulea** (Sweden), January 27, 2005.

Season	Club	League	GP	G	A	Pts	PIM	PP	SH	GW	S	%	+/-	TF	F%	Min	GP	G	A	Pts	PIM	PP	SH	GW	Min

RADULOV, Igor — (rah-DOO-lahf, EE-gohr)

Left wing. Shoots left. 6'1", 186 lbs. Born, Nizhny Tagil, USSR, August 23, 1982. Chicago's 4th choice, 74th overall, in 2000 Entry Draft.

Season	Club	League	GP	G	A	Pts	PIM	PP	SH	GW	S	%	+/-	TF	F%	Min	GP	G	A	Pts	PIM	PP	SH	GW	Min
1997-98	Yaroslavl	Russia	5	0	2	2	4	....	....	....	....	....	....	....	....	....	....	....	....	....	....	....	....	....	....
1998-99	Yaroslavl 2	Russia-3	21	2	3	5	4	....	....	....	....	....	....	....	....	....	....	....	....	....	....	....	....	....	....
99-2000	Yaroslavl 2	Russia-3	31	17	16	33	....	....	....	....	....	....	....	....	....	....	....	....	....	....	....	....	....	....	....
2000-01	Kristall Saratov	Russia-2	4	0	2	2	2	....	....	....	....	....	....	....	....	....	....	....	....	....	....	....	....	....	....
	St. Petersburg	Russia	8	1	0	1	6	....	....	....	....	....	....	....	....	....	....	....	....	....	....	....	....	....	....
2001-02	Mississauga	OHL	62	33	30	63	30	....	....	....	....	....	....	....	....	....	....	....	....	....	....	....	....	....	....
2002-03	**Chicago**	**NHL**	7	5	0	5	4	3	0	0	14	35.7	–3	0	0.0	15:06									
	Norfolk Admirals	AHL	62	18	9	27	26										9	2	2	4	8				
2003-04	**Chicago**	**NHL**	36	4	7	11	18	0	0	0	47	8.5	–2	0	0.0	12:15									
	Norfolk Admirals	AHL	38	9	14	23	26										8	0	1	1	4				
2004-05	Norfolk Admirals	AHL	16	0	0	0	16	....	....	....	....	....	....	....	....	....	....	....	....	....	....	....	....	....	....
	Spartak Moscow	Russia	25	2	2	4	22	....	....	....	....	....	....	....	....	....	....	....	....	....	....	....	....	....	....
	NHL Totals		**43**	**9**	**7**	**16**	**22**	**3**	**0**	**0**	**61**	**14.8**		**0**	**0.0**	**12:43**									

Assigned to **Spartak** (Russia) by **Chicago** (Norfolk-AHL), December 20, 2004.

RAFALSKI, Brian — (ra-FAWL-skee, BRIGH-uhn) — **N.J.**

Defense. Shoots right. 5'10", 190 lbs. Born, Dearborn, MI, September 28, 1973.

Season	Club	League	GP	G	A	Pts	PIM	PP	SH	GW	S	%	+/-	TF	F%	Min	GP	G	A	Pts	PIM	PP	SH	GW	Min
1990-91	Madison Capitols	USHL	47	12	11	23	28	....	....	....	....	....	....	....	....	....	....	....	....	....	....	....	....	....	....
1991-92	U. of Wisconsin	WCHA	34	3	14	17	34	....	....	....	....	....	....	....	....	....	....	....	....	....	....	....	....	....	....
1992-93	U. of Wisconsin	WCHA	32	0	13	13	10	....	....	....	....	....	....	....	....	....	....	....	....	....	....	....	....	....	....
1993-94	U. of Wisconsin	WCHA	37	6	17	23	26	....	....	....	....	....	....	....	....	....	....	....	....	....	....	....	....	....	....
1994-95	U. of Wisconsin	WCHA	43	11	34	45	48	....	....	....	....	....	....	....	....	....	....	....	....	....	....	....	....	....	....
1995-96	Brynas IF Gavle	Sweden	40	4	14	18	26	....	....	....	....	....	....	....	....	....	....	9	1	1	2					
1996-97	HPK Hameenlinna	Finland	49	11	24	35	26	....	....	....	....	....	....	....	....	....	....	10	6	5	11	4				
1997-98	HIFK Helsinki	Finland	40	13	10	23	20	....	....	....	....	....	....	....	....	....	....	9	5	6	11	0				
1998-99	HIFK Helsinki	Finland	53	19	34	53	18	....	....	....	....	....	....	....	....	....	....	11	5	*9	*14	4				
	HIFK Helsinki	EuroHL	6	4	6	10	10	....	....	....	....	....	....	....	....	....	....	4	1	1	2					
99-2000♦	**New Jersey**	**NHL**	75	5	27	32	28	1	0	1	128	3.9	21	1	0.0	18:51	23	2	6	8	8	0	0	1	21:25
2000-01	**New Jersey**	**NHL**	78	9	43	52	26	6	0	1	142	6.3	36	2100.0		21:41	25	7	11	18	7	1	0	3	22:08
2001-02	**New Jersey**	**NHL**	76	7	40	47	18	2	0	4	125	5.6	15	0	0.0	22:08	6	3	2	5	4	3	0	0	21:45
	United States	Olympics	6	1	2	3	2	....	....	....	....	....	....	....	....	....	....	....	....	....	....	....	....	....	....
2002-03♦	**New Jersey**	**NHL**	79	3	37	40	14	2	0	0	178	1.7	18	1	0.0	23:09	23	2	9	11	8	2	0	0	25:46
2003-04	**New Jersey**	**NHL**	69	6	30	36	24	2	0	1	130	4.6	6	0	0.0	22:48	5	0	1	1	0	0	0	0	22:22
2004-05					DID NOT PLAY																				
	NHL Totals		**377**	**30**	**177**	**207**	**110**	**13**	**0**	**7**	**703**	**4.3**		**4**	**50.0**	**21:43**	**82**	**14**	**29**	**43**	**27**	**6**	**0**	**4**	**22:56**

WCHA First All-Star Team (1995) • NCAA West First All-American Team (1995) • NHL All-Rookie Team (2000)
Played in NHL All-Star Game (2004)
Signed as a free agent by **New Jersey**, June 18, 1999.

RAGNARSSON, Marcus — (RAG-nahr-suhn, MAHR-kuhs)

Defense. Shoots left. 6'1", 215 lbs. Born, Ostervala, Sweden, August 13, 1971. San Jose's 5th choice, 99th overall, in 1992 Entry Draft.

Season	Club	League	GP	G	A	Pts	PIM	PP	SH	GW	S	%	+/-	TF	F%	Min	GP	G	A	Pts	PIM	PP	SH	GW	Min
1986-87	Ostervala IF	Sweden-3	28	1	6	7	....	....	....	....	....	....	....	....	....	....	....	....	....	....	....	....	....	....	....
1987-88	Ostervala IF	Sweden-3	25	3	12	15	....	....	....	....	....	....	....	....	....	....	....	....	....	....	....	....	....	....	....
1988-89	Ostervala IF	Sweden-3	30	15	14	29	....	....	....	....	....	....	....	....	....	....	....	....	....	....	....	....	....	....	....
1989-90	Nacka HK	Sweden-2	9	2	3	5	4	....	....	....	....	....	....	....	....	....	....	....	....	....	....	....	....	....	....
	Djurgarden	Sweden	13	0	2	2	0	....	....	....	....	....	....	....	....	....	....	1	0	0	0	0				
1990-91	Djurgarden	Sweden	35	4	1	5	12	....	....	....	....	....	....	....	....	....	....	7	0	0	0	6				
1991-92	Djurgarden	Sweden	40	8	5	13	14	....	....	....	....	....	....	....	....	....	....	10	0	1	1	4				
1992-93	Djurgarden	Sweden	35	3	3	6	53	....	....	....	....	....	....	....	....	....	....	6	0	3	3	8				
1993-94	Djurgarden	Sweden	19	0	4	4	24	....	....	....	....	....	....	....	....	....	....	....	....	....	....	....	....	....	....
1994-95	Djurgarden	Sweden	38	7	9	16	20	....	....	....	....	....	....	....	....	....	....	3	0	0	0	4				
1995-96	**San Jose**	**NHL**	71	8	31	39	42	4	0	0	94	8.5	–24	....	....	....	....	....	....	....	....	....	....	....	....
1996-97	**San Jose**	**NHL**	69	3	14	17	63	2	0	0	57	5.3	–18	....	....	....	....	....	....	....	....	....	....	....	....
1997-98	**San Jose**	**NHL**	79	5	20	25	65	3	0	2	91	5.5	–11	....	....	....	6	0	0	0	4	0	0	0	
	Sweden	Olympics	3	0	1	1	0	....	....	....	....	....	....	....	....	....	....	....	....	....	....	....	....	....	....
1998-99	**San Jose**	**NHL**	74	0	13	13	66	0	0	0	87	0.0	7	3	66.7	21:55	6	0	1	1	6	0	0	0	22:16
99-2000	**San Jose**	**NHL**	63	3	13	16	38	0	0	0	60	5.0	13	0	0.0	22:52	12	0	3	3	10	0	0	0	22:22
2000-01	**San Jose**	**NHL**	68	3	12	15	44	1	0	0	74	4.1	2	0	0.0	23:36	5	0	1	1	8	0	0	0	20:24
2001-02	**San Jose**	**NHL**	70	5	15	20	44	2	0	3	68	7.4	4	4	25.0	22:37	12	1	3	4	12	0	0	1	21:35
	Sweden	Olympics	4	0	2	2	2	....	....	....	....	....	....	....	....	....	....	....	....	....	....	....	....	....	....
2002-03	**San Jose**	**NHL**	25	1	7	8	30	0	0	0	27	3.7	2	2100.0		24:56	....	....	....	....	....	....	....	....	....
	Philadelphia	**NHL**	43	2	6	8	32	1	0	0	52	3.8	5	1100.0		21:10	13	0	1	1	6	0	0	0	25:23
2003-04	**Philadelphia**	**NHL**	70	7	9	16	58	2	0	2	82	8.5	12	0	0.0	20:55	14	1	4	5	14	0	0	1	21:58
2004-05	Almtuna	Sweden-2	....	....	....	....	....	....	....	....	....	....	....	....	....	....	1	1	0	1	0				
	NHL Totals		**632**	**37**	**140**	**177**	**482**	**15**	**0**	**7**	**692**	**5.3**		**10**	**60.0**	**22:24**	**68**	**2**	**13**	**15**	**60**	**0**	**0**	**1**	**22:35**

Played in NHL All-Star Game (2001)
Traded to **Philadelphia** by **San Jose** for Dan McGillis, December 6, 2002. Signed as a free agent by **Almtuna** (Sweden-2), January 30, 2005.

RASMUSSEN, Erik — (RAS-moo-suhn, AIR-ihk) — **N.J.**

Left wing/Center. Shoots left. 6'1", 210 lbs. Born, Minneapolis, MN, March 28, 1977. Buffalo's 1st choice, 7th overall, in 1996 Entry Draft.

Season	Club	League	GP	G	A	Pts	PIM	PP	SH	GW	S	%	+/-	TF	F%	Min	GP	G	A	Pts	PIM	PP	SH	GW	Min
1992-93	St. Louis Park	High-MN	23	16	24	40	50	....	....	....	....	....	....	....	....	....	....	....	....	....	....	....	....	....	....
1993-94	St. Louis Park	High-MN	18	25	18	43	80	....	....	....	....	....	....	....	....	....	....	....	....	....	....	....	....	....	....
1994-95	St. Louis Park	High-MN	23	19	33	52	80	....	....	....	....	....	....	....	....	....	....	....	....	....	....	....	....	....	....
1995-96	U. of Minnesota	WCHA	40	16	32	48	55	....	....	....	....	....	....	....	....	....	....	....	....	....	....	....	....	....	....
1996-97	U. of Minnesota	WCHA	34	15	12	27	*123	....	....	....	....	....	....	....	....	....	....	....	....	....	....	....	....	....	....
1997-98	**Buffalo**	**NHL**	21	2	3	5	14	0	0	0	28	7.1	2	....	....	....	....	....	....	....	....	....	....	....	....
	Rochester	AHL	53	9	14	23	83	....	....	....	....	....	....	....	....	....	1	0	0	0	5				
1998-99	**Buffalo**	**NHL**	42	3	7	10	37	0	0	0	40	7.5	6	67	40.3	12:22	21	2	4	6	18	0	0	1	12:51
	Rochester	AHL	37	12	14	26	47	....	....	....	....	....	....	....	....	....	....	....	....	....	....	....	....	....	....
99-2000	**Buffalo**	**NHL**	67	8	6	14	43	0	0	2	76	10.5	1	130	44.6	11:27	3	0	0	0	0	0	0	0	8:59
2000-01	**Buffalo**	**NHL**	82	12	19	31	51	1	0	3	95	12.6	0	565	43.7	13:47	3	0	1	1	0	0	0	0	16:26
2001-02	**Buffalo**	**NHL**	69	8	11	19	34	0	0	2	89	9.0	–1	236	39.8	13:03	....	....	....	....	....	....	....	....	....
2002-03	**Los Angeles**	**NHL**	57	4	12	16	28	0	0	1	75	5.3	–1	278	44.6	13:39	....	....	....	....	....	....	....	....	....
2003-04	**New Jersey**	**NHL**	69	7	6	13	41	0	0	0	68	10.3	5	423	44.4	11:34	5	0	2	2	2	0	0	0	14:44
2004-05					DID NOT PLAY																				
	NHL Totals		**407**	**44**	**64**	**108**	**248**	**1**	**0**	**8**	**471**	**9.3**		**1699**	**43.4**	**12:41**	**32**	**2**	**7**	**9**	**24**	**0**	**0**	**1**	**13:07**

Minnesota High School Player of the Year (1995)
Traded to **Los Angeles** by **Buffalo** for Adam Mair and Los Angeles' 5th round choice (Thomas Morrow) in 2003 Entry Draft, July 24, 2002. Signed as a free agent by **New Jersey**, July 25, 2003.

RATHJE, Mike — (RATH-jee, MIGHK) — **PHI.**

Defense. Shoots left. 6'5", 235 lbs. Born, Mannville, Alta., May 11, 1974. San Jose's 1st choice, 3rd overall, in 1992 Entry Draft.

Season	Club	League	GP	G	A	Pts	PIM	PP	SH	GW	S	%	+/-	TF	F%	Min	GP	G	A	Pts	PIM	PP	SH	GW	Min
1989-90	Sherwood Park	AMHL	33	6	11	17	30	....	....	....	....	....	....	....	....	....	6	1	1	2	2				
1990-91	Medicine Hat	WHL	64	1	16	17	28	....	....	....	....	....	....	....	....	....	12	0	4	4	2				
1991-92	Medicine Hat	WHL	67	11	23	34	99	....	....	....	....	....	....	....	....	....	4	0	1	1	2				
1992-93	Medicine Hat	WHL	57	12	37	49	103	....	....	....	....	....	....	....	....	....	10	3	3	6	12				
	Kansas City	IHL	....	....	....	....	....	....	....	....	....	....	....	....	....	....	5	0	0	0	12				
1993-94	**San Jose**	**NHL**	47	1	9	10	59	1	0	0	30	3.3	–9	....	....	....	1	0	0	0	0	0	0	0	
	Kansas City	IHL	6	0	2	2	0	....	....	....	....	....	....	....	....	....	....	....	....	....	....	....	....	....	....
1994-95	Kansas City	IHL	6	0	1	1	7	....	....	....	....	....	....	....	....	....	....	....	....	....	....	....	....	....	....
	San Jose	**NHL**	42	2	7	9	29	0	0	0	38	5.3	–1	....	....	....	11	5	2	7	4	5	0	0	
1995-96	**San Jose**	**NHL**	27	0	7	7	14	0	0	0	26	0.0	–16	....	....	....	....	....	....	....	....	....	....	....	....
	Kansas City	IHL	36	6	11	17	34	....	....	....	....	....	....	....	....	....	....	....	....	....	....	....	....	....	....

			Regular Season														Playoffs								
Season	Club	League	GP	G	A	Pts	PIM	PP	SH	GW	S	%	+/-	TF	F%	Min	GP	G	A	Pts	PIM	PP	SH	GW	Min
1996-97	San Jose	NHL	31	0	8	8	21	0	0	0	22	0.0	–1	....	....	....	....	....	....	....	....	....	....	....	....
1997-98	San Jose	NHL	81	3	12	15	59	1	0	0	61	4.9	–4	....	....	....	6	1	0	1	6	1	0	0	....
1998-99	San Jose	NHL	82	5	9	14	36	2	0	1	67	7.5	15	0	0.0	20:07	6	0	0	0	4	0	0	0	22:08
99-2000	San Jose	NHL	66	2	14	16	31	0	0	0	46	4.3	–2	0	0.0	22:11	12	1	3	4	8	0	0	0	21:32
2000-01	San Jose	NHL	81	0	11	11	48	0	0	0	89	0.0	7	0	0.0	22:20	6	0	1	1	4	0	0	0	24:20
2001-02	San Jose	NHL	52	5	12	17	48	4	0	0	56	8.9	23	0	0.0	21:31	12	1	3	4	6	1	0	0	23:29
2002-03	San Jose	NHL	82	7	22	29	48	3	0	1	147	4.8	–19	1	0.0	24:07	....	....	....	....	....	....	....	....	....
2003-04	San Jose	NHL	80	2	17	19	46	0	1	0	105	1.9	18	0	0.0	23:27	17	1	5	6	13	0	0	0	23:26
2004-05			Did not play																						
	NHL Totals		671	27	128	155	439	11	1	2	687	3.9		1	0.0	22:20	71	9	14	23	45	7	0	0	22:58

WHL East Second All-Star Team (1992, 1993)

• Missed majority of 1996-97 season recovering from groin injury suffered in game vs. Dallas, November 8, 1996. Signed as a free agent by **Philadelphia**, August 2, 2005.

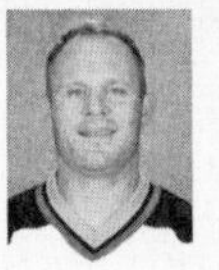

RAY, Rob

(RAY, RAWB)

Right wing. Shoots left. 6', 217 lbs. Born, Stirling, Ont., June 8, 1968. Buffalo's 5th choice, 97th overall, in 1988 Entry Draft.

1983-84	Trenton Bobcats	OHA-B	40	11	10	21	57	....	....	....	....	....	....	....	....	....	....	....	....	....	....	....	....	....	....
1984-85	Whitby Lawmen	OJHL	35	5	10	15	318	....	....	....	....	....	....	....	....	....	....	....	....	....	....	....	....	....	....
1985-86	Cornwall Royals	OHL	53	6	13	19	253	....	....	....	....	....	....	....	....	....	6	0	0	0	26	....	....	....	....
1986-87	Cornwall Royals	OHL	46	17	20	37	158	....	....	....	....	....	....	....	....	....	5	1	1	2	16	....	....	....	....
1987-88	Cornwall Royals	OHL	61	11	41	52	179	....	....	....	....	....	....	....	....	....	11	2	3	5	33	....	....	....	....
1988-89	Rochester	AHL	74	11	18	29	*446	....	....	....	....	....	....	....	....	....	....	....	....	....	....	....	....	....	....
1989-90	Buffalo	NHL	27	2	1	3	99	0	0	0	20	10.0	–2	....	....	....	....	....	....	....	....	....	....	....	....
	Rochester	AHL	43	2	13	15	335	....	....	....	....	....	....	....	....	....	17	1	3	4	115	....	....	....	....
1990-91	Buffalo	NHL	66	8	8	16	*350	0	0	1	54	14.8	–11	....	....	....	6	1	1	2	56	0	0	1	....
	Rochester	AHL	8	1	1	2	15	....	....	....	....	....	....	....	....	....	....	....	....	....	....	....	....	....	....
1991-92	Buffalo	NHL	63	5	3	8	354	0	0	0	29	17.2	–9	....	....	....	7	0	0	0	2	0	0	0	....
1992-93	Buffalo	NHL	68	3	2	5	211	1	0	0	28	10.7	–3	....	....	....	....	....	....	....	....	....	....	....	....
1993-94	Buffalo	NHL	82	3	4	7	274	0	0	0	34	8.8	2	....	....	....	7	1	0	1	43	0	0	0	....
1994-95	Buffalo	NHL	47	0	3	3	173	0	0	0	7	0.0	–4	....	....	....	5	0	0	0	14	0	0	0	....
1995-96	Buffalo	NHL	71	3	6	9	287	0	0	0	21	14.3	–8	....	....	....	....	....	....	....	....	....	....	....	....
1996-97	Buffalo	NHL	82	7	3	10	286	0	0	1	45	15.6	3	....	....	....	12	0	1	1	28	0	0	0	....
1997-98	Buffalo	NHL	63	2	4	6	234	1	0	1	19	10.5	2	....	....	....	10	0	0	0	24	0	0	0	....
1998-99	Buffalo	NHL	76	0	4	4	*261	0	0	0	23	0.0	–2	0	0.0	5:11	5	1	0	1	0	0	0	1	3:11
99-2000	Buffalo	NHL	69	1	3	4	158	0	0	0	17	5.9	0	0	0.0	4:13	....	....	....	....	....	....	....	....	....
2000-01	Buffalo	NHL	63	4	6	10	210	0	0	1	33	12.1	2	1	100.0	5:38	3	0	0	0	2	0	0	0	1:05
2001-02	Buffalo	NHL	71	2	3	5	200	0	0	0	23	8.7	–3	0	0.0	5:08	....	....	....	....	....	....	....	....	....
2002-03	Buffalo	NHL	41	0	0	0	92	0	0	0	14	0.0	–5	3	33.3	4:24	....	....	....	....	....	....	....	....	....
	Ottawa	NHL	5	0	0	0	4	0	0	0	0	0.0	0	0	0.0	4:53	....	....	....	....	....	....	....	....	....
2003-04	Ottawa	NHL	6	1	0	1	14	0	0	0	3	33.3	0	0	0.0	4:40	....	....	....	....	....	....	....	....	....
	Binghamton	AHL	5	2	0	2	11	....	....	....	....	....	....	....	....	....	....	....	....	....	....	....	....	....	....
2004-05			Did not play																						
	NHL Totals		900	41	50	91	3207	2	0	4	370	11.1		4	50.0	4:57	55	3	2	5	169	0	0	2	2:24

King Clancy Memorial Trophy (1999)

Traded to **Ottawa** by **Buffalo** for future considerations, March 10, 2003. Re-signed as a free agent by **Ottawa**, February 13, 2004.

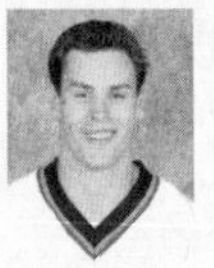

REASONER, Marty

(REE-sohn-uhr, MAHR-tee) **EDM.**

Center. Shoots left. 6'1", 200 lbs. Born, Honeoye Falls, NY, February 26, 1977. St. Louis' 1st choice, 14th overall, in 1996 Entry Draft.

1993-94	Deerfield	High-MA	22	27	25	52	....	....	....	....	....	....	....	....	....	....	....	....	....	....	....	....	....	....	....
1994-95	Deerfield	High-MA	26	25	32	57	14	....	....	....	....	....	....	....	....	....	....	....	....	....	....	....	....	....	....
1995-96	Boston College	H-East	34	16	29	45	32	....	....	....	....	....	....	....	....	....	....	....	....	....	....	....	....	....	....
1996-97	Boston College	H-East	35	20	24	44	31	....	....	....	....	....	....	....	....	....	....	....	....	....	....	....	....	....	....
1997-98	Boston College	H-East	42	*33	40	*73	56	....	....	....	....	....	....	....	....	....	....	....	....	....	....	....	....	....	....
1998-99	St. Louis	NHL	22	3	7	10	8	1	0	0	33	9.1	2	224	53.6	13:55	....	....	....	....	....	....	....	....	....
	Worcester IceCats	AHL	44	17	22	39	24	....	....	....	....	....	....	....	....	....	4	2	1	3	6	....	....	....	....
99-2000	St. Louis	NHL	32	10	14	24	20	3	0	0	51	19.6	9	379	49.6	15:20	7	2	1	3	4	1	0	0	13:12
	Worcester IceCats	AHL	44	23	28	51	39	....	....	....	....	....	....	....	....	....	....	....	....	....	....	....	....	....	....
2000-01	St. Louis	NHL	41	4	9	13	14	0	0	0	65	6.2	–5	454	53.1	14:00	10	3	1	4	0	0	0	1	12:21
	Worcester IceCats	AHL	34	17	18	35	25	....	....	....	....	....	....	....	....	....	....	....	....	....	....	....	....	....	....
2001-02	Edmonton	NHL	52	6	5	11	41	3	0	2	66	9.1	0	470	55.5	11:44	....	....	....	....	....	....	....	....	....
2002-03	Edmonton	NHL	70	11	20	31	28	2	2	0	102	10.8	19	968	53.5	14:50	6	1	0	1	2	1	0	0	14:22
	Hamilton	AHL	2	0	2	2	2	....	....	....	....	....	....	....	....	....	....	....	....	....	....	....	....	....	....
2003-04	Edmonton	NHL	17	2	6	8	10	0	1	0	28	7.1	5	321	52.7	16:30	....	....	....	....	....	....	....	....	....
2004-05	Salzburg	Austria	11	5	4	9	12	....	....	....	....	....	....	....	....	....	....	....	....	....	....	....	....	....	....
	NHL Totals		234	36	61	97	121	9	3	2	345	10.4		2816	53.2	14:06	23	6	2	8	6	2	0	1	13:08

Hockey East Rookie of the Year (1996) • Hockey East First All-Star Team (1997, 1998) • NCAA East First All-American Team (1998) • NCAA Championship All-Tournament Team (1998)

Traded to **Edmonton** by **St. Louis** with Jochen Hecht and Jan Horacek for Doug Weight and Michel Riesen, July 1, 2001. • Missed majority of 2003-04 season recovering from ankle (November 8, 2003 vs. Toronto) and knee (January 13, 2004 vs. Florida) injuries. Signed as a free agent by **Salzburg** (Austria), January 30, 2005.

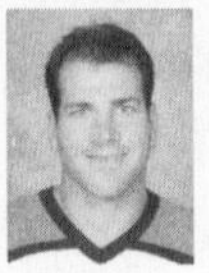

RECCHI, Mark

(REH-kee, MAHRK) **PIT.**

Right wing. Shoots left. 5'10", 190 lbs. Born, Kamloops, B.C., February 1, 1968. Pittsburgh's 4th choice, 67th overall, in 1988 Entry Draft.

1984-85	Langley Eagles	BCJHL	51	26	39	65	39	....	....	....	....	....	....	....	....	....	....	....	....	....	....	....	....	....	....
	New Westminster	WHL	4	1	0	1	0	....	....	....	....	....	....	....	....	....	....	....	....	....	....	....	....	....	....
1985-86	New Westminster	WHL	72	21	40	61	55	....	....	....	....	....	....	....	....	....	....	....	....	....	....	....	....	....	....
1986-87	Kamloops Chiefs	WHL	40	26	50	76	63	....	....	....	....	....	....	....	....	....	13	3	16	19	17	....	....	....	....
1987-88	Kamloops Chiefs	WHL	62	61	*93	154	75	....	....	....	....	....	....	....	....	....	17	10	*21	*31	18	....	....	....	....
1988-89	Pittsburgh	NHL	15	1	1	2	0	0	0	0	11	9.1	–2	....	....	....	....	....	....	....	....	....	....	....	....
	Muskegon	IHL	63	50	49	99	86	....	....	....	....	....	....	....	....	....	14	7	*14	*21	28	....	....	....	....
1989-90	Pittsburgh	NHL	74	30	37	67	44	6	2	4	143	21.0	6	....	....	....	....	....	....	....	....	....	....	....	....
	Muskegon	IHL	4	7	4	11	2	....	....	....	....	....	....	....	....	....	....	....	....	....	....	....	....	....	....
1990-91 ♦	Pittsburgh	NHL	78	40	73	113	48	12	0	9	184	21.7	0	....	....	....	24	10	24	34	33	5	0	2	....
1991-92	Pittsburgh	NHL	58	33	37	70	78	16	1	4	156	21.2	–16	....	....	....	....	....	....	....	....	....	....	....	....
	Philadelphia	NHL	22	10	17	27	18	4	0	1	54	18.5	–5	....	....	....	....	....	....	....	....	....	....	....	....
1992-93	Philadelphia	NHL	84	53	70	123	95	15	4	6	274	19.3	1	....	....	....	....	....	....	....	....	....	....	....	....
1993-94	Philadelphia	NHL	84	40	67	107	46	11	0	5	217	18.4	–2	....	....	....	....	....	....	....	....	....	....	....	....
1994-95	Philadelphia	NHL	10	2	3	5	12	1	0	2	17	11.8	–6	....	....	....	....	....	....	....	....	....	....	....	....
	Montreal	NHL	39	14	29	43	16	8	0	1	104	13.5	–3	....	....	....	....	....	....	....	....	....	....	....	....
1995-96	Montreal	NHL	82	28	50	78	69	11	2	6	191	14.7	20	....	....	....	6	3	3	6	0	3	0	0	....
1996-97	Montreal	NHL	82	34	46	80	58	7	2	3	202	16.8	–1	....	....	....	5	4	2	6	2	0	0	0	....
1997-98	Montreal	NHL	82	32	42	74	51	9	1	6	216	14.8	11	....	....	....	10	4	8	12	6	0	0	2	....
	Canada	Olympics	5	0	2	2	0	....	....	....	....	....	....	....	....	....	....	....	....	....	....	....	....	....	....
1998-99	Montreal	NHL	61	12	35	47	28	3	0	2	152	7.9	–4	239	44.8	20:37	....	....	....	....	....	....	....	....	....
	Philadelphia	NHL	10	4	2	6	6	0	0	0	19	21.1	–3	4	25.0	19:30	6	0	1	1	2	0	0	0	19:35
99-2000	Philadelphia	NHL	82	28	*63	91	50	7	1	5	223	12.6	20	353	49.6	21:43	18	6	12	18	6	2	0	1	23:10
2000-01	Philadelphia	NHL	69	27	50	77	33	7	1	8	191	14.1	15	138	42.8	21:40	6	2	2	4	2	1	0	1	23:00
2001-02	Philadelphia	NHL	80	22	42	64	46	7	2	4	205	10.7	5	82	53.7	20:40	4	0	0	0	2	0	0	0	21:10
2002-03	Philadelphia	NHL	79	20	32	52	35	8	1	3	171	11.7	0	168	52.4	18:50	13	7	3	10	2	1	0	1	18:00
2003-04	Philadelphia	NHL	82	26	49	75	47	14	1	5	167	15.6	18	298	52.4	17:12	18	4	2	6	4	2	0	0	16:46
2004-05			Did not play																						
	NHL Totals		1173	456	745	1201	780	146	18	74	2897	15.7		1282	49.1	20:03	110	40	57	97	59	14	0	7	19:53

WHL West First All-Star Team (1988) • IHL Second All-Star Team (1989) • NHL Second All-Star Team (1992)

Played in NHL All-Star Game (1991, 1993, 1994, 1997, 1998, 1999, 2000)

Traded to **Philadelphia** by **Pittsburgh** with Brian Benning and Los Angeles' 1st round choice (previously acquired, Philadelphia selected Jason Bowen) in 1992 Entry Draft for Rick Tocchet, Kjell Samuelsson, Ken Wregget and Philadelphia's 3rd round choice (Dave Roche) in 1993 Entry Draft, February 19, 1992. Traded to **Montreal** by **Philadelphia** with Philadelphia's 3rd round choice (Martin Hohenberger) in 1995 Entry Draft for Eric Desjardins, Gilbert Dionne and John LeClair, February 9, 1995. Traded to **Philadelphia** by **Montreal** for Danius Zubrus, Philadelphia's 2nd round choice (Matt Carkner) in 1999 Entry Draft and NY Islanders' 6th round choice (previously acquired, Montreal selected Scott Selig) in 2000 Entry Draft, March 10, 1999. Signed as a free agent by **Pittsburgh**, July 9, 2004.

REDDEN, Wade

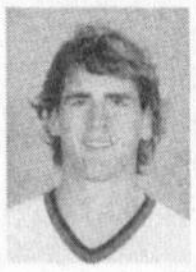

(REH-duhn, WAYD) **OTT.**

Defense. Shoots left. 6'2", 205 lbs. Born, Lloydminster, Sask., June 12, 1977. NY Islanders' 1st choice, 2nd overall, in 1995 Entry Draft.

			Regular Season														Playoffs								
Season	Club	League	GP	G	A	Pts	PIM	PP	SH	GW	S	%	+/-	TF	F%	Min	GP	G	A	Pts	PIM	PP	SH	GW	Min
1992-93	Lloydminster	AJHL	34	4	11	15	64	....	....	....	....	....	....	....	....	....	....	....	....	....	....	....	....	....	....
1993-94	Brandon	WHL	63	4	35	39	98	....	....	....	....	....	....	....	....	....	14	2	4	6	10	....	....	....	....
1994-95	Brandon	WHL	64	14	46	60	83	....	....	....	....	....	....	....	....	....	18	5	10	15	8	....	....	....	....
1995-96	Brandon	WHL	51	9	45	54	55	....	....	....	....	....	....	....	....	....	19	5	10	15	19	....	....	....	....
1996-97	**Ottawa**	**NHL**	**82**	**6**	**24**	**30**	**41**	**2**	**0**	**1**	**102**	**5.9**	**1**	....	....	....	**7**	**1**	**3**	**4**	**2**	**0**	**0**	**0**	....
1997-98	**Ottawa**	**NHL**	**80**	**8**	**14**	**22**	**27**	**3**	**0**	**2**	**103**	**7.8**	**17**	....	....	....	**9**	**0**	**2**	**2**	**2**	**0**	**0**	**0**	....
1998-99	**Ottawa**	**NHL**	**72**	**8**	**21**	**29**	**54**	**3**	**0**	**1**	**127**	**6.3**	**7**	**0**	**0.0**	**23:27**	**4**	**1**	**2**	**3**	**2**	**1**	**0**	**0**	**26:39**
99-2000	**Ottawa**	**NHL**	**81**	**10**	**26**	**36**	**49**	**3**	**0**	**2**	**163**	**6.1**	**−1**	**0**	**0.0**	**23:43**	....	....	....	....	....	....	....	....	....
2000-01	**Ottawa**	**NHL**	**78**	**10**	**37**	**47**	**49**	**4**	**0**	**0**	**159**	**6.3**	**22**	**0**	**0.0**	**25:17**	**4**	**0**	**0**	**0**	**0**	**0**	**0**	**0**	**27:29**
2001-02	**Ottawa**	**NHL**	**79**	**9**	**25**	**34**	**48**	**4**	**1**	**1**	**156**	**5.8**	**22**	**1**	**0.0**	**25:06**	**12**	**3**	**2**	**5**	**6**	**1**	**0**	**1**	**27:56**
2002-03	**Ottawa**	**NHL**	**76**	**10**	**35**	**45**	**70**	**4**	**0**	**3**	**154**	**6.5**	**23**	**0**	**0.0**	**25:24**	**18**	**1**	**8**	**9**	**10**	**0**	**0**	**1**	**25:28**
2003-04	**Ottawa**	**NHL**	**81**	**17**	**26**	**43**	**65**	**12**	**0**	**3**	**175**	**9.7**	**21**	**0**	**0.0**	**24:54**	**7**	**1**	**0**	**1**	**2**	**1**	**0**	**0**	**26:47**
2004-05			DID NOT PLAY																						
	NHL Totals		**629**	**78**	**208**	**286**	**403**	**35**	**1**	**13**	**1139**	**6.8**		**1**	**0.0**	**24:39**	**61**	**7**	**17**	**24**	**24**	**3**	**0**	**2**	**26:37**

WHL Rookie of the Year (1994) • WHL East Second All-Star Team (1995) • WHL East First All-Star Team (1996) • Memorial Cup Tournament All-Star Team (1996)
Played in NHL All-Star Game (2002)
Traded to **Ottawa** by **NY Islanders** with Damian Rhodes for Don Beaupre, Martin Straka and Bryan Berard, January 23, 1996.

REGEHR, Robyn

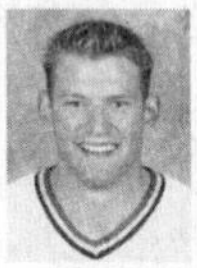

(reh-GEER, RAW-bihn) **CGY.**

Defense. Shoots left. 6'2", 226 lbs. Born, Recife, Brazil, April 19, 1980. Colorado's 3rd choice, 19th overall, in 1998 Entry Draft.

Season	Club	League	GP	G	A	Pts	PIM	PP	SH	GW	S	%	+/-	TF	F%	Min	GP	G	A	Pts	PIM	PP	SH	GW	Min
1995-96	Prince Albert	SMHL	59	8	24	32	157	....	....	....	....	....	....	....	....	....	....	....	....	....	....	....	....	....	....
1996-97	Kamloops Blazers	WHL	64	4	19	23	96	....	....	....	....	....	....	....	....	....	5	0	1	1	18	....	....	....	....
1997-98	Kamloops Blazers	WHL	65	4	10	14	120	....	....	....	....	....	....	....	....	....	5	0	3	3	8	....	....	....	....
1998-99	Kamloops Blazers	WHL	54	12	20	32	130	....	....	....	....	....	....	....	....	....	12	1	4	5	21	....	....	....	....
99-2000	**Calgary**	**NHL**	**57**	**5**	**7**	**12**	**46**	**2**	**0**	**0**	**64**	**7.8**	**−2**	**0**	**0.0**	**18:24**	....	....	....	....	....	....	....	....	....
	Saint John Flames	AHL	5	0	0	0	0	....	....	....	....	....	....	....	....	....	....	....	....	....	....	....	....	....	....
2000-01	**Calgary**	**NHL**	**71**	**1**	**3**	**4**	**70**	**0**	**0**	**0**	**62**	**1.6**	**−7**	**1**	**0.0**	**19:43**	....	....	....	....	....	....	....	....	....
2001-02	**Calgary**	**NHL**	**77**	**2**	**6**	**8**	**93**	**0**	**0**	**0**	**82**	**2.4**	**−24**	**0**	**0.0**	**20:54**	....	....	....	....	....	....	....	....	....
2002-03	**Calgary**	**NHL**	**76**	**0**	**12**	**12**	**87**	**0**	**0**	**0**	**109**	**0.0**	**−9**	**1**	**100.0**	**22:45**	....	....	....	....	....	....	....	....	....
2003-04	**Calgary**	**NHL**	**82**	**4**	**14**	**18**	**74**	**2**	**0**	**1**	**106**	**3.8**	**14**	**2**	**50.0**	**22:21**	**26**	**2**	**7**	**9**	**20**	**0**	**0**	**0**	**26:27**
2004-05			DID NOT PLAY																						
	NHL Totals		**363**	**12**	**42**	**54**	**370**	**4**	**0**	**1**	**423**	**2.8**		**4**	**50.0**	**20:59**	**26**	**2**	**7**	**9**	**20**	**0**	**0**	**0**	**26:27**

WHL West First All-Star Team (1999)
Traded to **Calgary** by **Colorado** with Rene Corbet, Wade Belak and Colorado's 2nd round compensatory choice (Jarret Stoll) in 2000 Entry Draft for Theoren Fleury and Chris Dingman, February 28, 1999.

REICH, Jeremy

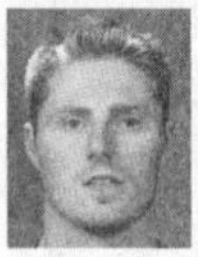

(REECH, JAIR-eh-MEE) **BOS.**

Left wing. Shoots left. 6'1", 204 lbs. Born, Craik, Sask., February 11, 1979. Chicago's 3rd choice, 39th overall, in 1997 Entry Draft.

Season	Club	League	GP	G	A	Pts	PIM	PP	SH	GW	S	%	+/-	TF	F%	Min	GP	G	A	Pts	PIM	PP	SH	GW	Min
1993-94	Pilote Butte	SAHA	80	70	65	135	120	....	....	....	....	....	....	....	....	....	....	....	....	....	....	....	....	....	....
1994-95	Sask. Contacts	SMHL	35	13	20	33	81	....	....	....	....	....	....	....	....	....	....	....	....	....	....	....	....	....	....
1995-96	Seattle	WHL	65	11	11	22	88	....	....	....	....	....	....	....	....	....	5	0	1	1	10	....	....	....	....
1996-97	Seattle	WHL	62	19	31	50	134	....	....	....	....	....	....	....	....	....	15	2	5	7	36	....	....	....	....
1997-98	Seattle	WHL	43	24	23	47	121	....	....	....	....	....	....	....	....	....	....	....	....	....	....	....	....	....	....
	Swift Current	WHL	22	8	8	16	47	....	....	....	....	....	....	....	....	....	12	5	6	11	37	....	....	....	....
1998-99	Swift Current	WHL	67	21	28	49	220	....	....	....	....	....	....	....	....	....	6	0	3	3	26	....	....	....	....
99-2000	Swift Current	WHL	72	33	58	91	167	....	....	....	....	....	....	....	....	....	12	2	10	12	19	....	....	....	....
2000-01	Syracuse Crunch	AHL	56	6	9	15	108	....	....	....	....	....	....	....	....	....	5	0	0	0	6	....	....	....	....
2001-02	Syracuse Crunch	AHL	59	9	7	16	178	....	....	....	....	....	....	....	....	....	10	4	0	4	16	....	....	....	....
2002-03	Syracuse Crunch	AHL	78	14	13	27	195	....	....	....	....	....	....	....	....	....	....	....	....	....	....	....	....	....	....
2003-04	**Columbus**	**NHL**	**9**	**0**	**1**	**1**	**20**	**0**	**0**	**0**	**3**	**0.0**	**−3**	**0**	**0.0**	**7:38**	....	....	....	....	....	....	....	....	....
	Syracuse Crunch	AHL	72	14	37	51	150	....	....	....	....	....	....	....	....	....	6	1	1	2	13	....	....	....	....
2004-05	Syracuse Crunch	AHL	50	4	5	9	189	....	....	....	....	....	....	....	....	....	....	....	....	....	....	....	....	....	....
	Houston Aeros	AHL	18	3	4	7	34	....	....	....	....	....	....	....	....	....	5	0	1	1	28	....	....	....	....
	NHL Totals		**9**	**0**	**1**	**1**	**20**	**0**	**0**	**0**	**3**	**0.0**		**0**	**0.0**	**7:38**	....	....	....	....	....	....	....	....	....

Signed as a free agent by **Columbus**, May 17, 2000. Loaned to **Houston** (AHL) by **Syracuse** (AHL) for the loan of Jason Beckett, March 10, 2005. Signed as a free agent by **Boston**, August 30, 2005.

REICHEL, Robert

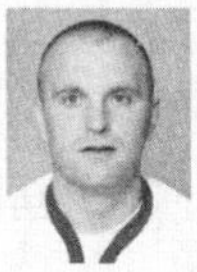

(RIGH-khul, RAW-buhrt)

Center. Shoots left. 5'10", 180 lbs. Born, Litvinov, Czech., June 25, 1971. Calgary's 5th choice, 70th overall, in 1989 Entry Draft.

Season	Club	League	GP	G	A	Pts	PIM	PP	SH	GW	S	%	+/-	TF	F%	Min	GP	G	A	Pts	PIM	PP	SH	GW	Min
1987-88	CHZ Litvinov	Czech	36	17	10	27	8	....	....	....	....	....	....	....	....	....	....	....	....	....	....	....	....	....	....
1988-89	CHZ Litvinov	Czech	44	23	25	48	32	....	....	....	....	....	....	....	....	....	....	....	....	....	....	....	....	....	....
1989-90	CHZ Litvinov	Czech	44	*43	28	*71	....	....	....	....	....	....	....	....	....	....	8	6	6	12	....	....	....	....	....
1990-91	**Calgary**	**NHL**	**66**	**19**	**22**	**41**	**22**	**3**	**0**	**3**	**131**	**14.5**	**17**	....	....	....	**6**	**1**	**1**	**2**	**0**	**1**	**0**	**0**	....
1991-92	**Calgary**	**NHL**	**77**	**20**	**34**	**54**	**32**	**8**	**0**	**3**	**181**	**11.0**	**1**	....	....	....	....	....	....	....	....	....	....	....	....
1992-93	**Calgary**	**NHL**	**80**	**40**	**48**	**88**	**54**	**12**	**0**	**5**	**238**	**16.8**	**25**	....	....	....	**6**	**2**	**4**	**6**	**2**	**2**	**0**	**0**	....
1993-94	**Calgary**	**NHL**	**84**	**40**	**53**	**93**	**58**	**14**	**0**	**6**	**249**	**16.1**	**20**	....	....	....	**7**	**0**	**5**	**5**	**0**	**0**	**0**	**0**	....
1994-95	Frankfurt Lions	Germany	21	19	24	43	41	....	....	....	....	....	....	....	....	....	....	....	....	....	....	....	....	....	....
	Calgary	**NHL**	**48**	**18**	**17**	**35**	**28**	**5**	**0**	**2**	**160**	**11.3**	**−2**	....	....	....	**7**	**2**	**4**	**6**	**4**	**0**	**0**	**1**	....
1995-96	Frankfurt Lions	Germany	46	47	54	101	84	....	....	....	....	....	....	....	....	....	3	1	3	4	0	....	....	....	....
1996-97	**Calgary**	**NHL**	**70**	**16**	**27**	**43**	**22**	**6**	**0**	**3**	**181**	**8.8**	**−2**	....	....	....	....	....	....	....	....	....	....	....	....
	NY Islanders	**NHL**	**12**	**5**	**14**	**19**	**4**	**0**	**1**	**0**	**33**	**15.2**	**7**	....	....	....	....	....	....	....	....	....	....	....	....
1997-98	**NY Islanders**	**NHL**	**82**	**25**	**40**	**65**	**32**	**8**	**0**	**2**	**201**	**12.4**	**−11**	....	....	....	....	....	....	....	....	....	....	....	....
	Czech Republic	Olympics	6	3	0	3	0	....	....	....	....	....	....	....	....	....	....	....	....	....	....	....	....	....	....
1998-99	**NY Islanders**	**NHL**	**70**	**19**	**37**	**56**	**50**	**5**	**1**	**1**	**186**	**10.2**	**−15**	**1241**	**51.7**	**19:36**	....	....	....	....	....	....	....	....	....
	Phoenix	**NHL**	**13**	**7**	**6**	**13**	**4**	**3**	**0**	**3**	**50**	**14.0**	**2**	**241**	**48.5**	**20:03**	**7**	**1**	**3**	**4**	**2**	**0**	**0**	**0**	**18:56**
99-2000	Litvinov	CzRep	45	25	32	57	24	....	....	....	....	....	....	....	....	....	7	3	4	7	2	....	....	....	....
2000-01	Litvinov	CzRep	49	23	33	56	72	....	....	....	....	....	....	....	....	....	5	1	2	3	4	....	....	....	....
2001-02	**Toronto**	**NHL**	**78**	**20**	**31**	**51**	**26**	**1**	**0**	**3**	**152**	**13.2**	**7**	**1045**	**49.6**	**15:11**	**18**	**0**	**3**	**3**	**4**	**0**	**0**	**0**	**12:40**
	Czech Republic	Olympics	4	1	0	1	2	....	....	....	....	....	....	....	....	....	....	....	....	....	....	....	....	....	....
2002-03	**Toronto**	**NHL**	**81**	**12**	**30**	**42**	**26**	**1**	**1**	**1**	**111**	**10.8**	**7**	**1123**	**52.2**	**14:33**	**7**	**2**	**1**	**3**	**0**	**0**	**0**	**0**	**20:54**
2003-04	**Toronto**	**NHL**	**69**	**11**	**19**	**30**	**30**	**2**	**0**	**2**	**100**	**11.0**	**2**	**1002**	**53.1**	**15:30**	**12**	**0**	**2**	**2**	**8**	**0**	**0**	**0**	**17:10**
2004-05	Litvinov	CzRep	32	9	19	28	32	....	....	....	....	....	....	....	....	....	....	....	....	....	....	....	....	....	....
	NHL Totals		**830**	**252**	**378**	**630**	**388**	**68**	**3**	**34**	**1973**	**12.8**		**4652**	**51.5**	**16:17**	**70**	**8**	**23**	**31**	**20**	**3**	**0**	**1**	**16:12**

Traded to **NY Islanders** by **Calgary** for Marty McInnis, Tyrone Garner and Calgary's 6th round choice (previously acquired, Calgary selected Ilja Demidov) in 1997 Entry Draft, March 18, 1997. Traded to **Phoenix** by **NY Islanders** with NY Islanders' 3rd round choice (Jason Jaspers) in 1999 Entry Draft and Ottawa's 4th round choice (previously acquired, Phoenix selected Preston Mizzi) in 1999 Entry Draft for Brad Isbister and Phoenix's 3rd round choice (Brian Collins) in 1999 Entry Draft, March 20, 1999. Traded to **Toronto** by **Phoenix** with Travis Green and Craig Mills for Danny Markov, June 12, 2001. Signed as a free agent by **Litvinov** (Czech), August 19, 2004.

REID, Brandon

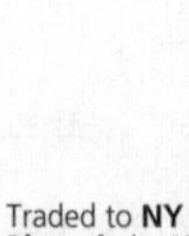

(REED, BRAN-duhn) **VAN.**

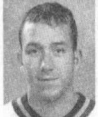

Center. Shoots right. 5'8", 185 lbs. Born, Kirkland, Que., March 9, 1981. Vancouver's 5th choice, 208th overall, in 2000 Entry Draft.

Season	Club	League	GP	G	A	Pts	PIM	PP	SH	GW	S	%	+/-	TF	F%	Min	GP	G	A	Pts	PIM	PP	SH	GW	Min
1996-97	Lac St-Louis Lions	QAAA	44	17	34	51	....	....	....	....	....	....	....	....	....	....	7	2	3	5	....	....	....	....	....
1997-98	Halifax	QMJHL	67	13	21	36	6	....	....	....	....	....	....	....	....	....	5	1	0	1	15	....	....	....	....
1998-99	Halifax	QMJHL	70	32	25	57	33	....	....	....	....	....	....	....	....	....	5	2	2	4	0	....	....	....	....
99-2000	Halifax	QMJHL	62	44	80	124	10	....	....	....	....	....	....	....	....	....	10	7	11	18	4	....	....	....	....
2000-01	Val-d'Or Foreurs	QMJHL	57	45	81	126	18	....	....	....	....	....	....	....	....	....	21	13	29	42	14	....	....	....	....
2001-02	Manitoba Moose	AHL	60	18	19	37	6	....	....	....	....	....	....	....	....	....	7	0	3	3	0	....	....	....	....
2002-03	**Vancouver**	**NHL**	**7**	**2**	**3**	**5**	**0**	**0**	**0**	**0**	**15**	**13.3**	**4**	**69**	**55.1**	**9:47**	**9**	**0**	**1**	**1**	**0**	**0**	**0**	**0**	**9:36**
	Manitoba Moose	AHL	73	18	36	54	18	....	....	....	....	....	....	....	....	....	1	1	1	2	0	....	....	....	....

			Regular Season														Playoffs								
Season	Club	League	GP	G	A	Pts	PIM	PP	SH	GW	S	%	+/-	TF	F%	Min	GP	G	A	Pts	PIM	PP	SH	GW	Min
2003-04	Vancouver	NHL	3	0	1	1	0	0	0	0	2	0.0	1	38	47.4	9:21	....	....	....	....	....	....	....	....	....
	Manitoba Moose	AHL	73	19	39	58	20	....	....	....	....	....	....	....	....	....	....	....	....	....	....	....	....	....	....
2004-05	Hamburg Freezers	Germany	45	18	29	47	41	....	....	....	....	....	....	....	....	....	6	0	3	3	4	....	....	....	....
	NHL Totals		10	2	4	6	0	0	0	0	17	11.8		107	52.3	9:40	9	0	1	1	0	0	0	0	9:36

QMJHL Second All-Star Team (2000) • George Parsons Trophy (Memorial Cup Tournament Most Sportsmanlike Player) (2000, 2001) • QMJHL First All-Star Team (2001) • Canadian Major Junior Sportsman of the Year (2001)

Signed as a free agent by **Hamburg** (Germany), July 7, 2004. Signed as a free agent by **Rapperswil** (Swiss), April 1, 2005.

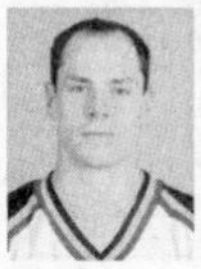

REINPRECHT, Steve

(REIGHN-prehkt, STEEV) **CGY.**

Center. Shoots left. 6', 195 lbs. Born, Edmonton, Alta., May 7, 1976.

			Regular Season														Playoffs								
Season	Club	League	GP	G	A	Pts	PIM	PP	SH	GW	S	%	+/-	TF	F%	Min	GP	G	A	Pts	PIM	PP	SH	GW	Min
1993-94	Edmonton SSAC	AMHL	71	48	77	125	....	....	....	....	....	....	....	....	....	....	....	....	....	....	....	....	....	....	....
1994-95	St. Albert Saints	AJHL	56	35	44	79	14	....	....	....	....	....	....	....	....	....	....	....	....	....	....	....	....	....	....
1995-96	St. Albert Saints	AJHL	39	24	33	57	16	....	....	....	....	....	....	....	....	....	....	....	....	....	....	....	....	....	....
1996-97	U. of Wisconsin	WCHA	38	11	9	20	12	....	....	....	....	....	....	....	....	....	....	....	....	....	....	....	....	....	....
1997-98	U. of Wisconsin	WCHA	41	19	24	43	18	....	....	....	....	....	....	....	....	....	....	....	....	....	....	....	....	....	....
1998-99	U. of Wisconsin	WCHA	38	16	17	33	14	....	....	....	....	....	....	....	....	....	....	....	....	....	....	....	....	....	....
99-2000	U. of Wisconsin	WCHA	37	26	40	*66	14	....	....	....	....	....	....	....	....	....	....	....	....	....	....	....	....	....	....
	Los Angeles	NHL	1	0	0	0	2	0	0	0	0	0.0	0	6	50.0	6:01	....	....	....	....	....	....	....	....	....
2000-01	Los Angeles	NHL	59	12	17	29	12	3	2	3	72	16.7	11	676	41.4	12:39	....	....	....	....	....	....	....	....	....
	♦ Colorado	NHL	21	3	4	7	2	0	0	0	28	10.7	–1	209	51.2	15:38	22	2	3	5	2	0	0	0	12:09
2001-02	Colorado	NHL	67	19	27	46	18	4	0	3	111	17.1	14	413	52.1	16:32	21	7	5	12	8	0	0	2	16:23
2002-03	Colorado	NHL	77	18	33	51	18	2	1	1	146	12.3	–6	928	46.4	17:22	7	1	2	3	0	0	0	0	15:32
2003-04	Calgary	NHL	44	7	22	29	4	3	0	1	68	10.3	1	120	40.0	17:05	....	....	....	....	....	....	....	....	....
2004-05	HC Mulhouse	France	22	20	27	47	6	....	....	....	....	....	....	....	....	....	10	7	6	13	2	....	....	....	....
	NHL Totals		269	59	103	162	56	12	3	8	425	13.9		2352	46.1	15:54	50	10	10	20	10	0	0	2	14:24

WCHA Second All-Star Team (1998) • WCHA First All-Star Team (2000) • WCHA Player of the Year (2000) • NCAA West First All-American Team (2000)

Signed as a free agent by **Los Angeles**, March 31, 2000. Traded to **Colorado** by **Los Angeles** with Rob Blake for Adam Deadmarsh, Aaron Miller, a player to be named later (Jared Aulin, March 22, 2001) and Colorado's 1st round choices in 2001 (Dave Steckel) and 2003 (Brian Boyle) Entry Drafts, February 21, 2001. Traded to **Buffalo** by **Colorado** for Keith Ballard, July 3, 2003. Traded to **Calgary** by **Buffalo** with Rhett Warrener for Chris Drury and Steve Begin, July 3, 2003. Signed as a free agent by **Mulhouse** (France), September 28, 2004.

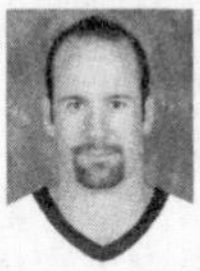

REIRDEN, Todd

(REER-dehn, TAWD)

Defense. Shoots left. 6'5", 225 lbs. Born, Deerfield, IL, June 25, 1971. New Jersey's 14th choice, 242nd overall, in 1990 Entry Draft.

			Regular Season														Playoffs								
Season	Club	League	GP	G	A	Pts	PIM	PP	SH	GW	S	%	+/-	TF	F%	Min	GP	G	A	Pts	PIM	PP	SH	GW	Min
1987-88	Deerfield	High-MA	22	19	32	51	....	....	....	....	....	....	....	....	....	....	....	....	....	....	....	....	....	....	....
1988-89	Tabor	High-MA	22	6	16	22	....	....	....	....	....	....	....	....	....	....	....	....	....	....	....	....	....	....	....
1989-90	Tabor	High-MA	22	10	28	38	....	....	....	....	....	....	....	....	....	....	....	....	....	....	....	....	....	....	....
1990-91	Bowling Green	CCHA	28	1	5	6	22	....	....	....	....	....	....	....	....	....	....	....	....	....	....	....	....	....	....
1991-92	Bowling Green	CCHA	33	8	7	15	34	....	....	....	....	....	....	....	....	....	....	....	....	....	....	....	....	....	....
1992-93	Bowling Green	CCHA	41	8	17	25	48	....	....	....	....	....	....	....	....	....	....	....	....	....	....	....	....	....	....
1993-94	Bowling Green	CCHA	38	7	23	30	56	....	....	....	....	....	....	....	....	....	....	....	....	....	....	....	....	....	....
1994-95	Albany River Rats	AHL	2	0	1	1	2	....	....	....	....	....	....	....	....	....	....	....	....	....	....	....	....	....	....
	Raleigh IceCaps	ECHL	26	2	13	15	33	....	....	....	....	....	....	....	....	....	....	....	....	....	....	....	....	....	....
	Tallahassee	ECHL	43	5	25	30	61	....	....	....	....	....	....	....	....	....	13	2	5	7	40	....	....	....	....
1995-96	Tallahassee	ECHL	7	1	3	4	10	....	....	....	....	....	....	....	....	....	....	....	....	....	....	....	....	....	....
	Jacksonville	ECHL	15	1	10	11	41	....	....	....	....	....	....	....	....	....	1	0	2	2	4	....	....	....	....
	Chicago Wolves	IHL	31	0	2	2	39	....	....	....	....	....	....	....	....	....	9	0	2	2	16	....	....	....	....
1996-97	Chicago Wolves	IHL	57	3	10	13	108	....	....	....	....	....	....	....	....	....	....	....	....	....	....	....	....	....	....
	San Antonio	IHL	23	2	5	7	51	....	....	....	....	....	....	....	....	....	9	0	1	1	17	....	....	....	....
1997-98	San Antonio	IHL	70	5	14	19	132	....	....	....	....	....	....	....	....	....	....	....	....	....	....	....	....	....	....
	Fort Wayne	IHL	11	2	2	4	16	....	....	....	....	....	....	....	....	....	4	0	2	2	4	....	....	....	....
1998-99	Edmonton	NHL	17	2	3	5	20	0	0	0	26	7.7	–1	0	0.0	17:17	....	....	....	....	....	....	....	....	....
	Hamilton	AHL	58	9	25	34	84	....	....	....	....	....	....	....	....	....	11	0	5	5	6	....	....	....	....
99-2000	St. Louis	NHL	56	4	21	25	32	0	0	1	77	5.2	18	1	0.0	18:18	4	0	1	1	0	0	0	0	13:43
2000-01	St. Louis	NHL	38	2	4	6	43	1	0	0	58	3.4	–2	2	50.0	16:50	1	0	0	0	0	0	0	0	2:52
	Worcester IceCats	AHL	7	2	6	8	20	....	....	....	....	....	....	....	....	....	....	....	....	....	....	....	....	....	....
2001-02	Atlanta	NHL	65	3	5	8	82	1	0	0	85	3.5	–25	1	0.0	18:02	....	....	....	....	....	....	....	....	....
2002-03	Cincinnati	AHL	58	7	13	20	97	....	....	....	....	....	....	....	....	....	....	....	....	....	....	....	....	....	....
2003-04	Phoenix	NHL	7	0	2	2	4	0	0	0	9	0.0	–4	0	0.0	15:22	....	....	....	....	....	....	....	....	....
	Cincinnati	AHL	39	3	8	11	42	....	....	....	....	....	....	....	....	....	....	....	....	....	....	....	....	....	....
	Springfield	AHL	34	6	7	13	42	....	....	....	....	....	....	....	....	....	....	....	....	....	....	....	....	....	....
2004-05	Houston Aeros	AHL	52	3	5	8	56	....	....	....	....	....	....	....	....	....	5	0	0	0	6	....	....	....	....
	NHL Totals		183	11	35	46	181	2	0	1	255	4.3		4	25.0	17:42	5	0	1	1	0	0	0	0	11:33

Signed as a free agent by **Edmonton**, September 17, 1998. Claimed on waivers by **St. Louis** from **Edmonton**, September 30, 1999. Signed as a free agent by **Atlanta**, July 16, 2001. Signed as a free agent by **Anaheim**, July 17, 2002. Traded to **Phoenix** by **Anaheim** for future considerations, January 17, 2004. Signed as a free agent by **Houston** (AHL), September 22, 2004.

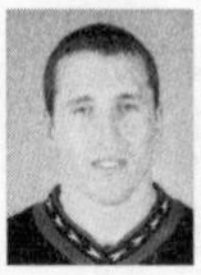

RHEAUME, Pascal

(RAY-awm, pas-KAL) **N.J.**

Center. Shoots left. 6'1", 220 lbs. Born, Quebec City, Que., June 21, 1973.

			Regular Season														Playoffs								
Season	Club	League	GP	G	A	Pts	PIM	PP	SH	GW	S	%	+/-	TF	F%	Min	GP	G	A	Pts	PIM	PP	SH	GW	Min
1990-91	Ste-Foy	QAAA	37	20	38	58	25	....	....	....	....	....	....	....	....	....	7	7	1	8	6	....	....	....	....
1991-92	Trois-Rivieres	QMJHL	65	17	20	37	84	....	....	....	....	....	....	....	....	....	14	5	4	9	23	....	....	....	....
1992-93	Sherbrooke	QMJHL	65	28	34	62	88	....	....	....	....	....	....	....	....	....	14	6	5	11	31	....	....	....	....
1993-94	Albany River Rats	AHL	55	17	18	35	43	....	....	....	....	....	....	....	....	....	5	0	1	1	0	....	....	....	....
1994-95	Albany River Rats	AHL	78	19	25	44	46	....	....	....	....	....	....	....	....	....	14	3	6	9	19	....	....	....	....
1995-96	Albany River Rats	AHL	68	26	42	68	50	....	....	....	....	....	....	....	....	....	4	1	2	3	2	....	....	....	....
1996-97	New Jersey	NHL	2	1	0	1	0	0	0	0	5	20.0	1	....	....	....	....	....	....	....	....	....	....	....	....
	Albany River Rats	AHL	51	22	23	45	40	....	....	....	....	....	....	....	....	....	16	2	8	10	16	....	....	....	....
1997-98	St. Louis	NHL	48	6	9	15	35	1	0	0	45	13.3	4	....	....	....	10	1	3	4	8	1	0	0	....
1998-99	St. Louis	NHL	60	9	18	27	24	2	0	0	85	10.6	10	21	71.4	13:19	5	1	0	1	4	0	0	0	11:36
99-2000	St. Louis	NHL	7	1	1	2	6	0	0	0	5	20.0	–2	2	0.0	10:08	....	....	....	....	....	....	....	....	....
	Worcester IceCats	AHL	7	1	1	2	4	....	....	....	....	....	....	....	....	....	....	....	....	....	....	....	....	....	....
2000-01	St. Louis	NHL	8	2	0	2	5	2	0	0	16	12.5	–1	7	42.9	11:56	3	0	1	1	0	0	0	0	11:30
	Worcester IceCats	AHL	56	23	35	58	63	....	....	....	....	....	....	....	....	....	11	2	4	6	2	....	....	....	....
2001-02	Chicago	NHL	19	0	2	2	4	0	0	0	19	0.0	–1	165	51.5	9:22	....	....	....	....	....	....	....	....	....
	Atlanta	NHL	42	11	9	20	25	6	0	2	61	18.0	–3	510	45.9	14:27	....	....	....	....	....	....	....	....	....
2002-03	Atlanta	NHL	56	4	9	13	24	0	2	1	70	5.7	–8	602	46.8	12:17	....	....	....	....	....	....	....	....	....
	♦ New Jersey	NHL	21	4	1	5	8	0	1	1	23	17.4	3	248	51.6	11:50	24	1	2	3	13	0	0	0	13:32
2003-04	NY Rangers	NHL	17	0	0	0	5	0	0	0	15	0.0	–3	46	56.5	10:02	....	....	....	....	....	....	....	....	....
	Hartford	AHL	3	1	0	1	0	....	....	....	....	....	....	....	....	....	....	....	....	....	....	....	....	....	....
	St. Louis	NHL	25	1	3	4	4	0	0	0	23	4.3	–3	26	38.5	10:19	3	0	0	0	2	0	0	0	6:55
2004-05	Albany River Rats	AHL	78	24	25	49	85	....	....	....	....	....	....	....	....	....	....	....	....	....	....	....	....	....	....
	NHL Totals		305	39	52	91	140	11	3	4	367	10.6		1627	48.1	12:13	45	3	6	9	27	1	0	0	12:31

Signed as a free agent by **New Jersey**, October 1, 1993. Claimed by **St. Louis** from **New Jersey** in Waiver Draft, September 28, 1997. • Missed majority of 1999-2000 season recovering from shoulder surgery, August, 1999. Signed as a free agent by **Chicago**, July 31, 2001. Claimed on waivers by **Atlanta** from **Chicago**, November 14, 2001. Traded to **New Jersey** by **Atlanta** for future considerations, February 24, 2003. Signed as a free agent by **NY Rangers**, October 22, 2003. Claimed on waivers by **St. Louis** from **NY Rangers**, January 29, 2004. Signed as a free agent by **New Jersey**, August 13, 2004.

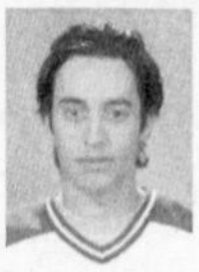

RIBEIRO, Mike

(rih-bee-AIR-roh, MIGHK) **MTL.**

Center. Shoots left. 6', 177 lbs. Born, Montreal, Que., February 10, 1980. Montreal's 2nd choice, 45th overall, in 1998 Entry Draft.

			Regular Season														Playoffs								
Season	Club	League	GP	G	A	Pts	PIM	PP	SH	GW	S	%	+/-	TF	F%	Min	GP	G	A	Pts	PIM	PP	SH	GW	Min
1996-97	Mtl-Bourassa	QAAA	43	32	57	89	48	....	....	....	....	....	....	....	....	....	16	15	23	38	14	....	....	....	....
1997-98	Rouyn-Noranda	QMJHL	67	40	*85	125	55	....	....	....	....	....	....	....	....	....	6	3	1	4	0	....	....	....	....
1998-99	Rouyn-Noranda	QMJHL	69	*67	*100	*167	137	....	....	....	....	....	....	....	....	....	11	5	11	16	12	....	....	....	....
	Fredericton	AHL	....	....	....	....	....	....	....	....	....	....	....	....	....	....	5	0	1	1	2	....	....	....	....
99-2000	Montreal	NHL	19	1	1	2	2	1	0	0	18	5.6	–6	95	34.7	10:40	....	....	....	....	....	....	....	....	....
	Quebec Citadelles	AHL	3	0	0	0	2	....	....	....	....	....	....	....	....	....	....	....	....	....	....	....	....	....	....
	Rouyn-Noranda	QMJHL	2	1	3	4	0	....	....	....	....	....	....	....	....	....	....	....	....	....	....	....	....	....	....
	Quebec Remparts	QMJHL	21	17	28	45	30	....	....	....	....	....	....	....	....	....	11	3	20	23	38	....	....	....	....
2000-01	Montreal	NHL	2	0	0	0	2	0	0	0	3	0.0	0	11	18.2	10:38	....	....	....	....	....	....	....	....	....
	Quebec Citadelles	AHL	74	26	40	66	44	....	....	....	....	....	....	....	....	....	9	1	5	6	23	....	....	....	....

			Regular Season														Playoffs								
Season	Club	League	GP	G	A	Pts	PIM	PP	SH	GW	S	%	+/-	TF	F%	Min	GP	G	A	Pts	PIM	PP	SH	GW	Min
2001-02	**Montreal**	**NHL**	**43**	**8**	**10**	**18**	**12**	**3**	**0**	**0**	**48**	**16.7**	**–11**	**141**	**44.0**	**13:55**									
	Quebec Citadelles	AHL	23	9	14	23	36										3	0	3	3	0				
2002-03	**Montreal**	**NHL**	**52**	**5**	**12**	**17**	**6**	**2**	**0**	**0**	**57**	**8.8**	**–3**	**358**	**50.3**	**11:07**									
	Hamilton	AHL	3	0	1	1	0																		
2003-04	**Montreal**	**NHL**	**81**	**20**	**45**	**65**	**34**	**7**	**0**	**5**	**103**	**19.4**	**15**	**913**	**44.8**	**17:05**	**11**	**2**	**1**	**3**	**18**	**0**	**0**	**0**	**16:31**
2004-05	Blues Espoo	Finland	17	8	9	17	4																		
	NHL Totals		**197**	**34**	**68**	**102**	**56**	**13**	**0**	**5**	**229**	**14.8**		**1518**	**45.2**	**14:08**	**11**	**2**	**1**	**3**	**18**	**0**	**0**	**0**	**16:31**

QMJHL Second All-Star Team (1998) • QMJHL First All-Star Team (1999) • Canadian Major Junior First All-Star Team (1999)

Signed as a free agent by **Blues** (Finland), January 17, 2005.

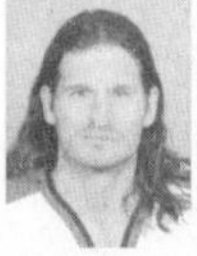

RICCI, Mike

(REE-CHEE, MIGHK) **PHX.**

Center. Shoots left. 6', 200 lbs. Born, Scarborough, Ont., October 27, 1971. Philadelphia's 1st choice, 4th overall, in 1990 Entry Draft.

Season	Club	League	GP	G	A	Pts	PIM	PP	SH	GW	S	%	+/-	TF	F%	Min	GP	G	A	Pts	PIM	PP	SH	GW	Min
1986-87	Toronto Marlies	MTHL	38	39	42	81	27																		
1987-88	Peterborough	OHL	41	24	37	61	20										8	5	5	10	4				
1988-89	Peterborough	OHL	60	54	52	106	43										17	19	16	35	18				
1989-90	Peterborough	OHL	60	52	64	116	39										12	5	7	12	26				
1990-91	**Philadelphia**	**NHL**	**68**	**21**	**20**	**41**	**64**	**9**	**0**	**4**	**121**	**17.4**	**–8**												
1991-92	**Philadelphia**	**NHL**	**78**	**20**	**36**	**56**	**93**	**11**	**2**	**0**	**149**	**13.4**	**–10**												
1992-93	**Quebec**	**NHL**	**77**	**27**	**51**	**78**	**123**	**12**	**1**	**10**	**142**	**19.0**	**8**				**6**	**0**	**6**	**6**	**8**	**0**	**0**	**0**	
1993-94	**Quebec**	**NHL**	**83**	**30**	**21**	**51**	**113**	**13**	**3**	**6**	**138**	**21.7**	**–9**												
1994-95	**Quebec**	**NHL**	**48**	**15**	**21**	**36**	**40**	**9**	**0**	**1**	**73**	**20.5**	**5**				**6**	**1**	**3**	**4**	**8**	**0**	**0**	**0**	
1995-96♦	**Colorado**	**NHL**	**62**	**6**	**21**	**27**	**52**	**3**	**0**	**1**	**73**	**8.2**	**1**				**22**	**6**	**11**	**17**	**18**	**3**	**0**	**1**	
1996-97	**Colorado**	**NHL**	**63**	**13**	**19**	**32**	**59**	**5**	**0**	**3**	**74**	**17.6**	**–3**				**17**	**2**	**4**	**6**	**17**	**0**	**0**	**1**	
1997-98	**Colorado**	**NHL**	**6**	**0**	**4**	**4**	**2**	**0**	**0**	**0**	**5**	**0.0**	**0**												
	San Jose	**NHL**	**59**	**9**	**14**	**23**	**30**	**5**	**0**	**2**	**86**	**10.5**	**–4**				**6**	**1**	**3**	**4**	**6**	**0**	**0**	**0**	
1998-99	**San Jose**	**NHL**	**82**	**13**	**26**	**39**	**68**	**2**	**1**	**2**	**98**	**13.3**	**1**	**1465**	**49.6**	**15:23**	**6**	**2**	**3**	**5**	**10**	**1**	**0**	**0**	**16:53**
99-2000	**San Jose**	**NHL**	**82**	**20**	**24**	**44**	**60**	**10**	**0**	**5**	**134**	**14.9**	**14**	**1522**	**50.7**	**16:52**	**12**	**5**	**1**	**6**	**2**	**3**	**0**	**1**	**17:37**
2000-01	**San Jose**	**NHL**	**81**	**22**	**22**	**44**	**60**	**9**	**2**	**4**	**141**	**15.6**	**3**	**1631**	**51.4**	**18:00**	**6**	**0**	**3**	**3**	**0**	**0**	**0**	**0**	**19:44**
2001-02	**San Jose**	**NHL**	**79**	**19**	**34**	**53**	**44**	**5**	**2**	**0**	**115**	**16.5**	**9**	**1501**	**49.0**	**17:04**	**12**	**4**	**6**	**10**	**4**	**0**	**0**	**1**	**19:51**
2002-03	**San Jose**	**NHL**	**75**	**11**	**23**	**34**	**53**	**5**	**1**	**2**	**101**	**10.9**	**–12**	**1152**	**51.6**	**16:31**									
2003-04	**San Jose**	**NHL**	**71**	**7**	**19**	**26**	**40**	**2**	**0**	**0**	**48**	**14.6**	**8**	**1116**	**54.8**	**14:21**	**17**	**2**	**3**	**5**	**4**	**0**	**0**	**0**	**15:31**
2004-05			DID NOT PLAY																						
	NHL Totals		**1014**	**233**	**355**	**588**	**901**	**100**	**12**	**40**	**1498**	**15.6**		**8387**	**51.0**	**16:24**	**110**	**23**	**43**	**66**	**77**	**7**	**0**	**4**	**17:36**

OHL Second All-Star Team (1989) • OHL First All-Star Team (1990) • OHL MVP (1990) • Canadian Major Junior Player of the Year (1990) • OHL First All-Star Team (1990)

Traded to **Quebec** by **Philadelphia** with Steve Duchesne, Peter Forsberg, Kerry Huffman, Ron Hextall, Philadelphia's 1st round choice (Jocelyn Thibault) in 1993 Entry Draft, $15,000,000 and future considerations (Chris Simon and Philadelphia's 1st round choice (later traded to Toronto – later traded to Washington – Washington selected Nolan Baumgartner) in 1994 Entry Draft, July 21, 1992) for Eric Lindros, June 30, 1992. Transferred to **Colorado** after **Quebec** franchise relocated, June 21, 1995. Traded to **San Jose** by **Colorado** with Colorado's 2nd round choice (later traded to Buffalo – Buffalo selected Jaroslav Kristek) in 1998 Entry Draft for Shean Donovan and San Jose's 1st round choice (Alex Tanguay) in 1998 Entry Draft, November 21, 1997. Signed as a free agent by **Phoenix**, July 9, 2004.

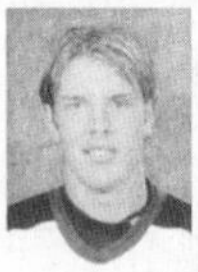

RICHARDS, Brad

(RIH-chahrds, BRAD) **T.B.**

Center. Shoots left. 6'1", 198 lbs. Born, Murray Harbour, P.E.I., May 2, 1980. Tampa Bay's 2nd choice, 64th overall, in 1998 Entry Draft.

Season	Club	League	GP	G	A	Pts	PIM	PP	SH	GW	S	%	+/-	TF	F%	Min	GP	G	A	Pts	PIM	PP	SH	GW	Min
1996-97	Notre Dame	SJHL	63	39	48	87	73																		
1997-98	Rimouski Oceanic	QMJHL	68	33	82	115	44										19	8	24	32	2				
1998-99	Rimouski Oceanic	QMJHL	59	39	92	131	55										11	9	12	21	6				
99-2000	Rimouski Oceanic	QMJHL	63	*71	*115	*186	69										12	13	*24	*37	16				
2000-01	**Tampa Bay**	**NHL**	**82**	**21**	**41**	**62**	**14**	**7**	**0**	**3**	**179**	**11.7**	**–10**	**955**	**41.4**	**16:54**									
2001-02	**Tampa Bay**	**NHL**	**82**	**20**	**42**	**62**	**13**	**5**	**0**	**0**	**251**	**8.0**	**–18**	**911**	**41.2**	**19:48**									
2002-03	**Tampa Bay**	**NHL**	**80**	**17**	**57**	**74**	**24**	**4**	**0**	**2**	**277**	**6.1**	**3**	**1007**	**47.5**	**19:56**	**11**	**0**	**5**	**5**	**12**	**0**	**0**	**0**	**22:21**
2003-04♦	**Tampa Bay**	**NHL**	**82**	**26**	**53**	**79**	**12**	**5**	**1**	**6**	**244**	**10.7**	**14**	**1167**	**46.7**	**20:26**	**23**	**12**	**14**	***26**	**4**	**7**	**0**	**7**	**23:28**
2004-05	Ak Bars Kazan	Russia	6	2	5	7	16																		
	NHL Totals		**326**	**84**	**193**	**277**	**63**	**21**	**1**	**11**	**951**	**8.8**		**4040**	**44.4**	**19:16**	**34**	**12**	**19**	**31**	**16**	**7**	**0**	**7**	**23:07**

QMJHL First All-Star Team (2000) • Canadian Major Junior First All-Star Team (2000) • Canadian Major Junior Player of the Year (2000) • Memorial Cup Tournament All-Star Team (2000) • Stafford Smythe Memorial Trophy (Memorial Cup Tournament MVP) (2000) • NHL All-Rookie Team (2001) • Lady Byng Trophy (2004) • Conn Smythe Trophy (2004)

Signed as a free agent by **Kazan** (Russia), November 8, 2004.

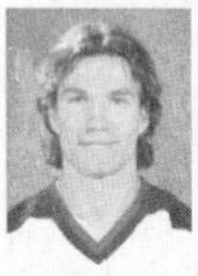

RICHARDSON, Luke

(RIH-chahrd-sohn, LEWK) **CBJ**

Defense. Shoots left. 6'4", 215 lbs. Born, Ottawa, Ont., March 26, 1969. Toronto's 1st choice, 7th overall, in 1987 Entry Draft.

Season	Club	League	GP	G	A	Pts	PIM	PP	SH	GW	S	%	+/-	TF	F%	Min	GP	G	A	Pts	PIM	PP	SH	GW	Min
1984-85	Ottawa Knights	OMHA	35	5	26	31	72																		
1985-86	Peterborough	OHL	63	6	18	24	57										16	2	1	3	50				
1986-87	Peterborough	OHL	59	13	32	45	70										12	0	5	5	24				
1987-88	**Toronto**	**NHL**	**78**	**4**	**6**	**10**	**90**	**0**	**0**	**0**	**49**	**8.2**	**–25**				**2**	**0**	**0**	**0**	**0**	**0**	**0**	**0**	
1988-89	**Toronto**	**NHL**	**55**	**2**	**7**	**9**	**106**	**0**	**0**	**0**	**59**	**3.4**	**–15**												
1989-90	**Toronto**	**NHL**	**67**	**4**	**14**	**18**	**122**	**0**	**0**	**0**	**80**	**5.0**	**–1**				**5**	**0**	**0**	**0**	**22**	**0**	**0**	**0**	
1990-91	**Toronto**	**NHL**	**78**	**1**	**9**	**10**	**238**	**0**	**0**	**0**	**68**	**1.5**	**–28**												
1991-92	**Edmonton**	**NHL**	**75**	**2**	**19**	**21**	**118**	**0**	**0**	**0**	**85**	**2.4**	**–9**				**16**	**0**	**5**	**5**	**45**	**0**	**0**	**0**	
1992-93	**Edmonton**	**NHL**	**82**	**3**	**10**	**13**	**142**	**0**	**2**	**0**	**78**	**3.8**	**–18**												
1993-94	**Edmonton**	**NHL**	**69**	**2**	**6**	**8**	**131**	**0**	**0**	**0**	**92**	**2.2**	**–13**												
1994-95	**Edmonton**	**NHL**	**46**	**3**	**10**	**13**	**40**	**1**	**1**	**1**	**51**	**5.9**	**–6**												
1995-96	**Edmonton**	**NHL**	**82**	**2**	**9**	**11**	**108**	**0**	**0**	**0**	**61**	**3.3**	**–27**												
1996-97	**Edmonton**	**NHL**	**82**	**1**	**11**	**12**	**91**	**0**	**0**	**0**	**67**	**1.5**	**9**				**12**	**0**	**2**	**2**	**14**	**0**	**0**	**0**	
1997-98	**Philadelphia**	**NHL**	**81**	**2**	**3**	**5**	**139**	**2**	**0**	**0**	**57**	**3.5**	**7**				**5**	**0**	**0**	**0**	**0**	**0**	**0**	**0**	
1998-99	**Philadelphia**	**NHL**	**78**	**0**	**6**	**6**	**106**	**0**	**0**	**0**	**49**	**0.0**	**–3**	**0**	**0.0**	**16:33**									
99-2000	**Philadelphia**	**NHL**	**74**	**2**	**5**	**7**	**140**	**0**	**0**	**1**	**50**	**4.0**	**14**	**0**	**0.0**	**16:11**	**18**	**0**	**1**	**1**	**41**	**0**	**0**	**0**	**21:58**
2000-01	**Philadelphia**	**NHL**	**82**	**2**	**6**	**8**	**131**	**0**	**1**	**0**	**75**	**2.7**	**23**	**1**	**0.0**	**20:42**	**6**	**0**	**0**	**0**	**4**	**0**	**0**	**0**	**24:39**
2001-02	**Philadelphia**	**NHL**	**72**	**1**	**8**	**9**	**102**	**0**	**0**	**0**	**65**	**1.5**	**18**	**0**	**0.0**	**18:17**	**5**	**0**	**0**	**0**	**4**	**0**	**0**	**0**	**19:18**
2002-03	**Columbus**	**NHL**	**82**	**0**	**13**	**13**	**73**	**0**	**0**	**0**	**56**	**0.0**	**–16**	**2**	**50.0**	**23:31**									
2003-04	**Columbus**	**NHL**	**64**	**1**	**5**	**6**	**48**	**0**	**0**	**1**	**34**	**2.9**	**–11**	**0**	**0.0**	**20:07**									
2004-05			DID NOT PLAY																						
	NHL Totals		**1247**	**32**	**147**	**179**	**1925**	**3**	**4**	**3**	**1076**	**3.0**		**3**	**33.3**	**19:17**	**69**	**0**	**8**	**8**	**130**	**0**	**0**	**0**	**22:04**

Traded to **Edmonton** by **Toronto** with Vincent Damphousse, Peter Ing and Scott Thornton for Grant Fuhr, Glenn Anderson and Craig Berube, September 19, 1991. Signed as a free agent by **Philadelphia**, July 23, 1997. Signed as a free agent by **Columbus**, July 4, 2002.

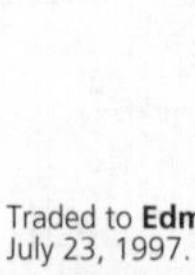

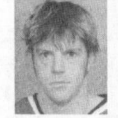

RISSMILLER, Pat

(RIGHZ-mih-luhr, PAT) **S.J.**

Left wing. Shoots left. 6'4", 210 lbs. Born, Belmont, MA, October 26, 1978.

Season	Club	League	GP	G	A	Pts	PIM	PP	SH	GW	S	%	+/-	TF	F%	Min	GP	G	A	Pts	PIM	PP	SH	GW	Min
1997-98	The Hill School	High-PA	STATISTICS NOT AVAILABLE																						
1998-99	Holy Cross	MAAC	34	13	28	41	23																		
99-2000	Holy Cross	MAAC	35	10	17	27	22																		
2000-01	Holy Cross	MAAC	29	14	15	29	40																		
2001-02	Holy Cross	MAAC	33	16	*30	*46	31																		
2002-03	Cleveland Barons	AHL	72	14	26	40	24																		
	Cincinnati	ECHL	2	2	2	4	0																		
2003-04	**San Jose**	**NHL**	**4**	**0**	**0**	**0**	**0**	**0**	**0**	**0**	**2**	**0.0**	**0**	**26**	**53.9**	**7:07**									
	Cleveland Barons	AHL	75	14	31	45	66										9	0	1	1	8				
2004-05	Cleveland Barons	AHL	69	21	23	44	50																		
	NHL Totals		**4**	**0**	**0**	**0**	**0**	**0**	**0**	**0**	**2**	**0.0**		**26**	**53.8**	**7:07**									

MAAC All-Rookie Team (1999) • MAAC First All-Star Team (2002) • MAAC Offensive Player of the Year (2002)

Signed as a free agent by **Cleveland** (AHL), September 23, 2002. Signed as a free agent by **San Jose**, June 30, 2003.

Season	Club	League	GP	G	A	Pts	PIM	PP	SH	GW	S	%	+/-	TF	F%	Min	GP	G	A	Pts	PIM	PP	SH	GW	Min
			Regular Season														Playoffs								

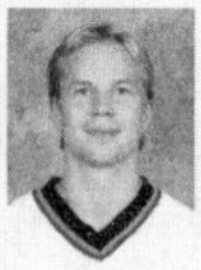

RITA, Jani

(REETA, YA-nee) **EDM.**

Left wing. Shoots left. 6'1", 206 lbs. Born, Helsinki, Finland, July 25, 1981. Edmonton's 1st choice, 13th overall, in 1999 Entry Draft.

Season	Club	League	GP	G	A	Pts	PIM	PP	SH	GW	S	%	+/-	TF	F%	Min	GP	G	A	Pts	PIM	PP	SH	GW	Min
1995-96	Jokerit U18	Fin-U18	5	0	0	0	0	....	....	....	....	....	....	....	....	....	....	....	....	....	....	....	....	....	....
1996-97	Jokerit U18	Fin-U18	27	22	7	29	4	....	....	....	....	....	....	....	....	....	....	....	....	....	....	....	....	....	....
1997-98	Jokerit U18	Fin-U18	7	7	4	11	2	....	....	....	....	....	....	....	....	....	....	....	....	....	....	....	....	....	....
	Jokerit Helsinki Jr.	Finland-Jr.	36	15	9	24	2	....	....	....	....	....	....	....	....	....	8	4	1	5	0	....	....	....	....
	Jokerit Helsinki	Finland	....	....	....	....	....	....	....	....	....	....	....	....	....	....	1	0	0	0	0	....	....	....	....
1998-99	Jokerit Helsinki Jr.	Finland-Jr.	20	9	13	22	8	....	....	....	....	....	....	....	....	....	....	....	....	....	....	....	....	....	....
	Jokerit Helsinki	Finland	41	3	2	5	39	....	....	....	....	....	....	....	....	....	....	....	....	....	....	....	....	....	....
	Jokerit Helsinki	EuroHL	3	0	0	0	0	....	....	....	....	....	....	....	....	....	....	....	....	....	....	....	....	....	....
99-2000	Jokerit Helsinki Jr.	Finland-Jr.	1	1	0	1	0	....	....	....	....	....	....	....	....	....	....	....	....	....	....	....	....	....	....
	Jokerit Helsinki	Finland	49	6	3	9	10	....	....	....	....	....	....	....	....	....	11	1	0	1	0	....	....	....	....
2000-01	Jokerit Helsinki Jr.	Finland-Jr.	3	3	2	5	0	....	....	....	....	....	....	....	....	....	....	....	....	....	....	....	....	....	....
	Jokerit Helsinki	Finland	50	5	10	15	18	....	....	....	....	....	....	....	....	....	5	0	0	0	2	....	....	....	....
2001-02	**Edmonton**	**NHL**	**1**	**0**	**0**	**0**	**0**	**0**	**0**	**0**	**0**	**0.0**	**0**	**0**	**0.0**	**6:09**	....	....	....	....	....	....	....	....	....
	Hamilton	AHL	76	25	17	42	32	....	....	....	....	....	....	....	....	....	15	8	4	12	0	....	....	....	....
2002-03	**Edmonton**	**NHL**	**12**	**3**	**1**	**4**	**0**	**0**	**0**	**0**	**18**	**16.7**	**2**	**1**	**0.0**	**9:32**	....	....	....	....	....	....	....	....	....
	Hamilton	AHL	64	21	27	48	18	....	....	....	....	....	....	....	....	....	23	3	4	7	2	....	....	....	....
2003-04	**Edmonton**	**NHL**	**2**	**0**	**0**	**0**	**0**	**0**	**0**	**0**	**1**	**0.0**	**0**	**0**	**0.0**	**4:34**	....	....	....	....	....	....	....	....	....
	Toronto	AHL	64	17	24	41	18	....	....	....	....	....	....	....	....	....	1	1	0	1	0	....	....	....	....
2004-05	HPK Hameenlinna	Finland	56	21	18	39	12	....	....	....	....	....	....	....	....	....	10	*7	4	11	4	....	....	....	....
	NHL Totals		**15**	**3**	**1**	**4**	**0**	**0**	**0**	**0**	**19**	**15.8**		**1**	**0.0**	**8:39**	....	....	....	....	....	....	....	....	....

Signed as a free agent by **HPK** (Finland), August 17, 2004.

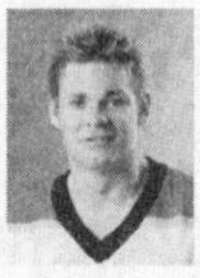

RITCHIE, Byron

(RIHT-chee, BIGH-rohn) **CGY.**

Center. Shoots left. 5'10", 195 lbs. Born, Burnaby, B.C., April 24, 1977. Hartford's 6th choice, 165th overall, in 1995 Entry Draft.

Season	Club	League	GP	G	A	Pts	PIM	PP	SH	GW	S	%	+/-	TF	F%	Min	GP	G	A	Pts	PIM	PP	SH	GW	Min
1992-93	North Delta	BCAHA	60	102	151	253	147	....	....	....	....	....	....	....	....	....	....	....	....	....	....	....	....	....	....
1993-94	Lethbridge	WHL	44	4	11	15	44	....	....	....	....	....	....	....	....	....	6	0	0	0	14	....	....	....	....
1994-95	Lethbridge	WHL	58	22	28	50	132	....	....	....	....	....	....	....	....	....	....	....	....	....	....	....	....	....	....
1995-96	Lethbridge	WHL	66	55	51	106	163	....	....	....	....	....	....	....	....	....	4	0	2	2	4	....	....	....	....
	Springfield	AHL	6	2	1	3	4	....	....	....	....	....	....	....	....	....	8	0	3	3	0	....	....	....	....
1996-97	Lethbridge	WHL	63	50	76	126	115	....	....	....	....	....	....	....	....	....	18	*16	12	*28	28	....	....	....	....
1997-98	New Haven	AHL	65	13	18	31	97	....	....	....	....	....	....	....	....	....	....	....	....	....	....	....	....	....	....
1998-99	**Carolina**	**NHL**	**3**	**0**	**0**	**0**	**0**	**0**	**0**	**0**	**0**	**0.0**	**0**	**5**	**20.0**	**3:25**	....	....	....	....	....	....	....	....	....
	New Haven	AHL	66	24	33	57	139	....	....	....	....	....	....	....	....	....	....	....	....	....	....	....	....	....	....
99-2000	**Carolina**	**NHL**	**26**	**0**	**2**	**2**	**17**	**0**	**0**	**0**	**13**	**0.0**	**–10**	**155**	**49.7**	**7:24**	....	....	....	....	....	....	....	....	....
	Cincinnati	IHL	34	8	13	21	81	....	....	....	....	....	....	....	....	....	10	1	6	7	32	....	....	....	....
2000-01	Cincinnati	IHL	77	31	35	66	166	....	....	....	....	....	....	....	....	....	5	3	2	5	10	....	....	....	....
2001-02	**Carolina**	**NHL**	**4**	**0**	**0**	**0**	**2**	**0**	**0**	**0**	**5**	**0.0**	**0**	**9**	**44.4**	**11:30**	....	....	....	....	....	....	....	....	....
	Lowell	AHL	43	25	30	55	38	....	....	....	....	....	....	....	....	....	....	....	....	....	....	....	....	....	....
	Florida	**NHL**	**31**	**5**	**6**	**11**	**34**	**2**	**0**	**0**	**55**	**9.1**	**–2**	**324**	**50.9**	**12:26**	....	....	....	....	....	....	....	....	....
2002-03	**Florida**	**NHL**	**30**	**0**	**3**	**3**	**19**	**0**	**0**	**0**	**29**	**0.0**	**–4**	**251**	**48.2**	**9:18**	....	....	....	....	....	....	....	....	....
	San Antonio	AHL	26	3	14	17	68	....	....	....	....	....	....	....	....	....	3	1	0	1	0	....	....	....	....
2003-04	**Florida**	**NHL**	**50**	**5**	**6**	**11**	**84**	**0**	**0**	**2**	**65**	**7.7**	**–10**	**168**	**48.8**	**13:54**	....	....	....	....	....	....	....	....	....
2004-05	Rogle	Sweden-2	30	17	16	33	111	....	....	....	....	....	....	....	....	....	2	0	0	0	4	....	....	....	....
	NHL Totals		**144**	**10**	**17**	**27**	**156**	**2**	**0**	**2**	**167**	**6.0**		**912**	**49.3**	**11:10**	....	....	....	....	....	....	....	....	....

WHL East Second All-Star Team (1996, 1997) • Memorial Cup Tournament All-Star Team (1997)

Rights transferred to **Carolina** after **Hartford** franchise relocated, June 25, 1997. Traded to **Florida** by **Carolina** with Sandis Ozolinsh for Bret Hedican, Kevyn Adams and Tomas Malec, January 16, 2002. Signed as a free agent by **Calgary**, July 2, 2004. Signed as a free agent by **Rogle** (Sweden-2) September 25, 2004.

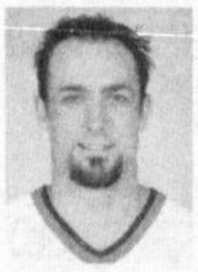

RIVERS, Jamie

(RIH-vuhrs, JAY-mee) **DET.**

Defense. Shoots left. 6', 195 lbs. Born, Ottawa, Ont., March 16, 1975. St. Louis' 2nd choice, 63rd overall, in 1993 Entry Draft.

Season	Club	League	GP	G	A	Pts	PIM	PP	SH	GW	S	%	+/-	TF	F%	Min	GP	G	A	Pts	PIM	PP	SH	GW	Min
1989-90	Ottawa South	ODMHA	50	26	46	72	46	....	....	....	....	....	....	....	....	....	....	....	....	....	....	....	....	....	....
1990-91	Ott. Jr. Senators	CJHL	55	4	30	34	74	....	....	....	....	....	....	....	....	....	....	....	....	....	....	....	....	....	....
1991-92	Sudbury Wolves	OHL	55	3	13	16	20	....	....	....	....	....	....	....	....	....	8	0	0	0	0	....	....	....	....
1992-93	Sudbury Wolves	OHL	62	12	43	55	20	....	....	....	....	....	....	....	....	....	14	7	19	26	4	....	....	....	....
1993-94	Sudbury Wolves	OHL	65	32	*89	121	58	....	....	....	....	....	....	....	....	....	10	1	9	10	14	....	....	....	....
1994-95	Sudbury Wolves	OHL	46	9	56	65	30	....	....	....	....	....	....	....	....	....	18	7	26	33	22	....	....	....	....
1995-96	**St. Louis**	**NHL**	**3**	**0**	**0**	**0**	**2**	**0**	**0**	**0**	**5**	**0.0**	**–1**				....	....	....	....	....	....	....	....	....
	Worcester IceCats	AHL	75	7	45	52	130	....	....	....	....	....	....				4	0	1	1	4	....	....	....	....
1996-97	**St. Louis**	**NHL**	**15**	**2**	**5**	**7**	**6**	**1**	**0**	**0**	**9**	**22.2**	**–4**				....	....	....	....	....	....	....	....	....
	Worcester IceCats	AHL	63	8	35	43	83	....	....	....	....	....	....				5	1	2	3	14	....	....	....	....
1997-98	**St. Louis**	**NHL**	**59**	**2**	**4**	**6**	**36**	**1**	**0**	**1**	**53**	**3.8**	**5**				....	....	....	....	....	....	....	....	....
1998-99	**St. Louis**	**NHL**	**76**	**2**	**5**	**7**	**47**	**1**	**0**	**0**	**78**	**2.6**	**–3**	**0**	**0.0**	**14:10**	**9**	**1**	**1**	**2**	**2**	**1**	**0**	**1**	**6:29**
99-2000	**NY Islanders**	**NHL**	**75**	**1**	**16**	**17**	**84**	**1**	**0**	**0**	**95**	**1.1**	**–4**	**0**	**0.0**	**19:39**	....	....	....	....	....	....	....	....	....
2000-01	**Ottawa**	**NHL**	**45**	**2**	**4**	**6**	**44**	**0**	**0**	**0**	**41**	**4.9**	**6**	**0**	**0.0**	**14:01**	**1**	**0**	**0**	**0**	**4**	**0**	**0**	**0**	**12:45**
	Grand Rapids	IHL	2	0	0	0	2	....	....	....	....	....	....	....	....	....	....	....	....	....	....	....	....	....	....
2001-02	**Ottawa**	**NHL**	**2**	**0**	**0**	**0**	**4**	**0**	**0**	**0**	**3**	**0.0**	**–3**	**0**	**0.0**	**11:37**	....	....	....	....	....	....	....	....	....
	Boston	**NHL**	**64**	**4**	**2**	**6**	**45**	**1**	**0**	**1**	**48**	**8.3**	**6**	**39**	**33.3**	**8:27**	**3**	**0**	**0**	**0**	**0**	**0**	**0**	**0**	**4:57**
2002-03	**Florida**	**NHL**	**1**	**0**	**0**	**0**	**2**	**0**	**0**	**0**	**2**	**0.0**	**–2**	**0**	**0.0**	**18:27**	....	....	....	....	....	....	....	....	....
	San Antonio	AHL	50	6	19	25	68	....	....	....	....	....	....	....	....	....	3	0	1	1	10	....	....	....	....
2003-04	**Detroit**	**NHL**	**50**	**3**	**4**	**7**	**41**	**0**	**0**	**0**	**31**	**9.7**	**9**	**1**	**0.0**	**10:14**	**2**	**0**	**0**	**0**	**2**	**0**	**0**	**0**	**5:40**
	Grand Rapids	AHL	2	0	0	0	4	....	....	....	....	....	....	....	....	....	....	....	....	....	....	....	....	....	....
2004-05	Hershey Bears	AHL	50	7	13	20	46	....	....	....	....	....	....	....	....	....	....	....	....	....	....	....	....	....	....
	NHL Totals		**390**	**16**	**40**	**56**	**311**	**5**	**0**	**2**	**365**	**4.4**		**40**	**32.5**	**13:40**	**15**	**1**	**1**	**2**	**8**	**1**	**0**	**1**	**6:29**

OHL First All-Star Team (1994) • Canadian Major Junior Second All-Star Team (1994) • OHL Second All-Star Team (1995) • AHL Second All-Star Team (1997)

Claimed by **NY Islanders** from **St. Louis** in Waiver Draft, September 27, 1999. Signed as a free agent by **Ottawa**, November 30, 2000. Claimed on waivers by **Boston** from **Ottawa**, October 13, 2001. Signed as a free agent by **San Antonio** (AHL), November 2, 2002. Signed as a free agent by **Florida**, December 16, 2002. Signed as a free agent by **Detroit**, July 29, 2003. Signed as a free agent by **Hershey** (AHL), November 3, 2004.

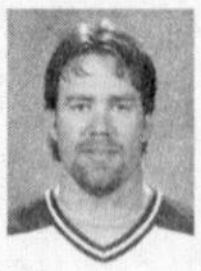

RIVET, Craig

(rih-VAY, KRAYG) **MTL.**

Defense. Shoots right. 6'2", 207 lbs. Born, North Bay, Ont., September 13, 1974. Montreal's 4th choice, 68th overall, in 1992 Entry Draft.

Season	Club	League	GP	G	A	Pts	PIM	PP	SH	GW	S	%	+/-	TF	F%	Min	GP	G	A	Pts	PIM	PP	SH	GW	Min
1990-91	Barrie Colts	OHA-B	42	9	17	26	55	....	....	....	....	....	....	....	....	....	....	....	....	....	....	....	....	....	....
1991-92	Kingston	OHL	66	5	21	26	97	....	....	....	....	....	....	....	....	....	....	....	....	....	....	....	....	....	....
1992-93	Kingston	OHL	64	19	55	74	117	....	....	....	....	....	....	....	....	....	16	5	7	12	39	....	....	....	....
1993-94	Kingston	OHL	61	12	52	64	100	....	....	....	....	....	....	....	....	....	6	0	3	3	6	....	....	....	....
	Fredericton	AHL	4	0	2	2	2	....	....	....	....	....	....	....	....	....	....	....	....	....	....	....	....	....	....
1994-95	Fredericton	AHL	78	5	27	32	126	....	....	....	....	....	....	....	....	....	12	0	4	4	17	....	....	....	....
	Montreal	**NHL**	**5**	**0**	**1**	**1**	**5**	**0**	**0**	**0**	**2**	**0.0**	**2**				....	....	....	....	....	....	....	....	....
1995-96	**Montreal**	**NHL**	**19**	**1**	**4**	**5**	**54**	**0**	**0**	**0**	**9**	**11.1**	**4**				....	....	....	....	....	....	....	....	....
	Fredericton	AHL	49	5	18	23	189	....	....	....	....	....	....				6	0	0	0	12	....	....	....	....
1996-97	**Montreal**	**NHL**	**35**	**0**	**4**	**4**	**54**	**0**	**0**	**0**	**24**	**0.0**	**7**				**5**	**0**	**1**	**1**	**14**	**0**	**0**	**0**	....
	Fredericton	AHL	23	3	12	15	99	....	....	....	....	....	....				....	....	....	....	....	....	....	....	....
1997-98	**Montreal**	**NHL**	**61**	**0**	**2**	**2**	**93**	**0**	**0**	**0**	**26**	**0.0**	**–3**				**5**	**0**	**0**	**0**	**2**	**0**	**0**	**0**	....
1998-99	**Montreal**	**NHL**	**66**	**2**	**8**	**10**	**66**	**0**	**0**	**0**	**39**	**5.1**	**–3**	**0**	**0.0**	**14:20**	....	....	....	....	....	....	....	....	....
99-2000	**Montreal**	**NHL**	**61**	**3**	**14**	**17**	**76**	**0**	**0**	**1**	**71**	**4.2**	**11**	**0**	**0.0**	**19:03**	....	....	....	....	....	....	....	....	....
2000-01	**Montreal**	**NHL**	**26**	**1**	**2**	**3**	**36**	**0**	**0**	**0**	**22**	**4.5**	**–8**	**0**	**0.0**	**19:04**	....	....	....	....	....	....	....	....	....
2001-02	**Montreal**	**NHL**	**82**	**8**	**17**	**25**	**76**	**0**	**0**	**0**	**90**	**8.9**	**1**	**1**	**0.0**	**19:00**	**12**	**0**	**3**	**3**	**4**	**0**	**0**	**0**	**21:26**
2002-03	**Montreal**	**NHL**	**82**	**7**	**15**	**22**	**71**	**3**	**0**	**2**	**118**	**5.9**	**1**	**0**	**0.0**	**22:00**	....	....	....	....	....	....	....	....	....
2003-04	**Montreal**	**NHL**	**80**	**4**	**8**	**12**	**98**	**2**	**0**	**1**	**96**	**4.2**	**–1**	**0**	**0.0**	**19:28**	**11**	**1**	**4**	**5**	**2**	**1**	**0**	**0**	**24:07**
2004-05	TPS Turku	Finland	18	3	1	4	28	....	....	....	....	....	....	....	....	....	6	0	0	0	39	....	....	....	....
	NHL Totals		**517**	**26**	**75**	**101**	**629**	**5**	**0**	**4**	**497**	**5.2**		**1**	**0.0**	**18:57**	**33**	**1**	**8**	**9**	**22**	**1**	**0**	**0**	**22:43**

• Missed majority of 2000-01 season recovering from shoulder injury suffered in game vs. Vancouver, October 30, 2000. Signed as a free agent by **TPS** (Finland), January 11, 2005.

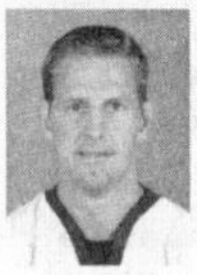

ROBERTS, Gary (RAW-buhrts, GAIR-ree) FLA.

Left wing. Shoots left. 6'2", 215 lbs. Born, North York, Ont., May 23, 1966. Calgary's 1st choice, 12th overall, in 1984 Entry Draft.

			Regular Season														Playoffs								
Season	Club	League	GP	G	A	Pts	PIM	PP	SH	GW	S	%	+/-	TF	F%	Min	GP	G	A	Pts	PIM	PP	SH	GW	Min
1980-81	Hamilton Kilty B's	OHA-B	3	0	1	1	0	....	....	....	....	....	....	....	....	....	....	....	....	....	....	....	....	....	....
1981-82	Whitby	OMHA	44	55	31	86	133	....	....	....	....	....	....	....	....	....	....	....	....	....	....	....	....	....	....
1982-83	Ottawa 67's	OHL	53	12	8	20	83	....	....	....	....	....	....	....	....	....	5	1	0	1	19	....	....	....	....
1983-84	Ottawa 67's	OHL	48	27	30	57	144	....	....	....	....	....	....	....	....	....	13	10	7	17	62	....	....	....	....
1984-85	Ottawa 67's	OHL	59	44	62	106	186	....	....	....	....	....	....	....	....	....	5	2	8	10	10	....	....	....	....
	Moncton	AHL	7	4	2	6	7	....	....	....	....	....	....	....	....	....	....	....	....	....	....	....	....	....	....
1985-86	Ottawa 67's	OHL	24	26	25	51	83	....	....	....	....	....	....	....	....	....	....	....	....	....	....	....	....	....	....
	Guelph Platers	OHL	23	18	15	33	65	....	....	....	....	....	....	....	....	....	20	18	13	31	43	....	....	....	....
1986-87	**Calgary**	**NHL**	**32**	**5**	**10**	**15**	**85**	**0**	**0**	**0**	**38**	**13.2**	**6**	....	....	....	**2**	**0**	**0**	**0**	**4**	**0**	**0**	**0**	....
	Moncton	AHL	38	20	18	38	72	....	....	....	....	....	....	....	....	....	....	....	....	....	....	....	....	....	....
1987-88	**Calgary**	**NHL**	**74**	**13**	**15**	**28**	**282**	**0**	**0**	**1**	**118**	**11.0**	**24**	....	....	....	**9**	**2**	**3**	**5**	**29**	**0**	**0**	**0**	....
1988-89♦	**Calgary**	**NHL**	**71**	**22**	**16**	**38**	**250**	**0**	**1**	**2**	**123**	**17.9**	**32**	....	....	....	**22**	**5**	**7**	**12**	**57**	**0**	**0**	**0**	....
1989-90	**Calgary**	**NHL**	**78**	**39**	**33**	**72**	**222**	**5**	**0**	**5**	**175**	**22.3**	**31**	....	....	....	**6**	**2**	**5**	**7**	**41**	**0**	**0**	**0**	....
1990-91	**Calgary**	**NHL**	**80**	**22**	**31**	**53**	**252**	**0**	**0**	**3**	**132**	**16.7**	**15**	....	....	....	**7**	**1**	**3**	**4**	**18**	**0**	**0**	**0**	....
1991-92	**Calgary**	**NHL**	**76**	**53**	**37**	**90**	**207**	**15**	**0**	**2**	**196**	**27.0**	**32**	....	....	....	....	....	....	....	....	....	....	....	....
1992-93	**Calgary**	**NHL**	**58**	**38**	**41**	**79**	**172**	**8**	**3**	**4**	**166**	**22.9**	**32**	....	....	....	**5**	**1**	**6**	**7**	**43**	**1**	**0**	**0**	....
1993-94	**Calgary**	**NHL**	**73**	**41**	**43**	**84**	**145**	**12**	**3**	**5**	**202**	**20.3**	**37**	....	....	....	**7**	**2**	**6**	**8**	**24**	**1**	**0**	**1**	....
1994-95	**Calgary**	**NHL**	**8**	**2**	**2**	**4**	**43**	**2**	**0**	**0**	**20**	**10.0**	**1**	....	....	....	....	....	....	....	....	....	....	....	....
1995-96	**Calgary**	**NHL**	**35**	**22**	**20**	**42**	**78**	**9**	**0**	**5**	**84**	**26.2**	**15**	....	....	....	....	....	....	....	....	....	....	....	....
1996-97	**Calgary**	**NHL**	DID NOT PLAY – INJURED																						
1997-98	**Carolina**	**NHL**	**61**	**20**	**29**	**49**	**103**	**4**	**0**	**2**	**106**	**18.9**	**3**	....	....	....	....	....	....	....	....	....	....	....	....
1998-99	**Carolina**	**NHL**	**77**	**14**	**28**	**42**	**178**	**1**	**1**	**4**	**138**	**10.1**	**2**	**15**	**46.7**	**19:36**	**6**	**1**	**1**	**2**	**8**	**0**	**0**	**0**	**21:01**
99-2000	**Carolina**	**NHL**	**69**	**23**	**30**	**53**	**62**	**12**	**0**	**1**	**150**	**15.3**	**-10**	**7**	**28.6**	**18:31**	....	....	....	....	....	....	....	....	....
2000-01	**Toronto**	**NHL**	**82**	**29**	**24**	**53**	**109**	**8**	**2**	**3**	**138**	**21.0**	**16**	**13**	**46.2**	**17:08**	**11**	**2**	**9**	**11**	**0**	**0**	**0**	**0**	**19:49**
2001-02	**Toronto**	**NHL**	**69**	**21**	**27**	**48**	**63**	**6**	**2**	**2**	**122**	**17.2**	**-4**	**6**	**33.3**	**17:23**	**19**	**7**	**12**	**19**	**56**	**3**	**0**	**1**	**19:28**
2002-03	**Toronto**	**NHL**	**14**	**5**	**3**	**8**	**10**	**3**	**0**	**0**	**22**	**22.7**	**-2**	**4**	**50.0**	**15:35**	**7**	**1**	**1**	**2**	**8**	**0**	**0**	**0**	**21:04**
2003-04	**Toronto**	**NHL**	**72**	**28**	**20**	**48**	**84**	**11**	**1**	**7**	**124**	**22.6**	**9**	**12**	**33.3**	**17:33**	**13**	**4**	**4**	**8**	**10**	**2**	**0**	**1**	**17:45**
2004-05			DID NOT PLAY																						
	NHL Totals		**1029**	**397**	**409**	**806**	**2345**	**96**	**13**	**46**	**2054**	**19.3**		**57**	**40.4**	**17:57**	**114**	**28**	**57**	**85**	**298**	**7**	**0**	**3**	**19:30**

OHL Second All-Star Team (1985, 1986) • Bill Masterton Memorial Trophy (1996)

Played in NHL All-Star Game (1992, 1993, 2004)

• Missed remainder of 1994-95 season and majority of 1995-96 season recovering from neck injury suffered in game vs. Toronto, February 4, 1995. • Missed remainder of 1995-96 season and entire 1996-97 season recovering from neck injury suffered in game vs. Vancouver, April 3, 1996. Traded to **Carolina** by **Calgary** with Trevor Kidd for Andrew Cassels and Jean-Sebastien Giguere, August 25, 1997. Signed as a free agent by **Toronto**, July 4, 2000. • Missed majority of 2002-03 season recovering from off-season shoulder surgery, August 13, 2002. Signed as a free agent by **Florida**, August 1, 2005.

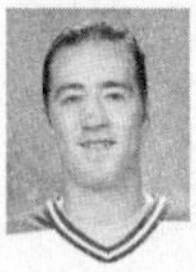

ROBIDAS, Stephane (ROH-bih-dah, STEH-fan) DAL.

Defense. Shoots right. 5'11", 188 lbs. Born, Sherbrooke, Que., March 3, 1977. Montreal's 7th choice, 164th overall, in 1995 Entry Draft.

			Regular Season														Playoffs								
Season	Club	League	GP	G	A	Pts	PIM	PP	SH	GW	S	%	+/-	TF	F%	Min	GP	G	A	Pts	PIM	PP	SH	GW	Min
1992-93	Magog	QAAA	41	3	12	15	16	....	....	....	....	....	....	....	....	....	5	1	1	2	2	....	....	....	....
1993-94	Shawinigan	QMJHL	67	3	18	21	33	....	....	....	....	....	....	....	....	....	1	0	0	0	0	....	....	....	....
1994-95	Shawinigan	QMJHL	71	13	56	69	44	....	....	....	....	....	....	....	....	....	15	7	12	19	4	....	....	....	....
1995-96	Shawinigan	QMJHL	67	23	56	79	53	....	....	....	....	....	....	....	....	....	6	1	5	6	10	....	....	....	....
1996-97	Shawinigan	QMJHL	67	24	51	75	59	....	....	....	....	....	....	....	....	....	7	4	6	10	14	....	....	....	....
1997-98	Fredericton	AHL	79	10	21	31	50	....	....	....	....	....	....	....	....	....	4	0	2	2	0	....	....	....	....
1998-99	Fredericton	AHL	79	8	33	41	59	....	....	....	....	....	....	....	....	....	15	1	5	6	10	....	....	....	....
99-2000	**Montreal**	**NHL**	**1**	**0**	**0**	**0**	**0**	**0**	**0**	**0**	**0**	**0.0**	**0**	**0**	**0.0**	**15:54**	....	....	....	....	....	....	....	....	....
	Quebec Citadelles	AHL	76	14	31	45	36	....	....	....	....	....	....	....	....	....	3	0	1	1	0	....	....	....	....
2000-01	**Montreal**	**NHL**	**65**	**6**	**6**	**12**	**14**	**1**	**0**	**0**	**77**	**7.8**	**0**	**1**	**100.0**	**20:44**	....	....	....	....	....	....	....	....	....
2001-02	**Montreal**	**NHL**	**56**	**1**	**10**	**11**	**14**	**1**	**0**	**0**	**68**	**1.5**	**-25**	**3**	**33.3**	**18:58**	**2**	**0**	**0**	**0**	**4**	**0**	**0**	**0**	**13:07**
2002-03	**Dallas**	**NHL**	**76**	**3**	**7**	**10**	**35**	**0**	**0**	**1**	**47**	**6.4**	**15**	**1**	**100.0**	**12:54**	**12**	**0**	**1**	**1**	**20**	**0**	**0**	**0**	**13:54**
2003-04	**Dallas**	**NHL**	**14**	**1**	**0**	**1**	**8**	**1**	**0**	**0**	**8**	**12.5**	**-2**	**1**	**100.0**	**12:57**	....	....	....	....	....	....	....	....	....
	Chicago	**NHL**	**45**	**2**	**10**	**12**	**33**	**0**	**1**	**1**	**55**	**3.6**	**6**	**0**	**0.0**	**20:56**	....	....	....	....	....	....	....	....	....
2004-05	Frankfurt Lions	Germany	51	15	32	47	64	....	....	....	....	....	....	....	....	....	6	1	2	3	6	....	....	....	....
	NHL Totals		**257**	**13**	**33**	**46**	**104**	**3**	**1**	**2**	**255**	**5.1**		**6**	**66.7**	**17:37**	**14**	**0**	**1**	**1**	**24**	**0**	**0**	**0**	**13:47**

QMJHL First All-Star Team (1996, 1997)

Claimed by **Atlanta** from **Montreal** in Waiver Draft, October 4, 2002. Traded to **Dallas** by **Atlanta** for future considerations, October 4, 2002. Traded to **Chicago** by **Dallas** with Dallas' 2nd round choice (Jakub Sindel) in 2004 Entry Draft for Jon Klemm and NY Rangers' 4th round choice (previously acquired, Dallas selected Fredrik Naslund) in 2004 Entry Draft, November 17, 2003. Signed as a free agent by **Frankfurt** (Germany), September 17, 2004.

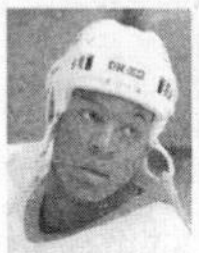

ROBINSON, Nathan BOS.

Center. Shoots left. 5'9", 181 lbs. Born, Scarborough, Ont., December 31, 1981.

			Regular Season														Playoffs								
Season	Club	League	GP	G	A	Pts	PIM	PP	SH	GW	S	%	+/-	TF	F%	Min	GP	G	A	Pts	PIM	PP	SH	GW	Min
1998-99	Belleville Bulls	OHL	50	11	8	19	23	....	....	....	....	....	....	....	....	....	21	4	4	8	14	....	....	....	....
99-2000	Belleville Bulls	OHL	61	19	18	37	45	....	....	....	....	....	....	....	....	....	15	3	4	7	10	....	....	....	....
2000-01	Belleville Bulls	OHL	66	32	37	69	57	....	....	....	....	....	....	....	....	....	10	6	10	16	7	....	....	....	....
2001-02	Belleville Bulls	OHL	67	47	63	*110	74	....	....	....	....	....	....	....	....	....	11	8	6	14	10	....	....	....	....
2002-03	Toledo Storm	ECHL	9	5	9	14	29	....	....	....	....	....	....	....	....	....	....	....	....	....	....	....	....	....	....
	Grand Rapids	AHL	53	3	14	17	24	....	....	....	....	....	....	....	....	....	8	0	3	3	0	....	....	....	....
2003-04	**Detroit**	**NHL**	**5**	**0**	**0**	**0**	**2**	**0**	**0**	**0**	**5**	**0.0**	**-1**	**0**	**0.0**	**6:01**	....	....	....	....	....	....	....	....	....
	Grand Rapids	AHL	69	24	26	50	41	....	....	....	....	....	....	....	....	....	3	0	0	0	2	....	....	....	....
2004-05	Grand Rapids	AHL	50	8	16	24	10	....	....	....	....	....	....	....	....	....	....	....	....	....	....	....	....	....	....
	Syracuse Crunch	AHL	19	6	14	20	18	....	....	....	....	....	....	....	....	....	....	....	....	....	....	....	....	....	....
	NHL Totals		**5**	**0**	**0**	**0**	**2**	**0**	**0**	**0**	**5**	**0.0**		**0**	**0.0**	**6:01**	....	....	....	....	....	....	....	....	....

OHL First All-Star Team (2002) • Canadian Major Junior First All-Star Team (2002)

Signed as a free agent by **Detroit**, October 12, 2002. Loaned to **Syracuse** (AHL) by **Grand Rapids** (AHL) for loan of Jeff Panzer, March 11, 2005. Signed as a free agent by **Boston**, August 15, 2005.

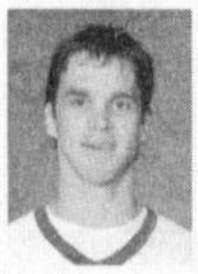

ROBITAILLE, Luc (ROH-buh-tigh, LEWK) L.A.

Left wing. Shoots left. 6'1", 215 lbs. Born, Montreal, Que., February 17, 1966. Los Angeles' 9th choice, 171st overall, in 1984 Entry Draft.

			Regular Season														Playoffs								
Season	Club	League	GP	G	A	Pts	PIM	PP	SH	GW	S	%	+/-	TF	F%	Min	GP	G	A	Pts	PIM	PP	SH	GW	Min
1982-83	Mtl-Bourassa	QAAA	48	36	57	93	28	....	....	....	....	....	....	....	....	....	7	9	6	15	14	....	....	....	....
1983-84	Hull Olympiques	QMJHL	70	32	53	85	48	....	....	....	....	....	....	....	....	....	....	....	....	....	....	....	....	....	....
1984-85	Hull Olympiques	QMJHL	64	55	94	149	115	....	....	....	....	....	....	....	....	....	5	4	2	6	27	....	....	....	....
1985-86	Hull Olympiques	QMJHL	63	68	123	191	91	....	....	....	....	....	....	....	....	....	15	17	27	44	28	....	....	....	....
1986-87	**Los Angeles**	**NHL**	**79**	**45**	**39**	**84**	**28**	**18**	**0**	**3**	**199**	**22.6**	**-18**	....	....	....	**5**	**1**	**4**	**5**	**2**	**0**	**0**	**0**	....
1987-88	**Los Angeles**	**NHL**	**80**	**53**	**58**	**111**	**82**	**17**	**0**	**6**	**220**	**24.1**	**-9**	....	....	....	**5**	**2**	**5**	**7**	**18**	**2**	**0**	**1**	....
1988-89	**Los Angeles**	**NHL**	**78**	**46**	**52**	**98**	**65**	**10**	**0**	**4**	**237**	**19.4**	**5**	....	....	....	**11**	**2**	**6**	**8**	**10**	**0**	**0**	**1**	....
1989-90	**Los Angeles**	**NHL**	**80**	**52**	**49**	**101**	**38**	**20**	**0**	**7**	**210**	**24.8**	**8**	....	....	....	**10**	**5**	**5**	**10**	**12**	**1**	**0**	**1**	....
1990-91	**Los Angeles**	**NHL**	**76**	**45**	**46**	**91**	**68**	**11**	**0**	**5**	**229**	**19.7**	**28**	....	....	....	**12**	**12**	**4**	**16**	**22**	**5**	**0**	**2**	....
1991-92	**Los Angeles**	**NHL**	**80**	**44**	**63**	**107**	**95**	**26**	**0**	**6**	**240**	**18.3**	**-4**	....	....	....	**6**	**3**	**4**	**7**	**12**	**1**	**0**	**1**	....
1992-93	**Los Angeles**	**NHL**	**84**	**63**	**62**	**125**	**100**	**24**	**2**	**8**	**265**	**23.8**	**18**	....	....	....	**24**	**9**	**13**	**22**	**28**	**4**	**0**	**2**	....
1993-94	**Los Angeles**	**NHL**	**83**	**44**	**42**	**86**	**86**	**24**	**0**	**3**	**267**	**16.5**	**-20**	....	....	....	....	....	....	....	....	....	....	....	....
1994-95	**Pittsburgh**	**NHL**	**46**	**23**	**19**	**42**	**37**	**5**	**0**	**3**	**109**	**21.1**	**10**	....	....	....	**12**	**7**	**4**	**11**	**26**	**0**	**0**	**2**	....
1995-96	**NY Rangers**	**NHL**	**77**	**23**	**46**	**69**	**80**	**11**	**0**	**4**	**223**	**10.3**	**13**	....	....	....	**11**	**1**	**5**	**6**	**8**	**0**	**0**	**0**	....
1996-97	**NY Rangers**	**NHL**	**69**	**24**	**24**	**48**	**48**	**5**	**0**	**4**	**200**	**12.0**	**16**	....	....	....	**15**	**4**	**7**	**11**	**4**	**0**	**0**	**0**	....
1997-98	**Los Angeles**	**NHL**	**57**	**16**	**24**	**40**	**66**	**5**	**0**	**7**	**130**	**12.3**	**5**	....	....	....	**4**	**1**	**2**	**3**	**6**	**0**	**0**	**0**	....
1998-99	**Los Angeles**	**NHL**	**82**	**39**	**35**	**74**	**54**	**11**	**0**	**7**	**292**	**13.4**	**-1**	**7**	**57.1**	**19:11**	....	....	....	....	....	....	....	....	....
99-2000	**Los Angeles**	**NHL**	**71**	**36**	**38**	**74**	**68**	**13**	**0**	**7**	**221**	**16.3**	**11**	**10**	**30.0**	**18:34**	**4**	**2**	**2**	**4**	**6**	**0**	**0**	**0**	**20:25**
2000-01	**Los Angeles**	**NHL**	**82**	**37**	**51**	**88**	**66**	**16**	**1**	**4**	**235**	**15.7**	**10**	**12**	**33.3**	**18:42**	**13**	**4**	**3**	**7**	**10**	**1**	**0**	**1**	**18:19**
2001-02♦	**Detroit**	**NHL**	**81**	**30**	**20**	**50**	**38**	**13**	**0**	**5**	**190**	**15.8**	**-2**	**12**	**41.7**	**14:51**	**23**	**4**	**5**	**9**	**10**	**1**	**0**	**1**	**13:16**
2002-03	**Detroit**	**NHL**	**81**	**11**	**20**	**31**	**50**	**3**	**0**	**0**	**148**	**7.4**	**4**	**18**	**50.0**	**12:49**	**4**	**1**	**0**	**1**	**0**	**0**	**0**	**0**	**11:30**
2003-04	**Los Angeles**	**NHL**	**80**	**22**	**29**	**51**	**56**	**12**	**0**	**4**	**221**	**10.0**	**4**	**2**	**0.0**	**16:41**	....	....	....	....	....	....	....	....	....

			Regular Season														Playoffs								
Season	Club	League	GP	G	A	Pts	PIM	PP	SH	GW	S	%	+/-	TF	F%	Min	GP	G	A	Pts	PIM	PP	SH	GW	Min
2004-05			DID NOT PLAY																						
	NHL Totals		**1366**	**653**	**717**	**1370**	**1125**	**244**	**3**	**87**	**3836**	**17.0**		**61**	**41.0**	**16:46**	**159**	**58**	**69**	**127**	**174**	**15**	**0**	**12**	**15:15**

QMJHL Second All-Star Team (1985) • QMJHL First All-Star Team (1986) • Canadian Major Junior Player of the Year (1986) • Memorial Cup Tournament All-Star Team (1986) • NHL All-Rookie Team (1987) • NHL Second All-Star Team (1987, 1992, 2001) • Calder Memorial Trophy (1987) • NHL First All-Star Team (1988, 1989, 1990, 1991, 1993)

Played in NHL All-Star Game (1988, 1989, 1990, 1991, 1992, 1993, 1999, 2001)

Traded to **Pittsburgh** by **Los Angeles** for Rick Tocchet and Pittsburgh's 2nd round choice (Pavel Rosa) in 1995 Entry Draft, July 29, 1994. Traded to **NY Rangers** by **Pittsburgh** with Ulf Samuelsson for Petr Nedved and Sergei Zubov, August 31, 1995. Traded to **Los Angeles** by **NY Rangers** for Kevin Stevens, August 28, 1997. Signed as a free agent by **Detroit**, July 5, 2001. Signed as a free agent by **Los Angeles**, July 24, 2003.

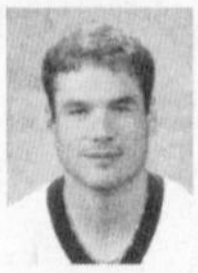

ROBITAILLE, Randy

(ROH-buh-tigh, RAN-dee) **NSH.**

Center. Shoots left. 5'11", 200 lbs. Born, Ottawa, Ont., October 12, 1975.

1993-94	Ott. Jr. Senators	CJHL	57	33	55	88	31																		
1994-95	Ott. Jr. Senators	CJHL	54	48	77	*125	111																		
1995-96	Miami-Ohio	CCHA	36	14	31	45	26																		
1996-97	Miami-Ohio	CCHA	39	27	34	61	44																		
	Boston	**NHL**	**1**	**0**	**0**	**0**	**0**	**0**	**0**	**0**	**0**	**0.0**	**0**												
1997-98	**Boston**	**NHL**	**4**	**0**	**0**	**0**	**0**	**0**	**0**	**0**	**5**	**0.0**	**–2**												
	Providence Bruins	AHL	48	15	29	44	16																		
1998-99	**Boston**	**NHL**	**4**	**0**	**2**	**2**	**0**	**0**	**0**	**0**	**5**	**0.0**	**–1**	**24**	**25.0**	**10:11**	**1**	**0**	**0**	**0**	**0**	**0**	**0**	**0**	**7:14**
	Providence Bruins	AHL	74	28	*74	102	34										19	6	*14	20	20				
99-2000	**Nashville**	**NHL**	**69**	**11**	**14**	**25**	**10**	**2**	**0**	**1**	**113**	**9.7**	**–13**	**528**	**51.5**	**12:52**									
2000-01	**Nashville**	**NHL**	**62**	**9**	**17**	**26**	**12**	**5**	**0**	**0**	**121**	**7.4**	**–11**	**481**	**48.4**	**14:10**									
	Milwaukee	IHL	19	10	23	33	4																		
2001-02	**Los Angeles**	**NHL**	**18**	**4**	**3**	**7**	**17**	**2**	**0**	**0**	**30**	**13.3**	**–9**	**60**	**65.0**	**12:54**									
	Manchester	AHL	6	7	3	10	0																		
	Pittsburgh	**NHL**	**40**	**10**	**20**	**30**	**16**	**3**	**0**	**1**	**91**	**11.0**	**–14**	**599**	**51.4**	**18:08**									
2002-03	**Pittsburgh**	**NHL**	**41**	**5**	**12**	**17**	**8**	**1**	**0**	**2**	**61**	**8.2**	**5**	**429**	**55.9**	**13:58**									
	NY Islanders	**NHL**	**10**	**1**	**2**	**3**	**2**	**1**	**0**	**0**	**8**	**12.5**	**0**	**68**	**48.5**	**12:28**	**5**	**1**	**1**	**2**	**0**	**1**	**0**	**0**	**13:03**
2003-04	**Atlanta**	**NHL**	**69**	**11**	**26**	**37**	**20**	**5**	**0**	**2**	**121**	**9.1**	**–12**	**1069**	**50.2**	**15:51**									
2004-05	ZSC Lions Zurich	Swiss	36	22	*45	*67	56										15	2	16	18	10				
	NHL Totals		**318**	**51**	**96**	**147**	**85**	**19**	**0**	**6**	**555**	**9.2**		**3258**	**51.2**	**14:33**	**6**	**1**	**1**	**2**	**0**	**1**	**0**	**0**	**12:05**

CCHA First All-Star Team (1997) • NCAA West First All-American Team (1997) • AHL First All-Star Team (1999) • Les Cunningham Award (MVP – AHL) (1999)

Signed as a free agent by **Boston**, March 27, 1997. Traded to **Atlanta** by **Boston** for Peter Ferraro, June 25, 1999. Traded to **Nashville** by **Atlanta** for Denny Lambert, August 16, 1999. Signed as a free agent by **Los Angeles**, July 6, 2001. Claimed on waivers by **Pittsburgh** from **Los Angeles**, January 4, 2002. Traded to **NY Islanders** by **Pittsburgh** for Philadelphia's 5th round choice (previously acquired, Pittsburgh selected Evgeni Isakov) in 2003 Entry Draft, March 9, 2003. Signed as a free agent by **Atlanta**, August 12, 2003. Signed as a free agent by **Zurich** (Swiss), April 26, 2004. Signed as a free agent by **Nashville**, August 19, 2005.

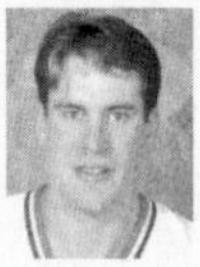

ROCHE, Dave

(ROHSH, DAYV)

Left wing. Shoots left. 6'4", 230 lbs. Born, Lindsay, Ont., June 13, 1975. Pittsburgh's 3rd choice, 62nd overall, in 1993 Entry Draft.

1990-91	Peterborough	OHA-B	40	22	17	39	86																		
1991-92	Peterborough	OHL	62	10	17	27	134										10	0	0	0	34				
1992-93	Peterborough	OHL	56	40	60	100	105										21	14	15	29	42				
1993-94	Peterborough	OHL	34	15	22	37	127																		
	Windsor Spitfires	OHL	29	14	20	34	73										4	1	1	2	15				
1994-95	Windsor Spitfires	OHL	66	55	59	114	180										10	9	6	15	16				
1995-96	**Pittsburgh**	**NHL**	**71**	**7**	**7**	**14**	**130**	**0**	**0**	**1**	**65**	**10.8**	**–5**				**16**	**2**	**7**	**9**	**26**	**0**	**0**	**0**	
1996-97	**Pittsburgh**	**NHL**	**61**	**5**	**5**	**10**	**155**	**2**	**0**	**0**	**53**	**9.4**	**–13**												
	Cleveland	IHL	18	5	5	10	25										13	6	3	9	*87				
1997-98	Syracuse Crunch	AHL	73	12	20	32	307										5	2	0	2	10				
1998-99	**Calgary**	**NHL**	**36**	**3**	**3**	**6**	**44**	**1**	**0**	**2**	**30**	**10.0**	**–1**	**0**	**0.0**	**7:15**									
	Saint John Flames	AHL	7	0	3	3	6																		
99-2000	**Calgary**	**NHL**	**2**	**0**	**0**	**0**	**5**	**0**	**0**	**0**	**3**	**0.0**	**–1**	**0**	**0.0**	**8:33**									
	Saint John Flames	AHL	67	22	21	43	130										3	0	1	1	8				
2000-01	Saint John Flames	AHL	79	32	26	58	179										19	3	6	9	43				
2001-02	Cincinnati	AHL	29	6	7	13	41																		
	NY Islanders	**NHL**	**1**	**0**	**0**	**0**	**0**	**0**	**0**	**0**	**0**	**0.0**	**0**	**1**	**0.0**	**2:51**									
	Bridgeport	AHL	48	25	14	39	64										20	3	0	3	20				
2002-03	Albany River Rats	AHL	76	21	16	37	89																		
2003-04	Toronto	AHL	60	7	13	20	88										3	0	0	0	0				
2004-05			DID NOT PLAY																						
	NHL Totals		**171**	**15**	**15**	**30**	**334**	**3**	**0**	**3**	**151**	**9.9**		**1**	**0.0**	**7:12**	**16**	**2**	**7**	**9**	**26**	**0**	**0**	**0**	

OHL First All-Star Team (1995)

Traded to **Calgary** by **Pittsburgh** with Ken Wregget for German Titov and Todd Hlushko, June 17, 1998. Signed as a free agent by **NY Islanders**, August 17, 2001. Traded to **Anaheim** by **NY Islanders** for Jim Cummins, January 14, 2002. Traded to **NY Islanders** by **Anaheim** for Ben Guite and the rights to Bjorn Mellin, March 19, 2002. Signed as a free agent by **New Jersey**, August 27, 2002. Signed as a free agent by **Toronto** (AHL), October 3, 2003.

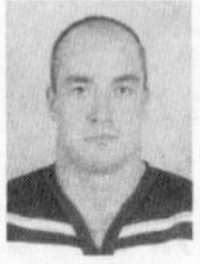

ROCHE, Travis

(ROHSH, TRA-vihs) **ATL.**

Defense. Shoots right. 6'1", 190 lbs. Born, Grand Cache, Alta., June 17, 1978.

1996-97	Trail	BCHL	49	17	40	57	159																		
1997-98	Trail	BCHL	38	11	31	42	104										11	0	8	8	21				
1998-99	North Dakota	WCHA	DID NOT PLAY – FRESHMAN																						
99-2000	North Dakota	WCHA	42	6	22	28	60																		
2000-01	North Dakota	WCHA	42	11	38	49	42																		
	Minnesota	**NHL**	**1**	**0**	**0**	**0**	**0**	**0**	**0**	**0**	**0**	**0.0**	**0**	**0**	**0.0**	**15:22**									
2001-02	**Minnesota**	**NHL**	**4**	**0**	**0**	**0**	**2**	**0**	**0**	**0**	**1**	**0.0**	**–1**	**0**	**0.0**	**12:30**									
	Houston Aeros	AHL	60	13	21	34	107										12	2	3	5	6				
2002-03	Houston Aeros	AHL	65	14	34	48	42										23	3	5	8	26				
2003-04	**Minnesota**	**NHL**	**5**	**0**	**1**	**1**	**0**	**0**	**0**	**0**	**5**	**0.0**	**–3**	**0**	**0.0**	**16:07**									
	Houston Aeros	AHL	60	8	30	38	18										2	0	0	0	2				
2004-05	Chicago Wolves	AHL	73	12	38	50	59										18	1	6	7	18				
	NHL Totals		**10**	**0**	**1**	**1**	**2**	**0**	**0**	**0**	**6**	**0.0**		**0**	**0.0**	**14:36**									

BCHL Second All-Star Team (1997) • BCHL Rookie of the Year Award (1997) • BCHL Playoff MVP Award (1997) • BCHL First All-Star Team (1998) • BCHL Best Defenseman Award (1998) • WCHA All-Rookie Team (2000) • WCHA First All-Star Team (2001) • NCAA West First All-American Team (2001) • NCAA Championship All-Tournament Team (2001) • AHL First All-Star Team (2005)

Signed as a free agent by **Minnesota**, April 8, 2001. Signed as a free agent by **Atlanta**, July 14, 2004.

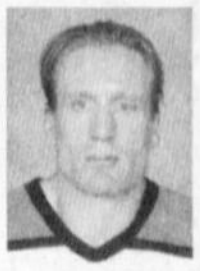

ROENICK, Jeremy

(ROH-nihk, JAIR-eh-mee) **L.A.**

Center. Shoots right. 6'1", 196 lbs. Born, Boston, MA, January 17, 1970. Chicago's 1st choice, 8th overall, in 1988 Entry Draft.

1986-87	Thayer Academy	High-MA	24	31	34	65																			
1987-88	Thayer Academy	High-MA	24	34	50	84																			
1988-89	Hull Olympiques	QMJHL	28	34	36	70	14																		
	Chicago	**NHL**	**20**	**9**	**9**	**18**	**4**	**2**	**0**	**0**	**52**	**17.3**	**4**				**10**	**1**	**3**	**4**	**7**	**1**	**0**	**1**	
1989-90	**Chicago**	**NHL**	**78**	**26**	**40**	**66**	**54**	**6**	**0**	**4**	**173**	**15.0**	**2**				**20**	**11**	**7**	**18**	**8**	**4**	**0**	**1**	
1990-91	**Chicago**	**NHL**	**79**	**41**	**53**	**94**	**80**	**15**	**4**	**10**	**194**	**21.1**	**38**				**6**	**3**	**5**	**8**	**4**	**1**	**0**	**1**	
1991-92	**Chicago**	**NHL**	**80**	**53**	**50**	**103**	**98**	**22**	**3**	**13**	**234**	**22.6**	**23**				**18**	**12**	**10**	**22**	**12**	**4**	**0**	**3**	
1992-93	**Chicago**	**NHL**	**84**	**50**	**57**	**107**	**86**	**22**	**3**	**3**	**255**	**19.6**	**15**				**4**	**1**	**2**	**3**	**2**	**0**	**0**	**0**	
1993-94	**Chicago**	**NHL**	**84**	**46**	**61**	**107**	**125**	**24**	**5**	**5**	**281**	**16.4**	**21**				**6**	**1**	**6**	**7**	**2**	**0**	**0**	**1**	
1994-95	Kolner Haie	Germany	3	3	1	4	2																		
	Chicago	**NHL**	**33**	**10**	**24**	**34**	**14**	**5**	**0**	**1**	**93**	**10.8**	**5**				**8**	**1**	**2**	**3**	**16**	**0**	**0**	**0**	
1995-96	**Chicago**	**NHL**	**66**	**32**	**35**	**67**	**109**	**12**	**4**	**2**	**171**	**18.7**	**9**				**10**	**5**	**7**	**12**	**2**	**1**	**0**	**1**	
1996-97	**Phoenix**	**NHL**	**72**	**29**	**40**	**69**	**115**	**10**	**3**	**7**	**228**	**12.7**	**–7**				**6**	**2**	**4**	**6**	**4**	**0**	**0**	**0**	
1997-98	**Phoenix**	**NHL**	**79**	**24**	**32**	**56**	**103**	**6**	**1**	**3**	**182**	**13.2**	**5**				**6**	**5**	**3**	**8**	**4**	**2**	**2**	**2**	
	United States	Olympics	4	0	1	1	6																		
1998-99	**Phoenix**	**NHL**	**78**	**24**	**48**	**72**	**130**	**4**	**0**	**3**	**203**	**11.8**	**7**	**956**	**47.6**	**20:10**	**1**	**0**	**0**	**0**	**0**	**0**	**0**	**0**	**26:55**
99-2000	**Phoenix**	**NHL**	**75**	**34**	**44**	**78**	**102**	**6**	**3**	**12**	**192**	**17.7**	**11**	**925**	**50.1**	**20:51**	**5**	**2**	**2**	**4**	**10**	**1**	**0**	**0**	**19:46**
2000-01	**Phoenix**	**NHL**	**80**	**30**	**46**	**76**	**114**	**13**	**0**	**7**	**192**	**15.6**	**–1**	**888**	**49.1**	**21:00**									

Season	Club	League	GP	G	A	Pts	PIM	PP	SH	GW	S	%	+/-	TF	F%	Min	GP	G	A	Pts	PIM	PP	SH	GW	Min
			Regular Season														Playoffs								
2001-02	**Philadelphia**	**NHL**	**75**	**21**	**46**	**67**	**74**	**5**	**0**	**3**	**167**	**12.6**	**32**	**1329**	**49.1**	**18:14**	**5**	**0**	**0**	**0**	**14**	**0**	**0**	**0**	**18:41**
	United States	Olympics	6	1	4	5	2	....	....	....	....	....	....	....	....	....	....	....	....	....	....	....	....	....	....
2002-03	**Philadelphia**	**NHL**	**79**	**27**	**32**	**59**	**75**	**8**	**1**	**6**	**197**	**13.7**	**20**	**1088**	**53.0**	**18:48**	**13**	**3**	**5**	**8**	**8**	**0**	**0**	**1**	**21:07**
2003-04	**Philadelphia**	**NHL**	**62**	**19**	**28**	**47**	**62**	**10**	**1**	**1**	**128**	**14.8**	**1**	**846**	**51.5**	**17:37**	**18**	**4**	**9**	**13**	**8**	**2**	**0**	**1**	**18:05**
2004-05			DID NOT PLAY																						
	NHL Totals		**1124**	**475**	**645**	**1120**	**1345**	**170**	**28**	**80**	**2942**	**16.1**		**6032**	**50.1**	**19:31**	**136**	**51**	**65**	**116**	**101**	**16**	**2**	**12**	**19:30**

QMJHL Second All-Star Team (1989)

Played in NHL All-Star Game (1991, 1992, 1993, 1994, 1999, 2000, 2002, 2003, 2004)

Traded to **Phoenix** by **Chicago** for Alex Zhamnov, Craig Mills and Phoenix's 1st round choice (Ty Jones) in 1997 Entry Draft, August 16, 1996. Signed as a free agent by **Philadelphia**, July 2, 2001. Traded to **Los Angeles** by **Philadelphia** with Nashville's 3rd round choice (previously acquired) in 2006 Entry Draft for future considerations, August 4, 2005.

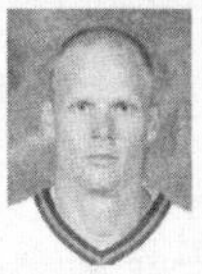

ROHLOFF, Todd

(ROH-lawf, TAWD) **T.B.**

Defense. Shoots left. 6'3", 213 lbs. Born, Grand Rapids, IL, January 16, 1974.

Season	Club	League	GP	G	A	Pts	PIM	PP	SH	GW	S	%	+/-	TF	F%	Min	GP	G	A	Pts	PIM	PP	SH	GW	Min
1992-93	St. Paul Vulcans	USHL	33	2	9	11	52	....	....	....	....	....	....	....	....	....	....	....	....	....	....	....	....	....	....
1993-94	St. Paul Vulcans	USHL	47	4	22	26	....	....	....	....	....	....	....	....	....	....	....	....	....	....	....	....	....	....	....
1994-95	Miami U.	CCHA	38	1	6	7	22	....	....	....	....	....	....	....	....	....	....	....	....	....	....	....	....	....	....
1995-96	Miami U.	CCHA	23	2	4	6	24	....	....	....	....	....	....	....	....	....	....	....	....	....	....	....	....	....	....
1996-97	Miami U.	CCHA	38	2	12	14	48	....	....	....	....	....	....	....	....	....	....	....	....	....	....	....	....	....	....
1997-98	Miami U.	CCHA	17	2	5	7	38	....	....	....	....	....	....	....	....	....	....	....	....	....	....	....	....	....	....
	Indianapolis Ice	IHL	5	0	1	1	6	....	....	....	....	....	....	....	....	....	1	0	0	0	0	....	....	....	....
1998-99	Portland Pirates	AHL	58	1	6	7	58	....	....	....	....	....	....	....	....	....	....	....	....	....	....	....	....	....	....
	Indianapolis Ice	IHL	12	2	0	2	8	....	....	....	....	....	....	....	....	....	5	1	1	2	6	....	....	....	....
99-2000	Cleveland	IHL	77	1	13	14	88	....	....	....	....	....	....	....	....	....	9	0	0	0	6	....	....	....	....
2000-01	Portland Pirates	AHL	58	3	8	11	59	....	....	....	....	....	....	....	....	....	3	0	0	0	2	....	....	....	....
2001-02	**Washington**	**NHL**	**16**	**0**	**1**	**1**	**14**	**0**	**0**	**0**	**6**	**0.0**	**–2**	**0**	**0.0**	**14:11**	....	....	....	....	....	....	....	....	....
	Portland Pirates	AHL	17	1	3	4	22	....	....	....	....	....	....	....	....	....	....	....	....	....	....	....	....	....	....
2002-03	Portland Pirates	AHL	64	2	10	12	65	....	....	....	....	....	....	....	....	....	3	0	0	0	2	....	....	....	....
2003-04	**Columbus**	**NHL**	**24**	**0**	**2**	**2**	**8**	**0**	**0**	**0**	**16**	**0.0**	**–12**	**2**	**50.0**	**19:15**	....	....	....	....	....	....	....	....	....
	Syracuse Crunch	AHL	14	1	5	6	16	....	....	....	....	....	....	....	....	....	....	....	....	....	....	....	....	....	....
	Washington	**NHL**	**35**	**0**	**3**	**3**	**18**	**0**	**0**	**0**	**19**	**0.0**	**–5**	**0**	**0.0**	**14:07**	....	....	....	....	....	....	....	....	....
2004-05	Rochester	AHL	12	0	1	1	4	....	....	....	....	....	....	....	....	....	....	....	....	....	....	....	....	....	....
	NHL Totals		**75**	**0**	**6**	**6**	**40**	**0**	**0**	**0**	**41**	**0.0**		**2**	**50.0**	**15:46**	....	....	....	....	....	....	....	....	....

Signed as a free agent by **Chicago**, March 24, 1998. Signed as a free agent by **Washington**, July 21, 2000. • Missed majority of 2001-02 season recovering from ankle injury suffered in off-season, September, 2001. Signed as a free agent by **Columbus**, September 5, 2003. Claimed on waivers by **Washington** from **Columbus**, January 9, 2004. Signed as a free agent by **Rochester** (AHL), September 10, 2004. Signed as a free agent by **Tampa Bay**, September 6, 2005.

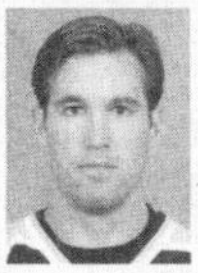

ROLSTON, Brian

(ROHL-stuhn, BRIGH-uhn) **MIN.**

Center/Right wing. Shoots left. 6'2", 210 lbs. Born, Flint, MI, February 21, 1973. New Jersey's 2nd choice, 11th overall, in 1991 Entry Draft.

Season	Club	League	GP	G	A	Pts	PIM	PP	SH	GW	S	%	+/-	TF	F%	Min	GP	G	A	Pts	PIM	PP	SH	GW	Min
1989-90	Det. Compuware	NAHL	40	36	37	73	57	....	....	....	....	....	....	....	....	....	....	....	....	....	....	....	....	....	....
1990-91	Det. Compuware	NAHL	36	49	46	95	14	....	....	....	....	....	....	....	....	....	....	....	....	....	....	....	....	....	....
1991-92	Lake Superior	CCHA	37	14	23	37	14	....	....	....	....	....	....	....	....	....	....	....	....	....	....	....	....	....	....
1992-93	Lake Superior	CCHA	39	33	31	64	20	....	....	....	....	....	....	....	....	....	....	....	....	....	....	....	....	....	....
1993-94	United States	Nat-Tm	41	20	28	48	36	....	....	....	....	....	....	....	....	....	....	....	....	....	....	....	....	....	....
	United States	Olympics	8	7	0	7	8	....	....	....	....	....	....	....	....	....	....	....	....	....	....	....	....	....	....
	Albany River Rats	AHL	17	5	5	10	8	....	....	....	....	....	....	....	....	....	5	1	2	3	0	....	....	....	....
1994-95	Albany River Rats	AHL	18	9	11	20	10	....	....	....	....	....	....	....	....	....	....	....	....	....	....	....	....	....	....
	♦ New Jersey	**NHL**	**40**	**7**	**11**	**18**	**17**	**2**	**0**	**3**	**92**	**7.6**	**5**	....	....	....	**6**	**2**	**1**	**3**	**4**	**1**	**0**	**0**	....
1995-96	**New Jersey**	**NHL**	**58**	**13**	**11**	**24**	**8**	**3**	**1**	**4**	**139**	**9.4**	**9**	....	....	....	....	....	....	....	....	....	....	....	....
1996-97	**New Jersey**	**NHL**	**81**	**18**	**27**	**45**	**20**	**2**	**2**	**3**	**237**	**7.6**	**6**	....	....	....	**10**	**4**	**1**	**5**	**6**	**1**	**2**	**0**	....
1997-98	**New Jersey**	**NHL**	**76**	**16**	**14**	**30**	**16**	**0**	**2**	**1**	**185**	**8.6**	**7**	....	....	....	**6**	**1**	**0**	**1**	**2**	**0**	**1**	**0**	....
1998-99	**New Jersey**	**NHL**	**82**	**24**	**33**	**57**	**14**	**5**	**5**	**3**	**210**	**11.4**	**11**	**51**	**45.1**	**18:49**	**7**	**1**	**0**	**1**	**2**	**0**	**1**	**0**	**17:36**
99-2000	**New Jersey**	**NHL**	**11**	**3**	**1**	**4**	**0**	**1**	**0**	**2**	**33**	**9.1**	**–2**	**37**	**37.8**	**19:09**	....	....	....	....	....	....	....	....	....
	Colorado	**NHL**	**50**	**8**	**10**	**18**	**12**	**1**	**0**	**3**	**107**	**7.5**	**–6**	**65**	**41.5**	**16:18**	....	....	....	....	....	....	....	....	....
	Boston	**NHL**	**16**	**5**	**4**	**9**	**6**	**3**	**0**	**1**	**66**	**7.6**	**–4**	**265**	**41.1**	**22:13**	....	....	....	....	....	....	....	....	....
2000-01	**Boston**	**NHL**	**77**	**19**	**39**	**58**	**28**	**5**	**0**	**4**	**286**	**6.6**	**6**	**666**	**45.7**	**19:19**	....	....	....	....	....	....	....	....	....
2001-02	**Boston**	**NHL**	**82**	**31**	**31**	**62**	**30**	**6**	**9**	**7**	**331**	**9.4**	**11**	**1289**	**46.6**	**20:24**	**6**	**4**	**1**	**5**	**0**	**1**	**1**	**0**	**20:37**
	United States	Olympics	6	0	3	3	0	....	....	....	....	....	....	....	....	....	....	....	....	....	....	....	....	....	....
2002-03	**Boston**	**NHL**	**81**	**27**	**32**	**59**	**32**	**6**	**5**	**5**	**281**	**9.6**	**1**	**1148**	**47.6**	**20:28**	**5**	**0**	**2**	**2**	**0**	**0**	**0**	**0**	**18:39**
2003-04	**Boston**	**NHL**	**82**	**19**	**29**	**48**	**40**	**3**	**2**	**3**	**257**	**7.4**	**9**	**1205**	**50.7**	**19:38**	**7**	**1**	**0**	**1**	**8**	**0**	**0**	**0**	**16:33**
2004-05			DID NOT PLAY																						
	NHL Totals		**736**	**190**	**242**	**432**	**223**	**37**	**26**	**39**	**2224**	**8.5**		**4726**	**47.3**	**19:26**	**47**	**13**	**5**	**18**	**22**	**3**	**5**	**0**	**18:15**

NCAA Championship All-Tournament Team (1992, 1993) • CCHA First All-Star Team (1993) • NCAA West Second All-American Team (1993)

Traded to **Colorado** by **New Jersey** with New Jersey's 1st round choice (later traded to Boston – Boston selected Martin Samuelsson) in 2000 Entry Draft for Claude Lemieux and Colorado's 1st (David Hale) and 2nd (Matt DeMarchi) round choices in 2000 Entry Draft, November 3, 1999. Traded to **Boston** by **Colorado** with Martin Grenier, Samuel Pahlsson and New Jersey's 1st round choice (previously acquired, Boston selected Martin Samuelsson) in 2000 Entry Draft for Raymond Bourque and Dave Andreychuk, March 6, 2000. Signed as a free agent by **Minnesota**, July 8, 2004.

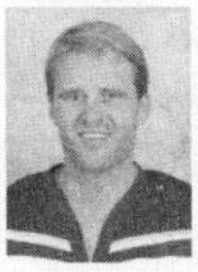

RONNING, Cliff

(RAWN-ihng, KLIHF)

Center. Shoots left. 5'8", 165 lbs. Born, Burnaby, B.C., October 1, 1965. St. Louis' 9th choice, 134th overall, in 1984 Entry Draft.

Season	Club	League	GP	G	A	Pts	PIM	PP	SH	GW	S	%	+/-	TF	F%	Min	GP	G	A	Pts	PIM	PP	SH	GW	Min
1982-83	New Westminster	BCJHL	52	83	68	151	22	....	....	....	....	....	....	....	....	....	....	....	....	....	....	....	....	....	....
1983-84	New Westminster	WHL	71	69	67	136	10	....	....	....	....	....	....	....	....	....	9	8	13	21	10	....	....	....	....
1984-85	New Westminster	WHL	70	*89	108	*197	20	....	....	....	....	....	....	....	....	....	11	10	14	24	4	....	....	....	....
1985-86	Canada	Nat-Tm	71	*55	*63	*118	53	....	....	....	....	....	....	....	....	....	....	....	....	....	....	....	....	....	....
	St. Louis	**NHL**	....	....	....	....	....	....	....	....	....	....	....	....	....	....	**5**	**1**	**1**	**2**	**2**	**1**	**0**	**0**	....
1986-87	Canada	Nat-Tm	26	17	16	33	12	....	....	....	....	....	....	....	....	....	....	....	....	....	....	....	....	....	....
	St. Louis	**NHL**	**42**	**11**	**14**	**25**	**6**	**2**	**0**	**2**	**68**	**16.2**	**–1**	....	....	....	**4**	**0**	**1**	**1**	**0**	**0**	**0**	**0**	....
1987-88	**St. Louis**	**NHL**	**26**	**5**	**8**	**13**	**12**	**1**	**0**	**1**	**38**	**13.2**	**6**	....	....	....	....	....	....	....	....	....	....	....	....
1988-89	**St. Louis**	**NHL**	**64**	**24**	**31**	**55**	**18**	**16**	**0**	**1**	**150**	**16.0**	**3**	....	....	....	**7**	**1**	**3**	**4**	**0**	**1**	**0**	**0**	....
	Peoria Rivermen	IHL	12	11	20	31	8	....	....	....	....	....	....	....	....	....	....	....	....	....	....	....	....	....	....
1989-90	HC Asiago	Italy	36	67	49	116	25	....	....	....	....	....	....	....	....	....	6	7	12	19	4	....	....	....	....
1990-91	**St. Louis**	**NHL**	**48**	**14**	**18**	**32**	**10**	**5**	**0**	**2**	**81**	**17.3**	**2**	....	....	....	....	....	....	....	....	....	....	....	....
	Vancouver	**NHL**	**11**	**6**	**6**	**12**	**0**	**2**	**0**	**0**	**32**	**18.8**	**–2**	....	....	....	**6**	**6**	**3**	**9**	**12**	**2**	**0**	**2**	....
1991-92	**Vancouver**	**NHL**	**80**	**24**	**47**	**71**	**42**	**6**	**0**	**2**	**216**	**11.1**	**18**	....	....	....	**13**	**8**	**5**	**13**	**6**	**1**	**0**	**1**	....
1992-93	**Vancouver**	**NHL**	**79**	**29**	**56**	**85**	**30**	**10**	**0**	**2**	**209**	**13.9**	**19**	....	....	....	**12**	**2**	**9**	**11**	**6**	**0**	**0**	**0**	....
1993-94	**Vancouver**	**NHL**	**76**	**25**	**43**	**68**	**42**	**10**	**0**	**4**	**197**	**12.7**	**7**	....	....	....	**24**	**5**	**10**	**15**	**16**	**2**	**0**	**2**	....
1994-95	**Vancouver**	**NHL**	**41**	**6**	**19**	**25**	**27**	**3**	**0**	**2**	**93**	**6.5**	**–4**	....	....	....	**11**	**3**	**5**	**8**	**2**	**1**	**0**	**2**	....
1995-96	**Vancouver**	**NHL**	**79**	**22**	**45**	**67**	**42**	**5**	**0**	**1**	**187**	**11.8**	**16**	....	....	....	**6**	**0**	**2**	**2**	**6**	**0**	**0**	**0**	....
1996-97	**Phoenix**	**NHL**	**69**	**19**	**32**	**51**	**26**	**8**	**0**	**2**	**171**	**11.1**	**–9**	....	....	....	**7**	**0**	**7**	**7**	**12**	**0**	**0**	**0**	....
1997-98	**Phoenix**	**NHL**	**80**	**11**	**44**	**55**	**36**	**3**	**0**	**0**	**197**	**5.6**	**5**	....	....	....	**6**	**1**	**3**	**4**	**4**	**0**	**0**	**0**	....
1998-99	**Phoenix**	**NHL**	**7**	**2**	**5**	**7**	**2**	**2**	**0**	**1**	**18**	**11.1**	**3**	**81**	**51.9**	**15:22**	....	....	....	....	....	....	....	....	....
	Nashville	**NHL**	**72**	**18**	**35**	**53**	**40**	**8**	**0**	**3**	**239**	**7.5**	**–6**	**1129**	**47.7**	**19:42**	....	....	....	....	....	....	....	....	....
99-2000	**Nashville**	**NHL**	**82**	**26**	**36**	**62**	**34**	**7**	**0**	**2**	**248**	**10.5**	**–13**	**611**	**45.7**	**18:11**	....	....	....	....	....	....	....	....	....
2000-01	**Nashville**	**NHL**	**80**	**19**	**43**	**62**	**28**	**6**	**0**	**4**	**237**	**8.0**	**4**	**331**	**45.0**	**17:23**	....	....	....	....	....	....	....	....	....
2001-02	**Nashville**	**NHL**	**67**	**18**	**31**	**49**	**24**	**4**	**0**	**0**	**164**	**11.0**	**0**	**98**	**51.0**	**16:44**	....	....	....	....	....	....	....	....	....
	Los Angeles	**NHL**	**14**	**1**	**4**	**5**	**8**	**1**	**0**	**0**	**35**	**2.9**	**0**	**14**	**50.0**	**16:53**	**4**	**0**	**1**	**1**	**2**	**0**	**0**	**0**	**11:09**
2002-03	**Minnesota**	**NHL**	**80**	**17**	**31**	**48**	**24**	**8**	**0**	**5**	**171**	**9.9**	**–6**	**566**	**47.0**	**17:25**	**17**	**2**	**7**	**9**	**4**	**1**	**0**	**0**	**16:39**
2003-04	**NY Islanders**	**NHL**	**40**	**9**	**15**	**24**	**2**	**2**	**0**	**0**	**55**	**16.4**	**3**	**174**	**45.4**	**11:56**	**4**	**0**	**0**	**0**	**0**	**0**	**0**	**0**	**5:44**
2004-05			DID NOT PLAY																						
	NHL Totals		**1137**	**306**	**563**	**869**	**453**	**109**	**0**	**34**	**2806**	**10.9**		**3004**	**47.0**	**17:16**	**126**	**29**	**57**	**86**	**72**	**9**	**0**	**7**	**14:01**

WHL Rookie of the Year (1984) • WHL West First All-Star Team (1985) • WHL Player of the Year (1985)

Traded to **Vancouver** by **St. Louis** with Geoff Courtnall, Robert Dirk, Sergio Momesso and St. Louis' 5th round choice (Brian Loney) in 1992 Entry Draft for Dan Quinn and Garth Butcher, March 5, 1991. Signed as a free agent by **Phoenix**, July 1, 1996. Traded to **Nashville** by **Phoenix** with Richard Lintner for future considerations, October 31, 1998. Traded to **Los Angeles** by **Nashville** for Jere Karalahti and Los Angeles' 4th round choice (Teemu Lassila) in 2003 Entry Draft, March 16, 2002. Traded to **Minnesota** by **Los Angeles** for Minnesota's 4th round choice (Aaron Rome) in 2002 Entry Draft, June 22, 2002. Signed as a free agent by **NY Islanders**, January 9, 2004.

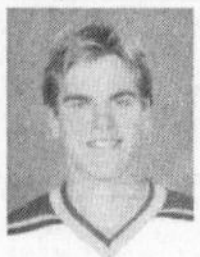

ROSA, Pavel

(ROHZA, PAH-vehl)

Right wing. Shoots right. 5'11", 188 lbs. Born, Most, Czech., June 7, 1977. Los Angeles' 3rd choice, 50th overall, in 1995 Entry Draft.

			Regular Season														Playoffs								
Season	Club	League	GP	G	A	Pts	PIM	PP	SH	GW	S	%	+/-	TF	F%	Min	GP	G	A	Pts	PIM	PP	SH	GW	Min
1994-95	Litvinov Jr.	CzRep-Jr.	40	56	42	98	....	....	....	....	....	....	....	....	....	....	....	....	....	....	....	....	....	....	....
	Litvinov	CzRep	2	0	0	0	0	....	....	....	....	....	....	....	....	....	1	0	0	0	0	....	....	....	....
1995-96	Hull Olympiques	QMJHL	61	46	70	116	39	....	....	....	....	....	....	....	....	....	18	14	22	36	25	....	....	....	....
1996-97	Hull Olympiques	QMJHL	68	*63	*90	*153	66	....	....	....	....	....	....	....	....	....	14	18	13	31	16	....	....	....	....
1997-98	Fredericton	AHL	1	0	0	0	0	....	....	....	....	....	....	....	....	....	....	....	....	....	....	....	....	....	....
	Long Beach	IHL	2	0	1	1	0	....	....	....	....	....	....	....	....	....	1	1	1	2	0	....	....	....	....
1998-99	**Los Angeles**	**NHL**	**29**	**4**	**12**	**16**	**6**	**0**	**0**	**0**	**61**	**6.6**	**0**	**0**	**0.0**	**13:34**	....	....	....	....	....	....	....	....	....
	Long Beach	IHL	31	17	13	30	28	....	....	....	....	....	....	....	....	....	6	1	2	3	0	....	....	....	....
99-2000	**Los Angeles**	**NHL**	**3**	**0**	**0**	**0**	**0**	**0**	**0**	**0**	**1**	**0.0**	**–1**	**0**	**0.0**	**11:21**	....	....	....	....	....	....	....	....	....
	Long Beach	IHL	74	22	31	53	76	....	....	....	....	....	....	....	....	....	6	2	2	4	4	....	....	....	....
2000-01	HPK Hameenlinna	Finland	54	25	25	50	53	....	....	....	....	....	....	....	....	....	....	....	....	....	....	....	....	....	....
2001-02	Jokerit Helsinki	Finland	46	21	22	43	37	....	....	....	....	....	....	....	....	....	12	3	5	8	18	....	....	....	....
2002-03	**Los Angeles**	**NHL**	**2**	**0**	**0**	**0**	**0**	**0**	**0**	**0**	**4**	**0.0**	**–1**	**0**	**0.0**	**13:57**	....	....	....	....	....	....	....	....	....
	Manchester	AHL	61	28	35	63	20	....	....	....	....	....	....	....	....	....	3	3	1	4	4	....	....	....	....
2003-04	**Los Angeles**	**NHL**	**2**	**1**	**1**	**2**	**0**	**0**	**0**	**0**	**4**	**25.0**	**1**	**0**	**0.0**	**12:41**	....	....	....	....	....	....	....	....	....
	Manchester	AHL	77	39	49	*88	32	....	....	....	....	....	....	....	....	....	6	3	6	9	6	....	....	....	....
2004-05	Dynamo Moscow	Russia	54	21	23	44	14	....	....	....	....	....	....	....	....	....	8	3	2	5	2	....	....	....	....
	NHL Totals		**36**	**5**	**13**	**18**	**6**	**0**	**0**	**0**	**70**	**7.1**		**0**	**0.0**	**13:21**	....	....	....	....	....	....	....	....	....

QMJHL All-Rookie Team (1996) • QMJHL Offensive Rookie of the Year (1996) • QMJHL First All-Star Team (1997) • Canadian Major Junior First All-Star Team (1997) • AHL Second All-Star Team (2004) • John P. Sollenger Award (Leading Scorer - AHL) (2004)

• Missed majority of 1997-98 season recovering from head injury suffered in training camp, September, 1997. Signed as a free agent by **Dynamo Moscow** (Russia), May 4, 2004.

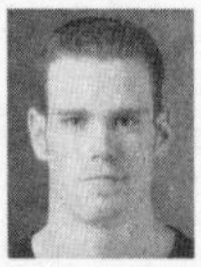

ROSSITER, Kyle

(RAWS-ih-tuhr, KIGHL)

Defense. Shoots left. 6'3", 220 lbs. Born, Edmonton, Alta., June 9, 1980. Florida's 1st choice, 30th overall, in 1998 Entry Draft.

			Regular Season														Playoffs								
Season	Club	League	GP	G	A	Pts	PIM	PP	SH	GW	S	%	+/-	TF	F%	Min	GP	G	A	Pts	PIM	PP	SH	GW	Min
1995-96	Edmonton SSAC	AMHL	34	5	19	24	116	....	....	....	....	....	....	....	....	....	....	....	....	....	....	....	....	....	....
1996-97	Spokane Chiefs	WHL	50	0	2	2	65	....	....	....	....	....	....	....	....	....	9	0	0	0	6	....	....	....	....
1997-98	Spokane Chiefs	WHL	61	6	16	22	190	....	....	....	....	....	....	....	....	....	15	0	3	3	28	....	....	....	....
1998-99	Spokane Chiefs	WHL	71	4	17	21	206	....	....	....	....	....	....	....	....	....	....	....	....	....	....	....	....	....	....
99-2000	Spokane Chiefs	WHL	63	11	22	33	155	....	....	....	....	....	....	....	....	....	15	1	4	5	25	....	....	....	....
2000-01	Louisville Panthers	AHL	78	2	5	7	110	....	....	....	....	....	....	....	....	....	....	....	....	....	....	....	....	....	....
2001-02	**Florida**	**NHL**	**2**	**0**	**0**	**0**	**2**	**0**	**0**	**0**	**0**	**0.0**	**–1**	**0**	**0.0**	**15:27**	....	....	....	....	....	....	....	....	....
	Utah Grizzlies	AHL	74	3	7	10	88	....	....	....	....	....	....	....	....	....	5	0	1	1	0	....	....	....	....
2002-03	**Florida**	**NHL**	**3**	**0**	**0**	**0**	**0**	**0**	**0**	**0**	**0**	**0.0**	**–2**	**0**	**0.0**	**10:09**	....	....	....	....	....	....	....	....	....
	San Antonio	AHL	67	0	7	7	107	....	....	....	....	....	....	....	....	....	3	0	0	0	0	....	....	....	....
2003-04	**Florida**	**NHL**	**4**	**0**	**0**	**0**	**7**	**0**	**0**	**0**	**1**	**0.0**	**–1**	**0**	**0.0**	**11:55**	....	....	....	....	....	....	....	....	....
	San Antonio	AHL	51	5	7	12	70	....	....	....	....	....	....	....	....	....	....	....	....	....	....	....	....	....	....
	Atlanta	**NHL**	**2**	**0**	**1**	**1**	**0**	**0**	**0**	**0**	**0**	**0.0**	**1**	**0**	**0.0**	**10:14**	....	....	....	....	....	....	....	....	....
	Chicago Wolves	AHL	12	0	1	1	25	....	....	....	....	....	....	....	....	....	6	0	0	0	19	....	....	....	....
2004-05	Chicago Wolves	AHL	33	1	5	6	43	....	....	....	....	....	....	....	....	....	....	....	....	....	....	....	....	....	....
	Wilkes-Barre	AHL	9	0	1	1	5	....	....	....	....	....	....	....	....	....	1	0	0	0	0	....	....	....	....
	NHL Totals		**11**	**0**	**1**	**1**	**9**	**0**	**0**	**0**	**1**	**0.0**		**0**	**0.0**	**11:46**	....	....	....	....	....	....	....	....	....

Canadian Major Junior Scholastic Player of the Year (1998)

Traded to **Atlanta** by **Florida** for Kamil Piros, March 8, 2004. Loaned to **Wilkes-Barre** (AHL) by **Chicago** (AHL) for cash, March 16, 2005.

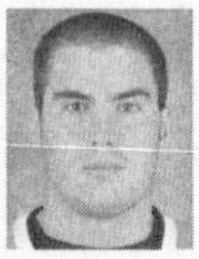

ROURKE, Allan

(RAWRK, AL-lan) **NYI**

Defense. Shoots left. 6'1", 214 lbs. Born, Mississauga, Ont., March 6, 1980. Toronto's 6th choice, 154th overall, in 1998 Entry Draft.

			Regular Season														Playoffs								
Season	Club	League	GP	G	A	Pts	PIM	PP	SH	GW	S	%	+/-	TF	F%	Min	GP	G	A	Pts	PIM	PP	SH	GW	Min
1995-96	Mississauga Reps	MTHL	38	15	25	40	173	....	....	....	....	....	....	....	....	....	....	....	....	....	....	....	....	....	....
1996-97	Kitchener Rangers	OHL	25	1	1	2	12	....	....	....	....	....	....	....	....	....	6	0	0	0	0	....	....	....	....
1997-98	Kitchener Rangers	OHL	48	5	17	22	59	....	....	....	....	....	....	....	....	....	6	1	1	2	6	....	....	....	....
1998-99	Kitchener Rangers	OHL	66	11	28	39	79	....	....	....	....	....	....	....	....	....	1	0	0	0	2	....	....	....	....
99-2000	Kitchener Rangers	OHL	67	31	43	74	57	....	....	....	....	....	....	....	....	....	5	0	6	6	13	....	....	....	....
2000-01	St. John's	AHL	64	9	19	28	36	....	....	....	....	....	....	....	....	....	....	....	....	....	....	....	....	....	....
2001-02	St. John's	AHL	62	2	9	11	48	....	....	....	....	....	....	....	....	....	10	0	2	2	6	....	....	....	....
2002-03	St. John's	AHL	65	12	19	31	49	....	....	....	....	....	....	....	....	....	....	....	....	....	....	....	....	....	....
2003-04	**Carolina**	**NHL**	**25**	**1**	**2**	**3**	**22**	**0**	**0**	**0**	**24**	**4.2**	**4**	**0**	**0.0**	**12:28**	....	....	....	....	....	....	....	....	....
	Lowell	AHL	45	5	9	14	45	....	....	....	....	....	....	....	....	....	....	....	....	....	....	....	....	....	....
2004-05	Lowell	AHL	60	7	9	16	75	....	....	....	....	....	....	....	....	....	11	1	2	3	40	....	....	....	....
	NHL Totals		**25**	**1**	**2**	**3**	**22**	**0**	**0**	**0**	**24**	**4.2**		**0**	**0.0**	**12:28**	....	....	....	....	....	....	....	....	....

OHL Second All-Star Team (2000)

Traded to **Carolina** by **Toronto** for Harold Druken, May 29, 2003. Signed as a free agent by **NY Islanders**, August 12, 2005.

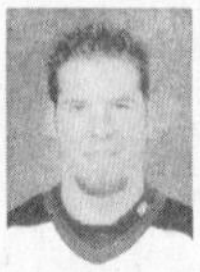

ROY, Andre

(WAH, AHN-dray) **PIT.**

Right wing. Shoots left. 6'4", 221 lbs. Born, Port Chester, NY, February 8, 1975. Boston's 5th choice, 151st overall, in 1994 Entry Draft.

			Regular Season														Playoffs								
Season	Club	League	GP	G	A	Pts	PIM	PP	SH	GW	S	%	+/-	TF	F%	Min	GP	G	A	Pts	PIM	PP	SH	GW	Min
1992-93	Nord Selects	QAHA	STATISTICS NOT AVAILABLE																						
1993-94	Goulbourn Royals	OHA-C	9	9	13	22	98	....	....	....	....	....	....	....	....	....	....	....	....	....	....	....	....	....	....
	Beauport	QMJHL	33	6	7	13	125	....	....	....	....	....	....	....	....	....	....	....	....	....	....	....	....	....	....
	Chicoutimi	QMJHL	32	4	14	18	152	....	....	....	....	....	....	....	....	....	25	3	6	9	94	....	....	....	....
1994-95	Chicoutimi	QMJHL	20	15	8	23	90	....	....	....	....	....	....	....	....	....	....	....	....	....	....	....	....	....	....
	Drummondville	QMJHL	34	18	13	31	233	....	....	....	....	....	....	....	....	....	4	2	0	2	34	....	....	....	....
1995-96	**Boston**	**NHL**	**3**	**0**	**0**	**0**	**0**	**0**	**0**	**0**	**0**	**0.0**	**0**	....	....	....	....	....	....	....	....	....	....	....	....
	Providence Bruins	AHL	58	7	8	15	167	....	....	....	....	....	....	....	....	....	1	0	0	0	10	....	....	....	....
1996-97	**Boston**	**NHL**	**10**	**0**	**2**	**2**	**12**	**0**	**0**	**0**	**12**	**0.0**	**–5**	....	....	....	....	....	....	....	....	....	....	....	....
	Providence Bruins	AHL	50	17	11	28	234	....	....	....	....	....	....	....	....	....	....	....	....	....	....	....	....	....	....
1997-98	Providence Bruins	AHL	36	3	11	14	154	....	....	....	....	....	....	....	....	....	....	....	....	....	....	....	....	....	....
	Charlotte	ECHL	27	10	8	18	132	....	....	....	....	....	....	....	....	....	7	2	3	5	34	....	....	....	....
1998-99	Fort Wayne	IHL	65	15	6	21	*395	....	....	....	....	....	....	....	....	....	2	0	0	0	11	....	....	....	....
99-2000	**Ottawa**	**NHL**	**73**	**4**	**3**	**7**	**145**	**0**	**0**	**1**	**39**	**10.3**	**3**	**3**	**33.3**	**6:29**	**5**	**0**	**0**	**0**	**2**	**0**	**0**	**0**	**5:54**
2000-01	**Ottawa**	**NHL**	**64**	**3**	**5**	**8**	**169**	**0**	**0**	**0**	**33**	**9.1**	**1**	**2**	**50.0**	**4:36**	**2**	**0**	**0**	**0**	**16**	**0**	**0**	**0**	**4:16**
2001-02	**Ottawa**	**NHL**	**56**	**6**	**8**	**14**	**148**	**0**	**0**	**0**	**60**	**10.0**	**3**	**1**	**100.0**	**8:23**	....	....	....	....	....	....	....	....	....
	Tampa Bay	**NHL**	**9**	**1**	**1**	**2**	**63**	**0**	**0**	**0**	**6**	**16.7**	**–5**	**0**	**0.0**	**8:58**	....	....	....	....	....	....	....	....	....
2002-03	**Tampa Bay**	**NHL**	**62**	**10**	**7**	**17**	**119**	**0**	**0**	**2**	**85**	**11.8**	**0**	**7**	**57.1**	**10:46**	**5**	**0**	**1**	**1**	**2**	**0**	**0**	**0**	**12:31**
2003-04♦	**Tampa Bay**	**NHL**	**33**	**1**	**1**	**2**	**78**	**0**	**0**	**0**	**24**	**4.2**	**–5**	**2**	**50.0**	**7:52**	**21**	**1**	**2**	**3**	**61**	**0**	**0**	**1**	**6:11**
2004-05			DID NOT PLAY																						
	NHL Totals		**310**	**25**	**27**	**52**	**734**	**0**	**0**	**3**	**259**	**9.7**		**15**	**53.3**	**7:33**	**33**	**1**	**3**	**4**	**81**	**0**	**0**	**1**	**6:59**

Signed as a free agent by **Ottawa**, April 28, 1999. Traded to **Tampa Bay** by **Ottawa** with Ottawa's 6th round choice (Paul Ranger) in 2002 Entry Draft for Juha Ylonen, March 15, 2002. • Spent majority of 2003-04 season as a healthy reserve. Signed as a free agent by **Pittsburgh**, August 4, 2005.

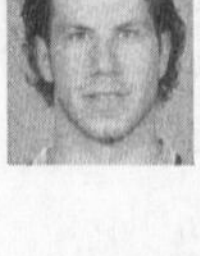

ROY, Derek

(ROI, DAIR-ihk) **BUF.**

Center. Shoots left. 5'9", 186 lbs. Born, Ottawa, Ont., May 4, 1983. Buffalo's 2nd choice, 32nd overall, in 2001 Entry Draft.

			Regular Season														Playoffs								
Season	Club	League	GP	G	A	Pts	PIM	PP	SH	GW	S	%	+/-	TF	F%	Min	GP	G	A	Pts	PIM	PP	SH	GW	Min
1998-99	Ontario East	OMHA	34	61	31	92	42	....	....	....	....	....	....	....	....	....	....	....	....	....	....	....	....	....	....
99-2000	Kitchener Rangers	OHL	66	34	53	87	44	....	....	....	....	....	....	....	....	....	5	4	1	5	6	....	....	....	....
2000-01	Kitchener Rangers	OHL	65	42	39	81	114	....	....	....	....	....	....	....	....	....	....	....	....	....	....	....	....	....	....
2001-02	Kitchener Rangers	OHL	62	43	46	89	92	....	....	....	....	....	....	....	....	....	4	1	2	3	2	....	....	....	....
2002-03	Kitchener Rangers	OHL	49	28	50	78	73	....	....	....	....	....	....	....	....	....	21	9	*23	32	14	....	....	....	....
2003-04	**Buffalo**	**NHL**	**49**	**9**	**10**	**19**	**12**	**1**	**0**	**4**	**71**	**12.7**	**–8**	**715**	**47.4**	**15:19**	....	....	....	....	....	....	....	....	....
	Rochester	AHL	26	10	16	26	20	....	....	....	....	....	....	....	....	....	16	6	8	14	18	....	....	....	....
2004-05	Rochester	AHL	67	16	45	61	60	....	....	....	....	....	....	....	....	....	9	6	5	11	6	....	....	....	....
	NHL Totals		**49**	**9**	**10**	**19**	**12**	**1**	**0**	**4**	**71**	**12.7**		**715**	**47.4**	**15:19**	....	....	....	....	....	....	....	....	....

OHL All-Rookie Team (2000) • OHL Rookie of the Year (2000) • CHL All-Rookie Team (2000) • CHL Plus/Minus Award (2000) • CHL Most Sportsmanlike Player (2000) • Memorial Cup Tournament All-Star Team (2003) • Stafford Smythe Memorial Trophy (Memorial Cup Tournament MVP) (2003)

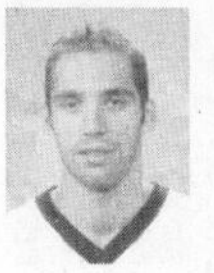

ROZSIVAL, Michal
(roh-ZIH-vahl, MEE-khahl)

Defense. Shoots right. 6'1", 212 lbs. Born, Vlasim, Czech., September 3, 1978. Pittsburgh's 5th choice, 105th overall, in 1996 Entry Draft.

			Regular Season														Playoffs								
Season	Club	League	GP	G	A	Pts	PIM	PP	SH	GW	S	%	+/-	TF	F%	Min	GP	G	A	Pts	PIM	PP	SH	GW	Min
1994-95	Jihlava Jr.	CzRep-Jr.	31	8	13	21	....	....	....	....	....	....	....	....	....	....	....	....	....	....	....	....	....	....	....
1995-96	HC Dukla Jihlava	CzRep	36	3	4	7	....	....	....	....	....	....	....	....	....	....	....	....	....	....	....	....	....	....	....
1996-97	Swift Current	WHL	63	8	31	39	80	....	....	....	....	....	....	....	....	....	10	0	6	6	15	....	....	....	....
1997-98	Swift Current	WHL	71	14	55	69	122	....	....	....	....	....	....	....	....	....	12	0	5	5	33	....	....	....	....
1998-99	Syracuse Crunch	AHL	49	3	22	25	72	....	....	....	....	....	....	....	....	....	....	....	....	....	....	....	....	....	....
99-2000	**Pittsburgh**	**NHL**	75	4	17	21	48	1	0	1	73	5.5	11	1	0.0	19:01	2	0	0	0	4	0	0	0	30:56
2000-01	**Pittsburgh**	**NHL**	30	1	4	5	26	0	0	0	17	5.9	3	1	100.0	17:06	....	....	....	....	....	....	....	....	....
	Wilkes-Barre	AHL	29	8	8	16	32	....	....	....	....	....	....	....	....	....	21	3	*19	22	23	....	....	....	....
2001-02	**Pittsburgh**	**NHL**	79	9	20	29	47	4	0	4	89	10.1	-6	0	0.0	20:01	....	....	....	....	....	....	....	....	....
2002-03	**Pittsburgh**	**NHL**	53	4	6	10	40	1	0	0	61	6.6	-5	0	0.0	20:25	....	....	....	....	....	....	....	....	....
2003-04	Wilkes-Barre	AHL	1	0	0	0	2	....	....	....	....	....	....	....	....	....	....	....	....	....	....	....	....	....	....
2004-05	HC Ocelari Trinec	CzRep	35	1	10	11	40	....	....	....	....	....	....	....	....	....	....	....	....	....	....	....	....	....	....
	Pardubice	CzRep	16	1	3	4	30	....	....	....	....	....	....	....	....	....	16	1	2	3	34	....	....	....	....
	NHL Totals		**237**	**18**	**47**	**65**	**161**	**6**	**0**	**5**	**240**	**7.5**		**2**	**50.0**	**19:25**	**2**	**0**	**0**	**0**	**4**	**0**	**0**	**0**	**30:56**

WHL East First All-Star Team (1998)

• Missed majority of 2003-04 season recovering from knee injury suffered in training camp, September 18, 2003. Signed as a free agent by **Trinec** (CzRep), September 17, 2004. Signed as a free agent by **Pardubice** (CzRep), January, 2005. Signed as a free agent by **NY Rangers**, August 29, 2005.

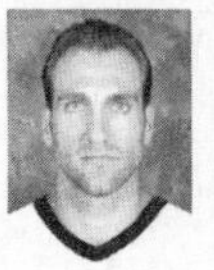

RUCCHIN, Steve
(ROO-chihn, STEEV) **NYR**

Center. Shoots left. 6'2", 211 lbs. Born, Thunder Bay, Ont., July 4, 1971. Anaheim's 1st choice, 2nd overall, in 1994 Supplemental Draft.

			Regular Season														Playoffs								
Season	Club	League	GP	G	A	Pts	PIM	PP	SH	GW	S	%	+/-	TF	F%	Min	GP	G	A	Pts	PIM	PP	SH	GW	Min
1989-90	Banting	High-ON	STATISTICS NOT AVAILABLE																						
	Thamesford	OHA-D	2	1	2	3	0	....	....	....	....	....	....	....	....	....	....	....	....	....	....	....	....	....	....
1990-91	Western Ontario	OUAA	34	13	16	29	14	....	....	....	....	....	....	....	....	....	....	....	....	....	....	....	....	....	....
1991-92	Western Ontario	OUAA	37	28	34	62	36	....	....	....	....	....	....	....	....	....	....	....	....	....	....	....	....	....	....
1992-93	Western Ontario	OUAA	34	22	26	48	16	....	....	....	....	....	....	....	....	....	....	....	....	....	....	....	....	....	....
1993-94	Western Ontario	OUAA	35	30	23	53	30	....	....	....	....	....	....	....	....	....	....	....	....	....	....	....	....	....	....
1994-95	San Diego Gulls	IHL	41	11	15	26	14	....	....	....	....	....	....	....	....	....	....	....	....	....	....	....	....	....	....
	Anaheim	**NHL**	43	6	11	17	23	0	0	1	59	10.2	7	....	....	....	....	....	....	....	....	....	....	....	....
1995-96	**Anaheim**	**NHL**	64	19	25	44	12	8	1	4	113	16.8	3	....	....	....	....	....	....	....	....	....	....	....	....
1996-97	**Anaheim**	**NHL**	79	19	48	67	24	6	1	2	153	12.4	26	....	....	....	8	1	2	3	10	0	0	0	....
1997-98	**Anaheim**	**NHL**	72	17	36	53	13	8	1	3	131	13.0	8	....	....	....	....	....	....	....	....	....	....	....	....
1998-99	**Anaheim**	**NHL**	69	23	39	62	22	5	1	5	145	15.9	11	1845	52.3	22:33	4	0	3	3	0	0	0	0	21:55
99-2000	**Anaheim**	**NHL**	71	19	38	57	16	10	0	2	131	14.5	9	1996	53.4	22:12	....	....	....	....	....	....	....	....	....
2000-01	**Anaheim**	**NHL**	16	3	5	8	0	2	0	0	19	15.8	-5	289	51.6	18:47	....	....	....	....	....	....	....	....	....
2001-02	**Anaheim**	**NHL**	38	7	16	23	6	4	0	1	57	12.3	-3	808	52.2	19:17	....	....	....	....	....	....	....	....	....
2002-03	**Anaheim**	**NHL**	82	20	38	58	12	6	1	4	194	10.3	-14	1613	54.2	21:05	21	7	3	10	2	1	0	2	23:35
2003-04	**Anaheim**	**NHL**	82	20	23	43	12	9	1	1	148	13.5	-14	1446	53.6	19:46	....	....	....	....	....	....	....	....	....
2004-05			DID NOT PLAY																						
	NHL Totals		**616**	**153**	**279**	**432**	**140**	**58**	**6**	**23**	**1150**	**13.3**		**7997**	**53.2**	**21:00**	**33**	**8**	**8**	**16**	**12**	**1**	**0**	**2**	**23:19**

• Missed majority of 2000-01 season recovering from jaw injury suffered in game vs. Colorado, November 15, 2000. • Missed majority of 2001-02 season recovering from leg injury suffered in game vs. San Jose, November 16, 2001. Traded to **NY Rangers** by **Anaheim** for Trevor Gillies and a conditional choice in 2007 Entry Draft, August 23, 2005.

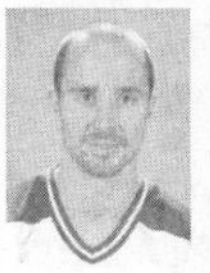

RUCINSKY, Martin
(roo-CHIHN-skee, MAHR-tihn) **NYR**

Left wing. Shoots left. 6'1", 205 lbs. Born, Most, Czech., March 11, 1971. Edmonton's 2nd choice, 20th overall, in 1991 Entry Draft.

			Regular Season														Playoffs								
Season	Club	League	GP	G	A	Pts	PIM	PP	SH	GW	S	%	+/-	TF	F%	Min	GP	G	A	Pts	PIM	PP	SH	GW	Min
1988-89	CHZ Litvinov	Czech	3	1	0	1	2	....	....	....	....	....	....	....	....	....	....	....	....	....	....	....	....	....	....
1989-90	CHZ Litvinov	Czech	39	12	6	18	....	....	....	....	....	....	....	....	....	....	8	5	3	8	....	....	....	....	....
1990-91	HC CHZ Litvinov	Czech	56	24	20	44	69	....	....	....	....	....	....	....	....	....	....	....	....	....	....	....	....	....	....
1991-92	**Edmonton**	**NHL**	2	0	0	0	0	0	0	0	1	0.0	-3	....	....	....	....	....	....	....	....	....	....	....	....
	Cape Breton	AHL	35	11	12	23	34	....	....	....	....	....	....	....	....	....	....	....	....	....	....	....	....	....	....
	Quebec	**NHL**	4	1	1	2	2	0	0	0	4	25.0	1	....	....	....	....	....	....	....	....	....	....	....	....
	Halifax Citadels	AHL	7	1	1	2	6	....	....	....	....	....	....	....	....	....	....	....	....	....	....	....	....	....	....
1992-93	**Quebec**	**NHL**	77	18	30	48	51	4	0	1	133	13.5	16	....	....	....	6	1	1	2	4	1	0	0	....
1993-94	**Quebec**	**NHL**	60	9	23	32	58	4	0	1	96	9.4	4	....	....	....	....	....	....	....	....	....	....	....	....
1994-95	Litvinov	CzRep	13	12	10	22	54	....	....	....	....	....	....	....	....	....	....	....	....	....	....	....	....	....	....
	Quebec	**NHL**	20	3	6	9	14	0	0	0	32	9.4	5	....	....	....	....	....	....	....	....	....	....	....	....
1995-96	HC Petra Vsetin	CzRep	1	1	1	2	0	....	....	....	....	....	....	....	....	....	....	....	....	....	....	....	....	....	....
	Colorado	**NHL**	22	4	11	15	14	0	0	1	39	10.3	10	....	....	....	....	....	....	....	....	....	....	....	....
	Montreal	**NHL**	56	25	35	60	54	9	2	3	142	17.6	8	....	....	....	....	....	....	....	....	....	....	....	....
1996-97	**Montreal**	**NHL**	70	28	27	55	62	6	3	3	172	16.3	1	....	....	....	5	0	0	0	4	0	0	0	....
1997-98	**Montreal**	**NHL**	78	21	32	53	84	5	3	3	192	10.9	13	....	....	....	10	3	0	3	4	1	0	0	....
	Czech Republic	Olympics	6	3	1	4	4	....	....	....	....	....	....	....	....	....	....	....	....	....	....	....	....	....	....
1998-99	Litvinov	CzRep	3	2	2	4	0	....	....	....	....	....	....	....	....	....	....	....	....	....	....	....	....	....	....
	Montreal	**NHL**	73	17	17	34	50	5	0	1	180	9.4	-25	12	50.0	18:12	....	....	....	....	....	....	....	....	....
99-2000	**Montreal**	**NHL**	80	25	24	49	70	7	1	4	242	10.3	1	31	54.8	18:54	....	....	....	....	....	....	....	....	....
2000-01	**Montreal**	**NHL**	57	16	22	38	66	5	1	4	141	11.3	-5	5	40.0	19:11	....	....	....	....	....	....	....	....	....
2001-02	**Montreal**	**NHL**	18	2	6	8	12	1	0	0	41	4.9	-1	5	80.0	16:15	....	....	....	....	....	....	....	....	....
	Dallas	**NHL**	42	6	11	17	24	2	0	1	63	9.5	3	7	57.1	14:33	....	....	....	....	....	....	....	....	....
	Czech Republic	Olympics	4	0	3	3	2	....	....	....	....	....	....	....	....	....	....	....	....	....	....	....	....	....	....
	NY Rangers	**NHL**	15	3	10	13	6	0	0	1	24	12.5	6	3	33.3	16:39	....	....	....	....	....	....	....	....	....
2002-03	Litvinov	CzRep	2	1	0	1	2	....	....	....	....	....	....	....	....	....	....	....	....	....	....	....	....	....	....
	St. Louis	**NHL**	61	16	14	30	38	4	4	3	135	11.9	-1	19	57.9	16:55	7	4	2	6	4	0	0	0	16:52
2003-04	**NY Rangers**	**NHL**	69	13	29	42	62	0	1	2	161	8.1	13	14	14.3	18:51	....	....	....	....	....	....	....	....	....
	Vancouver	**NHL**	13	1	2	3	10	0	0	0	45	2.2	2	2	0.0	19:03	7	1	1	2	6	1	0	0	17:02
2004-05	Litvinov	CzRep	38	15	26	41	87	....	....	....	....	....	....	....	....	....	....	....	....	....	....	....	....	....	....
	NHL Totals		**817**	**208**	**300**	**508**	**677**	**52**	**15**	**28**	**1843**	**11.3**		**98**	**48.0**	**17:55**	**35**	**9**	**4**	**13**	**22**	**3**	**0**	**0**	**16:57**

Played in NHL All-Star Game (2000)

Traded to **Quebec** by **Edmonton** for Ron Tugnutt and Brad Zavisha, March 10, 1992. Transferred to **Colorado** after **Quebec** franchise relocated, June 21, 1995. Traded to **Montreal** by **Colorado** with Andrei Kovalenko and Jocelyn Thibault for Patrick Roy and Mike Keane, December 6, 1995. Traded to **Dallas** by **Montreal** with Benoit Brunet for Donald Audette and Shaun Van Allen, November 21, 2001. Traded to **NY Rangers** by **Dallas** with Roman Lyashenko for Manny Malhotra and Barrett Heisten, March 12, 2002. Signed as a free agent by **St. Louis**, October 30, 2002. Signed as a free agent by **NY Rangers**, August 28, 2003. Traded to **Vancouver** by **NY Rangers** for R.J. Umberger and Martin Grenier, March 9, 2004. Signed as a free agent by **Litvinov** (CzRep), August 20, 2004. Signed as a free agent by **NY Rangers**, August 3, 2005.

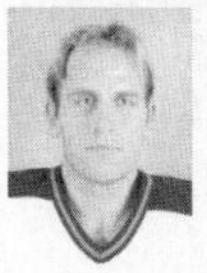

RUPP, Mike
(RUHP, MIGHK) **PHX.**

Center. Shoots left. 6'5", 230 lbs. Born, Cleveland, OH, January 13, 1980. New Jersey's 7th choice, 76th overall, in 2000 Entry Draft.

			Regular Season														Playoffs								
Season	Club	League	GP	G	A	Pts	PIM	PP	SH	GW	S	%	+/-	TF	F%	Min	GP	G	A	Pts	PIM	PP	SH	GW	Min
1996-97	St. Edward's	High-OH	20	26	24	50	....	....	....	....	....	....	....	....	....	....	....	....	....	....	....	....	....	....	....
1997-98	Windsor Spitfires	OHL	38	9	8	17	60	....	....	....	....	....	....	....	....	....	....	....	....	....	....	....	....	....	....
	Erie Otters	OHL	26	7	3	10	57	....	....	....	....	....	....	....	....	....	7	3	1	4	6	....	....	....	....
1998-99	Erie Otters	OHL	63	22	25	47	102	....	....	....	....	....	....	....	....	....	5	0	2	2	25	....	....	....	....
99-2000	Erie Otters	OHL	58	32	21	53	134	....	....	....	....	....	....	....	....	....	13	5	5	10	22	....	....	....	....
2000-01	Albany River Rats	AHL	71	10	10	20	63	....	....	....	....	....	....	....	....	....	....	....	....	....	....	....	....	....	....
2001-02	Albany River Rats	AHL	78	13	17	30	90	....	....	....	....	....	....	....	....	....	....	....	....	....	....	....	....	....	....
2002-03 ♦	**New Jersey**	**NHL**	26	5	3	8	21	2	0	3	34	14.7	0	150	44.7	11:39	4	1	3	4	0	0	0	1	11:28
	Albany River Rats	AHL	47	8	11	19	74	....	....	....	....	....	....	....	....	....	....	....	....	....	....	....	....	....	....
2003-04	**New Jersey**	**NHL**	51	6	5	11	41	1	0	1	64	9.4	-1	386	47.9	10:38	....	....	....	....	....	....	....	....	....
	Phoenix	**NHL**	6	0	1	1	6	0	0	0	12	0.0	-3	94	57.5	16:59	....	....	....	....	....	....	....	....	....
2004-05	Danbury Trashers	UHL	14	5	5	10	30	....	....	....	....	....	....	....	....	....	11	3	4	7	38	....	....	....	....
	NHL Totals		**83**	**11**	**9**	**20**	**68**	**3**	**0**	**4**	**110**	**10.0**		**630**	**48.6**	**11:25**	**4**	**1**	**3**	**4**	**0**	**0**	**0**	**1**	**11:28**

• Re-entered NHL Entry Draft. Originally NY Islanders' 1st choice, 9th overall, in 1998 Entry Draft.

Traded to **Phoenix** by **New Jersey** with New Jersey's 2nd round choice (later traded to Edmonton – Edmonton selected Geoff Paukovich) in 2004 Entry Draft for Jan Hrdina, March 5, 2004. Signed as a free agent by **Danbury** (UHL), February 10, 2005.

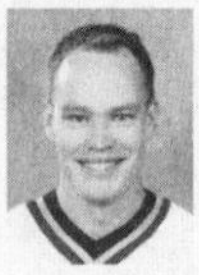

RUUTU, Jarkko
(ROO-too, YAHR-koh) **VAN.**

Right wing. Shoots left. 6'2", 195 lbs. Born, Vantaa, Finland, August 23, 1975. Vancouver's 3rd choice, 68th overall, in 1998 Entry Draft.

Season	Club	League	GP	G	A	Pts	PIM	PP	SH	GW	S	%	+/-	TF	F%	Min	GP	G	A	Pts	PIM	PP	SH	GW	Min
			Regular Season														Playoffs								
1991-92	HIFK Helsinki Jr.	Finland-Jr.	1	0	0	0	0																		
1992-93	HIFK Helsinki U18	Fin-U18	33	26	21	47	53																		
	HIFK Helsinki Jr.	Finland-Jr.	1	0	0	0	0																		
1993-94	HIFK Helsinki Jr.	Finland-Jr.	19	9	12	21	44																		
1994-95	HIFK Helsinki Jr.	Finland-Jr.	35	26	22	48	117																		
1995-96	Michigan Tech	WCHA	39	12	10	22	96																		
1996-97	HIFK Helsinki	Finland	48	11	10	21	*155																		
1997-98	HIFK Helsinki	Finland	37	10	10	20	87										8	*7	4	11	10				
1998-99	HIFK Helsinki	Finland	25	10	4	14	136										9	0	2	2	43				
	HIFK Helsinki	EuroHL	5	1	2	3	8																		
99-2000	**Vancouver**	**NHL**	**8**	**0**	**1**	**1**	**6**	**0**	**0**	**0**	**4**	**0.0**	**–1**	**0**	**0.0**	**8:47**									
	Syracuse Crunch	AHL	65	26	32	58	164										4	3	1	4	8				
2000-01	**Vancouver**	**NHL**	**21**	**3**	**3**	**6**	**32**	**0**	**1**	**0**	**23**	**13.0**	**1**	**0**	**0.0**	**10:39**	**4**	**0**	**1**	**1**	**8**	**0**	**0**	**0**	**10:18**
	Kansas City	IHL	46	11	18	29	111																		
2001-02	**Vancouver**	**NHL**	**49**	**2**	**7**	**9**	**74**	**0**	**0**	**0**	**37**	**5.4**	**–1**	**5**	**0.0**	**10:11**	**1**	**0**	**0**	**0**	**0**	**0**	**0**	**0**	**8:53**
	Finland	Olympics	4	0	0	0	4																		
2002-03	**Vancouver**	**NHL**	**36**	**2**	**2**	**4**	**66**	**0**	**0**	**1**	**36**	**5.6**	**–7**	**6**	**16.7**	**8:58**	**13**	**0**	**2**	**2**	**14**	**0**	**0**	**0**	**11:59**
2003-04	**Vancouver**	**NHL**	**71**	**6**	**8**	**14**	**133**	**1**	**0**	**0**	**70**	**8.6**	**–13**	**20**	**30.0**	**11:29**	**6**	**1**	**0**	**1**	**10**	**0**	**0**	**0**	**9:13**
2004-05	HIFK Helsinki	Finland	50	10	18	28	*215										3	0	0	0	41				
	NHL Totals		**185**	**13**	**21**	**34**	**311**	**1**	**1**	**1**	**170**	**7.6**		**31**	**22.6**	**10:26**	**24**	**1**	**3**	**4**	**32**	**0**	**0**	**0**	**10:53**

• Spent majority of 2002-03 season as a healthy reserve. Signed as a free agent by **HIFK** (Finland), September 23, 2004.

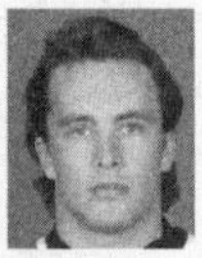

RUUTU, Tuomo
(ROO-too, TOO-oh-moh) **CHI.**

Center/Left wing. Shoots left. 6'2", 208 lbs. Born, Vantaa, Finland, February 16, 1983. Chicago's 1st choice, 9th overall, in 2001 Entry Draft.

Season	Club	League	GP	G	A	Pts	PIM	PP	SH	GW	S	%	+/-	TF	F%	Min	GP	G	A	Pts	PIM	PP	SH	GW	Min
1998-99	HIFK Helsinki U18	Fin-U18	25	9	11	20	88										2	1	1	2	2				
99-2000	HIFK Helsinki Jr.	Finland-Jr.	35	11	16	27	32										3	0	1	1	4				
	HIFK Helsinki	Finland	1	0	0	0	2																		
2000-01	HIFK Helsinki Jr.	Finland-Jr.	2	1	0	1	0																		
	Jokerit Helsinki	Finland	47	11	11	22	86										5	0	0	0	4				
2001-02	Jokerit Helsinki	Finland	51	7	16	23	69										10	0	6	6	29				
2002-03	HIFK Helsinki	Finland	30	12	15	27	24																		
2003-04	**Chicago**	**NHL**	**82**	**23**	**21**	**44**	**58**	**10**	**0**	**3**	**174**	**13.2**	**–31**	**317**	**46.4**	**16:24**									
2004-05			DID NOT PLAY																						
	NHL Totals		**82**	**23**	**21**	**44**	**58**	**10**	**0**	**3**	**174**	**13.2**		**317**	**46.4**	**16:24**									

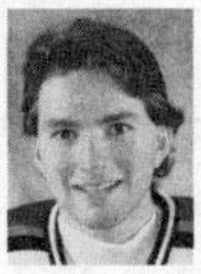

RYCROFT, Mark
(RIGH-krawft, MAHRK) **ST.L.**

Right wing. Shoots right. 5'11", 192 lbs. Born, Penticton, B.C., July 12, 1978.

Season	Club	League	GP	G	A	Pts	PIM	PP	SH	GW	S	%	+/-	TF	F%	Min	GP	G	A	Pts	PIM	PP	SH	GW	Min
1993-94	Penticton Ice	BCAHA	60	47	65	112	100																		
1994-95	Penticton Ice	BCAHA	43	33	43	76	90																		
1995-96	Nanaimo Clippers	BCHL	60	17	28	45	28																		
1996-97	Nanaimo Clippers	BCHL	58	32	35	67	79																		
1997-98	U. of Denver	WCHA	35	15	17	32	28																		
1998-99	U. of Denver	WCHA	41	19	18	37	36																		
99-2000	U. of Denver	WCHA	41	17	17	34	87																		
2000-01	Worcester IceCats	AHL	71	24	26	50	68										11	2	5	7	4				
2001-02	**St. Louis**	**NHL**	**9**	**0**	**3**	**3**	**4**	**0**	**0**	**0**	**14**	**0.0**	**0**	**1**	**0.0**	**9:50**									
	Worcester IceCats	AHL	66	12	19	31	68										3	0	1	1	0				
2002-03	Worcester IceCats	AHL	45	8	18	26	35										1	0	0	0	0				
2003-04	**St. Louis**	**NHL**	**71**	**9**	**12**	**21**	**32**	**0**	**0**	**0**	**110**	**8.2**	**2**	**11**	**63.6**	**14:23**	**3**	**0**	**0**	**0**	**2**	**0**	**0**	**0**	**9:41**
2004-05	HC Briancon	France	13	8	8	16	18										4	2	1	3	0				
	NHL Totals		**80**	**9**	**15**	**24**	**36**	**0**	**0**	**0**	**124**	**7.3**		**12**	**58.3**	**13:52**	**3**	**0**	**0**	**0**	**2**	**0**	**0**	**0**	**9:41**

WCHA All-Rookie Team (1998)

Signed as a free agent by **St. Louis**, May 15, 2000. Signed as a free agent by **Briancon** (France), November 9, 2004.

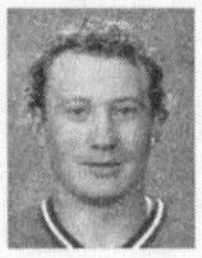

RYDER, Michael
(RIGH-duhr, MIGH-kuhl) **MTL.**

Right wing. Shoots right. 6'1", 196 lbs. Born, St. John's, Nfld., March 31, 1980. Montreal's 9th choice, 216th overall, in 1998 Entry Draft.

Season	Club	League	GP	G	A	Pts	PIM	PP	SH	GW	S	%	+/-	TF	F%	Min	GP	G	A	Pts	PIM	PP	SH	GW	Min
1996-97	Bonavista Saints	NFAHA	23	31	17	48																			
1997-98	Hull Olympiques	QMJHL	69	34	28	62	41										10	4	2	6	4				
1998-99	Hull Olympiques	QMJHL	69	44	43	87	65										23	*20	16	36	39				
99-2000	Hull Olympiques	QMJHL	63	50	58	108	50										15	11	17	28	28				
2000-01	Tallahassee	ECHL	5	4	5	9	6																		
	Quebec Citadelles	AHL	61	6	9	15	14																		
2001-02	Mississippi	ECHL	20	14	13	27	2																		
	Quebec Citadelles	AHL	50	11	17	28	9										3	0	1	1	2				
2002-03	Hamilton	AHL	69	34	33	67	43										23	11	6	17	8				
2003-04	**Montreal**	**NHL**	**81**	**25**	**38**	**63**	**26**	**10**	**0**	**4**	**215**	**11.6**	**10**	**25**	**24.0**	**16:00**	**11**	**1**	**2**	**3**	**4**	**0**	**0**	**0**	**16:52**
2004-05	Leksands IF	Sweden-2	42	34	27	61	32																		
	NHL Totals		**81**	**25**	**38**	**63**	**26**	**10**	**0**	**4**	**215**	**11.6**		**25**	**24.0**	**16:00**	**11**	**1**	**2**	**3**	**4**	**0**	**0**	**0**	**16:52**

NHL All-Rookie Team (2004)

Signed as a free agent by **Leksands** (Sweden-2), September 19, 2004.

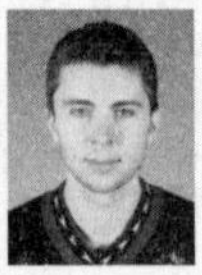

SAFRONOV, Kirill
(sah-FRAW-nawf, kih-RIHL) **NSH.**

Defense. Shoots left. 6'2", 215 lbs. Born, Leningrad, USSR, February 26, 1981. Phoenix's 2nd choice, 19th overall, in 1999 Entry Draft.

Season	Club	League	GP	G	A	Pts	PIM	PP	SH	GW	S	%	+/-	TF	F%	Min	GP	G	A	Pts	PIM	PP	SH	GW	Min
1996-97	St. Petersburg 2	Russia-3	9	0	0	0	6																		
	St. Petersburg	Russia	1	0	0	0	0																		
1997-98	St. Petersburg 2	Russia-3	34	4	3	7	36																		
	St. Petersburg	Russia	9	0	1	1	4										1	0	0	0	0				
1998-99	St. Petersburg 2	Russia-4	4	2	1	3	2																		
	St. Petersburg	Russia	45	1	3	4	32																		
99-2000	Quebec Remparts	QMJHL	55	11	32	43	95										11	2	4	6	14				
2000-01	Springfield	AHL	65	5	13	18	77																		
2001-02	**Phoenix**	**NHL**	**1**	**0**	**0**	**0**	**0**	**0**	**0**	**0**	**0**	**0.0**	**–2**	**0**	**0.0**	**6:08**									
	Springfield	AHL	68	3	19	22	26																		
	Atlanta	**NHL**	**2**	**0**	**0**	**0**	**2**	**0**	**0**	**0**	**2**	**0.0**	**–3**	**0**	**0.0**	**21:11**									
	Chicago Wolves	AHL	8	0	2	2	2										25	2	6	8	8				
2002-03	**Atlanta**	**NHL**	**32**	**2**	**2**	**4**	**14**	**0**	**0**	**0**	**21**	**9.5**	**–10**	**1**	**0.0**	**15:02**									
	Chicago Wolves	AHL	44	4	15	19	29										9	1	2	3	4				
2003-04	Chicago Wolves	AHL	21	1	4	5	8																		
	Milwaukee	AHL	59	4	16	20	41										21	0	6	6	20				
2004-05	Yaroslavl	Russia	19	0	1	1	49																		
	Voskresensk	Russia	35	5	8	13	34																		
	NHL Totals		**35**	**2**	**2**	**4**	**16**	**0**	**0**	**0**	**23**	**8.7**		**1**	**0.0**	**15:08**									

Traded to **Atlanta** by **Phoenix** with the rights to Ruslan Zainullin and Phoenix's 5th round choice (Patrick Dwyer) in 2002 Entry Draft for Darcy Hordichuk and Atlanta's 4th (Lance Monych) and 5th (John Zeiler) round choices in 2002 Entry Draft, March 19, 2002. Traded to **Nashville** by **Atlanta** with Simon Gamache for Ben Simon and Tomas Kloucek, December 2, 2003. Signed as a free agent by **Yaroslavl** (Russia), June 13, 2004. Signed as a free agent by **Voskresensk** (Russia), December, 2004. Signed as a free agent by **St. Petersburg** (Russia), July 22, 2005.

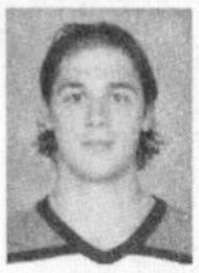

ST. JACQUES, Bruno (SAINT ZHAWK, BROO-noh) CAR.

Defense. Shoots left. 6'2", 210 lbs. Born, Montreal, Que., August 22, 1980. Philadelphia's 12th choice, 253rd overall, in 1998 Entry Draft.

			Regular Season														Playoffs								
Season	Club	League	GP	G	A	Pts	PIM	PP	SH	GW	S	%	+/-	TF	F%	Min	GP	G	A	Pts	PIM	PP	SH	GW	Min
1996-97	Mtl-Bourassa	QAAA	40	5	8	13											16	0	7	7					
1997-98	Baie-Comeau	QMJHL	63	1	11	12	140																		
1998-99	Baie-Comeau	QMJHL	49	8	13	21	85																		
99-2000	Baie-Comeau	QMJHL	60	8	28	36	120										6	0	2	2	10				
	Philadelphia	AHL	3	0	1	1	0										1	0	0	0	0				
2000-01	Philadelphia	AHL	45	1	16	17	83										10	1	0	1	16				
2001-02	**Philadelphia**	**NHL**	**7**	**0**	**0**	**0**	**2**	**0**	**0**	**0**	**4**	**0.0**	**4**	**0**	**0.0**	**13:51**									
	Philadelphia	AHL	55	3	11	14	59										4	0	0	0	0				
2002-03	**Philadelphia**	**NHL**	**6**	**0**	**0**	**0**	**2**	**0**	**0**	**0**	**5**	**0.0**	**–1**	**0**	**0.0**	**14:35**									
	Philadelphia	AHL	30	0	7	7	46																		
	Carolina	**NHL**	**18**	**2**	**5**	**7**	**12**	**0**	**0**	**0**	**14**	**14.3**	**–3**	**0**	**0.0**	**18:15**									
	Lowell	AHL	8	1	1	2	8																		
2003-04	**Carolina**	**NHL**	**35**	**0**	**2**	**2**	**31**	**0**	**0**	**0**	**16**	**0.0**	**–7**	**0**	**0.0**	**11:50**									
	Lowell	AHL	6	0	0	0	8																		
2004-05	Lowell	AHL	68	2	12	14	60										11	1	4	5	4				
	NHL Totals		**66**	**2**	**7**	**9**	**47**	**0**	**0**	**0**	**39**	**5.1**		**0**	**0.0**	**14:03**									

Traded to **Carolina** by **Philadelphia** with Pavel Brendl for Sami Kapanen and Ryan Bast, February 7, 2003. • Missed majority of 2003-04 season recovering from abdominal injury suffered in game vs. Philadelphia, November 28, 2003.

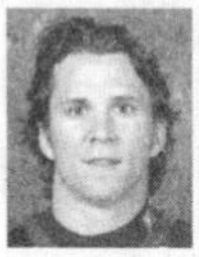

ST. LOUIS, Martin (sehn-loo-EE, mahr-TEHN) T.B.

Right wing. Shoots left. 5'9", 185 lbs. Born, Laval, Que., June 18, 1975.

Season	Club	League	GP	G	A	Pts	PIM	PP	SH	GW	S	%	+/-	TF	F%	Min	GP	G	A	Pts	PIM	PP	SH	GW	Min
1991-92	Laval-Laurentides	QAAA	42	29	*74	*103	38										12	7	15	22	16				
1992-93	Hawkesbury	CJHL	31	37	50	87	70																		
1993-94	U. of Vermont	ECAC	33	15	36	51	24																		
1994-95	U. of Vermont	ECAC	35	23	48	71	36																		
1995-96	U. of Vermont	ECAC	35	29	56	85	38																		
1996-97	U. of Vermont	ECAC	36	24	*36	60	65																		
1997-98	Cleveland	IHL	56	16	34	50	24																		
	Saint John Flames	AHL	25	15	11	26	20										20	5	15	20	16				
1998-99	**Calgary**	**NHL**	**13**	**1**	**1**	**2**	**10**	**0**	**0**	**0**	**14**	**7.1**	**–2**	**0**	**0.0**	**8:15**									
	Saint John Flames	AHL	53	28	34	62	30										7	4	4	8	2				
99-2000	**Calgary**	**NHL**	**56**	**3**	**15**	**18**	**22**	**0**	**0**	**1**	**73**	**4.1**	**–5**	**3**	**0.0**	**14:41**									
	Saint John Flames	AHL	17	15	11	26	14																		
2000-01	**Tampa Bay**	**NHL**	**78**	**18**	**22**	**40**	**12**	**3**	**3**	**4**	**141**	**12.8**	**–4**	**48**	**41.7**	**15:14**									
2001-02	**Tampa Bay**	**NHL**	**53**	**16**	**19**	**35**	**20**	**6**	**1**	**2**	**105**	**15.2**	**4**	**33**	**39.4**	**18:41**									
2002-03	**Tampa Bay**	**NHL**	**82**	**33**	**37**	**70**	**32**	**12**	**3**	**5**	**201**	**16.4**	**10**	**37**	**37.8**	**19:43**	**11**	**7**	**5**	**12**	**0**	**1**	**2**	**3**	**22:21**
2003-04♦	**Tampa Bay**	**NHL**	**82**	**38**	***56**	***94**	**24**	**8**	**8**	**7**	**212**	**17.9**	**35**	**24**	**33.3**	**20:35**	**23**	**9**	***15**	**24**	**14**	**3**	**1**	**3**	**22:52**
2004-05	Lausanne HC	Swiss	23	9	16	25	16																		
	NHL Totals		**364**	**109**	**150**	**259**	**120**	**29**	**15**	**19**	**746**	**14.6**		**145**	**37.9**	**17:37**	**34**	**16**	**20**	**36**	**14**	**4**	**3**	**6**	**22:42**

ECAC First All-Star Team (1995, 1996, 1997) • ECAC Player of the Year (1995) • NCAA East First All-American Team (1995, 1996, 1997) • NCAA Championship All-Tournament Team (1996) • NHL First All-Star Team (2004) • Art Ross Trophy (2004) • Lester B. Pearson Award (2004) • Hart Trophy (2004)

Played in NHL All-Star Game (2003, 2004)

Signed as a free agent by **Calgary**, February 19, 1998. Signed as a free agent by **Tampa Bay**, July 31, 2000. Signed as a free agent by **Lausanne** (Swiss), November 4, 2004.

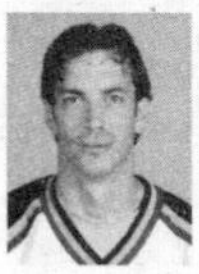

SAKIC, Joe (SAK-ihk, JOH) COL.

Center. Shoots left. 5'11", 195 lbs. Born, Burnaby, B.C., July 7, 1969. Quebec's 2nd choice, 15th overall, in 1987 Entry Draft.

Season	Club	League	GP	G	A	Pts	PIM	PP	SH	GW	S	%	+/-	TF	F%	Min	GP	G	A	Pts	PIM	PP	SH	GW	Min
1985-86	Burnaby	BCAHA	80	83	73	156	96																		
	Lethbridge	WHL	3	0	0	0	0																		
1986-87	Swift Current	WHL	72	60	73	133	31										4	0	1	1	0				
1987-88	Swift Current	WHL	64	*78	82	*160	64										10	11	13	24	12				
1988-89	**Quebec**	**NHL**	**70**	**23**	**39**	**62**	**24**	**10**	**0**	**2**	**148**	**15.5**	**–36**												
1989-90	**Quebec**	**NHL**	**80**	**39**	**63**	**102**	**27**	**8**	**1**	**2**	**234**	**16.7**	**–40**												
1990-91	**Quebec**	**NHL**	**80**	**48**	**61**	**109**	**24**	**12**	**3**	**7**	**245**	**19.6**	**–26**												
1991-92	**Quebec**	**NHL**	**69**	**29**	**65**	**94**	**20**	**6**	**3**	**1**	**217**	**13.4**	**5**												
1992-93	**Quebec**	**NHL**	**78**	**48**	**57**	**105**	**40**	**20**	**2**	**4**	**264**	**18.2**	**–3**				**6**	**3**	**3**	**6**	**2**	**1**	**0**	**0**	
1993-94	**Quebec**	**NHL**	**84**	**28**	**64**	**92**	**18**	**10**	**1**	**9**	**279**	**10.0**	**–8**												
1994-95	**Quebec**	**NHL**	**47**	**19**	**43**	**62**	**30**	**3**	**2**	**5**	**157**	**12.1**	**7**				**6**	**4**	**1**	**5**	**0**	**1**	**1**	**1**	
1995-96♦	**Colorado**	**NHL**	**82**	**51**	**69**	**120**	**44**	**17**	**6**	**7**	**339**	**15.0**	**14**				**22**	***18**	**16**	***34**	**14**	**6**	**0**	**6**	
1996-97	**Colorado**	**NHL**	**65**	**22**	**52**	**74**	**34**	**10**	**2**	**5**	**261**	**8.4**	**–10**				**17**	**8**	***17**	**25**	**14**	**3**	**0**	**0**	
1997-98	**Colorado**	**NHL**	**64**	**27**	**36**	**63**	**50**	**12**	**1**	**2**	**254**	**10.6**	**0**				**6**	**2**	**3**	**5**	**6**	**0**	**1**	**2**	
	Canada	Olympics	4	1	2	3	4																		
1998-99	**Colorado**	**NHL**	**73**	**41**	**55**	**96**	**29**	**12**	**5**	**6**	**255**	**16.1**	**23**	**1723**	**51.4**	**25:35**	**19**	**6**	**13**	**19**	**8**	**1**	**1**	**1**	**25:01**
99-2000	**Colorado**	**NHL**	**60**	**28**	**53**	**81**	**28**	**5**	**1**	**5**	**242**	**11.6**	**30**	**1392**	**53.8**	**23:16**	**17**	**2**	**7**	**9**	**8**	**2**	**0**	**0**	**23:50**
2000-01♦	**Colorado**	**NHL**	**82**	**54**	**64**	**118**	**30**	**19**	**3**	**12**	**332**	**16.3**	**45**	**2292**	**53.0**	**23:01**	**21**	***13**	**13**	***26**	**6**	**5**	**0**	**3**	**21:33**
2001-02	**Colorado**	**NHL**	**82**	**26**	**53**	**79**	**18**	**9**	**1**	**4**	**260**	**10.0**	**12**	**2148**	**52.2**	**22:00**	**21**	**9**	**10**	**19**	**4**	**4**	**0**	**1**	**22:44**
	Canada	Olympics	6	4	3	7	0																		
2002-03	**Colorado**	**NHL**	**58**	**26**	**32**	**58**	**24**	**8**	**0**	**1**	**190**	**13.7**	**4**	**1359**	**50.8**	**21:12**	**7**	**6**	**3**	**9**	**2**	**2**	**0**	**1**	**22:29**
2003-04	**Colorado**	**NHL**	**81**	**33**	**54**	**87**	**42**	**13**	**1**	**3**	**253**	**13.0**	**11**	**1705**	**52.6**	**20:16**	**11**	**7**	**5**	**12**	**8**	**1**	**1**	**2**	**21:15**
2004-05			DID NOT PLAY																						
	NHL Totals		**1155**	**542**	**860**	**1402**	**482**	**174**	**32**	**75**	**3930**	**13.8**		**10619**	**52.3**	**22:32**	**153**	**78**	**91**	**169**	**72**	**26**	**4**	**17**	**22:56**

WHL East Second All-Star Team (1987) • WHL East Rookie of the Year (1987) • WHL East Player of the Year (1987) • WHL East First All-Star Team (1988) • WHL Player of the Year (1988) • Canadian Major Junior Player of the Year (1988) • Conn Smythe Trophy (1996) • NHL First All-Star Team (2001, 2002, 2004) • Bud Light Plus/Minus Award (2001) (tied with Patrik Elias) • Lady Byng Trophy (2001) • Lester B. Pearson Award (2001) • Hart Trophy (2001)

Played in NHL All-Star Game (1990, 1991, 1992, 1993, 1994, 1996, 1998, 2000, 2001, 2002, 2004)

Transferred to **Colorado** after **Quebec** franchise relocated, June 21, 1995.

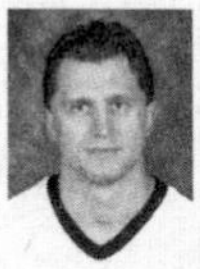

SALEI, Ruslan (sah-LAY, roos-LAHN) ANA.

Defense. Shoots left. 6'1", 213 lbs. Born, Minsk, USSR, November 2, 1974. Anaheim's 1st choice, 9th overall, in 1996 Entry Draft.

Season	Club	League	GP	G	A	Pts	PIM	PP	SH	GW	S	%	+/-	TF	F%	Min	GP	G	A	Pts	PIM	PP	SH	GW	Min
1992-93	Dynamo Moscow	CIS	9	1	0	1	10																		
1993-94	Tivali Minsk	CIS	39	2	3	5	50																		
1994-95	Tivali Minsk	CIS	51	4	2	6	44																		
1995-96	Las Vegas	IHL	76	7	23	30	123										15	3	7	10	18				
1996-97	**Anaheim**	**NHL**	**30**	**0**	**1**	**1**	**37**	**0**	**0**	**0**	**14**	**0.0**	**–8**												
	Baltimore Bandits	AHL	12	1	4	5	12																		
	Las Vegas	IHL	8	0	2	2	24										3	2	1	3	6				
1997-98	**Anaheim**	**NHL**	**66**	**5**	**10**	**15**	**70**	**1**	**0**	**0**	**104**	**4.8**	**7**												
	Cincinnati	AHL	6	3	6	9	14																		
	Belarus	Olympics	7	1	0	1	4																		
1998-99	**Anaheim**	**NHL**	**74**	**2**	**14**	**16**	**65**	**1**	**0**	**0**	**123**	**1.6**	**1**	**0**	**0.0**	**22:03**	**3**	**0**	**0**	**0**	**4**	**0**	**0**	**0**	**15:40**
99-2000	**Anaheim**	**NHL**	**71**	**5**	**5**	**10**	**94**	**1**	**0**	**0**	**116**	**4.3**	**3**	**0**	**0.0**	**20:21**									
2000-01	**Anaheim**	**NHL**	**50**	**1**	**5**	**6**	**70**	**0**	**0**	**0**	**73**	**1.4**	**–14**	**0**	**0.0**	**20:40**									
2001-02	**Anaheim**	**NHL**	**82**	**4**	**7**	**11**	**97**	**0**	**0**	**1**	**96**	**4.2**	**–10**	**0**	**0.0**	**21:25**									
	Belarus	Olympics	6	2	1	3	4																		
2002-03	**Anaheim**	**NHL**	**61**	**4**	**8**	**12**	**78**	**0**	**0**	**0**	**93**	**4.3**	**2**	**0**	**0.0**	**21:53**	**21**	**2**	**3**	**5**	**26**	**0**	**0**	**1**	**26:05**
2003-04	**Anaheim**	**NHL**	**82**	**4**	**11**	**15**	**110**	**0**	**1**	**2**	**145**	**2.8**	**–1**	**0**	**0.0**	**23:42**									
2004-05	Ak Bars Kazan	Russia	35	8	12	20	36										4	0	0	0	2				
	NHL Totals		**516**	**25**	**61**	**86**	**621**	**3**	**1**	**3**	**764**	**3.3**		**0**	**0.0**	**21:46**	**24**	**2**	**3**	**5**	**30**	**0**	**0**	**1**	**24:47**

Signed as a free agent by **Kazan** (Russia), October 20, 2004.

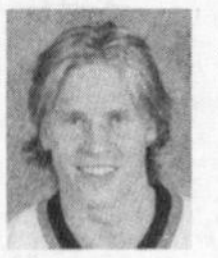

SALMELAINEN, Tony
(sal-meh-LIGH-nehn, TOH-nee) **EDM.**

Left wing. Shoots right. 5'9", 185 lbs. Born, Espoo, Finland, August 8, 1981. Edmonton's 3rd choice, 41st overall, in 1999 Entry Draft.

			Regular Season														Playoffs								
Season	Club	League	GP	G	A	Pts	PIM	PP	SH	GW	S	%	+/-	TF	F%	Min	GP	G	A	Pts	PIM	PP	SH	GW	Min
1996-97	Kiekko-Espoo Jr.	Finland-Jr.	30	8	5	13	38	....	....	....	....	....	....	....	....	....	....	....	....	....	....	....	....	....	....
1997-98	K-Espoo U18	Fin-U18	5	2	2	4	10	....	....	....	....	....	....	....	....	....	....	....	....	....	....	....	....	....	....
	HIFK Helsinki U18	Fin-U18	28	23	16	39	30	....	....	....	....	....	....	....	....	....	....	....	....	....	....	....	....	....	....
	HIFK Helsinki Jr.	Finland-Jr.	5	0	0	0	0	....	....	....	....	....	....	....	....	....	....	....	....	....	....	....	....	....	....
1998-99	HIFK Helsinki U18	Fin-U18	21	13	10	23	45	....	....	....	....	....	....	....	....	....	....	....	....	....	....	....	....	....	....
	HIFK Helsinki Jr.	Finland-Jr.	....	....	....	....	....	....	....	....	....	....	....	....	....	....	10	10	8	18	10	....	....	....	....
99-2000	HIFK Helsinki Jr.	Finland-Jr.	1	0	1	1	0	....	....	....	....	....	....	....	....	....	....	....	....	....	....	....	....	....	....
	HIFK Helsinki	Finland	1	1	0	1	0	....	....	....	....	....	....	....	....	....	....	....	....	....	....	....	....	....	....
	HIFK Helsinki	EuroHL	1	0	0	0	0	....	....	....	....	....	....	....	....	....	....	....	....	....	....	....	....	....	....
2000-01	HIFK Helsinki Jr.	Finland-Jr.	3	3	3	6	0	....	....	....	....	....	....	....	....	....	....	....	....	....	....	....	....	....	....
	HIFK Helsinki	Finland	19	1	0	1	6	....	....	....	....	....	....	....	....	....	....	....	....	....	....	....	....	....	....
	Ilves Tampere Jr.	Finland-Jr.	3	1	2	3	2	....	....	....	....	....	....	....	....	....	....	....	....	....	....	....	....	....	....
	Ilves Tampere	Finland	26	3	10	13	4	....	....	....	....	....	....	....	....	....	3	0	0	0	0	....	....	....	....
2001-02	Ilves Tampere Jr.	Finland-Jr.	6	2	2	4	27	....	....	....	....	....	....	....	....	....	....	....	....	....	....	....	....	....	....
	Ilves Tampere	Finland	49	10	9	19	30	....	....	....	....	....	....	....	....	....	3	0	0	0	2	....	....	....	....
2002-03	Hamilton	AHL	67	14	19	33	14	....	....	....	....	....	....	....	....	....	17	6	8	14	0	....	....	....	....
2003-04	**Edmonton**	**NHL**	**13**	**0**	**1**	**1**	**4**	**0**	**0**	**0**	**17**	**0.0**	**−1**	**0**	**0.0**	**9:39**	....	....	....	....	....	....	....	....	....
	Toronto	AHL	58	19	25	44	27	....	....	....	....	....	....	....	....	....	3	0	1	1	0	....	....	....	....
2004-05	Edmonton	AHL	76	22	24	46	26	....	....	....	....	....	....	....	....	....	....	....	....	....	....	....	....	....	....
	NHL Totals		**13**	**0**	**1**	**1**	**4**	**0**	**0**	**0**	**17**	**0.0**		**0**	**0.0**	**9:39**	....	....	....	....	....	....	....	....	....

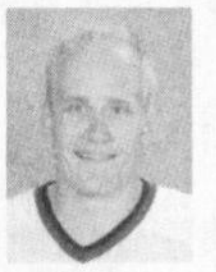

SALO, Sami
(SA-loh, SA-mee) **VAN.**

Defense. Shoots right. 6'3", 215 lbs. Born, Turku, Finland, September 2, 1974. Ottawa's 7th choice, 239th overall, in 1996 Entry Draft.

			Regular Season														Playoffs								
Season	Club	League	GP	G	A	Pts	PIM	PP	SH	GW	S	%	+/-	TF	F%	Min	GP	G	A	Pts	PIM	PP	SH	GW	Min
1991-92	Kiekko-67 Jr.	Finland-Jr.	23	4	5	9	26	....	....	....	....	....	....	....	....	....	....	....	....	....	....	....	....	....	....
1992-93	Kiekko-67 Jr.	Finland-Jr.	21	9	4	13	4	....	....	....	....	....	....	....	....	....	....	....	....	....	....	....	....	....	....
1993-94	TPS Turku Jr.	Finland-Jr.	36	7	13	20	16	....	....	....	....	....	....	....	....	....	7	0	1	1	10	....	....	....	....
1994-95	TPS Turku Jr.	Finland-Jr.	14	1	3	4	6	....	....	....	....	....	....	....	....	....	....	....	....	....	....	....	....	....	....
	Kiekko-67 Turku	Finland-2	19	4	2	6	4	....	....	....	....	....	....	....	....	....	....	....	....	....	....	....	....	....	....
	TPS Turku	Finland	7	1	2	3	8	....	....	....	....	....	....	....	....	....	1	0	0	0	0	....	....	....	....
1995-96	TPS Turku	Finland	47	7	14	21	32	....	....	....	....	....	....	....	....	....	11	1	3	4	8	....	....	....	....
1996-97	TPS Turku	Finland	48	9	6	15	10	....	....	....	....	....	....	....	....	....	10	2	3	5	4	....	....	....	....
	TPS Turku	EuroHL	6	0	2	2	6	....	....	....	....	....	....	....	....	....	2	0	0	0	2	....	....	....	....
1997-98	Jokerit Helsinki	Finland	35	3	5	8	10	....	....	....	....	....	....	....	....	....	8	0	1	1	2	....	....	....	....
	Jokerit Helsinki	EuroHL	6	1	1	2	2	....	....	....	....	....	....	....	....	....	....	....	....	....	....	....	....	....	....
1998-99	**Ottawa**	**NHL**	**61**	**7**	**12**	**19**	**24**	**2**	**0**	**1**	**106**	**6.6**	**20**	**0**	**0.0**	**19:42**	**4**	**0**	**0**	**0**	**0**	**0**	**0**	**0**	**21:32**
	Detroit Vipers	IHL	5	0	2	2	0	....	....	....	....	....	....	....	....	....	....	....	....	....	....	....	....	....	....
99-2000	**Ottawa**	**NHL**	**37**	**6**	**8**	**14**	**2**	**3**	**0**	**1**	**85**	**7.1**	**6**	**0**	**0.0**	**20:18**	**6**	**1**	**1**	**2**	**0**	**1**	**0**	**0**	**24:11**
2000-01	**Ottawa**	**NHL**	**31**	**2**	**16**	**18**	**10**	**1**	**0**	**0**	**61**	**3.3**	**9**	**0**	**0.0**	**19:44**	**4**	**0**	**0**	**0**	**0**	**0**	**0**	**0**	**22:30**
2001-02	**Ottawa**	**NHL**	**66**	**4**	**14**	**18**	**14**	**1**	**1**	**2**	**122**	**3.3**	**1**	**0**	**0.0**	**19:52**	**12**	**2**	**1**	**3**	**4**	**0**	**0**	**0**	**20:23**
	Finland	Olympics	4	0	0	0	0	....	....	....	....	....	....	....	....	....	....	....	....	....	....	....	....	....	....
2002-03	**Vancouver**	**NHL**	**79**	**9**	**21**	**30**	**10**	**4**	**0**	**1**	**126**	**7.1**	**9**	**0**	**0.0**	**20:08**	**12**	**1**	**3**	**4**	**0**	**0**	**0**	**0**	**20:52**
2003-04	**Vancouver**	**NHL**	**74**	**7**	**19**	**26**	**22**	**5**	**0**	**2**	**143**	**4.9**	**8**	**1**	**100.0**	**22:14**	**7**	**1**	**2**	**3**	**2**	**1**	**0**	**0**	**22:59**
2004-05	Frolunda	Sweden	41	6	8	14	18	....	....	....	....	....	....	....	....	....	14	1	6	7	2	....	....	....	....
	NHL Totals		**348**	**35**	**90**	**125**	**82**	**16**	**1**	**7**	**643**	**5.4**		**1**	**100.0**	**20:26**	**45**	**5**	**7**	**12**	**6**	**2**	**0**	**0**	**21:43**

NHL All-Rookie Team (1999)

• Missed majority of 1999-2000 season recovering from wrist injury suffered in game vs. Philadelphia, November 28, 1999. • Missed majority of 2000-01 season recovering from shoulder injury suffered in game vs. Atlanta, December 14, 2000. Traded to **Vancouver** by **Ottawa** for Peter Schaefer, September 21, 2002. Signed as a free agent by **Frolunda** (Sweden), September 24, 2004.

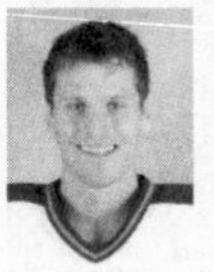

SALOMONSSON, Andreas
(sal-oh-MAWN-suhn, an-DRAY-uhs) **WSH.**

Right wing. Shoots left. 6'1", 200 lbs. Born, Ornskoldsvik, Sweden, December 19, 1973. New Jersey's 8th choice, 163rd overall, in 2001 Entry Draft.

			Regular Season														Playoffs								
Season	Club	League	GP	G	A	Pts	PIM	PP	SH	GW	S	%	+/-	TF	F%	Min	GP	G	A	Pts	PIM	PP	SH	GW	Min
1990-91	MoDo	Sweden	2	0	0	0	0	....	....	....	....	....	....	....	....	....	....	....	....	....	....	....	....	....	....
1991-92	MoDo	Sweden	20	1	1	2	26	....	....	....	....	....	....	....	....	....	....	....	....	....	....	....	....	....	....
1992-93	MoDo Jr.	Swe-Jr.	10	4	16	20	8	....	....	....	....	....	....	....	....	....	....	....	....	....	....	....	....	....	....
	MoDo	Sweden	33	1	1	2	0	....	....	....	....	....	....	....	....	....	....	....	....	....	....	....	....	....	....
1993-94	MoDo	Sweden	38	15	8	23	33	....	....	....	....	....	....	....	....	....	11	1	2	3	4	....	....	....	....
1994-95	MoDo	Sweden	40	5	9	14	34	....	....	....	....	....	....	....	....	....	....	....	....	....	....	....	....	....	....
1995-96	MoDo	Sweden	38	13	6	19	22	....	....	....	....	....	....	....	....	....	7	0	4	4	8	....	....	....	....
1996-97	MoDo	Sweden	23	6	6	12	22	....	....	....	....	....	....	....	....	....	....	....	....	....	....	....	....	....	....
	Ratingen Lowen	Germany	21	5	1	6	49	....	....	....	....	....	....	....	....	....	....	....	....	....	....	....	....	....	....
1997-98	MoDo	Sweden	45	6	15	21	69	....	....	....	....	....	....	....	....	....	8	4	3	7	4	....	....	....	....
1998-99	MoDo	Sweden	46	13	13	26	60	....	....	....	....	....	....	....	....	....	13	4	5	9	12	....	....	....	....
99-2000	MoDo	Sweden	48	9	15	24	38	....	....	....	....	....	....	....	....	....	12	0	4	4	12	....	....	....	....
	MoDo	EuroHL	5	2	2	4	4	....	....	....	....	....	....	....	....	....	3	1	1	2	4	....	....	....	....
2000-01	Djurgarden	Sweden	48	10	12	22	46	....	....	....	....	....	....	....	....	....	13	3	4	7	31	....	....	....	....
2001-02	**New Jersey**	**NHL**	**39**	**4**	**5**	**9**	**22**	**1**	**0**	**1**	**58**	**6.9**	**−12**	**6**	**33.3**	**13:30**	**4**	**0**	**1**	**1**	**0**	**0**	**0**	**0**	**12:16**
	Albany River Rats	AHL	19	3	10	13	6	....	....	....	....	....	....	....	....	....	....	....	....	....	....	....	....	....	....
2002-03	Portland Pirates	AHL	31	7	17	24	23	....	....	....	....	....	....	....	....	....	3	4	0	4	0	....	....	....	....
	Washington	**NHL**	**32**	**1**	**4**	**5**	**14**	**0**	**0**	**0**	**20**	**5.0**	**−1**	**29**	**37.9**	**8:50**	....	....	....	....	....	....	....	....	....
2003-04	MODO	Sweden	47	13	26	39	48	....	....	....	....	....	....	....	....	....	6	1	5	6	6	....	....	....	....
2004-05	MODO	Sweden	30	7	9	16	46	....	....	....	....	....	....	....	....	....	6	1	4	5	4	....	....	....	....
	NHL Totals		**71**	**5**	**9**	**14**	**36**	**1**	**0**	**1**	**78**	**6.4**		**35**	**37.1**	**11:24**	**4**	**0**	**1**	**1**	**0**	**0**	**0**	**0**	**12:15**

Claimed on waivers by **Washington** from **New Jersey**, October 15, 2002. Signed as a free agent by **MODO** (Sweden), August 7, 2003.

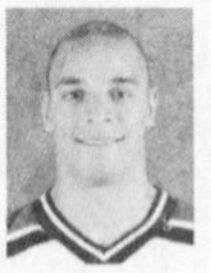

SALVADOR, Bryce
(SAL-vuh-dohr, BRIGHS) **ST.L.**

Defense. Shoots left. 6'2", 215 lbs. Born, Brandon, Man., February 11, 1976. Tampa Bay's 6th choice, 138th overall, in 1994 Entry Draft.

			Regular Season														Playoffs								
Season	Club	League	GP	G	A	Pts	PIM	PP	SH	GW	S	%	+/-	TF	F%	Min	GP	G	A	Pts	PIM	PP	SH	GW	Min
1991-92	Brandon	MAHA	52	6	23	29	38	....	....	....	....	....	....	....	....	....	....	....	....	....	....	....	....	....	....
1992-93	Lethbridge	WHL	64	1	4	5	29	....	....	....	....	....	....	....	....	....	4	0	0	0	0	....	....	....	....
1993-94	Lethbridge	WHL	61	4	14	18	36	....	....	....	....	....	....	....	....	....	9	0	1	1	2	....	....	....	....
1994-95	Lethbridge	WHL	67	1	9	10	88	....	....	....	....	....	....	....	....	....	....	....	....	....	....	....	....	....	....
1995-96	Lethbridge	WHL	56	4	12	16	75	....	....	....	....	....	....	....	....	....	3	0	1	1	2	....	....	....	....
1996-97	Lethbridge	WHL	63	8	32	40	81	....	....	....	....	....	....	....	....	....	19	0	7	7	14	....	....	....	....
1997-98	Worcester IceCats	AHL	46	2	8	10	74	....	....	....	....	....	....	....	....	....	11	0	1	1	45	....	....	....	....
1998-99	Worcester IceCats	AHL	69	5	13	18	129	....	....	....	....	....	....	....	....	....	4	0	1	1	2	....	....	....	....
99-2000	Worcester IceCats	AHL	55	0	13	13	53	....	....	....	....	....	....	....	....	....	9	0	1	1	2	....	....	....	....
2000-01	**St. Louis**	**NHL**	**75**	**2**	**8**	**10**	**69**	**0**	**0**	**1**	**60**	**3.3**	**−4**	**1**	**0.0**	**16:38**	**14**	**2**	**0**	**2**	**18**	**0**	**0**	**1**	**14:41**
2001-02	**St. Louis**	**NHL**	**66**	**5**	**7**	**12**	**78**	**1**	**0**	**2**	**37**	**13.5**	**3**	**0**	**0.0**	**16:55**	**10**	**0**	**1**	**1**	**4**	**0**	**0**	**0**	**12:34**
2002-03	**St. Louis**	**NHL**	**71**	**2**	**8**	**10**	**95**	**1**	**0**	**0**	**73**	**2.7**	**7**	**0**	**0.0**	**18:57**	**7**	**0**	**0**	**0**	**2**	**0**	**0**	**0**	**17:17**
2003-04	**St. Louis**	**NHL**	**69**	**3**	**5**	**8**	**47**	**0**	**0**	**1**	**60**	**5.0**	**−4**	**0**	**0.0**	**17:29**	**5**	**0**	**0**	**0**	**2**	**0**	**0**	**0**	**14:31**
	Worcester IceCats	AHL	2	0	1	1	0	....	....	....	....	....	....	....	....	....	....	....	....	....	....	....	....	....	....
2004-05	Missouri	UHL	7	0	0	0	16	....	....	....	....	....	....	....	....	....	3	0	0	0	0	....	....	....	....
	NHL Totals		**281**	**12**	**28**	**40**	**289**	**2**	**0**	**4**	**230**	**5.2**		**1**	**0.0**	**17:30**	**36**	**2**	**1**	**3**	**26**	**0**	**0**	**1**	**14:35**

Signed as a free agent by **St. Louis**, December 16, 1996. Signed as a free agent by **Missouri** (UHL), March 11, 2005.

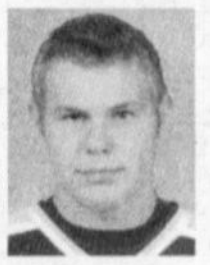

SAMSONOV, Sergei
(sam-SAWN-nahf, SAIR-gay) **BOS.**

Left wing. Shoots right. 5'8", 194 lbs. Born, Moscow, USSR, October 27, 1978. Boston's 2nd choice, 8th overall, in 1997 Entry Draft.

			Regular Season														Playoffs								
Season	Club	League	GP	G	A	Pts	PIM	PP	SH	GW	S	%	+/-	TF	F%	Min	GP	G	A	Pts	PIM	PP	SH	GW	Min
1994-95	CSKA Moscow 2	CIS-2	50	110	72	182	....	....	....	....	....	....	....	....	....	....	....	....	....	....	....	....	....	....	....
	CSKA Moscow	CIS	13	2	2	4	14	....	....	....	....	....	....	....	....	....	2	0	0	0	0	....	....	....	....
1995-96	CSKA Moscow	CIS	51	21	17	38	12	....	....	....	....	....	....	....	....	....	3	1	1	2	4	....	....	....	....
1996-97	Detroit Vipers	IHL	73	29	35	64	18	....	....	....	....	....	....	....	....	....	19	8	4	12	12	....	....	....	....
1997-98	**Boston**	**NHL**	**81**	**22**	**25**	**47**	**8**	**7**	**0**	**3**	**159**	**13.8**	**9**	....	....	....	**6**	**2**	**5**	**7**	**0**	**0**	**0**	**1**	....
1998-99	**Boston**	**NHL**	**79**	**25**	**26**	**51**	**18**	**6**	**0**	**8**	**160**	**15.6**	**−6**	**0**	**0.0**	**16:23**	**11**	**3**	**1**	**4**	**0**	**0**	**0**	**0**	**16:11**
99-2000	**Boston**	**NHL**	**77**	**19**	**26**	**45**	**4**	**6**	**0**	**3**	**145**	**13.1**	**−6**	**3**	**0.0**	**16:32**	....	....	....	....	....	....	....	....	....
2000-01	**Boston**	**NHL**	**82**	**29**	**46**	**75**	**18**	**3**	**0**	**3**	**215**	**13.5**	**6**	**14**	**42.9**	**19:23**	....	....	....	....	....	....	....	....	....

			Regular Season														Playoffs								
Season	Club	League	GP	G	A	Pts	PIM	PP	SH	GW	S	%	+/-	TF	F%	Min	GP	G	A	Pts	PIM	PP	SH	GW	Min
2001-02	**Boston**	**NHL**	**74**	**29**	**41**	**70**	**27**	**3**	**0**	**4**	**192**	**15.1**	**21**	**1**	**0.0**	**18:47**	**6**	**2**	**2**	**4**	**0**	**0**	**0**	**0**	**17:41**
	Russia	Olympics	6	1	2	3	4																		
2002-03	**Boston**	**NHL**	**8**	**5**	**6**	**11**	**2**	**1**	**0**	**3**	**23**	**21.7**	**8**	**0**	**0.0**	**20:20**	**5**	**0**	**2**	**2**	**0**	**0**	**0**	**0**	**17:07**
2003-04	**Boston**	**NHL**	**58**	**17**	**23**	**40**	**4**	**3**	**0**	**5**	**132**	**12.9**	**12**	**4**	**25.0**	**17:27**	**7**	**2**	**5**	**7**	**0**	**0**	**0**	**0**	**17:18**
2004-05	Dynamo Moscow	Russia	3	1	0	1	0										3	1	2	3	0				
	NHL Totals		**459**	**146**	**193**	**339**	**81**	**29**	**0**	**29**	**1026**	**14.2**		**22**	**31.8**	**17:47**	**35**	**9**	**15**	**24**	**0**	**0**	**0**	**1**	**16:55**

Garry F. Longman Memorial Trophy (Rookie of the Year – IHL) (1997) • NHL All-Rookie Team (1998) • Calder Memorial Trophy (1998)
Played in NHL All-Star Game (2001)

• Missed majority of 2002-03 season recovering from wrist injury suffered in game vs. Columbus, October 18, 2002. Signed as a free agent by **Dynamo Moscow** (Russia), February 2, 2005.

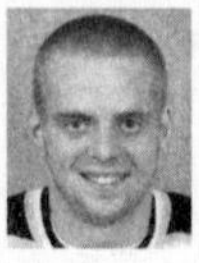

SAMUELSSON, Martin (SAM-yuhl-suhn, MAHR-tihn) BOS.

Right wing. Shoots left. 6'2", 200 lbs. Born, Upplands-Vasby, Sweden, January 25, 1982. Boston's 2nd choice, 27th overall, in 2000 Entry Draft.

Season	Club	League	GP	G	A	Pts	PIM	PP	SH	GW	S	%	+/-	TF	F%	Min	GP	G	A	Pts	PIM	PP	SH	GW	Min
1996-97	Hammarby Jr.	Swe-Jr.	6	1	1	2	0																		
1997-98	Hammarby Jr.	Swe-Jr.	20	13	12	25																			
	Hammarby	Sweden-2	2	0	0	0	0																		
1998-99	Malmo Jr.	Swe-Jr.	31	18	13	31	10																		
99-2000	MoDo U18	Swe-U18	6	3	0	3	4																		
	Malmo Jr.	Swe-Jr.	19	9	8	17	18										2	1	0	1	2				
2000-01	Hammarby	Sweden-2	24	13	4	17	8										5	0	0	0	2				
	Hammarby Jr.	Swe-Jr.	1	0	1	1	0																		
2001-02	Hammarby Jr.	Swe-Jr.	2	5	2	7	2																		
	Hammarby	Sweden-2	44	13	10	23	45										2	0	0	0	2				
2002-03	**Boston**	**NHL**	**8**	**0**	**1**	**1**	**2**	**0**	**0**	**0**	**3**	**0.0**	**–1**	**0**	**0.0**	**11:42**									
	Providence Bruins	AHL	64	24	15	39	34										4	0	0	0	0				
2003-04	**Boston**	**NHL**	**6**	**0**	**0**	**0**	**0**	**0**	**0**	**0**	**7**	**0.0**	**–1**	**1**	**0.0**	**5:38**									
	Providence Bruins	AHL	56	1	9	10	15										1	0	0	0	0				
2004-05	Providence Bruins	AHL	64	7	10	17	35										10	1	0	1	6				
	NHL Totals		**14**	**0**	**1**	**1**	**2**	**0**	**0**	**0**	**10**	**0.0**		**1**	**0.0**	**9:06**									

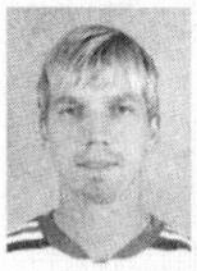

SAMUELSSON, Mikael (SAM-yuhl-suhn, MIH-kigh-ehl)

Right wing. Shoots left. 6'2", 211 lbs. Born, Mariefred, Sweden, December 23, 1976. San Jose's 7th choice, 145th overall, in 1998 Entry Draft.

Season	Club	League	GP	G	A	Pts	PIM	PP	SH	GW	S	%	+/-	TF	F%	Min	GP	G	A	Pts	PIM	PP	SH	GW	Min
1994-95	Sodertalje SK Jr.	Swe-Jr.	30	8	6	14	12																		
1995-96	Sodertalje SK Jr.	Swe-Jr.	22	13	12	25	20																		
	Sodertalje SK	Sweden-2	18	5	1	6	0										4	0	0	0	0				
1996-97	Sodertalje SK Jr.	Swe-Jr.	2	2	1	3																			
	Sodertalje SK	Sweden	29	3	2	5	10										10	0	0	0	4				
1997-98	Nykoping	Sweden-2	10	5	1	6	14																		
	Sodertalje SK	Sweden	41	11	9	20	66																		
1998-99	Sodertalje SK	Sweden-2	18	13	10	23	26										10	2	2	4	12				
	V.Frolunda	Sweden	27	0	5	5	10																		
99-2000	Brynas IF Gavle	Sweden	40	4	3	7	76										11	7	2	9	6				
	Brynas IF Gavle	EuroHL	4	0	2	2	4																		
2000-01	**San Jose**	**NHL**	**4**	**0**	**0**	**0**	**0**	**0**	**0**	**0**	**3**	**0.0**	**0**	**0**	**0.0**	**4:41**									
	Kentucky	AHL	66	32	46	78	58										3	1	0	1	0				
2001-02	**NY Rangers**	**NHL**	**67**	**6**	**10**	**16**	**23**	**1**	**2**	**1**	**94**	**6.4**	**10**	**5**	**40.0**	**11:52**									
	Hartford	AHL	8	3	6	9	12																		
2002-03	**NY Rangers**	**NHL**	**58**	**8**	**14**	**22**	**32**	**1**	**1**	**2**	**118**	**6.8**	**0**	**35**	**42.9**	**15:32**									
	Pittsburgh	**NHL**	**22**	**2**	**0**	**2**	**8**	**1**	**0**	**0**	**36**	**5.6**	**–21**	**8**	**75.0**	**14:04**									
2003-04	**Florida**	**NHL**	**37**	**3**	**6**	**9**	**35**	**0**	**0**	**1**	**50**	**6.0**	**0**	**28**	**28.6**	**12:15**									
2004-05	Geneve	Swiss	12	2	4	6	14																		
	Sodertalje SK	Sweden	29	7	13	20	45										10	3	3	6	24				
	NHL Totals		**188**	**19**	**30**	**49**	**98**	**3**	**3**	**4**	**301**	**6.3**		**76**	**40.8**	**13:11**									

Traded to **NY Rangers** by **San Jose** with Christian Gosselin for Adam Graves and future considerations, June 24, 2001. Traded to **Pittsburgh** by **NY Rangers** with Joel Bouchard, Richard Lintner, Rico Fata and future considerations for Mike Wilson, Alex Kovalev, Janne Laukkanen and Dan LaCouture, February 10, 2003. Traded to **Florida** by **Pittsburgh** with Pittsburgh's 1st round choice (Nathan Horton) and 2nd round compensatory choice (Stefan Meyer) in 2003 Entry Draft for Florida's 1st (Marc-Andre Fleury) and 3rd (Daniel Carcillo) round choices in 2003 Entry Draft, June 21, 2003. • Missed majority of 2003-04 season recovering from jaw (November 21, 2003 vs. Washington) and hand (January 21, 2004 vs. Columbus) injuries. Signed as a free agent by **Geneve** (Swiss), September 8, 2004. Signed as a free agent by **Sodertalje** (Sweden), October 26, 2004.

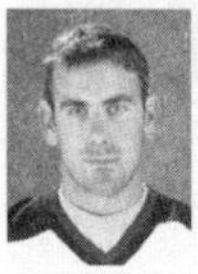

SANDERSON, Geoff (SAN-duhr-sohn, JEHF) CBJ

Left wing. Shoots left. 6', 190 lbs. Born, Hay River, N.W.T., February 1, 1972. Hartford's 2nd choice, 36th overall, in 1990 Entry Draft.

Season	Club	League	GP	G	A	Pts	PIM	PP	SH	GW	S	%	+/-	TF	F%	Min	GP	G	A	Pts	PIM	PP	SH	GW	Min
1987-88	St. Albert Royals	AMHL	45	65	55	120	175																		
1988-89	Swift Current	WHL	58	17	11	28	16										12	3	5	8	6				
1989-90	Swift Current	WHL	70	32	62	94	56										4	1	4	5	8				
1990-91	Swift Current	WHL	70	62	50	112	57										3	1	2	3	4				
	Hartford	**NHL**	**2**	**1**	**0**	**1**	**0**	**0**	**0**	**0**	**2**	**50.0**	**–2**				**3**	**0**	**0**	**0**	**0**	**0**	**0**	**0**	
	Springfield	AHL															1	0	0	0	2				
1991-92	**Hartford**	**NHL**	**64**	**13**	**18**	**31**	**18**	**2**	**0**	**1**	**98**	**13.3**	**5**				**7**	**1**	**0**	**1**	**2**	**0**	**0**	**0**	
1992-93	**Hartford**	**NHL**	**82**	**46**	**43**	**89**	**28**	**21**	**2**	**4**	**271**	**17.0**	**–21**												
1993-94	**Hartford**	**NHL**	**82**	**41**	**26**	**67**	**42**	**15**	**1**	**6**	**266**	**15.4**	**–13**												
1994-95	HPK Hameenlinna	Finland	12	6	4	10	24																		
	Hartford	**NHL**	**46**	**18**	**14**	**32**	**24**	**4**	**0**	**4**	**170**	**10.6**	**–10**												
1995-96	**Hartford**	**NHL**	**81**	**34**	**31**	**65**	**40**	**6**	**0**	**7**	**314**	**10.8**	**0**												
1996-97	**Hartford**	**NHL**	**82**	**36**	**31**	**67**	**29**	**12**	**1**	**4**	**297**	**12.1**	**–9**												
1997-98	**Carolina**	**NHL**	**40**	**7**	**10**	**17**	**14**	**2**	**0**	**0**	**96**	**7.3**	**–4**												
	Vancouver	**NHL**	**9**	**0**	**3**	**3**	**4**	**0**	**0**	**0**	**29**	**0.0**	**–1**												
	Buffalo	**NHL**	**26**	**4**	**5**	**9**	**20**	**0**	**0**	**2**	**72**	**5.6**	**6**				**14**	**3**	**1**	**4**	**4**	**1**	**0**	**1**	
1998-99	**Buffalo**	**NHL**	**75**	**12**	**18**	**30**	**22**	**1**	**0**	**1**	**155**	**7.7**	**8**	**4**	**50.0**	**12:55**	**19**	**4**	**6**	**10**	**14**	**0**	**0**	**1**	**13:52**
99-2000	**Buffalo**	**NHL**	**67**	**13**	**13**	**26**	**22**	**4**	**0**	**3**	**136**	**9.6**	**4**	**3**	**100.0**	**12:54**	**5**	**0**	**2**	**2**	**8**	**0**	**0**	**0**	**12:16**
2000-01	**Columbus**	**NHL**	**68**	**30**	**26**	**56**	**46**	**9**	**0**	**7**	**199**	**15.1**	**4**	**726**	**49.0**	**16:37**									
2001-02	**Columbus**	**NHL**	**42**	**11**	**5**	**16**	**12**	**5**	**0**	**2**	**112**	**9.8**	**–15**	**322**	**42.9**	**16:50**									
2002-03	**Columbus**	**NHL**	**82**	**34**	**33**	**67**	**34**	**15**	**2**	**2**	**286**	**11.9**	**–4**	**96**	**41.7**	**18:44**									
2003-04	**Columbus**	**NHL**	**67**	**13**	**16**	**29**	**34**	**5**	**0**	**1**	**191**	**6.8**	**–9**	**102**	**47.1**	**16:20**									
	Vancouver	**NHL**	**13**	**3**	**4**	**7**	**4**	**1**	**0**	**1**	**36**	**8.3**	**–1**	**14**	**21.4**	**14:46**	**7**	**1**	**1**	**2**	**4**	**0**	**0**	**0**	**12:54**
2004-05	Geneve	Swiss	9	4	1	5	29																		
	NHL Totals		**928**	**316**	**296**	**612**	**393**	**102**	**6**	**45**	**2730**	**11.6**		**1267**	**46.6**	**15:41**	**55**	**9**	**10**	**19**	**32**	**1**	**0**	**2**	**13:23**

Played in NHL All-Star Game (1994, 1997)

Transferred to **Carolina** after **Hartford** franchise relocated, June 25, 1997. Traded to **Vancouver** by **Carolina** with Sean Burke and Enrico Ciccone for Kirk McLean and Martin Gelinas, January 3, 1998. Traded to **Buffalo** by **Vancouver** for Brad May and Buffalo's 3rd round choice (later traded to Tampa Bay – Tampa Bay selected Jimmie Olvestad) in 1999 Entry Draft, February 4, 1998. Claimed by **Columbus** from **Buffalo** in Expansion Draft, June 23, 2000. Traded to **Vancouver** by **Columbus** for Vancouver's 3rd round choice (Daniel Lacosta) in 2004 Entry Draft, March 9, 2004. Claimed on waivers by **Columbus** from **Vancouver**, June 28, 2004. Signed as a free agent by **Geneve** (Swiss), January 5, 2005.

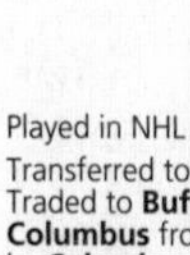

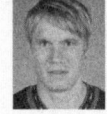

SANTALA, Tommi (SAHN-tah-luh, TAW-mee) ATL.

Center. Shoots right. 6'2", 210 lbs. Born, Helsinki, Finland, June 27, 1979. Atlanta's 10th choice, 245th overall, in 1999 Entry Draft.

Season	Club	League	GP	G	A	Pts	PIM	PP	SH	GW	S	%	+/-	TF	F%	Min	GP	G	A	Pts	PIM	PP	SH	GW	Min
1995-96	Jokerit U18	Fin-U18	25	8	4	12	12										6	1	2	3	4				
1996-97	Jokerit U18	Fin-U18	30	13	19	32	64																		
	Jokerit Helsinki Jr.	Finland-Jr.	20	0	2	2	10										5	0	0	0	0				
1997-98	Jokerit Helsinki Jr.	Finland-Jr.	36	10	28	38	48										8	0	1	1	4				
1998-99	Jokerit Helsinki Jr.	Finland-Jr.	30	20	24	44	20										8	1	3	4	22				
	Jokerit Helsinki	Finland	30	0	0	0	14										3	0	0	0	0				
	Jokerit Helsinki	EuroHL	1	0	2	2	0										1	0	0	0	0				
99-2000	Jokerit Helsinki	Finland	14	0	1	1	2																		
	HPK Hameenlinna	Finland	38	8	19	27	63										8	3	4	7	10				
	Jokerit Helsinki Jr.	Finland-Jr.	5	6	4	10	4																		
	HPK Jr.	Finland-Jr.	6	7	3	10	4																		
2000-01	HPK Hameenlinna	Finland	56	16	24	40	90																		
2001-02	HPK Hameenlinna	Finland	17	6	16	22	14																		

			Regular Season														Playoffs								
Season	Club	League	GP	G	A	Pts	PIM	PP	SH	GW	S	%	+/-	TF	F%	Min	GP	G	A	Pts	PIM	PP	SH	GW	Min
2002-03	HPK Hameenlinna	Finland	50	13	*38	51	92										13	6	6	12	18				
2003-04	Atlanta	NHL	33	1	2	3	22	0	0	1	23	4.3	–7	252	51.2	10:08									
	Chicago Wolves	AHL	50	15	22	37	34										10	1	6	7	31				
2004-05	Chicago Wolves	AHL	67	8	40	48	83										18	5	6	11	42				
	NHL Totals		33	1	2	3	22	0	0	1	23	4.3		252	51.2	10:08									

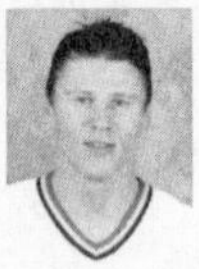

SAPRYKIN, Oleg

(sah-PRIH-kihn, OH-lehg) **PHX.**

Left wing. Shoots left. 6', 195 lbs. Born, Moscow, USSR, February 12, 1981. Calgary's 1st choice, 11th overall, in 1999 Entry Draft.

Season	Club	League	GP	G	A	Pts	PIM	PP	SH	GW	S	%	+/-	TF	F%	Min	GP	G	A	Pts	PIM	PP	SH	GW	Min
1997-98	HK CSKA Moscow	Russia-Q	15	0	3	3	6																		
	HK CSKA Moscow	Russia	20	0	2	2	8																		
1998-99	Seattle	WHL	66	47	46	93	107										11	5	11	16	36				
99-2000	Calgary	NHL	4	0	1	1	2	0	0	0	2	0.0	–4	0	0.0	12:35									
	Seattle	WHL	48	30	36	66	91										6	3	3	6	37				
2000-01	Calgary	NHL	59	9	14	23	43	2	0	0	95	9.5	4	2	50.0	12:10									
2001-02	Calgary	NHL	3	0	0	0	0	0	0	0	9	0.0	–2	0	0.0	13:25									
	Saint John Flames	AHL	52	5	19	24	53																		
2002-03	Calgary	NHL	52	8	15	23	46	1	0	1	116	6.9	5	1	0.0	11:53									
	Saint John Flames	AHL	21	12	9	21	22																		
2003-04	Calgary	NHL	69	12	17	29	41	4	0	0	151	7.9	1	13	23.1	13:48	26	3	3	6	14	1	0	1	14:01
2004-05	CSKA Moscow	Russia	40	15	8	23	105																		
	NHL Totals		187	29	47	76	132	7	0	1	373	7.8		16	25.0	12:43	26	3	3	6	14	1	0	1	14:01

WHL West Second All-Star Team (1999, 2000)

Traded to **Phoenix** by **Calgary** with Denis Gauthier for Daymond Langkow, August 26, 2004. Signed as a free agent by **CSKA** (Russia), September 25, 2004.

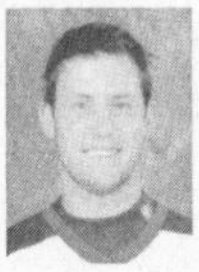

SARICH, Cory

(SAHR-ihch, KOH-ree) **T.B.**

Defense. Shoots right. 6'3", 204 lbs. Born, Saskatoon, Sask., August 16, 1978. Buffalo's 2nd choice, 27th overall, in 1996 Entry Draft.

Season	Club	League	GP	G	A	Pts	PIM	PP	SH	GW	S	%	+/-	TF	F%	Min	GP	G	A	Pts	PIM	PP	SH	GW	Min
1994-95	Sask. Contacts	SMHL	31	5	22	27	99																		
	Saskatoon Blades	WHL	6	0	0	0	4										3	0	1	1	0				
1995-96	Saskatoon Blades	WHL	59	5	18	23	54										3	0	0	0	4				
1996-97	Saskatoon Blades	WHL	58	6	27	33	158																		
1997-98	Saskatoon Blades	WHL	33	5	24	29	90																		
	Seattle	WHL	13	3	16	19	47																		
1998-99	Buffalo	NHL	4	0	0	0	0	0	0	0	2	0.0	3	0	0.0	13:11									
	Rochester	AHL	77	3	26	29	82										20	2	4	6	14				
99-2000	Buffalo	NHL	42	0	4	4	35	0	0	0	49	0.0	2	0	0.0	17:42									
	Rochester	AHL	15	0	6	6	44																		
	Tampa Bay	NHL	17	0	2	2	42	0	0	0	20	0.0	–8	0	0.0	20:42									
2000-01	Tampa Bay	NHL	73	1	8	9	106	0	0	1	66	1.5	–25	3	0.0	18:44									
	Detroit Vipers	IHL	3	0	2	2	2																		
2001-02	Tampa Bay	NHL	72	0	11	11	105	0	0	0	55	0.0	–4	2	50.0	16:06									
	Springfield	AHL	2	0	0	0	0																		
2002-03	Tampa Bay	NHL	82	5	9	14	63	0	0	2	79	6.3	–3	3	0.0	19:36	11	0	2	2	6	0	0	0	21:18
2003-04♦	Tampa Bay	NHL	82	3	16	19	89	0	1	1	93	3.2	5	1	0.0	18:31	23	0	2	2	25	0	0	0	19:11
2004-05		DID NOT PLAY																							
	NHL Totals		372	9	50	59	440	0	1	4	364	2.5		9	11.1	18:17	34	0	4	4	31	0	0	0	19:52

WHL West Second All-Star Team (1998) • AHL All-Rookie Team (1999)

Traded to **Tampa Bay** by **Buffalo** with Wayne Primeau, Brian Holzinger and Buffalo's 3rd round choice (Alexander Kharitonov) in 2000 Entry Draft for Chris Gratton and Tampa Bay's 2nd round choice (Derek Roy) in 2001 Entry Draft, March 9, 2000.

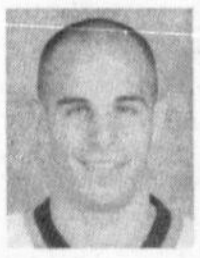

SARNO, Peter

(SAHR-noh, PEE-tuhr) **CBJ**

Center. Shoots left. 5'11", 185 lbs. Born, Toronto, Ont., July 26, 1979. Edmonton's 6th choice, 141st overall, in 1997 Entry Draft.

Season	Club	League	GP	G	A	Pts	PIM	PP	SH	GW	S	%	+/-	TF	F%	Min	GP	G	A	Pts	PIM	PP	SH	GW	Min
1995-96	North York	MTJHL	52	39	57	96	27																		
1996-97	Windsor Spitfires	OHL	66	20	63	83	59										5	0	3	3	6				
1997-98	Windsor Spitfires	OHL	64	33	*88	*121	18																		
	Hamilton	AHL	8	1	1	2	2																		
1998-99	Sarnia Sting	OHL	68	37	*93	*130	49										6	1	7	8	2				
99-2000	Hamilton	AHL	67	10	36	46	31																		
2000-01	Hamilton	AHL	79	19	46	65	64																		
2001-02	Hamilton	AHL	76	12	40	52	38										15	6	7	13	4				
2002-03	Blues Espoo	Finland	45	17	23	40	34										7	2	1	3	2				
2003-04	Edmonton	NHL	6	1	0	1	2	0	0	0	5	20.0	2	59	52.5	10:15									
	Toronto	AHL	31	6	12	18	29																		
	Manitoba Moose	AHL	23	5	9	14	6																		
2004-05	Manitoba Moose	AHL	80	16	66	82	53										14	1	8	9	4				
	NHL Totals		6	1	0	1	2	0	0	0	5	20.0		59	52.5	10:15									

OHL All-Rookie Team (1997) • OHL Rookie of the Year (1997)

Traded to **Vancouver** by **Edmonton** for Tyler Moss, February 16, 2004. Signed as a free agent by **Columbus**, August 22, 2005.

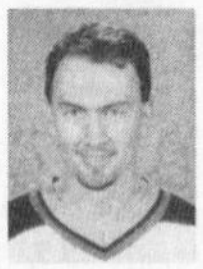

SATAN, Miroslav

(SHA-tuhn, MEER-oh-slav) **NYI**

Left wing. Shoots left. 6'3", 190 lbs. Born, Topolcany, Czech., October 22, 1974. Edmonton's 6th choice, 111th overall, in 1993 Entry Draft.

Season	Club	League	GP	G	A	Pts	PIM	PP	SH	GW	S	%	+/-	TF	F%	Min	GP	G	A	Pts	PIM	PP	SH	GW	Min
1991-92	Topolcany Jr.	Czech-Jr.	31	30	22	52																			
	VTJ Topolcany	Czech-2	9	2	1	3	6																		
1992-93	Dukla Trencin	Czech	38	11	6	17																			
1993-94	Dukla Trencin	Slovakia	30	32	16	48	16																		
	Slovakia	Olympics	8	*9	0	9	0																		
1994-95	Cape Breton	AHL	25	24	16	40	15																		
	Detroit Vipers	IHL	8	1	3	4	4																		
	San Diego Gulls	IHL	6	0	2	2	6																		
1995-96	Edmonton	NHL	62	18	17	35	22	6	0	4	113	15.9	0												
1996-97	Edmonton	NHL	64	17	11	28	22	5	0	2	90	18.9	–4												
	Buffalo	NHL	12	8	2	10	4	2	0	1	29	27.6	1				7	0	0	0	0	0	0	0	
1997-98	Buffalo	NHL	79	22	24	46	34	9	0	4	139	15.8	2				14	5	4	9	4	4	0	1	
1998-99	Buffalo	NHL	81	40	26	66	44	13	3	6	208	19.2	24	9	55.6	20:49	12	3	5	8	2	1	0	1	21:18
99-2000	Dukla Trencin	Slovakia	3	2	8	10	2																		
	Buffalo	NHL	81	33	34	67	32	5	3	5	265	12.5	16	7	14.3	20:35	5	3	2	5	0	0	0	0	19:52
2000-01	Buffalo	NHL	82	29	33	62	36	8	2	4	206	14.1	5	11	36.4	19:56	13	3	10	13	8	1	0	0	21:18
2001-02	Buffalo	NHL	82	37	36	73	33	15	5	5	267	13.9	14	4	50.0	21:10									
	Slovakia	Olympics	2	0	1	1	0																		
2002-03	Buffalo	NHL	79	26	49	75	20	11	1	3	240	10.8	–3	10	20.0	21:23									
2003-04	Bratislava	Slovakia	7	6	4	10	41																		
	Buffalo	NHL	82	29	28	57	30	11	1	5	206	14.1	–15	9	22.2	20:02									
2004-05	Bratislava	Slovakia	18	11	9	20	14										18	*15	7	*22	16				
	NHL Totals		704	259	260	519	277	85	15	39	1763	14.7		50	32.0	20:39	51	14	21	35	14	6	0	2	21:04

Played in NHL All-Star Game (2000, 2003)

Traded to **Buffalo** by **Edmonton** for Barrie Moore and Craig Millar, March 18, 1997. Signed as a free agent by **Bratislava** (Slovakia), December 29, 2004. Signed as a free agent by **NY Islanders**, August 3, 2005.

						Regular Season												Playoffs							
Season	Club	League	GP	G	A	Pts	PIM	PP	SH	GW	S	%	+/-	TF	F%	Min	GP	G	A	Pts	PIM	PP	SH	GW	Min

SAUER, Kurt   (SAW-uhr, KUHRT)   COL.

Defense. Shoots left. 6'4", 225 lbs.   Born, St. Cloud, MN, January 16, 1981. Colorado's 5th choice, 88th overall, in 2000 Entry Draft.

Season	Club	League	GP	G	A	Pts	PIM	PP	SH	GW	S	%	+/-	TF	F%	Min	GP	G	A	Pts	PIM	PP	SH	GW	Min
1998-99	North Iowa	USHL	52	1	4	5	67	....	....	....	....	....	....	....	....	....	....	....	....	....	....	....	....	....	....
99-2000	Spokane Chiefs	WHL	71	3	12	15	48	....	....	....	....	....	....	....	....	....	15	2	1	3	8	....	....	....	....
2000-01	Spokane Chiefs	WHL	48	5	10	15	85	....	....	....	....	....	....	....	....	....	3	1	0	1	2	....	....	....	....
2001-02	Spokane Chiefs	WHL	61	4	20	24	73	....	....	....	....	....	....	....	....	....	11	0	3	3	12	....	....	....	....
2002-03	**Anaheim**	**NHL**	80	1	2	3	74	0	0	0	50	2.0	−23	0	0.0	18:33	21	1	1	2	6	0	1	1	20:45
2003-04	**Anaheim**	**NHL**	55	1	4	5	32	0	0	0	32	3.1	−8	0	0.0	16:54	....	....	....	....	....	....	....	....	....
	Colorado	**NHL**	14	0	1	1	19	0	0	0	12	0.0	−3	0	0.0	15:04	3	0	0	0	0	0	0	0	11:56
2004-05			DID NOT PLAY																						
	NHL Totals		149	2	7	9	125	0	0	0	94	2.1		0	0.0	17:37	24	1	1	2	6	0	1	1	19:39

WHL West First All-Star Team (2002)
Signed as a free agent by **Anaheim**, July 6, 2002. Traded to **Colorado** by **Anaheim** with Anaheim's 4th round choice (Raymond Macias) in 2005 Entry Draft for Martin Skoula, February 21, 2004.

SAVAGE, Andre   (SA-vahj, AWN-dray)

Center. Shoots right. 6', 195 lbs.   Born, Ottawa, Ont., May 27, 1975.

Season	Club	League	GP	G	A	Pts	PIM	PP	SH	GW	S	%	+/-	TF	F%	Min	GP	G	A	Pts	PIM	PP	SH	GW	Min
1992-93	Gloucester	CJHL	54	34	34	68	38	....	....	....	....	....	....	....	....	....	....	....	....	....	....	....	....	....	....
1993-94	Gloucester	CJHL	57	43	74	117	44	....	....	....	....	....	....	....	....	....	....	....	....	....	....	....	....	....	....
1994-95	Michigan Tech	WCHA	39	7	17	24	56	....	....	....	....	....	....	....	....	....	....	....	....	....	....	....	....	....	....
1995-96	Michigan Tech	WCHA	38	13	27	40	42	....	....	....	....	....	....	....	....	....	....	....	....	....	....	....	....	....	....
1996-97	Michigan Tech	WCHA	37	18	20	38	34	....	....	....	....	....	....	....	....	....	....	....	....	....	....	....	....	....	....
1997-98	Michigan Tech	WCHA	33	14	27	41	34	....	....	....	....	....	....	....	....	....	....	....	....	....	....	....	....	....	....
1998-99	**Boston**	**NHL**	6	1	0	1	0	0	0	0	8	12.5	2	32	65.6	9:31	....	....	....	....	....	....	....	....	....
	Providence Bruins	AHL	63	27	42	69	54	....	....	....	....	....	....	....	....	....	5	0	1	1	0	....	....	....	....
99-2000	**Boston**	**NHL**	43	7	13	20	10	2	0	1	70	10.0	−8	619	55.1	14:40	....	....	....	....	....	....	....	....	....
	Providence Bruins	AHL	30	15	17	32	22	....	....	....	....	....	....	....	....	....	14	6	7	13	22	....	....	....	....
2000-01	**Boston**	**NHL**	1	0	0	0	0	0	0	0	1	0.0	0	3	100.0	4:38	....	....	....	....	....	....	....	....	....
	Providence Bruins	AHL	35	13	15	28	47	....	....	....	....	....	....	....	....	....	17	3	4	7	18	....	....	....	....
2001-02	Manitoba Moose	AHL	76	35	26	61	115	....	....	....	....	....	....	....	....	....	6	2	3	5	16	....	....	....	....
2002-03	**Philadelphia**	**NHL**	16	2	1	3	4	0	0	1	13	15.4	2	74	55.4	7:49	....	....	....	....	....	....	....	....	....
	Philadelphia	AHL	64	11	31	42	66	....	....	....	....	....	....	....	....	....	....	....	....	....	....	....	....	....	....
2003-04	Philadelphia	AHL	8	1	0	1	12	....	....	....	....	....	....	....	....	....	1	0	0	0	2	....	....	....	....
	Providence Bruins	AHL	63	16	30	46	94	....	....	....	....	....	....	....	....	....	....	....	....	....	....	....	....	....	....
2004-05	Hershey Bears	AHL	53	7	23	30	36	....	....	....	....	....	....	....	....	....	....	....	....	....	....	....	....	....	....
	San Antonio	AHL	20	1	4	5	12	....	....	....	....	....	....	....	....	....	....	....	....	....	....	....	....	....	....
	NHL Totals		66	10	14	24	14	2	0	2	92	10.9		728	55.8	12:23	....	....	....	....	....	....	....	....	....

WCHA First All-Star Team (1998) • AHL All-Rookie Team (1999)
Signed as a free agent by **Boston**, June 18, 1998. Signed as a free agent by **Vancouver**, August 2, 2001. Signed as a free agent by **Philadelphia**, August 20, 2002. Loaned to **Providence** (AHL) by **Philadelphia** (AHL) for the loan of P.J. Stock, October 29, 2003. Signed as a free agent by **Colorado**, July 22, 2004. Signed as a free agent by **Malmo** (Sweden), July 9, 2005. Loaned to **San Antonio** (AHL) by **Hershey** (AHL) for the loan of Josh Olson, February 25, 2005.

SAVAGE, Brian   (SA-vuhj, BRIGH-uhn)

Left wing. Shoots left. 6'1", 200 lbs.   Born, Sudbury, Ont., February 24, 1971. Montreal's 11th choice, 171st overall, in 1991 Entry Draft.

Season	Club	League	GP	G	A	Pts	PIM	PP	SH	GW	S	%	+/-	TF	F%	Min	GP	G	A	Pts	PIM	PP	SH	GW	Min
1989-90	Sudbury Cubs	NOJHA	32	45	40	85	61	....	....	....	....	....	....	....	....	....	....	....	....	....	....	....	....	....	....
1990-91	Miami-Ohio	CCHA	28	5	6	11	26	....	....	....	....	....	....	....	....	....	....	....	....	....	....	....	....	....	....
1991-92	Miami-Ohio	CCHA	40	24	16	40	43	....	....	....	....	....	....	....	....	....	....	....	....	....	....	....	....	....	....
1992-93	Miami U.	CCHA	38	*37	21	58	44	....	....	....	....	....	....	....	....	....	....	....	....	....	....	....	....	....	....
1993-94	Canada	Nat-Tm	51	20	26	46	38	....	....	....	....	....	....	....	....	....	....	....	....	....	....	....	....	....	....
	Canada	Olympics	8	2	2	4	6	....	....	....	....	....	....	....	....	....	....	....	....	....	....	....	....	....	....
	Montreal	**NHL**	3	1	0	1	0	0	0	0	3	33.3	0	....	....	....	3	0	2	2	0	0	0	0	....
	Fredericton	AHL	17	12	15	27	4	....	....	....	....	....	....	....	....	....	....	....	....	....	....	....	....	....	....
1994-95	**Montreal**	**NHL**	37	12	7	19	27	0	0	0	64	18.8	5	....	....	....	....	....	....	....	....	....	....	....	....
1995-96	**Montreal**	**NHL**	75	25	8	33	28	4	0	4	150	16.7	−8	....	....	....	6	0	2	2	2	0	0	0	....
1996-97	**Montreal**	**NHL**	81	23	37	60	39	5	0	2	219	10.5	−14	....	....	....	5	1	1	2	0	0	0	0	....
1997-98	**Montreal**	**NHL**	64	26	17	43	36	8	0	7	152	17.1	11	....	....	....	9	0	2	2	6	0	0	0	....
1998-99	**Montreal**	**NHL**	54	16	10	26	20	5	0	4	124	12.9	−14	70	44.3	16:30	....	....	....	....	....	....	....	....	....
99-2000	**Montreal**	**NHL**	38	17	12	29	19	6	1	5	107	15.9	−4	67	47.8	17:56	....	....	....	....	....	....	....	....	....
2000-01	**Montreal**	**NHL**	62	21	24	45	26	12	0	1	172	12.2	−13	30	56.7	18:50	....	....	....	....	....	....	....	....	....
2001-02	**Montreal**	**NHL**	47	14	15	29	30	7	0	2	117	12.0	−14	3	0.0	18:12	....	....	....	....	....	....	....	....	....
	Phoenix	**NHL**	30	6	6	12	8	2	0	2	47	12.8	1	4	50.0	15:02	5	0	0	0	0	0	0	0	11:13
2002-03	**Phoenix**	**NHL**	43	6	10	16	22	1	0	1	68	8.8	−5	14	35.7	13:22	....	....	....	....	....	....	....	....	....
2003-04	**Phoenix**	**NHL**	61	12	13	25	36	3	0	1	101	11.9	−5	13	38.5	14:19	....	....	....	....	....	....	....	....	....
	St. Louis	**NHL**	13	4	3	7	2	1	0	1	23	17.4	−3	0	0.0	16:15	5	1	1	2	0	0	0	0	15:10
2004-05			DID NOT PLAY																						
	NHL Totals		608	183	162	345	293	54	1	30	1347	13.6		201	45.8	16:24	33	2	8	10	8	0	0	0	13:11

CCHA First All-Star Team (1993) • CCHA Player of the Year (1993) • NCAA West Second All-American Team (1993)
• Missed majority of 1999-2000 season recovering from neck injury suffered in game vs. Los Angeles, November 20, 1999. Traded to **Phoenix** by **Montreal** with Montreal's 3rd round choice (Matt Jones) in 2002 Entry Draft and future considerations for Sergei Berezin, January 25, 2002. Traded to **St. Louis** by **Phoenix** for future considerations, March 9, 2004. Claimed on waivers by **Phoenix** from **St. Louis**, June 29, 2004.

SAVARD, Marc   (sa-VAHR, MAHRK)   ATL.

Center. Shoots left. 5'10", 195 lbs.   Born, Ottawa, Ont., July 17, 1977. NY Rangers' 3rd choice, 91st overall, in 1995 Entry Draft.

Season	Club	League	GP	G	A	Pts	PIM	PP	SH	GW	S	%	+/-	TF	F%	Min	GP	G	A	Pts	PIM	PP	SH	GW	Min
1992-93	Metcalfe Jets	OHA-B	36	*44	55	*99	38	....	....	....	....	....	....	....	....	....	....	....	....	....	....	....	....	....	....
1993-94	Oshawa Generals	OHL	61	18	39	57	20	....	....	....	....	....	....	....	....	....	5	4	3	7	8	....	....	....	....
1994-95	Oshawa Generals	OHL	66	43	96	*139	78	....	....	....	....	....	....	....	....	....	7	5	6	11	8	....	....	....	....
1995-96	Oshawa Generals	OHL	48	28	59	87	77	....	....	....	....	....	....	....	....	....	5	4	5	9	6	....	....	....	....
1996-97	Oshawa Generals	OHL	64	43	*87	*130	94	....	....	....	....	....	....	....	....	....	18	13	*24	*37	20	....	....	....	....
1997-98	**NY Rangers**	**NHL**	28	1	5	6	4	0	0	0	32	3.1	−4	....	....	....	....	....	....	....	....	....	....	....	....
	Hartford	AHL	58	21	53	74	66	....	....	....	....	....	....	....	....	....	15	8	19	27	24	....	....	....	....
1998-99	**NY Rangers**	**NHL**	70	9	36	45	38	4	0	1	116	7.8	−7	956	48.4	14:35	....	....	....	....	....	....	....	....	....
	Hartford	AHL	9	3	10	13	16	....	....	....	....	....	....	....	....	....	7	1	12	13	16	....	....	....	....
99-2000	**Calgary**	**NHL**	78	22	31	53	56	4	0	3	184	12.0	−2	1021	49.6	16:36	....	....	....	....	....	....	....	....	....
2000-01	**Calgary**	**NHL**	77	23	42	65	46	10	1	5	197	11.7	−12	1050	53.1	19:13	....	....	....	....	....	....	....	....	....
2001-02	**Calgary**	**NHL**	56	14	19	33	48	3	1	3	140	10.0	−18	577	54.8	17:20	....	....	....	....	....	....	....	....	....
2002-03	**Calgary**	**NHL**	10	1	2	3	8	0	0	0	21	4.8	−3	89	52.8	14:41	....	....	....	....	....	....	....	....	....
	Atlanta	**NHL**	57	16	31	47	77	6	0	4	127	12.6	−11	1247	50.9	19:50	....	....	....	....	....	....	....	....	....
2003-04	**Atlanta**	**NHL**	45	19	33	52	85	6	1	3	133	14.3	−8	1083	49.9	22:19	....	....	....	....	....	....	....	....	....
2004-05	HC Thurgau	Swiss-2	13	9	19	28	10	....	....	....	....	....	....	....	....	....	....	....	....	....	....	....	....	....	....
	SC Bern	Swiss	5	1	2	3	0	....	....	....	....	....	....	....	....	....	....	....	....	....	....	....	....	....	....
	NHL Totals		421	105	199	304	362	37	2	19	950	11.1		6023	50.9	17:56	....	....	....	....	....	....	....	....	....

OHL Second All-Star Team (1995)
Traded to **Calgary** by **NY Rangers** with NY Rangers 1st round choice (Oleg Saprykin) in 1999 Entry Draft for the rights to Jan Hlavac and Calgary's 1st (Jamie Lundmark) and 3rd (later traded back to Calgary – Calgary selected Craig Andersson) round choices in 1999 Entry Draft, June 26, 1999. Traded to **Atlanta** by **Calgary** for Ruslan Zainullin, November 15, 2002. Signed as a free agent by **Thurgau** (Swiss-2), October 11, 2004. Signed as a free agent by **Bern** (Swiss), November 23, 2004.

SCATCHARD, Dave   (SKAT-chuhrd, DAYV)   BOS.

Center. Shoots right. 6'3", 220 lbs.   Born, Hinton, Alta., February 20, 1976. Vancouver's 3rd choice, 42nd overall, in 1994 Entry Draft.

Season	Club	League	GP	G	A	Pts	PIM	PP	SH	GW	S	%	+/-	TF	F%	Min	GP	G	A	Pts	PIM	PP	SH	GW	Min
1991-92	Salmon Arm	BCAHA	65	98	100	198	167	....	....	....	....	....	....	....	....	....	....	....	....	....	....	....	....	....	....
1992-93	Kimberley	RMJHL	51	20	23	43	61	....	....	....	....	....	....	....	....	....	....	....	....	....	....	....	....	....	....
1993-94	Portland	WHL	47	9	11	20	46	....	....	....	....	....	....	....	....	....	10	2	1	3	4	....	....	....	....
1994-95	Portland	WHL	71	20	30	50	148	....	....	....	....	....	....	....	....	....	8	0	3	3	21	....	....	....	....
1995-96	Portland	WHL	59	19	28	47	146	....	....	....	....	....	....	....	....	....	7	1	8	9	14	....	....	....	....
	Syracuse Crunch	AHL	1	0	0	0	0	....	....	....	....	....	....	....	....	....	15	2	5	7	29	....	....	....	....
1996-97	Syracuse Crunch	AHL	26	8	7	15	65	....	....	....	....	....	....	....	....	....	....	....	....	....	....	....	....	....	....

			Regular Season														Playoffs								
Season	Club	League	GP	G	A	Pts	PIM	PP	SH	GW	S	%	+/-	TF	F%	Min	GP	G	A	Pts	PIM	PP	SH	GW	Min
1997-98	**Vancouver**	**NHL**	**76**	**13**	**11**	**24**	**165**	**0**	**0**	**1**	**85**	**15.3**	**–4**	....	....	....	....	....	....	....	....	....	....	....	....
1998-99	**Vancouver**	**NHL**	**82**	**13**	**13**	**26**	**140**	**0**	**2**	**2**	**130**	**10.0**	**–12**	**1007**	**56.3**	**13:46**	....	....	....	....	....	....	....	....	....
99-2000	**Vancouver**	**NHL**	**21**	**0**	**4**	**4**	**24**	**0**	**0**	**0**	**25**	**0.0**	**–3**	**190**	**59.5**	**10:12**	....	....	....	....	....	....	....	....	....
	NY Islanders	**NHL**	**44**	**12**	**14**	**26**	**93**	**0**	**1**	**1**	**103**	**11.7**	**0**	**710**	**55.8**	**13:42**	....	....	....	....	....	....	....	....	....
2000-01	**NY Islanders**	**NHL**	**81**	**21**	**24**	**45**	**114**	**4**	**0**	**5**	**176**	**11.9**	**–9**	**1322**	**55.1**	**16:50**	....	....	....	....	....	....	....	....	....
2001-02	**NY Islanders**	**NHL**	**80**	**12**	**15**	**27**	**111**	**3**	**1**	**4**	**117**	**10.3**	**–4**	**788**	**53.8**	**12:31**	**7**	**1**	**1**	**2**	**22**	**0**	**0**	**0**	**12:38**
2002-03	**NY Islanders**	**NHL**	**81**	**27**	**18**	**45**	**108**	**5**	**0**	**2**	**165**	**16.4**	**9**	**1147**	**52.7**	**14:30**	**5**	**1**	**0**	**1**	**6**	**0**	**0**	**1**	**15:58**
2003-04	**NY Islanders**	**NHL**	**61**	**9**	**16**	**25**	**78**	**1**	**1**	**1**	**111**	**8.1**	**12**	**1052**	**52.7**	**16:13**	**5**	**0**	**1**	**1**	**6**	**0**	**0**	**0**	**16:18**
2004-05		Did not play																							
	NHL Totals		**526**	**107**	**115**	**222**	**833**	**13**	**5**	**16**	**912**	**11.7**		**6216**	**54.5**	**14:23**	**17**	**2**	**2**	**4**	**34**	**0**	**0**	**1**	**14:41**

Traded to **NY Islanders** by **Vancouver** with Kevin Weekes and Bill Muckalt for Felix Potvin, NY Islanders' 2nd round compensatory choice (later traded to New Jersey – New Jersey selected Teemu Laine) in 2000 Entry Draft and NY Islanders' 3rd round choice (Thatcher Bell) in 2000 Entry Draft, December 19, 1999. Signed as a free agent by **Boston**, August 2, 2005.

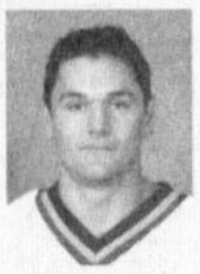

SCHAEFER, Peter

(SHAY-fuhr, PEE-tuhr) **OTT.**

Left wing. Shoots left. 5'11", 195 lbs. Born, Yellow Grass, Sask., July 12, 1977. Vancouver's 3rd choice, 66th overall, in 1995 Entry Draft.

1993-94	Yorkton Mallers	SMHL	32	27	14	41	133	....	....	....	....	....	....	....	....	....	....	....	....	....	....	....	....	....	....
	Brandon	WHL	2	1	0	1	0	....	....	....	....	....	....	....	....	....	....	....	....	....	....	....	....	....	....
1994-95	Brandon	WHL	68	27	32	59	34	....	....	....	....	....	....	....	....	....	18	5	3	8	18	....	....	....	....
1995-96	Brandon	WHL	69	47	61	108	53	....	....	....	....	....	....	....	....	....	19	10	13	23	5	....	....	....	....
1996-97	Brandon	WHL	61	49	74	123	85	....	....	....	....	....	....	....	....	....	6	1	4	5	4	....	....	....	....
	Syracuse Crunch	AHL	5	0	3	3	0	....	....	....	....	....	....	....	....	....	3	1	3	4	14	....	....	....	....
1997-98	Syracuse Crunch	AHL	73	19	44	63	41	....	....	....	....	....	....	....	....	....	5	2	1	3	2	....	....	....	....
1998-99	**Vancouver**	**NHL**	**25**	**4**	**4**	**8**	**8**	**1**	**0**	**1**	**24**	**16.7**	**–1**	**6**	**0.0**	**13:21**	....	....	....	....	....	....	....	....	....
	Syracuse Crunch	AHL	41	10	19	29	66	....	....	....	....	....	....	....	....	....	....	....	....	....	....	....	....	....	....
99-2000	**Vancouver**	**NHL**	**71**	**16**	**15**	**31**	**20**	**2**	**2**	**4**	**101**	**15.8**	**0**	**21**	**19.1**	**15:28**	....	....	....	....	....	....	....	....	....
	Syracuse Crunch	AHL	2	0	0	0	2	....	....	....	....	....	....	....	....	....	....	....	....	....	....	....	....	....	....
2000-01	**Vancouver**	**NHL**	**82**	**16**	**20**	**36**	**22**	**3**	**4**	**2**	**163**	**9.8**	**4**	**25**	**32.0**	**16:18**	**3**	**0**	**0**	**0**	**0**	**0**	**0**	**0**	**13:08**
2001-02	TPS Turku	Finland	33	16	15	31	93	....	....	....	....	....	....	....	....	....	8	1	2	3	2	....	....	....	....
2002-03	**Ottawa**	**NHL**	**75**	**6**	**17**	**23**	**32**	**0**	**0**	**1**	**93**	**6.5**	**11**	**44**	**20.5**	**14:59**	**16**	**2**	**3**	**5**	**6**	**0**	**1**	**0**	**11:51**
2003-04	**Ottawa**	**NHL**	**81**	**15**	**24**	**39**	**26**	**2**	**2**	**3**	**112**	**13.4**	**22**	**39**	**23.1**	**15:36**	**7**	**0**	**2**	**2**	**4**	**0**	**0**	**0**	**14:25**
2004-05	HC Forst Bolzano	Italy	15	11	14	25	10	....	....	....	....	....	....	....	....	....	10	1	7	8	12	....	....	....	....
	NHL Totals		**334**	**57**	**80**	**137**	**108**	**8**	**8**	**11**	**493**	**11.6**		**135**	**22.2**	**15:26**	**26**	**2**	**5**	**7**	**10**	**0**	**1**	**0**	**12:42**

WHL East First All-Star Team (1996, 1997) • WHL Player of the Year (1997) • Canadian Major Junior First All-Star Team (1997)

Signed as a free agent by **TPS** (Finland), October 18, 2001. Traded to **Ottawa** by **Vancouver** for Sami Salo, September 21, 2002. Signed as a free agent by **Bolzano** (Italy), November 30, 2004.

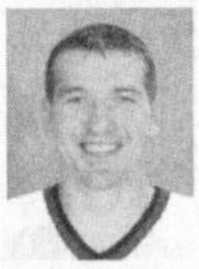

SCHASTLIVY, Petr

(schust-LEE-vee, PEH-tuhr)

Left wing. Shoots left. 6'1", 204 lbs. Born, Angarsk, USSR, April 18, 1979. Ottawa's 5th choice, 101st overall, in 1998 Entry Draft.

1997-98	Yaroslavl 2	Russia-2	47	15	9	24	34	....	....	....	....	....	....	....	....	....	....	....	....	....	....	....	....	....	....
	Yaroslavl	Russia	4	0	0	0	0	....	....	....	....	....	....	....	....	....	....	....	....	....	....	....	....	....	....
1998-99	Yaroslavl	Russia	40	6	1	7	28	....	....	....	....	....	....	....	....	....	6	0	0	0	2	....	....	....	....
99-2000	**Ottawa**	**NHL**	**13**	**2**	**5**	**7**	**2**	**1**	**0**	**1**	**22**	**9.1**	**4**	**0**	**0.0**	**12:18**	**1**	**0**	**0**	**0**	**0**	**0**	**0**	**0**	**13:09**
	Grand Rapids	IHL	46	16	12	28	10	....	....	....	....	....	....	....	....	....	17	8	7	15	6	....	....	....	....
2000-01	**Ottawa**	**NHL**	**17**	**3**	**2**	**5**	**6**	**0**	**0**	**0**	**32**	**9.4**	**–1**	**0**	**0.0**	**11:20**	....	....	....	....	....	....	....	....	....
	Grand Rapids	IHL	43	10	14	24	10	....	....	....	....	....	....	....	....	....	7	4	4	8	0	....	....	....	....
2001-02	**Ottawa**	**NHL**	**1**	**0**	**1**	**1**	**0**	**0**	**0**	**0**	**0**	**0.0**	**1**	**0**	**0.0**	**3:21**	....	....	....	....	....	....	....	....	....
	Grand Rapids	AHL	31	22	13	35	10	....	....	....	....	....	....	....	....	....	....	....	....	....	....	....	....	....	....
2002-03	**Ottawa**	**NHL**	**33**	**9**	**10**	**19**	**4**	**5**	**0**	**2**	**68**	**13.2**	**3**	**2**	**0.0**	**13:21**	....	....	....	....	....	....	....	....	....
2003-04	**Ottawa**	**NHL**	**43**	**2**	**4**	**6**	**14**	**1**	**0**	**1**	**37**	**5.4**	**–1**	**11**	**45.5**	**9:32**	....	....	....	....	....	....	....	....	....
	Anaheim	**NHL**	**22**	**2**	**0**	**2**	**4**	**0**	**0**	**1**	**48**	**4.2**	**–3**	**2**	**50.0**	**11:21**	....	....	....	....	....	....	....	....	....
2004-05	Yaroslavl	Russia	59	15	15	30	28	....	....	....	....	....	....	....	....	....	9	1	3	4	2	....	....	....	....
	NHL Totals		**129**	**18**	**22**	**40**	**30**	**7**	**0**	**5**	**207**	**8.7**		**15**	**40.0**	**11:17**	**1**	**0**	**0**	**0**	**0**	**0**	**0**	**0**	**13:09**

• Missed majority of 2001-02 season recovering from knee injury suffered in game vs. Chicago, December 31, 2001. • Missed majority of 2002-03 season recovering from groin injury suffered in practice, October 5, 2002. Traded to **Anaheim** by **Ottawa** for Todd Simpson, February 4, 2004. Signed as a free agent by **Yaroslavl** (Russia), September, 2004.

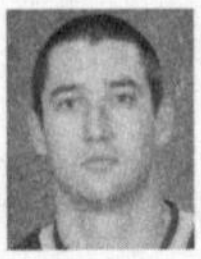

SCHMIDT, Chris

(SHMIHT, KRIHS)

Center. Shoots left. 6'3", 212 lbs. Born, Beaver Lodge, Alta., March 1, 1976. Los Angeles' 4th choice, 111th overall, in 1994 Entry Draft.

1992-93	Seattle	WHL	61	6	7	13	17	....	....	....	....	....	....	....	....	....	5	0	1	1	0	....	....	....	....
1993-94	Seattle	WHL	68	7	17	24	26	....	....	....	....	....	....	....	....	....	9	3	1	4	2	....	....	....	....
1994-95	Seattle	WHL	61	21	11	32	31	....	....	....	....	....	....	....	....	....	3	0	0	0	0	....	....	....	....
1995-96	Seattle	WHL	61	39	23	62	135	....	....	....	....	....	....	....	....	....	5	1	5	6	9	....	....	....	....
1996-97	Mississippi	ECHL	18	7	7	14	35	....	....	....	....	....	....	....	....	....	....	....	....	....	....	....	....	....	....
	Phoenix	IHL	37	3	6	9	60	....	....	....	....	....	....	....	....	....	....	....	....	....	....	....	....	....	....
1997-98	Fredericton	AHL	69	8	5	13	67	....	....	....	....	....	....	....	....	....	4	0	0	0	2	....	....	....	....
1998-99	Springfield	AHL	17	3	2	5	19	....	....	....	....	....	....	....	....	....	1	0	0	0	0	....	....	....	....
	Mississippi	ECHL	6	1	0	1	2	....	....	....	....	....	....	....	....	....	18	6	8	14	10	....	....	....	....
99-2000	Canada	Nat-Tm	33	1	9	10	28	....	....	....	....	....	....	....	....	....	....	....	....	....	....	....	....	....	....
	Lowell	AHL	38	8	10	18	38	....	....	....	....	....	....	....	....	....	7	2	1	3	8	....	....	....	....
2000-01	Lowell	AHL	79	21	32	53	84	....	....	....	....	....	....	....	....	....	4	2	2	4	2	....	....	....	....
2001-02	Manchester	AHL	62	9	12	21	43	....	....	....	....	....	....	....	....	....	5	0	2	2	0	....	....	....	....
2002-03	**Los Angeles**	**NHL**	**10**	**0**	**2**	**2**	**5**	**0**	**0**	**0**	**10**	**0.0**	**–1**	**2**	**100.0**	**10:01**	....	....	....	....	....	....	....	....	....
	Manchester	AHL	53	12	13	25	58	....	....	....	....	....	....	....	....	....	2	0	1	1	4	....	....	....	....
2003-04	Manchester	AHL	54	6	13	19	39	....	....	....	....	....	....	....	....	....	6	0	1	1	4	....	....	....	....
2004-05	Manchester	AHL	80	5	14	19	107	....	....	....	....	....	....	....	....	....	6	1	0	1	4	....	....	....	....
	NHL Totals		**10**	**0**	**2**	**2**	**5**	**0**	**0**	**0**	**10**	**0.0**		**2**	**100.0**	**10:01**	....	....	....	....	....	....	....	....	....

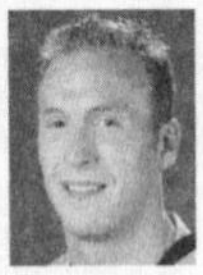

SCHNABEL, Robert

(SHNAH-buhl, RAW-buhrt)

Defense. Shoots left. 6'5", 230 lbs. Born, Prague, Czech., November 10, 1978. Phoenix's 7th choice, 129th overall, in 1998 Entry Draft.

1994-95	Slavia Jr.	CzRep-Jr.	35	11	6	17	14	....	....	....	....	....	....	....	....	....	....	....	....	....	....	....	....	....	....
1995-96	Slavia Jr.	CzRep-Jr.	38	3	5	8	....	....	....	....	....	....	....	....	....	....	....	....	....	....	....	....	....	....	....
1996-97	Slavia Jr.	CzRep-Jr.	36	5	2	7	....	....	....	....	....	....	....	....	....	....	....	....	....	....	....	....	....	....	....
	HC Slavia Praha	CzRep	4	0	0	0	4	....	....	....	....	....	....	....	....	....	1	0	0	0	0	....	....	....	....
1997-98	Red Deer Rebels	WHL	61	1	22	23	143	....	....	....	....	....	....	....	....	....	5	0	0	0	16	....	....	....	....
1998-99	Red Deer Rebels	WHL	1	0	0	0	2	....	....	....	....	....	....	....	....	....	....	....	....	....	....	....	....	....	....
	Springfield	AHL	77	1	7	8	155	....	....	....	....	....	....	....	....	....	3	1	0	1	4	....	....	....	....
99-2000	Springfield	AHL	40	2	8	10	133	....	....	....	....	....	....	....	....	....	5	0	0	0	4	....	....	....	....
2000-01	Springfield	AHL	22	1	2	3	38	....	....	....	....	....	....	....	....	....	....	....	....	....	....	....	....	....	....
	Timra IK	Sweden	16	0	2	2	72	....	....	....	....	....	....	....	....	....	....	....	....	....	....	....	....	....	....
2001-02	**Nashville**	**NHL**	**1**	**0**	**0**	**0**	**0**	**0**	**0**	**0**	**0**	**0.0**	**0**	**0**	**0.0**	**7:16**	....	....	....	....	....	....	....	....	....
	Milwaukee	AHL	67	2	7	9	130	....	....	....	....	....	....	....	....	....	....	....	....	....	....	....	....	....	....
2002-03	**Nashville**	**NHL**	**1**	**0**	**0**	**0**	**0**	**0**	**0**	**0**	**0**	**0.0**	**0**	**0**	**0.0**	**4:28**	....	....	....	....	....	....	....	....	....
	Milwaukee	AHL	62	3	6	9	178	....	....	....	....	....	....	....	....	....	6	0	0	0	34	....	....	....	....
2003-04	**Nashville**	**NHL**	**20**	**0**	**3**	**3**	**34**	**0**	**0**	**0**	**10**	**0.0**	**6**	**0**	**0.0**	**14:36**	....	....	....	....	....	....	....	....	....
	Milwaukee	AHL	11	1	0	1	27	....	....	....	....	....	....	....	....	....	0	0	0	0	0	....	....	....	....
2004-05	HC Sparta Praha	CzRep	47	1	4	5	85	....	....	....	....	....	....	....	....	....	4	0	0	0	12	....	....	....	....
	NHL Totals		**22**	**0**	**3**	**3**	**34**	**0**	**0**	**0**	**10**	**0.0**		**0**	**0.0**	**13:48**	....	....	....	....	....	....	....	....	....

• Re-entered NHL Entry Draft. Originally NY Islanders' 5th choice, 79th overall, in 1997 Entry Draft.

Claimed on waivers by **Nashville** from **Phoenix**, January 2, 2001. • Missed majority of 2003-04 season recovering from wrist injury suffered in game vs. Columbus, October 18, 2003. Signed as a free agent by **Sparta** (CzRep), May 19, 2004.

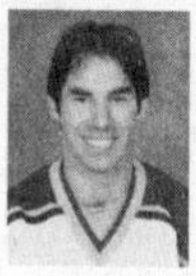

SCHNEIDER, Mathieu

(SHNIGH-duhr, MA-thew) **DET.**

Defense. Shoots left. 5'10", 192 lbs. Born, New York, NY, June 12, 1969. Montreal's 4th choice, 44th overall, in 1987 Entry Draft.

			Regular Season														Playoffs								
Season	Club	League	GP	G	A	Pts	PIM	PP	SH	GW	S	%	+/-	TF	F%	Min	GP	G	A	Pts	PIM	PP	SH	GW	Min
1985-86	Mount St. Charles	High-RI	19	3	27	30	....	....	....	....	....	....	....	....	....	....									
1986-87	Cornwall Royals	OHL	63	7	29	36	75	....	....	....	....	....	....	....	....	....	5	0	0	0	22	....	....	....	....
1987-88	Cornwall Royals	OHL	48	21	40	61	83	....	....	....	....	....	....	....	....	....	11	2	6	8	14	....	....	....	....
	Montreal	**NHL**	**4**	**0**	**0**	**0**	**2**	**0**	**0**	**0**	**2**	**0.0**	**–1**	....	....	....	....	....	....	....	....	....	....	....	....
	Sherbrooke	AHL	....	....	....	....	....	....	....	....	....	....	....	....	....	....	3	0	3	3	12	....	....	....	....
1988-89	Cornwall Royals	OHL	59	16	57	73	96	....	....	....	....	....	....	....	....	....	18	7	20	27	30	....	....	....	....
1989-90	**Montreal**	**NHL**	**44**	**7**	**14**	**21**	**25**	**5**	**0**	**1**	**84**	**8.3**	**2**	....	....	....	**9**	**1**	**3**	**4**	**31**	**1**	**0**	**0**	....
	Sherbrooke	AHL	28	6	13	19	20	....	....	....	....	....	....	....	....	....	....	....	....	....	....	....	....	....	....
1990-91	**Montreal**	**NHL**	**69**	**10**	**20**	**30**	**63**	**5**	**0**	**3**	**164**	**6.1**	**7**	....	....	....	**13**	**2**	**7**	**9**	**18**	**1**	**0**	**0**	....
1991-92	**Montreal**	**NHL**	**78**	**8**	**24**	**32**	**72**	**2**	**0**	**1**	**194**	**4.1**	**10**	....	....	....	**10**	**1**	**4**	**5**	**6**	**1**	**0**	**0**	....
1992-93♦	**Montreal**	**NHL**	**60**	**13**	**31**	**44**	**91**	**3**	**0**	**2**	**169**	**7.7**	**8**	....	....	....	**11**	**1**	**2**	**3**	**16**	**0**	**0**	**0**	....
1993-94	**Montreal**	**NHL**	**75**	**20**	**32**	**52**	**62**	**11**	**0**	**4**	**193**	**10.4**	**15**	....	....	....	**1**	**0**	**0**	**0**	**0**	**0**	**0**	**0**	....
1994-95	**Montreal**	**NHL**	**30**	**5**	**15**	**20**	**49**	**2**	**0**	**0**	**82**	**6.1**	**–3**	....	....	....	....	....	....	....	....	....	....	....	....
	NY Islanders	**NHL**	**13**	**3**	**6**	**9**	**30**	**1**	**0**	**2**	**36**	**8.3**	**–5**	....	....	....	....	....	....	....	....	....	....	....	....
1995-96	**NY Islanders**	**NHL**	**65**	**11**	**36**	**47**	**93**	**7**	**0**	**1**	**155**	**7.1**	**–18**	....	....	....	....	....	....	....	....	....	....	....	....
	Toronto	**NHL**	**13**	**2**	**5**	**7**	**10**	**0**	**0**	**0**	**36**	**5.6**	**–2**	....	....	....	**6**	**0**	**4**	**4**	**8**	**0**	**0**	**0**	....
1996-97	**Toronto**	**NHL**	**26**	**5**	**7**	**12**	**20**	**1**	**0**	**1**	**63**	**7.9**	**3**	....	....	....	....	....	....	....	....	....	....	....	....
1997-98	**Toronto**	**NHL**	**76**	**11**	**26**	**37**	**44**	**4**	**1**	**1**	**181**	**6.1**	**–12**	....	....	....	....	....	....	....	....	....	....	....	....
	United States	Olympics	4	0	0	0	6	....	....	....	....	....	....	....	....	....	....	....	....	....	....	....	....	....	....
1998-99	**NY Rangers**	**NHL**	**75**	**10**	**24**	**34**	**71**	**5**	**0**	**2**	**159**	**6.3**	**–19**	**0**	**0.0**	**24:35**	....	....	....	....	....	....	....	....	....
99-2000	**NY Rangers**	**NHL**	**80**	**10**	**20**	**30**	**78**	**3**	**0**	**1**	**228**	**4.4**	**–6**	**0**	**0.0**	**22:31**	....	....	....	....	....	....	....	....	....
2000-01	**Los Angeles**	**NHL**	**73**	**16**	**35**	**51**	**56**	**7**	**1**	**2**	**183**	**8.7**	**0**	**0**	**0.0**	**23:04**	**13**	**0**	**9**	**9**	**10**	**0**	**0**	**0**	**25:51**
2001-02	**Los Angeles**	**NHL**	**55**	**7**	**23**	**30**	**68**	**4**	**0**	**0**	**123**	**5.7**	**3**	**0**	**0.0**	**22:25**	**7**	**0**	**1**	**1**	**18**	**0**	**0**	**0**	**22:52**
2002-03	**Los Angeles**	**NHL**	**65**	**14**	**29**	**43**	**57**	**10**	**0**	**1**	**162**	**8.6**	**0**	**0**	**0.0**	**22:20**	....	....	....	....	....	....	....	....	....
	Detroit	**NHL**	**13**	**2**	**5**	**7**	**16**	**1**	**0**	**0**	**37**	**5.4**	**2**	**0**	**0.0**	**22:42**	**4**	**0**	**0**	**0**	**6**	**0**	**0**	**0**	**28:16**
2003-04	**Detroit**	**NHL**	**78**	**14**	**32**	**46**	**56**	**4**	**1**	**4**	**165**	**8.5**	**22**	**4**	**0.0**	**24:29**	**12**	**1**	**2**	**3**	**8**	**1**	**0**	**1**	**26:30**
2004-05			DID NOT PLAY																						
	NHL Totals		**992**	**168**	**384**	**552**	**963**	**75**	**3**	**26**	**2416**	**7.0**		**4**	**0.0**	**23:17**	**86**	**6**	**32**	**38**	**121**	**4**	**0**	**1**	**25:45**

OHL First All-Star Team (1988, 1989)
Played in NHL All-Star Game (1996, 2003)

Traded to **NY Islanders** by **Montreal** with Kirk Muller and Craig Darby for Pierre Turgeon and Vladimir Malakhov, April 5, 1995. Traded to **Toronto** by **NY Islanders** with Wendel Clark and D.J. Smith for Darby Hendrickson, Sean Haggerty, Kenny Jonsson and Toronto's 1st round choice (Roberto Luongo) in 1997 Entry Draft, March 13, 1996. • Missed majority of 1996-97 season recovering from groin injury suffered in game vs. St. Louis, December 27, 1996. Rights traded to **NY Rangers** by **Toronto** for Alexander Karpovtsev and NY Rangers' 4th round choice (Mirko Murovic) in 1999 Entry Draft, October 14, 1998. Claimed by **Columbus** from **NY Rangers** in Expansion Draft, June 23, 2000. Signed as a free agent by **Los Angeles**, August 14, 2000. Traded to **Detroit** by **Los Angeles** for Sean Avery, Maxim Kuznetsov, Detroit's 1st round choice (Jeff Tambellini) in 2003 Entry Draft and Detroit's 2nd round choice (later traded to Boston – Boston selected Martins Karsums) in 2004 Entry Draft, March 11, 2003.

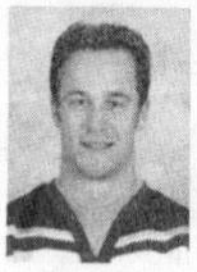

SCHULTZ, Nick

(SHUHLTZ, NIHK) **MIN.**

Defense. Shoots left. 6'1", 207 lbs. Born, Strasbourg, Sask., August 25, 1982. Minnesota's 2nd choice, 33rd overall, in 2000 Entry Draft.

			Regular Season														Playoffs								
Season	Club	League	GP	G	A	Pts	PIM	PP	SH	GW	S	%	+/-	TF	F%	Min	GP	G	A	Pts	PIM	PP	SH	GW	Min
1997-98	Yorkton Mallers	SMHL	59	10	30	40	74	....	....	....	....	....	....	....	....	....	....	....	....	....	....	....	....	....	....
1998-99	Prince Albert	WHL	58	5	18	23	37	....	....	....	....	....	....	....	....	....	14	0	7	7	0	....	....	....	....
99-2000	Prince Albert	WHL	72	11	33	44	38	....	....	....	....	....	....	....	....	....	6	0	3	3	2	....	....	....	....
2000-01	Prince Albert	WHL	59	17	30	47	120	....	....	....	....	....	....	....	....	....	....	....	....	....	....	....	....	....	....
	Cleveland	IHL	4	1	1	2	2	....	....	....	....	....	....	....	....	....	3	0	1	1	0	....	....	....	....
2001-02	**Minnesota**	**NHL**	**52**	**4**	**6**	**10**	**14**	**1**	**0**	**1**	**47**	**8.5**	**0**	**0**	**0.0**	**16:08**	....	....	....	....	....	....	....	....	....
	Houston Aeros	AHL	....	....	....	....	....	....	....	....	....	....	....	....	....	....	14	1	5	6	2	....	....	....	....
2002-03	**Minnesota**	**NHL**	**75**	**3**	**7**	**10**	**23**	**0**	**0**	**1**	**70**	**4.3**	**11**	**0**	**0.0**	**18:28**	**18**	**0**	**1**	**1**	**10**	**0**	**0**	**0**	**19:39**
2003-04	**Minnesota**	**NHL**	**79**	**6**	**10**	**16**	**16**	**1**	**0**	**0**	**72**	**8.3**	**12**	**0**	**0.0**	**20:19**	....	....	....	....	....	....	....	....	....
2004-05	Kassel Huskies	Germany	46	7	15	22	26	....	....	....	....	....	....	....	....	....	7	0	4	4	6	....	....	....	....
	NHL Totals		**206**	**13**	**23**	**36**	**53**	**2**	**0**	**2**	**189**	**6.9**		**0**	**0.0**	**18:35**	**18**	**0**	**1**	**1**	**10**	**0**	**0**	**0**	**19:39**

Signed as a free agent by **Kassel** (Germany), September 24, 2004.

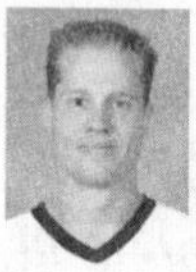

SCHULTZ, Ray

(SHUHLTZ, RAY) **N.J.**

Defense. Shoots left. 6'2", 215 lbs. Born, Red Deer, Alta., November 14, 1976. Ottawa's 8th choice, 184th overall, in 1995 Entry Draft.

			Regular Season														Playoffs								
Season	Club	League	GP	G	A	Pts	PIM	PP	SH	GW	S	%	+/-	TF	F%	Min	GP	G	A	Pts	PIM	PP	SH	GW	Min
1993-94	Edmonton SSAC	AMHL	31	3	24	27	94	....	....	....	....	....	....	....	....	....	....	....	....	....	....	....	....	....	....
	Tri-City	WHL	3	0	0	0	11	....	....	....	....	....	....	....	....	....	....	....	....	....	....	....	....	....	....
1994-95	Tri-City	WHL	63	1	8	9	209	....	....	....	....	....	....	....	....	....	11	0	0	0	16	....	....	....	....
1995-96	Calgary Hitmen	WHL	66	3	17	20	282	....	....	....	....	....	....	....	....	....	....	....	....	....	....	....	....	....	....
1996-97	Calgary Hitmen	WHL	32	3	17	20	141	....	....	....	....	....	....	....	....	....	....	....	....	....	....	....	....	....	....
	Kelowna Rockets	WHL	23	3	11	14	63	....	....	....	....	....	....	....	....	....	6	0	2	2	12	....	....	....	....
1997-98	**NY Islanders**	**NHL**	**13**	**0**	**1**	**1**	**45**	**0**	**0**	**0**	**4**	**0.0**	**3**	....	....	....	....	....	....	....	....	....	....	....	....
	Kentucky	AHL	51	2	4	6	179	....	....	....	....	....	....	....	....	....	1	0	0	0	25	....	....	....	....
1998-99	**NY Islanders**	**NHL**	**4**	**0**	**0**	**0**	**7**	**0**	**0**	**0**	**2**	**0.0**	**–2**	**1**	**0.0**	**15:21**	....	....	....	....	....	....	....	....	....
	Lowell	AHL	54	0	3	3	184	....	....	....	....	....	....	....	....	....	1	0	0	0	4	....	....	....	....
99-2000	**NY Islanders**	**NHL**	**9**	**0**	**1**	**1**	**30**	**0**	**0**	**0**	**2**	**0.0**	**1**	**0**	**0.0**	**14:18**	....	....	....	....	....	....	....	....	....
	Kansas City	IHL	65	5	5	10	208	....	....	....	....	....	....	....	....	....	....	....	....	....	....	....	....	....	....
2000-01	**NY Islanders**	**NHL**	**13**	**0**	**2**	**2**	**40**	**0**	**0**	**0**	**3**	**0.0**	**–1**	**0**	**0.0**	**10:50**	....	....	....	....	....	....	....	....	....
	Lowell	AHL	13	0	1	1	33	....	....	....	....	....	....	....	....	....	....	....	....	....	....	....	....	....	....
	Cleveland	IHL	44	3	5	8	127	....	....	....	....	....	....	....	....	....	3	1	0	1	16	....	....	....	....
2001-02	**NY Islanders**	**NHL**	**2**	**0**	**0**	**0**	**5**	**0**	**0**	**0**	**0**	**0.0**	**–1**	**0**	**0.0**	**3:22**	**2**	**0**	**0**	**0**	**2**	**0**	**0**	**0**	**9:11**
	Bridgeport	AHL	69	0	15	15	205	....	....	....	....	....	....	....	....	....	19	1	3	4	18	....	....	....	....
2002-03	**NY Islanders**	**NHL**	**4**	**0**	**0**	**0**	**28**	**0**	**0**	**0**	**1**	**0.0**	**–1**	**0**	**0.0**	**5:23**	....	....	....	....	....	....	....	....	....
	Bridgeport	AHL	51	2	8	10	105	....	....	....	....	....	....	....	....	....	9	1	0	1	14	....	....	....	....
2003-04	Milwaukee	AHL	73	2	10	12	153	....	....	....	....	....	....	....	....	....	22	1	2	3	31	....	....	....	....
2004-05	Albany River Rats	AHL	77	5	14	19	227	....	....	....	....	....	....	....	....	....	....	....	....	....	....	....	....	....	....
	NHL Totals		**45**	**0**	**4**	**4**	**155**	**0**	**0**	**0**	**12**	**0.0**		**1**	**0.0**	**11:13**	**2**	**0**	**0**	**0**	**2**	**0**	**0**	**0**	**9:11**

Signed as a free agent by **NY Islanders**, June 9, 1997. Signed as a free agent by **Nashville**, July 17, 2003. Signed as a free agent by **New Jersey**, July 6, 2004.

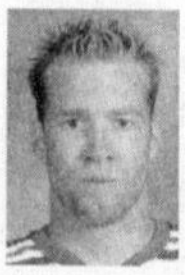

SCOTT, Richard

(SKAWT, RIH-chuhrd)

Left wing. Shoots left. 6'2", 195 lbs. Born, Orillia, Ont., August 1, 1978.

			Regular Season														Playoffs								
Season	Club	League	GP	G	A	Pts	PIM	PP	SH	GW	S	%	+/-	TF	F%	Min	GP	G	A	Pts	PIM	PP	SH	GW	Min
1996-97	Orillia Terriers	OPJHL	10	0	0	0	23	....	....	....	....	....	....	....	....	....	....	....	....	....	....	....	....	....	....
1997-98	Couchiching	OPJHL	45	13	19	32	166	....	....	....	....	....	....	....	....	....	....	....	....	....	....	....	....	....	....
1998-99	Oshawa Generals	OHL	54	12	12	24	193	....	....	....	....	....	....	....	....	....	....	....	....	....	....	....	....	....	....
99-2000	Charlotte	ECHL	55	1	5	6	317	....	....	....	....	....	....	....	....	....	....	....	....	....	....	....	....	....	....
2000-01	Charlotte	ECHL	4	1	1	2	22	....	....	....	....	....	....	....	....	....	....	....	....	....	....	....	....	....	....
	Hartford	AHL	64	2	5	7	320	....	....	....	....	....	....	....	....	....	1	0	0	0	0	....	....	....	....
2001-02	**NY Rangers**	**NHL**	**5**	**0**	**0**	**0**	**5**	**0**	**0**	**0**	**1**	**0.0**	**0**	**0**	**0.0**	**2:25**	....	....	....	....	....	....	....	....	....
	Hartford	AHL	39	2	3	5	211	....	....	....	....	....	....	....	....	....	....	....	....	....	....	....	....	....	....
2002-03	Hartford	AHL	32	0	5	5	150	....	....	....	....	....	....	....	....	....	2	0	0	0	16	....	....	....	....
	Charlotte	ECHL	3	0	1	1	4	....	....	....	....	....	....	....	....	....	....	....	....	....	....	....	....	....	....
2003-04	**NY Rangers**	**NHL**	**5**	**0**	**0**	**0**	**23**	**0**	**0**	**0**	**1**	**0.0**	**0**	**1**	**100.0**	**6:01**	....	....	....	....	....	....	....	....	....
	Hartford	AHL	15	2	2	4	79	....	....	....	....	....	....	....	....	....	....	....	....	....	....	....	....	....	....
2004-05			DID NOT PLAY																						
	NHL Totals		**10**	**0**	**0**	**0**	**28**	**0**	**0**	**0**	**2**	**0.0**		**1**	**100.0**	**4:13**	....	....	....	....	....	....	....	....	....

Signed as a free agent by **NY Rangers**, May 8, 2001. • Missed majority of 2003-04 season recovering from head injury suffered in game vs. NY Islanders, December 4, 2003.

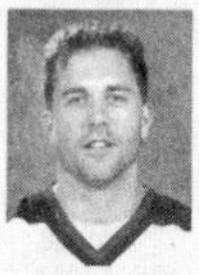

SCOVILLE, Darrel

(SKO-vihl, DAIR-uhl)

Defense. Shoots left. 6'3", 208 lbs. Born, Swift Current, Sask., October 13, 1975.

			Regular Season														Playoffs								
Season	Club	League	GP	G	A	Pts	PIM	PP	SH	GW	S	%	+/-	TF	F%	Min	GP	G	A	Pts	PIM	PP	SH	GW	Min
1994-95	Lebret Eagles	SJHL	61	15	50	65	....	....	....	....	....	....	....	....	....	....	....	....	....	....	....	....	....	....	....
1995-96	Merrimack	H-East	34	6	20	26	54	....	....	....	....	....	....	....	....	....	....	....	....	....	....	....	....	....	....
1996-97	Merrimack	H-East	35	7	16	23	71	....	....	....	....	....	....	....	....	....	....	....	....	....	....	....	....	....	....
1997-98	Merrimack	H-East	38	4	26	30	84	....	....	....	....	....	....	....	....	....	....	....	....	....	....	....	....	....	....
1998-99	Saint John Flames	AHL	61	1	7	8	66	....	....	....	....	....	....	....	....	....	7	1	2	3	13	....	....	....	....

			Regular Season														Playoffs								
Season	Club	League	GP	G	A	Pts	PIM	PP	SH	GW	S	%	+/-	TF	F%	Min	GP	G	A	Pts	PIM	PP	SH	GW	Min
99-2000	**Calgary**	**NHL**	**6**	**0**	**0**	**0**	**2**	**0**	**0**	**0**	**1**	**0.0**	**1**	**0**	**0.0**	**9:18**	....	....	....	....	....	....	....	....	....
	Saint John Flames	AHL	64	11	25	36	99	....	....	....	....	....	....	....	....	....	3	1	2	3	0	....	....	....	....
2000-01	Saint John Flames	AHL	76	11	32	47	125	....	....	....	....	....	....	....	....	....	11	2	6	8	8	....	....	....	....
2001-02	Syracuse Crunch	AHL	51	5	16	21	60	....	....	....	....	....	....	....	....	....	10	0	0	0	6	....	....	....	....
2002-03	**Columbus**	**NHL**	**2**	**0**	**0**	**0**	**4**	**0**	**0**	**0**	**1**	**0.0**	**0**	**0**	**0.0**	**14:31**	....	....	....	....	....	....	....	....	....
	Syracuse Crunch	AHL	24	4	9	13	26	....	....	....	....	....	....	....	....	....	....	....	....	....	....	....	....	....	....
2003-04	**Columbus**	**NHL**	**8**	**0**	**1**	**1**	**6**	**0**	**0**	**0**	**5**	**0.0**	**–4**	**0**	**0.0**	**19:14**	....	....	....	....	....	....	....	....	....
	Syracuse Crunch	AHL	70	10	32	42	73	....	....	....	....	....	....	....	....	....	6	0	2	2	4	....	....	....	....
2004-05	Hershey Bears	AHL	7	0	0	0	11	....	....	....	....	....	....	....	....	....	....	....	....	....	....	....	....	....	....
	Providence Bruins	AHL	43	1	6	7	26	....	....	....	....	....	....	....	....	....	....	....	....	....	....	....	....	....	....
	NHL Totals		**16**	**0**	**1**	**1**	**12**	**0**	**0**	**0**	**7**	**0.0**		**0**	**0.0**	**14:55**	....	....	....	....	....	....	....	....	....

Hockey East All-Rookie Team (1996)

Signed as a free agent by **Calgary**, June 12, 1998. Signed as a free agent by **Columbus**, July 10, 2001. • Missed majority of 2002-03 season recovering from abdominal (October 26, 2002 vs. Grand Rapids - AHL) and foot (January 6, 2003. vs. Philadelphia - AHL) injuries. Signed as a free agent by **Hershey** (AHL), September 28, 2004. Traded to **Providence** (AHL) by **Hershey** (AHL) for Carl Corazzini, November 15, 2004.

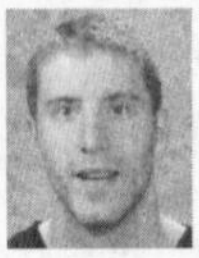

SCUDERI, Rob

(SKUD-uhree, RAWB) **PIT.**

Defense. Shoots left. 6', 214 lbs. Born, Syosset, NY, December 30, 1978. Pittsburgh's 5th choice, 134th overall, in 1998 Entry Draft.

Season	Club	League	GP	G	A	Pts	PIM	PP	SH	GW	S	%	+/-	TF	F%	Min	GP	G	A	Pts	PIM	PP	SH	GW	Min
1995-96	NY Apple Core	MJBHL	76	18	60	78	....	....	....	....	....	....	....	....	....	....	....	....	....	....	....	....	....	....	....
1996-97	NY Apple Core	MJBHL	82	42	70	112	64	....	....	....	....	....	....	....	....	....	....	....	....	....	....	....	....	....	....
1997-98	Boston College	H-East	42	0	24	24	12	....	....	....	....	....	....	....	....	....	....	....	....	....	....	....	....	....	....
1998-99	Boston College	H-East	41	2	8	10	20	....	....	....	....	....	....	....	....	....	....	....	....	....	....	....	....	....	....
99-2000	Boston College	H-East	42	1	12	13	22	....	....	....	....	....	....	....	....	....	....	....	....	....	....	....	....	....	....
2000-01	Boston College	H-East	43	4	19	23	42	....	....	....	....	....	....	....	....	....	....	....	....	....	....	....	....	....	....
2001-02	Wilkes-Barre	AHL	75	1	22	23	66	....	....	....	....	....	....	....	....	....	....	....	....	....	....	....	....	....	....
2002-03	Wilkes-Barre	AHL	74	4	17	21	44	....	....	....	....	....	....	....	....	....	6	0	1	1	4	....	....	....	....
2003-04	**Pittsburgh**	**NHL**	**13**	**1**	**2**	**3**	**4**	**0**	**0**	**0**	**4**	**25.0**	**2**	**0**	**0.0**	**20:06**	....	....	....	....	....	....	....	....	....
	Wilkes-Barre	AHL	64	1	15	16	54	....	....	....	....	....	....	....	....	....	24	0	3	3	14	....	....	....	....
2004-05	Wilkes-Barre	AHL	79	2	18	20	34	....	....	....	....	....	....	....	....	....	11	2	1	3	2	....	....	....	....
	NHL Totals		**13**	**1**	**2**	**3**	**4**	**0**	**0**	**0**	**4**	**25.0**		**0**	**0.0**	**20:06**	....	....	....	....	....	....	....	....	....

NCAA Championship All-Tournament Team (2001)

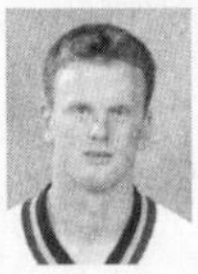

SEDIN, Daniel

(suh-DEEN, DAN-yehl) **VAN.**

Left wing. Shoots left. 6'1", 200 lbs. Born, Ornskoldsvik, Sweden, September 26, 1980. Vancouver's 1st choice, 2nd overall, in 1999 Entry Draft.

Season	Club	League	GP	G	A	Pts	PIM	PP	SH	GW	S	%	+/-	TF	F%	Min	GP	G	A	Pts	PIM	PP	SH	GW	Min
1997-98	MoDo Jr.	Swe-Jr.	26	26	14	40	....	....	....	....	....	....	....	....	....	....	....	....	....	....	....	....	....	....	....
	Malmo Jr.	Swe-Jr.	4	3	3	6	4	....	....	....	....	....	....	....	....	....	....	....	....	....	....	....	....	....	....
	MoDo	Sweden	45	4	8	12	26	....	....	....	....	....	....	....	....	....	9	0	0	0	2	....	....	....	....
1998-99	MoDo	Sweden	50	21	21	42	20	....	....	....	....	....	....	....	....	....	13	4	8	12	14	....	....	....	....
99-2000	MoDo	Sweden	50	19	26	45	28	....	....	....	....	....	....	....	....	....	13	*8	6	14	18	....	....	....	....
	MoDo	EuroHL	4	3	3	6	0	....	....	....	....	....	....	....	....	....	2	0	0	0	0	....	....	....	....
2000-01	**Vancouver**	**NHL**	**75**	**20**	**14**	**34**	**24**	**10**	**0**	**3**	**127**	**15.7**	**–3**	**10**	**60.0**	**13:00**	**4**	**1**	**2**	**3**	**0**	**0**	**0**	**0**	**16:15**
2001-02	**Vancouver**	**NHL**	**79**	**9**	**23**	**32**	**32**	**4**	**0**	**2**	**117**	**7.7**	**1**	**18**	**33.3**	**12:22**	**6**	**0**	**1**	**1**	**0**	**0**	**0**	**0**	**10:44**
2002-03	**Vancouver**	**NHL**	**79**	**14**	**17**	**31**	**34**	**4**	**0**	**2**	**134**	**10.4**	**8**	**24**	**45.8**	**12:26**	**14**	**1**	**5**	**6**	**8**	**1**	**0**	**1**	**12:23**
2003-04	**Vancouver**	**NHL**	**82**	**18**	**36**	**54**	**18**	**1**	**0**	**3**	**153**	**11.8**	**18**	**71**	**47.9**	**13:33**	**7**	**1**	**2**	**3**	**0**	**1**	**0**	**0**	**16:03**
2004-05	MODO	Sweden	49	13	20	33	40	....	....	....	....	....	....	....	....	....	6	0	3	3	6	....	....	....	....
	NHL Totals		**315**	**61**	**90**	**151**	**108**	**19**	**0**	**10**	**531**	**11.5**		**123**	**46.3**	**12:50**	**31**	**3**	**10**	**13**	**8**	**2**	**0**	**1**	**13:24**

Signed as a free agent by **MODO** (Sweden), September 18, 2004.

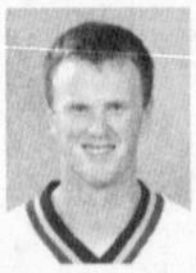

SEDIN, Henrik

(suh-DEEN, HEHN-rihk) **VAN.**

Center. Shoots left. 6'2", 200 lbs. Born, Ornskoldsvik, Sweden, September 26, 1980. Vancouver's 2nd choice, 3rd overall, in 1999 Entry Draft.

Season	Club	League	GP	G	A	Pts	PIM	PP	SH	GW	S	%	+/-	TF	F%	Min	GP	G	A	Pts	PIM	PP	SH	GW	Min
1997-98	MoDo Jr.	Swe-Jr.	26	14	22	36	....	....	....	....	....	....	....	....	....	....	....	....	....	....	....	....	....	....	....
	Malmo Jr.	Swe-Jr.	8	4	7	11	6	....	....	....	....	....	....	....	....	....	....	....	....	....	....	....	....	....	....
	MoDo	Sweden	39	1	4	5	8	....	....	....	....	....	....	....	....	....	7	0	0	0	0	....	....	....	....
1998-99	MoDo	Sweden	49	12	22	34	32	....	....	....	....	....	....	....	....	....	13	2	8	10	6	....	....	....	....
99-2000	MoDo	Sweden	50	9	38	47	22	....	....	....	....	....	....	....	....	....	13	5	9	14	2	....	....	....	....
2000-01	**Vancouver**	**NHL**	**82**	**9**	**20**	**29**	**38**	**2**	**0**	**1**	**98**	**9.2**	**–2**	**1020**	**44.1**	**13:31**	**4**	**0**	**4**	**4**	**0**	**0**	**0**	**0**	**16:31**
2001-02	**Vancouver**	**NHL**	**82**	**16**	**20**	**36**	**36**	**3**	**0**	**1**	**78**	**20.5**	**9**	**785**	**47.4**	**12:48**	**6**	**3**	**0**	**3**	**0**	**0**	**0**	**1**	**11:55**
2002-03	**Vancouver**	**NHL**	**78**	**8**	**31**	**39**	**38**	**4**	**1**	**1**	**81**	**9.9**	**9**	**995**	**48.2**	**13:58**	**14**	**3**	**2**	**5**	**8**	**1**	**0**	**0**	**13:01**
2003-04	**Vancouver**	**NHL**	**76**	**11**	**31**	**42**	**32**	**2**	**0**	**2**	**99**	**11.1**	**23**	**961**	**50.0**	**14:02**	**7**	**2**	**2**	**4**	**2**	**2**	**0**	**0**	**16:02**
2004-05	MODO	Sweden	44	14	22	36	50	....	....	....	....	....	....	....	....	....	6	1	3	4	6	....	....	....	....
	NHL Totals		**318**	**44**	**102**	**146**	**144**	**11**	**1**	**5**	**356**	**12.4**		**3761**	**47.4**	**13:34**	**31**	**8**	**8**	**16**	**10**	**3**	**0**	**1**	**13:56**

Signed as a free agent by **MODO** (Sweden), September 18, 2004.

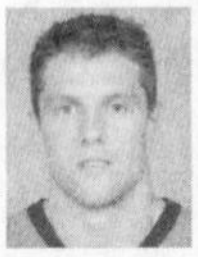

SEIDENBERG, Dennis

(ZIGH-dehn-buhrg, DEH-nihs) **PHI.**

Defense. Shoots left. 6', 200 lbs. Born, Schwenningen, West Germany, July 18, 1981. Philadelphia's 6th choice, 172nd overall, in 2001 Entry Draft.

Season	Club	League	GP	G	A	Pts	PIM	PP	SH	GW	S	%	+/-	TF	F%	Min	GP	G	A	Pts	PIM	PP	SH	GW	Min
99-2000	Mannheim Jr.	Ger-Jr.	52	12	28	40	28	....	....	....	....	....	....	....	....	....	....	....	....	....	....	....	....	....	....
	Adler Mannheim	Germany	3	0	0	0	0	....	....	....	....	....	....	....	....	....	....	....	....	....	....	....	....	....	....
2000-01	Mannheim Jr.	Ger-Jr.	9	3	8	11	20	....	....	....	....	....	....	....	....	....	....	....	....	....	....	....	....	....	....
	Adler Mannheim	Germany	55	2	5	7	6	....	....	....	....	....	....	....	....	....	12	0	1	1	10	....	....	....	....
2001-02	Adler Mannheim	Germany	55	7	13	20	56	....	....	....	....	....	....	....	....	....	8	0	0	0	2	....	....	....	....
2002-03	**Philadelphia**	**NHL**	**58**	**4**	**9**	**13**	**20**	**1**	**0**	**0**	**123**	**3.3**	**8**	**1**	**0.0**	**16:50**	....	....	....	....	....	....	....	....	....
	Philadelphia	AHL	19	5	6	11	17	....	....	....	....	....	....	....	....	....	....	....	....	....	....	....	....	....	....
2003-04	**Philadelphia**	**NHL**	**5**	**0**	**0**	**0**	**2**	**0**	**0**	**0**	**14**	**0.0**	**–4**	**0**	**0.0**	**17:20**	**3**	**0**	**0**	**0**	**0**	**0**	**0**	**0**	**7:36**
	Philadelphia	AHL	33	7	12	19	31	....	....	....	....	....	....	....	....	....	9	2	2	4	4	....	....	....	....
2004-05	Philadelphia	AHL	79	13	28	41	47	....	....	....	....	....	....	....	....	....	18	2	8	10	19	....	....	....	....
	NHL Totals		**63**	**4**	**9**	**13**	**22**	**1**	**0**	**0**	**137**	**2.9**		**1**	**0.0**	**16:52**	**3**	**0**	**0**	**0**	**0**	**0**	**0**	**0**	**7:36**

• Missed majority of 2003-04 season recovering from leg injury suffered in game vs. Edmonton, January 10, 2004.

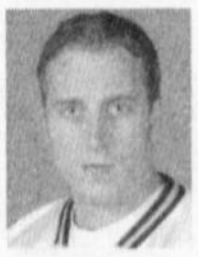

SEJNA, Peter

(SHAY-nah, PEE-tuhr) **ST.L.**

Left wing. Shoots left. 5'9", 198 lbs. Born, Liptovsky Mikulas, Czech., October 5, 1979.

Season	Club	League	GP	G	A	Pts	PIM	PP	SH	GW	S	%	+/-	TF	F%	Min	GP	G	A	Pts	PIM	PP	SH	GW	Min
1995-96	L. Mikulas U18	Svk-U18	44	40	23	63	20	....	....	....	....	....	....	....	....	....	....	....	....	....	....	....	....	....	....
1996-97	L. Mikulas U18	Svk-U18	40	32	19	51	6	....	....	....	....	....	....	....	....	....	....	....	....	....	....	....	....	....	....
	L. Mikulas	Slovakia	29	3	5	8	2	....	....	....	....	....	....	....	....	....	....	....	....	....	....	....	....	....	....
	L. Mikulas Jr.	Slovak-Jr.	17	14	10	24	8	....	....	....	....	....	....	....	....	....	....	....	....	....	....	....	....	....	....
1997-98	L. Mikulas	Slovakia	34	5	6	11	6	....	....	....	....	....	....	....	....	....	....	....	....	....	....	....	....	....	....
1998-99	Des Moines	USHL	52	40	23	63	26	....	....	....	....	....	....	....	....	....	14	11	6	17	8	....	....	....	....
99-2000	Des Moines	USHL	58	41	53	94	36	....	....	....	....	....	....	....	....	....	9	4	5	9	4	....	....	....	....
2000-01	Colorado College	WCHA	41	29	29	58	10	....	....	....	....	....	....	....	....	....	....	....	....	....	....	....	....	....	....
2001-02	Colorado College	WCHA	43	26	24	50	16	....	....	....	....	....	....	....	....	....	....	....	....	....	....	....	....	....	....
2002-03	Colorado College	WCHA	42	*36	46	*82	12	....	....	....	....	....	....	....	....	....	....	....	....	....	....	....	....	....	....
	St. Louis	**NHL**	**1**	**1**	**0**	**1**	**0**	**1**	**0**	**0**	**3**	**33.3**	**0**	**0**	**0.0**	**15:22**	....	....	....	....	....	....	....	....	....
2003-04	**St. Louis**	**NHL**	**20**	**2**	**2**	**4**	**4**	**2**	**0**	**0**	**36**	**5.6**	**–9**	**7**	**42.9**	**14:58**	....	....	....	....	....	....	....	....	....
	Worcester IceCats	AHL	59	12	29	41	13	....	....	....	....	....	....	....	....	....	10	3	3	6	10	....	....	....	....
2004-05	Worcester IceCats	AHL	64	17	21	38	24	....	....	....	....	....	....	....	....	....	....	....	....	....	....	....	....	....	....
	NHL Totals		**21**	**3**	**2**	**5**	**4**	**3**	**0**	**0**	**39**	**7.7**		**7**	**42.9**	**14:59**	....	....	....	....	....	....	....	....	....

WCHA Rookie of the Year (2001) • WCHA First All-Star Team (2003) • WCHA Player of the Year (2003) • NCAA West First All-American Team (2003) • Hobey Baker Memorial Award (Top U.S. Collegiate Player) (2003)

Signed as a free agent by **St. Louis**, April 6, 2003.

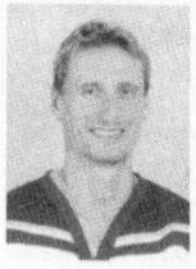

SEKERAS, Lubomir

(SEH-kuhr-ahsh, LOO-boh-mihr)

Defense. Shoots left. 6', 183 lbs. Born, Trencin, Czech., November 18, 1968. Minnesota's 8th choice, 232nd overall, in 2000 Entry Draft.

			Regular Season														Playoffs								
Season	Club	League	GP	G	A	Pts	PIM	PP	SH	GW	S	%	+/-	TF	F%	Min	GP	G	A	Pts	PIM	PP	SH	GW	Min
1987-88	Dukla Trencin Jr.	Czech-Jr.	STATISTICS NOT AVAILABLE																						
	Dukla Trencin	Czech															9	0	0	0	0				
1988-89	Dukla Trencin	Czech	16	2	5	7	22										11	0	4	4	0				
1989-90	Dukla Trencin	Czech	44	6	8	14											9	0	2	2					
1990-91	Dukla Trencin	Czech	52	6	16	22											6	0	1	1					
1991-92	Dukla Trencin	Czech	30	2	6	8	32										13	1	1	2	0				
1992-93	Dukla Trencin	Czech	40	5	19	24	48										11	4	9	13	0				
1993-94	Dukla Trencin	Slovakia	36	9	12	21	46										9	2	4	6	10				
1994-95	Dukla Trencin	Slovakia	36	11	11	22	24										9	2	7	9	8				
1995-96	Trinec	CzRep	40	11	13	24	44										3	0	0	0	0				
1996-97	Trinec	CzRep	52	14	21	35	56										4	1	0	1	2				
1997-98	Trinec	CzRep	50	11	33	44	42										13	2	10	12	4				
1998-99	Trinec	CzRep	50	8	15	23	38										10	2	6	8					
99-2000	HC Ocelari Trinec	CzRep	52	7	24	31	36										4	0	2	2	2				
2000-01	**Minnesota**	**NHL**	**80**	**11**	**23**	**34**	**52**	**4**	**0**	**2**	**102**	**10.8**	**–8**	**0**	**0.0**	**21:13**									
2001-02	**Minnesota**	**NHL**	**69**	**4**	**20**	**24**	**38**	**4**	**0**	**1**	**82**	**4.9**	**–7**	**0**	**0.0**	**22:37**									
2002-03	**Minnesota**	**NHL**	**60**	**2**	**9**	**11**	**30**	**1**	**0**	**1**	**50**	**4.0**	**–12**	**3**	**100.0**	**18:52**	**15**	**1**	**1**	**2**	**6**	**1**	**0**	**1**	**16:51**
2003-04	Yaroslavl	Russia	15	0	3	3	6																		
	Sodertalje SK	Sweden	33	4	13	17	30																		
	Dallas	**NHL**	**4**	**1**	**1**	**2**	**2**	**0**	**0**	**0**	**2**	**50.0**	**0**	**0**	**0.0**	**16:30**									
2004-05	Nurnberg	Germany	52	4	27	31	48										6	0	1	1	4				
	NHL Totals		**213**	**18**	**53**	**71**	**122**	**9**	**0**	**4**	**236**	**7.6**		**3**	**100.0**	**20:55**	**15**	**1**	**1**	**2**	**6**	**1**	**0**	**1**	**16:51**

Signed as a free agent by **Yaroslavl** (Russia), September 16, 2003. Signed as a free agent by **Sodertalje** (Sweden), December, 2003. Signed as a free agent by **Dallas**, March 9, 2004. Signed as a free agent by **Nurnberg** (Germany), July 8, 2004.

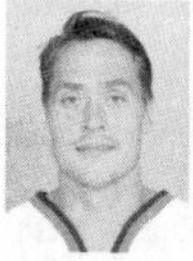

SELANNE, Teemu

(SEH-lahn-nay, TEE-moo) **ANA.**

Right wing. Shoots right. 6', 204 lbs. Born, Helsinki, Finland, July 3, 1970. Winnipeg's 1st choice, 10th overall, in 1988 Entry Draft.

1986-87	Jokerit Helsinki Jr.	Finland-Jr.	33	10	12	22	8																		
1987-88	Jokerit Helsinki Jr.	Finland-Jr.	33	*43	23	*66	18										5	4	3	7	2				
	Jokerit Helsinki	Finland-2	5	1	1	2	0																		
1988-89	PvUK Lahti Jr.	Finland-Jr.	3	3	1	4	2																		
	Jokerit Helsinki Jr.	Finland-Jr.	3	8	8	16	4																		
	Jokerit Helsinki	Finland-2	34	35	33	68	12										5	7	3	10	4				
1989-90	Jokerit Helsinki	Finland	11	4	8	12	0																		
1990-91	Jokerit Helsinki Jr.	Finland-Jr.	1	0	0	0	0																		
	Jokerit Helsinki	Finland	42	33	25	58	12																		
1991-92	Jokerit Helsinki	Finland	44	*39	23	62	20										10	*10	7	*17	18				
	Finland	Olympics	8	7	4	11	6																		
1992-93	**Winnipeg**	**NHL**	**84**	***76**	**56**	**132**	**45**	**24**	**0**	**7**	**387**	**19.6**	**8**				**6**	**4**	**2**	**6**	**2**	**2**	**0**	**2**	
1993-94	**Winnipeg**	**NHL**	**51**	**25**	**29**	**54**	**22**	**11**	**0**	**2**	**191**	**13.1**	**–23**												
1994-95	Jokerit Helsinki	Finland	20	7	12	19	6																		
	Winnipeg	**NHL**	**45**	**22**	**26**	**48**	**2**	**8**	**2**	**1**	**167**	**13.2**	**1**												
1995-96	**Winnipeg**	**NHL**	**51**	**24**	**48**	**72**	**18**	**6**	**1**	**4**	**163**	**14.7**	**3**												
	Anaheim	**NHL**	**28**	**16**	**20**	**36**	**4**	**3**	**0**	**1**	**104**	**15.4**	**2**												
1996-97	**Anaheim**	**NHL**	**78**	**51**	**58**	**109**	**34**	**11**	**1**	**8**	**273**	**18.7**	**28**				**11**	**7**	**3**	**10**	**4**	**3**	**0**	**1**	
1997-98	**Anaheim**	**NHL**	**73**	***52**	**34**	**86**	**30**	**10**	**1**	**10**	**268**	**19.4**	**12**												
	Finland	Olympics	5	4	6	*10	8																		
1998-99	**Anaheim**	**NHL**	**75**	***47**	**60**	**107**	**30**	**25**	**0**	**7**	**281**	**16.7**	**18**	**5**	**20.0**	**22:47**	**4**	**2**	**2**	**4**	**2**	**1**	**0**	**0**	**22:23**
99-2000	**Anaheim**	**NHL**	**79**	**33**	**52**	**85**	**12**	**8**	**0**	**6**	**236**	**14.0**	**6**	**13**	**23.1**	**22:44**									
2000-01	**Anaheim**	**NHL**	**61**	**26**	**33**	**59**	**36**	**10**	**0**	**5**	**202**	**12.9**	**–8**	**4**	**50.0**	**21:51**									
	San Jose	**NHL**	**12**	**7**	**6**	**13**	**0**	**2**	**0**	**2**	**31**	**22.6**	**1**	**4**	**75.0**	**18:14**	**6**	**0**	**2**	**2**	**2**	**0**	**0**	**0**	**17:13**
2001-02	**San Jose**	**NHL**	**82**	**29**	**25**	**54**	**40**	**9**	**1**	**8**	**202**	**14.4**	**–11**	**12**	**25.0**	**16:58**	**12**	**5**	**3**	**8**	**2**	**2**	**0**	**1**	**16:51**
	Finland	Olympics	4	3	0	3	2																		
2002-03	**San Jose**	**NHL**	**82**	**28**	**36**	**64**	**30**	**7**	**0**	**5**	**253**	**11.1**	**–6**	**107**	**42.1**	**19:14**									
2003-04	**Colorado**	**NHL**	**78**	**16**	**16**	**32**	**32**	**6**	**1**	**4**	**182**	**8.8**	**2**	**80**	**43.8**	**16:10**	**10**	**0**	**3**	**3**	**2**	**0**	**0**	**0**	**12:53**
2004-05			DID NOT PLAY																						
	NHL Totals		**879**	**452**	**499**	**951**	**335**	**140**	**7**	**70**	**2940**	**15.4**		**225**	**40.9**	**19:48**	**49**	**18**	**15**	**33**	**14**	**8**	**0**	**4**	**16:22**

NHL All-Rookie Team (1993) • NHL First All-Star Team (1993, 1997) • Calder Memorial Trophy (1993) • NHL Second All-Star Team (1998, 1999) • Maurice "Rocket" Richard Trophy (1999)

Played in NHL All-Star Game (1993, 1994, 1996, 1997, 1998, 1999, 2000, 2002, 2003)

• Missed majority of 1989-90 season recovering from leg injury suffered in game vs. HIFK (Finland), October 19, 1989. Traded to **Anaheim** by **Winnipeg** with Marc Chouinard and Winnipeg's 4th round choice (later traded to Toronto – later traded to Montreal – Montreal selected Kim Staal) in 1996 Entry Draft for Chad Kilger, Oleg Tverdovsky and Anaheim's 3rd round choice (Per-Anton Lundstrom) in 1996 Entry Draft, February 7, 1996. Traded to **San Jose** by **Anaheim** for Jeff Friesen, Steve Shields and San Jose's 2nd round choice (later traded to Dallas – Dallas selected Vojtech Polak) in 2003 Entry Draft, March 5, 2001. Signed as a free agent by **Colorado**, July 3, 2003. Signed as a free agent by **Anaheim**, August 22, 2005.

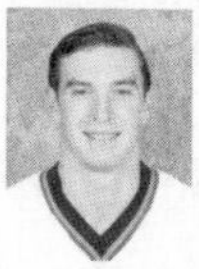

SEMENOV, Alexei

(seh-MEH-nahv, al-EHX-ay) **EDM.**

Defense. Shoots left. 6'6", 235 lbs. Born, Murmansk, USSR, April 10, 1981. Edmonton's 2nd choice, 36th overall, in 1999 Entry Draft.

1997-98	Krylja Sovetov 2	Russia-3	52	1	2	3	48																		
1998-99	St. Petersburg 2	Russia-4	19	0	1	1	20																		
	Sudbury Wolves	OHL	28	0	3	3	28										2	0	0	0	4				
99-2000	Sudbury Wolves	OHL	65	9	35	44	135										12	1	3	4	23				
	Hamilton	AHL															3	0	0	0	0				
2000-01	Sudbury Wolves	OHL	65	21	42	63	106										12	4	13	17	17				
2001-02	Hamilton	AHL	78	5	11	16	67																		
2002-03	**Edmonton**	**NHL**	**46**	**1**	**6**	**7**	**58**	**0**	**0**	**0**	**33**	**3.0**	**–7**	**0**	**0.0**	**19:41**	**6**	**0**	**0**	**0**	**0**	**0**	**0**	**0**	**13:05**
	Hamilton	AHL	37	4	3	7	45																		
2003-04	**Edmonton**	**NHL**	**46**	**2**	**3**	**5**	**32**	**1**	**0**	**0**	**36**	**5.6**	**8**	**0**	**0.0**	**17:16**									
2004-05	St. Petersburg	Russia	50	0	8	8	26																		
	NHL Totals		**92**	**3**	**9**	**12**	**90**	**1**	**0**	**0**	**69**	**4.3**		**0**	**0.0**	**18:28**	**6**	**0**	**0**	**0**	**0**	**0**	**0**	**0**	**13:05**

OHL First All-Star Team (2001)

Signed as a free agent by **St. Petersburg** (Russia), July 30, 2004.

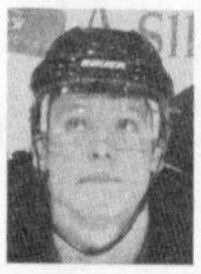

SEMIN, Alexander

(SEH-min, al-ehx-AN-duhr) **WSH.**

Left wing. Shoots left. 6', 181 lbs. Born, Krasnoyarsk, USSR, March 3, 1984. Washington's 2nd choice, 13th overall, in 2002 Entry Draft.

2001-02	Chelyabinsk	Russia-2	46	13	8	21	52										2	2	0	2	0				
2002-03	Lada Togliatti	Russia	47	10	7	17	36										10	*5	3	8	10				
2003-04	**Washington**	**NHL**	**52**	**10**	**12**	**22**	**36**	**4**	**0**	**2**	**92**	**10.9**	**–2**	**6**	**50.0**	**12:37**									
	Portland Pirates	AHL	4	3	1	4	6										7	4	7	11	19				
2004-05	Lada Togliatti	Russia	50	19	11	30	56										10	1	1	2	0				
	NHL Totals		**52**	**10**	**12**	**22**	**36**	**4**	**0**	**2**	**92**	**10.9**		**6**	**50.0**	**12:37**									

Signed as a free agent by **Togliatti** (Russia), September 25, 2004. • Suspended by **Washington** for failing to report to **Portland** (AHL), September 28, 2004.

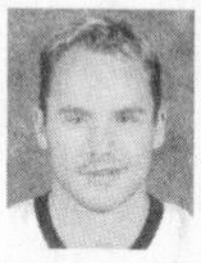

SEVERSON, Cam

(SEH-vuhr-SOHN, KAM) **CGY.**

Left wing. Shoots left. 6'1", 215 lbs. Born, Canora, Sask., January 15, 1978. San Jose's 6th choice, 192nd overall, in 1997 Entry Draft.

1996-97	Lethbridge	WHL	45	12	13	25	169																		
	Prince Albert	WHL	16	5	13	18	54										4	4	0	4	8				
1997-98	Prince Albert	WHL	41	23	25	48	129																		
	Spokane Chiefs	WHL	23	9	11	20	88										18	11	4	15	51				
1998-99	Spokane Chiefs	WHL	46	16	17	33	190																		
	Oklahoma City	CHL	5	6	3	9	4										10	4	0	4	26				
99-2000	Louisiana	ECHL	7	0	2	2	22																		
	Peoria Rivermen	ECHL	56	19	8	27	138										18	3	4	7	41				

			Regular Season														Playoffs								
Season	Club	League	GP	G	A	Pts	PIM	PP	SH	GW	S	%	+/-	TF	F%	Min	GP	G	A	Pts	PIM	PP	SH	GW	Min
2000-01	Portland Pirates	AHL	8	0	0	0	11	....	....	....	....	....	....	....	....	....	....	....	....	....	....	....	....	....	....
	Quad City	UHL	46	22	26	48	129	....	....	....	....	....	....	....	....	....	....	....	....	....	....	....	....	....	....
	Cincinnati	AHL	20	4	7	11	60	....	....	....	....	....	....	....	....	....	3	1	1	2	0	....	....	....	....
2001-02	Hartford	AHL	65	11	10	21	116	....	....	....	....	....	....	....	....	....	5	0	0	0	7	....	....	....	....
2002-03	**Anaheim**	**NHL**	**2**	**0**	**0**	**0**	**8**	**0**	**0**	**0**	**1**	**0.0**	**0**	**0**	**0.0**	**6:44**	**1**	**0**	**0**	**0**	**0**	**0**	**0**	**0**	**2:24**
	Cincinnati	AHL	71	12	9	21	156	....	....	....	....	....	....	....	....	....	....	....	....	....	....	....	....	....	....
2003-04	**Anaheim**	**NHL**	**31**	**3**	**0**	**3**	**50**	**1**	**0**	**0**	**24**	**12.5**	**–3**	**3**	**66.7**	**7:21**	....	....	....	....	....	....	....	....	....
	Cincinnati	AHL	38	7	7	14	145	....	....	....	....	....	....	....	....	....	....	....	....	....	....	....	....	....	....
2004-05	Milwaukee	AHL	63	6	8	14	255	....	....	....	....	....	....	....	....	....	4	0	0	0	12	....	....	....	....
	NHL Totals		**33**	**3**	**0**	**3**	**58**	**1**	**0**	**0**	**25**	**12.0**		**3**	**66.7**	**7:19**	**1**	**0**	**0**	**0**	**0**	**0**	**0**	**0**	**2:24**

Signed as a free agent by **Hartford** (AHL), September 24, 2001. Signed as a free agent by **Anaheim**, August 22, 2002. Signed as a free agent by **Nashville**, July 22, 2004. Signed as a free agent by **Calgary**, August 11, 2005.

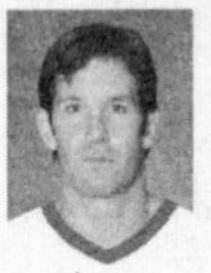

SHANAHAN, Brendan

(SHAN-na-HAN, BREHN-duhn) **DET.**

Left wing. Shoots right. 6'3", 218 lbs. Born, Mimico, Ont., January 23, 1969. New Jersey's 1st choice, 2nd overall, in 1987 Entry Draft.

Season	Club	League	GP	G	A	Pts	PIM	PP	SH	GW	S	%	+/-	TF	F%	Min	GP	G	A	Pts	PIM	PP	SH	GW	Min
1984-85	Mississauga Reps	MTHL	36	20	21	41	26	....	....	....	....	....	....	....	....	....	....	....	....	....	....	....	....	....	....
	Dixie Beehives	OJHL	1	0	0	0	0	....	....	....	....	....	....	....	....	....	....	....	....	....	....	....	....	....	....
1985-86	London Knights	OHL	59	28	34	62	70	....	....	....	....	....	....	....	....	....	5	5	5	10	5	....	....	....	....
1986-87	London Knights	OHL	56	39	53	92	92	....	....	....	....	....	....	....	....	....	....	....	....	....	....	....	....	....	....
1987-88	**New Jersey**	**NHL**	**65**	**7**	**19**	**26**	**131**	**2**	**0**	**2**	**72**	**9.7**	**–20**	....	....	....	**12**	**2**	**1**	**3**	**44**	**1**	**0**	**0**	....
1988-89	**New Jersey**	**NHL**	**68**	**22**	**28**	**50**	**115**	**9**	**0**	**0**	**152**	**14.5**	**2**	....	....	....	....	....	....	....	....	....	....	....	....
1989-90	**New Jersey**	**NHL**	**73**	**30**	**42**	**72**	**137**	**8**	**0**	**5**	**196**	**15.3**	**15**	....	....	....	**6**	**3**	**3**	**6**	**20**	**1**	**0**	**1**	....
1990-91	**New Jersey**	**NHL**	**75**	**29**	**37**	**66**	**141**	**7**	**0**	**2**	**195**	**14.9**	**4**	....	....	....	**7**	**3**	**5**	**8**	**12**	**2**	**0**	**0**	....
1991-92	**St. Louis**	**NHL**	**80**	**33**	**36**	**69**	**171**	**13**	**0**	**2**	**215**	**15.3**	**–3**	....	....	....	**6**	**2**	**3**	**5**	**14**	**1**	**0**	**0**	....
1992-93	**St. Louis**	**NHL**	**71**	**51**	**43**	**94**	**174**	**18**	**0**	**8**	**232**	**22.0**	**10**	....	....	....	**11**	**4**	**3**	**7**	**18**	**2**	**0**	**0**	....
1993-94	**St. Louis**	**NHL**	**81**	**52**	**50**	**102**	**211**	**15**	**7**	**8**	**397**	**13.1**	**–9**	....	....	....	**4**	**2**	**5**	**7**	**4**	**0**	**0**	**0**	....
1994-95	Dusseldorfer EG	Germany	3	5	3	8	4	....	....	....	....	....	....	....	....	....	....	....	....	....	....	....	....	....	....
	St. Louis	**NHL**	**45**	**20**	**21**	**41**	**136**	**6**	**2**	**6**	**153**	**13.1**	**7**	....	....	....	**5**	**4**	**5**	**9**	**14**	**1**	**0**	**1**	....
1995-96	**Hartford**	**NHL**	**74**	**44**	**34**	**78**	**125**	**17**	**2**	**6**	**280**	**15.7**	**2**	....	....	....	....	....	....	....	....	....	....	....	....
1996-97	**Hartford**	**NHL**	**2**	**1**	**0**	**1**	**0**	**0**	**1**	**0**	**13**	**7.7**	**1**	....	....	....	....	....	....	....	....	....	....	....	....
	♦ **Detroit**	**NHL**	**79**	**46**	**41**	**87**	**131**	**20**	**2**	**7**	**323**	**14.2**	**31**	....	....	....	**20**	**9**	**8**	**17**	**43**	**2**	**0**	**2**	....
1997-98 ♦	**Detroit**	**NHL**	**75**	**28**	**29**	**57**	**154**	**15**	**1**	**9**	**266**	**10.5**	**6**	....	....	....	**20**	**5**	**4**	**9**	**22**	**3**	**0**	**2**	....
	Canada	Olympics	6	2	0	2	0	....	....	....	....	....	....	....	....	....	....	....	....	....	....	....	....	....	....
1998-99	**Detroit**	**NHL**	**81**	**31**	**27**	**58**	**123**	**5**	**0**	**5**	**288**	**10.8**	**2**	**18**	**44.4**	**17:31**	**10**	**3**	**7**	**10**	**6**	**1**	**0**	**1**	**18:31**
99-2000	**Detroit**	**NHL**	**78**	**41**	**37**	**78**	**105**	**13**	**1**	**9**	**283**	**14.5**	**24**	**24**	**50.0**	**18:35**	**9**	**3**	**2**	**5**	**10**	**0**	**0**	**0**	**17:36**
2000-01	**Detroit**	**NHL**	**81**	**31**	**45**	**76**	**81**	**15**	**1**	**7**	**278**	**11.2**	**9**	**115**	**43.5**	**18:22**	**2**	**2**	**2**	**4**	**0**	**0**	**0**	**1**	**21:01**
2001-02 ♦	**Detroit**	**NHL**	**80**	**37**	**38**	**75**	**118**	**12**	**3**	**7**	**277**	**13.4**	**23**	**70**	**47.1**	**18:55**	**23**	**8**	**11**	**19**	**20**	**1**	**0**	**2**	**19:06**
	Canada	Olympics	6	0	1	1	0	....	....	....	....	....	....	....	....	....	....	....	....	....	....	....	....	....	....
2002-03	**Detroit**	**NHL**	**78**	**30**	**38**	**68**	**103**	**13**	**0**	**6**	**260**	**11.5**	**5**	**28**	**60.7**	**18:38**	**4**	**1**	**1**	**2**	**4**	**1**	**0**	**0**	**22:03**
2003-04	**Detroit**	**NHL**	**82**	**25**	**28**	**53**	**117**	**8**	**0**	**7**	**280**	**8.9**	**15**	**32**	**46.9**	**18:05**	**12**	**1**	**5**	**6**	**20**	**0**	**1**	**0**	**16:49**
2004-05			DID NOT PLAY																						
	NHL Totals		**1268**	**558**	**593**	**1151**	**2273**	**196**	**20**	**96**	**4160**	**13.4**		**287**	**47.0**	**18:21**	**151**	**52**	**65**	**117**	**251**	**16**	**1**	**10**	**18:35**

NHL First All-Star Team (1994, 2000) • NHL Second All-Star Team (2002) • King Clancy Memorial Trophy (2003)

Played in NHL All-Star Game (1994, 1996, 1997, 1998, 1999, 2000, 2002)

Signed as a free agent by **St. Louis**, July 25, 1991. Traded to **Hartford** by **St. Louis** for Chris Pronger, July 27, 1995. Traded to **Detroit** by **Hartford** with Brian Glynn for Paul Coffey, Keith Primeau and Detroit's 1st round choice (Nikos Tselios) in 1997 Entry Draft, October 9, 1996.

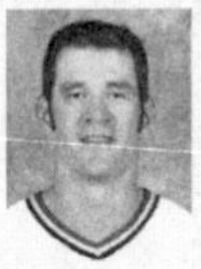

SHANTZ, Jeff

(SHAWNTS, JEHF)

Center. Shoots right. 6', 195 lbs. Born, Duchess, Alta., October 10, 1973. Chicago's 2nd choice, 36th overall, in 1992 Entry Draft.

Season	Club	League	GP	G	A	Pts	PIM	PP	SH	GW	S	%	+/-	TF	F%	Min	GP	G	A	Pts	PIM	PP	SH	GW	Min
1989-90	Medicine Hat	AMHL	36	18	31	49	30	....	....	....	....	....	....	....	....	....	....	....	....	....	....	....	....	....	....
	Regina Pats	WHL	1	0	0	0	0	....	....	....	....	....	....	....	....	....	....	....	....	....	....	....	....	....	....
1990-91	Regina Pats	WHL	69	16	21	37	22	....	....	....	....	....	....	....	....	....	8	2	2	4	2	....	....	....	....
1991-92	Regina Pats	WHL	72	39	50	89	35	....	....	....	....	....	....	....	....	....	....	....	....	....	....	....	....	....	....
1992-93	Regina Pats	WHL	64	29	54	83	75	....	....	....	....	....	....	....	....	....	13	2	12	14	14	....	....	....	....
1993-94	**Chicago**	**NHL**	**52**	**3**	**13**	**16**	**30**	**0**	**0**	**0**	**56**	**5.4**	**–14**	....	....	....	**6**	**0**	**0**	**0**	**6**	**0**	**0**	**0**	....
	Indianapolis Ice	IHL	19	5	9	14	20	....	....	....	....	....	....	....	....	....	....	....	....	....	....	....	....	....	....
1994-95	Indianapolis Ice	IHL	32	9	15	24	20	....	....	....	....	....	....	....	....	....	....	....	....	....	....	....	....	....	....
	Chicago	**NHL**	**45**	**6**	**12**	**18**	**33**	**0**	**2**	**0**	**58**	**10.3**	**11**	....	....	....	**16**	**3**	**1**	**4**	**2**	**0**	**0**	**0**	....
1995-96	**Chicago**	**NHL**	**78**	**6**	**14**	**20**	**24**	**1**	**2**	**0**	**72**	**8.3**	**12**	....	....	....	**10**	**2**	**3**	**5**	**6**	**0**	**0**	**0**	....
1996-97	**Chicago**	**NHL**	**69**	**9**	**21**	**30**	**28**	**0**	**1**	**1**	**86**	**10.5**	**11**	....	....	....	**6**	**0**	**4**	**4**	**6**	**0**	**0**	**0**	....
1997-98	**Chicago**	**NHL**	**61**	**11**	**20**	**31**	**36**	**1**	**2**	**2**	**69**	**15.9**	**0**	....	....	....	....	....	....	....	....	....	....	....	....
1998-99	**Chicago**	**NHL**	**7**	**1**	**0**	**1**	**4**	**0**	**0**	**0**	**5**	**20.0**	**–1**	**72**	**38.9**	**15:14**	....	....	....	....	....	....	....	....	....
	Calgary	**NHL**	**69**	**12**	**17**	**29**	**40**	**1**	**1**	**3**	**77**	**15.6**	**15**	**1112**	**48.4**	**16:47**	....	....	....	....	....	....	....	....	....
99-2000	**Calgary**	**NHL**	**74**	**13**	**18**	**31**	**30**	**6**	**0**	**1**	**112**	**11.6**	**–13**	**1576**	**51.1**	**18:15**	....	....	....	....	....	....	....	....	....
2000-01	**Calgary**	**NHL**	**73**	**5**	**15**	**20**	**58**	**0**	**0**	**0**	**88**	**5.7**	**–7**	**876**	**53.5**	**14:51**	....	....	....	....	....	....	....	....	....
2001-02	**Calgary**	**NHL**	**40**	**3**	**3**	**6**	**23**	**2**	**0**	**0**	**37**	**8.1**	**–3**	**298**	**53.0**	**11:26**	....	....	....	....	....	....	....	....	....
	Saint John Flames	AHL	2	0	1	1	0	....	....	....	....	....	....	....	....	....	....	....	....	....	....	....	....	....	....
2002-03	**Colorado**	**NHL**	**74**	**3**	**6**	**9**	**35**	**0**	**0**	**2**	**68**	**4.4**	**–12**	**874**	**52.1**	**11:28**	**6**	**0**	**0**	**0**	**4**	**0**	**0**	**0**	**9:42**
2003-04	Langnau	Swiss	48	18	27	45	40	....	....	....	....	....	....	....	....	....	....	....	....	....	....	....	....	....	....
2004-05	Langnau	Swiss	43	9	19	28	98	....	....	....	....	....	....	....	....	....	6	0	4	4	35	....	....	....	....
	Fribourg	Swiss	....	....	....	....	....	....	....	....	....	....	....	....	....	....	5	1	5	6	8	....	....	....	....
	NHL Totals		**642**	**72**	**139**	**211**	**341**	**11**	**8**	**9**	**728**	**9.9**		**4808**	**51.0**	**14:51**	**44**	**5**	**8**	**13**	**24**	**0**	**0**	**0**	**9:42**

WHL East First All-Star Team (1993)

Traded to **Calgary** by **Chicago** with Steve Dubinsky for Marty McInnis, Jamie Allison and Eric Andersson, October 27, 1998. Traded to **Colorado** by **Calgary** with Derek Morris and Dean McAmmond for Chris Drury and Stephane Yelle, October 1, 2002. Signed as a free agent by **Langnau** (Swiss), August 19, 2003. Loaned to **Fribourg** (Swiss) by **Langnau** (Swiss), March 14, 2005.

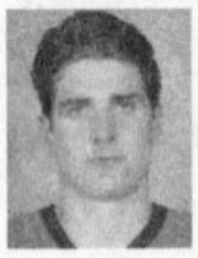

SHARP, Patrick

(SHAHRP, PAT-rihk) **PHI.**

Center. Shoots right. 6', 197 lbs. Born, Thunder Bay, Ont., December 27, 1981. Philadelphia's 2nd choice, 95th overall, in 2001 Entry Draft.

Season	Club	League	GP	G	A	Pts	PIM	PP	SH	GW	S	%	+/-	TF	F%	Min	GP	G	A	Pts	PIM	PP	SH	GW	Min
1998-99	Thunder Bay	USHL	55	19	24	43	48	....	....	....	....	....	....	....	....	....	3	1	1	2	0	....	....	....	....
99-2000	Thunder Bay	USHL	56	20	35	55	41	....	....	....	....	....	....	....	....	....	....	....	....	....	....	....	....	....	....
2000-01	U. of Vermont	ECAC	34	12	15	27	36	....	....	....	....	....	....	....	....	....	....	....	....	....	....	....	....	....	....
2001-02	U. of Vermont	ECAC	31	13	13	26	50	....	....	....	....	....	....	....	....	....	....	....	....	....	....	....	....	....	....
2002-03	**Philadelphia**	**NHL**	**3**	**0**	**0**	**0**	**2**	**0**	**0**	**0**	**3**	**0.0**	**0**	**7**	**42.9**	**5:59**	....	....	....	....	....	....	....	....	....
	Philadelphia	AHL	53	14	19	33	39	....	....	....	....	....	....	....	....	....	....	....	....	....	....	....	....	....	....
2003-04	**Philadelphia**	**NHL**	**41**	**5**	**2**	**7**	**55**	**0**	**0**	**1**	**44**	**11.4**	**–3**	**272**	**46.7**	**9:56**	**12**	**1**	**0**	**1**	**2**	**0**	**0**	**0**	**6:12**
	Philadelphia	AHL	35	15	14	29	45	....	....	....	....	....	....	....	....	....	1	2	0	2	0	....	....	....	....
2004-05	Philadelphia	AHL	75	23	29	52	80	....	....	....	....	....	....	....	....	....	21	8	13	*21	20	....	....	....	....
	NHL Totals		**44**	**5**	**2**	**7**	**57**	**0**	**0**	**1**	**47**	**10.6**		**279**	**46.6**	**9:40**	**12**	**1**	**0**	**1**	**2**	**0**	**0**	**0**	**6:12**

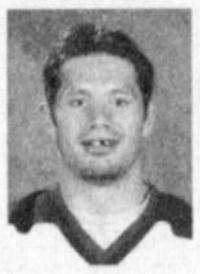

SHELLEY, Jody

(SHEH-lee, JOH-dee) **CBJ**

Left wing. Shoots left. 6'4", 225 lbs. Born, Thompson, Man., February 7, 1976.

Season	Club	League	GP	G	A	Pts	PIM	PP	SH	GW	S	%	+/-	TF	F%	Min	GP	G	A	Pts	PIM	PP	SH	GW	Min
1994-95	Halifax	QMJHL	72	10	12	22	194	....	....	....	....	....	....	....	....	....	7	0	1	1	12	....	....	....	....
1995-96	Halifax	QMJHL	50	13	19	32	319	....	....	....	....	....	....	....	....	....	6	0	2	2	36	....	....	....	....
1996-97	Halifax	QMJHL	58	25	19	44	*448	....	....	....	....	....	....	....	....	....	17	6	6	12	*123	....	....	....	....
1997-98	Dalhousie	AUAA	19	6	11	17	145	....	....	....	....	....	....	....	....	....	....	....	....	....	....	....	....	....	....
	Saint John Flames	AHL	18	1	1	2	50	....	....	....	....	....	....	....	....	....	....	....	....	....	....	....	....	....	....
1998-99	Saint John Flames	AHL	8	0	0	0	46	....	....	....	....	....	....	....	....	....	....	....	....	....	....	....	....	....	....
	Johnstown Chiefs	ECHL	52	12	17	29	325	....	....	....	....	....	....	....	....	....	....	....	....	....	....	....	....	....	....
99-2000	Johnstown Chiefs	ECHL	36	9	17	26	256	....	....	....	....	....	....	....	....	....	....	....	....	....	....	....	....	....	....
	Saint John Flames	AHL	22	1	4	5	93	....	....	....	....	....	....	....	....	....	3	0	0	0	2	....	....	....	....
2000-01	Syracuse Crunch	AHL	69	1	7	8	*357	....	....	....	....	....	....	....	....	....	5	0	0	0	21	....	....	....	....
	Columbus	**NHL**	**1**	**0**	**0**	**0**	**10**	**0**	**0**	**0**	**0**	**0.0**	**0**	**0**	**0.0**	**1:33**	....	....	....	....	....	....	....	....	....
2001-02	**Columbus**	**NHL**	**52**	**3**	**3**	**6**	**206**	**0**	**0**	**0**	**35**	**8.6**	**1**	**0**	**0.0**	**6:32**	....	....	....	....	....	....	....	....	....
	Syracuse Crunch	AHL	22	3	5	8	165	....	....	....	....	....	....	....	....	....	....	....	....	....	....	....	....	....	....
2002-03	**Columbus**	**NHL**	**68**	**1**	**4**	**5**	***249**	**0**	**0**	**0**	**39**	**2.6**	**–5**	**1**	**0.0**	**6:08**	....	....	....	....	....	....	....	....	....

			Regular Season														Playoffs								
Season	Club	League	GP	G	A	Pts	PIM	PP	SH	GW	S	%	+/-	TF	F%	Min	GP	G	A	Pts	PIM	PP	SH	GW	Min
2003-04	**Columbus**	**NHL**	**76**	**3**	**3**	**6**	**228**	**1**	**0**	**0**	**62**	**4.8**	**–10**	**3**	**0.0**	**7:14**									
2004-05	JYP Jyvaskyla	Finland	11	0	1	1	20										3	0	0	0	25				
	NHL Totals		**197**	**7**	**10**	**17**	**693**	**1**	**0**	**0**	**136**	**5.1**		**4**	**0.0**	**6:38**									

Signed as a free agent by **Calgary**, September 1, 1998. Signed as a free agent by **Syracuse** (AHL), September 15, 2000. Signed as a free agent by **Columbus**, January 31, 2001. Signed as a free agent by **JYP** (Finland), January 17, 2005.

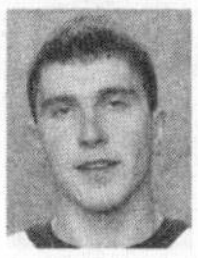

SHISHKANOV, Timofei (shihsh-KAHN-ahv, tee-moh-FAY) NSH.

Left wing. Shoots right. 6'1", 209 lbs. Born, Moscow, USSR, June 10, 1983. Nashville's 2nd choice, 33rd overall, in 2001 Entry Draft.

Season	Club	League	GP	G	A	Pts	PIM	PP	SH	GW	S	%	+/-	TF	F%	Min	GP	G	A	Pts	PIM	PP	SH	GW	Min
99-2000	Spartak 2	Russia-3	14	6	5	11	10																		
	Spartak Moscow	Russia-2	14	1	0	1	2																		
2000-01	Spartak 2	Russia-3	STATISTICS NOT AVAILABLE																						
2001-02	HK CSKA Moscow	Russia-2	23	7	6	13	8																		
	Spartak Moscow	Russia	12	0	0	0	2																		
	HK CSKA 2	Russia-3	13	7	9	16	14																		
2002-03	Quebec Remparts	QMJHL	51	36	46	82	60										11	5	12	17	14				
2003-04	**Nashville**	**NHL**	**2**	**0**	**0**	**0**	**0**	**0**	**0**	**0**	**0**	**0.0**	**–1**	**0**	**0.0**	**6:32**									
	Milwaukee	AHL	63	23	20	43	46										22	2	6	8	17				
2004-05	Milwaukee	AHL	70	20	15	35	31										6	1	0	1	2				
	NHL Totals		**2**	**0**	**0**	**0**	**0**	**0**	**0**	**0**	**0**	**0.0**		**0**	**0.0**	**6:32**									

QMJHL First All-Star Team (2003) • AHL All-Rookie Team (2004)

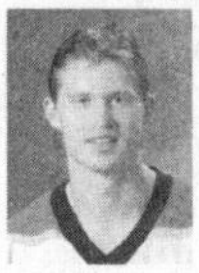

SHVIDKI, Denis (SHVIHD-kee, DEH-nihs) FLA.

Right wing. Shoots left. 6', 195 lbs. Born, Kharkov, USSR, November 21, 1980. Florida's 1st choice, 12th overall, in 1999 Entry Draft.

Season	Club	League	GP	G	A	Pts	PIM	PP	SH	GW	S	%	+/-	TF	F%	Min	GP	G	A	Pts	PIM	PP	SH	GW	Min
1996-97	Yaroslavl 2	Russia-3	35	21	12	33	32																		
	Yaroslavl	Russia	17	3	2	5	6																		
1997-98	Yaroslavl 2	Russia-2	32	20	13	33	20																		
	Yaroslavl	Russia	15	1	1	2	2																		
1998-99	Barrie Colts	OHL	61	35	59	94	8										12	7	9	16	2				
99-2000	Barrie Colts	OHL	61	41	65	106	55										9	3	1	4	2				
2000-01	**Florida**	**NHL**	**43**	**6**	**10**	**16**	**16**	**0**	**0**	**1**	**28**	**21.4**	**6**	**4**	**50.0**	**10:21**									
	Louisville Panthers	AHL	34	15	11	26	20																		
2001-02	**Florida**	**NHL**	**8**	**1**	**2**	**3**	**2**	**0**	**0**	**0**	**11**	**9.1**	**–4**	**1**	**0.0**	**11:57**									
	Utah Grizzlies	AHL	8	2	4	6	2																		
2002-03	San Antonio	AHL	54	8	18	26	28																		
	Florida	**NHL**	**23**	**4**	**2**	**6**	**12**	**2**	**0**	**1**	**29**	**13.8**	**–7**	**5**	**60.0**	**14:14**									
2003-04	**Florida**	**NHL**	**2**	**0**	**0**	**0**	**0**	**0**	**0**	**0**	**4**	**0.0**	**0**	**0**	**0.0**	**14:05**									
	San Antonio	AHL	77	15	39	54	30																		
2004-05			DID NOT PLAY																						
	NHL Totals		**76**	**11**	**14**	**25**	**30**	**2**	**0**	**2**	**72**	**15.3**		**10**	**50.0**	**11:47**									

OHL All-Rookie Team (1999) • OHL Second All-Star Team (1999)

• Missed majority of 2001-02 season recovering from head injury suffered in game vs. Philadelphia, October 4, 2001.

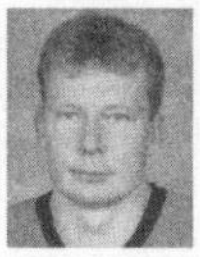

SIKLENKA, Mike (sih-KLEHN-kuh, MIGHK) DAL.

Right wing. Shoots right. 6'5", 224 lbs. Born, Meadow Lake, Sask., December 18, 1979. Washington's 5th choice, 118th overall, in 1998 Entry Draft.

Season	Club	League	GP	G	A	Pts	PIM	PP	SH	GW	S	%	+/-	TF	F%	Min	GP	G	A	Pts	PIM	PP	SH	GW	Min
1997-98	Lloydminster	AJHL	54	10	17	27	120																		
1998-99	Seattle	WHL	68	19	13	32	115										11	6	6	12	24				
99-2000	Portland Pirates	AHL	9	0	0	0	14																		
	Hampton Roads	ECHL	58	7	4	11	62										8	1	0	1	15				
2000-01	Richmond	ECHL	65	19	18	37	117										4	0	0	0	34				
	Portland Pirates	AHL	3	0	0	0	0																		
2001-02	Richmond	ECHL	55	13	21	34	111																		
	Portland Pirates	AHL	8	1	0	1	2																		
2002-03	**Philadelphia**	**NHL**	**1**	**0**	**0**	**0**	**0**	**0**	**0**	**0**	**1**	**0.0**	**0**	**0**	**0.0**	**4:26**									
	Philadelphia	AHL	64	6	6	12	169																		
2003-04	**NY Rangers**	**NHL**	**1**	**0**	**0**	**0**	**0**	**0**	**0**	**0**	**0**	**0.0**	**0**	**0**	**0.0**	**2:22**									
	Trenton Titans	ECHL	1	1	0	1	0																		
	Philadelphia	AHL	18	1	5	6	29																		
	Utah Grizzlies	AHL	26	3	6	9	74																		
2004-05	Klagenfurter AC	Austria	39	16	18	34	156										12	6	1	7	44				
	NHL Totals		**2**	**0**	**0**	**0**	**0**	**0**	**0**	**0**	**1**	**0.0**		**0**	**0.0**	**3:24**									

Signed as a free agent by **Philadelphia**, January 27, 2002. Claimed by **NY Rangers** from **Philadelphia** in Waiver Draft, October 3, 2003. Claimed on waivers by **Philadelphia** from **NY Rangers**, November 5, 2003. Traded to **Dallas** by **Philadelphia** for Steve Gainey, February 16, 2004. Signed as a free agent by **Klagenfurter** (Austria), October 8, 2004.

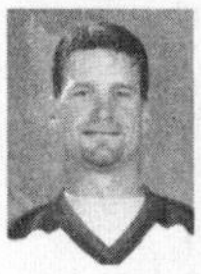

SILLINGER, Mike (sih-LIHN-juhr, MIGHK) ST.L.

Center. Shoots right. 5'11", 196 lbs. Born, Regina, Sask., June 29, 1971. Detroit's 1st choice, 11th overall, in 1989 Entry Draft.

Season	Club	League	GP	G	A	Pts	PIM	PP	SH	GW	S	%	+/-	TF	F%	Min	GP	G	A	Pts	PIM	PP	SH	GW	Min
1986-87	Regina Kings	SMHL	31	83	51	134																			
1987-88	Regina Pats	WHL	67	18	25	43	17										4	2	2	4	0				
1988-89	Regina Pats	WHL	72	53	78	131	52																		
1989-90	Regina Pats	WHL	70	57	72	129	41										11	12	10	22	2				
	Adirondack	AHL															1	0	0	0	0				
1990-91	Regina Pats	WHL	57	50	66	116	42										8	6	9	15	4				
	Detroit	**NHL**	**3**	**0**	**1**	**1**	**0**	**0**	**0**	**0**	**6**	**0.0**	**–2**				**3**	**0**	**1**	**1**	**0**	**0**	**0**	**0**	
1991-92	Adirondack	AHL	64	25	41	66	26										15	9	*19	*28	12				
	Detroit	**NHL**															**8**	**2**	**2**	**4**	**2**	**0**	**0**	**0**	
1992-93	**Detroit**	**NHL**	**51**	**4**	**17**	**21**	**16**	**0**	**0**	**0**	**47**	**8.5**	**0**												
	Adirondack	AHL	15	10	20	30	31										11	5	13	18	10				
1993-94	**Detroit**	**NHL**	**62**	**8**	**21**	**29**	**10**	**0**	**1**	**1**	**91**	**8.8**	**2**												
1994-95	CE Wien	Austria	13	13	14	27	10																		
	Detroit	**NHL**	**13**	**2**	**6**	**8**	**2**	**0**	**0**	**0**	**11**	**18.2**	**3**												
	Anaheim	**NHL**	**15**	**2**	**5**	**7**	**6**	**2**	**0**	**0**	**28**	**7.1**	**1**												
1995-96	**Anaheim**	**NHL**	**62**	**13**	**21**	**34**	**32**	**7**	**0**	**2**	**143**	**9.1**	**–20**												
	Vancouver	**NHL**	**12**	**1**	**3**	**4**	**6**	**0**	**1**	**0**	**16**	**6.3**	**2**				**6**	**0**	**0**	**0**	**2**	**0**	**0**	**0**	
1996-97	**Vancouver**	**NHL**	**78**	**17**	**20**	**37**	**25**	**3**	**3**	**2**	**112**	**15.2**	**–3**												
1997-98	**Vancouver**	**NHL**	**48**	**10**	**9**	**19**	**34**	**1**	**2**	**1**	**56**	**17.9**	**–14**												
	Philadelphia	**NHL**	**27**	**11**	**11**	**22**	**16**	**1**	**2**	**0**	**40**	**27.5**	**3**				**3**	**1**	**0**	**1**	**0**	**0**	**0**	**0**	
1998-99	**Philadelphia**	**NHL**	**25**	**0**	**3**	**3**	**8**	**0**	**0**	**0**	**23**	**0.0**	**–9**	**229**	**62.9**	**10:42**									
	Tampa Bay	**NHL**	**54**	**8**	**2**	**10**	**28**	**0**	**2**	**0**	**69**	**11.6**	**–20**	**320**	**57.8**	**13:57**									
99-2000	**Tampa Bay**	**NHL**	**67**	**19**	**25**	**44**	**86**	**6**	**3**	**1**	**126**	**15.1**	**–29**	**493**	**56.0**	**19:42**									
	Florida	**NHL**	**13**	**4**	**4**	**8**	**16**	**2**	**0**	**1**	**20**	**20.0**	**–1**	**248**	**61.3**	**19:33**	**4**	**2**	**1**	**3**	**2**	**0**	**0**	**0**	**20:24**
2000-01	**Florida**	**NHL**	**55**	**13**	**21**	**34**	**44**	**1**	**0**	**2**	**100**	**13.0**	**–12**	**1028**	**59.7**	**18:52**									
	Ottawa	**NHL**	**13**	**3**	**4**	**7**	**4**	**0**	**0**	**0**	**19**	**15.8**	**1**	**215**	**63.3**	**14:31**	**4**	**0**	**0**	**0**	**2**	**0**	**0**	**0**	**13:40**
2001-02	**Columbus**	**NHL**	**80**	**20**	**23**	**43**	**54**	**8**	**0**	**5**	**150**	**13.3**	**–35**	**2024**	**57.0**	**20:51**									
2002-03	**Columbus**	**NHL**	**75**	**18**	**25**	**43**	**52**	**9**	**3**	**3**	**128**	**14.1**	**–21**	**1490**	**56.5**	**19:08**									
2003-04	**Phoenix**	**NHL**	**60**	**8**	**6**	**14**	**54**	**0**	**1**	**0**	**66**	**12.1**	**–14**	**771**	**56.3**	**15:22**									
	St. Louis	**NHL**	**16**	**5**	**5**	**10**	**14**	**0**	**1**	**0**	**40**	**12.5**	**4**	**351**	**57.8**	**20:08**	**5**	**3**	**1**	**4**	**6**	**0**	**1**	**0**	**22:17**
2004-05			DID NOT PLAY																						
	NHL Totals		**829**	**166**	**232**	**398**	**507**	**40**	**19**	**18**	**1291**	**12.9**		**7169**	**57.7**	**17:50**	**33**	**8**	**5**	**13**	**14**	**0**	**1**	**0**	**19:03**

WHL East Second All-Star Team (1990) • WHL East First All-Star Team (1991)

Traded to **Anaheim** by **Detroit** with Jason York for Stu Grimson, Mark Ferner and Anaheim's 6th round choice (Magnus Nilsson) in 1996 Entry Draft, April 4, 1995. Traded to **Vancouver** by **Anaheim** for Roman Oksiuta, March 15, 1996. Traded to **Philadelphia** by **Vancouver** for Philadelphia's 5th round choice (later traded back to Philadelphia – Philadelphia selected Garrett Prosofsky) in 1998 Entry Draft, February 5, 1998. Traded to **Tampa Bay** by **Philadelphia** with Chris Gratton for Mikael Renberg and Daymond Langkow, December 12, 1998. Traded to **Florida** by **Tampa Bay** for Ryan Johnson and Dwayne Hay, March 14, 2000. Traded to **Ottawa** by **Florida** for future considerations, March 13, 2001. Signed as a free agent by **Columbus**, July 7, 2001. Traded to **Dallas** by **Columbus** with Columbus' 2nd round choice (Johan Fransson) in 2004 Entry Draft for Darryl Sydor, July 22, 2003. Traded to **Phoenix** by **Dallas** with future considerations for Teppo Numminen, July 22, 2003. Traded to **St. Louis** by **Phoenix** for Brent Johnson, March 4, 2004.

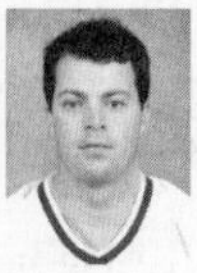

SIM, Jon
(SIHM, JAWN) **PHI.**

Left wing. Shoots left. 5'10", 190 lbs. Born, New Glasgow, N.S., September 29, 1977. Dallas' 2nd choice, 70th overall, in 1996 Entry Draft.

			Regular Season														Playoffs								
Season	Club	League	GP	G	A	Pts	PIM	PP	SH	GW	S	%	+/-	TF	F%	Min	GP	G	A	Pts	PIM	PP	SH	GW	Min
1994-95	Laval Titan	QMJHL	9	0	1	1	6	....	....	....	....	....	....	....	....	....	....	....	....	....	....	....	....	....	....
	Sarnia Sting	OHL	25	9	12	21	19	....	....	....	....	....	....	....	....	....	4	3	2	5	2	....	....	....	....
1995-96	Sarnia Sting	OHL	63	56	46	102	130	....	....	....	....	....	....	....	....	....	10	8	7	15	26	....	....	....	....
1996-97	Sarnia Sting	OHL	64	*56	39	95	109	....	....	....	....	....	....	....	....	....	12	9	5	14	32	....	....	....	....
1997-98	Sarnia Sting	OHL	59	44	50	94	95	....	....	....	....	....	....	....	....	....	5	1	4	5	14	....	....	....	....
1998-99♦	**Dallas**	**NHL**	**7**	**1**	**0**	**1**	**12**	**0**	**0**	**0**	**8**	**12.5**	**1**	**6**	**50.0**	**11:26**	**4**	**0**	**0**	**0**	**0**	**0**	**0**	**0**	**6:27**
	Michigan	IHL	68	24	27	51	91	....	....	....	....	....	....	....	....	....	5	3	1	4	18	....	....	....	....
99-2000	**Dallas**	**NHL**	**25**	**5**	**3**	**8**	**10**	**2**	**0**	**1**	**44**	**11.4**	**4**	**4**	**75.0**	**10:51**	**7**	**1**	**0**	**1**	**6**	**0**	**0**	**0**	**11:11**
	Michigan	IHL	35	14	16	30	65	....	....	....	....	....	....	....	....	....	....	....	....	....	....	....	....	....	....
2000-01	**Dallas**	**NHL**	**15**	**0**	**3**	**3**	**6**	**0**	**0**	**0**	**18**	**0.0**	**–2**	**1**	**100.0**	**8:47**	....	....	....	....	....	....	....	....	....
	Utah Grizzlies	IHL	39	16	13	29	44	....	....	....	....	....	....	....	....	....	....	....	....	....	....	....	....	....	....
2001-02	**Dallas**	**NHL**	**26**	**3**	**0**	**3**	**10**	**1**	**0**	**0**	**43**	**7.0**	**–3**	**3**	**0.0**	**9:30**	....	....	....	....	....	....	....	....	....
	Utah Grizzlies	AHL	31	21	6	27	63	....	....	....	....	....	....	....	....	....	....	....	....	....	....	....	....	....	....
2002-03	**Dallas**	**NHL**	**4**	**0**	**0**	**0**	**0**	**0**	**0**	**0**	**7**	**0.0**	**–1**	**2**	**50.0**	**9:10**	....	....	....	....	....	....	....	....	....
	Utah Grizzlies	AHL	42	16	31	47	85	....	....	....	....	....	....	....	....	....	....	....	....	....	....	....	....	....	....
	Nashville	**NHL**	**4**	**1**	**0**	**1**	**0**	**0**	**0**	**0**	**3**	**33.3**	**0**	**14**	**35.7**	**9:18**	....	....	....	....	....	....	....	....	....
	Los Angeles	**NHL**	**14**	**0**	**2**	**2**	**19**	**0**	**0**	**0**	**29**	**0.0**	**–3**	**3**	**33.3**	**12:05**	....	....	....	....	....	....	....	....	....
2003-04	**Los Angeles**	**NHL**	**48**	**6**	**7**	**13**	**27**	**0**	**0**	**1**	**73**	**8.2**	**0**	**19**	**31.6**	**10:01**	....	....	....	....	....	....	....	....	....
	Pittsburgh	**NHL**	**15**	**2**	**3**	**5**	**6**	**0**	**0**	**1**	**27**	**7.4**	**–4**	**0**	**0.0**	**13:39**	....	....	....	....	....	....	....	....	....
2004-05	Utah Grizzlies	AHL	10	2	2	4	12	....	....	....	....	....	....	....	....	....	....	....	....	....	....	....	....	....	....
	Philadelphia	AHL	63	35	26	61	66	....	....	....	....	....	....	....	....	....	21	*10	7	17	44	....	....	....	....
	NHL Totals		**158**	**18**	**18**	**36**	**90**	**3**	**0**	**3**	**252**	**7.1**		**52**	**38.5**	**10:30**	**11**	**1**	**0**	**1**	**6**	**0**	**0**	**0**	**9:27**

OHL Second All-Star Team (1998)

Traded to **Nashville** by **Dallas** for Bubba Berenzweig and future considerations, February 17, 2003. Claimed on waivers by **Los Angeles** from **Nashville**, March 8, 2003. Claimed on waivers by **Pittsburgh** from **Los Angeles**, March 4, 2004. Signed as a free agent by **Phoenix**, September 2, 2004. Loaned to **Philadelphia** (AHL) by **Utah** (AHL) for the loan of Peter White, November 14, 2004. Signed as a free agent by **Philadelphia**, August 2, 2005.

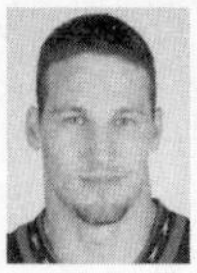

SIMON, Ben
(SIGH-mohn, BEN) **CBJ**

Left wing. Shoots left. 6', 195 lbs. Born, Shaker Heights, OH, June 14, 1978. Chicago's 5th choice, 110th overall, in 1997 Entry Draft.

Season	Club	League	GP	G	A	Pts	PIM	PP	SH	GW	S	%	+/-	TF	F%	Min	GP	G	A	Pts	PIM	PP	SH	GW	Min
1992-93	Shaker Heights	High-OH	25	15	21	36	....	....	....	....	....	....	....	....	....	....	....	....	....	....	....	....	....	....	....
1993-94	Shaker Heights	High-OH	24	45	41	86	....	....	....	....	....	....	....	....	....	....	....	....	....	....	....	....	....	....	....
1994-95	Shaker Heights	High-OH	25	61	68	129	....	....	....	....	....	....	....	....	....	....	....	....	....	....	....	....	....	....	....
1995-96	Cleveland Barons	NAHL	45	38	33	71	....	....	....	....	....	....	....	....	....	....	5	7	13	20	....	....	....	....	....
1996-97	U. of Notre Dame	CCHA	30	4	15	19	79	....	....	....	....	....	....	....	....	....	....	....	....	....	....	....	....	....	....
1997-98	U. of Notre Dame	CCHA	37	9	28	37	91	....	....	....	....	....	....	....	....	....	....	....	....	....	....	....	....	....	....
1998-99	U. of Notre Dame	CCHA	37	18	24	42	65	....	....	....	....	....	....	....	....	....	....	....	....	....	....	....	....	....	....
99-2000	U. of Notre Dame	CCHA	40	13	19	32	53	....	....	....	....	....	....	....	....	....	....	....	....	....	....	....	....	....	....
2000-01	Orlando	IHL	77	8	12	20	47	....	....	....	....	....	....	....	....	....	16	6	5	11	20	....	....	....	....
2001-02	**Atlanta**	**NHL**	**6**	**0**	**0**	**0**	**6**	**0**	**0**	**0**	**7**	**0.0**	**1**	**32**	**40.6**	**9:20**	....	....	....	....	....	....	....	....	....
	Chicago Wolves	AHL	74	11	23	34	56	....	....	....	....	....	....	....	....	....	25	2	3	5	24	....	....	....	....
2002-03	**Atlanta**	**NHL**	**10**	**0**	**1**	**1**	**9**	**0**	**0**	**0**	**7**	**0.0**	**0**	**54**	**31.5**	**9:25**	....	....	....	....	....	....	....	....	....
	Chicago Wolves	AHL	69	15	17	32	78	....	....	....	....	....	....	....	....	....	9	0	0	0	6	....	....	....	....
2003-04	Milwaukee	AHL	18	1	3	4	6	....	....	....	....	....	....	....	....	....	....	....	....	....	....	....	....	....	....
	Atlanta	**NHL**	**52**	**3**	**0**	**3**	**28**	**0**	**0**	**0**	**30**	**10.0**	**–10**	**203**	**33.0**	**6:05**	....	....	....	....	....	....	....	....	....
2004-05	Chicago Wolves	AHL	53	11	10	21	58	....	....	....	....	....	....	....	....	....	18	1	5	6	44	....	....	....	....
	NHL Totals		**68**	**3**	**1**	**4**	**43**	**0**	**0**	**0**	**44**	**6.8**		**289**	**33.6**	**6:51**	....	....	....	....	....	....	....	....	....

CCHA Second All-Star Team (1999)

Rights traded to **Atlanta** by **Chicago** for Atlanta's 9th round choice (Peter Flache) in 2000 Entry Draft, June 25, 2000. Signed as a free agent by **Nashville**, July 14, 2003. Traded to **Atlanta** by **Nashville** with Tomas Kloucek for Simon Gamache and Kirill Safronov, December 2, 2003. Signed as a free agent by **Columbus**, August 11, 2005.

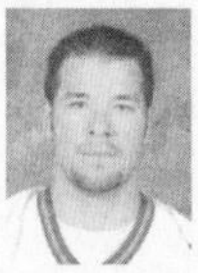

SIMON, Chris
(SIGH-mohn, KRIHS) **CGY.**

Left wing. Shoots left. 6'4", 235 lbs. Born, Wawa, Ont., January 30, 1972. Philadelphia's 2nd choice, 25th overall, in 1990 Entry Draft.

Season	Club	League	GP	G	A	Pts	PIM	PP	SH	GW	S	%	+/-	TF	F%	Min	GP	G	A	Pts	PIM	PP	SH	GW	Min
1986-87	Wawa Flyers	NOHA	36	12	20	32	108	....	....	....	....	....	....	....	....	....	....	....	....	....	....	....	....	....	....
1987-88	Soo Thunderbirds	NOHA	55	42	36	78	172	....	....	....	....	....	....	....	....	....	....	....	....	....	....	....	....	....	....
1988-89	Ottawa 67's	OHL	36	4	2	6	31	....	....	....	....	....	....	....	....	....	....	....	....	....	....	....	....	....	....
1989-90	Ottawa 67's	OHL	57	36	38	74	146	....	....	....	....	....	....	....	....	....	3	2	1	3	4	....	....	....	....
1990-91	Ottawa 67's	OHL	20	16	6	22	69	....	....	....	....	....	....	....	....	....	17	5	9	14	59	....	....	....	....
1991-92	Ottawa 67's	OHL	2	1	1	2	24	....	....	....	....	....	....	....	....	....	....	....	....	....	....	....	....	....	....
	Sault Ste. Marie	OHL	31	19	25	44	143	....	....	....	....	....	....	....	....	....	11	5	8	13	49	....	....	....	....
1992-93	**Quebec**	**NHL**	**16**	**1**	**1**	**2**	**67**	**0**	**0**	**1**	**15**	**6.7**	**–2**				**5**	**0**	**0**	**0**	**26**	**0**	**0**	**0**	
	Halifax Citadels	AHL	36	12	6	18	131	....	....	....	....	....	....	....	....	....	....	....	....	....	....	....	....	....	....
1993-94	**Quebec**	**NHL**	**37**	**4**	**4**	**8**	**132**	**0**	**0**	**1**	**39**	**10.3**	**–2**				....	....	....	....	....	....	....	....	....
1994-95	**Quebec**	**NHL**	**29**	**3**	**9**	**12**	**106**	**0**	**0**	**0**	**33**	**9.1**	**14**				**6**	**1**	**1**	**2**	**19**	**0**	**0**	**1**	
1995-96♦	**Colorado**	**NHL**	**64**	**16**	**18**	**34**	**250**	**4**	**0**	**1**	**105**	**15.2**	**10**				**12**	**1**	**2**	**3**	**11**	**0**	**0**	**0**	
1996-97	**Washington**	**NHL**	**42**	**9**	**13**	**22**	**165**	**3**	**0**	**1**	**89**	**10.1**	**–1**				....	....	....	....	....	....	....	....	....
1997-98	**Washington**	**NHL**	**28**	**7**	**10**	**17**	**38**	**4**	**0**	**1**	**71**	**9.9**	**–1**				**18**	**1**	**0**	**1**	**26**	**0**	**0**	**0**	
1998-99	**Washington**	**NHL**	**23**	**3**	**7**	**10**	**48**	**0**	**0**	**0**	**29**	**10.3**	**–4**	**2**	**50.0**	**12:08**	....	....	....	....	....	....	....	....	....
99-2000	**Washington**	**NHL**	**75**	**29**	**20**	**49**	**146**	**7**	**0**	**5**	**201**	**14.4**	**11**	**7**	**28.6**	**15:32**	**4**	**2**	**0**	**2**	**24**	**0**	**0**	**0**	**18:07**
2000-01	**Washington**	**NHL**	**60**	**10**	**10**	**20**	**109**	**4**	**0**	**2**	**123**	**8.1**	**–12**	**3**	**33.3**	**14:34**	**6**	**0**	**1**	**1**	**4**	**0**	**0**	**0**	**9:55**
2001-02	**Washington**	**NHL**	**82**	**14**	**17**	**31**	**137**	**1**	**0**	**1**	**121**	**11.6**	**–8**	**7**	**28.6**	**12:11**	....	....	....	....	....	....	....	....	....
2002-03	**Washington**	**NHL**	**10**	**0**	**2**	**2**	**23**	**0**	**0**	**0**	**16**	**0.0**	**–3**	**0**	**0.0**	**8:53**	....	....	....	....	....	....	....	....	....
	Chicago	**NHL**	**61**	**12**	**6**	**18**	**125**	**2**	**0**	**2**	**72**	**16.7**	**–4**	**5**	**20.0**	**11:06**	....	....	....	....	....	....	....	....	....
2003-04	**NY Rangers**	**NHL**	**65**	**14**	**9**	**23**	**225**	**3**	**0**	**0**	**116**	**12.1**	**14**	**3**	**0.0**	**11:56**	....	....	....	....	....	....	....	....	....
	Calgary	**NHL**	**13**	**3**	**2**	**5**	**25**	**1**	**0**	**0**	**31**	**9.7**	**1**	**2**	**100.0**	**16:38**	**16**	**5**	**2**	**7**	***74**	**4**	**0**	**1**	**15:06**
2004-05			DID NOT PLAY																						
	NHL Totals		**605**	**125**	**128**	**253**	**1596**	**29**	**0**	**15**	**1061**	**11.8**		**29**	**31.0**	**13:03**	**67**	**10**	**6**	**16**	**184**	**4**	**0**	**2**	**14:22**

• Missed majority of 1990-91 season recovering from shoulder surgery, October, 1990. Traded to **Quebec** by **Philadelphia** with Philadelphia's 1st round choice (later traded to Toronto – later traded to Washington – Washington selected Nolan Baumgartner) in 1994 Entry Draft to complete transaction that sent Eric Lindros to Philadelphia (June 30, 1992), July 21, 1992. Transferred to **Colorado** after **Quebec** franchise relocated, June 21, 1995. Traded to **Washington** by **Colorado** with Curtis Leschyshyn for Keith Jones and Washington's 1st (Scott Parker) and 4th (later traded back to Washington – Washington selected Krys Barch) round choices in 1998 Entry Draft, November 2, 1996. Traded to **Chicago** by **Washington** with Andrei Nikolishin for Michael Nylander, Chicago's 3rd round choice (Stephen Werner) in 2003 Entry Draft and future considerations, November 1, 2002. Signed as a free agent by **NY Rangers**, July 25, 2003. Traded to **Calgary** by **NY Rangers** with NY Rangers' 7th round choice (Matt Schneider) in 2004 Entry Draft for Jamie McLennan, Blair Betts and Greg Moore, March 6, 2004

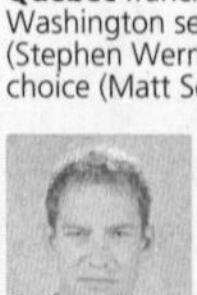

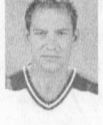

SIMPSON, Reid
(SIHMP-sohn, REED)

Left wing. Shoots left. 6'2", 216 lbs. Born, Flin Flon, Man., May 21, 1969. Philadelphia's 3rd choice, 72nd overall, in 1989 Entry Draft.

Season	Club	League	GP	G	A	Pts	PIM	PP	SH	GW	S	%	+/-	TF	F%	Min	GP	G	A	Pts	PIM	PP	SH	GW	Min
1984-85	Flin Flon Bombers	MMMHL	50	60	70	130	100	....	....	....	....	....	....	....	....	....	....	....	....	....	....	....	....	....	....
1985-86	Flin Flon Bombers	MJHL	40	20	21	41	200	....	....	....	....	....	....	....	....	....	....	....	....	....	....	....	....	....	....
	New Westminster	WHL	2	0	0	0	0	....	....	....	....	....	....	....	....	....	....	....	....	....	....	....	....	....	....
1986-87	Prince Albert	WHL	47	3	8	11	105	....	....	....	....	....	....	....	....	....	8	2	3	5	13	....	....	....	....
1987-88	Prince Albert	WHL	72	13	14	27	164	....	....	....	....	....	....	....	....	....	10	1	0	1	43	....	....	....	....
1988-89	Prince Albert	WHL	59	26	29	55	264	....	....	....	....	....	....	....	....	....	4	2	1	3	30	....	....	....	....
1989-90	Prince Albert	WHL	29	15	17	32	121	....	....	....	....	....	....	....	....	....	14	4	7	11	34	....	....	....	....
	Hershey Bears	AHL	28	2	2	4	175	....	....	....	....	....	....	....	....	....	....	....	....	....	....	....	....	....	....
1990-91	Hershey Bears	AHL	54	9	15	24	183	....	....	....	....	....	....	....	....	....	1	0	0	0	0	....	....	....	....
1991-92	**Philadelphia**	**NHL**	**1**	**0**	**0**	**0**	**0**	**0**	**0**	**0**	**0**	**0.0**	**0**				....	....	....	....	....	....	....	....	....
	Hershey Bears	AHL	60	11	7	18	145	....	....	....	....	....	....	....	....	....	....	....	....	....	....	....	....	....	....
1992-93	**Minnesota**	**NHL**	**1**	**0**	**0**	**0**	**5**	**0**	**0**	**0**	**0**	**0.0**	**0**				....	....	....	....	....	....	....	....	....
	Kalamazoo Wings	IHL	45	5	5	10	193	....	....	....	....	....	....	....	....	....	....	....	....	....	....	....	....	....	....
1993-94	Kalamazoo Wings	IHL	5	0	0	0	16	....	....	....	....	....	....	....	....	....	....	....	....	....	....	....	....	....	....
	Albany River Rats	AHL	37	9	5	14	135	....	....	....	....	....	....	....	....	....	5	1	1	2	18	....	....	....	....
1994-95	Albany River Rats	AHL	70	18	25	43	268	....	....	....	....	....	....	....	....	....	14	1	8	9	13	....	....	....	....
	New Jersey	**NHL**	**9**	**0**	**0**	**0**	**27**	**0**	**0**	**0**	**5**	**0.0**	**–1**				....	....	....	....	....	....	....	....	....
1995-96	**New Jersey**	**NHL**	**23**	**1**	**5**	**6**	**79**	**0**	**0**	**0**	**8**	**12.5**	**2**				....	....	....	....	....	....	....	....	....
	Albany River Rats	AHL	6	1	3	4	17	....	....	....	....	....	....	....	....	....	....	....	....	....	....	....	....	....	....

			Regular Season														Playoffs								
Season	Club	League	GP	G	A	Pts	PIM	PP	SH	GW	S	%	+/-	TF	F%	Min	GP	G	A	Pts	PIM	PP	SH	GW	Min
1996-97	**New Jersey**	**NHL**	**27**	**0**	**4**	**4**	**60**	**0**	**0**	**0**	**17**	**0.0**	**0**	....	....	....	**5**	**0**	**0**	**0**	**29**	**0**	**0**	**0**	....
	Albany River Rats	AHL	3	0	0	0	10	....	....	....	....	....	....	....	....	....	....	....	....	....	....	....	....	....	....
1997-98	**New Jersey**	**NHL**	**6**	**0**	**0**	**0**	**16**	**0**	**0**	**0**	**5**	**0.0**	**–2**	....	....	....	....	....	....	....	....	....	....	....	....
	Chicago	**NHL**	**38**	**3**	**2**	**5**	**102**	**1**	**0**	**0**	**19**	**15.8**	**–1**	....	....	....	....	....	....	....	....	....	....	....	....
1998-99	**Chicago**	**NHL**	**53**	**5**	**4**	**9**	**145**	**1**	**0**	**0**	**23**	**21.7**	**2**	**5**	**40.0**	**5:56**	....	....	....	....	....	....	....	....	....
99-2000	Cleveland	IHL	12	2	2	4	56	....	....	....	....	....	....	....	....	....	....	....	....	....	....	....	....	....	....
	Tampa Bay	**NHL**	**26**	**1**	**0**	**1**	**103**	**0**	**0**	**0**	**13**	**7.7**	**–3**	**1**	**100.0**	**4:33**	....	....	....	....	....	....	....	....	....
2000-01	**St. Louis**	**NHL**	**38**	**2**	**1**	**3**	**96**	**0**	**0**	**1**	**23**	**8.7**	**–3**	**1**	**0.0**	**6:57**	**5**	**0**	**0**	**0**	**2**	**0**	**0**	**0**	**6:13**
2001-02	**Montreal**	**NHL**	**25**	**1**	**1**	**2**	**63**	**0**	**0**	**1**	**9**	**11.1**	**0**	**0**	**0.0**	**4:22**	....	....	....	....	....	....	....	....	....
	Nashville	**NHL**	**26**	**5**	**0**	**5**	**69**	**0**	**0**	**0**	**13**	**38.5**	**–1**	**5**	**60.0**	**5:45**	....	....	....	....	....	....	....	....	....
	Milwaukee	AHL	2	1	0	1	37	....	....	....	....	....	....	....	....	....	....	....	....	....	....	....	....	....	....
2002-03	**Nashville**	**NHL**	**26**	**0**	**1**	**1**	**56**	**0**	**0**	**0**	**11**	**0.0**	**–4**	**1**	**0.0**	**5:04**	....	....	....	....	....	....	....	....	....
	Milwaukee	AHL	17	6	6	12	40	....	....	....	....	....	....	....	....	....	....	....	....	....	....	....	....	....	....
2003-04	**Pittsburgh**	**NHL**	**2**	**0**	**0**	**0**	**17**	**0**	**0**	**0**	**2**	**0.0**	**0**	**0**	**0.0**	**4:46**	....	....	....	....	....	....	....	....	....
	Wilkes-Barre	AHL	51	6	11	17	168	....	....	....	....	....	....	....	....	....	2	0	0	0	0	....	....	....	....
2004-05	Rockford IceHogs	UHL	15	1	3	4	46	....	....	....	....	....	....	....	....	....	7	0	0	0	18	....	....	....	....
	NHL Totals		**301**	**18**	**18**	**36**	**838**	**2**	**0**	**2**	**148**	**12.2**		**13**	**46.2**	**5:36**	**10**	**0**	**0**	**0**	**31**	**0**	**0**	**0**	**6:13**

Signed as a free agent by **Minnesota**, December 14, 1992. Transferred to **Dallas** after **Minnesota** franchise relocated, June 9, 1993. Traded to **New Jersey** by **Dallas** with Roy Mitchell for future considerations, March 21, 1994. Traded to **Chicago** by **New Jersey** for Chicago's 4th round choice (Mikko Jokela) in 1998 Entry Draft and future considerations, January 8, 1998. Traded to **Tampa Bay** by **Chicago** with Bryan Muir for Michael Nylander, November 12, 1999. • Missed majority of 1999-2000 season recovering from jaw injury suffered in game vs. NY Islanders, January 13, 2000. Signed as a free agent by **St. Louis**, August 24, 2000. • Missed majority of 2000-01 season recovering from groin injury suffered in game vs. Nashville, November 24, 2000. Signed as a free agent by **Montreal**, September 10, 2001. Claimed on waivers by **Nashville** from **Montreal**, January 28, 2002. Signed as a free agent by **Pittsburgh**, August 29, 2003. Signed as a free agent by **Rockford** (UHL), March 13, 2005.

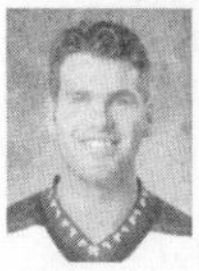

SIMPSON, Todd

(SIHMP-sohn, TAWD) **CHI.**

Defense. Shoots left. 6'3", 218 lbs. Born, North Vancouver, B.C., May 28, 1973.

Season	Club	League	GP	G	A	Pts	PIM	PP	SH	GW	S	%	+/-	TF	F%	Min	GP	G	A	Pts	PIM	PP	SH	GW	Min
1991-92	Brown U.	ECAC	18	1	4	5	38	....	....	....	....	....	....	....	....	....	....	....	....	....	....	....	....	....	....
1992-93	Tri-City	WHL	69	5	18	23	196	....	....	....	....	....	....	....	....	....	4	0	0	0	13	....	....	....	....
1993-94	Tri-City	WHL	12	2	3	5	32	....	....	....	....	....	....	....	....	....	....	....	....	....	....	....	....	....	....
	Saskatoon Blades	WHL	51	7	19	26	175	....	....	....	....	....	....	....	....	....	16	1	5	6	42	....	....	....	....
1994-95	Saint John Flames	AHL	80	3	10	13	321	....	....	....	....	....	....	....	....	....	5	0	0	0	4	....	....	....	....
1995-96	**Calgary**	**NHL**	**6**	**0**	**0**	**0**	**32**	**0**	**0**	**0**	**3**	**0.0**	**0**	....	....	....	....	....	....	....	....	....	....	....	....
	Saint John Flames	AHL	66	4	13	17	277	....	....	....	....	....	....	....	....	....	16	2	3	5	32	....	....	....	....
1996-97	**Calgary**	**NHL**	**82**	**1**	**13**	**14**	**208**	**0**	**0**	**0**	**85**	**1.2**	**–14**	....	....	....	....	....	....	....	....	....	....	....	....
1997-98	**Calgary**	**NHL**	**53**	**1**	**5**	**6**	**109**	**0**	**0**	**1**	**51**	**2.0**	**–10**	....	....	....	....	....	....	....	....	....	....	....	....
1998-99	**Calgary**	**NHL**	**73**	**2**	**8**	**10**	**151**	**0**	**0**	**0**	**52**	**3.8**	**18**	**1**	**100.0**	**17:19**	....	....	....	....	....	....	....	....	....
99-2000	**Florida**	**NHL**	**82**	**1**	**6**	**7**	**202**	**0**	**0**	**0**	**50**	**2.0**	**5**	**0**	**0.0**	**16:35**	**4**	**0**	**0**	**0**	**4**	**0**	**0**	**0**	**15:24**
2000-01	**Florida**	**NHL**	**25**	**1**	**3**	**4**	**74**	**0**	**0**	**1**	**26**	**3.8**	**0**	**0**	**0.0**	**16:29**	....	....	....	....	....	....	....	....	....
	Phoenix	**NHL**	**13**	**0**	**1**	**1**	**12**	**0**	**0**	**0**	**9**	**0.0**	**–4**	**0**	**0.0**	**13:56**	....	....	....	....	....	....	....	....	....
2001-02	**Phoenix**	**NHL**	**67**	**2**	**13**	**15**	**152**	**0**	**0**	**0**	**51**	**3.9**	**20**	**0**	**0.0**	**17:20**	**5**	**0**	**2**	**2**	**6**	**0**	**0**	**0**	**18:30**
2002-03	**Phoenix**	**NHL**	**66**	**2**	**7**	**9**	**135**	**0**	**0**	**0**	**67**	**3.0**	**7**	**0**	**0.0**	**16:59**	....	....	....	....	....	....	....	....	....
2003-04	**Anaheim**	**NHL**	**46**	**4**	**3**	**7**	**105**	**0**	**0**	**0**	**42**	**9.5**	**–6**	**0**	**0.0**	**14:18**	....	....	....	....	....	....	....	....	....
	Ottawa	**NHL**	**16**	**0**	**1**	**1**	**47**	**0**	**0**	**0**	**10**	**0.0**	**–1**	**1**	**0.0**	**14:21**	....	....	....	....	....	....	....	....	....
2004-05	Herning Blue Fox	Denmark	7	2	3	5	35	....	....	....	....	....	....	....	....	....	16	3	5	8	82	....	....	....	....
	NHL Totals		**529**	**14**	**60**	**74**	**1227**	**0**	**0**	**2**	**446**	**3.1**		**2**	**50.0**	**16:28**	**9**	**0**	**2**	**2**	**10**	**0**	**0**	**0**	**17:07**

Signed as free agent by **Calgary**, July 6, 1994. Traded to **Florida** by **Calgary** for Bill Lindsay, September 30, 1999. • Missed majority of 2000-01 season recovering from head injury suffered in game vs. NY Islanders, December 6, 2000. Traded to **Phoenix** by **Florida** for Phoenix's 2nd round choice (later traded to New Jersey – New Jersey selected Tuomas Pihlman) in 2001 Entry Draft, March 13, 2001. Claimed by **Anaheim** from **Phoenix** in Waiver Draft, October 3, 2003. Traded to **Ottawa** by **Anaheim** for Petr Schastlivy, February 4, 2004. Signed as a free agent by **Herning** (Denmark), December 16, 2004. Signed as a free agent by **Chicago**, August 23, 2005.

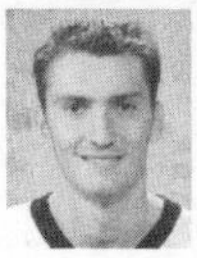

SIVEK, Michal

(sih-VIHK, MEE-khahl) **PIT.**

Center. Shoots left. 6'3", 214 lbs. Born, Nachod, Czech., January 21, 1981. Washington's 2nd choice, 29th overall, in 1999 Entry Draft.

Season	Club	League	GP	G	A	Pts	PIM	PP	SH	GW	S	%	+/-	TF	F%	Min	GP	G	A	Pts	PIM	PP	SH	GW	Min
1997-98	Sparta Jr.	CzRep-Jr.	31	13	8	21	....	....	....	....	....	....	....	....	....	....	....	....	....	....	....	....	....	....	....
	HC Sparta Praha	CzRep	25	1	1	2	10	....	....	....	....	....	....	....	....	....	5	1	0	1	0	....	....	....	....
1998-99	HC Sparta Praha	CzRep	1	1	0	1	....	....	....	....	....	....	....	....	....	....	....	....	....	....	....	....	....	....	....
	Kladno	CzRep	34	3	8	11	24	....	....	....	....	....	....	....	....	....	....	....	....	....	....	....	....	....	....
99-2000	Prince Albert	WHL	53	23	37	60	65	....	....	....	....	....	....	....	....	....	6	1	4	5	10	....	....	....	....
2000-01	HC Sparta Praha	CzRep	32	6	7	13	28	....	....	....	....	....	....	....	....	....	13	4	2	6	8	....	....	....	....
2001-02	Wilkes-Barre	AHL	25	4	8	12	30	....	....	....	....	....	....	....	....	....	....	....	....	....	....	....	....	....	....
	HC Sparta Praha	CzRep	17	5	3	8	20	....	....	....	....	....	....	....	....	....	12	0	1	1	10	....	....	....	....
2002-03	**Pittsburgh**	**NHL**	**38**	**3**	**3**	**6**	**14**	**1**	**0**	**0**	**45**	**6.7**	**–5**	**32**	**43.8**	**13:05**	....	....	....	....	....	....	....	....	....
	Wilkes-Barre	AHL	40	10	17	27	33	....	....	....	....	....	....	....	....	....	6	3	2	5	20	....	....	....	....
2003-04	Wilkes-Barre	AHL	22	4	7	11	6	....	....	....	....	....	....	....	....	....	....	....	....	....	....	....	....	....	....
2004-05	HC Sparta Praha	CzRep	37	1	5	6	48	....	....	....	....	....	....	....	....	....	5	0	0	0	2	....	....	....	....
	NHL Totals		**38**	**3**	**3**	**6**	**14**	**1**	**0**	**0**	**45**	**6.7**		**32**	**43.8**	**13:05**	....	....	....	....	....	....	....	....	....

Traded to **Pittsburgh** by **Washington** with Kris Beech, Ross Lupaschuk and future considerations for Jaromir Jagr and Frantisek Kucera, July 11, 2001. • Missed majority of 2003-04 season recovering from finger injury suffered in game vs. Syracuse (AHL), October 17, 2003. Signed as a free agent by **Sparta** (CzRep), May 19, 2004.

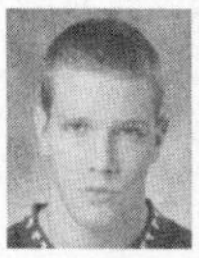

SJOSTROM, Fredrik

(SHAW-strahm, FREHD-rihk) **PHX.**

Right wing. Shoots left. 6'1", 217 lbs. Born, Fargelanda, Sweden, May 6, 1983. Phoenix's 1st choice, 11th overall, in 2001 Entry Draft.

Season	Club	League	GP	G	A	Pts	PIM	PP	SH	GW	S	%	+/-	TF	F%	Min	GP	G	A	Pts	PIM	PP	SH	GW	Min
99-2000	MoDo U18	Swe-U18	4	0	2	2	6	....	....	....	....	....	....	....	....	....	....	....	....	....	....	....	....	....	....
	Malmo Jr.	Swe-Jr.	18	4	6	10	8	....	....	....	....	....	....	....	....	....	....	....	....	....	....	....	....	....	....
2000-01	V.Frolunda Jr.	Swe-Jr.	11	3	7	10	12	....	....	....	....	....	....	....	....	....	4	1	2	3	6	....	....	....	....
	V.Frolunda	Sweden	31	3	2	5	6	....	....	....	....	....	....	....	....	....	5	0	0	0	2	....	....	....	....
2001-02	Calgary Hitmen	WHL	58	19	31	50	51	....	....	....	....	....	....	....	....	....	4	1	1	2	8	....	....	....	....
2002-03	Calgary Hitmen	WHL	63	34	43	77	95	....	....	....	....	....	....	....	....	....	5	1	3	4	4	....	....	....	....
	Springfield	AHL	2	1	0	1	0	....	....	....	....	....	....	....	....	....	6	2	0	2	12	....	....	....	....
2003-04	**Phoenix**	**NHL**	**57**	**7**	**6**	**13**	**22**	**0**	**0**	**1**	**73**	**9.6**	**–7**	**7**	**28.6**	**11:35**	....	....	....	....	....	....	....	....	....
	Springfield	AHL	17	0	7	7	8	....	....	....	....	....	....	....	....	....	....	....	....	....	....	....	....	....	....
2004-05	Utah Grizzlies	AHL	80	14	24	38	57	....	....	....	....	....	....	....	....	....	....	....	....	....	....	....	....	....	....
	NHL Totals		**57**	**7**	**6**	**13**	**22**	**0**	**0**	**1**	**73**	**9.6**		**7**	**28.6**	**11:35**	....	....	....	....	....	....	....	....	....

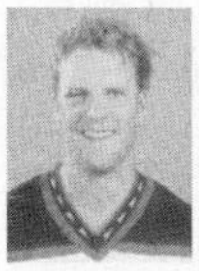

SKALDE, Jarrod

(SKAHL-dee, JAIR-ruhd) **PHX.**

Center. Shoots left. 6', 185 lbs. Born, Niagara Falls, Ont., February 26, 1971. New Jersey's 3rd choice, 26th overall, in 1989 Entry Draft.

Season	Club	League	GP	G	A	Pts	PIM	PP	SH	GW	S	%	+/-	TF	F%	Min	GP	G	A	Pts	PIM	PP	SH	GW	Min
1986-87	Fort Erie Meteors	OHA-B	41	27	34	61	36	....	....	....	....	....	....	....	....	....	....	....	....	....	....	....	....	....	....
1987-88	Oshawa Generals	OHL	60	12	16	28	24	....	....	....	....	....	....	....	....	....	7	2	1	3	2	....	....	....	....
1988-89	Oshawa Generals	OHL	65	38	38	76	36	....	....	....	....	....	....	....	....	....	6	1	5	6	2	....	....	....	....
1989-90	Oshawa Generals	OHL	62	40	52	92	66	....	....	....	....	....	....	....	....	....	17	10	7	17	6	....	....	....	....
1990-91	Oshawa Generals	OHL	15	8	14	22	14	....	....	....	....	....	....	....	....	....	....	....	....	....	....	....	....	....	....
	Belleville Bulls	OHL	40	30	52	82	21	....	....	....	....	....	....	....	....	....	6	9	6	15	10	....	....	....	....
	New Jersey	**NHL**	**1**	**0**	**1**	**1**	**0**	**0**	**0**	**0**	**2**	**0.0**	**0**	....	....	....	....	....	....	....	....	....	....	....	....
	Utica Devils	AHL	3	3	2	5	0	....	....	....	....	....	....	....	....	....	....	....	....	....	....	....	....	....	....
1991-92	**New Jersey**	**NHL**	**15**	**2**	**4**	**6**	**4**	**0**	**0**	**2**	**25**	**8.0**	**–1**	....	....	....	....	....	....	....	....	....	....	....	....
	Utica Devils	AHL	62	20	20	40	56	....	....	....	....	....	....	....	....	....	4	3	1	4	8	....	....	....	....
1992-93	**New Jersey**	**NHL**	**11**	**0**	**2**	**2**	**4**	**0**	**0**	**0**	**11**	**0.0**	**–3**	....	....	....	....	....	....	....	....	....	....	....	....
	Utica Devils	AHL	59	21	39	60	76	....	....	....	....	....	....	....	....	....	5	0	2	2	19	....	....	....	....
	Cincinnati	IHL	4	1	2	3	4	....	....	....	....	....	....	....	....	....	....	....	....	....	....	....	....	....	....
1993-94	**Anaheim**	**NHL**	**20**	**5**	**4**	**9**	**10**	**2**	**0**	**2**	**25**	**20.0**	**–3**	....	....	....	....	....	....	....	....	....	....	....	....
	San Diego Gulls	IHL	57	25	38	63	79	....	....	....	....	....	....	....	....	....	9	3	12	15	10	....	....	....	....
1994-95	Las Vegas	IHL	74	34	41	75	103	....	....	....	....	....	....	....	....	....	9	2	4	6	8	....	....	....	....
1995-96	Baltimore Bandits	AHL	11	2	6	8	55	....	....	....	....	....	....	....	....	....	....	....	....	....	....	....	....	....	....
	Calgary	**NHL**	**1**	**0**	**0**	**0**	**0**	**0**	**0**	**0**	**0**	**0.0**	**0**	....	....	....	....	....	....	....	....	....	....	....	....
	Saint John Flames	AHL	68	27	40	67	98	....	....	....	....	....	....	....	....	....	16	4	9	13	6	....	....	....	....
1996-97	Saint John Flames	AHL	65	32	36	68	94	....	....	....	....	....	....	....	....	....	3	0	0	0	14	....	....	....	....

			Regular Season														Playoffs								
Season	Club	League	GP	G	A	Pts	PIM	PP	SH	GW	S	%	+/-	TF	F%	Min	GP	G	A	Pts	PIM	PP	SH	GW	Min
1997-98	San Jose	NHL	22	4	6	10	14	0	0	0	30	13.3	–2	....	....	....	....	....	....	....	....	....	....	....	....
	Kentucky	AHL	6	2	6	8	10	....	....	....	....	....	....	....	....	....	....	....	....	....	....	....	....	....	....
	Chicago	NHL	4	0	1	1	2	0	0	0	4	0.0	0	....	....	....	....	....	....	....	....	....	....	....	....
	Indianapolis Ice	IHL	2	0	2	2	0	....	....	....	....	....	....	....	....	....	....	....	....	....	....	....	....	....	....
	Dallas	NHL	1	0	0	0	0	0	0	0	0	0.0	0	....	....	....	....	....	....	....	....	....	....	....	....
	Chicago	NHL	3	0	0	0	2	0	0	0	0	0.0	0	....	....	....	....	....	....	....	....	....	....	....	....
	Kentucky	AHL	17	3	9	12	38	....	....	....	....	....	....	....	....	....	3	3	0	3	6	....	....	....	....
1998-99	San Jose	NHL	17	1	1	2	4	0	0	0	17	5.9	–6	191	52.4	10:07	....	....	....	....	....	....	....	....	....
	Kentucky	AHL	54	17	40	57	75	....	....	....	....	....	....	....	....	....	12	4	5	9	16	....	....	....	....
99-2000	Utah Grizzlies	IHL	77	25	54	79	98	....	....	....	....	....	....	....	....	....	5	0	1	1	10	....	....	....	....
2000-01	Atlanta	NHL	19	1	2	3	20	0	0	0	24	4.2	–8	291	47.1	13:57	....	....	....	....	....	....	....	....	....
	Orlando	IHL	60	14	40	54	56	....	....	....	....	....	....	....	....	....	15	3	6	9	20	....	....	....	....
2001-02	Chicago Wolves	AHL	64	15	37	52	71	....	....	....	....	....	....	....	....	....	....	....	....	....	....	....	....	....	....
	Philadelphia	NHL	1	0	0	0	2	0	0	0	5	0.0	0	15	60.0	12:25	....	....	....	....	....	....	....	....	....
	Philadelphia	AHL	16	4	4	8	23	....	....	....	....	....	....	....	....	....	4	0	2	2	4	....	....	....	....
2002-03	Lausanne HC	Swiss	23	7	8	15	30	....	....	....	....	....	....	....	....	....	....	....	....	....	....	....	....	....	....
2003-04	Utah Grizzlies	AHL	77	23	35	58	55	....	....	....	....	....	....	....	....	....	....	....	....	....	....	....	....	....	....
2004-05	Springfield	AHL	15	1	5	6	16	....	....	....	....	....	....	....	....	....	....	....	....	....	....	....	....	....	....
	Utah Grizzlies	AHL	56	7	15	22	53	....	....	....	....	....	....	....	....	....	....	....	....	....	....	....	....	....	....
	NHL Totals		115	13	21	34	62	2	0	4	143	9.1		497	49.5	12:09	....	....	....	....	....	....	....	....	....

OHL Second All-Star Team (1991) • IHL First All-Star Team (2000)

Claimed by **Anaheim** from **New Jersey** in Expansion Draft, June 24, 1993. Traded to **Calgary** by **Anaheim** for Bobby Marshall, October 30, 1995. Signed as a free agent by **San Jose**, August 14, 1997. Claimed on waivers by **Chicago** from **San Jose**, January 8, 1998. Claimed on waivers by **San Jose** from **Chicago**, January 23, 1998. Claimed on waivers by **Dallas** from **San Jose**, January 27, 1998. Claimed on waivers by **Chicago** from **Dallas**, February 10, 1998. Claimed on waivers by **San Jose** from **Chicago**, March 6, 1998. Signed as a free agent by **Atlanta**, July 21, 2000. Traded to **Philadelphia** by **Atlanta** for Joe DiPenta, March 5, 2002. Signed as a free agent by **Lausanne** (Swiss), March 21, 2002. Signed as a free agent by **Dallas**, July 17, 2003. Signed as a free agent by **Tampa Bay**, July 28, 2004. Loaned to **Utah** (AHL) by **Springfield** (AHL) for cash, November 20, 2004.

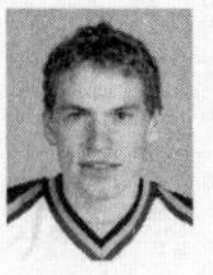

SKOULA, Martin (SHKOO-la, MAHR-tihn) DAL.

Defense. Shoots left. 6'2", 195 lbs. Born, Litomerice, Czech., October 28, 1979. Colorado's 2nd choice, 17th overall, in 1998 Entry Draft.

1995-96	Litvinov Jr.	CzRep-Jr.	38	0	4	4	....	....	....	....	....	....	....	....	....	....	....	....	....	....	....	....	....	....	....
	Litvinov	CzRep	....	....	....	....	....	....	....	....	....	....	....	....	....	....	1	0	0	0	0	....	....	....	....
1996-97	Litvinov Jr.	CzRep-Jr.	38	2	9	11	....	....	....	....	....	....	....	....	....	....	....	....	....	....	....	....	....	....	....
	Litvinov	CzRep	1	0	0	0	0	....	....	....	....	....	....	....	....	....	....	....	....	....	....	....	....	....	....
1997-98	Barrie Colts	OHL	66	8	36	44	36	....	....	....	....	....	....	....	....	....	6	1	3	4	4	....	....	....	....
1998-99	Barrie Colts	OHL	67	13	46	59	46	....	....	....	....	....	....	....	....	....	12	3	10	13	13	....	....	....	....
	Hershey Bears	AHL	....	....	....	....	....	....	....	....	....	....	....	....	....	....	1	0	0	0	0	....	....	....	....
99-2000	Colorado	NHL	80	3	13	16	20	2	0	0	66	4.5	5	0	0.0	18:15	17	0	2	2	4	0	0	0	18:45
2000-01♦	Colorado	NHL	82	8	17	25	38	3	0	2	108	7.4	8	1	100.0	20:41	23	1	4	5	8	0	0	0	11:59
2001-02	Colorado	NHL	82	10	21	31	42	5	0	1	100	10.0	–3	0	0.0	22:18	21	0	6	6	2	0	0	0	14:37
	Czech Republic	Olympics	4	0	0	0	0	....	....	....	....	....	....	....	....	....	....	....	....	....	....	....	....	....	....
2002-03	Colorado	NHL	81	4	21	25	68	2	0	0	93	4.3	11	1	100.0	18:27	7	0	1	1	4	0	0	0	11:05
2003-04	Colorado	NHL	58	2	14	16	30	0	0	0	54	3.7	2	0	0.0	17:21	....	....	....	....	....	....	....	....	....
	Anaheim	NHL	21	2	7	9	2	1	0	0	30	6.7	3	1	0.0	21:14	....	....	....	....	....	....	....	....	....
2004-05	Litvinov	CzRep	47	4	15	19	101	....	....	....	....	....	....	....	....	....	6	0	0	0	6	....	....	....	....
	NHL Totals		404	29	93	122	200	13	0	3	451	6.4		3	66.7	19:38	68	1	13	14	18	0	0	0	14:24

OHL All-Rookie Team (1998) • OHL Second All-Star Team (1999)

Traded to **Anaheim** by **Colorado** for Kurt Sauer and Anaheim's 4th round choice (Raymond Macias) in 2005 Entry Draft, February 21, 2004. Signed as a free agent by **Litvinov** (CzRep), September 17, 2004. Signed as a free agent by **Dallas**, August 3, 2005.

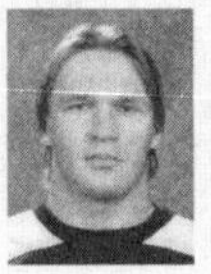

SKRASTINS, Karlis (SKRAS-tinsh, KAR-lihs) COL.

Defense. Shoots left. 6'1", 212 lbs. Born, Riga, USSR, July 9, 1974. Nashville's 8th choice, 230th overall, in 1998 Entry Draft.

1992-93	Pardaugava Riga	CIS	40	3	5	8	16	....	....	....	....	....	....	....	....	....	2	0	0	0	0	....	....	....	....
1993-94	Pardaugava Riga	CIS	42	7	5	12	18	....	....	....	....	....	....	....	....	....	2	1	0	1	4	....	....	....	....
1994-95	Pardaugava Riga	CIS	52	4	14	18	69	....	....	....	....	....	....	....	....	....	....	....	....	....	....	....	....	....	....
1995-96	TPS Turku	Finland	50	4	11	15	32	....	....	....	....	....	....	....	....	....	11	2	2	4	10	....	....	....	....
1996-97	TPS Turku	Finland	50	2	8	10	20	....	....	....	....	....	....	....	....	....	12	0	4	4	2	....	....	....	....
	TPS Turku	EuroHL	6	0	1	1	4	....	....	....	....	....	....	....	....	....	4	0	0	0	14	....	....	....	....
1997-98	TPS Turku	Finland	48	4	15	19	67	....	....	....	....	....	....	....	....	....	4	0	0	0	0	....	....	....	....
	TPS Turku	EuroHL	6	0	1	1	6	....	....	....	....	....	....	....	....	....	....	....	....	....	....	....	....	....	....
1998-99	Nashville	NHL	2	0	1	1	0	0	0	0	0	0.0	0	0	0.0	11:47	....	....	....	....	....	....	....	....	....
	Milwaukee	IHL	75	8	36	44	47	....	....	....	....	....	....	....	....	....	2	0	1	1	2	....	....	....	....
99-2000	Nashville	NHL	59	5	6	11	20	1	0	2	51	9.8	–7	0	0.0	20:51	....	....	....	....	....	....	....	....	....
	Milwaukee	IHL	19	3	8	11	10	....	....	....	....	....	....	....	....	....	....	....	....	....	....	....	....	....	....
2000-01	Nashville	NHL	82	1	11	12	30	0	0	1	66	1.5	–12	0	0.0	19:12	....	....	....	....	....	....	....	....	....
2001-02	Nashville	NHL	82	4	13	17	36	0	0	1	84	4.8	–12	0	0.0	20:29	....	....	....	....	....	....	....	....	....
	Latvia	Olympics	1	0	0	0	0	....	....	....	....	....	....	....	....	....	....	....	....	....	....	....	....	....	....
2002-03	Nashville	NHL	82	3	10	13	44	0	1	0	86	3.5	–18	0	0.0	20:17	....	....	....	....	....	....	....	....	....
2003-04	Colorado	NHL	82	5	8	13	26	0	1	1	102	4.9	18	0	0.0	21:49	11	0	2	2	2	0	0	0	23:07
2004-05	HK Riga 2000	Latvia	4	0	4	4	0	....	....	....	....	....	....	....	....	....	9	3	10	13	33	....	....	....	....
	HK Riga 2000	BelOpen	34	8	17	25	30	....	....	....	....	....	....	....	....	....	3	0	0	0	25	....	....	....	....
	NHL Totals		389	18	49	67	156	1	2	5	389	4.6		0	0.0	20:28	11	0	2	2	2	0	0	0	23:07

Traded to **Colorado** by **Nashville** for Colorado's 3rd round choice (later traded to Ottawa – Ottawa selected Peter Regin Jensen) in 2004 Entry Draft, June 30, 2003. Signed as a free agent by **Riga** (Latvia), September 25, 2004.

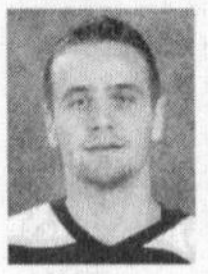

SKRBEK, Pavel (SKUHR-behk, PAH-vehl) NSH.

Defense. Shoots left. 6'3", 217 lbs. Born, Kladno, Czech., August 9, 1978. Pittsburgh's 2nd choice, 28th overall, in 1996 Entry Draft.

1994-95	HC Kladno Jr.	CzRep-Jr.	29	7	6	13	....	....	....	....	....	....	....	....	....	....	....	....	....	....	....	....	....	....	....
1995-96	Kladno Jr.	CzRep-Jr.	29	10	12	22	....	....	....	....	....	....	....	....	....	....	....	....	....	....	....	....	....	....	....
	HC Poldi Kladno	CzRep	13	0	1	1	....	....	....	....	....	....	....	....	....	....	5	0	0	0	....	....	....	....	....
1996-97	HC Poldi Kladno	CzRep	35	1	5	6	26	....	....	....	....	....	....	....	....	....	3	0	0	0	4	....	....	....	....
1997-98	Kladno	CzRep	47	4	10	14	126	....	....	....	....	....	....	....	....	....	....	....	....	....	....	....	....	....	....
1998-99	Pittsburgh	NHL	4	0	0	0	2	0	0	0	1	0.0	2	0	0.0	14:21	....	....	....	....	....	....	....	....	....
	Syracuse Crunch	AHL	64	6	16	22	38	....	....	....	....	....	....	....	....	....	....	....	....	....	....	....	....	....	....
99-2000	Wilkes-Barre	AHL	51	7	16	23	50	....	....	....	....	....	....	....	....	....	....	....	....	....	....	....	....	....	....
	Milwaukee	IHL	6	0	0	0	0	....	....	....	....	....	....	....	....	....	....	....	....	....	....	....	....	....	....
2000-01	Nashville	NHL	5	0	0	0	4	0	0	0	2	0.0	1	0	0.0	11:44	....	....	....	....	....	....	....	....	....
	Milwaukee	IHL	54	2	22	24	55	....	....	....	....	....	....	....	....	....	5	0	0	0	2	....	....	....	....
2001-02	Nashville	NHL	3	0	0	0	2	0	0	0	0	0.0	–2	0	0.0	10:18	....	....	....	....	....	....	....	....	....
	Kladno	CzRep	24	2	3	5	30	....	....	....	....	....	....	....	....	....	....	....	....	....	....	....	....	....	....
2002-03	Lulea HF	Sweden	39	2	2	4	61	....	....	....	....	....	....	....	....	....	4	0	0	0	10	....	....	....	....
2003-04	Lulea HF	Sweden	34	4	4	8	84	....	....	....	....	....	....	....	....	....	5	0	4	4	6	....	....	....	....
2004-05	Mora IK	Sweden	48	1	11	12	68	....	....	....	....	....	....	....	....	....	....	....	....	....	....	....	....	....	....
	NHL Totals		12	0	0	0	8	0	0	0	3	0.0		0	0.0	12:15	....	....	....	....	....	....	....	....	....

Traded to **Nashville** by **Pittsburgh** for Bob Boughner, March 13, 2000. Assigned to **Kladno** (CzRep) by **Nashville**, October 31, 2001. Signed as a free agent by **Lulea** (Sweden), June 20, 2002. Signed as a free agent by **Mora** (Sweden), August 23, 2004. Signed as a free agent by **Lulea** (Sweden), March 31, 2005.

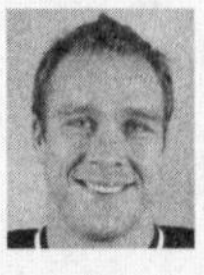

SKRLAC, Rob (SKUHR-lak, RAWB)

Left wing. Shoots left. 6'5", 245 lbs. Born, Port McNeill, B.C., June 10, 1976. Buffalo's 11th choice, 224th overall, in 1995 Entry Draft.

1993-94	Richmond	BCAHA	49	44	55	99	56	....	....	....	....	....	....	....	....	....	....	....	....	....	....	....	....	....	....
1994-95	Kamloops Blazers	WHL	23	0	1	1	177	....	....	....	....	....	....	....	....	....	....	....	....	....	....	....	....	....	....
1995-96	Kamloops Blazers	WHL	63	1	4	5	216	....	....	....	....	....	....	....	....	....	13	0	0	0	52	....	....	....	....
1996-97	Kamloops Blazers	WHL	61	8	10	18	278	....	....	....	....	....	....	....	....	....	5	0	0	0	35	....	....	....	....
1997-98	Albany River Rats	AHL	53	0	2	2	256	....	....	....	....	....	....	....	....	....	....	....	....	....	....	....	....	....	....
1998-99	Albany River Rats	AHL	61	1	1	2	213	....	....	....	....	....	....	....	....	....	1	0	0	0	0	....	....	....	....
99-2000	Albany River Rats	AHL	37	0	0	0	115	....	....	....	....	....	....	....	....	....	....	....	....	....	....	....	....	....	....
2000-01	Albany River Rats	AHL	38	0	0	0	105	....	....	....	....	....	....	....	....	....	....	....	....	....	....	....	....	....	....

			Regular Season														Playoffs								
Season	Club	League	GP	G	A	Pts	PIM	PP	SH	GW	S	%	+/-	TF	F%	Min	GP	G	A	Pts	PIM	PP	SH	GW	Min
2001-02	Albany River Rats	AHL	2	0	0	0	22	....	....	....	....	....	....	....	....	....	....	....	....	....	....	....	....	....	....
	Mississippi	ECHL	29	1	3	4	161	....	....	....	....	....	....	....	....	....	....	....	....	....	....	....	....	....	....
	Portland Pirates	AHL	33	0	3	3	87	....	....	....	....	....	....	....	....	....	....	....	....	....	....	....	....	....	....
2002-03	Albany River Rats	AHL	42	2	3	5	165	....	....	....	....	....	....	....	....	....	....	....	....	....	....	....	....	....	....
2003-04	**New Jersey**	**NHL**	**8**	**1**	**0**	**1**	**22**	**0**	**0**	**1**	**3**	**33.3**	**1**	**0**	**0.0**	**2:15**	....	....	....	....	....	....	....	....	....
	Albany River Rats	AHL	36	1	0	1	137	....	....	....	....	....	....	....	....	....	....	....	....	....	....	....	....	....	....
2004-05	Albany River Rats	AHL	52	0	2	2	184	....	....	....	....	....	....	....	....	....	....	....	....	....	....	....	....	....	....
	NHL Totals		**8**	**1**	**0**	**1**	**22**	**0**	**0**	**1**	**3**	**33.3**		**0**	**0.0**	**2:15**	....	....	....	....	....	....	....	....	....

Signed as a free agent by **New Jersey**, June 17, 1997.

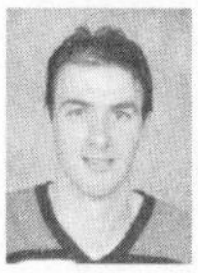

SLANEY, John

(SLAY-nee, JAWN) **PHI.**

Defense. Shoots left. 6', 189 lbs. Born, St. John's, Nfld., February 7, 1972. Washington's 1st choice, 9th overall, in 1990 Entry Draft.

Season	Club	League	GP	G	A	Pts	PIM	PP	SH	GW	S	%	+/-	TF	F%	Min	GP	G	A	Pts	PIM	PP	SH	GW	Min
1987-88	St. John's	NFAHA	65	41	69	110	70	....	....	....	....	....	....	....	....	....	....	....	....	....	....	....	....	....	....
1988-89	Cornwall Royals	OHL	66	16	43	59	23	....	....	....	....	....	....	....	....	....	18	8	16	24	10	....	....	....	....
1989-90	Cornwall Royals	OHL	64	38	59	97	68	....	....	....	....	....	....	....	....	....	6	0	8	8	11	....	....	....	....
1990-91	Cornwall Royals	OHL	34	21	25	46	28	....	....	....	....	....	....	....	....	....	....	....	....	....	....	....	....	....	....
1991-92	Cornwall Royals	OHL	34	19	41	60	43	....	....	....	....	....	....	....	....	....	6	3	8	11	0	....	....	....	....
	Baltimore	AHL	6	2	4	6	0	....	....	....	....	....	....	....	....	....	....	....	....	....	....	....	....	....	....
1992-93	Baltimore	AHL	79	20	46	66	60	....	....	....	....	....	....	....	....	....	7	0	7	7	8	....	....	....	....
1993-94	**Washington**	**NHL**	**47**	**7**	**9**	**16**	**27**	**3**	**0**	**1**	**70**	**10.0**	**3**	....	....	....	**11**	**1**	**1**	**2**	**2**	**1**	**0**	**0**	....
	Portland Pirates	AHL	29	14	13	27	17	....	....	....	....	....	....	....	....	....	....	....	....	....	....	....	....	....	....
1994-95	**Washington**	**NHL**	**16**	**0**	**3**	**3**	**6**	**0**	**0**	**0**	**21**	**0.0**	**–3**	....	....	....	....	....	....	....	....	....	....	....	....
	Portland Pirates	AHL	8	3	10	13	4	....	....	....	....	....	....	....	....	....	7	1	3	4	4	....	....	....	....
1995-96	**Colorado**	**NHL**	**7**	**0**	**3**	**3**	**4**	**0**	**0**	**0**	**12**	**0.0**	**2**	....	....	....	....	....	....	....	....	....	....	....	....
	Cornwall Aces	AHL	5	0	4	4	2	....	....	....	....	....	....	....	....	....	....	....	....	....	....	....	....	....	....
	Los Angeles	**NHL**	**31**	**6**	**11**	**17**	**10**	**3**	**1**	**0**	**63**	**9.5**	**5**	....	....	....	....	....	....	....	....	....	....	....	....
1996-97	**Los Angeles**	**NHL**	**32**	**3**	**11**	**14**	**4**	**1**	**0**	**1**	**60**	**5.0**	**–10**	....	....	....	....	....	....	....	....	....	....	....	....
	Phoenix	IHL	35	9	25	34	8	....	....	....	....	....	....	....	....	....	....	....	....	....	....	....	....	....	....
1997-98	**Phoenix**	**NHL**	**55**	**3**	**14**	**17**	**24**	**1**	**0**	**1**	**74**	**4.1**	**–3**	....	....	....	....	....	....	....	....	....	....	....	....
	Las Vegas	IHL	5	2	2	4	10	....	....	....	....	....	....	....	....	....	....	....	....	....	....	....	....	....	....
1998-99	**Nashville**	**NHL**	**46**	**2**	**12**	**14**	**14**	**0**	**0**	**1**	**84**	**2.4**	**–12**	**0**	**0.0**	**20:39**	....	....	....	....	....	....	....	....	....
	Milwaukee	IHL	7	0	1	1	0	....	....	....	....	....	....	....	....	....	....	....	....	....	....	....	....	....	....
99-2000	**Pittsburgh**	**NHL**	**29**	**1**	**4**	**5**	**10**	**1**	**0**	**0**	**27**	**3.7**	**–10**	**35**	**40.0**	**12:13**	**2**	**1**	**0**	**1**	**2**	**1**	**0**	**0**	**5:43**
	Wilkes-Barre	AHL	49	30	30	60	25	....	....	....	....	....	....	....	....	....	....	....	....	....	....	....	....	....	....
2000-01	Wilkes-Barre	AHL	40	12	38	50	4	....	....	....	....	....	....	....	....	....	....	....	....	....	....	....	....	....	....
	Philadelphia	AHL	25	6	11	17	10	....	....	....	....	....	....	....	....	....	10	2	6	8	6	....	....	....	....
2001-02	**Philadelphia**	**NHL**	**1**	**0**	**0**	**0**	**0**	**0**	**0**	**0**	**1**	**0.0**	**2**	**0**	**0.0**	**23:33**	**1**	**0**	**0**	**0**	**0**	**0**	**0**	**0**	**11:20**
	Philadelphia	AHL	64	20	39	59	26	....	....	....	....	....	....	....	....	....	5	2	1	3	0	....	....	....	....
2002-03	Philadelphia	AHL	55	9	33	42	36	....	....	....	....	....	....	....	....	....	....	....	....	....	....	....	....	....	....
2003-04	**Philadelphia**	**NHL**	**4**	**0**	**2**	**2**	**0**	**0**	**0**	**0**	**0**	**0.0**	**0**	**0**	**0.0**	**13:38**	....	....	....	....	....	....	....	....	....
	Philadelphia	AHL	59	19	29	48	31	....	....	....	....	....	....	....	....	....	12	3	4	7	6	....	....	....	....
2004-05	Philadelphia	AHL	78	14	30	44	39	....	....	....	....	....	....	....	....	....	21	3	7	10	12	....	....	....	....
	NHL Totals		**268**	**22**	**69**	**91**	**99**	**9**	**1**	**4**	**412**	**5.3**		**35**	**40.0**	**17:17**	**14**	**2**	**1**	**3**	**4**	**2**	**0**	**0**	**7:35**

OHL First All-Star Team (1990) • Canadian Major Junior Defenseman of the Year (1990) • OHL Second All-Star Team (1991) • AHL First All-Star Team (2001, 2002) • Eddie Shore Award (Outstanding Defenseman – AHL) (2001, 2002) • AHL Second All-Star Team (2004)

Traded to **Colorado** by **Washington** for Philadelphia's 3rd round choice (previously acquired, Washington selected Shawn McNeil) in 1996 Entry Draft, July 12, 1995. Traded to **Los Angeles** by **Colorado** for Winnipeg's 6th round choice (previously acquired, Colorado selected Brian Willsie) in 1996 Entry Draft, December 28, 1995. Signed as a free agent by **Phoenix**, August 19, 1997. Claimed by **Nashville** from **Phoenix** in Expansion Draft, June 26, 1998. Signed as a free agent by **Pittsburgh**, September 30, 1999. Traded to **Philadelphia** by **Pittsburgh** for Kevin Stevens, January 14, 2001.

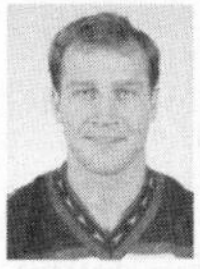

SLEGR, Jiri

(SLAY-guhr, YEE-ree) **BOS.**

Defense. Shoots left. 6'1", 210 lbs. Born, Jihlava, Czech., May 30, 1971. Vancouver's 3rd choice, 23rd overall, in 1990 Entry Draft.

Season	Club	League	GP	G	A	Pts	PIM	PP	SH	GW	S	%	+/-	TF	F%	Min	GP	G	A	Pts	PIM	PP	SH	GW	Min
1987-88	CHZ Litvinov	Czech	4	1	1	2	0	....	....	....	....	....	....	....	....	....	....	....	....	....	....	....	....	....	....
1988-89	CHZ Litvinov	Czech	8	0	0	0	4	....	....	....	....	....	....	....	....	....	....	....	....	....	....	....	....	....	....
1989-90	CHZ Litvinov	Czech	51	4	15	19	....	....	....	....	....	....	....	....	....	....	....	....	....	....	....	....	....	....	....
1990-91	HC CHZ Litvinov	Czech	47	11	36	47	26	....	....	....	....	....	....	....	....	....	....	....	....	....	....	....	....	....	....
1991-92	Litvinov	Czech	42	9	23	32	38	....	....	....	....	....	....	....	....	....	....	....	....	....	....	....	....	....	....
	Czechoslovakia	Olympics	8	1	1	2	14	....	....	....	....	....	....	....	....	....	....	....	....	....	....	....	....	....	....
1992-93	**Vancouver**	**NHL**	**41**	**4**	**22**	**26**	**109**	**2**	**0**	**0**	**89**	**4.5**	**16**	....	....	....	**5**	**0**	**3**	**3**	**4**	**0**	**0**	**0**	....
	Hamilton	AHL	21	4	14	18	42	....	....	....	....	....	....	....	....	....	....	....	....	....	....	....	....	....	....
1993-94	**Vancouver**	**NHL**	**78**	**5**	**33**	**38**	**86**	**1**	**0**	**0**	**160**	**3.1**	**0**	....	....	....	....	....	....	....	....	....	....	....	....
1994-95	Litvinov	CzRep	11	3	10	13	80	....	....	....	....	....	....	....	....	....	....	....	....	....	....	....	....	....	....
	Vancouver	**NHL**	**19**	**1**	**5**	**6**	**32**	**0**	**0**	**1**	**42**	**2.4**	**0**	....	....	....	....	....	....	....	....	....	....	....	....
	Edmonton	**NHL**	**12**	**1**	**5**	**6**	**14**	**1**	**0**	**0**	**27**	**3.7**	**–5**	....	....	....	....	....	....	....	....	....	....	....	....
1995-96	**Edmonton**	**NHL**	**57**	**4**	**13**	**17**	**74**	**0**	**1**	**1**	**91**	**4.4**	**–1**	....	....	....	....	....	....	....	....	....	....	....	....
	Cape Breton	AHL	4	1	2	3	4	....	....	....	....	....	....	....	....	....	....	....	....	....	....	....	....	....	....
1996-97	Litvinov	CzRep	1	0	0	0	0	....	....	....	....	....	....	....	....	....	....	....	....	....	....	....	....	....	....
	Sodertalje SK	Sweden	30	4	14	18	62	....	....	....	....	....	....	....	....	....	10	4	2	6	32	....	....	....	....
1997-98	**Pittsburgh**	**NHL**	**73**	**5**	**12**	**17**	**109**	**1**	**1**	**0**	**131**	**3.8**	**10**	....	....	....	**6**	**0**	**4**	**4**	**2**	**0**	**0**	**0**	....
	Czech Republic	Olympics	6	1	0	1	8	....	....	....	....	....	....	....	....	....	....	....	....	....	....	....	....	....	....
1998-99	**Pittsburgh**	**NHL**	**63**	**3**	**20**	**23**	**86**	**1**	**0**	**0**	**91**	**3.3**	**13**	**2**	**0.0**	**18:42**	**13**	**1**	**3**	**4**	**12**	**0**	**0**	**1**	**19:50**
99-2000	**Pittsburgh**	**NHL**	**74**	**11**	**20**	**31**	**82**	**0**	**0**	**2**	**144**	**7.6**	**20**	**3**	**66.7**	**21:22**	**10**	**2**	**3**	**5**	**19**	**0**	**0**	**1**	**20:02**
2000-01	**Pittsburgh**	**NHL**	**42**	**5**	**10**	**15**	**60**	**0**	**1**	**1**	**67**	**7.5**	**–9**	**0**	**0.0**	**17:37**	....	....	....	....	....	....	....	....	....
	Atlanta	**NHL**	**33**	**3**	**16**	**19**	**36**	**2**	**0**	**0**	**78**	**3.8**	**–1**	**1**	**0.0**	**21:34**	....	....	....	....	....	....	....	....	....
2001-02	**Atlanta**	**NHL**	**38**	**3**	**5**	**8**	**51**	**1**	**0**	**0**	**56**	**5.4**	**–21**	**0**	**0.0**	**21:21**	....	....	....	....	....	....	....	....	....
	♦ **Detroit**	**NHL**	**8**	**0**	**1**	**1**	**8**	**0**	**0**	**0**	**11**	**0.0**	**1**	**0**	**0.0**	**19:16**	**1**	**0**	**0**	**0**	**2**	**0**	**0**	**0**	**17:11**
2002-03	Litvinov	CzRep	10	2	3	5	14	....	....	....	....	....	....	....	....	....	....	....	....	....	....	....	....	....	....
	Avangard Omsk	Russia	6	1	2	3	8	....	....	....	....	....	....	....	....	....	9	0	3	3	*45	....	....	....	....
2003-04	**Vancouver**	**NHL**	**16**	**2**	**5**	**7**	**8**	**1**	**1**	**1**	**15**	**13.3**	**6**	**0**	**0.0**	**12:16**	....	....	....	....	....	....	....	....	....
	Boston	**NHL**	**36**	**4**	**15**	**19**	**27**	**0**	**0**	**1**	**83**	**4.8**	**5**	**0**	**0.0**	**20:03**	**7**	**1**	**1**	**2**	**0**	**0**	**0**	**0**	**18:08**
2004-05	Litvinov	CzRep	46	6	23	29	135	....	....	....	....	....	....	....	....	....	6	1	2	3	30	....	....	....	....
	NHL Totals		**590**	**51**	**182**	**233**	**782**	**10**	**4**	**7**	**1085**	**4.7**		**6**	**33.3**	**19:39**	**42**	**4**	**14**	**18**	**39**	**0**	**0**	**2**	**19:26**

Czechoslovakian First All-Star Team (1991)

Traded to **Edmonton** by **Vancouver** for Roman Oksiuta, April 7, 1995. Traded to **Pittsburgh** by **Edmonton** for Pittsburgh's 3rd round choice (later traded to New Jersey – New Jersey selected Brian Gionta) in 1998 Entry Draft, August 12, 1997. Traded to **Atlanta** by **Pittsburgh** for San Jose's 3rd round choice (previously acquired, later traded to Columbus – Columbus selected Aaron Johnson) in 2001 Entry Draft, January 14, 2001. Traded to **Detroit** by **Atlanta** for Yuri Butsayev and Detroit's 3rd round choice (later traded to Columbus – Columbus selected Jeff Genovy) in 2002 Entry Draft, March 19, 2002. Signed as a free agent by **Vancouver**, September 4, 2003. Traded to **Boston** by **Vancouver** for future considerations, January 17, 2004. Signed as a free agent by **Litvinov** (CzRep), August 20, 2004.

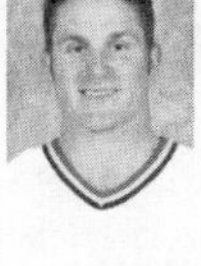

SLOAN, Blake

(SLOHN, BLAYK)

Right wing. Shoots right. 5'10", 196 lbs. Born, Park Ridge, IL, July 27, 1975.

Season	Club	League	GP	G	A	Pts	PIM	PP	SH	GW	S	%	+/-	TF	F%	Min	GP	G	A	Pts	PIM	PP	SH	GW	Min
1992-93	Tabor	High-MA	33	7	15	22	....	....	....	....	....	....	....	....	....	....	....	....	....	....	....	....	....	....	....
1993-94	U. of Michigan	CCHA	38	2	4	6	48	....	....	....	....	....	....	....	....	....	....	....	....	....	....	....	....	....	....
1994-95	U. of Michigan	CCHA	39	2	15	17	60	....	....	....	....	....	....	....	....	....	....	....	....	....	....	....	....	....	....
1995-96	U. of Michigan	CCHA	41	6	24	30	55	....	....	....	....	....	....	....	....	....	....	....	....	....	....	....	....	....	....
1996-97	U. of Michigan	CCHA	41	2	15	17	52	....	....	....	....	....	....	....	....	....	....	....	....	....	....	....	....	....	....
1997-98	Houston Aeros	IHL	70	2	13	15	86	....	....	....	....	....	....	....	....	....	2	0	0	0	0	....	....	....	....
1998-99 ♦	**Dallas**	**NHL**	**14**	**0**	**0**	**0**	**10**	**0**	**0**	**0**	**7**	**0.0**	**–1**	**0**	**0.0**	**9:01**	**19**	**0**	**2**	**2**	**8**	**0**	**0**	**0**	**9:58**
	Houston Aeros	IHL	62	8	10	18	76	....	....	....	....	....	....	....	....	....	....	....	....	....	....	....	....	....	....
99-2000	**Dallas**	**NHL**	**67**	**4**	**13**	**17**	**50**	**0**	**0**	**1**	**78**	**5.1**	**11**	**2**	**50.0**	**13:30**	**16**	**0**	**0**	**0**	**12**	**0**	**0**	**0**	**8:55**
2000-01	**Dallas**	**NHL**	**33**	**2**	**2**	**4**	**4**	**0**	**0**	**1**	**29**	**6.9**	**–2**	**4**	**25.0**	**9:56**	....	....	....	....	....	....	....	....	....
	Houston Aeros	IHL	20	7	4	11	18	....	....	....	....	....	....	....	....	....	....	....	....	....	....	....	....	....	....
	Columbus	**NHL**	**14**	**1**	**0**	**1**	**13**	**0**	**0**	**0**	**16**	**6.3**	**–2**	**7**	**28.6**	**13:19**	....	....	....	....	....	....	....	....	....
2001-02	**Columbus**	**NHL**	**60**	**2**	**7**	**9**	**46**	**0**	**0**	**0**	**49**	**4.1**	**–18**	**3**	**66.7**	**10:56**	....	....	....	....	....	....	....	....	....
	Calgary	**NHL**	**7**	**0**	**2**	**2**	**4**	**0**	**0**	**0**	**7**	**0.0**	**1**	**2**	**0.0**	**12:16**	....	....	....	....	....	....	....	....	....
2002-03	**Calgary**	**NHL**	**67**	**2**	**8**	**10**	**28**	**0**	**0**	**0**	**56**	**3.6**	**–5**	**31**	**12.9**	**12:23**	....	....	....	....	....	....	....	....	....

Season	Club	League	GP	G	A	Pts	PIM	PP	SH	GW	S	%	+/-	TF	F%	Min	GP	G	A	Pts	PIM	PP	SH	GW	Min
			Regular Season														Playoffs								
2003-04	Grand Rapids	AHL	7	4	2	6	4	....	....	....	....	....	....	....	....	....	....	....	....	....	....	....	....	....	....
	Dallas	**NHL**	**28**	**0**	**0**	**0**	**7**	**0**	**0**	**0**	**23**	**0.0**	**–1**	**4**	**0.0**	**7:11**	....	....	....	....	....	....	....	....	....
2004-05	Grand Rapids	AHL	78	15	11	26	68	....	....	....	....	....	....	....	....	....	....	....	....	....	....	....	....	....	....
	NHL Totals		**290**	**11**	**32**	**43**	**162**	**0**	**0**	**2**	**265**	**4.2**		**53**	**18.9**	**11:26**	**35**	**0**	**2**	**2**	**20**	**0**	**0**	**0**	**9:29**

Signed as a free agent by **Dallas**, March 10, 1998. Claimed on waivers by **Columbus** from **Dallas**, March 13, 2001. Traded to **Calgary** by **Columbus** for Jamie Allison, March 19, 2002. Signed as a free agent by **Grand Rapids** (AHL), November 18, 2003. Signed as a free agent by **Detroit**, December 1, 2003. Claimed on waivers by **Dallas** from **Detroit**, December 3, 2003. • Spent majority of 2003-04 season as a healthy reserve. Signed as a free agent by **Grand Rapids** (AHL), September 9, 2004.

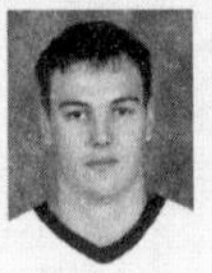

SMIRNOV, Alexei

(smihr-NAHV, al-EHX-ay)

Left wing. Shoots left. 6'3", 211 lbs. Born, Tver, USSR, January 28, 1982. Anaheim's 1st choice, 12th overall, in 2000 Entry Draft.

Season	Club	League	GP	G	A	Pts	PIM	PP	SH	GW	S	%	+/-	TF	F%	Min	GP	G	A	Pts	PIM	PP	SH	GW	Min
1997-98	Dynamo Mosc. 2	Russia-2	11	1	1	2	4	....	....	....	....	....	....	....	....	....	....	....	....	....	....	....	....	....	....
1998-99	Dyn'o Moscow 2	Russia-3	27	9	3	12	24	....	....	....	....	....	....	....	....	....	....	....	....	....	....	....	....	....	....
99-2000	Dyn'o Moscow 2	Russia-3	12	5	3	8	34	....	....	....	....	....	....	....	....	....	....	....	....	....	....	....	....	....	....
	THK Tver	Russia-2	35	3	5	8	24	....	....	....	....	....	....	....	....	....	....	....	....	....	....	....	....	....	....
	Dynamo Moscow	Russia	1	0	0	0	0	....	....	....	....	....	....	....	....	....	....	....	....	....	....	....	....	....	....
2000-01	Dynamo Moscow	Russia	29	2	0	2	16	....	....	....	....	....	....	....	....	....	....	....	....	....	....	....	....	....	....
2001-02	CSKA Moscow 2	Russia-3	2	1	0	1	0	....	....	....	....	....	....	....	....	....	....	....	....	....	....	....	....	....	....
	CSKA Moscow	Russia	51	5	11	16	42	....	....	....	....	....	....	....	....	....	....	....	....	....	....	....	....	....	....
2002-03	**Anaheim**	**NHL**	**44**	**3**	**2**	**5**	**18**	**0**	**0**	**1**	**46**	**6.5**	**–1**	**6**	**16.7**	**8:50**	**4**	**0**	**0**	**0**	**2**	**0**	**0**	**0**	**4:22**
	Cincinnati	AHL	19	7	3	10	12	....	....	....	....	....	....	....	....	....	....	....	....	....	....	....	....	....	....
2003-04	**Anaheim**	**NHL**	**8**	**0**	**1**	**1**	**2**	**0**	**0**	**0**	**8**	**0.0**	**0**	**3**	**0.0**	**7:17**	....	....	....	....	....	....	....	....	....
	Cincinnati	AHL	51	9	10	19	34	....	....	....	....	....	....	....	....	....	2	0	0	0	2	....	....	....	....
2004-05	Cincinnati	AHL	65	9	9	18	53	....	....	....	....	....	....	....	....	....	4	0	0	0	0	....	....	....	....
	NHL Totals		**52**	**3**	**3**	**6**	**20**	**0**	**0**	**1**	**54**	**5.6**		**9**	**11.1**	**8:36**	**4**	**0**	**0**	**0**	**2**	**0**	**0**	**0**	**4:22**

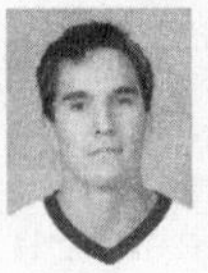

SMITH, Brandon

(SMIHTH, BRAN-duhn)

Defense. Shoots left. 6'1", 209 lbs. Born, Hazelton, B.C., February 25, 1973.

Season	Club	League	GP	G	A	Pts	PIM	PP	SH	GW	S	%	+/-	TF	F%	Min	GP	G	A	Pts	PIM	PP	SH	GW	Min
1989-90	Portland	WHL	59	2	17	19	16	....	....	....	....	....	....	....	....	....	....	....	....	....	....	....	....	....	....
1990-91	Portland	WHL	17	8	5	13	8	....	....	....	....	....	....	....	....	....	....	....	....	....	....	....	....	....	....
1991-92	Portland	WHL	70	12	32	44	63	....	....	....	....	....	....	....	....	....	....	....	....	....	....	....	....	....	....
1992-93	Portland	WHL	72	20	54	74	38	....	....	....	....	....	....	....	....	....	16	4	9	13	6	....	....	....	....
1993-94	Portland	WHL	72	19	63	82	47	....	....	....	....	....	....	....	....	....	10	2	10	12	8	....	....	....	....
1994-95	Dayton Bombers	ECHL	60	16	49	65	57	....	....	....	....	....	....	....	....	....	4	2	3	5	0	....	....	....	....
	Minnesota Moose	IHL	1	0	0	0	0	....	....	....	....	....	....	....	....	....	....	....	....	....	....	....	....	....	....
	Adirondack	AHL	14	1	2	3	7	....	....	....	....	....	....	....	....	....	3	0	0	0	2	....	....	....	....
1995-96	Adirondack	AHL	48	4	13	17	22	....	....	....	....	....	....	....	....	....	3	0	1	1	2	....	....	....	....
1996-97	Adirondack	AHL	80	8	26	34	30	....	....	....	....	....	....	....	....	....	4	0	0	0	0	....	....	....	....
1997-98	Adirondack	AHL	64	9	27	36	26	....	....	....	....	....	....	....	....	....	1	0	1	1	0	....	....	....	....
1998-99	**Boston**	**NHL**	**5**	**0**	**0**	**0**	**0**	**0**	**0**	**0**	**2**	**0.0**	**2**	**0**	**0.0**	**9:38**	....	....	....	....	....	....	....	....	....
	Providence Bruins	AHL	72	16	46	62	32	....	....	....	....	....	....	....	....	....	19	1	9	10	12	....	....	....	....
99-2000	**Boston**	**NHL**	**22**	**2**	**4**	**6**	**10**	**0**	**0**	**0**	**24**	**8.3**	**–4**	**0**	**0.0**	**19:29**	....	....	....	....	....	....	....	....	....
	Providence Bruins	AHL	55	8	30	38	20	....	....	....	....	....	....	....	....	....	14	1	11	12	2	....	....	....	....
2000-01	**Boston**	**NHL**	**3**	**1**	**0**	**1**	**0**	**1**	**0**	**0**	**2**	**50.0**	**–1**	**0**	**0.0**	**6:46**	....	....	....	....	....	....	....	....	....
	Providence Bruins	AHL	63	11	28	39	30	....	....	....	....	....	....	....	....	....	17	0	5	5	6	....	....	....	....
2001-02	Cleveland Barons	AHL	59	6	29	35	26	....	....	....	....	....	....	....	....	....	....	....	....	....	....	....	....	....	....
2002-03	**NY Islanders**	**NHL**	**3**	**0**	**0**	**0**	**0**	**0**	**0**	**0**	**1**	**0.0**	**–2**	**0**	**0.0**	**9:59**	....	....	....	....	....	....	....	....	....
	Bridgeport	AHL	63	9	32	41	37	....	....	....	....	....	....	....	....	....	9	1	3	4	5	....	....	....	....
2003-04	Bridgeport	AHL	74	5	23	28	39	....	....	....	....	....	....	....	....	....	7	1	3	4	9	....	....	....	....
2004-05	Rochester	AHL	67	4	14	18	32	....	....	....	....	....	....	....	....	....	8	1	1	2	4	....	....	....	....
	NHL Totals		**33**	**3**	**4**	**7**	**10**	**1**	**0**	**0**	**29**	**10.3**		**0**	**0.0**	**15:58**	....	....	....	....	....	....	....	....	....

WHL West Second All-Star Team (1993, 1994) • ECHL First All-Star Team (1995) • ECHL Defenseman of the Year (1995) • AHL First All-Star Team (1999)

Signed as a free agent by **Detroit**, July 22, 1997. Signed as a free agent by **Boston**, August 5, 1998. Signed as a free agent by **San Jose**, July 23, 2001. Signed as a free agent by **NY Islanders**, August 3, 2002. Signed as a free agent by **Rochester** (AHL), September 10, 2004.

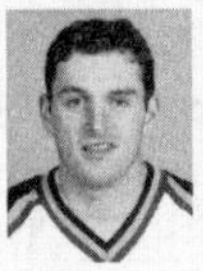

SMITH, D.J.

(SMIHTH, DEE-JAY)

Defense. Shoots left. 6'1", 205 lbs. Born, Windsor, Ont., May 13, 1977. NY Islanders' 3rd choice, 41st overall, in 1995 Entry Draft.

Season	Club	League	GP	G	A	Pts	PIM	PP	SH	GW	S	%	+/-	TF	F%	Min	GP	G	A	Pts	PIM	PP	SH	GW	Min
1992-93	Belle River	OHA-C	40	5	18	23	39	....	....	....	....	....	....	....	....	....	....	....	....	....	....	....	....	....	....
	Windsor Bulldogs	OHA-B	1	0	0	0	0	....	....	....	....	....	....	....	....	....	....	....	....	....	....	....	....	....	....
1993-94	Windsor Bulldogs	OHA-B	51	8	34	42	267	....	....	....	....	....	....	....	....	....	....	....	....	....	....	....	....	....	....
1994-95	Windsor Spitfires	OHL	61	4	13	17	201	....	....	....	....	....	....	....	....	....	10	1	3	4	41	....	....	....	....
1995-96	Windsor Spitfires	OHL	64	14	45	59	260	....	....	....	....	....	....	....	....	....	7	1	7	8	23	....	....	....	....
	St. John's	AHL	1	0	0	0	0	....	....	....	....	....	....	....	....	....	....	....	....	....	....	....	....	....	....
1996-97	Windsor Spitfires	OHL	63	15	52	67	190	....	....	....	....	....	....	....	....	....	5	1	7	8	11	....	....	....	....
	Toronto	**NHL**	**8**	**0**	**1**	**1**	**7**	**0**	**0**	**0**	**4**	**0.0**	**–5**	....	....	....	....	....	....	....	....	....	....	....	....
	St. John's	AHL	....	....	....	....	....	....	....	....	....	....	....	....	....	....	1	0	0	0	0	....	....	....	....
1997-98	St. John's	AHL	65	4	11	15	237	....	....	....	....	....	....	....	....	....	4	0	0	0	4	....	....	....	....
1998-99	St. John's	AHL	79	7	28	35	216	....	....	....	....	....	....	....	....	....	5	0	1	1	0	....	....	....	....
99-2000	**Toronto**	**NHL**	**3**	**0**	**0**	**0**	**5**	**0**	**0**	**0**	**2**	**0.0**	**–1**	**0**	**0.0**	**12:37**	....	....	....	....	....	....	....	....	....
	St. John's	AHL	74	6	22	28	197	....	....	....	....	....	....	....	....	....	....	....	....	....	....	....	....	....	....
2000-01	St. John's	AHL	59	7	12	19	106	....	....	....	....	....	....	....	....	....	4	0	0	0	11	....	....	....	....
2001-02	St. John's	AHL	59	6	10	16	152	....	....	....	....	....	....	....	....	....	....	....	....	....	....	....	....	....	....
	Hershey Bears	AHL	14	0	3	3	33	....	....	....	....	....	....	....	....	....	8	1	0	1	33	....	....	....	....
2002-03	**Colorado**	**NHL**	**34**	**1**	**0**	**1**	**55**	**0**	**0**	**0**	**7**	**14.3**	**2**	**0**	**0.0**	**3:49**	....	....	....	....	....	....	....	....	....
	Hershey Bears	AHL	2	0	0	0	4	....	....	....	....	....	....	....	....	....	....	....	....	....	....	....	....	....	....
2003-04	Hershey Bears	AHL	35	7	7	14	71	....	....	....	....	....	....	....	....	....	....	....	....	....	....	....	....	....	....
2004-05			DID NOT PLAY																						
	NHL Totals		**45**	**1**	**1**	**2**	**67**	**0**	**0**	**0**	**13**	**7.7**		**0**	**0.0**	**4:32**	....	....	....	....	....	....	....	....	....

OHL Second All-Star Team (1997)

Traded to **Toronto** by **NY Islanders** with Wendel Clark and Mathieu Schneider for Darby Hendrickson, Sean Haggerty, Kenny Jonsson and Toronto's 1st round choice (Roberto Luongo) in 1997 Entry Draft, March 13, 1996. Traded to **Nashville** by **Toronto** with Marty Wilford for Marc Moro, March 1, 2002. Traded to **Colorado** by **Nashville** for Tampa Bay's 9th round choice (previously acquired, Nashville selected Matt Davis) in 2002 Entry Draft, March 1, 2002. • Missed majority of 2002-03 season recovering from head injury suffered in game vs. San Jose, November 5, 2002. • Missed majority of 2003-04 season recovering from knee injury suffered in game vs. Norfolk (AHL), January 14, 2004.

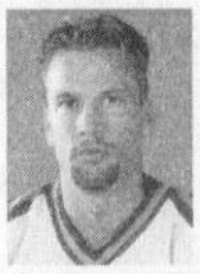

SMITH, Dan

(SMIHTH, DAN) **EDM.**

Defense. Shoots left. 6'3", 215 lbs. Born, Fernie, B.C., October 19, 1976. Colorado's 7th choice, 181st overall, in 1995 Entry Draft.

Season	Club	League	GP	G	A	Pts	PIM	PP	SH	GW	S	%	+/-	TF	F%	Min	GP	G	A	Pts	PIM	PP	SH	GW	Min
1994-95	U.B.C.	CWUAA	28	1	3	4	26	....	....	....	....	....	....	....	....	....	....	....	....	....	....	....	....	....	....
1995-96	Tri-City	WHL	58	1	21	22	70	....	....	....	....	....	....	....	....	....	11	1	3	4	14	....	....	....	....
1996-97	Tri-City	WHL	72	5	19	24	174	....	....	....	....	....	....	....	....	....	....	....	....	....	....	....	....	....	....
	Hershey Bears	AHL	8	0	1	1	6	....	....	....	....	....	....	....	....	....	15	0	1	1	25	....	....	....	....
1997-98	Hershey Bears	AHL	50	1	2	3	71	....	....	....	....	....	....	....	....	....	6	0	0	0	4	....	....	....	....
1998-99	**Colorado**	**NHL**	**12**	**0**	**0**	**0**	**9**	**0**	**0**	**0**	**6**	**0.0**	**5**	**0**	**0.0**	**12:14**	....	....	....	....	....	....	....	....	....
	Hershey Bears	AHL	54	5	7	12	72	....	....	....	....	....	....	....	....	....	5	0	1	1	0	....	....	....	....
99-2000	**Colorado**	**NHL**	**3**	**0**	**0**	**0**	**0**	**0**	**0**	**0**	**0**	**0.0**	**2**	**0**	**0.0**	**11:03**	....	....	....	....	....	....	....	....	....
	Hershey Bears	AHL	49	7	15	22	56	....	....	....	....	....	....	....	....	....	....	....	....	....	....	....	....	....	....
2000-01	Hershey Bears	AHL	58	2	12	14	34	....	....	....	....	....	....	....	....	....	12	0	1	1	4	....	....	....	....
2001-02	Colorado	WCHL	12	0	2	2	16	....	....	....	....	....	....	....	....	....	....	....	....	....	....	....	....	....	....
	Lukko Rauma	Finland	32	1	2	3	18	....	....	....	....	....	....	....	....	....	....	....	....	....	....	....	....	....	....
2002-03	Springfield	AHL	69	1	14	15	53	....	....	....	....	....	....	....	....	....	6	0	2	2	0	....	....	....	....
2003-04	Toronto	AHL	66	4	9	13	41	....	....	....	....	....	....	....	....	....	....	....	....	....	....	....	....	....	....
2004-05	Edmonton	AHL	72	5	10	15	72	....	....	....	....	....	....	....	....	....	....	....	....	....	....	....	....	....	....
	NHL Totals		**15**	**0**	**0**	**0**	**9**	**0**	**0**	**0**	**6**	**0.0**		**0**	**0.0**	**12:00**	....	....	....	....	....	....	....	....	....

Signed as a free agent by **Colorado** (WCHL), October 26, 2001. Signed as a free agent by **Lukko** (Finland) after receiving release from Colorado (WCHL), November 21, 2001. Signed as a free agent by **Edmonton**, August 21, 2003.

						Regular Season										Playoffs							
Season	Club	League	GP	G	A	Pts	PIM	PP	SH	GW	S	%	+/-	TF	F%	Min	GP	G	A	Pts	PIM	PP	SH	GW	Min

SMITH, Jason (SMIHTH, JAY-suhn) EDM.

Defense. Shoots right. 6'3", 215 lbs.   Born, Calgary, Alta., November 2, 1973. New Jersey's 1st choice, 18th overall, in 1992 Entry Draft.

Season	Club	League	GP	G	A	Pts	PIM	PP	SH	GW	S	%	+/-	TF	F%	Min	GP	G	A	Pts	PIM	PP	SH	GW	Min
1990-91	Calgary Canucks	AJHL	45	3	15	18	69	....	....	....	....	....	....				....	....	....	....	....				
	Regina Pats	WHL	2	0	0	0	7	....	....	....	....	....	....				4	0	0	0	2	....	....	....	
1991-92	Regina Pats	WHL	62	9	29	38	138	....	....	....	....	....	....				....	....	....	....	....				
1992-93	Regina Pats	WHL	64	14	52	66	175	....	....	....	....	....	....				13	4	8	12	39	....	....	....	
	Utica Devils	AHL	....	....	....	....	....	....	....	....	....	....	....				1	0	0	0	2	....	....	....	
1993-94	**New Jersey**	**NHL**	41	0	5	5	43	0	0	0	47	0.0	7				6	0	0	0	7	0	0	0	
	Albany River Rats	AHL	20	6	3	9	31	....	....	....	....	....	....				....	....	....	....	....				
1994-95	Albany River Rats	AHL	7	0	2	2	15	....	....	....	....	....	....				11	2	2	4	19	....	....	....	
	New Jersey	**NHL**	2	0	0	0	0	0	0	0	5	0.0	-3				....	....	....	....	....				
1995-96	**New Jersey**	**NHL**	64	2	1	3	86	0	0	0	52	3.8	5				....	....	....	....	....				
1996-97	**New Jersey**	**NHL**	57	1	2	3	38	0	0	0	48	2.1	-8				....	....	....	....	....				
	Toronto	**NHL**	21	0	5	5	16	0	0	0	26	0.0	-4				....	....	....	....	....				
1997-98	**Toronto**	**NHL**	81	3	13	16	100	0	0	0	97	3.1	-5				....	....	....	....	....				
1998-99	**Toronto**	**NHL**	60	2	11	13	40	0	0	0	53	3.8	-9	0	0.0	17:31	....	....	....	....	....				
	Edmonton	**NHL**	12	1	1	2	11	0	0	0	15	6.7	0	0	0.0	20:26	4	0	1	1	4	0	0	0	26:29
99-2000	**Edmonton**	**NHL**	80	3	11	14	60	0	0	1	96	3.1	16	1100	0.0	21:15	5	0	1	1	4	0	0	0	21:56
2000-01	**Edmonton**	**NHL**	82	5	15	20	120	1	1	0	140	3.6	14	1	0.0	21:40	6	0	2	2	6	0	0	0	25:27
2001-02	**Edmonton**	**NHL**	74	5	13	18	103	0	1	1	85	5.9	14	0	0.0	21:00	....	....	....	....	....				
2002-03	**Edmonton**	**NHL**	68	4	8	12	64	0	0	1	93	4.3	5	0	0.0	21:46	6	0	0	0	19	0	0	0	21:16
2003-04	**Edmonton**	**NHL**	68	7	12	19	98	0	1	1	84	8.3	13	2	50.0	21:21	....	....	....	....	....				
2004-05					DID NOT PLAY												....	....	....	....	....				
	NHL Totals		710	33	97	130	779	1	3	4	841	3.9		4	25.0	20:46	27	0	4	4	40	0	0	0	23:37

WHL East First All-Star Team (1993) • Canadian Major Junior First All-Star Team (1993)
• Missed majority of 1994-95 season recovering from knee injury suffered in practice, November 5, 1994. Traded to **Toronto** by **New Jersey** with Steve Sullivan and the rights to Alyn McCauley for Doug Gilmour, Dave Ellett and New Jersey's 4th round choice (previously acquired, New Jersey selected Andre Lakos) in 1999 Entry Draft, February 25, 1997. Traded to **Edmonton** by **Toronto** for Edmonton's 4th round choice (Jonathon Zion) in 1999 Entry Draft and Edmonton's 2nd round choice (Kris Vernarsky) in 2000 Entry Draft, March 23, 1999.

SMITH, Mark (SMIHTH, MAHRK) S.J.

Center. Shoots left. 5'10", 215 lbs.   Born, Edmonton, Alta., October 24, 1977. San Jose's 7th choice, 219th overall, in 1997 Entry Draft.

Season	Club	League	GP	G	A	Pts	PIM	PP	SH	GW	S	%	+/-	TF	F%	Min	GP	G	A	Pts	PIM	PP	SH	GW	Min
1993-94	Nipawin Hawks	SJHL	62	14	12	26	44	....	....	....	....	....	....				....	....	....	....	....				
1994-95	Lethbridge	WHL	49	3	4	7	25	....	....	....	....	....	....				....	....	....	....	....				
1995-96	Lethbridge	WHL	71	11	24	35	59	....	....	....	....	....	....				4	2	0	2	2	....	....	....	
1996-97	Lethbridge	WHL	62	19	38	57	125	....	....	....	....	....	....				19	7	13	20	51	....	....	....	
1997-98	Lethbridge	WHL	70	42	67	109	206	....	....	....	....	....	....				3	0	2	2	18	....	....	....	
	Kentucky	AHL	2	0	0	0	0	....	....	....	....	....	....				....	....	....	....	....				
1998-99	Kentucky	AHL	78	18	21	39	101	....	....	....	....	....	....				12	2	7	9	16	....	....	....	
99-2000	Kentucky	AHL	79	21	45	66	153	....	....	....	....	....	....				9	0	5	5	22	....	....	....	
2000-01	**San Jose**	**NHL**	42	2	2	4	51	0	0	0	39	5.1	2	308	52.9	8:48	....	....	....	....	....				
	Kentucky	AHL	6	2	6	8	23	....	....	....	....	....	....				....	....	....	....	....				
2001-02	**San Jose**	**NHL**	49	3	3	6	72	0	0	1	40	7.5	-1	368	54.1	8:03	....	....	....	....	....				
2002-03	**San Jose**	**NHL**	75	4	11	15	64	0	0	0	68	5.9	1	632	57.0	9:21	....	....	....	....	....				
2003-04	**San Jose**	**NHL**	36	1	3	4	72	0	0	0	31	3.2	-5	207	50.2	8:22	10	1	0	1	11	0	0	1	7:44
2004-05	Victoria	ECHL	20	6	9	15	41	....	....	....	....	....	....				....	....	....	....	....				
	NHL Totals		202	10	19	29	259	0	0	1	178	5.6		1515	54.5	8:45	10	1	0	1	11	0	0	1	7:44

WHL East Second All-Star Team (1998)
• Spent majority of 2003-04 season as a healthy reserve. Signed as a free agent by **Victoria** (ECHL), January 21, 2005.

SMITH, Nathan (SMIHTH, NAY-thun) VAN.

Center. Shoots left. 6'2", 192 lbs.   Born, Edmonton, Alta., February 9, 1982. Vancouver's 1st choice, 23rd overall, in 2000 Entry Draft.

Season	Club	League	GP	G	A	Pts	PIM	PP	SH	GW	S	%	+/-	TF	F%	Min	GP	G	A	Pts	PIM	PP	SH	GW	Min
1997-98	Sherwood Park	AMHL	35	15	13	28	24	....	....	....	....	....	....				....	....	....	....	....				
1998-99	Swift Current	WHL	47	5	8	13	26	....	....	....	....	....	....				....	....	....	....	....				
99-2000	Swift Current	WHL	70	21	28	49	72	....	....	....	....	....	....				12	1	6	7	4	....	....	....	
2000-01	Swift Current	WHL	67	28	62	90	78	....	....	....	....	....	....				19	4	3	7	20	....	....	....	
2001-02	Swift Current	WHL	47	22	38	60	52	....	....	....	....	....	....				12	3	6	9	18	....	....	....	
2002-03	Manitoba Moose	AHL	53	9	8	17	30	....	....	....	....	....	....				14	1	3	4	25	....	....	....	
2003-04	**Vancouver**	**NHL**	2	0	0	0	0	0	0	0	1	0.0	-1	12	33.3	5:16	....	....	....	....	....				
	Manitoba Moose	AHL	76	4	16	20	71	....	....	....	....	....	....				....	....	....	....	....				
2004-05	Manitoba Moose	AHL	72	7	9	16	67	....	....	....	....	....	....				14	2	4	6	20	....	....	....	
	NHL Totals		2	0	0	0	0	0	0	0	1	0.0		12	33.3	5:16	....	....	....	....	....				

SMITH, Nick (SMIHTH, NIHK)

Center. Shoots left. 6'2", 196 lbs.   Born, Hamilton, Ont., March 23, 1979. Florida's 4th choice, 74th overall, in 1997 Entry Draft.

Season	Club	League	GP	G	A	Pts	PIM	PP	SH	GW	S	%	+/-	TF	F%	Min	GP	G	A	Pts	PIM	PP	SH	GW	Min
1995-96	Shelburne	MTJHL	42	13	18	31	12	....	....	....	....	....	....				....	....	....	....	....				
1996-97	Barrie Colts	OHL	63	10	18	28	15	....	....	....	....	....	....				9	3	8	11	13	....	....	....	
1997-98	Barrie Colts	OHL	63	13	21	34	21	....	....	....	....	....	....				6	1	2	3	4	....	....	....	
1998-99	Barrie Colts	OHL	68	19	34	53	18	....	....	....	....	....	....				12	3	8	11	8	....	....	....	
99-2000	Louisville Panthers	AHL	53	8	4	12	8	....	....	....	....	....	....				4	0	0	0	0	....	....	....	
	Port Huron	UHL	2	1	1	2	0	....	....	....	....	....	....				....	....	....	....	....				
2000-01	Louisville Panthers	AHL	23	1	2	3	25	....	....	....	....	....	....				....	....	....	....	....				
2001-02	**Florida**	**NHL**	15	0	0	0	0	0	0	0	2	0.0	-1	53	47.2	4:09	....	....	....	....	....				
	Bridgeport	AHL	22	3	6	9	4	....	....	....	....	....	....				....	....	....	....	....				
	Saint John Flames	AHL	41	8	9	17	10	....	....	....	....	....	....				....	....	....	....	....				
2002-03	Cincinnati	AHL	79	12	26	38	28	....	....	....	....	....	....				....	....	....	....	....				
2003-04	Cincinnati	AHL	67	4	11	15	66	....	....	....	....	....	....				3	0	1	1	0	....	....	....	
2004-05					DID NOT PLAY												....	....	....	....	....				
	NHL Totals		15	0	0	0	0	0	0	0	2	0.0		53	47.2	4:09	....	....	....	....	....				

• Missed majority of 2000-01 season recovering from knee injury suffered in training camp, September 25, 2000. Signed as a free agent by **Anaheim**, August 22, 2002.

SMITH, Wyatt (SMIHTH, WIGH-uht) NYI

Center. Shoots left. 5'11", 200 lbs.   Born, Thief River Falls, MN, February 13, 1977. Phoenix's 6th choice, 233rd overall, in 1997 Entry Draft.

Season	Club	League	GP	G	A	Pts	PIM	PP	SH	GW	S	%	+/-	TF	F%	Min	GP	G	A	Pts	PIM	PP	SH	GW	Min
1994-95	Warroad Warriors	High-MN	28	29	31	60	28	....	....	....	....	....	....				....	....	....	....	....				
1995-96	U. of Minnesota	WCHA	32	4	5	9	32	....	....	....	....	....	....				....	....	....	....	....				
1996-97	U. of Minnesota	WCHA	38	16	14	30	44	....	....	....	....	....	....				....	....	....	....	....				
1997-98	U. of Minnesota	WCHA	39	24	23	47	62	....	....	....	....	....	....				....	....	....	....	....				
1998-99	U. of Minnesota	WCHA	43	23	20	43	37	....	....	....	....	....	....				....	....	....	....	....				
99-2000	**Phoenix**	**NHL**	2	0	0	0	0	0	0	0	0	0.0	-2	20	30.0	11:39	....	....	....	....	....				
	Springfield	AHL	60	14	26	40	26	....	....	....	....	....	....				5	2	3	5	13	....	....	....	
2000-01	**Phoenix**	**NHL**	42	3	7	10	13	0	1	0	40	7.5	7	335	40.9	12:20	....	....	....	....	....				
	Springfield	AHL	18	5	7	12	11	....	....	....	....	....	....				....	....	....	....	....				
2001-02	**Phoenix**	**NHL**	10	0	0	0	0	0	0	0	4	0.0	-5	81	48.2	10:36	....	....	....	....	....				
	Springfield	AHL	69	23	32	55	69	....	....	....	....	....	....				....	....	....	....	....				
2002-03	**Nashville**	**NHL**	11	1	0	1	0	0	0	0	8	12.5	-1	123	49.6	11:56	....	....	....	....	....				
	Milwaukee	AHL	56	24	27	51	89	....	....	....	....	....	....				4	1	0	1	4	....	....	....	
2003-04	**Nashville**	**NHL**	18	3	1	4	2	0	1	0	21	14.3	2	193	57.0	10:22	....	....	....	....	....				
	Milwaukee	AHL	40	9	7	16	40	....	....	....	....	....	....				22	5	7	12	25	....	....	....	
2004-05	Milwaukee	AHL	69	19	28	47	89	....	....	....	....	....	....				7	1	4	5	10	....	....	....	
	NHL Totals		83	7	8	15	15	0	2	0	73	9.6		752	46.9	11:38	....	....	....	....	....				

Signed as a free agent by **Nashville**, July 15, 2002. Signed as a free agent by **NY Islanders**, August 10, 2005.

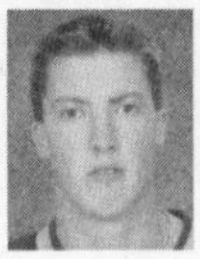

SMITHSON, Jerred

(SMIHTH-suhn, JEHR-rehd) **NSH.**

Center. Shoots right. 6'3", 194 lbs. Born, Vernon, B.C., February 4, 1979.

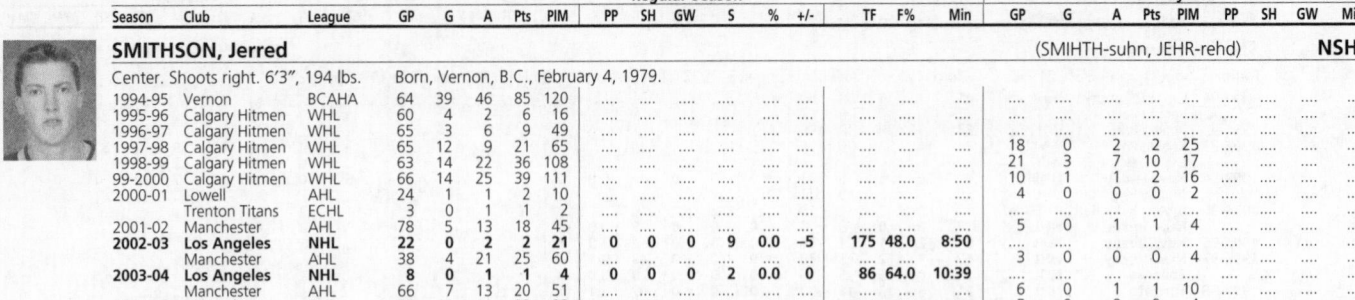

			Regular Season														Playoffs								
Season	Club	League	GP	G	A	Pts	PIM	PP	SH	GW	S	%	+/-	TF	F%	Min	GP	G	A	Pts	PIM	PP	SH	GW	Min
1994-95	Vernon	BCAHA	64	39	46	85	120																		
1995-96	Calgary Hitmen	WHL	60	4	2	6	16																		
1996-97	Calgary Hitmen	WHL	65	3	6	9	49																		
1997-98	Calgary Hitmen	WHL	65	12	9	21	65										18	0	2	2	25				
1998-99	Calgary Hitmen	WHL	63	14	22	36	108										21	3	7	10	17				
99-2000	Calgary Hitmen	WHL	66	14	25	39	111										10	1	1	2	16				
2000-01	Lowell	AHL	24	1	1	2	10										4	0	0	0	2				
	Trenton Titans	ECHL	3	0	1	1	2																		
2001-02	Manchester	AHL	78	5	13	18	45										5	0	1	1	4				
2002-03	**Los Angeles**	**NHL**	**22**	**0**	**2**	**2**	**21**	**0**	**0**	**0**	**9**	**0.0**	**-5**	**175**	**48.0**	**8:50**									
	Manchester	AHL	38	4	21	25	60										3	0	0	0	4				
2003-04	**Los Angeles**	**NHL**	**8**	**0**	**1**	**1**	**4**	**0**	**0**	**0**	**2**	**0.0**	**0**	**86**	**64.0**	**10:39**									
	Manchester	AHL	66	7	13	20	51										6	0	1	1	10				
2004-05	Milwaukee	AHL	80	11	11	22	92										5	0	0	0	4				
	NHL Totals		**30**	**0**	**3**	**3**	**25**	**0**	**0**	**0**	**11**	**0.0**		**261**	**53.3**	**9:19**									

Signed as a free agent by **Los Angeles**, February 18, 2000. Signed as a free agent by **Nashville**, July 22, 2004.

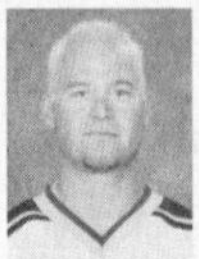

SMOLINSKI, Bryan

(smoh-LIHN-skee, BRIGH-uhn) **OTT.**

Center. Shoots right. 6'1", 208 lbs. Born, Toledo, OH, December 27, 1971. Boston's 1st choice, 21st overall, in 1990 Entry Draft.

Season	Club	League	GP	G	A	Pts	PIM	PP	SH	GW	S	%	+/-	TF	F%	Min	GP	G	A	Pts	PIM	PP	SH	GW	Min
1987-88	Det. Caesars	MNHL	80	43	77	120																			
1988-89	Stratford Cullitons	OHA-B	46	32	62	94	132																		
1989-90	Michigan State	CCHA	35	9	13	22	34																		
1990-91	Michigan State	CCHA	35	9	12	21	24																		
1991-92	Michigan State	CCHA	41	28	33	61	55																		
1992-93	Michigan State	CCHA	40	31	37	*68	93																		
	Boston	**NHL**	**9**	**1**	**3**	**4**	**0**	**0**	**0**	**0**	**10**	**10.0**	**3**				**4**	**1**	**0**	**1**	**2**	**0**	**0**	**0**	
1993-94	**Boston**	**NHL**	**83**	**31**	**20**	**51**	**82**	**4**	**3**	**5**	**179**	**17.3**	**4**				**13**	**5**	**4**	**9**	**4**	**2**	**0**	**0**	
1994-95	**Boston**	**NHL**	**44**	**18**	**13**	**31**	**31**	**6**	**0**	**5**	**121**	**14.9**	**-3**				**5**	**0**	**1**	**1**	**4**	**0**	**0**	**0**	
1995-96	**Pittsburgh**	**NHL**	**81**	**24**	**40**	**64**	**69**	**8**	**2**	**1**	**229**	**10.5**	**6**				**18**	**5**	**4**	**9**	**10**	**0**	**0**	**1**	
1996-97	Detroit Vipers	IHL	6	5	7	12	10																		
	NY Islanders	**NHL**	**64**	**28**	**28**	**56**	**25**	**9**	**0**	**1**	**183**	**15.3**	**9**												
1997-98	**NY Islanders**	**NHL**	**81**	**13**	**30**	**43**	**34**	**3**	**0**	**4**	**203**	**6.4**	**-16**												
1998-99	**NY Islanders**	**NHL**	**82**	**16**	**24**	**40**	**49**	**7**	**0**	**3**	**223**	**7.2**	**-7**	**1011**	**48.3**	**19:19**									
99-2000	**Los Angeles**	**NHL**	**79**	**20**	**36**	**56**	**48**	**2**	**0**	**0**	**160**	**12.5**	**2**	**1545**	**50.9**	**18:35**	**4**	**0**	**0**	**0**	**2**	**0**	**0**	**0**	**18:22**
2000-01	**Los Angeles**	**NHL**	**78**	**27**	**32**	**59**	**40**	**5**	**3**	**5**	**183**	**14.8**	**10**	**952**	**48.7**	**18:32**	**13**	**1**	**5**	**6**	**14**	**0**	**0**	**0**	**20:35**
2001-02	**Los Angeles**	**NHL**	**80**	**13**	**25**	**38**	**56**	**4**	**1**	**0**	**187**	**7.0**	**7**	**1316**	**45.7**	**19:23**	**7**	**2**	**0**	**2**	**2**	**1**	**0**	**0**	**18:15**
2002-03	**Los Angeles**	**NHL**	**58**	**18**	**20**	**38**	**18**	**6**	**1**	**8**	**150**	**12.0**	**-1**	**831**	**46.3**	**19:02**									
	Ottawa	**NHL**	**10**	**3**	**5**	**8**	**2**	**0**	**0**	**0**	**26**	**11.5**	**1**	**127**	**46.5**	**15:42**	**18**	**2**	**7**	**9**	**6**	**0**	**0**	**0**	**15:21**
2003-04	**Ottawa**	**NHL**	**80**	**19**	**27**	**46**	**49**	**4**	**0**	**3**	**182**	**10.4**	**22**	**880**	**44.7**	**16:39**	**7**	**1**	**1**	**2**	**4**	**0**	**0**	**0**	**16:04**
2004-05	Motor City	UHL	21	9	23	32	18																		
	NHL Totals		**829**	**231**	**303**	**534**	**503**	**58**	**10**	**35**	**2036**	**11.3**		**6662**	**47.7**	**18:30**	**89**	**17**	**22**	**39**	**48**	**3**	**0**	**1**	**17:30**

CCHA First All-Star Team (1993) • NCAA West First All-American Team (1993)

Traded to **Pittsburgh** by **Boston** with Glen Murray and Boston's 3rd round choice (Boyd Kane) in 1996 Entry Draft for Kevin Stevens and Shawn McEachern, August 2, 1995. Traded to **NY Islanders** by **Pittsburgh** for Darius Kasparaitis and Andreas Johansson, November 17, 1996. Traded to **Los Angeles** by **NY Islanders** with Ziggy Palffy, Marcel Cousineau and New Jersey's 4th round choice (previously acquired, Los Angeles selected Daniel Johansson) in 1999 Entry Draft for Olli Jokinen, Josh Green, Mathieu Biron and Los Angeles' 1st round choice (Taylor Pyatt) in 1999 Entry Draft, June 20, 1999. Traded to **Ottawa** by **Los Angeles** for the rights to Tim Gleason and future considerations, March 11, 2003. Signed as a free agent by **Motor City** (UHL), February 11, 2005.

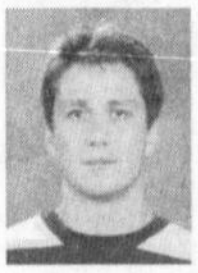

SMREK, Peter

(SMUHR-ehk, PEE-tuhr)

Defense. Shoots left. 6'1", 215 lbs. Born, Martin, Czech., February 16, 1979. St. Louis' 2nd choice, 85th overall, in 1999 Entry Draft.

Season	Club	League	GP	G	A	Pts	PIM	PP	SH	GW	S	%	+/-	TF	F%	Min	GP	G	A	Pts	PIM	PP	SH	GW	Min
1996-97	Martin	Slovakia	12	1	0	1											3	0	0	0					
1997-98	Martin Jr.	Slovak-Jr.	19	7	6	13	32																		
	Martin	Slovakia	23	0	5	5	24										1	0	0	0	0				
1998-99	Des Moines	USHL	52	6	26	32	59										14	2	7	9	8				
99-2000	Peoria Rivermen	ECHL	4	1	1	2	2																		
	Worcester IceCats	AHL	64	5	19	24	26										2	0	0	0	4				
2000-01	**St. Louis**	**NHL**	**6**	**2**	**0**	**2**	**2**	**0**	**0**	**1**	**5**	**40.0**	**1**	**0**	**0.0**	**13:01**									
	Worcester IceCats	AHL	50	2	7	9	71																		
	NY Rangers	**NHL**	**14**	**0**	**3**	**3**	**12**	**0**	**0**	**0**	**9**	**0.0**	**1**	**0**	**0.0**	**16:47**									
	Hartford	AHL															5	0	2	2	2				
2001-02	**NY Rangers**	**NHL**	**8**	**0**	**1**	**1**	**4**	**0**	**0**	**0**	**2**	**0.0**	**-7**	**0**	**0.0**	**14:28**									
	Hartford	AHL	50	2	5	7	36																		
	Slovakia	Olympics	4	0	0	0	0																		
	Milwaukee	AHL	8	0	2	2	4																		
2002-03	Milwaukee	AHL	68	3	20	23	70										5	0	0	0	0				
2003-04	Binghamton	AHL	80	5	18	23	91										2	0	0	0	4				
2004-05	Wolfsburg	Germany	51	13	14	27	70										7	0	2	2	6				
	NHL Totals		**28**	**2**	**4**	**6**	**18**	**0**	**0**	**1**	**16**	**12.5**		**0**	**0.0**	**15:19**									

Traded to **NY Rangers** by **St. Louis** for Alexei Gusarov, March 5, 2001. Traded to **Nashville** by **NY Rangers** for Richard Lintner, March 19, 2002. Traded to **Ottawa** by **Nashville** for Chris Bala, June 26, 2003. Signed as a free agent by **Wolfsburg** (Germany), May 7, 2004.

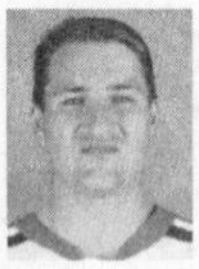

SMYTH, Brad

(SMIHTH, BRAD) **L.A.**

Right wing. Shoots right. 6', 200 lbs. Born, Ottawa, Ont., March 13, 1973.

Season	Club	League	GP	G	A	Pts	PIM	PP	SH	GW	S	%	+/-	TF	F%	Min	GP	G	A	Pts	PIM	PP	SH	GW	Min
1989-90	Nepean	OMHA	55	53	36	89	105																		
1990-91	London Knights	OHL	29	2	6	8	22																		
1991-92	London Knights	OHL	58	17	18	35	93										10	2	0	2	8				
1992-93	London Knights	OHL	66	54	55	109	118										12	7	8	15	25				
1993-94	Cincinnati	IHL	30	7	3	10	54																		
	Birmingham Bulls	ECHL	29	26	30	56	38										10	8	8	16	19				
1994-95	Springfield	AHL	3	0	0	0	7																		
	Birmingham Bulls	ECHL	36	33	35	68	52										3	5	2	7	0				
	Cincinnati	IHL	26	2	11	13	34										1	0	0	0	2				
1995-96	**Florida**	**NHL**	**7**	**1**	**1**	**2**	**4**	**1**	**0**	**0**	**12**	**8.3**	**-3**												
	Carolina Panthers	AHL	68	*68	58	*126	80																		
1996-97	**Florida**	**NHL**	**8**	**1**	**0**	**1**	**2**	**0**	**0**	**0**	**10**	**10.0**	**-3**												
	Los Angeles	**NHL**	**44**	**8**	**8**	**16**	**74**	**0**	**0**	**1**	**74**	**10.8**	**-7**												
	Phoenix	IHL	3	5	2	7	0																		
1997-98	**Los Angeles**	**NHL**	**9**	**1**	**3**	**4**	**4**	**0**	**0**	**0**	**12**	**8.3**	**-1**												
	NY Rangers	**NHL**	**1**	**0**	**0**	**0**	**0**	**0**	**0**	**0**	**1**	**0.0**	**0**												
	Hartford	AHL	57	29	33	62	79										15	12	8	20	11				
1998-99	**Nashville**	**NHL**	**3**	**0**	**0**	**0**	**6**	**0**	**0**	**0**	**5**	**0.0**	**-1**	**0**	**0.0**	**9:54**									
	Milwaukee	IHL	34	11	16	27	21																		
	Hartford	AHL	36	25	19	44	48										7	6	0	6	14				
99-2000	Hartford	AHL	80	39	37	76	62										23	*13	10	23	8				
2000-01	**NY Rangers**	**NHL**	**4**	**1**	**0**	**1**	**4**	**0**	**0**	**0**	**10**	**10.0**	**0**	**0**	**0.0**	**13:57**									
	Hartford	AHL	77	*50	29	79	110										5	2	3	5	8				
2001-02	Hartford	AHL	79	34	48	82	90										10	3	8	11	14				
2002-03	**Ottawa**	**NHL**	**12**	**3**	**1**	**4**	**15**	**2**	**0**	**0**	**16**	**18.8**	**-2**	**2**	**0.0**	**9:30**									
	Binghamton	AHL	69	24	32	56	77										14	7	6	13	12				

			Regular Season														Playoffs								
Season	Club	League	GP	G	A	Pts	PIM	PP	SH	GW	S	%	+/-	TF	F%	Min	GP	G	A	Pts	PIM	PP	SH	GW	Min
2003-04	Karpat Oulu	Finland	48	20	18	38	85	....	....	....	....	....	....	....	....	....	15	3	5	8	4	....	....	....	....
2004-05	Manchester	AHL	61	23	33	56	74	....	....	....	....	....	....	....	....	....	6	2	1	3	4	....	....	....	....
	NHL Totals		**88**	**15**	**13**	**28**	**109**	**3**	**0**	**1**	**140**	**10.7**		**2**	**0.0**	**10:30**	....	....	....	....	....	....	....	....	....

AHL First All-Star Team (1996, 2001, 2002) • John B. Sollenberger Trophy (Leading Scorer – AHL) (1996) • Les Cunningham Award (MVP – AHL) (1996)

Signed as a free agent by **Florida**, October 4, 1993. Traded to **Los Angeles** by **Florida** for Los Angeles' 3rd round choice (Vratislav Cech) in 1997 Entry Draft, November 28, 1996. Traded to **NY Rangers** by **Los Angeles** for future considerations, November 14, 1997. Signed as a free agent by **Nashville**, July 16, 1998. Traded to **NY Rangers** by **Nashville** for future considerations, May 3, 1999. Signed as a free agent by **Ottawa**, August 1, 2002. Signed as a free agent by **Karpat** (Finland), October 1, 2003. Signed as a free agent by **Los Angeles**, July 16, 2004.

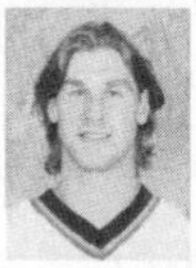

SMYTH, Ryan
(SMIHTH, RIGH-uhn) **EDM.**

Left wing. Shoots left. 6'1", 190 lbs. Born, Banff, Alta., February 21, 1976. Edmonton's 2nd choice, 6th overall, in 1994 Entry Draft.

Season	Club	League	GP	G	A	Pts	PIM	PP	SH	GW	S	%	+/-	TF	F%	Min	GP	G	A	Pts	PIM	PP	SH	GW	Min
1990-91	Banff Blazers	ABHL	25	100	50	150	....	....	....	....	....	....	....	....	....	....	....	....	....	....	....	....	....	....	....
	Lethbridge	AMHL	34	8	21	29	....	....	....	....	....	....	....	....	....	....	....	....	....	....	....	....	....	....	....
1991-92	Caronport	SMHL	35	55	61	116	98	....	....	....	....	....	....	....	....	....	....	....	....	....	....	....	....	....	....
	Moose Jaw	WHL	2	0	0	0	0	....	....	....	....	....	....	....	....	....	....	....	....	....	....	....	....	....	....
1992-93	Moose Jaw	WHL	64	19	14	33	59	....	....	....	....	....	....	....	....	....	....	....	....	....	....	....	....	....	....
1993-94	Moose Jaw	WHL	72	50	55	105	88	....	....	....	....	....	....	....	....	....	....	....	....	....	....	....	....	....	....
1994-95	Moose Jaw	WHL	50	41	45	86	66	....	....	....	....	....	....	....	....	....	10	6	9	15	22	....	....	....	....
	Edmonton	**NHL**	**3**	**0**	**0**	**0**	**0**	**0**	**0**	**0**	**2**	**0.0**	**–1**	....	....	....	....	....	....	....	....	....	....	....	....
1995-96	**Edmonton**	**NHL**	**48**	**2**	**9**	**11**	**28**	**1**	**0**	**0**	**65**	**3.1**	**–10**	....	....	....	....	....	....	....	....	....	....	....	....
	Cape Breton	AHL	9	6	5	11	4	....	....	....	....	....	....	....	....	....	....	....	....	....	....	....	....	....	....
1996-97	**Edmonton**	**NHL**	**82**	**39**	**22**	**61**	**76**	**20**	**0**	**4**	**265**	**14.7**	**–7**	....	....	....	**12**	**5**	**5**	**10**	**12**	**1**	**0**	**2**	....
1997-98	**Edmonton**	**NHL**	**65**	**20**	**13**	**33**	**44**	**10**	**0**	**2**	**205**	**9.8**	**–24**	....	....	....	**12**	**1**	**3**	**4**	**16**	**1**	**0**	**0**	....
1998-99	**Edmonton**	**NHL**	**71**	**13**	**18**	**31**	**62**	**6**	**0**	**2**	**161**	**8.1**	**0**	**5**	**20.0**	**14:26**	**3**	**3**	**0**	**3**	**0**	**2**	**0**	**0**	**24:35**
99-2000	**Edmonton**	**NHL**	**82**	**28**	**26**	**54**	**58**	**11**	**0**	**4**	**238**	**11.8**	**–2**	**24**	**54.2**	**19:12**	**5**	**1**	**0**	**1**	**6**	**0**	**1**	**0**	**19:18**
2000-01	**Edmonton**	**NHL**	**82**	**31**	**39**	**70**	**58**	**11**	**0**	**6**	**245**	**12.7**	**10**	**17**	**35.3**	**19:58**	**6**	**3**	**4**	**7**	**4**	**0**	**0**	**0**	**24:46**
2001-02	**Edmonton**	**NHL**	**61**	**15**	**35**	**50**	**48**	**7**	**1**	**5**	**150**	**10.0**	**7**	**12**	**41.7**	**19:27**	....	....	....	....	....	....	....	....	....
	Canada	Olympics	6	0	1	1	0	....	....	....	....	....	....	....	....	....	....	....	....	....	....	....	....	....	....
2002-03	**Edmonton**	**NHL**	**66**	**27**	**34**	**61**	**67**	**10**	**0**	**3**	**199**	**13.6**	**5**	**42**	**42.9**	**19:21**	**6**	**2**	**0**	**2**	**16**	**0**	**1**	**0**	**17:39**
2003-04	**Edmonton**	**NHL**	**82**	**23**	**36**	**59**	**70**	**8**	**2**	**6**	**245**	**9.4**	**11**	**484**	**47.1**	**19:39**	....	....	....	....	....	....	....	....	....
2004-05		DID NOT PLAY																							
	NHL Totals		**642**	**198**	**232**	**430**	**511**	**84**	**3**	**32**	**1775**	**11.2**		**584**	**46.4**	**18:43**	**44**	**15**	**12**	**27**	**54**	**4**	**2**	**2**	**21:15**

WHL East Second All-Star Team (1995)

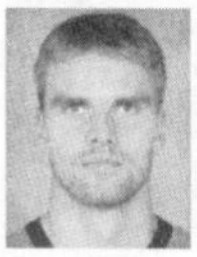

SOMIK, Radovan
(SAW-mihk, RAH-doh-vahn)

Right wing. Shoots right. 6'2", 194 lbs. Born, Martin, Czech., May 5, 1977. Philadelphia's 3rd choice, 100th overall, in 1995 Entry Draft.

Season	Club	League	GP	G	A	Pts	PIM	PP	SH	GW	S	%	+/-	TF	F%	Min	GP	G	A	Pts	PIM	PP	SH	GW	Min
1993-94	Martin	Slovakia	1	0	0	0	0	....	....	....	....	....	....	....	....	....	....	....	....	....	....	....	....	....	....
1994-95	Martin	Slovakia	25	3	0	3	39	....	....	....	....	....	....	....	....	....	3	1	0	1	2	....	....	....	....
1995-96	Martin	Slovakia	25	3	6	9	8	....	....	....	....	....	....	....	....	....	9	1	0	1	....	....	....	....	....
1996-97	Martin	Slovakia	35	3	5	8	....	....	....	....	....	....	....	....	....	....	3	0	0	0	....	....	....	....	....
1997-98	Martin	Slovakia	26	6	9	15	10	....	....	....	....	....	....	....	....	....	3	0	0	0	0	....	....	....	....
1998-99	Dukla Trencin	Slovakia	26	1	4	5	6	....	....	....	....	....	....	....	....	....	....	....	....	....	....	....	....	....	....
99-2000	Martin	Slovak-2	40	38	28	66	32	....	....	....	....	....	....	....	....	....	....	....	....	....	....	....	....	....	....
2000-01	Zlin	CzRep	46	15	10	25	22	....	....	....	....	....	....	....	....	....	6	1	0	1	0	....	....	....	....
2001-02	Zlin	CzRep	37	14	14	28	22	....	....	....	....	....	....	....	....	....	11	4	3	7	37	....	....	....	....
2002-03	**Philadelphia**	**NHL**	**60**	**8**	**10**	**18**	**10**	**0**	**1**	**2**	**95**	**8.4**	**9**	**20**	**35.0**	**15:49**	**5**	**1**	**1**	**2**	**6**	**0**	**0**	**0**	**11:39**
2003-04	**Philadelphia**	**NHL**	**53**	**4**	**10**	**14**	**17**	**0**	**0**	**0**	**41**	**9.8**	**–2**	**32**	**59.4**	**11:01**	**10**	**1**	**1**	**2**	**4**	**0**	**0**	**0**	**8:08**
	Philadelphia	AHL	1	0	0	0	2	....	....	....	....	....	....	....	....	....	....	....	....	....	....	....	....	....	....
2004-05	MHC Martin	Slovak-2	2	1	0	1	0	....	....	....	....	....	....	....	....	....	....	....	....	....	....	....	....	....	....
	HC Vsetin	CzRep	31	7	16	23	24	....	....	....	....	....	....	....	....	....	....	....	....	....	....	....	....	....	....
	Malmo	Sweden	8	1	0	1	6	....	....	....	....	....	....	....	....	....	....	....	....	....	....	....	....	....	....
	Malmo	Sweden-Q	10	1	3	4	2	....	....	....	....	....	....	....	....	....	....	....	....	....	....	....	....	....	....
	NHL Totals		**113**	**12**	**20**	**32**	**27**	**0**	**1**	**2**	**136**	**8.8**		**52**	**50.0**	**13:34**	**15**	**2**	**2**	**4**	**10**	**0**	**0**	**0**	**9:18**

Signed as a free agent by **Martin** (Slovak-2), October 2, 2004. Signed as a free agent by **Vsetin** (CzRep), October 7, 2004. Signed as a free agent by **Malmo** (Sweden), January 28, 2005.

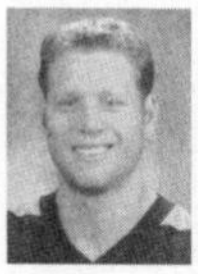

SONNENBERG, Martin
(SOHN-nehn-BUHRG, MAHR-tihn) **PHX.**

Left wing. Shoots left. 6', 197 lbs. Born, Wetaskiwin, Alta., January 23, 1978.

Season	Club	League	GP	G	A	Pts	PIM	PP	SH	GW	S	%	+/-	TF	F%	Min	GP	G	A	Pts	PIM	PP	SH	GW	Min
1994-95	Leduc Oil Barons	AMHL	35	28	40	68	34	....	....	....	....	....	....	....	....	....	....	....	....	....	....	....	....	....	....
1995-96	Saskatoon Blades	WHL	58	8	7	15	24	....	....	....	....	....	....	....	....	....	3	0	0	0	2	....	....	....	....
1996-97	Saskatoon Blades	WHL	72	38	26	64	79	....	....	....	....	....	....	....	....	....	....	....	....	....	....	....	....	....	....
1997-98	Saskatoon Blades	WHL	72	40	52	92	87	....	....	....	....	....	....	....	....	....	6	1	3	4	9	....	....	....	....
1998-99	**Pittsburgh**	**NHL**	**44**	**1**	**1**	**2**	**19**	**0**	**0**	**0**	**12**	**8.3**	**–2**	**2**	**0.0**	**4:00**	**7**	**0**	**0**	**0**	**0**	**0**	**0**	**0**	**3:03**
	Syracuse Crunch	AHL	36	15	9	24	31	....	....	....	....	....	....	....	....	....	....	....	....	....	....	....	....	....	....
99-2000	**Pittsburgh**	**NHL**	**14**	**1**	**2**	**3**	**0**	**1**	**0**	**0**	**19**	**5.3**	**0**	**7**	**28.6**	**7:26**	....	....	....	....	....	....	....	....	....
	Wilkes-Barre	AHL	62	20	33	53	109	....	....	....	....	....	....	....	....	....	....	....	....	....	....	....	....	....	....
2000-01	Wilkes-Barre	AHL	73	14	18	32	89	....	....	....	....	....	....	....	....	....	21	4	3	7	6	....	....	....	....
2001-02	Wilkes-Barre	AHL	78	20	30	50	127	....	....	....	....	....	....	....	....	....	....	....	....	....	....	....	....	....	....
2002-03	Saint John Flames	AHL	54	11	10	21	63	....	....	....	....	....	....	....	....	....	....	....	....	....	....	....	....	....	....
2003-04	**Calgary**	**NHL**	**5**	**0**	**0**	**0**	**2**	**0**	**0**	**0**	**7**	**0.0**	**–2**	**5**	**80.0**	**8:51**	....	....	....	....	....	....	....	....	....
	Lowell	AHL	48	20	22	42	46	....	....	....	....	....	....	....	....	....	....	....	....	....	....	....	....	....	....
2004-05	Utah Grizzlies	AHL	65	13	13	26	94	....	....	....	....	....	....	....	....	....	....	....	....	....	....	....	....	....	....
	NHL Totals		**63**	**2**	**3**	**5**	**21**	**1**	**0**	**0**	**38**	**5.3**		**14**	**42.9**	**5:09**	**7**	**0**	**0**	**0**	**0**	**0**	**0**	**0**	**3:03**

Signed as a free agent by **Pittsburgh**, October 9, 1998. Signed as a free agent by **Calgary**, July 9, 2002. Signed as a free agent by **Phoenix**, September 2, 2004.

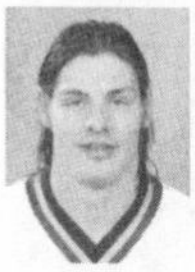

SOPEL, Brent
(SOH-puhl, BREHNT) **NYI**

Defense. Shoots right. 6'1", 205 lbs. Born, Calgary, Alta., January 7, 1977. Vancouver's 6th choice, 144th overall, in 1995 Entry Draft.

Season	Club	League	GP	G	A	Pts	PIM	PP	SH	GW	S	%	+/-	TF	F%	Min	GP	G	A	Pts	PIM	PP	SH	GW	Min
1992-93	Sask. Legion	SMHL	36	7	17	24	95	....	....	....	....	....	....	....	....	....	....	....	....	....	....	....	....	....	....
1993-94	Saskatoon Blazers	SMHL	34	9	30	39	180	....	....	....	....	....	....	....	....	....	....	....	....	....	....	....	....	....	....
	Saskatoon Blades	WHL	11	2	2	4	2	....	....	....	....	....	....	....	....	....	....	....	....	....	....	....	....	....	....
1994-95	Saskatoon Blades	WHL	22	1	10	11	31	....	....	....	....	....	....	....	....	....	....	....	....	....	....	....	....	....	....
	Swift Current	WHL	41	4	19	23	50	....	....	....	....	....	....	....	....	....	3	0	3	3	0	....	....	....	....
1995-96	Swift Current	WHL	71	13	48	61	87	....	....	....	....	....	....	....	....	....	6	1	2	3	4	....	....	....	....
	Syracuse Crunch	AHL	1	0	0	0	0	....	....	....	....	....	....	....	....	....	....	....	....	....	....	....	....	....	....
1996-97	Swift Current	WHL	62	15	41	56	109	....	....	....	....	....	....	....	....	....	10	5	11	16	32	....	....	....	....
	Syracuse Crunch	AHL	2	0	0	0	0	....	....	....	....	....	....	....	....	....	3	0	0	0	0	....	....	....	....
1997-98	Syracuse Crunch	AHL	76	10	33	43	70	....	....	....	....	....	....	....	....	....	5	0	7	7	12	....	....	....	....
1998-99	**Vancouver**	**NHL**	**5**	**1**	**0**	**1**	**4**	**1**	**0**	**0**	**5**	**20.0**	**–1**	**0**	**0.0**	**11:58**	....	....	....	....	....	....	....	....	....
	Syracuse Crunch	AHL	53	10	21	31	59	....	....	....	....	....	....	....	....	....	....	....	....	....	....	....	....	....	....
99-2000	**Vancouver**	**NHL**	**18**	**2**	**4**	**6**	**12**	**0**	**0**	**1**	**11**	**18.2**	**9**	**0**	**0.0**	**10:31**	....	....	....	....	....	....	....	....	....
	Syracuse Crunch	AHL	50	6	25	31	67	....	....	....	....	....	....	....	....	....	4	0	2	2	8	....	....	....	....
2000-01	**Vancouver**	**NHL**	**52**	**4**	**10**	**14**	**10**	**0**	**0**	**1**	**57**	**7.0**	**4**	**0**	**0.0**	**16:01**	**4**	**0**	**0**	**0**	**2**	**0**	**0**	**0**	**19:05**
	Kansas City	IHL	4	0	1	1	0	....	....	....	....	....	....	....	....	....	....	....	....	....	....	....	....	....	....
2001-02	**Vancouver**	**NHL**	**66**	**8**	**17**	**25**	**44**	**1**	**0**	**3**	**116**	**6.9**	**21**	**0**	**0.0**	**19:01**	**6**	**0**	**2**	**2**	**2**	**0**	**0**	**0**	**24:45**
2002-03	**Vancouver**	**NHL**	**81**	**7**	**30**	**37**	**23**	**6**	**0**	**1**	**167**	**4.2**	**–15**	**0**	**0.0**	**21:42**	**14**	**2**	**6**	**8**	**4**	**1**	**0**	**1**	**22:33**
2003-04	**Vancouver**	**NHL**	**80**	**10**	**32**	**42**	**36**	**6**	**0**	**2**	**173**	**5.8**	**11**	**0**	**0.0**	**21:56**	**7**	**0**	**1**	**1**	**0**	**0**	**0**	**0**	**23:55**
2004-05		DID NOT PLAY																							
	NHL Totals		**302**	**32**	**93**	**125**	**129**	**14**	**0**	**8**	**529**	**6.0**		**0**	**0.0**	**19:22**	**31**	**2**	**9**	**11**	**8**	**1**	**0**	**1**	**22:50**

Traded to **NY Islanders** by **Vancouver** for a conditional choice in 2006 Entry Draft, August 3, 2005.

						Regular Season														Playoffs						
Season	Club	League	GP	G	A	Pts	PIM	PP	SH	GW	S	%	+/-	TF	F%	Min	GP	G	A	Pts	PIM	PP	SH	GW	Min

SOURAY, Sheldon

(SUHR-ee, SHEHL-dohn) **MTL.**

Defense. Shoots left. 6'4", 227 lbs. Born, Elk Point, Alta., July 13, 1976. New Jersey's 3rd choice, 71st overall, in 1994 Entry Draft.

Season	Club	League	GP	G	A	Pts	PIM	PP	SH	GW	S	%	+/-	TF	F%	Min	GP	G	A	Pts	PIM	PP	SH	GW	Min
1990-91	Bonnyville Sabres	AAHA	30	15	20	35	100	....	....	....	....	....	....			....	....	....	....	....	....	....	....	....	....
1991-92	Quesnel	BCAHA	20	5	15	20	200	....	....	....	....	....	....			....	....	....	....	....	....	....	....	....	....
	Alberta Cycle	AMHL	11	0	5	5	67	....	....	....	....	....	....			....	....	....	....	....	....	....	....	....	....
1992-93	Ft. Saskatchewan	AJHL	35	0	12	12	125	....	....	....	....	....	....			....	....	....	....	....	....	....	....	....	....
	Tri-City	WHL	2	0	0	0	0	....	....	....	....	....	....			....	....	....	....	....	....	....	....	....	....
1993-94	Tri-City	WHL	42	3	6	9	122	....	....	....	....	....	....			....	....	....	....	....	....	....	....	....	....
1994-95	Tri-City	WHL	40	2	24	26	140	....	....	....	....	....	....			....	....	....	....	....	....	....	....	....	....
	Prince George	WHL	11	2	3	5	23	....	....	....	....	....	....			....	....	....	....	....	....	....	....	....	....
	Albany River Rats	AHL	7	0	2	2	8	....	....	....	....	....	....			....	....	....	....	....	....	....	....	....	....
1995-96	Prince George	WHL	32	9	18	27	91	....	....	....	....	....	....			....	....	....	....	....	....	....	....	....	....
	Kelowna Rockets	WHL	27	7	20	27	94	....	....	....	....	....	....			....	6	0	5	5	2	....	....	....	....
	Albany River Rats	AHL	6	0	2	2	12	....	....	....	....	....	....			....	4	0	1	1	4	....	....	....	....
1996-97	Albany River Rats	AHL	70	2	11	13	160	....	....	....	....	....	....			....	16	2	3	5	47	....	....	....	....
1997-98	**New Jersey**	**NHL**	60	3	7	10	85	0	0	1	74	4.1	18	0	0.0		3	0	1	1	2	0	0	0	
	Albany River Rats	AHL	6	0	0	0	8	....	....	....	....	....	....			....	....	....	....	....	....	....	....	....	....
1998-99	**New Jersey**	**NHL**	70	1	7	8	110	0	0	0	101	1.0	5	0	0.0	14:56	2	0	1	1	0	0	0	0	12:57
99-2000	**New Jersey**	**NHL**	52	0	8	8	70	0	0	0	74	0.0	−6	0	0.0	17:12	....	....	....	....	....	....	....	....	....
	Montreal	**NHL**	19	3	0	3	44	0	0	0	39	7.7	7	0	0.0	19:18	....	....	....	....	....	....	....	....	....
2000-01	**Montreal**	**NHL**	52	3	8	11	95	0	0	2	103	2.9	−11	0	0.0	20:36	....	....	....	....	....	....	....	....	....
2001-02	**Montreal**	**NHL**	34	3	5	8	62	1	0	0	56	5.4	−5	1100.0		18:11	12	0	1	1	16	0	0	0	19:01
2002-03	**Montreal**	**NHL**				DID NOT PLAY – INJURED											....	....	....	....	....	....	....	....	....
2003-04	**Montreal**	**NHL**	63	15	20	35	104	6	1	3	186	8.1	4	0	0.0	23:26	11	0	2	2	39	0	0	0	23:55
2004-05	Farjestad	Sweden	39	9	8	17	117	....	....	....	....	....	....			....	15	1	6	7	77	....	....	....	....
	NHL Totals		350	28	55	83	570	7	1	6	633	4.4		1100.0		18:52	28	0	5	5	57	0	0	0	20:41

WHL West Second All-Star Team (1996)
Played in NHL All-Star Game (2004)
Traded to **Montreal** by **New Jersey** with Josh DeWolf and New Jersey's 2nd round choice (later traded to Washington – later traded to Tampa Bay – Tampa Bay selected Andreas Holmqvist) in 2001 Entry Draft for Vladimir Malakhov, March 1, 2000. • Missed remainder of 2001-02 season and entire 2002-03 season recovering from wrist injury suffered in game vs. Tampa Bay, November 17, 2001. Signed as a free agent by **Farjestad** (Sweden), September 22, 2004.

SPACEK, Jaroslav

(SPAH-chehk, YA-roh-slahv) **CHI.**

Defense. Shoots left. 5'11", 206 lbs. Born, Rokycany, Czech., February 11, 1974. Florida's 5th choice, 117th overall, in 1998 Entry Draft.

Season	Club	League	GP	G	A	Pts	PIM	PP	SH	GW	S	%	+/-	TF	F%	Min	GP	G	A	Pts	PIM	PP	SH	GW	Min
1992-93	HC Skoda Plzen	Czech	16	1	3	4	....	....	....	....	....	....	....			....	....	....	....	....	....	....	....	....	....
1993-94	HC Skoda Plzen	CzRep	34	2	6	8	....	....	....	....	....	....	....			....	....	....	....	....	....	....	....	....	....
1994-95	Plzen	CzRep	38	4	8	12	14	....	....	....	....	....	....			....	3	1	0	1	2	....	....	....	....
1995-96	HC ZKZ Plzen	CzRep	40	3	10	13	42	....	....	....	....	....	....			....	3	0	1	1	4	....	....	....	....
1996-97	HC ZKZ Plzen	CzRep	52	9	29	38	44	....	....	....	....	....	....			....	....	....	....	....	....	....	....	....	....
1997-98	Farjestad	Sweden	45	10	16	26	63	....	....	....	....	....	....			....	12	2	5	7	14	....	....	....	....
	Farjestad	EuroHL	6	2	3	5	2	....	....	....	....	....	....			....	....	....	....	....	....	....	....	....	....
1998-99	**Florida**	**NHL**	63	3	12	15	28	2	1	0	92	3.3	15	1100.0		19:27	....	....	....	....	....	....	....	....	....
	New Haven	AHL	14	4	8	12	15	....	....	....	....	....	....			....	....	....	....	....	....	....	....	....	....
99-2000	**Florida**	**NHL**	82	10	26	36	53	4	0	1	111	9.0	7	1	0.0	22:40	4	0	0	0	0	0	0	0	20:29
2000-01	**Florida**	**NHL**	12	2	1	3	8	1	0	0	21	9.5	−4	0	0.0	19:12	....	....	....	....	....	....	....	....	....
	Chicago	**NHL**	50	5	18	23	20	2	0	1	85	5.9	7	0	0.0	21:31	....	....	....	....	....	....	....	....	....
2001-02	**Chicago**	**NHL**	60	3	10	13	29	0	0	1	64	4.7	5	0	0.0	16:25	....	....	....	....	....	....	....	....	....
	Czech Republic	Olympics	4	0	0	0	0	....	....	....	....	....	....			....	....	....	....	....	....	....	....	....	....
	Columbus	**NHL**	14	2	3	5	24	1	1	1	29	6.9	−9	0	0.0	23:35	....	....	....	....	....	....	....	....	....
2002-03	**Columbus**	**NHL**	81	9	36	45	70	5	0	1	166	5.4	−23	0	0.0	24:47	....	....	....	....	....	....	....	....	....
2003-04	**Columbus**	**NHL**	58	5	17	22	45	2	1	2	108	4.6	−13	0	0.0	23:26	....	....	....	....	....	....	....	....	....
2004-05	Plzen	CzRep	30	3	8	11	26	....	....	....	....	....	....			....	....	....	....	....	....	....	....	....	....
	HC Slavia Praha	CzRep	17	4	9	13	29	....	....	....	....	....	....			....	7	0	2	2	8	....	....	....	....
	NHL Totals		420	39	123	162	277	17	3	7	676	5.8		2	50.0	21:36	4	0	0	0	0	0	0	0	20:29

Traded to **Chicago** by **Florida** for Anders Eriksson, November 6, 2000. Traded to **Columbus** by **Chicago** with Chicago's 2nd round choice (Dan Fritsche) in 2003 Entry Draft for Lyle Odelein, March 19, 2002. Signed as a free agent by **Plzen** (CzRep), September 17, 2004. Signed as a free agent by **Slavia** (CzRep), January 4, 2005. Signed as a free agent by **Chicago**, August 3, 2005.

SPANHEL, Martin

(SPAN-hehl, MAHR-tihn) **CBJ.**

Left wing. Shoots left. 6'2", 206 lbs. Born, Zlin, Czech., July 1, 1977. Philadelphia's 6th choice, 152nd overall, in 1995 Entry Draft.

Season	Club	League	GP	G	A	Pts	PIM	PP	SH	GW	S	%	+/-	TF	F%	Min	GP	G	A	Pts	PIM	PP	SH	GW	Min
1994-95	AC ZPS Zlin Jr.	CzRep-Jr.	33	25	16	41	0	....	....	....	....	....	....			....	....	....	....	....	....	....	....	....	....
	AC ZPS Zlin	CzRep	1	1	0	1	0	....	....	....	....	....	....			....	....	....	....	....	....	....	....	....	....
1995-96	Lethbridge	WHL	6	1	0	1	0	....	....	....	....	....	....			....	....	....	....	....	....	....	....	....	....
	Moose Jaw	WHL	61	4	12	16	33	....	....	....	....	....	....			....	....	....	....	....	....	....	....	....	....
1996-97	AC ZPS Zlin	CzRep	22	3	6	9	20	....	....	....	....	....	....			....	....	....	....	....	....	....	....	....	....
1997-98	Zlin	CzRep	40	7	9	16	70	....	....	....	....	....	....			....	....	....	....	....	....	....	....	....	....
1998-99	Plzen	CzRep	49	12	12	24	60	....	....	....	....	....	....			....	5	2	1	3	27	....	....	....	....
99-2000	Plzen	CzRep	52	21	27	48	86	....	....	....	....	....	....			....	7	1	4	5	12	....	....	....	....
2000-01	**Columbus**	**NHL**	6	1	0	1	2	0	0	0	8	12.5	−1	1	0.0	12:29	....	....	....	....	....	....	....	....	....
	Syracuse Crunch	AHL	67	11	13	24	75	....	....	....	....	....	....			....	2	0	0	0	8	....	....	....	....
2001-02	**Columbus**	**NHL**	4	1	0	1	2	0	0	0	6	16.7	−2	0	0.0	11:12	....	....	....	....	....	....	....	....	....
	Syracuse Crunch	AHL	50	7	12	19	43	....	....	....	....	....	....			....	8	1	5	6	4	....	....	....	....
2002-03	HC Sparta Praha	CzRep	40	5	5	10	46	....	....	....	....	....	....			....	12	2	2	4	10	....	....	....	....
2003-04	HIFK Helsinki	Finland	36	2	11	13	22	....	....	....	....	....	....			0		....	....	....	....	....	....	....	....	....
	Plzen	CzRep	14	1	2	3	20	....	....	....	....	....	....			....	12	2	2	4	10	....	....	....	....
2004-05	Lillehammer IK	Norway	17	9	8	17	56	....	....	....	....	....	....			....	3	2	1	3	2	....	....	....	....
	NHL Totals		10	2	0	2	4	0	0	0	14	14.3		1	0.0	11:58	....	....	....	....	....	....	....	....	....

Traded to **San Jose** by **Philadelphia** with Philadelphia's 1st round choice (later traded to Buffalo – later traded to Phoenix – Phoenix selected Daniel Briere) in 1996 Entry Draft and Philadelphia's 4th round choice (later traded to Buffalo – Buffalo selected Mike Martone) in 1996 Entry Draft for Pat Falloon, November 16, 1995. Traded to **Buffalo** by **San Jose** with Vaclav Varada and Philadelphia's 1st (previously acquired, later traded to Phoenix – Phoenix selected Daniel Briere) and 4th (previously acquired, Buffalo selected Mike Martone) round choices in 1996 Entry Draft for Doug Bodger, November 16, 1995. Signed as a free agent by **Columbus**, May 30, 2000. Signed as a free agent by **Sparta** (CzRep) with Columbus retaining NHL rights, July 26, 2002. Signed as a free agent by **Lillehammer** (Norway), December 30, 2004.

SPEZZA, Jason

(SPEHT-zah, JAY-suhn) **OTT.**

Center. Shoots right. 6'2", 206 lbs. Born, Mississauga, Ont., June 13, 1983. Ottawa's 1st choice, 2nd overall, in 2001 Entry Draft.

Season	Club	League	GP	G	A	Pts	PIM	PP	SH	GW	S	%	+/-	TF	F%	Min	GP	G	A	Pts	PIM	PP	SH	GW	Min
1997-98	Toronto Marlies	MTHL	54	53	61	114	42	....	....	....	....	....	....			....	....	....	....	....	....	....	....	....	....
1998-99	Brampton	OHL	67	22	49	71	18	....	....	....	....	....	....			....	....	....	....	....	....	....	....	....	....
99-2000	Mississauga	OHL	52	24	37	61	33	....	....	....	....	....	....			....	....	....	....	....	....	....	....	....	....
2000-01	Mississauga	OHL	15	7	23	30	11	....	....	....	....	....	....			....	....	....	....	....	....	....	....	....	....
	Windsor Spitfires	OHL	41	36	50	86	32	....	....	....	....	....	....			....	9	4	5	9	10	....	....	....	....
2001-02	Windsor Spitfires	OHL	27	19	26	45	16	....	....	....	....	....	....			....	11	5	6	11	18	....	....	....	....
	Belleville Bulls	OHL	26	23	37	60	26	....	....	....	....	....	....			....	3	1	0	1	2	....	....	....	....
	Grand Rapids	AHL	....	....	....	....	....	....	....	....	....	....	....			....	3	1	1	2	0	....	....	....	....
2002-03	**Ottawa**	**NHL**	33	7	14	21	8	3	0	0	65	10.8	−3	330	45.8	12:40	3	1	1	2	0	1	0	0	11:34
	Binghamton	AHL	43	22	32	54	71	....	....	....	....	....	....			....	2	1	2	3	4	....	....	....	....
2003-04	**Ottawa**	**NHL**	78	22	33	55	71	5	0	3	142	15.5	22	956	47.7	14:38	3	0	0	0	2	0	0	0	9:44
2004-05	Binghamton	AHL	80	32	*85	*117	50	....	....	....	....	....	....			....	6	1	3	4	6	....	....	....	....
	NHL Totals		111	29	47	76	79	8	0	3	207	14.0		1286	47.2	14:03	6	1	1	2	2	1	0	0	10:39

OHL All-Rookie Team (1999) • AHL All-Rookie Team (2003) • AHL First All-Star Team (2005) • John P. Sollenberger Trophy (Top Scorer - AHL) (2005) • Les Cunningham Award (MVP – AHL) (2005)

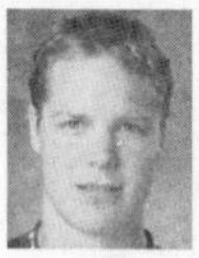

SPILLER, Matthew
(SPIHL-uhr, MA-thew) **PHX.**

Defense. Shoots left. 6'5", 233 lbs. Born, Daysland, Alta., February 7, 1983. Phoenix's 2nd choice, 31st overall, in 2001 Entry Draft.

Season	Club	League	Regular Season GP	G	A	Pts	PIM	PP	SH	GW	S	%	+/-	TF	F%	Min	Playoffs GP	G	A	Pts	PIM	PP	SH	GW	Min
1998-99	East Central Chill	AMBHL	36	8	19	27	140																		
99-2000	Seattle	WHL	60	1	10	11	108										7	0	0	0	25				
2000-01	Seattle	WHL	71	4	7	11	174																		
2001-02	Seattle	WHL	72	8	23	31	168										1	0	0	0	4				
2002-03	Seattle	WHL	68	11	24	35	198										15	2	7	9	36				
2003-04	**Phoenix**	**NHL**	**51**	**0**	**0**	**0**	**54**	**0**	**0**	**0**	**22**	**0.0**	**–11**	**0**	**0.0**	**10:42**									
	Springfield	AHL	21	1	2	3	32																		
2004-05	Utah Grizzlies	AHL	79	4	7	11	160																		
	NHL Totals		**51**	**0**	**0**	**0**	**54**	**0**	**0**	**0**	**22**	**0.0**		**0**	**0.0**	**10:42**									

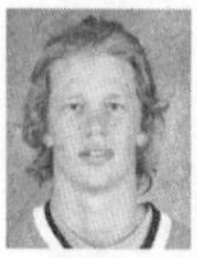

STAAL, Eric
(STAHL, AIR-ihk) **CAR.**

Center. Shoots left. 6'3", 200 lbs. Born, Thunder Bay, Ont., October 29, 1984. Carolina's 1st choice, 2nd overall, in 2003 Entry Draft.

Season	Club	League	GP	G	A	Pts	PIM	PP	SH	GW	S	%	+/-	TF	F%	Min	GP	G	A	Pts	PIM	PP	SH	GW	Min
99-2000	Thunder Bay	Exhib.	7	4	8	12	0																		
2000-01	Peterborough	OHL	63	19	30	49	23										7	2	5	7	4				
2001-02	Peterborough	OHL	56	23	39	62	40										6	3	6	9	10				
2002-03	Peterborough	OHL	66	39	59	98	36										7	9	5	14	6				
2003-04	**Carolina**	**NHL**	**81**	**11**	**20**	**31**	**40**	**2**	**1**	**3**	**164**	**6.7**	**–6**	**669**	**43.1**	**16:40**									
2004-05	Lowell	AHL	77	26	51	77	88										11	2	8	10	12				
	NHL Totals		**81**	**11**	**20**	**31**	**40**	**2**	**1**	**3**	**164**	**6.7**		**669**	**43.0**	**16:40**									

OHL Second All-Star Team (2003) • Canadian Major Junior First All-Star Team (2003)

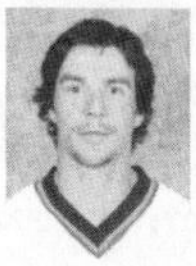

STAIOS, Steve
(STAY-uhs, STEEV) **EDM.**

Defense. Shoots right. 6'1", 200 lbs. Born, Hamilton, Ont., July 28, 1973. St. Louis' 1st choice, 27th overall, in 1991 Entry Draft.

Season	Club	League	GP	G	A	Pts	PIM	PP	SH	GW	S	%	+/-	TF	F%	Min	GP	G	A	Pts	PIM	PP	SH	GW	Min
1988-89	Hamilton Huskies	OMHA	58	13	39	52	78																		
1989-90	Hamilton Kilty B's	OHA-B	40	9	27	36	66																		
1990-91	Niagara Falls	OHL	66	17	29	46	115										12	2	3	5	10				
1991-92	Niagara Falls	OHL	65	11	42	53	122										17	7	8	15	27				
1992-93	Niagara Falls	OHL	12	4	14	18	30																		
	Sudbury Wolves	OHL	53	13	44	57	67										11	5	6	11	22				
1993-94	Peoria Rivermen	IHL	38	3	9	12	42																		
1994-95	Peoria Rivermen	IHL	60	3	13	16	64										6	0	0	0	10				
1995-96	Peoria Rivermen	IHL	6	0	1	1	14																		
	Worcester IceCats	AHL	57	1	11	12	114																		
	Boston	**NHL**	**12**	**0**	**0**	**0**	**4**	**0**	**0**	**0**	**4**	**0.0**	**–5**				**3**	**0**	**0**	**0**	**0**	**0**	**0**	**0**	
	Providence Bruins	AHL	7	1	4	5	8																		
1996-97	**Boston**	**NHL**	**54**	**3**	**8**	**11**	**71**	**0**	**0**	**0**	**56**	**5.4**	**–26**												
	Vancouver	**NHL**	**9**	**0**	**6**	**6**	**20**	**0**	**0**	**0**	**10**	**0.0**	**2**												
1997-98	**Vancouver**	**NHL**	**77**	**3**	**4**	**7**	**134**	**0**	**0**	**1**	**45**	**6.7**	**–3**												
1998-99	**Vancouver**	**NHL**	**57**	**0**	**2**	**2**	**54**	**0**	**0**	**0**	**33**	**0.0**	**–12**	**4**	**25.0**	**6:53**									
99-2000	**Atlanta**	**NHL**	**27**	**2**	**3**	**5**	**66**	**0**	**0**	**0**	**38**	**5.3**	**–5**	**2**	**50.0**	**13:01**									
2000-01	**Atlanta**	**NHL**	**70**	**9**	**13**	**22**	**137**	**4**	**0**	**0**	**156**	**5.8**	**–23**	**1**	**0.0**	**21:45**									
2001-02	**Edmonton**	**NHL**	**73**	**5**	**5**	**10**	**108**	**0**	**0**	**1**	**101**	**5.0**	**10**	**0**	**0.0**	**18:05**									
2002-03	**Edmonton**	**NHL**	**76**	**5**	**21**	**26**	**96**	**1**	**3**	**0**	**126**	**4.0**	**13**	**1**	**0.0**	**22:17**	**6**	**0**	**0**	**0**	**4**	**0**	**0**	**0**	**23:27**
2003-04	**Edmonton**	**NHL**	**82**	**6**	**22**	**28**	**86**	**1**	**0**	**1**	**153**	**3.9**	**17**	**0**	**0.0**	**23:03**									
2004-05	Lulea HF	Sweden	7	2	1	3	12																		
	NHL Totals		**537**	**33**	**84**	**117**	**776**	**6**	**3**	**3**	**722**	**4.6**		**8**	**25.0**	**18:37**	**9**	**0**	**0**	**0**	**4**	**0**	**0**	**0**	**23:27**

Traded to **Boston** by **St. Louis** with Kevin Sawyer for Steve Leach, March 8, 1996. Claimed on waivers by **Vancouver** from **Boston**, March 18, 1997. Claimed by **Atlanta** from **Vancouver** in Expansion Draft, June 25, 1999. • Missed majority of 1999-2000 season recovering from knee injury suffered in game vs. Colorado, October 23, 1999. Traded to **New Jersey** by **Atlanta** for New Jersey's 9th round choice (Simon Gamache) in 2000 Entry Draft, June 12, 2000. Traded to **Atlanta** by **New Jersey** for future considerations, July 10, 2000. Signed as a free agent by **Edmonton**, July 12, 2001. Signed as a free agent by **Lulea** (Sweden), January 28, 2005.

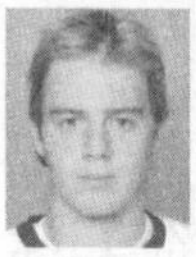

STAJAN, Matt
(STAY-juhn, MAHT) **TOR.**

Center. Shoots left. 6'1", 180 lbs. Born, Mississauga, Ont., December 19, 1983. Toronto's 2nd choice, 57th overall, in 2002 Entry Draft.

Season	Club	League	GP	G	A	Pts	PIM	PP	SH	GW	S	%	+/-	TF	F%	Min	GP	G	A	Pts	PIM	PP	SH	GW	Min
99-2000	Miss. Senators	GTHL	STATISTICS NOT AVAILABLE																						
2000-01	Belleville Bulls	OHL	57	9	18	27	27										7	1	6	7	5				
2001-02	Belleville Bulls	OHL	68	33	52	85	50										11	3	8	11	14				
2002-03	Belleville Bulls	OHL	57	34	60	94	75										7	5	8	13	16				
	St. John's	AHL	1	0	1	1	0																		
	Toronto	**NHL**	**1**	**1**	**0**	**1**	**0**	**0**	**0**	**0**	**1**	**100.0**	**1**	**12**	**33.3**	**11:00**									
2003-04	**Toronto**	**NHL**	**69**	**14**	**13**	**27**	**22**	**0**	**0**	**0**	**63**	**22.2**	**7**	**450**	**38.9**	**11:00**	**3**	**0**	**0**	**0**	**2**	**0**	**0**	**0**	**11:13**
2004-05	St. John's	AHL	80	23	43	66	43										5	2	2	4	6				
	NHL Totals		**70**	**15**	**13**	**28**	**22**	**0**	**0**	**0**	**64**	**23.4**		**462**	**38.7**	**11:00**	**3**	**0**	**0**	**0**	**2**	**0**	**0**	**0**	**11:13**

• Scored a goal in his first NHL game (April 5, 2003 vs. Ottawa).

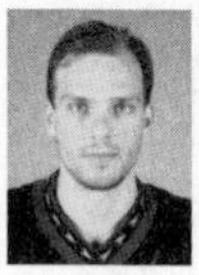

STEFAN, Patrik
(SHTEH-fan, PAT-rihk) **ATL.**

Center. Shoots left. 6'2", 210 lbs. Born, Pribram, Czech., September 16, 1980. Atlanta's 1st choice, 1st overall, in 1999 Entry Draft.

Season	Club	League	GP	G	A	Pts	PIM	PP	SH	GW	S	%	+/-	TF	F%	Min	GP	G	A	Pts	PIM	PP	SH	GW	Min
1996-97	HC Sparta Praha	CzRep	5	0	1	1	2										7	1	0	1	0				
1997-98	HC Sparta Praha	CzRep	27	2	6	8	16																		
	Long Beach	IHL	25	5	10	15	10										10	1	1	2	2				
1998-99	Long Beach	IHL	33	11	24	35	26																		
99-2000	**Atlanta**	**NHL**	**72**	**5**	**20**	**25**	**30**	**1**	**0**	**0**	**117**	**4.3**	**–20**	**988**	**41.4**	**14:49**									
2000-01	**Atlanta**	**NHL**	**66**	**10**	**21**	**31**	**22**	**0**	**0**	**1**	**93**	**10.8**	**–3**	**834**	**42.9**	**14:07**									
2001-02	**Atlanta**	**NHL**	**59**	**7**	**16**	**23**	**22**	**0**	**1**	**0**	**67**	**10.4**	**–4**	**628**	**41.9**	**15:58**									
	Chicago Wolves	AHL	5	3	0	3	0																		
2002-03	**Atlanta**	**NHL**	**71**	**13**	**21**	**34**	**12**	**3**	**0**	**2**	**96**	**13.5**	**–10**	**1125**	**45.7**	**16:50**									
2003-04	**Atlanta**	**NHL**	**82**	**14**	**26**	**40**	**26**	**3**	**2**	**2**	**110**	**12.7**	**–7**	**1446**	**45.6**	**16:29**									
2004-05	Ilves Tampere	Finland	37	13	28	41	47										7	1	6	7	4				
	NHL Totals		**350**	**49**	**104**	**153**	**112**	**7**	**3**	**5**	**483**	**10.1**		**5021**	**43.9**	**15:41**									

Signed as a free agent by **Ilves** (Finland), October 23, 2004.

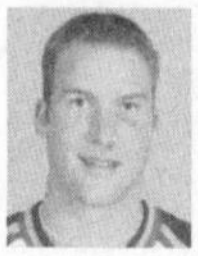

STEPHENS, Charlie
(STEE-vuhns, CHAHR-lee)

Center/Right wing. Shoots right. 6'3", 220 lbs. Born, London, Ont., April 5, 1981. Colorado's 9th choice, 196th overall, in 2001 Entry Draft.

Season	Club	League	GP	G	A	Pts	PIM	PP	SH	GW	S	%	+/-	TF	F%	Min	GP	G	A	Pts	PIM	PP	SH	GW	Min
1995-96	Elgin-Middlesex	MHAO	60	25	29	54	60																		
1996-97	Leamington Flyers	OHA-B	50	26	36	62	103																		
1997-98	St. Michael's	OHL	58	9	21	30	38																		
1998-99	St. Michael's	OHL	7	2	4	6	8																		
	Guelph Storm	OHL	61	24	28	52	72										11	3	5	8	19				
99-2000	Guelph Storm	OHL	56	16	34	50	87										6	1	3	4	15				
2000-01	Guelph Storm	OHL	67	38	38	76	53										4	0	2	2	2				
2001-02	Guelph Storm	OHL	4	1	2	3	2																		
	London Knights	OHL	56	23	33	56	55										12	6	10	16	18				
	Hershey Bears	AHL															1	0	0	0	0				
2002-03	**Colorado**	**NHL**	**2**	**0**	**0**	**0**	**0**	**0**	**0**	**0**	**1**	**0.0**	**0**	**0**	**0.0**	**5:20**									
	Hershey Bears	AHL	74	17	33	50	38										5	1	1	2	2				

			Regular Season														Playoffs								
Season	Club	League	GP	G	A	Pts	PIM	PP	SH	GW	S	%	+/-	TF	F%	Min	GP	G	A	Pts	PIM	PP	SH	GW	Min
2003-04	**Colorado**	**NHL**	6	0	2	2	4	0	0	0	1	0.0	−1	22	45.5	6:12	....	....	....	....	....	....	....	....	....
	Hershey Bears	AHL	32	5	9	14	21	....	....	....	....	....	....	....	....	....	....	....	....	....	....	....	....	....	....
	Quad City	UHL	7	0	1	1	0	....	....	....	....	....	....	....	....	....	....	....	....	....	....	....	....	....	....
	Binghamton	AHL	37	15	17	32	43	....	....	....	....	....	....	....	....	....	2	0	0	0	0	....	....	....	....
2004-05	Binghamton	AHL	80	7	21	28	64	....	....	....	....	....	....	....	....	....	6	3	0	3	19	....	....	....	....
	NHL Totals		8	0	2	2	4	0	0	0	2	0.0		22	45.5	5:59	....	....	....	....	....	....	....	....	....

• Re-entered NHL Entry Draft. Originally Washington's 3rd choice, 31st overall, in 1999 Entry Draft.

Traded to **Ottawa** by **Colorado** for Dennis Bonvie, January 23, 2004.

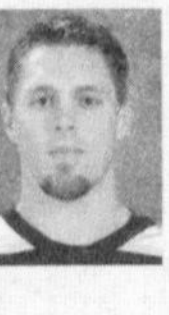

STEVENSON, Jeremy

(STEE-vehn-suhn, JAIR-eh-mee) **NSH.**

Left wing. Shoots left. 6'1", 215 lbs. Born, San Bernardino, CA, July 28, 1974. Anaheim's 10th choice, 262nd overall, in 1994 Entry Draft.

Season	Club	League	GP	G	A	Pts	PIM	PP	SH	GW	S	%	+/-	TF	F%	Min	GP	G	A	Pts	PIM	PP	SH	GW	Min
1989-90	Elliot Lake Vikings	NOHA	61	39	26	65	203	....	....	....	....	....	....	....	....	....	....	....	....	....	....	....	....	....	....
1990-91	Cornwall Royals	OHL	58	13	20	33	124	....	....	....	....	....	....	....	....	....	....	....	....	....	....	....	....	....	....
1991-92	Cornwall Royals	OHL	63	15	23	38	176	....	....	....	....	....	....	....	....	....	6	3	1	4	4	....	....	....	....
1992-93	Newmarket	OHL	54	28	28	56	144	....	....	....	....	....	....	....	....	....	5	5	1	6	28	....	....	....	....
1993-94	Newmarket	OHL	9	2	4	6	27	....	....	....	....	....	....	....	....	....	....	....	....	....	....	....	....	....	....
	Sault Ste. Marie	OHL	48	18	19	37	183	....	....	....	....	....	....	....	....	....	14	1	1	2	23	....	....	....	....
1994-95	Greensboro	ECHL	43	14	13	27	231	....	....	....	....	....	....	....	....	....	17	6	11	17	64	....	....	....	....
1995-96	**Anaheim**	**NHL**	3	0	1	1	12	0	0	0	1	0.0	1	....	....	....	....	....	....	....	....	....	....	....	....
	Baltimore Bandits	AHL	60	11	10	21	295	....	....	....	....	....	....	....	....	....	12	4	2	6	23	....	....	....	....
1996-97	**Anaheim**	**NHL**	5	0	0	0	14	0	0	0	1	0.0	−1	....	....	....	....	....	....	....	....	....	....	....	....
	Baltimore Bandits	AHL	25	8	8	16	125	....	....	....	....	....	....	....	....	....	3	0	0	0	8	....	....	....	....
1997-98	**Anaheim**	**NHL**	45	3	5	8	101	0	0	1	43	7.0	−4	....	....	....	....	....	....	....	....	....	....	....	....
	Cincinnati	AHL	10	5	0	5	34	....	....	....	....	....	....	....	....	....	....	....	....	....	....	....	....	....	....
1998-99	Cincinnati	AHL	22	4	4	8	83	....	....	....	....	....	....	....	....	....	3	1	0	1	2	....	....	....	....
99-2000	**Anaheim**	**NHL**	3	0	0	0	7	0	0	0	2	0.0	−1	0	0.0	6:50	....	....	....	....	....	....	....	....	....
	Cincinnati	AHL	41	11	14	25	100	....	....	....	....	....	....	....	....	....	....	....	....	....	....	....	....	....	....
2000-01	Milwaukee	IHL	60	16	13	29	262	....	....	....	....	....	....	....	....	....	5	2	0	2	12	....	....	....	....
	Nashville	**NHL**	8	1	0	1	39	0	0	0	6	16.7	−1	0	0.0	6:24	....	....	....	....	....	....	....	....	....
2001-02	**Nashville**	**NHL**	4	0	0	0	9	0	0	0	0	0.0	0	0	0.0	5:53	....	....	....	....	....	....	....	....	....
	Milwaukee	AHL	53	12	7	19	192	....	....	....	....	....	....	....	....	....	....	....	....	....	....	....	....	....	....
2002-03	**Minnesota**	**NHL**	32	5	6	11	69	1	0	1	29	17.2	6	0	0.0	10:48	14	0	5	5	12	0	0	0	12:32
	Houston Aeros	AHL	18	6	7	13	77	....	....	....	....	....	....	....	....	....	....	....	....	....	....	....	....	....	....
2003-04	**Minnesota**	**NHL**	3	0	0	0	2	0	0	0	5	0.0	−1	0	0.0	11:24	....	....	....	....	....	....	....	....	....
	Nashville	**NHL**	53	5	4	9	103	3	0	0	62	8.1	−2	4	50.0	10:03	6	0	0	0	8	0	0	0	6:43
2004-05	South Carolina	ECHL	42	9	20	29	140	....	....	....	....	....	....	....	....	....	3	1	0	1	2	....	....	....	....
	NHL Totals		156	14	16	30	356	4	0	2	149	9.4		4	50.0	9:47	20	0	5	5	20	0	0	0	10:48

• Re-entered NHL Entry Draft. Originally Winnipeg's 3rd choice, 60th overall, in 1992 Entry Draft.

Signed as a free agent by **Nashville**, September 25, 2000. Signed as a free agent by **Minnesota**, November 26, 2002. Claimed on waivers by **Nashville** from **Minnesota**, October 22, 2003. Signed as a free agent by **South Carolina** (ECHL), November 30, 2004.

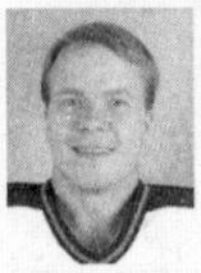

STEVENSON, Turner

(STEE-vehn-suhn, TUHR-nuhr) **PHI.**

Right wing. Shoots right. 6'3", 220 lbs. Born, Prince George, B.C., May 18, 1972. Montreal's 1st choice, 12th overall, in 1990 Entry Draft.

Season	Club	League	GP	G	A	Pts	PIM	PP	SH	GW	S	%	+/-	TF	F%	Min	GP	G	A	Pts	PIM	PP	SH	GW	Min
1987-88	Prince George	BCAHA	53	45	46	91	127	....	....	....	....	....	....	....	....	....	....	....	....	....	....	....	....	....	....
1988-89	Seattle	WHL	69	15	12	27	84	....	....	....	....	....	....	....	....	....	....	....	....	....	....	....	....	....	....
1989-90	Seattle	WHL	62	29	32	61	276	....	....	....	....	....	....	....	....	....	13	3	2	5	35	....	....	....	....
1990-91	Seattle	WHL	57	36	27	63	222	....	....	....	....	....	....	....	....	....	6	1	5	6	15	....	....	....	....
	Fredericton	AHL	....	....	....	....	....	....	....	....	....	....	....	....	....	....	4	0	0	0	5	....	....	....	....
1991-92	Seattle	WHL	58	20	32	52	264	....	....	....	....	....	....	....	....	....	15	9	3	12	55	....	....	....	....
1992-93	**Montreal**	**NHL**	1	0	0	0	0	0	0	0	1	0.0	−1	....	....	....	....	....	....	....	....	....	....	....	....
	Fredericton	AHL	79	25	34	59	102	....	....	....	....	....	....	....	....	....	5	2	3	5	11	....	....	....	....
1993-94	**Montreal**	**NHL**	2	0	0	0	2	0	0	0	0	0.0	−2	....	....	....	3	0	2	2	0	0	0	0	....
	Fredericton	AHL	66	19	28	47	155	....	....	....	....	....	....	....	....	....	....	....	....	....	....	....	....	....	....
1994-95	Fredericton	AHL	37	12	12	24	109	....	....	....	....	....	....	....	....	....	....	....	....	....	....	....	....	....	....
	Montreal	**NHL**	41	6	1	7	86	0	0	1	35	17.1	0	....	....	....	....	....	....	....	....	....	....	....	....
1995-96	**Montreal**	**NHL**	80	9	16	25	167	0	0	2	101	8.9	−2	....	....	....	6	0	1	1	2	0	0	0	....
1996-97	**Montreal**	**NHL**	65	8	13	21	97	1	0	0	76	10.5	−14	....	....	....	5	1	1	2	2	0	0	0	....
1997-98	**Montreal**	**NHL**	63	4	6	10	110	1	0	0	43	9.3	−8	....	....	....	10	3	4	7	12	0	0	0	....
1998-99	**Montreal**	**NHL**	69	10	17	27	88	0	0	2	102	9.8	6	29	37.9	12:57	....	....	....	....	....	....	....	....	....
99-2000	**Montreal**	**NHL**	64	8	13	21	61	0	0	2	94	8.5	−1	5	20.0	13:10	....	....	....	....	....	....	....	....	....
2000-01	**New Jersey**	**NHL**	69	8	18	26	97	2	0	1	92	8.7	11	0	0.0	11:00	23	1	3	4	20	0	0	1	9:27
2001-02	**New Jersey**	**NHL**	21	0	2	2	25	0	0	0	33	0.0	−3	0	0.0	11:38	1	0	0	0	4	0	0	0	10:13
2002-03♦	**New Jersey**	**NHL**	77	7	13	20	115	0	0	0	85	8.2	7	12	41.7	11:53	14	1	1	2	26	0	0	0	13:01
2003-04	**New Jersey**	**NHL**	61	14	13	27	76	4	0	2	76	18.4	0	5	60.0	12:42	5	0	0	0	0	0	0	0	13:29
2004-05			DID NOT PLAY																						
	NHL Totals		613	74	112	186	924	8	0	10	738	10.0		51	39.2	12:16	67	6	12	18	66	0	0	1	11:06

WHL West First All-Star Team (1992) • Memorial Cup Tournament All-Star Team (1992).

Claimed by **Columbus** from **Montreal** in Expansion Draft, June 23, 2000. Traded to **New Jersey** by **Columbus** to complete transaction that sent Krzysztof Oliwa (June 12, 2000) and Deron Quint (June 23, 2000) to **Columbus**, June 23, 2000. • Missed majority of 2001-02 season recovering from knee injury suffered in game vs. Vancouver, December 29, 2001. Signed as a free agent by **Philadelphia**, July 3, 2004.

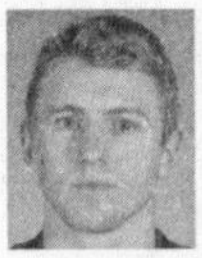

STEWART, Karl

(STEW-ahrt, KARL) **ATL.**

Center. Shoots left. 5'10", 175 lbs. Born, Aurora, Ont., June 30, 1983.

Season	Club	League	GP	G	A	Pts	PIM	PP	SH	GW	S	%	+/-	TF	F%	Min	GP	G	A	Pts	PIM	PP	SH	GW	Min
99-2000	Thornhill Rattlers	OPJHL	49	15	19	34	61	....	....	....	....	....	....	....	....	....	....	....	....	....	....	....	....	....	....
2000-01	Plymouth Whalers	OHL	68	9	14	23	87	....	....	....	....	....	....	....	....	....	19	3	4	7	14	....	....	....	....
2001-02	Plymouth Whalers	OHL	65	20	23	43	104	....	....	....	....	....	....	....	....	....	6	0	2	2	21	....	....	....	....
2002-03	Plymouth Whalers	OHL	68	35	50	85	120	....	....	....	....	....	....	....	....	....	17	7	10	17	31	....	....	....	....
2003-04	**Atlanta**	**NHL**	5	0	1	1	4	0	0	0	2	0.0	0	10	10.0	4:27	....	....	....	....	....	....	....	....	....
	Chicago Wolves	AHL	72	10	32	42	186	....	....	....	....	....	....	....	....	....	10	2	3	5	29	....	....	....	....
2004-05	Chicago Wolves	AHL	77	16	8	24	226	....	....	....	....	....	....	....	....	....	12	4	2	6	32	....	....	....	....
	NHL Totals		5	0	1	1	4	0	0	0	2	0.0		10	10.0	4:27	....	....	....	....	....	....	....	....	....

Signed as a free agent by **Atlanta**, September 28, 2001.

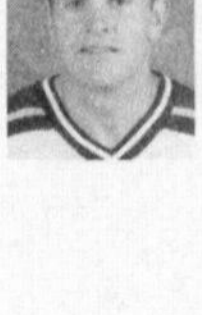

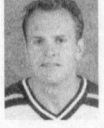

STILLMAN, Cory

(STIHL-mahn, KOHR-ee) **CAR.**

Left wing. Shoots left. 6', 194 lbs. Born, Peterborough, Ont., December 20, 1973. Calgary's 1st choice, 6th overall, in 1992 Entry Draft.

Season	Club	League	GP	G	A	Pts	PIM	PP	SH	GW	S	%	+/-	TF	F%	Min	GP	G	A	Pts	PIM	PP	SH	GW	Min
1989-90	Peterborough	OHA-B	41	30	*54	84	76	....	....	....	....	....	....	....	....	....	....	....	....	....	....	....	....	....	....
1990-91	Windsor Spitfires	OHL	64	31	70	101	31	....	....	....	....	....	....	....	....	....	11	3	6	9	8	....	....	....	....
1991-92	Windsor Spitfires	OHL	53	29	61	90	59	....	....	....	....	....	....	....	....	....	7	2	4	6	8	....	....	....	....
1992-93	Peterborough	OHL	61	25	55	80	55	....	....	....	....	....	....	....	....	....	18	3	8	11	18	....	....	....	....
1993-94	Saint John Flames	AHL	79	35	48	83	52	....	....	....	....	....	....	....	....	....	7	2	4	6	16	....	....	....	....
1994-95	Saint John Flames	AHL	63	28	53	81	70	....	....	....	....	....	....	....	....	....	5	0	2	2	2	....	....	....	....
	Calgary	**NHL**	10	0	2	2	2	0	0	0	7	0.0	1	....	....	....	....	....	....	....	....	....	....	....	....
1995-96	**Calgary**	**NHL**	74	16	19	35	41	4	1	3	132	12.1	−5	....	....	....	2	1	1	2	0	0	0	0	....
1996-97	**Calgary**	**NHL**	58	6	20	26	14	2	0	0	112	5.4	−6	....	....	....	....	....	....	....	....	....	....	....	....
1997-98	**Calgary**	**NHL**	72	27	22	49	40	9	4	1	178	15.2	−9	....	....	....	....	....	....	....	....	....	....	....	....
1998-99	**Calgary**	**NHL**	76	27	30	57	38	9	3	5	175	15.4	7	535	46.5	16:19	....	....	....	....	....	....	....	....	....
99-2000	**Calgary**	**NHL**	37	12	9	21	12	6	0	3	59	20.3	−9	283	54.4	17:45	....	....	....	....	....	....	....	....	....
2000-01	**Calgary**	**NHL**	66	21	24	45	45	7	0	4	148	14.2	−6	346	43.9	18:50	....	....	....	....	....	....	....	....	....
	St. Louis	**NHL**	12	3	4	7	6	3	0	0	26	11.5	−2	36	61.1	18:37	15	3	5	8	8	1	0	1	14:58
2001-02	**St. Louis**	**NHL**	80	23	22	45	36	6	0	4	140	16.4	8	196	46.4	0:00	9	0	2	2	2	0	0	0	....
2002-03	**St. Louis**	**NHL**	79	24	43	67	56	6	0	4	157	15.3	12	266	41.7	0:00	6	2	2	4	2	2	0	1	....
2003-04♦	**Tampa Bay**	**NHL**	81	25	55	80	36	11	1	6	178	14.0	18	38	31.6	19:31	21	2	5	7	15	0	1	0	0:00

			Regular Season														Playoffs								
Season	Club	League	GP	G	A	Pts	PIM	PP	SH	GW	S	%	+/-	TF	F%	Min	GP	G	A	Pts	PIM	PP	SH	GW	Min
2004-05			DID NOT PLAY																						
	NHL Totals		**645**	**184**	**250**	**434**	**326**	**63**	**9**	**30**	**1312**	**14.0**		**1700**	**33.9**	**9:37**	**53**	**8**	**15**	**23**	**27**	**3**	**1**	**2**	**6:14**

OHL Rookie of the Year (1991)

• Missed majority of 1999-2000 season recovering from shoulder injury suffered in game vs. Philadelphia, December 27, 1999. Traded to **St. Louis by Calgary** for Craig Conroy and St. Louis' 7th round choice (David Moss) in 2001 Entry Draft, March 13, 2001. Traded to **Tampa Bay** by **St. Louis** for Tampa Bay's 2nd round choice (David Backes) in 2003 Entry Draft, June 21, 2003. Signed as a free agent by **Carolina**, August 2, 2005.

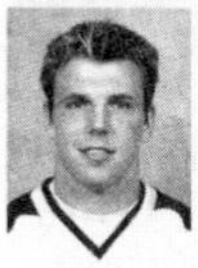

STOCK, P.J.

(STAWK, PEE-JAY)

Center. Shoots left. 5'10", 197 lbs. Born, Montreal, Que., May 26, 1975.

Season	Club	League	GP	G	A	Pts	PIM	PP	SH	GW	S	%	+/-	TF	F%	Min	GP	G	A	Pts	PIM	PP	SH	GW	Min
1992-93	Pembroke	CJHL	55	10	38	48	189																		
1993-94	Pembroke	CJHL	52	25	48	73	262																		
1994-95	Victoriaville Tigres	QMJHL	70	9	46	55	386										4	0	0	0	60				
1995-96	Victoriaville Tigres	QMJHL	67	19	43	62	432										12	5	4	9	79				
1996-97	St. FX University	AUAA	27	11	20	31	110										3	0	4	4	14				
1997-98	Hartford	AHL	41	8	8	16	202										11	1	3	4	79				
	NY Rangers	**NHL**	**38**	**2**	**3**	**5**	**114**	**0**	**0**	**1**	**9**	**22.2**	**4**												
1998-99	**NY Rangers**	**NHL**	**5**	**0**	**0**	**0**	**6**	**0**	**0**	**0**	**0**	**0.0**	**–1**	**8**	**50.0**	**2:42**									
	Hartford	AHL	55	4	14	18	250										6	0	1	1	35				
99-2000	**NY Rangers**	**NHL**	**11**	**0**	**1**	**1**	**11**	**0**	**0**	**0**	**2**	**0.0**	**1**	**63**	**31.8**	**6:13**									
	Hartford	AHL	64	13	23	36	290										23	1	11	12	69				
2000-01	**Montreal**	**NHL**	**20**	**1**	**2**	**3**	**32**	**0**	**0**	**0**	**9**	**11.1**	**–1**	**83**	**53.0**	**5:31**									
	Philadelphia	**NHL**	**31**	**1**	**3**	**4**	**78**	**0**	**0**	**0**	**18**	**5.6**	**–2**	**12**	**50.0**	**7:48**	**2**	**0**	**0**	**0**	**0**	**0**	**0**	**0**	**5:00**
	Philadelphia	AHL	9	1	2	3	37																		
2001-02	**Boston**	**NHL**	**58**	**0**	**3**	**3**	**122**	**0**	**0**	**0**	**12**	**0.0**	**–2**	**120**	**45.8**	**5:09**	**6**	**1**	**0**	**1**	**19**	**0**	**0**	**0**	**3:15**
2002-03	**Boston**	**NHL**	**71**	**1**	**9**	**10**	**160**	**1**	**0**	**0**	**38**	**2.6**	**–5**	**185**	**44.9**	**6:14**									
2003-04	**Boston**	**NHL**	**1**	**0**	**0**	**0**	**0**	**0**	**0**	**0**	**1**	**0.0**	**0**	**2**	**50.0**	**6:04**									
	Providence Bruins	AHL	4	1	0	1	2																		
	Philadelphia	AHL	66	5	18	23	207										12	0	2	2	34				
2004-05			DID NOT PLAY																						
	NHL Totals		**235**	**5**	**21**	**26**	**523**	**1**	**0**	**1**	**89**	**5.6**		**473**	**45.0**	**6:00**	**8**	**1**	**0**	**1**	**19**	**0**	**0**	**0**	**3:41**

Signed as a free agent by **NY Rangers**, November 18, 1997. Signed as a free agent by **Montreal**, July 7, 2000. Traded to **Philadelphia** by **Montreal** with Montreal's 6th round choice (Dennis Seidenberg) in 2001 Entry Draft for Gino Odjick, December 7, 2000. Signed as a free agent by **NY Rangers**, August 23, 2001. Claimed by **Boston** from **NY Rangers** in Waiver Draft, September 28, 2001. Loaned to **Philadelphia** (AHL) by **Providence** (AHL) for the loan of Andre Savage, October 29, 2003.

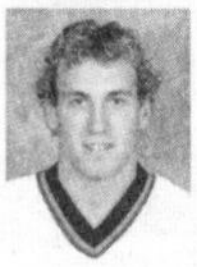

STOLL, Jarret

(STOHL, JEHR-eht) **EDM.**

Center. Shoots right. 6'1", 200 lbs. Born, Melville, Sask., June 25, 1982. Edmonton's 3rd choice, 36th overall, in 2002 Entry Draft.

Season	Club	League	GP	G	A	Pts	PIM	PP	SH	GW	S	%	+/-	TF	F%	Min	GP	G	A	Pts	PIM	PP	SH	GW	Min
1997-98	Saskatoon Blazers	SMHL	44	45	44	*89	78																		
	Edmonton Ice	WHL	8	2	3	5	4																		
1998-99	Kootenay Ice	WHL	57	13	21	34	38										4	0	0	0	2				
99-2000	Kootenay Ice	WHL	71	37	38	75	64										20	7	9	16	24				
2000-01	Kootenay Ice	WHL	62	40	66	106	105										11	5	9	14	22				
2001-02	Kootenay Ice	WHL	47	32	34	66	64										22	6	14	20	35				
2002-03	**Edmonton**	**NHL**	**4**	**0**	**1**	**1**	**0**	**0**	**0**	**0**	**5**	**0.0**	**–3**	**30**	**63.3**	**7:44**									
	Hamilton	AHL	76	21	33	54	86										23	5	8	13	25				
2003-04	**Edmonton**	**NHL**	**68**	**10**	**11**	**21**	**42**	**1**	**1**	**2**	**107**	**9.3**	**8**	**1019**	**54.1**	**13:54**									
2004-05	Edmonton	AHL	66	21	17	38	92																		
	NHL Totals		**72**	**10**	**12**	**22**	**42**	**1**	**1**	**2**	**112**	**8.9**		**1049**	**54.3**	**13:34**									

• Re-entered NHL Entry Draft. Originally Calgary's 3rd choice, 46th overall, in 2000 Entry Draft.

WHL East First All-Star Team (2001) • Canadian Major Junior First All-Star Team (2001) • WHL West First All-Star Team (2002)

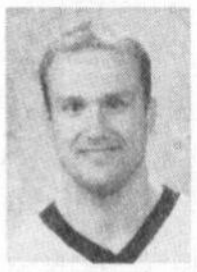

STRAKA, Martin

(STRAH-kuh, MAHR-tihn) **NYR**

Center. Shoots left. 5'9", 178 lbs. Born, Plzen, Czech., September 3, 1972. Pittsburgh's 1st choice, 19th overall, in 1992 Entry Draft.

Season	Club	League	GP	G	A	Pts	PIM	PP	SH	GW	S	%	+/-	TF	F%	Min	GP	G	A	Pts	PIM	PP	SH	GW	Min
1989-90	Skoda Plzen	Czech	1	0	3	3																			
1990-91	HC Skoda Plzen	Czech	47	7	24	31	6																		
1991-92	HC Skoda Plzen	Czech	50	27	28	55	20																		
1992-93	**Pittsburgh**	**NHL**	**42**	**3**	**13**	**16**	**29**	**0**	**0**	**1**	**28**	**10.7**	**2**				**11**	**2**	**1**	**3**	**2**	**0**	**0**	**0**	
	Cleveland	IHL	4	4	3	7	0																		
1993-94	**Pittsburgh**	**NHL**	**84**	**30**	**34**	**64**	**24**	**2**	**0**	**6**	**130**	**23.1**	**24**				**6**	**1**	**0**	**1**	**2**	**0**	**0**	**0**	
1994-95	Plzen	CzRep	19	10	11	21	18																		
	Pittsburgh	**NHL**	**31**	**4**	**12**	**16**	**16**	**0**	**0**	**0**	**36**	**11.1**	**0**												
	Ottawa	**NHL**	**6**	**1**	**1**	**2**	**0**	**0**	**0**	**0**	**13**	**7.7**	**–1**												
1995-96	**Ottawa**	**NHL**	**43**	**9**	**16**	**25**	**29**	**5**	**0**	**1**	**63**	**14.3**	**–14**												
	NY Islanders	**NHL**	**22**	**2**	**10**	**12**	**6**	**0**	**0**	**0**	**18**	**11.1**	**–6**												
	Florida	**NHL**	**12**	**2**	**4**	**6**	**6**	**1**	**0**	**0**	**17**	**11.8**	**1**				**13**	**2**	**2**	**4**	**2**	**0**	**0**	**0**	
1996-97	**Florida**	**NHL**	**55**	**7**	**22**	**29**	**12**	**2**	**0**	**1**	**94**	**7.4**	**9**				**4**	**0**	**0**	**0**	**0**	**0**	**0**	**0**	
1997-98	**Pittsburgh**	**NHL**	**75**	**19**	**23**	**42**	**28**	**4**	**3**	**4**	**117**	**16.2**	**–1**				**6**	**2**	**0**	**2**	**2**	**0**	**1**	**0**	
	Czech Republic	Olympics	6	1	2	3	0																		
1998-99	**Pittsburgh**	**NHL**	**80**	**35**	**48**	**83**	**26**	**5**	**4**	**4**	**177**	**19.8**	**12**	**845**	**43.6**	**23:35**	**13**	**6**	**9**	**15**	**6**	**1**	**0**	**0**	**25:00**
99-2000	**Pittsburgh**	**NHL**	**71**	**20**	**39**	**59**	**26**	**3**	**1**	**2**	**146**	**13.7**	**24**	**651**	**42.9**	**23:58**	**11**	**3**	**9**	**12**	**10**	**1**	**0**	**0**	**24:27**
2000-01	**Pittsburgh**	**NHL**	**82**	**27**	**68**	**95**	**38**	**7**	**1**	**4**	**185**	**14.6**	**19**	**331**	**43.2**	**23:01**	**18**	**5**	**8**	**13**	**8**	**3**	**0**	**2**	**21:24**
2001-02	**Pittsburgh**	**NHL**	**13**	**5**	**4**	**9**	**0**	**1**	**0**	**1**	**33**	**15.2**	**3**	**5**	**60.0**	**18:00**									
2002-03	**Pittsburgh**	**NHL**	**60**	**18**	**28**	**46**	**12**	**7**	**0**	**4**	**136**	**13.2**	**–18**	**115**	**45.2**	**20:37**									
2003-04	**Pittsburgh**	**NHL**	**22**	**4**	**8**	**12**	**16**	**1**	**0**	**0**	**34**	**11.8**	**–16**	**121**	**38.8**	**21:32**									
	Los Angeles	**NHL**	**32**	**6**	**8**	**14**	**4**	**1**	**1**	**0**	**34**	**17.6**	**–9**	**66**	**48.5**	**16:47**									
2004-05	Plzen	CzRep	45	16	18	34	76																		
	NHL Totals		**730**	**192**	**338**	**530**	**272**	**39**	**10**	**28**	**1261**	**15.2**		**2134**	**43.3**	**22:06**	**82**	**21**	**29**	**50**	**32**	**5**	**1**	**2**	**23:19**

Czechoslovakian First All-Star Team (1992)

Played in NHL All-Star Game (1999)

Traded to **Ottawa** by **Pittsburgh** for Troy Murray and Norm Maciver, April 7, 1995. Traded to **NY Islanders** by **Ottawa** with Don Beaupre and Bryan Berard for Damian Rhodes and Wade Redden, January 23, 1996. Claimed on waivers by **Florida** from **NY Islanders**, March 15, 1996. Signed as a free agent by **Pittsburgh**, August 6, 1997. • Missed majority of 2001-02 season recovering from leg injury suffered in game vs. Florida, October 28, 2001. Traded to **Los Angeles** by **Pittsburgh** for Martin Strbak and Sergei Anshakov, November 30, 2003. Signed as a free agent by **Plzen** (CzRep), September 17, 2004. Signed as a free agent by **NY Rangers**, August 2, 2005.

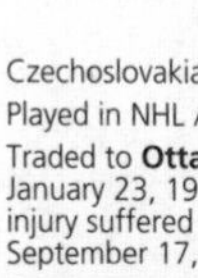

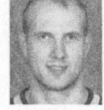

STRBAK, Martin

(SHTUHR-bak, MAHR-tehn) **PIT.**

Defense. Shoots left. 6'3", 210 lbs. Born, Presov, Czech., January 15, 1975. Los Angeles' 10th choice, 224th overall, in 1993 Entry Draft.

Season	Club	League	GP	G	A	Pts	PIM	PP	SH	GW	S	%	+/-	TF	F%	Min	GP	G	A	Pts	PIM	PP	SH	GW	Min
1994-95	Bratislava	Slovakia	26	3	4	7	10																		
1995-96	Bratislava	Slovakia	44	4	4	8	22																		
1996-97	Bratislava	Slovakia	38	3	2	5	24																		
	Bratislava	EuroHL	5	0	0	0	4																		
1997-98	Spis. N. Ves	Slovakia	33	1	1	2	18																		
1998-99	Bratislava	Slovakia	18	0	0	0	4										2	0	0	0	4				
	HC Trnava	Slovak-2	15	3	6	9	12																		
99-2000	Litvinov	CzRep	50	3	6	9	28																		
2000-01	HC Slovnaft Vsetin	CzRep	49	2	6	8	46										14	2	1	3	35				
2001-02	HC Vsetin	CzRep	33	8	9	17	46																		
	Yaroslavl	Russia	19	1	1	2	10										9	1	2	3	8				
2002-03	Yaroslavl	Russia	27	0	6	6	28																		
	HPK Hameenlinna	Finland	20	4	9	13	68										13	2	3	5	8				
2003-04	**Los Angeles**	**NHL**	**5**	**2**	**0**	**2**	**8**	**0**	**0**	**1**	**7**	**28.6**	**1**	**0**	**0.0**	**19:14**									
	Manchester	AHL	12	0	1	1	25																		
	Pittsburgh	**NHL**	**44**	**3**	**11**	**14**	**38**	**0**	**0**	**0**	**47**	**6.4**	**–11**	**2**	**50.0**	**19:31**									

Season	Club	League	GP	G	A	Pts	PIM	PP	SH	GW	S	%	+/-	TF	F%	Min	GP	G	A	Pts	PIM	PP	SH	GW	Min
			Regular Season														Playoffs								
2004-05	HC Kosice	Slovakia	14	1	4	5	14																		
	CSKA Moscow	Russia	36	2	11	13	34																		
	NHL Totals		**49**	**5**	**11**	**16**	**46**	**0**	**0**	**1**	**54**	**9.3**		**2**	**50.0**	**19:29**									

Traded to **Pittsburgh** by **Los Angeles** with Sergei Anshakov for Martin Straka, November 30, 2003. Signed as a free agent by **Kosice** (Slovakia), October 2, 2004. Signed as a free agent by **CSKA** (Russia), November 15, 2004.

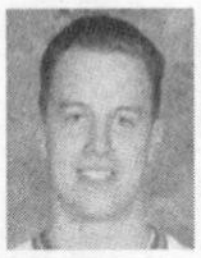

STROSHEIN, Garret

(STROH-shighn, GAIR-reht) **BOS.**

Right wing. Shoots right. 6'7", 245 lbs. Born, Edmonton, Alta., April 4, 1980.

Season	Club	League	GP	G	A	Pts	PIM	PP	SH	GW	S	%	+/-	TF	F%	Min	GP	G	A	Pts	PIM	PP	SH	GW	Min
1998-99	Seattle	WHL	11	0	0	0	32										4	0	0	0	7				
99-2000	Chilliwack Chiefs	BCHL	58	3	1	4	176																		
2000-01	San Diego Gulls	WCHL	3	0	0	0	5																		
	Chilliwack Chiefs	BCHL	55	7	8	15	187																		
2001-02	Mobile Mysticks	ECHL	3	0	0	0	13																		
	San Diego Gulls	WCHL	24	0	0	0	90																		
	Fresno	WCHL	20	1	0	1	67																		
	Bakersfield	WCHL															4	0	0	0	2				
2002-03	Richmond	ECHL	2	0	0	0	7																		
	Portland	WHL	28	0	1	1	86										2	0	0	0	6				
2003-04	**Washington**	**NHL**	**3**	**0**	**0**	**0**	**14**	**0**	**0**	**0**	**2**	**0.0**	**–1**	**0**	**0.0**	**7:16**									
	Portland Pirates	AHL	35	1	1	2	73																		
2004-05	Portland Pirates	AHL	42	0	1	1	109																		
	South Carolina	ECHL	1	0	0	0	5																		
	NHL Totals		**3**	**0**	**0**	**0**	**14**	**0**	**0**	**0**	**2**	**0.0**		**0**	**0.0**	**7:16**									

Signed as a free agent by **Washington**, July 14, 2003. Signed as a free agent by **Boston**, August 23, 2005.

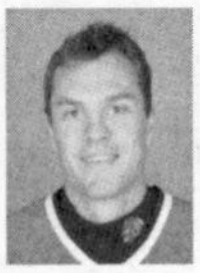

STRUDWICK, Jason

(STRUHD-wihk, JAY-suhn) **NYR**

Defense. Shoots left. 6'3", 210 lbs. Born, Edmonton, Alta., July 17, 1975. NY Islanders' 3rd choice, 63rd overall, in 1994 Entry Draft.

Season	Club	League	GP	G	A	Pts	PIM	PP	SH	GW	S	%	+/-	TF	F%	Min	GP	G	A	Pts	PIM	PP	SH	GW	Min
1991-92	Edmonton Legion	AMHL	35	3	8	11	67																		
1992-93	Edmonton Pats	AMHL	33	8	20	28	135																		
1993-94	Kamloops Blazers	WHL	61	6	8	14	118										19	0	4	4	24				
1994-95	Kamloops Blazers	WHL	72	3	11	14	183										21	1	1	2	39				
1995-96	**NY Islanders**	**NHL**	**1**	**0**	**0**	**0**	**7**	**0**	**0**	**0**	**0**	**0.0**	**0**												
	Worcester IceCats	AHL	60	2	7	9	119										4	0	1	1	0				
1996-97	Kentucky	AHL	80	1	9	10	198										4	0	0	0	0				
1997-98	**NY Islanders**	**NHL**	**17**	**0**	**1**	**1**	**36**	**0**	**0**	**0**	**3**	**0.0**	**1**												
	Kentucky	AHL	39	3	1	4	87																		
	Vancouver	**NHL**	**11**	**0**	**1**	**1**	**29**	**0**	**0**	**0**	**5**	**0.0**	**–3**												
	Syracuse Crunch	AHL															3	0	0	0	6				
1998-99	**Vancouver**	**NHL**	**65**	**0**	**3**	**3**	**114**	**0**	**0**	**0**	**25**	**0.0**	**–19**	**0**	**0.0**	**12:49**									
99-2000	**Vancouver**	**NHL**	**63**	**1**	**3**	**4**	**64**	**0**	**0**	**0**	**18**	**5.6**	**–13**	**0**	**0.0**	**15:12**									
2000-01	**Vancouver**	**NHL**	**60**	**1**	**4**	**5**	**64**	**0**	**0**	**1**	**21**	**4.8**	**16**	**0**	**0.0**	**9:59**	**2**	**0**	**0**	**0**	**0**	**0**	**0**	**0**	**2:15**
2001-02	**Vancouver**	**NHL**	**44**	**2**	**4**	**6**	**96**	**0**	**0**	**0**	**13**	**15.4**	**4**	**0**	**0.0**	**9:45**									
2002-03	**Chicago**	**NHL**	**48**	**2**	**3**	**5**	**87**	**0**	**0**	**0**	**19**	**10.5**	**–4**	**3**	**0.0**	**8:32**									
2003-04	**Chicago**	**NHL**	**54**	**1**	**3**	**4**	**73**	**0**	**0**	**0**	**32**	**3.1**	**–16**	**1**	**0.0**	**14:55**									
2004-05	Ferencvaros	Hungary	6	1	2	3	8																		
	NHL Totals		**363**	**7**	**22**	**29**	**570**	**0**	**0**	**1**	**136**	**5.1**		**4**	**0.0**	**12:05**	**2**	**0**	**0**	**0**	**0**	**0**	**0**	**0**	**2:15**

Traded to **Vancouver** by **NY Islanders** for Gino Odjick, March 23, 1998. Signed as a free agent by **Chicago**, July 15, 2002. Signed as a free agent by **NY Rangers**, July 20, 2004. Signed as a free agent by **Ferencvaros** (Hungary), January 17, 2005.

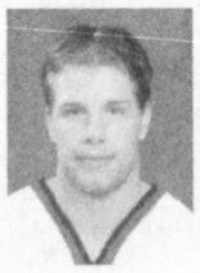

STUART, Brad

(STEW-ahrt, BRAD) **S.J.**

Defense. Shoots left. 6'2", 220 lbs. Born, Rocky Mountain House, Alta., November 6, 1979. San Jose's 1st choice, 3rd overall, in 1998 Entry Draft.

Season	Club	League	GP	G	A	Pts	PIM	PP	SH	GW	S	%	+/-	TF	F%	Min	GP	G	A	Pts	PIM	PP	SH	GW	Min
1995-96	Red Deer	AMHL	35	12	25	37	83																		
	Regina Pats	WHL	3	0	0	0	0																		
1996-97	Regina Pats	WHL	57	7	36	43	58										5	0	4	4	14				
1997-98	Regina Pats	WHL	72	20	45	65	82										9	3	4	7	10				
1998-99	Regina Pats	WHL	29	10	19	29	43																		
	Calgary Hitmen	WHL	30	11	22	33	26										21	8	15	23	59				
99-2000	**San Jose**	**NHL**	**82**	**10**	**26**	**36**	**32**	**5**	**1**	**3**	**133**	**7.5**	**3**	**0**	**0.0**	**20:24**	**12**	**1**	**0**	**1**	**6**	**1**	**0**	**0**	**16:30**
2000-01	**San Jose**	**NHL**	**77**	**5**	**18**	**23**	**56**	**1**	**0**	**2**	**119**	**4.2**	**10**	**0**	**0.0**	**20:06**	**5**	**1**	**0**	**1**	**0**	**0**	**0**	**0**	**20:19**
2001-02	**San Jose**	**NHL**	**82**	**6**	**23**	**29**	**39**	**2**	**0**	**2**	**96**	**6.3**	**13**	**0**	**0.0**	**21:41**	**12**	**0**	**3**	**3**	**8**	**0**	**0**	**0**	**19:42**
2002-03	**San Jose**	**NHL**	**36**	**4**	**10**	**14**	**46**	**2**	**0**	**1**	**63**	**6.3**	**–6**	**0**	**0.0**	**20:53**									
2003-04	**San Jose**	**NHL**	**77**	**9**	**30**	**39**	**34**	**5**	**0**	**0**	**129**	**7.0**	**9**	**0**	**0.0**	**22:09**	**17**	**1**	**5**	**6**	**13**	**0**	**0**	**0**	**23:23**
2004-05			DID NOT PLAY																						
	NHL Totals		**354**	**34**	**107**	**141**	**207**	**15**	**1**	**8**	**540**	**6.3**		**0**	**0.0**	**21:04**	**46**	**3**	**8**	**11**	**27**	**1**	**0**	**0**	**20:18**

WHL East Second All-Star Team (1998) • WHL East First All-Star Team (1999) • Canadian Major Junior First All-Star Team (1999) • Canadian Major Junior Defenseman of the Year (1999) • NHL All-Rookie Team (2000)

• Missed majority of 2002-03 season recovering from ankle (January 4, 2003 vs. Los Angeles) and head (February 21, 2003 vs. Columbus) injuries.

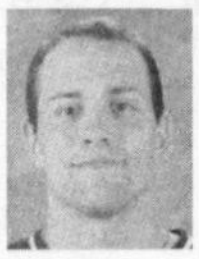

STUART, Mike

(STEW-ahrt, MIGHK) **ST.L.**

Defense. Shoots right. 6', 200 lbs. Born, Rochester, MN, August 31, 1980. Nashville's 6th choice, 137th overall, in 2000 Entry Draft.

Season	Club	League	GP	G	A	Pts	PIM	PP	SH	GW	S	%	+/-	TF	F%	Min	GP	G	A	Pts	PIM	PP	SH	GW	Min
1996-97	Rochester	USHL	46	4	9	13	22																		
1997-98	Rochester	USHL	50	4	15	19	40																		
1998-99	Colorado College	WCHA	40	2	12	14	44																		
99-2000	Colorado College	WCHA	32	2	5	7	26																		
2000-01	Colorado College	WCHA	33	1	13	14	36																		
2001-02	Colorado College	WCHA	35	3	9	12	46																		
2002-03	Peoria Rivermen	ECHL	19	2	7	9	12																		
	Worcester IceCats	AHL	41	1	5	6	19										3	0	0	0	2				
2003-04	**St. Louis**	**NHL**	**2**	**0**	**0**	**0**	**0**	**0**	**0**	**0**	**0**	**0.0**	**0**	**0**	**0.0**	**9:31**									
	Worcester IceCats	AHL	30	0	4	4	20																		
2004-05	Worcester IceCats	AHL	70	1	10	11	26																		
	NHL Totals		**2**	**0**	**0**	**0**	**0**	**0**	**0**	**0**	**0**	**0.0**		**0**	**0.0**	**9:31**									

USHL All-Rookie Team (1997)

Signed as a free agent by **St. Louis**, October 7, 2002. • Missed majority of 2003-04 season recovering from groin injury suffered in game vs. Hartford (AHL), January 28, 2004.

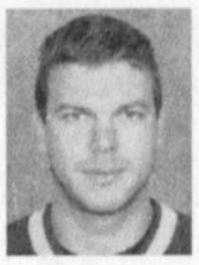

STUMPEL, Jozef

(STUM-puhl, JOH-zehf) **FLA.**

Center. Shoots right. 6'3", 225 lbs. Born, Nitra, Czech., July 20, 1972. Boston's 2nd choice, 40th overall, in 1991 Entry Draft.

Season	Club	League	GP	G	A	Pts	PIM	PP	SH	GW	S	%	+/-	TF	F%	Min	GP	G	A	Pts	PIM	PP	SH	GW	Min
1989-90	Plastika Nitra	Czech-2	38	12	11	23																			
1990-91	AC Nitra	Czech	49	23	22	45	14																		
1991-92	Kolner EC	Germany	33	19	18	37	35										4	1	1	2	0				
	Boston	**NHL**	**4**	**1**	**0**	**1**	**0**	**0**	**0**	**0**	**3**	**33.3**	**1**												
1992-93	**Boston**	**NHL**	**13**	**1**	**3**	**4**	**4**	**0**	**0**	**0**	**8**	**12.5**	**–3**												
	Providence Bruins	AHL	56	31	61	92	26										6	4	4	8	0				
1993-94	**Boston**	**NHL**	**59**	**8**	**15**	**23**	**14**	**0**	**0**	**1**	**62**	**12.9**	**4**				**13**	**1**	**7**	**8**	**4**	**0**	**0**	**0**	
	Providence Bruins	AHL	17	5	12	17	4																		
1994-95	Kolner Haie	Germany	25	16	23	39	18																		
	Boston	**NHL**	**44**	**5**	**13**	**18**	**8**	**1**	**0**	**2**	**46**	**10.9**	**4**				**5**	**0**	**0**	**0**	**0**	**0**	**0**	**0**	
1995-96	**Boston**	**NHL**	**76**	**18**	**36**	**54**	**14**	**5**	**0**	**2**	**158**	**11.4**	**–8**				**5**	**1**	**2**	**3**	**0**	**0**	**0**	**0**	
1996-97	**Boston**	**NHL**	**78**	**21**	**55**	**76**	**14**	**6**	**0**	**1**	**168**	**12.5**	**–22**												
1997-98	**Los Angeles**	**NHL**	**77**	**21**	**58**	**79**	**53**	**4**	**0**	**2**	**162**	**13.0**	**17**				**4**	**1**	**2**	**3**	**2**	**0**	**0**	**0**	
1998-99	**Los Angeles**	**NHL**	**64**	**13**	**21**	**34**	**10**	**1**	**0**	**1**	**131**	**9.9**	**–18**	**1484**	**54.0**	**19:44**									
99-2000	**Los Angeles**	**NHL**	**57**	**17**	**41**	**58**	**10**	**3**	**0**	**7**	**126**	**13.5**	**23**	**1088**	**50.6**	**19:16**	**4**	**0**	**4**	**4**	**8**	**0**	**0**	**0**	**21:05**
2000-01	Bratislava	Slovakia	9	2	4	6	16																		
	Los Angeles	**NHL**	**63**	**16**	**39**	**55**	**14**	**9**	**0**	**6**	**95**	**16.8**	**20**	**1278**	**52.7**	**19:35**	**13**	**3**	**5**	**8**	**10**	**2**	**0**	**1**	**21:56**

			Regular Season														Playoffs								
Season	Club	League	GP	G	A	Pts	PIM	PP	SH	GW	S	%	+/-	TF	F%	Min	GP	G	A	Pts	PIM	PP	SH	GW	Min
2001-02	Los Angeles	NHL	9	1	3	4	4	0	0	0	7	14.3	1	164	48.2	20:06									
	Boston	NHL	72	7	47	54	14	1	0	3	93	7.5	21	1346	49.7	18:36	6	0	2	2	0	0	0	0	16:43
	Slovakia	Olympics	2	2	1	3	0																		
2002-03	Boston	NHL	78	14	37	51	12	4	0	2	110	12.7	0	1601	54.7	18:27	5	0	2	2	0	0	0	0	17:31
2003-04	Los Angeles	NHL	64	8	29	37	16	4	0	0	78	10.3	5	1105	49.3	18:46									
2004-05	HC Slavia Praha	CzRep	52	13	26	39	41										7	4	2	6	10				
	NHL Totals		758	151	397	548	187	38	0	27	1247	12.1		8066	52.0	19:03	55	6	24	30	24	2	0	1	19:55

Traded to **Los Angeles** by **Boston** with Sandy Moger and Boston's 4th round choice (later traded to New Jersey – New Jersey selected Pierre Dagenais) in 1998 Entry Draft for Dmitri Kristich and Byron Dafoe, August 29, 1997. Traded to **Boston** by **Los Angeles** with Glen Murray for Jason Allison and Mikko Eloranta, October 24, 2001. Traded to **Los Angeles** by **Boston** with Boston's 7th round choice (later traded to Nashville – Nashville selected Miroslav Hanuljak) in 2003 Entry Draft for Philadelphia's 4th round choice (previously acquired, Boston selected Patrick Valcak) in 2003 Entry Draft and Detroit's 2nd round choice (previously acquired, Boston selected Martins Karsums) in 2004 Entry Draft, June 22, 2003. Signed as a free agent by **Slavia** (CzRep), August 28, 2004. Signed as a free agent by **Florida**, August 17, 2005.

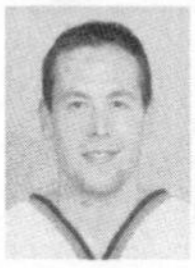

STURM, Marco
(STURHM, MAHR-koh) **S.J.**

Left wing. Shoots left. 6', 195 lbs. Born, Dingolfing, West Germany, September 8, 1978. San Jose's 2nd choice, 21st overall, in 1996 Entry Draft.

1995-96	EV Landshut	Germany	47	12	20	32	50										11	1	3	4	18				
1996-97	EV Landshut	Germany	46	16	27	43	40										7	1	4	5	6				
1997-98	San Jose	NHL	74	10	20	30	40	2	0	3	118	8.5	-2				2	0	0	0	0	0	0	0	
	Germany	Olympics	2	0	0	0	0																		
1998-99	San Jose	NHL	78	16	22	38	52	3	2	3	140	11.4	7	576	45.0	15:23	6	2	2	4	4	0	0	1	14:16
99-2000	San Jose	NHL	74	12	15	27	22	2	4	3	120	10.0	4	183	45.4	14:07	12	1	3	4	6	0	0	0	13:00
2000-01	San Jose	NHL	81	14	18	32	28	2	3	5	153	9.2	9	517	40.2	16:06	6	0	2	2	0	0	0	0	18:18
2001-02	San Jose	NHL	77	21	20	41	32	4	3	5	174	12.1	23	105	47.6	15:39	12	3	2	5	2	0	0	0	15:33
	Germany	Olympics	5	0	1	1	0																		
2002-03	San Jose	NHL	82	28	20	48	16	6	0	2	208	13.5	9	83	48.2	16:31									
2003-04	San Jose	NHL	64	21	20	41	36	10	2	6	158	13.3	0	7	42.9	16:25									
2004-05	ERC Ingolstadt	Germany	45	22	16	38	56										11	3	4	7	12				
	NHL Totals		530	122	135	257	226	29	14	27	1071	11.4		1471	43.7	15:42	38	6	9	15	12	0	0	1	14:56

Played in NHL All-Star Game (1999)

Signed as a free agent by **Ingolstadt** (Germany), August 8, 2004.

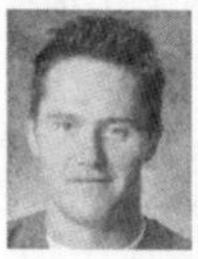

STUTZEL, Mike
(STUHT-zuhl, MIGHK)

Left wing. Shoots left. 6'2", 216 lbs. Born, Victoria, B.C., February 28, 1979.

1997-98	Powell River Kings	BCHL	24	7	5	12	38																		
	Prince George	BCHL	28	13	22	35	20										9	4	1	5	18				
1998-99	Prince George	BCHL	58	41	51	92	102																		
99-2000	Northern Mich.	CCHA	29	3	6	9	44																		
2000-01	Northern Mich.	CCHA	16	3	5	8	6																		
2001-02	Northern Mich.	CCHA	40	16	17	33	20																		
2002-03	Northern Mich.	CCHA	41	27	15	42	50																		
2003-04	Phoenix	NHL	9	0	0	0	0	0	0	0	3	0.0	-4	1	0.0	5:47									
	Springfield	AHL	62	12	12	24	39																		
2004-05	Utah Grizzlies	AHL	52	0	2	2	16																		
	Idaho Steelheads	ECHL	14	8	7	15	8										4	1	0	1	6				
	NHL Totals		9	0	0	0	0	0	0	0	3	0.0		1	0.0	5:47									

Signed as a free agent by **Phoenix**, April 10, 2003.

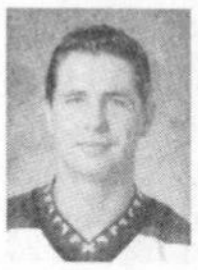

SUCHY, Radoslav
(soo-KHEE, RAD-oh-slav) **CBJ**

Defense. Shoots left. 6'2", 204 lbs. Born, Kezmarok, Czech., April 7, 1976.

1993-94	SKP PS Poprad Jr.	Slovak-Jr.	30	11	12	23	16																		
	SKP PS Poprad	Slovakia	3	0	0	0	0																		
1994-95	Sherbrooke	QMJHL	69	12	32	44	30										7	0	3	3	2				
1995-96	Sherbrooke	QMJHL	68	15	53	68	68										7	0	3	3	2				
1996-97	Sherbrooke	QMJHL	32	6	34	40	14																		
	Chicoutimi	QMJHL	28	5	24	29	26										19	6	15	21	12				
1997-98	Las Vegas	IHL	26	1	4	5	10																		
	Springfield	AHL	41	6	15	21	16										4	0	1	1	2				
1998-99	Springfield	AHL	69	4	32	36	10										3	0	1	1	0				
99-2000	Phoenix	NHL	60	0	6	6	16	0	0	0	36	0.0	2	0	0.0	15:09	5	0	1	1	0	0	0	0	16:18
	Springfield	AHL	2	0	1	1	0																		
2000-01	Phoenix	NHL	72	0	10	10	22	0	0	0	33	0.0	1	0	0.0	17:09									
2001-02	Phoenix	NHL	81	4	13	17	10	1	0	0	49	8.2	25	1	100.0	18:05	5	1	0	1	0	0	0	0	20:35
2002-03	Phoenix	NHL	77	1	8	9	18	1	0	0	48	2.1	2	1	0.0	16:26									
2003-04	Phoenix	NHL	82	7	14	21	8	2	0	2	82	8.5	1	1	100.0	19:40									
2004-05	HK SKP Poprad	Slovakia	34	5	10	15	24										5	0	0	0	2				
	NHL Totals		372	12	51	63	74	4	0	2	248	4.8		3	66.7	17:26	10	1	1	2	0	0	0	0	18:27

QMJHL All-Rookie Team (1995) • QMJHL Second All-Star Team (1997) • George Parsons Trophy (Memorial Cup Tournament Most Sportsmanlike Player) (1997)

Signed as a free agent by **Phoenix**, September 26, 1997. Traded to **Columbus** by **Phoenix** with Phoenix's 6th round choice (Derek Reinhart) in 2005 Entry Draft for Columbus' 4th round choice (later traded to Philadelphia - Philadelphia selected Jeremy Duchesne) in 2005 Entry Draft, July 6, 2004. Signed as a free agent by **Poprad** (Slovakia), October 4, 2004.

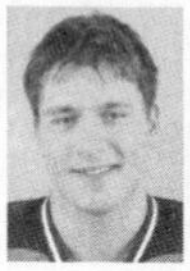

SUGLOBOV, Aleksander
(suh-GLOH-bahf, al-ehx-AN-duhr) **N.J.**

Right wing. Shoots left. 6', 200 lbs. Born, Elektrostal, USSR, January 15, 1982. New Jersey's 3rd choice, 56th overall, in 2000 Entry Draft.

1998-99	Spartak 2	Russia-4	1	0	0	0	0																		
	Spartak Moscow	Russia	1	0	0	0	0																		
99-2000	Yaroslavl 2	Russia-3	38	23	10	33	....																		
2000-01	St. Petersburg	Russia	8	1	0	1	6																		
	Ufa	Russia	6	0	0	0	4																		
	Yaroslavl	Russia	4	0	0	0	2										11	1	2	3	6				
2001-02	Yaroslavl 2	Russia-3	6	5	2	7	20																		
	Yaroslavl	Russia	25	4	2	6	26										5	1	1	2	18				
2002-03	Nizhnekamsk	Russia	6	0	0	0	4																		
	Yaroslavl	Russia	17	4	2	6	12										5	1	0	1	2				
2003-04	New Jersey	NHL	1	0	0	0	0	0	0	0	2	0.0	0	0	0.0	8:18									
	Albany River Rats	AHL	35	11	11	22	54																		
2004-05	Albany River Rats	AHL	72	25	21	46	77																		
	NHL Totals		1	0	0	0	0	0	0	0	2	0.0		0	0.0	8:18									

• Missed majority of 2003-04 season recovering from wrist injury suffered in game vs. Edmonton, January 5, 2004.

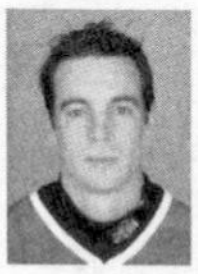

SULLIVAN, Steve
(SUHL-ih-vuhn, STEEV) **NSH.**

Right wing. Shoots right. 5'9", 155 lbs. Born, Timmins, Ont., July 6, 1974. New Jersey's 10th choice, 233rd overall, in 1994 Entry Draft.

1991-92	Timmins	NOJHA	47	66	55	121	141																		
1992-93	Sault Ste. Marie	OHL	62	36	27	63	44										16	3	8	11	18				
1993-94	Sault Ste. Marie	OHL	63	51	62	113	82										14	9	16	25	22				
1994-95	Albany River Rats	AHL	75	31	50	81	124										14	4	7	11	10				
1995-96	New Jersey	NHL	16	5	4	9	8	2	0	1	23	21.7	3												
	Albany River Rats	AHL	53	33	42	75	127										4	3	0	3	6				
1996-97	New Jersey	NHL	33	8	14	22	14	2	0	2	63	12.7	9												
	Albany River Rats	AHL	15	8	7	15	16																		
	Toronto	NHL	21	5	11	16	23	1	0	1	45	11.1	5												
1997-98	Toronto	NHL	63	10	18	28	40	1	0	1	112	8.9	-8												
1998-99	Toronto	NHL	63	20	20	40	28	4	0	5	110	18.2	12	685	44.4	14:12	13	3	3	6	14	2	0	0	16:20
99-2000	Toronto	NHL	7	0	1	1	4	0	0	0	11	0.0	-1	47	48.9	11:52									
	Chicago	NHL	73	22	42	64	52	2	1	6	169	13.0	20	692	48.0	18:05									
2000-01	Chicago	NHL	81	34	41	75	54	6	8	3	204	16.7	3	649	42.4	20:32									

			Regular Season														Playoffs								
Season	Club	League	GP	G	A	Pts	PIM	PP	SH	GW	S	%	+/-	TF	F%	Min	GP	G	A	Pts	PIM	PP	SH	GW	Min
2001-02	**Chicago**	**NHL**	**78**	**21**	**39**	**60**	**67**	**3**	**0**	**8**	**155**	**13.5**	**23**	**758**	**48.9**	**19:10**	**5**	**1**	**0**	**1**	**2**	**0**	**0**	**0**	**18:04**
2002-03	**Chicago**	**NHL**	**82**	**26**	**35**	**61**	**42**	**4**	**2**	**3**	**190**	**13.7**	**15**	**382**	**46.1**	**19:15**	....	....	....	....	....	....	....	....	....
2003-04	**Chicago**	**NHL**	**56**	**15**	**28**	**43**	**36**	**4**	**2**	**4**	**140**	**10.7**	**-7**	**103**	**44.7**	**21:19**	....	....	....	....	....	....	....	....	....
	Nashville	**NHL**	**24**	**9**	**21**	**30**	**12**	**7**	**0**	**0**	**78**	**11.5**	**8**	**124**	**43.6**	**20:02**	**6**	**1**	**1**	**2**	**6**	**0**	**0**	**1**	**18:58**
2004-05		DID NOT PLAY																							
	NHL Totals		**597**	**175**	**274**	**449**	**380**	**36**	**13**	**34**	**1300**	**13.5**		**3440**	**46.0**	**18:46**	**24**	**5**	**4**	**9**	**22**	**2**	**0**	**1**	**17:21**

AHL First All-Star Team (1996)

Traded to **Toronto** by **New Jersey** with Jason Smith and the rights to Alyn McCauley for Doug Gilmour, Dave Ellett and New Jersey's 3rd round choice (previously acquired, New Jersey selected Andre Lakos) in 1999 Entry Draft, February 25, 1997. Claimed on waivers by **Chicago** from **Toronto**, October 23, 1999. Traded to **Nashville** by **Chicago** for Nashville's 2nd round choices in 2004 (Ryan Garlock) and 2005 (Michael Blunden) Entry Drafts, February 16, 2004.

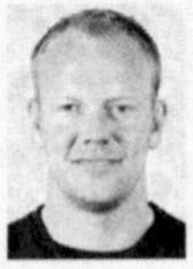

SUNDIN, Mats

(suhn-DEEN, MATS) **TOR.**

Center. Shoots right. 6'5", 231 lbs. Born, Bromma, Sweden, February 13, 1971. Quebec's 1st choice, 1st overall, in 1989 Entry Draft.

1988-89	Nacka HK	Sweden-2	25	10	8	18	18	....	....	....	....	....	....	....	....	....	....	....	....	....	....	....	....	....	....
1989-90	Djurgarden	Sweden	34	10	8	18	16	....	....	....	....	....	....	....	....	....	8	7	0	7	4	....	....	....	....
1990-91	**Quebec**	**NHL**	**80**	**23**	**36**	**59**	**58**	**4**	**0**	**0**	**155**	**14.8**	**-24**	....	....	....	....	....	....	....	....	....	....	....	....
1991-92	**Quebec**	**NHL**	**80**	**33**	**43**	**76**	**103**	**8**	**2**	**2**	**231**	**14.3**	**-19**	....	....	....	....	....	....	....	....	....	....	....	....
1992-93	**Quebec**	**NHL**	**80**	**47**	**67**	**114**	**96**	**13**	**4**	**9**	**215**	**21.9**	**21**	....	....	....	**6**	**3**	**1**	**4**	**6**	**1**	**0**	**0**	....
1993-94	**Quebec**	**NHL**	**84**	**32**	**53**	**85**	**60**	**6**	**2**	**4**	**226**	**14.2**	**1**	....	....	....	....	....	....	....	....	....	....	....	....
1994-95	Djurgarden	Sweden	12	7	2	9	14	....	....	....	....	....	....	....	....	....	....	....	....	....	....	....	....	....	....
	Toronto	**NHL**	**47**	**23**	**24**	**47**	**14**	**9**	**0**	**4**	**173**	**13.3**	**-5**	....	....	....	**7**	**5**	**4**	**9**	**4**	**2**	**0**	**1**	....
1995-96	**Toronto**	**NHL**	**76**	**33**	**50**	**83**	**46**	**7**	**6**	**7**	**301**	**11.0**	**8**	....	....	....	**6**	**3**	**1**	**4**	**4**	**2**	**0**	**1**	....
1996-97	**Toronto**	**NHL**	**82**	**41**	**53**	**94**	**59**	**7**	**4**	**8**	**281**	**14.6**	**6**	....	....	....	....	....	....	....	....	....	....	....	....
1997-98	**Toronto**	**NHL**	**82**	**33**	**41**	**74**	**49**	**9**	**1**	**5**	**219**	**15.1**	**-3**	....	....	....	....	....	....	....	....	....	....	....	....
	Sweden	Olympics	4	3	0	3	4	....	....	....	....	....	....	....	....	....	....	....	....	....	....	....	....	....	....
1998-99	**Toronto**	**NHL**	**82**	**31**	**52**	**83**	**58**	**4**	**0**	**6**	**209**	**14.8**	**22**	**1993**	**57.3**	**20:41**	**17**	**8**	**8**	**16**	**16**	**3**	**0**	**2**	**22:46**
99-2000	**Toronto**	**NHL**	**73**	**32**	**41**	**73**	**46**	**10**	**2**	**7**	**184**	**17.4**	**16**	**1619**	**50.8**	**20:11**	**12**	**3**	**5**	**8**	**10**	**0**	**0**	**1**	**21:27**
2000-01	**Toronto**	**NHL**	**82**	**28**	**46**	**74**	**76**	**9**	**0**	**6**	**226**	**12.4**	**15**	**1870**	**56.6**	**19:21**	**11**	**6**	**7**	**13**	**14**	**2**	**1**	**1**	**20:12**
2001-02	**Toronto**	**NHL**	**82**	**41**	**39**	**80**	**94**	**10**	**2**	**9**	**262**	**15.6**	**6**	**1812**	**57.5**	**19:20**	**8**	**2**	**5**	**7**	**4**	**0**	**0**	**0**	**20:07**
	Sweden	Olympics	4	5	4	*9	10	....	....	....	....	....	....	....	....	....	....	....	....	....	....	....	....	....	....
2002-03	**Toronto**	**NHL**	**75**	**37**	**35**	**72**	**58**	**16**	**3**	**8**	**223**	**16.6**	**1**	**1774**	**56.1**	**20:15**	**7**	**1**	**3**	**4**	**6**	**1**	**0**	**0**	**24:17**
2003-04	**Toronto**	**NHL**	**81**	**31**	**44**	**75**	**52**	**11**	**1**	**10**	**226**	**13.7**	**11**	**1705**	**53.0**	**19:52**	**9**	**4**	**5**	**9**	**8**	**0**	**0**	**1**	**18:24**
2004-05		DID NOT PLAY																							
	NHL Totals		**1086**	**465**	**624**	**1089**	**869**	**123**	**27**	**85**	**3131**	**14.9**		**10773**	**55.4**	**19:56**	**83**	**35**	**39**	**74**	**72**	**11**	**1**	**7**	**21:18**

NHL Second All-Star Team (2002, 2004)

Played in NHL All-Star Game (1996, 1997, 1998, 1999, 2000, 2001, 2002, 2004)

Traded to **Toronto** by **Quebec** with Garth Butcher, Todd Warriner and Philadelphia's 1st round choice (previously acquired, later traded to Washington – Washington selected Nolan Baumgartner) in 1994 Entry Draft for Wendel Clark, Sylvain Lefebvre, Landon Wilson and Toronto's 1st round choice (Jeffrey Kealty) in 1994 Entry Draft, June 28, 1994.

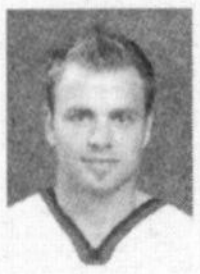

SUNDSTROM, Niklas

(SUHN-struhm, NIHK-las) **MTL.**

Right wing. Shoots left. 6', 191 lbs. Born, Ornskoldsvik, Sweden, June 6, 1975. NY Rangers' 1st choice, 8th overall, in 1993 Entry Draft.

1991-92	MoDo	Sweden	9	1	3	4	0	....	....	....	....	....	....	....	....	....	....	....	....	....	....	....	....	....	....
1992-93	MoDo Jr.	Swe-Jr.	2	3	1	4	0	....	....	....	....	....	....	....	....	....	....	....	....	....	....	....	....	....	....
	MoDo	Sweden	40	7	11	18	18	....	....	....	....	....	....	....	....	....	3	0	0	0	0	....	....	....	....
1993-94	MoDo Jr.	Swe-Jr.	3	3	4	7	2	....	....	....	....	....	....	....	....	....	....	....	....	....	....	....	....	....	....
	MoDo	Sweden	37	7	12	19	28	....	....	....	....	....	....	....	....	....	11	4	3	7	2	....	....	....	....
1994-95	MoDo	Sweden	33	8	13	21	30	....	....	....	....	....	....	....	....	....	....	....	....	....	....	....	....	....	....
1995-96	**NY Rangers**	**NHL**	**82**	**9**	**12**	**21**	**14**	**1**	**1**	**2**	**90**	**10.0**	**2**	....	....	....	**11**	**4**	**3**	**7**	**4**	**1**	**0**	**0**	....
1996-97	**NY Rangers**	**NHL**	**82**	**24**	**28**	**52**	**20**	**5**	**1**	**4**	**132**	**18.2**	**23**	....	....	....	**9**	**0**	**5**	**5**	**2**	**0**	**0**	**0**	....
1997-98	**NY Rangers**	**NHL**	**70**	**19**	**28**	**47**	**24**	**4**	**0**	**1**	**115**	**16.5**	**0**	....	....	....	....	....	....	....	....	....	....	....	....
	Sweden	Olympics	4	1	1	2	2	....	....	....	....	....	....	....	....	....	....	....	....	....	....	....	....	....	....
1998-99	**NY Rangers**	**NHL**	**81**	**13**	**30**	**43**	**20**	**1**	**2**	**3**	**89**	**14.6**	**-2**	**376**	**40.4**	**19:11**	....	....	....	....	....	....	....	....	....
99-2000	**San Jose**	**NHL**	**79**	**12**	**25**	**37**	**22**	**2**	**1**	**2**	**90**	**13.3**	**9**	**10**	**50.0**	**15:10**	**12**	**0**	**2**	**2**	**2**	**0**	**0**	**0**	**15:09**
2000-01	**San Jose**	**NHL**	**82**	**10**	**39**	**49**	**28**	**4**	**1**	**0**	**100**	**10.0**	**10**	**26**	**30.8**	**16:44**	**6**	**0**	**3**	**3**	**2**	**0**	**0**	**0**	**16:40**
2001-02	**San Jose**	**NHL**	**73**	**9**	**30**	**39**	**50**	**0**	**1**	**0**	**74**	**12.2**	**7**	**9**	**33.3**	**15:57**	**12**	**1**	**6**	**7**	**6**	**0**	**0**	**0**	**16:25**
	Sweden	Olympics	4	1	3	4	0	....	....	....	....	....	....	....	....	....	....	....	....	....	....	....	....	....	....
2002-03	**San Jose**	**NHL**	**47**	**2**	**10**	**12**	**22**	**0**	**0**	**0**	**36**	**5.6**	**-4**	**1**	**0.0**	**14:09**	....	....	....	....	....	....	....	....	....
	Montreal	**NHL**	**33**	**5**	**9**	**14**	**8**	**0**	**0**	**1**	**35**	**14.3**	**3**	**10**	**40.0**	**14:26**	....	....	....	....	....	....	....	....	....
2003-04	**Montreal**	**NHL**	**66**	**8**	**12**	**20**	**18**	**0**	**0**	**2**	**67**	**11.9**	**3**	**20**	**15.0**	**14:17**	**4**	**1**	**0**	**1**	**2**	**0**	**0**	**0**	**13:10**
2004-05	Milano	Italy	33	9	27	36	40	....	....	....	....	....	....	....	....	....	15	4	14	18	20	....	....	....	....
	NHL Totals		**695**	**111**	**223**	**334**	**226**	**17**	**7**	**15**	**828**	**13.4**		**452**	**38.7**	**16:00**	**54**	**6**	**19**	**25**	**18**	**1**	**0**	**0**	**15:38**

Traded to **Tampa Bay** by **NY Rangers** with Dan Cloutier and NY Rangers' 1st (Nikita Alexeev) and 3rd (later traded to San Jose – later traded to Chicago – Chicago selected Igor Radulov) round choices in 2000 Entry Draft for Chicago's 1st round choice (previously acquired, NY Rangers selected Pavel Brendl) in 1999 Entry Draft, June 26, 1999. Traded to **San Jose** by **Tampa Bay** with NY Rangers' 3rd round choice (previously acquired, later traded to Chicago – Chicago selected Igor Radulov) in 2000 Entry Draft for Bill Houlder, Andrei Zyuzin, Shawn Burr and Steve Guolla, August 4, 1999. Traded to **Montreal** by **San Jose** with San Jose's 3rd round choice (later traded to Los Angeles – Los Angeles selected Paul Baier) in 2004 Entry Draft for Jeff Hackett, January 23, 2003. Signed as a free agent by **Milano** (Italy), October 1, 2004.

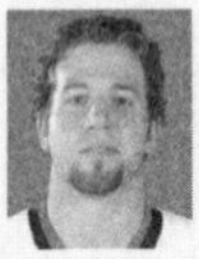

SURMA, Damian

(SUHR-ma, DAY-mee-an)

Center. Shoots left. 5'10", 200 lbs. Born, Lincoln Park, MI, January 22, 1981. Carolina's 5th choice, 174th overall, in 1999 Entry Draft.

1997-98	Det. Compuware	NAHL	54	12	18	30	54	....	....	....	....	....	....	....	....	....	7	1	4	5	10	....	....	....	....
1998-99	Plymouth Whalers	OHL	65	17	15	32	62	....	....	....	....	....	....	....	....	....	11	3	6	9	15	....	....	....	....
99-2000	Plymouth Whalers	OHL	66	34	44	78	114	....	....	....	....	....	....	....	....	....	20	9	8	17	10	....	....	....	....
2000-01	Plymouth Whalers	OHL	55	26	34	60	62	....	....	....	....	....	....	....	....	....	19	8	9	17	25	....	....	....	....
2001-02	Plymouth Whalers	OHL	55	28	27	55	68	....	....	....	....	....	....	....	....	....	6	3	0	3	10	....	....	....	....
	Lowell	AHL	1	0	0	0	0	....	....	....	....	....	....	....	....	....	4	0	0	0	0	....	....	....	....
2002-03	**Carolina**	**NHL**	**1**	**1**	**0**	**1**	**0**	**0**	**0**	**0**	**1**	**100.0**	**0**	**0**	**0.0**	**7:15**	....	....	....	....	....	....	....	....	....
	Lowell	AHL	68	11	11	22	46	....	....	....	....	....	....	....	....	....	....	....	....	....	....	....	....	....	....
2003-04	**Carolina**	**NHL**	**1**	**0**	**1**	**1**	**0**	**0**	**0**	**0**	**0**	**0.0**	**1**	**0**	**0.0**	**9:26**	....	....	....	....	....	....	....	....	....
	Lowell	AHL	48	3	5	8	21	....	....	....	....	....	....	....	....	....	....	....	....	....	....	....	....	....	....
	Florida Everblades	ECHL	18	6	9	15	20	....	....	....	....	....	....	....	....	....	16	5	4	9	20	....	....	....	....
2004-05	Florida Everblades	ECHL	72	32	28	60	74	....	....	....	....	....	....	....	....	....	19	7	6	13	14	....	....	....	....
	NHL Totals		**2**	**1**	**1**	**2**	**0**	**0**	**0**	**0**	**1**	**100.0**		**0**	**0.0**	**8:21**	....	....	....	....	....	....	....	....	....

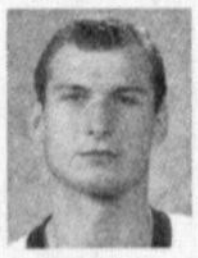

SUROVY, Tomas

(suh-ROH-vee, TAW-mahsh) **PIT.**

Center. Shoots left. 6'1", 205 lbs. Born, Banska Bystrica, Czech., September 24, 1981. Pittsburgh's 5th choice, 120th overall, in 2001 Entry Draft.

99-2000	B. Bystrica	Slovak-2	39	25	29	54	4	....	....	....	....	....	....	....	....	....	....	....	....	....	....	....	....	....	....
2000-01	HC SKP Poprad	Slovakia	53	22	28	50	30	....	....	....	....	....	....	....	....	....	6	2	1	3	14	....	....	....	....
2001-02	Wilkes-Barre	AHL	65	23	10	33	37	....	....	....	....	....	....	....	....	....	....	....	....	....	....	....	....	....	....
2002-03	**Pittsburgh**	**NHL**	**26**	**4**	**7**	**11**	**10**	**1**	**0**	**2**	**47**	**8.5**	**0**	**2**	**50.0**	**14:19**	....	....	....	....	....	....	....	....	....
	Wilkes-Barre	AHL	39	19	20	39	18	....	....	....	....	....	....	....	....	....	6	2	3	5	2	....	....	....	....
2003-04	**Pittsburgh**	**NHL**	**47**	**11**	**12**	**23**	**16**	**3**	**0**	**1**	**112**	**9.8**	**-8**	**4**	**25.0**	**12:28**	....	....	....	....	....	....	....	....	....
	Wilkes-Barre	AHL	30	14	15	29	14	....	....	....	....	....	....	....	....	....	24	6	10	16	8	....	....	....	....
2004-05	Wilkes-Barre	AHL	80	17	32	49	43	....	....	....	....	....	....	....	....	....	11	2	6	8	9	....	....	....	....
	NHL Totals		**73**	**15**	**19**	**34**	**26**	**4**	**0**	**3**	**159**	**9.4**		**6**	**33.3**	**13:08**	....	....	....	....	....	....	....	....	....

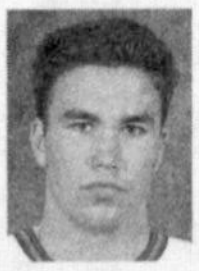

SUTHERBY, Brian

(SUH-thur-bee, BRIGH-uhn) **WSH.**

Center. Shoots left. 6'3", 205 lbs. Born, Edmonton, Alta., March 1, 1982. Washington's 1st choice, 26th overall, in 2000 Entry Draft.

1997-98	CAC Cement	AMHL	36	36	23	59	60	....	....	....	....	....	....	....	....	....	....	....	....	....	....	....	....	....	....
1998-99	Moose Jaw	WHL	66	9	12	21	47	....	....	....	....	....	....	....	....	....	11	0	1	1	0	....	....	....	....
99-2000	Moose Jaw	WHL	47	18	17	35	102	....	....	....	....	....	....	....	....	....	4	1	1	2	12	....	....	....	....
2000-01	Moose Jaw	WHL	59	34	43	77	138	....	....	....	....	....	....	....	....	....	4	2	1	3	10	....	....	....	....
2001-02	**Washington**	**NHL**	**7**	**0**	**0**	**0**	**2**	**0**	**0**	**0**	**3**	**0.0**	**-3**	**39**	**35.9**	**7:17**	....	....	....	....	....	....	....	....	....
	Moose Jaw	WHL	36	18	27	45	75	....	....	....	....	....	....	....	....	....	12	7	5	12	33	....	....	....	....

								Regular Season									Playoffs								
Season	Club	League	GP	G	A	Pts	PIM	PP	SH	GW	S	%	+/-	TF	F%	Min	GP	G	A	Pts	PIM	PP	SH	GW	Min
2002-03	**Washington**	**NHL**	**72**	**2**	**9**	**11**	**93**	**0**	**0**	**0**	**38**	**5.3**	**7**	**288**	**43.8**	**9:44**	**5**	**0**	**0**	**0**	**10**	**0**	**0**	**0**	**4:10**
	Portland Pirates	AHL	5	0	5	5	11	....	....	....	....	....	....	....	....	....	....	....	....	....	....	....	....	....	....
2003-04	**Washington**	**NHL**	**30**	**2**	**0**	**2**	**28**	**0**	**0**	**0**	**24**	**8.3**	**-5**	**116**	**41.4**	**10:15**	....	....	....	....	....	....	....	....	....
	Portland Pirates	AHL	6	2	4	6	16	....	....	....	....	....	....	....	....	....	....	....	....	....	....	....	....	....	....
2004-05	Portland Pirates	AHL	53	10	19	29	115	....	....	....	....	....	....	....	....	....	....	....	....	....	....	....	....	....	....
	NHL Totals		**109**	**4**	**9**	**13**	**123**	**0**	**0**	**0**	**65**	**6.2**		**443**	**42.4**	**9:43**	**5**	**0**	**0**	**0**	**10**	**0**	**0**	**0**	**4:10**

• Missed majority of 2003-04 season recovering from groin injury suffered in game vs. St. Louis, October 18, 2003.

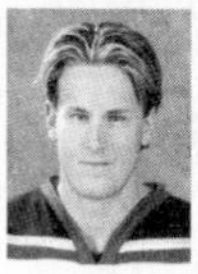

SUTTON, Andy

(SUH-tohn, AN-dee) **ATL.**

Defense. Shoots left. 6'6", 245 lbs. Born, Kingston, Ont., March 10, 1975.

1991-92	Gananoque	OHA-B	36	11	9	20	....	....	....	....	....	....	....	....	....	....	14	9	21	30	....	....	....	....	....
1992-93	Gananoque	OHA-B	38	14	9	23	....	....	....	....	....	....	....	....	....	....	12	16	13	29	....	....	....	....	....
1993-94	St. Mike's B's	MTJHL	48	17	23	40	161	....	....	....	....	....	....	....	....	....	3	0	0	0	20	....	....	....	....
1994-95	Michigan Tech	WCHA	19	2	1	3	42	....	....	....	....	....	....	....	....	....	....	....	....	....	....	....	....	....	....
1995-96	Michigan Tech	WCHA	33	2	2	4	58	....	....	....	....	....	....	....	....	....	....	....	....	....	....	....	....	....	....
1996-97	Michigan Tech	WCHA	32	2	7	9	73	....	....	....	....	....	....	....	....	....	....	....	....	....	....	....	....	....	....
1997-98	Michigan Tech	WCHA	38	16	24	40	97	....	....	....	....	....	....	....	....	....	....	....	....	....	....	....	....	....	....
	Kentucky	AHL	7	0	0	0	33	....	....	....	....	....	....	....	....	....	....	....	....	....	....	....	....	....	....
1998-99	**San Jose**	**NHL**	**31**	**0**	**3**	**3**	**65**	**0**	**0**	**0**	**24**	**0.0**	**-4**	**0**	**0.0**	**12:58**	....	....	....	....	....	....	....	....	....
	Kentucky	AHL	21	5	10	15	53	....	....	....	....	....	....	....	....	....	5	0	0	0	23	....	....	....	....
99-2000	**San Jose**	**NHL**	**40**	**1**	**1**	**2**	**80**	**0**	**0**	**0**	**29**	**3.4**	**-5**	**0**	**0.0**	**12:57**	....	....	....	....	....	....	....	....	....
	Kentucky	AHL	3	0	1	1	0	....	....	....	....	....	....	....	....	....	....	....	....	....	....	....	....	....	....
2000-01	**Minnesota**	**NHL**	**69**	**3**	**4**	**7**	**131**	**2**	**0**	**0**	**64**	**4.7**	**-11**	**3**	**33.3**	**12:55**	....	....	....	....	....	....	....	....	....
2001-02	**Minnesota**	**NHL**	**19**	**2**	**4**	**6**	**35**	**1**	**0**	**0**	**21**	**9.5**	**-4**	**2**	**0.0**	**10:57**	....	....	....	....	....	....	....	....	....
	Atlanta	**NHL**	**24**	**0**	**4**	**4**	**46**	**0**	**0**	**0**	**20**	**0.0**	**0**	**0**	**0.0**	**15:25**	....	....	....	....	....	....	....	....	....
2002-03	**Atlanta**	**NHL**	**53**	**3**	**18**	**21**	**114**	**1**	**1**	**0**	**65**	**4.6**	**-8**	**3**	**33.3**	**18:00**	....	....	....	....	....	....	....	....	....
2003-04	**Atlanta**	**NHL**	**65**	**8**	**13**	**21**	**94**	**7**	**1**	**1**	**102**	**7.8**	**0**	**1**	**0.0**	**23:21**	....	....	....	....	....	....	....	....	....
2004-05	GCK Lions Zurich	Swiss-2	18	8	18	26	58	....	....	....	....	....	....	....	....	....	6	2	4	6	16	....	....	....	....
	ZSC Lions Zurich	Swiss	8	2	2	4	32	....	....	....	....	....	....	....	....	....	1	0	1	1	2	....	....	....	....
	NHL Totals		**301**	**17**	**47**	**64**	**565**	**11**	**2**	**1**	**325**	**5.2**		**9**	**22.2**	**16:09**	....	....	....	....	....	....	....	....	....

WCHA Second All-Star Team (1998)

Signed as a free agent by **San Jose**, March 20, 1998. Traded to **Minnesota** by **San Jose** with San Jose's 7th round choice (Peter Bartos) in 2000 Entry Draft and 3rd round choice (later traded to Atlanta – later traded to Pittsburgh – later traded to Columbus – Columbus selected Aaron Johnson) in 2001 Entry Draft for Minnesota's 8th round choice (later traded to Calgary – Calgary selected Joe Campbell) in 2001 Entry Draft and future considerations, June 12, 2000. Traded to **Atlanta** by **Minnesota** for Hnat Domenichelli, January 22, 2002. Signed as a free agent by **GCK Zurich** (Swiss-2), September 24, 2004. Loaned to **ZSC Zurich** (Swiss) by **GCK Zurich** (Swiss-2), February 22, 2005.

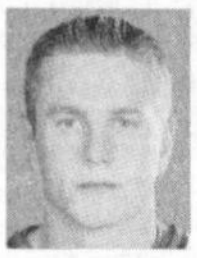

SVATOS, Marek

(SVA-tohsh, MAIR-ehk) **COL.**

Right wing. Shoots right. 5'9", 170 lbs. Born, Kosice, Czech., June 17, 1982. Colorado's 10th choice, 227th overall, in 2001 Entry Draft.

99-2000	HC VSZ Kosice Jr.	Slovak-Jr.	39	43	30	73	28	....	....	....	....	....	....	....	....	....	....	....	....	....	....	....	....	....	....
	HC VSZ Kosice	Slovakia	19	2	2	4	0	....	....	....	....	....	....	....	....	....	....	....	....	....	....	....	....	....	....
2000-01	Kootenay Ice	WHL	39	23	18	41	47	....	....	....	....	....	....	....	....	....	11	7	2	9	26	....	....	....	....
2001-02	Kootenay Ice	WHL	53	38	39	77	58	....	....	....	....	....	....	....	....	....	21	12	6	18	40	....	....	....	....
2002-03	Hershey Bears	AHL	30	9	4	13	10	....	....	....	....	....	....	....	....	....	....	....	....	....	....	....	....	....	....
2003-04	**Colorado**	**NHL**	**4**	**2**	**0**	**2**	**0**	**1**	**0**	**1**	**6**	**33.3**	**1**	**0**	**0.0**	**10:18**	**11**	**1**	**5**	**6**	**2**	**0**	**0**	**1**	**12:29**
2004-05	Hershey Bears	AHL	72	18	28	46	69	....	....	....	....	....	....	....	....	....	....	....	....	....	....	....	....	....	....
	NHL Totals		**4**	**2**	**0**	**2**	**0**	**1**	**0**	**1**	**6**	**33.3**		**0**	**0.0**	**10:18**	**11**	**1**	**5**	**6**	**2**	**0**	**0**	**1**	**12:29**

WHL West Second All-Star Team (2002)

• Missed majority of 2002-03 season recovering from shoulder injury that required surgery, January 28, 2003. • Missed majority of 2003-04 season recovering from shoulder injury suffered in game vs. St. Louis, October 12, 2003.

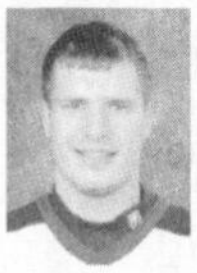

SVITOV, Alexander

(SVEE-tawf, al-ehx-AN-duhr) **CBJ**

Center. Shoots left. 6'3", 217 lbs. Born, Omsk, USSR, November 3, 1982. Tampa Bay's 1st choice, 3rd overall, in 2001 Entry Draft.

1997-98	Novokuznetsk 2	Russia-3	4	0	0	0	0	....	....	....	....	....	....	....	....	....	....	....	....	....	....	....	....	....	....
1998-99	Omsk 2	Russia-4	27	15	8	23	20	....	....	....	....	....	....	....	....	....	....	....	....	....	....	....	....	....	....
	Avangard Omsk	Russia	....	....	....	....	....	....	....	....	....	....	....	....	....	....	1	0	0	0	0	....	....	....	....
99-2000	Omsk 2	Russia-3	14	13	9	22	62	....	....	....	....	....	....	....	....	....	....	....	....	....	....	....	....	....	....
	Avangard Omsk	Russia	18	3	3	6	45	....	....	....	....	....	....	....	....	....	6	1	0	1	16	....	....	....	....
2000-01	Avangard Omsk	Russia	39	8	6	14	115	....	....	....	....	....	....	....	....	....	14	2	1	3	34	....	....	....	....
2001-02	CSKA Moscow 2	Russia-3	2	1	0	1	2	....	....	....	....	....	....	....	....	....	....	....	....	....	....	....	....	....	....
	Avangard Omsk	Russia	2	0	1	1	2	....	....	....	....	....	....	....	....	....	....	....	....	....	....	....	....	....	....
2002-03	**Tampa Bay**	**NHL**	**63**	**4**	**4**	**8**	**58**	**1**	**0**	**0**	**69**	**5.8**	**-4**	**395**	**42.8**	**8:50**	**7**	**0**	**0**	**0**	**6**	**0**	**0**	**0**	**7:19**
	Springfield	AHL	11	4	5	9	17	....	....	....	....	....	....	....	....	....	....	....	....	....	....	....	....	....	....
2003-04	**Tampa Bay**	**NHL**	**11**	**0**	**3**	**3**	**4**	**0**	**0**	**0**	**16**	**0.0**	**0**	**79**	**58.2**	**9:18**	....	....	....	....	....	....	....	....	....
	Hamilton	AHL	30	9	9	18	79	....	....	....	....	....	....	....	....	....	....	....	....	....	....	....	....	....	....
	Columbus	**NHL**	**29**	**2**	**6**	**8**	**16**	**0**	**0**	**0**	**36**	**5.6**	**-8**	**293**	**43.0**	**12:39**	....	....	....	....	....	....	....	....	....
2004-05	Syracuse Crunch	AHL	69	19	23	42	200	....	....	....	....	....	....	....	....	....	....	....	....	....	....	....	....	....	....
	NHL Totals		**103**	**6**	**13**	**19**	**78**	**1**	**0**	**0**	**121**	**5.0**		**767**	**44.5**	**9:58**	**7**	**0**	**0**	**0**	**6**	**0**	**0**	**0**	**7:19**

Traded to **Columbus** by **Tampa Bay** with Tampa Bay's 3rd round choice (later traded to Calgary – Calgary selected Dustin Boyd) in 2004 Entry Draft for Darryl Sydor and Columbus' 4th round choice (Mike Lundin) in 2004 Entry Draft, January 27, 2004.

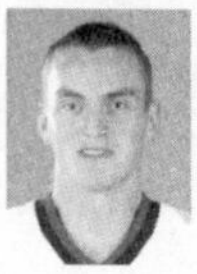

SVOBODA, Jaroslav

(svah-BOH-duh, YAR-oh-slawf) **DAL.**

Left wing. Shoots left. 6'2", 190 lbs. Born, Cervenka, Czech., June 1, 1980. Carolina's 8th choice, 208th overall, in 1998 Entry Draft.

1995-96	HC Olomouc Jr.	CzRep-Jr.	40	13	15	28	....	....	....	....	....	....	....	....	....	....	....	....	....	....	....	....	....	....	....
1996-97	HC Olomouc Jr.	CzRep-Jr.	39	19	14	33	....	....	....	....	....	....	....	....	....	....	....	....	....	....	....	....	....	....	....
1997-98	HC Olomouc Jr.	CzRep-Jr.	36	14	21	35	....	....	....	....	....	....	....	....	....	....	....	....	....	....	....	....	....	....	....
	HC Olomouc	CzRep-2	13	0	1	1	....	....	....	....	....	....	....	....	....	....	....	....	....	....	....	....	....	....	....
1998-99	Kootenay Ice	WHL	54	26	33	59	46	....	....	....	....	....	....	....	....	....	7	2	2	4	11	....	....	....	....
99-2000	Kootenay Ice	WHL	56	23	43	66	97	....	....	....	....	....	....	....	....	....	21	*15	13	*28	51	....	....	....	....
2000-01	Cincinnati	IHL	52	4	10	14	25	....	....	....	....	....	....	....	....	....	....	....	....	....	....	....	....	....	....
2001-02	**Carolina**	**NHL**	**10**	**2**	**2**	**4**	**2**	**0**	**0**	**0**	**12**	**16.7**	**0**	**1**	**0.0**	**9:23**	**23**	**1**	**4**	**5**	**28**	**1**	**0**	**1**	**14:45**
	Lowell	AHL	66	12	16	28	58	....	....	....	....	....	....	....	....	....	....	....	....	....	....	....	....	....	....
2002-03	**Carolina**	**NHL**	**48**	**3**	**11**	**14**	**32**	**1**	**0**	**0**	**63**	**4.8**	**-5**	**25**	**40.0**	**14:33**	....	....	....	....	....	....	....	....	....
	Lowell	AHL	9	1	1	2	10	....	....	....	....	....	....	....	....	....	....	....	....	....	....	....	....	....	....
2003-04	**Carolina**	**NHL**	**33**	**3**	**1**	**4**	**6**	**0**	**0**	**1**	**27**	**11.1**	**3**	**18**	**33.3**	**9:08**	....	....	....	....	....	....	....	....	....
	Lowell	AHL	9	2	2	4	4	....	....	....	....	....	....	....	....	....	....	....	....	....	....	....	....	....	....
2004-05	HC Olomouc	CzRep-2	18	7	6	13	67	....	....	....	....	....	....	....	....	....	....	....	....	....	....	....	....	....	....
	HC Ocelari Trinec	CzRep	9	0	2	2	14	....	....	....	....	....	....	....	....	....	....	....	....	....	....	....	....	....	....
	NHL Totals		**91**	**8**	**14**	**22**	**40**	**1**	**0**	**1**	**102**	**7.8**		**44**	**36.4**	**12:01**	**23**	**1**	**4**	**5**	**28**	**1**	**0**	**1**	**14:45**

Traded to **Dallas** by **Carolina** for Dallas' 4th round choice (Jakub Vojta) in 2005 Entry Draft, June 29, 2004. Signed as a free agent by **Olomouc** (CzRep-2), September 27, 2004. Signed as a free agent by **Trinec** (CzRep), January 6, 2005.

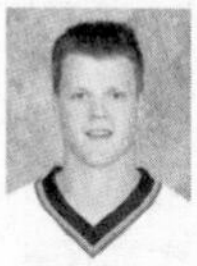

SWANSON, Brian

(SWAHN-suhn, BRIGH-uhn)

Center. Shoots left. 5'10", 185 lbs. Born, Eagle River, AK, March 24, 1976. San Jose's 5th choice, 115th overall, in 1994 Entry Draft.

1991-92	Anchorage	AAHL	50	35	40	75	10	....	....	....	....	....	....	....	....	....	....	....	....	....	....	....	....	....	....
1992-93	Anchorage	AAHL	45	40	50	90	12	....	....	....	....	....	....	....	....	....	....	....	....	....	....	....	....	....	....
1993-94	Omaha Lancers	USHL	47	38	42	80	40	....	....	....	....	....	....	....	....	....	....	....	....	....	....	....	....	....	....
1994-95	Omaha Lancers	USHL	33	14	35	49	12	....	....	....	....	....	....	....	....	....	....	....	....	....	....	....	....	....	....
1995-96	Colorado College	WCHA	40	26	33	59	24	....	....	....	....	....	....	....	....	....	....	....	....	....	....	....	....	....	....
1996-97	Colorado College	WCHA	43	19	32	51	47	....	....	....	....	....	....	....	....	....	....	....	....	....	....	....	....	....	....
1997-98	Colorado College	WCHA	42	18	*38	*56	26	....	....	....	....	....	....	....	....	....	....	....	....	....	....	....	....	....	....
1998-99	Colorado College	WCHA	42	25	*41	66	28	....	....	....	....	....	....	....	....	....	....	....	....	....	....	....	....	....	....
	Hartford	AHL	4	0	0	0	4	....	....	....	....	....	....	....	....	....	....	....	....	....	....	....	....	....	....
99-2000	Hamilton	AHL	69	19	40	59	18	....	....	....	....	....	....	....	....	....	10	2	5	7	6	....	....	....	....

			Regular Season														Playoffs								
Season	Club	League	GP	G	A	Pts	PIM	PP	SH	GW	S	%	+/-	TF	F%	Min	GP	G	A	Pts	PIM	PP	SH	GW	Min
2000-01	**Edmonton**	**NHL**	**16**	**1**	**1**	**2**	**6**	**0**	**0**	**0**	**8**	**12.5**	**–1**	**150**	**44.0**	**10:55**	....	....	....	....	....	....	....	....	....
	Hamilton	AHL	49	18	29	47	20	....	....	....	....	....	....	....	....	....	....	....	....	....	....	....	....	....	....
2001-02	**Edmonton**	**NHL**	**8**	**1**	**1**	**2**	**0**	**0**	**0**	**0**	**7**	**14.3**	**–1**	**59**	**54.2**	**10:10**	....	....	....	....	....	....	....	....	....
	Hamilton	AHL	65	34	39	73	26	....	....	....	....	....	....	....	....	....	15	7	6	13	6	....	....	....	....
2002-03	**Edmonton**	**NHL**	**44**	**2**	**10**	**12**	**10**	**1**	**0**	**1**	**67**	**3.0**	**–7**	**405**	**52.4**	**11:55**	....	....	....	....	....	....	....	....	....
2003-04	**Atlanta**	**NHL**	**2**	**0**	**1**	**1**	**0**	**0**	**0**	**0**	**0**	**0.0**	**0**	**17**	**29.4**	**6:35**	....	....	....	....	....	....	....	....	....
	Chicago Wolves	AHL	70	13	34	47	30	....	....	....	....	....	....	....	....	....	10	4	4	8	6	....	....	....	....
2004-05	Kassel Huskies	Germany	37	14	19	33	16	....	....	....	....	....	....	....	....	....	5	2	2	4	4	....	....	....	....
	NHL Totals		**70**	**4**	**13**	**17**	**16**	**1**	**0**	**1**	**82**	**4.9**		**631**	**49.9**	**11:20**	....	....	....	....	....	....	....	....	....

USHL First All-Star Team (1994) • USHL Second All-Star Team (1995) • WCHA Second All-Star Team (1996) • WCHA Rookie of the Year (1996) • WCHA First All-Star Team (1997, 1998, 1999) • NCAA West Second All-American Team (1998) • NCAA West First All-American Team (1999) • AHL Second All-Star Team (2002)

Traded to **NY Rangers** by **San Jose** with Jayson More and San Jose's 4th round choice (later traded back to San Jose – San Jose selected Adam Colagiacomo) in 1997 Entry Draft for Marty McSorley, August 20, 1996. Signed as a free agent by **Edmonton**, August 19, 1999. Signed as a free agent by **Atlanta**, July 24, 2003. Signed as a free agent by **Kassel** (Germany), April 20, 2004.

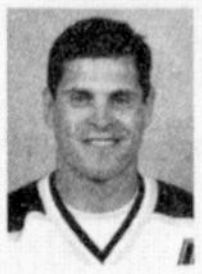

SWEENEY, Don

(SWEE-nee, DAWN)

Defense. Shoots left. 5'10", 185 lbs. Born, St. Stephen, N.B., August 17, 1966. Boston's 8th choice, 166th overall, in 1984 Entry Draft.

Season	Club	League	GP	G	A	Pts	PIM	PP	SH	GW	S	%	+/-	TF	F%	Min	GP	G	A	Pts	PIM	PP	SH	GW	Min
1983-84	South St. Paul	High-MN	22	33	26	59	....	....	....	....	....	....	....	....	....	....	....	....	....	....	....	....	....	....	....
1984-85	Harvard Crimson	ECAC	29	3	7	10	30	....	....	....	....	....	....	....	....	....	....	....	....	....	....	....	....	....	....
1985-86	Harvard Crimson	ECAC	31	4	5	9	12	....	....	....	....	....	....	....	....	....	....	....	....	....	....	....	....	....	....
1986-87	Harvard Crimson	ECAC	34	7	4	11	22	....	....	....	....	....	....	....	....	....	....	....	....	....	....	....	....	....	....
1987-88	Harvard Crimson	ECAC	30	6	23	29	37	....	....	....	....	....	....	....	....	....	....	....	....	....	....	....	....	....	....
	Maine Mariners	AHL	....	....	....	....	....	....	....	....	....	....	....	....	....	....	6	1	3	4	0	....	....	....	....
1988-89	**Boston**	**NHL**	**36**	**3**	**5**	**8**	**20**	**0**	**0**	**0**	**35**	**8.6**	**–6**	....	....	....	....	....	....	....	....	....	....	....	....
	Maine Mariners	AHL	42	8	17	25	24	....	....	....	....	....	....	....	....	....	....	....	....	....	....	....	....	....	....
1989-90	**Boston**	**NHL**	**58**	**3**	**5**	**8**	**58**	**0**	**0**	**0**	**49**	**6.1**	**11**	....	....	....	**21**	**1**	**5**	**6**	**18**	**1**	**0**	**0**	....
	Maine Mariners	AHL	11	0	8	8	8	....	....	....	....	....	....	....	....	....	....	....	....	....	....	....	....	....	....
1990-91	**Boston**	**NHL**	**77**	**8**	**13**	**21**	**67**	**0**	**1**	**3**	**102**	**7.8**	**2**	....	....	....	**19**	**3**	**0**	**3**	**25**	**0**	**0**	**0**	....
1991-92	**Boston**	**NHL**	**75**	**3**	**11**	**14**	**74**	**0**	**0**	**1**	**92**	**3.3**	**–9**	....	....	....	**15**	**0**	**0**	**0**	**10**	**0**	**0**	**0**	....
1992-93	**Boston**	**NHL**	**84**	**7**	**27**	**34**	**68**	**0**	**1**	**0**	**107**	**6.5**	**34**	....	....	....	**4**	**0**	**0**	**0**	**4**	**0**	**0**	**0**	....
1993-94	**Boston**	**NHL**	**75**	**6**	**15**	**21**	**50**	**1**	**2**	**2**	**136**	**4.4**	**29**	....	....	....	**12**	**2**	**1**	**3**	**4**	**0**	**0**	**1**	....
1994-95	**Boston**	**NHL**	**47**	**3**	**19**	**22**	**24**	**1**	**0**	**2**	**102**	**2.9**	**6**	....	....	....	**5**	**0**	**0**	**0**	**4**	**0**	**0**	**0**	....
1995-96	**Boston**	**NHL**	**77**	**4**	**24**	**28**	**42**	**2**	**0**	**3**	**142**	**2.8**	**–4**	....	....	....	**5**	**0**	**2**	**2**	**6**	**0**	**0**	**0**	....
1996-97	**Boston**	**NHL**	**82**	**3**	**23**	**26**	**39**	**0**	**0**	**0**	**113**	**2.7**	**–5**	....	....	....	....	....	....	....	....	....	....	....	....
1997-98	**Boston**	**NHL**	**59**	**1**	**15**	**16**	**24**	**0**	**0**	**0**	**55**	**1.8**	**12**	....	....	....	....	....	....	....	....	....	....	....	....
1998-99	**Boston**	**NHL**	**81**	**2**	**10**	**12**	**64**	**0**	**0**	**0**	**79**	**2.5**	**14**	**0**	**0.0**	**19:31**	**11**	**3**	**0**	**3**	**6**	**1**	**0**	**0**	**21:48**
99-2000	**Boston**	**NHL**	**81**	**1**	**13**	**14**	**48**	**0**	**0**	**0**	**82**	**1.2**	**–14**	**1**	**0.0**	**21:08**	....	....	....	....	....	....	....	....	....
2000-01	**Boston**	**NHL**	**72**	**2**	**10**	**12**	**26**	**1**	**0**	**1**	**60**	**3.3**	**–1**	**0**	**0.0**	**19:16**	....	....	....	....	....	....	....	....	....
2001-02	**Boston**	**NHL**	**81**	**3**	**15**	**18**	**35**	**1**	**0**	**0**	**70**	**4.3**	**22**	**0**	**0.0**	**20:09**	**6**	**0**	**1**	**1**	**2**	**0**	**0**	**0**	**17:44**
2002-03	**Boston**	**NHL**	**67**	**3**	**5**	**8**	**24**	**0**	**0**	**0**	**55**	**5.5**	**–1**	**0**	**0.0**	**13:13**	**5**	**0**	**1**	**1**	**0**	**0**	**0**	**0**	**14:40**
2003-04	**Dallas**	**NHL**	**63**	**0**	**11**	**11**	**18**	**0**	**0**	**0**	**39**	**0.0**	**22**	**0**	**0.0**	**15:53**	**5**	**0**	**0**	**0**	**2**	**0**	**0**	**0**	**16:59**
2004-05			DID NOT PLAY																						
	NHL Totals		**1115**	**52**	**221**	**273**	**681**	**6**	**4**	**12**	**1318**	**3.9**		**1**	**0.0**	**18:25**	**108**	**9**	**10**	**19**	**81**	**2**	**0**	**1**	**18:41**

ECAC First All-Star Team (1988) • NCAA East All-American Team (1988)

Signed as a free agent by **Dallas**, July 14, 2003.

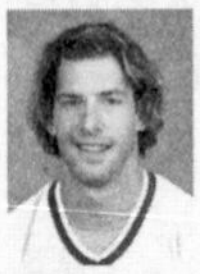

SYDOR, Darryl

(sih-DOHR, DAIR-ihl) **T.B.**

Defense. Shoots left. 6'1", 205 lbs. Born, Edmonton, Alta., May 13, 1972. Los Angeles' 1st choice, 7th overall, in 1990 Entry Draft.

Season	Club	League	GP	G	A	Pts	PIM	PP	SH	GW	S	%	+/-	TF	F%	Min	GP	G	A	Pts	PIM	PP	SH	GW	Min
1985-86	Genstar Cement	AAHA	34	20	17	37	60	....	....	....	....	....	....	....	....	....	....	....	....	....	....	....	....	....	....
1986-87	Genstar Cement	AAHA	36	15	20	35	60	....	....	....	....	....	....	....	....	....	....	....	....	....	....	....	....	....	....
1987-88	Edmonton Mets	AJHL	38	10	11	21	54	....	....	....	....	....	....	....	....	....	....	....	....	....	....	....	....	....	....
1988-89	Kamloops Blazers	WHL	65	12	14	26	86	....	....	....	....	....	....	....	....	....	15	1	4	5	19	....	....	....	....
1989-90	Kamloops Blazers	WHL	67	29	66	95	129	....	....	....	....	....	....	....	....	....	17	2	9	11	28	....	....	....	....
1990-91	Kamloops Blazers	WHL	66	27	78	105	88	....	....	....	....	....	....	....	....	....	12	3	*22	25	10	....	....	....	....
1991-92	Kamloops Blazers	WHL	29	9	39	48	33	....	....	....	....	....	....	....	....	....	17	3	15	18	18	....	....	....	....
	Los Angeles	**NHL**	**18**	**1**	**5**	**6**	**22**	**0**	**0**	**0**	**18**	**5.6**	**–3**	....	....	....	....	....	....	....	....	....	....	....	....
1992-93	**Los Angeles**	**NHL**	**80**	**6**	**23**	**29**	**63**	**0**	**0**	**1**	**112**	**5.4**	**–2**	....	....	....	**24**	**3**	**8**	**11**	**16**	**2**	**0**	**0**	....
1993-94	**Los Angeles**	**NHL**	**84**	**8**	**27**	**35**	**94**	**1**	**0**	**0**	**146**	**5.5**	**–9**	....	....	....	....	....	....	....	....	....	....	....	....
1994-95	**Los Angeles**	**NHL**	**48**	**4**	**19**	**23**	**36**	**3**	**0**	**0**	**96**	**4.2**	**–2**	....	....	....	....	....	....	....	....	....	....	....	....
1995-96	**Los Angeles**	**NHL**	**58**	**1**	**11**	**12**	**34**	**1**	**0**	**0**	**84**	**1.2**	**–11**	....	....	....	....	....	....	....	....	....	....	....	....
	Dallas	**NHL**	**26**	**2**	**6**	**8**	**41**	**1**	**0**	**0**	**33**	**6.1**	**–1**	....	....	....	....	....	....	....	....	....	....	....	....
1996-97	**Dallas**	**NHL**	**82**	**8**	**40**	**48**	**51**	**2**	**0**	**2**	**142**	**5.6**	**37**	....	....	....	**7**	**0**	**2**	**2**	**0**	**0**	**0**	**0**	....
1997-98	**Dallas**	**NHL**	**79**	**11**	**35**	**46**	**51**	**4**	**1**	**1**	**166**	**6.6**	**17**	....	....	....	**17**	**0**	**5**	**5**	**14**	**0**	**0**	**0**	....
1998-99♦	**Dallas**	**NHL**	**74**	**14**	**34**	**48**	**50**	**9**	**0**	**2**	**163**	**8.6**	**–1**	**1**	**100.0**	**21:16**	**23**	**3**	**9**	**12**	**16**	**1**	**0**	**1**	**22:20**
99-2000	**Dallas**	**NHL**	**74**	**8**	**26**	**34**	**32**	**5**	**0**	**1**	**132**	**6.1**	**6**	**1**	**0.0**	**23:09**	**23**	**1**	**6**	**7**	**6**	**0**	**0**	**0**	**20:48**
2000-01	**Dallas**	**NHL**	**81**	**10**	**37**	**47**	**34**	**8**	**0**	**1**	**140**	**7.1**	**5**	**1**	**0.0**	**21:25**	**10**	**1**	**3**	**4**	**0**	**1**	**0**	**0**	**22:42**
2001-02	**Dallas**	**NHL**	**78**	**4**	**29**	**33**	**50**	**2**	**0**	**0**	**183**	**2.2**	**3**	**0**	**0.0**	**21:07**	....	....	....	....	....	....	....	....	....
2002-03	**Dallas**	**NHL**	**81**	**5**	**31**	**36**	**40**	**2**	**0**	**1**	**132**	**3.8**	**22**	**0**	**0.0**	**18:19**	**12**	**0**	**6**	**6**	**6**	**0**	**0**	**0**	**19:14**
2003-04	**Columbus**	**NHL**	**49**	**2**	**13**	**15**	**26**	**1**	**0**	**0**	**80**	**2.5**	**–19**	**1**	**0.0**	**21:54**	....	....	....	....	....	....	....	....	....
	♦ **Tampa Bay**	**NHL**	**31**	**1**	**6**	**7**	**6**	**0**	**0**	**0**	**42**	**2.4**	**3**	**0**	**0.0**	**19:06**	**23**	**0**	**6**	**6**	**9**	**0**	**0**	**0**	**21:50**
2004-05			DID NOT PLAY																						
	NHL Totals		**943**	**85**	**342**	**427**	**630**	**39**	**1**	**9**	**1669**	**5.1**		**4**	**25.0**	**20:59**	**139**	**8**	**45**	**53**	**67**	**4**	**0**	**1**	**21:27**

WHL West First All-Star Team (1990, 1991, 1992)

Played in NHL All-Star Game (1998, 1999)

Traded to **Dallas** by **Los Angeles** with Los Angeles' 5th round choice (Ryan Christie) in 1996 Entry Draft for Shane Churla and Doug Zmolek, February 17, 1996. Traded to **Columbus** by **Dallas** for Mike Sillinger and Columbus' 2nd round choice (Johan Fransson) in 2004 Entry Draft, July 22, 2003. Traded to **Tampa Bay** by **Columbus** with Columbus' 4th round choice (Mike Lundin) in 2004 Entry Draft for Alexander Svitov and Tampa Bay's 3rd round choice (later traded to Calgary – Calgary selected Dustin Boyd) in 2004 Entry Draft, January 27, 2004.

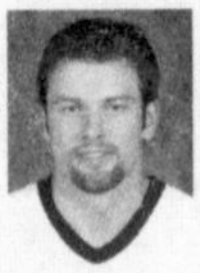

SYKORA, Petr

(SEE-koh-ra, PEE-tuhr) **ANA.**

Right wing. Shoots left. 6', 190 lbs. Born, Plzen, Czech., November 19, 1976. New Jersey's 1st choice, 18th overall, in 1995 Entry Draft.

Season	Club	League	GP	G	A	Pts	PIM	PP	SH	GW	S	%	+/-	TF	F%	Min	GP	G	A	Pts	PIM	PP	SH	GW	Min
1991-92	Plzen Jr.	Czech-Jr.	30	50	50	100	....	....	....	....	....	....	....	....	....	....	....	....	....	....	....	....	....	....	....
1992-93	HC Skoda Plzen	Czech	19	12	5	17	....	....	....	....	....	....	....	....	....	....	....	....	....	....	....	....	....	....	....
1993-94	HC Skoda Plzen	CzRep	37	10	16	26	....	....	....	....	....	....	....	....	....	....	4	0	1	1	....	....	....	....	....
	Cleveland	IHL	13	4	5	9	8	....	....	....	....	....	....	....	....	....	....	....	....	....	....	....	....	....	....
1994-95	Detroit Vipers	IHL	29	12	17	29	16	....	....	....	....	....	....	....	....	....	....	....	....	....	....	....	....	....	....
1995-96	**New Jersey**	**NHL**	**63**	**18**	**24**	**42**	**32**	**8**	**0**	**3**	**128**	**14.1**	**7**	....	....	....	....	....	....	....	....	....	....	....	....
	Albany River Rats	AHL	5	4	1	5	0	....	....	....	....	....	....	....	....	....	....	....	....	....	....	....	....	....	....
1996-97	**New Jersey**	**NHL**	**19**	**1**	**2**	**3**	**4**	**0**	**0**	**0**	**26**	**3.8**	**–8**	....	....	....	**2**	**0**	**0**	**0**	**2**	**0**	**0**	**0**	....
	Albany River Rats	AHL	43	20	25	45	48	....	....	....	....	....	....	....	....	....	4	1	4	5	2	....	....	....	....
1997-98	**New Jersey**	**NHL**	**58**	**16**	**20**	**36**	**22**	**3**	**1**	**4**	**130**	**12.3**	**0**	....	....	....	**2**	**0**	**0**	**0**	**0**	**0**	**0**	**0**	....
	Albany River Rats	AHL	2	4	1	5	0	....	....	....	....	....	....	....	....	....	....	....	....	....	....	....	....	....	....
1998-99	**New Jersey**	**NHL**	**80**	**29**	**43**	**72**	**22**	**15**	**0**	**7**	**222**	**13.1**	**16**	**33**	**33.3**	**16:14**	**7**	**3**	**3**	**6**	**4**	**0**	**0**	**1**	**18:11**
99-2000♦	**New Jersey**	**NHL**	**79**	**25**	**43**	**68**	**26**	**5**	**1**	**4**	**222**	**11.3**	**24**	**47**	**61.7**	**17:06**	**23**	**9**	**8**	**17**	**10**	**1**	**0**	**3**	**15:20**
2000-01	**New Jersey**	**NHL**	**73**	**35**	**46**	**81**	**32**	**9**	**2**	**3**	**249**	**14.1**	**36**	**15**	**33.3**	**17:44**	**25**	**10**	**12**	**22**	**12**	**2**	**2**	**2**	**18:40**
2001-02	**New Jersey**	**NHL**	**73**	**21**	**27**	**48**	**44**	**4**	**0**	**4**	**194**	**10.8**	**12**	**1**	**0.0**	**17:51**	**4**	**0**	**1**	**1**	**0**	**0**	**0**	**0**	**17:57**
	Czech Republic	Olympics	4	1	0	1	0	....	....	....	....	....	....	....	....	....	....	....	....	....	....	....	....	....	....
2002-03	**Anaheim**	**NHL**	**82**	**34**	**25**	**59**	**24**	**15**	**1**	**5**	**299**	**11.4**	**–7**	**23**	**39.1**	**0:00**	**21**	**4**	**9**	**13**	**12**	**1**	**0**	**2**	....
2003-04	**Anaheim**	**NHL**	**81**	**23**	**29**	**52**	**34**	**6**	**0**	**2**	**277**	**8.3**	**–9**	**9**	**22.2**	**17:57**	....	....	....	....	....	....	....	....	....
2004-05	Magnitogorsk	Russia	45	18	13	31	46	....	....	....	....	....	....	....	....	....	5	2	3	5	8	....	....	....	....
	NHL Totals		**608**	**202**	**259**	**461**	**240**	**65**	**5**	**32**	**1747**	**11.6**		**128**	**35.2**	**13:34**	**84**	**26**	**33**	**59**	**40**	**4**	**2**	**8**	**17:16**

NHL All-Rookie Team (1996)

Traded to **Anaheim** by **New Jersey** with Mike Commodore, Jean-Francois Damphousse and Igor Pohanka for Jeff Friesen, Oleg Tverdovsky and Maxim Balmochnykh, July 6, 2002. Signed as a free agent by **Magnitogorsk** (Russia), August 12, 2004.

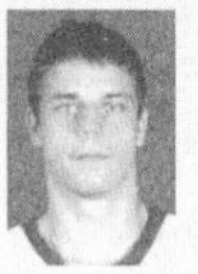

SYKORA, Petr

(SEE-koh-ra, PEE-tuhr) **WSH.**

Center. Shoots right. 6'3", 206 lbs. Born, Pardubice, Czech., December 21, 1978. Detroit's 2nd choice, 76th overall, in 1997 Entry Draft.

			Regular Season														Playoffs								
Season	Club	League	GP	G	A	Pts	PIM	PP	SH	GW	S	%	+/-	TF	F%	Min	GP	G	A	Pts	PIM	PP	SH	GW	Min
1994-95	HC Pardubice Jr.	CzRep-Jr.	38	35	33	68	....	....	....	....	....	....	....	....	....	....	....	....	....	....	....	....	....	....	....
1995-96	HC Pardubice Jr.	CzRep-Jr.	16	26	17	43	....	....	....	....	....	....	....	....	....	....	....	....	....	....	....	....	....	....	....
1996-97	HC Pardubice Jr.	CzRep-Jr.	12	14	4	18	....	....	....	....	....	....	....	....	....	....	....	....	....	....	....	....	....	....	....
	Pardubice	CzRep	29	1	3	4	4	....	....	....	....	....	....	....	....	....	....	....	....	....	....	....	....	....	....
1997-98	Pardubice	CzRep	39	4	5	9	8	....	....	....	....	....	....	....	....	....	3	0	0	0	....	....	....	....	....
1998-99	**Nashville**	**NHL**	**2**	**0**	**0**	**0**	**0**	**0**	**0**	**0**	**2**	**0.0**	**–1**	**11**	**45.5**	**8:19**	....	....	....	....	....	....	....	....	....
	Milwaukee	IHL	73	14	15	29	50	....	....	....	....	....	....	....	....	....	2	1	1	2	0	....	....	....	....
99-2000	Milwaukee	IHL	3	0	1	1	2	....	....	....	....	....	....	....	....	....	....	....	....	....	....	....	....	....	....
	Pardubice	CzRep	36	7	13	20	49	....	....	....	....	....	....	....	....	....	3	0	0	0	2	....	....	....	....
2000-01	Pardubice	CzRep	47	26	18	44	42	....	....	....	....	....	....	....	....	....	7	5	3	8	6	....	....	....	....
2001-02	Pardubice	CzRep	32	18	8	26	72	....	....	....	....	....	....	....	....	....	6	1	2	3	26	....	....	....	....
2002-03	Pardubice	CzRep	45	18	18	36	86	....	....	....	....	....	....	....	....	....	19	7	7	14	39	....	....	....	....
2003-04	Pardubice	CzRep	48	23	23	46	20	....	....	....	....	....	....	....	....	....	7	1	0	1	6	....	....	....	....
2004-05	Pardubice	CzRep	43	25	10	35	28	....	....	....	....	....	....	....	....	....	16	3	2	5	33	....	....	....	....
	NHL Totals		**2**	**0**	**0**	**0**	**0**	**0**	**0**	**0**	**2**	**0.0**		**11**	**45.5**	**8:19**	....	....	....	....	....	....	....	....	....

Traded to **Nashville** by **Detroit** with Detroit's 3rd round choice (later traded to Edmonton – Edmonton selected Mike Comrie) and 4th round compensatory choice (Alexander Krevsun) in 1999 Entry Draft for Doug Brown, July 14, 1998. Traded to **Washington** by **Nashville** for Washington's 3rd round choice (Paul Brown) in 2003 Entry Draft, June 22, 2002.

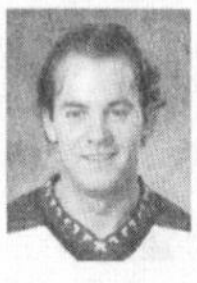

TAFFE, Jeff

(TAYF, JEHF) **PHX.**

Center. Shoots left. 6'3", 201 lbs. Born, Hastings, MN, February 19, 1981. St. Louis' 1st choice, 30th overall, in 2000 Entry Draft.

Season	Club	League	GP	G	A	Pts	PIM	PP	SH	GW	S	%	+/-	TF	F%	Min	GP	G	A	Pts	PIM	PP	SH	GW	Min
1996-97	Hastings Huskies	High-MN	25	21	37	58	....	....	....	....	....	....	....	....	....	....	....	....	....	....	....	....	....	....	....
1997-98	Hastings Huskies	High-MN	28	37	29	66	....	....	....	....	....	....	....	....	....	....	....	....	....	....	....	....	....	....	....
1998-99	Hastings Huskies	High-MN	28	39	51	90	....	....	....	....	....	....	....	....	....	....	....	....	....	....	....	....	....	....	....
	Rochester	USHL	17	12	9	21	26	....	....	....	....	....	....	....	....	....	....	....	....	....	....	....	....	....	....
99-2000	U. of Minnesota	WCHA	39	10	10	20	22	....	....	....	....	....	....	....	....	....	....	....	....	....	....	....	....	....	....
2000-01	U. of Minnesota	WCHA	38	12	23	35	56	....	....	....	....	....	....	....	....	....	....	....	....	....	....	....	....	....	....
2001-02	U. of Minnesota	WCHA	43	34	24	58	86	....	....	....	....	....	....	....	....	....	....	....	....	....	....	....	....	....	....
2002-03	**Phoenix**	**NHL**	**20**	**3**	**1**	**4**	**4**	**1**	**0**	**1**	**18**	**16.7**	**–4**	**113**	**29.2**	**11:34**	....	....	....	....	....	....	....	....	....
	Springfield	AHL	57	23	26	49	44	....	....	....	....	....	....	....	....	....	5	0	3	3	8	....	....	....	....
2003-04	**Phoenix**	**NHL**	**59**	**8**	**10**	**18**	**20**	**5**	**0**	**0**	**67**	**11.9**	**–8**	**219**	**43.4**	**11:02**	....	....	....	....	....	....	....	....	....
	Springfield	AHL	15	10	6	16	19	....	....	....	....	....	....	....	....	....	....	....	....	....	....	....	....	....	....
2004-05	Utah Grizzlies	AHL	27	9	10	19	35	....	....	....	....	....	....	....	....	....	....	....	....	....	....	....	....	....	....
	NHL Totals		**79**	**11**	**11**	**22**	**24**	**6**	**0**	**1**	**85**	**12.9**		**332**	**38.6**	**11:10**	....	....	....	....	....	....	....	....	....

Rights traded to **Phoenix** by **St. Louis** with Michal Handzus, Ladislav Nagy and St. Louis' 1st round choice (Ben Eager) in 2002 Entry Draft for Keith Tkachuk, March 13, 2001.

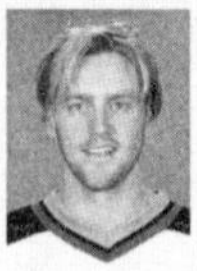

TALLINDER, Henrik

(tah-LIHN-duhr, HEHN-rihk) **BUF.**

Defense. Shoots left. 6'3", 215 lbs. Born, Stockholm, Sweden, January 10, 1979. Buffalo's 2nd choice, 48th overall, in 1997 Entry Draft.

Season	Club	League	GP	G	A	Pts	PIM	PP	SH	GW	S	%	+/-	TF	F%	Min	GP	G	A	Pts	PIM	PP	SH	GW	Min
1996-97	AIK Solna Jr.	Swe-Jr.	40	4	13	17	55	....	....	....	....	....	....	....	....	....	....	....	....	....	....	....	....	....	....
	AIK Solna	Sweden	1	0	0	0	0	....	....	....	....	....	....	....	....	....	....	....	....	....	....	....	....	....	....
1997-98	AIK Solna	Sweden	34	0	0	0	26	....	....	....	....	....	....	....	....	....	....	....	....	....	....	....	....	....	....
1998-99	AIK Solna	Sweden	36	0	0	0	30	....	....	....	....	....	....	....	....	....	....	....	....	....	....	....	....	....	....
99-2000	AIK Solna	Sweden	50	0	2	2	59	....	....	....	....	....	....	....	....	....	....	....	....	....	....	....	....	....	....
2000-01	TPS Turku	Finland	56	5	9	14	62	....	....	....	....	....	....	....	....	....	10	2	1	3	8	....	....	....	....
2001-02	**Buffalo**	**NHL**	**2**	**0**	**0**	**0**	**0**	**0**	**0**	**0**	**4**	**0.0**	**–1**	**0**	**0.0**	**18:10**	....	....	....	....	....	....	....	....	....
	Rochester	AHL	73	6	14	20	26	....	....	....	....	....	....	....	....	....	2	0	0	0	0	....	....	....	....
2002-03	**Buffalo**	**NHL**	**46**	**3**	**10**	**13**	**28**	**1**	**0**	**0**	**37**	**8.1**	**–3**	**0**	**0.0**	**19:53**	....	....	....	....	....	....	....	....	....
2003-04	**Buffalo**	**NHL**	**72**	**1**	**9**	**10**	**26**	**0**	**0**	**0**	**63**	**1.6**	**5**	**1**	**0.0**	**18:23**	....	....	....	....	....	....	....	....	....
2004-05	Linkopings HC	Sweden	44	6	10	16	63	....	....	....	....	....	....	....	....	....	....	....	....	....	....	....	....	....	....
	SC Bern	Swiss	....	....	....	....	....	....	....	....	....	....	....	....	....	....	10	1	1	2	4	....	....	....	....
	NHL Totals		**120**	**4**	**19**	**23**	**54**	**1**	**0**	**0**	**104**	**3.8**		**1**	**0.0**	**18:57**	....	....	....	....	....	....	....	....	....

Signed as a free agent by **Linkopings** (Sweden), September 9, 2004. Signed as a free agent by **Bern** (Swiss), February 22, 2005.

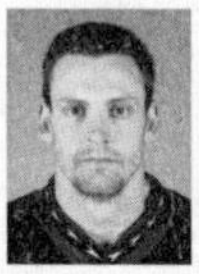

TAMER, Chris

(TAY-muhr, KRIHS)

Defense. Shoots left. 6'2", 205 lbs. Born, Dearborn, MI, November 17, 1970. Pittsburgh's 3rd choice, 68th overall, in 1990 Entry Draft.

Season	Club	League	GP	G	A	Pts	PIM	PP	SH	GW	S	%	+/-	TF	F%	Min	GP	G	A	Pts	PIM	PP	SH	GW	Min
1987-88	Redford Royals	NAHL	40	10	20	30	217	....	....	....	....	....	....	....	....	....	....	....	....	....	....	....	....	....	....
1988-89	Redford Royals	NAHL	31	6	13	19	79	....	....	....	....	....	....	....	....	....	....	....	....	....	....	....	....	....	....
1989-90	U. of Michigan	CCHA	42	2	7	9	147	....	....	....	....	....	....	....	....	....	....	....	....	....	....	....	....	....	....
1990-91	U. of Michigan	CCHA	45	8	19	27	130	....	....	....	....	....	....	....	....	....	....	....	....	....	....	....	....	....	....
1991-92	U. of Michigan	CCHA	43	4	15	19	125	....	....	....	....	....	....	....	....	....	....	....	....	....	....	....	....	....	....
1992-93	U. of Michigan	CCHA	39	5	18	23	113	....	....	....	....	....	....	....	....	....	....	....	....	....	....	....	....	....	....
1993-94	**Pittsburgh**	**NHL**	**12**	**0**	**0**	**0**	**9**	**0**	**0**	**0**	**10**	**0.0**	**3**	....	....	....	**5**	**0**	**0**	**0**	**2**	**0**	**0**	**0**	....
	Cleveland	IHL	53	1	2	3	160	....	....	....	....	....	....	....	....	....	....	....	....	....	....	....	....	....	....
1994-95	Cleveland	IHL	48	4	10	14	204	....	....	....	....	....	....	....	....	....	....	....	....	....	....	....	....	....	....
	Pittsburgh	**NHL**	**36**	**2**	**0**	**2**	**82**	**0**	**0**	**0**	**26**	**7.7**	**0**	....	....	....	**4**	**0**	**0**	**0**	**18**	**0**	**0**	**0**	....
1995-96	**Pittsburgh**	**NHL**	**70**	**4**	**10**	**14**	**153**	**0**	**0**	**1**	**75**	**5.3**	**20**	....	....	....	**18**	**0**	**7**	**7**	**24**	**0**	**0**	**0**	....
1996-97	**Pittsburgh**	**NHL**	**45**	**2**	**4**	**6**	**131**	**0**	**1**	**0**	**56**	**3.6**	**–25**	....	....	....	**4**	**0**	**0**	**0**	**4**	**0**	**0**	**0**	....
1997-98	**Pittsburgh**	**NHL**	**79**	**0**	**7**	**7**	**181**	**0**	**0**	**0**	**55**	**0.0**	**4**	....	....	....	**6**	**0**	**1**	**1**	**4**	**0**	**0**	**0**	....
1998-99	**Pittsburgh**	**NHL**	**11**	**0**	**0**	**0**	**32**	**0**	**0**	**0**	**2**	**0.0**	**–2**	**0**	**0.0**	**5:59**	....	....	....	....	....	....	....	....	....
	NY Rangers	**NHL**	**52**	**1**	**5**	**6**	**92**	**0**	**0**	**1**	**46**	**2.2**	**–12**	**0**	**0.0**	**15:25**	....	....	....	....	....	....	....	....	....
99-2000	**Atlanta**	**NHL**	**69**	**2**	**8**	**10**	**91**	**0**	**0**	**0**	**61**	**3.3**	**–32**	**5**	**40.0**	**18:29**	....	....	....	....	....	....	....	....	....
2000-01	**Atlanta**	**NHL**	**82**	**4**	**13**	**17**	**128**	**0**	**1**	**1**	**90**	**4.4**	**–1**	**1**	**0.0**	**19:42**	....	....	....	....	....	....	....	....	....
2001-02	**Atlanta**	**NHL**	**78**	**3**	**3**	**6**	**111**	**0**	**1**	**0**	**66**	**4.5**	**–11**	**0**	**0.0**	**18:30**	....	....	....	....	....	....	....	....	....
2002-03	**Atlanta**	**NHL**	**72**	**1**	**9**	**10**	**118**	**0**	**0**	**0**	**53**	**1.9**	**–10**	**0**	**0.0**	**15:41**	....	....	....	....	....	....	....	....	....
2003-04	**Atlanta**	**NHL**	**38**	**2**	**5**	**7**	**55**	**0**	**0**	**1**	**40**	**5.0**	**–9**	**0**	**0.0**	**17:58**	....	....	....	....	....	....	....	....	....
2004-05			DID NOT PLAY																						
	NHL Totals		**644**	**21**	**64**	**85**	**1183**	**0**	**3**	**4**	**580**	**3.6**		**6**	**33.3**	**17:27**	**37**	**0**	**8**	**8**	**52**	**0**	**0**	**0**	....

Traded to **NY Rangers** by **Pittsburgh** with Petr Nedved and Sean Pronger for Alex Kovalev and Harry York, November 25, 1998. Claimed by **Atlanta** from **NY Rangers** in Expansion Draft, June 25, 1999.
• Missed majority of 2003-04 season recovering from back injury suffered in game vs. Phoenix, January 11, 2004.

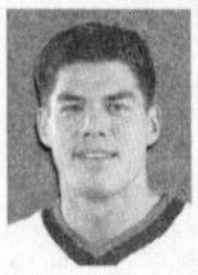

TANABE, David

(tuh-NA-bee, DAY-vihd) **PHX.**

Defense. Shoots right. 6'1", 212 lbs. Born, White Bear Lake, MN, July 19, 1980. Carolina's 1st choice, 16th overall, in 1999 Entry Draft.

Season	Club	League	GP	G	A	Pts	PIM	PP	SH	GW	S	%	+/-	TF	F%	Min	GP	G	A	Pts	PIM	PP	SH	GW	Min
1996-97	Hill-Murray	High-MN	28	12	14	26	....	....	....	....	....	....	....	....	....	....	....	....	....	....	....	....	....	....	....
1997-98	USA U-18	USDP	73	8	21	29	96	....	....	....	....	....	....	....	....	....	....	....	....	....	....	....	....	....	....
1998-99	U. of Wisconsin	WCHA	35	10	12	22	44	....	....	....	....	....	....	....	....	....	....	....	....	....	....	....	....	....	....
99-2000	**Carolina**	**NHL**	**31**	**4**	**0**	**4**	**14**	**3**	**0**	**0**	**28**	**14.3**	**–4**	**0**	**0.0**	**12:53**	....	....	....	....	....	....	....	....	....
	Cincinnati	IHL	32	0	13	13	14	....	....	....	....	....	....	....	....	....	11	1	4	5	6	....	....	....	....
2000-01	**Carolina**	**NHL**	**74**	**7**	**22**	**29**	**42**	**5**	**0**	**1**	**130**	**5.4**	**–9**	**0**	**0.0**	**17:55**	**6**	**2**	**0**	**2**	**12**	**2**	**0**	**0**	**20:47**
2001-02	**Carolina**	**NHL**	**78**	**1**	**15**	**16**	**35**	**0**	**0**	**0**	**113**	**0.9**	**–13**	**0**	**0.0**	**18:27**	**1**	**0**	**1**	**1**	**0**	**0**	**0**	**0**	**7:31**
2002-03	**Carolina**	**NHL**	**68**	**3**	**10**	**13**	**24**	**2**	**0**	**0**	**104**	**2.9**	**–27**	**0**	**0.0**	**18:12**	....	....	....	....	....	....	....	....	....
2003-04	**Phoenix**	**NHL**	**45**	**5**	**7**	**12**	**22**	**2**	**0**	**2**	**88**	**5.7**	**4**	**0**	**0.0**	**23:02**	....	....	....	....	....	....	....	....	....
2004-05	Rapperswil	Swiss	8	4	5	9	4	....	....	....	....	....	....	....	....	....	....	....	....	....	....	....	....	....	....
	Kloten Flyers	Swiss	20	3	7	10	18	....	....	....	....	....	....	....	....	....	5	1	4	5	8	....	....	....	....
	NHL Totals		**296**	**20**	**54**	**74**	**137**	**12**	**0**	**3**	**463**	**4.3**		**0**	**0.0**	**18:23**	**7**	**2**	**1**	**3**	**12**	**2**	**0**	**0**	**18:53**

WCHA All-Rookie Team (1999)

Traded to **Phoenix** by **Carolina** with Igor Knyazev for Danny Markov and future considerations (Edmonton's 3rd round choice (previously acquired, later traded to NY Rangers - NY Rangers selected Billy Ryan) in 2004 Entry Draft, June 26, 2004), June 21, 2003. Signed as a free agent by **Rapperswil** (Swiss), October 21, 2004. Signed as a free agent by **Kloten** (Swiss), November 29, 2004.

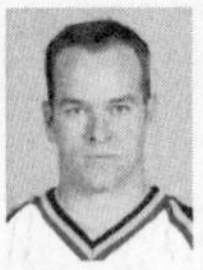

TANGUAY, Alex
(TAN-guay, AL-ehx) **COL.**

Left wing. Shoots left. 6', 190 lbs. Born, Ste-Justine, Que., November 21, 1979. Colorado's 1st choice, 12th overall, in 1998 Entry Draft.

			Regular Season														Playoffs								
Season	Club	League	GP	G	A	Pts	PIM	PP	SH	GW	S	%	+/-	TF	F%	Min	GP	G	A	Pts	PIM	PP	SH	GW	Min
1994-95	Cap-d-Madeleine	QAAA	1	0	1	1	0	....	....	....	....	....	....	....	....	....	....	....	....	....	....	....	....	....	....
1995-96	Cap-d-Madeleine	QAAA	44	29	34	63	64	....	....	....	....	....	....	....	....	....	5	2	4	6	14	....	....	....	....
1996-97	Halifax	QMJHL	70	27	41	68	60	....	....	....	....	....	....	....	....	....	12	5	8	13	8	....	....	....	....
1997-98	Halifax	QMJHL	51	47	38	85	32	....	....	....	....	....	....	....	....	....	5	7	6	13	4	....	....	....	....
1998-99	Halifax	QMJHL	31	27	34	61	30	....	....	....	....	....	....	....	....	....	5	1	2	3	2	....	....	....	....
	Hershey Bears	AHL	5	1	2	3	2	....	....	....	....	....	....	....	....	....	5	0	2	2	0	....	....	....	....
99-2000	**Colorado**	**NHL**	**76**	**17**	**34**	**51**	**22**	**5**	**0**	**3**	**74**	**23.0**	**6**	**11**	**45.5**	**15:38**	**17**	**2**	**1**	**3**	**2**	**1**	**0**	**1**	**10:49**
2000-01 ◆	**Colorado**	**NHL**	**82**	**27**	**50**	**77**	**37**	**7**	**1**	**3**	**135**	**20.0**	**35**	**30**	**43.3**	**17:51**	**23**	**6**	**15**	**21**	**8**	**1**	**0**	**2**	**19:18**
2001-02	**Colorado**	**NHL**	**70**	**13**	**35**	**48**	**36**	**7**	**0**	**2**	**90**	**14.4**	**8**	**37**	**40.5**	**18:20**	**19**	**5**	**8**	**13**	**0**	**3**	**0**	**0**	**17:25**
2002-03	**Colorado**	**NHL**	**82**	**26**	**41**	**67**	**36**	**3**	**0**	**5**	**142**	**18.3**	**34**	**123**	**39.0**	**17:48**	**7**	**1**	**2**	**3**	**4**	**0**	**0**	**1**	**19:06**
2003-04	**Colorado**	**NHL**	**69**	**25**	**54**	**79**	**42**	**7**	**0**	**5**	**117**	**21.4**	**30**	**71**	**40.9**	**18:21**	**8**	**2**	**2**	**4**	**2**	**1**	**0**	**1**	**15:46**
2004-05	HC Lugano	Swiss	6	3	3	6	4	....	....	....	....	....	....	....	....	....	....	....	....	....	....	....	....	....	....
	NHL Totals		**379**	**108**	**214**	**322**	**173**	**29**	**1**	**18**	**558**	**19.4**		**272**	**40.4**	**17:35**	**74**	**16**	**28**	**44**	**16**	**6**	**0**	**5**	**16:28**

QMJHL All-Rookie Team (1997)
Played in NHL All-Star Game (2004)
Signed as a free agent by **Lugano** (Swiss), October 7, 2004.

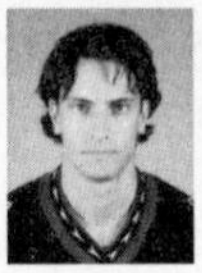

TAPPER, Brad
(TA-puhr, BRAD)

Right wing. Shoots right. 6', 185 lbs. Born, Scarborough, Ont., April 28, 1978.

Season	Club	League	GP	G	A	Pts	PIM	PP	SH	GW	S	%	+/-	TF	F%	Min	GP	G	A	Pts	PIM	PP	SH	GW	Min
1996-97	Wexford Raiders	MTJHL	50	42	70	112	169	....	....	....	....	....	....	....	....	....	....	....	....	....	....	....	....	....	....
1997-98	RPI Engineers	ECAC	34	14	11	25	62	....	....	....	....	....	....	....	....	....	....	....	....	....	....	....	....	....	....
1998-99	RPI Engineers	ECAC	35	20	20	40	60	....	....	....	....	....	....	....	....	....	....	....	....	....	....	....	....	....	....
99-2000	RPI Engineers	ECAC	37	*31	20	51	81	....	....	....	....	....	....	....	....	....	....	....	....	....	....	....	....	....	....
2000-01	**Atlanta**	**NHL**	**16**	**2**	**3**	**5**	**6**	**0**	**0**	**0**	**21**	**9.5**	**1**	**0**	**0.0**	**12:44**	....	....	....	....	....	....	....	....	....
	Orlando	IHL	45	7	9	16	39	....	....	....	....	....	....	....	....	....	2	0	0	0	2	....	....	....	....
2001-02	**Atlanta**	**NHL**	**20**	**2**	**4**	**6**	**43**	**0**	**0**	**0**	**34**	**5.9**	**–3**	**3**	**66.7**	**13:21**	....	....	....	....	....	....	....	....	....
	Chicago Wolves	AHL	50	14	12	26	62	....	....	....	....	....	....	....	....	....	19	3	4	7	42	....	....	....	....
2002-03	Chicago Wolves	AHL	28	9	14	23	42	....	....	....	....	....	....	....	....	....	9	1	3	4	10	....	....	....	....
	Atlanta	**NHL**	**35**	**10**	**4**	**14**	**23**	**1**	**0**	**3**	**68**	**14.7**	**2**	**4**	**25.0**	**13:03**	....	....	....	....	....	....	....	....	....
2003-04	Chicago Wolves	AHL	20	1	8	9	26	....	....	....	....	....	....	....	....	....	....	....	....	....	....	....	....	....	....
	Binghamton	AHL	29	9	12	21	26	....	....	....	....	....	....	....	....	....	....	....	....	....	....	....	....	....	....
2004-05	Nurnberg	Germany	50	26	23	49	101	....	....	....	....	....	....	....	....	....	6	0	2	2	18	....	....	....	....
	NHL Totals		**71**	**14**	**11**	**25**	**72**	**1**	**0**	**3**	**123**	**11.4**		**7**	**42.9**	**13:04**	....	....	....	....	....	....	....	....	....

ECAC First All-Star Team (2000) • NCAA East Second All-American Team (2000)
Signed as a free agent by **Atlanta**, April 11, 2000. Traded to **Ottawa** by **Atlanta** for Daniel Corso, January 6, 2004. Signed as a free agent by **Nurnberg** (Germany), July 22, 2004.

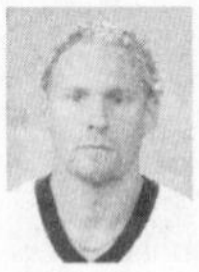

TARNSTROM, Dick
(TAHRN-struhm, DIHK) **PIT.**

Defense. Shoots left. 6'1", 205 lbs. Born, Sundbyberg, Sweden, January 20, 1975. NY Islanders' 12th choice, 272nd overall, in 1994 Entry Draft.

Season	Club	League	GP	G	A	Pts	PIM	PP	SH	GW	S	%	+/-	TF	F%	Min	GP	G	A	Pts	PIM	PP	SH	GW	Min
1992-93	AIK Solna	Sweden	3	0	0	0	0	....	....	....	....	....	....	....	....	....	....	....	....	....	....	....	....	....	....
1993-94	AIK Solna	Sweden-2	33	1	4	5	....	....	....	....	....	....	....	....	....	....	....	....	....	....	....	....	....	....	....
1994-95	AIK Solna	Sweden	37	8	4	12	26	....	....	....	....	....	....	....	....	....	....	....	....	....	....	....	....	....	....
1995-96	AIK Solna	Sweden	40	0	5	5	32	....	....	....	....	....	....	....	....	....	....	....	....	....	....	....	....	....	....
1996-97	AIK Solna	Sweden	49	5	3	8	38	....	....	....	....	....	....	....	....	....	7	0	1	1	6	....	....	....	....
1997-98	AIK Solna	Sweden	45	2	12	14	30	....	....	....	....	....	....	....	....	....	....	....	....	....	....	....	....	....	....
1998-99	AIK Solna	Sweden	47	9	14	23	36	....	....	....	....	....	....	....	....	....	....	....	....	....	....	....	....	....	....
99-2000	AIK Solna	Sweden	42	7	15	22	20	....	....	....	....	....	....	....	....	....	....	....	....	....	....	....	....	....	....
2000-01	AIK Solna	Sweden	50	10	18	28	28	....	....	....	....	....	....	....	....	....	5	0	0	0	8	....	....	....	....
2001-02	**NY Islanders**	**NHL**	**62**	**3**	**16**	**19**	**38**	**0**	**0**	**0**	**59**	**5.1**	**–12**	**0**	**0.0**	**17:39**	**5**	**0**	**0**	**0**	**2**	**0**	**0**	**0**	**7:13**
	Bridgeport	AHL	9	0	2	2	2	....	....	....	....	....	....	....	....	....	....	....	....	....	....	....	....	....	....
2002-03	**Pittsburgh**	**NHL**	**61**	**7**	**34**	**41**	**50**	**3**	**0**	**0**	**115**	**6.1**	**–11**	**0**	**0.0**	**23:54**	....	....	....	....	....	....	....	....	....
2003-04	**Pittsburgh**	**NHL**	**80**	**16**	**36**	**52**	**38**	**12**	**0**	**0**	**158**	**10.1**	**–37**	**0**	**0.0**	**24:03**	....	....	....	....	....	....	....	....	....
2004-05	Sodertalje SK	Sweden	50	7	18	25	46	....	....	....	....	....	....	....	....	....	9	1	0	1	6	....	....	....	....
	NHL Totals		**203**	**26**	**86**	**112**	**126**	**15**	**0**	**0**	**332**	**7.8**		**0**	**0.0**	**22:03**	**5**	**0**	**0**	**0**	**2**	**0**	**0**	**0**	**7:13**

Claimed on waivers by **Pittsburgh** from **NY Islanders**, August 6, 2002. Signed as a free agent by **Sodertalje** (Sweden), August 9, 2004.

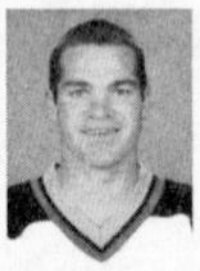

TAYLOR, Chris
(TAY-luhr, KRIHS) **BUF.**

Center. Shoots left. 6'2", 192 lbs. Born, Stratford, Ont., March 6, 1972. NY Islanders' 2nd choice, 27th overall, in 1990 Entry Draft.

Season	Club	League	GP	G	A	Pts	PIM	PP	SH	GW	S	%	+/-	TF	F%	Min	GP	G	A	Pts	PIM	PP	SH	GW	Min
1987-88	Stratford Cullitons	OHA-B	52	28	37	65	112	....	....	....	....	....	....	....	....	....	....	....	....	....	....	....	....	....	....
1988-89	London Knights	OHL	62	7	16	23	52	....	....	....	....	....	....	....	....	....	15	0	2	2	15	....	....	....	....
1989-90	London Knights	OHL	66	45	60	105	60	....	....	....	....	....	....	....	....	....	6	3	2	5	6	....	....	....	....
1990-91	London Knights	OHL	65	50	78	128	50	....	....	....	....	....	....	....	....	....	7	4	8	12	6	....	....	....	....
1991-92	London Knights	OHL	66	48	74	122	57	....	....	....	....	....	....	....	....	....	10	8	16	24	9	....	....	....	....
1992-93	Capital District	AHL	77	19	43	62	32	....	....	....	....	....	....	....	....	....	4	0	1	1	2	....	....	....	....
1993-94	Salt Lake	IHL	79	21	20	41	38	....	....	....	....	....	....	....	....	....	....	....	....	....	....	....	....	....	....
1994-95	Denver Grizzlies	IHL	78	38	48	86	47	....	....	....	....	....	....	....	....	....	14	7	6	13	10	....	....	....	....
	NY Islanders	**NHL**	**10**	**0**	**3**	**3**	**2**	**0**	**0**	**0**	**13**	**0.0**	**1**	....	....	....	....	....	....	....	....	....	....	....	....
1995-96	**NY Islanders**	**NHL**	**11**	**0**	**1**	**1**	**2**	**0**	**0**	**0**	**4**	**0.0**	**1**	....	....	....	....	....	....	....	....	....	....	....	....
	Utah Grizzlies	IHL	50	18	23	41	60	....	....	....	....	....	....	....	....	....	22	5	11	16	26	....	....	....	....
1996-97	**NY Islanders**	**NHL**	**1**	**0**	**0**	**0**	**0**	**0**	**0**	**0**	**1**	**0.0**	**0**	....	....	....	....	....	....	....	....	....	....	....	....
	Utah Grizzlies	IHL	71	27	40	67	24	....	....	....	....	....	....	....	....	....	7	1	2	3	0	....	....	....	....
1997-98	Utah Grizzlies	IHL	79	28	56	84	66	....	....	....	....	....	....	....	....	....	4	0	2	2	6	....	....	....	....
1998-99	**Boston**	**NHL**	**37**	**3**	**5**	**8**	**12**	**0**	**1**	**0**	**60**	**5.0**	**–3**	**512**	**53.7**	**14:24**	....	....	....	....	....	....	....	....	....
	Providence Bruins	AHL	21	6	11	17	6	....	....	....	....	....	....	....	....	....	....	....	....	....	....	....	....	....	....
	Las Vegas	IHL	14	3	12	15	2	....	....	....	....	....	....	....	....	....	....	....	....	....	....	....	....	....	....
99-2000	**Buffalo**	**NHL**	**11**	**1**	**1**	**2**	**2**	**0**	**0**	**0**	**15**	**6.7**	**–2**	**125**	**45.6**	**10:54**	**2**	**0**	**0**	**0**	**2**	**0**	**0**	**0**	**10:32**
	Rochester	AHL	49	21	28	49	21	....	....	....	....	....	....	....	....	....	....	....	....	....	....	....	....	....	....
2000-01	**Buffalo**	**NHL**	**14**	**0**	**2**	**2**	**6**	**0**	**0**	**0**	**21**	**0.0**	**1**	**138**	**50.7**	**11:08**	....	....	....	....	....	....	....	....	....
	Rochester	AHL	45	20	24	44	25	....	....	....	....	....	....	....	....	....	....	....	....	....	....	....	....	....	....
2001-02	Rochester	AHL	77	21	45	66	66	....	....	....	....	....	....	....	....	....	2	0	1	1	0	....	....	....	....
2002-03	**Buffalo**	**NHL**	**11**	**1**	**3**	**4**	**2**	**0**	**0**	**0**	**10**	**10.0**	**–1**	**152**	**47.4**	**13:55**	....	....	....	....	....	....	....	....	....
	Rochester	AHL	61	12	55	67	44	....	....	....	....	....	....	....	....	....	3	3	1	4	2	....	....	....	....
2003-04	**Buffalo**	**NHL**	**54**	**6**	**6**	**12**	**22**	**0**	**0**	**0**	**50**	**12.0**	**–2**	**531**	**51.0**	**10:10**	....	....	....	....	....	....	....	....	....
	Rochester	AHL	24	9	18	27	20	....	....	....	....	....	....	....	....	....	16	5	12	17	0	....	....	....	....
2004-05	Rochester	AHL	79	21	58	79	50	....	....	....	....	....	....	....	....	....	9	1	8	9	4	....	....	....	....
	NHL Totals		**149**	**11**	**21**	**32**	**48**	**0**	**1**	**0**	**174**	**6.3**		**1458**	**51.1**	**11:54**	**2**	**0**	**0**	**0**	**2**	**0**	**0**	**0**	**10:32**

Fred Hunt Memorial Trophy (Sportsmanship - AHL) (2005)
Signed as a free agent by **Los Angeles**, July 25, 1997. Signed as a free agent by **Boston**, August 5, 1998. Signed as a free agent by **Buffalo**, August 13, 1999.

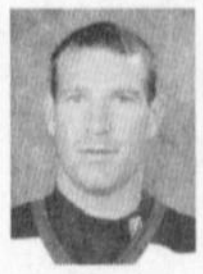

TAYLOR, Tim
(TAY-luhr, TIHM) **T.B.**

Center. Shoots left. 6'1", 190 lbs. Born, Stratford, Ont., February 6, 1969. Washington's 2nd choice, 36th overall, in 1988 Entry Draft.

Season	Club	League	GP	G	A	Pts	PIM	PP	SH	GW	S	%	+/-	TF	F%	Min	GP	G	A	Pts	PIM	PP	SH	GW	Min
1985-86	Stratford Cullitons	OHA-B	1	0	0	0	0	....	....	....	....	....	....	....	....	....	....	....	....	....	....	....	....	....	....
1986-87	Stratford Cullitons	OHA-B	31	25	26	51	51	....	....	....	....	....	....	....	....	....	....	....	....	....	....	....	....	....	....
	London Knights	OHL	34	7	9	16	11	....	....	....	....	....	....	....	....	....	....	....	....	....	....	....	....	....	....
1987-88	London Knights	OHL	64	46	50	96	66	....	....	....	....	....	....	....	....	....	12	9	9	18	26	....	....	....	....
1988-89	London Knights	OHL	61	34	80	114	93	....	....	....	....	....	....	....	....	....	21	*21	25	*46	58	....	....	....	....
1989-90	Baltimore	AHL	79	31	36	67	124	....	....	....	....	....	....	....	....	....	9	2	2	4	13	....	....	....	....
1990-91	Baltimore	AHL	79	25	42	67	75	....	....	....	....	....	....	....	....	....	5	0	1	1	4	....	....	....	....
1991-92	Baltimore	AHL	65	9	18	27	131	....	....	....	....	....	....	....	....	....	....	....	....	....	....	....	....	....	....
1992-93	Baltimore	AHL	41	15	16	31	49	....	....	....	....	....	....	....	....	....	....	....	....	....	....	....	....	....	....
	Hamilton	AHL	36	15	22	37	37	....	....	....	....	....	....	....	....	....	....	....	....	....	....	....	....	....	....
1993-94	**Detroit**	**NHL**	**1**	**1**	**0**	**1**	**0**	**0**	**0**	**0**	**4**	**25.0**	**–1**	....	....	....	....	....	....	....	....	....	....	....	....
	Adirondack	AHL	79	36	*81	*117	86	....	....	....	....	....	....	....	....	....	12	2	10	12	12	....	....	....	....

			Regular Season														Playoffs								
Season	Club	League	GP	G	A	Pts	PIM	PP	SH	GW	S	%	+/-	TF	F%	Min	GP	G	A	Pts	PIM	PP	SH	GW	Min
1994-95	Detroit	NHL	22	0	4	4	16	0	0	0	21	0.0	3	....	....	....	6	0	1	1	12	0	0	0	....
1995-96	Detroit	NHL	72	11	14	25	39	1	1	4	81	13.6	11	....	....	....	18	0	4	4	4	0	0	0	....
1996-97♦	Detroit	NHL	44	3	4	7	52	0	1	0	44	6.8	–6	....	....	....	2	0	0	0	0	0	0	0	....
1997-98	Boston	NHL	79	20	11	31	57	1	3	0	127	15.7	–16	....	....	....	6	0	0	0	10	0	0	0	....
1998-99	Boston	NHL	49	4	7	11	55	0	0	1	76	5.3	–10	834	58.3	15:56	12	0	3	3	8	0	0	0	15:09
99-2000	NY Rangers	NHL	76	9	11	20	72	0	0	2	79	11.4	–4	1276	58.9	14:09	....	....	....	....	....	....	....	....	....
2000-01	NY Rangers	NHL	38	2	5	7	16	0	0	1	34	5.9	–6	292	59.3	8:57	....	....	....	....	....	....	....	....	....
2001-02	Tampa Bay	NHL	48	4	4	8	25	0	1	0	50	8.0	–2	559	54.6	13:29	....	....	....	....	....	....	....	....	....
2002-03	Tampa Bay	NHL	82	4	8	12	38	0	0	1	95	4.2	–13	961	57.9	13:43	11	0	1	1	6	0	0	0	13:54
2003-04♦	Tampa Bay	NHL	82	7	15	22	25	0	0	1	95	7.4	–5	666	59.6	12:54	23	2	3	5	31	0	0	0	14:17
2004-05			DID NOT PLAY																						
	NHL Totals		593	65	83	148	395	2	6	10	706	9.2		4588	58.2	13:24	78	2	12	14	71	0	0	0	14:25

AHL First All-Star Team (1994) • John B. Sollenberger Trophy (Leading Scorer – AHL) (1994)

Traded to **Vancouver** by **Washington** for Eric Murano, January 29, 1993. Signed as a free agent by **Detroit**, July 28, 1993. Claimed by **Boston** from **Detroit** in Waiver Draft, September 28, 1997. Signed as a free agent by **NY Rangers**, July 30, 1999. • Missed majority of 2000-01 season recovering from abdominal injury suffered in game vs. Phoenix, January 4, 2001. Traded to **Tampa Bay** by **NY Rangers** for Kyle Freadrich and Nils Ekman, June 30, 2001.

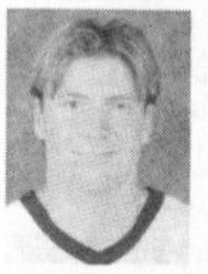

TENKRAT, Petr

(TEHN-krat, PEE-tuhr) **TOR.**

Right wing. Shoots right. 5'11", 200 lbs. Born, Kladno, Czech., May 31, 1977. Anaheim's 6th choice, 230th overall, in 1999 Entry Draft.

Season	Club	League	GP	G	A	Pts	PIM	PP	SH	GW	S	%	+/-	TF	F%	Min	GP	G	A	Pts	PIM	PP	SH	GW	Min
1994-95	HC Kladno	CzRep	1	0	0	0	0	....	....	....	....	....	....	....	....	....	....	....	....	....	....	....	....	....	....
1995-96	HC Poldi Kladno	CzRep	20	0	4	4	4	....	....	....	....	....	....	....	....	....	3	0	1	1	0	....	....	....	....
1996-97	HC Poldi Kladno	CzRep	43	5	9	14	6	....	....	....	....	....	....	....	....	....	3	0	1	1	0	....	....	....	....
1997-98	Kladno	CzRep	52	9	10	19	24	....	....	....	....	....	....	....	....	....	....	....	....	....	....	....	....	....	....
1998-99	Kladno	CzRep	50	21	14	35	32	....	....	....	....	....	....	....	....	....	....	....	....	....	....	....	....	....	....
99-2000	HPK Hameenlinna	Finland	32	20	9	29	31	....	....	....	....	....	....	....	....	....	....	....	....	....	....	....	....	....	....
	Ilves Tampere	Finland	22	15	5	20	44	....	....	....	....	....	....	....	....	....	3	1	1	2	14	....	....	....	....
2000-01	Anaheim	NHL	46	5	9	14	16	0	0	2	79	6.3	–11	0	0.0	12:48	....	....	....	....	....	....	....	....	....
	Cincinnati	AHL	25	9	9	18	24	....	....	....	....	....	....	....	....	....	4	3	2	5	0	....	....	....	....
2001-02	Anaheim	NHL	9	0	0	0	6	0	0	0	13	0.0	–6	1	0.0	11:47	....	....	....	....	....	....	....	....	....
	Cincinnati	AHL	3	2	3	5	2	....	....	....	....	....	....	....	....	....	....	....	....	....	....	....	....	....	....
	Nashville	NHL	58	8	16	24	28	0	1	2	82	9.8	–4	7	28.6	12:00	....	....	....	....	....	....	....	....	....
	Milwaukee	AHL	4	0	0	0	2	....	....	....	....	....	....	....	....	....	....	....	....	....	....	....	....	....	....
2002-03	Karpat Oulu	Finland	51	21	19	40	60	....	....	....	....	....	....	....	....	....	14	4	2	6	6	....	....	....	....
2003-04	Voskresensk	Russia	19	0	2	2	18	....	....	....	....	....	....	....	....	....	....	....	....	....	....	....	....	....	....
	Karpat Oulu	Finland	35	22	15	37	30	....	....	....	....	....	....	....	....	....	15	3	7	10	*45	....	....	....	....
2004-05	Karpat Oulu	Finland	53	18	20	38	46	....	....	....	....	....	....	....	....	....	12	*7	4	11	6	....	....	....	....
	NHL Totals		113	13	25	38	50	0	1	4	174	7.5		8	25.0	12:18	....	....	....	....	....	....	....	....	....

Traded to **Nashville** by **Anaheim** for Patrick Kjellberg, November 1, 2001. Claimed by **Florida** from **Nashville** in Waiver Draft, October 4, 2002. Traded to **Columbus** by **Florida** for Mathieu Biron, October 4, 2002. Signed as a free agent by **Karpat** (Finland), May 15, 2002. Claimed by **Toronto** from **Columbus** in Waiver Draft, October 3, 2003.

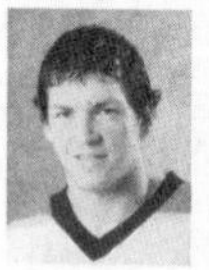

TETARENKO, Joey

(teh-tar-EHN-koh, JOH-ee) **MIN.**

Right wing. Shoots right. 6'2", 215 lbs. Born, Prince Albert, Sask., March 3, 1978. Florida's 4th choice, 82nd overall, in 1996 Entry Draft.

Season	Club	League	GP	G	A	Pts	PIM	PP	SH	GW	S	%	+/-	TF	F%	Min	GP	G	A	Pts	PIM	PP	SH	GW	Min
1993-94	North Battleford	SMHL	36	6	13	19	75	....	....	....	....	....	....	....	....	....	....	....	....	....	....	....	....	....	....
1994-95	Portland	WHL	59	0	1	1	134	....	....	....	....	....	....	....	....	....	9	0	0	0	8	....	....	....	....
1995-96	Portland	WHL	71	4	11	15	190	....	....	....	....	....	....	....	....	....	7	0	1	1	17	....	....	....	....
1996-97	Portland	WHL	68	8	18	26	182	....	....	....	....	....	....	....	....	....	2	0	0	0	2	....	....	....	....
1997-98	Portland	WHL	49	2	12	14	148	....	....	....	....	....	....	....	....	....	16	0	2	2	30	....	....	....	....
1998-99	New Haven	AHL	65	4	10	14	154	....	....	....	....	....	....	....	....	....	....	....	....	....	....	....	....	....	....
99-2000	Louisville Panthers	AHL	57	3	11	14	136	....	....	....	....	....	....	....	....	....	4	0	0	0	2	....	....	....	....
2000-01	Florida	NHL	29	3	1	4	44	0	0	0	21	14.3	–1	0	0.0	6:12	....	....	....	....	....	....	....	....	....
	Louisville Panthers	AHL	29	1	4	5	74	....	....	....	....	....	....	....	....	....	....	....	....	....	....	....	....	....	....
2001-02	Florida	NHL	38	1	0	1	123	0	0	0	10	10.0	–5	0	0.0	5:08	....	....	....	....	....	....	....	....	....
2002-03	San Antonio	AHL	50	4	12	16	123	....	....	....	....	....	....	....	....	....	....	....	....	....	....	....	....	....	....
	Florida	NHL	2	0	0	0	4	0	0	0	2	0.0	–1	0	0.0	6:19	....	....	....	....	....	....	....	....	....
	Ottawa	NHL	2	0	0	0	5	0	0	0	1	0.0	0	0	0.0	6:29	....	....	....	....	....	....	....	....	....
	Binghamton	AHL	14	2	2	4	33	....	....	....	....	....	....	....	....	....	14	0	0	0	36	....	....	....	....
2003-04	Carolina	NHL	2	0	0	0	0	0	0	0	0	0.0	0	1	0.0	3:31	....	....	....	....	....	....	....	....	....
	Lowell	AHL	57	1	6	7	167	....	....	....	....	....	....	....	....	....	....	....	....	....	....	....	....	....	....
2004-05	Houston Aeros	AHL	15	0	1	1	49	....	....	....	....	....	....	....	....	....	....	....	....	....	....	....	....	....	....
	NHL Totals		73	4	1	5	176	0	0	0	34	11.8		1	0.0	5:35	....	....	....	....	....	....	....	....	....

• Missed majority of 2001-02 season recovering from jaw injury suffered in game vs. NY Rangers, November 3, 2001. Traded to **Ottawa** by **Florida** for Simon Lajeunesse, March 4, 2003. Signed as a free agent by **Carolina**, July 2, 2003. Signed as a free agent by **Houston** (AHL), February 19, 2005.

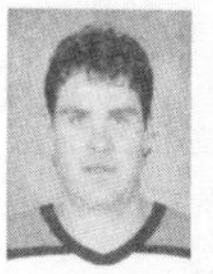

THERIEN, Chris

(TEH-ree-ehn, KRIHS) **PHI.**

Defense. Shoots left. 6'5", 235 lbs. Born, Ottawa, Ont., December 14, 1971. Philadelphia's 7th choice, 47th overall, in 1990 Entry Draft.

Season	Club	League	GP	G	A	Pts	PIM	PP	SH	GW	S	%	+/-	TF	F%	Min	GP	G	A	Pts	PIM	PP	SH	GW	Min
1988-89	Ott. Jr. Senators	CJHL	8	3	1	4	22	....	....	....	....	....	....	....	....	....	....	....	....	....	....	....	....	....	....
1989-90	Ott. Jr. Senators	CJHL	3	0	2	2	2	....	....	....	....	....	....	....	....	....	....	....	....	....	....	....	....	....	....
	Northwood	High-NY	31	35	37	72	54	....	....	....	....	....	....	....	....	....	....	....	....	....	....	....	....	....	....
1990-91	Providence	H-East	36	4	18	22	36	....	....	....	....	....	....	....	....	....	....	....	....	....	....	....	....	....	....
1991-92	Providence	H-East	36	16	25	41	38	....	....	....	....	....	....	....	....	....	....	....	....	....	....	....	....	....	....
1992-93	Providence	H-East	33	8	11	19	52	....	....	....	....	....	....	....	....	....	....	....	....	....	....	....	....	....	....
	Canada	Nat-Tm	8	1	4	5	8	....	....	....	....	....	....	....	....	....	....	....	....	....	....	....	....	....	....
1993-94	Canada	Nat-Tm	59	7	15	22	46	....	....	....	....	....	....	....	....	....	....	....	....	....	....	....	....	....	....
	Canada	Olympics	4	0	0	0	4	....	....	....	....	....	....	....	....	....	....	....	....	....	....	....	....	....	....
	Hershey Bears	AHL	6	0	0	0	2	....	....	....	....	....	....	....	....	....	....	....	....	....	....	....	....	....	....
1994-95	Hershey Bears	AHL	34	3	13	16	27	....	....	....	....	....	....	....	....	....	....	....	....	....	....	....	....	....	....
	Philadelphia	NHL	48	3	10	13	38	1	0	0	53	5.7	8	....	....	....	15	0	0	0	10	0	0	0	....
1995-96	Philadelphia	NHL	82	6	17	23	89	3	0	1	123	4.9	16	....	....	....	12	0	0	0	18	0	0	0	....
1996-97	Philadelphia	NHL	71	2	22	24	64	0	0	0	107	1.9	27	....	....	....	19	1	6	7	6	0	0	1	....
1997-98	Philadelphia	NHL	78	3	16	19	80	1	0	1	102	2.9	5	....	....	....	5	0	1	1	4	0	0	0	....
1998-99	Philadelphia	NHL	74	3	15	18	48	1	0	0	115	2.6	16	0	0.0	20:45	6	0	0	0	6	0	0	0	20:23
99-2000	Philadelphia	NHL	80	4	9	13	66	1	0	1	126	3.2	11	0	0.0	20:12	18	0	1	1	12	0	0	0	21:40
2000-01	Philadelphia	NHL	73	2	12	14	48	1	0	0	103	1.9	22	0	0.0	20:38	6	1	0	1	8	0	0	0	20:55
2001-02	Philadelphia	NHL	77	4	10	14	30	0	2	3	105	3.8	16	0	0.0	18:42	5	0	0	0	2	0	0	0	19:50
2002-03	Philadelphia	NHL	67	1	6	7	36	0	0	0	93	1.1	10	0	0.0	17:24	13	0	2	2	2	0	0	0	17:51
2003-04	Philadelphia	NHL	56	1	9	10	50	0	0	0	59	1.7	2	0	0.0	18:31	....	....	....	....	....	....	....	....	....
	Philadelphia	AHL	2	0	0	0	0	....	....	....	....	....	....	....	....	....	....	....	....	....	....	....	....	....	....
	Dallas	NHL	11	0	0	0	2	0	0	0	9	0.0	4	1	0.0	18:13	5	2	0	2	0	0	0	0	17:04
2004-05			DID NOT PLAY																						
	NHL Totals		717	29	126	155	551	8	2	6	995	2.9		1	0.0	19:25	104	4	10	14	68	0	0	1	19:54

Hockey East Second All-Star Team (1993) • NHL All-Rookie Team (1995)

Traded to **Dallas** by **Philadelphia** for Phoenix's 8th round choice (previously acquired, Philadelphia selected Martin Houle) in 2004 Entry Draft and Dallas' 3rd round choice (later traded to Tampa Bay - Tampa Bay selected Chris Lawrence) in 2005 Entry Draft, March 8, 2004. Signed as a free agent by **Philadelphia**, August 2, 2005.

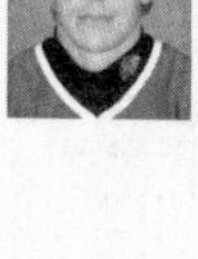

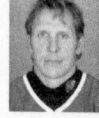

THOMAS, Steve

(TAW-mas, STEEV)

Left wing. Shoots left. 5'10", 185 lbs. Born, Stockport, England, July 15, 1963.

Season	Club	League	GP	G	A	Pts	PIM	PP	SH	GW	S	%	+/-	TF	F%	Min	GP	G	A	Pts	PIM	PP	SH	GW	Min
1980-81	Markham Waxers	OPJHL	42	22	25	47	76	....	....	....	....	....	....	....	....	....	....	....	....	....	....	....	....	....	....
	Toronto	OMJHL	1	0	0	0	0	....	....	....	....	....	....	....	....	....	....	....	....	....	....	....	....	....	....
1981-82	Markham Waxers	OPJHL	48	68	57	125	113	....	....	....	....	....	....	....	....	....	....	....	....	....	....	....	....	....	....
	Toronto	OHL	1	0	0	0	0	....	....	....	....	....	....	....	....	....	....	....	....	....	....	....	....	....	....
1982-83	Toronto	OHL	61	18	20	38	42	....	....	....	....	....	....	....	....	....	....	....	....	....	....	....	....	....	....
1983-84	Toronto	OHL	70	51	54	105	77	....	....	....	....	....	....	....	....	....	....	....	....	....	....	....	....	....	....
1984-85	Toronto	NHL	18	1	1	2	2	0	0	0	26	3.8	–13	....	....	....	....	....	....	....	....	....	....	....	....
	St. Catharines	AHL	64	42	48	90	56	....	....	....	....	....	....	....	....	....	....	....	....	....	....	....	....	....	....
1985-86	Toronto	NHL	65	20	37	57	36	5	0	5	197	10.2	–15	....	....	....	10	6	8	14	9	3	0	0	....
	St. Catharines	AHL	19	18	14	32	35	....	....	....	....	....	....	....	....	....	....	....	....	....	....	....	....	....	....

Season	Club	League	Regular Season GP	G	A	Pts	PIM	PP	SH	GW	S	%	+/-	TF	F%	Min	Playoffs GP	G	A	Pts	PIM	PP	SH	GW	Min
1986-87	**Toronto**	**NHL**	**78**	**35**	**27**	**62**	**114**	**3**	**0**	**7**	**245**	**14.3**	**–3**	....	....	....	**13**	**2**	**3**	**5**	**13**	**0**	**0**	**0**	....
1987-88	**Chicago**	**NHL**	**30**	**13**	**13**	**26**	**40**	**5**	**0**	**3**	**69**	**18.8**	**1**	....	....	....	**3**	**1**	**2**	**3**	**6**	**0**	**0**	**0**	....
1988-89	**Chicago**	**NHL**	**45**	**21**	**19**	**40**	**69**	**8**	**0**	**0**	**124**	**16.9**	**–2**	....	....	....	**12**	**3**	**5**	**8**	**10**	**1**	**0**	**2**	....
1989-90	**Chicago**	**NHL**	**76**	**40**	**30**	**70**	**91**	**13**	**0**	**7**	**235**	**17.0**	**–3**	....	....	....	**20**	**7**	**6**	**13**	**33**	**1**	**0**	**3**	....
1990-91	**Chicago**	**NHL**	**69**	**19**	**35**	**54**	**129**	**2**	**0**	**3**	**192**	**9.9**	**8**	....	....	....	**6**	**1**	**2**	**3**	**15**	**0**	**0**	**0**	....
1991-92	**Chicago**	**NHL**	**11**	**2**	**6**	**8**	**26**	**0**	**0**	**1**	**35**	**5.7**	**–3**	....	....	....	....	....	....	....	....	....	....	....	....
	NY Islanders	**NHL**	**71**	**28**	**42**	**70**	**71**	**3**	**0**	**2**	**210**	**13.3**	**11**	....	....	....	....	....	....	....	....	....	....	....	....
1992-93	**NY Islanders**	**NHL**	**79**	**37**	**50**	**87**	**111**	**12**	**0**	**7**	**264**	**14.0**	**3**	....	....	....	**18**	**9**	**8**	**17**	**37**	**0**	**0**	**0**	....
1993-94	**NY Islanders**	**NHL**	**78**	**42**	**33**	**75**	**139**	**17**	**0**	**5**	**249**	**16.9**	**–9**	....	....	....	**4**	**1**	**0**	**1**	**8**	**1**	**0**	**0**	....
1994-95	**NY Islanders**	**NHL**	**47**	**11**	**15**	**26**	**60**	**3**	**0**	**2**	**133**	**8.3**	**–14**	....	....	....	....	....	....	....	....	....	....	....	....
1995-96	**New Jersey**	**NHL**	**81**	**26**	**35**	**61**	**98**	**6**	**0**	**6**	**192**	**13.5**	**–2**	....	....	....	....	....	....	....	....	....	....	....	....
1996-97	**New Jersey**	**NHL**	**57**	**15**	**19**	**34**	**46**	**1**	**0**	**2**	**124**	**12.1**	**9**	....	....	....	**10**	**1**	**1**	**2**	**18**	**0**	**0**	**0**	....
1997-98	**New Jersey**	**NHL**	**55**	**14**	**10**	**24**	**32**	**3**	**0**	**4**	**111**	**12.6**	**4**	....	....	....	**6**	**0**	**3**	**3**	**2**	**0**	**0**	**0**	....
1998-99	**Toronto**	**NHL**	**78**	**28**	**45**	**73**	**33**	**11**	**0**	**7**	**209**	**13.4**	**26**	**4**	**25.0**	**18:23**	**17**	**6**	**3**	**9**	**12**	**2**	**0**	**1**	**20:37**
99-2000	**Toronto**	**NHL**	**81**	**26**	**37**	**63**	**68**	**9**	**0**	**9**	**151**	**17.2**	**1**	**8**	**50.0**	**16:19**	**12**	**6**	**3**	**9**	**10**	**0**	**0**	**1**	**18:21**
2000-01	**Toronto**	**NHL**	**57**	**8**	**26**	**34**	**46**	**1**	**0**	**1**	**140**	**5.7**	**0**	**3**	**33.3**	**16:02**	**11**	**6**	**3**	**9**	**4**	**4**	**0**	**0**	**16:22**
2001-02	**Chicago**	**NHL**	**34**	**11**	**4**	**15**	**17**	**3**	**0**	**0**	**66**	**16.7**	**0**	**0**	**0.0**	**17:21**	**5**	**1**	**1**	**2**	**0**	**0**	**0**	**0**	**15:45**
2002-03	**Chicago**	**NHL**	**69**	**4**	**13**	**17**	**51**	**0**	**0**	**1**	**91**	**4.4**	**0**	**19**	**36.8**	**12:45**	....	....	....	....	....	....	....	....	....
	Anaheim	**NHL**	**12**	**10**	**3**	**13**	**2**	**1**	**0**	**3**	**27**	**37.0**	**10**	**5**	**20.0**	**13:42**	**21**	**4**	**4**	**8**	**8**	**2**	**0**	**3**	**15:13**
2003-04	**Detroit**	**NHL**	**44**	**10**	**12**	**22**	**25**	**0**	**0**	**3**	**80**	**12.5**	**8**	**7**	**28.6**	**12:45**	**6**	**0**	**1**	**1**	**2**	**0**	**0**	**0**	**8:18**
2004-05		DID NOT PLAY																							
	NHL Totals		**1235**	**421**	**512**	**933**	**1306**	**106**	**0**	**78**	**3170**	**13.3**		**46**	**34.8**	**15:38**	**174**	**54**	**53**	**107**	**187**	**14**	**0**	**10**	**16:39**

AHL First All-Star Team (1985) • Dudley "Red" Garrett Memorial Award (Rookie of the Year – AHL) (1985)

Signed as a free agent by **Toronto,** May 12, 1984. Traded to **Chicago** by **Toronto** with Rick Vaive and Bob McGill for Al Secord and Ed Olczyk, September 3, 1987. Traded to **NY Islanders** by **Chicago** with Adam Creighton for Brent Sutter and Brad Lauer, October 25, 1991. Traded to **New Jersey** by **NY Islanders** for Claude Lemieux, October 3, 1995. Signed as a free agent by **Toronto**, July 30, 1998. Signed as a free agent by **Chicago**, July 17, 2001. • Missed majority of 2001-02 season recovering from ankle injury suffered in game vs. Calgary, November 15, 2001. Traded to **Anaheim** by **Chicago** for Anaheim's 5th round choice (Alexei Ivanov) in 2003 Entry Draft, March 11, 2003. Signed as a free agent by **Detroit**, November 5, 2003.

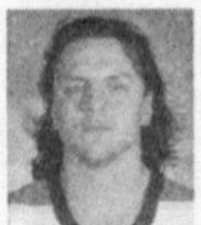

THOMPSON, Rocky

(TAWM-suhn, RAW-kee)

Defense. Shoots right. 6'2", 205 lbs. Born, Calgary, Alta., August 8, 1977. Calgary's 3rd choice, 72nd overall, in 1995 Entry Draft.

Season	Club	League	GP	G	A	Pts	PIM	PP	SH	GW	S	%	+/-	TF	F%	Min	GP	G	A	Pts	PIM	PP	SH	GW	Min
1992-93	Spruce Grove	AMHL	65	13	50	63	295	....	....	....	....	....	....	....	....	....	....	....	....	....	....	....	....	....	....
1993-94	Medicine Hat	WHL	68	1	4	5	166	....	....	....	....	....	....	....	....	....	3	0	0	0	2	....	....	....	....
1994-95	Medicine Hat	WHL	63	1	6	7	220	....	....	....	....	....	....	....	....	....	5	0	0	0	17	....	....	....	....
1995-96	Medicine Hat	WHL	71	9	20	29	260	....	....	....	....	....	....	....	....	....	5	2	3	5	26	....	....	....	....
	Saint John Flames	AHL	4	0	0	0	33	....	....	....	....	....	....	....	....	....	....	....	....	....	....	....	....	....	....
1996-97	Medicine Hat	WHL	47	6	9	15	170	....	....	....	....	....	....	....	....	....	....	....	....	....	....	....	....	....	....
	Swift Current	WHL	22	3	5	8	90	....	....	....	....	....	....	....	....	....	10	1	2	3	22	....	....	....	....
1997-98	**Calgary**	**NHL**	**12**	**0**	**0**	**0**	**61**	**0**	**0**	**0**	**3**	**0.0**	**0**	....	....	....	....	....	....	....	....	....	....	....	....
	Saint John Flames	AHL	51	3	0	3	187	....	....	....	....	....	....	....	....	....	18	1	1	2	47	....	....	....	....
1998-99	**Calgary**	**NHL**	**3**	**0**	**0**	**0**	**25**	**0**	**0**	**0**	**0**	**0.0**	**0**	**0**	**0.0**	**2:01**	....	....	....	....	....	....	....	....	....
	Saint John Flames	AHL	27	2	2	4	108	....	....	....	....	....	....	....	....	....	....	....	....	....	....	....	....	....	....
99-2000	Saint John Flames	AHL	53	2	8	10	125	....	....	....	....	....	....	....	....	....	....	....	....	....	....	....	....	....	....
	Louisville Panthers	AHL	3	0	1	1	54	....	....	....	....	....	....	....	....	....	4	0	0	0	4	....	....	....	....
2000-01	**Florida**	**NHL**	**4**	**0**	**0**	**0**	**19**	**0**	**0**	**0**	**0**	**0.0**	**0**	**0**	**0.0**	**1:28**	....	....	....	....	....	....	....	....	....
	Louisville Panthers	AHL	55	3	5	8	193	....	....	....	....	....	....	....	....	....	....	....	....	....	....	....	....	....	....
2001-02	**Florida**	**NHL**	**6**	**0**	**0**	**0**	**12**	**0**	**0**	**0**	**1**	**0.0**	**0**	**1**	**0.0**	**4:03**	....	....	....	....	....	....	....	....	....
	Hershey Bears	AHL	42	0	3	3	143	....	....	....	....	....	....	....	....	....	8	1	0	1	19	....	....	....	....
2002-03	San Antonio	AHL	79	1	11	12	275	....	....	....	....	....	....	....	....	....	3	0	0	0	4	....	....	....	....
2003-04	Toronto	AHL	69	1	8	9	196	....	....	....	....	....	....	....	....	....	3	1	1	2	0	....	....	....	....
2004-05	Edmonton	AHL	69	3	3	6	231	....	....	....	....	....	....	....	....	....	....	....	....	....	....	....	....	....	....
	NHL Totals		**25**	**0**	**0**	**0**	**117**	**0**	**0**	**0**	**4**	**0.0**		**1**	**0.0**	**2:47**	....	....	....	....	....	....	....	....	....

Traded to **Florida** by **Calgary** for Filip Kuba, March 16, 2000. Signed as a free agent by **Edmonton**, July 20, 2003.

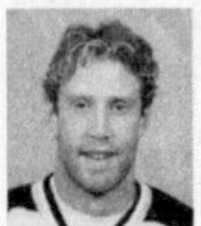

THORNTON, Joe

(THOHRN-tuhn, JOH) **BOS.**

Center. Shoots left. 6'4", 223 lbs. Born, London, Ont., July 2, 1979. Boston's 1st choice, 1st overall, in 1997 Entry Draft.

Season	Club	League	GP	G	A	Pts	PIM	PP	SH	GW	S	%	+/-	TF	F%	Min	GP	G	A	Pts	PIM	PP	SH	GW	Min
1993-94	Elgin-Middlesex	OMHA	67	*83	*85	*168	45	....	....	....	....	....	....	....	....	....	....	....	....	....	....	....	....	....	....
	St. Thomas Stars	OHA-B	6	2	6	8	2	....	....	....	....	....	....	....	....	....	....	....	....	....	....	....	....	....	....
1994-95	St. Thomas Stars	OHA-B	50	40	64	104	53	....	....	....	....	....	....	....	....	....	....	....	....	....	....	....	....	....	....
1995-96	Sault Ste. Marie	OHL	66	30	46	76	53	....	....	....	....	....	....	....	....	....	4	1	1	2	11	....	....	....	....
1996-97	Sault Ste. Marie	OHL	59	41	81	122	123	....	....	....	....	....	....	....	....	....	11	11	8	19	24	....	....	....	....
1997-98	**Boston**	**NHL**	**55**	**3**	**4**	**7**	**19**	**0**	**0**	**1**	**33**	**9.1**	**–6**	....	....	....	**6**	**0**	**0**	**0**	**9**	**0**	**0**	**0**	....
1998-99	**Boston**	**NHL**	**81**	**16**	**25**	**41**	**69**	**7**	**0**	**1**	**128**	**12.5**	**3**	**1073**	**48.7**	**15:21**	**11**	**3**	**6**	**9**	**4**	**2**	**0**	**2**	**19:52**
99-2000	**Boston**	**NHL**	**81**	**23**	**37**	**60**	**82**	**5**	**0**	**3**	**171**	**13.5**	**–5**	**1861**	**49.5**	**21:18**	....	....	....	....	....	....	....	....	....
2000-01	**Boston**	**NHL**	**72**	**37**	**34**	**71**	**107**	**19**	**1**	**5**	**181**	**20.4**	**–4**	**1651**	**52.1**	**21:45**	....	....	....	....	....	....	....	....	....
2001-02	**Boston**	**NHL**	**66**	**22**	**46**	**68**	**127**	**6**	**0**	**5**	**152**	**14.5**	**7**	**1341**	**49.1**	**19:59**	**6**	**2**	**4**	**6**	**10**	**0**	**0**	**0**	**21:09**
2002-03	**Boston**	**NHL**	**77**	**36**	**65**	**101**	**109**	**12**	**2**	**4**	**196**	**18.4**	**12**	**1766**	**49.5**	**22:33**	**5**	**1**	**2**	**3**	**4**	**1**	**0**	**0**	**20:13**
2003-04	**Boston**	**NHL**	**77**	**23**	**50**	**73**	**98**	**4**	**0**	**6**	**187**	**12.3**	**18**	**1671**	**56.3**	**21:38**	**7**	**0**	**0**	**0**	**14**	**0**	**0**	**0**	**21:30**
2004-05	HC Davos	Swiss	40	10	44	54	80	....	....	....	....	....	....	....	....	....	14	4	*20	*24	29	....	....	....	....
	NHL Totals		**509**	**160**	**261**	**421**	**611**	**53**	**3**	**25**	**1048**	**15.3**		**9363**	**51.0**	**20:23**	**35**	**6**	**12**	**18**	**41**	**3**	**0**	**2**	**20:35**

OHL All-Rookie Team (1996) • OHL Rookie of the Year (1996) • Canadian Major Junior Rookie of the Year (1996) • OHL Second All-Star Team (1997) • NHL Second All-Star Team (2003)
Played in NHL All-Star Game (2002, 2003, 2004)
Signed as a free agent by **Davos** (Swiss), July 8, 2004.

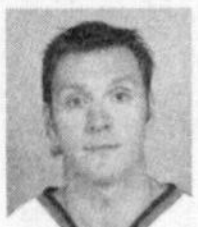

THORNTON, Scott

(THOHRN-tuhn, SKAWT) **S.J.**

Left wing. Shoots left. 6'3", 225 lbs. Born, London, Ont., January 9, 1971. Toronto's 1st choice, 3rd overall, in 1989 Entry Draft.

Season	Club	League	GP	G	A	Pts	PIM	PP	SH	GW	S	%	+/-	TF	F%	Min	GP	G	A	Pts	PIM	PP	SH	GW	Min
1986-87	London	OHA-B	31	10	7	17	10	....	....	....	....	....	....	....	....	....	....	....	....	....	....	....	....	....	....
1987-88	Belleville Bulls	OHL	62	11	19	30	54	....	....	....	....	....	....	....	....	....	6	0	1	1	2	....	....	....	....
1988-89	Belleville Bulls	OHL	59	28	34	62	103	....	....	....	....	....	....	....	....	....	5	1	1	2	6	....	....	....	....
1989-90	Belleville Bulls	OHL	47	21	28	49	91	....	....	....	....	....	....	....	....	....	11	2	10	12	15	....	....	....	....
1990-91	Belleville Bulls	OHL	3	2	1	3	2	....	....	....	....	....	....	....	....	....	6	0	7	7	14	....	....	....	....
	Toronto	**NHL**	**33**	**1**	**3**	**4**	**30**	**0**	**0**	**0**	**31**	**3.2**	**–15**	....	....	....	....	....	....	....	....	....	....	....	....
	Newmarket Saints	AHL	5	1	0	1	4	....	....	....	....	....	....	....	....	....	....	....	....	....	....	....	....	....	....
1991-92	**Edmonton**	**NHL**	**15**	**0**	**1**	**1**	**43**	**0**	**0**	**0**	**11**	**0.0**	**–6**	....	....	....	**1**	**0**	**0**	**0**	**0**	**0**	**0**	**0**	....
	Cape Breton	AHL	49	9	14	23	40	....	....	....	....	....	....	....	....	....	5	1	0	1	8	....	....	....	....
1992-93	**Edmonton**	**NHL**	**9**	**0**	**1**	**1**	**0**	**0**	**0**	**0**	**7**	**0.0**	**–4**	....	....	....	....	....	....	....	....	....	....	....	....
	Cape Breton	AHL	58	23	27	50	102	....	....	....	....	....	....	....	....	....	16	1	2	3	35	....	....	....	....
1993-94	**Edmonton**	**NHL**	**61**	**4**	**7**	**11**	**104**	**0**	**0**	**0**	**65**	**6.2**	**–15**	....	....	....	....	....	....	....	....	....	....	....	....
	Cape Breton	AHL	2	1	1	2	31	....	....	....	....	....	....	....	....	....	....	....	....	....	....	....	....	....	....
1994-95	**Edmonton**	**NHL**	**47**	**10**	**12**	**22**	**89**	**0**	**1**	**1**	**69**	**14.5**	**–4**	....	....	....	....	....	....	....	....	....	....	....	....
1995-96	**Edmonton**	**NHL**	**77**	**9**	**9**	**18**	**149**	**0**	**2**	**3**	**95**	**9.5**	**–25**	....	....	....	....	....	....	....	....	....	....	....	....
1996-97	**Montreal**	**NHL**	**73**	**10**	**10**	**20**	**128**	**1**	**1**	**1**	**110**	**9.1**	**–19**	....	....	....	**5**	**1**	**0**	**1**	**2**	**0**	**0**	**0**	....
1997-98	**Montreal**	**NHL**	**67**	**6**	**9**	**15**	**158**	**1**	**0**	**1**	**51**	**11.8**	**0**	....	....	....	**9**	**0**	**2**	**2**	**10**	**0**	**0**	**0**	....
1998-99	**Montreal**	**NHL**	**47**	**7**	**4**	**11**	**87**	**1**	**0**	**1**	**56**	**12.5**	**–2**	**466**	**52.8**	**12:24**	....	....	....	....	....	....	....	....	....
99-2000	**Montreal**	**NHL**	**35**	**2**	**3**	**5**	**70**	**0**	**0**	**1**	**36**	**5.6**	**–7**	**253**	**51.8**	**12:40**	....	....	....	....	....	....	....	....	....
	Dallas	**NHL**	**30**	**6**	**3**	**9**	**38**	**1**	**0**	**0**	**47**	**12.8**	**–5**	**14**	**14.3**	**13:03**	**23**	**2**	**7**	**9**	**28**	**0**	**0**	**1**	**14:11**
2000-01	**San Jose**	**NHL**	**73**	**19**	**17**	**36**	**114**	**4**	**0**	**1**	**159**	**11.9**	**4**	**29**	**41.4**	**13:54**	**6**	**3**	**0**	**3**	**8**	**0**	**0**	**1**	**15:50**
2001-02	**San Jose**	**NHL**	**77**	**26**	**16**	**42**	**116**	**6**	**0**	**5**	**144**	**18.1**	**11**	**18**	**61.1**	**13:31**	**12**	**3**	**3**	**6**	**6**	**0**	**0**	**0**	**15:52**
2002-03	**San Jose**	**NHL**	**41**	**9**	**12**	**21**	**41**	**4**	**0**	**1**	**64**	**14.1**	**–7**	**6**	**50.0**	**13:53**	....	....	....	....	....	....	....	....	....
2003-04	**San Jose**	**NHL**	**80**	**13**	**14**	**27**	**84**	**1**	**0**	**1**	**127**	**10.2**	**–6**	**27**	**40.7**	**13:57**	**12**	**2**	**2**	**4**	**22**	**0**	**0**	**0**	**12:31**
2004-05	Sodertalje SK	Sweden	12	2	5	7	10	....	....	....	....	....	....	....	....	....	10	0	3	3	27	....	....	....	....
	NHL Totals		**765**	**122**	**121**	**243**	**1251**	**19**	**4**	**16**	**1072**	**11.4**		**813**	**51.2**	**13:28**	**68**	**11**	**14**	**25**	**76**	**0**	**0**	**2**	**14:22**

Traded to **Edmonton** by **Toronto** with Vincent Damphousse, Peter Ing and Luke Richardson for Grant Fuhr, Glenn Anderson and Craig Berube, September 19, 1991. Traded to **Montreal** by **Edmonton** for Andrei Kovalenko, September 6, 1996. Traded to **Dallas** by **Montreal** for Juha Lind, January 22, 2000. Signed as a free agent by **San Jose**, July 1, 2000. • Missed majority of 2002-03 season recovering from shoulder (October 7, 2002 in training camp) and head (February 21, 2003 vs. Columbus) injuries. Signed as a free agent by **Sodertalje** (Sweden), January 13, 2005.

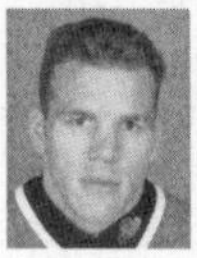

THORNTON, Shawn

(THOHRN-tohn, SHAWN) **CHI.**

Right wing. Shoots right. 6'1", 209 lbs. Born, Oshawa, Ont., July 23, 1977. Toronto's 6th choice, 190th overall, in 1997 Entry Draft.

Season	Club	League	Regular Season GP	G	A	Pts	PIM	PP	SH	GW	S	%	+/-	TF	F%	Min	Playoffs GP	G	A	Pts	PIM	PP	SH	GW	Min
1995-96	Peterborough	OHL	63	4	10	14	192	....	....	....	....	....	....	....	....	....	24	3	0	3	25	....	....	....	....
1996-97	Peterborough	OHL	61	19	10	29	204	....	....	....	....	....	....	....	....	....	11	2	4	6	20	....	....	....	....
1997-98	St. John's	AHL	59	0	3	3	225	....	....	....	....	....	....	....	....	....	....	....	....	....	....	....	....	....	....
1998-99	St. John's	AHL	78	8	11	19	354	....	....	....	....	....	....	....	....	....	5	0	0	0	9	....	....	....	....
99-2000	St. John's	AHL	60	4	12	16	316	....	....	....	....	....	....	....	....	....	....	....	....	....	....	....	....	....	....
2000-01	St. John's	AHL	79	5	12	17	320	....	....	....	....	....	....	....	....	....	3	1	2	3	2	....	....	....	....
2001-02	Norfolk Admirals	AHL	70	8	14	22	281	....	....	....	....	....	....	....	....	....	4	0	0	0	4	....	....	....	....
2002-03	**Chicago**	**NHL**	**13**	**1**	**1**	**2**	**31**	**0**	**0**	**0**	**15**	**6.7**	**–4**	**3**	**66.7**	**8:30**	....	....	....	....	....	....	....	....	....
	Norfolk Admirals	AHL	50	11	2	13	213	....	....	....	....	....	....	....	....	....	9	0	2	2	28	....	....	....	....
2003-04	**Chicago**	**NHL**	**8**	**1**	**0**	**1**	**23**	**0**	**0**	**0**	**14**	**7.1**	**2**	**19**	**42.1**	**11:14**	....	....	....	....	....	....	....	....	....
	Norfolk Admirals	AHL	64	6	11	17	259	....	....	....	....	....	....	....	....	....	8	1	1	2	6	....	....	....	....
2004-05	Norfolk Admirals	AHL	71	5	9	14	253	....	....	....	....	....	....	....	....	....	6	0	0	0	8	....	....	....	....
	NHL Totals		**21**	**2**	**1**	**3**	**54**	**0**	**0**	**0**	**29**	**6.9**		**22**	**45.5**	**9:32**	....	....	....	....	....	....	....	....	....

Traded to **Chicago** by **Toronto** for Marty Wilford, September 30, 2001.

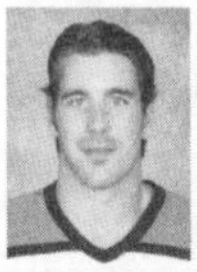

TILEY, Brad

(TIHL-ee, BRAD)

Defense. Shoots left. 6'1", 199 lbs. Born, Markdale, Ont., July 5, 1971. Boston's 4th choice, 84th overall, in 1991 Entry Draft.

Season	Club	League	Regular Season GP	G	A	Pts	PIM	PP	SH	GW	S	%	+/-	TF	F%	Min	Playoffs GP	G	A	Pts	PIM	PP	SH	GW	Min
1987-88	Owen Sound	OHA-B	45	18	25	43	69	....	....	....	....	....	....	....	....	....	....	....	....	....	....	....	....	....	....
1988-89	Sault Ste. Marie	OHL	50	4	11	15	31	....	....	....	....	....	....	....	....	....	....	....	....	....	....	....	....	....	....
1989-90	Sault Ste. Marie	OHL	66	9	32	41	47	....	....	....	....	....	....	....	....	....	....	....	....	....	....	....	....	....	....
1990-91	Sault Ste. Marie	OHL	66	11	55	66	29	....	....	....	....	....	....	....	....	....	14	4	15	19	12	....	....	....	....
1991-92	Maine Mariners	AHL	62	7	22	29	36	....	....	....	....	....	....	....	....	....	....	....	....	....	....	....	....	....	....
1992-93	Phoenix	IHL	46	11	27	38	35	....	....	....	....	....	....	....	....	....	....	....	....	....	....	....	....	....	....
	Binghamton	AHL	26	6	10	16	19	....	....	....	....	....	....	....	....	....	8	0	1	1	2	....	....	....	....
1993-94	Binghamton	AHL	29	6	10	16	6	....	....	....	....	....	....	....	....	....	....	....	....	....	....	....	....	....	....
	Phoenix	IHL	35	8	15	23	21	....	....	....	....	....	....	....	....	....	....	....	....	....	....	....	....	....	....
1994-95	Detroit Vipers	IHL	56	7	19	26	32	....	....	....	....	....	....	....	....	....	....	....	....	....	....	....	....	....	....
	Fort Wayne	IHL	14	1	6	7	2	....	....	....	....	....	....	....	....	....	3	1	2	3	0	....	....	....	....
1995-96	Orlando	IHL	69	11	23	34	82	....	....	....	....	....	....	....	....	....	23	2	4	6	16	....	....	....	....
1996-97	Phoenix	IHL	66	8	28	36	34	....	....	....	....	....	....	....	....	....	....	....	....	....	....	....	....	....	....
	Long Beach	IHL	3	1	0	1	2	....	....	....	....	....	....	....	....	....	....	....	....	....	....	....	....	....	....
1997-98	**Phoenix**	**NHL**	**1**	**0**	**0**	**0**	**0**	....	....	....	....	....	....	....	....	....	....	....	....	....	....	....	....	....	....
	Springfield	AHL	60	10	31	41	36	....	....	....	....	....	....	....	....	....	4	0	4	4	2	....	....	....	....
1998-99	**Phoenix**	**NHL**	**8**	**0**	**0**	**0**	**0**	**0**	**0**	**0**	**1**	**0.0**	**–1**	**0**	**0.0**	**11:29**	**1**	**0**	**0**	**0**	**0**	**0**	**0**	**0**	**13:11**
	Springfield	AHL	69	9	35	44	14	....	....	....	....	....	....	....	....	....	1	0	0	0	0	....	....	....	....
99-2000	Springfield	AHL	80	14	54	68	51	....	....	....	....	....	....	....	....	....	5	0	4	4	2	....	....	....	....
2000-01	**Philadelphia**	**NHL**	**2**	**0**	**0**	**0**	**0**	**0**	**0**	**0**	**1**	**0.0**	**–1**	**0**	**0.0**	**15:46**	....	....	....	....	....	....	....	....	....
	Philadelphia	AHL	56	11	19	30	10	....	....	....	....	....	....	....	....	....	10	1	2	3	2	....	....	....	....
2001-02	Philadelphia	AHL	56	6	15	21	14	....	....	....	....	....	....	....	....	....	....	....	....	....	....	....	....	....	....
2002-03	Philadelphia	AHL	79	8	28	36	28	....	....	....	....	....	....	....	....	....	....	....	....	....	....	....	....	....	....
2003-04	Milwaukee	AHL	75	13	34	47	14	....	....	....	....	....	....	....	....	....	22	1	6	7	6	....	....	....	....
2004-05	Milwaukee	AHL	77	8	17	25	23	....	....	....	....	....	....	....	....	....	6	0	5	5	2	....	....	....	....
	NHL Totals		**11**	**0**	**0**	**0**	**0**	**0**	**0**	**0**	**2**	**0.0**		**0**	**0.0**	**12:20**	**1**	**0**	**0**	**0**	**0**	**0**	**0**	**0**	**13:11**

Memorial Cup Tournament All-Star Team (1991) • AHL First All-Star Team (2000) • Eddie Shore Award (Outstanding Defenseman – AHL) (2000)

Signed as a free agent by **NY Rangers**, September 4, 1992. Traded to **Los Angeles** by **NY Rangers** for Los Angeles' 11th round choice (Jamie Butt) in 1994 Entry Draft, January 28, 1994. Signed as a free agent by **Phoenix**, September 4, 1997. Signed as a free agent by **Philadelphia**, July 14, 2000. Signed as a free agent by **Milwaukee** (AHL), October 22, 2003.

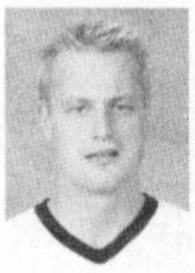

TIMANDER, Mattias

(tih-MAHN-duhr, MA-tee-uhs)

Defense. Shoots left. 6'2", 230 lbs. Born, Solleftea, Sweden, April 16, 1974. Boston's 7th choice, 208th overall, in 1992 Entry Draft.

Season	Club	League	Regular Season GP	G	A	Pts	PIM	PP	SH	GW	S	%	+/-	TF	F%	Min	Playoffs GP	G	A	Pts	PIM	PP	SH	GW	Min
1992-93	MoDo Jr.	Swe-Jr.	4	0	0	0	0	....	....	....	....	....	....	....	....	....	....	....	....	....	....	....	....	....	....
	Husums IF	Sweden-2	27	4	9	13	22	....	....	....	....	....	....	....	....	....	....	....	....	....	....	....	....	....	....
	MoDo	Sweden	1	0	0	0	0	....	....	....	....	....	....	....	....	....	....	....	....	....	....	....	....	....	....
1993-94	MoDo Jr.	Swe-Jr.	3	2	2	4	10	....	....	....	....	....	....	....	....	....	....	....	....	....	....	....	....	....	....
	MoDo	Sweden	23	2	2	4	6	....	....	....	....	....	....	....	....	....	11	2	0	2	10	....	....	....	....
1994-95	MoDo	Sweden	39	8	9	17	24	....	....	....	....	....	....	....	....	....	....	....	....	....	....	....	....	....	....
1995-96	MoDo	Sweden	37	4	10	14	34	....	....	....	....	....	....	....	....	....	7	1	1	2	8	....	....	....	....
1996-97	**Boston**	**NHL**	**41**	**1**	**8**	**9**	**14**	**0**	**0**	**0**	**62**	**1.6**	**–9**	....	....	....	....	....	....	....	....	....	....	....	....
	Providence Bruins	AHL	32	3	11	14	20	....	....	....	....	....	....	....	....	....	10	1	1	2	12	....	....	....	....
1997-98	**Boston**	**NHL**	**23**	**1**	**1**	**2**	**6**	**0**	**0**	**0**	**17**	**5.9**	**–9**	....	....	....	....	....	....	....	....	....	....	....	....
	Providence Bruins	AHL	31	3	7	10	25	....	....	....	....	....	....	....	....	....	....	....	....	....	....	....	....	....	....
1998-99	**Boston**	**NHL**	**22**	**0**	**6**	**6**	**10**	**0**	**0**	**0**	**22**	**0.0**	**4**	**0**	**0.0**	**12:54**	**4**	**1**	**1**	**2**	**2**	**0**	**0**	**0**	**13:03**
	Providence Bruins	AHL	43	2	22	24	24	....	....	....	....	....	....	....	....	....	....	....	....	....	....	....	....	....	....
99-2000	**Boston**	**NHL**	**60**	**0**	**8**	**8**	**22**	**0**	**0**	**0**	**39**	**0.0**	**–11**	**0**	**0.0**	**12:29**	....	....	....	....	....	....	....	....	....
	Hershey Bears	AHL	1	0	0	0	2	....	....	....	....	....	....	....	....	....	....	....	....	....	....	....	....	....	....
2000-01	**Columbus**	**NHL**	**76**	**2**	**9**	**11**	**24**	**0**	**0**	**1**	**68**	**2.9**	**–8**	**2**	**100.0**	**21:02**	....	....	....	....	....	....	....	....	....
2001-02	**Columbus**	**NHL**	**78**	**4**	**7**	**11**	**44**	**1**	**0**	**0**	**68**	**5.9**	**–34**	**1**	**0.0**	**19:52**	....	....	....	....	....	....	....	....	....
2002-03	**NY Islanders**	**NHL**	**80**	**3**	**13**	**16**	**24**	**0**	**0**	**1**	**83**	**3.6**	**–2**	**0**	**0.0**	**17:29**	**1**	**0**	**0**	**0**	**0**	**0**	**0**	**0**	**4:08**
2003-04	**NY Islanders**	**NHL**	**5**	**1**	**1**	**2**	**2**	**0**	**0**	**1**	**3**	**33.3**	**2**	**0**	**0.0**	**14:35**	....	....	....	....	....	....	....	....	....
	Bridgeport	AHL	35	2	6	8	12	....	....	....	....	....	....	....	....	....	....	....	....	....	....	....	....	....	....
	Philadelphia	**NHL**	**34**	**1**	**4**	**5**	**19**	**0**	**1**	**0**	**43**	**2.3**	**13**	**0**	**0.0**	**18:25**	**18**	**2**	**4**	**6**	**6**	**0**	**0**	**1**	**17:28**
2004-05	MODO	Sweden	47	3	7	10	60	....	....	....	....	....	....	....	....	....	6	0	1	1	4	....	....	....	....
	NHL Totals		**419**	**13**	**57**	**70**	**165**	**1**	**1**	**3**	**405**	**3.2**		**3**	**66.7**	**17:41**	**23**	**3**	**5**	**8**	**8**	**0**	**0**	**1**	**16:07**

Claimed by **Columbus** from **Boston** in Expansion Draft, June 23, 2000. Traded to **NY Islanders** by **Columbus** for NY Islanders' 4th round choice (Jekabs Redlihs) in 2002 Entry Draft, June 22, 2002. Traded to **Philadelphia** by **NY Islanders** for Tampa Bay's 7th round choice (previously acquired, NY Islanders selected Chris Campoli) in 2004 Entry Draft, January 22, 2004. Signed as a free agent by **MODO** (Sweden), June 3, 2004.

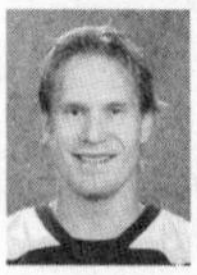

TIMONEN, Kimmo

(TEEM-oh-nehn, KEE-moh) **NSH.**

Defense. Shoots left. 5'10", 194 lbs. Born, Kuopio, Finland, March 18, 1975. Los Angeles' 11th choice, 250th overall, in 1993 Entry Draft.

Season	Club	League	Regular Season GP	G	A	Pts	PIM	PP	SH	GW	S	%	+/-	TF	F%	Min	Playoffs GP	G	A	Pts	PIM	PP	SH	GW	Min
1990-91	KalPa Kuopio Jr.	Finland-Jr.	4	0	1	1	2	....	....	....	....	....	....	....	....	....	....	....	....	....	....	....	....	....	....
1991-92	KalPa Kuopio Jr.	Finland-Jr.	32	7	10	17	4	....	....	....	....	....	....	....	....	....	....	....	....	....	....	....	....	....	....
	KalPa Kuopio	Finland	5	0	0	0	0	....	....	....	....	....	....	....	....	....	....	....	....	....	....	....	....	....	....
1992-93	KalPa Kuopio Jr.	Finland-Jr.	16	9	15	24	10	....	....	....	....	....	....	....	....	....	....	....	....	....	....	....	....	....	....
	KalPa Kuopio	Finland	33	0	2	2	4	....	....	....	....	....	....	....	....	....	....	....	....	....	....	....	....	....	....
1993-94	KalPa Kuopio Jr.	Finland-Jr.	5	4	7	11	0	....	....	....	....	....	....	....	....	....	....	....	....	....	....	....	....	....	....
	KalPa Kuopio	Finland	46	6	7	13	55	....	....	....	....	....	....	....	....	....	....	....	....	....	....	....	....	....	....
1994-95	TPS Turku Jr.	Finland-Jr.	1	0	0	0	0	....	....	....	....	....	....	....	....	....	....	....	....	....	....	....	....	....	....
	TPS Turku	Finland	45	3	4	7	10	....	....	....	....	....	....	....	....	....	13	0	1	1	6	....	....	....	....
1995-96	TPS Turku	Finland	48	3	21	24	22	....	....	....	....	....	....	....	....	....	9	1	2	3	12	....	....	....	....
1996-97	TPS Turku	Finland	50	10	14	24	18	....	....	....	....	....	....	....	....	....	12	2	7	9	8	....	....	....	....
	TPS Turku	EuroHL	6	1	0	1	27	....	....	....	....	....	....	....	....	....	4	0	1	1	0	....	....	....	....
1997-98	HIFK Helsinki	Finland	45	10	15	25	59	....	....	....	....	....	....	....	....	....	9	3	4	7	8	....	....	....	....
	Finland	Olympics	6	0	1	1	2	....	....	....	....	....	....	....	....	....	....	....	....	....	....	....	....	....	....
1998-99	**Nashville**	**NHL**	**50**	**4**	**8**	**12**	**30**	**1**	**0**	**0**	**75**	**5.3**	**–4**	**0**	**0.0**	**19:04**	....	....	....	....	....	....	....	....	....
	Milwaukee	IHL	29	2	13	15	22	....	....	....	....	....	....	....	....	....	....	....	....	....	....	....	....	....	....
99-2000	**Nashville**	**NHL**	**51**	**8**	**25**	**33**	**26**	**2**	**1**	**2**	**97**	**8.2**	**–5**	**0**	**0.0**	**21:06**	....	....	....	....	....	....	....	....	....
2000-01	**Nashville**	**NHL**	**82**	**12**	**13**	**25**	**50**	**6**	**0**	**3**	**151**	**7.9**	**–6**	**2**	**50.0**	**23:11**	....	....	....	....	....	....	....	....	....
2001-02	**Nashville**	**NHL**	**82**	**13**	**29**	**42**	**28**	**9**	**0**	**1**	**154**	**8.4**	**2**	**0**	**0.0**	**24:12**	....	....	....	....	....	....	....	....	....
	Finland	Olympics	4	0	1	1	2	....	....	....	....	....	....	....	....	....	....	....	....	....	....	....	....	....	....
2002-03	**Nashville**	**NHL**	**72**	**6**	**34**	**40**	**46**	**4**	**0**	**0**	**144**	**4.2**	**–3**	**0**	**0.0**	**22:25**	....	....	....	....	....	....	....	....	....
2003-04	**Nashville**	**NHL**	**77**	**12**	**32**	**44**	**52**	**8**	**0**	**1**	**180**	**6.7**	**–7**	**1**	**0.0**	**23:52**	**6**	**0**	**0**	**0**	**10**	**0**	**0**	**0**	**24:16**

			Regular Season														Playoffs								
Season	Club	League	GP	G	A	Pts	PIM	PP	SH	GW	S	%	+/-	TF	F%	Min	GP	G	A	Pts	PIM	PP	SH	GW	Min
2004-05	HC Lugano	Swiss	3	0	1	1	0																		
	Brynas IF Gavle	Sweden	10	5	3	8	8																		
	KalPa Kuopio	Finland-2	12	4	13	17	6										8	3	7	10	4				
	NHL Totals		**414**	**55**	**141**	**196**	**232**	**30**	**1**	**7**	**801**	**6.9**		**3**	**33.3**	**22:37**	**6**	**0**	**0**	**0**	**10**	**0**	**0**	**0**	**24:15**

Played in NHL All-Star Game (2004)

Traded to **Nashville** by **Los Angeles** with Jan Vopat for future considerations, June 26, 1998. Signed as a free agent by **Lugano** (Swiss), October 31, 2004. Signed as a free agent by **Brynas** (Sweden), November 8, 2004. Signed as a free agent by **KalPa Kuopio** (Finland-2), January 3, 2005.

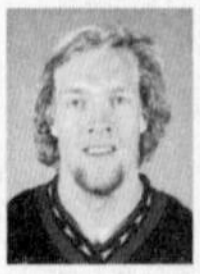

TJARNQVIST, Daniel (TUH-yahrn-kvihst, DAN-yehl) MIN.

Defense. Shoots left. 6'2", 200 lbs. Born, Umea, Sweden, October 14, 1976. Florida's 5th choice, 88th overall, in 1995 Entry Draft.

Season	Club	League	GP	G	A	Pts	PIM	PP	SH	GW	S	%	+/-	TF	F%	Min	GP	G	A	Pts	PIM	PP	SH	GW	Min
1992-93	Rogle Jr.	Swe-Jr.	7	1	0	1	0																		
1993-94	Rogle U18	Swe-U18	STATISTICS NOT AVAILABLE																						
1994-95	Rogle	Sweden	18	0	1	1	2																		
	Rogle	Sweden-Q	15	2	3	5	0																		
1995-96	Rogle	Sweden	22	1	7	8	6																		
1996-97	Jokerit Helsinki	Finland	44	3	8	11	4										9	0	3	3	4				
	Jokerit Helsinki	EuroHL	6	1	1	2	2																		
1997-98	Djurgarden	Sweden	40	5	9	14	12										15	1	1	2	2				
1998-99	Djurgarden	Sweden	40	4	3	7	16										4	0	0	0	2				
99-2000	Djurgarden	Sweden	42	3	16	19	8										5	0	0	0	2				
2000-01	Djurgarden	Sweden	45	9	17	26	26										16	6	5	11	2				
2001-02	**Atlanta**	**NHL**	**75**	**2**	**16**	**18**	**14**	**1**	**0**	**0**	**68**	**2.9**	**–22**	**4**	**25.0**	**21:32**									
2002-03	**Atlanta**	**NHL**	**75**	**3**	**12**	**15**	**26**	**1**	**0**	**0**	**65**	**4.6**	**–20**	**3**	**66.7**	**21:53**									
2003-04	**Atlanta**	**NHL**	**68**	**5**	**15**	**20**	**20**	**0**	**2**	**1**	**65**	**7.7**	**–4**	**4**	**25.0**	**22:17**									
2004-05	Djurgarden	Sweden	49	12	12	24	30										12	2	5	7	10				
	NHL Totals		**218**	**10**	**43**	**53**	**60**	**2**	**2**	**1**	**198**	**5.1**		**11**	**36.4**	**21:53**									

Traded to **Atlanta** by **Florida** with Gord Murphy, Herbert Vasiljevs and Ottawa's 6th round choice (previously acquired, later traded to Dallas – Dallas selected Justin Cox) in 1999 Entry Draft for Trevor Kidd, June 25, 1999. Signed as a free agent by **Djurgarden** (Sweden), September 16, 2004. Signed as a free agent by **Minnesota**, August 15, 2005.

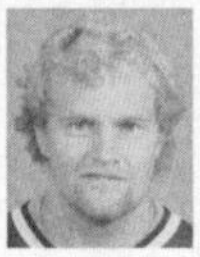

TJARNQVIST, Mathias (TUH-yahrn-kvihst, MAT-ee-uhs) DAL.

Right wing. Shoots left. 6'1", 183 lbs. Born, Umea, Sweden, April 15, 1979. Dallas' 3rd choice, 96th overall, in 1999 Entry Draft.

Season	Club	League	GP	G	A	Pts	PIM	PP	SH	GW	S	%	+/-	TF	F%	Min	GP	G	A	Pts	PIM	PP	SH	GW	Min
1995-96	Rogle Jr.	Swe-Jr.	4	2	0	2	0																		
1996-97	Rogle Jr.	Swe-Jr.	18	5	8	13																			
	Rogle	Sweden-2	15	1	4	5	4																		
1997-98	Rogle	Sweden-2	31	12	11	23	30										4	2	0	2	6				
1998-99	Rogle	Sweden-2	34	18	16	34	44										5	4	1	5	4				
99-2000	Djurgarden	Sweden	50	12	12	24	20										13	3	2	5	16				
2000-01	Djurgarden	Sweden	47	11	8	19	53										16	1	2	3	6				
2001-02	Djurgarden	Sweden	6	0	1	1	4										2	0	0	0	2				
2002-03	Djurgarden	Sweden	38	11	13	24	30										9	4	1	5	12				
2003-04	**Dallas**	**NHL**	**18**	**1**	**1**	**2**	**2**	**0**	**0**	**1**	**11**	**9.1**	**–6**	**4**	**25.0**	**9:43**									
	Utah Grizzlies	AHL	60	15	13	28	51																		
2004-05	HV 71 Jonkoping	Sweden	46	8	9	17	18																		
	NHL Totals		**18**	**1**	**1**	**2**	**2**	**0**	**0**	**1**	**11**	**9.1**		**4**	**25.0**	**9:43**									

Signed as a free agent by **HV 71** (Sweden), August 30, 2004. Signed as a free agent by **Linkoping** (Sweden), May 13, 2005.

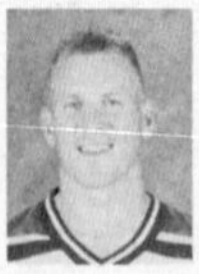

TKACHUK, Keith (kuh-CHUK, KEETH) ST.L.

Left wing. Shoots left. 6'2", 231 lbs. Born, Melrose, MA, March 28, 1972. Winnipeg's 1st choice, 19th overall, in 1990 Entry Draft.

Season	Club	League	GP	G	A	Pts	PIM	PP	SH	GW	S	%	+/-	TF	F%	Min	GP	G	A	Pts	PIM	PP	SH	GW	Min
1988-89	Malden Cath.	High-MA	21	30	16	46																			
1989-90	Malden Cath.	High-MA	6	12	14	26																			
1990-91	Boston University	H-East	36	17	23	40	70																		
1991-92	United States	Nat-Tm	45	10	10	20	141																		
	United States	Olympics	8	1	1	2	12																		
	Winnipeg	**NHL**	**17**	**3**	**5**	**8**	**28**	**2**	**0**	**0**	**22**	**13.6**	**0**				**7**	**3**	**0**	**3**	**30**	**0**	**0**	**0**	
1992-93	**Winnipeg**	**NHL**	**83**	**28**	**23**	**51**	**201**	**12**	**0**	**2**	**199**	**14.1**	**–13**				**6**	**4**	**0**	**4**	**14**	**1**	**0**	**0**	
1993-94	**Winnipeg**	**NHL**	**84**	**41**	**40**	**81**	**255**	**22**	**3**	**3**	**218**	**18.8**	**–12**												
1994-95	**Winnipeg**	**NHL**	**48**	**22**	**29**	**51**	**152**	**7**	**2**	**2**	**129**	**17.1**	**–4**												
1995-96	**Winnipeg**	**NHL**	**76**	**50**	**48**	**98**	**156**	**20**	**2**	**6**	**249**	**20.1**	**11**				**6**	**1**	**2**	**3**	**22**	**0**	**0**	**0**	
1996-97	**Phoenix**	**NHL**	**81**	***52**	**34**	**86**	**228**	**9**	**2**	**7**	**296**	**17.6**	**–1**				**7**	**6**	**0**	**6**	**7**	**2**	**0**	**0**	
1997-98	**Phoenix**	**NHL**	**69**	**40**	**26**	**66**	**147**	**11**	**0**	**8**	**232**	**17.2**	**9**				**6**	**3**	**3**	**6**	**10**	**0**	**0**	**0**	
	United States	Olympics	4	0	2	2	6																		
1998-99	**Phoenix**	**NHL**	**68**	**36**	**32**	**68**	**151**	**11**	**2**	**7**	**258**	**14.0**	**22**	**770**	**47.7**	**20:59**	**7**	**1**	**3**	**4**	**13**	**1**	**0**	**0**	**25:09**
99-2000	**Phoenix**	**NHL**	**50**	**22**	**21**	**43**	**82**	**5**	**1**	**1**	**183**	**12.0**	**7**	**500**	**50.4**	**19:21**	**5**	**1**	**1**	**2**	**4**	**1**	**0**	**0**	**18:46**
2000-01	**Phoenix**	**NHL**	**64**	**29**	**42**	**71**	**108**	**15**	**0**	**4**	**230**	**12.6**	**6**	**646**	**51.9**	**20:11**									
	St. Louis	**NHL**	**12**	**6**	**2**	**8**	**14**	**2**	**0**	**1**	**41**	**14.6**	**–3**	**87**	**54.0**	**19:39**	**15**	**2**	**7**	**9**	**20**	**2**	**0**	**1**	**19:17**
2001-02	**St. Louis**	**NHL**	**73**	**38**	**37**	**75**	**117**	**13**	**0**	**7**	**244**	**15.6**	**21**	**88**	**43.2**	**19:38**	**10**	**5**	**5**	**10**	**18**	**1**	**0**	**0**	**19:24**
	United States	Olympics	5	2	0	2	2																		
2002-03	**St. Louis**	**NHL**	**56**	**31**	**24**	**55**	**139**	**14**	**0**	**5**	**185**	**16.8**	**1**	**346**	**55.8**	**19:16**	**7**	**1**	**3**	**4**	**14**	**0**	**0**	**0**	**19:22**
2003-04	**St. Louis**	**NHL**	**75**	**33**	**38**	**71**	**83**	**18**	**0**	**8**	**233**	**14.2**	**8**	**410**	**49.5**	**19:39**	**5**	**0**	**2**	**2**	**10**	**0**	**0**	**0**	**19:18**
2004-05			DID NOT PLAY																						
	NHL Totals		**856**	**431**	**401**	**832**	**1861**	**161**	**12**	**61**	**2719**	**15.9**		**2847**	**50.4**	**19:52**	**81**	**27**	**26**	**53**	**162**	**8**	**0**	**1**	**20:06**

NHL Second All-Star Team (1995, 1998)

Played in NHL All-Star Game (1997, 1998, 1999, 2004)

Transferred to **Phoenix** after **Winnipeg** franchise relocated, July 1, 1996. Traded to **St. Louis** by **Phoenix** for Michal Handzus, Ladislav Nagy, the rights to Jeff Taffe and St. Louis' 1st round choice (Ben Eager) in 2002 Entry Draft, March 13, 2001.

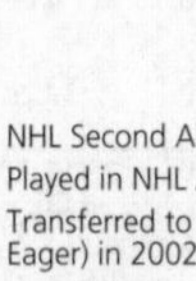

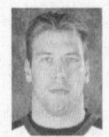

TOBLER, Ryan (TOH-bluhr, RIGH-uhn)

Left wing. Shoots left. 6'3", 227 lbs. Born, Calgary, Alta., May 13, 1976.

Season	Club	League	GP	G	A	Pts	PIM	PP	SH	GW	S	%	+/-	TF	F%	Min	GP	G	A	Pts	PIM	PP	SH	GW	Min
1993-94	Calgary Royals	AJHL	56	32	17	49	195																		
1994-95	Saskatoon Blades	WHL	61	11	19	30	81										10	1	2	3	8				
1995-96	Calgary Hitmen	WHL	16	10	3	13	8																		
	Swift Current	WHL	25	17	11	28	31										6	1	1	2	2				
1996-97	Swift Current	WHL	39	10	17	27	40																		
	Moose Jaw	WHL	24	6	15	21	16										12	1	6	7	16				
1997-98	Lake Charles	WPHL	66	22	34	56	204										4	2	3	5	18				
	Utah Grizzlies	IHL	3	1	0	1	2																		
1998-99	Adirondack	AHL	64	9	18	27	157										3	0	0	0	2				
99-2000	Milwaukee	IHL	78	19	28	47	293										2	0	0	0	0				
2000-01	Milwaukee	IHL	49	7	9	16	196																		
	Hartford	AHL	13	1	5	6	71										5	0	0	0	2				
2001-02	**Tampa Bay**	**NHL**	**4**	**0**	**0**	**0**	**5**	**0**	**0**	**0**	**1**	**0.0**	**–2**	**0**	**0.0**	**4:08**									
	Springfield	AHL	73	17	24	41	215																		
2002-03	Springfield	AHL	11	0	2	2	44																		
	Chicago Wolves	AHL	58	13	18	31	143										2	0	0	0	0				
2003-04	Colorado Eagles	CHL	51	30	49	79	93																		
	Wilkes-Barre	AHL	12	0	1	1	34										9	0	1	1	20				
2004-05	Colorado Eagles	CHL	51	26	37	63	119										16	6	*11	*17	37				
	NHL Totals		**4**	**0**	**0**	**0**	**5**	**0**	**0**	**0**	**1**	**0.0**		**0**	**0.0**	**4:08**									

Signed as a free agent by **Nashville**, May 1, 2000. Traded to **NY Rangers** by **Nashville** for Bert Robertsson, March 7, 2001. Signed as a free agent by **Tampa Bay**, August 21, 2001. Signed as a free agent by **Colorado** (CHL), September 1, 2003. Signed as a free agent by **Wilkes-Barre** (AHL), February 18, 2004.

						Regular Season												Playoffs							
Season	Club	League	GP	G	A	Pts	PIM	PP	SH	GW	S	%	+/-	TF	F%	Min	GP	G	A	Pts	PIM	PP	SH	GW	Min

TOMS, Jeff   (TAWMS, JEHF)

Center. Shoots left. 6'5", 200 lbs.   Born, Swift Current, Sask., June 4, 1974. New Jersey's 10th choice, 210th overall, in 1992 Entry Draft.

Season	Club	League	GP	G	A	Pts	PIM	PP	SH	GW	S	%	+/-	TF	F%	Min	GP	G	A	Pts	PIM	PP	SH	GW	Min
1990-91	Oakville	OMHA	58	34	47	81	72																		
1991-92	Sault Ste. Marie	OHL	36	9	5	14	0										16	0	1	1	2				
1992-93	Sault Ste. Marie	OHL	59	16	23	39	20										16	4	4	8	7				
1993-94	Sault Ste. Marie	OHL	64	52	45	97	19										14	11	4	15	2				
1994-95	Atlanta Knights	IHL	40	7	8	15	10										4	0	0	0	4				
1995-96	**Tampa Bay**	**NHL**	1	0	0	0	0	0	0	0	1	0.0	0												
	Atlanta Knights	IHL	68	16	18	34	18										1	0	0	0	0				
1996-97	**Tampa Bay**	**NHL**	34	2	8	10	10	0	0	1	53	3.8	2												
	Adirondack	AHL	37	11	16	27	8										4	1	2	3	0				
1997-98	**Tampa Bay**	**NHL**	13	1	2	3	7	0	0	0	14	7.1	-6												
	Washington	**NHL**	33	3	4	7	8	0	0	1	55	5.5	-11				1	0	0	0	0	0	0	0	0
1998-99	**Washington**	**NHL**	21	1	5	6	2	0	0	0	30	3.3	0	92	54.3	13:35									
	Portland Pirates	AHL	20	3	7	10	8																		
99-2000	**Washington**	**NHL**	20	1	2	3	4	0	0	1	18	5.6	-1	17	52.9	8:26									
	Portland Pirates	AHL	33	16	21	37	16										4	1	1	2	2				
2000-01	**NY Islanders**	**NHL**	39	2	4	6	10	0	0	0	37	5.4	-7	172	42.4	9:44									
	Springfield	AHL	5	6	5	11	0																		
	NY Rangers	**NHL**	15	1	1	2	0	0	0	0	12	8.3	-3	21	33.3	6:34									
	Hartford	AHL	12	4	9	13	2										5	6	0	6	2				
2001-02	**NY Rangers**	**NHL**	38	7	4	11	10	2	0	0	62	11.3	-4	243	45.3	10:31									
	Hartford	AHL	9	6	6	12	4																		
	Pittsburgh	**NHL**	14	2	1	3	4	0	0	0	22	9.1	-5	71	40.9	12:19									
2002-03	**Florida**	**NHL**	8	2	2	4	4	0	0	1	12	16.7	2	83	53.0	11:36									
	San Antonio	AHL	64	30	33	63	28										1	0	0	0	0				
2003-04	Cherepovets	Russia	14	0	2	2	8																		
	EHC Basel	Swiss	25	14	11	25	14																		
2004-05	HC Ambri-Piotta	Swiss	38	21	27	48	26										5	1	1	2	0				
	NHL Totals		**236**	**22**	**33**	**55**	**59**	**4**	**0**	**4**	**316**	**7.0**		**699**	**46.1**	**10:18**	**1**	**0**	**0**	**0**	**0**	**0**	**0**	**0**	**0**

Traded to **Tampa Bay** by **New Jersey** for Vancouver's 4th round choice (previously acquired, later traded to New Jersey – later traded to Calgary – Calgary selected Ryan Duthie) in 1994 Entry Draft, May 31, 1994. Claimed by on waivers by **Washington** from **Tampa Bay**, November 19, 1997. Signed as a free agent by **NY Islanders**, July 27, 2000. Claimed on waivers by **NY Rangers** from **NY Islanders**, January 13, 2001. Claimed on waivers by **Pittsburgh** from **NY Rangers**, March 16, 2002. Signed as a free agent by **Florida**, July 11, 2002. Assigned to **Cherepovets** (Russia) by **Florida**, July 1, 2003. Signed as a free agent by **Basel** (Swiss), November 11, 2003. Signed as a free agent by **Ambri-Piotta** (Swiss), September 15, 2004.

TOOTOO, Jordin   (TOO-TOO, JOHR-dihn)   **NSH.**

Right wing. Shoots right. 5'9", 194 lbs.   Born, Churchill, Man., February 2, 1983. Nashville's 6th choice, 98th overall, in 2001 Entry Draft.

Season	Club	League	GP	G	A	Pts	PIM	PP	SH	GW	S	%	+/-	TF	F%	Min	GP	G	A	Pts	PIM	PP	SH	GW	Min
1997-98	Spruce Grove	AMBHL					STATISTICS NOT AVAILABLE																		
1998-99	OCN Blizzard	MJHL	47	16	21	37	251																		
99-2000	Brandon	WHL	45	6	10	16	214																		
2000-01	Brandon	WHL	60	20	28	48	172										6	2	4	6	18				
2001-02	Brandon	WHL	64	32	39	71	272										16	4	3	7	*58				
2002-03	Brandon	WHL	51	35	39	74	216										17	6	3	9	49				
2003-04	**Nashville**	**NHL**	70	4	4	8	137	2	0	0	92	4.3	-6	18	55.6	8:29	5	0	0	0	4	0	0	0	5:09
2004-05	Milwaukee	AHL	59	10	12	22	266										6	0	0	0	41				
	NHL Totals		**70**	**4**	**4**	**8**	**137**	**2**	**0**	**0**	**92**	**4.3**		**18**	**55.6**	**8:29**	**5**	**0**	**0**	**0**	**4**	**0**	**0**	**0**	**5:09**

WHL East First All-Star Team (2003)

TORRES, Raffi   (TAW-rehs, RA-fee)   **EDM.**

Left wing. Shoots left. 6', 216 lbs.   Born, Toronto, Ont., October 8, 1981. NY Islanders' 2nd choice, 5th overall, in 2000 Entry Draft.

Season	Club	League	GP	G	A	Pts	PIM	PP	SH	GW	S	%	+/-	TF	F%	Min	GP	G	A	Pts	PIM	PP	SH	GW	Min
1997-98	Thornhill Rattlers	MTJHL	46	17	16	33	90																		
1998-99	Brampton	OHL	62	35	27	62	32																		
99-2000	Brampton	OHL	68	43	48	91	40										6	5	2	7	23				
2000-01	Brampton	OHL	55	33	37	70	76										8	7	4	11	19				
2001-02	**NY Islanders**	**NHL**	14	0	1	1	6	0	0	0	9	0.0	2	0	0.0	7:35									
	Bridgeport	AHL	59	20	10	30	45										20	8	9	17	26				
2002-03	**NY Islanders**	**NHL**	17	0	5	5	10	0	0	0	12	0.0	0	4	25.0	7:40									
	Bridgeport	AHL	49	17	15	32	54																		
	Hamilton	AHL	11	1	7	8	14										23	6	1	7	29				
2003-04	**Edmonton**	**NHL**	80	20	14	34	65	5	0	3	136	14.7	12	21	28.6	12:38									
2004-05	Edmonton	AHL	67	21	25	46	165																		
	NHL Totals		**111**	**20**	**20**	**40**	**81**	**5**	**0**	**3**	**157**	**12.7**		**25**	**28.0**	**11:14**									

OHL All-Rookie Team (1999) • OHL Second All-Star Team (2000, 2001)

Traded to **Edmonton** by **NY Islanders** with Brad Isbister for Janne Niinimaa and Washington's 2nd round choice (previously acquired, NY Islanders selected Evgeni Tunik) in 2003 Entry Draft, March 11, 2003.

TRAVERSE, Patrick   (tra-VAIRZ, PAT-rihk)   **DAL.**

Defense. Shoots left. 6'4", 207 lbs.   Born, Montreal, Que., March 14, 1974. Ottawa's 3rd choice, 50th overall, in 1992 Entry Draft.

Season	Club	League	GP	G	A	Pts	PIM	PP	SH	GW	S	%	+/-	TF	F%	Min	GP	G	A	Pts	PIM	PP	SH	GW	Min
1990-91	Mtl-Bourassa	QAAA	42	4	19	23	10										5	0	3	3	2				
1991-92	Shawinigan	QMJHL	59	3	11	14	12										10	0	0	0	4				
1992-93	Shawinigan	QMJHL	53	5	24	29	24																		
	St-Jean Lynx	QMJHL	15	1	6	7	0										4	0	1	1	2				
	New Haven	AHL	2	0	0	0	2																		
1993-94	St-Jean Lynx	QMJHL	66	15	37	52	30										5	0	4	4	4				
	P.E.I. Senators	AHL	3	0	1	1	2																		
1994-95	P.E.I. Senators	AHL	70	5	13	18	19										7	0	2	2	0				
1995-96	**Ottawa**	**NHL**	5	0	0	0	2	0	0	0	2	0.0	-1												
	P.E.I. Senators	AHL	55	4	21	25	32										5	1	2	3	2				
1996-97	Worcester IceCats	AHL	24	0	4	4	23																		
	Grand Rapids	IHL	10	2	1	3	10										2	0	1	1	2				
1997-98	Hershey Bears	AHL	71	14	15	29	67										7	1	3	4	4				
1998-99	**Ottawa**	**NHL**	46	1	9	10	22	0	0	0	35	2.9	12	0	0.0	14:56									
99-2000	**Ottawa**	**NHL**	66	6	17	23	21	1	0	0	73	8.2	17	0	0.0	18:43	6	0	0	0	2	0	0	0	17:50
2000-01	**Anaheim**	**NHL**	15	1	0	1	6	0	0	0	7	14.3	-6	0	0.0	17:19									
	Boston	**NHL**	37	2	6	8	14	1	0	1	39	5.1	4	0	0.0	16:38									
	Montreal	**NHL**	19	2	3	5	10	0	0	0	16	12.5	-8	0	0.0	21:36									
2001-02	Quebec Citadelles	AHL	4	0	2	2	4																		
	Montreal	**NHL**	25	2	3	5	14	2	0	0	24	8.3	-7	0	0.0	18:14									
2002-03	**Montreal**	**NHL**	65	0	13	13	24	0	0	0	63	0.0	-9	0	0.0	20:12									
2003-04	Hamilton	AHL	80	5	21	26	31										10	1	2	3	0				
2004-05	Houston Aeros	AHL	72	6	9	15	28										5	0	0	0	2				
	NHL Totals		**278**	**14**	**51**	**65**	**113**	**4**	**0**	**1**	**259**	**5.4**		**0**	**0.0**	**18:14**	**6**	**0**	**0**	**0**	**2**	**0**	**0**	**0**	**17:49**

Traded to **Anaheim** by **Ottawa** for Joel Kwiatkowski, June 12, 2000. Traded to **Boston** by **Anaheim** with Andrei Nazarov for Samuel Pahlsson, November 18, 2000. Traded to **Montreal** by **Boston** for Eric Weinrich, February 21, 2001. • Missed majority of 2001-02 season recovering from knee (November 3, 2001 vs. Calgary) and head (January 10, 2002 vs. NY Islanders) injuries. Signed as a free agent by **Dallas**, September 9, 2004.

TREMBLAY, Yannick   (TRAHM-blay, YA-nihk)

Defense. Shoots right. 6'2", 200 lbs.   Born, Pointe-aux-Trembles, Que., November 15, 1975. Toronto's 4th choice, 145th overall, in 1995 Entry Draft.

Season	Club	League	GP	G	A	Pts	PIM	PP	SH	GW	S	%	+/-	TF	F%	Min	GP	G	A	Pts	PIM	PP	SH	GW	Min
1991-92	Mtl-Bourassa	QAAA	35	2	5	7	55										8	0	4	4	2				
1992-93	Mtl-Bourassa	CEGEP	21	2	5	7	10										3	0	0	0	2				
1993-94	St. Thomas U.	AUAA	25	2	3	5	10																		
1994-95	Beauport	QMJHL	70	10	32	42	22										17	6	8	14	6				
1995-96	Beauport	QMJHL	61	12	33	45	42										20	3	16	19	18				
	St. John's	AHL	3	0	1	1	0																		

			Regular Season														Playoffs								
Season	Club	League	GP	G	A	Pts	PIM	PP	SH	GW	S	%	+/-	TF	F%	Min	GP	G	A	Pts	PIM	PP	SH	GW	Min
1996-97	Toronto	NHL	5	0	0	0	0	0	0	0	2	0.0	–4	....	....	....	....	....	....	....	....	....	....	....	....
	St. John's	AHL	67	7	25	32	34	....	....	....	....	....	....	....	....	....	11	2	9	11	0	....	....	....	....
1997-98	Toronto	NHL	38	2	4	6	6	1	0	0	45	4.4	–6	....	....	....	....	....	....	....	....	....	....	....	....
	St. John's	AHL	17	3	7	10	4	....	....	....	....	....	....	....	....	....	4	0	1	1	5	....	....	....	....
1998-99	Toronto	NHL	35	2	7	9	16	0	0	0	37	5.4	0	0	0.0	17:39	....	....	....	....	....	....	....	....	....
99-2000	Atlanta	NHL	75	10	21	31	22	4	1	2	139	7.2	–42	3	0.0	19:27	....	....	....	....	....	....	....	....	....
2000-01	Atlanta	NHL	46	4	8	12	30	1	0	1	102	3.9	–6	1	100.0	20:27	....	....	....	....	....	....	....	....	....
2001-02	Atlanta	NHL	66	9	15	24	47	1	0	1	115	7.8	–15	0	0.0	21:50	....	....	....	....	....	....	....	....	....
2002-03	Atlanta	NHL	75	8	22	30	32	5	0	1	151	5.3	–27	1	0.0	21:45	....	....	....	....	....	....	....	....	....
2003-04	Atlanta	NHL	38	2	8	10	13	1	0	1	47	4.3	–13	2	50.0	21:36	....	....	....	....	....	....	....	....	....
2004-05	Sherbrooke	QNAHL	36	26	25	51	40	....	....	....	....	....	....	....	....	....	....	....	....	....	....	....	....	....	....
	Adler Mannheim	Germany	14	1	4	5	16	....	....	....	....	....	....	....	....	....	14	2	6	8	6	....	....	....	....
	NHL Totals		378	37	85	122	166	13	1	6	638	5.8		7	28.6	20:38	....	....	....	....	....	....	....	....	....

Claimed by **Atlanta** from **Toronto** in Expansion Draft, June 25, 1999. • Missed majority of 2003-04 season recovering from foot (November 15, 2003 vs. Philadelphia) and hip (January 30, 2004 vs. Toronto) injuries. Signed as a free agent by **Sherbrooke** (QNAHL), November 16, 2004. Signed as a free agent by **Mannheim** (Germany), January 13, 2005.

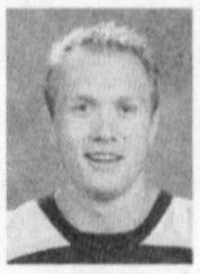

TREPANIER, Pascal

(TREHP-uhn-yay, pas-KAL)

Defense. Shoots right. 6', 210 lbs. Born, Gaspe, Que., September 4, 1973.

1989-90	Jonquiere Elites	QAAA	40	2	8	10	46	....	....	....	....	....	....	....	....	....	....	....	....	....	....	....	....	....	....
1990-91	Hull Olympiques	QMJHL	46	3	3	6	56	....	....	....	....	....	....	....	....	....	4	0	2	2	7	....	....	....	....
1991-92	Trois-Rivieres	QMJHL	53	4	18	22	125	....	....	....	....	....	....	....	....	....	15	3	5	8	21	....	....	....	....
1992-93	Sherbrooke	QMJHL	59	15	33	48	130	....	....	....	....	....	....	....	....	....	15	5	7	12	36	....	....	....	....
1993-94	Sherbrooke	QMJHL	48	16	41	57	67	....	....	....	....	....	....	....	....	....	12	1	8	9	14	....	....	....	....
1994-95	Dayton Bombers	ECHL	36	16	28	44	113	....	....	....	....	....	....	....	....	....	9	2	4	6	20	....	....	....	....
	Kalamazoo Wings	IHL	14	1	2	3	47	....	....	....	....	....	....	....	....	....	....	....	....	....	....	....	....	....	....
	Cornwall Aces	AHL	4	0	0	0	9	....	....	....	....	....	....	....	....	....	14	2	7	9	32	....	....	....	....
1995-96	Cornwall Aces	AHL	70	13	20	33	142	....	....	....	....	....	....	....	....	....	8	1	2	3	24	....	....	....	....
1996-97	Hershey Bears	AHL	73	14	39	53	151	....	....	....	....	....	....	....	....	....	23	6	13	19	59	....	....	....	....
1997-98	Colorado	NHL	15	0	1	1	18	0	0	0	9	0.0	–2	....	....	....	....	....	....	....	....	....	....	....	....
	Hershey Bears	AHL	43	13	18	31	105	....	....	....	....	....	....	....	....	....	7	4	2	6	8	....	....	....	....
1998-99	Anaheim	NHL	45	2	4	6	48	0	0	1	49	4.1	0	1	0.0	12:42	....	....	....	....	....	....	....	....	....
99-2000	Anaheim	NHL	37	0	4	4	54	0	0	0	33	0.0	2	1	0.0	11:18	....	....	....	....	....	....	....	....	....
2000-01	Anaheim	NHL	57	6	4	10	73	3	0	0	86	7.0	–12	1	100.0	16:47	....	....	....	....	....	....	....	....	....
2001-02	Colorado	NHL	74	4	9	13	59	2	0	0	87	4.6	4	0	0.0	14:37	2	0	0	0	0	0	0	0	5:43
2002-03	Nashville	NHL	1	0	0	0	0	0	0	0	1	0.0	0	0	0.0	9:55	....	....	....	....	....	....	....	....	....
	Milwaukee	AHL	52	9	15	24	33	....	....	....	....	....	....	....	....	....	....	....	....	....	....	....	....	....	....
	San Antonio	AHL	12	4	6	10	10	....	....	....	....	....	....	....	....	....	2	0	0	0	2	....	....	....	....
2003-04	Hershey Bears	AHL	75	11	33	44	53	....	....	....	....	....	....	....	....	....	....	....	....	....	....	....	....	....	....
2004-05	Nurnberg	Germany	52	15	39	54	66	....	....	....	....	....	....	....	....	....	6	3	1	4	6	....	....	....	....
	NHL Totals		229	12	22	34	252	5	0	1	265	4.5		3	33.3	14:12	2	0	0	0	0	0	0	0	5:43

AHL Second All-Star Team (1997)

Signed as a free agent by **Colorado**, August 30, 1995. Claimed by **Anaheim** from **Colorado** in Waiver Draft, October 5, 1998. Signed as a free agent by **Colorado**, September, 2001. Signed as a free agent by **Nashville**, July 16, 2002. Traded to **Florida** by **Nashville** for Wade Flaherty, March 9, 2003. Signed as a free agent by **Tampa Bay**, July 23, 2003. Signed as a free agent by **Nurnberg** (Germany), June 8, 2004.

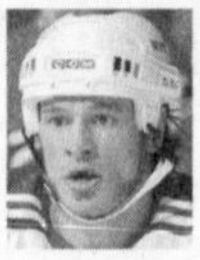

TRIPP, John

(TRIHP, JAWN)

Right wing. Shoots right. 6'2", 215 lbs. Born, Kingston, Ont., May 4, 1977. Calgary's 3rd choice, 42nd overall, in 1997 Entry Draft.

1993-94	St. Mary's Lincolns	OHA-B	42	15	29	44	116	....	....	....	....	....	....	....	....	....	....	....	....	....	....	....	....	....	....
1994-95	Oshawa Generals	OHL	58	6	11	17	53	....	....	....	....	....	....	....	....	....	7	0	1	1	4	....	....	....	....
1995-96	Oshawa Generals	OHL	56	13	14	27	95	....	....	....	....	....	....	....	....	....	5	1	1	2	13	....	....	....	....
1996-97	Oshawa Generals	OHL	59	28	20	48	126	....	....	....	....	....	....	....	....	....	18	*16	10	26	42	....	....	....	....
1997-98	Roanoke Express	ECHL	9	0	2	2	22	....	....	....	....	....	....	....	....	....	....	....	....	....	....	....	....	....	....
	Saint John Flames	AHL	61	1	11	12	66	....	....	....	....	....	....	....	....	....	2	0	1	1	0	....	....	....	....
1998-99	Saint John Flames	AHL	2	0	0	0	10	....	....	....	....	....	....	....	....	....	....	....	....	....	....	....	....	....	....
	Johnstown Chiefs	ECHL	7	2	0	2	12	....	....	....	....	....	....	....	....	....	....	....	....	....	....	....	....	....	....
99-2000	Johnstown Chiefs	ECHL	38	13	11	24	64	....	....	....	....	....	....	....	....	....	....	....	....	....	....	....	....	....	....
	Saint John Flames	AHL	29	8	7	15	38	....	....	....	....	....	....	....	....	....	3	0	0	0	2	....	....	....	....
2000-01	Pensacola	ECHL	36	19	14	33	110	....	....	....	....	....	....	....	....	....	....	....	....	....	....	....	....	....	....
	Houston Aeros	IHL	15	0	6	6	14	....	....	....	....	....	....	....	....	....	....	....	....	....	....	....	....	....	....
	Hershey Bears	AHL	5	0	1	1	0	....	....	....	....	....	....	....	....	....	....	....	....	....	....	....	....	....	....
	Milwaukee	IHL	12	0	1	1	31	....	....	....	....	....	....	....	....	....	....	....	....	....	....	....	....	....	....
2001-02	Pensacola	ECHL	49	25	27	52	114	....	....	....	....	....	....	....	....	....	....	....	....	....	....	....	....	....	....
	Hartford	AHL	23	4	9	13	22	....	....	....	....	....	....	....	....	....	10	4	2	6	17	....	....	....	....
2002-03	NY Rangers	NHL	9	1	2	3	2	0	0	0	16	6.3	1	0	0.0	8:43	....	....	....	....	....	....	....	....	....
	Hartford	AHL	57	29	21	50	68	....	....	....	....	....	....	....	....	....	2	0	0	0	2	....	....	....	....
2003-04	Los Angeles	NHL	34	1	5	6	33	0	0	0	45	2.2	–4	2	100.0	8:05	....	....	....	....	....	....	....	....	....
	Manchester	AHL	24	8	7	15	33	....	....	....	....	....	....	....	....	....	....	....	....	....	....	....	....	....	....
2004-05	Adler Mannheim	Germany	44	9	16	25	136	....	....	....	....	....	....	....	....	....	14	2	3	5	54	....	....	....	....
	NHL Totals		43	2	7	9	35	0	0	0	61	3.3		2	100.0	8:13	....	....	....	....	....	....	....	....	....

• Re-entered NHL Entry Draft. Originally Colorado's 3rd choice, 77th overall, in 1995 Entry Draft.

Signed to PTO (tryout) contract by **Hartford** (AHL), January 29, 2002. Signed as a free agent by **Hartford** (AHL), September 3, 2002. Signed as a free agent by **Los Angeles**, August 6, 2003. Signed as a free agent by **Mannheim** (Germany), April 20, 2004.

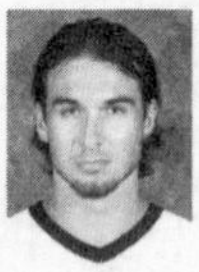

TRNKA, Pavel

(truhn-KAH, PAH-vehl)

Defense. Shoots left. 6'2", 206 lbs. Born, Plzen, Czech., July 27, 1976. Anaheim's 5th choice, 106th overall, in 1994 Entry Draft.

1993-94	HC Skoda Plzen	CzRep	12	0	1	1	....	....	....	....	....	....	....	....	....	....	....	....	....	....	....	....	....	....	....
1994-95	HC Kladno	CzRep	28	0	5	5	24	....	....	....	....	....	....	....	....	....	....	....	....	....	....	....	....	....	....
	Plzen	CzRep	6	0	0	0	0	....	....	....	....	....	....	....	....	....	....	....	....	....	....	....	....	....	....
1995-96	Baltimore Bandits	AHL	69	2	6	8	44	....	....	....	....	....	....	....	....	....	6	0	0	0	2	....	....	....	....
1996-97	Baltimore Bandits	AHL	69	6	14	20	86	....	....	....	....	....	....	....	....	....	3	0	0	0	2	....	....	....	....
1997-98	Anaheim	NHL	48	3	4	7	40	1	0	0	46	6.5	–4	....	....	....	....	....	....	....	....	....	....	....	....
	Cincinnati	AHL	23	3	5	8	28	....	....	....	....	....	....	....	....	....	....	....	....	....	....	....	....	....	....
1998-99	Anaheim	NHL	63	0	4	4	60	0	0	0	50	0.0	–6	0	0.0	16:06	4	0	1	1	2	0	0	0	21:26
99-2000	Anaheim	NHL	57	2	15	17	34	0	0	0	54	3.7	12	0	0.0	19:21	....	....	....	....	....	....	....	....	....
2000-01	Anaheim	NHL	59	1	7	8	42	0	0	0	59	1.7	–12	0	0.0	20:07	....	....	....	....	....	....	....	....	....
2001-02	Anaheim	NHL	71	2	11	13	66	1	0	0	78	2.6	–5	0	0.0	17:03	....	....	....	....	....	....	....	....	....
2002-03	Anaheim	NHL	24	3	6	9	6	1	0	0	33	9.1	2	0	0.0	16:00	....	....	....	....	....	....	....	....	....
	Florida	NHL	22	0	3	3	24	0	0	0	25	0.0	–1	0	0.0	17:24	....	....	....	....	....	....	....	....	....
2003-04	Florida	NHL	67	3	13	16	51	1	0	0	66	4.5	2	0	0.0	17:07	....	....	....	....	....	....	....	....	....
2004-05	Plzen	CzRep	47	7	10	17	103	....	....	....	....	....	....	....	....	....	....	....	....	....	....	....	....	....	....
	NHL Totals		411	14	63	77	323	4	0	0	411	3.4		0	0.0	17:43	4	0	1	1	2	0	0	0	21:26

Traded to **Florida** by **Anaheim** with Matt Cullen and Anaheim's 4th round choice (James Pemberton) in 2003 Entry Draft for Sandis Ozolinsh and Lance Ward, January 30, 2003. Signed as a free agent by **Plzen** (CzRep), August 2, 2004.

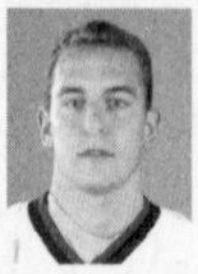

TSELIOS, Nikos

(TSEHL-ee-ohs, NEE-kohs)

Defense. Shoots left. 6'5", 226 lbs. Born, Oak Park, IL, January 20, 1979. Carolina's 1st choice, 22nd overall, in 1997 Entry Draft.

1995-96	Chicago	MEHL	27	5	8	13	40	....	....	....	....	....	....	....	....	....	....	....	....	....	....	....	....	....	....
1996-97	Belleville Bulls	OHL	64	9	37	46	61	....	....	....	....	....	....	....	....	....	6	1	1	2	2	....	....	....	....
1997-98	Belleville Bulls	OHL	20	2	10	12	16	....	....	....	....	....	....	....	....	....	....	....	....	....	....	....	....	....	....
	Plymouth Whalers	OHL	41	8	20	28	27	....	....	....	....	....	....	....	....	....	15	1	8	9	27	....	....	....	....
1998-99	Plymouth Whalers	OHL	60	21	39	60	60	....	....	....	....	....	....	....	....	....	11	4	10	14	8	....	....	....	....
99-2000	Cincinnati	IHL	80	3	19	22	75	....	....	....	....	....	....	....	....	....	10	0	2	2	4	....	....	....	....
2000-01	Cincinnati	IHL	79	7	18	25	98	....	....	....	....	....	....	....	....	....	5	0	3	3	0	....	....	....	....
2001-02	Carolina	NHL	2	0	0	0	6	0	0	0	3	0.0	–2	0	0.0	13:13	....	....	....	....	....	....	....	....	....
	Lowell	AHL	70	3	16	19	64	....	....	....	....	....	....	....	....	....	....	....	....	....	....	....	....	....	....

			Regular Season														Playoffs								
Season	Club	League	GP	G	A	Pts	PIM	PP	SH	GW	S	%	+/-	TF	F%	Min	GP	G	A	Pts	PIM	PP	SH	GW	Min
2002-03	Lowell	AHL	61	4	8	12	65	....	....	....	....	....	....	....	....	....	....	....	....	....	....	....	....	....	....
	Springfield	AHL	13	0	2	2	12	....	....	....	....	....	....	....	....	....	6	0	0	0	4	....	....	....	....
2003-04	Springfield	AHL	75	5	8	13	105	....	....	....	....	....	....	....	....	....	....	....	....	....	....	....	....	....	....
2004-05	Utah Grizzlies	AHL	5	1	1	2	4	....	....	....	....	....	....	....	....	....	....	....	....	....	....	....	....	....	....
	Springfield	AHL	35	3	6	9	37	....	....	....	....	....	....	....	....	....	....	....	....	....	....	....	....	....	....
	NHL Totals		**2**	**0**	**0**	**0**	**6**	**0**	**0**	**0**	**3**	**0.0**		**0**	**0.0**	**13:13**	....	....	....	....	....	....	....	....	....

OHL All-Rookie Team (1997)

Signed as a free agent by **Phoenix**, July 21, 2003. Loaned to **Springfield** (AHL) by **Utah** (AHL), November 22, 2004.

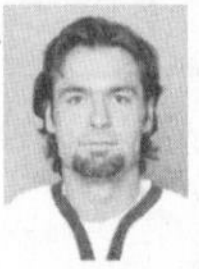

TUCKER, Darcy

(TUH-kuhr, DAHR-see) **TOR.**

Right wing. Shoots left. 5'10", 178 lbs. Born, Castor, Alta., March 15, 1975. Montreal's 8th choice, 151st overall, in 1993 Entry Draft.

Season	Club	League	GP	G	A	Pts	PIM	PP	SH	GW	S	%	+/-	TF	F%	Min	GP	G	A	Pts	PIM	PP	SH	GW	Min
1990-91	Red Deer	AMHL	47	70	90	160	48	....	....	....	....	....	....	....	....	....	....	....	....	....	....	....	....	....	....
1991-92	Kamloops Blazers	WHL	26	3	10	13	32	....	....	....	....	....	....	....	....	....	9	0	1	1	16	....	....	....	....
1992-93	Kamloops Blazers	WHL	67	31	58	89	155	....	....	....	....	....	....	....	....	....	13	7	6	13	34	....	....	....	....
1993-94	Kamloops Blazers	WHL	66	52	88	140	143	....	....	....	....	....	....	....	....	....	19	9	*18	*27	43	....	....	....	....
1994-95	Kamloops Blazers	WHL	64	64	73	137	94	....	....	....	....	....	....	....	....	....	21	*16	15	*31	19	....	....	....	....
1995-96	**Montreal**	**NHL**	**3**	**0**	**0**	**0**	**0**	**0**	**0**	**0**	**1**	**0.0**	**-1**	....	....	....	....	....	....	....	....	....	....	....	....
	Fredericton	AHL	74	29	64	93	174	....	....	....	....	....	....	....	....	....	7	7	3	10	14	....	....	....	....
1996-97	**Montreal**	**NHL**	**73**	**7**	**13**	**20**	**110**	**1**	**0**	**3**	**62**	**11.3**	**-5**	....	....	....	**4**	**0**	**0**	**0**	**0**	**0**	**0**	**0**	....
1997-98	**Montreal**	**NHL**	**39**	**1**	**5**	**6**	**57**	**0**	**0**	**0**	**19**	**5.3**	**-6**	....	....	....	....	....	....	....	....	....	....	....	....
	Tampa Bay	**NHL**	**35**	**6**	**8**	**14**	**89**	**1**	**1**	**0**	**44**	**13.6**	**-8**	....	....	....	....	....	....	....	....	....	....	....	....
1998-99	**Tampa Bay**	**NHL**	**82**	**21**	**22**	**43**	**176**	**8**	**2**	**3**	**178**	**11.8**	**-34**	**1470**	**45.6**	**19:24**	....	....	....	....	....	....	....	....	....
99-2000	**Tampa Bay**	**NHL**	**50**	**14**	**20**	**34**	**108**	**1**	**0**	**2**	**98**	**14.3**	**-15**	**152**	**48.7**	**19:58**	....	....	....	....	....	....	....	....	....
	Toronto	**NHL**	**27**	**7**	**10**	**17**	**55**	**0**	**2**	**3**	**40**	**17.5**	**3**	**11**	**54.6**	**16:41**	**12**	**4**	**2**	**6**	**15**	**1**	**0**	**2**	**17:23**
2000-01	**Toronto**	**NHL**	**82**	**16**	**21**	**37**	**141**	**2**	**0**	**4**	**122**	**13.1**	**6**	**413**	**47.0**	**16:09**	**11**	**0**	**2**	**2**	**6**	**0**	**0**	**0**	**13:59**
2001-02	**Toronto**	**NHL**	**77**	**24**	**35**	**59**	**92**	**7**	**0**	**5**	**124**	**19.4**	**24**	**138**	**43.5**	**16:59**	**17**	**4**	**4**	**8**	**38**	**1**	**0**	**1**	**16:50**
2002-03	**Toronto**	**NHL**	**77**	**10**	**26**	**36**	**119**	**4**	**1**	**2**	**108**	**9.3**	**-7**	**68**	**45.6**	**15:21**	**6**	**0**	**3**	**3**	**6**	**0**	**0**	**0**	**21:07**
2003-04	**Toronto**	**NHL**	**64**	**21**	**11**	**32**	**68**	**8**	**1**	**2**	**146**	**14.4**	**4**	**136**	**50.7**	**17:50**	**12**	**2**	**0**	**2**	**14**	**1**	**0**	**0**	**13:54**
2004-05			DID NOT PLAY																						
	NHL Totals		**609**	**127**	**171**	**298**	**1015**	**32**	**7**	**24**	**942**	**13.5**		**2388**	**46.2**	**17:25**	**62**	**10**	**11**	**21**	**79**	**3**	**0**	**3**	**16:15**

WHL West First All-Star Team (1994, 1995) • Canadian Major Junior First All-Star Team (1994) • Memorial Cup Tournament All-Star Team (1994, 1995) • Stafford Smythe Memorial Trophy (Memorial Cup Tournament MVP) (1994) • Dudley "Red" Garrett Memorial Award (Rookie of the Year – AHL) (1996)

Traded to **Tampa Bay** by **Montreal** with Stephane Richer and David Wilkie for Patrick Poulin, Mick Vukota and Igor Ulanov, January 15, 1998. Traded to **Toronto** by **Tampa Bay** with Tampa Bay's 4th round choice (Miguel Delisle) in 2000 Entry Draft for Mike Johnson, Marek Posmyk and Toronto's 5th (Pavel Sedov) and 6th (Aaron Gionet) round choices in 2000 Entry Draft, February 9, 2000.

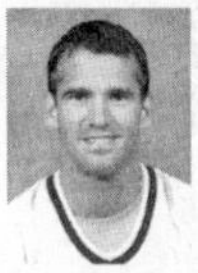

TURGEON, Pierre

(TUHR-zhaw, PEE-air) **COL.**

Center. Shoots left. 6'1", 199 lbs. Born, Rouyn, Que., August 28, 1969. Buffalo's 1st choice, 1st overall, in 1987 Entry Draft.

Season	Club	League	GP	G	A	Pts	PIM	PP	SH	GW	S	%	+/-	TF	F%	Min	GP	G	A	Pts	PIM	PP	SH	GW	Min
1984-85	Mtl-Bourassa	QAAA	41	49	52	101	26	....	....	....	....	....	....	....	....	....	5	3	8	11	2	....	....	....	....
1985-86	Granby Bisons	QMJHL	69	47	67	114	31	....	....	....	....	....	....	....	....	....	....	....	....	....	....	....	....	....	....
1986-87	Granby Bisons	QMJHL	58	69	85	154	8	....	....	....	....	....	....	....	....	....	7	9	6	15	15	....	....	....	....
1987-88	**Buffalo**	**NHL**	**76**	**14**	**28**	**42**	**34**	**8**	**0**	**3**	**101**	**13.9**	**-8**	....	....	....	**6**	**4**	**3**	**7**	**4**	**3**	**0**	**0**	....
1988-89	**Buffalo**	**NHL**	**80**	**34**	**54**	**88**	**26**	**19**	**0**	**5**	**182**	**18.7**	**-2**	....	....	....	**5**	**3**	**5**	**8**	**2**	**1**	**0**	**0**	....
1989-90	**Buffalo**	**NHL**	**80**	**40**	**66**	**106**	**29**	**17**	**1**	**10**	**193**	**20.7**	**10**	....	....	....	**6**	**2**	**4**	**6**	**2**	**0**	**0**	**1**	....
1990-91	**Buffalo**	**NHL**	**78**	**32**	**47**	**79**	**26**	**13**	**2**	**3**	**174**	**18.4**	**14**	....	....	....	**6**	**3**	**1**	**4**	**6**	**1**	**0**	**0**	....
1991-92	**Buffalo**	**NHL**	**8**	**2**	**6**	**8**	**4**	**0**	**0**	**0**	**14**	**14.3**	**-1**	....	....	....	....	....	....	....	....	....	....	....	....
	NY Islanders	**NHL**	**69**	**38**	**49**	**87**	**16**	**13**	**0**	**6**	**193**	**19.7**	**8**	....	....	....	....	....	....	....	....	....	....	....	....
1992-93	**NY Islanders**	**NHL**	**83**	**58**	**74**	**132**	**26**	**24**	**0**	**10**	**301**	**19.3**	**-1**	....	....	....	**11**	**6**	**7**	**13**	**0**	**0**	**0**	**0**	....
1993-94	**NY Islanders**	**NHL**	**69**	**38**	**56**	**94**	**18**	**10**	**4**	**6**	**254**	**15.0**	**14**	....	....	....	**4**	**0**	**1**	**1**	**0**	**0**	**0**	**0**	....
1994-95	**NY Islanders**	**NHL**	**34**	**13**	**14**	**27**	**10**	**3**	**2**	**2**	**93**	**14.0**	**-12**	....	....	....	....	....	....	....	....	....	....	....	....
	Montreal	**NHL**	**15**	**11**	**9**	**20**	**4**	**2**	**0**	**2**	**67**	**16.4**	**12**	....	....	....	....	....	....	....	....	....	....	....	....
1995-96	**Montreal**	**NHL**	**80**	**38**	**58**	**96**	**44**	**17**	**1**	**6**	**297**	**12.8**	**19**	....	....	....	**6**	**2**	**4**	**6**	**2**	**0**	**0**	**0**	....
1996-97	**Montreal**	**NHL**	**9**	**1**	**10**	**11**	**2**	**0**	**0**	**0**	**22**	**4.5**	**4**	....	....	....	....	....	....	....	....	....	....	....	....
	St. Louis	**NHL**	**69**	**25**	**49**	**74**	**12**	**5**	**0**	**7**	**194**	**12.9**	**4**	....	....	....	**5**	**1**	**1**	**2**	**2**	**1**	**0**	**0**	....
1997-98	**St. Louis**	**NHL**	**60**	**22**	**46**	**68**	**24**	**6**	**0**	**4**	**140**	**15.7**	**13**	....	....	....	**10**	**4**	**4**	**8**	**2**	**2**	**0**	**0**	....
1998-99	**St. Louis**	**NHL**	**67**	**31**	**34**	**65**	**36**	**10**	**0**	**5**	**193**	**16.1**	**4**	**1285**	**50.0**	**19:07**	**13**	**4**	**9**	**13**	**6**	**0**	**0**	**2**	**19:35**
99-2000	**St. Louis**	**NHL**	**52**	**26**	**40**	**66**	**8**	**8**	**0**	**3**	**139**	**18.7**	**30**	**1016**	**53.2**	**19:13**	**7**	**0**	**7**	**7**	**0**	**0**	**0**	**0**	**19:45**
2000-01	**St. Louis**	**NHL**	**79**	**30**	**52**	**82**	**37**	**11**	**0**	**6**	**171**	**17.5**	**14**	**1569**	**49.7**	**18:50**	**15**	**5**	**10**	**15**	**2**	**1**	**0**	**0**	**19:07**
2001-02	**Dallas**	**NHL**	**66**	**15**	**32**	**47**	**16**	**7**	**0**	**1**	**121**	**12.4**	**-4**	**822**	**48.4**	**16:31**	....	....	....	....	....	....	....	....	....
2002-03	**Dallas**	**NHL**	**65**	**12**	**30**	**42**	**18**	**3**	**0**	**5**	**76**	**15.8**	**4**	**290**	**53.8**	**14:38**	**5**	**0**	**1**	**1**	**0**	**0**	**0**	**0**	**12:21**
2003-04	**Dallas**	**NHL**	**76**	**15**	**25**	**40**	**20**	**6**	**0**	**1**	**104**	**14.4**	**17**	**578**	**49.3**	**14:13**	**5**	**1**	**3**	**4**	**2**	**0**	**0**	**0**	**15:53**
2004-05			DID NOT PLAY																						
	NHL Totals		**1215**	**495**	**779**	**1274**	**410**	**182**	**10**	**85**	**3029**	**16.3**		**5560**	**50.4**	**17:01**	**104**	**35**	**60**	**95**	**30**	**9**	**0**	**3**	**18:14**

QMJHL Offensive Rookie of the Year) (1986) • Lady Byng Memorial Trophy (1993)

Played in NHL All-Star Game (1990, 1993, 1994, 1996)

Traded to **NY Islanders** by **Buffalo** with Uwe Krupp, Benoit Hogue and Dave McLlwain for Pat LaFontaine, Randy Hillier, Randy Wood and NY Islanders' 4th round choice (Dean Melanson) in 1992 Entry Draft, October 25, 1991. Traded to **Montreal** by **NY Islanders** with Vladimir Malakhov for Kirk Muller, Mathieu Schneider and Craig Darby, April 5, 1995. Traded to **St. Louis** by **Montreal** with Rory Fitzpatrick and Craig Conroy for Murray Baron, Shayne Corson and St. Louis' 5th round choice (Gennady Razin) in 1997 Entry Draft, October 29, 1996. Signed as a free agent by **Dallas**, July 1, 2001. Signed as a free agent by **Colorado**, August 3, 2005.

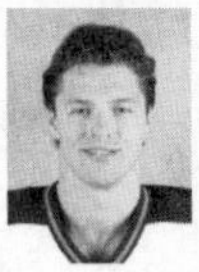

TVERDOVSKY, Oleg

(tvehr-DOHV-skee, OH-lehg) **CAR.**

Defense. Shoots left. 6'1", 205 lbs. Born, Donetsk, USSR, May 18, 1976. Anaheim's 1st choice, 2nd overall, in 1994 Entry Draft.

Season	Club	League	GP	G	A	Pts	PIM	PP	SH	GW	S	%	+/-	TF	F%	Min	GP	G	A	Pts	PIM	PP	SH	GW	Min
1992-93	Krylja Sovetov	CIS	21	0	1	1	6	....	....	....	....	....	....	....	....	....	6	0	0	0	0	....	....	....	....
1993-94	Krylja Sovetov	CIS	46	4	10	14	22	....	....	....	....	....	....	....	....	....	3	1	0	1	2	....	....	....	....
1994-95	Brandon	WHL	7	1	4	5	4	....	....	....	....	....	....	....	....	....	....	....	....	....	....	....	....	....	....
	Anaheim	**NHL**	**36**	**3**	**9**	**12**	**14**	**1**	**1**	**0**	**26**	**11.5**	**-6**	....	....	....	....	....	....	....	....	....	....	....	....
1995-96	**Anaheim**	**NHL**	**51**	**7**	**15**	**22**	**35**	**2**	**0**	**0**	**84**	**8.3**	**0**	....	....	....	....	....	....	....	....	....	....	....	....
	Winnipeg	**NHL**	**31**	**0**	**8**	**8**	**6**	**0**	**0**	**0**	**35**	**0.0**	**-7**	....	....	....	**6**	**0**	**1**	**1**	**0**	**0**	**0**	**0**	....
1996-97	**Phoenix**	**NHL**	**82**	**10**	**45**	**55**	**30**	**3**	**1**	**2**	**144**	**6.9**	**-5**	....	....	....	**7**	**0**	**1**	**1**	**0**	**0**	**0**	**0**	....
1997-98	Hamilton	AHL	9	8	6	14	2	....	....	....	....	....	....	....	....	....	....	....	....	....	....	....	....	....	....
	Phoenix	**NHL**	**46**	**7**	**12**	**19**	**12**	**4**	**0**	**1**	**83**	**8.4**	**1**	....	....	....	**6**	**0**	**7**	**7**	**0**	**0**	**0**	**0**	....
1998-99	**Phoenix**	**NHL**	**82**	**7**	**18**	**25**	**32**	**2**	**0**	**2**	**117**	**6.0**	**11**	**1**	**0.0**	**20:48**	**6**	**0**	**2**	**2**	**6**	**0**	**0**	**0**	**17:43**
99-2000	**Anaheim**	**NHL**	**82**	**15**	**36**	**51**	**30**	**5**	**0**	**5**	**153**	**9.8**	**5**	**1**	**0.0**	**22:46**	....	....	....	....	....	....	....	....	....
2000-01	**Anaheim**	**NHL**	**82**	**14**	**39**	**53**	**32**	**8**	**0**	**3**	**188**	**7.4**	**-11**	**0**	**0.0**	**24:25**	....	....	....	....	....	....	....	....	....
2001-02	**Anaheim**	**NHL**	**73**	**6**	**26**	**32**	**31**	**2**	**0**	**1**	**147**	**4.1**	**0**	**0**	**0.0**	**22:50**	....	....	....	....	....	....	....	....	....
	Russia	Olympics	6	1	1	2	0	....	....	....	....	....	....	....	....	....	....	....	....	....	....	....	....	....	....
2002-03♦	**New Jersey**	**NHL**	**50**	**5**	**8**	**13**	**22**	**2**	**0**	**1**	**76**	**6.6**	**2**	**0**	**0.0**	**16:48**	**15**	**0**	**3**	**3**	**0**	**0**	**0**	**0**	**15:06**
2003-04	Avangard Omsk	Russia	57	16	17	33	58	....	....	....	....	....	....	....	....	....	11	0	2	2	2	....	....	....	....
2004-05	Avangard Omsk	Russia	48	5	15	20	65	....	....	....	....	....	....	....	....	....	11	0	3	3	*35	....	....	....	....
	NHL Totals		**615**	**74**	**216**	**290**	**244**	**29**	**2**	**15**	**1053**	**7.0**		**2**	**0.0**	**21:54**	**40**	**0**	**14**	**14**	**6**	**0**	**0**	**0**	**15:51**

Played in NHL All-Star Game (1997)

Traded to **Winnipeg** by **Anaheim** with Chad Kilger and Anaheim's 3rd round choice (Per-Anton Lundstrom) in 1996 Entry Draft for Teemu Selanne, Marc Chouinard and Winnipeg's 4th round choice (later traded to Toronto – later traded to Montreal – Montreal selected Kim Staal) in 1996 Entry Draft, February 7, 1996. Transferred to **Phoenix** after **Winnipeg** franchise relocated, July 1, 1996. Traded to **Anaheim** by **Phoenix** for Travis Green and Anaheim's 1st round choice (Scott Kelman) in 1999 Entry Draft, June 26, 1999. Traded to **New Jersey** by **Anaheim** with Jeff Friesen and Maxim Balmochnykh for Petr Sykora, Mike Commodore, Jean-Francois Damphousse and Igor Pohanka, July 6, 2002. Signed as a free agent by **Omsk** (Russia), August 29, 2003. Signed as a free agent by **Carolina**, August 4, 2005.

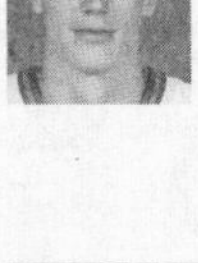

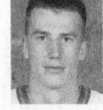

TVRDON, Roman

(t-vahr-DAWN, ROH-muhn)

Center. Shoots left. 6'1", 189 lbs. Born, Trencin, Czech., January 29, 1981. Washington's 6th choice, 132nd overall, in 1999 Entry Draft.

Season	Club	League	GP	G	A	Pts	PIM	PP	SH	GW	S	%	+/-	TF	F%	Min	GP	G	A	Pts	PIM	PP	SH	GW	Min
1995-96	Dukla Trencin U18	Svk-U18	46	25	15	40	32	....	....	....	....	....	....	....	....	....	....	....	....	....	....	....	....	....	....
1996-97	Dukla Trencin U18	Svk-U18	42	25	13	38	10	....	....	....	....	....	....	....	....	....	....	....	....	....	....	....	....	....	....
1997-98	Dukla Trencin Jr.	Slovak-Jr.	48	4	12	16	39	....	....	....	....	....	....	....	....	....	....	....	....	....	....	....	....	....	....
1998-99	Dukla Trencin Jr.	Slovak-Jr.	49	23	23	46	20	....	....	....	....	....	....	....	....	....	6	4	4	8	4	....	....	....	....
99-2000	Spokane Chiefs	WHL	69	26	44	70	40	....	....	....	....	....	....	....	....	....	15	4	7	11	16	....	....	....	....
2000-01	Spokane Chiefs	WHL	62	28	34	62	55	....	....	....	....	....	....	....	....	....	12	5	11	16	0	....	....	....	....
2001-02	Portland Pirates	AHL	49	5	9	14	22	....	....	....	....	....	....	....	....	....	....	....	....	....	....	....	....	....	....

			Regular Season															Playoffs								
Season	Club	League	GP	G	A	Pts	PIM	PP	SH	GW	S	%	+/-	TF	F%	Min	GP	G	A	Pts	PIM	PP	SH	GW	Min
2002-03	Portland Pirates	AHL	35	5	4	9	17	....	....	....	....	....	....	....	....	....	....	....	....	....	....	....	....	....	....
2003-04	**Washington**	**NHL**	**9**	**0**	**1**	**1**	**2**	**0**	**0**	**0**	**7**	**0.0**	**–3**	**45**	**35.6**	**10:41**	....	....	....	....	....	....	....	....	....
	Portland Pirates	AHL	51	2	4	6	20	....	....	....	....	....	....	....	....	....	7	0	0	0	2	....	....	....	....
2004-05	Nottingham	Britain	9	2	5	7	6	....	....	....	....	....	....	....	....	....	....	....	....	....	....	....	....	....	....
	NHL Totals		**9**	**0**	**1**	**1**	**2**	**0**	**0**	**0**	**7**	**0.0**		**45**	**35.6**	**10:41**	....	....	....	....	....	....	....	....	....

• Missed majority of 2002-03 season recovering from shoulder injury suffered in game vs. Saint John (AHL), December 28, 2002. Signed as a free agent by **Nottingham** (Britain), July 12, 2004.

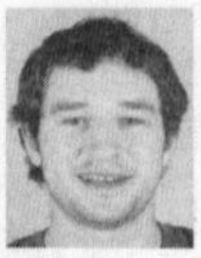

TYUTIN, Fedor

(TYOO-tihn, feh-DUHR) **NYR**

Defense. Shoots left. 6'2", 210 lbs. Born, Izhevsk, USSR, July 19, 1983. NY Rangers' 2nd choice, 40th overall, in 2001 Entry Draft.

Season	Club	League	GP	G	A	Pts	PIM	PP	SH	GW	S	%	+/-	TF	F%	Min	GP	G	A	Pts	PIM	PP	SH	GW	Min
1998-99	Magnitogorsk 2	Russia-4	7	0	1	1	2	....	....	....	....	....	....	....	....	....	....	....	....	....	....	....	....	....	....
99-2000	Izhstal Izhevsk 2	Russia-3	38	11	8	19	68	....	....	....	....	....	....	....	....	....	....	....	....	....	....	....	....	....	....
	Izhstal Izhevsk	Russia-2	10	0	1	1	12	....	....	....	....	....	....	....	....	....	....	....	....	....	....	....	....	....	....
2000-01	St. Petersburg	Russia	34	2	4	6	20	....	....	....	....	....	....	....	....	....	....	....	....	....	....	....	....	....	....
2001-02	Guelph Storm	OHL	53	19	40	59	54	....	....	....	....	....	....	....	....	....	9	2	8	10	8	....	....	....	....
2002-03	St. Petersburg	Russia	10	1	1	2	16	....	....	....	....	....	....	....	....	....	....	....	....	....	....	....	....	....	....
	Ak Bars Kazan	Russia	10	0	0	0	8	....	....	....	....	....	....	....	....	....	5	0	0	0	4	....	....	....	....
2003-04	**NY Rangers**	**NHL**	**25**	**2**	**5**	**7**	**14**	**0**	**1**	**0**	**33**	**6.1**	**–4**	**1**	**0.0**	**20:08**	....	....	....	....	....	....	....	....	....
	Hartford	AHL	43	5	9	14	50	....	....	....	....	....	....	....	....	....	16	0	5	5	18	....	....	....	....
2004-05	Hartford	AHL	13	2	1	3	10	....	....	....	....	....	....	....	....	....	....	....	....	....	....	....	....	....	....
	St. Petersburg	Russia	35	5	3	8	24	....	....	....	....	....	....	....	....	....	....	....	....	....	....	....	....	....	....
	NHL Totals		**25**	**2**	**5**	**7**	**14**	**0**	**1**	**0**	**33**	**6.1**		**1**	**0.0**	**20:08**	....	....	....	....	....	....	....	....	....

Signed as a free agent by **St. Petersburg** (Russia), November 11, 2004.

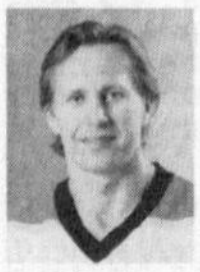

ULANOV, Igor

(yoo-LAH-nahf, EE-gohr) **EDM.**

Defense. Shoots left. 6'3", 220 lbs. Born, Krasnokamsk, USSR, October 1, 1969. Winnipeg's 8th choice, 203rd overall, in 1991 Entry Draft.

Season	Club	League	GP	G	A	Pts	PIM	PP	SH	GW	S	%	+/-	TF	F%	Min	GP	G	A	Pts	PIM	PP	SH	GW	Min
1990-91	Voskresensk	USSR	41	2	2	4	52	....	....	....	....	....	....	....	....	....	....	....	....	....	....	....	....	....	....
1991-92	Voskresensk	CIS	27	1	4	5	24	....	....	....	....	....	....	....	....	....	....	....	....	....	....	....	....	....	....
	Winnipeg	**NHL**	**27**	**2**	**9**	**11**	**67**	**0**	**0**	**0**	**23**	**8.7**	**5**	....	....	....	**7**	**0**	**0**	**0**	**39**	**0**	**0**	**0**	....
	Moncton Hawks	AHL	3	0	1	1	16	....	....	....	....	....	....	....	....	....	....	....	....	....	....	....	....	....	....
1992-93	**Winnipeg**	**NHL**	**56**	**2**	**14**	**16**	**124**	**0**	**0**	**0**	**26**	**7.7**	**6**	....	....	....	**4**	**0**	**0**	**0**	**4**	**0**	**0**	**0**	....
	Moncton Hawks	AHL	9	1	3	4	26	....	....	....	....	....	....	....	....	....	....	....	....	....	....	....	....	....	....
	Fort Wayne	IHL	3	0	1	1	29	....	....	....	....	....	....	....	....	....	....	....	....	....	....	....	....	....	....
1993-94	**Winnipeg**	**NHL**	**74**	**0**	**17**	**17**	**165**	**0**	**0**	**0**	**46**	**0.0**	**–11**	....	....	....	....	....	....	....	....	....	....	....	....
1994-95	**Winnipeg**	**NHL**	**19**	**1**	**3**	**4**	**27**	**0**	**0**	**0**	**13**	**7.7**	**–2**	....	....	....	....	....	....	....	....	....	....	....	....
	Washington	**NHL**	**3**	**0**	**1**	**1**	**2**	**0**	**0**	**0**	**0**	**0.0**	**3**	....	....	....	**2**	**0**	**0**	**0**	**4**	**0**	**0**	**0**	....
1995-96	**Chicago**	**NHL**	**53**	**1**	**8**	**9**	**92**	**0**	**0**	**0**	**24**	**4.2**	**12**	....	....	....	....	....	....	....	....	....	....	....	....
	Indianapolis Ice	IHL	1	0	0	0	0	....	....	....	....	....	....	....	....	....	....	....	....	....	....	....	....	....	....
	Tampa Bay	**NHL**	**11**	**2**	**1**	**3**	**24**	**0**	**0**	**1**	**13**	**15.4**	**–1**	....	....	....	**5**	**0**	**0**	**0**	**15**	**0**	**0**	**0**	....
1996-97	**Tampa Bay**	**NHL**	**59**	**1**	**7**	**8**	**108**	**0**	**0**	**0**	**56**	**1.8**	**2**	....	....	....	....	....	....	....	....	....	....	....	....
1997-98	**Tampa Bay**	**NHL**	**45**	**2**	**7**	**9**	**85**	**1**	**0**	**0**	**32**	**6.3**	**–5**	....	....	....	....	....	....	....	....	....	....	....	....
	Montreal	**NHL**	**4**	**0**	**1**	**1**	**12**	**0**	**0**	**0**	**4**	**0.0**	**–2**	....	....	....	**10**	**1**	**4**	**5**	**12**	**0**	**0**	**0**	....
1998-99	**Montreal**	**NHL**	**76**	**3**	**9**	**12**	**109**	**0**	**0**	**0**	**55**	**5.5**	**–3**	**0**	**0.0**	**17:35**	....	....	....	....	....	....	....	....	....
99-2000	**Montreal**	**NHL**	**43**	**1**	**5**	**6**	**76**	**0**	**0**	**0**	**33**	**3.0**	**–11**	**0**	**0.0**	**16:33**	....	....	....	....	....	....	....	....	....
	Edmonton	**NHL**	**14**	**0**	**3**	**3**	**10**	**0**	**0**	**0**	**6**	**0.0**	**–3**	**0**	**0.0**	**16:23**	**5**	**0**	**0**	**0**	**6**	**0**	**0**	**0**	**16:59**
2000-01	**Edmonton**	**NHL**	**67**	**3**	**20**	**23**	**90**	**1**	**0**	**0**	**74**	**4.1**	**15**	**0**	**0.0**	**23:01**	**6**	**0**	**0**	**0**	**4**	**0**	**0**	**0**	**24:25**
2001-02	**NY Rangers**	**NHL**	**39**	**0**	**6**	**6**	**53**	**0**	**0**	**0**	**17**	**0.0**	**–4**	**0**	**0.0**	**16:19**	....	....	....	....	....	....	....	....	....
	Hartford	AHL	6	1	1	2	2	....	....	....	....	....	....	....	....	....	....	....	....	....	....	....	....	....	....
	Florida	**NHL**	**14**	**0**	**4**	**4**	**11**	**0**	**0**	**0**	**9**	**0.0**	**–3**	**0**	**0.0**	**20:50**	....	....	....	....	....	....	....	....	....
2002-03	**Florida**	**NHL**	**56**	**1**	**1**	**2**	**39**	**0**	**0**	**0**	**20**	**5.0**	**7**	**0**	**0.0**	**16:42**	....	....	....	....	....	....	....	....	....
	San Antonio	AHL	5	1	0	1	4	....	....	....	....	....	....	....	....	....	....	....	....	....	....	....	....	....	....
2003-04	Toronto	AHL	10	0	5	5	8	....	....	....	....	....	....	....	....	....	....	....	....	....	....	....	....	....	....
	Edmonton	**NHL**	**42**	**5**	**13**	**18**	**28**	**1**	**0**	**3**	**49**	**10.2**	**19**	**0**	**0.0**	**19:51**	....	....	....	....	....	....	....	....	....
2004-05			DID NOT PLAY																						
	NHL Totals		**702**	**24**	**129**	**153**	**1122**	**3**	**0**	**4**	**500**	**4.8**		**0**	**0.0**	**18:34**	**39**	**1**	**4**	**5**	**84**	**0**	**0**	**0**	**21:02**

Traded to **Washington** by **Winnipeg** with Mike Eagles for Washington's 3rd (later traded to Dallas – Dallas selected Sergey Gusev) and 5th (Brian Elder) round choices in 1995 Entry Draft, April 7, 1995. Traded to **Chicago** by **Washington** for Chicago's 3rd round choice (Dave Weninger) in 1996 Entry Draft, October 17, 1995. Traded to **Tampa Bay** by **Chicago** with Patrick Poulin and Chicago's 2nd round choice (later traded to New Jersey – New Jersey selected Pierre Dagenais) in 1996 Entry Draft for Enrico Ciccone and Tampa Bay's 2nd round choice (Jeff Paul) in 1996 Entry Draft, March 20, 1996. Traded to **Montreal** by **Tampa Bay** with Patrick Poulin and Mick Vukota for Stephane Richer, Darcy Tucker and David Wilkie, January 15, 1998. Traded to **Edmonton** by **Montreal** with Alain Nasreddine for Christian Laflamme and Matthieu Descoteaux, March 9, 2000. Signed as a free agent by **NY Rangers**, July 20, 2001. Traded to **Florida** by **NY Rangers** with Filip Novak, NY Rangers' 1st (later traded to Calgary – Calgary selected Eric Nystrom) and 2nd (Rob Globke) round choices in 2002 Entry Draft and NY Rangers' 4th round choice (later traded to Atlanta – Atlanta selected Guillaume Desbiens) in 2003 Entry Draft for Pavel Bure and Florida's 2nd round choice (Lee Falardeau) in 2002 Entry Draft, March 18, 2002. Signed to a PTO (tryout) contract by **Toronto** (AHL), December 13, 2003. Signed as a free agent by **Edmonton**, January 5, 2004.

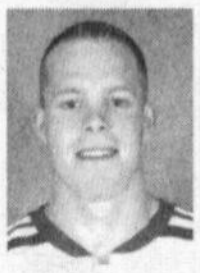

ULMER, Jeff

(UHL-muhr, JEHF)

Right wing. Shoots right. 5'11", 195 lbs. Born, Wilcox, Sask., April 27, 1977.

Season	Club	League	GP	G	A	Pts	PIM	PP	SH	GW	S	%	+/-	TF	F%	Min	GP	G	A	Pts	PIM	PP	SH	GW	Min
1994-95	Notre Dame	AJHL	63	25	35	60	....	....	....	....	....	....	....	....	....	....	....	....	....	....	....	....	....	....	....
1995-96	North Dakota	WCHA	29	5	3	8	26	....	....	....	....	....	....	....	....	....	....	....	....	....	....	....	....	....	....
1996-97	North Dakota	WCHA	26	6	11	17	16	....	....	....	....	....	....	....	....	....	....	....	....	....	....	....	....	....	....
1997-98	North Dakota	WCHA	32	12	12	24	44	....	....	....	....	....	....	....	....	....	....	....	....	....	....	....	....	....	....
1998-99	North Dakota	WCHA	38	16	20	36	46	....	....	....	....	....	....	....	....	....	....	....	....	....	....	....	....	....	....
99-2000	Canada	Nat-Tm	48	14	25	39	20	....	....	....	....	....	....	....	....	....	....	....	....	....	....	....	....	....	....
	Houston Aeros	IHL	5	1	0	1	0	....	....	....	....	....	....	....	....	....	11	2	4	6	6	....	....	....	....
2000-01	**NY Rangers**	**NHL**	**21**	**3**	**0**	**3**	**8**	**0**	**0**	**0**	**22**	**13.6**	**–6**	**16**	**31.3**	**10:23**	....	....	....	....	....	....	....	....	....
	Hartford	AHL	48	11	14	25	34	....	....	....	....	....	....	....	....	....	....	....	....	....	....	....	....	....	....
2001-02	Grand Rapids	AHL	73	9	17	26	65	....	....	....	....	....	....	....	....	....	5	0	1	1	11	....	....	....	....
2002-03	Binghamton	AHL	57	8	12	20	40	....	....	....	....	....	....	....	....	....	13	0	1	1	30	....	....	....	....
2003-04	Cardiff Devils	Britain	9	9	9	18	6	....	....	....	....	....	....	....	....	....	....	....	....	....	....	....	....	....	....
	Lukko Rauma	Finland	34	13	8	21	67	....	....	....	....	....	....	....	....	....	4	0	0	0	2	....	....	....	....
2004-05	Hershey Bears	AHL	80	22	29	51	47	....	....	....	....	....	....	....	....	....	....	....	....	....	....	....	....	....	....
	NHL Totals		**21**	**3**	**0**	**3**	**8**	**0**	**0**	**0**	**22**	**13.6**		**16**	**31.3**	**10:23**	....	....	....	....	....	....	....	....	....

Signed as a free agent by **Houston** (IHL), March 30, 2000. Signed as a free agent by **NY Rangers**, July 27, 2000. Traded to **Ottawa** by **NY Rangers** with Jason Doig for Sean Gagnon, June 29, 2001. Signed as a free agent by **Cardiff** (Britain), October 10, 2003. Signed as a free agent by **Lukko** (Finland), November 11, 2003. Signed as a free agent by **Colorado**, June 10, 2004.

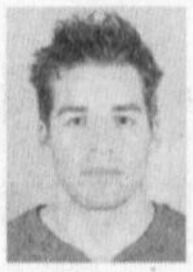

ULMER, Layne

(UHL-muhr, LAYN)

Center. Shoots left. 6'1", 205 lbs. Born, North Battleford, Sask., September 14, 1980. Ottawa's 8th choice, 209th overall, in 1999 Entry Draft.

Season	Club	League	GP	G	A	Pts	PIM	PP	SH	GW	S	%	+/-	TF	F%	Min	GP	G	A	Pts	PIM	PP	SH	GW	Min
1996-97	Swift Current	SMHL	43	35	49	84	71	....	....	....	....	....	....	....	....	....	....	....	....	....	....	....	....	....	....
1997-98	Swift Current	WHL	50	8	9	17	23	....	....	....	....	....	....	....	....	....	12	3	1	4	0	....	....	....	....
1998-99	Swift Current	WHL	72	40	35	75	34	....	....	....	....	....	....	....	....	....	6	2	1	3	4	....	....	....	....
99-2000	Swift Current	WHL	71	50	54	104	66	....	....	....	....	....	....	....	....	....	12	12	6	18	16	....	....	....	....
2000-01	Swift Current	WHL	68	*63	56	119	75	....	....	....	....	....	....	....	....	....	19	7	3	10	20	....	....	....	....
2001-02	Hartford	AHL	22	0	5	5	17	....	....	....	....	....	....	....	....	....	....	....	....	....	....	....	....	....	....
	Charlotte	ECHL	38	18	17	35	12	....	....	....	....	....	....	....	....	....	5	2	2	4	4	....	....	....	....
2002-03	Hartford	AHL	68	12	20	32	16	....	....	....	....	....	....	....	....	....	2	0	0	0	0	....	....	....	....
2003-04	**NY Rangers**	**NHL**	**1**	**0**	**0**	**0**	**0**	**0**	**0**	**0**	**1**	**0.0**	**–1**	**8**	**75.0**	**9:27**	....	....	....	....	....	....	....	....	....
	Hartford	AHL	76	22	16	38	26	....	....	....	....	....	....	....	....	....	7	2	5	7	0	....	....	....	....
2004-05	Hartford	AHL	65	7	30	37	23	....	....	....	....	....	....	....	....	....	6	0	0	0	2	....	....	....	....
	NHL Totals		**1**	**0**	**0**	**0**	**0**	**0**	**0**	**0**	**1**	**0.0**		**8**	**75.0**	**9:27**	....	....	....	....	....	....	....	....	....

WHL East First All-Star Team (2000, 2001)

Signed as a free agent by **NY Rangers**, June 13, 2001.

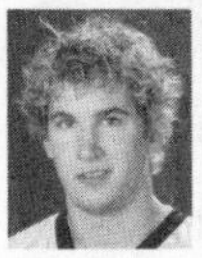

UPSHALL, Scottie
(UHP-shuhl, SKAW-tee) **NSH.**

Right wing. Shoots left. 6', 197 lbs. Born, Fort McMurray, Alta., October 7, 1983. Nashville's 1st choice, 6th overall, in 2002 Entry Draft.

			Regular Season														Playoffs								
Season	Club	League	GP	G	A	Pts	PIM	PP	SH	GW	S	%	+/-	TF	F%	Min	GP	G	A	Pts	PIM	PP	SH	GW	Min
1998-99	Fort McMurray	AMHL	28	62	40	102	100																		
99-2000	Fort McMurray	AJHL	52	26	26	52	65																		
2000-01	Kamloops Blazers	WHL	70	42	45	87	111										4	0	2	2	10				
2001-02	Kamloops Blazers	WHL	61	32	51	83	139										4	1	2	3	21				
2002-03	**Nashville**	**NHL**	**8**	**1**	**0**	**1**	**0**	**0**	**0**	**0**	**6**	**16.7**	**2**	**2**	**0.0**	**8:42**									
	Kamloops Blazers	WHL	42	25	31	56	111										6	0	2	2	34				
	Milwaukee	AHL	2	1	0	1	2										6	0	0	0	2				
2003-04	**Nashville**	**NHL**	**7**	**0**	**1**	**1**	**0**	**0**	**0**	**0**	**6**	**0.0**	**−2**	**8**	**37.5**	**9:11**									
	Milwaukee	AHL	31	13	11	24	42										8	3	0	3	4				
2004-05	Milwaukee	AHL	62	19	27	46	108										5	2	2	4	8				
	NHL Totals		**15**	**1**	**1**	**2**	**0**	**0**	**0**	**0**	**12**	**8.3**		**10**	**30.0**	**8:56**									

WHL All-Rookie Team (2001) • WHL Rookie of the Year (2001) • CHL All-Rookie Team (2001) • Canadian Major Junior Rookie of the Year (2001) • WHL West Second All-Star Team (2002)

• Missed majority of 2003-04 season recovering from knee injury suffered in game vs. Phoenix, December 22, 2003.

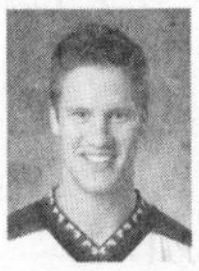

VAANANEN, Ossi
(VAN-ih-nehn, AW-see) **COL.**

Defense. Shoots left. 6'4", 215 lbs. Born, Vantaa, Finland, August 18, 1980. Phoenix's 2nd choice, 43rd overall, in 1998 Entry Draft.

Season	Club	League	GP	G	A	Pts	PIM	PP	SH	GW	S	%	+/-	TF	F%	Min	GP	G	A	Pts	PIM	PP	SH	GW	Min
1995-96	Jokerit U18	Fin-U18	1	0	0	0	0										1	0	0	0	0				
1996-97	Jokerit Helsinki Jr.	Finland-Jr.	17	1	2	3	43																		
1997-98	Jokerit Helsinki Jr.	Finland-Jr.	31	0	6	6	24																		
1998-99	Jokerit Helsinki Jr.	Finland-Jr.	12	1	6	7	16																		
	Jokerit Helsinki	EuroHL	5	0	0	0	2										1	0	1	1	2				
	Jokerit Helsinki	Finland	48	0	1	1	42										3	0	1	1	2				
99-2000	Jokerit Helsinki	Finland	49	1	6	7	46										11	1	1	2	2				
2000-01	**Phoenix**	**NHL**	**81**	**4**	**12**	**16**	**90**	**0**	**0**	**2**	**69**	**5.8**	**9**	**0**	**0.0**	**19:09**									
2001-02	**Phoenix**	**NHL**	**76**	**2**	**12**	**14**	**74**	**0**	**1**	**0**	**41**	**4.9**	**6**	**0**	**0.0**	**20:13**	**5**	**0**	**0**	**0**	**6**	**0**	**0**	**0**	**20:33**
	Finland	Olympics	2	0	1	1	0																		
2002-03	**Phoenix**	**NHL**	**67**	**2**	**7**	**9**	**82**	**0**	**0**	**0**	**49**	**4.1**	**1**	**0**	**0.0**	**19:15**									
2003-04	**Phoenix**	**NHL**	**67**	**2**	**4**	**6**	**87**	**0**	**0**	**1**	**39**	**5.1**	**−10**	**0**	**0.0**	**19:21**									
	Colorado	**NHL**	**12**	**0**	**0**	**0**	**2**	**0**	**0**	**0**	**6**	**0.0**	**−4**	**0**	**0.0**	**18:36**	**11**	**0**	**1**	**1**	**18**	**0**	**0**	**0**	**22:06**
2004-05	Jokerit Helsinki	Finland	28	2	2	4	30										12	0	0	0	26				
	NHL Totals		**303**	**10**	**35**	**45**	**335**	**0**	**1**	**3**	**204**	**4.9**		**0**	**0.0**	**19:28**	**16**	**0**	**1**	**1**	**24**	**0**	**0**	**0**	**21:37**

Traded to **Colorado** by **Phoenix** with Chris Gratton and Phoenix's 2nd round choice (Paul Stastny) in 2005 Entry Draft for Derek Morris and Keith Ballard, March 8, 2004. Signed as a free agent by **Jokerit** (Finland), December 1, 2004.

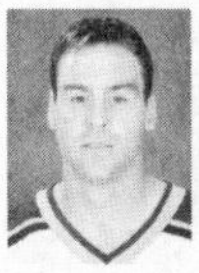

VALICEVIC, Rob
(val-IH-seh-VIK, RAWB)

Right wing. Shoots right. 6'1", 198 lbs. Born, Detroit, MI, January 6, 1971. NY Islanders' 6th choice, 114th overall, in 1991 Entry Draft.

Season	Club	League	GP	G	A	Pts	PIM	PP	SH	GW	S	%	+/-	TF	F%	Min	GP	G	A	Pts	PIM	PP	SH	GW	Min
1990-91	Det. Compuware	NAHL	39	31	44	75	54																		
1991-92	Lake Superior	CCHA	32	8	4	12	12																		
1992-93	Lake Superior	CCHA	43	21	20	41	28																		
1993-94	Lake Superior	CCHA	45	18	20	38	46																		
1994-95	Lake Superior	CCHA	37	10	21	31	40																		
1995-96	Louisiana	ECHL	60	42	20	62	85										5	2	3	5	8				
	Springfield	AHL	2	0	0	0	2																		
1996-97	Louisiana	ECHL	8	7	2	9	21																		
	Houston Aeros	IHL	58	11	12	23	42										12	1	3	4	11				
1997-98	Houston Aeros	IHL	72	29	28	57	47										4	2	0	2	2				
1998-99	**Nashville**	**NHL**	**19**	**4**	**2**	**6**	**2**	**0**	**0**	**2**	**23**	**17.4**	**4**	**17**	**29.4**	**11:01**									
	Houston Aeros	IHL	57	16	33	49	62										19	7	10	17	8				
99-2000	**Nashville**	**NHL**	**80**	**14**	**11**	**25**	**21**	**2**	**1**	**3**	**113**	**12.4**	**−11**	**50**	**44.0**	**14:31**									
2000-01	**Nashville**	**NHL**	**60**	**8**	**6**	**14**	**26**	**1**	**0**	**4**	**62**	**12.9**	**−2**	**35**	**40.0**	**14:06**									
2001-02	**Los Angeles**	**NHL**	**17**	**1**	**1**	**2**	**8**	**0**	**0**	**0**	**9**	**11.1**	**−4**	**166**	**41.6**	**9:34**									
	Manchester	AHL	59	11	23	34	25										5	1	0	1	4				
2002-03	**Anaheim**	**NHL**	**10**	**1**	**0**	**1**	**2**	**0**	**0**	**1**	**7**	**14.3**	**1**	**0**	**0.0**	**8:35**									
	Cincinnati	AHL	69	17	26	43	38																		
2003-04	**Dallas**	**NHL**	**7**	**0**	**0**	**0**	**2**	**0**	**0**	**0**	**4**	**0.0**	**−1**	**27**	**48.2**	**7:50**									
	Utah Grizzlies	AHL	67	11	26	37	44																		
2004-05	Flint Generals	UHL	78	36	60	96	38																		
	NHL Totals		**193**	**28**	**20**	**48**	**61**	**3**	**1**	**10**	**218**	**12.8**		**295**	**41.7**	**13:03**									

UHL Second All-Star Team (2005)

Signed as a free agent by **Nashville**, May 28, 1998. Signed as a free agent by **Los Angeles**, August 16, 2001. Signed as a free agent by **Anaheim**, July 24, 2002. Signed as a free agent by **Dallas**, August 28, 2003. Signed as a free agent by **Flint** (UHL), October 17, 2004.

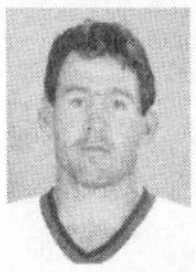

VAN ALLEN, Shaun
(VAN-AL-ehn, SHAWN)

Center. Shoots left. 6'1", 205 lbs. Born, Calgary, Alta., August 29, 1967. Edmonton's 5th choice, 105th overall, in 1987 Entry Draft.

Season	Club	League	GP	G	A	Pts	PIM	PP	SH	GW	S	%	+/-	TF	F%	Min	GP	G	A	Pts	PIM	PP	SH	GW	Min
1984-85	Swift Current	SJHL	61	12	20	32	136																		
1985-86	Saskatoon Blades	WHL	55	12	11	23	43										13	4	8	12	28				
1986-87	Saskatoon Blades	WHL	72	38	59	97	116										11	4	6	10	24				
1987-88	Milwaukee	IHL	40	14	28	42	34																		
	Nova Scotia Oilers	AHL	19	4	10	14	17										4	1	1	2	4				
1988-89	Cape Breton	AHL	76	32	42	74	81																		
1989-90	Cape Breton	AHL	61	25	44	69	83										4	0	2	2	8				
1990-91	**Edmonton**	**NHL**	**2**	**0**	**0**	**0**	**0**	**0**	**0**	**0**	**0**	**0.0**	**0**												
	Cape Breton	AHL	76	25	75	100	182										4	0	1	1	8				
1991-92	Cape Breton	AHL	77	29	*84	*113	80										5	3	7	10	14				
1992-93	**Edmonton**	**NHL**	**21**	**1**	**4**	**5**	**6**	**0**	**0**	**0**	**19**	**5.3**	**−2**												
	Cape Breton	AHL	43	14	62	76	68										15	8	9	17	18				
1993-94	**Anaheim**	**NHL**	**80**	**8**	**25**	**33**	**64**	**2**	**2**	**1**	**104**	**7.7**	**0**												
1994-95	**Anaheim**	**NHL**	**45**	**8**	**21**	**29**	**32**	**1**	**1**	**1**	**68**	**11.8**	**−4**												
1995-96	**Anaheim**	**NHL**	**49**	**8**	**17**	**25**	**41**	**0**	**0**	**2**	**78**	**10.3**	**13**												
1996-97	**Ottawa**	**NHL**	**80**	**11**	**14**	**25**	**35**	**1**	**1**	**2**	**123**	**8.9**	**−8**				**7**	**0**	**1**	**1**	**4**	**0**	**0**	**0**	
1997-98	**Ottawa**	**NHL**	**80**	**4**	**15**	**19**	**48**	**0**	**0**	**0**	**104**	**3.8**	**4**				**11**	**0**	**1**	**1**	**10**	**0**	**0**	**0**	
1998-99	**Ottawa**	**NHL**	**79**	**6**	**11**	**17**	**30**	**0**	**1**	**0**	**47**	**12.8**	**3**	**656**	**47.4**	**11:07**	**4**	**0**	**0**	**0**	**0**	**0**	**0**	**0**	**8:42**
99-2000	**Ottawa**	**NHL**	**75**	**9**	**19**	**28**	**37**	**0**	**2**	**4**	**75**	**12.0**	**20**	**911**	**48.6**	**11:49**	**6**	**0**	**1**	**1**	**9**	**0**	**0**	**0**	**12:09**
2000-01	**Dallas**	**NHL**	**59**	**7**	**16**	**23**	**16**	**0**	**2**	**3**	**51**	**13.7**	**5**	**559**	**47.1**	**12:05**	**8**	**0**	**2**	**2**	**8**	**0**	**0**	**0**	**13:56**
2001-02	**Dallas**	**NHL**	**19**	**2**	**4**	**6**	**6**	**0**	**0**	**0**	**20**	**10.0**	**−5**	**177**	**53.1**	**12:57**									
	Montreal	**NHL**	**54**	**6**	**9**	**15**	**20**	**0**	**1**	**1**	**28**	**21.4**	**5**	**381**	**47.8**	**10:08**	**7**	**0**	**1**	**1**	**2**	**0**	**0**	**0**	**9:25**
2002-03	**Ottawa**	**NHL**	**78**	**12**	**20**	**32**	**66**	**2**	**2**	**3**	**53**	**22.6**	**17**	**838**	**45.0**	**12:29**	**18**	**1**	**1**	**2**	**12**	**0**	**0**	**1**	**11:54**
2003-04	**Ottawa**	**NHL**	**73**	**2**	**10**	**12**	**80**	**0**	**1**	**0**	**41**	**4.9**	**6**	**792**	**52.3**	**11:29**									
2004-05			DID NOT PLAY																						
	NHL Totals		**794**	**84**	**185**	**269**	**481**	**6**	**13**	**17**	**811**	**10.4**		**4314**	**48.3**	**11:38**	**61**	**1**	**7**	**8**	**45**	**0**	**0**	**1**	**11:37**

AHL Second All-Star Team (1991) • AHL First All-Star Team (1992) • John B. Sollenberger Trophy (Leading Scorer – AHL) (1992)

Signed as a free agent by **Anaheim**, July 22, 1993. Traded to **Ottawa** by **Anaheim** with Jason York for Ted Drury and the rights to Marc Moro, October 1, 1996. Signed as a free agent by **Dallas**, July 12, 2000. Traded to **Montreal** by **Dallas** with Donald Audette for Martin Rucinsky and Benoit Brunet, November 21, 2001. Signed as a free agent by **Ottawa**, July 24, 2002.

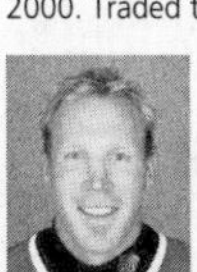

VANDENBUSSCHE, Ryan
(van-dehn-BUHSH, RIGH-yuhn) **PIT.**

Right wing. Shoots right. 6', 200 lbs. Born, Simcoe, Ont., February 28, 1973. Toronto's 9th choice, 173rd overall, in 1992 Entry Draft.

Season	Club	League	GP	G	A	Pts	PIM	PP	SH	GW	S	%	+/-	TF	F%	Min	GP	G	A	Pts	PIM	PP	SH	GW	Min
1988-89	Delhi Flames	OHA-D	3	1	1	2	2																		
1989-90	Norwich	OHA-C	21	12	10	22	146																		
	Tillsonburg Titans	OHA-B	24	0	5	5	113																		
1990-91	Massena	CJHL	10	2	3	5	46																		
	Cornwall Royals	OHL	49	3	8	11	139																		
1991-92	Cornwall Royals	OHL	61	13	15	28	232										6	0	2	2	9				

			Regular Season														Playoffs								
Season	Club	League	GP	G	A	Pts	PIM	PP	SH	GW	S	%	+/-	TF	F%	Min	GP	G	A	Pts	PIM	PP	SH	GW	Min
1992-93	Newmarket	OHL	30	15	12	27	161	....	....	....	....	....	....	....	....	....	....	....	....	....	....	....	....	....	....
	Guelph Storm	OHL	29	3	14	17	99	....	....	....	....	....	....	....	....	....	5	1	3	4	13	....	....	....	....
	St. John's	AHL	1	0	0	0	0	....	....	....	....	....	....	....	....	....	....	....	....	....	....	....	....	....	....
1993-94	St. John's	AHL	44	4	10	14	124	....	....	....	....	....	....	....	....	....	....	....	....	....	....	....	....	....	....
	Springfield	AHL	9	1	2	3	29	....	....	....	....	....	....	....	....	....	5	0	0	0	16	....	....	....	....
1994-95	St. John's	AHL	53	2	13	15	239	....	....	....	....	....	....	....	....	....	3	0	0	0	17	....	....	....	....
1995-96	Binghamton	AHL	68	3	17	20	240	....	....	....	....	....	....	....	....	....	4	0	0	0	9	....	....	....	....
1996-97	NY Rangers	NHL	11	1	0	1	30	0	0	0	4	25.0	–2	....	....	....	....	....	....	....	....	....	....	....	....
	Binghamton	AHL	38	8	11	19	133	....	....	....	....	....	....	....	....	....	....	....	....	....	....	....	....	....	....
1997-98	NY Rangers	NHL	16	1	0	1	38	0	0	0	2	50.0	–2	....	....	....	....	....	....	....	....	....	....	....	....
	Hartford	AHL	15	2	0	2	45	....	....	....	....	....	....	....	....	....	....	....	....	....	....	....	....	....	....
	Chicago	NHL	4	0	1	1	5	0	0	0	0	0.0	0	....	....	....	....	....	....	....	....	....	....	....	....
	Indianapolis Ice	IHL	3	1	1	2	4	....	....	....	....	....	....	....	....	....	....	....	....	....	....	....	....	....	....
1998-99	Chicago	NHL	6	0	0	0	17	0	0	0	3	0.0	0	0	0.0	9:29	....	....	....	....	....	....	....	....	....
	Indianapolis Ice	IHL	34	3	10	13	130	....	....	....	....	....	....	....	....	....	....	....	....	....	....	....	....	....	....
	Portland Pirates	AHL	37	4	1	5	119	....	....	....	....	....	....	....	....	....	....	....	....	....	....	....	....	....	....
99-2000	Chicago	NHL	52	0	1	1	143	0	0	0	19	0.0	–3	3	0.0	5:37	....	....	....	....	....	....	....	....	....
2000-01	Chicago	NHL	64	2	5	7	146	0	0	0	24	8.3	–8	2	0.0	7:46	....	....	....	....	....	....	....	....	....
2001-02	Chicago	NHL	50	1	2	3	103	0	0	0	22	4.5	–10	2	50.0	6:19	1	0	0	0	0	0	0	0	7:20
2002-03	Chicago	NHL	22	0	0	0	58	0	0	0	7	0.0	0	1	100.0	6:30	....	....	....	....	....	....	....	....	....
	Norfolk Admirals	AHL	4	0	1	1	5	....	....	....	....	....	....	....	....	....	....	....	....	....	....	....	....	....	....
2003-04	Chicago	NHL	65	4	1	5	120	2	0	0	25	16.0	–10	0	0.0	6:16	....	....	....	....	....	....	....	....	....
2004-05	Wilkes-Barre	AHL	23	4	7	11	67	....	....	....	....	....	....	....	....	....	11	2	2	4	11	....	....	....	....
	NHL Totals		290	9	10	19	660	2	0	0	106	8.5		8	25.0	6:37	1	0	0	0	0	0	0	0	7:20

Signed as a free agent by **NY Rangers**, August 22, 1995. Traded to **Chicago** by **NY Rangers** for Ryan Risidore, March 24, 1998. • Missed majority of 2002-03 season recovering from hand injury suffered in game vs. Detroit, January 5, 2003. Signed as a free agent by **Pittsburgh**, July 12, 2004. Signed as a free agent by **Wilkes-Barre** (AHL), February 17, 2005.

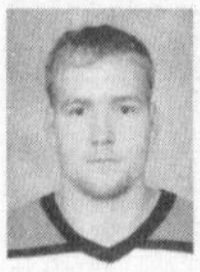

VANDERMEER, Jim (VAN-duhr-meer, JIHM) CHI.

Defense. Shoots left. 6'1", 218 lbs. Born, Caroline, Alta., February 21, 1980.

Season	Club	League	GP	G	A	Pts	PIM	PP	SH	GW	S	%	+/-	TF	F%	Min	GP	G	A	Pts	PIM	PP	SH	GW	Min
1997-98	Red Deer	AMHL	26	4	8	12	51	....	....	....	....	....	....	....	....	....	....	....	....	....	....	....	....	....	....
	Red Deer Rebels	WHL	35	0	3	3	55	....	....	....	....	....	....	....	....	....	2	0	0	0	0	....	....	....	....
1998-99	Red Deer Rebels	WHL	70	5	23	28	258	....	....	....	....	....	....	....	....	....	9	0	1	1	24	....	....	....	....
99-2000	Red Deer Rebels	WHL	71	8	30	38	221	....	....	....	....	....	....	....	....	....	4	0	1	1	16	....	....	....	....
2000-01	Red Deer Rebels	WHL	72	21	44	65	180	....	....	....	....	....	....	....	....	....	22	3	13	16	43	....	....	....	....
2001-02	Philadelphia	AHL	74	1	13	14	88	....	....	....	....	....	....	....	....	....	5	0	2	2	14	....	....	....	....
2002-03	Philadelphia	AHL	48	4	8	12	122	....	....	....	....	....	....	....	....	....	....	....	....	....	....	....	....	....	....
	Philadelphia	NHL	24	2	1	3	27	0	0	0	22	9.1	9	0	0.0	13:42	8	0	1	1	9	0	0	0	12:42
2003-04	Philadelphia	NHL	23	3	2	5	25	0	0	1	24	12.5	–5	0	0.0	15:47	....	....	....	....	....	....	....	....	....
	Philadelphia	AHL	26	1	6	7	120	....	....	....	....	....	....	....	....	....	....	....	....	....	....	....	....	....	....
	Chicago	NHL	23	2	10	12	58	1	1	0	37	5.4	–6	1	100.0	22:03	....	....	....	....	....	....	....	....	....
2004-05	Norfolk Admirals	AHL	52	3	10	13	164	....	....	....	....	....	....	....	....	....	....	....	....	....	....	....	....	....	....
	NHL Totals		70	7	13	20	110	1	1	1	83	8.4		1	100.0	17:08	8	0	1	1	9	0	0	0	12:42

WHL East First All-Star Team (2001) • Canadian Major Junior Humanitarian Player of the Year (2001)

Signed as a free agent by **Philadelphia**, December 21, 2000. Traded to **Chicago** by **Philadelphia** with the rights to Colin Fraser and Los Angeles' 2nd round choice (previously acquired, Chicago selected Bryan Bickell) in 2004 Entry Draft for Alex Zhamnov and Washington's 4th round choice (previously acquired, Philadelphia selected R.J. Anderson) in 2004 Entry Draft, February 19, 2004.

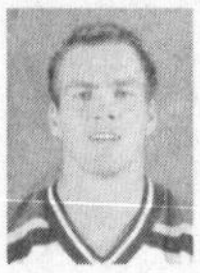

VAN RYN, Mike (VAN RIHN, MIGHK) FLA.

Defense. Shoots right. 6'1", 202 lbs. Born, London, Ont., May 14, 1979. New Jersey's 1st choice, 26th overall, in 1998 Entry Draft.

Season	Club	League	GP	G	A	Pts	PIM	PP	SH	GW	S	%	+/-	TF	F%	Min	GP	G	A	Pts	PIM	PP	SH	GW	Min
1995-96	London Nationals	OHA-B	44	9	14	23	24	....	....	....	....	....	....	....	....	....	....	....	....	....	....	....	....	....	....
1996-97	London Nationals	OHA-B	46	14	31	45	32	....	....	....	....	....	....	....	....	....	....	....	....	....	....	....	....	....	....
1997-98	U. of Michigan	CCHA	38	4	14	18	44	....	....	....	....	....	....	....	....	....	....	....	....	....	....	....	....	....	....
1998-99	U. of Michigan	CCHA	37	10	13	23	52	....	....	....	....	....	....	....	....	....	....	....	....	....	....	....	....	....	....
99-2000	Sarnia Sting	OHL	61	6	35	41	34	....	....	....	....	....	....	....	....	....	7	0	5	5	4	....	....	....	....
2000-01	St. Louis	NHL	1	0	0	0	0	0	0	0	1	0.0	–2	0	0.0	13:43	....	....	....	....	....	....	....	....	....
	Worcester IceCats	AHL	37	3	10	13	12	....	....	....	....	....	....	....	....	....	7	1	1	2	2	....	....	....	....
2001-02	St. Louis	NHL	48	2	8	10	18	0	0	1	52	3.8	10	0	0.0	16:23	9	0	0	0	0	0	0	0	16:04
	Worcester IceCats	AHL	24	2	7	9	17	....	....	....	....	....	....	....	....	....	....	....	....	....	....	....	....	....	....
2002-03	St. Louis	NHL	20	0	3	3	8	0	0	0	21	0.0	3	0	0.0	15:04	....	....	....	....	....	....	....	....	....
	Worcester IceCats	AHL	33	2	8	10	16	....	....	....	....	....	....	....	....	....	....	....	....	....	....	....	....	....	....
	San Antonio	AHL	11	0	3	3	20	....	....	....	....	....	....	....	....	....	3	0	0	0	0	....	....	....	....
2003-04	Florida	NHL	79	13	24	37	52	6	1	0	136	9.6	–16	3	33.3	24:26	....	....	....	....	....	....	....	....	....
2004-05		DID NOT PLAY																							
	NHL Totals		148	15	35	50	78	6	1	1	210	7.1		3	33.3	20:29	9	0	0	0	0	0	0	0	16:04

OJHL-B First All-Star Team (1997)

Signed as a free agent by **St. Louis**, June 30, 2000. • Missed majority of 2000-01 season recovering from shoulder injury suffered in game vs. Phoenix, October 5, 2000. Traded to **Florida** by **St. Louis** for Valeri Bure and Florida's 5th round choice (Nikita Nikitin) in 2004 Entry Draft, March 11, 2003.

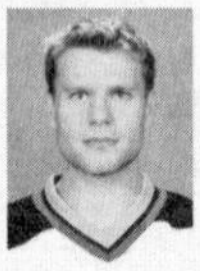

VARADA, Vaclav (vuh-RA-da, VAT-slav) OTT.

Right wing. Shoots left. 6', 208 lbs. Born, Vsetin, Czech., April 26, 1976. San Jose's 4th choice, 89th overall, in 1994 Entry Draft.

Season	Club	League	GP	G	A	Pts	PIM	PP	SH	GW	S	%	+/-	TF	F%	Min	GP	G	A	Pts	PIM	PP	SH	GW	Min
1993-94	HC Vitkovice	CzRep	24	6	7	13	....	....	....	....	....	....	....	....	....	....	5	1	1	2	....	....	....	....	....
1994-95	Tacoma Rockets	WHL	68	50	38	88	108	....	....	....	....	....	....	....	....	....	4	4	3	7	11	....	....	....	....
1995-96	Kelowna Rockets	WHL	59	39	46	85	100	....	....	....	....	....	....	....	....	....	6	3	3	6	16	....	....	....	....
	Buffalo	NHL	1	0	0	0	0	0	0	0	2	0.0	0	....	....	....	....	....	....	....	....	....	....	....	....
	Rochester	AHL	5	3	0	3	4	....	....	....	....	....	....	....	....	....	....	....	....	....	....	....	....	....	....
1996-97	Buffalo	NHL	5	0	0	0	2	0	0	0	2	0.0	0	....	....	....	....	....	....	....	....	....	....	....	....
	Rochester	AHL	53	23	25	48	81	....	....	....	....	....	....	....	....	....	10	1	6	7	27	....	....	....	....
1997-98	Buffalo	NHL	27	5	6	11	15	0	0	1	27	18.5	0	....	....	....	15	3	4	7	18	0	0	0	....
	Rochester	AHL	45	30	26	56	74	....	....	....	....	....	....	....	....	....	....	....	....	....	....	....	....	....	....
1998-99	Buffalo	NHL	72	7	24	31	61	1	0	1	123	5.7	11	1	0.0	14:30	21	5	4	9	14	1	0	0	16:31
99-2000	HC Vitkovice	CzRep	5	2	3	5	12	....	....	....	....	....	....	....	....	....	....	....	....	....	....	....	....	....	....
	Buffalo	NHL	76	10	27	37	62	0	0	0	140	7.1	12	1	0.0	14:58	5	0	0	0	8	0	0	0	14:19
2000-01	Buffalo	NHL	75	10	21	31	81	2	0	2	112	8.9	–2	2	0.0	15:57	13	0	4	4	8	0	0	0	18:08
2001-02	Buffalo	NHL	76	7	16	23	82	1	0	1	138	5.1	–7	3	0.0	16:33	....	....	....	....	....	....	....	....	....
2002-03	Buffalo	NHL	44	7	4	11	23	1	0	0	64	10.9	–2	13	53.9	16:07	....	....	....	....	....	....	....	....	....
	Ottawa	NHL	11	2	6	8	8	1	0	0	17	11.8	3	8	0.0	14:57	18	2	4	6	18	0	0	0	13:57
2003-04	Ottawa	NHL	30	5	5	10	26	0	0	1	47	10.6	2	14	35.7	14:21	7	1	1	2	4	0	0	0	12:03
2004-05	Vitkovice	CzRep	44	8	19	27	83	....	....	....	....	....	....	....	....	....	11	3	3	6	37	....	....	....	....
	NHL Totals		417	53	109	162	360	6	0	6	672	7.9		42	28.6	15:28	79	11	17	28	70	1	0	0	15:28

Traded to **Buffalo** by **San Jose** with Martin Spahnel and Philadelphia's 1st (previously acquired, later traded to Phoenix – Phoenix selected Daniel Briere) and 4th (previously acquired, Buffalo selected Mike Martone) round choices in 1996 Entry Draft for Doug Bodger, November 16, 1995. Traded to **Ottawa** by **Buffalo** with Buffalo's 5th round choice (Tim Cook) in 2003 Entry Draft for Jakub Klepis, February 25, 2003. • Missed majority of 2003-04 season recovering from knee injury suffered in game vs. Boston, December 13, 2003. Signed as a free agent by **Vitkovice** (CzRep), September 17, 2004.

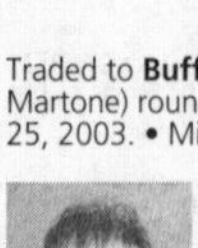

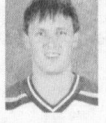

VARLAMOV, Sergei (vahr-LAHM-uhf, SAIR-gay)

Left wing. Shoots left. 5'11", 203 lbs. Born, Kiev, USSR, July 21, 1978.

Season	Club	League	GP	G	A	Pts	PIM	PP	SH	GW	S	%	+/-	TF	F%	Min	GP	G	A	Pts	PIM	PP	SH	GW	Min
1994-95	Nelson	RMJHL	26	11	15	26	56	....	....	....	....	....	....	....	....	....	....	....	....	....	....	....	....	....	....
1995-96	Swift Current	WHL	55	23	21	44	65	....	....	....	....	....	....	....	....	....	....	....	....	....	....	....	....	....	....
1996-97	Swift Current	WHL	72	46	39	85	94	....	....	....	....	....	....	....	....	....	10	3	8	11	10	....	....	....	....
	Saint John Flames	AHL	1	0	0	0	0	....	....	....	....	....	....	....	....	....	....	....	....	....	....	....	....	....	....
1997-98	Swift Current	WHL	72	*66	53	*119	132	....	....	....	....	....	....	....	....	....	12	10	5	15	28	....	....	....	....
	Calgary	NHL	1	0	0	0	0	0	0	0	0	0.0	0	....	....	....	....	....	....	....	....	....	....	....	....
	Saint John Flames	AHL	....	....	....	....	....	....	....	....	....	....	....	....	....	....	3	0	0	0	0	....	....	....	....
1998-99	Saint John Flames	AHL	76	24	33	57	66	....	....	....	....	....	....	....	....	....	7	0	4	4	8	....	....	....	....
99-2000	Calgary	NHL	7	3	0	3	0	0	0	1	11	27.3	0	1	0.0	10:22	....	....	....	....	....	....	....	....	....
	Saint John Flames	AHL	68	20	21	41	88	....	....	....	....	....	....	....	....	....	3	0	0	0	24	....	....	....	....
2000-01	Saint John Flames	AHL	55	21	30	51	56	....	....	....	....	....	....	....	....	....	19	*15	8	23	10	....	....	....	....

			Regular Season														Playoffs								
Season	Club	League	GP	G	A	Pts	PIM	PP	SH	GW	S	%	+/-	TF	F%	Min	GP	G	A	Pts	PIM	PP	SH	GW	Min
2001-02	St. Louis	NHL	52	5	7	12	26	0	0	0	83	6.0	4	1	0.0	11:10	1	0	0	0	2	0	0	0	8:45
	Ukraine	Olympics	2	0	1	1	14	....	....	....	....	....	....	....	....	....	....	....	....	....	....	....	....	....	....
2002-03	Worcester IceCats	AHL	72	23	38	61	79	....	....	....	....	....	....	....	....	....	3	2	0	2	0	....	....	....	....
	St. Louis	NHL	3	0	0	0	0	0	0	0	5	0.0	1	0	0.0	11:26	....	....	....	....	....	....	....	....	....
2003-04	Worcester IceCats	AHL	43	7	16	23	18	....	....	....	....	....	....	....	....	....	....	....	....	....	....	....	....	....	....
	Manitoba Moose	AHL	12	4	2	6	10	....	....	....	....	....	....	....	....	....	....	....	....	....	....	....	....	....	....
2004-05	Ak Bars Kazan	Russia	2	0	0	0	2	....	....	....	....	....	....	....	....	....	....	....	....	....	....	....	....	....	....
	Sibir Novosibirsk	Russia	27	2	2	4	55	....	....	....	....	....	....	....	....	....	....	....	....	....	....	....	....	....	....
	NHL Totals		**63**	**8**	**7**	**15**	**26**	**0**	**0**	**1**	**99**	**8.1**		**2**	**0.0**	**11:06**	**1**	**0**	**0**	**0**	**2**	**0**	**0**	**0**	**8:45**

WHL East First All-Star Team (1998) • WHL Player of the Year (1998) • Canadian Major Junior First All-Star Team (1998) • Canadian Major Junior Player of the Year (1998)

Signed as a free agent by **Calgary**, September 18, 1996. Traded to **St. Louis** by **Calgary** with Fred Brathwaite, Daniel Tkaczuk and Calgary's 9th round choice (Grant Jacobsen) in 2001 Entry Draft for Roman Turek and St. Louis' 4th round choice (Yegor Shastin) in 2001 Entry Draft, June 23, 2001. Traded to **Vancouver** by **St. Louis** for Ryan Ready, March 9, 2004. Signed as a free agent by **Kazan** (Russia), June 13, 2004. Loaned to **Novosibirsk** (Russia) by **Kazan** (Russia), November, 2004.

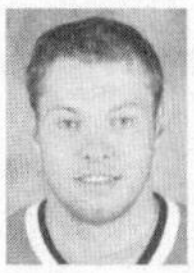

VASICEK, Josef

(VAHSH-ih-chehk, YOH-zehf) **CAR.**

Center. Shoots left. 6'4", 210 lbs. Born, Havlickuv Brod, Czech., September 12, 1980. Carolina's 4th choice, 91st overall, in 1998 Entry Draft.

1995-96	Havl. Brod U17	CzR-U17	36	25	25	50	....	....	....	....	....	....	....	....	....	....	....	....	....	....	....	....	....	....	....
1996-97	Slavia U17	CzR-U17	37	20	40	60	....	....	....	....	....	....	....	....	....	....	....	....	....	....	....	....	....	....	....
1997-98	Slavia Jr.	CzRep-Jr.	34	13	20	33	....	....	....	....	....	....	....	....	....	....	....	....	....	....	....	....	....	....	....
1998-99	Sault Ste. Marie	OHL	66	21	35	56	30	....	....	....	....	....	....	....	....	....	5	3	0	3	10	....	....	....	....
99-2000	Sault Ste. Marie	OHL	54	26	46	72	49	....	....	....	....	....	....	....	....	....	17	5	15	20	8	....	....	....	....
2000-01	Carolina	NHL	76	8	13	21	53	1	0	0	103	7.8	–8	786	46.6	11:49	6	2	0	2	0	0	0	0	13:56
	Cincinnati	IHL	....	....	....	....	....	....	....	....	....	....	....	....	....	....	3	0	0	0	0	....	....	....	....
2001-02	Carolina	NHL	78	14	17	31	53	3	0	3	117	12.0	–7	878	48.3	14:11	23	3	2	5	12	0	0	1	14:50
2002-03	Carolina	NHL	57	10	10	20	33	4	0	1	87	11.5	–19	652	49.5	15:57	....	....	....	....	....	....	....	....	....
2003-04	Carolina	NHL	82	19	26	45	60	6	0	5	161	11.8	–3	262	48.9	17:06	....	....	....	....	....	....	....	....	....
2004-05	HC Slavia Praha	CzRep	52	20	23	43	42	....	....	....	....	....	....	....	....	....	7	1	6	7	10	....	....	....	....
	NHL Totals		**293**	**51**	**66**	**117**	**199**	**14**	**0**	**9**	**468**	**10.9**		**2578**	**48.1**	**14:44**	**29**	**5**	**2**	**7**	**12**	**0**	**0**	**1**	**14:39**

Signed as a free agent by **Slavia** (CzRep), September 17, 2004.

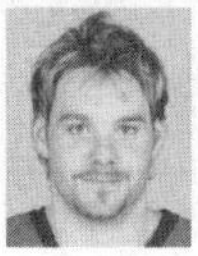

VAUCLAIR, Julien

(voh-KLAIR, JEW-lee-ehn)

Defense. Shoots left. 6', 205 lbs. Born, Delemont, Switz., October 2, 1979. Ottawa's 4th choice, 74th overall, in 1998 Entry Draft.

1995-96	HC Ajoie	Swiss-3	20	4	10	14	....	....	....	....	....	....	....	....	....	....	....	....	....	....	....	....	....	....	....
1996-97	HC Ajoie	Swiss-2	40	0	6	6	24	....	....	....	....	....	....	....	....	....	9	0	2	2	8	....	....	....	....
1997-98	HC Lugano Jr.	Swiss-Jr.	10	7	4	11	10	....	....	....	....	....	....	....	....	....	....	....	....	....	....	....	....	....	....
	HC Lugano	Swiss	36	1	2	3	12	....	....	....	....	....	....	....	....	....	7	0	0	0	25	....	....	....	....
1998-99	HC Lugano	Swiss	38	0	3	3	8	....	....	....	....	....	....	....	....	....	....	....	....	....	....	....	....	....	....
	HC Lugano Jr.	Swiss-Jr.	19	10	14	24	14	....	....	....	....	....	....	....	....	....	1	0	0	0	0	....	....	....	....
99-2000	HC Lugano	Swiss	45	3	3	6	16	....	....	....	....	....	....	....	....	....	14	0	0	0	0	....	....	....	....
	HC Lugano	EuroHL	6	1	0	1	0	....	....	....	....	....	....	....	....	....	4	1	0	1	2	....	....	....	....
2000-01	HC Lugano	Swiss	42	3	4	7	57	....	....	....	....	....	....	....	....	....	18	0	1	1	4	....	....	....	....
2001-02	Grand Rapids	AHL	71	5	14	19	18	....	....	....	....	....	....	....	....	....	4	0	1	1	4	....	....	....	....
	Switzerland	Olympics	4	1	0	1	2	....	....	....	....	....	....	....	....	....	....	....	....	....	....	....	....	....	....
2002-03	Binghamton	AHL	67	6	16	22	30	....	....	....	....	....	....	....	....	....	14	0	1	1	8	....	....	....	....
2003-04	Ottawa	NHL	1	0	0	0	2	0	0	0	0	0.0	1	0	0.0	12:48	....	....	....	....	....	....	....	....	....
	Binghamton	AHL	78	9	30	39	39	....	....	....	....	....	....	....	....	....	2	0	0	0	0	....	....	....	....
2004-05	HC Lugano	Swiss	42	4	7	11	26	....	....	....	....	....	....	....	....	....	3	0	0	0	2	....	....	....	....
	NHL Totals		**1**	**0**	**0**	**0**	**2**	**0**	**0**	**0**	**0**	**0.0**		**0**	**0.0**	**12:48**	....	....	....	....	....	....	....	....	....

Signed as a free agent by **Lugano** (Swiss), May 12, 2004.

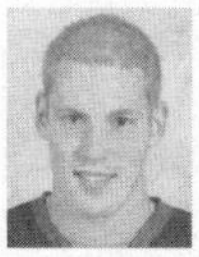

VEILLEUX, Stephane

(VAY-oo, STEH-fan) **MIN.**

Left wing. Shoots left. 6'1", 187 lbs. Born, Beauceville, Que., November 16, 1981. Minnesota's 4th choice, 93rd overall, in 2001 Entry Draft.

1997-98	Beauce-Amiante	QAAA	21	20	17	37	....	....	....	....	....	....	....	....	....	....	....	....	....	....	....	....	....	....	....
	Levis-Lauzon	QAAA	14	3	5	8	....	....	....	....	....	....	....	....	....	....	1	0	0	0	0	....	....	....	....
1998-99	Victoriaville Tigres	QMJHL	65	6	13	19	35	....	....	....	....	....	....	....	....	....	6	1	3	4	2	....	....	....	....
99-2000	Victoriaville Tigres	QMJHL	22	1	4	5	17	....	....	....	....	....	....	....	....	....	....	....	....	....	....	....	....	....	....
	Val-d'Or Foreurs	QMJHL	50	14	28	42	100	....	....	....	....	....	....	....	....	....	....	....	....	....	....	....	....	....	....
2000-01	Val-d'Or Foreurs	QMJHL	68	48	67	115	90	....	....	....	....	....	....	....	....	....	21	15	18	33	42	....	....	....	....
2001-02	Houston Aeros	AHL	77	13	22	35	113	....	....	....	....	....	....	....	....	....	14	2	4	6	20	....	....	....	....
2002-03	Minnesota	NHL	38	3	2	5	23	1	0	0	52	5.8	–6	13	7.7	12:08	....	....	....	....	....	....	....	....	....
	Houston Aeros	AHL	29	8	4	12	43	....	....	....	....	....	....	....	....	....	23	7	11	18	12	....	....	....	....
2003-04	Minnesota	NHL	19	2	8	10	20	1	1	1	37	5.4	0	10	40.0	14:20	....	....	....	....	....	....	....	....	....
	Houston Aeros	AHL	64	13	25	38	66	....	....	....	....	....	....	....	....	....	2	1	1	2	2	....	....	....	....
2004-05	Houston Aeros	AHL	59	15	24	39	35	....	....	....	....	....	....	....	....	....	....	....	....	....	....	....	....	....	....
	NHL Totals		**57**	**5**	**10**	**15**	**43**	**2**	**1**	**1**	**89**	**5.6**		**23**	**21.7**	**12:52**	....	....	....	....	....	....	....	....	....

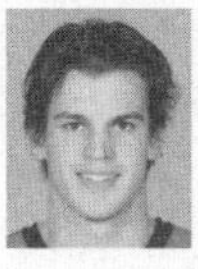

VERMETTE, Antoine

(vuhr-MEHT, AN-twuhn) **OTT.**

Center. Shoots left. 6'1", 184 lbs. Born, St-Agapit, Que., July 20, 1982. Ottawa's 3rd choice, 55th overall, in 2000 Entry Draft.

1997-98	Quebec Select	QAHA	19	11	20	31	36	....	....	....	....	....	....	....	....	....	....	....	....	....	....	....	....	....	....
	Levis-Lauzon	QAAA	8	1	1	2	4	....	....	....	....	....	....	....	....	....	1	0	0	0	0	....	....	....	....
1998-99	Quebec Remparts	QMJHL	57	9	17	26	32	....	....	....	....	....	....	....	....	....	13	0	0	0	2	....	....	....	....
99-2000	Victoriaville Tigres	QMJHL	71	30	41	71	87	....	....	....	....	....	....	....	....	....	6	0	1	1	6	....	....	....	....
2000-01	Victoriaville Tigres	QMJHL	71	57	62	119	102	....	....	....	....	....	....	....	....	....	9	4	6	10	14	....	....	....	....
2001-02	Victoriaville Tigres	QMJHL	4	0	2	2	6	....	....	....	....	....	....	....	....	....	22	10	16	26	10	....	....	....	....
2002-03	Binghamton	AHL	80	34	28	62	57	....	....	....	....	....	....	....	....	....	14	2	9	11	10	....	....	....	....
2003-04	Ottawa	NHL	57	7	7	14	16	0	1	0	63	11.1	5	100	44.0	11:59	4	0	1	1	4	0	0	0	11:35
	Binghamton	AHL	3	0	0	0	6	....	....	....	....	....	....	....	....	....	....	....	....	....	....	....	....	....	....
2004-05	Binghamton	AHL	78	28	45	73	36	....	....	....	....	....	....	....	....	....	6	1	4	5	10	....	....	....	....
	NHL Totals		**57**	**7**	**7**	**14**	**16**	**0**	**1**	**0**	**63**	**11.1**		**100**	**44.0**	**11:59**	**4**	**0**	**1**	**1**	**4**	**0**	**0**	**0**	**11:35**

AHL All-Rookie Team (2003)

• Missed majority of 2001-02 season recovering from neck injury suffered at Team Canada Jr. Selection Camp, June 3, 2001.

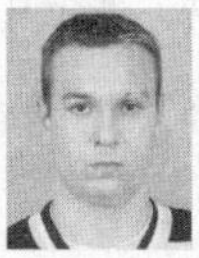

VERNARSKY, Kris

(veh-NAHR-skee, KRIHS)

Center. Shoots left. 6'3", 201 lbs. Born, Detroit, MI, April 5, 1982. Toronto's 2nd choice, 51st overall, in 2000 Entry Draft.

1997-98	USA U-18	USDP	69	11	18	29	97	....	....	....	....	....	....	....	....	....	....	....	....	....	....	....	....	....	....
1998-99	Plymouth Whalers	OHL	45	3	14	17	30	....	....	....	....	....	....	....	....	....	11	0	0	0	2	....	....	....	....
99-2000	Plymouth Whalers	OHL	64	16	22	38	63	....	....	....	....	....	....	....	....	....	19	3	6	9	24	....	....	....	....
2000-01	Plymouth Whalers	OHL	60	14	21	35	35	....	....	....	....	....	....	....	....	....	19	7	10	17	19	....	....	....	....
2001-02	Plymouth Whalers	OHL	59	19	36	55	98	....	....	....	....	....	....	....	....	....	6	1	2	3	15	....	....	....	....
2002-03	Boston	NHL	14	1	0	1	2	0	0	0	18	5.6	–2	22	54.6	10:15	....	....	....	....	....	....	....	....	....
	Providence Bruins	AHL	65	12	15	27	49	....	....	....	....	....	....	....	....	....	4	0	0	0	20	....	....	....	....
2003-04	Boston	NHL	3	0	0	0	0	0	0	0	0	0.0	–1	12	33.3	6:33	....	....	....	....	....	....	....	....	....
	Providence Bruins	AHL	55	8	9	17	61	....	....	....	....	....	....	....	....	....	2	0	0	0	4	....	....	....	....
2004-05	Providence Bruins	AHL	5	0	1	1	2	....	....	....	....	....	....	....	....	....	....	....	....	....	....	....	....	....	....
	Florida Everblades	ECHL	53	16	20	36	47	....	....	....	....	....	....	....	....	....	18	2	7	9	33	....	....	....	....
	NHL Totals		**17**	**1**	**0**	**1**	**2**	**0**	**0**	**0**	**18**	**5.6**		**34**	**47.1**	**9:36**	....	....	....	....	....	....	....	....	....

Rights traded to **Boston** by **Toronto** for Ric Jackman, May 13, 2002.

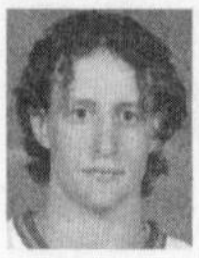

VEROT, Darcy
(vuhr-AWT, DAHR-see)

Left wing. Shoots left. 6', 199 lbs. Born, Radville, Sask., July 13, 1976.

Season	Club	League	GP	G	A	Pts	PIM	PP	SH	GW	S	%	+/-	TF	F%	Min	GP	G	A	Pts	PIM	PP	SH	GW	Min
			Regular Season														Playoffs								
1994-95	Weyburn	SJHL	57	8	18	26	240	....	....	....	....	....	....	....	....	....	16	5	2	7	50	....	....	....	....
1995-96	Weyburn	SJHL	64	15	30	45	191	....	....	....	....	....	....	....	....	....	3	1	0	1	20	....	....	....	....
1996-97	Weyburn	SJHL	61	26	51	77	218	....	....	....	....	....	....	....	....	....	13	3	8	11	24	....	....	....	....
1997-98	Lake Charles	WPHL	68	11	26	37	269	....	....	....	....	....	....	....	....	....	4	0	1	1	25	....	....	....	....
1998-99	Lake Charles	WPHL	68	17	23	40	236	....	....	....	....	....	....	....	....	....	9	2	4	6	53	....	....	....	....
99-2000	Wheeling Nailers	ECHL	44	7	12	19	240	....	....	....	....	....	....	....	....	....	....	....	....	....	....	....	....	....	....
	Wilkes-Barre	AHL	23	5	5	10	96	....	....	....	....	....	....	....	....	....	....	....	....	....	....	....	....	....	....
2000-01	Wilkes-Barre	AHL	78	10	15	25	347	....	....	....	....	....	....	....	....	....	21	2	3	5	40	....	....	....	....
2001-02	Wilkes-Barre	AHL	71	6	10	16	387	....	....	....	....	....	....	....	....	....	....	....	....	....	....	....	....	....	....
2002-03	Saint John Flames	AHL	73	5	11	16	299	....	....	....	....	....	....	....	....	....	....	....	....	....	....	....	....	....	....
2003-04	**Washington**	**NHL**	**37**	**0**	**2**	**2**	**135**	**0**	**0**	**0**	**11**	**0.0**	**–6**	**183**	**48.6**	**8:48**	....	....	....	....	....	....	....	....	....
	Portland Pirates	AHL	28	3	5	8	89	....	....	....	....	....	....	....	....	....	....	....	....	....	....	....	....	....	....
2004-05	Portland Pirates	AHL	36	0	1	1	189	....	....	....	....	....	....	....	....	....	....	....	....	....	....	....	....	....	....
	NHL Totals		**37**	**0**	**2**	**2**	**135**	**0**	**0**	**0**	**11**	**0.0**		**183**	**48.6**	**8:48**	....	....	....	....	....	....	....	....	....

Signed as a free agent by **Wilkes-Barre** (AHL), February 25, 2000. Signed as a free agent by **Pittsburgh**, July 28, 2000. Signed as a free agent by **Calgary**, July 9, 2002. Signed as a free agent by **Washingon**, September 5, 2003.

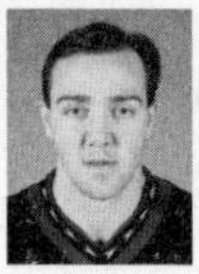

VIGIER, J.P.
(vih-ZHAY, JAY-pee) **ATL.**

Right wing. Shoots right. 6', 200 lbs. Born, Notre Dame de Lourdes, Man., September 11, 1976.

Season	Club	League	GP	G	A	Pts	PIM	PP	SH	GW	S	%	+/-	TF	F%	Min	GP	G	A	Pts	PIM	PP	SH	GW	Min
1995-96	Portage Terriers	MJHL	56	32	49	81	....	....	....	....	....	....	....	....	....	....	....	....	....	....	....	....	....	....	....
1996-97	Northern Mich.	WCHA	36	10	14	24	54	....	....	....	....	....	....	....	....	....	....	....	....	....	....	....	....	....	....
1997-98	Northern Mich.	CCHA	36	12	15	27	60	....	....	....	....	....	....	....	....	....	....	....	....	....	....	....	....	....	....
1998-99	Northern Mich.	CCHA	42	21	18	39	80	....	....	....	....	....	....	....	....	....	....	....	....	....	....	....	....	....	....
99-2000	Northern Mich.	CCHA	39	18	17	35	72	....	....	....	....	....	....	....	....	....	....	....	....	....	....	....	....	....	....
	Orlando	IHL	3	1	0	1	0	....	....	....	....	....	....	....	....	....	....	....	....	....	....	....	....	....	....
2000-01	**Atlanta**	**NHL**	**2**	**0**	**0**	**0**	**0**	**0**	**0**	**0**	**1**	**0.0**	**–2**	**1**	**100.0**	**9:56**	....	....	....	....	....	....	....	....	....
	Orlando	IHL	78	23	17	40	66	....	....	....	....	....	....	....	....	....	16	6	6	12	14	....	....	....	....
2001-02	**Atlanta**	**NHL**	**15**	**4**	**1**	**5**	**4**	**0**	**0**	**0**	**18**	**22.2**	**–5**	**3**	**66.7**	**13:13**	....	....	....	....	....	....	....	....	....
	Chicago Wolves	AHL	62	25	16	41	26	....	....	....	....	....	....	....	....	....	21	7	7	14	20	....	....	....	....
2002-03	**Atlanta**	**NHL**	**13**	**0**	**0**	**0**	**4**	**0**	**0**	**0**	**21**	**0.0**	**–13**	**1**	**0.0**	**14:07**	....	....	....	....	....	....	....	....	....
	Chicago Wolves	AHL	63	29	27	56	54	....	....	....	....	....	....	....	....	....	9	3	1	4	4	....	....	....	....
2003-04	**Atlanta**	**NHL**	**70**	**10**	**8**	**18**	**22**	**2**	**2**	**3**	**110**	**9.1**	**–18**	**53**	**47.2**	**14:36**	....	....	....	....	....	....	....	....	....
2004-05	Chicago Wolves	AHL	76	29	41	70	56	....	....	....	....	....	....	....	....	....	18	5	6	11	19	....	....	....	....
	NHL Totals		**100**	**14**	**9**	**23**	**30**	**2**	**2**	**3**	**150**	**9.3**		**58**	**48.3**	**14:14**	....	....	....	....	....	....	....	....	....

CCHA Second All-Star Team (1999) • CCHA All-Tournament Team (1999) • AHL Second All-Star Team (2005)

Signed as a free agent by **Atlanta**, April 20, 2000.

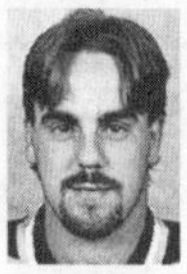

VIRTUE, Terry
(VIR-too, TAIR-ee)

Defense. Shoots right. 6', 198 lbs. Born, Scarborough, Ont., August 12, 1970.

Season	Club	League	GP	G	A	Pts	PIM	PP	SH	GW	S	%	+/-	TF	F%	Min	GP	G	A	Pts	PIM	PP	SH	GW	Min
1988-89	Hobbema Hawks	AJHL	56	6	31	37	339	....	....	....	....	....	....	....	....	....	....	....	....	....	....	....	....	....	....
	Victoria Cougars	WHL	8	1	1	2	13	....	....	....	....	....	....	....	....	....	....	....	....	....	....	....	....	....	....
1989-90	Victoria Cougars	WHL	24	1	9	10	85	....	....	....	....	....	....	....	....	....	....	....	....	....	....	....	....	....	....
	Tri-City	WHL	34	1	10	11	82	....	....	....	....	....	....	....	....	....	6	0	0	0	30	....	....	....	....
1990-91	Tri-City	WHL	11	1	8	9	24	....	....	....	....	....	....	....	....	....	....	....	....	....	....	....	....	....	....
	Portland	WHL	59	9	44	53	127	....	....	....	....	....	....	....	....	....	....	....	....	....	....	....	....	....	....
1991-92	Roanoke Valley	ECHL	38	4	22	26	165	....	....	....	....	....	....	....	....	....	....	....	....	....	....	....	....	....	....
	Louisville	ECHL	23	1	15	16	58	....	....	....	....	....	....	....	....	....	13	0	8	8	49	....	....	....	....
1992-93	Louisville	ECHL	28	0	17	17	84	....	....	....	....	....	....	....	....	....	....	....	....	....	....	....	....	....	....
	Wheeling	ECHL	31	3	15	18	86	....	....	....	....	....	....	....	....	....	16	3	5	8	18	....	....	....	....
1993-94	Wheeling	ECHL	34	5	28	33	61	....	....	....	....	....	....	....	....	....	6	2	2	4	4	....	....	....	....
	Cape Breton	AHL	26	4	6	10	10	....	....	....	....	....	....	....	....	....	5	0	0	0	17	....	....	....	....
1994-95	Worcester IceCats	AHL	73	14	25	39	183	....	....	....	....	....	....	....	....	....	....	....	....	....	....	....	....	....	....
	Atlanta Knights	IHL	1	0	0	0	2	....	....	....	....	....	....	....	....	....	....	....	....	....	....	....	....	....	....
1995-96	Worcester IceCats	AHL	76	7	31	38	234	....	....	....	....	....	....	....	....	....	4	0	0	0	4	....	....	....	....
1996-97	Worcester IceCats	AHL	80	16	26	42	220	....	....	....	....	....	....	....	....	....	5	0	4	4	8	....	....	....	....
1997-98	Worcester IceCats	AHL	74	8	26	34	233	....	....	....	....	....	....	....	....	....	11	1	4	5	41	....	....	....	....
1998-99	**Boston**	**NHL**	**4**	**0**	**0**	**0**	**0**	**0**	**0**	**0**	**2**	**0.0**	**2**	**0**	**0.0**	**9:41**	....	....	....	....	....	....	....	....	....
	Providence Bruins	AHL	76	8	48	56	117	....	....	....	....	....	....	....	....	....	17	2	12	14	29	....	....	....	....
99-2000	**NY Rangers**	**NHL**	**1**	**0**	**0**	**0**	**0**	**0**	**0**	**0**	**2**	**0.0**	**–2**	**0**	**0.0**	**12:32**	....	....	....	....	....	....	....	....	....
	Hartford	AHL	67	5	22	27	166	....	....	....	....	....	....	....	....	....	23	3	7	10	51	....	....	....	....
2000-01	Hartford	AHL	71	5	24	29	166	....	....	....	....	....	....	....	....	....	5	1	0	1	2	....	....	....	....
2001-02	Hartford	AHL	76	4	20	24	117	....	....	....	....	....	....	....	....	....	10	0	1	1	19	....	....	....	....
2002-03	Worcester IceCats	AHL	78	5	30	35	144	....	....	....	....	....	....	....	....	....	....	....	....	....	....	....	....	....	....
2003-04	Worcester IceCats	AHL	74	6	16	22	66	....	....	....	....	....	....	....	....	....	10	1	4	5	36	....	....	....	....
2004-05	Springfield	AHL	13	1	1	2	21	....	....	....	....	....	....	....	....	....	....	....	....	....	....	....	....	....	....
	Utah Grizzlies	AHL	65	3	18	21	112	....	....	....	....	....	....	....	....	....	....	....	....	....	....	....	....	....	....
	NHL Totals		**5**	**0**	**0**	**0**	**0**	**0**	**0**	**0**	**4**	**0.0**		**0**	**0.0**	**10:15**	....	....	....	....	....	....	....	....	....

AHL Second All-Star Team (1999)

Signed as a free agent by **St. Louis**, January 29, 1996. Signed as a free agent by **Boston**, August 28, 1998. Signed as a free agent by **NY Rangers**, July 29, 1999. Signed as a free agent by **St. Louis**, July 14, 2002. Signed as a free agent by **Springfield** (AHL), July 30, 2004. Loaned to **Utah** (AHL) by **Springfield** (AHL) for cash, November 22, 2004.

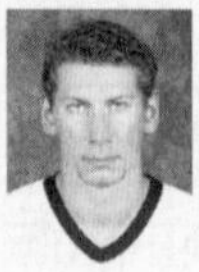

VISHNEVSKI, Vitaly
(vihsh-NEHV-skee, vih-TAL-ee) **ANA.**

Defense. Shoots left. 6'2", 203 lbs. Born, Kharkov, USSR, March 18, 1980. Anaheim's 1st choice, 5th overall, in 1998 Entry Draft.

Season	Club	League	GP	G	A	Pts	PIM	PP	SH	GW	S	%	+/-	TF	F%	Min	GP	G	A	Pts	PIM	PP	SH	GW	Min
1995-96	Yaroslavl 2	CIS-2	40	4	4	8	20	....	....	....	....	....	....	....	....	....	....	....	....	....	....	....	....	....	....
1996-97	Yaroslavl 2	Russia-3	45	0	2	2	30	....	....	....	....	....	....	....	....	....	....	....	....	....	....	....	....	....	....
1997-98	Yaroslavl 2	Russia-2	47	8	9	17	164	....	....	....	....	....	....	....	....	....	....	....	....	....	....	....	....	....	....
1998-99	Yaroslavl	Russia	34	3	4	7	38	....	....	....	....	....	....	....	....	....	10	0	0	0	4	....	....	....	....
99-2000	**Anaheim**	**NHL**	**31**	**1**	**1**	**2**	**26**	**1**	**0**	**0**	**17**	**5.9**	**0**	**0**	**0.0**	**16:38**	....	....	....	....	....	....	....	....	....
	Cincinnati	AHL	35	1	3	4	45	....	....	....	....	....	....	....	....	....	....	....	....	....	....	....	....	....	....
2000-01	**Anaheim**	**NHL**	**76**	**1**	**10**	**11**	**99**	**0**	**0**	**0**	**49**	**2.0**	**–1**	**0**	**0.0**	**19:14**	....	....	....	....	....	....	....	....	....
2001-02	**Anaheim**	**NHL**	**74**	**0**	**3**	**3**	**60**	**0**	**0**	**0**	**54**	**0.0**	**–10**	**0**	**0.0**	**17:36**	....	....	....	....	....	....	....	....	....
2002-03	**Anaheim**	**NHL**	**80**	**2**	**6**	**8**	**76**	**0**	**1**	**0**	**65**	**3.1**	**–8**	**0**	**0.0**	**14:10**	**21**	**0**	**1**	**1**	**6**	**0**	**0**	**0**	**10:02**
2003-04	**Anaheim**	**NHL**	**73**	**6**	**10**	**16**	**51**	**0**	**0**	**0**	**86**	**7.0**	**0**	**0**	**0.0**	**17:10**	....	....	....	....	....	....	....	....	....
2004-05	Voskresensk	Russia	51	7	17	24	92	....	....	....	....	....	....	....	....	....	....	....	....	....	....	....	....	....	....
	NHL Totals		**334**	**10**	**30**	**40**	**312**	**1**	**1**	**0**	**271**	**3.7**		**0**	**0.0**	**16:58**	**21**	**0**	**1**	**1**	**6**	**0**	**0**	**0**	**10:02**

Signed as a free agent by **Voskresensk** (Russia), August 25, 2004.

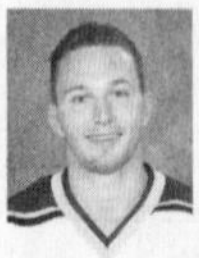

VISNOVSKY, Lubomir
(vihsh-NAWV-skee, LOO-boh-mihr) **L.A.**

Defense. Shoots left. 5'10", 188 lbs. Born, Topolcany, Czech., August 11, 1976. Los Angeles' 4th choice, 118th overall, in 2000 Entry Draft.

Season	Club	League	GP	G	A	Pts	PIM	PP	SH	GW	S	%	+/-	TF	F%	Min	GP	G	A	Pts	PIM	PP	SH	GW	Min
1994-95	Bratislava	Slovakia	36	11	12	23	10	....	....	....	....	....	....	....	....	....	9	1	3	4	2	....	....	....	....
1995-96	Bratislava	Slovakia	35	8	6	14	22	....	....	....	....	....	....	....	....	....	13	1	5	6	2	....	....	....	....
1996-97	Bratislava	Slovakia	44	11	12	23	....	....	....	....	....	....	....	....	....	....	2	0	1	1	....	....	....	....	....
	Bratislava	EuroHL	6	3	1	4	2	....	....	....	....	....	....	....	....	....	2	0	0	0	6	....	....	....	....
1997-98	Bratislava	Slovakia	36	7	9	16	16	....	....	....	....	....	....	....	....	....	11	2	4	6	8	....	....	....	....
	Bratislava	EuroHL	6	1	0	1	4	....	....	....	....	....	....	....	....	....	....	....	....	....	....	....	....	....	....
1998-99	Bratislava	Slovakia	40	9	10	19	31	....	....	....	....	....	....	....	....	....	10	5	5	10	0	....	....	....	....
	Bratislava	EuroHL	6	0	3	3	4	....	....	....	....	....	....	....	....	....	....	....	....	....	....	....	....	....	....
99-2000	Bratislava	Slovakia	52	21	24	45	38	....	....	....	....	....	....	....	....	....	8	5	3	8	16	....	....	....	....
2000-01	**Los Angeles**	**NHL**	**81**	**7**	**32**	**39**	**36**	**3**	**0**	**3**	**105**	**6.7**	**16**	**0**	**0.0**	**16:58**	**8**	**0**	**0**	**0**	**0**	**0**	**0**	**0**	**13:57**
2001-02	**Los Angeles**	**NHL**	**72**	**4**	**17**	**21**	**14**	**1**	**0**	**2**	**95**	**4.2**	**–5**	**0**	**0.0**	**16:15**	**4**	**0**	**1**	**1**	**0**	**0**	**0**	**0**	**8:22**
	Slovakia	Olympics	3	1	2	3	0	....	....	....	....	....	....	....	....	....	....	....	....	....	....	....	....	....	....
2002-03	**Los Angeles**	**NHL**	**57**	**8**	**16**	**24**	**28**	**1**	**0**	**1**	**85**	**9.4**	**2**	**0**	**0.0**	**19:20**	....	....	....	....	....	....	....	....	....

			Regular Season														Playoffs								
Season	Club	League	GP	G	A	Pts	PIM	PP	SH	GW	S	%	+/-	TF	F%	Min	GP	G	A	Pts	PIM	PP	SH	GW	Min
2003-04	**Los Angeles**	**NHL**	**58**	**8**	**21**	**29**	**26**	**5**	**0**	**0**	**114**	**7.0**	**8**	**0**	**0.0**	**24:02**	....	....	....	....	....	....	....	....	....
2004-05	Bratislava	Slovakia	43	13	25	38	40	....	....	....	....	....	....	....	....	....	14	2	10	12	10	....	....	....	....
	NHL Totals		**268**	**27**	**86**	**113**	**104**	**10**	**0**	**6**	**399**	**6.8**		**0**	**0.0**	**18:49**	**12**	**0**	**1**	**1**	**0**	**0**	**0**	**0**	**12:05**

NHL All-Rookie Team (2001)
Signed as a free agent by **Bratislava** (Slovakia), September 27, 2004.

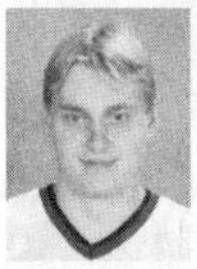

VOLCHENKOV, Anton

(vohl-chen-KAHF, AN-tawn) **OTT.**

Defense. Shoots left. 6'1", 227 lbs. Born, Moscow, USSR, February 25, 1982. Ottawa's 1st choice, 21st overall, in 2000 Entry Draft.

99-2000	HK Moscow 2	Russia-3	6	0	1	1	10	....	....	....	....	....	....	....	....	....	....	....	....	....	....	....	....	....	....
	HK Moscow	Russia-2	30	2	9	11	36	....	....	....	....	....	....	....	....	....	....	....	....	....	....	....	....	....	....
2000-01	Krylja Sovetov	Russia-2	34	3	4	7	56	....	....	....	....	....	....	....	....	....	....	....	....	....	....	....	....	....	....
2001-02	Krylja Sovetov 2	Russia-3	1	0	0	0	0	....	....	....	....	....	....	....	....	....	....	....	....	....	....	....	....	....	....
	Krylja Sovetov	Russia	47	4	16	20	50	....	....	....	....	....	....	....	....	....	3	0	0	0	29	....	....	....	....
2002-03	**Ottawa**	**NHL**	**57**	**3**	**13**	**16**	**40**	**0**	**0**	**0**	**75**	**4.0**	**–4**	**0**	**0.0**	**15:30**	**17**	**1**	**1**	**2**	**4**	**0**	**0**	**1**	**13:31**
2003-04	**Ottawa**	**NHL**	**19**	**1**	**2**	**3**	**8**	**0**	**0**	**0**	**15**	**6.7**	**1**	**0**	**0.0**	**13:04**	**5**	**0**	**0**	**0**	**6**	**0**	**0**	**0**	**11:52**
2004-05	Binghamton	AHL	69	10	35	45	62	....	....	....	....	....	....	....	....	....	6	0	3	3	0	....	....	....	....
	NHL Totals		**76**	**4**	**15**	**19**	**48**	**0**	**0**	**0**	**90**	**4.4**		**0**	**0.0**	**14:54**	**22**	**1**	**1**	**2**	**10**	**0**	**0**	**1**	**13:09**

• Missed majority of 2003-04 season recovering from shoulder injury suffered in game vs. Boston, December 8, 2003.

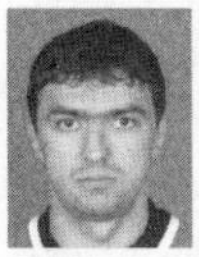

VOROBIEV, Pavel

(voh-roh-BEE-ehf, PAH-vehl) **CHI.**

Right wing. Shoots left. 6', 194 lbs. Born, Karaganda, USSR, May 5, 1982. Chicago's 2nd choice, 11th overall, in 2000 Entry Draft.

1996-97	Molot Perm 2	Russia-3	2	0	0	0	0	....	....	....	....	....	....	....	....	....	....	....	....	....	....	....	....	....	....
1997-98	Yaroslavl 2	Russia-2	16	2	0	2	6	....	....	....	....	....	....	....	....	....	....	....	....	....	....	....	....	....	....
1998-99	Yaroslavl 2	Russia-3	17	0	1	1	0	....	....	....	....	....	....	....	....	....	....	....	....	....	....	....	....	....	....
99-2000	Yaroslavl 2	Russia-3	40	19	15	34	20	....	....	....	....	....	....	....	....	....	....	....	....	....	....	....	....	....	....
	Yaroslavl	Russia	8	2	0	2	4	....	....	....	....	....	....	....	....	....	10	2	2	4	0	....	....	....	....
2000-01	Yaroslavl	Russia	36	8	8	16	28	....	....	....	....	....	....	....	....	....	10	4	1	5	8	....	....	....	....
2001-02	Yaroslavl	Russia	9	3	2	5	6	....	....	....	....	....	....	....	....	....	7	0	0	0	4	....	....	....	....
2002-03	Yaroslavl	Russia	44	10	18	28	10	....	....	....	....	....	....	....	....	....	7	0	1	1	2	....	....	....	....
2003-04	**Chicago**	**NHL**	**18**	**1**	**3**	**4**	**4**	**1**	**0**	**1**	**20**	**5.0**	**1**	**0**	**0.0**	**12:48**	....	....	....	....	....	....	....	....	....
	Norfolk Admirals	AHL	57	13	16	29	8	....	....	....	....	....	....	....	....	....	4	0	0	0	0	....	....	....	....
2004-05	Norfolk Admirals	AHL	79	19	25	44	48	....	....	....	....	....	....	....	....	....	6	2	1	3	4	....	....	....	....
	NHL Totals		**18**	**1**	**3**	**4**	**4**	**1**	**0**	**1**	**20**	**5.0**		**0**	**0.0**	**12:48**	....	....	....	....	....	....	....	....	....

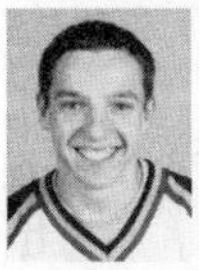

VRBATA, Radim

(vuhr-BA-tuh, RA-dihm) **CAR.**

Right wing. Shoots right. 6'1", 190 lbs. Born, Mlada Boleslav, Czech., June 13, 1981. Colorado's 10th choice, 212th overall, in 1999 Entry Draft.

1997-98	Ml. Boleslav Jr.	CzRep-Jr.	35	42	31	73	4	....	....	....	....	....	....	....	....	....	....	....	....	....	....	....	....	....	....
1998-99	Hull Olympiques	QMJHL	54	22	38	60	16	....	....	....	....	....	....	....	....	....	23	6	13	19	6	....	....	....	....
99-2000	Hull Olympiques	QMJHL	58	29	45	74	26	....	....	....	....	....	....	....	....	....	15	3	9	12	8	....	....	....	....
2000-01	Shawinigan	QMJHL	55	56	64	120	67	....	....	....	....	....	....	....	....	....	10	4	7	11	4	....	....	....	....
	Hershey Bears	AHL	....	....	....	....	....	....	....	....	....	....	....	....	....	....	1	0	1	1	2	....	....	....	....
2001-02	**Colorado**	**NHL**	**52**	**18**	**12**	**30**	**14**	**6**	**0**	**3**	**112**	**16.1**	**7**	**8**	**37.5**	**14:32**	**9**	**0**	**0**	**0**	**0**	**0**	**0**	**0**	**13:05**
	Hershey Bears	AHL	20	8	14	22	8	....	....	....	....	....	....	....	....	....	....	....	....	....	....	....	....	....	....
2002-03	**Colorado**	**NHL**	**66**	**11**	**19**	**30**	**16**	**3**	**0**	**4**	**171**	**6.4**	**0**	**14**	**50.0**	**13:55**	....	....	....	....	....	....	....	....	....
	Carolina	**NHL**	**10**	**5**	**0**	**5**	**2**	**3**	**0**	**0**	**44**	**11.4**	**–7**	**15**	**46.7**	**19:00**	....	....	....	....	....	....	....	....	....
2003-04	**Carolina**	**NHL**	**80**	**12**	**13**	**25**	**24**	**4**	**0**	**2**	**195**	**6.2**	**–10**	**21**	**38.1**	**13:42**	....	....	....	....	....	....	....	....	....
2004-05	Liberec	CzRep	45	18	21	39	91	....	....	....	....	....	....	....	....	....	12	3	2	5	0	....	....	....	....
	NHL Totals		**208**	**46**	**44**	**90**	**56**	**16**	**0**	**9**	**522**	**8.8**		**58**	**43.1**	**14:14**	**9**	**0**	**0**	**0**	**0**	**0**	**0**	**0**	**13:05**

QMJHL First All-Star Team (2001)
Traded to **Carolina** by **Colorado** for Bates Battaglia, March 11, 2003. Signed as a free agent by **Liberec** (CzRep), September 4, 2004.

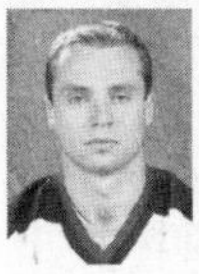

VYBORNY, David

(vih-BOHR-nee, DAY-vihd) **CBJ**

Right wing. Shoots left. 5'10", 189 lbs. Born, Jihlava, Czech., June 2, 1975. Edmonton's 3rd choice, 33rd overall, in 1993 Entry Draft.

1991-92	HC Sparta Praha	Czech	32	6	9	15	2	....	....	....	....	....	....	....	....	....	....	....	....	....	....	....	....	....	....
1992-93	HC Sparta Praha	Czech	52	20	24	44	....	....	....	....	....	....	....	....	....	....	....	....	....	....	....	....	....	....	....
1993-94	HC Sparta Praha	CzRep	44	15	20	35	0	....	....	....	....	....	....	....	....	....	6	4	7	11	0	....	....	....	....
1994-95	Cape Breton	AHL	76	23	38	61	30	....	....	....	....	....	....	....	....	....	....	....	....	....	....	....	....	....	....
1995-96	HC Sparta Praha	CzRep	40	12	18	30	....	....	....	....	....	....	....	....	....	....	12	6	5	11	....	....	....	....	....
1996-97	HC Sparta Praha	CzRep	47	20	29	49	14	....	....	....	....	....	....	....	....	....	10	7	7	14	6	....	....	....	....
1997-98	MoDo	Sweden	45	16	21	37	34	....	....	....	....	....	....	....	....	....	9	0	2	2	2	....	....	....	....
1998-99	HC Sparta Praha	CzRep	52	24	*46	*70	22	....	....	....	....	....	....	....	....	....	8	1	3	4	....	....	....	....	....
99-2000	HC Sparta Praha	CzRep	50	25	38	63	30	....	....	....	....	....	....	....	....	....	9	3	*8	*11	4	....	....	....	....
2000-01	**Columbus**	**NHL**	**79**	**13**	**19**	**32**	**22**	**5**	**0**	**1**	**125**	**10.4**	**–9**	**36**	**44.4**	**15:25**	....	....	....	....	....	....	....	....	....
2001-02	**Columbus**	**NHL**	**75**	**13**	**18**	**31**	**6**	**6**	**0**	**2**	**103**	**12.6**	**–14**	**25**	**44.0**	**15:27**	....	....	....	....	....	....	....	....	....
2002-03	**Columbus**	**NHL**	**79**	**20**	**26**	**46**	**16**	**4**	**1**	**4**	**125**	**16.0**	**12**	**46**	**32.6**	**16:20**	....	....	....	....	....	....	....	....	....
2003-04	**Columbus**	**NHL**	**82**	**22**	**31**	**53**	**40**	**8**	**4**	**2**	**158**	**13.9**	**–26**	**97**	**21.7**	**20:23**	....	....	....	....	....	....	....	....	....
2004-05	HC Sparta Praha	CzRep	51	12	34	46	10	....	....	....	....	....	....	....	....	....	5	2	5	7	4	....	....	....	....
	NHL Totals		**315**	**68**	**94**	**162**	**84**	**23**	**5**	**9**	**511**	**13.3**		**204**	**30.9**	**16:57**	....	....	....	....	....	....	....	....	....

Signed as a free agent by **Columbus**, June 8, 2000. Signed as a free agent by **Sparta** (CzRep), August 9, 2004.

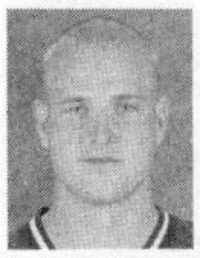

WALKER, Matt

(WAH-kuhr, MAT) **ST.L.**

Defense. Shoots right. 6'3", 227 lbs. Born, Beaverlodge, Alta., April 7, 1980. St. Louis' 3rd choice, 83rd overall, in 1998 Entry Draft.

1996-97	Grand Prairie	AAHA	68	22	62	74	186	....	....	....	....	....	....	....	....	....	....	....	....	....	....	....	....	....	....
1997-98	Portland	WHL	64	2	13	15	124	....	....	....	....	....	....	....	....	....	16	0	0	0	21	....	....	....	....
1998-99	Portland	WHL	64	1	10	11	151	....	....	....	....	....	....	....	....	....	4	0	1	1	6	....	....	....	....
99-2000	Portland	WHL	38	2	7	9	97	....	....	....	....	....	....	....	....	....	....	....	....	....	....	....	....	....	....
	Kootenay Ice	WHL	31	4	19	23	53	....	....	....	....	....	....	....	....	....	21	5	13	18	24	....	....	....	....
2000-01	Worcester IceCats	AHL	61	4	8	12	131	....	....	....	....	....	....	....	....	....	11	0	0	0	6	....	....	....	....
	Peoria Rivermen	ECHL	8	1	0	1	70	....	....	....	....	....	....	....	....	....	....	....	....	....	....	....	....	....	....
2001-02	Worcester IceCats	AHL	49	2	11	13	164	....	....	....	....	....	....	....	....	....	3	0	0	0	8	....	....	....	....
2002-03	**St. Louis**	**NHL**	**16**	**0**	**1**	**1**	**38**	**0**	**0**	**0**	**13**	**0.0**	**0**	**1**	**100.0**	**11:09**	....	....	....	....	....	....	....	....	....
	Worcester IceCats	AHL	40	1	8	9	58	....	....	....	....	....	....	....	....	....	....	....	....	....	....	....	....	....	....
2003-04	**St. Louis**	**NHL**	**14**	**0**	**1**	**1**	**25**	**0**	**0**	**0**	**8**	**0.0**	**0**	**0**	**0.0**	**11:23**	**4**	**0**	**0**	**0**	**0**	**0**	**0**	**0**	**9:43**
	Worcester IceCats	AHL	4	0	1	1	7	....	....	....	....	....	....	....	....	....	....	....	....	....	....	....	....	....	....
2004-05	Worcester IceCats	AHL	20	2	4	6	44	....	....	....	....	....	....	....	....	....	....	....	....	....	....	....	....	....	....
	NHL Totals		**30**	**0**	**2**	**2**	**63**	**0**	**0**	**0**	**21**	**0.0**		**1**	**100.0**	**11:15**	**4**	**0**	**0**	**0**	**0**	**0**	**0**	**0**	**9:43**

• Missed majority of 2003-04 season recovering from groin injury suffered in training camp, September 23, 2003.

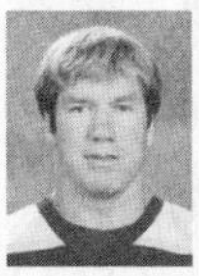

WALKER, Scott

(WAH-kuhr, SKAWT) **NSH.**

Right wing. Shoots right. 5'10", 196 lbs. Born, Cambridge, Ont., July 19, 1973. Vancouver's 4th choice, 124th overall, in 1993 Entry Draft.

1989-90	Kitchener	OHA-B	6	0	5	5	4	....	....	....	....	....	....	....	....	....	....	....	....	....	....	....	....	....	....
	Cambridge	OHA-B	27	7	22	29	87	....	....	....	....	....	....	....	....	....	....	....	....	....	....	....	....	....	....
1990-91	Cambridge	OHA-B	45	10	27	37	241	....	....	....	....	....	....	....	....	....	....	....	....	....	....	....	....	....	....
1991-92	Owen Sound	OHL	53	7	31	38	128	....	....	....	....	....	....	....	....	....	5	0	7	7	8	....	....	....	....
1992-93	Owen Sound	OHL	57	23	68	91	110	....	....	....	....	....	....	....	....	....	8	1	5	6	16	....	....	....	....
1993-94	Hamilton	AHL	77	10	29	39	272	....	....	....	....	....	....	....	....	....	4	0	1	1	25	....	....	....	....
1994-95	Syracuse Crunch	AHL	74	14	38	52	334	....	....	....	....	....	....	....	....	....	....	....	....	....	....	....	....	....	....
	Vancouver	**NHL**	**11**	**0**	**1**	**1**	**33**	**0**	**0**	**0**	**8**	**0.0**	**0**	....	....	....	....	....	....	....	....	....	....	....	....
1995-96	**Vancouver**	**NHL**	**63**	**4**	**8**	**12**	**137**	**0**	**1**	**1**	**45**	**8.9**	**–7**	....	....	....	....	....	....	....	....	....	....	....	....
	Syracuse Crunch	AHL	15	3	12	15	52	....	....	....	....	....	....	....	....	....	16	9	8	17	39	....	....	....	....
1996-97	**Vancouver**	**NHL**	**64**	**3**	**15**	**18**	**132**	**0**	**0**	**0**	**55**	**5.5**	**2**	....	....	....	....	....	....	....	....	....	....	....	....

			Regular Season														Playoffs								
Season	Club	League	GP	G	A	Pts	PIM	PP	SH	GW	S	%	+/-	TF	F%	Min	GP	G	A	Pts	PIM	PP	SH	GW	Min
1997-98	Vancouver	NHL	59	3	10	13	164	0	1	1	40	7.5	–8	....	....	....	....	....	....	....	....	....	....	....	....
1998-99	Nashville	NHL	71	15	25	40	103	0	1	2	96	15.6	0	265	48.3	16:21	....	....	....	....	....	....	....	....	....
99-2000	Nashville	NHL	69	7	21	28	90	0	1	0	98	7.1	–16	30	36.7	15:49	....	....	....	....	....	....	....	....	....
2000-01	Nashville	NHL	74	25	29	54	66	9	3	1	159	15.7	–2	541	51.4	19:17	....	....	....	....	....	....	....	....	....
2001-02	Nashville	NHL	28	4	5	9	18	1	0	0	46	8.7	–13	149	38.9	18:38	....	....	....	....	....	....	....	....	....
2002-03	Nashville	NHL	60	15	18	33	58	7	0	5	124	12.1	2	336	49.1	19:50	....	....	....	....	....	....	....	....	....
2003-04	Nashville	NHL	75	25	42	67	94	9	3	3	157	15.9	4	367	41.4	20:03	6	0	1	1	6	0	0	0	20:10
2004-05	Cambridge	OHA-Sr.	5	2	6	8	4	....	....	....	....	....	....	....	....	....	....	....	....	....	....	....	....	....	....
	Dundas	OHA-Sr.	3	3	2	5	8	....	....	....	....	....	....	....	....	....	....	....	....	....	....	....	....	....	....
	NHL Totals		574	101	174	275	895	26	10	13	828	12.2		1688	46.9	18:17	6	0	1	1	6	0	0	0	20:10

OHL Second All-Star Team (1993)

Claimed by **Nashville** from **Vancouver** in Expansion Draft, June 26, 1998. Signed as a free agent by **Cambridge** (OHA-Sr.), October 21, 2004. Signed as a free agent by **Dundas** (OHA-Sr.), February 10, 2005.

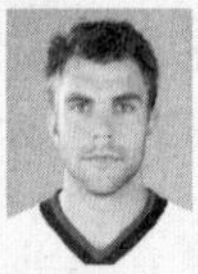

WALLIN, Niclas
(VAH-lihn, NIH-kluhs) **CAR.**

Defense. Shoots left. 6'3", 220 lbs. Born, Boden, Sweden, February 20, 1975. Carolina's 3rd choice, 97th overall, in 2000 Entry Draft.

Season	Club	League	GP	G	A	Pts	PIM	PP	SH	GW	S	%	+/-	TF	F%	Min	GP	G	A	Pts	PIM	PP	SH	GW	Min
1994-95	Bodens IK	Swe-Jr.	30	2	13	15	125	....	....	....	....	....	....	....	....	....	....	....	....	....	....	....	....	....	....
	Bodens IK	Sweden-2	13	0	0	0	0	....	....	....	....	....	....	....	....	....	2	0	0	0	0	....	....	....	....
1995-96	Bodens IK	Swe-Jr.	2	2	2	4	0	....	....	....	....	....	....	....	....	....	....	....	....	....	....	....	....	....	....
	Bodens IK	Sweden-2	30	2	7	9	26	....	....	....	....	....	....	....	....	....	2	0	1	1	2	....	....	....	....
1996-97	Brynas IF Gavle	Sweden	47	1	1	2	14	....	....	....	....	....	....	....	....	....	....	....	....	....	....	....	....	....	....
1997-98	Brynas IF Gavle	Sweden	44	2	3	5	57	....	....	....	....	....	....	....	....	....	3	0	1	1	4	....	....	....	....
1998-99	Brynas IF Gavle	Sweden	46	2	4	6	52	....	....	....	....	....	....	....	....	....	14	0	1	1	8	....	....	....	....
99-2000	Brynas IF Gavle	Sweden	48	7	9	16	73	....	....	....	....	....	....	....	....	....	11	2	1	3	14	....	....	....	....
	Brynas IF Gavle	EuroHL	5	1	1	2	10	....	....	....	....	....	....	....	....	....	....	....	....	....	....	....	....	....	....
2000-01	Carolina	NHL	37	2	3	5	21	0	0	0	19	10.5	–11	0	0.0	14:57	3	0	0	0	2	0	0	0	19:10
	Cincinnati	IHL	8	1	2	3	4	....	....	....	....	....	....	....	....	....	3	0	0	0	2	....	....	....	....
2001-02	Carolina	NHL	52	1	2	3	36	0	0	0	33	3.0	1	0	0.0	12:12	23	2	1	3	12	0	0	2	15:26
2002-03	Carolina	NHL	77	2	8	10	71	0	0	2	69	2.9	–19	0	0.0	16:12	....	....	....	....	....	....	....	....	....
2003-04	Carolina	NHL	57	3	7	10	51	0	0	0	74	4.1	–8	0	0.0	18:40	....	....	....	....	....	....	....	....	....
2004-05	Lulea HF	Sweden	39	6	7	13	89	....	....	....	....	....	....	....	....	....	3	0	1	1	6	....	....	....	....
	NHL Totals		223	8	20	28	179	0	0	2	195	4.1		0	0.0	15:41	26	2	1	3	14	0	0	2	15:52

Signed as a free agent by **Lulea** (Sweden), September 19, 2004.

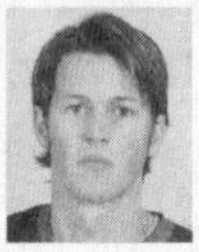

WALLIN, Rickard
(WAHL-in, RIH-kahrd) **MIN.**

Center. Shoots left. 6'2", 185 lbs. Born, Stockholm, Sweden, April 19, 1980. Phoenix's 8th choice, 160th overall, in 1998 Entry Draft.

Season	Club	League	GP	G	A	Pts	PIM	PP	SH	GW	S	%	+/-	TF	F%	Min	GP	G	A	Pts	PIM	PP	SH	GW	Min
1996-97	Vasteras IK Jr.	Swe-Jr.	26	3	3	6	....	....	....	....	....	....	....	....	....	....	....	....	....	....	....	....	....	....	....
1997-98	Farjestad Jr.	Swe-Jr.	29	20	30	50	32	....	....	....	....	....	....	....	....	....	2	1	1	2	2	....	....	....	....
1998-99	Farjestad Jr.	Swe-Jr.	21	11	15	26	30	....	....	....	....	....	....	....	....	....	....	....	....	....	....	....	....	....	....
	Farjestad	Sweden	5	0	0	0	0	....	....	....	....	....	....	....	....	....	....	....	....	....	....	....	....	....	....
99-2000	IF Troja-Ljungby	Sweden-2	46	15	22	37	54	....	....	....	....	....	....	....	....	....	....	....	....	....	....	....	....	....	....
2000-01	Farjestad	Sweden	47	9	22	31	24	....	....	....	....	....	....	....	....	....	16	11	3	14	4	....	....	....	....
2001-02	Farjestad	Sweden	50	12	31	43	56	....	....	....	....	....	....	....	....	....	10	4	9	13	8	....	....	....	....
2002-03	Minnesota	NHL	4	1	0	1	0	0	0	1	1	100.0	1	28	53.6	7:44	....	....	....	....	....	....	....	....	....
	Houston Aeros	AHL	52	13	22	35	70	....	....	....	....	....	....	....	....	....	23	4	11	15	22	....	....	....	....
2003-04	Minnesota	NHL	15	5	4	9	14	3	0	1	16	31.3	1	189	45.5	14:20	....	....	....	....	....	....	....	....	....
	Houston Aeros	AHL	47	14	18	32	36	....	....	....	....	....	....	....	....	....	2	0	0	0	2	....	....	....	....
2004-05	Houston Aeros	AHL	79	12	31	43	61	....	....	....	....	....	....	....	....	....	5	1	0	1	29	....	....	....	....
	NHL Totals		19	6	4	10	14	3	0	2	17	35.3		217	46.5	12:56	....	....	....	....	....	....	....	....	....

Rights traded to **Minnesota** by **Phoenix** for Joe Juneau, June 23, 2000.

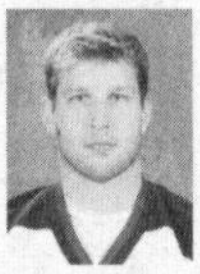

WALSER, Derrick
(WAHL-zuhr, DEHR-rihk) **CAR.**

Defense. Shoots left. 5'10", 196 lbs. Born, New Glasgow, N.S., May 12, 1978.

Season	Club	League	GP	G	A	Pts	PIM	PP	SH	GW	S	%	+/-	TF	F%	Min	GP	G	A	Pts	PIM	PP	SH	GW	Min
1994-95	Beauport	QMJHL	48	4	18	22	34	....	....	....	....	....	....	....	....	....	12	2	5	7	2	....	....	....	....
1995-96	Beauport	QMJHL	69	9	31	40	56	....	....	....	....	....	....	....	....	....	20	2	11	13	16	....	....	....	....
1996-97	Beauport	QMJHL	37	13	25	38	26	....	....	....	....	....	....	....	....	....	....	....	....	....	....	....	....	....	....
	Rimouski Oceanic	QMJHL	31	15	30	45	44	....	....	....	....	....	....	....	....	....	4	2	2	4	6	....	....	....	....
1997-98	Rimouski Oceanic	QMJHL	70	41	69	110	135	....	....	....	....	....	....	....	....	....	18	10	*26	36	49	....	....	....	....
1998-99	Saint John Flames	AHL	40	3	7	10	24	....	....	....	....	....	....	....	....	....	....	....	....	....	....	....	....	....	....
	Johnstown Chiefs	ECHL	24	8	12	20	29	....	....	....	....	....	....	....	....	....	....	....	....	....	....	....	....	....	....
99-2000	Saint John Flames	AHL	14	2	3	5	10	....	....	....	....	....	....	....	....	....	....	....	....	....	....	....	....	....	....
	Johnstown Chiefs	ECHL	54	17	26	43	104	....	....	....	....	....	....	....	....	....	7	3	3	6	8	....	....	....	....
2000-01	Saint John Flames	AHL	76	19	36	55	36	....	....	....	....	....	....	....	....	....	19	7	9	16	14	....	....	....	....
2001-02	Columbus	NHL	2	1	0	1	0	0	0	0	2	50.0	–2	0	0.0	16:18	....	....	....	....	....	....	....	....	....
	Syracuse Crunch	AHL	73	23	38	61	70	....	....	....	....	....	....	....	....	....	10	1	5	6	12	....	....	....	....
2002-03	Columbus	NHL	53	4	13	17	34	3	0	2	86	4.7	–9	1	100.0	14:52	....	....	....	....	....	....	....	....	....
	Syracuse Crunch	AHL	28	7	14	21	30	....	....	....	....	....	....	....	....	....	....	....	....	....	....	....	....	....	....
2003-04	Columbus	NHL	27	1	8	9	22	1	0	0	35	2.9	–6	0	0.0	18:23	....	....	....	....	....	....	....	....	....
	Syracuse Crunch	AHL	48	10	26	36	82	....	....	....	....	....	....	....	....	....	3	1	1	2	4	....	....	....	....
2004-05	Eisbaren Berlin	Germany	50	9	14	23	143	....	....	....	....	....	....	....	....	....	12	4	4	8	20	....	....	....	....
	NHL Totals		82	6	21	27	56	4	0	2	123	4.9		1	100.0	16:03	....	....	....	....	....	....	....	....	....

QMJHL First All-Star Team (1997, 1998) • Emile Bouchard Trophy (Top Defenseman – QMJHL) (1998) • Canadian Major Junior First All-Star Team (1998) • Canadian Major Junior Defenseman of the Year (1998)

Signed as a free agent by **Calgary**, October 16, 1998. Signed as a free agent by **Columbus**, September 17, 2001. Signed as a free agent by **Eisbaren Berlin** (Germany), May 13, 2004.

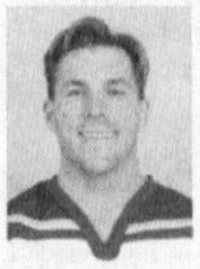

WALZ, Wes
(WAHLZ, WEHS) **MIN.**

Center. Shoots right. 5'10", 180 lbs. Born, Calgary, Alta., May 15, 1970. Boston's 3rd choice, 57th overall, in 1989 Entry Draft.

Season	Club	League	GP	G	A	Pts	PIM	PP	SH	GW	S	%	+/-	TF	F%	Min	GP	G	A	Pts	PIM	PP	SH	GW	Min
1987-88	Cgy. North Stars	AMHL	35	47	52	99	72	....	....	....	....	....	....	....	....	....	....	....	....	....	....	....	....	....	....
	Prince Albert	WHL	1	1	1	2	0	....	....	....	....	....	....	....	....	....	....	....	....	....	....	....	....	....	....
1988-89	Lethbridge	WHL	63	29	75	104	32	....	....	....	....	....	....	....	....	....	8	1	5	6	6	....	....	....	....
1989-90	Lethbridge	WHL	56	54	86	140	69	....	....	....	....	....	....	....	....	....	19	13	*24	*37	33	....	....	....	....
	Boston	NHL	2	1	1	2	0	1	0	0	1	100.0	–1	....	....	....	....	....	....	....	....	....	....	....	....
1990-91	Boston	NHL	56	8	8	16	32	1	0	1	57	14.0	–14	....	....	....	2	0	0	0	0	0	0	0	....
	Maine Mariners	AHL	20	8	12	20	19	....	....	....	....	....	....	....	....	....	2	0	0	0	21	....	....	....	....
1991-92	Boston	NHL	15	0	3	3	12	0	0	0	17	0.0	–3	....	....	....	....	....	....	....	....	....	....	....	....
	Maine Mariners	AHL	21	13	11	24	38	....	....	....	....	....	....	....	....	....	....	....	....	....	....	....	....	....	....
	Philadelphia	NHL	2	1	0	1	0	0	0	1	2	50.0	1	....	....	....	....	....	....	....	....	....	....	....	....
	Hershey Bears	AHL	41	13	28	41	37	....	....	....	....	....	....	....	....	....	6	1	2	3	0	....	....	....	....
1992-93	Hershey Bears	AHL	78	35	45	80	106	....	....	....	....	....	....	....	....	....	....	....	....	....	....	....	....	....	....
1993-94	Calgary	NHL	53	11	27	38	16	1	0	0	79	13.9	20	....	....	....	6	3	0	3	2	0	0	0	....
	Saint John Flames	AHL	15	6	6	12	14	....	....	....	....	....	....	....	....	....	....	....	....	....	....	....	....	....	....
1994-95	Calgary	NHL	39	6	12	18	11	4	0	1	73	8.2	7	....	....	....	1	0	0	0	0	0	0	0	....
1995-96	Detroit	NHL	2	0	0	0	0	0	0	0	2	0.0	0	....	....	....	....	....	....	....	....	....	....	....	....
	Adirondack	AHL	38	20	35	55	58	....	....	....	....	....	....	....	....	....	....	....	....	....	....	....	....	....	....
1996-97	EV Zug	Swiss	41	24	22	46	67	....	....	....	....	....	....	....	....	....	9	5	1	6	39	....	....	....	....
1997-98	EV Zug	Swiss	38	18	34	52	32	....	....	....	....	....	....	....	....	....	20	*16	*12	*28	18	....	....	....	....
	EV Zug	EuroHL	5	1	3	4	10	....	....	....	....	....	....	....	....	....	....	....	....	....	....	....	....	....	....
1998-99	EV Zug	Swiss	42	22	27	49	75	....	....	....	....	....	....	....	....	....	10	3	9	12	2	....	....	....	....
	EV Zug	EuroHL	6	7	5	12	4	....	....	....	....	....	....	....	....	....	2	0	0	0	12	....	....	....	....
99-2000	Long Beach	IHL	6	4	3	7	8	....	....	....	....	....	....	....	....	....	....	....	....	....	....	....	....	....	....
	HC Lugano	Swiss	13	7	11	18	14	....	....	....	....	....	....	....	....	....	5	3	4	7	4	....	....	....	....
2000-01	Minnesota	NHL	82	18	12	30	37	0	7	3	152	11.8	–8	1533	47.2	16:45	....	....	....	....	....	....	....	....	....
2001-02	Minnesota	NHL	64	10	20	30	43	0	2	5	97	10.3	0	1231	44.8	16:42	....	....	....	....	....	....	....	....	....
2002-03	Minnesota	NHL	80	13	19	32	63	0	0	4	115	11.3	11	1505	50.4	15:56	18	7	6	13	14	0	2	2	17:24
2003-04	Minnesota	NHL	57	12	13	25	32	0	3	2	70	17.1	5	909	46.3	16:18	....	....	....	....	....	....	....	....	....

			Regular Season														Playoffs								
Season	Club	League	GP	G	A	Pts	PIM	PP	SH	GW	S	%	+/-	TF	F%	Min	GP	G	A	Pts	PIM	PP	SH	GW	Min
2004-05			DID NOT PLAY																						
	NHL Totals		**452**	**80**	**115**	**195**	**246**	**7**	**12**	**17**	**665**	**12.0**		**5178**	**47.4**	**16:25**	**27**	**10**	**6**	**16**	**16**	**0**	**2**	**2**	**17:24**

WHL Rookie of the Year (1989) • WHL East First All-Star Team (1990)

Traded to **Philadelphia** by **Boston** with Garry Galley and Boston's 3rd round choice (Milos Holan) in 1993 Entry Draft for Gord Murphy, Brian Dobbin, Philadelphia's 3rd round choice (Sergei Zholtok) in 1992 Entry Draft and Philadelphia's 4th round choice (Charles Paquette) in 1993 Entry Draft, January 2, 1992. Signed as a free agent by **Calgary**, August 26, 1993. Signed as a free agent by **Detroit**, September 6, 1995. Signed as a free agent by **Long Beach** (IHL), October 12, 1999. Signed as a free agent by **Minnesota**, June 28, 2000.

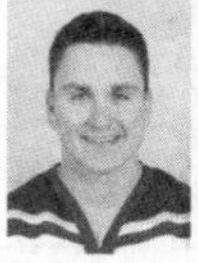

WANVIG, Kyle

(WEHN-vihg, KIGHL) **MIN.**

Right wing. Shoots right. 6'2", 219 lbs. Born, Calgary, Alta., January 29, 1981. Minnesota's 2nd choice, 36th overall, in 2001 Entry Draft.

Season	Club	League	GP	G	A	Pts	PIM	PP	SH	GW	S	%	+/-	TF	F%	Min	GP	G	A	Pts	PIM	PP	SH	GW	Min
1996-97	Calgary Blazers	AMHL	26	31	48	79	85	....	....	....	....	....	....	....	....	....	....	....	....	....	....	....	....	....	....
1997-98	Edmonton Ice	WHL	62	17	12	29	69	....	....	....	....	....	....	....	....	....	....	....	....	....	....	....	....	....	....
1998-99	Kootenay Ice	WHL	71	12	20	32	119	....	....	....	....	....	....	....	....	....	7	1	3	4	18	....	....	....	....
99-2000	Kootenay Ice	WHL	6	2	2	4	12	....	....	....	....	....	....	....	....	....	....	....	....	....	....	....	....	....	....
	Red Deer Rebels	WHL	58	21	18	39	123	....	....	....	....	....	....	....	....	....	4	1	0	1	4	....	....	....	....
2000-01	Red Deer Rebels	WHL	69	55	46	101	202	....	....	....	....	....	....	....	....	....	22	10	12	22	47	....	....	....	....
2001-02	Houston Aeros	AHL	34	6	7	13	43	....	....	....	....	....	....	....	....	....	9	0	1	1	23	....	....	....	....
2002-03	**Minnesota**	**NHL**	**7**	**1**	**0**	**1**	**13**	**0**	**0**	**0**	**5**	**20.0**	**0**	**1**	**100.0**	**9:14**	....	....	....	....	....	....	....	....	....
	Houston Aeros	AHL	57	13	16	29	137	....	....	....	....	....	....	....	....	....	21	6	4	10	27	....	....	....	....
2003-04	**Minnesota**	**NHL**	**6**	**0**	**1**	**1**	**10**	**0**	**0**	**0**	**16**	**0.0**	**–2**	**4**	**75.0**	**13:48**	....	....	....	....	....	....	....	....	....
	Houston Aeros	AHL	72	25	16	41	147	....	....	....	....	....	....	....	....	....	2	0	1	1	0	....	....	....	....
2004-05	Houston Aeros	AHL	76	13	17	30	158	....	....	....	....	....	....	....	....	....	5	1	2	3	8	....	....	....	....
	NHL Totals		**13**	**1**	**1**	**2**	**23**	**0**	**0**	**0**	**21**	**4.8**		**5**	**80.0**	**11:21**	....	....	....	....	....	....	....	....	....

• Re-entered NHL Entry Draft. Originally Boston's 3rd choice, 89th overall, in 1999 Entry Draft.

WHL East Second All-Star Team (2001) • Memorial Cup Tournament All-Star Team (2001) • Stafford Smythe Memorial Trophy (Memorial Cup Tournament MVP) (2001)

• Missed majority of 2001-02 season recovering from ankle injury suffered in game vs. Grand Rapids (AHL), December 30, 2001.

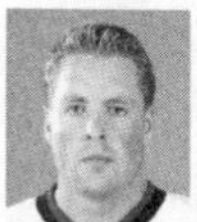

WARD, Aaron

(WOHRD, AIR-ruhn) **CAR.**

Defense. Shoots right. 6'2", 225 lbs. Born, Windsor, Ont., January 17, 1973. Winnipeg's 1st choice, 5th overall, in 1991 Entry Draft.

Season	Club	League	GP	G	A	Pts	PIM	PP	SH	GW	S	%	+/-	TF	F%	Min	GP	G	A	Pts	PIM	PP	SH	GW	Min
1988-89	Nepean Raiders	CJHL	54	1	14	15	40	....	....	....	....	....	....	....	....	....	....	....	....	....	....	....	....	....	....
1989-90	Nepean Raiders	CJHL	52	6	33	39	85	....	....	....	....	....	....	....	....	....	....	....	....	....	....	....	....	....	....
1990-91	U. of Michigan	CCHA	46	8	11	19	126	....	....	....	....	....	....	....	....	....	....	....	....	....	....	....	....	....	....
1991-92	U. of Michigan	CCHA	42	7	12	19	64	....	....	....	....	....	....	....	....	....	....	....	....	....	....	....	....	....	....
1992-93	U. of Michigan	CCHA	30	5	8	13	73	....	....	....	....	....	....	....	....	....	....	....	....	....	....	....	....	....	....
1993-94	**Detroit**	**NHL**	**5**	**1**	**0**	**1**	**4**	**0**	**0**	**0**	**3**	**33.3**	**2**	....	....	....	....	....	....	....	....	....	....	....	....
	Adirondack	AHL	58	4	12	16	87	....	....	....	....	....	....	....	....	....	9	2	6	8	6	....	....	....	....
1994-95	Adirondack	AHL	76	11	24	35	87	....	....	....	....	....	....	....	....	....	4	0	1	1	0	....	....	....	....
	Detroit	**NHL**	**1**	**0**	**1**	**1**	**2**	**0**	**0**	**0**	**0**	**0.0**	**1**	....	....	....	....	....	....	....	....	....	....	....	....
1995-96	Adirondack	AHL	74	5	10	15	133	....	....	....	....	....	....	....	....	....	3	0	0	0	6	....	....	....	....
1996-97♦	**Detroit**	**NHL**	**49**	**2**	**5**	**7**	**52**	**0**	**0**	**0**	**40**	**5.0**	**–9**	....	....	....	**19**	**0**	**0**	**0**	**17**	**0**	**0**	**0**	....
1997-98♦	**Detroit**	**NHL**	**52**	**5**	**5**	**10**	**47**	**0**	**0**	**1**	**47**	**10.6**	**–1**	....	....	....	....	....	....	....	....	....	....	....	....
1998-99	**Detroit**	**NHL**	**60**	**3**	**8**	**11**	**52**	**0**	**0**	**0**	**46**	**6.5**	**–5**	**0**	**0.0**	**13:55**	**8**	**0**	**1**	**1**	**8**	**0**	**0**	**0**	**10:15**
99-2000	**Detroit**	**NHL**	**36**	**1**	**3**	**4**	**24**	**0**	**0**	**0**	**25**	**4.0**	**–4**	**0**	**0.0**	**12:36**	**3**	**0**	**0**	**0**	**0**	**0**	**0**	**0**	**7:36**
2000-01	**Detroit**	**NHL**	**73**	**4**	**5**	**9**	**57**	**0**	**0**	**1**	**48**	**8.3**	**–4**	**0**	**0.0**	**17:00**	....	....	....	....	....	....	....	....	....
2001-02	**Carolina**	**NHL**	**79**	**3**	**11**	**14**	**74**	**0**	**0**	**2**	**69**	**4.3**	**0**	**1**	**100.0**	**19:40**	**23**	**1**	**1**	**2**	**22**	**0**	**0**	**0**	**21:12**
2002-03	**Carolina**	**NHL**	**77**	**3**	**6**	**9**	**90**	**0**	**0**	**1**	**66**	**4.5**	**–23**	**0**	**0.0**	**18:43**	....	....	....	....	....	....	....	....	....
2003-04	**Carolina**	**NHL**	**49**	**3**	**5**	**8**	**37**	**2**	**0**	**0**	**51**	**5.9**	**1**	**0**	**0.0**	**17:52**	....	....	....	....	....	....	....	....	....
2004-05	ERC Ingolstadt	Germany	8	0	3	3	16	....	....	....	....	....	....	....	....	....	11	1	1	2	16	....	....	....	....
	NHL Totals		**481**	**25**	**49**	**74**	**439**	**2**	**0**	**5**	**395**	**6.3**		**1**	**100.0**	**17:07**	**53**	**1**	**2**	**3**	**47**	**0**	**0**	**0**	**17:26**

Traded to **Detroit** by **Winnipeg** with Toronto's 4th round choice (previously acquired, Detroit selected John Jakopin) in 1993 Entry Draft for Paul Ysebaert and future considerations (Alan Kerr, June 18, 1993), June 11, 1993. • Missed majority of 1999-2000 season recovering from shoulder injury suffered in game vs. Vancouver, January 19, 2000. Traded to **Carolina** by **Detroit** for Carolina's 2nd round choice (Jiri Hudler) in 2002 Entry Draft, July 9, 2001. Signed as a free agent by **Ingolstadt** (Germany), February 15, 2005.

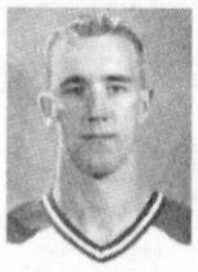

WARD, Jason

(WOHRD, JAY-suhn) **NYR**

Right wing. Shoots right. 6'3", 203 lbs. Born, Chapleau, Ont., January 16, 1979. Montreal's 1st choice, 11th overall, in 1997 Entry Draft.

Season	Club	League	GP	G	A	Pts	PIM	PP	SH	GW	S	%	+/-	TF	F%	Min	GP	G	A	Pts	PIM	PP	SH	GW	Min
1994-95	Oshawa	OHA-B	47	30	31	61	75	....	....	....	....	....	....	....	....	....	....	....	....	....	....	....	....	....	....
1995-96	Niagara Falls	OHL	64	15	35	50	139	....	....	....	....	....	....	....	....	....	10	6	4	10	23	....	....	....	....
1996-97	Erie Otters	OHL	58	25	39	64	137	....	....	....	....	....	....	....	....	....	5	1	2	3	2	....	....	....	....
1997-98	Erie Otters	OHL	21	7	9	16	42	....	....	....	....	....	....	....	....	....	....	....	....	....	....	....	....	....	....
	Windsor Spitfires	OHL	26	19	27	46	34	....	....	....	....	....	....	....	....	....	....	....	....	....	....	....	....	....	....
	Fredericton	AHL	7	1	0	1	2	....	....	....	....	....	....	....	....	....	1	0	0	0	2	....	....	....	....
1998-99	Windsor Spitfires	OHL	12	8	11	19	25	....	....	....	....	....	....	....	....	....	....	....	....	....	....	....	....	....	....
	Plymouth Whalers	OHL	23	14	13	27	28	....	....	....	....	....	....	....	....	....	11	6	8	14	12	....	....	....	....
	Fredericton	AHL	....	....	....	....	....	....	....	....	....	....	....	....	....	....	10	4	2	6	22	....	....	....	....
99-2000	**Montreal**	**NHL**	**32**	**2**	**1**	**3**	**10**	**1**	**0**	**0**	**24**	**8.3**	**–1**	**86**	**44.2**	**9:10**	....	....	....	....	....	....	....	....	....
	Quebec Citadelles	AHL	40	14	12	26	30	....	....	....	....	....	....	....	....	....	3	2	1	3	4	....	....	....	....
2000-01	**Montreal**	**NHL**	**12**	**0**	**0**	**0**	**12**	**0**	**0**	**0**	**4**	**0.0**	**3**	**2**	**50.0**	**8:16**	....	....	....	....	....	....	....	....	....
	Quebec Citadelles	AHL	23	7	12	19	69	....	....	....	....	....	....	....	....	....	....	....	....	....	....	....	....	....	....
2001-02	Quebec Citadelles	AHL	78	24	33	57	128	....	....	....	....	....	....	....	....	....	3	0	0	0	2	....	....	....	....
2002-03	**Montreal**	**NHL**	**8**	**3**	**2**	**5**	**0**	**0**	**0**	**0**	**10**	**30.0**	**3**	**6**	**50.0**	**11:17**	....	....	....	....	....	....	....	....	....
	Hamilton	AHL	69	31	41	72	78	....	....	....	....	....	....	....	....	....	23	*12	9	*21	20	....	....	....	....
2003-04	**Montreal**	**NHL**	**53**	**5**	**7**	**12**	**21**	**2**	**0**	**1**	**56**	**8.9**	**3**	**98**	**41.8**	**12:39**	**5**	**0**	**2**	**2**	**2**	**0**	**0**	**0**	**15:39**
	Hamilton	AHL	2	0	3	3	17	....	....	....	....	....	....	....	....	....	....	....	....	....	....	....	....	....	....
2004-05	Hamilton	AHL	77	20	34	54	66	....	....	....	....	....	....	....	....	....	4	2	1	3	2	....	....	....	....
	NHL Totals		**105**	**10**	**10**	**20**	**43**	**3**	**0**	**1**	**94**	**10.6**		**192**	**43.2**	**10:59**	**5**	**0**	**2**	**2**	**2**	**0**	**0**	**0**	**15:39**

AHL First All-Star Team (2003) • Les Cunningham Award (MVP – AHL) (2003)

• Missed majority of 2000-01 season recovering from knee injury suffered in game vs. Carolina, January 16, 2001. Signed as a free agent by **Hamilton** (AHL), October 19, 2004. Signed as a free agent by **NY Rangers**, August 4, 2005.

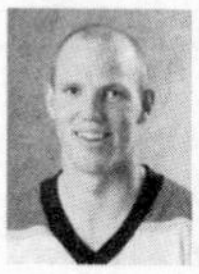

WARD, Lance

(WAWRD, LANTS) **OTT.**

Defense. Shoots left. 6'3", 210 lbs. Born, Lloydminster, Alta., June 2, 1978. Florida's 3rd choice, 63rd overall, in 1998 Entry Draft.

Season	Club	League	GP	G	A	Pts	PIM	PP	SH	GW	S	%	+/-	TF	F%	Min	GP	G	A	Pts	PIM	PP	SH	GW	Min
1993-94	Lloydminister	AAHA	20	8	12	20	68	....	....	....	....	....	....	....	....	....	....	....	....	....	....	....	....	....	....
1994-95	Red Deer Rebels	WHL	28	0	0	0	57	....	....	....	....	....	....	....	....	....	....	....	....	....	....	....	....	....	....
1995-96	Red Deer Rebels	WHL	72	4	13	17	127	....	....	....	....	....	....	....	....	....	10	0	4	4	10	....	....	....	....
1996-97	Red Deer Rebels	WHL	70	5	34	39	229	....	....	....	....	....	....	....	....	....	16	0	3	3	36	....	....	....	....
1997-98	Red Deer Rebels	WHL	71	8	25	33	233	....	....	....	....	....	....	....	....	....	5	0	0	0	16	....	....	....	....
1998-99	Miami Matadors	ECHL	6	1	0	1	12	....	....	....	....	....	....	....	....	....	....	....	....	....	....	....	....	....	....
	Fort Wayne	IHL	13	0	2	2	28	....	....	....	....	....	....	....	....	....	....	....	....	....	....	....	....	....	....
	New Haven	AHL	43	2	5	7	51	....	....	....	....	....	....	....	....	....	....	....	....	....	....	....	....	....	....
99-2000	Louisville Panthers	AHL	80	4	16	20	190	....	....	....	....	....	....	....	....	....	4	0	0	0	6	....	....	....	....
2000-01	**Florida**	**NHL**	**30**	**0**	**2**	**2**	**45**	**0**	**0**	**0**	**17**	**0.0**	**–3**	**0**	**0.0**	**15:50**	....	....	....	....	....	....	....	....	....
	Louisville Panthers	AHL	35	3	2	5	78	....	....	....	....	....	....	....	....	....	....	....	....	....	....	....	....	....	....
2001-02	**Florida**	**NHL**	**68**	**1**	**4**	**5**	**131**	**0**	**0**	**0**	**39**	**2.6**	**–20**	**1**	**0.0**	**14:31**	....	....	....	....	....	....	....	....	....
2002-03	**Florida**	**NHL**	**36**	**3**	**1**	**4**	**78**	**0**	**0**	**1**	**34**	**8.8**	**–4**	**0**	**0.0**	**9:07**	....	....	....	....	....	....	....	....	....
	Anaheim	**NHL**	**29**	**0**	**1**	**1**	**43**	**0**	**0**	**0**	**18**	**0.0**	**–2**	**0**	**0.0**	**7:08**	....	....	....	....	....	....	....	....	....
2003-04	**Anaheim**	**NHL**	**46**	**0**	**4**	**4**	**94**	**0**	**0**	**0**	**26**	**0.0**	**–1**	**0**	**0.0**	**8:41**	....	....	....	....	....	....	....	....	....
	Cincinnati	AHL	5	0	1	1	6	....	....	....	....	....	....	....	....	....	....	....	....	....	....	....	....	....	....
2004-05			DID NOT PLAY																						
	NHL Totals		**209**	**4**	**12**	**16**	**391**	**0**	**0**	**1**	**134**	**3.0**		**1**	**0.0**	**11:28**	....	....	....	....	....	....	....	....	....

• Re-entered NHL Entry Draft. Originally New Jersey's 1st choice, 10th overall, in 1996 Entry Draft.

Traded to **Anaheim** by **Florida** with Sandis Ozolinsh for Pavel Trnka, Matt Cullen and Anaheim's 4th round choice (James Pemberton) in 2003 Entry Draft, January 30, 2003. Signed as a free agent by **Ottawa**, August 26, 2005.

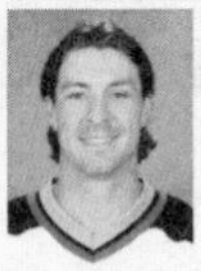

WARRENER, Rhett

(WAHR-ihn-uhr, REHT) **CGY.**

Defense. Shoots right. 6'2", 217 lbs. Born, Shaunavon, Sask., January 27, 1976. Florida's 2nd choice, 27th overall, in 1994 Entry Draft.

Season	Club	League	Regular Season														Playoffs								
Season	Club	League	GP	G	A	Pts	PIM	PP	SH	GW	S	%	+/-	TF	F%	Min	GP	G	A	Pts	PIM	PP	SH	GW	Min
1991-92	Saskatoon Blazers	SMHL	33	6	5	11	71	....	....	....	....	....	....	....	....	....	....	....	....	....	....	....	....	....	....
	Saskatoon Blades	WHL	2	0	0	0	0	....	....	....	....	....	....	....	....	....	....	....	....	....	....	....	....	....	....
1992-93	Saskatoon Blades	WHL	68	2	17	19	100	....	....	....	....	....	....	....	....	....	9	0	0	0	14	....	....	....	....
1993-94	Saskatoon Blades	WHL	61	7	19	26	131	....	....	....	....	....	....	....	....	....	16	0	5	5	33	....	....	....	....
1994-95	Saskatoon Blades	WHL	66	13	26	39	137	....	....	....	....	....	....	....	....	....	10	0	3	3	6	....	....	....	....
1995-96	**Florida**	**NHL**	28	0	3	3	46	0	0	0	19	0.0	4	....	....	....	21	0	1	1	0	0	0	0	....
	Carolina Panthers	AHL	9	0	0	0	4	....	....	....	....	....	....	....	....	....	....	....	....	....	....	....	....	....	....
1996-97	**Florida**	**NHL**	62	4	9	13	88	1	0	1	58	6.9	20	....	....	....	5	0	0	0	0	0	0	0	....
1997-98	**Florida**	**NHL**	79	0	4	4	99	0	0	0	66	0.0	–16	....	....	....	....	....	....	....	....	....	....	....	....
1998-99	**Florida**	**NHL**	48	0	7	7	64	0	0	0	33	0.0	–1	0	0.0	19:01	....	....	....	....	....	....	....	....	....
	Buffalo	**NHL**	13	1	0	1	20	0	0	0	11	9.1	3	0	0.0	18:13	20	1	3	4	32	0	0	0	22:08
99-2000	**Buffalo**	**NHL**	61	0	3	3	89	0	0	0	68	0.0	18	0	0.0	19:51	5	0	0	0	2	0	0	0	21:42
2000-01	**Buffalo**	**NHL**	77	3	16	19	78	0	0	2	103	2.9	10	0	0.0	20:24	13	0	2	2	4	0	0	0	22:37
2001-02	**Buffalo**	**NHL**	65	5	5	10	113	0	0	1	66	7.6	15	0	0.0	19:39	....	....	....	....	....	....	....	....	....
2002-03	**Buffalo**	**NHL**	50	0	9	9	63	0	0	0	47	0.0	1	0	0.0	18:14	....	....	....	....	....	....	....	....	....
2003-04	**Calgary**	**NHL**	77	3	14	17	97	0	1	1	82	3.7	8	1	0.0	19:52	24	0	1	1	6	0	0	0	24:06
2004-05			DID NOT PLAY																						
	NHL Totals		**560**	**16**	**70**	**86**	**757**	**1**	**1**	**5**	**553**	**2.9**		**1**	**0.0**	**19:34**	**88**	**1**	**7**	**8**	**44**	**0**	**0**	**0**	**22:57**

Traded to **Buffalo** by **Florida** with Florida's 5th round choice (Ryan Miller) in 1999 Entry Draft for Mike Wilson, March 23, 1999. Traded to **Calgary** by **Buffalo** with Steve Reinprecht for Chris Drury and Steve Begin, July 3, 2003.

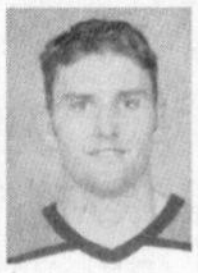

WATT, Mike

(WAHT, MIGHK)

Left wing. Shoots left. 6'2", 212 lbs. Born, Seaforth, Ont., March 31, 1976. Edmonton's 3rd choice, 32nd overall, in 1994 Entry Draft.

Season	Club	League	GP	G	A	Pts	PIM	PP	SH	GW	S	%	+/-	TF	F%	Min	GP	G	A	Pts	PIM	PP	SH	GW	Min
1990-91	Seaforth	OHA-D	39	15	23	38	43	....	....	....	....	....	....	....	....	....	....	....	....	....	....	....	....	....	....
1991-92	Stratford Cullitons	OHA-B	40	5	21	26	103	....	....	....	....	....	....	....	....	....	....	....	....	....	....	....	....	....	....
1992-93	Stratford Cullitons	OHA-B	45	20	35	55	100	....	....	....	....	....	....	....	....	....	....	....	....	....	....	....	....	....	....
1993-94	Stratford Cullitons	OHA-B	48	34	34	68	165	....	....	....	....	....	....	....	....	....	....	....	....	....	....	....	....	....	....
1994-95	Michigan State	CCHA	39	12	6	18	64	....	....	....	....	....	....	....	....	....	....	....	....	....	....	....	....	....	....
1995-96	Michigan State	CCHA	37	17	22	39	60	....	....	....	....	....	....	....	....	....	....	....	....	....	....	....	....	....	....
1996-97	Michigan State	CCHA	39	24	17	41	109	....	....	....	....	....	....	....	....	....	....	....	....	....	....	....	....	....	....
1997-98	**Edmonton**	**NHL**	14	1	2	3	4	0	0	1	14	7.1	–4	....	....	....	....	....	....	....	....	....	....	....	....
	Hamilton	AHL	63	24	25	49	65	....	....	....	....	....	....	....	....	....	9	2	2	4	8	....	....	....	....
1998-99	**NY Islanders**	**NHL**	75	8	17	25	12	0	0	4	75	10.7	–2	180	50.6	11:15	....	....	....	....	....	....	....	....	....
99-2000	**NY Islanders**	**NHL**	45	5	6	11	17	0	1	0	49	10.2	–8	81	48.2	12:02	....	....	....	....	....	....	....	....	....
	Lowell	AHL	16	6	11	17	6	....	....	....	....	....	....	....	....	....	7	1	1	2	4	....	....	....	....
2000-01	**Nashville**	**NHL**	18	1	1	2	8	0	0	1	18	5.6	–2	2	50.0	11:02	....	....	....	....	....	....	....	....	....
	Milwaukee	IHL	60	20	20	40	48	....	....	....	....	....	....	....	....	....	5	1	2	3	6	....	....	....	....
2001-02	Philadelphia	AHL	53	11	13	24	38	....	....	....	....	....	....	....	....	....	5	2	1	3	6	....	....	....	....
2002-03	**Carolina**	**NHL**	5	0	0	0	0	0	0	0	2	0.0	–1	19	47.4	7:30	....	....	....	....	....	....	....	....	....
	Lowell	AHL	61	9	14	23	35	....	....	....	....	....	....	....	....	....	....	....	....	....	....	....	....	....	....
2003-04	St. Petersburg	Russia	57	11	13	24	77	....	....	....	....	....	....	....	....	....	....	....	....	....	....	....	....	....	....
2004-05	St. Petersburg	Russia	47	6	6	12	54	....	....	....	....	....	....	....	....	....	....	....	....	....	....	....	....	....	....
	NHL Totals		**157**	**15**	**26**	**41**	**41**	**0**	**1**	**6**	**158**	**9.5**		**282**	**49.6**	**11:20**	....	....	....	....	....	....	....	....	....

Traded to **NY Islanders** by **Edmonton** for Eric Fichaud, June 18, 1998. Claimed on waivers by **Nashville** from **NY Islanders**, May 23, 2000. Traded to **Philadelphia** by **Nashville** for Mikhail Chernov, May 24, 2001. Signed as a free agent by **Carolina**, August 7, 2002. Signed as a free agent by **St. Petersburg** (Russia), June 27, 2003.

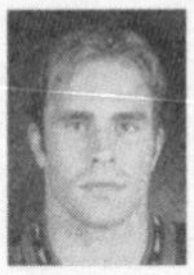

WEAVER, Mike

(WEE-vuhr, MIGHK) **L.A.**

Defense. Shoots right. 5'9", 180 lbs. Born, Bramalea, Ont., May 2, 1978.

Season	Club	League	GP	G	A	Pts	PIM	PP	SH	GW	S	%	+/-	TF	F%	Min	GP	G	A	Pts	PIM	PP	SH	GW	Min
1995-96	Bramalea Blues	OPJHL	48	10	39	49	103	....	....	....	....	....	....	....	....	....	....	....	....	....	....	....	....	....	....
1996-97	Michigan State	CCHA	39	0	7	7	46	....	....	....	....	....	....	....	....	....	....	....	....	....	....	....	....	....	....
1997-98	Michigan State	CCHA	44	4	22	26	68	....	....	....	....	....	....	....	....	....	....	....	....	....	....	....	....	....	....
1998-99	Michigan State	CCHA	42	1	6	7	54	....	....	....	....	....	....	....	....	....	....	....	....	....	....	....	....	....	....
99-2000	Michigan State	CCHA	26	0	7	7	20	....	....	....	....	....	....	....	....	....	....	....	....	....	....	....	....	....	....
2000-01	Orlando	IHL	68	0	8	8	34	....	....	....	....	....	....	....	....	....	16	0	2	2	8	....	....	....	....
2001-02	**Atlanta**	**NHL**	16	0	1	1	10	0	0	0	9	0.0	0	0	0.0	13:54	....	....	....	....	....	....	....	....	....
	Chicago Wolves	AHL	58	2	8	10	67	....	....	....	....	....	....	....	....	....	25	1	3	4	21	....	....	....	....
2002-03	**Atlanta**	**NHL**	40	0	5	5	20	0	0	0	21	0.0	–5	0	0.0	18:38	....	....	....	....	....	....	....	....	....
	Chicago Wolves	AHL	33	2	2	4	32	....	....	....	....	....	....	....	....	....	9	0	3	3	4	....	....	....	....
2003-04	**Atlanta**	**NHL**	1	0	0	0	0	0	0	0	0	0.0	–1	0	0.0	8:28	....	....	....	....	....	....	....	....	....
	Chicago Wolves	AHL	78	3	14	17	89	....	....	....	....	....	....	....	....	....	9	2	2	4	20	....	....	....	....
2004-05	Manchester	AHL	79	1	22	23	61	....	....	....	....	....	....	....	....	....	6	0	1	1	0	....	....	....	....
	NHL Totals		**57**	**0**	**6**	**6**	**30**	**0**	**0**	**0**	**30**	**0.0**		**0**	**0.0**	**17:08**	....	....	....	....	....	....	....	....	....

OPJHL Defenseman of the Year (1996) • CCHA All-Tournament Team (1997) • CCHA First All-Star Team (1999, 2000) • CCHA Best Defensive Defenseman Award (1999, 2000) • NCAA West Second All-American Team (1999, 2000)

Signed as a free agent by **Atlanta**, June 15, 2000. Signed as a free agent by **Los Angeles**, July 16, 2004.

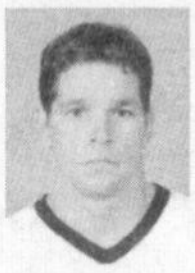

WEBB, Steve

(WEHB, STEEV)

Right wing. Shoots right. 6', 211 lbs. Born, Peterborough, Ont., April 30, 1975. Buffalo's 8th choice, 176th overall, in 1994 Entry Draft.

Season	Club	League	GP	G	A	Pts	PIM	PP	SH	GW	S	%	+/-	TF	F%	Min	GP	G	A	Pts	PIM	PP	SH	GW	Min
1991-92	Peterborough	OHA-B	37	9	9	18	195	....	....	....	....	....	....	....	....	....	....	....	....	....	....	....	....	....	....
1992-93	Windsor Spitfires	OHL	63	14	25	39	184	....	....	....	....	....	....	....	....	....	....	....	....	....	....	....	....	....	....
1993-94	Windsor Spitfires	OHL	2	0	1	1	9	....	....	....	....	....	....	....	....	....	....	....	....	....	....	....	....	....	....
	Peterborough	OHL	33	6	15	21	117	....	....	....	....	....	....	....	....	....	6	1	1	2	20	....	....	....	....
1994-95	Peterborough	OHL	42	8	16	24	109	....	....	....	....	....	....	....	....	....	11	3	3	6	22	....	....	....	....
1995-96	Muskegon Fury	ColHL	58	18	24	42	263	....	....	....	....	....	....	....	....	....	5	1	2	3	22	....	....	....	....
	Detroit Vipers	IHL	4	0	0	0	24	....	....	....	....	....	....	....	....	....	....	....	....	....	....	....	....	....	....
1996-97	**NY Islanders**	**NHL**	41	1	4	5	144	1	0	0	21	4.8	–10	....	....	....	....	....	....	....	....	....	....	....	....
	Kentucky	AHL	25	6	6	12	103	....	....	....	....	....	....	....	....	....	2	0	0	0	19	....	....	....	....
1997-98	**NY Islanders**	**NHL**	20	0	0	0	35	0	0	0	6	0.0	–2	....	....	....	....	....	....	....	....	....	....	....	....
	Kentucky	AHL	37	5	13	18	139	....	....	....	....	....	....	....	....	....	3	0	1	1	10	....	....	....	....
1998-99	**NY Islanders**	**NHL**	45	0	0	0	32	0	0	0	18	0.0	–10	0	0.0	4:13	....	....	....	....	....	....	....	....	....
	Lowell	AHL	23	2	4	6	80	....	....	....	....	....	....	....	....	....	....	....	....	....	....	....	....	....	....
99-2000	**NY Islanders**	**NHL**	65	1	3	4	103	0	0	0	27	3.7	–4	1	0.0	7:00	....	....	....	....	....	....	....	....	....
2000-01	**NY Islanders**	**NHL**	31	0	2	2	35	0	0	0	8	0.0	1	0	0.0	6:26	....	....	....	....	....	....	....	....	....
2001-02	**NY Islanders**	**NHL**	60	2	4	6	104	0	0	0	31	6.5	0	1	100.0	6:29	7	0	0	0	12	0	0	0	6:52
2002-03	**NY Islanders**	**NHL**	49	1	0	1	75	0	0	0	27	3.7	–5	0	0.0	6:02	5	0	0	0	10	0	0	0	6:46
2003-04	**Pittsburgh**	**NHL**	5	0	0	0	2	0	0	0	3	0.0	–3	0	0.0	5:20	....	....	....	....	....	....	....	....	....
	Wilkes-Barre	AHL	30	4	7	11	48	....	....	....	....	....	....	....	....	....	....	....	....	....	....	....	....	....	....
	NY Islanders	**NHL**	5	0	0	0	2	0	0	0	0	0.0	–1	1	0.0	4:57	2	0	0	0	6	0	0	0	4:01
	Bridgeport	AHL	7	0	1	1	29	....	....	....	....	....	....	....	....	....	5	0	0	0	4	....	....	....	....
2004-05			DID NOT PLAY																						
	NHL Totals		**321**	**5**	**13**	**18**	**532**	**1**	**0**	**0**	**141**	**3.5**		**3**	**33.3**	**6:05**	**14**	**0**	**0**	**0**	**28**	**0**	**0**	**0**	**6:25**

Signed as a free agent by **NY Islanders**, October 10, 1996. • Missed majority of 2000-01 season recovering from knee injury suffered in game vs. Anaheim, November 19, 2000. Signed as a free agent by **Philadelphia**, October 21, 2003. Claimed on waivers by **Pittsburgh** from **Philadelphia**, October 22, 2003. Traded to **NY Islanders** by **Pittsburgh** for Alain Nasreddine, March 8, 2004.

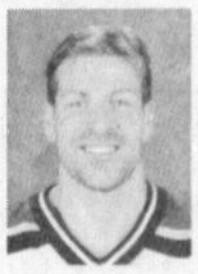

WEIGHT, Doug

(WAYT, DUHG) **ST.L.**

Center. Shoots left. 5'11", 200 lbs. Born, Warren, MI, January 21, 1971. NY Rangers' 2nd choice, 34th overall, in 1990 Entry Draft.

Season	Club	League	GP	G	A	Pts	PIM	PP	SH	GW	S	%	+/-	TF	F%	Min	GP	G	A	Pts	PIM	PP	SH	GW	Min
1988-89	Bloomfield Jets	NAHL	34	26	53	79	105	....	....	....	....	....	....	....	....	....	....	....	....	....	....	....	....	....	....
1989-90	Lake Superior	CCHA	46	21	48	69	44	....	....	....	....	....	....	....	....	....	....	....	....	....	....	....	....	....	....
1990-91	Lake Superior	CCHA	42	29	46	75	86	....	....	....	....	....	....	....	....	....	....	....	....	....	....	....	....	....	....
	NY Rangers	**NHL**	....	....	....	....	....	....	....	....	....	....	....	....	....	....	1	0	0	0	0	0	0	0	....
1991-92	**NY Rangers**	**NHL**	53	8	22	30	23	0	0	2	72	11.1	–3	....	....	....	7	2	2	4	0	1	0	0	....
	Binghamton	AHL	9	3	14	17	2	....	....	....	....	....	....	....	....	....	4	1	4	5	6	....	....	....	....

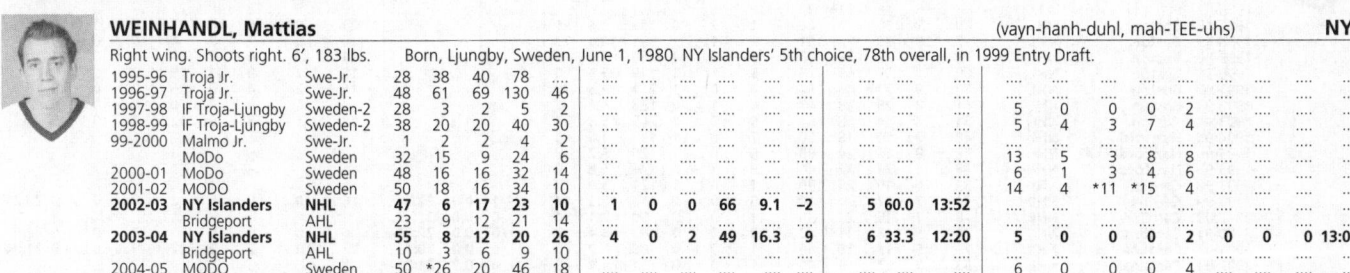

			Regular Season														Playoffs								
Season	Club	League	GP	G	A	Pts	PIM	PP	SH	GW	S	%	+/-	TF	F%	Min	GP	G	A	Pts	PIM	PP	SH	GW	Min
1992-93	NY Rangers	NHL	65	15	25	40	55	3	0	1	90	16.7	4	....	....	....	....	....	....	....	....	....	....	....	....
	Edmonton	NHL	13	2	6	8	10	0	0	0	35	5.7	–2	....	....	....	....	....	....	....	....	....	....	....	....
1993-94	Edmonton	NHL	84	24	50	74	47	4	1	1	188	12.8	–22	....	....	....	....	....	....	....	....	....	....	....	....
1994-95	Rosenheim	Germany	8	2	3	5	18	....	....	....	....	....	....	....	....	....	....	....	....	....	....	....	....	....	....
	Edmonton	NHL	48	7	33	40	69	1	0	1	104	6.7	–17	....	....	....	....	....	....	....	....	....	....	....	....
1995-96	Edmonton	NHL	82	25	79	104	95	9	0	2	204	12.3	–19	....	....	....	....	....	....	....	....	....	....	....	....
1996-97	Edmonton	NHL	80	21	61	82	80	4	0	2	235	8.9	1	....	....	....	12	3	8	11	8	0	0	0	....
1997-98	Edmonton	NHL	79	26	44	70	69	9	0	4	205	12.7	1	....	....	....	12	2	7	9	14	2	0	1	....
	United States	Olympics	4	0	2	2	2	....	....	....	....	....	....	....	....	....	....	....	....	....	....	....	....	....	....
1998-99	Edmonton	NHL	43	6	31	37	12	1	0	0	79	7.6	–8	853	49.5	19:51	4	1	1	2	15	0	0	0	14:43
99-2000	Edmonton	NHL	77	21	51	72	54	3	1	4	167	12.6	6	1588	50.4	20:35	5	3	2	5	4	2	0	1	21:05
2000-01	Edmonton	NHL	82	25	65	90	91	8	0	3	188	13.3	12	1514	51.3	22:08	6	1	5	6	17	0	0	0	22:45
2001-02	St. Louis	NHL	61	15	34	49	40	3	0	1	131	11.5	20	1123	49.2	19:48	10	1	1	2	4	1	0	1	16:26
	United States	Olympics	6	0	3	3	4	....	....	....	....	....	....	....	....	....	....	....	....	....	....	....	....	....	....
2002-03	St. Louis	NHL	70	15	52	67	52	7	0	3	182	8.2	–6	1048	50.4	20:23	7	5	8	13	2	5	0	1	22:26
2003-04	St. Louis	NHL	75	14	51	65	37	6	0	5	198	7.1	–3	1115	50.4	20:25	5	2	1	3	6	1	1	0	19:24
2004-05	Frankfurt Lions	Germany	7	6	9	15	26	....	....	....	....	....	....	....	....	....	11	2	10	12	8	....	....	....	....
	NHL Totals		912	224	604	828	734	58	2	29	2078	10.8		7241	50.3	20:38	69	20	35	55	70	12	1	4	19:26

CCHA First All-Star Team (1991) • NCAA West Second All-American Team (1991)

Played in NHL All-Star Game (1996, 1998, 2001, 2003)

Traded to **Edmonton** by **NY Rangers** for Esa Tikkanen, March 17, 1993. Traded to **St. Louis** by **Edmonton** with Michel Riesen for Marty Reasoner, Jochen Hecht and Jan Horacek, July 1, 2001. Signed as a free agent by **Frankfurt** (Germany), February 11, 2005.

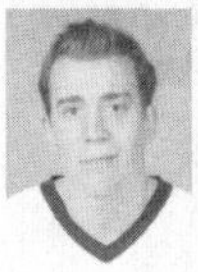

WEINHANDL, Mattias

(vayn-hanh-duhl, mah-TEE-uhs) **NYI**

Right wing. Shoots right. 6', 183 lbs. Born, Ljungby, Sweden, June 1, 1980. NY Islanders' 5th choice, 78th overall, in 1999 Entry Draft.

Season	Club	League	GP	G	A	Pts	PIM	PP	SH	GW	S	%	+/-	TF	F%	Min	GP	G	A	Pts	PIM	PP	SH	GW	Min
1995-96	Troja Jr.	Swe-Jr.	28	38	40	78	....	....	....	....	....	....	....	....	....	....	....	....	....	....	....	....	....	....	....
1996-97	Troja Jr.	Swe-Jr.	48	61	69	130	46	....	....	....	....	....	....	....	....	....	....	....	....	....	....	....	....	....	....
1997-98	IF Troja-Ljungby	Sweden-2	28	3	2	5	2	....	....	....	....	....	....	....	....	....	5	0	0	0	2	....	....	....	....
1998-99	IF Troja-Ljungby	Sweden-2	38	20	20	40	30	....	....	....	....	....	....	....	....	....	5	4	3	7	4	....	....	....	....
99-2000	Malmo Jr.	Swe-Jr.	1	2	2	4	2	....	....	....	....	....	....	....	....	....	....	....	....	....	....	....	....	....	....
	MoDo	Sweden	32	15	9	24	6	....	....	....	....	....	....	....	....	....	13	5	3	8	8	....	....	....	....
2000-01	MoDo	Sweden	48	16	16	32	14	....	....	....	....	....	....	....	....	....	6	1	3	4	6	....	....	....	....
2001-02	MODO	Sweden	50	18	16	34	10	....	....	....	....	....	....	....	....	....	14	4	*11	*15	4	....	....	....	....
2002-03	NY Islanders	NHL	47	6	17	23	10	1	0	0	66	9.1	–2	5	60.0	13:52	....	....	....	....	....	....	....	....	....
	Bridgeport	AHL	23	9	12	21	14	....	....	....	....	....	....	....	....	....	....	....	....	....	....	....	....	....	....
2003-04	NY Islanders	NHL	55	8	12	20	26	4	0	2	49	16.3	9	6	33.3	12:20	5	0	0	0	2	0	0	0	13:07
	Bridgeport	AHL	10	3	6	9	10	....	....	....	....	....	....	....	....	....	....	....	....	....	....	....	....	....	....
2004-05	MODO	Sweden	50	*26	20	46	18	....	....	....	....	....	....	....	....	....	6	0	0	0	4	....	....	....	....
	NHL Totals		102	14	29	43	36	5	0	2	115	12.2		11	45.5	13:02	5	0	0	0	2	0	0	0	13:07

Signed as a free agent by **MODO** (Sweden), September 18, 2004.

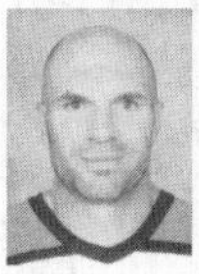

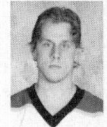

WEINRICH, Eric

(WIGHN-rihch, AIR-ihk) **ST.L.**

Defense. Shoots left. 6'1", 207 lbs. Born, Roanoke, VA, December 19, 1966. New Jersey's 3rd choice, 32nd overall, in 1985 Entry Draft.

Season	Club	League	GP	G	A	Pts	PIM	PP	SH	GW	S	%	+/-	TF	F%	Min	GP	G	A	Pts	PIM	PP	SH	GW	Min
1983-84	N. Yarmouth	High-ME	17	23	33	56	....	....	....	....	....	....	....	....	....	....	....	....	....	....	....	....	....	....	....
1984-85	N. Yarmouth	High-ME	20	6	21	27	....	....	....	....	....	....	....	....	....	....	....	....	....	....	....	....	....	....	....
1985-86	U. of Maine	H-East	34	0	14	14	26	....	....	....	....	....	....	....	....	....	....	....	....	....	....	....	....	....	....
1986-87	U. of Maine	H-East	41	12	32	44	59	....	....	....	....	....	....	....	....	....	....	....	....	....	....	....	....	....	....
1987-88	U. of Maine	H-East	8	4	7	11	22	....	....	....	....	....	....	....	....	....	....	....	....	....	....	....	....	....	....
	United States	Nat-Tm	38	3	9	12	24	....	....	....	....	....	....	....	....	....	....	....	....	....	....	....	....	....	....
	United States	Olympics	3	0	0	0	0	....	....	....	....	....	....	....	....	....	....	....	....	....	....	....	....	....	....
1988-89	New Jersey	NHL	2	0	0	0	0	0	0	0	3	0.0	–1	....	....	....	....	....	....	....	....	....	....	....	....
	Utica Devils	AHL	80	17	27	44	70	....	....	....	....	....	....	....	....	....	5	0	1	1	4	....	....	....	....
1989-90	New Jersey	NHL	19	2	7	9	11	1	0	1	16	12.5	1	....	....	....	6	1	3	4	17	0	0	0	....
	Utica Devils	AHL	57	12	48	60	38	....	....	....	....	....	....	....	....	....	....	....	....	....	....	....	....	....	....
1990-91	New Jersey	NHL	76	4	34	38	48	1	0	0	96	4.2	10	....	....	....	7	1	2	3	6	1	0	0	....
1991-92	New Jersey	NHL	76	7	25	32	55	5	0	0	97	7.2	10	....	....	....	7	0	2	2	4	0	0	0	....
1992-93	Hartford	NHL	79	7	29	36	76	0	2	2	104	6.7	–11	....	....	....	....	....	....	....	....	....	....	....	....
1993-94	Hartford	NHL	8	1	1	2	2	1	0	0	10	10.0	–5	....	....	....	....	....	....	....	....	....	....	....	....
	Chicago	NHL	54	3	23	26	31	1	0	2	105	2.9	6	....	....	....	6	0	2	2	6	0	0	0	....
1994-95	Chicago	NHL	48	3	10	13	33	1	0	2	50	6.0	1	....	....	....	16	1	5	6	4	0	0	0	....
1995-96	Chicago	NHL	77	5	10	15	65	0	0	0	76	6.6	14	....	....	....	10	1	4	5	10	1	0	0	....
1996-97	Chicago	NHL	81	7	25	32	62	1	0	0	115	6.1	19	....	....	....	6	0	1	1	4	0	0	0	....
1997-98	Chicago	NHL	82	2	21	23	106	0	0	0	85	2.4	10	....	....	....	....	....	....	....	....	....	....	....	....
1998-99	Chicago	NHL	14	1	3	4	12	0	0	0	24	4.2	–13	0	0.0	20:12	....	....	....	....	....	....	....	....	....
	Montreal	NHL	66	6	12	18	77	4	0	1	95	6.3	–12	0	0.0	24:44	....	....	....	....	....	....	....	....	....
99-2000	Montreal	NHL	77	4	25	29	39	2	0	0	120	3.3	4	0	0.0	25:21	....	....	....	....	....	....	....	....	....
2000-01	Montreal	NHL	60	6	19	25	34	2	0	1	81	7.4	–1	1	100.0	24:27	....	....	....	....	....	....	....	....	....
	Boston	NHL	22	1	5	6	10	1	0	1	28	3.6	–8	0	0.0	25:52	....	....	....	....	....	....	....	....	....
2001-02	Philadelphia	NHL	80	4	20	24	26	0	0	2	102	3.9	27	0	0.0	21:53	5	0	0	0	4	0	0	0	18:42
2002-03	Philadelphia	NHL	81	2	18	20	40	1	1	0	103	1.9	16	1	0.0	21:24	13	2	3	5	12	1	0	0	24:59
2003-04	Philadelphia	NHL	54	2	7	9	32	1	0	1	56	3.6	11	0	0.0	20:48	....	....	....	....	....	....	....	....	....
	St. Louis	NHL	26	2	8	10	14	1	0	0	27	7.4	1	0	0.0	23:05	5	0	1	1	0	0	0	0	23:36
2004-05	EC Villacher SV	Austria	10	3	8	11	8	....	....	....	....	....	....	....	....	....	3	0	1	1	6	....	....	....	....
	NHL Totals		1082	69	302	371	773	23	3	13	1393	5.0		2	50.0	23:09	81	6	23	29	67	3	0	0	23:19

Hockey East First All-Star Team (1987) • NCAA East Second All-American Team (1987) • AHL First All-Star Team (1990) • Eddie Shore Award (Outstanding Defenseman – AHL) (1990) • NHL All-Rookie Team (1991)

Traded to **Hartford** by **New Jersey** with Sean Burke for Bobby Holik and Hartford's 2nd round choice (Jay Pandolfo) in 1993 Entry Draft, August 28, 1992. Traded to **Chicago** by **Hartford** with Patrick Poulin for Steve Larmer and Bryan Marchment, November 2, 1993. Traded to **Montreal** by **Chicago** with Jeff Hackett, Alain Nasreddine and Tampa Bay's 4th round choice (previously acquired, Montreal selected Chris Dyment) in 1999 Entry Draft for Jocelyn Thibault, Dave Manson and Brad Brown, November 16, 1998. Traded to **Boston** by **Montreal** for Patrick Traverse, February 21, 2001. Signed as a free agent by **Philadelphia**, July 5, 2001. Traded to **St. Louis** by **Philadelphia** for St. Louis' 5th round choice (Gino Pisellini) in 2004 Entry Draft, February 9, 2004. Signed as a free agent by **Villacher** (Austria), February 14, 2005.

WEISS, Stephen

(WIGHS, STEEV-ehn) **FLA.**

Center. Shoots left. 5'11", 185 lbs. Born, Toronto, Ont., April 3, 1983. Florida's 1st choice, 4th overall, in 2001 Entry Draft.

Season	Club	League	GP	G	A	Pts	PIM	PP	SH	GW	S	%	+/-	TF	F%	Min	GP	G	A	Pts	PIM	PP	SH	GW	Min
1997-98	Tor. Young Nats	MTHL	48	51	58	109	....	....	....	....	....	....	....	....	....	....	....	....	....	....	....	....	....	....	....
1998-99	North York	OPJHL	35	15	22	37	10	....	....	....	....	....	....	....	....	....	....	....	....	....	....	....	....	....	....
99-2000	Plymouth Whalers	OHL	64	24	42	66	35	....	....	....	....	....	....	....	....	....	23	8	18	26	18	....	....	....	....
2000-01	Plymouth Whalers	OHL	62	40	47	87	45	....	....	....	....	....	....	....	....	....	18	7	16	23	10	....	....	....	....
2001-02	Florida	NHL	7	1	1	2	0	1	0	0	15	6.7	0	107	52.3	16:14	....	....	....	....	....	....	....	....	....
	Plymouth Whalers	OHL	46	25	45	70	69	....	....	....	....	....	....	....	....	....	6	2	7	9	13	....	....	....	....
2002-03	Florida	NHL	77	6	15	21	17	0	0	2	87	6.9	–13	1065	46.3	14:17	....	....	....	....	....	....	....	....	....
2003-04	Florida	NHL	50	12	17	29	10	3	0	2	82	14.6	–10	799	44.9	17:42	....	....	....	....	....	....	....	....	....
	San Antonio	AHL	10	6	3	9	14	....	....	....	....	....	....	....	....	....	....	....	....	....	....	....	....	....	....
2004-05	San Antonio	AHL	62	15	23	38	38	....	....	....	....	....	....	....	....	....	....	....	....	....	....	....	....	....	....
	Chicago Wolves	AHL	18	7	9	16	12	....	....	....	....	....	....	....	....	....	18	2	7	9	17	....	....	....	....
	NHL Totals		134	19	33	52	27	4	0	4	184	10.3		1971	46.1	15:40	....	....	....	....	....	....	....	....	....

OHL All-Rookie Team (2000)

Loaned to **Chicago** (AHL) by **San Antonio** (AHL) for cash, March 8, 2005.

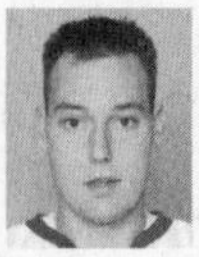

WELLWOOD, Kyle

(WEHL-wud, KIGHL) **TOR.**

Center. Shoots right. 5'10", 190 lbs. Born, Windsor, Ont., May 16, 1983. Toronto's 6th choice, 134th overall, in 2001 Entry Draft.

			Regular Season														Playoffs								
Season	Club	League	GP	G	A	Pts	PIM	PP	SH	GW	S	%	+/-	TF	F%	Min	GP	G	A	Pts	PIM	PP	SH	GW	Min
1998-99	Tecumseh	OHA-B	51	22	41	63	12	....	....	....	....	....	....	....	....	....	....	....	....	....	....	....	....	....	....
99-2000	Belleville Bulls	OHL	65	14	37	51	14	....	....	....	....	....	....	....	....	....	16	3	7	10	6	....	....	....	....
2000-01	Belleville Bulls	OHL	68	35	*83	*118	24	....	....	....	....	....	....	....	....	....	10	3	16	19	4	....	....	....	....
2001-02	Belleville Bulls	OHL	28	16	24	40	4	....	....	....	....	....	....	....	....	....	....	....	....	....	....	....	....	....	....
	Windsor Spitfires	OHL	26	14	21	35	0	....	....	....	....	....	....	....	....	....	16	12	12	24	0	....	....	....	....
2002-03	Windsor Spitfires	OHL	57	41	59	100	0	....	....	....	....	....	....	....	....	....	7	5	9	14	0	....	....	....	....
2003-04	**Toronto**	**NHL**	**1**	**0**	**0**	**0**	**0**	**0**	**0**	**0**	**1**	**0.0**	**–1**	**13**	**30.8**	**7:56**	....	....	....	....	....	....	....	....	....
	St. John's	AHL	76	20	35	55	6	....	....	....	....	....	....	....	....	....	....	....	....	....	....	....	....	....	....
2004-05	St. John's	AHL	80	38	49	87	20	....	....	....	....	....	....	....	....	....	5	2	2	4	2	....	....	....	....
	NHL Totals		**1**	**0**	**0**	**0**	**0**	**0**	**0**	**0**	**1**	**0.0**		**13**	**30.8**	**7:56**	....	....	....	....	....	....	....	....	....

OHL First All-Star Team (2001) • Canadian Major Junior Sportsman of the Year (2003)

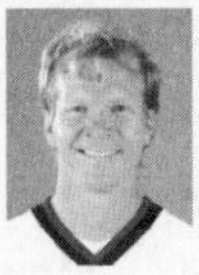

WESLEY, Glen

(WEH-slee, GLEHN) **CAR.**

Defense. Shoots left. 6'1", 205 lbs. Born, Red Deer, Alta., October 2, 1968. Boston's 1st choice, 3rd overall, in 1987 Entry Draft.

			Regular Season														Playoffs								
Season	Club	League	GP	G	A	Pts	PIM	PP	SH	GW	S	%	+/-	TF	F%	Min	GP	G	A	Pts	PIM	PP	SH	GW	Min
1983-84	Red Deer Rustlers	AJHL	57	9	20	29	40	....	....	....	....	....	....	....	....	....	....	....	....	....	....	....	....	....	....
	Portland	WHL	3	1	2	3	0	....	....	....	....	....	....	....	....	....	....	....	....	....	....	....	....	....	....
1984-85	Portland	WHL	67	16	52	68	76	....	....	....	....	....	....	....	....	....	6	1	6	7	8	....	....	....	....
1985-86	Portland	WHL	69	16	75	91	96	....	....	....	....	....	....	....	....	....	15	3	11	14	29	....	....	....	....
1986-87	Portland	WHL	63	16	46	62	72	....	....	....	....	....	....	....	....	....	20	8	18	26	27	....	....	....	....
1987-88	**Boston**	**NHL**	**79**	**7**	**30**	**37**	**69**	**1**	**2**	**0**	**158**	**4.4**	**21**	....	....	....	**23**	**6**	**8**	**14**	**22**	**4**	**1**	**0**	....
1988-89	**Boston**	**NHL**	**77**	**19**	**35**	**54**	**61**	**8**	**1**	**1**	**181**	**10.5**	**23**	....	....	....	**10**	**0**	**2**	**2**	**4**	**0**	**0**	**0**	....
1989-90	**Boston**	**NHL**	**78**	**9**	**27**	**36**	**48**	**5**	**0**	**4**	**166**	**5.4**	**6**	....	....	....	**21**	**2**	**6**	**8**	**36**	**0**	**0**	**1**	....
1990-91	**Boston**	**NHL**	**80**	**11**	**32**	**43**	**78**	**5**	**1**	**1**	**199**	**5.5**	**0**	....	....	....	**19**	**2**	**9**	**11**	**19**	**2**	**0**	**0**	....
1991-92	**Boston**	**NHL**	**78**	**9**	**37**	**46**	**54**	**4**	**0**	**1**	**211**	**4.3**	**–9**	....	....	....	**15**	**2**	**4**	**6**	**16**	**0**	**0**	**0**	....
1992-93	**Boston**	**NHL**	**64**	**8**	**25**	**33**	**47**	**4**	**1**	**0**	**183**	**4.4**	**–2**	....	....	....	**4**	**0**	**0**	**0**	**0**	**0**	**0**	**0**	....
1993-94	**Boston**	**NHL**	**81**	**14**	**44**	**58**	**64**	**6**	**1**	**1**	**265**	**5.3**	**1**	....	....	....	**13**	**3**	**3**	**6**	**12**	**1**	**0**	**0**	....
1994-95	**Hartford**	**NHL**	**48**	**2**	**14**	**16**	**50**	**1**	**0**	**1**	**125**	**1.6**	**–6**	....	....	....	....	....	....	....	....	....	....	....	....
1995-96	**Hartford**	**NHL**	**68**	**8**	**16**	**24**	**88**	**6**	**0**	**1**	**129**	**6.2**	**–9**	....	....	....	....	....	....	....	....	....	....	....	....
1996-97	**Hartford**	**NHL**	**68**	**6**	**26**	**32**	**40**	**3**	**1**	**0**	**126**	**4.8**	**0**	....	....	....	....	....	....	....	....	....	....	....	....
1997-98	**Carolina**	**NHL**	**82**	**6**	**19**	**25**	**36**	**1**	**0**	**1**	**121**	**5.0**	**7**	....	....	....	....	....	....	....	....	....	....	....	....
1998-99	**Carolina**	**NHL**	**74**	**7**	**17**	**24**	**44**	**0**	**0**	**2**	**112**	**6.3**	**14**	**1**	**0.0**	**22:31**	**6**	**0**	**0**	**0**	**2**	**0**	**0**	**0**	**28:21**
99-2000	**Carolina**	**NHL**	**78**	**7**	**15**	**22**	**38**	**1**	**0**	**0**	**99**	**7.1**	**–4**	**0**	**0.0**	**21:32**	....	....	....	....	....	....	....	....	....
2000-01	**Carolina**	**NHL**	**71**	**5**	**16**	**21**	**42**	**3**	**0**	**0**	**92**	**5.4**	**–2**	**0**	**0.0**	**22:21**	**6**	**0**	**0**	**0**	**0**	**0**	**0**	**0**	**22:07**
2001-02	**Carolina**	**NHL**	**77**	**5**	**13**	**18**	**56**	**1**	**0**	**0**	**88**	**5.7**	**–8**	**0**	**0.0**	**20:13**	**22**	**0**	**2**	**2**	**12**	**0**	**0**	**0**	**21:04**
2002-03	**Carolina**	**NHL**	**63**	**1**	**7**	**8**	**40**	**1**	**0**	**0**	**72**	**1.4**	**–5**	**0**	**0.0**	**21:24**	....	....	....	....	....	....	....	....	....
	Toronto	**NHL**	**7**	**0**	**3**	**3**	**4**	**0**	**0**	**0**	**5**	**0.0**	**3**	**0**	**0.0**	**20:41**	**5**	**0**	**1**	**1**	**2**	**0**	**0**	**0**	**27:39**
2003-04	**Carolina**	**NHL**	**74**	**0**	**6**	**6**	**32**	**0**	**0**	**0**	**82**	**0.0**	**18**	**0**	**0.0**	**21:22**	....	....	....	....	....	....	....	....	....
2004-05			DID NOT PLAY																						
	NHL Totals		**1247**	**124**	**382**	**506**	**891**	**50**	**7**	**13**	**2414**	**5.1**		**1**	**0.0**	**21:33**	**144**	**15**	**35**	**50**	**125**	**7**	**1**	**1**	**23:11**

WHL West First All-Star Team (1986, 1987) • NHL All-Rookie Team (1988)

Played in NHL All-Star Game (1989)

Traded to **Hartford** by **Boston** for Hartford's 1st round choices in 1995 (Kyle McLaren), 1996 (Johnathan Aitken) and 1997 (Sergei Samsonov) Entry Drafts, August 26, 1994. Transferred to **Carolina** after **Hartford** franchise relocated, June 25, 1997. Traded to **Toronto** by **Carolina** for Toronto's 2nd round choice (later traded to Columbus – Columbus selected Kyle Wharton) in 2004 Entry Draft, March 9, 2003. Signed as a free agent by **Carolina**, July 8, 2003.

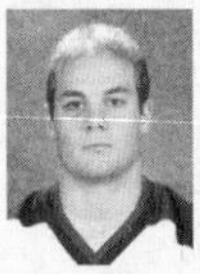

WESTCOTT, Duvie

(WEST-coht, DOO-vee) **CBJ**

Defense. Shoots right. 5'11", 192 lbs. Born, Winnipeg, Man., October 30, 1977.

			Regular Season														Playoffs								
Season	Club	League	GP	G	A	Pts	PIM	PP	SH	GW	S	%	+/-	TF	F%	Min	GP	G	A	Pts	PIM	PP	SH	GW	Min
1996-97	Winnipeg South	MJHL	52	12	47	59		....	....	....	....	....	....	....	....	....	....	....	....	....	....	....	....	....	....
1997-98	Alaska-Anchorage	WCHA	25	3	5	8	43	....	....	....	....	....	....	....	....	....	....	....	....	....	....	....	....	....	....
	Omaha Lancers	USHL	12	3	3	6	31	....	....	....	....	....	....	....	....	....	14	0	8	8	84	....	....	....	....
1998-99	St. Cloud State	WCHA	DID NOT PLAY – TRANSFERRED COLLEGES																						
99-2000	St. Cloud State	WCHA	36	1	18	19	67	....	....	....	....	....	....	....	....	....	....	....	....	....	....	....	....	....	....
2000-01	St. Cloud State	WCHA	38	10	24	34	116	....	....	....	....	....	....	....	....	....	....	....	....	....	....	....	....	....	....
2001-02	**Columbus**	**NHL**	**4**	**0**	**0**	**0**	**2**	**0**	**0**	**0**	**3**	**0.0**	**–2**	**0**	**0.0**	**15:08**	....	....	....	....	....	....	....	....	....
	Syracuse Crunch	AHL	68	4	29	33	99	....	....	....	....	....	....	....	....	....	10	0	1	1	12	....	....	....	....
2002-03	**Columbus**	**NHL**	**39**	**0**	**7**	**7**	**77**	**0**	**0**	**0**	**27**	**0.0**	**–3**	**0**	**0.0**	**18:41**	....	....	....	....	....	....	....	....	....
	Syracuse Crunch	AHL	22	1	10	11	54	....	....	....	....	....	....	....	....	....	....	....	....	....	....	....	....	....	....
2003-04	**Columbus**	**NHL**	**34**	**0**	**7**	**7**	**39**	**0**	**0**	**0**	**43**	**0.0**	**–15**	**0**	**0.0**	**21:11**	....	....	....	....	....	....	....	....	....
2004-05	JYP Jyvaskyla	Finland	46	11	7	18	106	....	....	....	....	....	....	....	....	....	1	2	0	2	25	....	....	....	....
	NHL Totals		**77**	**0**	**14**	**14**	**118**	**0**	**0**	**0**	**73**	**0.0**		**0**	**0.0**	**19:36**	....	....	....	....	....	....	....	....	....

WCHA Second All-Star Team (2001)

Signed as a free agent by **Columbus**, May 10, 2001. • Missed majority of 2003-04 season recovering from ankle (October 13, 2003 vs. Vancouver) and hand (January 31, 2004 vs. Minnesota) injuries. Signed as a free agent by **JYP** (Finland), September 30, 2004.

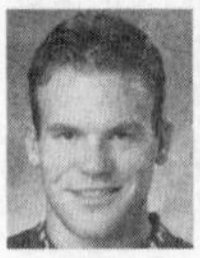

WESTRUM, Erik

(WEHST-ruhm, AIR-ihk) **MIN.**

Center. Shoots left. 6', 204 lbs. Born, Minneapolis, MN, July 26, 1979. Phoenix's 9th choice, 187th overall, in 1998 Entry Draft.

			Regular Season														Playoffs								
Season	Club	League	GP	G	A	Pts	PIM	PP	SH	GW	S	%	+/-	TF	F%	Min	GP	G	A	Pts	PIM	PP	SH	GW	Min
1995/97	Apple Valley	High-MN	78	56	84	140		....	....	....	....	....	....	....	....	....	....	....	....	....	....	....	....	....	....
1997-98	U. of Minnesota	WCHA	39	6	12	18	43	....	....	....	....	....	....	....	....	....	....	....	....	....	....	....	....	....	....
1998-99	U. of Minnesota	WCHA	41	10	26	36	81	....	....	....	....	....	....	....	....	....	....	....	....	....	....	....	....	....	....
99-2000	U. of Minnesota	WCHA	39	27	26	53	99	....	....	....	....	....	....	....	....	....	....	....	....	....	....	....	....	....	....
2000-01	U. of Minnesota	WCHA	42	26	35	61	84	....	....	....	....	....	....	....	....	....	....	....	....	....	....	....	....	....	....
2001-02	Springfield	AHL	73	13	29	42	116	....	....	....	....	....	....	....	....	....	....	....	....	....	....	....	....	....	....
2002-03	Springfield	AHL	70	10	22	32	65	....	....	....	....	....	....	....	....	....	6	0	4	4	6	....	....	....	....
2003-04	**Phoenix**	**NHL**	**15**	**1**	**1**	**2**	**20**	**0**	**0**	**0**	**29**	**3.4**	**–3**	**106**	**39.6**	**16:00**	....	....	....	....	....	....	....	....	....
	Springfield	AHL	56	14	18	32	91	....	....	....	....	....	....	....	....	....	....	....	....	....	....	....	....	....	....
2004-05	Utah Grizzlies	AHL	80	18	15	33	117	....	....	....	....	....	....	....	....	....	....	....	....	....	....	....	....	....	....
	NHL Totals		**15**	**1**	**1**	**2**	**20**	**0**	**0**	**0**	**29**	**3.4**		**106**	**39.6**	**16:00**	....	....	....	....	....	....	....	....	....

WCHA Second All-Star Team (2001)

• Statistics for **Apple Valley** (High-MN) are career totals for 1995-1997 seasons. Traded to **Minnesota** by **Phoenix** with Dustin Wood for Zbynek Michalek, August 26, 2005.

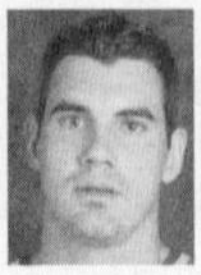

WHITE, Brian

(WIGHT, BRIGH-uhn)

Defense. Shoots right. 6'1", 195 lbs. Born, Winchester, MA, February 7, 1976. Tampa Bay's 11th choice, 268th overall, in 1994 Entry Draft.

			Regular Season														Playoffs								
Season	Club	League	GP	G	A	Pts	PIM	PP	SH	GW	S	%	+/-	TF	F%	Min	GP	G	A	Pts	PIM	PP	SH	GW	Min
1993-94	Arlington	High-MA	40	14	18	32	81	....	....	....	....	....	....	....	....	....	....	....	....	....	....	....	....	....	....
1994-95	U. of Maine	H-East	28	1	1	2	16	....	....	....	....	....	....	....	....	....	....	....	....	....	....	....	....	....	....
1995-96	U. of Maine	H-East	39	0	4	4	18	....	....	....	....	....	....	....	....	....	....	....	....	....	....	....	....	....	....
1996-97	U. of Maine	H-East	35	4	12	16	36	....	....	....	....	....	....	....	....	....	....	....	....	....	....	....	....	....	....
1997-98	U. of Maine	H-East	33	0	12	12	45	....	....	....	....	....	....	....	....	....	....	....	....	....	....	....	....	....	....
	Long Beach	IHL	1	0	0	0	0	....	....	....	....	....	....	....	....	....	....	....	....	....	....	....	....	....	....
1998-99	**Colorado**	**NHL**	**2**	**0**	**0**	**0**	**0**	**0**	**0**	**0**	**0**	**0.0**	**0**	**0**	**0.0**	**0:40**	....	....	....	....	....	....	....	....	....
	Hershey Bears	AHL	71	4	8	12	41	....	....	....	....	....	....	....	....	....	4	0	1	1	2	....	....	....	....
99-2000	Hershey Bears	AHL	79	3	19	22	78	....	....	....	....	....	....	....	....	....	14	0	3	3	21	....	....	....	....
2000-01	Hershey Bears	AHL	75	2	9	11	44	....	....	....	....	....	....	....	....	....	9	0	1	1	12	....	....	....	....
2001-02	Cincinnati	AHL	73	0	8	8	32	....	....	....	....	....	....	....	....	....	3	0	0	0	2	....	....	....	....
2002-03	Providence Bruins	AHL	51	2	5	7	34	....	....	....	....	....	....	....	....	....	4	0	1	1	8	....	....	....	....
2003-04	Providence Bruins	AHL	71	2	7	9	40	....	....	....	....	....	....	....	....	....	2	0	0	0	0	....	....	....	....
2004-05	Iserlohn Roosters	Germany	52	2	5	7	48	....	....	....	....	....	....	....	....	....	....	....	....	....	....	....	....	....	....
	NHL Totals		**2**	**0**	**0**	**0**	**0**	**0**	**0**	**0**	**0**	**0.0**		**0**	**0.0**	**0:40**	....	....	....	....	....	....	....	....	....

Signed as a free agent by **Colorado**, July 7, 1998. Signed as a free agent by **Anaheim**, August 14, 2001. Signed as a free agent by **Providence** (AHL), September 23, 2002. Signed as a free agent by **Iserlohn** (Germany), June 3, 2004.

								Regular Season									Playoffs								
Season	Club	League	GP	G	A	Pts	PIM	PP	SH	GW	S	%	+/-	TF	F%	Min	GP	G	A	Pts	PIM	PP	SH	GW	Min

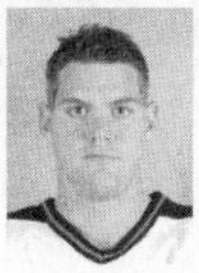

WHITE, Colin (WIGHT, CAWl-ihn) **N.J.**

Defense. Shoots left. 6'4", 215 lbs. Born, New Glasgow, N.S., December 12, 1977. New Jersey's 5th choice, 49th overall, in 1996 Entry Draft.

1994-95	Laval Titan	QMJHL	7	0	1	1	32	....	....	....	....	....	....	....	....	....	....	....	....	....	....	....	....	....	....
	Hull Olympiques	QMJHL	5	0	1	1	4	....	....	....	....	....	....	....	....	....	12	0	0	0	23	....	....	....	....
1995-96	Hull Olympiques	QMJHL	62	2	8	10	303	....	....	....	....	....	....	....	....	....	18	0	4	4	42	....	....	....	....
1996-97	Hull Olympiques	QMJHL	63	3	12	15	297	....	....	....	....	....	....	....	....	....	14	3	12	15	65	....	....	....	....
1997-98	Albany River Rats	AHL	76	3	13	16	235	....	....	....	....	....	....	....	....	....	13	0	0	0	55	....	....	....	....
1998-99	Albany River Rats	AHL	77	2	12	14	265	....	....	....	....	....	....	....	....	....	5	0	1	1	8	....	....	....	....
99-2000♦	**New Jersey**	**NHL**	**21**	**2**	**1**	**3**	**40**	**0**	**0**	**1**	**29**	**6.9**	**3**	**0**	**0.0**	**14:45**	**23**	**1**	**5**	**6**	**18**	**0**	**0**	**1**	**14:25**
	Albany River Rats	AHL	52	5	21	26	176	....	....	....	....	....	....	....	....	....	....	....	....	....	....	....	....	....	....
2000-01	**New Jersey**	**NHL**	**82**	**1**	**19**	**20**	**155**	**0**	**0**	**1**	**114**	**0.9**	**32**	**0**	**0.0**	**19:06**	**25**	**0**	**3**	**3**	**42**	**0**	**0**	**0**	**16:45**
2001-02	**New Jersey**	**NHL**	**73**	**2**	**3**	**5**	**133**	**0**	**0**	**0**	**81**	**2.5**	**6**	**0**	**0.0**	**20:06**	**6**	**0**	**0**	**0**	**2**	**0**	**0**	**0**	**21:50**
2002-03♦	**New Jersey**	**NHL**	**72**	**5**	**8**	**13**	**98**	**0**	**0**	**1**	**81**	**6.2**	**19**	**0**	**0.0**	**19:41**	**24**	**0**	**5**	**5**	**29**	**0**	**0**	**0**	**22:02**
2003-04	**New Jersey**	**NHL**	**75**	**2**	**11**	**13**	**96**	**0**	**0**	**0**	**61**	**3.3**	**10**	**0**	**0.0**	**21:02**	**5**	**0**	**0**	**0**	**4**	**0**	**0**	**0**	**19:40**
2004-05			DID NOT PLAY																						
	NHL Totals		**323**	**12**	**42**	**54**	**522**	**0**	**0**	**3**	**366**	**3.3**		**0**	**0.0**	**19:37**	**83**	**1**	**13**	**14**	**95**	**0**	**0**	**1**	**18:10**

QMJHL All-Rookie Team (1996) • NHL All-Rookie Team (2001)

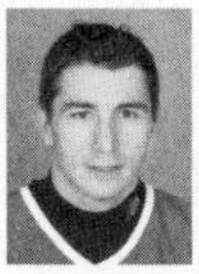

WHITE, Peter (WIGHT, PEE-tuhr)

Center. Shoots left. 5'11", 200 lbs. Born, Montreal, Que., March 15, 1969. Edmonton's 4th choice, 92nd overall, in 1989 Entry Draft.

1984-85	Lac St-Louis Lions	QAAA	42	16	32	48	18	....	....	....	....	....	....	....	....	....	11	4	3	7	4	....	....	....	....
1985-86	Lac St-Louis Lions	QAAA	42	38	62	100	28	....	....	....	....	....	....	....	....	....	2	3	1	4	2	....	....	....	....
1986-87	Pembroke	CJHL	55	20	34	54	20	....	....	....	....	....	....	....	....	....	....	....	....	....	....	....	....	....	....
1987-88	Pembroke	CJHL	56	*90	*136	*226	32	....	....	....	....	....	....	....	....	....	....	....	....	....	....	....	....	....	....
1988-89	Michigan State	CCHA	46	20	33	53	17	....	....	....	....	....	....	....	....	....	....	....	....	....	....	....	....	....	....
1989-90	Michigan State	CCHA	45	22	40	62	6	....	....	....	....	....	....	....	....	....	....	....	....	....	....	....	....	....	....
1990-91	Michigan State	CCHA	37	7	31	38	28	....	....	....	....	....	....	....	....	....	....	....	....	....	....	....	....	....	....
1991-92	Michigan State	CCHA	41	26	49	75	32	....	....	....	....	....	....	....	....	....	....	....	....	....	....	....	....	....	....
1992-93	Cape Breton	AHL	64	12	28	40	10	....	....	....	....	....	....	....	....	....	16	3	3	6	12	....	....	....	....
1993-94	**Edmonton**	**NHL**	**26**	**3**	**5**	**8**	**2**	**0**	**0**	**0**	**17**	**17.6**	**1**	....	....	....	....	....	....	....	....	....	....	....	....
	Cape Breton	AHL	45	21	49	70	12	....	....	....	....	....	....	....	....	....	5	2	3	5	2	....	....	....	....
1994-95	Cape Breton	AHL	65	36	*69	*105	30	....	....	....	....	....	....	....	....	....	....	....	....	....	....	....	....	....	....
	Edmonton	**NHL**	**9**	**2**	**4**	**6**	**0**	**2**	**0**	**0**	**13**	**15.4**	**1**	....	....	....	....	....	....	....	....	....	....	....	....
1995-96	**Edmonton**	**NHL**	**26**	**5**	**3**	**8**	**0**	**1**	**0**	**0**	**34**	**14.7**	**-14**	....	....	....	....	....	....	....	....	....	....	....	....
	Toronto	**NHL**	**1**	**0**	**0**	**0**	**0**	**0**	**0**	**0**	**0**	**0.0**	**0**	....	....	....	....	....	....	....	....	....	....	....	....
	St. John's	AHL	17	6	7	13	6	....	....	....	....	....	....	....	....	....	....	....	....	....	....	....	....	....	....
	Atlanta Knights	IHL	36	21	20	41	4	....	....	....	....	....	....	....	....	....	3	0	3	3	2	....	....	....	....
1996-97	Philadelphia	AHL	80	*44	61	*105	28	....	....	....	....	....	....	....	....	....	10	6	8	14	6	....	....	....	....
1997-98	Philadelphia	AHL	80	27	*78	*105	28	....	....	....	....	....	....	....	....	....	20	9	9	18	6	....	....	....	....
1998-99	**Philadelphia**	**NHL**	**3**	**0**	**0**	**0**	**0**	**0**	**0**	**0**	**0**	**0.0**	**0**	**8**	**37.5**	**2:02**	....	....	....	....	....	....	....	....	....
	Philadelphia	AHL	77	31	59	90	20	....	....	....	....	....	....	....	....	....	16	4	13	17	12	....	....	....	....
99-2000	**Philadelphia**	**NHL**	**21**	**1**	**5**	**6**	**6**	**0**	**0**	**0**	**24**	**4.2**	**1**	**277**	**54.5**	**13:04**	**16**	**0**	**2**	**2**	**0**	**0**	**0**	**0**	**11:54**
	Philadelphia	AHL	62	20	41	61	38	....	....	....	....	....	....	....	....	....	....	....	....	....	....	....	....	....	....
2000-01	**Philadelphia**	**NHL**	**77**	**9**	**16**	**25**	**16**	**1**	**0**	**1**	**68**	**13.2**	**1**	**1038**	**54.3**	**12:56**	**3**	**0**	**0**	**0**	**0**	**0**	**0**	**0**	**11:47**
2001-02	**Chicago**	**NHL**	**48**	**3**	**3**	**6**	**10**	**1**	**0**	**1**	**21**	**14.3**	**-8**	**513**	**53.0**	**10:31**	....	....	....	....	....	....	....	....	....
	Norfolk Admirals	AHL	24	4	19	23	18	....	....	....	....	....	....	....	....	....	4	0	1	1	0	....	....	....	....
2002-03	**Chicago**	**NHL**	**6**	**0**	**1**	**1**	**0**	**0**	**0**	**0**	**2**	**0.0**	**0**	**58**	**39.7**	**9:01**	....	....	....	....	....	....	....	....	....
	Norfolk Admirals	AHL	31	6	17	23	21	....	....	....	....	....	....	....	....	....	9	2	4	6	5	....	....	....	....
	Philadelphia	AHL	47	17	26	43	16	....	....	....	....	....	....	....	....	....	....	....	....	....	....	....	....	....	....
2003-04	**Philadelphia**	**NHL**	**3**	**0**	**0**	**0**	**2**	**0**	**0**	**0**	**2**	**0.0**	**-1**	**10**	**30.0**	**6:25**	....	....	....	....	....	....	....	....	....
	Philadelphia	AHL	75	12	48	60	39	....	....	....	....	....	....	....	....	....	12	2	1	3	10	....	....	....	....
2004-05	Philadelphia	AHL	10	2	6	8	6	....	....	....	....	....	....	....	....	....	....	....	....	....	....	....	....	....	....
	Utah Grizzlies	AHL	70	12	25	37	14	....	....	....	....	....	....	....	....	....	....	....	....	....	....	....	....	....	....
	NHL Totals		**220**	**23**	**37**	**60**	**36**	**5**	**0**	**2**	**181**	**12.7**		**1904**	**53.4**	**11:44**	**19**	**0**	**2**	**2**	**0**	**0**	**0**	**0**	**11:53**

AHL Second All-Star Team (1995, 1997) • John B. Sollenberger Trophy (Leading Scorer – AHL) (1995, 1997, 1998)

Traded to **Toronto** by **Edmonton** with Edmonton's 4th round choice (Jason Sessa) in 1996 Entry Draft for Kent Manderville, December 4, 1995. Signed as a free agent by **Philadelphia**, August 19, 1996. Signed as a free agent by **Chicago**, September 10, 2001. Traded to **Philadelphia** by **Chicago** for future considerations, March 11, 2003. Loaned to **Utah** (AHL) by **Philadelphia** (AHL) for the loan of Jon Sim, November 14, 2004.

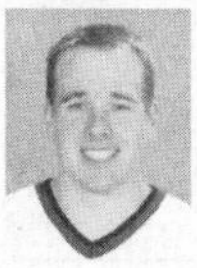

WHITE, Todd (WIGHT, TAWD) **MIN.**

Center. Shoots left. 5'10", 194 lbs. Born, Kanata, Ont., May 21, 1975.

1990-91	Powassan	NOJHA	38	34	38	72	118	....	....	....	....	....	....	....	....	....	....	....	....	....	....	....	....	....	....
1991-92	Kanata Valley	CJHL	55	39	49	88	30	....	....	....	....	....	....	....	....	....	....	....	....	....	....	....	....	....	....
1992-93	Kanata Valley	CJHL	49	51	87	138	46	....	....	....	....	....	....	....	....	....	....	....	....	....	....	....	....	....	....
1993-94	Clarkson Knights	ECAC	33	10	12	22	28	....	....	....	....	....	....	....	....	....	....	....	....	....	....	....	....	....	....
1994-95	Clarkson Knights	ECAC	34	13	16	29	44	....	....	....	....	....	....	....	....	....	....	....	....	....	....	....	....	....	....
1995-96	Clarkson Knights	ECAC	38	29	43	72	36	....	....	....	....	....	....	....	....	....	....	....	....	....	....	....	....	....	....
1996-97	Clarkson Knights	ECAC	37	*38	*36	*74	22	....	....	....	....	....	....	....	....	....	....	....	....	....	....	....	....	....	....
1997-98	**Chicago**	**NHL**	**7**	**1**	**0**	**1**	**2**	**0**	**0**	**0**	**3**	**33.3**	**0**	....	....	....	....	....	....	....	....	....	....	....	....
	Indianapolis Ice	IHL	65	46	36	82	28	....	....	....	....	....	....	....	....	....	5	2	3	5	4	....	....	....	....
1998-99	**Chicago**	**NHL**	**35**	**5**	**8**	**13**	**20**	**2**	**0**	**0**	**43**	**11.6**	**-1**	**452**	**46.0**	**13:39**	....	....	....	....	....	....	....	....	....
	Chicago Wolves	IHL	25	11	13	24	8	....	....	....	....	....	....	....	....	....	10	1	4	5	8	....	....	....	....
99-2000	**Chicago**	**NHL**	**1**	**0**	**0**	**0**	**0**	**0**	**0**	**0**	**0**	**0.0**	**0**	**9**	**55.6**	**13:02**	....	....	....	....	....	....	....	....	....
	Cleveland	IHL	42	21	30	51	32	....	....	....	....	....	....	....	....	....	....	....	....	....	....	....	....	....	....
	Philadelphia	**NHL**	**3**	**1**	**0**	**1**	**0**	**0**	**0**	**0**	**4**	**25.0**	**-1**	**25**	**40.0**	**10:29**	....	....	....	....	....	....	....	....	....
	Philadelphia	AHL	32	19	24	43	12	....	....	....	....	....	....	....	....	....	5	2	1	3	8	....	....	....	....
2000-01	**Ottawa**	**NHL**	**16**	**4**	**1**	**5**	**4**	**0**	**0**	**0**	**12**	**33.3**	**5**	**133**	**57.1**	**8:33**	**2**	**0**	**0**	**0**	**0**	**0**	**0**	**0**	**7:29**
	Grand Rapids	IHL	64	22	32	54	20	....	....	....	....	....	....	....	....	....	10	4	4	8	10	....	....	....	....
2001-02	**Ottawa**	**NHL**	**81**	**20**	**30**	**50**	**24**	**4**	**0**	**1**	**147**	**13.6**	**12**	**1508**	**50.5**	**18:22**	**12**	**2**	**2**	**4**	**6**	**0**	**0**	**0**	**18:57**
2002-03	**Ottawa**	**NHL**	**80**	**25**	**35**	**60**	**28**	**8**	**1**	**5**	**144**	**17.4**	**19**	**1396**	**50.5**	**17:58**	**18**	**5**	**1**	**6**	**6**	**1**	**1**	**2**	**16:59**
2003-04	**Ottawa**	**NHL**	**53**	**9**	**20**	**29**	**22**	**1**	**1**	**2**	**98**	**9.2**	**12**	**879**	**52.0**	**17:32**	**7**	**1**	**0**	**1**	**4**	**0**	**0**	**0**	**18:04**
2004-05	Sodertalje SK	Sweden	1	0	1	1	4	....	....	....	....	....	....	....	....	....	....	....	....	....	....	....	....	....	....
	NHL Totals		**276**	**65**	**94**	**159**	**100**	**15**	**2**	**8**	**451**	**14.4**		**4402**	**50.5**	**16:46**	**39**	**8**	**3**	**11**	**16**	**1**	**1**	**2**	**17:18**

ECAC Second All-Star Team (1996) • NCAA East Second All-American Team (1996) • ECAC First All-Star Team (1997) • ECAC Player of the Year (1997) • NCAA East First All-American Team (1997) • Garry F. Longman Memorial Trophy (Rookie of the Year – IHL) (1998)

Signed as a free agent by **Chicago**, August 27, 1997. Traded to **Philadelphia** by **Chicago** for future considerations, January 26, 2000. Signed as a free agent by **Ottawa**, July 12, 2000. Signed as a free agent by **Sodertalje** (Sweden), December 21, 2004. Traded to **Minnesota** by **Ottawa** for Colorado's 4th round choice (previously acquired, Ottawa selected Cody Bass) in 2005 Entry Draft, July 30, 2005.

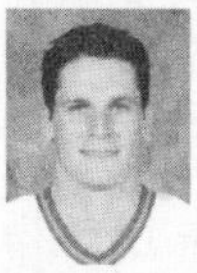

WHITFIELD, Trent (WHIHT-feeld, TREHNT) **ST.L.**

Center. Shoots left. 5'11", 204 lbs. Born, Estevan, Sask., June 17, 1977. Boston's 5th choice, 100th overall, in 1996 Entry Draft.

1993-94	Saskatoon Blazers	SMHL	36	26	22	48	42	....	....	....	....	....	....	....	....	....	....	....	....	....	....	....	....	....	....
	Spokane Chiefs	WHL	5	1	1	2	0	....	....	....	....	....	....	....	....	....	....	....	....	....	....	....	....	....	....
1994-95	Spokane Chiefs	WHL	48	8	17	25	26	....	....	....	....	....	....	....	....	....	11	7	6	13	5	....	....	....	....
1995-96	Spokane Chiefs	WHL	72	33	51	84	75	....	....	....	....	....	....	....	....	....	18	8	10	18	10	....	....	....	....
1996-97	Spokane Chiefs	WHL	58	34	42	76	74	....	....	....	....	....	....	....	....	....	9	5	7	12	10	....	....	....	....
1997-98	Spokane Chiefs	WHL	65	38	44	82	97	....	....	....	....	....	....	....	....	....	18	9	10	19	15	....	....	....	....
1998-99	Portland Pirates	AHL	50	10	8	18	20	....	....	....	....	....	....	....	....	....	....	....	....	....	....	....	....	....	....
	Hampton Roads	ECHL	19	13	12	25	12	....	....	....	....	....	....	....	....	....	4	2	0	2	14	....	....	....	....
99-2000	Portland Pirates	AHL	79	18	35	53	52	....	....	....	....	....	....	....	....	....	3	1	1	2	2	....	....	....	....
	Washington	**NHL**															**3**	**0**	**0**	**0**	**0**	**0**	**0**	**0**	**5:47**
2000-01	**Washington**	**NHL**	**61**	**2**	**4**	**6**	**35**	**0**	**0**	**0**	**47**	**4.3**	**3**	**520**	**51.9**	**9:39**	**5**	**0**	**0**	**0**	**2**	**0**	**0**	**0**	**7:07**
	Portland Pirates	AHL	19	9	11	20	27	....	....	....	....	....	....	....	....	....	....	....	....	....	....	....	....	....	....
2001-02	**Washington**	**NHL**	**24**	**0**	**1**	**1**	**28**	**0**	**0**	**0**	**15**	**0.0**	**-3**	**189**	**54.0**	**7:06**	....	....	....	....	....	....	....	....	....
	Portland Pirates	AHL	10	4	4	8	8	....	....	....	....	....	....	....	....	....	....	....	....	....	....	....	....	....	....
	NY Rangers	**NHL**	**1**	**0**	**0**	**0**	**0**	**0**	**0**	**0**	**0**	**0.0**	**1**	**18**	**50.0**	**12:44**	....	....	....	....	....	....	....	....	....
	Portland Pirates	AHL	24	10	16	26	16	....	....	....	....	....	....	....	....	....	....	....	....	....	....	....	....	....	....

			Regular Season														Playoffs								
Season	Club	League	GP	G	A	Pts	PIM	PP	SH	GW	S	%	+/-	TF	F%	Min	GP	G	A	Pts	PIM	PP	SH	GW	Min
2002-03	**Washington**	**NHL**	**14**	**1**	**1**	**2**	**6**	**0**	**0**	**1**	**4**	**25.0**	**1**	**124**	**57.3**	**8:30**	**6**	**0**	**0**	**0**	**10**	**0**	**0**	**0**	**11:01**
	Portland Pirates	AHL	64	27	34	61	42																		
2003-04	**Washington**	**NHL**	**44**	**6**	**5**	**11**	**14**	**0**	**1**	**2**	**38**	**15.8**	**–2**	**598**	**55.4**	**12:48**									
	Portland Pirates	AHL	24	8	7	15	22																		
2004-05	Portland Pirates	AHL	67	17	38	55	75																		
	NHL Totals		**144**	**9**	**11**	**20**	**83**	**0**	**1**	**3**	**104**	**8.7**		**1449**	**54.0**	**10:06**	**14**	**0**	**0**	**0**	**12**	**0**	**0**	**0**	**8:30**

WHL West First All-Star Team (1997) • WHL West Second All-Star Team (1998)

Signed as a free agent by **Washington**, September 1, 1998. Claimed on waivers by **NY Rangers** from **Washington**, January 16, 2002. Claimed on waivers by **Washington** from **NY Rangers**, February 1, 2002. Signed as a free agent by **St. Louis**, August 2, 2005.

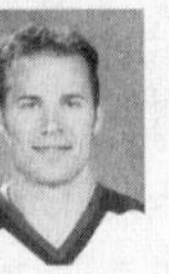

WHITNEY, Ray

(WHIHT-nee, RAY) **CAR.**

Left wing. Shoots right. 5'10", 178 lbs. Born, Fort Saskatchewan, Alta., May 8, 1972. San Jose's 2nd choice, 23rd overall, in 1991 Entry Draft.

Season	Club	League	GP	G	A	Pts	PIM	PP	SH	GW	S	%	+/-	TF	F%	Min	GP	G	A	Pts	PIM	PP	SH	GW	Min
1987-88	Ft. Saskatchewan	AMHL	71	80	155	235	119																		
1988-89	Spokane Chiefs	WHL	71	17	33	50	16																		
1989-90	Spokane Chiefs	WHL	71	57	56	113	50										6	3	4	7	6				
1990-91	Spokane Chiefs	WHL	72	67	118	*185	36										15	13	18	*31	12				
1991-92	Kolner EC	Germany	10	3	6	9	4																		
	Canada	Nat-Tm	5	1	0	1	6																		
	San Jose	**NHL**	**2**	**0**	**3**	**3**	**0**	**0**	**0**	**0**	**4**	**0.0**	**–1**												
	San Diego Gulls	IHL	63	36	54	90	12										4	0	0	0	0				
1992-93	**San Jose**	**NHL**	**26**	**4**	**6**	**10**	**4**	**1**	**0**	**0**	**24**	**16.7**	**–14**												
	Kansas City	IHL	46	20	33	53	14										12	5	7	12	2				
1993-94	**San Jose**	**NHL**	**61**	**14**	**26**	**40**	**14**	**1**	**0**	**0**	**82**	**17.1**	**2**				**14**	**0**	**4**	**4**	**8**	**0**	**0**	**0**	
1994-95	**San Jose**	**NHL**	**39**	**13**	**12**	**25**	**14**	**4**	**0**	**1**	**67**	**19.4**	**–7**				**11**	**4**	**4**	**8**	**2**	**0**	**0**	**1**	
1995-96	**San Jose**	**NHL**	**60**	**17**	**24**	**41**	**16**	**4**	**2**	**2**	**106**	**16.0**	**–23**												
1996-97	**San Jose**	**NHL**	**12**	**0**	**2**	**2**	**4**	**0**	**0**	**0**	**24**	**0.0**	**–6**												
	Kentucky	AHL	9	1	7	8	2																		
	Utah Grizzlies	IHL	43	13	35	48	34										7	3	1	4	6				
1997-98	**Edmonton**	**NHL**	**9**	**1**	**3**	**4**	**0**	**0**	**0**	**0**	**19**	**5.3**	**–1**												
	Florida	**NHL**	**68**	**32**	**29**	**61**	**28**	**12**	**0**	**2**	**156**	**20.5**	**10**												
1998-99	**Florida**	**NHL**	**81**	**26**	**38**	**64**	**18**	**7**	**0**	**6**	**193**	**13.5**	**–3**	**144**	**43.8**	**18:20**									
99-2000	**Florida**	**NHL**	**81**	**29**	**42**	**71**	**35**	**5**	**0**	**3**	**198**	**14.6**	**16**	**198**	**49.0**	**18:41**	**4**	**1**	**0**	**1**	**4**	**0**	**0**	**0**	**18:13**
2000-01	**Florida**	**NHL**	**43**	**10**	**21**	**31**	**28**	**5**	**0**	**0**	**117**	**8.5**	**–16**	**38**	**39.5**	**17:41**									
	Columbus	**NHL**	**3**	**0**	**3**	**3**	**2**	**0**	**0**	**0**	**3**	**0.0**	**–1**	**19**	**36.8**	**20:17**									
2001-02	**Columbus**	**NHL**	**67**	**21**	**40**	**61**	**12**	**6**	**0**	**3**	**210**	**10.0**	**–22**	**21**	**47.6**	**20:13**									
2002-03	**Columbus**	**NHL**	**81**	**24**	**52**	**76**	**22**	**8**	**2**	**2**	**235**	**10.2**	**–26**	**29**	**44.8**	**21:00**									
2003-04	**Detroit**	**NHL**	**67**	**14**	**29**	**43**	**22**	**3**	**1**	**4**	**119**	**11.8**	**7**	**18**	**38.9**	**16:24**	**12**	**1**	**3**	**4**	**4**	**0**	**0**	**1**	**11:56**
2004-05		DID NOT PLAY																							
	NHL Totals		**700**	**205**	**330**	**535**	**219**	**56**	**5**	**23**	**1557**	**13.2**		**467**	**45.4**	**18:51**	**41**	**6**	**11**	**17**	**18**	**0**	**0**	**2**	**13:30**

WHL West First All-Star Team (1991) • WHL Player of the Year (1991) • Memorial Cup Tournament All-Star Team (1991) • George Parsons Trophy (Memorial Cup Tournament Most Sportsmanlike Player) (1991)

Played in NHL All-Star Game (2000, 2003)

Signed as a free agent by **Edmonton**, October 1, 1997. Claimed on waivers by **Florida** from **Edmonton**, November 6, 1997. Traded to **Columbus** by **Florida** with future considerations for Kevyn Adams and Columbus's 4th round choice (Michael Woodford) in 2001 Entry Draft, March 13, 2001. Signed as a free agent by **Detroit**, July 30, 2003. Signed as a free agent by **Carolina**, August 7, 2005.

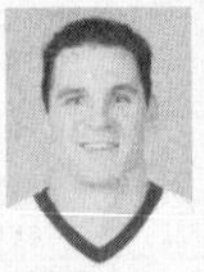

WIEMER, Jason

(WEE-muhr, JAY-suhn) **CGY.**

Center. Shoots left. 6'1", 225 lbs. Born, Kimberley, B.C., April 14, 1976. Tampa Bay's 1st choice, 8th overall, in 1994 Entry Draft.

Season	Club	League	GP	G	A	Pts	PIM	PP	SH	GW	S	%	+/-	TF	F%	Min	GP	G	A	Pts	PIM	PP	SH	GW	Min
1991-92	Kimberley	RMJHL	45	33	33	66	211																		
	Portland	WHL	2	0	1	1	0																		
1992-93	Portland	WHL	68	18	34	52	159										16	7	3	10	27				
1993-94	Portland	WHL	72	45	51	96	236										10	4	4	8	32				
1994-95	Portland	WHL	16	10	14	24	63																		
	Tampa Bay	**NHL**	**36**	**1**	**4**	**5**	**44**	**0**	**0**	**0**	**10**	**10.0**	**–2**												
1995-96	**Tampa Bay**	**NHL**	**66**	**9**	**9**	**18**	**81**	**4**	**0**	**1**	**89**	**10.1**	**–9**				**6**	**1**	**0**	**1**	**28**	**1**	**0**	**0**	
1996-97	**Tampa Bay**	**NHL**	**63**	**9**	**5**	**14**	**134**	**2**	**0**	**0**	**103**	**8.7**	**–13**												
	Adirondack	AHL	4	1	0	1	7																		
1997-98	**Tampa Bay**	**NHL**	**67**	**8**	**9**	**17**	**132**	**2**	**0**	**0**	**106**	**7.5**	**–9**												
	Calgary	**NHL**	**12**	**4**	**1**	**5**	**28**	**1**	**0**	**2**	**16**	**25.0**	**–1**												
1998-99	**Calgary**	**NHL**	**78**	**8**	**13**	**21**	**177**	**1**	**0**	**1**	**128**	**6.3**	**–12**	**867**	**40.9**	**13:17**									
99-2000	**Calgary**	**NHL**	**64**	**11**	**11**	**22**	**120**	**2**	**0**	**3**	**104**	**10.6**	**–10**	**955**	**47.6**	**14:41**									
2000-01	**Calgary**	**NHL**	**65**	**10**	**5**	**15**	**177**	**3**	**0**	**1**	**76**	**13.2**	**–15**	**599**	**51.1**	**13:56**									
2001-02	**Florida**	**NHL**	**70**	**11**	**20**	**31**	**178**	**5**	**1**	**1**	**115**	**9.6**	**–4**	**1241**	**44.1**	**17:09**									
2002-03	**NY Islanders**	**NHL**	**81**	**9**	**19**	**28**	**116**	**0**	**1**	**2**	**139**	**6.5**	**5**	**347**	**49.0**	**12:26**	**5**	**0**	**0**	**0**	**23**	**0**	**0**	**0**	**13:37**
2003-04	**NY Islanders**	**NHL**	**13**	**1**	**3**	**4**	**24**	**0**	**0**	**0**	**14**	**7.1**	**–1**	**72**	**47.2**	**11:36**									
	Minnesota	**NHL**	**62**	**7**	**11**	**18**	**106**	**1**	**0**	**0**	**89**	**7.9**	**–6**	**726**	**44.4**	**13:57**									
2004-05		DID NOT PLAY																							
	NHL Totals		**677**	**88**	**110**	**198**	**1317**	**21**	**2**	**11**	**989**	**8.9**		**4807**	**45.5**	**14:06**	**11**	**1**	**0**	**1**	**51**	**1**	**0**	**0**	**13:37**

Traded to **Calgary** by **Tampa Bay** for Sandy McCarthy and Calgary's 3rd (Brad Richards) and 5th (Curtis Rich) round choices in 1998 Entry Draft, March 24, 1998. Traded to **Florida** by **Calgary** with Valeri Bure for Rob Neidermayer and Philadelphia's 2nd round choice (previously acquired, Calgary selected Andrei Medvedev) in 2001 Entry Draft, June 24, 2001. Traded to **NY Islanders** by **Florida** for Branislav Mezei, July 3, 2002. Claimed on waivers by **Minnesota** from **NY Islanders**, November 13, 2003. Signed as a free agent by **Calgary**, August 5, 2004.

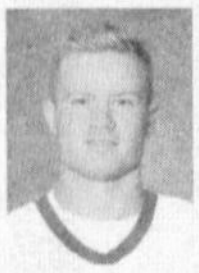

WILLIAMS, Jason

(WIHL-yuhms, JAY-suhn) **DET.**

Center. Shoots right. 5'11", 185 lbs. Born, London, Ont., August 11, 1980.

Season	Club	League	GP	G	A	Pts	PIM	PP	SH	GW	S	%	+/-	TF	F%	Min	GP	G	A	Pts	PIM	PP	SH	GW	Min
1995-96	Mount Brydges	OHA-D	36	31	28	59	18																		
1996-97	Peterborough	OHL	60	4	8	12	8										10	1	0	1	2				
1997-98	Peterborough	OHL	55	8	27	35	31										4	0	1	1	2				
1998-99	Peterborough	OHL	68	26	48	74	42										5	1	2	3	2				
99-2000	Peterborough	OHL	66	36	37	75	64										5	2	1	3	2				
2000-01	**Detroit**	**NHL**	**5**	**0**	**3**	**3**	**2**	**0**	**0**	**0**	**7**	**0.0**	**1**	**56**	**39.3**	**12:24**	**2**	**0**	**0**	**0**	**0**	**0**	**0**	**0**	**11:45**
	Cincinnati	AHL	76	24	45	69	48										1	0	0	0	2				
2001-02♦	**Detroit**	**NHL**	**25**	**8**	**2**	**10**	**4**	**4**	**0**	**0**	**32**	**25.0**	**2**	**208**	**47.6**	**10:50**	**9**	**0**	**0**	**0**	**2**	**0**	**0**	**0**	**6:12**
	Cincinnati	AHL	52	23	27	50	27										3	0	1	1	6				
2002-03	**Detroit**	**NHL**	**16**	**3**	**3**	**6**	**2**	**1**	**0**	**0**	**20**	**15.0**	**3**	**78**	**51.3**	**10:43**									
	Grand Rapids	AHL	45	23	22	45	18										15	1	7	8	16				
2003-04	**Detroit**	**NHL**	**49**	**6**	**7**	**13**	**15**	**0**	**0**	**0**	**44**	**13.6**	**1**	**315**	**49.2**	**9:27**	**3**	**0**	**0**	**0**	**2**	**0**	**0**	**0**	**6:11**
2004-05	Assat Pori	Finland	43	26	17	43	52										2	1	1	2	4				
	NHL Totals		**95**	**17**	**15**	**32**	**23**	**5**	**0**	**0**	**103**	**16.5**		**657**	**48.1**	**10:11**	**14**	**0**	**0**	**0**	**4**	**0**	**0**	**0**	**6:59**

Signed as a free agent by **Detroit**, September 18, 2000. Signed as a free agent by **Assat** (Finland), October 18, 2004.

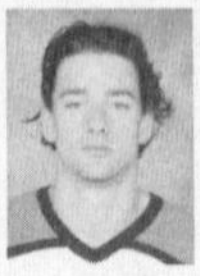

WILLIAMS, Justin

(WIHL-yuhms, JUHS-tihn) **CAR.**

Right wing. Shoots right. 6'1", 190 lbs. Born, Cobourg, Ont., October 4, 1981. Philadelphia's 1st choice, 28th overall, in 2000 Entry Draft.

Season	Club	League	GP	G	A	Pts	PIM	PP	SH	GW	S	%	+/-	TF	F%	Min	GP	G	A	Pts	PIM	PP	SH	GW	Min
1997-98	Colborne Colts	OHA-C	36	32	35	67	26																		
	Cobourg Cougars	OPJHL	17	0	3	3	5																		
1998-99	Plymouth Whalers	OHL	47	4	8	12	28										7	1	2	3	0				
99-2000	Plymouth Whalers	OHL	68	37	46	83	46										23	*14	16	*30	10				
2000-01	**Philadelphia**	**NHL**	**63**	**12**	**13**	**25**	**22**	**0**	**0**	**0**	**99**	**12.1**	**6**	**13**	**53.9**	**12:31**									
2001-02	**Philadelphia**	**NHL**	**75**	**17**	**23**	**40**	**32**	**0**	**0**	**1**	**162**	**10.5**	**11**	**16**	**25.0**	**14:27**	**5**	**0**	**0**	**0**	**4**	**0**	**0**	**0**	**16:42**
2002-03	**Philadelphia**	**NHL**	**41**	**8**	**16**	**24**	**22**	**0**	**0**	**2**	**105**	**7.6**	**15**	**16**	**50.0**	**15:57**	**12**	**1**	**5**	**6**	**8**	**0**	**0**	**1**	**14:11**
2003-04	**Philadelphia**	**NHL**	**47**	**6**	**20**	**26**	**32**	**3**	**0**	**1**	**107**	**5.6**	**10**	**38**	**31.6**	**15:30**									
	Carolina	**NHL**	**32**	**5**	**13**	**18**	**32**	**1**	**0**	**0**	**96**	**5.2**	**2**	**25**	**36.0**	**18:52**									
2004-05	Lulea HF	Sweden	49	14	18	32	61										4	0	1	1	29				
	NHL Totals		**258**	**48**	**85**	**133**	**140**	**4**	**0**	**4**	**569**	**8.4**		**108**	**37.0**	**14:58**	**17**	**1**	**5**	**6**	**12**	**0**	**0**	**1**	**14:56**

• Missed majority of 2002-03 season recovering from shoulder (November 15, 2002 vs. Carolina) and knee (January 18, 2003 vs. Tampa Bay) injuries. Traded to **Carolina** by **Philadelphia** for Danny Markov, January 20, 2004. Signed as a free agent by **Lulea** (Sweden), September 21, 2004.

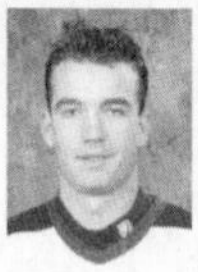

WILLIS, Shane

(WIH-lihs, SHAYN) **T.B.**

Right wing. Shoots right. 6'1", 195 lbs. Born, Edmonton, Alta., June 13, 1977. Carolina's 4th choice, 88th overall, in 1997 Entry Draft.

			Regular Season														Playoffs								
Season	Club	League	GP	G	A	Pts	PIM	PP	SH	GW	S	%	+/-	TF	F%	Min	GP	G	A	Pts	PIM	PP	SH	GW	Min
1992-93	Red Deer	ABHL	36	32	18	50	88	....	....	....	....	....	....	....	....	....	....	....	....	....	....	....	....	....	....
1993-94	Red Deer Royals	AMHL	34	40	26	66	103	....	....	....	....	....	....	....	....	....	....	....	....	....	....	....	....	....	....
1994-95	Prince Albert	WHL	65	24	19	43	38	....	....	....	....	....	....	....	....	....	13	3	4	7	6	....	....	....	....
1995-96	Prince Albert	WHL	69	41	40	81	47	....	....	....	....	....	....	....	....	....	18	11	10	21	18	....	....	....	....
1996-97	Prince Albert	WHL	41	34	22	56	63	....	....	....	....	....	....	....	....	....	....	....	....	....	....	....	....	....	....
	Lethbridge	WHL	26	22	17	39	24	....	....	....	....	....	....	....	....	....	19	13	11	24	20	....	....	....	....
1997-98	Lethbridge	WHL	64	58	54	112	73	....	....	....	....	....	....	....	....	....	4	2	3	5	6	....	....	....	....
	New Haven	AHL	1	0	1	1	2	....	....	....	....	....	....	....	....	....	....	....	....	....	....	....	....	....	....
1998-99	**Carolina**	**NHL**	**7**	**0**	**0**	**0**	**0**	**0**	**0**	**0**	**1**	**0.0**	**–2**	**0**	**0.0**	**2:14**	....	....	....	....	....	....	....	....	....
	New Haven	AHL	73	31	50	81	49	....	....	....	....	....	....	....	....	....	....	....	....	....	....	....	....	....	....
99-2000	**Carolina**	**NHL**	**2**	**0**	**0**	**0**	**0**	**0**	**0**	**0**	**1**	**0.0**	**–1**	**0**	**0.0**	**5:50**	....	....	....	....	....	....	....	....	....
	Cincinnati	IHL	80	35	25	60	64	....	....	....	....	....	....	....	....	....	11	5	3	8	8	....	....	....	....
2000-01	**Carolina**	**NHL**	**73**	**20**	**24**	**44**	**45**	**9**	**0**	**6**	**172**	**11.6**	**–6**	**10**	**20.0**	**15:58**	**2**	**0**	**0**	**0**	**0**	**0**	**0**	**0**	**12:56**
2001-02	**Carolina**	**NHL**	**59**	**7**	**10**	**17**	**24**	**2**	**0**	**0**	**126**	**5.6**	**–8**	**10**	**50.0**	**13:00**	....	....	....	....	....	....	....	....	....
	Tampa Bay	**NHL**	**21**	**4**	**3**	**7**	**6**	**0**	**0**	**0**	**29**	**13.8**	**0**	**12**	**8.3**	**11:18**	....	....	....	....	....	....	....	....	....
2002-03	Springfield	AHL	56	16	16	32	26	....	....	....	....	....	....	....	....	....	6	4	2	6	4	....	....	....	....
2003-04	**Tampa Bay**	**NHL**	**12**	**0**	**6**	**6**	**2**	**0**	**0**	**0**	**27**	**0.0**	**1**	**2**	**0.0**	**13:50**	....	....	....	....	....	....	....	....	....
	Hershey Bears	AHL	55	27	21	48	71	....	....	....	....	....	....	....	....	....	....	....	....	....	....	....	....	....	....
2004-05	Springfield	AHL	58	18	16	34	29	....	....	....	....	....	....	....	....	....	....	....	....	....	....	....	....	....	....
	NHL Totals		**174**	**31**	**43**	**74**	**77**	**11**	**0**	**6**	**356**	**8.7**		**34**	**23.5**	**13:35**	**2**	**0**	**0**	**0**	**0**	**0**	**0**	**0**	**12:56**

• Re-entered NHL Entry Draft. Originally Tampa Bay's 3rd choice, 56th overall, in 1995 Entry Draft.

WHL East First All-Star Team (1997, 1998) • AHL All-Rookie Team (1999) • AHL First All-Star Team (1999) • Dudley "Red" Garrett Memorial Award (Rookie of the Year – AHL) (1999) • NHL All-Rookie Team (2001)

Traded to **Tampa Bay** by **Carolina** with Chris Dingman for Kevin Weekes, March 5, 2002.

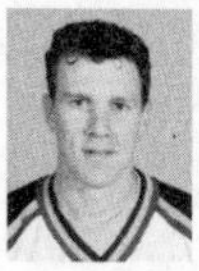

WILLSIE, Brian

(WIHL-see, BRIGH-uhn) **WSH.**

Right wing. Shoots right. 6'1", 195 lbs. Born, London, Ont., March 16, 1978. Colorado's 7th choice, 146th overall, in 1996 Entry Draft.

Season	Club	League	GP	G	A	Pts	PIM	PP	SH	GW	S	%	+/-	TF	F%	Min	GP	G	A	Pts	PIM	PP	SH	GW	Min
1993-94	Belmont Bombers	OHA-D	13	9	5	14	14	....	....	....	....	....	....	....	....	....	....	....	....	....	....	....	....	....	....
1994-95	St. Thomas Stars	OHA-B	45	35	47	82	47	....	....	....	....	....	....	....	....	....	....	....	....	....	....	....	....	....	....
1995-96	Guelph Storm	OHL	65	13	21	34	18	....	....	....	....	....	....	....	....	....	16	4	2	6	6	....	....	....	....
1996-97	Guelph Storm	OHL	64	37	31	68	37	....	....	....	....	....	....	....	....	....	18	15	4	19	10	....	....	....	....
1997-98	Guelph Storm	OHL	57	45	31	76	41	....	....	....	....	....	....	....	....	....	12	9	5	14	18	....	....	....	....
1998-99	Hershey Bears	AHL	72	19	10	29	28	....	....	....	....	....	....	....	....	....	3	1	0	1	0	....	....	....	....
99-2000	**Colorado**	**NHL**	**1**	**0**	**0**	**0**	**0**	**0**	**0**	**0**	**1**	**0.0**	**0**	**0**	**0.0**	**8:16**	....	....	....	....	....	....	....	....	....
	Hershey Bears	AHL	78	20	39	59	44	....	....	....	....	....	....	....	....	....	12	2	6	8	8	....	....	....	....
2000-01	Hershey Bears	AHL	48	18	23	41	20	....	....	....	....	....	....	....	....	....	12	7	2	9	14	....	....	....	....
2001-02	**Colorado**	**NHL**	**56**	**7**	**7**	**14**	**14**	**2**	**0**	**1**	**66**	**10.6**	**4**	**8**	**12.5**	**11:24**	**4**	**0**	**1**	**1**	**2**	**0**	**0**	**0**	**11:54**
2002-03	**Colorado**	**NHL**	**12**	**0**	**1**	**1**	**15**	**0**	**0**	**0**	**12**	**0.0**	**0**	**7**	**14.3**	**9:36**	**6**	**1**	**0**	**1**	**2**	**0**	**0**	**1**	**10:48**
	Hershey Bears	AHL	59	29	28	57	49	....	....	....	....	....	....	....	....	....	....	....	....	....	....	....	....	....	....
2003-04	**Washington**	**NHL**	**49**	**10**	**5**	**15**	**18**	**1**	**1**	**1**	**85**	**11.8**	**–7**	**46**	**34.8**	**12:42**	....	....	....	....	....	....	....	....	....
2004-05	Ljubljana	Interliga	12	7	6	13	34	....	....	....	....	....	....	....	....	....	....	....	....	....	....	....	....	....	....
	Ljubljana	Slovenia	2	0	3	3	4	....	....	....	....	....	....	....	....	....	....	....	....	....	....	....	....	....	....
	Portland Pirates	AHL	53	23	17	40	47	....	....	....	....	....	....	....	....	....	....	....	....	....	....	....	....	....	....
	NHL Totals		**118**	**17**	**13**	**30**	**47**	**3**	**1**	**2**	**164**	**10.4**		**61**	**29.5**	**11:44**	**10**	**1**	**1**	**2**	**4**	**0**	**0**	**1**	**11:14**

OHL First All-Star Team (1998)

Claimed by **Washington** from **Colorado** in Waiver Draft, October 3, 2003. Signed as a free agent by **Ljubljana** (Slovenia), October 8, 2004. Signed as a free agent by **Portland** (AHL), December 15, 2004.

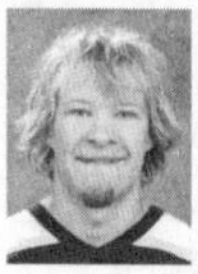

WILM, Clarke

(WIHLM, KLAHRK) **TOR.**

Center. Shoots left. 6', 202 lbs. Born, Central Butte, Sask., October 24, 1976. Calgary's 5th choice, 150th overall, in 1995 Entry Draft.

Season	Club	League	GP	G	A	Pts	PIM	PP	SH	GW	S	%	+/-	TF	F%	Min	GP	G	A	Pts	PIM	PP	SH	GW	Min
1991-92	Saskatoon Blazers	SMHL	36	18	28	46	16	....	....	....	....	....	....	....	....	....	....	....	....	....	....	....	....	....	....
	Saskatoon Blades	WHL	....	....	....	....	....	....	....	....	....	....	....	....	....	....	1	0	0	0	0	....	....	....	....
1992-93	Saskatoon Blades	WHL	69	14	19	33	71	....	....	....	....	....	....	....	....	....	9	4	2	6	13	....	....	....	....
1993-94	Saskatoon Blades	WHL	70	18	32	50	181	....	....	....	....	....	....	....	....	....	16	0	9	9	19	....	....	....	....
1994-95	Saskatoon Blades	WHL	71	20	39	59	179	....	....	....	....	....	....	....	....	....	10	6	1	7	21	....	....	....	....
1995-96	Saskatoon Blades	WHL	72	49	61	110	83	....	....	....	....	....	....	....	....	....	4	1	1	2	4	....	....	....	....
1996-97	Saint John Flames	AHL	62	9	19	28	107	....	....	....	....	....	....	....	....	....	5	2	0	2	15	....	....	....	....
1997-98	Saint John Flames	AHL	68	13	26	39	112	....	....	....	....	....	....	....	....	....	21	5	9	14	8	....	....	....	....
1998-99	**Calgary**	**NHL**	**78**	**10**	**8**	**18**	**53**	**2**	**2**	**0**	**94**	**10.6**	**11**	**609**	**40.9**	**11:32**	....	....	....	....	....	....	....	....	....
99-2000	**Calgary**	**NHL**	**78**	**10**	**12**	**22**	**67**	**1**	**3**	**0**	**81**	**12.3**	**–6**	**872**	**44.4**	**12:38**	....	....	....	....	....	....	....	....	....
2000-01	**Calgary**	**NHL**	**81**	**7**	**8**	**15**	**69**	**2**	**0**	**0**	**85**	**8.2**	**–11**	**992**	**51.9**	**14:11**	....	....	....	....	....	....	....	....	....
2001-02	**Calgary**	**NHL**	**66**	**4**	**14**	**18**	**61**	**0**	**1**	**0**	**83**	**4.8**	**–1**	**995**	**51.1**	**15:00**	....	....	....	....	....	....	....	....	....
2002-03	**Nashville**	**NHL**	**82**	**5**	**11**	**16**	**36**	**0**	**0**	**0**	**108**	**4.6**	**–11**	**339**	**50.4**	**11:58**	....	....	....	....	....	....	....	....	....
2003-04	**Toronto**	**NHL**	**10**	**0**	**0**	**0**	**7**	**0**	**0**	**0**	**10**	**0.0**	**0**	**43**	**46.5**	**11:45**	**5**	**0**	**1**	**1**	**2**	**0**	**0**	**0**	**12:45**
	St. John's	AHL	47	16	17	33	97	....	....	....	....	....	....	....	....	....	....	....	....	....	....	....	....	....	....
2004-05	St. John's	AHL	69	11	16	27	145	....	....	....	....	....	....	....	....	....	5	2	2	4	8	....	....	....	....
	NHL Totals		**395**	**36**	**53**	**89**	**293**	**5**	**6**	**0**	**461**	**7.8**		**3850**	**48.1**	**12:58**	**5**	**0**	**1**	**1**	**2**	**0**	**0**	**0**	**12:45**

Signed as a free agent by **Nashville**, July 11, 2002. Signed as a free agent by **Toronto**, October 28, 2003.

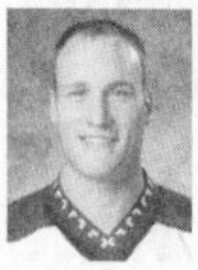

WILSON, Landon

(WIHL-suhn, LAN-duhn)

Right wing. Shoots right. 6'3", 226 lbs. Born, St. Louis, MO, March 13, 1975. Toronto's 2nd choice, 19th overall, in 1993 Entry Draft.

Season	Club	League	GP	G	A	Pts	PIM	PP	SH	GW	S	%	+/-	TF	F%	Min	GP	G	A	Pts	PIM	PP	SH	GW	Min
1991-92	California	WSJHL	38	50	42	92	135	....	....	....	....	....	....	....	....	....	....	....	....	....	....	....	....	....	....
1992-93	Dubuque	USHL	43	29	36	65	284	....	....	....	....	....	....	....	....	....	....	....	....	....	....	....	....	....	....
1993-94	North Dakota	WCHA	35	18	15	33	*147	....	....	....	....	....	....	....	....	....	....	....	....	....	....	....	....	....	....
1994-95	North Dakota	WCHA	31	7	16	23	141	....	....	....	....	....	....	....	....	....	....	....	....	....	....	....	....	....	....
	Cornwall Aces	AHL	8	4	4	8	25	....	....	....	....	....	....	....	....	....	13	3	4	7	68	....	....	....	....
1995-96	**Colorado**	**NHL**	**7**	**1**	**0**	**1**	**6**	**0**	**0**	**0**	**6**	**16.7**	**3**	....	....	....	....	....	....	....	....	....	....	....	....
	Cornwall Aces	AHL	53	21	13	34	154	....	....	....	....	....	....	....	....	....	8	1	3	4	22	....	....	....	....
1996-97	**Colorado**	**NHL**	**9**	**1**	**2**	**3**	**23**	**0**	**0**	**0**	**7**	**14.3**	**1**	....	....	....	....	....	....	....	....	....	....	....	....
	Boston	**NHL**	**40**	**7**	**10**	**17**	**49**	**0**	**0**	**0**	**76**	**9.2**	**–6**	....	....	....	....	....	....	....	....	....	....	....	....
	Providence Bruins	AHL	2	2	1	3	2	....	....	....	....	....	....	....	....	....	10	3	4	7	16	....	....	....	....
1997-98	**Boston**	**NHL**	**28**	**1**	**5**	**6**	**7**	**0**	**0**	**0**	**26**	**3.8**	**3**	....	....	....	**1**	**0**	**0**	**0**	**0**	**0**	**0**	**0**	....
	Providence Bruins	AHL	42	18	10	28	146	....	....	....	....	....	....	....	....	....	....	....	....	....	....	....	....	....	....
1998-99	**Boston**	**NHL**	**22**	**3**	**3**	**6**	**17**	**0**	**0**	**0**	**32**	**9.4**	**0**	**3**	**0.0**	**10:04**	**8**	**1**	**1**	**2**	**8**	**1**	**0**	**1**	**13:41**
	Providence Bruins	AHL	48	31	22	53	89	....	....	....	....	....	....	....	....	....	11	7	1	8	19	....	....	....	....
99-2000	**Boston**	**NHL**	**40**	**1**	**3**	**4**	**18**	**0**	**0**	**0**	**67**	**1.5**	**–6**	**14**	**42.9**	**10:09**	....	....	....	....	....	....	....	....	....
	Providence Bruins	AHL	17	5	5	10	45	....	....	....	....	....	....	....	....	....	9	2	3	5	38	....	....	....	....
2000-01	**Phoenix**	**NHL**	**70**	**18**	**13**	**31**	**92**	**2**	**0**	**3**	**123**	**14.6**	**3**	**13**	**46.2**	**11:26**	....	....	....	....	....	....	....	....	....
2001-02	**Phoenix**	**NHL**	**47**	**7**	**12**	**19**	**46**	**1**	**0**	**0**	**100**	**7.0**	**4**	**15**	**53.3**	**12:51**	**4**	**0**	**0**	**0**	**12**	**0**	**0**	**0**	**12:03**
	Springfield	AHL	2	2	1	3	2	....	....	....	....	....	....	....	....	....	....	....	....	....	....	....	....	....	....
2002-03	**Phoenix**	**NHL**	**31**	**6**	**8**	**14**	**26**	**0**	**0**	**3**	**92**	**6.5**	**1**	**35**	**54.3**	**12:11**	....	....	....	....	....	....	....	....	....
2003-04	**Phoenix**	**NHL**	**35**	**1**	**3**	**4**	**16**	**0**	**0**	**0**	**41**	**2.4**	**–3**	**44**	**31.8**	**9:51**	....	....	....	....	....	....	....	....	....
	Pittsburgh	**NHL**	**19**	**5**	**1**	**6**	**31**	**2**	**0**	**0**	**35**	**14.3**	**0**	**2**	**0.0**	**11:21**	....	....	....	....	....	....	....	....	....
2004-05	Blues Espoo	Finland	37	8	11	19	80	....	....	....	....	....	....	....	....	....	....	....	....	....	....	....	....	....	....
	NHL Totals		**348**	**51**	**60**	**111**	**331**	**5**	**0**	**6**	**605**	**8.4**		**126**	**42.1**	**11:15**	**13**	**1**	**1**	**2**	**20**	**1**	**0**	**1**	**13:08**

WCHA Rookie of the Year (1994) • AHL First All-Star Team (1999)

Traded to **Quebec** by **Toronto** with Wendel Clark, Sylvain Lefebvre and Toronto's 1st round choice (Jeffrey Kealty) in 1994 Entry Draft for Mats Sundin, Garth Butcher, Todd Warriner and Philadelphia's 1st round choice (previously acquired, later traded to Washington – Washington selected Nolan Baumgartner) in 1994 Entry Draft, June 28, 1994. Transferred to **Colorado** after **Quebec** franchise relocated, June 21, 1995. Traded to **Boston** by **Colorado** with Anders Myrvold for Boston's 1st round choice (Robyn Regehr) in 1998 Entry Draft, November 22, 1996. Signed as a free agent by **Phoenix**, July 7, 2000. • Missed majority of 2002-03 season recovering from eye injury suffered in game vs. Washington, December 13, 2002. Traded to **Pittsburgh** by **Phoenix** for future considerations, February 22, 2004. Signed as a free agent by **Blues** (Finland), June 23, 2004. Signed as a free agent by **Davos** (Swiss), August 31, 2005.

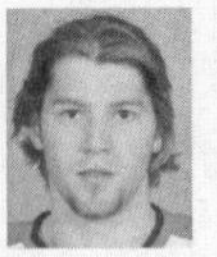

WISEMAN, Chad

(WIGHZ-man, CHAD) **NYR**

Left wing. Shoots left. 6', 205 lbs. Born, Burlington, Ont., March 25, 1981. San Jose's 8th choice, 246th overall, in 2000 Entry Draft.

			Regular Season														Playoffs								
Season	Club	League	GP	G	A	Pts	PIM	PP	SH	GW	S	%	+/-	TF	F%	Min	GP	G	A	Pts	PIM	PP	SH	GW	Min
1997-98	Burlington	OPJHL	50	28	36	64	31																		
1998-99	Mississauga	OHL	64	11	25	36	29																		
99-2000	Mississauga	OHL	68	23	45	68	53																		
2000-01	Mississauga	OHL	30	15	29	44	22																		
	Plymouth Whalers	OHL	32	11	16	27	12										19	12	8	20	22				
2001-02	Cleveland Barons	AHL	76	21	29	50	61																		
2002-03	**San Jose**	**NHL**	**4**	**0**	**0**	**0**	**4**	**0**	**0**	**0**	**1**	**0.0**	**–2**	**0**	**0.0**	**9:19**									
	Cleveland Barons	AHL	77	17	35	52	44																		
2003-04	**NY Rangers**	**NHL**	**4**	**1**	**0**	**1**	**0**	**0**	**0**	**0**	**3**	**33.3**	**–1**	**0**	**0.0**	**8:49**									
	Hartford	AHL	62	25	27	52	45										15	5	6	11	12				
2004-05	Hartford	AHL	60	17	16	33	74										6	1	1	2	6				
	NHL Totals		**8**	**1**	**0**	**1**	**4**	**0**	**0**	**0**	**4**	**25.0**		**0**	**0.0**	**9:04**									

Traded to **NY Rangers** by **San Jose** for Nils Ekman, August 12, 2003.

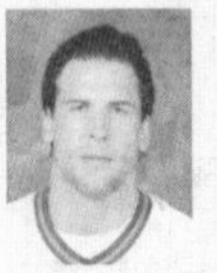

WITT, Brendan

(WIHT, BREHN-duhn) **WSH.**

Defense. Shoots left. 6'2", 219 lbs. Born, Humboldt, Sask., February 20, 1975. Washington's 1st choice, 11th overall, in 1993 Entry Draft.

Season	Club	League	GP	G	A	Pts	PIM	PP	SH	GW	S	%	+/-	TF	F%	Min	GP	G	A	Pts	PIM	PP	SH	GW	Min
1990-91	Saskatoon Blazers	SMHL	31	5	13	18	42																		
	Seattle	WHL															1	0	0	0	0				
1991-92	Seattle	WHL	67	3	9	12	212										15	1	1	2	84				
1992-93	Seattle	WHL	70	2	26	28	239										5	1	2	3	30				
1993-94	Seattle	WHL	56	8	31	39	235										9	3	8	11	23				
1994-95			DID NOT PLAY																						
1995-96	**Washington**	**NHL**	**48**	**2**	**3**	**5**	**85**	**0**	**0**	**1**	**44**	**4.5**	**–4**												
1996-97	**Washington**	**NHL**	**44**	**3**	**2**	**5**	**88**	**0**	**0**	**0**	**41**	**7.3**	**–20**												
	Portland Pirates	AHL	30	2	4	6	56										5	1	0	1	30				
1997-98	**Washington**	**NHL**	**64**	**1**	**7**	**8**	**112**	**0**	**0**	**0**	**68**	**1.5**	**–11**				**16**	**1**	**0**	**1**	**14**	**0**	**0**	**0**	
1998-99	**Washington**	**NHL**	**54**	**2**	**5**	**7**	**87**	**0**	**0**	**0**	**51**	**3.9**	**–6**	**0**	**0.0**	**15:50**									
99-2000	**Washington**	**NHL**	**77**	**1**	**7**	**8**	**114**	**0**	**0**	**0**	**64**	**1.6**	**5**	**2**	**50.0**	**20:56**	**3**	**0**	**0**	**0**	**0**	**0**	**0**	**0**	**20:52**
2000-01	**Washington**	**NHL**	**72**	**3**	**3**	**6**	**101**	**0**	**0**	**0**	**87**	**3.4**	**2**	**1**	**100.0**	**20:41**	**6**	**2**	**0**	**2**	**12**	**1**	**0**	**0**	**20:50**
2001-02	**Washington**	**NHL**	**68**	**3**	**7**	**10**	**78**	**0**	**0**	**0**	**81**	**3.7**	**–1**	**1**	**100.0**	**20:03**									
2002-03	**Washington**	**NHL**	**69**	**2**	**9**	**11**	**106**	**0**	**0**	**0**	**80**	**2.5**	**12**	**0**	**0.0**	**20:55**	**6**	**1**	**0**	**1**	**0**	**0**	**0**	**0**	**23:33**
2003-04	**Washington**	**NHL**	**72**	**2**	**10**	**12**	**123**	**0**	**0**	**0**	**91**	**2.2**	**–22**	**3**	**66.7**	**22:48**									
2004-05	Bracknell Bees	Britain-2	3	1	4	5	0																		
	NHL Totals		**568**	**19**	**53**	**72**	**894**	**0**	**0**	**1**	**607**	**3.1**		**7**	**71.4**	**20:24**	**31**	**4**	**0**	**4**	**26**	**1**	**0**	**0**	**21:55**

WHL West First All-Star Team (1993, 1994) • Canadian Major Junior First All-Star Team (1994)

• Missed entire 1994-95 season after failing to come to contract terms with **Washington**. Signed as a free agent by **Bracknell** (Britain-2), December 21, 2004.

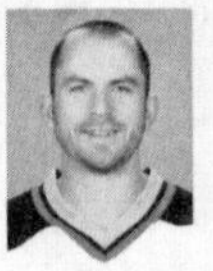

WOOLLEY, Jason

(WU-lee, JAY-suhn)

Defense. Shoots left. 6', 203 lbs. Born, Toronto, Ont., July 27, 1969. Washington's 4th choice, 61st overall, in 1989 Entry Draft.

Season	Club	League	GP	G	A	Pts	PIM	PP	SH	GW	S	%	+/-	TF	F%	Min	GP	G	A	Pts	PIM	PP	SH	GW	Min
1986-87	St. Mike's B's	OHA-B	35	13	22	35	40																		
1987-88	St. Mike's B's	OHA-B	31	19	37	56	22																		
1988-89	Michigan State	CCHA	47	12	25	37	26																		
1989-90	Michigan State	CCHA	45	10	38	48	26																		
1990-91	Michigan State	CCHA	40	15	44	59	24																		
1991-92	Canada	Nat-Tm	60	14	30	44	36																		
	Canada	Olympics	8	0	5	5	4																		
	Washington	**NHL**	**1**	**0**	**0**	**0**	**0**	**0**	**0**	**0**	**2**	**0.0**	**1**												
	Baltimore	AHL	15	1	10	11	6																		
1992-93	**Washington**	**NHL**	**26**	**0**	**2**	**2**	**10**	**0**	**0**	**0**	**11**	**0.0**	**3**												
	Baltimore	AHL	29	14	27	41	22										1	0	2	2	0				
1993-94	**Washington**	**NHL**	**10**	**1**	**2**	**3**	**4**	**0**	**0**	**0**	**15**	**6.7**	**2**				**4**	**1**	**0**	**1**	**4**	**0**	**0**	**1**	
	Portland Pirates	AHL	41	12	29	41	14										9	2	2	4	4				
1994-95	Detroit Vipers	IHL	48	8	28	36	38																		
	Florida	**NHL**	**34**	**4**	**9**	**13**	**18**	**1**	**0**	**0**	**76**	**5.3**	**–1**												
1995-96	**Florida**	**NHL**	**52**	**6**	**28**	**34**	**32**	**3**	**0**	**0**	**98**	**6.1**	**–9**				**13**	**2**	**6**	**8**	**14**	**1**	**0**	**1**	
1996-97	**Florida**	**NHL**	**3**	**0**	**0**	**0**	**2**	**0**	**0**	**0**	**7**	**0.0**	**1**												
	Pittsburgh	**NHL**	**57**	**6**	**30**	**36**	**28**	**2**	**0**	**1**	**79**	**7.6**	**3**				**5**	**0**	**3**	**3**	**0**	**0**	**0**	**0**	
1997-98	**Buffalo**	**NHL**	**71**	**9**	**26**	**35**	**35**	**3**	**0**	**2**	**129**	**7.0**	**8**				**15**	**2**	**9**	**11**	**12**	**1**	**0**	**1**	
1998-99	**Buffalo**	**NHL**	**80**	**10**	**33**	**43**	**62**	**4**	**0**	**2**	**154**	**6.5**	**16**	**0**	**0.0**	**18:43**	**21**	**4**	**11**	**15**	**10**	**2**	**0**	**1**	**17:54**
99-2000	**Buffalo**	**NHL**	**74**	**8**	**25**	**33**	**52**	**2**	**0**	**2**	**113**	**7.1**	**14**	**0**	**0.0**	**17:51**	**5**	**0**	**2**	**2**	**2**	**0**	**0**	**0**	**18:06**
2000-01	**Buffalo**	**NHL**	**67**	**5**	**18**	**23**	**46**	**4**	**0**	**3**	**92**	**5.4**	**0**	**0**	**0.0**	**17:22**	**8**	**1**	**5**	**6**	**2**	**0**	**0**	**1**	**18:30**
2001-02	**Buffalo**	**NHL**	**59**	**8**	**20**	**28**	**34**	**6**	**0**	**2**	**90**	**8.9**	**–6**	**0**	**0.0**	**17:11**									
2002-03	**Buffalo**	**NHL**	**14**	**0**	**3**	**3**	**29**	**0**	**0**	**0**	**29**	**0.0**	**–1**	**0**	**0.0**	**15:59**									
	Detroit	**NHL**	**62**	**6**	**17**	**23**	**22**	**1**	**0**	**2**	**52**	**11.5**	**12**	**0**	**0.0**	**16:59**	**4**	**1**	**0**	**1**	**0**	**0**	**0**	**0**	**15:25**
2003-04	**Detroit**	**NHL**	**55**	**4**	**15**	**19**	**28**	**0**	**0**	**1**	**60**	**6.7**	**19**	**2**	**50.0**	**15:42**	**4**	**0**	**0**	**0**	**0**	**0**	**0**	**0**	**17:00**
2004-05	Flint Generals	UHL	9	4	2	6	4																		
	NHL Totals		**665**	**67**	**228**	**295**	**402**	**26**	**0**	**15**	**1007**	**6.7**		**2**	**50.0**	**17:22**	**79**	**11**	**36**	**47**	**44**	**4**	**0**	**5**	**17:43**

CCHA First All-Star Team (1991) • NCAA West First All-American Team (1991)

Signed as a free agent by **Florida**, February 15, 1995. Traded to **Pittsburgh** by **Florida** with Stu Barnes for Chris Wells, November 19, 1996. Traded to **Buffalo** by **Pittsburgh** for Buffalo's 5th round choice (Robert Scuderi) in 1998 Entry Draft, September 24, 1997. Traded to **Detroit** by **Buffalo** for future considerations, November 16, 2002. Signed as a free agent by **Flint** (UHL), February 18, 2005.

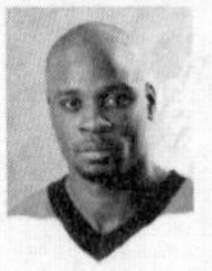

WORRELL, Peter

(woh-REHL, PEE-tuhr)

Left wing. Shoots left. 6'6", 235 lbs. Born, Pierrefonds, Que., August 18, 1977. Florida's 7th choice, 166th overall, in 1995 Entry Draft.

Season	Club	League	GP	G	A	Pts	PIM	PP	SH	GW	S	%	+/-	TF	F%	Min	GP	G	A	Pts	PIM	PP	SH	GW	Min
1993-94	Lac St-Louis Lions	QAAA	1	0	0	0	0										1	0	0	0	0				
1994-95	Hull Olympiques	QMJHL	56	1	8	9	243										21	0	1	1	91				
1995-96	Hull Olympiques	QMJHL	63	23	36	59	464										18	11	8	19	81				
1996-97	Hull Olympiques	QMJHL	62	17	46	63	437										14	3	13	16	83				
1997-98	**Florida**	**NHL**	**19**	**0**	**0**	**0**	**153**	**0**	**0**	**0**	**15**	**0.0**	**–4**												
	New Haven	AHL	50	15	12	27	309										1	0	1	1	6				
1998-99	**Florida**	**NHL**	**62**	**4**	**5**	**9**	**258**	**0**	**0**	**2**	**50**	**8.0**	**0**	**0**	**0.0**	**6:15**									
	New Haven	AHL	10	3	1	4	65																		
99-2000	**Florida**	**NHL**	**48**	**3**	**6**	**9**	**169**	**2**	**0**	**1**	**45**	**6.7**	**–7**	**1**	**100.0**	**8:25**	**4**	**1**	**0**	**1**	**8**	**0**	**0**	**0**	**11:17**
2000-01	**Florida**	**NHL**	**71**	**3**	**7**	**10**	**248**	**0**	**0**	**0**	**86**	**3.5**	**–10**	**3**	**33.3**	**9:28**									
2001-02	**Florida**	**NHL**	**79**	**4**	**5**	**9**	***354**	**0**	**0**	**1**	**65**	**6.2**	**–15**	**9**	**0.0**	**8:45**									
2002-03	**Florida**	**NHL**	**63**	**2**	**3**	**5**	**193**	**0**	**0**	**0**	**52**	**3.8**	**–14**	**13**	**15.4**	**9:16**									
2003-04	**Colorado**	**NHL**	**49**	**3**	**1**	**4**	**179**	**0**	**0**	**0**	**32**	**9.4**	**2**	**5**	**0.0**	**5:55**									
2004-05			DID NOT PLAY																						
	NHL Totals		**391**	**19**	**27**	**46**	**1554**	**2**	**0**	**4**	**345**	**5.5**		**31**	**12.9**	**8:08**	**4**	**1**	**0**	**1**	**8**	**0**	**0**	**0**	**11:17**

Traded to **Colorado** by **Florida** with Florida's 2nd round choice (later traded to NY Rangers – later traded back to Florida – Florida selected David Shantz) in 2004 Entry Draft for Eric Messier and Vaclav Nedorost, July 18, 2003.

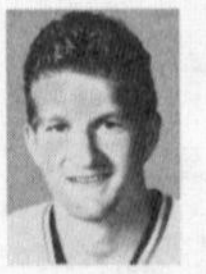

WOTTON, Mark

(WAH-tuhn, MAHRK) **WSH.**

Defense. Shoots left. 6'1", 195 lbs. Born, Foxwarren, Man., November 16, 1973. Vancouver's 11th choice, 237th overall, in 1992 Entry Draft.

Season	Club	League	GP	G	A	Pts	PIM	PP	SH	GW	S	%	+/-	TF	F%	Min	GP	G	A	Pts	PIM	PP	SH	GW	Min
1988-89	Foxwarren Blades	MAHA	60	10	30	40	70																		
1989-90	Saskatoon Blades	WHL	51	2	3	5	31										7	1	1	2	15				
1990-91	Saskatoon Blades	WHL	45	4	11	15	37																		
1991-92	Saskatoon Blades	WHL	64	11	25	36	62										21	2	6	8	22				
1992-93	Saskatoon Blades	WHL	71	15	51	66	90										9	6	5	11	18				
1993-94	Saskatoon Blades	WHL	65	12	34	46	108										16	3	12	15	32				
1994-95	Syracuse Crunch	AHL	75	12	29	41	50																		
	Vancouver	**NHL**	**1**	**0**	**0**	**0**	**0**	**0**	**0**	**0**	**2**	**0.0**	**1**				**5**	**0**	**0**	**0**	**4**	**0**	**0**	**0**	
1995-96	Syracuse Crunch	AHL	80	10	35	45	96										15	1	12	13	20				

			Regular Season														Playoffs								
Season	Club	League	GP	G	A	Pts	PIM	PP	SH	GW	S	%	+/-	TF	F%	Min	GP	G	A	Pts	PIM	PP	SH	GW	Min
1996-97	**Vancouver**	**NHL**	**36**	**3**	**6**	**9**	**19**	**0**	**1**	**0**	**41**	**7.3**	**8**	....	....	....	....	....	....	....	....	....	....	....	....
	Syracuse Crunch	AHL	27	2	8	10	25	....	....	....	....	....	....	....	....	....	2	0	0	0	4	....	....	....	....
1997-98	**Vancouver**	**NHL**	**5**	**0**	**0**	**0**	**6**	**0**	**0**	**0**	**3**	**0.0**	**–2**	....	....	....	....	....	....	....	....	....	....	....	....
	Syracuse Crunch	AHL	56	12	21	33	80	....	....	....	....	....	....	....	....	....	5	0	0	0	12	....	....	....	....
1998-99	Syracuse Crunch	AHL	72	4	31	35	74	....	....	....	....	....	....	....	....	....	....	....	....	....	....	....	....	....	....
99-2000	Michigan	IHL	70	3	7	10	72	....	....	....	....	....	....	....	....	....	....	....	....	....	....	....	....	....	....
2000-01	**Dallas**	**NHL**	**1**	**0**	**0**	**0**	**0**	**0**	**0**	**0**	**0**	**0.0**	**0**	**0**	**0.0**	**13:45**	....	....	....	....	....	....	....	....	....
	Utah Grizzlies	IHL	63	2	2	4	64	....	....	....	....	....	....	....	....	....	....	....	....	....	....	....	....	....	....
2001-02	Utah Grizzlies	AHL	57	9	18	27	68	....	....	....	....	....	....	....	....	....	4	0	1	1	6	....	....	....	....
2002-03	Utah Grizzlies	AHL	69	8	26	34	68	....	....	....	....	....	....	....	....	....	2	0	0	0	2	....	....	....	....
2003-04	Utah Grizzlies	AHL	23	1	3	4	25	....	....	....	....	....	....	....	....	....	....	....	....	....	....	....	....	....	....
2004-05	St. Petersburg	Russia	50	3	4	7	36	....	....	....	....	....	....	....	....	....	....	....	....	....	....	....	....	....	....
	NHL Totals		**43**	**3**	**6**	**9**	**25**	**0**	**1**	**0**	**46**	**6.5**		**0**	**0.0**	**13:45**	**5**	**0**	**0**	**0**	**4**	**0**	**0**	**0**	....

WHL East Second All-Star Team (1994)

Signed as a free agent by **Dallas**, July 9, 1999. • Missed majority of 2003-04 season recovering from knee injury suffered in game vs. Cincinnati (AHL), December 6, 2003. Signed as a free agent by **St. Petersburg** (Russia), July 9, 2004.

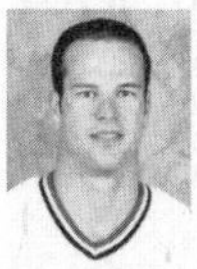

WRIGHT, Jamie

(RIGHT, JAY-mee)

Left wing. Shoots left. 6', 195 lbs. Born, Kitchener, Ont., May 13, 1976. Dallas' 3rd choice, 98th overall, in 1994 Entry Draft.

Season	Club	League	GP	G	A	Pts	PIM	PP	SH	GW	S	%	+/-	TF	F%	Min	GP	G	A	Pts	PIM	PP	SH	GW	Min
1991-92	Elmira	OHA-B	44	17	11	28	46	....	....	....	....	....	....	....	....	....	....	....	....	....	....	....	....	....	....
1992-93	Elmira	OHA-B	47	22	32	54	52	....	....	....	....	....	....	....	....	....	....	....	....	....	....	....	....	....	....
1993-94	Guelph Storm	OHL	65	17	15	32	34	....	....	....	....	....	....	....	....	....	8	2	1	3	10	....	....	....	....
1994-95	Guelph Storm	OHL	65	43	39	82	36	....	....	....	....	....	....	....	....	....	14	6	8	14	6	....	....	....	....
1995-96	Guelph Storm	OHL	55	30	36	66	45	....	....	....	....	....	....	....	....	....	16	10	12	22	35	....	....	....	....
1996-97	Michigan	IHL	60	6	8	14	34	....	....	....	....	....	....	....	....	....	1	0	0	0	0	....	....	....	....
1997-98	**Dallas**	**NHL**	**21**	**4**	**2**	**6**	**2**	**0**	**0**	**2**	**15**	**26.7**	**8**	....	....	....	**5**	**0**	**0**	**0**	**0**	**0**	**0**	**0**	....
	Michigan	IHL	53	15	11	26	31	....	....	....	....	....	....	....	....	....	....	....	....	....	....	....	....	....	....
1998-99	**Dallas**	**NHL**	**11**	**0**	**0**	**0**	**0**	**0**	**0**	**0**	**10**	**0.0**	**–3**	**0**	**0.0**	**7:37**	....	....	....	....	....	....	....	....	....
	Michigan	IHL	64	16	15	31	92	....	....	....	....	....	....	....	....	....	2	0	0	0	2	....	....	....	....
99-2000	**Dallas**	**NHL**	**23**	**1**	**4**	**5**	**16**	**0**	**0**	**0**	**15**	**6.7**	**4**	**2**	**50.0**	**9:50**	....	....	....	....	....	....	....	....	....
	Michigan	IHL	49	12	4	16	64	....	....	....	....	....	....	....	....	....	....	....	....	....	....	....	....	....	....
2000-01	**Dallas**	**NHL**	**2**	**1**	**0**	**1**	**0**	**0**	**0**	**0**	**4**	**25.0**	**–3**	**1**	**0.0**	**10:45**	....	....	....	....	....	....	....	....	....
	Utah Grizzlies	IHL	74	25	27	52	126	....	....	....	....	....	....	....	....	....	....	....	....	....	....	....	....	....	....
2001-02	**Calgary**	**NHL**	**44**	**4**	**12**	**16**	**20**	**0**	**0**	**0**	**64**	**6.3**	**6**	**10**	**60.0**	**13:44**	....	....	....	....	....	....	....	....	....
	Saint John Flames	AHL	34	11	13	24	34	....	....	....	....	....	....	....	....	....	....	....	....	....	....	....	....	....	....
2002-03	**Calgary**	**NHL**	**19**	**2**	**2**	**4**	**12**	**0**	**0**	**0**	**16**	**12.5**	**1**	**14**	**42.9**	**11:43**	....	....	....	....	....	....	....	....	....
	Saint John Flames	AHL	3	2	1	3	0	....	....	....	....	....	....	....	....	....	....	....	....	....	....	....	....	....	....
	Philadelphia	**NHL**	**4**	**0**	**0**	**0**	**4**	**0**	**0**	**0**	**2**	**0.0**	**–1**	**0**	**0.0**	**9:27**	....	....	....	....	....	....	....	....	....
	Philadelphia	AHL	33	10	14	24	31	....	....	....	....	....	....	....	....	....	....	....	....	....	....	....	....	....	....
2003-04	Toronto	AHL	78	25	30	55	101	....	....	....	....	....	....	....	....	....	....	....	....	....	....	....	....	....	....
2004-05	Edmonton	AHL	65	13	15	28	86	....	....	....	....	....	....	....	....	....	....	....	....	....	....	....	....	....	....
	NHL Totals		**124**	**12**	**20**	**32**	**54**	**0**	**0**	**2**	**126**	**9.5**		**27**	**48.1**	**11:37**	**5**	**0**	**0**	**0**	**0**	**0**	**0**	**0**	....

Signed as a free agent by **Calgary**, August 2, 2001. Traded to **Philadelphia** by **Calgary** for future considerations, January 22, 2003. Signed as a free agent by **Edmonton**, August 8, 2003.

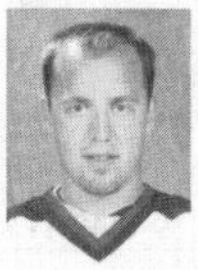

WRIGHT, Tyler

(RIGHT, TIGH-luhr) **CBJ**

Center. Shoots right. 6', 190 lbs. Born, Kamsack, Sask., April 6, 1973. Edmonton's 1st choice, 12th overall, in 1991 Entry Draft.

Season	Club	League	GP	G	A	Pts	PIM	PP	SH	GW	S	%	+/-	TF	F%	Min	GP	G	A	Pts	PIM	PP	SH	GW	Min
1988-89	Swift Current	SMHL	36	20	13	33	102	....	....	....	....	....	....	....	....	....	....	....	....	....	....	....	....	....	....
1989-90	Swift Current	WHL	67	14	18	32	119	....	....	....	....	....	....	....	....	....	4	0	0	0	12	....	....	....	....
1990-91	Swift Current	WHL	66	41	51	92	157	....	....	....	....	....	....	....	....	....	3	0	0	0	6	....	....	....	....
1991-92	Swift Current	WHL	63	36	46	82	185	....	....	....	....	....	....	....	....	....	8	2	5	7	16	....	....	....	....
1992-93	Swift Current	WHL	37	24	41	65	76	....	....	....	....	....	....	....	....	....	17	9	17	26	*49	....	....	....	....
	Edmonton	**NHL**	**7**	**1**	**1**	**2**	**19**	**0**	**0**	**0**	**7**	**14.3**	**–4**	....	....	....	....	....	....	....	....	....	....	....	....
1993-94	**Edmonton**	**NHL**	**5**	**0**	**0**	**0**	**4**	**0**	**0**	**0**	**2**	**0.0**	**–3**	....	....	....	....	....	....	....	....	....	....	....	....
	Cape Breton	AHL	65	14	27	41	160	....	....	....	....	....	....	....	....	....	5	2	0	2	11	....	....	....	....
1994-95	Cape Breton	AHL	70	16	15	31	184	....	....	....	....	....	....	....	....	....	....	....	....	....	....	....	....	....	....
	Edmonton	**NHL**	**6**	**1**	**0**	**1**	**14**	**0**	**0**	**0**	**6**	**16.7**	**1**	....	....	....	....	....	....	....	....	....	....	....	....
1995-96	**Edmonton**	**NHL**	**23**	**1**	**0**	**1**	**33**	**0**	**0**	**0**	**18**	**5.6**	**–7**	....	....	....	....	....	....	....	....	....	....	....	....
	Cape Breton	AHL	31	6	12	18	158	....	....	....	....	....	....	....	....	....	....	....	....	....	....	....	....	....	....
1996-97	**Pittsburgh**	**NHL**	**45**	**2**	**2**	**4**	**70**	**0**	**0**	**2**	**30**	**6.7**	**–7**	....	....	....	....	....	....	....	....	....	....	....	....
	Cleveland	IHL	10	4	3	7	34	....	....	....	....	....	....	....	....	....	14	4	2	6	44	....	....	....	....
1997-98	**Pittsburgh**	**NHL**	**82**	**3**	**4**	**7**	**112**	**1**	**0**	**0**	**46**	**6.5**	**–3**	....	....	....	**6**	**0**	**1**	**1**	**4**	**0**	**0**	**0**	....
1998-99	**Pittsburgh**	**NHL**	**61**	**0**	**0**	**0**	**90**	**0**	**0**	**0**	**16**	**0.0**	**–2**	**122**	**46.7**	**3:46**	**13**	**0**	**0**	**0**	**19**	**0**	**0**	**0**	**3:22**
99-2000	**Pittsburgh**	**NHL**	**50**	**12**	**10**	**22**	**45**	**0**	**0**	**1**	**68**	**17.6**	**4**	**698**	**47.1**	**13:24**	**11**	**3**	**1**	**4**	**17**	**0**	**0**	**0**	**16:12**
	Wilkes-Barre	AHL	25	5	15	20	86	....	....	....	....	....	....	....	....	....	....	....	....	....	....	....	....	....	....
2000-01	**Columbus**	**NHL**	**76**	**16**	**16**	**32**	**140**	**4**	**1**	**2**	**141**	**11.3**	**–9**	**999**	**45.1**	**17:41**	....	....	....	....	....	....	....	....	....
2001-02	**Columbus**	**NHL**	**77**	**13**	**11**	**24**	**100**	**4**	**0**	**1**	**120**	**10.8**	**–40**	**1036**	**43.9**	**17:12**	....	....	....	....	....	....	....	....	....
2002-03	**Columbus**	**NHL**	**70**	**19**	**11**	**30**	**113**	**3**	**2**	**3**	**108**	**17.6**	**–25**	**760**	**41.3**	**16:07**	....	....	....	....	....	....	....	....	....
2003-04	**Columbus**	**NHL**	**68**	**9**	**9**	**18**	**63**	**2**	**0**	**3**	**109**	**8.3**	**–19**	**316**	**43.7**	**14:34**	....	....	....	....	....	....	....	....	....
2004-05	EHC Biel-Bienne	Swiss-2	7	3	2	5	4	....	....	....	....	....	....	....	....	....	12	8	8	16	44	....	....	....	....
	NHL Totals		**570**	**77**	**64**	**141**	**803**	**14**	**3**	**12**	**671**	**11.5**		**3931**	**44.3**	**14:09**	**30**	**3**	**2**	**5**	**40**	**0**	**0**	**0**	**9:15**

Traded to **Pittsburgh** by **Edmonton** for Pittsburgh's 7th round choice (Brandon Lafrance) in 1996 Entry Draft, June 22, 1996. Claimed by **Columbus** from **Pittsburgh** in Expansion Draft, June 23, 2000. Signed as a free agent by **Biel-Bienne** (Swiss-2), January 6, 2005.

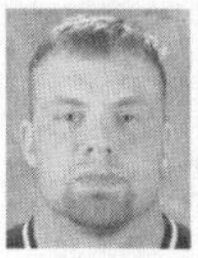

YABLONSKI, Jeremy

(ya-BLAWN-skee, JAIR-eh-mee) **NSH.**

Left wing. Shoots right. 6', 240 lbs. Born, Meadow Lake, Sask., March 21, 1980.

Season	Club	League	GP	G	A	Pts	PIM	PP	SH	GW	S	%	+/-	TF	F%	Min	GP	G	A	Pts	PIM	PP	SH	GW	Min
1996-97	Beardy's	SMHL	38	7	3	10	284	....	....	....	....	....	....	....	....	....	....	....	....	....	....	....	....	....	....
1997-98	Edmonton Ice	WHL	47	3	0	3	143	....	....	....	....	....	....	....	....	....	....	....	....	....	....	....	....	....	....
1998-99	Kootenay Ice	WHL	27	1	1	2	77	....	....	....	....	....	....	....	....	....	....	....	....	....	....	....	....	....	....
99-2000	Kootenay Ice	WHL	DID NOT PLAY – INJURED																						
2000-01	Phoenix	WCHL	44	2	1	3	169	....	....	....	....	....	....	....	....	....	....	....	....	....	....	....	....	....	....
2001-02	Idaho Steelheads	WCHL	69	2	1	3	303	....	....	....	....	....	....	....	....	....	....	....	....	....	....	....	....	....	....
2002-03	Peoria Rivermen	ECHL	24	1	2	3	154	....	....	....	....	....	....	....	....	....	....	....	....	....	....	....	....	....	....
	Cincinnati	AHL	9	0	0	0	42	....	....	....	....	....	....	....	....	....	....	....	....	....	....	....	....	....	....
	Worcester IceCats	AHL	20	1	0	1	50	....	....	....	....	....	....	....	....	....	....	....	....	....	....	....	....	....	....
2003-04	Worcester IceCats	AHL	6	0	0	0	19	....	....	....	....	....	....	....	....	....	....	....	....	....	....	....	....	....	....
	St. Louis	**NHL**	**1**	**0**	**0**	**0**	**5**	**0**	**0**	**0**	**1**	**0.0**	**–1**	**0**	**0.0**	**7:53**	....	....	....	....	....	....	....	....	....
	Peoria Rivermen	ECHL	13	0	2	2	62	....	....	....	....	....	....	....	....	....	....	....	....	....	....	....	....	....	....
	Milwaukee	AHL	2	0	0	0	11	....	....	....	....	....	....	....	....	....	....	....	....	....	....	....	....	....	....
2004-05	Milwaukee	AHL	32	3	2	5	116	....	....	....	....	....	....	....	....	....	....	....	....	....	....	....	....	....	....
	NHL Totals		**1**	**0**	**0**	**0**	**5**	**0**	**0**	**0**	**1**	**0.0**		**0**	**0.0**	**7:53**									

• Missed majority of 1998-99 season and entire 1999-2000 season recovering from head injury suffered in practice, January 3, 1999. Signed as a free agent by **Worcester** (AHL), July 17, 2003. Signed as a free agent by **St. Louis**, December 30, 2003. Claimed on waivers by **Nashville** from **St. Louis**, January 30, 2004.

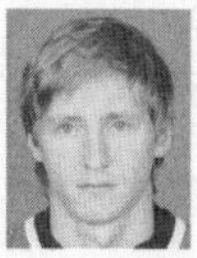

YAKUBOV, Mikhail

(yuh-KOO-bahf, mih-kigh-EHL) **CHI.**

Center. Shoots left. 6'3", 202 lbs. Born, Barnaul, USSR, February 16, 1982. Chicago's 1st choice, 10th overall, in 2000 Entry Draft.

Season	Club	League	GP	G	A	Pts	PIM	PP	SH	GW	S	%	+/-	TF	F%	Min	GP	G	A	Pts	PIM	PP	SH	GW	Min
1997-98	Lada Togliatti 2	Russia-3	7	0	0	0	0	....	....	....	....	....	....	....	....	....	....	....	....	....	....	....	....	....	....
1998-99	Lada Togliatti 2	Russia-4	38	11	4	15	32	....	....	....	....	....	....	....	....	....	....	....	....	....	....	....	....	....	....
99-2000	Lada Togliatti 2	Russia-3	26	12	19	31	14	....	....	....	....	....	....	....	....	....	....	....	....	....	....	....	....	....	....
2000-01	Lada Togliatti	Russia	25	0	0	0	4	....	....	....	....	....	....	....	....	....	4	0	0	0	0	....	....	....	....
2001-02	Red Deer Rebels	WHL	71	32	57	89	54	....	....	....	....	....	....	....	....	....	23	14	9	23	28	....	....	....	....
2002-03	Norfolk Admirals	AHL	62	6	5	11	36	....	....	....	....	....	....	....	....	....	9	0	0	0	8	....	....	....	....
2003-04	**Chicago**	**NHL**	**30**	**1**	**7**	**8**	**8**	**0**	**0**	**0**	**32**	**3.1**	**–12**	**337**	**45.7**	**13:44**	....	....	....	....	....	....	....	....	....
	Norfolk Admirals	AHL	51	9	18	27	22	....	....	....	....	....	....	....	....	....	8	0	3	3	2	....	....	....	....
2004-05	Norfolk Admirals	AHL	59	12	15	27	43	....	....	....	....	....	....	....	....	....	3	0	0	0	0	....	....	....	....
	NHL Totals		**30**	**1**	**7**	**8**	**8**	**0**	**0**	**0**	**32**	**3.1**		**337**	**45.7**	**13:44**	....	....	....	....	....	....	....	....	....

WHL East Second All-Star Team (2002)

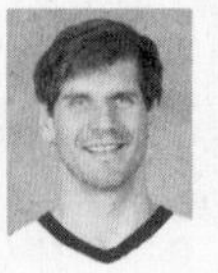

YASHIN, Alexei

(YAH-shin, al-EHX-ay) **NYI**

Center. Shoots right. 6'3", 225 lbs. Born, Sverdlovsk, USSR, November 5, 1973. Ottawa's 1st choice, 2nd overall, in 1992 Entry Draft.

			Regular Season														Playoffs								
Season	Club	League	GP	G	A	Pts	PIM	PP	SH	GW	S	%	+/-	TF	F%	Min	GP	G	A	Pts	PIM	PP	SH	GW	Min
1990-91	Sverdlovsk	USSR	26	2	1	3	10	....	....	....	....	....	....	....	....	....	....	....	....	....	....	....	....	....	....
1991-92	Dynamo Moscow	CIS	35	7	5	12	19	....	....	....	....	....	....	....	....	....	....	....	....	....	....	....	....	....	....
1992-93	Dynamo Moscow	CIS	27	10	12	22	18	....	....	....	....	....	....	....	....	....	10	7	3	10	18	....	....	....	....
1993-94	**Ottawa**	**NHL**	**83**	**30**	**49**	**79**	**22**	**11**	**2**	**3**	**232**	**12.9**	**–49**	....	....	....	....	....	....	....	....	....	....	....	....
1994-95	Las Vegas	IHL	24	15	20	35	32	....	....	....	....	....	....	....	....	....	....	....	....	....	....	....	....	....	....
	Ottawa	**NHL**	**47**	**21**	**23**	**44**	**20**	**11**	**0**	**1**	**154**	**13.6**	**–20**	....	....	....	....	....	....	....	....	....	....	....	....
1995-96	CSKA Moscow	CIS	4	2	2	4	4	....	....	....	....	....	....	....	....	....	....	....	....	....	....	....	....	....	....
	Ottawa	**NHL**	**46**	**15**	**24**	**39**	**28**	**8**	**0**	**1**	**143**	**10.5**	**–15**	....	....	....	....	....	....	....	....	....	....	....	....
1996-97	**Ottawa**	**NHL**	**82**	**35**	**40**	**75**	**44**	**10**	**0**	**5**	**291**	**12.0**	**–7**	....	....	....	**7**	**1**	**5**	**6**	**2**	**1**	**0**	**0**	....
1997-98	**Ottawa**	**NHL**	**82**	**33**	**39**	**72**	**24**	**5**	**0**	**6**	**291**	**11.3**	**6**	....	....	....	**11**	**5**	**3**	**8**	**8**	**3**	**0**	**2**	....
	Russia	Olympics	6	3	3	6	0	....	....	....	....	....	....	....	....	....	....	....	....	....	....	....	....	....	....
1998-99	**Ottawa**	**NHL**	**82**	**44**	**50**	**94**	**54**	**19**	**0**	**5**	**337**	**13.1**	**16**	**1428**	**41.9**	**22:05**	**4**	**0**	**0**	**0**	**10**	**0**	**0**	**0**	**26:06**
99-2000	**Ottawa**	**NHL**	DID NOT PLAY – SUSPENDED																						
2000-01	**Ottawa**	**NHL**	**82**	**40**	**48**	**88**	**30**	**13**	**2**	**10**	**263**	**15.2**	**10**	**1414**	**43.1**	**20:24**	**4**	**0**	**1**	**1**	**0**	**0**	**0**	**0**	**24:53**
2001-02	**NY Islanders**	**NHL**	**78**	**32**	**43**	**75**	**25**	**15**	**0**	**5**	**239**	**13.4**	**–3**	**828**	**46.7**	**20:37**	**7**	**3**	**4**	**7**	**2**	**1**	**0**	**0**	**21:54**
	Russia	Olympics	6	1	1	2	0	....	....	....	....	....	....	....	....	....	....	....	....	....	....	....	....	....	....
2002-03	**NY Islanders**	**NHL**	**81**	**26**	**39**	**65**	**32**	**14**	**0**	**7**	**274**	**9.5**	**–12**	**1074**	**47.2**	**18:32**	**5**	**2**	**2**	**4**	**2**	**0**	**0**	**0**	**21:06**
2003-04	**NY Islanders**	**NHL**	**47**	**15**	**19**	**34**	**10**	**3**	**0**	**1**	**148**	**10.1**	**–1**	**603**	**42.8**	**17:19**	**5**	**0**	**1**	**1**	**0**	**0**	**0**	**0**	**15:33**
2004-05	Yaroslavl	Russia	10	3	3	6	14	....	....	....	....	....	....	....	....	....	9	3	7	10	10	....	....	....	....
	NHL Totals		**710**	**291**	**374**	**665**	**289**	**109**	**4**	**44**	**2372**	**12.3**		**5347**	**44.1**	**20:01**	**43**	**11**	**16**	**27**	**24**	**5**	**0**	**2**	**21:37**

NHL Second All-Star Team (1999)

Played in NHL All-Star Game (1994, 1999, 2002)

• Suspended for entire 1999-2000 season by **Ottawa** for refusing to report to team, November 9, 1999. Traded to **NY Islanders** by **Ottawa** for Bill Muckalt, Zdeno Chara and NY Islanders' 1st round choice (Jason Spezza) in 2001 Entry Draft, June 23, 2001. Signed as a free agent by **Yaroslavl** (Russia), February 14, 2005.

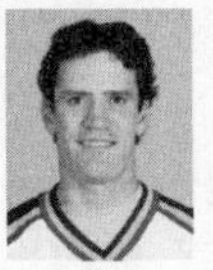

YELLE, Stephane

(YEHL, STEH-fan) **CGY.**

Center. Shoots left. 6'1", 190 lbs. Born, Ottawa, Ont., May 9, 1974. New Jersey's 9th choice, 186th overall, in 1992 Entry Draft.

Season	Club	League	GP	G	A	Pts	PIM	PP	SH	GW	S	%	+/-	TF	F%	Min	GP	G	A	Pts	PIM	PP	SH	GW	Min
1990-91	Cumberland	OHA-B	33	20	30	50	16	....	....	....	....	....	....	....	....	....	....	....	....	....	....	....	....	....	....
1991-92	Oshawa Generals	OHL	55	12	14	26	20	....	....	....	....	....	....	....	....	....	7	2	0	2	2	....	....	....	....
1992-93	Oshawa Generals	OHL	66	24	50	74	20	....	....	....	....	....	....	....	....	....	10	2	4	6	4	....	....	....	....
1993-94	Oshawa Generals	OHL	66	35	69	104	22	....	....	....	....	....	....	....	....	....	5	1	7	8	2	....	....	....	....
1994-95	Cornwall Aces	AHL	40	18	15	33	22	....	....	....	....	....	....	....	....	....	13	7	7	14	8	....	....	....	....
1995-96♦	**Colorado**	**NHL**	**71**	**13**	**14**	**27**	**30**	**0**	**2**	**1**	**93**	**14.0**	**15**	....	....	....	**22**	**1**	**4**	**5**	**8**	**0**	**1**	**0**	....
1996-97	**Colorado**	**NHL**	**79**	**9**	**17**	**26**	**38**	**0**	**1**	**1**	**89**	**10.1**	**1**	....	....	....	**12**	**1**	**6**	**7**	**2**	**0**	**0**	**0**	....
1997-98	**Colorado**	**NHL**	**81**	**7**	**15**	**22**	**48**	**0**	**1**	**0**	**93**	**7.5**	**–10**	....	....	....	**7**	**1**	**0**	**1**	**12**	**0**	**0**	**0**	....
1998-99	**Colorado**	**NHL**	**72**	**8**	**7**	**15**	**40**	**1**	**0**	**0**	**99**	**8.1**	**–8**	**1201**	**51.2**	**15:15**	**10**	**0**	**1**	**1**	**6**	**0**	**0**	**0**	**15:13**
99-2000	**Colorado**	**NHL**	**79**	**8**	**14**	**22**	**28**	**0**	**1**	**1**	**90**	**8.9**	**9**	**1294**	**52.2**	**15:51**	**17**	**1**	**2**	**3**	**4**	**0**	**0**	**0**	**15:38**
2000-01♦	**Colorado**	**NHL**	**50**	**4**	**10**	**14**	**20**	**0**	**1**	**0**	**54**	**7.4**	**–3**	**736**	**56.4**	**14:28**	**23**	**1**	**2**	**3**	**8**	**0**	**0**	**1**	**13:52**
2001-02	**Colorado**	**NHL**	**73**	**5**	**12**	**17**	**48**	**0**	**1**	**1**	**71**	**7.0**	**1**	**1036**	**51.8**	**14:02**	**20**	**0**	**2**	**2**	**14**	**0**	**0**	**0**	**13:26**
2002-03	**Calgary**	**NHL**	**82**	**10**	**15**	**25**	**50**	**3**	**0**	**3**	**121**	**8.3**	**–10**	**1494**	**53.4**	**18:06**	....	....	....	....	....	....	....	....	....
2003-04	**Calgary**	**NHL**	**53**	**4**	**13**	**17**	**24**	**1**	**0**	**0**	**76**	**5.3**	**1**	**996**	**56.6**	**15:48**	**23**	**3**	**3**	**6**	**16**	**0**	**1**	**1**	**17:04**
2004-05			DID NOT PLAY																						
	NHL Totals		**640**	**68**	**117**	**185**	**326**	**5**	**7**	**7**	**786**	**8.7**		**6757**	**53.4**	**15:42**	**134**	**8**	**20**	**28**	**70**	**0**	**2**	**2**	**15:02**

Traded to **Quebec** by **New Jersey** with New Jersey's 11th round choice (Steven Low) in 1994 Entry Draft for Quebec's 11th round choice (Mike Hanson) in 1994 Entry Draft, June 1, 1994. Transferred to **Colorado** after **Quebec** franchise relocated, June 21, 1995. Traded to **Calgary** by **Colorado** with Chris Drury for Derek Morris, Jeff Shantz and Dean McAmmond, October 1, 2002.

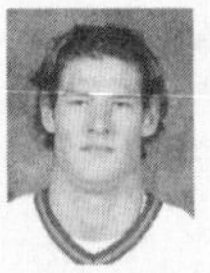

YONKMAN, Nolan

(YAWK-man, NOH-lan) **WSH.**

Defense. Shoots right. 6'6", 245 lbs. Born, Punnichy, Sask., April 1, 1981. Washington's 5th choice, 37th overall, in 1999 Entry Draft.

Season	Club	League	GP	G	A	Pts	PIM	PP	SH	GW	S	%	+/-	TF	F%	Min	GP	G	A	Pts	PIM	PP	SH	GW	Min
1996-97	Naicam Vikings	SAHA	64	15	23	38	36	....	....	....	....	....	....	....	....	....	....	....	....	....	....	....	....	....	....
	Kelowna Rockets	WHL	4	0	0	0	0	....	....	....	....	....	....	....	....	....	....	....	....	....	....	....	....	....	....
1997-98	Kelowna Rockets	WHL	65	0	2	2	36	....	....	....	....	....	....	....	....	....	7	0	0	0	2	....	....	....	....
1998-99	Kelowna Rockets	WHL	61	1	6	7	129	....	....	....	....	....	....	....	....	....	6	0	0	0	6	....	....	....	....
99-2000	Kelowna Rockets	WHL	71	5	7	12	153	....	....	....	....	....	....	....	....	....	5	0	0	0	8	....	....	....	....
2000-01	Kelowna Rockets	WHL	7	0	1	1	19	....	....	....	....	....	....	....	....	....	....	....	....	....	....	....	....	....	....
	Brandon	WHL	51	6	10	16	94	....	....	....	....	....	....	....	....	....	6	0	1	1	12	....	....	....	....
2001-02	**Washington**	**NHL**	**11**	**1**	**0**	**1**	**4**	**0**	**0**	**0**	**7**	**14.3**	**3**	**0**	**0.0**	**12:44**	....	....	....	....	....	....	....	....	....
	Portland Pirates	AHL	59	4	3	7	116	....	....	....	....	....	....	....	....	....	....	....	....	....	....	....	....	....	....
2002-03	Portland Pirates	AHL	24	1	4	5	40	....	....	....	....	....	....	....	....	....	3	0	1	1	2	....	....	....	....
2003-04	**Washington**	**NHL**	**1**	**0**	**0**	**0**	**0**	**0**	**0**	**0**	**0**	**0.0**	**0**	**0**	**0.0**	**5:00**	....	....	....	....	....	....	....	....	....
	Portland Pirates	AHL	4	0	0	0	11	....	....	....	....	....	....	....	....	....	....	....	....	....	....	....	....	....	....
2004-05	Portland Pirates	AHL	32	0	3	3	68	....	....	....	....	....	....	....	....	....	....	....	....	....	....	....	....	....	....
	NHL Totals		**12**	**1**	**0**	**1**	**4**	**0**	**0**	**0**	**7**	**14.3**		**0**	**0.0**	**12:05**	....	....	....	....	....	....	....	....	....

• Missed majority of 2002-03 season recovering from abdominal injury suffered in training camp, September 25, 2002. • Missed majority of 2003-04 and 2004-05 seasons recovering from knee injury suffered in game vs. Worcester (AHL), October 23, 2003.

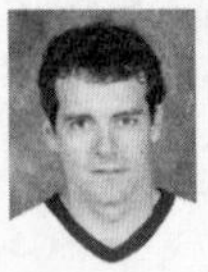

YORK, Jason

(YOHRK, JAY-suhn)

Defense. Shoots right. 6'1", 208 lbs. Born, Nepean, Ont., May 20, 1970. Detroit's 6th choice, 129th overall, in 1990 Entry Draft.

Season	Club	League	GP	G	A	Pts	PIM	PP	SH	GW	S	%	+/-	TF	F%	Min	GP	G	A	Pts	PIM	PP	SH	GW	Min
1986-87	Smiths Falls Bears	CJHL	46	6	13	19	86	....	....	....	....	....	....	....	....	....	....	....	....	....	....	....	....	....	....
1987-88	Hamilton	OHL	58	4	9	13	110	....	....	....	....	....	....	....	....	....	....	....	....	....	....	....	....	....	....
1988-89	Windsor Spitfires	OHL	65	19	44	63	105	....	....	....	....	....	....	....	....	....	....	....	....	....	....	....	....	....	....
1989-90	Windsor Spitfires	OHL	39	9	30	39	38	....	....	....	....	....	....	....	....	....	....	....	....	....	....	....	....	....	....
	Kitchener Rangers	OHL	25	11	25	36	17	....	....	....	....	....	....	....	....	....	17	3	19	22	10	....	....	....	....
1990-91	Windsor Spitfires	OHL	66	13	80	93	40	....	....	....	....	....	....	....	....	....	11	3	10	13	12	....	....	....	....
1991-92	Adirondack	AHL	49	4	20	24	32	....	....	....	....	....	....	....	....	....	5	0	1	1	0	....	....	....	....
1992-93	**Detroit**	**NHL**	**2**	**0**	**0**	**0**	**0**	**0**	**0**	**0**	**1**	**0.0**	**0**	....	....	....	....	....	....	....	....	....	....	....	....
	Adirondack	AHL	77	15	40	55	86	....	....	....	....	....	....	....	....	....	11	0	3	3	18	....	....	....	....
1993-94	**Detroit**	**NHL**	**7**	**1**	**2**	**3**	**2**	**0**	**0**	**0**	**9**	**11.1**	**0**	....	....	....	....	....	....	....	....	....	....	....	....
	Adirondack	AHL	74	10	56	66	98	....	....	....	....	....	....	....	....	....	12	3	11	14	22	....	....	....	....
1994-95	**Detroit**	**NHL**	**10**	**1**	**2**	**3**	**2**	**0**	**0**	**0**	**6**	**16.7**	**0**	....	....	....	....	....	....	....	....	....	....	....	....
	Adirondack	AHL	5	1	3	4	4	....	....	....	....	....	....	....	....	....	....	....	....	....	....	....	....	....	....
	Anaheim	**NHL**	**15**	**0**	**8**	**8**	**12**	**0**	**0**	**0**	**22**	**0.0**	**4**	....	....	....	....	....	....	....	....	....	....	....	....
1995-96	**Anaheim**	**NHL**	**79**	**3**	**21**	**24**	**88**	**0**	**0**	**0**	**106**	**2.8**	**–7**	....	....	....	....	....	....	....	....	....	....	....	....
1996-97	**Ottawa**	**NHL**	**75**	**4**	**17**	**21**	**67**	**1**	**0**	**0**	**121**	**3.3**	**–8**	....	....	....	**7**	**0**	**0**	**0**	**4**	**0**	**0**	**0**	....
1997-98	**Ottawa**	**NHL**	**73**	**3**	**13**	**16**	**62**	**0**	**0**	**0**	**109**	**2.8**	**8**	....	....	....	**7**	**1**	**1**	**2**	**7**	**1**	**0**	**0**	....
1998-99	**Ottawa**	**NHL**	**79**	**4**	**31**	**35**	**48**	**2**	**0**	**0**	**177**	**2.3**	**17**	**2**	**0.0**	**23:49**	**4**	**1**	**1**	**2**	**4**	**0**	**0**	**0**	**24:59**
99-2000	**Ottawa**	**NHL**	**79**	**8**	**22**	**30**	**60**	**1**	**0**	**1**	**159**	**5.0**	**–3**	**0**	**0.0**	**23:20**	**6**	**0**	**2**	**2**	**2**	**0**	**0**	**0**	**25:30**
2000-01	**Ottawa**	**NHL**	**74**	**6**	**16**	**22**	**72**	**3**	**0**	**2**	**133**	**4.5**	**7**	**0**	**0.0**	**23:49**	**4**	**0**	**0**	**0**	**4**	**0**	**0**	**0**	**20:58**
2001-02	**Anaheim**	**NHL**	**74**	**5**	**20**	**25**	**60**	**3**	**0**	**2**	**104**	**4.8**	**–11**	**0**	**0.0**	**19:19**	....	....	....	....	....	....	....	....	....
2002-03	**Nashville**	**NHL**	**74**	**4**	**15**	**19**	**52**	**2**	**0**	**0**	**107**	**3.7**	**13**	**0**	**0.0**	**19:57**	....	....	....	....	....	....	....	....	....
	Cincinnati	AHL	4	3	2	5	8	....	....	....	....	....	....	....	....	....	....	....	....	....	....	....	....	....	....
2003-04	**Nashville**	**NHL**	**67**	**2**	**13**	**15**	**64**	**0**	**0**	**1**	**80**	**2.5**	**–4**	**1**	**0.0**	**21:17**	**6**	**0**	**3**	**3**	**4**	**0**	**0**	**0**	**21:27**
2004-05			DID NOT PLAY																						
	NHL Totals		**708**	**41**	**180**	**221**	**589**	**12**	**0**	**6**	**1134**	**3.6**		**3**	**0.0**	**21:58**	**34**	**2**	**7**	**9**	**25**	**1**	**0**	**0**	**23:16**

AHL First All-Star Team (1994)

Traded to **Anaheim** by **Detroit** with Mike Sillinger for Stu Grimson, Mark Ferner and Anaheim's 6th round choice (Magnus Nilsson) in 1996 Entry Draft, April 4, 1995. Traded to **Ottawa** by **Anaheim** with Shaun Van Allen for Ted Drury and the rights to Marc Moro, October 1, 1996. Signed as a free agent by **Anaheim**, July 3, 2001. Traded to **Nashville** by **Anaheim** for future considerations, October 23, 2002.

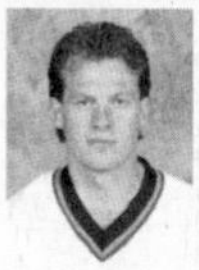

YORK, Mike

(YOHRK, MIGHK) **NYI**

Left wing. Shoots right. 5'10", 185 lbs. Born, Waterford, MI, January 3, 1978. NY Rangers' 7th choice, 136th overall, in 1997 Entry Draft.

			Regular Season														Playoffs								
Season	Club	League	GP	G	A	Pts	PIM	PP	SH	GW	S	%	+/-	TF	F%	Min	GP	G	A	Pts	PIM	PP	SH	GW	Min
1992-93	Michigan	MNHL	50	45	50	95	....	....	....	....	....	....	....	....	....	....	....	....	....	....	....	....	....	....	....
1993-94	Det. Compuware	MNHL	85	136	140	276	....	....	....	....	....	....	....	....	....	....	....	....	....	....	....	....	....	....	....
1994-95	Thornhill Islanders	MTJHL	49	39	54	*93	44	....	....	....	....	....	....	....	....	....	11	7	6	13	0	....	....	....	....
1995-96	Michigan State	CCHA	39	12	27	39	20	....	....	....	....	....	....	....	....	....	....	....	....	....	....	....	....	....	....
1996-97	Michigan State	CCHA	37	18	29	47	42	....	....	....	....	....	....	....	....	....	....	....	....	....	....	....	....	....	....
1997-98	Michigan State	CCHA	40	27	34	61	38	....	....	....	....	....	....	....	....	....	....	....	....	....	....	....	....	....	....
1998-99	Michigan State	CCHA	42	22	32	*54	41	....	....	....	....	....	....	....	....	....	....	....	....	....	....	....	....	....	....
	Hartford	AHL	3	2	2	4	0	....	....	....	....	....	....	....	....	....	6	3	1	4	0	....	....	....	....
99-2000	NY Rangers	NHL	82	26	24	50	18	8	0	4	177	14.7	-17	1131	48.1	1:35	....	....	....	....	....	....	....	....	....
2000-01	NY Rangers	NHL	79	14	17	31	20	3	2	4	171	8.2	1	1098	46.9	17:45	....	....	....	....	....	....	....	....	....
2001-02	NY Rangers	NHL	69	18	39	57	16	2	0	5	188	9.6	8	267	43.1	20:24	....	....	....	....	....	....	....	....	....
	United States	Olympics	6	0	1	1	0	....	....	....	....	....	....	....	....	....	....	....	....	....	....	....	....	....	....
	Edmonton	NHL	12	2	2	4	0	1	0	1	30	6.7	-1	100	56.0	16:35	....	....	....	....	....	....	....	....	....
2002-03	Edmonton	NHL	71	22	29	51	10	7	2	4	177	12.4	-8	390	43.9	19:04	6	0	2	2	2	0	0	0	14:20
2003-04	Edmonton	NHL	61	16	26	42	15	1	2	0	144	11.1	18	656	45.9	19:17	....	....	....	....	....	....	....	....	....
2004-05	Iserlohn Roosters	Germany	52	16	46	62	77	....	....	....	....	....	....	....	....	....	....	....	....	....	....	....	....	....	....
	NHL Totals		374	98	137	235	79	22	6	18	887	11.0		3642	46.7	15:10	6	0	2	2	2	0	0	0	14:20

CCHA Second All-Star Team (1998) • NCAA West First All-American Team (1998, 1999) • CCHA First All-Star Team (1999) • CCHA Player of the Year (1999) • NHL All-Rookie Team (2000)
Played in NHL All-Star Game (2002)

Traded to **Edmonton** by **NY Rangers** with NY Rangers' 4th round choice (Ivan Koltsov) in 2002 Entry Draft for Tom Poti and Rem Murray, March 19, 2002. Signed as a free agent by **Iserlohn** (Germany), February 25, 2005. Traded to **NY Islanders** by **Edmonton** with a conditional choice in 2006 Entry Draft for Michael Peca, August 3, 2005.

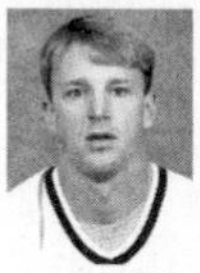

YOUNG, Scott

(YUHNG, SKAWT)

Right wing. Shoots right. 6'1", 200 lbs. Born, Clinton, MA, October 1, 1967. Hartford's 1st choice, 11th overall, in 1986 Entry Draft.

			Regular Season														Playoffs								
Season	Club	League	GP	G	A	Pts	PIM	PP	SH	GW	S	%	+/-	TF	F%	Min	GP	G	A	Pts	PIM	PP	SH	GW	Min
1984-85	St. Mark's	High-MA	23	28	41	69	....	....	....	....	....	....	....	....	....	....	....	....	....	....	....	....	....	....	....
1985-86	Boston University	H-East	38	16	13	29	31	....	....	....	....	....	....	....	....	....	....	....	....	....	....	....	....	....	....
1986-87	Boston University	H-East	33	15	21	36	24	....	....	....	....	....	....	....	....	....	....	....	....	....	....	....	....	....	....
1987-88	United States	Nat-Tm	56	11	47	58	31	....	....	....	....	....	....	....	....	....	....	....	....	....	....	....	....	....	....
	United States	Olympics	6	2	6	8	4	....	....	....	....	....	....	....	....	....	....	....	....	....	....	....	....	....	....
	Hartford	NHL	7	0	0	0	2	0	0	0	6	0.0	-6	....	....	....	4	1	0	1	0	0	0	0	....
1988-89	Hartford	NHL	76	19	40	59	27	6	0	2	203	9.4	-21	....	....	....	4	2	0	2	4	0	0	0	....
1989-90	Hartford	NHL	80	24	40	64	47	10	2	5	239	10.0	-24	....	....	....	7	2	0	2	2	0	0	0	....
1990-91	Hartford	NHL	34	6	9	15	8	3	1	2	94	6.4	-9	....	....	....	....	....	....	....	....	....	....	....	....
	♦ Pittsburgh	NHL	43	11	16	27	33	3	1	3	116	9.5	3	....	....	....	17	1	6	7	2	1	0	0	....
1991-92	HC Bolzano	Alpenliga	15	19	11	30	14	....	....	....	....	....	....	....	....	....	....	....	....	....	....	....	....	....	....
	HC Bolzano	Italy	18	22	17	39	6	....	....	....	....	....	....	....	....	....	5	4	3	7	7	....	....	....	....
	United States	Nat-Tm	10	2	4	6	21	....	....	....	....	....	....	....	....	....	....	....	....	....	....	....	....	....	....
	United States	Olympics	8	2	1	3	2	....	....	....	....	....	....	....	....	....	....	....	....	....	....	....	....	....	....
1992-93	Quebec	NHL	82	30	30	60	20	9	6	5	225	13.3	5	....	....	....	6	4	1	5	0	0	0	2	....
1993-94	Quebec	NHL	76	26	25	51	14	6	1	1	236	11.0	-4	....	....	....	....	....	....	....	....	....	....	....	....
1994-95	EV Landshut	Germany	4	6	1	7	6	....	....	....	....	....	....	....	....	....	....	....	....	....	....	....	....	....	....
	Frankfurt Lions	Germany	1	1	0	1	0	....	....	....	....	....	....	....	....	....	....	....	....	....	....	....	....	....	....
	Quebec	NHL	48	18	21	39	14	3	3	0	167	10.8	9	....	....	....	6	3	3	6	2	0	1	0	....
1995-96♦	Colorado	NHL	81	21	39	60	50	7	0	5	229	9.2	2	....	....	....	22	3	12	15	10	0	0	0	....
1996-97	Colorado	NHL	72	18	19	37	14	7	0	0	164	11.0	-5	....	....	....	17	4	2	6	14	2	0	0	....
1997-98	Anaheim	NHL	73	13	20	33	22	4	2	1	187	7.0	-13	....	....	....	....	....	....	....	....	....	....	....	....
1998-99	St. Louis	NHL	75	24	28	52	27	8	0	4	205	11.7	8	4	25.0	15:14	13	4	7	11	10	1	0	1	17:56
99-2000	St. Louis	NHL	75	24	15	39	18	6	1	7	244	9.8	12	2	50.0	16:06	6	6	2	8	8	3	0	0	17:18
2000-01	St. Louis	NHL	81	40	33	73	30	14	3	7	321	12.5	15	4	25.0	19:18	15	6	7	13	2	0	2	3	20:34
2001-02	St. Louis	NHL	67	19	22	41	26	5	0	1	210	9.0	11	4	0.0	18:31	10	3	0	3	2	1	1	0	17:40
	United States	Olympics	6	4	0	4	2	....	....	....	....	....	....	....	....	....	....	....	....	....	....	....	....	....	....
2002-03	Dallas	NHL	79	23	19	42	30	5	1	4	237	9.7	24	8	37.5	16:08	10	4	3	7	6	2	0	1	19:12
2003-04	Dallas	NHL	53	8	8	16	14	2	0	2	134	6.0	-15	5	20.0	14:45	4	1	0	1	2	1	0	0	15:05
2004-05	Memphis	CHL	3	2	1	3	0	....	....	....	....	....	....	....	....	....	....	....	....	....	....	....	....	....	....
	NHL Totals		1102	324	384	708	396	98	21	49	3217	10.1		27	25.9	16:46	141	44	43	87	64	11	4	7	18:32

Hockey East Rookie of the Year (1986) (co-winner - Al Loring)

Traded to **Pittsburgh** by **Hartford** for Rob Brown, December 21, 1990. Traded to **Quebec** by **Pittsburgh** for Bryan Fogarty, March 10, 1992. Transferred to **Colorado** after **Quebec** franchise relocated, June 21, 1995. Traded to **Anaheim** by **Colorado** for Anaheim's 3rd round choice (later traded to Florida – Florida selected Lance Ward) in 1998 Entry Draft, September 17, 1997. Signed as a free agent by **St. Louis**, July 28, 1998. Signed as a free agent by **Dallas**, July 5, 2002. Signed as a free agent by **Memphis** (CHL), January 7, 2005.

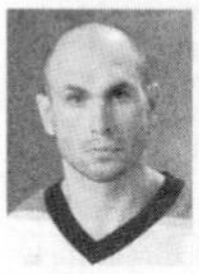

YUSHKEVICH, Dmitry

(yoosh-KAY-vihch, dih-MEE-tree)

Defense. Shoots right. 5'11", 208 lbs. Born, Cherepovets, USSR, November 19, 1971. Philadelphia's 6th choice, 122nd overall, in 1991 Entry Draft.

			Regular Season														Playoffs								
Season	Club	League	GP	G	A	Pts	PIM	PP	SH	GW	S	%	+/-	TF	F%	Min	GP	G	A	Pts	PIM	PP	SH	GW	Min
1988-89	Yaroslavl	USSR	23	2	1	3	8	....	....	....	....	....	....	....	....	....	....	....	....	....	....	....	....	....	....
1989-90	Yaroslavl	USSR	41	2	3	5	39	....	....	....	....	....	....	....	....	....	....	....	....	....	....	....	....	....	....
1990-91	Yaroslavl	USSR	41	10	4	14	22	....	....	....	....	....	....	....	....	....	....	....	....	....	....	....	....	....	....
1991-92	Dynamo Moscow	CIS	35	5	7	12	14	....	....	....	....	....	....	....	....	....	....	....	....	....	....	....	....	....	....
	Russia	Olympics	8	1	2	3	4	....	....	....	....	....	....	....	....	....	....	....	....	....	....	....	....	....	....
1992-93	Philadelphia	NHL	82	5	27	32	71	1	0	1	155	3.2	12	....	....	....	....	....	....	....	....	....	....	....	....
1993-94	Philadelphia	NHL	75	5	25	30	86	1	0	2	136	3.7	-8	....	....	....	....	....	....	....	....	....	....	....	....
1994-95	Yaroslavl	CIS	10	3	4	7	8	....	....	....	....	....	....	....	....	....	....	....	....	....	....	....	....	....	....
	Philadelphia	NHL	40	5	9	14	47	3	1	1	80	6.3	-4	....	....	....	15	1	5	6	12	0	0	0	....
1995-96	Toronto	NHL	69	1	10	11	54	1	0	0	96	1.0	-14	....	....	....	4	0	0	0	0	0	0	0	....
1996-97	Toronto	NHL	74	4	10	14	56	1	1	1	99	4.0	-24	....	....	....	....	....	....	....	....	....	....	....	....
1997-98	Toronto	NHL	72	0	12	12	78	0	0	0	92	0.0	-13	....	....	....	....	....	....	....	....	....	....	....	....
	Russia	Olympics	6	0	0	0	2	....	....	....	....	....	....	....	....	....	....	....	....	....	....	....	....	....	....
1998-99	Toronto	NHL	78	6	22	28	88	2	1	0	95	6.3	25	0	0.0	22:20	17	1	5	6	22	1	0	0	23:13
99-2000	Yaroslavl	Russia	7	2	3	5	2	....	....	....	....	....	....	....	....	....	....	....	....	....	....	....	....	....	....
	Toronto	NHL	77	3	24	27	55	2	1	1	103	2.9	2	0	0.0	23:18	12	1	1	2	4	0	0	0	24:45
2000-01	Toronto	NHL	81	5	19	24	52	1	0	0	110	4.5	-2	0	0.0	24:14	11	0	4	4	12	0	0	0	25:18
2001-02	Toronto	NHL	55	6	13	19	26	3	0	0	79	7.6	14	1	100.0	23:25	....	....	....	....	....	....	....	....	....
2002-03	Florida	NHL	23	1	6	7	14	0	0	0	23	4.3	-12	3	33.3	23:40	....	....	....	....	....	....	....	....	....
	Los Angeles	NHL	42	0	3	3	24	0	0	0	36	0.0	-4	2	0.0	19:57	....	....	....	....	....	....	....	....	....
	Philadelphia	NHL	18	2	2	4	8	0	0	0	16	12.5	7	0	0.0	18:05	13	1	4	5	2	0	0	1	24:20
2003-04	Yaroslavl	Russia	35	7	11	18	38	....	....	....	....	....	....	....	....	....	3	0	2	2	2	....	....	....	....
2004-05	Cherepovets	Russia	54	6	22	28	58	....	....	....	....	....	....	....	....	....	....	....	....	....	....	....	....	....	....
	NHL Totals		786	43	182	225	659	15	4	6	1120	3.8		6	33.3	22:43	72	4	19	23	52	1	0	1	24:16

Played in NHL All-Star Game (2000)

Traded to **Toronto** by **Philadelphia** with Philadelphia's 2nd round choice (Francis Larivee) in 1996 Entry Draft for Toronto's 1st round choice (Dainius Zubrus) in 1996 Entry Draft, Toronto's 2nd round choice (Jean-Marc Pelletier) in 1997 Entry Draft and Los Angeles' 4th round choice (previously acquired, later traded back to Los Angeles – Los Angeles selected Mikael Simons) in 1996 Entry Draft, August 30, 1995. Traded to **Florida** by **Toronto** for Robert Svehla, July 18, 2002. Traded to **Los Angeles** by **Florida** with NY Islanders' 5th round choice (previously acquired, Los Angeles selected Brady Murray) in 2003 Entry Draft for Jaroslav Bednar and Andreas Lilja, November 26, 2002. Traded to **Philadelphia** by **Los Angeles** for Philadelphia's 4th round choice (later traded to Boston – Boston selected Patrick Valcak) in 2003 Entry Draft and Philadelphia's 7th round choice (Daniel Taylor) in 2004 Entry Draft, March 1, 2003. Signed as a free agent by **Yaroslavl** (Russia), November 11, 2003.

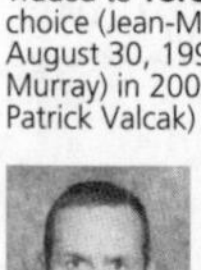

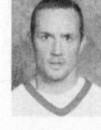

YZERMAN, Steve

(IGH-zuhr-muhn, STEEV) **DET.**

Center. Shoots right. 5'11", 185 lbs. Born, Cranbrook, B.C., May 9, 1965. Detroit's 1st choice, 4th overall, in 1983 Entry Draft.

			Regular Season														Playoffs								
Season	Club	League	GP	G	A	Pts	PIM	PP	SH	GW	S	%	+/-	TF	F%	Min	GP	G	A	Pts	PIM	PP	SH	GW	Min
1980-81	Nepean Raiders	CJHL	50	38	*54	92	44	....	....	....	....	....	....	....	....	....	....	....	....	....	....	....	....	....	....
1981-82	Peterborough	OHL	58	21	43	64	65	....	....	....	....	....	....	....	....	....	6	0	1	1	16	....	....	....	....
1982-83	Peterborough	OHL	56	42	49	91	33	....	....	....	....	....	....	....	....	....	4	1	4	5	0	....	....	....	....
1983-84	Detroit	NHL	80	39	48	87	33	13	0	2	177	22.0	-17	....	....	....	4	3	3	6	0	1	0	1	....
1984-85	Detroit	NHL	80	30	59	89	58	9	0	3	231	13.0	-17	....	....	....	3	2	1	3	2	0	0	0	....
1985-86	Detroit	NHL	51	14	28	42	16	3	0	3	132	10.6	-24	....	....	....	....	....	....	....	....	....	....	....	....
1986-87	Detroit	NHL	80	31	59	90	43	9	1	2	217	14.3	-1	....	....	....	16	5	13	18	8	1	0	0	....
1987-88	Detroit	NHL	64	50	52	102	44	10	6	6	242	20.7	30	....	....	....	3	1	3	4	6	0	0	0	....
1988-89	Detroit	NHL	80	65	90	155	61	17	3	7	388	16.8	17	....	....	....	6	5	5	10	2	2	0	0	....

Season	Club	League	GP	G	A	Pts	PIM	PP	SH	GW	S	%	+/-	TF	F%	Min	GP	G	A	Pts	PIM	PP	SH	GW	Min
			Regular Season														Playoffs								
1989-90	Detroit	NHL	79	62	65	127	79	16	7	8	332	18.7	-6												
1990-91	Detroit	NHL	80	51	57	108	34	12	6	4	326	15.6	-2				7	3	3	6	4	1	0	0	
1991-92	Detroit	NHL	79	45	58	103	64	9	8	9	295	15.3	26				11	3	5	8	12	0	1	1	
1992-93	Detroit	NHL	84	58	79	137	44	13	7	6	307	18.9	33				7	4	3	7	4	1	1	1	
1993-94	Detroit	NHL	58	24	58	82	36	7	3	3	217	11.1	11				3	1	3	4	0	0	0	0	
1994-95	Detroit	NHL	47	12	26	38	40	4	0	1	134	9.0	6				15	4	8	12	0	2	0	1	
1995-96	Detroit	NHL	80	36	59	95	64	16	2	8	220	16.4	29				18	8	12	20	4	4	0	1	
1996-97♦	Detroit	NHL	81	22	63	85	78	8	0	3	232	9.5	22				20	7	6	13	4	3	0	2	
1997-98♦	Detroit	NHL	75	24	45	69	46	6	2	0	188	12.8	3				22	6	*18	*24	22	3	1	0	
	Canada	Olympics	6	1	1	2	10																		
1998-99	Detroit	NHL	80	29	45	74	42	13	2	4	231	12.6	8	1600	56.9	21:35	10	9	4	13	0	4	0	2	21:49
99-2000	Detroit	NHL	78	35	44	79	34	15	2	6	234	15.0	28	1868	56.8	21:07	8	0	4	4	0	0	0	0	22:39
2000-01	Detroit	NHL	54	18	34	52	18	5	0	7	155	11.6	4	1197	59.6	22:14	1	0	0	0	0	0	0	0	5:58
2001-02♦	Detroit	NHL	52	13	35	48	18	5	1	5	104	12.5	11	1182	58.4	20:35	23	6	17	23	10	4	0	2	21:22
	Canada	Olympics	6	2	4	6	2																		
2002-03	Detroit	NHL	16	2	6	8	8	1	0	1	13	15.4	6	134	56.0	15:35	4	0	1	1	2	0	0	0	20:33
2003-04	Detroit	NHL	75	18	33	51	46	7	0	3	141	12.8	10	1134	55.3	17:32	11	3	2	5	0	0	0	1	17:02
2004-05			DID NOT PLAY																						
	NHL Totals		1453	678	1043	1721	906	198	50	91	4516	15.0		7115	57.3	20:18	192	70	111	181	80	26	3	12	20:28

NHL All-Rookie Team (1984) • Lester B. Pearson Award (1989) • Conn Smythe Trophy (1998) • NHL First All-Star Team (2000) • Frank J. Selke Trophy (2000) • Bill Masterton Memorial Trophy (2003)
Played in NHL All-Star Game (1984, 1988, 1989, 1990, 1991, 1992, 1993, 1997, 2000)
• Missed majority of 2002-03 season recovering from off-season knee surgery, August 2, 2002.

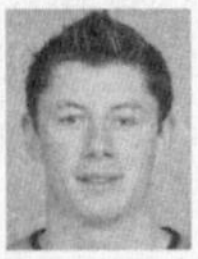

ZALESAK, Miroslav (zah-LIH-sahk, MEER-oh-slav) WSH.

Right wing. Shoots left. 6', 200 lbs. Born, Skalica, Czech., January 2, 1980. San Jose's 5th choice, 104th overall, in 1998 Entry Draft.

Season	Club	League	GP	G	A	Pts	PIM	PP	SH	GW	S	%	+/-	TF	F%	Min	GP	G	A	Pts	PIM	PP	SH	GW	Min
1995-96	HC Nitra Jr.	Slovak-Jr.	49	53	29	82	....																		
1996-97	Nitra Jr.	Slovak-Jr.	58	51	31	82	....																		
1997-98	Nitra Jr.	Slovak-Jr.	27	32	29	61	30																		
	Nitra	Slovakia	30	8	6	14	0																		
1998-99	Nitra	Slovakia	15	4	3	7	10																		
	Drummondville	QMJHL	45	24	27	51	18																		
99-2000	Drummondville	QMJHL	60	50	61	111	40										16	7	11	18	4				
2000-01	Kentucky	AHL	60	14	11	25	26										3	0	1	1	4				
2001-02	Cleveland Barons	AHL	74	22	20	42	44																		
2002-03	San Jose	NHL	10	1	2	3	0	0	0	0	8	12.5	-2	1	0.0	9:28									
	Cleveland Barons	AHL	50	27	22	49	35																		
2003-04	San Jose	NHL	2	0	0	0	0	0	0	0	3	0.0	-1	0	0.0	12:02									
	Cleveland Barons	AHL	72	35	40	75	80										9	1	4	5	14				
2004-05	HK 36 Skalica	Slovakia	18	11	14	25	18																		
	Litvinov	CzRep	30	6	6	12	26										6	1	1	2	0				
	NHL Totals		12	1	2	3	0	0	0	0	11	9.1		1	0.0	9:54									

Signed as a free agent by Skalica (Slovakia), September 17, 2004. Signed as a free agent by Litvinov (CzRep), November 19, 2004. Signed as a free agent by Washington, August 8, 2005.

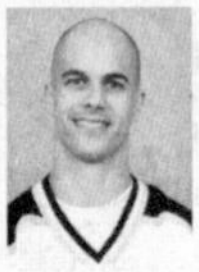

ZAMUNER, Rob (ZAM-nuhr, RAWB)

Left wing. Shoots left. 6'3", 203 lbs. Born, Oakville, Ont., September 17, 1969. NY Rangers' 3rd choice, 45th overall, in 1989 Entry Draft.

Season	Club	League	GP	G	A	Pts	PIM	PP	SH	GW	S	%	+/-	TF	F%	Min	GP	G	A	Pts	PIM	PP	SH	GW	Min
1985-86	Oakville Oaks	OMHA	48	43	50	93	66																		
1986-87	Guelph Jr. B's	OHA-B	3	6	7	13	15																		
	Guelph Platers	OHL	62	6	15	21	8																		
1987-88	Guelph Platers	OHL	58	20	41	61	18																		
1988-89	Guelph Platers	OHL	66	46	65	111	38										7	5	5	10	9				
1989-90	Flint Spirits	IHL	77	44	35	79	32										4	1	0	1	6				
1990-91	Binghamton	AHL	80	25	58	83	50										9	7	6	13	35				
1991-92	NY Rangers	NHL	9	1	2	3	2	0	0	0	11	9.1	0												
	Binghamton	AHL	61	19	53	72	42										11	8	9	17	8				
1992-93	Tampa Bay	NHL	84	15	28	43	74	1	0	0	183	8.2	-25												
1993-94	Tampa Bay	NHL	59	6	6	12	42	0	0	1	109	5.5	-9												
1994-95	Tampa Bay	NHL	43	9	6	15	24	0	3	1	74	12.2	-3												
1995-96	Tampa Bay	NHL	72	15	20	35	62	0	3	4	152	9.9	11				6	2	3	5	10	0	1	0	
1996-97	Tampa Bay	NHL	82	17	33	50	56	0	4	3	216	7.9	3												
1997-98	Tampa Bay	NHL	77	14	12	26	41	0	3	4	126	11.1	-31												
	Canada	Olympics	6	1	0	1	8																		
1998-99	Tampa Bay	NHL	58	8	11	19	24	1	1	2	89	9.0	-15	34	47.1	16:26									
99-2000	Ottawa	NHL	57	9	12	21	32	0	1	0	103	8.7	-6	29	37.9	14:56	6	2	0	2	2	0	0	1	12:59
2000-01	Ottawa	NHL	79	19	18	37	52	1	2	4	123	15.4	7	162	35.8	14:46	4	0	0	0	6	0	0	0	13:51
2001-02	Boston	NHL	66	12	13	25	24	1	2	0	98	12.2	6	192	41.7	13:13	6	0	2	2	4	0	0	0	12:35
2002-03	Boston	NHL	55	10	6	16	18	3	0	1	94	10.6	2	97	45.4	12:08	5	0	0	0	4	0	0	0	9:23
2003-04	Boston	NHL	57	4	5	9	16	0	0	0	49	8.2	3	58	50.0	9:43	7	0	0	0	0	0	0	0	5:35
	Providence Bruins	AHL	4	0	1	1	2																		
2004-05	EHC Basel	Swiss-2	40	10	24	34	91										12	7	7	14	24				
	NHL Totals		798	139	172	311	467	7	19	20	1427	9.7		572	41.6	13:37	34	4	5	9	26	0	1	1	10:32

Signed as a free agent by Tampa Bay, July 13, 1992. Traded to Ottawa by Tampa Bay with Tampa Bay's 2nd round choice (later traded to Philadelphia – later traded back to Tampa Bay – later traded to Dallas – Dallas selected Tobias Stephan) in 2002 Entry Draft for Andreas Johansson, June 29, 1999. Signed as a free agent by Boston, July 6, 2001. Signed as a free agent by Basel (Swiss-2), August 23, 2004.

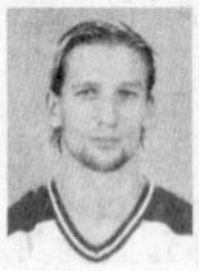

ZEDNIK, Richard (ZEHD-nihk, RIH-chuhrd) MTL.

Right wing. Shoots left. 6'1", 196 lbs. Born, Bystrica, Czech., January 6, 1976. Washington's 10th choice, 249th overall, in 1994 Entry Draft.

Season	Club	League	GP	G	A	Pts	PIM	PP	SH	GW	S	%	+/-	TF	F%	Min	GP	G	A	Pts	PIM	PP	SH	GW	Min
1993-94	B. Bystrica	Slovak-2	25	3	6	9	....																		
1994-95	Portland	WHL	65	35	51	86	89										9	5	5	10	20				
1995-96	Portland	WHL	61	44	37	81	154										7	8	4	12	23				
	Washington	NHL	1	0	0	0	0	0	0	0	0	0.0	0												
	Portland Pirates	AHL	1	1	1	2	0										21	4	5	9	26				
1996-97	Washington	NHL	11	2	1	3	4	1	0	0	21	9.5	-5												
	Portland Pirates	AHL	56	15	20	35	70										5	1	0	1	6				
1997-98	Washington	NHL	65	17	9	26	28	2	0	2	148	11.5	-2				17	7	3	10	16	2	0	0	
1998-99	Washington	NHL	49	9	8	17	50	1	0	2	115	7.8	-6	2	0.0	15:08									
99-2000	Washington	NHL	69	19	16	35	54	1	0	2	179	10.6	6	1	100.0	15:34	5	0	0	0	5	0	0	0	16:57
2000-01	Washington	NHL	62	16	19	35	61	4	0	3	155	10.3	-2	1	0.0	15:32									
	Montreal	NHL	12	3	6	9	10	1	0	0	23	13.0	-2	0	0.0	18:29									
2001-02	Montreal	NHL	82	22	22	44	59	4	0	3	249	8.8	-3	10	30.0	17:39	4	4	4	8	6	2	0	0	21:19
2002-03	Montreal	NHL	80	31	19	50	79	9	0	2	250	12.4	4	10	30.0	18:25									
2003-04	Montreal	NHL	81	26	24	50	63	7	0	9	218	11.9	5	6	50.0	17:30	11	3	3	6	2	0	0	1	18:52
2004-05	HKm Zvolen	Slovakia	36	15	19	34	56										17	9	10	19	12				
	NHL Totals		512	145	124	269	408	30	0	23	1358	10.7		30	33.3	16:52	37	14	10	24	29	4	0	1	18:53

WHL West Second All-Star Team (1996)
Traded to Montreal by Washington with Jan Bulis and Washington's 1st round choice (Alexander Perezhogin) in 2001 Entry Draft for Trevor Linden, Dainius Zubrus and New Jersey's 2nd round choice (previously acquired, later traded to Tampa Bay – Tampa Bay selected Andreas Holmqvist) in 2001 Entry Draft, March 13, 2001. Signed as a free agent by Zvolen (Slovakia), October 7, 2004.

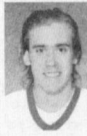

ZETTERBERG, Henrik (ZEH-tuhr-buhrg, HEHN-rihk) DET.

Left wing. Shoots left. 5'11", 176 lbs. Born, Njurunda, Sweden, October 9, 1980. Detroit's 4th choice, 210th overall, in 1999 Entry Draft.

Season	Club	League	GP	G	A	Pts	PIM	PP	SH	GW	S	%	+/-	TF	F%	Min	GP	G	A	Pts	PIM	PP	SH	GW	Min
1997-98	Timra IK Jr.	Swe-Jr.	18	9	5	14	4																		
	Timra IK	Sweden-2	16	1	2	3	4										4	0	1	1	0				
1998-99	Timra IK	Sweden-2	37	15	13	28	2										4	2	1	3	2				
99-2000	Timra IK	Sweden-2	32	20	14	34	20										10	10	4	14	4				
2000-01	Timra IK	Sweden	47	15	31	46	24																		
2001-02	Timra IK	Sweden	48	10	22	32	20																		
	Sweden	Olympics	4	0	1	1	0																		

			Regular Season														Playoffs								
Season	Club	League	GP	G	A	Pts	PIM	PP	SH	GW	S	%	+/-	TF	F%	Min	GP	G	A	Pts	PIM	PP	SH	GW	Min
2002-03	**Detroit**	**NHL**	79	22	22	44	8	5	1	4	135	16.3	6	401	46.1	16:19	4	1	0	1	0	0	0	0	18:19
2003-04	**Detroit**	**NHL**	61	15	28	43	14	7	1	2	137	10.9	15	627	45.6	18:15	12	2	2	4	4	0	0	0	17:17
2004-05	Timra IK	Sweden	50	19	31	*50	24	....	....	....	....	....	....	....	....	....	7	6	2	8	2	....	....	....	....
	NHL Totals		140	37	50	87	22	12	2	6	272	13.6		1028	45.8	17:09	16	3	2	5	4	0	0	0	17:32

Swedish Elite League Rookie of the Year (2001) • NHL All-Rookie Team (2003)

Signed as a free agent by **Timra** (Sweden), September 20, 2004.

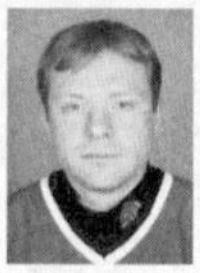

ZHAMNOV, Alex (ZHAHM-nahf, al-EHX) **BOS.**

Center. Shoots left. 6'1", 204 lbs. Born, Moscow, USSR, October 1, 1970. Winnipeg's 5th choice, 77th overall, in 1990 Entry Draft.

Season	Club	League	GP	G	A	Pts	PIM	PP	SH	GW	S	%	+/-	TF	F%	Min	GP	G	A	Pts	PIM	PP	SH	GW	Min
1988-89	Dynamo Moscow	USSR	4	0	0	0	0	....	....	....	....	....	....	....	....	....	....	....	....	....	....	....	....	....	....
1989-90	Dynamo Moscow	USSR	43	11	6	17	21	....	....	....	....	....	....	....	....	....	....	....	....	....	....	....	....	....	....
1990-91	Dynamo Moscow	USSR	46	16	12	28	24	....	....	....	....	....	....	....	....	....	....	....	....	....	....	....	....	....	....
1991-92	Dynamo Moscow	CIS	39	15	21	36	28	....	....	....	....	....	....	....	....	....	....	....	....	....	....	....	....	....	....
	Russia	Olympics	8	0	3	3	8	....	....	....	....	....	....	....	....	....	....	....	....	....	....	....	....	....	....
1992-93	**Winnipeg**	**NHL**	68	25	47	72	58	6	1	4	163	15.3	7	....	....	....	6	0	2	2	2	0	0	0	....
1993-94	**Winnipeg**	**NHL**	61	26	45	71	62	7	0	1	196	13.3	-20	....	....	....	....	....	....	....	....	....	....	....	....
1994-95	**Winnipeg**	**NHL**	48	30	35	65	20	9	0	4	155	19.4	5	....	....	....	....	....	....	....	....	....	....	....	....
1995-96	**Winnipeg**	**NHL**	58	22	37	59	65	5	0	2	199	11.1	-4	....	....	....	6	2	1	3	8	0	0	0	....
1996-97	**Chicago**	**NHL**	74	20	42	62	56	6	1	2	208	9.6	18	....	....	....	....	....	....	....	....	....	....	....	....
1997-98	**Chicago**	**NHL**	70	21	28	49	61	6	2	3	193	10.9	16	....	....	....	....	....	....	....	....	....	....	....	....
	Russia	Olympics	6	2	1	3	2	....	....	....	....	....	....	....	....	....	....	....	....	....	....	....	....	....	....
1998-99	**Chicago**	**NHL**	76	20	41	61	50	8	1	2	200	10.0	-10	1299	48.9	21:30	....	....	....	....	....	....	....	....	....
99-2000	**Chicago**	**NHL**	71	23	37	60	61	5	0	7	175	13.1	7	1171	45.8	22:08	....	....	....	....	....	....	....	....	....
2000-01	**Chicago**	**NHL**	63	13	36	49	40	3	1	3	117	11.1	-12	1486	48.1	21:15	....	....	....	....	....	....	....	....	....
2001-02	**Chicago**	**NHL**	77	22	45	67	67	6	0	3	173	12.7	8	1634	50.0	22:19	5	0	0	0	0	0	0	0	21:16
	Russia	Olympics	6	1	0	1	4	....	....	....	....	....	....	....	....	....	....	....	....	....	....	....	....	....	....
2002-03	**Chicago**	**NHL**	74	15	43	58	70	2	3	1	166	9.0	0	1345	51.3	21:06	....	....	....	....	....	....	....	....	....
2003-04	**Chicago**	**NHL**	23	6	12	18	14	1	0	1	63	9.5	-8	514	49.2	19:34	....	....	....	....	....	....	....	....	....
	Philadelphia	**NHL**	20	5	13	18	14	0	0	0	33	15.2	7	355	46.2	18:32	18	4	10	14	8	1	0	1	18:39
2004-05	Vityaz Chekhov	Russia-2	24	5	22	27	20	....	....	....	....	....	....	....	....	....	14	7	7	14	10	....	....	....	....
	NHL Totals		783	248	461	709	638	64	9	33	2041	12.2		7804	48.8	21:24	35	6	13	19	18	1	0	1	19:13

NHL Second All-Star Team (1995)

Played in NHL All-Star Game (2002)

Traded to **Chicago** by **Phoenix** with Craig Mills and Phoenix's 1st round choice (Ty Jones) in 1997 Entry Draft for Jeremy Roenick, August 16, 1996. Traded to **Philadelphia** by **Chicago** with Washington's 4th round choice (previously acquired, Philadelphia selected R.J. Anderson) in 2004 Entry Draft for Jim Vandermeer, the rights to Colin Fraser and Los Angeles' 2nd round choice (previously acquired, Chicago selected Bryan Bickell) in 2004 Entry Draft, February 19, 2004. Signed as a free agent by **Vityaz Chekhov** (Russia-2), November 15, 2004. Signed as a free agent by **Boston**, August 4, 2005.

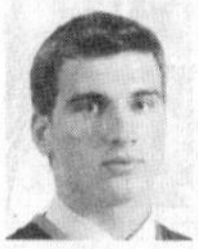

ZHERDEV, Nikolai (ZHAIR-dehv, NIH-koh-ligh) **CBJ**

Wing. Shoots right. 6'1", 186 lbs. Born, Kiev, USSR, November 5, 1984. Columbus' 1st choice, 4th overall, in 2003 Entry Draft.

Season	Club	League	GP	G	A	Pts	PIM	PP	SH	GW	S	%	+/-	TF	F%	Min	GP	G	A	Pts	PIM	PP	SH	GW	Min
99-2000	Elektrostal 2	Russia-3	21	10	7	17	26	....	....	....	....	....	....	....	....	....	7	0	0	0	0	....	....	....	....
2000-01	Elektrostal	Russia-2	18	5	8	13	12	....	....	....	....	....	....	....	....	....	....	....	....	....	....	....	....	....	....
	Russia	Exhib.	17	10	11	21	17	....	....	....	....	....	....	....	....	....	....	....	....	....	....	....	....	....	....
2001-02	Elektrostal	Russia-2	53	13	15	28	62	....	....	....	....	....	....	....	....	....	....	....	....	....	....	....	....	....	....
	Elektrostal 2	Russia-3	1	1	0	1	4	....	....	....	....	....	....	....	....	....	....	....	....	....	....	....	....	....	....
2002-03	CSKA Moscow	Russia	44	12	12	24	34	....	....	....	....	....	....	....	....	....	....	....	....	....	....	....	....	....	....
2003-04	CSKA Moscow	Russia	20	2	2	4	14	....	....	....	....	....	....	....	....	....	....	....	....	....	....	....	....	....	....
	Columbus	**NHL**	57	13	21	34	54	5	0	1	137	9.5	-11	9	11.1	16:11	....	....	....	....	....	....	....	....	....
2004-05	CSKA Moscow	Russia	51	19	21	40	62	....	....	....	....	....	....	....	....	....	....	....	....	....	....	....	....	....	....
	NHL Totals		57	13	21	34	54	5	0	1	137	9.5		9	11.1	16:11	....	....	....	....	....	....	....	....	....

Signed as a free agent by **CSKA** (Russia), July 27, 2004.

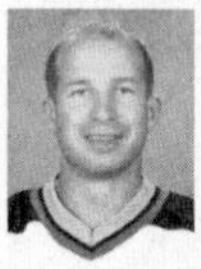

ZHITNIK, Alexei (ZHIHT-nihk, al-EHX-ay) **NYI**

Defense. Shoots left. 5'11", 215 lbs. Born, Kiev, USSR, October 10, 1972. Los Angeles' 3rd choice, 81st overall, in 1991 Entry Draft.

Season	Club	League	GP	G	A	Pts	PIM	PP	SH	GW	S	%	+/-	TF	F%	Min	GP	G	A	Pts	PIM	PP	SH	GW	Min
1989-90	Sokol Kiev	USSR	31	3	4	7	16	....	....	....	....	....	....	....	....	....	....	....	....	....	....	....	....	....	....
1990-91	Sokol Kiev	USSR	46	1	4	5	46	....	....	....	....	....	....	....	....	....	....	....	....	....	....	....	....	....	....
1991-92	CSKA Moscow	CIS	44	2	7	9	52	....	....	....	....	....	....	....	....	....	....	....	....	....	....	....	....	....	....
	Russia	Olympics	8	1	0	1	0	....	....	....	....	....	....	....	....	....	....	....	....	....	....	....	....	....	....
1992-93	**Los Angeles**	**NHL**	78	12	36	48	80	5	0	2	136	8.8	-3	....	....	....	24	3	9	12	26	2	0	1	....
1993-94	**Los Angeles**	**NHL**	81	12	40	52	101	11	0	1	227	5.3	-11	....	....	....	....	....	....	....	....	....	....	....	....
1994-95	**Los Angeles**	**NHL**	11	2	5	7	27	2	0	0	33	6.1	-3	....	....	....	....	....	....	....	....	....	....	....	....
	Buffalo	**NHL**	21	2	5	7	34	1	0	0	33	6.1	-3	....	....	....	5	0	1	1	14	0	0	0	....
1995-96	**Buffalo**	**NHL**	80	6	30	36	58	5	0	0	193	3.1	-25	....	....	....	....	....	....	....	....	....	....	....	....
1996-97	**Buffalo**	**NHL**	80	7	28	35	95	3	1	0	170	4.1	10	....	....	....	12	1	0	1	16	0	0	0	....
1997-98	**Buffalo**	**NHL**	78	15	30	45	102	2	3	3	191	7.9	19	....	....	....	15	0	3	3	36	0	0	0	....
	Russia	Olympics	6	0	2	2	2	....	....	....	....	....	....	....	....	....	....	....	....	....	....	....	....	....	....
1998-99	**Buffalo**	**NHL**	81	7	26	33	96	3	1	2	185	3.8	-6	0	0.0	25:39	21	4	11	15	*52	4	0	2	27:07
99-2000	**Buffalo**	**NHL**	74	2	11	13	95	1	0	0	139	1.4	-6	0	0.0	24:48	4	0	0	0	8	0	0	0	25:50
2000-01	**Buffalo**	**NHL**	78	8	29	37	75	5	0	1	149	5.4	-3	0	0.0	24:15	13	1	6	7	12	0	0	0	25:38
2001-02	**Buffalo**	**NHL**	82	1	33	34	80	1	0	0	150	0.7	-1	0	0.0	25:36	....	....	....	....	....	....	....	....	....
2002-03	**Buffalo**	**NHL**	70	3	18	21	85	0	0	1	138	2.2	-5	1	0.0	26:33	....	....	....	....	....	....	....	....	....
2003-04	**Buffalo**	**NHL**	68	4	24	28	102	2	0	0	134	3.0	-13	0	0.0	25:01	....	....	....	....	....	....	....	....	....
2004-05	Ak Bars Kazan	Russia	23	1	8	9	30	....	....	....	....	....	....	....	....	....	4	0	0	0	2	....	....	....	....
	NHL Totals		882	81	315	396	1030	41	5	10	1878	4.3		1	0.0	25:18	94	9	30	39	164	6	0	3	26:29

Played in NHL All-Star Game (1999, 2002)

Traded to **Buffalo** by **Los Angeles** with Robb Stauber, Charlie Huddy and Los Angeles' 5th round choice (Marian Menhart) in 1995 Entry Draft for Philippe Boucher, Denis Tsygurov and Grant Fuhr, February 14, 1995. Signed as a free agent by **Kazan** (Russia), December 6, 2004. Signed as a free agent by **NY Islanders**, August 2, 2005.

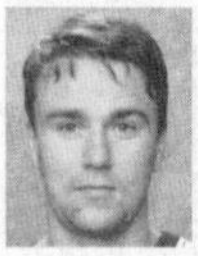

ZIDLICKY, Marek (zhihd-LIHTS-kee, MAIR-ehk) **NSH.**

Defense. Shoots right. 5'11", 190 lbs. Born, Most, Czech., February 3, 1977. NY Rangers' 6th choice, 176th overall, in 2001 Entry Draft.

Season	Club	League	GP	G	A	Pts	PIM	PP	SH	GW	S	%	+/-	TF	F%	Min	GP	G	A	Pts	PIM	PP	SH	GW	Min
1994-95	HC Kladno	CzRep	30	2	2	4	38	....	....	....	....	....	....	....	....	....	11	1	1	2	10	....	....	....	....
1995-96	HC Poldi Kladno	CzRep	37	4	5	9	74	....	....	....	....	....	....	....	....	....	7	1	1	2	8	....	....	....	....
1996-97	HC Poldi Kladno	CzRep	49	5	16	21	60	....	....	....	....	....	....	....	....	....	2	0	0	0	0	....	....	....	....
1997-98	Kladno	CzRep	51	2	13	15	121	....	....	....	....	....	....	....	....	....	....	....	....	....	....	....	....	....	....
1998-99	Kladno	CzRep	50	10	12	22	94	....	....	....	....	....	....	....	....	....	....	....	....	....	....	....	....	....	....
99-2000	HIFK Helsinki	Finland	47	4	16	20	66	....	....	....	....	....	....	....	....	....	9	3	2	5	24	....	....	....	....
	HIFK Helsinki	EuroHL	4	2	2	4	10	....	....	....	....	....	....	....	....	....	1	0	0	0	0	....	....	....	....
2000-01	HIFK Helsinki	Finland	51	12	25	37	146	....	....	....	....	....	....	....	....	....	5	0	1	1	6	....	....	....	....
2001-02	HIFK Helsinki	Finland	56	11	29	40	107	....	....	....	....	....	....	....	....	....	....	....	....	....	....	....	....	....	....
2002-03	HIFK Helsinki	Finland	54	10	37	47	79	....	....	....	....	....	....	....	....	....	4	0	0	0	4	....	....	....	....
2003-04	**Nashville**	**NHL**	82	14	39	53	82	9	0	4	143	9.8	-16	0	0.0	20:02	1	0	0	0	0	0	0	0	2:16
2004-05	HIFK Helsinki	Finland	49	11	20	31	91	....	....	....	....	....	....	....	....	....	5	0	3	3	14	....	....	....	....
	NHL Totals		82	14	39	53	82	9	0	4	143	9.8		0	0.0	20:02	1	0	0	0	0	0	0	0	2:16

Traded to **Nashville** by NY Rangers with Rem Murray and Tomas Kloucek for Mike Dunham, December 12, 2002. Signed as a free agent by **HIFK** (Finland), September 17, 2004.

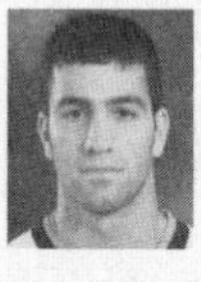

ZIGOMANIS, Mike (zih-goh-MAN-his, MIGHK) **CAR.**

Center. Shoots right. 6'1", 200 lbs. Born, North York, Ont., January 17, 1981. Carolina's 2nd choice, 46th overall, in 2001 Entry Draft.

Season	Club	League	GP	G	A	Pts	PIM	PP	SH	GW	S	%	+/-	TF	F%	Min	GP	G	A	Pts	PIM	PP	SH	GW	Min
1996-97	Wexford Raiders	MTHL	40	37	48	85	23	....	....	....	....	....	....	....	....	....	....	....	....	....	....	....	....	....	....
	Wexford Raiders	MTJHL	8	2	5	7	2	....	....	....	....	....	....	....	....	....	....	....	....	....	....	....	....	....	....
1997-98	Kingston	OHL	62	23	51	74	30	....	....	....	....	....	....	....	....	....	12	1	6	7	2	....	....	....	....
1998-99	Kingston	OHL	67	29	56	85	36	....	....	....	....	....	....	....	....	....	5	1	7	8	2	....	....	....	....
99-2000	Kingston	OHL	59	40	54	94	49	....	....	....	....	....	....	....	....	....	5	0	4	4	0	....	....	....	....
2000-01	Kingston	OHL	52	40	37	77	44	....	....	....	....	....	....	....	....	....	....	....	....	....	....	....	....	....	....
2001-02	Lowell	AHL	79	18	30	48	24	....	....	....	....	....	....	....	....	....	5	1	1	2	2	....	....	....	....

			Regular Season														Playoffs								
Season	Club	League	GP	G	A	Pts	PIM	PP	SH	GW	S	%	+/-	TF	F%	Min	GP	G	A	Pts	PIM	PP	SH	GW	Min
2002-03	**Carolina**	**NHL**	**19**	**2**	**1**	**3**	**0**	**1**	**1**	**0**	**19**	**10.5**	**–4**	**147**	**59.2**	**9:43**	....	....	....	....	....	....	....	....	....
	Lowell	AHL	38	13	18	31	19	....	....	....	....	....	....	....	....	....	....	....	....	....	....	....	....	....	....
2003-04	**Carolina**	**NHL**	**17**	**0**	**3**	**3**	**2**	**0**	**0**	**0**	**13**	**0.0**	**–1**	**108**	**53.7**	**8:37**	....	....	....	....	....	....	....	....	....
	Lowell	AHL	61	17	35	52	56	....	....	....	....	....	....	....	....	....	....	....	....	....	....	....	....	....	....
2004-05	Lowell	AHL	76	29	31	60	71	....	....	....	....	....	....	....	....	....	11	4	7	11	8	....	....	....	....
	NHL Totals		**36**	**2**	**4**	**6**	**2**	**1**	**1**	**0**	**32**	**6.3**		**255**	**56.9**	**9:12**	....	....	....	....	....	....	....	....	....

• Re-entered NHL Entry Draft. Originally Buffalo's 4th choice, 64th overall, in 1999 Entry Draft.

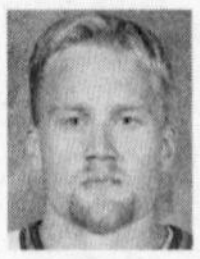

ZINGER, Dwayne

(ZIHN-guhr, DWAYN) **WSH.**

Defense. Shoots left. 6'4", 216 lbs. Born, Coronation, Alta., July 5, 1976.

Season	Club	League	GP	G	A	Pts	PIM	PP	SH	GW	S	%	+/-	TF	F%	Min	GP	G	A	Pts	PIM	PP	SH	GW	Min
1995-96	Melville	SJHL	64	7	17	24	....	....	....	....	....	....	....	....	....	....	....	....	....	....	....	....	....	....	....
1996-97	Alaska-Fairbanks	CCHA	32	1	5	6	45	....	....	....	....	....	....	....	....	....	....	....	....	....	....	....	....	....	....
1997-98	Alaska-Fairbanks	CCHA	32	1	3	4	91	....	....	....	....	....	....	....	....	....	....	....	....	....	....	....	....	....	....
1998-99	Alaska-Fairbanks	CCHA	33	4	14	18	42	....	....	....	....	....	....	....	....	....	....	....	....	....	....	....	....	....	....
99-2000	Alaska-Fairbanks	CCHA	34	10	4	14	34	....	....	....	....	....	....	....	....	....	....	....	....	....	....	....	....	....	....
	Cincinnati	AHL	13	0	2	2	33	....	....	....	....	....	....	....	....	....	....	....	....	....	....	....	....	....	....
2000-01	Cincinnati	AHL	68	6	9	15	120	....	....	....	....	....	....	....	....	....	4	1	1	2	2	....	....	....	....
2001-02	Cincinnati	AHL	67	6	13	19	156	....	....	....	....	....	....	....	....	....	3	0	1	1	2	....	....	....	....
2002-03	Portland Pirates	AHL	65	1	7	8	67	....	....	....	....	....	....	....	....	....	3	0	0	0	2	....	....	....	....
2003-04	**Washington**	**NHL**	**7**	**0**	**1**	**1**	**9**	**0**	**0**	**0**	**0**	**0.0**	**2**	**0**	**0.0**	**5:24**	....	....	....	....	....	....	....	....	....
	Portland Pirates	AHL	68	6	10	16	49	....	....	....	....	....	....	....	....	....	7	0	0	0	16	....	....	....	....
2004-05	Portland Pirates	AHL	58	0	4	4	118	....	....	....	....	....	....	....	....	....	....	....	....	....	....	....	....	....	....
	NHL Totals		**7**	**0**	**1**	**1**	**9**	**0**	**0**	**0**	**0**	**0.0**		**0**	**0.0**	**5:24**	....	....	....	....	....	....	....	....	....

SJHL First All-Star Team (1996)

Signed as a free agent by **Detroit**, March 13, 2000. Signed as a free agent by **Washington**, July 9, 2002.

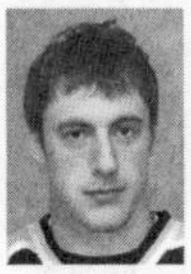

ZINOVJEV, Sergei

(zih-NOH-vee-ehv, SAIR-gay) **BOS.**

Center/Left wing. Shoots left. 5'10", 178 lbs. Born, Novokuznetsk, USSR, March 4, 1980. Boston's 6th choice, 73rd overall, in 2000 Entry Draft.

Season	Club	League	GP	G	A	Pts	PIM	PP	SH	GW	S	%	+/-	TF	F%	Min	GP	G	A	Pts	PIM	PP	SH	GW	Min
1995-96	Novokuznetsk 2	CIS-2	10	1	0	1	2	....	....	....	....	....	....	....	....	....	....	....	....	....	....	....	....	....	....
1996-97	Novokuznetsk 2	Russia-3	29	2	1	3	8	....	....	....	....	....	....	....	....	....	....	....	....	....	....	....	....	....	....
1997-98	Novokuznetsk 2	Russia-3	40	7	7	14	36	....	....	....	....	....	....	....	....	....	....	....	....	....	....	....	....	....	....
	Novokuznetsk 2	Russia-3	2	1	0	1	0	....	....	....	....	....	....	....	....	....	....	....	....	....	....	....	....	....	....
1998-99	Novokuznetsk 2	Russia-4	4	0	1	1	8	....	....	....	....	....	....	....	....	....	....	....	....	....	....	....	....	....	....
	Magnitogorsk	Russia	31	2	4	6	14	....	....	....	....	....	....	....	....	....	3	0	0	0	0	....	....	....	....
99-2000	Magnitogorsk	Russia	28	0	2	2	16	....	....	....	....	....	....	....	....	....	....	....	....	....	....	....	....	....	....
2000-01	Yaroslavl	Russia	27	2	10	12	36	....	....	....	....	....	....	....	....	....	....	....	....	....	....	....	....	....	....
	Ufa	Russia	8	4	5	9	6	....	....	....	....	....	....	....	....	....	....	....	....	....	....	....	....	....	....
2001-02	Spartak Moscow	Russia	51	12	18	30	43	....	....	....	....	....	....	....	....	....	....	....	....	....	....	....	....	....	....
2002-03	Ak Bars Kazan	Russia	47	14	17	31	50	....	....	....	....	....	....	....	....	....	5	1	1	2	6	....	....	....	....
2003-04	**Boston**	**NHL**	**10**	**0**	**1**	**1**	**2**	**0**	**0**	**0**	**8**	**0.0**	**1**	**72**	**41.7**	**9:48**	....	....	....	....	....	....	....	....	....
	Providence Bruins	AHL	4	1	2	3	0	....	....	....	....	....	....	....	....	....	....	....	....	....	....	....	....	....	....
	Ak Bars Kazan	Russia	27	5	9	14	75	....	....	....	....	....	....	....	....	....	8	0	1	1	12	....	....	....	....
2004-05	Ak Bars Kazan	Russia	54	17	21	38	82	....	....	....	....	....	....	....	....	....	4	1	0	1	12	....	....	....	....
	NHL Totals		**10**	**0**	**1**	**1**	**2**	**0**	**0**	**0**	**8**	**0.0**		**72**	**41.7**	**9:48**	....	....	....	....	....	....	....	....	....

Signed as a free agent by **Kazan** (Russia), December 9, 2003.

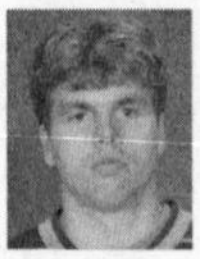

ZIZKA, Tomas

(ZHIHZH-kuh, TAW-mahsh) **L.A.**

Defense. Shoots left. 6'1", 198 lbs. Born, Sternberk, Czech., October 10, 1979. Los Angeles' 6th choice, 163rd overall, in 1998 Entry Draft.

Season	Club	League	GP	G	A	Pts	PIM	PP	SH	GW	S	%	+/-	TF	F%	Min	GP	G	A	Pts	PIM	PP	SH	GW	Min
1994-95	AC ZPS Zlin Jr.	CzRep-Jr.	39	1	10	11	....	....	....	....	....	....	....	....	....	....	....	....	....	....	....	....	....	....	....
1995-96	AC ZPS Zlin Jr.	CzRep-Jr.	47	2	8	10	....	....	....	....	....	....	....	....	....	....	....	....	....	....	....	....	....	....	....
1996-97	AC ZPS Zlin Jr.	CzRep-Jr.	14	1	0	1	....	....	....	....	....	....	....	....	....	....	....	....	....	....	....	....	....	....	....
1997-98	HC ZPS Zlin Jr.	CzRep-Jr.	11	3	4	7	....	....	....	....	....	....	....	....	....	....	....	....	....	....	....	....	....	....	....
	Zlin	CzRep	33	0	3	3	2	....	....	....	....	....	....	....	....	....	....	....	....	....	....	....	....	....	....
1998-99	Zlin	CzRep	44	3	7	10	14	....	....	....	....	....	....	....	....	....	11	1	2	3	....	....	....	....	....
99-2000	Zlin	CzRep	46	4	6	10	30	....	....	....	....	....	....	....	....	....	4	1	0	1	4	....	....	....	....
2000-01	Zlin	CzRep	43	2	11	13	16	....	....	....	....	....	....	....	....	....	6	0	0	0	6	....	....	....	....
2001-02	Manchester	AHL	58	4	17	21	22	....	....	....	....	....	....	....	....	....	4	1	0	1	14	....	....	....	....
2002-03	**Los Angeles**	**NHL**	**10**	**0**	**3**	**3**	**4**	**0**	**0**	**0**	**12**	**0.0**	**–4**	**0**	**0.0**	**15:24**	....	....	....	....	....	....	....	....	....
	Manchester	AHL	61	13	30	43	50	....	....	....	....	....	....	....	....	....	3	0	2	2	2	....	....	....	....
2003-04	**Los Angeles**	**NHL**	**15**	**2**	**3**	**5**	**12**	**1**	**0**	**0**	**24**	**8.3**	**–4**	**0**	**0.0**	**16:54**	....	....	....	....	....	....	....	....	....
	Manchester	AHL	58	4	24	28	31	....	....	....	....	....	....	....	....	....	5	0	3	3	10	....	....	....	....
2004-05	Spartak Moscow	Russia	23	0	3	3	32	....	....	....	....	....	....	....	....	....	....	....	....	....	....	....	....	....	....
	HC Slavia Praha	CzRep	26	2	4	6	26	....	....	....	....	....	....	....	....	....	2	0	0	0	2	....	....	....	....
	NHL Totals		**25**	**2**	**6**	**8**	**16**	**1**	**0**	**0**	**36**	**5.6**		**0**	**0.0**	**16:18**	....	....	....	....	....	....	....	....	....

Signed as a free agent by **Spartak** (Russia), August 31, 2004. Signed as a free agent by **Slavia** (CzRep), November, 2004.

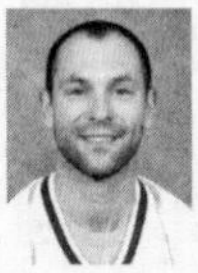

ZUBOV, Sergei

(ZOO-bahf, SAIR-gay) **DAL.**

Defense. Shoots right. 6'1", 200 lbs. Born, Moscow, USSR, July 22, 1970. NY Rangers' 6th choice, 85th overall, in 1990 Entry Draft.

Season	Club	League	GP	G	A	Pts	PIM	PP	SH	GW	S	%	+/-	TF	F%	Min	GP	G	A	Pts	PIM	PP	SH	GW	Min
1988-89	CSKA Moscow	USSR	29	1	4	5	10	....	....	....	....	....	....	....	....	....	....	....	....	....	....	....	....	....	....
1989-90	CSKA Moscow	USSR	48	6	2	8	16	....	....	....	....	....	....	....	....	....	....	....	....	....	....	....	....	....	....
1990-91	CSKA Moscow	USSR	41	6	5	11	12	....	....	....	....	....	....	....	....	....	....	....	....	....	....	....	....	....	....
1991-92	CSKA Moscow	CIS	44	4	7	11	8	....	....	....	....	....	....	....	....	....	....	....	....	....	....	....	....	....	....
	Russia	Olympics	8	0	1	1	0	....	....	....	....	....	....	....	....	....	....	....	....	....	....	....	....	....	....
1992-93	CSKA Moscow	CIS	1	0	1	1	0	....	....	....	....	....	....	....	....	....	....	....	....	....	....	....	....	....	....
	NY Rangers	**NHL**	**49**	**8**	**23**	**31**	**4**	**3**	**0**	**0**	**93**	**8.6**	**–1**	....	....	....	....	....	....	....	....	....	....	....	....
	Binghamton	AHL	30	7	29	36	14	....	....	....	....	....	....	....	....	....	11	5	5	10	2	....	....	....	....
1993-94♦	**NY Rangers**	**NHL**	**78**	**12**	**77**	**89**	**39**	**9**	**0**	**1**	**222**	**5.4**	**20**	....	....	....	**22**	**5**	**14**	**19**	**0**	**2**	**0**	**0**	....
	Binghamton	AHL	2	1	2	3	0	....	....	....	....	....	....	....	....	....	....	....	....	....	....	....	....	....	....
1994-95	**NY Rangers**	**NHL**	**38**	**10**	**26**	**36**	**18**	**6**	**0**	**0**	**116**	**8.6**	**–2**	....	....	....	**10**	**3**	**8**	**11**	**2**	**1**	**0**	**0**	....
1995-96	**Pittsburgh**	**NHL**	**64**	**11**	**55**	**66**	**22**	**3**	**2**	**1**	**141**	**7.8**	**28**	....	....	....	**18**	**1**	**14**	**15**	**26**	**1**	**0**	**0**	....
1996-97	**Dallas**	**NHL**	**78**	**13**	**30**	**43**	**24**	**1**	**0**	**3**	**133**	**9.8**	**19**	....	....	....	**7**	**0**	**3**	**3**	**2**	**0**	**0**	**0**	....
1997-98	**Dallas**	**NHL**	**73**	**10**	**47**	**57**	**16**	**5**	**1**	**2**	**148**	**6.8**	**16**	....	....	....	**17**	**4**	**5**	**9**	**2**	**3**	**0**	**1**	....
1998-99♦	**Dallas**	**NHL**	**81**	**10**	**41**	**51**	**20**	**5**	**0**	**3**	**155**	**6.5**	**9**	**0**	**0.0**	**24:14**	**23**	**1**	**12**	**13**	**4**	**0**	**0**	**0**	**30:16**
99-2000	**Dallas**	**NHL**	**77**	**9**	**33**	**42**	**18**	**3**	**1**	**3**	**179**	**5.0**	**–2**	**0**	**0.0**	**28:50**	**18**	**2**	**7**	**9**	**6**	**1**	**1**	**0**	**26:28**
2000-01	**Dallas**	**NHL**	**79**	**10**	**41**	**51**	**24**	**6**	**0**	**1**	**173**	**5.8**	**22**	**0**	**0.0**	**26:37**	**10**	**1**	**5**	**6**	**4**	**0**	**0**	**0**	**30:37**
2001-02	**Dallas**	**NHL**	**80**	**12**	**32**	**44**	**22**	**8**	**0**	**2**	**198**	**6.1**	**–4**	**0**	**0.0**	**26:46**	....	....	....	....	....	....	....	....	....
2002-03	**Dallas**	**NHL**	**82**	**11**	**44**	**55**	**26**	**8**	**0**	**2**	**158**	**7.0**	**21**	**0**	**0.0**	**25:50**	**12**	**4**	**10**	**14**	**4**	**2**	**0**	**0**	**30:45**
2003-04	**Dallas**	**NHL**	**77**	**7**	**35**	**42**	**20**	**4**	**1**	**1**	**154**	**4.5**	**0**	**0**	**0.0**	**25:50**	**5**	**1**	**1**	**2**	**0**	**1**	**0**	**0**	**28:01**
2004-05			DID NOT PLAY																						
	NHL Totals		**856**	**123**	**484**	**607**	**253**	**61**	**5**	**19**	**1870**	**6.6**		**0**	**0.0**	**26:20**	**142**	**22**	**79**	**101**	**50**	**11**	**1**	**1**	**29:14**

Played in NHL All-Star Game (1998, 1999, 2000)

Traded to **Pittsburgh** by **NY Rangers** with Petr Nedved for Luc Robitaille and Ulf Samuelsson, August 31, 1995. Traded to **Dallas** by **Pittsburgh** for Kevin Hatcher, June 22, 1996.

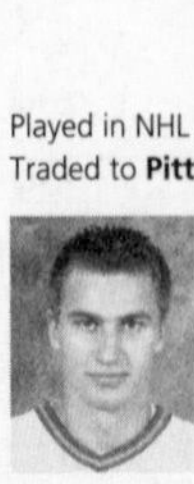

ZUBRUS, Dainius

(ZOO-bruhs, DAYN-ihs) **WSH.**

Right wing. Shoots left. 6'4", 226 lbs. Born, Elektrenai, USSR, June 16, 1978. Philadelphia's 1st choice, 15th overall, in 1996 Entry Draft.

Season	Club	League	GP	G	A	Pts	PIM	PP	SH	GW	S	%	+/-	TF	F%	Min	GP	G	A	Pts	PIM	PP	SH	GW	Min
1995-96	Pembroke	CJHL	28	19	13	32	73	....	....	....	....	....	....	....	....	....	....	....	....	....	....	....	....	....	....
	Caledon	MTJHL	7	3	7	10	2	....	....	....	....	....	....	....	....	....	17	11	12	23	4	....	....	....	....
1996-97	**Philadelphia**	**NHL**	**68**	**8**	**13**	**21**	**22**	**1**	**0**	**2**	**71**	**11.3**	**3**	....	....	....	**19**	**5**	**4**	**9**	**12**	**1**	**0**	**1**	....
1997-98	**Philadelphia**	**NHL**	**69**	**8**	**25**	**33**	**42**	**1**	**0**	**5**	**101**	**7.9**	**29**	....	....	....	**5**	**0**	**1**	**1**	**2**	**0**	**0**	**0**	....
1998-99	**Philadelphia**	**NHL**	**63**	**3**	**5**	**8**	**25**	**0**	**1**	**0**	**49**	**6.1**	**–5**	**29**	**51.7**	**11:00**	....	....	....	....	....	....	....	....	....
	Montreal	**NHL**	**17**	**3**	**5**	**8**	**4**	**0**	**0**	**1**	**31**	**9.7**	**–3**	**2**	**50.0**	**16:53**	....	....	....	....	....	....	....	....	....
99-2000	**Montreal**	**NHL**	**73**	**14**	**28**	**42**	**54**	**3**	**0**	**1**	**139**	**10.1**	**–1**	**212**	**39.2**	**17:37**	....	....	....	....	....	....	....	....	....
2000-01	**Montreal**	**NHL**	**49**	**12**	**12**	**24**	**30**	**3**	**0**	**0**	**70**	**17.1**	**–7**	**190**	**41.1**	**18:30**	....	....	....	....	....	....	....	....	....
	Washington	**NHL**	**12**	**1**	**1**	**2**	**7**	**1**	**0**	**0**	**13**	**7.7**	**–4**	**0**	**0.0**	**13:05**	**6**	**0**	**0**	**0**	**2**	**0**	**0**	**0**	**17:23**

Season	Club	League	GP	G	A	Pts	PIM	PP	SH	GW	S	%	+/-	TF	F%	Min	GP	G	A	Pts	PIM	PP	SH	GW	Min
2001-02	Washington	NHL	71	17	26	43	38	4	0	3	138	12.3	5	131	37.4	18:52	....	....	....	....	....	....	....	....	....
2002-03	Washington	NHL	63	13	22	35	43	2	0	0	104	12.5	15	565	50.3	16:26	6	2	2	4	4	1	0	0	21:30
2003-04	Washington	NHL	54	12	15	27	38	6	1	2	115	10.4	–16	916	48.0	19:31	....	....	....	....	....	....	....	....	....
2004-05	Lada Togliatti	Russia	42	8	11	19	85										10	3	1	4	22	....	....	....	....
	NHL Totals		539	91	152	243	303	21	2	14	831	11.0		2045	46.5	16:49	36	7	7	14	20	2	0	1	19:27

Traded to **Montreal** by **Philadelphia** with Philadelphia's 2nd round choice (Matt Carkner) in 1999 Entry Draft and NY Islanders' 6th round choice (previously acquired, Montreal selected Scott Selig) in 2000 Entry Draft for Mark Recchi, March 10, 1999. Traded to **Washington** by **Montreal** with Trevor Linden and New Jersey's 2nd round choice (previously acquired, later traded to Tampa Bay – Tampa Bay selected Andreas Holmqvist) in 2001 Entry Draft for Richard Zednik, Jan Bulis and Washington's 1st round choice (Alexander Perezhogin) in 2001 Entry Draft, March 13, 2001. Signed as a free agent by **Togliatti** (Russia), July 1, 2004.

ZYUZIN, Andrei

(ZYOO-zin, AWN-dray)   **MIN.**

Defense. Shoots left. 6'1", 215 lbs.   Born, Ufa, USSR, January 21, 1978. San Jose's 1st choice, 2nd overall, in 1996 Entry Draft.

Season	Club	League	GP	G	A	Pts	PIM	PP	SH	GW	S	%	+/-	TF	F%	Min	GP	G	A	Pts	PIM	PP	SH	GW	Min
1994-95	Ufa	CIS	30	3	0	3	16	....	....	....	....	....	....	....	....	....	....	....	....	....	....	....	....	....	....
1995-96	Ufa	CIS	41	6	3	9	24	....	....	....	....	....	....	....	....	....	....	....	....	....	....	....	....	....	....
1996-97	Ufa	Russia	32	7	10	17	28	....	....	....	....	....	....	....	....	....	7	1	1	2	4	....	....	....	....
1997-98	San Jose	NHL	56	6	7	13	66	2	0	2	72	8.3	8				6	1	0	1	14	0	0	1	
	Kentucky	AHL	17	4	5	9	28	....	....	....	....	....	....	....	....	....	....	....	....	....	....	....	....	....	....
1998-99	San Jose	NHL	25	3	1	4	38	2	0	0	44	6.8	5	0	0.0	15:56									
	Kentucky	AHL	23	2	12	14	42	....	....	....	....	....	....	....	....	....	....	....	....	....	....	....	....	....	....
99-2000	Tampa Bay	NHL	34	2	9	11	33	0	0	0	47	4.3	–11	0	0.0	20:28									
2000-01	Tampa Bay	NHL	64	4	16	20	76	2	1	1	92	4.3	–8	0	0.0	18:39									
	Detroit Vipers	IHL	2	0	1	1	0	....	....	....	....	....	....	....	....	....	....	....	....	....	....	....	....	....	....
2001-02	Tampa Bay	NHL	9	0	2	2	6	0	0	0	14	0.0	–6	0	0.0	19:41									
	New Jersey	NHL	38	1	2	3	25	1	0	0	47	2.1	1	0	0.0	15:04									
	Albany River Rats	AHL	3	0	1	1	2	....	....	....	....	....	....	....	....	....	....	....	....	....	....	....	....	....	....
2002-03	New Jersey	NHL	1	0	1	1	2	0	0	0	0	0.0	–1	0	0.0	20:03									
	Minnesota	NHL	66	4	12	16	34	2	0	0	113	3.5	–7	4	25.0	21:38	18	0	1	1	14	0	0	0	23:07
2003-04	Minnesota	NHL	65	8	13	21	48	4	0	1	104	7.7	4	0	0.0	20:22									
2004-05	Ufa	Russia	14	2	1	3	6	....	....	....	....	....	....	....	....	....	....	....	....	....	....	....	....	....	....
	Cherepovets	Russia	10	2	1	3	8	....	....	....	....	....	....	....	....	....	....	....	....	....	....	....	....	....	....
	NHL Totals		358	28	63	91	328	13	1	4	533	5.3		4	25.0	19:14	24	1	2	3	28	0	0	1	23:07

• Suspended for remainder of 1998-99 season by **San Jose** for leaving team without permission, April 1, 1999. Traded to **Tampa Bay** by **San Jose** with Bill Houlder, Shawn Burr and Steve Guolla for Niklas Sundstrom and NY Rangers' 3rd round choice (previously acquired, later traded to Chicago – Chicago selected Igor Radulov) in 2000 Entry Draft, August 4, 1999. • Missed majority of 1999-2000 season recovering from shoulder injury suffered in game vs. NY Islanders, January 13, 2000. Traded to **New Jersey** by **Tampa Bay** for Josef Boumedienne, Sascha Goc and the rights to Anton But, November 9, 2001. Claimed on waivers by **Minnesota** from **New Jersey**, November 2, 2002. Signed as a free agent by **Ufa** (Russia), September 25, 2004. Signed as a free agent by **Cherepovets** (Russia), December 20, 2004.

3,386 games, 2,335 points

The regular-season and playoff career totals of recently retired veteran players Vincent Damphousse and Scott Stevens are substantial. Stevens (right and bottom center) leads all NHL defensemen in regular-season games played with 1,635. He began his NHL career with Washington in 1982-83. He played in St. Louis in 1990-91 and joined the Devils the following season. He was a member of New Jersey's three Stanley Cup-winning teams in 1995, 2000 and 2003 and was awarded the Conn Smythe trophy as playoff MVP in 2000. The ultimate bodychecker, opposing forwards were keenly aware of his presence on the ice. Vincent Damphousse (left and top center) appeared in 1,378 regular-season games with Toronto, Edmonton, Montreal and San Jose. Drafted sixth overall in 1986, he never played a day in the minors and was a 21-goal teenage rookie with the Maple Leafs in 1986-87. He led three different teams in scoring in consecutive seasons beginning with the Leafs in 1990-91, Edmonton in 1991-92 and Montreal in 1992-93. He recorded six seasons with 80-or-more points and was a member of Montreal's Cup-winning team in 1993 when he led the club with 11 goals and 23 points in 20 playoff games.

NHL Goaltenders

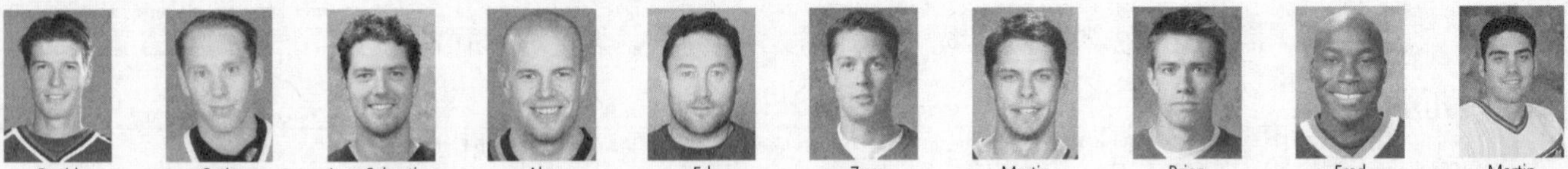

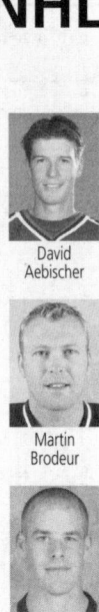

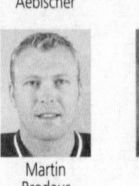

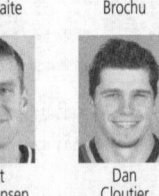

David Aebischer · Craig Anderson · Jean-Sebastien Aubin · Alex Auld · Ed Belfour · Zac Bierk · Martin Biron · Brian Boucher · Fred Brathwaite · Martin Brochu

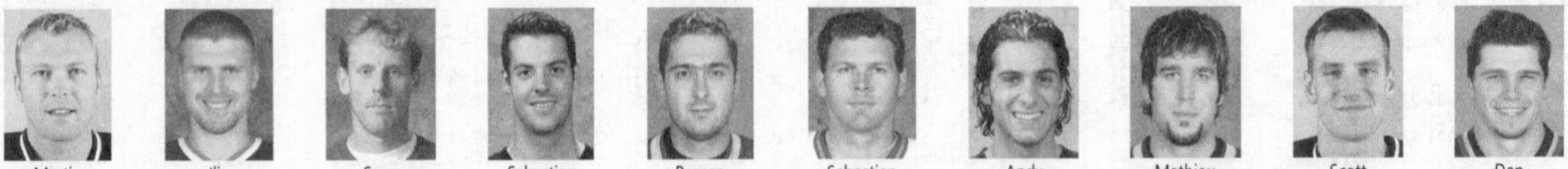

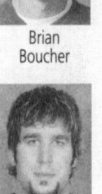

Martin Brodeur · Ilja Bryzgalov · Sean Burke · Sebastian Caron · Roman Cechmanek · Sebastien Charpentier · Andy Chiodo · Mathieu Chouinard · Scott Clemmensen · Dan Cloutier

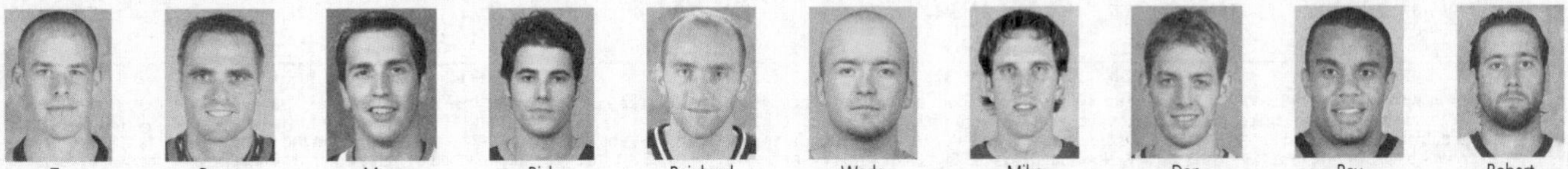

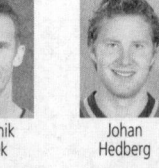

Ty Conklin · Byron Dafoe · Marc Denis · Rick DiPietro · Reinhard Divis · Wade Dubielewicz · Mike Dunham · Dan Ellis · Ray Emery · Robert Esche

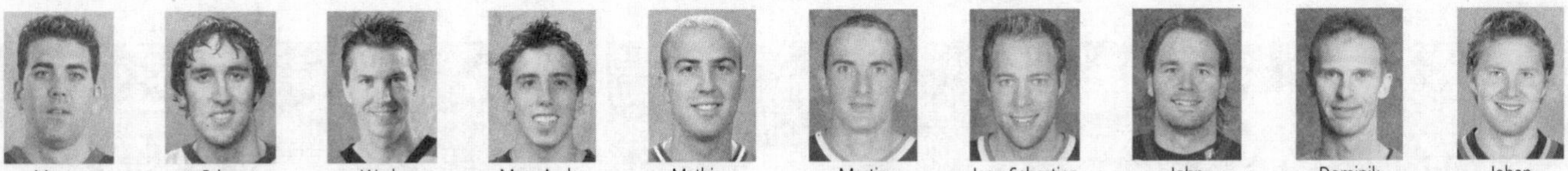

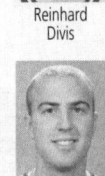

Manny Fernandez · Brian Finlay · Wade Flaherty · Marc-Andre Fleury · Mathieu Garon · Martin Gerber · Jean-Sebastien Giguere · John Grahame · Dominik Hasek · Johan Hedberg

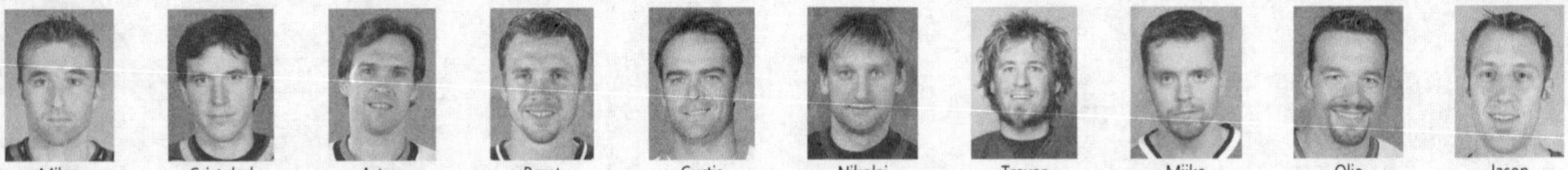

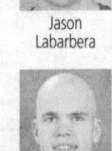

Milan Hnilicka · Cristobal Huet · Arturs Irbe · Brent Johnson · Curtis Joseph · Nikolai Khabibulin · Trevor Kidd · Miika Kiprusoff · Olie Kolzig · Jason Labarbera

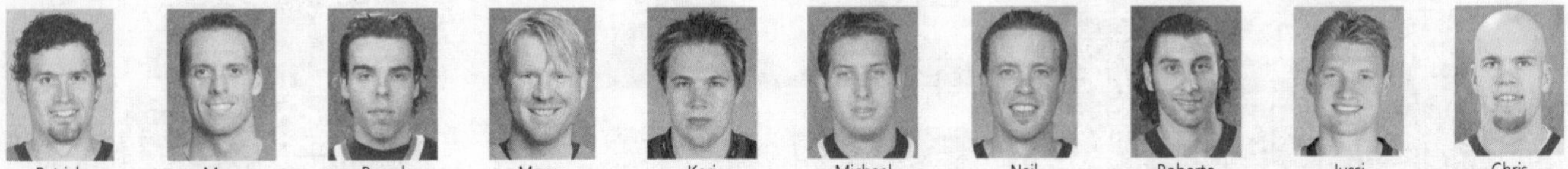

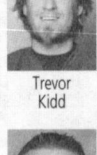

Patrick Lalime · Marc Lamothe · Pascal Leclaire · Manny Legace · Kari Lehtonin · Michael Leighton · Neil Little · Roberto Luongo · Jussi Markkanen · Chris Mason

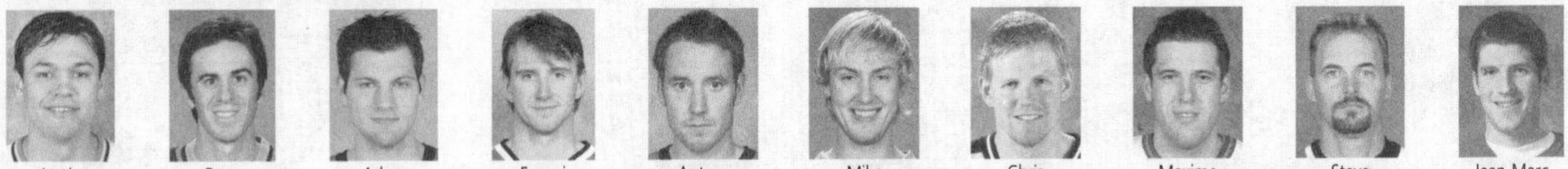

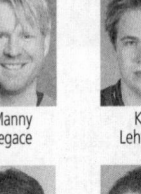

Jamie McLennan · Ryan Miller · Adam Munro · Evgeni Nabokov · Antero Niittymaki · Mika Noronen · Chris Osgood · Maxime Ouellet · Steve Passmore · Jean-Marc Pelletier

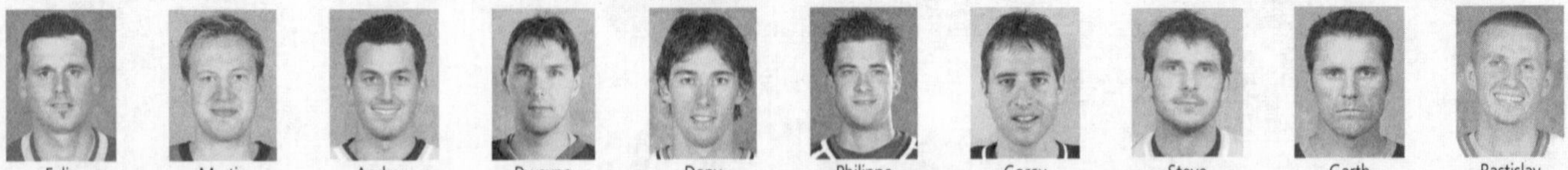

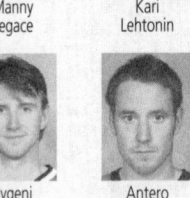

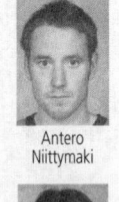

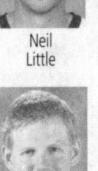

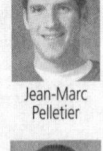

Felix Potvin · Martin Prusek · Andrew Raycroft · Dwayne Roloson · Dany Sabourin · Philippe Sauve · Corey Schwab · Steve Shields · Garth Snow · Rastislav Stana

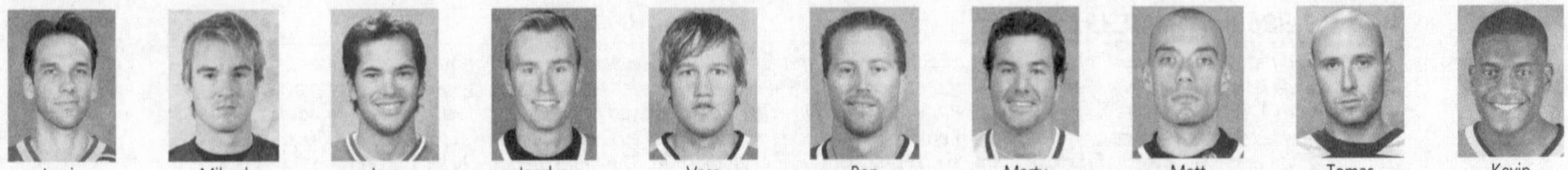

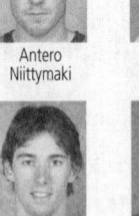

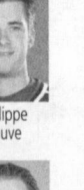

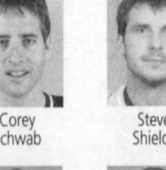

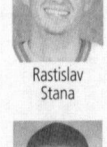

Jamie Storr · Mikael Tellqvist · Jose Theodore · Jocelyn Thibault · Vesa Toskala · Ron Tugnutt · Marty Turco · Matt Underhill · Tomas Vokoun · Kevin Weekes

2005-06 Goaltender Register

Note: The 2005-06 Goaltender Register lists all active NHL goaltenders, every goaltender drafted in the 2005 Entry Draft, goaltenders on NHL Reserve Lists and other goaltenders.

Trades and roster changes are current as of September 6, 2005.

To calculate a goaltender's goals-against per game average **(Avg)**, divide goals against **(GA)** by minutes played **(Mins)** and multiply this result by **60**.

Abbreviations: GP – games played; **W** – wins; **L** – losses; **T** – ties; **GA** – goals against; **SO** – shutouts; **Avg** – goals-against per game average.
♦ – member of Stanley Cup-winning team.

NHL Player Register begins on page 367.
Prospect Register begins on page 279.
League Abbreviations are listed on page 365.

AEBISCHER, David (A-bih-shuhr, DAY-vihd) COL.

Goaltender. Catches left. 6'1", 190 lbs. Born, Fribourg, Switz., February 7, 1978.
(Colorado's 7th choice, 161st overall, in 1997 Entry Draft).

			Regular Season								Playoffs						
Season	**Club**	**League**	**GP**	**W**	**L**	**T**	**Mins**	**GA**	**SO**	**Avg**	**GP**	**W**	**L**	**Mins**	**GA**	**SO**	**Avg**
1996-97	Fribourg	Swiss	10	....	....	....	577	34	0	3.54	3	1	2	184	13	0	4.24
1997-98	Chesapeake	ECHL	17	5	7	2	930	52	0	3.35	....	....	....	....	....	....	....
	Wheeling Nailers	ECHL	10	5	3	1	564	30	1	3.19	....	....	....	....	....	....	....
	Hershey Bears	AHL	2	0	0	1	79	5	0	3.76	....	....	....	....	....	....	....
	Fribourg	Swiss	1	1	0	0	60	1	0	1.00	4	....	....	240	17	....	4.25
1998-99	Hershey Bears	AHL	38	17	10	5	1932	79	2	2.45	3	1	2	152	6	0	2.37
99-2000	Hershey Bears	AHL	58	29	23	2	3259	180	1	3.31	14	7	6	788	40	2	3.05
2000-01♦	**Colorado**	**NHL**	**26**	**12**	**7**	**3**	**1393**	**52**	**3**	**2.24**	**1**	**0**	**0**	**1**	**0**	**0**	**0.00**
2001-02	**Colorado**	**NHL**	**21**	**13**	**6**	**0**	**1184**	**37**	**2**	**1.88**	**1**	**0**	**0**	**34**	**1**	**0**	**1.76**
	Switzerland	Olympics	2	1	0	0	81	6	0	4.43	....	....	....	....	....	....	....
2002-03	**Colorado**	**NHL**	**22**	**7**	**12**	**0**	**1235**	**50**	**1**	**2.43**	....	....	....	....	....	....	....
2003-04	**Colorado**	**NHL**	**62**	**32**	**19**	**9**	**3703**	**129**	**4**	**2.09**	**11**	**6**	**5**	**662**	**23**	**1**	**2.08**
2004-05	HC Lugano	Swiss	18	12	2	3	1019	41	0	2.41	4	1	3	240	10	0	2.50
	EHC Chur	Swiss-2	....	....	....	....	....	....	....	....	2	....	....	130	4	0	1.84
	NHL Totals		**131**	**64**	**44**	**12**	**7515**	**268**	**10**	**2.14**	**13**	**6**	**5**	**697**	**24**	**1**	**2.07**

Signed as a free agent by **Lugano** (Swiss), September 17, 2004.

AHONEN, Ari (ah-HOH-nuhn, AH-ree) N.J.

Goaltender. Catches left. 6'2", 195 lbs. Born, Jyvaskyla, Finland, February 6, 1981.
(New Jersey's 1st choice, 27th overall, in 1999 Entry Draft).

			Regular Season								Playoffs						
Season	**Club**	**League**	**GP**	**W**	**L**	**T**	**Mins**	**GA**	**SO**	**Avg**	**GP**	**W**	**L**	**Mins**	**GA**	**SO**	**Avg**
1997-98	JyP Jyvaskyla Jr.	Finland-Jr.	31	....	....	....	1853	64	....	2.09	....	....	....	....	....	....	....
1998-99	JyP Jyvaskyla Jr.	Finland-Jr.	24	....	....	....	1447	70	....	2.90	....	....	....	....	....	....	....
99-2000	HIFK Helsinki	Finland	24	11	7	1	1347	70	1	3.12	2	0	2	119	7	0	3.53
	HIFK Helsinki	EuroHL	5	4	1	0	285	15	1	3.16	....	....	....	....	....	....	....
2000-01	HIFK Helsinki	Finland	37	18	13	4	2101	97	2	2.77	5	2	3	395	9	1	1.37
2001-02	Albany River Rats	AHL	36	6	22	6	2106	106	0	3.02	....	....	....	....	....	....	....
2002-03	Albany River Rats	AHL	38	13	20	3	2171	110	1	3.04	....	....	....	....	....	....	....
2003-04	Albany River Rats	AHL	50	13	30	6	3012	150	2	2.99	....	....	....	....	....	....	....
2004-05	Albany River Rats	AHL	38	16	20	1	2195	114	4	3.12	....	....	....	....	....	....	....

Signed as a free agent by **HIFK** (Finland), April 21, 2005.

AKERLUND, Magnus (AK-uhr-luhnd, MAG-nuhs) CAR.

Goaltender. Catches right. 6'1", 183 lbs. Born, Osby, Sweden, April 25, 1986.
(Carolina's 5th choice, 137th overall, in 2004 Entry Draft).

			Regular Season								Playoffs						
Season	**Club**	**League**	**GP**	**W**	**L**	**T**	**Mins**	**GA**	**SO**	**Avg**	**GP**	**W**	**L**	**Mins**	**GA**	**SO**	**Avg**
2002-03	HV 71 Jr.	Swe-Jr.	18	....	....	....	861	44	1	3.07	2	....	....	80	6	0	4.50
2003-04	HV 71 Jr.	Swe-Jr.	26	....	....	....	1556	85	1	3.28	2	....	....	119	10	0	5.04
2004-05	HV 71 Jr.	Swe-Jr.	19	....	....	....	1096	48	1	2.63	....	....	....	....	....	....	....
	HV 71 Jonkoping	Sweden	3	....	....	....	185	9	0	2.92	....	....	....	....	....	....	....
	Skovde IK	Sweden-2	22	....	....	....	1290	55	1	2.56	....	....	....	....	....	....	....

ANDERSON, Craig (AN-duhr-suhn, KRAYG) CHI.

Goaltender. Catches left. 6'2", 174 lbs. Born, Park Ridge, IL, May 21, 1981.
(Chicago's 4th choice, 73rd overall, in 2001 Entry Draft).

			Regular Season								Playoffs						
Season	**Club**	**League**	**GP**	**W**	**L**	**T**	**Mins**	**GA**	**SO**	**Avg**	**GP**	**W**	**L**	**Mins**	**GA**	**SO**	**Avg**
1997-98	Chicago Jets	MEHL	50	....	....	....	2991	143	2	2.86	....	....	....	....	....	....	....
1998-99	Chicago Freeze	NAHL	14	11	3	0	840	40	0	2.56	....	....	....	....	....	....	....
	Guelph Storm	OHL	21	12	5	1	1006	52	1	3.10	3	0	2	114	9	0	4.74
99-2000	Guelph Storm	OHL	38	12	17	2	1955	117	0	3.59	3	0	1	110	5	0	2.73
2000-01	Guelph Storm	OHL	59	30	19	9	3555	156	3	2.63	4	0	4	240	17	0	4.25
2001-02	Norfolk Admirals	AHL	28	9	13	4	1568	77	2	2.95	1	0	1	21	1	0	2.83
2002-03	**Chicago**	**NHL**	**6**	**0**	**3**	**2**	**270**	**18**	**0**	**4.00**	....	....	....	....	....	....	....
	Norfolk Admirals	AHL	32	15	11	5	1795	58	4	1.94	5	2	3	345	15	0	2.61
2003-04	**Chicago**	**NHL**	**21**	**6**	**14**	**0**	**1205**	**57**	**1**	**2.84**	....	....	....	....	....	....	....
	Norfolk Admirals	AHL	37	17	20	0	2108	74	3	2.11	5	2	3	327	10	0	1.84
2004-05	Norfolk Admirals	AHL	15	9	4	1	886	27	2	1.83	6	2	4	356	14	0	2.36
	NHL Totals		**27**	**6**	**17**	**2**	**1475**	**75**	**1**	**3.05**	....	....	....	....	....	....	....

• Re-entered NHL Entry Draft. Originally Calgary's 3rd choice, 77th overall, in 1999 Entry Draft.

OHL First All-Star Team (2001)

ANDERSSON, Andreas (AN-duhr-suhn, an-DRAY-uhs) ANA.

Goaltender. Catches left. 6', 180 lbs. Born, Jonkoping, Sweden, April 9, 1979.
(Anaheim's 8th choice, 245th overall, in 1998 Entry Draft).

			Regular Season								Playoffs						
Season	**Club**	**League**	**GP**	**W**	**L**	**T**	**Mins**	**GA**	**SO**	**Avg**	**GP**	**W**	**L**	**Mins**	**GA**	**SO**	**Avg**
1997-98	HV 71 Jr.	Swe-Jr.	10	....	....	....	600	31	....	3.10	....	....	....	....	....	....	....
	HV 71 Jonkoping	Sweden	7	....	....	....	420	20	....	2.86	....	....	....	....	....	....	....
1998-99	Mora IK Jr.	Swe-Jr.	12	....	....	....	720	28	0	1.92	....	....	....	....	....	....	....
	HV 71 Jonkoping	Sweden	12	....	....	....	633	35	0	3.32	....	....	....	....	....	....	....
99-2000	Tranas AIF	Sweden-2	5	....	....	....	297	17	0	3.44	....	....	....	....	....	....	....
	HV 71 Jonkoping	Sweden	1	....	....	....	51	5	0	5.88	....	....	....	....	....	....	....
2000-01	IF Troja-Ljungby	Sweden-2	19	....	....	....	1076	66	0	3.68	2	1	1	120	5	0	2.50
2001-02	IF Troja-Ljungby	Sweden-2	6	....	....	....	360	27	0	4.50	....	....	....	....	....	....	....
2002-03	IF Troja-Ljungby	Sweden-2	9	....	....	....	419	20	0	2.86	2	....	....	116	3	0	1.55
2003-04	IF Troja-Ljungby	Sweden-2	32	....	....	....	1735	76	4	2.63	....	....	....	....	....	....	....
2004-05	IF Troja-Ljungby	Sweden-2	51	....	....	....	3042	144	0	2.84	....	....	....	....	....	....	....

ANTILA, Kristian (AN-tih-luh, KRIHS-tan) EDM.

Goaltender. Catches left. 6'3", 207 lbs. Born, Vammala, Finland, January 10, 1980.
(Edmonton's 4th choice, 113th overall, in 1998 Entry Draft).

			Regular Season								Playoffs						
Season	**Club**	**League**	**GP**	**W**	**L**	**T**	**Mins**	**GA**	**SO**	**Avg**	**GP**	**W**	**L**	**Mins**	**GA**	**SO**	**Avg**
1997-98	Ilves Tampere Jr.	Finland-Jr.	11	....	....	....	564	28	0	2.97	....	....	....	....	....	....	....
1998-99	Ilves Tampere Jr.	Finland-Jr.	18	8	8	1	1080	48	0	2.63	5	....	....	300	11	....	2.22
	Ilves Tampere	Finland	5	1	2	0	207	12	0	3.48	....	....	....	....	....	....	....
99-2000	Ilves Tampere Jr.	Finland-Jr.	6	4	2	0	360	21	0	3.56	....	....	....	....	....	....	....
	Diskos Jyvaskyla	Finland-2	5	1	4	0	300	23	0	4.67	....	....	....	....	....	....	....
	Ilves Tampere	Finland	25	4	11	4	1239	74	1	3.58	1	0	1	20	4	0	12.00
2000-01	Assat Pori	Finland	42	9	27	7	2417	146	1	3.62	....	....	....	....	....	....	....
2001-02	Assat Pori	Finland	35	7	22	3	1951	112	3	3.44	....	....	....	....	....	....	....
2002-03	Hamilton Bulldogs	AHL	2	1	1	0	97	6	0	3.71	....	....	....	....	....	....	....
	Wichita Thunder	CHL	21	10	7	2	1147	70	0	3.66	....	....	....	....	....	....	....
2003-04	Columbus	ECHL	9	1	5	0	334	17	1	3.06	....	....	....	....	....	....	....
	AIK Solna	Sweden-2	4	....	....	....	241	7	2	1.74	5	....	....	308	6	1	1.17
2004-05	Lulea HF	Sweden	18	....	....	....	1051	57	0	3.25	2	....	....	79	9	0	6.82

Loaned to **AIK Solna** (Sweden-2) by **Edmonton**, January 28, 2004.

ASKEY, Tom (AS-kee, TAWM)

Goaltender. Catches left. 6'1", 195 lbs. Born, Kenmore, NY, October 4, 1974.
(Anaheim's 8th choice, 186th overall, in 1993 Entry Draft).

			Regular Season								Playoffs						
Season	**Club**	**League**	**GP**	**W**	**L**	**T**	**Mins**	**GA**	**SO**	**Avg**	**GP**	**W**	**L**	**Mins**	**GA**	**SO**	**Avg**
1992-93	Ohio State	CCHA	25	2	19	0	1235	125	0	6.07	....	....	....	....	....	....	....
1993-94	Ohio State	CCHA	27	3	19	4	1488	103	0	4.15	....	....	....	....	....	....	....
1994-95	Ohio State	CCHA	26	4	19	2	1387	121	0	5.23	....	....	....	....	....	....	....
1995-96	Ohio State	CCHA	26	8	11	4	1340	68	0	3.05	....	....	....	....	....	....	....
1996-97	Baltimore Bandits	AHL	40	17	18	2	2238	140	1	3.75	3	0	3	137	11	0	4.79
1997-98	**Anaheim**	**NHL**	**7**	**0**	**1**	**2**	**273**	**12**	**0**	**2.64**	....	....	....	....	....	....	....
	Cincinnati	AHL	32	10	16	4	1753	104	3	3.56	....	....	....	....	....	....	....
1998-99	Cincinnati	AHL	53	21	22	3	2893	131	3	2.72	3	0	3	178	13	0	4.38
	Anaheim	**NHL**	....	....	....	....	....	....	....	....	**1**	**0**	**1**	**30**	**2**	**0**	**4.00**
99-2000	Kansas City Blades	IHL	13	3	5	3	658	43	0	3.92	....	....	....	....	....	....	....
	Houston Aeros	IHL	13	4	7	1	727	33	0	2.72	....	....	....	....	....	....	....
2000-01	Rochester	AHL	29	15	8	4	1671	71	1	2.55	....	....	....	....	....	....	....
2001-02	Rochester	AHL	34	16	15	3	2048	86	3	2.52	1	0	1	58	4	0	4.11
2002-03	Rochester	AHL	16	3	8	4	895	49	0	3.28	....	....	....	....	....	....	....
2003-04	Rochester	AHL	21	10	8	3	1273	48	1	2.26	2	2	0	120	5	1	2.50
2004-05	Rochester	AHL	20	10	6	2	1118	46	1	2.47	....	....	....	....	....	....	....
	NHL Totals		**7**	**0**	**1**	**2**	**273**	**12**	**0**	**2.64**	**1**	**0**	**1**	**30**	**2**	**0**	**4.00**

CCHA Second All-Star Team (1996) • Harry "Hap" Holmes Memorial Award (fewest goals against – AHL) (2001) (shared with Mika Noronen)

Signed as a free agent by **Rochester** (AHL), September 29, 2000. Signed as a free agent by **Buffalo**, August 10, 2001.

ASPLUND, Johan (AS-pluhnd, YOH-hahn) NYR

Goaltender. Catches left. 6'1", 180 lbs. Born, Slutskar, Sweden, December 15, 1980.
(NY Rangers' 4th choice, 79th overall, in 1999 Entry Draft).

			Regular Season								Playoffs						
Season	**Club**	**League**	**GP**	**W**	**L**	**T**	**Mins**	**GA**	**SO**	**Avg**	**GP**	**W**	**L**	**Mins**	**GA**	**SO**	**Avg**
1998-99	Brynas IF Gavle	Sweden	12	....	....	....	646	32	0	2.97	....	....	....	....	....	....	....
99-2000	Mora IK	Sweden-2	3	3	0	0	180	6	0	2.00	....	....	....	....	....	....	....
	Brynas IF Gavle	Sweden	10	....	....	....	622	30	0	2.89	....	....	....	....	....	....	....

2000-01	Brynas IF Gavle	Sweden	29	....	....	....	1761	79	2	2.69	3	0	3	177	11	0	3.73
2001-02	Brynas IF Gavle	Sweden	34	....	....	....	2069	102	1	2.96	3	0	3	188	16	0	5.11
2002-03	Brynas IF Gavle	Sweden	13	....	....	....	680	43	0	3.79	....	....	....	....	....	....	....
2003-04	Nykoping	Sweden-2	20	....	....	....	1092	48	2	2.64	2	....	....	100	4	0	2.40
2004-05	Nykoping	Sweden-2	38	....	....	....	2164	99	3	2.74	5	....	....	299	8	1	1.61

Signed as a free agent by **Nykoping** (Sweden-2), May 11, 2003.

AUBIN, Jean-Sebastien (OH-behn, ZHAWN-suh-BAS-tee-yeh) TOR.

Goaltender. Catches right. 5'11", 180 lbs. Born, Montreal, Que., July 19, 1977.
(Pittsburgh's 2nd choice, 76th overall, in 1995 Entry Draft).

			Regular Season								Playoffs						
Season	Club	League	GP	W	L	T	Mins	GA	SO	Avg	GP	W	L	Mins	GA	SO	Avg
1993-94	Montreal-Bourassa	QAAA	27	14	13	0	1524	96	1	3.74	4	1	3	222	19	0	5.14
1994-95	Sherbrooke	QMJHL	27	13	10	1	1287	73	1	3.40	3	1	2	185	11	0	3.57
1995-96	Sherbrooke	QMJHL	40	18	14	2	2140	127	0	3.57	4	1	3	238	23	0	5.55
1996-97	Sherbrooke	QMJHL	4	3	1	0	249	8	0	1.93	1	0	1	60	4	0	4.00
	Moncton Wildcats	QMJHL	22	9	12	0	1252	67	1	3.21	....	....	....	....	....	....	....
	Laval Titan	QMJHL	11	2	6	1	532	41	0	4.62	....	....	....	....	....	....	....
1997-98	Syracuse Crunch	AHL	8	2	4	1	380	26	0	4.10	....	....	....	....	....	....	....
	Dayton Bombers	ECHL	21	15	2	2	1177	59	1	3.01	3	1	1	142	4	0	1.69
1998-99	**Pittsburgh**	**NHL**	**17**	**4**	**3**	**6**	**756**	**28**	**2**	**2.22**	....	....	....	....	....	....	....
	Kansas City Blades	IHL	13	5	7	1	751	41	0	3.28	....	....	....	....	....	....	....
99-2000	**Pittsburgh**	**NHL**	**51**	**23**	**21**	**3**	**2789**	**120**	**2**	**2.58**	....	....	....	....	....	....	....
	Wilkes-Barre	AHL	11	2	8	0	538	39	0	4.35	....	....	....	....	....	....	....
2000-01	**Pittsburgh**	**NHL**	**36**	**20**	**14**	**1**	**2050**	**107**	**0**	**3.13**	**1**	**0**	**0**	**1**	**0**	**0**	**0.00**
2001-02	**Pittsburgh**	**NHL**	**21**	**3**	**12**	**1**	**1094**	**65**	**0**	**3.56**	....	....	....	....	....	....	....
2002-03	**Pittsburgh**	**NHL**	**21**	**6**	**13**	**0**	**1132**	**59**	**1**	**3.13**	....	....	....	....	....	....	....
	Wilkes-Barre	AHL	16	8	6	1	919	29	3	1.89	6	3	3	356	12	0	2.02
2003-04	**Pittsburgh**	**NHL**	**22**	**7**	**9**	**0**	**1067**	**53**	**1**	**2.98**	....	....	....	....	....	....	....
	Wilkes-Barre	AHL	13	4	5	2	670	31	0	2.78	....	....	....	....	....	....	....
2004-05	St. John's	AHL	23	12	9	0	1336	64	3	2.87	1	0	0	47	1	0	1.27
	NHL Totals		**168**	**63**	**72**	**11**	**8888**	**432**	**6**	**2.92**	**1**	**0**	**0**	**1**	**0**	**0**	**0.00**

Signed to a PTO (tryout) contract by **St. John's** (AHL), November 13, 2004. Signed as a free agent by **Toronto**, August 18, 2005.

AULD, Alex (AWLD, al-ehx) VAN.

Goaltender. Catches left. 6'4", 200 lbs. Born, Cold Lake, Alta., January 7, 1981.
(Florida's 2nd choice, 40th overall, in 1999 Entry Draft).

			Regular Season								Playoffs						
Season	Club	League	GP	W	L	T	Mins	GA	SO	Avg	GP	W	L	Mins	GA	SO	Avg
1996-97	Thunder Bay Kings	TBMHL	35	....	....	....	2100	46	10	1.35	....	....	....	....	....	....	....
1997-98	Sturgeon Falls Lynx	NOJHA	11	4	6	0	611	46	0	4.52	....	....	....	....	....	....	....
	North Bay	OHL	6	0	4	0	206	17	0	4.95	....	....	....	....	....	....	....
1998-99	North Bay	OHL	37	9	20	1	1894	106	1	3.36	3	0	3	170	10	0	3.53
99-2000	North Bay	OHL	55	21	26	6	3047	167	2	3.29	6	2	4	374	12	0	*1.93
2000-01	North Bay	OHL	40	22	11	5	2319	98	1	2.54	4	0	4	240	15	0	3.75
2001-02	**Vancouver**	**NHL**	**1**	**1**	**0**	**0**	**60**	**2**	**0**	**2.00**	....	....	....	....	....	....	....
	Columbia Inferno	ECHL	6	3	1	2	375	12	0	1.92	....	....	....	....	....	....	....
	Manitoba Moose	AHL	21	11	9	0	1104	65	1	3.53	1	0	0	20	0	0	0.00
2002-03	**Vancouver**	**NHL**	**7**	**3**	**3**	**0**	**382**	**10**	**1**	**1.57**	**1**	**0**	**0**	**20**	**1**	**0**	**3.00**
	Manitoba Moose	AHL	37	15	19	3	2209	97	3	2.64	....	....	....	....	....	....	....
2003-04	**Vancouver**	**NHL**	**6**	**2**	**2**	**2**	**349**	**12**	**0**	**2.06**	**3**	**1**	**2**	**222**	**9**	**0**	**2.43**
	Manitoba Moose	AHL	40	18	16	4	2329	99	4	2.55	....	....	....	....	....	....	....
2004-05	Manitoba Moose	AHL	50	25	18	4	2764	118	2	2.56	3	0	2	128	7	0	3.29
	NHL Totals		**14**	**6**	**5**	**2**	**791**	**24**	**1**	**1.82**	**4**	**1**	**2**	**242**	**10**	**0**	**2.48**

Rights traded to **Vancouver** by **Florida** for Vancouver's 2nd round compensatory choice (later traded to New Jersey – New Jersey selected Tuomas Pihlman) in 2001 Entry Draft and Vancouver's 3rd round choice (later traded to Atlanta – later traded to Buffalo – Buffalo selected John Adams) in 2002 Entry Draft, May 31, 2001.

BACASHIHUA, Jason (bak-ah-SHIH-hu-ah, JAY-suhn) ST.L.

Goaltender. Catches left. 5'11", 175 lbs. Born, Garden City, MI, September 20, 1982.
(Dallas' 1st choice, 26th overall, in 2001 Entry Draft).

			Regular Season								Playoffs						
Season	Club	League	GP	W	L	T	Mins	GA	SO	Avg	GP	W	L	Mins	GA	SO	Avg
99-2000	Chicago Freeze	NAHL	41	20	19	2	2432	118	2	2.91	2	0	2	103	12	0	6.97
2000-01	Chicago Freeze	NAJHL	39	24	14	0	2246	121	1	3.23	3	1	2	190	12	0	3.79
2001-02	Plymouth Whalers	OHL	46	26	12	7	2688	105	*5	2.34	6	2	4	360	15	0	2.50
	Utah Grizzlies	AHL	1	0	1	0	61	3	0	2.97	....	....	....	....	....	....	....
2002-03	Utah Grizzlies	AHL	39	18	18	2	2245	118	3	3.15	1	0	1	59	2	0	2.05
2003-04	Utah Grizzlies	AHL	39	13	19	5	2234	99	3	2.66	....	....	....	....	....	....	....
2004-05	Worcester IceCats	AHL	35	18	13	1	1909	80	2	2.51	....	....	....	....	....	....	....

Traded to **St. Louis** by **Dallas** for the rights to Shawn Belle, June 25, 2004.

BARULIN, Konstantin (bah-ROO-lihn, kawn-stuhn-TIHN) ST.L.

Goaltender. Catches left. 6', 180 lbs. Born, Karaganda, USSR, September 4, 1984.
(St. Louis' 3rd choice, 84th overall, in 2003 Entry Draft).

			Regular Season								Playoffs						
Season	Club	League	GP	W	L	T	Mins	GA	SO	Avg	GP	W	L	Mins	GA	SO	Avg
2001-02	Gazovik Tyumen	Russia-2	4	....	....	....	188	15	0	4.79	....	....	....	....	....	....	....
2002-03	Gazovik Tyumen	Russia-2	28	....	....	....	1672	47	5	1.69	....	....	....	....	....	....	....
2003-04	Gazovik Tyumen	Russia-2	11	....	....	....	663	24	....	2.17	....	....	....	....	....	....	....
	SKA St. Petersburg	Russia	1	....	....	....	1	0	0	0.00	....	....	....	....	....	....	....
	St. Petersburg 2	Russia-3	11	6	4	1	668	24	1	2.15	....	....	....	....	....	....	....
2004-05	Gazovik Tyumen	Russia-2	30	....	....	....	1773	59	6	2.00	3	....	....	136	9	0	3.97

BEAUCHEMIN, Rejean (boh-sheh-MEH, ray-JAWN) PHI.

Goaltender. Catches left. 6'1", 193 lbs. Born, Winnipeg, Man., May 3, 1985.
(Philadelphia's 10th choice, 191st overall, in 2003 Entry Draft).

			Regular Season								Playoffs						
Season	Club	League	GP	W	L	T	Mins	GA	SO	Avg	GP	W	L	Mins	GA	SO	Avg
2001-02	Winnipeg Warriors	MMMHL	29	6	8	4	1026	54	0	3.15	4	3	1	240	12	0	3.00
2002-03	Prince Albert	WHL	34	12	15	1	1618	86	1	3.19	....	....	....	....	....	....	....
2003-04	Prince Albert	WHL	62	30	21	6	3540	137	6	2.32	6	2	4	360	14	0	2.33
2004-05	Prince Albert	WHL	54	21	24	4	3052	133	5	2.61	17	11	6	1062	38	2	2.15

WHL East Second All-Star Team (2004)

BECKFORD-TSEU, Chris (BEHK-fuhrd-TSEW, KRIHS) ST.L.

Goaltender. Catches left. 6'2", 201 lbs. Born, Toronto, Ont., June 22, 1984.
(St. Louis' 8th choice, 159th overall, in 2003 Entry Draft).

			Regular Season								Playoffs						
Season	Club	League	GP	W	L	T	Mins	GA	SO	Avg	GP	W	L	Mins	GA	SO	Avg
2000-01	St. Mike's B's	OPJHL	26	....	....	....	1506	121	0	4.83	....	....	....	....	....	....	....
2001-02	Oshawa	OPJHL					STATISTICS NOT AVAILABLE										
	Guelph Storm	OHL	5	2	0	0	207	16	0	4.64	....	....	....	....	....	....	....
	Oshawa Generals	OHL	7	2	3	0	341	19	0	3.34	5	1	4	310	16	0	3.10
2002-03	Oshawa Generals	OHL	54	25	26	2	2978	157	4	3.16	13	6	7	727	48	1	3.96
2003-04	Oshawa Generals	OHL	9	1	5	2	495	28	0	3.39	....	....	....	....	....	....	....
	Kingston	OHL	40	16	19	2	2226	121	3	3.26	5	1	4	303	18	0	3.56
2004-05	Worcester IceCats	AHL	1	0	0	0	29	0	0	0.00	....	....	....	....	....	....	....
	Peoria Rivermen	ECHL	29	11	12	3	1594	72	1	2.71	....	....	....	....	....	....	....

BEECH, Kevin (BEECH, KEH-vihn) T.B.

Goaltender. Catches left. 6'4", 168 lbs. Born, London, Ont., September 23, 1986.
(Tampa Bay's 8th choice, 165th overall, in 2005 Entry Draft).

			Regular Season								Playoffs						
Season	Club	League	GP	W	L	T	Mins	GA	SO	Avg	GP	W	L	Mins	GA	SO	Avg
2003-04	Sudbury Wolves	OHL	16	3	9	0	811	48	0	3.55	1	1	0	56	0	0	0.00
2004-05	Sudbury Wolves	OHL	21	9	9	2	1132	50	2	2.65	6	2	1	276	12	0	2.61

BELFOUR, Ed (BEHL-fohr, EHD) TOR.

Goaltender. Catches left. 5'11", 202 lbs. Born, Carman, Man., April 21, 1965.

			Regular Season								Playoffs						
Season	Club	League	GP	W	L	T	Mins	GA	SO	Avg	GP	W	L	Mins	GA	SO	Avg
1983-84	Winkler Flyers	MJHL	14	....	....	....	818	68	0	4.99	....	....	....	....	....	....	....
1984-85	Winkler Flyers	MJHL	34	....	....	....	1973	145	1	4.41	7	3	4	528	41	0	4.66
1985-86	Winkler Flyers	MJHL	33	....	....	....	1943	124	1	3.83	....	....	....	....	....	....	....
1986-87	North Dakota	WCHA	34	29	4	0	2049	81	3	2.37	....	....	....	....	....	....	....
1987-88	Saginaw Hawks	IHL	61	32	25	0	*3446	183	3	3.19	9	4	5	561	33	0	3.53
1988-89	**Chicago**	**NHL**	**23**	**4**	**12**	**3**	**1148**	**74**	**0**	**3.87**	....	....	....	....	....	....	....
	Saginaw Hawks	IHL	29	12	10	0	1760	92	0	3.14	5	2	3	298	14	0	2.82
1989-90	Canada	Nat-Tm	33	13	12	6	1808	93	0	3.09	....	....	....	....	....	....	....
	Chicago	**NHL**	....	....	....	....	....	....	....	....	**9**	**4**	**2**	**409**	**17**	**0**	**2.49**
1990-91	**Chicago**	**NHL**	***74**	***43**	**19**	**7**	***4127**	**170**	**4**	***2.47**	**6**	**2**	**4**	**295**	**20**	**0**	**4.07**
1991-92	**Chicago**	**NHL**	**52**	**21**	**18**	**10**	**2928**	**132**	***5**	**2.70**	**18**	**12**	**4**	**949**	**39**	**1**	***2.47**
1992-93	**Chicago**	**NHL**	***71**	**41**	**18**	**11**	***4106**	**177**	***7**	**2.59**	**4**	**0**	**4**	**249**	**13**	**0**	**3.13**
1993-94	**Chicago**	**NHL**	**70**	**37**	**24**	**6**	**3998**	**178**	***7**	**2.67**	**6**	**2**	**4**	**360**	**15**	**0**	**2.50**
1994-95	**Chicago**	**NHL**	**42**	**22**	**15**	**3**	**2450**	**93**	***5**	**2.28**	**16**	**9**	**7**	**1014**	**37**	**1**	**2.19**
1995-96	**Chicago**	**NHL**	**50**	**22**	**17**	**10**	**2956**	**135**	**1**	**2.74**	**9**	**6**	**3**	**666**	**23**	**1**	***2.07**
1996-97	**Chicago**	**NHL**	**33**	**11**	**15**	**6**	**1966**	**88**	**1**	**2.69**	....	....	....	....	....	....	....
	San Jose	**NHL**	**13**	**3**	**9**	**0**	**757**	**43**	**1**	**3.41**	....	....	....	....	....	....	....
1997-98	**Dallas**	**NHL**	**61**	**37**	**12**	**10**	**3581**	**112**	**9**	***1.88**	**17**	**10**	**7**	**1039**	**31**	**1**	***1.79**
1998-99♦	**Dallas**	**NHL**	**61**	**35**	**15**	**9**	**3536**	**117**	**5**	**1.99**	***23**	***16**	**7**	***1544**	**43**	***3**	***1.67**
99-2000	**Dallas**	**NHL**	**62**	**32**	**21**	**7**	**3620**	**127**	**4**	**2.10**	***23**	**14**	**9**	**1443**	**45**	***4**	**1.87**
2000-01	**Dallas**	**NHL**	**63**	**35**	**20**	**7**	**3687**	**144**	**8**	**2.34**	**10**	**4**	**6**	**671**	**25**	**0**	**2.24**
2001-02	**Dallas**	**NHL**	**60**	**21**	**27**	**11**	**3467**	**153**	**1**	**2.65**	....	....	....	....	....	....	....
	Canada	Olympics					DID NOT PLAY – SPARE GOALTENDER										
2002-03	**Toronto**	**NHL**	**62**	**37**	**20**	**5**	**3738**	**141**	**7**	**2.26**	**7**	**3**	**4**	**532**	**24**	**0**	**2.71**
2003-04	**Toronto**	**NHL**	**59**	**34**	**19**	**6**	**3444**	**122**	**10**	**2.13**	**13**	**6**	**7**	**774**	**27**	**3**	**2.09**
2004-05								DID NOT PLAY									
	NHL Totals		**856**	**435**	**281**	**111**	**49509**	**2006**	**75**	**2.43**	**161**	**88**	**68**	**9945**	**359**	**14**	**2.17**

WCHA First All-Star Team (1987) • NCAA Championship All-Tournament Team (1987) • IHL First All-Star Team (1988) • Garry F. Longman Memorial Trophy (Rookie of the Year – IHL) (1988) (co-winner - John Cullen) • NHL All-Rookie Team (1991) • NHL First All-Star Team (1991, 1993) • Trico Goaltender Award (1991) • Calder Memorial Trophy (1991) • William M. Jennings Trophy (1991, 1993, 1995) • Vezina Trophy (1991, 1993) • NHL Second All-Star Team (1995) • William M. Jennings Trophy (1999) (shared with Roman Turek) • MBNA Roger Crozier Saving Grace Award (2000)

Played in NHL All-Star Game (1992, 1993, 1996, 1998, 1999)

Signed as a free agent by **Chicago**, September 25, 1987. Traded to **San Jose** by **Chicago** for Chris Terreri, Ulf Dahlen and Michal Sykora, January 25, 1997. Signed as a free agent by **Dallas**, July 2, 1997. Traded to **Nashville** by **Dallas** with Cameron Mann for David Gosselin and Nashville's 5th round choice (Eero Kilpelainen) in 2003 Entry Draft, June 29, 2002. Signed as a free agent by **Toronto**, July 2, 2002.

BERKHOEL, Adam (BUHRK-uhl, A-duhm) ATL.

Goaltender. Catches left. 5'11", 190 lbs. Born, St. Paul, MN, May 16, 1981.
(Chicago's 12th choice, 240th overall, in 2000 Entry Draft).

			Regular Season								Playoffs						
Season	Club	League	GP	W	L	T	Mins	GA	SO	Avg	GP	W	L	Mins	GA	SO	Avg
99-2000	Twin Cities	USHL	49	25	15	7	2848	129	0	2.72	13	7	6	797	43	0	3.24
2000-01	U. of Denver	WCHA	15	7	6	1	745	38	1	3.06	....	....	....	....	....	....	....
2001-02	U. of Denver	WCHA	18	12	4	1	1026	40	1	2.34	....	....	....	....	....	....	....
2002-03	U. of Denver	WCHA	26	12	6	4	1436	55	3	*2.30	....	....	....	....	....	....	....
2003-04	U. of Denver	WCHA	39	24	11	4	2225	91	*7	2.45	....	....	....	....	....	....	....
2004-05	Chicago Wolves	AHL	1	0	1	0	59	4	0	4.04	....	....	....	....	....	....	....
	Gwinnett	ECHL	24	9	10	5	1458	59	2	2.43	7	4	1	353	9	0	*1.53

USHL All-Rookie Team (2000) • USHL Second All-Star Team (2000) • NCAA Championship All-Tournament Team (2004) • NCAA Championship Tournament MVP (2004)

Traded to **Atlanta** by **Chicago** for Atlanta's 7th round choice (Adam Hobson) in 2005 Entry Draft, June 27, 2004.

BIERK, Zac (BUHRK, ZAK)

Goaltender. Catches left. 6'5", 205 lbs. Born, Peterborough, Ont., September 17, 1976.
(Tampa Bay's 8th choice, 212th overall, in 1995 Entry Draft).

			Regular Season								Playoffs						
Season	Club	League	GP	W	L	T	Mins	GA	SO	Avg	GP	W	L	Mins	GA	SO	Avg
1993-94	Peterborough	OPJHL	4	....	....	....	205	17	0	4.98	....	....	....	....	....	....	....
	Peterborough	OHL	9	0	4	2	423	37	0	5.22	1	0	0	33	7	0	12.70
1994-95	Peterborough	OHL	35	11	15	5	1779	117	0	3.95	6	2	3	301	24	0	4.78
1995-96	Peterborough	OHL	58	31	16	6	3292	174	2	3.17	*22	*14	7	*1383	83	0	3.60
1996-97	Peterborough	OHL	49	*28	16	0	2744	151	2	3.30	11	6	5	666	35	0	3.15
1997-98	**Tampa Bay**	**NHL**	**13**	**1**	**4**	**1**	**433**	**30**	**0**	**4.16**	....	....	....	....	....	....	....
	Adirondack	AHL	12	1	6	1	557	36	0	3.87	....	....	....	....	....	....	....
1998-99	**Tampa Bay**	**NHL**	**1**	**0**	**1**	**0**	**59**	**2**	**0**	**2.03**	....	....	....	....	....	....	....
	Cleveland	IHL	27	11	12	4	1556	79	0	3.05	....	....	....	....	....	....	....
99-2000	**Tampa Bay**	**NHL**	**12**	**4**	**4**	**1**	**509**	**31**	**0**	**3.65**	....	....	....	....	....	....	....
	Detroit Vipers	IHL	15	4	8	2	846	46	1	3.26	....	....	....	....	....	....	....
2000-01	**Minnesota**	**NHL**	**1**	**0**	**1**	**0**	**60**	**6**	**0**	**6.00**	....	....	....	....	....	....	....
	Cleveland	IHL	49	24	18	5	2785	134	6	2.89	4	0	3	182	10	0	3.29
2001-02	Augusta Lynx	ECHL	30	16	9	3	1748	68	1	2.33	....	....	....	....	....	....	....
	Springfield Falcons	AHL	1	0	1	0	20	4	0	12.00	....	....	....	....	....	....	....
2002-03	**Phoenix**	**NHL**	**16**	**4**	**9**	**1**	**884**	**32**	**1**	**2.17**	....	....	....	....	....	....	....
	Springfield Falcons	AHL	13	6	4	1	685	33	0	2.89	....	....	....	....	....	....	....
2003-04	**Phoenix**	**NHL**	**4**	**0**	**1**	**2**	**190**	**12**	**0**	**3.79**	....	....	....	....	....	....	....
	Springfield Falcons	AHL	2	0	1	1	106	6	0	3.38	....	....	....	....	....	....	....
2004-05								DID NOT PLAY									
	NHL Totals		**47**	**9**	**20**	**5**	**2135**	**113**	**1**	**3.18**	....	....	....	....	....	....	....

OHL First All-Star Team (1997) • Canadian Major Junior Second All-Star Team (1997)

• Missed remainder of 1998-99 season and majority of 1999-2000 season recovering from Meniere's Disease which was diagnosed on March 25, 1999. Claimed by **Minnesota** from **Tampa Bay** in Expansion Draft, June 23, 2000. Signed as a free agent by **Phoenix**, August 30, 2001.
• Missed majority of 2003-04 season recovering from hip injury suffered in game vs. Anaheim, November 9, 2003.

BIRON, Martin (BIH-rohn, MAHR-tihn) BUF.

Goaltender. Catches left. 6'2", 170 lbs. Born, Lac-St-Charles, Que., August 15, 1977.
(Buffalo's 2nd choice, 16th overall, in 1995 Entry Draft).

			Regular Season								Playoffs						
Season	Club	League	GP	W	L	T	Mins	GA	SO	Avg	GP	W	L	Mins	GA	SO	Avg
1993-94	Trois-Rivieres	QAAA	23	14	8	1	1412	80	1	3.40	2	1	1	112	7	0	3.73
1994-95	Beauport Harfangs	QMJHL	56	29	16	9	3193	132	3	*2.48	16	8	7	900	37	*4	2.47
1995-96	Beauport Harfangs	QMJHL	55	29	17	7	3201	152	1	2.85	*19	*12	7	1134	64	0	3.39
	Buffalo	**NHL**	**3**	**0**	**2**	**0**	**119**	**10**	**0**	**5.04**	....	....	....	....	....	....	....
1996-97	Beauport Harfangs	QMJHL	18	6	9	1	928	61	1	3.94	....	....	....	....	....	....	....
	Hull Olympiques	QMJHL	16	11	4	1	974	43	2	2.65	6	3	1	325	19	0	3.51
1997-98	South Carolina	ECHL	2	0	1	1	86	3	0	2.09	....	....	....	....	....	....	....
	Rochester	AHL	41	14	18	6	2312	113	*5	2.93	4	1	3	239	16	0	4.01
1998-99	**Buffalo**	**NHL**	**6**	**1**	**2**	**1**	**281**	**10**	**0**	**2.14**	....	....	....	....	....	....	....
	Rochester	AHL	52	36	13	3	3129	108	*6	*2.07	*20	12	8	1167	42	1	*2.16
99-2000	**Buffalo**	**NHL**	**41**	**19**	**18**	**2**	**2229**	**90**	**5**	**2.42**	....	....	....	....	....	....	....
	Rochester	AHL	6	6	0	0	344	12	1	2.09	....	....	....	....	....	....	....
2000-01	**Buffalo**	**NHL**	**18**	**7**	**7**	**1**	**918**	**39**	**2**	**2.55**	....	....	....	....	....	....	....
	Rochester	AHL	4	3	1	0	239	4	1	1.00	....	....	....	....	....	....	....
2001-02	**Buffalo**	**NHL**	**72**	**31**	**28**	**10**	**4085**	**151**	**4**	**2.22**	....	....	....	....	....	....	....
2002-03	**Buffalo**	**NHL**	**54**	**17**	**28**	**6**	**3170**	**135**	**4**	**2.56**	....	....	....	....	....	....	....
2003-04	**Buffalo**	**NHL**	**52**	**26**	**18**	**5**	**2972**	**125**	**2**	**2.52**	....	....	....	....	....	....	....
2004-05							DID NOT PLAY										
	NHL Totals		**246**	**101**	**103**	**25**	**13774**	**560**	**17**	**2.44**	....	....	....	....	....	....	....

QMJHL All-Rookie Team (1995) • Canadian Major Junior First All-Star Team (1995) • Canadian Major Junior Goaltender of the Year (1995) • AHL First All-Star Team (1999) • Harry "Hap" Holmes Memorial Award (fewest goals against – AHL) (1999) (shared with Tom Draper) • Aldege "Baz" Bastien Memorial Award (Outstanding Goaltender – AHL) (1999)

BISHOP, Ben (BIH-shuhp, BEHN) ST.L.

Goaltender. Catches left. 6'5", 205 lbs. Born, Denver, CO, November 21, 1986.
(St. Louis' 3rd choice, 85th overall, in 2005 Entry Draft).

			Regular Season								Playoffs						
Season	Club	League	GP	W	L	T	Mins	GA	SO	Avg	GP	W	L	Mins	GA	SO	Avg
2003-04	St.L. AAA Blues	MAHL	11	8	1	2	660	19	1	1.73	....	....	....	....	....	....	....
	St.L. AAA Blues	Exhib.	26	15	7	4	1480	62	3	2.51	....	....	....	....	....	....	....
2004-05	Texas Tornado	NAHL	45	*35	8	0	2577	83	5	1.93	*11	*9	2	*660	30	0	2.73

Signed Letter of Intent to attend **Maine** (H-East), April 28, 2005.

BJURLING, Bjorn (b-YUHR-lihng, b-YOHRN) EDM.

Goaltender. Catches left. 6', 205 lbs. Born, Stockholm, Sweden, August 21, 1979.
(Edmonton's 10th choice, 274th overall, in 2004 Entry Draft).

			Regular Season								Playoffs						
Season	Club	League	GP	W	L	T	Mins	GA	SO	Avg	GP	W	L	Mins	GA	SO	Avg
2000-01	Bodens IK	Sweden-2	32	....	....	....	1914	80	0	2.51	6	....	....	398	16	1	2.41
2001-02	Bodens IK	Sweden-2	43	....	....	....	2568	128	2	2.99	9	....	....	508	36	0	4.25
2002-03	Bodens IK	Sweden-2	3	....	....	....	179	7	1	2.35	....	....	....	....	....	....	....
	Djurgarden	Sweden	15	....	....	....	571	21	2	2.21	....	....	....	....	....	....	....
2003-04	Djurgarden	Sweden	45	....	....	....	2601	100	4	2.31	2	....	....	100	15	0	9.00
2004-05	Djurgarden	Sweden	24	....	....	....	1441	61	1	2.54	....	....	....	....	....	....	....

BLACKBURN, Dan (BLAK-buhrn, DAN)

Goaltender. Catches left. 6', 180 lbs. Born, Montreal, Que., May 20, 1983.
(NY Rangers' 1st choice, 10th overall, in 2001 Entry Draft).

			Regular Season								Playoffs						
Season	Club	League	GP	W	L	T	Mins	GA	SO	Avg	GP	W	L	Mins	GA	SO	Avg
1997-98	Bow Valley Eagles	AJHL	20	9	6	1	1039	58	1	3.35	3	0	0	97	8	0	4.95
1998-99	Bow Valley Eagles	AJHL	38	7	19	6	1941	146	0	4.51	2	0	2	118	8	0	4.07
99-2000	Kootenay Ice	WHL	51	34	8	7	3004	126	3	2.52	*21	*16	5	*1272	43	2	*2.03
2000-01	Kootenay Ice	WHL	50	*33	14	2	2922	135	1	2.77	11	7	4	706	23	1	1.95
2001-02	**NY Rangers**	**NHL**	**31**	**12**	**16**	**0**	**1737**	**95**	**0**	**3.28**	....	....	....	....	....	....	....
	Hartford Wolf Pack	AHL	4	2	1	1	244	11	0	2.71	....	....	....	....	....	....	....
2002-03	**NY Rangers**	**NHL**	**32**	**8**	**16**	**4**	**1762**	**93**	**1**	**3.17**	....	....	....	....	....	....	....
2003-04							DID NOT PLAY – INJURED										
2004-05	Victoria	ECHL	12	3	9	0	695	41	0	3.54	....	....	....	....	....	....	....
	NHL Totals		**63**	**20**	**32**	**4**	**3499**	**188**	**1**	**3.22**	....	....	....	....	....	....	....

WHL Rookie of the Year (2000) • WHL East First All-Star Team (2001) • WHL Goaltender of the Year (2001) • Canadian Major Junior First All-Star Team (2001) • Canadian Major Junior Goaltender of the Year (2001) • NHL All-Rookie Team (2002)

• Missed entire 2003-04 season recovering from shoulder injury suffered in training camp, September 2, 2003. Signed as a free agent by **Victoria** (ECHL), February 4, 2005.

BOUCHER, Brian (BOO-shay, BRIGH-uhn) PHX.

Goaltender. Catches left. 6'2", 198 lbs. Born, Woonsocket, RI, January 2, 1977.
(Philadelphia's 1st choice, 22nd overall, in 1995 Entry Draft).

			Regular Season								Playoffs						
Season	Club	League	GP	W	L	T	Mins	GA	SO	Avg	GP	W	L	Mins	GA	SO	Avg
1993-94	Mount St. Charles	High-RI	15	*14	0	1	*504	*8	*9	*0.57	4	*4	0	*180	*6	*1	*1.20
1994-95	Wexford Raiders	MTJHL	8	....	....	....	425	23	0	3.25	....	....	....	....	....	....	....
	Tri-City Americans	WHL	35	17	11	2	1969	108	1	3.29	13	6	5	795	50	0	3.77
1995-96	Tri-City Americans	WHL	55	33	19	2	3183	181	1	3.41	11	6	5	653	37	*2	3.40
1996-97	Tri-City Americans	WHL	41	10	24	6	2458	149	1	3.64	....	....	....	....	....	....	....
1997-98	Philadelphia	AHL	34	16	12	3	1901	101	0	3.19	2	0	0	30	1	0	1.95
1998-99	Philadelphia	AHL	36	20	8	5	2061	89	2	2.59	16	9	7	947	45	0	2.85
99-2000	**Philadelphia**	**NHL**	**35**	**20**	**10**	**3**	**2038**	**65**	**4**	***1.91**	**18**	**11**	**7**	**1183**	**40**	**1**	**2.03**
	Philadelphia	AHL	1	0	0	1	65	3	0	2.77	....	....	....	....	....	....	....
2000-01	**Philadelphia**	**NHL**	**27**	**8**	**12**	**5**	**1470**	**80**	**1**	**3.27**	**1**	**0**	**0**	**37**	**3**	**0**	**4.86**
2001-02	**Philadelphia**	**NHL**	**41**	**18**	**16**	**4**	**2295**	**92**	**2**	**2.41**	**2**	**0**	**1**	**88**	**2**	**0**	**1.36**
2002-03	**Phoenix**	**NHL**	**45**	**15**	**20**	**8**	**2544**	**128**	**0**	**3.02**	....	....	....	....	....	....	....
2003-04	**Phoenix**	**NHL**	**40**	**10**	**19**	**10**	**2364**	**108**	**5**	**2.74**	....	....	....	....	....	....	....
2004-05	HV 71 Jonkoping	Sweden	4	....	....	....	235	13	0	3.32	....	....	....	....	....	....	....
	NHL Totals		**188**	**71**	**77**	**30**	**10711**	**473**	**12**	**2.65**	**21**	**11**	**8**	**1308**	**45**	**1**	**2.06**

WHL West Second All-Star Team (1996) • WHL West First All-Star Team (1997) • WHL Goaltender of the Year (1997) • NHL All-Rookie Team (2000)

Traded to **Phoenix** by **Philadelphia** with Nashville's 3rd round choice (previously acquired, Phoenix selected Joe Callahan) in 2002 Entry Draft for Michal Handzus and Robert Esche, June 12, 2002. Signed as a free agent by **HV 71** (Sweden), October 20, 2004.

BOUTHILLETTE, Gabriel (boo-tih-LEHT, ga-BREE-ehl) ANA.

Goaltender. Catches left. 6'3", 193 lbs. Born, Sorel, Que., May 21, 1985.
(Anaheim's 6th choice, 203rd overall, in 2004 Entry Draft).

			Regular Season								Playoffs						
Season	Club	League	GP	W	L	T	Mins	GA	SO	Avg	GP	W	L	Mins	GA	SO	Avg
2003-04	Gatineau	QMJHL	27	17	2	4	1529	56	3	*2.20	2	0	1	59	2	0	2.03
2004-05	Acadie-Bathurst	QMJHL	58	15	33	5	3179	169	5	3.19	....	....	....	....	....	....	....

BOUTIN, Jonathan (boo-TEHN, JAWN-ah-thuhn) T.B.

Goaltender. Catches left. 6'2", 210 lbs. Born, Granby, Que., March 28, 1985.
(Tampa Bay's 3rd choice, 96th overall, in 2003 Entry Draft).

			Regular Season								Playoffs						
Season	Club	League	GP	W	L	T	Mins	GA	SO	Avg	GP	W	L	Mins	GA	SO	Avg
2001-02	Fort Saskatchewan	AJHL					STATISTICS NOT AVAILABLE										
	Halifax	QMJHL	11	4	1	1	459	18	0	2.35	2	0	0	15	0	0	0.00
2002-03	Halifax	QMJHL	47	22	11	2	2190	106	4	2.90	1	0	0	27	0	0	0.00
2003-04	PEI Rocket	QMJHL	30	13	12	2	1612	80	1	2.98	11	6	5	672	23	0	2.06
2004-05	PEI Rocket	QMJHL	32	15	14	2	1814	98	1	3.24	....	....	....	....	....	....	....
	Quebec Remparts	QMJHL	10	4	5	0	534	30	0	3.37	10	5	4	558	30	*1	3.22

BRATHWAITE, Fred (BRAYTH-wayt, FREHD)

Goaltender. Catches left. 5'7", 175 lbs. Born, Ottawa, Ont., November 24, 1972.

			Regular Season								Playoffs						
Season	Club	League	GP	W	L	T	Mins	GA	SO	Avg	GP	W	L	Mins	GA	SO	Avg
1988-89	Smiths Falls Bears	CJHL	38	16	18	1	2130	187	0	5.27	....	....	....	....	....	....	....
1989-90	Orillia Terriers	OJHL-B	15	....	....	....	782	47	0	3.61	....	....	....	....	....	....	....
	Oshawa Generals	OHL	20	11	2	1	886	43	1	2.91	10	4	2	451	22	0	*2.93
1990-91	Oshawa Generals	OHL	39	25	6	3	1986	112	1	3.38	13	*9	2	677	43	0	3.81
1991-92	Oshawa Generals	OHL	24	12	7	2	1248	81	0	3.89	....	....	....	....	....	....	....
	London Knights	OHL	23	15	6	2	1325	61	*4	2.76	10	5	5	615	36	0	3.51
1992-93	Detroit	OHL	37	23	10	4	2192	134	0	3.67	15	9	6	858	48	1	3.36
1993-94	**Edmonton**	**NHL**	**19**	**3**	**10**	**3**	**982**	**58**	**0**	**3.54**	....	....	....	....	....	....	....
	Cape Breton Oilers	AHL	2	1	1	0	119	6	0	3.04	....	....	....	....	....	....	....
1994-95	**Edmonton**	**NHL**	**14**	**2**	**5**	**1**	**601**	**40**	**0**	**3.99**	....	....	....	....	....	....	....
1995-96	**Edmonton**	**NHL**	**7**	**0**	**2**	**0**	**293**	**12**	**0**	**2.46**	....	....	....	....	....	....	....
	Cape Breton Oilers	AHL	31	12	16	0	1699	110	1	3.88	....	....	....	....	....	....	....
1996-97	Manitoba Moose	IHL	58	22	22	5	2945	167	1	3.40	....	....	....	....	....	....	....
1997-98	Manitoba Moose	IHL	51	23	18	4	2736	138	1	3.03	2	0	1	72	4	0	3.30
1998-99	Canada	Nat-Tm	24	6	8	3	989	47	2	2.85	....	....	....	....	....	....	....
	Calgary	**NHL**	**28**	**11**	**9**	**7**	**1663**	**68**	**1**	**2.45**	....	....	....	....	....	....	....
99-2000	**Calgary**	**NHL**	**61**	**25**	**25**	**7**	**3448**	**158**	**5**	**2.75**	....	....	....	....	....	....	....
	Saint John Flames	AHL	2	2	0	0	120	4	0	2.00	....	....	....	....	....	....	....
2000-01	**Calgary**	**NHL**	**49**	**15**	**17**	**10**	**2742**	**106**	**5**	**2.32**	....	....	....	....	....	....	....
2001-02	**St. Louis**	**NHL**	**25**	**9**	**11**	**4**	**1446**	**54**	**2**	**2.24**	**1**	**0**	**0**	**1**	**0**	**0**	**0.00**
2002-03	**St. Louis**	**NHL**	**30**	**12**	**9**	**4**	**1615**	**74**	**2**	**2.75**	....	....	....	....	....	....	....
2003-04	**Columbus**	**NHL**	**21**	**4**	**11**	**1**	**1050**	**59**	**0**	**3.37**	....	....	....	....	....	....	....
	Syracuse Crunch	AHL	3	0	2	1	188	7	1	2.23	....	....	....	....	....	....	....
2004-05	Ak Bars Kazan	Russia	34	....	....	....	1958	61	9	1.87	2	....	....	128	2	1	0.94
	NHL Totals		**254**	**81**	**99**	**37**	**13840**	**629**	**15**	**2.73**	**1**	**0**	**0**	**1**	**0**	**0**	**0.00**

• Scored a goal while with Detroit (OHL), April 20, 1993. Signed as a free agent by **Edmonton**, October 6, 1993. • Scored a goal while with Manitoba (IHL), November 9, 1996. Signed as a free agent by **Calgary**, January 6, 1999. Traded to **St. Louis** by **Calgary** with Daniel Tkaczuk, Sergei Varlamov and Calgary's 9th round choice (Grant Jacobsen) in 2001 Entry Draft for Roman Turek and St. Louis' 4th round choice (Yegor Shastin) in 2001 Entry Draft, June 23, 2001. • Played 6 seconds of playoff game vs. Detroit, May 4, 2002. Signed as a free agent by **Columbus**, June 2, 2003. Signed as a free agent by **Kazan** (Russia), June 19, 2004.

BROCHU, Martin (broh-SHOO, MAHR-tihn)

Goaltender. Catches left. 6', 199 lbs. Born, Anjou, Que., March 10, 1973.

			Regular Season								Playoffs						
Season	Club	League	GP	W	L	T	Mins	GA	SO	Avg	GP	W	L	Mins	GA	SO	Avg
1989-90	Montreal-Bourassa	QAAA	27	11	14	1	1471	103	3	4.20	3	1	2	193	10	1	3.10
1990-91	Granby Bisons	QMJHL	16	6	5	0	622	39	1	3.76	....	....	....	....	....	....	....
1991-92	Granby Bisons	QMJHL	52	15	29	2	2772	278	0	4.72	....	....	....	....	....	....	....
1992-93	Hull Olympiques	QMJHL	29	9	15	1	1453	137	0	5.66	2	0	1	69	7	0	6.07
1993-94	Fredericton	AHL	32	10	11	3	1505	76	2	3.03	....	....	....	....	....	....	....
1994-95	Fredericton	AHL	44	18	18	4	2475	145	0	3.51	....	....	....	....	....	....	....
1995-96	Fredericton	AHL	17	6	8	2	986	70	0	4.26	....	....	....	....	....	....	....
	Wheeling	ECHL	19	10	6	2	1060	51	1	2.89	....	....	....	....	....	....	....
	Portland Pirates	AHL	5	2	2	1	287	15	0	3.14	12	7	4	700	28	*2	*2.40
1996-97	Portland Pirates	AHL	55	23	17	7	2962	150	2	3.04	5	2	3	324	13	0	2.41
1997-98	Portland Pirates	AHL	37	16	14	1	1926	96	2	2.99	6	3	2	296	16	0	3.24
1998-99	**Washington**	**NHL**	**2**	**0**	**2**	**0**	**120**	**6**	**0**	**3.00**	....	....	....	....	....	....	....
	Portland Pirates	AHL	20	6	10	3	1164	57	2	2.94	....	....	....	....	....	....	....
	Utah Grizzlies	IHL	5	1	3	1	298	13	0	2.62	....	....	....	....	....	....	....
99-2000	Portland Pirates	AHL	54	32	15	6	3192	116	4	2.18	2	0	2	80	7	0	5.27
2000-01	Saint John Flames	AHL	55	27	19	5	3049	132	2	2.60	19	*14	4	1148	39	*4	2.04
2001-02	**Vancouver**	**NHL**	**6**	**0**	**3**	**0**	**216**	**15**	**0**	**4.17**	....	....	....	....	....	....	....
	Manitoba Moose	AHL	29	10	14	3	1625	91	1	3.36	....	....	....	....	....	....	....
2002-03	Verdun Dragons	QSPHL	1	1	0	0	60	2	0	2.00	....	....	....	....	....	....	....
	Cherepovets	Russia	8	....	....	....	480	15	2	1.88	....	....	....	....	....	....	....
2003-04	**Pittsburgh**	**NHL**	**1**	**0**	**0**	**0**	**33**	**1**	**0**	**1.82**	....	....	....	....	....	....	....
	Wilkes-Barre	AHL	15	4	9	1	731	31	1	2.55	....	....	....	....	....	....	....
	Wheeling Nailers	ECHL	9	6	2	1	521	23	1	2.65	....	....	....	....	....	....	....
2004-05							DID NOT PLAY										
	NHL Totals		**9**	**0**	**5**	**0**	**369**	**22**	**0**	**3.58**	....	....	....	....	....	....	....

AHL First All-Star Team (2000) • Aldege "Baz" Bastien Memorial Award (Outstanding Goaltender – AHL) (2000) • Les Cunningham Award (MVP – AHL) (2000)

Signed as a free agent by **Montreal**, September 22, 1992. Traded to **Washington** by **Montreal** for future considerations, March 15, 1996. Signed as a free agent by **Calgary**, August 25, 2000. Signed as a free agent by **Minnesota**, July 17, 2001. Claimed by **Vancouver** from **Minnesota** in Waiver Draft, September 28, 2001. Signed as a free agent by **Verdun** (QSPHL), October 22, 2002. Signed as a free agent by **Pittsburgh**, August 22, 2003.

BRODEUR, Martin (broh-DUHR, MAHR-tihn) N.J.

Goaltender. Catches left. 6'2", 210 lbs. Born, Montreal, Que., May 6, 1972.
(New Jersey's 1st choice, 20th overall, in 1990 Entry Draft).

			Regular Season								Playoffs						
Season	Club	League	GP	W	L	T	Mins	GA	SO	Avg	GP	W	L	Mins	GA	SO	Avg
1988-89	Montreal-Bourassa	QAAA	27	13	12	1	1580	98	0	3.72	3	0	3	210	14	0	3.99
1989-90	St-Hyacinthe Laser	QMJHL	42	23	13	2	2333	156	0	4.01	12	5	7	678	46	0	4.07
1990-91	St-Hyacinthe Laser	QMJHL	52	22	24	4	2946	162	2	3.30	4	0	4	232	16	0	4.14
1991-92	St-Hyacinthe Laser	QMJHL	48	27	16	4	2846	161	2	3.39	5	2	3	317	14	0	2.65
	New Jersey	**NHL**	**4**	**2**	**1**	**0**	**179**	**10**	**0**	**3.35**	**1**	**0**	**1**	**32**	**3**	**0**	**5.63**
1992-93	Utica Devils	AHL	32	14	13	5	1952	131	0	4.03	4	1	3	258	18	0	4.19
1993-94	**New Jersey**	**NHL**	**47**	**27**	**11**	**8**	**2625**	**105**	**3**	**2.40**	**17**	**8**	**9**	**1171**	**38**	**1**	**1.95**
1994-95♦	**New Jersey**	**NHL**	**40**	**19**	**11**	**6**	**2184**	**89**	**3**	**2.45**	***20**	***16**	**4**	***1222**	**34**	***3**	***1.67**
1995-96	**New Jersey**	**NHL**	**77**	**34**	**30**	**12**	***4433**	**173**	**6**	**2.34**	....	....	....	....	....	....	....
1996-97	**New Jersey**	**NHL**	**67**	**37**	**14**	**13**	**3838**	**120**	***10**	***1.88**	**10**	**5**	**5**	**659**	**19**	**2**	***1.73**
1997-98	**New Jersey**	**NHL**	**70**	***43**	**17**	**8**	**4128**	**130**	**10**	**1.89**	**6**	**2**	**4**	**366**	**12**	**0**	**1.97**
1998-99	**New Jersey**	**NHL**	***70**	***39**	**21**	**10**	***4239**	**162**	**4**	**2.29**	**7**	**3**	**4**	**425**	**20**	**0**	**2.82**
99-2000♦	**New Jersey**	**NHL**	**72**	***43**	**20**	**8**	**4312**	**161**	**6**	**2.24**	***23**	***16**	**7**	***1450**	**39**	**2**	***1.61**
2000-01	**New Jersey**	**NHL**	**72**	***42**	**17**	**11**	**4297**	**166**	**9**	**2.32**	***25**	**15**	**10**	***1505**	**52**	***4**	**2.07**
2001-02	**New Jersey**	**NHL**	***73**	**38**	**26**	**9**	***4347**	**156**	**4**	**2.15**	**6**	**2**	**4**	**381**	**9**	**1**	**1.42**
	Canada	Olympics	5	*4	0	1	300	9	0	*1.80	....	....	....	....	....	....	....
2002-03♦	**New Jersey**	**NHL**	**73**	***41**	**23**	**9**	**4374**	**147**	***9**	**2.02**	***24**	***16**	**8**	***1491**	**41**	***7**	**1.65**
2003-04	**New Jersey**	**NHL**	***75**	***38**	**26**	**11**	***4555**	**154**	***11**	**2.03**	**5**	**1**	**4**	**298**	**13**	**0**	**2.62**

Season	Club	League	GP	W	L	T	Mins	GA	SO	Avg	GP	W	L	Mins	GA	SO	Avg
2004-05							DID NOT PLAY										
NHL Totals			**740**	**403**	**217**	**105**	**43511**	**1573**	**75**	**2.17**	**144**	**84**	**60**	**9000**	**280**	**20**	**1.87**

QMJHL All-Rookie Team (1990) • QMJHL Second All-Star Team (1992) • NHL All-Rookie Team (1994) • Calder Memorial Trophy (1994) • NHL Second All-Star Team (1997, 1998) • William M. Jennings Trophy (1997) (shared with Mike Dunham) • William M. Jennings Trophy (1998, 2004) • NHL First All-Star Team (2003, 2004) • William M. Jennings Trophy (2003) (tied with Roman Cechmanek/Robert Esche) • Vezina Trophy (2003, 2004)

Played in NHL All-Star Game (1996, 1997, 1998, 1999, 2000, 2001, 2003, 2004)

• Scored a goal in playoffs vs. Montreal, April 17, 1997.

BRODEUR, Mike (broh-DUHR, MIGHK) CHI.

Goaltender. Catches left. 6'2", 170 lbs. Born, Calgary, Alta., March 30, 1983.
(Chicago's 7th choice, 211th overall, in 2003 Entry Draft).

			Regular Season								Playoffs						
Season	**Club**	**League**	**GP**	**W**	**L**	**T**	**Mins**	**GA**	**SO**	**Avg**	**GP**	**W**	**L**	**Mins**	**GA**	**SO**	**Avg**
2000-01	Cgy. AAA Flames	AMHL	21	11	8	3	1231	54	1	2.63	10	6	4	620	31	0	3.00
2001-02	Camrose Kodiaks	AJHL	24	13	9	1	1299	65	1	2.91	....	....	....	....	....	....	....
2002-03	Camrose Kodiaks	AJHL	48	28	16	2	2570	113	2	2.64	21	16	5	1378	48	4	2.09
2003-04	Moose Jaw	WHL	41	23	12	5	2385	84	5	2.11	10	6	4	624	18	1	*1.73
2004-05	Norfolk Admirals	AHL	1	0	1	0	39	4	0	6.17	....	....	....	....	....	....	....
	Greenville Grrrowl	ECHL	35	19	15	1	2081	93	2	2.68	5	2	3	302	10	1	1.98

BROWN, David (BROWN, DAY-vihd) PIT.

Goaltender. Catches left. 6', 185 lbs. Born, Stoney Creek, Ont., February 11, 1985.
(Pittsburgh's 11th choice, 228th overall, in 2004 Entry Draft).

			Regular Season								Playoffs						
Season	**Club**	**League**	**GP**	**W**	**L**	**T**	**Mins**	**GA**	**SO**	**Avg**	**GP**	**W**	**L**	**Mins**	**GA**	**SO**	**Avg**
2002-03	Hamilton Kilty B's	OPJHL	35	....	....	....	....	....	....	3.11	....	....	....	....	....	....	....
2003-04	U. of Notre Dame	CCHA	26	14	7	3	1445	56	5	2.32	....	....	....	....	....	....	....
2004-05	U. of Notre Dame	CCHA	15	2	10	1	767	55	0	4.30	....	....	....	....	....	....	....

BROWN, Mike (BROWN, MIGHK) BOS.

Goaltender. Catches left. 6', 177 lbs. Born, Syracuse, NY, March 4, 1985.
(Boston's 7th choice, 153rd overall, in 2003 Entry Draft).

			Regular Season								Playoffs						
Season	**Club**	**League**	**GP**	**W**	**L**	**T**	**Mins**	**GA**	**SO**	**Avg**	**GP**	**W**	**L**	**Mins**	**GA**	**SO**	**Avg**
2001-02	Baldwinsville Bees	High-NY	7	....	....	....	420	8	4	0.86	5	3	2	300	6	1	1.20
2002-03	Saginaw Spirit	OHL	39	8	23	3	2186	134	0	3.68	....	....	....	....	....	....	....
2003-04	Saginaw Spirit	OHL	51	14	32	3	2886	156	4	3.24	....	....	....	....	....	....	....
2004-05	Saginaw Spirit	OHL	26	7	17	1	1482	91	0	3.68	....	....	....	....	....	....	....
	Owen Sound	OHL	33	17	11	4	1956	81	3	2.48	8	4	4	485	19	*2	2.35

BRUST, Barry (BRUHST, BAIR-ree) L.A.

Goaltender. Catches left. 6'2", 210 lbs. Born, Swan River, Man., August 8, 1983.
(Minnesota's 4th choice, 73rd overall, in 2002 Entry Draft).

			Regular Season								Playoffs						
Season	**Club**	**League**	**GP**	**W**	**L**	**T**	**Mins**	**GA**	**SO**	**Avg**	**GP**	**W**	**L**	**Mins**	**GA**	**SO**	**Avg**
99-2000	Swan Valley	MJHL	19	10	9	0	1140	67	0	3.50	....	....	....	....	....	....	....
2000-01	Spokane Chiefs	WHL	16	4	6	1	777	42	0	3.24	....	....	....	....	....	....	....
2001-02	Spokane Chiefs	WHL	60	28	21	10	3540	152	1	2.58	11	6	5	677	23	0	2.04
2002-03	Spokane Chiefs	WHL	*59	22	31	4	*3385	194	0	3.44	11	4	7	722	37	0	3.07
2003-04	Spokane Chiefs	WHL	27	10	13	2	1505	75	0	2.99	....	....	....	....	....	....	....
	Calgary Hitmen	WHL	25	12	8	3	1448	54	2	2.24	7	3	4	457	15	2	1.97
2004-05	Reading Royals	ECHL	42	27	9	4	2413	79	4	1.96	8	4	4	481	14	2	1.74

WHL West First All-Star Team (2002)

Signed as a free agent by **Los Angeles**, June 10, 2004.

BRYZGALOV, Ilya (breez-GAH-lahf, ihl-YUH) ANA.

Goaltender. Catches left. 6'3", 198 lbs. Born, Togliatti, USSR, June 22, 1980.
(Anaheim's 2nd choice, 44th overall, in 2000 Entry Draft).

			Regular Season								Playoffs						
Season	**Club**	**League**	**GP**	**W**	**L**	**T**	**Mins**	**GA**	**SO**	**Avg**	**GP**	**W**	**L**	**Mins**	**GA**	**SO**	**Avg**
1997-98	Lada Togliatti 2	Russia-3	8	....	....	....	480	28	....	3.50	....	....	....	....	....	....	....
1998-99	Lada Togliatti 2	Russia-4	20	....	....	....	1200	43	....	2.15	....	....	....	....	....	....	....
99-2000	Spartak Moscow	Russia-2	9	....	....	....	500	21	....	2.52	....	....	....	....	....	....	....
	Lada Togliatti	Russia	14	....	....	....	796	18	3	1.36	7	....	....	407	10	1	1.47
2000-01	Lada Togliatti	Russia	34	....	....	....	1992	61	*8	1.84	5	....	....	249	8	0	1.93
2001-02	**Anaheim**	**NHL**	**1**	**0**	**0**	**0**	**32**	**1**	**0**	**1.88**	....	....	....	....	....	....	....
	Cincinnati	AHL	45	20	16	4	2399	99	4	2.48	....	....	....	....	....	....	....
	Russia	Olympics					DID NOT PLAY – SPARE GOALTENDER										
2002-03	Cincinnati	AHL	54	12	26	9	3020	142	1	2.82	....	....	....	....	....	....	....
2003-04	**Anaheim**	**NHL**	**1**	**1**	**0**	**0**	**60**	**2**	**0**	**2.00**	....	....	....	....	....	....	....
	Cincinnati	AHL	*64	27	25	10	*3748	145	6	2.32	9	5	4	536	27	1	3.02
2004-05	Cincinnati	AHL	36	17	13	1	2007	87	4	2.60	7	3	3	314	13	0	2.48
NHL Totals			**2**	**1**	**0**	**0**	**92**	**3**	**0**	**1.96**	....	....	....	....	....	....	....

BUDAJ, Peter (BOO-digh, PEE-tuhr) COL.

Goaltender. Catches left. 6'1", 200 lbs. Born, Bystrica, Czech., September 18, 1982.
(Colorado's 1st choice, 63rd overall, in 2001 Entry Draft).

			Regular Season								Playoffs						
Season	**Club**	**League**	**GP**	**W**	**L**	**T**	**Mins**	**GA**	**SO**	**Avg**	**GP**	**W**	**L**	**Mins**	**GA**	**SO**	**Avg**
99-2000	St. Michael's	OHL	34	6	18	1	1676	112	1	4.01	....	....	....	....	....	....	....
2000-01	St. Michael's	OHL	37	17	12	3	1996	95	3	2.86	11	6	4	621	26	1	2.51
2001-02	St. Michael's	OHL	42	26	9	5	2329	89	2	*2.29	12	5	6	620	34	*1	3.29
2002-03	Hershey Bears	AHL	28	10	10	2	1467	65	2	2.66	1	0	0	6	2	0	20.81
2003-04	Hershey Bears	AHL	46	17	20	6	2574	120	3	2.80	....	....	....	....	....	....	....
2004-05	Hershey Bears	AHL	59	29	25	2	3356	148	5	2.65	....	....	....	....	....	....	....

OHL Second All-Star Team (2002)

BURKE, Sean (BUHRK, SHAWN) T.B.

Goaltender. Catches left. 6'4", 211 lbs. Born, Windsor, Ont., January 29, 1967.
(New Jersey's 2nd choice, 24th overall, in 1985 Entry Draft).

			Regular Season								Playoffs						
Season	**Club**	**League**	**GP**	**W**	**L**	**T**	**Mins**	**GA**	**SO**	**Avg**	**GP**	**W**	**L**	**Mins**	**GA**	**SO**	**Avg**
1983-84	St. Mike's B's	MTJHL	25	....	....	....	1482	120	0	4.86	....	....	....	....	....	....	....
1984-85	Toronto Marlboros	OHL	49	25	21	3	2987	211	0	4.24	5	1	3	266	25	0	5.64
1985-86	Toronto Marlboros	OHL	47	16	27	3	2840	233	0	4.92	4	0	4	238	24	0	6.05
1986-87	Canada	Nat-Tm	42	27	13	2	2550	130	0	3.05	....	....	....	....	....	....	....
1987-88	Canada	Nat-Tm	37	19	9	2	1962	92	1	2.81	....	....	....	....	....	....	....
	Canada	Olympics	4	1	2	1	238	12	0	3.02	....	....	....	....	....	....	....
	New Jersey	**NHL**	**13**	**10**	**1**	**0**	**689**	**35**	**1**	**3.05**	**17**	**9**	**8**	**1001**	**57**	***1**	**3.42**
1988-89	**New Jersey**	**NHL**	**62**	**22**	**31**	**9**	**3590**	**230**	**3**	**3.84**	....	....	....	....	....	....	....
1989-90	**New Jersey**	**NHL**	**52**	**22**	**22**	**6**	**2914**	**175**	**0**	**3.60**	**2**	**0**	**2**	**125**	**8**	**0**	**3.84**
1990-91	**New Jersey**	**NHL**	**35**	**8**	**12**	**8**	**1870**	**112**	**0**	**3.59**	....	....	....	....	....	....	....
1991-92	Canada	Nat-Tm	31	18	6	4	1721	75	1	2.61	....	....	....	....	....	....	....
	Canada	Olympics	7	5	2	0	429	17	0	2.37	....	....	....	....	....	....	....
	San Diego Gulls	IHL	7	4	2	1	424	17	0	2.41	3	0	3	160	13	0	4.88
1992-93	**Hartford**	**NHL**	**50**	**16**	**27**	**3**	**2656**	**184**	**0**	**4.16**	....	....	....	....	....	....	....
1993-94	**Hartford**	**NHL**	**47**	**17**	**24**	**5**	**2750**	**137**	**2**	**2.99**	....	....	....	....	....	....	....
1994-95	**Hartford**	**NHL**	**42**	**17**	**19**	**4**	**2418**	**108**	**0**	**2.68**	....	....	....	....	....	....	....
1995-96	**Hartford**	**NHL**	**66**	**28**	**28**	**6**	**3669**	**190**	**4**	**3.11**	....	....	....	....	....	....	....
1996-97	**Hartford**	**NHL**	**51**	**22**	**22**	**6**	**2985**	**134**	**4**	**2.69**	....	....	....	....	....	....	....
1997-98	**Carolina**	**NHL**	**25**	**7**	**11**	**5**	**1415**	**66**	**1**	**2.80**	....	....	....	....	....	....	....
	Vancouver	**NHL**	**16**	**2**	**9**	**4**	**838**	**49**	**0**	**3.51**	....	....	....	....	....	....	....
	Philadelphia	**NHL**	**11**	**7**	**3**	**0**	**632**	**27**	**1**	**2.56**	**5**	**1**	**4**	**283**	**17**	**0**	**3.60**
1998-99	**Florida**	**NHL**	**59**	**21**	**24**	**14**	**3402**	**151**	**3**	**2.66**	....	....	....	....	....	....	....
99-2000	**Florida**	**NHL**	**7**	**2**	**5**	**0**	**418**	**18**	**0**	**2.58**	....	....	....	....	....	....	....
	Phoenix	**NHL**	**35**	**17**	**14**	**3**	**2074**	**88**	**3**	**2.55**	**5**	**1**	**4**	**296**	**16**	**0**	**3.24**
2000-01	**Phoenix**	**NHL**	**62**	**25**	**22**	**13**	**3644**	**138**	**4**	**2.27**	....	....	....	....	....	....	....
2001-02	**Phoenix**	**NHL**	**60**	**33**	**21**	**6**	**3587**	**137**	**5**	**2.29**	**5**	**1**	**4**	**297**	**13**	**0**	**2.63**
2002-03	**Phoenix**	**NHL**	**22**	**12**	**6**	**2**	**1248**	**44**	**2**	**2.12**	....	....	....	....	....	....	....
2003-04	**Phoenix**	**NHL**	**32**	**10**	**15**	**5**	**1795**	**84**	**1**	**2.81**	....	....	....	....	....	....	....
	Philadelphia	**NHL**	**15**	**6**	**5**	**2**	**825**	**35**	**1**	**2.55**	**1**	**0**	**0**	**40**	**1**	**0**	**1.50**
2004-05							DID NOT PLAY										
NHL Totals			**762**	**304**	**321**	**101**	**43419**	**2142**	**35**	**2.96**	**35**	**12**	**22**	**2042**	**112**	**1**	**3.29**

Played in NHL All-Star Game (1989, 2001, 2002)

Traded to **Hartford** by **New Jersey** with Eric Weinrich for Bobby Holik and Hartford's 2nd round choice (Jay Pandolfo) in 1993 Entry Draft, August 28, 1992. Transferred to **Carolina** after **Hartford** franchise relocated, June 25, 1997. Traded to **Vancouver** by **Carolina** with Geoff Sanderson and Enrico Ciccone for Kirk McLean and Martin Gelinas, January 3, 1998. Traded to **Philadelphia** by **Vancouver** for Garth Snow, March 4, 1998. Signed as a free agent by **Florida**, September 12, 1998. Traded to **Phoenix** by **Florida** with Florida's 5th round choice (Nate Kiser) in 2000 Entry Draft for Mikhail Shtalenkov and Phoenix's 4th round choice (Chris Eade) in 2000 Entry Draft, November 18, 1999. Traded to **Philadelphia** by **Phoenix** with Branko Radivojevic and Ben Eager for Mike Comrie, February 9, 2004. Signed as a free agent by **Tampa Bay**, August 9, 2005.

CARON, Sebastian (KAIR-aw, suh-BAS-tee-yeh) PIT.

Goaltender. Catches left. 6'1", 170 lbs. Born, Amqui, Que., June 25, 1980.
(Pittsburgh's 4th choice, 86th overall, in 1999 Entry Draft).

			Regular Season								Playoffs						
Season	**Club**	**League**	**GP**	**W**	**L**	**T**	**Mins**	**GA**	**SO**	**Avg**	**GP**	**W**	**L**	**Mins**	**GA**	**SO**	**Avg**
1997-98	TGV Pentagone	QAHA	17	....	....	....	762	48	1	2.84	....	....	....	....	....	....	....
1998-99	Rimouski Oceanic	QMJHL	30	13	10	3	1570	85	0	3.25	2	1	0	68	0	0	0.00
99-2000	Rimouski Oceanic	QMJHL	54	*38	11	3	3040	179	1	3.53	14	*12	2	828	50	0	3.62
2000-01	Wilkes-Barre	AHL	30	12	14	3	1746	103	4	3.54	....	....	....	....	....	....	....
2001-02	Wilkes-Barre	AHL	46	14	22	8	2671	139	1	3.12	....	....	....	....	....	....	....
2002-03	**Pittsburgh**	**NHL**	**24**	**7**	**14**	**2**	**1408**	**62**	**2**	**2.64**	....	....	....	....	....	....	....
	Wilkes-Barre	AHL	27	12	14	1	1561	81	1	3.11	....	....	....	....	....	....	....
2003-04	**Pittsburgh**	**NHL**	**40**	**9**	**24**	**5**	**2213**	**138**	**1**	**3.74**	....	....	....	....	....	....	....
	Wilkes-Barre	AHL	14	7	3	4	811	26	2	1.92	7	3	4	395	23	0	3.50
2004-05	Saguenay Fjord	QNAHL					STATISTICS NOT AVAILABLE										
NHL Totals			**64**	**16**	**38**	**7**	**3621**	**200**	**3**	**3.31**	....	....	....	....	....	....	....

Memorial Cup Tournament All-Star Team (2000) • Hap Emms Memorial Trophy (Memorial Cup Tournament Top Goaltender) (2000) • NHL All-Rookie Team (2003)

Signed as a free agent by **Saguenay** (QNAHL), September 21, 2004.

CASSIVI, Frederic (KASS-ih-vee, FREHD-uhr-ihk) WSH.

Goaltender. Catches left. 6'4", 215 lbs. Born, Sorel, Que., June 12, 1975.
(Ottawa's 7th choice, 210th overall, in 1994 Entry Draft).

			Regular Season								Playoffs						
Season	**Club**	**League**	**GP**	**W**	**L**	**T**	**Mins**	**GA**	**SO**	**Avg**	**GP**	**W**	**L**	**Mins**	**GA**	**SO**	**Avg**
1991-92	Abitibi Forestiers	QAAA	22	5	17	0	1320	106	0	4.84	3	1	2	180	15	0	5.06
1992-93							STATISTICS NOT AVAILABLE										
1993-94	St-Hyacinthe Laser	QMJHL	35	15	13	3	1751	127	1	4.35	....	....	....	....	....	....	....
1994-95	Halifax	QMJHL	24	9	12	1	1362	105	0	4.63	....	....	....	....	....	....	....
	St-Jean Lynx	QMJHL	19	12	6	0	1021	55	1	3.23	5	2	3	258	18	0	4.19
1995-96	Thunder Bay	ColHL	12	6	4	2	715	51	0	4.28	....	....	....	....	....	....	....
	P.E.I. Senators	AHL	41	20	14	3	2347	128	1	3.27	5	2	3	317	24	0	4.54
1996-97	Syracuse Crunch	AHL	55	23	22	8	3069	164	2	3.21	1	0	1	60	3	0	3.01
1997-98	Worcester IceCats	AHL	45	20	22	2	2593	140	1	3.24	6	3	3	326	18	0	3.31
1998-99	Cincinnati	IHL	44	21	17	2	2418	123	1	3.05	3	1	2	139	6	0	2.59
99-2000	Hershey Bears	AHL	31	14	9	3	1554	78	1	3.01	2	0	1	63	5	0	4.75
2000-01	Hershey Bears	AHL	49	17	24	3	2620	124	2	2.84	9	7	2	564	14	1	*1.49
2001-02	Hershey Bears	AHL	21	6	10	4	1201	50	0	2.50	....	....	....	....	....	....	....
	Atlanta	**NHL**	**6**	**2**	**3**	**0**	**307**	**17**	**0**	**3.32**	....	....	....	....	....	....	....
	Chicago Wolves	AHL	12	6	2	1	625	26	0	2.50	5	2	2	264	11	0	2.50
2002-03	**Atlanta**	**NHL**	**2**	**1**	**1**	**0**	**123**	**11**	**0**	**5.37**	....	....	....	....	....	....	....
	Chicago Wolves	AHL	21	10	8	1	1171	62	0	3.18	2	0	2	90	3	0	2.00
2003-04	Chicago Wolves	AHL	34	15	12	5	1911	82	1	2.57	....	....	....	....	....	....	....
2004-05	Cincinnati	AHL	46	25	18	2	2549	88	*10	2.07	8	2	4	444	21	0	2.84
NHL Totals			**8**	**3**	**4**	**0**	**430**	**28**	**0**	**3.91**	....	....	....	....	....	....	....

Signed as a free agent by **Colorado**, August 17, 1999. Traded to **Atlanta** by **Colorado** for Brett Clark, January 24, 2002. Signed as a free agent by **Cincinnati** (AHL), September 28, 2004.

CECHMANEK, Roman (chehkh-MAN-ehk, ROH-muhn)

Goaltender. Catches left. 6'3", 187 lbs. Born, Gottwaldov, Czech., March 2, 1971.
(Philadelphia's 3rd choice, 171st overall, in 2000 Entry Draft).

			Regular Season								Playoffs						
Season	**Club**	**League**	**GP**	**W**	**L**	**T**	**Mins**	**GA**	**SO**	**Avg**	**GP**	**W**	**L**	**Mins**	**GA**	**SO**	**Avg**
1988-89	TJ Gottwaldov	Czech	1	0	0	0	13	0	0	0.00	....	....	....	....	....	....	....
1989-90	TJ Zlin	Czech	2	0	0	0	89	5	0	3.37	....	....	....	....	....	....	....
1990-91	Dukla Jihlava	Czech	9	....	....	....	447	18	2	2.42	....	....	....	....	....	....	....
1991-92	DS Olomouc	Czech	13	....	....	....	731	54	0	4.43	....	....	....	....	....	....	....
	AC ZPS Zlin	Czech	2	0	1	0	67	8	0	7.73	....	....	....	....	....	....	....
1992-93	Banik Hodonin	Czech-2					STATISTICS NOT AVAILABLE										
1993-94	Zbrojovka Vsetin	CzRep-2					STATISTICS NOT AVAILABLE										
1994-95	HC Dadak Vsetin	CzRep	41	....	....	....	2413	98	5	2.44	11	....	....	619	23	1	2.23
1995-96	HC Petra Vsetin	CzRep	36	....	....	....	2142	77	4	2.16	13	....	....	783	17	2	1.30
1996-97	HC Petra Vsetin	CzRep	48	....	....	....	2762	98	3	2.13	10	....	....	602	11	2	1.10
1997-98	HC Petra Vsetin	CzRep	41	....	....	....	2306	76	....	*1.98	10	....	....	600	16	1	*1.60
1998-99	HC Slovnaft Vsetin	CzRep	45	....	....	....	2696	77	5	*1.71	12	8	4	*747	23	1	1.85
99-2000	Vsetin	CzRep	37	....	....	....	2141	88	0	2.47	9	5	4	545	15	3	1.65
2000-01	**Philadelphia**	**NHL**	**59**	**35**	**15**	**6**	**3431**	**115**	**10**	**2.01**	**6**	**2**	**4**	**347**	**18**	**0**	**3.11**
	Philadelphia	AHL	3	1	1	0	160	3	0	1.12	....	....	....	....	....	....	....
2001-02	**Philadelphia**	**NHL**	**46**	**24**	**13**	**6**	**2603**	**89**	**4**	**2.05**	**4**	**1**	**3**	**227**	**7**	**1**	**1.85**
	Czech Republic	Olympics					DID NOT PLAY – SPARE GOALTENDER										
2002-03	**Philadelphia**	**NHL**	**58**	**33**	**15**	**10**	**3350**	**102**	**6**	**1.83**	**13**	**6**	**7**	**867**	**31**	**2**	**2.15**
2003-04	**Los Angeles**	**NHL**	**49**	**18**	**21**	**6**	**2701**	**113**	**5**	**2.51**	....	....	....	....	....	....	....
2004-05	HC Vsetin	CzRep	35	....	....	....	1974	88	3	2.67	....	....	....	....	....	....	....
NHL Totals			**212**	**110**	**64**	**28**	**12085**	**419**	**25**	**2.08**	**23**	**9**	**14**	**1441**	**56**	**3**	**2.33**

NHL Second All-Star Team (2001) • William M. Jennings Trophy (2003) (shared with Robert Esche) (tied with Martin Brodeur)

Played in NHL All-Star Game (2001)

Traded to **Los Angeles** by **Philadelphia** for Los Angeles' 2nd round choice (later traded to Chicago – Chicago selected Bryan Bickell) in 2004 Entry Draft, May 28, 2003. Signed as a free agent by **Vsetin** (CzRep), September 17, 2004.

CENTOMO, Sebastien (sehn-TOH-moh, suh-BAS-tee-yeh)

Goaltender. Catches right. 6'1", 200 lbs. Born, Montreal, Que., March 26, 1981.

			Regular Season								Playoffs						
Season	Club	League	GP	W	L	T	Mins	GA	SO	Avg	GP	W	L	Mins	GA	SO	Avg
1996-97	Laval-Laurentides	QAAA	27	10	10	2	1298	102	0	4.71	5	2	3	348	18	0	3.10
1997-98	Laval-Laurentides	QAAA	30	16	11	2	1696	87	0	2.86	....	....	....	....	....	....	....
1998-99	Rouyn-Noranda	QMJHL	32	14	9	4	1658	104	1	3.76	2	0	1	28	5	0	10.71
99-2000	Rouyn-Noranda	QMJHL	50	24	17	3	2758	160	1	3.48	11	6	5	695	41	0	3.54
2000-01	Rouyn-Noranda	QMJHL	46	25	14	4	2599	158	3	3.65	1	0	1	60	4	0	4.00
2001-02	**Toronto**	**NHL**	**1**	**0**	**0**	**0**	**40**	**3**	**0**	**4.50**	....	....	....	....	....	....	....
	Memphis	CHL	19	16	1	0	1035	36	1	2.09	....	....	....	....	....	....	....
	St. John's	AHL	25	12	7	4	1429	60	2	2.52	11	4	6	691	29	2	2.52
2002-03	Greensboro	ECHL	10	3	3	3	565	24	1	2.55	....	....	....	....	....	....	....
	St. John's	AHL	19	7	10	1	1045	68	0	3.90	....	....	....	....	....	....	....
2003-04	St. John's	AHL	39	13	17	4	2097	110	2	3.15	....	....	....	....	....	....	....
2004-05	Las Vegas	ECHL	31	13	12	4	1845	80	2	2.60	....	....	....	....	....	....	....
	Long Beach	ECHL	9	6	1	1	460	17	1	2.22	6	3	3	378	13	0	2.06
	NHL Totals		**1**	**0**	**0**	**0**	**40**	**3**	**0**	**4.50**	....	....	....	....	....	....	....

CHL Rookie of the Year (2002)

Signed as a free agent by **Toronto**, September 10, 1999. Signed as a free agent by **Calgary**, September 7, 2004.

CEY, Morgan (SAY, MOHR-guhn) T.B.

Goaltender. Catches left. 6'3", 177 lbs. Born, Wilkie, Sask., October 27, 1981.

			Regular Season								Playoffs						
Season	Club	League	GP	W	L	T	Mins	GA	SO	Avg	GP	W	L	Mins	GA	SO	Avg
2000-01	Flin Flon Bombers	SJHL	53	*35	16	0	*3139	137	3	2.62	....	....	....	....	....	....	....
2001-02	U. of Notre Dame	CCHA	35	15	14	3	2027	92	2	2.72	....	....	....	....	....	....	....
2002-03	U. of Notre Dame	CCHA	36	15	15	6	2136	102	2	2.87	....	....	....	....	....	....	....
2003-04	U. of Notre Dame	CCHA	16	5	7	1	820	33	2	2.42	....	....	....	....	....	....	....
2004-05	U. of Notre Dame	CCHA	27	3	17	5	1483	74	0	2.99	....	....	....	....	....	....	....

Signed as a free agent by **Tampa Bay**, August 26, 2005.

CHARPENTIER, Sebastien (shahr-PUHNT-yay, suh-BAS-tee-yeh)

Goaltender. Catches left. 5'9", 177 lbs. Born, Drummondville, Que., April 18, 1977.
(Washington's 4th choice, 93rd overall, in 1995 Entry Draft).

			Regular Season								Playoffs						
Season	Club	League	GP	W	L	T	Mins	GA	SO	Avg	GP	W	L	Mins	GA	SO	Avg
1991-92	Drummondville	QAHA	14	....	....	....	840	34	2	2.42	....	....	....	....	....	....	....
1992-93	Drummondville	QAHA	20	....	....	....	1215	37	*7	*1.80	....	....	....	....	....	....	....
1993-94	Magog	QAAA	24	14	5	1	1443	75	1	3.16	....	....	....	....	....	....	....
1994-95	Laval Titan	QMJHL	41	25	12	1	2152	99	2	2.76	16	9	4	886	45	0	3.05
1995-96	Laval Titan	QMJHL	18	4	10	0	938	97	0	6.20	....	....	....	....	....	....	....
	Val-d'Or Foreurs	QMJHL	33	21	9	1	1906	87	1	2.74	13	7	5	740	45	0	3.64
1996-97	Shawinigan	QMJHL	*62	*37	17	4	*3480	177	1	3.05	4	2	1	196	13	0	3.98
1997-98	Portland Pirates	AHL	4	1	3	0	229	10	0	2.61	....	....	....	....	....	....	....
	Hampton Roads	ECHL	43	20	16	6	2388	114	0	2.86	18	*14	4	*1183	38	1	*1.93
1998-99	Quad City Mallards	UHL	6	0	0	0	4	0	0	0.00	....	....	....	....	....	....	....
	Portland Pirates	AHL	3	0	3	0	180	10	0	3.34	....	....	....	....	....	....	....
99-2000	Portland Pirates	AHL	18	10	4	3	1041	48	0	2.77	3	1	1	183	9	0	2.96
2000-01	Portland Pirates	AHL	34	16	16	1	1978	113	1	3.43	1	0	1	102	3	0	1.76
2001-02	**Washington**	**NHL**	**2**	**1**	**1**	**0**	**122**	**5**	**0**	**2.46**	....	....	....	....	....	....	....
	Portland Pirates	AHL	49	20	18	10	2941	131	3	2.67	....	....	....	....	....	....	....
2002-03	**Washington**	**NHL**	**17**	**5**	**7**	**1**	**859**	**40**	**0**	**2.79**	....	....	....	....	....	....	....
	Portland Pirates	AHL	12	3	7	2	727	28	2	2.31	....	....	....	....	....	....	....
2003-04	**Washington**	**NHL**	**7**	**0**	**6**	**0**	**369**	**21**	**0**	**3.41**	....	....	....	....	....	....	....
2004-05							DID NOT PLAY										
	NHL Totals		**26**	**6**	**14**	**1**	**1350**	**66**	**0**	**2.93**	....	....	....	....	....	....	....

ECHL Playoff MVP (1998)

• Missed majority of 2003-04 season recovering from leg injury suffered in practice, November 3, 2003.

CHIODO, Andy (KEE-aw-doh, AN-dee) PIT.

Goaltender. Catches left. 5'11", 192 lbs. Born, Toronto, Ont., April 25, 1983.
(Pittsburgh's 8th choice, 199th overall, in 2003 Entry Draft).

			Regular Season								Playoffs						
Season	Club	League	GP	W	L	T	Mins	GA	SO	Avg	GP	W	L	Mins	GA	SO	Avg
1998-99	Wexford Raiders	OPJHL	26	....	....	....	1519	105	0	4.05	....	....	....	....	....	....	....
99-2000	Wexford Raiders	OPJHL	24	....	....	....	1389	89	0	3.84	....	....	....	....	....	....	....
2000-01	St. Michael's	OHL	38	18	12	5	2069	86	*4	2.49	9	2	6	479	30	0	3.76
2001-02	St. Michael's	OHL	33	14	10	3	1743	79	2	2.72	7	3	1	288	17	*1	3.54
2002-03	St. Michael's	OHL	57	26	18	6	3065	154	3	3.01	18	10	8	1021	56	1	3.29
2003-04	**Pittsburgh**	**NHL**	**8**	**3**	**4**	**1**	**486**	**28**	**0**	**3.46**	....	....	....	....	....	....	....
	Wilkes-Barre	AHL	44	18	19	2	2448	98	4	2.40	18	9	7	1048	38	*3	2.18
	Wheeling Nailers	ECHL	2	0	2	0	86	9	0	6.26	....	....	....	....	....	....	....
2004-05	Wheeling Nailers	ECHL	22	9	10	2	1259	47	1	2.24	....	....	....	....	....	....	....
	Wilkes-Barre	AHL	14	5	7	1	788	43	2	3.27	9	5	4	556	23	1	2.48
	NHL Totals		**8**	**3**	**4**	**1**	**486**	**28**	**0**	**3.46**	....	....	....	....	....	....	....

• Re-entered NHL Entry Draft. Originally NY Islanders' 3rd choice, 166th overall, in 2001 Entry Draft.

OHL First All-Star Team (2003)

CHOUINARD, Mathieu (SHWEE-nuhr, MA-tyew)

Goaltender. Catches left. 6'1", 211 lbs. Born, Laval, Que., April 11, 1980.
(Ottawa's 2nd choice, 45th overall, in 2000 Entry Draft).

			Regular Season								Playoffs						
Season	Club	League	GP	W	L	T	Mins	GA	SO	Avg	GP	W	L	Mins	GA	SO	Avg
1995-96	Amos Foresters	QAAA	31	14	14	1	1613	114	1	4.24	1	1	2	190	11	0	3.48
1996-97	Shawinigan	QMJHL	17	4	7	1	795	51	0	3.85	4	1	3	264	15	0	3.41
1997-98	Shawinigan	QMJHL	55	*32	18	3	3055	142	2	2.79	6	2	4	348	24	0	4.14
1998-99	Shawinigan	QMJHL	56	36	16	4	3288	150	*5	2.74	6	2	4	392	27	0	4.13
99-2000	Shawinigan	QMJHL	*59	32	20	5	*3339	186	4	3.34	13	7	6	769	41	0	3.20
2000-01	Grand Rapids	IHL	28	17	7	1	1567	69	1	2.64	3	1	1	135	4	0	1.78
2001-02	Grand Rapids	AHL	25	11	12	1	1404	58	2	2.48	....	....	....	....	....	....	....
2002-03	Peoria Rivermen	ECHL	15	12	2	0	820	29	3	2.12	....	....	....	....	....	....	....
	Binghamton	AHL	4	2	0	0	152	5	0	1.98	1	0	0	2	0	0	0.00
2003-04	**Los Angeles**	**NHL**	**1**	**0**	**0**	**0**	**3**	**0**	**0**	**0.00**	....	....	....	....	....	....	....
	Manchester	AHL	22	10	6	0	1093	41	4	2.25	....	....	....	....	....	....	....
	Reading Royals	ECHL	3	1	1	1	185	7	0	2.27	....	....	....	....	....	....	....
2004-05	Cincinnati	AHL	3	1	1	0	153	4	1	1.57	....	....	....	....	....	....	....
	San Diego Gulls	ECHL	27	11	9	3	1453	73	1	3.01	....	....	....	....	....	....	....
	Peoria Rivermen	ECHL	1	0	1	0	58	2	0	2.07	....	....	....	....	....	....	....
	NHL Totals		**1**	**0**	**0**	**0**	**3**	**0**	**0**	**0.00**	....	....	....	....	....	....	....

• Re-entered NHL Entry Draft. Originally Ottawa's 1st choice, 15th overall, in 1998 Entry Draft.

QMJHL First All-Star Team (1999) • Harry "Hap" Holmes Memorial Award (fewest goals against – AHL) (2002) (shared with Martin Prusek and Simon Lajeunesse)

Signed as a free agent by **Los Angeles**, July 7, 2003. Signed as a free agent by **San Diego** (ECHL), September 29, 2004. Signed as a free agent by **Peoria** (ECHL), March 27, 2005.

CHURCHILL, Jason (CHUHR-chihl, JAY-suhn) S.J.

Goaltender. Catches left. 6'3", 184 lbs. Born, St. John's, Nfld., November 5, 1985.
(San Jose's 4th choice, 129th overall, in 2004 Entry Draft).

			Regular Season								Playoffs						
Season	Club	League	GP	W	L	T	Mins	GA	SO	Avg	GP	W	L	Mins	GA	SO	Avg
2002-03	Antigonish	MJrHL	36	16	18	1	2050	137	1	4.01	....	....	....	....	....	....	....
	Halifax	QMJHL	4	1	0	1	160	9	0	3.39	....	....	....	....	....	....	....
2003-04	Halifax	QMJHL	53	15	28	4	2894	180	2	3.73	....	....	....	....	....	....	....
2004-05	Halifax	QMJHL	54	28	18	8	3129	135	4	2.59	2	0	1	99	9	0	5.45

CLEMMENSEN, Scott (KLEH-mehn-sehn, SKAWT) N.J.

Goaltender. Catches left. 6'3", 205 lbs. Born, Des Moines, IA, July 23, 1977.
(New Jersey's 7th choice, 215th overall, in 1997 Entry Draft).

			Regular Season								Playoffs						
Season	Club	League	GP	W	L	T	Mins	GA	SO	Avg	GP	W	L	Mins	GA	SO	Avg
1995-96	Dubuque	USHL	20	10	7	1	1082	62	0	3.44	....	....	....	....	....	....	....
1996-97	Des Moines	USHL	36	22	9	2	2042	111	1	3.26	4	1	2	200	9	1	2.70
1997-98	Boston College	H-East	37	24	9	4	2205	102	*4	2.78	....	....	....	....	....	....	....
1998-99	Boston College	H-East	*42	26	12	4	*2507	120	1	2.87	....	....	....	....	....	....	....
99-2000	Boston College	H-East	29	19	7	0	1610	59	*5	2.20	....	....	....	....	....	....	....
2000-01	Boston College	H-East	*39	*30	7	2	*2312	82	3	2.13	....	....	....	....	....	....	....
2001-02	**New Jersey**	**NHL**	**2**	**0**	**0**	**0**	**20**	**1**	**0**	**3.00**	....	....	....	....	....	....	....
	Albany River Rats	AHL	29	5	19	4	1677	92	0	3.29	....	....	....	....	....	....	....
2002-03	Albany River Rats	AHL	47	12	24	8	2694	119	1	2.65	....	....	....	....	....	....	....
2003-04	**New Jersey**	**NHL**	**4**	**3**	**1**	**0**	**238**	**4**	**2**	**1.01**	....	....	....	....	....	....	....
	Albany River Rats	AHL	22	5	12	4	1309	67	0	3.07	....	....	....	....	....	....	....
2004-05	Albany River Rats	AHL	46	13	25	5	2645	124	2	2.81	....	....	....	....	....	....	....
	NHL Totals		**6**	**3**	**1**	**0**	**258**	**5**	**2**	**1.16**	....	....	....	....	....	....	....

NCAA Championship All-Tournament Team (2001)

CLOUTIER, Dan (KLOO-tyay, DAN) VAN.

Goaltender. Catches left. 6'1", 185 lbs. Born, Mont-Laurier, Que., April 22, 1976.
(NY Rangers' 1st choice, 26th overall, in 1994 Entry Draft).

			Regular Season								Playoffs						
Season	Club	League	GP	W	L	T	Mins	GA	SO	Avg	GP	W	L	Mins	GA	SO	Avg
1991-92	St. Thomas Stars	OJHL-B	14	....	....	....	823	80	0	5.83	....	....	....	....	....	....	....
1992-93	Timmins	NOJHA	5	4	0	0	255	10	0	2.35	....	....	....	....	....	....	....
	Sault Ste. Marie	OHL	12	4	6	0	572	44	0	4.62	4	1	2	231	12	0	3.12
1993-94	Sault Ste. Marie	OHL	55	28	14	6	2934	174	*2	3.56	14	*10	4	833	52	0	3.75
1994-95	Sault Ste. Marie	OHL	45	15	26	2	2518	185	1	4.41	....	....	....	....	....	....	....
1995-96	Sault Ste. Marie	OHL	13	9	3	0	641	43	0	4.02	....	....	....	....	....	....	....
	Guelph Storm	OHL	17	12	2	2	1004	35	2	2.09	16	11	5	993	52	*2	3.14
1996-97	Binghamton	AHL	60	23	28	8	3367	199	3	3.55	4	1	3	236	13	0	3.31
1997-98	**NY Rangers**	**NHL**	**12**	**4**	**5**	**1**	**551**	**23**	**0**	**2.50**	....	....	....	....	....	....	....
	Hartford Wolf Pack	AHL	24	12	8	3	1417	62	0	2.63	8	5	3	478	24	0	3.01
1998-99	**NY Rangers**	**NHL**	**22**	**6**	**8**	**3**	**1097**	**49**	**0**	**2.68**	....	....	....	....	....	....	....
99-2000	**Tampa Bay**	**NHL**	**52**	**9**	**30**	**3**	**2492**	**145**	**0**	**3.49**	....	....	....	....	....	....	....
2000-01	**Tampa Bay**	**NHL**	**24**	**3**	**13**	**3**	**1005**	**59**	**1**	**3.52**	....	....	....	....	....	....	....
	Detroit Vipers	IHL	1	0	1	0	59	3	0	3.05	....	....	....	....	....	....	....
	Vancouver	**NHL**	**16**	**4**	**6**	**5**	**914**	**37**	**0**	**2.43**	**2**	**0**	**2**	**117**	**9**	**0**	**4.62**
2001-02	**Vancouver**	**NHL**	**62**	**31**	**22**	**5**	**3502**	**142**	**7**	**2.43**	**6**	**2**	**3**	**273**	**16**	**0**	**3.52**
2002-03	**Vancouver**	**NHL**	**57**	**33**	**16**	**7**	**3376**	**136**	**2**	**2.42**	**14**	**7**	**7**	**833**	**45**	**0**	**3.24**
2003-04	**Vancouver**	**NHL**	**60**	**33**	**21**	**6**	**3539**	**134**	**5**	**2.27**	**3**	**1**	**1**	**138**	**5**	**0**	**2.17**
2004-05	Klagenfurter AC	Austria	13	7	0	5	772	25	1	1.94	10	6	4	590	27	1	2.75
	NHL Totals		**305**	**123**	**121**	**33**	**16476**	**725**	**15**	**2.64**	**25**	**10**	**13**	**1361**	**75**	**0**	**3.31**

OHL Second All-Star Team (1996) • AHL All-Rookie Team (1997)

Traded to **Tampa Bay** by **NY Rangers** with Niklas Sundstrom and NY Rangers' 1st (Nikita Alexeev) and 3rd (later traded to San Jose – later traded to Chicago – Chicago selected Igor Radulov) round choices in 2000 Entry Draft for Chicago's 1st round choice (previously acquired, NY Rangers selected Pavel Brendl) in 1999 Entry Draft, June 26, 1999. Traded to **Vancouver** by **Tampa Bay** for Adrian Aucoin and Vancouver's 2nd round choice (Alexander Polushin) in 2001 Entry Draft, February 7, 2001. Signed as a free agent by **Klagenfurter** (Austria), January 20, 2005.

COLEMAN, Gerald (KOHL-man, JAIR-uhld) T.B.

Goaltender. Catches left. 6'4", 205 lbs. Born, Romeoville, IL, April 3, 1985.
(Tampa Bay's 5th choice, 224th overall, in 2003 Entry Draft).

			Regular Season								Playoffs						
Season	Club	League	GP	W	L	T	Mins	GA	SO	Avg	GP	W	L	Mins	GA	SO	Avg
99-2000	Chicago	MEHL	26	....	....	....	1560	65	0	2.50	....	....	....	....	....	....	....
2000-01	USA U-17	USDP	45	11	23	5	2386	158	0	3.97	....	....	....	....	....	....	....
2001-02	USA U-17	USDP	26	9	13	4	1436	86	0	3.59	....	....	....	....	....	....	....
	USA U-18	USDP	11	5	3	1	570	31	1	3.28	....	....	....	....	....	....	....
2002-03	London Knights	OHL	26	6	9	3	1074	59	1	3.30	....	....	....	....	....	....	....
2003-04	London Knights	OHL	33	24	8	0	1852	68	*5	2.20	8	5	2	442	19	1	2.58
2004-05	London Knights	OHL	38	*32	2	2	2224	63	*8	*1.70	8	7	1	455	13	0	*1.71

CONKLIN, Ty (KAWN-klihn, TIGH) EDM.

Goaltender. Catches left. 6', 184 lbs. Born, Anchorage, AK, March 30, 1976.

			Regular Season								Playoffs						
Season	Club	League	GP	W	L	T	Mins	GA	SO	Avg	GP	W	L	Mins	GA	SO	Avg
1995-96	Green Bay	USHL	30	....	....	....	1727	82	1	2.85	....	....	....	....	....	....	....
1996-97	Alaska-Anchorage	WCHA					DID NOT PLAY – FRESHMAN										
	Green Bay	USHL	30	19	7	1	1609	86	1	3.21	17	8	9	980	56	1	3.43
1997-98	New Hampshire	H-East					DID NOT PLAY – TRANSFERRED COLLEGES										
1998-99	New Hampshire	H-East	22	18	3	1	1338	41	0	*1.84	....	....	....	....	....	....	....
99-2000	New Hampshire	H-East	*37	*22	8	6	*2194	91	2	2.49	....	....	....	....	....	....	....
2000-01	New Hampshire	H-East	34	17	12	5	2048	70	*5	*2.05	....	....	....	....	....	....	....
2001-02	**Edmonton**	**NHL**	**4**	**2**	**0**	**0**	**148**	**4**	**0**	**1.62**	....	....	....	....	....	....	....
	Hamilton Bulldogs	AHL	37	13	12	8	2043	89	1	2.61	7	4	2	416	18	0	2.60
2002-03	Hamilton Bulldogs	AHL	38	19	13	3	2140	91	4	2.55	17	9	6	1024	38	1	2.23
2003-04	**Edmonton**	**NHL**	**38**	**17**	**14**	**4**	**2086**	**84**	**1**	**2.42**	....	....	....	....	....	....	....
2004-05	Wolfsburg	Germany	11	....	....	....	623	31	0	2.99	7	....	....	414	11	2	1.59
	NHL Totals		**42**	**19**	**14**	**4**	**2234**	**88**	**1**	**2.36**	....	....	....	....	....	....	....

USHL Second All-Star Team (1996) • Hockey East All-Rookie Team (1999) • Hockey East Second All-Star Team (1999) • Hockey East First All-Star Team (2000, 2001) • Hockey East Player of the Year (2000) (co-winner - Mike Mottau) • NCAA East Second All-American Team (2000) • NCAA East First All-American Team (2001) • Walter Brown Award (New England's Outstanding American-born College player) (2001) (co-winner - Brian Gionta)

• Left **Alaska-Anchorage** (WCHA) and returned to **Green Bay** (USHL), November 14, 1996. Signed as a free agent by **Edmonton**, April 18, 2001. Signed as a free agent by **Wolfsburg** (Germany), January 25, 2005.

CRAWFORD, Corey (KRAW-fohrd, KOHR-ee) CHI.

Goaltender. Catches left. 6'2", 183 lbs. Born, Montreal, Que., December 31, 1984.
(Chicago's 2nd choice, 52nd overall, in 2003 Entry Draft).

			Regular Season								Playoffs						
Season	Club	League	GP	W	L	T	Mins	GA	SO	Avg	GP	W	L	Mins	GA	SO	Avg
2000-01	Gatineau Intrepide	QAAA	21	17	3	1	1260	40	2	1.92	....	....	....	....	....	....	....
2001-02	Moncton Wildcats	QMJHL	38	9	20	3	1863	116	1	3.74	....	....	....	....	....	....	....
2002-03	Moncton Wildcats	QMJHL	50	24	17	6	2855	130	2	2.73	6	2	3	303	20	0	3.97

2003-04	Moncton Wildcats	QMJHL	54	*35	15	3	3019	132	2	2.62	*20	*13	6	*1170	42	0	2.15
2004-05	Moncton Wildcats	QMJHL	51	28	16	6	2942	121	*6	2.47	12	6	6	725	33	*1	2.73

QMJHL Second All-Star Team (2004, 2005)

CRAWFORD-WEST, Brandon (KRAW-fohrd-WEHST, BRAN-duhn) PIT.

Goaltender. Catches right. 6', 180 lbs. Born, San Diego, CA, July 1, 1982.
(Pittsburgh's 9th choice, 250th overall, in 2001 Entry Draft).

			Regular Season								Playoffs						
Season	Club	League	GP	W	L	T	Mins	GA	SO	Avg	GP	W	L	Mins	GA	SO	Avg
2000-01	Texas Tornado	NAHL	43	30	9	3	2534	110	4	2.60	7	6	1	452	6	3	0.80
2001-02	Texas Tornado	NAHL	50	35	11	2	2825	109	4	2.32	6	3	3	389	13	0	2.01
2002-03	Tri-City Storm	USHL	22	7	12	1	1207	61	0	3.03	....	....	....	....	....	....	....
	Bozeman Icedogs	AWHL	15	7	7	1	825	47	0	3.42	5	2	3	309	14	0	2.71
2003-04	Miami U.	CCHA	33	21	8	3	1947	81	3	2.50	....	....	....	....	....	....	....
2004-05	Miami U.	CCHA	32	11	16	5	1885	78	2	2.48	....	....	....	....	....	....	....

DAFOE, Byron (duh-FOH, BIGH-ruhn)

Goaltender. Catches left. 5'11", 200 lbs. Born, Sussex, England, February 25, 1971.
(Washington's 2nd choice, 35th overall, in 1989 Entry Draft).

			Regular Season								Playoffs						
Season	Club	League	GP	W	L	T	Mins	GA	SO	Avg	GP	W	L	Mins	GA	SO	Avg
1987-88	Juan de Fuca	BCJHL	32	....	....	....	1716	129	0	4.51	....	....	....	....	....	....	....
1988-89	Portland	WHL	59	29	24	3	3279	291	1	5.32	*18	10	8	*1091	81	*1	4.45
1989-90	Portland	WHL	40	14	21	3	2265	193	0	5.11	....	....	....	....	....	....	....
1990-91	Portland	WHL	8	1	5	1	414	41	0	5.94	....	....	....	....	....	....	....
	Prince Albert	WHL	32	13	12	4	1839	124	0	4.05	....	....	....	....	....	....	....
1991-92	Baltimore Skipjacks	AHL	33	12	16	4	1847	119	0	3.87	....	....	....	....	....	....	....
	New Haven	AHL	7	3	2	1	364	22	0	3.63	....	....	....	....	....	....	....
	Hampton Roads	ECHL	10	6	4	0	562	26	0	2.78	....	....	....	....	....	....	....
1992-93	**Washington**	**NHL**	**1**	**0**	**0**	**0**	**1**	**0**	**0**	**0.00**	....	....	....	....	....	....	....
	Baltimore Skipjacks	AHL	48	16	20	7	2617	191	1	4.38	5	2	3	241	22	0	5.48
1993-94	**Washington**	**NHL**	**5**	**2**	**2**	**0**	**230**	**13**	**0**	**3.39**	**2**	**0**	**2**	**118**	**5**	**0**	**2.54**
	Portland Pirates	AHL	47	24	16	4	2661	148	1	3.34	1	0	0	9	1	0	6.79
1994-95	**Washington**	**NHL**	**4**	**1**	**1**	**1**	**187**	**11**	**0**	**3.53**	**1**	**0**	**0**	**20**	**1**	**0**	**3.00**
	Phoenix	IHL	49	25	16	6	2743	169	2	3.70	....	....	....	....	....	....	....
	Portland Pirates	AHL	6	5	0	0	330	16	0	2.91	7	3	4	416	29	0	4.18
1995-96	**Los Angeles**	**NHL**	**47**	**14**	**24**	**8**	**2666**	**172**	**1**	**3.87**	....	....	....	....	....	....	....
1996-97	**Los Angeles**	**NHL**	**40**	**13**	**17**	**5**	**2162**	**112**	**0**	**3.11**	....	....	....	....	....	....	....
1997-98	**Boston**	**NHL**	**65**	**30**	**25**	**9**	**3693**	**138**	**6**	**2.24**	**6**	**2**	**4**	**422**	**14**	**1**	**1.99**
1998-99	**Boston**	**NHL**	**68**	**32**	**23**	**11**	**4001**	**133**	***10**	**1.99**	**12**	**6**	**6**	**768**	**26**	**2**	**2.03**
99-2000	**Boston**	**NHL**	**41**	**13**	**16**	**10**	**2307**	**114**	**3**	**2.96**	....	....	....	....	....	....	....
2000-01	**Boston**	**NHL**	**45**	**22**	**14**	**7**	**2536**	**101**	**2**	**2.39**	....	....	....	....	....	....	....
2001-02	**Boston**	**NHL**	**64**	**35**	**26**	**3**	**3827**	**141**	**4**	**2.21**	**6**	**2**	**4**	**358**	**19**	**0**	**3.18**
2002-03	**Atlanta**	**NHL**	**17**	**5**	**11**	**1**	**895**	**65**	**0**	**4.36**	....	....	....	....	....	....	....
2003-04	**Atlanta**	**NHL**	**18**	**4**	**11**	**1**	**973**	**51**	**0**	**3.14**	....	....	....	....	....	....	....
2004-05							DID NOT PLAY										
	NHL Totals		**415**	**171**	**170**	**56**	**23478**	**1051**	**26**	**2.69**	**27**	**10**	**16**	**1686**	**65**	**3**	**2.31**

AHL First All-Star Team (1994) • Harry "Hap" Holmes Memorial Award (fewest goals against – AHL) (1994) (shared with Olaf Kolzig) • NHL Second All-Star Team (1999)

Traded to **Los Angeles** by **Washington** with Dmitri Khristich for Los Angeles' 1st round choice (Alexandre Volchkov) in 1996 Entry Draft and Dallas' 4th round choice (previously acquired, Washington selected Justin Davis) in 1996 Entry Draft, July 8, 1995. Traded to **Boston** by **Los Angeles** with Dimitri Khristich for Jozef Stumpel, Sandy Moger and Boston's 4th round choice (later traded to New Jersey – New Jersey selected Pierre Dagenais) in 1998 Entry Draft, August 29, 1997. Signed as a free agent by **Atlanta**, November 19, 2002.

DAIGNEAULT, Maxime (DAYN-yoh, mahx-EEM) WSH.

Goaltender. Catches left. 6'3", 202 lbs. Born, St-Jacques-le-Mineur, Que., January 23, 1984.
(Washington's 4th choice, 59th overall, in 2002 Entry Draft).

			Regular Season								Playoffs						
Season	Club	League	GP	W	L	T	Mins	GA	SO	Avg	GP	W	L	Mins	GA	SO	Avg
99-2000	Magog	QAAA	19	12	3	3	1108	53	3	2.87	18	12	5	945	42	1	2.67
2000-01	Val-d'Or Foreurs	QMJHL	28	14	8	1	1386	82	0	3.55	10	8	1	504	21	0	2.50
2001-02	Val-d'Or Foreurs	QMJHL	61	25	27	5	3270	184	3	3.38	7	3	4	431	23	0	3.20
2002-03	Val-d'Or Foreurs	QMJHL	48	23	18	3	2694	138	2	3.07	8	4	3	487	23	1	2.83
2003-04	Val-d'Or Foreurs	QMJHL	57	23	22	9	3250	158	2	2.92	7	3	4	416	16	0	2.31
2004-05	Portland Pirates	AHL	11	3	2	1	474	23	0	2.91	....	....	....	....	....	....	....
	South Carolina	ECHL	21	11	6	1	1172	59	1	3.02	....	....	....	....	....	....	....

Memorial Cup Tournament All-Star Team (2002) • Hap Emms Memorial Trophy (Memorial Cup Tournement Top Goaltender) (2002)

DAKERS, Taylor (DAK-uhrs, TAY-luhr) S.J.

Goaltender. Catches left. 6'1", 165 lbs. Born, Richmond, B.C., September 14, 1986.
(San Jose's 4th choice, 140th overall, in 2005 Entry Draft).

			Regular Season								Playoffs						
Season	Club	League	GP	W	L	T	Mins	GA	SO	Avg	GP	W	L	Mins	GA	SO	Avg
2002-03	Columbia Valley	KIJHL	37	....	....	....	2077	93	4	2.68	....	....	....	....	....	....	....
2003-04	Kootenay Ice	WHL	19	6	10	0	856	48	1	3.36	....	....	....	....	....	....	....
2004-05	Kootenay Ice	WHL	23	13	7	2	1303	44	4	2.03	....	....	....	....	....	....	....

DAMPHOUSSE, Jean-Francois (DAHM-fooz, ZHAWN-fran-SWUH)

Goaltender. Catches left. 6', 180 lbs. Born, St-Alexis-des-Monts, Que., July 21, 1979.
(New Jersey's 1st choice, 24th overall, in 1997 Entry Draft).

			Regular Season								Playoffs						
Season	Club	League	GP	W	L	T	Mins	GA	SO	Avg	GP	W	L	Mins	GA	SO	Avg
1993-94	Ste-Foy	QAHA	18	10	1	0	1078	53	0	2.95	14	10	4	842	50	0	3.52
1994-95	Ste-Foy	QAHA	16	....	....	....	958	48	0	3.01	....	....	....	....	....	....	....
	Ste-Foy	QAAA	2	1	0	1	120	8	0	3.84	....	....	....	....	....	....	....
1995-96	Ste-Foy	QAAA	32	18	10	1	1629	83	2	3.06	....	....	....	....	....	....	....
1996-97	Moncton Wildcats	QMJHL	39	6	25	2	2063	190	0	5.53	....	....	....	....	....	....	....
1997-98	Moncton Wildcats	QMJHL	59	24	26	6	3400	174	1	3.07	10	5	5	595	28	0	2.82
1998-99	Moncton Wildcats	QMJHL	40	19	17	2	2163	121	1	3.36	4	0	4	200	12	0	3.60
	Albany River Rats	AHL	1	0	1	0	59	3	0	3.06	....	....	....	....	....	....	....
99-2000	Augusta Lynx	ECHL	14	4	7	0	676	49	0	4.35	....	....	....	....	....	....	....
	Albany River Rats	AHL	26	9	11	2	1326	62	0	2.81	2	0	1	62	4	0	3.86
2000-01	Albany River Rats	AHL	55	24	23	3	2963	141	1	2.86	....	....	....	....	....	....	....
2001-02	**New Jersey**	**NHL**	**6**	**1**	**3**	**0**	**294**	**12**	**0**	**2.45**	....	....	....	....	....	....	....
	Albany River Rats	AHL	18	3	11	2	1001	57	0	3.42	....	....	....	....	....	....	....
2002-03	Cincinnati	AHL	31	12	14	4	1669	87	0	3.13	....	....	....	....	....	....	....
	Saint John Flames	AHL	10	5	5	0	591	23	0	2.33	....	....	....	....	....	....	....
2003-04	Hamilton Bulldogs	AHL	35	19	11	4	2010	77	2	2.30	10	4	6	592	25	1	2.54
2004-05	Quebec RadioX	QNAHL	39	27	8	0	2326	111	....	2.86	....	....	....	....	....	....	....
	NHL Totals		**6**	**1**	**3**	**0**	**294**	**12**	**0**	**2.45**	....	....	....	....	....	....	....

Traded to **Anaheim** by **New Jersey** with Petr Sykora, Mike Commodore and Igor Pohanka for Jeff Friesen, Oleg Tverdovsky and Maxim Balmochnykh, July 6, 2002. Traded to **Calgary** by **Anaheim** with Mike Commodore for Rob Niedermayer, March 11, 2003. Signed as a free agent by **Montreal**, July 4, 2003. Signed as a free agent by **Quebec** (QNAHL), September 21, 2004.

DANIS, Yann (DA-nihs, YAN) MTL.

Goaltender. Catches left. 6', 185 lbs. Born, Lafontaine, Que., June 21, 1981.

			Regular Season								Playoffs						
Season	Club	League	GP	W	L	T	Mins	GA	SO	Avg	GP	W	L	Mins	GA	SO	Avg
99-2000	St-Jerome	QJHL					STATISTICS NOT AVAILABLE										
	Cornwall Colts	CJHL	26	....	....	....	1367	71	0	3.12	....	....	....	....	....	....	....
2000-01	Brown U.	ECAC	12	2	8	1	667	40	0	3.60	....	....	....	....	....	....	....
2001-02	Brown U.	ECAC	24	11	10	2	1451	45	3	1.86	....	....	....	....	....	....	....
2002-03	Brown U.	ECAC	*34	15	14	5	*2074	80	5	2.31	....	....	....	....	....	....	....
2003-04	Brown U.	ECAC	30	15	11	4	1821	55	*5	*1.81	....	....	....	....	....	....	....
	Hamilton Bulldogs	AHL	2	2	0	0	120	3	1	1.50	1	0	0	12	0	0	0.00
2004-05	Hamilton Bulldogs	AHL	53	28	17	6	3075	120	5	2.34	4	0	4	237	13	0	3.29

ECAC Second All-Star Team (2002, 2003) • ECAC First All-Star Team (2004) • ECAC Goaltender of the Year (2004) • ECAC Player of the Year (2004) • NCAA East First All-American Team (2004)

Signed as a free agent by **Montreal**, March 19, 2004.

DENIS, Marc (deh-NEE, MAHRK) CBJ

Goaltender. Catches left. 6'1", 193 lbs. Born, Montreal, Que., August 1, 1977.
(Colorado's 1st choice, 25th overall, in 1995 Entry Draft).

			Regular Season								Playoffs						
Season	Club	League	GP	W	L	T	Mins	GA	SO	Avg	GP	W	L	Mins	GA	SO	Avg
1992-93	Montreal-Bourassa	QAAA	26	....	....	....	1559	74	5	2.87	....	....	....	....	....	....	....
1993-94	Trois-Rivieres	QAAA	36	10	22	3	2093	158	0	4.53	4	1	3	249	20	0	4.83
1994-95	Chicoutimi	QMJHL	32	17	9	1	1688	98	0	3.48	6	4	2	372	19	1	3.06
1995-96	Chicoutimi	QMJHL	51	23	21	4	2951	157	2	3.19	16	8	8	957	69	0	4.33
1996-97	Chicoutimi	QMJHL	41	22	15	2	2323	104	4	*2.69	*21	*11	10	*1229	70	*1	3.42
	Colorado	**NHL**	**1**	**0**	**1**	**0**	**60**	**3**	**0**	**3.00**	....	....	....	....	....	....	....
	Hershey Bears	AHL	....	....	....	....	....	....	....	....	4	1	0	56	1	0	1.08
1997-98	Hershey Bears	AHL	47	17	23	4	2588	125	1	2.90	6	3	3	346	15	0	2.59
1998-99	**Colorado**	**NHL**	**4**	**1**	**1**	**1**	**217**	**9**	**0**	**2.49**	....	....	....	....	....	....	....
	Hershey Bears	AHL	52	20	23	5	2908	137	4	2.83	3	1	1	143	7	0	2.93
99-2000	**Colorado**	**NHL**	**23**	**9**	**8**	**3**	**1203**	**51**	**3**	**2.54**	....	....	....	....	....	....	....
2000-01	**Columbus**	**NHL**	**32**	**6**	**20**	**4**	**1830**	**99**	**0**	**3.25**	....	....	....	....	....	....	....
2001-02	**Columbus**	**NHL**	**42**	**9**	**24**	**5**	**2335**	**121**	**1**	**3.11**	....	....	....	....	....	....	....
2002-03	**Columbus**	**NHL**	***77**	**27**	**41**	**8**	***4511**	**232**	**5**	**3.09**	....	....	....	....	....	....	....
2003-04	**Columbus**	**NHL**	**66**	**21**	**36**	**7**	**3796**	**162**	**5**	**2.56**	....	....	....	....	....	....	....
2004-05							DID NOT PLAY										
	NHL Totals		**245**	**73**	**131**	**28**	**13952**	**677**	**14**	**2.91**	....	....	....	....	....	....	....

QMJHL First All-Star Team (1997) • Canadian Major Junior First All-Star Team (1997) • Canadian Major Junior Goaltender of the Year (1997)

Traded to **Columbus** by **Colorado** for Columbus' 2nd round choice (later traded to Carolina – Carolina selected Tomas Kurka) in 2000 Entry Draft, June 7, 2000.

DENNIS, Adam (DEH-nihs, A-duhm) BUF.

Goaltender. Catches left. 5'11", 183 lbs. Born, Toronto, Ont., February 8, 1985.
(Buffalo's 6th choice, 182nd overall, in 2005 Entry Draft).

			Regular Season								Playoffs						
Season	Club	League	GP	W	L	T	Mins	GA	SO	Avg	GP	W	L	Mins	GA	SO	Avg
2002-03	Guelph Storm	OHL	18	6	7	1	846	45	0	3.19	....	....	....	....	....	....	....
2003-04	Guelph Storm	OHL	46	*33	10	2	2662	111	3	2.50	20	*15	5	1205	40	1	*1.99
2004-05	Guelph Storm	OHL	23	5	11	6	1372	57	3	2.49	....	....	....	....	....	....	....
	London Knights	OHL	16	12	4	0	920	23	3	1.50	11	9	1	629	22	*2	2.10

OHL First All-Star Team (2005) • Hap Emms Memorial Trophy (Memorial Cup Tournament Top Goaltender) (2005)

DesROCHERS, Patrick (duh-RAWSH-ay, PAT-rihk)

Goaltender. Catches left. 6'3", 209 lbs. Born, Penetanguishene, Ont., October 27, 1979.
(Phoenix's 1st choice, 14th overall, in 1998 Entry Draft).

			Regular Season								Playoffs						
Season	Club	League	GP	W	L	T	Mins	GA	SO	Avg	GP	W	L	Mins	GA	SO	Avg
1994-95	Barrie Colts	OPJHL	26	....	....	....	3205	179	3	3.08	....	....	....	....	....	....	....
1995-96	Sarnia Sting	OHL	29	12	6	2	1265	96	0	4.55	3	0	1	71	5	0	4.23
1996-97	Sarnia Sting	OHL	50	22	17	4	2667	154	*4	3.46	11	6	5	576	42	0	4.38
1997-98	Sarnia Sting	OHL	56	26	17	11	3205	179	1	3.35	4	1	2	160	12	0	4.50
1998-99	Sarnia Sting	OHL	8	3	5	0	425	26	0	3.67	....	....	....	....	....	....	....
	Kingston	OHL	44	14	22	3	2389	177	1	4.45	5	1	4	323	21	0	3.90
99-2000	Springfield Falcons	AHL	52	21	17	7	2710	137	1	3.03	2	1	1	120	7	1	3.50
2000-01	Springfield Falcons	AHL	50	17	24	5	2807	156	0	3.33	....	....	....	....	....	....	....
2001-02	**Phoenix**	**NHL**	**5**	**1**	**2**	**1**	**243**	**15**	**0**	**3.70**	....	....	....	....	....	....	....
	Springfield Falcons	AHL	34	12	18	1	1864	94	2	3.03	....	....	....	....	....	....	....
2002-03	**Phoenix**	**NHL**	**4**	**0**	**3**	**0**	**175**	**11**	**0**	**3.77**	....	....	....	....	....	....	....
	Springfield Falcons	AHL	8	2	4	1	454	20	0	2.64	....	....	....	....	....	....	....
	Carolina	**NHL**	**2**	**1**	**1**	**0**	**122**	**7**	**0**	**3.44**	....	....	....	....	....	....	....
	Lowell	AHL	17	4	12	1	1030	48	0	2.80	....	....	....	....	....	....	....
2003-04	Lowell	AHL	50	23	25	1	2838	138	0	2.92	....	....	....	....	....	....	....
2004-05	San Antonio	AHL	34	8	19	1	1487	79	2	3.19	....	....	....	....	....	....	....
	Texas Wildcatters	ECHL	2	0	2	0	120	10	0	5.00	....	....	....	....	....	....	....
	NHL Totals		**11**	**2**	**6**	**1**	**540**	**33**	**0**	**3.67**	....	....	....	....	....	....	....

Traded to **Carolina** by **Phoenix** for Jean-Marc Pelletier and future considerations, December 31, 2002. Signed as a free agent by **Florida**, August 25, 2004.

DiPIETRO, Rick (dee-pee-EHT-roh, RIHK) NYI

Goaltender. Catches right. 5'11", 185 lbs. Born, Winthrop, MA, September 19, 1981.
(NY Islanders' 1st choice, 1st overall, in 2000 Entry Draft).

			Regular Season								Playoffs						
Season	Club	League	GP	W	L	T	Mins	GA	SO	Avg	GP	W	L	Mins	GA	SO	Avg
1997-98	USA U-17	USDP	46	21	19	0	2526	131	2	3.11	....	....	....	....	....	....	....
1998-99	USA U-18	USDP	46	31	11	2	2760	113	2	2.46	....	....	....	....	....	....	....
99-2000	Boston University	H-East	29	18	5	5	1790	73	2	2.45	....	....	....	....	....	....	....
2000-01	**NY Islanders**	**NHL**	**20**	**3**	**15**	**1**	**1083**	**63**	**0**	**3.49**	....	....	....	....	....	....	....
	Chicago Wolves	IHL	14	4	5	2	778	44	0	3.39	....	....	....	....	....	....	....
2001-02	Bridgeport	AHL	59	*30	22	7	3472	134	4	2.32	20	12	8	*1270	45	*3	2.13
2002-03	**NY Islanders**	**NHL**	**10**	**2**	**5**	**2**	**585**	**29**	**0**	**2.97**	**1**	**0**	**0**	**15**	**0**	**0**	**0.00**
	Bridgeport	AHL	34	16	10	8	2044	73	3	2.14	5	2	3	299	10	1	2.01
2003-04	**NY Islanders**	**NHL**	**50**	**23**	**18**	**5**	**2844**	**112**	**5**	**2.36**	**5**	**1**	**4**	**303**	**11**	**1**	**2.18**
	Bridgeport	AHL	2	0	2	0	119	3	0	1.51	....	....	....	....	....	....	....
2004-05							DID NOT PLAY										
	NHL Totals		**80**	**28**	**38**	**8**	**4512**	**204**	**5**	**2.71**	**6**	**1**	**4**	**318**	**11**	**1**	**2.08**

Hockey East Second All-Star Team (2000) • Hockey East Rookie of the Year (2000)

DISHER, Josh (DIH-shur, JAWSH) N.J.

Goaltender. Catches left. 6'1", 170 lbs. Born, Chatham, Ont., June 24, 1985.
(New Jersey's 3rd choice, 185th overall, in 2004 Entry Draft).

			Regular Season								Playoffs						
Season	Club	League	GP	W	L	T	Mins	GA	SO	Avg	GP	W	L	Mins	GA	SO	Avg
2001-02	Oakville Rangers	OMHA	....	....	....	....	1170	....	2	2.55	....	....	....	....	....	....	....
2002-03	Burlington	OPJHL					STATISTICS NOT AVAILABLE										
2003-04	Erie Otters	OHL	*63	26	27	5	*3524	168	*5	2.86	9	4	5	506	29	0	3.44
2004-05	Erie Otters	OHL	51	25	21	3	2853	130	3	2.73	6	2	4	395	18	0	2.73

DIVIS, Reinhard (DIH-vihs, RIGHN-hard) ST.L.

Goaltender. Catches left. 6', 200 lbs. Born, Vienna, Austria, July 4, 1975.
(St. Louis' 8th choice, 261st overall, in 2000 Entry Draft).

			Regular Season								Playoffs						
Season	Club	League	GP	W	L	T	Mins	GA	SO	Avg	GP	W	L	Mins	GA	SO	Avg
1995-96	VEU Feldkirch	Austria	37	....	....	....	2200	85	0	2.32	....	....	....	....	....	....	....
1996-97	VEU Feldkirch	Alpenliga	45	....	....	....	2738	105	0	2.30	....	....	....	....	....	....	....
	VEU Feldkirch	Austria	....	....	....	....	....	....	....	....	11	....	....	620	27	0	2.61
1997-98	VEU Feldkirch	Alpenliga	13	....	....	....	779	22	0	1.69	....	....	....	....	....	....	....
	VEU Feldkirch	Austria	27	....	....	....	1620	55	0	2.07	....	....	....	....	....	....	....
1998-99	VEU Feldkirch	Austria	15	....	....	....	900	58	0	3.86	....	....	....	....	....	....	....
99-2000	Leksands IF	Sweden	48	....	....	....	2839	160	3	3.38	....	....	....	....	....	....	....
2000-01	Leksands IF	Sweden	41	....	....	....	2451	141	3	3.45	....	....	....	....	....	....	....
2001-02	**St. Louis**	**NHL**	**1**	**0**	**0**	**0**	**25**	**0**	**0**	**0.00**	....	....	....	....	....	....	....
	Worcester IceCats	AHL	55	28	20	5	3173	137	3	2.59	3	1	2	205	8	0	2.34
	Austria	Olympics	4	1	1	2	238	12	0	3.02	....	....	....	....	....	....	....
2002-03	**St. Louis**	**NHL**	**2**	**2**	**0**	**0**	**83**	**1**	**0**	**0.72**	....	....	....	....	....	....	....
	Worcester IceCats	AHL	9	6	1	0	453	17	0	2.25	....	....	....	....	....	....	....
2003-04	**St. Louis**	**NHL**	**13**	**4**	**4**	**2**	**629**	**29**	**0**	**2.77**	**1**	**0**	**0**	**18**	**0**	**0**	**0.00**
	Worcester IceCats	AHL	31	12	10	8	1709	63	3	2.21	....	....	....	....	....	....	....
2004-05	EC Villacher SV	Austria	26	10	10	4	1482	61	2	2.47	3	0	3	169	12	0	4.26
	NHL Totals		**16**	**6**	**4**	**2**	**737**	**30**	**0**	**2.44**	**1**	**0**	**0**	**18**	**0**	**0**	**0.00**

Signed as a free agent by **Villacher** (Austria), October 24, 2004.

DOYLE, Frank (DOIL, FRANK) N.J.

Goaltender. Catches . 6'1", 175 lbs. Born, Guelph, Ont., September 8, 1980.

			Regular Season								Playoffs						
Season	Club	League	GP	W	L	T	Mins	GA	SO	Avg	GP	W	L	Mins	GA	SO	Avg
2000-01	Cambridge	OHA-B	32	....	....	....	....	....	4	2.94	....	....	....	....	....	....	....
2001-02	University of Maine	H-East	DID NOT PLAY – FRESHMAN														
2002-03	University of Maine	H-East	21	10	4	5	1180	42	2	*2.14	....	....	....	....	....	....	....
2003-04	University of Maine	H-East	23	19	4	0	1325	40	5	1.81	....	....	....	....	....	....	....
2004-05	Utah Grizzlies	AHL	1	0	1	0	20	3	0	9.00	....	....	....	....	....	....	....
	Idaho Steelheads	ECHL	52	*32	13	4	2938	106	4	2.16	3	1	2	169	12	0	4.26

Signed as a free agent by **New Jersey**, August 12, 2005.

DROUIN-DESLAURIERS, Jeff droo-EHN-duh-LAW-ree-yay) EDM.

Goaltender. Catches right. 6'3", 175 lbs. Born, St-Jean-Richelieu, Que., May 15, 1984.
(Edmonton's 2nd choice, 31st overall, in 2002 Entry Draft).

			Regular Season								Playoffs						
Season	Club	League	GP	W	L	T	Mins	GA	SO	Avg	GP	W	L	Mins	GA	SO	Avg
2000-01	Gatineau Intrepide	QAAA	22	10	9	2	1194	61	2	3.07	2	1	0	125	6	0	2.89
2001-02	Chicoutimi	QMJHL	51	28	20	1	2909	170	1	3.51	4	0	3	197	20	0	6.11
2002-03	Chicoutimi	QMJHL	54	18	24	1	2582	164	0	3.81	4	0	4	240	15	0	9.00
2003-04	Chicoutimi	QMJHL	50	21	20	6	2701	129	1	2.87	18	10	8	956	50	1	3.14
2004-05	Edmonton	AHL	22	6	13	2	1258	62	0	2.96	....	....	....	....	....	....	....
	Greenville Grrrowl	ECHL	11	7	3	1	673	26	1	2.32	....	....	....	....	....	....	....

QMJHL All-Rookie Team (2002)

DUBA, Tomas (DOO-bah, TAW-mash) PIT.

Goaltender. Catches left. 6', 176 lbs. Born, Prague, Czech., July 2, 1981.
(Pittsburgh's 8th choice, 217th overall, in 2001 Entry Draft).

			Regular Season								Playoffs						
Season	Club	League	GP	W	L	T	Mins	GA	SO	Avg	GP	W	L	Mins	GA	SO	Avg
1998-99	Sparta Jr.	CzRep-Jr.	34	....	....	....	1850	95	....	3.08	....	....	....	....	....	....	....
99-2000	Sparta Jr.	CzRep-Jr.	30	....	....	....	1670	73	....	2.62	....	....	....	....	....	....	....
	HC CKD Slany	CzRep-3	1	0	1	0	60	5	0	5.00	....	....	....	....	....	....	....
2000-01	Sparta Jr.	CzRep-Jr.	14	....	....	....	774	41	0	3.18	2	....	....	60	6	0	6.00
	Beroun	CzRep-2	8	....	....	....	426	18	....	2.54	....	....	....	....	....	....	....
2001-02	SaiPa	Finland	47	10	31	4	2755	152	3	3.31	....	....	....	....	....	....	....
2002-03	SaiPa	Finland	34	9	17	5	1888	86	3	2.73	....	....	....	....	....	....	....
2003-04	Znojmo	CzRep	47	....	....	....	2568	103	4	2.41	7	3	4	412	20	0	2.91
2004-05	Plzen	CzRep	35	....	....	....	2008	83	1	2.48	....	....	....	....	....	....	....

DUBIELEWICZ, Wade (DOO-bih-wihtz, WAYD) NYI

Goaltender. Catches left. 5'10", 178 lbs. Born, Invermere, B.C., January 30, 1978.

			Regular Season								Playoffs						
Season	Club	League	GP	W	L	T	Mins	GA	SO	Avg	GP	W	L	Mins	GA	SO	Avg
1997-98	Trail Smoke Eaters	BCHL	41	....	....	....	2225	118	0	3.18	....	....	....	....	....	....	....
1998-99	Trail Smoke Eaters	BCHL	STATISTICS NOT AVAILABLE														
	Chilliwack Chiefs	BCHL	14	10	4	0	834	....	0	....	....	....	....	....	....	....	....
99-2000	U. of Denver	WCHA	13	3	5	1	596	27	1	2.72	....	....	....	....	....	....	....
2000-01	U. of Denver	WCHA	29	12	9	3	1542	59	2	2.30	....	....	....	....	....	....	....
2001-02	U. of Denver	WCHA	24	20	4	0	1431	41	2	*1.72	....	....	....	....	....	....	....
2002-03	U. of Denver	WCHA	19	9	8	2	1060	43	3	2.43	....	....	....	....	....	....	....
2003-04	**NY Islanders**	**NHL**	**2**	**1**	**0**	**1**	**105**	**3**	**0**	**1.71**	....	....	....	....	....	....	....
	Bridgeport	AHL	33	20	8	5	1959	45	9	*1.38	3	2	1	181	11	0	3.64
2004-05	Bridgeport	AHL	43	18	23	1	2539	113	1	2.67	....	....	....	....	....	....	....
	NHL Totals		**2**	**1**	**0**	**1**	**105**	**3**	**0**	**1.71**	....	....	....	....	....	....	....

WCHA Second All-Star Team (2001, 2003) • WCHA First All-Star Team (2002) • AHL All-Rookie Team (2004) • AHL Second All-Star Team (2004) • Dudley "Red" Garrett Memorial Award (Rookie of the Year - AHL) (2004) • Harry "Hap" Holmes Memorial Award (fewest goals against - AHL) (2004) (shared with Dieter Kochan)

Signed as a free agent by **NY Islanders**, May 25, 2003.

DUBNYK, Devan (DUHN-nihk, DEH-vuhn) EDM.

Goaltender. Catches left. 6'5", 194 lbs. Born, Regina, Sask., May 4, 1986.
(Edmonton's 1st choice, 14th overall, in 2004 Entry Draft).

			Regular Season								Playoffs						
Season	Club	League	GP	W	L	T	Mins	GA	SO	Avg	GP	W	L	Mins	GA	SO	Avg
2000-01	Calgary Bruins	CBHL	14	....	....	....	815	39	2	3.10	....	....	....	....	....	....	....
2001-02	Calgary Bruins	CBHL	18	7	9	2	1105	68	1	3.69	....	....	....	....	....	....	....
	Kamloops Blazers	WHL	3	1	1	0	143	13	0	5.45	....	....	....	....	....	....	....
2002-03	Kamloops Blazers	WHL	26	12	8	1	1279	68	2	3.19	....	....	....	....	....	....	....
2003-04	Kamloops Blazers	WHL	44	20	18	5	2533	106	6	2.51	4	1	3	245	12	0	2.94
2004-05	Kamloops Blazers	WHL	*65	23	34	7	3699	166	6	2.69	6	2	4	363	22	0	3.64

Canadian Major Junior Scholastic Player of the Year (2004)

DUCHESNE, Jeremy (DOO-shayn, JAIR-eh-mee) PHI.

Goaltender. Catches left. 6', 201 lbs. Born, Silver Spring, MD, October 17, 1986.
(Philadelphia's 3rd choice, 119th overall, in 2005 Entry Draft).

			Regular Season								Playoffs						
Season	Club	League	GP	W	L	T	Mins	GA	SO	Avg	GP	W	L	Mins	GA	SO	Avg
2002-03	St-Francois Blizzard	QAAA	26	7	11	5	1341	75	0	3.35	....	....	....	....	....	....	....
2003-04	Victoriaville Tigres	QMJHL	17	3	8	1	870	60	0	4.14	....	....	....	....	....	....	....
2004-05	Victoriaville Tigres	QMJHL	15	2	9	0	711	41	2	*3.46	....	....	....	....	....	....	....
	Halifax	QMJHL	18	12	0	2	921	23	3	*1.50	12	8	4	723	33	*1	2.74

DUNHAM, Mike (DUHN-uhm, MIGHK) ATL.

Goaltender. Catches left. 6'3", 200 lbs. Born, Johnson City, NY, June 1, 1972.
(New Jersey's 4th choice, 53rd overall, in 1990 Entry Draft).

			Regular Season								Playoffs						
Season	Club	League	GP	W	L	T	Mins	GA	SO	Avg	GP	W	L	Mins	GA	SO	Avg
1987-88	Canterbury	High-CT	29	....	....	....	1740	69	4	2.38	....	....	....	....	....	....	....
1988-89	Canterbury	High-CT	25	....	....	....	1500	63	2	2.52	....	....	....	....	....	....	....
1989-90	Canterbury School	High-CT	32	....	....	....	1558	68	3	1.96	....	....	....	....	....	....	....
1990-91	University of Maine	H-East	23	14	5	2	1275	63	0	*2.96	....	....	....	....	....	....	....
1991-92	University of Maine	H-East	7	6	0	0	382	14	1	2.20	....	....	....	....	....	....	....
	United States	Nat-Tm	3	0	1	1	157	10	0	3.82	....	....	....	....	....	....	....
1992-93	University of Maine	H-East	25	*21	1	1	1429	63	0	2.65	....	....	....	....	....	....	....
1993-94	United States	Nat-Tm	33	22	9	2	1983	125	2	3.78	....	....	....	....	....	....	....
	United States	Olympics	3	0	1	2	180	15	0	5.00	....	....	....	....	....	....	....
	Albany River Rats	AHL	5	2	2	1	304	26	0	5.12	....	....	....	....	....	....	....
1994-95	Albany River Rats	AHL	35	20	7	8	2120	99	1	2.80	7	6	1	419	20	1	2.86
1995-96	Albany River Rats	AHL	44	30	10	2	2592	109	1	2.52	3	1	2	182	5	1	1.65
1996-97	**New Jersey**	**NHL**	**26**	**8**	**7**	**1**	**1013**	**43**	**2**	**2.55**	....	....	....	....	....	....	....
	Albany River Rats	AHL	3	1	1	1	184	12	0	3.91	....	....	....	....	....	....	....
1997-98	**New Jersey**	**NHL**	**15**	**5**	**5**	**3**	**773**	**29**	**1**	**2.25**	....	....	....	....	....	....	....
1998-99	**Nashville**	**NHL**	**44**	**16**	**23**	**3**	**2472**	**127**	**1**	**3.08**	....	....	....	....	....	....	....
99-2000	**Nashville**	**NHL**	**52**	**19**	**27**	**6**	**3077**	**146**	**0**	**2.85**	....	....	....	....	....	....	....
	Milwaukee	IHL	1	1	0	0	60	1	0	1.00	....	....	....	....	....	....	....
2000-01	**Nashville**	**NHL**	**48**	**21**	**21**	**4**	**2810**	**107**	**4**	**2.28**	....	....	....	....	....	....	....
2001-02	**Nashville**	**NHL**	**58**	**23**	**24**	**9**	**3316**	**144**	**3**	**2.61**	....	....	....	....	....	....	....
	United States	Olympics	1	1	0	0	60	0	*1	0.00	....	....	....	....	....	....	....
2002-03	**Nashville**	**NHL**	**15**	**2**	**9**	**2**	**819**	**43**	**0**	**3.15**	....	....	....	....	....	....	....
	NY Rangers	**NHL**	**43**	**19**	**17**	**5**	**2467**	**94**	**5**	**2.29**	....	....	....	....	....	....	....
2003-04	**NY Rangers**	**NHL**	**57**	**16**	**30**	**6**	**3148**	**159**	**2**	**3.03**	....	....	....	....	....	....	....
2004-05	Skelleftea AIK HK	Sweden-2	13	....	....	....	726	36	4	2.97	....	....	....	....	....	....	....
	NHL Totals		**358**	**129**	**163**	**39**	**19895**	**892**	**18**	**2.69**	....	....	....	....	....	....	....

Hockey East First All-Star Team (1993) • NCAA East First All-American Team (1993) • Harry "Hap" Holmes Memorial Award (fewest goals against – AHL) (1995) (shared with Corey Schwab) • Jack A. Butterfield Trophy (Playoff MVP – AHL) (1995) (co-winner - Corey Schwab) • AHL Second All-Star Team (1996) • William M. Jennings Trophy (1997) (shared with Martin Brodeur)

Claimed by **Nashville** from **New Jersey** in Expansion Draft, June 26, 1998. Traded to **NY Rangers** by **Nashville** for Rem Murray, Tomas Kloucek and Marek Zidlicky, December 12, 2002. Signed as a free agent by **Skelleftea** (Sweden-2), January 31, 2005. Signed as a free agent by **Atlanta**, September 2, 2005.

EHELECHNER, Patrick (eh-heh-LEHCH-nuhr, PAT-rihk) S.J.

Goaltender. Catches left. 6'2", 169 lbs. Born, Rosenheim, West Germany, September 23, 1984.
(San Jose's 5th choice, 139th overall, in 2003 Entry Draft).

			Regular Season								Playoffs						
Season	Club	League	GP	W	L	T	Mins	GA	SO	Avg	GP	W	L	Mins	GA	SO	Avg
2000-01	Jung. Mannheim	German-4	40	....	....	....	2423	171	2	4.23	....	....	....	....	....	....	....
2001-02	EV Landshut	German-3	2	....	....	....	130	6	0	2.77	....	....	....	....	....	....	....
	Hannover	Germany	8	....	....	....	475	24	0	3.03	....	....	....	....	....	....	....
2002-03	ESC Wedemark	German-4	STATISTICS NOT AVAILABLE														
	Hannover	Germany	4	....	....	....	162	16	0	5.90	....	....	....	....	....	....	....
2003-04	Sudbury Wolves	OHL	56	22	26	6	3089	148	3	2.87	7	2	4	390	14	2	2.15
2004-05	Sudbury Wolves	OHL	51	23	21	4	2997	128	3	2.56	10	4	5	497	29	0	3.50

OHL Second All-Star Team (2004)

Signed as a free agent by **Mannheim** (Germany), April 25, 2005.

EKLUND, Brian (EHK-luhnd, BRIGH-uhn) T.B.

Goaltender. Catches left. 6'5", 205 lbs. Born, Braintree, MA, May 24, 1980.
(Tampa Bay's 8th choice, 226th overall, in 2000 Entry Draft).

			Regular Season								Playoffs						
Season	Club	League	GP	W	L	T	Mins	GA	SO	Avg	GP	W	L	Mins	GA	SO	Avg
1997-98	Archbishop Wms.	High-MA	22	....	....	....	1320	40	*6	*1.84	....	....	....	....	....	....	....
1998-99	Brown U.	ECAC	8	1	3	0	299	17	0	3.41	....	....	....	....	....	....	....
99-2000	Brown U.	ECAC	12	1	6	2	569	28	1	2.95	....	....	....	....	....	....	....
2000-01	Brown U.	ECAC	19	2	13	3	1084	62	0	3.43	....	....	....	....	....	....	....
2001-02	Brown U.	ECAC	9	3	5	0	454	30	0	3.97	....	....	....	....	....	....	....
2002-03	Pensacola Ice Pilots	ECHL	19	10	6	0	999	61	0	3.66	....	....	....	....	....	....	....
	Springfield Falcons	AHL	1	1	0	0	60	1	0	1.00	....	....	....	....	....	....	....
2003-04	Pensacola Ice Pilots	ECHL	*62	*38	17	7	*3725	187	1	3.01	5	2	3	333	16	0	2.88
2004-05	Springfield Falcons	AHL	43	14	23	0	2416	121	0	3.01	....	....	....	....	....	....	....

ELLIOTT, Brian (EHL-lee-awt, BRIGH-uhn) OTT.

Goaltender. Catches left. 6'3", 186 lbs. Born, Newmarket, Ont., April 9, 1985.
(Ottawa's 9th choice, 291st overall, in 2003 Entry Draft).

			Regular Season								Playoffs						
Season	Club	League	GP	W	L	T	Mins	GA	SO	Avg	GP	W	L	Mins	GA	SO	Avg
2002-03	Ajax Axemen	OPJHL	39	....	....	....	2097	135	0	3.86	....	....	....	....	....	....	....
2003-04	U. of Wisconsin	WCHA	6	3	3	0	336	12	0	2.14	....	....	....	....	....	....	....
2004-05	U. of Wisconsin	WCHA	9	6	2	1	467	9	3	1.16	....	....	....	....	....	....	....

ELLIS, Dan (EH-lihs, DAN) DAL.

Goaltender. Catches left. 6', 185 lbs. Born, Saskatoon, Sask., June 19, 1980.
(Dallas' 2nd choice, 60th overall, in 2000 Entry Draft).

			Regular Season								Playoffs						
Season	Club	League	GP	W	L	T	Mins	GA	SO	Avg	GP	W	L	Mins	GA	SO	Avg
1998-99	Newmarket	OPJHL	28	24	3	1	1670	63	3	2.25	....	....	....	....	....	....	....
99-2000	Omaha Lancers	USHL	55	*34	16	4	*3274	123	*11	*2.25	4	1	3	238	10	0	2.52
2000-01	Nebraska-Omaha	CCHA	40	21	14	3	2285	95	2	2.49	....	....	....	....	....	....	....
2001-02	Nebraska-Omaha	CCHA	40	20	15	4	2405	97	3	2.42	....	....	....	....	....	....	....
2002-03	Nebraska-Omaha	CCHA	39	11	21	5	2211	117	3	3.18	....	....	....	....	....	....	....
2003-04	**Dallas**	**NHL**	**1**	**1**	**0**	**0**	**60**	**3**	**0**	**3.00**	....	....	....	....	....	....	....
	Utah Grizzlies	AHL	20	5	14	0	1130	55	2	2.92	....	....	....	....	....	....	....
	Idaho Steelheads	ECHL	23	13	8	1	1334	57	2	2.56	*16	*13	3	*966	30	*3	*1.86
2004-05	Hamilton Bulldogs	AHL	31	10	19	0	1774	82	1	2.77	....	....	....	....	....	....	....
	NHL Totals		**1**	**1**	**0**	**0**	**60**	**3**	**0**	**3.00**	....	....	....	....	....	....	....

USHL First All-Star Team (2000) • USHL Goaltender of the Year (2000) • USHL Player of the Year (2000) • CCHA Second All-Star Team (2002) • ECHL Playoff MVP (2004)

ELLIS-PLANTE, Julien (EHL-ihs-PLAWNT, JEW-lee-ehn) VAN.

Goaltender. Catches left. 6', 194 lbs. Born, Sorel, Que., January 27, 1986.
(Vancouver's 5th choice, 189th overall, in 2004 Entry Draft).

			Regular Season								Playoffs						
Season	Club	League	GP	W	L	T	Mins	GA	SO	Avg	GP	W	L	Mins	GA	SO	Avg
2001-02	Antoine-Girouard	QAAA	22	16	2	1	1227	55	2	2.69	....	....	....	....	....	....	....
2002-03	Antoine-Girouard	QAAA	16	11	4	1	966	29	4	1.80	....	....	....	....	....	....	....
	Shawinigan	QMJHL	7	2	3	0	365	21	0	3.45	....	....	....	....	....	....	....
2003-04	Shawinigan	QMJHL	59	32	18	2	3287	156	1	2.85	10	3	6	569	33	0	3.48
2004-05	Shawinigan	QMJHL	59	27	21	11	3480	140	4	2.41	4	0	3	175	10	0	3.43

QMJHL First All-Star Team (2005)

EMERY, Ray (EH-muhr-ee, RAY) OTT.

Goaltender. Catches left. 6'2", 198 lbs. Born, Cayuga, Ont., September 28, 1982.
(Ottawa's 4th choice, 99th overall, in 2001 Entry Draft).

			Regular Season								Playoffs						
Season	Club	League	GP	W	L	T	Mins	GA	SO	Avg	GP	W	L	Mins	GA	SO	Avg
1998-99	Dunnville Terriers	OJHL-C	22	3	19	0	1320	140	0	6.37	....	....	....	....	....	....	....
99-2000	Welland Cougars	OHA-B	23	13	10	1	1323	62	1	2.68	....	....	....	....	....	....	....
	Sault Ste. Marie	OHL	16	9	3	0	716	36	1	3.02	15	8	7	883	33	*3	2.24
2000-01	Sault Ste. Marie	OHL	52	18	29	2	2938	174	1	3.55	....	....	....	....	....	....	....
2001-02	Sault Ste. Marie	OHL	*59	*33	17	9	*3477	158	4	2.73	6	2	4	360	19	*1	3.17
2002-03	**Ottawa**	**NHL**	**3**	**1**	**0**	**0**	**85**	**2**	**0**	**1.41**	....	....	....	....	....	....	....
	Binghamton	AHL	50	27	17	6	2924	118	*7	2.42	14	8	6	848	40	*2	2.83
2003-04	**Ottawa**	**NHL**	**3**	**2**	**0**	**0**	**126**	**5**	**0**	**2.38**	....	....	....	....	....	....	....
	Binghamton	AHL	53	21	23	7	3109	128	3	2.47	2	0	2	120	6	0	3.01
2004-05	Binghamton	AHL	51	28	18	5	2993	132	0	2.65	6	2	4	409	14	0	2.05
	NHL Totals		**6**	**3**	**0**	**0**	**211**	**7**	**0**	**1.99**	....	....	....	....	....	....	....

OHL First All-Star Team (2002) • Canadian Major Junior First All-Star Team (2002) • Canadian Major Junior Goaltender of the Year (2002) • AHL All-Rookie Team (2003)

ESCHE, Robert (EHSH, RAW-buhrt) PHI.

Goaltender. Catches left. 6'1", 210 lbs. Born, Whitesboro, NY, January 22, 1978.
(Phoenix's 5th choice, 139th overall, in 1996 Entry Draft).

			Regular Season								Playoffs						
Season	Club	League	GP	W	L	T	Mins	GA	SO	Avg	GP	W	L	Mins	GA	SO	Avg
1994-95	Gloucester	CJHL	20	10	6	0	1034	70	0	4.06	....	....	....	....	....	....	....
1995-96	Detroit Jr. Whalers	OHL	23	13	6	0	1219	76	1	3.74	3	0	2	105	4	0	2.29
1996-97	Detroit Jr. Whalers	OHL	58	24	28	2	3241	206	2	3.81	5	1	4	317	19	0	3.60
1997-98	Plymouth Whalers	OHL	48	29	13	4	2810	135	3	2.88	15	8	7	869	45	0	3.11
1998-99	**Phoenix**	**NHL**	**3**	**0**	**1**	**0**	**130**	**7**	**0**	**3.23**	....	....	....	....	....	....	....
	Springfield Falcons	AHL	55	24	20	6	2957	138	1	2.80	1	0	1	60	4	0	4.02
99-2000	**Phoenix**	**NHL**	**8**	**2**	**5**	**0**	**408**	**23**	**0**	**3.38**	....	....	....	....	....	....	....
	Houston Aeros	IHL	7	4	2	1	419	16	2	2.29	....	....	....	....	....	....	....
	Springfield Falcons	AHL	21	9	9	2	1207	61	2	3.03	3	1	2	180	12	0	4.01
2000-01	**Phoenix**	**NHL**	**25**	**10**	**8**	**4**	**1350**	**68**	**2**	**3.02**	....	....	....	....	....	....	....
2001-02	**Phoenix**	**NHL**	**22**	**6**	**10**	**2**	**1145**	**52**	**1**	**2.72**	....	....	....	....	....	....	....
	Springfield Falcons	AHL	1	1	0	0	60	0	1	0.00	....	....	....	....	....	....	....
2002-03	**Philadelphia**	**NHL**	**30**	**12**	**9**	**3**	**1638**	**60**	**2**	**2.20**	**1**	**0**	**0**	**30**	**1**	**0**	**2.00**
2003-04	**Philadelphia**	**NHL**	**40**	**21**	**11**	**7**	**2322**	**79**	**3**	**2.04**	**18**	**11**	**7**	**1061**	**41**	**1**	**2.32**
2004-05							DID NOT PLAY										
	NHL Totals		**128**	**51**	**44**	**16**	**6993**	**289**	**8**	**2.48**	**19**	**11**	**7**	**1091**	**42**	**1**	**2.31**

OHL Second All-Star Team (1998) • AHL All-Rookie Team (1999) • William M. Jennings Trophy (2003) (shared with Roman Cechmanek) (tied with Martin Brodeur)

Traded to **Philadelphia** by **Phoenix** with Michal Handzus for Brian Boucher and Nashville's 3rd round choice (previously acquired, Phoenix selected Joe Callahan) in 2002 Entry Draft, June 12, 2002.

FALLON, Joseph (FA-lohn, JOH-sehf) CHI.

Goaltender. Catches left. 6'3", 190 lbs. Born, Bemidji, MN, February 1, 1985.
(Chicago's 9th choice, 167th overall, in 2005 Entry Draft).

			Regular Season								Playoffs						
Season	Club	League	GP	W	L	T	Mins	GA	SO	Avg	GP	W	L	Mins	GA	SO	Avg
2001-02	Rochester	USHL	27	7	16	1	1484	93	0	3.76	....	....	....	....	....	....	....
2002-03	Cedar Rapids	USHL	42	20	15	6	2495	108	2	2.60	7	3	4	426	21	0	2.96
2003-04	Cedar Rapids	USHL	42	25	13	2	2370	108	4	2.73	4	1	3	237	9	0	2.28
2004-05	U. of Vermont	ECAC	32	17	10	4	1932	63	5	1.96	....	....	....	....	....	....	....

ECAC All-Rookie Team (2005) • ECAC Rookie of the Year (2005)

FERHI, Eddy (feh-REE, EH-dee)

Goaltender. Catches left. 6'3", 181 lbs. Born, Charenton, France, November 26, 1979.

			Regular Season								Playoffs						
Season	Club	League	GP	W	L	T	Mins	GA	SO	Avg	GP	W	L	Mins	GA	SO	Avg
1998-99	Levis Faucons	CEGEP					STATISTICS NOT AVAILABLE										
99-2000	Sacred Heart	MAAC	7	2	4	0	367	19	0	3.11	....	....	....	....	....	....	....
2000-01	Sacred Heart	MAAC	21	9	7	4	1248	50	2	*2.40	....	....	....	....	....	....	....
2001-02	Sacred Heart	MAAC	31	13	12	4	1775	90	2	3.04	....	....	....	....	....	....	....
2002-03	Sacred Heart	MAAC	29	12	12	5	1770	67	3	*2.27	....	....	....	....	....	....	....
	Cincinnati	AHL	1	1	0	0	60	2	0	2.00	....	....	....	....	....	....	....
2003-04	Cincinnati	AHL	19	2	12	3	1061	55	0	3.11	1	0	0	24	2	0	5.07
2004-05	San Diego Gulls	ECHL	30	13	13	2	1695	83	2	2.94	....	....	....	....	....	....	....

MAAC Second All-Star Team (2001, 2002) • MAAC First All-Star Team (2003) • MAAC Goaltender of the Year (2003) (co-winner - Brad Roberts)

Signed to amateur tryout contract by **Cincinnati** (AHL), April 3, 2003. Signed as a free agent by **Anaheim**, July 23, 2003.

FERNANDEZ, Manny (fuhr-NAN-dehz, MAN-ee) MIN.

Goaltender. Catches left. 6', 180 lbs. Born, Etobicoke, Ont., August 27, 1974.
(Quebec's 4th choice, 52nd overall, in 1992 Entry Draft).

			Regular Season								Playoffs						
Season	Club	League	GP	W	L	T	Mins	GA	SO	Avg	GP	W	L	Mins	GA	SO	Avg
1990-91	Lac St-Louis Lions	QAAA	20	13	5	0	1176	69	*3	3.52	3	2	1	181	12	0	3.98
1991-92	Laval Titan	QMJHL	31	14	13	2	1593	99	1	3.73	9	3	5	468	39	0	5.00
1992-93	Laval Titan	QMJHL	43	26	14	2	2347	141	1	3.60	13	*12	1	818	42	0	3.08
1993-94	Laval Titan	QMJHL	51	29	14	1	2776	143	*5	3.09	19	14	5	1116	49	*1	*2.63
1994-95	Kalamazoo Wings	IHL	46	21	10	9	2470	115	2	2.79	14	10	2	753	34	1	2.71
	Dallas	**NHL**	**1**	**0**	**1**	**0**	**59**	**3**	**0**	**3.05**	....	....	....	....	....	....	....
1995-96	**Dallas**	**NHL**	**5**	**0**	**1**	**1**	**249**	**19**	**0**	**4.58**	....	....	....	....	....	....	....
	Michigan K-Wings	IHL	47	22	15	9	2664	133	*4	3.00	6	5	1	372	14	0	*2.26
1996-97	Michigan K-Wings	IHL	48	20	24	2	2720	142	2	3.13	4	1	3	277	15	0	3.25
1997-98	**Dallas**	**NHL**	**2**	**1**	**0**	**0**	**69**	**2**	**0**	**1.74**	**1**	**0**	**0**	**2**	**0**	**0**	**0.00**
	Michigan K-Wings	IHL	55	27	17	5	3022	139	5	2.76	2	0	2	88	7	0	4.73
1998-99	**Dallas**	**NHL**	**1**	**0**	**1**	**0**	**60**	**2**	**0**	**2.00**	....	....	....	....	....	....	....
	Houston Aeros	IHL	50	34	6	9	2949	116	2	2.36	*19	*11	8	*1126	49	1	2.61
99-2000	**Dallas**	**NHL**	**24**	**11**	**8**	**3**	**1353**	**48**	**1**	**2.13**	**1**	**0**	**0**	**17**	**1**	**0**	**3.53**
2000-01	**Minnesota**	**NHL**	**42**	**19**	**17**	**4**	**2461**	**92**	**4**	**2.24**	....	....	....	....	....	....	....
2001-02	**Minnesota**	**NHL**	**44**	**12**	**24**	**5**	**2463**	**125**	**1**	**3.05**	....	....	....	....	....	....	....
2002-03	**Minnesota**	**NHL**	**35**	**19**	**13**	**2**	**1979**	**74**	**2**	**2.24**	**9**	**3**	**4**	**552**	**18**	**0**	**1.96**
2003-04	**Minnesota**	**NHL**	**37**	**11**	**14**	**9**	**2166**	**90**	**2**	**2.49**	....	....	....	....	....	....	....
2004-05	Lulea HF	Sweden	19	....	....	....	1083	50	2	2.77	3	....	....	159	13	0	4.90
	NHL Totals		**191**	**73**	**79**	**24**	**10859**	**455**	**10**	**2.51**	**11**	**3**	**4**	**571**	**19**	**0**	**2.00**

QMJHL First All-Star Team (1994) • QMJHL MVP (1994) • IHL Second All-Star Team (1995)

Rights traded to **Dallas** by **Quebec** for Tommy Sjodin and Dallas' 3rd round choice (Chris Drury) in 1994 Entry Draft, February 13, 1994. Traded to **Minnesota** by **Dallas** with Brad Lukowich for Minnesota's 3rd round choice (Joel Lundqvist) in 2000 Entry Draft and Minnesota's 4th round choice (later traded back to Minnesota – later traded to Los Angeles – Los Angeles selected Aaron Rome) in 2002 Entry Draft, June 12, 2000. Signed as a free agent by **Lulea** (Sweden), December 18, 2004.

FICHAUD, Eric (FEE-shoh, AIR-ihk)

Goaltender. Catches left. 5'11", 179 lbs. Born, Anjou, Que., November 4, 1975.
(Toronto's 1st choice, 16th overall, in 1994 Entry Draft).

			Regular Season								Playoffs						
Season	Club	League	GP	W	L	T	Mins	GA	SO	Avg	GP	W	L	Mins	GA	SO	Avg
1991-92	Montreal-Bourassa	QAAA	28	12	15	1	1678	110	0	3.95	9	5	4	567	32	0	3.39
1992-93	Chicoutimi	QMJHL	43	18	13	1	2039	149	0	4.38	....	....	....	....	....	....	....
1993-94	Chicoutimi	QMJHL	*63	*37	21	3	*3493	192	4	3.30	*26	*16	10	*1560	86	*1	3.31
1994-95	Chicoutimi	QMJHL	46	21	19	4	2637	151	4	3.44	7	2	5	428	20	0	2.80
1995-96	**NY Islanders**	**NHL**	**24**	**7**	**12**	**2**	**1234**	**68**	**1**	**3.31**	....	....	....	....	....	....	....
	Worcester IceCats	AHL	34	13	15	6	1989	97	1	2.93	2	1	1	127	7	0	3.30
1996-97	**NY Islanders**	**NHL**	**34**	**9**	**14**	**4**	**1759**	**91**	**0**	**3.10**	....	....	....	....	....	....	....
1997-98	**NY Islanders**	**NHL**	**17**	**3**	**8**	**3**	**807**	**40**	**0**	**2.97**	....	....	....	....	....	....	....
	Utah Grizzlies	IHL	1	0	0	0	40	3	0	4.45	....	....	....	....	....	....	....
1998-99	**Nashville**	**NHL**	**9**	**0**	**6**	**0**	**447**	**24**	**0**	**3.22**	....	....	....	....	....	....	....
	Milwaukee	IHL	8	5	2	1	480	25	0	3.13	....	....	....	....	....	....	....
99-2000	**Carolina**	**NHL**	**9**	**3**	**5**	**1**	**490**	**24**	**1**	**2.94**	....	....	....	....	....	....	....
	Quebec Citadelles	AHL	6	4	1	1	368	17	0	2.77	3	0	3	177	10	0	3.39
2000-01	**Montreal**	**NHL**	**2**	**0**	**2**	**0**	**62**	**4**	**0**	**3.87**	....	....	....	....	....	....	....
	Quebec Citadelles	AHL	42	19	19	2	2441	127	1	3.12	2	0	1	98	3	0	1.84
2001-02	Manitoba Moose	AHL	5	2	3	0	279	13	1	2.80	....	....	....	....	....	....	....
	Krefeld Pinguine	Germany	9	....	....	....	401	11	0	1.65	3	....	....	197	8	0	2.44
2002-03	Hamilton Bulldogs	AHL	27	14	7	3	1447	55	4	2.28	8	5	3	472	17	0	2.16
2003-04	Hamilton Bulldogs	AHL	31	16	11	3	1836	70	1	2.29	....	....	....	....	....	....	....
2004-05	Quebec RadioX	QNAHL	9	6	2	0	505	19	....	2.26	8	8	0	480	9	....	1.13
	NHL Totals		**95**	**22**	**47**	**10**	**4799**	**251**	**2**	**3.14**	....	....	....	....	....	....	....

Canadian Major Junior Second All-Star Team (1994) • Memorial Cup Tournament All-Star Team (1994) • Hap Emms Memorial Trophy (Memorial Cup Tournament Top Goaltender) (1994) • QMJHL First All-Star Team (1995)

Traded to **NY Islanders** by **Toronto** for Benoit Hogue, NY Islanders' 3rd round choice (Ryan Pepperall) in 1995 Entry Draft and NY Islanders' 5th round choice (Brandon Sugden) in 1996 Entry Draft, April 6, 1995. Traded to **Edmonton** by **NY Islanders** for Mike Watt, June 18, 1998. Traded to **Nashville** by **Edmonton** with Drake Berehowsky and Greg de Vries for Mikhail Shtalenkov and Jim Dowd, October 1, 1998. Traded to **Carolina** by **Nashville** for Toronto's 4th round choice (previously acquired, Nashville selected Yevgeny Pavlov) in 1999 Entry Draft and future considerations, June 26, 1999. Claimed on waivers by **Montreal** from **Carolina**, February 11, 2000. Signed as a free agent by **Krefeld** (Germany) following release by **Manitoba** (AHL), January 11, 2002. Signed as a free agent by **Montreal**, September 10, 2002.

FINLEY, Brian (FIHN-lee, BRIGH-uhn) NSH.

Goaltender. Catches right. 6'3", 201 lbs. Born, Sault Ste. Marie, Ont., July 13, 1981.
(Nashville's 1st choice, 6th overall, in 1999 Entry Draft).

			Regular Season								Playoffs						
Season	Club	League	GP	W	L	T	Mins	GA	SO	Avg	GP	W	L	Mins	GA	SO	Avg
1996-97	Soo Carlucci's	NOHA	45	....	....	....	1943	109	3	2.38	....	....	....	....	....	....	....
1997-98	Barrie Colts	OHL	41	23	14	1	2154	105	3	2.92	5	1	3	260	13	0	3.00
1998-99	Barrie Colts	OHL	52	*36	10	4	3063	136	3	2.66	5	4	1	323	15	0	2.79
99-2000	Barrie Colts	OHL	47	24	12	6	2540	130	2	3.07	*23	14	8	1353	58	1	2.57
2000-01	Barrie Colts	OHL	16	5	8	0	818	42	0	3.08	....	....	....	....	....	....	....
	Brampton Battalion	OHL	11	7	3	1	631	31	0	2.95	9	5	4	503	26	1	3.10
2001-02							DID NOT PLAY – INJURED										
2002-03	**Nashville**	**NHL**	**1**	**0**	**0**	**0**	**47**	**3**	**0**	**3.83**	....	....	....	....	....	....	....
	Milwaukee	AHL	22	7	11	2	1207	59	2	2.93	....	....	....	....	....	....	....
	Toledo Storm	ECHL	7	4	2	0	305	12	0	2.36	1	0	1	60	4	0	4.00
2003-04	Milwaukee	AHL	43	23	15	4	2561	100	2	2.34	1	0	1	59	2	0	2.05
2004-05	Milwaukee	AHL	64	36	22	4	3642	139	7	2.29	7	3	4	458	20	1	2.62
	NHL Totals		**1**	**0**	**0**	**0**	**47**	**3**	**0**	**3.83**	....	....	....	....	....	....	....

OHL All-Rookie Team (1998) • OHL First All-Star Team (1999) • OHL Playoff MVP (2000)

• Missed entire 2001-02 season recovering from groin injury suffered during 2000-01 season and re-injured in training camp, October 3, 2001.

FISHER, Glenn (FIH-shuhr, GLEHN) EDM.

Goaltender. Catches left. 6'1", 165 lbs. Born, Edmonton, Alta., April 25, 1983.
(Edmonton's 9th choice, 148th overall, in 2002 Entry Draft).

			Regular Season								Playoffs						
Season	Club	League	GP	W	L	T	Mins	GA	SO	Avg	GP	W	L	Mins	GA	SO	Avg
99-2000	Edm. Maple Leafs	AMBHL	16	9	5	2	944	62	0	3.94	....	....	....	....	....	....	....
2000-01	Edm. Maple Leafs	AMHL	19	6	9	3	1116	77	0	4.14	....	....	....	....	....	....	....
2001-02	Fort Saskatchewan	AJHL	47	14	26	2	2649	196	2	4.44	3	0	3	180	14	0	4.67
2002-03	Fort Saskatchewan	AJHL	51	17	27	6	2885	202	0	4.20	....	....	....	....	....	....	....
2003-04	U. of Denver	WCHA	9	3	1	1	436	26	0	3.58	....	....	....	....	....	....	....
2004-05	U. of Denver	WCHA	22	14	5	1	1247	59	0	2.84	....	....	....	....	....	....	....

FLAHERTY, Wade (FLAY-uhr-tee, WAYD) VAN.

Goaltender. Catches left. 6', 190 lbs. Born, Terrace, B.C., January 11, 1968.
(Buffalo's 10th choice, 181st overall, in 1988 Entry Draft).

			Regular Season								Playoffs						
Season	Club	League	GP	W	L	T	Mins	GA	SO	Avg	GP	W	L	Mins	GA	SO	Avg
1984-85	Kelowna Wings	WHL	1	0	0	0	55	5	0	5.45	....	....	....	....	....	....	....
1985-86	Seattle	WHL	9	1	3	0	271	36	0	7.97	....	....	....	....	....	....	....
	Spokane Chiefs	WHL	5	0	3	0	161	21	0	7.83	....	....	....	....	....	....	....
1986-87	Nanaimo Clippers	BCJHL	15	....	....	....	830	53	0	3.83	....	....	....	....	....	....	....
	Victoria Cougars	WHL	3	0	2	0	127	16	0	7.56	....	....	....	....	....	....	....
1987-88	Victoria Cougars	WHL	36	20	15	0	2052	135	0	3.95	5	2	3	300	18	0	3.60
1988-89	Victoria Cougars	WHL	42	21	19	0	2408	180	4	4.49	....	....	....	....	....	....	....
1989-90	Greensboro	ECHL	27	12	10	0	1308	96	0	4.40	....	....	....	....	....	....	....
1990-91	Kansas City Blades	IHL	*56	16	31	4	2990	224	0	4.49	....	....	....	....	....	....	....
1991-92	**San Jose**	**NHL**	**3**	**0**	**3**	**0**	**178**	**13**	**0**	**4.38**	....	....	....	....	....	....	....
	Kansas City Blades	IHL	43	26	14	3	2603	140	1	3.23	1	0	0	1	0	0	0.00
1992-93	**San Jose**	**NHL**	**1**	**0**	**1**	**0**	**60**	**5**	**0**	**5.00**	....	....	....	....	....	....	....
	Kansas City Blades	IHL	*61	*34	19	7	*3642	195	2	3.21	*12	6	6	733	34	*1	2.78
1993-94	Kansas City Blades	IHL	*60	32	19	9	*3564	202	0	3.40	....	....	....	....	....	....	....
1994-95	**San Jose**	**NHL**	**18**	**5**	**6**	**1**	**852**	**44**	**1**	**3.10**	**7**	**2**	**3**	**377**	**31**	**0**	**4.93**
1995-96	**San Jose**	**NHL**	**24**	**3**	**12**	**1**	**1137**	**92**	**0**	**4.85**	....	....	....	....	....	....	....
1996-97	**San Jose**	**NHL**	**7**	**2**	**4**	**0**	**359**	**31**	**0**	**5.18**	....	....	....	....	....	....	....
	Kentucky	AHL	19	8	6	2	1032	54	1	3.14	3	1	2	200	11	0	3.30
1997-98	**NY Islanders**	**NHL**	**16**	**4**	**4**	**3**	**694**	**23**	**3**	**1.99**	....	....	....	....	....	....	....
	Utah Grizzlies	IHL	24	16	5	3	1341	40	3	1.79	....	....	....	....	....	....	....
1998-99	**NY Islanders**	**NHL**	**20**	**5**	**11**	**2**	**1048**	**53**	**0**	**3.03**	....	....	....	....	....	....	....
	Lowell	AHL	5	1	3	1	305	16	0	3.15	....	....	....	....	....	....	....
99-2000	**NY Islanders**	**NHL**	**4**	**0**	**1**	**1**	**182**	**7**	**0**	**2.31**	....	....	....	....	....	....	....
2000-01	**NY Islanders**	**NHL**	**20**	**6**	**10**	**0**	**1017**	**56**	**1**	**3.30**	....	....	....	....	....	....	....
	Tampa Bay	**NHL**	**2**	**0**	**2**	**0**	**118**	**8**	**0**	**4.07**	....	....	....	....	....	....	....
2001-02	**Florida**	**NHL**	**4**	**2**	**1**	**1**	**245**	**12**	**0**	**2.94**	....	....	....	....	....	....	....
	Utah Grizzlies	AHL	45	22	13	5	2351	92	2	2.35	5	2	3	312	11	0	2.12
2002-03	**Nashville**	**NHL**	**1**	**0**	**1**	**0**	**51**	**4**	**0**	**4.71**	....	....	....	....	....	....	....
	San Antonio	AHL	30	11	13	5	1791	86	1	2.88	....	....	....	....	....	....	....
2003-04	Milwaukee	AHL	36	21	12	3	2146	78	3	2.18	*21	*16	5	*1371	44	1	1.93

2004-05	Manitoba Moose	AHL	36	19	10	3	2010	78	4	2.33	12	8	4	720	29	2	2.42
	NHL Totals		**120**	**27**	**56**	**9**	**5941**	**348**	**5**	**3.51**	**7**	**2**	**3**	**377**	**31**	**0**	**4.93**

WHL West Second All-Star Team (1988) • ECHL Playoff MVP (1990) • James Norris Memorial Trophy (fewest goals against – IHL) (1992) (shared with Arturs Irbe) • IHL Second All-Star Team (1993, 1994) • Jack A. Butterfield Trophy (Playoff MVP - AHL) (2004)

Signed as a free agent by **San Jose**, September 3, 1991. Signed as a free agent by **NY Islanders**, July 22, 1997. Traded to **Tampa Bay** by **NY Islanders** for future considerations, February 16, 2001. Signed as a free agent by **Florida**, August 2, 2001. Traded to **Nashville** by **Florida** for Pascal Trepanier, March 9, 2003. Signed as a free agent by **Vancouver**, July 7, 2004.

FLEURY, Marc-Andre (fluh-REE, MAHRK-AWN-dray) PIT.

Goaltender. Catches left. 6'1", 175 lbs. Born, Sorel, Que., November 28, 1984.
(Pittsburgh's 1st choice, 1st overall, in 2003 Entry Draft).

			Regular Season								Playoffs						
Season	**Club**	**League**	**GP**	**W**	**L**	**T**	**Mins**	**GA**	**SO**	**Avg**	**GP**	**W**	**L**	**Mins**	**GA**	**SO**	**Avg**
99-2000	Charles-Lemoyne	QAAA	15	4	9	0	780	36	1	2.77	....	....	....	....	....	....	....
2000-01	Cape Breton	QMJHL	35	12	13	2	1705	115	0	4.05	2	0	1	32	4	0	7.50
2001-02	Cape Breton	QMJHL	55	26	14	8	3043	141	2	2.78	16	9	7	1003	55	0	3.29
2002-03	Cape Breton	QMJHL	51	17	24	6	2889	162	2	3.36	4	0	4	228	17	0	4.47
2003-04	**Pittsburgh**	**NHL**	**21**	**4**	**14**	**2**	**1154**	**70**	**1**	**3.64**	....	....	....	....	....	....	....
	Cape Breton	QMJHL	10	8	1	1	606	20	0	1.98	4	1	3	251	13	0	3.10
	Wilkes-Barre	AHL	....	....	....	....	....	....	....	....	2	0	1	92	6	0	3.90
2004-05	Wilkes-Barre	AHL	54	26	19	4	3029	127	5	2.52	4	0	2	151	11	0	4.36
	NHL Totals		**21**	**4**	**14**	**2**	**1154**	**70**	**1**	**3.64**	....	....	....	....	....	....	....

QMJHL Second All-Star Team (2003)

Returned to **Cape Breton** (QMJHL) by **Pittsburgh**, January 29, 2004.

FORD, Todd (FOHRD, TAWD) TOR.

Goaltender. Catches left. 6'4", 176 lbs. Born, Calgary, Alta., May 1, 1984.
(Toronto's 3rd choice, 74th overall, in 2002 Entry Draft).

			Regular Season								Playoffs						
Season	**Club**	**League**	**GP**	**W**	**L**	**T**	**Mins**	**GA**	**SO**	**Avg**	**GP**	**W**	**L**	**Mins**	**GA**	**SO**	**Avg**
99-2000	Calgary Stamps	CBHL					STATISTICS NOT AVAILABLE										
2000-01	Swift Current	WHL	20	12	4	2	1066	53	0	2.98	1	0	0	26	2	0	4.62
2001-02	Swift Current	WHL	37	18	12	3	2003	99	2	2.97	10	5	5	603	28	0	2.79
2002-03	Swift Current	WHL	28	12	9	5	1588	71	2	2.68	....	....	....	....	....	....	....
	Prince George	WHL	17	4	9	2	936	70	0	4.49	1	0	1	60	7	0	7.00
2003-04	Prince George	WHL	28	8	14	4	1480	82	0	3.32	....	....	....	....	....	....	....
	Vancouver Giants	WHL	10	1	7	1	570	33	0	3.47	1	0	0	32	0	0	0.00
2004-05	Pensacola Ice Pilots	ECHL	28	19	4	2	1576	61	1	2.32	....	....	....	....	....	....	....

FOSTER, Brian (FAW-stuhr, BRIGH-uhn) FLA.

Goaltender. Catches left. 6'1", 155 lbs. Born, Pembroke, NH, February 4, 1987.
(Florida's 6th choice, 161st overall, in 2005 Entry Draft).

			Regular Season								Playoffs						
Season	**Club**	**League**	**GP**	**W**	**L**	**T**	**Mins**	**GA**	**SO**	**Avg**	**GP**	**W**	**L**	**Mins**	**GA**	**SO**	**Avg**
2003-04	N.H. Jr. Monarchs	EJHL					STATISTICS NOT AVAILABLE										
2004-05	N.H. Jr. Monarchs	EJHL	41	30	6	4	2339	....	3	2.51	....	....	....	....	....	....	....

FRANEK, Petr (FRAH-nehk, PEE-tuhr) COL.

Goaltender. Catches left. 5'11", 185 lbs. Born, Most, Czech., April 6, 1975.
(Quebec's 10th choice, 205th overall, in 1993 Entry Draft).

			Regular Season								Playoffs						
Season	**Club**	**League**	**GP**	**W**	**L**	**T**	**Mins**	**GA**	**SO**	**Avg**	**GP**	**W**	**L**	**Mins**	**GA**	**SO**	**Avg**
1992-93	Litvinov	Czech	5	....	....	....	273	15	0	3.29	....	....	....	....	....	....	....
1993-94	Litvinov	CzRep	11	....	....	....	535	34	0	3.81	2	0	1	61	10	0	9.83
1994-95	Litvinov	CzRep	12	....	....	....	657	47	0	4.29	1	0	0	16	0	0	0.00
1995-96	Litvinov	CzRep	36	....	....	....	2096	85	3	2.43	16	....	....	948	47	1	2.97
1996-97	Hershey Bears	AHL	15	4	1	0	457	23	3	3.02	....	....	....	....	....	....	....
	Brantford Smoke	ColHL	6	4	1	0	321	14	0	2.61	....	....	....	....	....	....	....
	Quebec Rafales	IHL	6	3	3	0	357	18	0	3.02	1	0	1	40	4	0	6.00
1997-98	Hershey Bears	AHL	43	19	14	2	2169	98	2	2.71	1	0	1	60	4	0	4.00
1998-99	Utah Grizzlies	IHL	8	1	6	1	446	26	0	3.50	....	....	....	....	....	....	....
	Las Vegas Thunder	IHL	37	17	13	2	1879	107	0	3.42	....	....	....	....	....	....	....
99-2000	Nurnberg	Germany	30	....	....	....	1603	73	2	2.73	....	....	....	....	....	....	....
2000-01	Karlovy Vary	CzRep	44	....	....	....	2507	121	....	2.90	....	....	....	....	....	....	....
2001-02	Karlovy Vary	CzRep	40	....	....	....	2189	109	....	2.99	....	....	....	....	....	....	....
2002-03	Karlovy Vary	CzRep	45	....	....	....	2570	107	5	2.50	....	....	....	....	....	....	....
2003-04	Karlovy Vary	CzRep	25	....	....	....	1471	58	2	2.37	....	....	....	....	....	....	....
	HC Slavia Praha	CzRep	4	....	....	....	245	8	0	1.96	*19	9	10	*1186	39	*3	1.97
2004-05	HC Slavia Praha	CzRep	42	....	....	....	2508	88	5	2.11	7	....	....	372	18	0	2.90

Rights transferred to **Colorado** after **Quebec** franchise relocated, June 21, 1995.

FRAZEE, Jeff (FRAY-zee, JEHF) N.J.

Goaltender. Catches left. 6', 184 lbs. Born, Edina, MN, May 13, 1987.
(New Jersey's 2nd choice, 38th overall, in 2005 Entry Draft).

			Regular Season								Playoffs						
Season	**Club**	**League**	**GP**	**W**	**L**	**T**	**Mins**	**GA**	**SO**	**Avg**	**GP**	**W**	**L**	**Mins**	**GA**	**SO**	**Avg**
2001-02	Holy Angels	High-MN	6	6	0	0	....	....	....	....	....	....	....	....	....	....	....
2002-03	Holy Angels	High-MN	16	14	1	1	....	....	....	....	....	....	....	....	....	....	....
2003-04	USA U-17	USDP	41	23	11	3	2244	102	2	2.73	....	....	....	....	....	....	....
2004-05	USA U-17&U-18	NAHL	9	8	1	0	500	18	1	2.16	....	....	....	....	....	....	....
	USA U-18	USDP	24	....	....	....	1309	59	3	2.71	....	....	....	....	....	....	....

Signed Letter of Intent to attend **Minnesota** (WCHA), November 18, 2004.

FUKUFUJI, Yutaka (foo-koo-FOO-jee, yoo-TA-ka) L.A.

Goaltender. Catches left. 6'1", 160 lbs. Born, Tokyo, Japan, September 17, 1982.
(Los Angeles' 9th choice, 238th overall, in 2004 Entry Draft).

			Regular Season								Playoffs						
Season	**Club**	**League**	**GP**	**W**	**L**	**T**	**Mins**	**GA**	**SO**	**Avg**	**GP**	**W**	**L**	**Mins**	**GA**	**SO**	**Avg**
2003-04	Kokudo Toyko	AsianHL	7	....	....	....	420	13	....	1.86	....	....	....	....	....	....	....
	Kokudo Toyko	Japan	7	....	....	....	430	12	....	1.67	....	....	....	....	....	....	....
2004-05	Bakersfield	ECHL	44	27	9	5	2517	104	3	2.48	....	....	....	....	....	....	....

GARNETT, Michael (gahr-NEHT, MIGH-kuhl) ATL.

Goaltender. Catches left. 6'1", 200 lbs. Born, Saskatoon, Sask., November 25, 1982.
(Atlanta's 2nd choice, 80th overall, in 2001 Entry Draft).

			Regular Season								Playoffs						
Season	**Club**	**League**	**GP**	**W**	**L**	**T**	**Mins**	**GA**	**SO**	**Avg**	**GP**	**W**	**L**	**Mins**	**GA**	**SO**	**Avg**
1997-98	Sask. Contacts	SMHL	3	1	1	0	82	8	0	5.85	....	....	....	....	....	....	....
1998-99	Sask. Contacts	SMHL					STATISTICS NOT AVAILABLE										
99-2000	Kindersley Klippers	SJHL	36	....	....	....	2067	140	1	3.57	....	....	....	....	....	....	....
	Red Deer Rebels	WHL	1	0	0	0	14	0	0	0.00	1	0	1	65	2	0	1.85
2000-01	Red Deer Rebels	WHL	21	14	5	1	1133	39	3	2.07	....	....	....	....	....	....	....
	Saskatoon Blades	WHL	28	7	17	2	1501	83	1	3.32	....	....	....	....	....	....	....
2001-02	Saskatoon Blades	WHL	*67	27	34	4	*3738	205	2	3.29	7	3	4	450	15	0	2.00
2002-03	Chicago Wolves	AHL	2	0	1	0	33	2	0	3.64	....	....	....	....	....	....	....
	Greenville Grrrowl	ECHL	38	16	15	3	2092	119	0	3.41	3	1	2	178	13	0	4.38
2003-04	Gwinnett	ECHL	33	21	10	2	1936	69	4	2.14	12	7	5	770	34	0	2.65
	Chicago Wolves	AHL	13	7	3	2	731	32	0	2.63	....	....	....	....	....	....	....
2004-05	Chicago Wolves	AHL	24	11	9	0	1321	63	1	2.86	2	2	0	119	3	0	1.51

GARON, Mathieu (gah-ROHN, MA-tyew) L.A.

Goaltender. Catches right. 6'2", 192 lbs. Born, Chandler, Que., January 9, 1978.
(Montreal's 2nd choice, 44th overall, in 1996 Entry Draft).

			Regular Season								Playoffs						
Season	**Club**	**League**	**GP**	**W**	**L**	**T**	**Mins**	**GA**	**SO**	**Avg**	**GP**	**W**	**L**	**Mins**	**GA**	**SO**	**Avg**
1993-94	Jonquiere Elites	QAAA	17	0	13	0	834	88	0	6.33	....	....	....	....	....	....	....
1994-95	Jonquiere Elites	QAAA	27	13	13	1	1554	94	0	3.63	9	6	2	467	26	0	3.34
1995-96	Victoriaville Tigres	QMJHL	51	18	27	0	2709	189	1	4.19	12	7	4	676	38	1	3.39
1996-97	Victoriaville Tigres	QMJHL	53	29	18	3	3032	150	*6	2.97	6	2	4	330	23	0	4.18
1997-98	Victoriaville Tigres	QMJHL	47	27	18	2	2802	125	5	2.68	6	2	4	345	22	0	3.82
1998-99	Fredericton	AHL	40	14	22	2	2222	114	3	3.08	6	1	1	208	12	0	3.47
99-2000	Quebec Citadelles	AHL	53	17	28	3	2884	149	2	3.10	1	0	0	20	3	0	8.82
2000-01	**Montreal**	**NHL**	**11**	**4**	**5**	**1**	**589**	**24**	**2**	**2.44**	....	....	....	....	....	....	....
	Quebec Citadelles	AHL	31	16	13	1	1768	86	1	2.92	8	4	4	459	22	1	2.88
2001-02	**Montreal**	**NHL**	**5**	**1**	**4**	**0**	**261**	**19**	**0**	**4.37**	....	....	....	....	....	....	....
	Quebec Citadelles	AHL	50	21	15	12	2988	136	2	2.73	3	0	3	198	12	0	3.63
2002-03	**Montreal**	**NHL**	**8**	**3**	**5**	**0**	**482**	**16**	**2**	**1.99**	....	....	....	....	....	....	....
	Hamilton Bulldogs	AHL	20	15	2	2	1150	34	4	1.77	....	....	....	....	....	....	....
2003-04	**Montreal**	**NHL**	**19**	**8**	**6**	**2**	**1003**	**38**	**0**	**2.27**	**1**	**0**	**0**	**12**	**0**	**0**	**0.00**
2004-05	Manchester	AHL	52	32	14	4	2969	105	8	2.12	6	2	4	285	17	0	3.58
	NHL Totals		**43**	**16**	**20**	**3**	**2335**	**97**	**4**	**2.49**	**1**	**0**	**0**	**12**	**0**	**0**	**0.00**

QMJHL All-Rookie Team (1996) • QMJHL Defensive Rookie of the Year (1996) • QMJHL First All-Star Team (1998) • Canadian Major Junior First All-Star Team (1998) • Canadian Major Junior Goaltender of the Year (1998)

Traded to **Los Angeles** by **Montreal** with San Jose's 3rd round choice (previously acquired, Los Angeles selected Paul Baier) in 2004 Entry Draft for Radek Bonk and Cristobal Huet, June 26, 2004.

GERBER, Martin (GUHR-buhr, MAHR-tihn) CAR.

Goaltender. Catches left. 6', 185 lbs. Born, Burgdorf, Switz., September 3, 1974.
(Anaheim's 10th choice, 232nd overall, in 2001 Entry Draft).

			Regular Season								Playoffs						
Season	**Club**	**League**	**GP**	**W**	**L**	**T**	**Mins**	**GA**	**SO**	**Avg**	**GP**	**W**	**L**	**Mins**	**GA**	**SO**	**Avg**
1996-97	SC Langnau	Swiss-2	38	....	....	....	2286	121	0	3.18	8	....	....	488	29	0	3.57
1997-98	SC Langnau	Swiss-2	40	....	....	....	2430	141	2	3.48	16	....	....	961	42	0	2.62
1998-99	SC Langnau	Swiss	42	....	....	....	2521	203	1	4.83	11	....	....	664	50	0	4.52
99-2000	SC Langnau	Swiss	44	....	....	....	2652	161	3	3.64	6	....	....	360	13	*2	*2.17
2000-01	SCL Tigers Langnau	Swiss	*44	....	....	....	2671	114	3	2.56	5	....	....	319	7	1	1.32
2001-02	Farjestad	Sweden	44	....	....	....	2664	87	*4	*1.96	*10	....	....	*657	18	*2	*1.64
	Switzerland	Olympics	3	1	1	1	158	4	0	1.52	....	....	....	....	....	....	....
2002-03	**Anaheim**	**NHL**	**22**	**6**	**11**	**3**	**1203**	**39**	**1**	**1.95**	**2**	**0**	**0**	**20**	**1**	**0**	**3.00**
	Cincinnati	AHL	1	1	0	0	60	2	0	2.00	....	....	....	....	....	....	....
2003-04	**Anaheim**	**NHL**	**32**	**11**	**12**	**4**	**1698**	**64**	**2**	**2.26**	....	....	....	....	....	....	....
2004-05	SCL Tigers Langnau	Swiss	20	6	10	4	1220	59	0	2.90	....	....	....	....	....	....	....
	Farjestad	Sweden	30	20	6	4	1827	58	4	1.90	*15	9	6	*900	36	1	2.40
	NHL Totals		**54**	**17**	**23**	**7**	**2901**	**103**	**3**	**2.13**	**2**	**0**	**0**	**20**	**1**	**0**	**3.00**

• Scored a goal in playoffs vs. Martigny (Swiss-2), February 27, 1997. Traded to **Carolina** by **Anaheim** for Tomas Malec and Carolina's 3rd round choice (Kyle Klubertanz) in 2004 Entry Draft, June 18, 2004. Signed as a free agent by **Langnau** (Swiss), September 17, 2004. Signed as a free agent by **Farjestad** (Sweden), November 7, 2004.

GIGUERE, Jean-Sebastien (ZHEE-gair, ZHAWN-suh-BAS-tee-yeh) ANA.

Goaltender. Catches left. 6'1", 199 lbs. Born, Montreal, Que., May 16, 1977.
(Hartford's 1st choice, 13th overall, in 1995 Entry Draft).

			Regular Season								Playoffs						
Season	**Club**	**League**	**GP**	**W**	**L**	**T**	**Mins**	**GA**	**SO**	**Avg**	**GP**	**W**	**L**	**Mins**	**GA**	**SO**	**Avg**
1992-93	Laval-Laurentides	QAAA	25	12	11	2	1498	76	0	3.02	11	6	5	654	38	0	3.49
1993-94	Verdun	QMJHL	25	13	5	2	1234	66	1	3.21	....	....	....	....	....	....	....
1994-95	Halifax	QMJHL	47	14	27	5	2755	181	2	3.94	7	3	4	417	17	1	*2.45
1995-96	Halifax	QMJHL	55	26	23	2	3230	185	1	3.44	6	1	5	354	24	0	4.07
1996-97	**Hartford**	**NHL**	**8**	**1**	**4**	**0**	**394**	**24**	**0**	**3.65**	....	....	....	....	....	....	....
	Halifax	QMJHL	50	28	19	3	3014	170	2	3.38	16	9	7	954	58	0	3.65
1997-98	Saint John Flames	AHL	31	16	10	3	1758	72	2	2.46	10	5	3	536	27	0	3.02
1998-99	**Calgary**	**NHL**	**15**	**6**	**7**	**1**	**860**	**46**	**0**	**3.21**	....	....	....	....	....	....	....
	Saint John Flames	AHL	39	18	16	3	2145	123	3	3.44	7	3	2	304	21	0	4.14
99-2000	**Calgary**	**NHL**	**7**	**1**	**3**	**1**	**330**	**15**	**0**	**2.73**	....	....	....	....	....	....	....
	Saint John Flames	AHL	41	17	17	3	2243	114	0	3.05	3	0	3	178	9	0	3.03
2000-01	**Anaheim**	**NHL**	**34**	**11**	**17**	**5**	**2031**	**87**	**4**	**2.57**	....	....	....	....	....	....	....
	Cincinnati	AHL	23	12	7	2	1306	53	0	2.43	....	....	....	....	....	....	....
2001-02	**Anaheim**	**NHL**	**53**	**20**	**25**	**6**	**3127**	**111**	**4**	**2.13**	....	....	....	....	....	....	....
2002-03	**Anaheim**	**NHL**	**65**	**34**	**22**	**6**	**3775**	**145**	**8**	**2.30**	**21**	**15**	**6**	**1407**	**38**	**5**	***1.62**
2003-04	**Anaheim**	**NHL**	**55**	**17**	**31**	**6**	**3210**	**140**	**3**	**2.62**	....	....	....	....	....	....	....
2004-05	Hamburg Freezers	Germany	6	....	....	....	301	12	0	2.39	2	....	....	100	7	0	4.20
	NHL Totals		**237**	**90**	**109**	**25**	**13727**	**568**	**19**	**2.48**	**21**	**15**	**6**	**1407**	**38**	**5**	**1.62**

QMJHL Second All-Star Team (1997) • AHL All-Rookie Team (1998) • Harry "Hap" Holmes Memorial Award (fewest goals against – AHL) (1998) (shared with Tyler Moss) • Conn Smythe Trophy (2003)

Transferred to **Carolina** after **Hartford** franchise relocated, June 25, 1997. Traded to **Calgary** by **Carolina** with Andrew Cassels for Gary Roberts and Trevor Kidd, August 25, 1997. Traded to **Anaheim** by **Calgary** for Anaheim's 2nd round choice (later traded to Washington – Washington selected Matt Pettinger) in 2000 Entry Draft, June 10, 2000. Signed as a free agent by **Hamburg** (Germany), January 31, 2005.

GLASS, Jeff (GLAS, JEHF) OTT.

Goaltender. Catches left. 6'2", 182 lbs. Born, Calgary, Alta., November 19, 1985.
(Ottawa's 5th choice, 89th overall, in 2004 Entry Draft).

			Regular Season								Playoffs						
Season	**Club**	**League**	**GP**	**W**	**L**	**T**	**Mins**	**GA**	**SO**	**Avg**	**GP**	**W**	**L**	**Mins**	**GA**	**SO**	**Avg**
2001-02	Crowsnest Pass	AJHL	34	....	....	....	1802	126	0	4.20	....	....	....	....	....	....	....
2002-03	Kootenay Ice	WHL	35	15	16	3	1884	77	4	2.45	9	4	5	643	23	0	2.15
2003-04	Kootenay Ice	WHL	57	26	20	6	3263	128	5	2.35	4	0	4	239	14	0	3.51
2004-05	Kootenay Ice	WHL	51	34	11	5	3061	90	8	1.76	16	10	6	1027	39	0	2.28

WHL West First All-Star Team (2005) • WHL Goaltender of the Year (2005) • Canadian Major Junior First All-Star Team (2005) • Canadian Major Junior Goaltender of the Year (2005)

GOEHRING, Karl (GAIR-ihng, KAHRL)

Goaltender. Catches left. 5'8", 160 lbs. Born, Apple Valley, MN, August 23, 1978.

			Regular Season								Playoffs						
Season	**Club**	**League**	**GP**	**W**	**L**	**T**	**Mins**	**GA**	**SO**	**Avg**	**GP**	**W**	**L**	**Mins**	**GA**	**SO**	**Avg**
1996-97	Fargo-Moorhead	USHL	32	13	18	1	1909	79	*4	*2.48	5	2	3	251	15	1	3.58
1997-98	North Dakota	WCHA	27	23	3	1	1504	57	1	*2.27	....	....	....	....	....	....	....
1998-99	North Dakota	WCHA	31	22	5	2	1774	71	3	2.40	....	....	....	....	....	....	....
99-2000	North Dakota	WCHA	30	19	6	4	1747	55	*8	*1.89	....	....	....	....	....	....	....
2000-01	North Dakota	WCHA	30	16	6	6	1662	66	*3	2.38	....	....	....	....	....	....	....
2001-02	Syracuse Crunch	AHL	15	5	6	3	891	37	1	2.49	....	....	....	....	....	....	....
	Dayton Bombers	ECHL	23	11	9	3	1393	52	2	2.24	*14	9	5	*866	35	1	2.43
2002-03	Syracuse Crunch	AHL	49	18	21	4	2608	116	4	2.67	....	....	....	....	....	....	....
2003-04	Syracuse Crunch	AHL	38	17	14	6	2234	97	1	2.60	5	2	2	295	16	0	3.26

2004-05	Syracuse Crunch	AHL	49	23	22	0	2788	128	3	2.75	....	....	....	....	....	....	....

WCHA First All-Star Team (1998, 2000) • WCHA Rookie of the Year (1998) • NCAA West First All-American Team (1998, 2000) • WCHA Second All-Star Team (1999)

Signed as a free agent by **Columbus**, May 7, 2001.

GOEPFERT, Robert (GEHP-fuhrt, RAW-buhrt) PIT.

Goaltender. Catches left. 5'10", 170 lbs. Born, Ozone Park, NY, May 9, 1983.
(Pittsburgh's 7th choice, 171st overall, in 2002 Entry Draft).

			Regular Season								Playoffs						
Season	Club	League	GP	W	L	T	Mins	GA	SO	Avg	GP	W	L	Mins	GA	SO	Avg
99-2000	Suffolk PAL	Metro-Jr.	38	....	....	....	2280	87	....	2.36	....	....	....	....	....	....	....
2000-01	Cedar Rapids	USHL	41	25	12	4	2565	125	1	2.92	4	1	3	188	18	0	5.73
2001-02	Cedar Rapids	USHL	51	27	16	5	2918	99	8	2.04	8	4	4	581	19	0	1.97
2002-03	Providence College	H-East	13	6	6	1	754	30	1	2.39	....	....	....	....	....	....	....
2003-04	Providence College	H-East	28	15	9	3	1641	68	2	2.49	....	....	....	....	....	....	....
2004-05	St. Cloud State	WCHA	DID NOT PLAY – TRANSFERRED COLLEGES														

USHL All-Rookie Team (2001) • USHL Goaltender of the Year (2001, 2002) • USHL First All-Star Team (2002) • USHL Player of the Year (2002)

GRAHAME, John (GRAY-uhm, JAWN) T.B.

Goaltender. Catches left. 6'2", 220 lbs. Born, Denver, CO, August 31, 1975.
(Boston's 7th choice, 229th overall, in 1994 Entry Draft).

			Regular Season								Playoffs						
Season	Club	League	GP	W	L	T	Mins	GA	SO	Avg	GP	W	L	Mins	GA	SO	Avg
1993-94	Sioux City	USHL	20	....	....	....	1200	73	0	3.70	....	....	....	....	....	....	....
1994-95	Lake Superior State	CCHA	28	16	7	3	1616	75	2	2.79	....	....	....	....	....	....	....
1995-96	Lake Superior State	CCHA	29	21	4	2	1558	66	2	2.54	....	....	....	....	....	....	....
1996-97	Lake Superior State	CCHA	37	19	13	4	2197	134	3	3.66	....	....	....	....	....	....	....
1997-98	Providence Bruins	AHL	55	15	31	4	3053	164	3	3.22	....	....	....	....	....	....	....
1998-99	Providence Bruins	AHL	48	*37	9	1	2771	134	3	2.90	19	*15	4	*1209	48	1	2.38
99-2000	**Boston**	**NHL**	**24**	**7**	**10**	**5**	**1344**	**55**	**2**	**2.46**	....	....	....	....	....	....	....
	Providence Bruins	AHL	27	11	13	2	1528	86	1	3.38	13	10	3	839	35	0	2.50
2000-01	**Boston**	**NHL**	**10**	**3**	**4**	**0**	**471**	**28**	**0**	**3.57**	....	....	....	....	....	....	....
	Providence Bruins	AHL	16	4	7	3	893	47	0	3.16	17	8	9	1043	46	2	2.65
2001-02	**Boston**	**NHL**	**19**	**8**	**7**	**2**	**1079**	**52**	**1**	**2.89**	....	....	....	....	....	....	....
2002-03	**Boston**	**NHL**	**23**	**11**	**9**	**2**	**1352**	**61**	**1**	**2.71**	....	....	....	....	....	....	....
	Tampa Bay	**NHL**	**17**	**6**	**5**	**4**	**914**	**34**	**2**	**2.23**	**1**	**0**	**1**	**111**	**2**	**0**	**1.08**
2003-04♦	**Tampa Bay**	**NHL**	**29**	**18**	**9**	**1**	**1688**	**58**	**1**	**2.06**	**1**	**0**	**0**	**34**	**2**	**0**	**3.53**
2004-05			DID NOT PLAY														
	NHL Totals		**122**	**53**	**44**	**14**	**6848**	**288**	**7**	**2.52**	**2**	**0**	**1**	**145**	**4**	**0**	**1.66**

Traded to **Tampa Bay** by **Boston** for Tampa Bay's 4th round choice (later traded to San Jose – San Jose selected Jason Churchill) in 2004 Entry Draft, January 13, 2003.

GRAHN, Carl (GRAHN, KARL) L.A.

Goaltender. Catches left. 6', 175 lbs. Born, Koupolo, Finland, January 8, 1981.
(Los Angeles' 11th choice, 282nd overall, in 2000 Entry Draft).

			Regular Season								Playoffs						
Season	Club	League	GP	W	L	T	Mins	GA	SO	Avg	GP	W	L	Mins	GA	SO	Avg
1998-99	KalPa Kuopio Jr.	Finland-Jr.	20	7	10	1	1153	63	1	3.28	....	....	....	....	....	....	....
	KalPa Kuopio	Finland	3	0	2	0	126	16	0	7.63	....	....	....	....	....	....	....
99-2000	KooKoo Jr.	Finland-Jr.	38	....	....	....	2165	124	1	3.44	....	....	....	....	....	....	....
2000-01	KooKoo Kouvola	Finland-2	14	2	8	1	631	41	0	3.90	....	....	....	....	....	....	....
2001-02	KooKoo Kouvola	Finland-2	36	19	10	6	2059	88	4	2.56	10	4	5	562	29	0	3.11
2002-03	KooKoo Kouvola	Finland-2	21	11	5	5	1276	49	2	2.30	8	4	3	466	21	1	2.71
2003-04	Pelicans Lahti	Finland	21	1	11	3	1121	72	0	3.85	....	....	....	....	....	....	....
	Kiekko-Vantaa	Finland-2	8	4	3	1	475	22	0	2.78	....	....	....	....	....	....	....
2004-05	KooKoo Kouvola	Finland-2	35	8	19	7	1971	101	2	3.07	....	....	....	....	....	....	....

GREISS, Thomas (GRIGHS, TAW-muhs) S.J.

Goaltender. Catches left. 6'1", 192 lbs. Born, Straubing, West Germany, January 29, 1986.
(San Jose's 2nd choice, 94th overall, in 2004 Entry Draft).

			Regular Season								Playoffs						
Season	Club	League	GP	W	L	T	Mins	GA	SO	Avg	GP	W	L	Mins	GA	SO	Avg
2001-02	EV Fussen Jr.	Ger-Jr.	STATISTICS NOT AVAILABLE														
2002-03	Koln Jr.	Ger-Jr.	25	....	....	....	1613	58	0	2.16	3	1	2	180	8	1	2.67
2003-04	Koln Jr.	Ger-Jr.	24	....	....	....	1286	56	....	2.61	....	....	....	....	....	....	....
	Kolner Haie	Germany	1	....	....	....	20	4	0	12.00	....	....	....	....	....	....	....
2004-05	Kolner Haie	Germany	8	....	....	....	459	16	0	2.09	....	....	....	....	....	....	....
	Regensburg	German-2	1	....	....	....	60	2	0	2.00	2	....	....	56	2	0	2.14

GUARD, Kelly (G'YEW-uhrd, KEHL-lee) OTT.

Goaltender. Catches left. 6'1", 203 lbs. Born, Prince Albert, Sask., June 10, 1983.

			Regular Season								Playoffs						
Season	Club	League	GP	W	L	T	Mins	GA	SO	Avg	GP	W	L	Mins	GA	SO	Avg
99-2000	Prince Albert	SMHL	STATISTICS NOT AVAILABLE														
2000-01	Prince Albert	SMHL	25	....	....	....	1488	81	0	3.27	....	....	....	....	....	....	....
	La Ronge	SJHL	STATISTICS NOT AVAILABLE														
2001-02	Kindersley Klippers	SJHL	45	29	11	4	2628	130	1	2.97	19	12	6	1145	60	1	3.14
2002-03	Kelowna Rockets	WHL	53	39	10	3	3018	97	*6	*1.93	19	*16	3	1233	36	*4	*1.75
2003-04	Kelowna Rockets	WHL	62	*44	14	4	3652	95	*13	*1.56	17	11	6	1042	31	1	1.79
2004-05	Charlotte Checkers	ECHL	26	12	11	2	1453	74	0	3.06	2	0	0	40	1	0	1.52

WHL West First All-Star Team (2003, 2004) • Memorial Cup Tournament All-Star Team (2004) • Hap Emms Memorial Trophy (Memorial Cup Tournament Top Goaltender) (2004) • Stafford Smythe Memorial Trophy (Memorial Cup Tournament MVP) (2004)

Signed as a free agent by **Ottawa**, May 11, 2004.

GUSTAFSON, Derek (GUHST-ahf-suhn, DAIR-ihk)

Goaltender. Catches left. 5'11", 210 lbs. Born, Gresham, OR, June 21, 1979.

			Regular Season								Playoffs						
Season	Club	League	GP	W	L	T	Mins	GA	SO	Avg	GP	W	L	Mins	GA	SO	Avg
1995-96	Seattle Ironmen	BCAHA	16	....	....	....	913	46	0	3.02	....	....	....	....	....	....	....
1996-97	Vernon Vipers	BCHL	23	....	....	....	1241	70	0	3.38	....	....	....	....	....	....	....
1997-98	Vernon Vipers	BCHL	42	27	13	2	2270	144	1	3.81	6	2	1	257	13	0	3.04
1998-99	Vernon Vipers	BCHL	42	39	3	0	2505	94	3	2.25	....	....	....	....	....	....	....
99-2000	St. Lawrence	ECAC	24	17	4	2	1475	51	2	2.07	....	....	....	....	....	....	....
2000-01	**Minnesota**	**NHL**	**4**	**1**	**3**	**0**	**239**	**10**	**0**	**2.51**	....	....	....	....	....	....	....
	Jackson Bandits	ECHL	7	4	3	0	404	15	1	2.23	....	....	....	....	....	....	....
	Cleveland	IHL	24	14	7	1	1293	59	2	2.74	2	0	1	53	5	0	5.64
2001-02	**Minnesota**	**NHL**	**1**	**0**	**0**	**0**	**26**	**0**	**0**	**0.00**	....	....	....	....	....	....	....
	Houston Aeros	AHL	38	14	13	6	2016	92	4	2.74	2	0	0	25	1	0	2.37
2002-03	Houston Aeros	AHL	41	23	14	2	2301	108	2	2.82	....	....	....	....	....	....	....
	Louisiana	ECHL	2	1	1	0	118	8	0	4.07	....	....	....	....	....	....	....
2003-04	Louisiana	ECHL	43	28	14	0	2499	87	*5	2.09	8	4	4	560	19	1	2.03
2004-05	Adirondack	UHL	57	32	18	6	3290	155	4	2.83	3	0	3	222	9	0	2.43
	NHL Totals		**5**	**1**	**3**	**0**	**265**	**10**	**0**	**2.26**	....	....	....	....	....	....	....

ECAC Second All-Star Team (2000) • ECAC Rookie of the Year (2000) • ECHL Second All-Star Team (2004)

Signed as a free agent by **Minnesota**, June 9, 2000. Signed as a free agent by **Louisiana** (ECHL), October 1, 2003. Signed as a free agent by **Adirondack** (UHL) , July 23, 2004.

HALAK, Jaroslav (HAH-lak, YAHR-roh-slav) MTL.

Goaltender. Catches left. 5'11", 171 lbs. Born, Bratislava, Slovakia, May 13, 1985.
(Montreal's 11th choice, 271st overall, in 2003 Entry Draft).

			Regular Season								Playoffs						
Season	Club	League	GP	W	L	T	Mins	GA	SO	Avg	GP	W	L	Mins	GA	SO	Avg
2001-02	Bratislava Jr.	Slovak-Jr.	22	....	....	....	1257	41	0	1.96	6	6	0	353	7	2	1.19
2002-03	Bratislava Jr.	Slovak-Jr.	20	13	3	3	1200	41	1	2.02	....	....	....	....	....	....	....
2003-04	Bratislava Jr.	Slovak-Jr.	29	....	....	....	1694	51	....	1.81	....	....	....	....	....	....	....
	HK 91 Senica	Slovak-2	21	....	....	....	1240	54	....	2.61	....	....	....	....	....	....	....
	Bratislava	Slovakia	12	....	....	....	650	18	0	1.66	1	....	....	45	6	0	8.00
2004-05	Lewiston	QMJHL	47	24	17	4	2697	125	4	2.78	8	4	4	460	27	0	3.52

HANULJAK, Miroslav (HA-nuhl-yak, MEER-oh-slav) NSH.

Goaltender. Catches left. 6'4", 197 lbs. Born, Litvinov, Czech., September 12, 1984.
(Nashville's 12th choice, 213th overall, in 2003 Entry Draft).

			Regular Season								Playoffs						
Season	Club	League	GP	W	L	T	Mins	GA	SO	Avg	GP	W	L	Mins	GA	SO	Avg
99-2000	Litvinov Jr.	CzRep-Jr.	42	....	....	....	2274	130	3	3.43	....	....	....	....	....	....	....
2000-01	Litvinov Jr.	CzRep-Jr.	48	....	....	....	2647	97	11	2.20	6	....	....	361	19	0	3.16
2001-02	Litvinov Jr.	CzRep-Jr.	5	....	....	....	274	9	0	1.97	....	....	....	....	....	....	....
2002-03	Litvinov Jr.	CzRep-Jr.	30	....	....	....	1515	67	1	2.65	....	....	....	....	....	....	....
2003-04	Litvinov Jr.	CzRep-Jr.	6	....	....	....	287	10	2	2.09	....	....	....	....	....	....	....
	HC Havirov Jr.	CzRep-Jr.	26	....	....	....	1494	66	3	2.65	....	....	....	....	....	....	....
2004-05	HC Havirov Jr.	CzRep-Jr.	16	9	4	3	894	40	1	2.68	....	....	....	....	....	....	....
	HC Havirov	CzRep-2	9	3	6	0	451	25	0	3.33	....	....	....	....	....	....	....
	SK HC Banik Most	CzRep-3	11	5	5	1	595	28	0	2.82	5	2	3	300	14	0	2.80

HARDING, Josh (HAHR-dihng, JAWSH) MIN.

Goaltender. Catches right. 6'1", 180 lbs. Born, Regina, Sask., June 18, 1984.
(Minnesota's 2nd choice, 38th overall, in 2002 Entry Draft).

			Regular Season								Playoffs						
Season	Club	League	GP	W	L	T	Mins	GA	SO	Avg	GP	W	L	Mins	GA	SO	Avg
2000-01	Reg. Pat Cdns.	SMHL	36	17	13	0	2106	96	2	2.75	3	1	2	170	11	0	3.88
2001-02	Regina Pats	WHL	42	27	13	1	2389	95	*4	2.39	6	2	4	325	16	0	2.95
2002-03	Regina Pats	WHL	57	18	24	13	*3385	155	3	2.75	5	1	4	321	13	0	2.43
2003-04	Regina Pats	WHL	28	12	14	2	1665	67	2	2.41	....	....	....	....	....	....	....
	Brandon	WHL	27	13	11	3	1612	65	5	2.42	11	5	6	660	36	0	3.27
2004-05	Houston Aeros	AHL	42	21	16	3	2388	80	4	2.01	2	0	2	119	8	0	4.03

WHL East Second All-Star Team (2002) • WHL East First All-Star Team (2003) • WHL Goaltender of the Year (2003) • WHL Player of the Year (2003)

HASEK, Dominik (HAH-shihk, DOHM-ihn-ihk) OTT.

Goaltender. Catches left. 5'11", 180 lbs. Born, Pardubice, Czech., January 29, 1965.
(Chicago's 11th choice, 207th overall, in 1983 Entry Draft).

			Regular Season								Playoffs						
Season	Club	League	GP	W	L	T	Mins	GA	SO	Avg	GP	W	L	Mins	GA	SO	Avg
1981-82	Tesla Pardubice	Czech	12	....	....	....	661	34	....	3.09	....	....	....	....	....	....	....
1982-83	Tesla Pardubice	Czech	42	....	....	....	2358	105	....	2.67	....	....	....	....	....	....	....
1983-84	Tesla Pardubice	Czech	40	....	....	....	2304	108	....	2.81	....	....	....	....	....	....	....
1984-85	Tesla Pardubice	Czech	42	....	....	....	2419	131	....	3.25	....	....	....	....	....	....	....
1985-86	Tesla Pardubice	Czech	45	....	....	....	2689	138	....	3.08	....	....	....	....	....	....	....
1986-87	Tesla Pardubice	Czech	43	....	....	....	2515	103	....	2.46	....	....	....	....	....	....	....
1987-88	Tesla Pardubice	Czech	31	....	....	....	1862	93	....	3.00	....	....	....	....	....	....	....
	Czechoslovakia	Olympics	5	3	2	0	217	18	1	4.98	....	....	....	....	....	....	....
1988-89	Tesla Pardubice	Czech	42	....	....	....	2507	114	....	2.73	....	....	....	....	....	....	....
1989-90	Dukla Jihlava	Czech	40	....	....	....	2251	80	....	2.13	....	....	....	....	....	....	....
1990-91	**Chicago**	**NHL**	**5**	**3**	**0**	**1**	**195**	**8**	**0**	**2.46**	**3**	**0**	**0**	**69**	**3**	**0**	**2.61**
	Indianapolis Ice	IHL	33	20	11	1	1903	80	*5	*2.52	1	1	0	60	3	0	3.00
1991-92	**Chicago**	**NHL**	**20**	**10**	**4**	**1**	**1014**	**44**	**1**	**2.60**	**3**	**0**	**2**	**158**	**8**	**0**	**3.04**
	Indianapolis Ice	IHL	20	7	10	3	1162	69	1	3.56	....	....	....	....	....	....	....
1992-93	**Buffalo**	**NHL**	**28**	**11**	**10**	**4**	**1429**	**75**	**0**	**3.15**	**1**	**1**	**0**	**45**	**1**	**0**	**1.33**
1993-94	**Buffalo**	**NHL**	**58**	**30**	**20**	**6**	**3358**	**109**	***7**	***1.95**	**7**	**3**	**4**	**484**	**13**	**2**	***1.61**
1994-95	HC Pardubice	CzRep	2	1	0	1	124	6	0	2.90	....	....	....	....	....	....	....
	Buffalo	**NHL**	**41**	**19**	**14**	**7**	**2416**	**85**	***5**	***2.11**	**5**	**1**	**4**	**309**	**18**	**0**	**3.50**
1995-96	**Buffalo**	**NHL**	**59**	**22**	**30**	**6**	**3417**	**161**	**2**	**2.83**	....	....	....	....	....	....	....
1996-97	**Buffalo**	**NHL**	**67**	**37**	**20**	**10**	**4037**	**153**	**5**	**2.27**	**3**	**1**	**1**	**153**	**5**	**0**	**1.96**
1997-98	**Buffalo**	**NHL**	***72**	**33**	**23**	**13**	***4220**	**147**	***13**	**2.09**	**15**	**10**	**5**	**948**	**32**	**1**	**2.03**
	Czech Republic	Olympics	6	*5	1	0	*369	6	*2	*0.97	....	....	....	....	....	....	....
1998-99	**Buffalo**	**NHL**	**64**	**30**	**18**	**14**	**3817**	**119**	**9**	**1.87**	**19**	**13**	**6**	**1217**	**36**	**2**	**1.77**
99-2000	**Buffalo**	**NHL**	**35**	**15**	**11**	**6**	**2066**	**76**	**3**	**2.21**	**5**	**1**	**4**	**301**	**12**	**0**	**2.39**
2000-01	**Buffalo**	**NHL**	**67**	**37**	**24**	**4**	**3904**	**137**	***11**	**2.11**	**13**	**7**	**6**	**833**	**29**	**1**	**2.09**
2001-02♦	**Detroit**	**NHL**	**65**	***41**	**15**	**8**	**3872**	**140**	**5**	**2.17**	***23**	***16**	**7**	***1455**	**45**	***6**	**1.86**
	Czech Republic	Olympics	4	1	2	1	239	8	0	2.01	....	....	....	....	....	....	....
2002-03			OUT OF HOCKEY – RETIRED														
2003-04	**Detroit**	**NHL**	**14**	**8**	**3**	**2**	**817**	**30**	**2**	**2.20**	....	....	....	....	....	....	....
2004-05			DID NOT PLAY														
	NHL Totals		**595**	**296**	**192**	**82**	**34562**	**1284**	**63**	**2.23**	**97**	**53**	**39**	**5972**	**202**	**12**	**2.03**

Czechoslovakian Goaltender of the Year (1986, 1987, 1988, 1989, 1990) • Czechoslovakian Player of the Year (1987, 1989, 1990) • Czechoslovakian First All-Star Team (1988, 1989, 1990) • IHL First All-Star Team (1991) • NHL All-Rookie Team (1992) • NHL First All-Star Team (1994, 1995, 1997, 1998, 1999, 2001) • William M. Jennings Trophy (1994) (shared with Grant Fuhr) • Vezina Trophy (1994, 1995, 1997, 1998, 1999, 2001) • Lester B. Pearson Award (1997, 1998) • Hart Trophy (1997, 1998) • William M. Jennings Trophy (2001)

Played in NHL All-Star Game (1996, 1997, 1998, 1999, 2001, 2002)

Traded to **Buffalo** by **Chicago** for Stephane Beauregard and Buffalo's 4th round choice (Eric Daze) in 1993 Entry Draft, August 7, 1992. Traded to **Detroit** by **Buffalo** for Vyacheslav Kozlov, Detroit's 1st round choice (later traded to Columbus – later traded to Atlanta – Atlanta selected Jim Slater) in 2002 Entry Draft and future considerations, July 1, 2001. • Officially announced retirement, June 25, 2002. • **Detroit** picked up the option on his contract, July 1, 2003. • Missed majority of 2003-04 season recovering from groin injury suffered in game vs. St. Louis, October 29, 2003. Signed as a free agent by **Ottawa**, July 6, 2004.

HAUSER, Adam (HOW-suhr, A-duhm) L.A.

Goaltender. Catches left. 6'2", 195 lbs. Born, Bovey, MN, May 27, 1980.
(Edmonton's 4th choice, 81st overall, in 1999 Entry Draft).

			Regular Season								Playoffs						
Season	Club	League	GP	W	L	T	Mins	GA	SO	Avg	GP	W	L	Mins	GA	SO	Avg
1996-97	Greenway Raiders	High-MN	25	....	....	....	1496	63	0	2.54	....	....	....	....	....	....	....
1997-98	USA U-18	USDP	38	19	10	7	2110	94	4	2.67	....	....	....	....	....	....	....
1998-99	U. of Minnesota	WCHA	*40	14	18	8	*2350	136	3	3.47	....	....	....	....	....	....	....
99-2000	U. of Minnesota	WCHA	36	20	14	2	2114	104	1	2.95	....	....	....	....	....	....	....
2000-01	U. of Minnesota	WCHA	40	*26	12	2	2366	101	*3	2.56	....	....	....	....	....	....	....
2001-02	U. of Minnesota	WCHA	35	*23	6	4	2003	80	1	2.40	....	....	....	....	....	....	....
2002-03	Jackson Bandits	ECHL	34	20	9	4	2021	83	*5	2.46	....	....	....	....	....	....	....
	Providence Bruins	AHL	1	0	0	1	64	3	0	2.80	....	....	....	....	....	....	....
2003-04	Manchester	AHL	43	20	15	7	2536	82	7	1.94	4	2	2	286	9	2	1.89
	Reading Royals	ECHL	4	3	0	1	245	7	1	1.71	....	....	....	....	....	....	....
2004-05	Manchester	AHL	32	19	11	0	1867	60	5	1.93	2	0	0	70	2	0	1.71

NCAA Championship All-Tournament Team (2002) • ECHL All-Rookie Team (2003)

Signed as a free agent by **Manchester** (AHL), August 19, 2003. Signed as a free agent by **Los Angeles**, July 8, 2004.

HEDBERG, Johan (HEHD-buhrg, YO-han) DAL.

Goaltender. Catches left. 6', 184 lbs. Born, Leksand, Sweden, May 5, 1973.
(Philadelphia's 8th choice, 218th overall, in 1994 Entry Draft).

			Regular Season								Playoffs						
Season	**Club**	**League**	**GP**	**W**	**L**	**T**	**Mins**	**GA**	**SO**	**Avg**	**GP**	**W**	**L**	**Mins**	**GA**	**SO**	**Avg**
1992-93	Leksands IF	Sweden	10	....	....	....	600	24	....	2.40	....	....	....	....	....	....	....
1993-94	Leksands IF	Sweden	17	....	....	....	1020	48	....	2.82	....	....	....	....	....	....	....
1994-95	Leksands IF	Sweden	17	....	....	....	986	58	....	3.53	....	....	....	....	....	....	....
1995-96	Leksands IF	Sweden	34	....	....	....	2013	95	....	2.83	4	....	....	240	13	....	3.25
1996-97	Leksands IF	Sweden	38	....	....	....	2260	95	3	2.52	8	....	....	581	18	1	1.86
1997-98	Baton Rouge	ECHL	2	1	1	0	100	7	0	4.20	....	....	....	....	....	....	....
	Detroit Vipers	IHL	16	7	2	2	726	32	1	2.64	....	....	....	....	....	....	....
	Manitoba Moose	IHL	14	8	4	1	745	32	1	2.58	2	0	2	105	6	0	3.40
1998-99	Leksands IF	Sweden	*48	....	....	....	*2940	140	0	2.86	4	....	....	255	15	0	3.53
99-2000	Kentucky	AHL	33	18	9	5	1973	88	3	2.68	5	3	2	311	10	1	1.93
2000-01	Manitoba Moose	IHL	46	23	13	7	2697	115	1	2.56	....	....	....	....	....	....	....
	Pittsburgh	**NHL**	**9**	**7**	**1**	**1**	**545**	**24**	**0**	**2.64**	**18**	**9**	**9**	**1123**	**43**	**2**	**2.30**
2001-02	**Pittsburgh**	**NHL**	**66**	**25**	**34**	**7**	**3877**	**178**	**6**	**2.75**	....	....	....	....	....	....	....
	Sweden	Olympics	1	1	0	0	60	1	0	1.00	....	....	....	....	....	....	....
2002-03	**Pittsburgh**	**NHL**	**41**	**14**	**22**	**4**	**2410**	**126**	**1**	**3.14**	....	....	....	....	....	....	....
2003-04	**Vancouver**	**NHL**	**21**	**8**	**6**	**2**	**1098**	**46**	**3**	**2.51**	**2**	**1**	**1**	**98**	**4**	**0**	**2.45**
	Manitoba Moose	AHL	2	0	2	0	125	9	0	4.32	....	....	....	....	....	....	....
2004-05	Leksands IF	Sweden-2	21	....	....	....	1274	45	1	2.12	....	....	....	....	....	....	....
	NHL Totals		**137**	**54**	**63**	**14**	**7930**	**374**	**10**	**2.83**	**20**	**10**	**10**	**1221**	**47**	**2**	**2.31**

Rights traded to **San Jose** by **Philadelphia** for San Jose's 7th round choice (Pavel Kasparik) in 1999 Entry Draft, August 6, 1998. Traded to **Pittsburgh** by **San Jose** with Bobby Dollas for Jeff Norton, March 12, 2001. Traded to **Vancouver** by **Pittsburgh** for Vancouver's 2nd round choice (Alex Goligoski) in 2004 Entry Draft, August 25, 2003. Signed as a free agent by **Leksands** (Sweden-2), August 1, 2004. Signed as a free agent by **Dallas**, August 5, 2005.

HEINO-LINDBERG, Chris (HAY-noh-LIHND-buhrg, KRIHS) MTL.

Goaltender. Catches right. 6', 163 lbs. Born, Helsingborg, Sweden, January 29, 1985.
(Montreal's 7th choice, 177th overall, in 2003 Entry Draft).

			Regular Season								Playoffs						
Season	**Club**	**League**	**GP**	**W**	**L**	**T**	**Mins**	**GA**	**SO**	**Avg**	**GP**	**W**	**L**	**Mins**	**GA**	**SO**	**Avg**
2001-02	Hammarby Jr.	Swe-Jr.	17	....	....	....	987	59	0	3.59	....	....	....	....	....	....	....
2002-03	Hammarby U18	Swe-U18	3	....	....	....	180	9	0	3.00	....	....	....	....	....	....	....
	Hammarby Jr.	Swe-Jr.	23	....	....	....	1383	80	0	3.47	2	....	....	128	6	0	2.81
	Hammarby	Sweden-2	1	....	....	....	60	2	0	2.00	....	....	....	....	....	....	....
2003-04	IF Vallentuna BK	Sweden-2	23	....	....	....	1157	92	0	4.77	....	....	....	....	....	....	....
	Hammarby	Sweden-2	3	....	....	....	105	8	0	4.57	....	....	....	....	....	....	....
	Hammarby Jr.	Swe-Jr.	8	....	....	....	483	20	0	2.48	2	....	....	122	10	0	4.92
2004-05	Hammarby Jr.	Swe-Jr.	3	....	....	....	189	7	0	2.22	....	....	....	....	....	....	....
	Hammarby	Sweden-2	41	....	....	....	2475	89	3	2.16	....	....	....	....	....	....	....

HNILICKA, Milan (huh-LEETCH-kuh, MEE-lan)

Goaltender. Catches left. 6'1", 190 lbs. Born, Pardubice, Czech., June 25, 1973.
(NY Islanders' 4th choice, 70th overall, in 1991 Entry Draft).

			Regular Season								Playoffs						
Season	**Club**	**League**	**GP**	**W**	**L**	**T**	**Mins**	**GA**	**SO**	**Avg**	**GP**	**W**	**L**	**Mins**	**GA**	**SO**	**Avg**
1989-90	Poldi Kladno	Czech	24	....	....	....	1113	70	....	3.77	....	....	....	....	....	....	....
1990-91	Poldi Kladno	Czech	40	....	....	....	2122	98	0	2.80	....	....	....	....	....	....	....
1991-92	Poldi Kladno	Czech	38	....	....	....	2066	128	0	3.73	....	....	....	....	....	....	....
1992-93	Swift Current	WHL	*65	*46	12	2	3679	206	2	3.36	*17	*12	5	*1017	54	*2	3.19
1993-94	Richmond	ECHL	43	18	16	5	2299	155	4	4.05	....	....	....	....	....	....	....
	Salt Lake	IHL	8	5	1	0	378	25	0	3.97	....	....	....	....	....	....	....
1994-95	Denver Grizzlies	IHL	15	9	4	1	798	47	1	3.53	....	....	....	....	....	....	....
1995-96	HC Poldi Kladno	CzRep	33	....	....	....	1959	93	1	2.84	8	....	....	493	24	....	2.92
1996-97	HC Poldi Kladno	CzRep	48	....	....	....	2736	120	*4	2.63	3	....	....	151	14	0	5.56
1997-98	HC Sparta Praha	CzRep	49	....	....	....	2847	99	....	2.09	11	....	....	632	31	....	3.00
1998-99	HC Sparta Praha	CzRep	*50	....	....	....	*2877	109	....	2.27	8	....	....	507	13	....	*1.54
99-2000	**NY Rangers**	**NHL**	**2**	**0**	**1**	**0**	**86**	**5**	**0**	**3.49**	....	....	....	....	....	....	....
	Hartford Wolf Pack	AHL	36	22	11	0	1979	71	5	*2.15	3	0	1	99	6	0	3.64
2000-01	**Atlanta**	**NHL**	**36**	**12**	**19**	**2**	**1879**	**105**	**2**	**3.35**	....	....	....	....	....	....	....
2001-02	**Atlanta**	**NHL**	**60**	**13**	**33**	**10**	**3367**	**179**	**3**	**3.19**	....	....	....	....	....	....	....
2002-03	**Atlanta**	**NHL**	**21**	**4**	**13**	**1**	**1097**	**65**	**0**	**3.56**	....	....	....	....	....	....	....
	Chicago Wolves	AHL	15	11	2	1	838	33	1	2.36	....	....	....	....	....	....	....
2003-04	**Los Angeles**	**NHL**	**2**	**0**	**1**	**0**	**80**	**5**	**0**	**3.75**	....	....	....	....	....	....	....
	Manchester	AHL	20	8	10	0	1022	44	1	2.58	2	0	2	127	5	0	2.37
2004-05	Liberec	CzRep	46	....	....	....	2740	106	5	2.32	12	....	....	702	32	0	2.74
	NHL Totals		**121**	**29**	**67**	**13**	**6509**	**359**	**5**	**3.31**	....	....	....	....	....	....	....

Harry "Hap" Holmes Memorial Award (fewest goals against – AHL) (2000) (shared with Jean-Francois Labbe)

Signed as a free agent by **NY Rangers**, July 15, 1999. Signed as a free agent by **Atlanta**, July 28, 2000. Traded to **Los Angeles** by **Atlanta** for future considerations, September 15, 2003. • Missed majority of 2003-04 season recovering from finger injury suffered in game vs. Phoenix, December 31, 2003. Signed as a free agent by **Liberec** (CzRep), May 18, 2004.

HOLMQVIST, Johan (HOHLM-kvihst, YOH-han)

Goaltender. Catches left. 6'3", 195 lbs. Born, Tolfta, Sweden, May 24, 1978.
(NY Rangers' 9th choice, 175th overall, in 1997 Entry Draft).

			Regular Season								Playoffs						
Season	**Club**	**League**	**GP**	**W**	**L**	**T**	**Mins**	**GA**	**SO**	**Avg**	**GP**	**W**	**L**	**Mins**	**GA**	**SO**	**Avg**
1996-97	Brynas IF Gavle	Sweden	2	0	0	0	80	4	0	3.00	....	....	....	....	....	....	....
1997-98	Brynas IF Gavle	Sweden	33	....	....	....	1897	82	....	2.59	3	0	3	180	14	....	4.67
1998-99	Brynas IF Gavle	Sweden	41	....	....	....	2383	111	4	2.79	*14	9	5	*855	34	0	2.39
99-2000	Brynas IF Gavle	Sweden	41	....	....	....	2402	104	4	2.60	11	....	....	671	30	1	2.68
2000-01	**NY Rangers**	**NHL**	**2**	**0**	**2**	**0**	**119**	**10**	**0**	**5.04**	....	....	....	....	....	....	....
	Hartford Wolf Pack	AHL	43	19	14	4	2305	111	2	2.89	5	2	3	314	13	0	2.48
2001-02	**NY Rangers**	**NHL**	**1**	**0**	**0**	**0**	**9**	**0**	**0**	**0.00**	....	....	....	....	....	....	....
	Hartford Wolf Pack	AHL	48	26	12	6	2734	140	1	3.07	4	1	2	163	12	0	4.41
2002-03	**NY Rangers**	**NHL**	**1**	**0**	**1**	**0**	**39**	**2**	**0**	**3.08**	....	....	....	....	....	....	....
	Hartford Wolf Pack	AHL	35	14	13	5	1904	84	2	2.65	....	....	....	....	....	....	....
	Charlotte Checkers	ECHL	1	1	0	0	60	2	0	2.00	....	....	....	....	....	....	....
	Houston Aeros	AHL	8	5	3	0	479	23	1	2.88	*23	*15	8	*1499	50	1	2.00
2003-04	Houston Aeros	AHL	59	23	27	7	3467	148	4	2.56	....	....	....	....	....	....	....
2004-05	Brynas IF Gavle	Sweden	42	....	....	....	2445	138	1	3.39	....	....	....	....	....	....	....
	NHL Totals		**4**	**0**	**3**	**0**	**167**	**12**	**0**	**4.31**	....	....	....	....	....	....	....

Jack A. Butterfield Trophy (Playoff MVP – AHL) (2003)

Traded to **Minnesota** by **NY Rangers** for Lawrence Nycholat, March 11, 2003. Signed as a free agent by **Brynas** (Sweden), July 29, 2004.

HOLT, Chris (HOHLT, KRIHS) NYR

Goaltender. Catches left. 6'2", 218 lbs. Born, Vancouver, B.C., June 5, 1985.
(NY Rangers' 8th choice, 180th overall, in 2003 Entry Draft).

			Regular Season								Playoffs						
Season	**Club**	**League**	**GP**	**W**	**L**	**T**	**Mins**	**GA**	**SO**	**Avg**	**GP**	**W**	**L**	**Mins**	**GA**	**SO**	**Avg**
2001-02	Billings Bulls	AWHL	24	13	7	1	1184	59	2	2.99	....	....	....	....	....	....	....
2002-03	USA U-18	USDP	32	9	15	2	1774	95	1	3.21	....	....	....	....	....	....	....
2003-04	Nebraska-Omaha	CCHA	27	5	17	2	1499	81	0	3.24	....	....	....	....	....	....	....
2004-05	Nebraska-Omaha	CCHA	37	19	14	4	2190	106	1	2.90	....	....	....	....	....	....	....

HOSTIKKA, Ville (HAWS-tih-kuh, VIHL-ee) PHI.

Goaltender. Catches left. 6'3", 209 lbs. Born, Lappeenranta, Finland, March 21, 1985.
(Philadelphia's 11th choice, 193rd overall, in 2003 Entry Draft).

			Regular Season								Playoffs						
Season	**Club**	**League**	**GP**	**W**	**L**	**T**	**Mins**	**GA**	**SO**	**Avg**	**GP**	**W**	**L**	**Mins**	**GA**	**SO**	**Avg**
2001-02	SaiPa Jr.	Finland-Jr.	4	4	0	0	240	9	1	2.25	2	0	0	68	5	0	4.41
	SaiPa U18	Fin-U18	24	11	8	4	1392	82	2	3.53	....	....	....	....	....	....	....
2002-03	SaiPa Jr.	Finland-Jr.	30	14	8	4	1750	79	2	2.71	1	0	1	58	5	0	5.17
2003-04	SaiPa Jr.	Finland-Jr.	12	1	6	3	645	41	0	3.81	....	....	....	....	....	....	....
2004-05	Lukko Rauma Jr.	Finland-Jr.	30	11	12	5	1808	96	1	3.19	....	....	....	....	....	....	....

HOULE, Martin (HOOL, MAHR-tehn) PHI.

Goaltender. Catches left. 5'10", 170 lbs. Born, Montreal, Que., February 12, 1985.
(Philadelphia's 8th choice, 232nd overall, in 2004 Entry Draft).

			Regular Season								Playoffs						
Season	**Club**	**League**	**GP**	**W**	**L**	**T**	**Mins**	**GA**	**SO**	**Avg**	**GP**	**W**	**L**	**Mins**	**GA**	**SO**	**Avg**
2001-02	Antoine-Girouard	QAAA	23	17	4	2	1309	45	1	2.06	....	....	....	....	....	....	....
	Cape Breton	QMJHL	1	1	0	0	38	0	0	0.00	....	....	....	....	....	....	....
2002-03	Cape Breton	QMJHL	30	4	18	3	1450	98	0	4.06	1	0	0	11	0	0	0.00
2003-04	Cape Breton	QMJHL	51	34	15	1	2951	114	3	2.32	1	0	1	59	4	0	4.10
2004-05	Cape Breton	QMJHL	56	26	18	5	3108	130	*6	2.51	4	1	3	246	10	0	*2.44

QMJHL First All-Star Team (2004)

HOWARD, James (HOW-uhrd, JAYMZ) DET.

Goaltender. Catches left. 6', 218 lbs. Born, Syracuse, NY, March 26, 1984.
(Detroit's 1st choice, 64th overall, in 2003 Entry Draft).

			Regular Season								Playoffs						
Season	**Club**	**League**	**GP**	**W**	**L**	**T**	**Mins**	**GA**	**SO**	**Avg**	**GP**	**W**	**L**	**Mins**	**GA**	**SO**	**Avg**
2001-02	USA U-17	USDP	9	6	3	0	484	29	1	3.67	....	....	....	....	....	....	....
	USA U-18	USDP	26	16	8	1	1492	47	3	1.89	....	....	....	....	....	....	....
2002-03	University of Maine	H-East	21	14	6	0	1151	47	3	2.45	....	....	....	....	....	....	....
2003-04	University of Maine	H-East	23	14	4	3	1364	27	*6	*1.19	....	....	....	....	....	....	....
2004-05	University of Maine	H-East	*39	*19	13	7	*2310	74	*6	1.92	....	....	....	....	....	....	....

Hockey East All-Rookie Team (2003) • Hockey East Rookie of the Year (2003) • Hockey East First All-Star Team (2004) • NCAA East Second All-American Team (2004)

HUET, Cristobal (oo-AY, KRIHS-toh-bahl) MTL.

Goaltender. Catches left. 6', 194 lbs. Born, St. Martin D'Heres, France, September 3, 1975.
(Los Angeles' 9th choice, 214th overall, in 2001 Entry Draft).

			Regular Season								Playoffs						
Season	**Club**	**League**	**GP**	**W**	**L**	**T**	**Mins**	**GA**	**SO**	**Avg**	**GP**	**W**	**L**	**Mins**	**GA**	**SO**	**Avg**
1997-98	CSG Grenoble	France					STATISTICS NOT AVAILABLE										
	France	Olympics	2	1	1	0	120	5	0	2.50	....	....	....	....	....	....	....
1998-99	HC Lugano	Swiss	21	....	....	....	1275	58	1	2.73	10	....	....	628	18	1	*1.72
99-2000	HC Lugano	Swiss	31	....	....	....	1886	50	*8	*1.59	13	....	....	783	29	0	2.22
2000-01	HC Lugano	Swiss	39	....	....	....	2365	77	*6	*1.95	*18	....	....	*1141	39	2	2.05
2001-02	HC Lugano	Swiss	39	....	....	....	2313	107	*4	2.78	1	0	1	60	3	0	3.00
	France	Olympics	3	0	2	1	179	10	0	3.36	....	....	....	....	....	....	....
2002-03	**Los Angeles**	**NHL**	**12**	**4**	**4**	**1**	**541**	**21**	**1**	**2.33**	....	....	....	....	....	....	....
	Manchester	AHL	30	16	8	5	1784	68	1	2.29	1	0	1	30	4	0	8.08
2003-04	**Los Angeles**	**NHL**	**41**	**10**	**16**	**10**	**2199**	**89**	**3**	**2.43**	....	....	....	....	....	....	....
2004-05	Adler Mannheim	Germany	36	....	....	....	2001	93	1	2.79	*14	....	....	*850	40	2	2.82
	NHL Totals		**53**	**14**	**20**	**11**	**2740**	**110**	**4**	**2.41**	....	....	....	....	....	....	....

Traded to **Montreal** by **Los Angeles** with Radek Bonk for Mathieu Garon and San Jose's 3rd round choice (previously acquired, Los Angeles selected Paul Baier) in 2004 Entry Draft, June 26, 2004. Signed as a free agent by **Mannheim** (Germany), September 14, 2004.

HURME, Jani (HOOR-meh, YAN-ee) ATL.

Goaltender. Catches left. 6', 190 lbs. Born, Turku, Finland, January 7, 1975.
(Ottawa's 2nd choice, 58th overall, in 1997 Entry Draft).

			Regular Season								Playoffs						
Season	**Club**	**League**	**GP**	**W**	**L**	**T**	**Mins**	**GA**	**SO**	**Avg**	**GP**	**W**	**L**	**Mins**	**GA**	**SO**	**Avg**
1992-93	TPS Turku Jr.	Finland-Jr.	12	....	....	....	669	47	0	4.22	1	....	....	60	0	1	0.00
1993-94	Kiekko-67 Jr.	Finland-Jr.	18	....	....	....	1082	57	0	3.16	....	....	....	....	....	....	....
	Kiekko-67 Turku	Finland-2	3	....	....	....	190	7	0	2.21	....	....	....	....	....	....	....
	TPS Turku	Finland	1	....	....	....	2	0	0	0.00	....	....	....	....	....	....	....
1994-95	TPS Turku Jr.	Finland-Jr.	2	....	....	....	125	5	0	2.40	....	....	....	....	....	....	....
	Kiekko-67 Jr.	Finland-Jr.	9	....	....	....	540	47	....	5.22	....	....	....	....	....	....	....
	Kiekko-67 Turku	Finland-2	19	....	....	....	1049	53	....	3.03	3	....	....	180	6	....	2.00
1995-96	TPS Turku Jr.	Finland-Jr.	13	....	....	....	777	34	1	2.63	....	....	....	....	....	....	....
	Kiekko-67 Turku	Finland-2	16	....	....	....	968	39	1	2.42	....	....	....	....	....	....	....
	TPS Turku	Finland	16	....	....	....	946	34	2	2.16	10	....	....	545	22	2	2.42
1996-97	TPS Turku	Finland	48	*31	11	6	*2917	101	*6	*2.08	*12	6	6	*722	39	0	3.24
1997-98	Detroit Vipers	IHL	6	2	2	2	290	20	0	4.13	....	....	....	....	....	....	....
	Indianapolis Ice	IHL	29	11	11	3	1506	83	1	3.30	3	1	0	129	10	0	4.62
1998-99	Detroit Vipers	IHL	12	7	3	1	643	26	1	2.43	....	....	....	....	....	....	....
	Cincinnati	IHL	26	14	9	2	1428	81	0	3.40	....	....	....	....	....	....	....
99-2000	**Ottawa**	**NHL**	**1**	**1**	**0**	**0**	**60**	**2**	**0**	**2.00**	....	....	....	....	....	....	....
	Grand Rapids	IHL	52	29	15	4	2948	107	4	2.18	*17	*10	7	*1028	37	1	2.16
2000-01	**Ottawa**	**NHL**	**22**	**12**	**5**	**4**	**1296**	**54**	**2**	**2.50**	....	....	....	....	....	....	....
2001-02	**Ottawa**	**NHL**	**25**	**12**	**9**	**1**	**1309**	**54**	**3**	**2.48**	....	....	....	....	....	....	....
	Finland	Olympics	3	1	2	0	179	9	0	3.01	....	....	....	....	....	....	....
2002-03	**Florida**	**NHL**	**28**	**4**	**11**	**6**	**1376**	**66**	**1**	**2.88**	....	....	....	....	....	....	....
2003-04							DID NOT PLAY – INJURED										
2004-05							DID NOT PLAY – INJURED										
	NHL Totals		**76**	**29**	**25**	**11**	**4041**	**176**	**6**	**2.61**	....	....	....	....	....	....	....

Finnish Elite League Rookie of the Year (1996) • Finnish Elite League Player of the Year (1997) • IHL Second All-Star Team (2000)

Traded to **Florida** by **Ottawa** for Billy Thompson and Greg Watson, October 1, 2002. Claimed by **Carolina** from **Florida** in Waiver Draft, October 3, 2003. Traded to **Atlanta** by **Carolina** for Atlanta's 4th round choice (Brett Carson) in 2004 Entry Draft, October 3, 2003. • Missed entire 2003-04 and 2004-05 seasons recovering from back injury suffered in training camp, October, 2003.

IRBE, Arturs (UHR-bay, AHR-tuhrs)

Goaltender. Catches left. 5'8", 190 lbs. Born, Riga, Latvia, February 2, 1967.
(Minnesota's 11th choice, 196th overall, in 1989 Entry Draft).

			Regular Season								Playoffs						
Season	**Club**	**League**	**GP**	**W**	**L**	**T**	**Mins**	**GA**	**SO**	**Avg**	**GP**	**W**	**L**	**Mins**	**GA**	**SO**	**Avg**
1986-87	Dynamo Riga	USSR	2	....	....	....	27	1	0	2.22	....	....	....	....	....	....	....
1987-88	Dynamo Riga	USSR	34	....	....	....	1870	86	4	2.76	....	....	....	....	....	....	....
1988-89	Dynamo Riga	USSR	40	....	....	....	2460	116	4	2.83	....	....	....	....	....	....	....
1989-90	Dynamo Riga	USSR	48	....	....	....	2880	115	2	2.40	....	....	....	....	....	....	....
1990-91	Dynamo Riga	USSR	46	....	....	....	2713	133	5	2.94	....	....	....	....	....	....	....
1991-92	**San Jose**	**NHL**	**13**	**2**	**6**	**3**	**645**	**48**	**0**	**4.47**	....	....	....	....	....	....	....
	Kansas City Blades	IHL	32	24	7	1	1955	80	0	*2.46	*15	*12	3	914	44	0	*2.89
1992-93	**San Jose**	**NHL**	**36**	**7**	**26**	**0**	**2074**	**142**	**1**	**4.11**	....	....	....	....	....	....	....
	Kansas City Blades	IHL	6	3	3	0	364	20	0	3.30	....	....	....	....	....	....	....
1993-94	**San Jose**	**NHL**	***74**	**30**	**28**	**16**	***4412**	**209**	**3**	**2.84**	**14**	**7**	**7**	**806**	**50**	**0**	**3.72**
1994-95	**San Jose**	**NHL**	**38**	**14**	**19**	**3**	**2043**	**111**	**4**	**3.26**	**6**	**2**	**4**	**316**	**27**	**0**	**5.13**

1995-96	**San Jose**	**NHL**	**22**	**4**	**12**	**4**	**1112**	**85**	**0**	**4.59**	....	....	....	....	....	....	....
	Kansas City Blades	IHL	4	1	2	1	226	16	0	4.24	....	....	....	....	....	....	....
1996-97	**Dallas**	**NHL**	**35**	**17**	**12**	**3**	**1965**	**88**	**3**	**2.69**	**1**	**0**	**0**	**13**	**0**	**0**	**0.00**
1997-98	**Vancouver**	**NHL**	**41**	**14**	**11**	**6**	**1999**	**91**	**2**	**2.73**	....	....	....	....	....	....	....
1998-99	**Carolina**	**NHL**	**62**	**27**	**20**	**12**	**3643**	**135**	**6**	**2.22**	**6**	**2**	**4**	**408**	**15**	**0**	**2.21**
99-2000	**Carolina**	**NHL**	***75**	**34**	**28**	**9**	**4345**	**175**	**5**	**2.42**	....	....	....	....	....	....	....
2000-01	**Carolina**	**NHL**	***77**	**37**	**29**	**9**	***4406**	**180**	**6**	**2.45**	**6**	**2**	**4**	**360**	**20**	**0**	**3.33**
2001-02	**Carolina**	**NHL**	**51**	**20**	**19**	**11**	**2974**	**126**	**3**	**2.54**	**18**	**10**	**8**	**1078**	**30**	**1**	**1.67**
	Latvia	Olympics	1	0	1	0	60	4	0	4.00	....	....	....	....	....	....	....
2002-03	**Carolina**	**NHL**	**34**	**7**	**24**	**2**	**1884**	**100**	**0**	**3.18**	....	....	....	....	....	....	....
	Lowell	AHL	7	3	3	1	427	21	0	2.95	....	....	....	....	....	....	....
2003-04	**Carolina**	**NHL**	**10**	**5**	**2**	**1**	**564**	**23**	**0**	**2.45**	....	....	....	....	....	....	....
	Johnstown Chiefs	ECHL	14	10	3	1	847	30	1	2.13	....	....	....	....	....	....	....
2004-05							DID NOT PLAY										
	NHL Totals		**568**	**218**	**236**	**79**	**32066**	**1513**	**33**	**2.83**	**51**	**23**	**27**	**2981**	**142**	**1**	**2.86**

IHL First All-Star Team (1992) • James Norris Memorial Trophy (fewest goals against – IHL) (1992) (shared with Wade Flaherty)

Played in NHL All-Star Game (1994, 1999)

Claimed by **San Jose** from **Minnesota** in Dispersal Draft, May 30, 1991. Signed as a free agent by **Dallas**, August 19, 1996. Signed as a free agent by **Vancouver**, August 25, 1997. Signed as a free agent by **Carolina**, September 14, 1998. Traded to **Columbus** by **Carolina** for future considerations, June 16, 2004.

JOHNSON, Brent (JAWN-suhn, BREHNT) VAN.

Goaltender. Catches left. 6'3", 205 lbs. Born, Farmington, MI, March 12, 1977.
(Colorado's 5th choice, 129th overall, in 1995 Entry Draft).

			Regular Season								Playoffs						
Season	**Club**	**League**	**GP**	**W**	**L**	**T**	**Mins**	**GA**	**SO**	**Avg**	**GP**	**W**	**L**	**Mins**	**GA**	**SO**	**Avg**
1993-94	Det. Compuware	NAJHL	18	....	....	....	1024	49	1	3.52	....	....	....	....	....	....	....
1994-95	Owen Sound	OHL	18	3	9	1	904	75	0	4.98	....	....	....	....	....	....	....
1995-96	Owen Sound	OHL	58	24	28	1	3211	243	1	4.54	6	2	4	371	29	0	4.69
1996-97	Owen Sound	OHL	50	20	28	1	2798	201	1	4.31	4	0	4	253	24	0	5.69
1997-98	Worcester IceCats	AHL	42	14	15	7	2240	119	0	3.19	6	3	2	332	19	0	3.43
1998-99	**St. Louis**	**NHL**	**6**	**3**	**2**	**0**	**286**	**10**	**0**	**2.10**	....	....	....	....	....	....	....
	Worcester IceCats	AHL	49	22	22	4	2925	146	2	2.99	4	1	3	238	12	0	3.02
99-2000	Worcester IceCats	AHL	58	24	27	5	3319	161	3	2.91	9	4	5	561	23	1	2.46
2000-01	**St. Louis**	**NHL**	**31**	**19**	**9**	**2**	**1744**	**63**	**4**	**2.17**	**2**	**0**	**1**	**62**	**2**	**0**	**1.94**
2001-02	**St. Louis**	**NHL**	**58**	**34**	**20**	**4**	**3491**	**127**	**5**	**2.18**	**10**	**5**	**5**	**590**	**18**	**3**	**1.83**
2002-03	**St. Louis**	**NHL**	**38**	**16**	**13**	**5**	**2042**	**84**	**2**	**2.47**	....	....	....	....	....	....	....
	Worcester IceCats	AHL	2	0	1	1	125	8	0	3.84	....	....	....	....	....	....	....
2003-04	**St. Louis**	**NHL**	**10**	**4**	**3**	**1**	**493**	**20**	**1**	**2.43**	....	....	....	....	....	....	....
	Worcester IceCats	AHL	8	2	2	2	365	14	0	2.30	....	....	....	....	....	....	....
	Phoenix	**NHL**	**8**	**1**	**6**	**1**	**486**	**21**	**0**	**2.59**	....	....	....	....	....	....	....
2004-05							DID NOT PLAY										
	NHL Totals		**151**	**77**	**53**	**13**	**8542**	**325**	**12**	**2.28**	**12**	**5**	**6**	**652**	**20**	**3**	**1.84**

Traded to **St. Louis** by **Colorado** for San Jose's 3rd round choice (previously acquired, Colorado selected Rick Berry) in 1997 Entry Draft, May 30, 1997. Traded to **Phoenix** by **St. Louis** for Mike Sillinger, March 4, 2004. Signed as a free agent by **Vancouver**, September 1, 2005.

JOSEPH, Curtis (JOH-sehf, KUR-tihs) PHX.

Goaltender. Catches left. 5'11", 190 lbs. Born, Keswick, Ont., April 29, 1967.

			Regular Season								Playoffs						
Season	**Club**	**League**	**GP**	**W**	**L**	**T**	**Mins**	**GA**	**SO**	**Avg**	**GP**	**W**	**L**	**Mins**	**GA**	**SO**	**Avg**
1984-85	King City Dukes	OHA-B	18	....	....	....	947	76	0	4.82	....	....	....	....	....	....	....
	Newmarket Flyers	OPJHL	2	1	1	0	120	16	0	8.00	....	....	....	....	....	....	....
1985-86	Richmond Hill	OPJHL	33	12	18	0	1716	156	1	5.45	....	....	....	....	....	....	....
1986-87	Richmond Hill	OPJHL	30	14	7	6	1764	128	1	4.35	....	....	....	....	....	....	....
1987-88	Notre Dame	SJHL	36	25	4	7	2174	94	1	2.59	....	....	....	....	....	....	....
1988-89	U. of Wisconsin	WCHA	38	21	11	5	2267	94	1	2.49	....	....	....	....	....	....	....
1989-90	Peoria Rivermen	IHL	23	10	8	2	1241	80	0	3.87	....	....	....	....	....	....	....
	St. Louis	**NHL**	**15**	**9**	**5**	**1**	**852**	**48**	**0**	**3.38**	**6**	**4**	**1**	**327**	**18**	**0**	**3.30**
1990-91	**St. Louis**	**NHL**	**30**	**16**	**10**	**2**	**1710**	**89**	**0**	**3.12**	....	....	....	....	....	....	....
1991-92	**St. Louis**	**NHL**	**60**	**27**	**20**	**10**	**3494**	**175**	**2**	**3.01**	**6**	**2**	**4**	**379**	**23**	**0**	**3.64**
1992-93	**St. Louis**	**NHL**	**68**	**29**	**28**	**9**	**3890**	**196**	**1**	**3.02**	**11**	**7**	**4**	**715**	**27**	***2**	**2.27**
1993-94	**St. Louis**	**NHL**	**71**	**36**	**23**	**11**	**4127**	**213**	**1**	**3.10**	**4**	**0**	**4**	**246**	**15**	**0**	**3.66**
1994-95	**St. Louis**	**NHL**	**36**	**20**	**10**	**1**	**1914**	**89**	**1**	**2.79**	**7**	**3**	**3**	**392**	**24**	**0**	**3.67**
1995-96	Las Vegas Thunder	IHL	15	12	2	1	874	29	1	1.99	....	....	....	....	....	....	....
	Edmonton	**NHL**	**34**	**15**	**16**	**2**	**1936**	**111**	**0**	**3.44**	....	....	....	....	....	....	....
1996-97	**Edmonton**	**NHL**	**72**	**32**	**29**	**9**	**4100**	**200**	**6**	**2.93**	**12**	**5**	**7**	**767**	**36**	**2**	**2.82**
1997-98	**Edmonton**	**NHL**	**71**	**29**	**31**	**9**	**4132**	**181**	**8**	**2.63**	**12**	**5**	**7**	**716**	**23**	**3**	**1.93**
1998-99	**Toronto**	**NHL**	**67**	**35**	**24**	**7**	**4001**	**171**	**3**	**2.56**	**17**	**9**	**8**	**1011**	**41**	**1**	**2.43**
99-2000	**Toronto**	**NHL**	**63**	**36**	**20**	**7**	**3801**	**158**	**4**	**2.49**	**12**	**6**	**6**	**729**	**25**	**1**	**2.06**
2000-01	**Toronto**	**NHL**	**68**	**33**	**27**	**8**	**4100**	**163**	**6**	**2.39**	**11**	**7**	**4**	**685**	**24**	**3**	**2.10**
2001-02	**Toronto**	**NHL**	**51**	**29**	**17**	**5**	**3065**	**114**	**4**	**2.23**	**20**	**10**	**10**	**1253**	**48**	**3**	**2.30**
	Canada	Olympics	1	0	1	0	60	5	0	5.00	....	....	....	....	....	....	....
2002-03	**Detroit**	**NHL**	**61**	**34**	**19**	**6**	**3566**	**148**	**5**	**2.49**	**4**	**0**	**4**	**289**	**10**	**0**	**2.08**
2003-04	**Detroit**	**NHL**	**31**	**16**	**10**	**3**	**1708**	**68**	**2**	**2.39**	**9**	**4**	**4**	**518**	**12**	**1**	***1.39**
	Grand Rapids	AHL	1	1	0	0	60	1	0	1.00	....	....	....	....	....	....	....
2004-05							DID NOT PLAY										
	NHL Totals		**798**	**396**	**289**	**90**	**46396**	**2124**	**43**	**2.75**	**131**	**62**	**66**	**8027**	**326**	**16**	**2.44**

WCHA First All-Star Team (1989) • WCHA Freshman of the Year (1989) • WCHA Most Valuable Player (1989) • NCAA West Second All-American Team (1989) • King Clancy Memorial Trophy (2000)

Played in NHL All-Star Game (1994, 2000)

Signed as a free agent by **St. Louis**, June 16, 1989. Traded to **Edmonton** by **St. Louis** with the rights to Mike Grier for St. Louis' 1st round choices (previously acquired) in 1996 (Marty Reasoner) and 1997 (later traded to Los Angeles – Los Angeles selected Matt Zultek) Entry Drafts, August 4, 1995. Signed as a free agent by **Toronto**, July 15, 1998. Traded to **Calgary** by **Toronto** for Calgary's 3rd round choice (later traded to Minnesota – Minnesota selected Danny Irmen) in 2003 Entry Draft and future considerations, June 30, 2002. Signed as a free agent by **Detroit**, July 2, 2002. Signed as a free agent by **Phoenix**, August 17, 2005.

KEETLEY, Matt (KEET-lee, MAT) CGY.

Goaltender. Catches right. 6', 175 lbs. Born, Medicine Hat, Alta., April 27, 1986.
(Calgary's 6th choice, 158th overall, in 2005 Entry Draft).

			Regular Season								Playoffs						
Season	**Club**	**League**	**GP**	**W**	**L**	**T**	**Mins**	**GA**	**SO**	**Avg**	**GP**	**W**	**L**	**Mins**	**GA**	**SO**	**Avg**
2003-04	Medicine Hat	AMHL	....	7	4	2	813	48	....	3.54	....	....	....	....	....	....	....
	Medicine Hat	WHL	3	0	1	0	72	5	0	4.17	2	0	0	15	1	0	4.00
2004-05	Medicine Hat	WHL	32	21	5	3	1846	51	6	*1.66	3	1	0	103	8	0	4.66

KESERICH, Ian (kuh-SAIR-ihch, EE-an) COL.

Goaltender. Catches left. 6'3", 180 lbs. Born, Cleveland, OH, January 6, 1986.
(Colorado's 6th choice, 215th overall, in 2004 Entry Draft).

			Regular Season								Playoffs						
Season	**Club**	**League**	**GP**	**W**	**L**	**T**	**Mins**	**GA**	**SO**	**Avg**	**GP**	**W**	**L**	**Mins**	**GA**	**SO**	**Avg**
2003-04	Cleveland Barons	NAHL					STATISTICS NOT AVAILABLE										
2004-05	Ohio State	CCHA	6	2	2	0	272	11	0	2.42	....	....	....	....	....	....	....

KETTLES, Kyle (KEH-tuhls, KIGHL)

Goaltender. Catches left. 6'3", 180 lbs. Born, Lac du Bonnet, Man., February 19, 1981.
(Nashville's 13th choice, 205th overall, in 1999 Entry Draft).

			Regular Season								Playoffs						
Season	**Club**	**League**	**GP**	**W**	**L**	**T**	**Mins**	**GA**	**SO**	**Avg**	**GP**	**W**	**L**	**Mins**	**GA**	**SO**	**Avg**
1997-98	Selkirk Steelers	MJHL	32	9	19	1	1613	119	0	4.43	....	....	....	....	....	....	....
	Brandon	WHL	....	....	....	....	....	....	....	....	1	0	0	10	2	0	12.00
1998-99	Selkirk Steelers	MJHL	17	7	8	0	939	65	0	4.15	....	....	....	....	....	....	....
	Neepawa Natives	MJHL	6	2	4	0	361	27	0	4.49	....	....	....	....	....	....	....
99-2000	Medicine Hat	WHL	57	16	33	5	3260	215	1	3.96	....	....	....	....	....	....	....
2000-01	Medicine Hat	WHL	47	15	24	2	2586	183	0	4.25	....	....	....	....	....	....	....
2001-02	Medicine Hat	WHL	5	1	4	0	274	23	0	5.04	....	....	....	....	....	....	....
	Moose Jaw	WHL	54	24	25	4	3089	160	*4	3.11	12	6	6	735	29	1	2.37
2002-03	Louisiana	ECHL	41	21	12	7	2439	106	*5	2.61	6	3	3	359	13	1	2.17
2003-04	Houston Aeros	AHL	22	4	9	5	1094	51	1	2.80	....	....	....	....	....	....	....
2004-05	Houston Aeros	AHL	3	0	1	0	62	3	0	2.90	....	....	....	....	....	....	....
	Louisiana	ECHL	19	5	9	2	983	59	1	3.60	....	....	....	....	....	....	....

Signed as a free agent by **Minnesota**, April 23, 2002.

KHABIBULIN, Nikolai (khah-bee-BOO-lihn, NIH-koh-ligh) CHI.

Goaltender. Catches left. 6'1", 203 lbs. Born, Sverdlovsk, USSR, January 13, 1973.
(Winnipeg's 8th choice, 204th overall, in 1992 Entry Draft).

			Regular Season								Playoffs						
Season	**Club**	**League**	**GP**	**W**	**L**	**T**	**Mins**	**GA**	**SO**	**Avg**	**GP**	**W**	**L**	**Mins**	**GA**	**SO**	**Avg**
1991-92	CSKA Moscow	CIS	2	0	0	0	34	2	0	3.53	....	....	....	....	....	....	....
1992-93	CSKA Moscow	CIS	13	....	....	....	491	27	....	3.29	....	....	....	....	....	....	....
1993-94	CSKA Moscow	CIS	46	....	....	....	2625	116	....	2.65	3	....	....	193	11	....	3.42
	Russian Penguins	IHL	12	2	7	2	639	47	0	4.41	....	....	....	....	....	....	....
1994-95	Springfield Indians	AHL	23	9	9	3	1240	80	0	3.87	....	....	....	....	....	....	....
	Winnipeg	**NHL**	**26**	**8**	**9**	**4**	**1339**	**76**	**0**	**3.41**	....	....	....	....	....	....	....
1995-96	**Winnipeg**	**NHL**	**53**	**26**	**20**	**3**	**2914**	**152**	**2**	**3.13**	**6**	**2**	**4**	**359**	**19**	**0**	**3.18**
1996-97	**Phoenix**	**NHL**	**72**	**30**	**33**	**6**	**4091**	**193**	**7**	**2.83**	**7**	**3**	**4**	**426**	**15**	**1**	**2.11**
1997-98	**Phoenix**	**NHL**	**70**	**30**	**28**	**10**	**4026**	**184**	**4**	**2.74**	**4**	**2**	**1**	**185**	**13**	**0**	**4.22**
1998-99	**Phoenix**	**NHL**	**63**	**32**	**23**	**7**	**3657**	**130**	**8**	**2.13**	**7**	**3**	**4**	**449**	**18**	**0**	**2.41**
99-2000	Long Beach	IHL	33	21	11	1	1936	59	5	*1.83	5	2	3	321	15	0	2.81
2000-01	**Tampa Bay**	**NHL**	**2**	**1**	**1**	**0**	**123**	**6**	**0**	**2.93**	....	....	....	....	....	....	....
2001-02	**Tampa Bay**	**NHL**	**70**	**24**	**32**	**10**	**3896**	**153**	**7**	**2.36**	....	....	....	....	....	....	....
	Russia	Olympics	6	3	2	1	*359	14	*1	2.34	....	....	....	....	....	....	....
2002-03	**Tampa Bay**	**NHL**	**65**	**30**	**22**	**11**	**3787**	**156**	**4**	**2.47**	**10**	**5**	**5**	**644**	**26**	**0**	**2.42**
2003-04♦	**Tampa Bay**	**NHL**	**55**	**28**	**19**	**7**	**3274**	**127**	**3**	**2.33**	**23**	***16**	**7**	**1401**	**40**	***5**	**1.71**
2004-05	Ak Bars Kazan	Russia	24	....	....	....	1457	40	5	1.65	2	....	....	118	6	0	3.04
	NHL Totals		**476**	**209**	**187**	**58**	**27107**	**1177**	**35**	**2.61**	**57**	**31**	**25**	**3464**	**131**	**6**	**2.27**

James Gatschene Memorial Trophy (MVP – IHL) (2000) (co-winner - Frederic Chabot)

Played in NHL All-Star Game (1998, 1999, 2002, 2003)

Transferred to **Phoenix** after **Winnipeg** franchise relocated, July 1, 1996. • Missed entire 1999-2000 NHL season and majority of 2000-01 season after failing to come to contract terms with **Phoenix**. Signed as a free agent by **Long Beach** (IHL) with **Phoenix** retaining NHL rights, January 14, 2000. Traded to **Tampa Bay** by **Phoenix** with Stan Neckar for Mike Johnson, Paul Mara, Ruslan Zainullin and NY Islanders' 2nd round choice (previously acquired, Phoenix selected Matthew Spiller) in 2001 Entry Draft, March 5, 2001. Signed as a free agent by **Kazan** (Russia), November 8, 2004. Signed as a free agent by **Chicago**, August 5, 2005.

KHUDOBIN, Anton (khuh-DAW-bihn, an-TAWN) MIN.

Goaltender. Catches left. 5'11", 176 lbs. Born, Ust-Kamenogorsk, USSR, May 7, 1986.
(Minnesota's 11th choice, 206th overall, in 2004 Entry Draft).

			Regular Season								Playoffs						
Season	**Club**	**League**	**GP**	**W**	**L**	**T**	**Mins**	**GA**	**SO**	**Avg**	**GP**	**W**	**L**	**Mins**	**GA**	**SO**	**Avg**
2003-04	Magnitogorsk 2	Russia-3	4	....	....	....	200	6	0	1.80	....	....	....	....	....	....	....
2004-05	Magnitogorsk	Russia	4	....	....	....	133	0	1	0.00	....	....	....	....	....	....	....
	Magnitogorsk 2	Russia-3					STATISTICS NOT AVAILABLE										

KIDD, Trevor (KIHD, TREH-vuhr)

Goaltender. Catches left. 6'2", 213 lbs. Born, Dugald, Man., March 26, 1972.
(Calgary's 1st choice, 11th overall, in 1990 Entry Draft).

			Regular Season								Playoffs						
Season	**Club**	**League**	**GP**	**W**	**L**	**T**	**Mins**	**GA**	**SO**	**Avg**	**GP**	**W**	**L**	**Mins**	**GA**	**SO**	**Avg**
1987-88	Eastman Selects	MAHA	14	....	....	....	840	66	0	4.72	....	....	....	....	....	....	....
1988-89	Brandon	WHL	32	11	13	1	1509	102	0	4.06	....	....	....	....	....	....	....
1989-90	Brandon	WHL	*63	24	32	2	*3676	254	2	4.15	....	....	....	....	....	....	....
1990-91	Brandon	WHL	30	10	19	1	1730	117	0	4.06	....	....	....	....	....	....	....
	Spokane Chiefs	WHL	14	8	3	0	749	44	0	3.52	15	*14	1	926	32	2	*2.07
1991-92	Canada	Nat-Tm	28	18	4	4	1349	79	2	3.51	....	....	....	....	....	....	....
	Canada	Olympics	1	1	0	0	60	0	1	0.00	....	....	....	....	....	....	....
	Calgary	**NHL**	**2**	**1**	**1**	**0**	**120**	**8**	**0**	**4.00**	....	....	....	....	....	....	....
1992-93	Salt Lake	IHL	29	10	16	1	1696	111	1	3.93	....	....	....	....	....	....	....
1993-94	**Calgary**	**NHL**	**31**	**13**	**7**	**6**	**1614**	**85**	**0**	**3.16**	....	....	....	....	....	....	....
1994-95	**Calgary**	**NHL**	***43**	**22**	**14**	**6**	***2463**	**107**	**3**	**2.61**	**7**	**3**	**4**	**434**	**26**	**1**	**3.59**
1995-96	**Calgary**	**NHL**	**47**	**15**	**21**	**8**	**2570**	**119**	**3**	**2.78**	**2**	**0**	**1**	**83**	**9**	**0**	**6.51**
1996-97	**Calgary**	**NHL**	**55**	**21**	**23**	**6**	**2979**	**141**	**4**	**2.84**	....	....	....	....	....	....	....
1997-98	**Carolina**	**NHL**	**47**	**21**	**21**	**3**	**2685**	**97**	**3**	**2.17**	....	....	....	....	....	....	....
1998-99	**Carolina**	**NHL**	**25**	**7**	**10**	**6**	**1358**	**61**	**2**	**2.70**	....	....	....	....	....	....	....
99-2000	**Florida**	**NHL**	**28**	**14**	**11**	**2**	**1574**	**69**	**1**	**2.63**	....	....	....	....	....	....	....
	Louisville Panthers	AHL	1	0	1	0	60	5	0	5.04	....	....	....	....	....	....	....
2000-01	**Florida**	**NHL**	**42**	**10**	**23**	**6**	**2354**	**130**	**1**	**3.31**	....	....	....	....	....	....	....
2001-02	**Florida**	**NHL**	**33**	**4**	**16**	**5**	**1683**	**90**	**1**	**3.21**	....	....	....	....	....	....	....
2002-03	**Toronto**	**NHL**	**19**	**6**	**10**	**2**	**1143**	**59**	**0**	**3.10**	....	....	....	....	....	....	....
2003-04	**Toronto**	**NHL**	**15**	**6**	**5**	**2**	**883**	**48**	**1**	**3.26**	**1**	**0**	**0**	**33**	**1**	**0**	**1.82**
	St. John's	AHL	1	1	0	0	60	1	0	1.00	....	....	....	....	....	....	....
2004-05	HC Orebro 90	Sweden-3	8	....	....	....	480	19	2	2.37	....	....	....	....	....	....	....
	NHL Totals		**387**	**140**	**162**	**52**	**21426**	**1014**	**19**	**2.84**	**10**	**3**	**5**	**550**	**36**	**1**	**3.93**

WHL East First All-Star Team (1990) • WHL Goaltender of the Year (1990) • Canadian Major Junior Goaltender of the Year (1990)

Traded to **Carolina** by **Calgary** with Gary Roberts for Andrew Cassels and Jean-Sebastien Giguere, August 25, 1997. Claimed by **Atlanta** from **Carolina** in Expansion Draft, June 25, 1999. Traded to **Florida** by **Atlanta** for Gord Murphy, Herbert Vasiljevs, Daniel Tjarnqvist and Ottawa's 6th round choice (previously acquired, later traded to Dallas – Dallas selected Justin Cox) in 1999 Entry Draft, June 25, 1999. Signed as a free agent by **Toronto**, August 26, 2002. Signed as a free agent by **Orebro** (Sweden-3), January 31, 2005.

KILPELAINEN, Eero (kih-pehl-AI-nehn, EE-roh) DAL.

Goaltender. Catches left. 5'11", 152 lbs. Born, Juva, Finland, May 7, 1985.
(Dallas' 6th choice, 144th overall, in 2003 Entry Draft).

			Regular Season								Playoffs						
Season	**Club**	**League**	**GP**	**W**	**L**	**T**	**Mins**	**GA**	**SO**	**Avg**	**GP**	**W**	**L**	**Mins**	**GA**	**SO**	**Avg**
2002-03	KalPa Kuopio Jr.	Finland-Jr.	20	8	6	1	991	57	0	3.45	....	....	....	....	....	....	....
	KalPa Kuopio	Finland-2	1	0	0	0	17	4	0	14.12	....	....	....	....	....	....	....
2003-04	KalPa Kuopio Jr.	Finland-Jr.	43	17	19	6	2528	118	2	2.80	2	0	2	116	4	0	2.07
2004-05	Peterborough	OHL	38	14	17	6	2218	121	0	3.27	1	0	1	78	4	0	3.08

KIPRUSOFF, Miikka (KIHP-ruh-sohf, MEE-kah) CGY.

Goaltender. Catches left. 6'2", 190 lbs. Born, Turku, Finland, October 26, 1976.
(San Jose's 5th choice, 116th overall, in 1995 Entry Draft).

			Regular Season								Playoffs						
Season	Club	League	GP	W	L	T	Mins	GA	SO	Avg	GP	W	L	Mins	GA	SO	Avg
1994-95	TPS Turku Jr.	Finland-Jr.	31	....	....	....	1896	92	....	2.91	....	....	....	....	....	....	....
	TPS Turku	Finland	4	....	....	....	240	12	0	3.00	2	....	....	120	7	....	3.50
1995-96	TPS Turku Jr.	Finland-Jr.	3	....	....	....	180	9	....	3.00	....	....	....	....	....	....	....
	Kiekko-67 Turku	Finland-2	5	....	....	....	300	7	....	1.40	....	....	....	....	....	....	....
	TPS Turku	Finland	12	....	....	....	550	38	0	4.14	3	....	....	114	4	....	2.11
1996-97	AIK Solna	Sweden	42	....	....	....	2466	104	3	2.53	7	....	....	420	23	0	3.28
1997-98	AIK Solna	Sweden	42	....	....	....	2457	110	....	2.69	....	....	....	....	....	....	....
1998-99	TPS Turku	Finland	39	*26	6	6	2259	70	4	1.86	10	*9	1	580	15	*3	*1.55
99-2000	Kentucky	AHL	47	23	19	4	2759	114	3	2.48	5	1	3	239	13	0	3.27
2000-01	**San Jose**	**NHL**	**5**	**2**	**1**	**0**	**154**	**5**	**0**	**1.95**	**3**	**1**	**1**	**149**	**5**	**0**	**2.01**
	Kentucky	AHL	36	19	9	6	2038	76	2	2.24	....	....	....	....	....	....	....
2001-02	**San Jose**	**NHL**	**20**	**7**	**6**	**3**	**1037**	**43**	**2**	**2.49**	**1**	**0**	**0**	**8**	**0**	**0**	**0.00**
	Cleveland Barons	AHL	4	4	0	0	242	7	0	1.73	....	....	....	....	....	....	....
2002-03	**San Jose**	**NHL**	**22**	**5**	**14**	**0**	**1199**	**65**	**1**	**3.25**	....	....	....	....	....	....	....
2003-04	**Calgary**	**NHL**	**38**	**24**	**10**	**4**	**2301**	**65**	**4**	***1.69**	***26**	**15**	**11**	***1655**	**51**	***5**	**1.85**
2004-05	Timra IK	Sweden	46	....	....	....	2719	97	5	2.14	6	....	....	356	13	0	2.19
	NHL Totals		**85**	**38**	**31**	**7**	**4691**	**178**	**7**	**2.28**	**30**	**16**	**12**	**1812**	**56**	**5**	**1.85**

Traded to **Calgary** by **San Jose** for Calgary's 2nd round choice (Marc-Edouard Vlasic) in 2005 Entry Draft, November 16, 2003. Signed as a free agent by **Timra** (Sweden), September 20, 2004.

KOCHAN, Dieter (KAH-kuhn, DEE-tuhr)

Goaltender. Catches left. 6'1", 180 lbs. Born, Saskatoon, Sask., May 11, 1974.
(Vancouver's 3rd choice, 98th overall, in 1993 Entry Draft).

			Regular Season								Playoffs						
Season	Club	League	GP	W	L	T	Mins	GA	SO	Avg	GP	W	L	Mins	GA	SO	Avg
1991-92	Sioux City	USHL	23	7	10	0	1131	100	0	5.31	....	....	....	....	....	....	....
1992-93	Kelowna Spartans	BCJHL	44	34	8	0	2582	137	1	3.18	15	12	3	927	48	1	3.10
1993-94	Northern Mich.	WCHA	20	9	7	0	985	57	2	3.47	....	....	....	....	....	....	....
1994-95	Northern Mich.	WCHA	29	8	17	3	1512	107	0	4.25	....	....	....	....	....	....	....
1995-96	Northern Mich.	WCHA	31	7	21	2	1627	123	0	4.54	....	....	....	....	....	....	....
1996-97	Northern Mich.	WCHA	26	8	15	2	1528	99	0	3.89	....	....	....	....	....	....	....
1997-98	Louisville	ECHL	18	7	9	2	980	61	1	3.73	....	....	....	....	....	....	....
1998-99	Binghamton	UHL	40	18	16	5	2322	115	2	2.97	4	1	2	208	9	0	2.60
99-2000	Binghamton	UHL	43	29	11	3	2544	110	4	2.59	....	....	....	....	....	....	....
	Orlando	IHL	4	4	0	0	240	4	1	1.00	....	....	....	....	....	....	....
	Springfield Falcons	AHL	2	1	1	0	120	5	1	2.50	....	....	....	....	....	....	....
	Tampa Bay	**NHL**	**5**	**1**	**4**	**0**	**238**	**17**	**0**	**4.29**	....	....	....	....	....	....	....
	Grand Rapids	IHL	2	1	0	1	93	1	0	0.64	....	....	....	....	....	....	....
2000-01	**Tampa Bay**	**NHL**	**10**	**0**	**3**	**0**	**314**	**18**	**0**	**3.44**	....	....	....	....	....	....	....
	Detroit Vipers	IHL	49	13	28	3	2606	154	0	3.55	....	....	....	....	....	....	....
2001-02	**Tampa Bay**	**NHL**	**5**	**0**	**3**	**1**	**237**	**16**	**0**	**4.05**	....	....	....	....	....	....	....
	Springfield Falcons	AHL	45	21	20	1	2518	112	2	2.67	....	....	....	....	....	....	....
2002-03	**Minnesota**	**NHL**	**1**	**0**	**1**	**0**	**60**	**5**	**0**	**5.00**	....	....	....	....	....	....	....
	Houston Aeros	AHL	25	15	6	3	1447	61	1	2.53	2	0	0	20	0	0	0.00
2003-04	Bridgeport	AHL	45	20	17	7	2728	85	6	1.87	4	1	3	281	12	0	2.57
2004-05	Bridgeport	AHL	39	19	19	0	2303	102	1	2.66	....	....	....	....	....	....	....
	NHL Totals		**21**	**1**	**11**	**1**	**849**	**56**	**0**	**3.96**	....	....	....	....	....	....	....

UHL Second All-Star Team (2000) • Harry "Hap" Holmes Memorial Award (fewest goals against - AHL) (2004) (shared with Wade Dubielewicz)

• Scored a goal vs. Winston-Salem (UHL), January 5, 1999. Signed as a free agent by **Tampa Bay**, March 27, 2000. Signed as a free agent by **Minnesota**, August 5, 2002. Signed as a free agent by **NY Islanders**, August 7, 2003.

KOLESNIK, Vitaly (koh-LEHZ-nihk, vih-TAL-ee) COL.

Goaltender. Catches left. 6'3", 198 lbs. Born, Ust-Kamenogorsk, USSR, August 20, 1979.

			Regular Season								Playoffs						
Season	Club	League	GP	W	L	T	Mins	GA	SO	Avg	GP	W	L	Mins	GA	SO	Avg
2002-03	Ust-Kamenogorsk	Russia-2	25	....	....	....	1308	46	2	2.11	....	....	....	....	....	....	....
2003-04	Ust-Kamenogorsk	Russia-2	35	....	....	....	1899	53	9	1.67	....	....	....	....	....	....	....
2004-05	Ust-Kamenogorsk	Russia-2	42	....	....	....	2329	65	8	1.67	....	....	....	....	....	....	....

Signed as a free agent by **Colorado**, August 16, 2005.

KOLZIG, Olie (KOHL-zihg, OH-lee) WSH.

Goaltender. Catches left. 6'3", 225 lbs. Born, Johannesburg, South Africa, April 6, 1970.
(Washington's 1st choice, 19th overall, in 1989 Entry Draft).

			Regular Season								Playoffs						
Season	Club	League	GP	W	L	T	Mins	GA	SO	Avg	GP	W	L	Mins	GA	SO	Avg
1986-87	Abbotsford Pilots	BCAHA	17	5	9	0	857	81	0	5.67	....	....	....	....	....	....	....
1987-88	New Westminster	WHL	15	6	5	0	650	48	1	4.43	3	0	3	149	11	0	4.43
1988-89	Tri-City Americans	WHL	30	16	10	2	1671	97	1	*3.48	....	....	....	....	....	....	....
1989-90	**Washington**	**NHL**	**2**	**0**	**2**	**0**	**120**	**12**	**0**	**6.00**	....	....	....	....	....	....	....
	Tri-City Americans	WHL	48	21	18	3	2504	187	1	4.48	6	4	0	318	27	0	5.09
1990-91	Baltimore Skipjacks	AHL	26	10	12	1	1367	72	0	3.16	....	....	....	....	....	....	....
	Hampton Roads	ECHL	21	11	9	1	1248	71	2	3.41	3	1	2	180	14	0	4.66
1991-92	Baltimore Skipjacks	AHL	28	5	17	2	1503	105	1	4.19	....	....	....	....	....	....	....
	Hampton Roads	ECHL	14	11	3	0	847	41	0	2.90	....	....	....	....	....	....	....
1992-93	**Washington**	**NHL**	**1**	**0**	**0**	**0**	**20**	**2**	**0**	**6.00**	....	....	....	....	....	....	....
	Rochester	AHL	49	25	16	4	2737	168	0	3.68	*17	9	8	*1040	61	0	3.52
1993-94	**Washington**	**NHL**	**7**	**0**	**3**	**0**	**224**	**20**	**0**	**5.36**	....	....	....	....	....	....	....
	Portland Pirates	AHL	29	16	8	5	1725	88	3	3.06	17	*12	5	1035	44	0	*2.55
1994-95	**Washington**	**NHL**	**14**	**2**	**8**	**2**	**724**	**30**	**0**	**2.49**	**2**	**1**	**0**	**44**	**1**	**0**	**1.36**
	Portland Pirates	AHL	2	1	0	1	125	3	0	1.44	....	....	....	....	....	....	....
1995-96	**Washington**	**NHL**	**18**	**4**	**8**	**2**	**897**	**46**	**0**	**3.08**	**5**	**2**	**3**	**341**	**11**	**0**	***1.94**
	Portland Pirates	AHL	5	5	0	0	300	7	1	1.40	....	....	....	....	....	....	....
1996-97	**Washington**	**NHL**	**29**	**8**	**15**	**4**	**1645**	**71**	**2**	**2.59**	....	....	....	....	....	....	....
1997-98	**Washington**	**NHL**	**64**	**33**	**18**	**10**	**3788**	**139**	**5**	**2.20**	**21**	**12**	**9**	**1351**	**44**	***4**	**1.95**
	Germany	Olympics	2	2	0	0	120	2	1	1.00	....	....	....	....	....	....	....
1998-99	**Washington**	**NHL**	**64**	**26**	**31**	**3**	**3586**	**154**	**4**	**2.58**	....	....	....	....	....	....	....
99-2000	**Washington**	**NHL**	**73**	**41**	**20**	**11**	***4371**	**163**	**5**	**2.24**	**5**	**1**	**4**	**284**	**16**	**0**	**3.38**
2000-01	**Washington**	**NHL**	**72**	**37**	**26**	**8**	**4279**	**177**	**5**	**2.48**	**6**	**2**	**4**	**375**	**14**	**1**	**2.24**
2001-02	**Washington**	**NHL**	**71**	**31**	**29**	**8**	**4131**	**192**	**6**	**2.79**	....	....	....	....	....	....	....
2002-03	**Washington**	**NHL**	**66**	**33**	**25**	**6**	**3894**	**156**	**4**	**2.40**	**6**	**2**	**4**	**404**	**14**	**1**	**2.08**
2003-04	**Washington**	**NHL**	**63**	**19**	**35**	**9**	**3738**	**180**	**2**	**2.89**	....	....	....	....	....	....	....
2004-05	Eisbaren Berlin	Germany	8	....	....	....	452	19	2	2.52	3	....	....	178	7	1	2.36
	NHL Totals		**544**	**234**	**220**	**63**	**31417**	**1342**	**33**	**2.56**	**45**	**20**	**24**	**2799**	**100**	**6**	**2.14**

WHL West Second All-Star Team (1989) • Harry "Hap" Holmes Memorial Award (fewest goals against – AHL) (1994) (shared with Byron Dafoe) • Jack A. Butterfield Trophy (Playoff MVP – AHL) (1994) • NHL First All-Star Team (2000) • Vezina Trophy (2000)

Played in NHL All-Star Game (1998, 2000)

• Scored a goal while with Tri-City (WHL), November 29, 1989. Signed as a free agent by **Eisbaren Berlin** (Germany), February 2, 2005.

KOOPMANS, Logan (KOOP-manz, LOH-guhn) DET.

Goaltender. Catches left. 6'2", 182 lbs. Born, Cranbrook, B.C., May 18, 1984.
(Detroit's 5th choice, 166th overall, in 2002 Entry Draft).

			Regular Season								Playoffs						
Season	Club	League	GP	W	L	T	Mins	GA	SO	Avg	GP	W	L	Mins	GA	SO	Avg
99-2000	Lethbridge	WHL	5	1	3	0	282	19	0	4.04	....	....	....	....	....	....	....
2000-01	Columbia Valley	KIJHL	37	....	....	....	2140	144	1	3.90	....	....	....	....	....	....	....
2001-02	Lethbridge	WHL	37	20	12	2	2057	97	3	2.83	4	0	4	237	14	0	3.54
2002-03	Lethbridge	WHL	34	9	17	0	1628	131	1	4.83	....	....	....	....	....	....	....
2003-04	Lethbridge	WHL	62	27	25	8	3565	155	5	2.61	....	....	....	....	....	....	....
2004-05	Toledo Storm	ECHL	25	12	10	1	1299	61	2	2.82	....	....	....	....	....	....	....

KOPRIVA, Miroslav (koh-PREE-vuh, MEER-oh-slav) MIN.

Goaltender. Catches left. 6'2", 176 lbs. Born, Kladno, Czech., December 5, 1983.
(Minnesota's 5th choice, 187th overall, in 2003 Entry Draft).

			Regular Season								Playoffs						
Season	Club	League	GP	W	L	T	Mins	GA	SO	Avg	GP	W	L	Mins	GA	SO	Avg
99-2000	HC Kladno Jr.	CzRep-Jr.	46	....	....	....	2510	121	4	2.89	4	....	....	249	13	0	3.13
2000-01	HC Kladno Jr.	CzRep-Jr.	26	....	....	....	1478	65	2	2.64	....	....	....	....	....	....	....
2001-02	HC Kladno Jr.	CzRep-Jr.	41	....	....	....	2367	124	6	3.14	....	....	....	....	....	....	....
2002-03	HC Kladno Jr.	CzRep-Jr.	42	....	....	....	2464	80	5	1.95	11	....	....	661	16	2	1.45
2003-04	HC Kladno Jr.	CzRep-Jr.	4	....	....	....	240	10	1	2.50	....	....	....	....	....	....	....
	Beroun	CzRep-2	31	....	....	....	1837	58	3	1.89	....	....	....	....	....	....	....
	HC Rabat Kladno	CzRep	13	....	....	....	687	46	2	4.02	....	....	....	....	....	....	....
2004-05	HC Rabat Kladno	CzRep	10	....	....	....	426	19	1	2.68	....	....	....	....	....	....	....
	Beroun	CzRep-2	31	....	....	....	1841	59	4	1.92	1	....	....	58	2	0	2.07

KOTYK, Seamus (koh-TIHK, SHAY-muhs)

Goaltender. Catches left. 5'11", 180 lbs. Born, London, Ont., October 7, 1980.
(Boston's 5th choice, 147th overall, in 1999 Entry Draft).

			Regular Season								Playoffs						
Season	Club	League	GP	W	L	T	Mins	GA	SO	Avg	GP	W	L	Mins	GA	SO	Avg
1996-97	Stratford Cullitons	OHA-B	28	....	....	....	1615	105	0	3.82	....	....	....	....	....	....	....
1997-98	Ottawa 67's	OHL	31	13	5	5	1422	63	4	2.66	7	3	2	332	11	0	1.99
1998-99	Ottawa 67's	OHL	41	26	7	4	2314	92	5	2.39	5	3	2	338	13	0	*2.31
99-2000	Ottawa 67's	OHL	26	12	6	2	1241	65	1	3.14	....	....	....	....	....	....	....
2000-01	Ottawa 67's	OHL	55	24	20	7	3087	141	2	2.74	*20	*16	4	*1157	46	*3	2.39
2001-02	Cleveland Barons	AHL	24	6	11	0	981	61	1	3.73	....	....	....	....	....	....	....
2002-03	Cleveland Barons	AHL	34	7	22	2	1838	118	2	3.85	....	....	....	....	....	....	....
2003-04	Cleveland Barons	AHL	30	13	10	5	1768	73	1	2.48	....	....	....	....	....	....	....
2004-05	Milwaukee	AHL	23	10	6	1	1138	56	0	2.95	1	0	0	2	0	0	0.00
	Rockford IceHogs	UHL	6	5	1	0	358	6	1	1.00	....	....	....	....	....	....	....

• Missed majority of 1999-2000 season recovering from surgery for cardiac arrhythmia, October 18, 1999. Signed as a free agent by **San Jose**, July 23, 2001. Signed as a free agent by **Milwaukee** (AHL), August 31, 2004.

KOWALSKI, Craig (koh-WAHL-skee, KRAYG) CAR.

Goaltender. Catches left. 5'10", 190 lbs. Born, Warren, MI, January 15, 1981.
(Carolina's 6th choice, 235th overall, in 2000 Entry Draft).

			Regular Season								Playoffs						
Season	Club	League	GP	W	L	T	Mins	GA	SO	Avg	GP	W	L	Mins	GA	SO	Avg
1998-99	Det. Compuware	NAHL	42	*34	7	6	2733	96	3	*2.10	7	*7	0	420	13	1	*1.86
99-2000	Det. Compuware	NAHL	49	33	12	3	2850	113	4	2.38	5	2	3	334	13	0	2.34
2000-01	Northern Mich.	CCHA	19	7	8	4	1078	49	1	2.73	....	....	....	....	....	....	....
2001-02	Northern Mich.	CCHA	38	24	11	2	2271	89	4	2.35	....	....	....	....	....	....	....
2002-03	Northern Mich.	CCHA	38	20	16	2	2213	104	3	2.82	....	....	....	....	....	....	....
2003-04	Northern Mich.	CCHA	37	17	14	4	2058	93	4	2.71	....	....	....	....	....	....	....
2004-05	Florida Everblades	ECHL	27	13	6	6	1503	72	1	2.87	6	3	0	238	13	0	3.27

KRAHN, Brent (KRAWN, BREHNT) CGY.

Goaltender. Catches left. 6'5", 220 lbs. Born, Winnipeg, Man., April 2, 1982.
(Calgary's 1st choice, 9th overall, in 2000 Entry Draft).

			Regular Season								Playoffs						
Season	Club	League	GP	W	L	T	Mins	GA	SO	Avg	GP	W	L	Mins	GA	SO	Avg
1997-98	Pembina Valley	MMMHL	22	20	0	1	1265	40	3	1.90	2	2	0	120	2	1	1.00
1998-99	Pembina Valley	MMMHL	13	10	3	0	770	30	2	2.34	....	....	....	....	....	....	....
99-2000	Calgary Hitmen	WHL	39	33	6	0	2315	92	4	2.38	5	2	2	266	13	0	2.93
2000-01	Calgary Hitmen	WHL	37	22	10	3	2087	104	1	2.99	....	....	....	....	....	....	....
2001-02	Calgary Hitmen	WHL	18	8	6	2	1033	61	0	3.54	2	1	1	119	6	0	3.03
2002-03	Calgary Hitmen	WHL	23	11	10	2	1343	72	2	3.22	....	....	....	....	....	....	....
	Seattle	WHL	5	5	0	0	302	9	2	1.79	15	9	6	960	38	2	2.38
2003-04	Lowell	AHL	7	2	3	0	344	15	0	2.62	....	....	....	....	....	....	....
	Las Vegas	ECHL	14	7	5	2	828	36	0	2.61	....	....	....	....	....	....	....
	San Antonio	AHL	14	3	7	1	715	41	0	3.44	....	....	....	....	....	....	....
2004-05	Lowell	AHL	35	20	11	2	1998	83	6	2.49	1	0	0	1	0	0	0.00

• Missed majority of 2001-02 season recovering from knee surgery, June, 2001.

LABARBERA, Jason (lah-BAR-buhr-uh, JAY-suhn) L.A.

Goaltender. Catches left. 6'2", 205 lbs. Born, Prince George, B.C., January 18, 1980.
(NY Rangers' 3rd choice, 66th overall, in 1998 Entry Draft).

			Regular Season								Playoffs						
Season	Club	League	GP	W	L	T	Mins	GA	SO	Avg	GP	W	L	Mins	GA	SO	Avg
1995-96	Prince George	BCAHA	31	....	....	....	1860	83	0	2.68	....	....	....	....	....	....	....
1996-97	Tri-City Americans	WHL	2	1	0	0	63	4	0	3.81	....	....	....	....	....	....	....
	Portland	WHL	9	5	1	1	443	18	0	2.44	....	....	....	....	....	....	....
1997-98	Portland	WHL	23	18	4	0	1305	72	1	3.31	....	....	....	....	....	....	....
1998-99	Portland	WHL	51	18	23	9	2991	170	4	3.41	4	0	4	252	19	0	4.52
99-2000	Portland	WHL	34	8	24	2	2005	123	1	3.68	....	....	....	....	....	....	....
	Spokane Chiefs	WHL	21	12	6	2	1146	50	0	2.62	9	6	1	435	18	1	2.48
2000-01	**NY Rangers**	**NHL**	**1**	**0**	**0**	**0**	**10**	**0**	**0**	**0.00**	....	....	....	....	....	....	....
	Hartford Wolf Pack	AHL	4	1	1	0	156	12	0	4.61	....	....	....	....	....	....	....
	Charlotte Checkers	ECHL	35	18	10	7	2100	112	1	3.20	2	1	1	143	5	0	2.09
2001-02	Charlotte Checkers	ECHL	13	9	3	1	744	29	0	2.34	4	2	2	212	12	0	3.39
	Hartford Wolf Pack	AHL	20	7	11	1	1058	55	0	3.12	....	....	....	....	....	....	....
2002-03	Hartford Wolf Pack	AHL	46	18	17	6	2452	105	2	2.57	2	0	2	117	6	0	3.07
2003-04	**NY Rangers**	**NHL**	**4**	**1**	**2**	**0**	**198**	**16**	**0**	**4.85**	....	....	....	....	....	....	....
	Hartford Wolf Pack	AHL	59	34	9	9	3393	90	*13	1.59	16	11	5	1043	30	*3	*1.73
2004-05	Hartford Wolf Pack	AHL	53	31	16	2	2937	90	6	1.84	4	1	3	238	9	0	2.27
	NHL Totals		**5**	**1**	**2**	**0**	**208**	**16**	**0**	**4.62**	....	....	....	....	....	....	....

AHL First All-Star Team (2004) • Aldege "Baz" Bastien Memorial Award (Outstanding Goaltender - AHL) (2004) • Les Cunningham Award (MVP - AHL) (2004) • Harry "Hap" Holmes Memorial Trophy (fewest goals against - AHL) (shared with Steve Valiquette) (2005)

Signed as a free agent by **Los Angeles**, August 2, 2005.

LABBE, Jean-Francois (lah-BAY, ZHAWN-fran-SWUH)

Goaltender. Catches left. 5'10", 175 lbs. Born, Sherbrooke, Que., June 15, 1972.

			Regular Season								Playoffs						
Season	Club	League	GP	W	L	T	Mins	GA	SO	Avg	GP	W	L	Mins	GA	SO	Avg
1988-89	Montreal L'est	QAAA	29	*22	7	0	1764	94	1	3.20	5	1	4	333	19	0	3.42
1989-90	Trois-Rivieres	QMJHL	28	13	10	0	1499	106	1	4.24	3	1	1	132	8	0	3.64

1990-91	Trois-Rivieres	QMJHL	54	*35	14	0	2870	158	5	3.30	5	1	4	230	19	0	4.96
1991-92	Trois-Rivieres	QMJHL	48	*31	13	3	2749	142	1	3.10	*15	*10	3	791	33	*1	*2.50
1992-93	Hull Olympiques	QMJHL	46	26	18	2	2701	156	2	3.46	10	6	3	518	24	*1	*2.78
1993-94	Thunder Bay	ColHL	52	*35	11	4	*2900	150	*2	*3.10	8	7	1	493	18	*2	*2.19
	P.E.I. Senators	AHL	7	4	3	0	389	22	0	3.39	....	....	....	....	....	....	....
1994-95	P.E.I. Senators	AHL	32	13	14	3	1817	94	2	3.10	....	....	....	....	....	....	....
1995-96	Cornwall Aces	AHL	55	25	21	5	2972	144	3	2.91	8	3	5	471	21	1	2.68
1996-97	Hershey Bears	AHL	66	*34	22	9	3811	160	*6	*2.52	*23	*14	8	*1364	59	1	2.60
1997-98	Hamilton Bulldogs	AHL	52	24	17	11	3138	149	2	2.85	7	3	4	413	20	0	2.90
1998-99	Hartford Wolf Pack	AHL	*59	28	26	3	*3392	182	2	3.22	7	3	4	447	22	0	2.95
99-2000	**NY Rangers**	**NHL**	**1**	**0**	**1**	**0**	**60**	**3**	**0**	**3.00**	....	....	....	....	....	....	....
	Hartford Wolf Pack	AHL	49	27	13	7	2853	120	1	2.52	*22	*15	7	*1320	48	3	2.18
2000-01	Hartford Wolf Pack	AHL	8	4	2	1	394	20	0	3.04	....	....	....	....	....	....	....
	Syracuse Crunch	AHL	37	15	15	5	2201	105	2	2.86	5	2	3	323	18	0	3.34
2001-02	**Columbus**	**NHL**	**3**	**1**	**1**	**0**	**117**	**6**	**0**	**3.08**	....	....	....	....	....	....	....
	Syracuse Crunch	AHL	51	27	16	7	2993	109	*9	2.18	10	6	4	596	19	2	*1.91
2002-03	**Columbus**	**NHL**	**11**	**2**	**4**	**0**	**451**	**27**	**0**	**3.59**	....	....	....	....	....	....	....
	Syracuse Crunch	AHL	4	1	2	1	247	11	0	2.68	....	....	....	....	....	....	....
2003-04	Lada Togliatti	Russia	30	....	....	....	1725	43	8	1.50	....	....	....	....	....	....	....
	Saint-Georges	QSPHL	11	8	1	2	669	22	2	1.97	....	....	....	....	....	....	....
2004-05	Augsburg	Germany	50	....	....	....	2970	139	3	2.81	5	....	....	298	17	0	3.42
	NHL Totals		**15**	**3**	**6**	**0**	**628**	**36**	**0**	**3.44**	....	....	....	....	....	....	....

QMJHL First All-Star Team (1992) • ColHL First All-Star Team (1994) • ColHL Rookie of the Year (1994) • ColHL Outstanding Goaltender (1994) • ColHL Playoff MVP (1994) • AHL First All-Star Team (1997) • Harry "Hap" Holmes Memorial Award (fewest goals against – AHL) (1997) • Aldege "Baz" Bastien Memorial Award (Outstanding Goaltender – AHL) (1997) • Les Cunningham Award (MVP – AHL) (1997) • Harry "Hap" Holmes Memorial Award (fewest goals against – AHL) (2000) (shared with Milan Hnilicka) • AHL Second All-Star Team (2002)

Signed as a free agent by **Ottawa**, May 12, 1994. Traded to **Colorado** by **Ottawa** for future considerations, September 20, 1995. Signed as a free agent by **Edmonton**, September 2, 1997. Signed as a free agent by **NY Rangers**, July 30, 1998. • Scored a goal vs. Quebec (AHL), February 5, 2000. Traded to **Columbus** by **NY Rangers** for Bert Robertsson, November 9, 2000. Signed as a free agent by **Togliatti** (Russia), July 1, 2003. Signed as a free agent by **Augsburg** (Germany), August 4, 2004. Signed as a free agent by **Nurnberg** (Germany), April 1, 2005.

LACASSE, Loic (luh-KAS, LOIK) MTL.

Goaltender. Catches left. 6'2", 175 lbs. Born, Granby, Que., April 23, 1986.
(Montreal's 5th choice, 181st overall, in 2004 Entry Draft).

			Regular Season								Playoffs						
Season	Club	League	GP	W	L	T	Mins	GA	SO	Avg	GP	W	L	Mins	GA	SO	Avg
2002-03	Antoine-Girouard	QAAA	24	22	1	1	1453	50	1	2.07	....	....	....	....	....	....	....
2003-04	Baie-Comeau	QMJHL	41	9	15	4	1758	117	0	3.99	4	0	4	172	16	0	5.57
2004-05	Baie-Comeau	QMJHL	39	10	22	2	2001	138	1	4.14	2	0	1	54	2	0	2.21

LACOSTA, Dan (luh-KAWS-tah, DAN) CBJ

Goaltender. Catches left. 6'1", 186 lbs. Born, Labrador City, Nfld., March 28, 1986.
(Columbus' 4th choice, 93rd overall, in 2004 Entry Draft).

			Regular Season								Playoffs						
Season	Club	League	GP	W	L	T	Mins	GA	SO	Avg	GP	W	L	Mins	GA	SO	Avg
2001-02	Wellington Dukes	OPJHL	24	19	2	3	1377	44	2	*1.92	....	....	....	....	....	....	....
2002-03	Owen Sound	OHL	28	8	10	3	1321	82	0	3.72	....	....	....	....	....	....	....
2003-04	Owen Sound	OHL	37	17	10	1	1810	82	4	2.72	....	....	....	....	....	....	....
2004-05	Owen Sound	OHL	25	15	7	2	1423	70	0	2.95	....	....	....	....	....	....	....
	Barrie Colts	OHL	21	10	5	2	1054	48	1	2.73	5	1	2	215	11	0	3.07

LALANDE, Kevin (lah-LAWND, KEH-vihn) CGY.

Goaltender. Catches left. 5'11", 175 lbs. Born, Kingston, Ont., February 19, 1987.
(Calgary's 5th choice, 128th overall, in 2005 Entry Draft).

			Regular Season								Playoffs						
Season	Club	League	GP	W	L	T	Mins	GA	SO	Avg	GP	W	L	Mins	GA	SO	Avg
2003-04	Hawkesbury	CJHL	35	....	....	....	2010	105	3	3.13	6	....	....	286	19	0	3.99
	Belleville Bulls	OHL	3	1	2	0	133	15	0	2.88	....	....	....	....	....	....	....
2004-05	Belleville Bulls	OHL	30	15	11	3	1797	79	1	2.64	2	0	2	120	8	0	4.00

LALIME, Patrick (lah-LEEM, PAT-rihk) ST.L.

Goaltender. Catches left. 6'2", 191 lbs. Born, St-Bonaventure, Que., July 7, 1974.
(Pittsburgh's 6th choice, 156th overall, in 1993 Entry Draft).

			Regular Season								Playoffs						
Season	Club	League	GP	W	L	T	Mins	GA	SO	Avg	GP	W	L	Mins	GA	SO	Avg
1990-91	Abitibi Forestiers	QAAA	26	9	17	0	1595	151	0	5.81	....	....	....	....	....	....	....
1991-92	Shawinigan	QMJHL	6	....	....	....	272	25	0	5.50	....	....	....	....	....	....	....
1992-93	Shawinigan	QMJHL	44	10	24	4	2467	192	0	4.67	....	....	....	....	....	....	....
1993-94	Shawinigan	QMJHL	48	22	20	0	2733	192	1	4.22	5	1	3	223	25	0	6.73
1994-95	Hampton Roads	ECHL	26	15	7	3	1470	82	2	3.35	....	....	....	....	....	....	....
	Cleveland	IHL	23	7	10	4	1230	91	0	4.44	....	....	....	....	....	....	....
1995-96	Cleveland	IHL	41	20	12	7	2314	149	0	3.86	....	....	....	....	....	....	....
1996-97	**Pittsburgh**	**NHL**	**39**	**21**	**12**	**2**	**2058**	**101**	**3**	**2.94**	....	....	....	....	....	....	....
	Cleveland	IHL	14	6	6	2	834	45	1	3.24	....	....	....	....	....	....	....
1997-98	Grand Rapids	IHL	31	10	10	9	1749	76	2	2.61	1	0	1	77	4	0	3.11
1998-99	Kansas City Blades	IHL	*66	*39	20	4	*3789	190	2	3.01	3	1	2	179	6	1	2.01
99-2000	**Ottawa**	**NHL**	**38**	**19**	**14**	**3**	**2038**	**79**	**3**	**2.33**	....	....	....	....	....	....	....
2000-01	**Ottawa**	**NHL**	**60**	**36**	**19**	**5**	**3607**	**141**	**7**	**2.35**	**4**	**0**	**4**	**251**	**10**	**0**	**2.39**
2001-02	**Ottawa**	**NHL**	**61**	**27**	**24**	**8**	**3583**	**148**	**7**	**2.48**	**12**	**7**	**5**	**778**	**18**	**4**	***1.39**
2002-03	**Ottawa**	**NHL**	**67**	**39**	**20**	**7**	**3943**	**142**	**8**	**2.16**	**18**	**11**	**7**	**1122**	**34**	**1**	**1.82**
2003-04	**Ottawa**	**NHL**	**57**	**25**	**23**	**7**	**3324**	**127**	**5**	**2.29**	**7**	**3**	**4**	**398**	**13**	**0**	**1.96**
2004-05								Did Not Play									
	NHL Totals		**322**	**167**	**112**	**32**	**18553**	**738**	**33**	**2.39**	**41**	**21**	**20**	**2549**	**75**	**5**	**1.77**

NHL All-Rookie Team (1997) • IHL First All-Star Team (1999)

Played in NHL All-Star Game (2003)

Rights traded to **Anaheim** by **Pittsburgh** for Sean Pronger, March 24, 1998. Traded to **Ottawa** by **Anaheim** for Ted Donato and the rights to Antti-Jussi Niemi, June 18, 1999. Traded to **St. Louis** by **Ottawa** for St. Louis' 4th round choice (Ilja Zubov) in 2005 Entry Draft, June 27, 2004.

LAMOTHE, Marc (luh-MAWTH, MAHRK)

Goaltender. Catches left. 6'2", 210 lbs. Born, New Liskeard, Ont., February 27, 1974.
(Montreal's 6th choice, 92nd overall, in 1992 Entry Draft).

			Regular Season								Playoffs						
Season	Club	League	GP	W	L	T	Mins	GA	SO	Avg	GP	W	L	Mins	GA	SO	Avg
1990-91	Ott. Jr. Senators	CJHL	25	13	7	0	1220	82	1	4.03	....	....	....	....	....	....	....
1991-92	Kingston	OHL	42	10	25	2	2378	189	1	4.77	....	....	....	....	....	....	....
1992-93	Kingston	OHL	45	23	12	6	2489	162	1	3.91	15	8	5	753	48	1	3.82
1993-94	Kingston	OHL	48	23	20	5	2828	177	*2	3.76	6	2	2	224	12	0	3.21
1994-95	Wheeling	ECHL	13	9	2	1	737	38	0	3.10	....	....	....	....	....	....	....
	Fredericton	AHL	9	2	5	0	428	32	0	4.48	....	....	....	....	....	....	....
1995-96	Fredericton	AHL	23	5	9	3	1166	73	1	3.76	3	1	2	161	9	0	3.36
1996-97	Indianapolis Ice	IHL	38	20	14	4	2271	100	1	2.64	1	0	0	20	1	0	3.00
1997-98	Indianapolis Ice	IHL	31	18	10	2	1772	72	3	2.44	4	1	3	177	10	0	3.38
1998-99	Indianapolis Ice	IHL	32	9	16	6	1823	115	1	3.78	6	3	3	338	10	*2	1.78
99-2000	**Chicago**	**NHL**	**2**	**1**	**1**	**0**	**116**	**10**	**0**	**5.17**	....	....	....	....	....	....	....
	Cleveland	IHL	44	19	18	4	2455	112	2	2.74	4	2	2	325	12	0	2.21
2000-01	Syracuse Crunch	AHL	42	17	15	7	2323	112	2	2.89	....	....	....	....	....	....	....
2001-02	Hamilton Bulldogs	AHL	45	22	19	2	2569	102	3	2.38	9	6	3	551	18	0	1.96
2002-03	Grand Rapids	AHL	*60	*33	18	8	*3438	122	6	2.13	15	10	5	945	29	1	1.84
2003-04	**Detroit**	**NHL**	**2**	**1**	**0**	**1**	**125**	**3**	**0**	**1.44**	....	....	....	....	....	....	....
	Grand Rapids	AHL	43	21	16	5	2535	87	4	2.06	4	0	3	200	12	0	3.60
2004-05	Yaroslavl	Russia	*55	....	....	....	*3357	90	6	1.61	9	....	....	521	21	0	2.42
	NHL Totals		**4**	**2**	**1**	**1**	**241**	**13**	**0**	**3.24**	....	....	....	....	....	....	....

AHL First All-Star Team (2003) • Harry "Hap" Holmes Memorial Award (fewest goals against – AHL) (2003) (shared with Joey MacDonald) • Aldege "Baz" Bastien Memorial Award (Outstanding Goaltender – AHL) (2003)

Signed as a free agent by **Chicago**, September 26, 1996. Signed as a free agent by **Edmonton**, August 16, 2001. Signed as a free agent by **Detroit**, August 5, 2002. Signed as a free agent by **Yaroslavl** (Russia), June 14, 2004.

LASSILA, Teemu (la-SIHL-uh, TEE-moo) NSH.

Goaltender. Catches left. 6'1", 200 lbs. Born, Helsinki, Finland, March 26, 1983.
(Nashville's 9th choice, 117th overall, in 2003 Entry Draft).

			Regular Season								Playoffs						
Season	Club	League	GP	W	L	T	Mins	GA	SO	Avg	GP	W	L	Mins	GA	SO	Avg
2001-02	TPS Turku Jr.	Finland-Jr.	43	26	12	5	2577	77	5	1.79	9	4	2	571	21	1	2.21
2002-03	Hermes Kokkola	Finland-2	21	9	5	6	1268	45	2	2.13	....	....	....	....	....	....	....
	TPS Turku	Finland	21	12	6	1	1190	38	*6	1.92	7	3	4	416	21	1	3.03
2003-04	Assat Pori	Finland	5	3	2	0	300	16	0	3.20	....	....	....	....	....	....	....
	TPS Turku	Finland	19	7	5	6	1079	31	3	*1.72	12	8	4	680	17	*4	1.50
2004-05	TPS Turku	Finland	52	21	14	16	3007	116	5	2.31	6	2	4	356	16	0	2.69

LAWSON, Tom (LAW-suhn, TAWM) COL.

Goaltender. Catches left. 6'5", 200 lbs. Born, Whitby, Ont., August 15, 1979.

			Regular Season								Playoffs						
Season	Club	League	GP	W	L	T	Mins	GA	SO	Avg	GP	W	L	Mins	GA	SO	Avg
1998-99	Markham Waxers	OPJHL	32	19	10	2	1793	101	....	3.38	....	....	....	....	....	....	....
99-2000	Bowling Green	CCHA	3	0	3	0	173	14	0	4.86	....	....	....	....	....	....	....
2000-01	Knoxville Speed	UHL	35	16	16	2	2002	116	0	3.48	....	....	....	....	....	....	....
	Cincinnati	AHL	1	0	0	0	23	1	0	2.58	....	....	....	....	....	....	....
2001-02	Anchorage Aces	WCHL	1	1	0	0	54	2	0	2.22	....	....	....	....	....	....	....
2002-03	Fort Wayne	UHL	56	29	15	10	3178	106	*7	*2.00	12	*11	1	750	21	*2	*1.68
2003-04	Hershey Bears	AHL	32	13	12	2	1693	65	4	2.30	....	....	....	....	....	....	....
	Reading Royals	ECHL	2	0	2	0	120	10	0	5.02	....	....	....	....	....	....	....
2004-05	Hershey Bears	AHL	27	10	14	0	1479	70	2	2.84	....	....	....	....	....	....	....

UHL First All-Star Team (2003)

Signed as a free agent by **Knoxville** (UHL) after leaving **Bowling Green** (CCHA), September 30, 2000. • Missed majority of 2001-02 season recovering from leg injury suffered in game vs. Colorado (WCHL), October 13, 2001. Signed as a free agent by **Fort Wayne** (UHL), October 13, 2002. Signed as a free agent by **Colorado**, June 3, 2003.

LECLAIRE, Pascal (lah-CLAIR, pas-KAL) CBJ

Goaltender. Catches left. 6'2", 190 lbs. Born, Repentigny, Que., November 7, 1982.
(Columbus' 1st choice, 8th overall, in 2001 Entry Draft).

			Regular Season								Playoffs						
Season	Club	League	GP	W	L	T	Mins	GA	SO	Avg	GP	W	L	Mins	GA	SO	Avg
1997-98	Cap-d-Madeleine	QAAA	26	6	17	3	1580	127	0	4.90	....	....	....	....	....	....	....
1998-99	Halifax	QMJHL	33	19	11	1	1828	96	2	3.15	1	0	0	17	2	0	7.06
99-2000	Halifax	QMJHL	31	16	8	4	1729	103	1	3.57	5	1	2	198	12	0	3.65
2000-01	Halifax	QMJHL	35	14	16	5	2111	126	1	3.58	2	0	2	109	10	0	5.49
2001-02	Montreal Rocket	QMJHL	45	15	23	4	2513	138	1	3.29	7	3	4	441	15	0	*2.04
2002-03	Syracuse Crunch	AHL	36	8	21	3	1886	112	0	3.56	....	....	....	....	....	....	....
2003-04	**Columbus**	**NHL**	**2**	**0**	**2**	**0**	**119**	**7**	**0**	**3.53**	....	....	....	....	....	....	....
	Syracuse Crunch	AHL	44	21	16	3	2447	125	2	3.06	3	1	2	142	12	0	5.07
2004-05	Syracuse Crunch	AHL	14	5	6	3	845	33	2	2.34	....	....	....	....	....	....	....
	NHL Totals		**2**	**0**	**2**	**0**	**119**	**7**	**0**	**3.53**	....	....	....	....	....	....	....

LEGACE, Manny (LEH-gah-see, MAN-nee) DET.

Goaltender. Catches left. 5'9", 162 lbs. Born, Toronto, Ont., February 4, 1973.
(Hartford's 5th choice, 188th overall, in 1993 Entry Draft).

			Regular Season								Playoffs						
Season	Club	League	GP	W	L	T	Mins	GA	SO	Avg	GP	W	L	Mins	GA	SO	Avg
1987-88	Alliston Hornets	OJHL-C	16	7	9	0	960	83	0	5.17	....	....	....	....	....	....	....
1988-89	Vaughan Raiders	MTJHL	23	....	....	....	1303	92	1	4.24	....	....	....	....	....	....	....
1989-90	Vaughan Raiders	MTJHL	21	8	11	1	1180	89	1	4.53	....	....	....	....	....	....	....
	Thornhill	OHA-B	8	3	3	2	480	30	0	3.75	....	....	....	....	....	....	....
1990-91	Niagara Falls	OHL	30	13	11	2	1515	107	0	4.24	4	1	1	119	10	0	5.04
1991-92	Niagara Falls	OHL	43	21	16	3	2384	143	0	3.60	14	8	5	791	56	0	4.25
1992-93	Niagara Falls	OHL	48	22	19	3	2630	171	0	3.90	4	0	4	240	18	0	4.50
1993-94	Canada	Nat-Tm	16	8	6	0	859	36	2	2.51	....	....	....	....	....	....	....
1994-95	Springfield Indians	AHL	39	12	17	6	2169	128	2	3.54	....	....	....	....	....	....	....
1995-96	Springfield Falcons	AHL	37	20	12	4	2196	83	*5	*2.27	4	1	3	220	18	0	4.91
1996-97	Springfield Falcons	AHL	36	17	14	5	2119	107	1	3.03	12	9	3	745	25	*2	2.01
	Richmond	ECHL	3	2	1	0	157	8	0	3.05	....	....	....	....	....	....	....
1997-98	Springfield Falcons	AHL	6	4	2	0	345	16	0	2.78	....	....	....	....	....	....	....
	Las Vegas Thunder	IHL	41	18	16	4	2106	111	1	3.16	4	1	3	237	16	0	4.05
1998-99	**Los Angeles**	**NHL**	**17**	**2**	**9**	**2**	**899**	**39**	**0**	**2.60**	....	....	....	....	....	....	....
	Long Beach	IHL	33	22	8	1	1796	67	2	2.24	6	4	2	338	9	0	*1.60
99-2000	**Detroit**	**NHL**	**4**	**4**	**0**	**0**	**240**	**11**	**0**	**2.75**	....	....	....	....	....	....	....
	Manitoba Moose	IHL	42	17	18	5	2409	104	2	2.59	2	0	2	141	7	0	2.97
2000-01	**Detroit**	**NHL**	**39**	**24**	**5**	**5**	**2136**	**73**	**2**	**2.05**	....	....	....	....	....	....	....
2001-02 ◆	**Detroit**	**NHL**	**20**	**10**	**6**	**2**	**1117**	**45**	**1**	**2.42**	**1**	**0**	**0**	**11**	**1**	**0**	**5.45**
2002-03	**Detroit**	**NHL**	**25**	**14**	**5**	**4**	**1406**	**51**	**0**	**2.18**	....	....	....	....	....	....	....
2003-04	**Detroit**	**NHL**	**41**	**23**	**10**	**5**	**2325**	**82**	**3**	**2.12**	**4**	**2**	**2**	**220**	**8**	**0**	**2.18**
2004-05	Voskresensk	Russia	2	....	....	....	89	10	0	6.73	....	....	....	....	....	....	....
	NHL Totals		**146**	**77**	**35**	**18**	**8123**	**301**	**6**	**2.22**	**5**	**2**	**2**	**231**	**9**	**0**	**2.34**

OHL First All-Star Team (1993) • AHL First All-Star Team (1996) • Harry "Hap" Holmes Memorial Award (fewest goals against – AHL) (1996) (shared with Scott Langkow) • Aldege "Baz" Bastien Memorial Award (Outstanding Goaltender – AHL) (1996)

Rights transferred to **Carolina** after **Hartford** franchise relocated, June 25, 1997. Traded to **Los Angeles** by **Carolina** for future considerations, July 31, 1998. Signed as a free agent by **Detroit**, August 9, 1999. Claimed on waivers by **Vancouver** from **Detroit**, September 30, 1999. Claimed on waivers by **Detroit** from **Vancouver**, October 13, 1999. Signed as a free agent by **Voskresensk** (Russia), December 20, 2004.

LEHTO, Mika (leh-TOH, MEE-kuh) PIT.

Goaltender. Catches left. 5'11", 175 lbs. Born, Vammala, Finland, April 12, 1979.
(Pittsburgh's 8th choice, 224th overall, in 1998 Entry Draft).

			Regular Season								Playoffs						
Season	Club	League	GP	W	L	T	Mins	GA	SO	Avg	GP	W	L	Mins	GA	SO	Avg
1996-97	Assat Pori Jr.	Finland-Jr.	6	....	....	....	304	17	0	3.35	....	....	....	....	....	....	....
1997-98	Assat Pori Jr.	Finland-Jr.	36	16	14	6	2160	103	2	2.86	....	....	....	....	....	....	....
	Assat Pori	Finland	1	0	0	0	35	1	0	1.71	1	0	0	17	0	0	0.00
1998-99	Assat Pori Jr.	Finland-Jr.	20	7	10	3	1202	68	....	3.39	....	....	....	....	....	....	....
	Assat Pori	Finland	15	4	6	1	773	38	1	2.95	....	....	....	....	....	....	....

99-2000	Assat Pori	Finland	23	4	11	3	1099	87	0	4.75	....	....	....	....	....	....	....
	Hermes Kokkola	Finland-2	6	3	2	1	339	19	1	3.36	....	....	....	....	....	....	....
	Assat Pori Jr.	Finland-Jr.	2	0	0	2	118	8	0	4.05	....	....	....	....	....	....	....
2000-01	JYP Jyvaskyla	Finland	41	12	20	8	2384	126	1	3.17	....	....	....	....	....	....	....
2001-02	JYP Jyvaskyla	Finland	37	10	17	10	2167	107	6	2.96	....	....	....	....	....	....	....
2002-03	Tappara Tampere	Finland	27	12	11	4	1512	45	3	*1.79	14	*10	3	928	23	*2	*1.49
2003-04	Tappara Tampere	Finland	*46	17	19	8	2639	111	3	2.52	3	1	2	190	5	0	1.58
2004-05	Tappara Tampere	Finland	42	12	17	9	2366	115	2	2.92	7	3	3	370	11	3	1.78

LEHTONEN, Kari (LEH-tuh-nehn, KAH-ree) ATL.

Goaltender. Catches left. 6'3", 200 lbs. Born, Helsinki, Finland, November 16, 1983.
(Atlanta's 1st choice, 2nd overall, in 2002 Entry Draft).

						Regular Season								Playoffs			
Season	Club	League	GP	W	L	T	Mins	GA	SO	Avg	GP	W	L	Mins	GA	SO	Avg
1998-99	Jokerit U18	Fin-U18	....	....	....	....	....	....	....	....	4	2	2	240	7	0	1.75
99-2000	Jokerit Helsinki Jr.	Finland-Jr.	33	21	9	3	1974	86	2	2.61	12	9	3	758	14	4	1.11
2000-01	Jokerit Helsinki Jr.	Finland-Jr.	31	20	9	1	1799	71	3	2.37	1	0	1	54	4	0	4.44
	Jokerit Helsinki	Finland	4	3	0	0	189	6	0	1.90	....	....	....	....	....	....	....
2001-02	Jokerit Helsinki Jr.	Finland-Jr.	6	5	1	0	360	11	1	1.83	....	....	....	....	....	....	....
	Jokerit Helsinki	Finland	23	13	5	3	1242	37	4	1.79	*11	*8	3	*623	18	*3	1.73
2002-03	Jokerit Helsinki	Finland	45	*23	14	6	2635	87	5	1.98	10	6	4	626	17	*2	1.63
2003-04	**Atlanta**	**NHL**	**4**	**4**	**0**	**0**	**240**	**5**	**1**	**1.25**	....	....	....	....	....	....	....
	Chicago Wolves	AHL	39	20	14	2	2192	88	3	2.41	10	6	4	663	23	1	2.08
2004-05	Chicago Wolves	AHL	57	38	17	2	3378	128	5	2.27	16	10	6	983	28	2	*1.71
	NHL Totals		**4**	**4**	**0**	**0**	**240**	**5**	**1**	**1.25**	....	....	....	....	....	....	....

AHL Second All-Star Team (2005)

LEIGHTON, Michael (LAY-tohn, MIGH-kuhl) CHI.

Goaltender. Catches left. 6'3", 186 lbs. Born, Petrolia, Ont., May 19, 1981.
(Chicago's 5th choice, 165th overall, in 1999 Entry Draft).

						Regular Season								Playoffs			
Season	Club	League	GP	W	L	T	Mins	GA	SO	Avg	GP	W	L	Mins	GA	SO	Avg
1997-98	Petrolia Jets	OHA-B	30	....	....	....	1583	87	2	3.30	....	....	....	....	....	....	....
1998-99	Windsor Spitfires	OHL	28	4	17	2	1389	112	0	4.84	3	0	1	80	10	0	7.50
99-2000	Windsor Spitfires	OHL	42	17	17	2	2272	118	1	3.12	12	5	6	616	32	0	3.12
2000-01	Windsor Spitfires	OHL	54	32	13	5	3035	138	2	2.73	9	4	5	519	27	1	3.12
2001-02	Norfolk Admirals	AHL	52	27	16	8	3114	111	6	2.14	4	1	2	238	8	0	2.02
2002-03	**Chicago**	**NHL**	**8**	**2**	**3**	**2**	**447**	**21**	**1**	**2.82**	....	....	....	....	....	....	....
	Norfolk Admirals	AHL	36	18	13	5	2185	91	4	2.50	4	3	1	240	7	1	1.75
2003-04	**Chicago**	**NHL**	**34**	**6**	**18**	**8**	**1988**	**99**	**2**	**2.99**	....	....	....	....	....	....	....
	Norfolk Admirals	AHL	18	10	7	1	1081	33	1	1.83	4	2	1	212	2	2	0.57
2004-05	Norfolk Admirals	AHL	41	20	16	3	2319	78	7	2.02	....	....	....	....	....	....	....
	NHL Totals		**42**	**8**	**21**	**10**	**2435**	**120**	**3**	**2.96**	....	....	....	....	....	....	....

AHL All-Rookie Team (2002)

LENEVEU, David (LEH-neh-voo, DAY-vihd) PHX.

Goaltender. Catches left. 6'1", 187 lbs. Born, Fernie, B.C., May 23, 1983.
(Phoenix's 3rd choice, 46th overall, in 2002 Entry Draft).

						Regular Season								Playoffs			
Season	Club	League	GP	W	L	T	Mins	GA	SO	Avg	GP	W	L	Mins	GA	SO	Avg
99-2000	Fernie Ghostriders	AWHL	22	15	2	0	1140	48	0	2.49	....	....	....	....	....	....	....
2000-01	Nanaimo Clippers	BCHL	41	....	....	....	2330	127	6	3.29	....	....	....	....	....	....	....
2001-02	Cornell Big Red	ECAC	14	11	2	1	842	21	2	*1.50	....	....	....	....	....	....	....
2002-03	Cornell Big Red	ECAC	32	*28	3	1	1946	39	*9	*1.20	....	....	....	....	....	....	....
2003-04	Springfield Falcons	AHL	38	16	19	3	2217	102	1	2.76	....	....	....	....	....	....	....
2004-05	Utah Grizzlies	AHL	48	11	32	3	2702	132	0	2.93	....	....	....	....	....	....	....

ECAC All-Rookie Team (2002) • ECAC First All-Star Team (2003) • ECAC Goaltender of the Year (2003) • ECAC Player of the Year (2003) (co-winner - Christopher Higgins) • NCAA East First All-American Team (2003)

LEVASSEUR, Jean-Philippe (leh-VAH-soor, ZHAWN-fihl-EEP) ANA.

Goaltender. Catches right. 6', 184 lbs. Born, Victoriaville, Que., January 15, 1987.
(Anaheim's 6th choice, 197th overall, in 2005 Entry Draft).

						Regular Season								Playoffs			
Season	Club	League	GP	W	L	T	Mins	GA	SO	Avg	GP	W	L	Mins	GA	SO	Avg
2002-03	Magog	QAAA	28	15	10	1	1563	71	3	2.73	....	....	....	....	....	....	....
2003-04	Magog	QAAA	24	12	11	2	1424	86	0	3.62	13	7	5	762	35	0	2.80
	Rouyn-Noranda	QMJHL	3	0	2	1	184	14	0	4.57	....	....	....	....	....	....	....
2004-05	Rouyn-Noranda	QMJHL	29	8	14	3	1393	89	0	3.83	3	0	0	48	3	0	3.76

LITTLE, Neil (LIH-tuhl, NEEL)

Goaltender. Catches left. 6'1", 193 lbs. Born, Medicine Hat, Alta., December 18, 1971.
(Philadelphia's 10th choice, 226th overall, in 1991 Entry Draft).

						Regular Season								Playoffs			
Season	Club	League	GP	W	L	T	Mins	GA	SO	Avg	GP	W	L	Mins	GA	SO	Avg
1989-90	Estevan Bruins	SJHL	46	21	19	4	2707	150	1	3.32	....	....	....	....	....	....	....
1990-91	RPI Engineers	ECAC	18	9	8	0	1032	71	0	4.13	....	....	....	....	....	....	....
1991-92	RPI Engineers	ECAC	28	11	11	3	1532	96	0	3.76	....	....	....	....	....	....	....
1992-93	RPI Engineers	ECAC	*31	*19	9	3	*1801	88	0	2.93	....	....	....	....	....	....	....
1993-94	RPI Engineers	ECAC	27	16	7	4	1570	88	0	3.36	....	....	....	....	....	....	....
	Hershey Bears	AHL	1	0	0	0	18	1	0	3.33	....	....	....	....	....	....	....
1994-95	Hershey Bears	AHL	19	5	7	3	919	60	0	3.91	....	....	....	....	....	....	....
	Johnstown Chiefs	ECHL	16	7	6	1	897	55	0	3.68	3	0	2	145	11	0	4.55
1995-96	Hershey Bears	AHL	48	21	18	6	2680	149	0	3.34	1	0	1	60	4	0	4.02
1996-97	Philadelphia	AHL	54	31	12	7	3007	145	0	2.89	10	6	4	620	20	1	*1.94
1997-98	Philadelphia	AHL	51	*31	11	7	2960	145	0	2.94	*20	*15	5	*1193	48	*3	2.41
1998-99	Grand Rapids	IHL	50	18	21	5	2740	144	3	3.15	....	....	....	....	....	....	....
99-2000	Philadelphia	AHL	51	26	18	2	2830	143	1	3.03	5	2	3	298	15	0	3.02
2000-01	Philadelphia	AHL	*58	22	27	4	3117	148	2	2.85	10	5	5	631	23	1	2.19
2001-02	**Philadelphia**	**NHL**	**1**	**0**	**1**	**0**	**60**	**4**	**0**	**4.00**	....	....	....	....	....	....	....
	Philadelphia	AHL	35	13	15	7	2079	70	2	2.02	5	2	3	298	13	0	2.62
2002-03	Philadelphia	AHL	42	18	19	4	2478	103	4	2.49	....	....	....	....	....	....	....
2003-04	**Philadelphia**	**NHL**	**1**	**0**	**1**	**0**	**33**	**2**	**0**	**3.64**	....	....	....	....	....	....	....
	Philadelphia	AHL	34	21	12	1	1900	62	6	1.96	....	....	....	....	....	....	....
2004-05	Philadelphia	AHL	26	15	7	0	1383	54	3	2.34	2	1	0	25	0	0	0.00
	NHL Totals		**2**	**0**	**2**	**0**	**93**	**6**	**0**	**3.87**	....	....	....	....	....	....	....

ECAC First All-Star Team (1993) • NCAA East Second All-American Team (1993)

LIV, Stefan (LIHV, STEH-fuhn) DET.

Goaltender. Catches left. 6', 172 lbs. Born, Jonkoping, Sweden, December 21, 1980.
(Detroit's 3rd choice, 102nd overall, in 2000 Entry Draft).

						Regular Season								Playoffs			
Season	Club	League	GP	W	L	T	Mins	GA	SO	Avg	GP	W	L	Mins	GA	SO	Avg
1997-98	HV 71 Jr.	Swe-Jr.	17	....	....	....	1020	47	....	2.76	....	....	....	....	....	....	....
1998-99	HV 71 Jonkoping	Sweden				DID NOT PLAY – SPARE GOALTENDER											
99-2000	HV 71 Jr.	Swe-Jr.	10	....	....	....	600	17	2	1.70	....	....	....	....	....	....	....
	Tranas AIF	Sweden-2	9	....	....	....	541	20	0	2.17	....	....	....	....	....	....	....
	HV 71 Jonkoping	Sweden	11	....	....	....	716	24	1	2.01	3	....	....	178	12	0	4.04
2000-01	HV 71 Jonkoping	Sweden	*46	....	....	....	*2752	127	4	2.77	....	....	....	....	....	....	....
2001-02	HV 71 Jonkoping	Sweden	38	....	....	....	2184	95	*4	2.61	8	....	....	517	27	0	3.13
2002-03	HV 71 Jonkoping	Sweden	46	....	....	....	2723	124	3	2.73	7	....	....	391	17	1	2.61
2003-04	HV 71 Jonkoping	Sweden	41	....	....	....	2450	91	6	2.23	*18	....	....	*1091	35	*5	1.92
2004-05	HV 71 Jonkoping	Sweden	40	....	....	....	2404	119	2	2.97	....	....	....	....	....	....	....

LUNDQVIST, Henrik (LUHND-kvihst, HEHN-rihk) NYR

Goaltender. Catches left. 6'1", 192 lbs. Born, Are, Sweden, March 2, 1982.
(NY Rangers' 7th choice, 205th overall, in 2000 Entry Draft).

						Regular Season								Playoffs			
Season	Club	League	GP	W	L	T	Mins	GA	SO	Avg	GP	W	L	Mins	GA	SO	Avg
1998-99	V.Frolunda Jr.	Swe-Jr.	35	....	....	....	2100	95	0	2.73	....	....	....	....	....	....	....
99-2000	V.Frolunda Jr.	Swe-Jr.	30	....	....	....	1726	73	0	2.54	5	4	1	300	7	2	1.40
2000-01	V.Frolunda U18	Swe-U18	2	....	....	....	120	5	0	2.50	3	2	1	182	5	0	1.62
	V.Frolunda Jr.	Swe-Jr.	19	....	....	....	1140	50	2	2.64	....	....	....	....	....	....	....
	IF Molndal Hockey	Sweden-2	7	....	....	....	420	29	0	4.22	....	....	....	....	....	....	....
	V.Frolunda	Sweden	4	....	....	....	190	11	0	3.47	....	....	....	....	....	....	....
2001-02	V.Frolunda	Sweden	20	....	....	....	1152	52	2	2.71	8	8	0	489	18	*2	2.21
	V.Frolunda Jr.	Swe-Jr.	1	1	0	0	60	4	0	4.00	....	....	....	....	....	....	....
2002-03	V.Frolunda	Sweden	28	....	....	....	1650	40	*6	*1.45	12	....	....	739	26	*2	2.11
	V.Frolunda Jr.	Swe-Jr.	1	1	0	0	60	4	0	4.00	....	....	....	....	....	....	....
2003-04	V.Frolunda	Sweden	*48	....	....	....	*2897	105	7	2.17	10	....	....	610	20	0	1.97
2004-05	Frolunda	Sweden	44	....	....	....	2642	79	*6	*1.79	14	....	....	854	15	*6	*1.05

LUONGO, Roberto (loo-WAHN-goh, roh-BUHR-toh) FLA.

Goaltender. Catches left. 6'3", 205 lbs. Born, Montreal, Que., April 4, 1979.
(NY Islanders' 1st choice, 4th overall, in 1997 Entry Draft).

						Regular Season								Playoffs			
Season	Club	League	GP	W	L	T	Mins	GA	SO	Avg	GP	W	L	Mins	GA	SO	Avg
1994-95	Montreal-Bourassa	QAAA	25	10	14	0	94	1465	0	3.85	....	....	....	....	....	....	....
1995-96	Val-d'Or Foreurs	QMJHL	23	6	11	4	1201	74	0	3.70	3	0	1	68	5	0	4.41
1996-97	Val-d'Or Foreurs	QMJHL	60	32	22	2	3305	171	2	3.10	13	8	5	777	44	0	3.40
1997-98	Val-d'Or Foreurs	QMJHL	54	27	20	5	3046	157	*7	3.09	*17	*14	3	*1019	37	*2	*2.18
1998-99	Val-d'Or Foreurs	QMJHL	21	6	10	2	1176	77	1	3.93	....	....	....	....	....	....	....
	Acadie-Bathurst	QMJHL	22	14	7	1	1340	74	0	3.31	*23	*16	6	*1400	64	0	2.74
99-2000	**NY Islanders**	**NHL**	**24**	**7**	**14**	**1**	**1292**	**70**	**1**	**3.25**	....	....	....	....	....	....	....
	Lowell	AHL	26	10	12	4	1517	74	1	2.93	6	3	3	359	18	0	3.01
2000-01	**Florida**	**NHL**	**47**	**12**	**24**	**7**	**2628**	**107**	**5**	**2.44**	....	....	....	....	....	....	....
	Louisville Panthers	AHL	3	1	2	0	178	10	0	3.38	....	....	....	....	....	....	....
2001-02	**Florida**	**NHL**	**58**	**16**	**33**	**4**	**3030**	**140**	**4**	**2.77**	....	....	....	....	....	....	....
2002-03	**Florida**	**NHL**	**65**	**20**	**34**	**7**	**3627**	**164**	**6**	**2.71**	....	....	....	....	....	....	....
2003-04	**Florida**	**NHL**	**72**	**25**	**33**	**14**	**4252**	**172**	**7**	**2.43**	....	....	....	....	....	....	....
2004-05							DID NOT PLAY										
	NHL Totals		**266**	**80**	**138**	**33**	**14829**	**653**	**23**	**2.64**	....	....	....	....	....	....	....

NHL Second All-Star Team (2004)

Played in NHL All-Star Game (2004)

Traded to **Florida** by **NY Islanders** with Olli Jokinen for Mark Parrish and Oleg Kvasha, June 24, 2000.

MacDONALD, Joey (mihk-DAWN-uhld, JOH-ee) DET.

Goaltender. Catches left. 6', 200 lbs. Born, Pictou, N.S., February 7, 1980.

						Regular Season								Playoffs			
Season	Club	League	GP	W	L	T	Mins	GA	SO	Avg	GP	W	L	Mins	GA	SO	Avg
1997-98	Halifax	QMJHL	17	3	12	0	815	54	0	3.97	3	1	2	140	15	0	6.43
1998-99	Peterborough	OHL	47	22	15	2	2483	123	3	2.97	3	0	2	145	13	0	5.38
99-2000	Peterborough	OHL	48	20	15	6	2641	125	2	2.84	5	1	4	280	16	1	3.43
2000-01	Peterborough	OHL	57	25	21	7	3284	161	1	2.94	7	3	4	425	18	0	2.54
2001-02	Toledo Storm	ECHL	38	12	15	7	2084	100	1	2.88	....	....	....	....	....	....	....
2002-03	Grand Rapids	AHL	25	14	6	0	1337	49	3	2.20	1	0	0	8	1	0	7.95
2003-04	Grand Rapids	AHL	39	22	12	3	2249	74	6	1.97	1	0	1	40	4	0	6.04
2004-05	Grand Rapids	AHL	*66	34	29	2	*3755	143	5	2.29	....	....	....	....	....	....	....

Harry "Hap" Holmes Memorial Award (fewest goals against – AHL) (2003) (shared with Marc Lamothe)

Signed as a free agent by **Detroit**, December 21, 2001.

MACHESNEY, Daren (muh-KEHS-nee, DAIR-ehn) WSH.

Goaltender. Catches left. 6', 163 lbs. Born, Hamilton, Ont., December 13, 1986.
(Washington's 5th choice, 143rd overall, in 2005 Entry Draft).

						Regular Season								Playoffs			
Season	Club	League	GP	W	L	T	Mins	GA	SO	Avg	GP	W	L	Mins	GA	SO	Avg
2003-04	Newmarket	OPJHL	32	....	....	....	1868	82	1	2.63	....	....	....	....	....	....	....
	Brampton Battalion	OHL	5	3	2	0	300	15	0	3.00	....	....	....	....	....	....	....
2004-05	Brampton Battalion	OHL	38	16	13	6	2166	99	1	2.74	5	2	3	331	15	0	2.72

OHL All-Rookie Team (2005)

MacINTYRE, Derek (MAK-ihn-tighr, DAIR-ihk) S.J.

Goaltender. Catches left. 6'2", 185 lbs. Born, Elgin, IL, November 1, 1985.
(San Jose's 8th choice, 234th overall, in 2004 Entry Draft).

						Regular Season								Playoffs			
Season	Club	League	GP	W	L	T	Mins	GA	SO	Avg	GP	W	L	Mins	GA	SO	Avg
2003-04	Soo Indians	NAJHL	39	31	3	2	2200	65	4	*1.77	4	1	1	153	10	0	3.92
2004-05	Ferris State	CCHA	17	5	8	1	883	47	0	3.19	....	....	....	....	....	....	....

MacINTYRE, Drew (MAK-ihn-tighr, DROO) DET.

Goaltender. Catches left. 6', 173 lbs. Born, Charlottetown, P.E.I., June 24, 1983.
(Detroit's 2nd choice, 121st overall, in 2001 Entry Draft).

						Regular Season								Playoffs			
Season	Club	League	GP	W	L	T	Mins	GA	SO	Avg	GP	W	L	Mins	GA	SO	Avg
1998-99	Trenton Sting	OPJHL	20	....	....	....	1173	71	2	3.63	....	....	....	....	....	....	....
99-2000	Sherbrooke	QMJHL	24	10	7	2	1253	67	0	3.21	....	....	....	....	....	....	....
2000-01	Sherbrooke	QMJHL	48	17	22	3	2552	139	4	3.27	4	0	4	238	19	0	4.78
2001-02	Sherbrooke	QMJHL	55	15	34	3	3028	201	1	3.98	....	....	....	....	....	....	....
2002-03	Sherbrooke	QMJHL	*61	31	24	5	*3515	161	2	2.75	12	5	7	767	52	0	4.07
2003-04	Toledo Storm	ECHL	11	6	4	0	574	25	0	2.61	....	....	....	....	....	....	....
2004-05	Grand Rapids	AHL	14	7	8	0	1049	47	1	2.69	....	....	....	....	....	....	....
	Toledo Storm	ECHL	2	0	1	0	87	6	0	4.12	....	....	....	....	....	....	....

• Missed majority of 2003-04 season recovering from thigh injury suffered in practice, December 27, 2003.

MAHONEY-WILSON, Brian (muh-HOH-nee-WIHL-suhn, BRIGH-uhn) S.J.

Goaltender. Catches left. 5'10", 150 lbs. Born, Boston, MA, April 7, 1986.
(San Jose's 9th choice, 288th overall, in 2004 Entry Draft).

						Regular Season								Playoffs			
Season	Club	League	GP	W	L	T	Mins	GA	SO	Avg	GP	W	L	Mins	GA	SO	Avg
2003-04	Catholic Memorial	High-MA	24	....	....	....	1280	....	7	1.16	....	....	....	....	....	....	....
2004-05	Walpole Stars	EJHL	40	17	20	2	2211	124	2	3.36	1	1	0	60	2	0	2.00

MALEK, Roman (MAHL-ehk, ROH-muhn) PHI.

Goaltender. Catches left. 5'11", 161 lbs. Born, Prague, Czech., September 25, 1977.
(Philadelphia's 5th choice, 158th overall, in 2001 Entry Draft).

			Regular Season								Playoffs						
Season	Club	League	GP	W	L	T	Mins	GA	SO	Avg	GP	W	L	Mins	GA	SO	Avg
1996-97	HC Slavia Praha Jr.	CzRep-Jr.	31	....	....	....	1820	55	....	1.81	....	....	....	....	....	....	....
	H+S Beroun	CzRep-2	9	....	....	....	469	28	....	3.50	....	....	....	....	....	....	....
1997-98	H+S Beroun	CzRep-2	36	....	....	....	2150	98	....	2.73	....	....	....	....	....	....	....
1998-99	HC Slavia Praha	CzRep	18	....	....	....	830	51	....	3.69	....	....	....	....	....	....	....
99-2000	HC Slavia Praha	CzRep	25	....	....	....	1342	59	....	2.64	....	....	....	....	....	....	....
	Beroun	CzRep-2	3	....	....	....	150	7	0	2.80	....	....	....	....	....	....	....
2000-01	HC Slavia Praha	CzRep	46	....	....	....	2550	100	....	2.35	11	....	....	665	28	....	2.53
2001-02	HC Slavia Praha	CzRep	33	....	....	....	1967	80	....	2.44	9	....	....	485	22	....	2.72
2002-03	HC Slavia Praha	CzRep	50	....	....	....	2844	77	*11	*1.62	17	....	....	1064	28	*5	1.58
2003-04	HC Slavia Praha	CzRep	23	....	....	....	1273	49	2	2.31	....	....	....	....	....	....	....
	Plzen	CzRep	17	....	....	....	1033	37	3	2.15	12	....	....	715	40	0	3.36
2004-05	Magnitogorsk	Russia	16	....	....	....	903	31	3	2.06	....	....	....	....	....	....	....
	Karlovy Vary	CzRep	23	....	....	....	1371	45	4	1.97	....	....	....	....	....	....	....

MANZATO, Daniel (man-ZA-toh, DAN-yehl) CAR.

Goaltender. Catches left. 6', 178 lbs. Born, Fribourg, Switz., January 17, 1984.
(Carolina's 3rd choice, 160th overall, in 2002 Entry Draft).

			Regular Season								Playoffs						
Season	Club	League	GP	W	L	T	Mins	GA	SO	Avg	GP	W	L	Mins	GA	SO	Avg
2000-01	Fribourg Jr.	Swiss-Jr.	36	....	....	....	2160	32	6	0.91	....	....	....	....	....	....	....
2001-02	Victoriaville Tigres	QMJHL	36	20	8	2	1894	102	0	3.23	6	3	0	249	17	0	4.09
2002-03	Victoriaville Tigres	QMJHL	48	23	18	5	2756	155	3	3.37	3	0	3	125	11	0	5.27
2003-04	Victoriaville Tigres	QMJHL	23	7	13	0	1170	78	0	4.00	....	....	....	....	....	....	....
	Kloten Flyers	Swiss	15	....	....	....	912	39	1	2.57	....	....	....	....	....	....	....
2004-05	HC Ambri-Piotta	Swiss	25	....	....	....	1446	65	1	2.70	....	....	....	....	....	....	....

Signed as a free agent by **Kloten** (Swiss), January 5, 2004, following release by **Victoriaville** (QMJHL), January 4, 2004. Signed as a free agent by **Ambri** (Swiss), August 5, 2004.

MARACLE, Norm (MAHR-ah-kuhl, NOHRM)

Goaltender. Catches left. 5'9", 195 lbs. Born, Belleville, Ont., October 2, 1974.
(Detroit's 6th choice, 126th overall, in 1993 Entry Draft).

			Regular Season								Playoffs						
Season	Club	League	GP	W	L	T	Mins	GA	SO	Avg	GP	W	L	Mins	GA	SO	Avg
1990-91	Cgy. North Stars	AMHL	29	....	....	....	1740	99	0	3.43	....	....	....	....	....	....	....
1991-92	Saskatoon Blades	WHL	29	13	6	3	1529	87	1	3.41	15	9	5	860	37	0	3.38
1992-93	Saskatoon Blades	WHL	53	27	18	3	1939	160	1	3.27	9	4	5	569	33	0	3.48
1993-94	Saskatoon Blades	WHL	56	*41	13	1	3219	148	2	2.76	16	*11	5	940	48	*1	3.06
1994-95	Adirondack	AHL	39	12	15	2	1997	119	0	3.57	....	....	....	....	....	....	....
1995-96	Adirondack	AHL	54	24	18	6	2949	135	2	2.75	1	0	1	30	4	0	8.11
1996-97	Adirondack	AHL	*68	*34	22	9	*3843	173	5	2.70	4	1	3	192	10	1	3.13
1997-98	**Detroit**	**NHL**	**4**	**2**	**0**	**1**	**178**	**6**	**0**	**2.02**	....	....	....	....	....	....	....
	Adirondack	AHL	*66	27	29	8	*3709	190	1	3.07	3	0	3	180	10	0	3.33
1998-99	**Detroit**	**NHL**	**16**	**6**	**5**	**2**	**821**	**31**	**0**	**2.27**	**2**	**0**	**0**	**58**	**3**	**0**	**3.10**
	Adirondack	AHL	6	3	3	0	359	18	0	3.01	....	....	....	....	....	....	....
99-2000	**Atlanta**	**NHL**	**32**	**4**	**19**	**2**	**1618**	**94**	**1**	**3.49**	....	....	....	....	....	....	....
2000-01	**Atlanta**	**NHL**	**13**	**2**	**8**	**3**	**753**	**43**	**0**	**3.43**	....	....	....	....	....	....	....
	Orlando	IHL	51	33	13	3	2963	100	*8	*2.02	*16	*12	4	*1003	37	1	2.21
2001-02	**Atlanta**	**NHL**	**1**	**0**	**1**	**0**	**60**	**3**	**0**	**3.00**	....	....	....	....	....	....	....
	Chicago Wolves	AHL	51	21	25	4	2919	141	3	2.90	2	0	1	55	4	0	4.36
2002-03	Chicago Wolves	AHL	49	22	18	6	2795	134	2	2.88	8	3	4	462	17	1	2.21
2003-04	Magnitogorsk	Russia	46	....	....	....	2463	84	8	2.05	*14	....	....	*857	22	2	1.54
2004-05	Avangard Omsk	Russia	28	....	....	....	1585	62	0	2.35	*10	....	....	568	30	0	3.17
	NHL Totals		**66**	**14**	**33**	**8**	**3430**	**177**	**1**	**3.10**	**2**	**0**	**0**	**58**	**3**	**0**	**3.10**

WHL East Second All-Star Team (1993) • WHL East First All-Star Team (1994) • WHL Goaltender of the Year (1994) • Canadian Major Junior First All-Star Team (1994) • Canadian Major Junior Goaltender of the Year (1994) • AHL Second All-Star Team (1997, 1998) • IHL First All-Star Team (2001) • James Norris Memorial Trophy (fewest goals against – IHL) (2001) (shared with Scott Fankhouser) • James Gatschene Memorial Trophy (MVP – IHL) (2001) • N.R. "Bud" Poile Trophy (Playoff MVP – IHL) (2001)

Claimed by **Atlanta** from **Detroit** in Expansion Draft, June 25, 1999. Signed as a free agent by **Magnitogorsk** (Russia), June 8, 2003. Signed as a free agent by **Omsk** (Russia), November 5, 2004.

MARKKANEN, Jussi (MAHR-kah-nehn, YOO-see) EDM.

Goaltender. Catches left. 6', 182 lbs. Born, Imatra, Finland, May 8, 1975.
(Edmonton's 5th choice, 133rd overall, in 2001 Entry Draft).

			Regular Season								Playoffs						
Season	Club	League	GP	W	L	T	Mins	GA	SO	Avg	GP	W	L	Mins	GA	SO	Avg
1991-92	SaiPa Jr.	Finland-Jr.	2	....	....	....	120	11	0	5.50	....	....	....	....	....	....	....
1992-93	SaiPa Jr.	Finland-Jr.	7	....	....	....	367	28	....	4.58	....	....	....	....	....	....	....
	SaiPa	Finland-2	16	....	....	....	798	60	....	4.51	....	....	....	....	....	....	....
1993-94	SaiPa	Finland-2	30	....	....	....	1726	97	....	3.37	....	....	....	....	....	....	....
1994-95	SaiPa	Finland-2	43	....	....	....	2493	122	....	2.94	3	....	....	179	5	....	1.68
1995-96	Tappara Jr.	Finland-Jr.	5	....	....	....	298	21	....	4.23	....	....	....	....	....	....	....
	Tappara Tampere	Finland	23	11	8	2	1238	59	1	2.86	....	....	....	....	....	....	....
1996-97	SaiPa	Finland	41	9	24	7	2340	132	0	3.38	....	....	....	....	....	....	....
1997-98	SaiPa	Finland	*48	21	20	5	*2870	138	4	2.89	3	0	3	164	11	0	4.02
1998-99	SaiPa	Finland	48	21	19	4	2633	105	4	2.39	7	3	3	366	21	0	3.44
99-2000	SaiPa	Finland	48	4	23	9	2794	150	2	3.22	....	....	....	....	....	....	....
2000-01	Tappara Tampere	Finland	52	*30	17	5	3076	107	*9	2.09	*10	7	3	*608	18	1	1.78
2001-02	**Edmonton**	**NHL**	**14**	**6**	**4**	**2**	**784**	**24**	**2**	**1.84**	....	....	....	....	....	....	....
	Hamilton Bulldogs	AHL	4	2	2	0	239	9	0	2.26	....	....	....	....	....	....	....
	Finland	Olympics				DID NOT PLAY – SPARE GOALTENDER											
2002-03	**Edmonton**	**NHL**	**22**	**7**	**8**	**3**	**1180**	**51**	**3**	**2.59**	**1**	**0**	**0**	**14**	**1**	**0**	**4.29**
2003-04	**NY Rangers**	**NHL**	**26**	**8**	**12**	**1**	**1244**	**53**	**2**	**2.56**	....	....	....	....	....	....	....
	Edmonton	**NHL**	**7**	**2**	**2**	**2**	**394**	**12**	**0**	**1.83**	....	....	....	....	....	....	....
2004-05	Lada Togliatti	Russia	54	....	....	....	3157	63	11	*1.20	*10	....	....	*627	15	1	1.44
	NHL Totals		**69**	**23**	**26**	**8**	**3602**	**140**	**7**	**2.33**	**1**	**0**	**0**	**14**	**1**	**0**	**4.29**

Traded to **NY Rangers** by **Edmonton** with Edmonton's 4th round choice (later traded to Toronto – Toronto selected Roman Kukumberg) for Brian Leetch, June 30, 2003. Traded to **Edmonton** by **NY Rangers** with Petr Nedved for Stephen Valiquette, Dwight Helminen, Edmonton's 2nd round compensatory choice (Dane Byers) in 2004 Entry Draft and future consideratons, March 3, 2004. Signed as a free agent by **Togliatti** (Russia), September 25, 2004.

MASON, Chris (MAY-sohn, KRIHS) NSH.

Goaltender. Catches left. 6', 195 lbs. Born, Red Deer, Alta., April 20, 1976.
(New Jersey's 7th choice, 122nd overall, in 1995 Entry Draft).

			Regular Season								Playoffs						
Season	Club	League	GP	W	L	T	Mins	GA	SO	Avg	GP	W	L	Mins	GA	SO	Avg
1992-93	Red Deer	AMHL	20	....	....	....	1280	76	0	3.35	....	....	....	....	....	....	....
1993-94	Victoria Cougars	WHL	5	1	4	0	237	27	0	6.84	....	....	....	....	....	....	....
1994-95	Prince George	WHL	44	8	30	1	2288	192	1	5.03	....	....	....	....	....	....	....
1995-96	Prince George	WHL	59	16	37	1	3289	236	1	4.31	....	....	....	....	....	....	....
1996-97	Prince George	WHL	50	19	24	4	2851	172	2	3.62	15	9	6	938	44	*1	2.81
1997-98	Cincinnati	AHL	47	13	19	7	2368	136	0	3.45	....	....	....	....	....	....	....
1998-99	**Nashville**	**NHL**	**3**	**0**	**0**	**0**	**69**	**6**	**0**	**5.22**	....	....	....	....	....	....	....
	Milwaukee	IHL	34	15	12	6	1901	92	1	2.90	....	....	....	....	....	....	....
99-2000	Milwaukee	IHL	53	20	21	8	2952	137	2	2.78	3	1	2	252	11	0	2.62
2000-01	**Nashville**	**NHL**	**1**	**0**	**1**	**0**	**59**	**2**	**0**	**2.03**	....	....	....	....	....	....	....
	Milwaukee	IHL	37	17	14	5	2226	87	5	2.35	4	1	3	239	12	0	3.02
2001-02	Milwaukee	AHL	48	17	21	7	2755	116	2	2.53	....	....	....	....	....	....	....
2002-03	San Antonio	AHL	50	25	18	6	2914	122	1	2.51	3	0	3	195	9	0	2.77
2003-04	**Nashville**	**NHL**	**17**	**4**	**4**	**1**	**744**	**27**	**1**	**2.18**	....	....	....	....	....	....	....
	Milwaukee	AHL	1	1	0	0	60	2	0	2.00	....	....	....	....	....	....	....
2004-05	Valerengen IF Oslo	Norway	20	....	....	....	1204	36	1	1.79	11	....	....	657	22	1	2.01
	NHL Totals		**21**	**4**	**5**	**1**	**872**	**35**	**1**	**2.41**	....	....	....	....	....	....	....

Signed as a free agent by **Anaheim**, June 27, 1997. Traded to **Nashville** by **Anaheim** with Marc Moro for Dominic Roussel, October 5, 1998. Signed as a free agent by **Florida**, August 20, 2002. Claimed by **Nashville** from **Florida** in Waiver Draft, October 3, 2003. Signed as a free agent by **Oslo** (Norway), November 30, 2004.

McELHINNEY, Curtis (MAK-IHL-ehn-ee, KUHR-this) CGY.

Goaltender. Catches left. 6'3", 207 lbs. Born, London, Ont., May 23, 1983.
(Calgary's 9th choice, 176th overall, in 2002 Entry Draft).

			Regular Season								Playoffs						
Season	Club	League	GP	W	L	T	Mins	GA	SO	Avg	GP	W	L	Mins	GA	SO	Avg
2000-01	Notre Dame	SJHL					STATISTICS NOT AVAILABLE										
2001-02	Colorado College	WCHA	9	6	0	1	441	15	1	2.04	....	....	....	....	....	....	....
2002-03	Colorado College	WCHA	*37	*25	6	5	*2147	85	*4	2.37	....	....	....	....	....	....	....
2003-04	Colorado College	WCHA	19	10	6	1	1015	41	2	2.42	....	....	....	....	....	....	....
2004-05	Colorado College	WCHA	26	*21	4	1	1550	58	2	2.24	....	....	....	....	....	....	....

WCHA First All-Star Team (2003, 2005) • NCAA West Second All-American Team (2003) • NCAA West First All-American Team (2005)

McGANN, Pat (mih-GAN, PAT) DAL.

Goaltender. Catches right. 5'11", 160 lbs. Born, Evergreen, IL, January 27, 1987.
(Dallas' 7th choice, 223rd overall, in 2005 Entry Draft).

			Regular Season								Playoffs						
Season	Club	League	GP	W	L	T	Mins	GA	SO	Avg	GP	W	L	Mins	GA	SO	Avg
2003-04	Chicago Chill	MAHL	31	14	16	1	....	....	....	3.40	....	....	....	....	....	....	....
2004-05	Team Illinois	MWEHL	50	31	18	1	....	91	5	2.21	....	....	....	....	....	....	....

McLENNAN, Jamie (muh-KLEH-nuhn, JAY-mee) FLA.

Goaltender. Catches left. 6', 190 lbs. Born, Edmonton, Alta., June 30, 1971.
(NY Islanders' 3rd choice, 48th overall, in 1991 Entry Draft).

			Regular Season								Playoffs						
Season	Club	League	GP	W	L	T	Mins	GA	SO	Avg	GP	W	L	Mins	GA	SO	Avg
1987-88	St. Albert Royals	AMHL	21	....	....	....	1224	80	0	3.92	....	....	....	....	....	....	....
1988-89	Spokane Chiefs	WHL	11	....	....	....	578	63	0	6.54	....	....	....	....	....	....	....
	Lethbridge	WHL	7	....	....	....	368	22	0	3.59	....	....	....	....	....	....	....
1989-90	Lethbridge	WHL	34	20	4	2	1690	110	1	3.91	13	6	5	677	44	0	3.90
1990-91	Lethbridge	WHL	56	32	18	4	3230	205	0	3.81	*16	8	8	*970	56	0	3.46
1991-92	Capital District	AHL	18	4	10	2	952	60	1	3.78	....	....	....	....	....	....	....
	Richmond	ECHL	32	16	12	2	1837	114	0	3.72	....	....	....	....	....	....	....
1992-93	Capital District	AHL	38	17	14	6	2171	117	1	3.23	1	0	1	20	5	0	15.00
1993-94	**NY Islanders**	**NHL**	**22**	**8**	**7**	**6**	**1287**	**61**	**0**	**2.84**	**2**	**0**	**1**	**82**	**6**	**0**	**4.39**
	Salt Lake	IHL	24	8	12	2	1320	80	0	3.64	....	....	....	....	....	....	....
1994-95	**NY Islanders**	**NHL**	**21**	**6**	**11**	**2**	**1185**	**67**	**0**	**3.39**	....	....	....	....	....	....	....
	Denver Grizzlies	IHL	4	3	0	1	239	12	0	3.00	11	8	2	640	23	1	*2.15
1995-96	**NY Islanders**	**NHL**	**13**	**3**	**9**	**1**	**636**	**39**	**0**	**3.68**	....	....	....	....	....	....	....
	Utah Grizzlies	IHL	14	9	2	2	728	29	0	2.39	....	....	....	....	....	....	....
	Worcester IceCats	AHL	22	14	7	1	1216	57	0	2.81	2	0	2	119	8	0	4.04
1996-97	Worcester IceCats	AHL	39	18	13	4	2152	100	2	2.79	4	2	2	262	16	0	3.67
1997-98	**St. Louis**	**NHL**	**30**	**16**	**8**	**2**	**1658**	**60**	**2**	**2.17**	**1**	**0**	**0**	**14**	**1**	**0**	**4.29**
1998-99	**St. Louis**	**NHL**	**33**	**13**	**14**	**4**	**1763**	**70**	**3**	**2.38**	**1**	**0**	**1**	**37**	**0**	**0**	**0.00**
99-2000	**St. Louis**	**NHL**	**19**	**9**	**5**	**2**	**1009**	**33**	**2**	**1.96**	....	....	....	....	....	....	....
2000-01	**Minnesota**	**NHL**	**38**	**5**	**23**	**9**	**2230**	**98**	**2**	**2.64**	....	....	....	....	....	....	....
2001-02	Houston Aeros	AHL	51	25	18	4	2852	130	3	2.74	14	8	6	880	31	2	2.11
2002-03	**Calgary**	**NHL**	**22**	**2**	**11**	**4**	**1165**	**58**	**0**	**2.99**	....	....	....	....	....	....	....
2003-04	**Calgary**	**NHL**	**26**	**12**	**9**	**3**	**1446**	**53**	**4**	**2.20**	....	....	....	....	....	....	....
	NY Rangers	**NHL**	**4**	**1**	**3**	**0**	**244**	**12**	**0**	**2.95**	....	....	....	....	....	....	....
2004-05	Guildford Flames	Britain-2	3	2	1	0	185	8	0	2.59	7	4	3	385	13	0	2.02
	NHL Totals		**228**	**75**	**100**	**33**	**12623**	**551**	**13**	**2.62**	**4**	**0**	**2**	**133**	**7**	**0**	**3.16**

WHL East First All-Star Team (1991) • WHL Goaltender of the Year (1991) • Bill Masterton Memorial Trophy (1998)

Signed as a free agent by **St. Louis**, July 15, 1996. Claimed by **Minnesota** from **St. Louis** in Expansion Draft, June 23, 2000. Traded to **Calgary** by **Minnesota** for Calgary's 9th round choice (Mika Hannula) in 2002 Entry Draft, June 22, 2002. Traded to **NY Rangers** by **Calgary** with Blair Betts and Greg Moore for Chris Simon and NY Rangers' 7th round choice (Matt Schneider) in 2004 Entry Draft, March 6, 2004. Signed as a free agent by **Florida**, July 2, 2004. Signed as a free agent by **Guildford** (Britain-2), February 17, 2005.

McVICAR, Rob (mihk-VIH-kuhr, RAWB) VAN.

Goaltender. Catches left. 6'4", 201 lbs. Born, Hay River, N.W.T., January 15, 1982.
(Vancouver's 6th choice, 151st overall, in 2002 Entry Draft).

			Regular Season								Playoffs						
Season	Club	League	GP	W	L	T	Mins	GA	SO	Avg	GP	W	L	Mins	GA	SO	Avg
1998-99	Brandon Kings	MMMHL	21	....	....	....	1217	69	0	3.40	....	....	....	....	....	....	....
99-2000	Brandon	WHL	14	5	6	0	687	43	0	3.76	....	....	....	....	....	....	....
2000-01	Brandon	WHL	27	12	10	2	1537	76	0	2.97	5	2	3	324	13	1	2.41
2001-02	Brandon	WHL	55	*33	18	2	3276	151	1	2.77	19	11	8	1255	44	1	2.10
2002-03	Brandon	WHL	51	31	14	5	3027	136	2	2.70	13	6	7	737	32	0	2.61
2003-04	Manitoba Moose	AHL	10	4	3	2	514	25	0	2.92	....	....	....	....	....	....	....
	Columbia Inferno	ECHL	19	11	5	2	1088	47	0	2.59	....	....	....	....	....	....	....
2004-05	Manitoba Moose	AHL	1	0	1	0	62	3	0	2.92	....	....	....	....	....	....	....
	Columbia Inferno	ECHL	34	14	14	5	2004	79	3	2.37	....	....	....	....	....	....	....

MEDVEDEV, Andrei (mehd-VEH-dehv, AN-dray) CGY.

Goaltender. Catches left. 6', 211 lbs. Born, Moscow, USSR, April 1, 1983.
(Calgary's 3rd choice, 56th overall, in 2001 Entry Draft).

			Regular Season								Playoffs						
Season	Club	League	GP	W	L	T	Mins	GA	SO	Avg	GP	W	L	Mins	GA	SO	Avg
1998-99	Spartak Moscow	Russia	2	....	....	....	80	2	1	1.50	....	....	....	....	....	....	....
99-2000	Spartak Moscow	Russia-2					STATISTICS NOT AVAILABLE										
2000-01	Spartak Moscow 2	Russia-3					STATISTICS NOT AVAILABLE										
2001-02	Spartak Moscow	Russia	11	....	....	....	208	8	0	2.31	....	....	....	....	....	....	....
	Spartak Moscow	Russia	2	....	....	....	61	4	0	3.93	....	....	....	....	....	....	....
2002-03	Spartak Moscow	Russia	17	....	....	....	810	28	1	2.07	....	....	....	....	....	....	....
2003-04	Spartak Moscow	Russia-2	29	....	....	....	1640	48	....	1.76	3	....	....	107	3	1	1.68
2004-05	Spartak Moscow	Russia	21	....	....	....	1061	56	0	3.17	....	....	....	....	....	....	....

MENSATOR, Lukas (MEHN-suh-tohr, loo-KAHSH) VAN.

Goaltender. Catches left. 5'8", 167 lbs. Born, Sokolov, Czech., August 18, 1984.
(Vancouver's 4th choice, 83rd overall, in 2002 Entry Draft).

			Regular Season								Playoffs						
Season	Club	League	GP	W	L	T	Mins	GA	SO	Avg	GP	W	L	Mins	GA	SO	Avg
99-2000	Karlovy Vary U17	CzR-U17	42	....	....	....	2406	160	0	3.99	....	....	....	....	....	....	....
	Karlovy Vary Jr.	CzRep-Jr.	1	1	0	0	60	3	0	3.00	....	....	....	....	....	....	....

2000-01	Karlovy Vary U17	CzR-U17	6	....	....	....	360	15	0	2.50	....	....	....	....	....	....	....
	Karlovy Vary Jr.	CzRep-Jr.	19	....	....	....	1085	60	0	3.32	....	....	....	....	....	....	....
2001-02	Karlovy Vary Jr.	CzRep-Jr.	31	....	....	....	1809	93	0	3.08	9	....	....	459	17	0	2.22
	Banik CHZ Sokolov	CzRep-3	3	....	....	....	180	12	0	4.00	....	....	....	....	....	....	....
2002-03	Ottawa 67's	OHL	42	26	8	5	2395	122	0	3.06	*23	13	8	*1381	63	*2	2.74
2003-04	Ottawa 67's	OHL	50	18	22	7	2924	162	0	3.32	7	3	4	447	23	0	3.09
2004-05	Karlovy Vary	CzRep	13	....	....	....	686	34	1	2.97	....	....	....	....	....	....	....
	IHC Pisek	CzRep-2	14	....	....	....	808	41	1	3.04	....	....	....	....	....	....	....
	BK Mlada Boleslav	CzRep-2	17	....	....	....	991	34	4	2.06	7	....	....	393	17	1	2.60

Signed as a free agent by **Karlovy Vary** (CzRep), May 17, 2004.

MICHAUD, Olivier (MEE-shoh, OH-lihv-ee-ay) MTL.

Goaltender. Catches left. 5'11", 179 lbs. Born, Beloeil, Que., September 14, 1983.

			Regular Season								Playoffs						
Season	**Club**	**League**	**GP**	**W**	**L**	**T**	**Mins**	**GA**	**SO**	**Avg**	**GP**	**W**	**L**	**Mins**	**GA**	**SO**	**Avg**
1998-99	Eclaireur Bantams	QAHA	23	14	4	5	1380	58	....	2.50	....	....	....	....	....	....	....
99-2000	Antoine-Girouard	QAAA	7	6	1	0	420	15	1	2.14	....	....	....	....	....	....	....
	Charles-Lemoyne	QAAA	16	8	4	2	886	57	0	3.86	16	8	8	1015	29	2	1.71
	Shawinigan	QMJHL	1	0	1	0	49	2	0	2.44	....	....	....	....	....	....	....
2000-01	Shawinigan	QMJHL	21	12	4	4	1096	54	1	2.96	3	1	2	150	6	0	2.41
2001-02	**Montreal**	**NHL**	**1**	**0**	**0**	**0**	**18**	**0**	**0**	**0.00**	....	....	....	....	....	....	....
	Shawinigan	QMJHL	46	29	11	3	2650	108	3	*2.45	12	7	5	744	36	0	2.91
2002-03	Shawinigan	QMJHL	27	8	13	3	1497	82	1	3.29	....	....	....	....	....	....	....
	Baie-Comeau	QMJHL	31	23	5	2	1775	90	3	3.04	12	7	5	748	38	0	3.05
2003-04	Columbus	ECHL	22	8	10	2	1234	62	1	3.01	....	....	....	....	....	....	....
	Hamilton Bulldogs	AHL	16	4	7	3	900	38	2	2.53	....	....	....	....	....	....	....
2004-05	Long Beach	ECHL	41	18	14	6	2315	98	1	2.54	1	0	1	59	4	0	4.10
	NHL Totals		**1**	**0**	**0**	**0**	**18**	**0**	**0**	**0.00**	....	....	....	....	....	....	....

Signed as a free agent by **Montreal**, September 18, 2001. • Promoted to **Montreal** from **Shawinigan** (QMJHL) and replaced injured Jose Theodore, October 26, 2001. • Returned to **Shawinigan** (QMJHL) by **Montreal**, November 5, 2001.

MILLER, Ryan (MIHL-luhr, RIGH-uhn) BUF.

Goaltender. Catches left. 6'2", 170 lbs. Born, East Lansing, MI, July 17, 1980.
(Buffalo's 7th choice, 138th overall, in 1999 Entry Draft).

			Regular Season								Playoffs						
Season	**Club**	**League**	**GP**	**W**	**L**	**T**	**Mins**	**GA**	**SO**	**Avg**	**GP**	**W**	**L**	**Mins**	**GA**	**SO**	**Avg**
1997-98	Soo Indians	NAJHL	37	21	14	0	2113	82	3	2.33	2	0	2	158	7	0	2.66
1998-99	Soo Indians	NAHL	47	31	14	1	2711	104	8	2.30	4	2	2	218	10	1	2.76
99-2000	Michigan State	CCHA	26	16	5	3	1525	39	*8	*1.53	....	....	....	....	....	....	....
2000-01	Michigan State	CCHA	40	*31	5	4	2447	54	*10	*1.32	....	....	....	....	....	....	....
2001-02	Michigan State	CCHA	40	26	9	5	2411	71	*8	*1.77	....	....	....	....	....	....	....
2002-03	**Buffalo**	**NHL**	**15**	**6**	**8**	**1**	**912**	**40**	**1**	**2.63**	....	....	....	....	....	....	....
	Rochester	AHL	47	23	18	5	2817	110	2	2.34	3	1	2	190	13	0	4.11
2003-04	**Buffalo**	**NHL**	**3**	**0**	**3**	**0**	**178**	**15**	**0**	**5.06**	....	....	....	....	....	....	....
	Rochester	AHL	60	27	25	7	3579	132	5	2.21	14	7	7	857	26	2	1.82
2004-05	Rochester	AHL	63	*41	17	4	3741	153	8	2.45	9	5	4	547	24	0	2.63
	NHL Totals		**18**	**6**	**11**	**1**	**1090**	**55**	**1**	**3.03**	....	....	....	....	....	....	....

CCHA Second All-Star Team (2000) • CCHA First All-Star Team (2001, 2002) • NCAA West First All-American Team (2001, 2002) • CCHA Player of the Year (2001, 2002) • Hobey Baker Memorial Award (Top U.S. Collegiate Player) (2001) • AHL First All-Star Team (2005) • Aldege "Baz" Bastien Memorial Trophy (Top Goaltender - AHL) (2005)

MOIR, Kyle (MOI-uhr, KIGHL) NSH.

Goaltender. Catches left. 6'3", 193 lbs. Born, Calgary, Alta., May 25, 1986.
(Nashville's 4th choice, 139th overall, in 2004 Entry Draft).

			Regular Season								Playoffs						
Season	**Club**	**League**	**GP**	**W**	**L**	**T**	**Mins**	**GA**	**SO**	**Avg**	**GP**	**W**	**L**	**Mins**	**GA**	**SO**	**Avg**
2002-03	Cgy. AAA Flames	AMHL	15	8	2	4	922	44	0	2.86	....	....	....	....	....	....	....
	Swift Current	WHL	7	4	1	0	283	14	1	2.97	1	0	1	60	7	0	7.00
2003-04	Swift Current	WHL	46	22	15	4	2460	119	3	2.90	1	0	0	20	2	0	6.00
2004-05	Swift Current	WHL	60	20	33	4	3339	152	3	2.73	....	....	....	....	....	....	....

MONTOYA, Al (mawn-TOI-uh, AL) NYR

Goaltender. Catches left. 6'1", 190 lbs. Born, Chicago, IL, February 13, 1985.
(NY Rangers' 1st choice, 6th overall, in 2004 Entry Draft).

			Regular Season								Playoffs						
Season	**Club**	**League**	**GP**	**W**	**L**	**T**	**Mins**	**GA**	**SO**	**Avg**	**GP**	**W**	**L**	**Mins**	**GA**	**SO**	**Avg**
99-2000	Loyola Academy	High-MN	28	12	13	3	1685	56	1	2.01	....	....	....	....	....	....	....
2000-01	Texas Tornado	NAHL	15	10	3	0	780	38	0	2.92	1	1	0	60	2	0	2.00
	United States	Nat-Tm	2	2	0	0	120	4	0	2.00	....	....	....	....	....	....	....
2001-02	USA U-17	USDP	34	11	16	2	1914	103	0	3.23	....	....	....	....	....	....	....
2002-03	U. of Michigan	CCHA	*43	*30	10	3	*2547	99	4	2.33	....	....	....	....	....	....	....
2003-04	U. of Michigan	CCHA	*40	*26	12	2	*2340	87	6	2.23	....	....	....	....	....	....	....
2004-05	U. of Michigan	CCHA	*40	*30	7	3	*2359	99	3	2.52	....	....	....	....	....	....	....

CCHA All-Rookie Team (2003) • NCAA West Second All-American Team (2004)

MORRISON, Mike (MOHR-ih-suhn, MIGHK) EDM.

Goaltender. Catches right. 6'3", 194 lbs. Born, Medford, MA, July 11, 1979.
(Edmonton's 8th choice, 186th overall, in 1998 Entry Draft).

			Regular Season								Playoffs						
Season	**Club**	**League**	**GP**	**W**	**L**	**T**	**Mins**	**GA**	**SO**	**Avg**	**GP**	**W**	**L**	**Mins**	**GA**	**SO**	**Avg**
1997-98	Exeter	High-NH	27	15	11	2	1632	64	1	2.35	....	....	....	....	....	....	....
1998-99	University of Maine	H-East	11	3	0	1	347	10	1	1.73	....	....	....	....	....	....	....
99-2000	University of Maine	H-East	12	7	2	1	608	27	1	2.67	....	....	....	....	....	....	....
2000-01	University of Maine	H-East	10	2	3	3	490	16	1	1.96	....	....	....	....	....	....	....
2001-02	University of Maine	H-East	30	20	3	4	1645	60	2	2.19	....	....	....	....	....	....	....
2002-03	Columbus	ECHL	38	9	18	6	1948	113	1	3.48	....	....	....	....	....	....	....
2003-04	Toronto	AHL	27	12	8	2	1309	55	3	2.52	....	....	....	....	....	....	....
2004-05	Greenville Grrrowl	ECHL	26	13	10	2	1576	72	1	2.74	3	1	1	150	9	0	3.61
	Edmonton	AHL	14	2	5	5	728	21	2	1.73	....	....	....	....	....	....	....

Hockey East First All-Star Team (2002)

MOSS, Tyler (MAWS, TIGH-luhr)

Goaltender. Catches right. 6', 185 lbs. Born, Ottawa, Ont., June 29, 1975.
(Tampa Bay's 2nd choice, 29th overall, in 1993 Entry Draft).

			Regular Season								Playoffs						
Season	**Club**	**League**	**GP**	**W**	**L**	**T**	**Mins**	**GA**	**SO**	**Avg**	**GP**	**W**	**L**	**Mins**	**GA**	**SO**	**Avg**
1991-92	Nepean Raiders	CJHL	26	7	12	1	1335	109	0	4.90	....	....	....	....	....	....	....
1992-93	Kingston	OHL	31	13	7	5	1537	97	0	3.79	6	1	2	228	19	0	5.00
1993-94	Kingston	OHL	13	6	4	3	795	42	1	3.17	3	0	2	136	8	0	3.53
1994-95	Kingston	OHL	*57	33	17	5	*3249	164	1	3.03	6	2	4	333	27	0	4.86
1995-96	Atlanta Knights	IHL	40	11	19	4	2030	138	1	4.08	3	0	3	213	11	0	3.10
1996-97	Adirondack	AHL	11	1	5	2	507	42	1	4.97	....	....	....	....	....	....	....
	Grand Rapids	IHL	15	5	6	1	715	35	0	2.94	....	....	....	....	....	....	....
	Muskegon Fury	ColHL	2	1	1	0	119	5	0	2.51	....	....	....	....	....	....	....
	Saint John Flames	AHL	9	6	1	1	534	17	0	1.91	5	2	3	242	15	0	3.72
1997-98	**Calgary**	**NHL**	**6**	**2**	**3**	**1**	**367**	**20**	**0**	**3.27**	....	....	....	....	....	....	....
	Saint John Flames	AHL	39	19	10	7	2194	91	0	2.49	15	8	5	761	37	0	2.91
1998-99	**Calgary**	**NHL**	**11**	**3**	**7**	**0**	**550**	**23**	**0**	**2.51**	....	....	....	....	....	....	....
	Saint John Flames	AHL	9	2	5	1	475	25	0	3.16	....	....	....	....	....	....	....
	Orlando	IHL	9	6	2	1	515	21	1	2.45	17	10	7	1017	53	0	3.13
99-2000	Wilkes-Barre	AHL	4	1	1	1	188	11	0	3.52	....	....	....	....	....	....	....
	Kansas City Blades	IHL	36	18	12	5	2116	105	3	2.98	....	....	....	....	....	....	....
2000-01	**Carolina**	**NHL**	**12**	**1**	**6**	**0**	**557**	**37**	**0**	**3.99**	....	....	....	....	....	....	....
	Cincinnati	IHL	9	5	3	1	506	24	2	2.85	....	....	....	....	....	....	....
2001-02	Lowell	AHL	43	20	16	7	2572	106	1	2.47	....	....	....	....	....	....	....
2002-03	**Vancouver**	**NHL**	**1**	**0**	**0**	**0**	**22**	**1**	**0**	**2.73**	....	....	....	....	....	....	....
	Manitoba Moose	AHL	42	21	15	5	2502	117	3	2.81	10	6	4	618	23	0	2.23
2003-04	Manitoba Moose	AHL	32	10	16	5	1883	91	3	2.90	....	....	....	....	....	....	....
	Toronto	AHL	16	7	9	0	932	41	3	2.64	3	1	2	211	8	0	2.28
2004-05	Edmonton	AHL	50	24	19	4	2870	126	5	2.63	....	....	....	....	....	....	....
	NHL Totals		**30**	**6**	**16**	**1**	**1496**	**81**	**0**	**3.25**	....	....	....	....	....	....	....

OHL All-Rookie Team (1993) • OHL First All-Star Team (1995) • Harry "Hap" Holmes Memorial Award (fewest goals against – AHL) (1998) (shared with Jean-Sebastien Giguere)

Traded to **Calgary** by **Tampa Bay** for Jamie Huscroft, March 18, 1997. Traded to **Pittsburgh** by **Calgary** with Rene Corbet for Brad Werenka, March 14, 2000. Signed as a free agent by **Carolina**, August 9, 2000. Signed as a free agent by **Vancouver**, July 5, 2002. Traded to **Edmonton** by **Vancouver** for Peter Sarno, February 16, 2004.

MRAZEK, Justin (muh-RA-zehk, JUHS-tihn) WSH.

Goaltender. Catches left. 6'3", 185 lbs. Born, Regina, Sask., July 21, 1985.
(Washington's 12th choice, 230th overall, in 2004 Entry Draft).

			Regular Season								Playoffs						
Season	**Club**	**League**	**GP**	**W**	**L**	**T**	**Mins**	**GA**	**SO**	**Avg**	**GP**	**W**	**L**	**Mins**	**GA**	**SO**	**Avg**
2003-04	Estevan Bruins	SJHL	38	14	16	5	2142	112	0	3.14	....	....	....	....	....	....	....
2004-05	Union College	ECAC	19	5	12	1	1080	39	1	2.17	....	....	....	....	....	....	....

MULLER, Robert (MEW-luhr, RAW-buhrt) WSH.

Goaltender. Catches left. 5'8", 165 lbs. Born, Rosenheim, West Germany, June 25, 1980.
(Washington's 9th choice, 275th overall, in 2001 Entry Draft).

			Regular Season								Playoffs						
Season	**Club**	**League**	**GP**	**W**	**L**	**T**	**Mins**	**GA**	**SO**	**Avg**	**GP**	**W**	**L**	**Mins**	**GA**	**SO**	**Avg**
1997-98	EHC Klostersee	German-3					STATISTICS NOT AVAILABLE										
1998-99	Rosenheim	Germany	33	....	....	....	1863	105	1	3.38	....	....	....	....	....	....	....
99-2000	Rosenheim	Germany	39	....	....	....	2228	131	1	3.53	....	....	....	....	....	....	....
2000-01	Adler Mannheim	Germany	23	....	....	....	1195	49	1	2.46	2	....	....	103	2	0	1.17
2001-02	Adler Mannheim	Germany	15	....	....	....	637	26	1	2.45	....	....	....	....	....	....	....
	Germany	Olympics	2	0	1	0	78	4	0	3.07	....	....	....	....	....	....	....
2002-03	Krefeld Pinguine	Germany	47	....	....	....	2762	107	5	2.32	14	....	....	843	28	*1	*1.99
2003-04	Krefeld Pinguine	Germany	49	....	....	....	2893	131	6	2.72	....	....	....	....	....	....	....
2004-05	Krefeld Pinguine	Germany	47	....	....	....	2769	136	1	2.95	....	....	....	....	....	....	....

MUNCE, Ryan (MUNTS, RIGH-uhn) L.A.

Goaltender. Catches left. 6'2", 180 lbs. Born, Mississauga, Ont., April 16, 1985.
(Los Angeles' 5th choice, 82nd overall, in 2003 Entry Draft).

			Regular Season								Playoffs						
Season	**Club**	**League**	**GP**	**W**	**L**	**T**	**Mins**	**GA**	**SO**	**Avg**	**GP**	**W**	**L**	**Mins**	**GA**	**SO**	**Avg**
2002-03	Sarnia Sting	OHL	27	15	7	0	1410	62	3	2.64	4	1	1	149	8	1	3.22
2003-04	Sarnia Sting	OHL	54	28	21	4	3160	158	2	3.00	5	1	4	298	17	0	3.42
2004-05	Sarnia Sting	OHL	55	12	32	6	3090	163	0	3.17	....	....	....	....	....	....	....

MUNRO, Adam (MUHN-roh, A-duhm) CHI.

Goaltender. Catches left. 6'2", 219 lbs. Born, St. George, Ont., November 12, 1982.
(Chicago's 1st choice, 29th overall, in 2001 Entry Draft).

			Regular Season								Playoffs						
Season	**Club**	**League**	**GP**	**W**	**L**	**T**	**Mins**	**GA**	**SO**	**Avg**	**GP**	**W**	**L**	**Mins**	**GA**	**SO**	**Avg**
1997-98	Brantford Classics	OMHA	15	13	2	0	660	20	*4	*1.36	....	....	....	....	....	....	....
1998-99	Brant County	OJHL-B	10	....	....	....	348	30	0	5.17	....	....	....	....	....	....	....
	Bowmanville	OPJHL	14	....	....	....	816	50	0	3.68	....	....	....	....	....	....	....
	Erie Otters	OHL	1	0	0	0	1	0	0	0.00	....	....	....	....	....	....	....
99-2000	Bowmanville	OPJHL	2	2	0	0	125	5	0	2.40	....	....	....	....	....	....	....
	Erie Otters	OHL	22	8	7	1	948	48	1	3.04	1	0	0	5	1	0	12.00
2000-01	Erie Otters	OHL	41	26	6	6	2283	88	*4	2.31	10	6	2	509	27	1	3.18
2001-02	Erie Otters	OHL	43	24	13	1	2277	128	3	3.37	6	4	2	361	17	0	2.83
2002-03	Erie Otters	OHL	8	2	6	0	426	24	1	3.38	....	....	....	....	....	....	....
	Sault Ste. Marie	OHL	42	20	20	2	2494	160	1	3.85	4	0	4	240	12	0	3.00
2003-04	**Chicago**	**NHL**	**7**	**1**	**5**	**1**	**426**	**26**	**0**	**3.66**	....	....	....	....	....	....	....
	Norfolk Admirals	AHL	12	5	4	1	695	26	0	2.24	....	....	....	....	....	....	....
	Gwinnett	ECHL	6	4	1	1	370	17	0	2.76	1	0	1	60	2	0	2.01
2004-05	Norfolk Admirals	AHL	30	14	10	2	1595	66	4	2.48	....	....	....	....	....	....	....
	Atlantic City	ECHL	5	2	2	1	272	9	0	1.99	....	....	....	....	....	....	....
	NHL Totals		**7**	**1**	**5**	**1**	**426**	**26**	**0**	**3.66**	....	....	....	....	....	....	....

NABOKOV, Evgeni (na-BAW-kahv, ehv-GEH-nee) S.J.

Goaltender. Catches left. 6', 200 lbs. Born, Ust-Kamenogorsk, USSR, July 25, 1975.
(San Jose's 9th choice, 219th overall, in 1994 Entry Draft).

			Regular Season								Playoffs						
Season	**Club**	**League**	**GP**	**W**	**L**	**T**	**Mins**	**GA**	**SO**	**Avg**	**GP**	**W**	**L**	**Mins**	**GA**	**SO**	**Avg**
1992-93	Ust-Kamenogorsk	CIS	4	1	0	0	109	5	0	2.75	....	....	....	....	....	....	....
1993-94	Ust-Kamenogorsk	CIS	11	....	....	....	539	29	0	3.23	....	....	....	....	....	....	....
1994-95	Dynamo Moscow	CIS	24	....	....	....	1265	40	....	1.90	13	....	....	810	30	....	2.22
1995-96	Dynamo Moscow	CIS	39	....	....	....	2008	67	5	2.00	6	....	....	298	7	....	1.41
1996-97	Dynamo Moscow	Russia	27	....	....	....	1588	56	2	2.12	4	....	....	255	12	0	2.82
1997-98	Kentucky	AHL	33	10	21	2	1866	122	0	3.92	1	0	0	23	1	0	2.59
1998-99	Kentucky	AHL	43	26	14	1	2429	106	5	2.62	11	6	5	599	30	*2	3.00
99-2000	**San Jose**	**NHL**	**11**	**2**	**2**	**1**	**414**	**15**	**1**	**2.17**	**1**	**0**	**0**	**20**	**0**	**0**	**0.00**
	Cleveland	IHL	20	12	4	3	1164	52	0	2.68	....	....	....	....	....	....	....
	Kentucky	AHL	2	1	1	0	120	3	1	1.50	....	....	....	....	....	....	....
2000-01	**San Jose**	**NHL**	**66**	**32**	**21**	**7**	**3700**	**135**	**6**	**2.19**	**4**	**1**	**3**	**218**	**10**	**1**	**2.75**
2001-02	**San Jose**	**NHL**	**67**	**37**	**24**	**5**	**3901**	**149**	**7**	**2.29**	**12**	**7**	**5**	**712**	**31**	**0**	**2.61**
2002-03	**San Jose**	**NHL**	**55**	**19**	**28**	**8**	**3227**	**146**	**3**	**2.71**	....	....	....	....	....	....	....
2003-04	**San Jose**	**NHL**	**59**	**31**	**19**	**8**	**3456**	**127**	**9**	**2.20**	**17**	**10**	**7**	**1052**	**30**	**3**	**1.71**
2004-05	Magnitogorsk	Russia	14	....	....	....	808	27	3	2.00	5	....	....	307	13	0	2.53
	NHL Totals		**258**	**121**	**94**	**29**	**14698**	**572**	**26**	**2.34**	**34**	**18**	**15**	**2002**	**71**	**4**	**2.13**

NHL All-Rookie Team (2001) • Calder Memorial Trophy (2001)

Played in NHL All-Star Game (2001)

• Scored a goal vs. Vancouver, March 10, 2002. Signed as a free agent by **Magnitogorsk** (Russia), December 2, 2004.

NASTIUK, Kevin (NAZ-tee-uhk, KEH-vihn) CAR.

Goaltender. Catches left. 6'2", 176 lbs. Born, Edmonton, Alta., July 20, 1985.
(Carolina's 4th choice, 126th overall, in 2003 Entry Draft).

			Regular Season								Playoffs						
Season	**Club**	**League**	**GP**	**W**	**L**	**T**	**Mins**	**GA**	**SO**	**Avg**	**GP**	**W**	**L**	**Mins**	**GA**	**SO**	**Avg**
99-2000	Inland Real Estate	EMHA	20	9	6	5	998	59	0	3.25	....	....	....	....	....	....	....
	CAC Cement	AMBHL	1	0	1	0	50	8	0	9.60	....	....	....	....	....	....	....

2000-01	CAC Cement	AMBHL	20	12	7	1	1233	64	0	3.11	1	1	0	60	2	0	2.00
2001-02	Medicine Hat	WHL	19	4	10	0	877	66	0	4.52	....	....	....	....	....	....	....
2002-03	Medicine Hat	WHL	42	15	20	2	2344	172	0	4.40	11	7	4	693	33	0	2.86
2003-04	Medicine Hat	WHL	*68	40	19	8	*4056	187	4	2.77	*20	*16	4	*1182	38	*4	1.93
2004-05	Medicine Hat	WHL	42	23	18	1	2426	88	7	2.18	12	5	7	715	27	0	2.27

WHL Playoff MVP (2004) • WHL East Second All-Star Team (2005)

NIITTYMAKI, Antero (NEE-too-mah-kee, AN-tehr-oh) PHI.

Goaltender. Catches left. 6', 195 lbs. Born, Turku, Finland, June 18, 1980.
(Philadelphia's 7th choice, 168th overall, in 1998 Entry Draft).

			Regular Season								Playoffs						
Season	Club	League	GP	W	L	T	Mins	GA	SO	Avg	GP	W	L	Mins	GA	SO	Avg
1998-99	TPS Turku Jr.	Finland-Jr.	35	....	....	....	2095	60	0	1.72	....	....	....	....	....	....	....
99-2000	TPS Turku Jr.	Finland-Jr.	1	1	0	0	60	1	0	1.00	....	....	....	....	....	....	....
	TPS Turku	Finland	32	23	6	2	1899	68	3	2.15	8	6	1	453	13	0	1.72
2000-01	TPS Turku	Finland	21	10	6	1	1112	46	2	2.48	....	....	....	....	....	....	....
2001-02	TPS Turku	Finland	27	16	8	1	1498	46	3	1.84	4	2	2	295	11	0	2.24
2002-03	Philadelphia	AHL	40	14	21	2	2283	98	0	2.58	....	....	....	....	....	....	....
2003-04	**Philadelphia**	**NHL**	**3**	**3**	**0**	**0**	**180**	**3**	**0**	**1.00**	....	....	....	....	....	....	....
	Philadelphia	AHL	49	24	13	6	2728	92	7	2.02	12	6	6	796	24	0	1.81
2004-05	Philadelphia	AHL	58	33	21	4	3453	119	6	2.07	*21	*15	5	*1269	37	*3	1.75
	NHL Totals		**3**	**3**	**0**	**0**	**180**	**3**	**0**	**1.00**	....	....	....	....	....	....	....

Jack A. Butterfield Trophy (Playoff - MVP) (2005)

NISSINEN, Tuomas (NIHS-ih-nehn, too-OH-muhs) ST.L.

Goaltender. Catches left. 6'1", 176 lbs. Born, Kuopio, Finland, July 17, 1983.
(St. Louis' 2nd choice, 89th overall, in 2001 Entry Draft).

			Regular Season								Playoffs						
Season	Club	League	GP	W	L	T	Mins	GA	SO	Avg	GP	W	L	Mins	GA	SO	Avg
2000-01	KalPa Kuopio Jr.	Finland-Jr.	40	15	14	5	2327	125	2	3.22	1	0	1	60	4	0	4.00
2001-02	KalPa Kuopio Jr.	Finland-Jr.	33	20	11	2	1988	81	3	2.44	1	0	1	59	4	0	4.04
	KalPa Kuopio	Finland-2	4	2	2	0	208	10	1	2.88	....	....	....	....	....	....	....
2002-03	Ilves Tampere	Finland	32	4	23	3	1750	108	1	3.70	....	....	....	....	....	....	....
2003-04	Hermes Kokkola	Finland-2	2	1	1	0	118	4	0	2.03	....	....	....	....	....	....	....
	Ilves Tampere	Finland	23	7	7	5	1267	56	2	2.65	1	0	0	40	0	0	0.00
	Ilves Tampere Jr.	Finland-Jr.	1	1	0	0	60	4	0	4.00	....	....	....	....	....	....	....
2004-05	TuTo Turku	Finland-2	3	2	0	1	185	7	1	2.27	....	....	....	....	....	....	....
	Assat Pori	Finland	16	1	12	1	817	54	0	3.97	....	....	....	....	....	....	....

NORONEN, Mika (NOH-rah-nehn, MEE-kah) BUF.

Goaltender. Catches left. 6'2", 200 lbs. Born, Tampere, Finland, June 17, 1979.
(Buffalo's 1st choice, 21st overall, in 1997 Entry Draft).

			Regular Season								Playoffs						
Season	Club	League	GP	W	L	T	Mins	GA	SO	Avg	GP	W	L	Mins	GA	SO	Avg
1995-96	Tappara Jr.	Finland-Jr.	16	....	....	....	962	37	2	2.31	....	....	....	....	....	....	....
1996-97	Tappara Tampere	Finland	5	1	3	0	215	17	0	4.73	....	....	....	....	....	....	....
1997-98	Tappara Tampere	Finland	37	14	12	3	1704	83	1	2.92	4	1	2	196	12	0	3.67
1998-99	Tappara Tampere	Finland	43	18	20	5	2494	135	2	3.25	....	....	....	....	....	....	....
99-2000	Rochester	AHL	54	*33	13	4	3089	112	*6	2.18	21	13	8	1235	37	*6	*1.80
2000-01	**Buffalo**	**NHL**	**2**	**2**	**0**	**0**	**108**	**5**	**0**	**2.78**	....	....	....	....	....	....	....
	Rochester	AHL	47	26	15	5	2753	100	4	2.18	4	1	3	250	11	0	2.64
2001-02	**Buffalo**	**NHL**	**10**	**4**	**3**	**1**	**518**	**23**	**0**	**2.66**	....	....	....	....	....	....	....
	Rochester	AHL	45	16	17	12	2764	115	3	2.50	1	0	1	59	3	0	3.06
2002-03	**Buffalo**	**NHL**	**16**	**4**	**9**	**3**	**891**	**36**	**1**	**2.42**	....	....	....	....	....	....	....
	Rochester	AHL	19	5	9	5	1169	55	2	2.82	....	....	....	....	....	....	....
2003-04	**Buffalo**	**NHL**	**35**	**11**	**17**	**2**	**1796**	**77**	**2**	**2.57**	....	....	....	....	....	....	....
2004-05	HPK Hameenlinna	Finland	27	14	8	4	1615	54	1	2.01	9	4	4	482	21	1	2.61
	NHL Totals		**63**	**21**	**29**	**6**	**3313**	**141**	**3**	**2.55**	....	....	....	....	....	....	....

AHL All-Rookie Team (2000) • AHL Second All-Star Team (2000, 2001) • Dudley "Red" Garrett Memorial Award (Rookie of the Year – AHL) (2000) • Harry "Hap" Holmes Memorial Award (fewest goals against – AHL) (2001) (shared with Tom Askey)

Signed as a free agent by **HPK** (Finland), November 2, 2004.

NORRENA, Fredrik (noh-REH-nah, FREHD-rihk) T.B.

Goaltender. Catches left. 6', 187 lbs. Born, Pietarsaari, Finland, November 29, 1973.
(Tampa Bay's 8th choice, 213th overall, in 2002 Entry Draft).

			Regular Season								Playoffs						
Season	Club	League	GP	W	L	T	Mins	GA	SO	Avg	GP	W	L	Mins	GA	SO	Avg
1992-93	TPS Turku	Finland	2	0	0	0	29	1	0	2.01	....	....	....	....	....	....	....
	TPS Turku Jr.	Finland-Jr.	25	....	....	....	1449	74	1	3.06	5	....	....	307	11	0	2.14
1993-94	TPS Turku Jr.	Finland-Jr.	2	0	1	0	80	5	0	3.75	1	0	1	58	4	0	4.10
	TPS Turku	Finland	10	3	3	0	387	19	0	2.95	....	....	....	....	....	....	....
	Kiekko-67 Turku	Finland-2	15	7	7	1	875	42	2	2.88	....	....	....	....	....	....	....
1994-95	TPS Turku	Finland	22	....	....	....	1328	60	....	2.71	....	....	....	....	....	....	....
	Kiekko-67 Turku	Finland-2	15	....	....	....	828	34	0	2.46	....	....	....	....	....	....	....
1995-96	TPS Turku	Finland	26	....	....	....	1540	68	0	2.65	....	....	....	....	....	....	....
1996-97	Kiekko-67 Turku	Finland-2	12	....	....	....	725	35	0	2.98	....	....	....	....	....	....	....
	AIK Solna	Sweden	5	....	....	....	274	15	1	3.28	....	....	....	....	....	....	....
1997-98	Lukko Rauma	Finland	48	12	19	4	2174	105	0	2.90	....	....	....	....	....	....	....
1998-99	TPS Turku	Finland	20	11	4	1	1010	35	2	2.08	1	0	0	20	2	0	6.00
99-2000	TPS Turku	Finland	21	15	4	0	1175	35	2	*1.79	4	3	1	234	10	0	2.56
	TuTo Turku	Finland-2	2	1	1	0	118	7	0	3.54	....	....	....	....	....	....	....
2000-01	TPS Turku	Finland	39	26	10	3	2266	66	6	*1.75	*10	*9	1	603	13	*2	*1.29
2001-02	TPS Turku	Finland	32	14	11	5	1877	62	2	1.98	4	1	3	256	7	1	*1.64
2002-03	V.Frolunda	Sweden	23	....	....	....	1386	56	1	2.42	4	....	....	287	6	1	*1.25
2003-04	Linkopings HC	Sweden	40	....	....	....	2414	68	*9	*1.69	3	....	....	176	6	0	2.05
2004-05	Linkopings HC	Sweden	43	....	....	....	2522	78	5	1.86	6	....	....	384	13	0	2.03

OSGOOD, Chris (AWS-gud, KRIHS) DET.

Goaltender. Catches left. 5'10", 175 lbs. Born, Peace River, Alta., November 26, 1972.
(Detroit's 3rd choice, 54th overall, in 1991 Entry Draft).

			Regular Season								Playoffs						
Season	Club	League	GP	W	L	T	Mins	GA	SO	Avg	GP	W	L	Mins	GA	SO	Avg
1988-89	Medicine Hat	AMHL	26	....	....	....	1441	88	0	3.66	....	....	....	....	....	....	....
1989-90	Medicine Hat	WHL	57	24	28	2	3094	228	0	4.42	3	0	3	173	17	0	5.91
1990-91	Medicine Hat	WHL	46	23	18	3	2630	173	2	3.95	12	7	5	712	42	0	3.54
1991-92	Medicine Hat	WHL	15	10	3	0	819	44	0	3.22	....	....	....	....	....	....	....
	Brandon	WHL	16	3	10	1	890	60	1	4.04	....	....	....	....	....	....	....
	Seattle	WHL	21	12	7	1	1217	65	1	3.20	15	9	6	904	51	0	3.38
1992-93	Adirondack	AHL	45	19	19	4	2438	159	0	3.91	1	0	1	59	2	0	2.03
1993-94	**Detroit**	**NHL**	**41**	**23**	**8**	**5**	**2206**	**105**	**2**	**2.86**	**6**	**3**	**2**	**307**	**12**	**1**	**2.35**
	Adirondack	AHL	4	3	1	0	239	13	0	3.26	....	....	....	....	....	....	....
1994-95	**Detroit**	**NHL**	**19**	**14**	**5**	**0**	**1087**	**41**	**1**	**2.26**	**2**	**0**	**0**	**68**	**2**	**0**	**1.76**
	Adirondack	AHL	2	1	1	0	120	6	0	3.00	....	....	....	....	....	....	....
1995-96	**Detroit**	**NHL**	**50**	***39**	**6**	**5**	**2933**	**106**	**5**	**2.17**	**15**	**8**	**7**	**936**	**33**	**2**	**2.12**
1996-97♦	**Detroit**	**NHL**	**47**	**23**	**13**	**9**	**2769**	**106**	**6**	**2.30**	**2**	**0**	**0**	**47**	**2**	**0**	**2.55**
1997-98♦	**Detroit**	**NHL**	**64**	**33**	**20**	**11**	**3807**	**140**	**6**	**2.21**	***22**	***16**	**6**	***1361**	**48**	**2**	**2.12**
1998-99	**Detroit**	**NHL**	**63**	**34**	**25**	**4**	**3691**	**149**	**3**	**2.42**	**6**	**4**	**2**	**358**	**14**	**1**	**2.35**
99-2000	**Detroit**	**NHL**	**53**	**30**	**14**	**8**	**3148**	**126**	**6**	**2.40**	**9**	**5**	**4**	**547**	**18**	**2**	**1.97**
2000-01	**Detroit**	**NHL**	**52**	**25**	**19**	**4**	**2834**	**127**	**1**	**2.69**	**6**	**2**	**4**	**365**	**15**	**1**	**2.47**
2001-02	**NY Islanders**	**NHL**	**66**	**32**	**25**	**6**	**3743**	**156**	**4**	**2.50**	**7**	**3**	**4**	**392**	**17**	**0**	**2.60**
2002-03	**NY Islanders**	**NHL**	**37**	**17**	**14**	**4**	**1993**	**97**	**2**	**2.92**	....	....	....	....	....	....	....
	St. Louis	**NHL**	**9**	**4**	**3**	**2**	**532**	**27**	**2**	**3.05**	**7**	**3**	**4**	**417**	**17**	**1**	**2.45**
2003-04	**St. Louis**	**NHL**	**67**	**31**	**25**	**8**	**3861**	**144**	**3**	**2.24**	**5**	**1**	**4**	**287**	**12**	**0**	**2.51**
2004-05							DID NOT PLAY										
	NHL Totals		**568**	**305**	**177**	**66**	**32604**	**1324**	**41**	**2.44**	**87**	**45**	**37**	**5085**	**190**	**10**	**2.24**

WHL East Second All-Star Team (1991) • NHL Second All-Star Team (1996) • William M. Jennings Trophy (1996) (shared with Mike Vernon)

Played in NHL All-Star Game (1996, 1997, 1998)

• Scored a goal while with Medicine Hat (WHL), January 3, 1991. • Scored a goal vs. Hartford, March 6, 1996. Claimed by **NY Islanders** from **Detroit** in Waiver Draft, September 28, 2001. Traded to **St. Louis** by **NY Islanders** with NY Islanders' 3rd round choice (Konstantin Barulin) in 2003 Entry Draft for Justin Papineau and St. Louis' 2nd round choice (Jeremy Colliton) in 2003 Entry Draft, March 11, 2003. Signed as a free agent by **Detroit**, August 8, 2005.

OUELLET, Maxime (OO-leht, MAX-eem) WSH.

Goaltender. Catches left. 6'2", 195 lbs. Born, Beauport, Que., June 17, 1981.
(Philadelphia's 1st choice, 22nd overall, in 1999 Entry Draft).

			Regular Season								Playoffs						
Season	Club	League	GP	W	L	T	Mins	GA	SO	Avg	GP	W	L	Mins	GA	SO	Avg
1996-97	Ste-Foy	QAAA	29	16	8	0	1470	81	0	2.75	9	4	5	555	31	0	3.37
1997-98	Quebec Remparts	QMJHL	24	12	7	1	1188	66	0	3.33	7	3	1	305	16	0	3.15
1998-99	Quebec Remparts	QMJHL	*59	*40	12	6	*3447	155	3	*2.70	13	6	7	803	41	*1	3.06
99-2000	Quebec Remparts	QMJHL	53	31	16	4	2984	133	2	2.67	11	7	4	638	28	*2	*2.63
2000-01	**Philadelphia**	**NHL**	**2**	**0**	**1**	**0**	**76**	**3**	**0**	**2.37**	....	....	....	....	....	....	....
	Rouyn-Noranda	QMJHL	25	18	6	1	1471	65	3	2.65	8	4	4	490	25	0	3.06
	Philadelphia	AHL	2	1	0	0	86	4	0	2.78	....	....	....	....	....	....	....
2001-02	Philadelphia	AHL	41	16	13	8	2294	104	1	2.72	....	....	....	....	....	....	....
	Portland Pirates	AHL	6	3	3	0	358	17	0	2.85	....	....	....	....	....	....	....
2002-03	Portland Pirates	AHL	48	22	16	7	2773	111	*7	2.40	2	1	1	120	8	0	4.00
2003-04	**Washington**	**NHL**	**6**	**2**	**3**	**1**	**365**	**19**	**1**	**3.12**	....	....	....	....	....	....	....
	Portland Pirates	AHL	52	15	29	8	3050	101	10	1.99	5	2	2	303	8	0	1.59
2004-05	Portland Pirates	AHL	40	15	20	3	2305	111	0	2.89	....	....	....	....	....	....	....
	NHL Totals		**8**	**2**	**4**	**1**	**441**	**22**	**1**	**2.99**	....	....	....	....	....	....	....

QMJHL Second All-Star Team (1999, 2000, 2001) • Jacques Plante Trophy (fewest goals against – QMJHL) (1999) • AHL Second All-Star Team (2003)

• Returned to **Rouyn-Noranda** (QMJHL) by **Philadelphia**, October 27, 2000. Traded to **Washington** by **Philadelphia** with Philadelphia's 1st (later traded to Dallas – Dallas selected Martin Vagner), 2nd (Maxime Daigneault) and 3rd (Derek Krestanovich) round choices in 2002 Entry Draft for Adam Oates, March 19, 2002.

PASSMORE, Steve (PAS-mohr, STEEV) PHX.

Goaltender. Catches left. 5'9", 165 lbs. Born, Thunder Bay, Ont., January 29, 1973.
(Quebec's 10th choice, 196th overall, in 1992 Entry Draft).

			Regular Season								Playoffs						
Season	Club	League	GP	W	L	T	Mins	GA	SO	Avg	GP	W	L	Mins	GA	SO	Avg
1988-89	Tri-City Americans	WHL	1	0	1	0	60	6	0	6.00	....	....	....	....	....	....	....
1989-90	West Island Deltas	BCAHA					STATISTICS NOT AVAILABLE										
	Tri-City Americans	WHL	4	....	....	....	215	17	0	4.74	....	....	....	....	....	....	....
1990-91	Victoria Cougars	WHL	35	3	25	1	1838	190	0	6.20	....	....	....	....	....	....	....
1991-92	Victoria Cougars	WHL	*71	15	50	5	*4228	347	0	4.92	....	....	....	....	....	....	....
1992-93	Victoria Cougars	WHL	43	14	24	2	2402	150	1	3.75	....	....	....	....	....	....	....
	Kamloops Blazers	WHL	25	19	6	0	1479	69	1	2.80	7	4	2	401	22	1	3.29
1993-94	Kamloops Blazers	WHL	36	22	9	2	1927	88	1	*2.74	*18	*11	7	*1099	60	0	3.28
1994-95	Cape Breton Oilers	AHL	25	8	13	3	1455	93	0	3.83	....	....	....	....	....	....	....
1995-96	Cape Breton Oilers	AHL	2	1	0	0	90	2	0	1.33	....	....	....	....	....	....	....
1996-97	Hamilton Bulldogs	AHL	27	12	12	3	1568	70	1	2.68	22	12	10	1325	61	*2	2.76
	Raleigh IceCaps	ECHL	2	1	1	0	118	13	0	6.56	....	....	....	....	....	....	....
1997-98	Hamilton Bulldogs	AHL	27	11	10	6	1655	87	2	3.15	3	0	2	132	14	0	6.33
	San Antonio	IHL	14	3	8	2	736	56	0	4.56	....	....	....	....	....	....	....
1998-99	**Edmonton**	**NHL**	**6**	**1**	**4**	**1**	**362**	**17**	**0**	**2.82**	....	....	....	....	....	....	....
	Hamilton Bulldogs	AHL	54	24	21	7	3148	117	4	2.23	11	5	6	680	31	0	2.74
99-2000	**Chicago**	**NHL**	**24**	**7**	**12**	**3**	**1388**	**63**	**1**	**2.72**	....	....	....	....	....	....	....
	Cleveland	IHL	2	1	0	1	120	3	1	1.50	....	....	....	....	....	....	....
2000-01	**Los Angeles**	**NHL**	**14**	**3**	**8**	**1**	**718**	**37**	**1**	**3.09**	....	....	....	....	....	....	....
	Lowell	AHL	6	2	4	0	334	24	0	4.32	....	....	....	....	....	....	....
	Chicago	**NHL**	**6**	**0**	**4**	**1**	**340**	**14**	**0**	**2.47**	....	....	....	....	....	....	....
	Chicago Wolves	IHL	6	2	2	2	340	22	0	3.88	....	....	....	....	....	....	....
2001-02	Norfolk Admirals	AHL	2	2	0	0	120	6	0	3.00	....	....	....	....	....	....	....
	Chicago	**NHL**	**23**	**8**	**5**	**4**	**1142**	**43**	**0**	**2.26**	**3**	**0**	**2**	**138**	**6**	**0**	**2.61**
2002-03	**Chicago**	**NHL**	**11**	**2**	**5**	**2**	**617**	**38**	**0**	**3.70**	....	....	....	....	....	....	....
	Norfolk Admirals	AHL	14	4	7	2	832	33	2	2.38	....	....	....	....	....	....	....
2003-04	**Chicago**	**NHL**	**9**	**2**	**6**	**0**	**478**	**23**	**0**	**2.89**	....	....	....	....	....	....	....
	Norfolk Admirals	AHL	15	3	10	2	889	39	2	2.63	....	....	....	....	....	....	....
2004-05	Adler Mannheim	Germany	21	....	....	....	1110	48	0	2.59	....	....	....	....	....	....	....
	NHL Totals		**93**	**23**	**44**	**12**	**5045**	**235**	**2**	**2.79**	**3**	**0**	**2**	**138**	**6**	**0**	**2.61**

WHL West First All-Star Team (1993, 1994) • Fred T. Hunt Memorial Award (Sportsmanship – AHL) (1997) • AHL Second All-Star Team (1999)

Traded to **Edmonton** by **Quebec** for Brad Werenka, March 21, 1994. • Missed majority of the 1995-96 season recovering from blood disorder, October, 1995. Signed as a free agent by **Chicago**, July 8, 1999. Traded to **Los Angeles** by **Chicago** for Los Angeles' 4th round choice (Olli Malmivaara) in 2000 Entry Draft, May 1, 2000. Traded to **Chicago** by **Los Angeles** for Chicago's 8th round choice (Mike Gabinet) in 2001 Entry Draft, February 28, 2001. Signed as a free agent by **Mannheim** (Germany), August 30, 2004. Signed as a free agent by **Phoenix**, August 19, 2005.

PATZOLD, Dimitri (PATZ-ohld, dih-MEE-tree) S.J.

Goaltender. Catches left. 6', 200 lbs. Born, Ust-Kamenogorsk, USSR, February 3, 1983.
(San Jose's 3rd choice, 107th overall, in 2001 Entry Draft).

			Regular Season								Playoffs						
Season	Club	League	GP	W	L	T	Mins	GA	SO	Avg	GP	W	L	Mins	GA	SO	Avg
99-2000	Kolner EC Jr.	Ger-Jr.	38	....	....	....	2131	73	0	2.06	....	....	....	....	....	....	....
	Kolner Haie 2	German-5	16	....	....	....	896	58	0	3.88	....	....	....	....	....	....	....
2000-01	EV Duisburg	German-3	6	....	....	....	360	17	0	2.83	....	....	....	....	....	....	....
	Erding Jets	German-2	24	....	....	....	1378	89	0	3.88	....	....	....	....	....	....	....
2001-02	EV Duisburg	German-2	6	....	....	....	360	17	0	2.83	....	....	....	....	....	....	....
	Kolner Haie	Germany	7	....	....	....	260	16	0	3.69	....	....	....	....	....	....	....
2002-03	Adler Mannheim	Germany	15	....	....	....	817	35	0	2.57	2	....	....	34	2	0	3.53
2003-04	Cleveland Barons	AHL	27	10	15	0	1457	70	3	2.88	....	....	....	....	....	....	....
	Johnstown Chiefs	ECHL	8	7	0	0	443	20	0	2.71	1	0	1	59	2	0	2.02
2004-05	Cleveland Barons	AHL	41	18	16	5	2418	104	1	2.58	....	....	....	....	....	....	....

PAVELEC, Ondrej (PAV-ehl-ehts, AWN-dray) ATL.

Goaltender. Catches left. 6'2", 180 lbs. Born, Kladno, Czechoslovakia, August 31, 1987.
(Atlanta's 2nd choice, 41st overall, in 2005 Entry Draft).

			Regular Season								Playoffs						
Season	Club	League	GP	W	L	T	Mins	GA	SO	Avg	GP	W	L	Mins	GA	SO	Avg
2003-04	HC Kladno U17	CzR-U17	38	....	....	....	2079	77	3	2.22	2	....	....	67	7	0	6.27
2004-05	HC Kladno Jr.	CzRep-Jr.	39	....	....	....	2218	85	7	2.30	10	....	....	587	24	1	2.45
	HK LEV Slany	CzRep-3	1	....	....	....	60	4	0	4.00	....	....	....	....	....	....	....

PELLETIER, Jean-Marc (PEHL-tyay, ZHAWN-MAHRK) FLA.

Goaltender. Catches left. 6'3", 209 lbs. Born, Atlanta, GA, March 4, 1978.
(Philadelphia's 1st choice, 30th overall, in 1997 Entry Draft).

			Regular Season								Playoffs						
Season	Club	League	GP	W	L	T	Mins	GA	SO	Avg	GP	W	L	Mins	GA	SO	Avg
1993-94	Richelieu Riverains	QAAA	24	14	8	2	1440	91	0	3.79	2	1	0	104	11	0	6.32
1994-95	Richelieu Riverains	QAAA	21	15	6	0	1260	71	0	3.36	2	1	1	153	11	0	4.32
1995-96	Cornell Big Red	ECAC	5	1	2	0	179	15	0	5.03	....	....	....	....	....	....	....
1996-97	Cornell Big Red	ECAC	11	5	2	3	679	28	1	2.47	....	....	....	....	....	....	....
1997-98	Rimouski Oceanic	QMJHL	34	17	11	3	1913	118	0	3.70	16	11	3	895	51	1	3.42
1998-99	**Philadelphia**	**NHL**	**1**	**0**	**1**	**0**	**60**	**5**	**0**	**5.00**	....	....	....	....	....	....	....
	Philadelphia	AHL	47	25	16	4	2636	122	2	2.78	1	0	0	27	0	0	0.00
99-2000	Philadelphia	AHL	24	14	10	0	1405	58	3	2.48	....	....	....	....	....	....	....
	Cincinnati	IHL	22	14	4	2	1278	52	2	2.44	3	1	1	160	8	1	3.00
2000-01	Cincinnati	IHL	39	18	14	5	2261	119	2	3.16	5	1	4	318	15	0	2.83
2001-02	Lowell	AHL	40	21	12	4	2284	98	2	2.57	5	2	3	298	13	0	2.62
2002-03	Lowell	AHL	17	6	10	0	861	51	1	3.55	....	....	....	....	....	....	....
	Phoenix	**NHL**	**2**	**0**	**2**	**0**	**119**	**6**	**0**	**3.03**	....	....	....	....	....	....	....
	Springfield Falcons	AHL	24	12	7	4	1391	55	2	2.37	6	3	3	368	16	1	2.61
2003-04	**Phoenix**	**NHL**	**4**	**1**	**1**	**0**	**175**	**12**	**0**	**4.11**	....	....	....	....	....	....	....
	Springfield Falcons	AHL	43	10	24	5	2433	109	2	2.69	....	....	....	....	....	....	....
2004-05	Utah Grizzlies	AHL	23	6	12	1	1231	77	0	3.75	....	....	....	....	....	....	....
	Springfield Falcons	AHL	13	2	10	1	715	35	0	2.94	....	....	....	....	....	....	....
	NHL Totals		**7**	**1**	**4**	**0**	**354**	**23**	**0**	**3.90**	....	....	....	....	....	....	....

Traded to **Carolina** by **Philadelphia** with Rod Brind'Amour and Philadelphia's 2nd round choice (later traded to Colorado – Colorado selected Argis Saviels) in 2000 Entry Draft for Keith Primeau and Carolina's 5th round choice (later traded to NY Islanders – NY Islanders selected Kristofer Ottosson) in 2000 Entry Draft, January 23, 2000. Traded to **Phoenix** by **Carolina** with future considerations for Patrick DesRochers, December 31, 2002. Signed as a free agent by **Florida**, August 19, 2005.

PELLETIER, Pier-Olivier (PEHL-tyay, PEE-yair-OH-lihv-ee-AY) PHX.

Goaltender. Catches left. 6'1", 175 lbs. Born, St-Louis, Que., April 8, 1987.
(Phoenix's 2nd choice, 59th overall, in 2005 Entry Draft).

			Regular Season								Playoffs						
Season	Club	League	GP	W	L	T	Mins	GA	SO	Avg	GP	W	L	Mins	GA	SO	Avg
2003-04	St-Francois Blizzard	QAAA	2	0	0	2	116	9	0	4.65	7	3	4	468	15	0	1.92
	Trois-Rivieres	QAAA	....	....	....	....	....	....	....	....	1	0	0	5	3	0	33.00
2004-05	Drummondville	QMJHL	40	15	17	4	2095	105	2	3.01	6	2	4	378	17	0	2.70

• Missed majority of 2003-04 season due to injury.

PENNER, Andrew (PEH-nuhr, AN-droo) CBJ

Goaltender. Catches left. 6'2", 205 lbs. Born, Scarborough, Ont., December 21, 1982.

			Regular Season								Playoffs						
Season	Club	League	GP	W	L	T	Mins	GA	SO	Avg	GP	W	L	Mins	GA	SO	Avg
1998-99	North York	OPJHL	26	....	....	....	1497	107	0	4.29	....	....	....	....	....	....	....
99-2000	North Bay	OHL	22	3	12	0	1070	79	0	4.43	....	....	....	....	....	....	....
2000-01	North Bay	OHL	32	10	19	1	1787	117	1	3.93	....	....	....	....	....	....	....
2001-02	North Bay	OHL	18	4	8	4	917	52	1	3.40	....	....	....	....	....	....	....
	Guelph Storm	OHL	36	18	12	5	2066	107	0	3.11	9	5	4	546	29	0	3.19
2002-03	Guelph Storm	OHL	51	21	21	7	2975	137	0	2.76	11	5	5	665	34	0	3.07
2003-04	Dayton Bombers	ECHL	50	15	27	2	2764	175	0	3.80	....	....	....	....	....	....	....
2004-05	Syracuse Crunch	AHL	23	8	12	1	1222	55	1	2.70	....	....	....	....	....	....	....
	Dayton Bombers	ECHL	15	6	8	1	893	49	0	3.29	....	....	....	....	....	....	....

Signed as a free agent by **Columbus**, September 17, 2001.

PETERS, Justin (PEE-tuhrs, JUHS-tihn) CAR.

Goaltender. Catches left. 6', 209 lbs. Born, Blyth, Ont., August 30, 1986.
(Carolina's 2nd choice, 38th overall, in 2004 Entry Draft).

			Regular Season								Playoffs						
Season	Club	League	GP	W	L	T	Mins	GA	SO	Avg	GP	W	L	Mins	GA	SO	Avg
2001-02	Huron-Perth	OMHA	17	11	2	4	810	32	1	1.89	13	9	4	285	30	1	2.31
2002-03	St. Michael's	OHL	23	6	10	1	1052	54	0	3.08	7	1	0	126	4	0	1.90
2003-04	St. Michael's	OHL	53	30	16	6	3149	139	4	2.65	18	10	8	1109	37	4	2.00
2004-05	St. Michael's	OHL	58	23	23	5	3150	146	3	2.78	10	4	4	524	25	0	2.86

PIETRASIAK, Jeff (peh-TRAZ-ee-ak, JEHF) PHX.

Goaltender. Catches left. 6'1", 180 lbs. Born, Marlboro, MA, April 5, 1983.
(Phoenix's 8th choice, 186th overall, in 2002 Entry Draft).

			Regular Season								Playoffs						
Season	Club	League	GP	W	L	T	Mins	GA	SO	Avg	GP	W	L	Mins	GA	SO	Avg
2000-01	Berkshire Bears	High-MA	25	....	....	....	1150	26	8	1.37	....	....	....	....	....	....	....
2001-02	Berkshire Bears	High-MA	32	....	....	....	1471	51	5	2.05	....	....	....	....	....	....	....
2002-03	New Hampshire	H-East	2	1	0	0	67	2	0	1.78	....	....	....	....	....	....	....
2003-04	New Hampshire	H-East	11	3	1	1	387	12	0	1.86	....	....	....	....	....	....	....
2004-05	New Hampshire	H-East	23	11	7	3	1280	62	2	2.91	....	....	....	....	....	....	....

PLANTE, Tyler (PLAWNT, TIGH-luhr) FLA.

Goaltender. Catches left. 6'2", 191 lbs. Born, Milwaukee, WI, April 16, 1987.
(Florida's 2nd choice, 32nd overall, in 2005 Entry Draft).

			Regular Season								Playoffs						
Season	Club	League	GP	W	L	T	Mins	GA	SO	Avg	GP	W	L	Mins	GA	SO	Avg
2003-04	Brandon	WHL	2	0	0	1	58	2	0	2.07	....	....	....	....	....	....	....
2004-05	Brandon	WHL	48	34	11	2	2833	122	6	2.58	*24	*13	11	*1408	69	0	2.94

WHL Rookie of the Year (2005) • Canadian Major Junior All-Rookie Team (2005)

POGGE, Justin (POHG, JUHS-tihn) TOR.

Goaltender. Catches left. 6'3", 183 lbs. Born, Ft. McMurray, Alta., April 22, 1986.
(Toronto's 1st choice, 90th overall, in 2004 Entry Draft).

			Regular Season								Playoffs						
Season	Club	League	GP	W	L	T	Mins	GA	SO	Avg	GP	W	L	Mins	GA	SO	Avg
2002-03	Summerland Sting	KIJHL	30	....	....	....	1761	91	0	3.13	....	....	....	....	....	....	....
2003-04	Prince George	WHL	44	17	18	2	2271	107	3	2.83	....	....	....	....	....	....	....
2004-05	Prince George	WHL	24	10	9	2	1198	56	4	2.80	....	....	....	....	....	....	....
	Calgary Hitmen	WHL	29	14	12	3	1727	66	2	2.29	12	7	5	742	24	1	1.94

POPPERLE, Tomas (PAW-puhr-lay, TAW-mash) CBJ

Goaltender. Catches left. 6'1", 187 lbs. Born, Broumov, Czech., October 10, 1984.
(Columbus' 5th choice, 131st overall, in 2005 Entry Draft).

			Regular Season								Playoffs						
Season	Club	League	GP	W	L	T	Mins	GA	SO	Avg	GP	W	L	Mins	GA	SO	Avg
2001-02	Sparta Jr.	CzRep-Jr.	29	....	....	....	1653	65	2	2.36	5	....	....	320	15	0	2.81
2002-03	Sparta Jr.	CzRep-Jr.	28	....	....	....	1500	52	2	2.08	....	....	....	....	....	....	....
2003-04	Sparta Jr.	CzRep-Jr.	30	....	....	....	1778	60	4	2.02	....	....	....	....	....	....	....
	HC Pribram	CzRep-3	2	....	....	....	60	2	0	2.00	....	....	....	....	....	....	....
	Beroun	CzRep-2	5	....	....	....	305	7	0	1.38	2	....	....	120	4	0	2.00
	HC Sparta Praha	CzRep	....	....	....	....	....	....	....	....	1	....	....	11	0	0	0.00
2004-05	Beroun	CzRep-2	16	....	....	....	966	29	1	1.80	2	....	....	120	5	0	2.50
	HC Sparta Praha	CzRep	25	....	....	....	1325	35	4	*1.58	2	....	....	12	4	0	20.00

POTVIN, Felix (PAHT-vihn, FEEL-ihx)

Goaltender. Catches left. 6'1", 190 lbs. Born, Anjou, Que., June 23, 1971.
(Toronto's 2nd choice, 31st overall, in 1990 Entry Draft).

			Regular Season								Playoffs						
Season	Club	League	GP	W	L	T	Mins	GA	SO	Avg	GP	W	L	Mins	GA	SO	Avg
1987-88	Montreal-Bourassa	QAAA	27	15	7	3	1585	103	3	3.90	6	2	4	341	20	0	3.51
1988-89	Chicoutimi	QMJHL	*65	25	31	1	*3489	271	*2	4.66	....	....	....	....	....	....	....
1989-90	Chicoutimi	QMJHL	*62	*31	26	2	*3478	231	*2	3.99	....	....	....	....	....	....	....
1990-91	Chicoutimi	QMJHL	54	33	15	4	3216	145	*6	*2.70	*16	*11	5	*992	46	0	*2.78
1991-92	**Toronto**	**NHL**	**4**	**0**	**2**	**1**	**210**	**8**	**0**	**2.29**	....	....	....	....	....	....	....
	St. John's	AHL	35	18	10	6	2070	101	2	2.93	11	7	4	642	41	0	3.83
1992-93	**Toronto**	**NHL**	**48**	**25**	**15**	**7**	**2781**	**116**	**2**	***2.50**	***21**	**11**	**10**	***1308**	**62**	**1**	**2.84**
	St. John's	AHL	5	3	0	2	309	18	0	3.50	....	....	....	....	....	....	....
1993-94	**Toronto**	**NHL**	**66**	**34**	**22**	**9**	**3883**	**187**	**3**	**2.89**	**18**	**9**	**9**	**1124**	**46**	**3**	**2.46**
1994-95	**Toronto**	**NHL**	**36**	**15**	**13**	**7**	**2144**	**104**	**0**	**2.91**	**7**	**3**	**4**	**424**	**20**	**1**	**2.83**
1995-96	**Toronto**	**NHL**	**69**	**30**	**26**	**11**	**4009**	**192**	**2**	**2.87**	**6**	**2**	**4**	**350**	**19**	**0**	**3.26**
1996-97	**Toronto**	**NHL**	***74**	**27**	**36**	**7**	***4271**	**224**	**0**	**3.15**	....	....	....	....	....	....	....
1997-98	**Toronto**	**NHL**	**67**	**26**	**33**	**7**	**3864**	**176**	**5**	**2.73**	....	....	....	....	....	....	....
1998-99	**Toronto**	**NHL**	**5**	**3**	**2**	**0**	**299**	**19**	**0**	**3.81**	....	....	....	....	....	....	....
	NY Islanders	**NHL**	**11**	**2**	**7**	**1**	**606**	**37**	**0**	**3.66**	....	....	....	....	....	....	....
99-2000	**NY Islanders**	**NHL**	**22**	**5**	**14**	**3**	**1273**	**68**	**1**	**3.21**	....	....	....	....	....	....	....
	Vancouver	**NHL**	**34**	**12**	**13**	**7**	**1966**	**85**	**0**	**2.59**	....	....	....	....	....	....	....
2000-01	**Vancouver**	**NHL**	**35**	**14**	**17**	**3**	**2006**	**103**	**1**	**3.08**	....	....	....	....	....	....	....
	Los Angeles	**NHL**	**23**	**13**	**5**	**5**	**1410**	**46**	**5**	**1.96**	**13**	**7**	**6**	**812**	**33**	**2**	**2.44**
2001-02	**Los Angeles**	**NHL**	**71**	**31**	**27**	**8**	**4071**	**157**	**6**	**2.31**	**7**	**3**	**4**	**417**	**15**	**1**	**2.16**
2002-03	**Los Angeles**	**NHL**	**42**	**17**	**20**	**3**	**2367**	**105**	**3**	**2.66**	....	....	....	....	....	....	....
2003-04	**Boston**	**NHL**	**28**	**12**	**8**	**6**	**1605**	**67**	**4**	**2.50**	....	....	....	....	....	....	....
2004-05			DID NOT PLAY														
	NHL Totals		**635**	**266**	**260**	**85**	**36765**	**1694**	**32**	**2.76**	**72**	**35**	**37**	**4435**	**195**	**8**	**2.64**

QMJHL All-Rookie Team (1989) • QMJHL Second All-Star Team (1990) • QMJHL First All-Star Team (1991) • Canadian Major Junior Goaltender of the Year (1991) • Memorial Cup Tournament All-Star Team (1991) • Hap Emms Memorial Trophy (Memorial Cup Tournament Top Goaltender) (1991) • AHL First All-Star Team (1992) • Dudley "Red" Garrett Memorial Award (Rookie of the Year – AHL) (1992) • Aldege "Baz" Bastien Memorial Award (Outstanding Goaltender – AHL) (1992) • NHL All-Rookie Team (1993)

Played in NHL All-Star Game (1994, 1996)

Traded to **NY Islanders** by **Toronto** with Toronto's 6th round choice (later traded to Tampa Bay – Tampa Bay selected Fedor Fedorov) in 1999 Entry Draft for Bryan Berard and NY Islanders' 6th round choice (Jan Sochor) in 1999 Entry Draft, January 9, 1999. Traded to **Vancouver** by **NY Islanders** with NY Islanders' 2nd round compensatory choice (later traded to New Jersey – New Jersey selected Teemu Laine) in 2000 Entry Draft and NY Islanders' 3rd round choice (Thatcher Bell) in 2000 Entry Draft for Kevin Weekes, Dave Scatchard and Bill Muckalt, December 19, 1999. Traded to **Los Angeles** by **Vancouver** for future considerations, February 15, 2001. Signed as a free agent by **Boston**, September 3, 2003.

PRICE, Carey (PRIGHS, KAIR-ee) MTL.

Goaltender. Catches left. 6'2", 222 lbs. Born, Vancouver, B.C., August 16, 1987.
(Montreal's 1st choice, 5th overall, in 2005 Entry Draft).

			Regular Season								Playoffs						
Season	Club	League	GP	W	L	T	Mins	GA	SO	Avg	GP	W	L	Mins	GA	SO	Avg
2002-03	Williams Lake	BCAHA	18	....	....	....	1050	48	1	2.70	....	....	....	....	....	....	....
	Tri-City Americans	WHL	1	0	0	0	20	2	0	6.00	....	....	....	....	....	....	....
2003-04	Tri-City Americans	WHL	28	8	9	3	1363	54	1	2.38	8	5	3	470	19	0	2.43
2004-05	Tri-City Americans	WHL	63	24	31	8	3712	145	8	2.34	5	1	4	325	12	0	2.22

PRUSEK, Martin (PREW-sehk, MAHR-tihn) CBJ

Goaltender. Catches left. 6'1", 176 lbs. Born, Ostrava, Czech., December 11, 1975.
(Ottawa's 6th choice, 164th overall, in 1999 Entry Draft).

			Regular Season								Playoffs						
Season	Club	League	GP	W	L	T	Mins	GA	SO	Avg	GP	W	L	Mins	GA	SO	Avg
1994-95	HC Vitkovice	CzRep	5	....	....	....	232	18	....	4.65	....	....	....	....	....	....	....
1995-96	HC Vitkovice	CzRep	40	....	....	....	2336	113	1	2.90	4	....	....	250	10	1	2.40
1996-97	HC Vitkovice	CzRep	49	....	....	....	2841	109	8	2.30	9	....	....	546	19	1	2.08
1997-98	HC Vitkovice	CzRep	50	....	....	....	2901	129	....	2.67	9	....	....	529	26	....	3.00
1998-99	HC Vitkovice	CzRep	37	....	....	....	1905	85	....	2.68	4	....	....	250	12	....	2.88
99-2000	HC Vitkovice	CzRep	50	....	....	....	2647	132	....	2.99	....	....	....	....	....	....	....
2000-01	HC Vitkovice	CzRep	30	....	....	....	1679	64	....	2.29	9	....	....	460	25	....	3.26
2001-02	**Ottawa**	**NHL**	**1**	**0**	**1**	**0**	**62**	**3**	**0**	**2.90**	....	....	....	....	....	....	....
	Grand Rapids	AHL	33	18	8	5	1903	58	4	*1.83	5	2	3	278	10	0	2.16
2002-03	**Ottawa**	**NHL**	**18**	**12**	**2**	**1**	**935**	**37**	**0**	**2.37**	....	....	....	....	....	....	....
	Binghamton	AHL	4	1	2	1	243	7	1	1.73	....	....	....	....	....	....	....
2003-04	**Ottawa**	**NHL**	**29**	**16**	**6**	**3**	**1528**	**54**	**3**	**2.12**	**1**	**0**	**0**	**40**	**1**	**0**	**1.50**
2004-05	HC Vitkovice Steel	CzRep	14	....	....	....	672	28	0	2.50	....	....	....	....	....	....	....
	Znojmo	CzRep	8	....	....	....	453	18	0	2.38	....	....	....	....	....	....	....
	NHL Totals		**48**	**28**	**9**	**4**	**2525**	**94**	**3**	**2.23**	**1**	**0**	**0**	**40**	**1**	**0**	**1.50**

AHL First All-Star Team (2002) • Harry "Hap" Holmes Memorial Award (fewest goals against – AHL) (2002) (shared with Simon Lajeunesse and Mathieu Chouinard) • Aldege "Baz" Bastien Memorial Award (Outstanding Goaltender – AHL) (2002)

Signed as a free agent by **Vitkovice** (CzRep), August 20, 2004. Loaned to **Znojmo** (CzRep) by **Vitkovice** (CzRep), December, 2004. Signed as a free agent by **Columbus**, August 4, 2005.

PUURULA, Joni (pu-u-ROO-luh, YOHN-ee) MTL.

Goaltender. Catches left. 5'11", 180 lbs. Born, Kokkola, Finland, August 4, 1982.
(Montreal's 10th choice, 243rd overall, in 2000 Entry Draft).

			Regular Season								Playoffs						
Season	Club	League	GP	W	L	T	Mins	GA	SO	Avg	GP	W	L	Mins	GA	SO	Avg
1998-99	Junkkarit Kalajoki	Finland-2	12	....	....	....	782	37	0	2.84	....	....	....	....	....	....	....
99-2000	Hermes Kokkola	Finland-2	23	8	12	2	1251	81	1	3.88	....	....	....	....	....	....	....
2000-01	FPS Forssa	Finland-2	39	13	22	2	2264	142	1	3.76	....	....	....	....	....	....	....
	FPS Forssa Jr.	Finland-Jr.	....	....	....	....	....	....	....	....	4	1	3	240	8	0	2.00
2001-02	HPK Jr.	Finland-Jr.	2	0	0	2	119	11	0	5.51	....	....	....	....	....	....	....
	FPS Forssa	Finland-2	5	2	2	1	305	18	0	3.54	....	....	....	....	....	....	....
	HPK Hameenlinna	Finland	9	8	0	1	515	18	0	2.10	8	4	3	453	13	0	1.72
2002-03	HPK Hameenlinna	Finland	34	19	6	9	1972	71	4	2.16	11	6	5	676	19	1	1.69
2003-04	Ahmat Hyvinkaa	Finland-2	3	2	0	1	182	9	0	2.97	....	....	....	....	....	....	....
	HPK Hameenlinna	Finland	33	16	9	7	1890	69	4	2.19	8	4	4	482	14	2	1.74
2004-05	Ufa	Russia	24	....	....	....	1222	61	3	2.99	....	....	....	....	....	....	....
	HPK Hameenlinna	Finland	7	1	0	6	447	19	0	2.55	....	....	....	....	....	....	....

QUICK, Jonathan (KWIHK, JAWN-ah-thuhn) L.A.

Goaltender. Catches left. 6', 180 lbs. Born, Milford, CT, January 21, 1986.
(Los Angeles' 4th choice, 72nd overall, in 2005 Entry Draft).

			Regular Season								Playoffs						
Season	Club	League	GP	W	L	T	Mins	GA	SO	Avg	GP	W	L	Mins	GA	SO	Avg
2002-03	Avon Old Farms	High-CT	13	8	5	0	780	38	0	2.92	....	....	....	....	....	....	....
2003-04	Avon Old Farms	High-CT	21	20	1	0	1260	26	2	1.71	....	....	....	....	....	....	....

2004-05	Avon Old Farms	High-CT	27	25	2	0	1413	1.14	9	1.14	....	....	....	....	....	....	....

Signed Letter of Intent to attend **Massachusetts** (H-East), December 2, 2004.

RACINE, Jean-Francois (RAY-seen, ZHAWN-fran-SWUH) TOR.

Goaltender. Catches left. 6'3", 194 lbs. Born, St-Hyacinthe, Que., April 27, 1982.
(Toronto's 4th choice, 90th overall, in 2000 Entry Draft).

			Regular Season								Playoffs						
Season	**Club**	**League**	**GP**	**W**	**L**	**T**	**Mins**	**GA**	**SO**	**Avg**	**GP**	**W**	**L**	**Mins**	**GA**	**SO**	**Avg**
1998-99	Magog	QAAA	36	19	12	1	2160	107	3	2.98	11	5	6	656	37	0	3.39
99-2000	Moncton Wildcats	QMJHL	10	3	3	1	410	28	0	4.10	....	....	....	....	....	....	....
	Drummondville	QMJHL	20	14	6	0	1152	63	1	3.28	3	0	0	65	5	0	4.60
2000-01	Drummondville	QMJHL	61	27	26	3	3362	189	4	3.37	5	2	3	303	20	0	3.97
2001-02	Drummondville	QMJHL	65	29	30	3	3640	208	2	3.43	12	5	7	720	42	1	3.50
2002-03	Memphis	CHL	35	22	9	3	2050	94	0	2.75	1	0	1	58	5	0	5.14
2003-04	Memphis	CHL	30	15	10	2	1645	74	2	2.70	....	....	....	....	....	....	....
	St. John's	AHL	9	4	5	0	496	24	1	2.90	....	....	....	....	....	....	....
2004-05	St. John's	AHL	17	10	4	0	893	41	0	2.76	....	....	....	....	....	....	....
	Memphis	CHL	19	9	6	1	951	57	0	3.60	....	....	....	....	....	....	....

RAMO, Karri (RAH-moh, KAH-ree) T.B.

Goaltender. Catches left. 6'2", 192 lbs. Born, Asikkala, Finland, July 1, 1986.
(Tampa Bay's 7th choice, 191st overall, in 2004 Entry Draft).

			Regular Season								Playoffs						
Season	**Club**	**League**	**GP**	**W**	**L**	**T**	**Mins**	**GA**	**SO**	**Avg**	**GP**	**W**	**L**	**Mins**	**GA**	**SO**	**Avg**
2002-03	Lukko Rauma Jr.	Finland-Jr.	19	....	....	....	1013	47	0	2.78	4	....	....	182	11	0	3.63
2003-04	Pelicans Lahti Jr.	Finland-Jr.	21	8	9	2	1140	60	0	3.16	7	4	2	388	11	1	1.70
	Pelicans Lahti	Finland	3	0	2	0	138	10	0	4.35	....	....	....	....	....	....	....
2004-05	Pelicans Lahti	Finland	26	4	12	4	1268	84	1	3.98	....	....	....	....	....	....	....
	Pelicans Lahti Jr.	Finland-Jr.	21	10	5	6	1269	36	6	1.70	4	1	3	206	16	0	4.66

RASK, Tuukka (RASK, TU-kah) TOR.

Goaltender. Catches left. 6'2", 165 lbs. Born, Savonlinna, Finland, March 10, 1987.
(Toronto's 1st choice, 21st overall, in 2005 Entry Draft).

			Regular Season								Playoffs						
Season	**Club**	**League**	**GP**	**W**	**L**	**T**	**Mins**	**GA**	**SO**	**Avg**	**GP**	**W**	**L**	**Mins**	**GA**	**SO**	**Avg**
2003-04	Ilves Tampere U18	Fin-U18	9	4	3	2	533	25	0	2.81	....	....	....	....	....	....	....
	Ilves Tampere Jr.	Finland-Jr.	30	12	10	7	1767	65	2	2.21	....	....	....	....	....	....	....
2004-05	Ilves Tampere Jr.	Finland-Jr.	26	17	3	4	1517	47	2	1.86	10	9	1	619	9	6	0.87
	Ilves Tampere	Finland	4	0	1	1	202	15	0	4.48	....	....	....	....	....	....	....

RAYCROFT, Andrew (RAY-krawft, AN-droo) BOS.

Goaltender. Catches left. 6', 185 lbs. Born, Belleville, Ont., May 4, 1980.
(Boston's 4th choice, 135th overall, in 1998 Entry Draft).

			Regular Season								Playoffs						
Season	**Club**	**League**	**GP**	**W**	**L**	**T**	**Mins**	**GA**	**SO**	**Avg**	**GP**	**W**	**L**	**Mins**	**GA**	**SO**	**Avg**
1996-97	Wellington Dukes	MTJHL	27	....	....	....	1402	92	0	3.94	....	....	....	....	....	....	....
1997-98	Sudbury Wolves	OHL	33	8	16	5	1802	125	0	4.16	2	0	1	89	8	0	5.39
1998-99	Sudbury Wolves	OHL	45	17	22	5	2528	173	1	4.11	3	0	2	96	13	0	8.13
99-2000	Kingston	OHL	*61	33	20	5	3340	191	0	3.43	5	1	4	300	21	0	4.20
2000-01	**Boston**	**NHL**	**15**	**4**	**6**	**0**	**649**	**32**	**0**	**2.96**	....	....	....	....	....	....	....
	Providence Bruins	AHL	26	8	14	4	1459	82	1	3.37	....	....	....	....	....	....	....
2001-02	**Boston**	**NHL**	**1**	**0**	**0**	**1**	**65**	**3**	**0**	**2.77**	....	....	....	....	....	....	....
	Providence Bruins	AHL	56	25	24	6	3317	142	4	2.57	2	0	2	119	5	0	2.52
2002-03	**Boston**	**NHL**	**5**	**2**	**3**	**0**	**300**	**12**	**0**	**2.40**	....	....	....	....	....	....	....
	Providence Bruins	AHL	39	23	10	3	2255	94	1	2.50	4	1	3	264	6	1	*1.36
2003-04	**Boston**	**NHL**	**57**	**29**	**18**	**9**	**3420**	**117**	**3**	**2.05**	**7**	**3**	**4**	**447**	**16**	**1**	**2.15**
2004-05	Tappara Tampere	Finland	11	4	5	2	658	32	1	2.92	3	0	2	104	11	0	6.36
	NHL Totals		**78**	**35**	**27**	**10**	**4434**	**164**	**3**	**2.22**	**7**	**3**	**4**	**447**	**16**	**1**	**2.15**

OHL First All-Star Team (2000) • Canadian Major Junior First All-Star Team (2000) • Canadian Major Junior Goaltender of the Year (2000) • NHL All-Rookie Team (2004) • Calder Memorial Trophy (2004)

Signed as a free agent by **Tappara** (Finland), January 17, 2005.

REGAN, Kevin (REE-guhn, KEH-vihn) BOS.

Goaltender. Catches left. 6', 190 lbs. Born, Boston, MA, July 25, 1984.
(Boston's 10th choice, 277th overall, in 2003 Entry Draft).

			Regular Season								Playoffs						
Season	**Club**	**League**	**GP**	**W**	**L**	**T**	**Mins**	**GA**	**SO**	**Avg**	**GP**	**W**	**L**	**Mins**	**GA**	**SO**	**Avg**
2001-02	St. Sebastian's	High-MA	31	27	4	0	1860	56	0	1.91	....	....	....	....	....	....	....
	USA U-18	USDP	1	0	0	0	12	0	0	0.00	....	....	....	....	....	....	....
	South Boston	USHA	3	3	0	0	158	8	0	2.58	....	....	....	....	....	....	....
2002-03	St. Sebastian's	High-MA	28	....	....	....	1215	47	4	1.81	....	....	....	....	....	....	....
2003-04	Waterloo	USHL	50	*28	19	1	0	111	*6	2.37	*12	*9	3	*735	19	*1	*1.55
2004-05	New Hampshire	H-East	23	15	4	2	1276	50	0	2.35	....	....	....	....	....	....	....

Hockey East All-Rookie Team (2005) (co-winners - Cory Schneider and Peter Vetri)

RINNE, Pekka (RIH-neh, PEH-kuh) NSH.

Goaltender. Catches left. 6'5", 207 lbs. Born, Kempele, Finland, November 3, 1982.
(Nashville's 10th choice, 258th overall, in 2004 Entry Draft).

			Regular Season								Playoffs						
Season	**Club**	**League**	**GP**	**W**	**L**	**T**	**Mins**	**GA**	**SO**	**Avg**	**GP**	**W**	**L**	**Mins**	**GA**	**SO**	**Avg**
2001-02	Karpat Oulu Jr.	Finland-Jr.	30	19	7	3	1724	61	3	2.12	3	1	2	184	10	0	3.26
2002-03	Karpat Oulu Jr.	Finland-Jr.	25	14	8	3	1479	48	5	1.95	4	1	3	238	7	0	1.76
	Karpat Oulu	Finland	1	0	1	0	60	7	0	7.00	....	....	....	....	....	....	....
2003-04	Karpat Oulu	Finland	14	5	4	4	824	41	0	2.99	2	1	0	22	0	0	0.00
	Hokki Kajaani	Finland-2	8	5	2	1	463	16	2	2.07	....	....	....	....	....	....	....
2004-05	Karpat Oulu	Finland	10	8	0	1	572	16	0	1.68	....	....	....	....	....	....	....

ROLOSON, Dwayne (ROH-loh-suhn, DWAYN) MIN.

Goaltender. Catches left. 6'1", 178 lbs. Born, Simcoe, Ont., October 12, 1969.

			Regular Season								Playoffs						
Season	**Club**	**League**	**GP**	**W**	**L**	**T**	**Mins**	**GA**	**SO**	**Avg**	**GP**	**W**	**L**	**Mins**	**GA**	**SO**	**Avg**
1984-85	Simcoe Penguins	OJHL-C	3	....	....	....	100	21	0	12.60	....	....	....	....	....	....	....
1985-86	Simcoe Rams	OJHL-C	1	....	....	....	60	6	0	6.00	....	....	....	....	....	....	....
1986-87	Norwich	OJHL-C	19	....	....	....	1091	55	0	*3.03	....	....	....	....	....	....	....
1987-88	Belleville Bobcats	OJHL-B	21	9	6	1	1070	60	*2	3.36	....	....	....	....	....	....	....
1988-89	Thorold	OJHL-B	27	15	6	4	1490	82	0	3.30	....	....	....	....	....	....	....
1989-90	Thorold	OHA-B	30	18	8	1	1683	108	0	3.85	....	....	....	....	....	....	....
1990-91	U. Mass-Lowell	H-East	15	5	9	0	823	63	0	4.59	....	....	....	....	....	....	....
1991-92	U. Mass-Lowell	H-East	12	3	8	0	660	52	0	4.73	....	....	....	....	....	....	....
1992-93	U. Mass-Lowell	H-East	*39	20	17	2	*2342	150	0	3.84	....	....	....	....	....	....	....
1993-94	U. Mass-Lowell	H-East	*40	*23	10	7	*2305	106	0	2.76	....	....	....	....	....	....	....
1994-95	Saint John Flames	AHL	46	16	21	8	2734	156	1	3.42	5	1	4	298	13	0	2.61
1995-96	Saint John Flames	AHL	67	*33	22	11	4026	190	1	2.83	16	10	6	1027	49	1	2.86
1996-97	**Calgary**	**NHL**	**31**	**9**	**14**	**3**	**1618**	**78**	**1**	**2.89**	....	....	....	....	....	....	....
	Saint John Flames	AHL	8	6	2	0	481	22	1	2.75	....	....	....	....	....	....	....
1997-98	**Calgary**	**NHL**	**39**	**11**	**16**	**8**	**2205**	**110**	**0**	**2.99**	....	....	....	....	....	....	....
	Saint John Flames	AHL	4	3	0	1	245	8	0	1.96	....	....	....	....	....	....	....
1998-99	**Buffalo**	**NHL**	**18**	**6**	**8**	**2**	**911**	**42**	**1**	**2.77**	**4**	**1**	**1**	**139**	**10**	**0**	**4.32**
	Rochester	AHL	2	2	0	0	120	4	0	2.00	....	....	....	....	....	....	....
99-2000	**Buffalo**	**NHL**	**14**	**1**	**7**	**3**	**677**	**32**	**0**	**2.84**	....	....	....	....	....	....	....
2000-01	Worcester IceCats	AHL	52	*32	15	5	*3127	113	*6	*2.17	11	6	5	697	23	1	1.98
2001-02	**Minnesota**	**NHL**	**45**	**14**	**20**	**7**	**2506**	**112**	**5**	**2.68**	....	....	....	....	....	....	....
2002-03	**Minnesota**	**NHL**	**50**	**23**	**16**	**8**	**2945**	**98**	**4**	**2.00**	**11**	**5**	**6**	**579**	**25**	**0**	**2.59**
2003-04	**Minnesota**	**NHL**	**48**	**19**	**18**	**11**	**2847**	**89**	**5**	**1.88**	....	....	....	....	....	....	....
2004-05	Lukko Rauma	Finland	34	20	10	4	2049	70	4	2.05	9	4	5	512	18	2	2.11
	NHL Totals		**245**	**83**	**99**	**42**	**13709**	**561**	**16**	**2.46**	**15**	**6**	**7**	**718**	**35**	**0**	**2.92**

Hockey East First All-Star Team (1994) • Hockey East Player of the Year (1994) • NCAA East First All-American Team (1994) • AHL First All-Star Team (2001) • Aldege "Baz" Bastien Memorial Award (Outstanding Goaltender – AHL) (2001) • MBNA/Mastercard Roger Crozier Saving Grace Award (2004)

Played in NHL All-Star Game (2004)

Signed as a free agent by **Calgary**, July 4, 1994. Signed as a free agent by **Buffalo**, July 15, 1998. Claimed by **Columbus** from **Buffalo** in Expansion Draft, June 23, 2000. Signed as a free agent by **St. Louis**, July 14, 2000. Signed as a free agent by **Minnesota**, July 2, 2001. Signed as a free agent by **Lukko** (Finland), October 18, 2004.

RUDKOWSKY, Cody (RUHD-kow-skee, KOH-dee)

Goaltender. Catches left. 6'1", 206 lbs. Born, Willingdon, Alta., July 21, 1978.

			Regular Season								Playoffs						
Season	**Club**	**League**	**GP**	**W**	**L**	**T**	**Mins**	**GA**	**SO**	**Avg**	**GP**	**W**	**L**	**Mins**	**GA**	**SO**	**Avg**
1995-96	Langley Thunder	BCJHL	23	....	....	....	1172	73	1	3.73	....	....	....	....	....	....	....
	Seattle	WHL	2	0	0	0	21	3	0	8.57	....	....	....	....	....	....	....
1996-97	Seattle	WHL	40	19	16	1	2162	124	0	3.44	1	1	0	30	0	0	0.00
1997-98	Seattle	WHL	53	20	22	3	2805	176	1	3.74	5	1	4	278	18	0	3.88
1998-99	Seattle	WHL	64	34	17	10	3665	177	*7	2.90	11	5	6	637	31	1	2.92
99-2000	Worcester IceCats	AHL	28	9	7	6	1405	75	0	3.20	....	....	....	....	....	....	....
	Peoria Rivermen	ECHL	10	6	4	0	599	32	0	3.20	2	1	1	119	6	0	3.02
2000-01	Worcester IceCats	AHL	25	13	8	3	1477	66	3	2.68	....	....	....	....	....	....	....
2001-02	Worcester IceCats	AHL	21	6	10	2	1108	50	1	2.71	....	....	....	....	....	....	....
	Peoria Rivermen	ECHL	12	5	2	4	709	24	3	2.03	2	0	1	78	4	0	3.08
2002-03	**St. Louis**	**NHL**	**1**	**1**	**0**	**0**	**30**	**0**	**0**	**0.00**	....	....	....	....	....	....	....
	Worcester IceCats	AHL	10	1	5	3	577	28	0	2.91	....	....	....	....	....	....	....
	Trenton Titans	ECHL	31	17	9	5	1867	85	2	2.73	3	0	3	178	14	0	4.72
2003-04	Worcester IceCats	AHL	1	0	0	0	49	3	0	3.67	1	0	1	58	2	0	2.07
	Reading Royals	ECHL	46	24	18	4	2728	108	1	2.38	14	8	6	834	28	1	2.02
2004-05	Providence Bruins	AHL	14	4	7	2	731	39	0	3.20	....	....	....	....	....	....	....
	Reading Royals	ECHL	20	8	11	1	1163	42	3	2.17	....	....	....	....	....	....	....
	NHL Totals		**1**	**1**	**0**	**0**	**30**	**0**	**0**	**0.00**	....	....	....	....	....	....	....

WHL West First All-Star Team (1999) • WHL Goaltender of the Year (1999) • WHL Player of the Year (1999) • Canadian Major Junior First All-Star Team (1999) • Canadian Major Junior Goaltender of the Year (1999)

Signed as a free agent by **St. Louis**, March 25, 1999. Signed as a free agent by **Providence** (AHL), December 1, 2004.

SABOURIN, Dany (SA-boo-rihn, DAN-ee) PIT.

Goaltender. Catches left. 6'2", 182 lbs. Born, Val-d'Or, Que., September 2, 1980.
(Calgary's 5th choice, 108th overall, in 1998 Entry Draft).

			Regular Season								Playoffs						
Season	**Club**	**League**	**GP**	**W**	**L**	**T**	**Mins**	**GA**	**SO**	**Avg**	**GP**	**W**	**L**	**Mins**	**GA**	**SO**	**Avg**
1996-97	Amos Forestiers	QAAA	24	6	16	0	1440	107	0	4.48	....	....	....	....	....	....	....
1997-98	Sherbrooke	QMJHL	37	15	15	2	1906	128	1	4.03	....	....	....	....	....	....	....
1998-99	Sherbrooke	QMJHL	30	8	13	2	1477	102	1	4.14	1	0	1	49	2	0	2.45
	Saint John Flames	AHL	....	....	....	....	....	....	....	....	1	0	1	57	4	0	4.19
99-2000	Sherbrooke	QMJHL	55	25	22	5	3067	181	1	3.54	5	1	4	324	18	0	3.33
2000-01	Saint John Flames	AHL	1	1	0	0	40	0	0	0.00	....	....	....	....	....	....	....
	Johnstown Chiefs	ECHL	19	4	9	1	903	56	0	3.72	1	0	0	40	2	0	3.00
2001-02	Johnstown Chiefs	ECHL	27	14	10	1	1539	84	0	3.28	3	0	2	137	5	0	2.18
2002-03	Saint John Flames	AHL	41	15	17	4	2220	100	4	2.70	....	....	....	....	....	....	....
2003-04	**Calgary**	**NHL**	**4**	**0**	**3**	**0**	**169**	**10**	**0**	**3.55**	....	....	....	....	....	....	....
	Lowell	AHL	14	5	7	2	821	39	0	2.85	....	....	....	....	....	....	....
	Las Vegas	ECHL	10	6	3	1	613	24	0	2.35	1	0	1	58	2	0	2.07
2004-05	Wilkes-Barre	AHL	20	8	8	2	1029	38	1	2.22	....	....	....	....	....	....	....
	Wheeling Nailers	ECHL	27	19	6	1	1579	44	5	*1.67	....	....	....	....	....	....	....
	NHL Totals		**4**	**0**	**3**	**0**	**169**	**10**	**0**	**3.55**	....	....	....	....	....	....	....

Signed as a free agent by **Pittsburgh**, August 10, 2005.

SANFORD, Curtis (SAN-fohrd, KUHR-this) ST.L.

Goaltender. Catches left. 5'10", 187 lbs. Born, Owen Sound, Ont., October 5, 1979.

			Regular Season								Playoffs						
Season	**Club**	**League**	**GP**	**W**	**L**	**T**	**Mins**	**GA**	**SO**	**Avg**	**GP**	**W**	**L**	**Mins**	**GA**	**SO**	**Avg**
1994-95	Wiarton Wolves	OJHL-C	18	....	....	....	949	98	0	6.20	....	....	....	....	....	....	....
1995-96	Collingwood	OJHL	21	....	....	....	2128	74	0	3.54	....	....	....	....	....	....	....
1996-97	Owen Sound	OHL	19	4	8	1	847	77	0	5.45	....	....	....	....	....	....	....
	Owen Sound	OJHL-B	6	....	....	....	360	28	0	4.68	....	....	....	....	....	....	....
1997-98	Owen Sound	OHL	30	13	10	2	1542	114	1	4.44	9	4	4	456	30	1	3.95
1998-99	Owen Sound	OHL	56	30	16	5	2998	191	2	3.82	16	9	7	960	58	0	3.63
99-2000	Owen Sound	OHL	53	18	26	6	3124	198	1	3.80	....	....	....	....	....	....	....
	Missouri	UHL	6	3	1	0	237	6	0	1.52	....	....	....	....	....	....	....
2000-01	Peoria Rivermen	ECHL	27	15	7	4	1511	48	3	*1.91	14	9	4	813	28	*2	2.07
	Worcester IceCats	AHL	5	3	0	1	237	16	0	4.06	....	....	....	....	....	....	....
2001-02	Peoria Rivermen	ECHL	24	13	8	2	1418	58	1	2.45	....	....	....	....	....	....	....
	Worcester IceCats	AHL	9	5	4	0	537	22	0	2.46	....	....	....	....	....	....	....
2002-03	**St. Louis**	**NHL**	**8**	**5**	**1**	**0**	**397**	**13**	**1**	**1.96**	....	....	....	....	....	....	....
	Worcester IceCats	AHL	41	18	14	8	2317	93	3	2.41	3	0	3	179	8	0	2.68
2003-04	Worcester IceCats	AHL	43	20	16	3	2367	84	5	2.13	9	4	5	569	24	0	2.53
2004-05	Worcester IceCats	AHL	50	19	25	2	2743	123	2	2.69	....	....	....	....	....	....	....
	NHL Totals		**8**	**5**	**1**	**0**	**397**	**13**	**1**	**1.96**	....	....	....	....	....	....	....

ECHL Second All-Star Team (2001)

Signed as a free agent by **St. Louis**, October 1, 2000.

SAUVE, Philippe (SOH-vay, FIHL-ihp) CGY.

Goaltender. Catches left. 6', 180 lbs. Born, Buffalo, NY, February 27, 1980.
(Colorado's 6th choice, 38th overall, in 1998 Entry Draft).

			Regular Season								Playoffs						
Season	**Club**	**League**	**GP**	**W**	**L**	**T**	**Mins**	**GA**	**SO**	**Avg**	**GP**	**W**	**L**	**Mins**	**GA**	**SO**	**Avg**
1995-96	Laval-Laurentides	QAAA	25	9	10	0	1184	87	1	4.11	15	7	8	900	54	0	3.58
1996-97	Rimouski Oceanic	QMJHL	26	11	9	2	1334	84	0	3.78	1	0	0	14	3	0	12.90
1997-98	Rimouski Oceanic	QMJHL	40	23	16	0	2326	131	1	3.38	7	0	5	262	33	0	7.55
1998-99	Rimouski Oceanic	QMJHL	44	16	19	4	2401	155	0	3.87	11	6	4	595	30	*1	3.03
99-2000	Drummondville	QMJHL	28	12	12	2	1526	106	0	4.17	....	....	....	....	....	....	....
	Hull Olympiques	QMJHL	17	9	7	1	992	57	0	3.45	12	6	6	735	47	0	3.84
2000-01	Hershey Bears	AHL	42	17	18	1	2182	100	3	2.75	3	0	3	218	10	0	2.75
2001-02	Hershey Bears	AHL	55	25	20	6	3130	111	6	2.13	8	3	5	486	21	0	2.59
2002-03	Hershey Bears	AHL	*60	26	20	12	3394	134	5	2.37	5	2	3	295	14	0	2.85
2003-04	**Colorado**	**NHL**	**17**	**7**	**7**	**3**	**986**	**50**	**0**	**3.04**	....	....	....	....	....	....	....
	Hershey Bears	AHL	10	3	7	0	578	25	2	2.59	....	....	....	....	....	....	....

Season	Club	League	GP	W	L	T	Mins	GA	SO	Avg	GP	W	L	Mins	GA	SO	Avg
2004-05	Mississippi	ECHL	21	13	4	4	1298	56	2	2.59	4	1	3	227	16	0	4.23
	NHL Totals		**17**	**7**	**7**	**3**	**986**	**50**	**0**	**3.04**	....	....	....	....	....	....	....

Canadian Major Junior Humanitarian Player of the Year (1999)

Signed as a free agent by **Mississippi** (ECHL), January 27, 2005. Traded to **Calgary** by **Colorado** for a conditional choice in 2006 Entry Draft, August 9, 2005.

SCHAEFER, Nolan (SHAY-fuhr, NOH-luhn) S.J.

Goaltender. Catches right. 6'2", 200 lbs. Born, Yellow Grass, Sask., January 15, 1980.
(San Jose's 4th choice, 166th overall, in 2000 Entry Draft).

							Regular Season							Playoffs			
Season	**Club**	**League**	**GP**	**W**	**L**	**T**	**Mins**	**GA**	**SO**	**Avg**	**GP**	**W**	**L**	**Mins**	**GA**	**SO**	**Avg**
1996-97	Yorkton Mallers	SMHL	36	....	....	....	1854	132	0	4.27	....	....	....	....	....	....	....
1997-98	Yorkton Mallers	SMHL	5	....	....	....	239	17	0	4.25	....	....	....	....	....	....	....
	Nipawin Hawks	SJHL	21	12	4	3	1080	42	*3	*2.33	....	....	....	....	....	....	....
1998-99	Nipawin Hawks	SJHL	46	....	....	....	2478	165	0	3.60	....	....	....	....	....	....	....
99-2000	Providence College	H-East	14	6	5	1	778	42	0	3.24	....	....	....	....	....	....	....
2000-01	Providence College	H-East	25	15	8	2	1529	63	3	2.47	....	....	....	....	....	....	....
2001-02	Providence College	H-East	*35	11	18	5	*2062	113	0	3.29	....	....	....	....	....	....	....
2002-03	Providence College	H-East	25	13	8	2	1440	71	0	2.96	....	....	....	....	....	....	....
2003-04	Cleveland Barons	AHL	27	14	9	3	1592	62	2	2.34	9	4	5	573	24	0	2.51
	Fresno Falcons	ECHL	12	5	5	0	654	34	1	3.12	....	....	....	....	....	....	....
2004-05	Cleveland Barons	AHL	43	17	23	1	2418	110	3	2.73	....	....	....	....	....	....	....

Hockey East Second All-Star Team (2001) • NCAA East Second All-American Team (2001)

SCHNEIDER, Cory (SHNIGH-duhr), KOHR-ee) VAN.

Goaltender. Catches left. 6'2", 195 lbs. Born, Salem, MA, March 18, 1986.
(Vancouver's 1st choice, 26th overall, in 2004 Entry Draft).

							Regular Season							Playoffs			
Season	**Club**	**League**	**GP**	**W**	**L**	**T**	**Mins**	**GA**	**SO**	**Avg**	**GP**	**W**	**L**	**Mins**	**GA**	**SO**	**Avg**
2002-03	Andover	High-MA	23	13	7	2	1385	39	3	1.69	....	....	....	....	....	....	....
2003-04	Andover	High-MA	24	17	5	2	1336	32	6	1.42	....	....	....	....	....	....	....
	USA U-18	USDP	12	11	1	0	679	21	1	1.86	....	....	....	....	....	....	....
2004-05	Boston College	H-East	18	13	1	4	1102	35	1	1.90	....	....	....	....	....	....	....

Hockey East All-Rookie Team (2005) (co-winners - Kevin Regan and Peter Vetri)

SCHWAB, Corey (SHWAHB, KOHR-ree)

Goaltender. Catches left. 6', 180 lbs. Born, North Battleford, Sask., November 4, 1970.
(New Jersey's 12th choice, 200th overall, in 1990 Entry Draft).

							Regular Season							Playoffs			
Season	**Club**	**League**	**GP**	**W**	**L**	**T**	**Mins**	**GA**	**SO**	**Avg**	**GP**	**W**	**L**	**Mins**	**GA**	**SO**	**Avg**
1988-89	Seattle	WHL	10	2	2	0	386	31	0	4.82	....	....	....	....	....	....	....
1989-90	Seattle	WHL	27	15	2	1	1150	69	1	3.60	3	0	0	49	2	0	2.45
1990-91	Seattle	WHL	*58	32	18	3	*3289	224	0	4.09	6	1	5	382	25	0	3.93
1991-92	Utica Devils	AHL	24	9	12	1	1322	95	0	4.31	....	....	....	....	....	....	....
	Cincinnati	ECHL	8	6	0	1	450	31	0	4.13	9	6	3	540	29	0	3.22
1992-93	Utica Devils	AHL	40	18	16	5	2387	169	*2	4.25	1	0	1	59	6	0	6.10
	Cincinnati	IHL	3	1	2	0	185	17	0	5.51	....	....	....	....	....	....	....
1993-94	Albany River Rats	AHL	51	27	21	3	3058	184	0	3.61	5	1	4	298	20	0	4.02
1994-95	Albany River Rats	AHL	45	25	10	9	2711	117	3	*2.59	7	6	1	425	19	0	2.68
1995-96	**New Jersey**	**NHL**	**10**	**0**	**3**	**0**	**331**	**12**	**0**	**2.18**	....	....	....	....	....	....	....
	Albany River Rats	AHL	5	3	2	0	299	13	0	2.61	....	....	....	....	....	....	....
1996-97	**Tampa Bay**	**NHL**	**31**	**11**	**12**	**1**	**1462**	**74**	**2**	**3.04**	....	....	....	....	....	....	....
1997-98	**Tampa Bay**	**NHL**	**16**	**2**	**9**	**1**	**821**	**40**	**1**	**2.92**	....	....	....	....	....	....	....
1998-99	**Tampa Bay**	**NHL**	**40**	**8**	**25**	**3**	**2146**	**126**	**0**	**3.52**	....	....	....	....	....	....	....
	Cleveland	IHL	8	1	6	1	477	31	0	3.90	....	....	....	....	....	....	....
99-2000	Orlando	IHL	16	9	4	2	868	31	1	2.14	....	....	....	....	....	....	....
	Vancouver	**NHL**	**6**	**2**	**1**	**1**	**269**	**16**	**0**	**3.57**	....	....	....	....	....	....	....
	Syracuse Crunch	AHL	12	7	5	0	720	42	0	3.50	4	1	3	246	11	1	2.69
2000-01	Kansas City Blades	IHL	50	22	24	1	2866	150	2	3.14	....	....	....	....	....	....	....
2001-02	**Toronto**	**NHL**	**30**	**12**	**10**	**5**	**1646**	**75**	**1**	**2.73**	**1**	**0**	**0**	**12**	**0**	**0**	**0.00**
2002-03♦	**New Jersey**	**NHL**	**11**	**5**	**3**	**1**	**614**	**15**	**1**	**1.47**	**2**	**0**	**0**	**28**	**0**	**0**	**0.00**
2003-04	**New Jersey**	**NHL**	**3**	**2**	**0**	**1**	**187**	**2**	**1**	**0.64**	....	....	....	....	....	....	....
2004-05							DID NOT PLAY										
	NHL Totals		**147**	**42**	**63**	**13**	**7476**	**360**	**6**	**2.89**	**3**	**0**	**0**	**40**	**0**	**0**	**0.00**

AHL Second All-Star Team (1995) • Harry "Hap" Holmes Memorial Award (fewest goals against – AHL) (1995) (shared with Mike Dunham) • Jack A. Butterfield Trophy (Playoff MVP – AHL) (1995) (co-winner - Mike Dunham)

Traded to **Tampa Bay** by **New Jersey** for Jeff Reese, Chicago's 2nd round choice (previously acquired, New Jersey selected Pierre Dagenais) in 1996 Entry Draft and Tampa Bay's 8th round choice (Jay Bertsch) in 1996 Entry Draft, June 22, 1996. Claimed by **Atlanta** from **Tampa Bay** in Expansion Draft, June 25, 1999. Traded to **Vancouver** by **Atlanta** for Vancouver's 4th round choice (Carl Mallette) in 2000 Entry Draft, October 29, 1999. Signed as a free agent by **Toronto**, October 1, 2001. Signed as a free agent by **New Jersey**, July 8, 2002. • Missed majority of the 2003-04 season recovering from groin injury suffered in game vs. NY Rangers, November 15, 2003.

SCHWARZ, Marek (SHWAHRTS, MAIR-ehk) ST.L.

Goaltender. Catches right. 5'11", 176 lbs. Born, Mlada Boleslav, Czech., April 1, 1986.
(St. Louis' 1st choice, 17th overall, in 2004 Entry Draft).

							Regular Season							Playoffs			
Season	**Club**	**League**	**GP**	**W**	**L**	**T**	**Mins**	**GA**	**SO**	**Avg**	**GP**	**W**	**L**	**Mins**	**GA**	**SO**	**Avg**
2000-01	Ml. Boleslav Jr.	CzRep-Jr.	45	....	....	....	1969	154	0	4.69	....	....	....	....	....	....	....
2001-02	Sparta Jr.	CzRep-Jr.	46	....	....	....	2692	86	9	1.92	6	....	....	368	16	0	2.61
2002-03	Sparta Jr.	CzRep-Jr.	34	....	....	....	1778	57	3	1.92	2	....	....	120	5	0	2.50
	HC Sparta Praha	CzRep	1	....	....	....	1	0	0	0.00	....	....	....	....	....	....	....
2003-04	Sparta Jr.	CzRep-Jr.	7	....	....	....	352	14	2	2.39	....	....	....	....	....	....	....
	Plzen	CzRep	10	....	....	....	603	33	0	3.28	....	....	....	....	....	....	....
	HC Sparta Praha	CzRep	8	....	....	....	335	20	0	3.58	....	....	....	....	....	....	....
	HC Ocelari Trinec	CzRep	5	....	....	....	280	12	0	2.57	....	....	....	....	....	....	....
	BK Mlada Boleslav	CzRep-2	1	....	....	....	63	6	0	5.71	....	....	....	....	....	....	....
2004-05	Vancouver Giants	WHL	56	26	24	4	3304	147	2	2.67	6	2	4	378	18	0	2.86

SCOTT, Travis (SKAWT, TRA-vihs)

Goaltender. Catches left. 6'2", 185 lbs. Born, Kanata, Ont., September 14, 1975.

							Regular Season							Playoffs			
Season	**Club**	**League**	**GP**	**W**	**L**	**T**	**Mins**	**GA**	**SO**	**Avg**	**GP**	**W**	**L**	**Mins**	**GA**	**SO**	**Avg**
1991-92	Nepean Raiders	CJHL	19	14	5	0	1065	71	1	4.00	....	....	....	....	....	....	....
1992-93	Nepean Raiders	CJHL	36	19	10	2	1968	133	0	4.05	....	....	....	....	....	....	....
1993-94	Windsor Spitfires	OHL	45	20	18	0	2312	158	1	4.10	4	0	4	240	16	0	4.00
1994-95	Windsor Spitfires	OHL	48	26	14	3	2644	147	3	3.34	3	0	1	94	6	1	3.83
1995-96	Oshawa Generals	OHL	31	15	9	4	1763	78	3	2.65	5	1	4	315	23	0	4.38
1996-97	Baton Rouge	ECHL	10	5	2	1	501	22	0	2.63	....	....	....	....	....	....	....
	Worcester IceCats	AHL	29	14	10	1	1482	75	1	3.04	....	....	....	....	....	....	....
1997-98	Baton Rouge	ECHL	36	14	11	6	1949	96	1	2.96	....	....	....	....	....	....	....
1998-99	Mississippi	ECHL	44	22	12	5	2337	112	1	2.88	*18	*14	4	*1252	42	3	2.01
99-2000	Lowell	AHL	46	15	23	3	2595	126	3	2.91	1	0	1	60	2	0	2.01
2000-01	**Los Angeles**	**NHL**	**1**	**0**	**0**	**0**	**25**	**3**	**0**	**7.20**	....	....	....	....	....	....	....
	Lowell	AHL	34	16	15	1	1977	83	2	2.52	4	1	2	209	7	1	2.01
2001-02	Manchester	AHL	39	21	12	3	2170	83	6	2.30	5	2	3	327	15	0	2.75
2002-03	Manchester	AHL	50	23	19	5	2829	116	4	2.46	3	0	2	148	9	0	3.65
2003-04	San Antonio	AHL	*64	26	31	6	3747	156	4	2.50	....	....	....	....	....	....	....
2004-05	San Antonio	AHL	59	18	28	4	3211	126	3	2.35	....	....	....	....	....	....	....
	NHL Totals		**1**	**0**	**0**	**0**	**25**	**3**	**0**	**7.20**	....	....	....	....	....	....	....

ECHL Playoff MVP (1999)

Signed as a free agent by **St. Louis**, December 30, 1996. Signed as a free agent by **Los Angeles**, February 18, 2000. Signed as a free agent by **Florida**, August 12, 2003.

SHANTZ, David (SHAWNTS, DAY-vihd) FLA.

Goaltender. Catches left. 6'1", 202 lbs. Born, Burlington, Ont., May 5, 1986.
(Florida's 2nd choice, 37th overall, in 2004 Entry Draft).

							Regular Season							Playoffs			
Season	**Club**	**League**	**GP**	**W**	**L**	**T**	**Mins**	**GA**	**SO**	**Avg**	**GP**	**W**	**L**	**Mins**	**GA**	**SO**	**Avg**
2002-03	Thorold	OJHL-B	36	30	3	3	2107	63	8	1.79	....	....	....	....	....	....	....
2003-04	Mississauga	OHL	43	21	18	3	2483	120	1	2.90	*24	12	12	*1449	49	*5	2.03
2004-05	Mississauga	OHL	27	10	11	3	1524	72	0	2.83	2	0	1	80	2	0	1.50

OHL All-Rookie Team (2004) • Canadian Major Junior All-Rookie Team (2004)

SHIELDS, Steve (SHEELDS, STEEV)

Goaltender. Catches left. 6'3", 215 lbs. Born, Toronto, Ont., July 19, 1972.
(Buffalo's 5th choice, 101st overall, in 1991 Entry Draft).

							Regular Season							Playoffs			
Season	**Club**	**League**	**GP**	**W**	**L**	**T**	**Mins**	**GA**	**SO**	**Avg**	**GP**	**W**	**L**	**Mins**	**GA**	**SO**	**Avg**
1989-90	St. Mary's Lincolns	OJHL-B	26	....	....	....	1512	121	0	4.80	....	....	....	....	....	....	....
1990-91	U. of Michigan	CCHA	37	26	6	3	1963	106	0	3.24	....	....	....	....	....	....	....
1991-92	U. of Michigan	CCHA	*37	*27	7	2	*2090	99	1	2.84	....	....	....	....	....	....	....
1992-93	U. of Michigan	CCHA	*39	*30	6	2	2027	75	2	*2.22	....	....	....	....	....	....	....
1993-94	U. of Michigan	CCHA	36	*28	6	1	1961	87	0	2.66	....	....	....	....	....	....	....
1994-95	Rochester	AHL	13	3	8	0	673	53	0	4.72	1	0	0	20	3	0	9.00
	South Carolina	ECHL	21	11	5	2	1158	52	2	2.69	3	0	2	144	11	0	4.58
1995-96	**Buffalo**	**NHL**	**2**	**1**	**0**	**0**	**75**	**4**	**0**	**3.20**	....	....	....	....	....	....	....
	Rochester	AHL	43	20	17	2	2357	140	1	3.56	*19	*15	3	*1127	47	1	2.50
1996-97	**Buffalo**	**NHL**	**13**	**3**	**8**	**2**	**789**	**39**	**0**	**2.97**	**10**	**4**	**6**	**570**	**26**	**1**	**2.74**
	Rochester	AHL	23	14	6	2	1331	60	1	2.70	....	....	....	....	....	....	....
1997-98	**Buffalo**	**NHL**	**16**	**3**	**6**	**4**	**785**	**37**	**0**	**2.83**	....	....	....	....	....	....	....
	Rochester	AHL	1	0	1	0	59	3	0	3.04	....	....	....	....	....	....	....
1998-99	**San Jose**	**NHL**	**37**	**15**	**11**	**8**	**2162**	**80**	**4**	**2.22**	**1**	**0**	**1**	**60**	**6**	**0**	**6.00**
99-2000	**San Jose**	**NHL**	**67**	**27**	**30**	**8**	**3797**	**162**	**4**	**2.56**	**12**	**5**	**7**	**696**	**36**	**0**	**3.10**
2000-01	**San Jose**	**NHL**	**21**	**6**	**8**	**5**	**1135**	**47**	**2**	**2.48**	....	....	....	....	....	....	....
2001-02	**Anaheim**	**NHL**	**33**	**9**	**20**	**2**	**1777**	**79**	**0**	**2.67**	....	....	....	....	....	....	....
2002-03	**Boston**	**NHL**	**36**	**12**	**13**	**9**	**2112**	**97**	**0**	**2.76**	**2**	**0**	**2**	**119**	**6**	**0**	**3.03**
2003-04	**Florida**	**NHL**	**16**	**3**	**6**	**1**	**732**	**42**	**0**	**3.44**	....	....	....	....	....	....	....
2004-05							DID NOT PLAY										
	NHL Totals		**241**	**79**	**102**	**39**	**13364**	**587**	**10**	**2.64**	**25**	**9**	**16**	**1445**	**74**	**1**	**3.07**

CCHA First All-Star Team (1993, 1994) • NCAA West Second All-American Team (1993, 1994)

Traded to **San Jose** by **Buffalo** with Buffalo's 4th round choice (Miroslav Zalesak) in 1998 Entry Draft for Kay Whitmore, Colorado's 2nd round choice (previously acquired, Buffalo selected Jaroslav Kristek) in 1998 Entry Draft and San Jose's 5th round choice (later traded to Columbus – Columbus selected Tyler Kolarik) in 2000 Entry Draft, June 18, 1998. Traded to **Anaheim** by **San Jose** with Jeff Friesen and San Jose's 2nd round choice (later traded to Dallas – Dallas selected Vojtech Polak) in 2003 Entry Draft for Teemu Selanne, March 5, 2001. Traded to **Boston** by **Anaheim** for Boston's 3rd round choice (Shane Hynes) in 2003 Entry Draft, June 25, 2002. Traded to **Florida** by **Boston** for future considerations, October 5, 2003.

SIDIKOV, Rustam (SIH-dih-kawf, ROOS-tuhm) NSH.

Goaltender. Catches left. 6', 158 lbs. Born, Moscow, USSR, July 5, 1985.
(Nashville's 10th choice, 133rd overall, in 2003 Entry Draft).

							Regular Season							Playoffs			
Season	**Club**	**League**	**GP**	**W**	**L**	**T**	**Mins**	**GA**	**SO**	**Avg**	**GP**	**W**	**L**	**Mins**	**GA**	**SO**	**Avg**
2000-01	CSKA Moscow 2	Russia-3	23	....	....	....	1204	50	....	2.50	....	....	....	103	4	0	2.33
2001-02	CSKA Moscow 2	Russia-3	1	....	....	....	60	5	0	5.00	....	....	....	....	....	....	....
2002-03	CSKA Moscow 2	Russia-3	2	....	....	....	120	2	0	1.00	....	....	....	....	....	....	....
2003-04	CSKA Moscow 2	Russia-3					STATISTICS NOT AVAILABLE										
2004-05	CSKA Moscow 2	Russia-3					STATISTICS NOT AVAILABLE										

SIGALET, Jordan (SIH-ga-leht, JOHR-duhn) BOS.

Goaltender. Catches left. 6'1", 180 lbs. Born, New Westminster, B.C., February 19, 1981.
(Boston's 6th choice, 209th overall, in 2001 Entry Draft).

							Regular Season							Playoffs			
Season	**Club**	**League**	**GP**	**W**	**L**	**T**	**Mins**	**GA**	**SO**	**Avg**	**GP**	**W**	**L**	**Mins**	**GA**	**SO**	**Avg**
99-2000	Victoria Salsa	BCHL	33	....	....	....	1980	108	0	3.28	....	....	....	....	....	....	....
2000-01	Victoria Salsa	BCHL	48	23	22	0	2820	142	0	3.03	18	12	5	1060	143	0	2.62
2001-02	Bowling Green	CCHA	13	2	6	2	657	38	0	3.47	....	....	....	....	....	....	....
2002-03	Bowling Green	CCHA	20	6	11	2	1208	66	1	3.28	....	....	....	....	....	....	....
2003-04	Bowling Green	CCHA	37	10	17	9	2210	101	2	2.74	....	....	....	....	....	....	....
2004-05	Bowling Green	CCHA	32	16	12	3	1849	89	1	2.89	....	....	....	....	....	....	....

CCHA First All-Star Team (2004) • CCHA Second All-Star Team (2005)

SKUDRA, Peter (SKOO-druh, PEE-tuhr)

Goaltender. Catches left. 6'1", 189 lbs. Born, Riga, Latvia, April 24, 1973.

							Regular Season							Playoffs			
Season	**Club**	**League**	**GP**	**W**	**L**	**T**	**Mins**	**GA**	**SO**	**Avg**	**GP**	**W**	**L**	**Mins**	**GA**	**SO**	**Avg**
1992-93	Pardaugava Riga	CIS	27	....	....	....	1498	74	....	2.96	1	....	....	60	5	0	5.00
1993-94	Pardaugava Riga	CIS	14	....	....	....	783	42	....	3.22	1	....	....	55	4	0	4.36
1994-95	Greensboro	ECHL	33	13	9	5	1612	113	0	4.20	6	2	2	341	28	0	4.92
	Memphis	CHL	2	0	1	0	80	8	0	6.00	....	....	....	....	....	....	....
1995-96	Erie Panthers	ECHL	12	3	8	1	681	47	0	4.14	....	....	....	....	....	....	....
	Johnstown Chiefs	ECHL	30	12	11	4	1657	98	0	3.55	....	....	....	....	....	....	....
1996-97	Hamilton Bulldogs	AHL	32	8	16	2	1615	101	0	3.75	....	....	....	....	....	....	....
	Johnstown Chiefs	ECHL	4	2	1	1	200	11	0	3.30	....	....	....	....	....	....	....
1997-98	**Pittsburgh**	**NHL**	**17**	**6**	**4**	**3**	**851**	**26**	**0**	**1.83**	....	....	....	....	....	....	....
	Houston Aeros	IHL	9	5	3	1	499	23	0	2.77	....	....	....	....	....	....	....
	Kansas City Blades	IHL	13	10	3	0	775	37	0	2.86	8	4	4	512	20	1	*2.34
1998-99	**Pittsburgh**	**NHL**	**37**	**15**	**11**	**5**	**1914**	**89**	**3**	**2.79**	....	....	....	....	....	....	....
99-2000	**Pittsburgh**	**NHL**	**20**	**5**	**7**	**3**	**922**	**48**	**1**	**3.12**	**1**	**0**	**0**	**20**	**1**	**0**	**3.00**
2000-01	**Buffalo**	**NHL**	**1**	**0**	**0**	**0**	**1**	**0**	**0**	**0.00**	....	....	....	....	....	....	....
	Rochester	AHL	2	2	0	0	120	5	0	2.50	....	....	....	....	....	....	....
	Boston	**NHL**	**25**	**6**	**12**	**1**	**1116**	**62**	**0**	**3.33**	....	....	....	....	....	....	....
	Providence Bruins	AHL	3	3	0	0	180	5	0	1.67	....	....	....	....	....	....	....
2001-02	**Vancouver**	**NHL**	**23**	**10**	**8**	**2**	**1166**	**47**	**1**	**2.42**	**2**	**0**	**1**	**96**	**5**	**0**	**3.13**
	Hartford Wolf Pack	AHL	3	2	1	0	179	8	0	2.69	....	....	....	....	....	....	....
2002-03	**Vancouver**	**NHL**	**23**	**9**	**5**	**6**	**1192**	**54**	**1**	**2.72**	....	....	....	....	....	....	....
	Manitoba Moose	AHL	1	1	0	0	60	3	0	3.00	....	....	....	....	....	....	....
2003-04	Ak Bars Kazan	Russia	9	....	....	....	545	20	0	2.20	....	....	....	....	....	....	....
	Voskresensk	Russia	34	....	....	....	2045	59	6	1.73	....	....	....	....	....	....	....

2004-05	Voskresensk	Russia	42	....	....	....	2339	97	3	2.49	....	....	....	....	....	....	....
	NHL Totals		**146**	**51**	**47**	**20**	**7162**	**326**	**6**	**2.73**	**3**	**0**	**1**	**116**	**6**	**0**	**3.10**

Signed as a free agent by **Pittsburgh**, September 25, 1997. Signed as a free agent by **Boston**, October 3, 2000. Claimed on waivers by **Buffalo** from **Boston**, October 6, 2000. • Played 27 seconds of game vs. Anaheim, October 20, 2000. Claimed on waivers by **Boston** from **Buffalo**, November 14, 2000. Signed as a free agent by **Vancouver**, November 7, 2001.

SMITH, Jason (SMIHTH, JAY-suhn) N.J.

Goaltender. Catches left. 6'1", 170 lbs. Born, St-Lambert, Que., July 17, 1985.
(New Jersey's 5th choice, 197th overall, in 2003 Entry Draft).

			Regular Season								Playoffs						
Season	Club	League	GP	W	L	T	Mins	GA	SO	Avg	GP	W	L	Mins	GA	SO	Avg
2002-03	Lennoxville	QJHL	29	22	4	1	1622	62	3	2.29	14	11	3	816	34	1	2.52
2003-04	Sacred Heart	AH	5	1	4	0	302	19	0	3.78	....	....	....	....	....	....	....
2004-05	Sacred Heart	AH	8	3	5	0	493	31	0	3.77	....	....	....	....	....	....	....

SMITH, Mike (SMIHTH, MIGHK) DAL.

Goaltender. Catches left. 6'3", 189 lbs. Born, Kingston, Ont., March 22, 1982.
(Dallas' 5th choice, 161st overall, in 2001 Entry Draft).

			Regular Season								Playoffs						
Season	Club	League	GP	W	L	T	Mins	GA	SO	Avg	GP	W	L	Mins	GA	SO	Avg
1998-99	Kingston	OPJHL	16	....	....	....	906	53	0	3.51	....	....	....	....	....	....	....
99-2000	Kingston	OHL	15	4	5	0	666	42	0	3.78	....	....	....	....	....	....	....
2000-01	Kingston	OHL	3	0	0	2	136	8	0	3.53	....	....	....	....	....	....	....
	Sudbury Wolves	OHL	43	22	13	7	2571	108	3	2.52	12	7	5	735	26	2	*2.12
2001-02	Sudbury Wolves	OHL	53	19	28	5	3082	157	3	3.06	5	1	4	302	15	0	2.98
2002-03	Utah Grizzlies	AHL	11	5	5	0	614	33	0	3.23	....	....	....	....	....	....	....
	Lexington	ECHL	27	11	10	4	1553	66	1	2.55	2	0	1	93	8	0	5.14
2003-04	Utah Grizzlies	AHL	21	8	11	0	1186	56	2	2.83	....	....	....	....	....	....	....
2004-05	Houston Aeros	AHL	45	19	17	3	2408	97	5	2.42	3	1	2	181	4	0	1.33

SNOW, Garth (SNOH, GAHRTH) NYI

Goaltender. Catches left. 6'3", 200 lbs. Born, Wrentham, MA, July 28, 1969.
(Quebec's 6th choice, 114th overall, in 1987 Entry Draft).

			Regular Season								Playoffs						
Season	Club	League	GP	W	L	T	Mins	GA	SO	Avg	GP	W	L	Mins	GA	SO	Avg
1986-87	Mount St. Charles	High-RI	30	....	....	....	1795	53	10	1.77	....	....	....	....	....	....	....
1987-88	Stratford Cullitons	OHA-B	30	20	6	0	1642	93	2	3.40	....	....	....	....	....	....	....
1988-89	University of Maine	H-East	5	2	2	0	241	14	1	3.49	....	....	....	....	....	....	....
1989-90	University of Maine	H-East	DID NOT PLAY – ACADEMICALLY INELIGIBLE														
1990-91	University of Maine	H-East	25	*18	4	0	1290	64	2	2.98	....	....	....	....	....	....	....
1991-92	University of Maine	H-East	31	*25	4	2	1792	73	*2	*2.44	....	....	....	....	....	....	....
1992-93	University of Maine	H-East	23	*21	0	1	1210	42	1	*2.08	....	....	....	....	....	....	....
1993-94	United States	Nat-Tm	23	13	5	3	1324	71	1	3.22	....	....	....	....	....	....	....
	United States	Olympics	5	1	3	1	299	17	0	3.41	....	....	....	....	....	....	....
	Quebec	**NHL**	**5**	**3**	**2**	**0**	**279**	**16**	**0**	**3.44**	....	....	....	....	....	....	....
	Cornwall Aces	AHL	16	6	5	3	927	51	0	3.30	13	8	5	790	42	0	3.19
1994-95	Cornwall Aces	AHL	*62	*32	20	7	*3558	162	3	2.73	8	4	3	402	14	*2	*2.09
	Quebec	**NHL**	**2**	**1**	**1**	**0**	**119**	**11**	**0**	**5.55**	**1**	**0**	**0**	**9**	**1**	**0**	**6.67**
1995-96	**Philadelphia**	**NHL**	**26**	**12**	**8**	**4**	**1437**	**69**	**0**	**2.88**	**1**	**0**	**0**	**1**	**0**	**0**	**0.00**
1996-97	**Philadelphia**	**NHL**	**35**	**14**	**8**	**8**	**1884**	**79**	**2**	**2.52**	**12**	**8**	**4**	**699**	**33**	**0**	**2.83**
1997-98	**Philadelphia**	**NHL**	**29**	**14**	**9**	**4**	**1651**	**67**	**1**	**2.43**	....	....	....	....	....	....	....
	Vancouver	**NHL**	**12**	**3**	**6**	**0**	**504**	**26**	**0**	**3.10**	....	....	....	....	....	....	....
1998-99	**Vancouver**	**NHL**	**65**	**20**	**31**	**8**	**3501**	**171**	**6**	**2.93**	....	....	....	....	....	....	....
99-2000	**Vancouver**	**NHL**	**32**	**10**	**15**	**3**	**1712**	**76**	**0**	**2.66**	....	....	....	....	....	....	....
2000-01	**Pittsburgh**	**NHL**	**35**	**14**	**15**	**4**	**2032**	**101**	**3**	**2.98**	....	....	....	....	....	....	....
	Wilkes-Barre	AHL	3	2	1	0	178	7	0	2.36	....	....	....	....	....	....	....
2001-02	**NY Islanders**	**NHL**	**25**	**10**	**7**	**2**	**1217**	**55**	**2**	**2.71**	**1**	**0**	**0**	**26**	**2**	**0**	**4.62**
2002-03	**NY Islanders**	**NHL**	**43**	**16**	**17**	**5**	**2390**	**92**	**1**	**2.31**	**5**	**1**	**4**	**305**	**12**	**1**	**2.36**
2003-04	**NY Islanders**	**NHL**	**39**	**14**	**15**	**5**	**2015**	**94**	**1**	**2.80**	....	....	....	....	....	....	....
2004-05	SKA St. Petersburg	Russia	16	....	....	....	893	41	1	2.75	....	....	....	....	....	....	....
	NHL Totals		**348**	**131**	**134**	**43**	**18741**	**857**	**16**	**2.74**	**20**	**9**	**8**	**1040**	**48**	**1**	**2.77**

Hockey East Second All-Star Team (1992, 1993) • NCAA Championship All-Tournament Team (1993)

Transferred to **Colorado** after **Quebec** franchise relocated, June 21, 1995. Traded to **Philadelphia** by **Colorado** for Philadelphia's 3rd (later traded to Washington – Washington selected Shawn McNeil) and 6th (Kai Fischer) round choices in 1996 Entry Draft, July 12, 1995. Traded to **Vancouver** by **Philadelphia** for Sean Burke, March 4, 1998. Signed as a free agent by **Pittsburgh**, October 10, 2000. Signed as a free agent by **NY Islanders**, July 14, 2001. Signed as a free agent by **St. Petersburg** (Russia), August 17, 2004.

SPRATT, James (SPRAT, JAYMZ) CGY.

Goaltender. Catches left. 6'1", 194 lbs. Born, Detroit, MI, November 10, 1985.
(Calgary's 9th choice, 213th overall, in 2004 Entry Draft).

			Regular Season								Playoffs						
Season	Club	League	GP	W	L	T	Mins	GA	SO	Avg	GP	W	L	Mins	GA	SO	Avg
2002-03	Sioux City	USHL	18	6	6	2	905	49	0	3.25	....	....	....	....	....	....	....
2003-04	Sioux City	USHL	34	19	6	5	1922	75	3	2.34	7	4	3	468	19	0	2.44
2004-05	Sioux City	USHL	42	24	11	3	2328	109	2	2.81	*13	*8	5	*752	32	*1	2.55

Signed Letter of Intent to attend **Bowling Green** (CCHA), May 26, 2005.

STALOCK, Alex (STAY-lahk, Al-ehx) S.J.

Goaltender. Catches left. 5'11", 170 lbs. Born, St. Paul, MN, July 28, 1987.
(San Jose's 3rd choice, 112th overall, in 2005 Entry Draft).

			Regular Season								Playoffs						
Season	Club	League	GP	W	L	T	Mins	GA	SO	Avg	GP	W	L	Mins	GA	SO	Avg
2003-04	South St. Paul	High-MN	31	23	7	1	....	....	....	2.20	....	....	....	....	....	....	....
2004-05	Cedar Rapids	USHL	32	19	9	3	1801	82	1	2.73	9	7	2	582	14	*1	*1.44

USHL Playoff MVP (2005)

Signed Letter of Intent to attend **Minnesota-Duluth** (WCHA), January 17, 2005.

STANA, Rastislav (STAN-ah, RAH-tih-slahv) WSH.

Goaltender. Catches left. 6'2", 184 lbs. Born, Kosice, Czech., January 10, 1980.
(Washington's 8th choice, 193rd overall, in 1998 Entry Draft).

			Regular Season								Playoffs						
Season	Club	League	GP	W	L	T	Mins	GA	SO	Avg	GP	W	L	Mins	GA	SO	Avg
1997-98	HC Kosice Jr.	Slovak-Jr.	32	....	....	....	1920	56	2	1.75	....	....	....	....	....	....	....
1998-99	Moose Jaw	WHL	36	21	14	1	2131	123	2	3.46	9	4	5	544	30	0	3.31
99-2000	Moose Jaw	WHL	14	4	9	0	730	48	0	3.95	....	....	....	....	....	....	....
	Calgary Hitmen	WHL	16	13	2	1	971	37	1	2.29	9	7	2	526	21	1	2.40
2000-01	Richmond	ECHL	38	15	16	2	2111	90	1	2.56	3	1	2	178	7	1	2.34
2001-02	Richmond	ECHL	36	20	12	3	2098	95	1	2.72	....	....	....	....	....	....	....
	Portland Pirates	AHL	3	1	2	0	180	11	0	3.66	....	....	....	....	....	....	....
	Slovakia	Olympics	1	1	0	0	60	1	0	1.00	....	....	....	....	....	....	....
2002-03	Portland Pirates	AHL	24	8	11	4	1355	49	2	2.17	1	0	1	59	3	0	3.08
2003-04	**Washington**	**NHL**	**6**	**1**	**2**	**0**	**211**	**11**	**0**	**3.13**	....	....	....	....	....	....	....
	Portland Pirates	AHL	24	14	5	4	1429	40	5	1.68	3	1	2	139	7	0	3.02
2004-05	Sodertalje SK	Sweden	45	....	....	....	2562	116	3	2.72	10	....	....	605	22	1	2.18
	NHL Totals		**6**	**1**	**2**	**0**	**211**	**11**	**0**	**3.13**	....	....	....	....	....	....	....

Signed as a free agent by **Sodertalje** (Sweden), May 26, 2004.

STEPHAN, Tobias (STEH-fan, toh-BEE-uhs) DAL.

Goaltender. Catches left. 6'3", 178 lbs. Born, Zurich, Switz., January 21, 1984.
(Dallas' 3rd choice, 34th overall, in 2002 Entry Draft).

			Regular Season								Playoffs						
Season	Club	League	GP	W	L	T	Mins	GA	SO	Avg	GP	W	L	Mins	GA	SO	Avg
2000-01	Kloten Flyers Jr.	Swiss-Jr.	STATISTICS NOT AVAILABLE														
2001-02	EHC Chur	Swiss	23	....	....	....	1396	80	0	3.44	10	....	....	604	39	0	3.87
2002-03	Kloten Flyers	Swiss	*44	....	....	....	2670	125	2	2.81	5	....	....	292	20	0	4.11
2003-04	Kloten Flyers	Swiss	26	....	....	....	1547	61	5	2.37	....	....	....	....	....	....	....
2004-05	Kloten Flyers	Swiss	*44	....	....	....	2580	123	4	2.86	5	....	....	301	11	0	2.19

STORR, Jamie (STOHR, JAY-mee) PHI.

Goaltender. Catches left. 6'2", 195 lbs. Born, Brampton, Ont., December 28, 1975.
(Los Angeles' 1st choice, 7th overall, in 1994 Entry Draft).

			Regular Season								Playoffs						
Season	Club	League	GP	W	L	T	Mins	GA	SO	Avg	GP	W	L	Mins	GA	SO	Avg
1990-91	Brampton Capitals	MTJHL	24	....	....	....	1145	91	0	4.77	15	....	....	885	60	0	4.07
1991-92	Owen Sound	OHL	34	11	16	1	1732	128	0	4.43	5	1	4	299	28	0	5.62
1992-93	Owen Sound	OHL	41	20	17	3	2362	180	0	4.57	8	4	4	454	35	0	4.63
1993-94	Owen Sound	OHL	35	21	11	1	2004	120	1	3.59	9	4	5	547	44	0	4.83
1994-95	Owen Sound	OHL	17	5	9	2	977	64	0	3.93	....	....	....	....	....	....	....
	Los Angeles	**NHL**	**5**	**1**	**3**	**1**	**263**	**17**	**0**	**3.88**	....	....	....	....	....	....	....
	Windsor Spitfires	OHL	4	3	1	0	241	8	1	1.99	10	6	3	520	34	1	3.92
1995-96	**Los Angeles**	**NHL**	**5**	**3**	**1**	**0**	**262**	**12**	**0**	**2.75**	....	....	....	....	....	....	....
	Phoenix	IHL	48	22	20	4	2711	139	2	3.08	2	1	1	118	4	1	2.03
1996-97	**Los Angeles**	**NHL**	**5**	**2**	**1**	**1**	**265**	**11**	**0**	**2.49**	....	....	....	....	....	....	....
	Phoenix	IHL	44	16	22	4	2441	147	0	3.61	....	....	....	....	....	....	....
1997-98	**Los Angeles**	**NHL**	**17**	**9**	**5**	**1**	**920**	**34**	**2**	**2.22**	**3**	**0**	**2**	**145**	**9**	**0**	**3.72**
	Long Beach	IHL	11	7	2	1	629	31	0	2.96	....	....	....	....	....	....	....
1998-99	**Los Angeles**	**NHL**	**28**	**12**	**12**	**2**	**1525**	**61**	**4**	**2.40**	....	....	....	....	....	....	....
99-2000	**Los Angeles**	**NHL**	**42**	**18**	**15**	**5**	**2206**	**93**	**1**	**2.53**	**1**	**0**	**1**	**36**	**2**	**0**	**3.33**
2000-01	**Los Angeles**	**NHL**	**45**	**19**	**18**	**6**	**2498**	**114**	**4**	**2.74**	....	....	....	....	....	....	....
2001-02	**Los Angeles**	**NHL**	**19**	**9**	**4**	**3**	**886**	**28**	**2**	**1.90**	**1**	**0**	**0**	**1**	**0**	**0**	**0.00**
2002-03	**Los Angeles**	**NHL**	**39**	**12**	**19**	**2**	**2027**	**86**	**3**	**2.55**	....	....	....	....	....	....	....
2003-04	**Carolina**	**NHL**	**14**	**0**	**8**	**2**	**660**	**32**	**0**	**2.91**	....	....	....	....	....	....	....
	Lowell	AHL	13	2	6	2	712	38	0	3.20	....	....	....	....	....	....	....
2004-05	Springfield Falcons	AHL	30	8	20	2	1697	91	0	3.22	....	....	....	....	....	....	....
	Utah Grizzlies	AHL	16	6	7	1	885	36	1	2.44	....	....	....	....	....	....	....
	NHL Totals		**219**	**85**	**86**	**23**	**11512**	**488**	**16**	**2.54**	**5**	**0**	**3**	**182**	**11**	**0**	**3.63**

OHL All-Rookie Team (1992) • OHL First All-Star Team (1994) • NHL All-Rookie Team (1998, 1999)

• Played 8 seconds of playoff game vs. Colorado, April 29, 2002. Signed as a free agent by **Carolina**, October 3, 2003. Signed as a free agent by **Springfield** (AHL), September 29, 2004. Signed as a free agent by **Philadelphia**, August 22, 2005.

TARASOV, Vadim (ta-RA-sahf, va-DEEM) MTL.

Goaltender. Catches left. 5'11", 187 lbs. Born, Ust-Kamenogorsk, USSR, December 31, 1976.
(Montreal's 9th choice, 196th overall, in 1999 Entry Draft).

			Regular Season								Playoffs						
Season	Club	League	GP	W	L	T	Mins	GA	SO	Avg	GP	W	L	Mins	GA	SO	Avg
1995-96	Novokuznetsk	CIS	26	....	....	....	1355	60	1	2.66	....	....	....	....	....	....	....
1996-97	Novokuznetsk	Russia	34	....	....	....	1971	87	0	2.65	....	....	....	....	....	....	....
1997-98	Novokuznetsk	Russia	23	....	....	....	1364	61	2	2.68	....	....	....	....	....	....	....
1998-99	Novokuznetsk	Russia	*41	....	....	....	*2346	56	*8	1.43	6	....	....	349	16	0	2.75
99-2000	Novokuznetsk	Russia	28	....	....	....	1583	66	1	2.50	14	....	....	791	26	1	1.97
2000-01	Novokuznetsk	Russia	33	....	....	....	1960	69	4	2.11	....	....	....	....	....	....	....
2001-02	Quebec Citadelles	AHL	14	7	4	2	801	42	0	3.15	....	....	....	....	....	....	....
2002-03	Novokuznetsk	Russia	29	....	....	....	1450	64	0	2.65	....	....	....	....	....	....	....
2003-04	Novokuznetsk	Russia	39	....	....	....	2165	63	4	1.75	3	....	....	169	9	0	3.20
2004-05	Novokuznetsk	Russia	35	....	....	....	1961	60	4	1.84	....	....	....	....	....	....	....

Russian League Best Goaltender (1999, 2000, 2001)

Signed as a free agent by **Novokuznetsk** (Russia) with Montreal retaining NHL rights, July 18, 2002.

TAYLOR, Daniel (TAY-luhr, DAN-yehl) L.A.

Goaltender. Catches left. 5'11", 179 lbs. Born, Plymouth, England, April 28, 1986.
(Los Angeles' 8th choice, 221st overall, in 2004 Entry Draft).

			Regular Season								Playoffs						
Season	Club	League	GP	W	L	T	Mins	GA	SO	Avg	GP	W	L	Mins	GA	SO	Avg
2002-03	Cumberland Grads	CJHL	23	13	3	0	1009	41	1	2.44	7	3	4	448	17	....	2.28
2003-04	Guelph Storm	OHL	26	16	4	3	1462	66	0	2.71	3	1	1	159	9	0	3.40
2004-05	Guelph Storm	OHL	31	13	14	3	1821	80	2	2.64	1	0	1	59	4	0	4.07

TELLQVIST, Mikael (TEHL-kvihst, MIGH-kuhl) TOR.

Goaltender. Catches left. 5'11", 194 lbs. Born, Sundbyberg, Sweden, September 19, 1979.
(Toronto's 3rd choice, 70th overall, in 2000 Entry Draft).

			Regular Season								Playoffs						
Season	Club	League	GP	W	L	T	Mins	GA	SO	Avg	GP	W	L	Mins	GA	SO	Avg
1997-98	Djurgarden Jr.	Swe-Jr.	23	....	....	....	1380	55	....	2.39	2	0	2	120	8	0	4.00
1998-99	Djurgarden	Sweden	3	1	2	0	124	8	0	3.87	4	....	....	240	11	0	2.75
	Djurgarden	EuroHL	3	2	1	0	180	8	....	2.33	....	....	....	....	....	....	....
99-2000	Huddinge IK	Sweden-2	11	4	7	0	660	33	....	3.30	....	....	....	....	....	....	....
	Djurgarden	Sweden	30	....	....	....	1909	66	2	*2.07	*13	....	....	*814	21	*3	*1.55
2000-01	Djurgarden	Sweden	43	....	....	....	2622	91	*5	*2.08	*16	....	....	*1006	45	*1	2.68
2001-02	St. John's	AHL	28	8	11	6	1521	79	0	3.12	1	1	0	15	0	0	0.00
	Sweden	Olympics	DID NOT PLAY – SPARE GOALTENDER														
2002-03	**Toronto**	**NHL**	**3**	**1**	**1**	**0**	**86**	**4**	**0**	**2.79**	....	....	....	....	....	....	....
	St. John's	AHL	47	17	25	3	2651	148	1	3.35	....	....	....	....	....	....	....
2003-04	**Toronto**	**NHL**	**11**	**5**	**3**	**2**	**647**	**31**	**0**	**2.87**	....	....	....	....	....	....	....
	St. John's	AHL	23	10	11	1	1343	59	1	2.64	....	....	....	....	....	....	....
2004-05	St. John's	AHL	45	24	16	4	2600	115	0	2.65	5	1	4	253	15	0	3.56
	NHL Totals		**14**	**6**	**4**	**2**	**733**	**35**	**0**	**2.86**	....	....	....	....	....	....	....

THEODORE, Jose (TEE-uh-dohr, joh-SAY) MTL.

Goaltender. Catches right. 5'11", 182 lbs. Born, Laval, Que., September 13, 1976.
(Montreal's 2nd choice, 44th overall, in 1994 Entry Draft).

			Regular Season								Playoffs						
Season	Club	League	GP	W	L	T	Mins	GA	SO	Avg	GP	W	L	Mins	GA	SO	Avg
1990-91	Richelieu	QAHA	42	....	....	....	2520	80	0	1.90	....	....	....	....	....	....	....
1991-92	Richelieu Riverains	QAAA	24	9	13	2	1440	96	0	3.99	5	2	3	295	26	0	5.28
1992-93	St-Jean Lynx	QMJHL	34	12	16	2	1776	112	0	3.78	3	0	2	175	11	0	3.77
1993-94	St-Jean Lynx	QMJHL	57	20	29	6	3225	194	0	3.61	5	1	4	296	18	0	3.65
1994-95	Hull Olympiques	QMJHL	*58	*32	22	2	*3348	193	5	3.46	*21	*15	6	*1263	59	*1	2.80
	Fredericton	AHL	....	....	....	....	....	....	....	....	1	0	1	60	3	0	3.00

1995-96	**Montreal**	**NHL**	**1**	**0**	**0**	**0**	**9**	**1**	**0**	**6.67**	....	....	....	....	....	....	....
	Hull Olympiques	QMJHL	48	33	11	2	2807	158	0	3.38	5	2	3	299	20	0	4.01
1996-97	**Montreal**	**NHL**	**16**	**5**	**6**	**2**	**821**	**53**	**0**	**3.87**	**2**	**1**	**1**	**168**	**7**	**0**	**2.50**
	Fredericton	AHL	26	12	12	0	1469	87	0	3.55	....	....	....	....	....	....	....
1997-98	Fredericton	AHL	53	20	23	8	3053	145	2	2.85	4	1	3	237	13	0	3.28
	Montreal	**NHL**	....	....	....	....	....	....	....	....	**3**	**0**	**1**	**120**	**1**	**0**	**0.50**
1998-99	**Montreal**	**NHL**	**18**	**4**	**12**	**0**	**913**	**50**	**1**	**3.29**	....	....	....	....	....	....	....
	Fredericton	AHL	27	12	13	2	1609	77	2	2.87	13	8	5	694	35	1	3.03
99-2000	**Montreal**	**NHL**	**30**	**12**	**13**	**2**	**1655**	**58**	**5**	**2.10**	....	....	....	....	....	....	....
2000-01	**Montreal**	**NHL**	**59**	**20**	**29**	**5**	**3298**	**141**	**2**	**2.57**	....	....	....	....	....	....	....
	Quebec Citadelles	AHL	3	3	0	0	180	9	0	3.00	....	....	....	....	....	....	....
2001-02	**Montreal**	**NHL**	**67**	**30**	**24**	**10**	**3864**	**136**	**7**	**2.11**	**12**	**6**	**6**	**686**	**35**	**0**	**3.06**
2002-03	**Montreal**	**NHL**	**57**	**20**	**31**	**6**	**3419**	**165**	**2**	**2.90**	....	....	....	....	....	....	....
2003-04	**Montreal**	**NHL**	**67**	**33**	**28**	**5**	**3961**	**150**	**6**	**2.27**	**11**	**4**	**7**	**678**	**27**	**1**	**2.39**
2004-05	Djurgarden	Sweden	17	....	....	....	1024	42	0	2.46	12	....	....	728	27	0	2.23
	NHL Totals		**315**	**124**	**143**	**30**	**17940**	**754**	**23**	**2.52**	**28**	**11**	**15**	**1652**	**70**	**1**	**2.54**

QMJHL Second All-Star Team (1995, 1996) • NHL Second All-Star Team (2002) • MBNA Roger Crozier Saving Grace Award (2002) • Vezina Trophy (2002) • Hart Trophy (2002)

Played in NHL All-Star Game (2002, 2004)

• Scored a goal vs. NY Islanders, January 2, 2001. Signed as a free agent by **Djurgarden** (Sweden), December 20, 2004.

THIBAULT, Jocelyn (TEE-boh, JAW-seh-lihn) PIT.

Goaltender. Catches left. 5'11", 169 lbs. Born, Montreal, Que., January 12, 1975.
(Quebec's 1st choice, 10th overall, in 1993 Entry Draft).

			Regular Season								Playoffs						
Season	**Club**	**League**	**GP**	**W**	**L**	**T**	**Mins**	**GA**	**SO**	**Avg**	**GP**	**W**	**L**	**Mins**	**GA**	**SO**	**Avg**
1990-91	Laval-Laurentides	QAAA	20	14	5	0	1178	78	1	3.94	5	2	3	300	20	0	4.00
1991-92	Trois-Rivieres	QMJHL	30	14	7	1	1496	77	0	3.09	3	1	1	110	4	0	2.19
1992-93	Sherbrooke	QMJHL	56	34	14	5	3190	159	3	2.99	15	9	6	882	57	0	3.87
1993-94	**Quebec**	**NHL**	**29**	**8**	**13**	**3**	**1504**	**83**	**0**	**3.31**	....	....	....	....	....	....	....
	Cornwall Aces	AHL	4	4	0	0	240	9	1	2.25	....	....	....	....	....	....	....
1994-95	Sherbrooke	QMJHL	13	6	6	1	776	38	1	2.94	....	....	....	....	....	....	....
	Quebec	**NHL**	**18**	**12**	**2**	**2**	**898**	**35**	**1**	**2.34**	**3**	**1**	**2**	**148**	**8**	**0**	**3.24**
1995-96	**Colorado**	**NHL**	**10**	**3**	**4**	**2**	**558**	**28**	**0**	**3.01**	....	....	....	....	....	....	....
	Montreal	**NHL**	**40**	**23**	**13**	**3**	**2334**	**110**	**3**	**2.83**	**6**	**2**	**4**	**311**	**18**	**0**	**3.47**
1996-97	**Montreal**	**NHL**	**61**	**22**	**24**	**11**	**3397**	**164**	**1**	**2.90**	**3**	**0**	**3**	**179**	**13**	**0**	**4.36**
1997-98	**Montreal**	**NHL**	**47**	**19**	**15**	**8**	**2652**	**109**	**2**	**2.47**	**2**	**0**	**0**	**43**	**4**	**0**	**5.58**
1998-99	**Montreal**	**NHL**	**10**	**3**	**4**	**2**	**529**	**23**	**1**	**2.61**	....	....	....	....	....	....	....
	Chicago	**NHL**	**52**	**21**	**26**	**5**	**3014**	**136**	**4**	**2.71**	....	....	....	....	....	....	....
99-2000	**Chicago**	**NHL**	**60**	**25**	**26**	**7**	**3438**	**158**	**3**	**2.76**	....	....	....	....	....	....	....
2000-01	**Chicago**	**NHL**	**66**	**27**	**32**	**7**	**3844**	**180**	**6**	**2.81**	....	....	....	....	....	....	....
2001-02	**Chicago**	**NHL**	**67**	**33**	**23**	**9**	**3838**	**159**	**6**	**2.49**	**3**	**1**	**2**	**159**	**7**	**0**	**2.64**
2002-03	**Chicago**	**NHL**	**62**	**26**	**28**	**7**	**3650**	**144**	**8**	**2.37**	....	....	....	....	....	....	....
2003-04	**Chicago**	**NHL**	**14**	**5**	**7**	**2**	**821**	**39**	**1**	**2.85**	....	....	....	....	....	....	....
2004-05							DID NOT PLAY										
	NHL Totals		**536**	**227**	**217**	**68**	**30477**	**1368**	**36**	**2.69**	**17**	**4**	**11**	**840**	**50**	**0**	**3.57**

QMJHL All-Rookie Team (1992) • QMJHL First All-Star Team (1993) • QMJHL MVP (1993) • Canadian Major Junior First All-Star Team (1993) • Canadian Major Junior Goaltender of the Year (1993)

Played in NHL All-Star Game (2003)

Transferred to **Colorado** after **Quebec** franchise relocated, June 21, 1995. Traded to **Montreal** by **Colorado** with Andrei Kovalenko and Martin Rucinsky for Patrick Roy and Mike Keane, December 6, 1995. Traded to **Chicago** by **Montreal** with Dave Manson and Brad Brown for Jeff Hackett, Eric Weinrich, Alain Nasreddine and Tampa Bay's 4th round choice (previously acquired, Montreal selected Chris Dyment) in 1999 Entry Draft, November 16, 1998. • Missed majority of 2003-04 season recovering from hip injury suffered in practice, November 9, 2003. Traded to **Pittsburgh** by **Chicago** for Pittsburgh's 4th round choice in 2006 Entry Draft, August 10, 2005.

THOMAS, Tim (TAW-mas, TIHM)

Goaltender. Catches left. 5'11", 181 lbs. Born, Flint, MI, April 15, 1974.
(Quebec's 11th choice, 217th overall, in 1994 Entry Draft).

			Regular Season								Playoffs						
Season	**Club**	**League**	**GP**	**W**	**L**	**T**	**Mins**	**GA**	**SO**	**Avg**	**GP**	**W**	**L**	**Mins**	**GA**	**SO**	**Avg**
1992-93	Davison High	High-MI	27	....	....	....	1580	87	....	3.30	....	....	....	....	....	....	....
1993-94	U. of Vermont	ECAC	*33	15	12	6	1864	94	0	3.03	....	....	....	....	....	....	....
1994-95	U. of Vermont	ECAC	34	18	13	2	2010	90	*4	*2.69	....	....	....	....	....	....	....
1995-96	U. of Vermont	ECAC	37	*26	7	4	*2254	88	*3	*2.34	....	....	....	....	....	....	....
1996-97	U. of Vermont	ECAC	36	22	11	3	2158	101	2	2.81	....	....	....	....	....	....	....
1997-98	HIFK Helsinki	Finland	18	13	4	1	1035	28	2	*1.62	*9	*9	0	*551	14	*3	*1.52
	Birmingham Bulls	ECHL	6	4	1	1	360	13	1	2.17	....	....	....	....	....	....	....
	Houston Aeros	IHL	1	0	1	0	59	4	0	4.01	....	....	....	....	....	....	....
1998-99	HIFK Helsinki	Finland	14	8	3	3	833	31	2	2.23	*11	7	4	*658	25	0	2.28
	Hamilton Bulldogs	AHL	15	6	8	0	837	45	0	3.23	....	....	....	....	....	....	....
99-2000	Detroit Vipers	IHL	36	10	21	3	2020	120	1	3.56	....	....	....	....	....	....	....
2000-01	AIK Solna	Sweden	43	....	....	....	2542	105	3	2.48	5	....	....	299	20	0	4.01
2001-02	Karpat Oulu	Finland	32	15	12	5	1937	79	4	2.45	3	1	2	180	12	0	4.00
2002-03	**Boston**	**NHL**	**4**	**3**	**1**	**0**	**220**	**11**	**0**	**3.00**	....	....	....	....	....	....	....
	Providence Bruins	AHL	35	18	12	5	2049	98	1	2.87	....	....	....	....	....	....	....
2003-04	Providence Bruins	AHL	43	20	16	6	2544	78	9	1.84	2	0	2	84	10	0	7.13
2004-05	Jokerit Helsinki	Finland	*54	*34	13	7	*3267	86	*15	*1.58	*12	8	4	*721	22	0	1.83
	NHL Totals		**4**	**3**	**1**	**0**	**220**	**11**	**0**	**3.00**	....	....	....	....	....	....	....

ECAC First All-Star Team (1995, 1996) • ECAC Goaltender of the Year (1996) • NCAA East Second All-American Team (1995) • NCAA East First All-American Team (1996)

Signed as a free agent by **Edmonton**, June 4, 1998. Signed as a free agent by **Boston**, August 8, 2002. Signed as a free agent by **Jokerit** (Finland), May 17, 2004.

THOMPSON, Billy (TAWM-suhn, BIHL-lee) OTT.

Goaltender. Catches left. 6'2", 200 lbs. Born, Saskatoon, Sask., September 24, 1982.
(Florida's 7th choice, 136th overall, in 2001 Entry Draft).

			Regular Season								Playoffs						
Season	**Club**	**League**	**GP**	**W**	**L**	**T**	**Mins**	**GA**	**SO**	**Avg**	**GP**	**W**	**L**	**Mins**	**GA**	**SO**	**Avg**
1997-98	Sask. Contacts	SMHL	23	14	5	3	1336	65	2	2.92	....	....	....	....	....	....	....
1998-99	Lebret Eagles	SJHL					STATISTICS NOT AVAILABLE										
99-2000	Estevan Bruins	SJHL	31	....	....	....	1763	132	1	4.49	5	1	3	328	17	0	3.11
	Prince George	WHL	1	0	1	0	60	5	0	5.00	....	....	....	....	....	....	....
2000-01	Prince George	WHL	57	24	24	3	3185	178	1	3.35	6	2	4	324	22	0	4.07
2001-02	Prince George	WHL	42	20	17	2	2375	108	2	2.73	7	3	4	402	21	0	3.13
2002-03	Prince George	WHL	50	20	26	0	2776	186	0	4.02	5	1	3	239	12	0	3.01
	Binghamton	AHL	1	1	0	0	60	5	0	5.00	....	....	....	....	....	....	....
2003-04	Binghamton	AHL	34	13	14	2	1725	83	2	2.89	....	....	....	....	....	....	....
2004-05	Binghamton	AHL	34	19	8	2	1869	76	1	2.44	....	....	....	....	....	....	....

WHL West Second All-Star Team (2003)

Traded to **Ottawa** by **Florida** with Greg Watson for Jani Hurme, October 1, 2002.

TOIVONEN, Hannu (TOI-voh-nuhn, HA-noo) BOS.

Goaltender. Catches left. 6'2", 191 lbs. Born, Kalvola, Finland, May 18, 1984.
(Boston's 1st choice, 29th overall, in 2002 Entry Draft).

			Regular Season								Playoffs						
Season	**Club**	**League**	**GP**	**W**	**L**	**T**	**Mins**	**GA**	**SO**	**Avg**	**GP**	**W**	**L**	**Mins**	**GA**	**SO**	**Avg**
2001-02	HPK Jr.	Finland-Jr.	31	15	12	4	1877	103	2	3.29	7	3	4	440	31	0	4.23
	HPK U18	Fin-U18	5	4	0	1	300	11	0	2.23	....	....	....	....	....	....	....
2002-03	HPK Hameenlinna	Finland	24	16	2	4	1432	54	2	2.26	2	1	1	118	3	1	1.53
2003-04	Providence Bruins	AHL	36	15	16	4	2162	83	2	2.30	0	0	0	0	0	0	0.00
2004-05	Providence Bruins	AHL	54	29	18	3	3017	103	7	2.05	17	10	7	1038	42	0	2.43

TOSKALA, Vesa (TAWS-kah-lah, VEH-sa) S.J.

Goaltender. Catches left. 5'10", 190 lbs. Born, Tampere, Finland, May 20, 1977.
(San Jose's 4th choice, 90th overall, in 1995 Entry Draft).

			Regular Season								Playoffs						
Season	**Club**	**League**	**GP**	**W**	**L**	**T**	**Mins**	**GA**	**SO**	**Avg**	**GP**	**W**	**L**	**Mins**	**GA**	**SO**	**Avg**
1994-95	Ilves Tampere Jr.	Finland-Jr.	17	....	....	....	956	36	....	2.26	....	....	....	....	....	....	....
1995-96	Ilves Tampere Jr.	Finland-Jr.	3	....	....	....	180	3	....	1.00	....	....	....	....	....	....	....
	KooVee Tampere	Finland-2	2	....	....	....	119	5	....	2.51	....	....	....	....	....	....	....
	Ilves Tampere	Finland	37	....	....	....	2073	109	1	3.16	2	....	....	78	11	....	8.49
1996-97	Ilves Tampere	Finland	40	22	12	5	2270	108	0	2.85	8	3	5	479	29	0	3.63
1997-98	Ilves Tampere	Finland	43	*26	13	3	2555	118	1	2.77	*9	6	3	519	18	1	2.08
1998-99	Ilves Tampere	Finland	33	21	12	0	1966	70	*5	2.14	4	1	3	248	14	0	3.39
99-2000	Farjestad	Sweden	44	....	....	....	2652	118	3	2.67	7	....	....	439	19	0	2.60
2000-01	Kentucky	AHL	44	22	13	5	2466	114	2	2.77	3	0	3	197	8	0	2.43
2001-02	**San Jose**	**NHL**	**1**	**0**	**0**	**0**	**10**	**0**	**0**	**0.00**	....	....	....	....	....	....	....
	Cleveland Barons	AHL	*62	19	33	7	*3574	178	3	2.99	....	....	....	....	....	....	....
2002-03	**San Jose**	**NHL**	**11**	**4**	**3**	**1**	**537**	**21**	**1**	**2.35**	....	....	....	....	....	....	....
	Cleveland Barons	AHL	49	15	30	2	2824	151	1	3.21	....	....	....	....	....	....	....
2003-04	**San Jose**	**NHL**	**28**	**12**	**8**	**4**	**1541**	**53**	**1**	**2.06**	....	....	....	....	....	....	....
2004-05	Ilves Tampere	Finland	3	0	1	2	186	8	0	2.58	6	3	3	358	19	0	3.19
	NHL Totals		**40**	**16**	**11**	**5**	**2088**	**74**	**2**	**2.13**	....	....	....	....	....	....	....

Signed as a free agent by **Ilves** (Finland), January 31, 2005.

TUGNUTT, Ron (TUHG-nuht, RAWN)

Goaltender. Catches left. 5'11", 160 lbs. Born, Scarborough, Ont., October 22, 1967.
(Quebec's 4th choice, 81st overall, in 1986 Entry Draft).

			Regular Season								Playoffs						
Season	**Club**	**League**	**GP**	**W**	**L**	**T**	**Mins**	**GA**	**SO**	**Avg**	**GP**	**W**	**L**	**Mins**	**GA**	**SO**	**Avg**
1983-84	Tor. Red Wings	MTHL	34	....	....	....	1690	91	3	2.67	....	....	....	....	....	....	....
	Weston Dukes	MTJHL	1	0	0	0	20	2	0	6.00	....	....	....	....	....	....	....
1984-85	Peterborough	OHL	18	7	4	2	938	59	0	3.77	....	....	....	....	....	....	....
1985-86	Peterborough	OHL	26	18	7	0	1543	74	1	2.88	3	2	0	133	6	0	2.71
1986-87	Peterborough	OHL	31	21	7	2	1891	88	2	*2.79	6	3	3	374	21	1	3.37
1987-88	**Quebec**	**NHL**	**6**	**2**	**3**	**0**	**284**	**16**	**0**	**3.38**	....	....	....	....	....	....	....
	Fredericton Express	AHL	34	20	9	4	1964	118	1	3.60	4	1	2	204	11	0	3.24
1988-89	**Quebec**	**NHL**	**26**	**10**	**10**	**3**	**1367**	**82**	**0**	**3.60**	....	....	....	....	....	....	....
	Halifax Citadels	AHL	24	14	7	2	1368	79	1	3.46	....	....	....	....	....	....	....
1989-90	**Quebec**	**NHL**	**35**	**5**	**24**	**3**	**1978**	**152**	**0**	**4.61**	....	....	....	....	....	....	....
	Halifax Citadels	AHL	6	1	5	0	366	23	0	3.77	....	....	....	....	....	....	....
1990-91	**Quebec**	**NHL**	**56**	**12**	**29**	**10**	**3144**	**212**	**0**	**4.05**	....	....	....	....	....	....	....
	Halifax Citadels	AHL	2	0	1	0	100	8	0	4.80	....	....	....	....	....	....	....
1991-92	**Quebec**	**NHL**	**30**	**6**	**17**	**3**	**1583**	**106**	**1**	**4.02**	....	....	....	....	....	....	....
	Halifax Citadels	AHL	8	3	3	1	447	30	0	4.03	....	....	....	....	....	....	....
	Edmonton	**NHL**	**3**	**1**	**1**	**0**	**124**	**10**	**0**	**4.84**	**2**	**0**	**0**	**60**	**3**	**0**	**3.00**
1992-93	**Edmonton**	**NHL**	**26**	**9**	**12**	**2**	**1338**	**93**	**0**	**4.17**	....	....	....	....	....	....	....
1993-94	**Anaheim**	**NHL**	**28**	**10**	**15**	**1**	**1520**	**76**	**1**	**3.00**	....	....	....	....	....	....	....
	Montreal	**NHL**	**8**	**2**	**3**	**1**	**378**	**24**	**0**	**3.81**	**1**	**0**	**1**	**59**	**5**	**0**	**5.08**
1994-95	**Montreal**	**NHL**	**7**	**1**	**3**	**1**	**346**	**18**	**0**	**3.12**	....	....	....	....	....	....	....
1995-96	Portland Pirates	AHL	58	21	23	6	3068	171	2	3.34	13	7	6	782	36	1	2.76
1996-97	**Ottawa**	**NHL**	**37**	**17**	**15**	**1**	**1991**	**93**	**3**	**2.80**	**7**	**3**	**4**	**425**	**14**	**1**	**1.98**
1997-98	**Ottawa**	**NHL**	**42**	**15**	**14**	**8**	**2236**	**84**	**3**	**2.25**	**2**	**0**	**1**	**74**	**6**	**0**	**4.86**
1998-99	**Ottawa**	**NHL**	**43**	**22**	**10**	**8**	**2508**	**75**	**3**	***1.79**	**2**	**0**	**2**	**118**	**6**	**0**	**3.05**
99-2000	**Ottawa**	**NHL**	**44**	**18**	**12**	**8**	**2435**	**103**	**4**	**2.54**	....	....	....	....	....	....	....
	Pittsburgh	**NHL**	**7**	**4**	**2**	**0**	**374**	**15**	**0**	**2.41**	**11**	**6**	**5**	**746**	**22**	**2**	**1.77**
2000-01	**Columbus**	**NHL**	**53**	**22**	**25**	**5**	**3129**	**127**	**4**	**2.44**	....	....	....	....	....	....	....
2001-02	**Columbus**	**NHL**	**44**	**12**	**27**	**3**	**2502**	**119**	**2**	**2.85**	....	....	....	....	....	....	....
2002-03	**Dallas**	**NHL**	**31**	**15**	**10**	**5**	**1701**	**70**	**4**	**2.47**	....	....	....	....	....	....	....
	Utah Grizzlies	AHL	5	1	3	1	281	14	0	2.99	....	....	....	....	....	....	....
2003-04	**Dallas**	**NHL**	**11**	**3**	**7**	**0**	**548**	**22**	**1**	**2.41**	....	....	....	....	....	....	....
	Utah Grizzlies	AHL	5	1	3	1	281	14	0	2.99	....	....	....	....	....	....	....
2004-05							DID NOT PLAY										
	NHL Totals		**537**	**186**	**239**	**62**	**29486**	**1497**	**26**	**3.05**	**25**	**9**	**13**	**1482**	**56**	**3**	**2.27**

OHL First All-Star Team (1987)

Played in NHL All-Star Game (1999)

Traded to **Edmonton** by **Quebec** with Brad Zavisha for Martin Rucinsky, March 10, 1992. Claimed by **Anaheim** from **Edmonton** in Expansion Draft, June 24, 1993. Traded to **Montreal** by **Anaheim** for Stephan Lebeau, February 20, 1994. Signed as a free agent by **Washington**, September 25, 1995. Signed as a free agent by **Ottawa**, August 14, 1996. Traded to **Pittsburgh** by **Ottawa** with Janne Laukkanen for Tom Barrasso, March 14, 2000. Signed as a free agent by **Columbus**, July 4, 2000. Traded to **Dallas** by **Columbus** with Columbus' 2nd round choice (Janos Vas) in 2002 Entry Draft for New Jersey's 1st round choice (previously acquired, later traded to Buffalo – Buffalo selected Dan Paille) in 2002 Entry Draft, June 18, 2002. • Missed majority of 2003-04 season recovering from knee (December 2, 2003 in practice) and groin (January 2, 2004 vs. Phoenix) injuries.

TURCO, Marty (TUHR-koh, MAHR-tee) DAL.

Goaltender. Catches left. 5'11", 183 lbs. Born, Sault Ste. Marie, Ont., August 13, 1975.
(Dallas' 4th choice, 124th overall, in 1994 Entry Draft).

			Regular Season								Playoffs						
Season	**Club**	**League**	**GP**	**W**	**L**	**T**	**Mins**	**GA**	**SO**	**Avg**	**GP**	**W**	**L**	**Mins**	**GA**	**SO**	**Avg**
1993-94	Cambridge	OJHL-B	34	19	10	3	1973	114	0	3.47	....	....	....	....	....	....	....
1994-95	U. of Michigan	CCHA	37	*27	7	1	2063	95	1	2.76	....	....	....	....	....	....	....
1995-96	U. of Michigan	CCHA	*42	*34	7	1	*2335	84	*5	*2.16	....	....	....	....	....	....	....
1996-97	U. of Michigan	CCHA	*41	*33	4	4	*2296	87	*4	*2.27	....	....	....	....	....	....	....
1997-98	U. of Michigan	CCHA	*45	*33	10	1	*2640	95	4	2.16	....	....	....	....	....	....	....
1998-99	Michigan K-Wings	IHL	54	24	17	10	3127	136	1	2.61	5	2	3	300	14	0	2.80
99-2000	Michigan K-Wings	IHL	60	23	27	*7	3399	139	*7	2.45	....	....	....	....	....	....	....
2000-01	**Dallas**	**NHL**	**26**	**13**	**6**	**1**	**1266**	**40**	**3**	***1.90**	....	....	....	....	....	....	....
2001-02	**Dallas**	**NHL**	**31**	**15**	**6**	**2**	**1519**	**53**	**2**	**2.09**	....	....	....	....	....	....	....
2002-03	**Dallas**	**NHL**	**55**	**31**	**10**	**10**	**3203**	**92**	**7**	***1.72**	**12**	**6**	**6**	**798**	**25**	**0**	**1.88**
2003-04	**Dallas**	**NHL**	**73**	**37**	**21**	**13**	**4359**	**144**	**9**	**1.98**	**5**	**1**	**4**	**325**	**18**	**0**	**3.32**

2004-05	Djurgarden	Sweden	6	....	....	....	356	12	1	2.02	....	....	....	....	....	....	....
	NHL Totals		**185**	**96**	**43**	**26**	**10347**	**329**	**21**	**1.91**	**17**	**7**	**10**	**1123**	**43**	**0**	**2.30**

CCHA Rookie of the Year (1995) • NCAA Championship All-Tournament Team (1996, 1998) • CCHA First All-Star Team (1997) • NCAA West First All-American Team (1997) • CCHA Second All-Star Team (1998) • NCAA Championship Tournament MVP (1998) • Garry F. Longman Memorial Trophy (Rookie of the Year – IHL) (1999) • MBNA Roger Crozier Saving Grace Award (2001, 2003) • NHL Second All-Star Team (2003)

Played in NHL All-Star Game (2003, 2004)

Signed as a free agent by **Djurgarden** (Sweden), November 13, 2004.

TURPLE, Dan (TUHR-puhl, DAN) ATL.

Goaltender. Catches left. 6'5", 220 lbs. Born, Oakville, Ont., January 1, 1985.
(Atlanta's 6th choice, 186th overall, in 2004 Entry Draft).

			Regular Season								Playoffs						
Season	**Club**	**League**	**GP**	**W**	**L**	**T**	**Mins**	**GA**	**SO**	**Avg**	**GP**	**W**	**L**	**Mins**	**GA**	**SO**	**Avg**
2002-03	Kingston	OHL	12	2	8	0	449	42	0	5.61	....	....	....	....	....	....	....
2003-04	Kingston	OHL	9	4	4	1	534	29	0	3.26	....	....	....	....	....	....	....
	Oshawa Generals	OHL	35	20	7	3	1843	81	2	2.64	7	3	4	443	19	1	2.57
2004-05	Oshawa Generals	OHL	10	4	4	0	469	29	0	3.71	....	....	....	....	....	....	....
	Kitchener Rangers	OHL	40	17	16	5	2335	92	3	2.36	3	0	2	162	9	0	3.33

UNDERHILL, Matt (UHN-duhr-hihl, MAT)

Goaltender. Catches left. 6'2", 195 lbs. Born, Merritt, B.C., September 16, 1979.
(Calgary's 8th choice, 170th overall, in 1999 Entry Draft).

			Regular Season								Playoffs						
Season	**Club**	**League**	**GP**	**W**	**L**	**T**	**Mins**	**GA**	**SO**	**Avg**	**GP**	**W**	**L**	**Mins**	**GA**	**SO**	**Avg**
1997-98	Notre Dame	SJHL	43	18	22	3	2573	132	2	3.07	....	....	....	....	....	....	....
1998-99	Cornell Big Red	ECAC	25	7	10	4	1320	65	1	2.95	....	....	....	....	....	....	....
99-2000	Cornell Big Red	ECAC	18	8	7	1	912	44	1	2.89	....	....	....	....	....	....	....
2000-01	Cornell Big Red	ECAC	25	13	8	3	1504	47	1	1.88	....	....	....	....	....	....	....
2001-02	Cornell Big Red	ECAC	21	14	6	1	1334	40	3	1.80	....	....	....	....	....	....	....
2002-03	Pee Dee Pride	ECHL	33	16	13	2	1878	88	0	2.81	....	....	....	....	....	....	....
	Providence Bruins	AHL	7	3	3	1	429	22	0	3.08	....	....	....	....	....	....	....
2003-04	Florence Pride	ECHL	29	10	14	4	1686	97	1	3.45	....	....	....	....	....	....	....
	Manchester	AHL	4	2	2	0	186	9	0	2.90	....	....	....	....	....	....	....
	Chicago	**NHL**	**1**	**0**	**1**	**0**	**61**	**4**	**0**	**3.93**	....	....	....	....	....	....	....
	Norfolk Admirals	AHL	1	0	0	0	20	0	0	0.00	....	....	....	....	....	....	....
2004-05	Mississippi	ECHL	24	13	8	3	1450	64	3	2.65	....	....	....	....	....	....	....
	St. John's	AHL	1	0	0	1	39	0	0	0.00	....	....	....	....	....	....	....
	Providence Bruins	AHL	5	1	2	1	244	12	1	2.95	....	....	....	....	....	....	....
	Alaska Aces	ECHL	3	3	0	0	180	6	0	2.00	3	1	1	145	8	0	3.31
	NHL Totals		**1**	**0**	**1**	**0**	**61**	**4**	**0**	**3.93**	....	....	....	....	....	....	....

ECAC First All-Star Team (2002) • ECAC Goaltender of the Year (2002)

Signed as a free agent by **Pee Dee** (ECHL), August 13, 2002. Signed as a free agent by **Chicago**, March 4, 2004. Signed as a free agent by **Mississippi** (ECHL), November 3, 2004. Signed to a PTO (tryout) contract by **St. John's** (AHL), February 3, 2005. Signed to a PTO (tryout) contract by **Providence** (AHL), February 21, 2005. Traded to **Alaska** (ECHL) by **Mississippi** (ECHL) for Lance Mayes and future considerations, March 22, 2005.

VALENT, Michal (VAH-lehnt, MEE-khahl) BUF.

Goaltender. Catches left. 6'2", 176 lbs. Born, Martin, Czech., March 5, 1986.
(Buffalo's 4th choice, 145th overall, in 2004 Entry Draft).

			Regular Season								Playoffs						
Season	**Club**	**League**	**GP**	**W**	**L**	**T**	**Mins**	**GA**	**SO**	**Avg**	**GP**	**W**	**L**	**Mins**	**GA**	**SO**	**Avg**
2002-03	MHC Martin U18	Svk-U18	24	....	....	....	1343	48	3	2.14	....	....	....	....	....	....	....
2003-04	MHC Martin Jr.	Slovak-Jr.	38	....	....	....	2188	118	1	3.24	....	....	....	....	....	....	....
2004-05	Sparta Jr.	CzRep-Jr.	24	....	....	....	1293	43	3	2.00	7	....	....	420	15	1	2.14
	Nymburk	CzRep-3	1	....	....	....	60	0	1	0.00	....	....	....	....	....	....	....

VALIQUETTE, Stephen (val-ih-KEHT, STEE-vehn)

Goaltender. Catches left. 6'5", 205 lbs. Born, Etobicoke, Ont., August 20, 1977.
(Los Angeles' 8th choice, 190th overall, in 1996 Entry Draft).

			Regular Season								Playoffs						
Season	**Club**	**League**	**GP**	**W**	**L**	**T**	**Mins**	**GA**	**SO**	**Avg**	**GP**	**W**	**L**	**Mins**	**GA**	**SO**	**Avg**
1993-94	Burlington	OPJHL	30	....	....	....	1663	112	1	4.04	....	....	....	....	....	....	....
1994-95	Rayside-Balfour	NOJHA	2	0	2	0	89	12	0	8.09	....	....	....	....	....	....	....
	Smiths Falls Bears	CJHL	21	10	8	3	1275	75	0	3.53	....	....	....	....	....	....	....
	Sudbury Wolves	OHL	4	2	0	0	138	6	0	2.61	....	....	....	....	....	....	....
1995-96	Sudbury Wolves	OHL	39	13	16	2	1887	123	0	3.91	....	....	....	....	....	....	....
1996-97	Sudbury Wolves	OHL	*61	21	29	7	3311	232	1	4.20	....	....	....	....	....	....	....
	Dayton Bombers	ECHL	3	1	0	0	89	6	0	4.03	2	1	1	118	5	0	2.54
1997-98	Sudbury Wolves	OHL	14	5	7	1	807	50	0	3.72	....	....	....	....	....	....	....
	Erie Otters	OHL	28	16	7	3	1525	65	3	2.56	7	3	4	467	15	1	1.93
1998-99	Hampton Roads	ECHL	31	18	7	3	1713	84	1	2.94	2	0	1	60	7	0	7.00
	Lowell	AHL	1	0	1	0	59	3	0	3.05	....	....	....	....	....	....	....
99-2000	**NY Islanders**	**NHL**	**6**	**2**	**0**	**0**	**193**	**6**	**0**	**1.87**	....	....	....	....	....	....	....
	Lowell	AHL	14	8	5	0	727	36	0	2.97	....	....	....	....	....	....	....
	Providence Bruins	AHL	1	1	0	0	60	3	0	3.00	....	....	....	....	....	....	....
	Trenton Titans	ECHL	12	5	6	1	692	36	1	3.12	....	....	....	....	....	....	....
2000-01	Springfield Falcons	AHL	20	7	10	1	1066	54	0	3.04	....	....	....	....	....	....	....
2001-02	Bridgeport	AHL	20	10	5	1	1071	45	2	2.52	1	0	0	18	1	0	3.30
2002-03	Bridgeport	AHL	34	15	14	3	1962	86	2	2.63	4	3	1	253	9	0	2.13
2003-04	**Edmonton**	**NHL**	**1**	**0**	**0**	**0**	**14**	**2**	**0**	**8.57**	....	....	....	....	....	....	....
	Toronto	AHL	35	14	14	5	2064	89	2	2.59	....	....	....	....	....	....	....
	NY Rangers	**NHL**	**2**	**1**	**1**	**0**	**120**	**6**	**0**	**3.00**	....	....	....	....	....	....	....
	Hartford Wolf Pack	AHL	7	2	4	1	400	15	1	2.25	1	0	0	11	0	0	0.00
2004-05	Hartford Wolf Pack	AHL	35	19	11	1	1900	56	7	*1.77	2	1	1	118	4	0	2.03
	NHL Totals		**9**	**3**	**1**	**0**	**327**	**14**	**0**	**2.57**	....	....	....	....	....	....	....

Shared Harry "Hap" Holmes Memorial Trophy (fewest goals against - AHL) with Jason LaBarbera (2005)

Signed as a free agent by **NY Islanders**, August 18, 1998. Signed as a free agent by **Edmonton**, July 20, 2003. Claimed by **Florida** from **Edmonton** in Waiver Draft, October 3, 2003. Claimed on waivers by **Edmonton** from **Florida**, October 9, 2003. Traded to **NY Rangers** by **Edmonton** with Dwight Helminen, Edmonton's 2nd round compensatory choice (Dane Byers) in 2004 Entry Draft and future considerations for Petr Nedved and Jussi Markkanen, March 3, 2004. Signed as a free agent by **Yaroslavl** (Russia), April 26, 2005.

VINCENT, Alexandre (VIHN-sihnt, al-ehx-AHN-druh) VAN.

Goaltender. Catches left. 6'4", 193 lbs. Born, Drummondville, Que., December 11, 1986.
(Vancouver's 3rd choice, 114th overall, in 2005 Entry Draft).

			Regular Season								Playoffs						
Season	**Club**	**League**	**GP**	**W**	**L**	**T**	**Mins**	**GA**	**SO**	**Avg**	**GP**	**W**	**L**	**Mins**	**GA**	**SO**	**Avg**
2001-02	Cap-d-Madeleine	QAAA	26	12	9	1	1264	85	0	4.04	....	....	....	....	....	....	....
2002-03	Jonquiere Elites	QAAA	31	7	17	2	1567	107	0	4.10	....	....	....	....	....	....	....
2003-04	Chicoutimi	QMJHL	34	11	11	1	1489	78	3	3.14	5	0	0	146	9	0	3.69
2004-05	Chicoutimi	QMJHL	49	24	13	4	2591	130	2	3.01	*14	7	6	765	40	*1	3.14

VOKOUN, Tomas (voh-KOON, TAW-mas) NSH.

Goaltender. Catches right. 6', 195 lbs. Born, Karlovy Vary, Czech., July 2, 1976.
(Montreal's 11th choice, 226th overall, in 1994 Entry Draft).

			Regular Season								Playoffs						
Season	**Club**	**League**	**GP**	**W**	**L**	**T**	**Mins**	**GA**	**SO**	**Avg**	**GP**	**W**	**L**	**Mins**	**GA**	**SO**	**Avg**
1993-94	HC Kladno	CzRep	1	0	0	0	20	2	0	6.01	....	....	....	....	....	....	....
1994-95	HC Kladno	CzRep	26	....	....	....	1368	70	....	3.07	5	....	....	240	19	....	4.75
1995-96	Wheeling	ECHL	35	20	10	2	1912	117	0	3.67	7	4	3	436	19	0	2.61
	Fredericton	AHL	....	....	....	....	....	....	....	....	1	0	1	59	4	0	4.09
1996-97	**Montreal**	**NHL**	**1**	**0**	**0**	**0**	**20**	**4**	**0**	**12.00**	....	....	....	....	....	....	....
	Fredericton	AHL	47	12	26	7	2645	154	2	3.49	....	....	....	....	....	....	....
1997-98	Fredericton	AHL	31	13	13	2	1735	90	0	3.11	....	....	....	....	....	....	....
1998-99	**Nashville**	**NHL**	**37**	**12**	**18**	**4**	**1954**	**96**	**1**	**2.95**	....	....	....	....	....	....	....
	Milwaukee	IHL	9	3	2	4	539	22	1	2.45	2	0	2	149	8	0	3.22
99-2000	**Nashville**	**NHL**	**33**	**9**	**20**	**1**	**1879**	**87**	**1**	**2.78**	....	....	....	....	....	....	....
	Milwaukee	IHL	7	5	2	0	364	17	0	2.80	....	....	....	....	....	....	....
2000-01	**Nashville**	**NHL**	**37**	**13**	**17**	**5**	**2088**	**85**	**2**	**2.44**	....	....	....	....	....	....	....
2001-02	**Nashville**	**NHL**	**29**	**5**	**14**	**4**	**1471**	**66**	**2**	**2.69**	....	....	....	....	....	....	....
2002-03	**Nashville**	**NHL**	**69**	**25**	**31**	**11**	**3974**	**146**	**3**	**2.20**	....	....	....	....	....	....	....
2003-04	**Nashville**	**NHL**	**73**	**34**	**29**	**10**	**4221**	**178**	**3**	**2.53**	**6**	**2**	**4**	**356**	**12**	**1**	**2.02**
2004-05	Znojmo	CzRep	27	....	....	....	1599	69	3	2.59	....	....	....	....	....	....	....
	HIFK Helsinki	Finland	19	11	4	4	1149	35	2	1.83	4	0	3	205	12	0	3.51
	NHL Totals		**279**	**98**	**129**	**35**	**15607**	**662**	**12**	**2.55**	**6**	**2**	**4**	**356**	**12**	**1**	**2.02**

Played in NHL All-Star Game (2004)

Claimed by **Nashville** from **Montreal** in Expansion Draft, June 26, 1998. Signed as a free agent by **Znojmo** (CzRep), September 6, 2004. Signed as a free agent by **HIFK** (Finland), December 20, 2004.

WARD, Cam (WOHRD, KAM) CAR.

Goaltender. Catches left. 6', 176 lbs. Born, Sherwood Park, Alta., February 29, 1984.
(Carolina's 1st choice, 25th overall, in 2002 Entry Draft).

			Regular Season								Playoffs						
Season	**Club**	**League**	**GP**	**W**	**L**	**T**	**Mins**	**GA**	**SO**	**Avg**	**GP**	**W**	**L**	**Mins**	**GA**	**SO**	**Avg**
1998-99	Sherwood Park	ABHL	24	13	7	4	1403	85	0	3.64	....	....	....	....	....	....	....
99-2000	Sherwood Park	AMHL	20	9	5	1	1194	71	0	3.57	7	4	3	262	22	0	3.57
2000-01	Sherwood Park	AMHL	25	14	6	3	1449	70	0	2.90	....	....	....	....	....	....	....
	Red Deer Rebels	WHL	1	1	0	0	60	0	1	0.00	....	....	....	....	....	....	....
2001-02	Red Deer Rebels	WHL	46	30	11	4	2694	102	1	*2.27	*23	14	9	*1502	53	*2	2.12
2002-03	Red Deer Rebels	WHL	57	*40	13	3	3368	118	5	2.10	*23	14	9	*1407	49	3	2.09
2003-04	Red Deer Rebels	WHL	56	31	16	8	3338	114	4	2.05	19	10	9	1200	37	3	1.85
2004-05	Lowell	AHL	50	27	17	3	2829	94	6	1.99	11	5	6	664	28	2	2.53

WHL East First All-Star Team (2002, 2004) • WHL East Second All-Star Team (2003) • WHL Goaltender of the Year (2002, 2004) • WHL Player of the Year (2004) • Canadian Major Junior First All-Star Team (2004) • Canadian Major Junior Goaltender of the Year (2004) • AHL All-Rookie Team (2005)

WEEKES, Kevin (WEEKS, KEH-vihn) NYR

Goaltender. Catches left. 6', 195 lbs. Born, Toronto, Ont., April 4, 1975.
(Florida's 2nd choice, 41st overall, in 1993 Entry Draft).

			Regular Season								Playoffs						
Season	**Club**	**League**	**GP**	**W**	**L**	**T**	**Mins**	**GA**	**SO**	**Avg**	**GP**	**W**	**L**	**Mins**	**GA**	**SO**	**Avg**
1990-91	Tor. Red Wings	MTHL	STATISTICS NOT AVAILABLE														
	St. Mike's B's	MTJHL	1	0	0	0	41	1	0	1.46	....	....	....	....	....	....	....
1991-92	Tor. Red Wings	MTHL	35	....	....	....	1575	68	4	1.94	....	....	....	....	....	....	....
	St. Mike's B's	MTJHL	2	0	1	1	127	11	0	5.20	4	1	2	214	15	1	4.21
1992-93	Owen Sound	OHL	29	9	12	5	1645	143	0	5.22	1	0	0	26	5	0	11.50
1993-94	Owen Sound	OHL	34	13	19	1	1974	158	0	4.80	....	....	....	....	....	....	....
1994-95	Ottawa 67's	OHL	41	13	23	4	2266	153	1	4.05	....	....	....	....	....	....	....
1995-96	Carolina Panthers	AHL	60	24	25	8	3404	229	2	4.04	....	....	....	....	....	....	....
1996-97	Carolina Monarchs	AHL	51	17	28	4	2899	172	1	3.56	....	....	....	....	....	....	....
1997-98	**Florida**	**NHL**	**11**	**0**	**5**	**1**	**485**	**32**	**0**	**3.96**	....	....	....	....	....	....	....
	Fort Wayne	IHL	12	9	2	1	719	34	1	2.84	....	....	....	....	....	....	....
1998-99	Detroit Vipers	IHL	33	19	5	7	1857	64	*4	*2.07	....	....	....	....	....	....	....
	Vancouver	**NHL**	**11**	**0**	**8**	**1**	**532**	**34**	**0**	**3.83**	....	....	....	....	....	....	....
99-2000	**Vancouver**	**NHL**	**20**	**6**	**7**	**4**	**987**	**47**	**1**	**2.86**	....	....	....	....	....	....	....
	NY Islanders	**NHL**	**36**	**10**	**20**	**4**	**2026**	**115**	**1**	**3.41**	....	....	....	....	....	....	....
2000-01	**Tampa Bay**	**NHL**	**61**	**20**	**33**	**3**	**3378**	**177**	**4**	**3.14**	....	....	....	....	....	....	....
2001-02	**Tampa Bay**	**NHL**	**19**	**3**	**9**	**0**	**830**	**40**	**2**	**2.89**	....	....	....	....	....	....	....
	Carolina	**NHL**	**2**	**2**	**0**	**0**	**120**	**3**	**0**	**1.50**	**8**	**3**	**2**	**408**	**11**	**2**	**1.62**
2002-03	**Carolina**	**NHL**	**51**	**14**	**24**	**9**	**2965**	**126**	**5**	**2.55**	....	....	....	....	....	....	....
2003-04	**Carolina**	**NHL**	**66**	**23**	**30**	**11**	**3765**	**146**	**6**	**2.33**	....	....	....	....	....	....	....
2004-05			DID NOT PLAY														
	NHL Totals		**277**	**78**	**136**	**33**	**15088**	**720**	**19**	**2.86**	**8**	**3**	**2**	**408**	**11**	**2**	**1.62**

James Norris Memorial Trophy (fewest goals against – IHL) (1999) (shared with Andrei Trefilov)

Traded to **Vancouver** by **Florida** with Ed Jovanovski, Dave Gagner, Mike Brown and Florida's 1st round choice (Nathan Smith) in 2000 Entry Draft for Pavel Bure, Bret Hedican, Brad Ference and Vancouver's 3rd round choice (Robert Fried) in 2000 Entry Draft, January 17, 1999. Traded to **NY Islanders** by **Vancouver** with Dave Scatchard and Bill Muckalt for Felix Potvin, NY Islanders' 2nd round compensatory choice (later traded to New Jersey – New Jersey selected Teemu Laine) in 2000 Entry Draft and NY Islanders' 3rd round choice (Thatcher Bell) in 2000 Entry Draft, December 19, 1999. Traded to **Tampa Bay** by **NY Islanders** with the rights to Kristian Kudroc and NY Islanders' 2nd round choice (later traded to Phoenix – Phoenix selected Matthew Spiller) in 2001 Entry Draft for Tampa Bay's 1st round choice (Raffi Torres) in 2000 Entry Draft, Calgary's 4th round choice (previously acquired, NY Islanders selected Vladimir Gorbunov) in 2000 Entry Draft and NY Islanders' 7th round choice (previously acquired, NY Islanders selected Ryan Caldwell) in 2000 Entry Draft, June 24, 2000. Traded to **Carolina** by **Tampa Bay** for Shane Willis and Chris Dingman, March 5, 2002. Signed as a free agent by **NY Rangers**, August 26, 2004.

WEIMAN, Tyler (WIGH-muhn, TIGH-luhr) COL.

Goaltender. Catches left. 5'11", 180 lbs. Born, Saskatoon, Sask., June 5, 1984.
(Colorado's 6th choice, 164th overall, in 2002 Entry Draft).

			Regular Season								Playoffs						
Season	**Club**	**League**	**GP**	**W**	**L**	**T**	**Mins**	**GA**	**SO**	**Avg**	**GP**	**W**	**L**	**Mins**	**GA**	**SO**	**Avg**
99-2000	Ft. Saskatchewan	AMBHL	21	15	4	2	1239	60	0	2.91	....	....	....	....	....	....	....
2000-01	Tri-City Americans	WHL	44	10	25	4	2464	155	0	3.77	....	....	....	....	....	....	....
2001-02	Tri-City Americans	WHL	47	18	17	5	2492	149	2	3.59	5	1	4	300	14	0	2.80
2002-03	Tri-City Americans	WHL	55	16	34	2	3129	207	1	3.97	....	....	....	....	....	....	....
2003-04	Tri-City Americans	WHL	54	23	21	7	3023	134	1	2.66	5	1	2	234	11	0	2.82
2004-05	Colorado Eagles	CHL	44	*33	6	5	2630	79	*8	*1.80	*13	*8	4	*744	32	1	2.58

WESTBLOM, Kristofer (WEHST-blahm, KRIHS-tuh-fuhr) MIN.

Goaltender. Catches left. 6'1", 155 lbs. Born, Meadow Lake, Sask., March 26, 1987.
(Minnesota's 3rd choice, 65th overall, in 2005 Entry Draft).

			Regular Season								Playoffs						
Season	**Club**	**League**	**GP**	**W**	**L**	**T**	**Mins**	**GA**	**SO**	**Avg**	**GP**	**W**	**L**	**Mins**	**GA**	**SO**	**Avg**
2002-03	Sask. Contacts	SMHL	21	14	3	2	1160	47	1	2.43	5	2	3	287	11	0	*2.30
2003-04	Sask. Contacts	SMHL	28	17	4	3	1513	50	2	*1.98	10	*7	2	625	17	*1	*1.63
2004-05	Kelowna Rockets	WHL	18	12	2	4	1094	33	4	1.81	4	3	1	251	8	0	1.91

YEATS, Matthew

(YAYTS, MA-thew)

Goaltender. Catches left. 5'11", 165 lbs. Born, Montreal, Que., April 6, 1979.
(Los Angeles' 9th choice, 248th overall, in 1998 Entry Draft).

						Regular Season						Playoffs				
Season	Club	League	GP	W	L	T	Mins	GA	SO	Avg	GP	W	L	Mins	GA	SO	Avg
1995-96	Lethbridge	WHL	1	0	0	0	20	3	0	9.00	....	....	....	....	....	....	....
1996-97	Olds Grizzlys	AJHL	32	....	....	....	1678	95	1	3.41	....	....	....	....	....	....	....
1997-98	Olds Grizzlys	AJHL	26	12	12	1	1498	96	0	3.85	....	....	....	....	....	....	....
1998-99	University of Maine	H-East					DID NOT PLAY – FRESHMAN										
99-2000	University of Maine	H-East	32	20	6	4	1821	79	0	2.60	....	....	....	....	....	....	....
2000-01	University of Maine	H-East	33	18	9	4	1897	76	2	2.40	....	....	....	....	....	....	....
2001-02	University of Maine	H-East	20	6	8	3	1048	54	0	3.09	....	....	....	....	....	....	....
2002-03	Philadelphia	AHL	2	1	1	0	90	4	0	2.67	....	....	....	....	....	....	....
	Atlantic City	ECHL	48	23	16	8	2811	141	4	3.01	8	4	1	397	16	1	2.42
2003-04	Portland Pirates	AHL	7	2	1	1	332	12	1	2.17	....	....	....	....	....	....	....
	Washington	**NHL**	**5**	**1**	**3**	**0**	**258**	**13**	**0**	**3.02**	....	....	....	....	....	....	....
2004-05	Reading Royals	ECHL	13	8	2	2	780	31	1	2.38	....	....	....	....	....	....	....
	Idaho Steelheads	ECHL	4	2	1	1	247	9	0	2.19	2	0	1	66	3	0	2.72
	NHL Totals		**5**	**1**	**3**	**0**	**258**	**13**	**0**	**3.02**							

• Ruled ineligible to play 1998-99 season by NCAA due to appearance with **Lethbridge** (WHL) in 1995-96. Signed as a free agent by **Portland** (AHL), November 6, 2003. Signed as a free agent by **Washington**, March 20, 2004. Signed as a free agent by **Reading** (ECHL), December 10, 2004.

ZABA, Matt

(ZA-buh, MAT) **L.A.**

Goaltender. Catches left. 6'1", 168 lbs. Born, Yorkton, Sask., July 14, 1983.
(Los Angeles' 8th choice, 231st overall, in 2003 Entry Draft).

						Regular Season						Playoffs				
Season	Club	League	GP	W	L	T	Mins	GA	SO	Avg	GP	W	L	Mins	GA	SO	Avg
2000-01	Yorkton Mallers	SMHL	26	13	10	3	1480	79	0	3.20	....	....	....	....	....	....	....
2001-02	Penticton Panthers	BCHL	33	....	....	....	1980	128	0	3.69	....	....	....	....	....	....	....
2002-03	Vernon Vipers	BCHL	44	34	9	0	2012	96	2	2.21	17	14	3	1006	25	3	1.49
2003-04	Colorado College	WCHA	23	10	10	2	1323	96	2	2.27	....	....	....	....	....	....	....
2004-05	Colorado College	WCHA	18	10	5	2	1050	43	2	2.46	....	....	....	....	....	....	....

WCHA All-Rookie Team (2004)

Game Savers...

First and Second All-Star Team goaltenders, 2002-03 and 2003-04. Martin Brodeur of the New Jersey Devils, above, has been named to the First All-Star Team in consecutive seasons. Earning Second Team honors were Marty Turco of the Dallas Stars, top right, in 2002-03 and Roberto Luongo of the Florida Panthers, right, in 2003-04. Brodeur was also named to the Second All-Star Team in 1996-97 and 1997-98.

Retired NHL Player Index

Abbreviations: Teams/Cities: – **Ana**. – Anaheim; **Atl**. – Atlanta; **Bos**. – Boston; **Bro**. – Brooklyn; **Buf**. – Buffalo; **Cal**. – California; **Cgy**. – Calgary; **Cle**. – Cleveland; **Col**. – Colorado; **CBJ** – Columbus; **Dal**. – Dallas; **Det**. – Detroit; **Edm**. – Edmonton; **Fla**. – Florida; **Ham**. – Hamilton; **Hfd**. – Hartford; **K.C.** – Kansas City; **L.A.** – Los Angeles; **Min**. – Minnesota; **Mtl**. – Montreal; **Mtl.M.** – Montreal Maroons; **Mtl.W.** – Montreal Wanderers; **N.J.** – New Jersey; **NYA** – NY Americans; **NYI** – NY Islanders; **NYR** – New York Rangers; – **Oak**. – Oakland; **Ott**. – Ottawa; – **Phi**. – Philadelphia; **Phx**. – Phoenix; **Pit**. – Pittsburgh; **Que**. – Quebec; **St.L.** – St. Louis; **S.J.** – San Jose; **T.B.** – Tampa Bay; **Tor.** – Toronto; **Van.** – Vancouver; **Wpg.** – Winnipeg; **Wsh.** – Washington

Total seasons are rounded off to the nearest full season. **A** – assists; **G** – goals; **GP** – games played; **PIM** – penalties in minutes; **TP** – total points.
● – deceased. Assists not recorded during 1917-18 season ‡ – Remains active in other leagues.

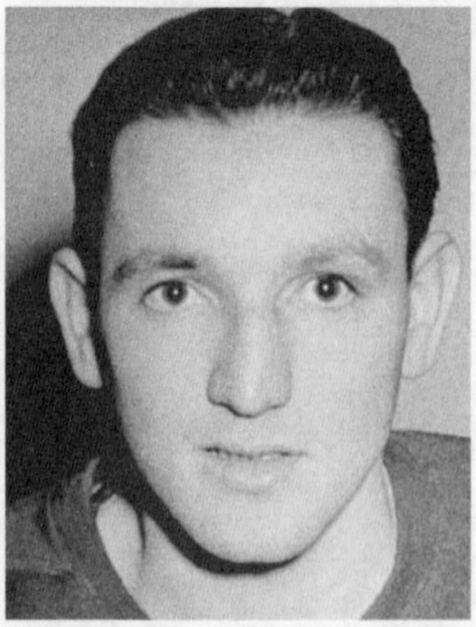
Sid Abel

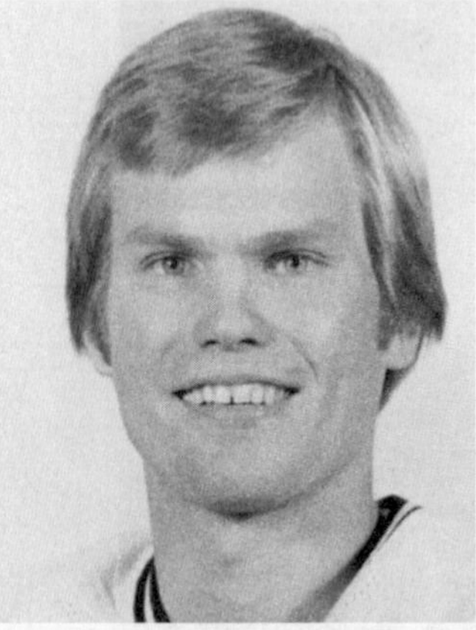
Steve Alley

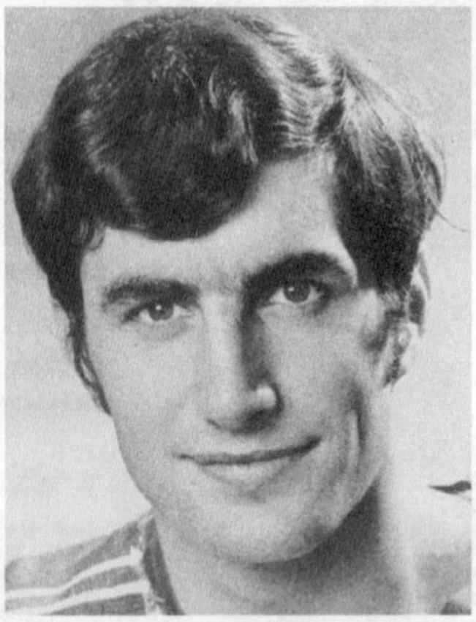
Syl Apps Jr.

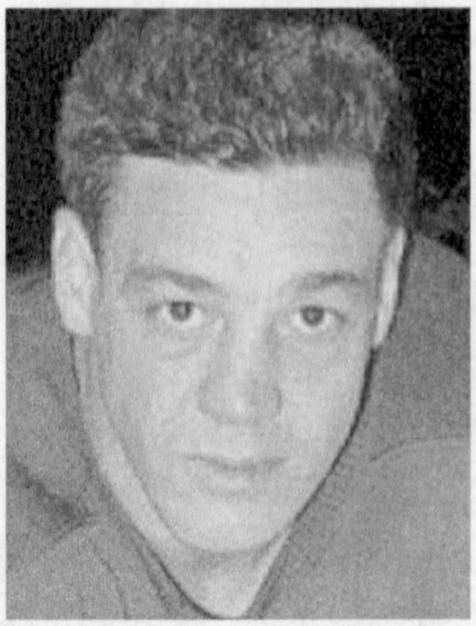
Walt Atanas

			Regular Schedule					Playoffs							
Name	NHL Teams	NHL Seasons	GP	G	A	TP	PIM	GP	G	A	TP	PIM	NHL Cup Wins	First NHL Season	Last NHL Season
A															
‡ Aalto, Antti	Ana.	4	151	11	17	28	52	4	0	0	0	2	....	1997-98	2000-01
Abbott, Reg	Mtl.	1	3	0	0	0	0	....	....	....	....	....	....	1952-53	1952-53
● Abel, Clarence	NYR, Chi.	8	333	19	18	37	359	38	1	1	2	58	2	1926-27	1933-34
Abel, Gerry	Det.	1	1	0	0	0	0	....	....	....	....	....	....	1966-67	1966-67
● Abel, Sid	Det., Chi.	14	612	189	283	472	376	97	28	30	58	79	3	1938-39	1953-54
Abgrall, Dennis	L.A.	1	13	0	2	2	4	....	....	....	....	....	....	1975-76	1975-76
Abrahamsson, Thommy	Hfd.	1	32	6	11	17	16	....	....	....	....	....	....	1980-81	1980-81
Achtymichuk, Gene	Mtl., Det.	4	32	3	5	8	2	....	....	....	....	....	....	1951-52	1958-59
Acomb, Doug	Tor.	1	2	0	1	1	0	....	....	....	....	....	....	1969-70	1969-70
Acton, Keith	Mtl., Min., Edm., Phi., Wsh., NYI	15	1023	226	358	584	1172	66	12	21	33	88	1	1979-80	1993-94
Adam, Douglas	NYR	1	4	0	1	1	0	....	....	....	....	....	....	1949-50	1949-50
Adam, Russ	Tor.	1	8	1	2	3	11	....	....	....	....	....	....	1982-83	1982-83
‡ Adams, Bryan	Atl.	2	11	0	1	1	2	....	....	....	....	....	....	1999-00	2000-01
Adams, Greg	Phi., Hfd., Wsh., Edm., Van., Que., Det.	10	545	84	143	227	1173	43	2	11	13	153	....	1980-81	1989-90
Adams, Greg	N.J., Van., Dal., Phx., Fla.	17	1056	355	388	743	326	81	20	22	42	16	....	1984-85	2000-01
● Adams, Jack	Tor., Ott.	7	173	83	32	115	366	10	2	0	2	13	2	1917-18	1926-27
Adams, John	Mtl.	1	42	6	12	18	11	3	0	0	0	0	....	1940-41	1940-41
● Adams, Stew	Chi., Tor.	4	95	9	26	35	60	11	3	3	6	14	....	1929-30	1932-33
Adduono, Rick	Bos., Atl.	2	4	0	0	0	2	....	....	....	....	....	....	1975-76	1979-80
Affleck, Bruce	St.L., Van., NYI	7	280	14	66	80	86	8	0	0	0	0	....	1974-75	1983-84
Agnew, Jim	Van., Hfd.	6	81	0	1	1	257	4	0	0	0	6	....	1986-87	1992-93
Ahern, Fred	Cal., Cle., Col.	4	146	31	30	61	130	2	0	1	1	2	....	1974-75	1977-78
Ahlin, Tony	Chi.	1	1	0	0	0	0	....	....	....	....	....	....	1937-38	1937-38
Ahola, Peter	L.A., Pit., S.J., Cgy.	3	123	10	17	27	137	6	0	0	0	2	....	1991-92	1993-94
Ahrens, Chris	Min.	6	52	0	3	3	84	1	0	0	0	0	....	1972-73	1977-78
Ailsby, Lloyd	NYR	1	3	0	0	0	2	....	....	....	....	....	....	1951-52	1951-52
Aitken, Brad	Pit., Edm.	2	14	1	3	4	25	....	....	....	....	....	....	1987-88	1990-91
Aivazoff, Micah	Det., Edm., NYI	3	92	4	6	10	46	....	....	....	....	....	....	1993-94	1995-96
‡ Alatalo, Mika	Phx.	2	152	17	29	46	58	5	0	0	0	2	....	1999-00	2000-01
Albelin, Tommy	Que., N.J., Cgy.	17	916	44	205	249	415	79	7	15	22	20	2	1987-88	2003-04
● Albright, Clint	NYR	1	59	14	5	19	19	....	....	....	....	....	....	1948-49	1948-49
Aldcorn, Gary	Tor., Det., Bos.	5	226	41	56	97	78	6	1	2	3	4	....	1956-57	1960-61
‡ Aldridge, Keith	Dal.	1	4	0	0	0	0	....	....	....	....	....	....	1999-00	1999-00
Alexander, Claire	Tor., Van.	4	155	18	47	65	36	16	2	4	6	4	....	1974-75	1977-78
● Alexandre, Art	Mtl.	2	11	0	2	2	8	4	0	0	0	0	....	1931-32	1932-33
Allan, Jeff	Cle.	1	4	0	0	0	2	....	....	....	....	....	....	1977-78	1977-78
‡ Allen, Chris	Fla.	2	2	0	0	0	2	....	....	....	....	....	....	1997-98	1998-99
Allen, George	NYR, Chi., Mtl.	8	339	82	115	197	179	41	9	10	19	32	....	1938-39	1946-47
Allen, Keith	Det.	2	28	0	4	4	8	5	0	0	0	0	1	1953-54	1954-55
Allen, Peter	Pit.	1	8	0	0	0	8	....	....	....	....	....	....	1995-96	1995-96
● Allen, Viv	NYA	1	6	0	1	1	0	....	....	....	....	....	....	1940-41	1940-41
Alley, Steve	Hfd.	2	15	3	3	6	11	3	0	1	1	0	....	1979-80	1980-81
Allison, Dave	Mtl.	1	3	0	0	0	12	....	....	....	....	....	....	1983-84	1983-84
Allison, Mike	NYR, Tor., L.A.	10	499	102	166	268	630	82	9	17	26	135	....	1980-81	1989-90
Allison, Ray	Hfd., Phi.	7	238	64	93	157	223	12	2	3	5	20	....	1979-80	1986-87
● Allum, Bill	NYR	1	1	0	1	1	0	....	....	....	....	....	....	1940-41	1940-41
● Amadio, Dave	Det., L.A.	3	125	5	11	16	163	16	1	2	3	18	....	1957-58	1968-69
‡ Ambroziak, Peter	Buf.	1	12	0	1	1	0	....	....	....	....	....	....	1994-95	1994-95
Amodeo, Mike	Wpg.	1	19	0	0	0	2	....	....	....	....	....	....	1979-80	1979-80
● Anderson, Bill	Bos.	1	....	....	....	....	....	1	0	0	0	0	....	1942-43	1942-43
Anderson, Dale	Det.	1	13	0	0	0	6	2	0	0	0	0	....	1956-57	1956-57
Anderson, Doug	Mtl.	1	....	....	....	....	....	2	0	0	0	0	1	1952-53	1952-53
Anderson, Earl	Det., Bos.	3	109	19	19	38	22	5	0	1	1	0	....	1974-75	1976-77
Anderson, Glenn	Edm., Tor., NYR, St.L.	16	1129	498	601	1099	1120	225	93	121	214	442	6	1980-81	1995-96
Anderson, Jim	L.A.	1	7	1	2	3	2	....	....	....	....	....	....	1967-68	1967-68
Anderson, John	Tor., Que., Hfd.	12	814	282	349	631	263	37	9	18	27	2	....	1977-78	1988-89
Anderson, Murray	Wsh.	1	40	0	1	1	68	....	....	....	....	....	....	1974-75	1974-75
Anderson, Perry	St.L., N.J., S.J.	10	400	50	59	109	1051	36	2	1	3	161	....	1981-82	1991-92
Anderson, Ron	Det., L.A., St.L., Buf.	5	251	28	30	58	146	5	0	0	0	4	....	1967-68	1971-72
Anderson, Ron	Wsh.	1	28	9	7	16	8	....	....	....	....	....	....	1974-75	1974-75
Anderson, Russ	Pit., Hfd., L.A.	9	519	22	99	121	1086	10	0	3	3	28	....	1976-77	1984-85
‡ Anderson, Shawn	Buf., Que., Wsh., Phi.	8	255	11	51	62	117	19	1	1	2	16	....	1986-87	1994-95
● Anderson, Tom	Det., NYA, Bro.	8	319	62	127	189	180	16	2	7	9	8	....	1934-35	1941-42
Andersson, Erik	Cgy.	1	12	2	1	3	8	....	....	....	....	....	....	1997-98	1997-98
Andersson, Kent-Erik	Min., NYR	7	456	72	103	175	78	50	4	11	15	4	....	1977-78	1983-84
Andersson, Mikael	Buf., Hfd., T.B., Phi., NYI	15	761	95	169	264	134	25	2	7	9	10	....	1985-86	1999-00
‡ Andersson, Niklas	Que., NYI, S.J., Nsh., Cgy.	6	164	29	53	82	85	....	....	....	....	....	....	1992-93	2000-01
Andersson, Peter	Wsh., Que.	3	172	10	41	51	81	7	0	2	2	2	....	1983-84	1985-86
‡ Andersson, Peter	NYR, Fla.	2	47	6	13	19	20	....	....	....	....	....	....	1992-93	1993-94
Andrascik, Steve	NYR	1	....	....	....	....	....	1	0	0	0	0	....	1971-72	1971-72
Andrea, Paul	NYR, Pit., Cal., Buf.	4	150	31	49	80	10	....	....	....	....	....	....	1965-66	1970-71
● Andrews, Lloyd	Tor.	4	53	8	5	13	10	2	0	0	0	0	1	1921-22	1924-25
Andrievski, Alexander	Chi.	1	1	0	0	0	0	....	....	....	....	....	....	1992-93	1992-93
Andruff, Ron	Mtl., Col.	5	153	19	36	55	54	2	0	0	0	0	....	1974-75	1978-79
Andrusak, Greg	Pit., Tor.	5	28	0	6	6	16	15	1	0	1	8	....	1993-94	1999-00
Angotti, Lou	NYR, Chi., Phi., Pit., St.L.	10	653	103	186	289	228	65	8	8	16	17	....	1964-65	1973-74
Anholt, Darrel	Chi.	1	1	0	0	0	0	....	....	....	....	....	....	1983-84	1983-84
Anslow, Hub	NYR	1	2	0	0	0	0	....	....	....	....	....	....	1947-48	1947-48
Antonovich, Mike	Min., Hfd., N.J.	5	87	10	15	25	37	....	....	....	....	....	....	1975-76	1983-84
Antoski, Shawn	Van., Phi., Pit., Ana.	8	183	3	5	8	599	36	1	3	4	74	....	1990-91	1997-98
● Apps, Syl	Tor.	10	423	201	231	432	56	69	25	29	54	8	3	1936-37	1947-48
Apps, Syl	NYR, Pit., L.A.	10	727	183	423	606	311	23	5	5	10	23	....	1970-71	1979-80
Arbour, Al	Det., Chi., Tor., St.L.	16	626	12	58	70	617	86	1	8	9	92	4	1953-54	1970-71
● Arbour, Amos	Mtl., Ham., Tor.	6	113	52	20	72	77	....	....	....	....	....	....	1918-19	1923-24
● Arbour, Jack	Det., Tor.	2	47	5	1	6	56	....	....	....	....	....	....	1926-27	1928-29
Arbour, John	Bos., Pit., Van., St.L.	5	106	1	9	10	149	5	0	0	0	0	....	1965-66	1971-72
● Arbour, Ty	Pit., Chi.	5	207	28	28	56	112	11	2	0	2	6	....	1926-27	1930-31
Archambault, Michel	Chi.	1	3	0	0	0	0	....	....	....	....	....	....	1976-77	1976-77
Archibald, Dave	Min., NYR, Ott., NYI	8	323	57	67	124	139	5	0	1	1	0	....	1987-88	1996-97
Archibald, Jim	Min.	3	16	1	2	3	45	....	....	....	....	....	....	1984-85	1986-87
Areshenkoff, Ron	Edm.	1	4	0	0	0	0	....	....	....	....	....	....	1979-80	1979-80
Armstrong, Bill	Phi.	1	1	0	1	1	0	....	....	....	....	....	....	1990-91	1990-91
● Armstrong, Bob	Bos.	12	542	13	86	99	671	42	1	7	8	28	....	1950-51	1961-62
Armstrong, George	Tor.	21	1187	296	417	713	721	110	26	34	60	52	4	1949-50	1970-71
Armstrong, Murray	Tor., NYA, Bro., Det.	8	270	67	121	188	72	30	4	6	10	2	....	1937-38	1945-46
● Armstrong, Norm	Tor.	1	7	1	1	2	2	....	....	....	....	....	....	1962-63	1962-63
Armstrong, Tim	Tor.	1	11	1	0	1	6	....	....	....	....	....	....	1988-89	1988-89
Arnason, Chuck	Mtl., Atl., Pit., K.C., Col., Cle., Min., Wsh.	8	401	109	90	199	122	9	2	4	6	4	....	1971-72	1978-79
Arniel, Scott	Wpg., Buf., Bos.	12	730	149	189	338	599	34	3	3	6	39	....	1981-82	1991-92
Arthur, Fred	Hfd., Phi.	3	80	1	8	9	49	4	0	0	0	2	....	1980-81	1982-83

Name	NHL Teams	NHL Seasons	Regular Schedule GP	G	A	TP	PIM	Playoffs GP	G	A	TP	PIM	NHL Cup Wins	First NHL Season	Last NHL Season
Arundel, John	Tor.	1	3	0	0	0	9	....	....	....	....	....	....	1949-50	1949-50
Arvedson, Magnus	Ott., Van.	7	434	100	125	225	241	52	3	8	11	34	....	1997-98	2003-04
• Ashbee, Barry	Bos., Phi.	5	284	15	70	85	291	17	0	4	4	22	1	1965-66	1973-74
• Ashby, Don	Tor., Col., Edm.	6	188	40	56	96	40	12	1	0	1	4	....	1975-76	1980-81
Ashton, Brent	Van., Col., N.J., Min., Que., Det., Wpg., Bos., Cgy.	14	998	284	345	629	635	85	24	25	49	70	....	1979-80	1992-93
Ashworth, Frank	Chi.	1	18	5	4	9	2	....	....	....	....	....	....	1946-47	1946-47
• Asmundson, Oscar	NYR, Det., St.L., NYA, Mtl.	5	111	11	23	34	30	9	0	2	2	4	1	1932-33	1937-38
‡ Astashenko, Kaspars	T.B.	2	23	1	2	3	8	....	....	....	....	....	....	1999-00	2000-01
‡ Astley, Mark	Buf.	3	75	4	19	23	92	2	0	0	0	0	....	1993-94	1995-96
• Atanas, Walt	NYR	1	49	13	8	21	40	....	....	....	....	....	....	1944-45	1944-45
Atcheynum, Blair	Ott., St.L., Nsh., Chi.	5	196	27	33	60	36	23	1	3	4	8	....	1992-93	2000-01
• Atkinson, Steve	Bos., Buf., Wsh.	6	302	60	51	111	104	1	0	0	0	0	....	1968-69	1974-75
Attwell, Bob	Col.	2	22	1	5	6	0	....	....	....	....	....	....	1979-80	1980-81
Attwell, Ron	St.L., NYR	1	22	1	7	8	8	....	....	....	....	....	....	1967-68	1967-68
Aubin, Norm	Tor.	2	69	18	13	31	30	1	0	0	0	0	....	1981-82	1982-83
Aubry, Pierre	Que., Det.	5	202	24	26	50	133	20	1	1	2	32	....	1980-81	1984-85
Aubuchon, Ossie	Bos., NYR	2	50	20	12	32	4	6	1	0	1	0	....	1942-43	1943-44
Audet, Philippe	Det.	1	4	0	0	0	0	....	....	....	....	....	....	1998-99	1998-99
Auge, Les	Col.	1	6	0	3	3	4	....	....	....	....	....	....	1980-81	1980-81
‡ Augusta, Patrik	Tor., Wsh.	2	4	0	0	0	0	....	....	....	....	....	....	1993-94	1998-99
• Aurie, Larry	Det.	12	489	147	129	276	279	24	6	9	15	10	2	1927-28	1938-39
Awrey, Don	Bos., St.L., Mtl., Pit., NYR, Col.	16	979	31	158	189	1065	71	0	18	18	150	2	1963-64	1978-79
• Ayres, Vern	NYA, Mtl.M., St.L., NYR	6	211	6	11	17	350	....	....	....	....	....	....	1930-31	1935-36

B

Name	NHL Teams	NHL Seasons	Regular Schedule GP	G	A	TP	PIM	Playoffs GP	G	A	TP	PIM	NHL Cup Wins	First NHL Season	Last NHL Season
Babando, Pete	Bos., Det., Chi., NYR	6	351	86	73	159	194	17	3	3	6	6	1	1947-48	1952-53
Babcock, Bobby	Wsh.	2	2	0	0	0	2	....	....	....	....	....	....	1990-91	1992-93
Babe, Warren	Min.	3	21	2	5	7	23	2	0	0	0	0	....	1987-88	1990-91
‡ Babenko, Yuri	Col.	1	3	0	0	0	0	....	....	....	....	....	....	2000-01	2000-01
Babin, Mitch	St.L.	1	8	0	0	0	0	....	....	....	....	....	....	1975-76	1975-76
Baby, John	Cle., Min.	2	26	2	8	10	26	....	....	....	....	....	....	1977-78	1978-79
Babych, Dave	Wpg., Hfd., Van., Phi., L.A.	19	1195	142	581	723	970	114	21	41	62	113	....	1980-81	1998-99
Babych, Wayne	St.L., Pit., Que., Hfd.	9	519	192	246	438	498	41	7	9	16	24	....	1978-79	1986-87
‡ Baca, Jergus	Hfd.	2	10	0	2	2	14	....	....	....	....	....	....	1990-91	1991-92
Backman, Mike	NYR	3	18	1	6	7	18	10	2	2	4	2	....	1981-82	1983-84
• Backor, Pete	Tor.	1	36	4	5	9	6	....	....	....	....	....	1	1944-45	1944-45
Backstrom, Ralph	Mtl., L.A., Chi.	17	1032	278	361	639	386	116	27	32	59	68	6	1956-57	1972-73
• Bailey, Ace	Tor.	8	313	111	82	193	472	21	3	4	7	12	1	1926-27	1933-34
• Bailey, Bob	Tor., Det., Chi.	5	150	15	21	36	207	15	0	4	4	22	....	1953-54	1957-58
• Bailey, Garnet	Bos., Det., St.L., Wsh.	10	568	107	171	278	633	15	2	4	6	28	1	1968-69	1977-78
Bailey, Reid	Phi., Tor., Hfd.	4	40	1	3	4	105	16	0	2	2	25	....	1980-81	1983-84
Baillargeon, Joel	Wpg., Que.	3	20	0	2	2	31	....	....	....	....	....	....	1986-87	1988-89
Baird, Ken	Cal.	1	10	0	2	2	15	....	....	....	....	....	....	1971-72	1971-72
Baker, Bill	Mtl., Col., St.L., NYR	3	143	7	25	32	175	6	0	0	0	0	....	1980-81	1982-83
Baker, Jamie	Que., S.J., Tor.	9	328	52	50	102	217	25	5	4	9	42	....	1989-90	1998-99
Bakovic, Peter	Van.	1	10	2	0	2	48	....	....	....	....	....	....	1987-88	1987-88
Balderis, Helmut	Min.	1	26	3	6	9	2	....	....	....	....	....	....	1989-90	1989-90
Baldwin, Doug	Tor., Det., Chi.	3	24	0	1	1	8	....	....	....	....	....	....	1945-46	1947-48
Balfour, Earl	Tor., Chi.	7	288	30	22	52	78	26	0	3	3	4	1	1951-52	1960-61
• Balfour, Murray	Mtl., Chi., Bos.	8	306	67	90	157	393	40	9	10	19	45	1	1956-57	1964-65
Ball, Terry	Phi., Buf.	4	74	7	19	26	26	....	....	....	....	....	....	1967-68	1971-72
Balon, Dave	NYR, Mtl., Min., Van.	14	776	192	222	414	607	78	14	21	35	109	2	1959-60	1972-73
Baltimore, Bryon	Edm.	1	2	0	0	0	4	....	....	....	....	....	....	1979-80	1979-80
Baluik, Stan	Bos.	1	7	0	0	0	2	....	....	....	....	....	....	1959-60	1959-60
‡ Bancroft, Steve	Chi., S.J.	2	6	0	1	1	2	....	....	....	....	....	....	1992-93	2001-02
Bandura, Jeff	NYR	1	2	0	1	1	0	....	....	....	....	....	....	1980-81	1980-81
‡ Banham, Frank	Ana., Phx.	4	32	9	2	11	16	....	....	....	....	....	....	1996-97	2002-03
Banks, Darren	Bos.	2	20	2	2	4	73	....	....	....	....	....	....	1992-93	1993-94
‡ Bannister, Drew	T.B., Edm., Ana., NYR	6	164	5	25	30	161	12	0	0	0	30	....	1995-96	2001-02
Barahona, Ralph	Bos.	2	6	2	2	4	0	....	....	....	....	....	....	1990-91	1991-92
• Barbe, Andy	Tor.	1	1	0	0	0	2	....	....	....	....	....	....	1950-51	1950-51
Barber, Bill	Phi.	14	903	420	463	883	623	129	53	55	108	109	2	1972-73	1983-84
Barber, Don	Min., Wpg., Que., S.J.	4	115	25	32	57	64	11	4	4	8	10	....	1988-89	1991-92
• Barilko, Bill	Tor.	5	252	26	36	62	456	47	5	7	12	104	4	1946-47	1950-51
Barkley, Doug	Chi., Det.	6	253	24	80	104	382	30	0	9	9	63	....	1957-58	1965-66
Barlow, Bob	Min.	2	77	16	17	33	10	6	2	2	4	6	....	1969-70	1970-71
Barnes, Blair	L.A.	1	1	0	0	0	0	....	....	....	....	....	....	1982-83	1982-83
Barnes, Norm	Phi., Hfd.	5	156	6	38	44	178	12	0	0	0	8	....	1976-77	1981-82
Baron, Normand	Mtl., St.L.	2	27	2	0	2	51	3	0	0	0	22	....	1983-84	1985-86
Barr, Dave	Bos., NYR, St.L., Hfd., Det., N.J., Dal.	13	614	128	204	332	520	71	12	10	22	70	....	1981-82	1993-94
Barrault, Doug	Min., Fla.	2	4	0	0	0	2	....	....	....	....	....	....	1992-93	1993-94
Barrett, Fred	Min., L.A.	13	745	25	123	148	671	44	0	2	2	60	....	1970-71	1983-84
Barrett, John	Det., Wsh., Min.	8	488	20	77	97	604	16	2	2	4	50	....	1980-81	1987-88
Barrie, Doug	Pit., Buf., L.A.	3	158	10	42	52	268	....	....	....	....	....	....	1968-69	1971-72
Barrie, Len	Phi., Fla., Pit., L.A.	7	184	19	45	64	290	8	1	0	1	8	....	1989-90	2000-01
Barry, Ed	Bos.	1	19	1	3	4	2	....	....	....	....	....	....	1946-47	1946-47
• Barry, Marty	NYA, Bos., Det., Mtl.	12	509	195	192	387	231	43	15	18	33	34	2	1927-28	1939-40
Barry, Ray	Bos.	1	18	1	2	3	6	....	....	....	....	....	....	1951-52	1951-52
Bartel, Robin	Cgy., Van.	2	41	0	1	1	14	6	0	0	0	16	....	1985-86	1986-87
Bartlett, Jim	Mtl., NYR, Bos.	5	191	34	23	57	273	2	0	0	0	0	....	1954-55	1960-61
• Barton, Cliff	Pit., Phi., NYR	3	85	10	9	19	22	....	....	....	....	....	....	1929-30	1939-40
‡ Bartos, Peter	Min.	1	13	4	2	6	6	....	....	....	....	....	....	2000-01	2000-01
‡ Bashkirov, Andrei	Mtl.	3	30	0	3	3	0	....	....	....	....	....	....	1998-99	2000-01
Bassen, Bob	NYI, Chi., St.L., Que., Dal., Cgy.	15	765	88	144	232	1004	93	9	15	24	134	....	1985-86	1999-00
‡ Bast, Ryan	Phi.	1	2	0	1	1	0	....	....	....	....	....	....	1998-99	1998-99
Bathe, Frank	Det., Phi.	9	224	3	28	31	542	27	1	3	4	42	....	1974-75	1983-84
Bathgate, Andy	NYR, Tor., Det., Pit.	17	1069	349	624	973	624	54	21	14	35	76	1	1952-53	1970-71
Bathgate, Frank	NYR	1	2	0	0	0	2	....	....	....	....	....	....	1952-53	1952-53
• Batters, Jeff	St.L.	2	16	0	0	0	28	....	....	....	....	....	....	1993-94	1994-95
‡ Batyrshin, Ruslan	L.A.	1	2	0	0	0	6	....	....	....	....	....	....	1995-96	1995-96
• Bauer, Bobby	Bos.	9	327	123	137	260	36	48	11	8	19	6	2	1936-37	1951-52
Baumgartner, Ken	L.A., NYI, Tor., Ana., Bos.	12	696	13	41	54	2244	51	1	2	3	106	....	1987-88	1998-99
Baumgartner, Mike	K.C.	1	17	0	0	0	0	....	....	....	....	....	....	1974-75	1974-75
Baun, Bob	Tor., Oak., Det.	17	964	37	187	224	1493	96	3	12	15	171	4	1956-57	1972-73
Bautin, Sergei	Wpg., Det., S.J.	3	132	5	25	30	176	6	0	0	0	2	....	1992-93	1995-96
Bawa, Robin	Wsh., Van., S.J., Ana.	4	61	6	1	7	60	1	0	0	0	0	....	1989-90	1993-94
Baxter, Paul	Que., Pit., Cgy.	8	472	48	121	169	1564	40	0	5	5	162	....	1979-80	1986-87
Beadle, Sandy	Wpg.	1	6	1	0	1	2	....	....	....	....	....	....	1980-81	1980-81
Beaton, Frank	NYR	2	25	1	1	2	43	....	....	....	....	....	....	1978-79	1979-80
• Beattie, Red	Bos., Det., NYA	9	334	62	85	147	137	24	4	2	6	8	....	1930-31	1938-39
Beaudin, Norm	St.L., Min.	2	25	1	2	3	4	....	....	....	....	....	....	1967-68	1970-71
Beaudoin, Serge	Atl.	1	3	0	0	0	0	....	....	....	....	....	....	1979-80	1979-80
Beaudoin, Yves	Wsh.	3	11	0	0	0	5	....	....	....	....	....	....	1985-86	1987-88
‡ Beaufait, Mark	S.J.	1	5	1	0	1	0	....	....	....	....	....	....	1992-93	1992-93
Beck, Barry	Col., NYR, L.A.	10	615	104	251	355	1016	51	10	23	33	77	....	1977-78	1989-90
Beckett, Bob	Bos.	4	68	7	6	13	18	....	....	....	....	....	....	1956-57	1963-64
Bedard, James	Chi.	2	22	1	1	2	8	....	....	....	....	....	....	1949-50	1950-51
Beddoes, Clayton	Bos.	2	60	2	8	10	57	....	....	....	....	....	....	1995-96	1996-97
Bednarski, John	NYR, Edm.	4	100	2	18	20	114	1	0	0	0	17	....	1974-75	1979-80
Beers, Bob	Bos., T.B., Edm., NYI	8	258	28	79	107	225	21	1	1	2	22	....	1989-90	1996-97
Beers, Eddy	Cgy., St.L.	5	250	94	116	210	256	41	7	10	17	47	....	1981-82	1985-86
• Behling, Dick	Det.	2	5	1	0	1	2	....	....	....	....	....	....	1940-41	1942-43
Beisler, Frank	NYA	2	2	0	0	0	0	....	....	....	....	....	....	1936-37	1939-40
Belanger, Alain	Tor.	1	9	0	1	1	6	....	....	....	....	....	....	1977-78	1977-78
‡ Belanger, Francis	Mtl.	1	10	0	0	0	29	....	....	....	....	....	....	2000-01	2000-01
‡ Belanger, Jesse	Mtl., Fla., Van., Edm., NYI	8	246	59	76	135	56	12	0	3	3	2	....	1991-92	2000-01
Belanger, Roger	Pit.	1	44	3	5	8	32	....	....	....	....	....	....	1984-85	1984-85
Belisle, Danny	NYR	1	4	2	0	2	0	....	....	....	....	....	....	1960-61	1960-61
Beliveau, Jean	Mtl.	20	1125	507	712	1219	1029	162	79	97	176	211	10	1950-51	1970-71
• Bell, Billy	Mtl.W., Mtl., Ott.	6	72	4	2	6	14	5	0	0	0	0	1	1917-18	1923-24
Bell, Bruce	Que., St.L., NYR, Edm.	5	209	12	64	76	113	34	3	5	8	41	....	1984-85	1989-90
Bell, Harry	NYR	1	1	0	1	1	0	....	....	....	....	....	....	1946-47	1946-47

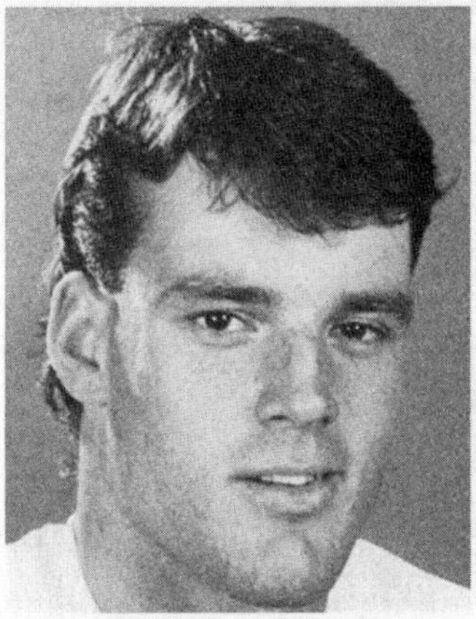
Bobby Babcock

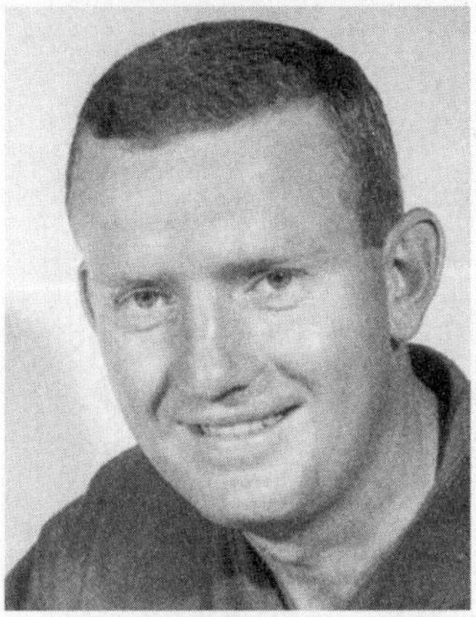
Doug Barkley

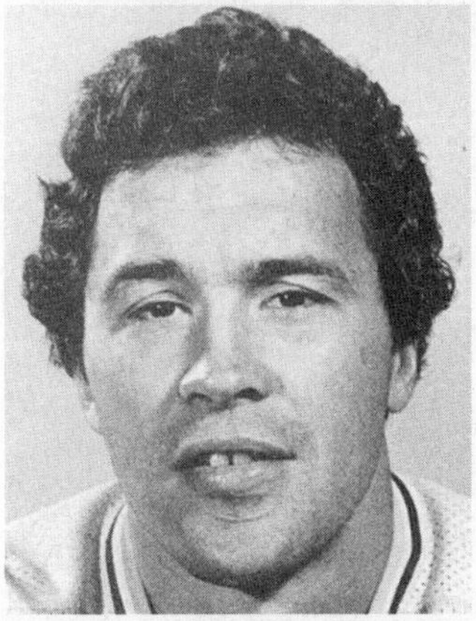
Fred Barrett

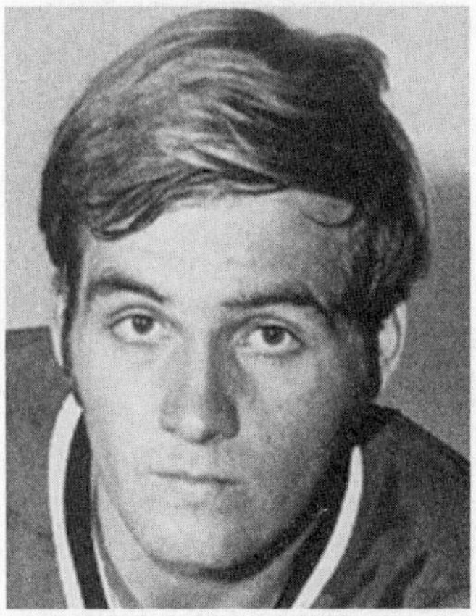
Mike Baumgartner

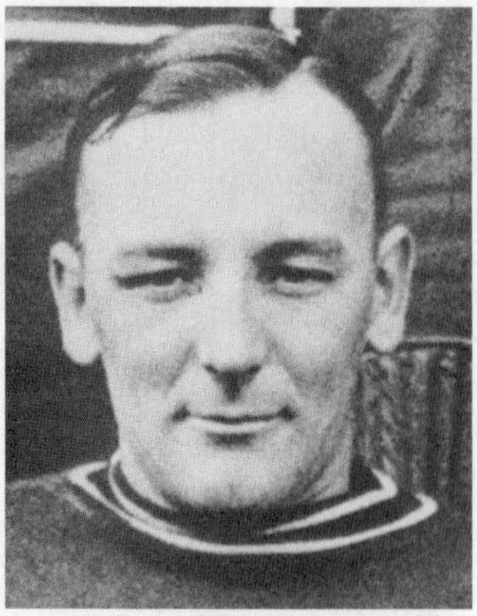

Pete Bellefeuille

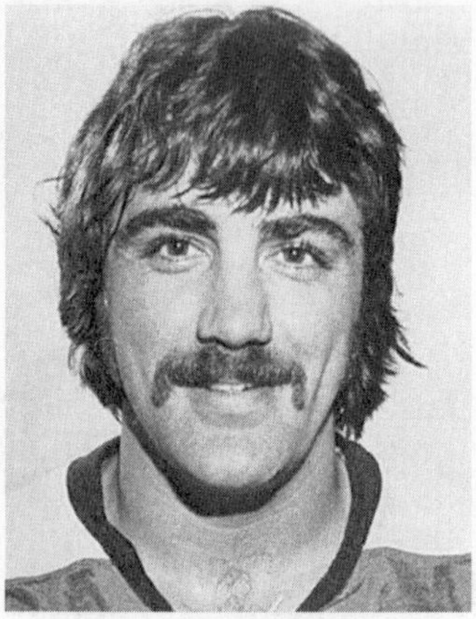

Yves Bergeron

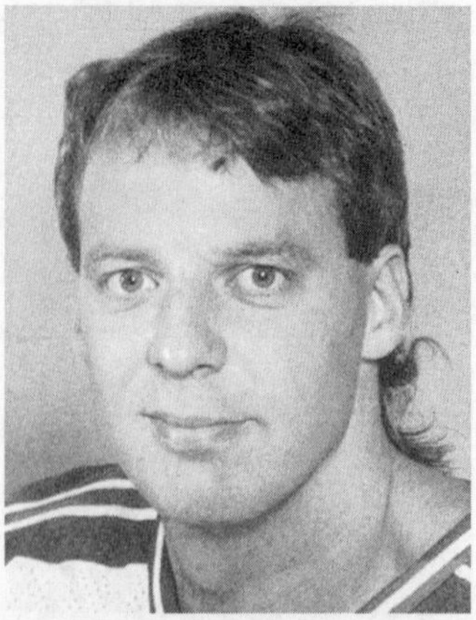

Bob Bodak

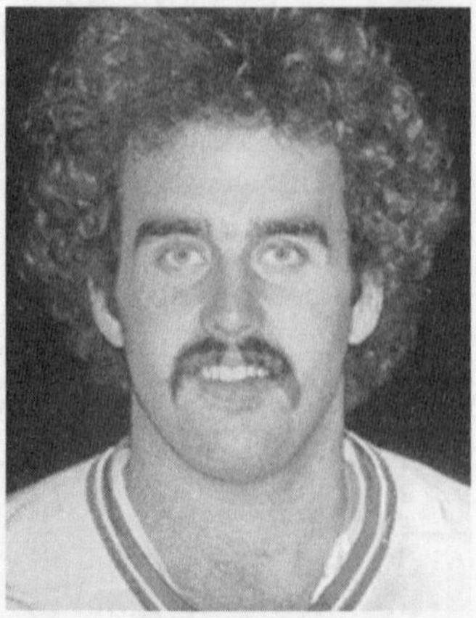

Jim Boo

			Regular Schedule					Playoffs							
Name	NHL Teams	NHL Seasons	GP	G	A	TP	PIM	GP	G	A	TP	PIM	NHL Cup Wins	First NHL Season	Last NHL Season
Bell, Joe	NYR	2	62	8	9	17	18	....	....	....	....	....	....	1942-43	1946-47
Belland, Neil	Van., Pit.	6	109	13	32	45	54	21	2	9	11	23	....	1981-82	1986-87
• Bellefeuille, Pete	Tor., Det.	4	92	26	4	30	58	....	....	....	....	....	....	1925-26	1929-30
• Bellemer, Andy	Mtl.M.	1	15	0	0	0	0	....	....	....	....	....	....	1932-33	1932-33
Bellows, Brian	Min., Mtl., T.B., Ana., Wsh.	17	1188	485	537	1022	718	143	51	71	122	143	1	1982-83	1998-99
• Bend, Lin	NYR	1	8	3	1	4	2	....	....	....	....	....	....	1942-43	1942-43
‡ Benda, Jan	Wsh.	1	9	0	3	3	6	....	....	....	....	....	....	1997-98	1997-98
Bennett, Adam	Chi., Edm.	3	69	3	8	11	69	....	....	....	....	....	....	1991-92	1993-94
Bennett, Bill	Bos., Hfd.	2	31	4	7	11	65	....	....	....	....	....	....	1978-79	1979-80
Bennett, Curt	St.L., NYR, Atl.	10	580	152	182	334	347	21	1	1	2	57	....	1970-71	1979-80
Bennett, Frank	Det.	1	7	0	1	1	2	....	....	....	....	....	....	1943-44	1943-44
Bennett, Harvey	Pit., Wsh., Phi., Min., St.L.	5	268	44	46	90	347	4	0	0	0	2	....	1974-75	1978-79
• Bennett, Max	Mtl.	1	1	0	0	0	0	....	....	....	....	....	....	1935-36	1935-36
Bennett, Rick	NYR	3	15	1	1	2	13	....	....	....	....	....	....	1989-90	1991-92
Benning, Brian	St.L., L.A., Phi., Edm., Fla.	11	568	63	233	296	963	48	3	20	23	74	....	1984-85	1994-95
Benning, Jim	Tor., Van.	9	605	52	191	243	461	7	1	1	2	2	....	1981-82	1989-90
• Benoit, Joe	Mtl.	5	185	75	69	144	94	11	6	3	9	11	1	1940-41	1946-47
Benson, Bill	NYA, Bro.	2	67	11	25	36	35	....	....	....	....	....	....	1940-41	1941-42
• Benson, Bobby	Bos.	1	8	0	1	1	4	....	....	....	....	....	....	1924-25	1924-25
• Bentley, Doug	Chi., NYR	13	566	219	324	543	217	23	9	8	17	12	....	1939-40	1953-54
• Bentley, Max	Chi., Tor., NYR	12	646	245	299	544	179	51	18	27	45	14	3	1940-41	1953-54
Bentley, Reg	Chi.	1	11	1	2	3	2	....	....	....	....	....	....	1942-43	1942-43
‡ Benysek, Ladislav	Edm., Min.	4	161	3	12	15	74	....	....	....	....	....	....	1997-98	2002-03
Beraldo, Paul	Bos.	2	10	0	0	0	4	....	....	....	....	....	....	1987-88	1988-89
‡ Beranek, Josef	Edm., Phi., Van., Pit.	9	531	118	144	262	398	57	5	8	13	24	....	1991-92	2000-01
Berenson, Red	Mtl., NYR, St.L., Det.	17	987	261	397	658	305	85	23	14	37	49	1	1961-62	1977-78
Berenzweig, Bubba	Nsh.	4	37	3	7	10	14	....	....	....	....	....	....	1999-00	2002-03
Berezan, Perry	Cgy., Min., S.J.	9	378	61	75	136	279	31	4	7	11	34	....	1984-85	1992-93
‡ Berezin, Sergei	Tor., Phx., Mtl., Chi., Wsh.	7	502	160	126	286	54	52	13	17	30	6	....	1996-97	2002-03
Berg, Bill	NYI, Tor., NYR, Ott.	10	546	55	67	122	488	61	3	4	7	34	....	1988-89	1998-99
• Bergdinon, Fred	Bos.	1	2	0	0	0	0	....	....	....	....	....	....	1925-26	1925-26
Bergen, Todd	Phi.	1	14	11	5	16	4	17	4	9	13	8	....	1984-85	1984-85
Berger, Mike	Min.	2	30	3	1	4	67	....	....	....	....	....	....	1987-88	1988-89
Bergeron, Michel	Det., NYI, Wsh.	5	229	80	58	138	165	....	....	....	....	....	....	1974-75	1978-79
Bergeron, Yves	Pit.	2	3	0	0	0	0	....	....	....	....	....	....	1974-75	1976-77
Bergevin, Marc	Chi., NYI, Hfd., T.B., Det., St.L., Pit., Van.	20	1191	36	145	181	1090	79	3	6	9	50	....	1984-85	2003-04
Bergkvist, Stefan	Pit.	2	7	0	0	0	9	4	0	0	0	2	....	1995-96	1996-97
Bergland, Tim	Wsh., T.B.	5	182	17	26	43	75	26	2	2	4	22	....	1989-90	1993-94
Bergloff, Bob	Min.	1	2	0	0	0	5	....	....	....	....	....	....	1982-83	1982-83
Berglund, Bo	Que., Min., Phi.	3	130	28	39	67	40	9	2	0	2	6	....	1983-84	1985-86
• Bergman, Gary	Det., Min., K.C.	12	838	68	299	367	1249	21	0	5	5	20	....	1964-65	1975-76
Bergman, Thommie	Det.	6	246	21	44	65	243	7	0	2	2	2	....	1972-73	1979-80
Bergqvist, Jonas	Cgy.	1	22	2	5	7	10	....	....	....	....	....	....	1989-90	1989-90
• Berlinquette, Louis	Mtl., Mtl.M., Pit.	8	193	45	33	78	129	11	0	5	5	9	....	1917-18	1925-26
Bernier, Serge	Phi., L.A., Que.	7	302	78	119	197	234	5	1	1	2	0	....	1968-69	1980-81
Berry, Bob	Mtl., L.A.	8	541	159	191	350	344	26	2	6	8	6	....	1968-69	1976-77
Berry, Brad	Wpg., Min., Dal.	8	241	4	28	32	323	13	0	1	1	16	....	1985-86	1993-94
Berry, Doug	Col.	2	121	10	33	43	25	....	....	....	....	....	....	1979-80	1980-81
Berry, Fred	Det.	1	3	0	0	0	0	....	....	....	....	....	....	1976-77	1976-77
Berry, Ken	Edm., Van.	4	55	8	10	18	30	....	....	....	....	....	....	1981-82	1988-89
‡ Bertrand, Eric	N.J., Atl., Mtl.	2	15	0	0	0	4	....	....	....	....	....	....	1999-00	2000-01
‡ Berube, Craig	Phi., Tor., Cgy., Wsh., NYI	17	1054	61	98	159	3149	89	3	1	4	211	....	1986-87	2002-03
• Besler, Phil	Bos., Chi., Det.	2	30	1	4	5	18	....	....	....	....	....	....	1935-36	1938-39
• Bessone, Pete	Det.	1	6	0	1	1	6	....	....	....	....	....	....	1937-38	1937-38
Bethel, John	Wpg.	1	17	0	2	2	4	....	....	....	....	....	....	1979-80	1979-80
Betik, Karel	T.B.	1	3	0	2	2	2	....	....	....	....	....	....	1998-99	1998-99
Bets, Maxim	Ana.	1	3	0	0	0	0	....	....	....	....	....	....	1993-94	1993-94
Bettio, Sam	Bos.	1	44	9	12	21	32	....	....	....	....	....	....	1949-50	1949-50
Beukeboom, Jeff	Edm., NYR	14	804	30	129	159	1890	99	3	16	19	197	4	1985-86	1998-99
Beverley, Nick	Bos., Pit., NYR, Min., L.A., Col.	11	502	18	94	112	156	7	0	1	1	0	....	1966-67	1979-80
Bialowas, Dwight	Atl., Min.	4	164	11	46	57	46	....	....	....	....	....	....	1973-74	1976-77
Bialowas, Frank	Tor.	1	3	0	0	0	12	....	....	....	....	....	....	1993-94	1993-94
Bianchin, Wayne	Pit., Edm.	7	276	68	41	109	137	3	0	1	1	6	....	1973-74	1979-80
Bicanek, Radim	Ott., Chi., CBJ	7	122	1	11	12	62	7	0	0	0	8	....	1994-95	2001-02
Bidner, Todd	Wsh.	1	12	2	1	3	7	....	....	....	....	....	....	1981-82	1981-82
Biggs, Don	Min., Phi.	2	12	2	0	2	8	....	....	....	....	....	....	1984-85	1989-90
Bignell, Larry	Pit.	2	20	0	3	3	2	3	0	0	0	2	....	1973-74	1974-75
Bilodeau, Gilles	Que.	1	9	0	1	1	25	....	....	....	....	....	....	1979-80	1979-80
• Bionda, Jack	Tor., Bos.	4	93	3	9	12	113	11	0	1	1	14	....	1955-56	1958-59
Bissett, Tom	Det.	1	5	0	0	0	0	....	....	....	....	....	....	1990-91	1990-91
Bjugstad, Scott	Min., Pit., L.A.	9	317	76	68	144	144	9	0	1	1	2	....	1983-84	1991-92
‡ Black, James	Hfd., Min., Dal., Buf., Chi., Wsh.	11	352	58	57	115	84	13	2	1	3	4	....	1989-90	2000-01
Black, Steve	Det., Chi.	2	113	11	20	31	77	13	0	0	0	13	1	1949-50	1950-51
Blackburn, Bob	NYR, Pit.	3	135	8	12	20	105	6	0	0	0	4	....	1968-69	1970-71
Blackburn, Don	Bos., Phi., NYR, NYI, Min.	6	185	23	44	67	87	12	3	0	3	10	....	1962-63	1972-73
Blade, Hank	Chi.	2	24	2	3	5	2	....	....	....	....	....	....	1946-47	1947-48
Bladon, Tom	Phi., Pit., Edm., Wpg., Det.	9	610	73	197	270	392	86	8	29	37	70	2	1972-73	1980-81
• Blaine, Garry	Mtl.	1	1	0	0	0	0	....	....	....	....	....	....	1954-55	1954-55
• Blair, Andy	Tor., Chi.	9	402	74	86	160	323	38	6	6	12	32	1	1928-29	1936-37
Blair, Chuck	Tor.	1	1	0	0	0	0	....	....	....	....	....	....	1948-49	1948-49
Blair, Dusty	Tor.	1	2	0	0	0	0	....	....	....	....	....	....	1950-51	1950-51
Blaisdell, Mike	Det., NYR, Pit., Tor.	9	343	70	84	154	166	6	1	2	3	10	....	1980-81	1988-89
Blake, Bob	Bos.	1	12	0	0	0	0	....	....	....	....	....	....	1935-36	1935-36
• Blake, Mickey	Mtl.M., St.L., Tor.	3	10	1	1	2	4	....	....	....	....	....	....	1932-33	1935-36
• Blake, Toe	Mtl.M., Mtl.	14	577	235	292	527	272	58	25	37	62	23	3	1934-35	1947-48
• Blight, Rick	Van., L.A.	7	326	96	125	221	170	5	0	5	5	2	....	1975-76	1982-83
• Blinco, Russ	Mtl.M., Chi.	6	268	59	66	125	24	19	3	3	6	4	1	1933-34	1938-39
Block, Ken	Van.	1	1	0	0	0	0	....	....	....	....	....	....	1970-71	1970-71
Bloemberg, Jeff	NYR	4	43	3	6	9	25	7	0	3	3	5	....	1988-89	1991-92
Blomqvist, Timo	Wsh., N.J.	5	243	4	53	57	293	13	0	0	0	24	....	1981-82	1986-87
Blomsten, Arto	Wpg., L.A.	3	25	0	4	4	8	....	....	....	....	....	....	1993-94	1995-96
Bloom, Mike	Wsh., Det.	3	201	30	47	77	215	....	....	....	....	....	....	1974-75	1976-77
Blum, John	Edm., Bos., Wsh., Det.	8	250	7	34	41	610	20	0	2	2	27	....	1982-83	1989-90
Bodak, Bob	Cgy., Hfd.	2	4	0	0	0	29	....	....	....	....	....	....	1987-88	1989-90
Boddy, Gregg	Van.	5	273	23	44	67	263	3	0	0	0	0	....	1971-72	1975-76
Bodger, Doug	Pit., Buf., S.J., N.J., L.A., Van.	16	1071	106	422	528	1007	47	6	18	24	25	....	1984-85	1999-00
• Bodnar, Gus	Tor., Chi., Bos.	12	667	142	254	396	207	32	4	3	7	10	2	1943-44	1954-55
Boehm, Ron	Oak.	1	16	2	1	3	10	....	....	....	....	....	....	1967-68	1967-68
• Boesch, Garth	Tor.	4	197	9	28	37	205	34	2	5	7	18	3	1946-47	1949-50
Boh, Rick	Min.	1	8	2	1	3	4	....	....	....	....	....	....	1987-88	1987-88
‡ Bohonos, Lonny	Van., Tor.	4	83	19	16	35	22	9	3	6	9	2	....	1995-96	1998-99
Boikov, Alexandre	Nsh.	2	10	0	0	0	15	....	....	....	....	....	....	1999-00	2000-01
Boileau, Marc	Det.	1	54	5	6	11	8	....	....	....	....	....	....	1961-62	1961-62
Boileau, Rene	NYA	1	7	0	0	0	0	....	....	....	....	....	....	1925-26	1925-26
Boimistruck, Fred	Tor.	2	83	4	14	18	45	....	....	....	....	....	....	1981-82	1982-83
Boisvert, Serge	Tor., Mtl.	5	46	5	7	12	8	23	3	7	10	4	1	1982-83	1987-88
Boivin, Claude	Phi., Ott.	4	132	12	19	31	364	....	....	....	....	....	....	1991-92	1994-95
Boivin, Leo	Tor., Bos., Det., Pit., Min.	19	1150	72	250	322	1192	54	3	10	13	59	....	1951-52	1969-70
Boland, Mike	K.C., Buf.	2	23	1	2	3	29	3	1	0	1	2	....	1974-75	1978-79
Boland, Mike	Phi.	1	2	0	0	0	0	....	....	....	....	....	....	1974-75	1974-75
Boldirev, Ivan	Bos., Cal., Chi., Atl., Van., Det.	15	1052	361	505	866	507	48	13	20	33	14	....	1970-71	1984-85
Bolduc, Danny	Det., Cgy.	3	102	22	19	41	33	1	0	0	0	0	....	1978-79	1983-84
Bolduc, Michel	Que.	2	10	0	0	0	6	....	....	....	....	....	....	1981-82	1982-83
• Boll, Buzz	Tor., NYA, Bro., Bos.	12	437	133	130	263	148	31	7	3	10	13	....	1932-33	1943-44
Bolonchuk, Larry	Van., Wsh.	4	74	3	9	12	97	....	....	....	....	....	....	1972-73	1977-78
• Bolton, Hugh	Tor.	8	235	10	51	61	221	17	0	5	5	14	1	1949-50	1956-57
Bonar, Dan	L.A.	3	170	25	39	64	208	14	3	4	7	22	....	1980-81	1982-83
Bonin, Brian	Pit., Min.	2	12	0	0	0	0	3	0	0	0	0	....	1998-99	2000-01
Bonin, Marcel	Det., Bos., Mtl.	9	454	97	175	272	336	50	11	14	25	51	4	1952-53	1961-62
‡ Bonsignore, Jason	Edm., T.B.	4	79	3	13	16	34	....	....	....	....	....	....	1994-95	1998-99
Boo, Jim	Min.	1	6	0	0	0	22	....	....	....	....	....	....	1977-78	1977-78
• Boone, Buddy	Bos.	2	34	5	3	8	28	22	2	1	3	25	....	1956-57	1957-58
Boothman, George	Tor.	2	58	17	19	36	18	5	2	1	3	2	....	1942-43	1943-44
Bordeleau, Christian	Mtl., St.L., Chi.	4	205	38	65	103	82	19	4	7	11	17	1	1968-69	1971-72

Name	NHL Teams	NHL Seasons	Regular Schedule GP	G	A	TP	PIM	Playoffs GP	G	A	TP	PIM	NHL Cup Wins	First NHL Season	Last NHL Season
Bordeleau, J.P.	Chi.	10	519	97	126	223	143	48	3	6	9	12	....	1969-70	1979-80
Bordeleau, Paulin	Van.	3	183	33	56	89	47	5	2	1	3	0	....	1973-74	1975-76
‡ Bordeleau, Sebastien	Mtl., Nsh., Min., Phx.	7	251	37	61	98	118	5	0	0	0	2	....	1995-96	2001-02
Borotsik, Jack	St.L.	1	1	0	0	0	0	....	....	....	....	....	....	1974-75	1974-75
Borsato, Luciano	Wpg.	5	203	35	55	90	113	7	1	0	1	4	....	1990-91	1994-95
Borschevsky, Nikolai	Tor., Cgy., Dal.	4	162	49	73	122	44	31	4	9	13	4	....	1992-93	1995-96
Boschman, Laurie	Tor., Edm., Wpg., N.J., Ott.	14	1009	229	348	577	2265	57	8	13	21	140	....	1979-80	1992-93
Bossy, Mike	NYI	10	752	573	553	1126	210	129	85	75	160	38	4	1977-78	1986-87
• Bostrom, Helge	Chi.	4	96	3	3	6	58	13	0	0	0	16	....	1929-30	1932-33
Botell, Mark	Phi.	1	32	4	10	14	31	....	....	....	....	....	....	1981-82	1981-82
Bothwell, Tim	NYR, St.L., Hfd.	12	502	28	93	121	382	49	0	3	3	56	....	1978-79	1988-89
Botting, Cam	Atl.	1	2	0	1	1	0	....	....	....	....	....	....	1975-76	1975-76
Boucha, Henry	Det., Min., K.C., Col.	6	247	53	49	102	157	....	....	....	....	....	....	1971-72	1976-77
Bouchard, Butch	Mtl.	15	785	49	144	193	863	113	11	21	32	121	4	1941-42	1955-56
Bouchard, Dick	NYR	1	1	0	0	0	0	....	....	....	....	....	....	1954-55	1954-55
• Bouchard, Edmond	Mtl., Ham., NYA, Pit.	8	211	19	21	40	117	....	....	....	....	....	....	1921-22	1928-29
Bouchard, Pierre	Mtl., Wsh.	12	595	24	82	106	433	76	3	10	13	56	5	1970-71	1981-82
• Boucher, Billy	Mtl., Bos., NYA	7	213	93	38	131	409	14	3	0	3	17	1	1921-22	1927-28
• Boucher, Bobby	Mtl.	1	11	1	0	1	0	2	0	0	0	0	1	1923-24	1923-24
• Boucher, Clarence	NYA	2	47	2	2	4	133	....	....	....	....	....	....	1926-27	1927-28
• Boucher, Frank	Ott., NYR	14	557	160	263	423	119	55	16	20	36	12	2	1921-22	1943-44
• Boucher, Georges	Ott., Mtl.M., Chi.	15	449	117	87	204	838	28	5	3	8	88	4	1917-18	1931-32
Boudreau, Bruce	Tor., Chi.	8	141	28	42	70	46	9	2	0	2	0	....	1976-77	1985-86
Boudrias, Andre	Mtl., Min., Chi., St.L., Van.	12	662	151	340	491	216	34	6	10	16	12	....	1963-64	1975-76
Boughner, Barry	Oak., Cal.	2	20	0	0	0	11	....	....	....	....	....	....	1969-70	1970-71
Bourbonnais, Dan	Hfd.	2	59	3	25	28	11	....	....	....	....	....	....	1981-82	1983-84
Bourbonnais, Rick	St.L.	3	71	9	15	24	29	4	0	1	1	0	....	1975-76	1977-78
• Bourcier, Conrad	Mtl.	1	6	0	0	0	0	....	....	....	....	....	....	1935-36	1935-36
Bourcier, Jean	Mtl.	1	9	0	1	1	0	....	....	....	....	....	....	1935-36	1935-36
• Bourgeault, Leo	Tor., NYR, Ott., Mtl.	8	307	24	20	44	269	24	1	1	2	18	1	1926-27	1934-35
Bourgeois, Charlie	Cgy., St.L., Hfd.	7	290	16	54	70	788	40	2	3	5	194	....	1981-82	1987-88
Bourne, Bob	NYI, L.A.	14	964	258	324	582	605	139	40	56	96	108	4	1974-75	1987-88
Bourque, Phil	Pit., NYR, Ott.	12	477	88	111	199	516	56	13	12	25	107	2	1983-84	1995-96
Bourque, Raymond	Bos., Col.	22	1612	410	1169	1579	1141	214	41	139	180	171	1	1979-80	2000-01
Boutette, Pat	Tor., Hfd., Pit.	10	756	171	282	453	1354	46	10	14	24	109	....	1975-76	1984-85
Boutilier, Paul	NYI, Bos., Min., NYR, Wpg.	8	288	27	83	110	358	41	1	9	10	45	1	1981-82	1988-89
Bowen, Jason	Phi., Edm.	6	77	2	6	8	109	....	....	....	....	....	....	1992-93	1997-98
Bowler, Bill	CBJ	1	9	0	2	2	8	....	....	....	....	....	....	2000-01	2000-01
Bowman, Kirk	Chi.	3	88	11	17	28	19	7	1	0	1	0	....	1976-77	1978-79
• Bowman, Ralph	Ott., St.L., Det.	7	274	8	17	25	260	22	2	2	4	6	2	1933-34	1939-40
Bownass, Jack	Mtl., NYR	4	80	3	8	11	58	....	....	....	....	....	....	1957-58	1961-62
Bowness, Rick	Atl., Det., St.L., Wpg.	7	173	18	37	55	191	5	0	0	0	2	....	1975-76	1981-82
• Boyd, Bill	NYR, NYA	4	138	15	7	22	72	10	0	0	0	4	1	1926-27	1929-30
Boyd, Irvin	Bos., Det.	4	96	10	10	20	30	5	0	1	1	4	....	1931-32	1943-44
Boyd, Randy	Pit., Chi., NYI, Van.	8	257	20	67	87	328	13	0	2	2	26	....	1981-82	1988-89
Boyer, Wally	Tor., Chi., Oak., Pit.	7	365	54	105	159	163	15	1	3	4	0	....	1965-66	1971-72
Boyer, Zac	Dal.	2	3	0	0	0	0	2	0	0	0	0	....	1994-95	1995-96
Boyko, Darren	Wpg.	1	1	0	0	0	0	....	....	....	....	....	....	1988-89	1988-89
Bozek, Steve	L.A., Cgy., St.L., Van., S.J.	11	641	164	167	331	309	58	12	11	23	69	....	1981-82	1991-92
‡ Bozon, Philippe	St.L.	4	144	16	25	41	101	19	2	0	2	31	....	1991-92	1994-95
• Brackenborough, John	Bos.	1	7	0	0	0	0	....	....	....	....	....	....	1925-26	1925-26
Brackenbury, Curt	Que., Edm., St.L.	4	141	9	17	26	226	2	0	0	0	0	....	1979-80	1982-83
Bradley, Bart	Bos.	1	1	0	0	0	0	....	....	....	....	....	....	1949-50	1949-50
Bradley, Brian	Cgy., Van., Tor., T.B.	13	651	182	321	503	528	13	3	7	10	16	....	1985-86	1997-98
Bradley, Lyle	Cal., Cle.	2	6	1	0	1	2	....	....	....	....	....	....	1973-74	1976-77
Brady, Neil	N.J., Ott., Dal.	5	89	9	22	31	95	....	....	....	....	....	....	1989-90	1993-94
Bragnalo, Rick	Wsh.	4	145	15	35	50	46	....	....	....	....	....	....	1975-76	1978-79
• Branigan, Andy	NYA, Bro.	2	27	1	2	3	31	....	....	....	....	....	....	1940-41	1941-42
Brasar, Per-Olov	Min., Van.	5	348	64	142	206	33	13	1	2	3	0	....	1977-78	1981-82
• Brayshaw, Russ	Chi.	1	43	5	9	14	24	....	....	....	....	....	....	1944-45	1944-45
Breault, Francois	L.A.	3	27	2	4	6	42	....	....	....	....	....	....	1990-91	1992-93
Breitenbach, Ken	Buf.	3	68	1	13	14	49	8	0	1	1	4	....	1975-76	1978-79
Brennan, Dan	L.A.	2	8	0	1	1	9	....	....	....	....	....	....	1983-84	1985-86
Brennan, Doug	NYR	3	123	9	7	16	152	16	1	0	1	21	1	1931-32	1933-34
• Brennan, Tom	Bos.	2	12	2	2	4	2	....	....	....	....	....	....	1943-44	1944-45
Brenneman, John	Chi., NYR, Tor., Det., Oak.	5	152	21	19	40	46	....	....	....	....	....	1	1964-65	1968-69
Bretto, Joe	Chi.	1	3	0	0	0	4	....	....	....	....	....	....	1944-45	1944-45
• Brewer, Carl	Tor., Det., St.L.	12	604	25	198	223	1037	72	3	17	20	146	3	1957-58	1979-80
Brickley, Andy	Phi., Pit., N.J., Bos., Wpg.	11	385	82	140	222	81	17	1	4	5	4	....	1982-83	1993-94
• Briden, Archie	Bos., Det., Pit.	2	71	9	5	14	56	....	....	....	....	....	....	1926-27	1929-30
Bridgman, Mel	Phi., Cgy., N.J., Det., Van.	14	977	252	449	701	1625	125	28	39	67	298	....	1975-76	1988-89
• Briere, Michel	Pit.	1	76	12	32	44	20	10	5	3	8	17	....	1969-70	1969-70
Brindley, Doug	Tor.	1	3	0	0	0	0	....	....	....	....	....	....	1970-71	1970-71
• Brink, Milt	Chi.	1	5	0	0	0	0	....	....	....	....	....	....	1936-37	1936-37
Brisson, Gerry	Mtl.	1	4	0	2	2	4	....	....	....	....	....	....	1962-63	1962-63
Britz, Greg	Tor., Hfd.	3	8	0	0	0	4	....	....	....	....	....	....	1983-84	1986-87
• Broadbent, Punch	Ott., Mtl.M., NYA	11	303	121	51	172	564	23	4	6	10	60	4	1918-19	1928-29
Brochu, Stephane	NYR	1	1	0	0	0	0	....	....	....	....	....	....	1988-89	1988-89
Broden, Connie	Mtl.	3	6	2	1	3	2	7	0	1	1	0	2	1955-56	1957-58
Brooke, Bob	NYR, Min., N.J.	7	447	69	97	166	520	34	9	9	18	59	....	1983-84	1989-90
Brooks, Gord	St.L., Wsh.	3	70	7	18	25	37	....	....	....	....	....	....	1971-72	1974-75
• Brophy, Bernie	Mtl.M., Det.	3	62	4	4	8	25	2	0	0	0	2	1	1925-26	1929-30
Brossart, Willie	Phi., Tor., Wsh.	6	129	1	14	15	88	1	0	0	0	0	....	1970-71	1975-76
Broten, Aaron	Col., N.J., Min., Que., Tor., Wpg.	12	748	186	329	515	441	34	7	18	25	40	....	1980-81	1991-92
Broten, Neal	Min., Dal., N.J., L.A.	17	1099	289	634	923	569	135	35	63	98	77	1	1980-81	1996-97
Broten, Paul	NYR, Dal., St.L.	7	322	46	55	101	264	38	4	6	10	18	....	1989-90	1995-96
‡ Brousseau, Paul	Col., T.B., Fla.	4	26	1	3	4	29	....	....	....	....	....	....	1995-96	2000-01
• Brown, Adam	Det., Chi., Bos.	10	391	104	113	217	378	26	2	4	6	14	1	1941-42	1951-52
Brown, Arnie	Tor., NYR, Det., NYI, Atl.	12	681	44	141	185	738	22	0	6	6	23	....	1961-62	1973-74
‡ Brown, Cam	Van.	1	1	0	0	0	7	....	....	....	....	....	....	1990-91	1990-91
• Brown, Connie	Det.	5	73	15	24	39	12	14	2	3	5	0	1	1938-39	1942-43
Brown, Dave	Phi., Edm., S.J.	14	729	45	52	97	1789	80	2	3	5	209	1	1982-83	1995-96
Brown, Doug	N.J., Pit., Det.	15	854	160	214	374	210	109	23	23	46	26	2	1986-87	2000-01
• Brown, Fred	Mtl.M.	1	19	1	0	1	0	9	0	0	0	0	....	1927-28	1927-28
Brown, George	Mtl.	3	79	6	22	28	34	7	0	0	0	2	....	1936-37	1938-39
• Brown, Gerry	Det.	2	23	4	5	9	2	12	2	1	3	4	....	1941-42	1945-46
Brown, Greg	Buf., Pit., Wpg.	4	94	4	14	18	86	6	0	1	1	4	....	1990-91	1994-95
Brown, Harold	NYR	1	13	2	1	3	2	....	....	....	....	....	....	1945-46	1945-46
Brown, Jeff	Que., St.L., Van., Hfd., Car., Tor., Wsh.	13	747	154	430	584	498	87	20	45	65	59	....	1985-86	1997-98
Brown, Jim	L.A.	1	3	0	1	1	5	....	....	....	....	....	....	1982-83	1982-83
Brown, Keith	Chi., Fla.	16	876	68	274	342	916	103	4	32	36	184	....	1979-80	1994-95
Brown, Kevin	L.A., Hfd., Car., Edm.	6	64	7	9	16	28	1	0	0	0	0	....	1994-95	1999-00
Brown, Larry	NYR, Det., Phi., L.A.	9	455	7	53	60	180	35	0	4	4	10	....	1969-70	1977-78
Brown, Rob	Pit., Hfd., Chi., Dal., L.A.	11	543	190	248	438	599	54	12	14	26	45	....	1987-88	1999-00
• Brown, Stan	NYR, Det.	2	48	8	2	10	18	2	0	0	0	0	....	1926-27	1927-28
Brown, Wayne	Bos.	1	....	....	....	....	....	4	0	0	0	2	....	1953-54	1953-54
• Browne, Cecil	Chi.	1	13	2	0	2	4	....	....	....	....	....	....	1927-28	1927-28
Brownschidle, Jack	St.L., Hfd.	9	494	39	162	201	151	26	0	5	5	18	....	1977-78	1985-86
Brownschidle, Jeff	Hfd.	2	7	0	1	1	2	....	....	....	....	....	....	1981-82	1982-83
Brubaker, Jeff	Hfd., Mtl., Cgy., Tor., Edm., NYR, Det.	8	178	16	9	25	512	2	0	0	0	27	....	1979-80	1988-89
Bruce, David	Van., St.L., S.J.	8	234	48	39	87	338	3	0	0	0	2	....	1985-86	1993-94
• Bruce, Gordie	Bos.	3	28	4	9	13	13	7	2	3	5	4	....	1940-41	1945-46
• Bruce, Morley	Ott.	4	71	8	3	11	27	3	0	0	0	2	2	1917-18	1921-22
Brumwell, Murray	Min., N.J.	7	128	12	31	43	70	2	0	0	0	2	....	1980-81	1987-88
Brunet, Benoit	Mtl., Dal., Ott.	13	539	101	161	262	229	54	5	20	25	32	1	1988-89	2001-02
• Bruneteau, Eddie	Det.	7	180	40	42	82	35	31	7	6	13	0	....	1940-41	1948-49
• Bruneteau, Mud	Det.	11	411	139	138	277	80	77	23	14	37	22	3	1935-36	1945-46
• Brydge, Bill	Tor., Det., NYA	9	368	26	52	78	506	2	0	0	0	4	....	1926-27	1935-36
Brydges, Paul	Buf.	1	15	2	2	4	6	....	....	....	....	....	....	1986-87	1986-87
• Brydson, Glenn	Mtl.M., St.L., NYR, Chi.	8	299	56	79	135	203	11	0	0	0	8	....	1930-31	1937-38
• Brydson, Gord	Tor.	1	8	2	0	2	8	....	....	....	....	....	....	1929-30	1929-30
Bubla, Jiri	Van.	5	256	17	101	118	202	6	0	0	0	7	....	1981-82	1985-86
• Buchanan, Al	Tor.	2	4	0	1	1	2	....	....	....	....	....	....	1948-49	1949-50
Buchanan, Bucky	NYR	1	2	0	0	0	0	....	....	....	....	....	....	1948-49	1948-49
Buchanan, Jeff	Col.	1	6	0	0	0	6	....	....	....	....	....	....	1998-99	1998-99

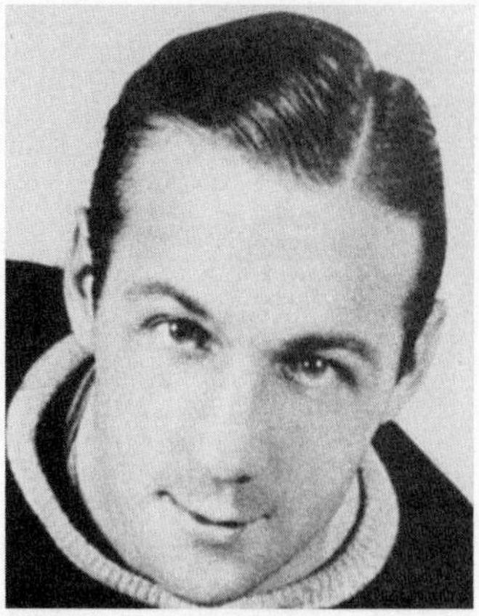

Leo Bourgeault

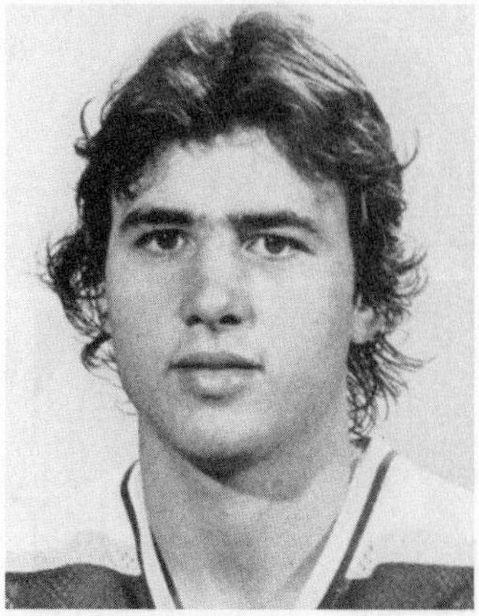

Neal Broten

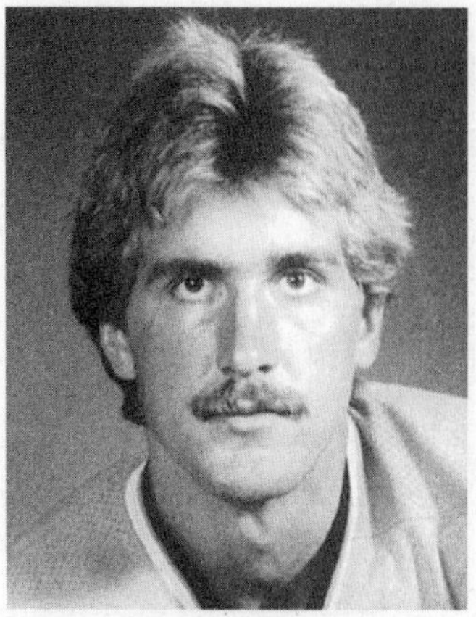

Rod Buskas

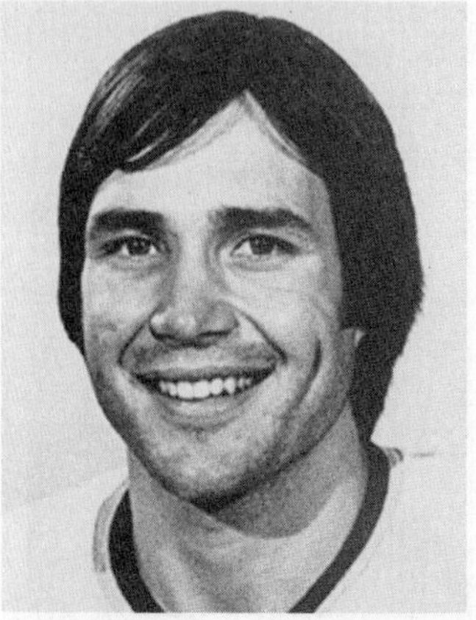

Bill Butters

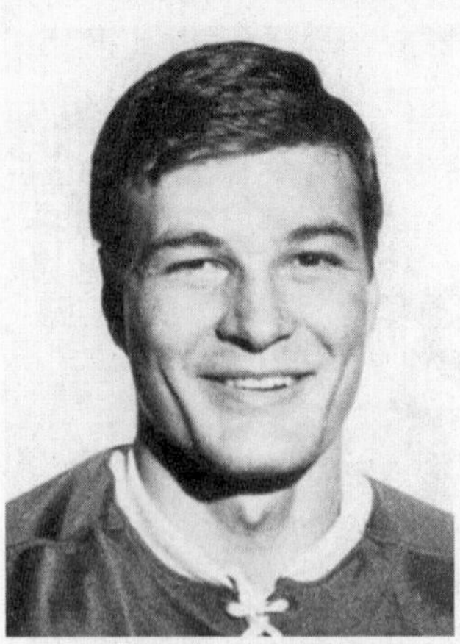

Mike Byers

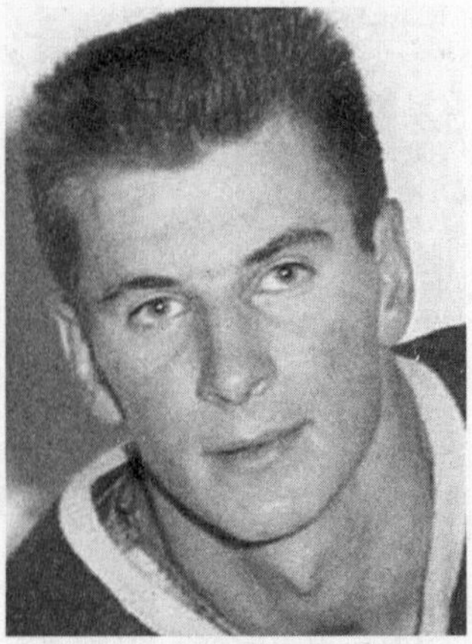

Larry Cahan

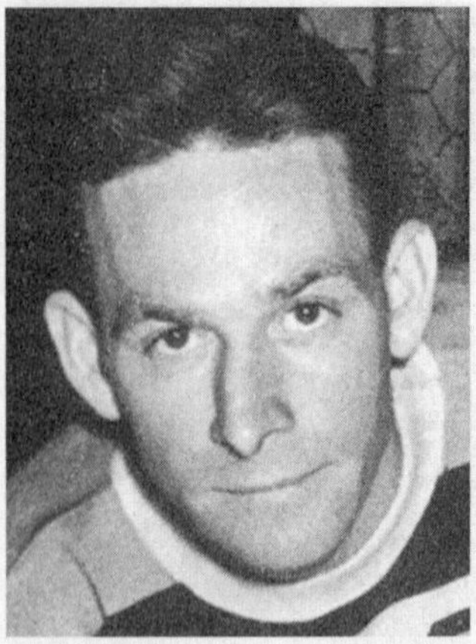

Norm Calladine

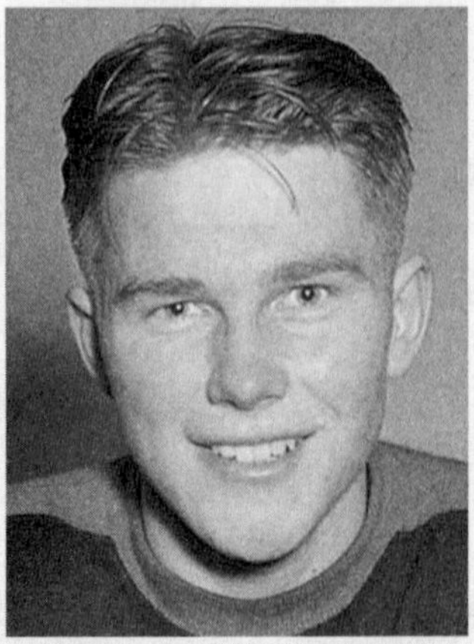

Don Campbell

			Regular Schedule					Playoffs					NHL	First	Last
Name	**NHL Teams**	**NHL Seasons**	**GP**	**G**	**A**	**TP**	**PIM**	**GP**	**G**	**A**	**TP**	**PIM**	**Cup Wins**	**NHL Season**	**NHL Season**
Buchanan, Mike	Chi.	1	1	0	0	0	0	....	....	....	....	....	....	1951-52	1951-52
Buchanan, Ron	Bos., St.L.	2	5	0	0	0	0	....	....	....	....	....	....	1966-67	1969-70
Bucyk, John	Det., Bos.	23	1540	556	813	1369	497	124	41	62	103	42	2	1955-56	1977-78
Bucyk, Randy	Mtl., Cgy.	2	19	4	2	6	8	2	0	0	0	0	....	1985-86	1987-88
Buhr, Doug	K.C.	1	6	0	2	2	4	....	....	....	....	....	....	1974-75	1974-75
Bukovich, Tony	Det.	2	17	7	3	10	6	6	0	1	1	0	....	1943-44	1944-45
Bullard, Mike	Pit., Cgy., St.L., Phi., Tor.	11	727	329	345	674	703	40	11	18	29	44	....	1980-81	1991-92
• Buller, Hy	Det., NYR	5	188	22	58	80	215	....	....	....	....	....	....	1943-44	1953-54
Bulley, Ted	Chi., Wsh., Pit.	8	414	101	113	214	704	29	5	5	10	24	....	1976-77	1983-84
Burakovsky, Robert	Ott.	1	23	2	3	5	6	....	....	....	....	....	....	1993-94	1993-94
• Burch, Billy	Ham., NYA, Bos., Chi.	11	390	137	61	198	255	2	0	0	0	0	....	1922-23	1932-33
• Burchell, Fred	Mtl.	2	4	0	0	0	2	....	....	....	....	....	....	1950-51	1953-54
Burdon, Glen	K.C.	1	11	0	2	2	0	....	....	....	....	....	....	1974-75	1974-75
Bure, Pavel	Van., Fla., NYR	12	702	437	342	779	484	64	35	35	70	74	....	1991-92	2002-03
Bureau, Marc	Cgy., Min., T.B., Mtl., Phi.	11	567	55	83	138	327	50	5	7	12	46	....	1989-90	1999-00
Burega, Bill	Tor.	1	4	0	1	1	4	....	....	....	....	....	....	1955-56	1955-56
• Burke, Eddie	Bos., NYA	4	106	29	20	49	55	....	....	....	....	....	....	1931-32	1934-35
• Burke, Marty	Mtl., Pit., Ott., Chi.	11	494	19	47	66	560	31	2	4	6	44	2	1927-28	1937-38
• Burmister, Roy	NYA	3	67	4	3	7	2	....	....	....	....	....	....	1929-30	1931-32
Burnett, Kelly	NYR	1	3	1	0	1	0	....	....	....	....	....	....	1952-53	1952-53
• Burns, Bobby	Chi.	3	20	1	0	1	8	....	....	....	....	....	....	1927-28	1929-30
Burns, Charlie	Det., Bos., Oak., Pit., Min.	11	749	106	198	304	252	31	5	4	9	6	....	1958-59	1972-73
Burns, Gary	NYR	2	11	2	2	4	18	5	0	0	0	2	....	1980-81	1981-82
• Burns, Norm	NYR	1	11	0	4	4	2	....	....	....	....	....	....	1941-42	1941-42
Burns, Robin	Pit., K.C.	5	190	31	38	69	139	....	....	....	....	....	....	1970-71	1975-76
Burr, Shawn	Det., T.B., S.J.	16	878	181	259	440	1069	91	16	19	35	95	....	1984-85	1999-00
Burridge, Randy	Bos., Wsh., L.A., Buf.	13	706	199	251	450	458	107	18	34	52	103	....	1985-86	1997-98
Burrows, Dave	Pit., Tor.	10	724	29	135	164	373	29	1	5	6	25	....	1971-72	1980-81
• Burry, Bert	Ott.	1	4	0	0	0	0	....	....	....	....	....	....	1932-33	1932-33
Burt, Adam	Hfd., Car., Phi., Atl.	13	737	37	115	152	961	21	0	1	1	8	....	1988-89	2000-01
Burton, Cummy	Det.	3	43	0	2	2	21	3	0	0	0	0	....	1955-56	1958-59
Burton, Nelson	Wsh.	2	8	1	0	1	21	....	....	....	....	....	....	1977-78	1978-79
• Bush, Eddie	Det.	2	26	4	6	10	40	11	1	6	7	23	....	1938-39	1941-42
Buskas, Rod	Pit., Van., L.A., Chi.	11	556	19	63	82	1294	18	0	3	3	45	....	1982-83	1992-93
Busniuk, Mike	Phi.	2	143	3	23	26	297	25	2	5	7	34	....	1979-80	1980-81
Busniuk, Ron	Buf.	2	6	0	3	3	13	....	....	....	....	....	....	1972-73	1973-74
• Buswell, Walt	Det., Mtl.	8	368	10	40	50	164	24	2	1	3	10	....	1932-33	1939-40
Butcher, Garth	Van., St.L., Que., Tor.	14	897	48	158	206	2302	50	6	5	11	122	....	1981-82	1994-95
Butler, Dick	Chi.	1	7	2	0	2	0	....	....	....	....	....	....	1947-48	1947-48
Butler, Jerry	NYR, St.L., Tor., Van., Wpg.	11	641	99	120	219	515	48	3	3	6	79	....	1972-73	1982-83
‡ Butsayev, Viacheslav	Phi., S.J., Ana., Fla., Ott., T.B.	6	132	17	26	43	133	....	....	....	....	....	....	1992-93	1999-00
Butters, Bill	Min.	2	72	1	4	5	77	....	....	....	....	....	....	1977-78	1978-79
Buttrey, Gord	Chi.	1	10	0	0	0	0	....	....	....	....	....	....	1943-44	1943-44
Buynak, Gord	St.L.	1	4	0	0	0	2	....	....	....	....	....	....	1974-75	1974-75
Byakin, Ilja	Edm., S.J.	2	57	8	25	33	44	....	....	....	....	....	....	1993-94	1994-95
Byce, John	Bos.	3	21	2	3	5	6	8	2	0	2	2	....	1989-90	1991-92
Byers, Gord	Bos.	1	1	0	1	1	0	....	....	....	....	....	....	1949-50	1949-50
Byers, Jerry	Min., Atl., NYR	4	43	3	4	7	15	....	....	....	....	....	....	1972-73	1977-78
Byers, Lyndon	Bos., S.J.	10	279	28	43	71	1081	37	2	2	4	96	....	1983-84	1992-93
Byers, Mike	Tor., Phi., L.A., Buf.	4	166	42	34	76	39	4	0	1	1	0	....	1967-68	1971-72
Byram, Shawn	NYI, Chi.	2	5	0	0	0	14	....	....	....	....	....	....	1990-91	1991-92

C

• Caffery, Jack	Tor., Bos.	3	57	3	2	5	22	10	1	0	1	4	....	1954-55	1957-58
Caffery, Terry	Chi., Min.	2	14	0	0	0	0	1	0	0	0	0	....	1969-70	1970-71
• Cahan, Larry	Tor., NYR, Oak., L.A.	13	666	38	92	130	700	29	1	1	2	38	....	1954-55	1970-71
• Cahill, Charles	Bos.	2	32	0	1	1	4	....	....	....	....	....	....	1925-26	1926-27
• Cain, Francis	Mtl.M., Tor.	2	61	4	0	4	35	....	....	....	....	....	....	1924-25	1925-26
• Cain, Herb	Mtl.M., Mtl., Bos.	13	570	206	194	400	178	67	16	13	29	13	2	1933-34	1945-46
Cairns, Don	K.C., Col.	2	9	0	1	1	2	....	....	....	....	....	....	1975-76	1976-77
Calder, Eric	Wsh.	2	2	0	0	0	0	....	....	....	....	....	....	1981-82	1982-83
• Calladine, Norm	Bos.	3	63	19	29	48	8	....	....	....	....	....	....	1942-43	1944-45
Callander, Drew	Phi., Van.	4	39	6	2	8	7	....	....	....	....	....	....	1976-77	1979-80
Callander, Jock	Pit., T.B.	5	109	22	29	51	116	22	3	8	11	12	1	1987-88	1992-93
Callighen, Brett	Edm.	3	160	56	89	145	132	14	4	6	10	8	....	1979-80	1981-82
Callighen, Patsy	NYR	1	36	0	0	0	32	9	0	0	0	0	1	1927-28	1927-28
‡ Caloun, Jan	S.J., CBJ	3	24	8	6	14	2	....	....	....	....	....	....	1995-96	2000-01
Camazzola, James	Chi.	2	3	0	0	0	0	....	....	....	....	....	....	1983-84	1986-87
Camazzola, Tony	Wsh.	1	3	0	0	0	4	....	....	....	....	....	....	1981-82	1981-82
Cameron, Al	Det., Wpg.	6	282	11	44	55	356	7	0	1	1	2	....	1975-76	1980-81
• Cameron, Billy	Mtl., NYA	2	39	0	0	0	2	2	0	0	0	0	1	1923-24	1925-26
Cameron, Craig	Det., St.L., Min., NYI	9	552	87	65	152	196	27	3	1	4	17	....	1966-67	1975-76
Cameron, Dave	Col., N.J.	3	168	25	28	53	238	....	....	....	....	....	....	1981-82	1983-84
• Cameron, Harry	Tor., Ott., Mtl.	6	128	88	51	139	189	11	5	4	9	16	2	1917-18	1922-23
• Cameron, Scotty	NYR	1	35	8	11	19	0	....	....	....	....	....	....	1942-43	1942-43
Campbell, Bryan	L.A., Chi.	5	260	35	71	106	74	22	3	4	7	2	....	1967-68	1971-72
Campbell, Colin	Pit., Col., Edm., Van., Det.	11	636	25	103	128	1292	45	4	10	14	181	....	1974-75	1984-85
• Campbell, Dave	Mtl.	1	2	0	0	0	0	....	....	....	....	....	....	1920-21	1920-21
Campbell, Don	Chi.	1	17	1	3	4	8	....	....	....	....	....	....	1943-44	1943-44
• Campbell, Earl	Ott., NYA	3	76	6	3	9	14	1	0	0	0	6	....	1923-24	1925-26
Campbell, Scott	Wpg., St.L.	3	80	4	21	25	243	....	....	....	....	....	....	1979-80	1981-82
Campbell, Wade	Wpg., Bos.	6	213	9	27	36	305	10	0	0	0	20	....	1982-83	1987-88
Campeau, Tod	Mtl.	3	42	5	9	14	16	1	0	0	0	0	....	1943-44	1948-49
Campedelli, Dom	Mtl.	1	2	0	0	0	0	....	....	....	....	....	....	1985-86	1985-86
Capuano, Dave	Pit., Van., T.B., S.J.	4	104	17	38	55	56	6	1	1	2	5	....	1989-90	1993-94
Capuano, Jack	Tor., Van., Bos.	3	6	0	0	0	0	....	....	....	....	....	....	1989-90	1991-92
Carbol, Leo	Chi.	1	6	0	1	1	4	....	....	....	....	....	....	1942-43	1942-43
Carbonneau, Guy	Mtl., St.L., Dal.	19	1318	260	403	663	820	231	38	55	93	161	3	1980-81	1999-00
Cardin, Claude	St.L.	1	1	0	0	0	0	....	....	....	....	....	....	1967-68	1967-68
Cardwell, Steve	Pit.	3	53	9	11	20	35	4	0	0	0	2	....	1970-71	1972-73
• Carey, George	Que., Ham., Tor.	5	72	21	12	33	20	....	....	....	....	....	....	1919-20	1923-24
Carkner, Terry	NYR, Que., Phi., Det., Fla.	13	858	42	188	230	1588	54	1	9	10	48	....	1986-87	1998-99
Carleton, Wayne	Tor., Bos., Cal.	7	278	55	73	128	172	18	2	4	6	14	1	1965-66	1971-72
Carlin, Brian	L.A.	1	5	1	0	1	0	....	....	....	....	....	....	1971-72	1971-72
Carlson, Jack	Min., St.L.	6	236	30	15	45	417	25	1	2	3	72	....	1978-79	1986-87
Carlson, Kent	Mtl., St.L., Wsh.	5	113	7	11	18	148	8	0	0	0	13	....	1983-84	1988-89
Carlson, Steve	L.A.	1	52	9	12	21	23	4	1	1	2	7	....	1979-80	1979-80
Carlsson, Anders	N.J.	3	104	7	26	33	34	3	1	0	1	2	....	1986-87	1988-89
Carlyle, Randy	Tor., Pit., Wpg.	18	1055	148	499	647	1400	69	9	24	33	120	....	1976-77	1992-93
Carnback, Patrik	Mtl., Ana.	4	154	24	38	62	122	....	....	....	....	....	....	1992-93	1995-96
• Caron, Alain	Oak., Mtl.	2	60	9	13	22	18	....	....	....	....	....	....	1967-68	1968-69
Carpenter, Bob	Wsh., NYR, L.A., Bos., N.J.	19	1178	320	408	728	919	140	21	38	59	136	1	1981-82	1998-99
• Carpenter, Ed	Que., Ham.	2	45	10	5	15	41	....	....	....	....	....	....	1919-20	1920-21
Carr, Gene	St.L., NYR, L.A., Pit., Atl.	8	465	79	136	215	365	35	5	8	13	66	....	1971-72	1978-79
Carr, Lorne	NYR, NYA, Tor.	13	580	204	222	426	132	53	10	9	19	13	2	1933-34	1945-46
Carr, Red	Tor.	1	5	0	1	1	2	....	....	....	....	....	....	1943-44	1943-44
Carriere, Larry	Buf., Atl., Van., L.A., Tor.	7	367	16	74	90	462	27	0	3	3	42	....	1972-73	1979-80
• Carrigan, Gene	NYR, Det., St.L.	3	37	2	1	3	13	4	0	0	0	0	....	1930-31	1934-35
Carroll, Billy	NYI, Edm., Det.	7	322	30	54	84	113	71	6	12	18	18	4	1980-81	1986-87
• Carroll, George	Mtl.M., Bos.	1	16	0	0	0	11	....	....	....	....	....	....	1924-25	1924-25
Carroll, Greg	Wsh., Det., Hfd.	2	131	20	34	54	44	....	....	....	....	....	....	1978-79	1979-80
Carruthers, Dwight	Det., Phi.	2	2	0	0	0	0	....	....	....	....	....	....	1965-66	1967-68
• Carse, Bill	NYR, Chi.	4	124	28	43	71	38	13	3	2	5	0	....	1938-39	1941-42
• Carse, Bob	Chi., Mtl.	5	167	32	55	87	52	10	0	2	2	2	....	1939-40	1947-48
• Carson, Bill	Tor., Bos.	4	159	54	24	78	156	11	3	0	3	14	1	1926-27	1929-30
• Carson, Frank	Mtl.M., NYA, Det.	7	248	42	48	90	166	27	0	2	2	9	1	1925-26	1933-34
• Carson, Gerry	Mtl., NYR, Mtl.M.	6	261	12	11	23	205	22	0	0	0	12	1	1928-29	1936-37
Carson, Jimmy	L.A., Edm., Det., Van., Hfd.	10	626	275	286	561	254	55	17	15	32	22	....	1986-87	1995-96
Carson, Lindsay	Phi., Hfd.	7	373	66	80	146	524	49	4	10	14	56	....	1981-82	1987-88
Carter, Billy	Mtl., Bos.	3	16	0	0	0	6	....	....	....	....	....	....	1957-58	1961-62
Carter, John	Bos., S.J.	8	244	40	50	90	201	31	7	5	12	51	....	1985-86	1992-93
Carter, Ron	Edm.	1	2	0	0	0	0	....	....	....	....	....	....	1979-80	1979-80
• Carveth, Joe	Det., Bos., Mtl.	11	504	150	189	339	81	69	21	16	37	28	2	1940-41	1950-51

Name	NHL Teams	NHL Seasons	Regular Schedule					Playoffs					NHL Cup Wins	First NHL Season	Last NHL Season
			GP	G	A	TP	PIM	GP	G	A	TP	PIM			
Cashman, Wayne	Bos.	17	1027	277	516	793	1041	145	31	57	88	250	2	1964-65	1982-83
‡ Casselman, Mike	Fla.	1	3	0	0	0	0	....	....	....	....	....	....	1995-96	1995-96
Cassidy, Bruce	Chi.	7	36	4	13	17	10	1	0	0	0	0	....	1983-84	1989-90
Cassidy, Tom	Pit.	1	26	3	4	7	15	....	....	....	....	....	....	1977-78	1977-78
Cassolato, Tony	Wsh.	3	23	1	6	7	4	....	....	....	....	....	....	1979-80	1981-82
Caufield, Jay	NYR, Min., Pit.	7	208	5	8	13	759	17	0	0	0	42	2	1986-87	1992-93
Cavallini, Gino	Cgy., St.L., Que.	9	593	114	159	273	507	74	14	19	33	66	....	1984-85	1992-93
Cavallini, Paul	Wsh., St.L., Dal.	10	564	56	177	233	750	69	8	27	35	114	....	1986-87	1995-96
Ceresino, Ray	Tor.	1	12	1	1	2	2	....	....	....	....	....	....	1948-49	1948-49
Cernik, Frantisek	Det.	1	49	5	4	9	13	....	....	....	....	....	....	1984-85	1984-85
Chabot, John	Mtl., Pit., Det.	8	508	84	228	312	85	33	6	20	26	2	....	1983-84	1990-91
• Chad, John	Chi.	3	80	15	22	37	29	10	0	1	1	2	....	1939-40	1945-46
• Chalmers, Chick	NYR	1	1	0	0	0	0	....	....	....	....	....	....	1953-54	1953-54
Chalupa, Milan	Det.	1	14	0	5	5	6	....	....	....	....	....	....	1984-85	1984-85
• Chamberlain, Murph	Tor., Mtl., Bro., Bos.	12	510	100	175	275	769	66	14	17	31	96	2	1937-38	1948-49
Chambers, Shawn	Min., Wsh., T.B., N.J., Dal.	13	625	50	185	235	364	94	7	26	33	72	2	1987-88	1999-00
Champagne, Andre	Tor.	1	2	0	0	0	0	....	....	....	....	....	....	1962-63	1962-63
Chapdelaine, Rene	L.A.	3	32	0	2	2	32	....	....	....	....	....	....	1990-91	1992-93
• Chapman, Art	Bos., NYA	10	438	62	176	238	140	26	1	5	6	9	....	1930-31	1939-40
Chapman, Blair	Pit., St.L.	7	402	106	125	231	158	25	4	6	10	15	....	1976-77	1982-83
‡ Chapman, Brian	Hfd.	1	3	0	0	0	29	....	....	....	....	....	....	1990-91	1990-91
Charbonneau, Jose	Mtl., Van.	4	71	9	13	22	67	11	1	0	1	8	....	1987-88	1994-95
Charbonneau, Stephane	Que.	1	2	0	0	0	0	....	....	....	....	....	....	1991-92	1991-92
Charlebois, Bob	Min.	1	7	1	0	1	0	....	....	....	....	....	....	1967-68	1967-68
Charlesworth, Todd	Pit., NYR	6	93	3	9	12	47	....	....	....	....	....	....	1983-84	1989-90
‡ Charron, Eric	Mtl., T.B., Wsh., Cgy.	8	130	2	7	9	127	6	0	0	0	8	....	1992-93	1999-00
Charron, Guy	Mtl., Det., K.C., Wsh.	12	734	221	309	530	146	....	....	....	....	....	....	1969-70	1980-81
Chartier, Dave	Wpg.	1	1	0	0	0	0	....	....	....	....	....	....	1980-81	1980-81
Chartraw, Rick	Mtl., L.A., NYR, Edm.	10	420	28	64	92	399	75	7	9	16	80	4	1974-75	1983-84
Chase, Kelly	St.L., Hfd., Tor.	11	458	17	36	53	2017	27	1	1	2	100	....	1989-90	1999-00
Chasse, Denis	St.L., Wsh., Wpg., Ott.	4	132	11	14	25	292	7	1	7	8	23	....	1993-94	1996-97
‡ Chebaturkin, Vladimir	NYI, St.L., Chi.	5	62	2	7	9	52	3	0	0	0	2	....	1997-98	2001-02
Check, Lude	Det., Chi.	2	27	6	2	8	4	....	....	....	....	....	....	1943-44	1944-45
Chernoff, Mike	Min.	1	1	0	0	0	0	....	....	....	....	....	....	1968-69	1968-69
Chernomaz, Rich	Col., N.J., Cgy.	7	51	9	7	16	18	....	....	....	....	....	....	1981-82	1991-92
Cherry, Dick	Bos., Phi.	3	145	12	10	22	45	4	1	0	1	4	....	1956-57	1969-70
Cherry, Don	Bos.	1	....	....	....	....	....	1	0	0	0	0	....	1954-55	1954-55
Chervyakov, Denis	Bos.	1	2	0	0	0	2	....	....	....	....	....	....	1992-93	1992-93
• Chevrefils, Real	Bos., Det.	8	387	104	97	201	185	30	5	4	9	20	....	1951-52	1958-59
• Chiasson, Steve	Det., Cgy., Hfd., Car.	13	751	93	305	398	1107	63	16	19	35	119	....	1986-87	1998-99
Chibirev, Igor	Hfd.	2	45	7	12	19	2	....	....	....	....	....	....	1993-94	1994-95
Chicoine, Dan	Cle., Min.	3	31	1	2	3	12	1	0	0	0	0	....	1977-78	1979-80
Chinnick, Rick	Min.	2	4	0	2	2	0	....	....	....	....	....	....	1973-74	1974-75
Chipperfield, Ron	Edm., Que.	2	83	22	24	46	34	....	....	....	....	....	....	1979-80	1980-81
Chisholm, Art	Bos.	1	3	0	0	0	0	....	....	....	....	....	....	1960-61	1960-61
Chisholm, Colin	Min.	1	1	0	0	0	0	....	....	....	....	....	....	1986-87	1986-87
• Chisholm, Lex	Tor.	2	54	10	8	18	19	3	1	0	1	0	....	1939-40	1940-41
Chorney, Marc	Pit., L.A.	4	210	8	27	35	209	7	0	1	1	2	....	1980-81	1983-84
Chorske, Tom	Mtl., N.J., Ott., NYI, Wsh., Cgy., Pit.	11	596	115	122	237	225	50	5	12	17	10	1	1989-90	1999-00
• Chouinard, Gene	Ott.	1	8	0	0	0	0	....	....	....	....	....	....	1927-28	1927-28
Chouinard, Guy	Atl., Cgy., St.L.	10	578	205	370	575	120	46	9	28	37	12	....	1974-75	1983-84
Christian, Dave	Wpg., Wsh., Bos., St.L., Chi.	15	1009	340	433	773	284	102	32	25	57	27	....	1979-80	1993-94
‡ Christian, Jeff	N.J., Pit., Phx.	5	18	2	2	4	17	....	....	....	....	....	....	1991-92	1997-98
Christie, Mike	Cal., Cle., Col., Van.	7	412	15	101	116	550	2	0	0	0	0	....	1974-75	1980-81
Christoff, Steve	Min., Cgy., L.A.	5	248	77	64	141	108	35	16	12	28	25	....	1979-80	1983-84
Chrystal, Bob	NYR	2	132	11	14	25	112	....	....	....	....	....	....	1953-54	1954-55
‡ Church, Brad	Wsh.	1	2	0	0	0	0	....	....	....	....	....	....	1997-98	1997-98
• Church, Jack	Tor., Bro., Bos.	5	130	4	19	23	154	25	1	1	2	18	....	1938-39	1945-46
Churla, Shane	Hfd., Cgy., Min., Dal., L.A., NYR	11	488	26	45	71	2301	78	5	7	12	282	....	1986-87	1996-97
Chychrun, Jeff	Phi., L.A., Pit., Edm.	8	262	3	22	25	744	19	0	2	2	65	1	1986-87	1993-94
Chynoweth, Dean	NYI, Bos.	9	241	4	18	22	667	6	0	0	0	26	....	1988-89	1997-98
Chyzowski, Dave	NYI, Chi.	6	126	15	16	31	144	2	0	0	0	0	....	1989-90	1996-97
Ciavaglia, Peter	Buf.	2	5	0	0	0	0	....	....	....	....	....	....	1991-92	1992-93
Ciccarelli, Dino	Min., Wsh., Det., T.B., Fla.	19	1232	608	592	1200	1425	141	73	45	118	211	....	1980-81	1998-99
Ciccone, Enrico	Min., Wsh., T.B., Chi., Car., Van., Mtl.	9	374	10	18	28	1469	13	1	0	1	48	....	1991-92	2000-01
Cichocki, Chris	Det., N.J.	4	68	11	12	23	27	....	....	....	....	....	....	1985-86	1988-89
Cierny, Jozef	Edm.	1	1	0	0	0	0	....	....	....	....	....	....	1993-94	1993-94
• Ciesla, Hank	Chi., NYR	4	269	26	51	77	87	6	0	2	2	0	....	1955-56	1958-59
‡ Ciger, Zdeno	N.J., Edm., NYR, T.B.	7	352	94	134	228	101	13	2	6	8	4	....	1990-91	2001-02
Cimellaro, Tony	Ott.	1	2	0	0	0	0	....	....	....	....	....	....	1992-93	1992-93
Cimetta, Rob	Bos., Tor.	4	103	16	16	32	66	1	0	0	0	15	....	1988-89	1991-92
Cirella, Joe	Col., N.J., Que., NYR, Fla., Ott.	15	828	64	211	275	1446	38	0	13	13	98	....	1981-82	1995-96
‡ Cirone, Jason	Wpg.	1	3	0	0	0	2	....	....	....	....	....	....	1991-92	1991-92
Clackson, Kim	Pit., Que.	2	106	0	8	8	370	8	0	0	0	70	....	1979-80	1980-81
• Clancy, King	Ott., Tor.	16	592	136	147	283	914	55	8	8	16	88	3	1921-22	1936-37
Clancy, Terry	Oak., Tor.	4	93	6	6	12	39	....	....	....	....	....	....	1967-68	1972-73
• Clapper, Dit	Bos.	20	833	228	246	474	462	82	13	17	30	50	3	1927-28	1946-47
Clark, Dan	NYR	1	4	0	1	1	6	....	....	....	....	....	....	1978-79	1978-79
Clark, Dean	Edm.	1	1	0	0	0	0	....	....	....	....	....	....	1983-84	1983-84
Clark, Gordie	Bos.	2	8	0	1	1	0	1	0	0	0	0	....	1974-75	1975-76
• Clark, Nobby	Bos.	1	5	0	0	0	0	....	....	....	....	....	....	1927-28	1927-28
Clark, Wendel	Tor., Que., NYI, T.B., Det., Chi.	15	793	330	234	564	1690	95	37	32	69	201	....	1985-86	1999-00
Clarke, Bobby	Phi.	15	1144	358	852	1210	1453	136	42	77	119	152	2	1969-70	1983-84
‡ Clarke, Dale	St.L.	1	3	0	0	0	0	....	....	....	....	....	....	2000-01	2000-01
• Cleghorn, Odie	Mtl., Pit.	10	181	95	34	129	142	12	7	2	9	5	1	1918-19	1927-28
• Cleghorn, Sprague	Ott., Tor., Mtl., Bos.	10	259	83	55	138	538	21	4	3	7	26	2	1918-19	1927-28
Clement, Bill	Phi., Wsh., Atl., Cgy.	11	719	148	208	356	383	50	5	3	8	26	2	1971-72	1981-82
Cline, Bruce	NYR	1	30	2	3	5	10	....	....	....	....	....	....	1956-57	1956-57
Clippingdale, Steve	L.A., Wsh.	2	19	1	2	3	9	1	0	0	0	0	....	1976-77	1979-80
Cloutier, Real	Que., Buf.	6	317	146	198	344	119	25	7	5	12	20	....	1979-80	1984-85
Cloutier, Rejean	Det.	2	5	0	2	2	2	....	....	....	....	....	....	1979-80	1981-82
Cloutier, Roland	Det., Que.	3	34	8	9	17	2	....	....	....	....	....	....	1977-78	1979-80
‡ Cloutier, Sylvain	Chi.	1	7	0	0	0	0	....	....	....	....	....	....	1998-99	1998-99
• Clune, Wally	Mtl.	1	5	0	0	0	6	....	....	....	....	....	....	1955-56	1955-56
Coalter, Gary	Cal., K.C.	2	34	2	4	6	2	....	....	....	....	....	....	1973-74	1974-75
Coates, Steve	Det.	1	5	1	0	1	24	....	....	....	....	....	....	1976-77	1976-77
Cochrane, Glen	Phi., Van., Chi., Edm.	10	411	17	72	89	1556	18	1	1	2	31	....	1978-79	1988-89
Coffey, Paul	Edm., Pit., L.A., Det., Hfd., Phi., Chi., Car., Bos.	21	1409	396	1135	1531	1802	194	59	137	196	264	4	1980-81	2000-01
Coflin, Hugh	Chi.	1	31	0	3	3	33	....	....	....	....	....	....	1950-51	1950-51
Cole, Danton	Wpg., T.B., N.J., NYI, Chi.	7	318	58	60	118	125	1	0	0	0	0	1	1989-90	1995-96
Colley, Tom	Min.	1	1	0	0	0	2	....	....	....	....	....	....	1974-75	1974-75
Collings, Norm	Mtl.	1	1	0	1	1	0	....	....	....	....	....	....	1934-35	1934-35
Collins, Bill	Min., Mtl., Det., St.L., NYR, Phi., Wsh.	11	768	157	154	311	415	18	3	5	8	12	....	1967-68	1977-78
Collins, Gary	Tor.	1	....	....	....	....	....	2	0	0	0	0	....	1958-59	1958-59
Collyard, Bob	St.L.	1	10	1	3	4	4	....	....	....	....	....	....	1973-74	1973-74
• Colman, Michael	S.J.	1	15	0	1	1	32	....	....	....	....	....	....	1991-92	1991-92
• Colville, Mac	NYR	9	353	71	104	175	130	40	9	10	19	14	1	1935-36	1946-47
• Colville, Neil	NYR	12	464	99	166	265	213	46	7	19	26	32	1	1935-36	1948-49
Colwill, Les	NYR	1	69	7	6	13	16	....	....	....	....	....	....	1958-59	1958-59
Comeau, Rey	Mtl., Atl., Col.	9	564	98	141	239	175	9	2	1	3	8	....	1971-72	1979-80
Comrie, Paul	Edm.	1	15	1	2	3	4	....	....	....	....	....	....	1999-00	1999-00
Conacher, Brian	Tor., Det.	5	155	28	28	56	84	12	3	2	5	21	1	1961-62	1971-72
• Conacher, Charlie	Tor., Det., NYA	12	459	225	173	398	523	49	17	18	35	49	1	1929-30	1940-41
Conacher, Jim	Det., Chi., NYR	8	328	85	117	202	91	19	5	2	7	4	....	1945-46	1952-53
• Conacher, Lionel	Pit., NYA, Mtl.M., Chi.	12	498	80	105	185	882	35	2	2	4	34	2	1925-26	1936-37
Conacher, Pat	NYR, Edm., N.J., L.A., Cgy., NYI	13	521	63	76	139	235	66	11	10	21	40	1	1979-80	1995-96
Conacher, Pete	Chi., NYR, Tor.	6	229	47	39	86	57	7	0	0	0	0	....	1951-52	1957-58
• Conacher, Roy	Bos., Det., Chi.	11	490	226	200	426	90	42	15	15	30	14	2	1938-39	1951-52
• Conn, Red	NYA	2	96	9	28	37	22	....	....	....	....	....	....	1933-34	1934-35
Conn, Rob	Chi., Buf.	2	30	2	5	7	20	....	....	....	....	....	....	1991-92	1995-96
• Connelly, Bert	NYR, Chi.	3	87	13	15	28	37	14	1	0	1	0	1	1934-35	1937-38
Connelly, Wayne	Mtl., Bos., Min., Det., St.L., Van.	10	543	133	174	307	156	24	11	7	18	4	....	1960-61	1971-72
Connor, Cam	Mtl., Edm., NYR	5	89	9	22	31	256	20	5	0	5	6	1	1978-79	1982-83
• Connor, Harry	Bos., NYA, Ott.	4	134	16	5	21	149	10	0	0	0	2	....	1927-28	1930-31

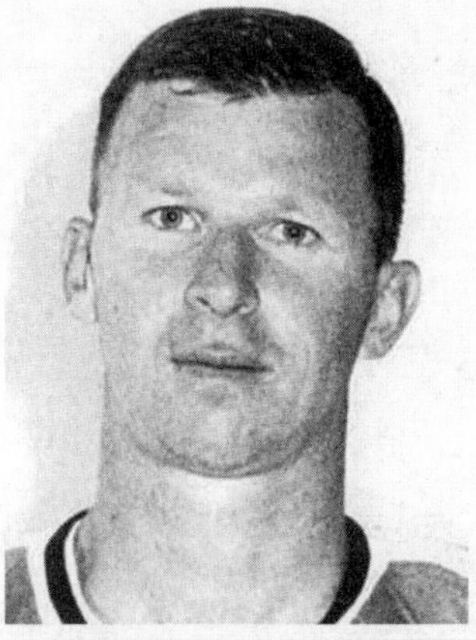
Dick Cherry

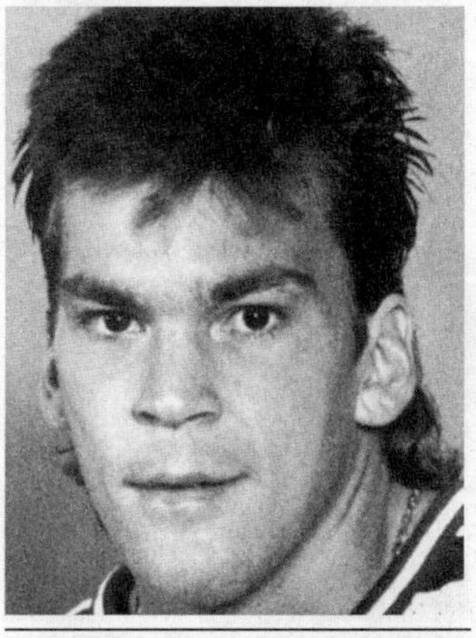
Chris Cichocki

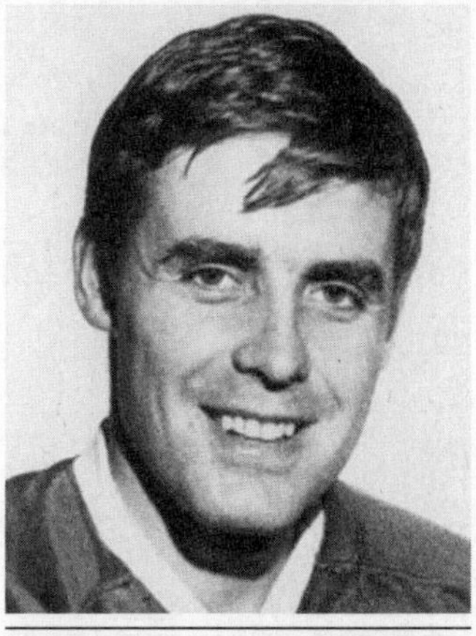
Terry Clancy

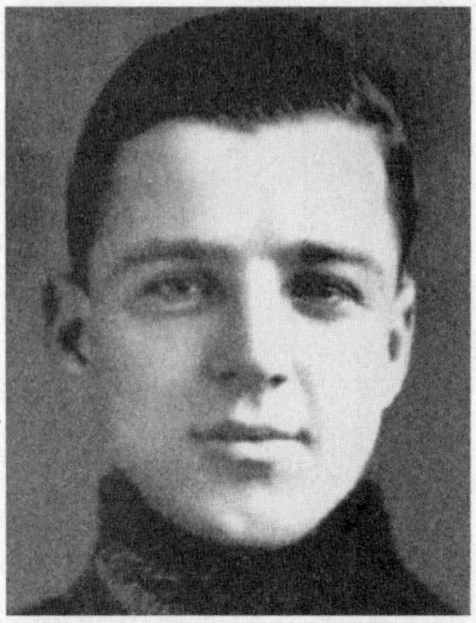
Odie Cleghorn

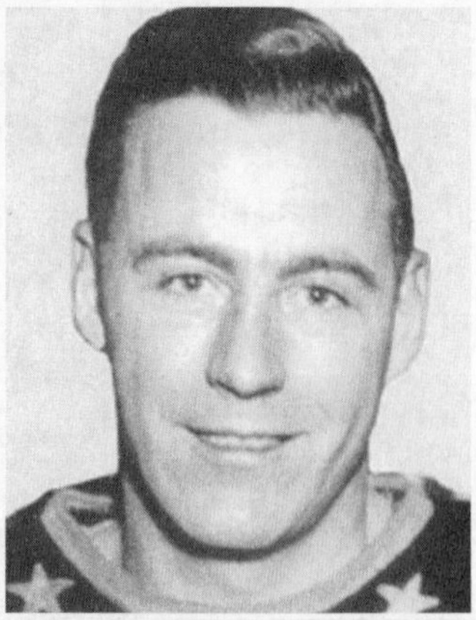

Eddie Convey

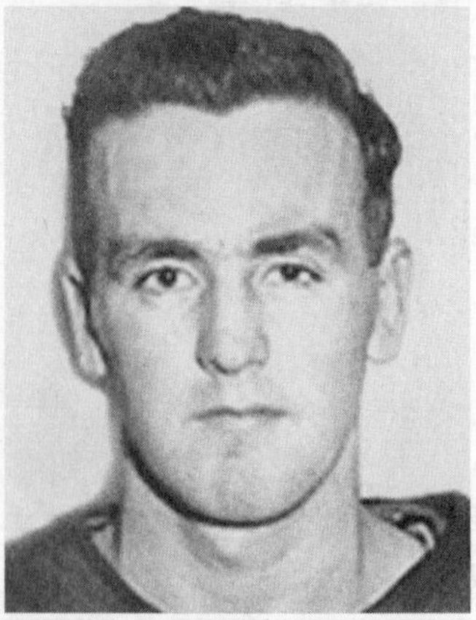

Murray Costello

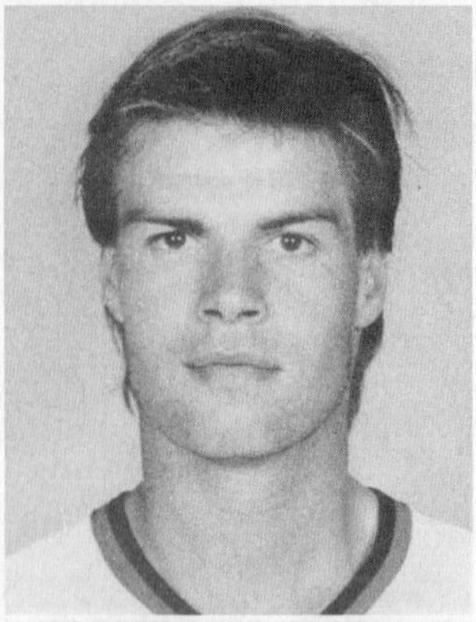

Adam Creighton

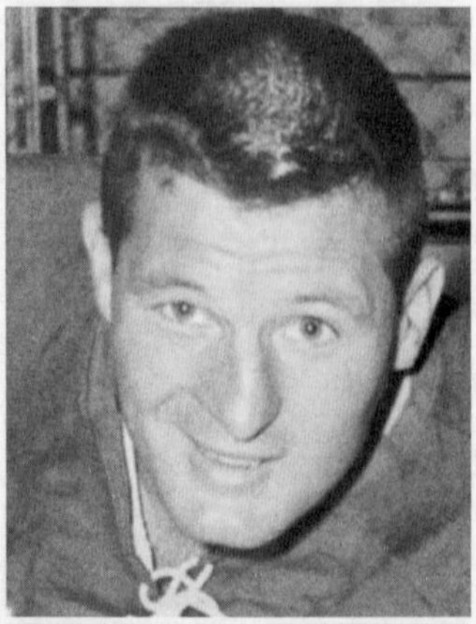

Ian Cushenan

			Regular Schedule					Playoffs							
Name	NHL Teams	NHL Seasons	GP	G	A	TP	PIM	GP	G	A	TP	PIM	NHL Cup Wins	First NHL Season	Last NHL Season
● Connors, Bob	NYA, Det.	3	78	17	10	27	110	2	0	0	0	10	....	1926-27	1929-30
Conroy, Al	Phi.	3	114	9	14	23	156	....	....	....	....	....	....	1991-92	1993-94
Contini, Joe	Col., Min.	3	68	17	21	38	34	2	0	0	0	0	....	1977-78	1980-81
‡ Convery, Brandon	Tor., Van., L.A.	4	72	9	19	28	36	5	0	0	0	2	....	1995-96	1998-99
● Convey, Eddie	NYA	3	36	1	1	2	33	....	....	....	....	....	....	1930-31	1932-33
● Cook, Bill	NYR	11	474	229	138	367	386	46	13	11	24	68	2	1926-27	1936-37
● Cook, Bob	Van., Det., NYI, Min.	4	72	13	9	22	22	....	....	....	....	....	....	1970-71	1974-75
● Cook, Bud	Bos., Ott., St.L.	3	50	5	4	9	22	....	....	....	....	....	....	1931-32	1934-35
● Cook, Bun	NYR, Bos.	11	473	158	144	302	444	46	15	3	18	50	2	1926-27	1936-37
● Cook, Lloyd	Bos.	1	4	1	0	1	0	....	....	....	....	....	....	1924-25	1924-25
● Cook, Tom	Chi., Mtl.M.	9	349	77	98	175	184	24	2	4	6	19	1	1929-30	1937-38
● Cooper, Carson	Bos., Mtl., Det.	8	294	110	57	167	111	7	0	0	0	2	....	1924-25	1931-32
‡ Cooper, David	Tor.	3	30	3	7	10	24	....	....	....	....	....	....	1996-97	2000-01
Cooper, Ed	Col.	2	49	8	7	15	46	....	....	....	....	....	....	1980-81	1981-82
● Cooper, Hal	NYR	1	8	0	0	0	2	....	....	....	....	....	....	1944-45	1944-45
● Cooper, Joe	NYR, Chi.	11	420	30	66	96	442	35	3	5	8	58	....	1935-36	1946-47
Copp, Bob	Tor.	2	40	3	9	12	26	....	....	....	....	....	....	1942-43	1950-51
● Corbeau, Bert	Mtl., Ham., Tor.	10	258	63	49	112	629	9	2	2	4	38	....	1917-18	1926-27
Corbet, Rene	Que., Col., Cgy., Pit.	8	362	58	74	132	420	53	7	6	13	52	1	1993-94	2000-01
● Corbett, Mike	L.A.	1	....	....	....	....	....	2	0	1	1	2	....	1967-68	1967-68
Corcoran, Norm	Bos., Det., Chi.	4	29	1	3	4	21	4	0	0	0	6	....	1949-50	1955-56
Corkum, Bob	Buf., Ana., Phi., Phx., L.A., N.J., Atl.	12	720	97	103	200	281	62	7	7	14	24	....	1989-90	2001-02
● Cormier, Roger	Mtl.	1	1	0	0	0	0	....	....	....	....	....	....	1925-26	1925-26
Cornforth, Mark	Bos.	1	6	0	0	0	4	....	....	....	....	....	....	1995-96	1995-96
Corrigan, Chuck	Tor., NYA	2	19	2	2	4	2	....	....	....	....	....	....	1937-38	1940-41
Corrigan, Mike	L.A., Van., Pit.	10	594	152	195	347	698	17	2	3	5	20	....	1967-68	1977-78
‡ Corrinet, Chris	Wsh.	1	8	0	1	1	6	....	....	....	....	....	....	2001-02	2001-02
● Corriveau, Andre	Mtl.	1	3	0	1	1	0	....	....	....	....	....	....	1953-54	1953-54
‡ Corriveau, Yvon	Wsh., Hfd., S.J.	9	280	48	40	88	310	29	5	7	12	50	....	1985-86	1993-94
Cory, Ross	Wpg.	2	51	2	10	12	41	....	....	....	....	....	....	1979-80	1980-81
Cossette, Jacques	Pit.	3	64	8	6	14	29	3	0	1	1	4	....	1975-76	1978-79
● Costello, Les	Tor.	3	15	2	3	5	11	6	2	2	4	2	1	1947-48	1949-50
Costello, Murray	Chi., Bos., Det.	4	162	13	19	32	54	5	0	0	0	2	....	1953-54	1956-57
Costello, Rich	Tor.	2	12	2	2	4	2	....	....	....	....	....	....	1983-84	1985-86
● Cotch, Charlie	Ham., Tor.	1	12	1	0	1	0	....	....	....	....	....	....	1924-25	1924-25
Cote, Alain	Que.	10	696	103	190	293	383	67	9	15	24	44	....	1979-80	1988-89
Cote, Alain	Bos., Wsh., Mtl., T.B., Que.	9	119	2	18	20	124	11	0	2	2	26	....	1985-86	1993-94
Cote, Patrick	Dal., Nsh., Edm.	6	105	1	2	3	377	....	....	....	....	....	....	1995-96	2000-01
Cote, Ray	Edm.	3	15	0	0	0	4	14	3	2	5	0	....	1982-83	1984-85
Cote, Sylvain	Hfd., Wsh., Tor., Chi., Dal.	19	1171	122	313	435	545	102	11	22	33	62	....	1984-85	2002-03
● Cotton, Baldy	Pit., Tor., NYA	12	503	101	103	204	419	43	4	9	13	46	1	1925-26	1936-37
● Coughlin, Jack	Tor., Que., Mtl., Ham.	3	19	2	0	2	3	....	....	....	....	....	1	1917-18	1920-21
Coulis, Tim	Wsh., Min.	4	47	4	5	9	138	3	1	0	1	2	....	1979-80	1985-86
Coulson, D'arcy	Phi.	1	28	0	0	0	103	....	....	....	....	....	....	1930-31	1930-31
● Coulter, Art	Chi., NYR	11	465	30	82	112	543	49	4	5	9	61	2	1931-32	1941-42
Coulter, Neal	NYI	3	26	5	5	10	11	....	....	....	....	....	....	1985-86	1987-88
Cournoyer, Yvan	Mtl.	16	968	428	435	863	255	147	64	63	127	47	10	1963-64	1978-79
Courteau, Yves	Cgy., Hfd.	3	22	2	5	7	4	1	0	0	0	0	....	1984-85	1986-87
‡ Courtenay, Ed	S.J.	2	44	7	13	20	10	....	....	....	....	....	....	1991-92	1992-93
Courtnall, Geoff	Bos., Edm., Wsh., St.L., Van.	17	1048	367	432	799	1465	156	39	70	109	262	1	1983-84	1999-00
Courtnall, Russ	Tor., Mtl., Min., Dal., Van., NYR, L.A.	16	1029	297	447	744	557	129	39	44	83	83	....	1983-84	1998-99
‡ Courville, Larry	Van.	3	33	1	2	3	16	....	....	....	....	....	....	1995-96	1997-98
● Coutu, Billy	Mtl., Ham., Bos.	10	244	33	21	54	478	19	1	1	2	39	1	1917-18	1926-27
● Couture, Gerry	Det., Mtl., Chi.	10	385	86	70	156	89	45	9	7	16	4	1	1944-45	1953-54
● Couture, Rosie	Chi., Mtl.	8	309	48	56	104	184	23	1	5	6	15	1	1928-29	1935-36
Couturier, Sylvain	L.A.	3	33	4	5	9	4	....	....	....	....	....	....	1988-89	1991-92
Cowick, Bruce	Phi., Wsh., St.L.	3	70	5	6	11	43	8	0	0	0	9	1	1973-74	1975-76
Cowie, Rob	L.A.	2	78	7	12	19	52	....	....	....	....	....	....	1994-95	1995-96
● Cowley, Bill	St.L., Bos.	13	549	195	353	548	143	64	12	34	46	22	2	1934-35	1946-47
● Cox, Danny	Tor., Ott., Det., NYR	8	319	47	49	96	128	10	0	1	1	6	....	1926-27	1933-34
Coxe, Craig	Van., Cgy., St.L., S.J.	8	235	14	31	45	713	5	1	0	1	18	....	1984-85	1991-92
‡ Craig, Mike	Min., Dal., Tor., S.J.	9	423	71	97	168	550	26	2	2	4	49	....	1990-91	2001-02
‡ Craighead, John	Tor.	1	5	0	0	0	10	....	....	....	....	....	....	1996-97	1996-97
Craigwell, Dale	S.J.	3	98	11	18	29	28	....	....	....	....	....	....	1991-92	1993-94
Crashley, Bart	Det., K.C., L.A.	6	140	7	36	43	50	....	....	....	....	....	....	1965-66	1975-76
Craven, Murray	Det., Phi., Hfd., Van., Chi., S.J.	18	1071	266	493	759	524	118	27	43	70	64	....	1982-83	1999-00
Crawford, Bob	St.L., Hfd., NYR, Wsh.	7	246	71	71	142	72	11	0	1	1	8	....	1979-80	1986-87
Crawford, Bobby	Col., Det.	2	16	1	3	4	6	....	....	....	....	....	....	1980-81	1982-83
● Crawford, Jack	Bos.	13	548	38	140	178	202	66	3	13	16	36	2	1937-38	1949-50
Crawford, Lou	Bos.	2	26	2	1	3	29	1	0	0	0	0	....	1989-90	1991-92
Crawford, Marc	Van.	6	176	19	31	50	229	20	1	2	3	44	....	1981-82	1986-87
● Crawford, Rusty	Ott., Tor.	2	38	10	8	18	117	2	2	1	3	9	1	1917-18	1918-19
Creighton, Adam	Buf., Chi., NYI, T.B., St.L.	14	708	187	216	403	1077	61	11	14	25	137	....	1983-84	1996-97
Creighton, Dave	Bos., Tor., Chi., NYR	12	616	140	174	314	223	51	11	13	24	20	....	1948-49	1959-60
● Creighton, Jimmy	Det.	1	11	1	0	1	2	....	....	....	....	....	....	1930-31	1930-31
Cressman, Dave	Min.	2	85	6	8	14	37	....	....	....	....	....	....	1974-75	1975-76
Cressman, Glen	Mtl.	1	4	0	0	0	2	....	....	....	....	....	....	1956-57	1956-57
Crisp, Terry	Bos., St.L., NYI, Phi.	11	536	67	134	201	135	110	15	28	43	40	2	1965-66	1976-77
Cristofoli, Ed	Mtl.	1	9	0	1	1	4	....	....	....	....	....	....	1989-90	1989-90
● Croghan, Maurice	Mtl.M.	1	16	0	0	0	4	....	....	....	....	....	....	1937-38	1937-38
Crombeen, Mike	Cle., St.L., Hfd.	8	475	55	68	123	218	27	6	2	8	32	....	1977-78	1984-85
Cronin, Shawn	Wsh., Wpg., Phi., S.J.	7	292	3	18	21	877	32	1	0	1	38	....	1988-89	1994-95
● Crossett, Stan	Phi.	1	21	0	0	0	10	....	....	....	....	....	....	1930-31	1930-31
Crossman, Doug	Chi., Phi., L.A., NYI, Hfd., Det., T.B., St.L.	14	914	105	359	464	534	97	12	39	51	105	....	1980-81	1993-94
Croteau, Gary	L.A., Det., Cal., K.C., Col.	12	684	144	175	319	143	11	3	2	5	8	....	1968-69	1979-80
Crowder, Bruce	Bos., Pit.	4	243	47	51	98	156	31	8	4	12	41	....	1981-82	1984-85
Crowder, Keith	Bos., L.A.	10	662	223	271	494	1354	85	14	22	36	218	....	1980-81	1989-90
Crowder, Troy	N.J., Det., L.A., Van.	7	150	9	7	16	433	4	0	0	0	22	....	1987-88	1996-97
‡ Crowe, Phil	L.A., Phi., Ott., Nsh.	6	94	4	5	9	173	3	0	0	0	16	....	1993-94	1999-00
Crowley, Mike	Ana.	3	67	5	15	20	44	....	....	....	....	....	....	1997-98	2000-01
‡ Crowley, Ted	Hfd., Col., NYI	2	34	2	4	6	12	....	....	....	....	....	....	1993-94	1998-99
‡ Crozier, Greg	Pit.	1	1	0	0	0	0	....	....	....	....	....	....	2000-01	2000-01
Crozier, Joe	Tor.	1	5	0	3	3	2	....	....	....	....	....	....	1959-60	1959-60
● Crutchfield, Nels	Mtl.	1	41	5	5	10	20	2	0	1	1	22	....	1934-35	1934-35
Culhane, Jim	Hfd.	1	6	0	1	1	4	....	....	....	....	....	....	1989-90	1989-90
Cullen, Barry	Tor., Det.	5	219	32	52	84	111	6	0	0	0	2	....	1955-56	1959-60
Cullen, Brian	Tor., NYR	7	326	56	100	156	92	19	3	0	3	2	....	1954-55	1960-61
Cullen, John	Pit., Hfd., Tor., T.B.	11	621	187	363	550	898	53	12	22	34	58	....	1988-89	1998-99
Cullen, Ray	NYR, Det., Min., Van.	6	313	92	123	215	120	20	3	10	13	2	....	1965-66	1970-71
Cummins, Barry	Cal.	1	36	1	2	3	39	....	....	....	....	....	....	1973-74	1973-74
Cummins, Jim	Det., Phi., T.B., Chi., Phx., Mtl., Ana., NYI, Col.	12	511	24	36	60	1538	37	1	2	3	43	....	1991-92	2003-04
Cunneyworth, Randy	Buf., Pit., Wpg., Hfd., Chi., Ott.	16	866	189	225	414	1280	45	7	7	14	61	....	1980-81	1998-99
Cunningham, Bob	NYR	2	4	0	1	1	0	....	....	....	....	....	....	1960-61	1961-62
Cunningham, Jim	Phi.	1	1	0	0	0	4	....	....	....	....	....	....	1977-78	1977-78
● Cunningham, Les	NYA, Chi.	2	60	7	19	26	21	1	0	0	0	0	....	1936-37	1939-40
Cupolo, Bill	Bos.	1	47	11	13	24	10	7	1	2	3	0	....	1944-45	1944-45
Curran, Brian	Bos., NYI, Tor., Buf., Wsh.	10	381	7	33	40	1461	24	0	1	1	122	....	1983-84	1993-94
Currie, Dan	Edm., L.A.	4	22	2	1	3	4	....	....	....	....	....	....	1990-91	1993-94
Currie, Glen	Wsh., L.A.	8	326	39	79	118	100	12	1	3	4	4	....	1979-80	1987-88
Currie, Hugh	Mtl.	1	1	0	0	0	0	....	....	....	....	....	....	1950-51	1950-51
Currie, Tony	St.L., Van., Hfd.	8	290	92	119	211	83	16	4	12	16	14	....	1977-78	1984-85
Curry, Floyd	Mtl.	11	601	105	99	204	147	91	23	17	40	38	4	1947-48	1957-58
Curtale, Tony	Cgy.	1	2	0	0	0	0	....	....	....	....	....	....	1980-81	1980-81
Curtis, Paul	Mtl., L.A., St.L.	4	185	3	34	37	161	5	0	0	0	2	....	1969-70	1972-73
Cushenan, Ian	Chi., Mtl., NYR, Det.	5	129	3	11	14	134	....	....	....	....	....	1	1956-57	1963-64
Cusson, Jean	Oak.	1	2	0	0	0	0	....	....	....	....	....	....	1967-68	1967-68
Cyr, Denis	Cgy., Chi., St.L.	6	193	41	43	84	36	4	0	0	0	0	....	1980-81	1985-86
Cyr, Paul	Buf., NYR, Hfd.	9	470	101	140	241	623	24	4	6	10	31	....	1982-83	1991-92

D

Name	NHL Teams	NHL Seasons	GP	G	A	TP	PIM	GP	G	A	TP	PIM	NHL Cup Wins	First NHL Season	Last NHL Season
‡ Dahl, Kevin	Cgy., Phx., Tor., CBJ	8	188	7	22	29	153	16	0	2	2	12	....	1992-93	2000-01
Dahlen, Ulf	NYR, Min., Dal., S.J., Chi., Wsh.	14	966	301	354	655	230	85	15	25	40	12	....	1987-88	2002-03

Name	NHL Teams	NHL Seasons	Regular Schedule GP	G	A	TP	PIM	Playoffs GP	G	A	TP	PIM	NHL Cup Wins	First NHL Season	Last NHL Season
Dahlin, Kjell	Mtl.	3	166	57	59	116	10	35	6	11	17	6	1	1985-86	1987-88
‡ Dahlman, Toni	Ott.	2	22	1	1	2	0	....	....	....	....	....	....	2001-02	2002-03
Dahlquist, Chris	Pit., Min., Cgy., Ott.	11	532	19	71	90	488	39	4	7	11	30	....	1985-86	1995-96
• Dahlstrom, Cully	Chi.	8	342	88	118	206	58	29	6	8	14	4	1	1937-38	1944-45
Daigle, Alain	Chi.	6	389	56	50	106	122	17	0	1	1	0	....	1974-75	1979-80
Daigneault, J.J.	Van., Phi., Mtl., St.L., Pit., Ana., NYI, Nsh., Phx., Min.	16	899	53	197	250	687	99	5	26	31	100	1	1984-85	2000-01
Dailey, Bob	Van., Phi.	9	561	94	231	325	814	63	12	34	46	105	....	1973-74	1981-82
• Daley, Frank	Det.	1	5	0	0	0	0	2	0	0	0	0	....	1928-29	1928-29
Daley, Pat	Wpg.	2	12	1	0	1	13	....	....	....	....	....	....	1979-80	1980-81
Dalgarno, Brad	NYI	10	321	49	71	120	332	27	2	4	6	37	....	1985-86	1995-96
Dallman, Marty	Tor.	2	6	0	1	1	0	....	....	....	....	....	....	1987-88	1988-89
Dallman, Rod	NYI, Phi.	4	6	1	0	1	26	1	0	1	1	0	....	1987-88	1991-92
Dame, Bunny	Mtl.	1	34	2	5	7	4	....	....	....	....	....	....	1941-42	1941-42
Damore, Hank	NYR	1	4	1	0	1	2	....	....	....	....	....	....	1943-44	1943-44
Damphousse, Vincent	Tor., Edm., Mtl., S.J.	18	1378	432	773	1205	1190	140	41	63	104	144	1	1986-87	2003-04
Daneyko, Ken	N.J.	20	1283	36	142	178	2519	175	5	17	22	296	3	1983-84	2002-03
Daniels, Jeff	Pit., Fla., Hfd., Car., Nsh.	12	425	17	26	43	83	41	3	5	8	2	1	1990-91	2002-03
‡ Daniels, Kimbi	Phi.	2	27	1	2	3	4	....	....	....	....	....	....	1990-91	1991-92
Daniels, Scott	Hfd., Phi., N.J.	6	149	8	12	20	667	1	0	0	0	0	....	1992-93	1998-99
Danton, Mike	N.J., St.L.	3	87	9	5	14	182	5	1	0	1	2	....	2000-01	2003-04
Daoust, Dan	Mtl., Tor.	8	522	87	167	254	544	32	7	5	12	83	....	1982-83	1989-90
Dark, Michael	St.L.	2	43	5	6	11	14	....	....	....	....	....	....	1986-87	1987-88
• Darragh, Harold	Pit., Phi., Bos., Tor.	8	308	68	49	117	50	16	1	3	4	4	1	1925-26	1932-33
• Darragh, Jack	Ott.	6	121	66	46	112	113	11	3	0	3	9	3	1917-18	1923-24
David, Richard	Que.	3	31	4	4	8	10	1	0	0	0	0	....	1979-80	1982-83
• Davidson, Bob	Tor.	12	491	94	160	254	398	79	5	17	22	76	2	1934-35	1945-46
• Davidson, Gord	NYR	2	51	3	6	9	8	....	....	....	....	....	....	1942-43	1943-44
‡ Davidsson, Johan	Ana., NYI	2	83	6	9	15	16	1	0	0	0	0	....	1998-99	1999-00
• Davie, Bob	Bos.	3	41	0	1	1	25	....	....	....	....	....	....	1933-34	1935-36
Davies, Buck	NYR	1	....	....	....	....	....	1	0	0	0	0	....	1947-48	1947-48
• Davis, Bob	Det.	1	3	0	0	0	0	....	....	....	....	....	....	1932-33	1932-33
Davis, Kim	Pit., Tor.	4	36	5	7	12	51	4	0	0	0	0	....	1977-78	1980-81
Davis, Lorne	Mtl., Chi., Det., Bos.	6	95	8	12	20	20	18	3	1	4	10	1	1951-52	1959-60
Davis, Mal	Det., Buf.	6	100	31	22	53	34	7	1	0	1	0	....	1978-79	1985-86
• Davison, Murray	Bos.	1	1	0	0	0	0	....	....	....	....	....	....	1965-66	1965-66
Davydov, Evgeny	Wpg., Fla., Ott.	4	155	40	39	79	120	11	2	2	4	2	....	1991-92	1994-95
‡ Dawe, Jason	Buf., NYI, Mtl., NYR	8	366	86	90	176	162	22	4	3	7	18	....	1993-94	2001-02
Dawes, Bob	Tor., Mtl.	4	32	2	7	9	6	10	0	0	0	2	1	1946-47	1950-51
• Day, Hap	Tor., NYA	14	581	86	116	202	601	53	4	7	11	56	1	1924-25	1937-38
Day, Joe	Hfd., NYI	3	72	1	10	11	87	....	....	....	....	....	....	1991-92	1993-94
Dea, Billy	NYR, Det., Chi., Pit.	8	397	67	54	121	44	11	2	1	3	6	....	1953-54	1970-71
• Deacon, Don	Det.	3	30	6	4	10	6	2	2	1	3	0	....	1936-37	1939-40
Deadmarsh, Butch	Buf., Atl., K.C.	5	137	12	5	17	155	4	0	0	0	17	....	1970-71	1974-75
Dean, Barry	Col., Phi.	3	165	25	56	81	146	....	....	....	....	....	....	1976-77	1978-79
Dean, Kevin	N.J., Atl., Dal., Chi.	7	331	7	48	55	138	16	2	2	4	2	1	1994-95	2000-01
Debenedet, Nelson	Det., Pit.	2	46	10	4	14	13	....	....	....	....	....	....	1973-74	1974-75
DeBlois, Lucien	NYR, Col., Wpg., Mtl., Que., Tor.	15	993	249	276	525	814	52	7	6	13	38	1	1977-78	1991-92
Debol, Dave	Hfd.	2	92	26	26	52	4	3	0	0	0	0	....	1979-80	1980-81
‡ DeBrusk, Louie	Edm., T.B., Phx., Chi.	11	401	24	17	41	1161	15	2	0	2	10	....	1991-92	2002-03
‡ DeFauw, Brad	Car.	1	9	3	0	3	2	....	....	....	....	....	....	2002-03	2002-03
Defazio, Dean	Pit.	1	22	0	2	2	28	....	....	....	....	....	....	1983-84	1983-84
DeGray, Dale	Cgy., Tor., L.A., Buf.	5	153	18	47	65	195	13	1	3	4	28	....	1985-86	1989-90
Delisle, Jonathan	Mtl.	1	1	0	0	0	0	....	....	....	....	....	....	1998-99	1998-99
‡ Delisle, Xavier	T.B., Mtl.	2	16	3	2	5	6	....	....	....	....	....	....	1998-99	2000-01
• Delmonte, Armand	Bos.	1	1	0	0	0	0	....	....	....	....	....	....	1945-46	1945-46
Delorme, Gilbert	Mtl., St.L., Que., Det., Pit.	9	541	31	92	123	520	56	1	9	10	56	....	1981-82	1989-90
Delorme, Ron	Col., Van.	9	524	83	83	166	667	25	1	2	3	59	....	1976-77	1984-85
Delory, Val	NYR	1	1	0	0	0	0	....	....	....	....	....	....	1948-49	1948-49
Delparte, Guy	Col.	1	48	1	8	9	18	....	....	....	....	....	....	1976-77	1976-77
Delvecchio, Alex	Det.	24	1549	456	825	1281	383	121	35	69	104	29	3	1950-51	1973-74
• DeMarco, Ab	Chi., Tor., Bos., NYR	7	209	72	93	165	53	11	3	0	3	2	....	1938-39	1946-47
DeMarco, Ab	NYR, St.L., Pit., Van., L.A., Bos.	9	344	44	80	124	75	25	1	2	3	17	....	1969-70	1978-79
• Demers, Tony	Mtl., NYR	6	83	20	22	42	23	2	0	0	0	0	....	1937-38	1943-44
Denis, Jean-Paul	NYR	2	10	0	2	2	2	....	....	....	....	....	....	1946-47	1949-50
Denis, Lulu	Mtl.	2	3	0	1	1	0	....	....	....	....	....	....	1949-50	1950-51
• Denneny, Corb	Tor., Ham., Chi.	9	176	103	42	145	148	6	1	0	1	7	2	1917-18	1927-28
• Denneny, Cy	Ott., Bos.	12	328	248	85	333	301	25	16	2	18	23	5	1917-18	1928-29
Dennis, Norm	St.L.	4	12	3	0	3	11	5	0	0	0	2	....	1968-69	1971-72
• Denoird, Gerry	Tor.	1	17	0	1	1	0	....	....	....	....	....	....	1922-23	1922-23
DePalma, Larry	Min., S.J., Pit.	7	148	21	20	41	408	3	0	0	0	6	....	1985-86	1993-94
Derlago, Bill	Van., Tor., Bos., Wpg., Que.	9	555	189	227	416	247	13	5	0	5	8	....	1978-79	1986-87
• Desaulniers, Gerard	Mtl.	3	8	0	2	2	4	....	....	....	....	....	....	1950-51	1953-54
‡ Descoteaux, Matthieu	Mtl.	1	5	1	1	2	4	....	....	....	....	....	....	2000-01	2000-01
• Desilets, Joffre	Mtl., Chi.	5	192	37	45	82	57	7	1	0	1	7	....	1935-36	1939-40
Desjardins, Martin	Mtl.	1	8	0	2	2	2	....	....	....	....	....	....	1989-90	1989-90
• Desjardins, Vic	Chi., NYR	2	87	6	15	21	27	16	0	0	0	0	....	1930-31	1931-32
Deslauriers, Jacques	Mtl.	1	2	0	0	0	0	....	....	....	....	....	....	1955-56	1955-56
Deuling, Jarrett	NYI	2	15	0	1	1	11	....	....	....	....	....	....	1995-96	1996-97
Devine, Kevin	NYI	1	2	0	1	1	8	....	....	....	....	....	....	1982-83	1982-83
• Dewar, Tom	NYR	1	9	0	2	2	4	....	....	....	....	....	....	1943-44	1943-44
Dewsbury, Al	Det., Chi.	9	347	30	78	108	365	14	1	5	6	16	1	1946-47	1955-56
Deziel, Michel	Buf.	1	....	....	....	....	....	1	0	0	0	0	....	1974-75	1974-75
Dheere, Marcel	Mtl.	1	11	1	2	3	2	5	0	0	0	6	....	1942-43	1942-43
Diachuk, Edward	Det.	1	12	0	0	0	19	....	....	....	....	....	....	1960-61	1960-61
Dick, Harry	Chi.	1	12	0	1	1	12	....	....	....	....	....	....	1946-47	1946-47
Dickens, Ernie	Tor., Chi.	6	278	12	44	56	98	13	0	0	0	4	1	1941-42	1950-51
Dickenson, Herb	NYR	2	48	18	17	35	10	....	....	....	....	....	....	1951-52	1952-53
Diduck, Gerald	NYI, Mtl., Van., Chi., Hfd., Phx., Tor., Dal.	17	932	56	156	212	1612	114	8	16	24	212	....	1984-85	2000-01
Dietrich, Don	Chi., N.J.	2	28	0	7	7	10	....	....	....	....	....	....	1983-84	1985-86
• Dill, Bob	NYR	2	76	15	15	30	135	....	....	....	....	....	....	1943-44	1944-45
• Dillabough, Bob	Det., Bos., Pit., Oak.	9	283	32	54	86	76	17	3	0	3	0	....	1961-62	1969-70
• Dillon, Cecil	NYR, Det.	10	453	167	131	298	105	43	14	9	23	14	1	1930-31	1939-40
Dillon, Gary	Col.	1	13	1	1	2	29	....	....	....	....	....	....	1980-81	1980-81
Dillon, Wayne	NYR, Wpg.	4	229	43	66	109	60	3	0	1	1	0	....	1975-76	1979-80
Dineen, Bill	Det., Chi.	5	323	51	44	95	122	37	1	1	2	18	2	1953-54	1957-58
Dineen, Gary	Min.	1	4	0	1	1	0	....	....	....	....	....	....	1968-69	1968-69
Dineen, Gord	NYI, Min., Pit., Ott.	13	528	16	90	106	695	40	1	7	8	68	....	1982-83	1994-95
Dineen, Kevin	Hfd., Phi., Car., Ott., CBJ	19	1188	355	405	760	2229	59	23	18	41	127	....	1984-85	2002-03
Dineen, Peter	L.A., Det.	2	13	0	2	2	13	....	....	....	....	....	....	1986-87	1989-90
• Dinsmore, Chuck	Mtl.M.	4	100	6	2	8	50	8	1	0	1	2	1	1924-25	1929-30
Dionne, Gilbert	Mtl., Phi., Fla.	6	223	61	79	140	108	39	10	12	22	34	1	1990-91	1995-96
Dionne, Marcel	Det., L.A., NYR	18	1348	731	1040	1771	600	49	21	24	45	17	....	1971-72	1988-89
‡ DiPietro, Paul	Mtl., Tor., L.A.	6	192	31	49	80	96	31	11	10	21	10	1	1991-92	1996-97
Dirk, Robert	St.L., Van., Chi., Ana., Mtl.	9	402	13	29	42	786	39	0	1	1	56	....	1987-88	1995-96
‡ Divisek, Tomas	Phi.	2	5	1	0	1	0	....	....	....	....	....	....	2000-01	2001-02
Djoos, Per	Det., NYR	3	82	2	31	33	58	....	....	....	....	....	....	1990-91	1992-93
Doak, Gary	Det., Bos., Van., NYR	16	789	23	107	130	908	78	2	4	6	121	1	1965-66	1980-81
Dobbin, Brian	Phi., Bos.	5	63	7	8	15	61	2	0	0	0	17	....	1986-87	1991-92
Dobson, Jim	Min., Col., Que.	4	12	0	0	0	6	....	....	....	....	....	....	1979-80	1983-84
• Doherty, Fred	Mtl.	1	1	0	0	0	0	....	....	....	....	....	....	1918-19	1918-19
Dollas, Bobby	Wpg., Que., Det., Ana., Edm., Pit., Ott., Cgy., S.J.	16	646	42	96	138	467	47	2	1	3	41	....	1983-84	2000-01
‡ Domenichelli, Hnat	Hfd., Cgy., Atl., Min.	7	267	52	61	113	104	....	....	....	....	....	....	1996-97	2002-03
Donaldson, Gary	Chi.	1	1	0	0	0	0	....	....	....	....	....	....	1973-74	1973-74
Donatelli, Clark	Min., Bos.	2	35	3	4	7	39	2	0	0	0	0	....	1989-90	1991-92
Donato, Ted	Bos., NYI, Ott., Ana., Dal., St.L., L.A., NYR	13	796	150	197	347	396	58	8	10	18	22	....	1991-92	2003-04
• Donnelly, Babe	Mtl.M.	1	34	0	1	1	14	2	0	0	0	0	....	1926-27	1926-27
Donnelly, Dave	Bos., Chi., Edm.	5	137	15	24	39	150	5	0	0	0	0	....	1983-84	1987-88
Donnelly, Gord	Que., Wpg., Buf., Dal.	12	554	28	41	69	2069	26	0	2	2	61	....	1983-84	1994-95
Donnelly, Mike	NYR, Buf., L.A., Dal., NYI	11	465	114	121	235	255	47	12	12	24	30	....	1986-87	1996-97
‡ Dopita, Jiri	Phi., Edm.	2	73	12	21	33	19	....	....	....	....	....	....	2001-02	2002-03
• Doran, John	NYA, Det., Mtl.	5	98	5	10	15	110	3	0	0	0	0	....	1933-34	1939-40

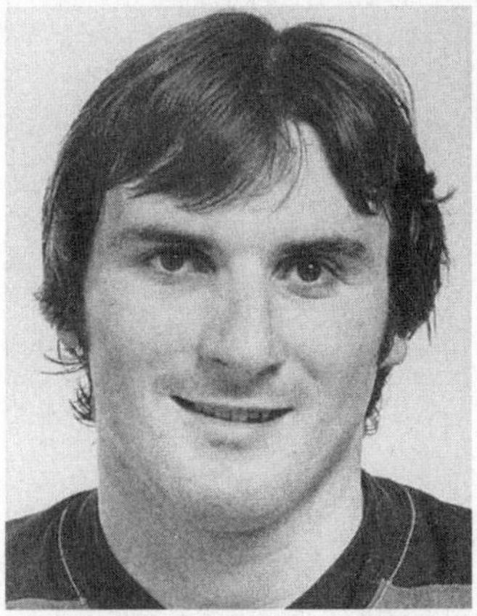

Lucien DeBlois

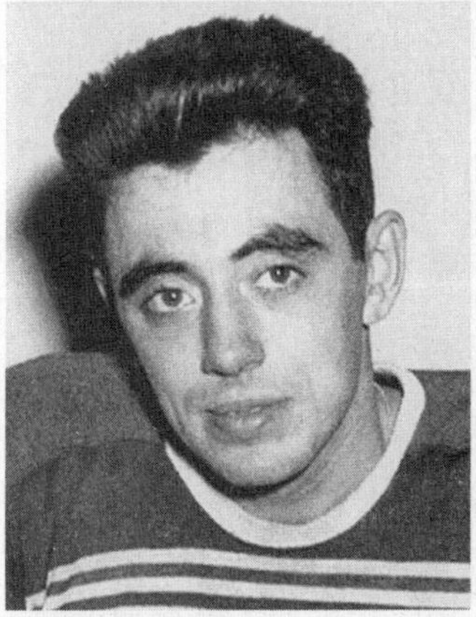

Jacques Deslauriers

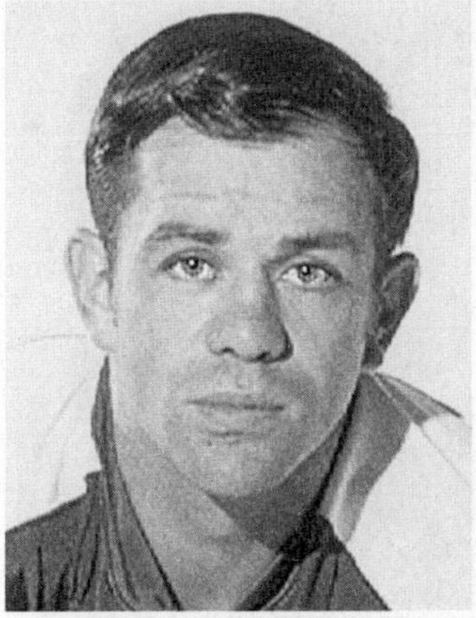

Bob Dillabough

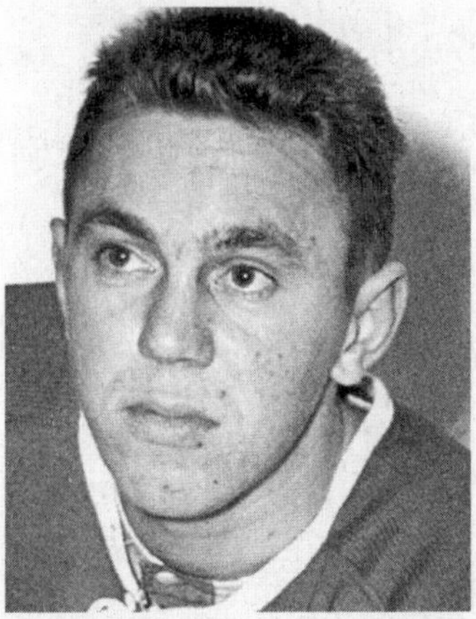

Eddie Dorohoy

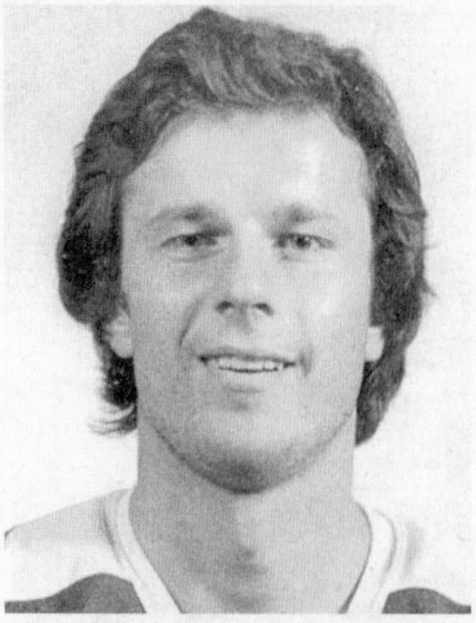

Vitezslav Duris

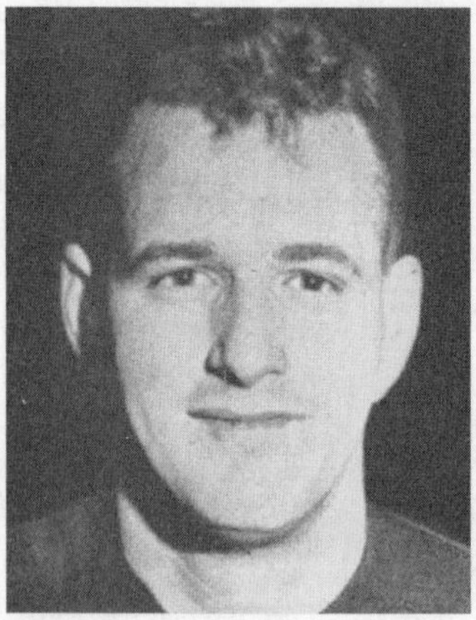

Jack Dyte

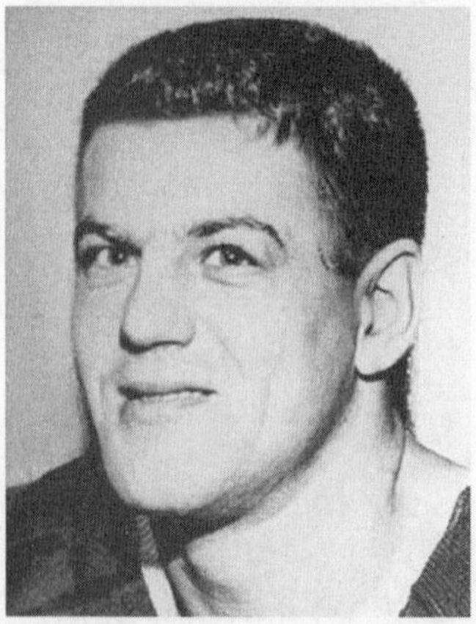

Bo Elik

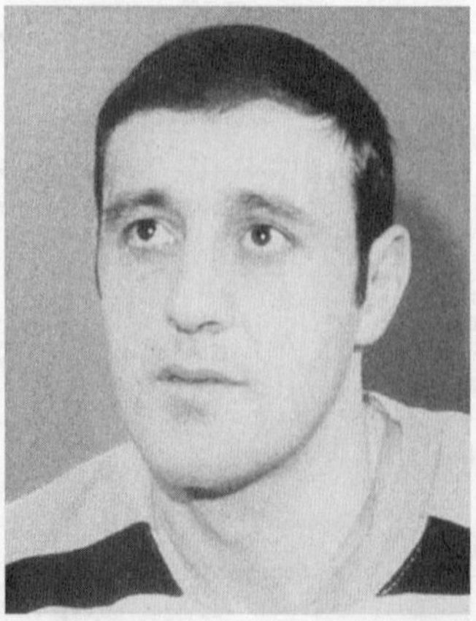

Phil Esposito

			Regular Schedule					Playoffs							
Name	NHL Teams	NHL Seasons	GP	G	A	TP	PIM	GP	G	A	TP	PIM	NHL Cup Wins	First NHL Season	Last NHL Season
Doran, Lloyd	Det.	1	24	3	2	5	10	....	....	....	....	....	....	1946-47	1946-47
• Doraty, Ken	Chi., Tor., Det.	5	103	15	26	41	24	15	7	2	9	2	....	1926-27	1937-38
Dore, Andre	NYR, St.L., Que.	7	257	14	81	95	261	23	1	2	3	32	....	1978-79	1984-85
Dore, Daniel	Que.	2	17	2	3	5	59	....	....	....	....	....	....	1989-90	1990-91
Dorey, Jim	Tor., NYR	4	232	25	74	99	553	11	0	2	2	40	....	1968-69	1971-72
Dorion, Dan	N.J.	2	4	1	1	2	2	....	....	....	....	....	....	1985-86	1987-88
Dornhoefer, Gary	Bos., Phi.	14	787	214	328	542	1291	80	17	19	36	203	2	1963-64	1977-78
Dorohoy, Eddie	Mtl.	1	16	0	0	0	6	....	....	....	....	....	....	1948-49	1948-49
Douglas, Jordy	Hfd., Min., Wpg.	6	268	76	62	138	160	6	0	0	0	4	....	1979-80	1984-85
Douglas, Kent	Tor., Oak., Det.	7	428	33	115	148	631	19	1	3	4	33	3	1962-63	1968-69
• Douglas, Les	Det.	4	52	6	12	18	8	10	3	2	5	2	1	1940-41	1946-47
Douris, Peter	Wpg., Bos., Ana., Dal.	11	321	54	67	121	80	27	3	5	8	14	....	1985-86	1997-98
• Downie, Dave	Tor.	1	11	0	1	1	2	....	....	....	....	....	....	1932-33	1932-33
‡ Doyon, Mario	Chi., Que.	3	28	3	4	7	16	....	....	....	....	....	....	1988-89	1990-91
• Draper, Bruce	Tor.	1	1	0	0	0	0	....	....	....	....	....	....	1962-63	1962-63
• Drillon, Gordie	Tor., Mtl.	7	311	155	139	294	56	50	26	15	41	10	1	1936-37	1942-43
Driscoll, Peter	Edm.	2	60	3	8	11	97	3	0	0	0	0	....	1979-80	1980-81
Driver, Bruce	N.J., NYR	15	922	96	390	486	670	108	10	40	50	64	1	1983-84	1997-98
Drolet, Rene	Phi., Det.	2	2	0	0	0	0	....	....	....	....	....	....	1971-72	1974-75
‡ Droppa, Ivan	Chi.	2	19	0	1	1	14	....	....	....	....	....	....	1993-94	1995-96
• Drouillard, Clarence	Det.	1	10	0	1	1	0	....	....	....	....	....	....	1937-38	1937-38
Drouin, Jude	Mtl., Min., NYI, Wpg.	12	666	151	305	456	346	72	27	41	68	33	....	1968-69	1980-81
Drouin, P.C.	Bos.	1	3	0	0	0	0	....	....	....	....	....	....	1996-97	1996-97
• Drouin, Polly	Mtl.	7	160	23	50	73	80	5	0	1	1	5	....	1934-35	1940-41
Druce, John	Wsh., Wpg., L.A., Phi.	10	531	113	126	239	347	53	17	6	23	38	....	1988-89	1997-98
Drulia, Stan	T.B.	3	126	15	27	42	52	....	....	....	....	....	....	1992-93	2000-01
• Drummond, Jim	NYR	1	2	0	0	0	0	....	....	....	....	....	....	1944-45	1944-45
• Drury, Herb	Pit., Phi.	6	213	24	13	37	203	4	1	1	2	0	....	1925-26	1930-31
‡ Drury, Ted	Cgy., Hfd., Ott., Ana., NYI, CBJ	8	414	41	52	93	367	14	1	0	1	4	....	1993-94	2000-01
‡ Dube, Christian	NYR	2	33	1	1	2	4	3	0	0	0	0	....	1996-97	1998-99
Dube, Gilles	Mtl., Det.	2	12	1	2	3	2	2	0	0	0	0	1	1949-50	1953-54
Dube, Norm	K.C.	2	57	8	10	18	54	....	....	....	....	....	....	1974-75	1975-76
Duberman, Justin	Pit.	1	4	0	0	0	0	....	....	....	....	....	....	1993-94	1993-94
‡ Dubinsky, Steve	Chi., Cgy., Nsh., St.L.	10	375	25	45	70	164	10	1	0	1	14	....	1993-94	2002-03
Duchesne, Gaetan	Wsh., Que., Min., S.J., Fla.	14	1028	179	254	433	617	84	14	13	27	97	....	1981-82	1994-95
Duchesne, Steve	L.A., Phi., Que., St.L., Ott., Det.	16	1113	227	525	752	824	121	16	61	77	96	1	1986-87	2001-02
Dudley, Rick	Buf., Wpg.	6	309	75	99	174	292	25	7	2	9	69	....	1972-73	1980-81
Duerden, Dave	Fla.	1	2	0	0	0	0	....	....	....	....	....	....	1999-00	1999-00
Duff, Dick	Tor., NYR, Mtl., L.A., Buf.	18	1030	283	289	572	743	114	30	49	79	78	6	1954-55	1971-72
Dufour, Luc	Bos., Que., St.L.	3	167	23	21	44	199	18	1	0	1	32	....	1982-83	1984-85
Dufour, Marc	NYR, L.A.	3	14	1	0	1	2	....	....	....	....	....	....	1963-64	1968-69
Dufresne, Donald	Mtl., T.B., L.A., St.L., Edm.	9	268	6	36	42	258	34	1	3	4	47	1	1988-89	1996-97
• Duggan, John	Ott.	1	27	0	0	0	0	2	0	0	0	0	....	1925-26	1925-26
Duggan, Ken	Min.	1	1	0	0	0	0	....	....	....	....	....	....	1987-88	1987-88
Duguay, Ron	NYR, Det., Pit., L.A.	12	864	274	346	620	582	89	31	22	53	118	....	1977-78	1988-89
• Duguid, Lorne	Mtl.M., Det., Bos.	6	135	9	15	24	57	4	1	0	1	6	....	1931-32	1936-37
• Dukowski, Duke	Chi., NYA, NYR	5	200	16	30	46	172	6	0	0	0	6	....	1926-27	1933-34
• Dumart, Woody	Bos.	16	772	211	218	429	99	88	12	15	27	23	2	1935-36	1953-54
Dunbar, Dale	Van., Bos.	2	2	0	0	0	2	....	....	....	....	....	....	1985-86	1988-89
• Duncan, Art	Det., Tor.	5	156	18	16	34	225	5	0	0	0	4	....	1926-27	1930-31
Duncan, Iain	Wpg.	4	127	34	55	89	149	11	0	3	3	6	....	1986-87	1990-91
Duncanson, Craig	L.A., Wpg., NYR	7	38	5	4	9	61	....	....	....	....	....	....	1985-86	1992-93
Dundas, Rocky	Tor.	1	5	0	0	0	14	....	....	....	....	....	....	1989-90	1989-90
• Dunlap, Frank	Tor.	1	15	0	1	1	2	....	....	....	....	....	....	1943-44	1943-44
Dunlop, Blake	Min., Phi., St.L., Det.	11	550	130	274	404	172	40	4	10	14	18	....	1973-74	1983-84
Dunn, Dave	Van., Tor.	3	184	14	41	55	313	10	1	1	2	41	....	1973-74	1975-76
Dunn, Richie	Buf., Cgy., Hfd.	12	483	36	140	176	314	36	3	15	18	24	....	1977-78	1988-89
Dupere, Denis	Tor., Wsh., St.L., K.C., Col.	8	421	80	99	179	66	16	1	0	1	0	....	1970-71	1977-78
Dupont, Andre	NYR, St.L., Phi., Que.	13	800	59	185	244	1986	140	14	18	32	352	2	1970-71	1982-83
Dupont, Jerome	Chi., Tor.	6	214	7	29	36	468	20	0	2	2	56	....	1981-82	1986-87
‡ DuPont, Micki	Cgy.	2	18	1	2	3	6	....	....	....	....	....	....	2001-02	2002-03
Dupont, Norm	Mtl., Wpg., Hfd.	5	256	55	85	140	52	13	4	2	6	0	....	1979-80	1983-84
• Dupre, Yanick	Phi.	3	35	2	0	2	16	....	....	....	....	....	....	1991-92	1995-96
• Durbano, Steve	St.L., Pit., K.C., Col.	6	220	13	60	73	1127	5	0	2	2	8	....	1972-73	1978-79
Duris, Vitezslav	Tor.	2	89	3	20	23	62	3	0	1	1	2	....	1980-81	1982-83
Dusablon, Benoit	NYR	1	3	0	0	0	2	....	....	....	....	....	....	2003-04	2003-04
Dussault, Norm	Mtl.	4	206	31	62	93	47	7	3	1	4	0	....	1947-48	1950-51
• Dutton, Red	Mtl.M., NYA	10	449	29	67	96	871	18	1	0	1	33	....	1926-27	1935-36
Dvorak, Miroslav	Phi.	3	193	11	74	85	51	18	0	2	2	6	....	1982-83	1984-85
Dwyer, Mike	Col., Cgy.	4	31	2	6	8	25	1	1	0	1	0	....	1978-79	1981-82
• Dyck, Henry	NYR	1	1	0	0	0	0	....	....	....	....	....	....	1943-44	1943-44
• Dye, Babe	Tor., Ham., Chi., NYA	11	271	201	47	248	221	10	2	0	2	11	1	1919-20	1930-31
Dykstra, Steve	Buf., Edm., Pit., Hfd.	5	217	8	32	40	545	1	0	0	0	2	....	1985-86	1989-90
Dyte, Jack	Chi.	1	27	1	0	1	31	....	....	....	....	....	....	1943-44	1943-44
Dziedzic, Joe	Pit., Phx.	3	130	14	14	28	131	21	1	3	4	23	....	1995-96	1998-99

E

Eagles, Mike	Que., Chi., Wpg., Wsh.	16	853	74	122	196	928	44	2	6	8	34	....	1982-83	1999-00
Eakin, Bruce	Cgy., Det.	4	13	2	2	4	4	....	....	....	....	....	....	1981-82	1985-86
Eakins, Dallas	Wpg., Fla., St.L., Phx., NYR, Tor., NYI, Cgy.	10	120	0	9	9	208	5	0	0	0	4	....	1992-93	2001-02
Eatough, Jeff	Buf.	1	1	0	0	0	0	....	....	....	....	....	....	1981-82	1981-82
Eaves, Mike	Min., Cgy.	8	324	83	143	226	80	43	7	10	17	14	....	1978-79	1985-86
Eaves, Murray	Wpg., Det.	8	57	4	13	17	9	4	0	1	1	2	....	1980-81	1989-90
Ecclestone, Tim	St.L., Det., Tor., Atl.	11	692	126	233	359	344	48	6	11	17	76	....	1967-68	1977-78
Edberg, Rolf	Wsh.	3	184	45	58	103	24	....	....	....	....	....	....	1978-79	1980-81
• Eddolls, Frank	Mtl., NYR	8	317	23	43	66	114	31	0	2	2	10	1	1944-45	1951-52
Edestrand, Darryl	St.L., Phi., Pit., Bos., L.A.	10	455	34	90	124	404	42	3	9	12	57	....	1967-68	1978-79
Edmundson, Garry	Mtl., Tor.	3	43	4	6	10	49	11	0	1	1	8	....	1951-52	1960-61
Edur, Tom	Col., Pit.	2	158	17	70	87	67	....	....	....	....	....	....	1976-77	1977-78
Egan, Pat	NYA, Bro., Det., Bos., NYR	11	554	77	153	230	776	46	9	4	13	48	....	1939-40	1950-51
‡ Egeland, Allan	T.B.	3	17	0	0	0	16	....	....	....	....	....	....	1995-96	1997-98
Egers, Jack	NYR, St.L., Wsh.	7	284	64	69	133	154	32	5	6	11	32	....	1969-70	1975-76
Ehman, Gerry	Bos., Det., Tor., Oak., Cal.	9	429	96	118	214	100	41	10	10	20	12	1	1957-58	1970-71
Eisenhut, Neil	Van., Cgy.	2	16	1	3	4	21	....	....	....	....	....	....	1993-94	1994-95
Eklund, Pelle	Phi., Dal.	9	594	120	335	455	109	66	10	36	46	8	....	1985-86	1993-94
Eldebrink, Anders	Van., Que.	2	55	3	11	14	29	14	0	0	0	10	....	1981-82	1982-83
‡ Elich, Matt	T.B.	2	16	1	1	2	0	....	....	....	....	....	....	1999-00	2000-01
Elik, Bo	Det.	1	3	0	0	0	0	....	....	....	....	....	....	1962-63	1962-63
‡ Elik, Todd	L.A., Min., Edm., S.J., St.L., Bos.	8	448	110	219	329	453	52	15	27	42	48	....	1989-90	1996-97
Ellett, Dave	Wpg., Tor., N.J., Bos., St.L.	16	1129	153	415	568	985	116	11	46	57	87	....	1984-85	1999-00
• Elliott, Fred	Ott.	1	43	2	0	2	6	....	....	....	....	....	....	1928-29	1928-29
Ellis, Ron	Tor.	16	1034	332	308	640	207	70	18	8	26	20	1	1963-64	1980-81
‡ Elomo, Miika	Wsh.	1	2	0	1	1	2	....	....	....	....	....	....	1999-00	1999-00
Eloranta, Kari	Cgy., St.L.	5	267	13	103	116	155	26	1	7	8	19	....	1981-82	1986-87
‡ Eloranta, Mikko	Bos., L.A.	4	264	32	44	76	186	7	1	1	2	2	....	1999-00	2002-03
Elynuik, Pat	Wpg., Wsh., T.B., Ott.	9	506	154	188	342	459	20	6	9	15	25	....	1987-88	1995-96
Emberg, Eddie	Mtl.	1	....	....	....	....	....	2	1	0	1	0	....	1944-45	1944-45
Emerson, Nelson	St.L., Wpg., Hfd., Car., Chi., Ott., Atl., L.A.	12	771	195	293	488	575	40	7	15	22	33	....	1990-91	2001-02
Emma, David	N.J., Bos., Fla.	5	34	5	6	11	2	....	....	....	....	....	....	1992-93	2000-01
Emmons, Gary	S.J.	1	3	1	0	1	0	....	....	....	....	....	....	1993-94	1993-94
Emmons, John	Ott., T.B., Bos.	3	85	2	4	6	64	....	....	....	....	....	....	1999-00	2001-02
• Emms, Hap	Mtl.M., NYA, Det., Bos.	10	320	36	53	89	311	14	0	0	0	12	....	1926-27	1937-38
Endean, Craig	Wpg.	1	2	0	1	1	0	....	....	....	....	....	....	1986-87	1986-87
Engblom, Brian	Mtl., Wsh., L.A., Buf., Cgy.	11	659	29	177	206	599	48	3	9	12	43	3	1976-77	1986-87
Engele, Jerry	Min.	3	100	2	13	15	162	2	0	1	1	0	....	1975-76	1977-78
English, John	L.A.	1	3	1	3	4	4	1	0	0	0	0	....	1987-88	1987-88
Ennis, Jim	Edm.	1	5	1	0	1	10	....	....	....	....	....	....	1987-88	1987-88
Erickson, Aut	Bos., Chi., Tor., Oak.	7	226	7	24	31	182	7	0	0	0	2	1	1959-60	1969-70
Erickson, Bryan	Wsh., L.A., Pit., Wpg.	9	351	80	125	205	141	14	3	4	7	7	....	1983-84	1993-94
Erickson, Grant	Bos., Min.	2	6	1	0	1	0	....	....	....	....	....	....	1968-69	1969-70
Eriksson, Peter	Edm.	1	20	3	3	6	24	....	....	....	....	....	....	1989-90	1989-90

Name	NHL Teams	NHL Seasons	Regular Schedule GP	G	A	TP	PIM	Playoffs GP	G	A	TP	PIM	NHL Cup Wins	First NHL Season	Last NHL Season
Eriksson, Roland	Min., Van.	3	193	48	95	143	26	2	1	0	1	0	....	1976-77	1978-79
Eriksson, Thomas	Phi.	5	208	22	76	98	107	19	0	3	3	12	....	1980-81	1985-86
Erixon, Jan	NYR	10	556	57	159	216	167	58	7	7	14	16	....	1983-84	1992-93
Errey, Bob	Pit., Buf., S.J., Det., Dal., NYR	15	895	170	212	382	1005	99	13	16	29	109	2	1983-84	1997-98
Esau, Len	Tor., Que., Cgy., Edm.	4	27	0	10	10	24	....	....	....	....	....	....	1991-92	1994-95
Esposito, Phil	Chi., Bos., NYR	18	1282	717	873	1590	910	130	61	76	137	138	2	1963-64	1980-81
• Evans, Chris	Tor., Buf., St.L., Det., K.C.	5	241	19	42	61	143	12	1	1	2	8	....	1969-70	1974-75
Evans, Daryl	L.A., Wsh., Tor.	6	113	22	30	52	25	11	5	8	13	12	....	1981-82	1986-87
Evans, Doug	St.L., Wpg., Phi.	8	355	48	87	135	502	22	3	4	7	38	....	1985-86	1992-93
• Evans, Jack	NYR, Chi.	14	752	19	80	99	989	56	2	2	4	97	1	1948-49	1962-63
Evans, John Paul	Phi.	3	103	14	25	39	34	1	0	0	0	0	....	1978-79	1982-83
Evans, Kevin	Min., S.J.	2	9	0	1	1	44	....	....	....	....	....	....	1990-91	1991-92
Evans, Paul	Tor.	2	11	1	1	2	21	2	0	0	0	0	....	1976-77	1977-78
Evans, Shawn	St.L., NYI	2	9	1	0	1	2	....	....	....	....	....	....	1985-86	1989-90
• Evans, Stewart	Det., Mtl.M., Mtl.	8	367	28	49	77	425	26	0	0	0	20	1	1930-31	1938-39
Evason, Dean	Wsh., Hfd., S.J., Dal., Cgy.	13	803	139	233	372	1002	55	9	20	29	132	....	1983-84	1995-96
Ewen, Todd	St.L., Mtl., Ana., S.J.	11	518	36	40	76	1911	26	0	0	0	87	1	1986-87	1996-97
Ezinicki, Bill	Tor., Bos., NYR	9	368	79	105	184	713	40	5	8	13	87	3	1944-45	1954-55

F

Name	NHL Teams	NHL Seasons	Regular Schedule GP	G	A	TP	PIM	Playoffs GP	G	A	TP	PIM	NHL Cup Wins	First NHL Season	Last NHL Season
Fahey, Trevor	NYR	1	1	0	0	0	0	....	....	....	....	....	....	1964-65	1964-65
Fairbairn, Bill	NYR, Min., St.L.	11	658	162	261	423	173	54	13	22	35	42	....	1968-69	1978-79
‡ Fairchild, Kelly	Tor., Dal., Col.	4	34	2	3	5	6	....	....	....	....	....	....	1995-96	2001-02
Falkenberg, Bob	Det.	5	54	1	5	6	26	....	....	....	....	....	....	1966-67	1971-72
Falloon, Pat	S.J., Phi., Ott., Edm., Pit.	9	575	143	179	322	141	66	11	7	18	16	....	1991-92	1999-00
Farkas, Jeff	Tor., Atl.	4	11	0	2	2	6	5	1	0	1	0	....	1999-00	2002-03
Farrant, Walt	Chi.	1	1	0	0	0	0	....	....	....	....	....	....	1943-44	1943-44
Farrish, Dave	NYR, Que., Tor.	7	430	17	110	127	440	14	0	2	2	24	....	1976-77	1983-84
Fashoway, Gordie	Chi.	1	13	3	2	5	14	....	....	....	....	....	....	1950-51	1950-51
Faubert, Mario	Pit.	7	231	21	90	111	292	10	2	2	4	6	....	1974-75	1981-82
Faulkner, Alex	Tor., Det.	3	101	15	17	32	15	12	5	0	5	2	....	1961-62	1963-64
Fauss, Ted	Tor.	2	28	0	2	2	15	....	....	....	....	....	....	1986-87	1987-88
Faust, Andre	Phi.	2	47	10	7	17	14	....	....	....	....	....	....	1992-93	1993-94
Feamster, Dave	Chi.	4	169	13	24	37	154	33	3	5	8	61	....	1981-82	1984-85
Featherstone, Glen	St.L., Bos., NYR, Hfd., Cgy.	9	384	19	61	80	939	28	0	2	2	103	....	1988-89	1996-97
Featherstone, Tony	Oak., Cal., Min.	3	130	17	21	38	65	2	0	0	0	0	....	1969-70	1973-74
Federko, Bernie	St.L., Det.	14	1000	369	761	1130	487	91	35	66	101	83	....	1976-77	1989-90
Fedotov, Anatoli	Wpg., Ana.	2	4	0	2	2	0	....	....	....	....	....	....	1992-93	1993-94
Fedyk, Brent	Det., Phi., Dal., NYR	10	470	97	112	209	308	16	3	2	5	12	....	1987-88	1998-99
Felix, Chris	Wsh.	4	35	1	12	13	10	2	0	1	1	0	....	1987-88	1990-91
‡ Felsner, Brian	Chi.	1	12	1	3	4	12	....	....	....	....	....	....	1997-98	1997-98
Felsner, Denny	St.L.	4	18	1	4	5	6	10	2	3	5	2	....	1991-92	1994-95
Feltrin, Tony	Pit., NYR	4	48	3	3	6	65	....	....	....	....	....	....	1980-81	1985-86
Fenton, Paul	Hfd., NYR, L.A., Wpg., Tor., Cgy., S.J.	8	411	100	83	183	198	17	4	1	5	27	....	1984-85	1991-92
Fenyves, David	Buf., Phi.	9	206	3	32	35	119	11	0	0	0	9	....	1982-83	1990-91
Fergus, Tom	Bos., Tor., Van.	12	726	235	346	581	499	65	21	17	38	48	....	1981-82	1992-93
‡ Ferguson, Craig	Mtl., Cgy., Fla.	5	27	1	1	2	6	....	....	....	....	....	....	1993-94	1999-00
Ferguson, George	Tor., Pit., Min.	12	797	160	238	398	431	86	14	23	37	44	....	1972-73	1983-84
Ferguson, John	Mtl.	8	500	145	158	303	1214	85	20	18	38	260	5	1963-64	1970-71
Ferguson, Lorne	Bos., Det., Chi.	8	422	82	80	162	193	31	6	3	9	24	....	1949-50	1958-59
Ferguson, Norm	Oak., Cal.	4	279	73	66	139	72	10	1	4	5	7	....	1968-69	1971-72
Ferner, Mark	Buf., Wsh., Ana., Det.	6	91	3	10	13	51	....	....	....	....	....	....	1986-87	1994-95
Ferraro, Ray	Hfd., NYI, NYR, L.A., Atl., St.L.	18	1258	408	490	898	1288	68	21	22	43	54	....	1984-85	2001-02
Fetisov, Viacheslav	N.J., Det.	9	546	36	192	228	656	116	2	26	28	147	2	1989-90	1997-98
Fidler, Mike	Cle., Min., Hfd., Chi.	7	271	84	97	181	124	....	....	....	....	....	....	1976-77	1982-83
• Field, Wilf	NYA, Bro., Mtl., Chi.	6	219	17	25	42	151	2	0	0	0	2	....	1936-37	1944-45
Fielder, Guyle	Chi., Det., Bos.	4	9	0	0	0	2	6	0	0	0	2	....	1950-51	1957-58
Filimonov, Dmitri	Ott.	1	30	1	4	5	18	....	....	....	....	....	....	1993-94	1993-94
Fillion, Bob	Mtl.	7	327	42	61	103	84	33	7	4	11	10	2	1943-44	1949-50
• Fillion, Marcel	Bos.	1	1	0	0	0	0	....	....	....	....	....	....	1944-45	1944-45
• Filmore, Tommy	Det., NYA, Bos.	4	117	15	12	27	33	....	....	....	....	....	....	1930-31	1933-34
• Finkbeiner, Lloyd	NYA	1	2	0	0	0	0	....	....	....	....	....	....	1940-41	1940-41
Finn, Steven	Que., T.B., L.A.	12	725	34	78	112	1724	23	0	4	4	39	....	1985-86	1996-97
Finney, Sid	Chi.	3	59	10	7	17	4	7	0	2	2	0	....	1951-52	1953-54
• Finnigan, Ed	St.L., Bos.	2	15	1	1	2	2	....	....	....	....	....	....	1934-35	1935-36
• Finnigan, Frank	Ott., Tor., St.L.	14	553	115	88	203	407	38	6	9	15	22	2	1923-24	1936-37
Fiorentino, Peter	NYR	1	1	0	0	0	0	....	....	....	....	....	....	1991-92	1991-92
Fischer, Ron	Buf.	2	18	0	7	7	6	....	....	....	....	....	....	1981-82	1982-83
• Fisher, Alvin	Tor.	1	9	1	0	1	4	....	....	....	....	....	....	1924-25	1924-25
Fisher, Craig	Phi., Wpg., Fla.	4	12	0	0	0	2	....	....	....	....	....	....	1989-90	1996-97
Fisher, Dunc	NYR, Bos., Det.	7	275	45	70	115	104	21	4	4	8	14	....	1947-48	1958-59
• Fisher, Joe	Det.	4	65	8	12	20	13	12	2	1	3	6	1	1939-40	1942-43
Fitchner, Bob	Que.	2	78	12	20	32	59	3	0	0	0	10	....	1979-80	1980-81
Fitzgerald, Rusty	Pit.	2	25	2	2	4	12	5	0	0	0	4	....	1994-95	1995-96
Fitzpatrick, Ross	Phi.	4	20	5	2	7	0	....	....	....	....	....	....	1982-83	1985-86
Fitzpatrick, Sandy	NYR, Min.	2	22	3	6	9	8	12	0	0	0	0	....	1964-65	1967-68
Flaman, Fern	Bos., Tor.	17	910	34	174	208	1370	63	4	8	12	93	1	1944-45	1960-61
Flatley, Pat	NYI, NYR	14	780	170	340	510	686	70	18	15	33	75	....	1983-84	1996-97
Fleming, Gerry	Mtl.	2	11	0	0	0	42	....	....	....	....	....	....	1993-94	1994-95
Fleming, Reggie	Mtl., Chi., Bos., NYR, Phi., Buf.	12	749	108	132	240	1468	50	3	6	9	106	1	1959-60	1970-71
Flesch, John	Min., Pit., Col.	4	124	18	23	41	117	....	....	....	....	....	....	1974-75	1979-80
Fletcher, Steven	Mtl., Wpg.	2	3	0	0	0	5	1	0	0	0	5	....	1987-88	1988-89
• Flett, Bill	L.A., Phi., Tor., Atl., Edm.	11	689	202	215	417	501	52	7	16	23	42	1	1967-68	1979-80
Fleury, Theoren	Cgy., Col., NYR, Chi.	15	1084	455	633	1088	1840	77	34	45	79	116	1	1988-89	2002-03
Flichel, Todd	Wpg.	3	6	0	1	1	4	....	....	....	....	....	....	1987-88	1989-90
Flockhart, Rob	Van., Min.	5	55	2	5	7	14	1	1	0	1	2	....	1976-77	1980-81
Flockhart, Ron	Phi., Pit., Mtl., St.L., Bos.	9	453	145	183	328	208	19	4	6	10	14	....	1980-81	1988-89
Floyd, Larry	N.J.	2	12	2	3	5	9	....	....	....	....	....	....	1982-83	1983-84
• Fogarty, Bryan	Que., Pit., Mtl.	6	156	22	52	74	119	....	....	....	....	....	....	1989-90	1994-95
• Fogolin, Lee	Det., Chi.	9	427	10	48	58	575	28	0	2	2	30	1	1947-48	1955-56
Fogolin Jr., Lee	Buf., Edm.	13	924	44	195	239	1318	108	5	19	24	173	2	1974-75	1986-87
Folco, Peter	Van.	1	2	0	0	0	0	....	....	....	....	....	....	1973-74	1973-74
Foley, Gerry	Tor., NYR, L.A.	4	142	9	14	23	99	9	0	1	1	2	....	1954-55	1968-69
Foley, Rick	Chi., Phi., Det.	3	67	11	26	37	180	4	0	1	1	4	....	1970-71	1973-74
Foligno, Mike	Det., Buf., Tor., Fla.	15	1018	355	372	727	2049	57	15	17	32	185	....	1979-80	1993-94
Folk, Bill	Det.	2	12	0	0	0	4	....	....	....	....	....	....	1951-52	1952-53
Fontaine, Len	Det.	2	46	8	11	19	10	....	....	....	....	....	....	1972-73	1973-74
Fontas, Jon	Min.	2	2	0	0	0	0	....	....	....	....	....	....	1979-80	1980-81
Fonteyne, Val	Det., NYR, Pit.	13	820	75	154	229	26	59	3	10	13	8	....	1959-60	1971-72
Fontinato, Lou	NYR, Mtl.	9	535	26	78	104	1247	21	0	2	2	42	....	1954-55	1962-63
Forbes, Dave	Bos., Wsh.	6	363	64	64	128	341	45	1	4	5	13	....	1973-74	1978-79
Forbes, Mike	Bos., Edm.	3	50	1	11	12	41	....	....	....	....	....	....	1977-78	1981-82
Forey, Connie	St.L.	1	4	0	0	0	2	....	....	....	....	....	....	1973-74	1973-74
• Forsey, Jack	Tor.	1	19	7	9	16	10	3	0	1	1	0	....	1942-43	1942-43
• Forslund, Gus	Ott.	1	48	4	9	13	2	....	....	....	....	....	....	1932-33	1932-33
Forslund, Tomas	Cgy.	2	44	5	11	16	12	....	....	....	....	....	....	1991-92	1992-93
Forsyth, Alex	Wsh.	1	1	0	0	0	0	....	....	....	....	....	....	1976-77	1976-77
Fortier, Dave	Tor., NYI, Van.	4	205	8	21	29	335	20	0	2	2	33	....	1972-73	1976-77
Fortier, Marc	Que., Ott., L.A.	6	212	42	60	102	135	....	....	....	....	....	....	1987-88	1992-93
Fortin, Ray	St.L.	3	92	2	6	8	33	6	0	0	0	8	....	1967-68	1969-70
Foster, Corey	N.J., Phi., Pit., NYI	4	45	5	6	11	24	3	0	0	0	4	....	1988-89	1996-97
Foster, Dwight	Bos., Col., N.J., Det.	10	541	111	163	274	420	35	5	12	17	4	....	1977-78	1986-87
Foster, Herb	NYR	2	6	1	0	1	5	....	....	....	....	....	....	1940-41	1947-48
• Foster, Yip	NYR, Bos., Det.	4	83	3	2	5	32	....	....	....	....	....	....	1929-30	1934-35
Fotiu, Nick	NYR, Hfd., Cgy., Phi., Edm.	13	646	60	77	137	1362	38	0	4	4	67	....	1976-77	1988-89
• Fowler, Jimmy	Tor.	3	135	18	29	47	39	18	0	3	3	2	....	1936-37	1938-39
Fowler, Tom	Chi.	1	24	0	1	1	18	....	....	....	....	....	....	1946-47	1946-47
Fox, Greg	Atl., Chi., Pit.	8	494	14	92	106	637	44	1	9	10	67	....	1977-78	1984-85
Fox, Jim	L.A.	9	578	186	293	479	143	22	4	8	12	0	....	1980-81	1989-90
• Foyston, Frank	Det.	2	64	17	7	24	32	....	....	....	....	....	....	1926-27	1927-28
Frampton, Bob	Mtl.	1	2	0	0	0	0	3	0	0	0	0	....	1949-50	1949-50
Franceschetti, Lou	Wsh., Tor., Buf.	10	459	59	81	140	747	44	3	2	5	111	....	1981-82	1991-92
Francis, Bobby	Det.	1	14	2	0	2	0	....	....	....	....	....	....	1982-83	1982-83

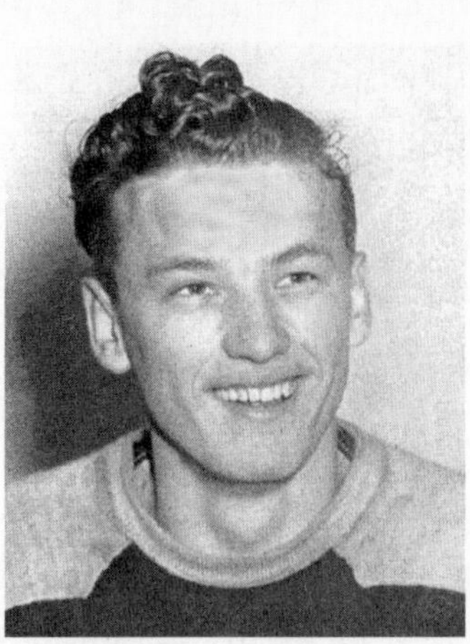
Gordie Fashoway

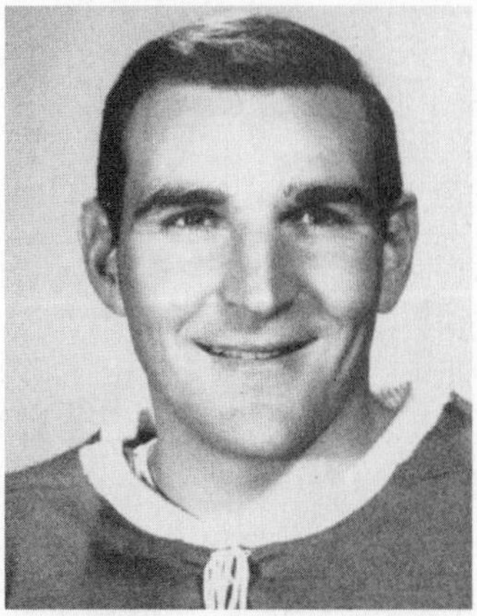
John Ferguson

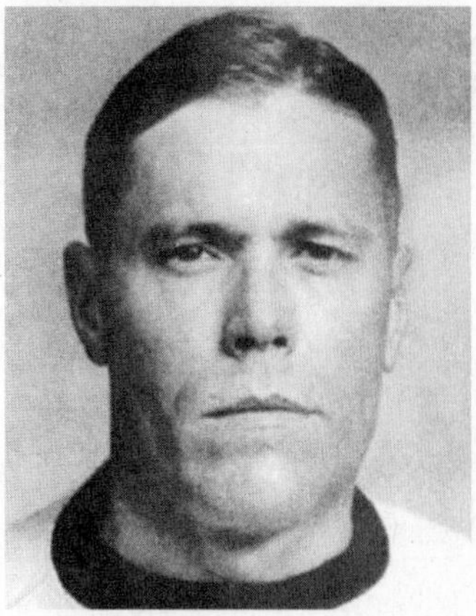
Frank Fredrickson

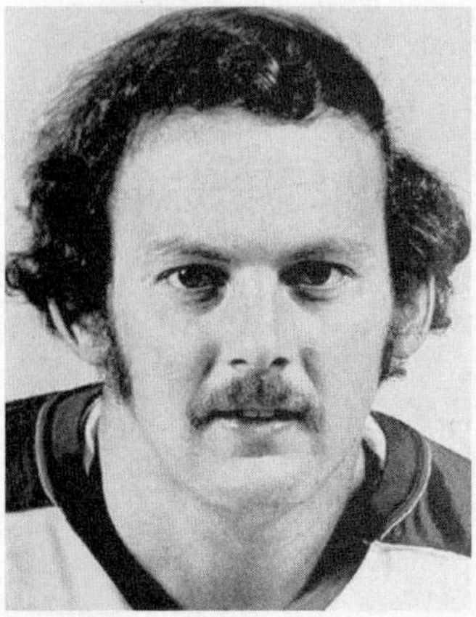
Larry Fullan

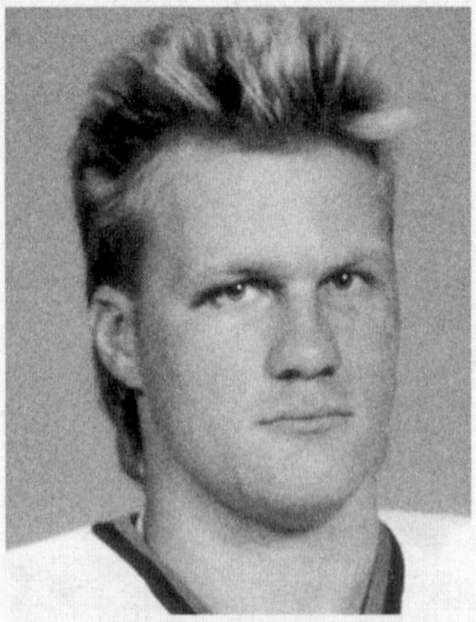
Link Gaetz

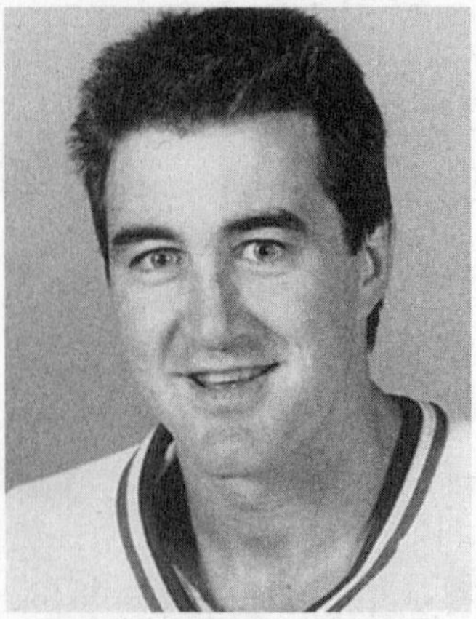
Stew Gavin

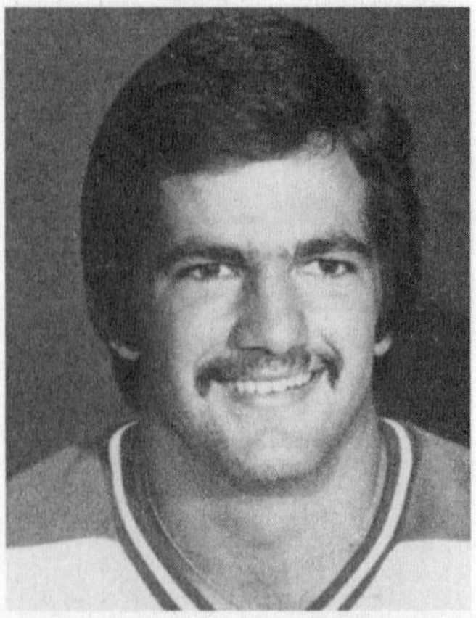
Danny Geoffrion

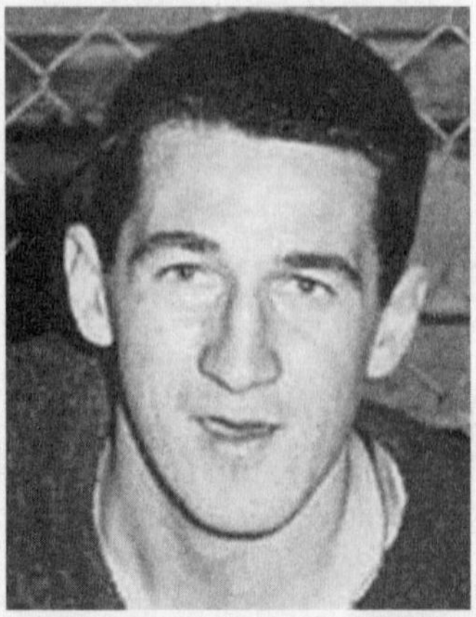
Jeannot Gilbert

Name	NHL Teams	NHL Seasons	Regular Schedule GP	G	A	TP	PIM	Playoffs GP	G	A	TP	PIM	NHL Cup Wins	First NHL Season	Last NHL Season
• Fraser, Archie	NYR	1	3	0	1	1	0	....	....	....	....	....	....	1943-44	1943-44
• Fraser, Charles	Ham.	1	1	0	0	0	0	....	....	....	....	....	....	1923-24	1923-24
Fraser, Curt	Van., Chi., Min.	12	704	193	240	433	1306	65	15	18	33	198	....	1978-79	1989-90
• Fraser, Gord	Chi., Det., Mtl., Pit., Phi.	5	144	24	12	36	224	2	1	0	1	6	....	1926-27	1930-31
Fraser, Harvey	Chi.	1	21	5	4	9	0	....	....	....	....	....	....	1944-45	1944-45
Fraser, Iain	NYI, Que., Dal., Edm., Wpg., S.J.	5	94	23	23	46	31	4	0	0	0	0	....	1992-93	1996-97
Fraser, Scott	Mtl., Edm., NYR	3	72	16	15	31	24	11	1	1	2	0	....	1995-96	1998-99
Frawley, Dan	Chi., Pit.	6	273	37	40	77	674	1	0	0	0	0	....	1983-84	1988-89
Freadrich, Kyle	T.B.	2	23	0	1	1	75	....	....	....	....	....	....	1999-00	2000-01
• Fredrickson, Frank	Det., Bos., Pit.	5	161	39	34	73	206	10	2	3	5	24	....	1926-27	1930-31
Freer, Mark	Phi., Ott., Cgy.	7	124	16	23	39	61	....	....	....	....	....	....	1986-87	1993-94
• Frew, Irv	Mtl.M., St.L., Mtl.	3	96	2	5	7	146	4	0	0	0	6	....	1933-34	1935-36
Friday, Tim	Det.	1	23	0	3	3	6	....	....	....	....	....	....	1985-86	1985-86
Fridgen, Dan	Hfd.	2	13	2	3	5	2	....	....	....	....	....	....	1981-82	1982-83
Friedman, Doug	Edm., Nsh.	2	18	0	1	1	34	....	....	....	....	....	....	1997-98	1998-99
Friest, Ron	Min.	3	64	7	7	14	191	6	1	0	1	7	....	1980-81	1982-83
Frig, Len	Chi., Cal., Cle., St.L.	7	311	13	51	64	479	14	2	1	3	0	....	1972-73	1979-80
Frost, Harry	Bos.	1	4	0	0	0	0	1	0	0	0	0	1	1938-39	1938-39
Frycer, Miroslav	Que., Tor., Det., Edm.	8	415	147	183	330	486	17	3	8	11	16	....	1981-82	1988-89
Fryday, Bob	Mtl.	2	5	1	0	1	0	....	....	....	....	....	....	1949-50	1951-52
Ftorek, Robbie	Det., Que., NYR	8	334	77	150	227	262	19	9	6	15	28	....	1972-73	1984-85
Fullan, Larry	Wsh.	1	4	1	0	1	0	....	....	....	....	....	....	1974-75	1974-75
Fusco, Mark	Hfd.	2	80	3	12	15	42	....	....	....	....	....	....	1983-84	1984-85

G

Name	NHL Teams	NHL Seasons	GP	G	A	TP	PIM	GP	G	A	TP	PIM	Cup Wins	First NHL Season	Last NHL Season
Gadsby, Bill	Chi., NYR, Det.	20	1248	130	438	568	1539	67	4	23	27	92	....	1946-47	1965-66
Gaetz, Link	Min., S.J.	3	65	6	8	14	412	....	....	....	....	....	....	1988-89	1991-92
Gage, Jody	Det., Buf.	6	68	14	15	29	26	....	....	....	....	....	....	1980-81	1991-92
• Gagne, Art	Mtl., Bos., Ott., Det.	6	228	67	33	100	257	11	2	1	3	20	....	1926-27	1931-32
Gagne, Paul	Col., N.J., Tor., NYI	8	390	110	101	211	127	....	....	....	....	....	....	1980-81	1989-90
Gagne, Pierre	Bos.	1	2	0	0	0	0	....	....	....	....	....	....	1959-60	1959-60
Gagner, Dave	NYR, Min., Dal., Tor., Cgy., Fla., Van.	15	946	318	401	719	1018	57	22	26	48	64	....	1984-85	1998-99
Gagnon, Germain	Mtl., NYI, Chi., K.C.	5	259	40	101	141	72	19	2	3	5	2	....	1971-72	1975-76
• Gagnon, Johnny	Mtl., Bos., NYA	10	454	120	141	261	295	32	12	12	24	37	1	1930-31	1939-40
‡ Gagnon, Sean	Phx., Ott.	3	12	0	1	1	34	....	....	....	....	....	....	1997-98	2000-01
Gainey, Bob	Mtl.	16	1160	239	262	501	585	182	25	48	73	151	5	1973-74	1988-89
• Gainor, Dutch	Bos., NYR, Ott., Mtl.M.	7	246	51	56	107	129	22	2	1	3	14	2	1927-28	1934-35
‡ Galanov, Maxim	NYR, Pit., Atl., T.B.	4	122	8	12	20	44	1	0	0	0	0	....	1997-98	2000-01
Galarneau, Michel	Hfd.	3	78	7	10	17	34	....	....	....	....	....	....	1980-81	1982-83
• Galbraith, Percy	Bos., Ott.	8	347	29	31	60	224	31	4	7	11	24	1	1926-27	1933-34
• Gallagher, John	Mtl.M., Det., NYA	7	205	14	19	33	153	24	2	3	5	27	1	1930-31	1938-39
Gallant, Gerard	Det., T.B.	11	615	211	269	480	1674	58	18	21	39	178	....	1984-85	1994-95
Galley, Garry	L.A., Wsh., Bos., Phi., Buf., NYI	17	1149	125	475	600	1218	89	7	23	30	119	....	1984-85	2000-01
Gallimore, Jamie	Min.	1	2	0	0	0	0	....	....	....	....	....	....	1977-78	1977-78
• Gallinger, Don	Bos.	5	222	65	88	153	89	23	5	5	10	19	....	1942-43	1947-48
Gamble, Dick	Mtl., Chi., Tor.	8	195	41	41	82	66	14	1	2	3	4	1	1950-51	1966-67
Gambucci, Gary	Min.	2	51	2	7	9	9	....	....	....	....	....	....	1971-72	1973-74
Ganchar, Perry	St.L., Mtl., Pit.	4	42	3	7	10	36	7	3	1	4	0	....	1983-84	1988-89
Gans, Dave	L.A.	2	6	0	0	0	2	....	....	....	....	....	....	1982-83	1985-86
‡ Gardiner, Bruce	Ott., T.B., CBJ, N.J.	6	312	34	54	88	263	21	1	4	5	8	....	1996-97	2001-02
• Gardiner, Herb	Mtl., Chi.	3	108	10	9	19	52	9	0	1	1	16	....	1926-27	1928-29
Gardner, Bill	Chi., Hfd.	9	380	73	115	188	68	45	3	8	11	17	....	1980-81	1988-89
• Gardner, Cal	NYR, Tor., Chi., Bos.	12	696	154	238	392	517	61	7	10	17	20	2	1945-46	1956-57
Gardner, Dave	Mtl., St.L., Cal., Cle., Phi.	7	350	75	115	190	41	....	....	....	....	....	....	1972-73	1979-80
Gardner, Paul	Col., Tor., Pit., Wsh., Buf.	10	447	201	201	402	207	16	2	6	8	14	....	1976-77	1985-86
Gare, Danny	Buf., Det., Edm.	13	827	354	331	685	1285	64	25	21	46	195	....	1974-75	1986-87
Gariepy, Ray	Bos., Tor.	2	36	1	6	7	43	....	....	....	....	....	....	1953-54	1955-56
• Garland, Scott	Tor., L.A.	3	91	13	24	37	115	7	1	2	3	35	....	1975-76	1978-79
Garner, Rob	Pit.	1	1	0	0	0	0	....	....	....	....	....	....	1982-83	1982-83
Garpenlov, Johan	Det., S.J., Fla., Atl.	10	609	114	197	311	276	44	10	9	19	22	....	1990-91	1999-00
• Garrett, Red	NYR	1	23	1	1	2	18	....	....	....	....	....	....	1942-43	1942-43
Gartner, Mike	Wsh., Min., NYR, Tor., Phx.	19	1432	708	627	1335	1159	122	43	50	93	125	....	1979-80	1997-98
• Gassoff, Bob	St.L.	4	245	11	47	58	866	9	0	1	1	16	....	1973-74	1976-77
Gassoff, Brad	Van.	4	122	19	17	36	163	3	0	0	0	0	....	1975-76	1978-79
Gatzos, Steve	Pit.	4	89	15	20	35	83	1	0	0	0	0	....	1981-82	1984-85
Gaudreau, Rob	S.J., Ott.	4	231	51	54	105	69	14	2	0	2	0	....	1992-93	1995-96
Gaudreault, Armand	Bos.	1	44	15	9	24	27	7	0	2	2	8	....	1944-45	1944-45
• Gaudreault, Leo	Mtl.	3	67	8	4	12	30	....	....	....	....	....	....	1927-28	1932-33
‡ Gaul, Mike	Col., CBJ	2	3	0	0	0	4	....	....	....	....	....	....	1998-99	2000-01
Gaulin, Jean-Marc	Que.	4	26	4	3	7	8	1	0	0	0	0	....	1982-83	1985-86
Gaume, Dallas	Hfd.	1	4	1	1	2	0	....	....	....	....	....	....	1988-89	1988-89
• Gauthier, Art	Mtl.	1	13	0	0	0	0	1	0	0	0	0	....	1926-27	1926-27
Gauthier, Daniel	Chi.	1	5	0	0	0	0	....	....	....	....	....	....	1994-95	1994-95
• Gauthier, Fern	NYR, Mtl., Det.	6	229	46	50	96	35	22	5	1	6	7	....	1943-44	1948-49
Gauthier, Jean	Mtl., Phi., Bos.	10	166	6	29	35	150	14	1	3	4	22	1	1960-61	1969-70
Gauthier, Luc	Mtl.	1	3	0	0	0	2	....	....	....	....	....	....	1990-91	1990-91
Gauvreau, Jocelyn	Mtl.	1	2	0	0	0	0	....	....	....	....	....	....	1983-84	1983-84
Gavin, Stew	Tor., Hfd., Min.	13	768	130	155	285	584	66	14	20	34	75	....	1980-81	1992-93
Geale, Bob	Pit.	1	1	0	0	0	2	....	....	....	....	....	....	1984-85	1984-85
• Gee, George	Chi., Det.	9	551	135	183	318	345	41	6	13	19	32	1	1945-46	1953-54
Geldart, Gary	Min.	1	4	0	0	0	5	....	....	....	....	....	....	1970-71	1970-71
Gendron, Jean-Guy	NYR, Bos., Mtl., Phi.	14	863	182	201	383	701	42	7	4	11	47	....	1955-56	1971-72
Gendron, Martin	Wsh., Chi.	3	30	4	2	6	10	....	....	....	....	....	....	1994-95	1997-98
Geoffrion, Bernie	Mtl., NYR	16	883	393	429	822	689	132	58	60	118	88	6	1950-51	1967-68
Geoffrion, Danny	Mtl., Wpg.	3	111	20	32	52	99	2	0	0	0	7	....	1979-80	1981-82
• Geran, Gerry	Mtl.W., Bos.	2	37	5	1	6	6	....	....	....	....	....	....	1917-18	1925-26
• Gerard, Eddie	Ott.	6	128	50	48	98	108	11	4	0	4	17	3	1917-18	1922-23
Germain, Eric	L.A.	1	4	0	1	1	13	1	0	0	0	4	....	1987-88	1987-88
Gernander, Ken	NYR	3	12	2	3	5	6	15	0	0	0	0	....	1995-96	2003-04
Getliffe, Ray	Bos., Mtl.	10	393	136	137	273	250	45	9	10	19	30	2	1935-36	1944-45
Giallonardo, Mario	Col.	2	23	0	3	3	6	....	....	....	....	....	....	1979-80	1980-81
Gibbs, Barry	Bos., Min., Atl., St.L., L.A.	13	797	58	224	282	945	36	4	2	6	67	....	1967-68	1979-80
Gibson, Don	Van.	1	14	0	3	3	20	....	....	....	....	....	....	1990-91	1990-91
Gibson, Doug	Bos., Wsh.	3	63	9	19	28	0	1	0	0	0	0	....	1973-74	1977-78
Gibson, John	L.A., Tor., Wpg.	3	48	0	2	2	120	....	....	....	....	....	....	1980-81	1983-84
Giesebrecht, Gus	Det.	4	135	27	51	78	13	17	2	3	5	0	....	1938-39	1941-42
Giffin, Lee	Pit.	2	27	1	3	4	9	....	....	....	....	....	....	1986-87	1987-88
Gilbert, Ed	K.C., Pit.	3	166	21	31	52	22	....	....	....	....	....	....	1974-75	1976-77
Gilbert, Greg	NYI, Chi., NYR, St.L.	15	837	150	228	378	576	133	17	33	50	162	3	1981-82	1995-96
Gilbert, Jeannot	Bos.	2	9	0	1	1	4	....	....	....	....	....	....	1962-63	1964-65
Gilbert, Rod	NYR	18	1065	406	615	1021	508	79	34	33	67	43	....	1960-61	1977-78
Gilbertson, Stan	Cal., St.L., Wsh., Pit.	6	428	85	89	174	148	3	1	1	2	2	....	1971-72	1976-77
Gilchrist, Brent	Mtl., Edm., Min., Dal., Det., Nsh.	15	792	135	170	305	400	90	17	14	31	48	1	1988-89	2002-03
Giles, Curt	Min., NYR, St.L.	14	895	43	199	242	733	103	6	16	22	118	....	1979-80	1992-93
Gilhen, Randy	Hfd., Wpg., Pit., L.A., NYR, T.B., Fla.	11	457	55	60	115	314	33	3	2	5	26	1	1982-83	1995-96
‡ Gill, Todd	Tor., S.J., St.L., Det., Phx., Col., Chi.	19	1007	82	272	354	1214	103	7	30	37	193	....	1984-85	2002-03
Gillen, Don	Phi., Hfd.	2	35	2	4	6	22	....	....	....	....	....	....	1979-80	1981-82
• Gillie, Farrand	Det.	1	1	0	0	0	0	....	....	....	....	....	....	1928-29	1928-29
Gillies, Clark	NYI, Buf.	14	958	319	378	697	1023	164	47	47	94	287	4	1974-75	1987-88
Gillis, Jere	Van., NYR, Que., Buf., Phi.	9	386	78	95	173	230	19	4	7	11	9	....	1977-78	1986-87
Gillis, Mike	Col., Bos.	6	246	33	43	76	186	27	2	5	7	10	....	1978-79	1983-84
Gillis, Paul	Que., Chi., Hfd.	11	624	88	154	242	1498	42	3	14	17	156	....	1982-83	1992-93
Gilmour, Doug	St.L., Cgy., Tor., N.J., Chi., Buf., Mtl.	20	1474	450	964	1414	1301	182	60	128	188	235	1	1983-84	2002-03
Gingras, Gaston	Mtl., Tor., St.L.	10	476	61	174	235	161	52	6	18	24	20	1	1979-80	1988-89
Girard, Bob	Cal., Cle., Wsh.	5	305	45	69	114	140	....	....	....	....	....	....	1975-76	1979-80
Girard, Kenny	Tor.	3	7	0	1	1	2	....	....	....	....	....	....	1956-57	1959-60
• Giroux, Art	Mtl., Bos., Det.	3	54	6	4	10	14	2	0	0	0	0	....	1932-33	1935-36
Giroux, Larry	St.L., K.C., Det., Hfd.	7	274	15	74	89	333	5	0	0	0	4	....	1973-74	1979-80
Giroux, Pierre	L.A.	1	6	1	0	1	17	....	....	....	....	....	....	1982-83	1982-83
Gladney, Bob	L.A., Pit.	2	14	1	5	6	4	....	....	....	....	....	....	1982-83	1983-84
Gladu, Jean-Paul	Bos.	1	40	6	14	20	2	7	2	2	4	0	....	1944-45	1944-45
Glennie, Brian	Tor., L.A.	10	572	14	100	114	621	32	0	1	1	66	....	1969-70	1978-79
Glennon, Matt	Bos.	1	3	0	0	0	2	....	....	....	....	....	....	1991-92	1991-92

Name	NHL Teams	NHL Seasons	Regular Schedule GP	G	A	TP	PIM	Playoffs GP	G	A	TP	PIM	NHL Cup Wins	First NHL Season	Last NHL Season
Gloeckner, Lorry	Det.	1	13	0	2	2	6	....	....	....	....	....	....	1978-79	1978-79
Gloor, Dan	Van.	1	2	0	0	0	0	....	....	....	....	....	....	1973-74	1973-74
• Glover, Fred	Det., Chi.	5	92	13	11	24	62	8	0	0	0	0	1	1948-49	1952-53
Glover, Howie	Chi., Det., NYR, Mtl.	5	144	29	17	46	101	11	1	2	3	2	....	1958-59	1968-69
Glynn, Brian	Cgy., Min., Edm., Ott., Van., Hfd.	10	431	25	79	104	410	57	6	10	16	40	....	1987-88	1996-97
Godden, Ernie	Tor.	1	5	1	1	2	6	....	....	....	....	....	....	1981-82	1981-82
• Godfrey, Warren	Bos., Det.	16	786	32	125	157	752	52	1	4	5	42	....	1952-53	1967-68
Godin, Eddy	Wsh.	2	27	3	6	9	12	....	....	....	....	....	....	1977-78	1978-79
• Godin, Sam	Ott., Mtl.	3	83	4	3	7	36	....	....	....	....	....	....	1927-28	1933-34
Godynyuk, Alexander	Tor., Cgy., Fla., Hfd.	7	223	10	39	49	224	....	....	....	....	....	....	1990-91	1996-97
Goegan, Pete	Det., NYR, Min.	11	383	19	67	86	365	33	1	3	4	61	....	1957-58	1967-68
Goertz, Dave	Pit.	1	2	0	0	0	2	....	....	....	....	....	....	1987-88	1987-88
• Goldham, Bob	Tor., Chi., Det.	12	650	28	143	171	400	66	3	14	17	53	5	1941-42	1955-56
‡ Goldmann, Erich	Ott.	1	1	0	0	0	0	....	....	....	....	....	....	1999-00	1999-00
• Goldsworthy, Bill	Bos., Min., NYR	14	771	283	258	541	793	40	18	19	37	30	....	1964-65	1977-78
• Goldsworthy, Leroy	NYR, Det., Chi., Mtl., Bos., NYA	10	336	66	57	123	79	24	1	0	1	4	1	1928-29	1938-39
Goldup, Glenn	Mtl., L.A.	9	291	52	67	119	303	16	4	3	7	22	....	1973-74	1981-82
Goldup, Hank	Tor., NYR	6	202	63	80	143	97	26	5	1	6	6	1	1939-40	1945-46
‡ Golubovsky, Yan	Det., Fla.	4	56	1	7	8	32	....	....	....	....	....	....	1997-98	2000-01
Goneau, Daniel	NYR	3	53	12	3	15	14	....	....	....	....	....	....	1996-97	1999-00
• Gooden, Bill	NYR	2	53	9	11	20	15	....	....	....	....	....	....	1942-43	1943-44
Goodenough, Larry	Phi., Van.	6	242	22	77	99	179	22	3	15	18	10	1	1974-75	1979-80
• Goodfellow, Ebbie	Det.	14	557	134	190	324	511	45	8	8	16	65	3	1929-30	1942-43
Gordiouk, Viktor	Buf.	2	26	3	8	11	0	....	....	....	....	....	....	1992-93	1994-95
Gordon, Fred	Det., Bos.	2	81	8	7	15	68	2	0	0	0	0	....	1926-27	1927-28
Gordon, Jack	NYR	3	36	3	10	13	0	9	1	1	2	7	....	1948-49	1950-51
Gordon, Robb	Van.	1	4	0	0	0	2	....	....	....	....	....	....	1998-99	1998-99
Gorence, Tom	Phi., Edm.	6	303	58	53	111	89	37	9	6	15	47	....	1978-79	1983-84
Goring, Butch	L.A., NYI, Bos.	16	1107	375	513	888	102	134	38	50	88	32	4	1969-70	1984-85
Gorman, Dave	Atl.	1	3	0	0	0	0	....	....	....	....	....	....	1979-80	1979-80
• Gorman, Ed	Ott., Tor.	4	111	14	6	20	108	8	0	0	0	2	1	1924-25	1927-28
Gosselin, Benoit	NYR	1	7	0	0	0	33	....	....	....	....	....	....	1977-78	1977-78
‡ Gosselin, David	Nsh.	2	13	2	1	3	11	....	....	....	....	....	....	1999-00	2001-02
Gosselin, Guy	Wpg.	1	5	0	0	0	6	....	....	....	....	....	....	1987-88	1987-88
Gotaas, Steve	Pit., Min.	3	49	6	9	15	53	3	0	1	1	5	....	1987-88	1990-91
• Gottselig, Johnny	Chi.	16	589	176	195	371	203	43	13	13	26	18	2	1928-29	1944-45
Gould, Bobby	Atl., Cgy., Wsh., Bos.	11	697	145	159	304	572	78	15	13	28	58	....	1979-80	1989-90
Gould, John	Buf., Van., Atl.	9	504	131	138	269	113	14	3	2	5	4	....	1971-72	1979-80
Gould, Larry	Van.	1	2	0	0	0	0	....	....	....	....	....	....	1973-74	1973-74
Goulet, Michel	Que., Chi.	15	1089	548	604	1152	825	92	39	39	78	110	....	1979-80	1993-94
• Goupille, Red	Mtl.	8	222	12	28	40	256	8	2	0	2	6	....	1935-36	1942-43
Govedaris, Chris	Hfd., Tor.	4	45	4	6	10	24	4	0	0	0	2	....	1989-90	1993-94
Goyer, Gerry	Chi.	1	40	1	2	3	4	3	0	0	0	2	....	1967-68	1967-68
Goyette, Phil	Mtl., NYR, St.L., Buf.	16	941	207	467	674	131	94	17	29	46	26	4	1956-57	1971-72
Graboski, Tony	Mtl.	3	66	6	10	16	24	3	0	0	0	6	....	1940-41	1942-43
• Gracie, Bob	Tor., Bos., NYA, Mtl.M., Mtl., Chi.	9	379	82	109	191	205	33	4	7	11	4	2	1930-31	1938-39
Gradin, Thomas	Van., Bos.	9	677	209	384	593	298	42	17	25	42	20	....	1978-79	1986-87
Graham, Dirk	Min., Chi.	12	772	219	270	489	917	90	17	27	44	92	....	1983-84	1994-95
• Graham, Leth	Ott., Ham.	6	27	3	0	3	0	1	0	0	0	0	1	1920-21	1925-26
Graham, Pat	Pit., Tor.	3	103	11	17	28	136	4	0	0	0	2	....	1981-82	1983-84
Graham, Rod	Bos.	1	14	2	1	3	7	....	....	....	....	....	....	1974-75	1974-75
• Graham, Ted	Chi., Mtl.M., Det., St.L., Bos., NYA	9	346	14	25	39	300	24	3	1	4	30	....	1927-28	1936-37
Granato, Tony	NYR, L.A., S.J.	14	773	248	244	492	1425	79	16	27	43	141	....	1988-89	2000-01
Grant, Danny	Mtl., Min., Det., L.A.	13	736	263	273	536	239	43	10	14	24	19	1	1965-66	1978-79
Gratton, Dan	L.A.	1	7	1	0	1	5	....	....	....	....	....	....	1987-88	1987-88
Gratton, Norm	NYR, Atl., Buf., Min.	5	201	39	44	83	64	6	0	1	1	2	....	1971-72	1975-76
Gravelle, Leo	Mtl., Det.	5	223	44	34	78	42	17	4	1	5	2	....	1946-47	1950-51
Graves, Adam	Det., Edm., NYR, S.J.	16	1152	329	287	616	1224	125	38	27	65	119	2	1987-88	2002-03
Graves, Hilliard	Cal., Atl., Van., Wpg.	9	556	118	163	281	209	2	0	0	0	0	....	1970-71	1979-80
Graves, Steve	Edm.	3	35	5	4	9	10	....	....	....	....	....	....	1983-84	1987-88
• Gray, Alex	NYR, Tor.	2	50	7	0	7	32	13	1	0	1	0	1	1927-28	1928-29
Gray, Terry	Bos., Mtl., L.A., St.L.	6	147	26	28	54	64	35	5	5	10	22	....	1961-62	1970-71
• Green, Red	Ham., NYA, Bos., Det.	6	195	59	26	85	290	1	0	0	0	0	1	1923-24	1928-29
Green, Rick	Wsh., Mtl., Det., NYI	15	845	43	220	263	588	100	3	16	19	73	1	1976-77	1991-92
• Green, Shorty	Ham., NYA	4	103	33	20	53	151	....	....	....	....	....	....	1923-24	1926-27
Green, Ted	Bos.	11	620	48	206	254	1029	31	4	8	12	54	1	1960-61	1971-72
Greenlaw, Jeff	Wsh., Fla.	6	57	3	6	9	108	2	0	0	0	21	....	1986-87	1993-94
Gregg, Randy	Edm., Van.	10	474	41	152	193	333	137	13	38	51	127	5	1981-82	1991-92
Greig, Bruce	Cal.	2	9	0	1	1	46	....	....	....	....	....	....	1973-74	1974-75
‡ Greig, Mark	Hfd., Tor., Cgy., Phi.	9	125	13	27	40	90	5	0	1	1	0	....	1990-91	2002-03
Grenier, Lucien	Mtl., L.A.	4	151	14	14	28	18	2	0	0	0	0	1	1968-69	1971-72
Grenier, Richard	NYI	1	10	1	1	2	2	....	....	....	....	....	....	1972-73	1972-73
Greschner, Ron	NYR	16	982	179	431	610	1226	84	17	32	49	106	....	1974-75	1989-90
‡ Gretzky, Brent	T.B.	2	13	1	3	4	2	....	....	....	....	....	....	1993-94	1994-95
Gretzky, Wayne	Edm., L.A., St.L., NYR	20	1487	894	1963	2857	577	208	122	260	382	66	4	1979-80	1998-99
Grieve, Brent	NYI, Edm., Chi., L.A.	4	97	20	16	36	87	....	....	....	....	....	....	1993-94	1996-97
Grigor, George	Chi.	1	2	1	0	1	0	1	0	0	0	0	....	1943-44	1943-44
Grimson, Stu	Cgy., Chi., Ana., Det., Hfd., Car., L.A., Nsh.	14	729	17	22	39	2113	42	1	1	2	120	....	1988-89	2001-02
Grisdale, John	Tor., Van.	6	250	4	39	43	346	10	0	1	1	15	....	1972-73	1978-79
‡ Groleau, Francois	Mtl.	3	8	0	1	1	6	....	....	....	....	....	....	1995-96	1997-98
‡ Gron, Stanislav	N.J.	1	1	0	0	0	0	....	....	....	....	....	....	2000-01	2000-01
Gronman, Tuomas	Chi., Pit.	2	38	1	3	4	38	1	0	0	0	0	....	1996-97	1997-98
Gronsdahl, Lloyd	Bos.	1	10	1	2	3	0	....	....	....	....	....	....	1941-42	1941-42
Gronstrand, Jari	Min., NYR, Que., NYI	5	185	8	26	34	135	3	0	0	0	4	....	1986-87	1990-91
Gross, Lloyd	Tor., NYA, Bos., Det.	3	62	11	5	16	20	1	0	0	0	0	....	1926-27	1934-35
• Grosso, Don	Det., Chi., Bos.	9	336	87	117	204	90	48	15	14	29	63	1	1938-39	1946-47
Grosvenor, Len	Ott., NYA, Mtl.	6	149	9	11	20	78	4	0	0	0	2	....	1927-28	1932-33
Groulx, Wayne	Que.	1	1	0	0	0	0	....	....	....	....	....	....	1984-85	1984-85
Gruen, Danny	Det., Col.	3	49	9	13	22	19	....	....	....	....	....	....	1972-73	1976-77
Gruhl, Scott	L.A., Pit.	3	20	3	3	6	6	....	....	....	....	....	....	1981-82	1987-88
Gryp, Bob	Bos., Wsh.	3	74	11	13	24	33	....	....	....	....	....	....	1973-74	1975-76
Guay, Francois	Buf.	1	1	0	0	0	0	....	....	....	....	....	....	1989-90	1989-90
Guay, Paul	Phi., L.A., Bos., NYI	7	117	11	23	34	92	9	0	1	1	12	....	1983-84	1990-91
Guerard, Daniel	Ott.	1	2	0	0	0	0	....	....	....	....	....	....	1994-95	1994-95
Guerard, Stephane	Que.	2	34	0	0	0	40	....	....	....	....	....	....	1987-88	1989-90
Guevremont, Jocelyn	Van., Buf., NYR	9	571	84	223	307	319	40	4	17	21	18	....	1971-72	1979-80
Guidolin, Aldo	NYR	4	182	9	15	24	117	....	....	....	....	....	....	1952-53	1955-56
Guidolin, Bep	Bos., Det., Chi.	9	519	107	171	278	606	24	5	7	12	35	....	1942-43	1951-52
Guindon, Bobby	Wpg.	1	6	0	1	1	0	....	....	....	....	....	....	1979-80	1979-80
Gusarov, Alexei	Que., Col., NYR, St.L.	11	607	39	128	167	313	68	0	14	14	38	1	1990-91	2000-01
Gusev, Sergey	Dal., T.B.	4	89	4	10	14	34	....	....	....	....	....	....	1997-98	2000-01
‡ Gusmanov, Ravil	Wpg.	1	4	0	0	0	0	....	....	....	....	....	....	1995-96	1995-96
Gustafsson, Bengt-Ake	Wsh.	9	629	196	359	555	196	32	9	19	28	16	....	1979-80	1988-89
‡ Gustafsson, Per	Fla., Tor., Ott.	2	89	8	27	35	38	1	0	0	0	0	....	1996-97	1997-98
Gustavsson, Peter	Col.	1	2	0	0	0	0	....	....	....	....	....	....	1981-82	1981-82
Guy, Kevan	Cgy., Van.	6	156	5	20	25	138	5	0	1	1	23	....	1986-87	1991-92

H

Name	NHL Teams	NHL Seasons	Regular Schedule GP	G	A	TP	PIM	Playoffs GP	G	A	TP	PIM	NHL Cup Wins	First NHL Season	Last NHL Season
Haanpaa, Ari	NYI	3	60	6	11	17	37	6	0	0	0	10	....	1985-86	1987-88
‡ Haas, David	Edm., Cgy.	2	7	2	1	3	7	....	....	....	....	....	....	1990-91	1993-94
Habscheid, Marc	Edm., Min., Det., Cgy.	11	345	72	91	163	171	12	1	3	4	13	....	1981-82	1991-92
Hachborn, Len	Phi., L.A.	3	102	20	39	59	29	7	0	3	3	7	....	1983-84	1985-86
Haddon, Lloyd	Det.	1	8	0	0	0	2	1	0	0	0	0	....	1959-60	1959-60
Hadfield, Vic	NYR, Pit.	16	1002	323	389	712	1154	73	27	21	48	117	....	1961-62	1976-77
• Haggarty, Jim	Mtl.	1	5	1	1	2	0	3	2	1	3	0	....	1941-42	1941-42
Haggerty, Sean	Tor., NYI, Nsh.	4	14	1	2	3	4	....	....	....	....	....	....	1995-96	2000-01
• Hagglund, Roger	Que.	1	3	0	0	0	0	....	....	....	....	....	....	1984-85	1984-85
Hagman, Matti	Bos., Edm.	4	237	56	89	145	36	20	5	2	7	6	....	1976-77	1981-82
Haidy, Gord	Det.	1	....	....	....	....	....	1	0	0	0	0	1	1949-50	1949-50
Hajdu, Richard	Buf.	2	5	0	0	0	4	....	....	....	....	....	....	1985-86	1986-87
Hajt, Bill	Buf.	14	854	42	202	244	433	80	2	16	18	70	....	1973-74	1986-87
Hakansson, Anders	Min., Pit., L.A.	5	330	52	46	98	141	6	0	0	0	2	....	1981-82	1985-86

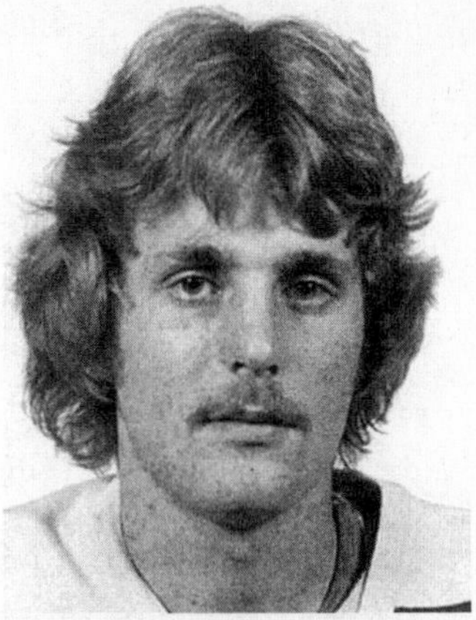
Ernie Godden

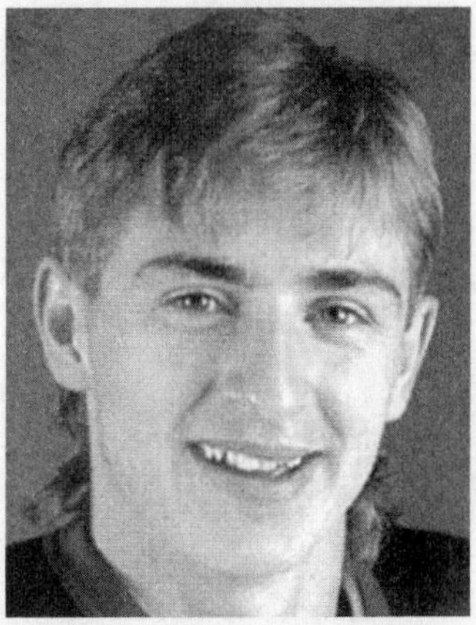
Brent Gretzky

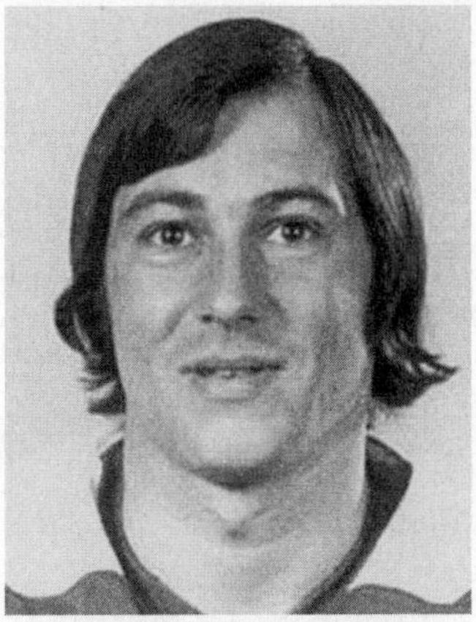
Bobby Guindon

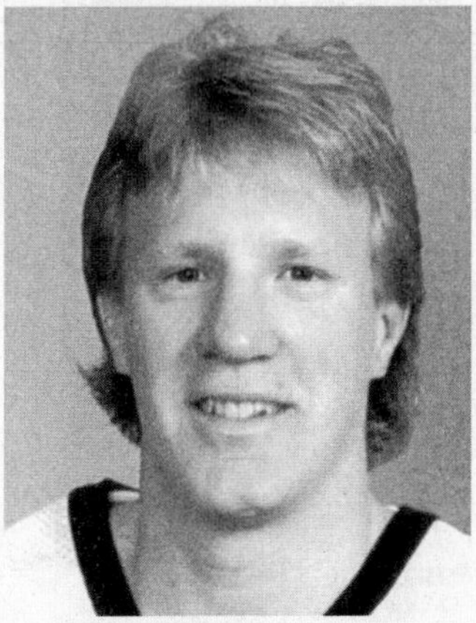
Len Hachborn

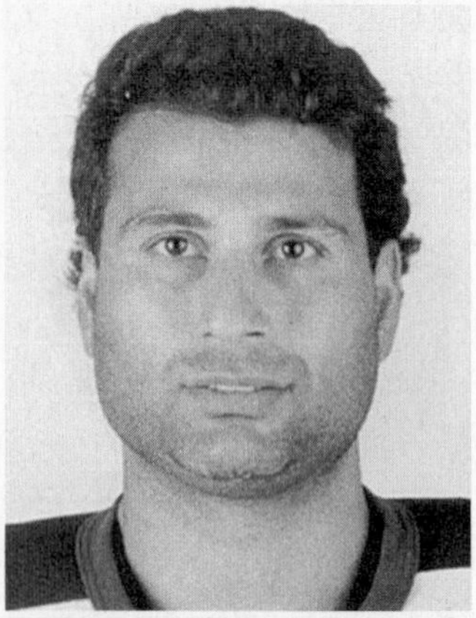

Bob Halkidis

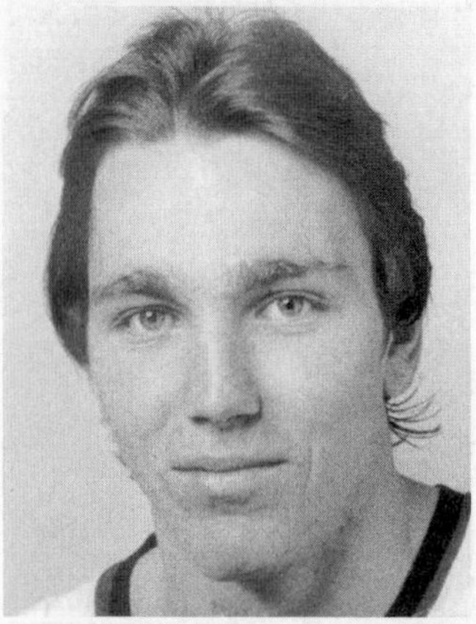

Steve Hazlett

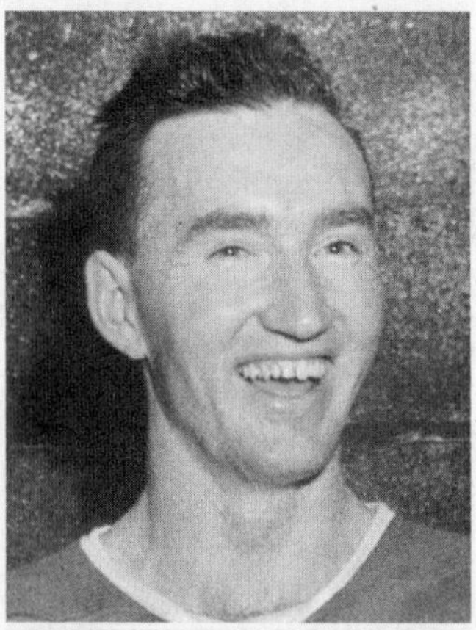

Gerry Heffernan

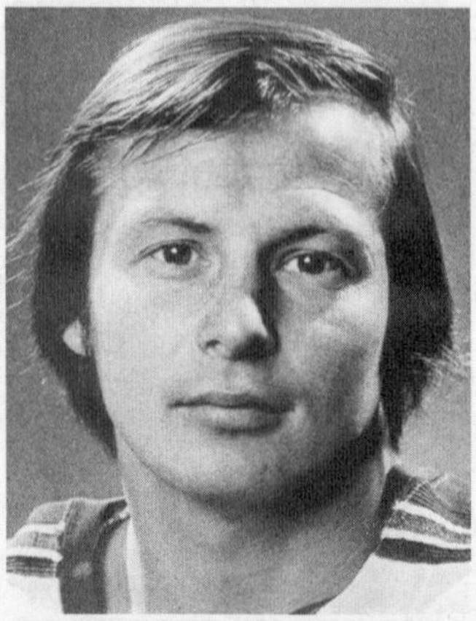

Bill Heindl

			Regular Schedule					Playoffs							
Name	NHL Teams	NHL Seasons	GP	G	A	TP	PIM	GP	G	A	TP	PIM	NHL Cup Wins	First NHL Season	Last NHL Season
• Halderson, Harold	Det., Tor.	1	44	3	2	5	65	....	....	....	....	....	....	1926-27	1926-27
Hale, Larry	Phi.	4	196	5	37	42	90	8	0	0	0	12	....	1968-69	1971-72
Haley, Len	Det.	2	30	2	2	4	14	6	1	3	4	6	....	1959-60	1960-61
Halkidis, Bob	Buf., L.A., Tor., Det., T.B., NYI	11	256	8	32	40	825	20	0	1	1	51	....	1984-85	1995-96
Halko, Steven	Car.	6	155	0	15	15	71	4	0	0	0	2	....	1997-98	2002-03
• Hall, Bob	NYA	1	8	0	0	0	0	....	....	....	....	....	....	1925-26	1925-26
Hall, Del	Cal.	3	9	2	0	2	2	....	....	....	....	....	....	1971-72	1973-74
• Hall, Joe	Mtl.	2	38	15	8	23	189	7	0	1	1	38	....	1917-18	1918-19
Hall, Murray	Chi., Det., Min., Van.	9	164	35	48	83	46	6	0	0	0	0	....	1961-62	1971-72
Hall, Taylor	Van., Bos.	5	41	7	9	16	29	....	....	....	....	....	....	1983-84	1987-88
Hall, Wayne	NYR	1	4	0	0	0	0	....	....	....	....	....	....	1960-61	1960-61
Haller, Kevin	Buf., Mtl., Phi., Hfd., Car., Ana., NYI	13	642	41	97	138	907	64	7	16	23	71	1	1989-90	2001-02
• Halliday, Milt	Ott.	3	67	1	0	1	4	6	0	0	0	0	1	1926-27	1928-29
Hallin, Mats	NYI, Min.	5	152	17	14	31	193	15	1	0	1	13	1	1982-83	1986-87
Halverson, Trevor	Wsh.	1	17	0	4	4	28	....	....	....	....	....	....	1998-99	1998-99
Halward, Doug	Bos., L.A., Van., Det., Edm.	14	653	69	224	293	774	47	7	10	17	113	....	1975-76	1988-89
Hamel, Gilles	Buf., Wpg., L.A.	9	519	127	147	274	276	27	4	5	9	10	....	1980-81	1988-89
• Hamel, Herb	Tor.	1	2	0	0	0	4	....	....	....	....	....	....	1930-31	1930-31
Hamel, Jean	St.L., Det., Que., Mtl.	12	699	26	95	121	766	33	0	2	2	44	....	1972-73	1983-84
• Hamill, Red	Bos., Chi.	12	419	128	94	222	160	24	1	2	3	20	1	1937-38	1950-51
Hamilton, Al	NYR, Buf., Edm.	7	257	10	78	88	258	7	0	0	0	2	....	1965-66	1979-80
Hamilton, Chuck	Mtl., St.L.	2	4	0	2	2	2	....	....	....	....	....	....	1961-62	1972-73
• Hamilton, Jack	Tor.	3	102	28	32	60	20	11	2	1	3	0	....	1942-43	1945-46
Hamilton, Jim	Pit.	8	95	14	18	32	28	6	3	0	3	0	....	1977-78	1984-85
• Hamilton, Reg	Tor., Chi.	12	424	21	87	108	412	64	3	8	11	46	2	1935-36	1946-47
Hammarstrom, Inge	Tor., St.L.	6	427	116	123	239	86	13	2	3	5	4	....	1973-74	1978-79
Hammond, Ken	L.A., Edm., NYR, Tor., Bos., S.J., Van., Ott.	8	193	18	29	47	290	15	0	0	0	24	....	1984-85	1992-93
Hampson, Gord	Cgy.	1	4	0	0	0	5	....	....	....	....	....	....	1982-83	1982-83
Hampson, Ted	Tor., NYR, Det., Oak., Cal., Min.	14	676	108	245	353	94	35	7	10	17	2	....	1959-60	1971-72
Hampton, Rick	Cal., Cle., L.A.	6	337	59	113	172	147	2	0	0	0	0	....	1974-75	1979-80
‡ Hamr, Radek	Ott.	2	11	0	0	0	0	....	....	....	....	....	....	1992-93	1993-94
Hamway, Mark	NYI	3	53	5	13	18	9	1	0	0	0	0	....	1984-85	1986-87
Handy, Ron	NYI, St.L.	2	14	0	3	3	0	....	....	....	....	....	....	1984-85	1987-88
Hangsleben, Al	Hfd., Wsh., L.A.	3	185	21	48	69	396	....	....	....	....	....	....	1979-80	1981-82
Hankinson, Ben	N.J., T.B.	3	43	3	3	6	45	2	1	0	1	4	....	1992-93	1994-95
Hanna, John	NYR, Mtl., Phi.	5	198	6	26	32	206	....	....	....	....	....	....	1958-59	1967-68
Hannan, Dave	Pit., Edm., Tor., Buf., Col., Ott.	16	841	114	191	305	942	63	6	7	13	46	2	1981-82	1996-97
• Hannigan, Gord	Tor.	4	161	29	31	60	117	9	2	0	2	8	....	1952-53	1955-56
Hannigan, Pat	Tor., NYR, Phi.	5	182	30	39	69	116	11	1	2	3	11	....	1959-60	1968-69
Hannigan, Ray	Tor.	1	3	0	0	0	2	....	....	....	....	....	....	1948-49	1948-49
Hansen, Richie	NYI, St.L.	4	20	2	8	10	4	....	....	....	....	....	....	1976-77	1981-82
Hanson, Dave	Det., Min.	2	33	1	1	2	65	....	....	....	....	....	....	1978-79	1979-80
• Hanson, Emil	Det.	1	7	0	0	0	6	....	....	....	....	....	....	1932-33	1932-33
Hanson, Keith	Cgy.	1	25	0	2	2	77	....	....	....	....	....	....	1983-84	1983-84
• Hanson, Oscar	Chi.	1	8	0	0	0	0	....	....	....	....	....	....	1937-38	1937-38
Harbaruk, Nick	Pit., St.L.	5	364	45	75	120	273	14	3	1	4	20	....	1969-70	1973-74
Harding, Jeff	Phi.	2	15	0	0	0	47	....	....	....	....	....	....	1988-89	1989-90
Hardy, Joe	Oak., Cal.	2	63	9	14	23	51	4	0	0	0	0	....	1969-70	1970-71
Hardy, Mark	L.A., NYR, Min.	15	915	62	306	368	1293	67	5	16	21	158	....	1979-80	1993-94
Hargreaves, Jim	Van.	2	66	1	7	8	105	....	....	....	....	....	....	1970-71	1972-73
‡ Harkins, Brett	Bos., Fla., CBJ	4	78	6	30	36	22	....	....	....	....	....	....	1994-95	2001-02
Harkins, Todd	Cgy., Hfd.	3	48	3	3	6	78	....	....	....	....	....	....	1991-92	1993-94
Harlock, David	Tor., Wsh., NYI, Atl.	8	212	2	14	16	188	....	....	....	....	....	....	1993-94	2001-02
Harlow, Scott	St.L.	1	1	0	1	1	0	....	....	....	....	....	....	1987-88	1987-88
Harmon, Glen	Mtl.	9	452	50	96	146	334	53	5	10	15	37	2	1942-43	1950-51
Harms, John	Chi.	2	44	5	5	10	21	4	3	0	3	2	....	1943-44	1944-45
• Harnott, Walter	Bos.	1	6	0	0	0	2	....	....	....	....	....	....	1933-34	1933-34
Harper, Terry	Mtl., L.A., Det., St.L., Col.	19	1066	35	221	256	1362	112	4	13	17	140	5	1962-63	1980-81
Harrer, Tim	Cgy.	1	3	0	0	0	2	....	....	....	....	....	....	1982-83	1982-83
• Harrington, Hago	Bos., Mtl.	3	72	9	3	12	15	4	1	0	1	2	....	1925-26	1932-33
• Harris, Billy	Tor., Det., Oak., Pit.	13	769	126	219	345	205	62	8	10	18	30	3	1955-56	1968-69
Harris, Billy	NYI, L.A., Tor.	12	897	231	327	558	394	71	19	19	38	48	....	1972-73	1983-84
Harris, Duke	Min., Tor.	1	26	1	4	5	4	....	....	....	....	....	....	1967-68	1967-68
• Harris, Henry	Bos.	1	32	2	4	6	20	....	....	....	....	....	....	1930-31	1930-31
Harris, Hugh	Buf.	1	60	12	26	38	17	3	0	0	0	0	....	1972-73	1972-73
Harris, Ron	Det., Oak., Atl., NYR	11	476	20	91	111	474	28	4	3	7	33	....	1962-63	1975-76
• Harris, Smokey	Bos.	1	6	3	1	4	8	....	....	....	....	....	....	1924-25	1924-25
Harris, Ted	Mtl., Min., Det., St.L., Phi.	12	788	30	168	198	1000	100	1	22	23	230	5	1963-64	1974-75
Harrison, Ed	Bos., NYR	4	194	27	24	51	53	9	1	0	1	2	....	1947-48	1950-51
Harrison, Jim	Bos., Tor., Chi., Edm.	8	324	67	86	153	435	13	1	1	2	43	....	1968-69	1979-80
Hart, Gerry	Det., NYI, Que., St.L.	15	730	29	150	179	1240	78	3	12	15	175	....	1968-69	1982-83
• Hart, Gizzy	Det., Mtl.	3	104	6	8	14	12	8	0	1	1	0	....	1926-27	1932-33
Hartman, Mike	Buf., Wpg., T.B., NYR	9	397	43	35	78	1388	21	0	0	0	106	1	1986-87	1994-95
Hartsburg, Craig	Min.	10	570	98	315	413	818	61	15	27	42	70	....	1979-80	1988-89
Harvey, Buster	Min., Atl., K.C., Det.	7	407	90	118	208	131	14	0	2	2	8	....	1970-71	1976-77
• Harvey, Doug	Mtl., NYR, Det., St.L.	20	1113	88	452	540	1216	137	8	64	72	152	6	1947-48	1968-69
Harvey, Hugh	K.C.	2	18	1	1	2	4	....	....	....	....	....	....	1974-75	1975-76
Hassard, Bob	Tor., Chi.	5	126	9	28	37	22	....	....	....	....	....	1	1949-50	1954-55
Hatcher, Kevin	Wsh., Dal., Pit., NYR, Car.	17	1157	227	450	677	1392	118	22	37	59	252	....	1984-85	2000-01
Hatoum, Ed	Det., Van.	3	47	3	6	9	25	....	....	....	....	....	....	1968-69	1970-71
‡ Hauer, Brett	Edm., Nsh.	3	37	4	4	8	38	....	....	....	....	....	....	1995-96	2001-02
Hawerchuk, Dale	Wpg., Buf., St.L., Phi.	16	1188	518	891	1409	730	97	30	69	99	67	....	1981-82	1996-97
‡ Hawgood, Greg	Bos., Edm., Phi., Fla., Pit., S.J., Van., Dal.	12	474	60	164	224	426	42	2	8	10	37	....	1987-88	2001-02
Hawkins, Todd	Van., Tor.	3	10	0	0	0	15	....	....	....	....	....	....	1988-89	1991-92
Haworth, Alan	Buf., Wsh., Que.	8	524	189	211	400	425	42	12	16	28	28	....	1980-81	1987-88
Haworth, Gord	NYR	1	2	0	1	1	0	....	....	....	....	....	....	1952-53	1952-53
Hawryliw, Neil	NYI	1	1	0	0	0	0	....	....	....	....	....	....	1981-82	1981-82
Hay, Bill	Chi.	8	506	113	273	386	244	67	15	21	36	62	1	1959-60	1966-67
• Hay, George	Chi., Det.	7	239	74	60	134	84	8	2	3	5	2	....	1926-27	1933-34
Hay, Jim	Det.	3	75	1	5	6	22	9	1	0	1	2	1	1952-53	1954-55
Hayek, Peter	Min.	1	1	0	0	0	0	....	....	....	....	....	....	1981-82	1981-82
Hayes, Chris	Bos.	1	....	....	....	....	....	1	0	0	0	0	1	1971-72	1971-72
• Haynes, Paul	Mtl.M., Bos., Mtl.	11	391	61	134	195	164	24	2	8	10	13	....	1930-31	1940-41
Hayward, Rick	L.A.	1	4	0	0	0	5	....	....	....	....	....	....	1990-91	1990-91
Hazlett, Steve	Van.	1	1	0	0	0	0	....	....	....	....	....	....	1979-80	1979-80
Head, Galen	Det.	1	1	0	0	0	0	....	....	....	....	....	....	1967-68	1967-68
• Headley, Fern	Bos., Mtl.	1	30	1	3	4	10	1	0	0	0	0	....	1924-25	1924-25
Healey, Rich	Det.	1	1	0	0	0	2	....	....	....	....	....	....	1960-61	1960-61
Heaphy, Shawn	Cgy.	1	1	0	0	0	0	....	....	....	....	....	....	1992-93	1992-93
Heaslip, Mark	NYR, L.A.	3	117	10	19	29	110	5	0	0	0	2	....	1976-77	1978-79
Heath, Randy	NYR	2	13	2	4	6	15	....	....	....	....	....	....	1984-85	1985-86
Hebenton, Andy	NYR, Bos.	9	630	189	202	391	83	22	6	5	11	8	....	1955-56	1963-64
‡ Hecl, Radoslav	Buf.	1	14	0	0	0	2	....	....	....	....	....	....	2002-03	2002-03
Hedberg, Anders	NYR	7	465	172	225	397	144	58	22	24	46	31	....	1978-79	1984-85
• Heffernan, Frank	Tor.	1	19	0	1	1	10	....	....	....	....	....	....	1919-20	1919-20
Heffernan, Gerry	Mtl.	3	83	33	35	68	27	11	3	3	6	8	1	1941-42	1943-44
Heidt, Mike	L.A.	1	6	0	1	1	7	....	....	....	....	....	....	1983-84	1983-84
• Heindl, Bill	Min., NYR	3	18	2	1	3	0	....	....	....	....	....	....	1970-71	1972-73
Heinrich, Lionel	Bos.	1	35	1	1	2	33	....	....	....	....	....	....	1955-56	1955-56
Heinze, Steve	Bos., CBJ, Buf., L.A.	12	694	178	158	336	379	69	11	15	26	48	....	1991-92	2002-03
Heiskala, Earl	Phi.	3	127	13	11	24	294	....	....	....	....	....	....	1968-69	1970-71
Helander, Peter	L.A.	1	7	0	1	1	0	....	....	....	....	....	....	1982-83	1982-83
‡ Helenius, Sami	Cgy., T.B., Col., Dal., Chi.	6	155	2	4	6	260	1	0	0	0	0	....	1996-97	2002-03
• Heller, Ott	NYR	15	647	55	176	231	465	61	6	8	14	61	2	1931-32	1945-46
Helman, Harry	Ott.	3	44	1	0	1	7	2	0	0	0	0	1	1922-23	1924-25
‡ Helminen, Raimo	NYR, Min., NYI	3	117	13	46	59	16	2	0	0	0	0	....	1985-86	1988-89
• Hemmerling, Tony	NYA	2	22	3	3	6	4	....	....	....	....	....	....	1935-36	1936-37
Henderson, Archie	Wsh., Min., Hfd.	3	23	3	1	4	92	....	....	....	....	....	....	1980-81	1982-83
‡ Henderson, Matt	Nsh., Chi.	2	6	0	1	1	2	....	....	....	....	....	....	1998-99	2001-02
Henderson, Murray	Bos.	8	405	24	62	86	305	41	2	3	5	23	....	1944-45	1951-52
Henderson, Paul	Det., Tor., Atl.	13	707	236	241	477	304	56	11	14	25	28	....	1962-63	1979-80
Hendrickson, John	Det.	3	5	0	0	0	4	....	....	....	....	....	....	1957-58	1961-62
Henning, Lorne	NYI	9	544	73	111	184	102	81	7	7	14	8	2	1972-73	1980-81

			Regular Schedule					Playoffs					NHL	First	Last
Name	NHL Teams	NHL Seasons	GP	G	A	TP	PIM	GP	G	A	TP	PIM	Cup Wins	NHL Season	NHL Season
● Henry, Camille	NYR, Chi., St.L.	14	727	279	249	528	88	47	6	12	18	7	....	1953-54	1969-70
Henry, Dale	NYI	6	132	13	26	39	263	14	1	0	1	19	....	1984-85	1989-90
Hepple, Alan	N.J.	3	3	0	0	0	7	....	....	....	....	....	....	1983-84	1985-86
‡ Herbers, Ian	Edm., T.B., NYI	2	65	0	5	5	79	....	....	....	....	....	....	1993-94	1999-00
● Herberts, Jimmy	Bos., Tor., Det.	6	206	83	31	114	253	9	3	0	3	10	....	1924-25	1929-30
Herchenratter, Art	Det.	1	10	1	2	3	2	....	....	....	....	....	....	1940-41	1940-41
Hergerts, Fred	NYA	2	20	2	4	6	2	....	....	....	....	....	....	1934-35	1935-36
● Hergesheimer, Phil	Chi., Bos.	4	125	21	41	62	19	6	0	0	0	2	....	1939-40	1942-43
Hergesheimer, Wally	NYR, Chi.	7	351	114	85	199	106	5	1	0	1	0	....	1951-52	1958-59
● Heron, Red	Tor., Bro., Mtl.	4	106	21	19	40	38	21	2	2	4	6	....	1938-39	1941-42
Heroux, Yves	Que.	1	1	0	0	0	0	....	....	....	....	....	....	1986-87	1986-87
‡ Herperger, Chris	Chi., Ott., Atl.	4	169	18	25	43	75	....	....	....	....	....	....	1999-00	2002-03
Herter, Jason	NYI	1	1	0	1	1	0	....	....	....	....	....	....	1995-96	1995-96
Hervey, Matt	Wpg., Bos., T.B.	3	35	0	5	5	97	5	0	0	0	6	....	1988-89	1992-93
Hess, Bob	St.L., Buf., Hfd.	8	329	27	95	122	178	4	1	1	2	2	....	1974-75	1983-84
● Heximer, Obs	NYR, Bos., NYA	3	84	13	7	20	16	5	0	0	0	2	....	1929-30	1934-35
● Hextall, Bryan	NYR	11	449	187	175	362	227	37	8	9	17	19	1	1936-37	1947-48
Hextall, Bryan	NYR, Pit., Atl., Det., Min.	8	549	99	161	260	738	18	0	4	4	59	....	1962-63	1975-76
Hextall, Dennis	NYR, L.A., Cal., Min., Det., Wsh.	13	681	153	350	503	1398	22	3	3	6	45	....	1967-68	1979-80
Heyliger, Vic	Chi.	2	33	2	3	5	2	....	....	....	....	....	....	1937-38	1943-44
● Hicke, Bill	Mtl., NYR, Oak., Cal., Pit.	14	729	168	234	402	395	42	3	10	13	41	2	1958-59	1971-72
Hicke, Ernie	Cal., Atl., NYI, Min., L.A.	8	520	132	140	272	407	2	1	0	1	0	....	1970-71	1977-78
Hickey, Greg	NYR	1	1	0	0	0	0	....	....	....	....	....	....	1977-78	1977-78
Hickey, Pat	NYR, Col., Tor., Que., St.L.	10	646	192	212	404	351	55	5	11	16	37	....	1975-76	1984-85
Hicks, Alex	Ana., Pit., S.J., Fla.	5	258	25	54	79	247	15	0	2	2	8	....	1995-96	1999-00
Hicks, Doug	Min., Chi., Edm., Wsh.	9	561	37	131	168	442	18	2	1	3	15	....	1974-75	1982-83
Hicks, Glenn	Det.	2	108	6	12	18	127	....	....	....	....	....	....	1979-80	1980-81
● Hicks, Henry	Mtl.M., Det.	3	96	7	2	9	72	....	....	....	....	....	....	1928-29	1930-31
Hicks, Wayne	Chi., Bos., Mtl., Phi., Pit.	5	115	13	23	36	22	2	0	1	1	2	1	1959-60	1967-68
Hidi, Andre	Wsh.	2	7	2	1	3	9	2	0	0	0	0	....	1983-84	1984-85
Hiemer, Uli	N.J.	3	143	19	54	73	176	....	....	....	....	....	....	1984-85	1986-87
‡ Higgins, Matt	Mtl.	4	57	1	2	3	6	....	....	....	....	....	....	1997-98	2000-01
Higgins, Paul	Tor.	2	25	0	0	0	152	1	0	0	0	0	....	1981-82	1982-83
Higgins, Tim	Chi., N.J., Det.	11	706	154	198	352	719	65	5	8	13	77	....	1978-79	1988-89
Hildebrand, Ike	NYR, Chi.	2	41	7	11	18	16	....	....	....	....	....	....	1953-54	1954-55
Hill, Al	Phi.	8	221	40	55	95	227	51	8	11	19	43	....	1976-77	1987-88
Hill, Brian	Hfd.	1	19	1	1	2	4	....	....	....	....	....	....	1979-80	1979-80
● Hill, Mel	Bos., Bro., Tor.	9	324	89	109	198	128	43	12	7	19	18	3	1937-38	1945-46
Hiller, Dutch	NYR, Det., Bos., Mtl.	9	383	91	113	204	163	48	9	8	17	21	2	1937-38	1945-46
Hiller, Jim	L.A., Det., NYR	2	63	8	12	20	116	2	0	0	0	4	....	1992-93	1993-94
Hillier, Randy	Bos., Pit., NYI, Buf.	11	543	16	110	126	906	28	0	2	2	93	1	1981-82	1991-92
Hillman, Floyd	Bos.	1	6	0	0	0	10	....	....	....	....	....	....	1956-57	1956-57
Hillman, Larry	Det., Bos., Tor., Min., Mtl., Phi., L.A., Buf.	19	790	36	196	232	579	74	2	9	11	30	6	1954-55	1972-73
● Hillman, Wayne	Chi., NYR, Min., Phi.	13	691	18	86	104	534	28	0	3	3	19	1	1960-61	1972-73
Hilworth, John	Det.	3	57	1	1	2	89	....	....	....	....	....	....	1977-78	1979-80
● Himes, Normie	NYA	9	402	106	113	219	127	2	0	0	0	0	....	1926-27	1934-35
Hindmarch, Dave	Cgy.	4	99	21	17	38	25	10	0	0	0	6	....	1980-81	1983-84
Hinse, Andre	Tor.	1	4	0	0	0	0	....	....	....	....	....	....	1967-68	1967-68
Hinton, Dan	Chi.	1	14	0	0	0	16	....	....	....	....	....	....	1976-77	1976-77
Hirsch, Tom	Min.	3	31	1	7	8	30	12	0	0	0	6	....	1983-84	1987-88
● Hirschfeld, Bert	Mtl.	2	33	1	4	5	2	5	1	0	1	0	....	1949-50	1950-51
Hislop, Jamie	Que., Cgy.	5	345	75	103	178	86	28	3	2	5	11	....	1979-80	1983-84
● Hitchman, Lionel	Ott., Bos.	12	417	28	34	62	523	35	3	1	4	73	2	1922-23	1933-34
● Hlinka, Ivan	Van.	2	137	42	81	123	28	16	3	10	13	8	....	1981-82	1982-83
‡ Hlushko, Todd	Phi., Cgy., Pit.	6	79	8	13	21	84	3	0	0	0	2	....	1993-94	1998-99
Hocking, Justin	L.A.	1	1	0	0	0	0	....	....	....	....	....	....	1993-94	1993-94
Hodge, Ken	Chi., Bos., NYR	14	881	328	472	800	779	97	34	47	81	120	2	1964-65	1977-78
Hodge Jr., Ken	Min., Bos., T.B.	4	142	39	48	87	32	15	4	6	10	6	....	1988-89	1992-93
‡ Hodgson, Dan	Tor., Van.	4	114	29	45	74	64	....	....	....	....	....	....	1985-86	1988-89
Hodgson, Rick	Hfd.	1	6	0	0	0	6	1	0	0	0	0	....	1979-80	1979-80
Hodgson, Ted	Bos.	1	4	0	0	0	0	....	....	....	....	....	....	1966-67	1966-67
Hoekstra, Cec	Mtl.	1	4	0	0	0	0	....	....	....	....	....	....	1959-60	1959-60
Hoekstra, Ed	Phi.	1	70	15	21	36	6	7	0	1	1	0	....	1967-68	1967-68
Hoene, Phil	L.A.	3	37	2	4	6	22	....	....	....	....	....	....	1972-73	1974-75
Hoffinger, Val	Chi.	2	28	0	1	1	30	....	....	....	....	....	....	1927-28	1928-29
Hoffman, Mike	Hfd.	3	9	1	3	4	2	....	....	....	....	....	....	1982-83	1985-86
Hoffmeyer, Bob	Chi., Phi., N.J.	6	198	14	52	66	325	3	0	1	1	25	....	1977-78	1984-85
Hofford, Jim	Buf., L.A.	3	18	0	0	0	47	....	....	....	....	....	....	1985-86	1988-89
Hogaboam, Bill	Atl., Det., Min.	8	332	80	109	189	100	2	0	0	0	0	....	1972-73	1979-80
Hoganson, Dale	L.A., Mtl., Que.	7	343	13	77	90	186	11	0	3	3	12	....	1969-70	1981-82
‡ Hoglund, Jonas	Cgy., Mtl., Tor.	7	545	117	145	262	112	59	8	11	19	8	....	1996-97	2002-03
Hogue, Benoit	Buf., NYI, Tor., Dal., T.B., Phx., Bos., Wsh.	15	863	222	321	543	877	92	17	16	33	124	1	1987-88	2001-02
Holan, Milos	Phi., Ana.	3	49	5	11	16	42	....	....	....	....	....	....	1993-94	1995-96
Holbrook, Terry	Min.	2	43	3	6	9	4	6	0	0	0	0	....	1972-73	1973-74
Holland, Jerry	NYR	2	37	8	4	12	6	....	....	....	....	....	....	1974-75	1975-76
● Hollett, Flash	Tor., Ott., Bos., Det.	13	562	132	181	313	358	79	8	26	34	38	2	1933-34	1945-46
‡ Hollinger, Terry	St.L.	2	7	0	0	0	2	....	....	....	....	....	....	1993-94	1994-95
● Hollingworth, Gord	Chi., Det.	4	163	4	14	18	201	3	0	0	0	2	....	1954-55	1957-58
Holloway, Bruce	Van.	1	2	0	0	0	0	....	....	....	....	....	....	1984-85	1984-85
● Holmes, Bill	Mtl., NYA	3	52	6	4	10	35	....	....	....	....	....	....	1925-26	1929-30
Holmes, Chuck	Det.	2	23	1	3	4	10	....	....	....	....	....	....	1958-59	1961-62
Holmes, Lou	Chi.	2	59	1	4	5	6	2	0	0	0	2	....	1931-32	1932-33
Holmes, Warren	L.A.	3	45	8	18	26	7	....	....	....	....	....	....	1981-82	1983-84
Holmgren, Paul	Phi., Min.	10	527	144	179	323	1684	82	19	32	51	195	....	1975-76	1984-85
● Holota, John	Det.	2	15	2	0	2	0	....	....	....	....	....	....	1942-43	1945-46
Holst, Greg	NYR	3	11	0	0	0	0	....	....	....	....	....	....	1975-76	1977-78
Holt, Gary	Cal., Cle., St.L.	5	101	13	11	24	133	....	....	....	....	....	....	1973-74	1977-78
Holt, Randy	Chi., Cle., Van., L.A., Cgy., Wsh., Phi.	10	395	4	37	41	1438	21	2	3	5	83	....	1974-75	1983-84
● Holway, Albert	Tor., Mtl.M., Pit.	5	112	7	2	9	48	6	0	0	0	0	1	1923-24	1928-29
Homenuke, Ron	Van.	1	1	0	0	0	0	....	....	....	....	....	....	1972-73	1972-73
Hoover, Ron	Bos., St.L.	3	18	4	0	4	31	8	0	0	0	18	....	1989-90	1991-92
Hopkins, Dean	L.A., Edm., Que.	6	223	23	51	74	306	18	1	5	6	29	....	1979-80	1988-89
Hopkins, Larry	Tor., Wpg.	4	60	13	16	29	26	6	0	0	0	2	....	1977-78	1982-83
Horacek, Tony	Phi., Chi.	5	154	10	19	29	316	2	1	0	1	2	....	1989-90	1994-95
Horava, Miloslav	NYR	3	80	5	17	22	38	2	0	1	1	0	....	1988-89	1990-91
Horbul, Doug	K.C.	1	4	1	0	1	2	....	....	....	....	....	....	1974-75	1974-75
Hordy, Mike	NYI	2	11	0	0	0	7	....	....	....	....	....	....	1978-79	1979-80
Horeck, Pete	Chi., Det., Bos.	8	426	106	118	224	340	34	6	8	14	43	....	1944-45	1951-52
● Horne, George	Mtl.M., Tor.	3	54	9	3	12	34	4	0	0	0	4	1	1925-26	1928-29
● Horner, Red	Tor.	12	490	42	110	152	1254	71	7	10	17	170	1	1928-29	1939-40
● Hornung, Larry	St.L.	2	48	2	9	11	10	11	0	2	2	2	....	1970-71	1971-72
● Horton, Tim	Tor., NYR, Pit., Buf.	24	1446	115	403	518	1611	126	11	39	50	183	4	1949-50	1973-74
Horvath, Bronco	NYR, Mtl., Bos., Chi., Tor., Min.	9	434	141	185	326	319	36	12	9	21	18	....	1955-56	1967-68
Hospodar, Ed	NYR, Hfd., Phi., Min., Buf.	9	450	17	51	68	1314	44	4	1	5	208	....	1979-80	1987-88
Hostak, Martin	Phi.	2	55	3	11	14	24	....	....	....	....	....	....	1990-91	1991-92
Hotham, Greg	Tor., Pit.	6	230	15	74	89	139	5	0	3	3	6	....	1979-80	1984-85
Houck, Paul	Min.	3	16	1	2	3	2	....	....	....	....	....	....	1985-86	1987-88
Houda, Doug	Det., Hfd., L.A., Buf., NYI, Ana.	15	561	19	63	82	1104	18	0	3	3	21	....	1985-86	2002-03
Houde, Claude	K.C.	2	59	3	6	9	40	....	....	....	....	....	....	1974-75	1975-76
Houde, Eric	Mtl.	3	30	2	3	5	4	....	....	....	....	....	....	1996-97	1998-99
Hough, Mike	Que., Fla., NYI	13	707	100	156	256	675	42	5	5	10	38	....	1986-87	1998-99
Houlder, Bill	Wsh., Buf., Ana., St.L., T.B., S.J., Nsh.	16	846	59	191	250	412	30	5	6	11	14	....	1987-88	2002-03
Houle, Rejean	Mtl.	11	635	161	247	408	395	90	14	34	48	66	5	1969-70	1982-83
Housley, Phil	Buf., Wpg., St.L., Cgy., N.J., Wsh., Chi., Tor.	21	1495	338	894	1232	822	85	13	43	56	36	....	1982-83	2002-03
Houston, Ken	Atl., Cgy., Wsh., L.A.	9	570	161	167	328	624	35	10	9	19	66	....	1975-76	1983-84
Howard, Jack	Tor.	1	2	0	0	0	0	....	....	....	....	....	....	1936-37	1936-37
Howatt, Garry	NYI, Hfd., N.J.	12	720	112	156	268	1836	87	12	14	26	289	2	1972-73	1983-84
Howe, Gordie	Det., Hfd.	26	1767	801	1049	1850	1685	157	68	92	160	220	4	1946-47	1979-80
Howe, Mark	Hfd., Phi., Det.	16	929	197	545	742	455	101	10	51	61	34	....	1979-80	1994-95
Howe, Marty	Hfd., Bos.	6	197	2	29	31	99	15	1	2	3	9	....	1979-80	1984-85
● Howe, Syd	Ott., Phi., Tor., St.L., Det.	17	698	237	291	528	212	70	17	27	44	10	3	1929-30	1945-46
Howe, Vic	NYR	3	33	3	4	7	10	....	....	....	....	....	....	1950-51	1954-55

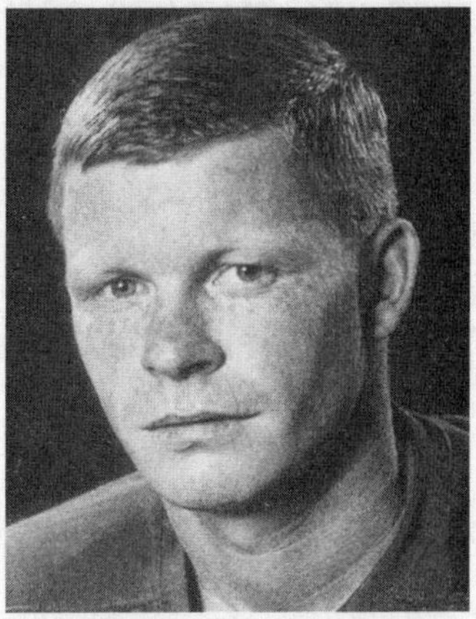

Dennis Hextall

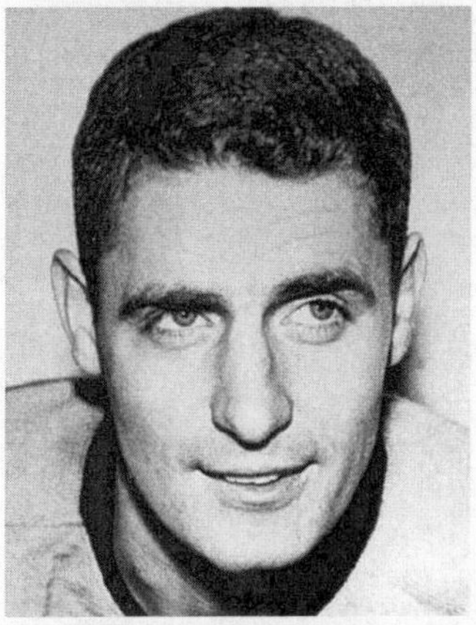

Floyd Hillman

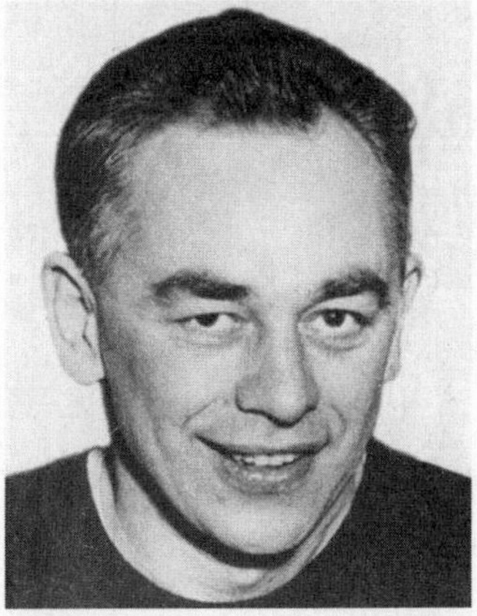

Flash Hollett

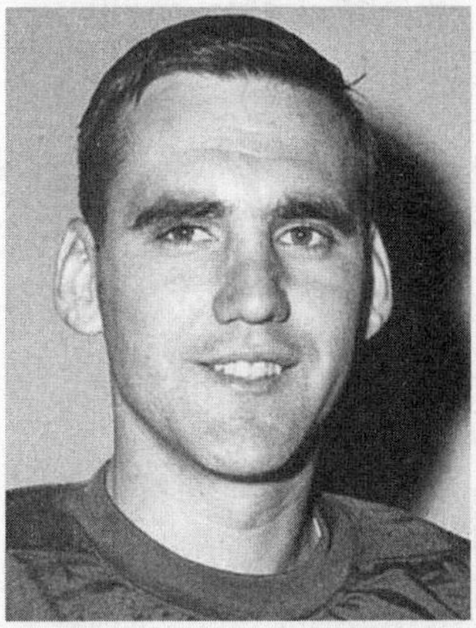

Brent Hughes

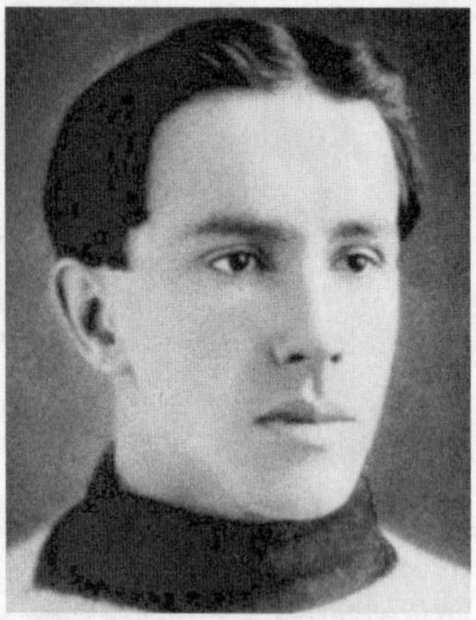
Harry Hyland

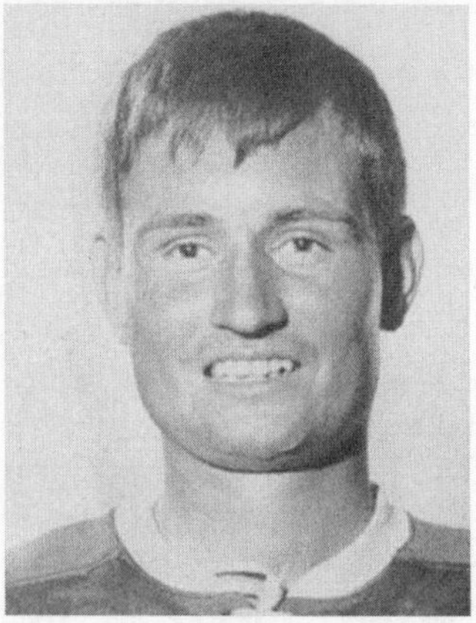
Brent Imlach

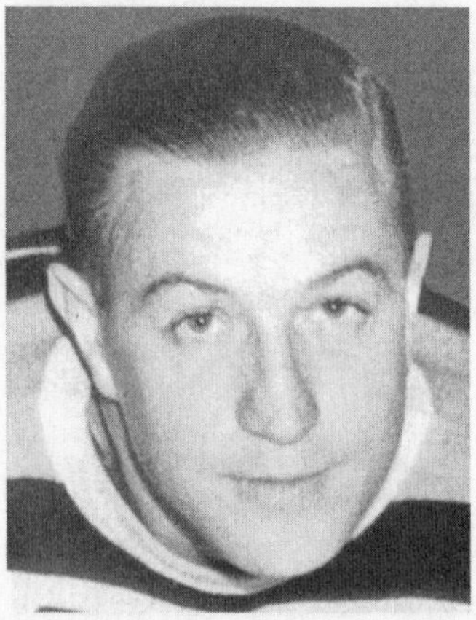
Art Jackson

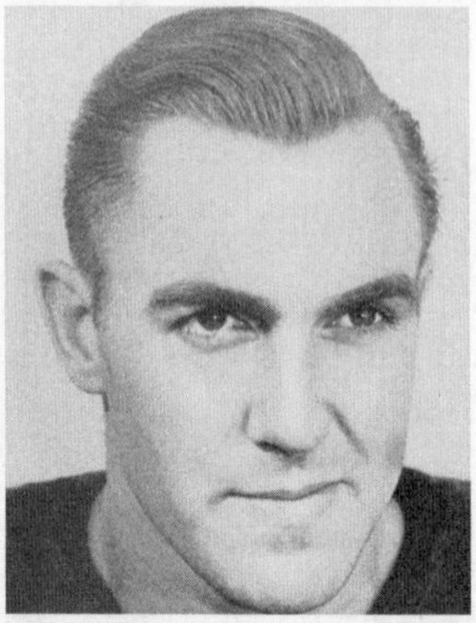
Bill Jennings

			Regular Schedule					Playoffs					NHL	First	Last
Name	NHL Teams	NHL Seasons	GP	G	A	TP	PIM	GP	G	A	TP	PIM	Cup Wins	NHL Season	NHL Season
Howell, Harry	NYR, Oak., Cal., L.A.	21	1411	94	324	418	1298	38	3	3	6	32	....	1952-53	1972-73
• Howell, Ron	NYR	2	4	0	0	0	0	....	....	....	....	....	....	1954-55	1955-56
Howse, Don	L.A.	1	33	2	5	7	6	2	0	0	0	0	....	1979-80	1979-80
Howson, Scott	NYI	2	18	5	3	8	4	....	....	....	....	....	....	1984-85	1985-86
Hoyda, Dave	Phi., Wpg.	4	132	6	17	23	299	12	0	0	0	17	....	1977-78	1980-81
Hrdina, Jiri	Cgy., Pit.	5	250	45	85	130	92	46	2	5	7	24	3	1987-88	1991-92
Hrechkosy, Dave	Cal., St.L.	4	140	42	24	66	41	3	1	0	1	2	....	1973-74	1976-77
Hrycuik, Jim	Wsh.	1	21	5	5	10	12	....	....	....	....	....	....	1974-75	1974-75
Hrymnak, Steve	Chi., Det.	2	18	2	1	3	4	2	0	0	0	0	....	1951-52	1952-53
Hrynewich, Tim	Pit.	2	55	6	8	14	82	....	....	....	....	....	....	1982-83	1983-84
Huard, Bill	Bos., Ott., Que., Dal., Edm., L.A.	8	223	16	18	34	594	5	0	0	0	2	....	1992-93	1999-00
Huard, Rolly	Tor.	1	1	1	0	1	0	....	....	....	....	....	....	1930-31	1930-31
Huber, Willie	Det., NYR, Van., Phi.	10	655	104	217	321	950	33	5	5	10	35	....	1978-79	1987-88
Hubick, Greg	Tor., Van.	2	77	6	9	15	10	....	....	....	....	....	....	1975-76	1979-80
Huck, Fran	Mtl., St.L.	3	94	24	30	54	38	11	3	4	7	2	....	1969-70	1972-73
Hucul, Fred	Chi., St.L.	5	164	11	30	41	113	6	1	0	1	10	....	1950-51	1967-68
Huddy, Charlie	Edm., L.A., Buf., St.L.	17	1017	99	354	453	785	183	19	66	85	135	5	1980-81	1996-97
Hudson, Dave	NYI, K.C., Col.	6	409	59	124	183	89	2	1	1	2	0	....	1972-73	1977-78
Hudson, Lex	Pit.	1	2	0	0	0	0	2	0	0	0	0	....	1978-79	1978-79
Hudson, Mike	Chi., Edm., NYR, Pit., Tor., St.L., Phx.	9	416	49	87	136	414	49	4	10	14	64	1	1988-89	1996-97
Hudson, Ron	Det.	2	33	5	2	7	2	....	....	....	....	....	....	1937-38	1939-40
Huffman, Kerry	Phi., Que., Ott.	10	401	37	108	145	361	11	0	0	0	2	....	1986-87	1995-96
Huggins, Al	Mtl.M.	1	20	1	1	2	2	....	....	....	....	....	....	1930-31	1930-31
Hughes, Albert	NYA	2	60	6	8	14	22	....	....	....	....	....	....	1930-31	1931-32
Hughes, Brent	L.A., Phi., St.L., Det., K.C.	8	435	15	117	132	440	22	1	3	4	53	....	1967-68	1974-75
Hughes, Brent	Wpg., Bos., Buf., NYI	8	357	41	39	80	831	29	4	1	5	53	....	1988-89	1996-97
Hughes, Frank	Cal.	1	5	0	0	0	0	....	....	....	....	....	....	1971-72	1971-72
Hughes, Howie	L.A.	3	168	25	32	57	30	14	2	0	2	2	....	1967-68	1969-70
Hughes, Jack	Col.	2	46	2	5	7	104	....	....	....	....	....	....	1980-81	1981-82
Hughes, James	Det.	1	40	0	1	1	48	....	....	....	....	....	....	1929-30	1929-30
Hughes, John	Van., Edm., NYR	2	70	2	14	16	211	7	0	1	1	16	....	1979-80	1980-81
Hughes, Pat	Mtl., Pit., Edm., Buf., St.L., Hfd.	10	573	130	128	258	646	71	8	25	33	77	3	1977-78	1986-87
Hughes, Ryan	Bos.	1	3	0	0	0	0	....	....	....	....	....	....	1995-96	1995-96
Hulbig, Joe	Edm., Bos.	5	55	4	4	8	16	6	0	1	1	2	....	1996-97	2000-01
Hull, Bobby	Chi., Wpg., Hfd.	16	1063	610	560	1170	640	119	62	67	129	102	1	1957-58	1979-80
Hull, Dennis	Chi., Det.	14	959	303	351	654	261	104	33	34	67	30	....	1964-65	1977-78
Hull, Jody	Hfd., NYR, Ott., Fla., T.B., Phi.	16	831	124	137	261	156	69	4	5	9	14	....	1988-89	2003-04
• Hunt, Fred	NYA, NYR	2	59	15	14	29	6	....	....	....	....	....	....	1940-41	1944-45
Hunter, Dale	Que., Wsh., Col.	19	1407	323	697	1020	3565	186	42	76	118	729	....	1980-81	1998-99
Hunter, Dave	Edm., Pit., Wpg.	10	746	133	190	323	918	105	16	24	40	211	3	1979-80	1988-89
Hunter, Mark	Mtl., St.L., Cgy., Hfd., Wsh.	12	628	213	171	384	1426	79	18	20	38	230	1	1981-82	1992-93
Hunter, Tim	Cgy., Que., Van., S.J.	16	815	62	76	138	3146	132	5	7	12	426	1	1981-82	1996-97
Huras, Larry	NYR	1	2	0	0	0	0	....	....	....	....	....	....	1976-77	1976-77
Hurlburt, Bob	Van.	1	1	0	0	0	2	....	....	....	....	....	....	1974-75	1974-75
Hurlbut, Mike	NYR, Que., Buf.	5	29	1	8	9	20	....	....	....	....	....	....	1992-93	1999-00
Hurley, Paul	Bos.	1	1	0	1	1	0	....	....	....	....	....	....	1968-69	1968-69
Hurst, Ron	Tor.	2	64	9	7	16	70	3	0	2	2	4	....	1955-56	1956-57
Huscroft, Jamie	N.J., Bos., Cgy., T.B., Van., Phx., Wsh.	10	352	5	33	38	1065	21	0	1	1	46	....	1988-89	1999-00
Huska, Ryan	Chi.	1	1	0	0	0	0	....	....	....	....	....	....	1997-98	1997-98
Huston, Ron	Cal.	2	79	15	31	46	8	....	....	....	....	....	....	1973-74	1974-75
Hutchinson, Ron	NYR	1	9	0	0	0	0	....	....	....	....	....	....	1960-61	1960-61
Hutchison, Dave	L.A., Tor., Chi., N.J.	10	584	19	97	116	1550	48	2	12	14	149	....	1974-75	1983-84
• Hutton, Bill	Bos., Ott., Phi.	2	64	3	2	5	8	2	0	0	0	0	....	1929-30	1930-31
• Hyland, Harry	Mtl.W., Ott.	1	17	14	2	16	65	....	....	....	....	....	....	1917-18	1917-18
Hynes, Dave	Bos.	2	22	4	0	4	2	....	....	....	....	....	....	1973-74	1974-75
Hynes, Gord	Bos., Phi.	2	52	3	9	12	22	12	1	2	3	6	....	1991-92	1992-93
I															
Iafrate, Al	Tor., Wsh., Bos., S.J.	12	799	152	311	463	1301	71	19	16	35	77	....	1984-85	1997-98
‡ Ignatjev, Victor	Pit.	1	11	0	1	1	6	1	0	0	0	2	....	1998-99	1998-99
‡ Ihnacak, Miroslav	Tor., Det.	3	56	8	9	17	39	1	0	0	0	0	....	1985-86	1988-89
Ihnacak, Peter	Tor.	8	417	102	165	267	175	28	4	10	14	25	....	1982-83	1989-90
Imlach, Brent	Tor.	2	3	0	0	0	0	....	....	....	....	....	....	1965-66	1966-67
Ingarfield, Earl	NYR, Pit., Oak., Cal.	13	746	179	226	405	239	21	9	8	17	10	....	1958-59	1970-71
Ingarfield, Earl	Atl., Cgy., Det.	2	39	4	4	8	22	2	0	1	1	0	....	1979-80	1980-81
Inglis, Billy	L.A., Buf.	3	36	1	3	4	4	11	1	2	3	4	....	1967-68	1970-71
• Ingoldsby, Johnny	Tor.	2	29	5	1	6	15	....	....	....	....	....	....	1942-43	1943-44
Ingram, Frank	Chi.	3	101	24	16	40	69	11	0	1	1	2	....	1929-30	1931-32
• Ingram, John	Bos.	1	1	0	0	0	0	....	....	....	....	....	....	1924-25	1924-25
Ingram, Ron	Chi., Det., NYR	4	114	5	15	20	81	2	0	0	0	0	....	1956-57	1964-65
Intranuovo, Ralph	Edm., Tor.	3	22	2	4	6	4	....	....	....	....	....	....	1994-95	1996-97
• Irvin, Dick	Chi.	3	94	29	23	52	78	2	2	0	2	4	....	1926-27	1928-29
Irvine, Ted	Bos., L.A., NYR, St.L.	11	724	154	177	331	657	83	16	24	40	115	....	1963-64	1976-77
Irwin, Ivan	Mtl., NYR	5	155	2	27	29	214	5	0	0	0	8	....	1952-53	1957-58
Isaksson, Ulf	L.A.	1	50	7	15	22	10	....	....	....	....	....	....	1982-83	1982-83
Issel, Kim	Edm.	1	4	0	0	0	0	....	....	....	....	....	....	1988-89	1988-89
J															
• Jackson, Art	Tor., Bos., NYA	11	468	123	178	301	144	52	8	12	20	29	2	1934-35	1944-45
• Jackson, Busher	Tor., NYA, Bos.	15	633	241	234	475	437	71	18	12	30	53	1	1929-30	1943-44
Jackson, Dane	Van., Buf., NYI	4	45	12	6	18	58	6	0	0	0	10	....	1993-94	1997-98
Jackson, Don	Min., Edm., NYR	10	311	16	52	68	640	53	4	5	9	147	2	1977-78	1986-87
• Jackson, Harold	Chi., Det.	8	219	17	34	51	208	31	1	2	3	33	2	1936-37	1946-47
Jackson, Jack	Chi.	1	48	2	5	7	38	....	....	....	....	....	....	1946-47	1946-47
Jackson, Jeff	Tor., NYR, Que., Chi.	8	263	38	48	86	313	6	1	1	2	16	....	1984-85	1991-92
Jackson, Jim	Cgy., Buf.	4	112	17	30	47	20	14	3	2	5	6	....	1982-83	1987-88
• Jackson, Lloyd	NYA	1	14	1	1	2	0	....	....	....	....	....	....	1936-37	1936-37
• Jackson, Stan	Tor., Bos., Ott.	5	86	9	6	15	75	....	....	....	....	....	1	1921-22	1926-27
Jackson, Walter	NYA, Bos.	4	84	16	11	27	18	....	....	....	....	....	....	1932-33	1935-36
• Jacobs, Paul	Tor.	1	1	0	0	0	0	....	....	....	....	....	....	1918-19	1918-19
Jacobs, Tim	Cal.	1	46	0	10	10	35	....	....	....	....	....	....	1975-76	1975-76
‡ Jakopin, John	Fla., Pit., S.J.	6	113	1	6	7	145	....	....	....	....	....	....	1997-98	2002-03
Jalo, Risto	Edm.	1	3	0	3	3	0	....	....	....	....	....	....	1985-86	1985-86
Jalonen, Kari	Cgy., Edm.	2	37	9	6	15	4	5	1	0	1	0	....	1982-83	1983-84
James, Gerry	Tor.	5	149	14	26	40	257	15	1	0	1	8	....	1954-55	1959-60
James, Val	Buf., Tor.	2	11	0	0	0	30	....	....	....	....	....	....	1981-82	1986-87
Jamieson, Jim	NYR	1	1	0	1	1	0	....	....	....	....	....	....	1943-44	1943-44
Jankowski, Lou	Det., Chi.	4	127	19	18	37	15	1	0	0	0	0	....	1950-51	1954-55
Janney, Craig	Bos., St.L., S.J., Wpg., Phx., T.B., NYI	12	760	188	563	751	170	120	24	86	110	53	....	1987-88	1998-99
Janssens, Mark	NYR, Min., Hfd., Ana., NYI, Phx., Chi.	14	711	40	73	113	1422	27	5	1	6	33	....	1987-88	2000-01
‡ Jantunen, Marko	Cgy.	1	3	0	0	0	0	....	....	....	....	....	....	1996-97	1996-97
Jarrett, Doug	Chi., NYR	13	775	38	182	220	631	99	7	16	23	82	....	1964-65	1976-77
Jarrett, Gary	Tor., Det., Oak., Cal.	7	341	72	92	164	131	11	3	1	4	9	....	1960-61	1971-72
Jarry, Pierre	NYR, Tor., Det., Min.	7	344	88	117	205	142	5	0	1	1	0	....	1971-72	1977-78
Jarvenpaa, Hannu	Wpg.	3	114	11	26	37	83	....	....	....	....	....	....	1986-87	1988-89
‡ Jarventie, Martti	Mtl.	1	1	0	0	0	0	....	....	....	....	....	....	2001-02	2001-02
Jarvi, Iiro	Que.	2	116	18	43	61	58	....	....	....	....	....	....	1988-89	1989-90
Jarvis, Doug	Mtl., Wsh., Hfd.	13	964	139	264	403	263	105	14	27	41	42	4	1975-76	1987-88
• Jarvis, James	Pit., Phi., Tor.	3	112	17	15	32	62	....	....	....	....	....	....	1929-30	1936-37
Jarvis, Wes	Wsh., Min., L.A., Tor.	9	237	31	55	86	98	2	0	0	0	2	....	1979-80	1987-88
Javanainen, Arto	Pit.	1	14	4	1	5	2	....	....	....	....	....	....	1984-85	1984-85
Jay, Bob	L.A.	1	3	0	1	1	0	....	....	....	....	....	....	1993-94	1993-94
Jeffrey, Larry	Det., Tor., NYR	8	368	39	62	101	293	38	4	10	14	42	1	1961-62	1968-69
Jelinek, Tomas	Ott.	1	49	7	6	13	52	....	....	....	....	....	....	1992-93	1992-93
Jenkins, Dean	L.A.	1	5	0	0	0	2	....	....	....	....	....	....	1983-84	1983-84
• Jenkins, Roger	Chi., Tor., Mtl., Bos., Mtl.M., NYA	8	325	15	39	54	253	25	1	7	8	12	2	1930-31	1938-39
Jennings, Bill	Det., Bos.	5	108	32	33	65	45	20	4	4	8	6	....	1940-41	1944-45
Jennings, Grant	Wsh., Hfd., Pit., Tor., Buf.	9	389	14	43	57	804	54	2	1	3	68	2	1987-88	1995-96
Jensen, Chris	NYR, Phi.	6	74	9	12	21	27	....	....	....	....	....	....	1985-86	1991-92
Jensen, David	Min.	3	18	0	2	2	11	....	....	....	....	....	....	1983-84	1985-86
Jensen, David	Hfd., Wsh.	4	69	9	13	22	22	11	0	0	0	2	....	1984-85	1987-88
Jensen, Steve	Min., L.A.	7	438	113	107	220	318	12	0	3	3	9	....	1975-76	1981-82

	Name	NHL Teams	NHL Seasons	Regular Schedule GP	G	A	TP	PIM	Playoffs GP	G	A	TP	PIM	NHL Cup Wins	First NHL Season	Last NHL Season
•	Jeremiah, Ed	NYA, Bos.	1	15	0	1	1	0	....	....	....	....	....	....	1931-32	1931-32
	Jerrard, Paul	Min.	1	5	0	0	0	4	....	....	....	....	....	....	1988-89	1988-89
•	Jerwa, Frank	Bos., St.L.	4	81	11	16	27	53	....	....	....	....	....	....	1931-32	1934-35
•	Jerwa, Joe	NYR, Bos., NYA	7	234	29	58	87	309	17	2	3	5	16	....	1930-31	1938-39
	Jirik, Jaroslav	St.L.	1	3	0	0	0	0	....	....	....	....	....	....	1969-70	1969-70
•	Joanette, Rosario	Mtl.	1	2	0	1	1	4	....	....	....	....	....	....	1944-45	1944-45
	Jodzio, Rick	Col., Cle.	1	70	2	8	10	71	....	....	....	....	....	....	1977-78	1977-78
	Johannesen, Glenn	NYI	1	2	0	0	0	0	....	....	....	....	....	....	1985-86	1985-86
	Johannson, John	N.J.	1	5	0	0	0	0	....	....	....	....	....	....	1983-84	1983-84
•	Johansen, Bill	Tor.	1	1	0	0	0	0	....	....	....	....	....	....	1949-50	1949-50
	Johansen, Trevor	Tor., Col., L.A.	5	286	11	46	57	282	13	0	3	3	21	....	1977-78	1981-82
	Johansson, Bjorn	Cle.	2	15	1	1	2	10	....	....	....	....	....	....	1976-77	1977-78
	Johansson, Calle	Buf., Wsh., Tor.	17	1109	119	416	535	519	105	12	43	55	44	....	1987-88	2003-04
‡	Johansson, Mathias	Cgy., Pit.	1	58	5	10	15	16	....	....	....	....	....	....	2002-03	2002-03
	Johansson, Roger	Cgy., Chi.	4	161	9	34	43	163	5	0	1	1	2	....	1989-90	1994-95
	Johns, Don	NYR, Mtl., Min.	6	153	2	21	23	76	....	....	....	....	....	....	1960-61	1967-68
	Johnson, Allan	Mtl., Det.	4	105	21	28	49	30	11	2	2	4	6	....	1956-57	1962-63
	Johnson, Brian	Det.	1	3	0	0	0	5	....	....	....	....	....	....	1983-84	1983-84
•	Johnson, Ching	NYR, NYA	12	436	38	48	86	808	61	5	2	7	161	2	1926-27	1937-38
•	Johnson, Danny	Tor., Van., Det.	3	121	18	19	37	24	....	....	....	....	....	....	1969-70	1971-72
	Johnson, Earl	Det.	1	1	0	0	0	0	....	....	....	....	....	....	1953-54	1953-54
	Johnson, Jim	NYR, Phi., L.A.	8	302	75	111	186	73	7	0	2	2	2	....	1964-65	1971-72
	Johnson, Jim	Pit., Min., Dal., Wsh., Phx.	13	829	29	166	195	1197	51	1	11	12	132	....	1985-86	1997-98
	Johnson, Mark	Pit., Min., Hfd., St.L., N.J.	11	669	203	305	508	260	37	16	12	28	10	....	1979-80	1989-90
	Johnson, Norm	Bos., Chi.	3	61	5	20	25	41	14	4	0	4	6	....	1957-58	1959-60
	Johnson, Terry	Que., St.L., Cgy., Tor.	9	285	3	24	27	580	38	0	4	4	118	....	1979-80	1987-88
	Johnson, Tom	Mtl., Bos.	17	978	51	213	264	960	111	8	15	23	109	6	1947-48	1964-65
•	Johnson, Virgil	Chi.	3	75	1	11	12	27	19	0	3	3	4	1	1937-38	1944-45
	Johnston, Bernie	Hfd.	2	57	12	24	36	16	3	0	1	1	0	....	1979-80	1980-81
	Johnston, George	Chi.	4	58	20	12	32	2	....	....	....	....	....	....	1941-42	1946-47
	Johnston, Greg	Bos., Tor.	9	187	26	29	55	124	22	2	1	3	12	....	1983-84	1991-92
	Johnston, Jay	Wsh.	2	8	0	0	0	13	....	....	....	....	....	....	1980-81	1981-82
	Johnston, Joey	Min., Cal., Chi.	6	331	85	106	191	320	....	....	....	....	....	....	1968-69	1975-76
	Johnston, Larry	L.A., Det., K.C., Col.	7	320	9	64	73	580	....	....	....	....	....	....	1967-68	1976-77
	Johnston, Marshall	Min., Cal.	7	251	14	52	66	58	6	0	0	0	2	....	1967-68	1973-74
	Johnston, Randy	NYI	1	4	0	0	0	4	....	....	....	....	....	....	1979-80	1979-80
	Johnstone, Eddie	NYR, Det.	10	426	122	136	258	375	55	13	10	23	83	....	1975-76	1986-87
	Johnstone, Ross	Tor.	2	42	5	4	9	14	3	0	0	0	0	1	1943-44	1944-45
•	Joliat, Aurel	Mtl.	16	655	270	190	460	771	46	9	13	22	66	3	1922-23	1937-38
•	Joliat, Rene	Mtl.	1	1	0	0	0	0	....	....	....	....	....	....	1924-25	1924-25
	Joly, Greg	Wsh., Det.	9	365	21	76	97	250	5	0	0	0	8	....	1974-75	1982-83
	Joly, Yvan	Mtl.	3	2	0	0	0	0	1	0	0	0	0	....	1979-80	1982-83
	Jomphe, Jean-Francois	Ana., Phx., Mtl.	4	111	10	29	39	102	....	....	....	....	....	....	1995-96	1998-99
	Jonathan, Stan	Bos., Pit.	8	411	91	110	201	751	63	8	4	12	137	....	1975-76	1982-83
	Jones, Bob	NYR	1	2	0	0	0	0	....	....	....	....	....	....	1968-69	1968-69
	Jones, Brad	Wpg., L.A., Phi.	6	148	25	31	56	122	9	1	1	2	2	....	1986-87	1991-92
	Jones, Buck	Det., Tor.	4	50	2	2	4	36	12	0	1	1	18	....	1938-39	1942-43
	Jones, Jim	Cal.	1	2	0	0	0	0	....	....	....	....	....	....	1971-72	1971-72
	Jones, Jimmy	Tor.	3	148	13	18	31	68	19	1	5	6	11	....	1977-78	1979-80
	Jones, Keith	Wsh., Col., Phi.	9	491	117	141	258	765	63	12	12	24	120	....	1992-93	2000-01
	Jones, Ron	Bos., Pit., Wsh.	5	54	1	4	5	31	....	....	....	....	....	....	1971-72	1975-76
‡	Jonsson, Jorgen	NYI, Ana.	1	81	12	19	31	16	....	....	....	....	....	....	1999-00	1999-00
	Jonsson, Tomas	NYI, Edm.	8	552	85	259	344	482	80	11	26	37	97	2	1981-82	1988-89
	Joseph, Chris	Pit., Edm., T.B., Van., Phi., Phx., Atl.	14	510	39	112	151	567	31	3	4	7	24	....	1987-88	2000-01
	Joseph, Tony	Wpg.	1	2	1	0	1	0	....	....	....	....	....	....	1988-89	1988-89
	Joyal, Eddie	Det., Tor., L.A., Phi.	9	466	128	134	262	103	50	11	8	19	18	....	1962-63	1971-72
	Joyce, Bob	Bos., Wsh., Wpg.	6	158	34	49	83	90	46	15	9	24	29	....	1987-88	1992-93
	Joyce, Duane	Dal.	1	3	0	0	0	0	....	....	....	....	....	....	1993-94	1993-94
•	Juckes, Bing	NYR	2	16	2	1	3	6	....	....	....	....	....	....	1947-48	1949-50
‡	Juhlin, Patrik	Phi.	2	56	7	6	13	23	13	1	0	1	2	....	1994-95	1995-96
	Julien, Claude	Que.	2	14	0	1	1	25	....	....	....	....	....	....	1984-85	1985-86
	Juneau, Joe	Bos., Wsh., Buf., Ott., Phx., Mtl.	13	828	156	416	572	272	112	25	54	79	69	....	1991-92	2003-04
‡	Junker, Steve	NYI	2	5	0	0	0	0	3	0	1	1	0	....	1992-93	1993-94
	Jutila, Timo	Buf.	1	10	1	5	6	13	....	....	....	....	....	....	1984-85	1984-85
	Juzda, Bill	NYR, Tor.	9	398	14	54	68	398	42	0	3	3	46	2	1940-41	1951-52

K

	Name	NHL Teams	NHL Seasons	Regular Schedule GP	G	A	TP	PIM	Playoffs GP	G	A	TP	PIM	NHL Cup Wins	First NHL Season	Last NHL Season
	Kabel, Bob	NYR	2	48	5	13	18	34	....	....	....	....	....	....	1959-60	1960-61
	Kachowski, Mark	Pit.	3	64	6	5	11	209	....	....	....	....	....	....	1987-88	1989-90
	Kachur, Ed	Chi.	2	96	10	14	24	35	....	....	....	....	....	....	1956-57	1957-58
	Kaese, Trent	Buf.	1	1	0	0	0	0	....	....	....	....	....	....	1988-89	1988-89
	Kaiser, Vern	Mtl.	1	50	7	5	12	33	2	0	0	0	0	....	1950-51	1950-51
•	Kalbfleish, Walter	Ott., St.L., NYA, Bos.	4	36	0	4	4	32	5	0	0	0	2	....	1933-34	1936-37
•	Kaleta, Alex	Chi., NYR	7	387	92	121	213	190	17	1	6	7	2	....	1941-42	1950-51
‡	Kallio, Tomi	Atl., CBJ, Phi.	3	140	24	31	55	48	....	....	....	....	....	....	2000-01	2002-03
	Kallur, Anders	NYI	6	383	101	110	211	149	78	12	23	35	32	4	1979-80	1984-85
‡	Kamensky, Valeri	Que., Col., NYR, Dal., N.J.	11	637	200	301	501	383	66	25	35	60	72	1	1991-92	2001-02
	Kaminski, Kevin	Min., Que., Wsh.	7	139	3	10	13	528	8	0	0	0	52	....	1988-89	1996-97
•	Kaminsky, Max	Ott., Bos., St.L., Mtl.M.	4	130	22	34	56	38	4	0	0	0	0	....	1933-34	1936-37
	Kaminsky, Yan	Wpg., NYI	2	26	3	2	5	4	2	0	0	0	4	....	1993-94	1994-95
•	Kampman, Bingo	Tor.	5	189	14	30	44	287	47	1	4	5	38	1	1937-38	1941-42
	Kane, Francis	Det.	1	2	0	0	0	0	....	....	....	....	....	....	1943-44	1943-44
	Kannegiesser, Gord	St.L.	2	23	0	1	1	15	....	....	....	....	....	....	1967-68	1971-72
	Kannegiesser, Sheldon	Pit., NYR, L.A., Van.	8	366	14	67	81	292	18	0	2	2	10	....	1970-71	1977-78
	Karabin, Ladislav	Pit.	1	9	0	0	0	2	....	....	....	....	....	....	1993-94	1993-94
‡	Karalahti, Jere	L.A., Nsh.	3	149	8	19	27	97	17	0	1	1	20	....	1999-00	2001-02
	Karamnov, Vitali	St.L.	3	92	12	20	32	65	2	0	0	0	2	....	1992-93	1994-95
	Karjalainen, Kyosti	L.A.	1	28	1	8	9	12	3	0	1	1	2	....	1991-92	1991-92
	Karlander, Al	Det.	4	212	36	56	92	70	4	0	1	1	0	....	1969-70	1972-73
‡	Karlsson, Andreas	Atl.	3	153	11	27	38	50	....	....	....	....	....	....	1999-00	2001-02
‡	Karpa, Dave	Que., Ana., Car., NYR	12	557	18	80	98	1374	19	1	1	2	39	....	1991-92	2002-03
‡	Karpov, Valeri	Ana.	3	76	14	15	29	32	....	....	....	....	....	....	1994-95	1996-97
	Kasatonov, Alexei	N.J., Ana., St.L., Bos.	7	383	38	122	160	326	33	4	7	11	40	....	1989-90	1995-96
	Kasper, Steve	Bos., L.A., Phi., T.B.	13	821	177	291	468	554	94	20	28	48	82	....	1980-81	1992-93
	Kastelic, Ed	Wsh., Hfd.	7	220	11	10	21	719	8	1	0	1	32	....	1985-86	1991-92
	Kaszycki, Mike	NYI, Wsh., Tor.	5	226	42	80	122	108	19	2	6	8	10	....	1977-78	1982-83
•	Kea, Ed	Atl., St.L.	10	583	30	145	175	508	32	2	4	6	39	....	1973-74	1982-83
	Kearns, Dennis	Van.	10	677	31	290	321	386	11	1	2	3	8	....	1971-72	1980-81
•	Keating, Jack	Det.	2	11	3	0	3	4	....	....	....	....	....	....	1938-39	1939-40
•	Keating, John	NYA	2	35	5	5	10	17	....	....	....	....	....	....	1931-32	1932-33
	Keating, Mike	NYR	1	1	0	0	0	0	....	....	....	....	....	....	1977-78	1977-78
•	Keats, Duke	Bos., Det., Chi.	3	82	30	19	49	113	....	....	....	....	....	....	1926-27	1928-29
	Keczmer, Dan	Min., Hfd., Cgy., Dal., Nsh.	10	235	8	38	46	212	12	0	1	1	8	....	1990-91	1999-00
•	Keeling, Butch	Tor., NYR	12	525	157	63	220	331	47	11	11	22	34	1	1926-27	1937-38
	Keenan, Larry	Tor., St.L., Buf., Phi.	6	233	38	64	102	28	46	15	16	31	12	....	1961-62	1971-72
	Kehoe, Rick	Tor., Pit.	14	906	371	396	767	120	39	4	17	21	4	....	1971-72	1984-85
	Kekalainen, Jarmo	Bos., Ott.	5	55	5	8	13	28	....	....	....	....	....	....	1989-90	1993-94
	Kelleher, Chris	Bos.	1	1	0	0	0	0	....	....	....	....	....	....	2001-02	2001-02
	Keller, Ralph	NYR	1	3	1	0	1	6	....	....	....	....	....	....	1962-63	1962-63
	Kellgren, Christer	Col.	1	5	0	0	0	0	....	....	....	....	....	....	1981-82	1981-82
	Kelly, Bob	Phi., Wsh.	12	837	154	208	362	1454	101	9	14	23	172	2	1970-71	1981-82
	Kelly, Bob	St.L., Pit., Chi.	6	425	87	109	196	687	23	6	3	9	40	....	1973-74	1978-79
	Kelly, Dave	Det.	1	16	2	0	2	4	....	....	....	....	....	....	1976-77	1976-77
	Kelly, John Paul	L.A.	7	400	54	70	124	366	18	1	1	2	41	....	1979-80	1985-86
•	Kelly, Pep	Tor., Chi., Bro.	8	288	74	53	127	105	38	7	6	13	10	....	1934-35	1941-42
	Kelly, Pete	St.L., Det., NYA, Bro.	7	177	21	38	59	68	19	3	1	4	2	2	1934-35	1941-42
	Kelly, Red	Det., Tor.	20	1316	281	542	823	327	164	33	59	92	51	8	1947-48	1966-67
•	Kemp, Kevin	Hfd.	1	3	0	0	0	4	....	....	....	....	....	....	1980-81	1980-81
	Kemp, Stan	Tor.	1	1	0	0	0	2	....	....	....	....	....	....	1948-49	1948-49
‡	Kenady, Chris	St.L., NYR	2	7	0	2	2	0	....	....	....	....	....	....	1997-98	1999-00
•	Kendall, Bill	Chi., Tor.	5	131	16	10	26	28	6	0	0	0	0	1	1933-34	1937-38
	Kennedy, Dean	L.A., NYR, Buf., Wpg., Edm.	12	717	26	108	134	1118	36	1	7	8	59	....	1982-83	1994-95
	Kennedy, Forbes	Chi., Det., Bos., Phi., Tor.	11	603	70	108	178	988	12	2	4	6	64	....	1956-57	1968-69

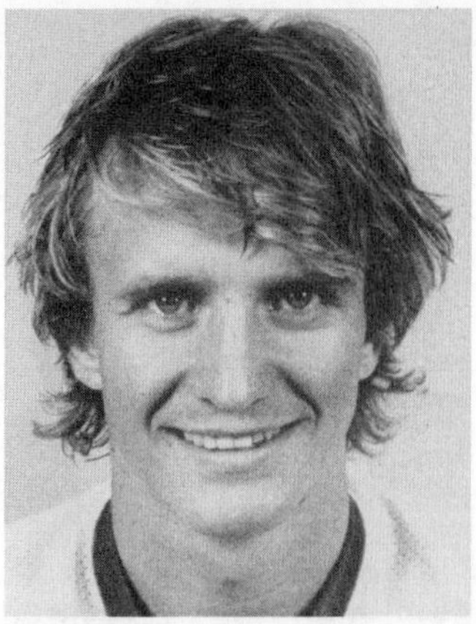

Tomas Jonsson

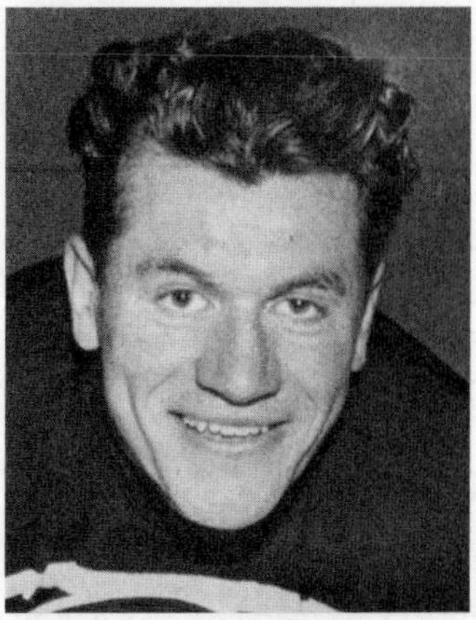

Alex Kaleta

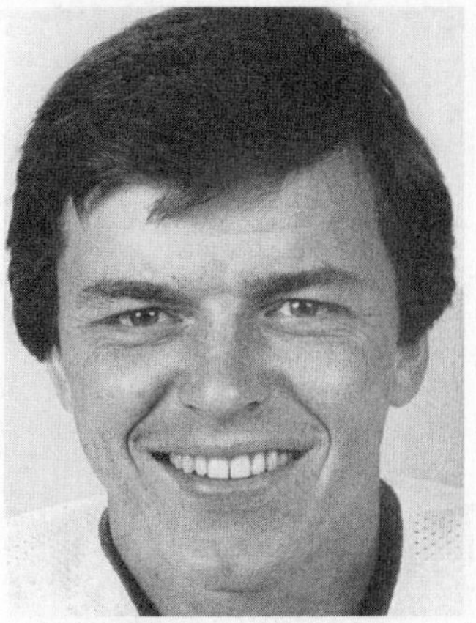

Anders Kallur

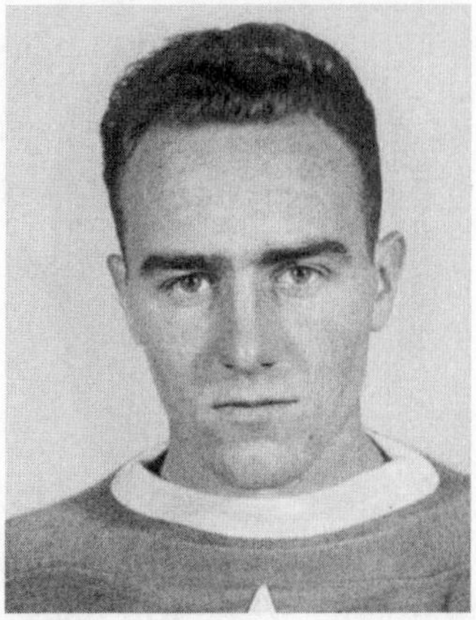

Pep Kelly

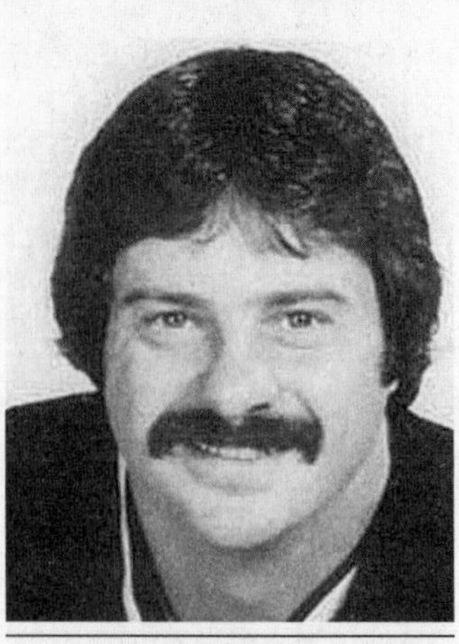

Orest Kindrachuk

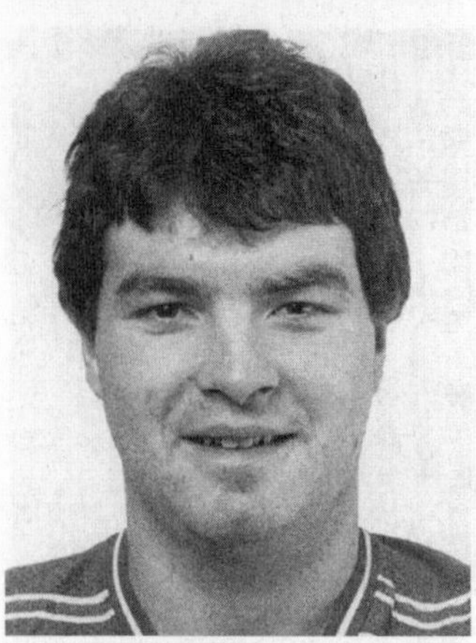

Chris Kotsopoulos

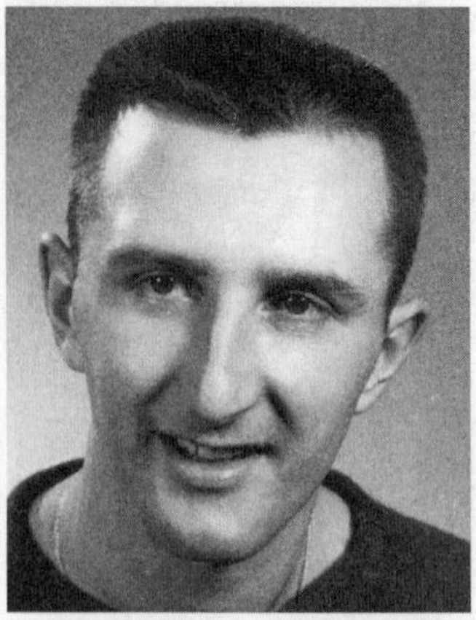

Aggie Kukulowicz

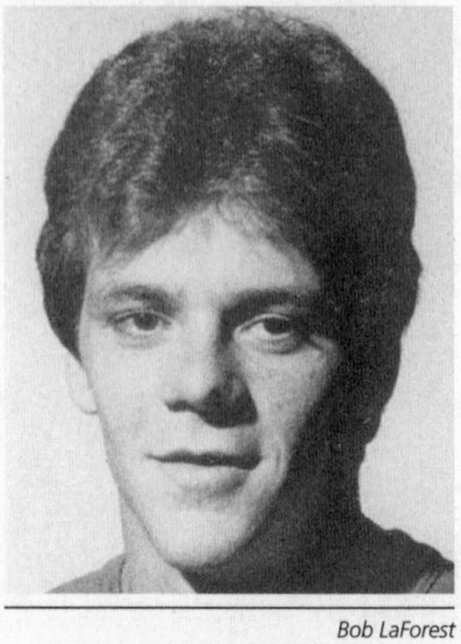

Bob LaForest

			Regular Schedule					Playoffs							
Name	**NHL Teams**	**NHL Seasons**	**GP**	**G**	**A**	**TP**	**PIM**	**GP**	**G**	**A**	**TP**	**PIM**	**NHL Cup Wins**	**First NHL Season**	**Last NHL Season**
‡ Kennedy, Mike	Dal., Tor., NYI	5	145	16	36	52	112	5	0	0	0	9	....	1994-95	1998-99
Kennedy, Sheldon	Det., Cgy., Bos.	8	310	49	58	107	233	24	6	4	10	20	....	1989-90	1996-97
Kennedy, Ted	Tor.	14	696	231	329	560	432	78	29	31	60	32	5	1942-43	1956-57
• Kenny, Ernest	NYR, Chi.	2	10	0	0	0	18	....	....	....	....	....	....	1930-31	1934-35
Keon, Dave	Tor., Hfd.	18	1296	396	590	986	117	92	32	36	68	6	4	1960-61	1981-82
‡ Kerch, Alexander	Edm.	1	5	0	0	0	2	....	....	....	....	....	....	1993-94	1993-94
Kerr, Alan	NYI, Det., Wpg.	9	391	72	94	166	826	38	5	4	9	70	....	1984-85	1992-93
Kerr, Reg	Cle., Chi., Edm.	6	263	66	94	160	169	7	1	0	1	7	....	1977-78	1983-84
Kerr, Tim	Phi., NYR, Hfd.	13	655	370	304	674	596	81	40	31	71	58	....	1980-81	1992-93
Kesa, Dan	Van., Dal., Pit., T.B.	4	139	8	22	30	66	13	1	0	1	0	....	1993-94	1999-00
Kessell, Rick	Pit., Cal.	5	135	4	24	28	6	....	....	....	....	....	....	1969-70	1973-74
Ketola, Veli-Pekka	Col.	1	44	9	5	14	4	....	....	....	....	....	....	1981-82	1981-82
Ketter, Kerry	Atl.	1	41	0	2	2	58	....	....	....	....	....	....	1972-73	1972-73
Kharin, Sergei	Wpg.	1	7	2	3	5	2	....	....	....	....	....	....	1990-91	1990-91
‡ Kharitonov, Alexander	T.B., NYI	2	71	7	15	22	12	....	....	....	....	....	....	2000-01	2001-02
Khmylev, Yuri	Buf., St.L.	5	263	64	88	152	133	26	8	6	14	24	....	1992-93	1996-97
‡ Khristich, Dmitri	Wsh., L.A., Bos., Tor.	12	811	259	337	596	422	75	15	25	40	41	....	1990-91	2001-02
Kidd, Ian	Van.	2	20	4	7	11	25	....	....	....	....	....	....	1987-88	1988-89
Kiessling, Udo	Min.	1	1	0	0	0	2	....	....	....	....	....	....	1981-82	1981-82
Kilrea, Brian	Det., L.A.	2	26	3	5	8	12	....	....	....	....	....	....	1957-58	1967-68
• Kilrea, Hec	Ott., Det., Tor.	15	633	167	129	296	438	48	8	7	15	18	3	1925-26	1939-40
• Kilrea, Ken	Det.	5	91	16	23	39	8	15	2	2	4	4	....	1938-39	1943-44
• Kilrea, Wally	Ott., Phi., NYA, Mtl.M., Det.	9	329	35	58	93	87	25	2	4	6	6	2	1929-30	1937-38
Kimble, Darin	Que., St.L., Bos., Chi.	7	311	23	20	43	1082	23	0	0	0	52	....	1988-89	1994-95
Kindrachuk, Orest	Phi., Pit., Wsh.	10	508	118	261	379	648	76	20	20	40	53	2	1972-73	1981-82
‡ King, Derek	NYI, Hfd., Tor., St.L.	14	830	261	351	612	417	47	4	17	21	24	....	1986-87	1999-00
King, Frank	Mtl.	1	10	1	0	1	2	....	....	....	....	....	....	1950-51	1950-51
King, Kris	Det., NYR, Wpg., Phx., Tor., Chi.	14	849	66	85	151	2030	67	8	5	13	142	....	1987-88	2000-01
King, Steven	NYR, Ana.	3	67	17	8	25	75	....	....	....	....	....	....	1992-93	1995-96
King, Wayne	Cal.	3	73	5	18	23	34	....	....	....	....	....	....	1973-74	1975-76
Kinnear, Geordie	Atl.	1	4	0	0	0	13	....	....	....	....	....	....	1999-00	1999-00
Kinsella, Brian	Wsh.	2	10	0	1	1	0	....	....	....	....	....	....	1975-76	1976-77
• Kinsella, Ray	Ott.	1	14	0	0	0	0	....	....	....	....	....	....	1930-31	1930-31
‡ Kiprusoff, Marko	Mtl., NYI	2	51	0	10	10	12	....	....	....	....	....	....	1995-96	2001-02
• Kirk, Bobby	NYR	1	39	4	8	12	14	....	....	....	....	....	....	1937-38	1937-38
Kirkpatrick, Bob	NYR	1	49	12	12	24	6	....	....	....	....	....	....	1942-43	1942-43
Kirton, Mark	Tor., Det., Van.	6	266	57	56	113	121	4	1	2	3	7	....	1979-80	1984-85
Kisio, Kelly	Det., NYR, S.J., Cgy.	13	761	229	429	658	768	39	6	15	21	52	....	1982-83	1994-95
Kitchen, Bill	Mtl., Tor.	4	41	1	4	5	40	3	0	1	1	0	....	1981-82	1984-85
• Kitchen, Hobie	Mtl.M., Det.	2	47	5	4	9	58	....	....	....	....	....	1	1925-26	1926-27
Kitchen, Mike	Col., N.J.	8	474	12	62	74	370	2	0	0	0	2	....	1976-77	1983-84
Kjellberg, Patric	Mtl., Nsh., Ana.	6	394	64	96	160	84	10	0	0	0	0	....	1992-93	2002-03
Klassen, Ralph	Cal., Cle., Col., St.L.	9	497	52	93	145	120	26	4	2	6	12	....	1975-76	1983-84
• Klein, Lloyd	Bos., NYA	8	164	30	24	54	68	5	0	0	0	2	1	1928-29	1937-38
Kleinendorst, Scot	NYR, Hfd., Wsh.	8	281	12	46	58	452	26	2	7	9	40	....	1982-83	1989-90
Klima, Petr	Det., Edm., T.B., L.A., Pit.	13	786	313	260	573	671	95	28	24	52	83	1	1985-86	1998-99
‡ Klimovich, Sergei	Chi.	1	1	0	0	0	2	....	....	....	....	....	....	1996-97	1996-97
• Klingbeil, Ike	Chi.	1	5	1	2	3	2	....	....	....	....	....	....	1936-37	1936-37
Klukay, Joe	Tor., Bos.	11	566	109	127	236	189	71	13	10	23	23	4	1942-43	1955-56
Kluzak, Gord	Bos.	7	299	25	98	123	543	46	6	13	19	129	....	1982-83	1990-91
Knibbs, Bill	Bos.	1	53	7	10	17	4	....	....	....	....	....	....	1964-65	1964-65
Knipscheer, Fred	Bos., St.L.	3	28	6	3	9	18	16	2	1	3	6	....	1993-94	1995-96
• Knott, Nick	Bro.	1	14	3	1	4	9	....	....	....	....	....	....	1941-42	1941-42
Knox, Paul	Tor.	1	1	0	0	0	0	....	....	....	....	....	....	1954-55	1954-55
‡ Knutsen, Espen	Ana., CBJ	5	207	30	81	111	105	....	....	....	....	....	....	1997-98	2003-04
Kocur, Joe	Det., NYR, Van.	15	820	80	82	162	2519	118	10	12	22	231	3	1984-85	1998-99
‡ Koehler, Greg	Car.	1	1	0	0	0	0	....	....	....	....	....	....	2000-01	2000-01
‡ Kohn, Ladislav	Cgy., Tor., Ana., Atl., Det.	7	186	14	28	42	125	2	0	0	0	5	....	1995-96	2002-03
‡ Kolarik, Pavel	Bos.	2	23	0	0	0	10	....	....	....	....	....	....	2000-01	2001-02
‡ Kolesar, Mark	Tor.	2	28	2	2	4	14	3	1	0	1	2	....	1995-96	1996-97
Kolstad, Dean	Min., S.J.	3	40	1	7	8	69	....	....	....	....	....	....	1988-89	1992-93
Komadoski, Neil	L.A., St.L.	8	502	16	76	92	632	23	0	2	2	47	....	1972-73	1979-80
Konik, George	Pit.	1	52	7	8	15	26	....	....	....	....	....	....	1967-68	1967-68
Konroyd, Steve	Cgy., NYI, Chi., Hfd., Det., Ott.	15	895	41	195	236	863	97	10	15	25	99	....	1980-81	1994-95
Konstantinov, Vladimir	Det.	6	446	47	128	175	838	82	5	14	19	107	1	1991-92	1996-97
Kontos, Chris	NYR, Pit., L.A., T.B.	8	230	54	69	123	103	20	11	0	11	12	....	1982-83	1992-93
• Kopak, Russ	Bos.	1	24	7	9	16	0	....	....	....	....	....	....	1943-44	1943-44
Korab, Jerry	Chi., Van., Buf., L.A.	15	975	114	341	455	1629	93	8	18	26	201	....	1970-71	1984-85
Kordic, Dan	Phi.	6	197	4	8	12	584	12	1	0	1	22	....	1991-92	1998-99
• Kordic, John	Mtl., Tor., Wsh., Que.	7	244	17	18	35	997	41	4	3	7	131	1	1985-86	1991-92
Korn, Jim	Det., Tor., Buf., N.J., Cgy.	10	597	66	122	188	1801	16	1	2	3	109	....	1979-80	1989-90
Korney, Mike	Det., NYR	4	77	9	10	19	59	....	....	....	....	....	....	1973-74	1978-79
Koroll, Cliff	Chi.	11	814	208	254	462	376	85	19	29	48	67	....	1969-70	1979-80
Kortko, Roger	NYI	2	79	7	17	24	28	10	0	3	3	17	....	1984-85	1985-86
Kostynski, Doug	Bos.	2	15	3	1	4	4	....	....	....	....	....	....	1983-84	1984-85
Kotanen, Dick	NYR	1	1	0	0	0	0	....	....	....	....	....	....	1950-51	1950-51
Kotsopoulos, Chris	NYR, Hfd., Tor., Det.	10	479	44	109	153	827	31	1	3	4	91	....	1980-81	1989-90
‡ Kovalenko, Andrei	Que., Col., Mtl., Edm., Phi., Car., Bos.	9	620	173	206	379	389	33	5	6	11	20	....	1992-93	2000-01
Kowal, Joe	Buf.	2	22	0	5	5	13	2	0	0	0	0	....	1976-77	1977-78
Kozak, Don	L.A., Van.	7	437	96	86	182	480	29	7	2	9	69	....	1972-73	1978-79
Kozak, Les	Tor.	1	12	1	0	1	2	....	....	....	....	....	....	1961-62	1961-62
• Kraftcheck, Stephen	Bos., NYR, Tor.	4	157	11	18	29	83	6	0	0	0	7	....	1950-51	1958-59
Krake, Skip	Bos., L.A., Buf.	7	249	23	40	63	182	10	1	0	1	17	....	1963-64	1970-71
Kravchuk, Igor	Chi., Edm., St.L., Ott., Cgy., Fla.	12	699	64	210	274	251	51	6	15	21	18	....	1991-92	2002-03
Kravets, Mikhail	S.J.	2	2	0	0	0	0	....	....	....	....	....	....	1991-92	1992-93
Krentz, Dale	Det.	3	30	5	3	8	9	2	0	0	0	0	....	1986-87	1988-89
‡ Kristek, Jaroslav	Buf.	1	6	0	0	0	4	....	....	....	....	....	....	2002-03	2002-03
‡ Krivokrasov, Sergei	Chi., Nsh., Cgy., Min., Ana.	10	450	86	109	195	288	21	2	0	2	14	....	1992-93	2001-02
• Krol, Joe	NYR, Bro.	3	26	10	4	14	8	....	....	....	....	....	....	1936-37	1941-42
Kromm, Richard	Cgy., NYI	9	372	70	103	173	138	36	2	6	8	22	....	1983-84	1992-93
Kron, Robert	Van., Hfd., Car., CBJ	12	771	144	194	338	119	16	3	2	5	2	....	1990-91	2001-02
Krook, Kevin	Col.	1	3	0	0	0	2	....	....	....	....	....	....	1978-79	1978-79
‡ Kroupa, Vlastimil	S.J., N.J.	5	105	4	19	23	66	20	1	2	3	25	....	1993-94	1997-98
Krulicki, Jim	NYR, Det.	1	41	0	3	3	6	....	....	....	....	....	....	1970-71	1970-71
Krupp, Uwe	Buf., NYI, Que., Col., Det., Atl.	15	729	69	212	281	660	81	6	23	29	86	1	1986-87	2002-03
Kruppke, Gord	Det.	3	23	0	0	0	32	....	....	....	....	....	....	1990-91	1993-94
Kruse, Paul	Cgy., NYI, Buf., S.J.	11	423	38	33	71	1074	28	5	2	7	36	....	1990-91	2000-01
Krushelnyski, Mike	Bos., Edm., L.A., Tor., Det.	14	897	241	328	569	699	139	29	43	72	106	3	1981-82	1994-95
Krutov, Vladimir	Van.	1	61	11	23	34	20	....	....	....	....	....	....	1989-90	1989-90
Krygier, Todd	Hfd., Wsh., Ana.	9	543	100	143	243	533	48	10	7	17	40	....	1989-90	1997-98
Kryskow, Dave	Chi., Wsh., Det., Atl.	4	231	33	56	89	174	12	2	0	2	4	....	1972-73	1975-76
Kryzanowski, Ed	Bos., Chi.	5	237	15	22	37	65	18	0	1	1	4	....	1948-49	1952-53
‡ Kucera, Frantisek	Chi., Hfd., Van., Phi., CBJ, Pit., Wsh.	9	465	24	95	119	251	12	0	1	1	0	....	1990-91	2001-02
‡ Kudashov, Alexei	Tor.	1	25	1	0	1	4	....	....	....	....	....	....	1993-94	1993-94
Kudelski, Bob	L.A., Ott., Fla.	9	442	139	102	241	218	22	4	4	8	4	....	1987-88	1995-96
• Kuhn, Gord	NYA	1	12	1	1	2	4	....	....	....	....	....	....	1932-33	1932-33
Kukulowicz, Aggie	NYR	2	4	1	0	1	0	....	....	....	....	....	....	1952-53	1953-54
Kulak, Stu	Van., Edm., NYR, Que., Wpg.	4	90	8	4	12	130	3	0	0	0	2	....	1982-83	1988-89
• Kullman, Arnie	Bos.	2	13	0	1	1	11	....	....	....	....	....	....	1947-48	1949-50
• Kullman, Eddie	NYR	6	343	56	70	126	298	6	1	0	1	2	....	1947-48	1953-54
Kumpel, Mark	Que., Det., Wpg.	6	288	38	46	84	113	39	6	4	10	14	....	1984-85	1990-91
• Kuntz, Alan	NYR	2	45	10	12	22	12	6	1	0	1	2	....	1941-42	1945-46
Kuntz, Murray	St.L.	1	7	1	2	3	0	....	....	....	....	....	....	1974-75	1974-75
Kurri, Jari	Edm., L.A., NYR, Ana., Col.	17	1251	601	797	1398	545	200	106	127	233	123	5	1980-81	1997-98
Kurtenbach, Orland	NYR, Bos., Tor., Van.	13	639	119	213	332	628	19	2	4	6	70	....	1960-61	1973-74
‡ Kurtz, Justin	Van.	1	27	3	5	8	14	....	....	....	....	....	....	2001-02	2001-02
Kurvers, Tom	Mtl., Buf., N.J., Tor., Van., NYI, Ana.	11	659	93	328	421	350	57	8	22	30	68	1	1984-85	1994-95
Kuryluk, Merv	Chi.	1	....	....	....	....	....	2	0	0	0	0	....	1961-62	1961-62
Kushner, Dale	NYI, Phi.	3	84	10	13	23	215	....	....	....	....	....	....	1989-90	1991-92
‡ Kuznik, Greg	Car.	1	1	0	0	0	0	....	....	....	....	....	....	2000-01	2000-01
Kuzyk, Ken	Cle.	2	41	5	9	14	8	....	....	....	....	....	....	1976-77	1977-78
‡ Kvartalnov, Dmitri	Bos.	2	112	42	49	91	26	4	0	0	0	0	....	1992-93	1993-94
Kwong, Larry	NYR	1	1	0	0	0	0	....	....	....	....	....	....	1947-48	1947-48
• Kyle, Bill	NYR	2	3	0	3	3	0	....	....	....	....	....	....	1949-50	1950-51
• Kyle, Gus	NYR, Bos.	3	203	6	20	26	362	14	1	2	3	34	....	1949-50	1951-52

Name	NHL Teams	NHL Seasons	Regular Schedule GP	G	A	TP	PIM	Playoffs GP	G	A	TP	PIM	NHL Cup Wins	First NHL Season	Last NHL Season
Kyllonen, Markku	Wpg.	1	9	0	2	2	2	....	....	....	....	....	....	1988-89	1988-89
Kypreos, Nick	Wsh., Hfd., NYR, Tor.	8	442	46	44	90	1210	34	1	3	4	65	1	1989-90	1996-97
Kyte, Jim	Wpg., Pit., Cgy., Ott., S.J.	13	598	17	49	66	1342	42	0	6	6	94	....	1982-83	1995-96

L

Name	NHL Teams	NHL Seasons	Regular Schedule GP	G	A	TP	PIM	Playoffs GP	G	A	TP	PIM	NHL Cup Wins	First NHL Season	Last NHL Season
Labadie, Mike	NYR	1	3	0	0	0	0	....	....	....	....	....	....	1952-53	1952-53
Labatte, Neil	St.L.	2	26	0	2	2	19	....	....	....	....	....	....	1978-79	1981-82
L'Abbe, Moe	Chi.	1	5	0	1	1	0	....	....	....	....	....	....	1972-73	1972-73
Labelle, Marc	Dal.	1	9	0	0	0	46	....	....	....	....	....	....	1996-97	1996-97
• Labine, Leo	Bos., Det.	11	643	128	193	321	730	60	12	11	23	82	....	1951-52	1961-62
Labossiere, Gord	NYR, L.A., Min.	6	215	44	62	106	75	10	2	3	5	28	....	1963-64	1971-72
Labovitch, Max	NYR	1	5	0	0	0	4	....	....	....	....	....	....	1943-44	1943-44
Labraaten, Dan	Det., Cgy.	4	268	71	73	144	47	8	1	0	1	4	....	1978-79	1981-82
Labre, Yvon	Pit., Wsh.	9	371	14	87	101	788	....	....	....	....	....	....	1970-71	1980-81
Labrie, Guy	Bos., NYR	2	42	4	9	13	16	....	....	....	....	....	....	1943-44	1944-45
Lach, Elmer	Mtl.	14	664	215	408	623	478	76	19	45	64	36	3	1940-41	1953-54
Lachance, Michel	Col.	1	21	0	4	4	22	....	....	....	....	....	....	1978-79	1978-79
Lacombe, Francois	Oak., Buf., Que.	4	78	2	17	19	54	3	1	0	1	0	....	1968-69	1979-80
Lacombe, Normand	Buf., Edm., Phi.	7	319	53	62	115	196	26	5	1	6	49	1	1984-85	1990-91
Lacroix, Andre	Phi., Chi., Hfd.	6	325	79	119	198	44	16	2	5	7	0	....	1967-68	1979-80
Lacroix, Daniel	NYR, Bos., Phi., Edm., NYI	7	188	11	7	18	379	16	0	1	1	26	....	1993-94	1999-00
Lacroix, Eric	Tor., L.A., Col., NYR, Ott.	8	472	67	70	137	361	30	1	5	6	25	....	1993-94	2000-01
Lacroix, Pierre	Que., Hfd.	4	274	24	108	132	197	8	0	2	2	10	....	1979-80	1982-83
Ladouceur, Randy	Det., Hfd., Ana.	14	930	30	126	156	1322	40	5	8	13	59	....	1982-83	1995-96
LaFayette, Nathan	St.L., Van., NYR, L.A.	6	187	17	20	37	103	32	2	7	9	8	....	1993-94	1998-99
Lafleur, Guy	Mtl., NYR, Que.	17	1126	560	793	1353	399	128	58	76	134	67	5	1971-72	1990-91
• Lafleur, Roland	Mtl.	1	1	0	0	0	0	....	....	....	....	....	....	1924-25	1924-25
LaFontaine, Pat	NYI, Buf., NYR	15	865	468	545	1013	552	69	26	36	62	36	....	1983-84	1997-98
Laforce, Ernie	Mtl.	1	1	0	0	0	0	....	....	....	....	....	....	1942-43	1942-43
LaForest, Bob	L.A.	1	5	1	0	1	2	....	....	....	....	....	....	1983-84	1983-84
Laforge, Claude	Mtl., Det., Phi.	8	193	24	33	57	82	5	1	2	3	15	....	1957-58	1968-69
Laforge, Marc	Hfd., Edm.	2	14	0	0	0	64	....	....	....	....	....	....	1989-90	1993-94
Laframboise, Pete	Cal., Wsh., Pit.	4	227	33	55	88	70	9	1	0	1	0	....	1971-72	1974-75
Lafrance, Adie	Mtl.	1	3	0	0	0	2	2	0	0	0	0	....	1933-34	1933-34
• Lafrance, Leo	Mtl., Chi.	2	33	2	0	2	6	....	....	....	....	....	....	1926-27	1927-28
Lafreniere, Jason	Que., NYR, T.B.	5	146	34	53	87	22	15	1	5	6	19	....	1986-87	1993-94
Lafreniere, Roger	Det., St.L.	2	13	0	0	0	4	....	....	....	....	....	....	1962-63	1972-73
Lagace, Jean-Guy	Pit., Buf., K.C.	6	197	9	39	48	251	....	....	....	....	....	....	1968-69	1975-76
Laidlaw, Tom	NYR, L.A.	10	705	25	139	164	717	69	4	17	21	78	....	1980-81	1989-90
Laird, Robbie	Min.	1	1	0	0	0	0	....	....	....	....	....	....	1979-80	1979-80
Lajeunesse, Serge	Det., Phi.	5	103	1	4	5	103	....	....	....	....	....	....	1970-71	1974-75
Lakovic, Sasha	Cgy., N.J.	3	37	0	4	4	118	....	....	....	....	....	....	1996-97	1998-99
Lalande, Hec	Chi., Det.	4	151	21	39	60	120	....	....	....	....	....	....	1953-54	1957-58
Lalonde, Bobby	Van., Atl., Bos., Cgy.	11	641	124	210	334	298	16	4	2	6	6	....	1971-72	1981-82
• Lalonde, Newsy	Mtl., NYA	6	99	124	41	165	183	7	15	4	19	32	....	1917-18	1926-27
Lalonde, Ron	Pit., Wsh.	7	397	45	78	123	106	....	....	....	....	....	....	1972-73	1978-79
Lalor, Mike	Mtl., St.L., Wsh., Wpg., S.J., Dal.	12	687	17	88	105	677	92	5	10	15	167	1	1985-86	1996-97
• Lamb, Joe	Mtl.M., Ott., NYA, Bos., Mtl., St.L., Det.	11	443	108	101	209	601	18	1	1	2	51	....	1927-28	1937-38
Lamb, Mark	Cgy., Det., Edm., Ott., Phi., Mtl.	11	403	46	100	146	291	70	7	19	26	51	1	1985-86	1995-96
‡ Lambert, Dan	Que.	2	29	6	9	15	22	....	....	....	....	....	....	1990-91	1991-92
Lambert, Denny	Ana., Ott., Nsh., Atl.	8	487	27	66	93	1391	17	0	1	1	28	....	1994-95	2001-02
Lambert, Lane	Det., NYR, Que.	6	283	58	66	124	521	17	2	4	6	40	....	1983-84	1988-89
Lambert, Yvon	Mtl., Buf.	10	683	206	273	479	340	90	27	22	49	67	4	1972-73	1981-82
Lamby, Dick	St.L.	3	22	0	5	5	22	....	....	....	....	....	....	1978-79	1980-81
• Lamirande, Jean-Paul	NYR, Mtl.	4	49	5	5	10	26	8	0	0	0	4	....	1946-47	1954-55
Lammens, Hank	Ott.	1	27	1	2	3	22	....	....	....	....	....	....	1993-94	1993-94
• Lamoureux, Leo	Mtl.	6	235	19	79	98	175	28	1	6	7	16	2	1941-42	1946-47
Lamoureux, Mitch	Pit., Phi.	3	73	11	9	20	59	....	....	....	....	....	....	1983-84	1987-88
Lampman, Mike	St.L., Van., Wsh.	4	96	17	20	37	34	....	....	....	....	....	....	1972-73	1976-77
Lancien, Jack	NYR	4	63	1	5	6	35	6	0	1	1	2	....	1946-47	1950-51
Landon, Larry	Mtl., Tor.	2	9	0	0	0	2	....	....	....	....	....	....	1983-84	1984-85
‡ Landry, Eric	Cgy., Mtl.	4	68	5	9	14	47	....	....	....	....	....	....	1997-98	2001-02
Lane, Gord	Wsh., NYI	10	539	19	94	113	1228	75	3	14	17	214	4	1975-76	1984-85
• Lane, Myles	NYR, Bos.	3	71	4	1	5	41	11	0	0	0	0	1	1928-29	1933-34
Langdon, Steve	Bos.	3	7	0	1	1	2	4	0	0	0	0	....	1974-75	1977-78
Langelle, Pete	Tor.	4	136	22	51	73	11	41	5	9	14	4	1	1938-39	1941-42
Langevin, Chris	Buf.	2	22	3	1	4	22	....	....	....	....	....	....	1983-84	1985-86
Langevin, Dave	NYI, Min., L.A.	8	513	12	107	119	530	87	2	17	19	106	4	1979-80	1986-87
Langlais, Alain	Min.	2	25	4	4	8	10	....	....	....	....	....	....	1973-74	1974-75
Langlois, Albert	Mtl., NYR, Det., Bos.	9	497	21	91	112	488	53	1	5	6	50	3	1957-58	1965-66
• Langlois, Charlie	Ham., NYA, Pit., Mtl.	4	151	22	5	27	189	2	0	0	0	0	....	1924-25	1927-28
Langway, Rod	Mtl., Wsh.	15	994	51	278	329	849	104	5	22	27	97	1	1978-79	1992-93
Lank, Jeff	Phi.	1	2	0	0	0	2	....	....	....	....	....	....	1999-00	1999-00
Lanthier, Jean-Marc	Van.	4	105	16	16	32	29	....	....	....	....	....	....	1983-84	1987-88
Lanyon, Ted	Pit.	1	5	0	0	0	4	....	....	....	....	....	....	1967-68	1967-68
Lanz, Rick	Van., Tor., Chi.	10	569	65	221	286	448	28	3	8	11	35	....	1980-81	1991-92
Laperriere, Daniel	St.L., Ott.	4	48	2	5	7	27	....	....	....	....	....	....	1992-93	1995-96
Laperriere, Jacques	Mtl.	12	691	40	242	282	674	88	9	22	31	101	6	1962-63	1973-74
‡ Laplante, Darryl	Det.	3	35	0	6	6	10	....	....	....	....	....	....	1997-98	1999-00
Lapointe, Guy	Mtl., St.L., Bos.	16	884	171	451	622	893	123	26	44	70	138	6	1968-69	1983-84
• Lapointe, Rick	Det., Phi., St.L., Que., L.A.	11	664	44	176	220	831	46	2	7	9	64	....	1975-76	1985-86
Lappin, Peter	Min., S.J.	2	7	0	0	0	2	....	....	....	....	....	....	1989-90	1991-92
Laprade, Edgar	NYR	10	500	108	172	280	42	18	4	9	13	4	....	1945-46	1954-55
• LaPrairie, Benjamin	Chi.	1	7	0	0	0	0	....	....	....	....	....	....	1936-37	1936-37
Larionov, Igor	Van., S.J., Det., Fla., N.J.	14	921	169	475	644	474	150	30	67	97	60	3	1989-90	2003-04
Lariviere, Garry	Que., Edm.	4	219	6	57	63	167	14	0	5	5	8	....	1979-80	1982-83
Larmer, Jeff	Col., N.J., Chi.	5	158	37	51	88	57	5	1	0	1	2	....	1981-82	1985-86
Larmer, Steve	Chi., NYR	15	1006	441	571	1012	532	140	56	75	131	89	1	1980-81	1994-95
• Larochelle, Wildor	Mtl., Chi.	12	474	92	74	166	211	34	6	4	10	24	2	1925-26	1936-37
Larocque, Denis	L.A.	1	8	0	1	1	18	....	....	....	....	....	....	1987-88	1987-88
‡ Larocque, Mario	T.B.	1	5	0	0	0	16	....	....	....	....	....	....	1998-99	1998-99
• Larose, Bonner	Bos.	1	6	0	0	0	0	....	....	....	....	....	....	1925-26	1925-26
Larose, Claude	Mtl., Min., St.L.	16	943	226	257	483	887	97	14	18	32	143	5	1962-63	1977-78
Larose, Claude	NYR	2	25	4	7	11	2	2	0	0	0	0	....	1979-80	1981-82
Larose, Guy	Wpg., Tor., Cgy., Bos.	6	70	10	9	19	63	4	0	0	0	0	....	1988-89	1994-95
Larouche, Pierre	Pit., Mtl., Hfd., NYR	14	812	395	427	822	237	64	20	34	54	16	2	1974-75	1987-88
‡ Larouche, Steve	Ott., NYR, L.A.	2	26	9	9	18	10	....	....	....	....	....	....	1994-95	1995-96
• Larson, Norm	NYA, Bro., NYR	3	89	25	18	43	12	....	....	....	....	....	....	1940-41	1946-47
Larson, Reed	Det., Bos., Edm., NYI, Min., Buf.	14	904	222	463	685	1391	32	4	7	11	63	....	1976-77	1989-90
Larter, Tyler	Wsh.	1	1	0	0	0	0	....	....	....	....	....	....	1989-90	1989-90
Latal, Jiri	Phi.	3	92	12	36	48	24	....	....	....	....	....	....	1989-90	1991-92
Latos, James	NYR	1	1	0	0	0	0	....	....	....	....	....	....	1988-89	1988-89
Latreille, Phil	NYR	1	4	0	0	0	2	....	....	....	....	....	....	1960-61	1960-61
Latta, David	Que.	4	36	4	8	12	4	....	....	....	....	....	....	1985-86	1990-91
Lauder, Martin	Bos.	1	3	0	0	0	2	....	....	....	....	....	....	1927-28	1927-28
Lauen, Mike	Wpg.	1	4	0	1	1	0	....	....	....	....	....	....	1983-84	1983-84
Lauer, Brad	NYI, Chi., Ott., Pit.	9	323	44	67	111	218	34	7	5	12	24	....	1986-87	1995-96
Laughlin, Craig	Mtl., Wsh., L.A., Tor.	8	549	136	205	341	364	33	6	6	12	20	....	1981-82	1988-89
Laughton, Mike	Oak., Cal.	4	189	39	48	87	101	11	2	4	6	0	....	1967-68	1970-71
Laukkanen, Janne	Que., Col., Ott., Pit., T.B.	9	407	22	99	121	335	59	7	9	16	46	....	1994-95	2002-03
Laurence, Don	Atl., St.L.	2	79	15	22	37	14	....	....	....	....	....	....	1978-79	1979-80
Laus, Paul	Fla.	9	530	14	58	72	1702	30	2	7	9	74	....	1993-94	2001-02
LaVallee, Kevin	Cgy., L.A., St.L., Pit.	7	366	110	125	235	85	32	5	8	13	21	....	1980-81	1986-87
LaVarre, Mark	Chi.	3	78	9	16	25	58	1	0	0	0	2	....	1985-86	1987-88
Lavender, Brian	St.L., NYI, Det., Cal.	4	184	16	26	42	174	3	0	0	0	2	....	1971-72	1974-75
Lavigne, Eric	L.A.	1	1	0	0	0	0	....	....	....	....	....	....	1994-95	1994-95
• Laviolette, Jack	Mtl.	1	18	2	1	3	6	2	0	0	0	0	....	1917-18	1917-18
Laviolette, Peter	NYR	1	12	0	0	0	6	....	....	....	....	....	....	1988-89	1988-89
Lavoie, Dominic	St.L., Ott., Bos., L.A.	6	38	5	8	13	32	....	....	....	....	....	....	1988-89	1993-94
Lawless, Paul	Hfd., Phi., Van., Tor.	7	239	49	77	126	54	3	0	2	2	2	....	1982-83	1989-90
Lawrence, Mark	Dal., NYI	6	142	18	26	44	115	....	....	....	....	....	....	1994-95	2000-01
Lawson, Danny	Det., Min., Buf.	5	219	28	29	57	61	16	0	1	1	2	....	1967-68	1971-72
Lawton, Brian	Min., NYR, Hfd., Que., Bos., S.J.	9	483	112	154	266	401	11	1	1	2	12	....	1983-84	1992-93

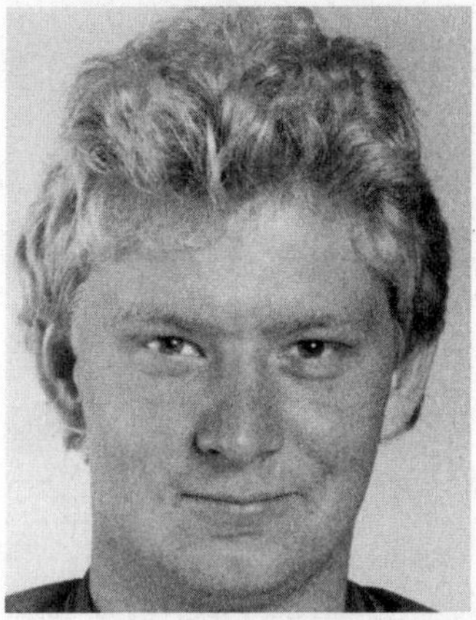
Jeff Larmer

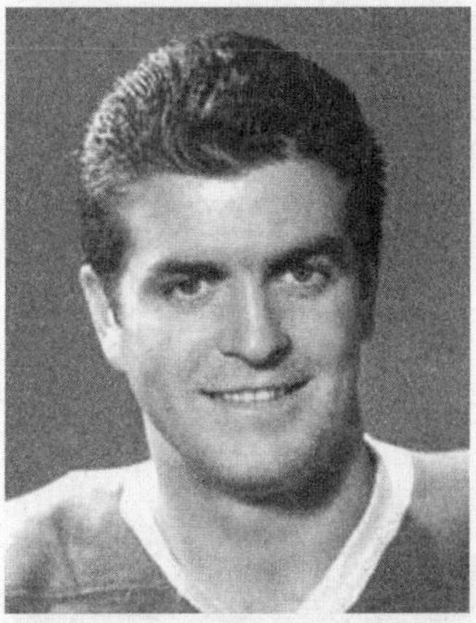
Jack LeClair

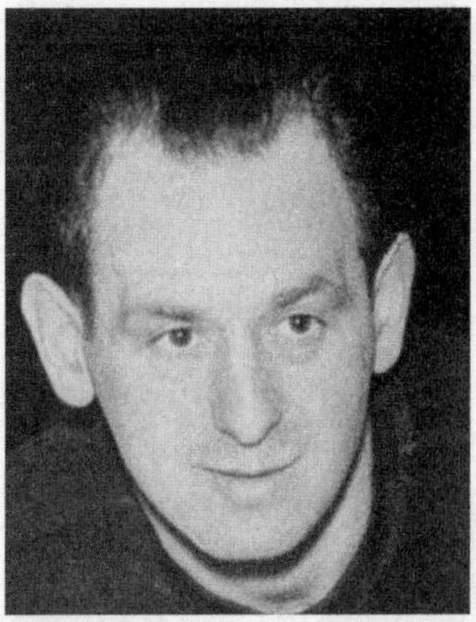
Alex Levinsky

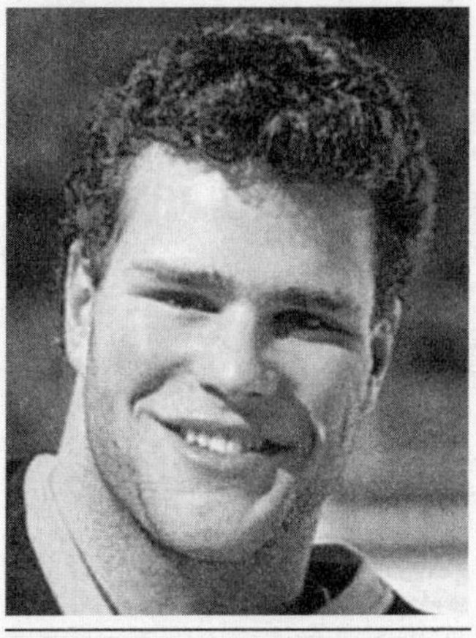
Brett Lindros

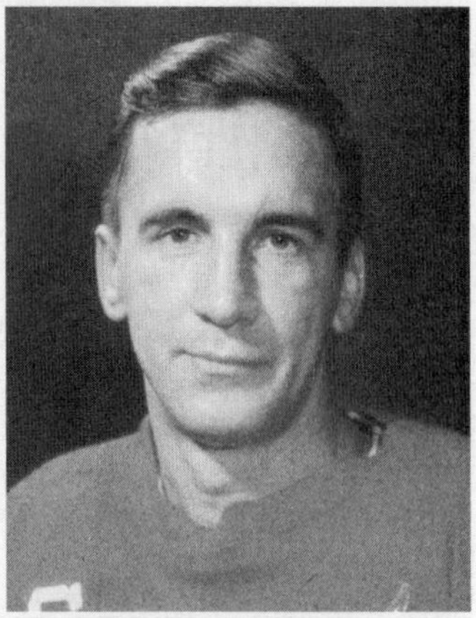

Ted Lindsay

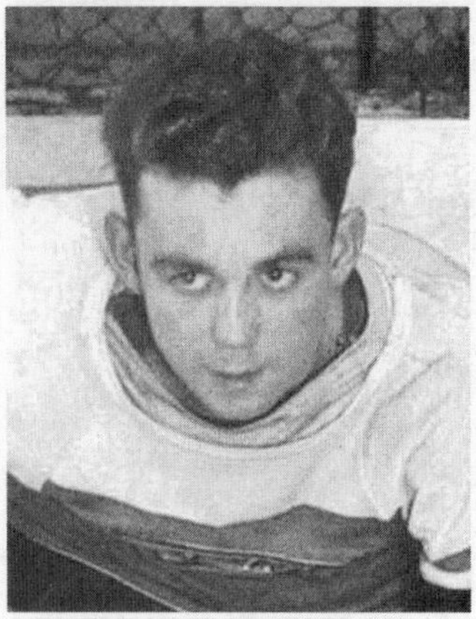

Norm Locking

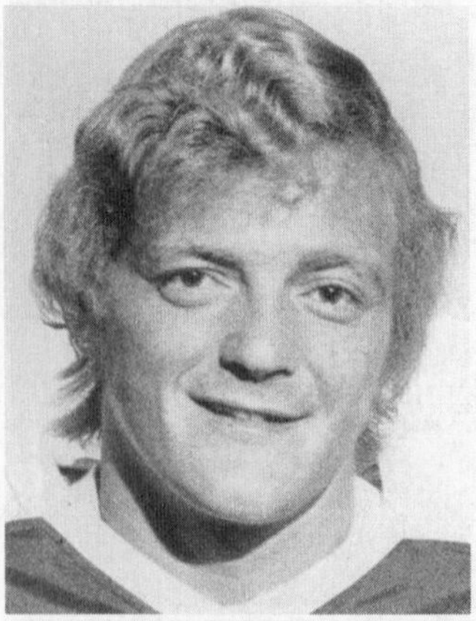

Joe Lundrigan

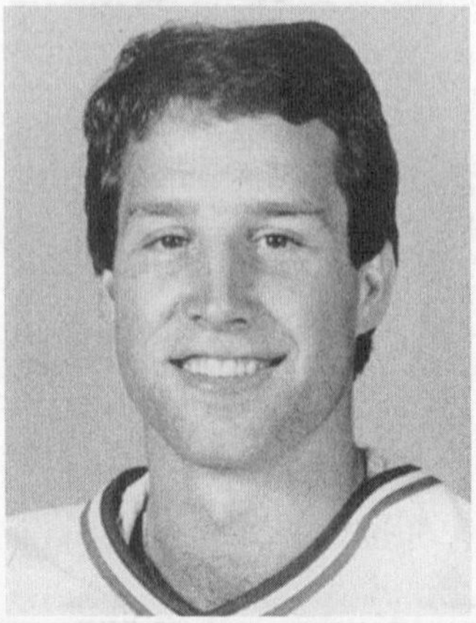

Paul MacDermid

			Regular Schedule					Playoffs							
Name	NHL Teams	NHL Seasons	GP	G	A	TP	PIM	GP	G	A	TP	PIM	NHL Cup Wins	First NHL Season	Last NHL Season
Laxdal, Derek	Tor., NYI	6	67	12	7	19	88	1	0	2	2	2	....	1984-85	1990-91
• Laycoe, Hal	NYR, Mtl., Bos.	11	531	25	77	102	292	40	2	5	7	39	....	1945-46	1955-56
Lazaro, Jeff	Bos., Ott.	3	102	14	23	37	114	28	3	3	6	32	....	1990-91	1992-93
Leach, Jamie	Pit., Hfd., Fla.	5	81	11	9	20	12	....	....	....	....	....	1	1989-90	1993-94
Leach, Larry	Bos.	3	126	13	29	42	91	7	1	1	2	8	....	1958-59	1961-62
Leach, Reggie	Bos., Cal., Phi., Det.	13	934	381	285	666	387	94	47	22	69	22	1	1970-71	1982-83
Leach, Stephen	Wsh., Bos., St.L., Car., Ott., Phx., Pit.	15	702	130	153	283	978	92	15	11	26	87	....	1985-86	1999-00
Leavins, Jim	Det., NYR	2	41	2	12	14	30	....	....	....	....	....	....	1985-86	1986-87
‡ Lebeau, Patrick	Mtl., Cgy., Fla., Pit.	4	15	3	2	5	6	....	....	....	....	....	....	1990-91	1998-99
Lebeau, Stephan	Mtl., Ana.	7	373	118	159	277	105	30	9	7	16	12	1	1988-89	1994-95
LeBlanc, Fern	Det.	3	34	5	6	11	0	....	....	....	....	....	....	1976-77	1978-79
LeBlanc, J.P.	Chi., Det.	5	153	14	30	44	87	2	0	0	0	0	....	1968-69	1978-79
LeBlanc, John	Van., Edm., Wpg.	7	83	26	13	39	28	1	0	0	0	0	....	1986-87	1994-95
LeBoutillier, Peter	Ana.	2	35	2	1	3	176	....	....	....	....	....	....	1996-97	1997-98
LeBrun, Al	NYR	2	6	0	2	2	4	....	....	....	....	....	....	1960-61	1965-66
Lecaine, Bill	Pit.	1	4	0	0	0	0	....	....	....	....	....	....	1968-69	1968-69
LeClair, Jack	Mtl.	3	160	20	40	60	56	20	6	1	7	6	2	1954-55	1956-57
Leclerc, Rene	Det.	2	87	10	11	21	105	....	....	....	....	....	....	1968-69	1970-71
Lecuyer, Doug	Chi., Wpg., Pit.	4	126	11	31	42	178	7	4	0	4	15	....	1978-79	1982-83
Ledingham, Walt	Chi., NYI	3	15	0	2	2	4	....	....	....	....	....	....	1972-73	1976-77
• Leduc, Albert	Mtl., Ott., NYR	10	383	57	35	92	614	28	5	6	11	32	2	1925-26	1934-35
LeDuc, Rich	Bos., Que.	4	130	28	38	66	69	5	0	0	0	9	....	1972-73	1980-81
Ledyard, Grant	NYR, L.A., Wsh., Buf., Dal., Van., Bos., Ott., T.B.	18	1028	90	276	366	766	83	6	12	18	96	....	1984-85	2001-02
• Lee, Bobby	Mtl.	1	1	0	0	0	0	....	....	....	....	....	....	1942-43	1942-43
Lee, Edward	Que.	1	2	0	0	0	5	....	....	....	....	....	....	1984-85	1984-85
Lee, Peter	Pit.	6	431	114	131	245	257	19	0	8	8	4	....	1977-78	1982-83
‡ Leeb, Greg	Dal.	1	2	0	0	0	0	....	....	....	....	....	....	2000-01	2000-01
Leeman, Gary	Tor., Cgy., Mtl., Van., St.L.	14	667	199	267	466	531	36	8	16	24	36	1	1982-83	1996-97
Lefebvre, Patrice	Wsh.	1	3	0	0	0	2	....	....	....	....	....	....	1998-99	1998-99
Lefebvre, Sylvain	Mtl., Tor., Que., Col., NYR	14	945	30	154	184	674	129	4	14	18	101	1	1989-90	2002-03
• Lefley, Bryan	NYI, K.C., Col.	5	228	7	29	36	101	2	0	0	0	0	....	1972-73	1977-78
Lefley, Chuck	Mtl., St.L.	9	407	128	164	292	137	29	5	8	13	10	2	1970-71	1980-81
• Leger, Roger	NYR, Mtl.	5	187	18	53	71	71	20	0	7	7	14	....	1943-44	1949-50
Legge, Barry	Que., Wpg.	3	107	1	11	12	144	....	....	....	....	....	....	1979-80	1981-82
Legge, Randy	NYR	1	12	0	2	2	2	....	....	....	....	....	....	1972-73	1972-73
Lehman, Tommy	Bos., Edm.	3	36	5	5	10	16	....	....	....	....	....	....	1987-88	1989-90
Lehto, Petteri	Pit.	1	6	0	0	0	4	....	....	....	....	....	....	1984-85	1984-85
Lehtonen, Antero	Wsh.	1	65	9	12	21	14	....	....	....	....	....	....	1979-80	1979-80
Lehvonen, Henri	K.C.	1	4	0	0	0	0	....	....	....	....	....	....	1974-75	1974-75
Leier, Edward	Chi.	2	16	2	1	3	2	....	....	....	....	....	....	1949-50	1950-51
Leinonen, Mikko	NYR, Wsh.	4	162	31	78	109	71	20	2	11	13	28	....	1981-82	1984-85
Leiter, Bobby	Bos., Pit., Atl.	10	447	98	126	224	144	8	3	0	3	2	....	1962-63	1975-76
Leiter, Ken	NYI, Min.	5	143	14	36	50	62	15	0	6	6	8	....	1984-85	1989-90
Lemaire, Jacques	Mtl.	12	853	366	469	835	217	145	61	78	139	63	8	1967-68	1978-79
Lemay, Moe	Van., Edm., Bos., Wpg.	8	317	72	94	166	442	28	6	3	9	55	1	1981-82	1988-89
Lemelin, Roger	K.C., Col.	4	36	1	2	3	27	....	....	....	....	....	....	1974-75	1977-78
Lemieux, Alain	St.L., Que., Pit.	6	119	28	44	72	38	19	4	6	10	0	....	1981-82	1986-87
Lemieux, Bob	Oak.	1	19	0	1	1	12	....	....	....	....	....	....	1967-68	1967-68
‡ Lemieux, Claude	Mtl., N.J., Col., Phx., Dal.	20	1197	379	406	785	1756	233	80	78	158	529	4	1983-84	2002-03
Lemieux, Jacques	L.A.	3	19	0	4	4	8	1	0	0	0	0	....	1967-68	1969-70
Lemieux, Jean	Atl., Wsh.	5	204	23	63	86	39	3	1	1	2	0	....	1973-74	1977-78
Lemieux, Jocelyn	St.L., Mtl., Chi., Hfd., N.J., Cgy., Phx.	12	598	80	84	164	740	60	5	10	15	88	....	1986-87	1997-98
• Lemieux, Real	Det., L.A., NYR, Buf.	8	456	51	104	155	262	18	2	4	6	10	....	1966-67	1973-74
Lemieux, Rich	Van., K.C., Atl.	5	274	39	82	121	132	2	0	0	0	0	....	1971-72	1975-76
Lenardon, Tim	N.J., Van.	2	15	2	1	3	4	....	....	....	....	....	....	1986-87	1989-90
• Lepine, Hec	Mtl.	1	33	5	2	7	2	....	....	....	....	....	....	1925-26	1925-26
• Lepine, Pit	Mtl.	13	526	143	98	241	392	41	7	5	12	26	2	1925-26	1937-38
Leroux, Francois	Edm., Ott., Pit., Col.	10	249	3	20	23	577	33	1	3	4	34	....	1988-89	1997-98
Leroux, Gaston	Mtl.	1	2	0	0	0	0	....	....	....	....	....	....	1935-36	1935-36
Leroux, Jean-Yves	Chi.	5	220	16	22	38	146	....	....	....	....	....	....	1996-97	2000-01
Lesieur, Art	Mtl., Chi.	4	100	4	2	6	50	14	0	0	0	4	1	1928-29	1935-36
Lessard, Rick	Cgy., S.J.	3	15	0	4	4	18	....	....	....	....	....	....	1988-89	1991-92
Lesuk, Bill	Bos., Phi., L.A., Wsh., Wpg.	8	388	44	63	107	368	9	1	0	1	12	1	1968-69	1979-80
• Leswick, Jack	Chi.	1	37	1	7	8	16	....	....	....	....	....	1	1933-34	1933-34
Leswick, Pete	NYA, Bos.	2	3	1	0	1	0	....	....	....	....	....	....	1936-37	1944-45
• Leswick, Tony	NYR, Det., Chi.	12	740	165	159	324	900	59	13	10	23	91	3	1945-46	1957-58
Levandoski, Joe	NYR	1	8	1	1	2	0	....	....	....	....	....	....	1946-47	1946-47
Leveille, Normand	Bos.	2	75	17	25	42	49	....	....	....	....	....	....	1981-82	1982-83
Leveque, Guy	L.A.	2	17	2	2	4	21	....	....	....	....	....	....	1992-93	1993-94
Lever, Don	Van., Atl., Cgy., Col., N.J., Buf.	15	1020	313	367	680	593	30	7	10	17	26	....	1972-73	1986-87
Levie, Craig	Wpg., Min., St.L., Van.	6	183	22	53	75	177	16	2	3	5	32	....	1981-82	1986-87
‡ Levins, Scott	Wpg., Fla., Ott., Phx.	5	124	13	20	33	316	....	....	....	....	....	....	1992-93	1997-98
• Levinsky, Alex	Tor., NYR, Chi.	9	367	19	49	68	307	37	2	1	3	26	2	1930-31	1938-39
Levo, Tapio	Col., N.J.	2	107	16	53	69	36	....	....	....	....	....	....	1981-82	1982-83
Lewicki, Danny	Tor., NYR, Chi.	9	461	105	135	240	177	28	0	4	4	8	1	1950-51	1958-59
Lewis, Dale	NYR	1	8	0	0	0	0	....	....	....	....	....	....	1975-76	1975-76
Lewis, Dave	NYI, L.A., N.J., Det.	15	1008	36	187	223	953	91	1	20	21	143	....	1973-74	1987-88
• Lewis, Doug	Mtl.	1	3	0	0	0	0	....	....	....	....	....	....	1946-47	1946-47
• Lewis, Herbie	Det.	11	483	148	161	309	248	38	13	10	23	6	2	1928-29	1938-39
Ley, Rick	Tor., Hfd.	6	310	12	72	84	528	14	0	2	2	20	....	1968-69	1980-81
Liba, Igor	NYR, L.A.	1	37	7	18	25	36	2	0	0	0	2	....	1988-89	1988-89
Libby, Jeff	NYI	1	1	0	0	0	0	....	....	....	....	....	....	1997-98	1997-98
Libett, Nick	Det., Pit.	14	982	237	268	505	472	16	6	2	8	2	....	1967-68	1980-81
Licari, Tony	Det.	1	9	0	1	1	0	....	....	....	....	....	....	1946-47	1946-47
Liddington, Bob	Tor.	1	11	0	1	1	2	....	....	....	....	....	....	1970-71	1970-71
Lidster, Doug	Van., NYR, St.L., Dal.	16	897	75	268	343	679	80	6	15	21	64	1	1983-84	1998-99
Lilley, John	Ana.	3	23	3	8	11	13	....	....	....	....	....	....	1993-94	1995-96
‡ Lind, Juha	Dal., Mtl.	3	133	9	13	22	20	15	2	2	4	8	....	1997-98	2000-01
Lindberg, Chris	Cgy., Que.	3	116	17	25	42	47	2	0	1	1	2	....	1991-92	1993-94
Lindbom, Johan	NYR	1	38	1	3	4	28	....	....	....	....	....	....	1997-98	1997-98
Linden, Jamie	Fla.	1	4	0	0	0	17	....	....	....	....	....	....	1994-95	1994-95
Lindgren, Lars	Van., Min.	6	394	25	113	138	325	40	5	6	11	20	....	1978-79	1983-84
Lindgren, Mats	Edm., NYI, Van.	8	387	54	74	128	146	24	1	5	6	10	....	1996-97	2003-04
Lindholm, Mikael	L.A.	1	18	2	2	4	2	....	....	....	....	....	....	1989-90	1989-90
Lindquist, Fredrik	Edm.	1	8	0	0	0	2	....	....	....	....	....	....	1998-99	1998-99
Lindros, Brett	NYI	2	51	2	5	7	147	....	....	....	....	....	....	1994-95	1995-96
Lindsay, Ted	Det., Chi.	17	1068	379	472	851	1808	133	47	49	96	194	4	1944-45	1964-65
Lindstrom, Willy	Wpg., Edm., Pit.	8	582	161	162	323	200	57	14	18	32	24	2	1979-80	1986-87
Linseman, Ken	Phi., Edm., Bos., Tor.	14	860	256	551	807	1727	113	43	77	120	325	1	1978-79	1991-92
‡ Lintner, Richard	Nsh., NYR, Pit.	3	112	8	12	20	54	....	....	....	....	....	....	1999-00	2002-03
Lipuma, Chris	T.B., S.J.	5	72	0	9	9	146	....	....	....	....	....	....	1992-93	1996-97
• Liscombe, Carl	Det.	9	373	137	140	277	117	59	22	19	41	20	1	1937-38	1945-46
Litzenberger, Ed	Mtl., Chi., Det., Tor.	12	618	178	238	416	283	40	5	13	18	34	4	1952-53	1963-64
Loach, Lonnie	Ott., L.A., Ana.	2	56	10	13	23	29	1	0	0	0	0	....	1992-93	1993-94
• Locas, Jacques	Mtl.	2	59	7	8	15	66	....	....	....	....	....	....	1947-48	1948-49
Lochead, Bill	Det., Col., NYR	6	330	69	62	131	180	7	3	0	3	6	....	1974-75	1979-80
• Locking, Norm	Chi.	2	48	2	6	8	26	....	....	....	....	....	....	1934-35	1935-36
Loewen, Darcy	Buf., Ott.	5	135	4	8	12	211	....	....	....	....	....	....	1989-90	1993-94
Lofthouse, Mark	Wsh., Det.	6	181	42	38	80	73	....	....	....	....	....	....	1977-78	1982-83
Logan, Dave	Chi., Van.	6	218	5	29	34	470	12	0	0	0	10	....	1975-76	1980-81
Logan, Robert	Buf., L.A.	3	42	10	5	15	0	....	....	....	....	....	....	1986-87	1988-89
Loiselle, Claude	Det., N.J., Que., Tor., NYI	13	616	92	117	209	1149	41	4	11	15	58	....	1981-82	1993-94
Lomakin, Andrei	Phi., Fla.	4	215	42	62	104	92	....	....	....	....	....	....	1991-92	1994-95
Loney, Brian	Van.	1	12	2	3	5	6	....	....	....	....	....	....	1995-96	1995-96
Loney, Troy	Pit., Ana., NYI, NYR	12	624	87	110	197	1091	67	8	14	22	97	2	1983-84	1994-95
Long, Barry	L.A., Det., Wpg.	5	280	11	68	79	250	5	0	1	1	18	....	1972-73	1981-82
• Long, Stan	Mtl.	1	....	....	....	....	....	3	0	0	0	0	....	1951-52	1951-52
Lonsberry, Ross	Bos., L.A., Phi., Pit.	15	968	256	310	566	806	100	21	25	46	87	2	1966-67	1980-81
Loob, Hakan	Cgy.	6	450	193	236	429	189	73	26	28	54	16	1	1983-84	1988-89
Loob, Peter	Que.	1	8	1	2	3	0	....	....	....	....	....	....	1984-85	1984-85
Lorentz, Jim	Bos., St.L., NYR, Buf.	10	659	161	238	399	208	54	12	10	22	30	1	1968-69	1977-78
Lorimer, Bob	NYI, Col., N.J.	10	529	22	90	112	431	49	3	10	13	83	2	1976-77	1985-86
• Lorrain, Rod	Mtl.	6	179	28	39	67	30	11	0	3	3	0	....	1935-36	1941-42
• Loughlin, Clem	Det., Chi.	3	101	8	6	14	77	....	....	....	....	....	....	1926-27	1928-29

			Regular Schedule					Playoffs					NHL	First	Last
Name	NHL Teams	NHL Seasons	GP	G	A	TP	PIM	GP	G	A	TP	PIM	Cup Wins	NHL Season	NHL Season
• Loughlin, Wilf	Tor.	1	14	0	0	0	2	....	....	....	....	....	....	1923-24	1923-24
Lovsin, Ken	Wsh.	1	1	0	0	0	0	....	....	....	....	....	....	1990-91	1990-91
Lowdermilk, Dwayne	Wsh.	1	2	0	1	1	2	....	....	....	....	....	....	1980-81	1980-81
Lowe, Darren	Pit.	1	8	1	2	3	0	....	....	....	....	....	....	1983-84	1983-84
Lowe, Kevin	Edm., NYR	19	1254	84	347	431	1498	214	10	48	58	192	6	1979-80	1997-98
Lowe, Odie	NYR	1	4	1	1	2	0	....	....	....	....	....	....	1949-50	1949-50
• Lowe, Ross	Bos., Mtl.	3	77	6	8	14	82	2	0	0	0	0	....	1949-50	1951-52
• Lowrey, Ed	Ott., Ham.	3	27	2	2	4	6	....	....	....	....	....	....	1917-18	1920-21
• Lowrey, Fred	Mtl.M., Pit.	2	53	1	1	2	10	2	0	0	0	6	....	1924-25	1925-26
• Lowrey, Gerry	Tor., Pit., Phi., Chi., Ott.	6	211	48	48	96	148	2	1	0	1	2	....	1927-28	1932-33
Lowry, Dave	Van., St.L., Fla., S.J., Cgy.	19	1084	164	187	351	1191	111	16	20	36	181	....	1985-86	2003-04
Lucas, Danny	Phi.	1	6	1	0	1	0	....	....	....	....	....	....	1978-79	1978-79
Lucas, Dave	Det.	1	1	0	0	0	0	....	....	....	....	....	....	1962-63	1962-63
Luce, Don	NYR, Det., Buf., L.A., Tor.	13	894	225	329	554	364	71	17	22	39	52	....	1969-70	1981-82
Ludvig, Jan	N.J., Buf.	7	314	54	87	141	418	....	....	....	....	....	....	1982-83	1988-89
Ludwig, Craig	Mtl., NYI, Min., Dal.	17	1256	38	184	222	1437	177	4	25	29	244	2	1982-83	1998-99
Ludzik, Steve	Chi., Buf.	9	424	46	93	139	333	44	4	8	12	70	....	1981-82	1989-90
Luhning, Warren	NYI, Dal.	3	29	0	1	1	21	....	....	....	....	....	....	1997-98	1999-00
Lukowich, Bernie	Pit., St.L.	2	79	13	15	28	34	2	0	0	0	0	....	1973-74	1974-75
Lukowich, Morris	Wpg., Bos., L.A.	8	582	199	219	418	584	11	0	2	2	24	....	1979-80	1986-87
Luksa, Charlie	Hfd.	1	8	0	1	1	4	....	....	....	....	....	....	1979-80	1979-80
Lumley, Dave	Mtl., Edm., Hfd.	9	437	98	160	258	680	61	6	8	14	131	2	1978-79	1986-87
Lumme, Jyrki	Mtl., Van., Phx., Dal., Tor.	15	985	114	354	468	620	105	9	35	44	52	....	1988-89	2002-03
Lund, Pentti	Bos., NYR	7	259	44	55	99	40	19	7	5	12	0	....	1946-47	1952-53
Lundberg, Brian	Pit.	1	1	0	0	0	2	....	....	....	....	....	....	1982-83	1982-83
Lunde, Len	Det., Chi., Min., Van.	8	321	39	83	122	75	20	3	2	5	2	....	1958-59	1970-71
Lundholm, Bengt	Wpg.	5	275	48	95	143	72	14	3	4	7	14	....	1981-82	1985-86
Lundrigan, Joe	Tor., Wsh.	2	52	2	8	10	22	....	....	....	....	....	....	1972-73	1974-75
Lundstrom, Tord	Det.	1	11	1	1	2	0	....	....	....	....	....	....	1973-74	1973-74
• Lundy, Pat	Det., Chi.	5	150	37	32	69	31	16	2	2	4	2	....	1945-46	1950-51
Luongo, Chris	Det., Ott., NYI	5	218	8	23	31	176	....	....	....	....	....	....	1990-91	1995-96
Lupien, Gilles	Mtl., Pit., Hfd.	5	226	5	25	30	416	25	0	0	0	21	2	1977-78	1981-82
Lupul, Gary	Van.	7	293	70	75	145	243	25	4	7	11	11	....	1979-80	1985-86
• Lyashenko, Roman	Dal., NYR	4	139	14	9	23	55	17	2	1	3	0	....	1999-00	2002-03
Lyle, George	Det., Hfd.	4	99	24	38	62	51	....	....	....	....	....	....	1979-80	1982-83
Lynch, Jack	Pit., Det., Wsh.	7	382	24	106	130	336	....	....	....	....	....	....	1972-73	1978-79
Lynn, Vic	NYR, Det., Mtl., Tor., Bos., Chi.	11	327	49	76	125	274	47	7	10	17	46	3	1942-43	1953-54
Lyon, Steve	Pit.	1	3	0	0	0	2	....	....	....	....	....	....	1976-77	1976-77
Lyons, Ron	Bos., Phi.	1	36	2	4	6	27	5	0	0	0	0	....	1930-31	1930-31
Lysiak, Tom	Atl., Chi.	13	919	292	551	843	567	76	25	38	63	49	....	1973-74	1985-86

M

MacAdam, Al	Phi., Cal., Cle., Min., Van.	12	864	240	351	591	509	64	20	24	44	21	1	1973-74	1984-85
MacDermid, Paul	Hfd., Wpg., Wsh., Que.	14	690	116	142	258	1303	43	5	11	16	116	....	1981-82	1994-95
MacDonald, Blair	Edm., Van.	4	219	91	100	191	65	11	0	6	6	2	....	1979-80	1982-83
MacDonald, Brett	Van.	1	1	0	0	0	0	....	....	....	....	....	....	1987-88	1987-88
MacDonald, Doug	Buf.	3	11	1	0	1	2	....	....	....	....	....	....	1992-93	1994-95
MacDonald, Kevin	Ott.	1	1	0	0	0	2	....	....	....	....	....	....	1993-94	1993-94
• MacDonald, Kilby	NYR	4	151	36	34	70	47	15	1	2	3	4	1	1939-40	1944-45
MacDonald, Lowell	Det., L.A., Pit.	13	506	180	210	390	92	30	11	11	22	12	....	1961-62	1977-78
MacDonald, Parker	Tor., NYR, Det., Bos., Min.	14	676	144	179	323	253	75	14	14	28	20	....	1952-53	1968-69
MacDougall, Kim	Min.	1	1	0	0	0	0	....	....	....	....	....	....	1974-75	1974-75
MacEachern, Shane	St.L.	1	1	0	0	0	0	....	....	....	....	....	....	1987-88	1987-88
Macey, Hub	NYR, Mtl.	3	30	6	9	15	0	8	0	0	0	0	....	1941-42	1946-47
MacGregor, Bruce	Det., NYR	14	893	213	257	470	217	107	19	28	47	44	....	1960-61	1973-74
MacGregor, Randy	Hfd.	1	2	1	1	2	2	....	....	....	....	....	....	1981-82	1981-82
MacGuigan, Garth	NYI	2	5	0	1	1	2	....	....	....	....	....	....	1979-80	1983-84
MacIntosh, Ian	NYR	1	4	0	0	0	4	....	....	....	....	....	....	1952-53	1952-53
MacIver, Don	Wpg.	1	6	0	0	0	2	....	....	....	....	....	....	1979-80	1979-80
Maciver, Norm	NYR, Hfd., Edm., Ott., Pit., Wpg., Phx.	12	500	55	230	285	350	56	3	11	14	32	....	1986-87	1997-98
MacKasey, Blair	Tor.	1	1	0	0	0	2	....	....	....	....	....	....	1976-77	1976-77
• MacKay, Calum	Det., Mtl.	8	237	50	55	105	214	38	5	13	18	20	1	1946-47	1954-55
MacKay, Dave	Chi.	1	29	3	0	3	26	5	0	1	1	2	....	1940-41	1940-41
• MacKay, Mickey	Chi., Pit., Bos.	4	147	44	19	63	79	11	0	0	0	6	1	1926-27	1929-30
• MacKay, Murdo	Mtl.	4	19	0	3	3	0	15	1	2	3	0	....	1945-46	1948-49
MacKell, Fleming	Tor., Bos.	13	665	149	220	369	562	80	22	41	63	75	2	1947-48	1959-60
• MacKell, Jack	Ott.	2	45	4	2	6	59	2	0	0	0	0	2	1919-20	1920-21
MacKenzie, Barry	Min.	1	6	0	1	1	6	....	....	....	....	....	....	1968-69	1968-69
• MacKenzie, Bill	Chi., Mtl.M., NYR, Mtl.	7	264	15	14	29	145	21	1	1	2	11	1	1932-33	1939-40
Mackey, David	Chi., Min., St.L.	6	126	8	12	20	305	3	0	0	0	2	....	1987-88	1993-94
• Mackey, Reg	NYR	1	34	0	0	0	16	1	0	0	0	0	....	1926-27	1926-27
• Mackie, Howie	Det.	2	20	1	0	1	4	8	0	0	0	0	1	1936-37	1937-38
MacKinnon, Paul	Wsh.	5	147	5	23	28	91	....	....	....	....	....	....	1979-80	1983-84
MacLean, John	N.J., S.J., NYR, Dal.	18	1194	413	429	842	1328	104	35	48	83	152	1	1983-84	2001-02
MacLean, Paul	St.L., Wpg., Det.	11	719	324	349	673	968	53	21	14	35	110	....	1980-81	1990-91
MacLeish, Rick	Phi., Hfd., Pit., Det.	14	846	349	410	759	434	114	54	53	107	38	2	1970-71	1983-84
MacLellan, Brian	L.A., NYR, Min., Cgy., Det.	10	606	172	241	413	551	47	5	9	14	42	1	1982-83	1991-92
MacLeod, Pat	Min., S.J., Dal.	4	53	5	13	18	14	....	....	....	....	....	....	1990-91	1995-96
MacMillan, Billy	Tor., Atl., NYI	7	446	74	77	151	184	53	6	6	12	40	....	1970-71	1976-77
MacMillan, Bob	NYR, St.L., Atl., Cgy., Col., N.J., Chi.	11	753	228	349	577	260	31	8	11	19	16	....	1974-75	1984-85
MacMillan, John	Tor., Det.	5	104	5	10	15	32	12	0	1	1	2	2	1960-61	1964-65
MacNeil, Al	Tor., Mtl., Chi., NYR, Pit.	11	524	17	75	92	617	37	0	4	4	67	....	1955-56	1967-68
MacNeil, Bernie	St.L.	1	4	0	0	0	0	....	....	....	....	....	....	1973-74	1973-74
Macoun, Jamie	Cgy., Tor., Det.	16	1128	76	282	358	1208	159	10	32	42	169	2	1982-83	1998-99
• MacPherson, Bud	Mtl.	7	259	5	33	38	233	29	0	3	3	21	1	1948-49	1956-57
• MacSweyn, Ralph	Phi.	5	47	0	5	5	10	8	0	0	0	6	....	1967-68	1971-72
MacTavish, Craig	Bos., Edm., NYR, Phi., St.L.	17	1093	213	267	480	891	193	20	38	58	218	4	1979-80	1996-97
MacWilliam, Mike	NYI	1	6	0	0	0	14	....	....	....	....	....	....	1995-96	1995-96
Madigan, Connie	St.L.	1	20	0	3	3	25	5	0	0	0	4	....	1972-73	1972-73
Madill, Jeff	N.J.	1	14	4	0	4	46	7	0	2	2	8	....	1990-91	1990-91
Magee, Dean	Min.	1	7	0	0	0	4	....	....	....	....	....	....	1977-78	1977-78
Maggs, Daryl	Chi., Cal., Tor.	3	135	14	19	33	54	4	0	0	0	0	....	1971-72	1979-80
Magnan, Marc	Tor.	1	4	0	1	1	5	....	....	....	....	....	....	1982-83	1982-83
• Magnuson, Keith	Chi.	11	589	14	125	139	1442	68	3	9	12	164	....	1969-70	1979-80
Maguire, Kevin	Tor., Buf., Phi.	6	260	29	30	59	782	11	0	0	0	86	....	1986-87	1991-92
Mahaffy, John	Mtl., NYR	3	37	11	25	36	4	1	0	1	1	0	....	1942-43	1944-45
Mahovlich, Frank	Tor., Det., Mtl.	18	1181	533	570	1103	1056	137	51	67	118	163	6	1956-57	1973-74
Mahovlich, Pete	Det., Mtl., Pit.	16	884	288	485	773	916	88	30	42	72	134	4	1965-66	1980-81
Mailhot, Jacques	Que.	1	5	0	0	0	33	....	....	....	....	....	....	1988-89	1988-89
Mailley, Frank	Mtl.	1	1	0	0	0	0	....	....	....	....	....	....	1942-43	1942-43
Mair, Jim	Phi., NYI, Van.	5	76	4	15	19	49	3	1	2	3	4	....	1970-71	1974-75
• Majeau, Fern	Mtl.	2	56	22	24	46	43	1	0	0	0	0	1	1943-44	1944-45
Major, Bruce	Que.	1	4	0	0	0	0	....	....	....	....	....	....	1990-91	1990-91
‡ Major, Mark	Det.	1	2	0	0	0	5	....	....	....	....	....	....	1996-97	1996-97
Makarov, Sergei	Cgy., S.J., Dal.	7	424	134	250	384	317	34	12	11	23	8	....	1989-90	1996-97
Makela, Mikko	NYI, L.A., Buf., Bos.	7	423	118	147	265	139	18	3	8	11	14	....	1985-86	1994-95
Maki, Chico	Chi.	15	841	143	292	435	345	113	17	36	53	43	1	1960-61	1975-76
• Maki, Wayne	Chi., St.L., Van.	6	246	57	79	136	184	2	1	0	1	2	....	1967-68	1972-73
Makkonen, Kari	Edm.	1	9	2	2	4	0	....	....	....	....	....	....	1979-80	1979-80
Maley, David	Mtl., N.J., Edm., S.J., NYI	9	466	43	81	124	1043	46	5	5	10	111	1	1985-86	1993-94
Malgunas, Stewart	Phi., Wpg., Wsh., Cgy.	7	129	1	5	6	144	....	....	....	....	....	....	1993-94	1999-00
Malinowski, Merlin	Col., N.J., Hfd.	5	282	54	111	165	121	....	....	....	....	....	....	1978-79	1982-83
Malkoc, Dean	Van., Bos., NYI	4	116	1	3	4	299	....	....	....	....	....	....	1995-96	1998-99
Mallette, Troy	NYR, Edm., N.J., Ott., Bos., T.B.	9	456	51	68	119	1226	15	2	2	4	99	....	1989-90	1997-98
Malone, Cliff	Mtl.	1	3	0	0	0	0	....	....	....	....	....	....	1951-52	1951-52
Malone, Greg	Pit., Hfd., Que.	11	704	191	310	501	661	20	3	5	8	32	....	1976-77	1986-87
• Malone, Joe	Mtl., Que., Ham.	7	126	143	32	175	57	9	6	2	8	6	1	1917-18	1923-24
Maloney, Dan	Chi., L.A., Det., Tor.	11	737	192	259	451	1489	40	4	7	11	35	....	1970-71	1981-82
Maloney, Dave	NYR, Buf.	11	657	71	246	317	1154	49	7	17	24	91	....	1974-75	1984-85
Maloney, Don	NYR, Hfd., NYI	13	765	214	350	564	815	94	22	35	57	101	....	1978-79	1990-91
Maloney, Phil	Bos., Tor., Chi.	5	158	28	43	71	16	6	0	0	0	0	....	1949-50	1959-60
‡ Maltais, Steve	Wsh., Min., T.B., Det., CBJ	6	120	9	18	27	53	1	0	0	0	0	....	1989-90	2000-01
Maluta, Ray	Bos.	2	25	2	3	5	6	2	0	0	0	0	....	1975-76	1976-77

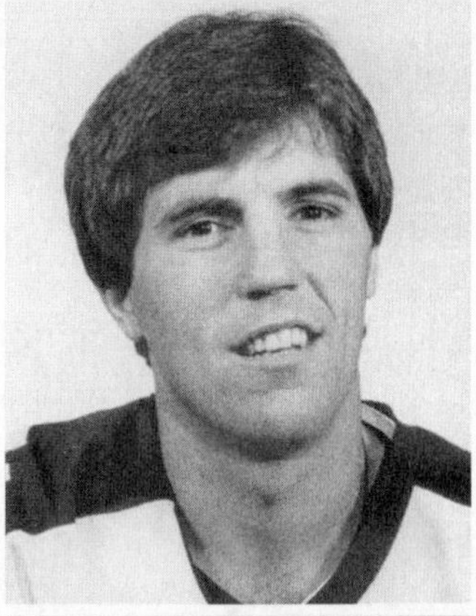
Terry Martin

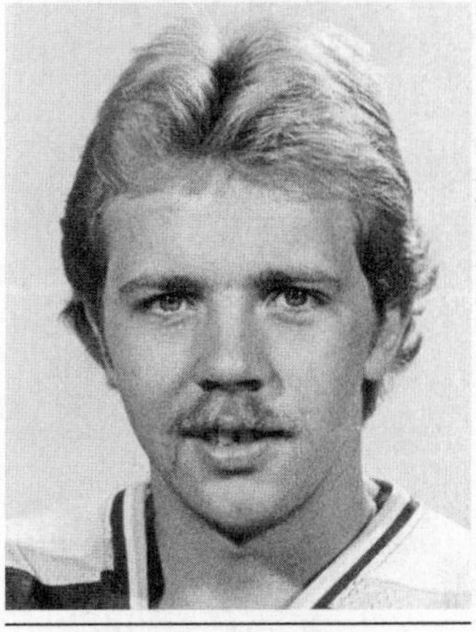
Kevin Maxwell

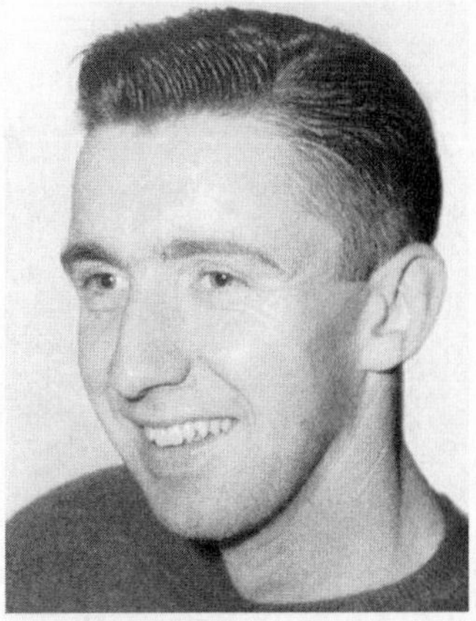
Max McNab

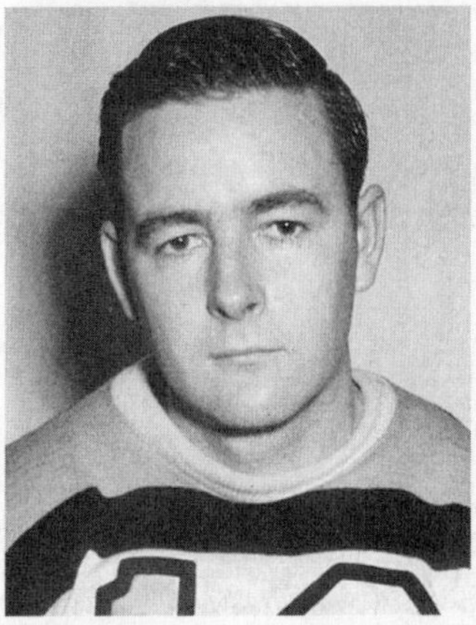
Pat McReavy

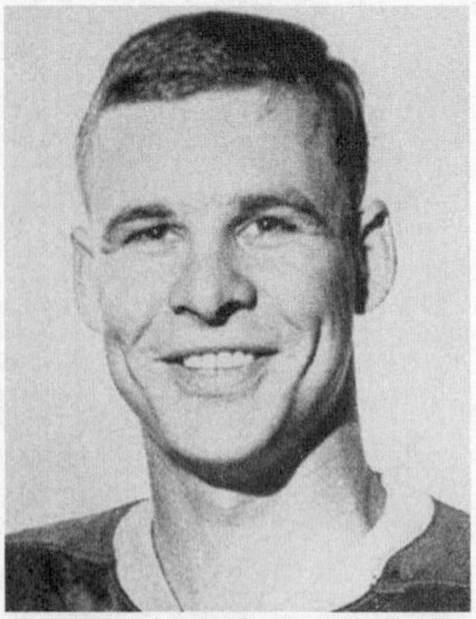

Barrie Meissner

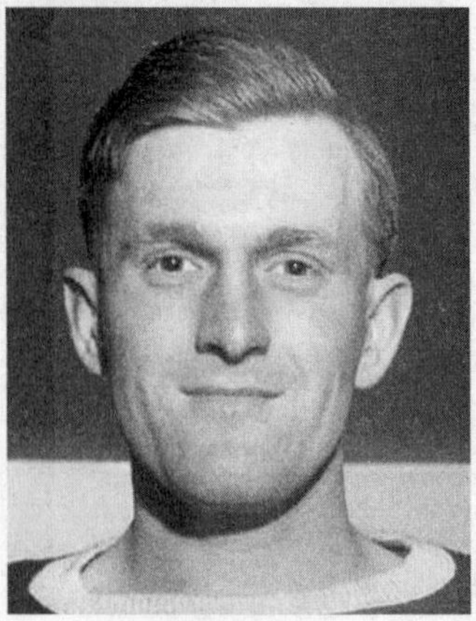

Don Metz

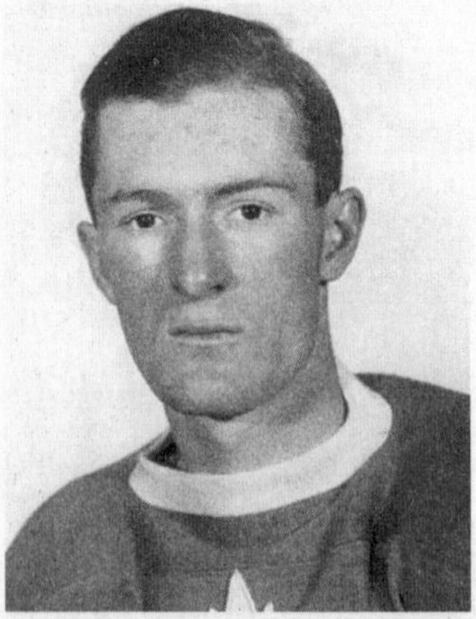

Nick Metz

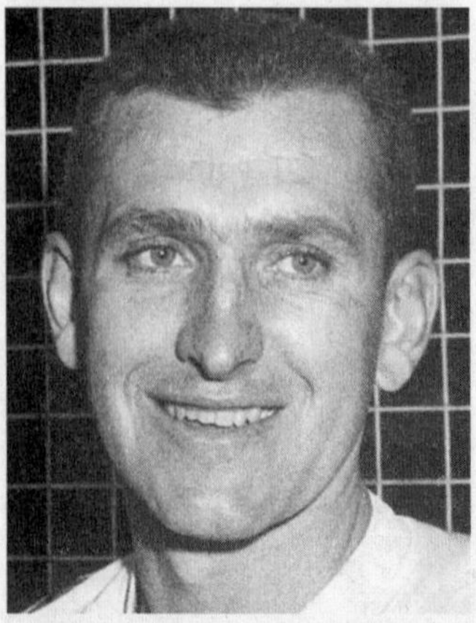

Rudy Migay

			Regular Schedule					Playoffs					NHL	First	Last
Name	NHL Teams	NHL Seasons	GP	G	A	TP	PIM	GP	G	A	TP	PIM	Cup Wins	NHL Season	NHL Season
Manastersky, Tom	Mtl.	1	6	0	0	0	11	....	....	....	....	....	....	1950-51	1950-51
Mancuso, Gus	Mtl., NYR	4	42	7	9	16	17	....	....	....	....	....	....	1937-38	1942-43
‡ Manderville, Kent	Tor., Edm., Hfd., Car., Phi., Pit.	12	646	37	67	104	348	67	3	3	6	44	....	1991-92	2002-03
Mandich, Dan	Min.	4	111	5	11	16	303	7	0	0	0	2	....	1982-83	1985-86
‡ Maneluk, Mike	Phi., Chi., NYR, CBJ	3	85	11	10	21	57	....	....	....	....	....	....	1998-99	2000-01
Manery, Kris	Cle., Min., Van., Wpg.	4	250	63	64	127	91	....	....	....	....	....	....	1977-78	1980-81
Manery, Randy	Det., Atl., L.A.	10	582	50	206	256	415	13	0	2	2	12	....	1970-71	1979-80
‡ Mann, Cameron	Bos., Nsh.	5	93	14	10	24	40	1	0	0	0	0	....	1997-98	2002-03
Mann, Jack	NYR	2	9	3	4	7	0	....	....	....	....	....	....	1943-44	1944-45
Mann, Jimmy	Wpg., Que., Pit.	8	293	10	20	30	895	22	0	0	0	89	....	1979-80	1987-88
Mann, Ken	Det.	1	1	0	0	0	0	....	....	....	....	....	....	1975-76	1975-76
• Mann, Norm	Tor.	3	31	0	3	3	4	2	0	0	0	0	....	1935-36	1940-41
• Manners, Rennison	Pit., Phi.	2	37	3	2	5	14	....	....	....	....	....	....	1929-30	1930-31
Manno, Bob	Van., Tor., Det.	8	371	41	131	172	274	17	2	4	6	12	....	1976-77	1984-85
Manson, Dave	Chi., Edm., Wpg., Phx., Mtl., Dal., Tor.	16	1103	102	288	390	2792	112	7	24	31	343	....	1986-87	2001-02
Manson, Ray	Bos., NYR	2	2	0	1	1	0	....	....	....	....	....	....	1947-48	1948-49
• Mantha, Georges	Mtl.	13	488	89	102	191	148	36	6	2	8	24	2	1928-29	1940-41
Mantha, Moe	Wpg., Pit., Edm., Min., Phi.	12	656	81	289	370	501	17	5	10	15	18	....	1980-81	1991-92
• Mantha, Sylvio	Mtl., Bos.	14	542	63	78	141	671	39	5	5	10	64	3	1923-24	1936-37
• Maracle, Bud	NYR	1	11	1	3	4	4	4	0	0	0	0	....	1930-31	1930-31
Marcetta, Milan	Tor., Min.	3	54	7	15	22	10	17	7	7	14	4	1	1966-67	1968-69
• March, Mush	Chi.	17	759	153	230	383	540	45	12	15	27	41	2	1928-29	1944-45
Marchinko, Brian	Tor., NYI	4	47	2	6	8	0	....	....	....	....	....	....	1970-71	1973-74
Marcinyshyn, Dave	N.J., Que., NYR	3	16	0	1	1	49	....	....	....	....	....	....	1990-91	1992-93
Marcon, Lou	Det.	3	60	0	4	4	42	....	....	....	....	....	....	1958-59	1962-63
Marcotte, Don	Bos.	15	868	230	254	484	317	132	34	27	61	81	2	1965-66	1981-82
‡ Marha, Josef	Col., Ana., Chi.	6	159	21	32	53	32	....	....	....	....	....	....	1995-96	2000-01
Marini, Hector	NYI, N.J.	5	154	27	46	73	246	10	3	6	9	14	2	1978-79	1983-84
‡ Marinucci, Chris	NYI, L.A.	2	13	1	4	5	2	....	....	....	....	....	....	1994-95	1996-97
• Mario, Frank	Bos.	2	53	9	19	28	24	....	....	....	....	....	....	1941-42	1944-45
• Mariucci, John	Chi.	5	223	11	34	45	308	12	0	3	3	26	....	1940-41	1947-48
Mark, Gordon	N.J., Edm.	4	85	3	10	13	187	....	....	....	....	....	....	1986-87	1994-95
Markell, John	Wpg., St.L., Min.	4	55	11	10	21	36	....	....	....	....	....	....	1979-80	1984-85
• Marker, Gus	Det., Mtl.M., Tor., Bro.	10	322	64	69	133	133	46	5	7	12	36	1	1932-33	1941-42
Markham, Ray	NYR	1	14	1	1	2	21	7	1	0	1	24	....	1979-80	1979-80
• Markle, Jack	Tor.	1	8	0	1	1	0	....	....	....	....	....	....	1935-36	1935-36
• Marks, Jack	Mtl.W., Tor., Que.	2	7	0	0	0	4	....	....	....	....	....	1	1917-18	1919-20
Marks, John	Chi.	10	657	112	163	275	330	57	5	9	14	60	....	1972-73	1981-82
Markwart, Nevin	Bos., Cgy.	8	309	41	68	109	794	19	1	0	1	33	....	1983-84	1991-92
Marois, Daniel	Tor., NYI, Bos., Dal.	8	350	117	93	210	419	19	3	3	6	28	....	1987-88	1995-96
Marois, Mario	NYR, Van., Que., Wpg., St.L.	15	955	76	357	433	1746	100	4	34	38	182	....	1977-78	1991-92
Marotte, Gilles	Bos., Chi., L.A., NYR, St.L.	12	808	56	265	321	919	29	3	3	6	26	....	1965-66	1976-77
Marquess, Mark	Bos.	1	27	5	4	9	6	4	0	0	0	0	....	1946-47	1946-47
Marsh, Brad	Atl., Cgy., Phi., Tor., Det., Ott.	15	1086	23	175	198	1241	97	6	18	24	124	....	1978-79	1992-93
Marsh, Gary	Det., Tor.	2	7	1	3	4	4	....	....	....	....	....	....	1967-68	1968-69
Marsh, Peter	Wpg., Chi.	5	278	48	71	119	224	26	1	5	6	33	....	1979-80	1983-84
Marshall, Bert	Det., Oak., Cal., NYR, NYI	14	868	17	181	198	926	72	4	22	26	99	....	1965-66	1978-79
Marshall, Don	Mtl., NYR, Buf., Tor.	19	1176	265	324	589	127	94	8	15	23	14	5	1951-52	1971-72
Marshall, Paul	Pit., Tor., Hfd.	4	95	15	18	33	17	1	0	0	0	0	....	1979-80	1982-83
Marshall, Willie	Tor.	4	33	1	5	6	2	....	....	....	....	....	....	1952-53	1958-59
Marson, Mike	Wsh., L.A.	6	196	24	24	48	233	....	....	....	....	....	....	1974-75	1979-80
• Martin, Clare	Bos., Det., Chi., NYR	6	237	12	28	40	78	27	0	2	2	6	1	1941-42	1951-52
Martin, Craig	Wpg., Fla.	2	21	0	1	1	24	....	....	....	....	....	....	1994-95	1996-97
Martin, Frank	Bos., Chi.	6	282	11	46	57	122	10	0	2	2	2	....	1952-53	1957-58
Martin, Grant	Van., Wsh.	4	44	0	4	4	55	1	1	0	1	2	....	1983-84	1986-87
Martin, Jack	Tor.	1	1	0	0	0	0	....	....	....	....	....	....	1960-61	1960-61
Martin, Matt	Tor.	4	76	0	5	5	71	....	....	....	....	....	....	1993-94	1996-97
Martin, Pit	Det., Bos., Chi., Van.	17	1101	324	485	809	609	100	27	31	58	56	....	1961-62	1978-79
Martin, Rick	Buf., L.A.	11	685	384	317	701	477	63	24	29	53	74	....	1971-72	1981-82
• Martin, Ron	NYA	2	94	13	16	29	36	....	....	....	....	....	....	1932-33	1933-34
Martin, Terry	Buf., Que., Tor., Edm., Min.	10	479	104	101	205	202	21	4	2	6	26	....	1975-76	1984-85
Martin, Tom	Tor.	1	3	1	0	1	0	....	....	....	....	....	....	1967-68	1967-68
Martin, Tom	Wpg., Hfd., Min.	6	92	12	11	23	249	4	0	0	0	6	....	1984-85	1989-90
Martineau, Don	Atl., Min., Det.	4	90	6	10	16	63	....	....	....	....	....	....	1973-74	1976-77
Martini, Darcy	Edm.	1	2	0	0	0	0	....	....	....	....	....	....	1993-94	1993-94
Martinson, Steve	Det., Mtl., Min.	4	49	2	1	3	244	1	0	0	0	10	....	1987-88	1991-92
Maruk, Dennis	Cal., Cle., Min., Wsh.	14	888	356	522	878	761	34	14	22	36	26	....	1975-76	1988-89
Masnick, Paul	Mtl., Chi., Tor.	6	232	18	41	59	139	33	4	5	9	27	1	1950-51	1957-58
• Mason, Charley	NYR, NYA, Det., Chi.	4	95	7	18	25	44	4	0	1	1	0	....	1934-35	1938-39
• Massecar, George	NYA	3	100	12	11	23	46	....	....	....	....	....	....	1929-30	1931-32
Masters, Jamie	St.L.	3	33	1	13	14	2	2	0	0	0	0	....	1975-76	1978-79
• Masterton, Bill	Min.	1	38	4	8	12	4	....	....	....	....	....	....	1967-68	1967-68
• Mathers, Frank	Tor.	3	23	1	3	4	4	....	....	....	....	....	....	1948-49	1951-52
Mathiasen, Dwight	Pit.	3	33	1	7	8	18	....	....	....	....	....	....	1985-86	1987-88
Mathieson, Jim	Wsh.	1	2	0	0	0	4	....	....	....	....	....	....	1989-90	1989-90
‡ Mathieu, Marquis	Bos.	3	16	0	2	2	14	....	....	....	....	....	....	1998-99	2000-01
‡ Matte, Christian	Col., Min.	5	25	2	3	5	12	....	....	....	....	....	....	1996-97	2000-01
• Matte, Joe	Tor., Ham., Bos., Mtl.	4	68	17	15	32	54	....	....	....	....	....	....	1919-20	1925-26
• Matte, Joe	Det., Chi.	2	24	0	3	3	8	....	....	....	....	....	....	1929-30	1942-43
Matteau, Stephane	Cgy., Chi., NYR, St.L., S.J., Fla.	13	848	144	172	316	742	109	12	22	34	80	1	1990-91	2002-03
Matteucci, Mike	Min.	2	6	0	0	0	4	....	....	....	....	....	....	2000-01	2001-02
Mattiussi, Dick	Pit., Oak., Cal.	4	200	8	31	39	124	8	0	1	1	6	....	1967-68	1970-71
• Matz, Johnny	Mtl.	1	30	2	3	5	0	1	0	0	0	0	....	1924-25	1924-25
Maxner, Wayne	Bos.	2	62	8	9	17	48	....	....	....	....	....	....	1964-65	1965-66
Maxwell, Brad	Min., Que., Tor., Van., NYR	10	612	98	270	368	1292	79	12	49	61	178	....	1977-78	1986-87
Maxwell, Bryan	Min., St.L., Wpg., Pit.	8	331	18	77	95	745	15	1	1	2	86	....	1977-78	1984-85
Maxwell, Kevin	Min., Col., N.J.	3	66	6	15	21	61	16	3	4	7	24	....	1980-81	1983-84
Maxwell, Wally	Tor.	1	2	0	0	0	0	....	....	....	....	....	....	1952-53	1952-53
May, Alan	Bos., Edm., Wsh., Dal., Cgy.	8	393	31	45	76	1348	40	1	2	3	80	....	1987-88	1994-95
Mayer, Derek	Ott.	1	17	2	2	4	8	....	....	....	....	....	....	1993-94	1993-94
Mayer, Jim	NYR	1	4	0	0	0	0	....	....	....	....	....	....	1979-80	1979-80
Mayer, Pat	Pit.	1	1	0	0	0	4	....	....	....	....	....	....	1987-88	1987-88
• Mayer, Shep	Tor.	1	12	1	2	3	4	....	....	....	....	....	....	1942-43	1942-43
• Mazur, Eddie	Mtl., Chi.	6	107	8	20	28	120	25	4	5	9	22	1	1950-51	1956-57
Mazur, Jay	Van.	4	47	11	7	18	20	6	0	1	1	8	....	1988-89	1991-92
McAdam, Gary	Buf., Pit., Det., Cgy., Wsh., N.J., Tor.	11	534	96	132	228	243	30	6	5	11	16	....	1975-76	1985-86
• McAdam, Sam	NYR	1	5	0	0	0	0	....	....	....	....	....	....	1930-31	1930-31
McAlpine, Chris	N.J., St.L., T.B., Atl., Chi., L.A.	8	289	6	24	30	245	28	0	1	1	18	1	1994-95	2002-03
• McAndrew, Hazen	Bro.	1	7	0	1	1	6	....	....	....	....	....	....	1941-42	1941-42
McAneeley, Ted	Cal.	3	158	8	35	43	141	....	....	....	....	....	....	1972-73	1974-75
McAtee, Jud	Det.	3	46	15	13	28	6	14	2	1	3	0	....	1942-43	1944-45
McAtee, Norm	Bos.	1	13	0	1	1	0	....	....	....	....	....	....	1946-47	1946-47
• McAvoy, George	Mtl.	1	....	....	....	....	....	4	0	0	0	0	....	1954-55	1954-55
McBain, Andrew	Wpg., Pit., Van., Ott.	11	608	129	172	301	633	24	5	7	12	39	....	1983-84	1993-94
‡ McBain, Jason	Hfd.	2	9	0	0	0	0	....	....	....	....	....	....	1995-96	1996-97
‡ McBain, Mike	T.B.	2	64	0	7	7	22	....	....	....	....	....	....	1997-98	1998-99
McBean, Wayne	L.A., NYI, Wpg.	6	211	10	39	49	168	2	1	1	2	0	....	1987-88	1993-94
McBride, Cliff	Mtl.M., Tor.	2	2	0	0	0	0	....	....	....	....	....	....	1928-29	1929-30
McBurney, Jim	Chi.	1	1	0	1	1	0	....	....	....	....	....	....	1952-53	1952-53
• McCabe, Stan	Det., Mtl.M.	4	78	9	4	13	49	....	....	....	....	....	....	1929-30	1933-34
• McCaffrey, Bert	Tor., Pit., Mtl.	7	260	43	30	73	202	8	2	1	3	10	1	1924-25	1930-31
McCahill, John	Col.	1	1	0	0	0	0	....	....	....	....	....	....	1977-78	1977-78
• McCaig, Doug	Det., Chi.	7	263	8	21	29	255	7	0	1	1	10	....	1941-42	1950-51
• McCallum, Dunc	NYR, Pit.	5	187	14	35	49	230	10	1	2	3	12	....	1965-66	1970-71
• McCalmon, Eddie	Chi., Phi.	2	39	5	0	5	14	....	....	....	....	....	....	1927-28	1930-31
McCann, Rick	Det.	6	43	1	4	5	6	....	....	....	....	....	....	1967-68	1974-75
McCarthy, Dan	NYR	1	5	4	0	4	4	....	....	....	....	....	....	1980-81	1980-81
McCarthy, Kevin	Phi., Van., Pit.	10	537	67	191	258	527	21	2	3	5	20	....	1977-78	1986-87
• McCarthy, Thomas	Que., Ham.	2	35	22	7	29	10	....	....	....	....	....	....	1919-20	1920-21
McCarthy, Tom	Det., Bos.	4	60	8	9	17	8	....	....	....	....	....	....	1956-57	1960-61
McCarthy, Tom	Min., Bos.	9	460	178	221	399	330	68	12	26	38	67	....	1979-80	1987-88
• McCartney, Walt	Mtl.	1	2	0	0	0	0	....	....	....	....	....	....	1932-33	1932-33
McCaskill, Ted	Min.	1	4	0	2	2	0	....	....	....	....	....	....	1967-68	1967-68
McClanahan, Rob	Buf., Hfd., NYR	5	224	38	63	101	126	34	4	12	16	31	....	1979-80	1983-84
McCleary, Trent	Ott., Bos., Mtl.	4	192	8	15	23	134	....	....	....	....	....	....	1995-96	1999-00

Name	NHL Teams	NHL Seasons	Regular Schedule					Playoffs					NHL Cup Wins	First NHL Season	Last NHL Season
			GP	G	A	TP	PIM	GP	G	A	TP	PIM			
McClelland, Kevin	Pit., Edm., Det., Tor., Wpg.	12	588	68	112	180	1672	98	11	18	29	281	4	1981-82	1993-94
McCord, Bob	Bos., Det., Min., St.L.	7	316	10	58	68	262	14	2	5	7	10	....	1963-64	1972-73
McCord, Dennis	Van.	1	3	0	0	0	6	....	....	....	....	....	....	1973-74	1973-74
McCormack, John	Tor., Mtl., Chi.	8	311	25	49	74	35	22	1	1	2	0	2	1947-48	1954-55
McCosh, Shawn	L.A., NYR	2	9	1	0	1	6	....	....	....	....	....	....	1991-92	1994-95
McCourt, Dale	Det., Buf., Tor.	7	532	194	284	478	124	21	9	7	16	6	....	1977-78	1983-84
McCreary, Bill	NYR, Det., Mtl., St.L.	8	309	53	62	115	108	48	6	16	22	14	....	1953-54	1970-71
McCreary, Bill	Tor.	1	12	1	0	1	4	....	....	....	....	....	....	1980-81	1980-81
• McCreary, Keith	Mtl., Pit., Atl.	10	532	131	112	243	294	16	0	4	4	6	....	1961-62	1974-75
• McCreedy, John	Tor.	2	64	17	12	29	25	21	4	3	7	16	2	1941-42	1944-45
McCrimmon, Brad	Bos., Phi., Cgy., Det., Hfd., Phx.	18	1222	81	322	403	1416	116	11	18	29	176	1	1979-80	1996-97
McCrimmon, Jim	St.L.	1	2	0	0	0	0	....	....	....	....	....	....	1974-75	1974-75
McCulley, Bob	Mtl.	1	1	0	0	0	0	....	....	....	....	....	....	1934-35	1934-35
• McCurry, Duke	Pit.	4	148	21	11	32	119	4	0	2	2	2	....	1925-26	1928-29
McCutcheon, Brian	Det.	3	37	3	1	4	7	....	....	....	....	....	....	1974-75	1976-77
McCutcheon, Darwin	Tor.	1	1	0	0	0	2	....	....	....	....	....	....	1981-82	1981-82
McDill, Jeff	Chi.	1	1	0	0	0	0	....	....	....	....	....	....	1976-77	1976-77
McDonagh, Bill	NYR	1	4	0	0	0	2	....	....	....	....	....	....	1949-50	1949-50
McDonald, Ab	Mtl., Chi., Bos., Det., Pit., St.L.	15	762	182	248	430	200	84	21	29	50	42	4	1957-58	1971-72
McDonald, Brian	Chi., Buf.	2	12	0	0	0	29	8	0	0	0	2	....	1967-68	1970-71
• McDonald, Bucko	Det., Tor., NYR	11	446	35	88	123	206	50	6	1	7	24	3	1934-35	1944-45
McDonald, Butch	Det., Chi.	2	66	8	20	28	2	5	0	2	2	10	....	1939-40	1944-45
McDonald, Gerry	Hfd.	2	8	0	0	0	4	....	....	....	....	....	....	1981-82	1983-84
• McDonald, Jack	Mtl.W., Mtl., Que., Tor.	5	69	26	14	40	30	7	1	3	4	3	....	1917-18	1921-22
McDonald, Jack	NYR	1	43	10	9	19	6	....	....	....	....	....	....	1943-44	1943-44
McDonald, Lanny	Tor., Col., Cgy.	16	1111	500	506	1006	899	117	44	40	84	120	1	1973-74	1988-89
McDonald, Robert	NYR	1	1	0	0	0	0	....	....	....	....	....	....	1943-44	1943-44
McDonald, Terry	K.C.	1	8	0	1	1	6	....	....	....	....	....	....	1975-76	1975-76
McDonnell, Joe	Van., Pit.	3	50	2	10	12	34	....	....	....	....	....	....	1981-82	1985-86
• McDonnell, Moylan	Ham.	1	22	1	2	3	2	....	....	....	....	....	....	1920-21	1920-21
McDonough, Al	L.A., Pit., Atl., Det.	5	237	73	88	161	73	8	0	1	1	2	....	1970-71	1977-78
McDonough, Hubie	L.A., NYI, S.J.	5	195	40	26	66	67	5	1	0	1	4	....	1988-89	1992-93
McDougal, Mike	NYR, Hfd.	4	61	8	10	18	43	....	....	....	....	....	....	1978-79	1982-83
McDougall, Bill	Det., Edm., T.B.	3	28	5	5	10	12	1	0	0	0	0	....	1990-91	1993-94
McElmury, Jim	Min., K.C., Col.	5	180	14	47	61	49	....	....	....	....	....	....	1972-73	1977-78
McEwen, Mike	NYR, Col., NYI, L.A., Wsh., Det., Hfd.	12	716	108	296	404	460	78	12	36	48	48	3	1976-77	1987-88
• McFadden, Jim	Det., Chi.	8	412	100	126	226	89	49	10	9	19	30	1	1946-47	1953-54
• McFadyen, Don	Chi.	4	179	12	33	45	77	11	2	2	4	5	1	1932-33	1935-36
McFall, Dan	Wpg.	2	9	0	1	1	0	....	....	....	....	....	....	1984-85	1985-86
• McFarlane, Gord	Chi.	1	2	0	0	0	0	....	....	....	....	....	....	1926-27	1926-27
McGeough, Jim	Wsh., Pit.	4	57	7	10	17	32	....	....	....	....	....	....	1981-82	1986-87
• McGibbon, Irv	Mtl.	1	1	0	0	0	2	....	....	....	....	....	....	1942-43	1942-43
McGill, Bob	Tor., Chi., S.J., Det., NYI, Hfd.	13	705	17	55	72	1766	49	0	0	0	88	....	1981-82	1993-94
• McGill, Jack	Mtl.	3	134	27	10	37	71	3	2	0	2	0	....	1934-35	1936-37
• McGill, Jack	Bos.	4	97	23	36	59	42	27	7	4	11	17	....	1941-42	1946-47
McGill, Ryan	Chi., Phi., Edm.	4	151	4	15	19	391	....	....	....	....	....	....	1991-92	1994-95
McGregor, Sandy	NYR	1	2	0	0	0	2	....	....	....	....	....	....	1963-64	1963-64
• McGuire, Mickey	Pit.	2	36	3	0	3	6	....	....	....	....	....	....	1926-27	1927-28
McHugh, Mike	Min., S.J.	4	20	1	0	1	16	....	....	....	....	....	....	1988-89	1991-92
McIlhargey, Jack	Phi., Van., Hfd.	8	393	11	36	47	1102	27	0	3	3	68	....	1974-75	1981-82
• McInenly, Bert	Det., NYA, Ott., Bos.	6	166	19	15	34	144	4	0	0	0	2	....	1930-31	1935-36
McInnis, Marty	NYI, Cgy., Ana., Bos.	12	796	170	250	420	330	22	3	2	5	4	....	1991-92	2002-03
McIntosh, Bruce	Min.	1	2	0	0	0	0	....	....	....	....	....	....	1972-73	1972-73
McIntosh, Paul	Buf.	2	48	0	2	2	66	2	0	0	0	7	....	1974-75	1975-76
• McIntyre, Jack	Bos., Chi., Det.	11	499	109	102	211	173	29	7	6	13	4	....	1949-50	1959-60
McIntyre, John	Tor., L.A., NYR, Van.	6	351	24	54	78	516	44	0	6	6	54	....	1989-90	1994-95
McIntyre, Larry	Tor.	2	41	0	3	3	26	....	....	....	....	....	....	1969-70	1972-73
McKay, Doug	Det.	1	....	....	....	....	....	1	0	0	0	0	1	1949-50	1949-50
McKay, Randy	Det., N.J., Dal., Mtl.	15	932	162	201	363	1731	123	20	23	43	123	2	1988-89	2002-03
McKay, Ray	Chi., Buf., Cal.	6	140	2	16	18	102	....	....	....	....	....	....	1968-69	1973-74
McKay, Scott	Ana.	1	1	0	0	0	0	....	....	....	....	....	....	1993-94	1993-94
McKechnie, Walt	Min., Cal., Bos., Det., Wsh., Cle., Tor., Col.	16	955	214	392	606	469	15	7	5	12	7	....	1967-68	1982-83
McKee, Mike	Que.	1	48	3	12	15	41	....	....	....	....	....	....	1993-94	1993-94
McKegney, Ian	Chi.	1	3	0	0	0	2	....	....	....	....	....	....	1976-77	1976-77
McKegney, Tony	Buf., Que., Min., NYR, St.L., Det., Chi.	13	912	320	319	639	517	79	24	23	47	56	....	1978-79	1990-91
McKendry, Alex	NYI, Cgy.	4	46	3	6	9	21	6	2	2	4	0	1	1977-78	1980-81
McKenna, Sean	Buf., L.A., Tor.	9	414	82	80	162	181	15	1	2	3	2	....	1981-82	1989-90
McKenney, Don	Bos., NYR, Tor., Det., St.L.	13	798	237	345	582	211	58	18	29	47	10	1	1954-55	1967-68
McKenny, Jim	Tor., Min.	14	604	82	247	329	294	37	7	9	16	10	....	1965-66	1978-79
McKenzie, Brian	Pit.	1	6	1	1	2	4	....	....	....	....	....	....	1971-72	1971-72
McKenzie, John	Chi., Det., NYR, Bos.	12	691	206	268	474	917	69	15	32	47	133	2	1958-59	1971-72
McKim, Andrew	Bos., Det.	3	38	1	4	5	6	....	....	....	....	....	....	1992-93	1994-95
• McKinnon, Alex	Ham., NYA, Chi.	5	193	19	11	30	237	....	....	....	....	....	....	1924-25	1928-29
• McKinnon, John	Mtl., Pit., Phi.	6	208	28	11	39	224	2	0	0	0	4	....	1925-26	1930-31
McLean, Don	Wsh.	1	9	0	0	0	6	....	....	....	....	....	....	1975-76	1975-76
• McLean, Fred	Que., Ham.	2	8	0	0	0	2	....	....	....	....	....	....	1919-20	1920-21
McLean, Jack	Tor.	3	67	14	24	38	76	13	2	2	4	8	1	1942-43	1944-45
McLean, Jeff	S.J.	1	6	1	0	1	0	....	....	....	....	....	....	1993-94	1993-94
• McLellan, John	Tor.	1	2	0	0	0	0	....	....	....	....	....	....	1951-52	1951-52
McLellan, Scott	Bos.	1	2	0	0	0	0	....	....	....	....	....	....	1982-83	1982-83
McLellan, Todd	NYI	1	5	1	1	2	0	....	....	....	....	....	....	1987-88	1987-88
• McLenahan, Rollie	Det.	1	9	2	1	3	10	2	0	0	0	0	....	1945-46	1945-46
McLeod, Al	Det.	1	26	2	2	4	24	....	....	....	....	....	....	1973-74	1973-74
McLeod, Jackie	NYR	5	106	14	23	37	12	7	0	0	0	0	....	1949-50	1954-55
McLlwain, Dave	Pit., Wpg., Buf., NYI, Tor., Ott.	10	501	100	107	207	292	20	0	2	2	2	....	1987-88	1996-97
• McMahon, Mike	Mtl., Bos.	3	57	7	18	25	102	13	1	2	3	30	1	1942-43	1945-46
McMahon, Mike Jr.	NYR, Min., Chi., Det., Pit., Buf.	8	224	15	68	83	171	14	3	7	10	4	....	1963-64	1971-72
McManama, Bob	Pit.	3	99	11	25	36	28	8	0	1	1	6	....	1973-74	1975-76
• McManus, Sammy	Mtl.M., Bos.	2	26	0	1	1	8	1	0	0	0	0	1	1934-35	1936-37
McMurchy, Tom	Chi., Edm.	4	55	8	4	12	65	....	....	....	....	....	....	1983-84	1987-88
McNab, Max	Det.	4	128	16	19	35	24	25	1	0	1	4	1	1947-48	1950-51
McNab, Peter	Buf., Bos., Van., N.J.	14	954	363	450	813	179	107	40	42	82	20	....	1973-74	1986-87
• McNabney, Sid	Mtl.	1	....	....	....	....	....	5	0	1	1	2	....	1950-51	1950-51
• McNamara, Howard	Mtl.	1	10	1	0	1	4	....	....	....	....	....	....	1919-20	1919-20
• McNaughton, George	Que.	1	1	0	0	0	0	....	....	....	....	....	....	1919-20	1919-20
McNeill, Billy	Det.	6	257	21	46	67	142	4	1	1	2	4	....	1956-57	1963-64
McNeill, Mike	Chi., Que.	2	63	5	11	16	18	....	....	....	....	....	....	1990-91	1991-92
McNeill, Stu	Det.	3	10	1	1	2	2	....	....	....	....	....	....	1957-58	1959-60
McPhee, George	NYR, N.J.	7	115	24	25	49	257	29	5	3	8	69	....	1982-83	1988-89
McPhee, Mike	Mtl., Min., Dal.	11	744	200	199	399	661	134	28	27	55	193	1	1983-84	1993-94
McRae, Basil	Que., Tor., Det., Min., T.B., St.L., Chi.	16	576	53	83	136	2457	78	8	4	12	349	....	1981-82	1996-97
McRae, Chris	Tor., Det.	3	21	1	0	1	122	....	....	....	....	....	....	1987-88	1989-90
McRae, Ken	Que., Tor.	7	137	14	21	35	364	6	0	0	0	4	....	1987-88	1993-94
• McReavy, Pat	Bos., Det.	4	55	5	10	15	4	22	3	3	6	9	1	1938-39	1941-42
McReynolds, Brian	Wpg., NYR, L.A.	3	30	1	5	6	8	....	....	....	....	....	....	1989-90	1993-94
McSheffrey, Bryan	Van., Buf.	3	90	13	7	20	44	....	....	....	....	....	....	1972-73	1974-75
McSorley, Marty	Pit., Edm., L.A., NYR, S.J., Bos.	17	961	108	251	359	3381	115	10	19	29	374	2	1983-84	1999-00
McSween, Don	Buf., Ana.	5	47	3	10	13	55	....	....	....	....	....	....	1987-88	1995-96
McTaggart, Jim	Wsh.	2	71	3	10	13	205	....	....	....	....	....	....	1980-81	1981-82
‡ McTavish, Dale	Cgy.	1	9	1	2	3	2	....	....	....	....	....	....	1996-97	1996-97
McTavish, Gord	St.L., Wpg.	2	11	1	3	4	2	....	....	....	....	....	....	1978-79	1979-80
• McVeigh, Charley	Chi., NYA	9	397	84	88	172	138	4	0	0	0	2	....	1926-27	1934-35
• McVicar, Jack	Mtl.M.	2	88	2	4	6	63	6	0	0	0	2	....	1930-31	1931-32
Meagher, Rick	Mtl., Hfd., N.J., St.L.	12	691	144	165	309	383	62	8	7	15	41	....	1979-80	1990-91
Meehan, Gerry	Tor., Phi., Buf., Van., Atl., Wsh.	10	670	180	243	423	111	10	0	1	1	0	....	1968-69	1978-79
Meeke, Brent	Cal., Cle.	5	75	9	22	31	8	....	....	....	....	....	....	1972-73	1976-77
Meeker, Howie	Tor.	8	346	83	102	185	329	42	6	9	15	50	4	1946-47	1953-54
Meeker, Mike	Pit.	1	4	0	0	0	5	....	....	....	....	....	....	1978-79	1978-79
• Meeking, Harry	Tor., Det., Bos.	3	64	18	12	30	66	9	3	0	3	6	....	1917-18	1926-27
Meger, Paul	Mtl.	6	212	39	52	91	118	35	3	8	11	16	1	1949-50	1954-55
Meighan, Ron	Min., Pit.	2	48	3	7	10	18	....	....	....	....	....	....	1981-82	1982-83
Meissner, Barrie	Min.	2	6	0	1	1	4	....	....	....	....	....	....	1967-68	1968-69
Meissner, Dick	Bos., NYR	5	171	11	15	26	37	....	....	....	....	....	....	1959-60	1964-65
Melametsa, Anssi	Wpg.	1	27	0	3	3	2	....	....	....	....	....	....	1985-86	1985-86

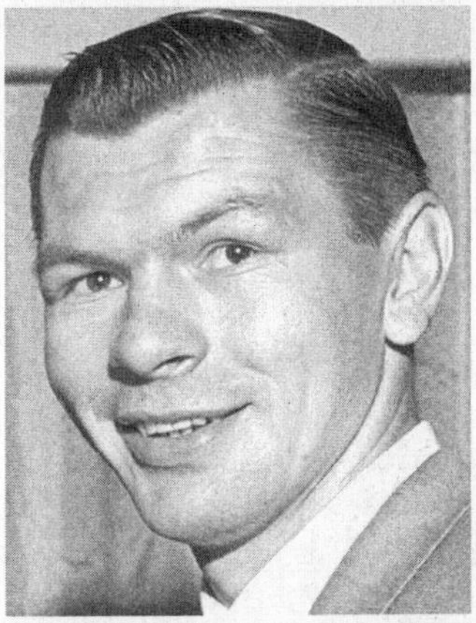

Stan Mikita

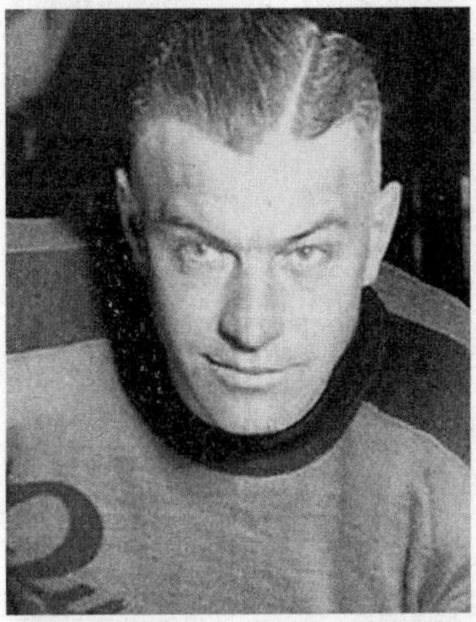

Hib Milks

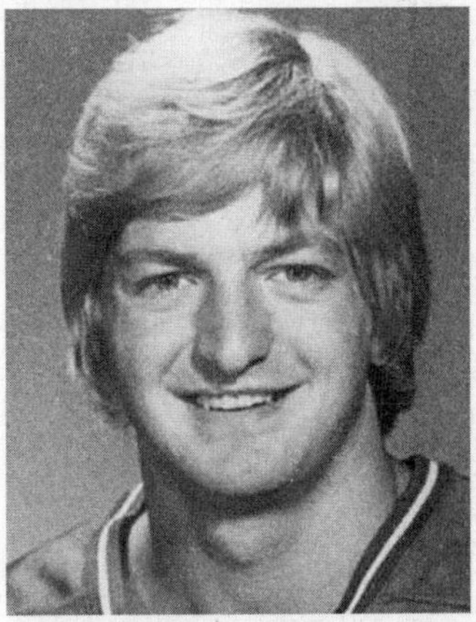

Pierre Mondou

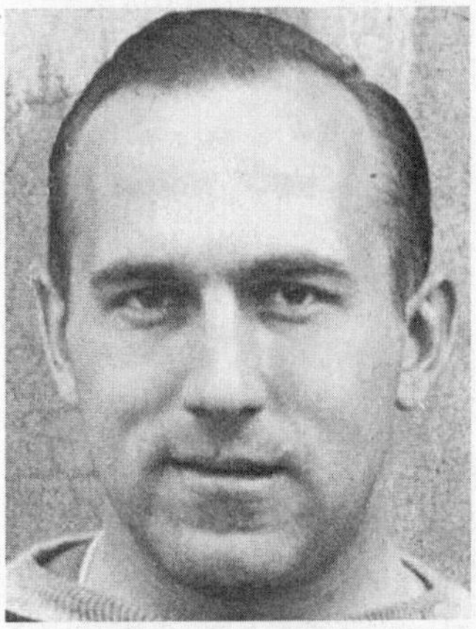

Howie Morenz

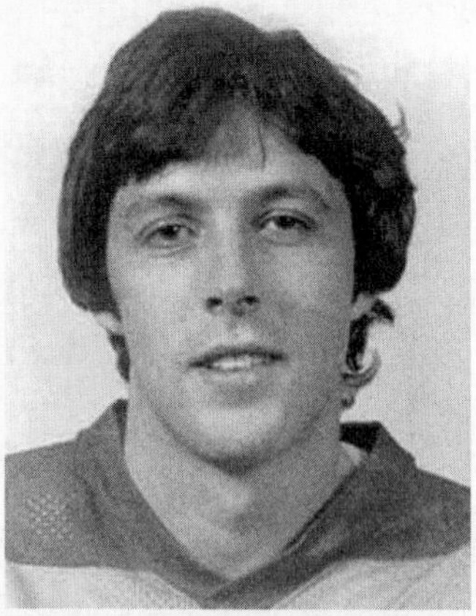

Angelo Moretto

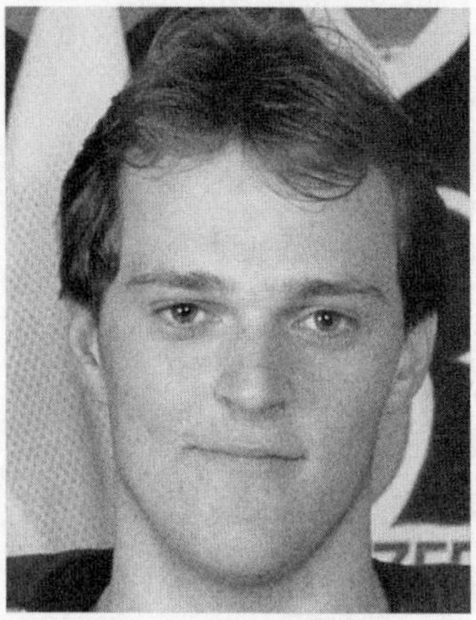

Glenn Mulvenna

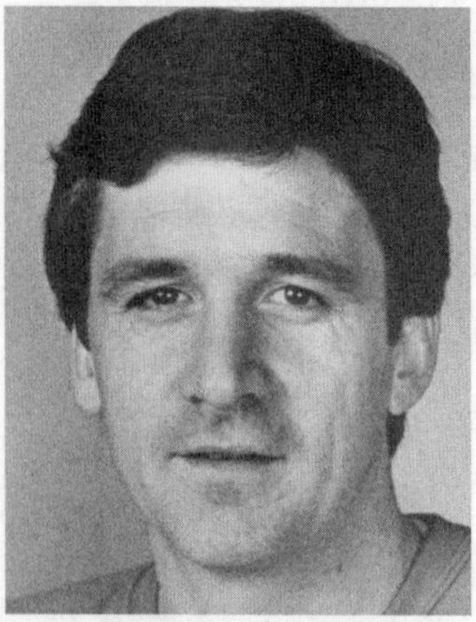

Terry Murray

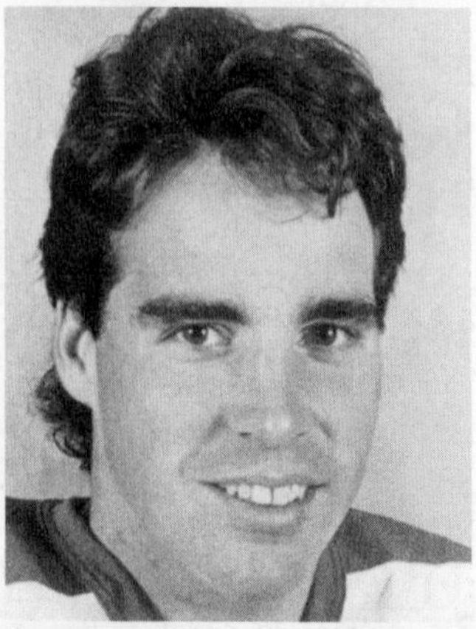

Todd Nelson

Name	NHL Teams	NHL Seasons	Regular Schedule GP	G	A	TP	PIM	Playoffs GP	G	A	TP	PIM	NHL Cup Wins	First NHL Season	Last NHL Season
‡ Melanson, Dean	Buf., Wsh.	2	9	0	0	0	8	....	....	....	....	....	....	1994-95	2001-02
Melin, Roger	Min.	2	3	0	0	0	0	....	....	....	....	....	....	1980-81	1981-82
Mellor, Tom	Det.	2	26	2	4	6	25	....	....	....	....	....	....	1973-74	1974-75
• Melnyk, Gerry	Det., Chi., St.L.	6	269	39	77	116	34	53	6	6	12	6	....	1955-56	1967-68
Melnyk, Larry	Bos., Edm., NYR, Van.	10	432	11	63	74	686	66	2	9	11	127	2	1980-81	1989-90
Melrose, Barry	Wpg., Tor., Det.	6	300	10	23	33	728	7	0	2	2	38	....	1979-80	1985-86
Menard, Hillary	Chi.	1	1	0	0	0	0	....	....	....	....	....	....	1953-54	1953-54
Menard, Howie	Det., L.A., Chi., Oak.	4	151	23	42	65	87	19	3	7	10	36	....	1963-64	1969-70
Mercredi, Vic	Atl.	1	2	0	0	0	0	....	....	....	....	....	....	1974-75	1974-75
Meredith, Greg	Cgy.	2	38	6	4	10	8	5	3	1	4	4	....	1980-81	1982-83
Merkosky, Glenn	Hfd., N.J., Det.	5	66	5	12	17	22	....	....	....	....	....	....	1981-82	1989-90
• Meronek, Bill	Mtl.	2	19	5	8	13	0	1	0	0	0	0	....	1939-40	1942-43
Merrick, Wayne	St.L., Cal., Cle., NYI	12	774	191	265	456	303	102	19	30	49	30	4	1972-73	1983-84
• Merrill, Horace	Ott.	2	8	0	0	0	3	....	....	....	....	....	1	1917-18	1919-20
Mertzig, Jan	NYR	1	23	0	2	2	8	....	....	....	....	....	....	1998-99	1998-99
Messier, Joby	NYR	3	25	0	4	4	24	....	....	....	....	....	....	1992-93	1994-95
Messier, Mitch	Min.	4	20	0	2	2	11	....	....	....	....	....	....	1987-88	1990-91
Messier, Paul	Col.	1	9	0	0	0	4	....	....	....	....	....	....	1978-79	1978-79
Metcalfe, Scott	Edm., Buf.	3	19	1	2	3	18	....	....	....	....	....	....	1987-88	1989-90
‡ Metropolit, Glen	Wsh., T.B.	4	103	10	37	47	26	3	0	0	0	2	....	1999-00	2002-03
Metz, Don	Tor.	9	172	20	35	55	42	42	7	8	15	12	5	1938-39	1948-49
• Metz, Nick	Tor.	12	518	131	119	250	149	76	19	20	39	31	4	1934-35	1947-48
Michaluk, Art	Chi.	1	5	0	0	0	0	....	....	....	....	....	....	1947-48	1947-48
Michaluk, John	Chi.	1	1	0	0	0	0	....	....	....	....	....	....	1950-51	1950-51
Michayluk, Dave	Phi., Pit.	3	14	2	6	8	8	7	1	1	2	0	1	1981-82	1991-92
Micheletti, Joe	St.L., Col.	3	158	11	60	71	114	11	1	11	12	10	....	1979-80	1981-82
Micheletti, Pat	Min.	1	12	2	0	2	8	....	....	....	....	....	....	1987-88	1987-88
• Mickey, Larry	Chi., NYR, Tor., Mtl., L.A., Phi., Buf.	11	292	39	53	92	160	9	1	0	1	10	....	1964-65	1974-75
• Mickoski, Nick	NYR, Chi., Det., Bos.	13	703	158	185	343	319	18	1	6	7	6	....	1947-48	1959-60
Middendorf, Max	Que., Edm.	4	13	2	4	6	6	....	....	....	....	....	....	1986-87	1990-91
Middleton, Rick	NYR, Bos.	14	1005	448	540	988	157	114	45	55	100	19	....	1974-75	1987-88
Miehm, Kevin	St.L.	2	22	1	4	5	8	2	0	1	1	0	....	1992-93	1993-94
Migay, Rudy	Tor.	10	418	59	92	151	293	15	1	0	1	20	....	1949-50	1959-60
‡ Mika, Petr	NYI	1	3	0	0	0	0	....	....	....	....	....	....	1999-00	1999-00
Mikita, Stan	Chi.	22	1394	541	926	1467	1270	155	59	91	150	169	1	1958-59	1979-80
Mikkelson, Bill	L.A., NYI, Wsh.	4	147	4	18	22	105	....	....	....	....	....	....	1971-72	1976-77
Mikol, Jim	Tor., NYR	2	34	1	4	5	8	....	....	....	....	....	....	1962-63	1964-65
Mikulchik, Oleg	Wpg., Ana.	3	37	0	3	3	33	....	....	....	....	....	....	1993-94	1995-96
Milbury, Mike	Bos.	12	754	49	189	238	1552	86	4	24	28	219	....	1975-76	1986-87
• Milks, Hib	Pit., Phi., NYR, Ott.	8	317	87	41	128	179	11	0	0	0	2	....	1925-26	1932-33
Millar, Craig	Edm., Nsh., T.B.	5	114	8	14	22	73	....	....	....	....	....	....	1996-97	2000-01
• Millar, Hugh	Det.	1	4	0	0	0	0	1	0	0	0	0	....	1946-47	1946-47
Millar, Mike	Hfd., Wsh., Bos., Tor.	5	78	18	18	36	12	....	....	....	....	....	....	1986-87	1990-91
Millen, Corey	NYR, L.A., N.J., Dal., Cgy.	8	335	90	119	209	236	47	5	7	12	22	....	1989-90	1996-97
• Miller, Bill	Mtl.M., Mtl.	3	95	7	3	10	16	12	0	0	0	0	1	1934-35	1936-37
Miller, Bob	Bos., Col., L.A.	6	404	75	119	194	220	36	4	7	11	27	....	1977-78	1984-85
Miller, Brad	Buf., Ott., Cgy.	6	82	1	5	6	321	....	....	....	....	....	....	1988-89	1993-94
• Miller, Earl	Chi., Tor.	5	109	19	14	33	124	10	1	0	1	6	1	1927-28	1931-32
Miller, Jack	Chi.	2	17	0	0	0	4	....	....	....	....	....	....	1949-50	1950-51
Miller, Jason	N.J.	3	6	0	0	0	0	....	....	....	....	....	....	1990-91	1992-93
Miller, Jay	Bos., L.A.	7	446	40	44	84	1723	48	2	3	5	243	....	1985-86	1991-92
Miller, Kelly	NYR, Wsh.	15	1057	181	282	463	512	119	20	34	54	65	....	1984-85	1998-99
Miller, Paul	Col.	1	3	0	3	3	0	....	....	....	....	....	....	1981-82	1981-82
Miller, Perry	Det.	4	217	10	51	61	387	....	....	....	....	....	....	1977-78	1980-81
Miller, Tom	Det., NYI	4	118	16	25	41	34	....	....	....	....	....	....	1970-71	1974-75
Miller, Warren	NYR, Hfd.	4	262	40	50	90	137	6	1	0	1	0	....	1979-80	1982-83
Mills, Craig	Wpg., Chi.	3	31	0	5	5	36	1	0	0	0	0	....	1995-96	1998-99
Miner, John	Edm.	1	14	2	3	5	16	....	....	....	....	....	....	1987-88	1987-88
Minor, Gerry	Van.	5	140	11	21	32	173	12	1	3	4	25	....	1979-80	1983-84
Mironov, Dmitri	Tor., Pit., Ana., Det., Wsh.	11	556	54	206	260	568	75	10	26	36	48	1	1991-92	2001-02
Miszuk, John	Det., Chi., Phi., Min.	6	237	7	39	46	232	19	0	3	3	19	....	1963-64	1969-70
Mitchell, Bill	Det.	1	1	0	0	0	0	....	....	....	....	....	....	1963-64	1963-64
• Mitchell, Herb	Bos.	2	44	6	0	6	36	....	....	....	....	....	....	1924-25	1925-26
‡ Mitchell, Jeff	Dal.	1	7	0	0	0	7	....	....	....	....	....	....	1997-98	1997-98
Mitchell, Red	Chi.	3	83	4	5	9	67	....	....	....	....	....	....	1941-42	1944-45
Mitchell, Roy	Min.	1	3	0	0	0	0	....	....	....	....	....	....	1992-93	1992-93
• Moe, Bill	NYR	5	261	11	42	53	163	1	0	0	0	0	....	1944-45	1948-49
Moffat, Lyle	Tor., Wpg.	3	97	12	16	28	51	....	....	....	....	....	....	1972-73	1979-80
• Moffat, Ron	Det.	3	37	1	1	2	8	7	0	0	0	0	....	1932-33	1934-35
Moger, Sandy	Bos., L.A.	5	236	41	38	79	212	5	2	2	4	12	....	1994-95	1998-99
Moher, Mike	N.J.	1	9	0	1	1	28	....	....	....	....	....	....	1982-83	1982-83
Mohns, Doug	Bos., Chi., Min., Atl., Wsh.	22	1390	248	462	710	1250	94	14	36	50	122	....	1953-54	1974-75
Mohns, Lloyd	NYR	1	1	0	0	0	0	....	....	....	....	....	....	1943-44	1943-44
Mokosak, Carl	Cgy., L.A., Phi., Pit., Bos.	6	83	11	15	26	170	1	0	0	0	0	....	1981-82	1988-89
Mokosak, John	Det.	2	41	0	2	2	96	....	....	....	....	....	....	1988-89	1989-90
Molin, Lars	Van.	3	172	33	65	98	37	19	2	9	11	7	....	1981-82	1983-84
Moller, Mike	Buf., Edm.	7	134	15	28	43	41	3	0	1	1	0	....	1980-81	1986-87
Moller, Randy	Que., NYR, Buf., Fla.	14	815	45	180	225	1692	78	6	16	22	197	....	1981-82	1994-95
Molloy, Mitch	Buf.	1	2	0	0	0	10	....	....	....	....	....	....	1989-90	1989-90
• Molyneaux, Larry	NYR	2	45	0	1	1	20	10	0	0	0	8	....	1937-38	1938-39
Momesso, Sergio	Mtl., St.L., Van., Tor., NYR	13	710	152	193	345	1557	119	18	26	44	311	....	1983-84	1996-97
Monahan, Garry	Mtl., Det., L.A., Tor., Van.	12	748	116	169	285	484	22	3	1	4	13	....	1967-68	1978-79
Monahan, Hartland	Cal., NYR, Wsh., Pit., L.A., St.L.	7	334	61	80	141	163	6	0	0	0	4	....	1973-74	1980-81
• Mondou, Armand	Mtl.	12	386	47	71	118	99	32	3	5	8	12	2	1928-29	1939-40
Mondou, Pierre	Mtl.	9	548	194	262	456	179	69	17	28	45	26	3	1976-77	1984-85
Mongeau, Michel	St.L., T.B.	4	54	6	19	25	10	2	0	1	1	0	....	1989-90	1992-93
Mongrain, Bob	Buf., L.A.	6	81	13	14	27	14	11	1	2	3	2	....	1979-80	1985-86
Monteith, Hank	Det.	3	77	5	12	17	6	4	0	0	0	0	....	1968-69	1970-71
‡ Montgomery, Jim	St.L., Mtl., Phi., S.J., Dal.	6	122	9	25	34	80	8	1	0	1	2	....	1993-94	2002-03
‡ Moore, Barrie	Buf., Edm., Wsh.	3	39	2	6	8	18	....	....	....	....	....	....	1995-96	1999-00
Moore, Dickie	Mtl., Tor., St.L.	14	719	261	347	608	652	135	46	64	110	122	6	1951-52	1967-68
• Moran, Amby	Mtl., Chi.	2	35	1	1	2	24	....	....	....	....	....	....	1926-27	1927-28
‡ Moravec, David	Buf.	1	1	0	0	0	0	....	....	....	....	....	....	1999-00	1999-00
More, Jay	NYR, Min., S.J., Phx., Chi., Nsh.	10	406	18	54	72	702	31	0	6	6	45	....	1988-89	1998-99
• Morenz, Howie	Mtl., Chi., NYR	14	550	271	201	472	546	39	13	9	22	58	3	1923-24	1936-37
Moretto, Angelo	Cle.	1	5	1	2	3	2	....	....	....	....	....	....	1976-77	1976-77
• Morin, Pete	Mtl.	1	31	10	12	22	7	1	0	0	0	0	....	1941-42	1941-42
• Morin, Stephane	Que., Van.	5	90	16	39	55	52	....	....	....	....	....	....	1989-90	1993-94
Morisset, Dave	Fla.	1	4	0	0	0	5	....	....	....	....	....	....	2001-02	2001-02
Morissette, Dave	Mtl.	2	11	0	0	0	57	....	....	....	....	....	....	1998-99	1999-00
• Morris, Bernie	Bos.	1	6	1	0	1	0	....	....	....	....	....	....	1924-25	1924-25
Morris, Jon	N.J., S.J., Bos.	6	103	16	33	49	47	11	1	7	8	25	....	1988-89	1993-94
• Morris, Moe	Tor., NYR	4	135	13	29	42	58	18	4	2	6	16	1	1943-44	1948-49
Morrison, Dave	L.A., Van.	4	39	3	3	6	4	....	....	....	....	....	....	1980-81	1984-85
Morrison, Don	Det., Chi.	3	112	18	28	46	12	3	0	1	1	0	....	1947-48	1950-51
Morrison, Doug	Bos.	4	23	7	3	10	15	....	....	....	....	....	....	1979-80	1984-85
Morrison, Gary	Phi.	3	43	1	15	16	70	5	0	1	1	2	....	1979-80	1981-82
Morrison, George	St.L.	2	115	17	21	38	13	3	0	0	0	0	....	1970-71	1971-72
Morrison, Jim	Bos., Tor., Det., NYR, Pit.	12	704	40	160	200	542	36	0	12	12	38	....	1951-52	1970-71
• Morrison, John	NYA	1	18	0	0	0	0	....	....	....	....	....	....	1925-26	1925-26
Morrison, Kevin	Col.	1	41	4	11	15	23	....	....	....	....	....	....	1979-80	1979-80
Morrison, Lew	Phi., Atl., Wsh., Pit.	9	564	39	52	91	107	17	0	0	0	2	....	1969-70	1977-78
Morrison, Mark	NYR	2	10	1	1	2	0	....	....	....	....	....	....	1981-82	1983-84
• Morrison, Rod	Det.	1	34	8	7	15	4	3	0	0	0	0	....	1947-48	1947-48
Morrow, Ken	NYI	10	550	17	88	105	309	127	11	22	33	97	4	1979-80	1988-89
Morrow, Scott	Cgy.	1	4	0	0	0	0	....	....	....	....	....	....	1994-95	1994-95
Morton, Dean	Det.	1	1	1	0	1	2	....	....	....	....	....	....	1989-90	1989-90
Mortson, Gus	Tor., Chi., Det.	13	797	46	152	198	1380	54	5	8	13	68	4	1946-47	1958-59
Mosdell, Ken	Bro., Mtl., Chi.	16	693	141	168	309	475	80	16	13	29	48	4	1941-42	1958-59
• Mosienko, Bill	Chi.	14	711	258	282	540	121	22	10	4	14	15	....	1941-42	1954-55
Mott, Morris	Cal.	3	199	18	32	50	49	....	....	....	....	....	....	1972-73	1974-75
• Motter, Alex	Bos., Det.	8	255	39	64	103	135	41	3	9	12	41	1	1934-35	1942-43
Moxey, Jim	Cal., Cle., L.A.	3	127	22	27	49	59	....	....	....	....	....	....	1974-75	1976-77
Mulhern, Richard	Atl., L.A., Tor., Wpg.	6	303	27	93	120	217	7	0	3	3	5	....	1975-76	1980-81
Mulhern, Ryan	Wsh.	1	3	0	0	0	0	....	....	....	....	....	....	1997-98	1997-98

			Regular Schedule					Playoffs					NHL	First	Last
Name	NHL Teams	NHL Seasons	GP	G	A	TP	PIM	GP	G	A	TP	PIM	Cup Wins	NHL Season	NHL Season
Mullen, Brian	Wpg., NYR, S.J., NYI	11	832	260	362	622	414	62	12	18	30	30	....	1982-83	1992-93
Mullen, Joe	St.L., Cgy., Pit., Bos.	17	1062	502	561	1063	241	143	60	46	106	42	3	1979-80	1996-97
Muller, Kirk	N.J., Mtl., NYI, Tor., Fla., Dal.	19	1349	357	602	959	1223	127	33	36	69	153	1	1984-85	2002-03
Muloin, Wayne	Det., Oak., Cal., Min.	3	147	3	21	24	93	11	0	0	0	2	....	1963-64	1970-71
Mulvenna, Glenn	Pit., Phi.	2	2	0	0	0	4	....	....	....	....	....	....	1991-92	1992-93
Mulvey, Grant	Chi., N.J.	10	586	149	135	284	816	42	10	5	15	70	....	1974-75	1983-84
Mulvey, Paul	Wsh., Pit., L.A.	4	225	30	51	81	613	....	....	....	....	....	....	1978-79	1981-82
• Mummery, Harry	Tor., Que., Mtl., Ham.	6	106	33	19	52	226	2	1	1	2	17	....	1917-18	1922-23
Muni, Craig	Tor., Edm., Chi., Buf., Wpg., Pit., Dal.	16	819	28	119	147	775	113	0	17	17	108	3	1981-82	1997-98
• Munro, Dunc	Mtl.M., Mtl.	8	239	28	18	46	172	21	2	2	4	18	1	1924-25	1931-32
• Munro, Gerry	Mtl.M., Tor.	2	34	1	0	1	37	....	....	....	....	....	....	1924-25	1925-26
Murdoch, Bob	Mtl., L.A., Atl., Cgy.	12	757	60	218	278	764	69	4	18	22	92	2	1970-71	1981-82
Murdoch, Bob	Cal., Cle., St.L.	4	260	72	85	157	127	....	....	....	....	....	....	1975-76	1978-79
Murdoch, Don	NYR, Edm., Det.	6	320	121	117	238	155	24	10	8	18	16	....	1976-77	1981-82
• Murdoch, Murray	NYR	11	508	84	108	192	197	55	9	12	21	28	2	1926-27	1936-37
Murphy, Brian	Det.	1	1	0	0	0	0	....	....	....	....	....	....	1974-75	1974-75
Murphy, Gord	Phi., Bos., Fla., Atl.	14	862	85	238	323	668	53	3	16	19	35	....	1988-89	2001-02
Murphy, Joe	Det., Edm., Chi., St.L., S.J., Bos., Wsh.	15	779	233	295	528	810	120	34	43	77	185	1	1986-87	2000-01
Murphy, Larry	L.A., Wsh., Min., Pit., Tor., Det.	21	1615	287	929	1216	1084	215	37	115	152	201	4	1980-81	2000-01
Murphy, Mike	St.L., NYR, L.A.	12	831	238	318	556	514	66	13	23	36	54	....	1971-72	1982-83
Murphy, Rob	Van., Ott., L.A.	7	125	9	12	21	152	4	0	0	0	2	....	1987-88	1993-94
Murphy, Ron	NYR, Chi., Det., Bos.	18	889	205	274	479	460	53	7	8	15	26	1	1952-53	1969-70
Murray, Allan	NYA	7	271	5	9	14	163	14	0	0	0	10	....	1933-34	1939-40
Murray, Bob	Atl., Van.	4	194	6	16	22	98	10	1	1	2	15	....	1973-74	1976-77
Murray, Bob	Chi.	15	1008	132	382	514	873	112	19	37	56	106	....	1975-76	1989-90
Murray, Chris	Mtl., Hfd., Car., Ott., Chi., Dal.	6	242	16	18	34	550	15	1	0	1	12	....	1994-95	1999-00
Murray, Jim	L.A.	1	30	0	2	2	14	....	....	....	....	....	....	1967-68	1967-68
Murray, Ken	Tor., NYI, Det., K.C.	5	106	1	10	11	135	....	....	....	....	....	....	1969-70	1975-76
• Murray, Leo	Mtl.	1	6	0	0	0	2	....	....	....	....	....	....	1932-33	1932-33
‡ Murray, Mike	Phi.	1	1	0	0	0	0	....	....	....	....	....	....	1987-88	1987-88
Murray, Pat	Phi.	2	25	3	1	4	15	....	....	....	....	....	....	1990-91	1991-92
Murray, Randy	Tor.	1	3	0	0	0	2	....	....	....	....	....	....	1969-70	1969-70
Murray, Rob	Wsh., Wpg., Phx.	8	107	4	15	19	111	9	0	0	0	18	....	1989-90	1998-99
Murray, Terry	Cal., Phi., Det., Wsh.	8	302	4	76	80	199	18	2	2	4	10	....	1972-73	1981-82
Murray, Troy	Chi., Wpg., Ott., Pit., Col.	15	915	230	354	584	875	113	17	26	43	145	1	1981-82	1995-96
Murzyn, Dana	Hfd., Cgy., Van.	14	838	52	152	204	1571	82	9	10	19	166	1	1985-86	1998-99
Musil, Frantisek	Min., Cgy., Ott., Edm.	15	797	34	106	140	1241	42	2	4	6	47	....	1986-87	2000-01
Myers, Hap	Buf.	1	13	0	0	0	6	....	....	....	....	....	....	1970-71	1970-71
Myles, Vic	NYR	1	45	6	9	15	57	....	....	....	....	....	....	1942-43	1942-43

N

Name	NHL Teams	NHL Seasons	GP	G	A	TP	PIM	GP	G	A	TP	PIM	Cup Wins	First NHL Season	Last NHL Season
‡ Nabokov, Dmitri	Chi., NYI	3	55	11	13	24	28	....	....	....	....	....	....	1997-98	1999-00
Nachbaur, Don	Hfd., Edm., Phi.	8	223	23	46	69	465	11	1	1	2	24	....	1980-81	1989-90
Nahrgang, Jim	Det.	3	57	5	12	17	34	....	....	....	....	....	....	1974-75	1976-77
Namestnikov, John	Van., NYI, Nsh.	6	43	0	9	9	24	2	0	0	0	2	....	1993-94	1999-00
Nanne, Lou	Min.	11	635	68	157	225	356	32	4	10	14	8	....	1967-68	1977-78
Nantais, Rich	Min.	3	63	5	4	9	79	....	....	....	....	....	....	1974-75	1976-77
Napier, Mark	Mtl., Min., Edm., Buf.	11	767	235	306	541	157	82	18	24	42	11	2	1978-79	1988-89
Naslund, Mats	Mtl., Bos.	9	651	251	383	634	111	102	35	57	92	33	1	1982-83	1994-95
Nattrass, Ralph	Chi.	4	223	18	38	56	308	....	....	....	....	....	....	1946-47	1949-50
Nattress, Ric	Mtl., St.L., Cgy., Tor., Phi.	11	536	29	135	164	377	67	5	10	15	60	1	1982-83	1992-93
Natyshak, Mike	Que.	1	4	0	0	0	0	....	....	....	....	....	....	1987-88	1987-88
‡ Ndur, Rumun	Buf., NYR, Atl.	4	69	2	3	5	137	....	....	....	....	....	....	1996-97	1999-00
Neaton, Pat	Pit.	1	9	1	1	2	12	....	....	....	....	....	....	1993-94	1993-94
Nechayev, Viktor	L.A.	1	3	1	0	1	0	....	....	....	....	....	....	1982-83	1982-83
Nedomansky, Vaclav	Det., NYR, St.L.	6	421	122	156	278	88	7	3	5	8	0	....	1977-78	1982-83
‡ Nedved, Zdenek	Tor.	3	31	4	6	10	14	....	....	....	....	....	....	1994-95	1996-97
Needham, Mike	Pit., Dal.	3	86	9	5	14	16	14	2	0	2	4	1	1991-92	1993-94
Neely, Bob	Tor., Col.	5	283	39	59	98	266	26	5	7	12	15	....	1973-74	1977-78
Neely, Cam	Van., Bos.	13	726	395	299	694	1241	93	57	32	89	168	....	1983-84	1995-96
Neilson, Jim	NYR, Cal., Cle.	16	1023	69	299	368	904	65	1	17	18	61	....	1962-63	1977-78
Nelson, Gordie	Tor.	1	3	0	0	0	11	....	....	....	....	....	....	1969-70	1969-70
‡ Nelson, Jeff	Wsh., Nsh.	3	52	3	8	11	20	3	0	0	0	4	....	1994-95	1998-99
Nelson, Todd	Pit., Wsh.	2	3	1	0	1	2	4	0	0	0	0	....	1991-92	1993-94
‡ Nemchinov, Sergei	NYR, Van., NYI, N.J.	11	761	152	193	345	251	105	11	20	31	24	2	1991-92	2001-02
Nemeth, Steve	NYR	1	12	2	0	2	2	....	....	....	....	....	....	1987-88	1987-88
‡ Nemirovsky, David	Fla.	4	91	16	22	38	42	3	1	0	1	0	....	1995-96	1998-99
Nesterenko, Eric	Tor., Chi.	21	1219	250	324	574	1273	124	13	24	37	127	1	1951-52	1971-72
Nethery, Lance	NYR, Edm.	2	41	11	14	25	14	14	5	3	8	9	....	1980-81	1981-82
Neufeld, Ray	Hfd., Wpg., Bos.	11	595	157	200	357	816	28	8	6	14	55	....	1979-80	1989-90
• Neville, Mike	Tor., NYA	3	65	5	5	10	14	2	0	0	0	0	....	1924-25	1930-31
Nevin, Bob	Tor., NYR, Min., L.A.	18	1128	307	419	726	211	84	16	18	34	24	2	1957-58	1975-76
Newberry, John	Mtl., Hfd.	4	22	0	4	4	6	2	0	0	0	0	....	1982-83	1985-86
Newell, Rick	Det.	2	6	0	0	0	0	....	....	....	....	....	....	1972-73	1973-74
Newman, Dan	NYR, Mtl., Edm.	4	126	17	24	41	63	3	0	0	0	4	....	1976-77	1979-80
• Newman, John	Det.	1	8	1	1	2	0	....	....	....	....	....	....	1930-31	1930-31
Nicholls, Bernie	L.A., NYR, Edm., N.J., Chi., S.J.	18	1127	475	734	1209	1292	118	42	72	114	164	....	1981-82	1998-99
Nicholson, Al	Bos.	2	19	0	1	1	4	....	....	....	....	....	....	1955-56	1956-57
• Nicholson, Ed	Det.	1	1	0	0	0	0	....	....	....	....	....	....	1947-48	1947-48
• Nicholson, Hickey	Chi.	1	2	1	0	1	0	....	....	....	....	....	....	1937-38	1937-38
Nicholson, Neil	Oak., NYI	4	39	3	1	4	23	2	0	0	0	0	....	1969-70	1977-78
Nicholson, Paul	Wsh.	3	62	4	8	12	18	....	....	....	....	....	....	1974-75	1976-77
Nicolson, Graeme	Bos., Col., NYR	3	52	2	7	9	60	....	....	....	....	....	....	1978-79	1982-83
Nieckar, Barry	Hfd., Cgy., Ana.	4	8	0	0	0	21	....	....	....	....	....	....	1992-93	1997-98
Niekamp, Jim	Det.	2	29	0	2	2	37	....	....	....	....	....	....	1970-71	1971-72
Nielsen, Jeff	NYR, Ana., Min.	5	252	20	27	47	70	4	0	0	0	2	....	1996-97	2000-01
Nielsen, Kirk	Bos.	1	6	0	0	0	0	....	....	....	....	....	....	1997-98	1997-98
‡ Niemi, Antti-Jussi	Ana.	2	29	1	1	2	22	....	....	....	....	....	....	2000-01	2001-02
Nienhuis, Kraig	Bos.	3	87	20	16	36	39	2	0	0	0	14	....	1985-86	1987-88
• Nighbor, Frank	Ott., Tor.	13	349	139	98	237	249	20	4	9	13	13	4	1917-18	1929-30
Nigro, Frank	Tor.	2	68	8	18	26	39	3	0	0	0	2	....	1982-83	1983-84
‡ Nikulin, Igor	Ana.	1	....	....	....	....	....	1	0	0	0	0	....	1996-97	1996-97
Nilan, Chris	Mtl., NYR, Bos.	13	688	110	115	225	3043	111	8	9	17	541	1	1979-80	1991-92
Nill, Jim	St.L., Van., Bos., Wpg., Det.	9	524	58	87	145	854	59	10	5	15	203	....	1981-82	1989-90
Nilsson, Kent	Atl., Cgy., Min., Edm.	9	553	264	422	686	116	59	11	41	52	14	1	1979-80	1994-95
Nilsson, Ulf	NYR	4	170	57	112	169	85	25	8	14	22	27	....	1978-79	1982-83
Nistico, Lou	Col.	1	3	0	0	0	0	....	....	....	....	....	....	1977-78	1977-78
• Noble, Reg	Tor., Mtl.M., Det.	16	510	168	106	274	916	18	2	2	4	33	3	1917-18	1932-33
Noel, Claude	Wsh.	1	7	0	0	0	0	....	....	....	....	....	....	1979-80	1979-80
• Nolan, Paddy	Tor.	1	2	0	0	0	0	....	....	....	....	....	....	1921-22	1921-22
Nolan, Ted	Det., Pit.	3	78	6	16	22	105	....	....	....	....	....	....	1981-82	1985-86
Nolet, Simon	Phi., K.C., Pit., Col.	10	562	150	182	332	187	34	6	3	9	8	1	1967-68	1976-77
Noonan, Brian	Chi., NYR, St.L., Van., Phx.	12	629	116	159	275	518	71	17	19	36	77	1	1987-88	1998-99
Nordmark, Robert	St.L., Van.	4	236	13	70	83	254	7	3	2	5	8	....	1987-88	1990-91
‡ Nordstrom, Peter	Bos.	1	2	0	0	0	0	....	....	....	....	....	....	1998-99	1998-99
Noris, Joe	Pit., St.L., Buf.	3	55	2	5	7	22	....	....	....	....	....	....	1971-72	1973-74
‡ Norris, Dwayne	Que., Ana.	3	20	2	4	6	8	....	....	....	....	....	....	1993-94	1995-96
Norrish, Rod	Min.	2	21	3	3	6	2	....	....	....	....	....	....	1973-74	1974-75
• Northcott, Baldy	Mtl.M., Chi.	11	446	133	112	245	273	31	8	5	13	14	1	1928-29	1938-39
Norton, Jeff	NYI, S.J., St.L., Edm., T.B., Fla., Pit., Bos.	15	799	52	332	384	615	65	4	21	25	89	....	1987-88	2001-02
Norwich, Craig	Wpg., St.L., Col.	2	104	17	58	75	60	....	....	....	....	....	....	1979-80	1980-81
Norwood, Lee	Que., Wsh., St.L., Det., N.J., Hfd., Cgy.	12	503	58	153	211	1099	65	6	22	28	171	....	1980-81	1993-94
Novy, Milan	Wsh.	1	73	18	30	48	16	2	0	0	0	0	....	1982-83	1982-83
Nowak, Hank	Pit., Det., Bos.	4	180	26	29	55	161	13	1	0	1	8	....	1973-74	1976-77
‡ Nurminen, Kai	L.A., Min.	2	69	17	11	28	24	....	....	....	....	....	....	1996-97	2000-01
Nykoluk, Mike	Tor.	1	32	3	1	4	20	....	....	....	....	....	....	1956-57	1956-57
Nylund, Gary	Tor., Chi., NYI	11	608	32	139	171	1235	24	0	6	6	63	....	1982-83	1992-93
• Nyrop, Bill	Mtl., Min.	4	207	12	51	63	101	35	1	7	8	22	3	1975-76	1981-82
Nystrom, Bob	NYI	14	900	235	278	513	1248	157	39	44	83	236	4	1972-73	1985-86

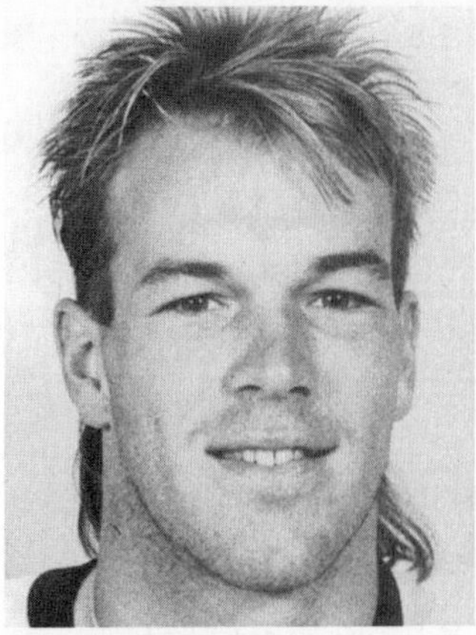

Kraig Nienhuis

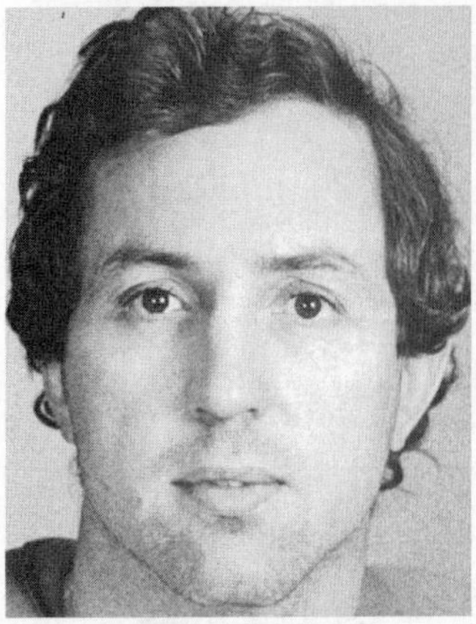

Milan Novy

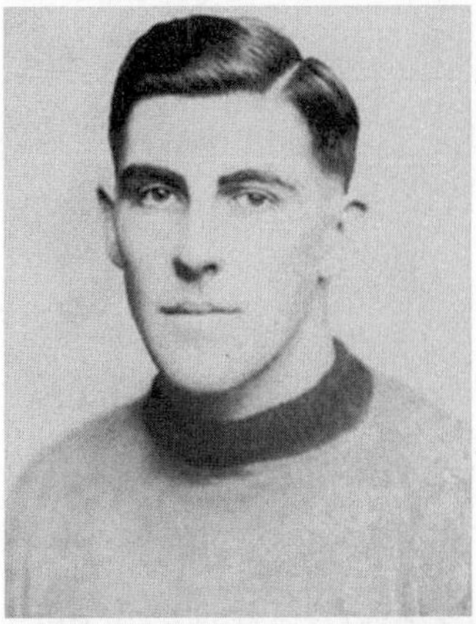

Russell Oatman

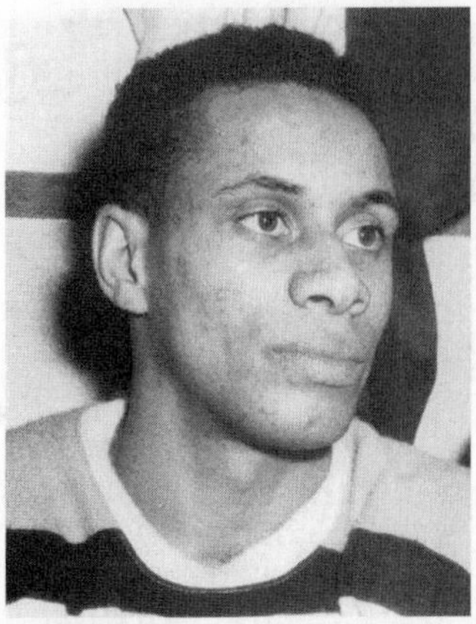

Willie O'Ree

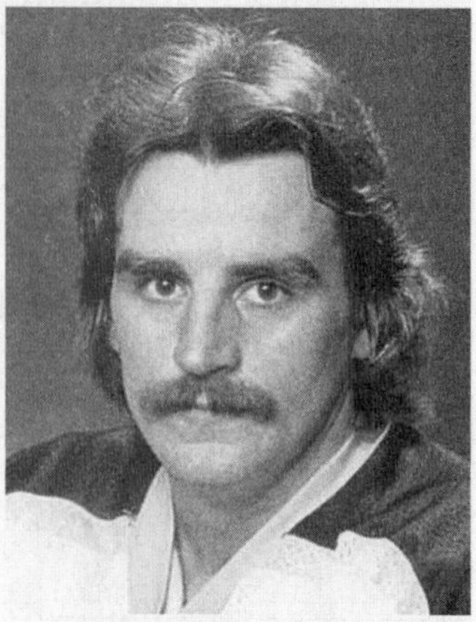

Clayton Pachal

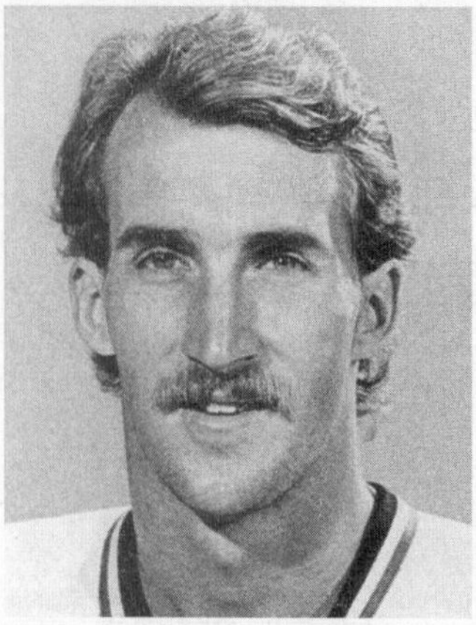

Steve Payne

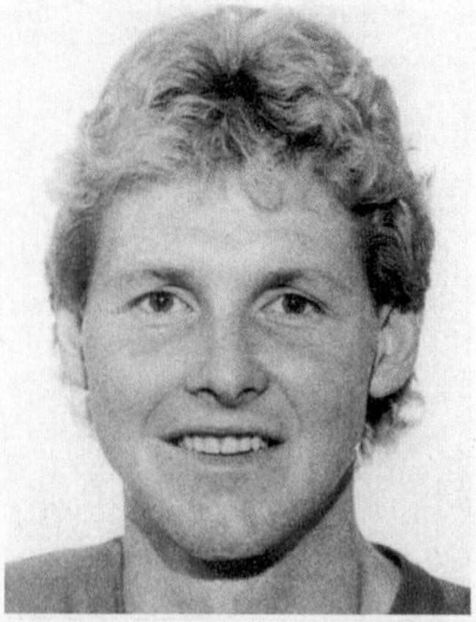

Lyle Phair

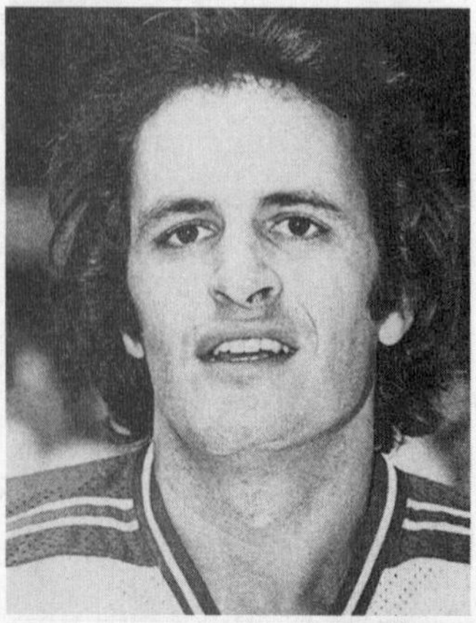

Pierre Plante

Name	NHL Teams	NHL Seasons	Regular Schedule GP	G	A	TP	PIM	Playoffs GP	G	A	TP	PIM	NHL Cup Wins	First NHL Season	Last NHL Season
O															
Oates, Adam	Det., St.L., Bos., Wsh., Phi., Ana., Edm.	19	1337	341	1079	1420	415	163	42	114	156	66	....	1985-86	2003-04
• Oatman, Russell	Det., Mtl.M., NYR	3	120	20	9	29	100	15	1	0	1	18	....	1926-27	1928-29
O'Brien, Dennis	Min., Col., Cle., Bos.	10	592	31	91	122	1017	34	1	2	3	101	....	1970-71	1979-80
O'Brien, Ellard	Bos.	1	2	0	0	0	0	....	....	....	....	....	....	1955-56	1955-56
O'Callahan, Jack	Chi., N.J.	7	389	27	104	131	541	32	4	11	15	41	....	1982-83	1988-89
O'Connell, Mike	Chi., Bos., Det.	13	860	105	334	439	605	82	8	24	32	64	....	1977-78	1989-90
• O'Connor, Buddy	Mtl., NYR	10	509	140	257	397	34	53	15	21	36	6	2	1941-42	1950-51
O'Connor, Myles	N.J., Ana.	4	43	3	4	7	69	....	....	....	....	....	....	1990-91	1993-94
Oddleifson, Chris	Bos., Van.	9	524	95	191	286	464	14	1	6	7	8	....	1972-73	1980-81
Odelein, Selmar	Edm.	3	18	0	2	2	35	....	....	....	....	....	....	1985-86	1988-89
Odgers, Jeff	S.J., Bos., Col., Atl.	12	821	75	70	145	2364	47	2	1	3	73	....	1991-92	2002-03
Odjick, Gino	Van., NYI, Phi., Mtl.	12	605	64	73	137	2567	44	4	1	5	142	....	1990-91	2001-02
O'Donnell, Fred	Bos.	2	115	15	11	26	98	5	0	1	1	5	....	1972-73	1973-74
O'Donoghue, Don	Oak., Cal.	3	125	18	17	35	35	3	0	0	0	0	....	1969-70	1971-72
Odrowski, Gerry	Det., Oak., St.L.	6	309	12	19	31	111	30	0	1	1	16	....	1960-61	1971-72
O'Dwyer, Bill	L.A., Bos.	5	120	9	13	22	108	10	0	0	0	2	....	1983-84	1989-90
O'Flaherty, Gerry	Tor., Van., Atl.	8	438	99	95	194	168	7	2	2	4	6	....	1971-72	1978-79
O'Flaherty, Peanuts	NYA, Bro.	2	21	5	1	6	0	....	....	....	....	....	....	1940-41	1941-42
Ogilvie, Brian	Chi., St.L.	6	90	15	21	36	29	....	....	....	....	....	....	1972-73	1978-79
• O'Grady, George	Mtl.W.	1	4	0	0	0	0	....	....	....	....	....	....	1917-18	1917-18
Ogrodnick, John	Det., Que., NYR	14	928	402	425	827	260	41	18	8	26	6	....	1979-80	1992-93
‡ Ojanen, Janne	N.J.	4	98	21	23	44	28	3	0	2	2	0	....	1988-89	1992-93
Okerlund, Todd	NYI	1	4	0	0	0	2	....	....	....	....	....	....	1987-88	1987-88
Oksiuta, Roman	Edm., Van., Ana., Pit.	4	153	46	41	87	100	10	2	3	5	0	....	1993-94	1996-97
‡ Olausson, Fredrik	Wpg., Edm., Ana., Pit., Det.	16	1022	147	434	581	450	71	6	23	29	28	1	1986-87	2002-03
Olczyk, Ed	Chi., Tor., Wpg., NYR, L.A., Pit.	16	1031	342	452	794	874	57	19	15	34	57	1	1984-85	1999-00
• Oliver, Harry	Bos., NYA	11	463	127	85	212	147	35	10	6	16	24	1	1926-27	1936-37
Oliver, Murray	Det., Bos., Tor., Min.	17	1127	274	454	728	320	35	9	16	25	10	....	1957-58	1974-75
Olmstead, Bert	Chi., Mtl., Tor.	14	848	181	421	602	884	115	16	43	59	101	5	1948-49	1961-62
Olsen, Darryl	Cgy.	1	1	0	0	0	0	....	....	....	....	....	....	1991-92	1991-92
Olson, Dennis	Det.	1	4	0	0	0	0	....	....	....	....	....	....	1957-58	1957-58
‡ Olsson, Christer	St.L., Ott.	2	56	4	12	16	24	3	0	0	0	0	....	1995-96	1996-97
• O'Neil, Jim	Bos., Mtl.	6	156	6	30	36	109	9	1	1	2	13	....	1933-34	1941-42
O'Neil, Paul	Van., Bos.	2	6	0	0	0	0	....	....	....	....	....	....	1973-74	1975-76
• O'Neill, Tom	Tor.	2	66	10	12	22	53	4	0	0	0	6	1	1943-44	1944-45
Orban, Bill	Chi., Min.	3	114	8	15	23	67	3	0	0	0	0	....	1967-68	1969-70
O'Ree, Willie	Bos.	2	45	4	10	14	26	....	....	....	....	....	....	1957-58	1960-61
O'Regan, Tom	Pit.	3	61	5	12	17	10	....	....	....	....	....	....	1983-84	1985-86
O'Reilly, Terry	Bos.	14	891	204	402	606	2095	108	25	42	67	335	....	1971-72	1984-85
Orlando, Gates	Buf.	3	98	18	26	44	51	5	0	4	4	14	....	1984-85	1986-87
• Orlando, Jimmy	Det.	6	199	6	25	31	375	36	0	9	9	105	1	1936-37	1942-43
Orleski, Dave	Mtl.	2	2	0	0	0	0	....	....	....	....	....	....	1980-81	1981-82
Orr, Bobby	Bos., Chi.	12	657	270	645	915	953	74	26	66	92	107	2	1966-67	1978-79
Osborne, Keith	St.L., T.B.	2	16	1	3	4	16	....	....	....	....	....	....	1989-90	1992-93
Osborne, Mark	Det., NYR, Tor., Wpg.	14	919	212	319	531	1152	87	12	16	28	141	....	1981-82	1994-95
Osburn, Randy	Tor., Phi.	2	27	0	2	2	0	....	....	....	....	....	....	1972-73	1974-75
O'Shea, Danny	Min., Chi., St.L.	5	369	64	115	179	265	39	3	7	10	61	....	1968-69	1972-73
O'Shea, Kevin	Buf., St.L.	3	134	13	18	31	85	12	2	1	3	10	....	1970-71	1972-73
Osiecki, Mark	Cgy., Ott., Wpg., Min.	2	93	3	11	14	43	....	....	....	....	....	....	1991-92	1992-93
O'Sullivan, Chris	Cgy., Van., Ana.	5	62	2	17	19	16	....	....	....	....	....	....	1996-97	2002-03
Otevrel, Jaroslav	S.J.	2	16	3	4	7	2	....	....	....	....	....	....	1992-93	1993-94
Otto, Joel	Cgy., Phi.	14	943	195	313	508	1934	122	27	47	74	207	1	1984-85	1997-98
Ouellette, Eddie	Chi.	1	43	3	2	5	11	1	0	0	0	0	....	1935-36	1935-36
Ouellette, Gerry	Bos.	1	34	5	4	9	0	....	....	....	....	....	....	1960-61	1960-61
Owchar, Dennis	Pit., Col.	6	288	30	85	115	200	10	1	1	2	8	....	1974-75	1979-80
• Owen, George	Bos.	5	183	44	33	77	151	21	2	5	7	25	1	1928-29	1932-33
P															
Pachal, Clayton	Bos., Col.	3	35	2	3	5	95	....	....	....	....	....	....	1976-77	1978-79
Paddock, John	Wsh., Phi., Que.	5	87	8	14	22	86	5	2	0	2	0	....	1975-76	1982-83
Paek, Jim	Pit., L.A., Ott.	5	217	5	29	34	155	27	1	4	5	8	2	1990-91	1994-95
Paiement, Rosaire	Phi., Van.	5	190	48	52	100	343	3	3	0	3	0	....	1967-68	1971-72
Paiement, Wilf	K.C., Col., Tor., Que., NYR, Buf., Pit.	14	946	356	458	814	1757	69	18	17	35	185	....	1974-75	1987-88
• Palangio, Pete	Mtl., Det., Chi.	5	71	13	10	23	28	7	0	0	0	0	1	1926-27	1937-38
Palazzari, Aldo	Bos., NYR	1	35	8	3	11	4	....	....	....	....	....	....	1943-44	1943-44
Palazzari, Doug	St.L.	4	108	18	20	38	23	2	0	0	0	0	....	1974-75	1978-79
Palmer, Brad	Min., Bos.	3	168	32	38	70	58	29	9	5	14	16	....	1980-81	1982-83
Palmer, Rob	Chi.	3	16	0	3	3	2	....	....	....	....	....	....	1973-74	1975-76
Palmer, Robert	L.A., N.J.	7	320	9	101	110	115	8	1	2	3	6	....	1977-78	1983-84
• Panagabko, Ed	Bos.	2	29	0	3	3	38	....	....	....	....	....	....	1955-56	1956-57
‡ Pankewicz, Greg	Ott., Cgy.	2	21	0	3	3	22	....	....	....	....	....	....	1993-94	1998-99
‡ Panteleev, Grigori	Bos., NYI	4	54	8	6	14	12	....	....	....	....	....	....	1992-93	1995-96
• Papike, Joe	Chi.	3	20	3	3	6	4	5	0	2	2	0	....	1940-41	1944-45
Pappin, Jim	Tor., Chi., Cal., Cle.	14	767	278	295	573	667	92	33	34	67	101	2	1963-64	1976-77
Paradise, Bob	Min., Atl., Pit., Wsh.	8	368	8	54	62	393	12	0	1	1	19	....	1971-72	1978-79
Pargeter, George	Mtl.	1	4	0	0	0	0	....	....	....	....	....	....	1946-47	1946-47
Parise, J.P.	Bos., Tor., Min., NYI, Cle.	14	890	238	356	594	706	86	27	31	58	87	....	1965-66	1978-79
Parizeau, Michel	St.L., Phi.	1	58	3	14	17	18	....	....	....	....	....	....	1971-72	1971-72
Park, Brad	NYR, Bos., Det.	17	1113	213	683	896	1429	161	35	90	125	217	....	1968-69	1984-85
Parker, Jeff	Buf., Hfd.	5	141	16	19	35	163	5	0	0	0	26	....	1986-87	1990-91
• Parkes, Ernie	Mtl.M.	1	17	0	0	0	2	....	....	....	....	....	....	1924-25	1924-25
Parks, Greg	NYI	3	23	1	2	3	6	2	0	0	0	0	....	1990-91	1992-93
• Parsons, George	Tor.	3	78	12	13	25	20	7	3	2	5	11	....	1936-37	1938-39
‡ Parssinen, Timo	Ana.	1	17	0	3	3	2	....	....	....	....	....	....	2001-02	2001-02
• Pasek, Dusan	Min.	1	48	4	10	14	30	2	1	0	1	0	....	1988-89	1988-89
Pasin, Dave	Bos., L.A.	2	76	18	19	37	50	3	0	1	1	0	....	1985-86	1988-89
Paslawski, Greg	Mtl., St.L., Wpg., Buf., Que., Phi., Cgy.	11	650	187	185	372	169	60	19	13	32	25	....	1983-84	1993-94
‡ Patera, Pavel	Dal., Min.	2	32	2	7	9	8	....	....	....	....	....	....	1999-00	2000-01
Paterson, Joe	Det., Phi., L.A., NYR	9	291	19	37	56	829	22	3	4	7	77	....	1980-81	1988-89
Paterson, Mark	Hfd.	4	29	3	3	6	33	....	....	....	....	....	....	1982-83	1985-86
Paterson, Rick	Chi.	9	430	50	43	93	136	61	7	10	17	51	....	1978-79	1986-87
Patey, Doug	Wsh.	3	45	4	2	6	8	....	....	....	....	....	....	1976-77	1978-79
Patey, Larry	Cal., St.L., NYR	12	717	153	163	316	631	40	8	10	18	57	....	1973-74	1984-85
Patrick, Craig	Cal., St.L., K.C., Wsh.	8	401	72	91	163	61	2	0	1	1	0	....	1971-72	1978-79
Patrick, Glenn	St.L., Cal., Cle.	4	38	2	3	5	72	....	....	....	....	....	....	1973-74	1976-77
• Patrick, Lester	NYR	1	1	0	0	0	2	....	....	....	....	....	....	1926-27	1926-27
• Patrick, Lynn	NYR	10	455	145	190	335	240	44	10	6	16	22	1	1934-35	1945-46
• Patrick, Muzz	NYR	5	166	5	26	31	133	25	4	0	4	34	1	1937-38	1945-46
Patrick, Steve	Buf., NYR, Que.	6	250	40	68	108	242	12	0	1	1	12	....	1980-81	1985-86
Patterson, Colin	Cgy., Buf.	10	504	96	109	205	239	85	12	17	29	57	1	1983-84	1992-93
Patterson, Dennis	K.C., Phi.	3	138	6	22	28	67	....	....	....	....	....	....	1974-75	1979-80
Patterson, Ed	Pit.	3	68	3	3	6	56	....	....	....	....	....	....	1993-94	1996-97
• Patterson, George	Tor., Mtl., NYA, Bos., Det., St.L.	9	284	51	27	78	218	3	0	0	0	2	....	1926-27	1934-35
• Paul, Butch	Det.	1	3	0	0	0	0	....	....	....	....	....	....	1964-65	1964-65
• Paulhus, Rollie	Mtl.	1	33	0	0	0	0	....	....	....	....	....	....	1925-26	1925-26
Pavelich, Mark	NYR, Min., S.J.	7	355	137	192	329	340	23	7	17	24	14	....	1981-82	1991-92
Pavelich, Marty	Det.	10	634	93	159	252	454	91	13	15	28	74	4	1947-48	1956-57
Pavese, Jim	St.L., NYR, Det., Hfd.	8	328	13	44	57	689	34	0	6	6	81	....	1981-82	1988-89
• Payer, Evariste	Mtl.	1	1	0	0	0	0	....	....	....	....	....	....	1917-18	1917-18
Payne, Davis	Bos.	2	22	0	1	1	14	....	....	....	....	....	....	1995-96	1996-97
Payne, Steve	Min.	10	613	228	238	466	435	71	35	35	70	60	....	1978-79	1987-88
Paynter, Kent	Chi., Wsh., Wpg., Ott.	7	37	1	3	4	69	4	0	0	0	10	....	1987-88	1993-94
Peake, Pat	Wsh.	5	134	28	41	69	105	13	2	2	4	20	....	1993-94	1997-98
• Pearson, Mel	NYR, Pit.	5	38	2	6	8	25	....	....	....	....	....	....	1959-60	1967-68
Pearson, Rob	Tor., Wsh., St.L.	6	269	56	54	110	645	33	4	2	6	94	....	1991-92	1996-97
Pearson, Scott	Tor., Que., Edm., Buf., NYI	10	292	56	42	98	615	10	2	0	2	14	....	1988-89	1999-00
Pedersen, Allen	Bos., Min., Hfd.	8	428	5	36	41	487	64	0	0	0	91	....	1986-87	1993-94
Pederson, Barry	Bos., Van., Pit., Hfd.	12	701	238	416	654	472	34	22	30	52	25	1	1980-81	1991-92
‡ Pederson, Mark	Mtl., Phi., S.J., Det.	5	169	35	50	85	77	2	0	0	0	0	....	1989-90	1993-94
Pederson, Tom	S.J., Tor.	5	240	20	49	69	142	24	1	11	12	10	....	1992-93	1996-97
• Peer, Bert	Det.	1	1	0	0	0	0	....	....	....	....	....	....	1939-40	1939-40

Name	NHL Teams	NHL Seasons	Regular Schedule GP	G	A	TP	PIM	Playoffs GP	G	A	TP	PIM	NHL Cup Wins	First NHL Season	Last NHL Season
Peirson, Johnny	Bos.	11	545	153	173	326	315	49	10	16	26	26	....	1946-47	1957-58
Pelensky, Perry	Chi.	1	4	0	0	0	5	....	....	....	....	....	....	1983-84	1983-84
Pelletier, Roger	Phi.	1	1	0	0	0	0	....	....	....	....	....	....	1967-68	1967-68
Peloffy, Andre	Wsh.	1	9	0	0	0	0	....	....	....	....	....	....	1974-75	1974-75
‡ Peltonen, Ville	S.J., Nsh.	5	175	18	42	60	40	....	....	....	....	....	....	1995-96	2000-01
Peluso, Mike	Chi., Ott., N.J., St.L., Cgy.	9	458	38	52	90	1951	62	3	4	7	107	1	1989-90	1997-98
Pelyk, Mike	Tor.	9	441	26	88	114	566	40	0	3	3	41	....	1967-68	1977-78
Penney, Chad	Ott.	1	3	0	0	0	2	....	....	....	....	....	....	1993-94	1993-94
Pennington, Cliff	Mtl., Bos.	3	101	17	42	59	6	....	....	....	....	....	....	1960-61	1962-63
Peplinski, Jim	Cgy.	11	711	161	263	424	1467	99	15	31	46	382	1	1980-81	1994-95
Perlini, Fred	Tor.	2	8	2	3	5	0	....	....	....	....	....	....	1981-82	1983-84
Perreault, Fern	NYR	2	3	0	0	0	0	....	....	....	....	....	....	1947-48	1949-50
Perreault, Gilbert	Buf.	17	1191	512	814	1326	500	90	33	70	103	44	....	1970-71	1986-87
Perry, Brian	Oak., Buf.	3	96	16	29	45	24	8	1	1	2	4	....	1968-69	1970-71
‡ Persson, Ricard	N.J., St.L., Ott.	7	229	10	44	54	262	26	1	3	4	59	....	1995-96	2001-02
Persson, Stefan	NYI	9	622	52	317	369	574	102	7	50	57	69	4	1977-78	1985-86
Pesut, George	Cal.	2	92	3	22	25	130	....	....	....	....	....	....	1974-75	1975-76
● Peters, Frank	NYR	1	43	0	0	0	59	4	0	0	0	2	....	1930-31	1930-31
Peters, Garry	Mtl., NYR, Phi., Bos.	8	311	34	34	68	261	9	2	2	4	31	1	1964-65	1971-72
Peters, Jimmy	Mtl., Bos., Det., Chi.	9	574	125	150	275	186	60	5	9	14	22	3	1945-46	1953-54
Peters, Jimmy	Det., L.A.	9	309	37	36	73	48	11	0	2	2	2	....	1964-65	1974-75
Peters, Steve	Col.	1	2	0	1	1	0	....	....	....	....	....	....	1979-80	1979-80
Peterson, Brent	Det., Buf., Van., Hfd.	11	620	72	141	213	484	31	4	4	8	65	....	1978-79	1988-89
‡ Peterson, Brent	T.B.	3	56	9	1	10	6	....	....	....	....	....	....	1996-97	1998-99
Petit, Michel	Van., NYR, Que., Tor., Cgy., L.A., T.B., Edm., Phi., Phx.	16	827	90	238	328	1839	19	0	2	2	61	....	1982-83	1997-98
‡ Petrenko, Sergei	Buf.	1	14	0	4	4	0	....	....	....	....	....	....	1993-94	1993-94
‡ Petrov, Oleg	Mtl., Nsh.	8	382	72	115	187	101	20	1	6	7	2	....	1992-93	2002-03
‡ Petrovicky, Robert	Hfd., Dal., St.L., T.B., NYI	8	208	27	38	65	118	2	0	0	0	0	....	1992-93	2000-01
Pettersson, Jorgen	St.L., Hfd., Wsh.	6	435	174	192	366	117	44	15	12	27	4	....	1980-81	1985-86
● Pettinger, Eric	Bos., Tor., Ott.	3	98	7	12	19	83	4	1	0	1	8	....	1928-29	1930-31
● Pettinger, Gord	NYR, Det., Bos.	8	292	42	74	116	77	47	4	5	9	11	4	1932-33	1939-40
Phair, Lyle	L.A.	3	48	6	7	13	12	1	0	0	0	0	....	1985-86	1987-88
Phillipoff, Harold	Atl., Chi.	3	141	26	57	83	267	6	0	2	2	9	....	1977-78	1979-80
● Phillips, Bill	Mtl.M.	1	27	1	1	2	6	4	0	0	0	2	....	1929-30	1929-30
● Phillips, Charlie	Mtl.	1	17	0	0	0	6	....	....	....	....	....	....	1942-43	1942-43
● Phillips, Merlyn	Mtl.M., NYA	8	302	52	31	83	232	24	5	1	6	19	1	1925-26	1932-33
Picard, Noel	Mtl., St.L., Atl.	7	335	12	63	75	616	50	2	11	13	167	1	1964-65	1972-73
Picard, Robert	Wsh., Tor., Mtl., Wpg., Que., Det.	13	899	104	319	423	1025	36	5	15	20	39	....	1977-78	1989-90
Picard, Roger	St.L.	1	15	2	2	4	21	....	....	....	....	....	....	1967-68	1967-68
Pichette, Dave	Que., St.L., N.J., NYR	7	322	41	140	181	348	28	3	7	10	54	....	1980-81	1987-88
Picketts, Hal	NYA	1	48	3	1	4	32	....	....	....	....	....	....	1933-34	1933-34
Pidhirny, Harry	Bos.	1	2	0	0	0	0	....	....	....	....	....	....	1957-58	1957-58
Pierce, Randy	Col., N.J., Hfd.	8	277	62	76	138	223	2	0	0	0	0	....	1977-78	1984-85
Pike, Alf	NYR	6	234	42	77	119	145	21	4	2	6	12	1	1939-40	1946-47
Pilon, Rich	NYI, NYR, St.L.	14	631	8	69	77	1745	15	0	0	0	50	....	1988-89	2001-02
Pilote, Pierre	Chi., Tor.	14	890	80	418	498	1251	86	8	53	61	102	1	1955-56	1968-69
Pinder, Gerry	Chi., Cal.	3	223	55	69	124	135	17	0	4	4	6	....	1969-70	1971-72
Pirus, Alex	Min., Det.	4	159	30	28	58	94	2	0	1	1	2	....	1976-77	1979-80
‡ Pisa, Ales	Edm., NYR	2	53	1	3	4	26	....	....	....	....	....	....	2001-02	2002-03
Pitlick, Lance	Ott., Fla.	8	393	16	33	49	298	24	0	2	2	21	....	1994-95	2001-02
● Pitre, Didier	Mtl.	6	127	64	34	98	84	9	2	4	6	16	....	1917-18	1922-23
Pivonka, Michal	Wsh.	13	825	181	418	599	478	95	19	36	55	86	....	1986-87	1998-99
● Plager, Barclay	St.L.	10	614	44	187	231	1115	68	3	20	23	182	....	1967-68	1976-77
Plager, Bill	Min., St.L., Atl.	9	263	4	34	38	294	31	0	2	2	26	....	1967-68	1975-76
Plager, Bob	NYR, St.L.	14	644	20	126	146	802	74	2	17	19	195	....	1964-65	1977-78
Plamondon, Gerry	Mtl.	5	74	7	13	20	10	11	5	2	7	2	1	1945-46	1950-51
Plante, Cam	Tor.	1	2	0	0	0	0	....	....	....	....	....	....	1984-85	1984-85
Plante, Dan	NYI	4	159	9	14	23	135	1	1	0	1	2	....	1993-94	1997-98
‡ Plante, Derek	Buf., Dal., Chi., Phi.	8	450	96	152	248	138	41	6	10	16	18	1	1993-94	2000-01
Plante, Pierre	Phi., St.L., Chi., NYR, Que.	9	599	125	172	297	599	33	2	6	8	51	....	1971-72	1979-80
Plantery, Mark	Wpg.	1	25	1	5	6	14	....	....	....	....	....	....	1980-81	1980-81
‡ Plavsic, Adrien	St.L., Van., T.B., Ana.	8	214	16	56	72	161	13	1	7	8	4	....	1989-90	1996-97
● Plaxton, Hugh	Mtl.M.	1	15	1	2	3	4	....	....	....	....	....	....	1932-33	1932-33
Playfair, Jim	Edm., Chi.	3	21	2	4	6	51	....	....	....	....	....	....	1983-84	1988-89
Playfair, Larry	Buf., L.A.	12	688	26	94	120	1812	43	0	6	6	111	....	1978-79	1989-90
Pleau, Larry	Mtl.	3	94	9	15	24	27	4	0	0	0	0	....	1969-70	1971-72
● Pletsch, Charles	Ham.	1	1	0	0	0	0	....	....	....	....	....	....	1920-21	1920-21
Plett, Willi	Atl., Cgy., Min., Bos.	13	834	222	215	437	2572	83	24	22	46	466	....	1975-76	1987-88
Plumb, Rob	Det.	2	14	3	2	5	2	....	....	....	....	....	....	1977-78	1978-79
Plumb, Ron	Hfd.	1	26	3	4	7	14	....	....	....	....	....	....	1979-80	1979-80
Pocza, Harvie	Wsh.	2	3	0	0	0	2	....	....	....	....	....	....	1979-80	1981-82
Poddubny, Walt	Edm., Tor., NYR, Que., N.J.	11	468	184	238	422	454	19	7	2	9	12	....	1981-82	1991-92
‡ Podein, Shjon	Edm., Phi., Col., St.L.	11	699	100	106	206	439	127	14	13	27	132	1	1992-93	2002-03
Podloski, Ray	Bos.	1	8	0	1	1	17	....	....	....	....	....	....	1988-89	1988-89
‡ Podollan, Jason	Fla., Tor., L.A., NYI	4	41	1	5	6	19	....	....	....	....	....	....	1996-97	2001-02
Podolsky, Nels	Det.	1	1	0	0	0	0	7	0	0	0	4	....	1948-49	1948-49
Poeschek, Rudy	NYR, Wpg., T.B., St.L.	12	364	6	25	31	817	5	0	0	0	18	....	1987-88	1999-00
● Poeta, Tony	Chi.	1	1	0	0	0	0	....	....	....	....	....	....	1951-52	1951-52
● Poile, Bud	Tor., Chi., Det., NYR, Bos.	7	311	107	122	229	91	23	4	5	9	8	1	1942-43	1949-50
Poile, Don	Det.	2	66	7	9	16	12	4	0	0	0	0	....	1954-55	1957-58
Poirier, Gordie	Mtl.	1	10	0	0	0	0	....	....	....	....	....	....	1939-40	1939-40
Polanic, Tom	Min.	2	19	0	2	2	53	5	1	1	2	4	....	1969-70	1970-71
● Polich, John	NYR	2	3	0	1	1	0	....	....	....	....	....	....	1939-40	1940-41
Polich, Mike	Mtl., Min.	5	226	24	29	53	57	23	2	1	3	2	1	1976-77	1980-81
Polis, Greg	Pit., St.L., NYR, Wsh.	10	615	174	169	343	391	7	0	2	2	6	....	1970-71	1979-80
Poliziani, Dan	Bos.	1	1	0	0	0	0	3	0	0	0	0	....	1958-59	1958-59
Polonich, Dennis	Det.	8	390	59	82	141	1242	7	1	0	1	19	....	1974-75	1982-83
Pooley, Paul	Wpg.	2	15	0	3	3	0	....	....	....	....	....	....	1984-85	1985-86
Popein, Larry	NYR, Oak.	8	449	80	141	221	162	16	1	4	5	6	....	1954-55	1967-68
Popiel, Poul	Bos., L.A., Det., Van., Edm.	7	224	13	41	54	210	4	1	0	1	4	....	1965-66	1979-80
‡ Popovic, Peter	Mtl., NYR, Pit., Bos.	8	485	10	63	73	291	35	1	4	5	18	....	1993-94	2000-01
● Portland, Jack	Mtl., Bos., Chi.	10	381	15	56	71	323	33	1	3	4	25	1	1933-34	1942-43
Porvari, Jukka	Col., N.J.	2	39	3	9	12	4	....	....	....	....	....	....	1981-82	1982-83
Posa, Victor	Chi.	1	2	0	0	0	2	....	....	....	....	....	....	1985-86	1985-86
Posavad, Mike	St.L.	2	8	0	0	0	0	....	....	....	....	....	....	1985-86	1986-87
‡ Posmyk, Marek	T.B.	2	19	1	2	3	20	....	....	....	....	....	....	1999-00	2000-01
Potomski, Barry	L.A., S.J.	3	68	6	5	11	227	....	....	....	....	....	....	1995-96	1997-98
Potvin, Denis	NYI	15	1060	310	742	1052	1356	185	56	108	164	253	4	1973-74	1987-88
Potvin, Jean	L.A., Phi., NYI, Cle., Min.	11	613	63	224	287	478	39	2	9	11	17	1	1970-71	1980-81
Potvin, Marc	Det., L.A., Hfd., Bos.	6	121	3	5	8	456	13	0	1	1	50	....	1990-91	1995-96
Poudrier, Daniel	Que.	3	25	1	5	6	10	....	....	....	....	....	....	1985-86	1987-88
Poulin, Daniel	Min.	1	3	1	1	2	2	....	....	....	....	....	....	1981-82	1981-82
Poulin, Dave	Phi., Bos., Wsh.	13	724	205	325	530	482	129	31	42	73	132	....	1982-83	1994-95
Poulin, Patrick	Hfd., Chi., T.B., Mtl.	11	634	101	134	235	299	32	6	2	8	8	....	1991-92	2001-02
Pouzar, Jaroslav	Edm.	4	186	34	48	82	135	29	6	4	10	16	3	1982-83	1986-87
● Powell, Ray	Chi.	1	31	7	15	22	2	....	....	....	....	....	....	1950-51	1950-51
● Powis, Geoff	Chi.	1	2	0	0	0	0	....	....	....	....	....	....	1967-68	1967-68
Powis, Lynn	Chi., K.C.	2	130	19	33	52	25	1	0	0	0	0	....	1973-74	1974-75
Prajsler, Petr	L.A., Bos.	4	46	3	10	13	51	4	0	0	0	0	....	1987-88	1991-92
● Pratt, Babe	NYR, Tor., Bos.	12	517	83	209	292	463	63	12	17	29	90	2	1935-36	1946-47
Pratt, Jack	Bos.	2	37	2	0	2	42	4	0	0	0	0	....	1930-31	1931-32
Pratt, Kelly	Pit.	1	22	0	6	6	15	....	....	....	....	....	....	1974-75	1974-75
Pratt, Tracy	Oak., Pit., Buf., Van., Col., Tor.	10	580	17	97	114	1026	25	0	1	1	62	....	1967-68	1976-77
Prentice, Dean	NYR, Bos., Det., Pit., Min.	22	1378	391	469	860	484	54	13	17	30	38	....	1952-53	1973-74
Prentice, Eric	Tor.	1	5	0	0	0	4	....	....	....	....	....	....	1943-44	1943-44
Presley, Wayne	Chi., S.J., Buf., NYR, Tor.	12	684	155	147	302	953	83	26	17	43	142	....	1984-85	1995-96
Preston, Rich	Chi., N.J.	8	580	127	164	291	348	47	4	18	22	56	....	1979-80	1986-87
Preston, Yves	Phi.	2	28	7	3	10	4	....	....	....	....	....	....	1978-79	1980-81
Priakin, Sergei	Cgy.	3	46	3	8	11	2	1	0	0	0	0	....	1988-89	1990-91
Price, Jack	Chi.	3	57	4	6	10	24	4	0	0	0	0	....	1951-52	1953-54
Price, Noel	Tor., NYR, Det., Mtl., Pit., L.A., Atl.	14	499	14	114	128	333	12	0	1	1	8	1	1957-58	1975-76
Price, Pat	NYI, Edm., Pit., Que., NYR, Min.	13	726	43	218	261	1456	74	2	10	12	195	....	1975-76	1987-88
Price, Tom	Cal., Cle., Pit.	5	29	0	2	2	12	....	....	....	....	....	....	1974-75	1978-79
Priestlay, Ken	Buf., Pit.	6	168	27	34	61	63	14	0	0	0	21	1	1986-87	1991-92

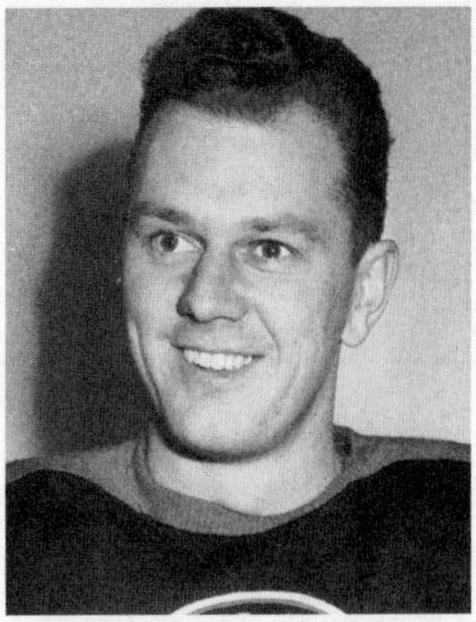
Bud Poile

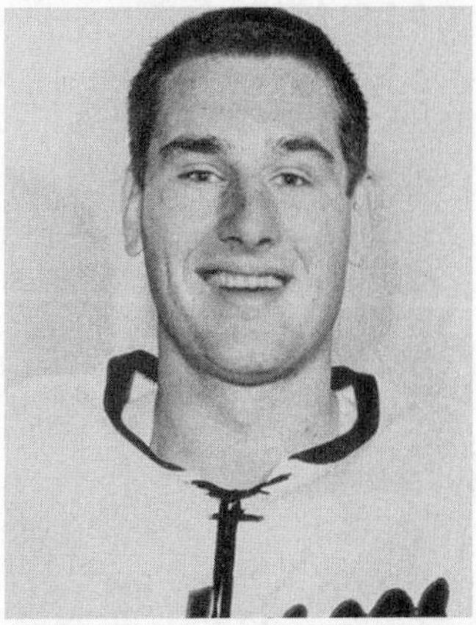
Tracy Pratt

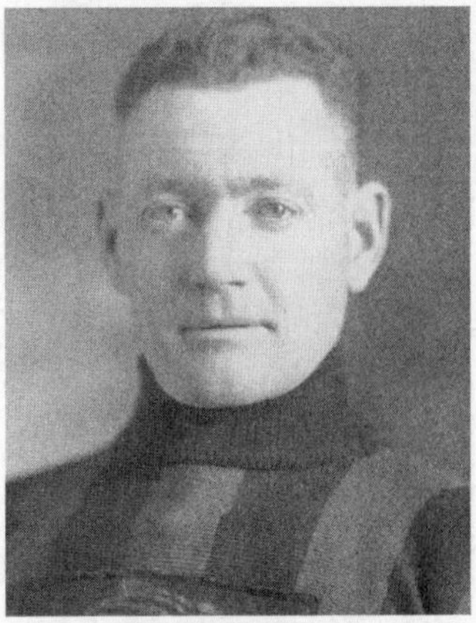
Goldie Prodgers

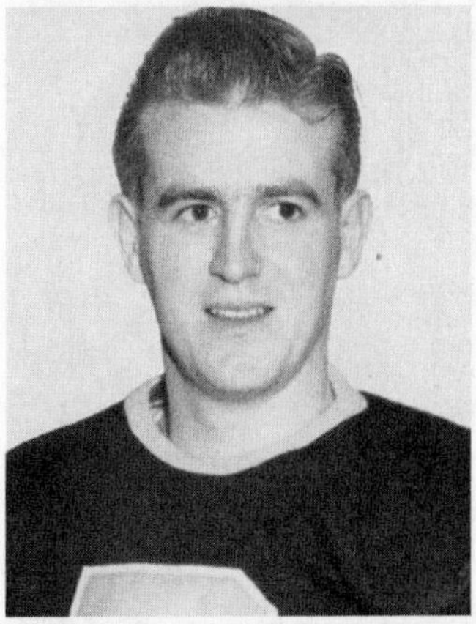
Max Quackenbush

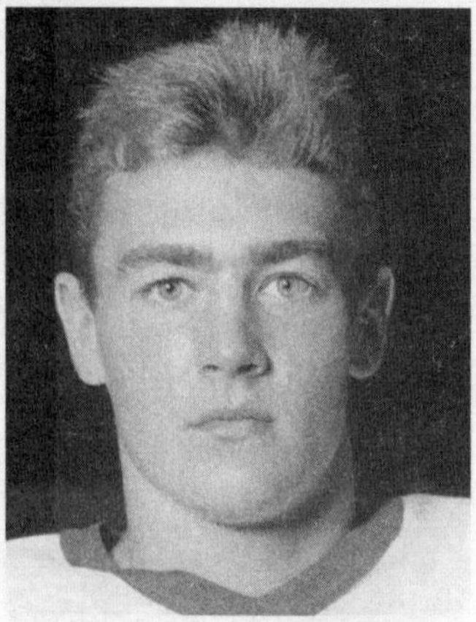

Dan Ratushny

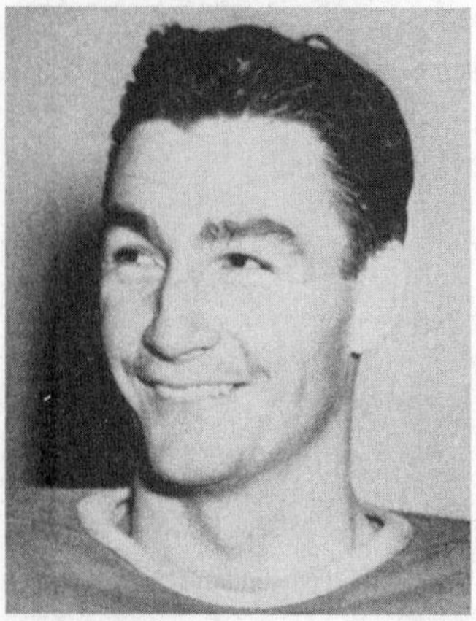

Terry Reardon

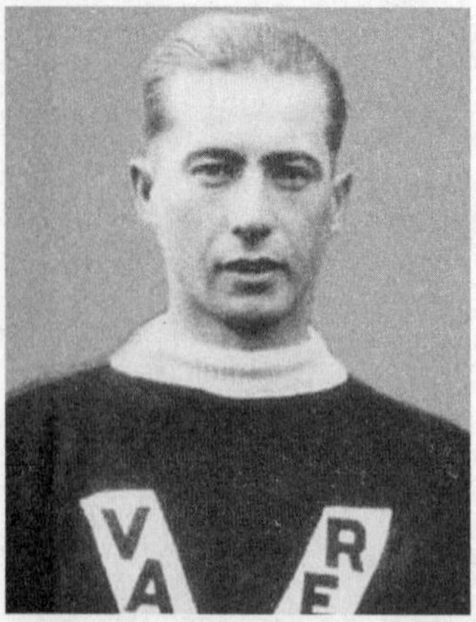

Ollie Reinikka

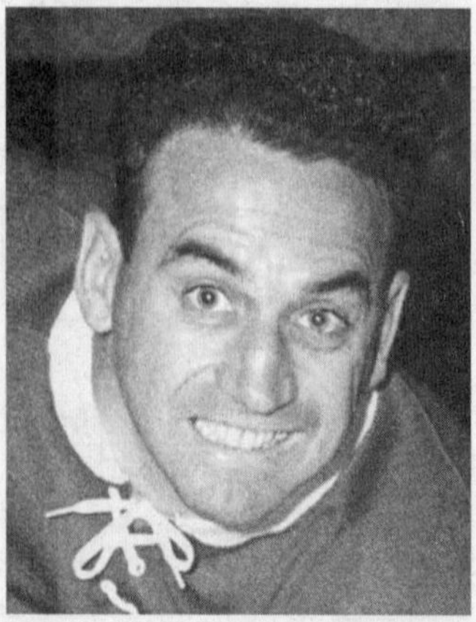

Rip Riopelle

			Regular Schedule					Playoffs					NHL	First	Last
Name	NHL Teams	NHL Seasons	GP	G	A	TP	PIM	GP	G	A	TP	PIM	Cup Wins	NHL Season	NHL Season
• Primeau, Joe	Tor.	9	310	66	177	243	105	38	5	18	23	12	1	1927-28	1935-36
Primeau, Kevin	Van.	1	2	0	0	0	4	....	....	....	....	....	....	1980-81	1980-81
• Pringle, Ellie	NYA	1	6	0	0	0	0	....	....	....	....	....	....	1930-31	1930-31
Probert, Bob	Det., Chi.	16	935	163	221	384	3300	81	16	32	48	274	....	1985-86	2001-02
‡ Prochazka, Martin	Tor., Atl.	2	32	2	5	7	8	....	....	....	....	....	....	1997-98	1999-00
• Prodgers, Goldie	Tor., Ham.	6	111	63	29	92	39	....	....	....	....	....	....	1919-20	1924-25
Prokhorov, Vitali	St.L.	3	83	19	11	30	35	4	0	0	0	0	....	1992-93	1994-95
Prokopec, Mike	Chi.	2	15	0	0	0	11	....	....	....	....	....	....	1995-96	1996-97
Pronovost, Andre	Mtl., Bos., Det., Min.	10	556	94	104	198	408	70	11	11	22	58	4	1956-57	1967-68
Pronovost, Jean	Pit., Atl., Wsh.	14	998	391	383	774	413	35	11	9	20	14	....	1968-69	1981-82
Pronovost, Marcel	Det., Tor.	21	1206	88	257	345	851	134	8	23	31	104	5	1949-50	1969-70
Propp, Brian	Phi., Bos., Min., Hfd.	15	1016	425	579	1004	830	160	64	84	148	151	....	1979-80	1993-94
Proulx, Christian	Mtl.	1	7	1	2	3	20	....	....	....	....	....	....	1993-94	1993-94
• Provost, Claude	Mtl.	15	1005	254	335	589	469	126	25	38	63	86	9	1955-56	1969-70
Prpic, Joel	Bos., Col.	3	18	0	3	3	4	....	....	....	....	....	....	1997-98	2000-01
Pryor, Chris	Min., NYI	6	82	1	4	5	122	....	....	....	....	....	....	1984-85	1989-90
Prystai, Metro	Chi., Det.	11	674	151	179	330	231	43	12	14	26	8	2	1947-48	1957-58
• Pudas, Al	Tor.	1	4	0	0	0	0	....	....	....	....	....	....	1926-27	1926-27
Pulford, Bob	Tor., L.A.	16	1079	281	362	643	792	89	25	26	51	126	4	1956-57	1971-72
Pulkkinen, Dave	NYI	1	2	0	0	0	0	....	....	....	....	....	....	1972-73	1972-73
• Purpur, Fido	St.L., Chi., Det.	5	144	25	35	60	46	16	1	2	3	4	....	1934-35	1944-45
Purves, John	Wsh.	1	7	1	0	1	0	....	....	....	....	....	....	1990-91	1990-91
• Pusie, Jean	Mtl., NYR, Bos.	5	61	1	4	5	28	7	0	0	0	0	1	1930-31	1935-36
Pyatt, Nelson	Det., Wsh., Col.	7	296	71	63	134	69	....	....	....	....	....	....	1973-74	1979-80

Q

• Quackenbush, Bill	Det., Bos.	14	774	62	222	284	95	80	2	19	21	8	....	1942-43	1955-56
Quackenbush, Max	Bos., Chi.	2	61	4	7	11	30	6	0	0	0	4	....	1950-51	1951-52
Quenneville, Joel	Tor., Col., N.J., Hfd., Wsh.	13	803	54	136	190	705	32	0	8	8	22	....	1978-79	1990-91
• Quenneville, Leo	NYR	1	25	0	3	3	10	3	0	0	0	0	....	1929-30	1929-30
• Quilty, John	Mtl., Bos.	4	125	36	34	70	81	13	3	5	8	9	....	1940-41	1947-48
Quinn, Dan	Cgy., Pit., Van., St.L., Phi., Min., Ott., L.A.	14	805	266	419	685	533	65	22	26	48	62	....	1983-84	1996-97
Quinn, Pat	Tor., Van., Atl.	9	606	18	113	131	950	11	0	1	1	21	....	1968-69	1976-77
Quinney, Ken	Que.	3	59	7	13	20	23	....	....	....	....	....	....	1986-87	1990-91
Quintal, Stephane	Bos., St.L., Wpg., Mtl., NYR, Chi.	16	1037	63	180	243	1320	52	2	10	12	51	....	1988-89	2003-04
Quintin, Jean-Francois	S.J.	2	22	5	5	10	4	....	....	....	....	....	....	1991-92	1992-93

R

‡ Racine, Yves	Det., Phi., Mtl., S.J., Cgy., T.B.	9	508	37	194	231	439	25	5	4	9	37	....	1989-90	1997-98
• Radley, Yip	NYA, Mtl.M.	2	18	0	1	1	13	....	....	....	....	....	....	1930-31	1936-37
Raglan, Herb	St.L., Que., T.B., Ott.	9	343	33	56	89	775	32	3	6	9	50	....	1985-86	1993-94
Raglan, Rags	Det., Chi.	3	100	4	9	13	52	3	0	0	0	0	....	1950-51	1952-53
Raleigh, Don	NYR	10	535	101	219	320	96	18	6	5	11	6	....	1943-44	1955-56
‡ Ralph, Brad	Phx.	1	1	0	0	0	0	....	....	....	....	....	....	2000-01	2000-01
Ramage, Rob	Col., St.L., Cgy., Tor., Min., T.B., Mtl., Phi.	15	1044	139	425	564	2226	84	8	42	50	218	2	1979-80	1993-94
• Ramsay, Beattie	Tor.	1	43	0	2	2	10	....	....	....	....	....	....	1927-28	1927-28
Ramsay, Craig	Buf.	14	1070	252	420	672	201	89	17	31	48	27	....	1971-72	1984-85
Ramsay, Les	Chi.	1	11	2	2	4	2	....	....	....	....	....	....	1944-45	1944-45
Ramsey, Mike	Buf., Pit., Det.	18	1070	79	266	345	1012	115	8	29	37	176	....	1979-80	1996-97
Ramsey, Wayne	Buf.	1	2	0	0	0	0	....	....	....	....	....	....	1977-78	1977-78
• Randall, Ken	Tor., Ham., NYA	10	218	68	50	118	533	6	2	1	3	27	2	1917-18	1926-27
Ranheim, Paul	Cgy., Hfd., Car., Phi., Phx.	15	1013	161	199	360	288	36	3	8	11	6	....	1988-89	2002-03
Ranieri, George	Bos.	1	2	0	0	0	0	....	....	....	....	....	....	1956-57	1956-57
‡ Ratchuk, Peter	Fla.	2	32	1	1	2	10	....	....	....	....	....	....	1998-99	2000-01
Ratelle, Jean	NYR, Bos.	21	1281	491	776	1267	276	123	32	66	98	24	....	1960-61	1980-81
Rathwell, Jake	Bos.	1	1	0	0	0	0	....	....	....	....	....	....	1974-75	1974-75
Ratushny, Dan	Van.	1	1	0	1	1	2	....	....	....	....	....	....	1992-93	1992-93
Rausse, Errol	Wsh.	3	31	7	3	10	0	....	....	....	....	....	....	1979-80	1981-82
Rautakallio, Pekka	Atl., Cgy.	3	235	33	121	154	122	23	2	5	7	8	....	1979-80	1981-82
Ravlich, Matt	Bos., Chi., Det., L.A.	10	410	12	78	90	364	24	1	5	6	16	....	1962-63	1972-73
• Raymond, Armand	Mtl.	2	22	0	2	2	10	....	....	....	....	....	....	1937-38	1939-40
• Raymond, Paul	Mtl.	4	76	2	3	5	6	5	0	0	0	2	....	1932-33	1938-39
Read, Mel	NYR	1	1	0	0	0	0	....	....	....	....	....	....	1946-47	1946-47
Reardon, Ken	Mtl.	7	341	26	96	122	604	31	2	5	7	62	1	1940-41	1949-50
• Reardon, Terry	Bos., Mtl.	7	193	47	53	100	73	30	8	10	18	12	1	1938-39	1946-47
Reaume, Marc	Tor., Det., Mtl., Van.	9	344	8	43	51	273	21	0	2	2	8	....	1954-55	1970-71
• Reay, Billy	Det., Mtl.	10	479	105	162	267	202	63	13	16	29	43	2	1943-44	1952-53
Redahl, Gord	Bos.	1	18	0	1	1	2	....	....	....	....	....	....	1958-59	1958-59
• Redding, George	Bos.	2	55	3	2	5	23	....	....	....	....	....	....	1924-25	1925-26
Redmond, Craig	L.A., Edm.	5	191	16	68	84	134	3	1	0	1	2	....	1984-85	1988-89
Redmond, Dick	Min., Cal., Chi., St.L., Atl., Bos.	13	771	133	312	445	504	66	9	22	31	27	....	1969-70	1981-82
Redmond, Keith	L.A.	1	12	1	0	1	20	....	....	....	....	....	....	1993-94	1993-94
Redmond, Mickey	Mtl., Det.	9	538	233	195	428	219	16	2	3	5	2	2	1967-68	1975-76
Reeds, Mark	St.L., Hfd.	8	365	45	114	159	135	53	8	9	17	23	....	1981-82	1988-89
Reekie, Joe	Buf., NYI, T.B., Wsh., Chi.	17	902	25	139	164	1326	51	3	4	7	63	....	1985-86	2001-02
• Regan, Bill	NYR, NYA	3	67	3	2	5	67	8	0	0	0	2	....	1929-30	1932-33
Regan, Larry	Bos., Tor.	5	280	41	95	136	71	42	7	14	21	18	....	1956-57	1960-61
Regier, Darcy	Cle., NYI	3	26	0	2	2	35	....	....	....	....	....	....	1977-78	1983-84
Reibel, Dutch	Det., Chi., Bos.	6	409	84	161	245	75	39	6	14	20	4	2	1953-54	1958-59
Reichert, Craig	Ana.	1	3	0	0	0	0	....	....	....	....	....	....	1996-97	1996-97
• Reid, Dave	Tor.	3	7	0	0	0	0	....	....	....	....	....	....	1952-53	1955-56
Reid, Dave	Bos., Tor., Dal., Col.	18	961	165	204	369	253	118	9	26	35	34	2	1983-84	2000-01
Reid, Gerry	Det.	1	....	....	....	....	....	2	0	0	0	2	....	1948-49	1948-49
Reid, Gord	NYA	1	1	0	0	0	2	....	....	....	....	....	....	1936-37	1936-37
• Reid, Reg	Tor.	2	39	1	0	1	4	2	0	0	0	0	....	1924-25	1925-26
Reid, Tom	Chi., Min.	11	701	17	113	130	654	42	1	13	14	49	....	1967-68	1977-78
Reierson, Dave	Cgy.	1	2	0	0	0	2	....	....	....	....	....	....	1988-89	1988-89
Reigle, Ed	Bos.	1	17	0	2	2	25	....	....	....	....	....	....	1950-51	1950-51
Reinhart, Paul	Atl., Cgy., Van.	11	648	133	426	559	277	83	23	54	77	42	....	1979-80	1989-90
• Reinikka, Ollie	NYR	1	16	0	0	0	0	....	....	....	....	....	....	1926-27	1926-27
• Reise, Leo	Ham., NYA, NYR	8	241	43	43	86	187	6	0	0	0	16	....	1920-21	1929-30
Reise, Leo	Chi., Det., NYR	9	494	28	81	109	399	52	8	5	13	68	2	1945-46	1953-54
Renaud, Mark	Hfd., Buf.	5	152	6	50	56	86	....	....	....	....	....	....	1979-80	1983-84
‡ Renberg, Mikael	Phi., T.B., Phx., Tor.	10	661	190	274	464	372	67	16	22	38	42	....	1993-94	2003-04
‡ Reynolds, Bobby	Tor.	1	7	1	1	2	0	....	....	....	....	....	....	1989-90	1989-90
Ribble, Pat	Atl., Chi., Tor., Wsh., Cgy.	8	349	19	60	79	365	8	0	1	1	12	....	1975-76	1982-83
Rice, Steven	NYR, Edm., Hfd., Car.	8	329	64	61	125	275	2	2	1	3	6	....	1990-91	1997-98
Richard, Henri	Mtl.	20	1256	358	688	1046	928	180	49	80	129	181	11	1955-56	1974-75
• Richard, Jacques	Atl., Buf., Que.	10	556	160	187	347	307	35	5	5	10	34	....	1972-73	1982-83
Richard, Jean-Marc	Que.	2	5	2	1	3	2	....	....	....	....	....	....	1987-88	1989-90
• Richard, Maurice	Mtl.	18	978	544	421	965	1285	133	82	44	126	188	8	1942-43	1959-60
‡ Richard, Mike	Wsh.	2	7	0	2	2	0	....	....	....	....	....	....	1987-88	1989-90
Richards, Todd	Hfd.	2	8	0	4	4	4	11	0	3	3	6	....	1990-91	1991-92
‡ Richards, Travis	Dal.	2	3	0	0	0	2	....	....	....	....	....	....	1994-95	1995-96
Richardson, Dave	NYR, Chi., Det.	4	45	3	2	5	27	....	....	....	....	....	....	1963-64	1967-68
Richardson, Glen	Van.	1	24	3	6	9	19	....	....	....	....	....	....	1975-76	1975-76
Richardson, Ken	St.L.	3	49	8	13	21	16	....	....	....	....	....	....	1974-75	1978-79
Richer, Bob	Buf.	1	3	0	0	0	0	....	....	....	....	....	....	1972-73	1972-73
Richer, Stephane	Mtl., N.J., T.B., St.L., Pit.	17	1054	421	398	819	614	134	53	45	98	61	2	1984-85	2001-02
Richer, Stephane	T.B., Bos., Fla.	3	27	1	5	6	20	3	0	0	0	0	....	1992-93	1994-95
Richmond, Steve	NYR, Det., N.J., L.A.	5	159	4	23	27	514	4	0	0	0	12	....	1983-84	1988-89
‡ Richter, Barry	NYR, Bos., NYI, Mtl.	5	151	11	34	45	76	....	....	....	....	....	....	1995-96	2000-01
Richter, Dave	Min., Phi., Van., St.L.	9	365	9	40	49	1030	22	1	0	1	80	....	1981-82	1989-90
Ridley, Mike	NYR, Wsh., Tor., Van.	12	866	292	466	758	424	104	28	50	78	70	....	1985-86	1996-97
‡ Riesen, Michel	Edm.	1	12	0	1	1	4	....	....	....	....	....	....	2000-01	2000-01
Riley, Bill	Wsh., Wpg.	5	139	31	30	61	320	....	....	....	....	....	....	1974-75	1979-80
Riley, Jack	Det., Mtl., Bos.	4	104	10	22	32	8	4	0	3	3	0	....	1932-33	1935-36
• Riley, Jim	Chi., Det.	1	9	0	2	2	14	....	....	....	....	....	....	1926-27	1926-27
Riopelle, Rip	Mtl.	3	169	27	16	43	73	8	1	1	2	2	....	1947-48	1949-50
Rioux, Gerry	Wpg.	1	8	0	0	0	6	....	....	....	....	....	....	1979-80	1979-80

Name	NHL Teams	NHL Seasons	Regular Schedule GP	G	A	TP	PIM	Playoffs GP	G	A	TP	PIM	NHL Cup Wins	First NHL Season	Last NHL Season
Rioux, Pierre	Cgy.	1	14	1	2	3	4	....	....	....	....	....	....	1982-83	1982-83
• Ripley, Vic	Chi., Bos., NYR, St.L.	7	278	51	49	100	173	20	4	1	5	10	....	1928-29	1934-35
Risebrough, Doug	Mtl., Cgy.	13	740	185	286	471	1542	124	21	37	58	238	4	1974-75	1986-87
Rissling, Gary	Wsh., Pit.	7	221	23	30	53	1008	5	0	1	1	4	....	1978-79	1984-85
Ritchie, Bob	Phi., Det.	2	29	8	4	12	10	....	....	....	....	....	....	1976-77	1977-78
• Ritchie, Dave	Mtl.W., Ott., Tor., Que., Mtl.	6	58	15	6	21	50	1	0	0	0	0	....	1917-18	1925-26
Ritson, Alex	NYR	1	1	0	0	0	0	....	....	....	....	....	....	1944-45	1944-45
Rittinger, Alan	Bos.	1	19	3	7	10	0	....	....	....	....	....	....	1943-44	1943-44
Rivard, Bob	Pit.	1	27	5	12	17	4	....	....	....	....	....	....	1967-68	1967-68
• Rivers, Gus	Mtl.	3	88	4	5	9	12	16	2	0	2	2	2	1929-30	1931-32
Rivers, Shawn	T.B.	1	4	0	2	2	2	....	....	....	....	....	....	1992-93	1992-93
Rivers, Wayne	Det., Bos., St.L., NYR	7	108	15	30	45	94	....	....	....	....	....	....	1961-62	1968-69
Rizzuto, Garth	Van.	1	37	3	4	7	16	....	....	....	....	....	....	1970-71	1970-71
• Roach, Mickey	Tor., Ham., NYA	8	211	77	34	111	54	....	....	....	....	....	....	1919-20	1926-27
Roberge, Mario	Mtl.	5	112	7	7	14	314	15	0	0	0	24	1	1990-91	1994-95
Roberge, Serge	Que.	1	9	0	0	0	24	....	....	....	....	....	....	1990-91	1990-91
Robert, Claude	Mtl.	1	23	1	0	1	9	....	....	....	....	....	....	1950-51	1950-51
Robert, Rene	Tor., Pit., Buf., Col.	12	744	284	418	702	597	50	22	19	41	73	....	1970-71	1981-82
Roberto, Phil	Mtl., St.L., Det., K.C., Col., Cle.	8	385	75	106	181	464	31	9	8	17	69	1	1969-70	1976-77
‡ Roberts, David	St.L., Edm., Van.	5	125	20	33	53	85	9	0	0	0	16	....	1993-94	1997-98
Roberts, Doug	Det., Oak., Cal., Bos.	10	419	43	104	147	342	16	2	3	5	46	....	1965-66	1974-75
Roberts, Gordie	Hfd., Min., Phi., St.L., Pit., Bos.	15	1097	61	359	420	1582	153	10	47	57	273	2	1979-80	1993-94
Roberts, Jim	Min.	3	106	17	23	40	33	2	0	0	0	0	....	1976-77	1978-79
Roberts, Jimmy	Mtl., St.L.	15	1006	126	194	320	621	153	20	16	36	160	5	1963-64	1977-78
• Robertson, Fred	Tor., Det.	2	34	1	0	1	35	7	0	0	0	0	1	1931-32	1933-34
Robertson, Geordie	Buf.	1	5	1	2	3	7	....	....	....	....	....	....	1982-83	1982-83
Robertson, George	Mtl.	2	31	2	5	7	6	....	....	....	....	....	....	1947-48	1948-49
Robertson, Torrie	Wsh., Hfd., Det.	10	442	49	99	148	1751	22	2	1	3	90	....	1980-81	1989-90
‡ Robertsson, Bert	Van., Edm., NYR	4	123	4	10	14	75	5	0	0	0	0	....	1997-98	2000-01
Robidoux, Florent	Chi.	3	52	7	4	11	75	....	....	....	....	....	....	1980-81	1983-84
Robinson, Doug	Chi., NYR, L.A.	7	239	44	67	111	34	11	4	3	7	0	....	1963-64	1970-71
• Robinson, Earl	Mtl.M., Chi., Mtl.	11	417	83	98	181	133	25	5	4	9	0	1	1928-29	1939-40
Robinson, Larry	Mtl., L.A.	20	1384	208	750	958	793	227	28	116	144	211	6	1972-73	1991-92
Robinson, Moe	Mtl.	1	1	0	0	0	0	....	....	....	....	....	....	1979-80	1979-80
Robinson, Rob	St.L.	1	22	0	1	1	8	....	....	....	....	....	....	1991-92	1991-92
Robinson, Scott	Min.	1	1	0	0	0	2	....	....	....	....	....	....	1989-90	1989-90
Robitaille, Mike	NYR, Det., Buf., Van.	8	382	23	105	128	280	13	0	1	1	4	....	1969-70	1976-77
• Roche, Des	Mtl.M., Ott., St.L., Mtl., Det.	4	113	20	18	38	44	....	....	....	....	....	....	1930-31	1934-35
• Roche, Earl	Mtl.M., Bos., Ott., St.L., Det.	4	147	25	27	52	48	2	0	0	0	0	....	1930-31	1934-35
Roche, Ernie	Mtl.	1	4	0	0	0	2	....	....	....	....	....	....	1950-51	1950-51
Rochefort, Dave	Det.	1	1	0	0	0	0	....	....	....	....	....	....	1966-67	1966-67
Rochefort, Leon	NYR, Mtl., Phi., L.A., Det., Atl., Van.	15	617	121	147	268	93	39	4	4	8	16	2	1960-61	1975-76
Rochefort, Normand	Que., NYR, T.B.	13	598	39	119	158	570	69	7	5	12	82	....	1980-81	1993-94
• Rockburn, Harvey	Det., Ott.	3	94	4	2	6	254	....	....	....	....	....	....	1929-30	1932-33
• Rodden, Eddie	Chi., Tor., Bos., NYR	4	97	6	14	20	60	2	0	1	1	0	....	1926-27	1930-31
Rodgers, Marc	Det.	1	21	1	1	2	10	....	....	....	....	....	....	1999-00	1999-00
‡ Roest, Stacy	Det., Min.	5	244	28	48	76	54	3	0	0	0	0	....	1998-99	2002-03
Rogers, John	Min.	2	14	2	4	6	0	....	....	....	....	....	....	1973-74	1974-75
Rogers, Mike	Hfd., NYR, Edm.	7	484	202	317	519	184	17	1	13	14	6	....	1979-80	1985-86
Rohlicek, Jeff	Van.	2	9	0	0	0	8	....	....	....	....	....	....	1987-88	1988-89
Rohlin, Leif	Van.	2	96	8	24	32	40	5	0	0	0	0	....	1995-96	1996-97
Rohloff, Jon	Bos.	3	150	7	25	32	129	10	1	2	3	8	....	1994-95	1996-97
Rolfe, Dale	Bos., L.A., Det., NYR	9	509	25	125	150	556	71	5	24	29	89	....	1959-60	1974-75
Romanchych, Larry	Chi., Atl.	6	298	68	97	165	102	7	2	2	4	4	....	1970-71	1976-77
Romaniuk, Russell	Wpg., Phi.	5	102	13	14	27	63	2	0	0	0	0	....	1991-92	1995-96
Rombough, Doug	Buf., NYI, Min.	4	150	24	27	51	80	....	....	....	....	....	....	1972-73	1975-76
Rominski, Dale	T.B.	1	3	0	1	1	2	....	....	....	....	....	....	1999-00	1999-00
• Romnes, Doc	Chi., Tor., NYA	10	360	68	136	204	42	45	7	18	25	4	2	1930-31	1939-40
Ronan, Ed	Mtl., Wpg., Buf.	6	182	13	23	36	101	27	4	3	7	16	1	1991-92	1996-97
• Ronan, Skene	Ott.	1	11	0	0	0	6	....	....	....	....	....	....	1918-19	1918-19
‡ Ronnqvist, Jonas	Ana.	1	38	0	4	4	14	....	....	....	....	....	....	2000-01	2000-01
Ronson, Len	NYR, Oak.	2	18	2	1	3	10	....	....	....	....	....	....	1960-61	1968-69
Ronty, Paul	Bos., NYR, Mtl.	8	488	101	211	312	103	21	1	7	8	6	....	1947-48	1954-55
Rooney, Steve	Mtl., Wpg., N.J.	5	154	15	13	28	496	25	3	2	5	86	1	1984-85	1988-89
Root, Bill	Mtl., Tor., St.L., Phi.	6	247	11	23	34	180	22	1	2	3	25	....	1982-83	1987-88
• Ross, Art	Mtl.W.	1	3	1	0	1	12	....	....	....	....	....	....	1917-18	1917-18
Ross, Jim	NYR	2	62	2	11	13	29	....	....	....	....	....	....	1951-52	1952-53
Rossignol, Roly	Det., Mtl.	3	14	3	5	8	6	1	0	0	0	2	....	1943-44	1945-46
Rota, Darcy	Chi., Atl., Van.	11	794	256	239	495	973	60	14	7	21	147	....	1973-74	1983-84
Rota, Randy	Mtl., L.A., K.C., Col.	5	212	38	39	77	60	5	0	1	1	0	....	1972-73	1976-77
• Rothschild, Sam	Mtl.M., Pit., NYA	4	100	8	6	14	25	6	0	0	0	0	1	1924-25	1927-28
• Roulston, Rolly	Det.	3	24	0	6	6	10	....	....	....	....	....	1	1935-36	1937-38
Roulston, Tom	Edm., Pit.	5	195	47	49	96	74	21	2	2	4	2	....	1980-81	1985-86
Roupe, Magnus	Phi.	2	40	3	5	8	42	....	....	....	....	....	....	1987-88	1988-89
Rouse, Bob	Min., Wsh., Tor., Det., S.J.	17	1061	37	181	218	1559	136	7	21	28	198	2	1983-84	1999-00
Rousseau, Bobby	Mtl., Min., NYR	15	942	245	458	703	359	128	27	57	84	69	4	1960-61	1974-75
Rousseau, Guy	Mtl.	2	4	0	1	1	0	....	....	....	....	....	....	1954-55	1956-57
Rousseau, Roland	Mtl.	1	2	0	0	0	0	....	....	....	....	....	....	1952-53	1952-53
Routhier, Jean-Marc	Que.	1	8	0	0	0	9	....	....	....	....	....	....	1989-90	1989-90
• Rowe, Bobby	Bos.	1	4	1	0	1	0	....	....	....	....	....	....	1924-25	1924-25
Rowe, Mike	Pit.	3	11	0	0	0	11	....	....	....	....	....	....	1984-85	1986-87
Rowe, Ron	NYR	1	5	1	0	1	0	....	....	....	....	....	....	1947-48	1947-48
Rowe, Tom	Wsh., Hfd., Det.	7	357	85	100	185	615	3	2	0	2	0	....	1976-77	1982-83
‡ Roy, Jean-Yves	NYR, Ott., Bos.	4	61	12	16	28	26	....	....	....	....	....	....	1994-95	1997-98
Roy, Stephane	Min.	1	12	1	0	1	0	....	....	....	....	....	....	1987-88	1987-88
‡ Royer, Gaetan	T.B.	1	3	0	0	0	2	....	....	....	....	....	....	2001-02	2001-02
‡ Royer, Remi	Chi.	1	18	0	0	0	67	....	....	....	....	....	....	1998-99	1998-99
Rozzini, Gino	Bos.	1	31	5	10	15	20	6	1	2	3	6	....	1944-45	1944-45
Rucinski, Mike	Chi.	2	1	0	0	0	0	2	0	0	0	0	....	1987-88	1988-89
Rucinski, Mike	Car.	3	26	0	2	2	10	....	....	....	....	....	....	1997-98	2000-01
Ruelle, Bernie	Det.	1	2	1	0	1	0	....	....	....	....	....	....	1943-44	1943-44
Ruff, Jason	St.L., T.B.	2	14	3	3	6	10	....	....	....	....	....	....	1992-93	1993-94
Ruff, Lindy	Buf., NYR	12	691	105	195	300	1264	52	11	13	24	193	....	1979-80	1990-91
Ruhnke, Kent	Bos.	1	2	0	1	1	0	....	....	....	....	....	....	1975-76	1975-76
Rumble, Darren	Phi., Ott., St.L., T.B.	8	193	10	26	36	216	....	....	....	....	....	....	1990-91	2003-04
Rundqvist, Thomas	Mtl.	1	2	0	1	1	0	....	....	....	....	....	....	1984-85	1984-85
• Runge, Paul	Bos., Mtl.M., Mtl.	7	140	18	22	40	57	7	0	0	0	6	....	1930-31	1937-38
Ruotsalainen, Reijo	NYR, Edm., N.J.	7	446	107	237	344	180	86	15	32	47	44	2	1981-82	1989-90
Rupp, Duane	NYR, Tor., Min., Pit.	10	374	24	93	117	220	10	2	2	4	8	....	1962-63	1972-73
Ruskowski, Terry	Chi., L.A., Pit., Min.	10	630	113	313	426	1354	21	1	6	7	86	....	1979-80	1988-89
Russell, Cam	Chi., Col.	10	396	9	21	30	872	44	0	5	5	16	....	1989-90	1998-99
• Russell, Church	NYR	3	90	20	16	36	12	....	....	....	....	....	....	1945-46	1947-48
Russell, Phil	Chi., Atl., Cgy., N.J., Buf.	15	1016	99	325	424	2038	73	4	22	26	202	....	1972-73	1986-87
Ruuttu, Christian	Buf., Chi., Van.	9	621	134	298	432	714	42	4	9	13	49	....	1986-87	1994-95
Ruzicka, Vladimir	Edm., Bos., Ott.	5	233	82	85	167	129	30	4	14	18	2	....	1989-90	1993-94
Ryan, Terry	Mtl.	3	8	0	0	0	36	....	....	....	....	....	....	1996-97	1998-99
Rychel, Warren	Chi., L.A., Tor., Col., Ana.	9	406	38	39	77	1422	70	8	13	21	121	1	1988-89	1998-99
Rymsha, Andy	Que.	1	6	0	0	0	23	....	....	....	....	....	....	1991-92	1991-92

S

Name	NHL Teams	NHL Seasons	Regular Schedule GP	G	A	TP	PIM	Playoffs GP	G	A	TP	PIM	NHL Cup Wins	First NHL Season	Last NHL Season
Saarinen, Simo	NYR	1	8	0	0	0	0	....	....	....	....	....	....	1984-85	1984-85
Sabol, Shaun	Phi.	1	2	0	0	0	0	....	....	....	....	....	....	1989-90	1989-90
Sabourin, Bob	Tor.	1	1	0	0	0	2	....	....	....	....	....	....	1951-52	1951-52
Sabourin, Gary	St.L., Tor., Cal., Cle.	10	627	169	188	357	397	62	19	11	30	58	....	1967-68	1976-77
Sabourin, Ken	Cgy., Wsh.	4	74	2	8	10	201	12	0	0	0	34	....	1988-89	1991-92
Sacco, David	Tor., Ana.	3	35	5	13	18	22	....	....	....	....	....	....	1993-94	1995-96
Sacco, Joe	Tor., Ana., NYI, Wsh., Phi.	13	738	94	119	213	421	26	2	0	2	8	....	1990-91	2002-03
Sacharuk, Larry	NYR, St.L.	5	151	29	33	62	42	2	1	1	2	2	....	1972-73	1976-77
Saganiuk, Rocky	Tor., Pit.	6	259	57	65	122	201	6	1	0	1	15	....	1978-79	1983-84
Saleski, Don	Phi., Col.	9	543	128	125	253	629	82	13	17	30	131	2	1971-72	1979-80
Salming, Borje	Tor., Det.	17	1148	150	637	787	1344	81	12	37	49	91	....	1973-74	1989-90
Salovaara, Barry	Det.	2	90	2	13	15	70	....	....	....	....	....	....	1974-75	1975-76
Salvian, Dave	NYI	1	....	....	....	....	....	1	0	1	1	2	....	1976-77	1976-77

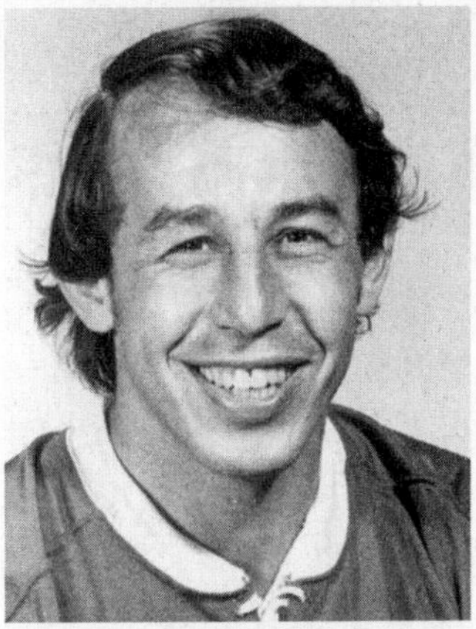
Jimmy Roberts

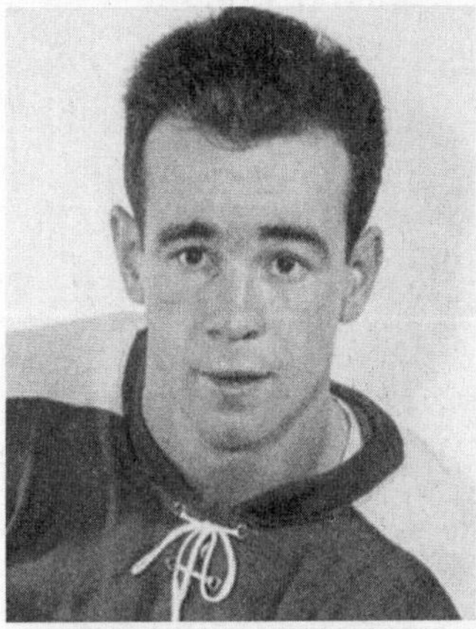
Roland Rousseau

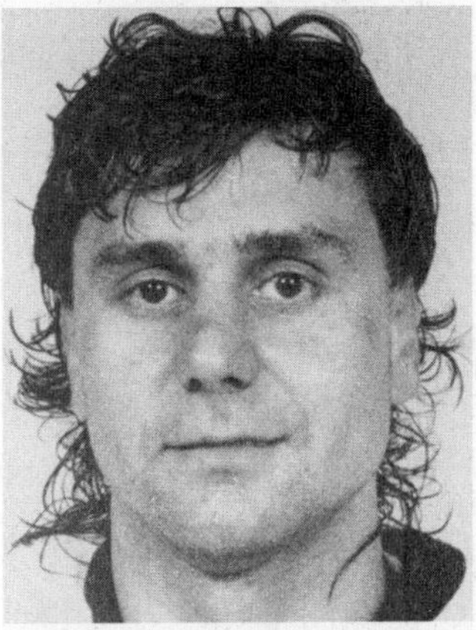
Vladimir Ruzicka

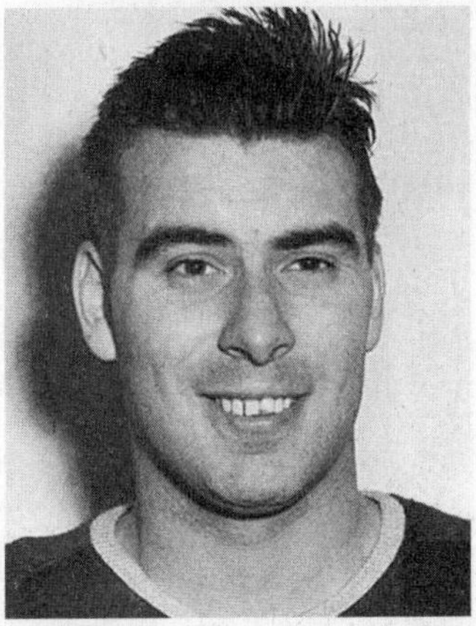
Bob Sabourin

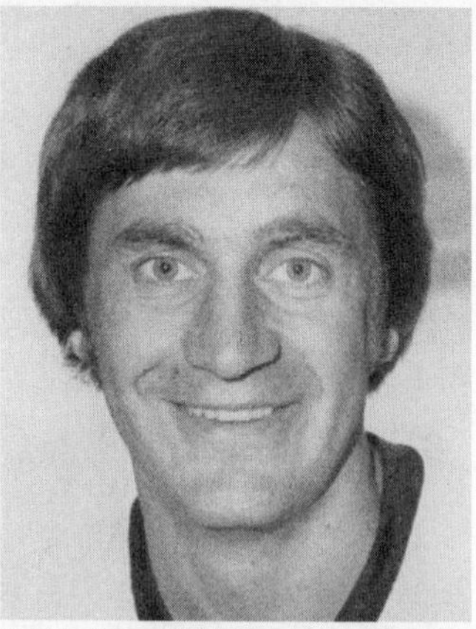

Bobby Schmautz

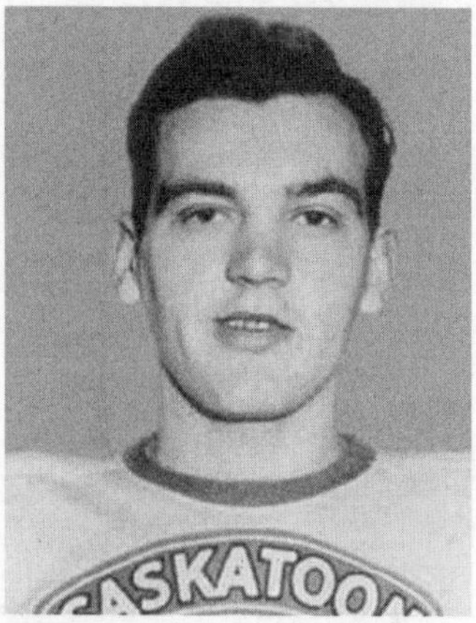

George Senick

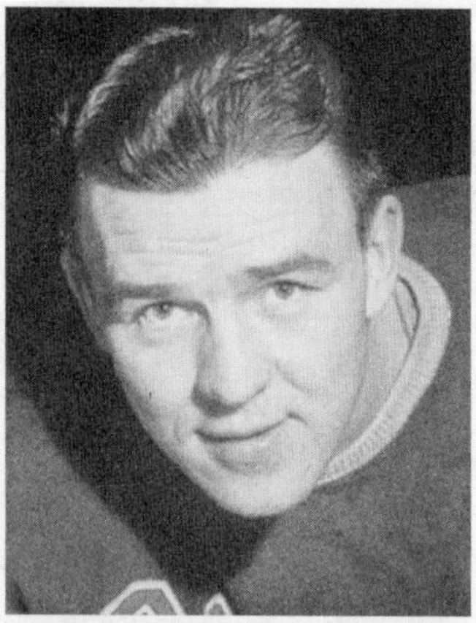

Alex Shibicky

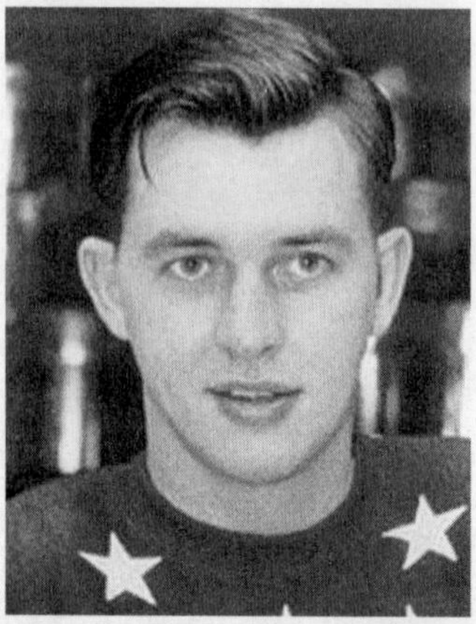

Cliff Simpson

			Regular Schedule					Playoffs					NHL	First	Last
Name	NHL Teams	NHL Seasons	GP	G	A	TP	PIM	GP	G	A	TP	PIM	Cup Wins	NHL Season	NHL Season
Samis, Phil	Tor.	2	2	0	0	0	0	5	0	1	1	2	1	1947-48	1949-50
Sampson, Gary	Wsh.	4	105	13	22	35	25	12	1	0	1	0	....	1983-84	1986-87
Samuelsson, Kjell	NYR, Phi., Pit., T.B.	14	813	48	138	186	1225	123	4	20	24	178	1	1985-86	1998-99
Samuelsson, Ulf	Hfd., Pit., NYR, Det., Phi.	16	1080	57	275	332	2453	132	7	27	34	272	2	1984-85	1999-00
Sandelin, Scott	Mtl., Phi., Min.	4	25	0	4	4	2	....	....	....	....	....	....	1986-87	1991-92
Sanderson, Derek	Bos., NYR, St.L., Van., Pit.	13	598	202	250	452	911	56	18	12	30	187	2	1965-66	1977-78
Sandford, Ed	Bos., Det., Chi.	9	502	106	145	251	355	42	13	11	24	27	....	1947-48	1955-56
Sandlak, Jim	Van., Hfd.	11	549	110	119	229	821	33	7	10	17	30	....	1985-86	1995-96
● Sands, Charlie	Tor., Bos., Mtl., NYR	12	427	99	109	208	58	34	6	6	12	4	1	1932-33	1943-44
Sandstrom, Tomas	NYR, L.A., Pit., Det., Ana.	15	983	394	462	856	1193	139	32	49	81	183	1	1984-85	1998-99
Sandwith, Terran	Edm.	1	8	0	0	0	6	....	....	....	....	....	....	1997-98	1997-98
Sanipass, Everett	Chi., Que.	5	164	25	34	59	358	5	2	0	2	4	....	1986-87	1990-91
‡ Sarault, Yves	Mtl., Cgy., Col., Ott., Atl., Nsh.	8	106	10	10	20	51	5	0	0	0	2	....	1994-95	2001-02
Sargent, Gary	L.A., Min.	8	402	61	161	222	273	20	5	7	12	8	....	1975-76	1982-83
Sarner, Craig	Bos.	1	7	0	0	0	0	....	....	....	....	....	....	1974-75	1974-75
Sarrazin, Dick	Phi.	3	100	20	35	55	22	4	0	0	0	0	....	1968-69	1971-72
Sasakamoose, Fred	Chi.	1	11	0	0	0	6	....	....	....	....	....	....	1953-54	1953-54
Sasser, Grant	Pit.	1	3	0	0	0	0	....	....	....	....	....	....	1983-84	1983-84
Sather, Glen	Bos., Pit., NYR, St.L., Mtl., Min.	10	658	80	113	193	724	72	1	5	6	86	....	1966-67	1975-76
Saunders, Bernie	Que.	2	10	0	1	1	8	....	....	....	....	....	....	1979-80	1980-81
Saunders, David	Van.	1	56	7	13	20	10	....	....	....	....	....	....	1987-88	1987-88
● Saunders, Ted	Ott.	1	18	1	3	4	4	....	....	....	....	....	....	1933-34	1933-34
Sauve, Jean-Francois	Buf., Que.	7	290	65	138	203	114	36	9	12	21	10	....	1980-81	1986-87
‡ Savage, Joel	Buf.	1	3	0	1	1	0	....	....	....	....	....	....	1990-91	1990-91
‡ Savage, Reggie	Wsh., Que.	3	34	5	7	12	28	....	....	....	....	....	....	1990-91	1993-94
● Savage, Tony	Bos., Mtl.	1	49	1	5	6	6	2	0	0	0	0	....	1934-35	1934-35
Savard, Andre	Bos., Buf., Que.	12	790	211	271	482	411	85	13	18	31	77	....	1973-74	1984-85
Savard, Denis	Chi., Mtl., T.B.	17	1196	473	865	1338	1336	169	66	109	175	256	1	1980-81	1996-97
Savard, Jean	Chi., Hfd.	3	43	7	12	19	29	....	....	....	....	....	....	1977-78	1979-80
Savard, Serge	Mtl., Wpg.	17	1040	106	333	439	592	130	19	49	68	88	8	1966-67	1982-83
‡ Savoia, Ryan	Pit.	1	3	0	0	0	0	....	....	....	....	....	....	1998-99	1998-99
Sawyer, Kevin	St.L., Bos., Phx., Ana.	6	110	3	3	6	403	....	....	....	....	....	....	1995-96	2002-03
Scamurra, Peter	Wsh.	4	132	8	25	33	59	....	....	....	....	....	....	1975-76	1979-80
Sceviour, Darin	Chi.	1	1	0	0	0	0	....	....	....	....	....	....	1986-87	1986-87
Schaeffer, Butch	Chi.	1	5	0	0	0	6	....	....	....	....	....	....	1936-37	1936-37
Schamehorn, Kevin	Det., L.A.	3	10	0	0	0	17	....	....	....	....	....	....	1976-77	1980-81
Schella, John	Van.	2	115	2	18	20	224	....	....	....	....	....	....	1970-71	1971-72
Scherza, Chuck	Bos., NYR	2	36	6	6	12	35	....	....	....	....	....	....	1943-44	1944-45
Schinkel, Ken	NYR, Pit.	12	636	127	198	325	163	19	7	2	9	4	....	1959-60	1972-73
‡ Schlegel, Brad	Wsh., Cgy.	3	48	1	8	9	10	7	0	1	1	2	....	1991-92	1993-94
Schliebener, Andy	Van.	3	84	2	11	13	74	6	0	0	0	0	....	1981-82	1984-85
Schmautz, Bobby	Chi., Van., Bos., Edm., Col.	13	764	271	286	557	988	84	28	33	61	92	....	1967-68	1980-81
● Schmautz, Cliff	Buf., Phi.	1	56	13	19	32	33	....	....	....	....	....	....	1970-71	1970-71
● Schmidt, Clarence	Bos.	1	7	1	0	1	2	....	....	....	....	....	....	1943-44	1943-44
Schmidt, Jackie	Bos.	1	45	6	7	13	6	5	0	0	0	0	....	1942-43	1942-43
Schmidt, Milt	Bos.	16	776	229	346	575	466	86	24	25	49	60	2	1936-37	1954-55
Schmidt, Norm	Pit.	4	125	23	33	56	73	....	....	....	....	....	....	1983-84	1987-88
Schmidt, Otto	Bos.	1	2	0	0	0	0	....	....	....	....	....	....	1943-44	1943-44
● Schnarr, Werner	Bos.	2	26	0	0	0	0	....	....	....	....	....	....	1924-25	1925-26
‡ Schneider, Andy	Ott.	1	10	0	0	0	15	....	....	....	....	....	....	1993-94	1993-94
Schock, Danny	Bos., Phi.	2	20	1	2	3	0	1	0	0	0	0	1	1969-70	1970-71
Schock, Ron	Bos., St.L., Pit., Buf.	15	909	166	351	517	260	55	4	16	20	29	....	1963-64	1977-78
Schoenfeld, Jim	Buf., Det., Bos.	13	719	51	204	255	1132	75	3	13	16	151	....	1972-73	1984-85
Schofield, Dwight	Det., Mtl., St.L., Wsh., Pit., Wpg.	7	211	8	22	30	631	9	0	0	0	55	....	1976-77	1987-88
Schreiber, Wally	Min.	2	41	8	10	18	12	....	....	....	....	....	....	1987-88	1988-89
● Schriner, Sweeney	NYA, Tor.	11	484	201	204	405	148	59	18	11	29	54	2	1934-35	1945-46
Schulte, Paxton	Que., Cgy.	2	2	0	0	0	4	....	....	....	....	....	....	1993-94	1996-97
Schultz, Dave	Phi., L.A., Pit., Buf.	9	535	79	121	200	2294	73	8	12	20	412	2	1971-72	1979-80
Schurman, Maynard	Hfd.	1	7	0	0	0	0	....	....	....	....	....	....	1979-80	1979-80
Schutt, Rod	Mtl., Pit., Tor.	8	286	77	92	169	177	22	8	6	14	26	....	1977-78	1985-86
Scissons, Scott	NYI	3	2	0	0	0	0	1	0	0	0	0	....	1990-91	1993-94
Sclisizzi, Enio	Det., Chi.	6	81	12	11	23	26	13	0	0	0	6	....	1946-47	1952-53
● Scott, Ganton	Tor., Ham., Mtl.M.	3	57	1	1	2	0	....	....	....	....	....	....	1922-23	1924-25
● Scott, Laurie	NYA, NYR	2	62	6	3	9	28	....	....	....	....	....	....	1926-27	1927-28
Scremin, Claudio	S.J.	2	17	0	1	1	29	....	....	....	....	....	....	1991-92	1992-93
Scruton, Howard	L.A.	1	4	0	4	4	9	....	....	....	....	....	....	1982-83	1982-83
Seabrooke, Glen	Phi.	3	19	1	6	7	4	....	....	....	....	....	....	1986-87	1988-89
Secord, Al	Bos., Chi., Tor., Phi.	12	766	273	222	495	2093	102	21	34	55	382	....	1978-79	1989-90
Sedlbauer, Ron	Van., Chi., Tor.	7	430	143	86	229	210	19	1	3	4	27	....	1974-75	1980-81
Seftel, Steve	Wsh.	1	4	0	0	0	2	....	....	....	....	....	....	1990-91	1990-91
Seguin, Dan	Min., Van.	2	37	2	6	8	50	....	....	....	....	....	....	1970-71	1973-74
Seguin, Steve	L.A.	1	5	0	0	0	9	....	....	....	....	....	....	1984-85	1984-85
● Seibert, Earl	NYR, Chi., Det.	15	645	89	187	276	746	66	11	8	19	76	2	1931-32	1945-46
Seiling, Ric	Buf., Det.	10	738	179	208	387	573	62	14	14	28	36	....	1977-78	1986-87
Seiling, Rod	Tor., NYR, Wsh., St.L., Atl.	17	979	62	269	331	601	77	4	8	12	55	....	1962-63	1978-79
Sejba, Jiri	Buf.	1	11	0	2	2	8	....	....	....	....	....	....	1990-91	1990-91
Selby, Brit	Tor., Phi., St.L.	8	350	55	62	117	163	16	1	1	2	8	....	1964-65	1971-72
Self, Steve	Wsh.	1	3	0	0	0	0	....	....	....	....	....	....	1976-77	1976-77
Selivanov, Alex	T.B., Edm., CBJ	7	459	121	114	235	379	13	2	3	5	16	....	1994-95	2000-01
Sellars, Luke	Atl.	1	1	0	0	0	2	....	....	....	....	....	....	2001-02	2001-02
Selmser, Sean	CBJ	1	1	0	0	0	5	....	....	....	....	....	....	2000-01	2000-01
Selwood, Brad	Tor., L.A.	3	163	7	40	47	153	6	0	0	0	4	....	1970-71	1979-80
‡ Semak, Alexander	N.J., T.B., NYI, Van.	6	289	83	91	174	187	8	1	1	2	0	....	1991-92	1996-97
Semchuk, Brandy	L.A.	1	1	0	0	0	2	....	....	....	....	....	....	1992-93	1992-93
Semenko, Dave	Edm., Hfd., Tor.	9	575	65	88	153	1175	73	6	6	12	208	2	1979-80	1987-88
Semenov, Anatoli	Edm., T.B., Van., Ana., Phi., Buf.	8	362	68	126	194	122	49	9	13	22	12	....	1989-90	1996-97
Senick, George	NYR	1	13	2	3	5	8	....	....	....	....	....	....	1952-53	1952-53
Seppa, Jyrki	Wpg.	1	13	0	2	2	6	....	....	....	....	....	....	1983-84	1983-84
Serafini, Ron	Cal.	1	2	0	0	0	2	....	....	....	....	....	....	1973-74	1973-74
Serowik, Jeff	Tor., Bos., Pit.	4	28	0	6	6	16	....	....	....	....	....	....	1990-91	1999-00
Servinis, George	Min.	1	5	0	0	0	0	....	....	....	....	....	....	1987-88	1987-88
Sevcik, Jaroslav	Que.	1	13	0	2	2	2	....	....	....	....	....	....	1989-90	1989-90
Severyn, Brent	Que., Fla., NYI, Col., Ana., Dal.	7	328	10	30	40	825	8	0	0	0	12	....	1989-90	1998-99
Sevigny, Pierre	Mtl., NYR	4	78	4	5	9	64	3	0	1	1	0	....	1993-94	1997-98
Shack, Eddie	NYR, Tor., Bos., L.A., Buf., Pit.	17	1047	239	226	465	1437	74	6	7	13	151	4	1958-59	1974-75
● Shack, Joe	NYR	2	70	9	27	36	20	....	....	....	....	....	....	1942-43	1944-45
Shafranov, Konstantin	St.L.	1	5	2	1	3	0	....	....	....	....	....	....	1996-97	1996-97
Shakes, Paul	Cal.	1	21	0	4	4	12	....	....	....	....	....	....	1973-74	1973-74
Shaldybin, Yevgeny	Bos.	1	3	1	0	1	0	....	....	....	....	....	....	1996-97	1996-97
Shanahan, Sean	Mtl., Col., Bos.	3	40	1	3	4	47	....	....	....	....	....	....	1975-76	1977-78
Shand, Dave	Atl., Tor., Wsh.	8	421	19	84	103	544	26	1	2	3	83	....	1976-77	1984-85
Shank, Daniel	Det., Hfd.	3	77	13	14	27	175	5	0	0	0	22	....	1989-90	1991-92
Shannon, Chuck	NYA	1	4	0	0	0	2	....	....	....	....	....	....	1939-40	1939-40
Shannon, Darrin	Buf., Wpg., Phx.	10	506	87	163	250	344	45	7	10	17	38	....	1988-89	1997-98
‡ Shannon, Darryl	Tor., Wpg., Buf., Atl., Cgy., Mtl.	13	544	28	111	139	523	29	4	7	11	16	....	1988-89	2000-01
● Shannon, Gerry	Ott., St.L., Bos., Mtl.M.	5	180	23	29	52	80	9	0	1	1	2	....	1933-34	1937-38
Sharifijanov, Vadim	N.J., Van.	3	92	16	21	37	50	4	0	0	0	0	....	1996-97	1999-00
Sharples, Jeff	Det.	3	105	14	35	49	70	7	0	3	3	6	....	1986-87	1988-89
Sharpley, Glen	Min., Chi.	6	389	117	161	278	199	27	7	11	18	24	....	1976-77	1981-82
Shaunessy, Scott	Que.	2	7	0	0	0	23	....	....	....	....	....	....	1986-87	1988-89
Shaw, Brad	Hfd., Ott., Wsh., St.L.	11	377	22	137	159	208	23	4	8	12	6	....	1985-86	1998-99
Shaw, David	Que., NYR, Edm., Min., Bos., T.B.	16	769	41	153	194	906	45	3	9	12	81	....	1982-83	1997-98
● Shay, Norm	Bos., Tor.	2	53	5	3	8	34	....	....	....	....	....	....	1924-25	1925-26
● Shea, Pat	Chi.	1	10	1	0	1	0	....	....	....	....	....	....	1931-32	1931-32
‡ Shearer, Rob	Col.	1	2	0	0	0	0	....	....	....	....	....	....	2000-01	2000-01
Shedden, Doug	Pit., Det., Que., Tor.	8	416	139	186	325	176	....	....	....	....	....	....	1981-82	1990-91
Sheehan, Bobby	Mtl., Cal., Chi., Det., NYR, Col., L.A.	9	310	48	63	111	40	25	4	3	7	8	1	1969-70	1981-82
Sheehy, Neil	Cgy., Hfd., Wsh.	9	379	18	47	65	1311	54	0	3	3	241	....	1983-84	1991-92
Sheehy, Tim	Det., Hfd.	2	27	2	1	3	0	....	....	....	....	....	....	1977-78	1979-80
Shelton, Doug	Chi.	1	5	0	1	1	2	....	....	....	....	....	....	1967-68	1967-68
● Sheppard, Frank	Det.	1	8	1	1	2	0	....	....	....	....	....	....	1927-28	1927-28
Sheppard, Gregg	Bos., Pit.	10	657	205	293	498	243	82	32	40	72	31	....	1972-73	1981-82
● Sheppard, Johnny	Det., NYA, Bos., Chi.	8	308	68	58	126	224	10	0	0	0	0	1	1926-27	1933-34
Sheppard, Ray	Buf., NYR, Det., S.J., Fla., Car.	13	817	357	300	657	212	81	30	20	50	21	....	1987-88	1999-00
● Sherf, John	Det.	5	19	0	0	0	8	8	0	1	1	2	1	1935-36	1943-44

			Regular Schedule					Playoffs					NHL	First	Last
Name	NHL Teams	NHL Seasons	GP	G	A	TP	PIM	GP	G	A	TP	PIM	Cup Wins	NHL Season	NHL Season
• Shero, Fred	NYR	3	145	6	14	20	137	13	0	2	2	8	....	1947-48	1949-50
• Sherritt, Gordon	Det.	1	8	0	0	0	12	....	....	....	....	....	....	1943-44	1943-44
Sherven, Gord	Edm., Min., Hfd.	5	97	13	22	35	33	3	0	0	0	0	....	1983-84	1987-88
Shevalier, Jeff	L.A., T.B.	3	32	5	9	14	8	....	....	....	....	....	....	1994-95	1999-00
• Shewchuk, Jack	Bos.	6	187	9	19	28	160	20	0	1	1	19	1	1938-39	1944-45
Shibicky, Alex	NYR	8	324	110	91	201	161	39	12	12	24	12	1	1935-36	1945-46
• Shields, Al	Ott., Phi., NYA, Mtl.M., Bos.	11	459	42	46	88	637	17	0	1	1	14	1	1927-28	1937-38
Shill, Bill	Bos.	3	79	21	13	34	18	7	1	2	3	2	....	1942-43	1946-47
• Shill, Jack	Tor., Bos., NYA, Chi.	6	160	15	20	35	70	25	1	6	7	23	1	1933-34	1938-39
Shinske, Rick	Cle., St.L.	3	63	5	16	21	10	....	....	....	....	....	....	1976-77	1978-79
Shires, Jim	Det., St.L., Pit.	3	56	3	6	9	32	....	....	....	....	....	....	1970-71	1972-73
• Shmyr, Paul	Chi., Cal., Min., Hfd.	7	343	13	72	85	528	34	3	3	6	44	....	1968-69	1981-82
Shoebottom, Bruce	Bos.	4	35	1	4	5	53	14	1	2	3	77	....	1987-88	1990-91
• Shore, Eddie	Bos., NYA	14	550	105	179	284	1047	55	6	13	19	181	2	1926-27	1939-40
• Shore, Hamby	Ott.	1	18	3	8	11	51	....	....	....	....	....	....	1917-18	1917-18
Short, Steve	L.A., Det.	2	6	0	0	0	2	....	....	....	....	....	....	1977-78	1978-79
‡ Shuchuk, Gary	Det., L.A.	5	142	13	26	39	70	20	2	2	4	12	....	1990-91	1995-96
Shudra, Ron	Edm.	1	10	0	5	5	6	....	....	....	....	....	....	1987-88	1987-88
Shutt, Steve	Mtl., L.A.	13	930	424	393	817	410	99	50	48	98	65	5	1972-73	1984-85
• Siebert, Babe	Mtl.M., NYR, Bos., Mtl.	14	592	140	156	296	982	49	7	5	12	62	2	1925-26	1938-39
Silk, Dave	NYR, Bos., Det., Wpg.	7	249	54	59	113	271	13	2	4	6	13	....	1979-80	1985-86
Siltala, Mike	Wsh., NYR	3	7	1	0	1	2	....	....	....	....	....	....	1981-82	1987-88
Siltanen, Risto	Edm., Hfd., Que.	8	562	90	265	355	266	32	6	12	18	30	....	1979-80	1986-87
Sim, Trevor	Edm.	1	3	0	1	1	2	....	....	....	....	....	....	1989-90	1989-90
Simard, Martin	Cgy., T.B.	3	44	1	5	6	183	....	....	....	....	....	....	1990-91	1992-93
‡ Simicek, Roman	Pit., Min.	2	63	7	10	17	59	....	....	....	....	....	....	2000-01	2001-02
Simmer, Charlie	Cal., Cle., L.A., Bos., Pit.	14	712	342	369	711	544	24	9	9	18	32	....	1974-75	1987-88
Simmons, Al	Cal., Bos.	3	11	0	1	1	21	1	0	0	0	0	....	1971-72	1975-76
• Simon, Cully	Det., Chi.	3	130	4	11	15	121	14	1	0	1	6	1	1942-43	1944-45
Simon, Jason	NYI, Phx.	2	5	0	0	0	34	....	....	....	....	....	....	1993-94	1996-97
Simon, Thain	Det.	1	3	0	0	0	0	....	....	....	....	....	....	1946-47	1946-47
Simon, Todd	Buf.	1	15	0	1	1	0	5	1	0	1	0	....	1993-94	1993-94
Simonetti, Frank	Bos.	4	115	5	8	13	76	12	0	1	1	8	....	1984-85	1987-88
Simpson, Bobby	Atl., St.L., Pit.	5	175	35	29	64	98	6	0	1	1	2	....	1976-77	1982-83
• Simpson, Cliff	Det.	2	6	0	1	1	0	2	0	0	0	2	....	1946-47	1947-48
Simpson, Craig	Pit., Edm., Buf.	10	634	247	250	497	659	67	36	32	68	56	2	1985-86	1994-95
• Simpson, Joe	NYA	6	228	21	19	40	156	2	0	0	0	0	....	1925-26	1930-31
Sims, Al	Bos., Hfd., L.A.	10	475	49	116	165	286	41	0	2	2	14	....	1973-74	1982-83
Sinclair, Reg	NYR, Det.	3	208	49	43	92	139	3	1	0	1	0	....	1950-51	1952-53
• Singbush, Alex	Mtl.	1	32	0	5	5	15	3	0	0	0	4	....	1940-41	1940-41
Sinisalo, Ilkka	Phi., Min., L.A.	11	582	204	222	426	208	68	21	11	32	6	....	1981-82	1991-92
Siren, Ville	Pit., Min.	5	290	14	68	82	276	7	0	0	0	6	....	1985-86	1989-90
Sirois, Bob	Phi., Wsh.	6	286	92	120	212	42	....	....	....	....	....	....	1974-75	1979-80
Sittler, Darryl	Tor., Phi., Det.	15	1096	484	637	1121	948	76	29	45	74	137	....	1970-71	1984-85
• Sjoberg, Lars-Erik	Wpg.	1	79	7	27	34	48	....	....	....	....	....	....	1979-80	1979-80
‡ Sjodin, Tommy	Min., Dal., Que.	2	106	8	40	48	52	....	....	....	....	....	....	1992-93	1993-94
• Skaare, Bjorn	Det.	1	1	0	0	0	0	....	....	....	....	....	....	1978-79	1978-79
Skarda, Randy	St.L.	2	26	0	5	5	11	....	....	....	....	....	....	1989-90	1991-92
• Skilton, Raymie	Mtl.W.	1	1	0	0	0	0	....	....	....	....	....	....	1917-18	1917-18
• Skinner, Alf	Tor., Bos., Mtl.M., Pit.	4	71	26	10	36	87	2	0	1	1	9	1	1917-18	1925-26
Skinner, Larry	Col.	4	47	10	12	22	8	2	0	0	0	0	....	1976-77	1979-80
‡ Skopintsev, Andrei	T.B., Atl.	3	40	2	4	6	32	....	....	....	....	....	....	1998-99	2000-01
Skov, Glen	Det., Chi., Mtl.	12	650	106	136	242	413	53	7	7	14	48	3	1949-50	1960-61
Skriko, Petri	Van., Bos., Wpg., S.J.	9	541	183	222	405	246	28	5	9	14	4	....	1984-85	1992-93
Skrudland, Brian	Mtl., Cgy., Fla., NYR, Dal.	15	881	124	219	343	1107	164	15	46	61	323	2	1985-86	1999-00
Sleaver, John	Chi.	2	13	1	0	1	6	....	....	....	....	....	....	1953-54	1956-57
Sleigher, Louis	Que., Bos.	6	194	46	53	99	146	17	1	1	2	64	....	1979-80	1985-86
Sloan, Tod	Tor., Chi.	13	745	220	262	482	831	47	9	12	21	47	2	1947-48	1960-61
• Slobodian, Peter	NYA	1	41	3	2	5	54	....	....	....	....	....	....	1940-41	1940-41
• Slowinski, Ed	NYR	6	291	58	74	132	63	16	2	6	8	6	....	1947-48	1952-53
Sly, Darryl	Tor., Min., Van.	4	79	1	2	3	20	....	....	....	....	....	....	1965-66	1970-71
Smail, Doug	Wpg., Min., Que., Ott.	13	845	210	249	459	602	42	9	2	11	49	....	1980-81	1992-93
Smart, Alex	Mtl.	1	8	5	2	7	0	....	....	....	....	....	....	1942-43	1942-43
Smedsmo, Dale	Tor.	1	4	0	0	0	0	....	....	....	....	....	....	1972-73	1972-73
Smehlik, Richard	Buf., Atl., N.J.	10	644	49	146	195	415	88	1	14	15	40	1	1992-93	2002-03
Smillie, Don	Bos.	1	12	2	2	4	4	....	....	....	....	....	....	1933-34	1933-34
• Smith, Alex	Ott., Det., Bos., NYA	11	443	41	50	91	645	19	0	2	2	26	1	1924-25	1934-35
• Smith, Art	Tor., Ott.	4	144	15	10	25	249	4	1	1	2	8	....	1927-28	1930-31
Smith, Barry	Bos., Col.	3	114	7	7	14	10	....	....	....	....	....	....	1975-76	1980-81
Smith, Bobby	Min., Mtl.	15	1077	357	679	1036	917	184	64	96	160	245	1	1978-79	1992-93
Smith, Brad	Van., Atl., Cgy., Det., Tor.	9	222	28	34	62	591	20	3	3	6	49	....	1978-79	1986-87
Smith, Brian	Det.	3	61	2	8	10	12	5	0	0	0	0	....	1957-58	1960-61
• Smith, Brian	L.A., Min.	2	67	10	10	20	33	7	0	0	0	0	....	1967-68	1968-69
• Smith, Carl	Det.	1	7	1	1	2	2	....	....	....	....	....	....	1943-44	1943-44
Smith, Clint	NYR, Chi.	11	483	161	236	397	24	42	10	14	24	2	1	1936-37	1946-47
Smith, Dallas	Bos., NYR	16	890	55	252	307	959	86	3	29	32	128	2	1959-60	1977-78
Smith, Dennis	Wsh., L.A.	2	8	0	0	0	4	....	....	....	....	....	....	1989-90	1990-91
Smith, Derek	Buf., Det.	8	335	78	116	194	60	30	9	14	23	13	....	1975-76	1982-83
Smith, Derrick	Phi., Min., Dal.	10	537	82	92	174	373	82	14	11	25	79	....	1984-85	1993-94
• Smith, Des	Mtl.M., Mtl., Chi., Bos.	5	196	22	25	47	236	25	1	4	5	18	1	1937-38	1941-42
• Smith, Don	Mtl.	1	12	1	0	1	6	....	....	....	....	....	....	1919-20	1919-20
Smith, Don	NYR	1	11	1	1	2	0	1	0	0	0	0	....	1949-50	1949-50
Smith, Doug	L.A., Buf., Edm., Van., Pit.	9	535	115	138	253	624	18	4	2	6	21	....	1981-82	1989-90
Smith, Floyd	Bos., NYR, Det., Tor., Buf.	13	616	129	178	307	207	48	12	11	23	16	....	1954-55	1971-72
Smith, Geoff	Edm., Fla., NYR	10	462	18	73	91	282	13	0	1	1	8	1	1989-90	1998-99
Smith, Glen	Chi.	1	2	0	0	0	0	....	....	....	....	....	....	1950-51	1950-51
• Smith, Glenn	Tor.	1	9	0	0	0	0	....	....	....	....	....	....	1921-22	1921-22
Smith, Gord	Wsh., Wpg.	6	299	9	30	39	284	....	....	....	....	....	....	1974-75	1979-80
Smith, Greg	Cal., Cle., Min., Det., Wsh.	13	829	56	232	288	1110	63	4	7	11	106	....	1975-76	1987-88
• Smith, Hooley	Ott., Mtl.M., Bos., NYA	17	715	200	225	425	1013	54	11	8	19	109	2	1924-25	1940-41
• Smith, Ken	Bos.	7	331	78	93	171	49	30	8	13	21	6	....	1944-45	1950-51
Smith, Nakina	Det.	1	10	1	2	3	0	....	....	....	....	....	....	1943-44	1943-44
Smith, Randy	Min.	2	3	0	0	0	0	....	....	....	....	....	....	1985-86	1986-87
Smith, Rick	Bos., Cal., St.L., Det., Wsh.	11	687	52	167	219	560	78	3	23	26	73	1	1968-69	1980-81
• Smith, Rodger	Pit., Phi.	6	210	20	4	24	172	4	3	0	3	0	....	1925-26	1930-31
Smith, Ron	NYI	1	11	1	1	2	14	....	....	....	....	....	....	1972-73	1972-73
• Smith, Sid	Tor.	12	601	186	183	369	94	44	17	10	27	2	3	1946-47	1957-58
Smith, Stan	NYR	2	9	2	1	3	0	1	0	0	0	0	1	1939-40	1940-41
Smith, Steve	Phi., Buf.	6	18	0	1	1	15	....	....	....	....	....	....	1981-82	1988-89
Smith, Steve	Edm., Chi., Cgy.	16	804	72	303	375	2139	134	11	41	52	288	3	1984-85	2000-01
Smith, Stu	Mtl.	2	4	2	2	4	2	1	0	0	0	0	....	1940-41	1941-42
Smith, Stu	Hfd.	4	77	2	10	12	95	....	....	....	....	....	....	1979-80	1982-83
• Smith, Tommy	Que.	1	10	0	1	1	11	....	....	....	....	....	....	1919-20	1919-20
Smith, Vern	NYI	1	1	0	0	0	0	....	....	....	....	....	....	1984-85	1984-85
Smith, Wayne	Chi.	1	2	1	1	2	2	1	0	0	0	0	....	1966-67	1966-67
Smrke, John	St.L., Que.	3	103	11	17	28	33	....	....	....	....	....	....	1977-78	1979-80
• Smrke, Stan	Mtl.	2	9	0	3	3	0	....	....	....	....	....	....	1956-57	1957-58
Smyl, Stan	Van.	13	896	262	411	673	1556	41	16	17	33	64	....	1978-79	1990-91
• Smylie, Rod	Tor., Ott.	6	74	4	2	6	12	4	0	0	0	2	1	1920-21	1925-26
Smyth, Greg	Phi., Que., Cgy., Fla., Tor., Chi.	10	229	4	16	20	783	12	0	0	0	40	....	1986-87	1996-97
Smyth, Kevin	Hfd.	3	58	6	8	14	31	....	....	....	....	....	....	1993-94	1995-96
Snell, Chris	Tor., L.A.	2	34	2	7	9	24	....	....	....	....	....	....	1993-94	1994-95
Snell, Ron	Pit.	2	7	3	2	5	6	....	....	....	....	....	....	1968-69	1969-70
Snell, Ted	Pit., K.C., Det.	2	104	7	18	25	22	....	....	....	....	....	....	1973-74	1974-75
Snepsts, Harold	Van., Min., Det., St.L.	17	1033	38	195	233	2009	93	1	14	15	231	....	1974-75	1990-91
Snow, Sandy	Det.	1	3	0	0	0	2	....	....	....	....	....	....	1968-69	1968-69
Snuggerud, Dave	Buf., S.J., Phi.	4	265	30	54	84	127	12	1	3	4	6	....	1989-90	1992-93
• Snyder, Dan	Atl.	3	49	11	5	16	64	....	....	....	....	....	....	2000-01	2002-03
Sobchuk, Dennis	Det., Que.	2	35	5	6	11	2	....	....	....	....	....	....	1979-80	1982-83
• Sobchuk, Gene	Van.	1	1	0	0	0	0	....	....	....	....	....	....	1973-74	1973-74
Solheim, Ken	Chi., Min., Det., Edm.	5	135	19	20	39	34	3	1	1	2	2	....	1980-81	1985-86
Solinger, Bob	Tor., Det.	5	99	10	11	21	19	....	....	....	....	....	....	1951-52	1959-60
• Somers, Art	Chi., NYR	6	222	33	56	89	189	30	1	5	6	20	1	1929-30	1934-35
Sommer, Roy	Edm.	1	3	1	0	1	7	....	....	....	....	....	....	1980-81	1980-81
Songin, Tom	Bos.	3	43	5	5	10	22	....	....	....	....	....	....	1978-79	1980-81

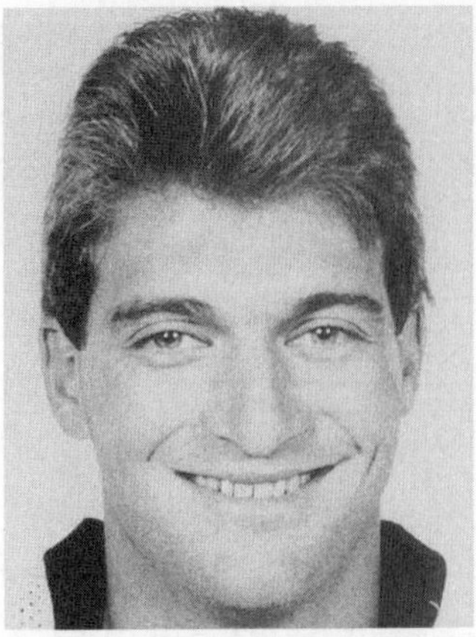
Louis Sleigher

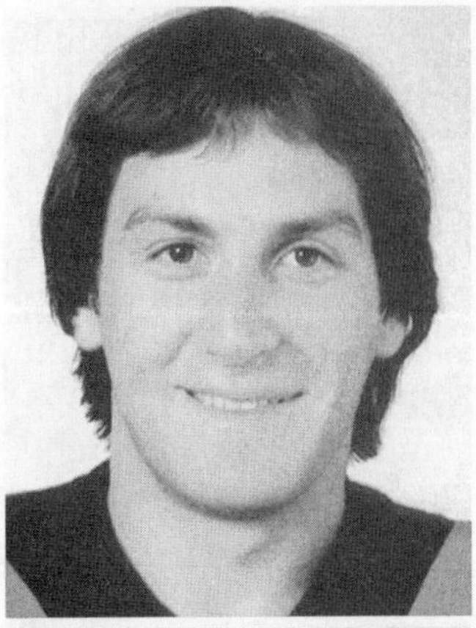
Stan Smyl

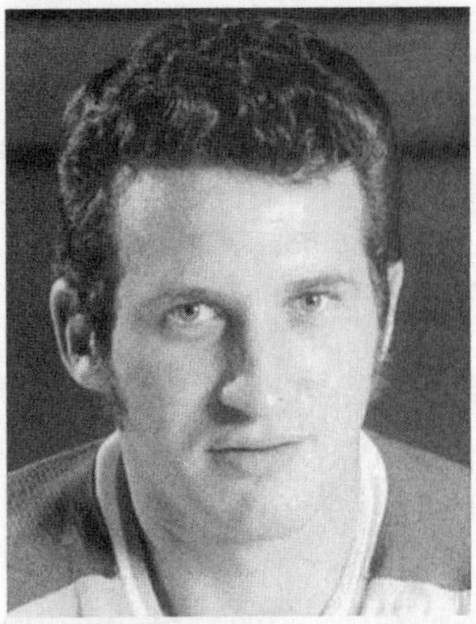
Sandy Snow

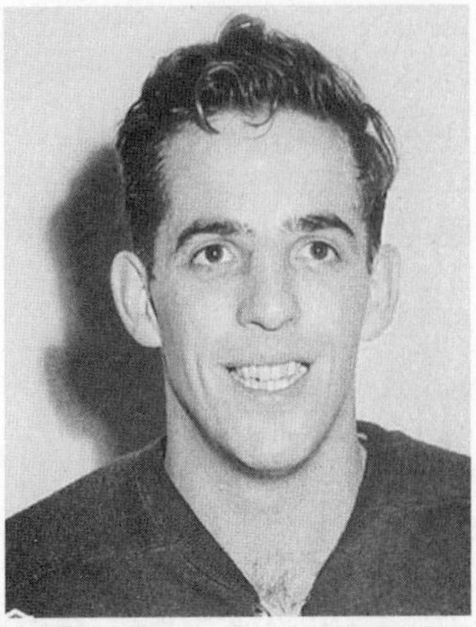
Glen Sonmor

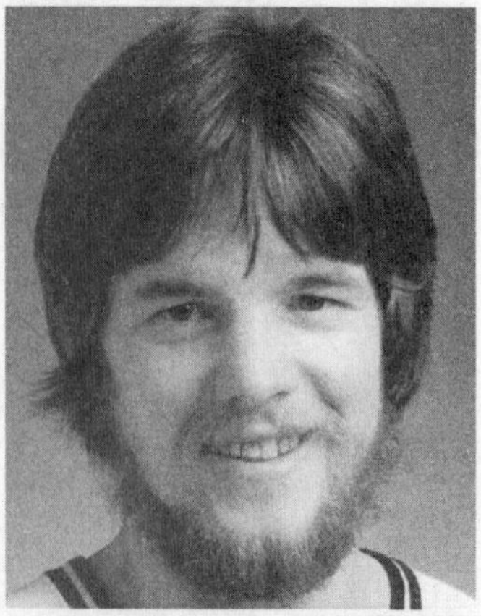

Andy Spruce

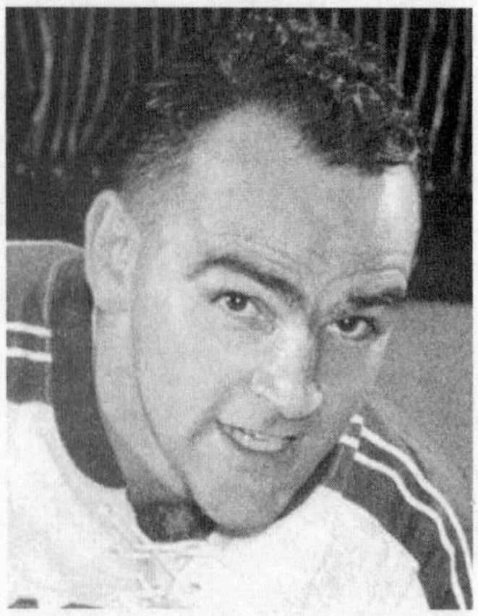

Neil Strain

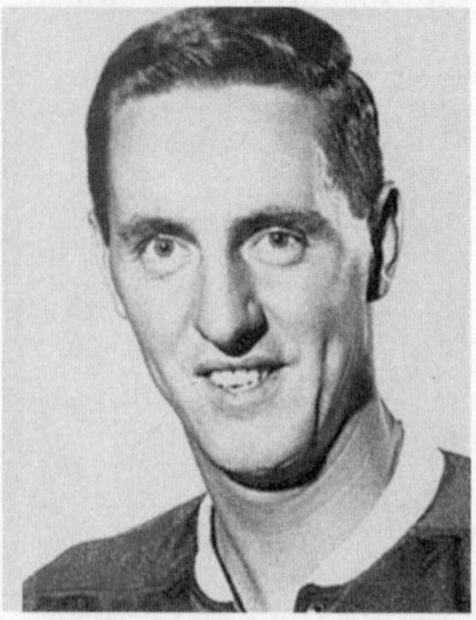

Joe Szura

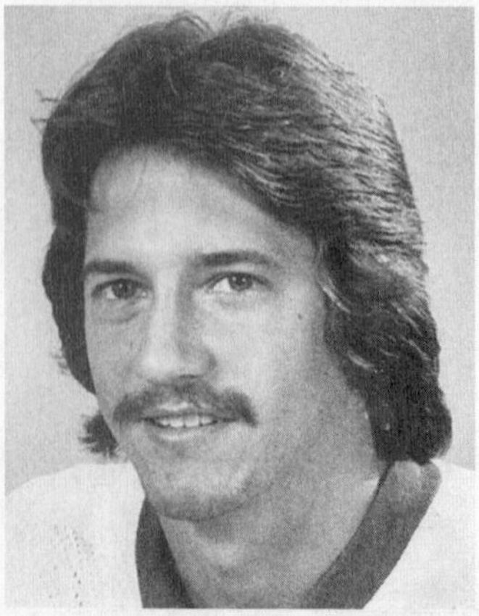

Steve Tambellini

Name	NHL Teams	NHL Seasons	Regular Schedule GP	G	A	TP	PIM	Playoffs GP	G	A	TP	PIM	NHL Cup Wins	First NHL Season	Last NHL Season
Sonmor, Glen	NYR	2	28	2	0	2	21	....	....	....	....	....	....	1953-54	1954-55
‡ Sorochan, Lee	Cgy.	2	3	0	0	0	0	....	....	....	....	....	....	1998-99	1999-00
• Sorrell, John	Det., NYA	11	490	127	119	246	100	42	12	15	27	10	2	1930-31	1940-41
• Sparrow, Emory	Bos.	1	8	0	0	0	4	....	....	....	....	....	....	1924-25	1924-25
Speck, Fred	Det., Van.	3	28	1	2	3	2	....	....	....	....	....	....	1968-69	1971-72
• Speer, Bill	Pit., Bos.	4	130	5	20	25	79	8	1	0	1	4	1	1967-68	1970-71
Speers, Ted	Det.	1	4	1	1	2	0	....	....	....	....	....	....	1985-86	1985-86
• Spence, Gordon	Tor.	1	3	0	0	0	0	....	....	....	....	....	....	1925-26	1925-26
• Spencer, Brian	Tor., NYI, Buf., Pit.	10	553	80	143	223	634	37	1	5	6	29	....	1969-70	1978-79
Spencer, Irv	NYR, Bos., Det.	8	230	12	38	50	127	16	0	0	0	8	....	1959-60	1967-68
• Speyer, Chris	Tor., NYA	3	14	0	0	0	0	....	....	....	....	....	....	1923-24	1933-34
Spring, Corey	T.B.	2	16	1	1	2	12	....	....	....	....	....	....	1997-98	1998-99
Spring, Don	Wpg.	4	259	1	54	55	80	6	0	0	0	10	....	1980-81	1983-84
Spring, Frank	Bos., St.L., Cal., Cle.	5	61	14	20	34	12	....	....	....	....	....	....	1969-70	1976-77
• Spring, Jesse	Ham., Pit., Tor., NYA	6	133	11	4	15	74	2	0	2	2	2	....	1923-24	1929-30
Spruce, Andy	Van., Col.	3	172	31	42	73	111	2	0	2	2	0	....	1976-77	1978-79
Srsen, Tomas	Edm.	1	2	0	0	0	0	....	....	....	....	....	....	1990-91	1990-91
St. Amour, Martin	Ott.	1	1	0	0	0	2	....	....	....	....	....	....	1992-93	1992-93
St. Laurent, Andre	NYI, Det., L.A., Pit.	11	644	129	187	316	749	59	8	12	20	48	....	1973-74	1983-84
St. Laurent, Dollard	Mtl., Chi.	12	652	29	133	162	496	92	2	22	24	87	5	1950-51	1961-62
St. Marseille, Frank	St.L., L.A.	10	707	140	285	425	242	88	20	25	45	18	....	1967-68	1976-77
St. Sauveur, Claude	Atl.	1	79	24	24	48	23	2	0	0	0	0	....	1975-76	1975-76
Stackhouse, Ron	Cal., Det., Pit.	12	889	87	372	459	824	32	5	8	13	38	....	1970-71	1981-82
• Stackhouse, Ted	Tor.	1	13	0	0	0	2	1	0	0	0	0	1	1921-22	1921-22
• Stahan, Butch	Mtl.	1	....	....	....	....	....	3	0	1	1	2	....	1944-45	1944-45
Stajduhar, Nick	Edm.	1	2	0	0	0	4	....	....	....	....	....	....	1995-96	1995-96
Staley, Al	NYR	1	1	0	1	1	0	....	....	....	....	....	....	1948-49	1948-49
Stamler, Lorne	L.A., Tor., Wpg.	4	116	14	11	25	16	....	....	....	....	....	....	1976-77	1979-80
Standing, George	Min.	1	2	0	0	0	0	....	....	....	....	....	....	1967-68	1967-68
Stanfield, Fred	Chi., Bos., Min., Buf.	14	914	211	405	616	134	106	21	35	56	10	2	1964-65	1977-78
Stanfield, Jack	Chi.	1	....	....	....	....	....	1	0	0	0	0	....	1965-66	1965-66
Stanfield, Jim	L.A.	3	7	0	1	1	0	....	....	....	....	....	....	1969-70	1971-72
Stankiewicz, Ed	Det.	2	6	0	0	0	2	....	....	....	....	....	....	1953-54	1955-56
Stankiewicz, Myron	St.L., Phi.	1	35	0	7	7	36	1	0	0	0	0	....	1968-69	1968-69
Stanley, Allan	NYR, Chi., Bos., Tor., Phi.	21	1244	100	333	433	792	109	7	36	43	80	4	1948-49	1968-69
• Stanley, Barney	Chi.	1	1	0	0	0	0	....	....	....	....	....	....	1927-28	1927-28
Stanley, Daryl	Phi., Van.	6	189	8	17	25	408	17	0	0	0	30	....	1983-84	1989-90
Stanowski, Wally	Tor., NYR	10	428	23	88	111	160	60	3	14	17	13	4	1939-40	1950-51
‡ Stanton, Paul	Pit., Bos., NYI	5	295	14	49	63	262	44	2	10	12	66	2	1990-91	1994-95
Stapleton, Brian	Wsh.	1	1	0	0	0	0	....	....	....	....	....	....	1975-76	1975-76
‡ Stapleton, Mike	Chi., Pit., Edm., Wpg., Phx., Atl., NYI, Van.	14	697	71	111	182	342	34	1	0	1	39	....	1986-87	2000-01
Stapleton, Pat	Bos., Chi.	10	635	43	294	337	353	65	10	39	49	38	....	1961-62	1972-73
Starikov, Sergei	N.J.	1	16	0	1	1	8	....	....	....	....	....	....	1989-90	1989-90
• Starr, Harold	Ott., Mtl.M., Mtl., NYR	7	205	6	5	11	186	15	1	0	1	4	....	1929-30	1935-36
Starr, Wilf	NYA, Det.	4	87	8	6	14	25	7	0	2	2	2	....	1932-33	1935-36
Stasiuk, Vic	Chi., Det., Bos.	14	745	183	254	437	669	69	16	18	34	40	3	1949-50	1962-63
Stastny, Anton	Que.	9	650	252	384	636	150	66	20	32	52	31	....	1980-81	1988-89
Stastny, Marian	Que., Tor.	5	322	121	173	294	110	32	5	17	22	7	....	1981-82	1985-86
Stastny, Peter	Que., N.J., St.L.	15	977	450	789	1239	824	93	33	72	105	123	....	1980-81	1994-95
Staszak, Ray	Det.	1	4	0	1	1	7	....	....	....	....	....	....	1985-86	1985-86
• Steele, Frank	Det.	1	1	0	0	0	0	....	....	....	....	....	....	1930-31	1930-31
Steen, Anders	Wpg.	1	42	5	11	16	22	....	....	....	....	....	....	1980-81	1980-81
Steen, Thomas	Wpg.	14	950	264	553	817	753	56	12	32	44	62	....	1981-82	1994-95
Stefaniw, Morris	Atl.	1	13	1	1	2	2	....	....	....	....	....	....	1972-73	1972-73
Stefanski, Bud	NYR	1	1	0	0	0	0	....	....	....	....	....	....	1977-78	1977-78
Stemkowski, Pete	Tor., Det., NYR, L.A.	15	967	206	349	555	866	83	25	29	54	136	1	1963-64	1977-78
Stenlund, Vern	Cle.	1	4	0	0	0	0	....	....	....	....	....	....	1976-77	1976-77
Stephenson, Bob	Hfd., Tor.	1	18	2	3	5	4	....	....	....	....	....	....	1979-80	1979-80
Stern, Ron	Van., Cgy., S.J.	12	638	75	86	161	2077	43	7	7	14	119	....	1987-88	1999-00
Sterner, Ulf	NYR	1	4	0	0	0	0	....	....	....	....	....	....	1964-65	1964-65
Stevens, John	Phi., Hfd.	5	53	0	10	10	48	....	....	....	....	....	....	1986-87	1993-94
Stevens, Kevin	Pit., Bos., L.A., NYR, Phi.	15	874	329	397	726	1470	103	46	60	106	170	2	1987-88	2001-02
‡ Stevens, Mike	Van., Bos., NYI, Tor.	4	23	1	4	5	29	....	....	....	....	....	....	1984-85	1989-90
• Stevens, Phil	Mtl.W., Mtl., Bos.	3	25	1	0	1	3	....	....	....	....	....	....	1917-18	1925-26
Stevens, Scott	Wsh., St.L., N.J.	22	1635	196	712	908	2785	233	26	92	118	402	3	1982-83	2003-04
Stevenson, Shayne	Bos., T.B.	3	27	0	2	2	35	....	....	....	....	....	....	1990-91	1992-93
Stewart, Allan	N.J., Bos.	6	64	6	4	10	243	....	....	....	....	....	....	1985-86	1991-92
Stewart, Bill	Buf., St.L., Tor., Min.	8	261	7	64	71	424	13	1	3	4	11	....	1977-78	1985-86
Stewart, Blair	Det., Wsh., Que.	7	229	34	44	78	326	....	....	....	....	....	....	1973-74	1979-80
Stewart, Bob	Bos., Cal., Cle., St.L., Pit.	9	575	27	101	128	809	5	1	1	2	2	....	1971-72	1979-80
Stewart, Cam	Bos., Fla., Min.	6	202	16	23	39	120	13	1	3	4	9	....	1993-94	2000-01
Stewart, Gaye	Tor., Chi., Det., NYR, Mtl.	11	502	185	159	344	274	25	2	9	11	16	2	1941-42	1953-54
• Stewart, Jack	Det., Chi.	12	565	31	84	115	765	80	5	14	19	143	2	1938-39	1951-52
Stewart, John	Pit., Atl., Cal.	5	258	58	60	118	158	4	0	0	0	10	....	1970-71	1974-75
Stewart, John	Que.	1	2	0	0	0	0	....	....	....	....	....	....	1979-80	1979-80
Stewart, Ken	Chi.	1	6	1	1	2	2	....	....	....	....	....	....	1941-42	1941-42
• Stewart, Nels	Mtl.M., Bos., NYA	15	650	324	191	515	953	50	9	12	21	47	1	1925-26	1939-40
Stewart, Paul	Que.	1	21	2	0	2	74	....	....	....	....	....	....	1979-80	1979-80
Stewart, Ralph	Van., NYI	7	252	57	73	130	28	19	4	4	8	2	....	1970-71	1977-78
Stewart, Ron	Tor., Bos., St.L., NYR, Van., NYI	21	1353	276	253	529	560	119	14	21	35	60	3	1952-53	1972-73
Stewart, Ryan	Wpg.	1	3	1	0	1	0	....	....	....	....	....	....	1985-86	1985-86
Stienburg, Trevor	Que.	4	71	8	4	12	161	1	0	0	0	0	....	1985-86	1988-89
Stiles, Tony	Cgy.	1	30	2	7	9	20	....	....	....	....	....	....	1983-84	1983-84
Stoddard, Jack	NYR	2	80	16	15	31	31	....	....	....	....	....	....	1951-52	1952-53
Stojanov, Alek	Van., Pit.	3	107	2	5	7	222	14	0	0	0	21	....	1994-95	1996-97
Stoltz, Roland	Wsh.	1	14	2	2	4	14	....	....	....	....	....	....	1981-82	1981-82
Stone, Steve	Van.	1	2	0	0	0	0	....	....	....	....	....	....	1973-74	1973-74
Storm, Jim	Hfd., Dal.	3	84	7	15	22	44	....	....	....	....	....	....	1993-94	1995-96
Stothers, Mike	Phi., Tor.	4	30	0	2	2	65	5	0	0	0	11	....	1984-85	1987-88
Stoughton, Blaine	Pit., Tor., Hfd., NYR	8	526	258	191	449	204	8	4	2	6	2	....	1973-74	1983-84
Stoyanovich, Steve	Hfd.	1	23	3	5	8	11	....	....	....	....	....	....	1983-84	1983-84
• Strain, Neil	NYR	1	52	11	13	24	12	....	....	....	....	....	....	1952-53	1952-53
Strate, Gord	Det.	3	61	0	0	0	34	....	....	....	....	....	....	1956-57	1958-59
Stratton, Art	NYR, Det., Chi., Pit., Phi.	4	95	18	33	51	24	5	0	0	0	0	....	1959-60	1967-68
Strobel, Art	NYR	1	7	0	0	0	0	....	....	....	....	....	....	1943-44	1943-44
Strong, Ken	Tor.	3	15	2	2	4	6	....	....	....	....	....	....	1982-83	1984-85
Struch, David	Cgy.	1	4	0	0	0	4	....	....	....	....	....	....	1993-94	1993-94
Strueby, Todd	Edm.	3	5	0	1	1	2	....	....	....	....	....	....	1981-82	1983-84
• Stuart, Billy	Tor., Bos.	7	195	30	20	50	151	12	1	1	2	6	1	1920-21	1926-27
Stumpf, Bob	St.L., Pit.	1	10	1	1	2	20	....	....	....	....	....	....	1974-75	1974-75
Sturgeon, Peter	Col.	2	6	0	1	1	2	....	....	....	....	....	....	1979-80	1980-81
Suikkanen, Kai	Buf.	2	2	0	0	0	0	....	....	....	....	....	....	1981-82	1982-83
Sulliman, Doug	NYR, Hfd., N.J., Phi.	11	631	160	168	328	175	16	1	3	4	2	....	1979-80	1989-90
Sullivan, Barry	Det.	1	1	0	0	0	0	....	....	....	....	....	....	1947-48	1947-48
Sullivan, Bob	Hfd.	1	62	18	19	37	18	....	....	....	....	....	....	1982-83	1982-83
Sullivan, Brian	N.J.	1	2	0	1	1	0	....	....	....	....	....	....	1992-93	1992-93
Sullivan, Frank	Tor., Chi.	4	8	0	0	0	2	....	....	....	....	....	....	1949-50	1955-56
Sullivan, Mike	S.J., Cgy., Bos., Phx.	11	709	54	82	136	203	34	4	8	12	14	....	1991-92	2001-02
Sullivan, Peter	Wpg.	2	126	28	54	82	40	....	....	....	....	....	....	1979-80	1980-81
Sullivan, Red	Bos., Chi., NYR	11	557	107	239	346	441	18	1	2	3	6	....	1949-50	1960-61
Summanen, Raimo	Edm., Van.	5	151	36	40	76	35	10	2	5	7	0	....	1983-84	1987-88
• Summerhill, Bill	Mtl., Bro.	4	72	14	17	31	70	3	0	0	0	2	....	1937-38	1941-42
‡ Sundblad, Niklas	Cgy.	1	2	0	0	0	0	....	....	....	....	....	....	1995-96	1995-96
‡ Sundin, Ronnie	NYR	1	1	0	0	0	0	....	....	....	....	....	....	1997-98	1997-98
Sundstrom, Patrik	Van., N.J.	10	679	219	369	588	349	37	9	17	26	25	....	1982-83	1991-92
Sundstrom, Peter	NYR, Wsh., N.J.	6	338	61	83	144	120	23	3	3	6	8	....	1983-84	1989-90
• Suomi, Al	Chi.	1	5	0	0	0	0	....	....	....	....	....	....	1936-37	1936-37
‡ Sushinsky, Maxim	Min.	1	30	7	4	11	29	....	....	....	....	....	....	2000-01	2000-01
Suter, Gary	Cgy., Chi., S.J.	17	1145	203	641	844	1349	108	17	56	73	120	1	1985-86	2001-02
Sutherland, Bill	Mtl., Phi., Tor., St.L., Det.	6	250	70	58	128	99	14	2	4	6	0	....	1962-63	1971-72
• Sutherland, Max	Bos.	1	2	0	0	0	0	....	....	....	....	....	....	1931-32	1931-32
Sutter, Brent	NYI, Chi.	18	1111	363	466	829	1054	144	30	44	74	164	2	1980-81	1997-98
Sutter, Brian	St.L.	12	779	303	333	636	1786	65	21	21	42	249	....	1976-77	1987-88
Sutter, Darryl	Chi.	8	406	161	118	279	288	51	24	19	43	26	....	1979-80	1986-87

Name	NHL Teams	NHL Seasons	Regular Schedule GP	G	A	TP	PIM	Playoffs GP	G	A	TP	PIM	NHL Cup Wins	First NHL Season	Last NHL Season
Sutter, Duane	NYI, Chi.	11	731	139	203	342	1333	161	26	32	58	405	4	1979-80	1989-90
Sutter, Rich	Pit., Phi., Van., St.L., Chi., T.B., Tor.	13	874	149	166	315	1411	78	13	5	18	133	....	1982-83	1994-95
Sutter, Ron	Phi., St.L., Que., NYI, Bos., S.J., Cgy.	19	1093	205	329	534	1352	104	8	32	40	193	....	1982-83	2000-01
‡ Sutton, Ken	Buf., Edm., St.L., N.J., S.J., NYI	11	388	23	80	103	338	32	3	4	7	29	1	1990-91	2001-02
Suzor, Mark	Phi., Col.	2	64	4	16	20	60	....	....	....	....	....	....	1976-77	1977-78
‡ Svartvadet, Per	Atl.	4	247	17	34	51	58	....	....	....	....	....	....	1999-00	2002-03
‡ Svehla, Robert	Fla., Tor.	9	655	68	267	335	649	38	1	14	15	42	....	1994-95	2002-03
Svejkovsky, Jaroslav	Wsh., T.B.	4	113	23	19	42	56	1	0	0	0	2	....	1996-97	1999-00
Svensson, Leif	Wsh.	2	121	6	40	46	49	....	....	....	....	....	....	1978-79	1979-80
Svensson, Magnus	Fla.	2	46	4	14	18	31	....	....	....	....	....	....	1994-95	1995-96
Svoboda, Petr	Mtl., Buf., Phi., T.B.	17	1028	58	341	399	1605	127	4	45	49	140	1	1984-85	2000-01
Svoboda, Petr	Tor.	1	18	1	2	3	10	....	....	....	....	....	....	2000-01	2000-01
Swain, Garry	Pit.	1	9	1	1	2	0	....	....	....	....	....	....	1968-69	1968-69
Swarbrick, George	Oak., Pit., Phi.	4	132	17	25	42	173	....	....	....	....	....	....	1967-68	1970-71
• Sweeney, Bill	NYR	1	4	1	0	1	0	....	....	....	....	....	....	1959-60	1959-60
Sweeney, Bob	Bos., Buf., NYI, Cgy.	10	639	125	163	288	799	103	15	18	33	197	....	1986-87	1995-96
Sweeney, Tim	Cgy., Bos., Ana., NYR	8	291	55	83	138	123	4	0	0	0	2	....	1990-91	1997-98
Sykes, Bob	Tor.	1	2	0	0	0	0	....	....	....	....	....	....	1974-75	1974-75
Sykes, Phil	L.A., Wpg.	10	456	79	85	164	519	26	0	3	3	29	....	1982-83	1991-92
‡ Sykora, Michal	S.J., Chi., T.B., Phi.	7	267	15	54	69	185	7	0	1	1	0	....	1993-94	2000-01
Sylvester, Dean	Buf., Atl.	3	96	21	16	37	32	4	0	0	0	0	....	1998-99	2000-01
Szura, Joe	Oak.	2	90	10	15	25	30	7	2	3	5	2	....	1967-68	1968-69

T

Name	NHL Teams	NHL Seasons	Regular Schedule GP	G	A	TP	PIM	Playoffs GP	G	A	TP	PIM	NHL Cup Wins	First NHL Season	Last NHL Season
Taft, John	Det.	1	15	0	2	2	4	....	....	....	....	....	....	1978-79	1978-79
Taglianetti, Peter	Wpg., Min., Pit., T.B.	11	451	18	74	92	1106	53	2	8	10	103	2	1984-85	1994-95
Talafous, Dean	Atl., Min., NYR	8	497	104	154	258	163	21	4	7	11	11	....	1974-75	1981-82
Talakoski, Ron	NYR	2	9	0	1	1	33	....	....	....	....	....	....	1986-87	1987-88
Talbot, Jean-Guy	Mtl., Min., Det., St.L., Buf.	17	1056	43	242	285	1006	150	4	26	30	142	7	1954-55	1970-71
Tallon, Dale	Van., Chi., Pit.	10	642	98	238	336	568	33	2	10	12	45	....	1970-71	1979-80
Tambellini, Steve	NYI, Col., N.J., Cgy., Van.	10	553	160	150	310	105	2	0	1	1	0	1	1978-79	1987-88
‡ Tancill, Chris	Hfd., Det., Dal., S.J.	8	134	17	32	49	54	11	1	1	2	8	....	1990-91	1997-98
Tanguay, Christian	Que.	1	2	0	0	0	0	....	....	....	....	....	....	1981-82	1981-82
Tannahill, Don	Van.	2	111	30	33	63	25	....	....	....	....	....	....	1972-73	1973-74
Tanti, Tony	Chi., Van., Pit., Buf.	11	697	287	273	560	661	30	3	12	15	27	....	1981-82	1991-92
Tardif, Marc	Mtl., Que.	8	517	194	207	401	443	62	13	15	28	75	2	1969-70	1982-83
Tardif, Patrice	St.L., L.A.	2	65	7	11	18	78	....	....	....	....	....	....	1994-95	1995-96
Tatarinov, Mikhail	Wsh., Que., Bos.	4	161	21	48	69	184	....	....	....	....	....	....	1990-91	1993-94
Tatchell, Spence	NYR	1	1	0	0	0	0	....	....	....	....	....	....	1942-43	1942-43
• Taylor, Billy	Tor., Det., Bos., NYR	7	323	87	180	267	120	33	6	18	24	13	1	1939-40	1947-48
• Taylor, Bob	Bos.	1	8	0	0	0	6	....	....	....	....	....	....	1929-30	1929-30
Taylor, Dave	L.A.	17	1111	431	638	1069	1589	92	26	33	59	145	....	1977-78	1993-94
Taylor, Harry	Tor., Chi.	3	66	5	10	15	30	1	0	0	0	0	1	1946-47	1951-52
Taylor, Mark	Phi., Pit., Wsh.	5	209	42	68	110	73	6	0	0	0	0	....	1981-82	1985-86
• Taylor, Ralph	Chi., NYR	3	99	4	1	5	169	4	0	0	0	10	....	1927-28	1929-30
Taylor, Ted	NYR, Det., Min., Van.	6	166	23	35	58	181	....	....	....	....	....	....	1964-65	1971-72
Taylor Jr., Billy	NYR	1	2	0	0	0	0	....	....	....	....	....	....	1964-65	1964-65
Teal, Jeff	Mtl.	1	6	0	1	1	0	....	....	....	....	....	....	1984-85	1984-85
Teal, Skip	Bos.	1	1	0	0	0	0	....	....	....	....	....	....	1954-55	1954-55
Teal, Vic	NYI	1	1	0	0	0	0	....	....	....	....	....	....	1973-74	1973-74
Tebbutt, Greg	Que., Pit.	2	26	0	3	3	35	....	....	....	....	....	....	1979-80	1983-84
Tepper, Stephen	Chi.	1	1	0	0	0	0	....	....	....	....	....	....	1992-93	1992-93
Terbenche, Paul	Chi., Buf.	5	189	5	26	31	28	12	0	0	0	0	....	1967-68	1973-74
Terrion, Greg	L.A., Tor.	8	561	93	150	243	339	35	2	9	11	41	....	1980-81	1987-88
Terry, Bill	Min.	1	5	0	0	0	0	....	....	....	....	....	....	1987-88	1987-88
• Tertyshny, Dmitri	Phi.	1	62	2	8	10	30	1	0	0	0	0	....	1998-99	1998-99
Tessier, Orval	Mtl., Bos.	3	59	5	7	12	6	....	....	....	....	....	....	1954-55	1960-61
‡ Tezikov, Alexei	Wsh., Van.	3	30	1	1	2	2	....	....	....	....	....	....	1998-99	2001-02
Theberge, Greg	Wsh.	5	153	15	63	78	73	4	0	1	1	0	....	1979-80	1983-84
Thelin, Mats	Bos.	3	163	8	19	27	107	5	0	0	0	6	....	1984-85	1986-87
Thelven, Michael	Bos.	5	207	20	80	100	217	34	4	10	14	34	....	1985-86	1989-90
Therrien, Gaston	Que.	3	22	0	8	8	12	9	0	1	1	4	....	1980-81	1982-83
Thibaudeau, Gilles	Mtl., NYI, Tor.	5	119	25	37	62	40	8	3	3	6	2	....	1986-87	1990-91
Thibeault, Lorrain	Det., Mtl.	2	5	0	2	2	2	....	....	....	....	....	....	1944-45	1945-46
Thiffault, Leo	Min.	1	....	....	....	....	....	5	0	0	0	0	....	1967-68	1967-68
Thomas, Cy	Chi., Tor.	1	14	2	2	4	12	....	....	....	....	....	....	1947-48	1947-48
Thomas, Reg	Que.	1	39	9	7	16	6	....	....	....	....	....	....	1979-80	1979-80
Thomas, Scott	Buf., L.A.	3	63	6	4	10	32	12	1	0	1	4	....	1992-93	2000-01
Thomlinson, Dave	St.L., Bos., L.A.	5	42	1	3	4	50	9	3	1	4	4	....	1989-90	1994-95
‡ Thompson, Brent	L.A., Wpg., Phx.	6	121	1	10	11	352	4	0	0	0	4	....	1991-92	1996-97
• Thompson, Cliff	Bos.	2	13	0	1	1	2	....	....	....	....	....	....	1941-42	1948-49
Thompson, Errol	Tor., Det., Pit.	10	599	208	185	393	184	34	7	5	12	11	....	1970-71	1980-81
• Thompson, Ken	Mtl.W.	1	1	0	0	0	0	....	....	....	....	....	....	1917-18	1917-18
• Thompson, Paul	NYR, Chi.	13	582	153	179	332	336	48	11	11	22	54	3	1926-27	1938-39
• Thoms, Bill	Tor., Chi., Bos.	13	548	135	206	341	154	44	6	10	16	6	....	1932-33	1944-45
• Thomson, Bill	Det.	2	9	2	2	4	0	2	0	0	0	0	....	1938-39	1943-44
Thomson, Floyd	St.L.	8	411	56	97	153	341	10	0	2	2	6	....	1971-72	1979-80
Thomson, Jim	Wsh., Hfd., N.J., L.A., Ott., Ana.	7	115	4	3	7	416	1	0	0	0	0	....	1986-87	1993-94
• Thomson, Jimmy	Tor., Chi.	13	787	19	215	234	920	63	2	13	15	135	4	1945-46	1957-58
• Thomson, Rhys	Mtl., Tor.	2	25	0	2	2	38	....	....	....	....	....	....	1939-40	1942-43
Thornbury, Tom	Pit.	1	14	1	8	9	16	....	....	....	....	....	....	1983-84	1983-84
• Thorsteinson, Joe	NYA	1	4	0	0	0	0	....	....	....	....	....	....	1932-33	1932-33
• Thurier, Fred	NYA, Bro., NYR	3	80	25	27	52	18	....	....	....	....	....	....	1940-41	1944-45
Thurlby, Tom	Oak.	1	20	1	1	2	4	....	....	....	....	....	....	1967-68	1967-68
Thyer, Mario	Min.	1	5	0	0	0	0	1	0	0	0	2	....	1989-90	1989-90
‡ Tibbetts, Billy	Pit., Phi., NYR	3	82	2	8	10	269	....	....	....	....	....	....	2000-01	2002-03
Tichy, Milan	Chi., NYI	3	23	0	5	5	40	....	....	....	....	....	....	1992-93	1995-96
Tidey, Alex	Buf., Edm.	3	9	0	0	0	8	2	0	0	0	0	....	1976-77	1979-80
Tikkanen, Esa	Edm., NYR, St.L., N.J., Van., Fla., Wsh.	15	877	244	386	630	1077	186	72	60	132	275	5	1984-85	1998-99
Tilley, Tom	St.L.	4	174	4	38	42	89	14	1	3	4	19	....	1988-89	1993-94
• Timgren, Ray	Tor., Chi.	6	251	14	44	58	70	30	3	9	12	6	2	1948-49	1954-55
Tinordi, Mark	NYR, Min., Dal., Wsh.	12	663	52	148	200	1514	70	7	11	18	165	....	1987-88	1998-99
Tippett, Dave	Hfd., Wsh., Pit., Phi.	12	721	93	169	262	317	62	6	16	22	34	....	1983-84	1993-94
Titanic, Morris	Buf.	2	19	0	0	0	0	....	....	....	....	....	....	1974-75	1975-76
Titov, German	Cgy., Pit., Edm., Ana.	9	624	157	220	377	311	34	11	12	23	18	....	1993-94	2001-02
‡ Tkaczuk, Daniel	Cgy.	1	19	4	7	11	14	....	....	....	....	....	....	2000-01	2000-01
Tkaczuk, Walt	NYR	14	945	227	451	678	556	93	19	32	51	119	....	1967-68	1980-81
Toal, Mike	Edm.	1	3	0	0	0	0	....	....	....	....	....	....	1979-80	1979-80
Tocchet, Rick	Phi., Pit., L.A., Bos., Wsh., Phx.	18	1144	440	512	952	2972	145	52	60	112	471	1	1984-85	2001-02
Todd, Kevin	N.J., Edm., Chi., L.A., Ana.	9	383	70	133	203	225	12	3	2	5	16	....	1988-89	1997-98
Tomalty, Glenn	Wpg.	1	1	0	0	0	0	....	....	....	....	....	....	1979-80	1979-80
Tomlak, Mike	Hfd.	4	141	15	22	37	103	10	0	1	1	4	....	1989-90	1993-94
‡ Tomlinson, Dave	Tor., Wpg., Fla.	4	42	1	3	4	28	....	....	....	....	....	....	1991-92	1994-95
Tomlinson, Kirk	Min.	1	1	0	0	0	0	....	....	....	....	....	....	1987-88	1987-88
• Tomson, Jack	NYA	3	15	1	1	2	0	2	0	0	0	0	....	1938-39	1940-41
Tonelli, John	NYI, Cgy., L.A., Chi., Que.	14	1028	325	511	836	911	172	40	75	115	200	4	1978-79	1991-92
Tookey, Tim	Wsh., Que., Pit., Phi., L.A.	7	106	22	36	58	71	10	1	3	4	2	....	1980-81	1988-89
Toomey, Sean	Min.	1	1	0	0	0	0	....	....	....	....	....	....	1986-87	1986-87
‡ Toporowski, Shayne	Tor.	1	3	0	0	0	7	....	....	....	....	....	....	1996-97	1996-97
Toppazzini, Jerry	Bos., Chi., Det.	12	783	163	244	407	436	40	13	9	22	13	....	1952-53	1963-64
• Toppazzini, Zellio	Bos., NYR, Chi.	5	123	21	22	43	49	2	0	0	0	0	....	1948-49	1956-57
Torgaev, Pavel	Cgy., T.B.	2	55	6	14	20	20	1	0	0	0	0	....	1995-96	1999-00
Torkki, Jari	Chi.	1	4	1	0	1	0	....	....	....	....	....	....	1988-89	1988-89
‡ Tormanen, Antti	Ott.	1	50	7	8	15	28	....	....	....	....	....	....	1995-96	1995-96
• Touhey, Bill	Mtl.M., Ott., Bos.	7	280	65	40	105	107	2	1	0	1	0	....	1927-28	1933-34
• Toupin, Jacques	Chi.	1	8	1	2	3	0	4	0	0	0	0	....	1943-44	1943-44
• Townsend, Art	Chi.	1	5	0	0	0	0	....	....	....	....	....	....	1926-27	1926-27
Townshend, Graeme	Bos., NYI, Ott.	5	45	3	7	10	28	....	....	....	....	....	....	1989-90	1993-94
Trader, Larry	Det., St.L., Mtl.	4	91	5	13	18	74	3	0	0	0	0	....	1982-83	1987-88
• Trainor, Wes	NYR	1	17	1	2	3	6	....	....	....	....	....	....	1948-49	1948-49
• Trapp, Bob	Chi.	2	82	4	4	8	129	2	0	0	0	4	....	1926-27	1927-28
Trapp, Doug	Buf.	1	2	0	0	0	0	....	....	....	....	....	....	1986-87	1986-87
• Traub, Percy	Chi., Det.	3	130	3	3	6	217	4	0	0	0	6	....	1926-27	1928-29

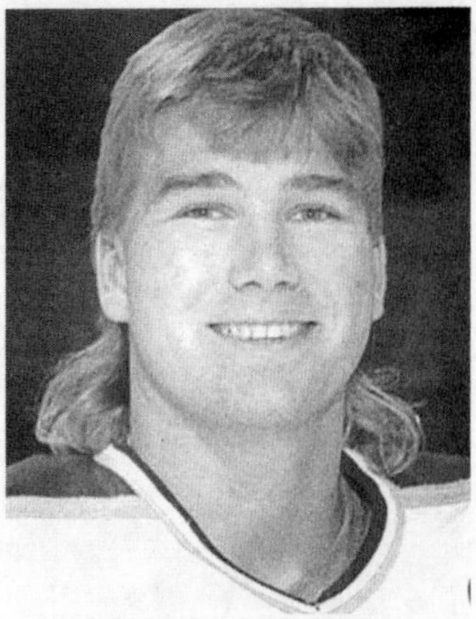
Stephen Tepper

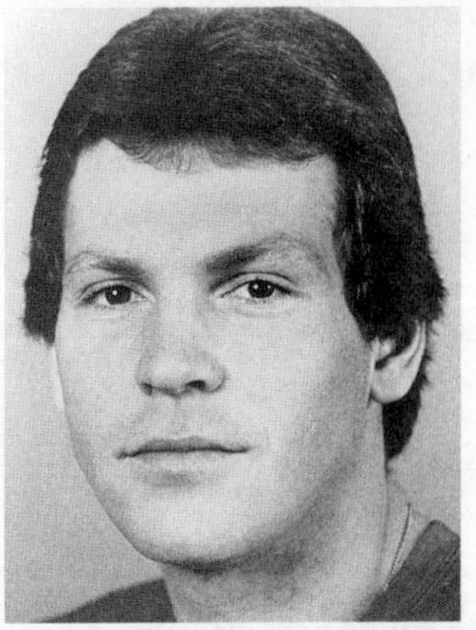
Greg Theberge

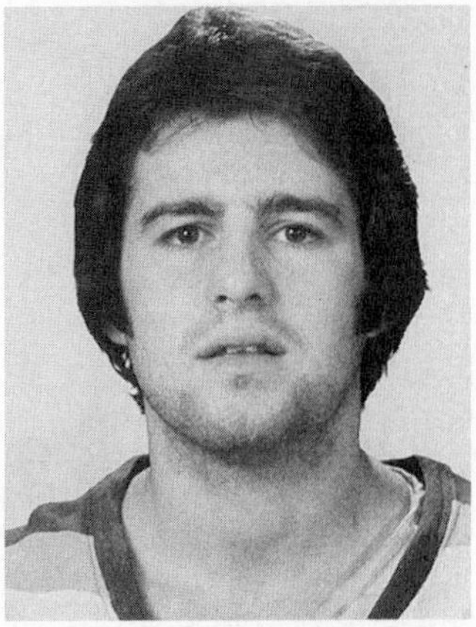
Morris Titanic

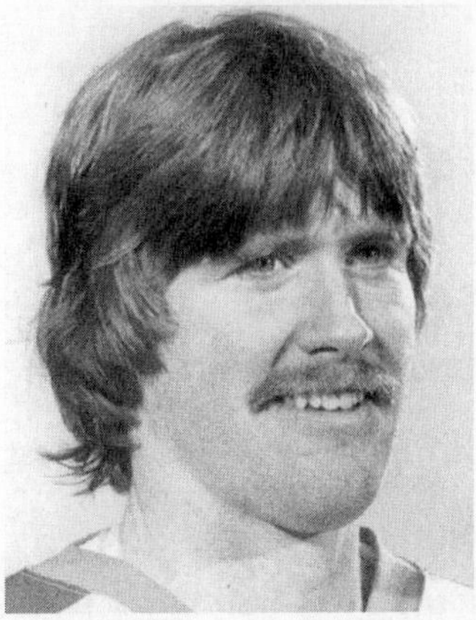
Glenn Tomalty

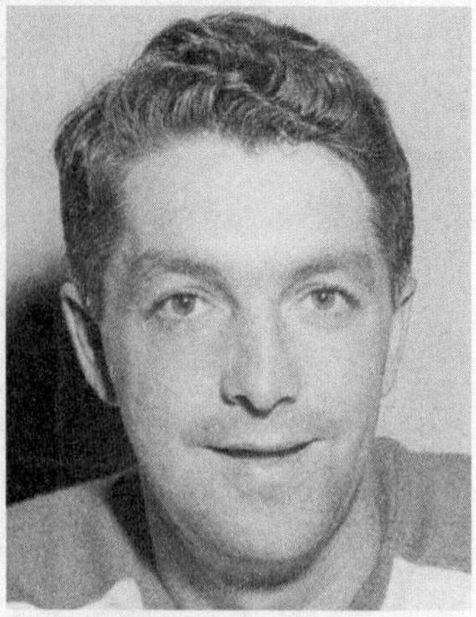

Nils Tremblay

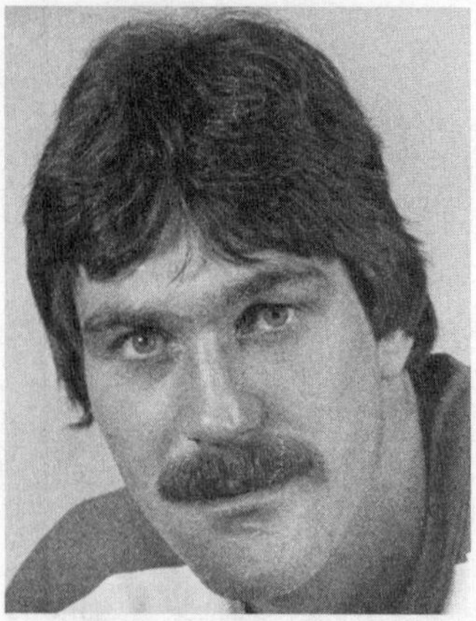

Den Ververgaert

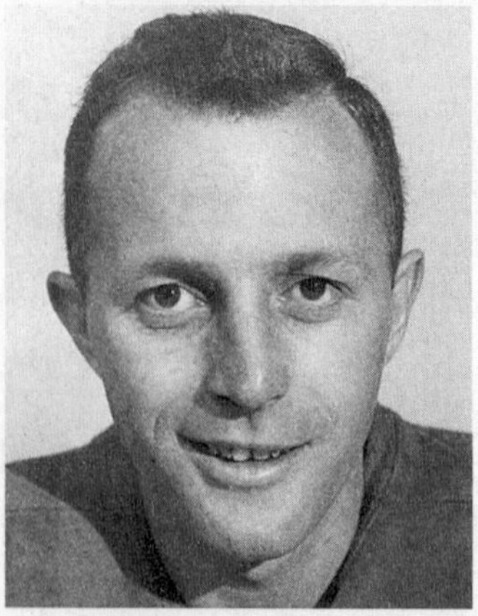

Bob Wall

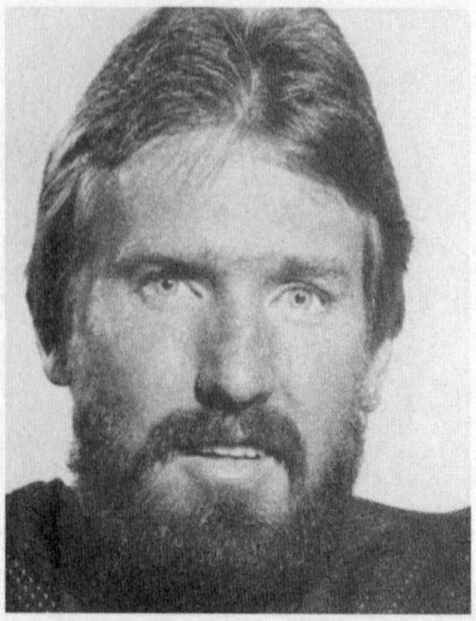

Stan Weir

Name	NHL Teams	NHL Seasons	Regular Schedule					Playoffs					NHL Cup Wins	First NHL Season	Last NHL Season
			GP	G	A	TP	PIM	GP	G	A	TP	PIM			
Trebil, Dan	Ana., Pit., St.L.	5	85	4	4	8	32	10	0	1	1	8	....	1996-97	2000-01
Tredway, Brock	L.A.	1	....	....	....	....	....	1	0	0	0	0	....	1981-82	1981-82
Tremblay, Brent	Wsh.	2	10	1	0	1	6	....	....	....	....	....	....	1978-79	1979-80
Tremblay, Gilles	Mtl.	9	509	168	162	330	161	48	9	14	23	4	3	1960-61	1968-69
• Tremblay, J.C.	Mtl.	13	794	57	306	363	204	108	14	51	65	58	5	1959-60	1971-72
Tremblay, Marcel	Mtl.	1	10	0	2	2	0	....	....	....	....	....	....	1938-39	1938-39
Tremblay, Mario	Mtl.	12	852	258	326	584	1043	101	20	29	49	187	5	1974-75	1985-86
• Tremblay, Nils	Mtl.	2	3	0	1	1	0	2	0	0	0	0	....	1944-45	1945-46
Trimper, Tim	Chi., Wpg., Min.	6	190	30	36	66	153	2	0	0	0	2	....	1979-80	1984-85
Trottier, Bryan	NYI, Pit.	18	1279	524	901	1425	912	221	71	113	184	277	6	1975-76	1993-94
• Trottier, Dave	Mtl.M., Det.	11	446	121	113	234	517	31	4	3	7	39	1	1928-29	1938-39
Trottier, Guy	NYR, Tor.	3	115	28	17	45	37	9	1	0	1	16	....	1968-69	1971-72
Trottier, Rocky	N.J.	2	38	6	4	10	2	....	....	....	....	....	....	1983-84	1984-85
‡ Trudel, Jean-Guy	Phx., Min.	3	5	0	0	0	4	....	....	....	....	....	....	1999-00	2002-03
• Trudel, Lou	Chi., Mtl.	8	306	49	69	118	122	24	1	3	4	4	2	1933-34	1940-41
Trudell, Rene	NYR	3	129	24	28	52	72	5	0	0	0	2	....	1945-46	1947-48
‡ Tsulygin, Nikolai	Ana.	1	22	0	1	1	8	....	....	....	....	....	....	1996-97	1996-97
Tsygurov, Denis	Buf., L.A.	3	51	1	5	6	45	....	....	....	....	....	....	1993-94	1995-96
‡ Tsyplakov, Vladimir	L.A., Buf.	6	331	69	101	170	90	18	1	2	3	16	....	1995-96	2000-01
Tucker, John	Buf., Wsh., NYI, T.B.	12	656	177	259	436	285	31	10	18	28	24	....	1983-84	1995-96
• Tudin, Connie	Mtl.	1	4	0	1	1	4	....	....	....	....	....	....	1941-42	1941-42
Tudor, Rob	Van., St.L.	3	28	4	4	8	19	3	0	0	0	0	....	1978-79	1982-83
Tuer, Allan	L.A., Min., Hfd.	4	57	1	1	2	208	....	....	....	....	....	....	1985-86	1989-90
‡ Tuomainen, Marko	Edm., L.A., NYI	4	79	9	9	18	84	1	0	0	0	0	....	1994-95	2001-02
Turcotte, Alfie	Mtl., Wpg., Wsh.	7	112	17	29	46	49	5	0	0	0	0	....	1983-84	1990-91
Turcotte, Darren	NYR, Hfd., Wpg., S.J., St.L., Nsh.	12	635	195	216	411	301	35	6	8	14	12	....	1988-89	1999-00
Turgeon, Sylvain	Hfd., N.J., Mtl., Ott.	12	669	269	226	495	691	36	4	7	11	22	....	1983-84	1994-95
Turlick, Gord	Bos.	1	2	0	0	0	2	....	....	....	....	....	....	1959-60	1959-60
Turnbull, Ian	Tor., L.A., Pit.	10	628	123	317	440	736	55	13	32	45	94	....	1973-74	1982-83
Turnbull, Perry	St.L., Mtl., Wpg.	9	608	188	163	351	1245	34	6	7	13	86	....	1979-80	1987-88
Turnbull, Randy	Cgy.	1	1	0	0	0	2	....	....	....	....	....	....	1981-82	1981-82
Turner, Bob	Mtl., Chi.	8	478	19	51	70	307	68	1	4	5	44	5	1955-56	1962-63
Turner, Brad	NYI	1	3	0	0	0	0	....	....	....	....	....	....	1991-92	1991-92
Turner, Dean	NYR, Col., L.A.	4	35	1	0	1	59	....	....	....	....	....	....	1978-79	1982-83
• Tustin, Norm	NYR	1	18	2	4	6	0	....	....	....	....	....	....	1941-42	1941-42
Tuten, Aud	Chi.	2	39	4	8	12	48	....	....	....	....	....	....	1941-42	1942-43
Tutt, Brian	Wsh.	1	7	1	0	1	2	....	....	....	....	....	....	1989-90	1989-90
Tuttle, Steve	St.L.	3	144	28	28	56	12	17	1	6	7	2	....	1988-89	1990-91
‡ Tuzzolino, Tony	Ana., NYR, Bos.	3	9	0	0	0	7	....	....	....	....	....	....	1997-98	2001-02
Twist, Tony	St.L., Que.	10	445	10	18	28	1121	18	1	1	2	22	....	1989-90	1998-99

U V

Name	NHL Teams	NHL Seasons	GP	G	A	TP	PIM	GP	G	A	TP	PIM	NHL Cup Wins	First NHL Season	Last NHL Season
Ubriaco, Gene	Pit., Oak., Chi.	3	177	39	35	74	50	11	2	0	2	4	....	1967-68	1969-70
Ullman, Norm	Det., Tor.	20	1410	490	739	1229	712	106	30	53	83	67	....	1955-56	1974-75
Unger, Garry	Tor., Det., St.L., Atl., L.A., Edm.	16	1105	413	391	804	1075	52	12	18	30	105	....	1967-68	1982-83
‡ Ustorf, Stefan	Wsh.	2	54	7	10	17	16	5	0	0	0	0	....	1995-96	1996-97
Vachon, Nick	NYI	1	1	0	0	0	0	....	....	....	....	....	....	1996-97	1996-97
Vadnais, Carol	Mtl., Oak., Cal., Bos., NYR, N.J.	17	1087	169	418	587	1813	106	10	40	50	185	2	1966-67	1982-83
‡ Vaic, Lubomir	Van.	2	9	1	1	2	2	....	....	....	....	....	....	1997-98	1999-00
Vail, Eric	Atl., Cgy., Det.	9	591	216	260	476	281	20	5	6	11	6	....	1973-74	1981-82
• Vail, Sparky	NYR	2	50	4	1	5	18	10	0	0	0	2	....	1928-29	1929-30
Vaive, Rick	Van., Tor., Chi., Buf.	13	876	441	347	788	1445	54	27	16	43	111	....	1979-80	1991-92
Valentine, Chris	Wsh.	3	105	43	52	95	127	2	0	0	0	4	....	1981-82	1983-84
Valiquette, Jack	Tor., Col.	7	350	84	134	218	79	23	3	6	9	4	....	1974-75	1980-81
Valk, Garry	Van., Ana., Pit., Tor., Chi.	13	777	100	156	256	747	61	6	7	13	79	....	1990-91	2002-03
Vallis, Lindsay	Mtl.	1	1	0	0	0	0	....	....	....	....	....	....	1993-94	1993-94
Van Boxmeer, John	Mtl., Col., Buf., Que.	11	588	84	274	358	465	38	5	15	20	37	1	1973-74	1983-84
Van Dorp, Wayne	Edm., Pit., Chi., Que.	6	125	12	12	24	565	27	0	1	1	42	....	1986-87	1991-92
Van Drunen, David	Ott.	1	1	0	0	0	0	....	....	....	....	....	....	1999-00	1999-00
‡ Van Impe, Darren	Ana., Bos., NYR, Fla., NYI, CBJ	9	411	25	90	115	397	33	3	9	12	28	....	1994-95	2002-03
Van Impe, Ed	Chi., Phi., Pit.	11	700	27	126	153	1025	66	1	12	13	131	2	1966-67	1976-77
‡ Varis, Petri	Chi.	1	1	0	0	0	0	....	....	....	....	....	....	1997-98	1997-98
Varvio, Jarkko	Dal.	2	13	3	4	7	4	....	....	....	....	....	....	1993-94	1994-95
Vasilevski, Alexander	St.L.	2	4	0	0	0	2	....	....	....	....	....	....	1995-96	1996-97
Vasiliev, Alexei	NYR	1	1	0	0	0	2	....	....	....	....	....	....	1999-00	1999-00
‡ Vasiljevs, Herbert	Fla., Atl., Van.	4	51	8	7	15	22	....	....	....	....	....	....	1998-99	2001-02
‡ Vasilyev, Andrei	NYI, Phx.	4	16	2	5	7	6	....	....	....	....	....	....	1994-95	1998-99
Vaske, Dennis	NYI, Bos.	9	235	5	41	46	253	22	0	7	7	16	....	1990-91	1998-99
• Vasko, Moose	Chi., Min.	13	786	34	166	200	719	78	2	7	9	73	1	1956-57	1969-70
Vasko, Rick	Det.	3	31	3	7	10	29	....	....	....	....	....	....	1977-78	1980-81
Vautour, Yvon	NYI, Col., N.J., Que.	6	204	26	33	59	401	....	....	....	....	....	....	1979-80	1984-85
Vaydik, Greg	Chi.	1	5	0	0	0	0	....	....	....	....	....	....	1976-77	1976-77
Veitch, Darren	Wsh., Det., Tor.	10	511	48	209	257	296	33	4	11	15	33	....	1980-81	1990-91
Velischek, Randy	Min., N.J., Que.	10	509	21	76	97	401	44	2	5	7	32	....	1982-83	1991-92
Vellucci, Mike	Hfd.	1	2	0	0	0	11	....	....	....	....	....	....	1987-88	1987-88
Venasky, Vic	L.A.	7	430	61	101	162	66	21	1	5	6	12	....	1972-73	1978-79
Veneruzzo, Gary	St.L.	2	7	1	1	2	0	9	0	2	2	2	....	1967-68	1971-72
Verbeek, Pat	N.J., Hfd., NYR, Dal., Det.	20	1424	522	541	1063	2905	117	26	36	62	225	1	1982-83	2001-02
Vermette, Mark	Que.	4	67	5	13	18	33	....	....	....	....	....	....	1988-89	1991-92
Verret, Claude	Buf.	2	14	2	5	7	2	....	....	....	....	....	....	1983-84	1984-85
Verstraete, Leigh	Tor.	3	8	0	1	1	14	....	....	....	....	....	....	1982-83	1987-88
Ververgaert, Dennis	Van., Phi., Wsh.	8	583	176	216	392	247	8	1	2	3	6	....	1973-74	1980-81
Vesey, Jim	St.L., Bos.	3	15	1	2	3	7	....	....	....	....	....	....	1988-89	1991-92
Veysey, Sid	Van.	1	1	0	0	0	0	....	....	....	....	....	....	1977-78	1977-78
‡ Vial, Dennis	NYR, Det., Ott.	8	242	4	15	19	794	....	....	....	....	....	....	1990-91	1997-98
Vickers, Steve	NYR	10	698	246	340	586	330	68	24	25	49	58	....	1972-73	1981-82
Vigneault, Alain	St.L.	2	42	2	5	7	82	4	0	1	1	26	....	1981-82	1982-83
‡ Viitakoski, Vesa	Cgy.	3	23	2	4	6	8	....	....	....	....	....	....	1993-94	1995-96
Vilgrain, Claude	Van., N.J., Phi.	5	89	21	32	53	78	11	1	1	2	17	....	1987-88	1993-94
Vincelette, Dan	Chi., Que.	6	193	20	22	42	351	12	0	0	0	4	....	1986-87	1991-92
Vipond, Pete	Cal.	1	3	0	0	0	0	....	....	....	....	....	....	1972-73	1972-73
Virta, Hannu	Buf.	5	245	25	101	126	66	17	1	3	4	6	....	1981-82	1985-86
‡ Virta, Tony	Min.	1	8	2	3	5	0	....	....	....	....	....	....	2001-02	2001-02
Visheau, Mark	Wpg., L.A.	2	29	1	3	4	107	....	....	....	....	....	....	1993-94	1998-99
Vitolinsh, Harijs	Wpg.	1	8	0	0	0	4	....	....	....	....	....	....	1993-94	1993-94
Viveiros, Emanuel	Min.	3	29	1	11	12	6	....	....	....	....	....	....	1985-86	1987-88
‡ Vlasak, Tomas	L.A.	1	10	1	3	4	2	....	....	....	....	....	....	2000-01	2000-01
• Vokes, Ed	Chi.	1	5	0	0	0	0	....	....	....	....	....	....	1930-31	1930-31
Volcan, Mickey	Hfd., Cgy.	4	162	8	33	41	146	....	....	....	....	....	....	1980-81	1983-84
Volchkov, Alexandre	Wsh.	1	3	0	0	0	0	....	....	....	....	....	....	1999-00	1999-00
Volek, David	NYI	6	396	95	154	249	201	15	5	5	10	2	....	1988-89	1993-94
Volmar, Doug	Det., L.A.	4	62	13	8	21	26	2	1	0	1	0	....	1969-70	1972-73
‡ Von Arx, Reto	Chi.	1	19	3	1	4	4	....	....	....	....	....	....	2000-01	2000-01
‡ Von Stefenelli, Phil	Bos., Ott.	2	33	0	5	5	23	....	....	....	....	....	....	1995-96	1996-97
Vopat, Jan	L.A., Nsh.	5	126	11	20	31	70	2	0	1	1	2	....	1995-96	1999-00
‡ Vopat, Roman	St.L., L.A., Chi., Phi.	4	133	6	14	20	253	....	....	....	....	....	....	1995-96	1998-99
Vorobiev, Vladimir	NYR, Edm.	3	33	9	7	16	14	1	0	0	0	0	....	1996-97	1998-99
• Voss, Carl	Tor., NYR, Det., Ott., St.L., NYA, Mtl.M., Chi.	8	261	34	70	104	50	24	5	3	8	0	1	1926-27	1937-38
‡ Vujtek, Vladimir	Mtl., Edm., T.B., Atl., Pit.	6	110	7	30	37	38	....	....	....	....	....	....	1991-92	2002-03
Vukota, Mick	NYI, T.B., Mtl.	11	574	17	29	46	2071	23	0	0	0	73	....	1987-88	1997-98
Vyazmikin, Igor	Edm.	1	4	1	0	1	0	....	....	....	....	....	....	1990-91	1990-91
‡ Vyshedkevich, Sergei	Atl.	2	30	2	5	7	16	....	....	....	....	....	....	1999-00	2000-01

W

Name	NHL Teams	NHL Seasons	GP	G	A	TP	PIM	GP	G	A	TP	PIM	NHL Cup Wins	First NHL Season	Last NHL Season
Waddell, Don	L.A.	1	1	0	0	0	0	....	....	....	....	....	....	1980-81	1980-81
• Waite, Frank	NYR	1	17	1	3	4	4	....	....	....	....	....	....	1930-31	1930-31
Walker, Gord	NYR, L.A.	4	31	3	4	7	23	....	....	....	....	....	....	1986-87	1989-90
Walker, Howard	Wsh., Cgy.	3	83	2	13	15	133	....	....	....	....	....	....	1980-81	1982-83
• Walker, Jack	Det.	2	80	5	8	13	18	....	....	....	....	....	....	1926-27	1927-28
Walker, Kurt	Tor.	3	71	4	5	9	142	16	0	0	0	34	....	1975-76	1977-78
Walker, Russ	L.A.	2	17	1	0	1	41	....	....	....	....	....	....	1976-77	1977-78

			Regular Schedule					Playoffs					NHL	First	Last
Name	NHL Teams	NHL Seasons	GP	G	A	TP	PIM	GP	G	A	TP	PIM	Cup Wins	NHL Season	NHL Season
Wall, Bob	Det., L.A., St.L.	8	322	30	55	85	155	22	0	3	3	2	....	1964-65	1971-72
Wallin, Jesse	Det.	4	49	0	2	2	34	....	....	....	....	....	....	1999-00	2002-03
Wallin, Peter	NYR	2	52	3	14	17	14	14	2	6	8	6	....	1980-81	1981-82
Walsh, Jim	Buf.	1	4	0	1	1	4	....	....	....	....	....	....	1981-82	1981-82
Walsh, Mike	NYI	2	14	2	0	2	4	....	....	....	....	....	....	1987-88	1988-89
Walter, Ryan	Wsh., Mtl., Van.	15	1003	264	382	646	946	113	16	35	51	62	1	1978-79	1992-93
• Walton, Bobby	Mtl.	1	4	0	0	0	0	....	....	....	....	....	....	1943-44	1943-44
Walton, Mike	Tor., Bos., Van., St.L., Chi.	12	588	201	247	448	357	47	14	10	24	45	2	1965-66	1978-79
Wappel, Gord	Atl., Cgy.	3	20	1	1	2	10	2	0	0	0	4	....	1979-80	1981-82
‡ Ward, Dixon	Van., L.A., Tor., Buf., Bos., NYR	10	537	95	129	224	431	62	14	20	34	46	....	1992-93	2002-03
Ward, Don	Chi., Bos.	2	34	0	1	1	16	....	....	....	....	....	....	1957-58	1959-60
Ward, Ed	Que., Cgy., Atl., Ana., N.J.	8	278	23	26	49	354	....	....	....	....	....	....	1993-94	2000-01
• Ward, Jimmy	Mtl.M., Mtl.	12	527	147	127	274	455	36	4	4	8	26	1	1927-28	1938-39
Ward, Joe	Col.	1	4	0	0	0	2	....	....	....	....	....	....	1980-81	1980-81
Ward, Ron	Tor., Van.	2	89	2	5	7	6	....	....	....	....	....	....	1969-70	1971-72
Ware, Jeff	Tor., Fla.	3	21	0	1	1	12	....	....	....	....	....	....	1996-97	1998-99
Ware, Michael	Edm.	2	5	0	1	1	15	....	....	....	....	....	....	1988-89	1989-90
• Wares, Eddie	NYR, Det., Chi.	9	321	60	102	162	161	45	5	7	12	34	1	1936-37	1946-47
Warner, Bob	Tor.	2	10	1	1	2	4	4	0	0	0	0	....	1975-76	1976-77
Warner, Jim	Hfd.	1	32	0	3	3	10	....	....	....	....	....	....	1979-80	1979-80
Warriner, Todd	Tor., T.B., Phx., Van., Phi., Nsh.	9	453	65	89	154	249	21	2	1	3	6	....	1994-95	2002-03
Warwick, Bill	NYR	2	14	3	3	6	16	....	....	....	....	....	....	1942-43	1943-44
• Warwick, Grant	NYR, Bos., Mtl.	9	395	147	142	289	220	16	2	4	6	6	....	1941-42	1949-50
‡ Washburn, Steve	Fla., Van., Phi.	6	93	14	15	29	42	1	0	1	1	0	....	1995-96	2000-01
• Wasnie, Nick	Chi., Mtl., NYA, Ott., St.L.	7	248	57	34	91	176	20	6	3	9	20	2	1927-28	1934-35
Watson, Bill	Chi.	4	115	23	36	59	12	6	0	2	2	0	....	1985-86	1988-89
Watson, Bryan	Mtl., Det., Oak., Pit., St.L., Wsh.	16	878	17	135	152	2212	32	2	0	2	70	....	1963-64	1978-79
Watson, Dave	Col.	2	18	0	1	1	10	....	....	....	....	....	....	1979-80	1980-81
• Watson, Harry	Bro., Det., Tor., Chi.	14	809	236	207	443	150	62	16	9	25	27	5	1941-42	1956-57
Watson, Jim	Det., Buf.	8	221	4	19	23	345	....	....	....	....	....	....	1963-64	1971-72
Watson, Jimmy	Phi.	10	613	38	148	186	492	101	5	34	39	89	2	1972-73	1981-82
Watson, Joe	Bos., Phi., Col.	14	835	38	178	216	447	84	3	12	15	82	2	1964-65	1978-79
• Watson, Phil	NYR, Mtl.	13	590	144	265	409	532	54	10	25	35	67	2	1935-36	1947-48
Watters, Tim	Wpg., L.A.	14	741	26	151	177	1289	82	1	5	6	115	....	1981-82	1994-95
Watts, Brian	Det.	1	4	0	0	0	0	....	....	....	....	....	....	1975-76	1975-76
• Webster, Aubrey	Phi., Mtl.M.	2	5	0	0	0	0	....	....	....	....	....	....	1930-31	1934-35
• Webster, Don	Tor.	1	27	7	6	13	28	5	0	0	0	12	....	1943-44	1943-44
Webster, John	NYR	1	14	0	0	0	4	....	....	....	....	....	....	1949-50	1949-50
Webster, Tom	Bos., Det., Cal.	5	102	33	42	75	61	1	0	0	0	0	....	1968-69	1979-80
• Weiland, Cooney	Bos., Ott., Det.	11	509	173	160	333	147	45	12	10	22	12	2	1928-29	1938-39
Weir, Stan	Cal., Tor., Edm., Col., Det.	10	642	139	207	346	183	37	6	5	11	4	....	1972-73	1982-83
Weir, Wally	Que., Hfd., Pit.	6	320	21	45	66	625	23	0	1	1	96	....	1979-80	1984-85
• Wellington, Alex	Que.	1	1	0	0	0	0	....	....	....	....	....	....	1919-20	1919-20
Wells, Chris	Pit., Fla.	5	195	9	20	29	193	3	0	0	0	0	....	1995-96	1999-00
Wells, Jay	L.A., Phi., Buf., NYR, St.L., T.B.	18	1098	47	216	263	2359	114	3	14	17	213	1	1979-80	1996-97
Wensink, John	St.L., Bos., Que., Col., N.J.	8	403	70	68	138	840	43	2	6	8	86	....	1973-74	1982-83
• Wentworth, Cy	Chi., Mtl.M., Mtl.	13	575	39	68	107	355	35	5	6	11	20	1	1927-28	1939-40
Werenka, Brad	Edm., Que., Chi., Pit., Cgy.	7	320	19	61	80	299	19	2	1	3	14	....	1992-93	2000-01
Wesenberg, Brian	Phi.	1	1	0	0	0	5	....	....	....	....	....	....	1998-99	1998-99
Wesley, Blake	Phi., Hfd., Que., Tor.	7	298	18	46	64	486	19	2	2	4	30	....	1979-80	1985-86
Westfall, Ed	Bos., NYI	18	1220	231	394	625	544	95	22	37	59	41	2	1961-62	1978-79
‡ Westlund, Tommy	Car.	4	203	9	13	22	48	25	1	0	1	17	....	1999-00	2002-03
Wharram, Kenny	Chi.	14	766	252	281	533	222	80	16	27	43	38	1	1951-52	1968-69
Wharton, Len	NYR	1	1	0	0	0	0	....	....	....	....	....	....	1944-45	1944-45
Wheeldon, Simon	NYR, Wpg.	3	15	0	2	2	10	....	....	....	....	....	....	1987-88	1990-91
• Wheldon, Don	St.L.	1	2	0	0	0	0	....	....	....	....	....	....	1974-75	1974-75
Whelton, Bill	Wpg.	1	2	0	0	0	0	....	....	....	....	....	....	1980-81	1980-81
Whistle, Rob	NYR, St.L.	2	51	7	5	12	16	4	0	0	0	2	....	1985-86	1987-88
White, Bill	L.A., Chi.	9	604	50	215	265	495	91	7	32	39	76	....	1967-68	1975-76
White, Moe	Mtl.	1	4	0	1	1	2	....	....	....	....	....	....	1945-46	1945-46
• White, Sherman	NYR	2	4	0	2	2	0	....	....	....	....	....	....	1946-47	1949-50
• White, Tex	Pit., NYA, Phi.	6	203	33	12	45	141	4	0	0	0	4	....	1925-26	1930-31
White, Tony	Wsh., Min.	5	164	37	28	65	104	....	....	....	....	....	....	1974-75	1979-80
Whitelaw, Bob	Det.	2	32	0	2	2	2	8	0	0	0	0	....	1940-41	1941-42
Whitlock, Bob	Min.	1	1	0	0	0	0	....	....	....	....	....	....	1969-70	1969-70
Whyte, Sean	L.A.	2	21	0	2	2	12	....	....	....	....	....	....	1991-92	1992-93
• Wickenheiser, Doug	Mtl., St.L., Van., NYR, Wsh.	10	556	111	165	276	286	41	4	7	11	18	....	1980-81	1989-90
• Widing, Juha	NYR, L.A., Cle.	8	575	144	226	370	208	8	1	2	3	2	....	1969-70	1976-77
Widmer, Jason	NYI, S.J.	3	7	0	1	1	7	....	....	....	....	....	....	1994-95	1996-97
• Wiebe, Art	Chi.	11	414	14	27	41	201	31	1	3	4	10	1	1932-33	1943-44
Wiemer, Jim	Buf., NYR, Edm., L.A., Bos.	11	325	29	72	101	378	62	5	8	13	63	....	1982-83	1993-94
• Wilcox, Archie	Mtl.M., Bos., St.L.	6	208	8	14	22	158	12	1	0	1	8	....	1929-30	1934-35
Wilcox, Barry	Van.	2	33	3	2	5	15	....	....	....	....	....	....	1972-73	1974-75
Wilder, Arch	Det.	1	18	0	2	2	2	....	....	....	....	....	....	1940-41	1940-41
Wiley, Jim	Pit., Van.	5	63	4	10	14	8	....	....	....	....	....	....	1972-73	1976-77
Wilkie, Bob	Det., Phi.	2	18	2	5	7	10	....	....	....	....	....	....	1990-91	1993-94
Wilkie, David	Mtl., T.B., NYR	6	167	10	26	36	165	8	1	2	3	14	....	1994-95	2000-01
Wilkins, Barry	Bos., Van., Pit.	9	418	27	125	152	663	6	0	1	1	4	....	1966-67	1975-76
• Wilkinson, John	Bos.	1	9	0	0	0	6	....	....	....	....	....	....	1943-44	1943-44
Wilkinson, Neil	Min., S.J., Chi., Wpg., Pit.	10	460	16	67	83	813	53	3	6	9	41	....	1989-90	1998-99
Wilks, Brian	L.A.	4	48	4	8	12	27	....	....	....	....	....	....	1984-85	1988-89
Willard, Rod	Tor.	1	1	0	0	0	0	....	....	....	....	....	....	1982-83	1982-83
• Williams, Burr	Det., St.L., Bos.	3	19	0	1	1	28	7	0	0	0	8	....	1933-34	1936-37
Williams, Butch	St.L., Cal.	3	108	14	35	49	131	....	....	....	....	....	....	1973-74	1975-76
Williams, Darryl	L.A.	1	2	0	0	0	10	....	....	....	....	....	....	1992-93	1992-93
Williams, David	S.J., Ana.	4	173	11	53	64	157	....	....	....	....	....	....	1991-92	1994-95
Williams, Fred	Det.	1	44	2	5	7	10	....	....	....	....	....	....	1976-77	1976-77
Williams, Gord	Phi.	2	2	0	0	0	2	....	....	....	....	....	....	1981-82	1982-83
Williams, Sean	Chi.	1	2	0	0	0	4	....	....	....	....	....	....	1991-92	1991-92
Williams, Tiger	Tor., Van., Det., L.A., Hfd.	14	962	241	272	513	3966	83	12	23	35	455	....	1974-75	1987-88
Williams, Tom	NYR, L.A.	8	397	115	138	253	73	29	8	7	15	4	....	1971-72	1978-79
• Williams, Tommy	Bos., Min., Cal., Wsh.	13	663	161	269	430	177	10	2	5	7	2	....	1961-62	1975-76
Willson, Don	Mtl.	2	22	2	7	9	0	3	0	0	0	0	....	1937-38	1938-39
Wilson, Behn	Phi., Chi.	9	601	98	260	358	1480	67	12	29	41	190	....	1978-79	1987-88
• Wilson, Bert	NYR, St.L., L.A., Cgy.	8	478	37	44	81	646	21	0	2	2	42	....	1973-74	1980-81
Wilson, Bob	Chi.	1	1	0	0	0	0	....	....	....	....	....	....	1953-54	1953-54
Wilson, Carey	Cgy., Hfd., NYR	10	552	169	258	427	314	52	11	13	24	14	....	1983-84	1992-93
• Wilson, Cully	Tor., Mtl., Ham., Chi.	5	127	59	28	87	243	2	1	0	1	6	....	1919-20	1926-27
Wilson, Doug	Chi., S.J.	16	1024	237	590	827	830	95	19	61	80	88	....	1977-78	1992-93
Wilson, Gord	Bos.	1	....	....	....	....	....	2	0	0	0	0	....	1954-55	1954-55
Wilson, Hub	NYA	1	2	0	0	0	0	....	....	....	....	....	....	1931-32	1931-32
Wilson, Jerry	Mtl.	1	3	0	0	0	2	....	....	....	....	....	....	1956-57	1956-57
Wilson, Johnny	Det., Chi., Tor., NYR	13	688	161	171	332	190	66	14	13	27	11	4	1949-50	1961-62
• Wilson, Larry	Det., Chi.	6	152	21	48	69	75	4	0	0	0	0	1	1949-50	1955-56
‡ Wilson, Mike	Buf., Fla., Pit., NYR	8	336	16	41	57	264	29	0	2	2	15	....	1995-96	2002-03
Wilson, Mitch	N.J., Pit.	2	26	2	3	5	104	....	....	....	....	....	....	1984-85	1986-87
Wilson, Murray	Mtl., L.A.	7	386	94	95	189	162	53	5	14	19	32	4	1972-73	1978-79
Wilson, Rick	Mtl., St.L., Det.	4	239	6	26	32	165	3	0	0	0	0	....	1973-74	1976-77
Wilson, Rik	St.L., Cgy., Chi.	6	251	25	65	90	220	22	0	4	4	23	....	1981-82	1987-88
Wilson, Roger	Chi.	1	7	0	2	2	6	....	....	....	....	....	....	1974-75	1974-75
Wilson, Ron	Tor., Min.	7	177	26	67	93	68	20	4	13	17	8	....	1977-78	1987-88
Wilson, Ron	Wpg., St.L., Mtl.	14	832	110	216	326	415	63	10	12	22	64	....	1979-80	1993-94
Wilson, Wally	Bos.	1	53	11	8	19	18	1	0	0	0	0	....	1947-48	1947-48
Wing, Murray	Det.	1	1	0	1	1	0	....	....	....	....	....	....	1973-74	1973-74
Winnes, Chris	Bos., Phi.	4	33	1	6	7	6	1	0	0	0	0	....	1990-91	1993-94
Wiseman, Brian	Tor.	1	3	0	0	0	0	....	....	....	....	....	....	1996-97	1996-97
• Wiseman, Eddie	Det., NYA, Bos.	10	456	115	165	280	136	43	10	10	20	16	1	1932-33	1941-42
Wiste, Jim	Chi., Van.	3	52	1	10	11	8	....	....	....	....	....	....	1968-69	1970-71
‡ Witehall, Johan	NYR, Mtl.	3	54	2	5	7	16	....	....	....	....	....	....	1998-99	2000-01
Witherspoon, Jim	L.A.	1	2	0	0	0	2	....	....	....	....	....	....	1975-76	1975-76
Witiuk, Steve	Chi.	1	33	3	8	11	14	....	....	....	....	....	....	1951-52	1951-52
Woit, Benny	Det., Chi.	7	334	7	26	33	170	41	2	6	8	18	3	1950-51	1956-57
Wojciechowski, Steve	Det.	2	54	19	20	39	17	6	0	1	1	0	....	1944-45	1946-47
Wolanin, Craig	N.J., Que., Col., T.B., Tor.	13	695	40	133	173	894	35	4	6	10	67	1	1985-86	1997-98
Wolf, Bennett	Pit.	3	30	0	1	1	133	....	....	....	....	....	....	1980-81	1982-83

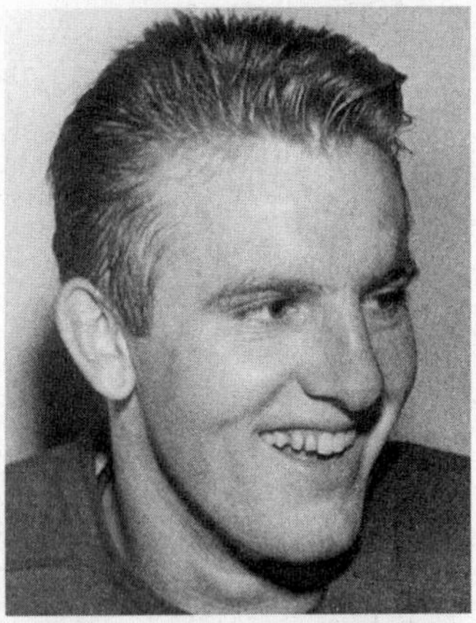
Larry Wilson

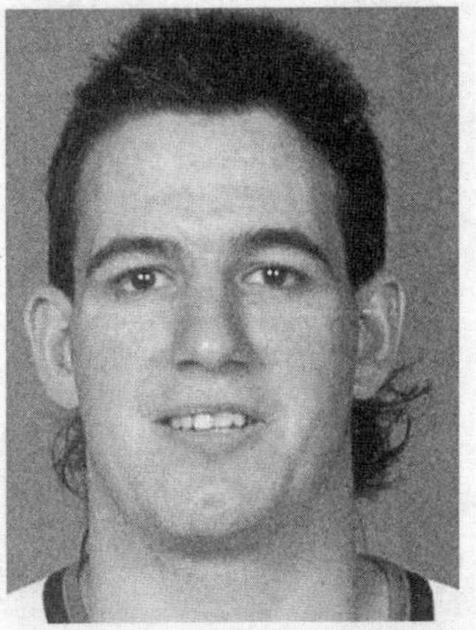
Kevin Wortman

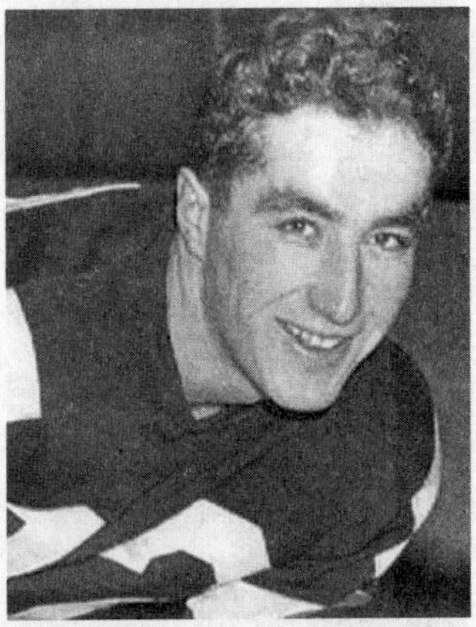
Ralph Wycherley

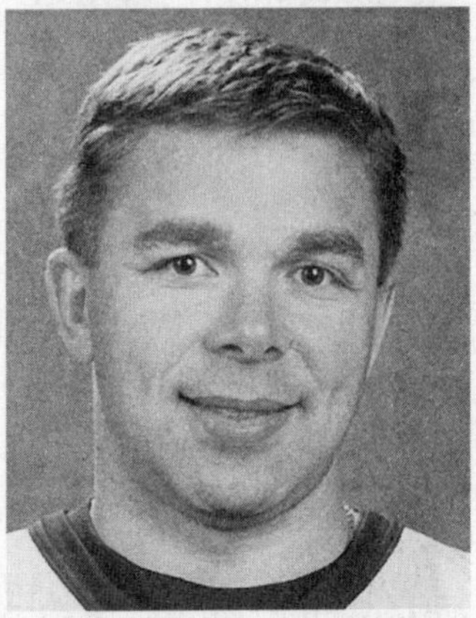
Vitali Yachmenev

Larry Zeidel

Ed Zeniuk

Name	NHL Teams	NHL Seasons	GP	G	A	TP	PIM	GP	G	A	TP	PIM	NHL Cup Wins	First NHL Season	Last NHL Season
			Regular Schedule					Playoffs							
Wong, Mike	Det.	1	22	1	1	2	12	....	....	....	....	....	....	1975-76	1975-76
‡ Wood, Dody	S.J.	5	106	8	10	18	471	....	....	....	....	....	....	1992-93	1997-98
Wood, Randy	NYI, Buf., Tor., Dal.	11	741	175	159	334	603	51	8	9	17	40	....	1986-87	1996-97
Wood, Robert	NYR	1	1	0	0	0	0	....	....	....	....	....	....	1950-51	1950-51
Woodley, Dan	Van.	1	5	2	0	2	17	....	....	....	....	....	....	1987-88	1987-88
Woods, Paul	Det.	7	501	72	124	196	276	7	0	5	5	4	....	1977-78	1983-84
Wortman, Kevin	Cgy.	1	5	0	0	0	2	....	....	....	....	....	....	1993-94	1993-94
• Woytowich, Bob	Bos., Min., Pit., L.A.	8	503	32	126	158	352	24	1	3	4	20	....	1964-65	1971-72
‡ Wren, Bob	Ana., Tor.	3	5	0	0	0	0	1	0	0	0	0	....	1997-98	2001-02
Wright, John	Van., St.L., K.C.	3	127	16	36	52	67	....	....	....	....	....	....	1972-73	1974-75
Wright, Keith	Phi.	1	1	0	0	0	0	....	....	....	....	....	....	1967-68	1967-68
Wright, Larry	Phi., Cal., Det.	5	106	4	8	12	19	....	....	....	....	....	....	1971-72	1977-78
Wycherley, Ralph	NYA, Bro.	2	28	4	7	11	6	....	....	....	....	....	....	1940-41	1941-42
• Wylie, Bill	NYR	1	1	0	0	0	0	....	....	....	....	....	....	1950-51	1950-51
Wylie, Duane	Chi.	2	14	3	3	6	2	....	....	....	....	....	....	1974-75	1976-77
Wyrozub, Randy	Buf.	4	100	8	10	18	10	....	....	....	....	....	....	1970-71	1973-74

Y Z

Name	NHL Teams	NHL Seasons	GP	G	A	TP	PIM	GP	G	A	TP	PIM	NHL Cup Wins	First NHL Season	Last NHL Season
‡ Yachmenev, Vitali	L.A., Nsh.	8	487	83	133	216	88	....	....	....	....	....	....	1995-96	2002-03
• Yackel, Ken	Bos.	1	6	0	0	0	2	2	0	0	0	2	....	1958-59	1958-59
‡ Yake, Terry	Hfd., Ana., Tor., St.L., Wsh.	11	403	77	120	197	220	32	4	4	8	36	....	1988-89	2000-01
‡ Yakushin, Dmitri	Tor.	1	2	0	0	0	2	....	....	....	....	....	....	1999-00	1999-00
Yaremchuk, Gary	Tor.	4	34	1	4	5	28	....	....	....	....	....	....	1981-82	1984-85
Yaremchuk, Ken	Chi., Tor.	6	235	36	56	92	106	31	6	8	14	49	....	1983-84	1988-89
Yates, Ross	Hfd.	1	7	1	1	2	4	....	....	....	....	....	....	1983-84	1983-84
Yawney, Trent	Chi., Cgy., St.L.	12	593	27	102	129	783	60	9	17	26	81	....	1987-88	1998-99
• Yegorov, Alexei	S.J.	2	11	3	3	6	2	....	....	....	....	....	....	1995-96	1996-97
‡ Ylonen, Juha	Phx., T.B., Ott.	6	341	26	76	102	90	15	0	7	7	4	....	1996-97	2001-02
York, Harry	St.L., NYR, Pit., Van.	4	244	29	46	75	99	5	0	0	0	2	....	1996-97	1999-00
Young, B.J.	Det.	1	1	0	0	0	0	....	....	....	....	....	....	1999-00	1999-00
Young, Brian	Chi.	1	8	0	2	2	6	....	....	....	....	....	....	1980-81	1980-81
Young, C.J.	Cgy., Bos.	1	43	7	7	14	32	....	....	....	....	....	....	1992-93	1992-93
• Young, Doug	Det., Mtl.	10	388	35	45	80	303	28	1	5	6	16	2	1931-32	1940-41
• Young, Howie	Det., Chi., Van.	8	336	12	62	74	851	19	2	4	6	46	....	1960-61	1970-71
Young, Tim	Min., Wpg., Phi.	10	628	195	341	536	438	36	7	24	31	27	....	1975-76	1984-85
Young, Warren	Min., Pit., Det.	7	236	72	77	149	472	....	....	....	....	....	....	1981-82	1987-88
Younghans, Tom	Min., NYR	6	429	44	41	85	373	24	2	1	3	21	....	1976-77	1981-82
Ysebaert, Paul	N.J., Det., Wpg., Chi., T.B.	11	532	149	187	336	217	30	4	3	7	20	....	1988-89	1998-99
‡ Zabransky, Libor	St.L.	2	40	1	6	7	50	....	....	....	....	....	....	1996-97	1997-98
Zaharko, Miles	Atl., Chi.	4	129	5	32	37	84	3	0	0	0	0	....	1977-78	1981-82
Zaine, Rod	Pit., Buf.	2	61	10	6	16	25	....	....	....	....	....	....	1970-71	1971-72
Zalapski, Zarley	Pit., Hfd., Cgy., Mtl., Phi.	12	637	99	285	384	684	48	4	23	27	47	....	1987-88	1999-00
Zanussi, Joe	NYR, Bos., St.L.	3	87	1	13	14	46	4	0	1	1	2	....	1974-75	1976-77
Zanussi, Ron	Min., Tor.	5	299	52	83	135	373	17	0	4	4	17	....	1977-78	1981-82
Zavisha, Brad	Edm.	1	2	0	0	0	0	....	....	....	....	....	....	1993-94	1993-94
‡ Zehr, Jeff	Bos.	1	4	0	0	0	2	....	....	....	....	....	....	1999-00	1999-00
Zeidel, Larry	Det., Chi., Phi.	5	158	3	16	19	198	12	0	1	1	12	1	1951-52	1968-69
‡ Zelepukin, Valeri	N.J., Edm., Phi., Chi.	10	595	117	177	294	527	85	13	13	26	48	1	1991-92	2000-01
Zemlak, Richard	Que., Min., Pit., Cgy.	5	132	2	12	14	587	1	0	0	0	10	....	1986-87	1991-92
Zeniuk, Ed	Det.	1	2	0	0	0	0	....	....	....	....	....	....	1954-55	1954-55
Zent, Jason	Ott., Phi.	3	27	3	3	6	13	....	....	....	....	....	....	1996-97	1998-99
Zetterstrom, Lars	Van.	1	14	0	1	1	2	....	....	....	....	....	....	1978-79	1978-79
Zettler, Rob	Min., S.J., Phi., Tor., Nsh., Wsh.	14	569	5	65	70	920	14	0	0	0	4	....	1988-89	2001-02
Zezel, Peter	Phi., St.L., Wsh., Tor., Dal., N.J., Van.	15	873	219	389	608	435	131	25	39	64	83	....	1984-85	1998-99
• Zholtok, Sergei	Bos., Ott., Mtl., Edm., Min., Nsh.	10	588	111	147	258	166	45	4	14	18	0	....	1992-93	2003-04
‡ Ziegler, Thomas	T.B.	1	5	0	0	0	0	....	....	....	....	....	....	2000-01	2000-01
Zmolek, Doug	S.J., Dal., L.A., Chi.	8	467	11	53	64	905	14	0	1	1	16	....	1992-93	1999-00
Zoborosky, Marty	Chi.	1	1	0	0	0	2	....	....	....	....	....	....	1944-45	1944-45
Zombo, Rick	Det., St.L., Bos.	12	652	24	130	154	728	60	1	11	12	127	....	1984-85	1995-96
Zuke, Mike	St.L., Hfd.	8	455	86	196	282	220	26	6	6	12	12	....	1978-79	1985-86
Zunich, Rudy	Det.	1	2	0	0	0	2	....	....	....	....	....	....	1943-44	1943-44

Retired Players, Goaltenders and Coaches Research Project

Throughout the Retired Players and Retired Goaltenders sections of this book, you will notice many players with a bullet (•) by their names. These players, according to our records, are deceased. The editors recognize that our information on the death dates of NHLers is incomplete. If you have documented information on the passing of any player not marked with a bullet (•) in this edition, we would like to hear from you. We also welcome information on deceased NHL head coaches. Please send this information to:

Retired Player
Research Project
c/o NHL Publishing
194 Dovercourt Road
Toronto, Ontario
M6J 3C8   Canada
Fax: 416/531-3939

Many thanks to the following contributors in 2004-05:

Tim Bateman, Corey Bryant, Paul R. Carroll, Jr., Bob Duff, Peter Fillman, Ernie Fitzsimmons, Gary J. Pearce, Drew "Whitey" White.

Retired NHL Goaltender Index

Abbreviations: Teams/Cities: – **Ana**. – Anaheim; **Atl**. – Atlanta; **Bos**. – Boston; **Bro**. – Brooklyn; **Buf**. – Buffalo; **Cal**. – California; **Cgy**. – Calgary; **Cle**. – Cleveland; **Col**. – Colorado; **CBJ** – Columbus; **Dal**. – Dallas; **Det**. – Detroit; **Edm**. – Edmonton; **Fla**. – Florida; **Ham**. – Hamilton; **Hfd**. – Hartford; **K.C.** – Kansas City; **L.A.** – Los Angeles; **Min**. – Minnesota; **Mtl**. – Montreal; **Mtl.M.** – Montreal Maroons; **Mtl.W.** – Montreal Wanderers; **N.J.** – New Jersey; **NYA** – NY Americans; **NYI** – NY Islanders; **NYR** – New York Rangers; – **Oak**. – Oakland; **Ott**. – Ottawa; – **Phi**. – Philadelphia; **Phx**. – Phoenix; **Pit**. – Pittsburgh; **Que**. – Quebec; **St.L.** – St. Louis; **S.J.** – San Jose; **T.B.** – Tampa Bay; **Tor**. – Toronto; **Van**. – Vancouver; **Wpg**. – Winnipeg; **Wsh**. – Washington

Avg. – goals against per 60 minutes played; **GA** – goals agains; **GP** – games played; **Mins** – minutes played; **SO** – shutouts.
• – deceased. § – Forward, defenseman or coach who appeared in goal. For complete career, see Retired Player Index. ‡ – Remains active in other leagues.

			Regular Schedule								Playoffs										
Name	NHL Teams	NHL Seasons	GP	W	L	T	Mins	GA	SO	Avg	GP	W	L	T	Mins	GA	SO	Avg	NHL Cup Wins	First NHL Season	Last NHL Season
Abbott, George	Bos.	1	1	0	1	0	60	7	0	7.00	....	....	....	....	....	....	....	....		1943-44	1943-44
Adams, John	Bos., Wsh.	2	22	9	10	1	1180	85	1	4.32	....	....	....	....	....	....	....	....		1972-73	1974-75
Aiken, Don	Mtl.	1	1	0	1	0	34	6	0	10.59	....	....	....	....	....	....	....	....		1957-58	1957-58
• Aitkenhead, Andy	NYR	3	106	47	43	16	6570	257	11	2.35	10	6	2	2	608	15	3	1.48	1	1932-33	1934-35
• Almas, Red	Det., Chi.	3	3	0	2	1	180	13	0	4.33	5	1	3	....	263	13	0	2.97		1946-47	1952-53
• Anderson, Lorne	NYR	1	3	1	2	0	180	18	0	6.00	....	....	....	....	....	....	....	....		1951-52	1951-52
Astrom, Hardy	NYR, Col.	3	83	17	44	12	4456	278	0	3.74	....	....	....	....	....	....	....	....		1977-78	1980-81
‡ Bach, Ryan	L.A.	1	3	0	3	0	108	8	0	4.44	....	....	....	....	....	....	....	....		1998-99	1998-99
Bailey, Scott	Bos.	2	19	6	6	2	965	55	0	3.42	....	....	....	....	....	....	....	....		1995-96	1996-97
Baker, Steve	NYR	4	57	20	20	11	3081	190	3	3.70	14	7	7	....	826	55	0	4.00		1979-80	1982-83
‡ Bales, Mike	Bos., Ott.	4	23	2	15	1	1120	77	0	4.13	....	....	....	....	....	....	....	....		1992-93	1996-97
Bannerman, Murray	Van., Chi.	8	289	116	125	33	16470	1051	8	3.83	40	20	18	....	2322	165	0	4.26		1977-78	1986-87
Baron, Marco	Bos., L.A., Edm.	6	86	34	38	9	4822	292	1	3.63	1	0	1	....	20	3	0	9.00		1979-80	1984-85
Barrasso, Tom	Buf., Pit., Ott., Car., Tor., St.L.	19	777	369	277	86	44180	2385	38	3.24	119	61	54	....	6953	349	6	3.01	2	1983-84	2002-03
Bassen, Hank	Chi., Det., Pit.	9	156	46	66	31	8759	434	5	2.97	5	1	3	....	274	11	0	2.41		1954-55	1967-68
• Bastien, Baz	Tor.	1	5	0	4	1	300	20	0	4.00	....	....	....	....	....	....	....	....		1945-46	1945-46
Bauman, Gary	Mtl., Min.	3	35	5	16	6	1719	102	0	3.56	....	....	....	....	....	....	....	....		1966-67	1968-69
Beaupre, Don	Min., Wsh., Ott., Tor.	17	667	268	277	75	37396	2151	17	3.45	72	33	31	....	3943	220	3	3.35		1980-81	1996-97
Beauregard, Stephane	Wpg., Phi.	5	90	19	39	11	4402	268	2	3.65	4	1	3	....	238	12	0	3.03		1989-90	1993-94
Bedard, Jim	Wsh.	2	73	17	40	13	4232	278	1	3.94	....	....	....	....	....	....	....	....		1977-78	1978-79
Behrend, Marc	Wpg.	3	39	12	19	3	1991	160	1	4.82	7	1	3	0	312	19	0	3.65		1983-84	1985-86
Belanger, Yves	St.L., Atl., Bos.	6	78	29	33	6	4134	259	2	3.76	....	....	....	....	....	....	....	....		1974-75	1979-80
Belhumeur, Michel	Phi., Wsh.	3	65	9	36	7	3306	254	0	4.61	1	0	0	....	10	1	0	6.00		1972-73	1975-76
• Bell, Gordie	Tor., NYR	2	8	3	5	0	480	31	0	3.88	2	1	1	....	120	9	0	4.50		1945-46	1955-56
• Benedict, Clint	Ott., Mtl.M.	13	362	190	143	28	22367	863	58	2.32	28	11	12	5	1707	53	9	1.86	4	1917-18	1929-30
Bennett, Harvey	Bos.	1	25	10	12	2	1470	103	0	4.20	....	....	....	....	....	....	....	....		1944-45	1944-45
Bergeron, Jean-Claude	Mtl., T.B., L.A.	6	72	21	33	7	3772	232	1	3.69	....	....	....	....	....	....	....	....		1990-91	1996-97
Bernhardt, Tim	Cgy., Tor.	4	67	17	36	7	3748	267	0	4.27	....	....	....	....	....	....	....	....		1982-83	1986-87
‡ Berthiaume, Daniel	Wpg., Min., L.A., Bos., Ott.	9	215	81	90	21	11662	714	5	3.67	14	5	9	....	807	50	0	3.72		1985-86	1993-94
Bester, Allan	Tor., Det., Dal.	10	219	73	99	17	11773	786	7	4.01	11	2	6	....	508	37	0	4.37		1983-84	1995-96
• Beveridge, Bill	Det., Ott., St.L., Mtl.M., NYR	9	297	87	166	42	18375	879	18	2.87	5	2	3	....	300	11	0	2.20		1929-30	1942-43
• Bibeault, Paul	Mtl., Tor., Bos., Chi.	7	214	81	107	25	12890	785	10	3.65	20	6	14	....	1237	71	2	3.44		1940-41	1946-47
Billington, Craig	N.J., Ott., Bos., Col., Wsh.	15	332	110	149	31	17097	1034	9	3.63	8	0	2	....	213	15	0	4.23		1985-86	2002-03
Binette, Andre	Mtl.	1	1	1	0	0	60	4	0	4.00	....	....	....	....	....	....	....	....		1954-55	1954-55
Binkley, Les	Pit.	5	196	58	94	34	11046	575	11	3.12	7	5	2	....	428	15	0	2.10		1967-68	1971-72
Bittner, Richard	Bos.	1	1	0	0	1	60	3	0	3.00	....	....	....	....	....	....	....	....		1949-50	1949-50
Blake, Mike	L.A.	3	40	13	15	5	2117	150	0	4.25	....	....	....	....	....	....	....	....		1981-82	1983-84
Blue, John	Bos., Buf.	3	46	16	18	7	2521	126	1	3.00	2	0	1	....	96	5	0	3.13		1992-93	1995-96
Boisvert, Gilles	Det.	1	3	0	3	0	180	9	0	3.00	....	....	....	....	....	....	....	....		1959-60	1959-60
Bouchard, Dan	Atl., Cgy., Que., Wpg.	14	655	286	232	113	37919	2061	27	3.26	43	13	30	....	2549	147	1	3.46		1972-73	1985-86
• Bourque, Claude	Mtl., Det.	2	62	16	38	8	3830	193	4	3.02	3	1	2	....	188	8	1	2.55		1938-39	1939-40
Boutin, Rollie	Wsh.	3	22	7	10	1	1137	75	0	3.96	....	....	....	....	....	....	....	....		1978-79	1980-81
• Bouvrette, Lionel	NYR	1	1	0	1	0	60	6	0	6.00	....	....	....	....	....	....	....	....		1942-43	1942-43
Bower, Johnny	NYR, Tor.	15	552	250	195	90	32016	1340	37	2.51	74	35	34	....	4378	180	5	2.47	4	1953-54	1969-70
§ • Branigan, Andy	NYA	1	1	0	0	0	7	0	0	0.00	....	....	....	....	....	....	....	....		1940-41	1940-41
• Brimsek, Frank	Bos., Chi.	10	514	252	182	80	31210	1404	40	2.70	68	32	36	....	4395	186	2	2.54	2	1938-39	1949-50
• Broda, Turk	Tor.	14	629	302	224	101	38167	1609	62	2.53	101	60	39	....	6389	211	13	1.98	5	1936-37	1951-52
Broderick, Ken	Min., Bos.	3	27	11	12	1	1464	74	1	3.03	....	....	....	....	....	....	....	....		1969-70	1974-75
Broderick, Len	Mtl.	1	1	1	0	0	60	2	0	2.00	....	....	....	....	....	....	....	....		1957-58	1957-58
Brodeur, Richard	NYI, Van., Hfd.	9	385	131	175	62	21968	1410	6	3.85	33	13	20	....	2009	111	1	3.32		1979-80	1987-88
Bromley, Gary	Buf., Van.	6	136	54	44	28	7427	425	7	3.43	7	2	5	....	360	25	0	4.17		1973-74	1980-81
• Brooks, Art	Tor.	1	4	2	2	0	220	23	0	6.27	....	....	....	....	....	....	....	....		1917-18	1917-18
Brooks, Ross	Bos.	3	54	37	7	6	3047	134	4	2.64	1	0	0	....	20	3	0	9.00		1972-73	1974-75
• Brophy, Frank	Que.	1	21	3	18	0	1249	148	0	7.11	....	....	....	....	....	....	....	....		1919-20	1919-20
Brown, Andy	Det., Pit.	3	62	22	26	9	3373	213	1	3.79	....	....	....	....	....	....	....	....		1971-72	1973-74
Brown, Ken	Chi.	1	1	0	0	0	18	1	0	3.33	....	....	....	....	....	....	....	....		1970-71	1970-71
Brunetta, Mario	Que.	3	40	12	17	1	1967	128	0	3.90	....	....	....	....	....	....	....	....		1987-88	1989-90
Bullock, Bruce	Van.	3	16	3	9	3	927	74	0	4.79	....	....	....	....	....	....	....	....		1972-73	1976-77
• Buzinski, Steve	NYR	1	9	2	6	1	560	55	0	5.89	....	....	....	....	....	....	....	....		1942-43	1942-43
Caley, Don	St.L.	1	1	0	0	0	30	3	0	6.00	....	....	....	....	....	....	....	....		1967-68	1967-68
Caprice, Frank	Van.	6	102	31	46	11	5589	391	1	4.20	....	....	....	....	....	....	....	....		1982-83	1987-88
Carey, Jim	Wsh., Bos., St.L.	5	172	79	65	16	9668	416	16	2.58	10	2	5	....	455	35	0	4.62		1994-95	1998-99
Caron, Jacques	L.A., St.L., Van.	5	72	24	29	11	3846	211	2	3.29	12	4	7	....	639	34	0	3.19		1967-68	1973-74
Carter, Lyle	Cal.	1	15	4	7	0	721	50	0	4.16	....	....	....	....	....	....	....	....		1971-72	1971-72
Casey, Jon	Min., Bos., St.L.	12	425	170	157	55	23255	1246	16	3.21	66	32	31	....	3743	192	3	3.08		1983-84	1996-97
‡ Chabot, Frederic	Mtl., Phi., L.A.	5	32	4	8	4	1262	62	0	2.95	....	....	....	....	....	....	....	....		1990-91	1998-99
• Chabot, Lorne	NYR, Tor., Mtl., Chi., Mtl.M., NYA	11	411	201	148	62	25307	860	72	2.04	37	13	17	6	2498	64	5	1.54	2	1926-27	1936-37
Chadwick, Ed	Tor., Bos.	6	184	57	92	35	11040	541	14	2.94	....	....	....	....	....	....	....	....		1955-56	1961-62
Champoux, Bob	Det., Cal.	2	17	2	11	3	923	80	0	5.20	1	1	0	....	55	4	0	4.36		1963-64	1973-74
Cheevers, Gerry	Tor., Bos.	13	418	230	102	74	24394	1174	26	2.89	88	53	34	....	5396	242	8	2.69	2	1961-62	1979-80
Cheveldae, Tim	Det., Wpg., Bos.	9	340	149	136	37	19172	1116	10	3.49	25	9	15	....	1418	71	2	3.00		1988-89	1996-97
Chevrier, Alain	N.J., Wpg., Chi., Pit., Det.	6	234	91	100	14	12202	845	2	4.16	16	9	7	....	1013	44	0	2.61		1985-86	1990-91
§ • Clancy, King	Ott., Tor.	2	2	0	0	0	3	1	0	20.00	....	....	....	....	....	....	....	....		1924-25	1931-32
§ • Cleghorn, Odie	Pit.	1	1	1	0	0	60	2	0	2.00	....	....	....	....	....	....	....	....		1925-26	1925-26
§ • Cleghorn, Sprague	Ott., Mtl.	2	2	0	0	0	5	0	0	0.00	....	....	....	....	....	....	....	....		1918-19	1921-22
Clifford, Chris	Chi.	2	2	0	0	0	24	0	0	0.00	....	....	....	....	....	....	....	....		1984-85	1988-89
Cloutier, Jacques	Buf., Chi., Que.	12	255	82	102	24	12826	778	3	3.64	8	1	5	....	413	18	1	2.62		1981-82	1993-94
Colvin, Les	Bos.	1	1	0	1	0	60	4	0	4.00	....	....	....	....	....	....	....	....		1948-49	1948-49
§ • Conacher, Charlie	Tor., Det.	3	4	0	0	0	10	0	0	0.00	....	....	....	....	....	....	....	....		1932-33	1938-39
• Connell, Alec	Ott., Det., NYA, Mtl.M.	12	417	193	156	67	26050	830	81	1.91	21	8	5	8	1309	26	4	1.19	2	1924-25	1936-37
Corsi, Jim	Edm.	1	26	8	14	3	1366	83	0	3.65	....	....	....	....	....	....	....	....		1979-80	1979-80
Courteau, Maurice	Bos.	1	6	2	4	0	360	33	0	5.50	....	....	....	....	....	....	....	....		1943-44	1943-44
Cousineau, Marcel	Tor., NYI, L.A.	4	26	4	10	1	1047	51	1	2.92	....	....	....	....	....	....	....	....		1996-97	1999-00
Cowley, Wayne	Edm.	1	1	0	1	0	57	3	0	3.16	....	....	....	....	....	....	....	....		1993-94	1993-94
Cox, Abbie	Mtl.M., NYA, Det., Mtl.	3	5	1	1	2	263	11	0	2.51	....	....	....	....	....	....	....	....		1929-30	1935-36
Craig, Jim	Atl., Bos., Min.	3	30	11	10	7	1588	100	0	3.78	....	....	....	....	....	....	....	....		1979-80	1983-84
Crha, Jiri	Tor.	2	69	28	27	11	3942	261	0	3.97	5	0	4	....	186	21	0	6.77		1979-80	1980-81
• Crozier, Roger	Det., Buf., Wsh.	14	518	206	197	70	28567	1446	30	3.04	32	14	16	....	1789	82	1	2.75		1963-64	1976-77
• Cude, Wilf	Phi., Bos., Chi., Mtl., Det.	10	282	100	132	49	17586	798	24	2.72	19	7	11	1	1257	51	1	2.43		1930-31	1940-41
Cutts, Don	Edm.	1	6	1	2	1	269	16	0	3.57	....	....	....	....	....	....	....	....		1979-80	1979-80
• Cyr, Claude	Mtl.	1	1	0	0	0	20	1	0	3.00	....	....	....	....	....	....	....	....		1958-59	1958-59
Dadswell, Doug	Cgy.	2	27	8	8	3	1346	99	0	4.41	....	....	....	....	....	....	....	....		1986-87	1987-88
D'Alessio, Corrie	Hfd.	1	1	0	0	0	11	0	0	0.00	....	....	....	....	....	....	....	....		1992-93	1992-93
Daley, Joe	Pit., Buf., Det.	4	105	34	44	19	5836	326	3	3.35	....	....	....	....	....	....	....	....		1968-69	1971-72
Damore, Nick	Bos.	1	1	1	0	0	60	3	0	3.00	....	....	....	....	....	....	....	....		1941-42	1941-42
D'Amour, Marc	Cgy., Phi.	2	16	2	4	2	579	32	0	3.32	....	....	....	....	....	....	....	....		1985-86	1988-89
§ • Darragh, Jack	Ott.	1	1	0	0	0	2	0	0	0.00	....	....	....	....	....	....	....	....		1919-20	1919-20

Name	NHL Teams	NHL Seasons	Regular Schedule								Playoffs								NHL Cup Wins	First NHL Season	Last NHL Season
			GP	W	L	T	Mins	GA	SO	Avg	GP	W	L	T	Mins	GA	SO	Avg			
Daskalakis, Cleon	Bos.	3	12	3	4	1	506	41	0	4.86	....	....	....	....	....	....	....	....		1984-85	1986-87
Davidson, John	St.L., NYR	10	301	123	124	39	17109	1004	7	3.52	31	16	14	....	1862	77	1	2.48		1973-74	1982-83
Decourcy, Bob	NYR	1	1	0	1	0	29	6	0	12.41	....	....	....	....	....	....	....	....		1947-48	1947-48
Defelice, Norm	Bos.	1	10	3	5	2	600	30	0	3.00	....	....	....	....	....	....	....	....		1956-57	1956-57
DeJordy, Denis	Chi., L.A., Mtl., Det.	12	316	124	128	51	17798	929	15	3.13	18	6	9	....	946	55	0	3.49	1	1960-61	1973-74
DelGuidice, Matt	Bos.	2	11	2	5	1	434	28	0	3.87	....	....	....	....	....	....	....	....		1990-91	1991-92
DeRouville, Philippe	Pit.	2	3	1	2	0	171	9	0	3.16	....	....	....	....	....	....	....	....		1994-95	1996-97
Desjardins, Gerry	L.A., Chi., NYI, Buf.	10	331	122	153	44	19014	1042	12	3.29	35	15	15	....	1874	108	0	3.46		1968-69	1977-78
• Dickie, Bill	Chi.	1	1	1	0	0	60	3	0	3.00	....	....	....	....	....	....	....	....		1941-42	1941-42
Dion, Connie	Det.	2	38	23	11	4	2280	119	1	3.13	5	1	4	....	300	17	0	3.40		1943-44	1944-45
Dion, Michel	Que., Wpg., Pit.	6	227	60	118	32	12695	898	2	4.24	5	2	3	....	304	22	0	4.34		1979-80	1984-85
Dolson, Dolly	Det.	3	93	35	41	17	5820	192	16	1.98	2	0	2	0	120	7	0	3.50		1928-29	1930-31
Dopson, Rob	Pit.	1	2	0	0	0	45	3	0	4.00	....	....	....	....	....	....	....	....		1993-94	1993-94
Dowie, Bruce	Tor.	1	2	0	1	0	72	4	0	3.33	....	....	....	....	....	....	....	....		1983-84	1983-84
‡ Draper, Tom	Wpg., Buf., NYI	6	53	19	23	5	2807	173	1	3.70	7	3	4	....	433	19	1	2.63		1988-89	1995-96
Dryden, Dave	NYR, Chi., Buf., Edm.	9	203	66	76	31	10424	555	9	3.19	3	0	2	....	133	9	0	4.06		1961-62	1979-80
Dryden, Ken	Mtl.	8	397	258	57	74	23352	870	46	2.24	112	80	32	....	6846	274	10	2.40	6	1970-71	1978-79
Duffus, Parris	Phx.	1	1	0	0	0	29	1	0	2.07	....	....	....	....	....	....	....	....		1996-97	1996-97
Dumas, Michel	Chi.	3	8	2	1	2	362	24	0	3.98	1	0	0	....	19	1	0	3.16		1974-75	1976-77
Dupuis, Bob	Edm.	1	1	0	1	0	60	4	0	4.00	....	....	....	....	....	....	....	....		1979-80	1979-80
• Durnan, Bill	Mtl.	7	383	208	112	62	22945	901	34	2.36	45	27	18	....	2871	99	2	2.07	2	1943-44	1949-50
Dyck, Ed	Van.	3	49	8	28	5	2453	178	1	4.35	....	....	....	....	....	....	....	....		1971-72	1973-74
Edwards, Don	Buf., Cgy., Tor.	10	459	208	155	74	26181	1449	16	3.32	42	16	21	....	2302	132	1	3.44		1976-77	1985-86
Edwards, Gary	St.L., L.A., Cle., Min., Edm., Pit.	13	286	88	125	51	16002	973	10	3.65	11	5	4	....	537	34	0	3.80		1968-69	1981-82
Edwards, Marv	Pit., Tor., Cal.	4	61	15	34	7	3467	218	2	3.77	....	....	....	....	....	....	....	....		1968-69	1973-74
• Edwards, Roy	Det., Pit.	7	236	97	88	38	13109	637	12	2.92	4	0	3	....	206	11	0	3.20		1967-68	1973-74
Eliot, Darren	L.A., Det., Buf.	5	89	25	41	12	4931	377	1	4.59	1	0	0	....	40	7	0	10.50		1984-85	1988-89
Ellacott, Ken	Van.	1	12	2	3	4	555	41	0	4.43	....	....	....	....	....	....	....	....		1982-83	1982-83
Erickson, Chad	N.J.	1	2	1	1	0	120	9	0	4.50	....	....	....	....	....	....	....	....		1991-92	1991-92
Esposito, Tony	Mtl., Chi.	16	886	423	306	151	52585	2563	76	2.92	99	45	53	....	6017	308	6	3.07	1	1968-69	1983-84
Essensa, Bob	Wpg., Det., Edm., Phx., Van., Buf.	12	446	173	176	47	24215	1270	18	3.15	16	4	9	0	864	51	0	3.54		1988-89	2001-02
• Evans, Claude	Mtl., Bos.	2	5	1	2	1	260	16	0	3.69	....	....	....	....	....	....	....	....		1954-55	1957-58
Exelby, Randy	Mtl., Edm.	2	2	0	1	0	63	5	0	4.76	....	....	....	....	....	....	....	....		1988-89	1989-90
‡ Fankhouser, Scott	Atl.	2	23	4	12	2	1180	65	0	3.31	....	....	....	....	....	....	....	....		1999-00	2000-01
Farr, Rocky	Buf.	3	19	2	6	3	722	42	0	3.49	....	....	....	....	....	....	....	....		1972-73	1974-75
Favell, Doug	Phi., Tor., Col.	12	373	123	153	69	20771	1096	18	3.17	21	6	15	....	1270	66	1	3.12		1967-68	1978-79
Fiset, Stephane	Que., Col., L.A., Mtl.	13	390	164	153	44	21785	1114	16	3.07	14	1	7	0	563	37	0	3.94	1	1989-90	2001-02
Fitzpatrick, Mark	L.A., NYI, Fla., T.B., Chi., Car.	12	329	113	136	49	18329	953	8	3.12	9	0	3	....	289	23	0	4.78		1988-89	1999-00
• Forbes, Jake	Tor., Ham., NYA, Phi.	13	210	85	114	11	12922	594	19	2.76	2	0	2	0	120	7	0	3.50		1919-20	1932-33
Ford, Brian	Que., Pit.	2	11	3	7	0	580	61	0	6.31	....	....	....	....	....	....	....	....		1983-84	1984-85
Foster, Norm	Bos., Edm.	2	13	7	4	0	623	34	0	3.27	....	....	....	....	....	....	....	....		1990-91	1991-92
‡ Fountain, Mike	Van., Car., Ott.	4	11	2	6	0	483	28	1	3.48	....	....	....	....	....	....	....	....		1996-97	2000-01
• Fowler, Hec	Bos.	1	7	1	6	0	409	42	0	6.16	....	....	....	....	....	....	....	....		1924-25	1924-25
Francis, Emile	Chi., NYR	6	95	31	52	11	5660	355	1	3.76	....	....	....	....	....	....	....	....		1946-47	1951-52
• Franks, Jimmy	Det., NYR, Bos.	4	42	12	23	7	2520	181	1	4.31	1	0	1	....	30	2	0	4.00	1	1936-37	1943-44
Frederick, Ray	Chi.	1	5	0	4	1	300	22	0	4.40	....	....	....	....	....	....	....	....		1954-55	1954-55
Friesen, Karl	N.J.	1	4	0	2	1	130	16	0	7.38	....	....	....	....	....	....	....	....		1986-87	1986-87
Froese, Bob	Phi., NYR	8	242	128	72	20	13451	694	13	3.10	18	3	9	....	830	55	0	3.98		1982-83	1989-90
Fuhr, Grant	Edm., Tor., Buf., L.A., St.L., Cgy.	19	868	403	295	114	48945	2756	25	3.38	150	92	50	....	8834	430	6	2.92	5	1981-82	1999-00
‡ Gage, Joaquin	Edm.	3	23	4	12	1	1076	67	0	3.74	....	....	....	....	....	....	....	....		1994-95	2000-01
Gagnon, David	Det.	1	2	0	1	0	35	6	0	10.29	....	....	....	....	....	....	....	....		1990-91	1990-91
• Gamble, Bruce	NYR, Bos., Tor., Phi.	10	327	110	150	46	18442	988	22	3.21	5	0	4	....	206	25	0	7.28	1	1958-59	1971-72
Gamble, Troy	Van.	4	72	22	29	9	3804	229	1	3.61	4	1	3	....	249	16	0	3.86		1986-87	1991-92
• Gardiner, Bert	NYR, Mtl., Chi., Bos.	6	144	49	68	27	8760	554	4	3.79	9	4	5	....	647	20	0	1.85		1935-36	1943-44
• Gardiner, Charlie	Chi.	7	316	112	152	52	19687	664	42	2.02	21	12	6	3	1472	35	5	1.43	1	1927-28	1933-34
Gardner, George	Det., Van.	5	66	16	30	6	3313	207	0	3.75	....	....	....	....	....	....	....	....		1965-66	1971-72
‡ Garner, Tyrone	Cgy.	1	3	0	2	0	139	12	0	5.18	....	....	....	....	....	....	....	....		1998-99	1998-99
Garrett, John	Hfd., Que., Van.	6	207	68	91	37	11763	837	1	4.27	9	4	3	....	461	33	0	4.30		1979-80	1984-85
Gatherum, Dave	Det.	1	3	2	0	1	180	3	1	1.00	....	....	....	....	....	....	....	....	1	1953-54	1953-54
Gauthier, Paul	Mtl.	1	1	0	0	1	70	2	0	1.71	....	....	....	....	....	....	....	....		1937-38	1937-38
Gauthier, Sean	S.J.	1	1	0	0	0	3	0	0	0.00	....	....	....	....	....	....	....	....		1998-99	1998-99
• Gelineau, Jack	Bos., Chi.	4	143	46	64	33	8580	447	7	3.13	4	1	2	....	260	7	1	1.62		1948-49	1953-54
Giacomin, Ed	NYR, Det.	13	609	289	209	96	35633	1672	54	2.82	65	29	35	....	3838	180	1	2.81		1965-66	1977-78
Gilbert, Gilles	Min., Bos., Det.	14	416	192	143	60	23677	1290	18	3.27	32	17	15	....	1919	97	3	3.03		1969-70	1982-83
Gill, Andre	Bos.	1	5	3	2	0	270	13	1	2.89	....	....	....	....	....	....	....	....		1967-68	1967-68
• Goodman, Paul	Chi.	3	52	23	20	9	3240	117	6	2.17	3	0	3	....	187	10	0	3.21	1	1937-38	1940-41
Gordon, Scott	Que.	2	23	2	16	0	1082	101	0	5.60	....	....	....	....	....	....	....	....		1989-90	1990-91
Gosselin, Mario	Que., L.A., Hfd.	9	241	91	107	14	12857	801	6	3.74	32	16	15	....	1816	99	0	3.27		1983-84	1993-94
Goverde, David	L.A.	3	5	1	4	0	278	29	0	6.26	....	....	....	....	....	....	....	....		1991-92	1993-94
Grahame, Ron	Bos., L.A., Que.	4	114	50	43	15	6472	409	5	3.79	4	2	1	....	202	7	0	2.08		1977-78	1980-81
• Grant, Benny	Tor., NYA, Bos.	6	50	17	26	4	2990	187	4	3.75	....	....	....	....	....	....	....	....		1928-29	1943-44
Grant, Doug	Det., St.L.	7	77	27	34	8	4199	280	2	4.00	....	....	....	....	....	....	....	....		1973-74	1979-80
Gratton, Gilles	St.L., NYR	2	47	13	18	9	2299	154	0	4.02	....	....	....	....	....	....	....	....		1975-76	1976-77
Gray, Gerry	Det., NYI	2	8	1	5	1	440	35	0	4.77	....	....	....	....	....	....	....	....		1970-71	1972-73
Gray, Harrison	Det.	1	1	0	1	0	40	5	0	7.50	....	....	....	....	....	....	....	....		1963-64	1963-64
Greenlay, Mike	Edm.	1	2	0	0	0	20	4	0	12.00	....	....	....	....	....	....	....	....		1989-90	1989-90
Guenette, Steve	Pit., Cgy.	5	35	19	16	0	1958	122	1	3.74	....	....	....	....	....	....	....	....		1986-87	1990-91
Hackett, Jeff	NYI, S.J., Chi., Mtl., Bos., Phi.	15	500	166	244	56	28125	1361	26	2.90	12	3	7	....	610	36	0	3.54		1988-89	2003-04
• Hainsworth, George	Mtl., Tor.	11	465	246	145	74	29087	937	94	1.93	52	22	25	5	3486	112	8	1.93	2	1926-27	1936-37
Hall, Glenn	Det., Chi., St.L.	19	906	407	326	163	53484	2222	84	2.49	115	49	65	....	6899	320	6	2.78	2	1951-52	1970-71
Hamel, Pierre	Tor., Wpg.	4	69	13	41	7	3766	276	0	4.40	....	....	....	....	....	....	....	....		1974-75	1980-81
Hanlon, Glen	Van., St.L., NYR, Det.	15	477	167	202	61	26037	1561	13	3.60	35	11	15	....	1756	92	4	3.14		1977-78	1990-91
Harrison, Paul	Min., Tor., Pit., Buf.	7	109	28	59	9	5806	408	2	4.22	4	0	1	....	157	9	0	3.44		1975-76	1981-82
Hayward, Brian	Wpg., Mtl., Min., S.J.	11	357	143	156	37	20025	1242	8	3.72	37	11	18	....	1803	104	0	3.46		1982-83	1992-93
Head, Don	Bos.	1	38	9	26	3	2280	158	2	4.16	....	....	....	....	....	....	....	....		1961-62	1961-62
Healy, Glenn	L.A., NYI, NYR, Tor.	15	437	166	190	47	24256	1361	13	3.37	37	13	15	....	1930	108	0	3.36	1	1985-86	2000-01
Hebert, Guy	St.L., Ana., NYR	10	491	191	222	56	27889	1307	28	2.81	14	4	7	....	744	33	1	2.66		1991-92	2000-01
• Hebert, Sammy	Tor., Ott.	2	4	2	1	0	200	19	0	5.70	....	....	....	....	....	....	....	....	1	1917-18	1923-24
Heinz, Rick	St.L., Van.	5	49	14	19	5	2356	159	2	4.05	1	0	0	....	8	1	0	7.50		1980-81	1984-85
Henderson, John	Bos.	2	46	15	15	15	2688	113	5	2.52	2	0	2	....	120	8	0	4.00		1954-55	1955-56
• Henry, Gord	Bos.	4	3	1	2	0	180	5	1	1.67	5	0	4	....	283	21	0	4.45		1948-49	1952-53
• Henry, Jim	NYR, Chi., Bos.	9	406	161	173	70	24355	1166	27	2.87	29	11	18	....	1741	81	2	2.79		1941-42	1954-55
Herron, Denis	Pit., K.C., Mtl.	14	462	146	203	76	25608	1579	10	3.70	15	5	10	....	901	50	0	3.33		1972-73	1985-86
Hextall, Ron	Phi., Que., NYI	13	608	296	214	69	34750	1723	23	2.97	93	47	43	....	5456	276	2	3.04		1986-87	1998-99
Highton, Hec	Chi.	1	24	10	14	0	1440	108	0	4.50	....	....	....	....	....	....	....	....		1943-44	1943-44
§ • Himes, Normie	NYA	2	2	0	1	0	79	3	0	2.28	....	....	....	....	....	....	....	....		1927-28	1928-29
‡ Hirsch, Corey	NYR, Van., Wsh., Dal.	7	108	34	45	14	5775	301	4	3.13	6	2	3	....	338	21	0	3.73		1992-93	2002-03
Hodge, Charlie	Mtl., Oak., Van.	14	358	150	125	61	20573	925	24	2.70	16	7	8	....	804	32	2	2.39	5	1954-55	1970-71
Hodson, Kevin	Det., T.B.	6	71	17	18	10	2910	134	4	2.76	1	0	0	....	1	0	0	0.00	2	1995-96	2002-03
Hoffort, Bruce	Phi.	2	9	4	0	3	368	22	0	3.59	....	....	....	....	....	....	....	....		1989-90	1990-91
Hoganson, Paul	Pit.	1	2	0	1	0	57	7	0	7.37	....	....	....	....	....	....	....	....		1970-71	1970-71
Hogosta, Goran	NYI, Que.	2	22	5	12	3	1208	83	1	4.12	....	....	....	....	....	....	....	....		1977-78	1979-80
Holden, Mark	Mtl., Wpg.	4	8	2	2	1	372	25	0	4.03	....	....	....	....	....	....	....	....		1981-82	1984-85
Holland, Ken	Hfd., Det.	2	4	0	2	1	206	17	0	4.95	....	....	....	....	....	....	....	....		1980-81	1983-84
Holland, Rob	Pit.	2	44	11	22	9	2513	171	1	4.08	....	....	....	....	....	....	....	....		1979-80	1980-81
• Holmes, Hap	Tor., Det.	4	103	39	54	10	6510	264	17	2.43	2	1	1	0	120	7	0	3.50	1	1917-18	1927-28
§ • Horner, Red	Tor.	1	1	0	0	0	1	1	0	60.00	....	....	....	....	....	....	....	....		1931-32	1931-32
Hrivnak, Jim	Wsh., Wpg., St.L.	5	85	34	30	3	4217	262	0	3.73	....	....	....	....	....	....	....	....		1989-90	1993-94
Hrudey, Kelly	NYI, L.A., S.J.	15	677	271	265	88	38084	2174	17	3.43	85	36	46	....	5163	283	0	3.29		1983-84	1997-98

Name	NHL Teams	NHL Seasons	Regular Schedule								Playoffs								NHL Cup Wins	First NHL Season	Last NHL Season
			GP	W	L	T	Mins	GA	SO	Avg	GP	W	L	T	Mins	GA	SO	Avg			
Ing, Peter	Tor., Edm., Det.	4	74	20	37	9	3941	266	1	4.05	....	....	....	....	....	....	....	....		1989-90	1993-94
Inness, Gary	Pit., Phi., Wsh.	7	162	58	61	27	8710	494	2	3.40	9	5	4	....	540	24	0	2.67		1973-74	1980-81
Ireland, Randy	Buf.	1	2	0	0	0	30	3	0	6.00	....	....	....	....	....	....	....	....		1978-79	1978-79
Irons, Robbie	St.L.	1	1	0	0	0	3	0	0	0.00	....	....	....	....	....	....	....	....		1968-69	1968-69
• Ironstone, Joe	Ott., NYA, Tor.	3	2	0	0	1	110	3	1	1.64	....	....	....	....	....	....	....	....		1924-25	1927-28
Jablonski, Pat	St.L., T.B., Mtl., Phx., Car.	8	128	28	62	18	6634	413	1	3.74	4	0	0	....	139	6	0	2.59		1989-90	1997-98
Jackson, Doug	Chi.	1	6	2	3	1	360	42	0	7.00	....	....	....	....	....	....	....	....		1947-48	1947-48
Jackson, Percy	Bos., NYA, NYR	4	7	1	3	1	392	26	0	3.98	....	....	....	....	....	....	....	....		1931-32	1935-36
‡ Jaks, Pauli	L.A.	1	1	0	0	0	40	2	0	3.00	....	....	....	....	....	....	....	....		1994-95	1994-95
Janaszak, Steve	Min., Col.	2	3	0	1	1	160	15	0	5.63	....	....	....	....	....	....	....	....		1979-80	1981-82
Janecyk, Bob	Chi., L.A.	6	110	43	47	13	6250	432	2	4.15	3	0	3	....	184	10	0	3.26		1983-84	1988-89
§ • Jenkins, Roger	NYA	1	1	0	1	0	30	7	0	14.00	....	....	....	....	....	....	....	....		1938-39	1938-39
Jensen, Al	Det., Wsh., L.A.	7	179	95	53	18	9974	557	8	3.35	12	5	5	....	598	32	0	3.21		1980-81	1986-87
Jensen, Darren	Phi.	2	30	15	10	1	1496	95	2	3.81	....	....	....	....	....	....	....	....		1984-85	1985-86
Johnson, Bob	St.L., Pit.	2	24	9	9	1	1059	66	0	3.74	....	....	....	....	....	....	....	....		1972-73	1974-75
Johnston, Eddie	Bos., Tor., St.L., Chi.	16	592	234	257	80	34216	1852	32	3.25	18	7	10	....	1023	57	1	3.34	2	1962-63	1977-78
‡ Jokela, Antti			....	....	....	....	....	....	....	....	....	....	....	....	....	....	....	....			
Junkin, Joe	Bos.	1	1	0	0	0	8	0	0	0.00	....	....	....	....	....	....	....	....		1968-69	1968-69
Kaarela, Jari	Col.	1	5	2	2	0	220	22	0	6.00	....	....	....	....	....	....	....	....		1980-81	1980-81
Kamppuri, Hannu	N.J.	1	13	1	10	1	645	54	0	5.02	....	....	....	....	....	....	....	....		1984-85	1984-85
• Karakas, Mike	Chi., Mtl.	8	336	114	169	53	20616	1002	28	2.92	23	11	12	0	1434	72	3	3.01	1	1935-36	1945-46
Keans, Doug	L.A., Bos.	9	210	96	64	26	11388	666	4	3.51	9	2	6	....	432	34	0	4.72		1979-80	1987-88
Keenan, Don	Bos.	1	1	0	1	0	60	4	0	4.00	....	....	....	....	....	....	....	....		1958-59	1958-59
• Kerr, Dave	Mtl.M., NYA, NYR	11	427	203	148	75	26639	954	51	2.15	40	18	19	3	2616	76	8	1.74	1	1930-31	1940-41
King, Scott	Det.	2	2	0	0	0	61	3	0	2.95	....	....	....	....	....	....	....	....		1990-91	1991-92
Kleisinger, Terry	NYR	1	4	0	2	0	191	14	0	4.40	....	....	....	....	....	....	....	....		1985-86	1985-86
Klymkiw, Julian	NYR	1	1	0	0	0	19	2	0	6.32	....	....	....	....	....	....	....	....		1958-59	1958-59
Knickle, Rick	L.A.	2	14	7	6	0	706	44	0	3.74	....	....	....	....	....	....	....	....		1992-93	1993-94
‡ Konstantinov, Evgeny	T.B.	2	2	0	0	0	21	1	0	2.86	....	....	....	....	....	....	....	....		2000-01	2002-03
Kuntar, Les	Mtl.	1	6	2	2	0	302	16	0	3.18	....	....	....	....	....	....	....	....		1993-94	1993-94
Kurt, Gary	Cal.	1	16	1	7	5	838	60	0	4.30	....	....	....	....	....	....	....	....		1971-72	1971-72
Labrecque, Patrick	Mtl.	1	2	0	1	0	98	7	0	4.29	....	....	....	....	....	....	....	....		1995-96	1995-96
Lacher, Blaine	Bos.	2	47	22	16	4	2636	123	4	2.80	5	1	4	....	283	12	0	2.54		1994-95	1995-96
• Lacroix, Frenchy	Mtl.	2	5	1	4	0	280	16	0	3.43	....	....	....	....	....	....	....	....		1925-26	1926-27
LaFerriere, Rick	Col.	1	1	0	0	0	20	1	0	3.00	....	....	....	....	....	....	....	....		1981-82	1981-82
LaForest, Mark	Det., Phi., Tor., Ott.	6	103	25	54	4	5032	354	2	4.22	2	1	0	....	48	1	0	1.25		1985-86	1993-94
‡ Lajeunesse, Simon	Ott.	1	1	0	0	0	24	0	0	0.00	....	....	....	....	....	....	....	....		2001-02	2001-02
‡ Langkow, Scott	Wpg., Phx., Atl.	4	20	3	12	1	943	68	0	4.33	....	....	....	....	....	....	....	....		1995-96	1999-00
• Larocque, Michel	Mtl., Tor., Phi., St.L.	11	312	160	89	45	17615	978	17	3.33	14	6	6	....	759	37	1	2.92	4	1973-74	1983-84
Larocque, Michel	Chi.	1	3	0	2	0	152	9	0	3.55	....	....	....	....	....	....	....	....		2000-01	2000-01
‡ Lasak, Jan	Nsh.	2	6	0	4	0	267	18	0	4.04	....	....	....	....	....	....	....	....		2001-02	2002-03
Laskowski, Gary	L.A.	2	59	19	27	5	2942	228	0	4.65	....	....	....	....	....	....	....	....		1982-83	1983-84
Laxton, Gord	Pit.	4	17	4	9	0	800	74	0	5.55	....	....	....	....	....	....	....	....		1975-76	1978-79
LeBlanc, Ray	Chi.	1	1	1	0	0	60	1	0	1.00	....	....	....	....	....	....	....	....		1991-92	1991-92
§ • Leduc, Albert	Mtl.	1	1	0	0	0	2	1	0	30.00	....	....	....	....	....	....	....	....		1931-32	1931-32
Legris, Claude	Det.	2	4	0	1	1	91	4	0	2.64	....	....	....	....	....	....	....	....		1980-81	1981-82
• Lehman, Hugh	Chi.	2	48	20	24	4	3047	136	6	2.68	2	0	1	1	120	10	0	5.00		1926-27	1927-28
Lemelin, Reggie	Atl., Cgy., Bos.	15	507	236	162	63	28006	1613	12	3.46	59	23	25	....	3119	186	2	3.58		1978-79	1992-93
Lenarduzzi, Mike	Hfd.	2	4	1	1	1	189	10	0	3.17	....	....	....	....	....	....	....	....		1992-93	1993-94
Lessard, Mario	L.A.	6	240	92	97	39	13529	843	9	3.74	20	6	12	....	1136	83	0	4.38		1978-79	1983-84
Levasseur, Jean-Louis	Min.	1	1	0	1	0	60	7	0	7.00	....	....	....	....	....	....	....	....		1979-80	1979-80
§ • Levinsky, Alex	Tor.	1	1	0	0	0	1	1	0	60.00	....	....	....	....	....	....	....	....		1931-32	1931-32
• Lindbergh, Pelle	Phi.	5	157	87	49	15	9150	503	7	3.30	23	12	10	....	1214	63	3	3.11		1981-82	1985-86
• Lindsay, Bert	Mtl.W., Tor.	2	20	6	14	0	1238	118	0	5.72	....	....	....	....	....	....	....	....		1917-18	1918-19
Littman, David	Buf., T.B.	3	3	0	2	0	141	14	0	5.96	....	....	....	....	....	....	....	....		1990-91	1992-93
Liut, Mike	St.L., Hfd., Wsh.	13	664	294	271	74	38215	2221	25	3.49	67	29	32	....	3814	215	2	3.38		1979-80	1991-92
Lockett, Ken	Van.	2	55	13	15	8	2348	131	2	3.35	1	0	1	....	60	6	0	6.00		1974-75	1975-76
• Lockhart, Howard	Tor., Que., Ham., Bos.	5	59	16	41	0	3413	287	1	5.05	....	....	....	....	....	....	....	....		1919-20	1924-25
LoPresti, Pete	Min., Edm.	6	175	43	102	20	9858	668	5	4.07	2	0	2	....	77	6	0	4.68		1974-75	1980-81
• LoPresti, Sam	Chi.	2	74	30	38	6	4530	236	4	3.13	8	3	5	....	530	17	1	1.92		1940-41	1941-42
‡ Lorenz, Danny	NYI	3	8	1	5	0	357	25	0	4.20	....	....	....	....	....	....	....	....		1990-91	1992-93
Loustel, Ron	Wpg.	1	1	0	1	0	60	10	0	10.00	....	....	....	....	....	....	....	....		1980-81	1980-81
Low, Ron	Tor., Wsh., Det., Que., Edm., N.J.	11	382	102	203	38	20502	1463	4	4.28	7	1	6	....	452	29	0	3.85		1972-73	1984-85
Lozinski, Larry	Det.	1	30	6	11	7	1459	105	0	4.32	....	....	....	....	....	....	....	....		1980-81	1980-81
• Lumley, Harry	Det., NYR, Chi., Tor., Bos.	16	803	330	329	142	48044	2206	71	2.75	76	29	47	....	4778	198	7	2.49	1	1943-44	1959-60
MacKenzie, Shawn	N.J.	1	4	0	1	0	130	15	0	6.92	....	....	....	....	....	....	....	....		1982-83	1982-83
Madeley, Darrin	Ott.	3	39	4	23	5	1928	140	0	4.36	....	....	....	....	....	....	....	....		1992-93	1994-95
Malarchuk, Clint	Que., Wsh., Buf.	11	338	141	130	45	19030	1100	12	3.47	15	2	9	0	781	56	0	4.30		1981-82	1991-92
Maneluk, George	NYI	1	4	1	1	0	140	15	0	6.43	....	....	....	....	....	....	....	....		1990-91	1990-91
Maniago, Cesare	Tor., Mtl., NYR, Min., Van.	15	568	190	257	97	32569	1773	30	3.27	36	15	21	....	2245	100	3	2.67		1960-61	1977-78
Marois, Jean	Tor., Chi.	2	3	1	2	0	180	15	0	5.00	....	....	....	....	....	....	....	....		1943-44	1953-54
Martin, Seth	St.L.	1	30	8	10	7	1552	67	1	2.59	2	0	0	....	73	5	0	4.11		1967-68	1967-68
Mason, Bob	Wsh., Chi., Que., Van.	8	145	55	65	16	7988	500	1	3.76	5	2	3	....	369	12	1	1.95		1983-84	1990-91
Mattsson, Markus	Wpg., Min., L.A.	4	92	21	46	14	5007	343	6	4.11	....	....	....	....	....	....	....	....		1979-80	1983-84
May, Darrell	St.L.	2	6	1	5	0	364	31	0	5.11	....	....	....	....	....	....	....	....		1985-86	1987-88
Mayer, Gilles	Tor.	4	9	2	6	1	540	24	0	2.67	....	....	....	....	....	....	....	....		1949-50	1955-56
• McAuley, Ken	NYR	2	96	17	64	15	5740	537	1	5.61	....	....	....	....	....	....	....	....		1943-44	1944-45
McCartan, Jack	NYR	2	12	2	7	3	680	42	1	3.71	....	....	....	....	....	....	....	....		1959-60	1960-61
• McCool, Frank	Tor.	2	72	34	31	7	4320	242	4	3.36	13	8	5	....	807	30	4	2.23	1	1944-45	1945-46
McDuffe, Peter	St.L., NYR, K.C., Det.	5	57	11	36	6	3207	218	0	4.08	1	0	1	....	60	7	0	7.00		1971-72	1975-76
McGrattan, Tom	Det.	1	1	0	0	0	8	1	0	7.50	....	....	....	....	....	....	....	....		1947-48	1947-48
McKay, Ross	Hfd.	1	1	0	0	0	35	3	0	5.14	....	....	....	....	....	....	....	....		1990-91	1990-91
McKenzie, Bill	Det., K.C., Col.	6	91	18	49	13	4776	326	2	4.10	....	....	....	....	....	....	....	....		1973-74	1979-80
McKichan, Steve	Van.	1	1	0	0	0	20	2	0	6.00	....	....	....	....	....	....	....	....		1990-91	1990-91
McLachlan, Murray	Tor.	1	2	0	1	0	25	4	0	9.60	....	....	....	....	....	....	....	....		1970-71	1970-71
McLean, Kirk	N.J., Van., Car., Fla., NYR	16	612	245	262	72	35090	1904	22	3.26	68	34	34	....	4189	198	6	2.84		1985-86	2000-01
McLelland, Dave	Van.	1	2	1	1	0	120	10	0	5.00	....	....	....	....	....	....	....	....		1972-73	1972-73
McLeod, Don	Det., Phi.	2	18	3	10	1	879	74	0	5.05	....	....	....	....	....	....	....	....		1970-71	1971-72
McLeod, Jim	St.L.	1	16	6	6	4	880	44	0	3.00	....	....	....	....	....	....	....	....		1971-72	1971-72
McNamara, Gerry	Tor.	2	7	2	2	1	323	14	0	2.60	....	....	....	....	....	....	....	....		1960-61	1969-70
• McNeil, Gerry	Mtl.	8	276	119	105	52	16535	649	28	2.36	35	17	18	....	2284	72	5	1.89	3	1947-48	1957-58
McRae, Gord	Tor.	5	71	30	22	10	3799	221	1	3.49	8	2	5	....	454	22	0	2.91		1972-73	1977-78
Melanson, Roland	NYI, Min., L.A., N.J., Mtl.	11	291	129	106	33	16452	995	6	3.63	23	4	9	....	801	59	0	4.42	3	1980-81	1991-92
Meloche, Gilles	Chi., Cal., Cle., Min., Pit.	18	788	270	351	131	45401	2756	20	3.64	45	21	19	....	2464	143	2	3.48		1970-71	1987-88
Micalef, Corrado	Det.	5	113	26	59	15	5794	409	2	4.24	3	0	0	....	49	8	0	9.80		1981-82	1985-86
‡ Michaud, Alfie	Van.	1	2	0	1	0	69	5	0	4.35	....	....	....	....	....	....	....	....		1999-00	1999-00
Middlebrook, Lindsay	Wpg., Min., N.J., Edm.	4	37	3	23	6	1845	152	0	4.94	....	....	....	....	....	....	....	....		1979-80	1982-83
• Millar, Al	Bos.	1	6	1	4	1	360	25	0	4.17	....	....	....	....	....	....	....	....		1957-58	1957-58
Millen, Greg	Pit., Hfd., St.L., Que., Chi., Det.	14	604	215	284	89	35377	2281	17	3.87	59	27	29	....	3383	193	0	3.42		1978-79	1991-92
• Miller, Joe	NYA, NYR, Pit., Phi.	4	127	24	87	16	7871	383	16	2.92	3	2	1	0	180	3	1	1.00	1	1927-28	1930-31
‡ Minard, Mike	Edm.	1	1	1	0	0	60	3	0	3.00	....	....	....	....	....	....	....	....		1999-00	1999-00
Mio, Eddie	Edm., NYR, Det.	7	192	64	73	30	10428	705	4	4.06	17	9	7	....	986	63	0	3.83		1979-80	1985-86
• Mitchell, Ivan	Tor.	3	22	10	9	0	1190	88	0	4.44	....	....	....	....	....	....	....	....	1	1919-20	1921-22
Moffat, Mike	Bos.	3	19	7	7	2	979	70	0	4.29	11	6	5	....	663	38	0	3.44		1981-82	1983-84
Moog, Andy	Edm., Bos., Dal., Mtl.	18	713	372	209	88	40151	2097	28	3.13	132	68	57	....	7452	377	4	3.04	3	1980-81	1997-98
• Moore, Alfie	NYA, Chi., Det.	4	21	7	14	0	1290	81	1	3.77	3	1	2	....	180	7	0	2.33	1	1936-37	1939-40
Moore, Robbie	Phi., Wsh.	2	6	3	1	1	257	8	2	1.87	5	3	2	....	268	18	0	4.03		1978-79	1982-83
Morissette, Jean-Guy	Mtl.	1	1	0	1	0	36	4	0	6.67	....	....	....	....	....	....	....	....		1963-64	1963-64
• Mowers, Johnny	Det.	4	152	65	61	26	9350	399	15	2.56	32	19	13	....	2000	85	2	2.55	1	1940-41	1946-47
Mrazek, Jerome	Phi.	1	1	0	0	0	6	1	0	10.00	....	....	....	....	....	....	....	....		1975-76	1975-76

Name	NHL Teams	NHL Seasons	Regular Schedule								Playoffs								NHL Cup Wins	First NHL Season	Last NHL Season
			GP	W	L	T	Mins	GA	SO	Avg	GP	W	L	T	Mins	GA	SO	Avg			
§ • Mummery, Harry	Que., Ham.	2	4	2	1	0	192	20	0	6.25	....	....	....	....	....	....	....	....		1919-20	1921-22
§ • Munro, Dunc	Mtl.M.	1	1	0	0	0	2	0	0	0.00	....	....	....	....	....	....	....	....		1924-25	1924-25
• Murphy, Hal	Mtl.	1	1	1	0	0	60	4	0	4.00	....	....	....	....	....	....	....	....		1952-53	1952-53
• Murray, Mickey	Mtl.	1	1	0	1	0	60	4	0	4.00	....	....	....	....	....	....	....	....		1929-30	1929-30
Muzzatti, Jason	Cgy., Hfd., NYR, S.J.	5	62	13	25	10	3014	167	1	3.32	....	....	....	....	....	....	....	....		1993-94	1997-98
‡ Myllys, Jarmo	Min., S.J.	4	39	4	27	1	1846	161	0	5.23	....	....	....	....	....	....	....	....		1988-89	1991-92
Mylnikov, Sergei	Que.	1	10	1	7	2	568	47	0	4.96	....	....	....	....	....	....	....	....		1989-90	1989-90
Myre, Phil	Mtl., Atl., St.L., Phi., Col., Buf.	14	439	149	198	76	25220	1482	14	3.53	12	6	5	....	747	41	1	3.29	1	1969-70	1982-83
‡ Naumenko, Gregg	Ana.	1	2	0	1	0	70	7	0	6.00	....	....	....	....	....	....	....	....		2000-01	2000-01
Newton, Cam	Pit.	2	16	4	7	1	814	51	0	3.76	....	....	....	....	....	....	....	....		1970-71	1972-73
Norris, Jack	Bos., Chi., L.A.	4	58	20	25	4	3119	202	2	3.89	....	....	....	....	....	....	....	....		1964-65	1970-71
Nurminen, Pasi	Atl.	3	125	48	54	12	7059	338	5	2.87	....	....	....	....	....	....	....	....		2001-02	2003-04
Oleschuk, Bill	K.C., Col.	4	55	7	28	10	2835	188	1	3.98	....	....	....	....	....	....	....	....		1975-76	1979-80
• Olesevich, Dan	NYR	1	1	0	0	1	29	2	0	4.14	....	....	....	....	....	....	....	....		1961-62	1961-62
O'Neill, Mike	Wpg., Ana.	4	21	0	9	2	855	61	0	4.28	....	....	....	....	....	....	....	....		1991-92	1996-97
Ouimet, Ted	St.L.	1	1	0	1	0	60	2	0	2.00	....	....	....	....	....	....	....	....		1968-69	1968-69
Pageau, Paul	L.A.	1	1	0	1	0	60	8	0	8.00	....	....	....	....	....	....	....	....		1980-81	1980-81
• Paille, Marcel	NYR	7	107	32	52	22	6342	362	2	3.42	....	....	....	....	....	....	....	....		1957-58	1964-65
Palmateer, Mike	Tor., Wsh.	8	356	149	138	52	20131	1183	17	3.53	29	12	17	....	1765	89	2	3.03		1976-77	1983-84
Pang, Darren	Chi.	3	81	27	35	7	4252	287	0	4.05	6	1	3	....	250	18	0	4.32		1984-85	1988-89
Parent, Bernie	Bos., Phi., Tor.	13	608	271	198	121	35136	1493	54	2.55	71	38	33	....	4302	174	6	2.43	2	1965-66	1978-79
Parent, Bob	Tor.	2	3	0	2	0	160	15	0	5.63	....	....	....	....	....	....	....	....		1981-82	1982-83
‡ Parent, Rich	St.L., T.B., Pit.	4	32	7	11	5	1561	82	1	3.15	....	....	....	....	....	....	....	....		1997-98	2000-01
Parro, Dave	Wsh.	4	77	21	36	10	4015	274	2	4.09	....	....	....	....	....	....	....	....		1980-81	1983-84
§ • Patrick, Lester	NYR	1	....	....	....	....	....	....	....	....	1	1	0	0	46	1	0	1.30	1	1927-28	1927-28
Peeters, Pete	Phi., Bos., Wsh.	13	489	246	155	51	27699	1424	21	3.08	71	35	35	....	4200	232	2	3.31		1978-79	1990-91
Pelletier, Marcel	Chi., NYR	2	8	1	6	0	395	32	0	4.86	....	....	....	....	....	....	....	....		1950-51	1962-63
Penney, Steve	Mtl., Wpg.	5	91	35	38	12	5194	313	1	3.62	27	15	12	....	1604	72	4	2.69		1983-84	1987-88
• Perreault, Bob	Mtl., Det., Bos.	3	31	8	16	7	1827	103	3	3.38	....	....	....	....	....	....	....	....		1955-56	1962-63
Pettie, Jim	Bos.	3	21	9	7	2	1157	71	1	3.68	....	....	....	....	....	....	....	....		1976-77	1978-79
Pietrangelo, Frank	Pit., Hfd.	7	141	46	59	6	7141	490	1	4.12	12	7	5	....	713	34	1	2.86	1	1987-88	1993-94
• Plante, Jacques	Mtl., NYR, St.L., Tor., Bos.	18	837	437	246	145	49533	1964	82	2.38	112	71	36	....	6651	237	14	2.14	6	1952-53	1972-73
Plasse, Michel	St.L., Mtl., K.C., Pit., Col., Que.	11	299	92	136	54	16760	1058	2	3.79	4	1	2	....	195	9	1	2.77	1	1970-71	1981-82
§ • Plaxton, Hugh	Mtl.M.	1	1	0	1	0	57	5	0	5.26	....	....	....	....	....	....	....	....		1932-33	1932-33
Pronovost, Claude	Bos., Mtl.	2	3	1	1	0	120	7	1	3.50	....	....	....	....	....	....	....	....		1955-56	1958-59
Puppa, Daren	Buf., Tor., T.B.	15	429	179	161	54	23819	1204	19	3.03	16	4	9	....	786	51	0	3.89		1985-86	1999-00
Pusey, Chris	Det.	1	1	0	0	0	40	3	0	4.50	....	....	....	....	....	....	....	....		1985-86	1985-86
Racicot, Andre	Mtl.	5	68	26	23	8	3357	196	2	3.50	4	0	1	....	31	4	0	7.74	1	1989-90	1993-94
Racine, Bruce	St.L.	1	11	0	3	0	230	12	0	3.13	1	0	0	....	1	0	0	0.00		1995-96	1995-96
‡ Ram, Jamie	NYR	1	1	0	0	0	27	0	0	0.00	....	....	....	....	....	....	....	....		1995-96	1995-96
Ranford, Bill	Bos., Edm., Wsh., T.B., Det.	15	647	240	279	76	35936	2042	15	3.41	53	28	25	....	3110	159	4	3.07	2	1985-86	1999-00
Raymond, Alain	Wsh.	1	1	0	1	0	40	2	0	3.00	....	....	....	....	....	....	....	....		1987-88	1987-88
• Rayner, Chuck	NYA, Bro., NYR	10	424	138	208	77	25491	1294	25	3.05	18	9	9	....	1135	46	1	2.43		1940-41	1952-53
Reaugh, Daryl	Edm., Hfd.	3	27	8	9	1	1246	72	1	3.47	....	....	....	....	....	....	....	....		1984-85	1990-91
Reddick, Pokey	Wpg., Edm., Fla.	6	132	46	58	16	7162	443	0	3.71	4	0	2	....	168	10	0	3.57	1	1986-87	1993-94
§ • Redding, George	Bos.	1	1	0	0	0	11	1	0	5.45	....	....	....	....	....	....	....	....		1924-25	1924-25
Redquest, Greg	Pit.	1	1	0	0	0	13	3	0	13.85	....	....	....	....	....	....	....	....		1977-78	1977-78
Reece, Dave	Bos.	1	14	7	5	2	777	43	2	3.32	....	....	....	....	....	....	....	....		1975-76	1975-76
Reese, Jeff	Tor., Cgy., Hfd., T.B., N.J.	11	174	53	65	17	8667	529	5	3.66	11	3	5	....	515	35	0	4.08		1987-88	1998-99
Resch, Glenn	NYI, Col., N.J., Phi.	14	571	231	224	82	32279	1761	26	3.27	41	17	17	....	2044	85	2	2.50	1	1973-74	1986-87
• Rheaume, Herb	Mtl.	1	31	10	20	1	1889	92	0	2.92	....	....	....	....	....	....	....	....		1925-26	1925-26
Rhodes, Damian	Tor., Ott., Atl.	10	309	99	140	48	17339	820	12	2.84	13	5	7	....	741	27	0	2.19		1990-91	2001-02
Ricci, Nick	Pit.	4	19	7	12	0	1087	79	0	4.36	....	....	....	....	....	....	....	....		1979-80	1982-83
Richardson, Terry	Det., St.L.	5	20	3	11	0	906	85	0	5.63	....	....	....	....	....	....	....	....		1973-74	1978-79
Richter, Mike	NYR	15	666	301	258	73	38183	1840	24	2.89	76	41	33	....	4514	202	9	2.68	1	1988-89	2002-03
Ridley, Curt	NYR, Van., Tor.	6	104	27	47	16	5498	355	1	3.87	2	0	2	....	120	8	0	4.00		1974-75	1980-81
Riendeau, Vincent	Mtl., St.L., Det., Bos.	8	184	85	65	20	10423	573	5	3.30	25	11	12	....	1277	71	1	3.34		1987-88	1994-95
Riggin, Dennis	Det.	2	18	6	10	2	999	52	1	3.12	....	....	....	....	....	....	....	....		1959-60	1962-63
Riggin, Pat	Atl., Cgy., Wsh., Bos., Pit.	9	350	153	120	52	19872	1135	11	3.43	25	8	13	....	1336	72	0	3.23		1979-80	1987-88
Ring, Bob	Bos.	1	1	0	0	0	33	4	0	7.27	....	....	....	....	....	....	....	....		1965-66	1965-66
Rivard, Fern	Min.	4	55	9	27	11	2865	190	2	3.98	....	....	....	....	....	....	....	....		1968-69	1974-75
• Roach, John Ross	Tor., NYR, Det.	14	492	219	204	68	30444	1246	58	2.46	29	12	14	3	1901	60	7	1.89	1	1921-22	1934-35
• Roberts, Moe	Bos., NYA, Chi.	4	10	3	5	0	501	31	0	3.71	....	....	....	....	....	....	....	....		1925-26	1951-52
• Robertson, Earl	Det., NYA, Bro.	6	190	60	95	34	11820	575	16	2.92	15	7	7	....	995	29	2	1.75	1	1936-37	1941-42
• Rollins, Al	Tor., Chi., NYR	9	430	141	205	83	25723	1192	28	2.78	13	6	7	....	755	30	0	2.38	1	1949-50	1959-60
Romano, Roberto	Pit., Bos.	6	126	46	63	8	7111	471	4	3.97	....	....	....	....	....	....	....	....		1982-83	1993-94
Rosati, Mike	Wsh.	1	1	1	0	0	28	0	0	0.00	....	....	....	....	....	....	....	....		1998-99	1998-99
Roussel, Dominic	Phi., Wpg., Ana., Edm.	8	205	77	70	23	10665	555	7	3.12	1	0	0	....	23	0	0	0.00		1991-92	2000-01
Roy, Patrick	Mtl., Col.	19	1029	551	315	131	60235	2546	66	2.54	247	151	94	....	15209	584	23	2.30	4	1984-85	2002-03
Rupp, Pat	Det.	1	1	0	1	0	60	4	0	4.00	....	....	....	....	....	....	....	....		1963-64	1963-64
Rutherford, Jim	Det., Pit., Tor., L.A.	13	457	151	227	59	25895	1576	14	3.65	8	2	5	....	440	28	0	3.82		1970-71	1982-83
• Rutledge, Wayne	L.A.	3	82	28	37	9	4325	241	2	3.34	8	2	4	....	378	20	0	3.17		1967-68	1969-70
St. Croix, Rick	Phi., Tor.	8	130	49	54	18	7295	451	2	3.71	11	4	6	....	562	29	1	3.10		1977-78	1984-85
St. Laurent, Sam	N.J., Det.	5	34	7	12	4	1572	92	1	3.51	1	0	0	....	10	1	0	6.00		1985-86	1989-90
‡ Salo, Tommy	NYI, Edm., Col.	10	526	210	225	73	30436	1296	37	2.55	22	5	16	0	1369	58	0	2.54		1994-95	2003-04
§ • Sands, Charlie	Mtl.	1	1	0	0	0	25	5	0	12.00	....	....	....	....	....	....	....	....		1939-40	1939-40
Sands, Mike	Min.	2	6	0	5	0	302	26	0	5.17	....	....	....	....	....	....	....	....		1984-85	1986-87
Sarjeant, Geoff	St.L., S.J.	2	8	1	2	1	291	20	0	4.12	....	....	....	....	....	....	....	....		1994-95	1995-96
Sauve, Bob	Buf., Det., Chi., N.J.	13	420	182	154	54	23711	1377	8	3.48	34	15	16	....	1850	95	4	3.08		1976-77	1988-89
• Sawchuk, Terry	Det., Bos., Tor., L.A., NYR	21	971	447	330	172	57194	2389	103	2.51	106	54	48	....	6290	266	12	2.54	4	1949-50	1969-70
• Schaefer, Joe	NYR	2	2	0	2	0	86	8	0	5.58	....	....	....	....	....	....	....	....		1959-60	1960-61
Schafer, Paxton	Bos.	1	3	0	0	0	77	6	0	4.68	....	....	....	....	....	....	....	....		1996-97	1996-97
Scott, Ron	NYR, L.A.	5	28	8	13	4	1450	91	0	3.77	1	0	0	....	32	4	0	7.50		1983-84	1989-90
Sevigny, Richard	Mtl., Que.	9	176	80	54	20	9485	507	5	3.21	4	0	3	....	208	13	0	3.75	1	1978-79	1986-87
Sharples, Scott	Cgy.	1	1	0	0	1	65	4	0	3.69	....	....	....	....	....	....	....	....		1991-92	1991-92
§ • Shields, Al	NYA	1	2	0	0	0	41	9	0	13.17	....	....	....	....	....	....	....	....		1931-32	1931-32
Shtalenkov, Mikhail	Ana., Edm., Phx., Fla.	7	190	62	82	19	9966	480	8	2.89	4	0	3	....	211	10	0	2.84		1993-94	1999-00
‡ Shulmistra, Richard	N.J., Fla.	2	2	1	1	0	122	3	0	1.48	....	....	....	....	....	....	....	....		1997-98	1999-00
Sidorkiewicz, Peter	Hfd., Ott., N.J.	8	246	79	128	27	13884	832	8	3.60	15	5	10	....	912	55	0	3.62		1987-88	1997-98
Simmons, Don	Bos., Tor., NYR	11	249	101	101	41	14555	701	20	2.89	24	13	11	....	1436	62	3	2.59	3	1956-57	1968-69
Simmons, Gary	Cal., Cle., L.A.	4	107	30	57	15	6162	366	5	3.56	1	0	0	....	20	1	0	3.00		1974-75	1977-78
Skidmore, Paul	St.L.	1	2	1	1	0	120	6	0	3.00	....	....	....	....	....	....	....	....		1981-82	1981-82
Skorodenski, Warren	Chi., Edm.	5	35	12	11	4	1732	100	2	3.46	2	0	0	....	33	6	0	10.91		1981-82	1987-88
• Smith, Al	Tor., Pit., Det., Buf., Hfd., Col.	10	233	74	99	36	12752	735	10	3.46	6	1	4	....	317	21	0	3.97		1965-66	1980-81
Smith, Billy	L.A., NYI	18	680	305	233	105	38431	2031	22	3.17	132	88	36	....	7645	348	5	2.73	4	1971-72	1988-89
Smith, Gary	Tor., Oak., Cal., Chi., Van., Min., Wsh., Wpg.	14	532	173	261	74	29619	1675	26	3.39	20	5	13	....	1153	62	1	3.23		1965-66	1979-80
• Smith, Normie	Mtl.M., Det.	8	199	81	83	35	12357	479	17	2.33	12	9	2	0	820	18	3	1.32	2	1931-32	1944-45
Sneddon, Bob	Cal.	1	5	0	2	0	225	21	0	5.60	....	....	....	....	....	....	....	....		1970-71	1970-71
Soderstrom, Tommy	Phi., NYI	5	156	45	69	19	8189	496	10	3.63	....	....	....	....	....	....	....	....		1992-93	1996-97
Soetaert, Doug	NYR, Wpg., Mtl.	12	284	110	104	42	15583	1030	6	3.97	5	1	2	....	180	14	0	4.67	1	1975-76	1986-87
Soucy, Christian	Chi.	1	1	0	0	0	3	0	0	0.00	....	....	....	....	....	....	....	....		1993-94	1993-94
• Spooner, Red	Pit.	1	1	0	1	0	60	6	0	6.00	....	....	....	....	....	....	....	....		1929-30	1929-30
§ • Spring, Jesse	Ham.	1	1	0	0	0	2	0	0	0.00	....	....	....	....	....	....	....	....		1924-25	1924-25
Staniowski, Ed	St.L., Wpg., Hfd.	10	219	67	104	21	12075	818	2	4.06	8	1	6	....	428	28	0	3.93		1975-76	1984-85
§ • Starr, Harold	Mtl.M.	1	1	0	0	0	3	0	0	0.00	....	....	....	....	....	....	....	....		1931-32	1931-32
Stauber, Robb	L.A., Buf.	4	62	21	23	9	3295	209	1	3.81	4	3	1	....	240	16	0	4.00		1989-90	1994-95
Stefan, Greg	Det.	9	299	115	127	30	16333	1068	5	3.92	30	12	17	....	1681	99	1	3.53		1981-82	1989-90
Stein, Phil	Tor.	1	1	0	0	1	70	2	0	1.71	....	....	....	....	....	....	....	....		1939-40	1939-40

		NHL Seasons	Regular Schedule								Playoffs								NHL Cup Wins	First NHL Season	Last NHL Season
Name	NHL Teams		GP	W	L	T	Mins	GA	SO	Avg	GP	W	L	T	Mins	GA	SO	Avg			
Stephenson, Wayne	St.L., Phi., Wsh.	10	328	146	103	49	18343	937	14	3.06	26	11	12	....	1522	79	2	3.11	1	1971-72	1980-81
Stevenson, Doug	NYR, Chi.	3	8	2	6	0	480	39	0	4.88	....									1944-45	1945-46
Stewart, Charles	Bos.	3	77	30	41	5	4742	194	10	2.45	....									1924-25	1926-27
Stewart, Jim	Bos.	1	1	0	1	0	20	5	0	15.00	....									1979-80	1979-80
• Stuart, Herb	Det.	1	3	1	2	0	180	5	0	1.67	....									1926-27	1926-27
Sylvestri, Don	Bos.	1	3	0	0	2	102	6	0	3.53	....									1984-85	1984-85
Tabaracci, Rick	Pit., Wpg., Wsh., Cgy., T.B., Atl., Col.	11	286	93	125	30	15255	760	15	2.99	17	4	12	....	1025	53	0	3.10		1988-89	1999-00
Takko, Kari	Min., Edm.	6	142	37	71	14	7317	475	1	3.90	4	0	1	....	109	7	0	3.85		1985-86	1990-91
‡ Tallas, Robbie	Bos., Chi.	6	99	28	42	10	5069	246	3	2.91	....									1995-96	2000-01
Tanner, John	Que.	3	21	2	11	5	1084	65	1	3.60	....									1989-90	1991-92
Tataryn, Dave	NYR	1	2	1	1	0	80	10	0	7.50	....									1976-77	1976-77
Taylor, Bobby	Phi., Pit.	5	46	15	17	6	2268	155	0	4.10	....								1	1971-72	1975-76
• Teno, Harvey	Det.	1	5	2	3	0	300	15	0	3.00	....									1938-39	1938-39
Terreri, Chris	N.J., S.J., Chi., NYI	14	406	151	172	43	22369	1143	9	3.07	29	12	12	....	1523	86	0	3.39	2	1986-87	2000-01
Thomas, Wayne	Mtl., Tor., NYR	9	243	103	93	34	13768	766	10	3.34	15	6	8	....	849	50	1	3.53		1972-73	1980-81
• Thompson, Tiny	Bos., Det.	12	553	284	194	75	34175	1183	81	2.08	44	20	24	0	2974	93	7	1.88	4	1928-29	1939-40
§ Toppazzini, Jerry	Bos.	1	1	0	0	0	1	0	0	0.00	....									1960-61	1960-61
Torchia, Mike	Dal.	1	6	3	2	1	327	18	0	3.30	....									1994-95	1994-95
‡ Trefilov, Andrei	Cgy., Buf., Chi.	7	54	12	25	4	2663	153	2	3.45	1	0	0	....	5	0	0	0.00		1992-93	1998-99
Tremblay, Vincent	Tor., Pit.	5	58	12	26	8	2785	223	1	4.80	....									1979-80	1983-84
Tucker, Ted	Cal.	1	5	1	1	1	177	10	0	3.39	....									1973-74	1973-74
‡ Turek, Roman	Dal., St.L., Cgy.	8	328	159	115	43	19095	734	27	2.31	22	12	9	0	1342	50	0	2.24	1	1996-97	2003-04
• Turner, Joe	Det.	1	1	0	0	1	70	3	0	2.57	....									1941-42	1941-42
Vachon, Rogie	Mtl., L.A., Det., Bos.	16	795	355	291	127	46298	2310	51	2.99	48	23	23	....	2876	133	2	2.77	3	1966-67	1981-82
Vanbiesbrouck, John	NYR, Fla., Phi., NYI, N.J.	20	882	374	346	119	50475	2503	40	2.98	71	28	38	....	3969	177	5	2.68		1981-82	2001-02
Veisor, Mike	Chi., Hfd., Wpg.	10	139	41	62	26	7806	532	5	4.09	4	0	2	....	180	15	0	5.00		1973-74	1983-84
Vernon, Mike	Cgy., Det., S.J., Fla.	19	781	385	273	92	44449	2206	27	2.98	138	77	56	....	8214	367	6	2.68	2	1982-83	2001-02
• Vezina, Georges	Mtl.	9	190	103	81	5	11592	633	13	3.28	13	10	3	0	780	35	2	2.69	1	1917-18	1925-26
Villemure, Gilles	NYR, Chi.	10	205	100	64	29	11581	542	13	2.81	14	5	5	....	656	32	0	2.93		1963-64	1976-77
‡ Waite, Jimmy	Chi., S.J., Phx.	11	106	28	41	12	5253	293	4	3.35	6	0	3	....	211	14	0	3.98		1988-89	1998-99
‡ Wakaluk, Darcy	Buf., Min., Dal., Phx.	8	191	67	75	21	9756	524	9	3.22	8	4	2	....	364	18	0	2.97		1988-89	1996-97
Wakely, Ernie	Mtl., St.L.	5	113	41	42	17	6244	290	8	2.79	10	2	6	....	509	37	1	4.36		1962-63	1971-72
• Walsh, Flat	Mtl.M., NYA	7	108	48	43	16	6641	256	12	2.31	8	2	4	2	570	16	2	1.68		1926-27	1932-33
Wamsley, Rick	Mtl., St.L., Cgy., Tor.	13	407	204	131	46	23123	1287	12	3.34	27	7	18	....	1397	81	0	3.48	1	1980-81	1992-93
Watt, Jim	St.L.	1	1	0	0	0	20	2	0	6.00	....									1973-74	1973-74
Weeks, Steve	NYR, Hfd., Van., NYI, L.A., Ott.	18	290	111	119	33	15879	989	5	3.74	12	3	5	....	486	27	0	3.33		1980-81	1992-93
Wetzel, Carl	Det., Min.	2	7	1	4	1	301	22	0	4.39	....									1964-65	1967-68
Whitmore, Kay	Hfd., Van., Bos., Cgy.	9	155	60	64	16	8596	508	4	3.55	4	0	2	....	174	13	0	4.48		1988-89	2001-02
Wilkinson, Derek	T.B.	4	22	3	12	3	933	57	0	3.67	....									1995-96	1998-99
Willis, Jordan	Dal.	1	1	0	1	0	19	1	0	3.16	....									1995-96	1995-96
Wilson, Dunc	Phi., Van., Tor., NYR, Pit.	10	287	80	150	33	15851	988	8	3.74	....									1969-70	1978-79
Wilson, Lefty	Det., Tor., Bos.	3	3	0	0	1	81	1	0	0.74	....									1953-54	1957-58
• Winkler, Hal	NYR, Bos.	2	75	35	26	14	4739	126	21	1.60	10	2	3	5	640	18	2	1.69		1926-27	1927-28
Wolfe, Bernie	Wsh.	4	120	20	61	21	6104	424	1	4.17	....									1975-76	1978-79
Wood, Alex	NYA	1	1	0	1	0	70	3	0	2.57	....									1936-37	1936-37
Worsley, Gump	NYR, Mtl., Min.	21	861	335	352	150	50183	2407	43	2.88	70	40	26	....	4084	189	5	2.78	4	1952-53	1973-74
• Worters, Roy	Pit., NYA, Mtl.	12	484	171	229	83	30175	1143	67	2.27	11	3	6	2	690	24	3	2.09		1925-26	1936-37
Worthy, Chris	Oak., Cal.	3	26	5	10	4	1326	98	0	4.43	....									1968-69	1970-71
Wregget, Ken	Tor., Phi., Pit., Cgy., Det.	17	575	225	248	53	31663	1917	9	3.63	56	28	25	....	3341	160	3	2.87	1	1983-84	1999-00
‡ Yeremeyev, Vitali	NYR	1	4	0	4	0	212	16	0	4.53	....									2000-01	2000-01
§ • Young, Doug	Det.	1	1	0	0	0	21	1	0	2.86	....									1933-34	1933-34
Young, Wendell	Van., Phi., Pit., T.B.	10	187	59	86	12	9410	618	2	3.94	2	0	1	....	99	6	0	3.64	2	1985-86	1994-95
Zanier, Mike	Edm.	1	3	1	1	1	185	12	0	3.89	....									1984-85	1984-85

Steve Baker

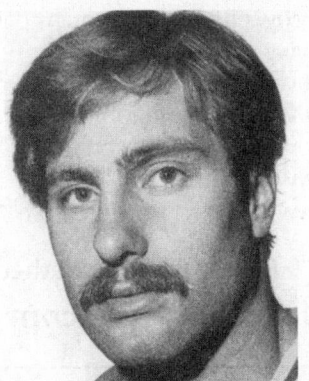

Steve Janaszak

Steve Penney

Wayne Thomas

Emile Francis

Mario Lessard

Pat Riggin

Hal Winkler

.com NHL League and Team Websites

National Hockey League ....www.nhl.com
NHL Site for Kids ....www.nhl.com/kids
NHL Merchandise Shop ....shop.nhl.com
NHL Job Postings........................hockeyjobs.nhl.com
Hockey Fights Cancer ....www.nhl.com/nhlhq/hockeyfightscancer/index.html

Official NHL Team Websites:

Anaheim...................................www.mightyducks.com
Atlanta ....www.atlantathrashers.com
Boston......................................www.bostonbruins.com
Buffalo ....www.sabres.com
Calgary.....................................www.calgaryflames.com
Carolina....................................www.carolinahurricanes.com
Chicago ....www.chicagoblackhawks.com
Colorado ....www.coloradoavalanche.com
Columbus ....www.bluejackets.com
Dallas ....www.dallasstars.com
Detroit......................................www.detroitredwings.com
Edmonton ....www.edmontonoilers.com
Florida ....www.floridapanthers.com
Los Angeles ....www.lakings.com
Minnesota ....www.wild.com
Montreal ....www.canadiens.com
Nashville...................................www.nashvillepredators.com
New Jersey ....www.newjerseydevils.com
NY Islanders ....www.newyorkislanders.com
NY Rangers ....www.newyorkrangers.com
Ottawa......................................www.ottawasenators.com
Philadelphia ....www.philadelphiaflyers.com
Phoenix ....www.phoenixcoyotes.com
Pittsburgh.................................www.pittsburghpenguins.com
St. Louis ....www.stlouisblues.com
San Jose ....www.sjsharks.com
Tampa Bay ....www.tampabaylightning.com
Toronto.....................................www.mapleleafs.com
Vancouver ....www.canucks.com
Washington...............................www.washingtoncaps.com

To order the *NHL Official Guide & Record Book* and other books about hockey:

www.nhlofficialguide.com

Contributors

The NHL Official Guide & Record Book is produced with the help of many.
Special thanks to: Rod Allison, Craig Allison, David Banks, Dwayne Barkley, Aaron Bell (OHL); Martin Bernard, Dan Benson, Ben Bishop, Bob Borgen, Scott Brand (USHL), Peter Brill, Jarrod Brodsky, Pete Cahill, Craig Campbell, Jack Carnefix (ECHL), Jason Chaimovitch (AHL), Steve Cherwonak (CHL), John Cooper, John Comerford, Robert Dalley, Arnold Dashney, Matt Davis, Denis Demers (QMJHL), Chris DePiero, Denis Dore, Al Doria, Steve Dove, Phil Doyle, Julia Drake, Jim Drinnan, Phil Ercolani, Jason Farris, Frank Faucon, Ernie Fitzsimmons, Peter Fillman, Lincoln Flagg, Mark Frankenfeld (NAHL), Kirk Fraser, Rob Gagnon, Randall Gambit, John Gardiner, Joe Gaul, Josh Gibbons, Bill Gibson, Sheri Grant, John Green, Stu Hackel (NAHL), Steve Hagwell (ECAC), Rob Hegberg, John Hellstrom, Hockey Hall of Fame, Chris Hurley, Peter Jagla, Karl Jahnke (QMJHL), Wally Johnson, Steve Kouleas, Brian Lavelle, Jon Litchfield, Andy Madden, Jean-Patrice Martel, Robert McAfee, Penny McEwen (SJHL), Dave McIntosh, Jim McKellar, Leroy McKinnon (WHL), John Moon, Herb Morell (OHL), John Moritsugu, NCAA Conference and School Sports Information Departments, NHL Broadcasters' Association, NHL Central Registry, NHL Officiating, NHL Players' Association, Joseph Nieforth, Zack Nutkevich, Steve Oddy, Adam Ottley, Dave Partridge, Lisa Peppin (UHL), Scott Pettigrew, Kenneth Pietrusiewicz, Fred Pletsch (CCHA), Mario Pouliot, Phil Pritchard, Valentina Riazanova, Craig Roberts (College Hockey America), Larry Rooney, Larry Sanderson, Scott Sanderson,

Ralph Slate, Noah Smith (Hockey East), SIHR, Doug Spencer (WCHA), Leonard Strandberg, Szymon Szemberg (IIHF), U.S. Hockey Hall of Fame, Bruce Vance, Eric Veilleux, Drew White, Paul Wilkinson (OPJHL), Andrew Will, Brett Williamson, Jeff Young.

Researchers and Historians: contact the Society for International Hockey Research
www.sihrhockey.org

Photo Credits

Graig Abel, Toronto; Scott Audette, Tampa; Steve and Brian Babineau, Boston; Bruce Bennett Studios; Andrew D. Bernstein Associates, Los Angeles; Mark Buckner, St. Louis; Scott Cunningham, Atlanta; Tim Defrisco, Colorado; Getty/NHL Images (Brian Bahr, Ronald Martinez, Doug Pensinger, Tom Pidgeon, Dave Sandford, Rick Stewart) Barry Gossage, Phoenix; Hockey Hall of Fame Collections; Glenn James, Dallas; Bruce Kluckhohn, Minnesota; Mitchell Layton, Washington; Richard Lewis, Florida; Dale McMillan, Edmonton; Matt Polk, Pittsburgh; Dave Reginek, Detroit; André Ringuette, Freestyle Photography, Ottawa; Debora Robinson, Anaheim; John Russell, Nashville; Jamie Sabau, Columbus; Bill Smith, Chicago; Don Smith, San Jose; Gerry Thomas, Calgary; Rocky Widner, San Jose; Bill Wippert, Buffalo.

Hockey Fights Cancer is a joint initiative founded in December 1998 by the National Hockey League and the National Hockey League Players' Association to raise money and awareness for hockey's most important fight. Hockey Fights Cancer is supported by NHL Member Clubs, NHL Alumni, the NHL Officials' Association, Professional Hockey Trainers and Equipment Managers, corporate marketing partners, broadcast partners and fans throughout North America. To date, more than $6.8 million has been raised to support local cancer research organizations as well as the American Cancer Society and Canadian Cancer Society national organizations.

The charity's largest fund-raising initiative is the annual Hockey Fights Cancer *On-Line Charity Auction.* Since it began in 2000, the Hockey Fights Cancer *On-Line Charity Auction* has raised more than $1.6 million to support cancer research and Children's Hospitals in North America.

Join the Fight! If you would like to make a contribution to Hockey Fights Cancer, please forward a check made payable to Hockey Fights Cancer to one of the following addresses:

<u>**For Canadian Residents**</u>:	<u>**For U.S. Residents:**</u>
Hockey Fights Cancer	Hockey Fights Cancer
P.O. Box 1282, Station B	P.O. Box 5037
Montreal, Quebec H3B 3K9	New York, NY 10185-5037

Please include your name and current address so that your donation can be acknowledged. All donations are tax-deductible.

For more information, log-on to www.nhl.com/nhlhq/hockeyfightscancer/index.html or call 1-800-540-6500.

FOUR STAR SELECTION...

NHL OFFICIAL GUIDE
IS PLEASED TO OFFER...

1. **THE NHL OFFICIAL GUIDE & RECORD BOOK**
The NHL's authoritative information source. 74th year in print. 672 pages. The "Bible of Hockey". Read worldwide.

2. **2006 OLYMPIC HOCKEY MEDIA GUIDE**
A limited edition 208-page, large-format softcover book with complete info on hockey's elite best-on-best competition.

3. **THE NHL YEARBOOK**
216-page, full-color magazine with features on each club. Award winners, All-Stars and special statistics.

4. **THE NHL RULE BOOK**
Complete playing rules, rink dimensions and officials' signals.

Free Book List with each order.